Food & Beverage
Market Place

Volume 1

2011

Tenth Edition

Food & Beverage Market Place

Volume 1

Food & Beverage Manufacturers

Product Categories

Company Profiles

Grey House
Publishing

AMENIA, NY 12501

PUBLISHER:	Leslie Mackenzie
EDITOR:	Richard Gottlieb
EDITORIAL DIRECTOR:	Laura Mars
PRODUCTION MANAGER:	Kristen Thatcher
COMPOSITION:	David Garoogian
PRODUCTION ASSISTANTS:	Diana Delgado; Erica Schneider; Donna Vanicky
MARKETING DIRECTOR:	Jessica Moody

Grey House Publishing, Inc.
4919 Route 22
Amenia, NY 12501
518.789.8700
FAX 845.373.6390
www.greyhouse.com
e-mail: books @greyhouse.com

Copyright © 2010 Grey House Publishing, Inc.
All rights reserved
First edition published 2001
Tenth edition published 2011
Printed in the USA

Food & beverage market place. - 9th ed. (2010) -
   3 v. ; 27.5 cm. Annual
  Includes index.
  ISSN: 1554-6334

1. Food industry and trade-United States-Directories. 2. Food industry and trade-Canada-Directories. 3. Beverage industry-United States-Directories. 4. Beverage industry-Canada-Directories. I. Grey House Publishing, Inc. II. Title: Food & beverage market place.

HD9003.T48
338-dc21

3-Volume Set	ISBN: 978-1-59237-577-6
Volume 1	**ISBN: 978-1-59237-578-3**
Volume 2	ISBN: 978-1-59237-579-0
Volume 3	ISBN: 978-1-59237-580-6

Table of Contents

VOLUME 1

VOLUME 2

VOLUME 3

Introduction

This tenth edition of the 3-volume *Food & Beverage Market Place* represents the largest, most comprehensive resource of food and beverage manufacturers and service suppliers. Not only one of the fastest growing industries, food and beverage companies also represent one of the most dynamic industry sectors. This 2011 *Food & Beverage Market Place* addresses all aspects of the food and beverage industry, with detailed profiles of 39,123 listings that cover major sectors – finished goods and ingredient manufacturers, equipment and supply manufacturers, food transport, warehousing, wholesalers, food brokers, importers and exporters.

As for many industry sectors affected by the economic downturn, the food and beverage industry saw prices continue to decline throughout most of 2009. Recent reports from the **Food Institute Report**, however, show that this deflationary period is coming to an end, and food prices for all major categories are seen rising in 2010. Other food and beverage news:

. . . number of new food products declined nearly 30% in 2009 from 2008 levels . . . sales of healthy snack foods and tea on the rise . . . restaurants industry improving . . . store brands more popular . . . digital coupon use increases . . . packaging continues to green . . . roasted ginger and rhubarb is a top flavor pair . . . consumers choosing more ethnic foods . . . pricier organic purchases decline . . .

Data Statistics

Each of the eight chapters in *Food & Beverage Market Place* reflects yearlong research. In addition to the hundreds of new company profiles in this new edition, you will find 87,559 key executives (1,168 more), 36,534 fax numbers (172 more), 26,527 web sites (350 more) and 21,585 e-mails (260 more). Plus, there are thousands of updates throughout all three volumes.

Volume 1   Food, Beverage & Ingredient Manufacturers, 15,898

Volume 2   Equipment, Supply & Service Providers, 13,563

Volume 3   Third Party Logistics
Brokers, 1,465
Importers & Exporters, 10,038
Transportation Firms, 1,018
Warehouse Companies, 1,719
Wholesalers & Distributors, 6,347

As the needs of the population change, this industry – and *Food & Beverage Market Place* –continues to keep pace. Whatever slice of the market you cater to, you will find your buyers, sellers, and users in this comprehensive reference tool – 3 volumes of the complete coverage our subscribers have come to expect. Our extensive indexing makes quick work of locating exactly the company, product or service you are looking for.

The product category sections for both food and beverage products in Volume 1 and equipment and supplies in Volume 2 begin with **Product Category Lists**. Here is where you will find 6,000 alphabetical terms for everything from Abalone to Zinc Citrate, from Adhesive Tapes to Zipper Application Systems. Use the detailed cross-references to find the full entry in the **Product Category** sections that immediately follow. Here you'll find layered categories, for example – **Fish & Seafood: Fish: Abalone** or **Ingredients, Flavors & Additives: Vitamins & Supplements: Zinc Citrate** – with the name, location, phone number and packaging format of companies who manufacturer/process the product you are looking for.

In addition to company profiles, this edition has 19 indexes, 17 chapter-specific, arranged by geographic region, product or company type, and two – **All Brands** and **All Companies** – that comprise all three volumes. See the Table of Contents for a complete list of specific indexes. Plus, chapters include **User Guides** that help you navigate chapter-specific data.

We are confident that this reference is the foremost research tool in the food and beverage industry. It will prove invaluable to manufacturers, buyers, specifiers, market researchers, consultants, and anyone working in food and beverage - one of the largest industries in the country.

Food & Beverage Market Place is also available for subscription on http://gold.greyhouse.com for even faster, easier access to this wealth of information. Subscribers can search by product category, state, sales volume, employee size, personnel name, title and much more. Plus, users can print out prospect sheets or download data into their own spreadsheet or database. This database is a must for anyone marketing a product or service to this vast industry. Visit the site, or call 800-562-2139 for a free trial.

MANUFACTURERS

User Guide
Product Category List
Product Categories
Company Profiles
Brand Name Index
Ethnic Food Index
Geographic Index
Parent/Child Index

Manufacturer User Guide

The **Food & Beverage Manufacturers Chapter** of *Thomas Food & Beverage Market Place* includes companies that manufacture food and beverage products, both finished goods and ingredients. The chapter begins with a **Product Category Listing** of food and beverage products that are manufactured by companies in this chapter. This category list is followed by a **Product Category Index**, organized by product. Each company listing includes packaging type, city and phone number.

Following the **Product Category Index** are the descriptive listings, which are organized alphabetically. Following the A – Z Food and Beverage Manufacturers listings are four indexes: **Brand Index**, which lists food and beverage brand names; **Ethnic Food Index**, which lists companies by ethnic type of food they manufacture; **Geographic Index**, which lists all companies by state, and **Parent Company Index**; which lists companies by their corporate parent. These Indexes refers to listing numbers, not page numbers.

Below is a sample listing illustrating the kind of information that is or might be included in a Food and Beverage Manufacturer listing. Each numbered item of information is described in the User Key on the following page.

---

1 ➤ 100000

2 ➤ **(HQ) AFF Specialties**

3 ➤ 555 Maplewood Drive

Cordova, TN 38016

4 ➤ 001-381-3222

5 ➤ 001-381-3223

6 ➤ 888-381-324

7 ➤ info@AFF.com

8 ➤ www.AFF.com

9 ➤ Manufacturer of Italian cheese and dried pasta and cooking oils. Exporter of olive oil.

10 ➤ President: Brian Miller
CFO: Philip George
COO: Blakeny Pinschell
Vice President: Kristin Rolls
Marketing: Melissa Backwith

11 ➤ *Estimated Sales*: $65 Million

12 ➤ *Number Employees*: 80

13 ➤ *Sq. Footage*: 30000

14 ➤ *Parent Co.*: Associated Foods

15 ➤ *Type of Packaging:* Consumer, Food Service, Bulk

16 ➤ *Company is also listed in the following section(s)*: Exporter

17 ➤ *Other Locations*: AFF Specialties, Atlanta, GA

18 ➤ *Brands:* Unique, Fiesta, Baking Rite, Carruso, Golden Dairy

Manufacturer User Key

1 ➤ **Record Number:** Entries are listed alphabetically within each category and numbered sequentially. The entry number, rather than the page number, is used in the indexes to refer to listings.

2 ➤ **Company Name:** Formal name of company. HQ indicates headquarter location. If names are completely capitalized, the listing will appear at the beginning of the alphabetized section.

3 ➤ **Address:** Location or permanent address of the company. If the mailing address differs from the street address, it will appear second. Companies are indexed by state.

4 ➤ **Phone Number:** The listed phone number is usually for the main office, but may also be for the sales, marketing, or public relations office as provided.

5 ➤ **Fax Number:** This is listed when provided by the company.

6 ➤ **Toll-Free Number:** This is listed when provided by the company.

7 ➤ **E-Mail:** This is listed when provided, and is generally the main office e-mail.

8 ➤ **Web Site:** This is listed when provided by the company and is also referred to as an URL address. These web sites are accessed through the Internet by typing http:// before the URL address.

9 ➤ **Description**: This paragraph contains a brief description of the food and beverages manufactured by the company, as well as other services they provide. Companies are indexed by the ethnic food they manufacture.

10 ➤ **Key Personnel:** Names and titles of company executives.

11 ➤ **Estimated Sales:** This is listed when provided by the company.

12 ➤ **Number of Employees:** Total number of employees within the company.

13 ➤ **Sq. Footage:** Size of facility.

14 ➤ **Parent Co.:** If the listing is a division of another company, the parent is listed here. Companies are indexed by the ethnic foods they manufacture.

15 ➤ **Type of Packaging:** Indicates the market that the food or beverage products are packaged for.

16 ➤ Indicates what other section in *Thomas Food & Beverage Market Place* this company is listed: Volume 1: Manufacturers. Volume 2: Equipment, Supplies & Services; Transportation; Warehouse; Wholesalers/Distributors. Volume 3: Brokers; Importers/Exporters.

17 ➤ **Other locations:** Indicates other company locations.

18 ➤ **Brands:** Listing of brand names that the company manufactures. Companies are indexed by brand names.

A

Abalone Fish *See Fish & Seafood: Fish: Abalone*
Aborio Rice *See Cereals, Grains, Rice & Flour: Rice: Aborio*
Acacia Gum *See Ingredients, Flavors & Additives: Gums: Acacia Gum*
Acetic Acidulants *See Ingredients, Flavors & Additives: Acidulants: Acetic*
Acidophilus Cultures *See Ingredients, Flavors & Additives: Cultures & Yeasts: Acidophilus Cultures*
Acids *See Ingredients, Flavors & Additives: Acids*
Acidulants *See Ingredients, Flavors & Additives: Acidulants*
Acorn Squash *See Fruits & Vegetables: Squash: Acorn*
Active Salt *See Spices, Seasonings & Seeds: Salt: Active*
Additives *See Ingredients, Flavors & Additives: Additives*
Additives Enzymes *See Ingredients, Flavors & Additives: Enzymes: Additives*
Ade Juices *See Beverages: Juices: Ade*
Adipic Acids *See Ingredients, Flavors & Additives: Acids: Adipic*
Adjuncts *See Ingredients, Flavors & Additives: Adjuncts*
Adobo Powders *See Ingredients, Flavors & Additives: Powders: Adobo*
Adzuki Beans *See Fruits & Vegetables: Beans: Adzuki*
Agar-Agar *See Ingredients, Flavors & Additives: Gums: Agar-Agar*
Agents *See Ingredients, Flavors & Additives: Agents*
Agnolotti *See Pasta & Noodles: Agnolotti*
Albacore Tuna Fish *See Fish & Seafood: Fish: Tuna: Albacore*
Albumen Solids *See Eggs & Egg Products: Solids: Albumen*
Alcoholic Beverages *See Beverages: Alcoholic Beverages*
Alcohols *See Ingredients, Flavors & Additives: Alcohols*
Alfalfa *See Cereals, Grains, Rice & Flour: Alfalfa*
Alfalfa Seeds *See Spices, Seasonings & Seeds: Seeds: Alfalfa*
Alfalfa Sprouts *See Fruits & Vegetables: Sprouts: Alfalfa*
Alfredo Sauces *See Sauces, Dips & Dressings: Sauces: Alfredo*
Algae *See Fruits & Vegetables: Algae*
Algin & Alginates *See Ingredients, Flavors & Additives: Gums: Algin & Alginates*
All Purpose Flour *See Cereals, Grains, Rice & Flour: Flour: All Purpose*
All Purpose Herbs Blends *See Ingredients, Flavors & Additives: Blends: Herbs: All Purpose*
Alligator Game *See Meats & Meat Products: Game: Alligator*
Allspice *See Spices, Seasonings & Seeds: Spices: Allspice*
Almond Biscotti *See Baked Goods: Cookies & Bars: Biscotti: Almond*
Almond Cookies *See Baked Goods: Cookies & Bars: Almond Cookies*
Almond Flavors *See Ingredients, Flavors & Additives: Flavors: Almond*
Almond Flour *See Cereals, Grains, Rice & Flour: Flour: Almond*
Almond Nut Butters *See Nuts & Nut Butters: Nut Butters: Almond*
Almond Nut Pastes *See Nuts & Nut Butters: Nut Pastes: Almond*
Almond Oils *See Oils, Shortening & Fats: Oils: Almond*
Almond Pastes *See Ingredients, Flavors & Additives: Pastes: Almond*
Almonds *See Nuts & Nut Butters: Nuts: Almonds*
Aloe Juices *See Beverages: Juices: Aloe*
Aloe Vera *See Fruits & Vegetables: Aloe Vera*
Amaranth *See Cereals, Grains, Rice & Flour: Grains: Amaranth*
Amaretto Cookies *See Baked Goods: Cookies & Bars: Amaretto Cookies*
Amaretto Flavors *See Ingredients, Flavors & Additives: Flavors: Amaretto*
Amaretto Liqueurs & Cordials *See Beverages: Spirits & Liqueurs: Liqueurs & Cordials: Amaretto*
Amber Ale *See Beverages: Beers: American & British Ale: Amber Ale*
Amber Jack *See Fish & Seafood: Fish: Amber Jack*
Amber Lager *See Beverages: Beers: Lager: Amber Lager*
American & British Ale *See Beverages: Beers: American & British Ale*
American Cheese *See Cheese & Cheese Products: Cheese: American*

American Cheese Imitations *See Cheese & Cheese Products: Imitation Cheeses & Substitutes: Imitation: American*
American Cheese Powders *See Ingredients, Flavors & Additives: Powders: Cheese: American*
American Cheese Substitutes *See Cheese & Cheese Products: Imitation Cheeses & Substitutes: Substitutes: American*
American/Skim Milk Cheese, Sliced Blend *See Cheese & Cheese Products: Cheese: Blend - American/Skim Milk: Sliced*
Aminoacetic Acids *See Ingredients, Flavors & Additives: Acids: Aminoacetic*
Ammonium Carbonate *See Ingredients, Flavors & Additives: Ammonium Carbonate*
Ammonium Phosphates *See Ingredients, Flavors & Additives: Phosphates: Ammonium Phosphates*
Analogs *See Ingredients, Flavors & Additives: Analogs*
Ancho Ground Chile Pepper *See Spices, Seasonings & Seeds: Spices: Chile Pepper: Ancho Ground*
Ancho Peppers *See Fruits & Vegetables: Peppers: Ancho*
Anchovies *See Fish & Seafood: Fish: Anchovies*
Anchovies Paste *See Fish & Seafood: Fish: Anchovies: Paste*
Andouille Sausage Seasonings *See Spices, Seasonings & Seeds: Seasonings: Sausage: Andouille*
Andouille Sausages *See Meats & Meat Products: Smoked, Cured & Deli Meats: Sausages: Andouille*
Angel Food Cake *See Baked Goods: Cakes & Pastries: Angel Food Cake*
Angel Hair *See Pasta & Noodles: Angel Hair*
Animal Crackers *See Baked Goods: Cookies & Bars: Animal Crackers*
Anise Flavors *See Ingredients, Flavors & Additives: Flavors: Anise; See also Spices/Anise Seed*
Anise Liqueur *See Beverages: Spirits & Liqueurs: Liqueurs & Cordials: Anise Liqueur*
Anise or Aniseed Oils *See Oils, Shortening & Fats: Oils: Anise or Aniseed*
Anise or Aniseed Seeds *See Spices, Seasonings & Seeds: Seeds: Anise or Aniseed*
Anise, Star *See Spices, Seasonings & Seeds: Spices: Anise - Star*
Annatto Colors *See Ingredients, Flavors & Additives: Colors: Annatto*
Annatto Natural Colors *See Ingredients, Flavors & Additives: Colors: Natural: Annatto*
Annatto Seeds *See Spices, Seasonings & Seeds: Seeds: Annatto*
Anthocyanins Grape Skin *See Ingredients, Flavors & Additives: Colors: Natural: Anthocyanins Grape Skin*
Anticaking Additives *See Ingredients, Flavors & Additives: Additives: Anticaking*
Anticaking Agents *See Ingredients, Flavors & Additives: Agents: Anticaking*
Antimicrobial Agents *See Ingredients, Flavors & Additives: Agents: Antimicrobial*
Antioxidants *See Specialty & Organic Foods: Organic Foods: Natural: Antioxidants; See also See Ingredients, Flavors & Additives: Antioxidants*
Antipasto *See Prepared Foods: Antipasto*
Antipasto Salads *See Prepared Foods: Prepared Salads: Antipasto*
Appaloosa Beans *See Fruits & Vegetables: Beans: Appaloosa*
Appetizers *See Prepared Foods: Appetizers; See also Prepared Foods: Appetizers: Fresh, Canned & Frozen*
Apple *See Fruits & Vegetables: Apple*
Apple Boysin Berry Juices *See Beverages: Juices: Apple Boysin Berry*
Apple Butter *See Jams, Jellies & Spreads: Spreads: Apple Butter*
Apple Cider Juices *See Beverages: Juices: Apple Cider*
Apple Cider Vinegar *See Sauces, Dips & Dressings: Vinegar: Apple Cider*
Apple Cobbler *See Baked Goods: Cakes & Pastries: Apple Cobbler*
Apple Cranberry Juices *See Beverages: Juices: Apple Cranberry*
Apple Flavors *See Ingredients, Flavors & Additives: Flavors: Apple*
Apple Grape Juices *See Beverages: Juices: Apple Grape*
Apple Juices *See Beverages: Juices: Apple*
Apple Pectins *See Ingredients, Flavors & Additives: Pectins: Apple*

Apple Pies *See Baked Goods: Pies: Apple*
Apple Rings *See Fruits & Vegetables: Apple: Rings*
Apple Sauces *See Fruits & Vegetables: Sauces: Apple*
Apple Sauces with Other Fruit or Spices *See Fruits & Vegetables: Sauces: Apple: with Other Fruit or Spices*
Apple Slices *See Fruits & Vegetables: Apple: Slices*
Apricot *See Fruits & Vegetables: Apricot*
Apricot Jams *See Jams, Jellies & Spreads: Jams: Apricot*
Apricot Juices *See Beverages: Juices: Apricot*
Apricot Kernals *See Fruits & Vegetables: Apricot: Kernals*
Aquaculture *See Specialty & Organic Foods: Aquaculture*
Arabic *See Ingredients, Flavors & Additives: Arabic*
Arctic Charr *See Fish & Seafood: Fish: Arctic Charr*
Ardouille Sausage *See Meats & Meat Products: Pork & Pork Products: Sausage: Ardouille*
Aroma Chemicals & Materials *See Ingredients, Flavors & Additives: Aroma Chemicals & Materials; See also See Ingredients, Flavors & Additives: Aroma Chemicals; See also See Ingredients, Flavors & Additives: Aroma Chemicals & Materials: Materials*
Arrowroot Flour *See Cereals, Grains, Rice & Flour: Flour: Arrowroot*
Arrowroot Starches *See Ingredients, Flavors & Additives: Starches: Arrowroot*
Arrowroot Thickening Agents *See Ingredients, Flavors & Additives: Agents: Thickening: Arrowroot*
Artichoke *See Fruits & Vegetables: Artichoke*
Artificial Flavors *See Ingredients, Flavors & Additives: Flavors: Artificial*
Artificial Sweeteners *See Sugars, Syrups & Sweeteners: Artificial*
Ascorbic Acid *See Ingredients, Flavors & Additives: Antioxidants: Ascorbic Acid; See also See Ingredients, Flavors & Additives: Vitamins & Supplements: C: Ascorbic Acid*
Aseptic Packed Capsicums Peppers *See Fruits & Vegetables: Peppers: Capsicums: Aseptic Packed*
Asiago Cheese *See Cheese & Cheese Products: Cheese: Asiago*
Asian *See Ethnic Foods: Asian*
Asian Pear *See Fruits & Vegetables: Pear: Asian*
Asparagus *See Fruits & Vegetables: Asparagus*
Aspartame *See Sugars, Syrups & Sweeteners: Sugar Substitutes: Aspartame*
Au Gratin Potatoes *See Fruits & Vegetables: Potatoes: Au Gratin*
Autolysates Yeast *See Ingredients, Flavors & Additives: Cultures & Yeasts: Yeast: Autolysates*
Avocado *See Fruits & Vegetables: Avocado*
Avocado Oils *See Oils, Shortening & Fats: Oils: Avocado*
Avocado Products *See Fruits & Vegetables: Avocado: Avocado Products*

B

Babka *See Baked Goods: Cakes & Pastries: Babka*
Baby Carrot *See Fruits & Vegetables: Carrot: Baby*
Baby Spinach *See Fruits & Vegetables: Spinach: Baby*
Bacillus Cultures *See Ingredients, Flavors & Additives: Cultures & Yeasts: Bacillus*
Bacon *See Meats & Meat Products: Smoked, Cured & Deli Meats: Bacon*
Bacon Pork Rinds *See Snack Foods: Pork Rinds: Bacon*
Bacon Slices *See Meats & Meat Products: Smoked, Cured & Deli Meats: Bacon: Slices*
Bacteria *See Ingredients, Flavors & Additives: Cultures & Yeasts: Bacteria*
Bacterial Cultures, Starter Media & Culture Replacements *See Ingredients, Flavors & Additives: Cultures & Yeasts: Bacterial Cultures, Starter Media & Culture Replacements*
Bacteriological Cultures & Yeasts *See Ingredients, Flavors & Additives: Cultures & Yeasts: Bacteriological*
Bagel Chips *See Snack Foods: Chips: Bagel Chips*
Bagels *See Baked Goods: Breads: Bagels*
Bagged Parboiled Rice *See Cereals, Grains, Rice & Flour: Rice: Parboiled: Bagged*
Bagged Specialty-Packaged Candy *See Candy & Confectionery: Specialty-Packaged Candy: Bagged*
Bagged Wheat *See Cereals, Grains, Rice & Flour: Wheat: Bagged*
Baguettes *See Baked Goods: Breads: Baguettes*
Baita Fruli Cheese *See Cheese & Cheese Products: Cheese: Baita Fruli*
Baked & Stuffed Potatoes *See Fruits & Vegetables: Potatoes: Baked & Stuffed*

EXAMPLE: Canadian Style Bacon *See Meats & Meat Products: Smoked, Cured & Deli Meats: Bacon: Canadian Style*

1. Product or Service you are looking for
2. Main Category, in alphabetical order, located in the page headers starting on page 23
3. Category Description, located in black bars and in page headers
4. Product Category, located in gray bars
5. Product Type, located under gray bars, centered in bold

Baked Beans *See Prepared Foods: Baked Beans (see also Pork & Beans); See also Fruits & Vegetables: Beans: Baked*

Baked Chips *See Snack Foods: Chips: Baked*

Baked Goods *See Baked Goods*

Baked Potato Chips *See Snack Foods: Chips: Potato: Baked*

Bakers Active Yeast *See Ingredients, Flavors & Additives: Cultures & Yeasts: Yeast: Bakers Active*

Bakers Cheese Powders *See Ingredients, Flavors & Additives: Powders: Cheese: Bakers*

Bakers' & Confectioners' Supplies *See Ingredients, Flavors & Additives: Confectionery: Bakers' & Confectioners' Supplies*

Bakers' Yeast *See Ingredients, Flavors & Additives: Cultures & Yeasts: Yeast: Bakers'*

Bakery Ingredients *See Ingredients, Flavors & Additives: Ingredients: Bakery*

Bakery Mix Flour *See Cereals, Grains, Rice & Flour: Flour: Bakery Mix*

Baking Bits *See Ingredients, Flavors & Additives: Bits: Baking*

Baking Chocolate *See Candy & Confectionery: Chocolate Products: Baking Chocolate*

Baking Decorations *See Candy & Confectionery: Decorations & Icings: Decorations: Baking*

Baking Doughs *See Doughs, Mixes & Fillings: Doughs: Baking*

Baking Fillings *See Doughs, Mixes & Fillings: Fillings: Baking*

Baking Mixes *See Doughs, Mixes & Fillings: Mixes: Baking*

Baking Mixes Flour *See Cereals, Grains, Rice & Flour: Flour: Baking Mixes*

Baking Powders *See Ingredients, Flavors & Additives: Powders: Baking*

Baking Seasonings *See Spices, Seasonings & Seeds: Seasonings: Baking*

Baking Shells *See Baked Goods: Pies: Baking Shells*

Baking Soda *See Ingredients, Flavors & Additives: Leaveners: Baking Soda*

Baklava *See Baked Goods: Cakes & Pastries: Baklava*

Balsamic Vinegar *See Sauces, Dips & Dressings: Vinegar: Balsamic*

Balsamic Vinegar Salad Dressings *See Sauces, Dips & Dressings: Salad Dressings: Balsamic Vinegar*

Bamboo Shoots *See Fruits & Vegetables: Bamboo Shoots*

Banana *See Fruits & Vegetables: Banana*

Banana Chips *See Snack Foods: Chips: Banana*

Banana Flakes *See Ingredients, Flavors & Additives: Flakes: Banana*

Banana Flavors *See Ingredients, Flavors & Additives: Flavors: Banana*

Banana Peppers *See Fruits & Vegetables: Peppers: Banana*

Banana Products *See Fruits & Vegetables: Banana: Banana Products*

Bar Mixers *See Beverages: Mixers: Bar Mixers*

Bar Syrups *See Sugars, Syrups & Sweeteners: Syrups: Bar*

Barbecue Potato Chips *See Snack Foods: Chips: Potato: Barbecue*

Barbecue Products *See Specialty Processed Foods: Barbecue Products (See also Specific Foods)*

Barbecue Sauces *See Sauces, Dips & Dressings: Sauces: Barbecue*

Barbecue Seasonings *See Spices, Seasonings & Seeds: Seasonings: Barbecue*

Barbecued Beef *See Meats & Meat Products: Beef & Beef Products: Barbecued*

Barbecued Chicken *See Meats & Meat Products: Poultry: Chicken: Barbecued*

Barbecued Chicken, Frozen *See Meats & Meat Products: Poultry: Chicken: Barbecued Frozen*

Barbecued Pork *See Meats & Meat Products: Pork & Pork Products: Barbecued*

Barley *See Cereals, Grains, Rice & Flour: Barley*

Barley Bran Fiber *See Cereals, Grains, Rice & Flour: Fiber: Barley Bran*

Barley Flour *See Cereals, Grains, Rice & Flour: Flour: Barley*

Bars, Cereal *See Cereals, Grains, Rice & Flour: Cereal: Bars*

Bars, Cookies *See Baked Goods: Cookies & Bars: Bars*

Bartlett Pear *See Fruits & Vegetables: Pear: Bartlett*

Bases *See Ingredients, Flavors & Additives: Bases*

Bases, Ice Cream *See Dairy Products: Ice Cream: Bases*

Basil Leaf *See Spices, Seasonings & Seeds: Spices: Basil Leaf*

Basil Spices *See Spices, Seasonings & Seeds: Spices: Basil*

Basmati Rice *See Cereals, Grains, Rice & Flour: Rice: Basmati*

Bass *See Fish & Seafood: Fish: Bass*

Batters *See Doughs, Mixes & Fillings: Batters*

Bay Leaves *See Spices, Seasonings & Seeds: Spices: Bay Leaves*

Bean Dips *See Sauces, Dips & Dressings: Dips: Bean*

Bean Flour *See Cereals, Grains, Rice & Flour: Flour: Bean*

Bean Oils *See Oils, Shortening & Fats: Oils: Bean*

Bean Sprouts *See Fruits & Vegetables: Sprouts: Bean*

Beans *See Fruits & Vegetables: Beans*

Bearnaise Sauces *See Sauces, Dips & Dressings: Sauces: Bearnaise*

Bee Pollen & Propolis *See Sugars, Syrups & Sweeteners: Honey: Bee Pollen & Propolis*

Beech Mushrooms *See Fruits & Vegetables: Mushrooms: Beech*

Beef & Beef Products *See Meats & Meat Products: Beef & Beef Products*

Beef & Beef Products, Sliced *See Meats & Meat Products: Beef & Beef Products: Sliced*

Beef & Beef Products, Special Trim *See Meats & Meat Products: Beef & Beef Products: Special Trim*

Beef Bases *See Ingredients, Flavors & Additives: Bases: Beef*

Beef Bouillon *See Ingredients, Flavors & Additives: Bases: Bouillon: Beef*

Beef Casings *See Meats & Meat Products: Smoked, Cured & Deli Meats: Sausages: Casings: Sausage, Pork, Beef*

Beef Certified Organic *See Specialty & Organic Foods: Organic Foods: Certified: Beef*

Beef Dinners *See Meats & Meat Products: Beef & Beef Products: Dinners*

Beef Dinners, Prepared Meals *See Prepared Foods: Prepared Meals: Beef Dinner*

Beef Extracts *See Ingredients, Flavors & Additives: Extracts: Beef*

Beef Frankfurters *See Meats & Meat Products: Frankfurters: Beef*

Beef Jerky *See Meats & Meat Products: Smoked, Cured & Deli Meats: Beef Jerky*

Beef Marinades *See Sauces, Dips & Dressings: Marinades: Beef*

Beef Soup *See Prepared Foods: Soups & Stews: Beef Soup*

Beef Stew *See Meats & Meat Products: Beef & Beef Products: Stew; See also See Prepared Foods: Soups & Stews: Beef Stew*

Beef Stock Powders *See Ingredients, Flavors & Additives: Powders: Beef Stock*

Beef, Frozen Rolls *See Meats & Meat Products: Beef & Beef Products: Rolls - Frozen*

Beer Flavors *See Ingredients, Flavors & Additives: Flavors: Beer*

Beers *See Beverages: Beers*

Bees Wax *See Sugars, Syrups & Sweeteners: Honey: Bees Wax*

Beet Jellies *See Jams, Jellies & Spreads: Jellies: Beets*

Beet Juices *See Beverages: Juices: Beet*

Beet Powder *See Fruits & Vegetables: Dried & Dehydrated Vegetables: Beet Powder*

Beet Relishes *See Relishes & Pickled Products: Relishes: Beets*

Beets *See Fruits & Vegetables: Beets*

Belgian & French Ale *See Beverages: Beers: Belgian & French Ale*

Bell Peppers *See Fruits & Vegetables: Peppers: Bell*

Bell Peppers, Dehydrated *See Fruits & Vegetables: Dried & Dehydrated Vegetables: Bell Peppers*

Benzoate of Soda *See Ingredients, Flavors & Additives: Benzoate of Soda*

Benzoic Acids *See Ingredients, Flavors & Additives: Acids: Benzoic*

Berries *See Fruits & Vegetables: Berries*

Berries, Frozen *See Fruits & Vegetables: Frozen Fruit: Berries*

Beta Carotene *See Ingredients, Flavors & Additives: Vitamins & Supplements: Beta Carotene*

Betaine Beet *See Ingredients, Flavors & Additives: Colors: Natural: Betaine Beet*

Beverage Bases *See Ingredients, Flavors & Additives: Bases: Beverage*

Beverage Extracts *See Ingredients, Flavors & Additives: Extracts: Beverages*

Beverage Flavors *See Ingredients, Flavors & Additives: Flavors: Beverage*

Beverage Mixes *See Doughs, Mixes & Fillings: Mixes: Beverage*

Beverage Powders *See Ingredients, Flavors & Additives: Powders: Beverage*

Beverage Syrups *See Sugars, Syrups & Sweeteners: Syrups: Beverages*

Beverages *See Beverages*

Bialys *See Baked Goods: Breads: Bialys*

Binders *See Ingredients, Flavors & Additives: Binders*

Binders for Meat Products *See Ingredients, Flavors & Additives: Binders: for Meat Products*

Bing Cherries *See Fruits & Vegetables: Cherries: Bing*

Bioflavinoids *See Ingredients, Flavors & Additives: Bioflavinoids*

Biopolymers *See Ingredients, Flavors & Additives: Biopolymers*

Biotin *See Ingredients, Flavors & Additives: Vitamins & Supplements: Biotin*

Biscotti *See Baked Goods: Cookies & Bars: Biscotti*

Biscuit Mixes *See Doughs, Mixes & Fillings: Mixes: Biscuit*

Biscuits *See Baked Goods: Breads: Biscuits*

Bits *See Ingredients, Flavors & Additives: Bits*

Bits, Imitation Bacon *See Meats & Meat Products: Smoked, Cured & Deli Meats: Bacon: Bits Imitation*

Bits, Real Bacon *See Meats & Meat Products: Smoked, Cured & Deli Meats: Bacon: Bits Real*

Bitters *See Beverages: Bitters*

Black & Tan Ale *See Beverages: Beers: American & British Ale: Black & Tan*

Black Bean Sauces *See Sauces, Dips & Dressings: Sauces: Black Bean*

Black Beans *See Fruits & Vegetables: Beans: Black*

Black Cod Fish *See Fish & Seafood: Fish: Cod: Black*

Black Currant Tea *See Beverages: Coffee & Tea: Tea: Black Currant*

Black Forest Ham *See Meats & Meat Products: Smoked, Cured & Deli Meats: Ham: Black Forest*

Black Olives *See Fruits & Vegetables: Olives: Black*

Black Pepper *See Spices, Seasonings & Seeds: Spices: Pepper: Black - White - Red; See also See Spices, Seasonings & Seeds - Spices: Black Pepper - Ground*

Black Pepper Oils *See Oils, Shortening & Fats: Oils: Black Pepper*

Black Puinoa Rice *See Cereals, Grains, Rice & Flour: Rice: Black Puinoa*

Black Sesame Seeds *See Spices, Seasonings & Seeds: Seeds: Sesame: Black*

Black Sliced Truffles *See Fruits & Vegetables: Mushrooms: Truffles: Black Sliced*

Black Tea *See Beverages: Coffee & Tea: Tea: Black*

Black Thai Rice *See Cereals, Grains, Rice & Flour: Rice: Black Thai*

Black Tiger Shrimp *See Fish & Seafood: Shellfish: Shrimp: Black Tiger*

Black Trumpet Mushrooms *See Fruits & Vegetables: Mushrooms: Black Trumpet*

Black Trumpet Mushrooms, Dehydrated *See Fruits & Vegetables: Dried & Dehydrated Vegetables: Mushrooms: Black Trumpets*

Black Walnuts *See Nuts & Nut Butters: Nuts: Walnuts: Black*

Black Whole Truffles *See Fruits & Vegetables: Mushrooms: Truffles: Black Whole*

Black-eyed Peas *See Fruits & Vegetables: Peas: Black-eyed*

Blackberry *See Fruits & Vegetables: Berries: Blackberry*

Blackberry Flavors *See Ingredients, Flavors & Additives: Flavors: Blackberry*

Blackening Seasonings *See Spices, Seasonings & Seeds: Seasonings: Blackening*

Blackeye Beans *See Fruits & Vegetables: Beans: Blackeye (Cowpeas)*

Blended Scotch Whiskey *See Beverages: Spirits & Liqueurs: Scotch Whiskey: Blended*

Blends *See Ingredients, Flavors & Additives: Blends*

Blends, Butter *See Dairy Products: Butter: Blends*

Blends, Corn Syrups *See Sugars, Syrups & Sweeteners: Syrups: Corn: Blends*

Blintzes *See Baked Goods: Cakes & Pastries: Blintzes*

Blood Orange *See Fruits & Vegetables: Orange: Blood*

Blood Orange Juice *See Beverages: Juices: Orange: Blood*

Blood Sausages *See Meats & Meat Products: Smoked, Cured & Deli Meats: Sausages: Blood*

Blue Cheese *See Cheese & Cheese Products: Cheese: Blue*

Blue Cheese Salad Dressings *See Sauces, Dips & Dressings: Salad Dressings: Blue Cheese*

Blue Cheese Salad Dressings, Mixes *See Sauces, Dips & Dressings: Salad Dressings: Mixes: Blue Cheese*

Blue Crab *See Fish & Seafood: Shellfish: Crab: Blue*

Blue Lake Beans *See Fruits & Vegetables: Beans: Blue Lake*

Blueberry *See Fruits & Vegetables: Berries: Blueberry*

Blueberry Flavors *See Ingredients, Flavors & Additives: Flavors: Blueberry*

Blueberry Juices *See Beverages: Juices: Blueberry*

Blueberry Pies *See Baked Goods: Pies: Blueberry*

Bluefish *See Fish & Seafood: Fish: Bluefish*

Boar *See Meats & Meat Products: Game: Boar*

Bock Lager *See Beverages: Beers: Lager: Bock*

Bockwurst Sausages *See Meats & Meat Products: Smoked, Cured & Deli Meats: Sausages: Bockwurst*

Boiled Eggs *See Eggs & Egg Products: Boiled*

Bok Choy Cabbage *See Fruits & Vegetables: Cabbage: Bok Choy*

Boletes Mushrooms *See Fruits & Vegetables: Mushrooms: Boletes*

Bologna Smoked, Cured & Deli Meats *See Meats & Meat Products: Smoked, Cured & Deli Meats: Bologna*

Bon Bons *See Candy & Confectionery: Candy: Bon Bons*

Boned Herring *See Fish & Seafood: Fish: Herring: Boned*

Borage Oils *See Oils, Shortening & Fats: Oils: Borage*

Bordeaux Vinegar *See Sauces, Dips & Dressings: Vinegar: Bordeaux*

Boric/Boracic Acids *See Ingredients, Flavors & Additives: Acids: Boric/Boracic*

Borscht *See Prepared Foods: Soups & Stews: Borscht*

Bosc Pear *See Fruits & Vegetables: Pear: Bosc*

Boston Butterhead Lettuce *See Fruits & Vegetables: Lettuce: Butterhead: Boston*

Botanical Extracts *See Ingredients, Flavors & Additives: Extracts: Botanical*

Bottled Apple Juices *See Beverages: Juices: Apple: Bottled*

Bottled Beers *See Beverages: Beers: Bottled*

Bottled Cherry Juices *See Beverages: Juices: Cherry: Bottled*

Bottled Cranberry Juices *See Beverages: Juices: Cranberry: Bottled*

Bottled Fruit & Vegetable Juices *See Beverages: Juices: Fruit & Vegetable: Bottled*

Bottled Fruit Juices *See Beverages: Juices: Fruit: Bottled*

Bottled Grape Juices *See Beverages: Juices: Grape: Bottled*

Bottled Grapefruit Juices *See Beverages: Juices: Grapefruit: Bottled*

Bottled Lemon Juices *See Beverages: Juices: Lemon: Bottled*

Bottled Water *See Beverages: Water: Bottled*

Bottomfish *See Fish & Seafood: Fish: Bottomfish*

Boudin Sausages *See Meats & Meat Products: Smoked, Cured & Deli Meats: Sausages: Boudin*

Bouillon Bases *See Ingredients, Flavors & Additives: Bases: Bouillon*

Bourbon Whiskey *See Beverages: Spirits & Liqueurs: Whiskey, American: Bourbon*

Bows *See Pasta & Noodles: Bows*

Boxed Apple Juices *See Beverages: Juices: Apple: Boxed*

Boxed Cherry Juices *See Beverages: Juices: Cherry: Boxed*

Boxed Chocolate *See Candy & Confectionery: Chocolate Products: Boxed Chocolate*

Boxed Cranberry Juices *See Beverages: Juices: Cranberry: Boxed*

Boxed Grape Juices *See Beverages: Juices: Grape: Boxed*

Boxed Grapefruit Juices *See Beverages: Juices: Grapefruit: Boxed*

Boxed Pineapple Juices *See Beverages: Juices: Pineapple: Boxed*

Boxed Specialty-Packaged Candy *See Candy & Confectionery: Specialty-Packaged Candy: Boxed*

Boxed Specialty-Packaged Candy, Non-Chocolate *See Candy & Confectionery: Specialty-Packaged Candy: Non-Chocolate - Boxed*

Boxed Tomato Juices *See Beverages: Juices: Tomato: Boxed*

Boysenberry *See Fruits & Vegetables: Berries: Boysenberry*

Bra Cheese *See Cheese & Cheese Products: Cheese: Bra*

Bran *See Cereals, Grains, Rice & Flour: Bran*

Brandied Fruits *See Fruits & Vegetables: Brandied Fruits*

Brandy *See Beverages: Spirits & Liqueurs: Brandy*

Brandy Liqueur *See Beverages: Spirits & Liqueurs: Liqueurs & Cordials: Brandy Liqueur*

Bratwurst *See Meats & Meat Products: Smoked, Cured & Deli Meats: Bratwurst*

Bratwurst Sausages *See Meats & Meat Products: Smoked, Cured & Deli Meats: Sausages: Bratwurst*

Braunschweiger Sausages *See Meats & Meat Products: Smoked, Cured & Deli Meats: Sausages: Braunschweiger*

Brazil Nuts *See Nuts & Nut Butters: Nuts: Brazil*

Bread Crumbs & Croutons *See Baked Goods: Bread Crumbs & Croutons; See also Baked Goods: Bread Crumbs & Croutons: Bread Crumbs*

Bread Doughs *See Doughs, Mixes & Fillings: Doughs: Bread*

Bread Mixes *See Doughs, Mixes & Fillings: Mixes: Bread*

Bread Sticks *See Baked Goods: Bread Sticks*

Bread Stuffing *See Baked Goods: Stuffing: Bread*

Bread, Wheat *See Cereals, Grains, Rice & Flour: Wheat: Bread*

Breaded Chicken *See Meats & Meat Products: Poultry: Chicken: Breaded*

Breaded Clam Strips *See Fish & Seafood: Shellfish: Clam: Breaded Strips*

Breaded Frozen Veal *See Meats & Meat Products: Beef & Beef Products: Veal: Breaded Frozen*

Breaded Pork *See Meats & Meat Products: Pork & Pork Products: Breaded*

Breaded Shrimp *See Fish & Seafood: Shellfish: Shrimp: Breaded*

Breaded Vegetables *See Prepared Foods: Breaded Vegetables*

Breading *See Doughs, Mixes & Fillings: Breading*

Breading Batters *See Doughs, Mixes & Fillings: Batters: Breading*

Breading Mixes *See Doughs, Mixes & Fillings: Mixes: Breading*

Breads *See Baked Goods: Breads*

Breakfast Cereal *See Cereals, Grains, Rice & Flour: Cereal: Breakfast*

Breakfast, Instant *See Prepared Foods: Breakfast Foods: Instant*

Breakfast, Prepared Meals *See Prepared Foods: Prepared Meals: Breakfast*

Breast Turkey *See Meats & Meat Products: Poultry: Turkey: Breast*

Breath Tablets *See Candy & Confectionery: Candy: Breath Tablets*

Brewers' Active Yeast *See Ingredients, Flavors & Additives: Cultures & Yeasts: Yeast: Brewers Active*

Brewers' Rice *See Cereals, Grains, Rice & Flour: Rice: Brewers'*

Brewers' Yeast *See Ingredients, Flavors & Additives: Cultures & Yeasts: Yeast: Brewers'*

Brewing Adjuncts *See Ingredients, Flavors & Additives: Adjuncts: Brewing*

Brie *See Cheese & Cheese Products: Cheese: Brie*

Brisket of Beef *See Meats & Meat Products: Beef & Beef Products: Brisket*

Brittles *See Candy & Confectionery: Candy: Brittles*

Broad Beans *See Fruits & Vegetables: Beans: Broad*

Broccoli *See Fruits & Vegetables: Broccoli*

Broccoli & Cauliflower Mixed Vegetables *See Fruits & Vegetables: Vegetables Mixed: Broccoli & Cauliflower*

Broccoli, Dried *See Fruits & Vegetables: Dried & Dehydrated Vegetables: Broccoli*

Broccoli, Peas & Carrots Mixed Vegetables *See Fruits & Vegetables: Vegetables Mixed: Broccoli, Peas & Carrots*

Broilers *See Meats & Meat Products: Poultry: Chicken: Broilers*

Brook Trout *See Fish & Seafood: Fish: Trout: Brook*

Broth *See Prepared Foods: Broth*

Broth Powders *See Ingredients, Flavors & Additives: Powders: Broth*

Brown Bettys *See Baked Goods: Cakes & Pastries: Brown Bettys*

Brown Breads *See Baked Goods: Breads: Brown*

Brown Mustard *See Sauces, Dips & Dressings: Mustard: Brown*

Brown Rice *See Cereals, Grains, Rice & Flour: Rice: Brown*

Brown Rice Crisps *See Cereals, Grains, Rice & Flour: Crisps: Brown Rice*

Brown Sugar *See Sugars, Syrups & Sweeteners: Sugar: Brown*

Brownie Mixes *See Doughs, Mixes & Fillings: Mixes: Brownie*

Brownie Pies *See Baked Goods: Pies: Brownie*

Brownies with Nuts *See Baked Goods: Cookies & Bars: Brownies: with Nuts*

Brownies, Baking Mixes *See Doughs, Mixes & Fillings: Mixes: Baking: Brownies*

Brownies, Cookies & Bars *See Baked Goods: Cookies & Bars: Brownies*

Brussel Sprouts *See Fruits & Vegetables: Brussel Sprouts*

Buckwheat Flour *See Cereals, Grains, Rice & Flour: Flour: Buckwheat*

Buffalo *See Meats & Meat Products: Game: Buffalo*

Bulgar Wheat *See Cereals, Grains, Rice & Flour: Wheat: Bulgar*

Bulk Wines *See Beverages: Wines: Bulk*

Bulking Additives *See Ingredients, Flavors & Additives: Additives: Bulking*

Bulking Agents *See Ingredients, Flavors & Additives: Agents: Bulking*

Buns *See Baked Goods: Breads: Buns*

Burgers, Veal *See Meats & Meat Products: Beef & Beef Products: Veal: Burgers*

Burgers, Vegetarian *See Specialty & Organic Foods: Vegetarian Products: Burgers*

Burnt Sugar Colors *See Ingredients, Flavors & Additives: Colors: Burnt Sugar*

Burritos *See Ethnic Foods: Burritos*

Burritos, Prepared Meals *See Prepared Foods: Prepared Meals: Burritos*

Butter *See Dairy Products: Butter*

Butter & Cheese Colors *See Ingredients, Flavors & Additives: Colors: Butter & Cheese*

Butter Beans *See Fruits & Vegetables: Beans: Butter*

Butter, Flavors *See Ingredients, Flavors & Additives: Flavors: Butter*

Butter, Honey *See Sugars, Syrups & Sweeteners: Honey: Butter*

Butter, Maple Flavors *See Ingredients, Flavors & Additives: Flavors: Maple: Butter*

Butter, Maple Sugar *See Sugars, Syrups & Sweeteners: Sugar: Maple: Butter*

Butter, Milk Flavors *See Ingredients, Flavors & Additives: Flavors: Milk: Butter*

Butter, Snack Seasonings *See Spices, Seasonings & Seeds: Seasonings: Snack: Butter*

Butter, Toffee Rum Flavors *See Ingredients, Flavors & Additives: Flavors: Rum: Butter Toffee*

Butterfish *See Fish & Seafood: Fish: Butterfish*

Butterhead Lettuce *See Fruits & Vegetables: Lettuce: Butterhead*

Buttermilk *See Dairy Products: Buttermilk & Buttermilk Products: Buttermilk*

Buttermilk & Buttermilk Products *See Dairy Products: Buttermilk & Buttermilk Products*

Buttermilk Bacteria *See Ingredients, Flavors & Additives: Cultures & Yeasts: Bacteria: Buttermilk*

Buttermilk Flavors *See Ingredients, Flavors & Additives: Flavors: Buttermilk*

Buttermilk Powders *See Ingredients, Flavors & Additives: Powders: Buttermilk*

Buttermilk Products *See Dairy Products: Buttermilk & Buttermilk Products: Buttermilk Products*

Butterscotch Candy *See Candy & Confectionery: Candy: Butterscotch*

Butterscotch Flavors *See Ingredients, Flavors & Additives: Flavors: Butterscotch*

C

Cabbage *See Fruits & Vegetables: Cabbage*

Cabbage Flakes *See Fruits & Vegetables: Dried & Dehydrated Vegetables: Cabbage Flakes*

Cabbage Seeds *See Spices, Seasonings & Seeds: Seeds: Cabbage*

Cabernet Sauvignon *See Beverages: Wines: Red Grape Wines: Cabernet Sauvignon*

Cacciatore Sausages *See Meats & Meat Products: Smoked, Cured & Deli Meats: Sausages: Cacciatore*

Caciotta Cheese *See Cheese & Cheese Products: Cheese: Caciotta*

Cactus *See Fruits & Vegetables: Cactus*

Caffeine *See Ingredients, Flavors & Additives: Caffeine*

Cajeta Flavors *See Ingredients, Flavors & Additives: Flavors: Cajeta*

Cajun Fried Porkskins *See Prepared Foods: Porkskins: Fried: Cajun*

Cajun Sausages *See Meats & Meat Products: Smoked, Cured & Deli Meats: Sausages: Cajun*

Cajun Spice Snack Seasonings *See Spices, Seasonings & Seeds: Seasonings: Snack: Cajun Spice*

Cajun Style Seasonings *See Spices, Seasonings & Seeds: Seasonings: Cajun Style*

Cake Batters *See Doughs, Mixes & Fillings: Batters: Cake*

Cake Decorations *See Candy & Confectionery: Decorations & Icings: Decorations: Cake*

Cake Fillings *See Doughs, Mixes & Fillings: Fillings: Cake*

Cake Flour *See Cereals, Grains, Rice & Flour: Flour: Cake*

Cake Icings *See Candy & Confectionery: Decorations & Icings: Icings: Cake*

Cake Mixes *See Doughs, Mixes & Fillings: Mixes: Cake*

Cakes *See Baked Goods: Cakes & Pastries: Cakes*

1	2	3	4	5

EXAMPLE: Canadian Style Bacon *See Meats & Meat Products: Smoked, Cured & Deli Meats: Bacon: Canadian Style*

1. Product or Service you are looking for
2. Main Category, in alphabetical order, located in the page headers starting on page 23
3. Category Description, located in black bars and in page headers
4. Product Category, located in gray bars
5. Product Type, located under gray bars, centered in bold

Product Category List

Cakes & Donut Toppings *See Ingredients, Flavors & Additives: Toppings: Cakes & Donuts*

Cakes & Pastries *See Baked Goods: Cakes & Pastries*

Cakes, Crab *See Fish & Seafood: Shellfish: Crab: Cakes*

Cakes, Fish *See Fish & Seafood: Fish: Cakes*

Cakes, Frozen Crab *See Fish & Seafood: Shellfish: Crab: Cakes Frozen*

Calcium *See Ingredients, Flavors & Additives: Vitamins & Supplements: Calcium*

Calcium & Nutritionally Fortified Pellets *See Ingredients, Flavors & Additives: Half-Products: Calcium & Nutritionally Fortified Pellets*

Calcium Phosphate *See Ingredients, Flavors & Additives: Phosphates: Calcium Phosphate*

Camembert *See Cheese & Cheese Products: Cheese: Camembert*

Canadian Style Bacon *See Meats & Meat Products: Smoked, Cured & Deli Meats: Bacon: Canadian Style*

Candied Fruits *See Fruits & Vegetables: Candied Fruits*

Candy *See Candy & Confectionery: Candy*

Candy Bars *See Candy & Confectionery: Candy: Candy Bars*

Candy Canes *See Candy & Confectionery: Candy: Canes*

Candy Coatings *See Candy & Confectionery: Candy Coatings*

Candy Makers' Waxes *See Ingredients, Flavors & Additives: Waxes: Candy Makers'*

Cane Sugar *See Sugars, Syrups & Sweeteners: Sugar: Cane*

Cane Syrup *See Sugars, Syrups & Sweeteners: Syrups: Cane*

Caneberries *See Fruits & Vegetables: Caneberries*

Canned & Frozen Chili *See Prepared Foods: Chili: Canned & Frozen*

Canned & Frozen Collard Greens *See Fruits & Vegetables: Collard Greens: Canned & Frozen*

Canned & Frozen Corn *See Fruits & Vegetables: Corn: Canned & Frozen*

Canned & Frozen Enchiladas *See Ethnic Foods: Enchiladas: Canned & Frozen*

Canned & Frozen Guava *See Fruits & Vegetables: Guava: Canned & Frozen*

Canned & Frozen Hash *See Prepared Foods: Hash: Canned & Frozen*

Canned & Frozen Mustard Greens *See Fruits & Vegetables: Mustard: Greens: Canned & Frozen*

Canned & Frozen Tomato Pastes *See Ingredients, Flavors & Additives: Pastes: Tomato: Canned & Frozen*

Canned Anchovies *See Fish & Seafood: Fish: Anchovies: Canned*

Canned Apple *See Fruits & Vegetables: Apple: Canned*

Canned Apple Juices *See Beverages: Juices: Apple: Canned*

Canned Apple Sauces *See Fruits & Vegetables: Sauces: Apple: Canned*

Canned Apple Slices *See Fruits & Vegetables: Apple: Slices: Canned*

Canned Apricot *See Fruits & Vegetables: Apricot: Canned*

Canned Apricot Juices *See Beverages: Juices: Apricot: Canned*

Canned Artichoke *See Fruits & Vegetables: Artichoke: Canned*

Canned Asparagus *See Fruits & Vegetables: Asparagus: Canned*

Canned Baked Beans *See Prepared Foods: Baked Beans (see also Pork & Beans): Canned*

Canned Beans *See Fruits & Vegetables: Beans: Canned*

Canned Beef with Natural Juices *See Meats & Meat Products: Beef & Beef Products: Canned with Natural Juices*

Canned Beers *See Beverages: Beers: Canned*

Canned Beets *See Fruits & Vegetables: Beets: Canned*

Canned Berries *See Fruits & Vegetables: Berries: Canned*

Canned Black-eyed Peas *See Fruits & Vegetables: Peas: Black-eyed: Canned*

Canned Blue Lake Beans *See Fruits & Vegetables: Beans: Blue Lake: Canned*

Canned Blueberry *See Fruits & Vegetables: Berries: Blueberry: Canned*

Canned Boned Chicken *See Meats & Meat Products: Poultry: Chicken: Canned Boned*

Canned Boysenberry *See Fruits & Vegetables: Berries: Boysenberry: Canned*

Canned Broth *See Prepared Foods: Broth: Canned, Frozen, Powdered*

Canned Brussel Sprouts *See Fruits & Vegetables: Brussel Sprouts: Canned*

Canned Butter Beans *See Fruits & Vegetables: Beans: Butter: Canned*

Canned Cabbage *See Fruits & Vegetables: Cabbage: Canned*

Canned Carrot *See Fruits & Vegetables: Carrot: Canned*

Canned Cauliflower *See Fruits & Vegetables: Cauliflower: Canned*

Canned Celery *See Fruits & Vegetables: Celery: Canned*

Canned Cherries *See Fruits & Vegetables: Cherries: Canned*

Canned Cherry Juices *See Beverages: Juices: Cherry: Canned*

Canned Chili *See Prepared Foods: Chili: Canned*

Canned Chop Suey *See Ethnic Foods: Chop Suey: Canned*

Canned Clam *See Fish & Seafood: Shellfish: Clam: Canned*

Canned Corn *See Fruits & Vegetables: Corn: Canned*

Canned Crab *See Fish & Seafood: Shellfish: Crab: Canned*

Canned Crab Meat *See Fish & Seafood: Shellfish: Crab: Meat Canned*

Canned Cranberry *See Fruits & Vegetables: Berries: Cranberry: Canned*

Canned Cranberry Juices *See Beverages: Juices: Cranberry: Canned*

Canned Dry Beans *See Fruits & Vegetables: Beans: Dry: Canned*

Canned Figs *See Fruits & Vegetables: Figs: Canned*

Canned Fish *See Fish & Seafood: Fish: Canned*

Canned Fish Cakes *See Fish & Seafood: Fish: Cakes: Canned*

Canned French Fries *See Prepared Foods: French Fries: Canned*

Canned Fruit & Vegetable Juices *See Beverages: Juices: Fruit & Vegetable: Canned*

Canned Fruit Juices *See Beverages: Juices: Fruit: Canned*

Canned Fruits *See Fruits & Vegetables: Canned Fruits*

Canned Grape Juices *See Beverages: Juices: Grape: Canned*

Canned Grapefruit Juices *See Beverages: Juices: Grapefruit: Canned*

Canned Greek Beans *See Fruits & Vegetables: Beans: Greek: Canned*

Canned Green Beans *See Fruits & Vegetables: Beans: Green: Canned*

Canned Ham *See Meats & Meat Products: Smoked, Cured & Deli Meats: Ham: Canned*

Canned Hominy *See Cereals, Grains, Rice & Flour: Hominy: Canned*

Canned Kidney Beans *See Fruits & Vegetables: Beans: Kidney: Canned*

Canned Lemon Juices *See Beverages: Juices: Lemon: Canned*

Canned Lentil Beans *See Fruits & Vegetables: Beans: Lentil: Canned*

Canned Lima Beans *See Fruits & Vegetables: Beans: Lima: Canned*

Canned Luncheon Meat *See Meats & Meat Products: Smoked, Cured & Deli Meats: Luncheon Meat: Canned*

Canned Mandarin Orange *See Fruits & Vegetables: Orange: Mandarin: Canned*

Canned Meat Balls *See Prepared Foods: Meat Balls: Canned*

Canned Mushrooms *See Fruits & Vegetables: Mushrooms: Canned*

Canned Navy Beans *See Fruits & Vegetables: Beans: Navy: Canned*

Canned Nectar *See Fruits & Vegetables: Nectar: Canned*

Canned Noodles *See Pasta & Noodles: Noodles: Canned*

Canned Okra *See Fruits & Vegetables: Okra: Canned*

Canned Onion *See Fruits & Vegetables: Onion: Canned*

Canned Orange Sections *See Fruits & Vegetables: Orange: Sections: Canned*

Canned Oriental Vegetables *See Fruits & Vegetables: Oriental: Canned*

Canned Oysters *See Fish & Seafood: Shellfish: Oysters: Canned*

Canned Pasta *See Pasta & Noodles: Canned*

Canned Peach *See Fruits & Vegetables: Peach: Canned; See also Fruits & Vegetables: Peach: Klingstone: Canned - Sliced & Diced*

Canned Pear *See Fruits & Vegetables: Pear: Canned*

Canned Peas *See Fruits & Vegetables: Peas: Canned*

Canned Peas & Carrots *See Fruits & Vegetables: Vegetables Mixed: Peas & Carrots: Canned*

Canned Peppers *See Fruits & Vegetables: Peppers: Canned*

Canned Pigs' Feet *See Meats & Meat Products: Pork & Pork Products: Pigs' Feet: Canned*

Canned Pineapple *See Fruits & Vegetables: Pineapple: Canned*

Canned Pineapple Chunks *See Fruits & Vegetables: Pineapple: Canned: Chunks*

Canned Pineapple Juices *See Beverages: Juices: Pineapple: Canned*

Canned Plums *See Fruits & Vegetables: Plums: Canned*

Canned Pork & Beans *See Prepared Foods: Pork & Beans (see also Baked Beans): Canned*

Canned Pork with Natural Juices *See Meats & Meat Products: Pork & Pork Products: Canned with Natural Juices*

Canned Potatoes *See Fruits & Vegetables: Potatoes: Canned*

Canned Prepared Meals *See Prepared Foods: Prepared Meals: Canned*

Canned Prunes *See Fruits & Vegetables: Prunes: Canned*

Canned Pumpkin *See Fruits & Vegetables: Pumpkin: Canned*

Canned Ravioli *See Pasta & Noodles: Ravioli: Canned*

Canned Refried Beans *See Fruits & Vegetables: Beans: Refried: Canned*

Canned Rhubarb *See Fruits & Vegetables: Rhubarb: Canned*

Canned Rutabaga *See Fruits & Vegetables: Rutabaga: Canned*

Canned Salsa *See Sauces, Dips & Dressings: Salsa: Canned*

Canned Sardines *See Fish & Seafood: Fish: Sardines: Canned*

Canned Seafood *See Fish & Seafood: Seafood: Canned*

Canned Shellfish *See Fish & Seafood: Shellfish: Canned*

Canned Shrimp *See Fish & Seafood: Shellfish: Shrimp: Canned*

Canned Soup *See Prepared Foods: Soups & Stews: Canned Soup*

Canned Spaghetti *See Prepared Foods: Prepared Meals: Spaghetti: Canned; See also Pasta & Noodles: Spaghetti: Canned*

Canned Spanish Rice *See Cereals, Grains, Rice & Flour: Rice: Spanish: Canned*

Canned Spinach *See Fruits & Vegetables: Spinach: Canned*

Canned Squash *See Fruits & Vegetables: Squash: Canned*

Canned Stew *See Prepared Foods: Soups & Stews: Canned Stew*

Canned Strawberry *See Fruits & Vegetables: Berries: Strawberry: Canned*

Canned Succotash *See Fruits & Vegetables: Succotash: Canned*

Canned Tomato *See Fruits & Vegetables: Tomato: Canned*

Canned Tomato Juices *See Beverages: Juices: Tomato: Canned*

Canned Tomato Pulps & Purees *See Fruits & Vegetables: Pulps & Purees: Tomato: Canned*

Canned Tomato Sauces *See Sauces, Dips & Dressings: Sauces: Tomato: Canned*

Canned Tuna *See Fish & Seafood: Fish: Tuna: Canned*

Canned Tuna - Chunk Light in Oil *See Fish & Seafood: Fish: Tuna: Canned - Chunk Light in Oil*

Canned Tuna - Chunk Light in Water *See Fish & Seafood: Fish: Tuna: Canned - Chunk Light in Water*

Canned Tuna - Chunk Solid in Oil *See Fish & Seafood: Fish: Tuna: Canned - Chunk Solid in Oil*

Canned Tuna - Chunk Solid in Water *See Fish & Seafood: Fish: Tuna: Canned - Chunk Solid in Water*

Canned Turkey *See Meats & Meat Products: Poultry: Turkey: Canned*

Canned Turnip *See Fruits & Vegetables: Turnip: Canned*

Canned Vegetables *See Fruits & Vegetables: Canned Vegetables*

Canned Vegetables, Mixed *See Fruits & Vegetables: Vegetables Mixed: Canned*

Canned Venison *See Meats & Meat Products: Game: Venison: Canned*

Canned Water Pack Cherries *See Fruits & Vegetables: Cherries: Water Pack: Canned*

Canned Wax Beans *See Fruits & Vegetables: Beans: Wax: Canned*

Canned Yams *See Fruits & Vegetables: Yams: Canned*

Cannellini Beans *See Fruits & Vegetables: Beans: Cannellini*

Cannelloni *See Pasta & Noodles: Cannelloni*

Cannoli *See Baked Goods: Cakes & Pastries: Cannoli*

Canola Oils *See Oils, Shortening & Fats: Oils: Canola*

Cantaloupe *See Fruits & Vegetables: Melon: Cantaloupe*

Capellini *See Pasta & Noodles: Capellini*

Capers *See Spices, Seasonings & Seeds: Spices: Capers*

Capon Chicken *See Meats & Meat Products: Poultry: Chicken: Capon*

Cappuccino *See Beverages: Coffee & Tea: Cappuccino; See also Beverages: Coffee & Tea: Coffee: Cappuccino*

Cappuccino Mixes *See Doughs, Mixes & Fillings: Mixes: Cappuccino*

Cappuccino Powders *See Ingredients, Flavors & Additives: Powders: Cappuccino*

Capsicums Peppers *See Fruits & Vegetables: Peppers: Capsicums*

Caramel Apple *See Fruits & Vegetables: Apple: Caramel*

Caramel Burnt Sugar Colors *See Ingredients, Flavors & Additives: Colors: Burnt Sugar: Caramel*

Caramel Candy *See Candy & Confectionery: Candy: Caramel*

Caramel Colors *See Ingredients, Flavors & Additives: Colors: Caramel*

Caramel Covered Apple *See Fruits & Vegetables: Apple: Covered: Caramel*

Caramel Flavors *See Ingredients, Flavors & Additives: Flavors: Caramel*

Caraway Oils *See Oils, Shortening & Fats: Oils: Caraway*

Caraway Seeds *See Spices, Seasonings & Seeds: Seeds: Caraway*

Carboxymethylcellulose *See Ingredients, Flavors & Additives: Gums: Carboxymethylcellulose*

Cardamom Oils *See Oils, Shortening & Fats: Oils: Cardamom*

Cardamom Seeds *See Spices, Seasonings & Seeds: Seeds: Cardamom*

Cardamom Spices *See Spices, Seasonings & Seeds: Spices: Cardamom*

Caribou *See Meats & Meat Products: Game: Caribou*

Carmine *See Ingredients, Flavors & Additives: Colors: Natural: Carmine*

Carob Candy *See Candy & Confectionery: Candy: Carob*

Carob Candy Coatings *See Candy & Confectionery: Candy Coatings: Carob*

Carob Ingredients *See Candy & Confectionery: Chocolate Products: Carob Ingredients*

Carob Powder Spices *See Spices, Seasonings & Seeds: Spices: Carob Powder*

Carob Powders *See Ingredients, Flavors & Additives: Powders: Carob*

Carotenoids *See Ingredients, Flavors & Additives: Colors: Natural: Carotenoids*

Carp *See Fish & Seafood: Fish: Carp*

Carrageenan *See Ingredients, Flavors & Additives: Gums: Carrageenan*

Carrot *See Fruits & Vegetables: Carrot*

Carrot Cake *See Baked Goods: Cakes & Pastries: Carrot Cake*

Carrot Juices *See Beverages: Juices: Carrot*

Cascabel Peppers *See Fruits & Vegetables: Peppers: Cascabel*

Casein *See Ingredients, Flavors & Additives: Casein & Caseinates; See also Ingredients, Flavors & Additives: Casein & Caseinates: Casein*

Cashews *See Nuts & Nut Butters: Nuts: Cashews*

Casings *See Meats & Meat Products: Smoked, Cured & Deli Meats: Sausages: Casings: Sausage, Pork, Beef*

Cassava Chips *See Snack Foods: Chips: Cassava*

Cassava Powders *See Ingredients, Flavors & Additives: Powders: Cassava*

Cassava Starches *See Ingredients, Flavors & Additives: Starches: Cassava*

Cassava Tapioca *See Cereals, Grains, Rice & Flour: Tapioca: Cassava*

Casseroles, Prepared Meals *See Prepared Foods: Prepared Meals: Casseroles*

Cassia *See Spices, Seasonings & Seeds: Spices: Cassia (Cinnamon); See also Spices, Seasonings & Seeds: Spices: Cinnamon: Cassia*

Cassia Oils *See Oils, Shortening & Fats: Oils: Cassia*

Castor Oils *See Oils, Shortening & Fats: Oils: Castor*

Catfish *See Fish & Seafood: Fish: Catfish*

Cauliflower *See Fruits & Vegetables: Cauliflower*

Cauliflower, Pickled *See Relishes & Pickled Products: Pickled Products: Cauliflower*

Cavatappi *See Pasta & Noodles: Cavatappi*

Cavatelli *See Pasta & Noodles: Cavatelli*

Caviar *See Fish & Seafood: Caviar (Roe)*

Cayenne Pepper *See Spices, Seasonings & Seeds: Spices: Cayenne Pepper*

Cayenne Spices *See Spices, Seasonings & Seeds: Spices: Cayenne*

Ceasar Salad Dressings *See Sauces, Dips & Dressings: Salad Dressings: Ceasar*

Ceasar Salad Dressings, Mixes *See Sauces, Dips & Dressings: Salad Dressings: Mixes: Ceasar*

Celery *See Fruits & Vegetables: Celery*

Celery Flakes *See Fruits & Vegetables: Dried & Dehydrated Vegetables: Celery Flakes; See also Spices, Seasonings & Seeds: Spices: Celery Flakes*

Celery Oils *See Oils, Shortening & Fats: Oils: Celery*

Celery Powders *See Ingredients, Flavors & Additives: Powders: Celery*

Celery Salt *See Spices, Seasonings & Seeds: Salt: Celery*

Celery Seeds *See Spices, Seasonings & Seeds: Seeds: Celery*

Celery Sticks *See Fruits & Vegetables: Celery: Sticks*

Cellulose Fiber *See Cereals, Grains, Rice & Flour: Fiber: Cellulose*

Cellulose Gel *See Ingredients, Flavors & Additives: Cellulose Gel*

Cereal *See Cereals, Grains, Rice & Flour: Cereal*

Cereal Bars *See Cereals, Grains, Rice & Flour: Cereal: Bars*

Cereal Binders *See Ingredients, Flavors & Additives: Binders: Cereal*

Cereal Crisps *See Cereals, Grains, Rice & Flour: Crisps: Cereal*

Cereal Solids Hydrolyzed Anticaking Agents *See Ingredients, Flavors & Additives: Agents: Anticaking: Cereal Solids Hydrolyzed*

Cereal Solids Hydrolyzed Products *See Ingredients, Flavors & Additives: Hydrolyzed Products: Cereal Solids*

Certified Dyes *See Ingredients, Flavors & Additives: Colors: Dyes: Certified*

Certified Organic Foods *See Specialty & Organic Foods: Organic Foods: Certified*

Chai Tea *See Beverages: Coffee & Tea: Tea: Chai*

Challah *See Baked Goods: Breads: Challah*

Chalupa Shells *See Ethnic Foods: Shells: Chalupa*

Chamomile Tea *See Beverages: Coffee & Tea: Tea: Chamomile*

Champagne *See Beverages: Wines: French: Champagne*

Champagne Vinegar *See Sauces, Dips & Dressings: Vinegar: Champagne*

Chanterelle *See Fruits & Vegetables: Mushrooms: Chanterelle*

Chardonnay *See Beverages: Wines: White Grape Varieties: Chardonnay*

Cheddar Cheese *See Cheese & Cheese Products: Cheese: Cheddar*

Cheddar Cheese, Imitation *See Cheese & Cheese Products: Imitation Cheeses & Substitutes: Imitation: Cheddar*

Cheddar Cheese, Powders *See Ingredients, Flavors & Additives: Powders: Cheese: Cheddar*

Cheddar Snack Seasonings *See Spices, Seasonings & Seeds: Seasonings: Snack: Cheddar*

Cheese *See Cheese & Cheese Products: Cheese; See also Cheese & Cheese Products: Cheese*

Cheese Bacteria *See Ingredients, Flavors & Additives: Cultures & Yeasts: Bacteria: Cheese*

Cheese Blends *See Ingredients, Flavors & Additives: Blends: Cheese*

Cheese Cake *See Baked Goods: Cakes & Pastries: Cheese Cake*

Cheese Curls *See Snack Foods: Cheese Curls*

Cheese Dips *See Sauces, Dips & Dressings: Dips: Cheese*

Cheese Flavors *See Ingredients, Flavors & Additives: Flavors: Cheese*

Cheese Foods & Substitutes *See Cheese & Cheese Products: Imitation Cheeses & Substitutes: Cheese Foods & Substitutes*

Cheese Loaves, Yellow Process *See Cheese & Cheese Products: Process Loaves: Yellow*

Cheese Pizza *See Prepared Foods: Pizza & Pizza Products: Pizza: Cheese*

Cheese Powders *See Ingredients, Flavors & Additives: Powders: Cheese*

Cheese Ravioli *See Pasta & Noodles: Ravioli: Cheese*

Cheese Sauces *See Sauces, Dips & Dressings: Sauces: Cheese*

Cheese Seasonings *See Spices, Seasonings & Seeds: Seasonings: Cheese*

Cheese Starter Media *See Ingredients, Flavors & Additives: Starter Media: Cheese*

Cheese Substitutes *See Cheese & Cheese Products: Imitation Cheeses & Substitutes: Substitutes*

Cheese Twists *See Snack Foods: Cheese Twists*

Cheese, Blend - American/Skim Milk *See Cheese & Cheese Products: Cheese: Blend - American/Skim Milk*

Cheese, No-Fat *See Cheese & Cheese Products: Cheese: No-Fat*

Cheese, White/Yellow Process Sliced *See Cheese & Cheese Products: Cheese: Process Sliced: White/Yellow*

Cheesecake Flavors *See Ingredients, Flavors & Additives: Flavors: Cheesecake*

Chelating Agents *See Ingredients, Flavors & Additives: Chelating Agents*

Chemicals *See Ingredients, Flavors & Additives: Chemicals*

Chemicals, Aroma *See Ingredients, Flavors & Additives: Aroma Chemicals & Materials: Chemicals*

Cherries *See Fruits & Vegetables: Cherries*

Cherry Flavors *See Ingredients, Flavors & Additives: Flavors: Cherry*

Cherry Juices *See Beverages: Juices: Cherry*

Cherry Peppers *See Fruits & Vegetables: Peppers: Cherry*

Cherry Pies *See Baked Goods: Pies: Cherry*

Cherry Tomato *See Fruits & Vegetables: Tomato: Cherry*

Chervil *See Spices, Seasonings & Seeds: Spices: Chervil*

Chestnut Flower Flour *See Cereals, Grains, Rice & Flour: Flour: Chestnut Flower*

Chestnuts *See Nuts & Nut Butters: Nuts: Chestnuts*

Chewing Gum *See Candy & Confectionery: Candy: Chewing Gum*

Chianti *See Beverages: Wines: Italian: Chianti*

Chick Beans *See Fruits & Vegetables: Beans: Chick*

Chicken *See Meats & Meat Products: Poultry: Chicken*

Chicken & Dumplings Soups & Stews *See Prepared Foods: Soups & Stews: Chicken & Dumplings*

Chicken & Noodles Soups & Stews *See Prepared Foods: Soups & Stews: Chicken & Noodles*

Chicken Bases *See Ingredients, Flavors & Additives: Bases: Chicken*

Chicken Broth *See Prepared Foods: Broth: Chicken*

Chicken Bulk *See Meats & Meat Products: Poultry: Chicken: Bulk (Leg Quarters, Legs, Thighs)*

Chicken Extenders *See Ingredients, Flavors & Additives: Extenders: Chicken*

Chicken Extracts *See Ingredients, Flavors & Additives: Extracts: Chicken*

Chicken Fats & Lard *See Oils, Shortening & Fats: Fats & Lard: Chicken*

Chicken Frankfurters *See Meats & Meat Products: Frankfurters: Chicken*

Chicken Marinades *See Sauces, Dips & Dressings: Marinades: Chicken*

Chicken Nuggets *See Meats & Meat Products: Poultry: Chicken: Nuggets*

Chicken Sausages *See Meats & Meat Products: Smoked, Cured & Deli Meats: Sausages: Chicken*

Chicken, Cut-Up Frozen *See Meats & Meat Products: Poultry: Chicken: Cut-Up Frozen*

Chicken, Cut-Up IQF *See Meats & Meat Products: Poultry: Chicken: Cut-Up IQF (Individually Quick Frozen)*

Chicken, Prepared Meals *See Prepared Foods: Prepared Meals: Chicken*

Chicken, Prepared Salads *See Prepared Foods: Prepared Salads: Chicken*

Chicks Hatcheries *See Eggs & Egg Products: Hatcheries: Chicks*

Chicory *See Fruits & Vegetables: Chicory*

Chile Pepper Spices *See Spices, Seasonings & Seeds: Spices: Chile Pepper*

Chile Peppers *See Fruits & Vegetables: Peppers: Chile*

Chili *See Prepared Foods: Chili*

Chili Beans *See Fruits & Vegetables: Beans: Chili*

Chili Crush *See Spices, Seasonings & Seeds: Spices: Chili Crush*

Chili Dips *See Sauces, Dips & Dressings: Dips: Chili*

Chili Mixes *See Doughs, Mixes & Fillings: Mixes: Chili*

Chili Pods *See Spices, Seasonings & Seeds: Spices: Chili Pods*

Chili Powder *See Spices, Seasonings & Seeds: Spices: Chili Powder; See also Ingredients, Flavors & Additives: Powders: Chili*

Chili Sauces *See Sauces, Dips & Dressings: Sauces: Chili*

Chili with Cheese *See Prepared Foods: Chili: with Cheese*

Chilled Apple Juices *See Beverages: Juices: Apple: Chilled*

Chilled Cherry Juices *See Beverages: Juices: Cherry: Chilled*

Chilled Grape Juices *See Beverages: Juices: Grape: Chilled*

Chimichangas *See Prepared Foods: Prepared Meals: Burritos: Chimichangas*

Chinese *See Ethnic Foods: Chinese*

Chinese Black Rice *See Cereals, Grains, Rice & Flour: Rice: Chinese Black*

Chinese Cabbage *See Fruits & Vegetables: Cabbage: Chinese*

EXAMPLE: **Canadian Style Bacon** *See Meats & Meat Products: Smoked, Cured & Deli Meats: Bacon: Canadian Style*

1. Product or Service you are looking for
2. Main Category, in alphabetical order, located in the page headers starting on page 23
3. Category Description, located in black bars and in page headers
4. Product Category, located in gray bars
5. Product Type, located under gray bars, centered in bold

Chinese Spices *See Spices, Seasonings & Seeds: Spices: Chinese*

Chinese Style Seasonings *See Spices, Seasonings & Seeds: Seasonings: Chinese Style*

Chip Dips *See Sauces, Dips & Dressings: Dips: Chip*

Chipotle Peppers *See Fruits & Vegetables: Peppers: Chipotle*

Chipped Beef *See Meats & Meat Products: Beef & Beef Products: Chipped*

Chips *See Snack Foods: Chips*

Chives *See Spices, Seasonings & Seeds: Spices: Chives; See also Fruits & Vegetables: Chives*

Chlorophyll *See Ingredients, Flavors & Additives: Chlorophyll*

Chocolate Almond Biscotti *See Baked Goods: Cookies & Bars: Biscotti: Chocolate Almond*

Chocolate Bars *See Candy & Confectionery: Chocolate Products: Chocolate Bars*

Chocolate Bases *See Ingredients, Flavors & Additives: Bases: Chocolate*

Chocolate Candy *See Candy & Confectionery: Chocolate Products: Chocolate Candy*

Chocolate Candy Coatings *See Candy & Confectionery: Candy Coatings: Chocolate*

Chocolate Cherries *See Candy & Confectionery: Chocolate Products: Chocolate Cherries*

Chocolate Chip Compound for Ice Cream *See Ingredients, Flavors & Additives: Chocolate Products: Chocolate Chip Compound for Ice Cream*

Chocolate Chip Cookies *See Baked Goods: Cookies & Bars: Chocolate Chip Cookies*

Chocolate Chips *See Candy & Confectionery: Chocolate Products: Chocolate Chips; See also Snack Foods: Chips: Chocolate*

Chocolate Chunks *See Candy & Confectionery: Chocolate Products: Chocolate Chunks*

Chocolate Coated Nuts *See Nuts & Nut Butters: Nuts: Coated: Chocolate*

Chocolate Coated Raisins *See Fruits & Vegetables: Raisins: Chocolate Coated*

Chocolate Covered Apple *See Fruits & Vegetables: Apple: Covered: Chocolate*

Chocolate Dessert Fillings *See Doughs, Mixes & Fillings: Fillings: Dessert: Chocolate*

Chocolate Dipped Biscotti *See Baked Goods: Cookies & Bars: Biscotti: Chocolate Dipped*

Chocolate Drinks *See Beverages: Cocoa & Chocolate Drinks: Chocolate Drinks*

Chocolate Fillings *See Doughs, Mixes & Fillings: Fillings: Chocolate*

Chocolate Flavors *See Ingredients, Flavors & Additives: Flavors: Chocolate*

Chocolate Liqueur *See Beverages: Spirits & Liqueurs: Liqueurs & Cordials: Chocolate Liqueur*

Chocolate Milk *See Dairy Products: Milk & Milk Products: Milk: Chocolate*

Chocolate Products *See Candy & Confectionery: Chocolate Products; See also Ingredients, Flavors & Additives: Chocolate Products*

Chocolate Pudding *See Dairy Products: Pudding: Chocolate*

Chop Suey *See Ethnic Foods: Chop Suey*

Chopped Broccoli *See Fruits & Vegetables: Broccoli: Chopped*

Chopped Broccoli, Dehydrated *See Fruits & Vegetables: Dried & Dehydrated Vegetables: Broccoli: Chopped*

Chopped Celery *See Fruits & Vegetables: Celery: Chopped*

Chopped Clam *See Fish & Seafood: Shellfish: Clam: Chopped*

Chopped Garlic *See Spices, Seasonings & Seeds: Spices: Garlic: Chopped*

Chopped Onion *See Spices, Seasonings & Seeds: Spices: Onion: Chopped*

Chopped Shellfish *See Fish & Seafood: Shellfish: Chopped*

Chorizo Sausages *See Meats & Meat Products: Smoked, Cured & Deli Meats: Sausages: Chorizo*

Chourico Sausages *See Meats & Meat Products: Smoked, Cured & Deli Meats: Sausages: Chourico*

Chow Chow *See Ethnic Foods: Chow Chow*

Chow Fun Noodles *See Pasta & Noodles: Noodles: Chow Fun*

Chow Mein *See Ethnic Foods: Chow Mein*

Chow Mein Noodles *See Pasta & Noodles: Noodles: Chow Mein*

Chowder *See Fish & Seafood: Fish: Chowder; See also Prepared Foods: Soups & Stews: Chowder; See also Prepared Foods: Chowder*

Christmas Specialty-Packaged Candy *See Candy & Confectionery: Specialty-Packaged Candy: Christmas*

Chub *See Fish & Seafood: Fish: Chub*

Chum Salmon *See Fish & Seafood: Fish: Salmon: Chum*

Chunky Salsa *See Sauces, Dips & Dressings: Salsa: Chunky*

Churros *See Baked Goods: Cakes & Pastries: Churros*

Chutney *See Prepared Foods: Chutney*

Cider & Vinegar Colors *See Ingredients, Flavors & Additives: Colors: Cider & Vinegar*

Cinnamon Flavors *See Ingredients, Flavors & Additives: Flavors: Cinnamon*

Cinnamon Leaf & Bark Oils *See Oils, Shortening & Fats: Oils: Cinnamon - Leaf & Bark*

Cinnamon Rolls *See Baked Goods: Breads: Rolls: Cinnamon*

Cinnamon Spices *See Spices, Seasonings & Seeds: Spices: Cinnamon*

Cinnamon Toast *See Baked Goods: Breads: Cinnamon Toast*

Cinnamon Toast, Snack Seasonings *See Spices, Seasonings & Seeds: Seasonings: Snack: Cinnamon Toast*

Citric Acidulants *See Ingredients, Flavors & Additives: Acidulants: Citric*

Citron *See Spices, Seasonings & Seeds: Spices: Citron*

Citrus Blends Juices *See Beverages: Juices: Citrus Blends*

Citrus Flavors *See Ingredients, Flavors & Additives: Flavors: Citrus*

Citrus Fruits *See Fruits & Vegetables: Citrus Fruits*

Citrus Oils *See Oils, Shortening & Fats: Oils: Citrus*

Citrus Pectins *See Ingredients, Flavors & Additives: Pectins: Citrus*

Citrus Peel Products *See Fruits & Vegetables: Citrus Peel Products*

Citrus Pulps & Purees *See Fruits & Vegetables: Pulps & Purees: Citrus*

Clam *See Fish & Seafood: Shellfish: Clam*

Clam & Fish Chowder *See Prepared Foods: Chowder: Clam & Fish*

Clam Juice *See Fish & Seafood: Shellfish: Clam: Juice*

Clam Sauces *See Sauces, Dips & Dressings: Sauces: Clam*

Clarifying Agents *See Ingredients, Flavors & Additives: Agents: Clarifying*

Cloudear Mushrooms *See Fruits & Vegetables: Mushrooms: Cloudear*

Clove Oils *See Oils, Shortening & Fats: Oils: Clove*

Cloves *See Spices, Seasonings & Seeds: Spices: Cloves*

Club Soda *See Beverages: Soft Drinks & Sodas: Club Soda*

Coagulants *See Ingredients, Flavors & Additives: Coagulants*

Coarse Frozen Ground Beef *See Meats & Meat Products: Beef & Beef Products: Ground: Coarse Frozen*

Coated Candy Bars *See Candy & Confectionery: Candy: Candy Bars: Coated*

Coated Nuts *See Nuts & Nut Butters: Nuts: Coated*

Coated Popcorn *See Snack Foods: Popcorn: Coated*

Coatings *See Ingredients, Flavors & Additives: Coatings*

Cocktail Fruit *See Fruits & Vegetables: Fruit: Cocktail*

Cocktail Mixes *See Doughs, Mixes & Fillings: Mixes: Cocktail*

Cocktail Onion *See Fruits & Vegetables: Onion: Cocktail*

Cocktail Sauces *See Sauces, Dips & Dressings: Sauces: Cocktail*

Cocktail Seafood *See Fish & Seafood: Seafood: Cocktail*

Cocktail Shrimp *See Fish & Seafood: Shellfish: Shrimp: Cocktail*

Cocktail Tomato *See Fruits & Vegetables: Tomato: Cocktail*

Cocktail Tomato Juices *See Beverages: Juices: Tomato: Cocktail*

Cocoa & Chocolate Drinks *See Beverages: Cocoa & Chocolate Drinks*

Cocoa & Cocoa Products *See Candy & Confectionery: Chocolate Products: Cocoa & Cocoa Products*

Cocoa & Rice Pellets *See Ingredients, Flavors & Additives: Half-Products: Cocoa & Rice Pellets*

Cocoa Butter *See Ingredients, Flavors & Additives: Cocoa Butter*

Cocoa Flavors *See Ingredients, Flavors & Additives: Flavors: Cocoa*

Cocoa Powders *See Ingredients, Flavors & Additives: Powders: Cocoa*

Cocoa Replacers *See Ingredients, Flavors & Additives: Replacers: Cocoa*

Cocoa Rice Crisps *See Cereals, Grains, Rice & Flour: Crisps: Cocoa Rice*

Cocoa Soy Crisps *See Cereals, Grains, Rice & Flour: Crisps: Cocoa Soy*

Coconut & Coconut Products *See Fruits & Vegetables: Coconut & Coconut Products*

Coconut Candy *See Candy & Confectionery: Candy: Coconut*

Coconut Flavors *See Ingredients, Flavors & Additives: Flavors: Coconut*

Coconut Juices *See Beverages: Juices: Coconut*

Coconut Oils *See Oils, Shortening & Fats: Oils: Coconut*

Cod *See Fish & Seafood: Fish: Cod*

Cod Liver Oils *See Oils, Shortening & Fats: Oils: Cod Liver*

Coffee *See Beverages: Coffee & Tea; See also Beverages: Coffee & Tea: Coffee*

Coffee Cake *See Baked Goods: Cakes & Pastries: Coffee Cake*

Coffee Creamers *See Dairy Products: Creamers: Coffee*

Coffee Extenders *See Ingredients, Flavors & Additives: Extenders: Coffee*

Coffee Extracts *See Ingredients, Flavors & Additives: Extracts: Coffee*

Coffee Flavors *See Ingredients, Flavors & Additives: Flavors: Coffee*

Coffee Liqueur *See Beverages: Spirits & Liqueurs: Liqueurs & Cordials: Coffee Liqueur*

Coho Salmon *See Fish & Seafood: Fish: Salmon: Coho*

Cola Soft Drinks *See Beverages: Soft Drinks & Sodas: Soft Drinks: Cola*

Colby *See Cheese & Cheese Products: Cheese: Colby*

Cold Smoked Seafood *See Fish & Seafood: Seafood: Smoked: Cold*

Cole Slaw *See Prepared Foods: Prepared Salads: Cole Slaw*

Collard Greens *See Fruits & Vegetables: Collard Greens*

Colloids Stabilizers *See Ingredients, Flavors & Additives: Stabilizers: Colloids*

Colored Crisps *See Cereals, Grains, Rice & Flour: Crisps: Colored*

Colored Pellets *See Ingredients, Flavors & Additives: Half-Products: Colored Pellets*

Colored Starch Bits *See Ingredients, Flavors & Additives: Toppings: Colored Starch Bits; See also Ingredients, Flavors & Additives: Bits: Colored Starch*

Colors *See Ingredients, Flavors & Additives: Colors*

Compacting Agents *See Ingredients, Flavors & Additives: Agents: Compacting*

Compound Coatings *See Ingredients, Flavors & Additives: Coatings: Compound*

Compounds *See Ingredients, Flavors & Additives: Compounds*

Concentrate Ade Juices *See Beverages: Juices: Ade: Concentrate*

Concentrate Apple Juices *See Beverages: Juices: Apple: Concentrate*

Concentrate Apricot Juices *See Beverages: Juices: Apricot: Concentrate*

Concentrate Cherry Juices *See Beverages: Juices: Cherry: Concentrate*

Concentrate Cranberry Juices *See Beverages: Juices: Cranberry: Concentrate*

Concentrate Drink Juices *See Beverages: Juices: Drink: Concentrate*

Concentrate Fruit & Vegetable Juices *See Beverages: Juices: Fruit & Vegetable: Concentrate*

Concentrate Fruit Juices *See Beverages: Juices: Fruit: Concentrate*

Concentrate Fruit Punch Juices *See Beverages: Juices: Fruit Punch: Concentrate*

Concentrate Fruit Puree Juices *See Beverages: Juices: Vegetable: Concentrates - Fruit Puree*

Concentrate Grape Juices *See Beverages: Juices: Grape: Concentrate*

Concentrate Grapefruit Juices *See Beverages: Juices: Grapefruit: Concentrate*

Concentrate Lemon Juices *See Beverages: Juices: Lemon: Concentrate*

Concentrate Lemonade Juices *See Beverages: Juices: Lemonade: Concentrate*

Concentrate Orange Juices *See Beverages: Juices: Orange: Concentrate*

Concentrate Orange Juices, Frozen *See Beverages: Juices: Orange: Concentrate - Frozen*

Concentrate Pineapple Juices *See Beverages: Juices: Pineapple: Concentrate*

Concentrate Soy Protein *See Fruits & Vegetables: Soy: Soy Protein: Concentrate*

Concentrates *See Ingredients, Flavors & Additives: Concentrates*

Conch Fish *See Fish & Seafood: Fish: Conch*

Conch Shellfish *See Fish & Seafood: Shellfish: Conch*

Conchigite Rigate *See Pasta & Noodles: Conchigite Rigate*

Condensed Buttermilk *See Dairy Products: Buttermilk & Buttermilk Products: Buttermilk: Condensed*

Condensed Milk *See Dairy Products: Milk & Milk Products: Milk: Condensed*

Condensed Milk, Bulk Only *See Dairy Products: Milk & Milk Products: Milk: Condensed - Bulk Only*

Condiments *See Sauces, Dips & Dressings: Condiments*

Cones *See Baked Goods: Cones*

Confectioners Crunch *See Candy & Confectionery: Confectionery: Confectioners Crunch*

Confectioners Dipping Fruit *See Fruits & Vegetables: Dipping Fruit: Confectioners'*

Confectionery *See Candy & Confectionery: Confectionery; See also Candy & Confectionery: Confectionery; See also Ingredients, Flavors & Additives: Confectionery*

Confectionery Candy Coatings *See Candy & Confectionery: Candy Coatings: Confectionery*

Confectionery Toppings *See Ingredients, Flavors & Additives: Toppings: Confectionery*

Convenience Food *See Prepared Foods: Convenience Food*

Convenience Prepared Meals *See Prepared Foods: Prepared Meals: Convenience*

Cooked *See Eggs & Egg Products: Cooked*

Cooked Chicken, Breaded - Frozen *See Meats & Meat Products: Poultry: Chicken: Cooked - Breaded - Frozen*

Cooked Corn-on-the-Cob *See Fruits & Vegetables: Corn: Corn-on-the-Cob: Cooked*

Cooked Crab *See Fish & Seafood: Shellfish: Crab: Cooked*

Cooked Frozen Hamburger *See Meats & Meat Products: Beef & Beef Products: Hamburger: Cooked Frozen*

Cooked Frozen Patties *See Meats & Meat Products: Beef & Beef Products: Patties: Cooked Frozen*

Cooked Ham, Water-added Chilled *See Meats & Meat Products: Smoked, Cured & Deli Meats: Ham: Cooked - Water-added Chilled*

Cooked Oysters *See Fish & Seafood: Shellfish: Oysters: Cooked*

Cooked Shrimp *See Fish & Seafood: Shellfish: Shrimp: Cooked*

Cookie Batters *See Doughs, Mixes & Fillings: Batters: Cookie*

Cookie Bits *See Ingredients, Flavors & Additives: Bits: Cookie*

Cookie Doughs *See Doughs, Mixes & Fillings: Doughs: Cookie*

Cookie Fillings *See Doughs, Mixes & Fillings: Fillings: Cookie*

Cookie Mixes *See Doughs, Mixes & Fillings: Mixes: Cookie*

Cookies *See Baked Goods: Cookies & Bars: Cookies*

Cookies & Bars *See Baked Goods: Cookies & Bars*

Cookies & Biscuits *See Baked Goods: Cookies & Bars: Cookies & Biscuits*

Cookies Bars *See Baked Goods: Cookies & Bars: Bars*

Cooking Compounds *See Ingredients, Flavors & Additives: Compounds: Cooking*

Cooking Compounds, Fats & Lard *See Oils, Shortening & Fats: Fats & Lard: Lard: Cooking Compounds*

Cooking Oils *See Oils, Shortening & Fats: Oils: Cooking*

Cooking Wines *See Beverages: Wines: Cooking*

Coriander *See Spices, Seasonings & Seeds: Spices: Coriander (Cilantro)*

Coriander Seed Oils *See Oils, Shortening & Fats: Oils: Coriander Seed*

Coriander Seeds *See Spices, Seasonings & Seeds: Seeds: Coriander*

Corn *See Fruits & Vegetables: Corn*

Corn Bran Fiber *See Cereals, Grains, Rice & Flour: Fiber: Corn Bran*

Corn Breads *See Baked Goods: Breads: Corn*

Corn Candy *See Candy & Confectionery: Candy: Corn*

Corn Chips *See Snack Foods: Chips: Corn*

Corn Dogs *See Meats & Meat Products: Frankfurters: Corn Dogs*

Corn Flour *See Cereals, Grains, Rice & Flour: Flour: Corn*

Corn Fritters *See Prepared Foods: Prepared Meals: Corn Fritters*

Corn Meal *See Cereals, Grains, Rice & Flour: Corn Meal*

Corn Nuts *See Snack Foods: Corn Nuts*

Corn Oils *See Oils, Shortening & Fats: Oils: Corn*

Corn Starches *See Ingredients, Flavors & Additives: Starches: Corn*

Corn Syrups *See Sugars, Syrups & Sweeteners: Syrups: Corn*

Corn-Based Cereal *See Cereals, Grains, Rice & Flour: Cereal: Corn-Based*

Corn-on-the-Cob *See Fruits & Vegetables: Corn: Corn-on-the-Cob*

Corned Beef *See Meats & Meat Products: Smoked, Cured & Deli Meats: Corned Beef*

Cornish Game Hens *See Meats & Meat Products: Poultry: Cornish Game Hens*

Corsignano *See Cheese & Cheese Products: Cheese: Corsignano*

Cottage Cheese *See Cheese & Cheese Products: Cheese: Cottage*

Cotton Candy *See Candy & Confectionery: Candy: Cotton*

Cottonseed Oils *See Oils, Shortening & Fats: Oils: Cottonseed*

Couscous *See Ethnic Foods: Couscous*

Covered Apple *See Fruits & Vegetables: Apple: Covered*

Crab *See Fish & Seafood: Shellfish: Crab; See also Prepared Foods: Prepared Meals: Crab*

Crab Extracts *See Ingredients, Flavors & Additives: Extracts: Crab*

Crab Meat *See Fish & Seafood: Shellfish: Crab: Meat*

Crackers *See Baked Goods: Crackers; See also Baked Goods: Crackers: Crackers*

Cranberry *See Fruits & Vegetables: Berries: Cranberry*

Cranberry Juices *See Beverages: Juices: Cranberry*

Cranberry Orange Biscotti *See Baked Goods: Cookies & Bars: Biscotti: Cranberry Orange*

Cranberry Sauces *See Fruits & Vegetables: Sauces: Cranberry*

Crayfish *See Fish & Seafood: Shellfish: Crayfish*

Cream *See Dairy Products: Cream*

Cream Ale *See Beverages: Beers: American & British Ale: Cream Ale*

Cream Cheese *See Cheese & Cheese Products: Cheese: Cream*

Cream Cheese Powders *See Ingredients, Flavors & Additives: Powders: Cheese: Cream*

Cream Dessert Fillings *See Doughs, Mixes & Fillings: Fillings: Dessert: Cream*

Cream from Milk *See Dairy Products: Cream: from Milk*

Cream of Broccoli Soups & Stews *See Prepared Foods: Soups & Stews: Cream of Broccoli*

Cream of Mushroom Soups & Stews *See Prepared Foods: Soups & Stews: Cream of Mushroom*

Cream of Potato Soups & Stews *See Prepared Foods: Soups & Stews: Cream of Potato*

Cream of Tartar *See Spices, Seasonings & Seeds: Spices: Tartar: Cream*

Cream Puff *See Baked Goods: Cakes & Pastries: Cream Puff*

Cream Soda *See Beverages: Soft Drinks & Sodas: Soft Drinks: Cream Soda - Vanilla; See also Beverages: Soft Drinks & Sodas: Soft Drinks: Cream Soda*

Creamers *See Dairy Products: Creamers*

Creamy Dijon Salad Dressings *See Sauces, Dips & Dressings: Salad Dressings: Mixes: Creamy Dijon; See also Sauces, Dips & Dressings: Salad Dressings: Creamy Dijon*

Creme Fillings *See Doughs, Mixes & Fillings: Fillings: Creme*

Cremes Candy *See Candy & Confectionery: Candy: Cremes*

Creole Chicken *See Prepared Foods: Prepared Meals: Chicken: Creole*

Crepes *See Prepared Foods: Crepes*

Criminis Mushrooms *See Fruits & Vegetables: Mushrooms: Criminis*

Crisp Rice Toppings *See Ingredients, Flavors & Additives: Toppings: Crisp Rice*

Crisped Bran Crisps *See Cereals, Grains, Rice & Flour: Crisps: Crisped Bran*

Crisped Corn Crisps *See Cereals, Grains, Rice & Flour: Crisps: Crisped Corn*

Crisped Oat Crisps *See Cereals, Grains, Rice & Flour: Crisps: Crisped Oat*

Crisped Rice Crisps *See Cereals, Grains, Rice & Flour: Crisps: Crisped Rice*

Crisped Soy Crisps *See Cereals, Grains, Rice & Flour: Crisps: Crisped Soy*

Crisped Wheat Crisps *See Cereals, Grains, Rice & Flour: Crisps: Crisped Wheat*

Crisps *See Cereals, Grains, Rice & Flour: Crisps*

Criterion Apple *See Fruits & Vegetables: Apple: Criterion*

Croaker *See Fish & Seafood: Fish: Croaker*

Croissant Sesame Crackers *See Baked Goods: Crackers: Croissant Sesame Crackers*

Croissants *See Baked Goods: Breads: Croissants*

Croquettes *See Prepared Foods: Croquettes*

Croutons *See Baked Goods: Bread Crumbs & Croutons: Croutons; See also Baked Goods: Bread Crumbs & Croutons: Crumbs*

Crumpets *See Baked Goods: Cakes & Pastries: Crumpets*

Crunch Toppings *See Ingredients, Flavors & Additives: Toppings: Crunch*

Crunches *See Baked Goods: Crunches*

Crunchy Peanut Butter *See Nuts & Nut Butters: Nut Butters: Peanut Butter: Crunchy*

Crushed Canned Tomato *See Fruits & Vegetables: Tomato: Canned: Crushed*

Crushed Fruits & Vegetables *See Fruits & Vegetables: Crushed*

Crushed Onion *See Fruits & Vegetables: Onion: Crushed*

Crushed Red Pepper *See Spices, Seasonings & Seeds: Spices: Red Pepper: Crushed*

Crysanthemums *See Fruits & Vegetables: Crysanthemums*

Crystalline Fructose *See Sugars, Syrups & Sweeteners: Fructose: Crystalline*

Crystallized Ginger *See Spices, Seasonings & Seeds: Spices: Ginger: Crystallized; See also Fruits & Vegetables: Ginger: Crystallized*

Crystallized, Glace Candied Fruits *See Fruits & Vegetables: Candied Fruits: Crystallized, Glace*

Cucumber *See Fruits & Vegetables: Cucumber*

Cucumber for Pickling *See Fruits & Vegetables: Cucumber: for Pickling*

Cultured Flavors *See Ingredients, Flavors & Additives: Flavors: Cultured*

Cultures *See Ingredients, Flavors & Additives: Cultures & Yeasts: Cultures*

Cultures & Yeasts *See Ingredients, Flavors & Additives: Cultures & Yeasts*

Cumin Seeds *See Spices, Seasonings & Seeds: Seeds: Cumin*

Cumin Spices *See Spices, Seasonings & Seeds: Spices: Cumin*

Cupcake *See Baked Goods: Cakes & Pastries: Cupcakes*

Curd Seasonings *See Spices, Seasonings & Seeds: Seasonings: Curd*

Cured Smoked Seafood *See Fish & Seafood: Seafood: Smoked: Cured*

Curing Preparations *See Ingredients, Flavors & Additives: Curing Preparations*

Currants Berries *See Fruits & Vegetables: Berries: Currants*

Curry Powder *See Spices, Seasonings & Seeds: Spices: Curry Powder; See also Ingredients, Flavors & Additives: Powders: Curry*

Curry Sauces *See Sauces, Dips & Dressings: Sauces: Curry*

Cusk *See Fish & Seafood: Fish: Cusk*

Custard *See Dairy Products: Custard*

Custard Dessert Fillings *See Doughs, Mixes & Fillings: Fillings: Dessert: Custard*

Custard Powders *See Ingredients, Flavors & Additives: Powders: Custard*

Custom Blends *See Ingredients, Flavors & Additives: Blends: Custom*

Custom Designed Colloid Stabilizers *See Ingredients, Flavors & Additives: Stabilizers: Colloids: Custom Designed*

D

D'Anjou/Bosc Pear *See Fruits & Vegetables: Pear: D'Anjou/Bosc*

Dairy Bases *See Ingredients, Flavors & Additives: Bases: Dairy*

Dairy Butter *See Dairy Products: Butter: Dairy*

Dairy Coagulants *See Ingredients, Flavors & Additives: Coagulants: Dairy*

Dairy Drinks *See Dairy Products: Dairy Drinks*

Dairy Flavors *See Ingredients, Flavors & Additives: Flavors: Dairy*

Dairy Ingredients *See Ingredients, Flavors & Additives: Ingredients: Dairy*

Dairy Products *See Dairy Products*

Dairy Seasonings *See Spices, Seasonings & Seeds: Seasonings: Dairy Products*

Dairy Whipped Toppings *See Ingredients, Flavors & Additives: Toppings: Whipped: Dairy*

Danish *See Baked Goods: Cakes & Pastries: Danish*

Darjeeling Tea *See Beverages: Coffee & Tea: Tea: Darjeeling*

Dark Green Zucchini *See Fruits & Vegetables: Zucchini: Dark Green*

Dark Red Kidney Beans *See Fruits & Vegetables: Beans: Kidney: Dark Red*

Dark Rum *See Beverages: Spirits & Liqueurs: Rum: Dark*

EXAMPLE: **Canadian Style Bacon** *See Meats & Meat Products: Smoked, Cured & Deli Meats: Bacon: Canadian Style*

1. Product or Service you are looking for
2. Main Category, in alphabetical order, located in the page headers starting on page 23
3. Category Description, located in black bars and in page headers
4. Product Category, located in gray bars
5. Product Type, located under gray bars, centered in bold

DarkLager/Dunkel Lager *See Beverages: Beers: Lager: DarkLager/Dunkel*

Dates *See Fruits & Vegetables: Dates*

De Arbol Peppers *See Fruits & Vegetables: Peppers: De Arbol*

Decaffeinated Coffee *See Beverages: Coffee & Tea: Coffee: Decaffeinated*

Decaffeinated Coffee, Naturally *See Beverages: Coffee & Tea: Coffee Decaffeinated Naturally*

Decaffeinated Espresso *See Beverages: Coffee & Tea: Espresso: Decaffeinated*

Decaffeinated Tea *See Beverages: Coffee & Tea: Tea: Decaffeinated*

Decorations *See Candy & Confectionery: Decorations & Icings; See also Candy & Confectionery: Decorations & Icings: Decorations*

Decorative Items *See Ingredients, Flavors & Additives: Decorative Items*

Defatted Wheat Germ *See Cereals, Grains, Rice & Flour: Wheat: Germ: Defatted*

Defoamers *See Ingredients, Flavors & Additives: Defoamers*

Dehydrated Capsicums Peppers *See Fruits & Vegetables: Peppers: Capsicums: Dehydrated*

Dehydrated Carrot *See Fruits & Vegetables: Carrot: Dehydrated*

Dehydrated Celery *See Fruits & Vegetables: Celery: Dehydrated*

Dehydrated Egg *See Eggs & Egg Products: Dehydrated*

Dehydrated Food *See Specialty Processed Foods: Dehydrated Food (See also Specific Foods)*

Dehydrated Fruit *See Fruits & Vegetables: Dried & Dehydrated Fruits: Dehydrated Fruit; See also Fruits & Vegetables: Dehydrated*

Dehydrated Mushrooms *See Fruits & Vegetables: Mushrooms: Dehydrated*

Dehydrated Onion *See Fruits & Vegetables: Dried & Dehydrated Vegetables: Onion: Dehydrated*

Dehydrated Parsley *See Spices, Seasonings & Seeds: Spices: Parsley: Dehydrated*

Dehydrated Potatoes *See Fruits & Vegetables: Potatoes: Dehydrated*

Dehydrated Shellfish *See Fish & Seafood: Shellfish: Dehydrated*

Dehydrated Soup *See Prepared Foods: Soups & Stews: Dehydrated Soup*

Dehydrated Vegetables *See Fruits & Vegetables: Dried & Dehydrated Vegetables: Dehydrated Vegetables; See also Fruits & Vegetables: Dehydrated*

Deli Foods *See Meats & Meat Products: Smoked, Cured & Deli Meats: Deli Foods*

Deli Meats *See Meats & Meat Products: Smoked, Cured & Deli Meats: Deli Meats*

Deli Meats, Fresh Turkey Breast *See Meats & Meat Products: Smoked, Cured & Deli Meats: Turkey: Deli Breast - Fresh*

Deli Meats, Frozen Turkey Breast *See Meats & Meat Products: Smoked, Cured & Deli Meats: Turkey: Deli Breast - Frozen*

Deli Meats, Smoked Turkey Breast *See Meats & Meat Products: Smoked, Cured & Deli Meats: Turkey: Deli Breast - Smoked*

Desiccated & Shredded Coconut *See Fruits & Vegetables: Coconut & Coconut Products: Desiccated & Shredded*

Desiccated Egg *See Eggs & Egg Products: Dried: Desiccated*

Desiccated Fruit *See Fruits & Vegetables: Dried & Dehydrated Fruits: Desiccated Fruit*

Desiccated Vegetables *See Fruits & Vegetables: Dried & Dehydrated Vegetables: Desiccated Vegetables*

Dessert Fillings *See Doughs, Mixes & Fillings: Fillings: Dessert*

Dessert Mixes *See Doughs, Mixes & Fillings: Mixes: Dessert*

Dessert Mixes, Frozen *See Doughs, Mixes & Fillings: Mixes: Frozen: Dessert*

Dessert Sauces *See Sauces, Dips & Dressings: Sauces: Dessert*

Dessert Tarts *See Baked Goods: Cakes & Pastries: Dessert Tarts*

Dessert Toppings *See Ingredients, Flavors & Additives: Toppings: Dessert*

Desserts *See Baked Goods: Desserts*

Dextrin Starches *See Ingredients, Flavors & Additives: Starches: Dextrin*

Dextrose Corn Syrups *See Sugars, Syrups & Sweeteners: Syrups: Corn: Dextrose*

Dextrose Sweeteners *See Ingredients, Flavors & Additives: Sweeteners: Dextrose*

Diced & Cooked Chicken *See Meats & Meat Products: Poultry: Chicken: Diced & Cooked*

Diced Canned Pear *See Fruits & Vegetables: Pear: Canned: Diced*

Diced Frozen Chicken *See Meats & Meat Products: Poultry: Chicken: Diced Frozen*

Diced Tomato *See Fruits & Vegetables: Tomato: Diced*

Diet & Weight Loss Aids *See Specialty & Organic Foods: Dietary Products: Diet & Weight Loss Aids*

Dietary Products *See Specialty & Organic Foods: Dietary Products*

Dietary Supplements *See Specialty & Organic Foods: Dietary Products: Dietary Supplements*

Dietetic Candy *See Candy & Confectionery: Candy: Dietetic*

Dietetic Juices *See Beverages: Juices: Dietetic*

Digestive Aids *See Ingredients, Flavors & Additives: Digestive Aids*

Dijon Mixes *See Sauces, Dips & Dressings: Salad Dressings: Mixes: Dijon*

Dill Pickles *See Relishes & Pickled Products: Pickled Products: Pickles: Dill*

Dill Seeds *See Spices, Seasonings & Seeds: Seeds: Dill*

Dill Spices *See Spices, Seasonings & Seeds: Spices: Dill*

Dill Weed Spices *See Spices, Seasonings & Seeds: Spices: Dill Weed*

Dillweed Oils *See Oils, Shortening & Fats: Oils: Dillweed*

Dim Sum *See Ethnic Foods: Dim Sum*

Dip Mixes *See Doughs, Mixes & Fillings: Mixes: Dip*

Dipping Fruit *See Fruits & Vegetables: Dipping Fruit*

Dips *See Sauces, Dips & Dressings: Dips*

Distilled Water *See Beverages: Water: Distilled*

Divinity Candy *See Candy & Confectionery: Candy: Divinity*

Dogfish *See Fish & Seafood: Fish: Dogfish*

Dolcetto *See Beverages: Wines: Red Grape Wines: Dolcetto*

Dolphin *See Fish & Seafood: Fish: Dolphin*

Donut Mixes *See Doughs, Mixes & Fillings: Mixes: Donut*

Doughnut Doughs *See Doughs, Mixes & Fillings: Doughs: Doughnuts*

Doughnut Fillings *See Doughs, Mixes & Fillings: Fillings: Doughnuts*

Doughnuts *See Baked Goods: Cakes & Pastries: Doughnuts*

Doughs *See Doughs, Mixes & Fillings: Doughs*

Dressing Flavors *See Ingredients, Flavors & Additives: Flavors: Flavors: Dressing*

Dried & Dehydrated Fruits *See Fruits & Vegetables: Dried & Dehydrated Fruits*

Dried & Dehydrated Vegetables *See Fruits & Vegetables: Dried & Dehydrated Vegetables*

Dried Apple *See Fruits & Vegetables: Apple: Dried*

Dried Apricot *See Fruits & Vegetables: Apricot: Dried*

Dried Banana *See Fruits & Vegetables: Banana: Dried*

Dried Beans *See Fruits & Vegetables: Beans: Dried*

Dried Beet Pulp *See Fruits & Vegetables: Pulps & Purees: Pulp: Dried Beet*

Dried Blueberry *See Fruits & Vegetables: Berries: Blueberry: Dried*

Dried Cantaloupe *See Fruits & Vegetables: Melon: Cantaloupe: Dried*

Dried Cayenne Pepper *See Spices, Seasonings & Seeds: Spices: Cayenne Pepper: Dried*

Dried Cherries *See Fruits & Vegetables: Cherries: Dried*

Dried Chicken Fats *See Oils, Shortening & Fats: Fats: Lard: Chicken: Dried*

Dried Chile Peppers *See Fruits & Vegetables: Peppers: Chile: Dried Pods*

Dried Chives *See Fruits & Vegetables: Dried & Dehydrated Vegetables: Dried Chives*

Dried Coconut *See Fruits & Vegetables: Coconut & Coconut Products: Dried*

Dried Cranberry *See Fruits & Vegetables: Berries: Cranberry: Dried*

Dried Cream *See Dairy Products: Cream: Dried*

Dried Egg *See Eggs & Egg Products: Dried*

Dried Fruit *See Fruits & Vegetables: Dried & Dehydrated Fruits: Dried Fruit*

Dried Honey *See Sugars, Syrups & Sweeteners: Honey: Dried*

Dried Mango *See Fruits & Vegetables: Mango: Dried*

Dried Molasses *See Sugars, Syrups & Sweeteners: Molasses: Dried*

Dried Papaya *See Fruits & Vegetables: Papaya: Dried*

Dried Peach *See Fruits & Vegetables: Peach: Dried*

Dried Pear *See Fruits & Vegetables: Pear: Dried*

Dried Pineapple *See Fruits & Vegetables: Pineapple: Dried*

Dried Plums *See Fruits & Vegetables: Plums: Dried*

Dried Prunes *See Fruits & Vegetables: Prunes: Dried*

Dried Raisins *See Fruits & Vegetables: Raisins: Dried*

Dried Refried Beans *See Fruits & Vegetables: Beans: Refried: Dried*

Dried Sliced Beef *See Meats & Meat Products: Beef & Beef Products: Sliced: Dried*

Dried Spices *See Spices, Seasonings & Seeds: Spices: Dried*

Dried Strawberry *See Fruits & Vegetables: Berries: Strawberry: Dried*

Dried Tomato *See Fruits & Vegetables: Tomato: Dried*

Drink Mixes *See Doughs, Mixes & Fillings: Mixes: Drink*

Dry Beans *See Fruits & Vegetables: Beans: Dry*

Dry Buttermilk *See Dairy Products: Buttermilk & Buttermilk Products: Buttermilk Products: Dry*

Dry Malt *See Cereals, Grains, Rice & Flour: Malt: Dry*

Dry Pancake Batters *See Doughs, Mixes & Fillings: Batters: Pancake: Dry*

Dry Peas *See Fruits & Vegetables: Peas: Dry*

Dry Raisin Juice *See Ingredients, Flavors & Additives: Replacers: Raisin Juice: Dry*

Dry Sweetcream Buttermilk *See Dairy Products: Buttermilk & Buttermilk Products: Buttermilk Products: Dry Sweetcream*

Duck *See Meats & Meat Products: Poultry: Duck*

Duck Sauces *See Sauces, Dips & Dressings: Sauces: Duck*

Dumpling Mixes *See Doughs, Mixes & Fillings: Mixes: Dumplings*

Dumplings *See Baked Goods: Cakes & Pastries: Dumplings*

Dungeness Crab *See Fish & Seafood: Shellfish: Crab: Dungeness*

Dusting Starches *See Ingredients, Flavors & Additives: Starches: Dusting*

Dutch *See Ethnic Foods: Dutch*

Dyes *See Ingredients, Flavors & Additives: Colors: Dyes*

E

E - Tocopherol *See Ingredients, Flavors & Additives: Vitamins & Supplements: E - Tocopherol*

Earl Grey Tea *See Beverages: Coffee & Tea: Tea: Earl Grey*

Earl Grey Tea, Decaffeinated *See Beverages: Coffee & Tea: Tea: Earl Grey Decaffeinated*

Easter Specialty-Packaged Candy *See Candy & Confectionery: Specialty-Packaged Candy: Easter*

Eastern Oregon Dry Bulb Onion *See Fruits & Vegetables: Onion: Eastern Oregon Dry Bulb Onion*

Echinacea Purpurea Powders *See Ingredients, Flavors & Additives: Powders: Echinacea Purpurea*

Eclairs *See Baked Goods: Cakes & Pastries: Eclairs*

Edam *See Cheese & Cheese Products: Cheese: Edam*

Edible Coatings *See Ingredients, Flavors & Additives: Coatings: Edible*

Edible Dry Beans *See Fruits & Vegetables: Beans: Dry: Edible*

Edible Oils *See Oils, Shortening & Fats: Oils: Edible*

Edible Release, Grease Agents *See Ingredients, Flavors & Additives: Agents: Release,Grease: Edible*

Eel *See Fish & Seafood: Fish: Eel*

Egg Drop Soup *See Prepared Foods: Soups & Stews: Egg Drop Soup*

Egg Nog *See Dairy Products: Egg Nog*

Egg Noodles *See Pasta & Noodles: Noodles: Egg*

Egg Powders *See Ingredients, Flavors & Additives: Powders: Egg*

Egg Replacers *See Ingredients, Flavors & Additives: Replacers: Egg*

Egg Rolls *See Ethnic Foods: Egg Rolls*

Egg Substitutes *See Eggs & Egg Products: Substitutes*

Egg Tomato *See Fruits & Vegetables: Tomato: Roma (Egg)*

Eggplant *See Fruits & Vegetables: Eggplant*

Eggplant Parmigiana *See Prepared Foods: Prepared Meals: Eggplant Parmigiana*

Eggplant, Dried & Dehydrated *See Fruits & Vegetables: Dried & Dehydrated Vegetables: Eggplant*

Eggs & Egg Products *See Eggs & Egg Products*

Eggs, Pickled Products *See Relishes & Pickled Products: Pickled Products: Eggs*

Eggs, Prepared Meals *See Prepared Foods: Prepared Meals: Eggs*

Elbow Macaroni *See Pasta & Noodles: Elbow Macaroni*

Emu *See Meats & Meat Products: Game: Emu*

Emulsifiers *See Ingredients, Flavors & Additives: Emulsifiers*

Enchiladas *See Ethnic Foods: Enchiladas*

Endive *See Spices, Seasonings & Seeds: Spices: Endive*

Energy Bars *See Specialty & Organic Foods: Health & Dietary: Energy Bars*

English Breakfast Tea *See Beverages: Coffee & Tea: Tea: English Breakfast*

English Breakfast Tea, Decaffeinated *See Beverages: Coffee & Tea: Tea: English Breakfast Decaffeinated*

English Muffins *See Baked Goods: Breads: English Muffins*

English Style B Ale *See Beverages: Beers: American & British Style: English Style B*

Enhancers *See Ingredients, Flavors & Additives: Enhancers*

Enokis Mushrooms *See Fruits & Vegetables: Mushrooms: Enokis*

Enrichment & Nutrient Additives *See Ingredients, Flavors & Additives: Additives: Enrichment & Nutrient*

Enrichment Blends *See Ingredients, Flavors & Additives: Blends: Enrichment*

Entrees Prepared Meals *See Prepared Foods: Prepared Meals: Entrees*

Enzymes *See Ingredients, Flavors & Additives: Enzymes*

Enzymes Additives *See Ingredients, Flavors & Additives: Additives: Enzymes*

Epazote Herb *See Spices, Seasonings & Seeds: Spices: Epazote Herb*

Escargot *See Prepared Foods: Prepared Meals: Escargot*

Escarole *See Spices, Seasonings & Seeds: Spices: Escarole*

Espresso *See Beverages: Coffee & Tea: Espresso*

Essential Fatty Acids *See Ingredients, Flavors & Additives: Fatty Acids: Essential*

Essential Oils *See Oils, Shortening & Fats: Oils: Essential*

Ethnic Foods *See Ethnic Foods*

Ethyleneamines *See Ingredients, Flavors & Additives: Ethyleneamines*

Etoufee *See Prepared Foods: Prepared Meals: Etoufee*

Evaporated Milk *See Dairy Products: Milk & Milk Products: Milk: Evaporated*

Extenders *See Ingredients, Flavors & Additives: Extenders*

Extra Virgin Olive Oils *See Oils, Shortening & Fats: Oils: Olive: Extra Virgin*

Extract Flavors *See Ingredients, Flavors & Additives: Flavors: Extract*

Extracts *See Ingredients, Flavors & Additives: Extracts*

Extracts, Spices *See Spices, Seasonings & Seeds: Spices: Extracts*

Extracts, Yeast *See Ingredients, Flavors & Additives: Cultures & Yeasts: Yeast: Extracts*

F

Fair-Trade Tea *See Beverages: Coffee & Tea: Tea: Fair-Trade*

Fajita Chicken Strips *See Meats & Meat Products: Poultry: Chicken: Fajita Strips*

Fajita Marinades *See Sauces, Dips & Dressings: Marinades: Fajita*

Fajita Seasonings *See Spices, Seasonings & Seeds: Seasonings: Fajita*

Farfalle *See Pasta & Noodles: Farfalle*

Farina Cereal *See Cereals, Grains, Rice & Flour: Cereal: Farina*

Farm-Raised Game *See Meats & Meat Products: Game: Farm-Raised*

Fat & Cholesterol Free *See Eggs & Egg Products: Fat & Cholesterol Free*

Fat Flavors *See Ingredients, Flavors & Additives: Flavors: Fat*

Fat Replacers *See Ingredients, Flavors & Additives: Replacers: Fat*

Fat-Free Ice Cream *See Dairy Products: Ice Cream: Fat-Free*

Fat-Free Milk *See Dairy Products: Milk & Milk Products: Milk: Fat-Free*

Fats *See Oils, Shortening & Fats*

Fats & Lard *See Oils, Shortening & Fats: Fats & Lard*

Fatty Acids *See Ingredients, Flavors & Additives: Fatty Acids*

Fava Beans *See Fruits & Vegetables: Beans: Fava*

Fennel Seeds *See Spices, Seasonings & Seeds: Seeds: Fennel*

Fennel Spices *See Spices, Seasonings & Seeds: Spices: Fennel*

Fenugreek Seeds *See Spices, Seasonings & Seeds: Seeds: Fenugreek*

Fenugreek Spices *See Spices, Seasonings & Seeds: Spices: Fenugreek*

Fermented Products *See Specialty Processed Foods: Fermented Products (See also Specific Foods)*

Feta Cheese *See Cheese & Cheese Products: Cheese: Feta*

Fettuccine *See Pasta & Noodles: Fettuccine*

Feverfew Powders *See Ingredients, Flavors & Additives: Powders: Feverfew*

Fiber *See Cereals, Grains, Rice & Flour: Fiber*

Fig Pastes *See Ingredients, Flavors & Additives: Pastes: Fig*

Fig, Dried *See Fruits & Vegetables: Dried & Dehydrated Fruits: Fig*

Figs *See Fruits & Vegetables: Figs*

Filberts *See Nuts & Nut Butters: Nuts: Filberts*

Filet Mignon *See Meats & Meat Products: Beef & Beef Products: Filet Mignon*

Filled Candy *See Candy & Confectionery: Candy: Filled*

Filled Doughnuts *See Baked Goods: Cakes & Pastries: Doughnuts: Filled*

Fillers *See Ingredients, Flavors & Additives: Fillers*

Fillets, Chicken *See Meats & Meat Products: Poultry: Chicken: Fillets*

Fillets, Fish *See Fish & Seafood: Fish: Fillets*

Fillets, Herring *See Fish & Seafood: Fish: Herring: Fillets*

Fillets, Turkey *See Meats & Meat Products: Poultry: Turkey: Fillets*

Fillings *See Doughs, Mixes & Fillings: Fillings*

Finfish *See Fish & Seafood: Fish: Finfish*

Fire Roasted Vegetables *See Fruits & Vegetables: Fire Roasted Vegetables*

Firming Agents *See Ingredients, Flavors & Additives: Agents: Firming*

Fish *See Fish & Seafood: Fish; See also Prepared Foods: Prepared Meals: Fish*

Fish & Chips *See Prepared Foods: Prepared Meals: Fish & Chips*

Fish Oils *See Oils, Shortening & Fats: Oils: Fish*

Fish Paste *See Fish & Seafood: Fish: Paste*

Fish Patties *See Prepared Foods: Prepared Meals: Fish Patties*

Fish Powders *See Ingredients, Flavors & Additives: Powders: Fish*

Fish Sauces *See Sauces, Dips & Dressings: Sauces: Fish*

Fish Steaks *See Fish & Seafood: Fish: Steaks*

Fish Sticks *See Prepared Foods: Prepared Meals: Fish Sticks; See also See Fish & Seafood: Fish: Sticks*

Flakes *See Ingredients, Flavors & Additives: Flakes*

Flat Breads *See Baked Goods: Breads: Flat*

Flavor Bases *See Ingredients, Flavors & Additives: Bases: Flavor*

Flavor Bits *See Ingredients, Flavors & Additives: Bits: Flavor*

Flavor Enhancers *See Ingredients, Flavors & Additives: Flavors: Flavors: Enhancers; See also See Ingredients, Flavors & Additives: Flavor Enhancers*

Flavored Cheese Cake *See Baked Goods: Cakes & Pastries: Cheese Cake: Flavored*

Flavored Coffee *See Beverages: Coffee & Tea: Coffee: Flavored*

Flavored Ice Cream *See Dairy Products: Ice Cream: Flavored*

Flavored Liquid Vinegar *See Sauces, Dips & Dressings: Vinegar: Liquid: Flavored*

Flavored Milk *See Dairy Products: Milk & Milk Products: Milk: Flavored*

Flavored Pellets *See Ingredients, Flavors & Additives: Half-Products: Flavored Pellets*

Flavored Popcorn *See Snack Foods: Popcorn: Flavored*

Flavored Pretzels *See Snack Foods: Pretzels: Flavored*

Flavored Stout *See Beverages: Beers: Stout & Porter: Flavored Stout*

Flavored Sugar Bits *See Ingredients, Flavors & Additives: Bits: Flavored Sugar*

Flavored Tea *See Beverages: Coffee & Tea: Tea: Flavored*

Flavored Water *See Beverages: Water: Flavored*

Flavored Wraps *See Baked Goods: Wraps: Flavored*

Flavoring Extracts *See Ingredients, Flavors & Additives: Extracts: Flavoring*

Flavors *See Ingredients, Flavors & Additives: Flavors; See also Ingredients, Flavors & Additives: Flavors: Flavors*

Flax Crisps *See Cereals, Grains, Rice & Flour: Crisps: Flax*

Flax Seeds *See Spices, Seasonings & Seeds: Seeds: Flax*

Flounder *See Fish & Seafood: Fish: Flounder*

Flour *See Cereals, Grains, Rice & Flour: Flour*

Flour, Rice Starch, Organic *See Specialty & Organic Foods: Organic Foods: Rice Starch: Flour*

Flowers, Edible *See Fruits & Vegetables: Flowers - Edible*

Fluid Shortening *See Oils, Shortening & Fats: Shortening: Fluid*

Fluke *See Fish & Seafood: Fish: Fluke*

Foaming & Whipping Agents *See Ingredients, Flavors & Additives: Agents: Foaming & Whipping*

Focaccia *See Baked Goods: Breads: Focaccia*

Foie Gras *See Meats & Meat Products: Pates & Fois Gras: Foie Gras*

Fondant *See Sugars, Syrups & Sweeteners: Sugar: Fondant*

Fondants *See Candy & Confectionery: Candy: Fondants*

Fontina Cheese *See Cheese & Cheese Products: Cheese: Fontina*

Food Bases *See Ingredients, Flavors & Additives: Bases: Food*

Food Ingredients *See Ingredients, Flavors & Additives: Ingredients: Food*

Food Preservatives *See Ingredients, Flavors & Additives: Preservatives: Food*

Food Releases *See Ingredients, Flavors & Additives: Releases: Food*

Foodservice, Individual Packets *See Prepared Foods: Individual Packets: Foodservice*

Formula *See Baby Foods: Formula*

Fortification Protein *See Ingredients, Flavors & Additives: Vitamins & Supplements: Protein Supplements: Fortification Protein*

Fortified Refined Vegetable Oils *See Oils, Shortening & Fats: Oils: Vegetable: Fortified Refined*

Fortune Cookies *See Baked Goods: Cookies & Bars: Fortune Cookies*

Fra Diavolo Sauces *See Sauces, Dips & Dressings: Sauces: Fra Diavolo*

Fragrances *See Ingredients, Flavors & Additives: Aroma Chemicals & Materials: Fragrances*

Frankfurters *See Meats & Meat Products: Frankfurters*

Frankfurters, Mini *See Meats & Meat Products: Frankfurters: Mini*

Free Flow Additives *See Ingredients, Flavors & Additives: Additives: Free Flow*

Freeze-Dried Food *See Specialty Processed Foods: Freeze Dried Food (See also Specific Foods)*

Freeze-Dried Fruits & Vegetables *See Fruits & Vegetables: Dehydrated: Freeze Dried; See also Fruits & Vegetables: Dried & Dehydrated Fruits: Freeze Dried; See also Fruits & Vegetables: Dried & Dehydrated Vegetables: Freeze Dried*

Freeze-Dried Mushrooms *See Fruits & Vegetables: Dried & Dehydrated Vegetables: Mushrooms: Freeze Dried*

Freeze-Dried Seafood *See Fish & Seafood: Seafood: Freeze-Dried*

French Breads *See Baked Goods: Breads: French*

French Fries *See Prepared Foods: French Fries*

French Salad Dressings *See Sauces, Dips & Dressings: Salad Dressings: French; See also Sauces, Dips & Dressings: Salad Dressings: Mixes: French*

French Toast *See Prepared Foods: French Toast*

French Wines *See Beverages: Wines: French*

Fresh Apple *See Fruits & Vegetables: Apple: Fresh*

Fresh Bagels *See Baked Goods: Breads: Bagels: Fresh*

Fresh Bakes Goods *See Baked Goods: Fresh*

Fresh Beef *See Meats & Meat Products: Beef & Beef Products: Fresh*

Fresh Biscuits *See Baked Goods: Breads: Biscuits: Fresh*

Fresh Breads *See Baked Goods: Breads: Fresh*

Fresh Chicken *See Meats & Meat Products: Poultry: Chicken: Fresh*

Fresh Clam *See Fish & Seafood: Shellfish: Clam: Fresh*

Fresh Crab *See Fish & Seafood: Shellfish: Crab: Fresh*

Fresh Cream *See Dairy Products: Cream: Fresh*

Fresh Eggs *See Eggs & Egg Products: Fresh*

Fresh Fish *See Fish & Seafood: Fish: Fresh*

Fresh Fish Cakes *See Fish & Seafood: Fish: Cakes: Fresh*

Fresh Fruit *See Fruits & Vegetables: Fresh Fruit*

Fresh Ham *See Meats & Meat Products: Smoked, Cured & Deli Meats: Ham: Fresh*

Fresh Herring *See Fish & Seafood: Fish: Herring: Fresh*

Fresh Lamb *See Meats & Meat Products: Lamb: Fresh*

Fresh Lobster *See Fish & Seafood: Shellfish: Lobster: Fresh*

Fresh Milk *See Dairy Products: Milk & Milk Products: Milk: Fresh*

Fresh Mushrooms *See Fruits & Vegetables: Mushrooms: Fresh*

Fresh Oysters *See Fish & Seafood: Shellfish: Oysters: Fresh*

Fresh Peas *See Fruits & Vegetables: Peas: Fresh*

Fresh Pies *See Baked Goods: Pies: Fresh*

Fresh Pork *See Meats & Meat Products: Pork & Pork Products: Fresh*

Fresh Potatoes *See Fruits & Vegetables: Potatoes: Fresh*

Fresh Prepared Foods *See Prepared Foods: Fresh*

Fresh Rolls *See Baked Goods: Breads: Rolls: Fresh*

Fresh Sardines *See Fish & Seafood: Fish: Sardines: Fresh*

Fresh Seafood *See Fish & Seafood: Seafood: Fresh*

Fresh Shellfish *See Fish & Seafood: Shellfish: Fresh*

Fresh Shrimp *See Fish & Seafood: Shellfish: Shrimp: Fresh*

Fresh Soy *See Fruits & Vegetables: Soy: Fresh*

Fresh Stew *See Prepared Foods: Soups & Stews: Fresh Stew*
Fresh Succotash *See Fruits & Vegetables: Succotash: Fresh*
Fresh Tomato *See Fruits & Vegetables: Tomato: Fresh*
Fresh Turkey *See Meats & Meat Products: Poultry: Turkey: Fresh*
Fresh Veal *See Meats & Meat Products: Beef & Beef Products: Veal: Fresh*
Fresh Vegetables *See Fruits & Vegetables: Fresh Vegetables*
Fresh Yeast *See Ingredients, Flavors & Additives: Cultures & Yeasts: Yeast: Fresh*
Freshwater Fish *See Fish & Seafood: Fish: Freshwater*
Fried Chips *See Snack Foods: Chips: Fried*
Fried Oysters *See Fish & Seafood: Shellfish: Oysters: Fried*
Fried Porkskins *See Prepared Foods: Porkskins: Fried*
Fried Rice, Prepared Meals *See Prepared Foods: Prepared Meals: Fried Rice*
Fried Rice, Seasonings *See Spices, Seasonings & Seeds: Seasonings: Fried Rice*
Frozen Appetizers *See Prepared Foods: Appetizers: Frozen*
Frozen Apple *See Fruits & Vegetables: Apple: Frozen*
Frozen Apple Juices *See Beverages: Juices: Apple: Frozen*
Frozen Apricot *See Fruits & Vegetables: Apricot: Frozen*
Frozen Apricot Juices *See Beverages: Juices: Apricot: Frozen*
Frozen Artichoke *See Fruits & Vegetables: Artichoke: Frozen*
Frozen Asparagus *See Fruits & Vegetables: Asparagus: Frozen*
Frozen Au Gratin Potatoes *See Fruits & Vegetables: Potatoes: Au Gratin: Frozen*
Frozen Bagels *See Baked Goods: Breads: Bagels: Frozen*
Frozen Baked & Stuffed Potatoes *See Fruits & Vegetables: Potatoes: Baked & Stuffed: Frozen*
Frozen Baked Goods *See Baked Goods: Frozen*
Frozen Baking Doughs *See Doughs, Mixes & Fillings: Doughs: Baking*
Frozen Barbecued Beef *See Meats & Meat Products: Beef & Beef Products: Barbecued: Frozen*
Frozen Barbecued Pork *See Meats & Meat Products: Pork & Pork Products: Barbecued: Frozen*
Frozen Beans *See Fruits & Vegetables: Beans: Frozen*
Frozen Beef & Beef Products *See Meats & Meat Products: Beef & Beef Products: Frozen*
Frozen Beef Stew *See Meats & Meat Products: Beef & Beef Products: Stew: Frozen*
Frozen Beets *See Fruits & Vegetables: Beets: Frozen*
Frozen Berries *See Fruits & Vegetables: Berries: Frozen*
Frozen Beverage Mixes *See Doughs, Mixes & Fillings: Mixes: Beverage: Frozen*
Frozen Biscuits *See Baked Goods: Breads: Biscuits: Frozen*
Frozen Black-eyed Peas *See Fruits & Vegetables: Peas: Black-eyed: Frozen*
Frozen Blackberry *See Fruits & Vegetables: Berries: Blackberry: Frozen*
Frozen Blintzes *See Baked Goods: Cakes & Pastries: Blintzes: Frozen*
Frozen Blue Lake Beans *See Fruits & Vegetables: Beans: Blue Lake: Frozen*
Frozen Blueberry *See Fruits & Vegetables: Berries: Blueberry: Frozen*
Frozen Boysenberry *See Fruits & Vegetables: Berries: Boysenberry: Frozen*
Frozen Breads *See Baked Goods: Breads: Frozen*
Frozen Broccoli *See Fruits & Vegetables: Broccoli: Frozen*
Frozen Broth *See Prepared Foods: Broth: Frozen*
Frozen Brussel Sprouts *See Fruits & Vegetables: Brussel Sprouts: Frozen*
Frozen Buns *See Baked Goods: Breads: Buns: Frozen*
Frozen Butter Beans *See Fruits & Vegetables: Beans: Butter: Frozen*
Frozen Cabbage *See Fruits & Vegetables: Cabbage: Frozen*
Frozen Cake Batters *See Doughs, Mixes & Fillings: Batters: Cake: Frozen*
Frozen Cakes *See Baked Goods: Cakes & Pastries: Frozen Cakes*
Frozen Cappuccino Mixes *See Doughs, Mixes & Fillings: Mixes: Cappuccino: Frozen*
Frozen Capsicums Peppers *See Fruits & Vegetables: Peppers: Capsicums: Frozen*
Frozen Carrot *See Fruits & Vegetables: Carrot: Frozen*
Frozen Cauliflower *See Fruits & Vegetables: Cauliflower: Frozen*
Frozen Celery *See Fruits & Vegetables: Celery: Frozen*
Frozen Cheese Cake *See Baked Goods: Cakes & Pastries: Cheese Cake: Frozen*
Frozen Cherries *See Fruits & Vegetables: Cherries: Frozen*
Frozen Cherry Juices *See Beverages: Juices: Cherry: Frozen*
Frozen Chicken *See Meats & Meat Products: Poultry: Chicken: Frozen*

Frozen Chicken Fats & Lard *See Oils, Shortening & Fats: Fats & Lard: Chicken: Frozen*
Frozen Chili *See Prepared Foods: Chili: Frozen*
Frozen Chop Suey *See Ethnic Foods: Chop Suey: Frozen*
Frozen Clam *See Fish & Seafood: Shellfish: Clam: Frozen*
Frozen Clam Strips *See Fish & Seafood: Shellfish: Clam: Frozen Strips*
Frozen Coconut & Coconut Products *See Fruits & Vegetables: Coconut & Coconut Products: Frozen*
Frozen Convenience Food *See Prepared Foods: Convenience Food: Frozen*
Frozen Cookies *See Baked Goods: Cookies & Bars: Frozen Cookies*
Frozen Corn *See Fruits & Vegetables: Corn: Frozen*
Frozen Corn-on-the-Cob *See Fruits & Vegetables: Corn: Corn-on-the-Cob: Frozen*
Frozen Crab *See Fish & Seafood: Shellfish: Crab: Frozen; See also See Prepared Foods: Prepared Meals: Crab: Frozen*
Frozen Crab Meat *See Fish & Seafood: Shellfish: Crab: Meat Frozen*
Frozen Cranberry *See Fruits & Vegetables: Berries: Cranberry: Frozen*
Frozen Cranberry Juices *See Beverages: Juices: Cranberry: Frozen*
Frozen Crayfish *See Fish & Seafood: Shellfish: Crayfish: Frozen*
Frozen Crepes *See Prepared Foods: Crepes: Frozen*
Frozen Dehydrated Potatoes *See Fruits & Vegetables: Potatoes: Dehydrated: Frozen*
Frozen Doughnuts *See Baked Goods: Cakes & Pastries: Doughnuts: Frozen*
Frozen Doughs *See Doughs, Mixes & Fillings: Doughs: Frozen*
Frozen Eggs *See Eggs & Egg Products: Frozen*
Frozen Enchiladas *See Ethnic Foods: Enchiladas: Frozen*
Frozen Entrees *See Prepared Foods: Prepared Meals: Entrees: Frozen*
Frozen Figs *See Fruits & Vegetables: Figs: Frozen*
Frozen Fish *See Fish & Seafood: Fish: Frozen*
Frozen Fish Cakes *See Fish & Seafood: Fish: Cakes: Frozen*
Frozen Fish Sticks *See Prepared Foods: Prepared Meals: Fish Sticks: Frozen*
Frozen Foods *See Specialty Processed Foods: Frozen Foods (See also Specific Foods)*
Frozen French Fries *See Prepared Foods: French Fries: Frozen*
Frozen French Toast *See Prepared Foods: French Toast: Frozen*
Frozen Fruit *See Fruits & Vegetables: Frozen Fruit*
Frozen Fruit & Vegetable Juices *See Beverages: Juices: Fruit & Vegetable: Frozen*
Frozen Fruit Juices *See Beverages: Juices: Fruit: Frozen*
Frozen Fruit Pies *See Baked Goods: Pies: Fruit: Frozen*
Frozen Garlic Breads *See Baked Goods: Breads: Garlic: Frozen*
Frozen Gnocchi *See Pasta & Noodles: Gnocchi: Frozen*
Frozen Grape Juices *See Beverages: Juices: Grape: Frozen*
Frozen Grapefruit Juices *See Beverages: Juices: Grapefruit: Frozen*
Frozen Green Beans *See Fruits & Vegetables: Beans: Green: Frozen*
Frozen Ground Beef & Beef Products *See Meats & Meat Products: Beef & Beef Products: Ground: Frozen*
Frozen Ham *See Meats & Meat Products: Smoked, Cured & Deli Meats: Ham: Frozen*
Frozen Herring *See Fish & Seafood: Fish: Herring: Frozen*
Frozen Kale *See Fruits & Vegetables: Kale: Frozen*
Frozen Kidney Beans *See Fruits & Vegetables: Beans: Kidney: Frozen*
Frozen Lamb *See Meats & Meat Products: Lamb: Frozen*
Frozen Lasagna *See Pasta & Noodles: Lasagna: Frozen*
Frozen Lemon Juices *See Beverages: Juices: Lemon: Frozen*
Frozen Lima Beans *See Fruits & Vegetables: Beans: Lima: Frozen*
Frozen Lobster *See Fish & Seafood: Shellfish: Lobster: Frozen*
Frozen Mashed Sweet Potatoes *See Fruits & Vegetables: Sweet Potatoes: Mashed: Frozen*
Frozen Meat Balls *See Prepared Foods: Meat Balls: Frozen*
Frozen Meat Pies *See Baked Goods: Pies: Meat: Frozen*
Frozen Melon Balls *See Fruits & Vegetables: Melon: Balls: Frozen*
Frozen Mixes *See Doughs, Mixes & Fillings: Mixes: Frozen*
Frozen Mozzarella Cheese, Lite Shredded *See Cheese & Cheese Products: Cheese: Mozzarella: Lite Shredded - Frozen*

Frozen Muffins *See Baked Goods: Cakes & Pastries: Muffins: Frozen*
Frozen Mushrooms *See Fruits & Vegetables: Mushrooms: Frozen*
Frozen Non-Dairy Desserts *See Baked Goods: Desserts: Non-Dairy: Frozen*
Frozen Non-Fruit Pies *See Baked Goods: Pies: Non-Fruit: Frozen*
Frozen Okra *See Fruits & Vegetables: Okra: Frozen*
Frozen Onion *See Fruits & Vegetables: Onion: Frozen*
Frozen Onion Rings *See Prepared Foods: Onion Rings: Frozen*
Frozen Oven Type Potatoes *See Fruits & Vegetables: Potatoes: Oven Type: Frozen*
Frozen Oysters *See Fish & Seafood: Shellfish: Oysters: Frozen*
Frozen Pancakes *See Prepared Foods: Pancakes: Frozen*
Frozen Pasta *See Pasta & Noodles: Pasta: Frozen*
Frozen Patties Beef & Beef Products *See Meats & Meat Products: Beef & Beef Products: Patties: Frozen*
Frozen Peach *See Fruits & Vegetables: Peach: Frozen*
Frozen Pear *See Fruits & Vegetables: Pear: Frozen*
Frozen Peas *See Fruits & Vegetables: Peas: Frozen*
Frozen Peas & Carrots *See Fruits & Vegetables: Vegetables Mixed: Peas & Carrots: Frozen*
Frozen Peppers *See Fruits & Vegetables: Peppers: Frozen*
Frozen Pineapple *See Fruits & Vegetables: Pineapple: Frozen*
Frozen Pineapple Juices *See Beverages: Juices: Pineapple: Frozen*
Frozen Pizza *See Prepared Foods: Pizza & Pizza Products: Pizza: Frozen*
Frozen Pizza Doughs *See Doughs, Mixes & Fillings: Doughs: Pizza: Frozen*
Frozen Pizza Shells *See Prepared Foods: Pizza & Pizza Products: Shells: Frozen*
Frozen Plums *See Fruits & Vegetables: Plums: Frozen*
Frozen Pork & Pork Products *See Meats & Meat Products: Pork & Pork Products: Frozen*
Frozen Potato Rounds *See Fruits & Vegetables: Potatoes: Frozen: Rounds*
Frozen Potatoes *See Fruits & Vegetables: Potatoes: Frozen*
Frozen Prepared Foods *See Prepared Foods: Frozen*
Frozen Prepared Meals *See Prepared Foods: Prepared Meals: Frozen*
Frozen Prepared Pork & Pork Products *See Meats & Meat Products: Pork & Pork Products: Prepared: Frozen*
Frozen Prunes *See Fruits & Vegetables: Prunes: Frozen*
Frozen Pumpkin *See Fruits & Vegetables: Pumpkin: Frozen*
Frozen Rabbit *See Meats & Meat Products: Game: Rabbit: Frozen*
Frozen Raspberries *See Fruits & Vegetables: Berries: Raspberries: Frozen*
Frozen Ravioli *See Pasta & Noodles: Ravioli: Frozen*
Frozen Rhubarb *See Fruits & Vegetables: Rhubarb: Frozen*
Frozen Rice *See Cereals, Grains, Rice & Flour: Rice: Frozen*
Frozen Rolls *See Baked Goods: Breads: Rolls: Frozen*
Frozen Rutabaga *See Fruits & Vegetables: Rutabaga: Frozen*
Frozen Sauces *See Sauces, Dips & Dressings: Sauces: Frozen*
Frozen Scampi *See Fish & Seafood: Shellfish: Scampi: Frozen*
Frozen Seafood *See Fish & Seafood: Seafood: Frozen*
Frozen Shellfish *See Fish & Seafood: Shellfish: Frozen*
Frozen Shrimp *See Fish & Seafood: Shellfish: Shrimp: Frozen*
Frozen Sliced Beef & Beef Products *See Meats & Meat Products: Beef & Beef Products: Sliced: Frozen*
Frozen Slices Apple *See Fruits & Vegetables: Apple: Slices: Frozen*
Frozen Soup *See Prepared Foods: Soups & Stews: Frozen Soup*
Frozen Spaghetti *See Pasta & Noodles: Spaghetti: Frozen*
Frozen Special Trim Beef & Beef Products *See Meats & Meat Products: Beef & Beef Products: Special Trim: Frozen*
Frozen Spinach *See Fruits & Vegetables: Spinach: Frozen*
Frozen Squash *See Fruits & Vegetables: Squash: Frozen*
Frozen Stew *See Prepared Foods: Soups & Stews: Frozen Stew*
Frozen Strawberry *See Fruits & Vegetables: Berries: Strawberry: Frozen*
Frozen Stuffed Cabbage *See Prepared Foods: Prepared Meals: Stuffed Cabbage: Frozen*
Frozen Substitutes *See Eggs & Egg Products: Substitutes: Frozen*
Frozen Succotash *See Fruits & Vegetables: Succotash: Frozen*

Frozen Sweet Potatoes *See Fruits & Vegetables: Sweet Potatoes: Frozen*

Frozen Tamales *See Ethnic Foods: Tamales: Frozen*

Frozen Tomato *See Fruits & Vegetables: Tomato: Frozen*

Frozen Tomato Juices *See Beverages: Juices: Tomato: Frozen*

Frozen Tomato Sauces *See Sauces, Dips & Dressings: Sauces: Tomato: Frozen*

Frozen Tuna *See Fish & Seafood: Fish: Tuna: Frozen*

Frozen Turkey *See Meats & Meat Products: Poultry: Turkey: Frozen*

Frozen Turnip *See Fruits & Vegetables: Turnip: Frozen*

Frozen Veal *See Meats & Meat Products: Beef & Beef Products: Veal: Frozen*

Frozen Vegetables *See Fruits & Vegetables: Frozen Vegetables*

Frozen Vegetables Mixed *See Fruits & Vegetables: Vegetables Mixed: Frozen*

Frozen Venison *See Meats & Meat Products: Game: Venison: Frozen*

Frozen Waffles *See Baked Goods: Waffles: Frozen*

Frozen Wax Beans *See Fruits & Vegetables: Beans: Wax: Frozen*

Frozen Yams *See Fruits & Vegetables: Yams: Frozen*

Frozen Yogurt *See Dairy Products: Yogurt: Frozen*

Frozen Yogurt Powders *See Ingredients, Flavors & Additives: Powders: Yogurt: Frozen*

Fructose *See Sugars, Syrups & Sweeteners: Fructose*

Fruit *See Fruits & Vegetables: Fruit*

Fruit & Vegetable Coating Waxes *See Ingredients, Flavors & Additives: Waxes: Fruit & Vegetable Coating*

Fruit & Vegetable Juices *See Beverages: Juices: Fruit & Vegetable*

Fruit & Vegetable Pulps & Purees *See Fruits & Vegetables: Pulps & Purees: Fruit & Vegetable*

Fruit & Vegetable Puree *See Fruits & Vegetables: Pulps & Purees: Puree: Fruit & Vegetable*

Fruit Bases *See Ingredients, Flavors & Additives: Bases: Fruit*

Fruit Butter Spreads *See Jams, Jellies & Spreads: Spreads: Fruit Butter*

Fruit Cake *See Baked Goods: Cakes & Pastries: Fruit Cake*

Fruit Cobbler *See Baked Goods: Cakes & Pastries: Fruit Cobbler*

Fruit Cocktail *See Fruits & Vegetables: Fruit Cocktail*

Fruit Concentrates *See Ingredients, Flavors & Additives: Concentrates: Fruit*

Fruit Extracts *See Ingredients, Flavors & Additives: Extracts: Fruit*

Fruit Fillings *See Doughs, Mixes & Fillings: Fillings: Fruit*

Fruit Flavors *See Ingredients, Flavors & Additives: Flavors: Fruit*

Fruit Juices *See Beverages: Juices: Fruit*

Fruit Oils *See Oils, Shortening & Fats: Oils: Fruit*

Fruit Pastes *See Ingredients, Flavors & Additives: Pastes: Fruit*

Fruit Pectins *See Ingredients, Flavors & Additives: Pectins: Fruit*

Fruit Pies *See Baked Goods: Pies: Fruit*

Fruit Powders *See Ingredients, Flavors & Additives: Powders: Fruit*

Fruit Pulp *See Fruits & Vegetables: Pulps & Purees: Pulp: Fruit*

Fruit Pulps & Purees *See Fruits & Vegetables: Pulps & Purees: Fruit*

Fruit Punch Juices *See Beverages: Juices: Fruit Punch*

Fruit Puree *See Fruits & Vegetables: Pulps & Purees: Puree: Fruit*

Fruit Puree Concentrates *See Ingredients, Flavors & Additives: Concentrates: Fruit Puree*

Fruit Salad *See Fruits & Vegetables: Fruit: Salad*

Fruit Syrups *See Sugars, Syrups & Sweeteners: Syrups: Fruit*

Fruit Toppings *See Ingredients, Flavors & Additives: Toppings: Fruit*

Fruit, Certified Organic *See Specialty & Organic Foods: Organic Foods: Certified: Fruit*

Fruits & Vegetables *See Fruits & Vegetables*

Fruits, Organic *See Specialty & Organic Foods: Organic Foods: Fruits*

Fryer Rabbit *See Meats & Meat Products: Game: Rabbit: Fryer*

Fudge Candy *See Candy & Confectionery: Candy: Fudge*

Fudge Chocolate Products *See Candy & Confectionery: Chocolate Products: Fudge*

Fudge Sauces *See Sauces, Dips & Dressings: Sauces: Fudge*

Fudgesicles *See Dairy Products: Ice Cream: Fudgesicles*

Fumaric Acidulants *See Ingredients, Flavors & Additives: Acidulants: Fumaric*

Fund Raising Specialty-Packaged Candy *See Candy & Confectionery: Specialty-Packaged Candy: Fund Raising*

Funnel Cake *See Baked Goods: Cakes & Pastries: Funnel Cake*

G

Galangal *See Fruits & Vegetables: Galangal*

Game Meat & Poultry *See Meats & Meat Products: Game: Meat & Poultry; See also See Meats & Meat Products: Game*

Garbanzo Beans *See Fruits & Vegetables: Beans: Garbanzo*

Garlic *See Fruits & Vegetables: Garlic*

Garlic Bread Sticks *See Baked Goods: Bread Sticks: Garlic*

Garlic Breads *See Baked Goods: Breads: Garlic*

Garlic Juices *See Beverages: Juices: Garlic*

Garlic Oils *See Oils, Shortening & Fats: Oils: Garlic*

Garlic Powders *See Ingredients, Flavors & Additives: Powders: Garlic (See also Spices/Garlic Powder)*

Garlic Salt *See Spices, Seasonings & Seeds: Salt: Garlic; See also Spices, Seasonings & Seeds: Spices: Garlic Salt*

Garlic Sauces *See Sauces, Dips & Dressings: Sauces: Garlic*

Garlic Spices *See Spices, Seasonings & Seeds: Spices: Garlic*

Gefilte Fish *See Fish & Seafood: Fish: Gefilte*

Gelatin Thickeners *See Ingredients, Flavors & Additives: Thickeners: Gelatin*

Gelato *See Dairy Products: Ice Cream: Gelato*

Gellan *See Ingredients, Flavors & Additives: Gums: Gellan*

General Grocery *See General Grocery*

Geoduck Clams *See Fish & Seafood: Shellfish: Geoduck Clams*

Gewurztraminer *See Beverages: Wines: White Grape Varieties: Gewurztraminer*

Ghatti *See Ingredients, Flavors & Additives: Gums: Ghatti*

Gherkins Pickles *See Relishes & Pickled Products: Pickled Products: Pickles: Gherkins*

Giardiniera *See Prepared Foods: Giardiniera*

Gin *See Beverages: Spirits & Liqueurs: Gin*

Ginger *See Fruits & Vegetables: Ginger*

Ginger Ale *See Beverages: Soft Drinks & Sodas: Soft Drinks: Ginger Ale*

Ginger Oils *See Oils, Shortening & Fats: Oils: Ginger*

Ginger Pieces *See Spices, Seasonings & Seeds: Spices: Ginger: Pieces*

Ginger Sauces *See Sauces, Dips & Dressings: Sauces: Ginger*

Ginger Snaps *See Baked Goods: Cookies & Bars: Ginger Snaps*

Ginger Spices *See Spices, Seasonings & Seeds: Spices: Ginger*

Gingko Powders *See Ingredients, Flavors & Additives: Powders: Gingko*

Ginseng Powders *See Ingredients, Flavors & Additives: Powders: Ginseng*

Ginseng Spices *See Spices, Seasonings & Seeds: Spices: Ginseng*

Glace *See Fruits & Vegetables: Glace*

Glandulars *See Ingredients, Flavors & Additives: Glandulars*

Glass-Packed Apple Juices *See Beverages: Juices: Apple: Glass-Packed*

Glass-Packed Apricot Juices *See Beverages: Juices: Apricot: Glass-Packed*

Glass-Packed Cherry Juices *See Beverages: Juices: Cherry: Glass-Packed*

Glass-Packed Chilled Tomato Juices *See Beverages: Juices: Tomato: Glass-Packed Chilled*

Glass-Packed Cranberry Juices *See Beverages: Juices: Cranberry: Glass-Packed*

Glass-Packed Fish *See Fish & Seafood: Fish: Packed: Glass*

Glass-Packed Fruit & Vegetable Juices *See Beverages: Juices: Fruit & Vegetable: Glass-Packed*

Glass-Packed Fruit Juices *See Beverages: Juices: Fruit: Glass-Packed*

Glass-Packed Grape Juices *See Beverages: Juices: Grape: Glass-Packed*

Glass-Packed Grapefruit Juices *See Beverages: Juices: Grapefruit: Glass-Packed*

Glass-Packed Lemon Juices *See Beverages: Juices: Lemon: Glass-Packed*

Glass-Packed Pineapple Juices *See Beverages: Juices: Pineapple: Glass-Packed*

Glazed & Coated Nuts *See Nuts & Nut Butters: Nuts: Glazed & Coated*

Glazes *See Sauces, Dips & Dressings: Glazes*

Gluconates *See Ingredients, Flavors & Additives: Flavor Enhancers: Gluconates*

Gluconic Acids (Gluconolactone) *See Ingredients, Flavors & Additives: Acids: Gluconic (Gluconolactone)*

Glucose *See Sugars, Syrups & Sweeteners: Syrups: Corn: Glucose - Etc.*

Glutamic Acids *See Ingredients, Flavors & Additives: Acids: Glutamic*

Gluten Flour *See Cereals, Grains, Rice & Flour: Flour: Gluten*

Gluten Wheat *See Cereals, Grains, Rice & Flour: Wheat: Gluten*

Glycine *See Ingredients, Flavors & Additives: Glycine*

Gnocchi *See Pasta & Noodles: Gnocchi*

Goat *See Meats & Meat Products: Goat*

Goat Milk *See Dairy Products: Milk & Milk Products: Milk: Goat*

Goat's Cheese *See Cheese & Cheese Products: Cheese: Goat's*

Gold Kiwi *See Fruits & Vegetables: Kiwi: Gold*

Golden Delicious Apple *See Fruits & Vegetables: Apple: Golden Delicious*

Golden Scallopino Squash *See Fruits & Vegetables: Squash: Golden Scallopino*

Golden Trout *See Fish & Seafood: Fish: Trout: Golden*

Goose Berries *See Fruits & Vegetables: Berries: Goose*

Goose Poultry *See Meats & Meat Products: Poultry: Goose*

Gorgonzola Cheese *See Cheese & Cheese Products: Cheese: Gorgonzola*

Gotu Kola Powders *See Ingredients, Flavors & Additives: Powders: Gotu Kola*

Gouda Cheese *See Cheese & Cheese Products: Cheese: Gouda*

Gourmet & Specialty Foods *See Specialty & Organic Foods: Gourmet & Specialty Foods; See also Specialty & Organic Foods: Gourmet & Specialty Foods: Gourmet & Specialty Foods*

Gourmet Flavored Lollypops *See Candy & Confectionery: Candy: Lollypops: Gourmet Flavored*

Gourmet Potato Chips *See Snack Foods: Chips: Potato: Gourmet*

Gourmet Salad Dressings *See Sauces, Dips & Dressings: Salad Dressings: Gourmet*

Graham Toppings *See Ingredients, Flavors & Additives: Toppings: Graham*

Grain Flavors *See Ingredients, Flavors & Additives: Flavors: Grain*

Grain-Based Ingredients *See Ingredients, Flavors & Additives: Grain-Based*

Grains *See Cereals, Grains, Rice & Flour: Grains*

Granita Ice Cream *See Dairy Products: Ice Cream: Granita*

Granita Mixes *See Doughs, Mixes & Fillings: Mixes: Granita*

Granny Smith Apple *See Fruits & Vegetables: Apple: Granny Smith*

Granola *See Cereals, Grains, Rice & Flour: Granola*

Granola Toppings *See Ingredients, Flavors & Additives: Toppings: Granola*

Granulated Garlic *See Fruits & Vegetables: Garlic: Granulated; See also Spices, Seasonings & Seeds: Spices: Garlic: Granulated*

Granulated Onion *See Fruits & Vegetables: Dried & Dehydrated Vegetables: Onion: Granulated; See also Spices, Seasonings & Seeds: Spices: Onion: Granulated*

Granulated Peanuts *See Nuts & Nut Butters: Nuts: Peanuts: Granulated*

Granulated Starch Pearl Tapioca *See Cereals, Grains, Rice & Flour: Tapioca: Pearl: Granulated, Starch*

Granulated Sugar *See Sugars, Syrups & Sweeteners: Sugar: Granulated*

Granules Honey *See Sugars, Syrups & Sweeteners: Honey: Granules*

Grape *See Fruits & Vegetables: Grape*

Grape Ade Juices *See Beverages: Juices: Ade: Grape*

Grape Jams *See Jams, Jellies & Spreads: Jams: Grape*

Grape Juices *See Beverages: Juices: Grape*

Grape Leaves *See Fruits & Vegetables: Grape: Leaves*

1	2	3	4	5

EXAMPLE: Canadian Style Bacon *See Meats & Meat Products: Smoked, Cured & Deli Meats: Bacon: Canadian Style*

1. Product or Service you are looking for
2. Main Category, in alphabetical order, located in the page headers starting on page 23
3. Category Description, located in black bars and in page headers
4. Product Category, located in gray bars
5. Product Type, located under gray bars, centered in bold

Grape Skin Extract Color *See Ingredients, Flavors & Additives: Colors: Grape Skin Extract Color*
Grapefruit *See Fruits & Vegetables: Grapefruit*
Grapefruit Juices *See Beverages: Juices: Grapefruit*
Grapefruit Oils *See Oils, Shortening & Fats: Oils: Grapefruit*
Grapeseed Oils *See Oils, Shortening & Fats: Oils: Grapeseed*
Grated Cheese *See Cheese & Cheese Products: Cheese: Grated*
Gravy *See Sauces, Dips & Dressings: Gravy*
Gravy Bases *See Ingredients, Flavors & Additives: Bases: Gravy*
Gravy Mixes *See Doughs, Mixes & Fillings: Mixes: Gravy*
Great Northern Beans *See Fruits & Vegetables: Beans: Great Northern*
Greek Beans *See Fruits & Vegetables: Beans: Greek*
Greek Olives *See Fruits & Vegetables: Olives: Greek*
Greek Oregano *See Spices, Seasonings & Seeds: Spices: Oregano: Greek*
Greek Style Seasonings *See Spices, Seasonings & Seeds: Seasonings: Greek Style*
Green & Yellow Split Peas, Dried *See Fruits & Vegetables: Peas: Green & Yellow Split - Dried*
Green Beans *See Fruits & Vegetables: Beans: Green*
Green Bell Peppers, Dried *See Fruits & Vegetables: Dried & Dehydrated Vegetables: Bell Peppers: Green*
Green Cabbage *See Fruits & Vegetables: Cabbage: Green*
Green Kiwi *See Fruits & Vegetables: Kiwi: Green*
Green Looseleaf Lettuce *See Fruits & Vegetables: Lettuce: Looseleaf: Green*
Green Mung Beans *See Fruits & Vegetables: Beans: Green Mung; See also Fruits & Vegetables: Beans: Mung: Green*
Green Olives *See Fruits & Vegetables: Olives: Green*
Green Olives with Pimiento *See Fruits & Vegetables: Olives: Green: with Pimiento*
Green Onion *See Fruits & Vegetables: Onion: Green*
Green Peas *See Fruits & Vegetables: Peas: Green*
Green Tea *See Beverages: Coffee & Tea: Tea: Green*
Greens Mustard *See Fruits & Vegetables: Mustard: Greens*
Grilled Patties Chicken *See Meats & Meat Products: Poultry: Chicken: Grilled Patties*
Grits *See Cereals, Grains, Rice & Flour: Grits; See also Cereals, Grains, Rice & Flour: Grits: Corn White & Yellow*
Groats *See Cereals, Grains, Rice & Flour: Oats & Oat Products: Groats*
Ground Allspice *See Spices, Seasonings & Seeds: Spices: Allspice: Ground*
Ground Bay Leaves *See Spices, Seasonings & Seeds: Spices: Bay Leaves: Ground*
Ground Beef & Beef Products *See Meats & Meat Products: Beef & Beef Products: Ground*
Ground Cardamom *See Spices, Seasonings & Seeds: Spices: Cardamom: Ground*
Ground Cayenne Pepper *See Spices, Seasonings & Seeds: Spices: Cayenne Pepper: Ground*
Ground Celery Seeds *See Spices, Seasonings & Seeds: Seeds: Celery: Ground*
Ground Cinnamon *See Spices, Seasonings & Seeds: Spices: Cinnamon: Ground*
Ground Cloves *See Spices, Seasonings & Seeds: Spices: Cloves: Ground*
Ground Coriander Seeds *See Spices, Seasonings & Seeds: Seeds: Coriander: Ground*
Ground Fennel Seeds *See Spices, Seasonings & Seeds: Seeds: Fennel: Ground*
Ground Ginger *See Spices, Seasonings & Seeds: Spices: Ginger: Ground*
Ground Mace *See Spices, Seasonings & Seeds: Spices: Mace (See also Nutmeg): Ground*
Ground Nutmeg *See Spices, Seasonings & Seeds: Spices: Nutmeg (See also Mace): Ground*
Ground Peppercorns *See Spices, Seasonings & Seeds: Spices: Peppercorns: Ground*
Ground Rosemary *See Spices, Seasonings & Seeds: Spices: Rosemary: Ground*
Ground Star Anise *See Spices, Seasonings & Seeds: Spices: Anise - Star: Ground*
Ground Thyme *See Spices, Seasonings & Seeds: Spices: Thyme: Ground*
Ground Turkey *See Meats & Meat Products: Poultry: Turkey: Ground*
Ground Turmeric *See Spices, Seasonings & Seeds: Spices: Turmeric: Ground*
Ground Veal *See Meats & Meat Products: Beef & Beef Products: Veal: Ground*
Ground White Pepper *See Spices, Seasonings & Seeds: Spices: White Pepper: Ground*
Grouper *See Fish & Seafood: Fish: Grouper*

Gruyere A1802 *See Cheese & Cheese Products: Cheese: Gruyere*
Guacamole *See Ethnic Foods: Guacamole*
Guacamole Dips *See Sauces, Dips & Dressings: Dips: Guacamole*
Guajillo Peppers *See Fruits & Vegetables: Peppers: Guajillo*
Guar Gum *See Ingredients, Flavors & Additives: Gums: Guar Gum*
Guava *See Fruits & Vegetables: Guava*
Guava Juices *See Beverages: Juices: Guava*
Guinea Hen *See Meats & Meat Products: Game: Guinea Hen*
Gumbo *See Prepared Foods: Soups & Stews: Gumbo*
Gums *See Ingredients, Flavors & Additives: Gums*
Gums & Jellies *See Candy & Confectionery: Candy: Gums & Jellies*
Gyros *See Prepared Foods: Prepared Meals: Gyros*

H

Habanero Peppers *See Fruits & Vegetables: Peppers: Habanero*
Habanero Sauces *See Sauces, Dips & Dressings: Sauces: Habanero*
Haddock *See Fish & Seafood: Fish: Haddock*
Hake *See Fish & Seafood: Fish: Hake*
Halal Foods *See Ethnic Foods: Halal Foods*
Half & Half *See Dairy Products: Milk & Milk Products: Milk: Half & Half*
Half & Half Flavors *See Ingredients, Flavors & Additives: Flavors: Half & Half*
Half-Products *See Ingredients, Flavors & Additives: Half-Products*
Half-Products, Calcium & Nutritionally Fortified Pellets *See Ingredients, Flavors & Additives: Half-Products: Calcium & Nutritionally Fortified Pellets*
Half-Products, Cocoa & Rice Pellets *See Ingredients, Flavors & Additives: Half-Products: Cocoa & Rice Pellets*
Half-Products, Colored Pellets *See Ingredients, Flavors & Additives: Half-Products: Colored Pellets*
Half-Products, Organic Pellets *See Ingredients, Flavors & Additives: Half-Products: Organic Pellets*
Half-Products, Veggie & Rice Pellets *See Ingredients, Flavors & Additives: Half-Products: Veggie & Rice Pellets*
Half_Products, Flavored Pellets *See Ingredients, Flavors & Additives: Half-Products: Flavored Pellets*
Halibut *See Fish & Seafood: Fish: Halibut*
Halloween Specialty-Packaged Candy *See Candy & Confectionery: Specialty-Packaged Candy: Halloween*
Ham *See Meats & Meat Products: Smoked, Cured & Deli Meats: Ham*
Ham Steak *See Meats & Meat Products: Smoked, Cured & Deli Meats: Ham: Steak*
Hamburger *See Meats & Meat Products: Beef & Beef Products: Hamburger*
Hard Candy *See Candy & Confectionery: Candy: Hard*
Hard-Boiled Eggs *See Eggs & Egg Products: Hard-Boiled*
Hash *See Prepared Foods: Hash*
Hash Browned Potatoes *See Prepared Foods: Potato Products: Hash Browned Potatoes*
Hatcheries *See Eggs & Egg Products: Hatcheries*
Hatcheries, Turkey Chicks *See Eggs & Egg Products: Hatcheries: Chicks: Turkey*
Havarti Cheese *See Cheese & Cheese Products: Cheese: Havarti*
Hazelnut Biscotti *See Baked Goods: Cookies & Bars: Biscotti: Hazelnut*
Hazelnut Flavors *See Ingredients, Flavors & Additives: Flavors: Hazelnut*
Hazelnut Flour *See Cereals, Grains, Rice & Flour: Flour: Hazelnut*
Hazelnut Nut Butters *See Nuts & Nut Butters: Nut Butters: Hazelnut*
Hazelnut Oils *See Oils, Shortening & Fats: Oils: Hazelnut*
Hazelnuts *See Nuts & Nut Butters: Nuts: Hazelnuts*
Head Cheese *See Meats & Meat Products: Smoked, Cured & Deli Meats: Head Cheese*
Health & Dietary *See Specialty & Organic Foods: Health & Dietary*
Health Products *See Specialty & Organic Foods: Dietary Products: Health Products*
Hearts Artichoke *See Fruits & Vegetables: Artichoke: Hearts*
Heat Stable Flavors *See Ingredients, Flavors & Additives: Flavors: Heat Stable*
Heather *See Spices, Seasonings & Seeds: Spices: Heather*
Hemp Nut Oils *See Oils, Shortening & Fats: Oils: Hemp Nut*
Herbal Supplements *See Spices, Seasonings & Seeds: Herbs: Herbal Supplements*

Herbal Tea *See Beverages: Coffee & Tea: Tea: Herbal*
Herbes de Provence *See Spices, Seasonings & Seeds: Spices: Herbes de Provence*
Herbs *See Spices, Seasonings & Seeds: Herbs*
Herbs & Spices Blends *See Ingredients, Flavors & Additives: Blends: Herbs & Spices*
Herbs Blends *See Ingredients, Flavors & Additives: Blends: Herbs*
Herbs for Beef *See Spices, Seasonings & Seeds: Herbs: for Beef*
Herbs for Pork *See Spices, Seasonings & Seeds: Herbs: for Pork*
Herbs for Poultry *See Spices, Seasonings & Seeds: Herbs: for Poultry*
Herbs for Seafood *See Spices, Seasonings & Seeds: Herbs: for Seafood*
Herring *See Fish & Seafood: Fish: Herring*
Herring Caviar *See Fish & Seafood: Caviar (Roe): Herring*
Hickory Smoke Oil Flavors *See Ingredients, Flavors & Additives: Flavors: Hickory Smoke Oil*
High Amylose Starches *See Ingredients, Flavors & Additives: Starches: High Amylose*
High Bush Blueberry *See Fruits & Vegetables: Berries: Blueberry: High Bush*
High Fructose Corn Syrups *See Sugars, Syrups & Sweeteners: Syrups: Corn: High Fructose*
Hoisin Sauces *See Sauces, Dips & Dressings: Sauces: Hoisin*
Hoki *See Fish & Seafood: Fish: Hoki*
Hollandaise *See Sauces, Dips & Dressings: Sauces: Hollandaise*
Hominy *See Cereals, Grains, Rice & Flour: Hominy*
Honey *See Sugars, Syrups & Sweeteners: Honey*
Honeydew *See Fruits & Vegetables: Melon: Honeydew*
Hops *See Cereals, Grains, Rice & Flour: Hops*
Horse *See Meats & Meat Products: Horse*
Horseradish *See Spices, Seasonings & Seeds: Spices: Horseradish; See also Sauces, Dips & Dressings: Sauces: Horseradish*
Hot Chili Powders *See Ingredients, Flavors & Additives: Powders: Chili: Hot*
Hot Chocolate *See Beverages: Cocoa & Chocolate Drinks: Hot Chocolate*
Hot Chocolate Mixes *See Doughs, Mixes & Fillings: Mixes: Hot Chocolate*
Hot Cocoa *See Beverages: Cocoa & Chocolate Drinks: Hot Cocoa*
Hot Cocoa with Marshmallows *See Beverages: Cocoa & Chocolate Drinks: Hot Cocoa: with Marshmallows*
Hot Cross Buns *See Baked Goods: Breads: Buns: Hot Cross*
Hot Curry Powders *See Ingredients, Flavors & Additives: Powders: Curry: Hot*
Hot Dogs *See Meats & Meat Products: Frankfurters: Hot Dogs*
Hot Italian Sausage Seasonings *See Spices, Seasonings & Seeds: Seasonings: Sausage: Hot Italian*
Hot Italian Sausages *See Meats & Meat Products: Smoked, Cured & Deli Meats: Sausages: Hot Italian*
Hot Pepper Sauces *See Sauces, Dips & Dressings: Sauces: Pepper: Hot*
Hot Salami *See Meats & Meat Products: Smoked, Cured & Deli Meats: Salami: Hot*
Hot Sauces *See Sauces, Dips & Dressings: Sauces: Hot*
Hot Sausages *See Meats & Meat Products: Smoked, Cured & Deli Meats: Sausages: Hot*
Hulled Sesame Seeds *See Spices, Seasonings & Seeds: Seeds: Sesame: Hulled*
Hulls Rice *See Cereals, Grains, Rice & Flour: Rice: Hulls*
Humectants *See Ingredients, Flavors & Additives: Humectants*
Hummus *See Cereals, Grains, Rice & Flour: Hummus*
Hush Puppies *See Prepared Foods: Hush Puppies*
Hush Puppies, Frozen & Mixes *See Prepared Foods: Hush Puppies: Frozen & Mixes*
Husks Corn *See Fruits & Vegetables: Corn: Husks*
Hydrocolloids *See Ingredients, Flavors & Additives: Hydrocolloids*
Hydrogenated Fats & Lard *See Oils, Shortening & Fats: Fats & Lard: Hydrogenated*
Hydrolyzed Products *See Ingredients, Flavors & Additives: Hydrolyzed Products*
Hydroxypropyl Methylcellulose *See Ingredients, Flavors & Additives: Gums: Hydroxypropyl Methylcellulose*

I

Ice Cream *See Dairy Products: Ice Cream*
Ice Cream Bases *See Dairy Products: Ice Cream: Bases*
Ice Cream Mixes *See Doughs, Mixes & Fillings: Mixes: Ice Cream*

Ice Cream Powders *See Ingredients, Flavors & Additives: Powders: Ice Cream*

Ice Cream, Ribbons *See Dairy Products: Ice Cream: Ribbons*

Ice Cream, Roll *See Dairy Products: Ice Cream: Roll*

Ice Milk *See Dairy Products: Ice Cream: Ice Milk*

Iceberg Lettuce Based Prepared Salads *See Prepared Foods: Prepared Salads: Iceberg Lettuce Based*

Iced Coffee *See Beverages: Coffee & Tea: Coffee: Iced*

Iced Tea *See Beverages: Coffee & Tea: Tea: Iced*

Ices *See Dairy Products: Ice Cream: Ices*

Icing Sugar *See Sugars, Syrups & Sweeteners: Sugar: Icing*

Icings *See Candy & Confectionery: Decorations & Icings: Icings*

Imitation Cheeses & Substitutes *See Cheese & Cheese Products: Imitation Cheeses & Substitutes; See also Cheese & Cheese Products: Imitation Cheeses & Substitutes: Imitation*

Imitation Crab *See Fish & Seafood: Shellfish: Crab: Imitation*

Imitation Fish *See Fish & Seafood: Fish: Imitation*

Improvers Doughs *See Doughs, Mixes & Fillings: Doughs: Improvers*

Inclusions *See Ingredients, Flavors & Additives: Inclusions*

India Pale Ale *See Beverages: Beers: American & British Ale: India Pale Ale*

Individual Packets *See Prepared Foods: Individual Packets*

Individual Quick Frozen Food *See Prepared Foods: Individual Quick Frozen Food*

Individually Packaged Cookies & Bars *See Baked Goods: Cookies & Bars: Individually Packaged*

Ingredients *See Ingredients, Flavors & Additives: Ingredients; See also Baked Goods: Ingredients*

Ingredients, Flavors & Additives *See Ingredients, Flavors & Additives*

Ingredients, Flavors & Additives, Almond Pastes *See Ingredients, Flavors & Additives: Pastes: Almond*

Ingredients, Organic Foods *See Specialty & Organic Foods: Organic Foods: Ingredients*

Ink Squid *See Fish & Seafood: Shellfish: Squid: Ink*

Inositol *See Ingredients, Flavors & Additives: Vitamins & Supplements: Inositol*

Instant Cereal *See Cereals, Grains, Rice & Flour: Cereal: Instant*

Instant Coffee *See Beverages: Coffee & Tea: Coffee: Instant*

Instant Coffee, Decaffeinated *See Beverages: Coffee & Tea: Coffee: Instant - Decaffeinated*

Instant Potatoes *See Fruits & Vegetables: Potatoes: Instant*

Instant Rice *See Cereals, Grains, Rice & Flour: Rice: Instant*

Instant Tea *See Beverages: Coffee & Tea: Tea: Instant*

Instantized Flour *See Cereals, Grains, Rice & Flour: Flour: Instantized*

Invert Sugar *See Sugars, Syrups & Sweeteners: Sugar: Invert*

IQF Frozen Cherries *See Fruits & Vegetables: Cherries: Frozen: IQF (Individually Quick Frozen)*

IQF Rice *See Cereals, Grains, Rice & Flour: Rice: IQF (Individual Quick Frozen)*

IQF Vegetables *See Fruits & Vegetables: Vegetables: IQF (Individual Quick Frozen)*

Irish Breakfast Tea *See Beverages: Coffee & Tea: Tea: Irish Breakfast*

Irish Creme Flavors *See Ingredients, Flavors & Additives: Flavors: Irish Creme*

Irish Whiskey *See Beverages: Spirits & Liqueurs: Irish Whiskey*

Isolate Soy Protein *See Fruits & Vegetables: Soy: Soy Protein: Isolate*

Italian *See Ethnic Foods: Italian*

Italian Beans *See Fruits & Vegetables: Beans: Italian*

Italian Beef & Beef Products *See Meats & Meat Products: Beef & Beef Products: Italian*

Italian Breads *See Baked Goods: Breads: Italian*

Italian Herbs Seasonings *See Spices, Seasonings & Seeds: Seasonings: Italian Herbs*

Italian Olives *See Fruits & Vegetables: Olives: Italian*

Italian Style Salad Dressings *See Sauces, Dips & Dressings: Salad Dressings: Italian Style*

Italian Style Salad Dressings, Mixes *See Sauces, Dips & Dressings: Salad Dressings: Mixes: Italian Style*

Italian Style Seasonings *See Spices, Seasonings & Seeds: Seasonings: Italian Style*

Italian Wines *See Beverages: Wines: Italian*

J

Jalapeno & Chiles Peppers *See Fruits & Vegetables: Peppers: Jalapeno & Chiles*

Jalapeno Peppers *See Fruits & Vegetables: Peppers: Jalapeno*

Jamacain Beef Patties *See Meats & Meat Products: Beef & Beef Products: Patties: Jamacain*

Jambalaya *See Ethnic Foods: Jambalaya*

Jambalaya Mixes *See Doughs, Mixes & Fillings: Mixes: Jambalaya*

Jams *See Jams, Jellies & Spreads: Jams*

Japanese *See Ethnic Foods: Japanese*

Japanese Wines *See Beverages: Wines: Japanese*

Japones Peppers *See Fruits & Vegetables: Peppers: Japones*

Jarred or Cupped Fruit *See Fruits & Vegetables: Fruit: Jarred or Cupped*

Jasmati Rice *See Cereals, Grains, Rice & Flour: Rice: Jasmati*

Jasmine Rice *See Cereals, Grains, Rice & Flour: Rice: Jasmine*

Jasmine Tea *See Beverages: Coffee & Tea: Tea: Jasmine*

Jellied Cranberry Sauces *See Fruits & Vegetables: Sauces: Cranberry: Jellied*

Jellies *See Jams, Jellies & Spreads: Jellies*

Jelly Beans *See Candy & Confectionery: Candy: Jelly Beans*

Jelly Powders *See Ingredients, Flavors & Additives: Powders: Jelly*

Jerk Sauces *See Sauces, Dips & Dressings: Sauces: Jerk*

Juice Bases *See Ingredients, Flavors & Additives: Bases: Juice*

Juice Concentrates *See Beverages: Juices: Concentrates*

Juice Drinks *See Beverages: Juices: Drink*

Juice, Tropical Fruit *See Beverages: Juices: Tropical Fruits*

Juices *See Beverages: Juices*

Juniper Berries *See Fruits & Vegetables: Berries: Juniper; See also Spices, Seasonings & Seeds: Spices: Juniper Berries*

K

Kale *See Fruits & Vegetables: Kale*

Karaya Gum *See Ingredients, Flavors & Additives: Gums: Karaya Gum*

Kasmati Rice *See Cereals, Grains, Rice & Flour: Rice: Kasmati*

Kefir *See Dairy Products: Milk & Milk Products: Kefir*

Kegged Beers *See Beverages: Beers: Kegged*

Kelp Products *See Fruits & Vegetables: Kelp Products*

Ketchup *See Sauces, Dips & Dressings: Ketchup*

Key Lime Juices *See Beverages: Juices: Key Lime*

Key Lime Pies *See Baked Goods: Pies: Key Lime*

Kidney Beans *See Fruits & Vegetables: Beans: Kidney*

Kielbasa Sausage Seasonings *See Spices, Seasonings & Seeds: Seasonings: Sausage: Kielbasa*

Kielbasa Sausages *See Meats & Meat Products: Smoked, Cured & Deli Meats: Sausages: Kielbasa*

Kiev Chicken *See Prepared Foods: Prepared Meals: Chicken: Kiev*

King Cod *See Fish & Seafood: Fish: King Cod*

King Crab *See Fish & Seafood: Shellfish: Crab: King*

King Salmon *See Fish & Seafood: Fish: Salmon: King*

Kingfish *See Fish & Seafood: Fish: Kingfish*

Kisses *See Candy & Confectionery: Candy: Kisses*

Kiwi *See Fruits & Vegetables: Kiwi*

Klingstone Peach *See Fruits & Vegetables: Peach: Klingstone*

Knishes *See Prepared Foods: Knishes*

Knockwurst *See Meats & Meat Products: Smoked, Cured & Deli Meats: Knockwurst*

Knockwurst Sausages *See Meats & Meat Products: Smoked, Cured & Deli Meats: Sausages: Knockwurst*

Kohlrabi *See Fruits & Vegetables: Kohlrabi*

Kolsch Belgian & French Ale *See Beverages: Beers: Belgian & French Ale: Kolsch*

Kosher Foods *See Ethnic Foods: Kosher Foods*

Kosher Frankfurters *See Meats & Meat Products: Frankfurters: Kosher*

Kosher Pickles *See Relishes & Pickled Products: Pickled Products: Pickles: Kosher*

Kumquat *See Fruits & Vegetables: Kumquat*

L

Lactic Acidulants *See Ingredients, Flavors & Additives: Acidulants: Lactic*

Lactobacillus Acidophilus *See Ingredients, Flavors & Additives: Cultures & Yeasts: Lactobacillus Acidophilus*

Lactoferrin *See Ingredients, Flavors & Additives: Lactoferrin*

Lactose Sweeteners *See Ingredients, Flavors & Additives: Sweeteners: Lactose*

Lactose-Free Milk *See Dairy Products: Milk & Milk Products: Milk: Lactose-Free*

Lady Fingers *See Baked Goods: Cookies & Bars: Lady Fingers; See also Baked Goods: Cakes & Pastries: Ladyfingers*

Lager Beers *See Beverages: Beers: Lager*

Lamb *See Meats & Meat Products: Lamb*

Lamb Marinades *See Sauces, Dips & Dressings: Marinades: Lamb*

Langostinos *See Fish & Seafood: Shellfish: Langostinos*

Lard *See Oils, Shortening & Fats: Fats & Lard: Lard*

Lasagna *See Pasta & Noodles: Lasagna; See also Prepared Foods: Prepared Meals: Lasagna*

Latte Coffee *See Beverages: Coffee & Tea: Coffee: Latte*

Lavender *See Spices, Seasonings & Seeds: Spices: Lavender*

Lavender Flowers *See Spices, Seasonings & Seeds: Spices: Lavender Flowers*

Leaveners *See Ingredients, Flavors & Additives: Leaveners*

Lecithin Emulsifiers *See Ingredients, Flavors & Additives: Emulsifiers: Lecithin*

Lecithinated Stabilizers *See Ingredients, Flavors & Additives: Stabilizers: Lecithinated*

Leek *See Fruits & Vegetables: Leek*

Leeks, Chopped Dried *See Fruits & Vegetables: Dried & Dehydrated Vegetables: Leeks - Chopped*

Leg of Lamb *See Meats & Meat Products: Lamb: Leg of*

Lemon *See Fruits & Vegetables: Lemon*

Lemon & Basil Seasonings *See Spices, Seasonings & Seeds: Seasonings: Lemon & Basil*

Lemon & Dill Seasonings *See Spices, Seasonings & Seeds: Seasonings: Lemon & Dill*

Lemon Ade Juices *See Beverages: Juices: Ade: Lemon*

Lemon Flavors *See Ingredients, Flavors & Additives: Flavors: Lemon*

Lemon Grass Oils *See Oils, Shortening & Fats: Oils: Lemon Grass*

Lemon Grass Spices *See Spices, Seasonings & Seeds: Spices: Lemon Grass*

Lemon Juices *See Beverages: Juices: Lemon*

Lemon Oils *See Oils, Shortening & Fats: Oils: Lemon*

Lemon Peel *See Spices, Seasonings & Seeds: Spices: Lemon Peel*

Lemon Pepper Seasonings *See Spices, Seasonings & Seeds: Seasonings: Lemon Pepper*

Lemon Sauces *See Sauces, Dips & Dressings: Sauces: Lemon*

Lemon Tea *See Beverages: Coffee & Tea: Tea: Lemon*

Lemon-Lime Soda *See Beverages: Soft Drinks & Sodas: Soft Drinks: Lemon-Lime Soda*

Lemon-Meringue Pies *See Baked Goods: Pies: Lemon-Meringue*

Lemonade Juices *See Beverages: Juices: Lemonade*

Lentil Beans *See Fruits & Vegetables: Beans: Lentil; See also Fruits & Vegetables: Dried: Lentil Blend*

Lentil Soup *See Prepared Foods: Soups & Stews: Lentil Soup*

Lettuce *See Fruits & Vegetables: Lettuce*

Licorice Candy *See Candy & Confectionery: Candy: Licorice*

Licorice Flavors *See Ingredients, Flavors & Additives: Flavors: Licorice*

Light Red Kidney Beans *See Fruits & Vegetables: Beans: Kidney: Light Red*

Lima Beans *See Fruits & Vegetables: Beans: Lima*

Limburger Cheese *See Cheese & Cheese Products: Cheese: Limburger*

Lime *See Fruits & Vegetables: Lime*

Lime Flavors *See Ingredients, Flavors & Additives: Flavors: Lime*

Lime Juices *See Beverages: Juices: Lime*

Lime Oils *See Oils, Shortening & Fats: Oils: Lime*

Lingonberries *See Fruits & Vegetables: Berries: Lingonberries*

Linguica Sausages *See Meats & Meat Products: Smoked, Cured & Deli Meats: Sausages: Linguica*

---

1 2 3 4 5

EXAMPLE: **Canadian Style Bacon** *See Meats & Meat Products: Smoked, Cured & Deli Meats: Bacon: Canadian Style*

1. Product or Service you are looking for
2. Main Category, in alphabetical order, located in the page headers starting on page 23
3. Category Description, located in black bars and in page headers
4. Product Category, located in gray bars
5. Product Type, located under gray bars, centered in bold

Link Sausages *See Meats & Meat Products: Smoked, Cured & Deli Meats: Sausages: Link*

Liqueur Cake *See Baked Goods: Cakes & Pastries: Liqueur Cake*

Liqueur Flavors *See Ingredients, Flavors & Additives: Flavors: Liqueur*

Liqueurs & Cordials *See Beverages: Spirits & Liqueurs: Liqueurs & Cordials*

Liquid *See Eggs & Egg Products: Liquid*

Liquid & Granulated Sugar *See Sugars, Syrups & Sweeteners: Sugar: Liquid & Granulated*

Liquid Beverage Mixes *See Doughs, Mixes & Fillings: Mixes: Beverage: Liquid*

Liquid Chicken Fats & Lard *See Oils, Shortening & Fats: Fats & Lard: Chicken: Liquid*

Liquid Egg Whites *See Eggs & Egg Products: Liquid: Whites*

Liquid Honey *See Sugars, Syrups & Sweeteners: Honey: Liquid*

Liquid Mixes *See Doughs, Mixes & Fillings: Mixes: Liquid*

Liquid Spices *See Spices, Seasonings & Seeds: Spices: Liquid*

Liquid Sugar *See Sugars, Syrups & Sweeteners: Sugar: Liquid*

Liquid Vegetable Shortening *See Oils, Shortening & Fats: Shortening: Vegetable: Liquid*

Liquid Vinegar *See Sauces, Dips & Dressings: Vinegar: Liquid*

Live Crab *See Fish & Seafood: Shellfish: Crab: Live*

Live Crayfish *See Fish & Seafood: Shellfish: Crayfish: Live*

Live Lobster *See Fish & Seafood: Shellfish: Lobster: Live*

Live Shellfish *See Fish & Seafood: Shellfish: Live*

Liver *See Meats & Meat Products: Beef & Beef Products: Liver*

Liver Extracts *See Ingredients, Flavors & Additives: Extracts: Liver*

Liverwurst *See Meats & Meat Products: Smoked, Cured & Deli Meats: Liverwurst*

Lobster *See Fish & Seafood: Shellfish: Lobster*

Lobster Meat *See Fish & Seafood: Shellfish: Lobster: Meat*

Lobster Mushrooms *See Fruits & Vegetables: Mushrooms: Lobster*

Lobster Tails *See Fish & Seafood: Shellfish: Lobster: Tails*

Locust Bean Gum *See Ingredients, Flavors & Additives: Gums: Locust Bean Gum*

Loganberries *See Fruits & Vegetables: Loganberries*

Loin Chop, Lamb *See Meats & Meat Products: Lamb: Loin Chop*

Loin Chop, Pork *See Meats & Meat Products: Pork & Pork Products: Loin Chop; See also Meats & Meat Products: Pork & Pork Products: Loins*

Loin Chop, Veal *See Meats & Meat Products: Beef & Beef Products: Veal: Loin Chop*

Lollypops *See Candy & Confectionery: Candy: Lollypops*

London Broil *See Meats & Meat Products: Beef & Beef Products: London Broil*

Loose Leaf Tea *See Beverages: Coffee & Tea: Tea: Loose Leaf*

Looseleaf Lettuce *See Fruits & Vegetables: Lettuce: Looseleaf*

Low Carb Bread Mixes *See Doughs, Mixes & Fillings: Mixes: Bread: Low Carb*

Low Carb Dessert Mixes *See Doughs, Mixes & Fillings: Mixes: Dessert: Low Carb*

Low Carb Desserts *See Baked Goods: Desserts: Low Carb*

Low Carb Ice Cream Mixes *See Doughs, Mixes & Fillings: Mixes: Ice Cream: Low Carb*

Low Fat Butter *See Dairy Products: Butter: Low Fat*

Low Moisture Part Skim Mozzarella Cheese *See Cheese & Cheese Products: Cheese: Mozzarella: Low Moisture Part Skim*

Low Moisture Part Skim Mozzarella Cheese, Shredded - Frozen *See Cheese & Cheese Products: Cheese: Mozzarella: Low Moisture Part Skim Shredded - Frozen*

Low-Calorie Desserts *See Specialty & Organic Foods: Dietary Products: Low-Calorie Desserts; See also See Baked Goods: Desserts: Low-Calorie*

Low-Calorie Non-Dairy Ice Cream *See Dairy Products: Ice Cream: Non-Dairy: Low-Calorie*

Low-Fat Cheese *See Cheese & Cheese Products: Cheese: Low-Fat*

Low-Fat Ice Cream *See Dairy Products: Ice Cream: Low-Fat*

Low-Fat Milk *See Dairy Products: Milk & Milk Products: Milk: Low-Fat*

Low-Fat Potato Chips *See Snack Foods: Chips: Potato: Low-Fat*

Low-Fat Yogurt *See Dairy Products: Yogurt: Low-Fat*

Lox Smoked Seafood *See Fish & Seafood: Seafood: Smoked: Lox*

Lozenges Candy *See Candy & Confectionery: Candy: Lozenges*

Lumpfish *See Fish & Seafood: Fish: Lumpfish*

Luncheon Meat *See Meats & Meat Products: Smoked, Cured & Deli Meats: Luncheon Meat*

Lupini Beans *See Fruits & Vegetables: Beans: Lupini*

Luxury Cognac Brandy *See Beverages: Spirits & Liqueurs: Brandy: Luxury Cognac*

M

Macadamia Flavors *See Ingredients, Flavors & Additives: Flavors: Macadamia*

Macadamia Nuts *See Nuts & Nut Butters: Nuts: Macadamia*

Macaroni, Prepared Meals *See Prepared Foods: Prepared Meals: Macaroni*

Macaroni, Prepared Salads *See Prepared Foods: Prepared Salads: Macaroni*

Macaroons *See Baked Goods: Cookies & Bars: Macaroons*

Mace Spices *See Spices, Seasonings & Seeds: Spices: Mace (See also Nutmeg)*

Mackerel *See Fish & Seafood: Fish: Mackerel*

Mahi-Mahi *See Fish & Seafood: Fish: Mahi-Mahi*

Maitakes *See Fruits & Vegetables: Mushrooms: Maitakes*

Malic Acidulants *See Ingredients, Flavors & Additives: Acidulants: Malic*

Malt *See Cereals, Grains, Rice & Flour: Malt*

Malt Extract Syrups *See Sugars, Syrups & Sweeteners: Syrups: Malt Extract*

Malt Liquor *See Beverages: Beers: Lager: Malt Liquor*

Malt Vinegar *See Sauces, Dips & Dressings: Vinegar: Malt*

Maltodextrin *See Ingredients, Flavors & Additives: Maltodextrin*

Mandarin Orange *See Fruits & Vegetables: Orange: Mandarin*

Mango *See Fruits & Vegetables: Mango*

Mango Juices *See Beverages: Juices: Mango*

Manhattan Chowder *See Prepared Foods: Soups & Stews: Chowder: Manhattan*

Maple Candy *See Candy & Confectionery: Candy: Maple*

Maple Flavors *See Ingredients, Flavors & Additives: Flavors: Maple*

Maple Sugar *See Sugars, Syrups & Sweeteners: Sugar: Maple*

Maple Syrups *See Sugars, Syrups & Sweeteners: Syrups: Maple*

Maraschino Cherries *See Fruits & Vegetables: Cherries: Maraschino*

Margarine *See Oils, Shortening & Fats: Margarine*

Marinades *See Sauces, Dips & Dressings: Marinades*

Marinara Sauces *See Sauces, Dips & Dressings: Sauces: Marinara*

Marinated Shellfish *See Fish & Seafood: Shellfish: Marinated*

Marinated Tomato *See Fruits & Vegetables: Tomato: Marinated*

Marjoram Spices *See Spices, Seasonings & Seeds: Spices: Marjoram*

Marlin *See Fish & Seafood: Fish: Marlin*

Marmalades & Preserves *See Jams, Jellies & Spreads: Marmalades & Preserves*

Marsala Cooking Wines *See Beverages: Wines: Cooking: Marsala*

Marshmallow Candy *See Candy & Confectionery: Candy: Marshmallow*

Marshmallow Creme Candy *See Candy & Confectionery: Candy: Marshmallow Creme*

Marshmallows *See Candy & Confectionery: Candy: Marshmallows*

Marzipan *See Candy & Confectionery: Candy: Marzipan*

Masa Flour *See Cereals, Grains, Rice & Flour: Flour: Masa*

Mascarpone Cheese *See Cheese & Cheese Products: Cheese: Mascarpone*

Mashed Sweet Potatoes *See Fruits & Vegetables: Sweet Potatoes: Mashed*

Masking Flavors *See Ingredients, Flavors & Additives: Flavors: Masking*

Mature Rabbit *See Meats & Meat Products: Game: Rabbit: Mature*

Matzo *See Ethnic Foods: Matzo*

Matzo Meal *See Ethnic Foods: Matzo: Meal*

Mayonaise *See Sauces, Dips & Dressings: Mayonaise*

Meal *See Fish & Seafood: Fish: Meal*

Meal Crackers *See Baked Goods: Crackers: Meal*

Meal Fillers *See Ingredients, Flavors & Additives: Fillers: Meal*

Meat Analogs *See Ingredients, Flavors & Additives: Analogs: Meat*

Meat Balls *See Prepared Foods: Meat Balls*

Meat Curing Preparations *See Ingredients, Flavors & Additives: Curing Preparations: Meat*

Meat Extenders *See Ingredients, Flavors & Additives: Extenders: Meat*

Meat Flavors *See Ingredients, Flavors & Additives: Flavors: Meat*

Meat Loaf *See Prepared Foods: Meat Loaf*

Meat Marinades *See Sauces, Dips & Dressings: Marinades: Meat*

Meat Meal *See Meats & Meat Products: Meat Meal*

Meat Pies *See Baked Goods: Pies: Meat*

Meat Powders *See Ingredients, Flavors & Additives: Powders: Meat*

Meat Products Seasonings *See Spices, Seasonings & Seeds: Seasonings: Meat Products*

Meat Ravioli *See Pasta & Noodles: Ravioli: Meat*

Meat Sauces *See Sauces, Dips & Dressings: Sauces: Meat*

Meat Spaghetti Sauces *See Sauces, Dips & Dressings: Sauces: Spaghetti: Meat*

Meat Stock Powders *See Ingredients, Flavors & Additives: Powders: Meat Stock*

Meat Stuffing *See Prepared Foods: Stuffing: Meat*

Meat Tenderizers *See Ingredients, Flavors & Additives: Tenderizers: Meat*

Meatless Spaghetti Sauces *See Sauces, Dips & Dressings: Sauces: Spaghetti: Meatless*

Meats & Meat Products *See Meats & Meat Products*

Medical Nutritionals *See Ingredients, Flavors & Additives: Vitamins & Supplements: Medical Nutritionals*

Mediterranean Sauces *See Sauces, Dips & Dressings: Sauces: Mediterranean*

Melba Toast *See Baked Goods: Breads: Melba Toast*

Melon *See Fruits & Vegetables: Melon*

Melon Balls *See Fruits & Vegetables: Melon: Balls*

Meringue Dessert Fillings *See Doughs, Mixes & Fillings: Fillings: Dessert: Meringue*

Meringue Powders *See Ingredients, Flavors & Additives: Powders: Meringue*

Meringue Toppings *See Ingredients, Flavors & Additives: Toppings: Meringue*

Merlot *See Beverages: Wines: Red Grape Wines: Merlot*

Mesquite BBQ Snack Seasonings *See Spices, Seasonings & Seeds: Seasonings: Snack: Mesquite BBQ*

Methoxypolyethylene Glycols *See Ingredients, Flavors & Additives: Methoxypolyethylene Glycols*

Methyl Salicylate *See Ingredients, Flavors & Additives: Aroma Chemicals & Materials: Chemicals: Methyl Salicylate*

Methylcellulose *See Ingredients, Flavors & Additives: Gums: Methylcellulose*

Mexican *See Ethnic Foods: Mexican*

Mexican Food Sauces *See Sauces, Dips & Dressings: Sauces: Mexican Food*

Mexican Oregano *See Spices, Seasonings & Seeds: Spices: Oregano: Mexican*

Mexican Style Seasonings *See Spices, Seasonings & Seeds: Seasonings: Mexican Style*

Microwavable Entrees *See Prepared Foods: Prepared Meals: Entrees: Microwavable*

Microwave Flavors *See Ingredients, Flavors & Additives: Flavors: Microwave*

Milano Salami *See Meats & Meat Products: Smoked, Cured & Deli Meats: Salami: Milano*

Mild Salsa *See Sauces, Dips & Dressings: Salsa: Mild*

Milk *See Dairy Products: Milk & Milk Products: Milk*

Milk & Milk Products *See Dairy Products: Milk & Milk Products*

Milk Calcium *See Ingredients, Flavors & Additives: Milk Calcium*

Milk Coconut *See Fruits & Vegetables: Coconut & Coconut Products: Milk*

Milk Enzyme *See Dairy Products: Milk & Milk Products: Milk Products: Milk & Milk Fat: Enzyme*

Milk Flavors *See Ingredients, Flavors & Additives: Flavors: Milk*

Milk Powders *See Ingredients, Flavors & Additives: Powders: Milk*

Milk Productss *See Dairy Products: Milk & Milk Products: Milk Products*

Milk Proteins *See Ingredients, Flavors & Additives: Hydrolyzed Products: Milk Proteins; See also Dairy Products: Milk & Milk Products: Milk Products: Milk Proteins*

Milk Rice Powders *See Ingredients, Flavors & Additives: Powders: Rice: Milk*

Milk Solids *See Dairy Products: Milk & Milk Products: Milk Solids*

Milk, Modified - Dry Blends *See Dairy Products: Milk & Milk Products: Milk Products: Modified - Dry Blends*

Milled Rice *See Cereals, Grains, Rice & Flour: Rice: Milled*

Millet *See Cereals, Grains, Rice & Flour: Millet*
Millet Flour *See Cereals, Grains, Rice & Flour: Flour: Millet*
Milo *See Beverages: Cocoa & Chocolate Drinks: Milo*
Minced Clam *See Fish & Seafood: Shellfish: Clam: Minced*
Minced Garlic *See Spices, Seasonings & Seeds: Spices: Garlic: Minced*
Minced Onion *See Fruits & Vegetables: Dried & Dehydrated Vegetables: Onion: Minced; See also Spices, Seasonings & Seeds: Spices: Onion: Minced; See also Fruits & Vegetables: Onion: Minced*
Mineral Blends *See Ingredients, Flavors & Additives: Vitamins & Supplements: Mineral Blends*
Mineral Supplements *See Ingredients, Flavors & Additives: Vitamins & Supplements: Supplements: Minerals; See also Ingredients, Flavors & Additives: Vitamins & Supplements: Minerals*
Mineral Water *See Beverages: Water: Mineral*
Miners Lettuce *See Fruits & Vegetables: Lettuce: Miners*
Mini Frankfurters *See Meats & Meat Products: Frankfurters: Mini*
Mint Herb Tea *See Beverages: Coffee & Tea: Tea: Mint Herb*
Mint Leaves *See Spices, Seasonings & Seeds: Spices: Mint Leaves*
Mint Sauces *See Sauces, Dips & Dressings: Sauces: Mint*
Mint Spices *See Spices, Seasonings & Seeds: Spices: Mint*
Mint Tea *See Beverages: Coffee & Tea: Tea: Mint*
Mints Candy *See Candy & Confectionery: Candy: Mints*
Miso *See Fruits & Vegetables: Miso*
Mix *See Eggs & Egg Products: Mix*
Mixed Nuts *See Nuts & Nut Butters: Nuts: Mixed Nuts*
Mixers *See Beverages: Mixers*
Mixes *See Doughs, Mixes & Fillings: Mixes*
Mixes, Salad Dressings *See Sauces, Dips & Dressings: Salad Dressings: Mixes*
Mixes, Sauces *See Sauces, Dips & Dressings: Sauces: Mixes*
Mocha Biscotti *See Baked Goods: Cookies & Bars: Biscotti: Mocha*
Mocha Coffee & Tea *See Beverages: Coffee & Tea: Mocha*
Modified Food Starches *See Ingredients, Flavors & Additives: Agents: Anticaking: Modified Food Starch*
Modified Rice Starches *See Ingredients, Flavors & Additives: Starches: Rice: Modified*
Modified Starches *See Ingredients, Flavors & Additives: Starches: Modified*
Modifiers Agents *See Ingredients, Flavors & Additives: Agents: Modifiers*
Molasses *See Sugars, Syrups & Sweeteners: Molasses*
Molasses Flakes *See Ingredients, Flavors & Additives: Flakes: Molasses*
Molasses Powders *See Ingredients, Flavors & Additives: Powders: Molasses*
Molding Starches *See Ingredients, Flavors & Additives: Starches: Molding*
Mole Sauces *See Sauces, Dips & Dressings: Sauces: Mole*
Monkfish *See Fish & Seafood: Fish: Monkfish*
Montasio *See Cheese & Cheese Products: Cheese: Montasio*
Monte Veronese *See Cheese & Cheese Products: Cheese: Monte Veronese*
Monterey Jack *See Cheese & Cheese Products: Cheese: Monterey Jack*
Morel Mushrooms *See Fruits & Vegetables: Mushrooms: Morel; See also Fruits & Vegetables: Dried & Dehydrated Vegetables: Mushrooms: Morels Whole*
Mortadella Sausages *See Meats & Meat Products: Smoked, Cured & Deli Meats: Sausages: Mortadella*
Mousse Candy *See Candy & Confectionery: Candy: Mousse*
Mousseron *See Fruits & Vegetables: Mushrooms: Mousseron*
Mozzarella *See Cheese & Cheese Products: Cheese: Mozzarella*
Mozzarella Cheese, Low Moisture Part Skim *See Cheese & Cheese Products: Cheese: Mozzarella: Low Moisture Part Skim*
Mozzarella Cheese, Low Moisture Part Skim, Shredded - Frozen *See Cheese & Cheese Products: Cheese: Mozzarella: Low Moisture Part Skim Shredded - Frozen*
Mozzarella Sticks *See Prepared Foods: Prepared Meals: Mozzarella Sticks*
Mozzarella, Imitation *See Cheese & Cheese Products: Imitation Cheeses & Substitutes: Imitation: Mozzarella*
MSG & Salt Mixture *See Spices, Seasonings & Seeds: Salt: MSG & Salt Mixture*

Muenster *See Cheese & Cheese Products: Cheese: Muenster*
Muesli Cereal *See Cereals, Grains, Rice & Flour: Cereal: Muesli*
Muffin Batters *See Doughs, Mixes & Fillings: Batters: Muffin*
Muffin Loaves *See Baked Goods: Cakes & Pastries: Muffin Loaves*
Muffin Mixes *See Doughs, Mixes & Fillings: Mixes: Muffin*
Muffins *See Baked Goods: Cakes & Pastries: Muffins*
Mulato Peppers *See Fruits & Vegetables: Peppers: Mulato*
Mulberries *See Fruits & Vegetables: Berries: Mulberries*
Mulled Wine Spice *See Spices, Seasonings & Seeds: Spices: Mulled Wine Spice*
Mullet *See Fish & Seafood: Fish: Mullet*
Mulling *See Spices, Seasonings & Seeds: Spices: Mulling*
Multi-Grain Breads *See Baked Goods: Breads: Multi-Grain*
Multi-Packs Specialty-Packaged Candy *See Candy & Confectionery: Specialty-Packaged Candy: Multi-Packs*
Mung Bean Noodles *See Pasta & Noodles: Noodles: Mung Bean*
Mung Bean Sprouts *See Fruits & Vegetables: Sprouts: Mung Bean*
Mung Beans *See Fruits & Vegetables: Beans: Mung*
Muscovy Duck *See Meats & Meat Products: Game: Muscovy Duck*
Mushroom Sauces *See Sauces, Dips & Dressings: Sauces: Mushroom*
Mushrooms *See Fruits & Vegetables: Dried & Dehydrated Vegetables: Mushrooms; See also Fruits & Vegetables: Mushrooms*
Muskox *See Meats & Meat Products: Game: Muskox*
Mussels *See Fish & Seafood: Shellfish: Mussels*
Mustard *See Sauces, Dips & Dressings: Mustard; See also Fruits & Vegetables: Mustard*
Mustard Bran *See Cereals, Grains, Rice & Flour: Bran: Mustard*
Mustard Flour *See Cereals, Grains, Rice & Flour: Flour: Mustard*
Mustard Oils *See Oils, Shortening & Fats: Oils: Mustard*
Mustard Powder *See Spices, Seasonings & Seeds: Spices: Mustard Powder; See also Ingredients, Flavors & Additives: Powders: Mustard*
Mustard Seeds *See Spices, Seasonings & Seeds: Seeds: Mustard*
Mustard Spices *See Spices, Seasonings & Seeds: Spices: Mustards; See also Spices, Seasonings & Seeds: Spices: Mustard*
Mustard Spices, Dry - Prepared *See Spices, Seasonings & Seeds: Spices: Mustard: Dry - Prepared*
Mutton *See Meats & Meat Products: Mutton*

N

Nacho Cheese Sauces *See Sauces, Dips & Dressings: Sauces: Cheese: Nacho*
Nacho Cheese Snack Seasonings *See Spices, Seasonings & Seeds: Seasonings: Snack: Nacho Cheese*
Nacho Chips *See Snack Foods: Chips: Nacho*
Napoli Salami *See Meats & Meat Products: Smoked, Cured & Deli Meats: Salami: Napoli*
Natural Chemicals *See Ingredients, Flavors & Additives: Chemicals: Natural*
Natural Colors *See Ingredients, Flavors & Additives: Colors: Natural; See also See Ingredients, Flavors & Additives: Colors: Natural: Others*
Natural Flavorings Spices *See Spices, Seasonings & Seeds: Spices: Natural Flavorings*
Natural Granules Honey *See Sugars, Syrups & Sweeteners: Honey: Granules: Natural*
Natural Gums *See Ingredients, Flavors & Additives: Gums: Natural*
Natural Organic Foods *See Specialty & Organic Foods: Organic Foods: Natural*
Natural Sweeteners *See Sugars, Syrups & Sweeteners: Natural Sweeteners*
Naval Orange *See Fruits & Vegetables: Orange: Naval*
Navy Beans *See Fruits & Vegetables: Beans: Navy*
Nectar *See Fruits & Vegetables: Nectar*
Nectarines *See Fruits & Vegetables: Nectarines*
Neutral Spirits & Liqueurs *See Beverages: Spirits & Liqueurs: Neutral*
New England Chowder *See Prepared Foods: Soups & Stews: Chowder: New England*

New York Style Cheese Cake *See Baked Goods: Cakes & Pastries: Cheese Cake: New York Style*
Niacin *See Ingredients, Flavors & Additives: Vitamins & Supplements: Niacin*
No Salt Potato Chips *See Snack Foods: Chips: Potato: No Salt*
No-Fat Cheese *See Cheese & Cheese Products: Cheese: No-Fat*
No-Fat Yogurt *See Dairy Products: Yogurt: No-Fat*
Non-Alcoholic Beers *See Beverages: Beers: Non-Alcoholic*
Non-Alcoholic Beverages *See Beverages: Non-Alcoholic Beverages*
Non-Alcoholic Wines *See Beverages: Wines: Non-Alcoholic*
Non-Dairy & Imitation Dairy Bases *See Ingredients, Flavors & Additives: Bases: Dairy: Non-Dairy & Imitation*
Non-Dairy Coffee Creamers *See Dairy Products: Creamers: Coffee: Non-Dairy*
Non-Dairy Cream *See Dairy Products: Cream: Non-Dairy*
Non-Dairy Desserts *See Baked Goods: Desserts: Non-Dairy*
Non-Dairy Ice Cream *See Dairy Products: Ice Cream: Non-Dairy*
Non-Dairy Whipped Toppings *See Ingredients, Flavors & Additives: Toppings: Whipped: Non-Dairy*
Non-Fat Cheese Cake *See Baked Goods: Cakes & Pastries: Cheese Cake: Non-Fat*
Non-Fat Milk Solids *See Dairy Products: Milk & Milk Products: Milk Solids: Non-Fat*
Non-Fat Salad Dressings *See Sauces, Dips & Dressings: Salad Dressings: Non-Fat*
Non-Fruit Pies *See Baked Goods: Pies: Non-Fruit*
Non-Fruit Toppings *See Ingredients, Flavors & Additives: Toppings: Non-Fruit*
Non-Stick Coatings *See Ingredients, Flavors & Additives: Coatings: Non-Stick*
Nonpareils *See Candy & Confectionery: Candy: Nonpareils*
Noodles *See Pasta & Noodles: Noodles*
Nougats *See Candy & Confectionery: Candy: Nougats*
Novelties, Candy *See Candy & Confectionery: Candy: Novelties*
Novelties, Ice Cream *See Dairy Products: Ice Cream: Novelties*
Nut Breads *See Baked Goods: Breads: Nut*
Nut Butters *See Nuts & Nut Butters: Nut Butters*
Nut Flavors *See Ingredients, Flavors & Additives: Flavors: Nut*
Nut Flour *See Cereals, Grains, Rice & Flour: Flour: Nut*
Nut Meats *See Nuts & Nut Butters: Nuts: Nut Meats*
Nut Pastes *See Nuts & Nut Butters: Nut Pastes*
Nutmeg *See Spices, Seasonings & Seeds: Spices: Nutmeg (See also Mace)*
Nutmeg Oils *See Oils, Shortening & Fats: Oils: Nutmeg*
Nutraceuticals *See Ingredients, Flavors & Additives: Vitamins & Supplements: Nutraceuticals*
Nutritional Supplements *See Ingredients, Flavors & Additives: Vitamins & Supplements: Nutritional Supplements*
Nuts *See Nuts & Nut Butters: Nuts*
NY Strip Steak *See Meats & Meat Products: Beef & Beef Products: NY Strip Steak*

O

Oat Bran *See Cereals, Grains, Rice & Flour: Oats & Oat Products: Oat Bran*
Oat Bran Fiber *See Cereals, Grains, Rice & Flour: Fiber: Oat Bran*
Oat Fiber Crisps *See Cereals, Grains, Rice & Flour: Crisps: Oat Fiber*
Oat Flour *See Cereals, Grains, Rice & Flour: Flour: Oat*
Oatmeal *See Cereals, Grains, Rice & Flour: Oats & Oat Products: Oatmeal*
Oatmeal & Chocolate Chip Cookies *See Baked Goods: Cookies & Bars: Oatmeal & Chocolate Chip Cookies*
Oatmeal Cereal *See Cereals, Grains, Rice & Flour: Cereal: Oatmeal*
Oatmeal Cookies *See Baked Goods: Cookies & Bars: Oatmeal Cookies*
Oatmeal Raisin Cookies *See Baked Goods: Cookies & Bars: Oatmeal Raisin Cookies*
Oats & Oat Products *See Cereals, Grains, Rice & Flour: Oats & Oat Products*
Oats Fiber *See Cereals, Grains, Rice & Flour: Fiber: Oats*
Oats Flakes *See Ingredients, Flavors & Additives: Flakes: Oats*
Ocean Perch *See Fish & Seafood: Fish: Perch: Ocean*

EXAMPLE: **Canadian Style Bacon** *See Meats & Meat Products: Smoked, Cured & Deli Meats: Bacon: Canadian Style*

1. Product or Service you are looking for
2. Main Category, in alphabetical order, located in the page headers starting on page 23
3. Category Description, located in black bars and in page headers
4. Product Category, located in gray bars
5. Product Type, located under gray bars, centered in bold

Octopus See Fish & Seafood: Shellfish: Octopus

Oil & Vinegar Salad Dressings See Sauces, Dips & Dressings: Salad Dressings: Oil & Vinegar

Oil & Vinegar Salad Dressings, Mixes See Sauces, Dips & Dressings: Salad Dressings: Mixes: Oil & Vinegar

Oils, Shortening & Fats; See also See Oils, Shortening & Fats: Oils

Okra See Fruits & Vegetables: Okra

Olive Loaf See Meats & Meat Products: Smoked, Cured & Deli Meats: Olive Loaf

Olive Oil Anchovies See Fish & Seafood: Fish: Anchovies: Olive Oil

Olive Oil Bread Sticks See Baked Goods: Bread Sticks: Olive Oil

Olive Oils See Oils, Shortening & Fats: Oils: Olive

Olive Spreads See Jams, Jellies & Spreads: Spreads: Olive

Olives See Fruits & Vegetables: Olives

One Percent Milk See Dairy Products: Milk & Milk Products: Milk: 1 Percent

Onion See Fruits & Vegetables: Onion

Onion Bread Sticks See Baked Goods: Bread Sticks: Onion

Onion for Dehydration See Fruits & Vegetables: Dried & Dehydrated Vegetables: Onion: for Dehydration

Onion Juices See Beverages: Juices: Onion

Onion Oils See Oils, Shortening & Fats: Oils: Onion

Onion Powders See Ingredients, Flavors & Additives: Powders: Onion (See also Spices/Onion Powder)

Onion Rings See Prepared Foods: Onion Rings

Onion Salt See Spices, Seasonings & Seeds: Salt: Onion

Onion Spices See Spices, Seasonings & Seeds: Spices: Onion

Onion, Dried & Dehydrated See Fruits & Vegetables: Dried & Dehydrated Vegetables: Onion

Oolong Tea See Beverages: Coffee & Tea: Tea: Oolong

Orange See Fruits & Vegetables: Orange

Orange Ade Juices See Beverages: Juices: Ade: Orange

Orange Flavors See Ingredients, Flavors & Additives: Flavors: Orange

Orange Juices See Beverages: Juices: Orange

Orange Juices, Not Concentrated See Beverages: Juices: Orange: Not Concentrated

Orange Oils See Oils, Shortening & Fats: Oils: Orange

Orange Peel Pieces See Fruits & Vegetables: Orange: Peels: Pieces

Orange Pekoe Tea See Beverages: Coffee & Tea: Tea: Orange Pekoe

Orange Puree See Fruits & Vegetables: Pulps & Purees: Puree: Orange

Orange Roughy See Fish & Seafood: Fish: Orange Roughy

Orange Sauces See Sauces, Dips & Dressings: Sauces: Orange

Orange Sections See Fruits & Vegetables: Orange: Sections

Oregano Spices See Spices, Seasonings & Seeds: Spices: Oregano

Organic See Baby Foods: Organic

Organic Carrot See Fruits & Vegetables: Carrot: Organic

Organic Foods See Specialty & Organic Foods: Organic Foods

Organic Pellets See Ingredients, Flavors & Additives: Half-Products: Organic Pellets

Organic Rice See Cereals, Grains, Rice & Flour: Rice: Organic

Organic Sauces See Sauces, Dips & Dressings: Sauces: Organic

Oriental See Ethnic Foods: Oriental

Oriental Mustard See Sauces, Dips & Dressings: Mustard: Oriental

Oriental Noodles See Pasta & Noodles: Noodles: Oriental

Oriental Vegetables See Fruits & Vegetables: Oriental Vegetables

Orzo Pasta See Pasta & Noodles: Pasta: Orzo

Osaka Purple Mustard See Fruits & Vegetables: Mustard: Osaka Purple

Ostrich See Meats & Meat Products: Game: Ostrich

Oven Type Potatoes See Fruits & Vegetables: Potatoes: Oven Type

Oyster Mushrooms See Fruits & Vegetables: Mushrooms: Oyster

Oyster Mushrooms, Dried See Fruits & Vegetables: Dried & Dehydrated Vegetables: Mushrooms: Oyster

Oyster Sauces See Sauces, Dips & Dressings: Sauces: Oyster

Oysters See Fish & Seafood: Shellfish: Oysters

P

Packaged Meats See Meats & Meat Products: Packaged

Packed Fish See Fish & Seafood: Fish: Packed

Paella See Ethnic Foods: Paella

Pale Ale See Beverages: Beers: American & British Ale: Pale Ale

Palm Kernel Oils See Oils, Shortening & Fats: Oils: Palm: Kernel

Palm Oils See Oils, Shortening & Fats: Oils: Palm

Pan Coatings & Sprays See Oils, Shortening & Fats: Pan Coatings & Sprays

Pancake Batters See Doughs, Mixes & Fillings: Batters: Pancake

Pancake Flour See Cereals, Grains, Rice & Flour: Flour: Pancake

Pancake Mixes See Doughs, Mixes & Fillings: Mixes: Pancake

Pancake Syrups See Sugars, Syrups & Sweeteners: Syrups: Pancake

Pancakes See Prepared Foods: Pancakes

Pancakes with Fruit See Prepared Foods: Pancakes: with Fruit

Panettones See Baked Goods: Cakes & Pastries: Panettones

Pantothenic Acid See Ingredients, Flavors & Additives: Vitamins & Supplements: Pantothenic Acid

Papaya See Fruits & Vegetables: Papaya

Papaya Juices See Beverages: Juices: Papaya

Paprika See Spices, Seasonings & Seeds: Spices: Paprika

Paraffin Waxes See Ingredients, Flavors & Additives: Waxes: Paraffin

Parboiled Rice See Cereals, Grains, Rice & Flour: Rice: Parboiled

Parmesan Cheese See Cheese & Cheese Products: Cheese: Parmesan

Parmesan Cheese, Imitation See Cheese & Cheese Products: Imitation Cheeses & Substitutes: Imitation: Parmesan

Parmesan Salad Dressing Mixes See Sauces, Dips & Dressings: Salad Dressings: Mixes: Parmesan

Parsley Spices See Spices, Seasonings & Seeds: Spices: Parsley

Particulates See Ingredients, Flavors & Additives: Particulates

Partridge See Meats & Meat Products: Game: Partridge

Parve Foods See Ethnic Foods: Parve Foods

Passion Fruit Flavors See Ingredients, Flavors & Additives: Flavors: Passion Fruit

Passion Fruit Juices See Beverages: Juices: Passion Fruit

Pasta See Pasta & Noodles: Pasta

Pasta & Noodle Dishes See Prepared Foods: Prepared Meals: Pasta & Noodle Dishes

Pasta & Noodles See Pasta & Noodles

Pasta Prepared Salads See Prepared Foods: Prepared Salads: Pasta

Pasta Sauces See Sauces, Dips & Dressings: Sauces: Pasta

Pastes See Ingredients, Flavors & Additives: Pastes

Pastrami See Meats & Meat Products: Smoked, Cured & Deli Meats: Pastrami

Pastries See Baked Goods: Cakes & Pastries: Pastries

Pastry Flour See Cereals, Grains, Rice & Flour: Flour: Pastry

Pates See Meats & Meat Products: Pates & Fois Gras: Pates

Pates & Fois Gras See Meats & Meat Products: Pates & Fois Gras

Patti Sausages See Meats & Meat Products: Smoked, Cured & Deli Meats: Sausages: Patti

Patties, Beef See Meats & Meat Products: Beef & Beef Products: Patties

Patties, Breaded Chicken See Meats & Meat Products: Poultry: Chicken: Patties Breaded

Patties, Chicken See Meats & Meat Products: Poultry: Chicken: Patties

Patties, Fish See Fish & Seafood: Fish: Patties

Patties, Vegetarian See Specialty & Organic Foods: Vegetarian Products: Patties

Pau D'Arco Bark Powders See Ingredients, Flavors & Additives: Powders: Pau D'Arco Bark

Peach See Fruits & Vegetables: Peach

Peach Flavors See Ingredients, Flavors & Additives: Flavors: Peach

Peach Juices See Beverages: Juices: Peach

Peach Pies See Baked Goods: Pies: Peach

Peaches, Sliced See Fruits & Vegetables: Peach: Sliced

Peanut Brittle See Candy & Confectionery: Candy: Peanut Brittle

Peanut Butter See Nuts & Nut Butters: Nut Butters: Peanut Butter

Peanut Butter Chips See Snack Foods: Chips: Peanut Butter

Peanut Butter, No Additives See Nuts & Nut Butters: Nut Butters: Peanut Butter: No Additives

Peanut Butter, Smooth See Nuts & Nut Butters: Nut Butters: Peanut Butter: Smooth

Peanut Flour See Cereals, Grains, Rice & Flour: Flour: Peanut

Peanut Oils See Oils, Shortening & Fats: Oils: Peanut

Peanut Sauces See Sauces, Dips & Dressings: Sauces: Peanut

Peanut Seeds See Spices, Seasonings & Seeds: Seeds: Peanut

Peanuts See Nuts & Nut Butters: Nuts: Peanuts

Pear See Fruits & Vegetables: Pear

Pear Flavors See Ingredients, Flavors & Additives: Flavors: Pear

Pear Juices See Beverages: Juices: Pear

Pear, Canned Halves See Fruits & Vegetables: Pear: Canned: Halves

Pearl & Cocktail Onions See Fruits & Vegetables: Onion: Pearl & Cocktail Onions

Pearl Tapioca See Cereals, Grains, Rice & Flour: Tapioca: Pearl

Peas See Fruits & Vegetables: Peas

Peas & Carrots See Fruits & Vegetables: Vegetables Mixed: Peas & Carrots

Peas, Air-dried See Fruits & Vegetables: Dried & Dehydrated Vegetables: Peas - Air-dried

Pecan Butter Flavors See Ingredients, Flavors & Additives: Flavors: Butter: Pecan

Pecan Log See Baked Goods: Cakes & Pastries: Pecan Log

Pecan Nuts See Nuts & Nut Butters: Nuts: Pecan

Pecorino See Cheese & Cheese Products: Cheese: Pecorino

Pectin Gums See Ingredients, Flavors & Additives: Gums: Pectin

Pectins See Ingredients, Flavors & Additives: Pectins

Peeled Carrot See Fruits & Vegetables: Carrot: Peeled

Peeled Eggs See Eggs & Egg Products: Peeled

Peeled Shrimp See Fish & Seafood: Shellfish: Shrimp: Peeled

Peels, Citrus Fruits See Fruits & Vegetables: Citrus Fruits: Peels

Peels, Lemon See Fruits & Vegetables: Lemon: Peels

Peels, Orange See Fruits & Vegetables: Orange: Peels

Peking Duck See Meats & Meat Products: Game: Peking Duck

Penne See Pasta & Noodles: Penne

Pentanol See Ingredients, Flavors & Additives: Alcohols: Pentanol

Pepatello See Cheese & Cheese Products: Cheese: Pepatello

Pepper See Spices, Seasonings & Seeds: Spices: Pepper

Pepper Blends See Ingredients, Flavors & Additives: Blends: Pepper

Pepper Mash See Spices, Seasonings & Seeds: Spices: Pepper Mash

Pepper Oils See Oils, Shortening & Fats: Oils: Pepper

Pepper Sauces See Sauces, Dips & Dressings: Sauces: Pepper

Peppercorn Salad Dressing Mixes See Sauces, Dips & Dressings: Salad Dressings: Mixes: Peppercorn

Peppercorns See Spices, Seasonings & Seeds: Spices: Peppercorns

Peppermint See Spices, Seasonings & Seeds: Spices: Peppermint

Peppermint Flavors See Ingredients, Flavors & Additives: Flavors: Peppermint

Peppermint Leaf Tea See Beverages: Coffee & Tea: Tea: Peppermint Leaf

Peppermint Oils See Oils, Shortening & Fats: Oils: Peppermint

Pepperoncini Peppers See Fruits & Vegetables: Peppers: Pepperoncini

Pepperoni See Meats & Meat Products: Smoked, Cured & Deli Meats: Pepperoni

Pepperoni Salami See Meats & Meat Products: Smoked, Cured & Deli Meats: Salami: Pepperoni

Peppers See Fruits & Vegetables: Peppers

Peppers, Pickled See Relishes & Pickled Products: Pickled Products: Peppers

Perch See Fish & Seafood: Fish: Perch

Persimmons See Fruits & Vegetables: Persimmons

Pesto Sauces See Sauces, Dips & Dressings: Sauces: Pesto

Petit Fours See Baked Goods: Cakes & Pastries: Petit Fours

Pheasant See Meats & Meat Products: Game: Pheasant

Phosphates See Ingredients, Flavors & Additives: Phosphates

Phosphoric Acidulants See Ingredients, Flavors & Additives: Acidulants: Phosphoric

Picante Salsa See Sauces, Dips & Dressings: Salsa: Picante

Pickerel See Fish & Seafood: Fish: Pickerel

Pickled Ginger See Fruits & Vegetables: Ginger: Pickled

Pickled Meat Products See Relishes & Pickled Products: Meats

Pickled Products See Relishes & Pickled Products: Pickled Products

Pickles *See Relishes & Pickled Products: Pickled Products: Pickles*

Pickling Spices *See Spices, Seasonings & Seeds: Spices: Pickling Spices*

Pie Crust Mixes *See Doughs, Mixes & Fillings: Mixes: Pie Crust*

Pie Fillings *See Doughs, Mixes & Fillings: Fillings: Pie*

Pierogies *See Prepared Foods: Pierogies*

Pies *See Baked Goods: Pies*

Pignolias Nuts *See Nuts & Nut Butters: Nuts: Pignolias*

Pigs' Feet *See Meats & Meat Products: Pork & Pork Products: Pigs' Feet*

Pike *See Fish & Seafood: Fish: Pike*

Pilsner Lager *See Beverages: Beers: Lager: Pilsner*

Pimiento Oils *See Oils, Shortening & Fats: Oils: Pimiento*

Pimientos *See Fruits & Vegetables: Pimientos*

Pine Nuts *See Nuts & Nut Butters: Nuts: Pine*

Pineapple *See Fruits & Vegetables: Pineapple*

Pineapple Flavors *See Ingredients, Flavors & Additives: Flavors: Pineapple*

Pineapple Juices *See Beverages: Juices: Pineapple*

Pink Beans *See Fruits & Vegetables: Beans: Pink*

Pink Grapefruit *See Fruits & Vegetables: Grapefruit: Pink*

Pink Salmon *See Fish & Seafood: Fish: Salmon: Pink*

Pinot Blanc *See Beverages: Wines: White Grape Varieties: Pinot Blanc*

Pinot Gris *See Beverages: Wines: White Grape Varieties: Pinot Gris*

Pinot Noir *See Beverages: Wines: Red Grape Wines: Pinot Noir*

Pinto Beans *See Fruits & Vegetables: Beans: Pinto*

Pistachio Nuts *See Nuts & Nut Butters: Nuts: Pistachio*

Pita Breads *See Baked Goods: Breads: Pita*

Pita Chips *See Snack Foods: Chips: Pita*

Pizelle *See Prepared Foods: Pizelle*

Pizza *See Prepared Foods: Pizza & Pizza Products: Pizza*

Pizza & Pizza Products *See Prepared Foods: Pizza & Pizza Products*

Pizza Bagels *See Prepared Foods: Pizza & Pizza Products: Pizza Bagels*

Pizza Crust *See Prepared Foods: Pizza & Pizza Products: Pizza: Crust*

Pizza Doughs *See Doughs, Mixes & Fillings: Doughs: Pizza*

Pizza Sauces *See Sauces, Dips & Dressings: Sauces: Pizza*

Pizza Seasonings *See Spices, Seasonings & Seeds: Seasonings: Pizza*

Pizza Shells *See Prepared Foods: Pizza & Pizza Products: Shells*

Pizza Toppings *See Prepared Foods: Pizza & Pizza Products: Pizza Toppings*

Plantain Chips *See Snack Foods: Chips: Plantain*

Plantains *See Fruits & Vegetables: Banana: Plantain*

Plum Pudding *See Dairy Products: Pudding: Plum*

Plum Sauces *See Sauces, Dips & Dressings: Sauces: Plum*

Plum Tomato *See Fruits & Vegetables: Tomato: Plum*

Plums *See Fruits & Vegetables: Plums*

Pocket Sandwiches *See Prepared Foods: Prepared Meals: Sandwiches: Pocket*

Poi *See Cereals, Grains, Rice & Flour: Poi*

Polenta *See Pasta & Noodles: Pasta: Polenta*

Polish Sausages *See Meats & Meat Products: Smoked, Cured & Deli Meats: Sausages: Polish*

Pollack *See Fish & Seafood: Fish: Pollack*

Polythylene Glycols *See Ingredients, Flavors & Additives: Polythylene Glycols*

Pomace Apple *See Fruits & Vegetables: Apple: Pomace*

Pomace Olive Oils *See Oils, Shortening & Fats: Oils: Olive: Pomace*

Pomegranate *See Fruits & Vegetables: Pomegranate*

Pompano *See Fish & Seafood: Fish: Pompano*

Popcorn *See Snack Foods: Popcorn*

Popcorn Specialties *See Candy & Confectionery: Candy: Popcorn Specialties*

Popping Corn Oils *See Oils, Shortening & Fats: Oils: Popping Corn*

Poppy & Sesame Crackers *See Baked Goods: Crackers: Poppy & Sesame Crackers*

Poppy Seed Oils *See Oils, Shortening & Fats: Oils: Poppy Seed*

Poppy Seeds *See Spices, Seasonings & Seeds: Seeds: Poppy*

Popsicles *See Dairy Products: Ice Cream: Popsicles*

Porcini Mushrooms *See Fruits & Vegetables: Mushrooms: Porcini*

Porcini Mushrooms, Dried *See Fruits & Vegetables: Dried & Dehydrated Vegetables: Mushrooms: Porcini*

Pork & Beans *See Prepared Foods: Pork & Beans (see also Baked Beans)*

Pork & Pork Products *See Meats & Meat Products: Pork & Pork Products*

Pork Casings *See Meats & Meat Products: Smoked, Cured & Deli Meats: Sausages: Casings: Sausage, Pork, Beef*

Pork Frankfurters *See Meats & Meat Products: Frankfurters: Pork*

Pork Rinds *See Snack Foods: Pork Rinds*

Pork Sausages *See Meats & Meat Products: Smoked, Cured & Deli Meats: Sausages: Pork*

Porkskins *See Prepared Foods: Porkskins*

Porter *See Beverages: Beers: Stout & Porter: Porter*

Porterhouse Beef *See Meats & Meat Products: Beef & Beef Products: Porterhouse*

Portion Contol & Packaged Foods *See Prepared Foods: Portion Contol & Packaged Foods*

Portioned Juices *See Beverages: Juices: Portioned*

Portobello Mushrooms *See Fruits & Vegetables: Mushrooms: Portobello*

Portuguese Port Wines *See Beverages: Wines: Portuguese: Port*

Portuguese Wines *See Beverages: Wines: Portuguese*

Pot Pies *See Prepared Foods: Pot Pies*

Pot Roast *See Meats & Meat Products: Beef & Beef Products: Pot Roast*

Pot Stickers *See Prepared Foods: Pot Stickers*

Potassium Bitartrate *See Ingredients, Flavors & Additives: Potassium Bitartrate (Cream of Tartar)*

Potassium Bromate *See Ingredients, Flavors & Additives: Potassium Bromate*

Potassium Citrate *See Ingredients, Flavors & Additives: Potassium Citrate*

Potassium Lactate *See Ingredients, Flavors & Additives: Potassium Lactate*

Potassium Sorbate *See Ingredients, Flavors & Additives: Potassium Sorbate*

Potato Chips *See Snack Foods: Chips: Potato*

Potato Chips, No Salt *See Snack Foods: Chips: Potato: No Salt*

Potato Flakes *See Ingredients, Flavors & Additives: Flakes: Potato*

Potato Flour *See Cereals, Grains, Rice & Flour: Flour: Potato*

Potato Products *See Prepared Foods: Potato Products*

Potato Puffs, Frozen Products *See Prepared Foods: Potato Products: Puffs - Frozen*

Potato Starches *See Ingredients, Flavors & Additives: Starches: Potato*

Potato Sticks *See Snack Foods: Potato Sticks*

Potato, Prepared Salads *See Prepared Foods: Prepared Salads: Potato*

Potatoes *See Fruits & Vegetables: Potatoes; See also See Fruits & Vegetables: Potatoes: Potatoes*

Potatoes, Frozen Wedges *See Fruits & Vegetables: Potatoes: Frozen: Wedges*

Pouch-Packed Fish *See Fish & Seafood: Fish: Packed: Pouch*

Pouch-Packed Tuna Fish *See Fish & Seafood: Fish: Tuna: Pouch-Packed*

Poultry *See Meats & Meat Products: Poultry*

Poultry & Game *See Meats & Meat Products: Smoked, Cured & Deli Meats: Smoked Meat: Poultry & Game*

Poultry Flavors *See Ingredients, Flavors & Additives: Flavors: Poultry*

Poultry, Certified Organic *See Specialty & Organic Foods: Organic Foods: Certified: Poultry*

Pound Cake *See Baked Goods: Cakes & Pastries: Pound Cake*

Powdered Broth *See Prepared Foods: Broth: Powdered*

Powdered Chicken Fats & Lard *See Oils, Shortening & Fats: Fats & Lard: Chicken: Powdered*

Powdered Fruit Juices *See Beverages: Juices: Powdered Fruit*

Powdered Garlic *See Spices, Seasonings & Seeds: Spices: Garlic: Powdered*

Powdered Mixes *See Doughs, Mixes & Fillings: Mixes: Powdered*

Powdered Sugar *See Sugars, Syrups & Sweeteners: Sugar: Powdered*

Powdered Vegetables *See Fruits & Vegetables: Powdered Vegetables*

Powders *See Ingredients, Flavors & Additives: Powders*

Powders Prepared for Further Processing *See Ingredients, Flavors & Additives: Powders: Prepared for Further Processing*

Pralines *See Nuts & Nut Butters: Nuts: Pralines (See also Confectionery)*

Prawns *See Fish & Seafood: Shellfish: Prawns*

Precooked Rice *See Cereals, Grains, Rice & Flour: Rice: Precooked*

Preformed Snack Pellets *See Snack Foods: Snack Pellets: Preformed*

Pregelatinized Powders *See Ingredients, Flavors & Additives: Powders: Pregelatinized*

Pregelatinized Starches *See Ingredients, Flavors & Additives: Starches: Pregelatinized*

Prepared Bases *See Ingredients, Flavors & Additives: Bases: Prepared*

Prepared Chicken *See Meats & Meat Products: Poultry: Chicken: Prepared*

Prepared Cocktail Mixes *See Beverages: Mixers: Prepared Cocktail Mixes*

Prepared Eggs *See Eggs & Egg Products: Prepared*

Prepared Foods *See Prepared Foods*

Prepared Frozen Chicken *See Meats & Meat Products: Poultry: Chicken: Prepared Frozen*

Prepared Gravy *See Sauces, Dips & Dressings: Gravy: Prepared*

Prepared Meals *See Prepared Foods: Prepared Meals*

Prepared Mustard *See Spices, Seasonings & Seeds: Spices: Mustard: Prepared*

Prepared Pork & Pork Products *See Meats & Meat Products: Pork & Pork Products: Prepared*

Prepared Salads *See Prepared Foods: Prepared Salads*

Prepared Yams *See Fruits & Vegetables: Yams: Prepared*

Preservatives *See Ingredients, Flavors & Additives: Preservatives*

Pressed Dextrose Candy *See Candy & Confectionery: Candy: Pressed Dextrose*

Pretzels *See Snack Foods: Pretzels*

Pretzels, Sticks or Rods *See Snack Foods: Pretzels: Sticks or Rods*

Primary Dried Yeast *See Ingredients, Flavors & Additives: Cultures & Yeasts: Yeast: Primary Dried*

Primavera Sauces *See Sauces, Dips & Dressings: Sauces: Primavera*

Process Cheese Loaves *See Cheese & Cheese Products: Cheese: Process Cheese Loaves*

Process Sliced Cheese *See Cheese & Cheese Products: Cheese: Process Sliced*

Processed American Cheese *See Cheese & Cheese Products: Cheese: Processed American*

Processed Beef & Beef Products *See Meats & Meat Products: Beef & Beef Products: Processed*

Processed Coconut & Coconut Products *See Fruits & Vegetables: Coconut & Coconut Products: Processed*

Processed Swiss Cheese *See Cheese & Cheese Products: Cheese: Processed Swiss*

Processed Tomato *See Fruits & Vegetables: Tomato: Processed*

Produce *See Fruits & Vegetables: Produce*

Produce, Certified Organic *See Specialty & Organic Foods: Organic Foods: Certified: Produce*

Products, Beef & Beef *See Meats & Meat Products: Beef & Beef Products: Products*

Products, Cranberry *See Fruits & Vegetables: Berries: Cranberry: Products*

Products, Tomato *See Fruits & Vegetables: Tomato: Products*

Propanol Alcohols *See Ingredients, Flavors & Additives: Alcohols: Propanol*

Propylene Glycols *See Ingredients, Flavors & Additives: Alcohols: Propylene Glycols*

Prosciutto *See Meats & Meat Products: Smoked, Cured & Deli Meats: Prosciutto*

Protein Clusters Toppings *See Ingredients, Flavors & Additives: Toppings: Protein Clusters*

Protein Powders *See Ingredients, Flavors & Additives: Powders: Protein*

Protein Supplements *See Ingredients, Flavors & Additives: Vitamins & Supplements: Protein Supplements*

Protein, Rice *See Cereals, Grains, Rice & Flour: Rice: Protein*

Protein, Soy *See Fruits & Vegetables: Soy: Protein*

Proteins *See Ingredients, Flavors & Additives: Proteins*

Provolone *See Cheese & Cheese Products: Cheese: Provolone*

EXAMPLE: Canadian Style Bacon *See Meats & Meat Products: Smoked, Cured & Deli Meats: Bacon: Canadian Style*

1 ⎴ 2 ⎴ 3 ⎴ 4 ⎴ 5

1. Product or Service you are looking for
2. Main Category, in alphabetical order, located in the page headers starting on page 23
3. Category Description, located in black bars and in page headers
4. Product Category, located in gray bars
5. Product Type, located under gray bars, centered in bold

Prune Juices *See Beverages: Juices: Prune*
Prunes *See Fruits & Vegetables: Prunes*
Pudding *See Dairy Products: Pudding*
Puff Pastry *See Baked Goods: Cakes & Pastries: Puff Pastry*
Puff Pastry Doughs *See Doughs, Mixes & Fillings: Doughs: Puff Pastry*
Pulp *See Fruits & Vegetables: Pulps & Purees: Pulp*
Pulps & Purees *See Fruits & Vegetables: Pulps & Purees*
Pumpernickel *See Baked Goods: Breads: Pumpernickel*
Pumpkin *See Fruits & Vegetables: Pumpkin*
Pumpkin Seed Oils *See Oils, Shortening & Fats: Oils: Pumpkin Seed*
Pumpkin Seeds *See Spices, Seasonings & Seeds: Seeds: Pumpkin*
Punch Mixes *See Doughs, Mixes & Fillings: Mixes: Punch*
Punch Powders *See Ingredients, Flavors & Additives: Powders: Punch*
Puree *See Fruits & Vegetables: Pulps & Purees: Puree*
Purple Sticky Rice *See Cereals, Grains, Rice & Flour: Rice: Purple Sticky*
Puttanesca Sauces *See Sauces, Dips & Dressings: Sauces: Puttanesca*

Q

Quail *See Meats & Meat Products: Game: Quail (See also Eggs: Quail)*
Quail Eggs *See Eggs & Egg Products: Quail*
Quiche *See Prepared Foods: Quiche*
Quince *See Fruits & Vegetables: Quince*
Quinoa *See Cereals, Grains, Rice & Flour: Quinoa*

R

Rabbit *See Meats & Meat Products: Game: Rabbit*
Radish *See Fruits & Vegetables: Radish*
Rainbow Trout *See Fish & Seafood: Fish: Trout: Rainbow*
Raisin Breads *See Baked Goods: Breads: Raisin*
Raisin Juice Replacers *See Ingredients, Flavors & Additives: Replacers: Raisin Juice*
Raisin Juices *See Beverages: Juices: Raisin*
Raisins *See Fruits & Vegetables: Raisins*
Ramen Noodles *See Pasta & Noodles: Noodles: Ramen*
Ranch Salad Dressing *See Sauces, Dips & Dressings: Salad Dressings: Ranch*
Ranch Salad Dressing Mixes *See Sauces, Dips & Dressings: Salad Dressings: Mixes: Ranch*
Ranch Snack Seasonings *See Spices, Seasonings & Seeds: Seasonings: Snack: Ranch*
Rape Seeds *See Spices, Seasonings & Seeds: Seeds: Rape*
Raschera *See Cheese & Cheese Products: Cheese: Raschera*
Raspberries *See Fruits & Vegetables: Berries: Raspberries*
Raspberry Flavors *See Ingredients, Flavors & Additives: Flavors: Raspberry*
Raspberry Juices *See Beverages: Juices: Raspberry*
Raspberry Vinegar *See Sauces, Dips & Dressings: Vinegar: Raspberry*
Raspberry Vinegrette Salad Dressing *See Sauces, Dips & Dressings: Salad Dressings: Raspberry Vinegrette*
Raspberry Vinegrette Salad Dressing Mixes *See Sauces, Dips & Dressings: Salad Dressings: Mixes: Raspberry Vinegrette*
Ravioli *See Pasta & Noodles: Ravioli*
Raw & Shelled Peanuts *See Nuts & Nut Butters: Nuts: Peanuts: Raw & Shelled*
Raw Beef & Beef Products *See Meats & Meat Products: Beef & Beef Products: Raw*
Raw Chicken *See Meats & Meat Products: Poultry: Chicken: Raw*
Raw Crayfish *See Fish & Seafood: Shellfish: Crayfish: Raw*
Raw Peanuts *See Nuts & Nut Butters: Nuts: Peanuts: Raw*
Raw Pork & Pork Products *See Meats & Meat Products: Pork & Pork Products: Raw*
Raw Turkey *See Meats & Meat Products: Poultry: Turkey: Raw*
Raw Veal *See Meats & Meat Products: Beef & Beef Products: Veal: Raw*
Ready to Use Icings *See Candy & Confectionery: Decorations & Icings: Icings: Ready to Use*
Red Bell Peppers, Dried *See Fruits & Vegetables: Dried & Dehydrated Vegetables: Bell Peppers: Red*
Red Bordeaux *See Beverages: Wines: French: Red Bordeaux*
Red Burgundy *See Beverages: Wines: French: Red Burgundy*
Red Cabbage *See Fruits & Vegetables: Cabbage: Red*
Red Currants *See Fruits & Vegetables: Berries: Currants: Red*
Red Delicious Apple *See Fruits & Vegetables: Apple: Red Delicious*

Red Grape Wines *See Beverages: Wines: Red Grape Wines; See also Beverages: Wines: Red Grapes*
Red Looseleaf Lettuce *See Fruits & Vegetables: Lettuce: Looseleaf: Red*
Red Meritage/Bordeaux *See Beverages: Wines: Red Grape Wines: Red Meritage/Bordeaux*
Red Onion *See Fruits & Vegetables: Onion: Red*
Red Pear *See Fruits & Vegetables: Pear: Red*
Red Pepper *See Spices, Seasonings & Seeds: Spices: Red Pepper; See also Spices, Seasonings & Seeds: Spices: Pepper: Black - White - Red*
Red Potatoes *See Fruits & Vegetables: Potatoes: Red*
Reduced-Calorie Beer *See Beverages: Beers: Specialty &Cider: Reduced Calorie Beer*
Reduced-Calorie Salad Dressing Mixes *See Sauces, Dips & Dressings: Salad Dressings: Mixes: Reduced-Calorie*
Reduced-Fat Cheddar Cheese *See Cheese & Cheese Products: Cheese: Cheddar: Reduced Fat*
Reduced-Fat Milk *See Dairy Products: Milk & Milk Products: Milk: Reduced-Fat*
Reduced-Fat Shredded Cheddar Cheese *See Cheese & Cheese Products: Cheese: Cheddar: Reduced Fat - Shredded*
Refried Beans *See Fruits & Vegetables: Beans: Refried*
Refrigerated Appetizers *See Prepared Foods: Appetizers: Refrigerated*
Refrigerated Apple Juices *See Beverages: Juices: Apple: Refrigerated*
Refrigerated Apricot Juices *See Beverages: Juices: Apricot: Refrigerated*
Refrigerated Buns *See Baked Goods: Breads: Buns: Refrigerated*
Refrigerated Cherry Juices *See Beverages: Juices: Cherry: Refrigerated*
Refrigerated Cranberry Juices *See Beverages: Juices: Cranberry: Refrigerated*
Refrigerated Egg Substitutes *See Eggs & Egg Products: Substitutes: Refrigerated*
Refrigerated Fruit Juices *See Beverages: Juices: Fruit: Refrigerated*
Refrigerated Grape Juices *See Beverages: Juices: Grape: Refrigerated*
Refrigerated Grapefruit Juices *See Beverages: Juices: Grapefruit: Refrigerated*
Refrigerated Juices *See Beverages: Juices: Refrigerated*
Refrigerated Lemon Juices *See Beverages: Juices: Lemon: Refrigerated*
Refrigerated Pancakes *See Prepared Foods: Pancakes: Refrigerated*
Refrigerated Pineapple Juices *See Beverages: Juices: Pineapple: Refrigerated*
Regular & Lowfat Bakery Mix *See Cereals, Grains, Rice & Flour: Flour: Bakery Mix: Regular & Lowfat*
Regular Chili Powders *See Ingredients, Flavors & Additives: Powders: Chili: Regular*
Release, Grease Agents *See Ingredients, Flavors & Additives: Agents: Release, Grease*
Releases *See Ingredients, Flavors & Additives: Releases*
Relishes *See Relishes & Pickled Products: Relishes*
Relishes & Condiments *See Relishes & Pickled Products: Relishes: Relishes & Condiments*
Replacers *See Ingredients, Flavors & Additives: Replacers*
Replacers, Milk Solids *See Dairy Products: Milk & Milk Products: Milk Solids: Replacers*
Resistant Starch Fiber *See Cereals, Grains, Rice & Flour: Fiber: Resistant Starch*
Rhubarb *See Fruits & Vegetables: Rhubarb*
Rhubarb Pie *See Baked Goods: Pies: Rhubarb Pie*
Rib Center Cut Pork *See Meats & Meat Products: Pork & Pork Products: Rib Center Cut*
Rib Chop Lamb *See Meats & Meat Products: Lamb: Rib Chop*
Rib Chop Veal *See Meats & Meat Products: Beef & Beef Products: Veal: Rib Chop*
Rib Eye Roast Beef *See Meats & Meat Products: Beef & Beef Products: Rib Eye Roast*
Rib Eye Steak *See Meats & Meat Products: Beef & Beef Products: Rib Eye Steak*
Rib Rub Seasonings *See Spices, Seasonings & Seeds: Seasonings: Rib Rub*
Rib Steak *See Meats & Meat Products: Beef & Beef Products: Rib Steak*
Rice *See Cereals, Grains, Rice & Flour: Rice*
Rice Bran *See Cereals, Grains, Rice & Flour: Bran: Rice*
Rice Bran Oils *See Oils, Shortening & Fats: Oils: Rice Bran*
Rice Cakes *See Snack Foods: Rice Cakes*
Rice Crisps *See Cereals, Grains, Rice & Flour: Crisps: Rice*
Rice Flour *See Cereals, Grains, Rice & Flour: Flour: Rice*
Rice Mixes *See Doughs, Mixes & Fillings: Mixes: Rice*

Rice Pilaf *See Cereals, Grains, Rice & Flour: Rice: Pilaf*
Rice Powders *See Ingredients, Flavors & Additives: Powders: Rice*
Rice Pudding *See Dairy Products: Pudding: Rice*
Rice Starches *See Ingredients, Flavors & Additives: Starches: Rice*
Rice Starches, Organic *See Specialty & Organic Foods: Organic Foods: Rice Starch*
Rice, Bagged Parboiled *See Cereals, Grains, Rice & Flour: Rice: Parboiled: Bagged*
Rice, Parboiled, US #1 Long Grain *See Cereals, Grains, Rice & Flour: Rice: Parboiled: US #1 Long Grain*
Rice, Prepared Meals *See Prepared Foods: Prepared Meals: Rice*
Rice-Based Cereal *See Cereals, Grains, Rice & Flour: Cereal: Rice-Based*
Ricotta *See Cheese & Cheese Products: Cheese: Ricotta*
Riesling *See Beverages: Wines: White Grape Varieties: Riesling*
Rigatoni *See Pasta & Noodles: Rigatoni*
Riso *See Pasta & Noodles: Riso*
Risotto Rice *See Cereals, Grains, Rice & Flour: Rice: Risotto*
Roast Beef *See Meats & Meat Products: Beef & Beef Products: Roast Beef*
Roast Pork Tenderloin *See Meats & Meat Products: Pork & Pork Products: Tenderloin Roast*
Roasted Coffee *See Beverages: Coffee & Tea: Coffee: Roasted*
Roasted Garlic & Herb Crackers *See Baked Goods: Crackers: Roasted Garlic & Herb Crackers*
Roasted Nuts *See Nuts & Nut Butters: Nuts: Roasted*
Roasted Peanuts *See Nuts & Nut Butters: Nuts: Peanuts: Roasted*
Roasted Peppers *See Fruits & Vegetables: Peppers: Roasted*
Roasted Vegetables *See Fruits & Vegetables: Roasted Vegetables*
Rock Candy *See Candy & Confectionery: Candy: Rock*
Rock Fish *See Fish & Seafood: Fish: Rock Fish*
Rock Salt *See Spices, Seasonings & Seeds: Salt: Rock*
Rolled Oats *See Cereals, Grains, Rice & Flour: Oats & Oat Products: Rolled*
Rolls *See Baked Goods: Breads: Rolls*
Roma Tomato *See Fruits & Vegetables: Tomato: Roma (Egg)*
Romaine Lettuce *See Fruits & Vegetables: Lettuce: Romaine*
Romano *See Cheese & Cheese Products: Cheese: Romano*
Rome Beauty *See Fruits & Vegetables: Apple: Rome Beauty*
Root Beer Extracts *See Ingredients, Flavors & Additives: Extracts: Root Beer*
Root Beer Flavors *See Ingredients, Flavors & Additives: Flavors: Root Beer*
Roots & Tubers *See Fruits & Vegetables: Roots & Tubers*
Roquefort *See Cheese & Cheese Products: Cheese: Roquefort*
Rosellino *See Cheese & Cheese Products: Cheese: Rosellino*
Rosemary *See Spices, Seasonings & Seeds: Spices: Rosemary*
Rosemary Spices, Cut *See Spices, Seasonings & Seeds: Spices: Rosemary: Cut*
Rotelle *See Pasta & Noodles: Rotelle*
Rotini *See Pasta & Noodles: Rotini*
Royal Jellies *See Jams, Jellies & Spreads: Jellies: Royal*
Rubbed Sage *See Spices, Seasonings & Seeds: Spices: Sage: Rubbed*
Rugulach *See Baked Goods: Cakes & Pastries: Rugulach*
Rum *See Beverages: Spirits & Liqueurs: Rum*
Rum Cake *See Baked Goods: Cakes & Pastries: Rum Cake*
Rum Flavors *See Ingredients, Flavors & Additives: Flavors: Rum*
Rusk *See Baked Goods: Cakes & Pastries: Rusk*
Russet Potatoes, Fresh *See Fruits & Vegetables: Potatoes: Fresh: Russet*
Rutabaga *See Fruits & Vegetables: Rutabaga*
Rye *See Cereals, Grains, Rice & Flour: Rye*
Rye Breads *See Baked Goods: Breads: Rye*
Rye Flour *See Cereals, Grains, Rice & Flour: Flour: Rye*

S

Sablefish *See Fish & Seafood: Fish: Sablefish*
Saccharin *See Sugars, Syrups & Sweeteners: Sugar Substitutes: Saccharin*
Safflower Oils *See Oils, Shortening & Fats: Oils: Safflower*
Saffron *See Spices, Seasonings & Seeds: Spices: Saffron*
Sage *See Spices, Seasonings & Seeds: Spices: Sage*
Sage Leaves *See Spices, Seasonings & Seeds: Spices: Sage: Leaves*
Sage Oils *See Oils, Shortening & Fats: Oils: Sage*

Sake *See Beverages: Wines: Japanese: Sake*

Salad Dressings *See Sauces, Dips & Dressings: Salad Dressings*

Salad Greens *See Fruits & Vegetables: Salad Greens*

Salad Oils *See Oils, Shortening & Fats: Oils: Salad*

Salad, Prepared Meals *See Prepared Foods: Prepared Meals: Salad*

Salami *See Meats & Meat Products: Smoked, Cured & Deli Meats: Salami*

Salmon *See Fish & Seafood: Fish: Salmon*

Salmon Caviar *See Fish & Seafood: Caviar (Roe): Salmon*

Salmon Sausages *See Meats & Meat Products: Smoked, Cured & Deli Meats: Sausages: Salmon*

Salmon Steak *See Fish & Seafood: Fish: Salmon: Steak*

Salmon, Prepared Salads *See Prepared Foods: Prepared Salads: Salmon*

Salsa *See Sauces, Dips & Dressings: Salsa*

Salsa Dips *See Sauces, Dips & Dressings: Dips: Salsa*

Salsa with Cheese *See Sauces, Dips & Dressings: Salsa: with Cheese*

Salt *See Spices, Seasonings & Seeds: Salt*

Salt Anchovies *See Fish & Seafood: Fish: Anchovies: Salt*

Salt Substitutes *See Spices, Seasonings & Seeds: Salt: Substitutes*

Salt-free Chili Powders *See Ingredients, Flavors & Additives: Powders: Chili: Salt-free*

Salted & Marinated Herring *See Fish & Seafood: Fish: Herring: Salted & Marinated*

Salted Almonds *See Nuts & Nut Butters: Nuts: Almonds: Salted*

Salted Butter *See Dairy Products: Butter: Salted*

Salted Fish *See Fish & Seafood: Fish: Salted*

Salted Peanuts *See Nuts & Nut Butters: Nuts: Peanuts: Salted*

Salted Pecans *See Nuts & Nut Butters: Nuts: Pecan: Salted*

Salted Potato Chips *See Snack Foods: Chips: Potato: Salted*

Sandwich Creme Cookies *See Baked Goods: Cookies & Bars: Sandwich Creme Cookies*

Sandwiches, Prepared Meals *See Prepared Foods: Prepared Meals: Sandwiches*

Sangiovese *See Beverages: Wines: Red Grape Wines: Sangiovese*

Sardines *See Fish & Seafood: Fish: Sardines*

Sarsaparilla *See Beverages: Soft Drinks & Sodas: Soft Drinks: Sarsaparilla*

Sassafras Oils *See Oils, Shortening & Fats: Oils: Sassafras*

Sauce Bases *See Ingredients, Flavors & Additives: Bases: Sauce*

Sauces *See Fruits & Vegetables: Sauces; See also Sauces, Dips & Dressings: Sauces*

Sauerkraut *See Relishes & Pickled Products: Sauerkraut*

Sauerkraut Juice *See Relishes & Pickled Products: Sauerkraut: Juice*

Sausage Binders *See Ingredients, Flavors & Additives: Binders: Sausage*

Sausage Casings *See Meats & Meat Products: Smoked, Cured & Deli Meats: Sausages: Casings: Sausage, Pork, Beef*

Sausage Seasonings *See Spices, Seasonings & Seeds: Seasonings: Sausage*

Sausage, Pork *See Meats & Meat Products: Pork & Pork Products: Sausage*

Sausage, Smoked *See Meats & Meat Products: Smoked, Cured & Deli Meats: Sausages*

Sausage, Turkey *See Meats & Meat Products: Poultry: Turkey: Sausage*

Sauvignon Blanc *See Beverages: Wines: White Grape Varieties: Sauvignon Blanc*

Savory *See Spices, Seasonings & Seeds: Spices: Savory*

Saw Palmetto Berry Powders *See Ingredients, Flavors & Additives: Powders: Saw Palmetto Berry*

Scallions *See Fruits & Vegetables: Scallions*

Scallops *See Fish & Seafood: Shellfish: Scallops*

Scampi *See Fish & Seafood: Shellfish: Scampi*

Scampi, Prepared Meals *See Prepared Foods: Prepared Meals: Scampi*

Schnapps Liqueuer *See Beverages: Spirits & Liqueurs: Liqueurs & Cordials: Schnapps Liqueuer*

Scones *See Baked Goods: Breads: Scones*

Scotch Whiskey *See Beverages: Spirits & Liqueurs: Scotch Whiskey*

Scrapple *See Meats & Meat Products: Pork & Pork Products: Scrapple*

Sea Bass *See Fish & Seafood: Fish: Sea Bass*

Sea Salt *See Spices, Seasonings & Seeds: Salt: Sea*

Sea Trout *See Fish & Seafood: Fish: Sea Trout*

Seafood *See Fish & Seafood: Seafood*

Seafood Bases *See Ingredients, Flavors & Additives: Bases: Seafood*

Seafood Extracts *See Ingredients, Flavors & Additives: Extracts: Seafood*

Seafood Flavors *See Ingredients, Flavors & Additives: Flavors: Seafood*

Seafood Powders *See Ingredients, Flavors & Additives: Powders: Seafood*

Seafood Ravioli *See Pasta & Noodles: Ravioli: Seafood*

Seafood Salad *See Fish & Seafood: Seafood: Salad*

Seafood Sauces *See Sauces, Dips & Dressings: Sauces: Seafood*

Seafood Soup Bases *See Ingredients, Flavors & Additives: Bases: Soup: Seafood*

Seafood, Prepared Meals *See Prepared Foods: Prepared Meals: Seafood*

Seafood, Prepared Salads *See Prepared Foods: Prepared Salads: Seafood*

Seasoning Powders *See Ingredients, Flavors & Additives: Powders: Seasoning*

Seasonings *See Spices, Seasonings & Seeds: Seasonings*

Seasonings for Corned Beef *See Spices, Seasonings & Seeds: Seasonings: for Corned Beef*

Seasonings for Tacos *See Spices, Seasonings & Seeds: Seasonings: for Tacos*

Seaweeds & Sea Vegetables *See Fruits & Vegetables: Seaweeds & Sea Vegetables*

Seedless Watermelon *See Fruits & Vegetables: Melon: Watermelon: Seedless*

Seeds *See Spices, Seasonings & Seeds: Seeds*

Self-Rising Flour *See Cereals, Grains, Rice & Flour: Flour: Self-Rising*

Semolina *See Pasta & Noodles: Semolina*

Semolina Flour *See Cereals, Grains, Rice & Flour: Flour: Semolina*

Serrano Peppers *See Fruits & Vegetables: Peppers: Serrano*

Sesame Bread Sticks *See Baked Goods: Bread Sticks: Sesame*

Sesame Oils *See Oils, Shortening & Fats: Oils: Sesame*

Sesame Seeds *See Spices, Seasonings & Seeds: Seeds: Sesame*

Shad *See Fish & Seafood: Fish: Shad*

Shad Caviar *See Fish & Seafood: Caviar (Roe): Shad*

Shallot *See Fruits & Vegetables: Shallot*

Shallots *See Spices, Seasonings & Seeds: Spices: Shallots*

Shallots, Freeze-Dried *See Fruits & Vegetables: Dried & Dehydrated Vegetables: Shallots - Freeze Dried*

Shark *See Fish & Seafood: Fish: Shark*

Sheephead *See Fish & Seafood: Fish: Sheephead*

Shelf Stable Entrees *See Prepared Foods: Prepared Meals: Entrees: Shelf Stable*

Shelled Nuts *See Nuts & Nut Butters: Nuts: Shelled*

Shellfish *See Fish & Seafood: Shellfish: Shellfish; See also Fish & Seafood: Shellfish*

Shells *See Ethnic Foods: Shells; See also Pasta & Noodles: Shells*

Sherbet *See Dairy Products: Ice Cream: Sherbet*

Sherry *See Beverages: Wines: Spanish: Sherry*

Sherry Vinegar *See Sauces, Dips & Dressings: Vinegar: Sherry*

Shiitake *See Fruits & Vegetables: Mushrooms: Shiitake; See also Fruits & Vegetables: Dried & Dehydrated Vegetables: Mushrooms: Shiitake Whole*

Shoestring French Fries *See Prepared Foods: French Fries: Shoestring*

Shoofly Mixes *See Doughs, Mixes & Fillings: Mixes: Shoofly*

Shoofly Pie *See Baked Goods: Pies: Shoofly Pie*

Short Breads *See Baked Goods: Breads: Short*

Shortening *See Oils, Shortening & Fats; See also See Oils, Shortening & Fats: Shortening*

Shredded Cheddar Cheese *See Cheese & Cheese Products: Cheese: Cheddar: Shredded*

Shrimp *See Fish & Seafood: Shellfish: Shrimp*

Shrimp, Frozen Scampi *See Prepared Foods: Prepared Meals: Scampi: Shrimp Frozen*

Sicilian Style Sausages *See Meats & Meat Products: Smoked, Cured & Deli Meats: Sausages: Sicilian Style (with Cheese)*

Siciliano Salami *See Meats & Meat Products: Smoked, Cured & Deli Meats: Salami: Siciliano*

Single & Blended Enrichment & Nutrient Additives *See Ingredients, Flavors & Additives: Additives: Enrichment & Nutrient: Single & Blended*

Sirloin Cubes *See Meats & Meat Products: Beef & Beef Products: Sirloin Cubes*

Skim Milk *See Dairy Products: Milk & Milk Products: Milk: Skim*

Sliced Beef & Beef Products *See Meats & Meat Products: Beef & Beef Products: Sliced*

Sliced Blend, American/Skim Milk Cheese *See Cheese & Cheese Products: Cheese: Blend - American/Skim Milk: Sliced*

Sliced Peaches *See Fruits & Vegetables: Peach: Sliced*

Slushes *See Dairy Products: Ice Cream: Slushes*

Small Red Beans *See Fruits & Vegetables: Beans: Small Red*

Smelt *See Fish & Seafood: Fish: Smelt*

Smoke Flavors *See Ingredients, Flavors & Additives: Flavors: Smoke*

Smoked & Cured Fish *See Fish & Seafood: Fish: Smoked & Cured*

Smoked Ham *See Meats & Meat Products: Smoked, Cured & Deli Meats: Ham: Smoked*

Smoked Meat *See Meats & Meat Products: Smoked, Cured & Deli Meats: Smoked Meat*

Smoked Salmon *See Fish & Seafood: Fish: Salmon: Smoked*

Smoked Sausages *See Meats & Meat Products: Smoked, Cured & Deli Meats: Sausages: Smoked*

Smoked Seafood *See Fish & Seafood: Seafood: Smoked*

Smoked Shellfish *See Fish & Seafood: Shellfish: Smoked*

Smoked Turkey *See Meats & Meat Products: Smoked, Cured & Deli Meats: Turkey: Smoked*

Smoked, Cured & Deli Meats *See Meats & Meat Products: Smoked, Cured & Deli Meats*

Smooth Peanut Butter *See Nuts & Nut Butters: Nut Butters: Peanut Butter: Smooth*

Smoothie Powder Mixes *See Doughs, Mixes & Fillings: Mixes: Smoothie Powder*

Smoothie Powders *See Ingredients, Flavors & Additives: Powders: Smoothie*

Smoothies *See Beverages: Smoothies*

Snack Foods *See Snack Foods*

Snack Pellets *See Snack Foods: Snack Pellets*

Snack Seasonings *See Spices, Seasonings & Seeds: Seasonings: Snack*

Snails *See Fish & Seafood: Shellfish: Snails*

Snake Beans *See Fruits & Vegetables: Beans: Snake*

Snap Peas *See Fruits & Vegetables: Peas: Snap*

Snapper *See Fish & Seafood: Fish: Snapper*

Snow Crab *See Fish & Seafood: Shellfish: Crab: Snow*

Sockeye Salmon *See Fish & Seafood: Fish: Salmon: Sockeye*

Soda Water *See Beverages: Soft Drinks & Sodas: Soda Water*

Sodium *See Ingredients, Flavors & Additives: Sodium*

Sodium Alginates *See Ingredients, Flavors & Additives: Sodium Alginates*

Sodium Benzoate *See Ingredients, Flavors & Additives: Sodium Benzoate*

Sodium Citrate *See Ingredients, Flavors & Additives: Sodium Citrate*

Sodium Phosphate *See Ingredients, Flavors & Additives: Phosphates: Sodium Phosphate*

Soft Cookies *See Baked Goods: Cookies & Bars: Soft Cookies*

Soft Drinks & Sodas *See Beverages: Soft Drinks & Sodas; See also Beverages: Soft Drinks & Sodas: Soft Drinks*

Soft Pretzels *See Snack Foods: Pretzels: Soft*

Soft Shell Crab *See Fish & Seafood: Shellfish: Crab: Soft Shell*

Sole *See Fish & Seafood: Fish: Sole*

Solids *See Eggs & Egg Products: Solids*

Solubilizers *See Ingredients, Flavors & Additives: Surfactants & Solubilizers: Solubilizers*

Sorbet *See Dairy Products: Ice Cream: Sorbet*

Sorbic Acidulants *See Ingredients, Flavors & Additives: Acidulants: Sorbic*

Sorbitol *See Ingredients, Flavors & Additives: Sweeteners: Sorbitol*

Sorghum *See Cereals, Grains, Rice & Flour: Sorghum*

Sorrel *See Spices, Seasonings & Seeds: Spices: Sorrel*

Soup Bases *See Ingredients, Flavors & Additives: Bases: Soup*

	1	2	3	4	5

EXAMPLE: **Canadian Style Bacon** *See Meats & Meat Products: Smoked, Cured & Deli Meats: Bacon: Canadian Style*

1. Product or Service you are looking for

2. Main Category, in alphabetical order, located in the page headers starting on page 23

3. Category Description, located in black bars and in page headers

4. Product Category, located in gray bars

5. Product Type, located under gray bars, centered in bold

Soup Blend *See Fruits & Vegetables: Dried & Dehydrated Vegetables: Soup Blend*
Soup Mixes *See Doughs, Mixes & Fillings: Mixes: Soup*
Soups & Stews *See Prepared Foods: Soups & Stews*
Sour Cream *See Dairy Products: Sour Cream*
Sour Cream & Onion Potato Chips *See Snack Foods: Chips: Potato: Sour Cream & Onion*
Sour Cream & Onion Snack Seasonings *See Spices, Seasonings & Seeds: Seasonings: Snack: Sour Cream & Onion*
Sour Cream Flavors *See Ingredients, Flavors & Additives: Flavors: Sour: Cream*
Sour Flavors *See Ingredients, Flavors & Additives: Flavors: Sour*
Sourdough Breads *See Baked Goods: Breads: Sourdough*
Southern Peas *See Fruits & Vegetables: Peas: Southern*
Southwest Seasonings *See Spices, Seasonings & Seeds: Seasonings: Southwest*
Soy *See Fruits & Vegetables: Soy*
Soy Bean *See Fruits & Vegetables: Soy: Soy Bean*
Soy Bean Meal *See Cereals, Grains, Rice & Flour: Soy Bean Meal*
Soy Bran Fiber *See Cereals, Grains, Rice & Flour: Fiber: Soy Bran*
Soy Crisps *See Cereals, Grains, Rice & Flour: Crisps: Soy*
Soy Crumbs Toppings *See Ingredients, Flavors & Additives: Toppings: Soy Crumbs*
Soy Flakes *See Ingredients, Flavors & Additives: Flakes: Soy*
Soy Frankfurters *See Meats & Meat Products: Frankfurters: Soy*
Soy Milk *See Fruits & Vegetables: Soy: Soy Milk*
Soy Milk Powders *See Ingredients, Flavors & Additives: Powders: Soy Milk*
Soy Nuts *See Nuts & Nut Butters: Nuts: Soy*
Soy Powders *See Ingredients, Flavors & Additives: Powders: Soy*
Soy Protein *See Fruits & Vegetables: Soy: Soy Protein*
Soy Protein Flour *See Cereals, Grains, Rice & Flour: Flour: Soy Protein*
Soy Sauces *See Sauces, Dips & Dressings: Sauces: Soy*
Soybean Flour *See Cereals, Grains, Rice & Flour: Flour: Soybean*
Soybean Oils *See Oils, Shortening & Fats: Oils: Soybean*
Spaghetti *See Pasta & Noodles: Spaghetti*
Spaghetti Sauces *See Sauces, Dips & Dressings: Sauces: Spaghetti*
Spaghetti with Meatballs *See Prepared Foods: Prepared Meals: Spaghetti: with Meatballs*
Spaghetti, Prepared Meals *See Prepared Foods: Prepared Meals: Spaghetti*
Spanish Onion *See Fruits & Vegetables: Onion: Spanish*
Spanish Rice *See Cereals, Grains, Rice & Flour: Rice: Spanish*
Spanish Wines *See Beverages: Wines: Spanish*
Spareribs *See Meats & Meat Products: Pork & Pork Products: Spareribs*
Sparkling Apple Boysenberry Juices *See Beverages: Juices: Apple Boysenberry: Sparkling*
Sparkling Apple Cider Juices *See Beverages: Juices: Apple Cider: Sparkling*
Sparkling Apple Cranberry Juices *See Beverages: Juices: Apple Cranberry: Sparkling*
Sparkling Apple Grape Juices *See Beverages: Juices: Apple Grape: Sparkling*
Sparkling Apple Juices *See Beverages: Juices: Apple: Sparkling*
Sparkling Water *See Beverages: Soft Drinks & Sodas: Sparkling Water*
Sparkling Wines *See Beverages: Wines: Sparkling (See also French/Champagne)*
Spearmint *See Spices, Seasonings & Seeds: Spices: Spearmint*
Spearmint Flavors *See Ingredients, Flavors & Additives: Flavors: Spearmint*
Spearmint Leaves *See Spices, Seasonings & Seeds: Spices: Mint Leaves: Spearmint*
Specialty & Cider Beers *See Beverages: Beers: Specialty & Cider*
Specialty Bread Crumbs *See Ingredients, Flavors & Additives: Toppings: Specialty Bread Crumbs*
Specialty-Packaged Candy *See Candy & Confectionery: Specialty-Packaged Candy*
Specialty-Packaged Candy, Bagged *See Candy & Confectionery: Specialty-Packaged Candy: Bagged*
Specialty-Packaged Candy, Boxed *See Candy & Confectionery: Specialty-Packaged Candy: Boxed*
Specialty-Packaged Candy, Boxed Non-Chocolate *See Candy & Confectionery: Specialty-Packaged Candy: Non-Chocolate - Boxed*

Specialty-Packaged Candy, Christmas *See Candy & Confectionery: Specialty-Packaged Candy: Christmas*
Specialty-Packaged Candy, Easter *See Candy & Confectionery: Specialty-Packaged Candy: Easter*
Specialty-Packaged Candy, Fund-Raising *See Candy & Confectionery: Specialty-Packaged Candy: Fund Raising*
Specialty-Packaged Candy, Halloween *See Candy & Confectionery: Specialty-Packaged Candy: Halloween*
Specialty-Packaged Candy, Multi-Packs *See Candy & Confectionery: Specialty-Packaged Candy: Multi-Packs*
Specialty-Packaged Candy, Packaged for Racks *See Candy & Confectionery: Specialty-Packaged Candy: Packaged for Racks*
Specialty-Packaged Candy, Packaged for Theaters *See Candy & Confectionery: Specialty-Packaged Candy: Packaged for Theaters*
Specialty-Packaged Candy, Valentine *See Candy & Confectionery: Specialty-Packaged Candy: Valentine*
Specialty-Packaged Candy, Vending *See Candy & Confectionery: Specialty-Packaged Candy: Vending*
Spelt *See Pasta & Noodles: Spelt*
Spelt Flour *See Cereals, Grains, Rice & Flour: Flour: Spelt*
Spice Seeds *See Spices, Seasonings & Seeds: Spice*
Spiced Herring *See Fish & Seafood: Fish: Herring: Spiced*
Spices *See Spices, Seasonings & Seeds: Spices*
Spinach *See Fruits & Vegetables: Spinach*
Spinach Pasta *See Pasta & Noodles: Spinach*
Spinach Powder *See Fruits & Vegetables: Dried & Dehydrated Vegetables: Spinach Powder*
Spirits & Liqueurs *See Spirits & Liqueurs*
Spirulina *See Ingredients, Flavors & Additives: Spirulina*
Sponge Cake *See Baked Goods: Cakes & Pastries: Sponge Cake*
Sponge Gourd *See Fruits & Vegetables: Sponge Gourd*
Sports Drinks *See Beverages: Sports Drinks*
Spray Cooking Oils *See Oils, Shortening & Fats: Oils: Cooking: Spray*
Spreads *See Jams, Jellies & Spreads: Spreads*
Spring Rolls *See Ethnic Foods: Egg Rolls: Spring Rolls*
Spring Water *See Beverages: Water: Spring*
Spring Wheat *See Cereals, Grains, Rice & Flour: Wheat: Spring*
Sprinkles *See Ingredients, Flavors & Additives: Toppings: Sprinkles*
Sprouts *See Fruits & Vegetables: Sprouts*
Squab *See Meats & Meat Products: Game: Squab*
Squash *See Fruits & Vegetables: Squash*
Squid *See Fish & Seafood: Shellfish: Squid*
St. John's Wort *See Ingredients, Flavors & Additives: Powders: St. John's Wort*
Stabilizers *See Ingredients, Flavors & Additives: Stabilizers*
Star Anise *See Spices, Seasonings & Seeds: Spices: Star Anise; See also See Spices, Seasonings & Seeds: Spices: Anise - Star*
Star Fruit *See Fruits & Vegetables: Star Fruit*
Starches *See Ingredients, Flavors & Additives: Starches*
Starter Media *See Ingredients, Flavors & Additives: Starter Media*
Steak *See Meats & Meat Products: Beef & Beef Products: Steak*
Steak Sauces *See Sauces, Dips & Dressings: Sauces: Steak*
Steaks *See Meats & Meat Products: Steaks*
Stewed Tomato *See Fruits & Vegetables: Tomato: Stewed*
Sticky Buns *See Baked Goods: Breads: Buns: Sticky*
Stir-Fry Sauces *See Sauces, Dips & Dressings: Sauces: Stir-Fry*
Stone Crab *See Fish & Seafood: Shellfish: Crab: Stone*
Stone Crab Claws *See Fish & Seafood: Shellfish: Crab: Claws Stone*
Stored Corn *See Fruits & Vegetables: Corn: Stored*
Stout & Porter Beers *See Beverages: Beers: Stout & Porter*
Strawberry *See Fruits & Vegetables: Berries: Strawberry*
Strawberry Flavors *See Ingredients, Flavors & Additives: Flavors: Strawberry*
Strawberry Jams *See Jams, Jellies & Spreads: Jams: Strawberry*
Strawberry Juices *See Beverages: Juices: Strawberry*
Strawberry Milk *See Dairy Products: Milk & Milk Products: Milk: Strawberry*
Strawberry Shortcake *See Baked Goods: Cakes & Pastries: Strawberry Shortcake*
String Cheese *See Cheese & Cheese Products: Cheese: String*
Striped Bass *See Fish & Seafood: Fish: Bass: Striped*
Strudel *See Baked Goods: Cakes & Pastries: Strudel*
Stuffed Cabbage, Prepared Meals *See Prepared Foods: Prepared Meals: Stuffed Cabbage*
Stuffed Crab *See Fish & Seafood: Shellfish: Crab: Stuffed*
Stuffed Crab, Prepared Meals *See Prepared Foods: Prepared Meals: Crab: Stuffed*

Stuffed Fish, Prepared Meals *See Prepared Foods: Prepared Meals: Fish: Stuffed*
Stuffed Peppers, Prepared Meals *See Prepared Foods: Prepared Meals: Stuffed Peppers*
Stuffed Shells *See Pasta & Noodles: Stuffed Shells*
Stuffed Shells Prepared Meals *See Prepared Foods: Prepared Meals: Stuffed Shells*
Stuffing *See Baked Goods: Stuffing; See also Prepared Foods: Stuffing*
Stuffing for Meat *See Baked Goods: Stuffing: for Meat*
Stuffing for Poultry *See Baked Goods: Stuffing: for Poultry*
Sturgeon *See Fish & Seafood: Fish: Sturgeon*
Substitutes, Cheese *See Cheese & Cheese Products: Imitation Cheeses & Substitutes: Substitutes*
Substitutes, Egg *See Eggs & Egg Products: Substitutes*
Substitutes, Salt *See Spices, Seasonings & Seeds: Salt: Substitutes*
Succotash *See Fruits & Vegetables: Succotash*
Sucrose *See Sugars, Syrups & Sweeteners: Sucrose*
Sugar *See Sugars, Syrups & Sweeteners: Sugar*
Sugar Alternatives *See Sugars, Syrups & Sweeteners: Sugar Substitutes: Sugar Alternatives*
Sugar Beets *See Fruits & Vegetables: Beets: Sugar*
Sugar Cookies *See Baked Goods: Cookies & Bars: Sugar Cookies*
Sugar Substitutes *See Sugars, Syrups & Sweeteners: Sugar Substitutes*
Sugar Wafers *See Baked Goods: Cookies & Bars: Wafers: Sugar*
Sugar-Free Foods *See Specialty & Organic Foods: Dietary Products: Sugar-Free Foods*
Sugars, Syrups & Sweeteners *See Sugars, Syrups & Sweeteners*
Sumac Berries *See Spices, Seasonings & Seeds: Spices: Sumac Berries*
Sun Tea *See Beverages: Coffee & Tea: Tea: Sun*
Sun-Dried Fruit *See Fruits & Vegetables: Sun Dried Fruit*
Sun-Dried Tomato *See Fruits & Vegetables: Tomato: Sun-Dried*
Sundae Toppings *See Sugars, Syrups & Sweeteners: Syrups: Toppings: Sundae*
Sunflower *See Fruits & Vegetables: Sunflower*
Sunflower Oils *See Oils, Shortening & Fats: Oils: Sunflower*
Sunflower Seeds *See Spices, Seasonings & Seeds: Seeds: Sunflower*
Supplements *See Ingredients, Flavors & Additives: Vitamins & Supplements: Supplements*
Supplements, Fiber *See Cereals, Grains, Rice & Flour: Fiber: Supplements*
Surfactants & Solubilizers *See Ingredients, Flavors & Additives: Surfactants & Solubilizers*
Survival Foods *See Specialty & Organic Foods: Survival Foods*
Sushi *See Fish & Seafood: Sushi*
Swamp Cabbage *See Fruits & Vegetables: Cabbage: Swamp*
Swedish Meat Balls *See Prepared Foods: Meat Balls: Swedish*
Sweet & Sour Sauces *See Sauces, Dips & Dressings: Sauces: Sweet & Sour*
Sweet Cherries *See Fruits & Vegetables: Cherries: Sweet*
Sweet Corn *See Fruits & Vegetables: Corn: Sweet*
Sweet Italian Sausage Seasonings *See Spices, Seasonings & Seeds: Seasonings: Sausage: Sweet Italian*
Sweet Italian Sausages *See Meats & Meat Products: Smoked, Cured & Deli Meats: Sausages: Sweet Italian*
Sweet Peppers *See Fruits & Vegetables: Peppers: Sweet*
Sweet Pickles *See Relishes & Pickled Products: Pickled Products: Pickles: Sweet*
Sweet Potatoes *See Fruits & Vegetables: Sweet Potatoes*
Sweet Processed Corn *See Fruits & Vegetables: Corn: Sweet Processed*
Sweet Rolls *See Baked Goods: Breads: Rolls: Sweet*
Sweet Salami *See Meats & Meat Products: Smoked, Cured & Deli Meats: Salami: Sweet*
Sweet Sausages *See Meats & Meat Products: Smoked, Cured & Deli Meats: Sausages: Sweet*
Sweet Stout *See Beverages: Beers: Stout & Porter: Sweet Stout*
Sweetened & Condensed Milk *See Dairy Products: Milk & Milk Products: Milk: Sweetened & Condensed*
Sweetened Milk *See Dairy Products: Milk & Milk Products: Milk: Sweetened*
Sweeteners *See Ingredients, Flavors & Additives: Sweeteners*
Swiss Cheese *See Cheese & Cheese Products: Cheese: Swiss*
Swordfish *See Fish & Seafood: Fish: Swordfish*

Synthetic Glycerine *See Ingredients, Flavors & Additives: Synthetic Glycerine*
Syrah Red Grape Wines *See Beverages: Wines: Red Grape Wines: Syrah*
Syrup Malt *See Cereals, Grains, Rice & Flour: Malt: Syrup*
Syrups *See Sugars, Syrups & Sweeteners: Syrups*
Szechuan Sauces *See Sauces, Dips & Dressings: Sauces: Szechuan*

T

Tabbouleh *See Ethnic Foods: Tabbouleh*
Table Grape *See Fruits & Vegetables: Grape: Table*
Tabletizing Compacting Agents *See Ingredients, Flavors & Additives: Agents: Compacting: Tabletizing*
Taco Chips *See Snack Foods: Chips: Taco*
Taco Fillings *See Ethnic Foods: Tacos: Fillings*
Taco Sauces *See Sauces, Dips & Dressings: Sauces: Taco*
Taco Shells *See Ethnic Foods: Shells: Taco*
Tacos *See Ethnic Foods: Tacos*
Taffy *See Candy & Confectionery: Candy: Taffy*
Tagliatelle *See Pasta & Noodles: Tagliatelle*
Tahini Sauces *See Sauces, Dips & Dressings: Sauces: Tahini*
Taleggio *See Cheese & Cheese Products: Cheese: Taleggio*
Tamales *See Ethnic Foods: Tamales*
Tamarind *See Fruits & Vegetables: Tamarind*
Tandoori *See Spices, Seasonings & Seeds: Spices: Tandoori*
Tangelos *See Fruits & Vegetables: Tangelos*
Tangerine Juices *See Beverages: Juices: Tangerine*
Tangerine Oils *See Oils, Shortening & Fats: Oils: Tangerine*
Tangerines *See Fruits & Vegetables: Tangerines*
Tapioca *See Cereals, Grains, Rice & Flour: Tapioca*
Tapioca Flour *See Cereals, Grains, Rice & Flour: Flour: Tapioca*
Tapioca Pudding *See Dairy Products: Pudding: Tapioca*
Tapioca Starches *See Ingredients, Flavors & Additives: Starches: Tapioca*
Taquitos *See Ethnic Foods: Taquitos*
Tara *See Ingredients, Flavors & Additives: Gums: Tara*
Taro *See Fruits & Vegetables: Taro*
Tarragon *See Spices, Seasonings & Seeds: Spices: Tarragon*
Tart Cherries *See Fruits & Vegetables: Cherries: Tart*
Tartar *See Spices, Seasonings & Seeds: Spices: Tartar*
Tartar Sauces *See Sauces, Dips & Dressings: Sauces: Tartar*
Tartaric Acidulants *See Ingredients, Flavors & Additives: Acidulants: Tartaric*
Tarts *See Baked Goods: Cakes & Pastries: Tarts*
Tartufo *See Baked Goods: Cakes & Pastries: Tartufo*
Tasso *See Meats & Meat Products: Smoked, Cured & Deli Meats: Tasso*
Tater Tots *See Prepared Foods: French Fries: Tater Tots*
Tea *See Beverages: Coffee & Tea: Tea*
Tea Bags *See Beverages: Coffee & Tea: Tea: Bags*
Tea Cookies *See Baked Goods: Cookies & Bars: Tea Cookies*
Tea Extracts *See Ingredients, Flavors & Additives: Extracts: Tea*
Tea Flavors *See Ingredients, Flavors & Additives: Flavors: Tea*
Tea, Fair-Trade *See Beverages: Coffee & Tea: Tea: Fair-Trade*
Teas *See Spices, Seasonings & Seeds: Spices: Teas*
Tempeh *See Ethnic Foods: Tempeh*
Tenderizers *See Ingredients, Flavors & Additives: Tenderizers*
Tenderizing Compounds *See Ingredients, Flavors & Additives: Compounds: Tenderizing*
Tequila and Mezcal *See Beverages: Spirits & Liqueurs: Tequila and Mezcal*
Teriyaki Sauces *See Sauces, Dips & Dressings: Sauces: Teriyaki*
Texture Modifiers Agents *See Ingredients, Flavors & Additives: Agents: Modifiers: Texture*
Textured Vegetable Protein *See Fruits & Vegetables: Textured Vegetable Protein*
Texturized Soy Protein *See Fruits & Vegetables: Soy: Protein: Texturized; See also Fruits & Vegetables: Soy: Soy Protein: Texturized*
Thick Bacon Slices *See Meats & Meat Products: Smoked, Cured & Deli Meats: Bacon: Slices Thick*
Thickeners *See Ingredients, Flavors & Additives: Thickeners*

Thickening Agents *See Ingredients, Flavors & Additives: Agents: Thickening*
Thin Boiling Starches *See Ingredients, Flavors & Additives: Starches: Thin Boiling*
Thousand Island Salad Dressing *See Sauces, Dips & Dressings: Salad Dressings: Thousand Island*
Thousand Island Salad Dressing Mixes *See Sauces, Dips & Dressings: Salad Dressings: Mixes: Thousand Island*
Thyme *See Spices, Seasonings & Seeds: Spices: Thyme*
Thyme Oils *See Oils, Shortening & Fats: Oils: Thyme*
Tilapia *See Fish & Seafood: Fish: Tilapia*
Tiramisu *See Baked Goods: Cakes & Pastries: Tiramisu*
Toasted Breads *See Baked Goods: Breads: Toasted*
Toffee *See Candy & Confectionery: Candy: Toffee*
Tofu Powders *See Ingredients, Flavors & Additives: Powders: Tofu*
Tomatillos *See Fruits & Vegetables: Tomatillos*
Tomato *See Fruits & Vegetables: Tomato*
Tomato Concentrates *See Ingredients, Flavors & Additives: Concentrates: Tomato*
Tomato Juices *See Beverages: Juices: Tomato*
Tomato Pastes *See Ingredients, Flavors & Additives: Pastes: Tomato*
Tomato Pesto Seasonings *See Spices, Seasonings & Seeds: Seasonings: Tomato Pesto*
Tomato Powder *See Fruits & Vegetables: Dried & Dehydrated Vegetables: Tomatoes: Tomato Powder; See also Ingredients, Flavors & Additives: Powders: Tomato*
Tomato Pulps & Purees *See Fruits & Vegetables: Pulps & Purees: Tomato; See also Fruits & Vegetables: Pulps & Purees: Puree: Tomato*
Tomato Sauce with Spices *See Sauces, Dips & Dressings: Sauces: Tomato: with Spices*
Tomato Sauces *See Sauces, Dips & Dressings: Sauces: Tomato*
Tomatoes, Dried *See Fruits & Vegetables: Dried & Dehydrated Vegetables: Tomatoes*
Tomatoes, Dried Halves *See Fruits & Vegetables: Dried & Dehydrated Vegetables: Tomatoes: Halves*
Tongue *See Meats & Meat Products: Beef & Beef Products: Tongue*
Toppings *See Sugars, Syrups & Sweeteners: Syrups: Toppings; See also Ingredients, Flavors & Additives: Toppings*
Tortellini *See Pasta & Noodles: Tortellini*
Tortes *See Baked Goods: Cakes & Pastries: Tortes*
Tortilla & Tortilla Products *See Ethnic Foods: Tortilla & Tortilla Products*
Tortilla Chips *See Snack Foods: Chips: Tortilla*
Tortillas *See Ethnic Foods: Tortilla & Tortilla Products: Tortillas*
Tortoni *See Dairy Products: Ice Cream: Tortoni*
Torula *See Ingredients, Flavors & Additives: Cultures & Yeasts: Yeast: Torula Dried*
Toscano Salami *See Meats & Meat Products: Smoked, Cured & Deli Meats: Salami: Toscano*
Tostadas *See Ethnic Foods: Tostadas*
Tragacanth *See Ingredients, Flavors & Additives: Gums: Tragacanth*
Trail Mix *See Snack Foods: Trail Mix*
Trail Mixes *See Doughs, Mixes & Fillings: Mixes: Trail*
Tricalcium Phosphate *See Ingredients, Flavors & Additives: Agents: Anticaking: Tricalcium Phosphate*
Tripe *See Meats & Meat Products: Tripe*
Tropical & Exotic Fruit *See Fruits & Vegetables: Tropical & Exotic Fruit*
Tropical Fruit Juices *See Beverages: Juices: Tropical Fruits*
Trout *See Fish & Seafood: Fish: Trout*
Truffles, Candy *See Candy & Confectionery: Candy: Truffles*
Truffles, Mushrooms *See Fruits & Vegetables: Mushrooms: Truffles*
Tubetti *See Pasta & Noodles: Tubetti*
Tuffoli *See Pasta & Noodles: Tuffoli*
Tuna *See Fish & Seafood: Fish: Tuna*
Tuna, Prepared Salads *See Prepared Foods: Prepared Salads: Tuna*
Turbot *See Fish & Seafood: Fish: Turbot*
Turkey *See Meats & Meat Products: Poultry: Turkey*
Turkey Dinner, Prepared Meals *See Prepared Foods: Prepared Meals: Turkey Dinner*
Turkey Frankfurters *See Meats & Meat Products: Frankfurters: Turkey*

Turkey Leg *See Meats & Meat Products: Poultry: Turkey: Leg*
Turkey Sausages *See Meats & Meat Products: Smoked, Cured & Deli Meats: Sausages: Turkey*
Turkey, Game *See Meats & Meat Products: Game: Turkey*
Turkey, Prepared Salads *See Prepared Foods: Prepared Salads: Turkey*
Turkey, Smoked *See Meats & Meat Products: Smoked, Cured & Deli Meats: Turkey*
Turmeric Natural Colors *See Ingredients, Flavors & Additives: Colors: Natural: Turmeric*
Turmeric Spices *See Spices, Seasonings & Seeds: Spices: Turmeric*
Turnip *See Fruits & Vegetables: Turnip*
Turnip Greens *See Fruits & Vegetables: Turnip: Turnip Greens: Canned*
Turnovers *See Baked Goods: Cakes & Pastries: Turnovers*
Turtle Seafood *See Fish & Seafood: Seafood: Turtle*
Twists Pretzels *See Snack Foods: Pretzels: Twists*
Two Percent Milk *See Dairy Products: Milk & Milk Products: Milk: 2 Percent*

U

Uncompounded Aroma Materials *See Ingredients, Flavors & Additives: Aroma Chemicals & Materials: Materials: Uncompounded*
Uncooked Frozen Hamburger *See Meats & Meat Products: Beef & Beef Products: Hamburger: Uncooked Frozen*
Unsalted Butter *See Dairy Products: Butter: Unsalted*

V

V.S. Cognac Three Star Brandy *See Beverages: Spirits & Liqueurs: Brandy: V.S. Cognac Three Star*
V.S.O.P. Cognac Brandy *See Beverages: Spirits & Liqueurs: Brandy: V.S.O.P. Cognac*
Vacuum Packed Coffee *See Beverages: Coffee & Tea: Coffee: Vacuum Packed*
Valencia Orange *See Fruits & Vegetables: Orange: Valencia*
Valentine Specialty-Packaged Candy *See Candy & Confectionery: Specialty-Packaged Candy: Valentine*
Valerian Root Powders *See Ingredients, Flavors & Additives: Powders: Valerian Root*
Vanilla Beans *See Spices, Seasonings & Seeds: Spices: Vanilla Beans*
Vanilla Butter Flavors *See Ingredients, Flavors & Additives: Flavors: Butter: Vanilla*
Vanilla Extracts *See Ingredients, Flavors & Additives: Extracts: Vanilla*
Vanilla Flavors *See Ingredients, Flavors & Additives: Flavors: Vanilla*
Vanilla Powders *See Ingredients, Flavors & Additives: Powders: Vanilla*
Vanilla Pudding *See Dairy Products: Pudding: Vanilla*
Vanilla Spices *See Spices, Seasonings & Seeds: Spices: Vanilla*
Vanillin Flavors *See Ingredients, Flavors & Additives: Flavors: Vanillin*
Variegates Flavors *See Ingredients, Flavors & Additives: Flavors: Variegates*
Veal *See Meats & Meat Products: Beef & Beef Products: Veal*
Veal Cutlet *See Meats & Meat Products: Beef & Beef Products: Veal: Cutlet*
Veal Sausages *See Meats & Meat Products: Smoked, Cured & Deli Meats: Sausages: Veal*
Vegetable Bases *See Ingredients, Flavors & Additives: Bases: Vegetable*
Vegetable Colors *See Ingredients, Flavors & Additives: Colors: Vegetable*
Vegetable Concentrates *See Ingredients, Flavors & Additives: Concentrates: Vegetable*
Vegetable Extracts *See Ingredients, Flavors & Additives: Extracts: Vegetable*
Vegetable Flavors *See Ingredients, Flavors & Additives: Flavors: Vegetable*
Vegetable Gum *See Ingredients, Flavors & Additives: Gums: Vegetable Gum*
Vegetable Juices *See Beverages: Juices: Vegetable*
Vegetable Mixes *See Doughs, Mixes & Fillings: Mixes: Vegetable*
Vegetable Oils *See Oils, Shortening & Fats: Oils: Vegetable*
Vegetable Proteins *See Ingredients, Flavors & Additives: Hydrolyzed Products: Vegetable Proteins*

EXAMPLE: **Canadian Style Bacon** *See Meats & Meat Products: Smoked, Cured & Deli Meats: Bacon: Canadian Style*

1. Product or Service you are looking for
2. Main Category, in alphabetical order, located in the page headers starting on page 23
3. Category Description, located in black bars and in page headers
4. Product Category, located in gray bars
5. Product Type, located under gray bars, centered in bold

Vegetable Pulp *See Fruits & Vegetables: Pulps & Purees: Pulp: Vegetable*

Vegetable Puree *See Fruits & Vegetables: Pulps & Purees: Puree: Vegetable*

Vegetable Ravioli *See Pasta & Noodles: Ravioli: Vegetable*

Vegetable Seeds *See Spices, Seasonings & Seeds: Seeds: Vegetable*

Vegetable Shortening *See Oils, Shortening & Fats: Shortening: Vegetable*

Vegetable Stuffing *See Prepared Foods: Stuffing: Vegetable*

Vegetables *See Fruits & Vegetables: Vegetables*

Vegetables, Mixed *See Fruits & Vegetables: Vegetables Mixed*

Vegetables, Organic *See Specialty & Organic Foods: Organic Foods: Vegetables*

Vegetables, Pickled *See Relishes & Pickled Products: Pickled Products: Vegetables*

Vegetarian Products *See Specialty & Organic Foods: Vegetarian Products*

Vegetarian, Prepared Meals *See Prepared Foods: Prepared Meals: Vegetarian*

Veggie & Rice Pellets *See Ingredients, Flavors & Additives: Half-Products: Veggie & Rice Pellets*

Vending Specialty-Packaged Candy *See Candy & Confectionery: Specialty-Packaged Candy: Vending*

Venison *See Meats & Meat Products: Game: Venison*

Venison Sausages *See Meats & Meat Products: Smoked, Cured & Deli Meats: Sausages: Venison*

Vermicelli *See Pasta & Noodles: Vermicelli*

Vinegar *See Sauces, Dips & Dressings: Vinegar*

Viognier *See Beverages: Wines: White Grape Varieties: Viognier*

Vitamin A *See Ingredients, Flavors & Additives: Vitamins & Supplements: A*

Vitamin C *See Ingredients, Flavors & Additives: Vitamins & Supplements: C*

Vitamin E *See Ingredients, Flavors & Additives: Vitamins & Supplements: E - Tocopherol*

Vitamin Oils *See Oils, Shortening & Fats: Oils: Vitamin*

Vitamins & Supplements *See Ingredients, Flavors & Additives: Vitamins & Supplements; See also Ingredients, Flavors & Additives: Vitamins & Supplements: Supplements: Vitamins; See also Ingredients, Flavors & Additives: Vitamins & Supplements: Vit*

Vodka *See Beverages: Spirits & Liqueurs: Vodka*

Volpino Salami *See Meats & Meat Products: Smoked, Cured & Deli Meats: Salami: Volpino*

W

Wafers *See Baked Goods: Cookies & Bars: Wafers*

Waffle Mixes *See Doughs, Mixes & Fillings: Mixes: Waffle*

Waffle Syrups *See Sugars, Syrups & Sweeteners: Syrups: Waffle*

Waffles *See Baked Goods: Waffles*

Walnut Oils *See Oils, Shortening & Fats: Oils: Walnut*

Walnuts Nuts *See Nuts & Nut Butters: Nuts: Walnuts*

Wasabi *See Spices, Seasonings & Seeds: Spices: Wasabi*

Water *See Beverages: Water*

Water Chestnuts *See Fruits & Vegetables: Water Chestnuts*

Water Pack Cherries *See Fruits & Vegetables: Cherries: Water Pack*

Watercress *See Fruits & Vegetables: Watercress*

Watermelon *See Fruits & Vegetables: Melon: Watermelon*

Watermelon, Seedless *See Fruits & Vegetables: Melon: Watermelon: Seedless*

Wax Beans *See Fruits & Vegetables: Beans: Wax*

Waxes *See Ingredients, Flavors & Additives: Waxes*

Waxy Maize Starches *See Ingredients, Flavors & Additives: Starches: Waxy Maize*

Waxy Starches *See Ingredients, Flavors & Additives: Starches: Waxy*

Wehani Rice *See Cereals, Grains, Rice & Flour: Rice: Wehani*

Wheat *See Cereals, Grains, Rice & Flour: Wheat*

Wheat Ale *See Beverages: Beers: Wheat: Wheat Ale*

Wheat Beers *See Beverages: Beers: Wheat*

Wheat Bran *See Cereals, Grains, Rice & Flour: Bran: Wheat*

Wheat Bran Fiber *See Cereals, Grains, Rice & Flour: Fiber: Wheat Bran*

Wheat Breads *See Baked Goods: Breads: Wheat*

Wheat Flakes *See Cereals, Grains, Rice & Flour: Wheat: Flakes*

Wheat Flour *See Cereals, Grains, Rice & Flour: Flour: Wheat*

Wheat Germ *See Cereals, Grains, Rice & Flour: Wheat: Germ*

Wheat Germ Oils *See Oils, Shortening & Fats: Oils: Wheat Germ*

Wheat Starches *See Ingredients, Flavors & Additives: Starches: Wheat*

Wheat, Bagged *See Cereals, Grains, Rice & Flour: Wheat: Bagged*

Wheat-Based Cereal *See Cereals, Grains, Rice & Flour: Cereal: Wheat-Based*

Whey & Whey Products *See Cereals, Grains, Rice & Flour: Whey & Whey Products*

Whey Crisps *See Cereals, Grains, Rice & Flour: Crisps: Whey*

Whey Protein Concentrates & Isolates *See Ingredients, Flavors & Additives: Concentrates: Whey Protein Concentrates & Isolates*

Whipped Cream *See Dairy Products: Cream: Whipped*

Whipped Toppings *See Ingredients, Flavors & Additives: Toppings: Whipped*

Whiskey, American *See Beverages: Spirits & Liqueurs: Whiskey, American*

Whiskey, Canadian *See Beverages: Spirits & Liqueurs: Whiskey, Canadian*

White Breads *See Baked Goods: Breads: White*

White Burgundy *See Beverages: Wines: French: White Burgundy*

White Chocolate Dipped Biscotti *See Baked Goods: Cookies & Bars: Biscotti: White Chocolate Dipped*

White Distilled Vinegar *See Sauces, Dips & Dressings: Vinegar: White Distilled*

White Fresh Potatoes *See Fruits & Vegetables: Potatoes: Fresh: White*

White Grape Wines *See Beverages: Wines: White Grape Varieties; See also See Beverages: Wines: White Grapes*

White Grapefruit *See Fruits & Vegetables: Grapefruit: White*

White Ground Pepper *See Spices, Seasonings & Seeds: Spices: Pepper: White Ground*

White Mushrooms *See Fruits & Vegetables: Mushrooms: White*

White Pepper *See Spices, Seasonings & Seeds: Spices: White Pepper; See also Spices, Seasonings & Seeds: Spices: Pepper: Black - White - Red*

White Rice *See Cereals, Grains, Rice & Flour: Rice: White*

White Sesame Seeds *See Spices, Seasonings & Seeds: Seeds: Sesame: White*

White Silver Rum *See Beverages: Spirits & Liqueurs: Rum: White Silver*

White Unbleached Flour *See Cereals, Grains, Rice & Flour: Flour: White Unbleached*

White Whole Truffles *See Fruits & Vegetables: Mushrooms: Truffles: White Whole*

White/Yellow Process Sliced Cheese *See Cheese & Cheese Products: Cheese: Process Sliced: White/Yellow*

Whitefish *See Fish & Seafood: Fish: Whitefish*

Whiting *See Fish & Seafood: Fish: Whiting*

Whole & Dried Chili Pods *See Spices, Seasonings & Seeds: Spices: Chili Pods: Whole & Dried*

Whole Allspice *See Spices, Seasonings & Seeds: Spices: Allspice: Whole*

Whole Black Olives *See Fruits & Vegetables: Olives: Black: Whole*

Whole Broccoli *See Fruits & Vegetables: Broccoli: Whole*

Whole Cayenne Pepper *See Spices, Seasonings & Seeds: Spices: Cayenne Pepper: Whole*

Whole Cinnamon *See Spices, Seasonings & Seeds: Spices: Cinnamon: Whole*

Whole Clam *See Fish & Seafood: Shellfish: Clam: Whole*

Whole Coriander Seeds *See Spices, Seasonings & Seeds: Seeds: Coriander: Whole*

Whole Corn *See Fruits & Vegetables: Corn: Whole*

Whole Egg Solids *See Eggs & Egg Products: Solids: Whole Egg*

Whole Frozen Turkey *See Meats & Meat Products: Poultry: Turkey: Whole Frozen*

Whole Grain Muffins *See Baked Goods: Cakes & Pastries: Muffins: Whole Grain*

Whole Maraschino Cherries *See Fruits & Vegetables: Cherries: Maraschino: Whole*

Whole Milk *See Dairy Products: Milk & Milk Products: Milk: Whole*

Whole Milk Solids *See Dairy Products: Milk & Milk Products: Milk Solids: Whole*

Whole Nutmeg Spices *See Spices, Seasonings & Seeds: Spices: Nutmeg (See also Mace): Whole*

Whole Shiitake Mushrooms *See Fruits & Vegetables: Mushrooms: Shiitake: Whole*

Whole Threads Saffron *See Spices, Seasonings & Seeds: Spices: Saffron: Whole Threads*

Whole Wheat Bread Sticks *See Baked Goods: Bread Sticks: Whole Wheat*

Whole Wheat Flour *See Cereals, Grains, Rice & Flour: Flour: Whole wheat*

Whole wheat Pastry Flour *See Cereals, Grains, Rice & Flour: Flour: Whole wheat: Pastry*

Whole Yellow Mustard Seeds *See Spices, Seasonings & Seeds: Seeds: Mustard: Whole Yellow*

Wild Game *See Meats & Meat Products: Game: Wild*

Wild Mushrooms *See Fruits & Vegetables: Mushrooms: Wild*

Wild Rice *See Cereals, Grains, Rice & Flour: Rice: Wild*

Wild Turkey *See Meats & Meat Products: Game: Turkey: Wild*

Wine Flavors *See Ingredients, Flavors & Additives: Flavors: Wine*

Wine Grape *See Fruits & Vegetables: Grape: Wine*

Wine Vinegar *See Sauces, Dips & Dressings: Vinegar: Wine*

Wine Yeast *See Ingredients, Flavors & Additives: Cultures & Yeasts: Yeast: Wine*

Wines *See Beverages: Wines*

Winter Squash Pumpkin *See Fruits & Vegetables: Pumpkin: Winter Squash*

Winter Wheat *See Cereals, Grains, Rice & Flour: Wheat: Winter*

Wonton Chips *See Ethnic Foods: Wonton Chips*

Wonton Soup *See Prepared Foods: Soups & Stews: Wonton Soup*

Wontons *See Ethnic Foods: Wontons*

Wood Ear Mushrooms *See Fruits & Vegetables: Mushrooms: Wood Ear*

Wood Ear Mushrooms, Dried *See Fruits & Vegetables: Dried & Dehydrated Vegetables: Mushrooms: Wood Ears*

Wood Pigeon *See Meats & Meat Products: Game: Wood Pigeon*

Worcestershire Sauces *See Sauces, Dips & Dressings: Sauces: Worcestershire*

Wrappers, Egg Roll *See Ethnic Foods: Egg Rolls: Wrappers*

Wraps *See Baked Goods: Wraps*

X

X.O. Cognac Brandy *See Beverages: Spirits & Liqueurs: Brandy: X.O. Cognac*

Xanthan Gum *See Ingredients, Flavors & Additives: Gums: Xanthan Gum*

Y

Yams *See Fruits & Vegetables: Yams*

Yeast *See Ingredients, Flavors & Additives: Cultures & Yeasts: Yeast*

Yeast Extracts *See Ingredients, Flavors & Additives: Extracts: Yeast*

Yellow Cherry Tomato *See Fruits & Vegetables: Tomato: Yellow Cherry*

Yellow Mustard *See Sauces, Dips & Dressings: Mustard: Yellow*

Yellow Process Cheese Loaves *See Cheese & Cheese Products: Cheese: Process Loaves: Yellow*

Yellow Split Peas *See Fruits & Vegetables: Peas: Yellow Split*

Yellowfin Tuna *See Fish & Seafood: Fish: Tuna: Yellowfin*

Yogurt *See Dairy Products: Yogurt*

Yogurt Bacteria *See Ingredients, Flavors & Additives: Cultures & Yeasts: Bacteria: Yogurt*

Yogurt Bases *See Ingredients, Flavors & Additives: Bases: Yogurt*

Yogurt Bases, Flavors, Stabilizers *See Dairy Products: Yogurt: Bases, Flavors, Stabilizers*

Yogurt Coated Nuts *See Nuts & Nut Butters: Nuts: Coated: Yogurt*

Yogurt Coated Raisins *See Fruits & Vegetables: Raisins: Yogurt Coated*

Yogurt Cultures *See Ingredients, Flavors & Additives: Cultures & Yeasts: Yogurt*

Yogurt Flavors *See Ingredients, Flavors & Additives: Flavors: Yogurt*

Yogurt Powder Mixes *See Doughs, Mixes & Fillings: Mixes: Yogurt Powder*

Yogurt Powders *See Ingredients, Flavors & Additives: Powders: Yogurt*

Yogurt Stabilizers *See Ingredients, Flavors & Additives: Stabilizers: Yogurt*

Yogurt with Fruit *See Dairy Products: Yogurt: with Fruit*

Yogurt, No-Fat *See Dairy Products: Yogurt: No-Fat*

Yolk *See Eggs & Egg Products: Yolk*

Z

Zinc Citrate *See Ingredients, Flavors & Additives: Vitamins & Supplements: Zinc Citrate*

Zinfandel, Red *See Beverages: Wines: Red Grape Wines: Zinfandel*

Zucchini *See Fruits & Vegetables: Zucchini*

Baked Goods

General

A & M Cookie Company Canada
Kitchener, ON .800-265-6508
A Southern Season
Chapel Hill, NC 800-253-5317
Adam Matthews, Inc.
Jeffersontown, KY 502-499-1244
Adams Foods
Dothan, AL .334-983-4233
Adrian's Bakery
Edmonton, AB 800-668-3533
Ak-Mak Bakeries
Sanger, CA .559-264-4145
Aladdin Bakers
Brooklyn, NY 718-499-1818
Alaska Pride Baking Company
Anchorage, AK 907-278-2867
Alati-Caserta Desserts
Montreal, QC 514-271-3013
Albertson's Bakery
Palm Desert, CA 760-360-6322
Alfred & Sam Italian Bakery
Lancaster, PA 717-392-6311
Almondina®/YZ Enterprises, Inc.
Maumee, OH 800-736-8779
Alois J. Binder Bakery
New Orleans, LA 504-947-1111
Alpha Baking Company
La Porte, IN 219-324-7440
Alpha Baking Company
Chicago, IL 773-261-6000
Alpha Baking Company
Chicago, IL 773-489-5400
Amalfitano's Italian Bakery
New Castle, DE 302-324-9005
Ambassador Foods
Van Nuys, CA 800-338-3369
Amberwave Foods
Oakmont, PA 412-828-3040
Amcan Industries
Elmsford, NY 914-347-4838
American Copak Corporation
Chatsworth, CA 818-576-1000
Ames International
Fife, WA 888-469-2637
Amoroso's Baking Company
Philadelphia, PA 800-377-6557
Andre French Bakery Retail
Fort Myers, FL 239-482-2011
Andre-Boudin Bakeries
San Francisco, CA 415-882-1849
Anthony & Sons Italian Bakery
Fairfield, NJ 973-244-9669
Antonio's Bakery
Ozone Park, NY 718-322-1314
April Hill
Grand Rapids, MI 616-245-0595
Archway & Mother's Cookie Company
Oakland, CA 800-369-3997
Archway Cookies
Ashland, OH 888-427-2492
Artel
Boisbriand, QC 450-433-1322
Arturo's Bakery
Waterbury, CT 203-754-3056
Artuso Pastry Foods
Mt Vernon, NY 914-663-8806
Artuso Pastry Shop
Bronx, NY .718-367-2515
Athens Baking Company
Fresno, CA 559-485-3024
Athens Pastries & Frozen Foods
Cleveland, OH 800-837-5683
Atkinson Milling Company
Selma, NC 800-948-5707
Atlanta Bread Company International, Inc.
Smyrna, GA 800-398-3728
Atlas Biscuit Company
Verona, NJ 973-239-8300
August Food Limited
Lubbock, TX 806-744-1918
August Foods
Lubbock, TX 806-744-1918
Aunt Bea Bakery
Saint Louis, MO 636-225-8808

Aunt Gussie Cookies & Crackers
Garfield, NJ 973-340-4480
Aunt Heddy's Bakery
Brooklyn, NY 718-782-0582
Aunt Millies Bakeries
Fort Wayne, IN 260-424-8245
Automatic Rolls of New Jersey
Edison, NJ 732-549-2243
Award Baking International
New Germany, MN 952-353-2533
Awrey Bakeries
Livonia, MI 800-950-2253
Azteca Foods
Summit Argo, IL 708-563-6600
B&A Bakery
Scarborough, ON 800-263-2878
B&M
Portland, ME 207-772-8341
Bagel Guys
Brooklyn, NY 718-222-4361
Bagels By Bell
Brooklyn, NY 718-272-2780
Bailey Street Bakery
Atlanta, GA 800-822-4634
Bake Crafters Food
Collegedale, TN 800-296-8935
Bake Masters of Atlanta
Doraville, GA 770-447-6823

To advertise in the
Food & Beverage Market Place
Online Database call
(800) 562-2139
or log on to
http://gold.greyhouse.com
and click on "Advertise."

Bake Rite Rolls
Bensalem, PA 215-638-2400
Bakehouse
Hallandale Beach, FL 954-458-1600
BakeMark
Schaumburg, IL 562-949-1054
Baker Boy Bake Shop
Dickinson, ND 800-437-2008
Baker Boys
Calgary, AB 877-246-6036
Baker's Choice
Birmingham, MI 248-827-7500
Baker's Dozen
Herkimer, NY 315-866-6770
Bakerhaus Veit Limited
Woodbridge, ON 800-387-8860
Bakers of Paris
Brisbane, CA 415-468-9100
Bakery Chef
Chicago, IL 773-384-1900
Bakery Corp
Miami, FL 800-521-4345
Bakery Europa
Honolulu, HI 808-845-5011
Bakery Management Corporation
Miami, FL 305-623-3838
Baldinger Bakery
St Paul, MN 651-224-5761
Baltic Bakery
Chicago, IL 773-523-1510
Baltimore Bakery
Norfolk, VA 757-855-4731
Banquet Schuster Bakery
Pueblo, CO 719-544-1062
Baptista's Bakery
Franklin, WI 877-261-3157
Barbara's Bakery
Petaluma, CA 707-765-2273
Barbero Bakery, Inc.
Trenton, NJ 609-394-5122

Barker System Bakery
Mt Carmel, PA 570-339-3380
Basque French Bakery
Fresno, CA 559-268-7088
Bay Star Baking Company
Alameda, CA 510-523-4202
BBU Bakeries
Denver, CO 303-691-6342
Beach Bagel Bakeries
Miami, FL 305-691-3514
Beatrice Bakery Company
Beatrice, NE 800-228-4030
Beatrice Bakery Company/Grandma's Bake Shoppe
Beatrice, NE 800-228-4030
Beck's Waffles of Oklahoma
Shawnee, OK 800-646-6254
Beckmann's Old World Bakery
Santa Cruz, CA 831-423-2566
Bee Wayne Bakery
Saint Joseph, MO 816-232-8483
Bella Napoli Italian Bakery
Troy, NY .888-800-0103
Bellacicco Distribution Company
Brooklyn, NY 800-561-1705
Benson's Bakery
Bogart, GA 800-888-6059
Berkshire Mountain Bakery
Housatonic, MA 866-274-6124
Berlin Natural Bakery
Berlin, OH 800-686-5334
Best Brands Corporation
Dallas, TX 800-969-2253
Best Foods Baking Group
Frederick, MD 800-635-1700
Best Harvest Bakeries
Kansas City, KS 800-811-5715
Best Maid Cookie Company
River Falls, WI 888-444-0322
Beth's Fine Desserts
Cotati, CA 415-464-1891
Better Bagel Bakery
Sarasota, FL 941-924-0393
Betty Lou's Golden Smackers
McMinnville, OR 800-242-5205
Bimbo Bakeries
Montebello, CA 323-720-6000
Bimbo Bakeries
Montebello, CA 877-224-7374
Birkholm's Jr Danish Bakery
Solvang, CA 805-688-3872
Bishop Baking Company
Cleveland, TN 423-472-1561
Blackey's Bakery
Minneapolis, MN 612-789-5326
Blue Dog Bakery
Seattle, WA 888-749-7229
Blue Planet Foods, Inc.
Collegedale, TN 877-396-3145
Bluepoint Bakery
Denver, CO 303-298-1100
Boboli International Inc
Stockton, CA 209-473-3507
Boca Foods Company
Madison, WI 608-285-6950
Bodacious Food Company
Jasper, GA 800-391-1979
Bonert's Slice of Pie
Santa Ana, CA 714-540-3535
Bonnie Baking Company
La Porte, IN 219-362-4561
Borden's Bread
Regina, SK 306-525-3341
Borinquen Biscuit Corporation
Yauco, PR 787-856-3030
Boudreaux's Foods
New Orleans, LA 504-733-8440
BP Gourmet
Hauppauge, NY 631-234-5200
Bread Alone Bakery
Shokan, NY 800-769-3328
Bread Box
Virden, NB 204-748-1513
Breadsmith
Cincinnati, OH 513-791-8817
Breadworks Bakery & Deli
Charlottesville, VA 434-296-4663

Breakfast at Brennan's
New Orleans, LA 800-888-9932
Bremner Company
Poteau, OK 918-647-8630
Brenner's Bakery of Arlington
Arlington, VA 703-534-0211
Brenntag Pacific
Santa Fe Springs, CA 562-903-9626
Bridgford Foods Corporation Superior Foods Division
Anaheim, CA 800-527-2105
Brightwood Baking Company
Cicero, IN 317-356-2449
Brooklyn Bagel Company
Staten Island, NY 800-349-3055
Brooklyn Baking Company
Waterbury, CT...................203-574-9198
Brother's Bakery
Southington, CT 860-628-5455
Brothers Juniper Bakery
Santa Rosa, CA..................707-542-6546
Brown's Bakery
Defiance, OH 419-784-3330
Brownie Products Company
Gardner, IL 815-237-2163
Bruce Baking Company
New Rochelle, NY 914-636-0808
Bubbles Baking Company
Van Nuys, CA 800-777-4970
Bunge Foods
Tustin, CA 714-258-1223
Bunny Bread
Covington, LA 504-241-1206
Bunny Bread Company
Cape Girardeau, MO.............573-332-7349
Buns & Roses Organic Wholegrain Bakery
Edmonton, AB 780-438-0098
Buns Master Bakery
Lethbridge, AB 403-320-2966
Buns Master Bakery
North Hamilton, ON 905-560-5011
Buon Italia
New York, NY 212-633-9090
Busken Bakery
Cincinnati, OH 513-871-2114
Butter Krust Baking Company
Sunbury, PA.....................570-286-5845
Butternut Bread
Grand Rapids, MI 616-245-8292
Byrnes & Kiefer Company
Callery, PA......................877-444-2240
Cains Foods/Olde Cape Cod
Ayer, MA 800-225-0601
Calgary Italian Bakery
Calgary, AB.....................800-661-6868
California Pie Company
Livermore, CA 925-373-7700
California Smart Foods
San Francisco, CA 415-826-0449
Calise & Sons Bakery
Lincoln, RI 800-225-4737
Calmar Bakery
Calmar, AB......................780-985-3583
Campagna-Turano Bakery
Berwyn, IL 708-788-9220
Campbell Soup Company
Camden, NJ.....................800-257-8443
Canada Bread
Etobicoke, ON 416-622-2040
Canada Bread Atlantic
St. John's, NL 709-722-5410
Canada Bread Company
Edmonton, AB 780-451-4663
Canada Bread Company
Langley, BC 800-465-5515
Caravan Trading Company
Union City, CA 510-487-2600
Caribbean Food Delights
Tappan, NY 845-398-3000
Carmine's Bakery
Sanford, FL 407-324-1200
Carole's Cheesecake Company
Toronto, ON 416-256-0000
Carolina Cupboard
Hillsborough, NC 800-400-3441
Carolina Foods
Charlotte, NC 800-234-0441
Cascade Cookie Company
St Louis, MO 314-877-7000
Case Side Holdings Company
Kensington, PE 902-836-4214
Casino Bakery
Tampa, FL 813-242-0311

Catania Bakery
Washington, DC 202-332-5135
Cateraid
Howell, MI 800-508-8217
CBC Foods Inc
Little River, KS...................800-276-4770
Cedarlane Foods
Carson, CA 800-826-3322
Celebrity Cheesecake
Davie, FL 877-986-2253
Cellone Bakery
Pittsburgh, PA 800-334-8438
Cemac Foods Corporation
Philadelphia, PA 800-724-0179
Central Bakery
Fall River, MA 508-675-7620
CGI Desserts
Sugar Land, TX..................281-240-1200
Chalet Desserts
Union City, CA 510-783-8300
Charles Heitzman Bakery
Louisville, KY 502-635-2651
Charles J. Ross
Reading, PA 610-685-5161
Charlie's Specialties
Hermitage, PA 724-346-2350
Chattanooga Bakery
Chattanooga, TN.................800-251-3404
Cheesecake Aly
Glen Rock, NJ 800-555-8862
Cheesecake Etc. Desserts
Miami Springs, FL 305-887-0258
Chella's Dutch Delicacies
Lake Oswego, OR................800-458-3331
Chelsea Market Baskets
New York, NY 888-727-7887
Cheri's Desert Harvest
Tucson, AZ 800-743-1141
Chewys Rugulach
San Diego, CA...................800-241-3456
Chex Finer Foods
Attleboro, MA...................800-322-2434
Chicago Baking Company
Chicago, IL 773-536-7700
Chisholm Bakery
Chisholm, MN 218-254-4006
Chloe Foods Corporation
Brooklyn, NY 718-827-3600
Chmuras Bakery
Indian Orchard, MA 413-543-2521
Chocolate Chix
Waxahachie, TX 214-744-2442
Chudleigh's
Milton, ON 800-387-4028
Cinderella Cheese Cake Company
Riverside, NJ 856-461-6302
City Baker
Calgary, AB.....................403-263-8578
City Bakery
Hallettsville, TX 800-272-9416
City Cafe Bakery
Fayetteville, GA 770-461-6800
Clarkson Scottish Bakery
Mississauga, ON 905-823-1500
Claudio Pastry Company
Elmwood Park, IL 708-453-0598
Claxton Bakery
Claxton, GA 800-841-4211
Clear Lake Bakery
Saint Louis, MO 641-357-5264
Clements Pastry Shop
Hyattsville, MD 800-444-7428
Cloverhill Bakery-Vend Corporation
Chicago, IL 773-745-9800
Cloverland Sweets/Priester's Pecan Company
Fort Deposit, AL 800-523-3505
Clydes Delicious Donuts
Addison, IL 630-628-6555
Cobi Foods
Hantsport, NS 800-565-8229
Coby's Cookies
North York, ON..................416-633-1567
Cohen's Bakery
Buffalo, NY 716-892-8149
Colchester Bakery
Colchester, CT 860-537-2415
Cold Spring Bakery
Cold Spring, MN 320-685-8681
Cole's Quality Foods
Muskegon, MI 231-722-1651
Collin Street Bakery
Corsicana, TX 800-504-1896

Colombo Bakery
Sacramento, CA 916-648-1011
Colorado Baking Company
West Chicago, IL 630-231-6804
Colors Gourmet Pizza
Carlsbad, CA 760-431-2203
Columbus Bakery
Columbus, OH 614-645-2275
Community Bakeries
Chicago, IL 773-384-1900
Community Orchard
Fort Dodge, IA 515-573-8212
Con Agra Foods
Holly Ridge, NC 910-329-9061
Confection Solutions
Sylmar, CA 800-284-2422
Consolidated Biscuit Company
Mc Comb, OH...................800-537-9544
Continental Food Products
Flushing, NY 718-358-7894
Cookie Cupboard Baking Corporation
Fairfield, NJ 800-217-2938
Cookie Kingdom
Oglesby, IL 815-883-3331
Cookie Specialties
Wheeling, IL 847-537-3888
Cookie Tree Bakeries
Salt Lake City, UT 800-998-0111
Cookies & More
Lewiston, ME 207-923-4227
Corfu Foods
Bensenville, IL 630-595-2510
Cottage Bakery
Lodi, CA 209-333-8044
Cotton Baking Company
Bossier City, LA 800-777-1832
Cougar Mountain Baking Company
Seattle, WA 206-467-5044
Country Club Bakery
Fairmont, WV 304-363-5690
Country Hearth Bread
Murfreesboro, TN 615-893-6041
Country Home Bakers
Torrance, CA 800-672-6277
Creative Bakers
Brooklyn, NY 800-247-7864
Creative Spices
Union City, CA 510-471-4956
Creme Curls Bakery
Hudsonville, MI 800-466-1219
Crestwood Bakery
Pleasant Prairie, WI 414-453-4790
Crispy Bagel Company
Baltimore, MD 800-522-7655
Crum Creek Mills
Springfield, PA 888-607-3500
Culinar Canada
Ste. Marie De Beauce, QC 418-387-5421
Culinary Masters Corporation
Alpharetta, GA 800-261-5261
Cupoladua Oven
Wexford, PA 412-592-5378
Cusano's Baking Company
Hallandale Beach, FL 954-458-1010
Cutie Pie Corporation
Salt Lake City, UT 800-453-4575
CW Resources
New Britain, CT 860-229-7700
Dairy State Foods
Milwaukee, WI 800-435-4499
Dakota Brands International
Jamestown, ND 800-844-5073
Dancing Deer Baking Company
Hyde Park, MA 888-699-3337
Daniel's Bagel & Baguette Corporation
Calgary, AB.....................403-243-3207
Danish Baking Company
Van Nuys, CA 800-777-4970
Dare Foods
Kitchener, ON 800-865-8225
Dave's Bakery
Honesdale, PA 570-253-1660
David's Cookies
Fairfield, NJ 973-808-8248
Davis Bakery & Delicatessen
Cleveland, OH 216-464-5599
Davis Bread & Desserts
Davis, CA 530-757-2700
Davis Cookie Company
Rimersburg, PA 814-473-8181
Dawn Food Products
Jackson, MI 800-248-1144

Dawn Food Products
York, PA 800-405-6282

Dawn Food Products
Louisville, KY 800-626-2542

Day's Bakery
Honesdale, PA. 570-253-1660

De Bas Chocolatier
Fresno, CA 559-294-7638

De Beukelaer Corporation
Madison, MS 601-856-7454

Dee Lite Bakery
Honolulu, HI 808-847-5396

Dee's Cheesecake Factory/Dee's Foodservice
Albuquerque, NM 505-884-1777

Deerfield Bakery
Buffalo Grove, IL 847-520-0068

Del Campo Baking Company
Wilmington, DE 302-656-6676

Del's Pastry
Etobicoke, ON 416-231-4383

Dengler's Bakery
Souderton, PA 215-723-2706

Derst Baking Company
Savannah, GA. 912-233-2235

Desserts by David Glass
Bloomfield, CT. 860-769-5570

Desserts of Distinction
Milwaukie, OR 503-654-8370

Dewey's Bakery
Winston-Salem, NC 800-274-2994

DF Stauffer Biscuit Company
York, PA 800-673-2473

Di Camillo Bakery
Niagara Falls, NY 800-634-4363

Di Paolo Baking Company
Rochester, NY 585-232-3510

Diamond Bakery Company
Honolulu, HI 808-845-8200

DiCarlo's Bakery
San Pedro, CA. 310-831-2524

Dimitria Delights
North Grafton, MA 800-763-1113

Dimpflmeier Bakery
Toronto, ON 416-239-3031

Dinkel's Bakery
Chicago, IL 800-822-8817

Division Baking Corporation
New York, NY 800-934-9238

Dolly Madison Bakery
Columbus, IN 812-376-7432

Dong Kee Company
Chicago, IL 312-225-6340

Dough Delight
Concord, ON 800-465-5515

Dough Works Company
Horicon, WI 800-383-8808

Dough-To-Go
Santa Clara, CA 408-727-4094

Dover Industries Limited
Burlington, ON 800-387-7316

Drader Manufacturing Industries
Edmonton, AB 800-661-4122

Dufflet Pastries
Toronto, ON 416-536-1330

Dunford Bakers
Fayetteville, AR 479-521-3000

Dunford Bakers Company
West Jordan, UT 801-304-0400

Dunham Hill Bakery
Woodstock, VT 800-218-3121

Dutch Ann Foods Company
Natchez, MS 601-445-5566

Dutch Girl Donuts
Detroit, MI 313-368-3020

Dutchess Bakery
Charleston, WV 304-346-3210

Dynamic Foods
Lubbock, TX 806-762-0780

Earth Mother Foods Company
Arcata, CA 707-825-6723

Earthgrains Company
St. Louis, MO 314-259-7000

East Balt Bakery
Denver, CO 303-377-5533

East Balt Bakery
Kissimmee, FL 407-933-2222

East Balt Commissary
Chicago, IL 773-376-4444

Eddy's Bakery
Boise, ID .208-377-8100

Edelweiss Patisserie
Charlestown, MA 617-628-0225

Eden Vineyards Winery
Alva, FL 239-728-9463

Edner Corporation
Hayward, CA 510-441-8504

Edwards Baking Company
Atlanta, GA. 800-241-0559

El Charro Mexican Food Industries
Roswell, NM 575-622-8590

El Peto Products
Cambridge, ON 800-387-4064

El Segundo Bakery
El Segundo, CA 310-322-3422

Elegant Desserts
Lyndhurst, NJ 201-933-0770

Eli's Cheesecake Company
Chicago, IL 800-999-8300

Ellison Bakery
Fort Wayne, IN 800-711-8091

Elmwood Pastry
West Hartford, CT. 860-233-2029

Empress Foods
Winnipeg, NB 204-775-0344

Ener-G Foods
Seattle, WA 800-331-5222

Engel's Bakeries
Calgary, AB. 403-250-9560

Entenmann's-Oroweat/BestFoods
S San Francisco, CA. 650-875-3100

EPI Breads
Atlanta, GA. 800-325-1014

Erba Food Products
Brooklyn, NY 718-272-7700

Esco Foods
San Francisco, CA 415-864-2147

EuroAm
Federal Way, WA 888-839-2702

European Bakers
Tucker, GA 770-723-6180

European Style Bakery
Beverly Hills, CA 818-368-6876

Evans Bakery
Cozad, NE. 800-222-5641

Everix Bakery
Fond Du Lac, WI 920-921-2250

F R LePage Bakeries
Auburn, ME 207-783-9161

Falcone's Cookieland
Brooklyn, NY 718-236-4200

Fancy Lebanese Bakery
Halifax, NS 902-429-0400

Fantasia
Sedalia, MO 660-827-1172

Fantasy Cookie Company
Sylmar, CA 800-354-4488

Fantini Baking Company
Haverhill, MA 800-343-2110

Fantis Foods
Carlstadt, NJ 201-933-6200

Farm Fresh Bakery
Lawton, OK. 580-355-3485

Farrell Baking Company
West Middlesex, PA 724-342-7906

Father Sam's Syrian Bread
Buffalo, NY. 800-521-6719

Fayes Bakery Products
Dexter, MO 573-624-4920

Federal Pretzel Baking Company
Philadelphia, PA 215-467-0505

Felix Roma & Sons
Endicott, NY 800-640-3336

Ferrara Bakery & Cafe
New York, NY 212-226-6150

Field's
Pauls Valley, OK 405-238-7381

Fiera Foods
North York, ON. 416-744-1010

Finkemeier Bakery
Kansas City, KS 913-831-3103

Fireside Kitchen
Halifax, NS 902-454-7387

Fisher Rex Sandwiches
Raleigh, NC 919-832-6494

Fisher's Bakery
Ellicott City, MD. 410-461-9275

Flamin' Red's Woodfired
Pawlet, VT 802-325-3641

Fleischer's Bagels
Macedon, NY 315-986-9999

Flower Bakeries
London, KY 800-568-3476

Flower Foods, Inc.
Thomasville, GA. 229-226-9110

Flowers Bakeries
Thomasville, GA. 800-226-2429

Flowers Bakeries
Bluefield, WV. 800-327-1630

Flowers Bakeries
Thomasville, GA. 800-568-3476

Flowers Bakery of Montgomery
Montgomery, AL. 334-281-7030

Flowers Bakery of Winston-Salem
Winston Salem, NC 800-334-5260

Flowers Baking
San Antonio, TX. 210-661-2361

Flowers Baking Company
Jamestown, NC 336-841-8840

Flowers Baking Company
Morristown, TN 423-586-2471

Flowers Baking Company
Pine Bluff, AR 870-534-0221

Flowers Baking Company
Jacksonville, FL 904-353-8293

Flowers Foods Bakeries
Thomasville, GA. 229-226-9110

Flowers Snack of Tennessee
Crossville, TN. 931-484-6101

Food for Life Baking Company
Corona, CA 951-279-5090

Food Mill
Oakland, CA 510-482-3848

Food of Our Own Design
Maplewood, NJ 973-762-0985

Foodbrands America
Oklahoma City, OK 405-290-4000

Fortella Fortune Cookies
Chicago, IL 312-567-9000

Fortune Cookie Factory
Oakland, CA 510-832-5552

Forty Second Street Bagel Cafe
Upland, CA 909-949-7334

Foxtail Foods
Fairfield, OH. 800-323-6944

France Croissant
New York, NY 212-888-1210

France Delices
Montreal, QC 514-259-2291

Franklin Baking Company
Kinston, NC 800-248-7494

Frankly Natural Bakers
San Diego, CA 800-727-7229

Franz Bakery
Portland, OR 503-232-2191

Fred Meyer Bakery
Clackamas, OR 503-650-2000

Freedman's Bakery
Belmar, NJ 732-681-2334

French Baking
Stratford, CT. 203-378-7381

Fresh Start Bakeries
City of Industry, CA 626-961-2525

Fresh Start Bakeries
Brea, CA .714-256-8900

Freund Baking Company
Glendale, CA 818-502-1400

Frisco Baking Company
Los Angeles, CA 323-225-6111

Frito-Lay
Dallas, TX .800-352-4477

Frookie
Des Plaines, IL 847-699-3200

Frostbite
Toledo, OH 800-968-7711

Fujiya
Honolulu, HI 808-845-2921

Future Bakery & Cafe
Etobicoke, ON 416-231-1491

G H Bent Company
Milton, MA 617-698-5945

G H Leidenheimer Baking Company
New Orleans, LA 800-259-9099

Gabilas Knishes
Brooklyn, NY 718-387-0750

Gadoua Bakery
Napierville, QC 450-245-3326

Gai's Northwest Bakeries
Seattle, WA 206-322-0931

Galassos Baking Company
Mira Loma, CA 951-360-1211

Gambino's
Kenner, LA 504-712-0809

Gardner Pie Company
Akron, OH. 330-245-2030

Gemini Food Industries
Fiskdale, MA 508-347-2800

General Henry Biscuit Company
Du Quoin, IL 618-542-6222
General Mills
Federalsburg, MD 410-479-4800
General Mills
Chelsea, MA 800-370-7834
General Taste Bakery
Commerce, CA 323-888-2170
George H Leidenheimer Baking
New Orleans, LA 800-259-9099
George Weston Bakeries
Riviera Beach, FL 561-848-9705
George Weston Bakeries
Northlake, IL 708-562-6311
George Weston Bakeries
Bay Shore, NY 800-356-3314
George Weston Bakeries
Albany, NY 800-531-4002
Georgia Fruit Cake Company
Claxton, GA 912-739-2683
Gerard's French Bakery
Longmont, CO 303-772-4710
German Bakery at Village Corner
Stone Mountain, GA 866-476-6443
Giant Food
Lanham, MD 888-469-4426
Glencourt
Napa, CA 707-944-4444
Global Bakeries
Pacoima, CA 818-896-0525
Glutino
Laval, QC 800-363-3438
Goglanian Bakeries
Santa Ana, CA 714-444-3500
Gold Coast Baking Company
Santa Ana, CA 714-545-2253
Gold Medal Bakery
Fall River, MA 800-642-7568
Gold Medal Baking Company
Philadelphia, PA 215-627-4787
Gold Standard Baking
Chicago, IL 800-648-7904
Golden Boys Pies of San Diego
San Diego, CA 800-746-0280
Golden Brown Bakery
South Haven, MI 269-637-3418
Golden Glow Cookie Company
Bronx, NY 718-379-6223
Goll's Bakery
Havre De Grace, MD 410-939-4321
Gonnella Frozen Products
Schaumburg, IL 847-884-8829
Good Old Days Foods
Little Rock, AR 501-565-1257
Gould's Maple Sugarhouse
Shelburne Falls, MA 413-625-6170
Gourmet Baker
Burnaby, BC 800-663-1972
Gourmet Croissant
Brooklyn, NY 718-499-4911
Grain Bin Bakers
Carmel, CA 831-624-3883
Grainbakers Bakery
Chicago Heights, IL 708-758-8900
Grandma Beth's Cookies
Alliance, NE 308-762-8433
Granello Bakery
Las Vegas, NV 702-361-0311
Great Cakes
Los Angeles, CA 310-287-0228
Great San Saba River Pecan Company
San Saba, TX 800-621-9121
Grebe's Bakery & Delicatessen
Milwaukee, WI 800-356-9377
Grecian Delight Foods
Elk Grove Vlg, IL 800-621-4387
Greenhills Irish Bakery
Dorchester, MA 617-825-8187
Gregory's Foods
Eagan, MN 800-231-4734
Greyston Bakery
Yonkers, NY 800-289-2253
Grossinger's Home Bakery
New York, NY 800-479-6996
Grote Bakery
Hamilton, OH 513-874-7436
Guttenplan's Frozen Dough
Middletown, NJ 888-422-4357
GWB Foods Corporation
Brooklyn, NY 718-686-9600
H Cantin
Beauport, QC 800-463-5268

H&H Bagels
New York, NY 800-692-2435
H&S Bakery
Baltimore, MD 800-959-7655
H.E. Butt Grocery Company
San Antonio, TX 800-432-3113
Haas Baking Company
St Louis, MO 800-325-3171
Haby's Alsatian Bakery
Castroville, TX 830-931-2118
Hafner
Stone Mountain, GA 888-725-4605
Hahn's Old Fashioned Cake Company
Farmingdale, NY 631-249-3456
Handy Pax
Randolph, MA 781-963-8300
Harbar Corporation
Canton, MA 800-881-7040
Hardin's Bakery
Tuscaloosa, AL 205-344-6690
Harlan Bakeries
Avon, IN 317-272-3600
Harlan Bakeries, Inc.
Avon, IN 317-272-3600
Harold Food Company
Charlotte, NC 704-588-8061
Harris Baking Company
Rogers, AR 479-636-3313
Harting's Bakery
Bowmansville, PA 717-445-5644
Harvest Bakery
Bristol, CT 860-589-8800
Harvest Day Bakery
Buena Park, CA 714-739-6318
Harvest Valley Bakery
La Salle, IL 815-224-9030
Havi Food Services Worldwide
Oak Park, IL 708-445-1700
Hawaii Baking Company
Honolulu, HI 808-694-8198
Hawaii Candy
Honolulu, HI 808-836-8955
Hawaii Star Bakery
Honolulu, HI 808-841-3602
Hawaiian Bagel
Honolulu, HI 808-596-0638
Hazelwood Farms Bakery
Rochester, NY 585-424-1240
Health Valley Company
Irwindale, CA 800-334-3204
Hedgehaven Specialty Foods
Ilwaco, WA 800-642-4711
Heidi's Gourmet Desserts
Tucker, GA 800-241-4166
Heinemann's
Milwaukee, WI 414-265-1900
Heinemann's Bakeries
Chicago, IL 312-239-5592
Heiner's Bakery
Huntington, WV 800-776-8411
Heino's German-Style Wholesale Bakery
Naples, FL 941-643-3911
Heinz Bakery Products
Old Bethpage, NY 631-249-3170
Heinz Company of Canada
North York, ON 800-268-6641
Heinz North America
Fort Myers, FL 239-694-3663
Heisler Food Enterprises
Bronx, NY 718-543-0855
Heitzman Bakery
Louisville, KY 502-452-1891
Herman's Bakery Coffee Shop
Cambridge, MN 763-689-1515
Hershey International
Weston, FL 954-385-2600
Heyerly Bakery
Ossian, IN 260-622-4196
Highlandville Packing
Highlandville, MO 417-443-3365
Holsum Bakery
Toa Baja, PR 787-798-8282
Holsum Bakery
Phoenix, AZ 800-755-8167
Holsum Bread
Kenosha, WI 262-658-1396
Holt's Bakery
Douglas, GA 912-384-2202
Home Baked Group
Boca Raton, FL 561-995-0767
Home Bakery
Laramie, WY 307-742-2721

Home Baking Company
Birmingham, AL 205-252-1161
Home Maid Bakery
Wailuku, HI 808-244-7015
Home Style Bakery
Grand Junction, CO 970-243-1233
Homes Packaging Company
Millersburg, OH 800-401-2529
Homestead Baking Company
Rumford, RI 800-556-7216
Homestyle Bread
Phoenix, AZ 602-268-0677
Hommus Factory
Haverhill, MA 508-460-0212
Honey Rose Baking Company
Encinitas, CA 760-942-8996
Hunt Country Foods
Middleburg, VA 540-364-2622
Huval Baking Company
Lafayette, LA 337-232-1611
Hye Quality Bakery
Fresno, CA 877-445-1778
I & K Distributors
Delphos, OH 800-869-6337
IBC Holsum
Atlanta, GA 800-465-7861
Il Gelato
Astoria, NY 718-937-3033
Il Giardino Bakery
Chicago, IL 773-889-2388
Immaculate Consumption
Flat Rock, NC 888-826-6567
Independent Bakers Association
Washington, DC 202-333-8190
Innovative Health Products
Largo, FL 800-654-2347
Innovative Ingredients
Reisterstown, MD 888-403-2907
Interbake Foods
Canby, OR 503-651-3003
Interbake Foods Corporate Office
Richmond, VA 804-755-7107
International Baking Company
Vernon, CA 323-583-9841
International Brownie
Weymouth, MA 800-230-1588
International Equipment
Arecibo, PR 787-879-3151
Interstate Bakeries Corporation
Los Angeles, CA 323-750-7204
Interstate Bakeries Corporation
Cincinnati, OH 513-721-0212
Interstate Bakeries Corporation
Jacksonville, FL 904-696-1400
Interstate Brands
Biddeford, ME 207-286-1200
Interstate Brands
Alexandria, LA 318-448-6600
Interstate Brands Company/Drake Bakeries
Wayne, NJ 973-696-5010
Interstate Brands Corporation
Birmingham, AL 205-841-6301
Interstate Brands Corporation
Rocky Mount, NC 252-977-3400
Interstate Brands Corporation
Peoria, IL 309-674-9221
Interstate Brands Corporation
Monroe, LA 318-388-2244
Interstate Brands Corporation
Billings, MT 406-248-4800
Interstate Brands Corporation
Emporia, KS 620-342-6811
Interstate Brands Corporation
Charlotte, NC 704-398-2051
Interstate Brands Corporation
Kansas City, MO 800-777-8067
Interstate Brands Corporation
Kansas City, MO 816-502-4000
Interstate Brands Corporation
Florence, SC 843-393-8895
Interstate Brands Corporation
Knoxville, TN 865-947-6191
Interstate Brands Corporation/Butternut Bread Bakeries
Springfield, MO 417-869-0711
Interstate Brands Corporation/Butternut Bread Company
Boonville, MO 660-882-6107
Interstate Brands Corporation/Dolly Madison Cakes
Columbus, GA 706-257-7000
Interstate Brands Corporation/Merita Bread Bakery
Orlando, FL 407-843-5110
Interstate Brands Corporation/Wonder Bread Bakery
St Louis, MO 314-385-1600

Interstate Brands Corporation/Wonder/Hostess
Philadelphia, PA 215-969-1200
Irresistible Cookie Jar
Hayden Lake, ID 208-664-1261
Isabella's Healthy Bakery
Cuyahoga Falls, OH 800-476-6328
Italian Bakery
Virginia, MN 218-741-3464
Italian Baking Company
Youngstown, OH 330-782-1358
Italian Baking Company
Edmonton, AB 780-424-4830
Italian Peoples Bakery
Ewing, NJ 609-771-1369
Iversen Baking Company
Bedminster, PA 215-636-5904
J J Gandy's Pies
Palm Harbor, FL 727-938-7437
J W Allen Company
Wheeling, IL 847-459-5400
J&J Snack Foods Corporation
Vernon, CA 800-486-7622
J&J Snack Foods Corporation
Pennsauken, NJ 856-665-9533
J&J Wall Baking Company
Sacramento, CA 916-381-1410
J.P. Sunrise Bakery
Edmonton, AB 780-454-5797
Jacques' Bakery
San Juan Capistrano, CA 949-496-5322
Jaeger Bakery
Milwaukee, WI 414-263-1700
Jamae Natural Foods
Los Angeles, CA 800-343-0052
James Skinner Company
Omaha, NE 800-358-7428
Jay Hoyt of California
Petaluma, CA .707-762-1881
JC'S Natural Bakery
El Cajon, CA 619-239-4043
Jenny Lee Bakery
Mc Kees Rocks, PA 412-331-8900
Jerabek's New Bohemian Coffee House
St Paul, MN 651-228-1245
Jerusalem House
Eugene, OR 541-485-1012
Jewel Bakery
Melrose Park, IL 708-531-6000
Jim's Cheese Pantry
Waterloo, WI .800-345-3571
Jimmy's Cookies
Fair Lawn, NJ .201-797-8900
JMP Bakery Company
Brooklyn, NY .718-272-5400
Joe Fazio's Bakery
St Louis, MO 314-645-6239
Joey's Fine Foods
Newark, NJ 973-482-1400
John J. Nissen Baking Company
Portland, ME .207-775-3460
John J. Nissen Baking Company
Brewer, ME 207-989-7654
John Wm. Macy's Cheesesticks
Elmwood Park, NJ 800-643-0573
Jon Donaire Pastry
Santa Fe Springs, CA 877-366-2473
Jonathan Lord Corporation
Bohemia, NY .800-814-7517
Jones Bakeries
Winston Salem, NC 800-849-5663
Jou Jou's Pita Bakery
Birmingham, AL 205-945-7482
Joyce Food Products
Elmwood Park, NJ 201-791-4300
Jubelt Variety Bakeries
Mount Olive, IL 217-999-7312
Jubilations
Columbus, MS 662-328-9210
Just Desserts
San Francisco, CA 415-602-9245
Just Off Melrose
Palm Springs, CA 800-743-4109
K&S Bakery Products
Edmonton, AB 780-481-8155
Kahns Bakery Company
El Paso, TX 915-544-6950
Kammeh International Trade Co
Chicago, IL 312-804-0800
Kangaroo Brands
Milwaukee, WI 800-798-0857
Kapaa Bakery
Kapaa, HI 808-822-4541

Karam Elsaha Baking Company
Manlius, NY 315-682-2780
Karp's
Georgetown, MA 800-373-5277
Karp's
Schaumburg, IL. 800-593-5277
Karsh's Bakery
Phoenix, AZ 602-264-4874
Keebler Company
Macon, GA 478-781-4620
Keebler Company
Branchburg, NJ 973-254-2000
Keller's Bakery
Lafayette, LA .337-235-1568
Kellogg Canada Inc
Mississauga, ON 888-876-3750
Kellogg Company
Battle Creek, MI 800-962-1413
Kellogg Company Grand Rapids Bakery
Grand Rapids, MI 616-247-4841
Kellogg Snacks
Kansas City, KS 800-229-4414
Kemach Food Products   Corporation
Brooklyn, NY .888-453-6224
Kemoo Farm Foods
Wahiawa, HI 808-622-8004
Kerrobert Bakery
Kerrobert, SK .306-834-2461
Key Lime
Smyrna, GA 770-333-0840
Keystone Pretzel Bakery
Lititz, PA 888-572-4500
KHS-Bartelt
Sarasota, FL 800-829-9980
Kid's Kookie Company
San Clemente, CA. 800-350-7577
King Soopers Bakery
Denver, CO 303-778-3128
King's Hawaiian
Torrance, CA .800-800-5461
Klosterman Baking Company
Springfield, OH 937-322-9588
Koehler Bakery Company
North Little Rock, AR 800-262-5900
Koepplinger Bakery
Detroit, MI 248-967-2020
Koffee Kup Bakery
Burlington, VT 802-863-2696
Kollar Cookies
Woodbridge, NJ 732-229-3364
Korbs Baking Company
Pawtucket, RI .401-726-4422
Kosher French Baguettes
Brooklyn, NY .718-633-4994
Kossar's Bialystoker Kuchen Bakery
New York, NY .877-424-2597
Kotarides Baking Company of Virginia
Norfolk, VA. 757-461-1000
Kraft
Parsippany, NJ. 973-292-1755
Kraft Food Ingredients
Memphis, TN .901-381-6500
Kraft Foods
Atlanta, GA. 404-756-6000
Kraft Foods
East Hanover, NJ 973-503-2000
Kraft Foods   kery
Chicago, IL 800-572-3847
Kreamo Bakers
South Bend, IN 574-234-0188
Krispy Bakery
West Palm Beach, FL 561-585-5504
Krispy Kreme Doughnut Company
Winston Salem, NC 800-457-4779
Kroger Anderson Bakery
Anderson, SC .864-226-9135
Kupris Home Bakery
Manchester, CT 860-649-4746
Kyger Bakery Products
Lafayette, IN .765-447-1252
L&M Bakery
Lawrence, MA 978-687-7346
La Boulangerie
San Diego, CA 858-578-4040
La Buena Mexican Foods Products
Tucson, AZ 520-624-1796
La Cigale Bakery
Opa Locka, FL 800-333-8578
La Francaise Bakery
Northlake, IL. .800-654-7220
La Parisienne Bakery
Manassas, VA .800-727-4790

La Patisserie
Phoenix, AZ 602-254-5868
La Piccolina
Decatur, GA 800-626-1624
La Rosa Bakery
New York, NY .212-281-1500
La Tempesta
S San Francisco, CA. 800-762-8330
La Tortilla Factory
Santa Rosa, CA 800-446-1516
Lady Walton's and Bronco Bob's Cowboy Brand
Specialty Foods
Dallas, TX. 800-552-8006
Lady Walton's Cookies
Dallas, TX. 800-552-8006
Laguna Cookie & Dessert Company
Santa Ana, CA 800-673-2473
Lake States Yeast
Rhinelander, WI 918-535-2676
Lakeview Bakery
Calgary, AB. 403-246-6127
Lamb-Weston
Pasco, WA 800-766-7783
Lamonaca Bakery
Windber, PA 814-467-4909
Landolfi Food Products
Trenton, NJ 609-392-1830
Lang Bakery
Worthington, MN 507-372-7909
Lanthier Bakery
Alexandria, ON. 613-525-2435
Laronga Bakery
Somerville, MA 617-625-8600
LaRosa Bakery
Shrewsbury, NJ 800-527-6722
Latonia Bakery
Covington, KY 859-491-8855
Laura's French Baking Company
Los Angeles, CA 888-353-5144
Lavash Corporation
Los Angeles, CA 323-663-5249
Lawrences Delights
Doraville, GA .800-568-0021
Lax & Mandel Bakery
Cleveland, OH 216-382-8877
Le Chic French Bakery
Miami Beach, FL 305-673-5522
Ledonne Brothers Bakery
Roseto, PA. 610-588-0423
Lefse House
Camrose, AB. .780-672-7555
Leidenheimer Baking Company
New Orleans, LA 504-525-1575
Lenchner Bakery
Concord, ON. .905-738-8811
Lender's Bagel Bakery
Mattoon, IL 217-235-3181
Lender's Bagel Bakery
West Seneca, NY 716-668-6761
Leo's Bakery
Marshfield, MA 781-837-3300
LePage Bakeries
Auburn, ME 207-783-9161
Lepage Bakeries
Auburn, ME 207-783-9161
Lewis Bakeries
London, ON 519-434-5252
Lewis Brothers Bakeries
Sikeston, MO .573-471-1650
Lewis Brothers Bakeries
Vincennes, IN .812-886-6533
Lewis Brothers Bakery
La Porte, IN 219-362-4561
Lewis Brothers Bakery
Murfreesboro, TN 615-893-6041
Lewis Brothers Bakery
Evansville, IN .812-425-4642
Lewis-Vincennes Bakery
Vincennes, IN .812-886-6533
Liberty Richter
Saddle Brook, NJ 201-291-8749
Linden Cookies
Congers, NY 800-660-5051
Little Angel Foods
Daytona Beach, FL 904-257-3040
Little Dutch Boy Bakeries
Draper, UT 801-571-3800
Livermore Falls Baking Company
Livermore Falls, ME. 207-897-3442
Loafin' Around
Laytonsville, MD 301-570-4513

Log House Foods
Plymouth, MN.................763-546-8395

Lombardi's Bakery
Torrington, CT................860-489-4766

Lone Star Bakery
Round Rock, TX...............512-255-3629

Lone Star Consolidated Foods
Dallas, TX....................800-658-5637

Longo's Bakery
Hazleton, PA..................570-454-5825

Lotus Bakery
Santa Rosa, CA................800-875-6887

Louis Bakeries
La Porte, IN..................219-362-4561

Louis Swiss Pastry
Aspen, CO.....................970-925-8592

Love & Quiches Desserts
Freeport, NY..................800-525-5251

Love's Bakery
Honolulu, HI..................888-455-6837

Lucerne Foods
Calgary, AB...................403-287-4080

Lucy's Sweet Surrender
Cleveland, OH.................216-752-0828

Ludwick's Frozen Donuts
Grand Rapids, MI..............800-366-8816

Luna's Tortillas
Dallas, TX....................214-747-2661

Lupi Marchigiano Bakery
New Haven, CT.................203-562-9491

Lusitania Bakery
Blandon, PA...................610-926-1311

M.M. Bake Shop
Laurel, MS....................601-428-5153

Mac's Donut Shop
Aliquippa, PA.................724-375-6776

MacFarms of Hawaii
Captain Cook, HI..............808-328-2435

Maggiora Baking Company
Richmond, CA..................510-235-0274

Magna Foods Corporation
City of Industry, CA..........800-995-4394

Main Street Custom Foods
Cuyahoga Falls, OH............800-533-6246

Main Street Gourmet
Cuyahoga Falls, OH............800-533-6246

Main Street Gourmet Fundraising
Cuyahoga Falls, OH............800-533-6246

Main Street Muffins
Cuyahoga Falls, OH............800-533-6246

Main Street's Cambritt Cookies
Cuyahoga Falls, OH............800-533-6246

Mancuso Cheese Company
Joliet, IL....................815-722-2475

Manderfield Home Bakery
Menasha, WI...................920-725-7794

Maple Leaf Bakery
Toronto, ON...................800-805-3460

Maple Leaf Foods
Franklin Park, IL.............847-451-8100

Maplehurst Bakeries
Carrollton, GA................800-482-4810

Marika's Kitchen
Hancock, ME...................800-694-9400

Marin Food Specialties
Byron, CA.....................925-634-6126

Market Day Corporation
Itasca, IL....................877-632-7753

Marshall Biscuits
Saraland, AL..................251-679-6226

Marshall's Biscuit Company
Saraland, AL..................800-368-9811

Martin Brothers Distributing Company
Cedar Falls, IA...............319-266-1775

Martino's Bakery
Burbank, CA...................818-842-0715

Mary Ann's Baking Company
Sacramento, CA................916-681-7444

Mary of Puddin Hill
Greenville, TX................800-545-8889

Maryland Baking Company
Atlanta, GA...................404-622-1731

Maui Bagel
Kahului, HI...................808-270-7561

Maurice Lenell Cooky Company
Chicago, IL...................800-323-1760

Mayer's Cider Mill
Webster, NY...................800-543-0043

Mazelle's Cheesecakes Concoctions Creations
Dallas, TX....................903-737-4315

McGlynn Bakeries, LLC
Minneapolis, MN...............763-574-2423

Mediterranean Gyros Products
Long Island City, NY..........718-786-3399

Mehaffie Pies
Dayton, OH....................937-253-1163

Mercado Latino
City of Industry, CA..........626-333-6862

Merlino Italian Baking Company
Seattle, WA...................800-207-2997

Metropolitan Baking Company
Hamtramck, MI.................313-875-7246

Metz Baking Company
Pekin, IL.....................309-347-7315

Meyer's Bakeries
Casa Grande, AZ...............800-528-5770

Meyer's Bakeries
Hope, AR......................800-643-1542

Meyer's Bakeries
Orlando, FL...................887-859-2006

Mi-Lady Bakery
Tifton, GA....................229-382-1955

Michael D's Cookies & Cakes
Aurora, IL....................630-892-2525

Michel's Bakery
Philadelphia, PA..............215-725-4328

Mikawaya Bakery
Los Angeles, CA...............213-628-6514

Milano Baking Company
Joliet, IL....................815-727-4872

Mill City Sourdough Bakery
Saint Paul, MN................612-224-8871

Millie's Pierogi
Chicopee Falls, MA............800-743-7641

Mineo's Pies
Scranton, PA..................570-347-8278

Mississippi Bakery
Burlington, IA................319-752-6315

Modern Italian Bakery of West Babylon
Oakdale, NY...................631-589-7300

Molinaro's Fine Italian Foods
Mississauga, ON...............800-268-4959

Mom's Bakery
Atlanta, GA...................404-344-4189

Mom's Famous
Boca Raton, FL................561-750-1903

Mom's Food Company
South El Monte, CA............800-969-6667

Monaco Baking Company
Santa Fe Springs, CA..........800-569-4640

Mondo Baking Company
Rome, GA......................706-291-8439

Monk's Bread
Victor, NY....................585-243-0660

Monster Cone
Montreal, QC..................800-542-9801

Montana Bakery
Stamford, CT..................203-969-7700

Montione's Biscotti & Baked Goods
Mansfield, MA.................800-559-1010

Morabito Baking Company
Norristown, PA................800-525-7747

Morningstar Foods
Dallas, TX....................225-273-2803

Morrison Meat Pies
West Valley, UT...............801-977-0181

Mother's Home Bakery
Denver, CO....................303-825-3641

Mothers Kitchen Inc
Burlington, NJ................609-387-7200

Mozzicato De Pasquale Bakery Pastry
Hartford, CT..................860-296-0426

Mozzicato Depasquale Bakery & Pastry Shop
Hartford, CT..................860-296-0426

Mrs Baird's Bakery
Fort Worth, TX................817-864-2500

Mrs. Baird's Bakeries
Waco, TX......................254-750-2500

Mrs. Baird's Bakeries
Abilene, TX...................325-692-3141

Mrs. Baird's Bakeries
Fort Worth, TX................806-763-9304

Mrs. Fly's Bakery
Collegeville, PA..............610-489-7288

Mrs. Smith's Bakeries
Spartanburg, SC...............864-503-9588

Mt View Bakery
Mountain View, HI.............808-968-6353

Multi Marques
Montreal, QC..................514-255-9492

Murray Biscuit Company
Atlanta, GA...................800-745-5582

Murray Biscuit Company/Kellogg
Alpharetta, GA................800-745-5582

Murray Biscuit Company/Kellogg Snacks
Charlotte, NC.................704-334-7611

My Bagel Chips
Long Beach, NY................516-889-0732

My Grandma's Coffee Cake of New England
Hyde Park, MA.................800-847-2636

Nabisco Biscuit Company
Philadelphia, PA..............215-673-4800

Nabisco Biscuit Company
Richmond, VA..................804-222-8802

Naleway Foods
Winnipeg, MB..................800-665-7448

Nancy's Specialty Foods
Newark, CA....................510-494-1100

Nardi Bakery & Deli
East Hartford, CT.............860-289-5458

National Bakers Services
Plantation, FL................954-920-7666

National Food Corporation
Medley, FL....................305-884-2020

Natural Ovens Bakery
Manitowoc, WI.................800-558-3535

Naturally Delicious
Oakland Park, FL..............954-485-6730

Nature's Hilights
Chico, CA.....................800-313-6454

Nature's Path Foods
Delta, BC.....................604-940-0505

Ne-Mo's Bakery
Escondido, CA.................800-325-2692

Nestle' Handheld Foods Group
Englewood, CO.................800-225-2270

Neuman Bakery Specialties
Addison, IL...................800-253-5298

Nevada Baking Company
Las Vegas, NV.................702-384-8950

New Bakery Company of Ohio
Zanesville, OH................800-848-9845

New England Country Bakers
Watertown, CT.................800-225-3779

New England Muffin Company
Fall River, MA................508-675-2833

New Horizons Baking Company
Fremont, IN...................260-495-7055

New Morning
Needham, MA...................781-444-0440

New Salem Tea-Bread Company
New Salem, MA.................800-897-5910

New White Palace Bakery
Philadelphia, PA..............215-324-9852

New York Bagel Boys
West Sacramento, CA...........916-739-6540

New York Bakeries
Hialeah, FL...................305-882-1355

New York Bakery & Bagelry
Saint Louis, MO...............314-731-0080

New York Frozen Foods
Cleveland, OH.................216-292-5655

New York International Bread Company
Orlando, FL...................407-843-9744

Newly Weds Foods
Watertown, MA.................800-621-7521

Nickles Bakery of Indiana
Elkhart, IN...................574-293-0608

Nickles Bakery of Ohio
Lima, OH......................419-224-7080

Nickles Bakery of Ohio
Martins Ferry, OH.............740-633-1711

Nickles Bakery of Ohio
Navarre, OH...................800-362-9775

Nicole's Divine Crackers
Chicago, IL...................312-640-8883

Nikki's Cookies
Milwaukee, WI.................800-776-7107

Nonni's Food Company
Tulsa, OK.....................877-295-0289

North American Enterprises
Tucson, AZ....................800-817-8666

North East Foods
Baltimore, MD.................410-558-1050

North's Bakery California
North Hollywood, CA...........818-761-2892

Norths Bakery California Inc
North Hollywood, CA...........818-761-2892

Northside Bakery
Richmond, VA..................804-329-6851

Northwest Candy Emporium
Everett, WA...................800-404-7266

Notre Dame Bakery
Lewisporte, NL................709-535-2738

Novelty Kosher Pastry
Spring Valley, NY.............845-356-0428

Nustef Foods
Mississauga, ON 905-896-3060
Nuthouse Company
Mobile, AL 251-433-1689
Nutrilicious Natural Bakery
Countryside, IL 800-835-8097
Nylander's Vantage Products
Lakeport, CA 916-929-5200
Oak State Products
Wenona, IL .815-853-4348
Oakrun Farm Bakery
Ancaster, ON. 905-648-1818
Oh Boy! Corporation
San Fernando, CA. 818-361-1128
OH Chocolate
Calgary, AB. 403-283-4612
Ohta Wafer Factory
Honolulu, HI. 808-949-2775
Old Country Bakery
North Hollywood, CA 818-838-2302
Old Fashioned Kitchen
Lakewood, NJ. 732-364-4100
Olivia's Croutons
New Haven, VT 888-425-3080
Orange Bakery
Irvine, CA 949-863-1377
Original Ya-hoo! Baking Company
Sherman, TX. 800-575-9373
Orlando Baking Company
Cleveland, OH 800-362-5504
Orlando's Pastries
Collingdale, PA 610-532-9300
Oroweat Baking Company
Montebello, CA 323-721-5161
Orwasher's Bakery Handmade Bread
New York, NY 212-288-6569
Osman's Pies
Stow, OH. 330-655-2919
Otis Spunkmeyer
San Leandro, CA. 800-938-1900
Ottenberg's Bakers
Washington, DC 800-334-7264
Our Thyme Garden
Cleburne, TX 800-482-4372
Oven Fresh Baking Company
Chicago, IL. 773-638-1234
Pacific Ocean Produce
Santa Cruz, CA. 831-423-2654
Palermo Bakery
Seaside, CA. 831-394-8212
Palm Springs Baking Company
Palm Springs, CA. 760-320-7414
Pan Pepin
Bayamon, PR 787-787-1717
Pan-O-Gold Baking Company
St Cloud, MN 320-251-9361
Parco Foods
Blue Island, IL 708-371-9200
Paris Pastry
Los Angeles, CA. 310-474-8888
Pasco Corporation of America
Torrance, CA. 310-516-1918
Pasta Shoppe
Nashville, TN 800-247-0188
Pastry Chef
Pawtucket, RI 800-639-8606
Pati-Petite Cookies
Bridgeville, PA 800-253-5805
Patisserie Wawel
Montreal, QC 614-524-3348
PB&S Chemicals
Henderson, KY 800-950-7267
Pechters Baking
Harrison, NJ 800-525-5779

Peggy Lawton Kitchens
East Walpole, MA. 800-843-7325
Peking Noodle Company
Los Angeles, CA. 323-223-2023
Pellman Foods
New Holland, PA 717-354-8070
Pennant Foods Company
Northlake, IL 800-877-1157
Pepperidge Farm
Downingtown, PA. 610-269-2500
Pepperidge Farm
Lakeland, FL. 863-688-4000
Pepperidge Farm
Norwalk, CT 888-737-7374
Pete & Joy's Bakery
Little Falls, MN. 320-632-6388
Petri Baking Products Inc
Silver Creek, NY. 800-346-1981
Petrofsky's Bakery Products
Maryland Heights, MO. 314-432-5101
Phipps Desserts
Toronto, ON 416-481-9111
Piantedosi Baking Company
Malden, MA 800-339-0080
Pie Piper Products
Bensenville, IL 800-621-8183
Piemonte's Bakery
Rockford, IL 815-962-4833
Pierre Foods
Cincinnati, OH 513-874-8741
Pierre's French Bakery
Portland, OR 503-233-8871
Pillsbury
Medford, MA 800-289-2732
Pillsbury
McMinnville, OR 800-325-5439
Pillsbury Bakeries & Food Services
Sherwood Park, AB 780-464-1544
Pillsbury Frozen Foods
Lithonia, GA 770-482-5092
Pinnacle Foods Group
Cherry Hill, NJ 877-852-7424
Pioneer French Baking
Venice, CA .310-392-4128
Pioneer Frozen Foods
Duncanville, TX 972-298-4281
Pita King Bakery
Everett, MA. 425-258-4040
Pittsfield Rye Bakery
Pittsfield, MA 413-443-9141
Plaidberry Company
Vista, CA. 760-727-5403
Plehn's Bakery
St Matthews, KY. 502-896-4438
Plumlife Company
Newbury, MA 978-462-8458
Pocono Cheesecake Factory
Swiftwater, PA 570-839-6844
Pollman's Bake Shops
Mobile, AL .251-438-1511
Portuguese Baking Company
Newark, NJ .973-589-8875
Positively Third Street Bakery
Duluth, MN. 218-724-8619
Powers Baking Company
Sunrise, FL .305-681-7000
Pratzel's Bakery
St Louis, MO. 314-993-5511
President's Choice International
Toronto, ON 416-967-2501
Preuss Bake Shop
Waseca, MN 507-835-4320
Priester Pecan Company
Fort Deposit, AL 800-277-3226

Prime Pastry
Brooklyn, NY 888-771-2464
Primos Northgate
Flowood, MS 601-936-3398
Prince of Peace Enterprises
Hayward, CA 800-732-2328
Protano's Bakery
Hollywood, FL 954-925-3474
Pure's Food Specialties
Broadview, IL 708-344-8884
Purity Factories
St.John's, NL. 800-563-3411
Quality Bakery
Invermere, BC. 888-681-9977
Quality Bakery Products
Fort Lauderdale, FL 954-779-3663
Quality Bakery/MM Deli
Port Colborne, ON 905-834-4911
Quality Croutons
Chicago, IL .800-334-2796
Quality Naturally! Foods
City of Industry, CA 888-498-6986
Quiche & Tell
Flushing, NY. 718-381-7562
Quinzani Bakery
Boston, MA. 800-999-1062
R&B Quality Foods
Scottsdale, AZ. 480-443-1415
R.M. Palmer Company
Reading, PA 610-372-8971
R.W. Frookies
Sag Harbor, NY. 800-913-3663
Ralph's Grocery Company
Los Angeles, CA. 310-884-9000
Ranaldi Bros Frozen Food Products Inc
Warwick, RI 401-738-3444
Randag & Associates Inc
Elmhurst, IL 630-530-2830
Real Food Marketing
Kansas City, MO. 816-221-4100
Renaissance Baking Company
North Miami, FL. 305-893-2144
Renaissance Foods
Saint Louis, MO 314-961-6554
Rentschler's Bakery
Kutztown, PA 610-683-3506
Reser's Fine Foods
Beaverton, OR 800-333-6431
Rhodes Bake-N-Serv
Salt Lake City, UT 800-695-0122
Rhodes International
Columbus, WI. 800-876-7333
Rich Ice Cream Company
West Palm Beach, FL 561-833-7585
Rich Products Corporation
Winchester, VA 540-667-1955
Rich Products Corporation
Fresno, CA .559-486-7380
Rich Products Corporation
Hilliard, OH. 614-771-1117
Rich Products Corporation
Buffalo, NY. 800-356-7094
Rich Products Corporation
Buffalo, NY. 800-828-2021
Rich Products of Canada
Fort Erie, ON 800-263-8174
Richmond Baking Company
Richmond, IN 765-962-8535
Rising Dough Bakery
Sacramento, CA 916-387-9700
Robert's Bakery
Minnetonka, MN. 612-473-9719
Rockland Bakery
Nanuet, NY. 800-734-4376

Rogers Bakery
Plainville, CT 860-747-1686
Rolling Pin Bakery
Great Bend, KS 316-793-5381
Rolling Pin Bakery
Bow Island, AB 403-545-2434
Roma & Ray's Italian Bakery
Valley Stream, NY 516-825-7610
Roma Bakeries
Rockford, IL 815-964-6737
Roma Bakery
San Jose, CA 408-294-0123
Romero's Food Products
Santa Fe Springs, CA 562-802-1858
Rosemark Bakery
St Paul, MN 651-698-3838
Roskam Baking Company
Grand Rapids, MI 616-574-5757
Rotella's Italian Bakery
La Vista, NE 402-592-6600
Rovira Biscuit Corporation
Ponce, PR 787-844-8585
Rowena's
Norfolk, VA 800-627-8699
Royal Court Cookie Company
North Hollywood, CA 800-730-2545
Royal Home Bakery
Newmarket, ON 905-715-7044
Royal Pie Bakery
San Diego, CA 619-233-6393
Royal Wine Company
Bayonne, NJ 201-437-9131
Rubschlager Baking Corporation
Chicago, IL 773-826-1245
Rudolph's Specialty Bakery
Toronto, ON 416-763-4315
Ruiz Mexican Foods
Ontario, CA 909-947-7811
Run-A-Ton Group
Morristown, NJ 800-247-6580
Russell & Kohne
Corona Del Mar, CA 949-675-0994
Ruth Ashbrook Bakery
Portland, OR 503-240-7437
Ryals Bakery
Milledgeville, GA 478-452-0321
Ryke's Bakery
Muskegon, MI 231-557-8011
S&M Communion Bread Company
Nashville, TN 615-292-1969
Sacramento Baking Company
Sacramento, CA 916-361-2000
Safeway Dairy Products
Walnut Creek, CA 925-944-4000
Saint Amour/Powerline Foods
Stanton, CA 714-827-5366
Saint Armands Baking Company
Bradenton, FL 941-753-7494
Salem Baking Company
Winston Salem, NC. 800-274-2994
Salerno Foods
Des Plaines, IL 800-247-2848
Salvatore's Pizza Shells
Utica, NY 315-735-7919
San Anselmo's Cookies & Biscotti
San Anselmo, CA 800-229-1249
San Francisco Bread Company
San Jose, CA 408-298-6919
San Francisco Fine Bakery
Redwood City, CA 650-369-8573
San Francisco French Bread
Oakland, CA 510-638-3252
San Luis Sourdough
San Luis Obispo, CA 800-266-7687
San-J International
Richmond, VA 800-446-5500
Sanborn Sourdough Bakery
Las Vegas, NV 702-795-1030
Sandors Bakeries
Miami, FL 305-642-8484
Sanitary Bakery
Little Falls, MN 320-632-6388
Santa Fe Bite-Size Bakery
Albuquerque, NM 505-342-1119
Sara Lee Bakery
Salt Lake City, UT 801-487-4677
Sara Lee Bakery   The Earth Grains Baking
Companies HQ
Neenah, WI 866-613-2784
Sara Lee Bakery Group
Birmingham, AL 205-322-8000

Sara Lee Bakery Group
Earth City, MO 314-291-5480
Sara Lee Bakery Group
Phoenix, AZ 602-252-6881
Sara Lee Bakery Group
Rapid City, SD 605-343-3512
Sara Lee Bakery Group
Orangeburg, SC 800-476-3536
Sara Lee Bakery Group
Hastings, NE 800-669-4395
Sara Lee Bakery Group
Greenville, SC. 864-299-0604
Sara Lee Bakery Group   Bakery
Denver, CO
Sara Lee Bakery Group   The EarthGrains - Bakery
Saint Paul, MN
Sara Lee Bakery Group   The EarthGrains - Bakery
Traverse City, MI 231-922-3296
Sara Lee Bakery Group   The EarthGrains - Bakery
Wichita, KS. 316-943-3176
Sara Lee Bakery Group   The EarthGrains - Bakery
Corpus Christi, TX 361-884-6311
Sara Lee Bakery Group   The EarthGrains - Bakery
Beaumont, TX. 409-842-9150
Sara Lee Bakery Group   The EarthGrains - Bakery
Springfield, MO 417-865-0929
Sara Lee Bakery Group   The EarthGrains - Bakery
Jasper, TN 423-837-8856
Sara Lee Bakery Group   The EarthGrains - Bakery
Louisville, KY 502-491-7499
Sara Lee Bakery Group   The EarthGrains - Bakery
Oakland, CA 510-635-4343
Sara Lee Bakery Group   The EarthGrains - Bakery
Chico, CA 530-343-9631
Sara Lee Bakery Group   The EarthGrains - Bakery
Fresno, CA 559-495-3571
Sara Lee Bakery Group   The EarthGrains - Bakery
Hattiesburg, MS 601-545-3781
Sara Lee Bakery Group   The EarthGrains - Bakery
Nashville, TN 615-298-3001
Sara Lee Bakery Group   The EarthGrains - Bakery
St Louis, MO 800-323-7117
Sara Lee Bakery Group   The EarthGrains - Bakery
Memphis, TN 800-627-0921
Sara Lee Bakery Group   The EarthGrains - Bakery
Tulsa, OK 918-254-5468
Sara Lee Corporation
Downers Grove, IL 630-598-8100
Sara Lee Wholesome Bakery
Oak Lawn, IL 708-499-5711
Sara Lee/Old Home
South Sioux City, NE 402-494-5474
Sarabeth's Bakery
Bronx, NY. 800-773-7378
Sarah Lingwood's Kitchen
Cape Coral, FL 360-293-7181
Sarilii
Knoxville, TN 865-573-1941
Sarsfield Foods
Kentville, NS 902-678-2241
SASIB Biscuits and Snacks Division
Hudson, OH 330-656-3317
Saxby Bakery
Edmonton, AB 780-440-4177
Schadel's Bakery
Silver City, NM 505-538-3031
Schaller's Bakery Inc
Greensburg, PA 800-241-1777
Schat's Dutch Bakeries
Bishop, CA 760-873-7156
Schisa Brothers
Manlius, NY 315-463-0213
Schmidt Baking Company
Baltimore, MD 800-456-2253
Schott's Bakery
Houston, TX 713-869-5701
Schulze & Burch Biscuit Company
Chicago, IL 773-927-6622
Schwan's Consumer Brands North America
Bloomington, MN 952-832-4300
Schwan's Sales Enterprises
Marshall, MN 800-533-5290
Schwans Bakeries
Stilwell, OK 918-696-8325
Schwans Food Company
Norcross, GA 800-241-0559
Schwans Frozen Foods
Marshall, MN 800-533-5290
Schwebel Baking Company
Youngstown, OH. 330-783-2860
Schwebel Baking Company
Youngstown, OH. 800-860-2867

Scialo Brothers
Providence, RI 877-421-0986
Scot Paris Fine Desserts
New York, NY 212-807-1802
Scotty Wotty's Creamy Cheescake
Hillsborough, NJ 908-281-9720
Seavers Bakery
Johnson City, TN 423-928-8131
Seckinger-Lee Company
Savannah, GA 800-291-2973
Shamrock Foods Company
Phoenix, AZ 800-289-3663
Shashy's Fine Foods
Montgomery, AL. 334-263-7341
Shaw Baking Company
Thunder Bay, ON 807-345-7327
Sheila's Select Gourmet Recipe
Heber City, UT 800-516-7286
Sherwood Brands
Rockville, MD 301-309-6161
Sheryl's Chocolate Creations
Hicksville, NY 888-882-2462
Shipley Baking Company
Fort Smith, AR 479-452-1933
Siljans Crispy Cup Company
Calgary, AB 403-275-0135
Silver Lake Cookie Company
Islip, NY 631-581-4000
Silver Tray Cookies
Fort Lauderdale, FL 305-883-0800
Simon Hubig Company
New Orleans, LA 504-945-2181
Sinbad Sweets
Fresno, CA 800-350-7933
SJR Foods
New Bedford, MA 781-821-3090
Smith's Bakery
Hattiesburg, MS 601-288-7000
Smoak's Bakery & Catering Service
Augusta, GA 706-738-1792
Solana Beach Baking Company
Carlsbad, CA 760-931-0148
Soloman Baking Company
Denver, CO 303-371-2777
Solvang Bakery
Solvang, CA 800-377-4253
South West Foods Tasty Bakery
Tyler, TX. 903-877-3481
Southchem
Durham, NC 800-849-7000
Spanish Gardens Food Manufacturing
Kansas City, KS 913-831-4242
Specialty Bakers
Marysville, PA 800-233-0778
Specialty Baking Products
Dunkirk, NY 716-366-0938
Spilke's Baking Company
Brooklyn, NY 718-384-2150
Spohrers Bakeries
Collingdale, PA 610-532-9959
Spot Bagel Bakery
Seattle, WA 206-623-0066
Spring Glen Fresh Foods
Ephrata, PA 800-641-2853
St. Cloud Bakery
St Cloud, MN 320-251-8055
St. Francis Pie Shop
Clayton, CA 510-655-0136
Stacy's Pita Chip Company
Randolph, MA 888-332-4477
Stagnos Bakery
East Liberty, PA 412-441-3485
Standard Bakery
Kealakekua, HI 808-322-3688
Stangl's Bakeries
Ambridge, PA 724-266-5080
Starbucks Coffee Company
Seattle, WA 800-782-7282
Stauffer's
Cuba, NY 585-968-2700
Stella Baking Company
Rockford, IL 815-398-5191
Stella D'Oro Biscuit Company
Bronx, NY. 718-549-3700
Sterling Foods
San Antonio, TX 210-490-1669
Steve's Mom
Bronx, NY. 800-362-4545
Sticky Fingers Bakeries
Spokane Valley, WA 800-458-5826
Strauss Bakeries
Elkhart, IN. 219-295-4373

Stroehmann Bakeries
Horsham, PA 215-672-8010
Stroehmann Bakeries
West Hazleton, PA 570-455-2066
Stroehmann Bakeries
Harrisburg, PA 800-220-2867
Stroehmann Bakeries
Horsham, PA 800-984-0989
Stroehmann Bakery
Horsham, PA 800-984-0989
Strossner's Bakery
Greenville, SC 864-233-3996
Sturgis Pretzel House
Lititz, PA 717-626-4354
Sugar Bowl Bakery
Hayward, CA 510-782-2118
Sugar Kake Cookie
Tonawanda, NY 800-775-5180
Summerfield Foods
Santa Rosa, CA 707-579-3938
Sun Pac Foods
Brampton, ON. 905-792-2700
Sunbeam
New Bedford, MA 800-458-8407
Sunbeam Baking Company
El Paso, TX 800-328-6111
Suncoast Foods Corporation
San Diego, CA 619-299-0475
Sunray Bakery Corporation
Salem, NH. 603-898-3079
Sunset Specialty Foods
Sunset Beach, CA 562-592-4976
Superior Bakery
North Grosvenordale, CT 860-923-9555
Superior Cake Products
Southbridge, MA 508-764-3276
Supermoms
St Paul Park, MN 800-944-7276
Svenhard's Swedish Bakery
Oakland, CA 800-333-7836
Swatt Baking Company
Olean, NY .800-370-6656
Sweet Endings
West Palm Beach, FL 888-635-1177
Sweet Gallery Exclusive Pastry
Toronto, ON 416-232-1539
Sweet Life Enterprises
Santa Ana, CA 949-417-3205
Sweet Sam's Baking Company
Bronx, NY. 718-822-0599
Sweetery
Anderson, SC 800-752-1188
T. Marzetti Company
Columbus, OH 614-846-2232
Table de France
Ontario, CA. 909-923-5205
Table Pride
Atlanta, GA. 770-455-7464
Table Talk Pie
Worcester, MA 508-798-8811
Tasty Baking Company
Philadelphia, PA 800-338-2789
Tasty Mix Quality Foods
Brooklyn, NY. 866-TAS-TYMX
Tastykake
Philadelphia, PA 215-221-8500
Taystee Bakeries
Marquette, MI 906-226-2587
Teeny Foods Corporation
Portland, OR 503-252-3006
Tennessee Bun Company
Dickson, TN 888-486-2867
Terra Harvest Foods
Rockford, IL 815-636-9500
Terranetti's Italian Bakery
Mechanicsburg, PA. 717-697-5434
Teti Bakery
Etobicoke, ON 800-465-0123
Texas Crumb & Food Products
Farmers Branch, TX 800-522-7862
The Bama Company
Tulsa, OK .800-756-2262
The Cheesecake Factory
Calabasas Hills, CA 818-871-3000
Thornton Bakery
Memphis, TN 901-324-2118
Tina's
Anaheim, CA 714-630-4123
Titterington's Olde English Bake Shop
Woburn, MA 781-938-7600
Tom Cat Bakery
Long Island City, NY 718-786-4224

Tom's Foods
Corsicana, TX 903-874-6553
Tomaro's Bakery
Clarksburg, WV 304-622-0691
Toufayan Bakeries
Orlando, FL. 407-295-2257
Traditional Baking
Bloomington, CA 909-421-0391
Treasure Foods
West Valley, UT. 801-974-0911
Tripoli Bakery
Lawrence, MA 978-682-7754
Tripp Bakers
Wheeling, IL 800-621-3702
Troppers
Santa Barbara, CA 805-969-4054
Tsue Chong Noodle Company
Seattle, WA 206-623-0801
Turano Pastry Shops
Bloomingdale, IL 630-529-6161
Turnbull Bakeries of Lousiana
New Orleans, LA 504-581-5383
Tuscan Bakery
Portland, OR 800-887-2261
Twin City Bagels/National Choice Bakery
South St Paul, MN 651-554-0200
Twin Marquis
Brooklyn, NY. 800-367-6868
Two Chefs on a Roll
Carson, CA 800-842-3025
ULDO USA
Lexington, MA 781-860-7800
Ultimate Biscotti
Eugene, OR 541-344-8220
Uncle Andy's Pic & Pay Bakery
South Portland, ME 207-799-7199
Uncle Ralph's Cookie Company
Frederick, MD. 800-422-0626
Unified Western Grocers
Los Angeles, CA. 323-232-6124
Unique Bakery Company
Toronto, ON 416-751-8200
United Noodle Manufacturing Company
Salt Lake City, UT 801-485-0951
United Pie Company
Elkhart, IN. 574-294-3419
United States Bakery
Portland, OR 503-731-5679
Upper Crust Bakery
Phoenix, AZ 602-255-0464
Upper Crust Baking Company
Pismo Beach, CA 800-676-1691
Upper Crust Biscotti
Pismo Beach, CA 866-972-6879
Uptown Bakers
Washington, DC 202-546-6500
Valley Bakery
Rock Valley, IA 712-476-5386
Valley Lahvosh Baking Company
Fresno, CA 800-480-2704
Valley Pie Company
Phoenix, AZ 602-943-4512
Vallos Baking Company
Bethlehem, PA 610-866-1012
Van de Kamp's
Chambersburg, PA 570-263-4127
Vande Walle's Candies
Appleton, WI 920-738-7799
Venus Wafers
Hingham, MA 800-545-4538
Vermont Bread Company
Brattleboro, VT. 802-254-4600
Vie de France Bakery
Bensenville, IL 630-595-9521
Vie de France Bakery
Vienna, VA 800-446-4404
Vie de France Bakery
Atlanta, GA. 800-933-5486
Vie de France Yamazaki
Denver, CO 303-371-6280
Vie de France Yamazaki
Vernon, LA 323-582-1241
Vie de France Yamazaki
Vienna, VA 800-393-8926
Vie de France Yamazaki
Vienna, VA 800-446-4404
Vigneri Confections
Rochester, NY. 585-254-6160
Vilotti & Marinelli Baking Company
Philadelphia, PA 215-627-5038
VIP Foodservice
Kahului, HI 808-877-5055

Vista Bakery
Burlington, IA 800-553-2343
Vocatura Bakery
Norwich, CT 860-887-2220
Voortman Cookies
Bloomington, CA 909-877-8471
Waldensian Bakeries
Valdese, NC. 828-874-2136
Wally Biscotti
Denver, CO 866-659-2559
Way Baking Company
Jackson, MI. 800-347-7373
Wedding Cake Studio
Williamsfield, OH. 440-667-1765
Wedemeyer's Bakery
S San Francisco, CA 650-873-1000
Well-Bred Loaf
Valley Cottage, NY. 800-444-5623
WendySue & Tobey's
Gardena, CA 310-516-9705
Wenger's Bakery
Reading, PA 610-372-6545
Wenner Bread Products
Bayport, NY 800-869-6262
Wenzel's Bakery
Tamaqua, PA 570-668-2360
Westco Bakemark
Pico Rivera, CA 800-695-5061
Weston Bakeries
Calgary, AB. 403-259-1500
Weston Bakeries
Etobicoke, ON 416-252-7323
Weston Bakeries
Sudbury, ON 705-673-4185
Weston Bakeries
Kingston, ON 800-267-0229
Weston Bakeries
Toronto, ON 800-590-6861
Wheat Montana Farms & Bakery
Three Forks, MT 800-535-2798
White Castle System
Columbus, OH 866-272-8372
Whole Earth Bakery
New York, NY 212-677-7597
Wick's Pies
Winchester, IN 800-642-5880
Widoffs Modern Bakery
Worcester, MA 508-752-7200

William Poll
  New York, NY 800-993-7655
Williamsburg Chocolatier
  Williamsburg, VA 804-966-9000
Willmar Cookie & Nut Company
  Willmar, MN 320-235-0600
Willmark Sales Company
  West Hempstead, NY 718-388-7141
Winder Dairy
  West Valley, UT 800-946-3371
Wolferman's
  Medford, OR 913-888-4499
Wonder Bread
  Provo, UT .801-373-8192
Wonder Bread
  Tampa, FL .813-253-2813
Wonton Food
  Brooklyn, NY 800-776-8889
Woodie Pie Company
  Artesia, NM 505-746-2132
World of Chantilly
  Brooklyn, NY 718-859-1110
Wow! Factor Desserts
  Sherwood Park, AB 800-604-2253
WSMP
  Claremont, NC 828-459-7626
Wuollet Bakery
  Minneapolis, MN 612-381-9400
Yost's Dutch Maid Bakery
  Johnstown, PA. 814-266-3191
Young's Bakery
  Uniontown, PA 724-437-6361
Yrica's Rugelach & Baking Company
  Brooklyn, NY 718-965-3657
YZ Enterprises
  Maumee, OH. 800-736-8779
Zeppys Bakery
  Lawrence, MA 781-963-7022
Zoelsmanns Bakery & Deli
  Pueblo, CO 719-543-0407

Bread Crumbs & Croutons

General Mills
  Federalsburg, MD 410-479-4800
Griffith Laboratories
  Scarborough, ON 416-288-3050
H&S Edible Products Corporation
  Mount Vernon, NY 800-253-3364
Heinz Company of Canada
  North York, ON. 800-268-6641
Just Off Melrose
  Palm Springs, CA 800-743-4109
Olivia's Croutons
  New Haven, VT 888-425-3080
Quality Bakery Products
  Fort Lauderdale, FL 954-779-3663
Quality Croutons
  Chicago, IL 800-334-2796
Roskam Baking Company
  Grand Rapids, MI 616-574-5757
Sara Lee Bakery
  Neenah, WI 800-323-7117
Sugar Foods Corporation
  New York, NY 212-753-6900
Sun Pac Foods
  Brampton, ON. 905-792-2700

Bread Crumbs

Bellacicco Distribution Company
  Brooklyn, NY 800-561-1705
Colonna Brothers
  North Bergen, NJ 201-864-1115
Duval Bakery Products
  Jacksonville, FL 904-354-7878
Four C Foods Corporation
  Brooklyn, NY 718-272-4242
Griffith Laboratories
  Scarborough, ON 416-288-3050
Kerry Ingredients
  Evansville, IN 812-464-9151
Lakeview Bakery
  Calgary, AB. 403-246-6127
Newly Weds Foods
  Chicago, IL 800-621-7521
Quality Bakery Products
  Fort Lauderdale, FL 954-779-3663
Richmond Baking Company
  Richmond, IN 765-962-8535
Sara Lee Bakery
  Neenah, WI 800-323-7117

Sun Pac Foods
  Brampton, ON. 905-792-2700
Texas Crumb & Food Products
  Farmers Branch, TX 800-522-7862
Turnbull Bakeries of Lousiana
  New Orleans, LA 504-581-5383
Vigo Importing Company
  Tampa, FL. 813-884-3491

Croutons

Aladdin Bakers
  Brooklyn, NY 718-499-1818
Heaven Scent Natural Foods
  Santa Monica, CA. 310-829-9050
Icco Cheese Company
  Orangeburg, NY 845-398-9800
Just Off Melrose
  Palm Springs, CA 800-743-4109
Lakeview Bakery
  Calgary, AB. 403-246-6127
Live A Little Gourmet Foods
  Newark, CA 888-744-2300
Olivia's Croutons
  New Haven, VT 888-425-3080
Pepperidge Farm
  Bedford, NH 800-562-8340
Pepperidge Farm
  San Antonio, TX 888-737-7374
Pepperidge Farms
  Norwalk, CT 888-737-7374
Progresso Quality Foods
  Vineland, NJ 800-200-9377
Quality Bakery Products
  Fort Lauderdale, FL 954-779-3663
Quality Croutons
  Chicago, IL 800-334-2796
Roskam Baking Company
  Grand Rapids, MI 616-574-5757
San Francisco French Bread
  Oakland, CA 510-638-3252
Sugar Foods
  Sun Valley, CA 818-768-7900
Sun Pac Foods
  Brampton, ON. 905-792-2700

Crumbs

Aladdin Bakers
  Brooklyn, NY 718-499-1818
Bellacicco Distribution Company
  Brooklyn, NY 800-561-1705
Four C Foods Corporation
  Brooklyn, NY 718-272-4242
Gonnella Frozen Products
  Schaumburg, IL. 847-884-8829
Griffith Laboratories
  Scarborough, ON 416-288-3050
Heaven Scent Natural Foods
  Santa Monica, CA. 310-829-9050
Icco Cheese Company
  Orangeburg, NY 845-398-9800
Newly Weds Foods
  Chicago, IL 800-621-7521
Progresso Quality Foods
  Vineland, NJ 800-200-9377
Quality Bakery Products
  Fort Lauderdale, FL 954-779-3663
Richmond Baking Company
  Richmond, IN 765-962-8535
Sun Pac Foods
  Brampton, ON. 905-792-2700
Texas Crumb & Food Products
  Farmers Branch, TX 800-522-7862
Vigo Importing Company
  Tampa, FL. 813-884-3491

Seasoned

Kellogg US Snack   Division
  Battlecreek, MI 269-961-2000

Bread Sticks

Adrian's Bakery
  Edmonton, AB 800-668-3533
Andre-Boudin Bakeries
  San Francisco, CA 415-882-1849
Bake Crafters Food
  Collegedale, TN 800-296-8935
Baker & Baker
  Schaumburg, IL. 800-593-5777

Baker & Baker, Inc.
  Schaumburg, IL. 800-593-5777
Clown-Gysin Brands
  Northbrook, IL 800-323-5778
Colonna Brothers
  North Bergen, NJ 201-864-1115
Dwayne Keith Brooks Company
  Orangevale, CA 916-988-1030
Falcone's Cookieland
  Brooklyn, NY 718-236-4200
John Wm. Macy's Cheesesticks
  Elmwood Park, NJ 800-643-0573
Kemach Food Products   Corporation
  Brooklyn, NY 888-453-6224
La Piccolina
  Decatur, GA 800-626-1624
Nature's Hilights
  Chico, CA .800-313-6454
Orlando Baking Company
  Cleveland, OH 800-362-5504
Real Food Marketing
  Kansas City, MO 816-221-4100
Stella D'Oro Biscuit Company
  Bronx, NY. 718-549-3700
Teeny Foods Corporation
  Portland, OR 503-252-3006
Tomanetti Food Products
  Oakmont, PA. 800-875-3040
Toufayan Bakeries
  Orlando, FL 407-295-2257
Tropical
  Columbus, OH 800-538-3941
Turnbull Bakeries of Lousiana
  New Orleans, LA 504-581-5383

Breads

1-2-3 Gluten Inc
  Pittsburgh, PA 843-768-7231
Aunt Millies Bakeries
  Fort Wayne, IN 260-424-8245
Bake Masters of Atlanta
  Doraville, GA 770-447-6823
Bakemark Ingredients Canada
  Richmond, BC 800-665-9441
Baker
  Milford, NJ 800-995-3989
Baptista's Bakery
  Franklin, WI 877-261-3157
Bella Chi-Cha Products
  Santa Cruz, CA 831-423-1851
Berkshire Mountain Bakery
  Housatonic, MA 866-274-6124
Bridgford Foods Corpora tion
  Anaheim, CA 800-527-2105
Buns Master Bakery
  North Hamilton, ON 905-560-5011
Butter Krust Baking Company
  Sunbury, PA. 800-282-8093
Chatila's Bakery
  Salem, NH 603-898-5459
Chella's Dutch Delicacies
  Lake Oswego, OR 800-458-3331
Clarmil Manufacturing Corporation
  Hayward, CA 888-252-7645
Colchester Bakery
  Colchester, CT 860-537-2415
Grandma's Recipe Ruglactch
  New York, NY 212-627-2775
Haby's Alsatian Bakery
  Castroville, TX 830-931-2118
Holsum Bakery
  Phoenix, AZ 800-755-8167
Klosterman Baking Company
  Cincinnati, OH 513-242-1109
Lakeview Bakery
  Calgary, AB. 403-246-6127
LePage Bakeries
  Auburn, ME 207-783-9161
Metropolitan Bakery
  Philadelphia, PA 877-412-7323
Morabito Baking Company
  Norristown, PA 800-525-7747
Morse's Sauerkraut
  Waldoboro, ME. 866-832-5569
Mozzicato Depasquale Bakery & Pastry Shop
  Hartford, CT 860-296-0426
Mrs Baird's Bakery
  Fort Worth, TX 817-864-2500
Naturally Delicious
  Oakland Park, FL 954-485-6730
Nature's Hilights
  Chico, CA .800-313-6454

Neuman Bakery Specialties
Addison, IL 800-253-5298
New Horizon Foods
Union City, CA 510-489-8600
Oasis Breads
Escondido, CA 760-747-7390
Old World Bakery
Baltimore, MD 513-931-1411
Orwasher's Bakery Handmade Bread
New York, NY 212-288-6569
Pepperidge Farm Bread Distributor
Grand Blanc, MI 810-743-9640
Pepperidge Farms
Norwalk, CT 888-737-7374
Plehn's Bakery
St Matthews, KY 502-896-4438
Ralph's Grocery Company
Los Angeles, CA 310-884-9000
Royal Caribbean Bakery
Mt Vernon, NY 888-818-0971
Sandors Bakeries
Miami, FL 305-642-8484
Southeast Baking Corporation
Greer, SC 864-627-1380
Sunbeam Baking Company
El Paso, TX 800-328-6111
Superior Baking Company
Brockton, MA 800-696-2253
Taste Maker Foods
Memphis, TN 800-467-1407
Vantage USA
Chicago, IL 773-247-1086
Vermont Bread Company
Brattleboro, VT 802-254-4600
Wuollet Bakery
Minneapolis, MN 612-381-9400

Bagels

Aladdin Bakers
Brooklyn, NY 718-499-1818
Amoroso's Baking Company
Philadelphia, PA 800-377-6557
Andre-Boudin Bakeries
San Francisco, CA 415-882-1849
Awrey Bakeries
Livonia, MI 800-950-2253
Bagel Factory
Birmingham, AL 205-969-0000
Bagel Guys
Brooklyn, NY 718-222-4361
Bagel King
Walnut Creek, CA 925-938-5464
Bagel Works
Boynton Beach, FL 704-553-8822
Bagelworks
New York, NY 212-744-6444
Bake Crafters Food
Collegedale, TN 800-296-8935
Baker Boy Bake Shop
Dickinson, ND 800-437-2008
BBU Bakeries
Denver, CO 303-691-6342
Beach Bagel Bakeries
Miami, FL 305-691-3514
Better Bagel Bakery
Sarasota, FL 941-924-0393
Bocconcino Food Products
Moonachie, NJ 201-933-7474
Brooklyn Bagel Company
Staten Island, NY 800-349-3055
Buckhead Gourmet
Atlanta, GA 800-605-5754
Chatila's Bakery
Salem, NH 603-898-5459
Crispy Bagel Company
Baltimore, MD 800-522-7655
Dakota Brands International
Jamestown, ND 800-844-5073
Dough Delight
Concord, ON 800-465-5515
Entenmann's-Oroweat/BestFoods
S San Francisco, CA 650-875-3100
Evans Bakery
Cozad, NE 800-222-5641
F R LePage Bakeries
Auburn, ME 207-783-9161
Felix Roma & Sons
Endicott, NY 800-640-3336
Fleischer's Bagels
Macedon, NY 315-986-9999

H&H Bagels
New York, NY 800-692-2435
Harlan Bakeries
Avon, IN 317-272-3600
Harlan Bakeries, Inc.
Avon, IN 317-272-3600
JMP Bakery Company
Brooklyn, NY 718-272-5400
Kellogg Company
Battle Creek, MI 800-962-1413
Kerrobert Bakery
Kerrobert, SK 306-834-2461
La Francaise Bakery
Northlake, IL 800-654-7220
Lakeview Bakery
Calgary, AB 403-246-6127
Lenchner Bakery
Concord, ON 905-738-8811
Lender's Bagel Bakery
Mattoon, IL 217-235-3181
Lender's Bagel Bakery
West Seneca, NY 716-668-6761
Maple Leaf Foods
Franklin Park, IL 847-451-8100
Maui Bagel
Kahului, HI 808-270-7561
Meyer's Bakeries
Hope, AR 800-643-1542
Modern Baked Products
Oakdale, NY 877-727-2253
My Bagel Chips
Long Beach, NY 516-889-0732
New York Bagel Boys
West Sacramento, CA 916-739-6540
New York Bakery & Bagelry
Saint Louis, MO 314-731-0080
Oroweat Baking Company
Montebello, CA 323-721-5161
Otis Spunkmeyer
San Leandro, CA 800-938-1900
Pechters Baking
Harrison, NJ 800-525-5779
Petrofsky's Bagels
Saint Louis, MO 314-432-4177
Petrofsky's Bakery Products
Maryland Heights, MO 314-432-5101
Pinnacle Foods Group
Cherry Hill, NJ 877-852-7424
Positively Third Street Bakery
Duluth, MN 218-724-8619
Prairie Malt
Biggar, SK 306-948-3500
Quality Naturally! Foods
City of Industry, CA 888-498-6986
Sara Lee Bakery Group
Greenville, SC 864-299-0604
Sara Lee Corporation
Downers Grove, IL 630-598-8100
SJR Foods
New Bedford, MA 781-821-3090
Spot Bagel Bakery
Seattle, WA 206-623-0066
Toufayan Bakeries
Orlando, FL 407-295-2257
Twin City Bagels/National Choice Bakery
South St Paul, MN 651-554-0200
Ultimate Bagel
Altoona, PA 814-942-2435
Upper Crust Baking Company
Pismo Beach, CA 800-676-1691
W&G Flavors
Hunt Valley, MD 410-771-6606
Wenner Bread Products
Bayport, NY 800-869-6262
Western Bagel Baking Corporation
Van Nuys, CA 818-786-5847
Zeppys Bakery
Lawrence, MA 781-963-7022

Fresh

Bagel Guys
Brooklyn, NY 718-222-4361
Canada Bread
North Bay, ON 800-461-6122
Felix Roma & Sons
Endicott, NY 800-640-3336
Fleischer's Bagels
Macedon, NY 315-986-9999
Harlan Bakeries
Avon, IN 317-272-3600
New York Bagel Boys
West Sacramento, CA 916-739-6540

Pechters Baking
Harrison, NJ 800-525-5779
Russ & Daughters
New York, NY 800-787-7229
Western Bagel Baking Corporation
Van Nuys, CA 818-786-5847

Frozen

Aladdin Bakers
Brooklyn, NY 718-499-1818
Andre-Boudin Bakeries
San Francisco, CA 415-882-1849
Awrey Bakeries
Livonia, MI 800-950-2253
Bake Crafters Food
Collegedale, TN 800-296-8935
Bocconcino Food Products
Moonachie, NJ 201-933-7474
Brooklyn Bagel Company
Staten Island, NY 800-349-3055
Evans Bakery
Cozad, NE 800-222-5641
Fleischer's Bagels
Macedon, NY 315-986-9999
Guttenplan's Frozen Dough
Middletown, NJ 888-422-4357
Harlan Bakeries
Avon, IN 317-272-3600
Heinz North America
Fort Myers, FL 239-694-3663
Lender's Bagel Bakery
Mattoon, IL 217-235-3181
Lender's Bagel Bakery
West Seneca, NY 716-668-6761
New York Bagel Boys
West Sacramento, CA 916-739-6540
Ore-Ida Foods
Pittsburgh, PA 412-237-3450
Oroweat Baking Company
Montebello, CA 323-721-5161
Petrofsky's Bakery Products
Maryland Heights, MO 314-432-5101
Quality Naturally! Foods
City of Industry, CA 888-498-6986
Sara Lee Bakery Group
Greenville, SC 864-299-0604
Sara Lee Corporation
Downers Grove, IL 630-598-8100
Wenner Bread Products
Bayport, NY 800-869-6262
Western Bagel Baking Corporation
Van Nuys, CA 818-786-5847

Baguettes

Kosher French Baguettes
Brooklyn, NY 718-633-4994
Orlando Baking Company
Cleveland, OH 800-362-5504
Tom Cat Bakery
Long Island City, NY 718-786-4224

Bialys

Harlan Bakeries
Avon, IN 317-272-3600
Russ & Daughters
New York, NY 800-787-7229

Biscuits

Almondina®/YZ Enterprises, Inc.
Maumee, OH 800-736-8779
American Vintage Wine Biscuits
Long Island City, NY 718-361-1003
Awrey Bakeries
Livonia, MI 800-950-2253
Bake Crafters Food
Collegedale, TN 800-296-8935
Baker Boy Bake Shop
Dickinson, ND 800-437-2008
Bakery Chef
Louisville, KY 800-594-0203
Blue Chip Group
Salt Lake City, UT 800-878-0099
Bob Evans Farms
Hillsdale, MI 517-437-3349
Borinquen Biscuit Corporation
Yauco, PR 787-856-3030
Bremner Biscuit Company
Denver, CO 800-722-1871

Bridgford Foods
Anaheim, CA 800-527-2105
Bridgford Foods Corporation Superior Foods Division
Anaheim, CA 800-527-2105
Buon Italia
New York, NY 212-633-9090
Callie's Charleston Biscuits LLC
Charleston, SC 843-577-1198
Chelsea Market Baskets
New York, NY 888-727-7887
Chelsea Milling Company
Chelsea, MI..................734-475-1361
Chex Finer Foods
Attleboro, MA.................800-322-2434
Consolidated Biscuit Company
Mc Comb, OH.................800-537-9544
Dare Foods
Kitchener, ON 800-865-8225
Del's Pastry
Etobicoke, ON 416-231-4383
Di Camillo Bakery
Niagara Falls, NY 800-634-4363
Dolly Madison Bakery
Columbus, IN 812-376-7432
Ener-G Company
Seattle, WA 800-331-5222
Falcone's Cookieland
Brooklyn, NY 718-236-4200
Flowers Bakeries
Thomasville, GA..............800-568-3476
Flowers Baking
San Antonio, TX..............210-661-2361
Franklin Baking Company
Goldsboro, NC 800-248-7494
Fresh Start Bakeries
Brea, CA 714-256-8900
General Henry Biscuit Company
Du Quoin, IL.................618-542-6222
Godiva Chocolatier
New York, NY 800-946-3482
Grebe's Bakery & Delicatessen
Milwaukee, WI................800-356-9377
GWB Foods Corporation
Brooklyn, NY 718-686-9600
Heitzman Bakery
Louisville, KY 502-452-1891
Hershey International
Weston, FL 954-385-2600
Interstate Brands Corporation
Kansas City, MO..............800-777-8067
Interstate Brands Corporation
Kansas City, MO..............816-502-4000
Interstate Brands Corporation
Florence, SC 843-393-8895
Keebler Company
Macon, GA 478-781-4620
Keebler Company
Branchburg, NJ...............973-254-2000
Kellogg Snacks
Kansas City, KS 800-229-4414
KHS-Bartelt
Sarasota, FL 800-829-9980
Kraft Foods
East Hanover, NJ..............973-503-2000
Lewis Brothers Bakery
La Porte, IN..................219-362-4561
Lewis Brothers Bakery
Evansville, IN.................812-425-4642
Lone Star Bakery
Round Rock, TX...............512-255-3629
Marshall Biscuits
Saraland, AL 251-679-6226
Merlino Italian Baking Company
Seattle, WA 800-207-2997
Mom's Bakery
Atlanta, GA..................404-344-4189
Mom's Food Company
South El Monte, CA 800-969-6667
Native South Services
Fredericksburg, TX 800-236-2848
Pacific Ocean Produce
Santa Cruz, CA 831-423-2654
Pett Spice Products
Atlanta, GA..................404-691-5235
Pierre Foods
Cincinnati, OH 513-874-8741
Pioneer Frozen Foods
Duncanville, TX 972-298-4281
Purity Factories
St.John's, NL.................800-563-3411
Quality Naturally! Foods
City of Industry, CA 888-498-6986

Rovira Biscuit Corporation
Ponce, PR 787-844-8585
Royal Home Bakery
Newmarket, ON 905-715-7044
Royal Wine Company
Bayonne, NJ 201-437-9131
Saputo
Montreal, QC 514-328-6662
Sara Lee Bakery Group   Bakery
Denver, CO
Sara Lee Bakery Group   The EarthGrains - Bakery
Wichita, KS..................316-943-3176
Sara Lee Bakery Group   The EarthGrains - Bakery
Louisville, KY 502-491-7499
Sara Lee Wholesome Bakery
Oak Lawn, IL.................708-499-5711
Sarilii
Knoxville, TN.................865-573-1941
Schulze & Burch Biscuit Company
Chicago, IL 773-927-6622
Seckinger-Lee Company
Savannah, GA................800-291-2973
Southernfood Specialties
Atlanta, GA..................800-255-5323
Stella Baking Company
Rockford, IL 815-398-5191
Stella D'Oro Biscuit Company
Bronx, NY 718-549-3700
The Bama Company
Tulsa, OK 800-756-2262
TIPIAK INC
Stamford, CT.................203-961-9117
Ultimate Biscotti
Eugene, OR..................541-344-8220
Unique Bakery Company
Toronto, ON 416-751-8200
Wedemeyer's Bakery
S San Francisco, CA 650-873-1000

Fresh

Automatic Rolls of New Jersey
Edison, NJ 732-549-2243
Ener-G Foods
Seattle, WA 800-331-5222
Interstate Bakeries Corporation
Jacksonville, FL 904-696-1400
Interstate Brands Corporation
Kansas City, MO..............800-777-8067
Mrs. Kavanagh's English Muffins
Rumford, RI 800-556-7216
New Bakery Company of Ohio
Zanesville, OH 800-848-9845
Quinzani Bakery
Boston, MA..................800-999-1062
Sara Lee Bakery Group
Phoenix, AZ 602-252-6881
Sara Lee Bakery Group   The EarthGrains - Bakery
Corpus Christi, TX 361-884-6311
Sara Lee Bakery Group   The EarthGrains - Bakery
Tulsa, OK 918-254-5468

Frozen

Awrey Bakeries
Livonia, MI..................800-950-2253
Bake Crafters Food
Collegedale, TN 800-296-8935
Bridgford Foods Corporation Superior Foods Division
Anaheim, CA 800-527-2105
Dynamic Foods
Lubbock, TX.................806-762-0780
Fresh Start Bakeries
Brea, CA 714-256-8900
Lone Star Bakery
Round Rock, TX...............512-255-3629
Pacific Ocean Produce
Santa Cruz, CA 831-423-2654
Sara Lee Bakery Group   The EarthGrains - Bakery
Corpus Christi, TX 361-884-6311
The Bama Company
Tulsa, OK 800-756-2262

Brown

B&M
Portland, ME.................207-772-8341
Jou Jou's Pita Bakery
Birmingham, AL...............205-945-7482
Lewis Brothers Bakery
Evansville, IN.................812-425-4642
Schmidt Baking Company
Baltimore, MD 800-456-2253

Terranetti's Italian Bakery
Mechanicsburg, PA.............717-697-5434

Buns

Alois J. Binder Bakery
New Orleans, LA...............504-947-1111
Alpha Baking Company
La Porte, IN..................219-324-7440
Athens Baking Company
Fresno, CA 559-485-3024
Aunt Bea Bakery
Saint Louis, MO 636-225-8808
Aunt Millies Bakeries
Fort Wayne, IN 260-424-8245
Baker's Choice
Birmingham, MI...............248-827-7500
Baldinger Bakery
St Paul, MN..................651-224-5761
Best Harvest Bakeries
Kansas City, KS 800-811-5715
Bimbo Bakeries
Montebello, CA 877-224-7374
Bread Box
Virden, NB 204-748-1513
Buns Master Bakery
North Hamilton, ON 905-560-5011
Calgary Italian Bakery
Calgary, AB. 800-661-6868
Caribbean Food Delights
Tappan, NY 845-398-3000
Colombo Bakery
Sacramento, CA 916-648-1011
Columbus Bakery
Columbus, OH 614-645-2275
Country Club Bakery
Fairmont, WV 304-363-5690
DiCarlo's Bakery
San Pedro, CA 310-831-2524
Dimpflmeier Bakery
Toronto, ON 416-239-3031
Earthgrains Company
St. Louis, MO 314-259-7000
East Balt Bakery
Denver, CO 303-377-5533
East Balt Bakery
Kissimmee, FL 407-933-2222
El Peto Products
Cambridge, ON...............800-387-4064
European Bakers
Tucker, GA 770-723-6180
Evans Bakery
Cozad, NE 800-222-5641
F R LePage Bakeries
Auburn, ME 207-783-9161
Fancy Lebanese Bakery
Halifax, NS 902-429-0400
Flowers Bakeries
Thomasville, GA. 800-226-2429
Flowers Bakeries
Bluefield, WV 800-327-1630
Flowers Bakeries
Thomasville, GA. 800-568-3476
Flowers Bakery of Montgomery
Montgomery, AL. 334-281-7030
Flowers Baking Company
Jamestown, NC 336-841-8840
Flowers Baking Company
Morristown, TN 423-586-2471
Flowers Baking Company
Pine Bluff, AR 870-534-0221
Flowers Baking Company
Jacksonville, FL 904-353-8293
Fresh Start Bakeries
Stockton, CA.................209-943-9200
Fresh Start Bakeries
City of Industry, CA 626-961-2525
Gadoua Bakery
Napierville, QC 450-245-3326
Gai's Northwest Bakeries
Seattle, WA 206-322-0931
George Weston Bakeries
Albany, NY 800-531-4002
Gourmet Baker
Burnaby, BC 800-663-1972
Hardin's Bakery
Tuscaloosa, AL 205-344-6690
Harris Baking Company
Rogers, AR 479-636-3313
Harting's Bakery
Bowmansville, PA..............717-445-5644

Heiner's Bakery
Huntington, WV 800-776-8411
Holsum Bakery
Phoenix, AZ 800-755-8167
Home Baking Company
Birmingham, AL 205-252-1161
Huval Baking Company
Lafayette, LA 337-232-1611
Interstate Brands Corporation
Birmingham, AL 205-841-6301
Interstate Brands Corporation
Kansas City, MO 800-777-8067
Interstate Brands Corporation
Kansas City, MO 816-502-4000
Interstate Brands Corporation/Butternut Bread Company
Boonville, MO 660-882-6107
Interstate Brands Corporation/Merita Bread Bakery
Orlando, FL 407-843-5110
Interstate Brands Corporation/Wonder Bread Bakery
St Louis, MO 314-385-1600
J.P. Sunrise Bakery
Edmonton, AB 780-454-5797
Jenny Lee Bakery
Mc Kees Rocks, PA 412-331-8900
Kerrobert Bakery
Kerrobert, SK 306-834-2461
Lakeview Bakery
Calgary, AB 403-246-6127
Lewis Brothers Bakeries
Sikeston, MO 573-471-1650
Louis Bakeries
La Porte, IN 219-362-4561
Mrs Baird's Bakery
Fort Worth, TX 817-864-2500
Mrs. Baird's Bakeries
Waco, TX 254-750-2500
Mrs. Baird's Bakeries
Abilene, TX 325-692-3141
Nardi Bakery & Deli
East Hartford, CT 860-289-5458
New Horizons Baking Company
Fremont, IN 260-495-7055
Nickles Bakery of Ohio
Lima, OH 419-224-7080
Nickles Bakery of Ohio
Martins Ferry, OH 740-633-1711

Ottenberg's Bakers
Washington, DC 800-334-7264
Pan-O-Gold Baking Company
St Cloud, MN 320-251-9361
Pierre Foods
Cincinnati, OH 513-874-8741
Quality Bakery/MM Deli
Port Colborne, ON 905-834-4911
Roma Bakery
San Jose, CA 408-294-0123
Rotella's Italian Bakery
La Vista, NE 402-592-6600
Royal Home Bakery
Newmarket, ON 905-715-7044
Rudi's Organic Bakery
Boulder, CO 877-293-0876
Sara Lee Bakery Group
Stockton, CA 209-946-0772
Sara Lee Bakery Group
Phoenix, AZ 602-252-6881
Sara Lee Bakery Group
Hastings, NE 800-669-4395
Sara Lee Bakery Group   Bakery
Denver, CO
Sara Lee Bakery Group   The EarthGrains - Bakery
Saint Paul, MN
Sara Lee Bakery Group   The EarthGrains - Bakery
Wichita, KS 316-943-3176
Sara Lee Bakery Group   The EarthGrains - Bakery
Springfield, MO 417-865-0929
Sara Lee Bakery Group   The EarthGrains - Bakery
Louisville, KY 502-491-7499
Sara Lee Bakery Group   The EarthGrains - Bakery
Oakland, CA 510-635-4343
Sara Lee Bakery Group   The EarthGrains - Bakery
Chico, CA 530-343-9631
Sara Lee Bakery Group   The EarthGrains - Bakery
Fresno, CA 559-495-3571
Sara Lee Bakery Group   The EarthGrains - Bakery
Hattiesburg, MS 601-545-3781
Sara Lee Bakery Group   The EarthGrains - Bakery
Nashville, TN 615-298-3001
Sara Lee Bakery Group   The EarthGrains - Bakery
Memphis, TN 800-627-0921
Sara Lee Bakery Group   The EarthGrains - Bakery
Tulsa, OK 918-254-5468

Sara Lee Wholesome Bakery
Oak Lawn, IL 708-499-5711
Sara Lee/Old Home
South Sioux City, NE 402-494-5474
Schott's Bakery
Houston, TX 713-869-5701
Schwan's Consumer Brands North America
Bloomington, MN 952-832-4300
Shipley Baking Company
Fort Smith, AR 479-452-1933
Tennessee Bun Company
Dickson, TN 888-486-2867
Twin Marquis
Brooklyn, NY 800-367-6868
United States Bakery
Portland, OR 503-731-5679
Wenger's Bakery
Reading, PA 610-372-6545
Wonder Bread
Tampa, FL 813-253-2813

Frozen

Sara Lee Bakery Group   The EarthGrains - Bakery
Corpus Christi, TX 361-884-6311

Hot Cross

Baker's Choice
Birmingham, MI 248-827-7500

Sticky

Cinnamon Bakery
Braintree, MA 800-886-2867

Challah

Atlanta Bread Company International, Inc.
Smyrna, GA 800-398-3728
Orwasher's Bakery Handmade Bread
New York, NY 212-288-6569

Cinnamon Toast

Log House Foods
Plymouth, MN 763-546-8395

Corn

Bake Crafters Food
Collegedale, TN 800-296-8935
Dynamic Foods
Lubbock, TX 806-762-0780
Main Street Gourmet
Cuyahoga Falls, OH 800-533-6246
Mom's Food Company
South El Monte, CA 800-969-6667
Pinahs Company
Waukesha, WI 800-967-2447
Shiloh Foods
Savannah, TN 800-795-2550
Tova Industries
Louisville, KY 888-532-8682

Croissants

Andre-Boudin Bakeries
San Francisco, CA 415-882-1849
Bake Crafters Food
Collegedale, TN 800-296-8935
BakeMark Canada
Laval, QC 800-361-4998
Bakery Europa
Honolulu, HI .808-845-5011
Bridor
Boucherville, QC 450-641-1265
Edner Corporation
Hayward, CA .510-441-8504
France Croissant
New York, NY 212-888-1210
Norths Bakery California Inc
North Hollywood, CA 818-761-2892
Vie de France Yamazaki
Vienna, VA 800-446-4404

English Muffins

Aunt Millies Bakeries
Fort Wayne, IN 260-424-8245
Canada Bread Company
Langley, BC .800-465-5515
Fresh Start Bakeries
City of Industry, CA 626-961-2525
Fresh Start Bakeries
Brea, CA 714-256-8900
George Weston Bakeries
Bay Shore, NY 800-356-3314
Gourmet Baker
Burnaby, BC .800-663-1972
Homestead Baking Company
Rumford, RI .800-556-7216
LePage Bakeries
Auburn, ME .207-783-9161
Matthew's All Natural
Woburn, MA .978-458-7858
Meyer's Bakeries
Casa Grande, AZ 800-528-5770
Meyer's Bakeries
Hope, AR 800-643-1542
Meyer's Bakeries
Orlando, FL .887-859-2006
Mrs. Kavanagh's English Muffins
Rumford, RI .800-556-7216
New Horizons Baking Company
Fremont, IN .260-495-7055
Norths Bakery California Inc
North Hollywood, CA 818-761-2892
Oakrun Farm Bakery
Ancaster, ON 905-648-1818
Sara Lee Corporation
Downers Grove, IL 630-598-8100
Weston Bakeries
Toronto, ON .800-590-6861
Wolferman's
Medford, OR 913-888-4499

Flat

Aladdin Bakers
Brooklyn, NY 718-499-1818
American Flatbread
Waitsfield, VT 802-496-8856
Baker & Baker
Schaumburg, IL 800-593-5777
Baker & Baker, Inc.
Schaumburg, IL 800-593-5777
Cosa de Rio Foods
Louisville, KY 502-772-2500
Di Camillo Bakery
Niagara Falls, NY 800-634-4363

Dough Delight
Concord, ON 800-465-5515
Dr Kracker
Dallas, TX 214-503-1971
Falcone's Cookieland
Brooklyn, NY 718-236-4200
George Weston Bakeries
Hollywood, FL 800-356-3314
Goglanian Bakeries
Santa Ana, CA 714-444-3500
Good Wives
Lynn, MA 800-521-8160
Harbar Corporation
Canton, MA .800-881-7040
Kemach Food Products   Corporation
Brooklyn, NY 888-453-6224
Molinaro's Fine Italian Foods
Mississauga, ON 800-268-4959
Nu-World Amaranth
Naperville, IL 630-369-6851
Real Food Marketing
Kansas City, MO 816-221-4100
Rudolph's Specialty Bakery
Toronto, ON 416-763-4315
Teeny Foods Corporation
Portland, OR 503-252-3006
Teti Bakery
Etobicoke, ON 800-465-0123
Toufayan Bakeries
Orlando, FL .407-295-2257
Valley Lahvosh Baking Company
Fresno, CA .800-480-2704

Focaccia

Amberwave Foods
Oakmont, PA 412-828-3040
Atlanta Bread Company International, Inc.
Smyrna, GA .800-398-3728
Baker & Baker
Schaumburg, IL 800-593-5777
Baker & Baker, Inc.
Schaumburg, IL 800-593-5777
Clarmil Manufacturing Corporation
Hayward, CA 888-252-7645
Colors Gourmet Pizza
Carlsbad, CA 760-431-2203
Molinaro's Fine Italian Foods
Mississauga, ON 800-268-4959
Orlando Baking Company
Cleveland, OH 800-362-5504
Real Food Marketing
Kansas City, MO 816-221-4100
Teeny Foods Corporation
Portland, OR 503-252-3006
Windsor Frozen Foods
Houston, TX .800-437-6936

French

Atlanta Bread Company International, Inc.
Smyrna, GA .800-398-3728
Galassos Baking Company
Mira Loma, CA 951-360-1211
General Mills
Chelsea, MA 800-370-7834
Hawaii Star Bakery
Honolulu, HI .808-841-3602
Ledonne Brothers Bakery
Roseto, PA .610-588-0423
Leidenheimer Baking Company
New Orleans, LA 504-525-1575
Maple Leaf Foods
Franklin Park, IL 847-451-8100
Orlando Baking Company
Cleveland, OH 800-362-5504
Oroweat Baking Company
Montebello, CA 323-721-5161
Piemonte's Bakery
Rockford, IL .815-962-4833
Pioneer French Baking
Venice, CA .310-392-4128
Quinzani Bakery
Boston, MA .800-999-1062
Tom Cat Bakery
Long Island City, NY 718-786-4224
Vantage USA
Chicago, IL .773-247-1086
Vermont Bread Company
Brattleboro, VT 802-254-4600
Vie de France Yamazaki
Denver, CO .303-371-6280

Fresh

Adrian's Bakery
Edmonton, AB 800-668-3533
Alfred & Sam Italian Bakery
Lancaster, PA 717-392-6311
Alois J. Binder Bakery
New Orleans, LA 504-947-1111
Alpha Baking Company
La Porte, IN .219-324-7440
Alpha Baking Company
Chicago, IL .773-261-6000
Amoroso's Baking Company
Philadelphia, PA 800-377-6557
Andre-Boudin Bakeries
San Francisco, CA 415-882-1849
Bakery Europa
Honolulu, HI .808-845-5011
Baldinger Bakery
St Paul, MN .651-224-5761
Bellacicco Distribution Company
Brooklyn, NY 800-561-1705
Benson's Bakery
Bogart, GA .800-888-6059
Bimbo Bakeries
Montebello, CA 877-224-7374
Borden's Bread
Regina, SK .306-525-3341
Bread Alone Bakery
Shokan, NY .800-769-3328
Brooklyn Baking Company
Waterbury, CT 203-574-9198
Brown's Bakery
Defiance, OH 419-784-3330
Bunny Bread Company
Cape Girardeau, MO 573-332-7349
Canada Bread
North Bay, ON 800-461-6122
Canada Bread Atlantic
St. John's, NL 709-722-5410
Canada Bread Company
Edmonton, AB 780-451-4663
Canada Bread Company
Langley, BC 800-465-5515
Casino Bakery
Tampa, FL .813-242-0311
Cole's Quality Foods
Muskegon, MI 231-722-1651
Colombo Bakery
Sacramento, CA 916-648-1011
Crestwood Bakery
Pleasant Prairie, WI 414-453-4790
Danish Baking Company
Van Nuys, CA 800-777-4970
Dave's Bakery
Honesdale, PA 570-253-1660
Del Campo Baking Company
Wilmington, DE 302-656-6676
Empress Foods
Winnipeg, NB 204-775-0344
Ener-G Foods
Seattle, WA .800-331-5222
EPI De France Bakery
Atlanta, GA .800-325-1014
F R LePage Bakeries
Auburn, ME .207-783-9161
Father Sam's Syrian Bread
Buffalo, NY .800-521-6719
Felix Roma & Sons
Endicott, NY 800-640-3336
Flowers Bakeries
Thomasville, GA 800-568-3476
Flowers Foods Bakeries
Thomasville, GA 229-226-9110
Galassos Baking Company
Mira Loma, CA 951-360-1211
Glazier Packing Company
Potsdam, NY 315-265-2500
Goglanian Bakeries
Santa Ana, CA 714-444-3500
Gold Standard Baking
Chicago, IL .800-648-7904
Harlan Bakeries
Avon, IN 317-272-3600
Highlandville Packing
Highlandville, MO 417-443-3365
Homestead Baking Company
Rumford, RI .800-556-7216
Huval Baking Company
Lafayette, LA 337-232-1611
International Baking Company
Vernon, CA .323-583-9841

Interstate Bakeries Corporation
Cincinnati, OH 513-721-0212
Interstate Bakeries Corporation
Jacksonville, FL 904-696-1400
Interstate Brands Corporation
Peoria, IL 309-674-9221
Interstate Brands Corporation
Monroe, LA. 318-388-2244
Interstate Brands Corporation
Billings, MT 406-248-4800
Interstate Brands Corporation
Knoxville, TN. 865-947-6191
Interstate Brands Corporation/Wonder Bread Bakery
St Louis, MO. 314-385-1600
Interstate Brands Corporation/Wonder/Hostess
Philadelphia, PA 215-969-1200
JMP Bakery Company
Brooklyn, NY 718-272-5400
John J. Nissen Baking Company
Portland, ME. 207-775-3460
Jones Bakeries
Winston Salem, NC. 800-849-5663
Jou Jou's Pita Bakery
Birmingham, AL. 205-945-7482
Jubelt Variety Bakeries
Mount Olive, IL 217-999-7312
Karam Elsaha Baking Company
Manlius, NY 315-682-2780
Klosterman Baking Company
Springfield, OH. 937-322-9588
Kosher French Baguettes
Brooklyn, NY 718-633-4994
L&M Bakery
Lawrence, MA. 978-687-7346
Landolfi Food Products
Trenton, NJ 609-392-1830
Lanthier Bakery
Alexandria, ON. 613-525-2435
Leidenheimer Baking Company
New Orleans, LA 504-525-1575
Lewis Bakeries
London, ON 519-434-5252
Lewis Brothers Bakeries
Vincennes, IN 812-886-6533
Lewis Brothers Bakery
Evansville, IN 812-425-4642
Lucerne Foods
Calgary, AB. 403-287-4080
Meyer's Bakeries
Hope, AR 800-643-1542
Mississippi Bakery
Burlington, IA. 319-752-6315
Mrs. Baird's Bakeries
Fort Worth, TX 806-763-9304
Multi Marques
Montreal, QC 514-255-9492
Natural Ovens Bakery
Manitowoc, WI. 800-558-3535
Nevada Baking Company
Las Vegas, NV 702-384-8950
New White Palace Bakery
Philadelphia, PA 215-324-9852
Norths Bakery California Inc
North Hollywood, CA 818-761-2892
Orlando Baking Company
Cleveland, OH 800-362-5504
Oroweat Baking Company
Montebello, CA 323-721-5161
Ottenberg's Bakers
Washington, DC 800-334-7264
Pechters Baking
Harrison, NJ 800-525-5779
Penny Curtiss Baking Company
Syracuse, NY 315-454-3241
Pepperidge Farm
Lakeland, FL. 863-688-4000
Piemonte's Bakery
Rockford, IL 815-962-4833
Pillsbury
McMinnville, OR 800-325-5439
Pioneer French Baking
Venice, CA 310-392-4128
Pittsfield Rye Bakery
Pittsfield, MA 413-443-9141
Positively Third Street Bakery
Duluth, MN. 218-724-8619
Quinzani Bakery
Boston, MA 800-999-1062
Real Food Marketing
Kansas City, MO. 816-221-4100
Renaissance Baking Company
North Miami, FL. 305-893-2144

Roma Bakery
San Jose, CA. 408-294-0123
Saint Armands Baking Company
Bradenton, FL. 941-753-7494
San Francisco French Bread
Oakland, CA 510-638-3252
Sara Lee Bakery Group
Phoenix, AZ 602-252-6881
Sara Lee Bakery Group   The EarthGrains - Bakery
Jasper, TN 423-837-8856
Sara Lee Bakery Group   The EarthGrains - Bakery
Tulsa, OK 918-254-5468
Schmidt Baking Company
Martinsburg, WV 800-456-2253
Schwebel Baking Company
Youngstown, OH. 800-860-2867
Shaw Baking Company
Thunder Bay, ON 807-345-7327
Sterling Foods
San Antonio, TX 210-490-1669
Stroehmann Bakeries
Harrisburg, PA 800-220-2867
Stroehmann Bakeries
Horsham, PA 800-984-0989
Superior Bakery
North Grosvenordale, CT 860-923-9555
Swatt Baking Company
Olean, NY 800-370-6656
Teeny Foods Corporation
Portland, OR 503-252-3006
Terranetti's Italian Bakery
Mechanicsburg, PA 717-697-5434
Turano Pastry Shops
Bloomingdale, IL 630-529-6161
Vermont Bread Company
Brattleboro, VT 802-254-4600
Vie de France Bakery
Bensenville, IL 630-595-9521
Vie de France Bakery
Atlanta, GA. 800-933-5486
Vie de France Yamazaki
Vienna, VA 800-393-8926
Weston Bakeries
Calgary, AB. 403-259-1500
Weston Bakeries
Sudbury, ON 705-673-4185
Weston Bakeries
Kingston, ON 800-267-0229
Weston Bakeries
Toronto, ON 800-590-6861
Wolferman's
Medford, OR. 913-888-4499
Wonder Bread
Tampa, FL. 813-253-2813
Yost's Dutch Maid Bakery
Johnstown, PA. 814-266-3191

Frozen

American Flatbread
Waitsfield, VT. 802-496-8856
Andre-Boudin Bakeries
San Francisco, CA 415-882-1849
Awrey Bakeries
Livonia, MI. 800-950-2253
Benson's Bakery
Bogart, GA 800-888-6059
Bridor
Boucherville, QC 450-641-1265
Caribbean Food Delights
Tappan, NY 845-398-3000
Cedarlane Foods
Carson, CA 800-826-3322
Cole's Quality Foods
Muskegon, MI. 231-722-1651
Danish Baking Company
Van Nuys, CA. 800-777-4970
Del Campo Baking Company
Wilmington, DE 302-656-6676
EPI De France Bakery
Atlanta, GA. 800-325-1014
Evans Bakery
Cozad, NE 800-222-5641
General Mills
Chelsea, MA 800-370-7834
Glazier Packing Company
Potsdam, NY 315-265-2500
Guttenplan's Frozen Dough
Middletown, NJ 888-422-4357
Harlan Bakeries
Avon, IN 317-272-3600

J&J Wall Baking Company
Sacramento, CA 916-381-1410
Leidenheimer Baking Company
New Orleans, LA 504-525-1575
Meyer's Bakeries
Hope, AR 800-643-1542
Mothers Kitchen Inc
Burlington, NJ. 609-387-7200
New York Frozen Foods
Cleveland, OH 216-292-5655
Penny Curtiss Baking Company
Syracuse, NY 315-454-3241
Pillsbury
McMinnville, OR 800-325-5439
Positively Third Street Bakery
Duluth, MN. 218-724-8619
Real Food Marketing
Kansas City, MO. 816-221-4100
Rich Products Corporation
Winchester, VA 540-667-1955
Rich Products Corporation
Fresno, CA 559-486-7380
Rich Products Corporation
Buffalo, NY 800-356-7094
Rich Products Corporation
Buffalo, NY 800-828-2021
Sara Lee Bakery Group   The EarthGrains - Bakery
Corpus Christi, TX 361-884-6311
Sara Lee Corporation
Downers Grove, IL 630-598-8100
Wenner Bread Products
Bayport, NY 800-869-6262
Winder Dairy
West Valley, UT 800-946-3371
Wolferman's
Medford, OR. 913-888-4499

Garlic

Bellacicco Distribution Company
Brooklyn, NY 800-561-1705
Cole's Quality Foods
Muskegon, MI. 231-722-1651
Dabruzzi's Italian Foods
Hudson, WI. 715-386-3653
George Weston Bakeries
Bay Shore, NY 800-356-3314
Landolfi Food Products
Trenton, NJ 609-392-1830
Oh Boy! Corporation
San Fernando, CA 818-361-1128
Piemonte's Bakery
Rockford, IL 815-962-4833
Real Food Marketing
Kansas City, MO. 816-221-4100
T. Marzetti Company
Columbus, OH 614-846-2232

Frozen

Cole's Quality Foods
Grand Rapids, MI. 616-975-0081
Oh Boy Corporation
San Fernando, CA 818-361-1128

Italian

Armanino Foods of Distinction
Hayward, CA 510-441-9300
Butter Krust Baking Company
Sunbury, PA. 800-282-8093
Cusano's Baking Company
Hallandale Beach, FL. 954-458-1010
Dough Delight
Concord, ON. 800-465-5515
JMP Bakery Company
Brooklyn, NY 718-272-5400
Ledonne Brothers Bakery
Roseto, PA 610-588-0423
Milano Baking Company
Joliet, IL .815-727-4872
Orlando Baking Company
Cleveland, OH 800-362-5504
Piemonte's Bakery
Rockford, IL 815-962-4833
Quinzani Bakery
Boston, MA 800-999-1062
Scialo Brothers
Providence, RI 877-421-0986
Teeny Foods Corporation
Portland, OR 503-252-3006
Tom Cat Bakery
Long Island City, NY 718-786-4224

Vantage USA
Chicago, IL 773-247-1086
Wenner Bread Products
Bayport, NY 800-869-6262

Melba Toast

Turnbull Bakeries of Lousiana
New Orleans, LA 504-581-5383
Turnbull Cone Baking Company
Chattanooga, TN 423-265-4551

Multi-Grain

Harvest Innovations
Indianola, IA 515-962-5063
Jones Bakeries
Winston Salem, NC. 800-849-5663
Mother Nature's Goodies
Yucaipa, CA 909-795-6018
Orlando Baking Company
Cleveland, OH 800-362-5504

Nut

L&M Bakery
Lawrence, MA 978-687-7346

Pita

Athens Pastries & Frozen Foods
Cleveland, OH 800-837-5683
Bake Crafters Food
Collegedale, TN 800-296-8935
Byblos Bakery
Calgary, AB. 403-250-3711
Corfu Foods
Bensenville, IL 630-595-2510
Dough Delight
Concord, ON. 800-465-5515
Fancy Lebanese Bakery
Halifax, NS 902-429-0400
Father Sam's Syrian Bread
Buffalo, NY. 800-521-6719
Goglanian Bakeries
Santa Ana, CA 714-444-3500
Harlan Bakeries, Inc.
Avon, IN 317-272-3600
Jou Jou's Pita Bakery
Birmingham, AL 205-945-7482
Kangaroo Brands
Milwaukee, WI 800-798-0857
Karam Elsaha Baking Company
Manlius, NY 315-682-2780
Konto's Foods
Paterson, NJ 973-278-2800
Mediterranean Gyros Products
Long Island City, NY 718-786-3399
Mediterranean Pita Bakery
Edmonton, AB 780-476-6666
Ozery's Pita Break
Toronto, ON. 888-556-5560
Pechters Baking
Harrison, NJ 800-525-5779
Pita King Bakery
Everett, WA. 425-258-4040
Pita Products
Farmington Hills, MI 800-600-7482
Sara Lee Corporation
Downers Grove, IL 630-598-8100
Soloman Baking Company
Denver, CO 303-371-2777
Stacy's Pita Chip Company
Randolph, MA 888-332-4477
Teeny Foods Corporation
Portland, OR 503-252-3006
Toufayan Bakeries
Ridgefield, NJ 201-941-2000
Toufayan Bakeries
Orlando, FL. 407-295-2257

Pumpernickel

Atlanta Bread Company International, Inc.
Smyrna, GA 800-398-3728
Colchester Bakery
Colchester, CT 860-537-2415
Dimpflmeier Bakery
Toronto, ON. 416-239-3031
New White Palace Bakery
Philadelphia, PA 215-324-9852
Orwasher's Bakery Handmade Bread
New York, NY 212-288-6569

Raisin

Clarmil Manufacturing Corporation
Hayward, CA 888-252-7645
Lewis Brothers Bakeries
Vincennes, IN 812-886-6533
Orwasher's Bakery Handmade Bread
New York, NY 212-288-6569

Rolls

Adrian's Bakery
Edmonton, AB 800-668-3533
Alois J. Binder Bakery
New Orleans, LA. 504-947-1111
Alpha Baking Company
Chicago, IL 773-261-6000
Amoroso's Baking Company
Philadelphia, PA 800-377-6557
April Hill
Grand Rapids, MI 616-245-0595
Atlanta Bread Company International, Inc.
Smyrna, GA 800-398-3728
Aunt Millies Bakeries
Fort Wayne, IN 260-424-8245
Automatic Rolls of New Jersey
Edison, NJ 732-549-2243
Awrey Bakeries
Livonia, MI 800-950-2253
B&A Bakery
Scarborough, ON 800-263-2878
Bake Rite Rolls
Bensalem, PA 215-638-2400
Baker
Milford, NJ 800-995-3989
Baker & Baker
Schaumburg, IL 800-593-5777
Baker & Baker, Inc.
Schaumburg, IL. 800-593-5777
Baker Boy Bake Shop
Dickinson, ND 800-437-2008
Baker's Dozen
Herkimer, NY 315-866-6770
Bakers of Paris
Brisbane, CA. 415-468-9100
Bakery Chef
Louisville, KY 800-594-0203
Baldinger Bakery
St Paul, MN. 651-224-5761
Basque French Bakery
Fresno, CA 559-268-7088
Bay Star Baking Company
Alameda, CA. 510-523-4202
Bellacicco Distribution Company
Brooklyn, NY 800-561-1705
Berlin Natural Bakery
Berlin, OH 800-686-5334
Best Harvest Bakeries
Kansas City, KS 800-811-5715
Better Bagel Bakery
Sarasota, FL 941-924-0393
Bimbo Bakeries
Montebello, CA 877-224-7374
Birkholm's Jr Danish Bakery
Solvang, CA 805-688-3872
Bonnie Baking Company
La Porte, IN. 219-362-4561
Borden's Bread
Regina, SK 306-525-3341
Brenner's Bakery of Arlington
Arlington, VA 703-534-0211
Bridgford Foods Corporation Superior Foods Division
Anaheim, CA 800-527-2105
Brightwood Baking Company
Cicero, IN 317-356-2449
Brother's Bakery
Southington, CT 860-628-5455
Brown's Bakery
Defiance, OH 419-784-3330
Bunge Foods
Tustin, CA 714-258-1223
Bunny Bread Company
Cape Girardeau, MO 573-332-7349
Buns Master Bakery
North Hamilton, ON 905-560-5011
Busken Bakery
Cincinnati, OH 513-871-2114
Butter Krust Baking Company
Sunbury, PA. 800-282-8093
California Smart Foods
San Francisco, CA 415-826-0449
Canada Bread Atlantic
St. John's, NL 709-722-5410

Canada Bread Company
Edmonton, AB 780-451-4663
Canada Bread Company
Langley, BC 800-465-5515
Cellone Bakery
Pittsburgh, PA 800-334-8438
Chicago Baking Company
Chicago, IL 773-536-7700
Clarmil Manufacturing Corporation
Hayward, CA 888-252-7645
Clydes Delicious Donuts
Addison, IL 630-628-6555
Cohen's Bakery
Buffalo, NY. 716-892-8149
Colombo Bakery
Sacramento, CA 916-648-1011
Country Club Bakery
Fairmont, WV 304-363-5690
Dakota Brands International
Jamestown, ND 800-844-5073
Dave's Bakery
Honesdale, PA 570-253-1660
Davis Bread & Desserts
Davis, CA 530-757-2700
Dee Lite Bakery
Honolulu, HI 808-847-5396
Dee's Cheesecake Factory/Dee's Foodservice
Albuquerque, NM 505-884-1777
Del Campo Baking Company
Wilmington, DE 302-656-6676
Di Paolo Baking Company
Rochester, NY 585-232-3510
Dimpflmeier Bakery
Toronto, ON. 416-239-3031
Dolly Madison Bakery
Columbus, IN 812-376-7432
East Balt Bakery
Denver, CO 303-377-5533
Eden Vineyards Winery
Alva, FL 239-728-9463
Egypt Star Bakery
Whitehall, PA 610-434-3762
El Segundo Bakery
El Segundo, CA 310-322-3422
Empress Foods
Winnipeg, NB 204-775-0344
Ener-G Foods
Seattle, WA 800-331-5222
Evans Bakery
Cozad, NE. 800-222-5641
F R LePage Bakeries
Auburn, ME 207-783-9161
Felix Roma & Sons
Endicott, NY 800-640-3336
Flowers Bakeries
Thomasville, GA 800-226-2429
Flowers Bakeries
Bluefield, WV 800-327-1630
Flowers Bakeries
Thomasville, GA. 800-568-3476
Flowers Bakery of Montgomery
Montgomery, AL 334-281-7030
Flowers Baking Company
Jamestown, NC 336-841-8840
Flowers Baking Company
Morristown, TN 423-586-2471
Flowers Baking Company
Pine Bluff, AR 870-534-0221
Flowers Baking Company
Jacksonville, FL 904-353-8293
Flowers Foods Bakeries
Thomasville, GA. 229-226-9110
Flowers Snack of Tennessee
Crossville, TN. 931-484-6101
Forty Second Street Bagel Cafe
Upland, CA 909-949-7334
Franklin Baking Company
Goldsboro, NC 800-248-7494
Fresh Start Bakeries
Brea, CA 714-256-8900
G H Leidenheimer Baking Company
New Orleans, LA 800-259-9099
Gai's Northwest Bakeries
Seattle, WA 206-322-0931
Galassos Baking Company
Mira Loma, CA. 951-360-1211
General Henry Biscuit Company
Du Quoin, IL 618-542-6222
George H Leidenheimer Baking
New Orleans, LA 800-259-9099
German Bakery at Village Corner
Stone Mountain, GA 866-476-6443

Giant Food
Lanham, MD 888-469-4426
Glazier Packing Company
Potsdam, NY 315-265-2500
Global Bakeries
Pacoima, CA 818-896-0525
Gold Medal Bakery
Fall River, MA 800-642-7568
Gold Medal Baking Company
Philadelphia, PA 215-627-4787
Golden Brown Bakery
South Haven, MI 269-637-3418
Gonnella Frozen Products
Schaumburg, IL 847-884-8829
Great Cakes
Los Angeles, CA 310-287-0228
Grebe's Bakery & Delicatessen
Milwaukee, WI 800-356-9377
Grote Bakery
Hamilton, OH 513-874-7436
Guttenplan's Frozen Dough
Middletown, NJ 888-422-4357
Hardin's Bakery
Tuscaloosa, AL 205-344-6690
Havi Food Services Worldwide
Oak Park, IL 708-445-1700
Hawaii Star Bakery
Honolulu, HI 808-841-3602
Heitzman Bakery
Louisville, KY 502-452-1891
Holsum Bakery
Phoenix, AZ 800-755-8167
Homestead Baking Company
Rumford, RI 800-556-7216
Huval Baking Company
Lafayette, LA 337-232-1611
IBC Holsum
Atlanta, GA 800-465-7861
International Baking Company
Vernon, CA 323-583-9841
International Equipment
Arecibo, PR. 787-879-3151
Interstate Bakeries Corporation
Jacksonville, FL 904-696-1400
Interstate Brands
Biddeford, ME 207-286-1200
Interstate Brands Corporation
Rocky Mount, NC 252-977-3400
Interstate Brands Corporation
Billings, MT 406-248-4800
Interstate Brands Corporation
Emporia, KS 620-342-6811
Interstate Brands Corporation
Kansas City, MO 800-777-8067
Interstate Brands Corporation
Kansas City, MO 816-502-4000
Interstate Brands Corporation
Knoxville, TN 865-947-6191
Interstate Brands Corporation/Butternut Bread Company
Boonville, MO 660-882-6107
Interstate Brands Corporation/Merita Bread Bakery
Orlando, FL 407-843-5110
Interstate Brands Corporation/Wonder Bread Bakery
St Louis, MO 314-385-1600
J&J Wall Baking Company
Sacramento, CA 916-381-1410
James Skinner Company
Omaha, NE 800-358-7428
Jenny Lee Bakery
Mc Kees Rocks, PA 412-331-8900
John J. Nissen Baking Company
Brewer, ME 207-989-7654
Koepplinger Bakery
Detroit, MI 248-967-2020
Kotarides Baking Company of Virginia
Norfolk, VA 757-461-1000
Kreamo Bakers
South Bend, IN 574-234-0188
Lake States Yeast
Rhinelander, WI 918-535-2676
Lanthier Bakery
Alexandria, ON 613-525-2435
Leidenheimer Baking Company
New Orleans, LA 504-525-1575
Lepage Bakeries
Auburn, ME 207-783-9161
Lewis Bakeries
London, ON 519-434-5252
Lewis Brothers Bakeries
Sikeston, MO 573-471-1650
Lewis Brothers Bakery
Evansville, IN 812-425-4642

Livermore Falls Baking Company
Livermore Falls, ME 207-897-3442
Lone Star Consolidated Foods
Dallas, TX 800-658-5637
Longo's Bakery
Hazleton, PA 570-454-5825
Lucerne Foods
Calgary, AB 403-287-4080
M.M. Bake Shop
Laurel, MS 601-428-5153
Maggiora Baking Company
Richmond, CA 510-235-0274
Marshall's Biscuit Company
Saraland, AL 800-368-9811
Mary Ann's Baking Company
Sacramento, CA 916-681-7444
Maui Bagel
Kahului, HI 808-270-7561
McGlynn Bakeries, LLC
Minneapolis, MN 763-574-2423
Meyer's Bakeries
Hope, AR 800-643-1542
Milano Baking Company
Joliet, IL 815-727-4872
Mom's Food Company
South El Monte, CA 800-969-6667
Morabito Baking Company
Norristown, PA 800-525-7747
Mrs Baird's Bakery
Fort Worth, TX 817-864-2500
Mrs. Baird's Bakeries
Abilene, TX 325-692-3141
Mrs. Baird's Bakeries
Fort Worth, TX 806-763-9304
Mrs. Kavanagh's English Muffins
Rumford, RI 800-556-7216
Mt View Bakery
Mountain View, HI 808-968-6353
Multi Marques
Montreal, QC 514-255-9492
Nevada Baking Company
Las Vegas, NV 702-384-8950
New Bakery Company of Ohio
Zanesville, OH 800-848-9845
New White Palace Bakery
Philadelphia, PA 215-324-9852
New York Bagel Boys
West Sacramento, CA 916-739-6540
New York Bakeries
Hialeah, FL 305-882-1355
New York Frozen Foods
Cleveland, OH 216-292-5655
Nickles Bakery of Ohio
Lima, OH 419-224-7080
Novelty Kosher Pastry
Spring Valley, NY 845-356-0428
Orlando Baking Company
Cleveland, OH 800-362-5504
Oroweat Baking Company
Montebello, CA 323-721-5161
Orwasher's Bakery Handmade Bread
New York, NY 212-288-6569
Oven Ready Products
Guelph, ON 519-767-2415
Pechters Baking
Harrison, NJ 800-525-5779
Pepperidge Farm
Lakeland, FL 863-688-4000
Pepperidge Farm
Downers Grove, IL 888-737-7374
Piantedosi Baking Company
Malden, MA 800-339-0080
Piemonte's Bakery
Rockford, IL 815-962-4833
Pittsfield Rye Bakery
Pittsfield, MA 413-443-9141
Portuguese Baking Company
Newark, NJ 973-589-8875
Powers Baking Company
Sunrise, FL 305-681-7000
Quinzani Bakery
Boston, MA 800-999-1062
Renaissance Baking Company
North Miami, FL 305-893-2144
Rentschler's Bakery
Kutztown, PA 610-683-3506
Rich Products Corporation
Winchester, VA 540-667-1955
Rich Products Corporation
Buffalo, NY 800-356-7094
Rogers Bakery
Plainville, CT 860-747-1686

Roma Bakeries
Rockford, IL 815-964-6737
Roma Bakery
San Jose, CA 408-294-0123
Rudi's Organic Bakery
Boulder, CO 877-293-0876
Ryals Bakery
Milledgeville, GA 478-452-0321
Saint Armands Baking Company
Bradenton, FL 941-753-7494
San Francisco French Bread
Oakland, CA 510-638-3252
Sara Lee Bakery   The Earth Grains Baking
Companies HQ
Neenah, WI 866-613-2784
Sara Lee Bakery Group
Birmingham, AL 205-322-8000
Sara Lee Bakery Group
Orangeburg, SC 800-476-3536
Sara Lee Bakery Group   Bakery
Denver, CO
Sara Lee Bakery Group   The EarthGrains - Bakery
Saint Paul, MN
Sara Lee Bakery Group   The EarthGrains - Bakery
Wichita, KS 316-943-3176
Sara Lee Bakery Group   The EarthGrains - Bakery
Louisville, KY 502-491-7499
Sara Lee Bakery Group   The EarthGrains - Bakery
Hattiesburg, MS 601-545-3781
Sara Lee Wholesome Bakery
Oak Lawn, IL 708-499-5711
Schmidt Baking Company
Martinsburg, WV 800-456-2253
Schott's Bakery
Houston, TX 713-869-5701
Schwebel Baking Company
Youngstown, OH 330-783-2860
Schwebel Baking Company
Youngstown, OH 800-860-2867
Shaw Baking Company
Thunder Bay, ON 807-345-7327
Simon Hubig Company
New Orleans, LA 504-945-2181
Stagnos Bakery
East Liberty, PA 412-441-3485
Stroehmann Bakeries
Horsham, PA 800-984-0989
Stroehmann Bakery
Horsham, PA 800-984-0989
Sunbeam
New Bedford, MA 800-458-8407
Superior Bakery
North Grosvenordale, CT 860-923-9555
Swatt Baking Company
Olean, NY 800-370-6656
Table Pride
Atlanta, GA 770-455-7464
Terranetti's Italian Bakery
Mechanicsburg, PA 717-697-5434
Tom Cat Bakery
Long Island City, NY 718-786-4224
Tomaro's Bakery
Clarksburg, WV 304-622-0691
Tripoli Bakery
Lawrence, MA 978-682-7754
Turano Pasty Shops
Berwyn, IL 708-788-5320
Unified Western Grocers
Los Angeles, CA 323-232-6124
United States Bakery
Portland, OR 503-731-5679
Upper Crust Baking Company
Pismo Beach, CA 800-676-1691
Valley Bakery
Rock Valley, IA 712-476-5386
Vallos Baking Company
Bethlehem, PA 610-866-1012
Vermont Bread Company
Brattleboro, VT 802-254-4600
Vie de France Bakery
Atlanta, GA 800-933-5486
Vie de France Yamazaki
Vienna, VA 800-393-8926
Vilotti & Marinelli Baking Company
Philadelphia, PA 215-627-5038
Wedemeyer's Bakery
S San Francisco, CA 650-873-1000
Wenner Bread Products
Bayport, NY 800-869-6262
Weston Bakeries
Calgary, AB 403-259-1500

Weston Bakeries
Sudbury, ON 705-673-4185
Weston Bakeries
Kingston, ON 800-267-0229
Weston Bakeries
Toronto, ON 800-590-6861
Wonder Bread
Tampa, FL 813-253-2813
Zeppys Bakery
Lawrence, MA 781-963-7022
Zoelsmanns Bakery & Deli
Pueblo, CO 719-543-0407

Cinnamon

Baker & Baker
Schaumburg, IL 800-593-5777
Baker & Baker, Inc.
Schaumburg, IL 800-593-5777
Cinnamon Bakery
Braintree, MA 800-886-2867
Clarmil Manufacturing Corporation
Hayward, CA 888-252-7645
Honeybake Farms
Kansas City, KS 913-371-7777
James Skinner Company
Omaha, NE 800-358-7428
La Francaise Bakery
Northlake, IL 800-654-7220
Lone Star Bakery
Round Rock, TX 512-255-3629
Mrs Baird's Bakery
Fort Worth, TX 817-864-2500
Pacific Ocean Produce
Santa Cruz, CA 831-423-2654
Sara Lee Corporation
Downers Grove, IL 630-598-8100
Schwan's Consumer Brands North America
Bloomington, MN 952-832-4300
Svenhard's Swedish Bakery
Oakland, CA 800-333-7836

Fresh

Adrian's Bakery
Edmonton, AB 800-668-3533
Best Harvest Bakeries
Kansas City, KS 800-811-5715
Borden's Bread
Regina, SK 306-525-3341
Brown's Bakery
Defiance, OH 419-784-3330
Canada Bread
North Bay, ON 800-461-6122
Canada Bread Atlantic
St. John's, NL 709-722-5410
Canada Bread Company
Edmonton, AB 780-451-4663
Canada Bread Company
Langley, BC 800-465-5515
East Balt Bakery
Denver, CO 303-377-5533
Empress Foods
Winnipeg, NB 204-775-0344
Felix Roma & Sons
Endicott, NY 800-640-3336
Flowers Bakeries
Thomasville, GA 800-568-3476
Flowers Baking Company
Jamestown, NC 336-841-8840
Flowers Foods Bakeries
Thomasville, GA 229-226-9110
Galassos Baking Company
Mira Loma, CA 951-360-1211
Homestead Baking Company
Rumford, RI 800-556-7216
Interstate Brands Corporation
Kansas City, MO 800-777-8067
Interstate Brands Corporation
Knoxville, TN 865-947-6191
Lanthier Bakery
Alexandria, ON 613-525-2435
Leidenheimer Baking Company
New Orleans, LA 504-525-1575
Lewis Bakeries
London, ON 519-434-5252
Lucerne Foods
Calgary, AB 403-287-4080
Mrs. Baird's Bakeries
Fort Worth, TX 806-763-9304
Multi Marques
Montreal, QC 514-255-9492

New York Frozen Foods
Cleveland, OH 216-292-5655
Ottenberg's Bakers
Washington, DC 800-334-7264
Pechters Baking
Harrison, NJ 800-525-5779
Penny Curtiss Baking Company
Syracuse, NY 315-454-3241
Pepperidge Farm
Lakeland, FL 863-688-4000
Quinzani Bakery
Boston, MA 800-999-1062
Roma Bakery
San Jose, CA 408-294-0123
Sara Lee Bakery Group
Phoenix, AZ 602-252-6881
Sara Lee Bakery Group   The EarthGrains - Bakery
Corpus Christi, TX 361-884-6311
Sara Lee Bakery Group   The EarthGrains - Bakery
Tulsa, OK 918-254-5468
Schmidt Baking Company
Martinsburg, WV 800-456-2253
Schwebel Baking Company
Youngstown, OH 800-860-2867
Shaw Baking Company
Thunder Bay, ON 807-345-7327
Terranetti's Italian Bakery
Mechanicsburg, PA 717-697-5434
Vie de France Yamazaki
Vienna, VA 800-393-8926
Weston Bakeries
Calgary, AB 403-259-1500
Weston Bakeries
Sudbury, ON 705-673-4185
Weston Bakeries
Kingston, ON 800-267-0229
Weston Bakeries
Toronto, ON 800-590-6861

Frozen

Awrey Bakeries
Livonia, MI 800-950-2253
Bake Crafters Food
Collegedale, TN 800-296-8935
Bridgford Foods Corporation Superior Foods Division
Anaheim, CA 800-527-2105
Brightwood Baking Company
Cicero, IN 317-356-2449
Del Campo Baking Company
Wilmington, DE 302-656-6676
Dwayne Keith Brooks Company
Orangevale, CA 916-988-1030
Dynamic Foods
Lubbock, TX 806-762-0780
Evans Bakery
Cozad, NE 800-222-5641
Flowers Foods Bakeries
Thomasville, GA 229-226-9110
Fresh Start Bakeries
Brea, CA 714-256-8900
Guttenplan's Frozen Dough
Middletown, NJ 888-422-4357
J&J Wall Baking Company
Sacramento, CA 916-381-1410
James Skinner Company
Omaha, NE 800-358-7428
Leidenheimer Baking Company
New Orleans, LA 504-525-1575
Lone Star Bakery
Round Rock, TX 512-255-3629
Pacific Ocean Produce
Santa Cruz, CA 831-423-2654
Penny Curtiss Baking Company
Syracuse, NY 315-454-3241
Rich Products Corporation
Winchester, VA 540-667-1955
Rich Products Corporation
Buffalo, NY 800-356-7094
Sara Lee Bakery Group   The EarthGrains - Bakery
Corpus Christi, TX 361-884-6311
Sara Lee Corporation
Downers Grove, IL 630-598-8100

Sweet

Awrey Bakeries
Livonia, MI 800-950-2253
Baker Boy Bake Shop
Dickinson, ND 800-437-2008
Brightwood Baking Company
Cicero, IN 317-356-2449

Bunny Bread Company
Cape Girardeau, MO 573-332-7349
Clydes Delicious Donuts
Addison, IL 630-628-6555
Dawn Food Products
Jackson, MI 800-248-1144
Flowers Baking
San Antonio, TX 210-661-2361
Flowers Snack of Tennessee
Crossville, TN 931-484-6101
International Baking Company
Vernon, CA 323-583-9841
Interstate Brands Corporation
Emporia, KS 620-342-6811
Saint Armands Baking Company
Bradenton, FL 941-753-7494
Sara Lee Bakery   The Earth Grains Baking
Companies HQ
Neenah, WI 866-613-2784
Sara Lee Wholesome Bakery
Oak Lawn, IL 708-499-5711
Zoelsmanns Bakery & Deli
Pueblo, CO 719-543-0407

Rye

Adrian's Bakery
Edmonton, AB 800-668-3533
Alfred & Sam Italian Bakery
Lancaster, PA 717-392-6311
Amoroso's Baking Company
Philadelphia, PA 800-377-6557
Atlanta Bread Company International, Inc.
Smyrna, GA 800-398-3728
Butternut Bread
Grand Rapids, MI 616-245-8292
Chmuras Bakery
Indian Orchard, MA 413-543-2521
Colchester Bakery
Colchester, CT 860-537-2415
Cybros
Waukesha, WI 800-876-2253
Dimpflmeier Bakery
Toronto, ON 416-239-3031
Hawaii Star Bakery
Honolulu, HI 808-841-3602
Highlandville Packing
Highlandville, MO 417-443-3365
Holsum Bakery
Fort Wayne, IN 260-456-2130
Interstate Bakeries Corporation
Cincinnati, OH 513-721-0212
Interstate Brands Corporation
Peoria, IL 309-674-9221
Interstate Brands Corporation/Butternut Bread Bakeries
Springfield, MO 417-869-0711
John J. Nissen Baking Company
Portland, ME 207-775-3460
Kreamo Bakers
South Bend, IN 574-234-0188
New White Palace Bakery
Philadelphia, PA 215-324-9852
Orlando Baking Company
Cleveland, OH 800-362-5504
Orwasher's Bakery Handmade Bread
New York, NY 212-288-6569
Patisserie Wawel
Montreal, QC 614-524-3348
Piemonte's Bakery
Rockford, IL 815-962-4833
Pyrenees French Bakery
Bakersfield, CA 888-898-7159
Quality Bakery
Invermere, BC 888-681-9977
Rudolph's Specialty Bakery
Toronto, ON 416-763-4315
Terranetti's Italian Bakery
Mechanicsburg, PA 717-697-5434
Tribeca Oven
Carlstadt, NJ 201-935-8800
Turano Pastry Shops
Bloomingdale, IL 630-529-6161
Waldensian Bakeries
Valdese, NC 828-874-2136

Scones

Baker & Baker
Schaumburg, IL 800-593-5777
Baker & Baker, Inc.
Schaumburg, IL 800-593-5777
Bette's Diner Products
Berkeley, CA 510-644-3230

Butter Baked Goods
Vancouver, BC 604-221-4333
Case Side Holdings Company
Kensington, PE 902-836-4214
Immaculate Consumption
Flat Rock, NC 888-826-6567
Main Street Gourmet
Cuyahoga Falls, OH 800-533-6246
Poppie's Dough
Chicago, IL 312-949-0404
Sticky Fingers Bakeries
San Francisco, CA 800-458-5826
Treasure Foods
West Valley, UT. 801-974-0911
Uptown Bakers
Washington, DC 202-546-6500

Short

Biscottea
Issaquah, WA 425-313-1993
Crookes & Hanson
Bedford, OH 800-999-0263
Golden West Specialty Foods
Brisbane, CA 800-584-4481
Merlino Italian Baking Company
Seattle, WA 800-207-2997
R.M. Palmer Company
Reading, PA 610-372-8971
Royal Court Cookie Company
North Hollywood, CA 800-730-2545
Sugar Kake Cookie
Tonawanda, NY 800-775-5180
Vermont Chocolatiers
Northfield, VT 877-485-4226
Walkers Shortbread
Hauppauge, NY 800-521-0141

Sourdough

Atlanta Bread Company International, Inc.
Smyrna, GA 800-398-3728
Berkshire Mountain Bakery
Housatonic, MA 866-274-6124
Hawaii Star Bakery
Honolulu, HI 808-841-3602
Mill City Sourdough Bakery
Saint Paul, MN 612-224-8871
Morabito Baking Company
Norristown, PA 800-525-7747
Orlando Baking Company
Cleveland, OH 800-362-5504
Orwasher's Bakery Handmade Bread
New York, NY 212-288-6569
Ottenberg's Bakers
Washington, DC 800-334-7264
San Luis Sourdough
San Luis Obispo, CA 800-266-7687

Toasted

National Food Corporation
Medley, FL 305-884-2020

Wheat

Atlanta Bread Company International, Inc.
Smyrna, GA 800-398-3728
Butter Krust Baking Company
Sunbury, PA. 800-282-8093
Butternut Bread
Grand Rapids, MI 616-245-8292
Entenmann's-Oroweat/BestFoods
S San Francisco, CA 650-875-3100
Highlandville Packing
Highlandville, MO 417-443-3365
Holsum Bakery
Fort Wayne, IN 260-456-2130
Interstate Bakeries Corporation
Cincinnati, OH 513-721-0212
Interstate Brands Corporation
Peoria, IL. 309-674-9221
Interstate Brands Corporation/Butternut Bread Bakeries
Springfield, MO 417-869-0711
John J. Nissen Baking Company
Portland, ME. 207-775-3460
Jones Bakeries
Winston Salem, NC. 800-849-5663
Jou Jou's Pita Bakery
Birmingham, AL 205-945-7482
Kreamo Bakers
South Bend, IN 574-234-0188

Lewis Brothers Bakery
Evansville, IN 812-425-4642
Orwasher's Bakery Handmade Bread
New York, NY 212-288-6569
Pechters Baking
Harrison, NJ 800-525-5779
Pyrenees French Bakery
Bakersfield, CA 888-898-7159
Shaw Baking Company
Thunder Bay, ON 807-345-7327
Tribeca Oven
Carlstadt, NJ 201-935-8800

White

Butternut Bread
Grand Rapids, MI 616-245-8292
Highlandville Packing
Highlandville, MO 417-443-3365
Holsum Bakery
Fort Wayne, IN 260-456-2130
Interstate Bakeries Corporation
Cincinnati, OH 513-721-0212
Interstate Brands Corporation
Peoria, IL. 309-674-9221
Interstate Brands Corporation/Butternut Bread Bakeries
Springfield, MO 417-869-0711
John J. Nissen Baking Company
Portland, ME 207-775-3460
Jones Bakeries
Winston Salem, NC 800-849-5663
Kreamo Bakers
South Bend, IN 574-234-0188
Lewis Brothers Bakery
Evansville, IN 812-425-4642
Mrs. Baird's Bakeries
Waco, TX 254-750-2500
Orwasher's Bakery Handmade Bread
New York, NY 212-288-6569
Pan-O-Gold Baking Company
St Cloud, MN 320-251-9361
Pechters Baking
Harrison, NJ 800-525-5779
Pyrenees French Bakery
Bakersfield, CA 888-898-7159
Schmidt Baking Company
Baltimore, MD 800-456-2253
Shaw Baking Company
Thunder Bay, ON 807-345-7327
Terranetti's Italian Bakery
Mechanicsburg, PA. 717-697-5434
Waldensian Bakeries
Valdese, NC. 828-874-2136

Cakes & Pastries

BakeMark Canada
Laval, QC 800-361-4998

Angel Food Cake

Kyger Bakery Products
Lafayette, IN 765-447-1252
Orlando's Pastries
Collingdale, PA 610-532-9300
Specialty Bakers
Marysville, PA 800-233-0778
Unique Bakery Company
Toronto, ON 416-751-8200

Apple Cobbler

Main Street Gourmet
Cuyahoga Falls, OH 800-533-6246

Babka

Aunt Heddy's Bakery
Brooklyn, NY 718-782-0582
Morse's Sauerkraut
Waldoboro, ME. 866-832-5569

Baklava

Athens Baking Company
Fresno, CA 559-485-3024
Fillo Factory
Dumont, NJ. 800-653-4556
Hommus Factory
Haverhill, MA 508-460-0212
Lawrences Delights
Doraville, GA 800-568-0021

Marika's Kitchen
Hancock, ME 800-694-9400
Sinbad Sweets
Fresno, CA 800-350-7933

Blintzes

Frozen

Echo Lake Farm Produce Company
Burlington, WI 262-763-9551
Old Fashioned Kitchen
Lakewood, NJ 732-364-4100
Old Fashioned Kitchen
Newport Beach, CA 800-833-4635

Brown Bettys

Euro Chocolate Fountain
San Diego, CA 800-423-9303

Cakes

Adams Foods
Dothan, AL 334-983-4233
Alati-Caserta Desserts
Montreal, QC 514-271-3013
Amendt Corporation
Monroe, MI. 734-242-2411
AMK Specialty Gourmet Products
De Pere, WI. 888-317-2649
Angel's Bakeries
Brooklyn, NY 718-389-1400
Athena's Silverland®Desserts
Forest Park, IL 800-737-3636
Atkins Elegant Desserts
Fishers, IN. 800-887-8808
Awrey Bakeries
Livonia, MI 800-950-2253
Bake Crafters Food
Collegedale, TN 800-296-8935
BakeMark Canada
Laval, QC 800-361-4998
Baker Boy Bake Shop
Dickinson, ND 800-437-2008
Baker's Choice
Birmingham, MI 248-827-7500
Bakery Chef
Chicago, IL 773-384-1900
Bakery Corp
Miami, FL 800-521-4345
Balboa Dessert Company
Santa Ana, CA 800-974-9699
Banquet Schuster Bakery
Pueblo, CO 719-544-1062
Bauducco Foods Inc
Miami, FL. 305-477-9270
BBU Bakeries
Denver, CO 303-691-6342
Beatrice Bakery Company
Beatrice, NE 800-228-4030
Benson's Bakery
Bogart, GA 800-888-6059
Berke-Blake Fancy Foods, Inc.
Longwood, FL 888-386-2253
Best Brands Corporation
Dallas, TX 800-969-2253
Big Fatty's Flaming Foods
Valley View, TX 888-248-6332
Birkholm's Jr Danish Bakery
Solvang, CA 805-688-3872
Bishop Baking Company
Cleveland, TN. 423-472-1561
Bittersweet Pastries
Norwood, NJ. 800-537-7791
Borden's Bread
Regina, SK 306-525-3341
Boulder Brownie Company
New Canaan, CT. 800-309-9995
Breadworks Bakery & Deli
Charlottesville, VA 434-296-4663
Brenner's Bakery of Arlington
Arlington, VA 703-534-0211
Brownie Baker
Fresno, CA 800-598-6501
Busken Bakery
Cincinnati, OH 513-871-2114
Cal Java International
Northridge, CA 800-207-2750
Calmar Bakery
Calmar, AB 780-985-3583
Caribbean Food Delights
Tappan, NY. 845-398-3000

Carole's Cheesecake Company
Toronto, ON 416-256-0000
Carolina Foods
Charlotte, NC 800-234-0441
Case Side Holdings Company
Kensington, PE 902-836-4214
Cateraid
Howell, MI 800-508-8217
Celebrity Cheesecake
Davie, FL 877-986-2253
Cemac Foods Corporation
Philadelphia, PA 800-724-0179
CGI Desserts
Sugar Land, TX 281-240-1200
Chalet Desserts
Union City, CA 510-783-8300
Chattanooga Bakery
Chattanooga, TN 800-251-3404
Cheesecake Etc. Desserts
Miami Springs, FL 305-887-0258
Cheesecake Factory
Calabasas Hills, CA 818-871-3000
Cheryl & Company
Westerville, OH 614-891-8822
Chocolate Chix
Waxahachie, TX 214-744-2442
Cinderella Cheese Cake Company
Riverside, NJ 856-461-6302
City Baker
Calgary, AB 403-263-8578
City Bakery
New York, NY 877-328-3687
Clarmil Manufacturing Corporation
Hayward, CA 888-252-7645
Claudio Pastry Company
Elmwood Park, IL 708-453-0598
Cloverhill Bakery-Vend Corporation
Chicago, IL 773-745-9800
Clydes Delicious Donuts
Addison, IL 630-628-6555
Collin Street Bakery
Corsicana, TX 800-504-1896
Columbus Gourmet
Columbus, GA 800-356-1858
Comanzo & Company Specialty Bakers
Smithfield, RI 888-352-5455
Crane's Pie Pantry Restaurant
Fennville, MI 269-561-2297
Creative Bakers
Brooklyn, NY 800-247-7864
Creme Glacee Gelati
St Leonard, QC 888-322-0116
Crestwood Bakery
Pleasant Prairie, WI 414-453-4790
Culinar Canada
Ste. Marie De Beauce, QC 418-387-5421
Dancing Deer Baking Company
Hyde Park, MA 888-699-3337
Danish Baking Company
Van Nuys, CA 800-777-4970
Danvers Bakery
Danvers, MA 978-774-9186
Dave's Bakery
Honesdale, PA 570-253-1660
Davis Bakery & Delicatessen
Cleveland, OH 216-464-5599
Dawn Food Products
Jackson, MI 800-248-1144
Dawn Food Products
York, PA 800-405-6282
Decadent Desserts
Calgary, AB 403-245-5535
Dee's Cheesecake Factory/Dee's Foodservice
Albuquerque, NM 505-884-1777
Deerfield Bakery
Buffalo Grove, IL 847-520-0068
Del's Pastry
Etobicoke, ON 416-231-4383
Delicious Brands
Des Plaines, IL 800-247-2848
Derst Baking Company
Savannah, GA 912-233-2235
Desserts by David Glass
Bloomfield, CT 860-769-5570
Di Camillo Bakery
Niagara Falls, NY 800-634-4363
Dinkel's Bakery
Chicago, IL 800-822-8817
Division Baking Corporation
New York, NY 800-934-9238
Dolly Madison Bakery
Columbus, IN 812-376-7432

Dough Works Company
Horicon, WI 800-383-8808
Dr. Cookie
Seattle, WA 206-389-9321
Dufflet Pastries
Toronto, ON 416-536-1330
Dunford Bakers
Fayetteville, AR 479-521-3000
Dutch Kitchen Bakery
Fitchburg, MA 978-345-1393
Dynamic Foods
Lubbock, TX 806-762-0780
Eddy's Bakery
Boise, ID 208-377-8100
Edelweiss Patisserie
Charlestown, MA 617-628-0225
Eilenberger Bakery
Palestine, TX 800-831-2544
El Peto Products
Cambridge, ON 800-387-4064
El Segundo Bakery
El Segundo, CA 310-322-3422
Elmwood Pastry
West Hartford, CT 860-233-2029
European Style Bakery
Beverly Hills, CA 818-368-6876
Evans Bakery
Cozad, NE 800-222-5641
Fantasia
Sedalia, MO 660-827-1172
Ferrara Bakery & Cafe
New York, NY 212-226-6150
Fireside Kitchen
Halifax, NS 902-454-7387
Fisher's Bakery
Ellicott City, MD 410-461-9275
Flowers Baking
San Antonio, TX 210-661-2361
Flowers Snack of Tennessee
Crossville, TN 931-484-6101
Food of Our Own Design
Maplewood, NJ 973-762-0985
Foxtail Foods
Fairfield, OH 800-323-6944
France Delices
Montreal, QC 514-259-2291
Future Bakery & Cafe
Etobicoke, ON 416-231-1491
Garden & Orchard Foods
Fargo, ND 800-370-3682
George Weston Bakeries
Riviera Beach, FL 561-848-9705
George Weston Bakeries
Northlake, IL 708-562-6311
George Weston Bakeries
Bay Shore, NY 800-356-3314
George Weston Bakeries
Albany, NY 800-531-4002
Georgia Fruit Cake Company
Claxton, GA 912-739-2683
Giant Food
Lanham, MD 888-469-4426
Gold Medal Baking Company
Philadelphia, PA 215-627-4787
Golden Brown Bakery
South Haven, MI 269-637-3418
Golden Glow Cookie Company
Bronx, NY 718-379-6223
Golden Walnut Specialty Foods
Zion, IL 800-843-3645
Gourmet Baker
Burnaby, BC 800-663-1972
Gourmet Ice Cream
Palmer, MA 413-283-3740
Gourmet Treats
Torrance, CA 800-444-9549
Grand Avenue Chocolates
Concord, CA 877-934-1800
Great Cakes
Los Angeles, CA 310-287-0228
Great San Saba River Pecan Company
San Saba, TX 800-621-9121
Great Western Products Company
Assumption, IL 217-226-3241
Great Western Products Company
Bremen, IN 217-546-4010
Great Western Products Company
Bismarck, ND 573-734-2210
Grebe's Bakery & Delicatessen
Milwaukee, WI 800-356-9377
Greyston Bakery
Yonkers, NY 800-289-2253

Grossinger's Home Bakery
New York, NY 800-479-6996
Grote Bakery
Hamilton, OH 513-874-7436
GWB Foods Corporation
Brooklyn, NY 718-686-9600
Haby's Alsatian Bakery
Castroville, TX 830-931-2118
Hahn's Old Fashioned Cake Company
Farmingdale, NY 631-249-3456
Harrington's of Vermont
Richmond, VT 802-434-7500
Hawaii Candy
Honolulu, HI 808-836-8955
Haydel's Bakery
Jefferson, LA 800-442-1342
Heidi's Gourmet Desserts
Tucker, GA 800-241-4166
Heinemann's Bakeries
Chicago, IL 312-239-5592
Heitzman Bakery
Louisville, KY 502-452-1891
Holton Food Products Company
La Grange, IL 708-352-5599
Hunt Country Foods
Middleburg, VA 540-364-2622
Interstate Brands
Biddeford, ME 207-286-1200
Interstate Brands
Alexandria, LA 318-448-6600
Interstate Brands Company/Drake Bakeries
Wayne, NJ 973-696-5010
Interstate Brands Corporation
Emporia, KS 620-342-6811
Interstate Brands Corporation/Dolly Madison Cakes
Columbus, GA 706-257-7000
Interstate Brands Corporation/Wonder Bread Bakery
St Louis, MO 314-385-1600
Italian Baking Company
Edmonton, AB 780-424-4830
Ivy Cottage Scone Mixes
South Pasadena, CA 626-441-2761
James Skinner Company
Omaha, NE 800-358-7428
Jay Hoyt of California
Petaluma, CA 707-762-1881
Joey's Fine Foods
Newark, NJ 973-482-1400
John J. Nissen Baking Company
Brewer, ME 207-989-7654
Jon Donaire Pastry
Santa Fe Springs, CA 877-366-2473
Just Desserts
San Francisco, CA 415-602-9245
K&S Bakery Products
Edmonton, AB 780-481-8155
Kemoo Farm Foods
Wahiawa, HI 808-622-8004
Kennedy Gourmet
Houston, TX 800-882-6253
King's Hawaiian
Torrance, CA 800-800-5461
Koehler Bakery Company
North Little Rock, AR 800-262-5900
Kyger Bakery Products
Lafayette, IN 765-447-1252
L&M Bakery
Lawrence, MA 978-687-7346
Laura's French Baking Company
Los Angeles, CA 888-353-5144
Lax & Mandel Bakery
Cleveland, OH 216-382-8877
Little Miss Muffin
Chicago, IL 800-456-9328
Lone Star Bakery
Round Rock, TX 512-255-3629
Love & Quiches Desserts
Freeport, NY 800-525-5251
M/S Smears
Pembroke, NC 910-521-1641
Mac's Donut Shop
Aliquippa, PA 724-375-6776
Maplehurst Bakeries
Carrollton, GA 800-482-4810
Maridee's Country Kitchen Cakes
Lindsay, OK 800-798-7730
Market Fare Foods
Saint Louis, MO 888-669-6420
Martino's Bakery
Burbank, CA 818-842-0715
Mary of Puddin Hill
Greenville, TX 800-545-8889

Matthews 1812 House
    Cornwall Bridge, CT 800-662-1812
Maurice French Pastries
    Metairie, LA 888-285-8261
McKee Foods Corporation
    Collegedale, TN 423-238-7111
Mehaffie Pies
    Dayton, OH .937-253-1163
Michel's Bakery
    Philadelphia, PA 215-725-4328
Mid-Atlantic Foods
    Easton, MD .800-922-4688
Millers Ice Cream
    Houston, TX .713-861-3138
Moravian Cookies Shop
    Winston Salem, NC 800-274-2994
Morningstar Foods
    Dallas, TX 225-273-2803
Mothers Kitchen Inc
    Burlington, NJ 609-387-7200
Mozzicato De Pasquale Bakery Pastry
    Hartford, CT .860-296-0426
Mrs. Fields' Famous Brands
    Salt Lake City, UT 800-343-5377
Mrs. Smith's Bakeries
    Spartanburg, SC 864-503-9588
Multi Marques
    Montreal, QC 514-255-9492
My Daddy's Cheesecake
    Cape Girardeau, MO 800-735-6765
My Grandma's Coffee Cak e of New England
    Hyde Park, MA 800-847-2636
Naturally Delicious
    Oakland Park, FL 954-485-6730
New Glarus Bakery
    New Glarus, WI 866-805-5536
New York Bakeries
    Hialeah, FL .305-882-1355
Nickles Bakery of Ohio
    Columbus, OH 800-335-9775
Northside Bakery
    Richmond, VA 804-329-6851
O&H Danish Bakery
    Racine, WI 262-637-8895
Ohta Wafer Factory
    Honolulu, HI .808-949-2775
Old Country Bakery
    North Hollywood, CA 818-838-2302
Original Ya-hoo! Baking Company
    Sherman, TX 800-575-9373
Orlando's Pastries
    Collingdale, PA 610-532-9300
Osman's Pies
    Stow, OH 330-655-2919
Ouma's Bakery
    Poultney, VT 802-287-9310
Our Lady of Guadalupe Abbey
    Lafayette, OR 503-852-7148
Pacific Ocean Produce
    Santa Cruz, CA 831-423-2654
Parco Foods
    Blue Island, IL 708-371-9200
Pastry Chef
    Pawtucket, RI 800-639-8606
Patti's Plum Puddings
    Lawndale, CA 310-376-1463
Pearl River Pastry & Chocolates
    Pearl River, NY 800-632-2639
Pellman Foods
    New Holland, PA 717-354-8070
Pepperidge Farm
    Downingtown, PA 610-269-2500
Pie Piper Products
    Bensenville, IL 800-621-8183
Pillsbury
    McMinnville, OR 800-325-5439
Plaza Sweets
    Mamaroneck, NY 914-698-0233
Plehn's Bakery
    St Matthews, KY 502-896-4438
Plumlife Company
    Newbury, MA 978-462-8458
Pocono Cheesecake Factory
    Swiftwater, PA 570-839-6844
Quaker
    Barrington, IL 800-333-8027
Quality Bakery/MM Deli
    Port Colborne, ON 905-834-4911
Quiche & Tell
    Flushing, NY 718-381-7562
RCB Baking
    Fargo, ND 701-282-2300

Real Food Marketing
    Kansas City, MO 816-221-4100
Red Mill Farms
    Brooklyn, NY 800-344-2253
Rentschler's Bakery
    Kutztown, PA 610-683-3506
Rich Ice Cream Company
    West Palm Beach, FL 561-833-7585
Rising Dough Bakery
    Sacramento, CA 916-387-9700
Rolling Pin Bakery
    Bow Island, AB 403-545-2434
Rowena's
    Norfolk, VA .800-627-8699
Royal Caribbean Bakery
    Mt Vernon, NY 888-818-0971
Royal Home Bakery
    Newmarket, ON 905-715-7044
Rudolph's Specialty Bakery
    Toronto, ON .416-763-4315
Ruth Ashbrook Bakery
    Portland, OR 503-240-7437
Ryals Bakery
    Milledgeville, GA 478-452-0321
Ryke's Bakery
    Muskegon, MI 231-557-8011
Sacramento Baking Company
    Sacramento, CA 916-361-2000
Samadi Sweets Cafe
    Falls Church, VA 703- 57-8 06
Santa Fe Bite-Size Bakery
    Moriarty, NM 800-342-1119
Sara Lee Bakery
    Salt Lake City, UT 801-487-4677
Sara Lee Bakery Group
    Phoenix, AZ .602-252-6881
Sara Lee Bakery Group
    Rapid City, SD 605-343-3512
Sara Lee Bakery Group   The EarthGrains - Bakery
    Saint Paul, MN
Sara Lee Bakery Group   The EarthGrains - Bakery
    Beaumont, TX 409-842-9150
Sara Lee Bakery Group   The EarthGrains - Bakery
    Oakland, CA .510-635-4343
Sara Lee Bakery Group   The EarthGrains - Bakery
    Fresno, CA 559-495-3571
Sara Lee Bakery Group   The EarthGrains - Bakery
    Rome, GA 706-295-4499
Sara Lee Bakery Group   The EarthGrains - Bakery
    St Louis, MO 800-323-7117
Sara Lee Corporation
    Downers Grove, IL 630-598-8100
Sarabeth's Kitchen
    Bronx, NY 718-589-2900
Saxby Foods
    Edmonton, AB 780-440-4177
Schwan's Consumer Brands North America
    Bloomington, MN 952-832-4300
Schwans Food Company
    Norcross, GA 800-241-0559
Scialo Brothers
    Providence, RI 877-421-0986
Scot Paris Fine Desserts
    New York, NY 212-807-1802
Seckinger-Lee Company
    Savannah, GA 800-291-2973
Sessions Company
    Enterprise, AL 334-393-0200
Silver Tray Cookies
    Fort Lauderdale, FL 305-883-0800
Smoak's Bakery & Catering Service
    Augusta, GA 706-738-1792
Solvang Bakery
    Solvang, CA .800-377-4253
Southeast Dairy Processors
    Tampa, FL 813-621-3233
Specialty Bakers
    Marysville, PA 800-233-0778
Specialty Foods Corporation
    Deerfield, IL .847-405-5300
Spilke's Baking Company
    Brooklyn, NY 718-384-2150
Standard Bakery
    Kealakekua, HI 808-322-3688
Sterling Foods
    San Antonio, TX 210-490-1669
Steve's Mom
    Bronx, NY 800-362-4545
Stroehmann Bakeries
    Norristown, PA 800-984-0989
Strossner's Bakery
    Greenville, SC 864-233-3996

Sunbeam Baking Company
    El Paso, TX .800-328-6111
Superior Cake Products
    Southbridge, MA 508-764-3276
Swagger Foods Corporation
    Vernon Hills, IL 847-913-1200
Sweet Endings
    West Palm Beach, FL 888-635-1177
Sweet Gallery Exclusive Pastry
    Toronto, ON .416-232-1539
Tasty Baking Company
    Philadelphia, PA 800-338-2789
Tastykake
    Philadelphia, PA 215-221-8500
Tate's Bake Shop
    Southampton, NY 631-283-9830
The Cheesecake Factory
    Calabasas Hills, CA 818-871-3000
Thymly Products
    Colora, MD .410-658-4820
Two Chicks and a Ladle
    New York, NY 212-251-0025
Uncle Ralph's Cookie Company
    Frederick, MD 800-422-0626
Unique Bakery Company
    Toronto, ON .416-751-8200
Uniquely Together
    Chicago, IL .800-613-7276
Uptown Bakers
    Washington, DC 202-546-6500
Vickey's Vittles
    North Hills, CA 818-841-1944
Vie de France Bakery
    Bensenville, IL 630-595-9521
Vie de France Yamazaki
    Denver, CO .303-371-6280
Vigneri Confections
    Rochester, NY 585-254-6160
Waldensian Bakeries
    Valdese, NC .828-874-2136
Warwick Ice Cream Company
    Warwick, RI .401-821-8403
Wedding Cake Studio
    Williamsfield, OH 440-667-1765
Weiss Homemade Kosher Bakery
    Brooklyn, NY 800-498-3477
Wenger's Bakery
    Reading, PA .610-372-6545
White Oak Farms
    Sandown, NH 800-473-8869
Williamsburg Chocolatier
    Williamsburg, VA 804-966-9000
Winder Dairy
    West Valley, UT 800-946-3371
Wonder Bread
    Provo, UT 801-373-8192
Wonder/Hostess
    Jamaica, NY 718-526-3184
World of Chantilly
    Brooklyn, NY 718-859-1110
Wow! Factor Desserts
    Sherwood Park, AB 800-604-2253
Yost's Dutch Maid Bakery
    Johnstown, PA 814-266-3191
Young's Bakery
    Uniontown, PA 724-437-6361
Zeppys Bakery
    Lawrence, MA 781-963-7022
Zoelsmanns Bakery & Deli
    Pueblo, CO .719-543-0407

Cannoli

Artuso Pastry Foods
    Mt Vernon, NY 914-663-8806
Artuso Pastry Shop
    Bronx, NY 718-367-2515

Carrot Cake

Clarmil Manufacturing Corporation
    Hayward, CA 888-252-7645
Dee's Cheesecake Factory/Dee's Foodservice
    Albuquerque, NM 505-884-1777
Eli's Cheesecake Company
    Chicago, IL .800-999-8300
Main Street Gourmet
    Cuyahoga Falls, OH 800-533-6246

Cheese Cake

Atkins Elegant Desserts
    Fishers, IN .800-887-8808

Balboa Dessert Company
Santa Ana, CA 800-974-9699
Berke-Blake Fancy Foods, Inc.
Longwood, FL 888-386-2253
Brownie Baker
Fresno, CA 800-598-6501
Carberry's Home Made Ice Cream
Merritt Island, FL 321-452-8900
Carole's Cheesecake Company
Toronto, ON 416-256-0000
Cateraid
Howell, MI 800-508-8217
Celebrity Cheesecake
Davie, FL 877-986-2253
Cemac Foods Corporation
Philadelphia, PA 800-724-0179
CGI Desserts
Sugar Land, TX. 281-240-1200
Chatila's Bakery
Salem, NH. 603-898-5459
Cheesecake Aly
Glen Rock, NJ 800-555-8862
Cheesecake Etc. Desserts
Miami Springs, FL 305-887-0258
Cheesecake Momma
Ukiah, CA 707-462-2253
Cinderella Cheese Cake Company
Riverside, NJ. 856-461-6302
Creative Bakers
Brooklyn, NY 800-247-7864
Dee's Cheesecake Factory/Dee's Foodservice
Albuquerque, NM 505-884-1777
Desserts by David Glass
Bloomfield, CT 860-769-5570
Division Baking Corporation
New York, NY 800-934-9238
Eli's Cheesecake Company
Chicago, IL 800-999-8300
Future Bakery & Cafe
Etobicoke, ON 416-231-1491
Golden Walnut Specialty Foods
Zion, IL 800-843-3645
Gourmet Baker
Burnaby, BC 800-663-1972
Heidi's Gourmet Desserts
Tucker, GA 800-241-4166
Hoff's Bakery
Medford, MA 888-871-5100
Holey Moses Cheesecake
Westhampton Beach, NY 800-225-2253
Jay Hoyt of California
Petaluma, CA 707-762-1881
Jon Donaire Pastry
Santa Fe Springs, CA 877-366-2473
Jubilations
Columbus, MS 662-328-9210
Little Angel Foods
Daytona Beach, FL. 904-257-3040
Love & Quiches Desserts
Freeport, NY 800-525-5251
Mazelle's Cheesecakes Concoctions Creations
Dallas, TX. 903-737-4315
Mehaffie Pies
Dayton, OH. 937-253-1163
Morningstar Foods
Dallas, TX. 225-273-2803
New England Country Bakers
Watertown, CT 800-225-3779
Pie Piper Products
Bensenville, IL 800-621-8183
Pocono Cheesecake Factory
Swiftwater, PA 570-839-6844
Sam's Homemade Cheesecake
San Diego, CA 858-578-3460
Sara Lee Corporation
Downers Grove, IL 630-598-8100
Schwans Food Company
Norcross, GA 800-241-0559
Scot Paris Fine Desserts
New York, NY 212-807-1802
Scotty Wotty's Creamy Cheescake
Hillsborough, NJ. 908-281-9720
Steve's Mom
Bronx, NY 800-362-4545
The Cheesecake Factory
Calabasas Hills, CA 818-871-3000
Two Chicks and a Ladle
New York, NY 212-251-0025
Wow! Factor Desserts
Sherwood Park, AB 800-604-2253

Flavored

Cemac Foods Corporation
Philadelphia, PA 800-724-0179
Jon Donaire Pastry
Santa Fe Springs, CA 877-366-2473
Junior's Cheesecake
Maspeth, NY 800-458-6467

Frozen

Balboa Dessert Company
Santa Ana, CA 800-974-9699
Cateraid
Howell, MI 800-508-8217
Cemac Foods Corporation
Philadelphia, PA 800-724-0179
CGI Desserts
Sugar Land, TX. 281-240-1200
Chalet Desserts
Union City, CA 510-783-8300
Cinderella Cheese Cake Company
Riverside, NJ. 856-461-6302
Creative Bakers
Brooklyn, NY 800-247-7864
Dee's Cheesecake Factory/Dee's Foodservice
Albuquerque, NM 505-884-1777
Desserts of Distinction
Milwaukie, OR 503-654-8370
Division Baking Corporation
New York, NY 800-934-9238
Galaxy Desserts
Richmond, CA 800-225-3523
Heidi's Gourmet Desserts
Tucker, GA 800-241-4166
Jay Hoyt of California
Petaluma, CA 707-762-1881
Lawler Foods
Humble, TX 281-446-0059
Love & Quiches Desserts
Freeport, NY 800-525-5251
Mehaffie Pies
Dayton, OH. 937-253-1163
Morningstar Foods
Dallas, TX. 225-273-2803
Sam's Homemade Cheesecake
San Diego, CA 858-578-3460
Sara Lee Corporation
Downers Grove, IL 630-598-8100
Schwans Food Company
Norcross, GA 800-241-0559

NewYork Style

Cannoli Factory
Wyandanch, NY 631-643-2700

Non-Fat

Cemac Foods Corporation
Philadelphia, PA 800-724-0179
Two Chicks and a Ladle
New York, NY 212-251-0025

Churros

J&J Snack Foods Corporation
Pennsauken, NJ. 856-665-9533

Coffee Cake

Awrey Bakeries
Livonia, MI 800-950-2253
Clydes Delicious Donuts
Addison, IL 630-628-6555
Dough Delight
Concord, ON 800-465-5515
Dough Works Company
Horicon, WI 800-383-8808
James Skinner Company
Omaha, NE 800-358-7428
Jenny Lee Bakery
Mc Kees Rocks, PA 412-331-8900
L&M Bakery
Lawrence, MA 978-687-7346
Main Street Gourmet
Cuyahoga Falls, OH 800-533-6246

Cream Puff

Creme Curls Bakery
Hudsonville, MI 800-466-1219
Hafner
Stone Mountain, GA 888-725-4605

Jenny Lee Bakery
Mc Kees Rocks, PA 412-331-8900
Rich Ice Cream Company
West Palm Beach, FL 561-833-7585

Crumpets

Gourmet Baker
Burnaby, BC 800-663-1972
Norths Bakery California Inc
North Hollywood, CA 818-761-2892
Sara Lee Corporation
Downers Grove, IL 630-598-8100
Wolferman's
Medford, OR 913-888-4499

Cupcakes

Butter Baked Goods
Vancouver, BC 604-221-4333
Interstate Bakeries Corporation
Los Angeles, CA 323-750-7204
Jenny Lee Bakery
Mc Kees Rocks, PA 412-331-8900
Maplehurst Bakeries
Carrollton, GA 800-482-4810
Mrs Baird's Bakery
Fort Worth, TX 817-864-2500
Schwan's Consumer Brands North America
Bloomington, MN 952-832-4300
Yost's Dutch Maid Bakery
Johnstown, PA. 814-266-3191

Danish

Atlanta Bread Company International, Inc.
Smyrna, GA 800-398-3728
Awrey Bakeries
Livonia, MI 800-950-2253
BakeMark Canada
Laval, QC 800-361-4998
Baker & Baker
Schaumburg, IL 800-593-5777
Baker & Baker, Inc.
Schaumburg, IL 800-593-5777
Baker's Choice
Birmingham, MI 248-827-7500
Brownie Baker
Fresno, CA 800-598-6501
Bunny Bread Company
Cape Girardeau, MO. 573-332-7349
Clydes Delicious Donuts
Addison, IL 630-628-6555
Del's Pastry
Etobicoke, ON 416-231-4383
Dimitria Delights
North Grafton, MA 800-763-1113
El Segundo Bakery
El Segundo, CA 310-322-3422
Fiera Foods
North York, ON. 416-744-1010
France Croissant
New York, NY 212-888-1210
George Weston Bakeries
Northlake, IL 708-562-6311
George Weston Bakeries
Albany, NY 800-531-4002
Gourmet Baker
Burnaby, BC 800-663-1972
Gourmet Croissant
Brooklyn, NY 718-499-4911
Heitzman Bakery
Louisville, KY 502-452-1891
James Skinner Company
Omaha, NE 800-358-7428
Jenny Lee Bakery
Mc Kees Rocks, PA 412-331-8900
Joey's Fine Foods
Newark, NJ 973-482-1400
La Francaise Bakery
Northlake, IL. 800-654-7220
Laura's French Baking Company
Los Angeles, CA. 888-353-5144
Lusitania Bakery
Blandon, PA 610-926-1311
Mary Ann's Baking Company
Sacramento, CA 916-681-7444
Michel's Bakery
Philadelphia, PA 215-725-4328
Norths Bakery California Inc
North Hollywood, CA 818-761-2892
Roma Bakeries
Rockford, IL 815-964-6737

Sara Lee Corporation
   Downers Grove, IL 630-598-8100
Schwan's Consumer Brands North America
   Bloomington, MN. 952-832-4300
Shaw Baking Company
   Thunder Bay, ON 807-345-7327
Strossner's Bakery
   Greenville, SC. 864-233-3996
Svenhard's Swedish Bakery
   Oakland, CA 800-333-7836
Turano Pastry Shops
   Bloomingdale, IL 630-529-6161
Unique Bakery Company
   Toronto, ON 416-751-8200
Uptown Bakers
   Washington, DC 202-546-6500
Vie de France Bakery
   Bensenville, IL 630-595-9521
Vie de France Yamazaki
   Vienna, VA 800-446-4404
Well-Bred Loaf
   Valley Cottage, NY 800-444-5623

Dessert Tarts

Solvang Bakery
   Solvang, CA 800-377-4253

Doughnuts

All Round Foods
   Westbury, NY 516-338-1888
Artel
   Boisbriand, QC 450-433-1322
Awrey Bakeries
   Livonia, MI 800-950-2253
Bake Crafters Food
   Collegedale, TN 800-296-8935
Baker Boy Bake Shop
   Dickinson, ND 800-437-2008
Baker's Dozen
   Herkimer, NY 315-866-6770
BBU Bakeries
   Denver, CO 303-691-6342
Brenner's Bakery of Arlington
   Arlington, VA 703-534-0211
Brightwood Baking Company
   Cicero, IN .317-356-2449
Bunny Bread Company
   Cape Girardeau, MO 573-332-7349
Busken Bakery
   Cincinnati, OH 513-871-2114
Butter Krust Baking Company
   Sunbury, PA. 800-282-8093
Carolina Foods
   Charlotte, NC 800-234-0441
Case Side Holdings Company
   Kensington, PE 902-836-4214
Chatila's Bakery
   Salem, NH .603-898-5459
Cloverhill Bakery-Vend Corporation
   Chicago, IL 773-745-9800
Clydes Delicious Donuts
   Addison, IL 630-628-6555
Davis Bakery & Delicatessen
   Cleveland, OH 216-464-5599
Dawn Food Products
   Jackson, MI 800-248-1144
Dunford Bakers
   Fayetteville, AR 479-521-3000
Dunford Bakers Company
   West Jordan, UT 801-304-0400
Dutch Girl Donuts
   Detroit, MI 313-368-3020
Earthgrains Company
   St. Louis, MO 314-259-7000
Elmwood Pastry
   West Hartford, CT. 860-233-2029
Flowers Baking
   San Antonio, TX 210-661-2361
Flowers Snack of Tennessee
   Crossville, TN. 931-484-6101
George Weston Bakeries
   Hollywood, FL 800-356-3314
Giant Food
   Lanham, MD. 888-469-4426
Glazier Packing Company
   Potsdam, NY. 315-265-2500
Granny's Kitchens
   Frankfort, NY 315-735-5000
Grebe's Bakery & Delicatessen
   Milwaukee, WI 800-356-9377

Haas Baking Company
   St Louis, MO. 800-325-3171
Harting's Bakery
   Bowmansville, PA. 717-445-5644
Heitzman Bakery
   Louisville, KY 502-452-1891
Interstate Brands Corporation
   Emporia, KS 620-342-6811
Interstate Brands Corporation
   Charlotte, NC 704-398-2051
Interstate Brands Corporation/Dolly Madison Cakes
   Columbus, GA 706-257-7000
Interstate Brands Corporation/Merita Bread Bakery
   Orlando, FL. 407-843-5110
Interstate Brands Corporation/Wonder/Hostess
   Philadelphia, PA 215-969-1200
Jenny Lee Bakery
   Mc Kees Rocks, PA 412-331-8900
Jubelt Variety Bakeries
   Mount Olive, IL 217-999-7312
Kerrobert Bakery
   Kerrobert, SK 306-834-2461
Koffee Kup Bakery
   Burlington, VT 802-863-2696
Kristy Kremarie
   Huntsville, AL 256-536-7475
LePage Bakeries
   Auburn, ME 207-783-9161
Lepage Bakeries
   Auburn, ME 207-783-9161
Lone Star Consolidated Foods
   Dallas, TX. 800-658-5637
Ludwick's Frozen Donuts
   Grand Rapids, MI 800-366-8816
Mac's Donut Shop
   Aliquippa, PA 724-375-6776
Maple Donuts
   York, PA 800-627-5348
Maui Bagel
   Kahului, HI 808-270-7561
Mrs. Willman's Baking
   Burnaby, BC 403-250-9105
Mt View Bakery
   Mountain View, HI 808-968-6353
Nutrilicious Natural Bakery
   Countryside, IL 800-835-8097
Orlando's Pastries
   Collingdale, PA. 610-532-9300
Penny Curtiss Baking Company
   Syracuse, NY 315-454-3241
Plehn's Bakery
   St Matthews, KY 502-896-4438
Quality Naturally! Foods
   City of Industry, CA 888-498-6986
Rich Products Corporation
   Hilliard, OH. 614-771-1117
Rolling Pin Bakery
   Bow Island, AB. 403-545-2434
Ruth Ashbrook Bakery
   Portland, OR. 503-240-7437
Sara Lee Corporation
   Downers Grove, IL 630-598-8100
Sara Lee Wholesome Bakery
   Oak Lawn, IL 708-499-5711
Schwan's Consumer Brands North America
   Bloomington, MN. 952-832-4300
Shaw Baking Company
   Thunder Bay, ON 807-345-7327
Steve's Doughnut Shop
   Somerset, MA. 508-672-0865
Stroehmann Bakeries
   Horsham, PA. 800-984-0989
Tastykake
   Philadelphia, PA 215-221-8500
United States Bakery
   Portland, OR 503-731-5679
Vallos Baking Company
   Bethlehem, PA 610-866-1012

Filled

Ocean Spray Cranberries
   Kenosha, WI 262-694-0621

Frozen

All Round Foods
   Westbury, NY 516-338-1888
Artel
   Boisbriand, QC 450-433-1322
Awrey Bakeries
   Livonia, MI 800-950-2253

Bake Crafters Food
   Collegedale, TN 800-296-8935
Bridor
   Boucherville, QC 450-641-1265
Brightwood Baking Company
   Cicero, IN .317-356-2449
Carolina Foods
   Charlotte, NC 800-234-0441
Clydes Delicious Donuts
   Addison, IL 630-628-6555
Glazier Packing Company
   Potsdam, NY 315-265-2500
Granny's Kitchens
   Frankfort, NY 315-735-5000
Haas Baking Company
   St Louis, MO 800-325-3171
Lone Star Consolidated Foods
   Dallas, TX. 800-658-5637
Ludwick's Frozen Donuts
   Grand Rapids, MI 800-366-8816
Mel-O-Cream Donuts International
   Springfield, IL. 217-483-7272
Pillsbury
   McMinnville, OR 800-325-5439
Rich Products Corporation
   Hilliard, OH. 614-771-1117
Sara Lee Corporation
   Downers Grove, IL 630-598-8100

Dumplings

Aristocrat International Corporation
   Secaucus, NJ 201-866-1900
Atkinson Milling Company
   Selma, NC 800-948-5707
Chang Food Company
   Garden Grove, CA 714-265-9990
Chateau Food Products
   Cicero, IL .708-863-4207
Chinese Spaghetti Factory
   Boston, MA. 617-445-7714
Community Orchard
   Fort Dodge, IA 515-573-8212
Dimitria Delights
   North Grafton, MA 800-763-1113
Harvest Food Products Company
   Concord, CA 925-676-8208
Harvest Time Foods
   Ayden, NC. 252-746-6675
Jewel Date Company
   Thermal, CA 760-399-4474
La Tang Cuisine Manufacturing
   Houston, TX 713-780-4876
Mandoo
   Englewood, NJ 201-568-9337
Marcetti Frozen Pasta
   Altoona, IA 515-967-4254
Mayfield Farms
   Brampton, ON. 905-846-0506
Millie's Pierogi
   Chicopee Falls, MA 800-743-7641
Naleway Foods
   Winnipeg, MB. 800-665-7448
On-Cor Foods Products
   Northbrook, IL 847-205-1040
Pierre Foods
   Cincinnati, OH 513-874-8741
Prime Food Processing Corporation
   Brooklyn, NY 888-639-2323
Shine Food
   Torrance, CA. 310-533-6010
Sweet Sue Kitchens
   Athens, AL 256-216-0500
Twin Marquis
   Brooklyn, NY 800-367-6868
Wei-Chuan
   Bell Gardens, CA 562-927-6681

Eclairs

Creme Curls Bakery
   Hudsonville, MI 800-466-1219

Jenny Lee Bakery
Mc Kees Rocks, PA 412-331-8900
Rich Ice Cream Company
West Palm Beach, FL 561-833-7585

Frozen Cakes

Alati-Caserta Desserts
Montreal, QC 514-271-3013
Awrey Bakeries
Livonia, MI 800-950-2253
Benson's Bakery
Bogart, GA 800-888-6059
BODEGA Chocolates
Costa Mesa, CA 888-326-3342
Carolina Foods
Charlotte, NC 800-234-0441
Carousel Cakes
Nanuet, NY 800-659-2253
Cemac Foods Corporation
Philadelphia, PA 800-724-0179
CGI Desserts
Sugar Land, TX 281-240-1200
Chalet Desserts
Union City, CA 510-783-8300
Cinderella Cheese Cake Company
Riverside, NJ 856-461-6302
Creative Bakers
Brooklyn, NY 800-247-7864
Creme Glacee Gelati
St Leonard, QC 888-322-0116
Danish Baking Company
Van Nuys, CA 800-777-4970
Daphne Baking Company
Kent, CT 860-927-1818
Division Baking Corporation
New York, NY 800-934-9238
Dynamic Foods
Lubbock, TX 806-762-0780
Evans Bakery
Cozad, NE 800-222-5641
Fantasia
Sedalia, MO 660-827-1172
French Patisserie
Pacifica, CA 800-300-2253
Grossinger's Home Bakery
New York, NY 800-479-6996
Heidi's Gourmet Desserts
Tucker, GA 800-241-4166
James Skinner Company
Omaha, NE 800-358-7428
Jay Hoyt of California
Petaluma, CA 707-762-1881
Koehler Bakery Company
North Little Rock, AR 800-262-5900
Kyger Bakery Products
Lafayette, IN 765-447-1252
Little Miss Muffin
Chicago, IL 800-456-9328
Lone Star Bakery
Round Rock, TX 512-255-3629
Love & Quiches Desserts
Freeport, NY 800-525-5251
Main Street Gourmet
Cuyahoga Falls, OH 800-533-6246
Mehaffie Pies
Dayton, OH 937-253-1163
Morningstar Foods
Dallas, TX 225-273-2803
Mothers Kitchen Inc
Burlington, NJ 609-387-7200
My Grandma's Coffee Cak e of New England
Hyde Park, MA 800-847-2636
Pacific Ocean Produce
Santa Cruz, CA 831-423-2654
Parco Foods
Blue Island, IL 708-371-9200
Pastry Chef
Pawtucket, RI 800-639-8606
Pellman Foods
New Holland, PA 717-354-8070
Pepperidge Farm
Downingtown, PA 610-269-2500
Pillsbury
McMinnville, OR 800-325-5439
Real Food Marketing
Kansas City, MO 816-221-4100
Rowena's
Norfolk, VA 800-627-8699
Sara Lee Bakery Group   The EarthGrains - Bakery
Beaumont, TX 409-842-9150

Sara Lee Corporation
Downers Grove, IL 630-598-8100
Saxby Foods
Edmonton, AB 780-440-4177
Schwans Food Company
Norcross, GA 800-241-0559
Uncle Ralph's Cookie Company
Frederick, MD 800-422-0626
Warwick Ice Cream Company
Warwick, RI 401-821-8403
Winder Dairy
West Valley, UT 800-946-3371

Fruit Cake

Beatrice Bakery Company
Beatrice, NE 800-228-4030
Caribbean Food Delights
Tappan, NY 845-398-3000
Claxton Bakery
Claxton, GA 800-841-4211
Fireside Kitchen
Halifax, NS 902-454-7387
Multi Marques
Montreal, QC 514-255-9492
Neuman Bakery Specialties
Addison, IL 800-253-5298
Old Cavendish Products
Cavendish, VT 800-536-7899

Fruit Cobbler

Good Old Days Foods
Little Rock, AR 501-565-1257
Harold Food Company
Charlotte, NC 704-588-8061
Lone Star Bakery
Round Rock, TX 512-255-3629
Original Ya-hoo! Baking Company
Sherman, TX 800-575-9373
Pacific Ocean Produce
Santa Cruz, CA 831-423-2654
Spring Glen Fresh Foods
Ephrata, PA 800-641-2853

Ladyfingers

Jenny Lee Bakery
Mc Kees Rocks, PA 412-331-8900
Lawrences Delights
Doraville, GA 800-568-0021
Specialty Bakers
Marysville, PA 800-233-0778

Liqueur Cake

Beatrice Bakery Company
Beatrice, NE 800-228-4030
Dinkel's Bakery
Chicago, IL 800-822-8817

Muffin Loaves

Main Street Gourmet
Cuyahoga Falls, OH 800-533-6246

Muffins

Andre-Boudin Bakeries
San Francisco, CA 415-882-1849
Angel's Bakeries
Brooklyn, NY 718-389-1400
Atlanta Bread Company International, Inc.
Smyrna, GA 800-398-3728
Awrey Bakeries
Livonia, MI 800-950-2253
Bake Crafters Food
Collegedale, TN 800-296-8935
Bake Rite Rolls
Bensalem, PA 215-638-2400
BakeMark Canada
Laval, QC 800-361-4998
Bakemark Ingredients Canada
Richmond, BC 800-665-9441
Baker & Baker
Schaumburg, IL 800-593-5777
Baker & Baker, Inc.
Schaumburg, IL 800-593-5777
Baker Boy Bake Shop
Dickinson, ND 800-437-2008
Baker's Choice
Birmingham, MI 248-827-7500

Bakery Chef
Chicago, IL 773-384-1900
BBU Bakeries
Denver, CO 303-691-6342
Breakfast at Brennan's
New Orleans, LA 800-888-9932
Brownie Baker
Fresno, CA 800-598-6501
Busken Bakery
Cincinnati, OH 513-871-2114
Calgary Italian Bakery
Calgary, AB 800-661-6868
Canada Bread Company
Langley, BC 800-465-5515
Case Side Holdings Company
Kensington, PE 902-836-4214
Central Bakery
Fall River, MA 508-675-7620
Chatila's Bakery
Salem, NH 603-898-5459
Cloverhill Bakery-Vend Corporation
Chicago, IL 773-745-9800
Community Bakeries
Chicago, IL 773-384-1900
Danish Baking Company
Van Nuys, CA 800-777-4970
Del's Pastry
Etobicoke, ON 416-231-4383
DiCarlo's Bakery
San Pedro, CA 310-831-2524
Dolly Madison Bakery
Columbus, IN 812-376-7432
Dough Works Company
Horicon, WI 800-383-8808
Dunford Bakers
Fayetteville, AR 479-521-3000
Edelweiss Patisserie
Charlestown, MA 617-628-0225
Edner Corporation
Hayward, CA 510-441-8504
El Peto Products
Cambridge, ON 800-387-4064
Enterprises Pates et Croutes
Boucherville, QC 450-655-7790
Fireside Kitchen
Halifax, NS 902-454-7387
Fisher's Bakery
Ellicott City, MD 410-461-9275
Flowers Bakery of Winston-Salem
Winston Salem, NC 800-334-5260
Foxtail Foods
Fairfield, OH 800-323-6944
France Croissant
New York, NY 212-888-1210
Fresh Start Bakeries
City of Industry, CA 626-961-2525
Fresh Start Bakeries
Brea, CA 714-256-8900
George Weston Bakeries
Northlake, IL 708-562-6311
George Weston Bakeries
Bay Shore, NY 800-356-3314
Gold Medal Baking Company
Philadelphia, PA 215-627-4787
Gourmet Baker
Burnaby, BC 800-663-1972
Gourmet Croissant
Brooklyn, NY 718-499-4911
Greyston Bakery
Yonkers, NY 800-289-2253
Hawaii Star Bakery
Honolulu, HI 808-841-3602
Heitzman Bakery
Louisville, KY 502-452-1891
Homestead Baking Company
Rumford, RI 800-556-7216
International Brownie
Weymouth, MA 800-230-1588
Interstate Bakeries Corporation
Los Angeles, CA 323-750-7204
Interstate Brands
Biddeford, ME 207-286-1200
Irresistible Cookie Jar
Hayden Lake, ID 208-664-1261
Isabella's Healthy Bakery
Cuyahoga Falls, OH 800-476-6328
J&J Snack Foods Corporation
Pennsauken, NJ 856-665-9533
James Skinner Company
Omaha, NE 800-358-7428
Jenny Lee Bakery
Mc Kees Rocks, PA 412-331-8900

Joey's Fine Foods
  Newark, NJ 973-482-1400
Kerrobert Bakery
  Kerrobert, SK 306-834-2461
Lone Star Bakery
  Round Rock, TX 512-255-3629
Lusitania Bakery
  Blandon, PA 610-926-1311
Mac's Donut Shop
  Aliquippa, PA 724-375-6776
Magnificent Muffin Corporation
  Farmingdale, NY 631-454-8022
Main Street Gourmet
  Cuyahoga Falls, OH 800-533-6246
Main Street Gourmet Fundraising
  Cuyahoga Falls, OH 800-533-6246
Main Street Muffins
  Cuyahoga Falls, OH 800-533-6246
Meyer's Bakeries
  Casa Grande, AZ 800-528-5770
Meyer's Bakeries
  Orlando, FL 887-859-2006
Michel's Bakery
  Philadelphia, PA 215-725-4328
Mt View Bakery
  Mountain View, HI 808-968-6353
New England Muffin Company
  Fall River, MA 508-675-2833
New Horizons Baking Company
  Fremont, IN 260-495-7055
Norths Bakery California Inc
  North Hollywood, CA 818-761-2892
Notre Dame Bakery
  Lewisporte, NL 709-535-2738
Oakrun Farm Bakery
  Ancaster, ON 905-648-1818
Oroweat Baking Company
  Montebello, CA 323-721-5161
Osman's Pies
  Stow, OH 330-655-2919
Otis Spunkmeyer
  San Leandro, CA 800-938-1900
Otis Spunkmeyer Company
  Norcross, GA 800-438-9251
Oven Fresh Baking Company
  Chicago, IL 773-638-1234
Pacific Ocean Produce
  Santa Cruz, CA 831-423-2654

Plaidberry Company
  Vista, CA 760-727-5403
Rich Products Corporation
  Buffalo, NY 800-828-2021
Rising Dough Bakery
  Sacramento, CA 916-387-9700
Sara Lee Bakery Group   The EarthGrains - Bakery
  Saint Paul, MN
Sara Lee Bakery Group   The EarthGrains - Bakery
  Oakland, CA 510-635-4343
Sara Lee Corporation
  Downers Grove, IL 630-598-8100
Shaw Baking Company
  Thunder Bay, ON 807-345-7327
Unique Bakery Company
  Toronto, ON 416-751-8200
Uptown Bakers
  Washington, DC 202-546-6500
Vie de France Bakery
  Bensenville, IL 630-595-9521
Vitalicious
  New York, NY 877-848-2877
Well-Bred Loaf
  Valley Cottage, NY 800-444-5623
Weston Bakeries
  Toronto, ON 800-590-6861

Frozen

Dynamic Foods
  Lubbock, TX 806-762-0780
Isabella's Healthy Bakery
  Cuyahoga Falls, OH 800-476-6328
Main Street Gourmet
  Cuyahoga Falls, OH 800-533-6246
Main Street Gourmet Fundraising
  Cuyahoga Falls, OH 800-533-6246
Main Street Muffins
  Cuyahoga Falls, OH 800-533-6246

Whole Grain

Isabella's Healthy Bakery
  Cuyahoga Falls, OH 800-476-6328
Main Street Gourmet
  Cuyahoga Falls, OH 800-533-6246
Main Street Muffins
  Cuyahoga Falls, OH 800-533-6246

Panettones

Vigneri Confections
  Rochester, NY 585-254-6160

Pastries

Alessi Bakery
  Tampa, FL 813-879-4544
Artuso Pastry Foods
  Mt Vernon, NY 914-663-8806
Artuso Pastry Shop
  Bronx, NY 718-367-2515
Athens Pastries & Frozen Foods
  Cleveland, OH 800-837-5683
Atlanta Bread Company International, Inc.
  Smyrna, GA 800-398-3728
Bakery Europa
  Honolulu, HI 808-845-5011
Banquet Schuster Bakery
  Pueblo, CO 719-544-1062
Big Fatty's Flaming Foods
  Valley View, TX 888-248-6332
Birkholm's Jr Danish Bakery
  Solvang, CA 805-688-3872
BODEGA Chocolates
  Costa Mesa, CA 888-326-3342
Borden's Bread
  Regina, SK 306-525-3341
Brenner's Bakery of Arlington
  Arlington, VA 703-534-0211
Calgary Italian Bakery
  Calgary, AB 800-661-6868
Campbell Soup Company of Canada
  Listowel, ON 800-575-7687
Caribbean Food Delights
  Tappan, NY 845-398-3000
Case Side Holdings Company
  Kensington, PE 902-836-4214
Castella Imports
  Hauppauge, NY 866-227-8355
Chatila's Bakery
  Salem, NH 603-898-5459
Chella's Dutch Delicacies
  Lake Oswego, OR 800-458-3331

City Baker
  Calgary, AB 403-263-8578
Clarkson Scottish Bakery
  Mississauga, ON 905-823-1500
Claudio Pastry Company
  Elmwood Park, IL 708-453-0598
Clements Pastry Shop
  Hyattsville, MD 800-444-7428
Cohen's Bakery
  Buffalo, NY 716-892-8149
Columbus Bakery
  Columbus, OH 614-645-2275
Creme Curls Bakery
  Hudsonville, MI 800-466-1219
Danish Baking Company
  Van Nuys, CA 800-777-4970
Dawn Food Products
  Jackson, MI 800-248-1144
Di Paolo Baking Company
  Rochester, NY 585-232-3510
Dimitria Delights
  North Grafton, MA 800-763-1113
Dufour Pastry Kitchens
  New York, NY 212-929-2800
Dunham Hill Bakery
  Woodstock, VT 800-218-3121
Edelweiss Patisserie
  Charlestown, MA 617-628-0225
Elegant Desserts
  Lyndhurst, NJ 201-933-0770
Fantis Foods
  Carlstadt, NJ 201-933-6200
Ferrara Bakery & Cafe
  New York, NY 212-226-6150
Fiera Foods
  North York, ON 416-744-1010
Fillo Factory
  Dumont, NJ 800-653-4556
Flower Foods, Inc.
  Thomasville, GA 229-226-9110
Flowers Bakery of Winston-Salem
  Winston Salem, NC 800-334-5260
Food of Our Own Design
  Maplewood, NJ 973-762-0985
Foodbrands America
  Oklahoma City, OK 405-290-4000
France Croissant
  New York, NY 212-888-1210
Future Bakery & Cafe
  Etobicoke, ON 416-231-1491
George Weston Bakeries
  Albany, NY 800-531-4002
Golden Glow Cookie Company
  Bronx, NY 718-379-6223
Gourmet Baker
  Burnaby, BC 800-663-1972
Hafner
  Stone Mountain, GA 888-725-4605
Heinemann's Bakeries
  Chicago, IL 312-239-5592
Holt's Bakery
  Douglas, GA 912-384-2202
International Equipment
  Arecibo, PR 787-879-3151
James Skinner Company
  Omaha, NE 800-358-7428
John J. Nissen Baking Company
  Brewer, ME 207-989-7654
Just Desserts
  San Francisco, CA 415-602-9245
Kerrobert Bakery
  Kerrobert, SK 306-834-2461
King Soopers Bakery
  Denver, CO 303-778-3128
Laura's French Baking Company
  Los Angeles, CA 888-353-5144
Lax & Mandel Bakery
  Cleveland, OH 216-382-8877
Lenchner Bakery
  Concord, ON 905-738-8811
Let Them Eat Cake
  Tampa, FL 813-837-6888
Lewis Bakeries
  London, ON 519-434-5252
Little Miss Muffin
  Chicago, IL 800-456-9328
Lone Star Consolidated Foods
  Dallas, TX 800-658-5637
Lucy's Sweet Surrender
  Cleveland, OH 216-752-0828
Mac's Donut Shop
  Aliquippa, PA 724-375-6776

Main Street Gourmet
Cuyahoga Falls, OH 800-533-6246
Main Street Gourmet Fundraising
Cuyahoga Falls, OH 800-533-6246
Mary Ann's Baking Company
Sacramento, CA 916-681-7444
Michel's Bakery
Philadelphia, PA 215-725-4328
Mikawaya Bakery
Los Angeles, CA 213-628-6514
Moravian Cookies Shop
Winston Salem, NC 800-274-2994
Morse's Sauerkraut
Waldoboro, ME 866-832-5569
Mozzicato Depasquale Bakery & Pastry Shop
Hartford, CT 860-296-0426
Mrs. Willman's Baking
Burnaby, BC 403-250-9105
Nancy's Specialty Foods
Newark, CA 510-494-1100
National Food Corporation
Medley, FL 305-884-2020
Northside Bakery
Richmond, VA 804-329-6851
Oakrun Farm Bakery
Ancaster, ON 905-648-1818
Old Country Bakery
North Hollywood, CA 818-838-2302
Orange Bakery
Irvine, CA 949-863-1377
Pauline's Pastries
Concord, ON 877-292-6826
Pepperidge Farm
Downingtown, PA 610-269-2500
Prime Pastries
Concord, ON 905-669-5883
Quaker Bonnet
Buffalo, NY 800-283-2447
Quality Naturally! Foods
City of Industry, CA 888-498-6986
Ranaldi Bros Frozen Food Products Inc
Warwick, RI 401-738-3444
Rogers Bakery
Plainville, CT 860-747-1686
Rolling Pin Bakery
Bow Island, AB 403-545-2434
Royal Caribbean Bakery
Mt Vernon, NY 888-818-0971
Royal Court Cookie Company
North Hollywood, CA 800-730-2545
Ryke's Bakery
Muskegon, MI 231-557-8011
Saputo
Montreal, QC 514-328-6662
Sara Lee Bakery Group   The EarthGrains - Bakery
Beaumont, TX 409-842-9150
Sara Lee Bakery Group   The EarthGrains - Bakery
St Louis, MO 800-323-7117
Schulze & Burch Biscuit Company
Chicago, IL 773-927-6622
Scialo Brothers
Providence, RI 877-421-0986
Shaw Baking Company
Thunder Bay, ON 807-345-7327
Solana Beach Baking Company
Carlsbad, CA 760-931-0148
Specialty Baking Products
Dunkirk, NY 716-366-0938
Spohrers Bakeries
Collingdale, PA 610-532-9959
St. Cloud Bakery
St Cloud, MN 320-251-8055
Standard Bakery
Kealakekua, HI 808-322-3688
Starbucks Coffee Company
Seattle, WA 800-782-7282
Strossner's Bakery
Greenville, SC 864-233-3996
Svenhard's Swedish Bakery
Oakland, CA 800-333-7836
Sweet Gallery Exclusive Pastry
Toronto, ON 416-232-1539
Taste It Presents
Kenilworth, NJ 908-241-0672
Teawolf Industries, Ltd
Pine Brook, NJ 973-575-4600
Turano Pastry Shops
Bloomingdale, IL 630-529-6161
Turano Pasty Shops
Berwyn, IL 708-788-5320
United States Bakery
Portland, OR 503-731-5679

Uptown Bakers
Washington, DC 202-546-6500
Valley Bakery
Rock Valley, IA 712-476-5386
Vie de France Yamazaki
Denver, CO 303-371-6280
Vie de France Yamazaki
Vienna, VA 800-393-8926
Vie de France Yamazaki
Vienna, VA 800-446-4404
Vienna Bakery
Edmonton, AB 780-436-8211
Vigneri Confections
Rochester, NY 585-254-6160
Weiss Homemade Kosher Bakery
Brooklyn, NY 800-498-3477
Wenger's Bakery
Reading, PA 610-372-6545
Zeppys Bakery
Lawrence, MA 781-963-7022

Pecan Log

Lawrences Delights
Doraville, GA 800-568-0021

Petit Fours

Ferrara Bakery & Cafe
New York, NY 212-226-6150
Mazelle's Cheesecakes Concoctions Creations
Dallas, TX 903-737-4315
Silver Lake Cookie Company
Islip, NY 631-581-4000

Pound Cake

Adams Foods
Dothan, AL 334-983-4233
Bakery Chef
Chicago, IL 773-384-1900
Brownie Baker
Fresno, CA 800-598-6501
Clarmil Manufacturing Corporation
Hayward, CA 888-252-7645
McDuffies Bakery
Clarence, NY 800-875-1598
New England Country Bakers
Watertown, CT 800-225-3779
Rowena's
Norfolk, VA 800-627-8699
Sara Lee Corporation
Downers Grove, IL 630-598-8100
Silver Tray Cookies
Fort Lauderdale, FL 305-883-0800
Unique Bakery Company
Toronto, ON 416-751-8200
Waldensian Bakeries
Valdese, NC 828-874-2136
Well-Bred Loaf
Valley Cottage, NY 800-444-5623

Puff Pastry

BakeMark
Schaumburg, IL 562-949-1054
Baker & Baker
Schaumburg, IL 800-593-5777
Baker & Baker, Inc.
Schaumburg, IL 800-593-5777
Dutchland Frozen Foods
Lester, IA 888-497-7243
France Croissant
New York, NY 212-888-1210
Gourmet Baker
Burnaby, BC 800-663-1972
Pepperidge Farm
Downingtown, PA 610-269-2500
Specialty Baking Products
Dunkirk, NY 716-366-0938

Rugulach

Baker & Baker
Schaumburg, IL 800-593-5777
Baker & Baker, Inc.
Schaumburg, IL 800-593-5777
Chewys Rugulach
San Diego, CA 800-241-3456
Morse's Sauerkraut
Waldoboro, ME 866-832-5569
Neuman Bakery Specialties
Addison, IL 800-253-5298

Steve's Mom
Bronx, NY 800-362-4545
Suzanne's Sweets
Katonah, NY 914-301-5307
Yrica's Rugelach & Baking Company
Brooklyn, NY 718-965-3657

Rusk

House-Autry Mills
Four Oaks, NC 800-849-0802

Sponge Cake

Clarmil Manufacturing Corporation
Hayward, CA 888-252-7645
Multi Marques
Montreal, QC 514-255-9492
Patisserie Wawel
Montreal, QC 614-524-3348
Specialty Bakers
Marysville, PA 800-233-0778
Sweet Gallery Exclusive Pastry
Toronto, ON 416-232-1539

Strawberry Shortcake

Penn Maid Crowley Foods
Philadelphia, PA 800-247-6269

Strudel

Athens Pastries & Frozen Foods
Cleveland, OH 800-837-5683
Creme Curls Bakery
Hudsonville, MI 800-466-1219
Dee's Cheesecake Factory/Dee's Foodservice
Albuquerque, NM 505-884-1777
Dimitria Delights
North Grafton, MA 800-763-1113
Fillo Factory
Dumont, NJ 800-653-4556
Gourmet Baker
Burnaby, BC 800-663-1972
Jenny Lee Bakery
Mc Kees Rocks, PA 412-331-8900
Le Notre, Alain & Marie Baker
Houston, TX 800-536-6873
Rising Dough Bakery
Sacramento, CA 916-387-9700
Sinbad Sweets
Fresno, CA 800-350-7933
Svenhard's Swedish Bakery
Oakland, CA 800-333-7836

Tarts

CGI Desserts
Sugar Land, TX 281-240-1200
Clarmil Manufacturing Corporation
Hayward, CA 888-252-7645
Daphne Baking Company
Kent, CT 860-927-1818
Dufflet Pastries
Toronto, ON 416-536-1330
Dufour Pastry Kitchens
New York, NY 212-929-2800
Elegant Desserts
Lyndhurst, NJ 201-933-0770
Greyston Bakery
Yonkers, NY 800-289-2253
Health Valley Company
Irwindale, CA 800-334-3204
Honey Rose Baking Company
Encinitas, CA 760-942-8996
J.P. Sunrise Bakery
Edmonton, AB 780-454-5797
Jenny Lee Bakery
Mc Kees Rocks, PA 412-331-8900
Joey's Fine Foods
Newark, NJ 973-482-1400
Kellogg Canada Inc
Mississauga, ON 888-876-3750
Love & Quiches Desserts
Freeport, NY 800-525-5251
Royal Home Bakery
Newmarket, ON 905-715-7044
Sinbad Sweets
Fresno, CA 800-350-7933
Unique Bakery Company
Toronto, ON 416-751-8200

Tiramisu

Schwans Food Company
Norcross, GA 800-241-0559
Vantage USA
Chicago, IL 773-247-1086
Vigneri Confections
Rochester, NY 585-254-6160

Tortes

Alessi Bakery
Tampa, FL 813-879-4544
Balboa Dessert Company
Santa Ana, CA .800-974-9699
Danish Baking Company
Van Nuys, CA 800-777-4970
Dufflet Pastries
Toronto, ON 416-536-1330
Gourmet Baker
Burnaby, BC 800-663-1972
Heidi's Gourmet Desserts
Tucker, GA 800-241-4166
Hoff's Bakery
Medford, MA 888-871-5100
Jenny Lee Bakery
Mc Kees Rocks, PA 412-331-8900
Scot Paris Fine Desserts
New York, NY 212-807-1802
Strossner's Bakery
Greenville, SC 864-233-3996
Sweet Endings
West Palm Beach, FL 888-635-1177
Sweet Gallery Exclusive Pastry
Toronto, ON 416-232-1539
Vigneri Confections
Rochester, NY 585-254-6160

Turnovers

BakeMark
Schaumburg, IL 562-949-1054
BakeMark Canada
Laval, QC 800-361-4998
Con Agra Foods
Holly Ridge, NC 910-329-9061

Creme Curls Bakery
Hudsonville, MI 800-466-1219
Del's Pastry
Etobicoke, ON .416-231-4383
Fiera Foods
North York, ON 416-744-1010
Jenny Lee Bakery
Mc Kees Rocks, PA 412-331-8900
Oven Ready Products
Guelph, ON 519-767-2415
Unique Bakery Company
Toronto, ON 416-751-8200

Cones

Ace Baking Company
Wadsworth, IL .800-879-2231
Derby Cone Company
Louisville, KY 502-491-1220
Dover Industries Limited
Burlington, ON .800-387-7316
Edy's Grand Ice Cream
Rockaway, NJ 800-362-7899
Foothills Creamery
Calgary, AB 403-263-7725
Great Western Products Company
Assumption, IL .217-226-3241
Great Western Products Company
Bremen, IN 217-546-4010
Great Western Products Company
Bismarck, MO 573-734-2210
Harlan Bakeries
Avon, IN 317-272-3600
Ice Cream Specialties
Lafayette, IN 765-474-2989
Interbake Foods
Green Bay, WI .804-576-3459
Joy Cone Company
Hermitage, PA .800-242-2663
Kemach Food Products   Corporation
Brooklyn, NY 888-453-6224
Kraft Foods
East Hanover, NJ 973-503-2000
Marshmallow Cone Company
Cincinnati, OH .800-641-8551

Monster Cone
Montreal, QC 800-542-9801
Norse Dairy Systems
Columbus, OH .614-294-4931
O'Boyle's Ice Cream Company
Bristol, PA 215-788-0421
Olde Tyme Food Corporation
East Longmeadow, MA 800-356-6533
Ono Cones of Hawaii
Pearl City, HI 808-487-8690
Sargeant's Army Marketing
Bowmanville, ON 905-623-2888
Table de France
Ontario, CA 909-923-5205
Turnbull Cone Baking Company
Chattanooga, TN 423-265-4551
Zimmer Custom Made Packaging
Columbus, OH .800-338-7465

Cookies & Bars

Almond Cookies

Andre-Boudin Bakeries
San Francisco, CA 415-882-1849
Dong Kee Company
Chicago, IL 312-225-6340
Erba Food Products
Brooklyn, NY 718-272-7700
Fortella Fortune Cookies
Chicago, IL 312-567-9000
Mamma Says
Butler, NJ 877-283-6282
YZ Enterprises
Maumee, OH 800-736-8779

Animal Crackers

Old Colony Baking Company
Lake Bluff, IL 847-283-9292

Bars

Agricore United
Winnipeg, MB .204-944-5411

AMT Labs
North Salt Lake, UT 801-299-1661
Bake Crafters Food
Collegedale, TN 800-296-8935
Barbara's Bakery
Petaluma, CA 707-765-2273
Betty Lou's Golden Smackers
McMinnville, OR 800-242-5205
Cambridge Food
Monterey, CA 800-433-2584
Carrie's Chocolates
Edmonton, AB 877-778-2462
Chase Candy Company
St Joseph, MO 800-786-1625
Cliff Bar
Berkeley, CA 800-884-5254
Con Agra Store Brands
Edina, MN 952-835-6900
ConAgra Food Store Brands
Edina, MN 952-469-4981
Cream of the West
Harlowton, MT 800-477-2383
Edner Corporation
Hayward, CA 510-441-8504
Edy's Grand Ice Cream
Rockaway, NJ 800-362-7899
Fieldbrook Farms
Dunkirk, NY 800-333-0805
Food of Our Own Design
Maplewood, NJ 973-762-0985
Frankly Natural Bakers
San Diego, CA 800-727-7229
Frozfruit Corporation
Gardena, CA 310-217-1034
Global Health Laboratories
Melville, NY 631-293-0030
Gourmet Baker
Burnaby, BC 800-663-1972
Govadinas Fitness Foods
San Diego, CA 800-900-0108
Health Valley Company
Irwindale, CA 800-334-3204
Hershey Chocolate & Confectionery Division
Pleasanton, CA 925-460-0359
High Country Snack Food
Lincoln, MT 800-433-3916
Honey Acres
Ashippun, WI 800-558-7745
Increda-Meal
Cato, NY 315-626-2111
Jamae Natural Foods
Los Angeles, CA 800-343-0052
JSL Foods
Los Angeles, CA 800-745-3236
Kellogg Company
Battle Creek, MI 800-962-1413
Kraft Foods
East Hanover, NJ 973-503-2000
L&M Bakery
Lawrence, MA 978-687-7346
Lotus Bakery
Santa Rosa, CA 800-875-6887
Marin Food Specialties
Byron, CA 925-634-6126
Mars M&M
Henderson, NV 888-265-6788
Merlino Italian Baking Company
Seattle, WA 800-207-2997
MLO/GeniSoy Products Company
Tulas, OK 866-606-3829
Murray Biscuit Company
Atlanta, GA 800-745-5582
Nature's Plus
Long Beach, CA 800-525-0200
Nellson Candies
Baldwin Park, CA 626-334-4508
Nestle Food Group
Toronto, ON 416-535-2181
Oberweis Dairy
North Aurora, IL 888-645-5868
Personal Health Developm
Ventura, CA 800-988-4465
Prairie Sun Grains
Calgary, AB 800-556-6807
Premier Nutrition
Carlsbad, CA 888-836-8972
Quaker Oats Company
Danville, IL 217-443-3990
Randag & Associates Inc
Elmhurst, IL 630-530-2830
Sacharen Brothers
Montreal, QC 514-277-8205

Schulze & Burch Biscuit Company
Chicago, IL 773-927-6622
Severn Peanut Company
Severn, NC 800-642-4064
Sturm Foods
Manawa, WI 800-347-8876
Sucesores de Pedro Cortes
San Juan, PR 787-754-7040
Sugar Kake Cookie
Tonawanda, NY 800-775-5180
Sweet Productions
Jericho, NY 631-842-0548
Sweety Novelty
Monterey Park, CA 626-282-4482
Ultimate Nutrition
Plainville, CT 330-405-5008
Weaver Nut Company
Ephrata, PA 717-738-3781
York Barbell Company
York, PA 800-358-9675

Biscotti

All About Lollipops
Poway, CA 866-475-6554
Award Baking International
New Germany, MN 952-353-2533
Baker & Baker
Schaumburg, IL 800-593-5777
Baker & Baker, Inc.
Schaumburg, IL 800-593-5777
Be-Bop Biscotti
Bend, OR 888-545-7487
Bernadette Baking Company
Medford, MA 781-393-8700
Biscotti Goddess
Richmond, VA 804-745-9490
Crunchy Foods
Oakland, CA 800-211-5903
Daniele Imports
Rochester, NY 800-298-9410
De Bas Chocolatier
Fresno, CA 559-294-7638
Di Camillo Bakery
Niagara Falls, NY 800-634-4363
Elliott Bay Baking Co.
Seattle, WA 206-762-7690
Ferrara Bakery & Cafe
New York, NY 212-226-6150
Godiva Chocolatier
New York, NY 800-946-3482
Grain-Free JK Gourmet
Toronto, ON 800-608-0465
Hansen's Juices
Azusa, CA 626-812-6022
Immaculate Consumption
Flat Rock, NC 888-826-6567
Just Off Melrose
Palm Springs, CA 800-743-4109
La Tempesta
S San Francisco, CA 800-762-8330
LaRosa Bakery
Shrewsbury, NJ 800-527-6722
Mamma Says
Butler, NJ 877-283-6282
Merlino Italian Baking Company
Seattle, WA 800-207-2997
Montione's Biscotti & Baked Goods
Mansfield, MA 800-559-1010
Moosewood Hollow LLC
Plainfield, VT 866-463-8733
My Boy's Baking LLC
Allentown, PA 610-759-4552
North American Enterprises
Tucson, AZ 800-817-8666
Our Thyme Garden
Cleburne, TX 800-482-4372
Poppie's Dough
Chicago, IL 312-949-0404
Royal Wine Company
Bayonne, NJ 201-437-9131
Touche Bakery
London, ON 518-455-0044
Tuscan Bakery
Portland, OR 800-887-2261
Ultimate Biscotti
Eugene, OR 541-344-8220
Upper Crust Biscotti
Pismo Beach, CA 866-972-6879
Wally Biscotti
Denver, CO 866-659-2559

Almond
Main Street Gourmet
Cuyahoga Falls, OH 800-533-6246

Chocolate Almond
Main Street Gourmet
Cuyahoga Falls, OH 800-533-6246

Chocolate Dipped
Main Street Gourmet
Cuyahoga Falls, OH 800-533-6246

Hazelnut
Main Street Gourmet
Cuyahoga Falls, OH 800-533-6246

Mocha
Main Street Gourmet
Cuyahoga Falls, OH 800-533-6246

White Chocolate Dipped
Main Street Gourmet
Cuyahoga Falls, OH 800-533-6246

Brownies

Andre-Boudin Bakeries
San Francisco, CA 415-882-1849
Athena's Silverland®Desserts
Forest Park, IL 800-737-3636
Bake Crafters Food
Collegedale, TN 800-296-8935
BakeMark Canada
Laval, QC 800-361-4998
Baker & Baker
Schaumburg, IL 800-593-5777
Baker & Baker, Inc.
Schaumburg, IL 800-593-5777
Baker Boy Bake Shop
Dickinson, ND 800-437-2008
Bakers Breakfast Cookie
Bellingham, WA 877-889-1090
Boca Bons, Inc.
Coral Springs, FL 800-314-2835
Brownie Baker
Fresno, CA 800-598-6501
Browniepops LLC
Leawood, KS 816-797-0715
Chalet Desserts
Union City, CA 510-783-8300
Cheryl & Company
Westerville, OH 614-891-8822
Christie Cookie Company
Nashville, TN 615-242-3817
Coby's Cookies
North York, ON 416-633-1567
Danish Baking Company
Van Nuys, CA 800-777-4970
Dee's Cheesecake Factory/Dee's Foodservice
Albuquerque, NM 505-884-1777
Dough Works Company
Horicon, WI 800-383-8808
Dufflet Pastries
Toronto, ON 416-536-1330
Dynamic Foods
Lubbock, TX 806-762-0780
Eilenberger Bakery
Palestine, TX 800-831-2544
Fairytale Brownies
Phoenix, AZ 800-324-7982
Food of Our Own Design
Maplewood, NJ 973-762-0985
Frankly Natural Bakers
San Diego, CA 800-727-7229
George Weston Bakeries
Albany, NY 800-531-4002
Handy Pax
Randolph, MA 781-963-8300
Harvest Valley Bakery
La Salle, IL 815-224-9030
Heavenscent Edibles
New York, NY 212-369-0310
Heidi's Gourmet Desserts
Tucker, GA 800-241-4166
Home Baked Group
Boca Raton, FL 561-995-0767
Jenny Lee Bakery
Mc Kees Rocks, PA 412-331-8900

Lawler Foods
Humble, TX 281-446-0059
Lone Star Bakery
Round Rock, TX............512-255-3629
Mac's Donut Shop
Aliquippa, PA 724-375-6776
Main Street Gourmet
Cuyahoga Falls, OH 800-533-6246
Main Street Gourmet Fundraising
Cuyahoga Falls, OH 800-533-6246
Maplehurst Bakeries
Carrollton, TX 800-482-4810
Mari's New York
Brooklyn, NY 212-253-2014
McDuffies Bakery
Clarence, NY..............800-875-1598
Michel's Bakery
Philadelphia, PA 215-725-4328
Murray Biscuit Company/Kellogg Snacks
Lake Bluff, IL............847-689-8400
Osman's Pies
Stow, OH.................330-655-2919
Otis Spunkmeyer Company
Norcross, GA 800-438-9251
Pacific Ocean Produce
Santa Cruz, CA 831-423-2654
Parco Foods
Blue Island, IL 708-371-9200
Peggy Lawton Kitchens
East Walpole, MA..........800-843-7325
Pie Piper Products
Bensenville, IL 800-621-8183
Sara Lee Bakery Group   The EarthGrains - Bakery
Rome, GA 706-295-4499
Selma's Cookies
Apopka, FL...............800-922-6654
Sterling Foods
San Antonio, TX 210-490-1669
Sticky Fingers Bakeries
Spokane Valley, WA 800-458-5826
Tate's Bake Shop
Southampton, NY 631-283-9830
Vitalicious
New York, NY 877-848-2877
Well-Bred Loaf
Valley Cottage, NY 800-444-5623
William Poll
New York, NY 800-993-7655

with Nuts

Dinkel's Bakery
Chicago, IL...............800-822-8817
Main Street Gourmet
Cuyahoga Falls, OH 800-533-6246

Chocolate Chip Cookies

Christie Cookie Company
Nashville, TN 615-242-3817
Confection Solutions
Sylmar, CA 800-284-2422
Country Choice Naturals
Eden Prairie, MN 952-829-8824
Dinkel's Bakery
Chicago, IL...............800-822-8817
Erba Food Products
Brooklyn, NY 718-272-7700
Kellogg Snacks
Kansas City, KS 800-229-4414
Main Street Gourmet
Cuyahoga Falls, OH 800-533-6246
Main Street's Cambritt Cookies
Cuyahoga Falls, OH 800-533-6246
Mississippi Cheese StrawFactory
Yazoo City, MS............866-830-9415
Murray Biscuit Company
Atlanta, GA 800-745-5582
Peggy Lawton Kitchens
East Walpole, MA..........800-843-7325
Sunset Specialty Foods
Sunset Beach, CA 562-592-4976

Cookies

A & M Cookie Company Canada
Kitchener, ON 800-265-6508
A La Carte
Chicago, IL...............800-722-2370
Abraham's Natural Foods
Long Branch, NJ 800-327-9903
Alessi Bakery
Tampa, FL................813-879-4544

All Wrapped Up
Lauderhill, FL.............800-891-2194
Almondina®/YZ Enterprises, Inc.
Maumee, OH..............800-736-8779
Ambassador Foods
Van Nuys, CA 800-338-3369
American Brittle
Sandusky, OH.............800-274-8853
Ames International
Fife, WA 888-469-2637
Andre-Boudin Bakeries
San Francisco, CA 415-882-1849
Angel's Bakeries
Brooklyn, NY 718-389-1400
ARA Food Corporation
Miami, FL................800-533-8831
Archway & Mother's Cookie Company
Oakland, CA 800-369-3997
Archway Cookies
Ashland, OH..............888-427-2492
Arcor USA
Coral Gables, FL...........800-572-7267
Arturo's Bakery
Waterbury, CT.............203-754-3056
Atlas Biscuit Company
Verona, NJ...............973-239-8300
Aunt Gussie Cookies & Crackers
Garfield, NJ...............973-340-4480
Austin Special Foods Company
Austin, TX................866-372-8663
Authentic Marotti Biscotti
Lewisville, TX..............972-221-7295
Bake Crafters Food
Collegedale, TN 800-296-8935
BakeMark
Schaumburg, IL............562-949-1054
BakeMark Canada
Laval, QC 800-361-4998
Bakemark Ingredients Canada
Richmond, BC 800-665-9441
Baker & Baker
Schaumburg, IL............800-593-5777
Baker & Baker, Inc.
Schaumburg, IL............800-593-5777
Baker Boy Bake Shop
Dickinson, ND 800-437-2008
Baker's Choice
Birmingham, MI 248-827-7500
Bakers Breakfast Cookie
Bellingham, WA 877-889-1090
Barbara's Bakery
Petaluma, CA 707-765-2273
Berkshire Mountain Bakery
Housatonic, MA 866-274-6124
Best Maid Cookie Company
River Falls, WI 888-444-0322
Beth's Fine Desserts
Cotati, CA 415-464-1891
Betty Lou's Golden Smackers
McMinnville, OR 800-242-5205
Big Fatty's Flaming Foods
Valley View, TX 888-248-6332
Big Shoulders Baking
Chicago, IL...............800-456-9328
Bloomfield Bakers
Los Alamitos, CA 800-594-4111
Blue Chip Group
Salt Lake City, UT 800-878-0099
Boca Foods Company
Madison, WI 608-285-6950
Borden's Bread
Regina, SK 306-525-3341
Borinquen Biscuit Corporation
Yauco, PR 787-856-3030
Boston America Corporation
Woburn, MA 617-923-1111
BP Gourmet
Hauppauge, NY 631-234-5200
Breakfast at Brennan's
New Orleans, LA 800-888-9932
Bremner Company
Poteau, OK 918-647-8630
Brent & Sam's Cookies
N Little Rock, AR...........800-825-1613
Brooklyn Baking Company
Waterbury, CT............203-574-9198
Brownie Baker
Fresno, CA 800-598-6501
Buckeye Pretzel Company
Williamsport, PA...........800-257-6029
Buon Italia
New York, NY 212-633-9090

Busken Bakery
Cincinnati, OH 513-871-2114
Byrd Cookie Company
Savannah, GA 800-291-2973
Carolina Cupboard
Hillsborough, NC 800-400-3441
Cascade Cookie Company
St Louis, MO..............314-877-7000
Case Side Holdings Company
Kensington, PE 902-836-4214
CGI Desserts
Sugar Land, TX............281-240-1200
Charlie's Specialties
Hermitage, PA.............724-346-2350
Chatila's Bakery
Salem, NH................603-898-5459
Chelsea Market Baskets
New York, NY 888-727-7887
Chocoholics Divine Desserts
Clements, CA 800-760-2462
Chocolate Chix
Waxahachie, TX 214-744-2442
Chocolate Moon
Asheville, NC 800-723-1236
Chocolates a la Carte
Valencia, CA 800-818-2462
Christie Cookie Company
Nashville, TN 615-242-3817
CJ Vitner Company
Chicago, IL...............773-523-7900
Clarmil Manufacturing Corporation
Hayward, CA 888-252-7645
Columbus Bakery
Columbus, OH 614-645-2275
Columbus Gourmet
Columbus, GA 800-356-1858
Confection Solutions
Sylmar, CA 800-284-2422
Consolidated Biscuit Company
Mc Comb, OH.............800-537-9544
Cookie Specialties
Wheeling, IL..............847-537-3888
Cookie Tree Bakeries
Salt Lake City, UT..........800-998-0111
Cookies & More
Lewiston, ME 207-923-4227
Cookietree Bakeries
Salt Lake City, UT..........800-998-0111
Cooperstown Cookie Company
Cooperstown, NY 888-269-7315
Country Choice Naturals
Eden Prairie, MN 952-829-8824
Country Home Bakers
Torrance, CA..............800-672-6277
Cuisinary Fine Foods
Dallas, TX................888-283-5303
Cybros
Waukesha, WI 800-876-2253
Dainty Confections
Valley Stream, NY 516-825-0943
Dairy State Foods
Milwaukee, WI 800-435-4499
Dancing Deer Baking Company
Hyde Park, MA 888-699-3337
Dangold
Flushing, NY..............718-591-5286
Dare Foods
Toronto, ON 800-665-5817
Dare Foods
Denver, CO 800-722-1871
Dare Foods
Kitchener, ON.............800-865-8225
Dare Foods Incorporated
Kitchener, ON.............800-265-8222
Dave's Bakery
Honesdale, PA.............570-253-1660
Davis Cookie Company
Rimersburg, PA............814-473-8181
Dayhoff
Clearwater, FL.............800-354-3372
De Beukelaer Corporation
Madison, MS..............601-856-7454
Delicious Frookie Company
Des Plaines, IL.............847-699-5900
DF Stauffer Biscuit Company
York, PA.................800-673-2473
Di Camillo Bakery
Niagara Falls, NY 800-634-4363
Diamond Bakery Company
Honolulu, HI 808-845-8200
Dinkel's Bakery
Chicago, IL...............800-822-8817

Dong Kee Company
Chicago, IL 312-225-6340
Donsuemor Madeleines
Alameda, CA 888-420-4441
Dufflet Pastries
Toronto, ON 416-536-1330
Dunford Bakers
Fayetteville, AR 479-521-3000
Dutchess Bakery
Charleston, WV 304-346-3210
Edelweiss Patisserie
Charlestown, MA 617-628-0225
El Segundo Bakery
El Segundo, CA 310-322-3422
Elegant Gourmet
Kirkland, WA 425-814-2500
Eleni's Cookies
New York, NY 212-255-6804
Elite Bakery
Rochester, NY 877-791-7376
Elliott Bay Baking Co.
Seattle, WA 206-762-7690
Ellison Bakery
Fort Wayne, IN 800-711-8091
Elmwood Pastry
West Hartford, CT 860-233-2029
Ener-G Foods
Seattle, WA 800-331-5222
Erba Food Products
Brooklyn, NY 718-272-7700
Ethnic Edibles
New York, NY 718-320-0147
Evans Bakery
Cozad, NE 800-222-5641
Falcone's Cookieland
Brooklyn, NY 718-236-4200
Fantasy Cookie Company
Sylmar, CA 800-354-4488
Fauchon
New York, NY 877-605-0130
Federal Pretzel Baking Company
Philadelphia, PA 215-467-0505
Fernando C Pujals & Bros
San Juan, PR 787-792-3080
Ferrara Bakery & Cafe
New York, NY 212-226-6150
Firefly Fandango
Seattle, WA 206-760-3700
Fireside Kitchen
Halifax, NS 902-454-7387
Flathau's Fine Foods
Hattiesburg, MS 888-263-1299
Flowers Bakery of Winston-Salem
Winston Salem, NC 800-334-5260
Flowers Baking
San Antonio, TX 210-661-2361
FNI Group LLC
Sherborn, MA 508-655-8816
Food Mill
Oakland, CA 510-482-3848
Fortella Fortune Cookies
Chicago, IL 312-567-9000
Fortunate Cookie
Stowe, VT 866-266-5337
Fortune Cookie Factory
Oakland, CA 510-832-5552
Foxtail Foods
Fairfield, OH 800-323-6944
Frankly Natural Bakers
San Diego, CA 800-727-7229
Frookie
Des Plaines, IL 847-699-3200
Fujiya
Honolulu, HI 808-845-2921
G H Bent Company
Milton, MA 617-698-5945
George Weston Bakeries
Northlake, IL 708-562-6311
George Weston Bakeries
Bay Shore, NY 800-356-3314
Giant Food
Lanham, MD 888-469-4426
Gift Factory/Beverly Hills
Sylmar, CA 800-365-6619
Gladder's Gourmet Cookies
Lockhart, TX 888-398-4523
Glazier Packing Company
Potsdam, NY 315-265-2500
Glennys
Freeport, NY 888-864-1243
Glutino
Laval, QC 800-363-3438

Golden Glow Cookie Company
Bronx, NY 718-379-6223
Golden Walnut Specialty Foods
Zion, IL 800-843-3645
Golden West Specialty Foods
Brisbane, CA 800-584-4481
Good Health Natural Foods
Northport, NY 631-261-2111
Gourmet Treats
Torrance, CA 800-444-9549
Grand Avenue Chocolates
Concord, CA 877-934-1800
Grandma Beth's Cookies
Alliance, NE 308-762-8433
Greyston Bakery
Yonkers, NY 800-289-2253
GWB Foods Corporation
Brooklyn, NY 718-686-9600
H.B. Trading
Totowa, NJ 973-812-1022
H.E. Butt Grocery Company
San Antonio, TX 800-432-3113
Haby's Alsatian Bakery
Castroville, TX 830-931-2118
Handy Pax
Randolph, MA 781-963-8300
Harvest Valley Bakery
La Salle, IL 815-224-9030
Hawaii Candy
Honolulu, HI 808-836-8955
Hawaiian King Candies
Honolulu, HI 800-570-1902
Hazelwood Farm Bakeries
Minneapolis, MN 314-595-4150
Health Valley Company
Irwindale, CA 800-334-3204
Heaven Scent Natural Foods
Santa Monica, CA 310-829-9050
Heavenscent Edibles
New York, NY 212-369-0310
Hedgehaven Specialty Foods
Ilwaco, WA 800-642-4711
Heinemann's Bakeries
Chicago, IL 312-239-5592
Heitzman Bakery
Louisville, KY 502-452-1891
HempNut
Henderson, NV 707-576-7050
Heritage Shortbread
Hilton Head Island, SC 843-342-7268
Hershey International
Weston, FL 954-385-2600
Heyerly Bakery
Ossian, IN 260-622-4196
Holt's Bakery
Douglas, GA 912-384-2202
Holton Food Products Company
La Grange, IL 708-352-5599
Honey Rose Baking Company
Encinitas, CA 760-942-8996
Hop Kee
Chicago, IL 312-791-9111
Hunt Country Foods
Middleburg, VA 540-364-2622
Immaculate Baking Company
Flat Rock, NC 828-696-1655
Immaculate Consumption
Flat Rock, NC 888-826-6567
Indianola Pecan House
Indianola, MS 800-541-6252
Innovative Health Products
Largo, FL 800-654-2347
Interbake Foods
Canby, OR 503-651-3003
Interbake Foods Corporate Office
Richmond, VA 804-755-7107
Irresistible Cookie Jar
Hayden Lake, ID 208-664-1261
Iversen Baking Company
Bedminster, PA 215-636-5904
J&J Snack Foods Corporation
Vernon, CA 800-486-7622
J&J Snack Foods Corporation
Pennsauken, NJ 856-665-9533
Jaeger Bakery
Milwaukee, WI 414-263-1700
Jamae Natural Foods
Los Angeles, CA 800-343-0052
Jenny Lee Bakery
Mc Kees Rocks, PA 412-331-8900
JFC International
Commerce, CA 800-633-1004

Jimmy's Cookies
Fair Lawn, NJ 201-797-8900
Joey's Fine Foods
Newark, NJ 973-482-1400
Joseph's Lite Cookies
Deming, NM 575-546-2839
JSL Foods
Los Angeles, CA 800-745-3236
Jubelt Variety Bakeries
Mount Olive, IL 217-999-7312
Just Desserts
San Francisco, CA 415-602-9245
K&F Select Fine Coffees
Portland, OR 800-558-7788
Karen's Fabulous Biscotti
White Plains, NY 914-682-2165
Kauai Kookie Kompany
Eleele, HI 800-361-1126
Keebler Company
Macon, GA 478-781-4620
Keebler Company
Branchburg, NJ 973-254-2000
Kellogg Company
Battle Creek, MI 800-962-1413
Kellogg Company Grand Rapids Bakery
Grand Rapids, MI 616-247-4841
Kellogg Food Away From Home
Elmhurst, IL 630-956-9645
Kellogg Snacks
Kansas City, KS 800-229-4414
Kellogg US Snack   Division
Battlecreek, MI 269-961-2000
Kelsen Bisca
Melville, NY 888-253-5736
Kemach Food Products   Corporation
Brooklyn, NY 888-453-6224
Kid's Kookie Company
San Clemente, CA. 800-350-7577
Kollar Cookies
Woodbridge, NJ 732-229-3364
Kraft
Parsippany, NJ. 973-292-1755
Kraft Food Ingredients
Memphis, TN 901-381-6500
Kraft Foods
East Hanover, NJ 973-503-2000
Kraft Foods Biscuit Confections & Snacks
East Hanover, NJ 973-503-2000
La Boulangerie
San Diego, CA 858-578-4040
Lady Walton's and Bronco Bob's Cowboy Brand
Specialty Foods
Dallas, TX 800-552-8006
Lady Walton's Cookies
Dallas, TX 800-552-8006
Laguna Cookie & Dessert Company
Santa Ana, CA 800-673-2473
Lance Inc
Charlotte, NC 800-438-1880
LaRosa Bakery
Shrewsbury, NJ 800-527-6722
Lazzaroni USA
Saddle Brook, NJ 201-368-1240
Liberty Richter
Saddle Brook, NJ 201-291-8749
Linden Cookies
Congers, NY 800-660-5051
Little Dutch Boy Bakeries
Draper, UT 801-571-3800
Lotte USA
Battle Creek, MI 269-963-6664
Lotus Bakery
Santa Rosa, CA 800-875-6887
Lovin' Oven
Hertford, NC 888-775-0099
Ludwick's Frozen Donuts
Grand Rapids, MI 800-366-8816
Luv Yu Bakery
Louisville, KY 502-451-4511
LWC Brands Inc
Dallas, TX 214-630-9101
Mac's Donut Shop
Aliquippa, PA 724-375-6776
MacFarms of Hawaii
Captain Cook, HI 808-328-2435
Magna Foods Corporation
City of Industry, CA 800-995-4394
Main Street Gourmet
Cuyahoga Falls, OH 800-533-6246
Main Street's Cambritt Cookies
Cuyahoga Falls, OH 800-533-6246

Mamma Says
Butler, NJ . . . 877-283-6282

Marin Food Specialties
Byron, CA . . . 925-634-6126

Maurice Lenell Cooky Company
Chicago, IL . . . 800-323-1760

Mayfair Sales
Buffalo, NY . . . 800-248-2881

McDuffies Bakery
Clarence, NY . . . 800-875-1598

McKee Foods Corporation
Collegedale, TN . . . 423-238-7111

McTavish Company
Portland, OR . . . 800-256-9844

Mercado Latino
City of Industry, CA . . . 626-333-6862

Merlino Italian Baking Company
Seattle, WA . . . 800-207-2997

Michael D's Cookies & Cakes
Aurora, IL . . . 630-892-2525

Michael's Cookies
San Diego, CA . . . 800-822-5384

Miss Meringue
San Marcos, CA . . . 800-561-6516

Monaco Baking Company
Santa Fe Springs, CA . . . 800-569-4640

Moravian Cookies Shop
Winston Salem, NC . . . 800-274-2994

Mozzicato De Pasquale Bakery Pastry
Hartford, CT . . . 860-296-0426

Mozzicato Depasquale Bakery & Pastry Shop
Hartford, CT . . . 860-296-0426

Mrs. Denson's Cookie Company
Ukiah, CA . . . 800-219-3199

Mt View Bakery
Mountain View, HI . . . 808-968-6353

Murray Biscuit Company
Atlanta, GA . . . 800-745-5582

Murray Biscuit Company/Kellogg Snacks
Charlotte, NC . . . 704-334-7611

Murray Biscuit Company/Kellogg Snacks
Clearwater, FL . . . 727-524-6000

Murray Biscuit Company/Kellogg Snacks
Augusta, GA . . . 800-776-2667

Murray Biscuit Company/Kellogg Snacks
Lake Bluff, IL . . . 847-689-8400

My Boy's Baking LLC
Allentown, PA . . . 610-759-4552

Nabisco Biscuit Company
Richmond, VA . . . 804-222-8802

National Food Corporation
Medley, FL . . . 305-884-2020

Natural Nectar
Huntington, NY . . . 631-367-7280

Nikki's Cookies
Milwaukee, WI . . . 800-776-7107

Northwest Candy Emporium
Everett, WA . . . 800-404-7266

Notre Dame Bakery
Lewisporte, NL . . . 709-535-2738

Nustef Foods
Mississauga, ON . . . 905-896-3060

Nutrilicious Natural Bakery
Countryside, IL . . . 800-835-8097

Oak State Products
Wenona, IL . . . 815-853-4348

Oh, Sugar! LLC
Roswell, GA . . . 866-557-8427

Old Colony Baking Company
Lake Bluff, IL . . . 847-283-9292

Olde Colony Bakery
Mt Pleasant, SC . . . 800-722-9932

Original Ya-hoo! Baking Company
Sherman, TX . . . 800-575-9373

Orlando's Pastries
Collingdale, PA . . . 610-532-9300

Osman's Pies
Stow, OH . . . 330-655-2919

Otis Spunkmeyer Company
Norcross, GA . . . 800-438-9251

Our Cookie
Oakland Park, FL . . . 877-885-2715

Our Thyme Garden
Cleburne, TX . . . 800-482-4372

Pamela's Products
Ukiah, CA . . . 707-462-6605

Parco Foods
Blue Island, IL . . . 708-371-9200

Paris Pastry
Los Angeles, CA . . . 310-474-8888

Parmalat
Toronto, ON . . . 800-563-1515

Partners, A Tastful Cracker
Seattle, WA . . . 800-632-7477

Pati-Petite Cookies
Bridgeville, PA . . . 800-253-5805

Peggy Lawton Kitchens
East Walpole, MA . . . 800-843-7325

Peking Noodle Company
Los Angeles, CA . . . 323-223-2023

Penny Curtiss Baking Company
Syracuse, NY . . . 315-454-3241

Pepperidge Farm
Norwalk, CT . . . 888-737-7374

Pepperidge Farms
Norwalk, CT . . . 888-737-7374

Pepsi
Chicago, IL . . . 312-821-1000

Petri Baking Products Inc
Silver Creek, NY . . . 800-346-1981

Pillsbury
McMinnville, OR . . . 800-325-5439

Pillsbury Frozen Foods
Lithonia, GA . . . 770-482-5092

Plehn's Bakery
St Matthews, KY . . . 502-896-4438

Poppie's Dough
Chicago, IL . . . 888-767-7431

Positively Third Street Bakery
Duluth, MN . . . 218-724-8619

Pure's Food Specialties
Broadview, IL . . . 708-344-8884

Quaker Bonnet
Buffalo, NY . . . 800-283-2447

Quality Naturally! Foods
City of Industry, CA . . . 888-498-6986

R.W. Frookies
Sag Harbor, NY . . . 800-913-3663

Ralcorp Holdings
St Louis, MO . . . 800-772-6757

Real Cookies
Merrick, NY . . . 800-822-5113

Redi-Froze
South Bend, IN . . . 574-237-5111

Rene Rey Chocolates Ltd
North Vancouver, BC . . . 888-985-0949

Rich Products Corporation
Buffalo, NY . . . 800-356-7094

Rich Products Corporation
Buffalo, NY . . . 800-828-2021

Richmond Baking Company
Richmond, IN . . . 765-962-8535

Rogers Bakery
Plainville, CT . . . 860-747-1686

Royal Court Cookie Company
North Hollywood, CA . . . 800-730-2545

Ryke's Bakery
Muskegon, MI . . . 231-557-8011

Sacramento Cookie Factory
Sacramento, CA . . . 877-877-2646

Saint Amour/Powerline Foods
Stanton, CA . . . 714-827-5366

Salem Baking Company
Winston Salem, NC . . . 800-274-2994

Salerno Foods
Des Plaines, IL . . . 800-247-2848

San Anselmo's Cookies & Biscotti
San Anselmo, CA . . . 800-229-1249

Sanitary Bakery
Little Falls, MN . . . 320-632-6388

Santa Fe Bite-Size Bakery
Albuquerque, NM . . . 505-342-1119

Sara Lee Bakery Group The EarthGrains - Bakery
Rome, GA . . . 706-295-4499

Sara Lee Corporation
Downers Grove, IL . . . 630-598-8100

Sarabeth's Kitchen
Bronx, NY . . . 718-589-2900

Sarabeth's Kitchen
Bronx, NY . . . 800-773-7378

Sarah Lingwood's Kitchen
Cape Coral, FL . . . 360-293-7181

Schulze & Burch Biscuit Company
Chicago, IL . . . 773-927-6622

Schwans Food Company
Norcross, GA . . . 800-241-0559

Schwans Frozen Foods
Marshall, MN . . . 800-533-5290

Scialo Brothers
Providence, RI . . . 877-421-0986

Selma's Cookies
Apopka, FL . . . 800-922-6654

Shepherdsfield Bakery
Fulton, MO . . . 573-642-1439

Sherwood Brands
Rockville, MD . . . 301-309-6161

Sheryl's Chocolate Creations
Hicksville, NY . . . 888-882-2462

Shur-Good Biscuit Co.
Cincinnati, OH . . . 513-458-6200

Silver Lake Cookie Company
Islip, NY . . . 631-581-4000

Silver Tray Cookies
Fort Lauderdale, FL . . . 305-883-0800

Simply Gourmet Confections
Irvine, CA . . . 714-505-3955

Sister's Gourmet
Dacula, GA . . . 877-338-1388

Smoak's Bakery & Catering Service
Augusta, GA . . . 706-738-1792

Somerset Industries
Spring House, PA . . . 800-883-8728

Sorbee International
Philadelphia, PA . . . 800-654-3997

Southernfood Specialties
Atlanta, GA . . . 800-255-5323

Specialty Foods Corporation
Deerfield, IL . . . 847-405-5300

Spilke's Baking Company
Brooklyn, NY . . . 718-384-2150

Sporting Colors LLC
Manhattan, KS . . . 888-394-2292

Spruce Foods
San Clemente, CA . . . 949-366-9457

Sprucewood Handmade Cookie Company
Warkworth, ON . . . 877-632-1300

St. Cloud Bakery
St Cloud, MN . . . 320-251-8055

Stauffer Biscuit Company
York, PA . . . 800-673-2473

Stauffer's
Cuba, NY . . . 585-968-2700

Stella Baking Company
Rockford, IL . . . 815-398-5191

Stella D'Oro Biscuit Company
Bronx, NY . . . 718-549-3700

Sterling Foods
San Antonio, TX . . . 210-490-1669

Steve's Mom
Bronx, NY . . . 800-362-4545

Stroehmann Bakeries
Norristown, PA . . . 800-984-0989

Sugar Kake Cookie
Tonawanda, NY . . . 800-775-5180

Sunset Specialty Foods
Sunset Beach, CA . . . 562-592-4976

Table de France
Ontario, CA . . . 909-923-5205

Taste of Nature
Beverly Hills, CA . . . 310-396-4433

Tastykake
Philadelphia, PA . . . 215-221-8500

Tate's Bake Shop
Southampton, NY . . . 631-283-9830

Tea Aura
Toronto, ON . . . 416-225-8868

The Bama Company
Tulsa, OK . . . 800-756-2262

Todd's
Vernon, CA . . . 800-938-6337

Torn Ranch
Novato, CA . . . 415-506-3000

Touche Bakery
London, ON . . . 518-455-0044

Traverse Bay Confections
Tukwila, WA . . . 206-725-0099

Tsue Chong Noodle Company
Seattle, WA . . . 206-623-0801

Turkey Hill Sugarbush
Waterloo, QC . . . 450-539-4822

Turnbull Bakeries
Chattanooga, TN . . . 800-488-7628

Uncle Ralph's Cookie Company
Frederick, MD . . . 800-422-0626

United Noodle Manufacturing Company
Salt Lake City, UT . . . 801-485-0951

United States Bakery
Portland, OR . . . 503-731-5679

Upper Crust Baking Company
Pismo Beach, CA . . . 800-676-1691

Uptown Bakers
Washington, DC . . . 202-546-6500

V L Foods
White Plains, NY . . . 914-697-4851

Valley Bakery
Rock Valley, IA . . . 712-476-5386

Vickey's Vittles
North Hills, CA..............818-841-1944
Vie de France Bakery
Bensenville, IL.............630-595-9521
Vista Bakery
Burlington, IA.............800-553-2343
Voortman Cookies
Burlington, ON............905-335-9500
Voortman Cookies
Bloomington, CA...........909-877-8471
Walkers Shortbread
Hauppauge, NY............800-521-0141
Wenger's Bakery
Reading, PA..............610-372-6545
Westbrae Natural Foods
Garden City, NY...........800-434-4246
Wildlife Cookie Company
Saint Charles, IL..........630-377-6196
Willmar Cookie & Nut Company
Willmar, MN..............320-235-0600
Wonton Food
Brooklyn, NY.............800-776-8889
Yohay Baking Company
Lindenhurst, NY...........631-225-0300
Yost's Dutch Maid Bakery
Johnstown, PA............814-266-3191
Young's Bakery
Uniontown, PA............724-437-6361
Yrica's Rugelach & Baking Company
Brooklyn, NY.............718-965-3657
YZ Enterprises
Maumee, OH..............800-736-8779
Zazi Baking Company
Petaluma, CA.............888-778-6399
Zeppys Bakery
Lawrence, MA.............781-963-7022

Cookies & Biscuits

A & M Cookie Company Canada
Kitchener, ON............800-265-6508
Almondina®/YZ Enterprises, Inc.
Maumee, OH..............800-736-8779
American Brittle
Sandusky, OH.............800-274-8853
Ames International
Fife, WA................888-469-2637
ARA Food Corporation
Miami, FL...............800-533-8831
Archway & Mother's Cookie Company
Oakland, CA..............800-369-3997
Archway Cookies
Ashland, OH..............888-427-2492
Arcor USA
Coral Gables, FL..........800-572-7267
Arturo's Bakery
Waterbury, CT............203-754-3056
Atlantic Baking Company
Pittsburgh, PA............412-361-2516
Atlas Biscuit Company
Verona, NJ..............973-239-8300
Aunt Gussie Cookies & Crackers
Garfield, NJ.............973-340-4480
Baker's Choice
Birmingham, MI...........248-827-7500
Barbara's Bakery
Petaluma, CA.............707-765-2273
Best Maid Cookie Company
River Falls, WI...........888-444-0322
Betty Lou's Golden Smackers
McMinnville, OR...........800-242-5205
Blue Chip Group
Salt Lake City, UT.........800-878-0099
Blue Dog Bakery
Seattle, WA..............888-749-7229
Boca Foods Company
Madison, WI.............608-285-6950
Borden's Bread
Regina, SK..............306-525-3341
Borinquen Biscuit Corporation
Yauco, PR...............787-856-3030
Breakfast at Brennan's
New Orleans, LA...........800-888-9932
Bremner Biscuit Company
Denver, CO..............800-722-1871
Bremner Company
Poteau, OK..............918-647-8630
Bridgford Foods Corporation Superior Foods Division
Anaheim, CA.............800-527-2105
Brooklyn Baking Company
Waterbury, CT............203-574-9198

Buckeye Pretzel Company
Williamsport, PA..........800-257-6029
Buon Italia
New York, NY............212-633-9090
Busken Bakery
Cincinnati, OH............513-871-2114
Cains Foods/Olde Cape Cod
Ayer, MA...............800-225-0601
Carolina Cupboard
Hillsborough, NC..........800-400-3441
Cascade Cookie Company
St Louis, MO.............314-877-7000
Case Side Holdings Company
Kensington, PE...........902-836-4214
CGI Desserts
Sugar Land, TX...........281-240-1200
Charlie's Specialties
Hermitage, PA............724-346-2350
Chelsea Market Baskets
New York, NY............888-727-7887
Chocolate Chix
Waxahachie, TX...........214-744-2442
CJ Vitner Company
Chicago, IL..............773-523-7900
Columbus Bakery
Columbus, OH............614-645-2275
Confection Solutions
Sylmar, CA..............800-284-2422
Consolidated Biscuit Company
Mc Comb, OH.............800-537-9544
Cookie Specialties
Wheeling, IL.............847-537-3888
Cookie Tree Bakeries
Salt Lake City, UT.........800-998-0111
Country Home Bakers
Torrance, CA.............800-672-6277
Dairy State Foods
Milwaukee, WI............800-435-4499
Dancing Deer Baking Company
Hyde Park, MA............888-699-3337
Dare Foods
Toronto, ON.............800-665-5817
Dare Foods
Kitchener, ON............800-865-8225
Dave's Bakery
Honesdale, PA............570-253-1660
Davis Cookie Company
Rimersburg, PA...........814-473-8181
De Bas Chocolatier
Fresno, CA..............559-294-7638
De Beukelaer Corporation
Madison, MS.............601-856-7454
Delicious Frookie Company
Des Plaines, IL...........847-699-5900
DF Stauffer Biscuit Company
York, PA...............800-673-2473
Di Camillo Bakery
Niagara Falls, NY..........800-634-4363
Diamond Bakery Company
Honolulu, HI.............808-845-8200
Dinkel's Bakery
Chicago, IL..............800-822-8817
Dong Kee Company
Chicago, IL..............312-225-6340
Dough Works Company
Horicon, WI.............800-383-8808
Dufflet Pastries
Toronto, ON.............416-536-1330
Dunford Bakers
Fayetteville, AR...........479-521-3000
Dutchess Bakery
Charleston, WV...........304-346-3210
Edelweiss Patisserie
Charlestown, MA..........617-628-0225
Edward & Sons Trading Company
Carpinteria, CA...........805-684-8500
El Segundo Bakery
El Segundo, CA...........310-322-3422
Elmwood Pastry
West Hartford, CT.........860-233-2029
Erba Food Products
Brooklyn, NY............718-272-7700
Evans Bakery
Cozad, NE..............800-222-5641
Falcone's Cookieland
Brooklyn, NY............718-236-4200
Fantasy Cookie Company
Sylmar, CA..............800-354-4488
Federal Pretzel Baking Company
Philadelphia, PA..........215-467-0505
Fernando C Pujals & Bros
San Juan, PR............787-792-3080

Ferrara Bakery & Cafe
New York, NY............212-226-6150
Fireside Kitchen
Halifax, NS..............902-454-7387
Flowers Baking
San Antonio, TX...........210-661-2361
Food Mill
Oakland, CA.............510-482-3848
Fortella Fortune Cookies
Chicago, IL..............312-567-9000
Fortune Cookie Factory
Oakland, CA.............510-832-5552
Foxtail Foods
Fairfield, OH.............800-323-6944
Frankly Natural Bakers
San Diego, CA............800-727-7229
Fujiya
Honolulu, HI.............808-845-2921
G H Bent Company
Milton, MA..............617-698-5945
George Weston Bakeries
Northlake, IL.............708-562-6311
George Weston Bakeries
Hollywood, FL............800-356-3314
Giant Food
Lanham, MD.............888-469-4426
Glazier Packing Company
Potsdam, NY.............315-265-2500
Golden Glow Cookie Company
Bronx, NY..............718-379-6223
GPR Company
Stowe, PA..............610-326-4777
Grandma Beth's Cookies
Alliance, NE.............308-762-8433
Granowska's
Toronto, ON.............416-533-7755
Greyston Bakery
Yonkers, NY.............800-289-2253
GWB Foods Corporation
Brooklyn, NY............718-686-9600
H.E. Butt Grocery Company
San Antonio, TX...........800-432-3113
Hain Celestial Group
Melville, NY.............800-434-4246
Handy Pax
Randolph, MA............781-963-8300
Harvest Valley Bakery
La Salle, IL.............815-224-9030
Hawaii Candy
Honolulu, HI.............808-836-8955
Health Valley Company
Irwindale, CA............800-334-3204
Hedgehaven Specialty Foods
Ilwaco, WA.............800-642-4711
Heinemann's Bakeries
Chicago, IL..............312-239-5592
Hershey International
Weston, FL..............954-385-2600
Heyerly Bakery
Ossian, IN..............260-622-4196
Holland-American Wafer Company
Wyoming, MI............800-253-8350
Holt's Bakery
Douglas, GA.............912-384-2202
Honey Rose Baking Company
Encinitas, CA............760-942-8996
Hunt Country Foods
Middleburg, VA...........540-364-2622
Hye Quality Bakery
Fresno, CA..............877-445-1778
Immaculate Consumption
Flat Rock, NC............888-826-6567
Innovative Health Products
Largo, FL...............800-654-2347
Interbake Foods
Canby, OR..............503-651-3003
Interbake Foods Corporate Office
Richmond, VA............804-755-7107
Irresistible Cookie Jar
Hayden Lake, ID...........208-664-1261
Iversen Baking Company
Bedminster, PA...........215-636-5904
J&J Snack Foods Corporation
Vernon, CA..............800-486-7622
J&J Snack Foods Corporation
Pennsauken, NJ...........856-665-9533
Jaeger Bakery
Milwaukee, WI...........414-263-1700
Jamae Natural Foods
Los Angeles, CA...........800-343-0052
James Candy Company
Atlantic City, NJ..........800-441-1404

JFC International
Commerce, CA 800-633-1004
Jim's Cheese Pantry
Waterloo, WI 800-345-3571
Jimmy's Cookies
Fair Lawn, NJ 201-797-8900
Joey's Fine Foods
Newark, NJ 973-482-1400
Jubelt Variety Bakeries
Mount Olive, IL 217-999-7312
Just Desserts
San Francisco, CA 415-602-9245
Karp's
Schaumburg, IL. 800-593-5277
Keebler Company
Macon, GA 478-781-4620
Keebler Company
Branchburg, NJ 973-254-2000
Kellogg Company Grand Rapids Bakery
Grand Rapids, MI 616-247-4841
Kellogg Snacks
Kansas City, KS 800-229-4414
Kellogg US Snack   Division
Battlecreek, MI 269-961-2000
Kemach Food Products   Corporation
Brooklyn, NY 888-453-6224
KHS-Bartelt
Sarasota, FL 800-829-9980
Kid's Kookie Company
San Clemente, CA. 800-350-7577
Kinnikinnick Foods
Edmonton, AB 877-503-4466
Kollar Cookies
Woodbridge, NJ 732-229-3364
Koyo Foods
Richmond, CA 510-527-7066
Kraft
Parsippany, NJ. 973-292-1755
Kraft Food Ingredients
Memphis, TN 901-381-6500
Kraft Foods
Atlanta, GA 404-756-6000
Kraft Foods
East Hanover, NJ 973-503-2000
Kraft Foods   kery
Chicago, IL 800-572-3847
Kraft Foods Biscuit Confections & Snacks
East Hanover, NJ 973-503-2000
La Boulangerie
San Diego, CA 858-578-4040
Lady Walton's and Bronco Bob's Cowboy Brand
Specialty Foods
Dallas, TX. 800-552-8006
Lady Walton's Cookies
Dallas, TX 800-552-8006
Laguna Cookie & Dessert Company
Santa Ana, CA 800-673-2473
Lance Inc
Charlotte, NC 800-438-1880
LaRosa Bakery
Shrewsbury, NJ 800-527-6722
Liberty Richter
Saddle Brook, NJ 201-291-8749
Linden Cookies
Congers, NY 800-660-5051
Little Dutch Boy Bakeries
Draper, UT 801-571-3800
Log House Foods
Plymouth, MN. 763-546-8395
Lotus Bakery
Santa Rosa, CA 800-875-6887
Ludwick's Frozen Donuts
Grand Rapids, MI 800-366-8816
Mac's Donut Shop
Aliquippa, PA 724-375-6776
MacFarms of Hawaii
Captain Cook, HI 808-328-2435
Magna Foods Corporation
City of Industry, CA 800-995-4394
Marin Food Specialties
Byron, CA 925-634-6126
Marshall Biscuits
Saraland, AL 251-679-6226
Maurice Lenell Cooky Company
Chicago, IL 800-323-1760
Mercado Latino
City of Industry, CA 626-333-6862
Merlino International Baking Company
Seattle, WA 800-207-2997
Michael D's Cookies & Cakes
Aurora, IL 630-892-2525

Mom's Food Company
South El Monte, CA 800-969-6667
Mozzicato De Pasquale Bakery Pastry
Hartford, CT 860-296-0426
Mozzicato Depasquale Bakery & Pastry Shop
Hartford, CT 860-296-0426
Mt View Bakery
Mountain View, HI 808-968-6353
Murray Biscuit Company
Atlanta, GA 800-745-5582
Murray Biscuit Company/Kellogg Snacks
Charlotte, NC 704-334-7611
Murray Biscuit Company/Kellogg Snacks
Clearwater, FL 727-524-6000
Murray Biscuit Company/Kellogg Snacks
Augusta, GA 800-776-2667
Nabisco Biscuit Company
Philadelphia, PA 215-673-4800
Nabisco Biscuit Company
Richmond, VA. 804-222-8802
National Food Corporation
Medley, FL 305-884-2020
New Morning
Needham, MA. 781-444-0440
Nicole's Divine Crackers
Chicago, IL 312-640-8883
Nikki's Cookies
Milwaukee, WI 800-776-7107
Northwest Candy Emporium
Everett, WA. 800-404-7266
Notre Dame Bakery
Lewisporte, NL 709-535-2738
Nustef Foods
Mississauga, ON 905-896-3060
Nutrilicious Natural Bakery
Countryside, IL 800-835-8097
Oak State Products
Wenona, IL 815-853-4348
Ohta Wafer Factory
Honolulu, HI 808-949-2775
Original Ya-hoo! Baking Company
Sherman, TX 800-575-9373
Orlando's Pastries
Collingdale, PA 610-532-9300
Osman's Pies
Stow, OH 330-655-2919
Our Thyme Garden
Cleburne, TX 800-482-4372
Parco Foods
Blue Island, IL 708-371-9200
Paris Pastry
Los Angeles, CA. 310-474-8888
Parmalat
Toronto, ON 800-563-1515
Pati-Petite Cookies
Bridgeville, PA 800-253-5805
Peggy Lawton Kitchens
East Walpole, MA. 800-843-7325
Peking Noodle Company
Los Angeles, CA. 323-223-2023
Pepperidge Farm
Norwalk, CT 888-737-7374
Petri Baking Products Inc
Silver Creek, NY 800-346-1981
Pillsbury Frozen Foods
Lithonia, GA 770-482-5092
Pioneer Frozen Foods
Duncanville, TX 972-298-4281
Positively Third Street Bakery
Duluth, MN. 218-724-8619
Pure's Food Specialties
Broadview, IL 708-344-8884
Purity Factories
St.John's, NL. 800-563-3411
R.M. Palmer Company
Reading, PA 610-372-8971
R.W. Frookies
Sag Harbor, NY. 800-913-3663
Ralcorp Holdings
St Louis, MO. 800-772-6757
Rich Products Corporation
Buffalo, NY. 800-356-7094
Rich Products Corporation
Buffalo, NY. 800-828-2021
Richmond Baking Company
Richmond, IN 765-962-8535
Rogers Bakery
Plainville, CT 860-747-1686
Rovira Biscuit Corporation
Ponce, PR 787-844-8585
Royal Court Cookie Company
North Hollywood, CA 800-730-2545

Royal Wine Company
Bayonne, NJ 201-437-9131
Ryke's Bakery
Muskegon, MI. 231-557-8011
S&M Communion Bread Company
Nashville, TN 615-292-1969
Saint Amour/Powerline Foods
Stanton, CA. 714-827-5366
Salem Baking Company
Winston Salem, NC 800-274-2994
Salerno Foods
Des Plaines, IL 800-247-2848
San Anselmo's Cookies & Biscotti
San Anselmo, CA 800-229-1249
San-J International
Richmond, VA. 800-446-5500
Sanitary Bakery
Little Falls, MN. 320-632-6388
Santa Fe Bite-Size Bakery
Albuquerque, NM 505-342-1119
Sara Lee Bakery Group The EarthGrains - Bakery
Rome, GA 706-295-4499
Sara Lee Corporation
Downers Grove, IL 630-598-8100
Sarah Lingwood's Kitchen
Cape Coral, FL 360-293-7181
Schulze & Burch Biscuit Company
Chicago, IL 773-927-6622
Schwans Food Company
Norcross, GA 800-241-0559
Schwans Frozen Foods
Marshall, MN 800-533-5290
Scialo Brothers
Providence, RI 877-421-0986
Seckinger-Lee Company
Savannah, GA 800-291-2973
Sherwood Brands
Rockville, MD 301-309-6161
Sheryl's Chocolate Creations
Hicksville, NY 888-882-2462
Silver Lake Cookie Company
Islip, NY 631-581-4000
Silver Tray Cookies
Fort Lauderdale, FL 305-883-0800
Smoak's Bakery & Catering Service
Augusta, GA 706-738-1792
Spilke's Baking Company
Brooklyn, NY 718-384-2150
Sporting Colors LLC
Manhattan, KS 888-394-2292
St. Cloud Bakery
St Cloud, MN 320-251-8055
Stauffer's
Cuba, NY 585-968-2700
Stella Baking Company
Rockford, IL 815-398-5191
Stella D'Oro Biscuit Company
Bronx, NY. 718-549-3700
Sterling Foods
San Antonio, TX 210-490-1669
Stroehmann Bakeries
Norristown, PA 800-984-0989
Sugar Kake Cookie
Tonawanda, NY 800-775-5180
Sunset Specialty Foods
Sunset Beach, CA 562-592-4976
Table de France
Ontario, CA. 909-923-5205
Tastykake
Philadelphia, PA 215-221-8500
Terra Harvest Foods
Rockford, IL 815-636-9500
The Bama Company
Tulsa, OK 800-756-2262
Treasure Foods
West Valley, UT. 801-974-0911
Triple-C
Hamilton, ON 800-263-9105
Tsue Chong Noodle Company
Seattle, WA 206-623-0801
Turano Pastry Shops
Bloomingdale, IL 630-529-6161
Turnbull Cone Baking Company
Chattanooga, TN. 423-265-4551
Tuscan Bakery
Portland, OR 800-887-2261
Ultimate Biscotti
Eugene, OR 541-344-8220
Uncle Ralph's Cookie Company
Frederick, MD. 800-422-0626
United Noodle Manufacturing Company
Salt Lake City, UT. 801-485-0951

Upper Crust Baking Company
Pismo Beach, CA 800-676-1691
Uptown Bakers
Washington, DC 202-546-6500
Utz Quality Foods
Hanover, PA 800-367-7629
V L Foods
White Plains, NY 914-697-4851
Venus Wafers
Hingham, MA 800-545-4538
Vista Bakery
Burlington, IA 800-553-2343
Voortman Cookies
Bloomington, CA 909-877-8471
Wenger's Bakery
Reading, PA 610-372-6545
Westbrae Natural Foods
Garden City, NY 800-434-4246
Willmar Cookie & Nut Company
Willmar, MN 320-235-0600
Wise Foods
Kennesaw, GA 770-426-5821
Wonder Bread
Provo, UT .801-373-8192
Wonton Food
Brooklyn, NY 800-776-8889
Yost's Dutch Maid Bakery
Johnstown, PA 814-266-3191
Young's Bakery
Uniontown, PA 724-437-6361
Yrica's Rugelach & Baking Company
Brooklyn, NY 718-965-3657
YZ Enterprises
Maumee, OH 800-736-8779
Zeppys Bakery
Lawrence, MA 781-963-7022

Fortune Cookies

Dong Kee Company
Chicago, IL 312-225-6340
Fortella Fortune Cookies
Chicago, IL 312-567-9000
Fortune Cookie Factory
Oakland, CA 510-832-5552
Hawaii Candy
Honolulu, HI 808-836-8955
JFC International
Commerce, CA 800-633-1004
Ohta Wafer Factory
Honolulu, HI 808-949-2775
Peking Noodle Company
Los Angeles, CA 323-223-2023
Tsue Chong Noodle Company
Seattle, WA 206-623-0801
United Noodle Manufacturing Company
Salt Lake City, UT 801-485-0951
Wings Foods of Alberta
Edmonton, AB 780-433-6406
Wonton Food
Brooklyn, NY 800-776-8889

Frozen Cookies

Baker & Baker, Inc.
Schaumburg, IL 800-593-5777
Evans Bakery
Cozad, NE 800-222-5641
Glazier Packing Company
Potsdam, NY 315-265-2500
GWB Foods Corporation
Brooklyn, NY 718-686-9600
McGlynn Bakeries, LLC
Minneapolis, MN 763-574-2423
Parco Foods
Blue Island, IL 708-371-9200
Rich Products Corporation
Buffalo, NY 800-356-7094
Rich Products Corporation
Buffalo, NY 800-828-2021
Sara Lee Corporation
Downers Grove, IL 630-598-8100
Sunset Specialty Foods
Sunset Beach, CA 562-592-4976
The Bama Company
Tulsa, OK .800-756-2262

Ginger Snaps

Country Choice Naturals
Eden Prairie, MN 952-829-8824

Individually Packaged

Big Shoulders Baking
Chicago, IL 800-456-9328

Lady Fingers

Ambassador Foods
Van Nuys, CA 800-338-3369

Macaroons

Erba Food Products
Brooklyn, NY 718-272-7700
L&M Bakery
Lawrence, MA 978-687-7346
Red Mill Farms
Brooklyn, NY 800-344-2253
Steve's Mom
Bronx, NY 800-362-4545

Mini Cookies

Bauducco Foods Inc
Miami, FL .305-477-9270

Oatmeal & Chocolate Chip Cookies

Main Street Gourmet
Cuyahoga Falls, OH 800-533-6246
Main Street's Cambritt Cookies
Cuyahoga Falls, OH 800-533-6246

Oatmeal Cookies

Country Choice Naturals
Eden Prairie, MN 952-829-8824
Hazelwood Farm Bakeries
Minneapolis, MN 314-595-4150
Main Street Gourmet
Cuyahoga Falls, OH 800-533-6246
Main Street's Cambritt Cookies
Cuyahoga Falls, OH 800-533-6246
Mississippi Cheese StrawFactory
Yazoo City, MS 866-830-9415
Murray Biscuit Company
Atlanta, GA 800-745-5582
Peggy Lawton Kitchens
East Walpole, MA 800-843-7325
Wampler Foods
Dallas, TX 717-624-2191

Oatmeal Raisin Cookies

Hazelwood Farm Bakeries
Minneapolis, MN 314-595-4150
Main Street Gourmet
Cuyahoga Falls, OH 800-533-6246
Main Street's Cambritt Cookies
Cuyahoga Falls, OH 800-533-6246

Sandwich Creme Cookies

Country Choice Naturals
Eden Prairie, MN 952-829-8824
Kellogg Snacks
Kansas City, KS 800-229-4414
Sugar Kake Cookie
Tonawanda, NY 800-775-5180
Vista Bakery
Burlington, IA 800-553-2343

Soft Cookies

Oak State Products
Wenona, IL 815-853-4348

Sugar Cookies

Falcone's Cookieland
Brooklyn, NY 718-236-4200
Main Street Gourmet
Cuyahoga Falls, OH 800-533-6246
Main Street's Cambritt Cookies
Cuyahoga Falls, OH 800-533-6246
Murray Biscuit Company
Atlanta, GA 800-745-5582
Young's Bakery
Uniontown, PA 724-437-6361

Tea Cookies

Hawaii Candy
Honolulu, HI 808-836-8955

Ohta Wafer Factory
Honolulu, HI 808-949-2775

Wafers

Arcor USA
Coral Gables, FL 800-572-7267
Castella Imports
Hauppauge, NY 866-227-8355
Ce De Candy
Union, NJ .800-631-7968
Dayhoff
Clearwater, FL 800-354-3372
Fernando C Pujals & Bros
San Juan, PR 787-792-3080
Functional Foods
Roseville, MI 877-372-0550
Gold Star Chocolate
Brooklyn, NY 718-330-0187
Holland-American Wafer Company
Wyoming, MI 800-253-8350
Honey Wafer Baking Company
Crestwood, IL 800-261-2984
Kitchen Table Bakers
Syosset, NY. 800-486-4582
Lady Walton's Cookies
Dallas, TX 800-552-8006
Lance Inc
Charlotte, NC 800-438-1880
Mayfair Sales
Buffalo, NY 800-248-2881
PEZ Candy
Orange, CT 203-795-0531
Q Bell Foods
Nyack, NY 845-358-1475
Royal Wine Company
Bayonne, NJ 201-437-9131
Sherwood Brands
Rockville, MD 301-309-6161
Table de France
Ontario, CA. 909-923-5205
Turnbull Bakeries
Chattanooga, TN 800-488-7628
V L Foods
White Plains, NY 914-697-4851
Yohay Baking Company
Lindenhurst, NY 631-225-0300

Sugar

Abitec Corporation
Columbus, OH 800-555-1255
ACATRIS
Oakville, ON. 905-829-2414
ADM Cocoa
Milwaukee, WI 800-558-9958
ADM Milling Company
Shawnee Mission, KS. 913-266-6300
Alfred L. Wolff, Inc.
Park Ridge, IL 312-265-9889
American Culinary Gardens
Springfield, MO 888-831-2433
Annie's Frozen Yogurt
Minneapolis, MN 800-969-9648
Aunt Aggie De's Pralines
Sinton, TX 888-772-5463
BakeMark Canada
Laval, QC .800-361-4998
Bakery Crafts
West Chester, OH 800-543-1673
Barry Callebaut USA, Inc.
Pennsauken, NJ 800-836-2626
Bouchard Family Farm
Fort Kent, ME 800-239-3237
Brookside Foods
Abbotsford, BC 877-793-3866
Calico Cottage
Amityville, NY 800-645-5345
California Cereal Products
Oakland, CA 510-452-4500
Canada Bread
Etobicoke, ON 416-622-2040
Cargill Flour Milling
Minneapolis, MN 800-227-4455
Chelsea Milling Company
Chelsea, MI. 734-475-1361
City Bakery
Hallettsville, TX 800-272-9416
Country Choice Naturals
Eden Prairie, MN 952-829-8824
Crown Processing Company
Bellflower, CA 562-865-0293

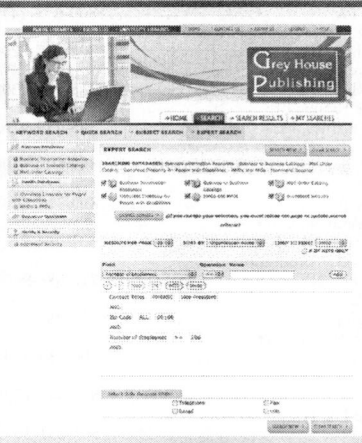

Dutch Ann Foods Company
Natchez, MS 601-445-5566
Ellison Milling Company
Lethbridge, AB 403-328-6622
Embassy Flavours Ltd.
Brampton, ON. 800-334-3371
Flavormatic Industries
Wappingers Falls, NY 845-297-9100
Flavtek
Los Angeles, CA 800-562-5880
Foley's Candies
Richmond, BC 888-236-5397
French's Ingredients
Springfield, MO 417-837-1813
Georgia Nut Ingredients
Skokie, IL 877-674-2993
Ghirardelli Chocolate Company
Short Hills, NJ 800-877-9338
Gold Coast Ingredients
Commerce, CA 800-352-8673
Golden Foods
Commerce, CA 800-350-2462
Great Recipes Company
Beaverton, OR 800-273-2331
Gregory's Foods
Eagan, MN 800-231-4734
GWB Foods Corporation
Brooklyn, NY 718-686-9600
Halton Flour Milling
Acton, ON. 800-608-7694
Ingredients, Inc.
Buffalo Grove, IL 847-419-9595
Karp's
Georgetown, MA 800-373-5277
Kerry Sweets Ingredients
Gridley, IL 309-747-3534
La Cookie
Houston, TX 713-784-2722
Marie Callender's Gourmet Products/Goldrush Products
San Jose, CA. 800-729-5428
Martha Olson's Great Foods
Sutter Creek, CA. 800-973-3966
Mimac Glaze
Brampton, ON. 877-990-9975
Natrium Products
Cortland, NY 800-962-4203
Ottens Flavors
Philadelphia, PA 800-523-0767
Paradise Island Foods
Nanaimo, BC 800-889-3370
Petra International
Hamilton, ON 800-261-7226
Petrofsky's Bagels
Saint Louis, MO 314-432-4177
Pillsbury
Minneapolis, MN 800-845-3103
Pillsbury Bakeries & Food Services
Sherwood Park, AB 780-464-1544
Produits Alimentaire
St Lambert De Lauzon, QC 800-463-1787
Purato's
Seattle, WA 206-762-5400
Riceland Foods   Rice Milling Operations
Little Rock, AR. 888-532-4844
Rich Products Corporation
Hilliard, OH. 614-771-1117
Rich Products Corporation
Cameron, WI. 715-458-4556
Royal Wine Company
Bayonne, NJ 201-437-9131
Sanford Milling Company
Henderson, NC 252-438-4526
Saputo Cheese
Lincolnshire, IL 800-558-9714
Schwans Frozen Foods
Marshall, MN 800-533-5290
Southern Brown Rice
Weiner, AR 800-421-7423
Southern Style Nuts
Sherman, TX 800-624-8242
Sugar Flowers Plus
Glendale, CA 800-972-2935
Tastee Fare
Little Rock, AR. 501-568-7870
Tasty Selections
Concord, ON 905-760-2353
Teff Company
Caldwell, ID 888-822-2221
Vanco Products Company
Dorchester, MA 617-265-3400
Westco-Bake Mark
Pico Rivera, CA 562-949-1054

Wilbur Chocolate
Lititz, PA 800-233-0139
WILD Flavors
Cincinnati, OH 888-945-3352
Wilsonhill Farm
Underhill, VT 802-899-2154
Yorktown Baking Company
Yorktown Heights, NY 800-235-3961

Crackers

Crackers

American Vintage Wine Biscuits
Long Island City, NY 718-361-1003
Archway & Mother's Cookie Company
Oakland, CA 800-369-3997
Aunt Gussie Cookies & Crackers
Garfield, NJ 973-340-4480
Bake Crafters Food
Collegedale, TN 800-296-8935
Blue Dog Bakery
Seattle, WA 888-749-7229
Borinquen Biscuit Corporation
Yauco, PR 787-856-3030
Bremner Company
Poteau, OK 918-647-8630
Cains Foods
Ayer, MA 978-772-0300
Christie-Brown
East Hanover, NJ 973-503-4000
Columbus Bakery
Columbus, OH 614-645-2275
Confection Solutions
Sylmar, CA 800-284-2422
Dairyfood USA Inc
Blue Mounds, WI 800-236-3300
Dare Foods
Denver, CO 800-722-1871
Dare Foods Incorporated
Kitchener, ON 800-265-8222
Dave's Bakery
Honesdale, PA. 570-253-1660
Dengler's Bakery
Souderton, PA 215-723-2706
DF Stauffer Biscuit Company
York, PA 800-673-2473
Diamond Bakery Company
Honolulu, HI 808-845-8200
Falcone's Cookieland
Brooklyn, NY 718-236-4200
Fortitude Brands LLC
Coral Gables, FL 305-439-9763
Frookie
Des Plaines, IL 847-699-3200
Glutino
Laval, QC 800-363-3438
Good Health Natural Foods
Northport, NY 631-261-2111
GWB Foods Corporation
Brooklyn, NY 718-686-9600
Handy Pax
Randolph, MA 781-963-8300
Health Valley Company
Irwindale, CA 800-334-3204
Hye Quality Bakery
Fresno, CA 877-445-1778
Interbake Foods
Canby, OR. 503-651-3003
Interbake Foods Corporate Office
Richmond, VA. 804-755-7107
Jim's Cheese Pantry
Waterloo, WI. 800-345-3571
Keebler Company
Macon, GA 478-781-4620
Keebler Company
Branchburg, NJ 973-254-2000
Kellogg Company
Battle Creek, MI 800-962-1413
Kellogg Company Grand Rapids Bakery
Grand Rapids, MI 616-247-4841
Kellogg Snacks
Kansas City, KS 800-229-4414
Kellogg US Snack   Division
Battlecreek, MI 269-961-2000
Kemach Food Products   Corporation
Brooklyn, NY 888-453-6224
KHS-Bartelt
Sarasota, FL 800-829-9980
Kraft
Parsippany, NJ. 973-292-1755

Kraft Food Ingredients
Memphis, TN 901-381-6500
Kraft Foods
East Hanover, NJ 973-503-2000
La Panzanella
Tukwila, WA 206-903-0500
La Piccolina
Decatur, GA 800-626-1624
Liberty Richter
Saddle Brook, NJ 201-291-8749
Linden Cookies
Congers, NY 800-660-5051
Magna Foods Corporation
City of Industry, CA 800-995-4394
Mary's Gone Crackers
Gridley, CA 888-258-1250
Murray Biscuit Company
Atlanta, GA 800-745-5582
Murray Biscuit Company/Kellogg
Alpharetta, GA 800-745-5582
Nabisco Biscuit Company
Richmond, VA. 804-222-8802
New Morning
Needham, MA. 781-444-0440
Nicole's Divine Crackers
Chicago, IL 312-640-8883
Oberweis Dairy
North Aurora, IL 888-645-5868
Pepperidge Farms
Norwalk, CT 888-737-7374
Pinahs Company
Waukesha, WI 800-967-2447
R.A.B. Food Group LLC
Secaucus, NJ 201-453-5200
Ralcorp Holdings
St Louis, MO. 800-772-6757
Richmond Baking Company
Richmond, IN 765-962-8535
Rovira Biscuit Corporation
Ponce, PR 787-844-8585
Royal Wine Company
Bayonne, NJ 201-437-9131
Salerno Foods
Des Plaines, IL 800-247-2848
Santa Fe Bite-Size Bakery
Albuquerque, NM 505-342-1119
Schulze & Burch Biscuit Company
Chicago, IL 773-927-6622
Stauffer Biscuit Company
York, PA 800-673-2473
Stella Baking Company
Rockford, IL 815-398-5191
Terra Harvest Foods
Rockford, IL 815-636-9500
The Bama Company
Tulsa, OK 800-756-2262
Urban Accents
Chicago, IL 877-872-7742
Urban Oven
Tempe, AZ 866-770-6836
Venus Wafers
Hingham, MA 800-545-4538
Vision Pack Brands
El Segundo, CA 877-477-8500
Vista Bakery
Burlington, IA 800-553-2343
Willmar Cookie & Nut Company
Willmar, MN 320-235-0600

Meal

Newly Weds Foods
Chicago, IL 800-621-7521
Richmond Baking Company
Richmond, IN 765-962-8535
Sugar Foods Corporation
New York, NY 212-753-6900

Crunches

Nuvex Ingredients
Blue Earth, MN 507-526-4331

Desserts

Adams Foods
Dothan, AL 334-983-4233
AFP Advanced Food Products, LLC
Visalia, CA 559-627-2070
Aglamesis Brothers
Cincinnati, OH 513-531-5196
Agropur Cooperative Agro-Alimentaire
Granby, QC 800-363-5686

Akenhead's Ice Cream Company
East Palestine, OH 330-426-9553
Al Gelato Bornay
Franklin Park, IL. 847-455-5355
Alamance Foods/Triton Water Company
Burlington, NC 800-476-9111
Alati-Caserta Desserts
Montreal, QC .514-271-3013
Albertson's Ice-Cream
Boise, ID 877-932-7948
Alinosi French Superfine Candies
Detroit, MI 313-527-3195
Alpenrose Dairy
Portland, OR .503-244-1133
AlpineAire Foods
Rocklin, CA 800-322-6325
Ambassador Foods
Van Nuys, CA 800-338-3369
Amboy Specialty Foods Company
Dixon, IL. 800-892-0400
American Classic Ice Cream Company
Bay Shore, NY 631-666-1000
Americana Foods
Dallas, TX. 972-709-7100
Andre-Boudin Bakeries
San Francisco, CA 415-882-1849
Anke Kruse Organics
Guelph, ON. .519-824-6161
ASK Foods
Palmyra, PA. .800-879-4275
Athens Pastries & Frozen Foods
Cleveland, OH 800-837-5683
Atlanta Flagship Dairy
Atlanta, GA 800-224-0669
Awrey Bakeries
Livonia, MI. 800-950-2253
Baker & Baker
Schaumburg, IL. 800-593-5777
Baker's Choice
Birmingham, MI 248-827-7500
Bakery Chef
Chicago, IL 773-384-1900
Bakery Corp
Miami, FL 800-521-4345
Bakery Europa
Honolulu, HI .808-845-5011
Balboa Dessert Company
Santa Ana, CA 800-974-9699
Banquet Schuster Bakery
Pueblo, CO 719-544-1062
Barnes Ice Cream Company
Augusta, ME. 207-622-0827
Baskin-Robbins Flavors
Burbank, CA. 800-859-5339
BBU Bakeries
Denver, CO. .303-691-6342
Beatrice Bakery Company
Beatrice, NE .800-228-4030
Benson Creamery
Decatur, IL 217-429-2351
Benson's Bakery
Bogart, GA 800-888-6059
Bernie's Foods
Brooklyn, NY 718-417-6677
Best Brands Corporation
Dallas, TX. 800-969-2253
Best Maid Cookie Company
River Falls, WI 888-444-0322
Bestfoods Foodservice
Somerset, NJ 732-627-8722
Beth's Fine Desserts
Cotati, CA 415-464-1891
Bill Mack's Homemade Ice Cream
Dover, PA 717-292-1931
Birdsall Ice Cream Company
Mason City, IA 641-423-5365
Birkholm's Jr Danish Bakery
Solvang, CA .805-688-3872
Bittersweet Pastries
Norwood, NJ 800-537-7791
Black's Barbecue
Lockhart, TX. 512-398-2712
Blue Bell Creameries
Brenham, TX .979-836-7977
Blue Ridge Farms
Chicago, IL 708-748-4405
Blue Ridge Farms
Brooklyn, NY 718-827-9000
Bonnie Doon Ice Cream Corporation
Elkhart, IN. 574-264-3390
Borden's Bread
Regina, SK 306-525-3341

Bottineau Cooperative Creamery
Bottineau, ND 701-228-2216
Brenner's Bakery of Arlington
Arlington, VA .703-534-0211
Brighams
Arlington, MA 800-274-4426
Broughton Foods
Marietta, OH .800-283-2479
Brown's Ice Cream
Minneapolis, MN 612-378-1075
Browns Dairy
Valparaiso, IN 219-464-4141
Browns' Ice Cream Company
Bowling Green, KY 270-843-9882
Bubbies Homemade Ice Cream
Aiea, HI. 808-487-7218
Buck's Spumoni Company
Milford, CT. 203-874-2007
Bunny Bread Company
Cape Girardeau, MO. 573-332-7349
Busken Bakery
Cincinnati, OH 513-871-2114
California Brands Flavors
Oakland, CA .800-348-0111
Calmar Dairy
Calmar, AB 780-985-3583
Cannoli Factory
Wyandanch, NY 631-643-2700
Caprine Estates
Bellbrook, OH. 937-848-7406
Carbolite Foods
Evansville, IN 888-524-3314
Caribbean Food Delights
Tappan, NY 845-398-3000
Carole's Cheesecake Company
Toronto, ON .416-256-0000
Carolina Foods
Charlotte, NC 800-234-0441
Carousel Cakes
Nanuet, NY 800-659-2253
Cascadian Farm & MUIR Glen; Division of General
Mills
Sedro Woolley, WA. 360-855-0100
Case Side Holdings Company
Kensington, PE 902-836-4214
Cateraid
Howell, MI 800-508-8217
CBC Foods Inc
Little River, KS 800-276-4770
Cedar Crest Specialties
Cedarburg, WI. 800-877-8341
Cedarlane Natural Foods
Carson, CA 310-886-7720
Celebrity Cheesecake
Davie, FL 877-986-2253
Cemac Foods Corporation
Philadelphia, PA 800-724-0179
Centreside Dairy
Renfrew, ON .613-432-2914
CGI Desserts
Sugar Land, TX. 281-240-1200
Chalet Desserts
Union City, CA 510-783-8300
Chattanooga Bakery
Chattanooga, TN. 800-251-3404
Cheesecake Aly
Glen Rock, NJ 800-555-8862
Cheesecake Etc. Desserts
Miami Springs, FL 305-887-0258
Chef Hans Gourmet Foods
Monroe, LA. .800-890-4267
Chella's Dutch Delicacies
Lake Oswego, OR. 800-458-3331
Chelsea Milling Company
Chelsea, MI. .734-475-1361
Chewys Rugulach
San Diego, CA 800-241-3456
Chloe Foods Corporation
Brooklyn, NY 718-827-3600
Chocolaterie Bernard Callebaut
Calgary, AB. .800-661-8367
Chudleigh's
Milton, ON 800-387-4028
Ciao Bella Gelato Company
Irvington, NJ .800-435-2863
Clarkson Scottish Bakery
Mississauga, ON 905-823-1500
Claudio Pastry Company
Elmwood Park, IL. 708-453-0598
Claxton Bakery
Claxton, GA .800-841-4211

Clements Pastry Shop
Hyattsville, MD 800-444-7428
Cloverhill Bakery-Vend Corporation
Chicago, IL 773-745-9800
Cloverland Sweets/Priester's Pecan Company
Fort Deposit, AL. 800-523-3505
Clydes Delicious Donuts
Addison, IL. .630-628-6555
Cobi Foods
Hantsport, NS 800-565-8229
Coby's Cookies
North York, ON. 416-633-1567
Cold Fusion Foods
West Hollywood, CA 310-287-3244
Collin Street Bakery
Corsicana, TX. 800-504-1896
Columbus Bakery
Columbus, OH 614-645-2275
Community Orchard
Fort Dodge, IA 515-573-8212
Compact Industries
St Charles, IL 800-513-4262
Con Agra Foods
Holly Ridge, NC 910-329-9061
ConAgra Grocery Products
Irvine, CA 714-680-1000
ConAgra Grocery Products
Fullerton, CA 800-736-2212
Conifer Specialties Inc
Woodinville, WA. 800-588-9160
Consun Food Industries
Elyria, OH. 440-233-7501
Country Choice Naturals
Eden Prairie, MN 952-829-8824
Country Fresh
Grand Rapids, MI 800-748-0480
Country Home Bakers
Torrance, CA 800-672-6277
Cream O'Weaver Dairy
Salt Lake City, UT 801-973-9922
Creative Bakers
Brooklyn, NY 800-247-7864
Creme Curls Bakery
Hudsonville, MI 800-466-1219
Creme Glacee Gelati
St Leonard, QC 888-322-0116
Crestwood Bakery
Pleasant Prairie, WI 414-453-4790
Crowley Foods
Arkport, NY .800-637-0019
Crystal Cream & Butter Company
Sacramento, CA 916-447-6455
Culinar Canada
Ste. Marie De Beauce, QC 418-387-5421
Cummings Studio Chocolates
Salt Lake City, UT 800-537-3957
Curly's Dairy
Stayton, OR. .800-785-1335
Dairy Fresh Corporation
Greensboro, AL. 800-239-5114
Dairy Land
Macon, GA 478-742-6461
Dairy Queen of Georgia
Decatur, GA .404-292-3553
Dancing Deer Baking Company
Hyde Park, MA 888-699-3337
Danish Baking Company
Van Nuys, CA 800-777-4970
Dave's Bakery
Honesdale, PA. 570-253-1660
Dave's Hawaiian Ice Cream
Pearl City, HI .808-453-0500
Davis Bakery & Delicatessen
Cleveland, OH 216-464-5599
Davis Bread & Desserts
Davis, CA 530-757-2700
Dawn Food Products
Jackson, MI .800-248-1144
Dean Foods Company
Dallas, TX. 214-303-3400
Dee's Cheesecake Factory/Dee's Foodservice
Albuquerque, NM 505-884-1777

Deep Foods
  Union, NJ 908-810-7500
Deerfield Bakery
  Buffalo Grove, IL 847-520-0068
Del Monte Foods
  San Francisco, CA 800-543-3090
Del's Pastry
  Etobicoke, ON 416-231-4383
Delicious Desserts
  Brooklyn, NY 718-680-1156
Deluxe Ice Cream Company
  Salem, OR 800-304-7172
Dengler's Bakery
  Souderton, PA 215-723-2706
Desserts by David Glass
  Bloomfield, CT 860-769-5570
Desserts of Distinction
  Milwaukie, OR 503-654-8370
Di Camillo Bakery
  Niagara Falls, NY 800-634-4363
Di Paolo Baking Company
  Rochester, NY 585-232-3510
Dianne's Gourmet Desserts
  Le Center, MN 800-289-7437
Dimitria Delights
  North Grafton, MA 800-763-1113
Dinkel's Bakery
  Chicago, IL 800-822-8817
Divine Delights
  Petaluma, CA 800-443-2836
Division Baking Corporation
  New York, NY 800-934-9238
Dolly Madison Bakery
  Columbus, IN 812-376-7432
Don's Food Products
  Schwenksville, PA 888-321-3667
Dough Delight
  Concord, ON 800-465-5515
Dough Works Company
  Horicon, WI 800-383-8808
Dreyer's Grand Ice Cream
  Oakland, CA 877-437-3937
Dreyers Grand Ice Cream
  Oakland, CA 510-652-8187
Dufflet Pastries
  Toronto, ON 416-536-1330
Dunford Bakers
  Fayetteville, AR 479-521-3000
Dunham Hill Bakery
  Woodstock, VT 800-218-3121
Dunkin Brands Inc.
  Canton, MA 800-458-7731
Dynamic Foods
  Lubbock, TX 806-762-0780
Eddy's Bakery
  Boise, ID 208-377-8100
Edelweiss Patisserie
  Charlestown, MA 617-628-0225
Edwards Baking Company
  Atlanta, GA 800-241-0559
Edy's Grand Ice Cream
  Rockaway, NJ 800-362-7899
Edy's Grand Ice Cream
  Glendale Heights, IL 888-377-3397
El Segundo Bakery
  El Segundo, CA 310-322-3422
Elegant Desserts
  Lyndhurst, NJ 201-933-0770
Eli's Cheesecake Company
  Chicago, IL 800-999-8300
Elmwood Pastry
  West Hartford, CT 860-233-2029
Eskimo Pie Corporation
  Ronkonkoma, NY 631-737-9700
European Style Bakery
  Beverly Hills, CA 818-368-6876
Evans Bakery
  Cozad, NE 800-222-5641
Faith Dairy
  Tacoma, WA 253-531-3398
Famous Pacific Dessert Company
  Seattle, WA 800-666-1950
Fantasia
  Sedalia, MO 660-827-1172
Fantis Foods
  Carlstadt, NJ 201-933-6200
Farr Candy Company
  Idaho Falls, ID 208-522-8215
Fendall Ice Cream Company
  Salt Lake City, UT 801-355-3583
Field's
  Pauls Valley, OK 405-238-7381

Fieldbrook Farms
  Dunkirk, NY 800-333-0805
Fiera Foods
  North York, ON 416-744-1010
Fillo Factory
  Dumont, NJ 800-653-4556
Fireside Kitchen
  Halifax, NS 902-454-7387
Fisher Rex Sandwiches
  Raleigh, NC 919-832-6494
Fisher's Bakery
  Ellicott City, MD 410-461-9275
Flavor Right Foods Group
  Columbus, OH 888-464-3734
Flavors from Florida
  Bartow, FL 863-533-0408
Flowers Bakery of Winston-Salem
  Winston Salem, NC 800-334-5260
Flowers Baking
  San Antonio, TX 210-661-2361
Flowers Snack of Tennessee
  Crossville, TN 931-484-6101
FNI Group LLC
  Sherborn, MA 508-655-8816
Food of Our Own Design
  Maplewood, NJ 973-762-0985
Foodbrands America
  Oklahoma City, OK 405-290-4000
Foothills Creamery
  Calgary, AB 403-263-7725
Foxtail Foods
  Fairfield, OH 800-323-6944
France Delices
  Montreal, QC 514-259-2291
Frankly Natural Bakers
  San Diego, CA 800-727-7229
French Patisserie
  Pacifica, CA 800-300-2253
Friendly Ice Cream Corporation
  Wilbraham, MA 800-966-9970
Friuli Sorbet
  New York, NY 212-966-3073
Frostbite
  Toledo, OH 800-968-7711
Frozfruit Corporation
  Gardena, CA 310-217-1034
FrutStix Company
  Santa Barbara, CA 805-965-1656
Furst-McNess Company/Terrapin Ridge
  Freeport, IL 800-999-4052
Future Bakery & Cafe
  Etobicoke, ON 416-231-1491
G A Food Service
  St Petersburg, FL 727-573-2211
G H Bent Company
  Milton, MA 617-698-5945
Galliker Dairy
  Johnstown, PA 800-477-6455
Garber Ice Cream Company
  Winchester, VA 800-662-5422
Gardner Pie Company
  Akron, OH 330-245-2030
Garelick Farms
  Lynn, MA 800-487-8700
Gelato Fresco
  Toronto, ON 416-785-5415
George L. Wells Meat Company
  Philadelphia, PA 800-523-1730
George Weston Bakery
  Riviera Beach, FL 561-848-9705
George Weston Bakeries
  Northlake, IL 708-562-6311
George Weston Bakeries
  Bay Shore, NY 800-356-3314
George Weston Bakeries
  Albany, NY 800-531-4002
Georgia Fruit Cake Company
  Claxton, GA 912-739-2683
Giant Food
  Lanham, MD 888-469-4426
Gifford's Dairy
  Skowhegan, ME 207-474-9821
Gimbal's Fine Candies
  S San Francisco, CA 800-344-6225
Gindi Gourmet
  Boulder, CO 303-473-9177
Glover's Ice Cream
  Frankfort, IN 800-686-5163
Golden Boys Pies of San Diego
  San Diego, CA 800-746-0280
Golden Brown Bakery
  South Haven, MI 269-637-3418

Golden Glow Cookie Company
  Bronx, NY 718-379-6223
Good Humor Breyers Ice Cream Company
  Hagerstown, MD 301-797-9603
Good Humor Breyers Ice Cream Company
  Framingham, MA 508-620-4300
Good Humor Breyers Ice Cream Company
  Henderson, NV 702-564-0020
Good Humor Breyers Ice Cream Company
  Green Bay, WI 866-204-9750
Good Humor Breyers Ice Cream Company
  Green Bay, WI 920-499-5151
Good Old Days Foods
  Little Rock, AR 501-565-1257
Gourmet Baker
  Burnaby, BC 800-663-1972
Gourmet Croissant
  Brooklyn, NY 718-499-4911
Gourmet Ice Cream
  Palmer, MA 413-283-3740
Govatos
  Wilmington, DE 888-799-5252
Grainaissance
  Emeryville, CA 800-472-4697
Granowska's
  Toronto, ON 416-533-7755
Great American Dessert
  Flushing, NY 718-894-3494
Great Cakes
  Los Angeles, CA 310-287-0228
Great Northern Maple Products
  Saint Honor, De Shenley, QC 418-485-7777
Great San Saba River Pecan Company
  San Saba, TX 800-621-9121
Grebe's Bakery & Delicatessen
  Milwaukee, WI 800-356-9377
Grecian Delight Foods
  Elk Grove Vlg, IL 800-621-4387
Greyston Bakery
  Yonkers, NY 800-289-2253
Groezinger Provisions
  Neptune, NJ 800-927-9473
Grossinger's Home Bakery
  New York, NY 800-479-6996
Grote Bakery
  Hamilton, OH 513-874-7436
Gumpert's Canada
  Mississauga, ON 800-387-9324
H.E. Butt Grocery Company
  San Antonio, TX 800-432-3113
H.P. Hood
  Agawam, MA 413-786-7166
Haby's Alsatian Bakery
  Castroville, TX 830-931-2118
Hafner
  Stone Mountain, GA 888-725-4605
Hahn's Old Fashioned Cake Company
  Farmingdale, NY 631-249-3456
Handy Pax
  Randolph, MA 781-963-8300
Hanover Foods Corporation
  Hanover, PA 717-632-6000
Happy & Healthy Products
  Boca Raton, FL 561-367-0739
Harold Food Company
  Charlotte, NC 704-588-8061
Harry & David
  Medford, OR 877-322-1200
Harvest Bakery
  Bristol, CT 860-589-8800
Harvest Valley Bakery
  La Salle, IL 815-224-9030
Hazelwood Farms Bakery
  Rochester, NY 585-424-1240
Health Valley Company
  Irwindale, CA 800-334-3204
Heidi's Gourmet Desserts
  Tucker, GA 800-241-4166
Heinemann's Bakeries
  Chicago, IL 312-239-5592
Heinz North America
  Pittsburgh, PA 412-237-5700
Heitzman Bakery
  Louisville, KY 502-452-1891
Hershey Creamery Company
  Harrisburg, PA 888-240-1905
HFI Foods
  Redmond, WA 425-883-1320
Hiland Roberts Ice Cream Company
  Norfolk, NE 402-371-3660
Holt's Bakery
  Douglas, GA 912-384-2202

Holton Food Products Company
La Grange, IL 708-352-5599
Home Made Brand Foods Company
Newburyport, MA.................978-462-3663
Homer's Ice Cream
Wilmette, IL 847-251-0477
Honey Bar/Creme de la Creme
Kingston, NY 845-331-4643
Honey Rose Baking Company
Encinitas, CA 760-942-8996
Honeybake Farms
Kansas City, KS 913-371-7777
Hormel Foods Corporation
Omaha, NE 402-493-8470
Hormel Foods Corporation
Oklahoma City, OK 405-745-3471
Hormel Foods Corporation
Oklahoma City, OK 405-843-5643
Hormel Foods Corporation
West Allis, WI.................414-604-0570
Hormel Foods Corporation
Cincinnati, OH 513-563-0211
Hormel Foods Corporation
Urbandale, IA 515-276-8872
Hormel Foods Corporation
Phoenix, AZ 602-230-2400
Hormel Foods Corporation
Charlotte, NC 704-527-4388
Hormel Foods Corporation
Austin, MN 800-523-4635
Hormel Foods Corporation
Lisle, IL 800-533-2000
Hormel Foods Corporation
Salt Lake City, UT 801-487-8251
Hormel Foods Corporation
Lubbock, TX.................806-796-3630
Hormel Foods Corporation
Lebanon, NJ 908-236-7009
Hormel Foods Corporation
Shawnee Mission, KS.................913-888-8744
HP Hood
Lynnfield, MA 800-343-6592
Humble Cremery
Los Angeles, CA.................800-697-9925
Hunt Country Foods
Middleburg, VA 540-364-2622
Hunter Farms
High Point, NC 800-446-8035
Hygeia Dairy Company
McAllen, TX.................956-686-0511
Ice Cream & Yogurt Club
Boynton Beach, FL.................561-731-3331
Ice Cream Specialties
St Louis, MO.................314-962-3935
Ice Cream Specialties
Lafayette, IN.................765-474-2989
Icy Bird
Sparta, TN.................931-738-3557
Il Gelato
Astoria, NY 718-937-3033
Il Tiramisu
Valley Stream, NY 516-599-1010
Incredible Cheesecake Company
San Diego, CA 619-563-9722
International Equipment
Arecibo, PR.................787-879-3151
International Multifoods Corporation
Orrville, OH 800-664-2942
International Yogurt Company
Portland, OR 800-962-7326
Interstate Bakeries Corporation
Los Angeles, CA.................323-750-7204
Interstate Brands
Alexandria, LA 318-448-6600
Interstate Brands Company/Drake Bakeries
Wayne, NJ 973-696-5010
Interstate Brands Corporation
Emporia, KS 620-342-6811
Interstate Brands Corporation
Kansas City, MO.................816-502-4000
Interstate Brands Corporation/Dolly Madison Cakes
Columbus, GA 706-257-7000
Interstate Brands Corporation/Wonder Bread Bakery
St Louis, MO.................314-385-1600
It's It Ice Cream Company
Burlingame, CA 800-345-1928
Italian Bakery
Virginia, MN 218-741-3464
Italian Baking Company
Edmonton, AB 780-424-4830
J&J Snack Foods Corporation
Pennsauken, NJ.................856-665-9533

J.A.M.B. Low Carb Distributor
Pompano Beach, FL.................800-708-6738
J.P. Sunrise Bakery
Edmonton, AB 780-454-5797
J.W. Haywood & Sons Dairy
Louisville, KY.................502-774-2311
Jack & Jill Ice Cream Company
Moorestown, NJ 856-813-2300
Jackson Ice Cream Company
Denver, CO.................303-534-2454
Jackson Milk & Ice CreamCompany
Hutchinson, KS.................620-663-1244
James Skinner Company
Omaha, NE 800-358-7428
Jay Hoyt of California
Petaluma, CA 707-762-1881
Joey's Fine Foods
Newark, NJ.................973-482-1400
John J. Nissen Baking Company
Brewer, ME.................207-989-7654
Johnson's Real Ice Cream
Columbus, OH 614-231-0014
Jon Donaire Pastry
Santa Fe Springs, CA 877-366-2473
Josh & John's Ice Cream
Colorado Springs, CO.................800-530-2855
Joyva Corporation
Brooklyn, NY.................718-497-0170
Jubelt Variety Bakeries
Mount Olive, IL 217-999-7312
Just Desserts
San Francisco, CA 415-602-9245
Kan-Pac
Arkansas City, KS.................620-442-6820
Kapaa Poi Factory
Kapaa, HI 808-822-5426
Karp's
Georgetown, MA 800-373-5277
Katrina's Tartufo
Port Jeffrsn Sta, NY 800-480-8836
Kellogg Snacks
Kansas City, KS 800-229-4414
Kemoo Farm Foods
Wahiawa, HI 808-622-8004
Kemp Foods
York, PA 800-233-2007
Kerrobert Bakery
Kerrobert, SK 306-834-2461
King's Hawaiian
Torrance, CA 800-800-5461
Klinke Brothers Ice Cream Company
Memphis, TN 901-743-8250
Knoll Creek Dairy
Harrison, NY 718-892-4500
Knouse Foods
Peach Glen, PA 717-677-8181
Koehler Bakery Company
North Little Rock, AR 800-262-5900
Kohler Mix Specialties
White Bear Lake, MN.................651-426-1633
Kohler Mix Specialties
Newington, CT 860-666-1511
Kokinos Purity Ice CreamCompany
Monroe, LA.................318-322-2930
Kozy Shack
Hicksville, NY 516-870-3000
Kyger Bakery Products
Lafayette, IN.................765-447-1252
L&M Bakery
Lawrence, MA 978-687-7346
La Francaise Bakery
Northlake, IL.................800-654-7220
Labrada Nutrition
Houston, TX.................281-209-2137
Laguna Cookie & Dessert Company
Santa Ana, CA 800-673-2473
Lamb-Weston
Weston, OR.................800-766-7783
LaRosa Bakery
Shrewsbury, NJ 800-527-6722
Lawrences Delights
Doraville, GA 800-568-0021
Lax & Mandel Bakery
Cleveland, OH 216-382-8877
Leader Candies
Brooklyn, NY 718-366-6900
Lenchner Bakery
Concord, ON 905-738-8811
Lewis Bakeries
London, ON 519-434-5252
Lewis Brothers Bakeries
Vincennes, IN 812-886-6533

Lewis Brothers Bakery
Evansville, IN 812-425-4642
Little Angel Foods
Daytona Beach, FL 904-257-3040
London Farm Dairy
Port Huron, MI 800-284-5111
Lone Star Bakery
Round Rock, TX.................512-255-3629
Lone Star Consolidated Foods
Dallas, TX.................800-658-5637
Louis Trauth Dairy
Newport, KY.................800-544-6455
Love & Quiches Desserts
Freeport, NY.................800-525-5251
Lucy's Sweet Surrender
Cleveland, OH 216-752-0828
Lusitania Bakery
Blandon, PA 610-926-1311
M&L Gourmet Ice Cream
Baltimore, MD 410-276-4880
Mac's Donut Shop
Aliquippa, PA 724-375-6776
Mack's Homemade Ice Cream
York, PA 717-741-2027
Mackie International
Commerce, CA 800-733-9762
Main Street Custom Foods
Cuyahoga Falls, OH 800-533-6246
Main Street Gourmet
Cuyahoga Falls, OH 800-533-6246
Main Street Gourmet Fundraising
Cuyahoga Falls, OH 800-533-6246
Main Street's Cambritt Cookies
Cuyahoga Falls, OH 800-533-6246
Mama Lee's Gourmet Hot Chocolate
Nashville, TN 888-626-2533
Maola Milk & Ice Cream Company
New Bern, NC.................252-638-1131
Maple Island
St Paul, MN.................800-369-1022
Maplehurst Bakeries
Carrollton, GA 800-482-4810
Mar-Key Foods
Vidalia, GA 912-537-4204
Mario's Gelati
Vancouver, BC 604-879-9411
Mars M&M
Henderson, NV 888-265-6788
Martino's Bakery
Burbank, CA 818-842-0715
Mary Ann's Baking Company
Sacramento, CA 916-681-7444
Matador Processors
Blanchard, OK 800-847-0797
Matterhorn Ice Cream Company
Caldwell, ID 800-822-1635
Mayer's Cider Mill
Webster, NY 800-543-0043
Mazelle's Cheesecakes Concoctions Creations
Dallas, TX.................903-737-4315
McArthur Dairy
Miami, FL.................877-803-6565
McConnell's Fine Ice Cream
Santa Barbara, CA 805-963-2958
Meadow Gold Dairy
Lewiston, ID 208-746-9006
Meadows Country Products
Hollidaysburg, PA.................888-499-1001
Mehaffie Pies
Dayton, OH 937-253-1163
Mia Products
Scranton, PA 570-457-7431
Michel's Bakery
Philadelphia, PA 215-725-4328
Michele's Family Bakery
York, PA 717-741-2027
Michelle Chocolatiers
Colorado Springs, CO.................888-447-3654
Michigan Dairy
Livonia, MI 734-367-5390
Mid States Dairy
Hazelwood, MO.................314-731-1150
Mikawaya Bakery
Los Angeles, CA.................213-628-6514
Millers Ice Cream
Houston, TX.................713-861-3138
Millie's Pierogi
Chicopee Falls, MA 800-743-7641
Mineo's Pies
Scranton, PA 570-347-8278
Mississippi Bakery
Burlington, IA.................319-752-6315

Mississippi Cheese StrawFactory
Yazoo City, MS 866-830-9415
Mister Cookie Face
Lakewood, NJ 732-370-5533
Model Dairy
Reno, NV 800-433-2030
Monaco Baking Company
Santa Fe Springs, CA 800-569-4640
Mooresville Ice Cream Company
Mooresville, NC 704-664-5456
Morningstar Foods
Dallas, TX 225-273-2803
Mothers Kitchen Inc
Burlington, NJ 609-387-7200
Mozzicato De Pasquale Bakery Pastry
Hartford, CT 860-296-0426
Mozzicato Depasquale Bakery & Pastry Shop
Hartford, CT 860-296-0426
Mrs Baird's Bakery
Fort Worth, TX 817-864-2500
Mrs. Baird's Bakeries
Abilene, TX. 325-692-3141
Mrs. Smith's Bakeries
Spartanburg, SC 864-503-9588
Mrs. Sullivan's Pies
Jackson, TN 800-456-2205
Mt View Bakery
Mountain View, HI 808-968-6353
Multi Marques
Montreal, QC 514-255-9492
Multiflex Company
Wyckoff, NJ 201-447-3888
My Daddy's Cheesecake
Cape Girardeau, MO. 800-735-6765
My Grandma's Coffee Cak e of New England
Hyde Park, MA 800-847-2636
Najila's
Binghamton, NY 607-722-4287
Nancy's Pies
Rock Island, IL 800-480-0055
National Food Corporation
Medley, FL 305-884-2020
Natural Fruit Corporation
Hialeah, FL 305-887-7525
Natural Quick Foods
Seattle, WA 206-365-5757
Naturally Delicious
Oakland Park, FL 954-485-6730
Nature's Hilights
Chico, CA 800-313-6454
New York Bakeries
Hialeah, FL 305-882-1355
Nickles Bakery of Ohio
Columbus, OH 800-335-9775
Nikki's Cookies
Milwaukee, WI 800-776-7107
NOH Foods of Hawaii
Gardena, CA 310-324-6770
Northside Bakery
Richmond, VA. 804-329-6851
Notre Dame Bakery
Lewisporte, NL 709-535-2738
O'Boyle's Ice Cream Company
Bristol, PA 215-788-0421
Oak Leaf Confections
Scarborough, ON 800-338-3631
OH Chocolate
Calgary, AB. 403-283-4612
Old Country Bakery
North Hollywood, CA 818-838-2302
Old Fashioned Kitchen
Lakewood, NJ 732-364-4100
Orange Bakery
Irvine, CA 949-863-1377
Original Ya-hoo! Baking Company
Sherman, TX. 800-575-9373
Orlando's Pastries
Collingdale, PA. 610-532-9300
Orval Kent Food Company
Wheeling, IL 847-459-9000
Osman's Pies
Stow, OH. 330-655-2919
Out of a Flower
Lancaster, TX 800-743-4696
Pacific Ocean Produce
Santa Cruz, CA 831-423-2654
Parco Foods
Blue Island, IL 708-371-9200
Parker Products
Fort Worth, TX 800-433-5749
Pasta Factory
Northlake, IL 800-615-6951

Pastry Chef
Pawtucket, RI 800-639-8606
Patisserie Wawel
Montreal, QC 614-524-3348
Pearl River Pastry & Chocolates
Pearl River, NY. 800-632-2639
Peggy Lawton Kitchens
East Walpole, MA. 800-843-7325
Pellman Foods
New Holland, PA 717-354-8070
Pepperidge Farm
Downingtown, PA. 610-269-2500
Perry's Ice Cream Company
Akron, NY. 800-873-7797
Pet Dairy
Portsmouth, VA. 757-397-2387
Pet Dairy
Spartanburg, SC 864-576-6280
Petersen Ice Cream Company
Oak Park, IL 708-386-6130
Pevely Dairy Company
St Louis, MO. 314-771-4400
Phipps Desserts
Toronto, ON 416-481-9111
Pie Piper Products
Bensenville, IL 800-621-8183
Piedmont Candy Corporation
Lexington, NC 336-248-2477
Pillsbury
McMinnville, OR 800-325-5439
Pinocchio Italian Ice Cream Company
Edmonton, AB 780-455-1905
Plains Creamery
Amarillo, TX. 806-374-0385
Platte Valley Creamery
Scottsbluff, NE 308-632-4225
Plehn's Bakery
St Matthews, KY 502-896-4438
Plumlife Company
Newbury, MA 978-462-8458
Pocono Cheesecake Factory
Swiftwater, PA 570-839-6844
Poudre Valley Creamery
Fort Collins, CO 970-482-8475
Prairie Farms Dairy
Carlinville, IL 217-854-2547
Prairie Farms Dairy
O Fallon, IL. 618-632-3632
Precision Foods
Melrose Park, IL 800-333-0003
Price Cold Storage & Packing Company
Yakima, WA 509-966-4110
Price's Creameries
El Paso, TX. 915-565-2711
Puritan/ATZ Ice Cream
Kendallville, IN 260-347-2700
Purity Dairies
Nashville, TN 615-244-1900
Purity Ice Cream Company
Ithaca, NY. 607-272-1545
Quality Bakery/MM Deli
Port Colborne, ON 905-834-4911
Quality Naturally! Foods
City of Industry, CA 888-498-6986
Quiche & Tell
Flushing, NY. 718-381-7562
Real Food Marketing
Kansas City, MO. 816-221-4100
Refrigerated Foods Association
Chamblee, GA. 770-452-0660
Reinhold Ice Cream Company
Pittsburgh, PA. 412-321-7600
Reiter Dairy
Akron, OH. 800-362-0825
Rentschler's Bakery
Kutztown, PA 610-683-3506
Reser's Fine Foods
Salt Lake City, UT 801-972-5633
Rhino Foods
Burlington, VT 800-639-3350
Rhodes Bake-N-Serv
Salt Lake City, UT 800-695-0122
Rich Ice Cream Company
West Palm Beach, FL 561-833-7585
Rich Products Corporation
Hilliard, OH. 614-771-1117
Richman Festival Ice Cream Company
Paterson, NJ 973-684-8935
Rising Dough Bakery
Sacramento, CA 916-387-9700
Roberts Dairy Company
Kansas City, MO. 800-279-1692

Robinson Dairy
Denver, CO. 800-332-6355
Rogers Bakery
Plainville, CT 860-747-1686
Rolling Pin Bakery
Bow Island, AB. 403-545-2434
Roma Bakeries
Rockford, IL 815-964-6737
Roney Oatman
Aurora, IL 630-859-2800
Rosati Italian Water Ice
Clifton Heights, PA. 610-626-1818
Roselani Tropics Ice Cream
Wailuku, HI 808-244-7951
Rowena's
Norfolk, VA. 800-627-8699
Royal Court Cookie Company
North Hollywood, CA 800-730-2545
Royal Home Bakery
Newmarket, ON 905-715-7044
Royal Pie Bakery
San Diego, CA 619-233-6393
RW Delights
Millington, NJ 866-892-1096
Ryals Bakery
Milledgeville, GA 478-452-0321
Ryke's Bakery
Muskegon, MI 231-557-8011
Sacramento Baking Company
Sacramento, CA 916-361-2000
Safeway Dairy Products
Capitol Heights, MD 301-341-9555
Safeway Stores
Tempe, AZ 877-723-3929
Sam's Homemade Cheesecake
San Diego, CA 858-578-3460
Sara Lee Bakery
Salt Lake City, UT 801-487-4677
Sara Lee Bakery Group
Earth City, MO 314-291-5480
Sara Lee Bakery Group
Phoenix, AZ 602-252-6881
Sara Lee Bakery Group
Rapid City, SD 605-343-3512
Sara Lee Bakery Group   The EarthGrains - Bakery
Saint Paul, MN
Sara Lee Bakery Group   The EarthGrains - Bakery
Traverse City, MI 231-922-3296
Sara Lee Bakery Group   The EarthGrains - Bakery
Beaumont, TX. 409-842-9150
Sara Lee Bakery Group   The EarthGrains - Bakery
Fresno, CA 559-495-3571
Sara Lee Bakery Group   The EarthGrains - Bakery
Rome, GA 706-295-4499
Sara Lee Corporation
Downers Grove, IL 630-598-8100
Sara Lee/Old Home
South Sioux City, NE 402-494-5474
Sarabeth's Bakery
Bronx, NY 800-773-7378
Savino's Italian Ices
Deerfield Beach, FL 954-426-4119
Saxby Foods
Edmonton, AB 780-440-4177
Schneider Valley Farms Dairy
Williamsport, PA 570-326-2021
Schneider's Dairy Holdings Inc
Pittsburgh, PA. 412-881-3525
Schoep's Ice Cream Company
Madison, WI 800-236-0032
Schulze & Burch Biscuit Company
Chicago, IL 773-927-6622
Schwan's Consumer Brands North America
Bloomington, MN. 952-832-4300
Schwans Bakeries
Stilwell, OK 918-696-8325
Schwans Food Company
Norcross, GA. 800-241-0559
Scialo Brothers
Providence, RI 877-421-0986
Scot Paris Fine Desserts
New York, NY. 212-807-1802
Scotsburn Dairy Group
Truro, NS 902-895-4412
Scotty Wotty's Creamy Cheescake
Hillsborough, NJ. 908-281-9720
Seavers Bakery
Johnson City, TN 423-928-8131
Seckinger-Lee Company
Savannah, GA. 800-291-2973
Serv-Agen Corporation
Cherry Hill, NJ 856-663-6966

Sessions Company
  Enterprise, AL 334-393-0200
Shaw Baking Company
  Thunder Bay, ON 807-345-7327
Shef Products
  Las Vegas, NV 702-873-2275
Silver Tray Cookies
  Fort Lauderdale, FL 305-883-0800
Sinbad Sweets
  Fresno, CA .800-350-7933
Sisler's Ice & Ice Cream
  Ohio, IL 888-891-3856
Smart Ice
  Fort Myers, FL 239-334-3123
Smith Dairy Products Company
  Orrville, OH 800-776-7076
Smoak's Bakery & Catering Service
  Augusta, GA 706-738-1792
Snelgrove Ice Cream Company
  Salt Lake City, UT 800-569-0005
Snyder's Ice Cream
  Ashland, PA 570-875-3320
Solana Beach Baking Company
  Carlsbad, CA 760-931-0148
Solvang Bakery
  Solvang, CA 800-377-4253
Southern Ice Cream Specialties
  Marietta, GA 770-428-0452
Specialty Bakers
  Marysville, PA 800-233-0778
Specialty Baking Products
  Dunkirk, NY 716-366-0938
Spilke's Baking Company
  Brooklyn, NY 718-384-2150
Spohrers Bakeries
  Collingdale, PA 610-532-9959
Spring Glen Fresh Foods
  Ephrata, PA 800-641-2853
St. Cloud Bakery
  St Cloud, MN 320-251-8055
Standard Bakery
  Kealakekua, HI 808-322-3688
Starbucks Coffee Company
  Seattle, WA 800-782-7282
Steese Ice Cream
  Grove City, PA 724-748-4115
Sterling Foods
  San Antonio, TX 210-490-1669
Stewart's Ice Cream
  Saratoga Springs, NY 518-581-1000
Sticky Fingers Bakeries
  Spokane Valley, WA 800-458-5826
Stone's Home Made Candy Shop
  Oswego, NY 888-223-3928
Stroehmann Bakeries
  Norristown, PA 800-984-0989
Strossner's Bakery
  Greenville, SC 864-233-3996
Sugar Creek/Eskimo Pie
  Russellville, AR 800-445-2715
Sunbeam Baking Company
  El Paso, TX 800-328-6111
Sunshine Dairy Foods
  Portland, OR 503-234-7526
Sunshine Farms Dairy
  Elyria, OH .440-322-6301
Superior Cake Products
  Southbridge, MA 508-764-3276
Superstore Industries
  Fairfield, CA 707-864-0502
Svenhard's Swedish Bakery
  Oakland, CA 800-333-7836
Sweenor Chocolate
  Wakefield, RI 800-834-3123
Sweet Endings
  West Palm Beach, FL 888-635-1177
Sweet Gallery Exclusive Pastry
  Toronto, ON 416-232-1539
Sweet Shop
  La Crosse, WI 608-784-7724
Sweet Street Desserts
  Reading, PA 800-793-3897
Sweety Novelty
  Monterey Park, CA 626-282-4482
Table de France
  Ontario, CA 909-923-5205
Table Talk Pie
  Worcester, MA 508-798-8811
Taste It Presents
  Kenilworth, NJ 908-241-0672
Tastykake
  Philadelphia, PA 215-221-8500

Teawolf Industries, Ltd
  Pine Brook, NJ 973-575-4600
Tebay Dairy Company
  Parkersburg, WV 304-863-3705
The Bama Company
  Tulsa, OK 800-756-2262
The Cheesecake Factory
  Calabasas Hills, CA 818-871-3000
Thrifty Ice Cream
  El Monte, CA 626-571-0122
Tillamook County Creamery Association
  Tillamook, OR 503-842-4481
Tipiak
  Stamford, CT 203-961-9117
Toft Dairy
  Sandusky, OH 800-521-4606
Tofutti Brands
  Cranford, NJ 908-272-2400
Tom's Ice Cream Bowl
  Zanesville, OH 740-452-5267
Tony's Ice Cream Company
  Gastonia, NC 704-867-7085
Top Hat Company
  Wilmette, IL 847-256-6565
Treat Ice Cream Company
  San Jose, CA 408-292-9321
Tropical Treets
  North York, ON 888-424-8229
Tsue Chong Noodle Company
  Seattle, WA 206-623-0801
Turano Pastry Shops
  Bloomingdale, IL 630-529-6161
Turkey Hill Dairy
  Conestoga, PA 800-693-2479
Turner Dairies
  Jackson, TN 731-427-6012
Turner Dairies
  Covington, TN 901-476-2643
Turtle Mountain
  Eugene, OR 541-338-9400
Tuscan Dairy Farms
  Dallas, TX .800-526-4416
Two Chefs on a Roll
  Carson, CA 800-842-3025
Two Chicks and a Ladle
  New York, NY 212-251-0025
Umpqua Dairy Products Company
  Roseburg, OR 541-672-2638
Uncle Ralph's Cookie Company
  Frederick, MD 800-422-0626
Unique Bakery Company
  Toronto, ON 416-751-8200
United Dairy
  Martins Ferry, OH 800-252-1542
United Dairy
  Uniontown, PA 800-966-6455
United Pie Company
  Elkhart, IN .574-294-3419
Universal Flavor Corporation
  Indianapolis, IN 317-243-3521
Uptown Bakers
  Washington, DC 202-546-6500
Valley Dairy Fairview Dairy
  Windber, PA 814-467-5537
Valley Maid Ice Cream
  Aurora, IL .630-851-2241
Van de Kamp's
  Chambersburg, PA 570-263-4127
Varda Chocolatier
  Elizabeth, NJ 800-448-2732
Velda Farms
  Lakeland, FL 800-279-4166
Velda Farms
  North Miami Bch, FL 800-795-4649
Velvet Ice Cream Company
  Utica, OH .800-589-5000
Venice Spumoni/Spring Valley Ice Cream
  Philadelphia, PA 800-784-0312
Vickey's Vittles
  North Hills, CA 818-841-1944
Vie de France Yamazaki
  Denver, CO 303-371-6280
Vie de France Yamazaki
  Vienna, VA 800-393-8926
Vie de France Yamazaki
  Vienna, VA 800-446-4404
Vienna Sausage Company
  Chicago, IL 800-326-6652
Vigneri Confections
  Rochester, NY 585-254-6160
VIP Foods
  Flushing, NY 718-821-3942

Vitamilk Dairy
  Bellingham, WA 206-529-4128
Waldensian Bakeries
  Valdese, NC 828-874-2136
Warwick Ice Cream Company
  Warwick, RI 401-821-8403
Wayne Dairy Products
  Richmond, IN 800-875-9294
Wedding Cake Studio
  Williamsfield, OH 440-667-1765
Weiss Provisions
  Pittsburgh, PA 800-458-6328
Welch's Foods Inc
  Concord, MA 800-340-6870
Weldon Ice Cream Company
  Millersport, OH 740-467-2400
Well-Bred Loaf
  Valley Cottage, NY 800-444-5623
Wells' Dairy
  Le Mars, IA 800-942-3800
Welsh Farms
  Clifton, NJ .973-772-2388
Wenger's Bakery
  Reading, PA 610-372-6545
White Coffee Corporation
  Long Island City, NY 800-221-0140
Whitey's Ice Cream Manufacturing
  Moline, IL .888-594-4839
Wick's Pies
  Winchester, IN 800-642-5880
Williamsburg Chocolatier
  Williamsburg, VA 804-966-9000
Winder Dairy
  West Valley, UT 800-946-3371
Winmix/Natural Care Products
  Englewood, FL 941-475-7432
Wonder Bread
  Provo, UT .801-373-8192
Woodie Pie Company
  Artesia, NM 505-746-2132
Wright Ice Cream
  Cayuga, IN 800-686-9561
Wuollet Bakery
  Minneapolis, MN 612-381-9400
Yarnell Ice Cream Company
  Searcy, AR .800-766-2414
Yost's Dutch Maid Bakery
  Johnstown, PA 814-266-3191
Young's Bakery
  Uniontown, PA 724-437-6361
Zeppys Bakery
  Lawrence, MA 781-963-7022
Ziegenfelder Company
  Wheeling, WV 304-232-6360
Zoelsmanns Bakery & Deli
  Pueblo, CO 719-543-0407

Low Carb

Real Food Marketing
  Kansas City, MO 816-221-4100

Low-Calorie

Cedar Crest Specialties
  Cedarburg, WI 800-877-8341
ConAgra Grocery Products
  Irvine, CA .714-680-1000
Fendall Ice Cream Company
  Salt Lake City, UT 801-355-3583
G A Food Service
  St Petersburg, FL 727-573-2211
George Weston Bakeries
  Albany, NY 800-531-4002
Health Valley Company
  Irwindale, CA 800-334-3204
J&J Snack Foods Corporation
  Pennsauken, NJ 856-665-9533
Jackson Ice Cream Company
  Denver, CO 303-534-2454
Kemp Foods
  York, PA 800-233-2007
Master Mix
  Placentia, CA 714-524-1698
O'Boyle's Ice Cream Company
  Bristol, PA .215-788-0421
Price Cold Storage & Packing Company
  Yakima, WA 509-966-4110
Real Food Marketing
  Kansas City, MO 816-221-4100
Tova Industries
  Louisville, KY 888-532-8682

Wells' Dairy
Le Mars, IA 800-942-3800

Non-Dairy

Frozen
A&B Ingredients
Fairfield, NJ 973-227-1390

Fresh
Fresh Start Bakeries
Brea, CA 714-256-8900

Frozen
Aladdin Bakers
Brooklyn, NY 718-499-1818
Alati-Caserta Desserts
Montreal, QC 514-271-3013
All Round Foods
Westbury, NY 516-338-1888
Andre-Boudin Bakeries
San Francisco, CA 415-882-1849
Artel
Boisbriand, QC 450-433-1322
Athens Pastries & Frozen Foods
Cleveland, OH 800-837-5683
Atkins Elegant Desserts
Fishers, IN 800-887-8808
Awrey Bakeries
Livonia, MI 800-950-2253
Bake Crafters Food
Collegedale, TN 800-296-8935
Baker Boy Bake Shop
Dickinson, ND 800-437-2008
Beck's Waffles of Oklahoma
Shawnee, OK 800-646-6254
Benson's Bakery
Bogart, GA 800-888-6059
Best Maid Cookie Company
River Falls, WI 888-444-0322
Boboli International Inc
Stockton, CA 209-473-3507
BODEGA Chocolates
Costa Mesa, CA 888-326-3342
Bridgford Foods Corporation Superior Foods Division
Anaheim, CA 800-527-2105
Brightwood Baking Company
Cicero, IN 317-356-2449
Brooklyn Bagel Company
Staten Island, NY 800-349-3055
Brownie Products Company
Gardner, IL 815-237-2163
Campbell Soup Company of Canada
Listowel, ON 800-575-7687
Caribbean Food Delights
Tappan, NY 845-398-3000
Carolina Foods
Charlotte, NC 800-234-0441
CBC Foods Inc
Little River, KS 800-276-4770
Cedarlane Foods
Carson, CA 800-826-3322
Cemac Foods Corporation
Philadelphia, PA 800-724-0179
CGI Desserts
Sugar Land, TX 281-240-1200
Chalet Desserts
Union City, CA 510-783-8300
Chewys Rugulach
San Diego, CA 800-241-3456
Chloe Foods Corporation
Brooklyn, NY 718-827-3600
Cinderella Cheese Cake Company
Riverside, NJ 856-461-6302
Cobi Foods
Hantsport, NS 800-565-8229
Cole's Quality Foods
Muskegon, MI 231-722-1651
Con Agra Foods
Holly Ridge, NC 910-329-9061

Concept 2 Bakers
Minneapolis, MN 800-266-2782
Continental Food Products
Flushing, NY 718-358-7894
Cookie Tree Bakeries
Salt Lake City, UT 800-998-0111
Danish Baking Company
Van Nuys, CA 800-777-4970
Dawn Food Products
Louisville, KY 800-626-2542
Dee's Cheesecake Factory/Dee's Foodservice
Albuquerque, NM 505-884-1777
Del Campo Baking Company
Wilmington, DE 302-656-6676
Desserts of Distinction
Milwaukie, OR 503-654-8370
Dimitria Delights
North Grafton, MA 800-763-1113
Division Baking Corporation
New York, NY 800-934-9238
Dunham Hill Bakery
Woodstock, VT 800-218-3121
Dutch Ann Foods Company
Natchez, MS 601-445-5566
Dynamic Foods
Lubbock, TX 806-762-0780
Edner Corporation
Hayward, CA 510-441-8504
Edwards Baking Company
Atlanta, GA 800-241-0559
Eli's Cheesecake Company
Chicago, IL 800-999-8300
Engel's Bakeries
Calgary, AB 403-250-9560
English Bay Batter
Dublin, OH 614-760-9921
Evans Bakery
Cozad, NE 800-222-5641
Fantasia
Sedalia, MO 660-827-1172
Fantis Foods
Carlstadt, NJ 201-933-6200
Field's
Pauls Valley, OK 405-238-7381
Fiera Foods
North York, ON 416-744-1010
Fleischer's Bagels
Macedon, NY 315-986-9999
Flower Bakeries
London, KY 800-568-3476
France Croissant
New York, NY 212-888-1210
France Delices
Montreal, QC 514-259-2291
Fresh Start Bakeries
Brea, CA 714-256-8900
Gabilas Knishes
Brooklyn, NY 718-387-0750
Gardner Pie Company
Akron, OH 330-245-2030
Gemini Food Industries
Fiskdale, MA 508-347-2800
General Mills
Chelsea, MA 800-370-7834
Good Old Days Foods
Little Rock, AR 501-565-1257
Gourmet Croissant
Brooklyn, NY 718-499-4911
Grecian Delight Foods
Elk Grove Vlg, IL 800-621-4387
Gregory's Foods
Eagan, MN 800-231-4734
Grossinger's Home Bakery
New York, NY 800-479-6996
Guttenplan's Frozen Dough
Middletown, NJ 888-422-4357
GWB Foods Corporation
Brooklyn, NY 718-686-9600
H&H Bagels
New York, NY 800-692-2435
Haas Baking Company
St Louis, MO. 800-325-3171
Harlan Bakeries
Avon, IN 317-272-3600
Harold Food Company
Charlotte, NC 704-588-8061
Hazelwood Farms Bakery
Rochester, NY 585-424-1240
Heinz North America
Fort Myers, FL 239-694-3663
Isabella's Healthy Bakery
Cuyahoga Falls, OH 800-476-6328

J&J Wall Baking Company
Sacramento, CA 916-381-1410
James Skinner Company
Omaha, NE 800-358-7428
Jay Hoyt of California
Petaluma, CA 707-762-1881
Karp's
Georgetown, MA 800-373-5277
Karp's
Schaumburg, IL. 800-593-5277
Koehler Bakery Company
North Little Rock, AR 800-262-5900
Kyger Bakery Products
Lafayette, IN 765-447-1252
Lamb-Weston
Weston, OR 800-766-7783
Le Notre, Alain & Marie Baker
Houston, TX 800-536-6873
Leidenheimer Baking Company
New Orleans, LA 504-525-1575
Lenchner Bakery
Concord, ON 905-738-8811
Lender's Bagel Bakery
Mattoon, IL 217-235-3181
Lender's Bagel Bakery
West Seneca, NY 716-668-6761
Lewis Brothers Bakeries
Vincennes, IN 812-886-6533
Lone Star Bakery
Round Rock, TX 512-255-3629
Lone Star Consolidated Foods
Dallas, TX 800-658-5637
Love & Quiches Desserts
Freeport, NY 800-525-5251
Ludwick's Frozen Donuts
Grand Rapids, MI 800-366-8816
Main Street Custom Foods
Cuyahoga Falls, OH 800-533-6246
Main Street Gourmet
Cuyahoga Falls, OH 800-533-6246
Main Street Gourmet Fundraising
Cuyahoga Falls, OH 800-533-6246
Main Street Muffins
Cuyahoga Falls, OH 800-533-6246
Main Street's Cambritt Cookies
Cuyahoga Falls, OH 800-533-6246
Mehaffie Pies
Dayton, OH 937-253-1163
Merkel McDonald
Austin, TX. 800-356-0229
Meyer's Bakeries
Hope, AR 800-643-1542
Morningstar Foods
Dallas, TX 225-273-2803
Mother Nature's Goodies
Yucaipa, CA 909-795-6018
Mothers Kitchen Inc
Burlington, NJ. 609-387-7200
Mozzicato Depasquale Bakery & Pastry Shop
Hartford, CT 860-296-0426
Mrs. Kavanagh's English Muffins
Rumford, RI 800-556-7216
Mrs. Sullivan's Pies
Jackson, TN 800-456-2205
My Grandma's Coffee Cak e of New England
Hyde Park, MA 800-847-2636
Naleway Foods
Winnipeg, MB. 800-665-7448
Nancy's Specialty Foods
Newark, CA 510-494-1100
Nestle' Handheld Foods Group
Englewood, CO. 800-225-2270
New England Muffin Company
Fall River, MA 508-675-2833
New York Bagel Boys
West Sacramento, CA 916-739-6540
Oh Boy Corporation
San Fernando, CA 818-361-1128
Old Fashioned Kitchen
Lakewood, NJ 732-364-4100
Orange Bakery
Irvine, CA 949-863-1377
Ore-Ida Foods
Pittsburgh, PA 412-237-3450
Oroweat Baking Company
Montebello, CA 323-721-5161
Pacific Ocean Produce
Santa Cruz, CA 831-423-2654
Parco Foods
Blue Island, IL 708-371-9200
Pastry Chef
Pawtucket, RI 800-639-8606

Pellman Foods
New Holland, PA 717-354-8070
Pepperidge Farm
Downingtown, PA 610-269-2500
Petrofsky's Bakery Products
Maryland Heights, MO 314-432-5101
Pillsbury
McMinnville, OR 800-325-5439
Pillsbury Bakeries & Food Services
Sherwood Park, AB 780-464-1544
Positively Third Street Bakery
Duluth, MN 218-724-8619
Prairie City Bakery
Vernon Hills, IL 800-338-5122
Prime Pastry
Brooklyn, NY 888-771-2464
Ramona's Mexican Food Products
Gardena, CA 310-323-1950
Ranaldi Bros Frozen Food Products Inc
Warwick, RI 401-738-3444
Randag & Associates Inc
Elmhurst, IL 630-530-2830
Ready Bake Foods
Mississauga, ON 905-567-0660
Real Food Marketing
Kansas City, MO 816-221-4100
Rhodes Bake-N-Serv
Salt Lake City, UT 800-695-0122
Rhodes International
Columbus, WI 800-876-7333
Rich Products Corporation
Winchester, VA 540-667-1955
Rich Products Corporation
Fresno, CA 559-486-7380
Rich Products Corporation
Hilliard, OH 614-771-1117
Rich Products Corporation
Buffalo, NY 800-356-7094
Rich Products Corporation
Buffalo, NY 800-828-2021
Rich Products of Canada
Fort Erie, ON 800-263-8174
Rowena's
Norfolk, VA 800-627-8699
Rubschlager Baking Corporation
Chicago, IL 773-826-1245
Sara Lee Bakery Group
Earth City, MO 314-291-5480
Sara Lee Bakery Group
Greenville, SC 864-299-0604
Sara Lee Bakery Group   The EarthGrains - Bakery
Traverse City, MI 231-922-3296
Sara Lee Bakery Group   The EarthGrains - Bakery
Corpus Christi, TX 361-884-6311
Sara Lee Bakery Group   The EarthGrains - Bakery
Beaumont, TX 409-842-9150
Saxby Foods
Edmonton, AB 780-440-4177
Schwans Bakeries
Stilwell, OK 918-696-8325
Schwans Food Company
Norcross, GA 800-241-0559
Sunset Specialty Foods
Sunset Beach, CA 562-592-4976
Table de France
Ontario, CA 909-923-5205
Tasty Mix Quality Foods
Brooklyn, NY 866-TAS-TYMX
The Bama Company
Tulsa, OK 800-756-2262
Tripp Bakers
Wheeling, IL 800-621-3702
Two Chefs on a Roll
Carson, CA 800-842-3025
Uncle Ralph's Cookie Company
Frederick, MD 800-422-0626
Unique Bakery Company
Toronto, ON 416-751-8200
Wenner Bread Products
Bayport, NY 800-869-6262
Wick's Pies
Winchester, IN 800-642-5880
Winder Dairy
West Valley, UT 800-946-3371
Wolferman's
Medford, OR 913-888-4499

Ingredients

ADM Food Ingredients
Olathe, KS 800-255-6637
Al-Rite Fruits & Syrups
Miami, FL 305-652-2540

AnaCon Foods Company
Atchison, KS 800-328-0291
Bake Mark
Pico Rivera, CA 562-949-1054
Brolite Products
Streamwood, IL 888-276-5483
Burnette Foods
Hartford, MI 616-621-3181
California Blending Corpany
El Monte, CA 626-448-1918
California Brands Flavors
Oakland, CA 800-348-0111
Caravan Products Company
Totowa, NJ 800-526-5261
Castella Imports
Hauppauge, NY 866-227-8355
Clofine Dairy & Food Products
Linwood, NJ 800-441-1001
Creme Curls Bakery
Hudsonville, MI 800-466-1219
Dawn Food Products
Louisville, KY 800-626-2542
Deer Creek Honey Farms
London, OH 740-852-0899
Dorothy Dawson Foods Products
Jackson, MI 517-788-9830
DSM Specialties
Norristown, PA 800-662-4478
Dufour Pastry Kitchens
New York, NY 212-929-2800
Eden Processing
Poplar Grove, IL 815-765-2000
Flavorchem
Downers Grove, IL 800-323-1301
Fleischmann's Yeast
Chesterfield, MO 800-247-7473
Holton Food Products Company
La Grange, IL 708-352-5599
Hulman & Company
Terre Haute, IN 812-232-9446
Indiana Sugar
Burr Ridge, IL 630-986-9150
Interstate Brands
Biddeford, ME 207-286-1200
Kellogg US Snack   Division
Battlecreek, MI 269-961-2000
Lake States Yeast
Rhinelander, WI 918-535-2676
Lucas Meyer
Decatur, IL 800-769-3660
Lyoferm & Vivolac Cultures
Indianapolis, IN 800-844-8649
Main Street Ingredients
La Crosse, WI 800-359-2345
Master Taste International
Plant City, FL 800-237-7629
Nature's Hand
Burnsville, MN 952-890-6033
NZMP
Santa Rosa, CA 800-358-9096
Pacific Westcoast Foods
Portland, OR 800-874-9333
QA Products
Elk Grove Vlg, IL 800-635-7907
Roland Industries
Saint Louis, MO 800-325-1183
Vrymeer Commodities
St Charles, IL 630-584-0069
Watson Foods Company
West Haven, CT 800-388-3481
Wiggin Farms
Arbuckle, CA 530-476-2288

Pies

Bake Crafters Food
Collegedale, TN 800-296-8935
Baker Boy Bake Shop
Dickinson, ND 800-437-2008
Bear Creek Smokehouse
Marshall, TX 800-950-2327
Berke-Blake Fancy Foods, Inc.
Longwood, FL 888-386-2253
Bonert's Slice of Pie
Santa Ana, CA 714-540-3535
Chatila's Bakery
Salem, NH 603-898-5459
Cheryl & Company
Westerville, OH 614-891-8822
Clarmil Manufacturing Corporation
Hayward, CA 888-252-7645
Cookies & More
Lewiston, ME 207-923-4227

Interstate Bakeries Corporation
Los Angeles, CA 323-750-7204
Jenny Lee Bakery
Mc Kees Rocks, PA 412-331-8900
Mrs Baird's Bakery
Fort Worth, TX 817-864-2500
Primos Northgate
Flowood, MS 601-936-3398
Shawnee Canning Company
Cross Junction, VA 800-713-1414

Apple

Cheryl & Company
Westerville, OH 614-891-8822
Gould's Maple Sugarhouse
Shelburne Falls, MA 413-625-6170
Mayer's Cider Mill
Webster, NY 800-543-0043
Mehaffie Pies
Dayton, OH 937-253-1163
Orlando's Pastries
Collingdale, PA 610-532-9300
The Bama Company
Tulsa, OK 800-756-2262

Baking Shells

Calise & Sons Bakery
Lincoln, RI 800-225-4737
Canada Bread
Etobicoke, ON 416-622-2040
Classic Confections
Atlanta, GA 800-359-7351
Con Agra Store Brands
Edina, MN 952-835-6900
Del Rey Tortilleria
Chicago, IL 800-446-1459
Dufour Pastry Kitchens
New York, NY 212-929-2800
Dutch Ann Foods Company
Natchez, MS 601-445-5566
Father Sam's Syrian Bread
Buffalo, NY 800-521-6719
Hafner
Stone Mountain, GA 888-725-4605
Hong Kong Noodle Company
Chicago, IL 312-842-0480
Kellogg Company
Battle Creek, MI 800-962-1413
Kellogg US Snack   Division
Battlecreek, MI 269-961-2000
Lamonaca Bakery
Windber, PA 814-467-4909
Livermore Falls Baking Company
Livermore Falls, ME 207-897-3442
Lone Star Bakery
Round Rock, TX 512-255-3629
Molinaro's Fine Italian Foods
Mississauga, ON 800-268-4959
Pacific Ocean Produce
Santa Cruz, CA 831-423-2654
Pasta Factory
Northlake, IL 800-615-6951
Pidy Gourmet Pastry Shells
Inwood, NY 516-239-6057
Pidy Gourmet Pastry Shells
Inwood, NY 800-231-7439
Pillsbury Bakeries & Food Services
Sherwood Park, AB 780-464-1544
Pillsbury Frozen Foods
Lithonia, GA 770-482-5092
Proferas Pizza Bakery
Scranton, PA 570-342-4181
Richmond Baking Company
Richmond, IN 765-962-8535
Salvatore's Pizza Shells
Utica, NY 315-735-7919
Schwans Bakeries
Stilwell, OK 918-696-8325
Specialty Bakers
Marysville, PA 800-233-0778
Sterling Foods
San Antonio, TX 210-490-1669
The Bama Company
Tulsa, OK 800-756-2262
Tomaro's Bakery
Clarksburg, WV 304-622-0691
Wick's Pies
Winchester, IN 800-642-5880

Blueberry

Mehaffie Pies
Dayton, OH 937-253-1163

Brownie

The Bama Company
Tulsa, OK 800-756-2262

Cherry

Mehaffie Pies
Dayton, OH 937-253-1163
Orlando's Pastries
Collingdale, PA 610-532-9300
The Bama Company
Tulsa, OK 800-756-2262

Fresh

August Food Limited
Lubbock, TX .806-744-1918
August Foods
Lubbock, TX .806-744-1918
Banquet Schuster Bakery
Pueblo, CO 719-544-1062
BBU Bakeries
Denver, CO 303-691-6342
Borden's Bread
Regina, SK 306-525-3341
Brenner's Bakery of Arlington
Arlington, VA 703-534-0211
Busken Bakery
Cincinnati, OH 513-871-2114
California Pie Company
Livermore, CA 925-373-7700
Carole's Cheesecake Company
Toronto, ON .416-256-0000
Case Side Holdings Company
Kensington, PE 902-836-4214
Celebrity Cheesecake
Davie, FL 877-986-2253
CGI Desserts
Sugar Land, TX. 281-240-1200
Clarkson Scottish Bakery
Mississauga, ON 905-823-1500
Cloverland Sweets/Priester's Pecan Company
Fort Deposit, AL. 800-523-3505
Del's Pastry
Etobicoke, ON 416-231-4383
Dolly Madison Bakery
Columbus, IN 812-376-7432
Dufflet Pastries
Toronto, ON .416-536-1330
El Peto Products
Cambridge, ON 800-387-4064
Flower Bakeries
London, KY .800-568-3476
Foxtail Foods
Fairfield, OH 800-323-6944
George Weston Bakeries
Northlake, IL. 708-562-6311
Giant Food
Lanham, MD .888-469-4426
Golden Boys Pies of San Diego
San Diego, CA 800-746-0280
Gourmet Baker
Burnaby, BC .800-663-1972
Great San Saba River Pecan Company
San Saba, TX 800-621-9121
Greyston Bakery
Yonkers, NY .800-289-2253
Honey Rose Baking Company
Encinitas, CA 760-942-8996
Interstate Brands
Biddeford, ME 207-286-1200
Interstate Brands Corporation/Dolly Madison Cakes
Columbus, GA 706-257-7000
Italian Bakery
Virginia, MN 218-741-3464
L&M Bakery
Lawrence, MA 978-687-7346
Love & Quiches Desserts
Freeport, NY 800-525-5251
Mehaffie Pies
Dayton, OH. .937-253-1163
Michel's Bakery
Philadelphia, PA 215-725-4328
Mineo's Pies
Scranton, PA 570-347-8278
Mrs. Baird's Bakeries
Abilene, TX. .325-692-3141

Mrs. Sullivan's Pies
Jackson, TN .800-456-2205
Mt View Bakery
Mountain View, HI 808-968-6353
New England Country Bakers
Watertown, CT 800-225-3779
Northside Bakery
Richmond, VA. 804-329-6851
Notre Dame Bakery
Lewisporte, NL 709-535-2738
Orlando's Pastries
Collingdale, PA 610-532-9300
Osman's Pies
Stow, OH. 330-655-2919
Plaidberry Company
Vista, CA 760-727-5403
Rentschler's Bakery
Kutztown, PA 610-683-3506
Rising Dough Bakery
Sacramento, CA 916-387-9700
Roma Bakeries
Rockford, IL. 815-964-6737
Royal Pie Bakery
San Diego, CA 619-233-6393
Ryke's Bakery
Muskegon, MI. 231-557-8011
Sara Lee Bakery Group
Rapid City, SD 605-343-3512
Sara Lee Bakery Group   The EarthGrains - Bakery
Saint Paul, MN
Sara Lee Corporation
Downers Grove, IL 630-598-8100
Sara Lee/Old Home
South Sioux City, NE 402-494-5474
Schwan's Consumer Brands North America
Bloomington, MN. 952-832-4300
Scialo Brothers
Providence, RI 877-421-0986
Scot Paris Fine Desserts
New York, NY 212-807-1802
Seavers Bakery
Johnson City, TN 423-928-8131
Sinbad Sweets
Fresno, CA 800-350-7933
Spring Glen Fresh Foods
Ephrata, PA .800-641-2853
St. Cloud Bakery
St Cloud, MN 320-251-8055
Standard Bakery
Kealakekua, HI 808-322-3688
Sweet Endings
West Palm Beach, FL 888-635-1177
Table Talk Pie
Worcester, MA 508-798-8811
Tastykake
Philadelphia, PA 215-221-8500
United Pie Company
Elkhart, IN. .574-294-3419
Valley Pie Company
Phoenix, AZ .602-943-4512
Van de Kamp's
Chambersburg, PA 570-263-4127
Wenger's Bakery
Reading, PA .610-372-6545
Yost's Dutch Maid Bakery
Johnstown, PA 814-266-3191
Zoelsmanns Bakery & Deli
Pueblo, CO 719-543-0407

Fruit

Bonert's Slice of Pie
Santa Ana, CA 714-540-3535

Frozen

Cutie Pie Corporation
Salt Lake City, UT 800-453-4575
Dynamic Foods
Lubbock, TX. 806-762-0780
Edwards Baking Company
Atlanta, GA .800-241-0559
Field's
Pauls Valley, OK. 405-238-7381
Gardner Pie Company
Akron, OH. 330-245-2030
Gourmet Ice Cream
Palmer, MA. .413-283-3740
Harold Food Company
Charlotte, NC 704-588-8061
Mehaffie Pies
Dayton, OH. .937-253-1163

Mothers Kitchen Inc
Burlington, NJ. 609-387-7200
Pastry Chef
Pawtucket, RI 800-639-8606
Pellman Foods
New Holland, PA 717-354-8070
Sara Lee Bakery Group
Earth City, MO 314-291-5480
Sara Lee Bakery Group   The EarthGrains - Bakery
Traverse City, MI 231-922-3296
Sara Lee Corporation
Downers Grove, IL 630-598-8100
Schwans Food Company
Norcross, GA 800-241-0559
The Bama Company
Tulsa, OK 800-756-2262
Wick's Pies
Winchester, IN 800-642-5880

Key Lime

Cheesecake Etc. Desserts
Miami Springs, FL 305-887-0258

Lemon-Meringue

Kyger Bakery Products
Lafayette, IN 765-447-1252
Mehaffie Pies
Dayton, OH. .937-253-1163

Meat

Cobi Foods
Hantsport, NS 800-565-8229
London Pantry Foods
Mt Pleasant, SC. 888-208-7787
Mexi-Frost Specialties Company
Brooklyn, NY 718-625-3324
Morrison Lamothe
Toronto, ON .416-291-6762
Mortimer's Fine Foods
Burlington, ON 905-336-0000

Frozen

Cobi Foods
Hantsport, NS 800-565-8229
Country Pies
Coombs, BC .250-248-6415
Mexi-Frost Specialties Company
Brooklyn, NY 718-625-3324
Unique Bakery Company
Toronto, ON .416-751-8200
Wick's Pies
Winchester, IN 800-642-5880

Non-Fruit

Ledonne Brothers Bakery
Roseto, PA. 610-588-0423
MacEwan's Meats
Calgary, AB. .403-228-9999
Snyder Foods
Port Perry, ON. 905-985-7373
T. Marzetti Company
Columbus, OH 614-846-2232

Frozen

CGI Desserts
Sugar Land, TX. 281-240-1200
Dimitria Delights
North Grafton, MA 800-763-1113
Dynamic Foods
Lubbock, TX. 806-762-0780
Edwards Baking Company
Atlanta, GA .800-241-0559
Field's
Pauls Valley, OK. 405-238-7381
Gardner Pie Company
Akron, OH. 330-245-2030
Gourmet Ice Cream
Palmer, MA. .413-283-3740
Kyger Bakery Products
Lafayette, IN 765-447-1252
Mothers Kitchen Inc
Burlington, NJ. 609-387-7200
Nancy's Specialty Foods
Newark, CA .510-494-1100
Pastry Chef
Pawtucket, RI 800-639-8606
Pellman Foods
New Holland, PA 717-354-8070

Sara Lee Bakery Group
   Earth City, MO 314-291-5480
Sara Lee Bakery Group   The EarthGrains - Bakery
   Traverse City, MI 231-922-3296
Sara Lee Corporation
   Downers Grove, IL 630-598-8100
The Bama Company
   Tulsa, OK 800-756-2262
Wick's Pies
   Winchester, IN 800-642-5880

Peach

Mehaffie Pies
   Dayton, OH 937-253-1163
Orlando's Pastries
   Collingdale, PA 610-532-9300
The Bama Company
   Tulsa, OK 800-756-2262

Rhubarb Pie

Bear Stewart Corporation
   Chicago, IL 800-697-2327
Best Brands Corporation
   Dallas, TX .800-969-2253

Stuffing

Amalgamated Produce
   Bridgeport, CT 800-358-3808
Bodin Foods
   New Iberia, LA 337-367-1344
Coastal Seafoods
   Ridgefield, CT 203-431-0453
Good Old Days Foods
   Little Rock, AR 501-565-1257
Griffith Laboratories
   Scarborough, ON 416-288-3050
Kellogg Company
   Battle Creek, MI 800-962-1413
Kraft Food Ingredients
   Memphis, TN 901-381-6500
Pepperidge Farm
   Bedford, NH 800-562-8340
Pepperidge Farm
   Norwalk, CT 888-737-7374
Quality Bakery Products
   Fort Lauderdale, FL 954-779-3663
Roskam Baking Company
   Grand Rapids, MI 616-574-5757
Stroehmann Bakery
   Horsham, PA 800-984-0989
Sturm Foods
   Manawa, WI 800-347-8876
Texas Crumb & Food Products
   Farmers Branch, TX 800-522-7862
Weston Bakeries
   Calgary, AB. 403-259-1500
Zatarain's
   Gretna, LA 800-435-6639

Bread

Oroweat Baking Company
   Montebello, CA 323-721-5161

for Meat

Blue Chip Group
   Salt Lake City, UT 800-878-0099
Boekhout Farms
   Ontario, NY. 315-524-4041
Leelanau Fruit Company
   Suttons Bay, MI 231-271-3514
Savoie's Sausage & Food Products
   Opelousas, LA. 337-948-4115
Scotsburn Dairy Group
   Truro, NS .902-895-4412
Texas Crumb & Food Products
   Farmers Branch, TX 800-522-7862
Weston Bakeries
   Calgary, AB. 403-259-1500
World Flavors
   Warminster, PA 215-672-4400

for Poultry

Boekhout Farms
   Ontario, NY. 315-524-4041
Leelanau Fruit Company
   Suttons Bay, MI 231-271-3514

Savoie's Sausage & Food Products
   Opelousas, LA. 337-948-4115
Scotsburn Dairy Group
   Truro, NS .902-895-4412
Weston Bakeries
   Calgary, AB. 403-259-1500
World Flavors
   Warminster, PA 215-672-4400

Waffles

Bake Crafters Food
   Collegedale, TN 800-296-8935
ConAgra Snack Foods Group/Act II Popcorn
   Edina, MN. 800-328-6286
Continental Mills
   Seattle, WA. 253-872-8400
Kellogg Company
   San Jose, CA. 408-295-8656
Kellogg Company
   Hammonton, NJ 609-567-2300
Kellogg Company
   Battle Creek, MI 800-962-1413
Kloss Manufacturing Company
   Allentown, PA. 800-445-7100
Meyer's Bakeries
   Hope, AR .800-643-1542
Nature's Path Foods
   Delta, BC. .604-940-0505
Nestle' Handheld Foods Group
   Englewood, CO. 800-225-2270
Pillsbury
   Allentown, PA. 610-797-5947
Shepherdsfield Bakery
   Fulton, MO 573-642-1439
Van's International Foods
   Torrance, CA. 310-320-9559

Frozen

Bake Crafters Food
   Collegedale, TN 800-296-8935
Beck's Waffles of Oklahoma
   Shawnee, OK 800-646-6254
ConAgra Snack Foods Group/Act II Popcorn
   Edina, MN. 800-328-6286
Continental Mills
   Seattle, WA. 253-872-8400
Echo Lake Farm Produce Company
   Burlington, WI 262-763-9551
Kellogg Canada Inc
   Mississauga, ON 888-876-3750
Kellogg Company
   San Jose, CA. 408-295-8656
Kellogg Company
   Hammonton, NJ 609-567-2300
Kellogg Company
   Battle Creek, MI 800-962-1413
Meyer's Bakeries
   Hope, AR .800-643-1542
Nestle' Handheld Foods Group
   Englewood, CO. 800-225-2270
Pillsbury
   Allentown, PA. 610-797-5947
Van's International Foods
   Torrance, CA. 310-320-9559

Wraps

La Tortilla Factory
   Santa Rosa, CA. 800-446-1516
Nanka Seimen Company
   Vernon, CA 323-585-9967
Scott Adams Foods
   Newton, NJ. 973-300-2091
Toufayan Bakeries
   Orlando, FL. 407-295-2257
Valley Lahvosh Baking Company
   Fresno, CA 800-480-2704

Flavored

La Tortilla Factory
   Santa Rosa, CA. 800-446-1516

Beverages

General

A. Duda & Sons
  Labelle, FL 800-440-3265
A. Lassonde, Inc.
  Rougemont, QC 514-878-1057
ABC Tea House
  Baldwin Park, CA 888-220-3988
Abita Brewing Company
  Abita Springs, LA 800-737-2311
Absopure Water Company
  Champaign, IL 800-422-7678
Abunda Life Laboratories
  Asbury Park, NJ 732-775-4141
Acacia Vineyard
  Napa, CA. 707-226-9991
Ackerman Winery
  Amana, IA. 319-622-6513
Acqua Blox LLC
  Santa Fe Springs, CA 562-693-9599
Adirondack Beverages
  Scotia, NY. 800-316-6096
Admiral Beverages
  Worland, WY 307-347-4201
AFP Advanced Food Products, LLC
  Visalia, CA 559-627-2070
After-the-Fall Products
  Havre De Grace, MD 410-939-1403
Agri-Mark
  Lawrence, MA 978-687-4936
Aimonetto and Sons
  Seattle, WA 866-823-2777
Al-Rite Fruits & Syrups
  Miami, FL 305-652-2540
Alacer Corporation
  Foothill Ranch, CA 800-854-0249
Alamance Foods/Triton Water Company
  Burlington, NC 800-476-9111
Alexander & Baldwin
  Honolulu, HI 808-525-6611
Alfer Laboratories
  Chatsworth, CA 818-709-0737
Alfresh Beverages Canada
  Rexdale, ON 800-465-1516
Aliments Lexus Foods
  Rougemont, QC 800-227-4891
All American Foods, Inc.
  Mankato, MN 800-833-2661
All Juice Food & Beverage
  Hendersonville, NC 800-736-5674
Allegro Coffee Company
  Thornton, CO 800-666-4869
Aloe Farms
  Harlingen, TX 800-262-6771
Aloe Laboratories, Inc.
  Harlingen, TX 800-258-5380
Aloha Distillers
  Honolulu, HI 808-841-5787
Alpine Valley Water
  Harvey, IL 708-333-3910
Alternative Health & Herbs
  Albany, OR 800-345-4152
Ambootia Tea Estate
  Chicago, IL 312-661-1550
Amcan Industries
  Elmsford, NY 914-347-4838
America's Best Beverage Company
  Whitestone, NY 800-736-7338
American Food Traders
  Miami, FL 305-670-6250
American Fruit Processors
  Pacoima, CA 818-899-9574
American Mercantile Corporation
  Groveland, FL 901-454-1900

American Purpac Technologies, LLC
  Beloit, WI 877-787-7221
American Soy Products
  Saline, MI 734-429-2310
Andalusia Distributing Company
  Andalusia, AL 334-222-3671
Andrew Peller Limited
  Grimsby, ON 905-643-4131
Anheuser-Busch
  Columbus, OH 614-888-6644
Apple & Eve
  Roslyn, NY 800-969-8018
Aqua Clara Bottling & Distribution
  Clearwater, FL 727-446-2999
Arbuckle Coffee
  Pittsburgh, PA 800-533-8278
Arcadian Estate Winery
  Rock Stream, NY 800-298-1346
Ariel Vineyards
  Napa, CA. 800-456-9472
Arizona Beverage Company
  New Hyde Park, NY 800-832-3775

Asiamerica Ingredients
  Westwood, NJ 201-497-5531

Processor, importer, exporter and distributor of
bulk vitamins, amino acids, nutraceuticals, aromatic chemicals, food additives, herbs, mineral
nutrients and pharmaceuticals.

Atlanta Coffee Roasters
  Atlanta, GA 800-252-8211
Atlanta Flagship Dairy
  Atlanta, GA 800-224-0669
August Schell Brewing Company
  New Ulm, MN. 800-770-5020
Avalon Foodservice, Inc.
  Canal Fulton, OH 800-362-0622
B.M. Lawrence & Company
  San Francisco, CA 415-981-3650
Bacardi Canada, Inc.
  Brampton, ON. 905-451-6100
Banfi Vintners
  Glen Head, NY 800-645-6511
Barkers Farm Dairy
  Pecks Mill, WV. 304-855-4512
Barq's Beverages of Baton Rouge
  Baton Rouge, LA 225-928-3971
Barrows Tea Company
  New Bedford, MA 800-832-5024
Barton Brands
  Chicago, IL 800-598-6352
Batavia Wine Cellars
  Canandaigua, NY 800-879-9463
Baywood Cellars
  Lodi, CA 800-214-0445
Bean Forge
  Coos Bay, OR 888-292-1632
Beckmen Vineyards
  Los Olivos, CA 805-688-8664
Belton Foods
  Dayton, OH 800-443-2266
Belvedere Winery
  Healdsburg, CA 800-433-8296
Benmarl Wine Company
  Marlboro, NY 845-236-4265
Berkeley Farms
  Hayward, CA 510-265-8600
Berry Citrus Products
  Labelle, FL 863-675-2769
Bevco
  Surrey, BC 800-663-0090
Beverage Capital Corporation
  Halethorpe, MD 410-242-7003
Bianchi Winery
  Newport Beach, CA 949-646-9100
Big Red Bottling
  Waco, TX 254-772-7791

Birdseye Dairy
  Green Bay, WI. 920-494-5388
Black Prince Distillery, Inc.
  Clifton, NJ 973-365-2050
Blue Sky Natural Beverage Company
  Santa Fe, NM 505-995-9761
Bolthouse Farms
  Bakersfield, CA 800-467-4683
Borgnine Beverage Company
  Sherman Oaks, CA 818-501-5312
Boston's Best Coffee Roasters
  South Easton, MA 800-323-4889
Bottineau Cooperative Creamery
  Bottineau, ND. 701-228-2216
Brander Vineyard
  Los Olivos, CA 800-970-9979
Brenntag Pacific
  Santa Fe Springs, CA 562-903-9626
Briar's USA
  North Brunswick, NJ 887-327-4277
Brick Brewery
  Waterloo, ON 800-505-8971
Brimstone Hill Vineyard
  Pine Bush, NY 845-744-2231
Brooklyn Bottling Company
  Milton, NY 845-795-2171
Broughton Foods
  Marietta, OH 800-283-2479
Buckmaster Coffee
  Hillsboro, OR 800-962-9148
Buena Vista Carneros Winery
  Sonoma, CA 800-678-8504
Buffalo Trace Distillery
  Frankfort, KY 800-654-8471
Bull Run Roasting Company
  Hayward, WI. 715-634-3646
Bully Hill Vineyards
  Hammondsport, NY 607-868-3610
Burnette Foods
  Hartford, MI 616-621-3181
C-B Beverage Corporation
  Hopkins, MN 952-935-9905
C.F. Burger Creamery
  Detroit, MI 800-229-2322
Cadillac Coffee Company
  Madison Heights, MI 800-438-6900
Cafe Du Monde
  New Orleans, LA 504-587-0835
Cafe Yaucono/Jimenez & Fernandez
  Santurce, PR 787-721-3337
Cain's Coffee Company
  Springfield, MO 800-641-4025
California Brands Flavors
  Oakland, CA 800-348-0111
California Day Fresh
  Glendora, CA 800-800-0986
California Farms & Canners
  San Francisco, CA 415-433-3522
California Natural Products
  Lathrop, CA 209-858-2525
Callaway Vineyards & Winery
  Temecula, CA 800-472-2377
Canada Dry Bottling Company
  Flushing, NY 718-661-4265
Canadian Mist Distillers
  Collingwood, ON 705-445-4690
Canandaigua Wine Concentrate
  Madera, CA. 559-673-7071
Caracollillo Coffee Mills
  Tampa, FL. 800-682-0023
Caravan Company
  Worcester, MA 508-752-3777
Cargill Juice Products
  Frostproof, FL 800-227-4455
Carolina Products
  Greer, SC. 864-879-3084
Carolina Treet
  Wilmington, NC 800-616-6344
Cascade Mountain Winery & Restaurant
  Amenia, NY 845-373-9021
Cass Clay Creamery
  Fargo, ND 701-293-6455
Castello Di Borghese
  Cutchogue, NY 800-734-5158
Catamount Brewing Company
  Windsor, VT 802-674-6700

Cawy Bottling Company
Miami, FL 877-917-2299
Cecchetti Sebastiani Cellar
Sonoma, CA 707-996-8463
Cedar Creek Winery
Cedarburg, WI. 800-827-8020
Cedar Lake Foods
Cedar Lake, MI 800-246-5039
Central Coca-Cola Bottling Company
Richmond, VA. 800-359-3759
Central Dairies
St Johns, NL 800-563-6455
Chadler
Swedesboro, NJ 856-467-0099
Chartrand Imports
Rockland, ME 800-473-7307
Chase Brothers Dairy
Oxnard, CA 800-438-6455
Chateau des Charmes Wines
St. Davids, ON 800-263-2541
Chateau Julien Winery
Carmel, CA 831-624-2600
Chateau Sassenage
Truth or Consequences, NM........505-894-7244
Chateau St. Jean Vineyards
Kenwood, CA 707-833-4134
Chestnut Mountain Winery
Hoschton, GA 770-867-6914
Chi Company/Tabor Hill Winery
Buchanan, MI 800-283-3363
Chicago Coffee Roastery
Huntley, IL 800-762-5402
Chicama Vineyards
West Tisbury, MA. 888-244-2262
Chimere
Santa Maria, CA 805-922-9097
China Bowl Trading Company
Westport, CT 203-222-0381
Chiquita Brands International
Cincinnati, OH 800-438-0015
Chocolat
Bellevue, WA 800-808-2462
Chouinard Vineyards
Castro Valley, CA 510-582-9900
Christine Woods Winery
Philo, CA. 707-895-2115
Christopher Creek Winery
Healdsburg, CA 707-433-6992
Chukar Cherries
Prosser, WA. 800-624-9544
Chung's Gourmet Foods
Houston, TX 800-824-8647
Cienega Valley Winery/DeRose
Hollister, CA 831-636-9143
Cimarron Cellars
Caney, OK 580-889-5997
Cinnabar Vineyards & Winery
Saratoga, CA...................408-741-5858
Citrus Citrosuco North America
Lake Wales, FL 800-356-4592
Citrus International
Winter Park, FL. 407-629-8037
Citrus Service
Winter Garden, FL 407-656-4999
City Bean
Stevenson Ranch, CA 888-248-9232
City Brewery Latrobe
Latrobe, PA 724-537-5545
City Brewing Company
La Crosse, WI 608-785-4200
Claiborne & Churchill Vintners
San Luis Obispo, CA 805-544-4066
Claire's Grand River Winery
Madison, OH 440-298-9838
Classic Tea
Libertyville, IL 630-680-9934
Claudia Springs Winery
San Jose, CA...................408-895-3926
Clayton's Coffee & Tea
Modesto, CA...................209-522-7811
Clean Foods
Santa Paula, CA 800-526-8328
Clear Creek Distillery
Portland, OR 503-248-9470
Clear Mountain Coffee Company
Silver Spring, MD. 301-587-2233
Clearwater Coffee Company
Lake Zurich, IL 847-540-7711
Cliffstar Corporation
Dunkirk, NY 800-777-2389
Cline Cellars
Sonoma, CA 800-543-2070

Clinton Milk Company
Newark, NJ 973-642-3000
Clinton Vineyards
Clinton Corners, NY 845-266-5372
Clos Du Bois
Geyserville, CA 800-222-3189
Clos du Lac Cellars
Ione, CA 209-274-2238
Clos Du Muriel
Temecula, CA 951-296-5400
Clos du Val Wine Company
Napa, CA 800-993-9463
Clos Pegase Winery
Calistoga, CA 800-866-8583
Cloudstone Vineyards
Los Altos Hills, CA 650-948-8621
Clover Hill Vineyards & Winery
Breinigsville, PA. 800-256-8374
Coastlog Industries
Novi, MI 248-344-9556
Cobi Foods
Hantsport, NS 800-565-8229
Cobraz Brazilian Coffee
New York, NY 212-759-7700
Coburg Dairy
North Charleston, SC 843-554-4870
Coca-Cola Bottling Company
El Paso, TX.....................800-288-3228
Coca-Cola Bottling Company
Charlotte, NC 800-777-2653
Coca-Cola Bottling Company
Honolulu, HI 808-839-6711
Coca-Cola Bottling Company
West Memphis, AR...............870-732-1460
Cocolalla Winery
Cocolalla, ID....................208-263-3774
Coffee & Tea
Bloomington, MN 952-853-1148
Coffee Barrel
Okemos, MI 517-349-3888
Coffee Bean
Englewood, CO. 303-922-1238
Coffee Bean International
Portland, OR 800-877-0474
Coffee Bean of Leesburg
Leesburg, VA 800-232-6872
Coffee Beanery
Flushing, MI 800-728-2326
Coffee Butler Service
Alexandria, VA 703-823-0028
Coffee Concepts
Dallas, TX. 214-363-9331
Coffee Creations
Portland, OR 800-245-5856
Coffee Creations
Lahaina, HI 808-575-9735
Coffee Culture-A House
Lincoln, NE. 402-438-8456
Coffee Holding Company
Brooklyn, NY 800-458-2233
Coffee Masters
Spring Grove, IL 800-334-6485
Coffee Masters
Barrington, IL 847-382-9786
Coffee Mill Roastery
Elon, NC 800-729-1727
Coffee Millers & Roasting
Cape Coral, FL 239-573-6800
Coffee People
Beaverton, OR 800-354-5282
Coffee Process Technology
Houston, TX 713-695-7530
Coffee Reserve
Phoenix, AZ 623-434-0939
Coffee Roasters
Oakland, NJ 201-337-8221
Coffee Roasters of New Orleans
New Orleans, LA 800-737-5464
Coffee Up
Chicago, IL 847-288-9330
Coffee Works
Sacramento, CA 800-275-3335
Cold Hollow Cider Mill
Waterbury Center, VT.............800-327-7537
College Coffee Roasters
Mountville, PA 717-285-9561
Coloma Frozen Foods
Coloma, MI 800-642-2723
Colombian Coffee Federation
New York, NY 212-421-8300
Colonial Coffee Roasters
Miami, FL 305-638-0885

Colorado Cellars Winery
Palisade, CO 970-464-7921
Colorado Spice
Boulder, CO 800-677-7423
Columbia Winery
Woodinville, WA. 425-488-2776
Comfort Food's
North Andover, MA 978-557-0009
Commodities Marketing, Inc.
Edison, NJ 732-516-0700
Commonwealth Fish & Beer Company
Boston, MA.....................617-523-8383
Community Coffee Specialty
Baton Rouge, LA 800-525-5583
Compact Industries
St Charles, IL 800-513-4262
Compass Foods/Eight O'Clock Coffee
Montvale, NJ 800-299-2739
ConAgra Grocery Products
Irvine, CA......................714-680-1000
Concannon Vineyard
Livermore, CA 800-258-9866
Condaxis Coffee Company
Jacksonville, FL 904-356-5330
Conn Creek Winery
St Helena, CA 800-793-7960
Conneaut Cellars Winery
Conneaut Lake, PA 877-229-9463
Conrotto A. Winery
Gilroy, CA......................408-847-2233
Consolidated Distilled Products
Chicago, IL 773-927-4161
Consolidated Tea Company
Lynbrook, NY 516-887-1144
Consun Food Industries
Elyria, OH......................440-233-7501
Contact International
Skokie, IL 847-324-4411
Continental Coffee Products Company
Houston, TX 800-323-6178
Cool
Richardson, TX. 972-437-9352
Cooper Mountain Vineyards
Beaverton, OR 503-649-0027
Coors Brewing Company
Golden, CO 800-642-6116
Corim International Coffee
Brick, NJ 800-942-4201
Corus Brands
Woodinville, WA. 425-806-2600
Cosentino Winery
Yountville, CA 800-764-1220
Cotswold Cottage Foods
Arvada, CO 800-208-1977
Cott Beverages
Tampa, FL 813-313-1800
Cott Concentrates/Royal Crown Cola International
Columbus, GA 800-652-5642
Cottonwood Canyon Vineyards
Santa Maria, CA 805-937-8463
Country Pure Foods
Akron, OH.....................330-753-2293
Country Pure Foods
Akron, OH.....................877-995-8423
Cow Palace Too
Granger, WA 509-829-5777
Cowie Wine Cellars
Paris, AR.......................479-963-3990
Crescini Wines
Soquel, CA 831-462-1466
Cristom Vineyards
Salem, OR 503-375-3068
Cronin Vineyards
Woodside, CA 650-851-1452
Crowley Foods
Binghamton, NY 800-637-0019
Crown Regal Wine Cellars
Brooklyn, NY 718-604-1430
Cruse Vineyards
Chester, SC 803-377-3944
Crystal & Vigor Beverages
Kearny, NJ 201-991-2342
Crystal Geyser Roxanne LLC
Pensacola, FL 850-476-8844
Crystal Springs Water Company
Fort Lauderdale, FL 800-432-1321
Crystal Water Company
Orlando, FL.....................800-444-7873
CTL Foods
Colfax, WI. 800-962-5227
Culligan Water Technologies
Northbrook, IL 847-205-6000

Cuneo Cellars
Amity, OR 503-835-2782
Custom Brands Unlimited
Solebury, PA 215-297-9842
Custom Food Service
Phoenix, AZ 602-254-1876
Custom House Coffee Roasters
Miami, FL 888-563-5282
Cutrale Citrus Juices
Leesburg, FL 352-728-7800
Cutrale Citrus Juices
Auburndale, FL 863-965-5000
Cuvaison Vineyard
Calistoga, CA 707-942-6266
Cygnet Cellars
Hollister, CA 831-637-7559
Dairy Farmers of America
Springfield, MO 800-243-2479
Dairy Fresh Corporation
Greensboro, AL 800-239-5114
Dairy Fresh Foods
Taylor, MI 313-295-6300
Dairy Land
Macon, GA 478-742-6461
Dairy Maid Dairy
Frederick, MD 301-663-5114
Dairyman's/Land O' Lakes
Tulare, CA 559-687-8287
Dalla Valle Vineyards
Oakville, CA 707-944-2676
Dallis Brothers
Jamaica, NY 800-424-4252
Damron Corporation
Chicago, IL 800-333-1860
Danone Waters of North America
Pasadena, CA 626-585-1000
Dark Mountain Winery and Brewery
Vail, AZ 520-762-5777
Daume Winery
Camarillo, CA 800-559-9922
David Bruce Winery
Los Gatos, CA 800-397-9972
David Rio Coffee & Tea
San Francisco, CA 800-454-9605
Davis Bynum Winery
Healdsburg, CA 800-826-1073

Daybreak Coffee Roasters
Glastonbury, CT 800-882-5282
Daymar Select Fine Coffees
El Cajon, CA 800-466-7590
Dazbog Coffee Company
Denver, CO 303-892-9999
De Coty Coffee Company
San Angelo, TX 800-588-8001
De Lima Company
Syracuse, NY 800-962-8864
De Loach Vineyards
Santa Rosa, CA 707-526-9111
De Lorimier Winery
Geyserville, CA 800-546-7718
Dean Foods/Land O'Lakes
Bismarck, ND 701-222-3131
Dean Foods/Verifine Dairy Products
Sheboygan, WI 800-236-6455
Deaver Vineyards
Plymouth, CA 209-245-4099
Decoty Coffee Company
San Angelo, TX 800-588-8001
Deep Rock Fontenelle Water Company
Omaha, NE 800-433-1303
Deep Rock Water Company
Denver, CO 800-695-2020
Deep Rock Water Company
Minneapolis, MN 800-800-8986
Deer Meadow Vineyard
Winchester, VA 800-653-6632
Deer Park Winery
Elk Creek, MO 707-963-5411
Dehlinger Winery
Sebastopol, CA 707-823-2378
Del's Lemonade & Refreshments
Cranston, RI 401-463-6190
Delicato Vineyards
Napa, CA 707-265-1700
Delicato Vineyards
Napa, CA 877-824-3600
Denatale Vineyards
Healdsburg, CA 707-431-8460
Destileria Serralles
Mercedita, PR 787-723-0107
Devansoy
Carroll, IA 800-747-8605

Devine Foods
Media, PA 888-338-4631
Devlin Wine Cellars
Soquel, CA 831-476-7288
DG Yuengling & Son
Pottsville, PA 570-622-4141
Di Grazia Vineyards
Brookfield, CT 800-230-8853
Diageo United Distillers
Norwalk, CT 203-602-5000
Diamond Creek Vineyards
Calistoga, CA 707-942-6926
Diamond Oaks Vineyard
Cloverdale, CA 707-894-3191
Diamond Water
Hot Springs, AR 501-623-1251
Diehl Food Ingredients
Defiance, OH 800-251-3033
Distant Lands Coffee Roaster
Tyler, TX 800-346-5459
Distillata Company
Cleveland, OH 800-999-2906
Distillerie Stock USA
New York, NY 800-323-1884
Dixie Brewing Company
New Orleans, LA 504-822-8711
Dixie Dairy Company
Gary, IN 219-885-6101
DMH Ingredients
Libertyville, IL 847-362-9977
Dole Food Company
Westlake Village, CA 818-879-6600
Domaine Chandon
Yountville, CA 800-242-6366
Domaine Montreaux
Napa, CA 800-743-6668
Domaine St. George Winery
Healdsburg, CA 707-433-5508
Don Francisco Coffee Traders
Los Angeles, CA 800-697-5282
Don Hilario Estate Coffee
Tampa, FL 800-799-1903
Don Jose Foods
Oceanside, CA 760-631-0243
Donatoni Winery
Inglewood, CA 310-645-5445

Door-Peninsula Winery
Sturgeon Bay, WI 800-551-5049
Downeast Coffee
Pawtucket, RI 800-922-6287
Dr. Frank's Vinifera Wine Cellar
Hammondsport, NY 800-320-0735
Dr. Konstantin Frank Vinifera Wine Cellars
Hammondsport, NY 800-320-0735
Dr. Pepper/Seven-Up
Racine, WI 800-696-5891
Dreyer Sonoma
Woodside, CA 650-851-9448
Droubi's Imports
Houston, TX 713-988-7138
Dry Creek Vineyard
Healdsburg, CA 800-864-9463
DS Waters of America
Atlanta, GA 800-728-5508
Duck Pond Cellars
Dundee, OR 800-437-3213
Duckhorn Vineyards
St Helena, CA 888-354-8885
Duncan Peak Vineyards
Hopland, CA 707-744-1129
Dundee Wine Company
Dundee, OR 888-427-4953
Dunn Vineyards
Angwin, CA 707-965-3642
Duplin Wine Cellars
Rose Hill, NC 800-774-9634
Durney Vineyards
Carmel Valley, CA 800-625-8466
Dutch Henry Winery
Calistoga, CA 888-224-5879
E&J Gallo Winery
Modesto, CA 209-341-3111
E&J Gallo Winery
Livingston, CA .209-394-6219
E&J Gallo Winery
Fresno, CA 559-458-2480
Eagle Coffee Company
Baltimore, MD .800-545-4015
Eagle Crest Vineyards
Conesus, NY 585-346-2321
Earth Ade Beverages
Charlotte, NC 704-343-9990
Easley Winery
Indianapolis, IN 317-636-4516
East India Coffee & Tea Company
San Leandro, CA 800-829-1300
East Side Winery/Oak Ridge Vineyards
Lodi, CA 209-369-4768
Eastern Tea Corporation
Monroe Township, NJ 800-221-0865
Eastrise Trading Corporation
City of Industry, CA 626-330-0933
Eberle Winery
Paso Robles, CA 805-238-9607
Ed Oliveira Winery
Arcata, CA 707-822-3023
Eden Foods Inc
Clinton, MI 800-248-0320
Edgewood Estate Winery
Napa, CA 800-755-2374
Edmunds St. John
Berkeley, CA 510-981-1510
Edna Valley Vineyard
San Luis Obispo, CA 805-544-5855
El Dorado Coffee
Flushing, NY 800-635-2566
El Paso Winery
Ulster Park, NY 845-331-8642
Eldorado Artesian Springs
Eldorado Springs, CO 303-499-1316
Eldorado Coffee Distributors
New Orleans, LA 504-949-8416
Elk Cove Vineyards
Gaston, OR 503-985-7760
Elk Run Vineyards
Mt Airy, MD 800-414-2513
Ellis Coffee Company
Philadelphia, PA 800-822-3984
Elliston Vineyards
Sunol, CA 925-862-2377
Ellsworth Cooperative Creamery
Ellsworth, WI 715-273-4311
Emilio Guglielmo Winery
Morgan Hill, CA 408-779-2145
Empire Tea Services
Columbus, IN 800-790-0246
Empresas La Famosa/Coco Lopez
Toa Baja, PR 787-251-0060

Ener-G Foods
Seattle, WA 800-331-5222
Enz Vineyards
Hollister, CA 831-637-3956
Eola Hills Wine Cellars
Rickreall, OR 800-291-6730
EOS Estate Winery
Paso Robles, CA 800-349-9463
Erath Vineyards Winery
Dundee, OR 800-539-5463
Erba Food Products
Brooklyn, NY 718-272-7700
Espresso Vivace
Seattle, WA 206-860-5869
Essentia Water
Phoenix, AZ 877-293-2239
Eureka Springs Winery
Eureka Springs, AR 479-253-8754
Eureka Water Company
Oklahoma City, OK 800-310-8474
Eurobubblies
Santa Monica, CA 800-273-0750
European Coffee
Cherry Hill, NJ .856-428-7202
European Roasterie
Le Center, MN .888-469-2233
Evans Properties
Dade City, FL 352-567-5662
Evco Wholesale Foods
Emporia, KS 620-343-7000
Evensen Vineyards
Oakville, CA 707-944-2396
Everfresh Beverages
Warren, MI 586-755-9500
Evesham Wood Vineyard & Winery
Salem, OR 503-371-8478
Excellent Coffee Company
Pawtucket, RI 800-345-2007
Excelso Coffee Company
Norcross, GA 800-241-2138
Eyrie Vineyards
Dundee, OR 503-472-6315
F. Gavina & Sons
Vernon, CA 323-582-0671
F.X. Matt Brewing Company
Utica, NY 800-690-3181
Fall Creek Vineyards
Austin, TX 512-476-4477
Fantis Foods
Carlstadt, NJ 201-933-6200
Far Niente Winery
Oakville, CA 707-944-2861
Farella-Park Vineyards
Napa, CA 707-254-9489
Farfelu Vineyards
Flint Hill, VA 540-364-2930
Farmer Brothers Company
Torrance, CA 800-735-2878
Farmland Dairies
Wallington, NJ .888-727-6252
Farmland Dairies
Wallington, NJ .973-777-2500
FCC Coffee Packers
Doral, FL 305-591-1128
Fee Brothers
Rochester, NY 800-961-3337
Fellom Ranch Vineyards
Cupertino, CA .408-741-0307
Fenestra Winery
Livermore, CA .800-789-9463
Fenn Valley Vineyards
Fennville, MI 800-432-6265
Ferolito Vultaggio & Sons
New Hyde Park, NY 800-832-3775
Ferrante Winery & Ristorante
Geneva, OH 440-466-6046
Ferrara Bakery & Cafe
New York, NY 212-226-6150
Ferrara Winery
Escondido, CA .760-745-7632
Ferrari-Carano Vineyards& Winery
Healdsburg, CA 800-831-0381
Ferrigno Vineyard & Winery
St James, MO 573-265-7742
Ferrigno Vineyards & Winry
St James, MO 573-265-7742
Fess Parker Winery
Los Olivos, CA .800-446-2455
Festive Finer Foods
Jamaica, NY 718-341-2100
Ficklin Vineyards
Madera, CA 559-674-4598

Fidalgo Bay Coffee
Burlington, WA 800-310-5540
Field Stone Winery & Vineyard
Healdsburg, CA 800-544-7273
Fieldbrook Valley Winery
McKinleyville, CA 707-839-4140
Fields of Fair Whiskey
Paxico, KS 785-636-5460
Fife Vineyards
Redwood Valley, CA 707-485-0323
Fiji Water Company
Basalt, CO 877-426-3454
Filsinger Vineyards & Winery
Temecula, CA .951-302-6363
Fine Foods Northwest
Seattle, WA 800-862-3965
Finlay Tea Solutions
Morristown, NJ 973-538-1701
Fiore Winery
Pylesville, MD .410-452-0132
Firelands Wine Company
Sandusky, OH .800-548-9463
Firestone Vineyard
Los Olivos, CA .805-688-3940
First Colony Coffee & Tea Company
Norfolk, VA 800-446-8555
First Roasters of Central Florida
Longwood, FL .407-699-6364
Fisher Ridge Wine Company
Charleston, WV 304-342-8702
Fisher Vineyards
Santa Rosa, CA 707-539-7511
Fitzpatrick Winery & Lodge
Somerset, CA 800-245-9166
Fizz-O Water Company
Tulsa, OK 918-834-3691
Fizzy Lizzy
New York, NY 800-203-9336
Flavor Innovations
South Plainfield, NJ 800-536-2030
Flavouressence Products
Mississauga, ON 866-209-7778
Flora Springs Wine Company
St Helena, CA 707-967-8032
Florida Distillers Company
Lake Alfred, FL 863-956-3477
Florida Food Products
Eustis, FL 800-874-2331
Florida Fruit Juices
Chicago, IL 773-586-6200
Florida Juice Products
Lakeland, FL 863-802-4040
Florida Key West
Fort Myers, FL .239-694-8787
Florida's Natural Growers
Umatilla, FL 800-366-4440
Flynn Vineyards Winery
Rickreall, OR 888-427-4953
Fmali Herb
Santa Cruz, CA 831-423-7913
Foley Estates Vineyards & Winery
Solvang, CA 805-688-8554
Folgers Coffee Company
Orrville, OH 877-693-6543
Folie a Deux Winery
St Helena, CA 800-473-4454
Folklore Foods
Toppenish, WA 509-865-4772
Foltz Coffee Tea & Spice Company
New Orleans, LA 504-486-1545
Foppiano Vineyard
Healdsburg, CA 707-433-7272
Foremost Dairies-Hawaii
Honolulu, HI 808-841-5831
Foremost Farms
Fitchburg, WI .608-271-3000
Foremost Farms
Waukesha, WI .800-289-7787
Foris Vineyards
Cave Junction, OR 541-592-3752
Forman Vineyards
St Helena, CA 707-963-3900
Fortino Winery
Gilroy, CA 888-617-6606
Fortuna Cellars
Davis, CA 530-756-6686
Fortunes International Teas
Mc Kees Rocks, PA 800-551-8327
Fountainhead Water Company
Norcross, GA 864-944-1993
Four Chimneys Farm Winery Trust
Himrod, NY 607-243-7502

Four Sisters Winery
Belvidere, NJ 908-475-3671
Fox Run Vineyards
Penn Yan, NY 800-636-9786
Fox Vineyards Winery
Social Circle, GA 770-787-5402
Foxen Vineyard
Santa Maria, CA 805-937-4251
Franciscan Oakville Estates
Rutherford, CA 800-529-9463
Franciscan Vineyards
Rutherford, CA 800-529-9463
Franco's Cocktail Mixes
Pompano Beach, FL 800-782-4508
Frank Family Vineyard
Calistoga, CA 707-942-0859
Frank-Lin Distillers
San Jose, CA 408-259-8900
Franklin Hill Vineyards
Bangor, PA 888-887-2839
Franzia Winery
Ripon, CA 209-599-4111
Fratelli Perata
Paso Robles, CA 805-238-2809
Frederick Wildman & Sons
New York, NY 800-733-9463
Freed, Teller & Freed
Burlingame, CA 800-370-7371
Freemark Abbey Winery
Helena, CA 800-963-9698
Freixenet
Sonoma, CA 707-996-4981
Fresh Roast Systems
Petaluma, CA 707-763-1050
Fresh Squeezed Juice Company
Sebastian, FL 561-589-0390
Frey Vineyards
Redwood Valley, CA. 800-760-3739
Frick Winery
Sacramento, CA 415-776-7331
Frisinger Cellars
Napa, CA. 707-255-3749
Frog's Leap Winery
Rutherford, CA 800-959-4704
Frontenac Point Vineyard
Trumansburg, NY 607-387-9619
Frontier Natural Co-op
Norway, IA 303-449-8137
Full Service Beverage Company
Wichita, KS 800-540-0001
G&J Pepsi-Cola Bottlers
Columbus, OH 614-253-8771
Gadsden Coffee/Caffe
Arivaca, AZ. 888-514-5282
Gainey Vineyard
Santa Ynez, CA. 805-688-0558
Galante Vineyards
Carmel Valley, CA 800-425-2683
Galena Cellars Winery
Galena, IL 800-397-9463
Galleano Winery
Mira Loma, CA. 951-685-5376
Galliker Dairy
Johnstown, PA. 800-477-6455
Galluccio Estate Vineyards
Cutchogue, NY 631-734-7089
Garelick Farms
Lynn, MA 800-487-8700
Gary Farrell Wines
Santa Rosa, CA 707-433-6616
Gehl Guernsey Farms
Germantown, WI. 800-434-5713
George A Dickel & Company
Tullahoma, TN 931-857-9313
George H Hathaway Coffee Company
Summit Argo, IL. 708-458-7668
Georgia Sun
Newnan, GA 770-251-2500
Georgia Winery
Ringgold, GA 706-937-2177
Georis Winery
Carmel Valley, CA 831-659-1050
Germanton Winery
Germanton, NC 800-322-2894
Geyser Peak Winery
Geyserville, CA 800-945-4447
Giacorelli Imports
Boca Raton, FL. 561-451-1415
Giasi Winery
Rock Stream, NY 607-535-7785
Gibson Wine Company
Sanger, CA 559-875-2505

Gilette Foods
Union, NJ 908-688-0500
Ginseng Up Corporation
New York, NY 212-696-1930
Girard Spring Water
North Providence, RI 800-477-9287
Girard Winery/Rudd Estates
Oakville, CA. 707-944-8577
Girardet Wine Cellars
Roseburg, OR 541-679-7252
Giumarra Vineyards
Bakersfield, CA 661-395-7000
Givaudan Flavors
Bridgeton, MO 800-422-5444
Glen Summit Springs Water Company
Mountain Top, PA. 800-621-7596
Glencourt
Napa, CA. 707-944-4444
Glenora Wine Cellars
Dundee, NY 800-243-5513
Global Beverage Company
Rochester, NY 585-381-3560
Global Food Industries
Townville, SC 800-225-4152
Global Health Laboratories
Melville, NY 631-293-0030
Global Marketing Associates
Schaumburg, IL 847-490-6481
GlobeTrends
Morris Plains, NJ 800-416-8327
Globus Coffee
Manhasset, NY 516-304-5780
Gloria Ferrer Champagne
Sonoma, CA 707-996-7256
Gloria Jean's Gourmet Coffees
Rcho Sta Marg, CA. 800-354-5258
Gloria Winery & Vineyard
Springfield, MO 417-926-6263
Glunz Family Winery & Cellars
Grayslake, IL. 847-548-9463
Gold Star Coffee Company
Salem, MA 888-505-5233
Golden Creek Vineyard
Santa Rosa, CA 707-538-2350
Golden Moon Tea
Herndon, VA 877-327-5473
Golden Town Apple Products
Thornbury, ON 519-599-6300
Good Earth® Teas
Santa Cruz, CA 831-423-7913
Good Harbor Vineyards
Lake Leelanau, MI 231-256-7165
Good-O-Beverages Company
Bronx, NY 718-328-6400
Goodson Brothers Coffee Company
Knoxville, TN 865-693-3572
Goosecross Cellars
Yountville, CA 800-276-9210
Goya Foods
Secaucus, NJ 201-348-4900
Grace Tea Company
New York, NY 212-678-2008
Grainaissance
Emeryville, CA. 800-472-4697
Grande River Vineyards
Palisade, CO 800-264-7696
Granite Springs Winery
Somerset, CA 800-638-6041
Great Eastern Sun
Asheville, NC 800-334-5809
Great Spring Waters
Richmond, CA 800-950-9393
Great Western Juice Company
Cleveland, OH 800-321-9180
Green Mountain Chocolates
Franklin, MA 508-520-7160
Green Mountain Cidery
Middlebury, VT. 802-388-0700
Green Spot Packaging
Claremont, CA 800-456-3210
Greenfield Wine Company
Saint Helena, CA 707-963-2335
Greenwood Ridge Vineyards
Philo, CA. 707-895-2002
Gregory Packaging
Newark, NJ 973-465-1113
Groth Vineyards & Winery
Oakville, CA. 707-944-0290
Groupe Paul Masson
Longueuil, QC 514-878-3050
Gruet Winery
Albuquerque, NM 888-897-9463

Guilliams Winery
St Helena, CA 707-963-9059
Guinness-Bass Import Company
Stamford, CT. 800-521-1591
Gundlach Bundschu Winery
Sonoma, CA 707-938-5277
GWB Foods Corporation
Brooklyn, NY 718-686-9600
H Coturri & Sons Winery
Glen Ellen, CA 866-268-8774
H&H Products Company
Orlando, FL. 407-299-5410
H&K Products-Pappy's Sassafras Teas
Columbus Grove, OH 877-659-5110
H. Meyer Dairy Company
Cincinnati, OH 800-347-6455
H.P. Hood
Lynnfield, ME. 800-343-6592
H.P. Hood
Barre, VT 800-622-4468
H.R. Nicholson Company
Sykesville, MD 800-638-3514
Haas Coffee Group
Miami, FL. 305-371-7473
Habersham Winery
Helen, GA 706-878-9463
Hafner Vineyard
Healdsburg, CA 707-433-4606
Hahn Estates and Smith &Hook
Soledad, CA 831-678-4555
Haight-Brown Vineyard
Litchfield, CT. 800-577-9463
Hains Celestial Group
Melville, NY 877-612-4246
Hallcrest Vineyards
Felton, CA. 831-335-4441
Handley Cellars
Philo, CA. 800-733-3151
Hank's Beverage Company
Feastervl Trvs, PA. 800-289-4722
Hanover Foods Corporation
Hanover, PA 717-632-6000
Hansen Beverage
Corona, CA 800-426-7367
Hanzell Vineyards
Sonoma, CA 707-996-3860
Harbor Winery
West Sacramento, CA 916-371-6776
Harmony Cellars
Harmony, CA 800-432-9239
Harney & Sons Tea Company
Salisbury, CT. 888-427-6398
Harold L. King & Company
Redwood City, CA 888-368-2233
Harpersfield Vineyard
Geneva, OH. 440-466-4739
Harrisburg Dairies
Harrisburg, PA 800-692-7429
Hart Winery
Temecula, CA 877-638-8788
Hartford Family Winery
Forestville, CA 800-588-0234
Has Beans Coffee & Tea Company
Mount Shasta, CA 800-427-2326
Hastings Cooperative Creamery
Hastings, MN 651-437-9414
Hawaii Coffee Company
Honolulu, HI 800-338-8353
Hawaiian Isles Kona Coffee Co
Honolulu, HI 808-833-2244
Hawaiian Natural Water Company
Pearl City, HI 808-483-0520
Hawk Pacific Freight
Napa, CA. 707-259-0266
Haydenergy Health
New York, NY 800-255-1660
Hazlitt's 1852 Vineyard
Hector, NY 888-750-0494
Heartland Vineyards
Cleveland, OH 440-871-0701
Heaven Hill Distilleries
Bardstown, KY 502-348-3921
Heck Cellars
Arvin, CA. 661-854-6120
Hecker Pass Winery
Gilroy, CA. 408-842-8755
Hegy's South Hills Vineyard & Winery
Twin Falls, ID. 208-599-0074
Heineman's Winery
Put In Bay, OH 419-285-2811
Heitz Wine Cellar
St Helena, CA 707-963-3542

Helena View/Johnston Vineyard
Calistoga, CA 707-942-4956
Hells Canyon Winery
Caldwell, ID 800-318-7873
Hemisphere Associated
Huntington, NY 631-673-3840
Henry Estate Winery
Umpqua, OR 800-782-2686
Henry Hill & Company
Napa, CA. 707-224-6565
Heritage Farms Dairy
Murfreesboro, TN 615-895-2790
Heritage Northwest
Juneau, AK .907-586-1088
Heritage Store
Virginia Beach, VA 757-428-0110
Heritage Wine Cellars
North East, PA. 800-747-0083
Hermann J. Wiemer Vineyard
Dundee, NY 800-371-7971
Hermann Wiemer Vineyards
Dundee, NY 800-371-7971
Hermannhof Winery
Hermann, MO. 800-393-0100
Heron Hill Winery
Hammondsport, NY 800-441-4241
Hershey
Mississauga, ON. 800-468-1714
Hess Collection Winery
Napa, CA. 877-707-4377
Hi-Country Corona
Selah, WA 909-272-2600
Hi-Country Foods Corporation
Selah, WA 509-697-7292
High Coffee Corporation
Houston, TX 713-465-2230
High Rise Coffee Roasters
Colorado Springs, CO. 719-633-1833
Highland Manor Winery
Jamestown, TN 931-879-9519
Highwood Distillers
High River, AB. 403-652-3202
Hiland Dairy Foods Company
Wichita, KS. 316-267-4221
Hiland Dairy Foods Company
Springfield, MO 417-862-9311

Hill of Beans Coffee Roasters
Los Angeles, CA. 888-527-6278
Hillcrest Vineyard
Roseburg, OR 541-673-3709
Hiller Cranberries
Rochester, MA 508-763-5257
Hillsboro Coffee Company
Tampa, FL. .813-877-2126
Hinckley Springs Water Company
Chicago, IL .773-586-8600
Hinzerling Winery
Prosser, WA 800-722-6702
Hiram Walker & Sons
Fort Smith, AR 479-783-4191
Home Roast Coffee
Lutz, FL. 813-949-0807
Homewood Winery
Sonoma, CA 707-996-6353
Honest Tea
Bethesda, MD 800-865-4736
Honeywood Winery
Salem, OR 800-726-4101
Honig Vineyard and Winery
Rutherford, CA 800-929-2217
Hood River Coffee Company
Hood River, OR 800-336-2954
Hood River Distillers
Hood River, OR 541-386-1588
Hood River Vineyards and Winery
Hood River, OR 541-386-3772
Hoodsport Winery
Hoodsport, WA. 800-580-9894
Hop Kiln Winery
Healdsburg, CA 707-433-6491
Hopkins Vineyard
Warren, CT .860-868-7954
Horizon Winery
Santa Rosa, CA. 707-544-2961
House of Coffee Beans
Houston, TX 800-422-1799
Huber's Orchard Winery
Borden, IN. 800-345-9463
Hudson Valley Fruit Juice
Highland, NY 845-691-8061
Hunt-Wesson Foods
Rochester, NY. 209-847-0321

Hunter Farms
High Point, NC 800-446-8035
Hurst Vineyards
Bosque, NM 505-864-1831
Husch Vineyards
Philo, CA. 800-554-8724
Hygeia Dairy Company
Corpus Christi, TX 361-854-4561
Ideal Distributing Company
Bothell, WA. 425-488-6121
IL HWA American Corporation
Belleville, NJ 800-446-7364
Imperial Foods
Long Island City, NY 718-784-3400
In Ranchito
Zillah, WA. .509-829-5880
Indian Hollow Farms
Richland Center, WI. 800-236-3944
Indian River Foods
Fort Pierce, FL 561-462-2222
Indian Rock Vineyards
Murphys, CA. 209-728-8514
Indian Springs Vineyards
Browns Valley, CA 800-375-9311
Indigo Coffee Roasters
Florence, MA 800-447-5450
Ingleside Plantation Winery
Colonial Beach, VA 804-224-8687
Inland Northwest Dairies
Spokane, WA. 509-489-8600
Inn Foods
Watsonville, CA 831-724-2026
Inniskillin Wines
Niagara-On-The-Lake, ON. 888-466-4754
Innovative Food Solutions LLC
Columbus, OH 800-884-3314
Innovative Health Products
Largo, FL 800-654-2347
Innovative Ingredients
Reisterstown, MD. 888-403-2907
Inter-American Products
Cincinnati, OH 800-645-2233
Inter-Continental Imports Company
Newington, CT 800-424-4422
International Coffee Corporation
New Orleans, LA 504-586-8700

International Trademarks
  Darien, CT. 203-656-4046
Interstate Foods
  Lansing, MI. 517-372-5500
Irani & Company
  Indianapolis, IN 317-894-4465
Iron Horse Ranch & Vineyard
  Sebastopol, CA. 707-887-1212
Ironstone Vineyards
  Murphys, CA. 209-728-1251
Island Sweetwater Beverage Company
  Bryn Mawr, PA. 610-525-7444
J Vineyards & Winery
  Healdsburg, CA 800-885-9463
J&J Snack Foods Corporation
  Pennsauken, NJ 856-665-9533
J. Filippi Winery
  Etiwanda, CA 909-899-5755
J. Fritz Winery
  Cloverdale, CA. 707-894-3389
J. Stonestreet & Sons Vineyard
  Healdsburg, CA 800-723-6336
J.B. Peel Coffee Roasters
  Red Hook, NY 800-231-7372
J.G. British Imports
  Sarasota, FL 888-965-1700
Jack Daniel's Distillery
  Lynchburg, TN 931-759-4221
Jackson Milk & Ice CreamCompany
  Hutchinson, KS. 620-663-1244
Jackson Valley Vineyards
  Ione, CA 916-354-3200
Jamaica John
  Franklin Park, IL. 847-451-1730
Jamesport Vineyards
  Jamesport, NY. 631-722-5256
Java Jungle
  Visalia, CA 559-732-5282
Java Sun Coffee Roasters
  Marblehead, MA. 781-631-7788
JBR Coffee & Tea
  San Leandro, CA. 800-829-1300
Jenny's Country Kitchen
  Dover, MN 800-357-3497
Jeremiah's Pick Coffee Company
  San Francisco, CA 800-537-3642
Jo Mints
  Corona Del Mar, CA. 877-566-4687
Jodar Vineyard & Winery
  Placerville, CA 530-621-0324
Jogue Inc
  Northville, MI. 800-521-3888
Johlin Century Winery
  Oregon, OH. 419-693-6288
John A. Vassilaros & Son
  Flushing, NY. 718-886-4140
John C. Meier Juice Company
  Cincinnati, OH 800-346-2941
John Conti Coffee Company
  Louisville, KY. 800-928-5282
Johnson Estate Wines
  Westfield, NY. 800-374-6569
Johnson's Alexander Valley Wines
  Healdsburg, CA. 800-888-5532
Johnston's Winery
  Ballston Spa, NY 518-882-6310
Jones Brewing Company
  Smithton, PA 800-237-2337
Joseph Filippi Winery
  Etiwanda, CA 909-899-5755
Joseph Phelps Vineyards
  St Helena, CA. 707-963-2745
Josuma Coffee Corporation
  Menlo Park, CA. 650-366-5453
Joullian Vineyards
  Carmel Valley, CA. 877-659-2800
Juice Bowl Products
  Lakeland, FL. 863-665-5515
Juice Guys
  Cambridge, MA 508-228-4464
Juice Mart
  West Hills, CA 877-888-1011
Juicy Whip
  La Verne, CA 909-392-7500
Julac
  Rougemont, QC 514-861-2404
Justin Lloyd Premium Tea Company
  Carson, CA 310-834-4000
Justin Winery & Vineyard
  Paso Robles, CA 800-726-0049
Kaffe Magnum Opus
  Vineland, NJ 800-652-5282

Kagome
  Los Banos, CA 209-826-8850
Kalin Cellars
  Novato, CA 415-883-3543
Kan-Pac
  Arkansas City, KS. 620-442-6820
Kate's Vineyard
  Napa, CA. .707-255-2644
Kathryn Kennedy Winery
  Saratoga, CA. 408-867-4170
Kauai Coffee Company
  Kalaheo, HI 800-545-8605
Kava King
  Ormond Beach, FL 888-670-5282
KDK Inc
  Draper, UT 801-571-3506
Kelleys Island Wine Company
  Kelleys Island, OH 419-746-2678
Kemach Food Products   Corporation
  Brooklyn, NY 888-453-6224
Kemp Foods
  York, PA 800-233-2007
Kemps
  Cedarburg, WI. 262-377-5040
Kendall Citrus Corporation
  Goulds, FL 305-258-1628
Kendall-Jackson Wine
  Windsor, CA. 800-544-4413
Kenlake Foods
  Murray, KY. 800-632-6900
Kenwood Vineyards
  Kenwood, CA. 707-833-5891
King Brewing Company
  Fairfield, CA 707-428-4503
King Estate Winery
  Eugene, OR. 800-884-4441
King Juice
  Milwaukee, WI 414-482-0303
Kiona Vineyards Winery
  Benton City, WA 509-588-6716
Kirigin Cellars
  Gilroy, CA .408-847-8827
Kistler Vineyards
  Sebastopol, CA 707-823-5603
Kittling Ridge Estate Wines & Spirits
  Grimsby, ON. 905-945-9225
Kittridge & Fredrickson Fine Coffees
  Portland, OR. 800-558-7788
Klein Family Vintners
  Healdsburg, CA. 707-433-6511
Klingshirn Winery
  Avon Lake, OH 440-933-6666
Knapp Vineyards
  Romulus, NY 800-869-9271
Knoll Creek Dairy
  Harrison, NY 718-892-4500
Knouse Foods
  Peach Glen, PA 717-677-8181
Knoxage Water Company
  San Diego, CA 619-234-3333
Kobricks Coffee Company
  Jersey City, NJ 800-562-3662
Kohler Mix Specialties
  White Bear Lake, MN. 651-426-1633
Kona Coffee Council
  Kealakekua, HI 808-323-2911
Kona Kava Coffee Company
  Philo, CA. .707-985-3913
Koryo Winery Company
  Gardena, CA 310-532-3240
Kraft Foods
  Northfield, IL. 800-323-0768
Kraft Foods
  Northfield, IL. 847-646-2000
Kramer Vineyards
  Gaston, OR. 800-619-4637
Krier Foods
  Milwaukee, WI 414-355-5400
Kunde Estate Winery
  Kenwood, CA. 707-833-5501
La Abra Farm & Winery
  Lovingston, VA. 434-263-5392
La Buena Vida Vineyards
  Grapevine, TX 817-481-9463
La Chiripada Winery
  Dixon, NM 800-528-7801
La Costa Coffee Roasting
  Carlsbad, CA 760-434-3233
La Jota Vineyard Company
  Angwin, CA. 877-222-0292
La Rocca Vineyards
  Forest Ranch, CA 800-808-9463

La Rochelle Winery
  Livermore, CA 888-647-7768
La Vans Coffee Company
  Bordentown, NJ 609-298-5400
La Vina Winery
  Anthony, NM 575-882-7632
Labatt Breweries
  Toronto, ON 416-361-5050
Labatt Breweries
  Lasalle, QC 514-366-5050
Lacas Coffee Company
  Pennsauken, NJ 800-220-1133
Laci Le Beau Corporation
  Fresno, CA 800-356-0490
Laetitia Vineyard
  Arroyo Grande, CA. 888-809-8463
Lafollette Vineyard & Winery
  Belle Mead, NJ 908-359-5018
Laird & Company
  North Garden, VA 877-438-5247
Lake Arrowhead
  Twin Peaks, CA. 877-237-8528
Lake Sonoma Winery
  Healdsburg, CA 877-850-9463
Lakeridge Winery & Vineyards
  Clermont, FL. 800-768-9463
Lakeshore Winery
  Romulus, NY 315-549-7075
Lakespring Winery
  Yountville, CA 707-944-2475
Lakewood Juices
  Miami, FL. 305-324-5900
Lakewood Vineyards
  Watkins Glen, NY. 607-535-9252
Lambert Bridge Winery
  Healdsburg, CA 800-975-0555
Lamoreaux Landing Wine Cellar
  Lodi, NY 607-582-6011
Lancaster County Winery
  Willow Street, PA 717-464-3555
Land O Lakes Milk
  Sioux Falls, SD 605-330-9526
Land O'Lakes
  St Paul, MN. 651-730-2100
Land O'Lakes
  St Paul, MN. 800-328-9680
Land O'Lakes, Inc
  Arden Hills, MN 800-328-9680
Land-O-Sun Dairies
  O Fallon, IL. 618-632-6381
Landmark Vineyards
  Kenwood, CA. 800- 45- 636
Landshire
  Belleville, IL. 618-398-8122
Lange Winery
  Dundee, OR. 503-538-6476
Langer Juice Company
  City of Industry, CA 626-336-1666
Langtry Estate & Vineyards
  Middletown, CA 707-987-9127
Larry's Vineyards & Winery
  Schenectady, NY. 518-355-7365
Latah Creek Wine Cellars
  Spokane Valley, WA 509-926-0164
Latcham Vineyards
  Mt Aukum, CA. 800-750-5591
Laurel Glen Vineyard
  Glen Ellen, CA 707-526-3914
Lava Cap Winery
  Placerville, CA 530-621-0175
Lavazza Premium Coffee Corporation
  New York, NY 800-466-3287
Lazy Creek Vineyard
  Philo, CA. .707-895-2021
Le Bleu Corporation
  Advance, NC. 800-854-4471
Le Boeuf & Associates
  North Falmouth, MA. 800-444-5666
Leaves Pure Teas
  Scottsdale, AZ. 800-242-8807
Leelanau Wine Cellars
  Omena, MI 800-782-8128
Leeward Winery
  Ventura, CA. 805-656-5054
Leidenfrost Vineyards
  Hector, NY 607-546-2800
Leisure Time Ice & Spring Water
  Kiamesha Lake, NY 800-443-1412
Lemon Creek Winery
  Berrien Springs, MI 269-471-1321
Lemon-X Corporation
  Huntington Sta, NY 800-220-1061

Lenox-Martell
Jamaica Plain, MA 617-442-7777
Leonetti Cellar
Walla Walla, WA 509-525-1428
Leroy Hill Coffee Company
Mobile, AL 800-866-5282
Les Bourgeois Vineyards
Rocheport, MO 573-698-2300
Level Valley Creamery
Antioch, TN 800-251-1292
Lewis Cellars
Hillsborough, CA 415-445-7884
Lexington Coffee & Tea Company
Lexington, KY 859-277-1102
Liberty Dairy
Evart, MI 800-632-5552
Lifeway Foods Inc
Morton Grove, IL 847-967-1010
Light Rock Beverage Company
Danbury, CT 203-743-3410
Limur Winery
San Francisco, CA 415-781-8691
Lin Court Vineyards
Solvang, CA 805-688-8554
Linden Beverage Company
Linden, VA 540-635-2118
Lindsay's Tea
S San Francisco, CA 800-624-7031
Lingle Brothers Coffee
Bell Gardens, CA 562-927-3317
Lion Brewery
Wilkes Barre, PA 800-233-8327
Lipsey Mountain Spring Water
Norcross, GA 770-449-0001
Little Amana Winery
Amana, IA 319-668-9664
Live Oaks Winery
Gilroy, CA 408-842-2401
Lockcoffee
Larchmont, NY 914-273-7838
Lola Savannah
Houston, TX 888-663-9166
Longo Coffee & Tea
New York, NY 212-477-6783
Lost Trail Root Beer Com
Louisburg, KS 800-748-7765
Louis Dreyfus Citrus
Winter Garden, FL 407-656-1000
Louis Dreyfus Corporation - Coffee Division
Wilton, CT 203-761-2000
Louisburg Cider Mill
Louisburg, KS 800-748-7765
Love Creek Orchards
Medina, TX 800-449-0882
Lucas Vineyards
Interlaken, NY 800-682-9463
Lucas Winery
Lodi, CA 209-368-2006
Ludwigshof Winery
Eskridge, KS 785-449-2498
LUXCO
St Louis, MO 314-772-2627
Lynfred Winery
Roselle, IL 888-298-9463
Lyons-Magnus
Fresno, CA 559-268-5966
M.E. Swing Company
Alexandria, VA 800-485-4019
M.H. Zeigler & Sons
Lansdale, PA 215-855-5161
M.S. Walker
Somerville, MA 617-776-6700
Mackie International
Commerce, CA 800-733-9762
MacKinlay Teas
Ann Arbor, MI 734-747-9012
Madison Foods
St Paul, MN 651-265-8212
Madys Company
San Francisco, CA 415-822-2227
Magnetic Springs Water Company
Columbus, OH 800-572-2990
Magnum Coffee Roastery
Nunica, MI 888-937-5282

Majestic Coffee & Tea
San Carlos, CA 650-591-5678
Majestic Distilling Company
Baltimore, MD 410-242-0200
Makers Mark Distillery
Loretto, KY 270-865-2881
Mama Lee's Gourmet Hot Chocolate
Nashville, TN 888-626-2533
Manhattan Coffee Company
Earth City, MO 800-926-3333
Manhattan Special Bottling Corporation
Brooklyn, NY 718-388-4144
Mar-Key Foods
Vidalia, GA 912-537-4204
Marie Brizard Wines & Spirits
Sausalito, CA 800-878-1123
Markham Vineyards
St Helena, CA 707-963-5292
Mars Chocolates
Hackettstown, NJ 908-852-1000
Martini & Prati Wines
Santa Rosa, CA 707-823-2404
Marva Maid Dairy
Newport News, VA 800-544-4439
Maryland & Virginia Milk Producers Cooperative
Reston, VA 703-742-7443
Masala Chai Company
Santa Cruz, CA 831-475-8881
Matilija Water Company
Ventura, CA 805-322-7212
Maui Pineapple Company
Kahului, HI 808-877-3351
Maui Pineapple Company
Concord, CA 925-798-0240
Mayacamas Vineyards
Napa, CA 707-224-4030
Mayer Brothers Apple Products
Barker, NY 716-795-9930
Mayer Brothers Apple Products
West Seneca, NY 800-696-2937
Mayer's Cider Mill
Webster, NY 800-543-0043
Mayfield Farms
Brampton, ON 905-846-0506
McArthur Dairy
Miami, FL 305-576-2880
McClancy Seasoning Company
Fort Mill, SC 800-843-1968
McCutcheon's Apple Products
Frederick, MD 800-888-7537
McDonald Dairy Company
Flint, MI 810-232-9193
McGregor Vineyard Winery
Dundee, NY 800-272-0192
Meadow Brook Dairy
Erie, PA 800-352-4010
Meadowbrook Distributing Corporation
Amityville, NY 631-226-9000
Melitta
Clearwater, FL 727-535-2111
Mendocino Beverages International
Comptche, CA 707-937-0547
Meramec Vineyards
St James, MO 877-216-9463
Merci Spring Water
Saint Louis, MO 314-812-4812
Meridian Beverage Company
Atlanta, GA 800-728-1481
Merlinos
Canon City, CO 719-275-5558
Merritt Estate Wines
Forestville, NY 888-965-4800
Michigan Dairy
Livonia, MI 734-367-5390
Mid States Dairy
Hazelwood, MO 314-731-1150
Miller Brewing Company
Milwaukee, WI 414-931-2000
Milsolv Corporation
Butler, WI 800-558-8501
Minnehaha Spring Water Company
Cleveland, OH 216-431-0243
Minute Maid Company
Sugar Land, TX 713-888-5000
Minute Maid Company
Dunedin, FL 800-237-0159
Mogen David Wine Corporation
Westfield, NY 716-326-7100
Mojave Foods Corporation
Commerce, CA 323-890-8900
Molson Breweries
Regina, SK 306-359-1786

Molson Breweries
Montreal, QC 514-521-1786
Monarch Beverage Company
Atlanta, GA 800-241-3732
Mondial Foods Company
Los Angeles, CA 213-383-3531
Montebello Brands
Baltimore, MD 410-282-8800
Moran Coffee Company
Dublin, OH 614-889-2500
Morningstar Foods
Mt Crawford, VA 540-434-7328
Mother Parker's Tea & Coffee
Mississauga, ON 905-279-9100
Mount Olympus Waters
Salt Lake City, UT 800-628-6056
Mountain Valley ProductsInc
Sunnyside, WA 509-837-8084
Mrs. Clark's Foods
Ankeny, IA 800-736-5674

Juices, salad dressings and sauces.

Murray Cider Company
Roanoke, VA 540-977-9000
Music Mountain Water Company
Birmingham, AL 800-349-6555
Nagel's Beverages Company
East Nampa, ID 208-475-1250
Naterl
St. Bruno, QC 800- 50- 115
National Beverage Corporation
Fort Lauderdale, FL 888-462-2349
National Fruit Product Company
Lincolnton, NC 704-735-2531
Natural Spring Water Company
Johnson City, TN 423-926-7905
Nature's Plus
Long Beach, CA 800-525-0200
Navarro Vineyards & Winery
Philo, CA 800-537-9463
NAYA
Stamford, CT 800-566-6292
NC Mountain Water
Marion, NC 800-220-4718
Neenah Springs
Oxford, WI 608-586-5605
Nehalem Bay Winery
Nehalem, OR 888-368-9463
Newly Weds Foods
Memphis, TN 800-647-9314
Newman's Own
Westport, CT 203-222-0136
Niagara Brewing Company
Niagara Falls, ON 800-267-3392
Nicholas G. Verry
Parlier, CA 209-646-2785
NOH Foods of Hawaii
Gardena, CA 310-324-6770
North Country Natural Spring Water
Port Kent, NY 518-834-9400
North Salem Vineyard
North Salem, NY 914-669-5518
Northern Breweries
Sault St. Marie, ON 800-461-2258
Northland Cranberries
Jackson, WI 262-677-2221
Northland Cranberries
Mountain Home, NC 828-693-0711
Northwest Naturals Corporation
Bothell, WA 425-881-2200
Northwestern Coffee Mills
Washburn, WI 800-243-5283
Northwestern Foods
St Paul, MN 800-236-4937
Novartis Nutrition Corporation
Minneapolis, MN 952-848-6000
NTC Foods Corporation
Williamsville, NY 800-333-1637
Nutritional Counselors of America
Spencer, TN 931-946-3600
O-At-Ka Milk Products Cooperative
Batavia, NY 800-828-8152
Ocean Spray Cranberries
Kenosha, WI 262-694-0621

Ocean Spray Cranberries
Bordentown, NJ 609-298-0905
Ocean Spray Cranberries
Vero Beach, FL 772-562-0800
Ocean Spray Cranberries
Lakeville-Middleboro, MA 800-662-3263
Odwalla
Denver, CO 303-282-0500
Office General des Eaux Minerales
Montreal, QC 514-482-7221
Old Dutch Mustard Company
Great Neck, NY 516-466-0522
Old Fashioned Natural Products
Santa Ana, CA 800-552-9045
Old Orchard Brands
Sparta, MI 616-887-1745
Omar Coffee Company
Newington, CT 800-394-6627
One World Enterprises
Los Angeles, CA 888-663-2626
Orange-Co of Florida
Arcadia, FL 863-494-4939
Orleans Coffee Exchange
Kenner, LA 800-737-5464
Ormand Peugeog Corporation
Miami, FL 305-624-6834
Pak Technologies
Milwaukee, WI 414-438-8600
Paramount Coffee Company
Lansing, MI 800-968-1222
Paramount Distillers
Cleveland, OH 216-671-6300
Parducci Wine Estates
Ukiah, CA 888-362-9463
Paris Foods Corporation
Camden, NJ 856-964-0915
Parmalat Canada
Toronto, ON 800-563-1515
Parman-Kendall Corporation
Goulds, FL 305-258-1628
Partners Coffee Company
Atlanta, GA 800-341-5282
Paul de Lima Company
Syracuse, NY 800-962-8864
PB&S Chemicals
Henderson, KY 800-950-7267
Pearl Coffee Company
Akron, OH 800-822-5282
Peerless Coffee Company
Oakland, CA 800-310-5662
Pepsi
Chicago, IL 312-821-1000
Pepsi Bottling Group
Mesquite, TX 214-324-8500
Pepsi Bottling Group
Fort Smith, AR 479-646-7881
Pepsi Bottling Group
Redding, CA 530-245-2100
Pepsi Bottling Group
Houston, TX 713-645-4111
Pepsi Bottling Group
Buffalo, NY 800-235-1131
Pepsi Bottling Group
Burnsville, MN 800-433-8109
Pepsi Bottling Group
San Antonio, TX 800-933-5311
Pepsi Bottling Group
Tulsa, OK 800-963-2424
Pepsi Bottling Group
Pleasanton, CA 925-416-2500
Pepsi-Cola Bottling Company
St Louis, MO 314-679-7000
Pepsi-Cola Bottling Company
Brooklyn, NY 718-649-2401
Pepsi-Cola General Bottlers
Arlington Hts, IL 847-483-6880
PepsiAmericas
New Orleans, LA 504-467-3774
PepsiAmericas
Reserve, LA 985-536-1191
PepsiCo
Philadelphia, PA 215-961-4000
PepsiCo
Barrington, IL 847-842-4652
PepsiCo Inc
Purchase, NY 914-253-2000
Perfect Foods
Monroe, NY 800-933-3288
Perfection Fine Products
Maple Heights, OH 216-475-5744
Pernod Ricard USA
White Plains, NY 914-539-4500

Pernod Ricard USA Seagram Lawrenceburg Distillery
Greendale, IN 812-537-0700
Perricone Juices
Beaumont, CA 951-769-7171
Perry Creek Winery
Telford, PA 800-880-4026
Personal Edge Nutrition
Ballwin, MO 877-982-3343
Pet Dairy
Spartanburg, SC 864-576-6280
Pet Milk
Florence, SC 800-735-3066
Pete's Brewing Company
San Antonio, TX 800-877-7383
Pevely Dairy Company
St Louis, MO 314-771-4400
Pfefferkorn's Coffee
Baltimore, MD 800-682-4665
Phamous Phloyd's Barbeque Sauce
Denver, CO 303-757-3285
Phillips Beverage Company
Minneapolis, MN 612-362-7500
Phillips Syrup Corporation
Cleveland, OH 216-661-4800
Pleasant Valley Wine Company
Hammondsport, NY 607-569-6111
Pleasant View Dairy
Highland, IN 219-838-0155
Pod Pack International
Baton Rouge, LA 225-752-1110
Pokka Beverages
American Canyon, CA 800-972-5962
Poland Spring Water
Brea, CA .800-950-9396
Polar Beverage
Worcester, MA 800-734-9800
Polar Water Company
Carnegie, PA 800-444-7873
Pontiac Coffee Break
Pontiac, MI 248-332-9403
Post Familie Vineyards
Altus, AR 800-275-8423
Prairie Farms Dairy
Carlinville, IL 217-854-2547
Premier Blending
Wichita, KS 316-267-5533
Premier Juices
Clearwater, FL 727-533-8200
Premium Coffee Company
Eatontown, NJ 800-524-2743
Premium Water
Orange Springs, FL 800-243-1163
Prince of Peace Enterprises
Hayward, CA 800-732-2328
Progenix Corporation
Wausau, WI 800-233-3356
Purity Dairies
Nashville, TN 615-244-1900
Q.E. Tea
Bridgeville, PA 800-622-8327
Quaker Oats Company
Mountain Top, PA 800-367-6287
Quality Brands
Deland, FL 386-738-3808
Quality Kitchen Corporation
Danbury, CT 203-744-2000
Quality Naturally! Foods
City of Industry, CA 888-498-6986
R C Bigelow
Fairfield, CT 800-243-5587
R.J. Corr Naturals
Posen, IL 708-389-4200
Rainbow Valley Orchards
Fallbrook, CA 760-723-3911
Ray Brothers & Noble Canning Company
Hobbs, IN 765-675-7451
Rebound
Newburgh, NY 845-562-5400
Red Diamond
Birmingham, AL 800-292-4651
Red Gold
Elwood, IN 877-748-9798
Redhook Ale Breweries
Newington, NH 603-430-8600
Regency Coffee & VendingCompany
Olathe, KS 913-829-1994
Regent Champagne Cellars
New York, NY 845-691-7296
Reilly Dairy & Food Company
Tampa, FL 813-839-8458
Reily Foods/JFG Coffee Company
Knoxville, TN 800-535-1961

Reiter Dairy
Springfield, OH 937-323-5777
Renault Winery
Egg Harbor City, NJ 609-965-2111
Rex Wine Vinegar Company
Newark, NJ 973-589-6911
Richland Beverage Associates
Carrollton, TX 214-357-0248
Robert Keenan Winery
St Helena, CA 707-963-9177
Robert Mondavi Winery
Oakville, CA 888-766-6328
Roberts Dairy Company
Omaha, NE 402-344-4321
Roberts Dairy Company
Kansas City, MO 800-279-1692
Rockies Brewing Company
Boulder, CO 303-444-8448
Rohstein Corporation
Woburn, MA 781-935-8300
Ronnoco Coffee Company
St Louis, MO 800-428-2287
Ronzoni Foods Canada
Etobicoke, ON 800-387-5032
Roos Foods
Kenton, DE 800-343-3642
Roselani Tropics Ice Cream
Wailuku, HI 808-244-7951
Rosenberger's Dairies
Hatfield, PA 800-355-9074
Royal Coffee & Tea Company
Mississauga, ON 800-667-6226
Royal Crown Bottling Company
Bowling Green, KY 270-842-8106
Royal Cup Coffee
Birmingham, AL 800-366-5836
Royal Wine Company
Bayonne, NJ 201-437-9131
Royal Wine Company
Bayonne, NJ 800-382-8299
Rubicon/Niebaum-Coppola Estate & Winery
Rutherford, CA 800-782-4266
Russo Farms
Vineland, NJ 856-692-5942
Rutherford Hill Winery
Rutherford, CA 707-963-1871
S&D Coffee, Inc
Concord, NC 704-339-0917
S&D Coffee, Inc
Concord, NC 704-782-3121
Safeway Beverage
Denver, CO 303-320-7960
Safeway Beverage
Bellevue, WA 425-455-6444
Safeway Dairy Products
Walnut Creek, CA 925-944-4000
Safeway Milk Plant
Tempe, AZ 480-894-4391
Saint Arnold Brewing Company
Houston, TX 713-686-9494
San Antonio Winery
Los Angeles, CA 800-626-7722
San Joaquin Valley Dairymen
Los Banos, CA 209-826-4901
San-Ei Gen FFI
New York, NY 212-315-7840
Sandstone Winery
Amana, IA 319-622-3081
Saputo
Montreal, QC 514-328-6662
Saputo Cheese
Fond Du Lac, WI 800-824-3373
Sara Lee Coffee & Tea
Rochester, NY
Sara Lee Coffee & Tea
Minneapolis, MN 888-246-2598
Sara Lee Corporation
Downers Grove, IL 630-598-8100
Saratoga Beverage Group
Saratoga Springs, NY 888-426-8642
Satori Teas
Salinas, CA 800-444-7286
Schapiro's Kosher Winery
New York, NY 212-755-5066
Schirf Brewing Company
Park City, UT 435-649-0900
Schneider's Dairy Holdings Inc
Pittsburgh, PA 412-881-3525
Schramsberg Vineyards
Calistoga, CA 800-877-3623
Scotian Gold Cooperative
Coldbrook, NS 902-679-2191

Seco & Golden 100
Deland, FL 386-734-3906
Seller Kirk & Company
Schwenksville, PA 215-480-7342
Seltzer & Rydholm
Auburn, ME 207-784-5791
Sesinco Foods
New York, NY 212-243-1306
Seven Up/RC Bottling Company
Paragould, AR. 870-236-8765
SEW Friel
Queenstown, MD 410-827-8841
Shasta Beverages
Shawnee Mission, KS. 913-888-6777
Silvan Ridge
Eugene, OR. 541-345-1945
Silver Oak Cellars
Oakville, CA 800-273-8805
Silver Springs Citrus
Howey In Hills, FL. 800-940-2277
SimmaLoosa Company
Covington, LA 985-892-1400
Simpson & Vail
Brookfield, CT 800-282-8327
Sinton Dairy Foods Company
Colorado Springs, CO. 800-388-4970
Sinton Dairy Foods Company
Denver, CO 800-666-4808
Skjodt-Barrett Foods
Mississauga, ON 877-600-1200
Smart Ice
Fort Myers, FL 239-334-3123
Smeltzer Orchard Company
Frankfort, MI 231-882-4421
Smith Dairy Products Company
Orrville, OH 800-776-7076
SnowBird Corporation
Bayonne, NJ 800-576-1616
Solana Gold Organics
Sebastopol, CA 800-459-1121
Somerset Syrup & Beverage
Edison, NJ. 800-526-8865
Sourthern Tea
Marietta, GA 800-241-0896
Southchem
Durham, NC 800-849-7000
Southern Beverage Packers
Appling, GA 800-326-2469
Spangler Vineyards
Roseburg, OR 541-679-9654
Specialty Beverages
Indian Wells, CA. 626-963-5536
Specialty Coffee Roasters
Miami, FL 800-253-9363
Spoetzl Brewery
Shiner, TX 361-594-3383
Spring Mountain Vineyards
Saint Helena, CA 877-769-4637
Spring Water Company
Chesapeake, VA 800-832-0271
St. Julian Wine Company
Paw Paw, MI. 800-732-6002
Starbucks Coffee Company
Seattle, WA 800-782-7282
Stash Tea Company
Portland, OR 800-547-1514
Stevens Point Brewery
Stevens Point, WI 800-369-4911
Stevens Tropical Plantation
West Palm Beach, FL 561-683-4701
Stewart's Private Blend Foods
Chicago, IL 800-654-2862
Stimson Lane Vineyards &Estate
Woodinville, WA. 800-267-6793
Stimson Lane Winery
Prosser, WA. 509-882-3928
Stockton Graham & Company
Raleigh, NC 800-835-5943
Stone Hill Wine Company
Hermann, MO 573-486-2221
Stop & Shop Manufacturing
Readville, MA. 617-361-8400
Straub Brewery Industries
St Marys, PA 814-834-2875
Sturm Foods
Manawa, WI 800-347-8876
Suiza Dairy Corporation
Rio Piedras, PR 787-792-7300
Summit Brewing Company
Saint Paul, MN 651-265-7800
Sun Orchard of Florida
Haines City, FL. 877-875-8423

Sun Pac Foods
Brampton, ON. 905-792-2700
Sunflower Restaurant Supply
Salina, KS 785-823-6394
SunkiStreet Growers
Ontario, CA. 800-225-3727
Sunlike Juice
Scarborough, ON 416-297-1140
Sunshine Farms
Portage, WI. 608-742-2016
Sunshine Farms Dairy
Elyria, OH 440-322-6301
Sunsweet Growers
Yuba City, CA 800-417-2253
Suntory International
New York, NY 212-891-6600
Suntory Water Group
Atlanta, GA 770-933-1400
Superbrand Dairies
Miami, FL. 305-685-8079
Superior Trading Company
San Francisco, CA 415-982-8722
Superstore Industries
Fairfield, CA 707-864-0502
Sutter Home Winery
St Helena, CA 707-963-3104
Swan Joseph Vineyards
Forestville, CA 707-573-3747
Swire Coca-Cola
Draper, UT 801-816-5300
Swiss Valley Farms Company
Cedar Rapids, IA. 319-364-8153
SYFO Beverage Company ofFlorida
Jacksonville, FL 904-381-9002
Talbott Farms
Palisade, CO 970-464-5656
Tamarack Farms Dairy
Newark, OH 866-221-4141
Tastee Apple Inc
Newcomerstown, OH 800-262-7753
Tatra Herb Company
Morrisville, PA 888-828-7248
Templar Food Products
New Providence, NJ 800-883-6752
Tequila XQ
Guadalajara Jalisco, ... 333-587-7799
Texas Coffee Company
Beaumont, TX. 800-259-3400
Thomas Canning/Maidstone
Maidstone, ON 519-737-1531
Thomas Kruse Winery
Gilroy, CA. 408-842-7016
Three Lakes Winery
Three Lakes, WI 800-944-5434
Todhunter Foods
Lake Alfred, FL. 863-956-1116
Todhunter International
West Palm Beach, FL 561-655-8977
Toft Dairy
Sandusky, OH 800-521-4606
Torke Coffee Roasting Company
Sheboygan, WI 800-242-7671
Traditional Medicinals
Sebastopol, CA 800-543-4372
Tree Top
Selah, WA 800-367-6571
Tree Top
Selah, WA 800-542-4055
Trefethen Vineyards
Napa, CA. 800-556-4847
Trigo Corporation
Toa Baja, PR 787-794-1300
Triple D Orchards
Empire, MI 866-781-9410
Triple Springs Spring Water
Meriden, CT 203-235-8374
Tropicana
Bradenton, FL. 800-828-2102
True Organic Products International
Miami, FL. 800-487-0379
Truesdale Packaging Company
Warrenton, MO 636-456-6800
Turkey Hill Dairy
Conestoga, PA. 800-693-2479
Turkey Hill Sugarbush
Waterloo, QC 450-539-4822
Turn on Beverages Inc
Spring Valley, NY 866-739-2387
Turner Dairies
Covington, TN 901-476-2643
UDV Canada
Etobicoke, ON 416-626-2000

UDV Wines
San Francisco, CA 415-835-7300
Unilever
Mont-Royal, QC 514-735-1141
Unilever Bestfoods
Englewood Cliffs, NJ 201-894-4000
United Dairy
Martins Ferry, OH. 800-252-1542
United Dairymen of Arizona
Tempe, AZ. 480-966-7211
Upstate Farms Cooperative
Rochester, NY. 585-458-1880
Upstate Farms Cooperative
Buffalo, NY. 866-874-6455
US Filter
East Orange, NJ 973-677-8946
USA Sunrise Beverage
Spearfish, SD 605-723-0690
V. Sattui Winery
St Helena, CA 800-799-8888
Valley Fig Growers
Fresno, CA 559-237-3893
Valley View Packing Company
San Jose, CA. 408-289-8300
Van Roy Coffee
Cleveland, OH 877-826-7669
Vancouver Island Brewing Company
Victoria, BC 250-361-0007
Varni Brothers/7-Up Bottling
Modesto, CA. 209-521-1777
Vegetable Juices
Chicago, IL 888-776-9752
Velda Farms
Lakeland, FL. 800-279-4166
Velda Farms
North Miami Bch, FL. 800-795-4649
Ventura Coastal Corporation
Ventura, CA. 805-653-7000
Venture Vineyards
Lodi, NY 888-635-6277
Vie-Del Company
Fresno, CA 559-834-2525
Viking Distillery
Albany, GA 229-436-0181
Villa Mt. Eden Winery
St Helena, CA 707-944-2414
Vincor International
Mississauga, ON. 800-265-9463

Vitality Foodservice
  Barrie, ON 800-668-5463
Vitality Foodservice
  Tampa, FL 888-863-6726
Vitamilk Dairy
  Bellingham, WA 206-529-4128
Von Stiehl Winery
  Algoma, WI 800-955-5208
W.J. Stearns & Sons/Mountain Dairy
  Storrs Mansfield, CT 860-423-9289
Wagner Vineyards
  Lodi, NY 866-924-6378
Wah Yet Group
  Hayward, CA 800-229-3392
Water Concepts
  Des Plaines, IL 847-699-9797
Wayne Dairy Products
  Richmond, IN 800-875-9294
Weaver Nut Company
  Ephrata, PA 717-738-3781
Wechsler Coffee Corporation
  Moonachie, NJ 800-800-2633
Welch's Foods Inc
  Lawton, MI 269-624-1308
Welch's Foods Inc
  Kennewick, WA 509-582-2131
Welch's Foods Inc
  Concord, MA 800-340-6870
Welch's Foods Inc
  North East, PA 814-725-4577
Welsh Farms
  Newark, NJ 800-221-0663
Wengert's Dairy
  Lebanon, PA 800-222-2129
Went's Dairy
  Niagara Falls, NY 716-692-6543
Westbrae Natural Foods
  Garden City, NY 800-434-4246
WestFarm Foods
  Boise, ID 208-375-3062
Wheeling Coffee & Spice Company
  Wheeling, WV 800-500-0141
White Coffee Corporation
  Long Island City, NY 800-221-0140
White Rock Products Corporation
  Whitestone, NY 800-969-7625
White Wave
  Broomfield, CO 800-488-9283
Whittaker & Associates
  Atlanta, GA 404-266-1265
Whole Herb Company
  Sonoma, CA 707-935-1077
Widmer's Wine Cellars
  Naples, NY 585-374-6311
Winchester Farms Dairy
  Winchester, KY 859-745-5500
Windmill Water
  Edgewood, NM 505-281-9287
Windsor Vineyards
  Windsor, CA 800-333-9987
Windsor Vineyards
  Windsor, CA 800-992-4233
Winmix/Natural Care Products
  Englewood, FL 941-475-7432
Winnsboro Beverage Packers
  Winnsboro, LA 318-435-9404
Woodbury Vineyards
  Fredonia, NY 866-691-9463
World Citrus West
  Lake Wales, FL 863-676-1411
World of Coffee, World of Tea
  Stirling, NJ 908-647-1218
Yakima Brewing Company
  Yakima, WA 509-575-1900
Yoder Dairies
  Chesapeake, VA 757-497-3518
Yoo-Hoo Chocolate Beverage Company
  Carlstadt, NJ 201-933-0070
Yoo-Hoo Chocolate Beverage Company
  Port Chester, NY 800-966-4669
York Mountain Winery
  Paso Robles, CA 805-238-3925
Young Winfield
  Kleinburg, ON 905-893-2536
Z.D. Wines LLC
  Napa, CA 800-487-7757
Zephyr Hills
  Tamarac, FL 954-597-7852

Alcoholic Beverages

A&G Food & Liquors
  Chicago, IL 773-994-1541

A. Nonini Winery
  Fresno, CA 559-275-1936
A. Rafanelli Winery
  Healdsburg, CA 707-433-1385
Abita Brewing Company
  Abita Springs, LA 800-737-2311
Acacia Vineyard
  Napa, CA 707-226-9991
Ackerman Winery
  Amana, IA 319-622-3379
Ackerman Winery
  Amana, IA 319-622-6513
Adair Vineyards
  New Paltz, NY 845-255-1377
Adam Puchta Winery
  Hermann, MO 573-486-5596
Adams County Winery
  Orrtanna, PA 717-334-4631
Adelaida Cellars
  Paso Robles, CA 800-676-1232
Adelsheim Vineyard
  Newberg, OR 503-538-5222
Adler Fels Vineyards & Winery
  Santa Rosa, CA 707-569-1493
Admiral Wine Merchants
  Irvington, NJ 800-582-9463
Aetna Springs Cellars
  Pope Valley, CA 707-965-2675
Afton Mountain Vineyards
  Afton, VA 540-456-8667
Ahlgren Vineyard
  Boulder Creek, CA 800-338-6071
Airlie Winery
  Monmouth, OR 503-838-6013
Alba Vineyard
  Milford, NJ 908-995-7800
Alexander Johnson's Valley Wines
  Healdsburg, CA 800-888-5532
Alexis Bailly Vineyard
  Hastings, MN 651-437-1413
Allegro Vineyards
  Brogue, PA 717-927-9148
Almarla Vineyards & Winery
  Shubuta, MS 601-687-5548
Aloha Distillers
  Honolulu, HI 808-841-5787
Alpen Cellars
  Trinity Center, CA 530-266-9513
Alpine Vineyards
  Monroe, OR 541-424-5851
Alta Vineyard Cellar
  Calistoga, CA 707-942-6708
Altamura Vineyards & Winery
  Napa, CA 707-253-2000
Alto Vineyards
  Alto Pass, IL 618-893-4898
Amador Foothill Winery
  Plymouth, CA 800-778-9463
Amalthea Cellars Farm Winery
  Atco, NJ 856-768-8585
Amberg Wine Cellars
  Clifton Springs, NY 315-462-3455
Americana Vineyards
  Interlaken, NY 607-387-6801
Amity Vineyards
  Amity, OR 888-264-8966
Amizetta Vineyards
  St Helena, CA 707-963-1460
Amwell Valley Vineyard
  Ringoes, NJ 908-788-5852
Anchor Brewing Company
  San Francisco, CA 415-863-8350
Anderson Valley Brewing
  Boonville, CA 707-895-2337
Anderson's Conn Valley Vineyards
  St Helena, CA 800-946-3497
Andrew Peller Limited
  Grimsby, ON 905-643-4131
Annapolis Winery
  Annapolis, CA 707-886-5460
Antelope Valley Winery
  Lancaster, CA 800-282-8332
Anthony Road Wine Company
  Penn Yan, NY 800-559-2182
Arbor Crest Wine Cellars
  Spokane, WA 509-927-8571
Arbor Hill Grapery & Winery
  Naples, NY 800-554-7553
Argonaut Winery
  Ione, CA 209-245-5567
Argyle Wines
  Dundee, OR 888-427-4953

Arizona Vineyards
  Nogales, AZ 520-287-7972
Arns Winery
  Saint Helena, CA 707-963-3429
Arrowood Vineyards & Winery
  Glen Ellen, CA 800-938-5170
Artesa Vineyards & Winery
  Napa, CA 707-224-1668
Ashland Vineyards
  Ashland, OR 541-488-0088
ASV Wines
  Delano, CA 661-792-3159
Au Bon Climat Winery
  Los Olivos, CA 805-937-9801
Audubon Cellars
  Berkeley, CA 510-540-5384
August Schell Brewing Company
  New Ulm, MN 800-770-5020
Augusta Winery
  Augusta, MO 888-667-9463
Autumn Wind Vineyard
  Newberg, OR 503-538-6931
Babcock Winery & Vineyards
  Lompoc, CA 805-736-1455
Bacardi Canada, Inc.
  Brampton, ON 905-451-6100
Bacardi USA
  Miami, FL 800-222-2734
Baily Vineyard & Winery
  Temecula, CA 951-676-9463
Balagna Winery Company
  Los Alamos, NM 505-672-3678
Baldwin Vineyards
  Pine Bush, NY 845-744-2226
Balic Winery
  Mays Landing, NJ 609-625-1903
Bandiera Winery
  Cloverdale, CA 707-894-4295
Banfi Vintners
  Glen Head, NY 800-645-6511
Barca Wine Cellars
  Roseville, CA 916-967-0770
Bargetto's Winery
  Soquel, CA 800-422-7438
Baron Vineyards
  Paso Robles, CA 805-239-3313
Barton Brands
  Chicago, IL 800-598-6352
Basignani Winery
  Sparks Glencoe, MD 410-472-0703
Baxter's Vineyard
  Nauvoo, IL 800-854-1396
Baywood Cellars
  Lodi, CA 800-214-0445
Beachaven Vineyards & Winery
  Clarksville, TN 931-645-8867
Beam Global Spirits & Wine
  Deerfield, IL 847-948-8888
Bear Creek Winery
  Cave Junction, OR 541-592-3977
Beaucanon Estate Wines
  Napa, CA 800-660-3520
Beckmen Vineyards
  Los Olivos, CA 805-688-8664
Bedell North Fork, LLC
  Cutchogue, NY 631-734-7537
Bell Mountain Vineyards
  Fredericksburg, TX. 830-685-3297
Bellerose Vineyard
  Healdsburg, CA 707-433-1637
Belvedere Vineyards & Winery
  Healdsburg, CA 800-433-8296
Belvedere Winery
  Healdsburg, CA 800-433-8296
Benziger Family Winery
  Glen Ellen, CA 888-490-2739
Bernardo Winery
  San Diego, CA 858-487-1866
Bernardus Winery & Vineyards
  Carmel Valley, CA 888-648-9463
Bernheim Distilling Company
  Louisville, KY 800-303-0053
Bethel Heights Vineyard,Inc.
  Salem, OR 503-581-2262
Bianchi Winery
  Newport Beach, CA 949-646-9100
Bias Vineyards & Winery
  Berger, MO 573-834-5475
Bidwell Vineyard
  Cutchogue, NY 631-734-5200
Biltmore Estate Wine Company
  Asheville, NC 800-411-3812

Binns Vineyards & Winery
Las Cruces, NM 575-522-2211
Bishop Farms Winery
Cheshire, CT .203-272-8243
Black Mesa Winery
Velarde, NM .800-852-6372
Black Prince Distillery, Inc.
Clifton, NJ 973-365-2050
Black Sheep Vintners
Murphys, CA .209-728-2157
Blackwell Wine Company
Lost Hills, CA 661-397-2622
Blumenhof Vineyards-Winery
Dutzow, MO .800-419-2245
Boeger Winery
Placerville, CA 800-655-2634
Bogle Vineyards
Clarksburg, CA 916-744-1139
Bohemian Brewery
Midvale, UT .801-566-5474
Boisset America
Sausalito, CA 800-878-1123
Bonny Doon Vineyard
Santa Cruz, CA 831-425-3625
Boordy Vineyards
Hydes, MD 410-592-5015
Bordoni Vineyards
Vallejo, CA 707-642-1504
Boskydel Vineyard
Lake Leelanau, MI 231-256-7272
Bouchaine Vineyards
Napa, CA 800-654-9463
BR Cohn Winery
Glen Ellen, CA 707-938-4064
Brander Vineyard
Los Olivos, CA 800-970-9979
Braren Pauli Winery
Redwood Valley, CA 800-423-6519
Braswell's Winery
Dora, AL 205-648-8335
Bravard Vineyards & Winery
Hopkinsville, KY 270-269-2583
Breitenbach Wine Cellars
Dover, OH 330-343-3603
Briceland Vineyards
Redway, CA .707-923-2429
Brick Brewery
Waterloo, ON 800-505-8971
Brimstone Hill Vineyard
Pine Bush, NY 845-744-2231
Bristle Ridge Vineyard
Knob Noster, MO 800-994-9463
Broad Run Vineyards
Louisville, KY 502-231-0372
Broadley Vineyards
Monroe, OR .541-847-5934
Bronco Wine Company
Ceres, CA 800-692-5780
Brookmere Vineyards
Belleville, PA 717-935-5380
Brotherhood Winery
Washingtonville, NY 845-496-3661
Brown County Wine Company
Nashville, IN 888-298-2984
Brutocao Cellars
Hopland, CA .800-433-3689
Bryant Vineyard
Talladega, AL 256-268-2638
Buccia Vineyard
Conneaut, OH 440-593-5976
Buckingham Valley Vineyards
Buckingham, PA 215-794-7188
Buehler Vineyards
St Helena, CA 707-963-2155
Burnley Vineyards and Daniel Cellars
Barboursville, VA 540-832-2828
Butler Winery
Bloomington, IN 812-339-7233
Butterfly Creek Winery
Mariposa, CA 209-966-2097
Buttonwood Farm Winery
Solvang, CA .800-715-1404
Byington Winery & Vineyards
Los Gatos, CA 408-354-1111
Byron Vineyard & Winery
Santa Maria, CA 805-934-4770
Cache Cellars
Davis, CA 530-756-6068
Cain Vineyard & Winery
St Helena, CA 707-963-1616
Cakebread Cellars
Rutherford, CA 800-588-0298

Calafia Cellars
St Helena, CA 707-963-0114
Calera Wine Company
Hollister, CA 831-637-9170
Callahan Ridge Winery
Roseburg, OR 800-695-4946
Callaway Vineyards & Winery
Temecula, CA 800-472-2377
Camas Prairie Winery
Moscow, ID .800-616-0214
Cambria Winery & Vineyard
Santa Maria, CA 888-339-9463
Campari
New York, NY 212-891-3600
Canada Dry Bottling Company
Flushing, NY 718-661-4265
Canandaigua Wine Concentrate
Madera, CA .559-673-7071
Cantwell's Old Mill Winery
Geneva, OH .440-466-5560
Cap Rock Winery
Lubbock, TX 800-546-9463
Caparone Winery
Paso Robles, CA 805-467-3827
Caporale Winery
Napa, CA 707-253-9230
Cardinale Winery
Oakville, CA .707-944-2807
Carlson Vineyards
Palisade, CO 888-464-5554
Carmela Vineyards
Glenns Ferry, ID 208-366-2539
Carneros Creek Winery
Napa, CA 707-253-9464
Carrousel Cellars
Gilroy, CA 408-847-2060
Casa Larga Vineyards
Fairport, NY .585-223-4210
Casa Nuestra
St Helena, CA 866-844-9463
Casco Bay Brewing
Portland, ME 207-797-2020
Castello Di Borghese
Cutchogue, NY 800-734-5158
Catamount Brewing Company
Windsor, VT .802-674-6700
Catoctin Vineyards
Brookeville, MD 301-774-2310
Cavender Castle Winery
Atlanta, GA .706-864-4759
Caymus Vineyards
Rutherford, CA 707-967-3010
Cayuga Ridge Estate Winery
Ovid, NY 800-598-9463
Cedar Creek Winery
Cedarburg, WI 800-827-8020
Cedar Mountain Winery
Livermore, CA 925-373-6636
Chaddsford Winery
Chadds Ford, PA 610-388-6221
Chadler
Swedesboro, NJ 856-467-0099
Chalet Debonne Vineyards
Madison, OH 440-466-3485
Chalk Hill Estate Vineyards & Winery
Healdsburg, CA 707-838-4306
Chalone Wine Group
Napa, CA 707-254-4200
Champoeg Wine Cellars
Aurora, OR .503-678-2144
Channing Rudd Cellars
Middletown, CA 707-987-2209
Chappellet Winery
St Helena, CA 800-494-6379
Charles B. Mitchell Vineyards
Somerset, CA 800-704-9463
Charles Jacquin Et Cie
Philadelphia, PA 800-523-3811
Charles Spinetta Winery
Plymouth, CA 209-245-3384
Chartrand Imports
Rockland, ME 800-473-7307
Chateau Anne Marie
Carlton, OR .503-864-2991
Chateau Boswell
St Helena, CA 707-963-5472
Chateau Chevre Winery
Napa, CA 707-944-2184
Chateau des Charmes Wines
St. Davids, ON 800-263-2541
Chateau Diana Winery
Healdsburg, CA 707-433-6992

Chateau Grand Traverse
Traverse City, MI 231-223-7355
Chateau Julien Winery
Carmel, CA .831-624-2600
Chateau LaFayette Reneau
Hector, NY .800-469-9463
Chateau Montelena Winery
Calistoga, CA 707-942-5105
Chateau Morisette Winery
Meadows of Dan, VA 540-593-2865
Chateau Potelle Winery
Napa, CA 707-255-9440
Chateau Ra-Ha
Jerseyville, IL 866-639-4832
Chateau Sassenage
Truth or Consequences, NM 505-894-7244
Chateau Souverain
Geyserville, CA 707-433-3141
Chateau St. Jean Vineyards
Kenwood, CA 707-833-4134
Chateau Thomas Winery
Plainfield, IN 888-761-9463
Chatom Vineyards
Murphys, CA 800-435-8852
Chermont Winery
Esmont, VA .804-286-2211
Chestnut Mountain Winery
Hoschton, GA 770-867-6914
Chi Company/Tabor Hill Winery
Buchanan, MI 800-283-3363
Chicama Vineyards
West Tisbury, MA 888-244-2262
Chimere
Santa Maria, CA 805-922-9097
Chouinard Vineyards
Castro Valley, CA 510-582-9900
Christine Woods Winery
Philo, CA 707-895-2115
Christopher Creek Winery
Healdsburg, CA 707-433-6992
Cienega Valley Winery/DeRose
Hollister, CA 831-636-9143
Cimarron Cellars
Caney, OK 580-889-5997
Cinnabar Vineyards & Winery
Saratoga, CA 408-741-5858
City Brewery Latrobe
Latrobe, PA .724-537-5545
CK Mondavi Vineyards
St Helena, CA 707-967-2200
Claiborne & Churchill Vintners
San Luis Obispo, CA 805-544-4066
Claire's Grand River Winery
Madison, OH 440-298-9838
Claudia Springs Winery
San Jose, CA 408-895-3926
Clear Creek Distillery
Portland, OR 503-248-9470
Cline Cellars
Sonoma, CA 800-543-2070
Clos Du Bois
Geyserville, CA 800-222-3189
Clos du Lac Cellars
Ione, CA 209-274-2238
Clos Du Muriel
Temecula, CA 951-296-5400
Clos du Val Wine Company
Napa, CA 800-993-9463
Clos Pegase Winery
Calistoga, CA 800-866-8583
Cloudstone Vineyards
Los Altos Hills, CA 650-948-8621
Clover Hill Vineyards & Winery
Breinigsville, PA 800-256-8374
Cocolalla Winery
Cocolalla, ID 208-263-3774
Colorado Cellars Winery
Palisade, CO 970-464-7921
Commonwealth Fish & Beer Company
Boston, MA .617-523-8383
Concannon Vineyard
Livermore, CA 800-258-9866
Conn Creek Winery
St Helena, CA 800-793-7960
Conneaut Cellars Winery
Conneaut Lake, PA 877-229-9463
Conrotto A. Winery
Gilroy, CA 408-847-2233
Consolidated Distilled Products
Chicago, IL .773-927-4161
Cooper Mountain Vineyards
Beaverton, OR 503-649-0027

Coors Brewing Company
Golden, CO 800-642-6116
Corby Distilleries
Toronto, ON 800-367-9079
Corus Brands
Woodinville, WA 425-806-2600
Cosentino Winery
Yountville, CA 800-764-1220
Cottonwood Canyon Vineyards
Santa Maria, CA 805-937-8463
Cowie Wine Cellars
Paris, AR 479-963-3990
Crescini Wines
Soquel, CA 831-462-1466

Cribari Vineyards
Fresno, CA 800-277-9095

Processor and exporter of high quality California bulk wine. Cribari Vineyards, Inc. has been involved in the California wine industry for more than four generations. Our commitment to quality and service is unsurpassed. We are competitive in our pricing and can furnish many varieties of California wine blended to our customers' specifications. Some of our most popular products are Cabernet Sauvignon, Merlot, Chardonnay, Sauterne, Sherry, Chablis, Marsala, and Chianti.

Cristom Vineyards
Salem, OR 503-375-3068
Cronin Vineyards
Woodside, CA 650-851-1452
Crown Regal Wine Cellars
Brooklyn, NY 718-604-1430
Cruse Vineyards
Chester, SC 803-377-3944
Crystal Geyser Roxanne LLC
Pensacola, FL 850-476-8844
Cuneo Cellars
Amity, OR 503-835-2782
Cuvaison Vineyard
Calistoga, CA 707-942-6266
Cygnet Cellars
Hollister, CA 831-637-7559
Dalla Valle Vineyards
Oakville, CA 707-944-2676
Dark Mountain Winery and Brewery
Vail, AZ .520-762-5777
Daume Winery
Camarillo, CA 800-559-9922
David Bruce Winery
Los Gatos, CA 800-397-9972
Davis Bynum Winery
Healdsburg, CA 800-826-1073
De Loach Vineyards
Santa Rosa, CA 707-526-9111
De Lorimier Winery
Geyserville, CA 800-546-7718
Deaver Vineyards
Plymouth, CA 209-245-4099
Deer Meadow Vineyard
Winchester, VA 800-653-6632
Deer Park Winery
Elk Creek, MO 707-963-5411
Dehlinger Winery
Sebastopol, CA 707-823-2378
Delicato Vineyards
Napa, CA 707-265-1700
Denatale Vineyards
Healdsburg, CA 707-431-8460
Devlin Wine Cellars
Soquel, CA 831-476-7288
DG Yuengling & Son
Pottsville, PA 570-622-4141
Di Grazia Vineyards
Brookfield, CT 800-230-8853
Diageo United Distillers
Norwalk, CT 203-602-5000
Diamond Creek Vineyards
Calistoga, CA 707-942-6926
Diamond Oaks Vineyard
Cloverdale, CA 707-894-3191

Diamond Water
Hot Springs, AR 501-623-1251
Distant Lands Coffee Roaster
Tyler, TX 800-346-5459
Distillerie Stock USA
New York, NY 800-323-1884
Dixie Brewing Company
New Orleans, LA 504-822-8711
Domaine Montreaux
Napa, CA 800-743-6668
Domaine St. George Winery
Healdsburg, CA 707-433-5508
Donatoni Winery
Inglewood, CA 310-645-5445
Door-Peninsula Winery
Sturgeon Bay, WI 800-551-5049
Dr. Konstantin Frank Vinifera Wine Cellars
Hammondsport, NY 800-320-0735
Dreyer Sonoma
Woodside, CA 650-851-9448
Dry Creek Vineyard
Healdsburg, CA 800-864-9463
Duck Pond Cellars
Dundee, OR 800-437-3213
Duckhorn Vineyards
St Helena, CA 888-354-8885
Duncan Peak Vineyards
Hopland, CA 707-744-1129
Dundee Wine Company
Dundee, OR 888-427-4953
Dunn Vineyards
Angwin, CA 707-965-3642
Duplin Wine Cellars
Rose Hill, NC 800-774-9634
Dutch Henry Winery
Calistoga, CA 888-224-5879
E&J Gallo Winery
Livingston, CA 209-394-6219
E&J Gallo Winery
Fresno, CA 559-458-2480
Eagle Crest Vineyards
Conesus, NY 585-346-2321
East Side Winery/Oak Ridge Vineyards
Lodi, CA 209-369-4768
Eberle Winery
Paso Robles, CA 805-238-9607
Ed Oliveira Winery
Arcata, CA 707-822-3023
Edgewood Estate Winery
Napa, CA 800-755-2374
Edmunds St. John
Berkeley, CA 510-981-1510
Edna Valley Vineyard
San Luis Obispo, CA 805-544-5855
El Molino Winery
St Helena, CA 707-963-3632
Elk Cove Vineyards
Gaston, OR 503-985-7760
Elk Run Vineyards
Mt Airy, MD 800-414-2513
Elliston Vineyards
Sunol, CA 925-862-2377
Emilio Guglielmo Winery
Morgan Hill, CA 408-779-2145
Enz Vineyards
Hollister, CA 831-637-3956
Eola Hills Wine Cellars
Rickreall, OR 800-291-6730
EOS Estate Winery
Paso Robles, CA 800-349-9463
Erath Vineyards Winery
Dundee, OR 800-539-5463
Esterlina Vineyard & Winery
Philo, CA 707-895-2920
Eureka Springs Winery
Eureka Springs, AR 479-253-8754
Evensen Vineyards
Oakville, CA 707-944-2396
Evesham Wood Vineyard & Winery
Salem, OR 503-371-8478
Eyrie Vineyards
Dundee, OR 503-472-6315
F.X. Matt Brewing Company
Utica, NY 800-690-3181
Fall Creek Vineyards
Austin, TX 512-476-4477
Far Niente Winery
Oakville, CA 707-944-2861
Farella-Park Vineyards
Napa, CA 707-254-9489
Farfelu Vineyards
Flint Hill, VA 540-364-2930

Fellom Ranch Vineyards
Cupertino, CA 408-741-0307
Fenestra Winery
Livermore, CA 800-789-9463
Fenn Valley Vineyards
Fennville, MI 800-432-6265
Ferrante Winery & Ristorante
Geneva, OH 440-466-6046
Ferrara Winery
Escondido, CA 760-745-7632
Ferrari-Carano Vineyards& Winery
Healdsburg, CA 800-831-0381
Ferrigno Vineyard & Winery
St James, MO 573-265-7742
Ferrigno Vineyards & Winry
St James, MO 573-265-7742
Fess Parker Winery
Los Olivos, CA 800-446-2455
Ficklin Vineyards
Madera, CA 559-674-4598
Field Stone Winery & Vineyard
Healdsburg, CA 800-544-7273
Fieldbrook Valley Winery
McKinleyville, CA 707-839-4140
Fields of Fair Whiskey
Paxico, KS 785-636-5460
Fife Vineyards
Redwood Valley, CA 707-485-0323
Filsinger Vineyards & Winery
Temecula, CA 951-302-6363
Fiore Winery
Pylesville, MD 410-452-0132
Firelands Wine Company
Sandusky, OH 800-548-9463
Firestone Vineyard
Los Olivos, CA 805-688-3940
Fisher Ridge Wine Company
Charleston, WV 304-342-8702
Fisher Vineyards
Santa Rosa, CA 707-539-7511
Fitzpatrick Winery & Lodge
Somerset, CA 800-245-9166
Flora Springs Wine Company
St Helena, CA 707-967-8032
Florida Distillers Company
Lake Alfred, FL 863-956-3477
Flynn Vineyards Winery
Rickreall, OR 888-427-4953
Foley Estates Vineyards & Winery
Solvang, CA 805-688-8554
Folie a Deux Winery
St Helena, CA 800-473-4454
Foris Vineyards
Cave Junction, OR 541-592-3752
Forman Vineyards
St Helena, CA 707-963-3900
Fortino Winery
Gilroy, CA 888-617-6606
Fortuna Cellars
Davis, CA 530-756-6686
Four Sisters Winery
Belvidere, NJ 908-475-3671
Fox Run Vineyards
Penn Yan, NY 800-636-9786
Fox Vineyards Winery
Social Circle, GA 770-787-5402
Foxen Vineyard
Santa Maria, CA 805-937-4251
Franciscan Oakville Estates
Rutherford, CA 800-529-9463
Franciscan Vineyards
Rutherford, CA 800-529-9463
Frank Family Vineyard
Calistoga, CA 707-942-0859
Frank-Lin Distillers
San Jose, CA 408-259-8900
Franklin Hill Vineyards
Bangor, PA 888-887-2839
Franzia Winery
Ripon, CA 209-599-4111
Fratelli Perata
Paso Robles, CA 805-238-2809
Frederick Wildman & Sons
New York, NY 800-733-9463
Freemark Abbey Winery
Helena, CA 800-963-9698
Freixenet
Sonoma, CA 707-996-4981
Frey Vineyards
Redwood Valley, CA 800-760-3739
Frick Winery
Sacramento, CA 415-776-7331

Frisinger Cellars
Napa, CA 707-255-3749

Frog's Leap Winery
Rutherford, CA 800-959-4704

Frontenac Point Vineyard
Trumansburg, NY 607-387-9619

Gainey Vineyard
Santa Ynez, CA. 805-688-0558

Galante Vineyards
Carmel Valley, CA 800-425-2683

Galena Cellars Winery
Galena, IL. .800-397-9463

Galluccio Estate Vineyards
Cutchogue, NY 631-734-7089

Gallup Sales Company
Gallup, NM 505-863-5241

Gary Farrell Wines
Santa Rosa, CA 707-433-6616

George A Dickel & Company
Tullahoma, TN 931-857-9313

Georgia Winery
Ringgold, GA 706-937-2177

Georis Winery
Carmel Valley, CA 831-659-1050

Germanton Winery
Germanton, NC. 800-322-2894

Geyser Peak Winery
Geyserville, CA 800-945-4447

Giasi Winery
Rock Stream, NY 607-535-7785

Girard Winery/Rudd Estates
Oakville, CA. 707-944-8577

Girardet Wine Cellars
Roseburg, OR 541-679-7252

Gloria Ferrer Champagne
Sonoma, CA 707-996-7256

Gloria Winery & Vineyard
Springfield, MO 417-926-6263

Glunz Family Winery & Cellars
Grayslake, IL. 847-548-9463

Golden Creek Vineyard
Santa Rosa, CA 707-538-2350

Good Harbor Vineyards
Lake Leelanau, MI 231-256-7165

Goodson Brothers Coffee Company
Knoxville, TN. 865-693-3572

Grand Teton Brewing
Victor, ID. .888-899-1656

Grande River Vineyards
Palisade, CO 800-264-7696

Granite Springs Winery
Somerset, CA 800-638-6041

Great Divide Brewing Company
Denver, CO 303-296-9460

Greenfield Wine Company
Saint Helena, CA 707-963-2335

Greenwood Ridge Vineyards
Philo, CA. .707-895-2002

Groth Vineyards & Winery
Oakville, CA. 707-944-0290

Groupe Paul Masson
Longueuil, QC 514-878-3050

Gruet Winery
Albuquerque, NM 888-897-9463

Guilliams Winery
St Helena, CA 707-963-9059

Gundlach Bundschu Winery
Sonoma, CA 707-938-5277

H Coturri & Sons Winery
Glen Ellen, CA 866-268-8774

Habersham Winery
Helen, GA .706-878-9463

Hafner Vineyard
Healdsburg, CA 707-433-4606

Hahn Estates and Smith &Hook
Soledad, CA 831-678-4555

Haight-Brown Vineyard
Litchfield, CT 800-577-9463

Hallcrest Vineyards
Felton, CA .831-335-4441

Handley Cellars
Philo, CA. .800-733-3151

Hanzell Vineyards
Sonoma, CA 707-996-3860

Harbor Winery
West Sacramento, CA 916-371-6776

Harmony Cellars
Harmony, CA 800-432-9239

Harpersfield Vineyard
Geneva, OH. 440-466-4739

Hart Winery
Temecula, CA 877-638-8788

Hartford Family Winery
Forestville, CA 800-588-0234

Hawk Pacific Freight
Napa, CA. .707-259-0266

Hazlitt's 1852 Vineyard
Hector, NY 888-750-0494

Heartland Vineyards
Cleveland, OH 440-871-0701

Heck Cellars
Arvin, CA. .661-854-6120

Hecker Pass Winery
Gilroy, CA .408-842-8755

Hegy's South Hills Vineyard & Winery
Twin Falls, ID. 208-599-0074

Heineman's Winery
Put In Bay, OH 419-285-2811

Helena View/Johnston Vineyard
Calistoga, CA 707-942-4956

Hells Canyon Winery
Caldwell, ID 800-318-7873

Henry Estate Winery
Umpqua, OR 800-782-2686

Henry Hill & Company
Napa, CA. .707-224-6565

Heritage Wine Cellars
North East, PA. 800-747-0083

Hermann J. Wiemer Vineyard
Dundee, NY 800-371-7971

Hermannhof Winery
Hermann, MO 800-393-0100

Heron Hill Winery
Hammondsport, NY 800-441-4241

Hess Collection Winery
Napa, CA. .877-707-4377

Hidden Mountain Ranch Winery
Paso Robles, CA. 805-226-9907

Highland Manor Winery
Jamestown, TN 931-879-9519

Highwood Distillers
High River, AB 403-652-3202

Hillcrest Vineyard
Roseburg, OR 541-673-3709

Hinzerling Winery
Prosser, WA. 800-722-6702

Hiram Walker & Sons
Fort Smith, AR 479-783-4191

Hiram Walker & Sons
Windsor, ON 519-254-5171

Homewood Winery
Sonoma, CA 707-996-6353

Honeywood Winery
Salem, OR. 800-726-4101

Honig Vineyard and Winery
Rutherford, CA 800-929-2217

Hood River Distillers
Hood River, OR 541-386-1588

Hood River Vineyards and Winery
Hood River, OR 541-386-3772

Hoodsport Winery
Hoodsport, WA. 800-580-9894

Hop Kiln Winery
Healdsburg, CA 707-433-6491

Hopkins Vineyard
Warren, CT 860-868-7954

Horizon Winery
Santa Rosa, CA 707-544-2961

Huber's Orchard Winery
Borden, IN. 800-345-9463

Hunt Country Vineyards
Branchport, NY. 800-946-3289

Hurst Vineyards
Bosque, NM 505-864-1831

Husch Vineyards
Philo, CA. .800-554-8724

Ingleside Plantation Winery
Colonial Beach, VA 804-224-8687

Inniskillin Wines
Niagara-On-The-Lake, ON. 888-466-4754

Iron Horse Ranch & Vineyard
Sebastopol, CA 707-887-1212

Ironstone Vineyards
Murphys, CA 209-728-1251

J Vineyards & Winery
Healdsburg, CA 800-885-9463

J. Filippi Winery
Etiwanda, CA 909-899-5997

J. Fritz Winery
Cloverdale, CA 707-894-3389

J. Stonestreet & Sons Vineyard
Healdsburg, CA 800-723-6336

Jack Daniel's Distillery
Lynchburg, TN 931-759-4221

Jackson Valley Vineyards
Ione, CA 916-354-3200

Jamesport Vineyards
Jamesport, NY. 631-722-5256

Jodar Vineyard & Winery
Placerville, CA 530-621-0324

Johlin Century Winery
Oregon, OH 419-693-6288

Johnson's Alexander Valley Wines
Healdsburg, CA 800-888-5532

Johnston's Winery
Ballston Spa, NY. 518-882-6310

Jones Brewing Company
Smithton, PA 800-237-2337

Joseph Filippi Winery
Etiwanda, CA 909-899-5755

Joullian Vineyards
Carmel Valley, CA 877-659-2800

Julac
Rougemont, QC 514-861-2404

Justin Winery & Vineyard
Paso Robles, CA. 800-726-0049

Kalin Cellars
Novato, CA 415-883-3543

Kate's Vineyard
Napa, CA. .707-255-2644

Kathryn Kennedy Winery
Saratoga, CA 408-867-4170

Kelleys Island Wine Company
Kelleys Island, OH 419-746-2678

Kelson Creek Winery
Plymouth, CA 209-245-4700

Kendall-Jackson Wine
Windsor, CA 800-544-4413

King Brewing Company
Fairfield, CA 707-428-4503

King Estate Winery
Eugene, OR 800-884-4441

Kiona Vineyards Winery
Benton City, WA 509-588-6716

Kirigin Cellars
Gilroy, CA .408-847-8827

Kistler Vineyards
Sebastopol, CA 707-823-5603

Kittling Ridge Estate Wines & Spirits
Grimsby, ON 905-945-9225

Klein Family Vintners
Healdsburg, CA. 707-433-6511

Klingshirn Winery
Avon Lake, OH 440-933-6666

Knapp Vineyards
Romulus, NY. 800-869-9271

Koryo Winery Company
Gardena, CA 310-532-3240

Kramer Vineyards
Gaston, OR 800-619-4637

Kunde Estate Winery
Kenwood, CA 707-833-5501

L. Mawby Vineyards
Suttons Bay, MI 231-271-3522

La Abra Farm & Winery
Lovingston, VA. 434-263-5392

La Buena Vida Vineyards
Grapevine, TX 817-481-9463

La Chiripada Winery
Dixon, NM 800-528-7801

La Rocca Vineyards
Forest Ranch, CA 800-808-9463

La Vina Winery
Anthony, NM 575-882-7632

Labatt Breweries
Toronto, ON 416-361-5050

Labatt Breweries
Lasalle, QC 514-366-5050

Laetitia Vineyard
Arroyo Grande, CA. 888-809-8463

Lafollette Vineyard & Winery
Belle Mead, NJ 908-359-5018

Laird & Company
Eatontown, NJ. 877-438-5247

Lake Sonoma Winery
Healdsburg, CA 877-850-9463

Lakeridge Winery & Vineyards
Clermont, FL 800-768-9463

Lakeshore Winery
Romulus, NY. 315-549-7075

Lakespring Winery
Yountville, CA 707-944-2475

Lakewood Vineyards
Watkins Glen, NY. 607-535-9252

Lambert Bridge Winery
Healdsburg, CA 800-975-0555

Lamoreaux Landing Wine Cellar
Lodi, NY 607-582-6011
Lancaster County Winery
Willow Street, PA 717-464-3555
Landmark Vineyards
Kenwood, CA 800- 45- 636
Lange Winery
Dundee, OR. 503-538-6476
Langtry Estate & Vineyards
Middletown, CA 707-987-9127
Larry's Vineyards & Winery
Schenectady, NY. 518-355-7365
Latah Creek Wine Cellars
Spokane Valley, WA 509-926-0164
Latcham Vineyards
Mt Aukum, CA 800-750-5591
Laurel Glen Vineyard
Glen Ellen, CA 707-526-3914
Lava Cap Winery
Placerville, CA 530-621-0175
Lazy Creek Vineyard
Philo, CA. .707-895-2021
Le Boeuf & Associates
North Falmouth, MA 800-444-5666
Leelanau Wine Cellars
Omena, MI 800-782-8128
Leidenfrost Vineyards
Hector, NY 607-546-2800
Lemon Creek Winery
Berrien Springs, MI 269-471-1321
Leonetti Cellar
Walla Walla, WA. 509-525-1428
Les Bourgeois Vineyards
Rocheport, MO. 573-698-2300
Lewis Cellars
Hillsborough, CA 415-445-7884
Limur Winery
San Francisco, CA 415-781-8691
Lin Court Vineyards
Solvang, CA 805-688-8554
Little Amana Winery
Amana, IA. 319-668-9664
Little Hills Winery
St Charles, MO 877-584-4557
Live Oaks Winery
Gilroy, CA. 408-842-2401
Livermore Valley Cellars
Livermore, CA 925-447-1751
Livingston Moffett Winery
Saint Helena, CA 800-788-0370
Llano Estacado Winery
Lubbock, TX. 800-634-3854
Lockwood Vineyards
Monterey, CA 831-642-9200
Loew Vineyards
Mt Airy, MD 301-831-5464
Lohr Winery
San Jose, CA 408-288-5057
Lolonis Winery
Walnut Creek, CA 925-938-8066
Long Vineyards
St Helena, CA 707-963-2496
Lonz Winery
Middle Bass, OH. 419-285-5411
Los Olivos Vintners
Los Olivos, CA 800-824-8584
Lost Hills Winery
Acampo, CA. 209-369-2746
Lost Mountain Winery
Sequim, WA 888-683-5229
Louis M. Martini
St Helena, CA 800-321-9463
Lucas Winery
Lodi, CA. 209-368-2006
Ludwigshof Winery
Eskridge, KS 785-449-2498
LUXCO
St Louis, MO. 314-772-2627
Lynfred Winery
Roselle, IL. 888-298-9463
M.S. Walker
Somerville, MA 617-776-6700
Madison Foods
St Paul, MN. 651-265-8212
Madison Vineyard
Ribera, NM 575-421-8028
Madonna Estate Mont St John
Napa, CA. .707-255-8864
Madrona Vineyards
Camino, CA. 530-644-5948
Magnanini Winery
Wallkill, NY 845-895-2767

Magnotta Winery Corporation
Woodbridge, ON. 800-461-9463
Maisons Marques & Domaines USA
Oakland, CA 510-286-2000
Mama Rap's & Winery
Gilroy, CA. 800-842-6262
Manfred Vierthaler Winery
Sumner, WA 888-663-9463
Marie Brizard Wines & Spirits
Sausalito, CA 800-878-1123
Marietta Cellars
Hopland, CA 707-433-2747
Marimar Torres Estate
Sebastopol, CA 707-823-4365
Marin Brewing Company
Larkspur, CA 415-461-4677
Mark West Vineyards
Forestville, CA 707-836-9647
Markham Vineyards
St Helena, CA 707-963-5292
Markko Vineyard
Conneaut, OH 800-252-3197
Marlow Wine Cellars
Monteagle, TN 931-924-2120
Martin & Weyrich Winery
Paso Robles, CA 805-238-2520
Martz Vineyards
Yorkville, CA 707-895-2334
Mastantuono Winery
Templeton, CA 805-238-0676
Matanzas Creek Winery
Santa Rosa, CA 800-500-6464
Matson Vineyards
Redding, CA 530-222-2833
Maurice Carrie Winery
Temecula, CA 800-716-1711
Mayacamas Vineyards
Napa, CA. .707-224-4030
Mazzocco Vineyards
Healdsburg, CA 707-857-3240
McCormick Distilling Company
Weston, MO 888-640-3082
McDowell Valley Vineyards & Cellars
Hopland, CA 707-744-1774
McHenry Vineyard
Davis, CA .530-756-3202
McIntosh's Ohio Valley Wines
Bethel, OH 937-379-1159
McKinlay Vineyards
Newberg, OR 503-625-2534
Meeker Vineyard
Healdsburg, CA 707-433-2500
Menghini Winery
Julian, CA .760-765-2072
Mercury Brewing Company
Ipswich, MA 978-356-3329
Meredyth Vineyard
Middleburg, VA 540-687-6277
Meridian Vineyards
Paso Robles, CA 805-237-6000
Merryvale Vineyards
St Helena, CA 800-326-6069
Messina Hof Wine Cellars & Vineyards
Bryan, TX .800-736-9463
Michel-Schlumberger
Healdsburg, CA 800-447-3060
Milano Winery
Hopland, CA 800-564-2582
Milat Vineyards
St Helena, CA 707-963-0758
Mill Creek Vineyards
Healdsburg, CA 877-349-2121
Millbrook Vineyard and Winery
Millbrook, NY 800-662-9463
Miller Brewing Company
Milwaukee, WI 414-931-2000
Milliaire Winery
Murphys, CA 209-728-1658
Mission Mountain Winery
Dayton, MT. 406-849-5524
Missouri Winery Warehouse Outlet
Cuba, MO .573-885-2168
Mohawk Distilled Products
North Miami, FL. 305-892-3460
Molson Breweries
Regina, SK 306-359-1786
Molson Breweries
Montreal, QC 514-521-1786
Molson Coors Brewing
Denver, CO 800-642-6116
Mon Ami Champagne Company
Port Clinton, OH 800-777-4266

Montelle Winery
Augusta, MO. 888-595-9463
Monterey Vineyard
Gonzales, CA 831-675-4000
Montevina Winery
Plymouth, CA 209-245-6942
Montmorenci Vineyards
Aiken, SC .803-649-4870
Moonlight Brewing Company
Windsor, CA 707-528-2537
Moresco Vineyards
Stockton, CA. 209-467-3081
Morrione Vineyards
Wetumpka, AL 334-567-9957
Mosby Winery
Buellton, CA 800-706-6729
Moss Creek Winery
Napa, CA. .707-252-1295
Mount Baker Vineyards
Everson, WA 360-592-2300
Mount Bethel Winery
Altus, AR .479-468-2444
Mount Eden Vineyards
Saratoga, CA 408-867-5832
Mount Hope Estate Winery
Manheim, PA 717-665-7021
Mount Palomar Winery
Temecula, CA 800-854-5177
Mount Pleasant Winery
Augusta, MO. 800-467-9463
Mt. Nittany Vineyard
Centre Hall, PA 814-466-6373
Murphy Goode Estate Winery
Healdsburg, CA 707-431-7644
Naked Mountain Vineyard & Winery
Markham, VA 540-364-1609
Nalle Winery
Healdsburg, CA 707-433-1040
Nantucket Vineyards
Nantucket, MA 508-325-5929
Napa Cellars
Oakville, CA 800-848-9630
Napa Creek Winery
Saint Helena, CA 707-963-9456
Napa Valley Port Cellars
Napa, CA. .707-257-7777
Napa Wine Company
Oakville, CA 800-848-9630
Nashoba Valley Winery
Bolton, MA 978-779-5521
Navarro Vineyards & Winery
Philo, CA. .800-537-9463
Naylor Wine Cellars
Stewartstown, PA 800-292-3370
Nevada City Winery
Nevada City, CA 800-203-9463
Nevada County Wine Guild
Nevada City, CA 530-265-3662
New Belgium Brewing Company
Fort Collins, CO 888-622-4044
New Hope Winery
New Hope, PA. 800-592-9463
New Land Vineyard
Geneva, NY. 315-585-4432
Newport Vineyards & Winery
Middletown, RI. 401-848-5161
Newton Vineyard
St Helena, CA 707-963-9000
Niagara Brewing Company
Niagara Falls, ON 800-267-3392
Nicasio Vineyards
Soquel, CA 831-423-1073
Nichelini Winery
St Helena, CA 707-963-0717
Niebaum-Coppola Estate Winery
Rutherford, CA 707-963-9099
Nissley Vineyards
Bainbridge, PA 800-522-2387
Nordman of California
Sanger, CA 559-638-9923
Northern Breweries
Sault St. Marie, ON. 800-461-2258
Northern Lights Brewing Company
Airway Heights, WA. 509-244-4909
Northern Vineyards Winery
Stillwater, MN. 651-430-1032
Northville Winery
Northville, MI. 248-349-3181
Nutmeg Vineyard
Andover, CT 860-742-8402
O'Vallon Winery
Washburn, MO 417-826-5830

Oak Grove Orchards Winery
Rickreall, OR 503-364-7052
Oak Hill Farm
Glen Ellen, CA 800-878-7808
Oak Knoll Winery
Hillsboro, OR 800-625-5665
Oak Ridge Winery
Lodi, CA 209-369-4758
Oak Ridge Winery
Lodi, CA 209-369-4768
Oak Spring Winery
Altoona, PA 814-946-3799
Oasis Winery
Hume, VA .800-304-7656
Obester Winery
Half Moon Bay, CA 650-726-9463
Oceania Cellars
Arroyo Grande, CA. 805-481-5434
Ojai Vineyard
Oak View, CA 805-649-1674
Old Creek Ranch Winery
Ventura, CA. 805-649-4132
Old Rip Van Winkle Distillery
Louisville, KY. 502-897-9113
Old South Winery
Natchez, MS 601-445-9924
Old Wine Cellar
Amana, IA .319-622-3116
Olde Heurich Brewing Company
Washington, DC 202-333-2313
Oliver Wine Company
Bloomington, IN 800-258-2783
Olympic Cellars
Port Angeles, WA 360-452-0160
One Vineyard and Winery
St Helena, CA 707-963-1123
Optima Wine Cellars
Healdsburg, CA 707-431-8222
Opus One
Oakville, CA. 800-292-6787
Orchard Heights Winery
Salem, OR .503-391-7308
Orfila Vineyards
Escondido, CA 760-738-6500
Organic Wine Company
San Francisco, CA 888-326-9463
Orleans Hill Vineyard Association
Woodland, CA. 530-661-6538
Ormand Peugeog Corporation
Miami, FL. 305-624-6834
Orr Mountain Winery
Nashville, TN 615-741-2159
Ozeki Sake
Hollister, CA. 831-630-1101
Pabst Brewing Company
San Antonio, TX. 800-935-2337
Pacheco Ranch Winery
Novato, CA. 415-883-5583
Pacific Echo Cellars
Philo, CA. .707-895-2065
Pacific Hop Exchange Brewing Company
Novato, CA. 415-884-2820
Page Mill Winery
Livermore, CA 925-456-7676
Pahlmeyer Winery
Napa, CA 707-255-2321
Pahrump Valley Vineyards
Pahrump, NV 800-368-9463
Palmer Vineyards
Riverhead, NY 800-901-8783
Panther Creek Cellars
McMinnville, OR 503-472-8080
Paper City Brewery
Holyoke, MA 413-535-1588
Paradise Valley Vineyards
Phoenix, AZ 602-233-8727
Paragon Vineyards
San Luis Obispo, CA 805-544-9080
Parasio Springs Vineyards
Soledad, CA 831-678-0300
Pastori Winery
Cloverdale, CA 707-857-3418
Paumanok Vineyards
Aquebogue, NY 631-722-8800
Peaceful Bend Vineyard
Steelville, MO 573-775-3000
Peconic Bay Winery
Cutchogue, NY 631-734-7361
Pedrizzetti Winery
Morgan Hill, CA 408-779-7389
Pedroncelli Winery
Geyserville, CA 800-836-3894

Peju Winery
Rutherford, CA 800-446-7358
Pellegrini Family Vineyards
Fulton, CA 800-891-0244
Penn-Shore Vineyards
North East, PA. 814-725-8688
Pernod Ricard USA
White Plains, NY 914-539-4500
Perry Creek Winery
Telford, PA 800-880-4026
Pete's Brewing Company
San Antonio, TX. 800-877-7383
Peter Michael Winery
Calistoga, CA 800-354-4459
Peterson & Sons Winery
Kalamazoo, MI 269-626-9755
Pheasant Ridge Winery
Lubbock, TX. 806-746-6033
Philip Togni Vineyard
St Helena, CA 707-963-3731
Phillips Beverage Company
Minneapolis, MN 612-362-7500
Phillips Farms & Michael David Vineyards
Lodi, CA 888-707-9463
Piedmont Vineyards & Winery
Middleburg, VA 540-687-5528
Piedra Creek Winery
San Luis Obispo, CA 805-541-1281
Pikes Peak Vineyards
Colorado Springs, CO. 719-576-0075
Pindar Vineyards
Peconic, NY 631-734-6200
Pine Ridge Winery
Yountville, CA 800-575-9777
Plam Vineyards & Winery
Solvang, CA 800-978-2633
Plum Creek Cellars
Palisade, CO 970-464-7586
Plymouth Colony Winery
Plymouth, MA. 508-747-3334
Pommeraie Winery
Sebastopol, CA 707-823-9463
Pompei Winery
Cleveland, OH 216-883-9370
Ponderosa Valley Vineyard & Winery
Ponderosa, NM 575-834-7487
Ponzi Vineyards
Beaverton, OR 503-628-1227
Poplar Ridge Vineyards
Hector, NY 607-582-6421
Porter Creek Vineyards
Healdsburg, CA 707-433-6321
Prager Winery & Port Works
St Helena, CA 800-969-7678
Presque Isle Wine Cellar
North East, PA. 800-488-7492
Preston Premium Wines
Pasco, WA 509-545-1990
Preston Vineyards
Healdsburg, CA 800-305-9707
Prince Michael Vineyards
Leon, VA. .800-869-8242
Quady Winery
Madera, CA. 800-733-8068
Quail Ridge Cellars & Vineyards
Saint Helena, CA 800-706-9463
Quilceda Creek Vintners
Snohomish, WA 360-568-2389
Quivira Vineyards
Healdsburg, CA 800-292-8339
R.H. Phillips
Esparto, CA. 530-662-3504
Rabbit Ridge
Healdsburg, CA 707-431-7128
Radanovich Vineyards & Winery
Mariposa, CA. 209-966-3187
Rainbow Hill Vineyards
Newcomerstown, OH 740-545-9305
Rancho De Philo
Alta Loma, CA 909-987-4208
Rancho Sisquoc Winery
Santa Maria, CA 805-937-3616
Rapazzini Winery
Gilroy, CA. 408-842-5649
Ravenswood
Sonoma, CA 800-669-4679
Raymond Vineyard & Cellar
St Helena, CA 800-525-2659
Rebec Vineyards
Amherst, VA 434-946-5168
Redhawk Vineyard
Salem, OR. 503-362-1596

Redhook Ale Breweries
Newington, NH. 603-430-8600
Reeves Winery
Middletown, CA. 707-987-9650
Regent Champagne Cellars
New York, NY. 845-691-7296
Renaissance Vineyard & Winery
Oregon House, CA 800-655-3277
Renault Winery
Egg Harbor City, NJ 609-965-2111
Renwood Winery
Sacramento, CA 800-348-8466
Retzlaff Vineyards
Livermore, CA 925-447-8941
Rex Wine Vinegar Company
Newark, NJ 973-589-6911
Richard L. Graeser Winery
Calistoga, CA 707-942-4437
Richardson Vineyards
Sonoma, CA 707-938-2610
Richland Beverage Associates
Carrollton, TX. 214-357-0248
Ridge Vineyards
Cupertino, CA 408-867-3233
Ritchie Creek Vineyard
St Helena, CA 707-963-4661
Rivendell Winery
New Paltz, NY 845-255-2494
River Road Vineyards
Sebastopol, CA. 707-887-2243
River Run Vintners
Watsonville, CA 831-726-3112
Roberian Vineyards
Forestville, NY 716-673-9255
Robert F Pliska & Company Winery
Purgitsville, WV 877-747-2737
Robert Keenan Winery
St Helena, CA 707-963-9177
Robert Mondavi Winery
Oakville, CA 888-766-6238
Robert Mondavi Winery
Oakville, CA 888-766-6328
Robert Mueller Cellars
Windsor, CA 707-837-7399
Robert Pecota Winery
Calistoga, CA 707-942-6625
Robert Sinskey Vineyards
Napa, CA. .800-869-2030
Robller Vineyard
New Haven, MO. 573-237-3986
Roche Caneros Estate Winry
Sonoma, CA 800-825-9475
Rockies Brewing Company
Boulder, CO 303-444-8448
Rodney Strong Vineyards
Healdsburg, CA 800-474-9463
Rogue Ales
Newport, OR. 541-265-3188
Rolling Hills Vineyards
Camarillo, CA. 805-484-8100
Rombauer Vineyards
St Helena, CA 800- 62- 220
Rose Creek Vineyards
Hagerman, ID 208-837-4353
Rosenblum Cellars
Alameda, CA. 510-865-7007
Ross Keller Winery
Nipomo, CA 805-929-3627
Roudon-Smith Vineyards
Scotts Valley, CA 831-438-1244
Round Hill Vineyards
St Helena, CA 800-778-0424
Royal Kedem Food & Wine Company
Bayonne, NJ 201-437-9131
Rudd Winery
Oakville, CA. 707-944-8577
Rutherford Hill Winery
Rutherford, CA 707-963-1871
Saddleback Cellars
Oakville, CA 707-944-8808
Saint Arnold Brewing Company
Houston, TX 713-686-9494
Sainte Genevieve Winery
Ste Genevieve, MO. 800-398-1298
Saintsbury
Napa, CA. .707-252-0592
Sakeone Corporation
Forest Grove, OR 800-550-7253
Salamandre Wine Cellars
Aptos, CA. 831-685-0321
Salishan Vineyards
La Center, WA. 360-263-2713

San Dominique Winery
Camp Verde, AZ 480-945-8583
San Francisco Brewing Company
San Francisco, CA 415-434-3344
Sand Castle Winery
Erwinna, PA 800-722-9463
Sandia Shadows Vineyard & Winery
Albuquerque, NM 505-856-1006
Sanford Winery
Buellton, CA 805-688-3300
Santa Barbara Winery
Santa Barbara, CA 805-963-3633
Santa Cruz Mountain Vineyard
Felton, CA 831-335-4242
Santa Fe Vineyards
Espanola, NM 505-753-8100
Santa Margarita Vineyard & Winery
Temecula, CA 909-676-4431
Sarah's Vineyard
Gilroy, CA 408-842-4278
Satiety
Davis, CA 530-757-2699
Saucilito Canyon Vineyard
San Luis Obispo, CA 805-543-2111
Sausal Winery
Healdsburg, CA 800-500-2285
Savannah Chanelle Vineyards
Saratoga, CA 408-741-2934
Sawtooth Winery
Nampa, ID. 208-467-1200
Sazerac Company
New Orleans, LA 800-899-9450
Scenic Valley Winery
Lanesboro, MN 507-467-2958
Schapiro's Kosher Winery
New York, NY 212-755-5066
Schirf Brewing Company
Park City, UT 435-649-0900
Schloss Doepken Winery
Ripley, NY 716-326-3636
Schoppaul Hill Winery at Ivanhoe
Denton, TX 940-380-9463
Schramsberg Vineyards
Calistoga, CA 800-877-3623
Schug Carneros Estate Winery
Sonoma, CA 800-966-9365
Sea Ridge Winery
Occidental, CA 707-874-1707
Seavey Vineyard
St Helena, CA 707-963-8339
Secret House Vineyards
Veneta, OR 800-497-1574
Seghesio Family Vineyards
Healdsburg, CA 707-433-3579
Sellards Winery
Sebastopol, CA 707-823-8293
Sequoia Grove Vineyards
Rutherford, CA 800-851-7841
Serendipity Cellars
Monmouth, OR 503-838-4284
Serra Mission Winery
Saint Louis, MO 314-991-2559
Seven Hills Winery
Walla Walla, WA 877-777-7870
Seven Lakes Vineyards
Fenton, MI 810-629-5686
Shafer Vineyards
Napa, CA 707-944-2877
Shallon Winery
Astoria, OR 503-325-5978
Sharon Mill Winery
Manchester, MI 734-971-6337
Shenandoah Vineyards
Plymouth, CA 209-245-4455

Sierra Vista Winery
Placerville, CA 530-622-7221
Signore Winery
Brooktondale, NY. 607-539-7935
Signorello Vineyards
Napa, CA. 707-255-5990
Silvan Ridge
Eugene, OR. 541-345-1945
Silver Creek Distillers
Rigby, ID. 208-754-0042
Silver Fox Vineyard
Mariposa, CA 209-966-4800
Silver Mountain Vineyards
Santa Cruz, CA 408-353-2278
Silver Oak Cellars
Oakville, CA 800-273-8805
Silverado Hill Cellars
Napa, CA 707-253-9306
Silverado Vineyards
Napa, CA 707-257-1770
Simon Levi Cellars
Kenwood, CA 888-315-0040
Six Mile Creek Vineyard
Ithaca, NY. 800-260-0612
Sky Vineyards
Glen Ellen, CA 707-935-1391
Slate Quarry Winery
Nazareth, PA 610-759-0286
Smart Ice
Fort Myers, FL 239-334-3123
Smith Vineyard & Winery
Grass Valley, CA 530-273-7032
Smith-Madrone Vineyards & Winery
St Helena, CA 707-963-2283
Smothers Winery/Remick Ridge
Glen Ellen, CA 800-795-9463
Sobon Estate
Plymouth, CA 209-245-4455
Sokol Blosser Winery
Dundee, OR. 800-582-6668
Sonoita Vineyards
Elgin, AZ. 520-455-5893
Sonoma Wine Services
Vineburg, CA 707-996-9773
Sonoma-Cutrer Vineyards
Fulton, CA. 707-528-1181
Southern California Brewing Company
Torrance, CA 310-329-8881
Sow's Ear Winery
Brooksville, ME 207-326-4649
Spangler Vineyards
Roseburg, OR 541-679-9654
Spoetzl Brewery
Shiner, TX. 361-594-3383
Spottswoode Winery
St Helena, CA 707-963-0134
Spring Mountain Vineyard
Saint Helena, CA 877-769-4637
Springhill Cellars
Albany, OR 541-928-1009
Spurgeon Vineyards & Winery
Highland, WI 800-236-5555
St. Francis Vineyards
Santa Rosa, CA. 707-833-2148
St. Innocent Winery
Salem, OR 503-378-1526
St. James Winery
St James, MO 800-280-9463
St. Julian Wine Company
Paw Paw, MI 800-732-6002
Stags' Leap Winery
Napa, CA. 800-640-5327
Star Hill Winery
Napa, CA. 707-255-1957

Starr & Brown
Portland, OR 503-287-1775
Ste. Chapelle Winery
Caldwell, ID 877-783-2427
Stearns Wharf Vintners
Santa Barbara, CA 805-966-6624
Steltzner Vineyards
Napa, CA. 707-252-7272
Steuk's Country Market & Winery
Sandusky, OH 419-625-8324
Stevenot Winery & Imports
Murphys, CA. 209-728-0638
Stevens Point Brewery
Stevens Point, WI 800-369-4911
Stimson Lane Winery
Prosser, WA. 509-882-3928
Stone Hill Wine Company
Hermann, MO 573-486-2221
Stonegate
St Helena, CA 707-603-2203
Stoneridge Winery
Sutter Creek, CA. 209-223-1761
Stonington Vineyards
Stonington, CT 800-421-9463
Stony Hill Vineyard
St Helena, CA 707-963-2636
Stony Ridge Winery
Livermore, CA 925-449-0458
Storrs Winery
Santa Cruz, CA 831-458-5030
Story Winery
Plymouth, CA 800-712-6390
Storybook Mountain Winery
Calistoga, CA 707-942-5282
Straub Brewery Industries
St Marys, PA 814-834-2875
Streblow Vineyards
Saint Helena, CA 707-963-5892
Stryker Sonoma Winery Vineyards
Geyserville, CA 800-433-1944
Sudwerk Privatbrauerei Hubsch
Davis, CA 530-758-8700
Sugar Creek Winery
Defiance, MO 636-987-2400
Sullivan Vineyards Winery
Rutherford, CA 877-277-7337
Summit Brewing Company
Saint Paul, MN 651-265-7800
Summit Lake Vineyards & Winery
Angwin, CA 707-965-2488
Summum Winery
Salt Lake City, UT 801-355-0137
Sunrise Winery
San Jose, CA. 408-741-1310
Sutter Home Winery
St Helena, CA 707-963-3104
Swan Joseph Vineyards
Forestville, CA 707-573-3747
Sweet Traders
Huntington Beach, CA 714-903-6800
Sycamore Vineyards
Saint Helena, CA 800-963-9698
Sylvester Winery
Paso Robles, CA. 805-227-4000
Talbott Vineyards
Gonzales, CA 831-675-3000
Talley Vineyards
Arroyo Grande, CA. 805-489-2508
Tamuzza Vineyards
Hope, NJ 908-459-5878
Tarara Winery
Leesburg, VA 703-771-7100
Tartan Hill Winery
New Era, MI 231-861-4657

Tedeschi Vineyards
Kula, HI. 808-878-6058
Tempest Vineyards
Amity, OR. 503-835-2600
Tequila XQ
Guadalajara Jalisco, ... 333-587-7799
Thoma Vineyards
Dallas, OR. 503-623-6420
Thomas Fogarty Winery
Portola Valley, CA 800-247-4163
Thomas Kruse Winery
Gilroy, CA. 408-842-7016
Thornton Winery
Temecula, CA 951-699-0099
Thorpe Vineyard
Wolcott, NY 315-594-2502
TKC Vineyards
Plymouth, CA 888-627-2356
Todhunter International
West Palm Beach, FL 561-655-8977
Tomasello Winery
Hammonton, NJ 800-666-9463
Topolos at Russian River Vine
Forestville, CA 707-887-1575
Transamerica Wine Corporation
Brooklyn, NY 718-875-4017
Trefethen Vineyards
Napa, CA. 800-556-4847
Trentadue Winery
Geyserville, CA 888-332-3032
Triple Rock Brewing Company
Berkeley, CA. 510-549-5999
Troy Winery
Troy, OH 937-339-3655
Truchard Vineyards
Napa, CA. 707-253-7153
Truckee River Winery
Truckee, CA 530-587-4626
Tucker Cellars
Sunnyside, WA 509-837-8701
Tudal Winery
St Helena, CA 707-963-3947
Tularosa Vineyards
Tularosa, NM 800-687-4467
Tyee Wine Cellars
Corvallis, OR 541-753-8754
UDV Canada
Etobicoke, ON 416-626-2000
UDV Wines
San Francisco, CA 415-835-7300
Uinta Brewing
Salt Lake City, UT 801-467-0909
Union Beverage Company
Chicago, IL 800-685-6868
United Distillers & Vintners
Norwalk, CT 203-323-3311
US Distilled Products
Princeton, MN. 763-389-4903
UST
Danbury, CT 800-650-7411
Val Verde Winery
Del Rio, TX. 830-775-9714
Valley of the Moon Winery
Glen Ellen, CA 707-996-6941
Valley View Winery
Jacksonville, OR. 800-781-9463
Van Der Heyden Vineyards
Napa, CA. 800-948-9463
Vancouver Island Brewing Company
Victoria, BC 250-361-0007
Varni Brothers/7-Up Bottling
Modesto, CA 209-521-1777
Ventana Vineyards Winery
Monterey, CA 800-237-8846
Vetter Vineyards Winery
Westfield, NY 716-326-3100
Via Della Chiesa Vineyards
Raynham, MA. 508-822-7775
Viader Vineyards & Winery
Deer Park, CA. 707-963-3816
Viano Winery
Martinez, CA 925-228-6465
Viansa Winery
Sonoma, CA 800-995-4740
Vie-Del Company
Fresno, CA 559-834-2525
Villa Helena/Arger-Martucci Winery
St Helena, CA 707-963-4334
Villa Milan Vineyard
Milan, IN. 812-654-3419
Villa Mt. Eden Winery
St Helena, CA 707-944-2414

Villar Vintners of Valdese
Valdese, NC. 828-879-3202
Vina Vista Vineyard & Winery
San Carlos, CA 707-857-3722
Vincent Arroyo Winery
Calistoga, CA 707-942-9231
Vincor International
Mississauga, ON. 800-265-9463
Vinoklet Winery & Vineyard
Cincinnati, OH 513-385-9309
Von Stiehl Winery
Algoma, WI. 800-955-5208
Von Strasser Winery
Calistoga, CA 888-359-9463
Vynecrest Vineyards and Winery
Breinigsville, PA. 800-361-0725
Wachusett Brewing Company
Westminster, MA 978-874-9965
Walker Valley Vineyards
Walker Valley, NY 845-744-3449
Warner Vineyards Winery
Paw Paw, MI. 800-756-5357
Wasson Brothers Winery
Sandy, OR. 503-668-3124
Weibel Champagne Vineyards
Fremont, CA 510-656-2340
Wente Brothers Estate Winery
Livermore, CA 925-456-2300
Wermuth Winery
Calistoga, CA 707-942-5924
West Park Wine Cellars
West Park, NY. 845-384-6709
Westbend Vinyards
Lewisville, NC 866-901-5032
Westport Rivers Vineyard& Winery
Westport, MA 800-993-9695
Westwood Winery
Sonoma, CA 707-935-3246
Whaler Vineyard Winery
Ukiah, CA. 707-462-6355
What's Brewing
San Antonio, TX. 210-648-6470
Whitcraft Wines
Santa Barbara, CA 805-730-1680
White Oak Vineyards & Winery
Healdsburg, CA 707-433-8429
White Rock Distilleries
Lewiston, ME 207-783-1433
White Rock Vineyards
Napa, CA. 707-257-7922
Whitehall Lane Winery
St Helena, CA 707-963-9454
Whitford Cellars
Napa, CA. 707-942-0840
Wiederkehr Wine Cellars
Altus, AR 800-622-9463
Wild Hog Vineyard
Cazadero, CA 707-847-3687
Wild Horse Winery
Templeton, CA 805-434-2541
Wild Winds Farms
Naples, NY 800-836-5253
Wildhurst
Kelseyville, CA. 800-595-9463
William Grant & Sons
New York, NY 212-594-4848
William Harrison Vineyards & Winery LLC
St Helena, CA 707-963-8762
William Hill Winery
Napa, CA. 707-224-5424
Williams-Selym Winery
Healdsburg, CA 707-433-6425
Williamsburg Winery
Williamsburg, VA 757-229-0999
Willow Hill Vineyards
Johnstown, OH 740-587-4622
Wimberley Valley Winery
Driftwood, TX 512-847-2592
Windsor Vineyards
Windsor, CA. 800-992-4233
Windwalker Vineyards
Somerset, CA 530-620-4054
Winters Winery
Winters, CA 530-795-3201
Witness Tree Vineyard
Salem, OR. 888-478-8766
Wolf Creek Vineyards
Norton, OH 800-436-0426
Wollersheim Winery
Prairie Du Sac, WI 800-847-9463
Wooden Valley Winery
Fairfield, CA. 707-864-0730

Woodside Vineyards
Woodside, CA. 650-851-3144
Woodward Canyon Winery
Touchet, WA 509-525-4129
Worden
Spokane, WA. 509-455-7835
Wyandotte Winery
Gahanna, OH. 614-476-3624
Yakima Brewing Company
Yakima, WA 509-575-1900
Yakima River Winery
Prosser, WA. 509-786-2805
Yamhill Valley Vineyards
McMinnville, OR 800-825-4845
York Mountain Winery
Paso Robles, CA 805-238-3925
Z.D. Wines LLC
Napa, CA. 800-487-7757
Zaca Mesa Winery
Los Olivos, CA. 800-350-7972
Zayante Vineyards
Felton, CA. 831-335-7992
Ziem Vineyards
Fairplay, MD. 301-223-8352

Beers

Abita Brewing Company
Abita Springs, LA. 800-737-2311
Alaskan Brewing Company
Juneau, AK 907-780-5866
AleSmith Brewing Company
San Diego, CA 858-549-9888
Alley Kat Brewing Company
Edmonton, AB 780-436-8922
Amstell Holding
New Bedford, MA 508-995-6100
Amsterdam Brewing Company
Toronto, ON 416-504-1040
Anchor Brewing Company
San Francisco, CA 415-863-8350
Anderson Valley Brewing
Boonville, CA. 707-895-2337
Andrew's Brewing
Lincolnville, ME 207-763-3305
Anheuser-Busch
Baldwinsville, NY 315-635-4000
Anheuser-Busch
Columbus, OH 614-888-6644
Anheuser-Busch
Fairfield, CA. 707-429-2000
Anheuser-Busch
Houston, TX 713-675-2311
Anheuser-Busch
Cartersville, GA 770-386-2000
Anheuser-Busch
Van Nuys, CA. 818-989-5300
Anheuser-Busch
Jacksonville, FL 904-751-0700
Anheuser-Busch
Newark, NJ 973-645-7700
Anheuser-Busch Inc
St Louis, MO. 800-342-5283
Apani Southwest
Abilene, TX. 325-690-1550
Arnold Foods Company
Greenwich, CT 203-531-2000
Assets Grille & Southwest Brewing Company
Albuquerque, NM 505-889-6400
Atlanta Brewing Company
Bar Harbor, ME. 800-475-5417
Atwater Block Brewing Company
Detroit, MI 313-877-9205
August Schell Brewing Company
New Ulm, MN. 800-770-5020
Avery Brewing Company
Boulder, CO 877-844-5679
Bad Frog Brewing
Saint Augustine, FL 888-223-3764
Baltimore Brewing Company
Baltimore, MD 410-837-5000
Bar Harbor Brewing Company
Bar Harbor, ME. 207-288-4592
Bay Brewery Company
Benicia, CA. 707-747-6961
Bay Hawk Ales
Irvine, CA 949-442-7565
Bear Brewing Company
Kamloops, BC. 250-851-2543
Beaver Street Brewery
Flagstaff, AZ 928-779-0079
Belmont Brewing Company
Long Beach, CA 562-433-3891

 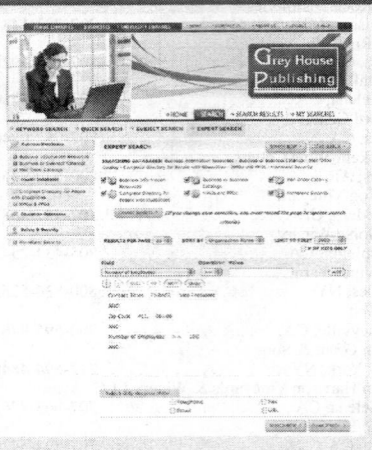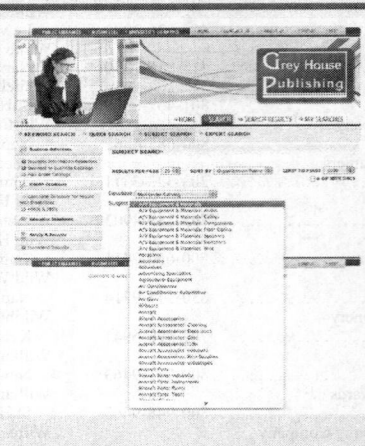

Berkshire Brewing Company, Inc.
South Deerfield, MA 877-222-7468
Big Bucks Brewery & Steakhouse
Auburn Hills, MI 989-732-5781
Big Rock Brewery
Calgary, AB. 800-242-3107
Big Sky Brewing Company
Missoula, MT 800-559-2774
Bird Creek Brewery
Indian, AK. 907-344-2473
Bison Brewing Company
Berkeley, CA 510-697-1537
Black Mountain Brewing Company
Cave Creek, AZ 480-488-3553
Bloomington Brewing Company
Bloomington, IN 812-323-2112
Bluegrass Brewing Company
St Matthews, KY. 502-899-7070
Bohemian Brewery
Midvale, UT 801-566-5474
Boston Beer Company
Boston, MA. 800-372-1131
Boston Stoker
Vandalia, OH. 800-745-5282
Boulder Creek Brewing Company
Boulder Creek, CA 831-338-7882
Boulder Street Coffee Roaster
Colorado Springs, CO. 719-577-4291
Boulevard Brewing Company
Kansas City, MO. 816-474-7095
Bow Valley Brewing Company
Canmore, AB 403-678-2739
Brasserie Brasel Brewery
Lasalle, QC 800-463-2728
Breckenridge Brewery
Denver, CO 303-623-2739
Brewski's Brewing Company
El Segundo, CA 310-202-9400
Brick Brewery
Waterloo, ON 800-505-8971
Bristol Brewing Company
Colorado Springs, CO. 719-633-2555
Brooklyn Brewery
Brooklyn, NY 718-486-7422
Buffalo Bill Brewing Company
Hayward, CA 510-886-9823
Butterfields Brewing Company
Fresno, CA 559-264-5521
Canada Dry Bottling Company
Flushing, NY. 718-661-4265
Capital Brewery
Middleton, WI. 608-836-7100
Carolina Brewery
Chapel Hill, NC 919-942-1800
Carta Blanca
El Paso, TX. 915-544-6367
Casco Bay Brewing
Portland, ME. 207-797-2020
Catamount Brewing Company
Windsor, VT 802-674-6700
Champion Beverages
Darien, CT. 203-655-9026
Chicago Pizza & Brewery
Huntington Beach, CA 714-848-3747
Christopher Joseph Brewing Company
Tempe, AZ 480-966-4438
Cisco Brewers
Nantucket, MA 508-325-5929
City Brewery Latrobe
Latrobe, PA 724-537-5545
City Brewing Company
La Crosse, WI 608-785-4200
Clipper City Brewing
Baltimore, MD 410-247-7822
Cold Spring Brewing Company
Cold Spring, MN 320-685-8686
Columbia Brewery
Creston, BC. 250-428-9344
Columbus Brewing Company
Columbus, OH 614-464-2739
Commonwealth Brewing Company
Boston, MA. 617-523-8383
Commonwealth Fish & Beer Company
Boston, MA. 617-523-8383
Concord Brewery
Lowell, MA 978-937-1200
Coors Brewing Company
Golden, CO 800-642-6116
Copper Tank Brewing Company
Austin, TX. 512-854-9380
Creemore Springs Brewery
Creemore, ON. 800-267-2240

Crooked River Brewing Company
Cleveland, OH 216-771-2337
Crowley Beverage Corporation
Wayland, MA 800-997-3337
Crown City Brewery
Pasadena, CA 626-577-5548
Crystal Geyser Roxanne LLC
Pensacola, FL 850-476-8844
Dark Mountain Winery and Brewery
Vail, AZ .520-762-5777
Dempseys Restaurant
Petaluma, CA 707-765-9694
Deschutes Brewery
Bend, OR. 541-385-8606
DG Yuengling & Son
Pottsville, PA. 570-622-4141
Dixie Brewing Company
New Orleans, LA 504-822-8711
DL Geary Brewing
Portland, ME. 207-878-2337
Dogfish Head Craft Brewery
Lewes, DE. 888-834-3474
Dogwood Brewing Company
Atlanta, GA. 404-367-0500
Drakes Brewing
San Leandro, CA. 510-562-0866
Durango Brewing
Durango, CO. 970-247-3396
Eastern Brewing Corporation
Hammonton, NJ 609-561-2700
Etna Brewing Company
Etna, CA .530-467-5277
F&M Brewery
Waterloo, ON 877-316-2337
F.X. Matt Brewing Company
Utica, NY 800-690-3181
Falla Imports
Greenville, ME 609-476-4106
Flagstaff Brewing Company
Flagstaff, AZ. 928-773-1442
Florida Brewery
Auburndale, FL. 863-965-1825
Flying Dog Brewery
Denver, CO 303-292-5027
Fort Garry Brewing Company
Winnipeg, NB 204-487-3678
Frederick Brewing Company
Frederick, MD. 888-258-7434
French's Coffee
Walnut Creek, CA. 925-978-6105
Full Sail Brewing Company
Hood River, OR 541-386-2281
Gambrinus Company
San Antonio, TX. 210-490-9128
Gentle Ben's Brewing Company
Tucson, AZ 520-624-4177
Giumarra Vineyards
Bakersfield, CA 661-395-7000
Golden City Brewery
Golden, CO 303-279-8092
Goose Island Brewing
Chicago, IL 312-915-0071
Gordon Biersch Brewing Company
San Jose, CA 408-294-6785
Grand Rapids Brewing Company
Grand Rapids, MI 616-285-5970
Grand Teton Brewing
Victor, ID. 888-899-1656
Grant's Yakima Brewery
Yakima, WA 509-575-1900
Gray Brewing Company
Janesville, WI 608-754-5150
Great Divide Brewing Company
Denver, CO 303-296-9460
Great Lakes Brewing
Etobicoke, ON 800-463-5435
Great Lakes Brewing Company
Cleveland, OH 216-771-4404
Great Northern Brewing Company
Whitefish, MT. 406-863-1000
Great Western Brewing Company
Saskatoon, SK. 800-764-4492
Guinness-Bass Import Company
Stamford, CT. 800-521-1591
H.C. Berger Brewing
Fort Collins, CO 970-493-9044
Hair of the Dog Brewing Company
Portland, OR 503-232-6585
Hale's Ales
Seattle, WA 206-706-1544
Harpoon Brewery
Boston, MA. 800-427-7666

Heartland Brewery
New York, NY 212-645-3400
High Falls Brewing
Rochester, NY. 585-546-1030
High Falls Brewing Company
Rochester, NY. 800-729-4366
Hog Haus Brewing Company
Fayetteville, AR 479-521-2739
Hogtown Brewing Company
Mississauga, ON 905-855-9065
Hornell Brewing Company
New Hyde Park, NY 516-812-0300
Humbolt Brewing Company
Arcata, CA 707-826-1734
Il Vicino Pizzeria
Salida, CO 719-539-5219
Jones Brewing Company
Smithton, PA. 800-237-2337
Kalamazoo Brewing Company
Galesburg, MI. 269-382-2338
Karl Strauss Breweries
San Diego, CA. 858-273-2739
Kevton Gourmet Tea
Streetman, TX 888-538-8668
Kona Brewing
Kailua Kona, HI 808-334-2739
La Brasserie McAuslan Brewing
Montreal, QC 514-939-3060
Labatt Breweries
Toronto, ON 416-361-5050
Labatt Breweries
Lasalle, QC 514-366-5050
Labatt Breweries
London, ON 519-663-5050
Labatt Breweries
Etobicoke, ON 800-268-2337
Labatt Breweries
Edmonton, AB 800-268-2997
Lafayette Brewing Company
Lafayette, IN. 765-742-2591
Laguna Beach Brewing Company
Laguna Beach, CA 949-494-2739
Lake St. George Brewing
Liberty, ME. 207-589-4690
Lake Titus Brewery
Malone, NY. 518-483-2337
Lakefront Brewery
Milwaukee, WI. 414-372-8800
Lakeport Brewing Corporation
Hamilton, ON 905-523-4200
Lang Creek Brewery
Marion, MT. 406-858-2200
Left Hand Brewing Company
Longmont, CO 303-772-0258
Legend Brewing Company
Richmond, VA. 804-232-3446
Leininkugel Brewing Company
Chippewa Falls, WI 715-720-1471
Les Brasseurs Du Nord
Blainville, QC 800-378-3733
Les Brasseurs GMT
Montreal, QC 888-253-8330
Lion Brewery
Wilkes Barre, PA. 800-233-8327
Lone Wolfe Brewing
Carbondale, CO 970-963-9757
Long Trail Brewing Company
Bridgewater Corners, VT 802-672-5011
Los Gatos Brewing Company
Los Gatos, CA. 408-395-9929
Lost Coast Brewery
Eureka, CA 707-445-4480
Mad River Brewing
Blue Lake, CA 707-668-4151
Magnotta Winery Corporation
Woodbridge, ON 800-461-9463
Main Street Brewery
Cincinnati, OH 513-665-4678
Manhattan Beach Brewing Company
Manhattan Beach, CA. 310-798-2744
Marin Brewing Company
Larkspur, CA. 415-461-4677
Maritime Pacific Brewing Company
Seattle, WA. 206-782-6181
Mayer's Cider Mill
Webster, NY 800-543-0043
McNeill's Brewery
Brattleboro, VT. 802-254-2553
Meier's Wine Cellars
Cincinnati, OH 800-346-2941
Mendocino Brewing Company
Ukiah, CA. 707-463-2087

Mercury Brewing Company
Ipswich, MA....978-356-3329
Mid-America Brewing Supply
Shakopee, MN....507-934-4975
Mill City Brewing Company
Lowell, MA....978-937-2690
Miller Brewing Company
St Louis, MO....314-822-5483
Miller Brewing Company
Eden, NC....336-635-1198
Miller Brewing Company
Milwaukee, WI....414-931-2000
Miller Brewing Company
Bellevue, WA....425-641-6775
Miller Brewing Company
Edison, NJ....732-635-1400
Miller Brewing Company
Fort Worth, TX....800-645-5376
Miller Brewing Company
Trenton, OH....800-944-5483
Miller Brewing Company
Elk Grove Vlg, IL....847-758-9941
Millrose Brewing Company
South Barrington, IL....800-464-5576
Millstream Brewing
Amana, IA....319-622-3672
Mishawaka Brewing Company
Granger, IN....574-256-9993
MJ Barleyhoppers
Tampa, FL....813-287-0907
Moet Hennessy USA
New York, NY....212-888-7575
Molson Breweries
Regina, SK....306-359-1786
Molson Breweries
Toronto, ON....416-675-1786
Molson Breweries
Montreal, QC....514-521-1786
Molson Breweries
North York, ON....800-665-7661
Molson Coors Brewing
Denver, CO....800-642-6116
Moonlight Brewing Company
Windsor, CA....707-528-2537
Moosehead Breweries
St. John, NB....506-635-7000
Mountain Crest Brewing SRL LLC
Monroe, WI....608-325-3191
Mountain Sun Brewery
Boulder, CO....303-546-0886
Multnomah Brewing
Portland, OR....503-236-3106
Murphys Creek Brewing
Murphys, CA....209-736-2739
Nevada City Brewing
Nevada City, CA....530-265-2446
New Belgium Brewing Company
Fort Collins, CO....888-622-4044
New Glarus Brewing
New Glarus, WI....608-527-5850
Niagara Brewing Company
Niagara Falls, ON....800-267-3392
Northampton Brewing Company
Northampton, MA....413-584-9903
Northern Breweries
Sudbury, ON....705-675-7561
Northern Breweries
Sault St. Marie, ON....800-461-2258
Northern Lights Brewing Company
Airway Heights, WA....509-244-4909
Nutfield Brewing Company
Derry, NH....603-434-9678
Oak Creek Brewing Company
Sedona, AZ....928-204-1300
Odell Brewing Company
Fort Collins, CO....970-498-9070
Okanagan Spring Brewery
Vernon, BC....800-663-7037
Oland Breweries
Halifax, NS....800-268-2337
Old Credit Brewing Company
Port Credit, ON....905-271-9888
Olde Heurich Brewing Company
Washington, DC....202-333-2313
Onalaska Brewing
Onalaska, WA....360-978-4253
Oregon Trader Brewing
Albany, OR....541-928-1931
Pabst Brewing Company
San Antonio, TX....800-935-2337
Pacific Coast Brewing Company
Oakland, CA....510-836-2739
Pacific Hop Exchange Brewing Company
Novato, CA....415-884-2820
Pacific Western Brewing Company
Prince George, BC....250-562-1131
Palmetto Brewing
Charleston, SC....843-937-0903
Paper City Brewery
Holyoke, MA....413-535-1588
Pennsylvania Brewing Company
Pittsburgh, PA....412-237-9400
Pete's Brewing Company
San Antonio, TX....800-877-7383
Pike Place Brewery
Seattle, WA....206-622-3373
Pittsburgh Brewing Company
Pittsburgh, PA....412-682-7400
Portland Brewing Company
Portland, OR....503-226-7623
Prescott Brewing Company
Prescott, AZ....928-771-2795
Pyramid Brewing
Seattle, WA....206-682-3377
Red Bell Brewing
Foxcroft Square, PA....888-733-2355
Red White & Brew
Redding, CA....530-222-5891
Redhook Ale Breweries
Woodinville, WA....425-483-3232
Redhook Ale Breweries
Newington, NH....603-430-8600
Richland Beverage Associates
Carrollton, TX....214-357-0248
River Market Brewing Company
Kansas City, MO....816-471-6300
Rock Bottom Brewery
Denver, CO....303-534-7616
Rockies Brewing Company
Boulder, CO....303-444-8448
Rogue Ales
Newport, OR....541-265-3188
Rohrbach Brewing Company
Rochester, NY....585-594-9800
Russell Brewing Company
Surrey, BC....604-599-1190
S&P
Mill Valley, CA....800-935-2337
Saint Arnold Brewing Company
Houston, TX....713-686-9494
San Andreas Brewing Company
Hollister, CA....831-637-7074
San Francisco Brewing Company
San Francisco, CA....415-434-3344
Santa Cruz Brewing Company
Santa Cruz, CA....831-429-8838
Santa Fe Brewing
Santa Fe, NM....505-424-3333
Sapporo
New York, NY....800-827-8234
Schafley Tap Room
St Louis, MO....314-241-2337
Schirf Brewing Company
Park City, UT....435-649-0900
Sea Dog Brewing Company
Bangor, ME....207-947-8004
Seven Barrell Brewery
West Lebanon, NH....603-298-5566
Shipyard Brewing Company
Portland, ME....207-761-0807
Sierra Nevada Brewing Company
Chico, CA....530-345-2739
Sleeman Breweries
Delta, BC....604-940-2887
Sleeman Brewing & Malting Company
Guelph, ON....800-268-8537
Smuttynose Brewing
Portsmouth, NH....603-436-4026
Snake River Brewing Company
Jackson, WY....307-739-2337
Southern California Brewing Company
Torrance, CA....310-329-8881
Spaten West
S San Francisco, CA....650-794-0800
Spoetzl Brewery
Shiner, TX....361-594-3383
Sprecher Brewing
Milwaukee, WI....888-650-2739
St. Croix Beer Company
Saint Paul, MN....651-387-0708
St. Stan's Brewing Company
Modesto, CA....209-524-2337
Star Creek Brewing Company
Dallas, TX....214-999-0999
Star Union Brewing Company
Hennepin, IL....815-925-7400
Stevens Point Brewery
Stevens Point, WI....800-369-4911
Stoudt Brewing Company
Adamstown, PA....717-484-4387
Straub Brewery Industries
St Marys, PA....814-834-2875
Sudwerk Privatbrauerei Hubsch
Davis, CA....530-758-8700
Summit Brewing Company
Saint Paul, MN....651-265-7800
Sweetwater Brewing Company
Atlanta, GA....404-691-2537
Tabernash Brewing Company
Longmont, CO....303-772-0258
Taos Trails Brewery
Ranchos De Taos, NM....505-758-0099
Thymly Products
Colora, MD....410-658-4820
Tin Wistle
Penticton, BC....250-770-1122
Toro Brewing
Morgan Hill, CA....408-778-2739
Trafalgar Brewing Company
Oakville, ON....905-337-0133
Triple Rock Brewing Company
Berkeley, CA....510-549-5999
Triumph Brewing Company
Princeton, NJ....609-924-7855
Troy Brewing Company
Troy, NY....518-273-2337
Tuscan Brewing
Red Bluff, CA....530-529-9318
Uinta Brewing
Salt Lake City, UT....801-467-0909
Unibroue/Unibrew
Chambly, QC....450-658-7658
Vancouver Island Brewing Company
Victoria, BC....250-361-0007
Vino's
Little Rock, AR....501-375-8466
Wachusett Brewing Company
Westminster, MA....978-874-9965
Wagner Vineyards
Lodi, NY....866-924-6378
Wellington Brewing
Guelph, ON....800-576-3853
Westside Brewing Company
New York, NY....212-721-2161
What's Brewing
San Antonio, TX....210-648-6470
Whistler Brewing Company
Burnaby, BC....604-438-2337
Whistler Brewing Company
Vancouver, BC....604-932-6185
Whitefish Brewing
Whitefish, MT....406-862-2684
Widmer Brothers Brewing Company
Portland, OR....503-281-2437
William B. Reily & Company
Baltimore, MD....410-675-9550
Wilson Corn Products
Rochester, IN....574-223-3177
Yakima Brewing Company
Yakima, WA....509-575-1900
Yellow Rose Brewing Company
San Antonio, TX....210-496-6669
Yuengling Brewery
Pottsville, PA....570-622-4141

American & British Ale

Amber Ale

Grand Teton Brewing
Victor, ID....888-899-1656
Pete's Brewing Company
San Antonio, TX....800-877-7383
Saint Arnold Brewing Company
Houston, TX....713-686-9494

Black & Tan

DG Yuengling & Son
Pottsville, PA....570-622-4141

Cream Ale

Northern Lights Brewing Company
Airway Heights, WA....509-244-4909

English Style B
Catamount Brewing Company
Windsor, VT 802-674-6700

India Pale Ale
Saint Arnold Brewing Company
Houston, TX 713-686-9494

Pale Ale
DG Yuengling & Son
Pottsville, PA. 570-622-4141
Northern Lights Brewing Company
Airway Heights, WA. 509-244-4909
Pete's Brewing Company
San Antonio, TX 800-877-7383

Belgian & French Ale

Kolsch
Saint Arnold Brewing Company
Houston, TX 713-686-9494

Bottled
Arizona Beverage Company
New Hyde Park, NY 800-832-3775
August Schell Brewing Company
New Ulm, MN. 800-770-5020
Catamount Brewing Company
Windsor, VT 802-674-6700
DG Yuengling & Son
Pottsville, PA. 570-622-4141
Jones Brewing Company
Smithton, PA. 800-237-2337
Molson Coors Brewing
Denver, CO 800-642-6116
Spaten Beer
Little Neck, NY 718-281-1912
Straub Brewery Industries
St Marys, PA 814-834-2875

Canned
Arizona Beverage Company
New Hyde Park, NY 800-832-3775
Jones Brewing Company
Smithton, PA. 800-237-2337
Molson Coors Brewing
Denver, CO 800-642-6116

Kegged
Bohemian Brewery
Midvale, UT 801-566-5474
DG Yuengling & Son
Pottsville, PA. 570-622-4141
Jones Brewing Company
Smithton, PA. 800-237-2337

Lager

Amber Lager
DG Yuengling & Son
Pottsville, PA. 570-622-4141
Karl Strauss Breweries
San Diego, CA 858-273-2739

Bock
Saint Arnold Brewing Company
Houston, TX 713-686-9494

DarkLager/Dunkel
Brick Brewery
Waterloo, ON 800-505-8971

Malt Liquor
Bad Frog Brewing
Saint Augustine, FL 888-223-3764
Jones Brewing Company
Smithton, PA. 800-237-2337
Miller Brewing Company
Milwaukee, WI 414-931-2000

Pilsner
Anderson Valley Brewing
Boonville, CA. 707-895-2337

Saint Arnold Brewing Company
Houston, TX 713-686-9494

Non-Alcoholic
B.M. Lawrence & Company
San Francisco, CA 415-981-3650
Coors Brewing Company
Golden, CO 800-642-6116
Jones Brewing Company
Smithton, PA. 800-237-2337
Lion Brewery
Wilkes Barre, PA 800-233-8327
Miller Brewing Company
Milwaukee, WI 414-931-2000
Molson Coors Brewing
Denver, CO 800-642-6116
Richland Beverage Associates
Carrollton, TX. 214-357-0248
Safeway Dairy Products
Walnut Creek, CA 925-944-4000

Specialty &Cider

Reduced Calorie Beer
DG Yuengling & Son
Pottsville, PA. 570-622-4141

Stout & Porter

Flavored Stout
Saint Arnold Brewing Company
Houston, TX 713-686-9494

Porter
DG Yuengling & Son
Pottsville, PA. 570-622-4141

Sweet Stout
Pete's Brewing Company
San Antonio, TX. 800-877-7383

Wheat

Wheat Ale
Alley Kat Brewing Company
Edmonton, AB 780-436-8922
Grand Teton Brewing
Victor, ID. 888-899-1656

Bitters
Fee Brothers
Rochester, NY 800-961-3337
Flora
Lynden, WA. 800-446-2110
Instantwhip: Florida
Tampa, FL. 813-621-3233
Kittling Ridge Estate Wines & Spirits
Grimsby, ON 905-945-9225

Cocoa & Chocolate Drinks

Chocolate Drinks
America's Best Beverage Company
Whitestone, NY 800-736-7338
Central Coca-Cola Bottling Company
Richmond, VA. 800-359-3759
North American Beverage Company
Ocean City, NJ 609-399-1486
Richard's Gourmet Coffee
West Bridgewater, MA 800-370-2633
Seller Kirk & Company
Schwenksville, PA 215-480-7342
Yoo-Hoo Chocolate Beverage Company
Carlstadt, NJ 201-933-0070

Hot Chocolate
Elegant Gourmet
Kirkland, WA 425-814-2500
Gourmet Village
Morin Heights, QC 800-668-2314
S.J. McCullagh
Buffalo, NY. 800-753-3473

Hot Cocoa
Associated Brands
Toronto, ON 800-265-0050
Brewfresh Coffee Company
South Salt Lake, UT 888-486-3334
Caffe D'Amore Gourmet Beverages
Monrovia, CA 800-999-0171
Chatz Roasting Company
Ceres, CA 800-792-6333
Chicago Coffee Roastery
Huntley, IL 800-762-5402
Coffee Masters
Spring Grove, IL. 800-334-6485
Country Choice Naturals
Eden Prairie, MN 952-829-8824
Flavor Innovations
South Plainfield, NJ 800-536-2030
Gloria Jean's Gourmet Coffees
Rcho Sta Marg, CA. 800-354-5258
Jenny's Country Kitchen
Dover, MN 800-357-3497
Mama Lee's Gourmet Hot Chocolate
Nashville, TN 888-626-2533
Nantucket Tea Traders
Nantucket, MA 508-325-0203
Neighbors Coffee
Oklahoma City, OK 800-299-9016
Nestle USA Inc
Glendale, CA 800-633-2330
Northwestern Foods
St Paul, MN. 800-236-4937
Omanhene Cocoa Bean Company
Milwaukee, WI 800-588-2462
Royal Coffee & Tea Company
Mississauga, ON 800-667-6226
S&D Coffee, Inc
Concord, NC 704-339-0917
S.J. McCullagh
Buffalo, NY. 800-753-3473
Sara Lee Corporation
Downers Grove, IL 630-598-8100
Sara Lee Foodservice
Rolling Meadows, IL 847-595-6000
Seller Kirk & Company
Schwenksville, PA 215-480-7342
Stephen's Gourmet Kitchens
Farmington, UT 800-845-2400
Subco Foods Inc
West Chicago, IL 630-231-0003
Swagger Foods Corporation
Vernon Hills, IL 847-913-1200
Techni-Brew International
Portland, OR 800-454-4077
White Coffee Corporation
Long Island City, NY 800-221-0140

with Marshmallows
Snapple Beverage Group
Port Chester, NY 800-762-7753
Todd's
Des Moines, IA. 800-247-5363

Milo
Archer Daniels Midland Company
Decatur, IL 800-637-5843

Coffee & Tea
A Southern Season
Chapel Hill, NC 800-253-5317
Amelia Bay Beverage Systems
Alpharetta, GA 800-650-8327
Aroma Coffee Company
Forest Park, IL 708-488-8340

Atlanta Bread Company International, Inc.
Smyrna, GA 800-398-3728
Borgnine Beverage Company
Sherman Oaks, CA 818-501-5312
Burke Brands
Miami, FL 877-436-6722
Fairwinds Gourmet Coffee
Auburn, NH 800-645-4515
La Crema Coffee Company
West Chester, OH 513-779-6278
Massimo Zanetti Beverage Company
Suffolk, VA 757-538-8083
Point Group
Satellite Beach, FL 888-272-1249
Queen City Coffee Company
West Chester, OH 800-487-7460
R C Bigelow
Fairfield, CT 800-243-5587
Sara Lee Coffee & Tea
Earth City, MO 314-731-2500
Sara Lee Coffee & Tea   Wholesale Coffee & Tea Location
Minneapolis, MN 888-246-2598
Tetley Tea
Shelton, CT 800-728-0084
Texas Spice Company
Cedar Park, TX 800-880-8007
Zephyr Hills Bottled Watter Corporation
Tampa, FL 800-950-9398

Cappuccino

Advance Food Brokers
West Bloomfield, MI 248-851-9045
Agropur Cooperative Agro-Alimentaire
Granby, QC 800-363-5686
Alljuice
Hendersonville, NC 800-736-5674
Aloe'Ha Drink Products
Houston, TX 713-978-6359
American Instants
Flanders, NJ 973-584-8811
Anheuser-Busch
Cartersville, GA 770-386-2000
Aquafina
Wichita, KS 316-522-4100
Arcadia Dairy Farms
Arden, NC 828-684-3556
Arctic Beverages
Flin Flon, MB 204-687-7517
Atlanta Coffee & Tea Company
Decatur, GA 800-426-4781
Autocrat Coffee & Extracts
Lincoln, RI 800-288-6272
Baltimore Brewing Company
Baltimore, MD 410-837-5000
Barbe's Dairy
Westwego, LA 504-347-6201
Beacon Drive In
Spartanburg, SC 864-585-9387
Bear Brewing Company
Kamloops, BC 250-851-2543
Beaulieu Vineyard
Rutherford, CA 800-264-6918
Beaver Street Brewery
Flagstaff, AZ 928-779-0079
Beckman & Gast Company
St Henry, OH 419-678-4195
Belmar Spring Water Company
Glen Rock, NJ 201-444-1010
Better Beverages
Cerritos, CA 562-924-8321
Bigelow Tea
Shelton, CT 800-235-7072
Blenheim Bottling Company
Hamer, SC 800-270-9344
Blue Chip Group
Salt Lake City, UT 800-878-0099
Boissons Miami Pomor
Longueuil, QC 877-977-3744
Bottle Green Drinks Company
Mississauga, ON 905-273-6137
Bow Valley Brewing Company
Canmore, AB 403-678-2739
Brasserie Brasel Brewery
Lasalle, QC 800-463-2728
Brenntag
Reading, PA 888-926-4151
Bunge Beverage & Dairy Ingredients
St Louis, MO 314-292-2000
Caffe D'Oro
Chino, CA 800-200-5005

Caffe D'Vita
Chino, CA 800-200-5005
California Dairies
Fresno, CA 559-233-5154
Campbell Soup Company
Camden, NJ 800-257-8443
Celestial Seasonings Teas
Boulder, CO 303-530-5300
Chicago Coffee Roastery
Huntley, IL 800-762-5402
Christie Food Products
Randolph, NJ 800-727-2523
Clark Spring Water Company
Pueblo, CO 719-543-1594
Clipper Spring Brewing
Baltimore, MD 410-247-7822
Coca-Cola Bottling Company
Brampton, ON 800-926-5301
Cold Spring Brewing Company
Cold Spring, MN 320-685-8686
Coleman Dairy
Little Rock, AR 501-748-1700
Columbia Brewery
Creston, BC 250-428-9344
Compact Industries
St Charles, IL 800-513-4262
Consolidated Mills
Houston, TX 713-896-4196
Cott Beverage West
Calgary, AB 403-279-6677
Cream O'Weaver Dairy
Salt Lake City, UT 801-973-9922
Creemore Springs Brewery
Creemore, ON 800-267-2240
Creme D'Lite
Dallas, TX 214-637-1010
Crosby Molasses Company
St. John, NB 506-634-7515
Crystal Foods
Brick, NJ 732-477-0073
Dean Dairy Products
Sharpsville, PA 800-942-8096
Dean Foods Company
Dallas, TX 214-303-3400
Dean Milk Company
Louisville, KY 800-451-3326
Decoty Coffee Company
San Angelo, TX 800-588-8001
Del Monte Foods
San Francisco, CA 800-543-3090
Delta Distributors
Longview, TX 800-945-1858
Dogfish Head Craft Brewery
Lewes, DE 888-834-3474
Energy Drinks
West Hempstead, NY 516-481-0872
Ensemble Beverages
Montgomery, AL 334-324-7719
Faygo Beverages
Detroit, MI 800-347-6591
Flora
Lynden, WA 800-446-2110
Florida Natural Flavors
Casselberry, FL 800-872-5979
Florida's Natural Brand
Lake Wales, FL 888-657-6600
Foster Farms Dairy
Fresno, CA 800-241-0008
Fresh Juice Company
Newark, NJ 973-465-7100
Fresh Samantha
Saco, ME 800-658-4635
Freshco
Stuart, FL 772-595-0070
G A Food Service
St Petersburg, FL 727-573-2211
G H Ford Tea Company
Wappingers Falls, NY 845-298-8900
Gerhart Coffee Company
Lancaster, PA 800-536-4310
Ghirardelli Chocolate Company
Short Hills, NJ 800-877-9338
Golden Drop
Los Angeles, CA 323-225-9161
Great Lakes Brewing
Etobicoke, ON 800-463-5435
Great Northern Brewing Company
Whitefish, MT 406-863-1000
Great Western Brewing Company
Saskatoon, SK 800-764-4492
Gulf States Canners
Clinton, MS 601-924-0511

Halifax Group
Doraville, GA 770-452-8828
Hansen's Juices
Azusa, CA 626-812-6022
Healthmate Products
Highland Park, IL 800-584-8642
Heritage Foods
Santa Ana, CA 714-775-5000
Hobarama Corporation
Miami, FL 880-439-2295
Hogtown Brewing Company
Mississauga, ON 905-855-9065
Honickman Affiliates
Pennsauken, NJ 800-573-7745
Humboldt Creamery Association
Fortuna, CA 707-725-6182
Hygeia Dairy Company
McAllen, TX 956-686-0511
Icy Bird
Sparta, TN 931-738-3557
Ideal American
Holland, IN 812-424-3351
Ideal Dairy
Richfield, UT 435-896-5061
IMS Food Service
Shelton, CT 800-235-7072
INCA Kola Golden Kola
Bloomfield, NJ 973-680-9700
Jianlibao America
New York, NY 800-526-1688
Key Colony/Red Parrot Juices
Lyons, IL 800-424-0868
King's Cupboard
Red Lodge, MT 800-962-6555
Knoll Creek Dairy
Harrison, NY 718-892-4500
Labatt Breweries
Edmonton, AB 800-268-2997
Lacto Milk Products Corporation
Flemington, NJ 908-788-2200
Lake Country Foods
Oconomowoc, WI 262-567-5521
Lakefront Brewery
Milwaukee, WI 414-372-8800
Land O'Pines Company
Lufkin, TX 936-634-5537
LeHigh Valley Dairies
Lansdale, PA 215-855-8205
Louis Trauth Dairy
Newport, KY 800-544-6455
Lucerne Foods
Taber, AB 403-223-3546
M.A. Gedney
Chaska, MN 952-448-2612
Mafco Natural Products
Richmond, VA 804-222-1600
Magic Valley Quality Milk Producers
Jerome, ID 208-324-7519
Makers Mark Distillery
Loretto, KY 270-865-2881
Mama Lee's Gourmet Hot Chocolate
Nashville, TN 888-626-2533
Maola Milk & Ice Cream Company
New Bern, NC 252-638-1131
Martin Coffee Company
Jacksonville, FL 904-355-9661
McArthur Dairy
Miami, FL 877-803-6565
McCain Foods Canada
Florenceville, NB 506-392-5541
McCormick Ingredients
Hunt Valley, MD 800-632-5847
Meadow Gold Dairy
Lewiston, ID 208-746-9006
Mendocino Brewing Company
Ukiah, CA 707-463-2087
MEYENBERG Goat Milk Products
Turlock, CA 800-891-4628
Miller Brewing Company
St Louis, MO 314-822-5483
Miller Brewing Company
Eden, NC 336-635-1198
Miller Brewing Company
Milwaukee, WI 414-931-2000
Miller Brewing Company
Bellevue, WA 425-641-6775
Miller Brewing Company
Edison, NJ 732-635-1400
Miller Brewing Company
Fort Worth, TX 800-645-5376
Miller Brewing Company
Trenton, OH 800-944-5483

Miller Brewing Company
Elk Grove Vlg, IL..................847-758-9941
Millstream Brewing
Amana, IA.........................319-622-3672
Minute Maid Company
Bombay, BC.......................800-438-2653
Minute Maid Company
Houston, TX.......................888-884-8952
Monticello Cellars
Napa, CA..........................707-253-2802
Moosehead Breweries
St. John, NB.......................506-635-7000
Neighbors Coffee
Oklahoma City, OK..............800-299-9016
Nestle Canada Inc
North York, ON...................800-563-7853
Noel Corporation
Yakima, WA.......................509-248-1313
Nor-Cal Beverage Company
West Sacramento, CA.............916-374-2621
Northumberland Cooperative
Miramichi, NB....................800-332-3328
Northwestern Foods
St Paul, MN.......................800-236-4937
NSpired Natural Foods
Melville, NY......................631-845-4689
Oak Farms
Dallas, TX........................214-941-0302
Oak Farms
San Antonio, TX..................800-292-2169
Ocean Spray Cranberries
Middleboro, MA...................508-946-1000
Ocean Spray Cranberries
Middleboro, MA...................800-662-3263
Ojai Cook
Los Angeles, CA...................886-571-1551
Olympic Foods
Spokane, WA.......................509-455-8059
Our Thyme Garden
Cleburne, TX......................800-482-4372
Peace River Citrus Products
Arcadia, FL.......................863-494-0440
Pennsylvania Brewing Company
Pittsburgh, PA....................412-237-9400
Pepsi Bottling Group Canada
Mississauga, ON...................800-387-9546
Pepsi-Cola Canada
Winnipeg, NB......................800-387-9546
PepsiAmericas
Fort Wayne, IN....................800-388-2235
Portland Brewing Company
Portland, OR......................503-226-7623
Premier Blending
Wichita, KS.......................316-267-5533
Premium Waters
Minneapolis, MN..................800-332-3332
Price's Creameries
El Paso, TX.......................915-565-2711
Quaker Oats Company
Dallas, TX........................214-330-8681
Quality Naturally! Foods
City of Industry, CA..............888-498-6986
Randag & Associates Inc
Elmhurst, IL......................630-530-2830
Redco Foods
Windsor, CT.......................800-645-1190
Redwood Vintners
Novato, CA........................415-892-6949
Richard's Gourmet Coffee
West Bridgewater, MA............800-370-2633
Royale International   Beverage Co Inc
Davenport, IA.....................563-386-5222
Saint Albans CooperativeCreamy
Saint Albans, VT..................800-559-0343
San Marco Coffee,Inc.
Charlotte, NC.....................800-715-9298
Sandusky Cooperative Milk Producers Association
Castalia, OH......................419-684-5812
Santa Cruz Brewing Company
Santa Cruz, CA....................831-429-8838
Sapporo
New York, NY.....................800-827-8234
Sara Lee Coffee & Tea
Earth City, MO....................314-731-2500
Sara Lee Coffee & Tea   Wholesale Coffee & Tea
Location
Minneapolis, MN..................888-246-2598
Sara Lee Foodservice
Rolling Meadows, IL..............800-261-4754
Schepps Dairy
Dallas, TX........................800-428-6455

Scotsburn Dairy Group
Truro, NS.........................902-895-4412
Sebastiani Vineyards
Sonoma, CA.......................800-888-5532
Shipyard Brewing Company
Portland, ME......................207-761-0807
Smucker Quality Beverages
Havre De Grace, MD...............410-939-1403
Smucker Quality Beverages
Chico, CA.........................530-899-5000
Southeast Canners
Columbus, GA.....................706-324-0040
Southern Gardens Citrus Processing
Clewiston, FL.....................863-983-3030
Southern Heritage Coffee Company
Indianapolis, IN..................800-486-1198
Steelback Brewery
Tiverton, ON......................800-879-0541
Stephen's Gourmet Kitchens
Farmington, UT...................800-845-2400
Stewart's Beverages
White Plains, NY..................914-397-9200
Swiss Dairy
Riverside, CA.....................951-898-9427
Swiss Valley Farms Company
Dubuque, IA......................800-397-9156
Tabernash Brewing Company
Longmont, CO.....................303-772-0258
Taos Brewing Supply
Santa Fe, NM......................505-983-0505
Tianfu China Cola
Katonah, NY......................914-232-3102
Tonex
Wallington, NJ....................973-773-5135
Tova Industries
Louisville, KY.....................888-532-8682
Tri-States Coca-Cola Bottling Company
Cincinnati, OH....................800-543-2653
Triple H Food Processors
Riverside, CA.....................951-352-5700
True Beverages
O Fallon, MO......................800-325-6152
Turner Dairies
Jackson, TN.......................731-427-6012
Tuscan Dairy Farms
Dallas, TX........................800-526-4416
Ultra Seal
New Paltz, NY.....................845-255-2496
Unibroue/Unibrew
Chambly, QC......................450-658-7658
Unilever Canada
Toronto, ON.......................416-964-1857
United Dairy
Uniontown, PA....................800-966-6455
Virgil's Root Beer
Los Angeles, CA...................800-997-3337
Warren Laboratories
Abbott, TX........................800-421-2563
WestFarm Foods
Seattle, WA.......................206-286-6832
WestFarm Foods
Seattle, WA.......................509-837-8000
Winder Dairy
West Valley, UT...................800-946-3371
Yosemite Waters
Los Angeles, CA...................800-427-8420

Coffee

Alakef Coffee Roasters
Duluth, MN.......................800-438-9228
Alaska Coffee Company
Anchorage, AK....................907-333-3626
Alexander & Baldwin
Honolulu, HI......................808-525-6611
All Goode Organics
Santa Barbara, CA.................805-683-3370
Allann Brothers Coffee Company
Albany, OR........................800-926-6886
Allegro Coffee Company
Thornton, CO.....................800-666-4869
Alpen Sierra Coffee Company
Minden, NV.......................800-531-1405
Alpine Coffee Roasters
Leavenworth, WA.................800-246-2761
America's Best Beverage Company
Whitestone, NY...................800-736-7338
American Coffee Company
New Orleans, LA..................800-554-7234
American Food & Equipment
Miami, FL.........................305-361-6517

Ancora Coffee Roasters
Madison, WI......................800-260-0217
Andresen Ryan Coffee Com
Superior, WI......................715-395-3793
Anke Kruse Organics
Guelph, ON.......................519-824-6161
Arbuckle Coffee
Pittsburgh, PA....................800-533-8278
Armenia Coffee Corporation
Purchase, NY.....................914-694-6100
Armeno Coffee Roasters
Northborough, MA................508-393-2821
Aroma Coffee Roasters
Hoboken, NJ......................201-792-1730
Aroma Ridge
Marietta, GA......................800-528-2123
Artist Coffee
Londonderry, NH.................866-440-4511
Astor Products
Jacksonville, FL...................904-783-5000
Atlanta Coffee Roasters
Atlanta, GA.......................800-252-8211
Atlantic
New York, NY.....................212-480-2255
Austin Chase Coffee
Seattle, WA.......................888-502-2333
Avalon Foodservice, Inc.
Canal Fulton, OH.................800-362-0622
Avalon Organic Coffees
Albuquerque, NM.................800-662-2575
B.B. Bean Coffee
Monument, CO....................719-481-1170
B.K. Coffee
Oneonta, NY......................800-432-1499
Baby's Coffee
Key West, FL......................800-523-2326
Back Bay Trading
Alpharetta, GA....................800-650-8327
Baltimore Coffee & Tea Company
Timonium, MD....................800-823-1408
Barefoot Contessa Pantry
York, ME..........................207-351-2713
Barnie's Coffee & Tea Company
Orlando, FL.......................800-284-1416
Baronet Coffee
Hartford, CT......................800-227-6638
Barrie House Gourmet Coffee
Yonkers, NY......................800-876-2233
Barrington Coffee Roasting Company
Lee, MA...........................800-528-0998
Batdorf and Bronson Roasters
Olympia, WA......................800-955-5282
Bay View Farm
Honaunau, HI.....................800-662-5880
Bean Forge
Coos Bay, OR.....................888-292-1632
Benbow's Coffee Roasters
Bar Harbor, ME...................207-288-5271
Berardi's Fresh Roast
Cleveland, OH....................800-876-9109
Big Train
Foothill Ranch, CA................800-244-8724
Blackbear Coffee Company
Hendersonville, NC...............828-692-6333
Blaser & Wolthers Specialty
Miami, FL.........................305-374-7111
Boston's Best Coffee Roasters
South Easton, MA.................800-323-4889
Bountiful Pantry
Nantucket, MA....................888-832-6466
Boyd Coffee Company
Portland, OR......................800-545-4077
Boyer Coffee Company
Denver, CO........................800-452-5282
Breakfast at Brennan's
New Orleans, LA..................800-888-9932
Brewfresh Coffee Company
South Salt Lake, UT...............888-486-3334
Bridgetown Coffee
Portland, OR......................800-726-0320
Brisk Coffee Company
Tampa, FL.........................800-899-5282
Broad Street Coffee Roasers
Durham, NC.......................800-733-9916
Brown & Jenkins Trading Company
Cambridge, VT....................800-456-5282
Buckmaster Coffee
Hillsboro, OR.....................800-962-9148
Bucks County Coffee Company
Langhorne, PA....................800-844-8790
Bull Run Roasting Company
Hayward, WI......................715-634-3646

Bustelo Coffee Roasting Company
Miami, FL 305-592-7302
BuyWell Coffee
Colorado Springs, CO. 719-598-7870
Cadillac Coffee Company
Madison Heights, MI 800-438-6900
Cafe Appassionato Coffee Company
Seattle, WA 888-522-2333
Cafe Cartago
Denver, CO 800-443-8666
Cafe Del Mundo
Anchorage, AK 907-562-2326
Cafe Descafeinado de Chiapas
Doral, FL 305-499-9775
Cafe Du Monde
New Orleans, LA 504-587-0835
Cafe La Semeuse
Brooklyn, NY 800-242-6333
Cafe Moak
Rockford, MI 800-757-8776
Cafe Moto
San Diego, CA 800-818-3363
Cafe Salvador
San Francisco, CA 415-751-7630
Cafe Society Coffee Company
Dallas, TX. 800-717-6000
Cafe Sol de Oro International
Toronto, ON 416-322-8182
Cafe Yaucono/Jimenez & Fernandez
Santurce, PR 787-721-3337
Caffe D'Oro
Chino, CA 800-200-5005
Caffe Darte
Seattle, WA 800-999-5334
Caffe Luca
Tukwila, WA 800-728-9116
Caffe Trieste Superb Coffees
San Francisco, CA 415-550-1107
Cajun Creole Products
New Iberia, LA 800-946-8688
Cal Trading Company
Burlingame, CA 650-697-4615
Cape Cod Coffee Roasters
Mashpee, MA 508-477-2400
Capricorn Coffees
San Francisco, CA 800-541-0758
Captain Cook Coffee Company
Captain Cook, HI 808-322-2087
Caracollillo Coffee Mills
Tampa, FL 800-682-0023
Caravan Company
Worcester, MA 508-752-3777
Caribbean Coffee Company
Santa Barbara, CA 805-962-3201
Caribou Coffee Company
Brooklyn Center, MN 888-227-4268
Carrabassett Coffee Roasters
Kingfield, ME 888-292-2326
Cascade Coffee
Everett, WA 425-347-3995
Cave Creek Coffee Company
Cave Creek, AZ 480-488-0603
Central Coast Coffee Roasting
Los Osos, CA 800-382-6837
Chatz Roasting Company
Ceres, CA 800-792-6333
Chauvin Coffee Corporation
St Louis, MO. 800-455-5282
Chicago Coffee Roastery
Huntley, IL 800-762-5402
Chock Full O'Nuts
, NY 888-246-2598
City Bean
Stevenson Ranch, CA 888-248-9232
Clayton's Coffee & Tea
Modesto, CA. 209-522-7811
Clean Foods
Santa Paula, CA 800-526-8328
Clear Mountain Coffee Company
Silver Spring, MD. 301-587-2233
Clearwater Coffee Company
Lake Zurich, IL 847-540-7711
Cobraz Brazilian Coffee
New York, NY 212-759-7700
Coca-Cola Enterprises
Atlanta, GA 800-233-7210
Coffee & Tea
Bloomington, MN 952-853-1148
Coffee Associates
Edgewater, NJ 201-945-1060
Coffee Barrel
Okemos, MI 517-349-3888

Coffee Bean
Englewood, CO. 303-922-1238
Coffee Bean & Tea Leaf
Los Angeles, CA 800-832-5323
Coffee Bean International
Portland, OR 800-877-0474
Coffee Bean of Leesburg
Leesburg, VA 800-232-6872
Coffee Beanery
Flushing, MI 800-728-2326
Coffee Brothers
Colton, NC 888-443-5282
Coffee Butler Service
Alexandria, VA 703-823-0028
Coffee Concepts
Dallas, TX. 214-363-9331
Coffee Creations
Portland, OR 800-245-5856
Coffee Creations
Lahaina, HI 808-575-9735
Coffee Culture-A House
Lincoln, NE. 402-438-8456
Coffee Exchange
Providence, RI 800-263-3339
Coffee Express Company
Plymouth, MI 800-466-9000
Coffee Holding Company
Brooklyn, NY 800-458-2233
Coffee Masters
Spring Grove, IL 800-334-6485
Coffee Masters
Barrington, IL 847-382-9786
Coffee Mill Roastery
Elon, NC 800-729-1727
Coffee Mill Roasting Company
Sudbury, ON 705-525-2700
Coffee Millers & Roasting
Cape Coral, FL 239-573-6800
Coffee People
Beaverton, OR 800-354-5282
Coffee Process Technology
Houston, TX 713-695-7530
Coffee Reserve
Phoenix, AZ 623-434-0939
Coffee Roasters
Oakland, NJ 201-337-8221
Coffee Roasters of New Orleans
New Orleans, LA 800-737-5464
Coffee Up
Chicago, IL 847-288-9330
Coffee Works
Sacramento, CA 800-275-3335
College Coffee Roasters
Mountville, PA 717-285-9561
Colonial Coffee Roasters
Miami, FL 305-638-0885
Columbia Coffee & Tea Company
Weston, ON. 416-745-4235
Comfort Food's
North Andover, MA 978-557-0009
Community Coffee Specialty
Baton Rouge, LA 800-525-5583
Compass Foods/Eight O'Clock Coffee
Montvale, NJ. 800-299-2739
Condaxis Coffee Company
Jacksonville, FL 904-356-5330
Continental Coffee Products Company
Houston, TX 800-323-6178
Corim International Coffee
Brick, NJ 800-942-4201
Country Pure Foods
Akron, OH 877-995-8423
Cupper's Coffee Company
Lethbridge, AB 403-380-4555
Custom House Coffee Roasters
Miami, FL 888-563-5282
Dallis Brothers
Jamaica, NY 800-424-4252
David Rio Coffee & Tea
San Francisco, CA 800-454-9605
Daybreak Coffee Roasters
Glastonbury, CT 800-882-5282
Daymar Select Fine Coffees
El Cajon, CA. 800-466-7590
Dazbog Coffee Company
Denver, CO 303-892-9999
De Coty Coffee Company
San Angelo, TX 800-588-8001
De Lima Company
Syracuse, NY 800-962-8864
Decoy Coffee Company
San Angelo, TX 800-588-8001

Diedrich Coffee
Irvine, CA 800-354-5282
Dillanos Coffee Roasters
Sumner, WA 800-234-5282
Distant Lands Coffee Roaster
Tyler, TX. 800-346-5459
DMH Ingredients
Libertyville, IL 847-362-9977
Don Francisco Coffee Traders
Los Angeles, CA 800-697-5282
Don Hilario Estate Coffee
Tampa, FL 800-799-1903
Downeast Coffee
Pawtucket, RI 800-922-6287
Droubi's Imports
Houston, TX 713-988-7138
Eagle Coffee Company
Baltimore, MD 800-545-4015
East India Coffee & Tea Company
San Leandro, CA 800-829-1300
East Indies Coffee & Tea Company
Lebanon, PA 800-220-2326
El Dorado Coffee
Flushing, NY 800-635-2566
Eldorado Coffee Distributors
New Orleans, LA 504-949-8416
Ellis Coffee Company
Philadelphia, PA 800-822-3984
Equal Exchange
West Bridgewater, MA 774-776-7400
Erba Food Products
Brooklyn, NY 718-272-7700
Espresso Vivace
Seattle, WA 206-860-5869
European Coffee
Cherry Hill, NJ 856-428-7202
European Roasterie
Le Center, MN 888-469-2233
Evco Wholesale Foods
Emporia, KS 620-343-7000
Excellent Coffee Company
Pawtucket, RI 800-345-2007
Excelso Coffee Company
Norcross, GA 800-241-2138
F Gavina & Sons Inc
Vernon, CA 800-428-4627
F. Gavina & Sons
Vernon, CA 323-582-0671
Fama Sales
New York, NY 212-757-9433
Farmer Brothers Company
Torrance, CA. 800-735-2878
FCC Coffee Packers
Doral, FL 305-591-1128
Ferrara Bakery & Cafe
New York, NY 212-226-6150
Fidalgo Bay Coffee
Burlington, WA. 800-310-5540
Fine Foods Northwest
Seattle, WA 800-862-3965
First Colony Coffee & Tea Company
Norfolk, VA. 800-446-8555
First Roasters of Central Florida
Longwood, FL 407-699-6364
Folgers Coffee Company
Orrville, OH 877-693-6543
Foltz Coffee Tea & Spice Company
New Orleans, LA 504-486-1545
Fratello Coffee
Calgary, AB 800-465-7227
Freed, Teller & Freed
Burlingame, CA 800-370-7371
Fresh Roast Systems
Petaluma, CA 707-763-1050
Frontier Natural Co-op
Norway, IA 303-449-8137
Gadsden Coffee/Caffe
Arivaca, AZ. 888-514-5282
Gardner's Gourmet
Fremont, CA 800-676-8558
George H Hathaway Coffee Company
Summit Argo, IL 708-458-7668
Gerhart Coffee Company
Lancaster, PA 800-536-4310
Global Food Industries
Townville, SC 800-225-4152
Globus Coffee
Manhasset, NY 516-304-5780
Gloria Jean's Gourmet Coffees
Rcho Sta Marg, CA 800-354-5258
Godiva Chocolatier
New York, NY 800-946-3482

Gold Star Coffee Company
Salem, MA 888-505-5233
Gondwanaland
Corrales, NM 505-899-5660
GPR Company
Stowe, PA 610-326-4777
Green Mountain Chocolates
Franklin, MA 508-520-7160
Greene Brothers Specialty Coffee Roaster
Hackettstown, NJ 908-979-0022
Greenwell Farms
Morganfield, KY 270-389-3289
Haas Coffee Group
Miami, FL 305-371-7473
Harold L. King & Company
Redwood City, CA 888-368-2233
Has Beans Coffee & Tea Company
Mount Shasta, CA 800-427-2326
Hawaii Coffee Company
Honolulu, HI 800-338-8353
Hawaiian Isles Kona Coffee Co
Honolulu, HI 808-833-2244
Hena Coffee
Brooklyn, NY 718-272-8237
Herbal Coffee International
Jacksonville Beach, FL 800-743-8774
Heritage Northwest
Juneau, AK 907-586-1088
High Coffee Corporation
Houston, TX 713-465-2230
High Rise Coffee Roasters
Colorado Springs, CO 719-633-1833
Hill of Beans Coffee Roasters
Los Angeles, CA 888-527-6278
Hillsboro Coffee Company
Tampa, FL 813-877-2126
Home Roast Coffee
Lutz, FL 813-949-0807
Hood River Coffee Company
Hood River, OR 800-336-2954
House of Coffee Beans
Houston, TX 800-422-1799
House of Tsang
San Francisco, CA 415-282-9952
Ideal Distributing Company
Bothell, WA 425-488-6121

Indigo Coffee Roasters
Florence, MA 800-447-5450
Instant Products of America
Columbus, IN 812-372-9100
Inter-American Products
Cincinnati, OH 800-645-2233
Inter-Continental Imports Company
Newington, CT 800-424-4422
International Coffee Corporation
New Orleans, LA 504-586-8700
Internova
St Lambert-De-Levis, QC 418-889-9929
Interstate Foods
Lansing, MI 517-372-5500
Itoen
Honolulu, HI 808-847-4477
J.B. Peel Coffee Roasters
Red Hook, NY 800-231-7372
Jaguar Yerba Company
Ashland, OR 800-839-0775
Jamaica John
Franklin Park, IL 847-451-1730
Jamaican Gourmet Coffee Company
New Haven, CT 203-239-5633
James Finley & Company
Florham Park, NJ 973-539-8030
Jasper Products LLC
Joplin, MO 877-769-7367
Java Cabana
Miami, FL 305-592-7302
Java Jungle
Visalia, CA 559-732-5282
Java Sun Coffee Roasters
Marblehead, MA 781-631-7788
Java-Gourmet/Keuka Lake Coffee Roaster
Penn Yan, NY 888-478-2739
JBR Coffee & Tea
San Leandro, CA 800-829-1300
Jelks Coffee Roasters
Shreveport, LA 318-636-6391
Jenny's Country Kitchen
Dover, MN 800-357-3497
Jeremiah's Pick Coffee Company
San Francisco, CA 800-537-3642
John A. Vassilaros & Son
Flushing, NY 718-886-4140

John Conti Coffee Company
Louisville, KY 800-928-5282
Josuma Coffee Corporation
Menlo Park, CA 650-366-5453
Kaffe Magnum Opus
Vineland, NJ 800-652-5282
Kauai Coffee Company
Kalaheo, HI 800-545-8605
Keystone Coffee Company
San Jose, CA 408-998-2221
Kittridge & Fredrickson Fine Coffees
Portland, OR 800-558-7788
Kobricks Coffee Company
Jersey City, NJ 800-562-3662
Kona Coffee Council
Kealakekua, HI 808-323-2911
Kona Kava Coffee Company
Philo, CA 707-985-3913
Kona Premium Coffee Company
Keauhou, HI 888-322-9550
Kraft Foods
Northfield, IL 847-646-2000
La Costa Coffee Roasting
Carlsbad, CA 760-434-3233
La Vans Coffee Company
Bordentown, NJ 609-298-5400
Lacas Coffee Company
Pennsauken, NJ 800-220-1133
Lake Arrowhead
Twin Peaks, CA 877-237-8528
Landshire
Belleville, IL 618-398-8122
Larry's Beans Inc
Raleigh, NC 919-828-1234
Lavazza Premium Coffee Corporation
New York, NY 800-466-3287
Leavenworth Coffee Roast
Leavenworth, WA 800-246-2761
Lenson Coffee & Tea Company
Pleasantville, NJ 609-646-3003
Leroy Hill Coffee Company
Mobile, AL 800-866-5282
Lexington Coffee & Tea Company
Lexington, KY 859-277-1102
Lindsay's Tea
S San Francisco, CA 800-624-7031

Lingle Brothers Coffee
Bell Gardens, CA 562-927-3317
Lockcoffee
Larchmont, NY 914-273-7838
Lola Savannah
Houston, TX 888-663-9166
Long Expected Coffee Co mpany
Yonkers, NY 914-969-7933
Longbottom Coffee & Tea
Hillsboro, OR 800-288-1271
Longo Coffee & Tea
New York, NY 212-477-6783
Louis Dreyfus Corporation - Coffee Division
Wilton, CT 203-761-2000
Love Creek Orchards
Medina, TX 800-449-0882
Lowery's Premium Roast Coffee
Snohomish, WA 800-767-1783
M.E. Swing Company
Alexandria, VA 800-485-4019
Magnum Coffee Roastery
Nunica, MI 888-937-5282
Majestic Coffee & Tea
San Carlos, CA 650-591-5678
Manhattan Coffee Company
Earth City, MO 800-926-3333
Maui Coffee Roasters
Kahului, HI 800-645-2877
Maui's Kaanapali Estate Coffee
Lahaina, HI 808-661-1802
Mazzoli Coffee
Brooklyn, NY 718-259-6194
Melitta
Clearwater, FL 727-535-2111
Mercon Coffee Corporation
Hoboken, NJ 201-418-9400
Mills Coffee Roasting Company
Providence, RI 888-781-5282
Milone Brothers Coffee
Modesto, CA 800-974-8500
Moka D'Oro Coffee
Farmingdale, NY 888-665-2367
Monarch Beverage Company
Atlanta, GA 800-241-3732
Montana Coffee Traders
Whitefish, MT 800-345-5282
Moran Coffee Company
Dublin, OH 614-889-2500
Morning Star Coffee
West Chester, PA 888-854-2233
Mother Parker's Tea & Coffee
Mississauga, ON 905-279-9100
Mountain City Coffee Roasters
Enka, NC 888-730-0869
Mountain Roastery Coffee Company
Port Huron, MI 416-256-2727
Moutanos Brothers Coffee Company
S San Francisco, CA 800-624-7031
Mr. Espresso
Oakland, CA 510-287-5200
Muqui Coffee Company
San Jose, CA 408-929-4405
Mystic Coffee Roasters
Mystic, CT 860-536-2999
Nantucket Tea Traders
Nantucket, MA 508-325-0203
Native American Tea & Cofee
Aberdeen, SD 605-226-2006
New Harmony Coffee Roasters
Philadelphia, PA 215-925-6770
New Jamaican Gold
Hayward, CA 800-672-9956
New York Coffee & Bagels
New York, NY 212-986-6116
Newly Weds Foods
Memphis, TN 800-647-9314
North American Coffees
Laredo, TX 973-359-0300
Northwest Naturals Corporation
Bothell, WA 425-881-2200
Northwestern Coffee Mills
Washburn, WI 800-243-5283
O'Neill Coffee Company
West Middlesex, PA 724-528-9281
Oasis Coffee Company
Norwalk, CT 203-847-0554
Ocean Coffee Roasters
Pawtucket, RI 800-598-5282
Old Mansion Foods
Petersburg, VA 800-476-1877
Old Town Coffee & Tea Company
Baltimore, MD 410-752-1229

Olympic Coffee & Roasting
Bellevue, WA 888-244-8313
Omar Coffee Company
Newington, CT 800-394-6627
Orleans Coffee Exchange
Kenner, LA 800-737-5464
Oskri Organics
Thiensville, WI 800-628-1110
Pan American Coffee Company
Hoboken, NJ 800-229-1883
Paramount Coffee Company
Lansing, MI 800-968-1222
Partners Coffee Company
Atlanta, GA 800-341-5282
Pascal Coffee
Yonkers, NY 914-969-7933
Paul de Lima Company
Syracuse, NY 800-962-8864
Peaberry's Coffee & Tea
Oakland, CA 510-653-0450
Pear's Coffee
Omaha, NE 800-317-1773
Pearl Coffee Company
Akron, OH 800-822-5282
Peerless Coffee Company
Oakland, CA 800-310-5662
Peet's Coffee & Tea
Berkeley, CA 800-999-2132
Pett's Coffee & Tea
Berkeley, CA 510-594-2100
Pfefferkorn's Coffee
Baltimore, MD 800-682-4665
PJ's Coffee & Tea
New Orleans, LA 800-527-1055
Plantation Coffee
Elk Grove, CA 916-686-2633
Plaza House Coffee
Staten Island, NY 718-979-9555
Po'okela Enterprises
Kailua Kona, HI 866-328-9753
Pod Pack International
Baton Rouge, LA 225-752-1110
Pokka Beverages
American Canyon, CA 800-972-5962
Polly's Gourmet Coffee
Long Beach, CA 562-433-2996
Pontiac Coffee Break
Pontiac, MI 248-332-9403
Pontiac Foods
Columbia, SC 803-699-1600
Port Vue Coffee Company
Pottsville, PA 570-429-2690
Premier Roasters
Daly City, CA 415-337-4040
Premium Coffee Company
Eatontown, NJ 800-524-2743
Private Brands Coffee & Tea Company
Saint Louis, MO 314-652-0851
Puroast Coffee
Woodland, CA 877-569-2243
Q.E. Tea
Bridgeville, PA 800-622-8327
Queen Anne Coffee Roaster
Seattle, WA 206-284-9396
Randag & Associates Inc
Elmhurst, IL 630-530-2830
Reading Coffee Roasters
Birdsboro, PA 800-331-6713
Red Diamond
Birmingham, AL 800-292-4651
Regency Coffee & VendingCompany
Olathe, KS 913-829-1994
Reily Foods Company
New Orleans, LA 504-524-6132
Reily Foods/JFG Coffee Company
Knoxville, TN 800-535-1961
Rethemeyer Coffee Company
St Louis, MO 314-231-0990
Richard's Gourmet Coffee
West Bridgewater, MA 800-370-2633
Riffel's Coffee Company
Wichita, KS 888-399-4567
River Road Coffee
Lake Clear, NY 315-769-9941
Roasterie
Kansas City, MO 800-376-0245
Rocky Mountain Coffee Roasters
Carbondale, CO 800-666-3465
Rodda Coffee Company
Yachats, OR 541-547-4132
Ronnoco Coffee Company
St Louis, MO 800-428-2287

Rostov's Coffee & Tea Company
Richmond, VA. 800-637-6772
Rowland Coffee Roasters
Doral, FL 800-990-9039
Royal Coffee
Emeryville, CA 510-652-4256
Royal Coffee & Tea Company
Mississauga, ON 800-667-6226
Royal Coffee New York
Staten Island, NY 888-769-2569
Royal Cup Coffee
Birmingham, AL 800-366-5836
Royal Swedish Classic Coffee
Arlington Hts, IL 847-364-9704
S A Piazza & Associates
Clackamas, OR 503-657-3123
S&D Coffee, Inc
Concord, NC 704-339-0917
S&D Coffee, Inc
Concord, NC 704-782-3121
S.J. McCullagh
Buffalo, NY 800-753-3473
Sahara Coffee
Reno, NV 775-825-5033
Sambets Cajun Deli
Austin, TX 800-472-6238
San Francisco Bay Coffee Company
San Leandro, CA 800-829-1300
San Jose Coffee Company
San Jose, CA 408-272-3311
San Juan Coffee RoastingCompany
Friday Harbor, WA 800-858-4276
San Marco Coffee,Inc.
Charlotte, NC 800-715-9298
SANGARIA USA
Torrance, CA 310-530-2202
Santa Barbara Roasting Company
Santa Barbara, CA 800-321-5282
Santa Elena Coffee Company
Hutto, TX 512-846-2908
Sara Lee Coffee & Tea
Rochester, NY
Sara Lee Coffee & Tea
Minneapolis, MN 888-246-2598
Sara Lee Corporation
Downers Grove, IL 630-598-8100
Schuil Coffee Company
Kentwood, MI 616-956-1881
Seattle's Best Coffee
Seattle, WA 206-903-8010
Seven Hills Coffee Company
Cincinnati, OH 513-489-5220
Sierra Madre Organic Coffee
Denver, CO 303-446-0050
Simpson & Vail
Brookfield, CT 800-282-8327
Sivetz Coffee
Corvallis, OR 541-753-9713
Societe Cafe
Montreal-Nord, QC 514-325-9130
South Beach Coffee Company
Miami Beach, FL 305-576-9696
Southern Heritage Coffee Company
Indianapolis, IN 800-486-1198
Specialty Coffee Roasters
Miami, FL 800-253-9363
Spices of Life Gourmet Coffee
Fort Myers, FL 239-334-8004
Spinelli Coffee Company
Seattle, WA 415-821-7100
Starbucks Coffee Company
Seattle, WA 800-782-7282
Stasero International
Seattle, WA 888-929-2378
Steep & Brew Coffee Roasters
Monona, WI 800-876-1986
Stewart's Private Blend Foods
Chicago, IL 800-654-2862
Stockton Graham & Company
Raleigh, NC 800-835-5943
Subco Foods Inc
West Chicago, IL 630-231-0003
Sugai Kona Coffee
Kealakekua, HI 808-322-7717
Sundance Roasting Company
Sandpoint, ID 208-265-2445
Sunflower Restaurant Supply
Salina, KS 785-823-6394
Sweeney's Gourmet Coffee Roast
Henderson, NV 702-558-0505
Tadin Herb & Tea Company
Commerce, CA 323-728-5100

Techni-Brew International
Portland, OR 800-454-4077
Texas Coffee Company
Beaumont, TX. 800-259-3400
Thanksgiving Coffee Company
Fort Bragg, CA 800-462-1999
Toddy Products
Houston, TX 713-225-2066
Tom & Dave's Specialty Coffee
San Rafael, CA 800-249-5050
Torke Coffee Roasting Company
Sheboygan, WI 800-242-7671
Torrefazione Italia
Seattle, WA 800-827-2333
Torreo Coffee Company
Philadelphia, PA 888-286-7736
Tostino Coffee Roasters
Tucson, AZ .800-678-3519
Tradewinds Coffee Company
Raleigh, NC 800-457-0406
Tristao Trading
New York, NY 212-285-8120
Uncommon Grounds Coffee
Berkeley, CA. 800-600-5282
United Intertrade
Houston, TX 800-969-2233
Valley Tea & Coffee
Alhambra, CA 626-281-5799
Van Roy Coffee
Cleveland, OH 877-826-7669
Vassilaros & Son
Flushing, NY 718-886-4140
Victor Allen Coffee Company
Albuquerque, NM 800-662-2575
Victor Allen's Coffee and Tea
Little Chute, WI 800-394-5282
Village Roaster
Lakewood, CO 800-237-3822
Vitality Foodservice
Barrie, ON. .800-668-5463
Wabash Coffee
Vincennes, IN 812-882-6066
Wallingford Coffee Company
Cleveland, OH 800-714-0944
Wallingford Coffee Mills
Cincinnati, OH 800-533-3690
Walsh's Coffee Roasters
San Mateo, CA 650-347-5112
Weaver Nut Company
Ephrata, PA 717-738-3781
Wechsler Coffee Corporation
Moonachie, NJ 800-800-2633
West Coast Specialty Coffee
Campbell, CA 650-259-9308
Wheeling Coffee & Spice Company
Wheeling, WV 800-500-0141
White Cloud Coffee
Boise, ID 800-627-0309
White Coffee Corporation
Long Island City, NY 800-221-0140
William Turner
Frederick, MD. 301-620-1135
Willoughby's Coffee & Tea
Branford, CT. 800-388-8400
Winn-Dixie Stores
Jacksonville, FL 800-946-6349
World Cup Roasters
Portland, OR 503-228-5503
World of Coffee
Stirling, NJ 800-543-0062
World of Coffee, World of Tea
Stirling, NJ 908-647-1218
Yosemite Coffee & Roasting
Oakhurst, CA 559-683-8815
Young Winfield
Kleinburg, ON. 905-893-2536

Cappuccino

American Purpac Technologies, LLC
Beloit, WI .877-787-7221
AREL Group
Atlanta, GA. 800-737-3094
Caffe D'Amore
Monrovia, CA 800-999-0171
Caffe D'Amore Gourmet Beverages
Monrovia, CA 800-999-0171
Flavor Waves
Novato, CA 415-899-0084
GPR Company
Stowe, PA .610-326-4777
Instant Products of America
Columbus, IN 812-372-9100

Decaffeinated

American Coffee Company
New Orleans, LA 800-554-7234
Arbuckle Coffee
Pittsburgh, PA 800-533-8278
Brewfresh Coffee Company
South Salt Lake, UT 888-486-3334
Caffe Luca
Tukwila, WA 800-728-9116
Chock Full O'Nuts
, NY 888-246-2598
Coffee Exchange
Providence, RI 800-263-3339
Compact Industries
St Charles, IL 800-513-4262
DMH Ingredients
Libertyville, IL 847-362-9977
Folgers Coffee Company
Orrville, OH 877-693-6543
GPR Company
Stowe, PA .610-326-4777
Heritage Northwest
Juneau, AK 907-586-1088
Jelks Coffee Roasters
Shreveport, LA 318-636-6391
Kaffe Magnum Opus
Vineland, NJ 800-652-5282
Orleans Coffee Exchange
Kenner, LA 800-737-5464
Puroast Coffee
Woodland, CA. 877-569-2243
San Francisco Bay Coffee Company
San Leandro, CA. 800-829-1300
Sara Lee Corporation
Downers Grove, IL 630-598-8100
Stewart's Private Blend Foods
Chicago, IL 800-654-2862
Thanksgiving Coffee Company
Fort Bragg, CA 800-462-1999
Van Roy Coffee
Cleveland, OH 877-826-7669
Vitality Foodservice
Barrie, ON. .800-668-5463
Weaver Nut Company
Ephrata, PA 717-738-3781
Wechsler Coffee Corporation
Moonachie, NJ 800-800-2633

Decaffeinated Naturally

GPR Company
Stowe, PA .610-326-4777

Flavored

American Coffee Company
New Orleans, LA 800-554-7234
Andresen Ryan Coffee Com
Superior, WI 715-395-3793
Arbuckle Coffee
Pittsburgh, PA 800-533-8278
Aroma Coffee Company
Forest Park, IL 708-488-8340
Brewfresh Coffee Company
South Salt Lake, UT 888-486-3334
Cafe Society Coffee Company
Dallas, TX. 800-717-6000
Custom House Coffee Roasters
Miami, FL. 888-563-5282
Daymar Select Fine Coffees
El Cajon, CA. 800-466-7590
Decoty Coffee Company
San Angelo, TX 800-588-8001
Distant Lands Coffee Roaster
Tyler, TX. .800-346-5459
East Indies Coffee & Tea Company
Lebanon, PA 800-220-2326
GPR Company
Stowe, PA .610-326-4777
Greene Brothers Specialty Coffee Roaster
Hackettstown, NJ 908-979-0022
Harold L. King & Company
Redwood City, CA 888-368-2233
Hawaii Coffee Company
Honolulu, HI 800-338-8353
Heritage Northwest
Juneau, AK 907-586-1088
Jelks Coffee Roasters
Shreveport, LA 318-636-6391
Kaffe Magnum Opus
Vineland, NJ 800-652-5282
Kauai Coffee Company
Kalaheo, HI. 800-545-8605

Longbottom Coffee & Tea
Hillsboro, OR 800-288-1271
Love Creek Orchards
Medina, TX. 800-449-0882
Lowery's Premium Roast Coffee
Snohomish, WA 800-767-1783
Magnum Coffee Roastery
Nunica, MI 888-937-5282
Orleans Coffee Exchange
Kenner, LA 800-737-5464
Pearl Coffee Company
Akron, OH. 800-822-5282
Premium Coffee Company
Eatontown, NJ. 800-524-2743
Puroast Coffee
Woodland, CA. 877-569-2243
Riffel's Coffee Company
Wichita, KS 888-399-4567
San Francisco Bay Coffee Company
San Leandro, CA. 800-829-1300
San Juan Coffee RoastingCompany
Friday Harbor, WA 800-858-4276
Sara Lee Corporation
Downers Grove, IL 630-598-8100
Starbucks Coffee Company
Seattle, WA 800-782-7282
Stewart's Private Blend Foods
Chicago, IL 800-654-2862
Thanksgiving Coffee Company
Fort Bragg, CA 800-462-1999
Weaver Nut Company
Ephrata, PA 717-738-3781
Wechsler Coffee Corporation
Moonachie, NJ 800-800-2633

Iced

Arizona Beverage Company
New Hyde Park, NY. 800-832-3775

Instant

Chock Full O'Nuts
, NY. 888-246-2598
Coffee Holding Company
Brooklyn, NY 800-458-2233
Compact Industries
St Charles, IL 800-513-4262
Daymar Select Fine Coffees
El Cajon, CA. 800-466-7590
FCC Coffee Packers
Doral, FL. .305-591-1128
GPR Company
Stowe, PA .610-326-4777
Instant Products of America
Columbus, IN 812-372-9100
Tonex
Wallington, NJ 973-773-5135
Vitality Foodservice
Barrie, ON. .800-668-5463

Instant - Decaffeinated

GPR Company
Stowe, PA .610-326-4777
Reily Foods Company
New Orleans, LA 504-524-6132
Swagger Foods Corporation
Vernon Hills, IL 847-913-1200

Latte

GPR Company
Stowe, PA .610-326-4777

Roasted

Alakef Coffee Roasters
Duluth, MN. 800-438-9228
Allegro Coffee Company
Thornton, CO 800-666-4869
Arbuckle Coffee
Pittsburgh, PA 800-533-8278
Boyd Coffee Company
Portland, OR 800-545-4077
Brewfresh Coffee Company
South Salt Lake, UT 888-486-3334
Brisk Coffee Company
Tampa, FL .800-899-5282
Buckmaster Coffee
Hillsboro, OR 800-962-9148
Cafe Moto
San Diego, CA 800-818-3363
Cain's Coffee Company
Springfield, MO 800-641-4025

Clear Mountain Coffee Company
Silver Spring, MD.................301-587-2233
Coffee Bean International
Portland, OR.....................800-877-0474
Coffee Reserve
Phoenix, AZ.....................623-434-0939
Colonial Coffee Roasters
Miami, FL........................305-638-0885
Daymar Select Fine Coffees
El Cajon, CA....................800-466-7590
Distant Lands Coffee Roaster
Tyler, TX........................800-346-5459
DMH Ingredients
Libertyville, IL..................847-362-9977
El Dorado Coffee
Flushing, NY....................800-635-2566
Finger Lakes Coffee Roasters
Farmington, NY..................800-420-6154
Folgers Coffee Company
Orrville, OH.....................877-693-6543
GPR Company
Stowe, PA.......................610-326-4777
Grounds for Thought
Bowling Green, OH...............419-354-2326
Heritage Northwest
Juneau, AK......................907-586-1088
House of Coffee Beans
Houston, TX.....................800-422-1799
Indigo Coffee Roasters
Florence, MA....................800-447-5450
JBR Coffee & Tea
San Leandro, CA.................800-829-1300
Jeremiah's Pick Coffee Company
San Francisco, CA...............800-537-3642
Kauai Coffee Company
Kalaheo, HI.....................800-545-8605
Lola Savannah
Houston, TX.....................888-663-9166
Lucile's Famous Creole Seasonings
Boulder, CO.....................800-727-3653
M.E. Swing Company
Alexandria, VA..................800-485-4019
Magnum Coffee Roastery
Nunica, MI......................888-937-5282
Maui Coffee Roasters
Kahului, HI.....................800-645-2877
Milone Brothers Coffee
Modesto, CA.....................800-974-8500
Montana Coffee Traders
Whitefish, MT...................800-345-5282
Morning Star Coffee
West Chester, PA................888-854-2233
New Harmony Coffee Roasters
Philadelphia, PA................215-925-6770
Oasis Coffee Company
Norwalk, CT.....................203-847-0554
Olympic Coffee & Roasting
Bellevue, WA....................888-244-8313
Pan American Coffee Company
Hoboken, NJ.....................800-229-1883
Pfefferkorn's Coffee
Baltimore, MD...................800-682-4665
Puroast Coffee
Woodland, CA....................877-569-2243
Rowland Coffee Roasters
Doral, FL.......................800-990-9039
Royal Blend Coffee Company
Bend, OR........................541-388-8164
Royal Coffee & Tea Company
Mississauga, ON.................800-667-6226
San Juan Coffee RoastingCompany
Friday Harbor, WA...............800-858-4276
Sara Lee Corporation
Downers Grove, IL...............630-598-8100
Southern Heritage Coffee Company
Indianapolis, IN................800-486-1198
Steep & Brew Coffee Roasters
Monona, WI......................800-876-1986
Stewart's Private Blend Foods
Chicago, IL.....................800-654-2862
Sunflower Restaurant Supply
Salina, KS......................785-823-6394
Texas Coffee Company
Beaumont, TX....................800-259-3400
Torke Coffee Roasting Company
Sheboygan, WI...................800-242-7671
U Roast Em
Hayward, WI.....................715-634-6255
Van Roy Coffee
Cleveland, OH...................877-826-7669
Weaver Nut Company
Ephrata, PA.....................717-738-3781

Wheeling Coffee & Spice Company
Wheeling, WV....................800-500-0141
White Cloud Coffee
Boise, ID.......................800-627-0309
Young Winfield
Kleinburg, ON...................905-893-2536

Vacuum Packed

GPR Company
Stowe, PA.......................610-326-4777

Espresso

Advance Food Brokers
West Bloomfield, MI.............248-851-9045
AREL Group
Atlanta, GA.....................800-737-3094
Aroma Coffee Company
Forest Park, IL.................708-488-8340
Blue Chip Group
Salt Lake City, UT..............800-878-0099
Caffe Darte
Seattle, WA.....................800-999-5334
Caffe Luca
Tukwila, WA.....................800-728-9116
Chock Full O'Nuts
, NY...........................888-246-2598
Coca-Cola Bottling Company
Brampton, ON....................800-926-5301
Cream O'Weaver Dairy
Salt Lake City, UT..............801-973-9922
Curly's Dairy
Stayton, OR.....................800-785-1335
Distant Lands Coffee Roaster
Tyler, TX........................800-346-5459
Fama Sales
New York, NY....................212-757-9433
Folklore Foods
Toppenish, WA...................509-865-4772
GPR Company
Stowe, PA.......................610-326-4777
Heritage Northwest
Juneau, AK......................907-586-1088
Hygeia Dairy Company
McAllen, TX.....................956-686-0511
Ideal Dairy
Richfield, UT...................435-896-5061
Knoll Creek Dairy
Harrison, NY....................718-892-4500
Kobricks Coffee Company
Jersey City, NJ.................800-562-3662
Lacto Milk Products Corporation
Flemington, NJ..................908-788-2200
Louis Trauth Dairy
Newport, KY.....................800-544-6455
Maola Milk & Ice Cream Company
New Bern, NC....................252-638-1131
Martin Coffee Company
Jacksonville, FL................904-355-9661
McCormick Ingredients
Hunt Valley, MD.................800-632-5847
Meadow Gold Dairy
Lewiston, ID....................208-746-9006
Moka D'Oro Coffee
Farmingdale, NY.................888-665-2367
Monticello Cellars
Napa, CA........................707-253-2802
Nestle Canada Inc
North York, ON..................800-563-7853
Oak Farms
Dallas, TX......................214-941-0302
Pepsi Bottling Group Canada
Mississauga, ON.................800-387-9546
Price's Creameries
El Paso, TX.....................915-565-2711
Puroast Coffee
Woodland, CA....................877-569-2243
S A Piazza & Associates
Clackamas, OR...................503-657-3123
Saint Albans CooperativeCreamy
Saint Albans, VT................800-559-0343
San Marco Coffee,Inc.
Charlotte, NC...................800-715-9298
Sara Lee Coffee & Tea
Earth City, MO..................314-731-2500
Sara Lee Coffee & Tea   Wholesale Coffee & Tea
Location
Minneapolis, MN.................888-246-2598
Sebastiani Vineyards
Sonoma, CA......................800-888-5532
Smucker Quality Beverages
Havre De Grace, MD..............410-939-1403

Smucker Quality Beverages
Chico, CA.......................530-899-5000
Sopralco
Plantation, FL..................954-584-2225
Southern Heritage Coffee Company
Indianapolis, IN................800-486-1198
Starbucks Coffee Company
Seattle, WA.....................800-782-7282
Swiss Valley Farms Company
Dubuque, IA.....................800-397-9156
Tuscan Dairy Farms
Dallas, TX......................800-526-4416
Ultra Seal
New Paltz, NY...................845-255-2496
Unilever Canada
Toronto, ON.....................416-964-1857
Winder Dairy
West Valley, UT.................800-946-3371

Decaffeinated

GPR Company
Stowe, PA.......................610-326-4777

Mocha

Foremost Farms
Waukesha, WI....................800-289-7787
Jones Brewing Company
Smithton, PA....................800-237-2337

Tea

Abunda Life Laboratories
Asbury Park, NJ.................732-775-4141
Ahmad Tea
Deer Park, TX...................800-637-7704
Al-Rite Fruits & Syrups
Miami, FL........................305-652-2540
Alaska Herb Tea Company
Anchorage, AK...................800-654-2764
Alexander Gourmet Imports
Mississauga, ON.................800-265-5081
Allen Flavors
Edison, NJ......................908-561-5995
Alpine Pure USA
Accord, MA......................866-832-7997
Alternative Health & Herbs
Albany, OR......................800-345-4152
American Instants
Flanders, NJ....................973-584-8811
American Soy Products
Saline, MI......................734-429-2310
Artist Coffee
Londonderry, NH.................866-440-4511
Astor Products
Jacksonville, FL................904-783-5000
Atlanta Coffee & Tea Company
Decatur, GA.....................800-426-4781
Atlanta Flagship Dairy
Atlanta, GA.....................800-224-0669
Bagai Tea Company
San Marcos, CA..................760-591-3084
Barnes & Watson Fine Teas
Seattle, WA.....................800-447-8832
Barrows Tea Company
New Bedford, MA.................800-832-5024
Beacon Drive In
Spartanburg, SC.................864-585-9387
Bigelow Tea
Shelton, CT.....................800-235-7072
Blue Willow Tea Company
Emeryville, CA..................800-328-0353
Boston Tea Company
Hackensack, NJ..................800-800-2633
Bountiful Pantry
Nantucket, MA...................888-832-6466
Boyd Coffee Company
Portland, OR....................800-545-4077
Bread & Chocolate
Wells River, VT.................800-524-6715
Cadillac Coffee Company
Madison Heights, MI.............800-438-6900
Carolina Treet
Wilmington, NC..................800-616-6344
Celestial Seasonings Teas
Boulder, CO.....................303-530-5300
Central Coca-Cola Bottling Company
Richmond, VA....................800-359-3759
Charleston Tea Plantation
Wadmalaw Island, SC.............800-443-5987
Chicago Coffee Roastery
Huntley, IL.....................800-762-5402

China Mist Tea Company
Scottsdale, AZ. 800-242-8807
Choice Organic Teas
Seattle, WA 206-525-0051
City Bean
Stevenson Ranch, CA. 888-248-9232
Clayton's Coffee & Tea
Modesto, CA. 209-522-7811
Clear Mountain Coffee Company
Silver Spring, MD. 301-587-2233
Coffee & Tea
Bloomington, MN. 952-853-1148
Coffee Bean International
Portland, OR. 800-877-0474
Coffee Masters
Barrington, IL. 847-382-9786
Coffee Mill Roastery
Elon, NC 800-729-1727
Colorado Spice
Boulder, CO .800-677-7423
Community Coffee Specialty
Baton Rouge, LA 800-525-5583
Company of a Philadelphia Gentleman
Philadelphia, PA. 215-427-2827
Consolidated Tea Company
Lynbrook, NY. 516-887-1144
Contact International
Skokie, IL. 847-324-4411
Continental Coffee Products Company
Houston, TX .800-323-6178
Cora Italian Specialties
Countryside, IL. 800-696-2672
Cotswold Cottage Foods
Arvada, CO. .800-208-1977
Crosby Molasses Company
St. John, NB .506-634-7515
Crystal Geyser Water Company
Calistoga, CA 800-726-6121
Custom Brands Unlimited
Solebury, PA .215-297-9842
Da Vinci Gourmet
Seattle, WA 800-640-6779
Dallis Brothers
Jamaica, NY .800-424-4252
Damron Corporation
Chicago, IL 800-333-1860
David Rio Coffee & Tea
San Francisco, CA 800-454-9605
Davidson's Organic Tea
Reno, NV 800-882-5888
Davidsons
Reno, NV 800-882-5888
De Coty Coffee Company
San Angelo, TX 800-588-8001
Decoty Coffee Company
San Angelo, TX 800-588-8001
DMH Ingredients
Libertyville, IL 847-362-9977
Droubi's Imports
Houston, TX .713-988-7138
East India Coffee & Tea Company
San Leandro, CA. 800-829-1300
East Indies Coffee & Tea Company
Lebanon, PA .800-220-2326
Eastern Tea Corporation
Monroe Township, NJ 800-221-0865
Eastrise Trading Corporation
City of Industry, CA 626-330-0933
Eden Foods Inc
Clinton, MI 800-248-0320
Empire Tea Services
Columbus, OH 800-790-0246
F Gavina & Sons Inc
Vernon, CA 800-428-4627
Father's Country Hams
Bremen, KY .270-525-3554
Fauchon
New York, NY 877-605-0130
Fee Brothers
Rochester, NY. 800-961-3337
Finlay Tea Solutions
Morristown, NJ. 973-538-1701
Flavor Innovations
South Plainfield, NJ 800-536-2030
Flavor Specialties
Corona, CA 951-734-6620
Flavorbank
Tampa, FL. 813-885-1797
Flora
Lynden, WA. .800-446-2110
Fmali Herb
Santa Cruz, CA 831-423-7913

Foltz Coffee Tea & Spice Company
New Orleans, LA 504-486-1545
Fortunes International Teas
Mc Kees Rocks, PA 800-551-8327
G H Ford Tea Company
Wappingers Falls, NY. 845-298-8900
G.L. Mezzetta Inc
American Canyon, CA 707-648-1050
Generation Tea
Spring Valley, NY. 866-742-5668
GlobeTrends
Morris Plains, NJ 800-416-8327
Gloria Jean's Gourmet Coffees
Rcho Sta Marg, CA. 800-354-5258
Golden Moon Tea
Herndon, VA .877-327-5473
Good Earth® Teas
Santa Cruz, CA 831-423-7913
Grace Tea Company
New York, NY 212-678-2008
Great Eastern Sun
Asheville, NC 800-334-5809
H&H Products Company
Orlando, FL. .407-299-5410
H&K Products-Pappy's Sassafras Teas
Columbus Grove, OH 877-659-5110
Harney & Sons Tea Company
Salisbury, CT. 888-427-6398
Has Beans Coffee & Tea Company
Mount Shasta, CA. 800-427-2326
Herbs, Etc.
Santa Fe, NM 888-694-3727
Heritage Store
Virginia Beach, VA 757-428-0110
House of Coffee Beans
Houston, TX .800-422-1799
Ideal Distributing Company
Bothell, WA. .425-488-6121
IL HWA American Corporation
Belleville, NJ .800-446-7364
IMS Food Service
Shelton, CT. .800-235-7072
India Tea Importers
Pico Rivera, CA 562-801-9600
India Tree Gourmet Spices & Specialties
Seattle, WA 800-369-4848
Indochina Tea Company
Los Angeles, CA. 323-650-8020
Ineeka Inc
Chicago, IL 312-661-1550
Irani & Company
Indianapolis, IN 317-894-4465
J.G. British Imports
Sarasota, FL. 888-965-1700
John A. Vassilaros & Son
Flushing, NY. 718-886-4140
Justin Lloyd Premium Tea Company
Carson, CA 310-834-4000
Laci Le Beau Corporation
Fresno, CA 800-356-0490
Leaves Pure Teas
Scottsdale, AZ. 800-242-8807
Leroy Hill Coffee Company
Mobile, AL 800-866-5282
Lyons-Magnus
Fresno, CA 559-268-5966
MacKinlay Teas
Ann Arbor, MI 734-747-9012
Madys Company
San Francisco, CA 415-822-2227
Mafco Natural Products
Richmond, VA. 804-222-1600
Masala Chai Company
Santa Cruz, CA 831-475-8881
McCormick Ingredients
Hunt Valley, MD. 800-632-5847
Metropolitan Tea Company
Toronto, ON .800-388-0351
Mighty Leaf Tea
San Rafael, CA 415-491-2650
Mojave Foods Corporation
Commerce, CA 323-890-8900
Mother Parker's Tea & Coffee
Mississauga, ON. 905-279-9100
Nestle Canada Inc
North York, ON. 800-563-7853
Newly Weds Foods
Memphis, TN 800-647-9314
NOH Foods of Hawaii
Gardena, CA .310-324-6770
Northwestern Foods
St Paul, MN. .800-236-4937

NSpired Natural Foods
Melville, NY .631-845-4689
Numi Tea
Oakland, CA .866-972-6879
Nutraceutical Corporation
Park City, UT 800-669-8877
O'Mona International Tea
Rye Brook, NY 914-937-8858
O'Neil's Distributors
Goodland, IN 219-297-4521
O'Neill Coffee Company
West Middlesex, PA 724-528-9281
Old Town Coffee & Tea Company
Baltimore, MD 410-752-1229
Orleans Coffee Exchange
Kenner, LA 800-737-5464
Our Thyme Garden
Cleburne, TX 800-482-4372
Pepsi Bottling Group
Tulsa, OK 800-963-2424
Pepsi-Cola General Bottlers
Arlington Hts, IL 847-483-6880
Pet Milk
Florence, SC .800-735-3066
Plantextrakt/Martin Bower
Jersey City, NJ 201-659-3100
Pokka Beverages
American Canyon, CA 800-972-5962
Prince of Peace Enterprises
Hayward, CA 800-732-2328
Progenix Corporation
Wausau, WI. .800-233-3356
Q.E. Tea
Bridgeville, PA 800-622-8327
R C Bigelow
Fairfield, CT .800-243-5587
Randag & Associates Inc
Elmhurst, IL .630-530-2830
Redco Foods
Windsor, CT .800-645-1190
Reily Foods Company
New Orleans, LA 504-524-6132
Richard's Gourmet Coffee
West Bridgewater, MA 800-370-2633
Royal Food Distributors
Scottsdale, AZ. 602-971-4910
Royal Pacific Tea & Coffee
Scottsdale, AZ. 480-951-8251

Sampac Enterprises
S San Francisco, CA 650-876-0808
Sara Lee Coffee & Tea
Rochester, NY
Sara Lee Coffee & Tea
Earth City, MO 314-731-2500
Sara Lee Coffee & Tea
Houston, TX 888-246-2598
Sara Lee Corporation
Downers Grove, IL 630-598-8100
Sara Lee Foodservice
Rolling Meadows, IL 800-261-4754
Schneider's Dairy Holdings Inc
Pittsburgh, PA 412-881-3525
Secret Tea Garden
Vancouver, BC 604-261-3070
Serendipitea
Long Island City, NY 888-832-5433
Simpson & Vail
Brookfield, CT 800-282-8327
Southern Tea
Marietta, GA 800-241-0896
Southern Tea Company
Marietta, GA 770-428-3528
SpecialTeas
Norwalk, CT 888-365-6983
Stewart's Private Blend Foods
Chicago, IL 800-654-2862
Sturm Foods
Manawa, WI 800-347-8876
Sunlike Juice
Scarborough, ON 416-297-1140
Superior Trading Company
San Francisco, CA 415-982-8722
Tata Tea
Plant City, FL 813-754-2602
Tatra Herb Company
Morrisville, PA 888-828-7248
Tea Beyond
West Caldwell, NJ 973-226-0327
Tea Forte
Concord, MA 978-369-7777
Tea Needs Inc
Boca Raton, FL 561-237-5237
Templar Food Products
New Providence, NJ 800-883-6752
Ten Ren Tea & Ginseng Company
New York, NY 800-292-2049
Thirs-Tea Corporation
Miami, FL 305-651-4350
Traditional Medicinals
Sebastopol, CA 800-543-4372
Tri-Sun International
Santa Ana, CA 800-387-4786
Truesdale Packaging Company
Warrenton, MO 636-456-6800
Twining R & Company
Greensboro, NC 336-275-8634
Two Leaves and a Bud
Basalt, CO 866-631-7973
U Roast Em
Hayward, WI................... 715-634-6255
Ultra Seal
New Paltz, NY 845-255-2496
Uncle Bum's Gourmet Foods
Riverside, CA 800-486-2867
Uncle Lee's Tea
South El Monte, CA 800-732-8830
Unilever
Mont-Royal, QC 514-735-1141
Unilever Canada
Toronto, ON 416-964-1857
Unilever United States
Englewood Cliffs, NJ 201-567-8000
Universal Commodities
Bronxville, NY 914-779-5700
Van Roy Coffee
Cleveland, OH 877-826-7669
VIP Foods
Flushing, NY 718-821-3942
Vita Specialty Foods
Inwood, WV 800-974-4778
Weaver Nut Company
Ephrata, PA 717-738-3781
Wechsler Coffee Corporation
Moonachie, NJ 800-800-2633
White Coffee Corporation
Long Island City, NY 800-221-0140
White Rock Products Corporation
Whitestone, NY 800-969-7625
Whole Herb Company
Sonoma, CA 707-935-1077

Winn-Dixie Dairies
Hammond, LA 985-549-6870
World Ginseng Center
San Francisco, CA 800-747-8808
Yellow Emperor
Eugene, OR 877-485-6664
Zhena's Gypsy Tea
Ojai, CA 800-448-0803

Bags

ABC Tea House
Baldwin Park, CA 888-220-3988
Barrows Tea Company
New Bedford, MA 800-832-5024
Blue Ridge Tea & Herb Company
Brooklyn, NY 718-625-3100
Choice Organic Teas
Seattle, WA 206-525-0051
Eastern Shore Tea
Lutherville, MD 800-823-1408
Eastern Tea Corporation
Monroe Township, NJ 800-221-0865
Empire Tea Services
Columbus, IN 800-790-0246
Harris Freeman & Company
Anaheim, CA 800-275-2378
Modern Tea Packers
Brooklyn, NY 718-417-1060
Southern Tea
Marietta, GA 800-241-0896
Tetley Tea
Shelton, CT 800-728-0084
World of Coffee, World of Tea
Stirling, NJ 908-647-1218

Black

Alpine Pure USA
Accord, MA 866-832-7997
Chieftain Wild Rice Company
Spooner, WI 800-262-6368
Harney & Sons Tea Company
Salisbury, CT.................. 888-427-6398
SpecialTeas
Norwalk, CT 888-365-6983
Talbott Teas
Chicago, IL 888-809-6062
Universal Commodities
Bronxville, NY 914-779-5700

Chai

Alpine Pure USA
Accord, MA 866-832-7997
Choice Organic Teas
Seattle, WA 206-525-0051
Da Vinci Gourmet
Seattle, WA 800-640-6779
David Rio Coffee & Tea
San Francisco, CA 800-454-9605
Father's Country Hams
Bremen, KY 270-525-3554
Masala Chai Company
Santa Cruz, CA 831-475-8881
Oregon Chai
Portland, OR 888-874-2424
Sattwa Chai
Newberg, OR 503-538-4715
Templar Food Products
New Providence, NJ 800-883-6752
Toddy Products
Houston, TX 713-225-2066

Chamomile

Castella Imports
Hauppauge, NY 866-227-8355
Choice Organic Teas
Seattle, WA 206-525-0051

Darjeeling

Choice Organic Teas
Seattle, WA 206-525-0051

Decaffeinated

Alexander Gourmet Imports
Mississauga, ON 800-265-5081
Ancora Coffee Roasters
Madison, WI 800-260-0217
Boston Tea Company
Hackensack, NJ................. 800-800-2633

Castella Imports
Hauppauge, NY 866-227-8355
Choice Organic Teas
Seattle, WA 206-525-0051
DMH Ingredients
Libertyville, IL 847-362-9977
Harney & Sons Tea Company
Salisbury, CT.................. 888-427-6398
Masala Chai Company
Santa Cruz, CA 831-475-8881
Mother Parker's Tea & Coffee
Mississauga, ON 905-279-9100
Plantextrakt/Martin Bower
Jersey City, NJ 201-659-3100
SpecialTeas
Norwalk, CT 888-365-6983
Stash Tea Company
Portland, OR 800-547-1514
Universal Commodities
Bronxville, NY 914-779-5700
Weaver Nut Company
Ephrata, PA 717-738-3781

Earl Grey

Alpine Pure USA
Accord, MA 866-832-7997
Blue Willow Tea Company
Emeryville, CA 800-328-0353
Choice Organic Teas
Seattle, WA 206-525-0051

Earl Grey Decaffeinated

Choice Organic Teas
Seattle, WA 206-525-0051

English Breakfast

Choice Organic Teas
Seattle, WA 206-525-0051

Fair-Trade

Chieftain Wild Rice Company
Spooner, WI 800-262-6368

Flavored

Alaska Herb Tea Company
Anchorage, AK 800-654-2764
Aqua Vie Beverage Corporation
Ketchum, ID 800-744-7500
Arbuckle Coffee
Pittsburgh, PA 800-533-8278
Belmar Spring Water Company
Glen Rock, NJ 201-444-1010
Boston Tea Company
Hackensack, NJ................. 800-800-2633
Cafe Society Coffee Company
Dallas, TX 800-717-6000
Central Coca-Cola Bottling Company
Richmond, VA.................. 800-359-3759
Choice Organic Teas
Seattle, WA 206-525-0051
Cold Spring Brewing Company
Cold Spring, MN 320-685-8686
Daymar Select Fine Coffees
El Cajon, CA................... 800-466-7590
East Indies Coffee & Tea Company
Lebanon, PA 800-220-2326
Empire Tea Services
Columbus, IN 800-790-0246
Father's Country Hams
Bremen, KY 270-525-3554
First Colony Coffee & Tea Company
Norfolk, VA................... 800-446-8555
Fortunes International Teas
Mc Kees Rocks, PA 800-551-8327
Frair & Grimes
Kent, WA 206-935-0134
H&K Products-Pappy's Sassafras Teas
Columbus Grove, OH 877-659-5110
Harney & Sons Tea Company
Salisbury, CT.................. 888-427-6398
Houston Tea & Beverage
Houston, TX 800-585-4549
Laci Le Beau Corporation
Fresno, CA 800-356-0490
Masala Chai Company
Santa Cruz, CA 831-475-8881
Mother Parker's Tea & Coffee
Mississauga, ON 905-279-9100
NOH Foods of Hawaii
Gardena, CA 310-324-6770

Plantextrakt/Martin Bower
Jersey City, NJ .201-659-3100
Premium Waters
Minneapolis, MN 800-332-3332
R C Bigelow
Fairfield, CT 800-243-5587
Royal Coffee & Tea Company
Mississauga, ON 800-667-6226
San Francisco Bay Coffee Company
San Leandro, CA. 800-829-1300
SpecialTeas
Norwalk, CT 888-365-6983
Starbucks Coffee Company
Seattle, WA 800-782-7282
Stewart's Private Blend Foods
Chicago, IL 800-654-2862
Unilever Bestfoods
Englewood Cliffs, NJ 201-894-4000
Universal Commodities
Bronxville, NY 914-779-5700
Weaver Nut Company
Ephrata, PA 717-738-3781
Yosemite Waters
Los Angeles, CA. 800-427-8420

Green

AIYA
New York, NY 212-499-0610
AIYA America, Inc.
Torrance, CA. 310-212-1395
Alexander Gourmet Imports
Mississauga, ON 800-265-5081
Alpine Pure USA
Accord, MA 866-832-7997
Ancora Coffee Roasters
Madison, WI .800-260-0217
AOI Tea Company - North America Office
Huntington Beach, CA 877-264-0877
Baycliff Company
New York, NY 212-772-6078
Boston Tea Company
Hackensack, NJ. 800-800-2633
China Mist Tea Company
Scottsdale, AZ. 800-242-8807
Choice Organic Teas
Seattle, WA 206-525-0051
Da Vinci Gourmet
Seattle, WA 800-640-6779
Eden Foods Inc
Clinton, MI 800-248-0320
Empire Tea Services
Columbus, IN 800-790-0246
Flavor Specialties
Corona, CA 951-734-6620
Fmali Herb
Santa Cruz, CA. 831-423-7913
Fortunes International Teas
Mc Kees Rocks, PA 800-551-8327
Harney & Sons Tea Company
Salisbury, CT. 888-427-6398
NuNaturals
Eugene, OR. .800-753-4372
Plantextrakt/Martin Bower
Jersey City, NJ 201-659-3100
R C Bigelow
Fairfield, CT 800-243-5587
RFI Ingredients
Blauvelt, NY .800-962-7663
Sencha Naturals
Los Angeles, CA. 888-473-6242
SpecialTeas
Norwalk, CT 888-365-6983
Talbott Teas
Chicago, IL 888-809-6062
Templar Food Products
New Providence, NJ 800-883-6752
The Long Life Beverage Company
Mission Hills, CA 800-848-7331
Universal Commodities
Bronxville, NY 914-779-5700

Herbal

Abunda Life Laboratories
Asbury Park, NJ 732-775-4141
Agrinom LLC
Hakalau, HI. .808-963-6771
Alternative Health & Herbs
Albany, OR. .800-345-4152
Ancora Coffee Roasters
Madison, WI .800-260-0217

Berardi's Fresh Roast
Cleveland, OH 800-876-9109
Body Breakthrough
Deer Park, NY. 800-874-6299
Boston Spice & Tea Company
Boston, VA 800-966-4372
Boston Tea Company
Hackensack, NJ. 800-800-2633
China Mist Tea Company
Scottsdale, AZ. 800-242-8807
Choice Organic Teas
Seattle, WA 206-525-0051
Coffee Bean International
Portland, OR .800-877-0474
Common Folk Farm
Naples, ME 207-787-2764
Empire Tea Services
Columbus, IN 800-790-0246
Fmali Herb
Santa Cruz, CA. 831-423-7913
Fortunes International Teas
Mc Kees Rocks, PA 800-551-8327
Ginkgoton
Gardena, CA. 310-538-8383
Hansen's Natural
Fullerton, CA 714-870-0310
Herb Tea Company
Oxnard, CA. .805-486-6477
HerbaSway Laboratories
Wallingford, CT 800-672-7322
Heritage Store
Virginia Beach, VA 757-428-0110
Hobe Laboratories
Tempe, AZ 800-528-4482
IL HWA American Corporation
Belleville, NJ 800-446-7364
Kandia's Fine Teas
Lewiston, ME 207-782-6300
Laci Le Beau Corporation
Fresno, CA 800-356-0490
Madys Company
San Francisco, CA 415-822-2227
Mafco Natural Products
Richmond, VA. 804-222-1600
Maharishi Ayurveda Products International
Colorado Springs, CO. 800-255-8332
Montana Tea & Spice Trading
Missoula, MT 406-721-4882
Mother Parker's Tea & Coffee
Mississauga, ON 905-279-9100
Native Scents
Taos, NM. 800-645-3471
Now Foods
Bloomingdale, IL 888-669-3663
Nutritional Counselors of America
Spencer, TN .931-946-3600
Old Fashioned Natural Products
Santa Ana, CA 800-552-9045
Organic India USA
Boulder, CO .888-550-8332
P.C. Teas Company
Burlingame, CA 800-423-8728
PC Teas Company
Burlingame, CA 800-423-8728
Plantextrakt/Martin Bower
Jersey City, NJ 201-659-3100
Progenix Corporation
Wausau, WI. .800-233-3356
R C Bigelow
Fairfield, CT 800-243-5587
San Francisco Bay Coffee Company
San Leandro, CA. 800-829-1300
San Francisco Herb & Natural Food Company
Fremont, CA .800-227-2830
Satori Teas
Salinas, CA 800-444-7286
Stash Tea Company
Portland, OR .800-547-1514
Sugai Kona Coffee
Kealakekua, HI 808-322-7717
Superior Trading Company
San Francisco, CA 415-982-8722
Tatra Herb Company
Morrisville, PA 888-828-7248
Templar Food Products
New Providence, NJ 800-883-6752
Traditional Medicinals
Sebastopol, CA 800-543-4372
Triple Leaf Tea
S San Francisco, CA 800-552-7448
Unilever Bestfoods
Englewood Cliffs, NJ 201-894-4000

Vermont Liberty Tea Company
Waterbury, VT. 802-244-6102
Wah Yet Group
Hayward, CA .800-229-3392
Whole Herb Company
Sonoma, CA .707-935-1077

Iced

Al-Rite Fruits & Syrups
Miami, FL. 305-652-2540
Arizona Beverage Company
New Hyde Park, NY. 800-832-3775
Bay Pac Beverages
Walnut Creek, CA. 925-279-0800
Boyd Coffee Company
Portland, OR .800-545-4077
Brooklyn Bottling Company
Milton, NY 845-795-2171
Central Coca-Cola Bottling Company
Richmond, VA. 800-359-3759
China Mist Tea Company
Scottsdale, AZ. 800-242-8807
Clement Pappas & Company
Seabrook, NJ. 800-257-7019
Coca-Cola Enterprises
Atlanta, GA. .800-233-7210
Droubi's Imports
Houston, TX .713-988-7138
Energy Drinks
West Hempstead, NY 516-481-0872
Ensemble Beverages
Montgomery, AL. 334-324-7719
Farmland Dairies
Wallington, NJ 888-727-6252
Flavor Innovations
South Plainfield, NJ 800-536-2030
Florida's Natural Growers
Lake Wales, FL 863-676-1411
Galliker Dairy
Johnstown, PA. 800-477-6455
Global Beverage Company
Rochester, NY 585-381-3560
Harney & Sons Tea Company
Salisbury, CT. 888-427-6398
Harris Freeman & Company
Anaheim, CA 800-275-2378
Honest Tea
Bethesda, MD 800-865-4736
Inko's White Iced Tea
Englewood, NJ 866-747-4656
Itoen
Honolulu, HI. 808-847-4477
Northwestern Foods
St Paul, MN .800-236-4937
Pokka Beverages
American Canyon, CA 800-972-5962
PR Nutrition
San Diego, CA 800-397-5556
Quaker Oats Company
Dallas, TX. 214-330-8681
Rosenberger's Dairies
Hatfield, PA. .800-355-9074
Rupari Food Service
Deerfield Beach, FL 800-578-7274
Schneider Valley Farms Dairy
Williamsport, PA. 570-326-2021
Schneider's Dairy Holdings Inc
Pittsburgh, PA. 412-881-3525
Serengeti Tea
Gardena, CA .888-604-2040
Snapple Beverage Group
Port Chester, NY. 800-762-7753
Stash Tea Company
Portland, OR .800-547-1514
Sturm Foods
Manawa, WI. 800-347-8876
Sunlike Juice
Scarborough, ON 416-297-1140
Sweet Leaf Tea Company
Austin, TX. 512-328-7775
Templar Food Products
New Providence, NJ 800-883-6752
Tradewinds-Tea Company
Cincinnati, OH 800-599-8434
Turkey Hill Dairy
Conestoga, PA. 800-693-2479
Unilever Bestfoods
Englewood Cliffs, NJ 201-894-4000
Wengert's Dairy
Lebanon, PA .800-222-2129
White Rock Products Corporation
Whitestone, NY 800-969-7625

Instant

American Instants
Flanders, NJ 973-584-8811
Castella Imports
Hauppauge, NY 866-227-8355
Crosby Molasses Company
St. John, NB 506-634-7515
Daymar Select Fine Coffees
El Cajon, CA..................... 800-466-7590
Finlay Tea Solutions
Morristown, NJ 973-538-1701
H&K Products-Pappy's Sassafras Teas
Columbus Grove, OH 877-659-5110
Nestle Canada Inc
North York, ON 800-563-7853
Northwestern Foods
St Paul, MN...................... 800-236-4937
Plantextrakt/Martin Bower
Jersey City, NJ 201-659-3100
Prince of Peace Enterprises
Hayward, CA..................... 800-732-2328
Robertet Flavors
Piscataway, NJ 732-981-8300
Unilever Bestfoods
Englewood Cliffs, NJ 201-894-4000
Universal Commodities
Bronxville, NY 914-779-5700
VIP Foods
Flushing, NY 718-821-3942
Weaver Nut Company
Ephrata, PA...................... 717-738-3781
Whole Herb Company
Sonoma, CA 707-935-1077

Irish Breakfast

Choice Organic Teas
Seattle, WA 206-525-0051

Jasmine

Alpine Pure USA
Accord, MA 866-832-7997
Blue Willow Tea Company
Emeryville, CA.................... 800-328-0353
Choice Organic Teas
Seattle, WA 206-525-0051

Lemon

Da Vinci Gourmet
Seattle, WA 800-640-6779
Father's Country Hams
Bremen, KY 270-525-3554

Loose Leaf

Choice Organic Teas
Seattle, WA 206-525-0051
David Rio Coffee & Tea
San Francisco, CA 800-454-9605
Great Lakes Tea & Spice Company
Glen Arbor, MI 877-645-9363
Rishi Tea
Milwaukee, WI 866-747-4483
Vermont Tea & Trading Company
Middlebury, VT. 802-388-4005

Mint

Choice Organic Teas
Seattle, WA 206-525-0051
Father's Country Hams
Bremen, KY 270-525-3554
Laci Le Beau Corporation
Fresno, CA 800-356-0490

Mint Herb

Choice Organic Teas
Seattle, WA 206-525-0051

Oolong

Astral Extracts Ltd
Syosset, NY 516-496-2505
Choice Organic Teas
Seattle, WA 206-525-0051
Harney & Sons Tea Company
Salisbury, CT. 888-427-6398
Plantextrakt/Martin Bower
Jersey City, NJ 201-659-3100
SpecialTeas
Norwalk, CT 888-365-6983

Templar Food Products
New Providence, NJ 800-883-6752
Whole Herb Company
Sonoma, CA 707-935-1077

Orange Pekoe

Choice Organic Teas
Seattle, WA 206-525-0051

Peppermint Leaf

Choice Organic Teas
Seattle, WA 206-525-0051
Plantextrakt/Martin Bower
Jersey City, NJ 201-659-3100
Satori Teas
Salinas, CA 800-444-7286
Whole Herb Company
Sonoma, CA 707-935-1077

Sun

American Instants
Flanders, NJ 973-584-8811
Atlanta Coffee & Tea Company
Decatur, GA 800-426-4781
Crosby Molasses Company
St. John, NB 506-634-7515
McCormick Ingredients
Hunt Valley, MD. 800-632-5847
Nestle Canada Inc
North York, ON. 800-563-7853
Redco Foods
Windsor, CT 800-645-1190
Sara Lee Coffee & Tea
Earth City, MO 314-731-2500
Sara Lee Foodservice
Rolling Meadows, IL 800-261-4754
Stash Tea Company
Portland, OR 800-547-1514
Thirs-Tea Corporation
Miami, FL 305-651-4350
Unilever Canada
Toronto, ON 416-964-1857

Juices

A. Duda & Sons
Labelle, FL 800-440-3265
A. Duda Farm Fresh Foods
Belle Glade, FL................... 561-996-7621
AFP Advanced Food Products, LLC
Visalia, CA 559-627-2070
After-the-Fall Products
Havre De Grace, MD 410-939-1403
Alfer Laboratories
Chatsworth, CA 818-709-0737
Alfresh Beverages Canada
Rexdale, ON 800-465-1516
Aliments Lexus Foods
Rougemont, QC 800-227-4891
All Juice Food & Beverage
Hendersonville, NC 800-736-5674
Aloe Farms
Harlingen, TX..................... 800-262-6771
Aloe Laboratories, Inc.
Harlingen, TX..................... 800-258-5380
Amcan Industries
Elmsford, NY 914-347-4838
American Food Traders
Miami, FL 305-670-6250
American Fruit Processors
Pacoima, CA...................... 818-899-9574
American Soy Products
Saline, MI 734-429-2310
Ameripec
Buena Park, CA 714-690-9191
Aseltine Cider Company
Comstock Park, MI 616-784-7676
Atlanta Flagship Dairy
Atlanta, GA...................... 800-224-0669
Avalon Foodservice, Inc.
Canal Fulton, OH 800-362-0622
Berkeley Farms
Hayward, CA 510-265-8600
Beverage Capital Corporation
Halethorpe, MD 410-242-7003
Birdseye Dairy
Green Bay, WI. 920-494-5388
Bowman Apple Products Company
Mt Jackson, VA................... 877-426-9626
Bully Hill Vineyards
Hammondsport, NY 607-868-3610

Burnette Foods
Hartford, MI 616-621-3181
Byesville Aseptics
Byesville, OH 740-685-2548
California Custom Fruits & Flavors
Irwindale, CA 877-558-0056
Cargill Juice Products
Frostproof, FL.................... 800-227-4455
Carolina Products
Greer, SC 864-879-3084
Cascadian Farm & MUIR Glen; Division of General
Mills
Sedro Woolley, WA. 360-855-0100
Central Coca-Cola Bottling Company
Richmond, VA.................... 800-359-3759
Chase Brothers Dairy
Oxnard, CA 800-438-6455
Chiquita Brands International
Cincinnati, OH 800-438-0015
Chung's Gourmet Foods
Houston, TX 800-824-8647
Citrus Citrosuco North America
Lake Wales, FL 800-356-4592
Citrus International
Winter Park, FL 407-629-8037
Citrus Service
Winter Garden, FL 407-656-4999
Cliffstar Corporation
Dunkirk, NY 800-777-2389
Clinton Milk Company
Newark, NJ 973-642-3000
Coastlog Industries
Novi, MI 248-344-9556
Coca-Cola Bottling Company
Honolulu, HI 808-839-6711
Cold Hollow Cider Mill
Waterbury Center, VT. 800-327-7537
Commodities Marketing, Inc.
Edison, NJ 732-516-0700
Consun Food Industries
Elyria, OH 440-233-7501
Country Life
Hauppauge, NY 800-645-5768
Country Pure Foods
Akron, OH 330-753-2293
Crown Regal Wine Cellars
Brooklyn, NY 718-604-1430
Cumberland Dairy
Rosenhayn, NJ 856-451-1300
Cutrale Citrus Juices
Leesburg, FL 352-728-7800
Cyclone Enterprises
Houston, TX 281-872-0087
Dairy Land
Macon, GA 478-742-6461
Dairy Maid Dairy
Frederick, MD 301-663-5114
Damon Industries
Sparks, NV 775-331-3200
Del's Lemonade & Refreshments
Cranston, RI 401-463-6190
Dole Food Company
Westlake Village, CA 818-879-6600
Empresa La Famosa
Toa Baja, PR..................... 787-251-0060
Empresas La Famosa/Coco Lopez
Toa Baja, PR..................... 787-251-0060
Evans Properties
Dade City, FL 352-567-5662
Everfresh Beverages
Warren, MI 586-755-9500
Farmland Dairies
Grand Rapids, MI 616-538-3822
Farmland Dairies
Wallington, NJ 888-727-6252
Farmland Dairies
Wallington, NJ 973-777-2500
Flavouressence Products
Mississauga, ON 866-209-7778
Florida Bottling
Miami, FL........................ 305-324-5900
Florida Juice Products
Lakeland, FL..................... 863-802-4040
Florida Key West
Fort Myers, FL 239-694-8787
Florida's Natural Growers
Umatilla, FL 800-366-4440
Florida's Natural Growers
Lake Wales, FL 863-676-1411
Foremost Farms
Fitchburg, WI 608-271-3000

Four Chimneys Farm Winery Trust
Himrod, NY 607-243-7502
Fresh Squeezed Juice Company
Sebastian, FL .561-589-0390
Garelick Farms
Lynn, MA 800-487-8700
Giacorelli Imports
Boca Raton, FL. 561-451-1415
Gilette Foods
Union, NJ 908-688-0500
GLCC Company
Paw Paw, MI .269-657-3167
Global Beverage Company
Rochester, NY. 585-381-3560
Global Marketing Associates
Schaumburg, IL. 847-490-6481
Green Spot Packaging
Claremont, CA 800-456-3210
H.P. Hood
Lynnfield, ME. 800-343-6592
Hains Celestial Group
Melville, NY. .877-612-4246
Hallcrest Vineyards
Felton, CA. 831-335-4441
Hansen Beverage
Corona, CA 800-426-7367
Harrisburg Dairies
Harrisburg, PA 800-692-7429
Hawaii Coffee Company
Honolulu, HI. .800-338-8353
Heck Cellars
Arvin, CA 661-854-6120
Heritage Farms Dairy
Murfreesboro, TN. 615-895-2790
Hi-Country Corona
Selah, WA 909-272-2600
Hi-Country Foods Corporation
Selah, WA 509-697-7292
Hiller Cranberries
Rochester, MA 508-763-5257
Howard Foods
Danvers, MA. .978-774-6207
Hudson Valley Fruit Juice
Highland, NY .845-691-8061
Hunt-Wesson Foods
Rochester, NY. 209-847-0321
Hygeia Dairy Company
Corpus Christi, TX 361-854-4561
Inn Foods
Watsonville, CA 831-724-2026
Johanna Foods
Flemington, NJ 800-727-6700
John C. Meier Juice Company
Cincinnati, OH 800-346-2941
Juice Bowl Products
Lakeland, FL. .863-665-5515
Juice Mart
West Hills, CA 877-888-1011
Juice Tyme
Chicago, IL 800-236-5823
Juicy Whip
La Verne, CA .909-392-7500
Kagome
Los Banos, CA 209-826-8850
Kan-Pac
Arkansas City, KS. 620-442-6820
Kemach Food Products   Corporation
Brooklyn, NY .888-453-6224

Kemps
Cedarburg, WI. 262-377-5040
Kendall Citrus Corporation
Goulds, FL 305-258-1628
King Juice
Milwaukee, WI. 414-482-0303
Knouse Foods
Peach Glen, PA 717-677-8181
Knouse Foods Cooperative
Paw Paw, MI .269-657-5524
Krier Foods
Milwaukee, WI. 414-355-5400
Land O Lakes Milk
Sioux Falls, SD. 605-330-9526
Land O'Lakes
St Paul, MN. 651-730-2100
Langer Juice Company
City of Industry, CA 626-336-1666
Lemon-X Corporation
Huntington Sta, NY 800-220-1061
Lenox-Martell
Jamaica Plain, MA 617-442-7777
Liberty Dairy
Evart, MI 800-632-5552
Louis Dreyfus Citrus
Winter Garden, FL 407-656-1000
LPO/ LaDolc
Overland Park, KS 913-681-7757
Lyons-Magnus
Fresno, CA 559-268-5966
M&B Products
Tampa, FL. 800-899-7255
Magnotta Winery Corporation
Woodbridge, ON. 800-461-9463
Manzanita Ranch
Julian, CA 760-765-0102
Marva Maid Dairy
Newport News, VA. 800-544-4439
Matanuska Maid Dairy
Anchorage, AK 907-561-5223
Maui Pineapple Company
Kahului, HI. 808-877-3351
Maui Pineapple Company
Concord, CA .925-798-0240
Mayer Brothers Apple Products
Barker, NY 716-795-9930
Mayer Brothers Apple Products
West Seneca, NY 800-696-2937
Mayer's Cider Mill
Webster, NY 800-543-0043
Mayfield Dairy Farms
Athens, TN 800-362-9546
Mayfield Farms
Brampton, ON. 905-846-0506
McArthur Dairy
Miami, FL. 305-576-2880
McCutcheon's Apple Products
Frederick, MD. 800-888-7537
Meduri Farms Inc
Dallas, OR. 503-831-1097
Meramec Vineyards
St James, MO .877-216-9463
Minute Maid Company
Sugar Land, TX. 713-888-5000
Minute Maid Company
Dunedin, FL 800-237-0159
Mission San Juan Juices
Dana Point, CA. 949-495-7929

Mott's
Port Chester, NY. 800-964-7842
Mott's
Port Chester, NY. 914-612-4000
Mountain Sun Organic & Natural Juices
Dolores, CO 970-882-2283
Mountain Valley ProductsInc
Sunnyside, WA 509-837-8084

Mrs. Clark's Foods
Ankeny, IA 800-736-5674

Juices, salad dressings and sauces.

Nana Mae's Organics
Sebastopol, CA. 707-829-7359
Nantucket Nectars
Port Chester, NY. 617-868-3600
Natalie's Orchard Island Juice
Fort Pierce, FL 772-465-1122
National Fruit Product Company
Winchester, VA. 540-662-3401
National Fruit Product Company
Lincolnton, NC. 704-735-2531
National Grape Cooperative
Westfield, NY .716-326-5200
Northland Cranberries
Jackson, WI. 262-677-2221
Northland Cranberries
Wisconsin Rapids, WI 715-424-4444
Northland Cranberries
Mountain Home, NC. 828-693-0711
Northwest Naturals Corporation
Bothell, WA. 425-881-2200
Oberweis Dairy
North Aurora, IL. 888-645-5868
Ocean Spray Cranberries
Bordentown, NJ 609-298-0905
Ocean Spray Cranberries
Vero Beach, FL. 772-562-0800
Odwalla
Denver, CO 303-282-0500
Orchard Island Juice Company
Fort Pierce, FL 888-373-7444
Parmalat Canada
Toronto, ON 800-563-1515
Peace Mountain Natural Beverages Corporation
Springfield, MA 413-567-4942
Pepsi Bottling Group
Mesquite, TX .214-324-8500
Pepsi Bottling Group
Tulsa, OK 800-963-2424
Pepsi-Cola General Bottlers
Arlington Hts, IL 847-483-6880
Perfect Foods
Monroe, NY 800-933-3288
Pet Milk
Florence, SC 800-735-3066
Pilgrim Foods
Greenville, NH 603-878-2100
Pokka Beverages
American Canyon, CA 800-972-5962

Prairie Farms Dairy
Carlinville, IL 217-854-2547
Premier Juices
Clearwater, FL 727-533-8200
Purity Dairies
Nashville, TN 615-244-1900
Pyramid Juice Company
Ashland, OR 541-482-2292
Quality Brands
Deland, FL 386-738-3808
R.J. Corr Naturals
Posen, IL 708-389-4200
R.W. Knudsen
Chico, CA 530-899-5000
Rainbow Valley Orchards
Fallbrook, CA 760-723-3911
Rapunzel Pure Organics
Chatham, NY 800-207-2814
Regent Champagne Cellars
New York, NY 845-691-7296
Reiter Dairy
Akron, OH 800-362-0825
Reiter Dairy
Springfield, OH. 937-323-5777
Roberts Dairy Company
Omaha, NE 402-344-4321
Rohtstein Corporation
Woburn, MA 781-935-8300
Ronzoni Foods Canada
Etobicoke, ON 800-387-5032
Royal Kedem Food & Wine Company
Bayonne, NJ 201-437-9131
SANGARIA USA
Torrance, CA. 310-530-2202
Saputo
Montreal, QC 514-328-6662
Saratoga Beverage Group
Saratoga Springs, NY 888-426-8642
Schneider Valley Farms Dairy
Williamsport, PA 570-326-2021
Schneider's Dairy Holdings Inc
Pittsburgh, PA 412-881-3525
SEW Friel
Queenstown, MD 410-827-8841
Sherrill Orchards
Arvin, CA 661-858-2035
Shonan USA
Grandview, WA 509-882-5583
Silver Springs Citrus
Howey In Hills, FL 800-940-2277
Sinton Dairy Foods Company
Colorado Springs, CO. 800-388-4970
Sir Real Foods
White Plains, NY 914-948-9342
Smeltzer Orchard Company
Frankfort, MI 231-882-4421
Snapple Beverage Group
Port Chester, NY 800-762-7753
Solana Gold Organics
Sebastopol, CA 800-459-1121
St. James Winery
St James, MO 800-280-9463
St. Julian Wine Company
Paw Paw, MI 800-732-6002
Stevens Tropical Plantation
West Palm Beach, FL 561-683-4701
Stevens Tropical Plantation
West Palm Beach, FL 800-785-1355
Stop & Shop Manufacturing
Readville, MA 617-361-8400
Suiza Dairy Corporation
Rio Piedras, PR 787-792-7300
Sun Orchard
Tempe, AZ 800-505-8423
Sun Pac Foods
Brampton, ON. 905-792-2700
Sundance Industries
Newburgh, NY 845-565-6065
SunkiStreet Growers
Ontario, CA 800-225-3727
Sunlike Juice
Scarborough, ON 416-297-1140
Sunny Avocado
Jamul, CA 800-999-2862
Sunshine Farms Dairy
Elyria, OH 440-322-6301
Superbrand Dairies
Miami, FL. 305-685-8079
Superstore Industries
Fairfield, CA 707-864-0502
Swiss Valley Farms Company
Cedar Rapids, IA 319-364-8153

Switch Beverage
Darien, CT. 203-202-7383
Tamarack Farms Dairy
Newark, OH 866-221-4141
Tastee Apple Inc
Newcomerstown, OH 800-262-7753
Tazo Tea
Portland, OR 800-299-9445
Thomas Canning/Maidstone
Maidstone, ON 519-737-1531
Titusville Dairy Products
Titusville, PA 800-352-0101
Todhunter Foods
Lake Alfred, FL 863-956-1116
Todhunter International
West Palm Beach, FL 561-655-8977
Toft Dairy
Sandusky, OH 800-521-4606
Tradewinds-Tea Company
Cincinnati, OH 800-599-8434
Trailblazer Food Products
Portland, OR 800-777-7179
Tree Top
Selah, WA 800-542-4055
Treesweet Products
Houston, TX 281-876-3759
Tri-Boro Fruit Company
Fresno, CA 559-486-4141
Triple D Orchards
Empire, MI 866-781-9410
True Organic Products International
Miami, FL 800-487-0379
Truesdale Packaging Company
Warrenton, MO 636-456-6800
Turner Dairies
Covington, TN 901-476-2643
Upstate Farms Cooperative
Buffalo, NY. 866-874-6455
Valley Fig Growers
Fresno, CA 559-237-3893
Valley View Packing Company
San Jose, CA 408-289-8300
Vegetable Juices
Chicago, IL 888-776-9752
Velda Farms
North Miami Bch, FL 800-795-4649
Ventura Coastal Corporation
Ventura, CA. 805-653-7000
Veryfine Products
Littleton, MA 800-837-9346
Vitality Foodservice
Barrie, ON. 800-668-5463
Vitality Foodservice
Tampa, FL 888-863-6726
Washington State Juice
Pacoima, CA 818-899-1195
Welch's Foods Inc
Lawton, MI 269-624-1308
Welch's Foods Inc
Concord, MA 800-340-6870
Welsh Farms
Newark, NJ 800-221-0663
White Rock Products Corporation
Whitestone, NY 800-969-7625
Wholesome Sweeteners
Savannah, GA 800-680-1896
William Bolthouse Farms
Bakersfield, CA 661-366-7205
Winmix/Natural Care Products
Englewood, FL 941-475-7432
Winn-Dixie Dairies
Hammond, LA 985-549-6870
Winter Garden Citrus
Winter Garden, FL 407-656-4423
World Citrus
Winston Salem, NC. 336-723-1861
Yoder Dairies
Chesapeake, VA 757-497-3518

Ade

Country Pure Foods
Akron, OH. 877-995-8423
Optimal Nutrients
Foster City, CA 707-528-1800
S&D Coffee, Inc
Concord, NC 704-339-0917

Concentrate

American Purpac Technologies, LLC
Beloit, WI 877-787-7221

California Custom Fruits & Flavors
Irwindale, CA 877-558-0056

Grape

Arizona Beverage Company
New Hyde Park, NY 800-832-3775

Lemon

Arizona Beverage Company
New Hyde Park, NY 800-832-3775

Orange

Arizona Beverage Company
New Hyde Park, NY 800-832-3775

Aloe

Alfer Laboratories
Chatsworth, CA 818-709-0737
Aloe Farms
Harlingen, TX 800-262-6771
Aloe Laboratories, Inc.
Harlingen, TX 800-258-5380

EMERLING INTERNATIONAL FOODS, INC.

Emerling International Foods
Buffalo, NY. 716-833-7381

We supply food manufacturers and food service
customers worldwide (since 1988) with bulk ingredients including: Fruits & Vegetables; Juice
Concentrates; Herbs & Spices; Oils & Vinegars;
Flavors & Colors; Honey & Molasses. We also
produce PURE MAPLE SYRUP.

Superbrand Dairies
Miami, FL. 305-685-8079

Apple

All Juice Food & Beverage
Hendersonville, NC 800-736-5674
Apple & Eve
Roslyn, NY 800-969-8018
Aseltine Cider Company
Comstock Park, MI 616-784-7676
Birdseye Dairy
Green Bay, WI 920-494-5388
Bowman Apple Products Company
Mt Jackson, VA 877-426-9626
Brooklyn Bottling Company
Milton, NY 845-795-2171
Burnette Foods
Elk Rapids, MI 231-264-8116
Burnette Foods
Hartford, MI 616-621-3181
Cal India Foods International
Chino, CA 909-613-1660
Carolina Products
Greer, SC 864-879-3084
Cherry Central Cooperative Inc
Traverse City, MI 231-946-1860
Citrus Citrosuco North America
Lake Wales, FL 800-356-4592
Clement Pappas & Company
Seabrook, NJ 800-257-7019
Cliffstar Corporation
Dunkirk, NY 800-777-2389
Cold Hollow Cider Mill
Waterbury Center, VT. 800-327-7537
Coloma Frozen Foods
Coloma, MI. 800-642-2723
Country Pure Foods
Akron, OH. 330-753-2293
Country Pure Foods
Ellington, CT 860-872-8346
Country Pure Foods
Akron, OH. 877-995-8423
Erba Food Products
Brooklyn, NY 718-272-7700
Florida Fruit Juices
Chicago, IL 773-586-6200
Florida's Natural Growers
Lake Wales, FL 863-676-1411
Golden Town Apple Products
Thornbury, ON 519-599-6300
Green Spot Packaging
Claremont, CA 800-456-3210
Gregory Packaging
Newark, NJ 973-465-1113

Hazel Creek Orchards
  Mt Airy, GA 706-754-4899
Heritage Farms Dairy
  Murfreesboro, TN..................615-895-2790
Hi-Country Foods Corporation
  Selah, WA 509-697-7292
Knouse Foods
  Peach Glen, PA 717-677-8181
Knouse Foods Cooperative
  Paw Paw, MI.......................269-657-5524
LPO/ LaDolc
  Overland Park, KS 913-681-7757
M&B Products
  Tampa, FL.........................800-899-7255
Madera Enterprises
  Madera, CA........................800-507-9555
Manzanita Ranch
  Julian, CA.........................760-765-0102
Marva Maid Dairy
  Newport News, VA.................800-544-4439
Mayer Brothers Apple Products
  Barker, NY 716-795-9930
Mayer Brothers Apple Products
  West Seneca, NY 716-696-2937
Mayfield Farms
  Brampton, ON......................905-846-0506
McCutcheon's Apple Products
  Frederick, MD......................800-888-7537
Merlinos
  Canon City, CO....................719-275-5558
Minute Maid Company
  Sugar Land, TX.....................713-888-5000
Minute Maid Company
  Dunedin, FL 800-237-0159
Mott's
  Port Chester, NY...................800-964-7842
Mott's
  Port Chester, NY...................914-612-4000
Mountain Valley ProductsInc
  Sunnyside, WA.....................509-837-8084
Murray Cider Company
  Roanoke, VA.......................540-977-9000
Nana Mae's Organics
  Sebastopol, CA.....................707-829-7359
National Fruit Product Company
  Winchester, VA.....................540-662-3401
National Fruit Product Company
  Lincolnton, NC.....................704-735-2531
Northland Cranberries
  Mountain Home, NC................828-693-0711
Old Dutch Mustard Company
  Great Neck, NY 516-466-0522
Old Orchard Brands
  Sparta, MI.........................616-887-1745
Quality Brands
  Deland, FL 386-738-3808
Rosenberger's Dairies
  Hatfield, PA........................800-355-9074
Royal Kedem Food & Wine Company
  Bayonne, NJ 201-437-9131
SEW Friel
  Queenstown, MD 410-827-8841
Sinton Dairy Foods Company
  Colorado Springs, CO..............800-388-4970
Smeltzer Orchard Company
  Frankfort, MI 231-882-4421
Solana Gold Organics
  Sebastopol, CA.....................800-459-1121
Sunlike Juice
  Scarborough, ON 416-297-1140
Tastee Apple Inc
  Newcomerstown, OH 800-262-7753
Tree Top
  Selah, WA 800-367-6571
Tree Top
  Selah, WA 800-542-4055
Triple D Orchards
  Empire, MI 866-781-9410
True Organic Products International
  Miami, FL..........................800-487-0379
Valley View Packing Company
  San Jose, CA.......................408-289-8300
Vitality Foodservice
  Barrie, ON.........................800-668-5463
Yoder Dairies
  Chesapeake, VA 757-497-3518

Bottled

Apple & Eve
  Roslyn, NY 800-969-8018
Aseltine Cider Company
  Comstock Park, MI 616-784-7676

Carolina Products
  Greer, SC..........................864-879-3084
Cliffstar Corporation
  Dunkirk, NY 800-777-2389
Northland Cranberries
  Wisconsin Rapids, WI 715-424-4444

Boxed

Cloverland Green Spring Dairy
  Baltimore, MD 800-876-6455

EMERLING INTERNATIONAL FOODS, INC.

Emerling International Foods
  Buffalo, NY........................716-833-7381

We supply food manufacturers and food service customers worldwide (since 1988) with bulk ingredients including: Fruits & Vegetables; Juice Concentrates; Herbs & Spices; Oils & Vinegars; Flavors & Colors; Honey & Molasses. We also produce PURE MAPLE SYRUP.

Tree Top
  Selah, WA 800-367-6571

Canned

Alljuice
  Hendersonville, NC 800-736-5674
Bowman Apple Products Company
  Mt Jackson, VA....................877-426-9626
Burnette Foods
  Hartford, MI 616-621-3181
Cliffstar Corporation
  Dunkirk, NY 800-777-2389
Country Pure Foods
  Akron, OH.........................877-995-8423

EMERLING INTERNATIONAL FOODS, INC.

Emerling International Foods
  Buffalo, NY........................716-833-7381

We supply food manufacturers and food service customers worldwide (since 1988) with bulk ingredients including: Fruits & Vegetables; Juice Concentrates; Herbs & Spices; Oils & Vinegars; Flavors & Colors; Honey & Molasses. We also produce PURE MAPLE SYRUP.

Florida's Natural Brand
  Lake Wales, FL 888-657-6600
Greenwood Associates
  Highland Park, IL 847-242-7900
Hansen's Juices
  Azusa, CA.........................626-812-6022
Langer Juice Company
  City of Industry, CA 626-336-3100
Manzana Products Company
  Sebastopol, CA....................707-823-5313
Mason County Fruit Packers Cooperative
  Ludington, MI......................231-845-6248
McCutcheon's Apple Products
  Frederick, MD......................800-888-7537
Noel Corporation
  Yakima, WA 509-248-1313
Old Dutch Mustard Company
  Great Neck, NY 516-466-0522
Quality Brands
  Deland, FL 386-738-3808
San Benito Foods
  Vancouver, WA 800-453-7832
SEW Friel
  Queenstown, MD 410-827-8841
Steelback Brewery
  Tiverton, ON.......................800-879-0541
Sunlike Juice
  Scarborough, ON 416-297-1140
Tree Top
  Selah, WA 800-367-6571
Triple D Orchards
  Empire, MI 866-781-9410

Chilled

EMERLING INTERNATIONAL FOODS, INC.

Emerling International Foods
  Buffalo, NY........................716-833-7381

We supply food manufacturers and food service customers worldwide (since 1988) with bulk ingredients including: Fruits & Vegetables; Juice Concentrates; Herbs & Spices; Oils & Vinegars; Flavors & Colors; Honey & Molasses. We also produce PURE MAPLE SYRUP.

Tree Top
  Selah, WA 800-367-6571

Concentrate

A. Duda Farm Fresh Foods
  Belle Glade, FL.....................561-996-7621
Citrus Citrosuco North America
  Lake Wales, FL.....................800-356-4592
Cliffstar Corporation
  Dunkirk, NY 800-777-2389
Georgia Sun
  Newnan, GA.......................770-251-2500
GLCC Company
  Paw Paw, MI.......................269-657-3167
Green Spot Packaging
  Claremont, CA.....................800-456-3210
Hemisphere Associated
  Huntington, NY 631-673-3840
Mayer Brothers Apple Products
  Barker, NY 716-795-9930
Mountain Valley ProductsInc
  Sunnyside, WA.....................509-837-8084
Pacific Coast Fruit Company
  Portland, OR 503-234-6411
Sun Pac Foods
  Brampton, ON.....................905-792-2700
Tree Top
  Selah, WA 800-542-4055
Valley View Packing Company
  San Jose, CA.......................408-289-8300

Frozen

Bowman Apple Products Company
  Mt Jackson, VA....................877-426-9626
Country Pure Foods
  Akron, OH.........................330-753-2293
Country Pure Foods
  Akron, OH.........................877-995-8423
Greenwood Associates
  Highland Park, IL 847-242-7900
Gregory Packaging
  Newark, NJ 973-465-1113
Old Dutch Mustard Company
  Great Neck, NY 516-466-0522
Old Orchard Brands
  Sparta, MI.........................616-887-1745
Quality Brands
  Deland, FL 386-738-3808
Smeltzer Orchard Company
  Frankfort, MI 231-882-4421
Tree Top
  Selah, WA 800-367-6571
Triple D Orchards
  Empire, MI 866-781-9410

Glass-Packed

Bowman Apple Products Company
  Mt Jackson, VA....................877-426-9626
Country Pure Foods
  Akron, OH.........................877-995-8423

EMERLING INTERNATIONAL FOODS, INC.

Emerling International Foods
  Buffalo, NY........................716-833-7381

We supply food manufacturers and food service customers worldwide (since 1988) with bulk ingredients including: Fruits & Vegetables; Juice Concentrates; Herbs & Spices; Oils & Vinegars; Flavors & Colors; Honey & Molasses. We also produce PURE MAPLE SYRUP.

Tree Top
  Selah, WA 800-367-6571

Refrigerated

Bowman Apple Products Company
  Mt Jackson, VA 877-426-9626
Country Pure Foods
  Akron, OH 877-995-8423

Apple Cider

American Purpac Technologies, LLC
  Beloit, WI 877-787-7221
Clement Pappas & Company
  Seabrook, NJ 800-257-7019
Lost Trail Root Beer Com
  Louisburg, KS 800-748-7765
Shawnee Canning Company
  Cross Junction, VA 800-713-1414
Spotted Tavern Winery & Dodd's Cider Mill
  Hartwood, VA 540-752-4453
Tree Top
  Selah, WA 800-367-6571

Sparkling

Lost Trail Root Beer Com
  Louisburg, KS 800-748-7765

Apricot

Country Pure Foods
  Akron, OH 877-995-8423
Valley View Packing Company
  San Jose, CA 408-289-8300
Vitality Foodservice
  Barrie, ON 800-668-5463

Canned

Country Pure Foods
  Akron, OH 877-995-8423

EMERLING INTERNATIONAL FOODS, INC.

Emerling International Foods
  Buffalo, NY 716-833-7381

We supply food manufacturers and food service
customers worldwide (since 1988) with bulk ingredients including: Fruits & Vegetables; Juice
Concentrates; Herbs & Spices; Oils & Vinegars;
Flavors & Colors; Honey & Molasses. We also
produce PURE MAPLE SYRUP.

Greenwood Associates
  Highland Park, IL 847-242-7900

Concentrate

Valley View Packing Company
  San Jose, CA 408-289-8300

Frozen

Country Pure Foods
  Akron, OH 877-995-8423
Greenwood Associates
  Highland Park, IL 847-242-7900

Glass-Packed

Country Pure Foods
  Akron, OH 877-995-8423

EMERLING INTERNATIONAL FOODS, INC.

Emerling International Foods
  Buffalo, NY 716-833-7381

We supply food manufacturers and food service
customers worldwide (since 1988) with bulk ingredients including: Fruits & Vegetables; Juice
Concentrates; Herbs & Spices; Oils & Vinegars;
Flavors & Colors; Honey & Molasses. We also
produce PURE MAPLE SYRUP.

Greenwood Associates
  Highland Park, IL 847-242-7900

Refrigerated

Country Pure Foods
  Akron, OH 877-995-8423

Beet

EMERLING INTERNATIONAL FOODS, INC.

Emerling International Foods
  Buffalo, NY 716-833-7381

We supply food manufacturers and food service
customers worldwide (since 1988) with bulk ingredients including: Fruits & Vegetables; Juice
Concentrates; Herbs & Spices; Oils & Vinegars;
Flavors & Colors; Honey & Molasses. We also
produce PURE MAPLE SYRUP.

Vegetable Juices
  Chicago, IL 888-776-9752

Blueberry

Blueberry Store
  Grand Junction, MI 877-654-2400
Clement Pappas & Company
  Seabrook, NJ 800-257-7019
Hazel Creek Orchards
  Mt Airy, GA 706-754-4899

Carrot

EMERLING INTERNATIONAL FOODS, INC.

Emerling International Foods
  Buffalo, NY 716-833-7381

We supply food manufacturers and food service
customers worldwide (since 1988) with bulk ingredients including: Fruits & Vegetables; Juice
Concentrates; Herbs & Spices; Oils & Vinegars;
Flavors & Colors; Honey & Molasses. We also
produce PURE MAPLE SYRUP.

Post Familie Vineyards
  Altus, AR 800-275-8423
Vegetable Juices
  Chicago, IL 888-776-9752
William Bolthouse Farms
  Bakersfield, CA 661-366-7205

Cherry

Cliffstar Corporation
  Dunkirk, NY 800-777-2389
Erba Food Products
  Brooklyn, NY 718-272-7700
Greenwood Associates
  Highland Park, IL 847-242-7900
Hazel Creek Orchards
  Mt Airy, GA 706-754-4899
Knouse Foods Cooperative
  Paw Paw, MI 269-657-5524
Langer Juice Company
  City of Industry, CA 626-336-3100
M&B Fruit Juice Company
  Akron, OH 330-253-7465
Manzana Products Company
  Sebastopol, CA 707-823-5313

Manzanita Ranch
  Julian, CA 760-765-0102
Merlinos
  Canon City, CO 719-275-5558
Sunlike Juice
  Scarborough, ON 416-297-1140
Tree Top
  Selah, WA 800-367-6571

Bottled

Cliffstar Corporation
  Dunkirk, NY 800-777-2389

Boxed

Tree Top
  Selah, WA 800-367-6571

Canned

Cliffstar Corporation
  Dunkirk, NY 800-777-2389

EMERLING INTERNATIONAL FOODS, INC.

Emerling International Foods
  Buffalo, NY 716-833-7381

We supply food manufacturers and food service
customers worldwide (since 1988) with bulk ingredients including: Fruits & Vegetables; Juice
Concentrates; Herbs & Spices; Oils & Vinegars;
Flavors & Colors; Honey & Molasses. We also
produce PURE MAPLE SYRUP.

Tree Top
  Selah, WA 800-367-6571

Chilled

Tree Top
  Selah, WA 800-367-6571

Concentrate

Cliffstar Corporation
  Dunkirk, NY 800-777-2389
GLCC Company
  Paw Paw, MI 269-657-3167
Hemisphere Associated
  Huntington, NY 631-673-3840

Frozen

EMERLING INTERNATIONAL FOODS, INC.

Emerling International Foods
  Buffalo, NY 716-833-7381

We supply food manufacturers and food service
customers worldwide (since 1988) with bulk ingredients including: Fruits & Vegetables; Juice
Concentrates; Herbs & Spices; Oils & Vinegars;
Flavors & Colors; Honey & Molasses. We also
produce PURE MAPLE SYRUP.

Milne Fruit Products
  Prosser, WA 509-786-2611
Tree Top
  Selah, WA 800-367-6571

Glass-Packed

EMERLING INTERNATIONAL FOODS, INC.

Emerling International Foods
  Buffalo, NY 716-833-7381

We supply food manufacturers and food service
customers worldwide (since 1988) with bulk ingredients including: Fruits & Vegetables; Juice
Concentrates; Herbs & Spices; Oils & Vinegars;
Flavors & Colors; Honey & Molasses. We also
produce PURE MAPLE SYRUP.

Greenwood Associates
  Highland Park, IL 847-242-7900
Minute Maid Company
  Houston, TX 888-884-8952
Peace River Citrus Products
  Arcadia, FL 863-494-0440

Tree Top
Selah, WA 800-367-6571

Refrigerated

Country Pure Foods
Akron, OH. 877-995-8423

Citrus Blends

A. Duda & Sons
Labelle, FL 800-440-3265

American Mercantile Corporation
Groveland, FL. 901-454-1900

Apple & Eve
Roslyn, NY 800-969-8018

Atlanta Flagship Dairy
Atlanta, GA 800-224-0669

Berry Citrus Products
Labelle, FL 863-675-2769

Byesville Aseptics
Byesville, OH 740-685-2548

Citrus International
Winter Park, FL. 407-629-8037

Citrus Service
Winter Garden, FL 407-656-4999

Country Pure Foods
Akron, OH. 877-995-8423

Dairy Land
Macon, GA 478-742-6461

EMERLING INTERNATIONAL FOODS, INC.

Emerling International Foods
Buffalo, NY. 716-833-7381

We supply food manufacturers and food service customers worldwide (since 1988) with bulk ingredients including: Fruits & Vegetables; Juice Concentrates; Herbs & Spices; Oils & Vinegars; Flavors & Colors; Honey & Molasses. We also produce PURE MAPLE SYRUP.

Evans Properties
Dade City, FL 352-567-5662

Florida's Natural Brand
Lake Wales, FL 888-657-6600

Fresh Juice Company
Newark, NJ 973-465-7100

Galliker Dairy
Johnstown, PA. 800-477-6455

Green Spot Packaging
Claremont, CA 800-456-3210

Hansen's Juices
Azusa, CA 626-812-6022

Hi-Country Corona
Selah, WA 909-272-2600

Icy Bird
Sparta, TN 931-738-3557

Johanna Foods
Flemington, NJ 800-727-6700

Kendall Citrus Corporation
Goulds, FL 305-258-1628

Kennesaw Fruit & Juice
Pompano Beach, FL 800-949-0371

Key Colony/Red Parrot Juices
Lyons, IL. 800-424-0868

Minute Maid Company
Houston, TX 888-884-8952

Mrs. Clark's Foods
Ankeny, IA 800-736-5674

Juices, salad dressings and sauces.

Orange-Co of Florida
Arcadia, FL 863-494-4939

Sales USA
Salado, TX 800-766-7344

Saratoga Beverage Group
Saratoga Springs, NY 888-426-8642

Silver Springs Citrus
Howey In Hills, FL. 800-940-2277

Southern Gardens Citrus Processing
Clewiston, FL 863-983-3030

Sun Orchard of Florida
Haines City, FL 877-875-8423

SunkiStreet Growers
Ontario, CA 800-225-3727

Sunlike Juice
Scarborough, ON 416-297-1140

Superbrand Dairies
Miami, FL 305-685-8079

T.G Lee Dairy
Orlando, FL 407-894-4941

Ventura Coastal Corporation
Ventura, CA. 805-653-7000

Winter Garden Citrus
Winter Garden, FL 407-656-4423

World Citrus
Winston Salem, NC. 336-723-1861

World Citrus West
Lake Wales, FL 863-676-1411

Coconut

Coco Lopez
Miramar, FL 800-341-2242

Commodities Marketing, Inc.
Edison, NJ 732-516-0700

Concentrates

Aloe Life
San Diego, CA 800-414-2563

Central Michigan Foods
Owosso, MI. 517-723-3846

Chase Brothers Dairy
Oxnard, CA. 800-438-6455

Citrus Citrosuco North America
Lake Wales, FL 800-356-4592

Citrus Service
Winter Garden, FL 407-656-4999

Cliffstar Corporation
Dunkirk, NY 800-777-2389

Cobi Foods
Hantsport, NS 800-565-8229

Coca-Cola Enterprises
Atlanta, GA 800-233-7210

Daily Juice Products
Verona, PA 800-245-2929

David Michael & Company
Philadelphia, PA 800-363-5286

Del's Lemonade & Refreshments
Cranston, RI 401-463-6190

Delano Growers Grape Products
Delano, CA 661-725-3255

Fee Brothers
Rochester, NY 800-961-3337

Georgia Sun
Newnan, GA 770-251-2500

Gilette Foods
Union, NJ 908-688-0500

GLCC Company
Paw Paw, MI. 269-657-3167

Global Citrus Resources
Lakeland, FL 863-647-9020

Green Spot Packaging
Claremont, CA 800-456-3210

Hemisphere Associated
Huntington, NY 631-673-3840

Hi-Country Corona
Selah, WA 909-272-2600

Imperial Flavors Beverage Company
Milwaukee, WI 414-536-7788

Indian River Foods
Fort Pierce, FL 561-462-2222

Kerr Concentrates
Salem, OR 800-910-5377

Lion Raisins
Selma, CA 559-834-6677

Louis Dreyfus Citrus
Winter Garden, FL 407-656-1000

Main Squeeze
Columbia, MO 573-817-5616

Maui Pineapple Company
Kahului, HI 808-877-3351

Maui Pineapple Company
Concord, CA 925-798-0240

Mayer Brothers Apple Products
Barker, NY 716-795-9930

Merci Spring Water
Saint Louis, MO 314-812-4812

Minute Maid Company
Houston, TX 888-884-8952

Mountain Valley ProductsInc
Sunnyside, WA 509-837-8084

Newman's Own
Westport, CT 203-222-0136

Northwest Naturals Corporation
Bothell, WA. 425-881-2200

NTC Foods Corporation
Williamsville, NY 800-333-1637

Ocean Spray Cranberries
Vero Beach, FL 772-562-0800

Orange Bang
Sylmar, CA 818-833-1000

Pacific Coast Fruit Company
Portland, OR 503-234-6411

Parman-Kendall Corporation
Goulds, FL 305-258-1628

RFI Ingredients
Blauvelt, NY 800-962-7663

Rocket Products Company
Fenton, MO 800-325-9567

S&D Coffee, Inc
Concord, NC 704-339-0917

Sea Breeze Fruit Flavors
Towaco, NJ 800-732-2733

Silver Springs Citrus
Howey In Hills, FL. 800-940-2277

SimmaLoosa Company
Covington, LA 985-892-1400

Sun Pac Foods
Brampton, ON. 905-792-2700

Sun-Maid Growers of California
Kingsburg, CA 800-272-4746

Sunsweet Growers
Yuba City, CA 800-417-2253

Tone Products Company
Melrose Park, IL 708-681-3660

Tova Industries
Louisville, KY 888-532-8682

Tree Top
Selah, WA 800-367-6571

Tropicana
Bradenton, FL. 800-828-2102

Valley Fig Growers
Fresno, CA 559-237-3893

Valley View Packing Company
San Jose, CA. 408-289-8300

Vegetable Juices
Chicago, IL 888-776-9752

Vie-Del Company
Fresno, CA 559-834-2525

Vita-Pakt Citrus Company
Covina, CA. 626-332-1101

Vitality Foodservice
Barrie, ON. 800-668-5463

Welch's Foods Inc
Lawton, MI 269-624-1308

Welch's Foods Inc
Concord, MA 800-340-6870

Welch's Foods Inc
North East, PA. 814-725-4577

Cranberry

Apple & Eve
Roslyn, NY 800-969-8018

Atoka Cranberries, Inc.
Manseau, Quebec, CN 819-356-2001

Clement Pappas & Company
Seabrook, NJ. 800-257-7019

Cliffstar Corporation
Dunkirk, NY 800-777-2389

Country Pure Foods
Akron, OH. 330-753-2293

Country Pure Foods
Akron, OH. 877-995-8423

Delectable Gourmet LLC
Lindenhurst, NY 800-696-1350

Erba Food Products
Brooklyn, NY 718-272-7700

Florida's Natural Growers
Lake Wales, FL 863-676-1411

Gregory Packaging
Newark, NJ 973-465-1113

Key Colony/Red Parrot Juices
Lyons, IL. 800-424-0868

Langer Juice Company
City of Industry, CA 626-336-3100

McCutcheon's Apple Products
Frederick, MD. 800-888-7537

Northland Cranberries
Wisconsin Rapids, WI 715-424-4444

Northland Cranberries
Mountain Home, NC 828-693-0711

Ocean Spray Cranberries
Kenosha, WI 262-694-0621

Ocean Spray Cranberries
  Middleboro, MA 508-946-1000
Ocean Spray Cranberries
  Bordentown, NJ 609-298-0905
Ocean Spray Cranberries
  Middleboro, MA 800-662-3263
Royal Kedem Food & Wine Company
  Bayonne, NJ 201-437-9131
Smucker Quality Beverages
  Havre De Grace, MD 410-939-1403
Sunlike Juice
  Scarborough, ON 416-297-1140
Welch's Foods Inc
  Concord, MA 800-340-6870

Bottled

Apple & Eve
  Roslyn, NY 800-969-8018
Cliffstar Corporation
  Dunkirk, NY 800-777-2389
Northland Cranberries
  Wisconsin Rapids, WI 715-424-4444

Boxed

EMERLING INTERNATIONAL FOODS, INC.

Emerling International Foods
  Buffalo, NY 716-833-7381

> **We supply food manufacturers and food service customers worldwide (since 1988) with bulk ingredients including: Fruits & Vegetables; Juice Concentrates; Herbs & Spices; Oils & Vinegars; Flavors & Colors; Honey & Molasses. We also produce PURE MAPLE SYRUP.**

Ocean Spray Cranberries
  Kenosha, WI 262-694-0621

Canned

Cliffstar Corporation
  Dunkirk, NY 800-777-2389
Country Pure Foods
  Akron, OH 877-995-8423

EMERLING INTERNATIONAL FOODS, INC.

Emerling International Foods
  Buffalo, NY 716-833-7381

> **We supply food manufacturers and food service customers worldwide (since 1988) with bulk ingredients including: Fruits & Vegetables; Juice Concentrates; Herbs & Spices; Oils & Vinegars; Flavors & Colors; Honey & Molasses. We also produce PURE MAPLE SYRUP.**

McCutcheon's Apple Products
  Frederick, MD 800-888-7537
Ocean Spray Cranberries
  Kenosha, WI 262-694-0621

Concentrate

Cliffstar Corporation
  Dunkirk, NY 800-777-2389
GLCC Company
  Paw Paw, MI 269-657-3167
Hemisphere Associated
  Huntington, NY 631-673-3840
Ocean Spray Cranberries
  Middleboro, MA 800-662-3263
Pacific Coast Fruit Company
  Portland, OR 503-234-6411
Sea Breeze Fruit Flavors
  Towaco, NJ 800-732-2733

Frozen

Country Pure Foods
  Akron, OH 330-753-2293
Country Pure Foods
  Akron, OH 877-995-8423
Gregory Packaging
  Newark, NJ 973-465-1113
Milne Fruit Products
  Prosser, WA 509-786-2611
Ocean Spray Cranberries
  Kenosha, WI 262-694-0621

Glass-Packed

Country Pure Foods
  Akron, OH 877-995-8423

EMERLING INTERNATIONAL FOODS, INC.

Emerling International Foods
  Buffalo, NY 716-833-7381

> **We supply food manufacturers and food service customers worldwide (since 1988) with bulk ingredients including: Fruits & Vegetables; Juice Concentrates; Herbs & Spices; Oils & Vinegars; Flavors & Colors; Honey & Molasses. We also produce PURE MAPLE SYRUP.**

Ocean Spray Cranberries
  Kenosha, WI 262-694-0621

Refrigerated

Country Pure Foods
  Akron, OH 877-995-8423
Ocean Spray Cranberries
  Kenosha, WI 262-694-0621

Dietetic

Boissons Miami Pomor
  Longueuil, QC 877-977-3744
Florida Natural Flavors
  Casselberry, FL 800-872-5979
H R Nicholson Company
  Baltimore, MD 800-638-3514
Healthmate Products
  Highland Park, IL 800-584-8642
Pride Beverages
  Alpharetta, GA 770-663-0990
Southern Gardens Citrus Processing
  Clewiston, FL 863-983-3030
Systems Bio-Industries
  Langhorne, PA 215-702-1000

Drink

Concentrate

American Purpac Technologies, LLC
  Beloit, WI 877-787-7221
Commodities Marketing, Inc.
  Edison, NJ 732-516-0700

Fruit

A. Duda & Sons
  Labelle, FL 800-440-3265
A. Lassonde, Inc.
  Rougemont, QC 514-878-1057
Alca Trading Company
  Miami, FL 305-265-8331
Alfresh Beverages Canada
  Rexdale, ON 800-465-1516
All Juice Food & Beverage
  Hendersonville, NC 800-736-5674
American Fruit Processors
  Pacoima, CA 818-899-9574
American Mercantile Corporation
  Groveland, FL 901-454-1900
Apple & Eve
  Roslyn, NY 800-969-8018
Aseltine Cider Company
  Comstock Park, MI 616-784-7676
Atlanta Flagship Dairy
  Atlanta, GA 800-224-0669
B.M. Lawrence & Company
  San Francisco, CA 415-981-3650
Batavia Wine Cellars
  Canandaigua, NY 800-879-9463
Berry Citrus Products
  Labelle, FL 863-675-2769
Birdseye Dairy
  Green Bay, WI 920-494-5388
Bully Hill Vineyards
  Hammondsport, NY 607-868-3610
Burnette Foods
  Hartford, MI 616-621-3181
Byesville Aseptics
  Byesville, OH 740-685-2548
Cal India Foods International
  Chino, CA 909-613-1660
California Day Fresh
  Glendora, CA 800-800-0986

Carolina Products
  Greer, SC 864-879-3084
Central Coca-Cola Bottling Company
  Richmond, VA 800-359-3759
Century Foods International
  Sparta, WI 800-269-1901
Ceres Fruit Juices
  Markham, ON 800-905-1116
Chase Brothers Dairy
  Oxnard, CA 800-438-6455
Chiquita Brands International
  Cincinnati, OH 800-438-0015
Citrus Citrusoco North America
  Lake Wales, FL 800-356-4592
Cliffstar Corporation
  Dunkirk, NY 800-777-2389
Cobi Foods
  Hantsport, NS 800-565-8229
Coca-Cola Bottling Company
  Honolulu, HI 808-839-6711
Cold Hollow Cider Mill
  Waterbury Center, VT 800-327-7537
Consun Food Industries
  Elyria, OH 440-233-7501
Country Pure Foods
  Akron, OH 330-753-2293
Crown Regal Wine Cellars
  Brooklyn, NY 718-604-1430
Cutrale Citrus Juices
  Leesburg, FL 352-728-7800
Cutrale Citrus Juices
  Auburndale, FL 863-965-5000
Del's Lemonade & Refreshments
  Cranston, RI 401-463-6190
Erba Food Products
  Brooklyn, NY 718-272-7700
Everfresh Beverages
  Warren, MI 586-755-9500
Fizzy Lizzy
  New York, NY 800-203-9336
Florida Fruit Juices
  Chicago, IL 773-586-6200
Florida Juice Products
  Lakeland, FL 863-802-4040
Florida Key West
  Fort Myers, FL 239-694-8787
Four Chimneys Farm Winery Trust
  Himrod, NY 607-243-7502
Galliker Dairy
  Johnstown, PA 800-477-6455
Giacorelli Imports
  Boca Raton, FL 561-451-1415
Global Beverage Company
  Rochester, NY 585-381-3560
Global Marketing Associates
  Schaumburg, IL 847-490-6481
Golden Town Apple Products
  Thornbury, ON 519-599-6300
Great Western Juice Company
  Cleveland, OH 800-321-9180
Gregory Packaging
  Newark, NJ 973-465-1113
Hale Indian River Groves
  Wabasso, FL 800-562-4502
Harrisburg Dairies
  Harrisburg, PA 800-692-7429
Hawaii Coffee Company
  Honolulu, HI 800-338-8353
Heck Cellars
  Arvin, CA 661-854-6120
Heineman's Winery
  Put In Bay, OH 419-285-2811
Heritage Farms Dairy
  Murfreesboro, TN 615-895-2790
Hi-Country Corona
  Selah, WA 909-272-2600
Hi-Country Foods Corporation
  Selah, WA 509-697-7292
Hudson Valley Fruit Juice
  Highland, NY 845-691-8061
Hygeia Dairy Company
  Corpus Christi, TX 361-854-4561

Indian River Foods
Fort Pierce, FL .561-462-2222
Inn Foods
Watsonville, CA 831-724-2026
Jackson Milk & Ice CreamCompany
Hutchinson, KS. 620-663-1244
Jersey Juice
Lebanon, NJ .609-406-0500
Kagome
Los Banos, CA 209-826-8850
Knouse Foods
Peach Glen, PA 717-677-8181
Knouse Foods Cooperative
Paw Paw, MI. 269-657-5524
Lakewood Juices
Miami, FL 305-324-5900
Langer Juice Company
City of Industry, CA 626-336-1666
Leeward Resources
Baltimore, MD 410-837-9003
Louis Dreyfus Citrus
Winter Garden, FL 407-656-1000
LPO/ LaDolc
Overland Park, KS 913-681-7757
Ludfords
Rancho Cucamonga, CA 909-948-0797
Madera Enterprises
Madera, CA. .800-507-9555
Manzanita Ranch
Julian, CA 760-765-0102
Marva Maid Dairy
Newport News, VA 800-544-4439
Matanuska Maid Dairy
Anchorage, AK 907-561-5223
Maui Pineapple Company
Kahului, HI. .808-877-3351
Maui Pineapple Company
Concord, CA .925-798-0240
Mayer Brothers Apple Products
Barker, NY 716-795-9930
Mayer Brothers Apple Products
West Seneca, NY 800-696-2937
Mayer's Cider Mill
Webster, NY .800-543-0043
Mayfield Farms
Brampton, ON. 905-846-0506
McArthur Dairy
Miami, FL 305-576-2880
McCutcheon's Apple Products
Frederick, MD. 800-888-7537
Meduri Farms Inc
Dallas, OR. 503-831-1097
Meramec Vineyards
St James, MO 877-216-9463
Merlinos
Canon City, CO. 719-275-5558
Minute Maid Company
Sugar Land, TX. 713-888-5000
Minute Maid Company
Dunedin, FL .800-237-0159
Monarch Beverage Company
Atlanta, GA. .800-241-3732
Mott's
Port Chester, NY. 914-612-4000
Mountain Valley ProductsInc
Sunnyside, WA 509-837-8084
Mrs. Denson's Cookie Company
Ukiah, CA. 800-219-3199
Murray Cider Company
Roanoke, VA. 540-977-9000
Nana Mae's Organics
Sebastopol, CA 707-829-7359
Natalie's Orchard Island Juice
Fort Pierce, FL 772-465-1122
National Fruit Product Company
Lincolnton, NC. 704-735-2531
National Grape Cooperative
Westfield, NY 716-326-5200
Northland Cranberries
Jackson, WI. .262-677-2221
Northland Cranberries
Wisconsin Rapids, WI 715-424-4444
Northwest Naturals Corporation
Bothell, WA. .425-881-2200
NTC Foods Corporation
Williamsville, NY 800-333-1637
Ocean Spray Cranberries
Bordentown, NJ 609-298-0905
Ocean Spray Cranberries
Vero Beach, FL 772-562-0800
Ocean Spray Cranberries
Aberdeen, WA. 800-662-3263

Oceana Foods
Shelby, MI. 231-861-2141
Odwalla
Denver, CO 303-282-0500
Old Orchard Brands
Sparta, MI. 616-887-1745
Paris Foods Corporation
Camden, NJ. .856-964-0915
Parman-Kendall Corporation
Goulds, FL 305-258-1628
Pepsi Bottling Group
Mesquite, TX 214-324-8500
Pepsi-Cola General Bottlers
Arlington Hts, IL 847-483-6880
Perfection Fine Products
Maple Heights, OH 216-475-5744
Point Group
Satellite Beach, FL 888-272-1249
Pokka Beverages
American Canyon, CA 800-972-5962
Prairie Farms Dairy
Carlinville, IL 217-854-2547
Prairie Farms Dairy Inc
Carlinville, IL 217-854-2547
Premier Blending
Wichita, KS. .316-267-5533
Premier Juices
Clearwater, FL 727-533-8200
Purity Dairies
Nashville, TN 615-244-1900
Quality Kitchen Corporation
Danbury, CT .203-744-2000
R.J. Corr Naturals
Posen, IL 708-389-4200
Rainbow Valley Orchards
Fallbrook, CA 760-723-3911
Ravifruit
Hackensack, NJ 201-939-5656
Reiter Dairy
Akron, OH. 800-362-0825
Reiter Dairy
Springfield, OH. 937-323-5777
Roberts Dairy Company
Omaha, NE 402-344-4321
Rohtstein Corporation
Woburn, MA. 781-935-8300
Rosenberger's Dairies
Hatfield, PA. .800-355-9074
Royal Kedem Food & Wine Company
Bayonne, NJ .201-437-9131
Royal Wine Company
Bayonne, NJ .201-437-9131
Royal Wine Company
Bayonne, NJ .800-382-8299
SANGARIA USA
Torrance, CA .310-530-2202
Saratoga Beverage Group
Saratoga Springs, NY 888-426-8642
Schneider Valley Farms Dairy
Williamsport, PA. 570-326-2021
Schneider's Dairy Holdings Inc
Pittsburgh, PA. 412-881-3525
Silver Springs Citrus
Howey In Hills, FL. 800-940-2277
Smart Juices
Bethlehem, PA. 484-257-7080
Smeltzer Orchard Company
Frankfort, MI 231-882-4421
Smith Dairy Products Company
Orrville, OH. .800-776-7076
Snapple Beverage Group
Port Chester, NY. 800-762-7753
Solana Gold Organics
Sebastopol, CA 800-459-1121
St. James Winery
St James, MO 800-280-9463
St. Julian Wine Company
Paw Paw, MI. 800-732-6002
Stevens Tropical Plantation
West Palm Beach, FL 561-683-4701

Stevens Tropical Plantation
West Palm Beach, FL 800-785-1355
Stone Hill Wine Company
Hermann, MO 573-486-2221
Suiza Dairy Corporation
Rio Piedras, PR 787-792-7300
Sun Pac Foods
Brampton, ON. 905-792-2700
SunkiStreet Growers
Ontario, CA. .800-225-3727
Sunlike Juice
Scarborough, ON 416-297-1140
Sunny Avocado
Jamul, CA. 800-999-2862
Sunshine Farms Dairy
Elyria, OH. 440-322-6301
Sunsweet Growers
Yuba City, CA 800-417-2253
Superbrand Dairies
Miami, FL. 305-685-8079
Superstore Industries
Fairfield, CA .707-864-0502
Swiss Valley Farms Company
Cedar Rapids, IA. 319-364-8153
Tamarack Farms Dairy
Newark, OH. .866-221-4141
Tastee Apple Inc
Newcomerstown, OH. 800-262-7753
Three Vee Food & Syrup Company
Brooklyn, NY 800-801-7330
Titusville Dairy Products
Titusville, PA 800-352-0101
Todhunter Foods
Lake Alfred, FL. 863-956-1116
Todhunter International
West Palm Beach, FL 561-655-8977
Toft Dairy
Sandusky, OH 800-521-4606
Tree Top
Selah, WA 800-542-4055
Treesweet Products
Houston, TX .281-876-3759
Tri-Boro Fruit Company
Fresno, CA 559-486-4141
Triple D Orchards
Empire, MI 866-781-9410
True Organic Products International
Miami, FL. 800-487-0379
Turner Dairies
Covington, TN 901-476-2643
Valley Fig Growers
Fresno, CA 559-237-3893
Valley View Packing Company
San Jose, CA .408-289-8300
Velda Farms
North Miami Bch, FL. 800-795-4649
Ventura Coastal Corporation
Ventura, CA. .805-653-7000
Venture Vineyards
Lodi, NY. 888-635-6277
Veryfine Products
Littleton, MA 800-837-9346
Vitality Foodservice
Barrie, ON. 800-668-5463
Vitality Foodservice
Tampa, FL. 888-863-6726
Welch's Foods Inc
Lawton, MI 269-624-1308
Welch's Foods Inc
Concord, MA .800-340-6870
Welch's Foods Inc
North East, PA. 814-725-4577
Wengert's Dairy
Lebanon, PA .800-222-2129
White Rock Products Corporation
Whitestone, NY 800-969-7625
Widmer's Wine Cellars
Naples, NY 585-374-6311
Winmix/Natural Care Products
Englewood, FL 941-475-7432
World Citrus
Winston Salem, NC. 336-723-1861
World Citrus West
Lake Wales, FL 863-676-1411
Yoder Dairies
Chesapeake, VA 757-497-3518

Bottled

Apple & Eve
Roslyn, NY 800-969-8018
Aseltine Cider Company
Comstock Park, MI. 616-784-7676

Bully Hill Vineyards
Hammondsport, NY 607-868-3610
Carolina Products
Greer, SC. 864-879-3084
Chiquita Brands International
Cincinnati, OH 800-438-0015
Cliffstar Corporation
Dunkirk, NY 800-777-2389
Langer Juice Company
City of Industry, CA 626-336-1666
Stevens Tropical Plantation
West Palm Beach, FL 800-785-1355
Turner Dairies
Covington, TN 901-476-2643

Canned

Alfresh Beverages Canada
Rexdale, ON 800-465-1516
B.M. Lawrence & Company
San Francisco, CA 415-981-3650
Cliffstar Corporation
Dunkirk, NY. 800-777-2389
Hi-Country Corona
Selah, WA 909-272-2600
Langer Juice Company
City of Industry, CA 626-336-1666
McCutcheon's Apple Products
Frederick, MD. 800-888-7537
Northland Cranberries
Jackson, WI. 262-677-2221
Oceana Foods
Shelby, MI. 231-861-2141
SANGARIA USA
Torrance, CA 310-530-2202
SEW Friel
Queenstown, MD 410-827-8841
Silver Springs Citrus
Howey In Hills, FL. 800-940-2277
Sun Pac Foods
Brampton, ON. 905-792-2700
Sunshine Farms Dairy
Elyria, OH. 440-322-6301
Triple D Orchards
Empire, MI 866-781-9410

Concentrate

Citrus Citrosuco North America
Lake Wales, FL. 800-356-4592
Cutrale Citrus Juices
Leesburg, FL. 352-728-7800
GLCC Company
Paw Paw, MI 269-657-3167
Green Spot Packaging
Claremont, CA 800-456-3210
Hemisphere Associated
Huntington, NY 631-673-3840
Hi-Country Corona
Selah, WA 909-272-2600
Louis Dreyfus Citrus
Winter Garden, FL 407-656-1000
Mayer Brothers Apple Products
Barker, NY 716-795-9930
Mountain Valley ProductsInc
Sunnyside, WA 509-837-8084
Ocean Spray Cranberries
Vero Beach, FL 772-562-0800
Pacific Coast Fruit Company
Portland, OR 503-234-6411
Sea Breeze Fruit Flavors
Towaco, NJ 800-732-2733
Tree Top
Selah, WA 800-542-4055
Valley Fig Growers
Fresno, CA 559-237-3893
Valley View Packing Company
San Jose, CA. 408-289-8300

Frozen

California Day Fresh
Glendora, CA 800-800-0986
Citrus Citrosuco North America
Lake Wales, FL 800-356-4592
Cobi Foods
Hantsport, NS 800-565-8229
Country Pure Foods
Akron, OH. 330-753-2293
Del's Lemonade & Refreshments
Cranston, RI 401-463-6190

EMERLING INTERNATIONAL FOODS, INC.

Emerling International Foods
Buffalo, NY. 716-833-7381

> We supply food manufacturers and food service customers worldwide (since 1988) with bulk ingredients including: Fruits & Vegetables; Juice Concentrates; Herbs & Spices; Oils & Vinegars; Flavors & Colors; Honey & Molasses. We also produce PURE MAPLE SYRUP.

Florida Natural Flavors
Casselberry, FL 800-872-5979
Florida's Natural Brand
Lake Wales, FL 888-657-6600
Greenwood Associates
Highland Park, IL 847-242-7900
Gregory Packaging
Newark, NJ 973-465-1113
Harrisburg Dairies
Harrisburg, PA 800-692-7429
Hi-Country Corona
Selah, WA 909-272-2600
Indian River Foods
Fort Pierce, FL 561-462-2222
Inn Foods
Watsonville, CA 831-724-2026
Jackson Milk & Ice CreamCompany
Hutchinson, KS 620-663-1244
Maui Pineapple Company
Concord, CA 925-798-0240
McCain Foods Canada
Florenceville, NB 506-392-5541
Minute Maid Company
Bombay, BC 800-438-2653
Minute Maid Company
Houston, TX 888-884-8952
Ocean Spray Cranberries
Aberdeen, WA. 800-662-3263
Ocean Spray Ingredient Technology Group
Middleboro, MA 800-662-3263
Old Orchard Brands
Sparta, MI. 616-887-1745
Paris Foods Corporation
Camden, NJ. 856-964-0915
Saratoga Beverage Group
Saratoga Springs, NY 888-426-8642
Smeltzer Orchard Company
Frankfort, MI 231-882-4421
Tree Top
Selah, WA 800-367-6571
Triple D Orchards
Empire, MI 866-781-9410
Unique Ingredients
Naches, WA. 509-653-1991
Wild Fruitz Beverages
Ambler, PA 888-688-7632

Glass-Packed

Alfresh Beverages Canada
Rexdale, ON 800-465-1516
Northland Cranberries
Jackson, WI. 262-677-2221

Refrigerated

Chiquita Brands International
Cincinnati, OH 800-438-0015
Silver Springs Citrus
Howey In Hills, FL. 800-940-2277
Sunshine Farms Dairy
Elyria, OH. 440-322-6301

Fruit & Vegetable

After-the-Fall Products
Havre De Grace, MD 410-939-1403
Aileen Quirk & Sons
Kansas City, MO. 816-471-4580
Alamance Foods/Triton Water Company
Burlington, NC 800-476-9111
Alljuice
Hendersonville, NC 800-736-5674
Apple & Eve
Roslyn, NY 800-969-8018
Arcadia Dairy Farms
Arden, NC. 828-684-3556
Astral Extracts Ltd
Syosset, NY. 516-496-2505
Barbe's Dairy
Westwego, LA. 504-347-6201

Beckman & Gast Company
St Henry, OH. 419-678-4195
Bevco
Surrey, BC. 800-663-0090
Beverage Capital Corporation
Halethorpe, MD 410-242-7003
Blue Moon Foods
White River Junction, VT. 802-295-1165
Bowman Apple Products Company
Mt Jackson, VA. 877-426-9626
Brooklyn Bottling Company
Milton, NY 845-795-2171
Burnette Foods
Hartford, MI 616-621-3181
Byesville Aseptics
Byesville, OH 740-685-2548
Cal-Tex Citrus Juice
Houston, TX 800-231-0133
California Day Fresh
Glendora, CA 800-800-0986
Campbell Soup Company
Camden, NJ. 800-257-8443
Citrus Citrosuco North America
Lake Wales, FL 800-356-4592
Community Orchard
Fort Dodge, IA 515-573-8212
ConAgra Grocery Products
Irvine, CA 714-680-1000
Country Pure Foods
Akron, OH 330-753-2293
Country Pure Foods
Akron, OH 877-995-8423
Dean Dairy Products
Sharpsville, PA 800-942-8096
Del Monte Foods
San Francisco, CA 800-543-3090
Florida Bottling
Miami, FL. 305-324-5900
Florida's Natural Brand
Lake Wales, FL 888-657-6600
Fresh Juice Company
Newark, NJ 973-465-7100
Fresh Samantha
Saco, ME. 800-658-4635
Freshco
Stuart, FL 772-595-0070
Golden State Vintners
Cutler, CA 559-528-3033
Greenwood Associates
Highland Park, IL 847-242-7900
H.P. Hood
Lynnfield, ME. 800-343-6592
H.R. Nicholson Company
Sykesville, MD 800-638-3514
Hanover Foods Corporation
Hanover, PA 717-632-6000
Hansen's Juices
Azusa, CA. 626-812-6022
Hudson Valley Fruit Juice
Highland, NY 845-691-8061
Icy Bird
Sparta, TN. 931-738-3557
Jackson Milk & Ice CreamCompany
Hutchinson, KS 620-663-1244
Jel-Sert Company
West Chicago, IL 800-323-2592
Key Colony/Red Parrot Juices
Lyons, IL 800-424-0868
Lane's Dairy
El Paso, TX 915-772-6700
Langer Juice Company
City of Industry, CA 626-336-3100
LeHigh Valley Dairies
Lansdale, PA 215-855-8205
Lenox-Martell
Jamaica Plain, MA 617-442-7777
Leonard Fountain Specialties
Detroit, MI 313-891-4141
Louis Trauth Dairy
Newport, KY 800-544-6455
Lucerne Foods
Taber, AB 403-223-3546
M&B Fruit Juice Company
Akron, OH. 330-253-7465
Manzana Products Company
Sebastopol, CA 707-823-5313
Marcus Dairy
Danbury, CT 800-243-2511
Mayfield Farms
Brampton, ON. 905-846-0506
McArthur Dairy
Miami, FL. 877-803-6565

McCain Foods Canada
Florenceville, NB 506-392-5541
Meier's Wine Cellars
Cincinnati, OH 800-346-2941
Minute Maid Company
Bombay, BC 800-438-2653
Minute Maid Company
Houston, TX 888-884-8952

Mrs. Clark's Foods
Ankeny, IA 800-736-5674

Juices, salad dressings and sauces.

Noel Corporation
Yakima, WA 509-248-1313
Ocean Spray Cranberries
Kenosha, WI 262-694-0621
Ocean Spray Cranberries
Middleboro, MA 508-946-1000
Ocean Spray Cranberries
Lakeville-Middleboro, MA 800-662-3263
Odwalla
Denver, CO 303-282-0500
Old Dutch Mustard Company
Great Neck, NY 516-466-0522
Olympic Foods
Spokane, WA. 509-455-8059
Pavich Family Farms
Terra Bella, CA 661-391-1000
Peace River Citrus Products
Arcadia, FL 863-494-0440
Perfection Fine Products
Maple Heights, OH 216-475-5744
Plaidberry Company
Vista, CA 760-727-5403
Post Familie Vineyards
Altus, AR 800-275-8423
Quality Brands
Deland, FL 386-738-3808
Ray Brothers & Noble Canning Company
Hobbs, IN 765-675-7451
Red Gold
Elwood, IN 877-748-9798
RFI Ingredients
Blauvelt, NY 800-962-7663
Sales USA
Salado, TX 800-766-7344
Schepps Dairy
Dallas, TX. 800-428-6455
SEW Friel
Queenstown, MD 410-827-8841
Smucker Quality Beverages
Havre De Grace, MD 410-939-1403
Smucker Quality Beverages
Chico, CA 530-899-5000
Southern Gardens Citrus Processing
Clewiston, FL 863-983-3030
SunkiStreet Growers
Ontario, CA. 800-225-3727
Tamarack Farms Dairy
Newark, OH 866-221-4141
Tastee Apple Inc
Newcomerstown, OH 800-262-7753
Tree Top
Selah, WA 800-367-6571
Truesdale Packaging Company
Warrenton, MO 636-456-6800
Ultra Seal
New Paltz, NY 845-255-2496
Unique Ingredients
Naches, WA 509-653-1991
United Dairy
Uniontown, PA 800-966-6455

Vegetable Juices
Chicago, IL 888-776-9752
Welch's Foods Inc
Kennewick, WA 509-582-2131
Welch's Foods Inc
Westfield, NY 716-326-5252
WestFarm Foods
Seattle, WA 206-286-6832
Winder Dairy
West Valley, UT 800-946-3371

Bottled

Apple & Eve
Roslyn, NY 800-969-8018
Beverage Capital Corporation
Halethorpe, MD 410-242-7003
Clement Pappas & Company
Seabrook, NJ. 800-257-7019
Odwalla
Denver, CO 303-282-0500
Polar Beverage
Worcester, MA 800-734-9800
Truesdale Packaging Company
Warrenton, MO 636-456-6800

Canned

B.M. Lawrence & Company
San Francisco, CA 415-981-3650
Beverage Capital Corporation
Halethorpe, MD 410-242-7003
Burnette Foods
Hartford, MI 616-621-3181
Polar Beverage
Worcester, MA 800-734-9800
SEW Friel
Queenstown, MD 410-827-8841
Truesdale Packaging Company
Warrenton, MO 636-456-6800

Concentrate

American Purpac Technologies, LLC
Beloit, WI 877-787-7221
Astral Extracts Ltd
Syosset, NY. 516-496-2505
Citrus Citrosuco North America
Lake Wales, FL 800-356-4592

EMERLING INTERNATIONAL FOODS, INC.

Emerling International Foods
Buffalo, NY. 716-833-7381

We supply food manufacturers and food service
customers worldwide (since 1988) with bulk ingredients including: Fruits & Vegetables; Juice
Concentrates; Herbs & Spices; Oils & Vinegars;
Flavors & Colors; Honey & Molasses. We also
produce PURE MAPLE SYRUP.

Frozen

Citrus Citrosuco North America
Lake Wales, FL 800-356-4592
Country Pure Foods
Akron, OH. 330-753-2293
Ludfords
Rancho Cucamonga, CA 909-948-0797

Glass-Packed

Burnette Foods
Hartford, MI 616-621-3181

Fruit Punch

Arizona Beverage Company
New Hyde Park, NY 800-832-3775
Barber's Dairy
Birmingham, AL. 205-942-2351
Erba Food Products
Brooklyn, NY 718-272-7700
Minute Maid Company
Dunedin, FL 800-237-0159
Pepsi Bottling Group
Mesquite, TX 214-324-8500
Reiter Dairy
Springfield, OH. 937-323-5777
Rocket Products Company
Fenton, MO. 800-325-9567
Sinton Dairy Foods Company
Colorado Springs, CO. 800-388-4970

Sunlike Juice
Scarborough, ON 416-297-1140
Trailblazer Food Products
Portland, OR 800-777-7179
Winn-Dixie Dairies
Hammond, LA 985-549-6870

Concentrate

Mayer Brothers Apple Products
West Seneca, NY 800-696-2937

Garlic

EMERLING INTERNATIONAL FOODS, INC.

Emerling International Foods
Buffalo, NY. 716-833-7381

We supply food manufacturers and food service
customers worldwide (since 1988) with bulk ingredients including: Fruits & Vegetables; Juice
Concentrates; Herbs & Spices; Oils & Vinegars;
Flavors & Colors; Honey & Molasses. We also
produce PURE MAPLE SYRUP.

Howard Foods
Danvers, MA. 978-774-6207
Vegetable Juices
Chicago, IL 888-776-9752

Grape

A.W. Jantzi & Sons
Wellesley, ON 519-656-2400
Arcadia Dairy Farms
Arden, NC. 828-684-3556
Bully Hill Vineyards
Hammondsport, NY 607-868-3610
Clement Pappas & Company
Seabrook, NJ. 800-257-7019
Cliffstar Corporation
Dunkirk, NY 800-777-2389
Country Pure Foods
Ellington, CT 860-872-8346
Country Pure Foods
Akron, OH. 877-995-8423
Crown Regal Wine Cellars
Brooklyn, NY 718-604-1430
Everfresh Beverages
Warren, MI 586-755-9500
Florida Fruit Juices
Chicago, IL. 773-586-6200
Florida's Natural Brand
Lake Wales, FL 888-657-6600
Four Chimneys Farm Winery Trust
Himrod, NY 607-243-7502
Golden State Vintners
Cutler, CA 559-528-3033
Green Spot Packaging
Claremont, CA 800-456-3210
Greenwood Associates
Highland Park, IL 847-242-7900
Growers Cooperative Grape Juice Company
Westfield, NY 716-326-3161
Hillcrest Orchard
Lake Placid, FL. 865-397-5273
Knouse Foods
Peach Glen, PA 717-677-8181
Langer Juice Company
City of Industry, CA 626-336-3100
M&B Fruit Juice Company
Akron, OH. 330-253-7465
Madera Enterprises
Madera, CA. 800-507-9555
Manzana Products Company
Sebastopol, CA 707-823-5313
Manzanita Ranch
Julian, CA 760-765-0102
Mayer Brothers Apple Products
West Seneca, NY 800-696-2937
Mayer's Cider Mill
Webster, NY 800-543-0043
McArthur Dairy
Miami, FL 305-576-2880
McCutcheon's Apple Products
Frederick, MD. 800-888-7537
Meier's Wine Cellars
Cincinnati, OH 800-346-2941
Meramec Vineyards
St James, MO 877-216-9463

Merlinos
Canon City, CO..............719-275-5558
Minute Maid Company
Houston, TX..............888-884-8952
Northland Cranberries
Mountain Home, NC............828-693-0711
Paklab Products
Boucherville, QC.............450-449-1224
Post Familie Vineyards
Altus, AR.................800-275-8423
Royal Kedem Food & Wine Company
Bayonne, NJ................201-437-9131
Royal Wine Company
Bayonne, NJ................201-437-9131
Royal Wine Company
Bayonne, NJ................800-382-8299
SEW Friel
Queenstown, MD..............410-827-8841
Smucker Quality Beverages
Havre De Grace, MD...........410-939-1403
St. James Winery
St James, MO...............800-280-9463
St. Julian Wine Company
Paw Paw, MI...............800-732-6002
Sunlike Juice
Scarborough, ON.............416-297-1140
Tree Top
Selah, WA.................800-542-4055
True Organic Products International
Miami, FL.................800-487-0379
Venture Vineyards
Lodi, NY.................888-635-6277
Welch's Foods Inc
Kennewick, WA..............509-582-2131
Welch's Foods Inc
Concord, MA...............800-340-6870
Widmer's Wine Cellars
Naples, NY................585-374-6311

Bottled

Cliffstar Corporation
Dunkirk, NY................800-777-2389
Northland Cranberries
Wisconsin Rapids, WI...........715-424-4444
R.A.B. Food Group LLC
Secaucus, NJ...............201-453-5200
Sunlike Juice
Scarborough, ON.............416-297-1140
Welch's Foods Inc
Kennewick, WA..............509-582-2131
Widmer's Wine Cellars
Naples, NY................585-374-6311

Boxed

American Purpac Technologies, LLC
Beloit, WI................877-787-7221
Cloverland Green Spring Dairy
Baltimore, MD..............800-876-6455
Royal Wine Company
Bayonne, NJ................800-382-8299
Welch's Foods Inc
Kennewick, WA..............509-582-2131

Canned

American Purpac Technologies, LLC
Beloit, WI................877-787-7221
Cliffstar Corporation
Dunkirk, NY................800-777-2389
Country Pure Foods
Akron, OH.................877-995-8423

EMERLING INTERNATIONAL FOODS, INC.

Emerling International Foods
Buffalo, NY................716-833-7381

We supply food manufacturers and food service customers worldwide (since 1988) with bulk ingredients including: Fruits & Vegetables; Juice Concentrates; Herbs & Spices; Oils & Vinegars; Flavors & Colors; Honey & Molasses. We also produce PURE MAPLE SYRUP.

Growers Cooperative Grape Juice Company
Westfield, NY...............716-326-3161
McCutcheon's Apple Products
Frederick, MD..............800-888-7537
SEW Friel
Queenstown, MD..............410-827-8841
Unique Ingredients
Naches, WA................509-653-1991

Welch's Foods Inc
Kennewick, WA..............509-582-2131

Chilled

American Purpac Technologies, LLC
Beloit, WI................877-787-7221

EMERLING INTERNATIONAL FOODS, INC.

Emerling International Foods
Buffalo, NY................716-833-7381

We supply food manufacturers and food service customers worldwide (since 1988) with bulk ingredients including: Fruits & Vegetables; Juice Concentrates; Herbs & Spices; Oils & Vinegars; Flavors & Colors; Honey & Molasses. We also produce PURE MAPLE SYRUP.

Welch's Foods Inc
Kennewick, WA..............509-582-2131

Concentrate

Cliffstar Corporation
Dunkirk, NY................800-777-2389
GLCC Company
Paw Paw, MI...............269-657-3167
Green Spot Packaging
Claremont, CA..............800-456-3210
Hemisphere Associated
Huntington, NY.............631-673-3840
Louis Dreyfus Citrus
Winter Garden, FL............407-656-1000
Mayer Brothers Apple Products
West Seneca, NY.............800-696-2937
Mountain Valley ProductsInc
Sunnyside, WA..............509-837-8084
Ocean Spray Cranberries
Middleboro, MA.............800-662-3263
Paklab Products
Boucherville, QC.............450-449-1224
Sun Pac Foods
Brampton, ON...............905-792-2700
Tree Top
Selah, WA.................800-542-4055

Frozen

American Purpac Technologies, LLC
Beloit, WI................877-787-7221
Country Pure Foods
Akron, OH.................877-995-8423

EMERLING INTERNATIONAL FOODS, INC.

Emerling International Foods
Buffalo, NY................716-833-7381

We supply food manufacturers and food service customers worldwide (since 1988) with bulk ingredients including: Fruits & Vegetables; Juice Concentrates; Herbs & Spices; Oils & Vinegars; Flavors & Colors; Honey & Molasses. We also produce PURE MAPLE SYRUP.

Growers Cooperative Grape Juice Company
Westfield, NY...............716-326-3161
Louis Dreyfus Citrus
Winter Garden, FL............407-656-1000
Milne Fruit Products
Prosser, WA................509-786-2611
Welch's Foods Inc
Kennewick, WA..............509-582-2131

Glass-Packed

American Purpac Technologies, LLC
Beloit, WI................877-787-7221
Country Pure Foods
Akron, OH.................877-995-8423

EMERLING INTERNATIONAL FOODS, INC.

Emerling International Foods
Buffalo, NY................716-833-7381

We supply food manufacturers and food service customers worldwide (since 1988) with bulk ingredients including: Fruits & Vegetables; Juice Concentrates; Herbs & Spices; Oils & Vinegars; Flavors & Colors; Honey & Molasses. We also produce PURE MAPLE SYRUP.

Growers Cooperative Grape Juice Company
Westfield, NY...............716-326-3161
Royal Wine Company
Bayonne, NJ................800-382-8299
Unique Ingredients
Naches, WA................509-653-1991
Welch's Foods Inc
Kennewick, WA..............509-582-2131

Refrigerated

Country Pure Foods
Akron, OH.................877-995-8423

Grapefruit

American Mercantile Corporation
Groveland, FL..............901-454-1900
Clement Pappas & Company
Seabrook, NJ...............800-257-7019
Cliffstar Corporation
Dunkirk, NY................800-777-2389
Country Pure Foods
Akron, OH.................330-753-2293
Country Pure Foods
Akron, OH.................877-995-8423
Cropp Cooperative-Organic Valley
La Farge, WI...............888-444-6455
Cutrale Citrus Juices
Auburndale, FL.............863-965-5000
Florida Fruit Juices
Chicago, IL................773-586-6200
Florida Juice Products
Lakeland, FL...............863-802-4040
Florida's Natural Growers
Lake Wales, FL.............863-676-1411
Freshco
Stuart, FL.................772-595-0070
Gene's Citrus Ranch
Palmetto, FL...............888-723-2006
Great Western Juice Company
Cleveland, OH..............800-321-9180
Greenwood Associates
Highland Park, IL............847-242-7900
Gregory Packaging
Newark, NJ................973-465-1113
Hi-Country Corona
Selah, WA.................909-272-2600
Indian River Foods
Fort Pierce, FL.............561-462-2222
Kennesaw Fruit & Juice
Pompano Beach, FL...........800-949-0371
Louis Dreyfus Citrus
Winter Garden, FL............407-656-1000
Marva Maid Dairy
Newport News, VA............800-544-4439
Mayer Brothers Apple Products
West Seneca, NY.............800-696-2937
Minute Maid Company
Sugar Land, TX.............713-888-5000
Minute Maid Company
Dunedin, FL...............800-237-0159
Minute Maid Company
Houston, TX...............888-884-8952
Natalie's Orchard Island Juice
Fort Pierce, FL.............772-465-1122
Ocean Spray Cranberries
Vero Beach, FL.............772-562-0800
Ocean Spray Cranberries
Lakeville-Middleboro, MA........800-662-3263
Perricone Juices
Beaumont, CA...............951-769-7171
Quality Kitchen Corporation
Danbury, CT................203-744-2000
Rainbow Valley Orchards
Fallbrook, CA..............760-723-3911
Reiter Dairy
Springfield, OH.............937-323-5777
Saratoga Beverage Group
Saratoga Springs, NY..........888-426-8642
Silver Springs Citrus
Howey In Hills, FL...........800-940-2277
Sun Orchard
Tempe, AZ................800-505-8423
Sunlike Juice
Scarborough, ON.............416-297-1140
Superbrand Dairies
Miami, FL.................305-685-8079
Tropicana
Bradenton, FL..............800-828-2102
World Citrus West
Lake Wales, FL.............863-676-1411

Yoder Dairies
  Chesapeake, VA .757-497-3518

Bottled

Cliffstar Corporation
  Dunkirk, NY 800-777-2389
Northland Cranberries
  Wisconsin Rapids, WI 715-424-4444

Boxed

American Purpac Technologies, LLC
  Beloit, WI 877-787-7221

EMERLING INTERNATIONAL FOODS, INC.

Emerling International Foods
  Buffalo, NY 716-833-7381

We supply food manufacturers and food service customers worldwide (since 1988) with bulk ingredients including: Fruits & Vegetables; Juice Concentrates; Herbs & Spices; Oils & Vinegars; Flavors & Colors; Honey & Molasses. We also produce PURE MAPLE SYRUP.

Canned

American Purpac Technologies, LLC
  Beloit, WI 877-787-7221
Country Pure Foods
  Akron, OH. 877-995-8423

EMERLING INTERNATIONAL FOODS, INC.

Emerling International Foods
  Buffalo, NY 716-833-7381

We supply food manufacturers and food service customers worldwide (since 1988) with bulk ingredients including: Fruits & Vegetables; Juice Concentrates; Herbs & Spices; Oils & Vinegars; Flavors & Colors; Honey & Molasses. We also produce PURE MAPLE SYRUP.

Hi-Country Corona
  Selah, WA 909-272-2600
Ocean Spray Cranberries
  Lakeville-Middleboro, MA 800-662-3263

Concentrate

Cliffstar Corporation
  Dunkirk, NY 800-777-2389
Georgia Sun
  Newnan, GA 770-251-2500
Hi-Country Corona
  Selah, WA 909-272-2600
Ocean Spray Cranberries
  Vero Beach, FL 772-562-0800
Sea Breeze Fruit Flavors
  Towaco, NJ 800-732-2733
Sun Pac Foods
  Brampton, ON .905-792-2700

Frozen

A. Duda Farm Fresh Foods
  Belle Glade, FL 561-996-7621
American Purpac Technologies, LLC
  Beloit, WI 877-787-7221

Country Pure Foods
  Akron, OH. 330-753-2293
Country Pure Foods
  Akron, OH. 877-995-8423

EMERLING INTERNATIONAL FOODS, INC.

Emerling International Foods
  Buffalo, NY 716-833-7381

We supply food manufacturers and food service customers worldwide (since 1988) with bulk ingredients including: Fruits & Vegetables; Juice Concentrates; Herbs & Spices; Oils & Vinegars; Flavors & Colors; Honey & Molasses. We also produce PURE MAPLE SYRUP.

Hi-Country Corona
  Selah, WA 909-272-2600
Ocean Spray Cranberries
  Lakeville-Middleboro, MA 800-662-3263

Glass-Packed

American Purpac Technologies, LLC
  Beloit, WI 877-787-7221
Country Pure Foods
  Akron, OH. 877-995-8423

EMERLING INTERNATIONAL FOODS, INC.

Emerling International Foods
  Buffalo, NY 716-833-7381

We supply food manufacturers and food service customers worldwide (since 1988) with bulk ingredients including: Fruits & Vegetables; Juice Concentrates; Herbs & Spices; Oils & Vinegars; Flavors & Colors; Honey & Molasses. We also produce PURE MAPLE SYRUP.

Ocean Spray Cranberries
  Lakeville-Middleboro, MA 800-662-3263

Refrigerated

American Purpac Technologies, LLC
  Beloit, WI 877-787-7221
Country Pure Foods
  Akron, OH. 877-995-8423
Ocean Spray Cranberries
  Lakeville-Middleboro, MA 800-662-3263

Guava

Meadow Gold Dairies
  Honolulu, HI 808-949-6161
Parman-Kendall Corporation
  Goulds, FL 305-258-1628
Stevens Tropical Plantation
  West Palm Beach, FL 561-683-4701

Key Lime

Florida Key West
  Fort Myers, FL 239-694-8787

Lemon

Agrocan
  Toronto, ON 877-247-6226
American Purpac Technologies, LLC
  Beloit, WI 877-787-7221
Castella Imports
  Hauppauge, NY 866-227-8355
Clement Pappas & Company
  Seabrook, NJ .800-257-7019
Erba Food Products
  Brooklyn, NY .718-272-7700
Florida Key West
  Fort Myers, FL 239-694-8787
Greenwood Associates
  Highland Park, IL 847-242-7900
Hansen's Juices
  Azusa, CA 626-812-6022
Hi-Country Corona
  Selah, WA 909-272-2600
Jus-Made
  Dallas, TX 800-969-3746
Louis Dreyfus Citrus
  Winter Garden, FL 407-656-1000
Minute Maid Company
  Houston, TX 888-884-8952
Natalie's Orchard Island Juice
  Fort Pierce, FL 772-465-1122

Nielsen Citrus Products
  Huntington Beach, CA 714-892-5586
Perricone Juices
  Beaumont, CA. 951-769-7171
Rainbow Valley Orchards
  Fallbrook, CA .760-723-3911
Reiter Dairy
  Springfield, OH. 937-323-5777
Sun Orchard
  Tempe, AZ 800-505-8423
Todhunter International
  West Palm Beach, FL 561-655-8977
Village Imports
  Brisbane, CA. .888-865-8714

Bottled

Cliffstar Corporation
  Dunkirk, NY 800-777-2389

Canned

American Purpac Technologies, LLC
  Beloit, WI 877-787-7221
Cliffstar Corporation
  Dunkirk, NY 800-777-2389

EMERLING INTERNATIONAL FOODS, INC.

Emerling International Foods
  Buffalo, NY. 716-833-7381

We supply food manufacturers and food service customers worldwide (since 1988) with bulk ingredients including: Fruits & Vegetables; Juice Concentrates; Herbs & Spices; Oils & Vinegars; Flavors & Colors; Honey & Molasses. We also produce PURE MAPLE SYRUP.

Hi-Country Corona
  Selah, WA 909-272-2600

Concentrate

Citrico
  Northbrook, IL 888-625-8516
Cliffstar Corporation
  Dunkirk, NY 800-777-2389
Hi-Country Corona
  Selah, WA 909-272-2600
Louis Dreyfus Citrus
  Winter Garden, FL 407-656-1000

Frozen

American Purpac Technologies, LLC
  Beloit, WI 877-787-7221

EMERLING INTERNATIONAL FOODS, INC.

Emerling International Foods
  Buffalo, NY. 716-833-7381

We supply food manufacturers and food service customers worldwide (since 1988) with bulk ingredients including: Fruits & Vegetables; Juice Concentrates; Herbs & Spices; Oils & Vinegars; Flavors & Colors; Honey & Molasses. We also produce PURE MAPLE SYRUP.

Hi-Country Corona
  Selah, WA 909-272-2600
Louis Dreyfus Citrus
  Winter Garden, FL 407-656-1000
Nielsen Citrus Products
  Huntington Beach, CA 714-892-5586

Glass-Packed

American Purpac Technologies, LLC
  Beloit, WI 877-787-7221

EMERLING INTERNATIONAL FOODS, INC.

Emerling International Foods
  Buffalo, NY. 716-833-7381

We supply food manufacturers and food service customers worldwide (since 1988) with bulk ingredients including: Fruits & Vegetables; Juice Concentrates; Herbs & Spices; Oils & Vinegars; Flavors & Colors; Honey & Molasses. We also produce PURE MAPLE SYRUP.

Refrigerated

American Purpac Technologies, LLC
  Beloit, WI 877-787-7221

Lemonade

Anderson Erickson Dairy
  Des Moines, IA 515-265-2521
Calvert's
  El Paso, TX 915-544-3434
Clement Pappas & Company
  Seabrook, NJ 800-257-7019
Del's Lemonade & Refreshments
  Cranston, RI 401-463-6190
Florida's Natural Growers
  Lake Wales, FL 863-676-1411
Jones Soda Company
  Seattle, WA 800-656-6050
M&B Fruit Juice Company
  Akron, OH 330-253-7465
M.H. Zeigler & Sons
  Lansdale, PA 215-855-5161
Naterl
  St. Bruno, QC 800- 50- 115
Newman's Own
  Westport, CT 203-222-0136
Rocket Products Company
  Fenton, MO 800-325-9567
Sunlike Juice
  Scarborough, ON 416-297-1140
Sweet Leaf Tea Company
  Austin, TX 512-328-7775
Techni-Brew International
  Portland, OR 800-454-4077

Concentrate

A. Duda Farm Fresh Foods
  Belle Glade, FL 561-996-7621
ADM Ethanol Sales
  Decatur, IL 217-424-2565
Advance Food Brokers
  West Bloomfield, MI 248-851-9045
Anheuser-Busch
  Cartersville, GA 770-386-2000
Baltimore Brewing Company
  Baltimore, MD 410-837-5000
Bear Brewing Company
  Kamloops, BC 250-851-2543
Beaulieu Vineyard
  Rutherford, CA 800-264-6918
Beaver Street Brewery
  Flagstaff, AZ 928-779-0079
Bow Valley Brewing Company
  Canmore, AB 403-678-2739
Brasserie Brasel Brewery
  Lasalle, QC 800-463-2728
Bravard Vineyards & Winery
  Hopkinsville, KY 270-269-2583
Clipper City Brewing
  Baltimore, MD 410-247-7822
Cold Spring Brewing Company
  Cold Spring, MN 320-685-8686
Columbia Brewery
  Creston, BC 250-428-9344
Creemore Springs Brewery
  Creemore, ON 800-267-2240
Dogfish Head Craft Brewery
  Lewes, DE 888-834-3474
Golden State Vintners
  Cutler, CA 559-528-3033
Great Lakes Brewing
  Etobicoke, ON 800-463-5435
Great Northern Brewing Company
  Whitefish, MT 406-863-1000
Great Western Brewing Company
  Saskatoon, SK 800-764-4492
Hogtown Brewing Company
  Mississauga, ON 905-855-9065
Labatt Breweries
  Edmonton, AB 800-268-2997
Lakefront Brewery
  Milwaukee, WI 414-372-8800
Makers Mark Distillery
  Loretto, KY 270-865-2881
Mayer Brothers Apple Products
  West Seneca, NY 800-696-2937
Mendocino Brewing Company
  Ukiah, CA 707-463-2087
Miller Brewing Company
  St Louis, MO 314-822-5483

Miller Brewing Company
  Eden, NC 336-635-1198
Miller Brewing Company
  Milwaukee, WI 414-931-2000
Miller Brewing Company
  Edison, NJ 732-635-1400
Miller Brewing Company
  Fort Worth, TX 800-645-5376
Miller Brewing Company
  Trenton, OH 800-944-5483
Miller Brewing Company
  Elk Grove Vlg, IL 847-758-9941
Millstream Brewing
  Amana, IA 319-622-3672
Minute Maid Company
  Houston, TX 888-884-8952
Monticello Cellars
  Napa, CA 707-253-2802
Moosehead Breweries
  St. John, NB 506-635-7000
Natural Wonder Foods
  Brooklyn, NY 718-436-6811
Pennsylvania Brewing Company
  Pittsburgh, PA 412-237-9400
Portland Brewing Company
  Portland, OR 503-226-7623
Santa Cruz Brewing Company
  Santa Cruz, CA 831-429-8838
Sapporo
  New York, NY 800-827-8234
Sebastiani Vineyards
  Sonoma, CA 800-888-5532
Shipyard Brewing Company
  Portland, ME 207-761-0807
Tabernash Brewing Company
  Longmont, CO 303-772-0258
Unibroue/Unibrew
  Chambly, QC 450-658-7658

Lime

American Purpac Technologies, LLC
  Beloit, WI 877-787-7221
Castella Imports
  Hauppauge, NY 866-227-8355
Clement Pappas & Company
  Seabrook, NJ 800-257-7019

EMERLING INTERNATIONAL FOODS, INC.

Emerling International Foods
  Buffalo, NY 716-833-7381

> We supply food manufacturers and food service customers worldwide (since 1988) with bulk ingredients including: Fruits & Vegetables; Juice Concentrates; Herbs & Spices; Oils & Vinegars; Flavors & Colors; Honey & Molasses. We also produce PURE MAPLE SYRUP.

Florida's Natural Brand
  Lake Wales, FL 888-657-6600
Greenwood Associates
  Highland Park, IL 847-242-7900
Hi-Country Corona
  Selah, WA 909-272-2600
M&B Fruit Juice Company
  Akron, OH 330-253-7465
Mott's
  Port Chester, NY 914-612-4000
Natalie's Orchard Island Juice
  Fort Pierce, FL 772-465-1122
Nielsen Citrus Products
  Huntington Beach, CA 714-892-5586
Parman-Kendall Corporation
  Goulds, FL 305-258-1628
Perricone Juices
  Beaumont, CA 951-769-7171
Reiter Dairy
  Springfield, OH 937-323-5777
Sun Orchard
  Tempe, AZ 800-505-8423
True Organic Products International
  Miami, FL 800-487-0379

Mango

Stevens Tropical Plantation
  West Palm Beach, FL 561-683-4701
Sunlike Juice
  Scarborough, ON 416-297-1140

Onion

EMERLING INTERNATIONAL FOODS, INC.

Emerling International Foods
  Buffalo, NY 716-833-7381

> We supply food manufacturers and food service customers worldwide (since 1988) with bulk ingredients including: Fruits & Vegetables; Juice Concentrates; Herbs & Spices; Oils & Vinegars; Flavors & Colors; Honey & Molasses. We also produce PURE MAPLE SYRUP.

Howard Foods
  Danvers, MA 978-774-6207
Vegetable Juices
  Chicago, IL 888-776-9752

Orange

A. Duda & Sons
  Labelle, FL 800-440-3265
Alta Dena Certified Dairy
  City of Industry, CA 800-535-1369
American Mercantile Corporation
  Groveland, FL 901-454-1900
American Purpac Technologies, LLC
  Beloit, WI 877-787-7221
Anderson Erickson Dairy
  Des Moines, IA 515-265-2521
Arcadia Dairy Farms
  Arden, NC 828-684-3556
Atlanta Flagship Dairy
  Atlanta, GA 800-224-0669
Barbe's Dairy
  Westwego, LA 504-347-6201
Barber's Dairy
  Birmingham, AL 205-942-2351
Birdseye Dairy
  Green Bay, WI 920-494-5388
Byrne Dairy
  Syracuse, NY 800-899-1535
Cass Clay Creamery
  Fargo, ND 701-293-6455
Chase Brothers Dairy
  Oxnard, CA 800-438-6455
Citrus Citrosuco North America
  Lake Wales, FL 800-356-4592
Clement Pappas & Company
  Seabrook, NJ 800-257-7019
Cliffstar Corporation
  Dunkirk, NY 800-777-2389
Cloverland Green Spring Dairy
  Baltimore, MD 800-876-6455
Country Pure Foods
  Akron, OH 330-753-2293
Country Pure Foods
  Ellington, CT 860-872-8346
Country Pure Foods
  Akron, OH 877-995-8423
Cropp Cooperative-Organic Valley
  La Farge, WI 888-444-6455
Cutrale Citrus Juices
  Leesburg, FL 352-728-7800
Cutrale Citrus Juices
  Auburndale, FL 863-965-5000
Dean Foods Company/Country Fresh
  Grand Rapids, MI 616-243-0173

EMERLING INTERNATIONAL FOODS, INC.

Emerling International Foods
  Buffalo, NY 716-833-7381

> We supply food manufacturers and food service customers worldwide (since 1988) with bulk ingredients including: Fruits & Vegetables; Juice Concentrates; Herbs & Spices; Oils & Vinegars; Flavors & Colors; Honey & Molasses. We also produce PURE MAPLE SYRUP.

Erba Food Products
  Brooklyn, NY 718-272-7700
Everfresh Beverages
  Warren, MI 586-755-9500
Florida Fruit Juices
  Chicago, IL 773-586-6200
Florida Juice Products
  Lakeland, FL 863-802-4040

Florida's Natural Brand
Lake Wales, FL 888-657-6600
Florida's Natural Growers
Lake Wales, FL 863-676-1411
Freshco
Stuart, FL 772-595-0070
Galliker Dairy
Johnstown, PA. 800-477-6455
Gene's Citrus Ranch
Palmetto, FL .888-723-2006
Great Western Juice Company
Cleveland, OH 800-321-9180
Green Spot Packaging
Claremont, CA 800-456-3210
Greenwood Associates
Highland Park, IL 847-242-7900
Harrisburg Dairies
Harrisburg, PA 800-692-7429
Heritage Farms Dairy
Murfreesboro, TN 615-895-2790
Hi-Country Corona
Selah, WA 909-272-2600
Hygeia Dairy Company
Corpus Christi, TX 361-854-4561
Indian River Foods
Fort Pierce, FL 561-462-2222
Inn Foods
Watsonville, CA 831-724-2026
Jackson Milk & Ice CreamCompany
Hutchinson, KS. 620-663-1244
Jus-Made
Dallas, TX. 800-969-3746
Key Colony/Red Parrot Juices
Lyons, IL 800-424-0868
Knouse Foods
Peach Glen, PA 717-677-8181
Louis Dreyfus Citrus
Winter Garden, FL 407-656-1000
Louis Trauth Dairy
Newport, KY. 800-544-6455
M&B Fruit Juice Company
Akron, OH. 330-253-7465
M&B Products
Tampa, FL. 800-899-7255
Marcus Dairy
Danbury, CT .800-243-2511
Marva Maid Dairy
Newport News, VA 800-544-4439
Matanuska Maid Dairy
Anchorage, AK 907-561-5223
Mayer Brothers Apple Products
West Seneca, NY 800-696-2937
McArthur Dairy
Miami, FL 877-803-6565
Meadow Gold Dairies
Honolulu, HI .808-949-6161
Minute Maid Company
Sugar Land, TX 713-888-5000
Minute Maid Company
Dunedin, FL .800-237-0159
Minute Maid Company
Bombay, BC .800-438-2653
Minute Maid Company
Houston, TX .888-884-8952
Natalie's Orchard Island Juice
Fort Pierce, FL 772-465-1122
Noel Corporation
Yakima, WA .509-248-1313
Northland Cranberries
Wisconsin Rapids, WI 715-424-4444
Peace River Citrus Products
Arcadia, FL 863-494-0440
Perricone Juices
Beaumont, CA. 951-769-7171
Prairie Farms Dairy
Carlinville, IL .217-854-2547
Prairie Farms Dairy
Granite City, IL 618-451-5600
Prairie Farms Dairy Inc
Carlinville, IL .217-854-2547
Quality Kitchen Corporation
Danbury, CT .203-744-2000

Rainbow Valley Orchards
Fallbrook, CA 760-723-3911
Reiter Dairy
Akron, OH. 800-362-0825
Reiter Dairy
Springfield, OH. 937-323-5777
Roberts Dairy Company
Omaha, NE 402-344-4321
Rocket Products Company
Fenton, MO .800-325-9567
Saratoga Beverage Group
Saratoga Springs, NY 888-426-8642
Sinton Dairy Foods Company
Colorado Springs, CO. 800-388-4970
Sun Orchard
Tempe, AZ 800-505-8423
Sunlike Juice
Scarborough, ON 416-297-1140
Sunshine Farms Dairy
Elyria, OH. 440-322-6301
Superbrand Dairies
Miami, FL 305-685-8079
Superstore Industries
Fairfield, CA .707-864-0502
Swiss Valley Farms Company
Cedar Rapids, IA. 319-364-8153
Toft Dairy
Sandusky, OH 800-521-4606
Treesweet Products
Houston, TX .281-876-3759
Tropicana
Bradenton, FL 800-828-2102
True Organic Products International
Miami, FL 800-487-0379
Turner Dairies
Covington, TN 901-476-2643
Tuscan/Lehigh Valley Dais
Lansdale, PA 800-937-3233
Velda Farms
North Miami Bch, FL 800-795-4649
Wengert's Dairy
Lebanon, PA .800-222-2129
World Citrus West
Lake Wales, FL 863-676-1411
Yoder Dairies
Chesapeake, VA 757-497-3518

Blood

Gregory Packaging
Newark, NJ .973-465-1113

Concentrate

CCPI/Valley Foods
Lindsay, CA .559-562-5169
Chase Brothers Dairy
Oxnard, CA. .800-438-6455
Cliffstar Corporation
Dunkirk, NY .800-777-2389
Country Pure Foods
Ellington, CT 860-872-8346
Cutrale Citrus Juices
Leesburg, FL 352-728-7800
Georgia Sun
Newnan, GA 770-251-2500
Green Spot Packaging
Claremont, CA 800-456-3210
Greenwood Associates
Highland Park, IL 847-242-7900
Hi-Country Corona
Selah, WA 909-272-2600
Indian River Foods
Fort Pierce, FL 561-462-2222
Louis Dreyfus Citrus
Winter Garden, FL 407-656-1000
Mayer Brothers Apple Products
West Seneca, NY 800-696-2937
Minute Maid Company
Houston, TX .888-884-8952
Sea Breeze Fruit Flavors
Towaco, NJ .800-732-2733
Sun Pac Foods
Brampton, ON. 905-792-2700

Concentrate - Frozen

A. Duda Farm Fresh Foods
Belle Glade, FL 561-996-7621
Indian River Foods
Fort Pierce, FL 561-462-2222
Louis Dreyfus Citrus
Winter Garden, FL 407-656-1000

Not Concentrated

Citrus Citrosuco North America
Lake Wales, FL 800-356-4592
Greenwood Associates
Highland Park, IL 847-242-7900
Minute Maid Company
Houston, TX .888-884-8952
Silver Springs Citrus
Howey In Hills, FL 800-940-2277

Papaya

Stevens Tropical Plantation
West Palm Beach, FL 561-683-4701
Sunlike Juice
Scarborough, ON 416-297-1140

Passion Fruit

Meadow Gold Dairies
Honolulu, HI .808-949-6161

Peach

Green Spot Packaging
Claremont, CA 800-456-3210
Hazel Creek Orchards
Mt Airy, GA .706-754-4899
Sunlike Juice
Scarborough, ON 416-297-1140
Valley View Packing Company
San Jose, CA. 408-289-8300

Pear

San Benito Foods
Vancouver, WA 800-453-7832
Valley View Packing Company
San Jose, CA. 408-289-8300

Pineapple

Alfresh Beverages Canada
Rexdale, ON .800-465-1516
American Purpac Technologies, LLC
Beloit, WI 877-787-7221
Cal India Foods International
Chino, CA 909-613-1660
Clement Pappas & Company
Seabrook, NJ 800-257-7019
Commodities Marketing, Inc.
Edison, NJ 732-516-0700
Country Pure Foods
Ellington, CT 860-872-8346
Country Pure Foods
Akron, OH. 877-995-8423
Del Monte Foods
San Francisco, CA 800-543-3090

EMERLING INTERNATIONAL FOODS, INC.

Emerling International Foods
Buffalo, NY. .716-833-7381

Florida Fruit Juices
Chicago, IL 773-586-6200
Greenwood Associates
Highland Park, IL 847-242-7900
Langer Juice Company
City of Industry, CA 626-336-3100
M&B Products
Tampa, FL. 800-899-7255
Maui Pineapple Company
Kahului, HI 808-877-3351
Maui Pineapple Company
Concord, CA .925-798-0240
Mondial Foods Company
Los Angeles, CA. 213-383-3531
NTC Foods Corporation
Williamsville, NY 800-333-1637
Rohtstein Corporation
Woburn, MA .781-935-8300
SEW Friel
Queenstown, MD 410-827-8841

Smucker Quality Beverages
Havre De Grace, MD 410-939-1403
Sunlike Juice
Scarborough, ON 416-297-1140
True Organic Products International
Miami, FL 800-487-0379

Boxed

American Purpac Technologies, LLC
Beloit, WI 877-787-7221
Country Pure Foods
Akron, OH 877-995-8423

Canned

Alfresh Beverages Canada
Rexdale, ON 800-465-1516
American Purpac Technologies, LLC
Beloit, WI 877-787-7221
Country Pure Foods
Akron, OH 877-995-8423
NTC Foods Corporation
Williamsville, NY 800-333-1637
SEW Friel
Queenstown, MD 410-827-8841

Concentrate

Georgia Sun
Newnan, GA 770-251-2500
Maui Pineapple Company
Kahului, HI 808-877-3351
Maui Pineapple Company
Concord, CA 925-798-0240
Pacific Coast Fruit Company
Portland, OR 503-234-6411
Sun Pac Foods
Brampton, ON 905-792-2700

Frozen

American Purpac Technologies, LLC
Beloit, WI 877-787-7221
Country Pure Foods
Akron, OH 877-995-8423
Maui Pineapple Company
Concord, CA 925-798-0240

Glass-Packed

Alfresh Beverages Canada
Rexdale, ON 800-465-1516
American Purpac Technologies, LLC
Beloit, WI 877-787-7221
Country Pure Foods
Akron, OH 877-995-8423

Refrigerated

American Purpac Technologies, LLC
Beloit, WI 877-787-7221
Country Pure Foods
Akron, OH 877-995-8423

Portioned

Arcadia Dairy Farms
Arden, NC 828-684-3556

Powdered Fruit

GPR Company
Stowe, PA 610-326-4777

Prune

American Purpac Technologies, LLC
Beloit, WI 877-787-7221
Clement Pappas & Company
Seabrook, NJ 800-257-7019
Del Monte Foods
San Francisco, CA 800-543-3090

EMERLING INTERNATIONAL FOODS, INC.

Emerling International Foods
Buffalo, NY 716-833-7381

We supply food manufacturers and food service
customers worldwide (since 1988) with bulk ingredients including: Fruits & Vegetables; Juice
Concentrates; Herbs & Spices; Oils & Vinegars;
Flavors & Colors; Honey & Molasses. We also
produce PURE MAPLE SYRUP.

Erba Food Products
Brooklyn, NY 718-272-7700
Knouse Foods
Peach Glen, PA 717-677-8181
Madera Enterprises
Madera, CA 800-507-9555
Mayfair Packing Company
San Jose, CA 408-280-2349
McArthur Dairy
Miami, FL 305-576-2880
SEW Friel
Queenstown, MD 410-827-8841
Sunsweet Growers
Yuba City, CA 800-417-2253
Valley View Packing Company
San Jose, CA 408-289-8300

Raisin

Mayfair Packing Company
San Jose, CA 408-280-2349
Victor Packing Company
Madera, CA 559-673-5908

Raspberry

Hazel Creek Orchards
Mt Airy, GA 706-754-4899
Manzanita Ranch
Julian, CA 760-765-0102
Meduri Farms Inc
Dallas, OR 503-831-1097
Merlinos
Canon City, CO 719-275-5558
Stone Hill Wine Company
Hermann, MO 573-486-2221

Refrigerated

Apple & Eve
Roslyn, NY 800-969-8018
Foremost Farms
Fitchburg, WI 608-271-3000
Perfect Foods
Monroe, NY 800-933-3288
Wengert's Dairy
Lebanon, PA 800-222-2129
World Citrus West
Lake Wales, FL 863-676-1411

Strawberry

Green Spot Packaging
Claremont, CA 800-456-3210
Madera Enterprises
Madera, CA 800-507-9555
Merlinos
Canon City, CO 719-275-5558

Tangerine

American Mercantile Corporation
Groveland, FL 901-454-1900
American Purpac Technologies, LLC
Beloit, WI 877-787-7221

EMERLING INTERNATIONAL FOODS, INC.

Emerling International Foods
Buffalo, NY 716-833-7381

We supply food manufacturers and food service
customers worldwide (since 1988) with bulk ingredients including: Fruits & Vegetables; Juice
Concentrates; Herbs & Spices; Oils & Vinegars;
Flavors & Colors; Honey & Molasses. We also
produce PURE MAPLE SYRUP.

Greenwood Associates
Highland Park, IL 847-242-7900
Louis Dreyfus Citrus
Winter Garden, FL 407-656-1000
Minute Maid Company
Houston, TX 888-884-8952
True Organic Products International
Miami, FL 800-487-0379

Tomato

Alimentaire Whyte's Inc
Laval, QC 800-625-1979
American Purpac Technologies, LLC
Beloit, WI 877-787-7221

Beckman & Gast Company
St Henry, OH 419-678-4195
Burnette Foods
Hartford, MI 616-621-3181
Cal-Tex Citrus Juice
Houston, TX 800-231-0133
ConAgra Grocery Products
Irvine, CA 714-680-1000
Country Pure Foods
Akron, OH 330-753-2293
Country Pure Foods
Akron, OH 877-995-8423
Del Monte Foods
San Francisco, CA 800-543-3090
Erba Food Products
Brooklyn, NY 718-272-7700
Hunt-Wesson Foods
Rochester, NY 209-847-0321
Ocean Spray Cranberries
Lakeville-Middleboro, MA 800-662-3263
Ray Brothers & Noble Canning Company
Hobbs, IN 765-675-7451
Red Gold
Elwood, IN 877-748-9798
SEW Friel
Queenstown, MD 410-827-8841
Sun Pac Foods
Brampton, ON 905-792-2700
Thomas Canning/Maidstone
Maidstone, ON 519-737-1531
Welch's Foods Inc
Concord, MA 800-340-6870

Boxed

American Purpac Technologies, LLC
Beloit, WI 877-787-7221

Canned

Agrocan
Toronto, ON 877-247-6226
American Purpac Technologies, LLC
Beloit, WI 877-787-7221

EMERLING INTERNATIONAL FOODS, INC.

Emerling International Foods
Buffalo, NY 716-833-7381

We supply food manufacturers and food service
customers worldwide (since 1988) with bulk ingredients including: Fruits & Vegetables; Juice
Concentrates; Herbs & Spices; Oils & Vinegars;
Flavors & Colors; Honey & Molasses. We also
produce PURE MAPLE SYRUP.

Hirzel Canning Company &Farms
Northwood, OH 419-693-0531

Cocktail

EMERLING INTERNATIONAL FOODS, INC.

Emerling International Foods
Buffalo, NY 716-833-7381

We supply food manufacturers and food service
customers worldwide (since 1988) with bulk ingredients including: Fruits & Vegetables; Juice
Concentrates; Herbs & Spices; Oils & Vinegars;
Flavors & Colors; Honey & Molasses. We also
produce PURE MAPLE SYRUP.

Mayfair Packing Company
San Jose, CA 408-280-2349
Vegetable Juices
Chicago, IL 888-776-9752

Frozen

American Purpac Technologies, LLC
Beloit, WI 877-787-7221
Vegetable Juices
Chicago, IL 888-776-9752

Glass-Packed Chilled

American Purpac Technologies, LLC
Beloit, WI 877-787-7221

EMERLING INTERNATIONAL FOODS, INC.

Emerling International Foods
Buffalo, NY........................716-833-7381

We supply food manufacturers and food service
customers worldwide (since 1988) with bulk ingredients including: Fruits & Vegetables; Juice
Concentrates; Herbs & Spices; Oils & Vinegars;
Flavors & Colors; Honey & Molasses. We also
produce PURE MAPLE SYRUP.

Tropical Fruits

American Purpac Technologies, LLC
Beloit, WI....................877-787-7221
Clement Pappas & Company
Seabrook, NJ..................800-257-7019
Cliffstar Corporation
Dunkirk, NY..................800-777-2389
Country Pure Foods
Akron, OH....................877-995-8423

EMERLING INTERNATIONAL FOODS, INC.

Emerling International Foods
Buffalo, NY........................716-833-7381

We supply food manufacturers and food service
customers worldwide (since 1988) with bulk ingredients including: Fruits & Vegetables; Juice
Concentrates; Herbs & Spices; Oils & Vinegars;
Flavors & Colors; Honey & Molasses. We also
produce PURE MAPLE SYRUP.

Furmano Foods
Northumberland, PA.............877-877-6032
Green Spot Packaging
Claremont, CA.................800-456-3210
Hawaiian Sun Products
Honolulu, HI..................808-845-3211
Healthmate Products
Highland Park, IL.............800-584-8642
International Trade Impa
Lawrenceville, NJ.............800-223-5484
Langer Juice Company
City of Industry, CA..........626-336-3100
Mondial Foods Company
Los Angeles, CA...............213-383-3531
Parman-Kendall Corporation
Goulds, FL...................305-258-1628
Sinton Dairy Foods Company
Colorado Springs, CO..........800-388-4970
Stevens Tropical Plantation
West Palm Beach, FL...........561-683-4701
Sunlike Juice
Scarborough, ON...............416-297-1140
True Organic Products International
Miami, FL....................800-487-0379

Vegetable

Apple & Eve
Roslyn, NY...................800-969-8018
B.M. Lawrence & Company
San Francisco, CA.............415-981-3650
Beckman & Gast Company
St Henry, OH.................419-678-4195
Byesville Aseptics
Byesville, OH.................740-685-2548
California Day Fresh
Glendora, CA.................800-800-0986
Campbell Soup Company
Camden, NJ...................800-257-8443
Carriage House Companies
Fredonia, NY.................800-828-8915
Century Foods International
Sparta, WI...................800-269-1901
Florida Food Products
Eustis, FL...................800-874-2331
Greenwood Associates
Highland Park, IL.............847-242-7900
Howard Foods
Danvers, MA..................978-774-6207
Hudson Valley Fruit Juice
Highland, NY.................845-691-8061
Hunt-Wesson Foods
Rochester, NY................209-847-0321
Ludfords
Rancho Cucamonga, CA..........909-948-0797
Rapunzel Pure Organics
Chatham, NY..................800-207-2814

RFI Ingredients
Blauvelt, NY.................800-962-7663
SEW Friel
Queenstown, MD...............410-827-8841
Tamarack Farms Dairy
Newark, OH...................866-221-4141
Thomas Canning/Maidstone
Maidstone, ON................519-737-1531
Vegetable Juices
Chicago, IL..................888-776-9752
William Bolthouse Farms
Bakersfield, CA..............661-366-7205

Concentrates - Fruit Puree

GLCC Company
Paw Paw, MI..................269-657-3167
Greenwood Associates
Highland Park, IL.............847-242-7900
RFI Ingredients
Blauvelt, NY.................800-962-7663

Mixers

Bar Mixers

Coastal Promotions
West Palm Beach, FL...........561-202-5915
La Jota Vineyard Company
Angwin, CA...................877-222-0292

Prepared Cocktail Mixes

A.C. Calderoni & Company
Brisbane, CA.................866-468-1897
Al-Rite Fruits & Syrups
Miami, FL....................305-652-2540
Aliments Lexus Foods
Rougemont, QC................800-227-4891
American Beverage Marketers
New Albany, IN...............812-944-3585
American Beverage Marketers
Shawnee Mission, KS...........913-451-8311
American Purpac Technologies, LLC
Beloit, WI...................877-787-7221
Bacardi Canada, Inc.
Brampton, ON.................905-451-6100
Bacardi USA
Miami, FL....................800-222-2734
Bartush-Schnitzius Foods Company
Lewisville, TX...............972-219-1270
Beam Global Spirits & Wine
Deerfield, IL................847-948-8888
Beverage Specialties
Fredonia, NY.................800-828-8915
Blue Crab Bay Company
Melfa, VA....................800-221-2722
Brown-Forman Beverages Worldwide
Louisville, KY...............502-585-1100
Byesville Aseptics
Byesville, OH.................740-685-2548
Carolina Treet
Wilmington, NC...............800-616-6344
Commodities Marketing, Inc.
Edison, NJ...................732-516-0700
Daily Juice Products
Verona, PA...................800-245-2929
Demitri's Bloody Mary Seasonings
Seattle, WA..................800-627-9649
Fee Brothers
Rochester, NY................800-961-3337
Flavouressence Products
Mississauga, ON..............866-209-7778
Franciscan Oakville Estates
Rutherford, CA...............800-529-9463
Franco's Cocktail Mixes
Pompano Beach, FL............800-782-4508
Frank & Dean's Cocktail Mixes
Pasadena, CA.................626-351-4272
Giumarra Vineyards
Bakersfield, CA..............661-395-7000
Great Western Juice Company
Cleveland, OH................800-321-9180
Island Oasis Frozen Cocktail Company
Walpole, MA..................800-777-4752
Jus-Made
Dallas, TX...................800-969-3746
Kennedy Candy Company
Kilgore, TX..................800-657-5258
Key Colony/Red Parrot Juices
Lyons, FL....................800-424-0868
Kittling Ridge Estate Wines & Spirits
Grimsby, ON..................905-945-9225

La Paz Products
Brea, CA.....................714-990-0982
Lemate of New England
Sharon, MA...................781-784-7369
Lemix
Canton, OH...................330-488-3072
Lemon-X Corporation
Huntington Sta, NY............800-220-1061
Main Squeeze
Columbia, MO.................573-817-5616
Margarita Man
San Antonio, TX..............800-950-8149
Master Taste International
Plant City, FL...............800-237-7629
McIlhenny Company
New Orleans, LA..............504-523-7370
Mele-Koi Farms
Newport Beach, CA............949-660-9000
Miramar Fruit Trading Company
Medley, FL...................305-883-4774
Misty
Lincoln, NE..................402-466-8424
Mott's
Port Chester, NY.............914-612-4000
Perfection Fine Products
Maple Heights, OH............216-475-5744
Prima Foods International
Ocala, FL....................800-774-8751
Reser's Fine Foods
Beaverton, OR................800-333-6431
Royale International Beverage Co Inc
Davenport, IA................563-386-5222
Ruffner's
Wayne, PA....................610-687-9800
S.J. McCullagh
Buffalo, NY..................800-753-3473
Sea Breeze Fruit Flavors
Towaco, NJ...................800-732-2733
Sirocco Enterprises
Jefferson, LA................504-834-1549
St. Julian Wine Company
Paw Paw, MI..................800-732-6002
Toucan Enterprises
Marrero, LA..................800-736-9289
Trader Vic's Food Products
Emeryville, CA...............877-762-4824
Tree Ripe Products
East Hanover, NJ.............800-873-3747
Tropical Illusions
Trenton, MO..................660-359-6849
Vegetable Juices
Chicago, IL..................888-776-9752
Vitality Foodservice
Tampa, FL....................888-863-6726
W&G Flavors
Hunt Valley, MD..............410-771-6606
Wagner Excello Food Products
Broadview, IL................708-338-4488

Non-Alcoholic Beverages

Aliments Lexus Foods
Rougemont, QC................800-227-4891
American Instants
Flanders, NJ.................973-584-8811
Anheuser-Busch Inc
St Louis, MO.................800-342-5283
Ariel Vineyards
Napa, CA.....................800-456-9472
Atlanta Coffee & Tea Company
Decatur, GA..................800-426-4781
Autocrat Coffee & Extracts
Lincoln, RI..................800-288-6272
B.M. Lawrence & Company
San Francisco, CA.............415-981-3650
Coca-Cola Enterprises
Atlanta, GA..................800-233-7210
Coors Brewing Company
Golden, CO...................800-642-6116
Fee Brothers
Rochester, NY................800-961-3337
Florida Distillers Company
Lake Alfred, FL..............863-956-3477
Franco's Cocktail Mixes
Pompano Beach, FL............800-782-4508
Gerhart Coffee Company
Lancaster, PA................800-536-4310
Kristian Regale
Hudson, WI...................715-386-8388
Lion Brewery
Wilkes Barre, PA.............800-233-8327
Martin Coffee Company
Jacksonville, FL.............904-355-9661

119

Meier's Wine Cellars
Cincinnati, OH 800-346-2941
Mercury Brewing Company
Ipswich, MA 978-356-3329
Miller Brewing Company
Milwaukee, WI 414-931-2000
Natural Group
Oxnard, CA 805-485-3420
Nestle Canada Inc
North York, ON 800-563-7853
Richland Beverage Associates
Carrollton, TX 214-357-0248
Safeway Dairy Products
Walnut Creek, CA 925-944-4000
Sara Lee Coffee & Tea
Earth City, MO 314-731-2500
Sara Lee Coffee & Tea   Wholesale Coffee & Tea
Location
Minneapolis, MN 888-246-2598
Sara Lee Foodservice
Rolling Meadows, IL 800-261-4754
Sweet Traders
Huntington Beach, CA 714-903-6800

Smoothies

Blue Chip Group
Salt Lake City, UT 800-878-0099
Caffe D'Amore Gourmet Beverages
Monrovia, CA 800-999-0171
California Dairies
Fresno, CA 559-233-5154
Cascade Fresh
Seattle, WA 800-511-0057
Coleman Dairy
Little Rock, AR 501-748-1700
Cream O'Weaver Dairy
Salt Lake City, UT 801-973-9922
Curly's Dairy
Stayton, OR 800-785-1335
Dairy Farmers of America
Sulphur Springs, TX 903-885-6518
Dannon Company
Fort Worth, TX 800-211-6565
Gardner's Gourmet
Fremont, CA 800-676-8558
GPI USA LLC.
Athens, GA 706-850-7826
Hunter Farms
High Point, NC 800-446-8035
Ideal Dairy
Richfield, UT 435-896-5061
Jus-Made
Dallas, TX 800-969-3746
K&F Select Fine Coffees
Portland, OR 800-558-7788
Lane's Dairy
El Paso, TX 915-772-6700
Maola Milk & Ice Cream Company
New Bern, NC 252-638-1131
Marcus Dairy
Danbury, CT 800-243-2511
Meadow Gold Dairy
Lewiston, ID 208-746-9006
MEYENBERG Goat Milk Products
Turlock, CA 800-891-4628
Mission San Juan Juices
Dana Point, CA 949-495-7929
Oak Farms
Dallas, TX 214-941-0302
Oak Farms
San Antonio, TX 800-292-2169
Plains Creamery
Amarillo, TX 806-374-0385
Price's Creameries
El Paso, TX 915-565-2711
Saint Albans CooperativeCreamy
Saint Albans, VT 800-559-0343
Saratoga Beverage Group
Saratoga Springs, NY 888-426-8642
Scotsburn Dairy Group
Truro, NS 902-895-4412
Sheila's Select Gourmet Recipe
Heber City, UT 800-516-7286
Smucker Quality Beverages
Havre De Grace, MD 410-939-1403
Smucker Quality Beverages
Chico, CA 530-899-5000
Sunshine Dairy Foods
Portland, OR 503-234-7526
Swiss Valley Farms Company
Davenport, IA 563-468-6600

Swiss Valley Farms Company
Dubuque, IA 800-397-9156
Tuscan Dairy Farms
Dallas, TX 800-526-4416
Valley of the Rogue Dairy
Grants Pass, OR 541-476-2020
Victor Packing Company
Madera, CA 559-673-5908
Winder Dairy
West Valley, UT 800-946-3371
YoCream International
Portland, OR 800-962-7326
Yoplait USA
Minneapolis, MN 800-967-5248

Soft Drinks & Sodas

Aliments Lexus Foods
Rougemont, QC 800-227-4891
Beverage Capital Corporation
Halethorpe, MD 410-242-7003
Big Red Bottling
Waco, TX 254-772-7791
BN Soda
Watertown, MA 617-731-6720
Briar's USA
North Brunswick, NJ 887-327-4277
Canada Dry Bottling Company
Flushing, NY 718-661-4265
Cool
Richardson, TX 972-437-9352
Fentimans North America
Danville, CA 925-837-9995
Grand Teton Brewing
Victor, ID. 888-899-1656
GuS Grown-up Soda
New York, NY 212-355-7454
Jones Soda Vancouver
Richmond, BC 800-656-6050
Laurel Hill
Santa Monica, CA 310-395-6630
Mercury Brewing Company
Ipswich, MA 978-356-3329
Nagel's Beverages Company
East Nampa, ID 208-475-1250
Snow Beverages
New York, NY 212-353-3270
Southwest Canners of Texas
Nacogdoches, TX 936-569-9737

Club Soda

Mercury Brewing Company
Ipswich, MA 978-356-3329

Soda Water

Central Coca-Cola Bottling Company
Richmond, VA. 800-359-3759

Soft Drinks

A-Treat Bottling Company
Allentown, PA. 800-220-1531
Abita Brewing Company
Abita Springs, LA 800-737-2311
Admiral Beverages
Worland, WY 307-347-4201
American Food Traders
Miami, FL 305-670-6250
B.M. Lawrence & Company
San Francisco, CA 415-981-3650
Barq's Beverages of Baton Rouge
Baton Rouge, LA 225-928-3971
Beverage Capital Corporation
Halethorpe, MD 410-242-7003
Blue Sky Natural Beverage Company
Santa Fe, NM 505-995-9761
BN Soda
Watertown, MA 617-731-6720
Brooklyn Bottling Company
Milton, NY 845-795-2171
California Farms & Canners
San Francisco, CA 415-433-3522
Canada Dry Bottling Company
Flushing, NY 718-661-4265
Cawy Bottling Company
Miami, FL 877-917-2299
Central Coca-Cola Bottling Company
Richmond, VA. 800-359-3759
Coca-Cola Bottling Company
El Paso, TX 800-288-3228

Coca-Cola Bottling Company
Charlotte, NC 800-777-2653
Coca-Cola Bottling Company
Honolulu, HI 808-839-6711
Coca-Cola Bottling Company
West Memphis, AR. 870-732-1460
Coca-Cola Bottling Company
Lenexa, KS 913-492-8100
Coca-Cola Enterprises
Atlanta, GA 800-233-7210
Contact International
Skokie, IL 847-324-4411
Cool Mountain Beverages
Des Plaines, IL 847-759-9330
Cott Concentrates/Royal Crown Cola International
Columbus, GA 800-652-5642
Crystal & Vigor Beverages
Kearny, NJ 201-991-2342
CTL Foods
Colfax, WI. 800-962-5227
Dr. Pepper/Seven-Up
Racine, WI 800-696-5891
Everfresh Beverages
Warren, MI 586-755-9500
F.X. Matt Brewing Company
Utica, NY 800-690-3181
Full Service Beverage Company
Wichita, KS. 800-540-0001
Functional Products LLC
Atlantic Beach, FL 800-628-5908
G&J Pepsi-Cola Bottlers
Columbus, OH 614-253-8771
Ginseng Up Corporation
New York, NY 212-696-1930
Global Beverage Company
Rochester, NY 585-381-3560
Good-O-Beverages Company
Bronx, NY. 718-328-6400
Hank's Beverage Company
Feastervl Trvs, PA. 800-289-4722
Haydenergy Health
New York, NY 800-255-1660
International Trademarks
Darien, CT. 203-656-4046
Iron Horse Products
Edina, MN. 952-920-7722
Island Sweetwater Beverage Company
Bryn Mawr, PA 610-525-7444
J&J Snack Foods Corporation
Pennsauken, NJ 856-665-9533
Krier Foods
Milwaukee, WI 414-355-5400
Langer Juice Company
City of Industry, CA 626-336-1666
Lenox-Martell
Jamaica Plain, MA 617-442-7777
Lost Trail Root Beer Com
Louisburg, KS 800-748-7765
Louisiana Coca-Cola Bottling Company
Harahan, LA 800-362-6996
Manhattan Special Bottling Corporation
Brooklyn, NY 718-388-4144
Mar-Key Foods
Vidalia, GA 912-537-4204
Meadowbrook Distributing Corporation
Amityville, NY 631-226-9000
Monarch Beverage Company
Atlanta, GA 800-241-3732
Mount Claire Spring Water
Torrington, CT 888-525-2473
National Beverage Corporation
Fort Lauderdale, FL 888-462-2349
Original American Beverage Company
North Stonington, CT 800-625-3767
Pepsi Bottling Group
Mesquite, TX 214-324-8500
Pepsi Bottling Group
Fort Smith, AR 479-646-7881

Pepsi Bottling Group
Redding, CA 530-245-2100
Pepsi Bottling Group
Houston, TX 713-645-4111
Pepsi Bottling Group
Buffalo, NY 800-235-1131
Pepsi Bottling Group
Burnsville, MN 800-433-8109
Pepsi Bottling Group
San Antonio, TX 800-933-5311
Pepsi Bottling Group
Tulsa, OK 800-963-2424
Pepsi Bottling Group
Pleasanton, CA 925-416-2500
Pepsi-Cola Bottling Company
St Louis, MO. 314-679-7000
Pepsi-Cola Bottling Company
Brooklyn, NY 718-649-2401
Pepsi-Cola General Bottlers
Arlington Hts, IL 847-483-6880
PepsiAmericas
New Orleans, LA 504-467-3774
PepsiAmericas
Reserve, LA 985-536-1191
PepsiCo
Philadelphia, PA 215-961-4000
PepsiCo Inc
Purchase, NY 914-253-2000
Polar Beverage
Worcester, MA 800-734-9800
R.J. Corr Naturals
Posen, IL 708-389-4200
R.W. Knudsen
Chico, CA 530-899-5000
Regent Champagne Cellars
New York, NY 845-691-7296
Roselani Tropics Ice Cream
Wailuku, HI 808-244-7951
Royal Crown Bottling Company
Bowling Green, KY 270-842-8106
Safeway Beverage
Denver, CO 303-320-7960
Safeway Beverage
Bellevue, WA 425-455-6444
SANGARIA USA
Torrance, CA. 310-530-2202
Seltzer & Rydholm
Auburn, ME 207-784-5791
Seven Up/RC Bottling Company
Paragould, AR. 870-236-8765
Shasta Beverages
Shawnee Mission, KS 913-888-6777
Soho Beverages
Vienna, VA 703-689-2800
Southern Beverage Packers
Appling, GA 800-326-2469
Sparkling Water Distributors
Merrick, NY 800-277-2755
Spear Packing
New Brunswick, NJ 732-247-4212
Specialty Beverages
Indian Wells, CA. 626-963-5536
Stop & Shop Manufacturing
Readville, MA 617-361-8400
Swire Coca-Cola
Draper, UT 801-816-5300
Todhunter Foods
Lake Alfred, FL. 863-956-1116
Truesdale Packaging Company
Warrenton, MO 636-456-6800
USA Sunrise Beverage
Spearfish, SD 605-723-0690
Varni Brothers/7-Up Bottling
Modesto, CA 209-521-1777
Vermont Sweetwater Bottling Company
Poultney, VT 800-974-9877
Vitality Foodservice
Tampa, FL. 888-863-6726
Wet Planet Beverage
Rochester, NY. 585-381-3560
White Rock Products Corporation
Whitestone, NY 800-969-7625
Winnsboro Beverage Packers
Winnsboro, LA 318-435-9404
Yoo-Hoo Chocolate Beverage Company
Port Chester, NY. 800-966-4669

Cola

A-Treat Bottling Company
Allentown, PA. 800-220-1531
Adirondack Beverages
Scotia, NY. 800-316-6096

Al's Beverage Company
East Windsor, CT 888-257-7632
Aloe'Ha Drink Products
Houston, TX 713-978-6359
American Bottling & Beverage
Walterboro, SC 843-538-7709
Bar Harbor Brewing Company
Bar Harbor, ME. 207-288-4592
Better Beverages
Cerritos, CA 562-924-8321
Beverage America
Holland, MI. 616-396-1281
Beverage House
Cartersville, GA 888-367-8327
Beverage Specialties
Fredonia, NY 800-828-8915
Boylan Bottling Company
Haledon, NJ 800-289-7978
Cable Car Beverage Corporation
Denver, CO 303-298-9038
Cadbury Schweppes
Plano, TX 800-696-5891
Castle Beverages
Ansonia, CT 203-734-0883
Catawissa Bottling Company
Catawissa, PA 800-892-4419
Central Coca-Cola Bottling Company
Richmond, VA. 800-359-3759
Champion Beverages
Darien, CT. 203-655-9026
Coca-Cola Bottling Company
Brampton, ON. 800-926-5301
Coca-Cola Enterprises
Atlanta, GA. 800-233-7210
Cornell Beverages
Brooklyn, NY 718-381-3000
Cott Beverage
Tampa, FL. 888-260-3776
Crowley Beverage Corporation
Wayland, MA 800-997-3337
Double-Cola Company
Chattanooga, TN. 423-267-5691
Dr Pepper/Seven Up
Dallas, TX. 800-527-7096
Egg Cream America
Northbrook, IL 847-559-2703
Faygo Beverages
Detroit, MI 800-347-6591
Giumarra Vineyards
Bakersfield, CA 661-395-7000
Gulf States Canners
Clinton, MS. 601-924-0511
Hampton Associates & Sons
Fairfax, VA 703-968-5847
Honickman Affiliates
Pennsauken, NJ. 800-573-7745
Hosmer Mountain Bottling
Willimantic, CT 800-763-2445
INCA Kola Golden Kola
Bloomfield, NJ 973-680-9700
Inca Kola/Golden Kola
New York, NY 973-688-0970
Indiana Beverage 7UP
Gary, IN. 219-882-3100
Kennebec Fruit Company
Lisbon Falls, ME 207-353-8173
Lenox-Martell
Jamaica Plain, MA 617-442-7777
Millstream Brewing
Amana, IA. 319-622-3672
Moceri South Western
San Diego, CA 619-297-7900
New Age Canadian Beverage
Hollywood, FL 954-438-1484
New York Bottling Company
Bronx, NY. 718-378-2525
Noel Corporation
Yakima, WA 509-248-1313
North Shore Bottling Company
Brooklyn, NY 718-272-8900
Northern Neck Bottling Company
Montross, VA 800-431-2693
Pennsylvania Dutch BirchBeer
Huntingdon Valley, PA 215-396-2012
Pepsi Bottling Co of Buffalo
Buffalo, NY 800-235-1131
Pepsi Bottling Group Canada
Mississauga, ON 800-387-9546
Pepsi-Cola Canada
Winnipeg, NB 800-387-9546
PepsiAmericas
Fort Wayne, IN 800-388-2235

Pocono Mountain Bottling Company
Wilkes Barre, PA. 570-822-7695
Premier Beverages
Plano, TX 972-547-6295
Reed's Original Beverage Corporation
Los Angeles, CA 800-997-3337
Rivella USA
Boca Raton, FL 561-417-5810
Sarum Tea Company
Lakeville, CT 860-435-2086
Shasta Beverages
Shawnee Mission, KS 913-888-6777
Smucker Quality Beverages
Chico, CA 530-899-5000
SoBe Beverages
Norwalk, CT 800-588-0548
Southeast Canners
Columbus, GA 706-324-0040
Specialty Beverages
Indian Wells, CA. 626-963-5536
Stewart's Beverages
White Plains, NY 914-397-9200
Sun State Beverage
Atlanta, GA 770-451-3990
Taos Brewing Supply
Santa Fe, NM 505-983-0505
Thomas Kemper Soda Company
Seattle, WA 206-381-8712
Tianfu China Cola
Katonah, NY 914-232-3102
Tri-States Coca-Cola Bottling Company
Cincinnati, OH 800-543-2653
Triple XXX Root Beer Com
Houston, TX 713-780-9203
USA Beverage
Warrenton, MO 636-456-5468
Virgil's Root Beer
Los Angeles, CA 800-997-3337

Cream Soda

Central Coca-Cola Bottling Company
Richmond, VA. 800-359-3759
Cool Mountain Beverages
Des Plaines, IL 847-759-9330
Mercury Brewing Company
Ipswich, MA 978-356-3329
PepsiCo
Philadelphia, PA 215-961-4000
Sparkling Water Distributors
Merrick, NY 800-277-2755

Cream Soda - Vanilla

Thomas Kemper Soda Company
Seattle, WA 206-381-8712
Tri-States Coca-Cola Bottling Company
Cincinnati, OH 800-543-2653

Ginger Ale

Adirondack Beverages
Scotia, NY. 800-316-6096
Central Coca-Cola Bottling Company
Richmond, VA. 800-359-3759
Cool Mountain Beverages
Des Plaines, IL 847-759-9330
Grand Teton Brewing
Victor, ID. 888-899-1656
Specialty Beverages
Indian Wells, CA. 626-963-5536
Thomas Kemper Soda Company
Seattle, WA 206-381-8712

Lemon-Lime Soda

Cool Mountain Beverages
Des Plaines, IL 847-759-9330
Manhattan Special Bottling Corporation
Brooklyn, NY 718-388-4144
Mercury Brewing Company
Ipswich, MA 978-356-3329

Sarsaparilla

Manhattan Special Bottling Corporation
Brooklyn, NY 718-388-4144
Specialty Beverages
Indian Wells, CA 626-963-5536

Sparkling Water

Absopure Water Company
Champaign, IL 800-422-7678

Bevco
Surrey, BC............................800-663-0090
Blue Sky Natural Beverage Company
Santa Fe, NM.......................505-995-9761
Crystal Geyser Roxanne LLC
Pensacola, FL.......................850-476-8844
Crystal Geyser Water Company
San Francisco, CA 415-616-9590
Crystal Geyser Water Company
Calistoga, CA 800-726-6121
Crystal Rock Spring Water Company
Waterford, CT 860-443-5000
Giumarra Vineyards
Bakersfield, CA 661-395-7000
Hinckley Springs Water Company
Chicago, IL 773-586-8600
Jackson Milk & Ice CreamCompany
Hutchinson, KS.....................620-663-1244
Matilija Water Company
Ventura, CA.........................805-322-7212
Mount Olympus Waters
Salt Lake City, UT 800-628-6056
National Beverage Corporation
Fort Lauderdale, FL 888-462-2349
Poland Spring Water
Brea, CA 800-950-9396
Polar Beverage
Worcester, MA 800-734-9800
Polar Water Company
Carnegie, PA 800-444-7873
R.J. Corr Naturals
Posen, IL 708-389-4200
Regent Champagne Cellars
New York, NY 845-691-7296
Saratoga Beverage Group
Saratoga Springs, NY 888-426-8642
Southern Beverage Packers
Appling, GA 800-326-2469
Sparkling Water Distributors
Merrick, NY 800-277-2755
Sweet Earth Natural Foods
Pacific Grove, CA 800-737-3311
Universal Beverages
Ponte Vedra Bch, FL 904-280-7795
Yosemite Waters
Los Angeles, CA...................800-427-8420

Spirits & Liqueurs

Brandy

Corby Distilleries
Toronto, ON 800-367-9079
E&J Gallo Winery
Modesto, CA 209-341-3111
Germain-Robin
Ukiah, CA 800-782-8145
Golden State Vintners
Cutler, CA 559-528-3033
Heaven Hill Distilleries
Bardstown, KY 502-348-3921
Heck Cellars
Arvin, CA 661-854-6120
Hood River Distillers
Hood River, OR 541-386-1588
Ironstone Vineyards
Murphys, CA........................209-728-1251
Kittling Ridge Estate Wines & Spirits
Grimsby, ON........................905-945-9225
Laird & Company
North Garden, VA 877-438-5247
M.S. Walker
Somerville, MA 617-776-6700
Majestic Distilling Company
Baltimore, MD......................410-242-0200
Marie Brizard Wines & Spirits
Sausalito, CA 800-878-1123
Oak Ridge Winery
Lodi, CA.............................209-369-4768
Pernod Ricard USA
White Plains, NY 914-539-4500
Todhunter Foods & Monarch Wine Company
West Palm Beach, FL 800-336-9463
Vie-Del Company
Fresno, CA 559-834-2525

Luxury Cognac

Heaven Hill Distilleries
Bardstown, KY 502-348-3921

V.S. Cognac Three Star

Corby Distilleries
Toronto, ON 800-367-9079

V.S.O.P. Cognac

Corby Distilleries
Toronto, ON 800-367-9079

X.O. Cognac

Corby Distilleries
Toronto, ON 800-367-9079

Gin

A. Smith Bowman Distillery
Fredericksburg, VA 540-373-4555
Beam Global Spirits & Wine
Deerfield, IL 847-948-8888
Brown-Forman Beverages Worldwide
Louisville, KY.......................502-585-1100
Corby Distilleries
Toronto, ON 800-367-9079
Destileria Serralles
Mercedita, PR.......................787-723-0107
E&J Gallo Winery
Modesto, CA 209-341-3111
Heaven Hill Distilleries
Bardstown, KY 502-348-3921
Hiram Walker & Sons
Fort Smith, AR 479-783-4191
Hiram Walker & Sons
Windsor, ON 519-254-5171
Hood River Distillers
Hood River, OR 541-386-1588
Laird & Company
Eatontown, NJ 877-438-5247
Majestic Distilling Company
Baltimore, MD......................410-242-0200
Marie Brizard Wines & Spirits
Sausalito, CA 800-878-1123
Pernod Ricard USA
White Plains, NY 914-539-4500
Pernod Ricard USA Seagram Lawrenceburg Distillery
Greendale, IN 812-537-0700
UDV Canada
Etobicoke, ON 416-626-2000
Viking Distillery
Albany, GA 229-436-0181
Vincor International
Mississauga, ON....................800-265-9463

Irish Whiskey

Beam Global Spirits & Wine
Deerfield, IL 847-948-8888
Corby Distilleries
Toronto, ON 800-367-9079
Fortune Brands
Lincolnshire, IL 847-541-9500
George A Dickel & Company
Tullahoma, TN 931-857-9313
Heaven Hill Distilleries
Bardstown, KY 502-348-3921
Hiram Walker & Sons
Fort Smith, AR 479-783-4191
Hiram Walker & Sons
Windsor, ON 519-254-5171
Jack Daniel's Distillery
Lynchburg, TN 931-759-4221
Kittling Ridge Estate Wines & Spirits
Grimsby, ON........................905-945-9225
Laird & Company
Eatontown, NJ 877-438-5247
Makers Mark Distillery
Loretto, KY..........................270-865-2881
Pernod Ricard USA
White Plains, NY 914-539-4500
Pernod Ricard USA Seagram Lawrenceburg Distillery
Greendale, IN 812-537-0700

Liqueurs & Cordials

Aloha Distillers
Honolulu, HI........................808-841-5787
Bacardi Canada, Inc.
Brampton, ON.......................905-451-6100
Beam Global Spirits & Wine
Deerfield, IL 847-948-8888
Black Prince Distillery, Inc.
Clifton, NJ...........................973-365-2050

Bottle Green Drinks
Mississauga, ON....................905-273-6137
Brown-Forman Beverages Worldwide
Louisville, KY.......................502-585-1100
Charles Jacquin Et Cie
Philadelphia, PA....................800-523-3811
Clear Creek Distillery
Portland, OR 503-248-9470
Consolidated Distilled Products
Chicago, IL 773-927-4161
Destileria Serralles
Mercedita, PR.......................787-723-0107
Distillerie Stock USA
New York, NY 800-323-1884
Franciscan Oakville Estates
Rutherford, CA......................800-529-9463
Hawk Pacific Freight
Napa, CA.............................707-259-0266
Heaven Hill Distilleries
Bardstown, KY 502-348-3921
Highwood Distillers
High River, AB 403-652-3202
Hiram Walker & Sons
Fort Smith, AR 479-783-4191
Hiram Walker & Sons
Windsor, ON 519-254-5171
Kittling Ridge Estate Wines & Spirits
Grimsby, ON........................905-945-9225
M.S. Walker
Somerville, MA 617-776-6700
Marie Brizard Wines & Spirits
Sausalito, CA 800-878-1123
Paramount Distillers
Cleveland, OH 216-671-6300
Pernod Ricard USA
White Plains, NY 914-539-4500
Phillips Beverage Company
Minneapolis, MN 612-362-7500
Renault Winery
Egg Harbor City, NJ 609-965-2111
Royal Wine Company
Bayonne, NJ.........................201-437-9131
Sakeone Corporation
Forest Grove, OR 800-550-7253
Todhunter Foods & Monarch Wine Company
West Palm Beach, FL 800-336-9463
United Distillers & Vintners
Norwalk, CT.........................203-323-3311

Amaretto

Heaven Hill Distilleries
Bardstown, KY 502-348-3921

Anise Liqueur

Pernod Ricard USA
White Plains, NY 914-539-4500

Brandy Liqueur

Majestic Distilling Company
Baltimore, MD......................410-242-0200

Chocolate Liqueur

Aloha Distillers
Honolulu, HI........................808-841-5787

Coffee Liqueur

Aloha Distillers
Honolulu, HI........................808-841-5787
Heaven Hill Distilleries
Bardstown, KY 502-348-3921

Schnapps Liqueuer

Marie Brizard Wines & Spirits
Sausalito, CA 800-878-1123

Neutral

Buffalo Trace Distillery
Frankfort, KY 800-654-8471
M.S. Walker
Somerville, MA 617-776-6700
Paramount Distillers
Cleveland, OH 216-671-6300

Rum

A. Smith Bowman Distillery
Fredericksburg, VA 540-373-4555
Bacardi Canada, Inc.
Brampton, ON.......................905-451-6100

Bacardi USA
  Miami, FL 800-222-2734
Beam Global Spirits & Wine
  Deerfield, IL 847-948-8888
Buffalo Trace Distillery
  Frankfort, KY 800-654-8471
Corby Distilleries
  Toronto, ON 800-367-9079
Destileria Serralles
  Mercedita, PR 787-723-0107
Heaven Hill Distilleries
  Bardstown, KY 502-348-3921
Highwood Distillers
  High River, AB 403-652-3202
Hiram Walker & Sons
  Windsor, ON 519-254-5171
Hood River Distillers
  Hood River, OR 541-386-1588
Kittling Ridge Estate Wines & Spirits
  Grimsby, ON 905-945-9225
Majestic Distilling Company
  Baltimore, MD 410-242-0200
Marie Brizard Wines & Spirits
  Sausalito, CA 800-878-1123
Mohawk Distilled Products
  North Miami, FL 305-892-3460
Todhunter International
  West Palm Beach, FL 561-655-8977
Trigo Corporation
  Toa Baja, PR 787-794-1300

Dark

Bacardi Canada, Inc.
  Brampton, ON 905-451-6100
Corby Distilleries
  Toronto, ON 800-367-9079

White Silver

Corby Distilleries
  Toronto, ON 800-367-9079

Scotch Whiskey

A. Smith Bowman Distillery
  Fredericksburg, VA 540-373-4555
Bacardi Canada, Inc.
  Brampton, ON. 905-451-6100
Beam Global Spirits & Wine
  Deerfield, IL 847-948-8888
Brown-Forman Beverages Worldwide
  Louisville, KY. 502-585-1100
Canadian Mist Distillers
  Collingwood, ON 705-445-4690
George A Dickel & Company
  Tullahoma, TN 931-857-9313
Heaven Hill Distilleries
  Bardstown, KY 502-348-3921
Hiram Walker & Sons
  Windsor, ON 519-254-5171
Hood River Distillers
  Hood River, OR 541-386-1588
Jack Daniel's Distillery
  Lynchburg, TN 931-759-4221
Kittling Ridge Estate Wines & Spirits
  Grimsby, ON 905-945-9225
Laird & Company
  Eatontown, NJ 877-438-5247
Majestic Distilling Company
  Baltimore, MD 410-242-0200
Makers Mark Distillery
  Loretto, KY 270-865-2881
Marie Brizard Wines & Spirits
  Sausalito, CA 800-878-1123
Montebello Brands
  Baltimore, MD 410-282-8800
Pernod Ricard USA
  White Plains, NY 914-539-4500
Pernod Ricard USA Seagram Lawrenceburg Distillery
  Greendale, IN 812-537-0700

Blended

Hiram Walker & Sons
  Fort Smith, AR 479-783-4191

Tequila and Mezcal

A. Smith Bowman Distillery
  Fredericksburg, VA. 540-373-4555
Beam Global Spirits & Wine
  Deerfield, IL 847-948-8888

Corby Distilleries
  Toronto, ON 800-367-9079
Heaven Hill Distilleries
  Bardstown, KY 502-348-3921
Highwood Distillers
  High River, AB 403-652-3202
Hiram Walker & Sons
  Fort Smith, AR 479-783-4191
Hood River Distillers
  Hood River, OR 541-386-1588
Majestic Distilling Company
  Baltimore, MD 410-242-0200
Marie Brizard Wines & Spirits
  Sausalito, CA 800-878-1123
Tequila XQ
  Guadalajara Jalisco, ... 333-587-7799
Vincor International
  Mississauga, ON 800-265-9463

Anejo Tequila

Tequila XQ
  Guadalajara Jalisco, ... 333-587-7799

Reposado Tequila

Tequila XQ
  Guadalajara Jalisco, ... 333-587-7799

Vodka

A. Smith Bowman Distillery
  Fredericksburg, VA 540-373-4555
Bacardi Canada, Inc.
  Brampton, ON. 905-451-6100
Bacardi USA
  Miami, FL 800-222-2734
Beam Global Spirits & Wine
  Deerfield, IL 847-948-8888
Brown-Forman Beverages Worldwide
  Louisville, KY. 502-585-1100
Corby Distilleries
  Toronto, ON 800-367-9079
Crillon Importers
  Paramus, NJ 201-368-8878
Destileria Serralles
  Mercedita, PR 787-723-0107
Heaven Hill Distilleries
  Bardstown, KY 502-348-3921
Highwood Distillers
  High River, AB 403-652-3202
Hiram Walker & Sons
  Fort Smith, AR 479-783-4191
Hiram Walker & Sons
  Windsor, ON 519-254-5171
Hood River Distillers
  Hood River, OR 541-386-1588
Kittling Ridge Estate Wines & Spirits
  Grimsby, ON 905-945-9225
Laird & Company
  Eatontown, NJ 877-438-5247
Majestic Distilling Company
  Baltimore, MD 410-242-0200
Marie Brizard Wines & Spirits
  Sausalito, CA 800-878-1123
Pernod Ricard USA
  White Plains, NY 914-539-4500
R&A Imports
  Pacific Plsds, CA 310-454-2247
Trigo Corporation
  Toa Baja, PR 787-794-1300
Viking Distillery
  Albany, GA. 229-436-0181
Vincor International
  Mississauga, ON 800-265-9463

Whiskey, American

Barton Brands
  Chicago, IL 800-598-6352
Beam Global Spirits & Wine
  Deerfield, IL 847-948-8888
Corby Distilleries
  Toronto, ON 800-367-9079
George A Dickel & Company
  Tullahoma, TN 931-857-9313
Heaven Hill Distilleries
  Bardstown, KY 502-348-3921
Hiram Walker & Sons
  Fort Smith, AR 479-783-4191
Hiram Walker & Sons
  Windsor, ON 519-254-5171
Jack Daniel's Distillery
  Lynchburg, TN 931-759-4221

Kittling Ridge Estate Wines & Spirits
  Grimsby, ON 905-945-9225
Laird & Company
  Eatontown, NJ. 877-438-5247
Makers Mark Distillery
  Loretto, KY 270-865-2881
Pernod Ricard USA Seagram Lawrenceburg Distillery
  Greendale, IN 812-537-0700

Bourbon

A. Smith Bowman Distillery
  Fredericksburg, VA. 540-373-4555
Barton Brands
  Chicago, IL. 800-598-6352
Brown-Forman Beverages Worldwide
  Louisville, KY. 502-585-1100
Buffalo Trace Distillery
  Frankfort, KY 800-654-8471
Corby Distilleries
  Toronto, ON 800-367-9079
Heaven Hill Distilleries
  Bardstown, KY 502-348-3921
Laird & Company
  Eatontown, NJ 877-438-5247
Majestic Distilling Company
  Baltimore, MD 410-242-0200
Marie Brizard Wines & Spirits
  Sausalito, CA 800-878-1123
Old Rip Van Winkle Distillery
  Louisville, KY 502-897-9113
Pernod Ricard USA
  White Plains, NY 914-539-4500
Viking Distillery
  Albany, GA. 229-436-0181

Whiskey, Canadian

Beam Global Spirits & Wine
  Deerfield, IL 847-948-8888
Corby Distilleries
  Toronto, ON 800-367-9079

Sports Drinks

AC Gunter
  Clear Brook, VA 540-662-5484
American Purpac Technologies, LLC
  Beloit, WI 877-787-7221

asiamerica

Asiamerica Ingredients
  Westwood, NJ 201-497-5531

Processor, importer, exporter and distributor of
bulk vitamins, amino acids, nutraceuticals, aromatic chemicals, food additives, herbs, mineral
nutrients and pharmaceuticals.

Captiva
  Augusta, NJ. 973-579-7883
Central Coca-Cola Bottling Company
  Richmond, VA. 800-359-3759
Century Foods International
  Sparta, WI 800-269-1901
China Food Merchant Corporation
  Fullerton, CA 877-465-2582
Choice Organic Teas
  Seattle, WA 206-525-0051
Clement Pappas & Company
  Seabrook, NJ 800-257-7019
Cool
  Richardson, TX. 972-437-9352

123

Crystal Star Herbal Nutrition
Salinas, CA 831-422-7500
Eclipse Sports Supplements
Scranton, PA 800-320-0062
I Rice & Company
Philadelphia, PA 800-232-6022
Innovative Food Solutions LLC
Columbus, OH 800-884-3314
Itoen
Honolulu, HI 808-847-4477
Jo Mints
Corona Del Mar, CA. 877-566-4687
Masala Chai Company
Santa Cruz, CA 831-475-8881
Monarch Beverage Company
Atlanta, GA. 800-241-3732
Natures Best
Hauppauge, NY 800-345-2378
Nutriwest
Douglas, WY. 800-443-3333
Optimum Nutrition
Walterboro, SC 800-763-3444
QK Corporation
Baton Rouge, LA 225-753-8292
Quaker Oats Company
Mountain Top, PA. 800-367-6287
Randag & Associates Inc
Elmhurst, IL 630-530-2830
Tova Industries
Louisville, KY 888-532-8682
Uncle Bum's Gourmet Foods
Riverside, CA 800-486-2867

Water

Abita Springs Water Company
Metairie, LA 504-828-2500
Absopure Water Company
Plymouth, MI 800-422-7678
Acqua Blox LLC
Santa Fe Springs, CA 562-693-9599
Adobe Springs
Patterson, CA 408-897-3023
Alpine Valley Water
Harvey, IL 708-333-3910
Aqua Clara Bottling & Distribution
Clearwater, FL 727-446-2999
Arbor Springs Water Company
Ferndale, MI 800-343-7003
Blue Hills Spring Water Company
Quincy, MA. 617-472-4200
Blue Sky Natural Beverage Company
Santa Fe, NM 505-995-9761
Camp Holly Springs
Richmond, VA. 804-795-2096
Canada Dry Bottling Company
Flushing, NY. 718-661-4265
Captiva
Augusta, NJ. 973-579-7883
Cascade Clear Water
Burlington, WA. 360-757-4441
Clearly Canadian Beverage Corporation
Vancouver, BC 800-663-0227
Coca-Cola Bottling Company
Honolulu, HI 808-839-6711
Coca-Cola Enterprises
Atlanta, GA. 800-233-7210
Crystal Geyser Roxanne LLC
Pensacola, FL 850-476-8844
Crystal Springs
Mississauga, ON. 800-822-5889
Crystal Springs Water Company
Fort Lauderdale, FL 800-432-1321

Crystal Water Company
Orlando, FL. 800-444-7873
Culligan Water Technologies
Northbrook, IL 847-205-6000
Danone Waters of North America
Pasadena, CA 626-585-1000
Deep Rock Fontenelle Water Company
Omaha, NE 800-433-1303
Deep Rock Water Company
Denver, CO 800-695-2020
Deep Rock Water Company
Minneapolis, MN 800-800-8986
Distillata Company
Cleveland, OH 800-999-2906
DS Waters of America
Atlanta, GA. 800-728-5508
Eldorado Artesian Springs
Eldorado Springs, CO. 303-499-1316
Essentia Water
Phoenix, AZ 877-293-2239
Eureka Water Company
Oklahoma City, OK 800-310-8474
Fiji Water Company
Basalt, CO. 877-426-3454
Fizz-O Water Company
Tulsa, OK 918-834-3691
Fizzy Lizzy
New York, NY 800-203-9336
Fountainhead Water Company
Norcross, GA 864-944-1993
Full Service Beverage Company
Wichita, KS. 800-540-0001
Girard Spring Water
North Providence, RI 800-477-9287
Glen Summit Springs Water Company
Mountain Top, PA. 800-621-7596
Global Beverage Company
Rochester, NY. 585-381-3560
Great Spring Waters
Richmond, CA 800-950-9393
GWB Foods Corporation
Brooklyn, NY 718-686-9600
Harrisburg Dairies
Harrisburg, PA 800-692-7429
Hawaiian Natural Water Company
Pearl City, HI 808-483-0520
Healing Light
Catskill, NY 518-537-8800
Heck Cellars
Arvin, CA 661-854-6120
Island Sweetwater Beverage Company
Bryn Mawr, PA 610-525-7444
Jackson Milk & Ice CreamCompany
Hutchinson, KS. 620-663-1244
Knoxage Water Company
San Diego, CA 619-234-3333
Le Bleu Corporation
Advance, NC. 800-854-4471
Leisure Time Ice & Spring Water
Kiamesha Lake, NY 800-443-1412
Light Rock Beverage Company
Danbury, CT 203-743-3410
Lipsey Mountain Spring Water
Norcross, GA 770-449-0001
Mayer Brothers Apple Products
Barker, NY 716-795-9930
Mayer Brothers Apple Products
West Seneca, NY 800-696-2937
Metro Mint
San Francisco, CA 415-979-0781
Minnehaha Spring Water Company
Cleveland, OH 216-431-0243
Monarch Beverage Company
Atlanta, GA. 800-241-3732

Mount Claire Spring Water
Torrington, CT 888-525-2473
Mountain Valley Spring Company
Hot Springs, AR 800-643-1501
Music Mountain Water Company
Birmingham, AL 800-349-6555
Nantze Springs
Dothan, AL 800-239-7873
Natural Group
Oxnard, CA 805-485-3420
Natural Spring Water Company
Johnson City, TN 423-926-7905
NAYA
Stamford, CT. 800-566-6292
Naya
Mirabel, QC 450-562-7911
NC Mountain Water
Marion, NC. 800-220-4718
Neenah Springs
Oxford, WI 608-586-5605
North American Water Group
Overland Park, KS 913-469-1156
North Country Natural Spring Water
Port Kent, NY 518-834-9400
Northern Falls
Grand Rapids, MI 616-954-2061
Office General des Eaux Minerales
Montreal, QC 514-482-7221
Peace Mountain Natural Beverages Corporation
Springfield, MA 413-567-4942
Pepsi Bottling Group
Mesquite, TX 214-324-8500
Pepsi Bottling Group
Tulsa, OK 800-963-2424
Pocono Spring Company
Mt Pocono, PA 800-634-4584
Poland Spring Water
Brea, CA 800-950-9396
Premium Water
Orange Springs, FL 800-243-1163
Pure-Flo Water Company
Santee, CA 800-787-3356
Q Tonic
Brooklyn, NY 718-398-6642
Quibell Spring Water Beverage
Martinsville, VA 540-632-0100
R.J. Corr Naturals
Posen, IL 708-389-4200
Rebound
Newburgh, NY 845-562-5400
Regent Champagne Cellars
New York, NY 845-691-7296
Reiter Dairy
Springfield, OH. 937-323-5777
Sand Springs Springwater
Williamstown, MA 413-458-8281
Saratoga Beverage Group
Saratoga Springs, NY 888-426-8642
Schneider's Dairy Holdings Inc
Pittsburgh, PA 412-881-3525
Sinton Dairy Foods Company
Colorado Springs, CO. 800-388-4970
SnowBird Corporation
Bayonne, NJ. 800-576-1616
Sparkling Spring Water Company
Vernon Hills, IL 800-772-7554
St. Clair Industries
Fort Lauderdale, FL 954-491-0400
Suntory Water Group
Atlanta, GA. 770-933-1400
Talking Rain Beverage Company
Preston, WA 800-734-0748
Three Springs Water Company
Laurel Run, PA 800-332-7873

TRC Nutritional Laboratories
Tulsa, OK 800-421-7310
Triple Springs Spring Water
Meriden, CT 203-235-8374
Triton Water Company
Burlington, NC 800-476-9111
Universal Beverages
Leesburg, FL 352-315-1010
US Filter
East Orange, NJ 973-677-8946
USA Sunrise Beverage
Spearfish, SD 605-723-0690
Varni Brothers/7-Up Bottling
Modesto, CA 209-521-1777
Vichy Springs Mineral Water Corporation
Ukiah, CA 707-462-9515
Water Concepts
Des Plaines, IL 847-699-9797
White Rock Products Corporation
Whitestone, NY 800-969-7625
Windmill Water
Edgewood, NM 505-281-9287
Winterbrook Beverage Group
Greendale, IN 812-537-7348
Wissahickon Spring Water International
Philadelphia, PA 800-394-3733
Zephyr Hills
Tamarac, FL 954-597-7852

Bottled

Absopure Water Company
Plymouth, MI 800-422-7678
All Seasons International Distributors
Louisville, KY 502-473-1709
Alpine Valley Water
Harvey, IL 708-333-3910
Aqua Clara Bottling & Distribution
Clearwater, FL 727-446-2999
Arbor Springs Water Company
Ferndale, MI 800-343-7003
Assouline & Ting
Philadelphia, PA 800-521-4491
Bevco
Surrey, BC 800-663-0090
Bio-Hydration Research Lab
Carlsbad, CA 800-531-5088
Calcium Springs Water Company
Park City, UT 435-615-7700
Camp Holly Springs
Richmond, VA 804-795-2096
Canada Dry Bottling Company
Flushing, NY 718-661-4265
Captiva
Augusta, NJ 973-579-7883
Central Coca-Cola Bottling Company
Richmond, VA 800-359-3759
Coca-Cola Bottling Company
Honolulu, HI 808-839-6711
Country Pure Foods
Ellington, CT 860-872-8346
Crystal Geyser Roxanne LLC
Pensacola, FL 850-476-8844
Crystal Rock Spring Water Company
Waterford, CT 860-443-5000
Crystal Springs
Mississauga, ON 800-822-5889
Crystal Springs Water Company
Fort Lauderdale, FL 800-432-1321
Crystal Water Company
Orlando, FL 800-444-7873
Danone Waters of North America
Pasadena, CA 626-585-1000
Deep Rock Fontenelle Water Company
Omaha, NE 800-433-1303
Deep Rock Water Company
Minneapolis, MN 800-800-8986
Distillata Company
Cleveland, OH 800-999-2906
DS Waters of America
Atlanta, GA 800-728-5508
Eldorado Artesian Springs
Eldorado Springs, CO 303-499-1316
Eureka Water Company
Oklahoma City, OK 800-310-8474
Figuerola Laboratories
Santa Ynez, CA 800-219-1147
Fiji Water Company
Basalt, CO 877-426-3454
Fiji Water LLC
Los Angeles, CA 888-426-3454

Fountainhead Water Company
Norcross, GA 864-944-1993
Full Service Beverage Company
Wichita, KS 800-540-0001
Functional Products LLC
Atlantic Beach, FL 800-628-5908
Girard Spring Water
North Providence, RI 800-477-9287
Giumarra Vineyards
Bakersfield, CA 661-395-7000
Glen Summit Springs Water Company
Mountain Top, PA 800-621-7596
Global Beverage Company
Rochester, NY 585-381-3560
GWB Foods Corporation
Brooklyn, NY 718-686-9600
H3O
Beckley, WV 888-436-9287
Hansen's Natural
Fullerton, CA 714-870-0310
Hawaiian Natural Water Company
Pearl City, HI 808-483-0520
Heck Cellars
Arvin, CA 661-854-6120
Hi-Country Foods Corporation
Selah, WA 509-697-7292
Hinckley Springs Water Company
Chicago, IL 773-586-8600
Island Sweetwater Beverage Company
Bryn Mawr, PA 610-525-7444
J. Weil & Company
Boise, ID 800-755-3885
Jackson Milk & Ice CreamCompany
Hutchinson, KS 620-663-1244
Le Bleu Corporation
Advance, NC 800-854-4471
Leisure Time Ice & Spring Water
Kiamesha Lake, NY 800-443-1412
Light Rock Beverage Company
Danbury, CT 203-743-3410
Lipsey Mountain Spring Water
Norcross, GA 770-449-0001
Matilija Water Company
Ventura, CA 805-322-7212
Merci Spring Water
Saint Louis, MO 314-812-4812
Mount Olympus Waters
Salt Lake City, UT 800-628-6056
Mountain Valley Spring Company
Hot Springs, AR 800-643-1501
Music Mountain Water Company
Birmingham, AL 800-349-6555
National Beverage Corporation
Fort Lauderdale, FL 888-462-2349
Natural Spring Water Company
Johnson City, TN 423-926-7905
Naya
Mirabel, QC 450-562-7911
NC Mountain Water
Marion, NC 800-220-4718
North American Water Group
Overland Park, KS 913-469-1156
Peace Mountain Natural Beverages Corporation
Springfield, MA 413-567-4942
Pepsi Bottling Group
Mesquite, TX 214-324-8500
Pepsi Bottling Group
Pleasanton, CA 925-416-2500
Pocono Mountain Bottling Company
Wilkes Barre, PA 570-822-7695
Pocono Spring Company
Mt Pocono, PA 800-634-4584
Poland Spring Water
Brea, CA 800-950-9396
Polar Beverage
Worcester, MA 800-734-9800
Polar Water Company
Carnegie, PA 800-444-7873
Premium Water
Orange Springs, FL 800-243-1163
Pure-Flo Water Company
Santee, CA 800-787-3356
Quibell Spring Water Beverage
Martinsville, VA 540-632-0100
Regent Champagne Cellars
New York, NY 845-691-7296
Reiter Dairy
Springfield, OH 937-323-5777
Royal Crown Bottling Company
Bowling Green, KY 270-842-8106
SnowBird Corporation
Bayonne, NJ 800-576-1616

Southern Beverage Packers
Appling, GA 800-326-2469
Sparkling Spring Water Company
Vernon Hills, IL 800-772-7554
Spring Water Company
Chesapeake, VA 800-832-0271
Suntory Water Group
Atlanta, GA 770-933-1400
Titusville Dairy Products
Titusville, PA 800-352-0101
Triton Water Company
Burlington, NC 800-476-9111
Universal Beverages
Leesburg, FL 352-315-1010
Universal Beverages
Ponte Vedra Bch, FL 904-280-7795
US Filter
East Orange, NJ 973-677-8946
USA Sunrise Beverage
Spearfish, SD 605-723-0690
Vichy Springs Mineral Water Corporation
Ukiah, CA 707-462-9515
Water Concepts
Des Plaines, IL 847-699-9797
Windmill Water
Edgewood, NM 505-281-9287
Winterbrook Beverage Group
Greendale, IN 812-537-7348
Wissahickon Spring Water International
Philadelphia, PA 800-394-3733
Yosemite Waters
Los Angeles, CA 800-427-8420

Distilled

Absopure Water Company
Plymouth, MI 800-422-7678
Alacer Corporation
Foothill Ranch, CA 800-854-0249
Alamance Foods/Triton Water Company
Burlington, NC 800-476-9111
Alpine Valley Water
Harvey, IL 708-333-3910
Aquafina
Wichita, KS 316-522-4100
Arcadia Dairy Farms
Arden, NC 828-684-3556
Belmar Spring Water Company
Glen Rock, NJ 201-444-1010
Bevco
Surrey, BC 800-663-0090
Clark Spring Water Company
Pueblo, CO 719-543-1594
Cold Spring Brewing Company
Cold Spring, MN 320-685-8686
Conquest International LLC
Plainville, KS 785-434-2483
Crystal Rock Spring Water Company
Waterford, CT 860-443-5000
Crystal Springs Water Company
Fort Lauderdale, FL 800-432-1321
Deep Rock Fontenelle Water Company
Omaha, NE 800-433-1303
Deep Rock Water Company
Denver, CO 800-695-2020
Distillata Company
Cleveland, OH 800-999-2906
Energy Brands/Haute Source
Flushing, NY 800-746-0087
Fizz-O Water Company
Tulsa, OK 918-834-3691
Giumarra Vineyards
Bakersfield, CA 661-395-7000
Hinckley Springs Water Company
Chicago, IL 773-586-8600
Jackson Milk & Ice CreamCompany
Hutchinson, KS 620-663-1244
Land O'Pines Company
Lufkin, TX 936-634-5537
Le Bleu Corporation
Advance, NC 800-854-4471
Louis Trauth Dairy
Newport, KY 800-544-6455
Matilija Water Company
Ventura, CA 805-322-7212
Merci Spring Water
Saint Louis, MO 314-812-4812
Mount Olympus Waters
Salt Lake City, UT 800-628-6056
Mountain Valley Spring Company
Hot Springs, AR 800-643-1501

National Beverage Corporation
Fort Lauderdale, FL 888-462-2349
Poland Spring Water
Brea, CA 800-950-9396
Polar Beverage
Worcester, MA 800-734-9800
Polar Water Company
Carnegie, PA 800-444-7873
Premium Water
Orange Springs, FL 800-243-1163
Premium Waters
Minneapolis, MN 800-332-3332
SnowBird Corporation
Bayonne, NJ 800-576-1616
Southern Beverage Packers
Appling, GA 800-326-2469
Sparkling Spring Water Company
Vernon Hills, IL 800-772-7554
Spring Water Company
Chesapeake, VA 800-832-0271
US Filter
East Orange, NJ 973-677-8946
Yosemite Waters
Los Angeles, CA 800-427-8420
Zephyr Hills
Tamarac, FL 954-597-7852
Zephyr Hills Bottled Watter Corporation
Tampa, FL 800-950-9398

Flavored

Captiva
Augusta, NJ 973-579-7883
Clearly Canadian Beverage Corporation
Vancouver, BC 800-663-0227
Heritage Shortbread
Hilton Head Island, SC 843-342-7268
Hi Ball Energy
San Francisco, CA 415-420-4801
Hint
San Francisco, CA 415-513-4050
Northern Falls
Grand Rapids, MI 616-954-2061
Saratoga Beverage Group
Saratoga Springs, NY 888-426-8642
Watermark Innovation
Southampton, NY 201-693-8285

Mineral

Adobe Springs
Patterson, CA 408-897-3023
Beaulieu Vineyard
Rutherford, CA 800-264-6918
Canada Dry Bottling Company
Flushing, NY 718-661-4265
Clearly Canadian Beverage Corporation
Vancouver, BC 800-663-0227
Crystal Geyser Water Company
Calistoga, CA 800-726-6121
Deep Rock Fontenelle Water Company
Omaha, NE 800-433-1303
Golden State Vintners
Cutler, CA 559-528-3033
Matilija Water Company
Ventura, CA 805-322-7212
Moka D'Oro Coffee
Farmingdale, NY 888-665-2367
Monticello Cellars
Napa, CA 707-253-2802
Office General des Eaux Minerales
Montreal, QC 514-482-7221
R.J. Corr Naturals
Posen, IL 708-389-4200
Sebastiani Vineyards
Sonoma, CA 800-888-5532
Three Springs Water Company
Laurel Run, PA 800-332-7873
USA Sunrise Beverage
Spearfish, SD 605-723-0690

Spring

Abita Springs Water Company
Metairie, LA 504-828-2500
Absopure Water Company
Plymouth, MI 800-422-7678
Alamance Foods/Triton Water Company
Burlington, NC 800-476-9111
Amanda Hills Spring Water
Pataskala, OH 800-375-0885
Arizona Beverage Company
New Hyde Park, NY 800-832-3775

Bevco
Surrey, BC 800-663-0090
Camp Holly Springs
Richmond, VA 804-795-2096
Contact International
Skokie, IL 847-324-4411
Country Pure Foods
Ellington, CT 860-872-8346
Crystal Geyser Water Company
San Francisco, CA 415-616-9590
Crystal Geyser Water Company
Calistoga, CA 800-726-6121
Crystal Rock Spring Water Company
Waterford, CT 860-443-5000
Crystal Springs Water Company
Fort Lauderdale, FL 800-432-1321
Deep Rock Water Company
Denver, CO 800-695-2020
Fizz-O Water Company
Tulsa, OK 918-834-3691
Garelick Farms
Franklin, MA 800-343-4982
Girard Spring Water
North Providence, RI 800-477-9287
Glen Summit Springs Water Company
Mountain Top, PA 800-621-7596
Great Spring Waters
Richmond, VA 800-950-9393
Harrisburg Dairies
Harrisburg, PA 800-692-7429
Hawaiian Natural Water Company
Pearl City, HI 808-483-0520
Hinckley Springs Water Company
Chicago, IL 773-586-8600
Jackson Milk & Ice CreamCompany
Hutchinson, KS 620-663-1244
Matilija Water Company
Ventura, CA 805-322-7212
Mayer Brothers Apple Products
Barker, NY 716-795-9930
Mayer Brothers Apple Products
West Seneca, NY 800-696-2937
Merci Spring Water
Saint Louis, MO 314-812-4812
Meridian Beverage Company
Atlanta, GA 800-728-1481
Minnehaha Spring Water Company
Cleveland, OH 216-431-0243
Miscoe Springs
Mendon, MA 508-473-0550
Mount Olympus Waters
Salt Lake City, UT 800-628-6056
Mountain Valley Spring Company
Hot Springs, AR 800-643-1501
Music Mountain Water Company
Birmingham, AL 800-349-6555
National Beverage Corporation
Fort Lauderdale, FL 888-462-2349
Natural Spring Water Company
Johnson City, TN 423-926-7905
NAYA
Stamford, CT 800-566-6292
Naya
Mirabel, QC 450-562-7911
North Country Natural Spring Water
Port Kent, NY 518-834-9400
Northern Falls
Grand Rapids, MI 616-954-2061
Poland Spring Water
Greenwich, CT 203-531-4100
Poland Spring Water
Brea, CA 800-950-9396
Polar Beverage
Worcester, MA 800-734-9800
Polar Water Company
Carnegie, PA 800-444-7873
Premium Water
Orange Springs, FL 800-243-1163
Regent Champagne Cellars
New York, NY 845-691-7296
Sand Springs Springwater
Williamstown, MA 413-458-8281
Saratoga Beverage Group
Saratoga Springs, NY 888-426-8642
SnowBird Corporation
Bayonne, NJ 800-576-1616
Southern Beverage Packers
Appling, GA 800-326-2469
Sparkling Spring Water Company
Vernon Hills, IL 800-772-7554
Sparkling Water Distributors
Merrick, NY 800-277-2755

Spring Water Company
Chesapeake, VA 800-832-0271
Triple Springs Spring Water
Meriden, CT 203-235-8374
US Filter
East Orange, NJ 973-677-8946
USA Sunrise Beverage
Spearfish, SD 605-723-0690
White Rock Products Corporation
Whitestone, NY 800-969-7625
Windmill Water
Edgewood, NM 505-281-9287
Yoder Dairies
Chesapeake, VA 757-497-3518
Zephyr Hills
Tamarac, FL 954-597-7852
Zephyr Hills Bottled Watter Corporation
Tampa, FL 800-950-9398

Wines

A. Nonini Winery
Fresno, CA 559-275-1936
A. Rafanelli Winery
Healdsburg, CA 707-433-1385
Abingdon Vineyard & Winery
Abingdon, VA 276-623-1255
Acacia Vineyard
Napa, CA 707-226-9991
Ackerman Winery
Amana, IA 319-622-3379
Ackerman Winery
Amana, IA 319-622-6513
Adair Vineyards
New Paltz, NY 845-255-1377
Adam Puchta Winery
Hermann, MO 573-486-5596
Adams County Winery
Orrtanna, PA 717-334-4631
Adelaida Cellars
Paso Robles, CA 800-676-1232
Adelsheim Vineyard
Newberg, OR 503-538-5222
Adler Fels Vineyards & Winery
Santa Rosa, CA 707-569-1493
Admiral Wine Merchants
Irvington, NJ 800-582-9463
Aetna Springs Cellars
Pope Valley, CA 707-965-2675
Afton Mountain Vineyards
Afton, VA 540-456-8667
Ahlgren Vineyard
Boulder Creek, CA 800-338-6071
Airlie Winery
Monmouth, OR 503-838-6013
Alba Vineyard
Milford, NJ 908-995-7800
Alexander Johnson's Valley Wines
Healdsburg, CA 800-888-5532
Alexis Bailly Vineyard
Hastings, MN 651-437-1413
Allegro Vineyards
Brogue, PA 717-927-9148
Allied Wine Corporation
Monticello, NY 845-796-4160
Almarla Vineyards & Winery
Shubuta, MS 601-687-5548
Alpen Cellars
Trinity Center, CA 530-266-9513
Alpine Vineyards
Monroe, OR 541-424-5851
Alta Vineyard Cellar
Calistoga, CA 707-942-6708
Altamura Vineyards & Winery
Napa, CA 707-253-2000
Alto Vineyards
Alto Pass, IL 618-893-4898
Amador Foothill Winery
Plymouth, CA 800-778-9463
Amalthea Cellars Farm Winery
Atco, NJ 856-768-8585
Amberg Wine Cellars
Clifton Springs, NY 315-462-3455
Americana Vineyards
Interlaken, NY 607-387-6801
Amity Vineyards
Amity, OR 888-264-8966
Amizetta Vineyards
St Helena, CA 707-963-1460
AmRhein Wine Cellars
Bent Mountain, VA 540-929-4632
Amwell Valley Vineyard
Ringoes, NJ 908-788-5852

Anchor Brewing Company
San Francisco, CA 415-863-8350
Anderson's Conn Valley Vineyards
St Helena, CA 800-946-3497
Andrew Peller Limited
Grimsby, ON 905-643-4131
Annapolis Winery
Annapolis, CA 707-886-5460
Antelope Valley Winery
Lancaster, CA 800-282-8332
Anthony Road Wine Company
Penn Yan, NY 800-559-2182
Arbor Crest Wine Cellars
Spokane, WA. 509-927-8571
Arbor Hill Grapery & Winery
Naples, NY 800-554-7553
Arbor Mist Winery
Canandaigua, NY 866-396-7394
Arcadian Estate Winery
Rock Stream, NY 800-298-1346
Argonaut Winery
Ione, CA 209-245-5567
Argyle Wines
Dundee, OR. .888-427-4953
Ariel Vineyards
Napa, CA. 800-456-9472
Arizona Vineyards
Nogales, AZ .520-287-7972
Arns Winery
Saint Helena, CA 707-963-3429
Arrowood Vineyards & Winery
Glen Ellen, CA 800-938-5170
Artesa Vineyards & Winery
Napa, CA. 707-224-1668
Ashland Vineyards
Ashland, OR .541-488-0088
ASV Wines
Delano, CA 661-792-3159
Atlas Peak Vineyards
Sonoma, CA .866-522-9463
Atwater Block Brewing Company
Detroit, MI 313-877-9205
Au Bon Climat Winery
Los Olivos, CA 805-937-9801
Audubon Cellars
Berkeley, CA. 510-540-5384
Augusta Winery
Augusta, MO. 888-667-9463
Autumn Hill Vineyards/Blue Ridge Wine
Stanardsville, VA 434-985-6100
Autumn Wind Vineyard
Newberg, OR 503-538-6931
Avalon Organic Coffees
Albuquerque, NM. 800-662-2575
Babcock Winery & Vineyards
Lompoc, CA .805-736-1455
Baily Vineyard & Winery
Temecula, CA 951-676-9463
Balagna Winery Company
Los Alamos, NM. 505-672-3678
Baldwin Vineyards
Pine Bush, NY 845-744-2226
Balic Winery
Mays Landing, NJ. 609-625-1903
Bandiera Winery
Cloverdale, CA 707-894-4295
Banfi Vintners
Glen Head, NY 800-645-6511
Barboursville Vineyards
Barboursville, VA 540-832-3824
Barca Wine Cellars
Roseville, CA 916-967-0770
Bargetto's Winery
Soquel, CA 800-422-7438

Baron Vineyards
Paso Robles, CA. 805-239-3313
Basignani Winery
Sparks Glencoe, MD. 410-472-0703
Batavia Wine Cellars
Canandaigua, NY 800-879-9463
Baxter's Vineyard
Nauvoo, IL 800-854-1396
Baywood Cellars
Lodi, CA 800-214-0445
Beachaven Vineyards & Winery
Clarksville, TN 931-645-8867
Bear Creek Winery
Cave Junction, OR 541-592-3977
Beaucanon Estate Wines
Napa, CA. 800-660-3520
Beaulieu Vineyard
Rutherford, CA 800-264-6918
Beckmen Vineyards
Los Olivos, CA 805-688-8664
Bedell North Fork, LLC
Cutchogue, NY 631-734-7537
Bell Mountain Vineyards
Fredericksburg, TX. 830-685-3297
Bellerose Vineyard
Healdsburg, CA 707-433-1637
Belvedere Vineyards & Winery
Healdsburg, CA 800-433-8296
Belvedere Winery
Healdsburg, CA 800-433-8296
Benmarl Wine Company
Marlboro, NY 845-236-4265
Benziger Family Winery
Glen Ellen, CA 888-490-2739
Bernardo Winery
San Diego, CA 858-487-1866
Bernardus Winery & Vineyards
Carmel Valley, CA 888-648-9463
Bethel Heights Vineyard,Inc.
Salem, OR. 503-581-2262
Bianchi Winery
Newport Beach, CA 949-646-9100
Bias Vineyards & Winery
Berger, MO 573-834-5475
Bidwell Vineyard
Cutchogue, NY 631-734-5200
Biltmore Estate Wine Company
Asheville, NC 800-411-3812
Binns Vineyards & Winery
Las Cruces, NM 575-522-2211
Bishop Farms Winery
Cheshire, CT. 203-272-8243
Black Mesa Winery
Velarde, NM .800-852-6372
Black Sheep Vintners
Murphys, CA 209-728-2157
Blackwell Wine Company
Lost Hills, CA 661-397-2622
Blalock Seafood
Orange Beach, AL 251-974-5811
Blue Hills Spring Water Company
Quincy, MA. .617-472-4200
Blue Mountain Vineyards
New Tripoli, PA 610-298-3068
Blumenhof Vineyards-Winery
Dutzow, MO .800-419-2245
Boeger Winery
Placerville, CA 800-655-2634
Bogle Vineyards
Clarksburg, CA 916-744-1139
Boisset America
Sausalito, CA 800-878-1123
Bonny Doon Vineyard
Santa Cruz, CA 831-425-3625

Bonterra Vineyard
Hopland, CA .707-744-7575
Boordy Vineyards
Hydes, MD 410-592-5015
Bordoni Vineyards
Vallejo, CA 707-642-1504
Borra Vineyards
Lodi, CA 209-368-2446
Boskydel Vineyard
Lake Leelanau, MI 231-256-7272
Bouchaine Vineyards
Napa, CA. 800-654-9463
BR Cohn Winery
Glen Ellen, CA 707-938-4064
Brandborg Cellars
Elkton, OR 510-215-9553
Brander Vineyard
Los Olivos, CA 800-970-9979
Braren Pauli Winery
Redwood Valley, CA. 800-423-6519
Braswell's Winery
Dora, AL 205-648-8335
Bravard Vineyards & Winery
Hopkinsville, KY 270-269-2583
Breaux Vineyards
Purcellville, VA. 800-492-9961
Breitenbach Wine Cellars
Dover, OH. 330-343-3603
Briceland Vineyards
Redway, CA .707-923-2429
Bridgeview Winery
Cave Junction, OR 877-273-4843
Brimstone Hill Vineyard
Pine Bush, NY 845-744-2231
Bristle Ridge Vineyard
Knob Noster, MO 800-994-9463
Broad Run Vineyards
Louisville, KY 502-231-0372
Broadley Vineyards
Monroe, OR .541-847-5934
Bronco Wine Company
Ceres, CA 800-692-5780
Brookmere Vineyards
Belleville, PA 717-935-5380
Brotherhood Winery
Washingtonville, NY 845-496-3661
Brown County Wine Company
Nashville, IN. 888-298-2984
Brutocao Cellars
Hopland, CA. 800-433-3689
Bryant Vineyard
Talladega, AL 256-268-2638
Buccia Winery
Conneaut, OH 440-593-5976
Buckingham Valley Vineyards
Buckingham, PA 215-794-7188
Buehler Vineyards
St Helena, CA 707-963-2155
Buena Vista Carneros Winery
Sonoma, CA .800-678-8504
Buffalo Trace Distillery
Frankfort, KY 800-654-8471
Bully Hill Vineyards
Hammondsport, NY 607-868-3610
Burnley Vineyards and Daniel Cellars
Barboursville, VA. 540-832-2828
Butler Winery
Bloomington, IN. 812-339-7233
Butterfly Creek Winery
Mariposa, CA 209-966-2097
Buttonwood Farm Winery
Solvang, CA .800-715-1404
Byington Winery & Vineyards
Los Gatos, CA. 408-354-1111

Byron Vineyard & Winery
Santa Maria, CA 805-934-4770
Cache Cellars
Davis, CA 530-756-6068
Cain Vineyard & Winery
St Helena, CA 707-963-1616
Cakebread Cellars
Rutherford, CA 800-588-0298
Calafia Cellars
St Helena, CA 707-963-0114
Calera Wine Company
Hollister, CA 831-637-9170
California Olive Oil Corporation
Salem, MA 800-386-6457
Callahan Ridge Winery
Roseburg, OR 800-695-4946
Callaway Vineyards & Winery
Temecula, CA 800-472-2377
Camas Prairie Winery
Moscow, ID 800-616-0214
Cambria Winery & Vineyard
Santa Maria, CA 888-339-9463
Campagana Winery
Redwood Valley, CA 707-485-1221
Campari
New York, NY 212-891-3600
Canandaigua Wine Concentrate
Madera, CA 559-673-7071
Cantwell's Old Mill Winery
Geneva, OH 440-466-5560
Cap Rock Winery
Lubbock, TX 800-546-9463
Caparone Winery
Paso Robles, CA 805-467-3827
Caporale Winery
Napa, CA 707-253-9230
Cardinale Winery
Oakville, CA 707-944-2807
Carlson Vineyards
Palisade, CO 888-464-5554
Carmela Vineyards
Glenns Ferry, ID 208-366-2539
Carneros Creek Winery
Napa, CA 707-253-9464
Carrousel Cellars
Gilroy, CA 408-847-2060
Casa Larga Vineyards
Fairport, NY 585-223-4210
Casa Nuestra
St Helena, CA 866-844-9463
Cascade Mountain Winery & Restaurant
Amenia, NY 845-373-9021
Castello Di Borghese
Cutchogue, NY 800-734-5158
Catoctin Vineyards
Brookeville, MD 301-774-2310
Cavender Castle Winery
Atlanta, GA 706-864-4759
Caymus Vineyards
Rutherford, CA 707-967-3010
Cayuga Ridge Estate Winery
Ovid, NY 800-598-9463
Cecchetti Sebastiani Cellar
Sonoma, CA 707-996-8463
Cedar Creek Winery
Cedarburg, WI 800-827-8020
Cedar Mountain Winery
Livermore, CA 925-373-6636
Chaddsford Winery
Chadds Ford, PA 610-388-6221
Chalet Debonne Vineyards
Madison, OH 440-466-3485
Chalk Hill Estate Vineyards & Winery
Healdsburg, CA 707-838-4306
Chalone Wine Group
Napa, CA 707-254-4200
Champoeg Wine Cellars
Aurora, OR 503-678-2144
Channing Rudd Cellars
Middletown, CA 707-987-2209
Chappellet Winery
St Helena, CA 800-494-6379
Charles B. Mitchell Vineyards
Somerset, CA 800-704-9463
Charles Jacquin Et Cie
Philadelphia, PA 800-523-3811
Charles Krug Winery
St Helena, CA 707-967-2200
Charles Spinetta Winery
Plymouth, CA 209-245-3384
Chartrand Imports
Rockland, ME 800-473-7307

Chateau Anne Marie
Carlton, OR 503-864-2991
Chateau Boswell
St Helena, CA 707-963-5472
Chateau Chevre Winery
Napa, CA 707-944-2184
Chateau des Charmes Wines
St. Davids, ON 800-263-2541
Chateau Diana Winery
Healdsburg, CA 707-433-6992
Chateau Grand Traverse
Traverse City, MI 231-223-7355
Chateau Julien Winery
Carmel, CA 831-624-2600
Chateau LaFayette Reneau
Hector, NY 800-469-9463
Chateau Montelena Winery
Calistoga, CA 707-942-5105
Chateau Morisette Winery
Meadows of Dan, VA 540-593-2865
Chateau Potelle Winery
Napa, CA 707-255-9440
Chateau Ra-Ha
Jerseyville, IL 866-639-4832
Chateau Sassenage
Truth or Consequences, NM 505-894-7244
Chateau Souverain
Geyserville, CA 707-433-3141
Chateau St. Jean Vineyards
Kenwood, CA 707-833-4134
Chateau Thomas Winery
Plainfield, IN 888-761-9463
Chatom Vineyards
Murphys, CA 800-435-8852
Chermont Winery
Esmont, VA 804-286-2211
Chestnut Mountain Winery
Hoschton, GA 770-867-6914
Chi Company/Tabor Hill Winery
Buchanan, MI 800-283-3363
Chicama Vineyards
West Tisbury, MA 888-244-2262
Chimere
Santa Maria, CA 805-922-9097
China Bowl Trading Company
Westport, CT 203-222-0381
Chouinard Vineyards
Castro Valley, CA 510-582-9900
Christensen Ridge
Madison, VA 540-923-4800
Christine Woods Winery
Philo, CA 707-895-2115
Christopher Creek Winery
Healdsburg, CA 707-433-6992
Cienega Valley Winery/DeRose
Hollister, CA 831-636-9143
Cimarron Cellars
Caney, OK 580-889-5997
Cinnabar Vineyards & Winery
Saratoga, CA 408-741-5858
CK Mondavi Vineyards
St Helena, CA 707-967-2200
Claiborne & Churchill Vintners
San Luis Obispo, CA 805-544-4066
Claire's Grand River Winery
Madison, OH 440-298-9838
Claudia Springs Winery
San Jose, CA 408-895-3926
Clear Creek Distillery
Portland, OR 503-248-9470
Cline Cellars
Sonoma, CA 800-543-2070
Clinton Vineyards
Clinton Corners, NY 845-266-5372
Clos Du Bois
Geyserville, CA 800-222-3189
Clos du Lac Cellars
Ione, CA 209-274-2238
Clos Du Muriel
Temecula, CA 951-296-5400
Clos du Val Wine Company
Napa, CA 800-993-9463
Clos Pegase Winery
Calistoga, CA 800-866-8583
Cloudstone Vineyards
Los Altos Hills, CA 650-948-8621
Clover Hill Vineyards & Winery
Breinigsville, PA 800-256-8374
Cocolalla Winery
Cocolalla, ID 208-263-3774
Colorado Cellars Winery
Palisade, CO 970-464-7921

Columbia Winery
Woodinville, WA 425-488-2776
Concannon Vineyard
Livermore, CA 800-258-9866
Conn Creek Winery
St Helena, CA 800-793-7960
Conneaut Cellars Winery
Conneaut Lake, PA 877-229-9463
Conrotto A. Winery
Gilroy, CA 408-847-2233
Cooper Mountain Vineyards
Beaverton, OR 503-649-0027
Cooper Vineyards
Louisa, VA 540-894-5253
Corus Brands
Woodinville, WA 425-806-2600
Cosentino Winery
Yountville, CA 800-764-1220
Cottonwood Canyon Vineyards
Santa Maria, CA 805-937-8463
Country Life
Hauppauge, NY 800-645-5768
Cowie Wine Cellars
Paris, AR 479-963-3990
Crescini Wines
Soquel, CA 831-462-1466

Cribari Vineyards
Fresno, CA 800-277-9095

Processor and exporter of high quality California bulk wine. Cribari Vineyards, Inc. has been involved in the California wine industry for more than four generations. Our commitment to quality and service is unsurpassed. We are competitive in our pricing and can furnish many varieties of California wine blended to our customers' specifications. Some of our most popular products are Cabernet Sauvignon, Merlot, Chardonnay, Sauterne, Sherry, Chablis, Marsala, and Chianti.

Cristom Vineyards
Salem, OR 503-375-3068
Cronin Vineyards
Woodside, CA 650-851-1452
Crown Regal Wine Cellars
Brooklyn, NY 718-604-1430
Cruse Vineyards
Chester, SC 803-377-3944
Cuneo Cellars
Amity, OR 503-835-2782
Cuvaison Vineyard
Calistoga, CA 707-942-6266
Cygnet Cellars
Hollister, CA 831-637-7559
Dalla Valle Vineyards
Oakville, CA 707-944-2676
Dark Mountain Winery and Brewery
Vail, AZ 520-762-5777
Daume Winery
Camarillo, CA 800-559-9922
David Bruce Winery
Los Gatos, CA 800-397-9972
Davis Bynum Winery
Healdsburg, CA 800-826-1073
De Loach Vineyards
Santa Rosa, CA 707-526-9111
De Lorimier Winery
Geyserville, CA 800-546-7718
Deaver Vineyards
Plymouth, CA 209-245-4099
Deer Meadow Vineyard
Winchester, VA 800-653-6632
Deer Park Winery
Elk Creek, MO 707-963-5411
Dehlinger Winery
Sebastopol, CA 707-823-2378
Delicato Vineyards
Napa, CA 707-265-1700
Delicato Vineyards
Napa, CA 877-824-3600
Denatale Vineyards
Healdsburg, CA 707-431-8460

Destileria Serralles
Mercedita, PR 787-723-0107
Devlin Wine Cellars
Soquel, CA .831-476-7288
Di Grazia Vineyards
Brookfield, CT 800-230-8853
Diamond Creek Vineyards
Calistoga, CA 707-942-6926
Diamond Oaks Vineyard
Cloverdale, CA 707-894-3191
Diamond Water
Hot Springs, AR 501-623-1251
Distant Lands Coffee Roaster
Tyler, TX 800-346-5459
Domaine Chandon
Yountville, CA 800-242-6366
Domaine Montreaux
Napa, CA 800-743-6668
Domaine St. George Winery
Healdsburg, CA 707-433-5508
Dominion Wine Cellars
Culpeper, VA 540-825-8772
Don Sebastiani & Sons
Sonoma, CA .707-933-1704
Donatoni Winery
Inglewood, CA 310-645-5445
Door-Peninsula Winery
Sturgeon Bay, WI 800-551-5049
Dr. Frank's Vinifera Wine Cellar
Hammondsport, NY 800-320-0735
Dr. Konstantin Frank Vinifera Wine Cellars
Hammondsport, NY 800-320-0735
Dreyer Sonoma
Woodside, CA 650-851-9448
Dry Creek Vineyard
Healdsburg, CA 800-864-9463
Duck Pond Cellars
Dundee, OR .800-437-3213
Duckhorn Vineyards
St Helena, CA 888-354-8885
Duncan Peak Vineyards
Hopland, CA 707-744-1129
Dundee Wine Company
Dundee, OR .888-427-4953
Dunn Vineyards
Angwin, CA .707-965-3642
Duplin Wine Cellars
Rose Hill, NC 800-774-9634
Durney Vineyards
Carmel Valley, CA 800-625-8466
Dutch Henry Winery
Calistoga, CA 888-224-5879
E&J Gallo Winery
Modesto, CA 209-341-3111
E&J Gallo Winery
Livingston, CA 209-394-6219
E&J Gallo Winery
Fresno, CA 559-458-2480
E&J Gallo Winery
Mississauga, ON 905-602-4575
Eagle Crest Vineyards
Conesus, NY 585-346-2321
Easley Winery
Indianapolis, IN 317-636-4516
East Side Winery/Oak Ridge Vineyards
Lodi, CA 209-369-4768
Ed Oliveira Winery
Arcata, CA 707-822-3023
Edgewood Estate Winery
Napa, CA 800-755-2374
Edmunds St. John
Berkeley, CA 510-981-1510
Edna Valley Vineyard
San Luis Obispo, CA 805-544-5855
Ehrle Brothers Winery
Homestead, IA 319-622-3241
El Molino Winery
St Helena, CA 707-963-3632
El Paso Winery
Ulster Park, NY 845-331-8642
Elk Cove Vineyards
Gaston, OR .503-985-7760
Elk Run Vineyards
Mt Airy, MD .800-414-2513
Elliston Vineyards
Sunol, CA 925-862-2377
Embassy Wine Company
Brooklyn, NY 718-272-0600
Emilio Guglielmo Winery
Morgan Hill, CA 408-779-2145
Enz Vineyards
Hollister, CA 831-637-3956

Eola Hills Wine Cellars
Rickreall, OR 800-291-6730
EOS Estate Winery
Paso Robles, CA 800-349-9463
Erath Vineyards Winery
Dundee, OR .800-539-5463
Esterlina Vineyard & Winery
Philo, CA 707-895-2920
Eureka Springs Winery
Eureka Springs, AR 479-253-8754
Evensen Vineyards
Oakville, CA .707-944-2396
Evergreen Juices
Ontario, CA .877-915-8423
Evesham Wood Vineyard & Winery
Salem, OR 503-371-8478
Eyrie Vineyards
Dundee, OR .503-472-6315
Fall Creek Vineyards
Austin, TX 512-476-4477
Fantis Foods
Carlstadt, NJ 201-933-6200
Far Niente Winery
Oakville, CA .707-944-2861
Farella-Park Vineyards
Napa, CA 707-254-9489
Farfelu Vineyards
Flint Hill, VA 540-364-2930
Fellom Ranch Vineyards
Cupertino, CA 408-741-0307
Fenestra Winery
Livermore, CA 800-789-9463
Fenn Valley Vineyards
Fennville, MI 800-432-6265
Ferrante Winery & Ristorante
Geneva, OH .440-466-6046
Ferrara Winery
Escondido, CA 760-745-7632
Ferrari-Carano Vineyards& Winery
Healdsburg, CA 800-831-0381
Ferrigno Vineyard & Winery
St James, MO 573-265-7742
Ferrigno Vineyards & Winry
St James, MO 573-265-7742
Fess Parker Winery
Los Olivos, CA 800-446-2455
Ficklin Vineyards
Madera, CA .559-674-4598
Field Stone Winery & Vineyard
Healdsburg, CA 800-544-7273
Fieldbrook Valley Winery
McKinleyville, CA 707-839-4140
Fife Vineyards
Redwood Valley, CA 707-485-0323
Filsinger Vineyards & Winery
Temecula, CA 951-302-6363
Fiore Winery
Pylesville, MD 410-452-0132
Firelands Wine Company
Sandusky, OH 800-548-9463
Firestone Vineyard
Los Olivos, CA 805-688-3940
First Colony Winery
Charlottesville, VA 877-979-7105
Fisher Ridge Wine Company
Charleston, WV 304-342-8702
Fisher Vineyards
Santa Rosa, CA 707-539-7511
Fitzpatrick Winery & Lodge
Somerset, CA 800-245-9166
Flora Springs Wine Company
St Helena, CA 707-967-8032
Flynn Vineyards Winery
Rickreall, OR 888-427-4953
Foley Estates Vineyards & Winery
Solvang, CA .805-688-8554
Folie a Deux Winery
St Helena, CA 800-473-4454
Foppiano Vineyard
Healdsburg, CA 707-433-7272
Foris Vineyards
Cave Junction, OR 541-592-3752
Forman Vineyards
St Helena, CA 707-963-3900
Fortino Winery
Gilroy, CA 888-617-6606
Fortuna Cellars
Davis, CA 530-756-6686
Four Sisters Winery
Belvidere, NJ 908-475-3671
Fox Run Vineyards
Penn Yan, NY 800-636-9786

Fox Vineyards Winery
Social Circle, GA 770-787-5402
Foxen Vineyard
Santa Maria, CA 805-937-4251
Franciscan Oakville Estates
Rutherford, CA 800-529-9463
Franciscan Vineyards
Rutherford, CA 800-529-9463
Frank Family Vineyard
Calistoga, CA 707-942-0859
Franklin Hill Vineyards
Bangor, PA .888-887-2839
Franzia Winery
Ripon, CA 209-599-4111
Fratelli Perata
Paso Robles, CA 805-238-2809
Frederick Wildman & Sons
New York, NY 800-733-9463
Freemark Abbey Winery
Helena, CA .800-963-9698
Freixenet
Sonoma, CA 707-996-4981
Frey Vineyards
Redwood Valley, CA 800-760-3739
Frick Winery
Sacramento, CA 415-776-7331
Frisinger Cellars
Napa, CA 707-255-3749
Frog's Leap Winery
Rutherford, CA 800-959-4704
Frontenac Point Vineyard
Trumansburg, NY 607-387-9619
Gainey Vineyard
Santa Ynez, CA 805-688-0558
Galante Vineyards
Carmel Valley, CA 800-425-2683
Galena Cellars Winery
Galena, IL 800-397-9463
Galleano Winery
Mira Loma, CA 951-685-5376
Galluccio Estate Vineyards
Cutchogue, NY 631-734-7089
Gary Farrell Wines
Santa Rosa, CA 707-433-6616
Georgia Winery
Ringgold, GA 706-937-2177
Georis Winery
Carmel Valley, CA 831-659-1050
Germanton Winery
Germanton, NC 800-322-2894
Geyser Peak Winery
Geyserville, CA 800-945-4447
Giasi Winery
Rock Stream, NY 607-535-7785
Gibson Wine Company
Sanger, CA .559-875-2505
Girard Winery/Rudd Estates
Oakville, CA 707-944-8577
Girardet Wine Cellars
Roseburg, OR 541-679-7252
Giumarra Vineyards
Bakersfield, CA 661-395-7000
Glenora Wine Cellars
Dundee, NY .800-243-5513
Gloria Ferrer Champagne
Sonoma, CA 707-996-7256
Gloria Winery & Vineyard
Springfield, MO 417-926-6263
Glunz Family Winery & Cellars
Grayslake, IL 847-548-9463
Golden Creek Vineyard
Santa Rosa, CA 707-538-2350
Golden State Vintners
Cutler, CA 559-528-3033
Good Harbor Vineyards
Lake Leelanau, MI 231-256-7165
Goodson Brothers Coffee Company
Knoxville, TN 865-693-3572
Goosecross Cellars
Yountville, CA 800-276-9210
Grand View Winery
East Calais, VT 802-456-7012
Grande River Vineyards
Palisade, CO 800-264-7696
Granite Springs Winery
Somerset, CA 800-638-6041
Greenfield Wine Company
Saint Helena, CA 707-963-2335
Greenwood Ridge Vineyards
Philo, CA 707-895-2002
Groth Vineyards & Winery
Oakville, CA 707-944-0290

129

Groupe Paul Masson
Longueuil, QC 514-878-3050
Gruet Winery
Albuquerque, NM 888-897-9463
Guilliams Winery
St Helena, CA 707-963-9059
Gundlach Bundschu Winery
Sonoma, CA 707-938-5277
H Coturri & Sons Winery
Glen Ellen, CA 866-268-8774
Habersham Winery
Helen, GA 706-878-9463
Hafner Vineyard
Healdsburg, CA 707-433-4606
Hahn Estates and Smith &Hook
Soledad, CA 831-678-4555
Haight-Brown Vineyard
Litchfield, CT 800-577-9463
Hallcrest Vineyards
Felton, CA 831-335-4441
Handley Cellars
Philo, CA 800-733-3151
Hanzell Vineyards
Sonoma, CA 707-996-3860
Harbor Winery
West Sacramento, CA 916-371-6776
Harmony Cellars
Harmony, CA 800-432-9239
Harpersfield Vineyard
Geneva, OH 440-466-4739
Hart Winery
Temecula, CA 877-638-8788
Hartford Family Winery
Forestville, CA 800-588-0234
Hazlitt's 1852 Vineyard
Hector, NY 888-750-0494
Heartland Vineyards
Cleveland, OH 440-871-0701
Heaven Hill Distilleries
Bardstown, KY 502-348-3921
Heck Cellars
Arvin, CA 661-854-6120
Hecker Pass Winery
Gilroy, CA 408-842-8755
Hegy's South Hills Vineyard & Winery
Twin Falls, ID 208-599-0074
Heineman's Winery
Put In Bay, OH 419-285-2811
Heitz Wine Cellar
St Helena, CA 707-963-3542
Helena View/Johnston Vineyard
Calistoga, CA 707-942-4956
Hells Canyon Winery
Caldwell, ID 800-318-7873
Henry Estate Winery
Umpqua, OR 800-782-2686
Henry Hill & Company
Napa, CA 707-224-6565
Heritage Wine Cellars
North East, PA 800-747-0083
Hermann J. Wiemer Vineyard
Dundee, NY 800-371-7971
Hermann Wiemer Vineyards
Dundee, NY 800-371-7971
Hermannhof Winery
Hermann, MO 800-393-0100
Heron Hill Winery
Hammondsport, NY 800-441-4241
Hess Collection Winery
Napa, CA 877-707-4377
Hidden Mountain Ranch Winery
Paso Robles, CA 805-226-9907
Highland Manor Winery
Jamestown, TN 931-879-9519
Hill Top Berry Farm & Winery
Nellysford, VA 434-361-1266
Hillcrest Vineyard
Roseburg, OR 541-673-3709
Hinzerling Winery
Prosser, WA 800-722-6702
Homewood Winery
Sonoma, CA 707-996-6353
Honeywood Winery
Salem, OR 800-726-4101
Honig Vineyard and Winery
Rutherford, CA 800-929-2217
Hood River Vineyards and Winery
Hood River, OR 541-386-3772
Hoodsport Winery
Hoodsport, WA 800-580-9894
Hop Kiln Winery
Healdsburg, CA 707-433-6491

Hopkins Vineyard
Warren, CT 860-868-7954
Horizon Winery
Santa Rosa, CA 707-544-2961
Horton Cellars Winery
Gordonsville, VA 800-829-4633
Houdini
Fullerton, CA 714-525-0325
Huber's Orchard Winery
Borden, IN. 800-345-9463
Hunt Country Vineyards
Branchport, NY 800-946-3289
Hurst Vineyards
Bosque, NM 505-864-1831
Husch Vineyards
Philo, CA 800-554-8724
Indian Rock Vineyards
Murphys, CA 209-728-8514
Indian Springs Vineyards
Browns Valley, CA 800-375-9311
Ingleside Plantation Winery
Colonial Beach, VA 804-224-8687
Inniskillin Wines
Niagara-On-The-Lake, ON 888-466-4754
Iron Horse Ranch & Vineyard
Sebastopol, CA 707-887-1212
Ironstone Vineyards
Murphys, CA 209-728-1251
J Vineyards & Winery
Healdsburg, CA 800-885-9463
J. Filippi Winery
Etiwanda, CA 909-899-5755
J. Fritz Winery
Cloverdale, CA 707-894-3389
J. Stonestreet & Sons Vineyard
Healdsburg, CA 800-723-6336
Jackson Valley Vineyards
Ione, CA 916-354-3200
Jamaican Gourmet Coffee Company
New Haven, CT 203-239-5633
Jamesport Vineyards
Jamesport, NY 631-722-5256
Jefferson Vineyards
Charlottesville, VA 800-272-3042
Jodar Vineyard & Winery
Placerville, CA 530-621-0324
Johlin Century Winery
Oregon, OH 419-693-6288
Johnson Estate Wines
Westfield, NY 800-374-6569
Johnson's Alexander Valley Wines
Healdsburg, CA 800-888-5532
Johnston's
Ballston Spa, NY 518-882-6310
Joseph Filippi Winery
Etiwanda, CA 909-899-5755
Joseph Phelps Vineyards
St Helena, CA 707-963-2745
Joullian Vineyards
Carmel Valley, CA 877-659-2800
Justin Winery & Vineyard
Paso Robles, CA 800-726-0049
Kalin Cellars
Novato, CA 415-883-3543
Karly Wines
Plymouth, CA 209-245-3922
Kate's Vineyard
Napa, CA 707-255-2644
Kathryn Kennedy Winery
Saratoga, CA 408-867-4170
Kelleys Island Wine Company
Kelleys Island, OH 419-746-2678
Kelson Creek Winery
Plymouth, CA 209-245-4700
Kendall-Jackson Wine
Windsor, CA 800-544-4413
Kenwood Vineyards
Kenwood, CA 707-833-5891
King Brewing Company
Fairfield, CA 707-428-4503
King Estate Winery
Eugene, OR 800-884-4441
Kiona Vineyards Winery
Benton City, WA 509-588-6716
Kirigin Cellars
Gilroy, CA 408-847-8827
Kistler Vineyards
Sebastopol, CA 707-823-5603
Kittling Ridge Estate Wines & Spirits
Grimsby, ON 905-945-9225
Klein Family Vintners
Healdsburg, CA. 707-433-6511

Klingshirn Winery
Avon Lake, OH 440-933-6666
Kluge Estate Winery & Vineyard
Charlottesville, VA 434-977-3895
Knapp Vineyards
Romulus, NY 800-869-9271
Koryo Winery Company
Gardena, CA 310-532-3240
Kramer Vineyards
Gaston, OR 800-619-4637
Kristin Hill Winery
Amity, OR 503-835-4012
Kunde Estate Winery
Kenwood, CA 707-833-5501
L. Mawby Vineyards
Suttons Bay, MI 231-271-3522
La Abra Farm & Winery
Lovingston, VA 434-263-5392
La Buena Vida Vineyards
Grapevine, TX 817-481-9463
La Chiripada Winery
Dixon, NM 800-528-7801
La Jota Vineyard Company
Angwin, CA 877-222-0292
La Rocca Vineyards
Forest Ranch, CA 800-808-9463
La Rochelle Winery
Livermore, CA 888-647-7768
La Vina Winery
Anthony, NM 575-882-7632
Laetitia Vineyard
Arroyo Grande, CA 888-809-8463
Lafollette Vineyard & Winery
Belle Mead, NJ 908-359-5018
Laird & Company
North Garden, VA 877-438-5247
Lake Sonoma Winery
Healdsburg, CA 877-850-9463
Lakeridge Winery & Vineyards
Clermont, FL. 800-768-9463
Lakeshore Winery
Romulus, NY 315-549-7075
Lakespring Winery
Yountville, CA 707-944-2475
Lakewood Vineyards
Watkins Glen, NY 607-535-9252
Lambert Bridge Winery
Healdsburg, CA 800-975-0555
Lamoreaux Landing Wine Cellar
Lodi, NY 607-582-6011
Lancaster County Winery
Willow Street, PA 717-464-3555
Landmark Vineyards
Kenwood, CA 800- 45- 636
Lange Winery
Dundee, OR. 503-538-6476
Langtry Estate & Vineyards
Middletown, CA 707-987-9127
Larry's Vineyards & Winery
Schenectady, NY 518-355-7365
Latah Creek Wine Cellars
Spokane Valley, WA 509-926-0164
Latcham Vineyards
Mt Aukum, CA 800-750-5591
Laurel Glen Vineyard
Glen Ellen, CA 707-526-3914
Lava Cap Winery
Placerville, CA 530-621-0175
Lazy Creek Vineyard
Philo, CA. 707-895-2021
Le Boeuf & Associates
North Falmouth, MA 800-444-5666
Leelanau Wine Cellars
Omena, MI 800-782-8128
Leeward Winery
Ventura, CA 805-656-5054
Leidenfrost Vineyards
Hector, NY 607-546-2800
Lemon Creek Winery
Berrien Springs, MI 269-471-1321
Leonetti Cellar
Walla Walla, WA 509-525-1428
Les Bourgeois Vineyards
Rocheport, MO 573-698-2300
Lewis Cellars
Hillsborough, CA 415-445-7884
Life Force Winery
Moscow, ID 208-882-9158
Limur Winery
San Francisco, CA 415-781-8691
Lin Court Vineyards
Solvang, CA 805-688-8554

Little Amana Winery
Amana, IA 319-668-9664
Little Hills Winery
St Charles, MO 877-584-4557
Live Oaks Winery
Gilroy, CA 408-842-2401
Livermore Valley Cellars
Livermore, CA 925-447-1751
Livingston Moffett Winery
Saint Helena, CA 800-788-0370
Llano Estacado Winery
Lubbock, TX 800-634-3854
Lockwood Vineyards
Monterey, CA 831-642-9200
Loew Vineyards
Mt Airy, MD 301-831-5464
Lohr Winery
San Jose, CA 408-288-5057
Lolonis Winery
Walnut Creek, CA 925-938-8066
Long Vineyards
St Helena, CA 707-963-2496
Lonz Winery
Middle Bass, OH 419-285-5411
Los Olivos Vintners
Los Olivos, CA 800-824-8584
Lost Hills Winery
Acampo, CA 209-369-2746
Lost Mountain Winery
Sequim, WA 888-683-5229
Louis M. Martini
St Helena, CA 800-321-9463
Lucas Vineyards
Interlaken, NY 800-682-9463
Lucas Winery
Lodi, CA 209-368-2006
Ludwigshof Winery
Eskridge, KS 785-449-2498
LUXCO
St Louis, MO 314-772-2627
Lynfred Winery
Roselle, IL 888-298-9463
M.S. Walker
Somerville, MA 617-776-6700
Madison Foods
St Paul, MN 651-265-8212
Madison Vineyard
Ribera, NM 575-421-8028
Madonna Estate Mont St John
Napa, CA 707-255-8864
Madrona Vineyards
Camino, CA 530-644-5948
Magnanini Winery
Wallkill, NY 845-895-2767
Maisons Marques & Domaines USA
Oakland, CA 510-286-2000
Mama Rap's & Winery
Gilroy, CA 800-842-6262
Manfred Vierthaler Winery
Sumner, WA 888-663-9463
Marie Brizard Wines & Spirits
Sausalito, CA 800-878-1123
Marietta Cellars
Hopland, CA 707-433-2747
Marimar Torres Estate
Sebastopol, CA 707-823-4365
Mark West Vineyards
Forestville, CA 707-836-9647
Markham Vineyards
St Helena, CA 707-963-5292
Markko Vineyard
Conneaut, OH 800-252-3197
Marlow Wine Cellars
Monteagle, TN 931-924-2120
Martin & Weyrich Winery
Paso Robles, CA 805-238-2520
Martini & Prati Wines
Santa Rosa, CA 707-823-2404
Martz Vineyards
Yorkville, CA 707-895-2334
Mastantuono Winery
Templeton, CA 805-238-0676
Matanzas Creek Winery
Santa Rosa, CA 800-500-6464
Matson Vineyards
Redding, CA 530-222-2833
Maurice Carrie Winery
Temecula, CA 800-716-1711
Mayacamas Vineyards
Napa, CA 707-224-4030
Mazzocco Vineyards
Healdsburg, CA 707-857-3240

McDowell Valley Vineyards & Cellars
Hopland, CA 707-744-1774
McGregor Vineyard Winery
Dundee, NY 800-272-0192
McHenry Vineyard
Davis, CA 530-756-3202
McIntosh's Ohio Valley Wines
Bethel, OH 937-379-1159
McKinlay Vineyards
Newberg, OR 503-625-2534
Meeker Vineyard
Healdsburg, CA 707-433-2500
Meier's Wine Cellars
Cincinnati, OH 800-346-2941
Menghini Winery
Julian, CA 760-765-2072
Meredyth Vineyard
Middleburg, VA 540-687-6277
Meridian Vineyards
Paso Robles, CA 805-237-6000
Merritt Estate Wines
Forestville, NY 888-965-4800
Merryvale Vineyards
St Helena, CA 800-326-6069
Messina Hof Wine Cellars & Vineyards
Bryan, TX 800-736-9463
Michel-Schlumberger
Healdsburg, CA 800-447-3060
Milano Winery
Hopland, CA 800-564-2582
Milat Vineyards
St Helena, CA 707-963-0758
Mill Creek Vineyards
Healdsburg, CA 877-349-2121
Millbrook Vineyard and Winery
Millbrook, NY 800-662-9463
Milliaire Winery
Murphys, CA 209-728-1658
Mission Mountain Winery
Dayton, MT 406-849-5524
Missouri Winery Warehouse Outlet
Cuba, MO 573-885-2168
Mogen David Wine Corporation
Westfield, NY 716-326-7100
Montelle Winery
Augusta, MO 888-595-9463
Monterey Vineyard
Gonzales, CA 831-675-4000
Montevina Winery
Plymouth, CA 209-245-6942
Monticello Cellars
Napa, CA 707-253-2802
Montmorenci Vineyards
Aiken, SC 803-649-4870
Moresco Vineyards
Stockton, CA 209-467-3081
Morgan Winery
Salinas, CA 831-751-7777
Morrione Vineyards
Wetumpka, AL 334-567-9957
Mosby Winery
Buellton, CA 800-706-6729
Moss Creek Winery
Napa, CA 707-252-1295
Mount Baker Vineyards
Everson, WA 360-592-2300
Mount Bethel Winery
Altus, AR 479-468-2444
Mount Eden Vineyards
Saratoga, CA 408-867-5832
Mount Hope Estate Winery
Manheim, PA 717-665-7021
Mount Palomar Winery
Temecula, CA 800-854-5177
Mount Pleasant Winery
Augusta, MO 800-467-9463
Mountain Cove Vineyards & Winegarden
Lovingston, VA 434-263-5392
Mt. Nittany Vineyard
Centre Hall, PA 814-466-6373
Murphy Goode Estate Winery
Healdsburg, CA 707-431-7644
Naked Mountain Vineyard & Winery
Markham, VA 540-364-1609
Nalle Winery
Healdsburg, CA 707-433-1040
Nantucket Vineyards
Nantucket, MA 508-325-5929
Napa Cellars
Oakville, CA 800-848-9630
Napa Creek Winery
Saint Helena, CA 707-963-9456

Napa Valley Port Cellars
Napa, CA 707-257-7777
Napa Wine Company
Oakville, CA 800-848-9630
Nashoba Valley Winery
Bolton, MA 978-779-5521
Navarro Vineyards & Winery
Philo, CA 800-537-9463
Naylor Wine Cellars
Stewartstown, PA 800-292-3370
Nevada City Winery
Nevada City, CA 800-203-9463
Nevada County Wine Guild
Nevada City, CA 530-265-3662
New Hope Winery
New Hope, PA 800-592-9463
New Land Vineyard
Geneva, NY 315-585-4432
Newport Vineyards & Winery
Middletown, RI 401-848-5161
Newton Vineyard
St Helena, CA 707-963-9000
Nicasio Vineyards
Soquel, CA 831-423-1073
Nichelini Winery
St Helena, CA 707-963-0717
Nicholas G. Verry
Parlier, CA 209-646-2785
Niebaum-Coppola Estate Winery
Rutherford, CA 707-963-9099
Nissley Vineyards
Bainbridge, PA 800-522-2387
Nordman of California
Sanger, CA 559-638-9923
North Salem Vineyard
North Salem, NY 914-669-5518
Northern Vineyards Winery
Stillwater, MN 651-430-1032
Northville Winery
Northville, MI 248-349-3181
Nutmeg Vineyard
Andover, CT 860-742-8402
O'Vallon Winery
Washburn, MO 417-826-5830
Oak Grove Orchards Winery
Rickreall, OR 503-364-7052
Oak Knoll Winery
Hillsboro, OR 800-625-5665
Oak Ridge Winery
Lodi, CA 209-369-4758
Oak Spring Winery
Altoona, PA 814-946-3799
Oakencroft Vineyard & Winery
Charlottesville, VA 434-296-4188
Oasis Winery
Hume, VA 800-304-7656
Obester Winery
Half Moon Bay, CA 650-726-9463
Oceania Cellars
Arroyo Grande, CA 805-481-5434
Ojai Vineyard
Oak View, CA 805-649-1674
Old Creek Ranch Winery
Ventura, CA 805-649-4132
Old Firehouse Winery
Geneva, OH 800-362-6751
Old House Vineyards
Culpeper, VA 540-423-1032
Old South Winery
Natchez, MS 601-445-9924
Old Wine Cellar
Amana, IA 319-622-3116
Oliver Wine Company
Bloomington, IN 800-258-2783
Olympic Cellars
Port Angeles, WA 360-452-0160
One Vineyard and Winery
St Helena, CA 707-963-1123
Optima Wine Cellars
Healdsburg, CA 707-431-8222
Opus One
Oakville, CA 800-292-6787
Orchard Heights Winery
Salem, OR 503-391-7308
Orfila Vineyards
Escondido, CA 760-738-6500
Organic Wine Company
San Francisco, CA 888-326-9463
Orleans Hill Vineyard Association
Woodland, CA 530-661-6538
Ormand Peugeog Corporation
Miami, FL 305-624-6834

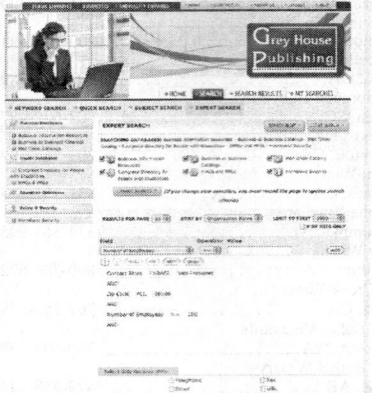

Orr Mountain Winery
Nashville, TN 615-741-2159
Pacheco Ranch Winery
Novato, CA 415-883-5583
Pacific Echo Cellars
Philo, CA. .707-895-2065
Page Mill Winery
Livermore, CA 925-456-7676
Pahlmeyer Winery
Napa, CA. .707-255-2321
Pahrump Valley Vineyards
Pahrump, NV 800-368-9463
Palm Bay Imports
Boca Raton, FL 800-872-5622
Palmer Vineyards
Riverhead, NY 800-901-8783
Panther Creek Cellars
McMinnville, OR 503-472-8080
Paradise Valley Vineyards
Phoenix, AZ 602-233-8727
Paragon Vineyards
San Luis Obispo, CA 805-544-9080
Parasio Springs Vineyards
Soledad, CA 831-678-0300
Parducci Wine Estates
Ukiah, CA. .888-362-9463
Pastori Winery
Cloverdale, CA 707-857-3418
Paumanok Vineyards
Aquebogue, NY 631-722-8800
Pazdar Winery
Scotchtown Branch, NY 845-695-1903
Peaceful Bend Vineyard
Steelville, MO. 573-775-3000
Peconic Bay Winery
Cutchogue, NY 631-734-7361
Pedrizzetti Winery
Morgan Hill, CA. 408-779-7389
Pedroncelli Winery
Geyserville, CA 800-836-3894
Peju Winery
Rutherford, CA 800-446-7358
Pellegrini Family Vineyards
Fulton, CA .800-891-0244
Penn-Shore Vineyards
North East, PA. 814-725-8688
Pernod Ricard USA
White Plains, NY 914-539-4500
Perry Creek Winery
Telford, PA 800-880-4026
Peter Michael Winery
Calistoga, CA 800-354-4459
Peterson & Sons Winery
Kalamazoo, MI. 269-626-9755
Pheasant Ridge Winery
Lubbock, TX 806-746-6033
Philip Togni Vineyard
St Helena, CA 707-963-3731
Phillips Farms & Michael David Vineyards
Lodi, CA 888-707-9463
Piedmont Vineyards & Winery
Middleburg, VA 540-687-5528
Piedra Creek Winery
San Luis Obispo, CA 805-541-1281
Pikes Peak Vineyards
Colorado Springs, CO. 719-576-0075
Pindar Vineyards
Peconic, NY 631-734-6200
Pine Ridge Winery
Yountville, CA 800-575-9777
Plam Vineyards & Winery
Solvang, CA 800-978-2633
Pleasant Valley Wine Company
Hammondsport, NY 607-569-6111
Plum Creek Cellars
Palisade, CO 970-464-7586
Plymouth Colony Winery
Plymouth, MA. 508-747-3334
Pommeraie Winery
Sebastopol, CA 707-823-9463
Pompei Winery
Cleveland, OH 216-883-9370
Ponderosa Valley Vineyard & Winery
Ponderosa, NM 575-834-7487
Ponzi Vineyards
Beaverton, OR 503-628-1227
Poplar Ridge Vineyards
Hector, NY 607-582-6421
Porter Creek Vineyards
Healdsburg, CA 707-433-6321
Post Familie Vineyards
Altus, AR .800-275-8423

Prager Winery & Port Works
St Helena, CA 800-969-7678
Presque Isle Wine Cellar
North East, PA. 800-488-7492
Preston Premium Wines
Pasco, WA 509-545-1990
Preston Vineyards
Healdsburg, CA 800-305-9707
Prince Michael Vineyards
Leon, VA .800-869-8242
Quady Winery
Madera, CA 800-733-8068
Quail Ridge Cellars & Vineyards
Saint Helena, CA 800-706-9463
Quilceda Creek Vintners
Snohomish, WA 360-568-2389
Quivira Vineyards
Healdsburg, CA 800-292-8339
R.A.B. Food Group LLC
Secaucus, NJ. 201-453-5200
R.H. Phillips
Esparto, CA. 530-662-3504
Rabbit Ridge
Healdsburg, CA 707-431-7128
Radanovich Vineyards & Winery
Mariposa, CA 209-966-3187
Rahco International
St Augustine, FL 800-851-7681
Rainbow Hill Vineyards
Newcomerstown, OH 740-545-9305
Rancho De Philo
Alta Loma, CA 909-987-4208
Rancho Sisquoc Winery
Santa Maria, CA 805-937-3616
Rapazzini Winery
Gilroy, CA. 408-842-5649
Ravenswood
Sonoma, CA 800-669-4679
Raymond Vineyard & Cellar
St Helena, CA 800-525-2659
Rebec Vineyards
Amherst, VA 434-946-5168
Redhawk Vineyard
Salem, OR 503-362-1596
Reeves Winery
Middletown, CA 707-987-9650
Regent Champagne Cellars
New York, NY 845-691-7296
Renaissance Vineyard & Winery
Oregon House, CA 800-655-3277
Renault Winery
Egg Harbor City, NJ 609-965-2111
Renwood Winery
Sacramento, CA 800-348-8466
Retzlaff Vineyards
Livermore, CA 925-447-8941
Rex Wine Vinegar Company
Newark, NJ 973-589-6911
Richard L. Graeser Winery
Calistoga, CA 707-942-4437
Richardson Vineyards
Sonoma, CA 707-938-2610
Ridge Vineyards
Cupertino, CA 408-867-3233
Ritchie Creek Vineyard
St Helena, CA 707-963-4661
Rivendell Winery
New Paltz, NY 845-255-2494
River Road Vineyards
Sebastopol, CA 707-887-2243
River Run Vintners
Watsonville, CA 831-726-3112
Riverland Vineyards
Gonzales, CA 831-675-2481
Roberian Vineyards
Forestville, NY 716-673-9255
Robert F Pliska & Company Winery
Purgitsville, WV 877-747-2737
Robert Keenan Winery
St Helena, CA 707-963-9177
Robert Mondavi Winery
Oakville, CA. 888-766-6238
Robert Mondavi Winery
Oakville, CA. 888-766-6328
Robert Mueller Cellars
Windsor, CA 707-837-7399
Robert Pecota Winery
Calistoga, CA 707-942-6625
Robert Sinskey Vineyards
Napa, CA. .800-869-2030
Robller Vineyard
New Haven, MO 573-237-3986

Roche Caneros Estate Winry
Sonoma, CA 800-825-9475
Rockbridge Vineyard
Raphine, VA 540-377-6204
Rodney Strong Vineyards
Healdsburg, CA 800-474-9463
Rogue Ales
Newport, OR. 541-265-3188
Rolling Hills Vineyards
Camarillo, CA 805-484-8100
Rombauer Vineyards
St Helena, CA 800- 62- 220
Rose Creek Vineyards
Hagerman, ID 208-837-4353
Rosenblum Cellars
Alameda, CA. 510-865-7007
Ross Keller Winery
Nipomo, CA 805-929-3627
Roudon-Smith Vineyards
Scotts Valley, CA 831-438-1244
Round Hill Vineyards
St Helena, CA 800-778-0424
Royal Kedem Food & Wine Company
Bayonne, NJ 201-437-9131
Royal Wine Company
Bayonne, NJ 201-437-9131
Royal Wine Company
Bayonne, NJ 800-382-8299
Rubicon/Niebaum-Coppola Estate & Winery
Rutherford, CA 800-782-4266
Rudd Winery
Oakville, CA. 707-944-8577
Rutherford Hill Winery
Rutherford, CA 707-963-1871
S. Anderson Vineyard
Yountville, CA 800-428-2259
Saddleback Cellars
Oakville, CA. 707-944-8808
Sainte Genevieve Winery
Ste Genevieve, MO. 800-398-1298
Saintsbury
Napa, CA. .707-252-0592
Salamandre Wine Cellars
Aptos, CA .831-685-0321
Salishan Vineyards
La Center, WA. 360-263-2713
San Antonio Winery
Los Angeles, CA 800-626-7722
San Dominique Winery
Camp Verde, AZ 480-945-8583
Sand Castle Winery
Erwinna, PA 800-722-9463
Sandia Shadows Vineyard & Winery
Albuquerque, NM 505-856-1006
Sandstone Winery
Amana, IA .319-622-3081
Sanford Winery
Buellton, CA 805-688-3300
Santa Barbara Winery
Santa Barbara, CA 805-963-3633
Santa Cruz Mountain Vineyard
Felton, CA .831-335-4242
Santa Fe Vineyards
Espanola, NM 505-753-8100
Santa Margarita Vineyard & Winery
Temecula, CA 909-676-4431
Sarah's Vineyard
Gilroy, CA. 408-842-4278
Satiety
Davis, CA .530-757-2699
Saucilito Canyon Vineyard
San Luis Obispo, CA 805-543-2111
Sausal Winery
Healdsburg, CA 800-500-2285
Savannah Chanelle Vineyards
Saratoga, CA. 408-741-2934
Sawtooth Winery
Nampa, ID. 208-467-1200
Scenic Valley Winery
Lanesboro, MN 507-467-2958
Schapiro's Kosher Winery
New York, NY 212-755-5066
Schloss Doepken Winery
Ripley, NY 716-326-3636
Schoppaul Hill Winery at Ivanhoe
Denton, TX. 940-380-9463
Schramsberg Vineyards
Calistoga, CA 800-877-3623
Schug Carneros Estate Winery
Sonoma, CA 800-966-9365
Sea Ridge Winery
Occidental, CA 707-874-1707

Seavey Vineyard
St Helena, CA 707-963-8339

Sebastiani Vineyards
Sonoma, CA 800-888-5532

Secret House Vineyards
Veneta, OR 800-497-1574

Seghesio Family Vineyards
Healdsburg, CA 707-433-3579

Sellards Winery
Sebastopol, CA 707-823-8293

Sequoia Grove Vineyards
Rutherford, CA 800-851-7841

Serendipity Cellars
Monmouth, OR 503-838-4284

Serra Mission Winery
Saint Louis, MO 314-991-2559

Seven Hills Winery
Walla Walla, WA 877-777-7870

Seven Lakes Vineyards
Fenton, MI 810-629-5686

Shafer Vineyards
Napa, CA 707-944-2877

Shallon Winery
Astoria, OR 503-325-5978

Sharon Mill Winery
Manchester, MI 734-971-6337

Sharp Rock Vineyards
Sperryville, VA 540-987-9700

Shenandoah Vineyards
Plymouth, CA 209-245-4455

Sierra Vista Winery
Placerville, CA 530-622-7221

Signore Winery
Brooktondale, NY 607-539-7935

Signorello Vineyards
Napa, CA 707-255-5990

Silvan Ridge
Eugene, OR 541-345-1945

Silver Fox Vineyard
Mariposa, CA 209-966-4800

Silver Mountain Vineyards
Santa Cruz, CA 408-353-2278

Silver Oak Cellars
Oakville, CA 800-273-8805

Silverado Hill Cellars
Napa, CA 707-253-9306

Silverado Vineyards
Napa, CA 707-257-1770

Simon Levi Cellars
Kenwood, CA 888-315-0040

Six Mile Creek Vineyard
Ithaca, NY 800-260-0612

Sky Vineyards
Glen Ellen, CA 707-935-1391

Slate Quarry Winery
Nazareth, PA 610-759-0286

Smith Vineyard & Winery
Grass Valley, CA 530-273-7032

Smith-Madrone Vineyards & Winery
St Helena, CA 707-963-2283

Smokehouse Winery
Sperryville, VA 540-987-3194

Smothers Winery/Remick Ridge
Glen Ellen, CA 800-795-9463

Sobon Estate
Plymouth, CA 209-245-4455

Sokol Blosser Winery
Dundee, OR 800-582-6668

Sonoita Vineyards
Elgin, AZ 520-455-5893

Sonoma Wine Services
Vineburg, CA 707-996-9773

Sonoma-Cutrer Vineyards
Fulton, CA 707-528-1181

Sow's Ear Winery
Brooksville, ME 207-326-4649

Spangler Vineyards
Roseburg, OR 541-679-9654

Spottswoode Winery
St Helena, CA 707-963-0134

Spring Mountain Vineyard
Saint Helena, CA 877-769-4637

Spring Mountain Vineyards
Saint Helena, CA 877-769-4637

Springhill Cellars
Albany, OR 541-928-1009

Spurgeon Vineyards & Winery
Highland, WI 800-236-5555

St. Francis Vineyards
Santa Rosa, CA 707-833-2148

St. Innocent Winery
Salem, OR 503-378-1526

St. James Winery
St James, MO 800-280-9463

St. Julian Wine Company
Paw Paw, MI 800-732-6002

Stags' Leap Winery
Napa, CA 800-640-5327

Star Hill Winery
Napa, CA 707-255-1957

Starr & Brown
Portland, OR 503-287-1775

Ste. Chapelle Winery
Caldwell, ID 877-783-2427

Stearns Wharf Vintners
Santa Barbara, CA 805-966-6624

Steltzner Vineyards
Napa, CA 707-252-7272

Steuk's Country Market & Winery
Sandusky, OH 419-625-8324

Stevenot Winery & Imports
Murphys, CA 209-728-0638

Stimson Lane Vineyards & Estate
Woodinville, WA 800-267-6793

Stimson Lane Winery
Prosser, WA 509-882-3928

Stone Hill Wine Company
Hermann, MO 573-486-2221

Stonegate
St Helena, CA 707-603-2203

Stoneridge Winery
Sutter Creek, CA 209-223-1761

Stonington Vineyards
Stonington, CT 800-421-9463

Stony Hill Vineyard
St Helena, CA 707-963-2636

Stony Ridge Winery
Livermore, CA 925-449-0458

Storrs Winery
Santa Cruz, CA 831-458-5030

Story Winery
Plymouth, CA 800-712-6390

Storybook Mountain Winery
Calistoga, CA 707-942-5282

Streblow Vineyards
Saint Helena, CA 707-963-5892

Stryker Sonoma Winery Vineyards
Geyserville, CA 800-433-1944

Sugar Creek Winery
Defiance, MO 636-987-2400

Sullivan Vineyards Winery
Rutherford, CA 877-277-7337

Summit Lake Vineyards & Winery
Angwin, CA 707-965-2488

Summum Winery
Salt Lake City, UT 801-355-0137

Sunrise Winery
San Jose, CA 408-741-1310

Sunstone Vineyards & Winery
Santa Ynez, CA 800-313-9463

Susquehanna Valley Winery
Danville, PA 570-275-2364

Sutter Home Winery
St Helena, CA 707-963-3104

Swan Joseph Vineyards
Forestville, CA 707-573-3747

Swanson Vineyards & Winery
Rutherford, CA 800-942-0809

Swedish Hill Vineyard
Romulus, NY 888-549-9463

Sweet Traders
Huntington Beach, CA 714-903-6800

Sycamore Vineyards
Saint Helena, CA 800-963-9698

Sylvester Winery
Paso Robles, CA 805-227-4000

Sylvin Farms Winery
Egg Harbor City, NJ 609-965-1548

Talbott Vineyards
Gonzales, CA 831-675-3000

Talley Vineyards
Arroyo Grande, CA 805-489-2508

Tamuzza Vineyards
Hope, NJ 908-459-5878

Tarara Winery
Leesburg, VA 703-771-7100

Tartan Hill Winery
New Era, MI 231-861-4657

Tedeschi Vineyards
Kula, HI 808-878-6058

Tempest Vineyards
Amity, OR 503-835-2600

Thoma Vineyards
Dallas, OR 503-623-6420

Thomas Fogarty Winery
Portola Valley, CA 800-247-4163

Thomas Kruse Winery
Gilroy, CA 408-842-7016

Thornton Winery
Temecula, CA 951-699-0099

Thorpe Vineyard
Wolcott, NY 315-594-2502

Three Lakes Winery
Three Lakes, WI 800-944-5434

TKC Vineyards
Plymouth, CA 888-627-2356

Todhunter Foods
Lake Alfred, FL 863-956-1116

Todhunter Foods & Monarch Wine Company
West Palm Beach, FL 800-336-9463

Todhunter International
West Palm Beach, FL 561-655-8977

Tomasello Winery
Hammonton, NJ 800-666-9463

Topolos at Russian River Vine
Forestville, CA 707-887-1575

Transamerica Wine Corporation
Brooklyn, NY 718-875-4017

Trefethen Vineyards
Napa, CA 800-556-4847

Trentadue Winery
Geyserville, CA 888-332-3032

Trigo Corporation
Toa Baja, PR 787-794-1300

Troy Winery
Troy, OH 937-339-3655

Truchard Vineyards
Napa, CA 707-253-7153

Truckee River Winery
Truckee, CA 530-587-4626

Tucker Cellars
Sunnyside, WA 509-837-8701

Tudal Winery
St Helena, CA 707-963-3947

Tularosa Vineyards
Tularosa, NM 800-687-4467

Tyee Wine Cellars
Corvallis, OR 541-753-8754

UDV Canada
Etobicoke, ON 416-626-2000

UDV Wines
San Francisco, CA 415-835-7300

United Distillers & Vintners
Norwalk, CT 203-323-3311

UST
Danbury, CT 800-650-7411

V. Sattui Winery
St Helena, CA 800-799-8888

Val Verde Winery
Del Rio, TX 830-775-9714

Valley of the Moon Winery
Glen Ellen, CA 707-996-6941

Valley View Winery
Jacksonville, OR 800-781-9463

Van Der Heyden Vineyards
Napa, CA 800-948-9463

Ventana Vineyards Winery
Monterey, CA 800-237-8846

Veramar Vineyard
Berryville, VA 540-955-5510

Vetter Vineyards Winery
Westfield, NY 716-326-3100

Via Della Chiesa Vineyards
Raynham, MA 508-822-7775

Viader Vineyards & Winery
Deer Park, CA 707-963-3816

Viano Winery
Martinez, CA 925-228-6465

Viansa Winery
Sonoma, CA 800-995-4740

Vie-Del Company
Fresno, CA 559-834-2525

Villa Helena/Arger-Martucci Winery
St Helena, CA 707-963-4334

Villa Milan Vineyard
Milan, IN 812-654-3419

Villa Mt. Eden Winery
St Helena, CA 707-944-2414

Village Imports
Brisbane, CA 888-865-8714

Villar Vintners of Valdese
Valdese, NC 828-879-3202

Vina Vista Vineyard & Winery
San Carlos, CA 707-857-3722

Vincent Arroyo Winery
Calistoga, CA 707-942-9231

Vinoklet Winery & Vineyard
Cincinnati, OH 513-385-9309
Von Stiehl Winery
Algoma, WI. .800-955-5208
Von Strasser Winery
Calistoga, CA 888-359-9463
Vynecrest Vineyards and Winery
Breinigsville, PA. 800-361-0725
Wagner Vineyards
Lodi, NY. 866-924-6378
Walker Valley Vineyards
Walker Valley, NY 845-744-3449
Warner Vineyards Winery
Paw Paw, MI. .800-756-5357
Wasson Brothers Winery
Sandy, OR 503-668-3124
Weibel Champagne Vineyards
Fremont, CA .510-656-2340
Wente Brothers Estate Winery
Livermore, CA 925-456-2300
Wermuth Winery
Calistoga, CA 707-942-5924
West Park Wine Cellars
West Park, NY 845-384-6709
Westbend Vinyards
Lewisville, NC 866-901-5032
Westport Rivers Vineyard& Winery
Westport, MA 800-993-9695
Westwood Winery
Sonoma, CA .707-935-3246
Whaler Vineyard Winery
Ukiah, CA 707-462-6355
Whitcraft Wines
Santa Barbara, CA 805-730-1680
White Hall Vineyards
Crozet, VA. 434-823-8615
White Oak Vineyards & Winery
Healdsburg, CA 707-433-8429
White Rock Vineyards
Napa, CA. 707-257-7922
Whitehall Lane Winery
St Helena, CA 707-963-9454
Whitford Cellars
Napa, CA. 707-942-0840
Widmer's Wine Cellars
Naples, NY 585-374-6311
Wiederkehr Wine Cellars
Altus, AR 800-622-9463
Wild Hog Vineyard
Cazadero, CA 707-847-3687
Wild Horse Winery
Templeton, CA 805-434-2541
Wild Winds Farms
Naples, NY 800-836-5253
Wildhurst
Kelseyville, CA. 800-595-9463
William Grant & Sons
New York, NY 212-594-4848
William Harrison Vineyards & Winery LLC
St Helena, CA 707-963-8762
William Hill Winery
Napa, CA. 707-224-5424
Williams of Vermont
Portland, ME. 207-774-3355
Williams-Selym Winery
Healdsburg, CA 707-433-6425
Williamsburg Winery
Williamsburg, VA 757-229-0999
Willow Hill Vineyards
Johnstown, OH 740-587-4622
Willowcroft Farm Vineyards
Leesburg, VA 703-777-8161
Wimberley Valley Winery
Driftwood, TX 512-847-2592
Windham Winery
Purcellville, VA. 540-668-6464
Windsor Vineyards
Windsor, CA .800-333-9987
Windsor Vineyards
Windsor, CA .800-992-4233
Windwalker Vineyards
Somerset, CA 530-620-4054
Wine Group
San Francisco, CA 415-986-8700
Wine-A-Rita
Texarkana, TX. 903-832-7309
Wintergreen Winery
Nellysford, VA 434-361-2519
Winters Winery
Winters, CA. .530-795-3201
Wishnev Wine Management
Walnut Creek, CA 925-930-6374

Witness Tree Vineyard
Salem, OR 888-478-8766
Wolf Creek Vineyards
Norton, OH 800-436-0426
Wollersheim Winery
Prairie Du Sac, WI 800-847-9463
Woodbury Vineyards
Fredonia, NY 866-691-9463
Wooden Valley Winery
Fairfield, CA .707-864-0730
Woodside Vineyards
Woodside, CA. 650-851-3144
Woodward Canyon Winery
Touchet, WA 509-525-4129
Worden
Spokane, WA. 509-455-7835
Wyandotte Winery
Gahanna, OH. 614-476-3624
Yakima River Winery
Prosser, WA. 509-786-2805
Yamhill Valley Vineyards
McMinnville, OR 800-825-4845
York Mountain Winery
Paso Robles, CA 805-238-3925
Z.D. Wines LLC
Napa, CA 800-487-7757
Zaca Mesa Winery
Los Olivos, CA. 800-350-7972
Zayante Vineyards
Felton, CA. 831-335-7992
Ziem Vineyards
Fairplay, MD. 301-223-8352

Bulk

Cribari Vineyards
Fresno, CA 800-277-9095

Processor and exporter of high quality California bulk wine. Cribari Vineyards, Inc. has been involved in the California wine industry for more than four generations. Our commitment to quality and service is unsurpassed. We are competitive in our pricing and can furnish many varieties of California wine blended to our customers' specifications. Some of our most popular products are Cabernet Sauvignon, Merlot, Chardonnay, Sauterne, Sherry, Chablis, Marsala, and Chianti.

Cooking

Batavia Wine Cellars
Canandaigua, NY 800-879-9463
California Olive Oil Corporation
Salem, MA 800-386-6457

Cribari Vineyards
Fresno, CA 800-277-9095

Processor and exporter of high quality California bulk wine. Cribari Vineyards, Inc. has been involved in the California wine industry for more than four generations. Our commitment to quality and service is unsurpassed. We are competitive in our pricing and can furnish many varieties of California wine blended to our customers' specifications. Some of our most popular products are Cabernet Sauvignon, Merlot, Chardonnay, Sauterne, Sherry, Chablis, Marsala, and Chianti.

EMERLING INTERNATIONAL FOODS, INC.

Emerling International Foods
Buffalo, NY. .716-833-7381

We supply food manufacturers and food service customers worldwide (since 1988) with bulk ingredients including: Fruits & Vegetables; Juice Concentrates; Herbs & Spices; Oils & Vinegars; Flavors & Colors; Honey & Molasses. We also produce PURE MAPLE SYRUP.

Fleischmanns Vinegar
Cerritos, CA .800-443-1067
Four Chimneys Farm Winery Trust
Himrod, NY .607-243-7502
Kari-Out Company
White Plains, NY 800-433-8799
Mizkan Americas
Mt Prospect, IL. 800-323-4358
Rapazzini Winery
Gilroy, CA. 408-842-5649
Rex Wine Vinegar Company
Newark, NJ .973-589-6911
San Antonio Winery
Los Angeles, CA. 800-626-7722
Todhunter Foods
Lake Alfred, FL. 863-956-1116
Todhunter Foods & Monarch Wine Company
West Palm Beach, FL 800-336-9463
Todhunter International
West Palm Beach, FL 561-655-8977

Marsala

Cribari Vineyards
Fresno, CA 800-277-9095

Processor and exporter of high quality California bulk wine. Cribari Vineyards, Inc. has been involved in the California wine industry for more than four generations. Our commitment to quality and service is unsurpassed. We are competitive in our pricing and can furnish many varieties of California wine blended to our customers' specifications. Some of our most popular products are Cabernet Sauvignon, Merlot, Chardonnay, Sauterne, Sherry, Chablis, Marsala, and Chianti.

French

Brown-Forman Beverages Worldwide
Louisville, KY. 502-585-1100

Champagne

Briceland Vineyards
Redway, CA .707-923-2429
Brimstone Hill Vineyard
Pine Bush, NY 845-744-2231
Buena Vista Carneros Winery
Sonoma, CA .800-678-8504
Bully Hill Vineyards
Hammondsport, NY 607-868-3610
Chateau des Charmes Wines
St. Davids, ON 800-263-2541
Chi Company/Tabor Hill Winery
Buchanan, MI 800-283-3363
Chicama Vineyards
West Tisbury, MA 888-244-2262
Chouinard Vineyards
Castro Valley, CA 510-582-9900
Clinton Vineyards
Clinton Corners, NY 845-266-5372
Domaine Chandon
Yountville, CA 800-242-6366
Dr. Frank's Vinifera Wine Cellar
Hammondsport, NY 800-320-0735
Dr. Konstantin Frank Vinifera Wine Cellars
Hammondsport, NY 800-320-0735
Fenn Valley Vineyards
Fennville, MI 800-432-6265
Glenora Wine Cellars
Dundee, NY .800-243-5513

Marie Brizard Wines & Spirits
Sausalito, CA 800-878-1123
Meier's Wine Cellars
Cincinnati, OH 800-346-2941
Mon Ami Champagne Company
Port Clinton, OH 800-777-4266
North Salem Vineyard
North Salem, NY 914-669-5518
Regent Champagne Cellars
New York, NY 845-691-7296
Royal Wine Company
Bayonne, NJ 201-437-9131
Schramsberg Vineyards
Calistoga, CA 800-877-3623
St. Julian Wine Company
Paw Paw, MI 800-732-6002
Stone Hill Wine Company
Hermann, MO 573-486-2221
Thornton Winery
Temecula, CA 951-699-0099
Westport Rivers Vineyard& Winery
Westport, MA 800-993-9695
Windsor Vineyards
Windsor, CA 800-333-9987
Woodbury Vineyards
Fredonia, NY 866-691-9463
York Mountain Winery
Paso Robles, CA 805-238-3925

Red Bordeaux

Babcock Winery & Vineyards
Lompoc, CA 805-736-1455

Red Burgundy

Cribari Vineyards
Fresno, CA 800-277-9095

Processor and exporter of high quality California bulk wine. Cribari Vineyards, Inc. has been involved in the California wine industry for more than four generations. Our commitment to quality and service is unsurpassed. We are competitive in our pricing and can furnish many varieties of California wine blended to our customers' specifications. Some of our most popular products are Cabernet Sauvignon, Merlot, Chardonnay, Sauterne, Sherry, Chablis, Marsala, and Chianti.

Heineman's Winery
Put In Bay, OH 419-285-2811

White Burgundy

Buena Vista Carneros Winery
Sonoma, CA 800-678-8504

Italian

Buena Vista Carneros Winery
Sonoma, CA 800-678-8504
E&J Gallo Winery
Modesto, CA 209-341-3111

Chianti

E&J Gallo Winery
Modesto, CA 209-341-3111

Red

E&J Gallo Winery
Modesto, CA 209-341-3111

Japanese

Sake

Ozeki Sake
Hollister, CA 831-630-1101

Non-Alcoholic

Ariel Vineyards
Napa, CA 800-456-9472

Cedar Creek Winery
Cedarburg, WI. 800-827-8020
Safeway Dairy Products
Walnut Creek, CA. 925-944-4000

Portuguese

Port

Alto Vineyards
Alto Pass, IL 618-893-4898
Chateau Grand Traverse
Traverse City, MI 231-223-7355
Chouinard Vineyards
Castro Valley, CA 510-582-9900
Cienega Valley Winery/DeRose
Hollister, CA 831-636-9143
Fenestra Winery
Livermore, CA 800-789-9463
Fenn Valley Vineyards
Fennville, MI 800-432-6265
Ficklin Vineyards
Madera, CA 559-674-4598

Red Grape Wines

Hazlitt's 1852 Vineyard
Hector, NY 888-750-0494
Hermann Wiemer Vineyards
Dundee, NY 800-371-7971
Hermannhof Winery
Hermann, MO 800-393-0100
Heron Hill Winery
Hammondsport, NY 800-441-4241

Cabernet Sauvignon

A. Rafanelli Winery
Healdsburg, CA 707-433-1385
AmRhein Wine Cellars
Bent Mountain, VA. 540-929-4632
Autumn Hill Vineyards/Blue Ridge Wine
Stanardsville, VA 434-985-6100
Babcock Winery & Vineyards
Lompoc, CA 805-736-1455
Barboursville Vineyards
Barboursville, VA. 540-832-3824
Black Mesa Winery
Velarde, NM 800-852-6372

Breaux Vineyards
Purcellville, VA. 800-492-9961
Burnley Vineyards and Daniel Cellars
Barboursville, VA. 540-832-2828
Catoctin Vineyards
Brookeville, MD. 301-774-2310
Cedar Creek Winery
Cedarburg, WI. 800-827-8020
Chateau Morisette Winery
Meadows of Dan, VA 540-593-2865
Chatom Vineyards
Murphys, CA. 800-435-8852
Chicama Vineyards
West Tisbury, MA 888-244-2262
Chouinard Vineyards
Castro Valley, CA 510-582-9900
Cienega Valley Winery/DeRose
Hollister, CA 831-636-9143
Cooper Vineyards
Louisa, VA 540-894-5253
Corus Brands
Woodinville, WA. 425-806-2600
Cosentino Winery
Yountville, CA 800-764-1220

Cribari Vineyards
Fresno, CA 800-277-9095

Processor and exporter of high quality California bulk wine. Cribari Vineyards, Inc. has been involved in the California wine industry for more than four generations. Our commitment to quality and service is unsurpassed. We are competitive in our pricing and can furnish many varieties of California wine blended to our customers' specifications. Some of our most popular products are Cabernet Sauvignon, Merlot, Chardonnay, Sauterne, Sherry, Chablis, Marsala, and Chianti.

Cuvaison Vineyard
Calistoga, CA 707-942-6266
Delicato Vineyards
Napa, CA. 877-824-3600
E&J Gallo Winery
Modesto, CA 209-341-3111
Farfelu Vineyards
Flint Hill, VA 540-364-2930
Fenestra Winery
Livermore, CA 800-789-9463
Ficklin Vineyards
Madera, CA. 559-674-4598
First Colony Winery
Charlottesville, VA 877-979-7105
Foris Vineyards
Cave Junction, OR 541-592-3752
Freemark Abbey Winery
Helena, CA 800-963-9698
Greenwood Ridge Vineyards
Philo, CA. 707-895-2002
Groth Vineyards & Winery
Oakville, CA 707-944-0290
Hazlitt's 1852 Vineyard
Hector, NY 888-750-0494
Heineman's Winery
Put In Bay, OH 419-285-2811
Honig Vineyard and Winery
Rutherford, CA 800-929-2217
Mayacamas Vineyards
Napa, CA. 707-224-4030
Oakencroft Vineyard & Winery
Charlottesville, VA 434-296-4188
Oasis Winery
Hume, VA 800-304-7656
Obester Winery
Half Moon Bay, CA 650-726-9463
Old House Vineyards
Culpeper, VA. 540-423-1032
Piedmont Vineyards & Winery
Middleburg, VA 540-687-5528
Plum Creek Cellars
Palisade, CO 970-464-7586
Retzlaff Vineyards
Livermore, CA 925-447-8941

Ritchie Creek Vineyard
St Helena, CA 707-963-4661
Robert Pecota Winery
Calistoga, CA 707-942-6625
Rodney Strong Vineyards
Healdsburg, CA 800-474-9463
Secret House Vineyards
Veneta, OR 800-497-1574
Seven Hills Winery
Walla Walla, WA 877-777-7870
Shafer Vineyards
Napa, CA 707-944-2877
Signorello Vineyards
Napa, CA 707-255-5990
Silver Fox Vineyard
Mariposa, CA 209-966-4800
Silver Oak Cellars
Oakville, CA 800-273-8805
Smith Vineyard & Winery
Grass Valley, CA 530-273-7032
Smothers Winery/Remick Ridge
Glen Ellen, CA 800-795-9463
Sonoita Vineyards
Elgin, AZ. .520-455-5893
Spottswoode Winery
St Helena, CA 707-963-0134
Stone Mountain Vineyards
Dyke, VA .434-990-9463
Sycamore Vineyards
Saint Helena, CA 800-963-9698
Sylvester Winery
Paso Robles, CA 805-227-4000
Tularosa Vineyards
Tularosa, NM 800-687-4467
Veramar Vineyard
Berryville, VA 540-955-5510
Veritas Vineyards & Winery
Afton, VA .540-456-8000
Vincent Arroyo Winery
Calistoga, CA 707-942-9231
Von Stiehl Winery
Algoma, WI. 800-955-5208
Westbend Vinyards
Lewisville, NC 866-901-5032
White Hall Vineyards
Crozet, VA. 434-823-8615
White Oak Vineyards & Winery
Healdsburg, CA 707-433-8429
Whitehall Lane Winery
St Helena, CA 707-963-9454
Willowcroft Farm Vineyards
Leesburg, VA 703-777-8161
Windham Winery
Purcellville, VA. 540-668-6464
Wintergreen Winery
Nellysford, VA 434-361-2519
Woodside Vineyards
Woodside, CA. 650-851-3144
York Mountain Winery
Paso Robles, CA 805-238-3925
Z.D. Wines LLC
Napa, CA. .800-487-7757

Dolcetto

Cosentino Winery
Yountville, CA 800-764-1220
Witness Tree Vineyard
Salem, OR. 888-478-8766

Malbec

E&J Gallo Winery
Modesto, CA 209-341-3111

Merlot

A. Rafanelli Winery
Healdsburg, CA 707-433-1385
Autumn Hill Vineyards/Blue Ridge Wine
Stanardsville, VA 434-985-6100
Babcock Winery & Vineyards
Lompoc, CA 805-736-1455
Barboursville Vineyards
Barboursville, VA. 540-832-3824
Breaux Vineyards
Purcellville, VA. 800-492-9961
Chateau Grand Traverse
Traverse City, MI 231-223-7355
Chateau Morisette Winery
Meadows of Dan, VA 540-593-2865
Chateau Souverain
Geyserville, CA 707-433-3141

Chicama Vineyards
West Tisbury, MA 888-244-2262
Cienega Valley Winery/DeRose
Hollister, CA. 831-636-9143
Cooper Winery
Louisa, VA 540-894-5253
Corus Brands
Woodinville, WA. 425-806-2600
Cosentino Winery
Yountville, CA 800-764-1220

Cribari Vineyards
Fresno, CA 800-277-9095

Processor and exporter of high quality California bulk wine. Cribari Vineyards, Inc. has been involved in the California wine industry for more than four generations. Our commitment to quality and service is unsurpassed. We are competitive in our pricing and can furnish many varieties of California wine blended to our customers' specifications. Some of our most popular products are Cabernet Sauvignon, Merlot, Chardonnay, Sauterne, Sherry, Chablis, Marsala, and Chianti.

Cuvaison Vineyard
Calistoga, CA 707-942-6266
Delicato Vineyards
Napa, CA. 877-824-3600
E&J Gallo Winery
Modesto, CA 209-341-3111
Fenestra Winery
Livermore, CA 800-789-9463
First Colony Winery
Charlottesville, VA 877-979-7105
Foris Vineyards
Cave Junction, OR 541-592-3752
Greenwood Ridge Vineyards
Philo, CA. 707-895-2002
Groth Vineyards & Winery
Oakville, CA. 707-944-0290
Gundlach Bundschu Winery
Sonoma, CA. 707-938-5277
Hazlitt's 1852 Vineyard
Hector, NY 888-750-0494
Heron Hill Winery
Hammondsport, NY 800-441-4241
Jefferson Vineyards
Charlottesville, VA 800-272-3042
Nevada City Winery
Nevada City, CA. 800-203-9463
Oakencroft Vineyard & Winery
Charlottesville, VA 434-296-4188
Oasis Winery
Hume, VA 800-304-7656
Old House Vineyards
Culpeper, VA. 540-423-1032
Plum Creek Cellars
Palisade, CO 970-464-7586
Retzlaff Vineyards
Livermore, CA 925-447-8941
Robert Pecota Winery
Calistoga, CA 707-942-6625
Rodney Strong Vineyards
Healdsburg, CA 800-474-9463
Seven Hills Winery
Walla Walla, WA 877-777-7870
Shafer Vineyards
Napa, CA. 707-944-2877
Signorello Vineyards
Napa, CA. 707-255-5990
Silver Fox Vineyard
Mariposa, CA 209-966-4800
Smith Vineyard & Winery
Grass Valley, CA 530-273-7032
Smothers Winery/Remick Ridge
Glen Ellen, CA 800-795-9463
Sycamore Vineyards
Saint Helena, CA 800-963-9698
Sylvester Winery
Paso Robles, CA 805-227-4000
Tularosa Vineyards
Tularosa, NM 800-687-4467

Veritas Vineyards & Winery
Afton, VA .540-456-8000
Vincent Arroyo Winery
Calistoga, CA 707-942-9231
Von Stiehl Winery
Algoma, WI. 800-955-5208
Westbend Vinyards
Lewisville, NC 866-901-5032
White Hall Vineyards
Crozet, VA. 434-823-8615
White Oak Vineyards & Winery
Healdsburg, CA 707-433-8429
Whitehall Lane Winery
St Helena, CA 707-963-9454
Windham Winery
Purcellville, VA. 540-668-6464
York Mountain Winery
Paso Robles, CA 805-238-3925

Pinot Noir

Babcock Winery & Vineyards
Lompoc, CA 805-736-1455
Barboursville Vineyards
Barboursville, VA. 540-832-3824
Buena Vista Carneros Winery
Sonoma, CA. 800-678-8504
Byron Vineyard & Winery
Santa Maria, CA 805-934-4770
Chateau Grand Traverse
Traverse City, MI 231-223-7355
Corus Brands
Woodinville, WA. 425-806-2600
Cosentino Winery
Yountville, CA 800-764-1220
Cristom Vineyards
Salem, OR. 503-375-3068
Cuvaison Vineyard
Calistoga, CA 707-942-6266
E&J Gallo Winery
Modesto, CA 209-341-3111
Edna Valley Vineyard
San Luis Obispo, CA 805-544-5855
Fenestra Winery
Livermore, CA 800-789-9463
Fess Parker Winery
Los Olivos, CA 800-446-2455
Foris Vineyards
Cave Junction, OR 541-592-3752
Greenwood Ridge Vineyards
Philo, CA. 707-895-2002
Gundlach Bundschu Winery
Sonoma, CA. 707-938-5277
Hermann Wiemer Vineyards
Dundee, NY 800-371-7971
Heron Hill Winery
Hammondsport, NY 800-441-4241
Mayacamas Vineyards
Napa, CA. 707-224-4030
McGregor Vineyard Winery
Dundee, NY 800-272-0192
Nalle Winery
Healdsburg, CA 707-433-1040
Navarro Vineyards & Winery
Philo, CA. 800-537-9463
Nehalem Bay Winery
Nehalem, OR. 888-368-9463
Ritchie Creek Vineyard
St Helena, CA 707-963-4661
Rodney Strong Vineyards
Healdsburg, CA 800-474-9463
Secret House Vineyards
Veneta, OR 800-497-1574
Tualatin Estate Vineyards
Forest Grove, OR 503-357-5005
Westwood Winery
Sonoma, CA. 707-935-3246
Whitford Cellars
Napa, CA. 707-942-0840
Williams-Selym Winery
Healdsburg, CA 707-433-6425
Witness Tree Vineyard
Salem, OR. 888-478-8766
Woodside Vineyards
Woodside, CA. 650-851-3144
York Mountain Winery
Paso Robles, CA 805-238-3925
Z.D. Wines LLC
Napa, CA. 800-487-7757

Red Meritage/Bordeaux
Fenn Valley Vineyards
    Fennville, MI 800-432-6265

Sangiovese
Babcock Winery & Vineyards
    Lompoc, CA 805-736-1455
Corus Brands
    Woodinville, WA. 425-806-2600
Cosentino Winery
    Yountville, CA 800-764-1220
E&J Gallo Winery
    Modesto, CA 209-341-3111
Fenestra Winery
    Livermore, CA 800-789-9463
Nevada City Winery
    Nevada City, CA. 800-203-9463
Plum Creek Cellars
    Palisade, CO 970-464-7586
Sylvester Winery
    Paso Robles, CA 805-227-4000
Tularosa Vineyards
    Tularosa, NM 800-687-4467
Vincent Arroyo Winery
    Calistoga, CA 707-942-9231

Syrah
Babcock Winery & Vineyards
    Lompoc, CA 805-736-1455
Black Mesa Winery
    Velarde, NM 800-852-6372
Cedar Creek Winery
    Cedarburg, WI. 800-827-8020
Chouinard Vineyards
    Castro Valley, CA 510-582-9900
Cooper Vineyards
    Louisa, VA 540-894-5253
Corus Brands
    Woodinville, WA. 425-806-2600
Cosentino Winery
    Yountville, CA 800-764-1220
Cuvaison Vineyard
    Calistoga, CA 707-942-6266
Fenestra Winery
    Livermore, CA 800-789-9463
Fess Parker Winery
    Los Olivos, CA 800-446-2455
Nevada City Winery
    Nevada City, CA. 800-203-9463
Plum Creek Cellars
    Palisade, CO 970-464-7586
Signorello Vineyards
    Napa, CA. .707-255-5990
Sky Vineyards
    Glen Ellen, CA 707-935-1391
Sylvester Winery
    Paso Robles, CA 805-227-4000
Tularosa Vineyards
    Tularosa, NM 800-687-4467
Westwood Winery
    Sonoma, CA 707-935-3246
Whitford Cellars
    Napa, CA. .707-942-0840

Zinfandel
A. Nonini Winery
    Fresno, CA 559-275-1936
A. Rafanelli Winery
    Healdsburg, CA 707-433-1385
Burnley Vineyards and Daniel Cellars
    Barboursville, VA. 540-832-2828
Chateau Souverain
    Geyserville, CA 707-433-3141
Chatom Vineyards
    Murphys, CA. 800-435-8852
Chouinard Vineyards
    Castro Valley, CA 510-582-9900
Cienega Valley Winery/DeRose
    Hollister, CA 831-636-9143
Corus Brands
    Woodinville, WA. 425-806-2600
Cosentino Winery
    Yountville, CA 800-764-1220

Cribari Vineyards
    Fresno, CA 800-277-9095

> Processor and exporter of high quality California bulk wine. Cribari Vineyards, Inc. has been involved in the California wine industry for more than four generations. Our commitment to quality and service is unsurpassed. We are competitive in our pricing and can furnish many varieties of California wine blended to our customers' specifications. Some of our most popular products are Cabernet Sauvignon, Merlot, Chardonnay, Sauterne, Sherry, Chablis, Marsala, and Chianti.

Cuvaison Vineyard
    Calistoga, CA 707-942-6266
Delicato Vineyards
    Napa, CA. .877-824-3600
E&J Gallo Winery
    Modesto, CA 209-341-3111
Fenestra Winery
    Livermore, CA 800-789-9463
Fess Parker Winery
    Los Olivos, CA 800-446-2455
Gundlach Bundschu Winery
    Sonoma, CA 707-938-5277
Livermore Valley Cellars
    Livermore, CA 925-447-1751
Nalle Winery
    Healdsburg, CA 707-433-1040
Nevada City Winery
    Nevada City, CA. 800-203-9463
Old Wine Cellar
    Amana, IA. 319-622-3116
Rodney Strong Vineyards
    Healdsburg, CA 800-474-9463
Silver Fox Vineyard
    Mariposa, CA 209-966-4800
Sky Vineyards
    Glen Ellen, CA 707-935-1391
Storybook Mountain Winery
    Calistoga, CA 707-942-5282
Sylvester Winery
    Paso Robles, CA 805-227-4000
Vincent Arroyo Winery
    Calistoga, CA 707-942-9231
Von Stiehl Winery
    Algoma, WI. 800-955-5208
White Oak Vineyards & Winery
    Healdsburg, CA 707-433-8429
Williams-Selym Winery
    Healdsburg, CA 707-433-6425
Woodside Vineyards
    Woodside, CA. 650-851-3144
York Mountain Winery
    Paso Robles, CA 805-238-3925

Red Grapes
Alto Vineyards
    Alto Pass, IL. 618-893-4898
Babcock Winery & Vineyards
    Lompoc, CA 805-736-1455
Brown-Forman Beverages Worldwide
    Louisville, KY. 502-585-1100
Chateau Grand Traverse
    Traverse City, MI 231-223-7355
Chicama Vineyards
    West Tisbury, MA. 888-244-2262
Chouinard Vineyards
    Castro Valley, CA 510-582-9900
Cienega Valley Winery/DeRose
    Hollister, CA. 831-636-9143
Corus Brands
    Woodinville, WA. 425-806-2600
Cosentino Winery
    Yountville, CA 800-764-1220

Cribari Vineyards
    Fresno, CA 800-277-9095

> Processor and exporter of high quality California bulk wine. Cribari Vineyards, Inc. has been involved in the California wine industry for more than four generations. Our commitment to quality and service is unsurpassed. We are competitive in our pricing and can furnish many varieties of California wine blended to our customers' specifications. Some of our most popular products are Cabernet Sauvignon, Merlot, Chardonnay, Sauterne, Sherry, Chablis, Marsala, and Chianti.

E&J Gallo Winery
    Modesto, CA 209-341-3111
Fess Parker Winery
    Los Olivos, CA 800-446-2455
Galleano Winery
    Mira Loma, CA. 951-685-5376
Heineman's Winery
    Put In Bay, OH 419-285-2811
Newport Vineyards & Winery
    Middletown, RI. 401-848-5161
Wildhurst
    Kelseyville, CA. 800-595-9463
Wooden Valley Winery
    Fairfield, CA 707-864-0730

Spanish

Sherry

Cribari Vineyards
    Fresno, CA 800-277-9095

> Processor and exporter of high quality California bulk wine. Cribari Vineyards, Inc. has been involved in the California wine industry for more than four generations. Our commitment to quality and service is unsurpassed. We are competitive in our pricing and can furnish many varieties of California wine blended to our customers' specifications. Some of our most popular products are Cabernet Sauvignon, Merlot, Chardonnay, Sauterne, Sherry, Chablis, Marsala, and Chianti.

Pleasant Valley Wine Company
    Hammondsport, NY 607-569-6111

Sparkling (See also French/Champagne)
Brimstone Hill Vineyard
    Pine Bush, NY 845-744-2231
Brown-Forman Beverages Worldwide
    Louisville, KY. 502-585-1100
Buena Vista Carneros Winery
    Sonoma, CA 800-678-8504
Bully Hill Vineyards
    Hammondsport, NY 607-868-3610
Clinton Vineyards
    Clinton Corners, NY. 845-266-5372
Diamond Water
    Hot Springs, AR 501-623-1251
Domaine Chandon
    Yountville, CA 800-242-6366
Dr. Frank's Vinifera Wine Cellar
    Hammondsport, NY 800-320-0735
E&J Gallo Winery
    Modesto, CA 209-341-3111
Glenora Wine Cellars
    Dundee, NY 800-243-5513
Hazlitt's 1852 Vineyard
    Hector, NY 888-750-0494

Hermann Wiemer Vineyards
Dundee, NY 800-371-7971
Hermannhof Winery
Hermann, MO 800-393-0100
Heron Hill Winery
Hammondsport, NY 800-441-4241
La Rochelle Winery
Livermore, CA 888-647-7768
Meier's Wine Cellars
Cincinnati, OH 800-346-2941
Mon Ami Champagne Company
Port Clinton, OH 800-777-4266
North Salem Vineyard
North Salem, NY 914-669-5518
Riverland Vineyards
Gonzales, CA 831-675-2481
Royal Wine Company
Bayonne, NJ 201-437-9131
Royal Wine Company
Bayonne, NJ 800-382-8299
Schramsberg Vineyards
Calistoga, CA 800-877-3623
St. Innocent Winery
Salem, OR 503-378-1526
Tualatin Estate Vineyard
Forest Grove, OR 503-357-5005
Windsor Vineyards
Windsor, CA 800-333-9987
Woodbury Vineyards
Fredonia, NY 866-691-9463

White Grape Varieties

Alto Vineyards
Alto Pass, IL 618-893-4898
Babcock Winery & Vineyards
Lompoc, CA 805-736-1455
Cienega Valley Winery/DeRose
Hollister, CA 831-636-9143
Hazlitt's 1852 Vineyard
Hector, NY 888-750-0494
Hermann Wiemer Vineyards
Dundee, NY 800-371-7971
Hermannhof Winery
Hermann, MO 800-393-0100
Heron Hill Winery
Hammondsport, NY 800-441-4241

Chardonnay

AmRhein Wine Cellars
Bent Mountain, VA 540-929-4632
Autumn Hill Vineyards/Blue Ridge Wine
Stanardsville, VA 434-985-6100
Babcock Winery & Vineyards
Lompoc, CA 805-736-1455
Barboursville Vineyards
Barboursville, VA 540-832-3824
Benmarl Wine Company
Marlboro, NY 845-236-4265
Breaux Vineyards
Purcellville, VA 800-492-9961
Buena Vista Carneros Winery
Sonoma, CA 800-678-8504
Burnley Vineyards and Daniel Cellars
Barboursville, VA 540-832-2828
Byron Vineyard & Winery
Santa Maria, CA 805-934-4770
Catoctin Vineyards
Brookeville, MD 301-774-2310
Cedar Creek Winery
Cedarburg, WI 800-827-8020
Chateau Grand Traverse
Traverse City, MI 231-223-7355
Chateau Morisette Winery
Meadows of Dan, VA 540-593-2865
Chateau Souverain
Geyserville, CA 707-433-3141
Chicama Vineyards
West Tisbury, MA 888-244-2262
Chouinard Vineyards
Castro Valley, CA 510-582-9900
Cienega Valley Winery/DeRose
Hollister, CA 831-636-9143
Cooper Vineyards
Louisa, VA 540-894-5253
Corus Brands
Woodinville, WA 425-806-2600
Cosentino Winery
Yountville, CA 800-764-1220

CVI BULK WINES

Cribari Vineyards
Fresno, CA 800-277-9095

Processor and exporter of high quality California bulk wine. Cribari Vineyards, Inc. has been involved in the California wine industry for more than four generations. Our commitment to quality and service is unsurpassed. We are competitive in our pricing and can furnish many varieties of California wine blended to our customers' specifications. Some of our most popular products are Cabernet Sauvignon, Merlot, Chardonnay, Sauterne, Sherry, Chablis, Marsala, and Chianti.

Cristom Vineyards
Salem, OR 503-375-3068
Cuvaison Vineyard
Calistoga, CA 707-942-6266
Delicato Vineyards
Napa, CA 877-824-3600
E&J Gallo Winery
Modesto, CA 209-341-3111
Edna Valley Vineyard
San Luis Obispo, CA 805-544-5855
Fenestra Winery
Livermore, CA 800-789-9463
Fenn Valley Vineyards
Fennville, MI 800-432-6265
Fess Parker Winery
Los Olivos, CA 800-446-2455
First Colony Winery
Charlottesville, VA 877-979-7105
Foris Vineyards
Cave Junction, OR 541-592-3752
Freemark Abbey Winery
Helena, CA 800-963-9698
Groth Vineyards & Winery
Oakville, CA 707-944-0290
Gundlach Bundschu Winery
Sonoma, CA 707-938-5277
Hazlitt's 1852 Vineyard
Hector, NY 888-750-0494
Heineman's Winery
Put In Bay, OH 419-285-2811
Hermann Wiemer Vineyards
Dundee, NY 800-371-7971
Heron Hill Winery
Hammondsport, NY 800-441-4241
Mayacamas Vineyards
Napa, CA 707-224-4030
McGregor Vineyard Winery
Dundee, NY 800-272-0192
Nalle Winery
Healdsburg, CA 707-433-1040
Nehalem Bay Winery
Nehalem, OR 888-368-9463
Nevada City Winery
Nevada City, CA 800-203-9463
Oakencroft Vineyard & Winery
Charlottesville, VA 434-296-4188
Oasis Winery
Hume, VA 800-304-7656
Obester Winery
Half Moon Bay, CA 650-726-9463
Old House Vineyards
Culpeper, VA 540-423-1032
Plum Creek Cellars
Palisade, CO 970-464-7586
Retzlaff Vineyards
Livermore, CA 925-447-8941
Rodney Strong Vineyards
Healdsburg, CA 800-474-9463
Secret House Vineyards
Veneta, OR 800-497-1574
Shafer Vineyards
Napa, CA 707-944-2877
Signorello Vineyards
Napa, CA 707-255-5990
Sky Vineyards
Glen Ellen, CA 707-935-1391
Smith Vineyard & Winery
Grass Valley, CA 530-273-7032
Stone Mountain Vineyards
Dyke, VA 434-990-9463

Stonington Vineyards
Stonington, CT 800-421-9463
Sylvester Winery
Paso Robles, CA 805-227-4000
Tularosa Vineyards
Tularosa, NM 800-687-4467
Veramar Vineyard
Berryville, VA 540-955-5510
Veritas Vineyards & Winery
Afton, VA 540-456-8000
Vincent Arroyo Winery
Calistoga, CA 707-942-9231
White Hall Vineyards
Crozet, VA 434-823-8615
White Oak Vineyards & Winery
Healdsburg, CA 707-433-8429
Whitehall Lane Winery
St Helena, CA 707-963-9454
Whitford Cellars
Napa, CA 707-942-0840
Williams-Selym Winery
Healdsburg, CA 707-433-6425
Willowcroft Farm Vineyards
Leesburg, VA 703-777-8161
Windham Winery
Purcellville, VA 540-668-6464
Wintergreen Winery
Nellysford, VA 434-361-2519
Witness Tree Vineyard
Salem, OR 888-478-8766
Woodside Vineyards
Woodside, CA 650-851-3144
Z.D. Wines LLC
Napa, CA 800-487-7757

Gewrurztraminer

Babcock Winery & Vineyards
Lompoc, CA 805-736-1455
Chouinard Vineyards
Castro Valley, CA 510-582-9900
Corus Brands
Woodinville, WA 425-806-2600
Cosentino Winery
Yountville, CA 800-764-1220
Fenn Valley Vineyards
Fennville, MI 800-432-6265
Foris Vineyards
Cave Junction, OR 541-592-3752
Gundlach Bundschu Winery
Sonoma, CA 707-938-5277
Hazlitt's 1852 Vineyard
Hector, NY 888-750-0494
Hermann Wiemer Vineyards
Dundee, NY 800-371-7971
McGregor Vineyard Winery
Dundee, NY 800-272-0192
Nevada City Winery
Nevada City, CA 800-203-9463
Stonington Vineyards
Stonington, CT 800-421-9463
Tualatin Estate Vineyards
Forest Grove, OR 503-357-5005
White Hall Vineyards
Crozet, VA 434-823-8615

Pinot Blanc

Byron Vineyard & Winery
Santa Maria, CA 805-934-4770
Foris Vineyards
Cave Junction, OR 541-592-3752
Nehalem Bay Winery
Nehalem, OR 888-368-9463
Tualatin Estate Vineyards
Forest Grove, OR 503-357-5005
Witness Tree Vineyard
Salem, OR 888-478-8766

Pinot Gris

Babcock Winery & Vineyards
Lompoc, CA 805-736-1455
Byron Vineyard & Winery
Santa Maria, CA 805-934-4770
Corus Brands
Woodinville, WA 425-806-2600
Cosentino Winery
Yountville, CA 800-764-1220
Cristom Vineyards
Salem, OR 503-375-3068
Foris Vineyards
Cave Junction, OR 541-592-3752

Hazlitt's 1852 Vineyard
Hector, NY 888-750-0494
Heineman's Winery
Put In Bay, OH 419-285-2811
Jefferson Vineyards
Charlottesville, VA 800-272-3042
Secret House Vineyards
Veneta, OR 800-497-1574
Seven Hills Winery
Walla Walla, WA 877-777-7870
White Hall Vineyards
Crozet, VA 434-823-8615

Riesling

Abingdon Vineyard & Winery
Abingdon, VA 276-623-1255
Autumn Hill Vineyards/Blue Ridge Wine
Stanardsville, VA 434-985-6100
Barboursville Vineyards
Barboursville, VA 540-832-3824
Burnley Vineyards and Daniel Cellars
Barboursville, VA 540-832-2828
Catoctin Vineyards
Brookeville, MD 301-774-2310
Chateau Grand Traverse
Traverse City, MI 231-223-7355
Chouinard Vineyards
Castro Valley, CA 510-582-9900
Corus Brands
Woodinville, WA. 425-806-2600
E&J Gallo Winery
Modesto, CA 209-341-3111
Fenestra Winery
Livermore, CA 800-789-9463
Fenn Valley Vineyards
Fennville, MI 800-432-6265
Fess Parker Winery
Los Olivos, CA 800-446-2455
Freemark Abbey Winery
Helena, CA 800-963-9698
Greenwood Ridge Vineyards
Philo, CA. 707-895-2002
Gundlach Bundschu Winery
Sonoma, CA 707-938-5277
Hazlitt's 1852 Vineyard
Hector, NY 888-750-0494
Heineman's Winery
Put In Bay, OH 419-285-2811
Hermann Wiemer Vineyards
Dundee, NY 800-371-7971
Heron Hill Winery
Hammondsport, NY 800-441-4241
Jefferson Vineyards
Charlottesville, VA 800-272-3042
McGregor Vineyard Winery
Dundee, NY 800-272-0192
Oasis Winery
Hume, VA 800-304-7656
Obester Winery
Half Moon Bay, CA 650-726-9463
Plum Creek Cellars
Palisade, CO 970-464-7586
Secret House Vineyards
Veneta, OR 800-497-1574
Seven Hills Winery
Walla Walla, WA. 877-777-7870
Tualatin Estate Vineyards
Forest Grove, OR 503-357-5005
Veramar Vineyard
Berryville, VA 540-955-5510
Westbend Vinyards
Lewisville, NC 866-901-5032

Willowcroft Farm Vineyards
Leesburg, VA 703-777-8161
Windham Winery
Purcellville, VA. 540-668-6464
Wintergreen Winery
Nellysford, VA 434-361-2519

Sauvignon Blanc

Babcock Winery & Vineyards
Lompoc, CA 805-736-1455
Chateau Souverain
Geyserville, CA 707-433-3141
Chicama Vineyards
West Tisbury, MA 888-244-2262
Chouinard Vineyards
Castro Valley, CA 510-582-9900
Cosentino Winery
Yountville, CA 800-764-1220
Delicato Vineyards
Napa, CA 877-824-3600
E&J Gallo Winery
Modesto, CA 209-341-3111
Fenestra Winery
Livermore, CA 800-789-9463
Groth Vineyards & Winery
Oakville, CA 707-944-0290
Honig Vineyard and Winery
Rutherford, CA 800-929-2217
Mayacamas Vineyards
Napa, CA 707-224-4030
Nalle Winery
Healdsburg, CA 707-433-1040
Nevada City Winery
Nevada City, CA 800-203-9463
Plum Creek Cellars
Palisade, CO 970-464-7586
Retzlaff Vineyards
Livermore, CA 925-447-8941
Rodney Strong Vineyards
Healdsburg, CA 800-474-9463
Signorello Vineyards
Napa, CA 707-255-5990
Spottswoode Winery
St Helena, CA 707-963-0134
Westbend Vinyards
Lewisville, NC 866-901-5032
White Oak Vineyards & Winery
Healdsburg, CA 707-433-8429
Whitehall Lane Winery
St Helena, CA 707-963-9454

Viognier

AmRhein Wine Cellars
Bent Mountain, VA. 540-929-4632
Breaux Vineyards
Purcellville, VA. 800-492-9961
Chicama Vineyards
West Tisbury, MA 888-244-2262
Cienega Valley Winery/DeRose
Hollister, CA. 831-636-9143
Corus Brands
Woodinville, WA. 425-806-2600
Cosentino Winery
Yountville, CA 800-764-1220
Cristom Vineyards
Salem, OR 503-375-3068
Fenestra Winery
Livermore, CA 800-789-9463
Fess Parker Winery
Los Olivos, CA 800-446-2455
Seven Hills Winery
Walla Walla, WA 877-777-7870

Signorello Vineyards
Napa, CA. 707-255-5990
Tularosa Vineyards
Tularosa, NM 800-687-4467
Witness Tree Vineyard
Salem, OR 888-478-8766

White Grapes

Brown-Forman Beverages Worldwide
Louisville, KY 502-585-1100
Chateau Grand Traverse
Traverse City, MI 231-223-7355
Chicama Vineyards
West Tisbury, MA 888-244-2262
Chouinard Vineyards
Castro Valley, CA 510-582-9900
Corus Brands
Woodinville, WA. 425-806-2600

Cribari Vineyards
Fresno, CA 800-277-9095

Galleano Winery
Mira Loma, CA. 951-685-5376
Heineman's Winery
Put In Bay, OH 419-285-2811
Newport Vineyards & Winery
Middletown, RI. 401-848-5161
Wildhurst
Kelseyville, CA. 800-595-9463
Wooden Valley Winery
Fairfield, CA 707-864-0730

Candy & Confectionery

Candy

A La Carte
Chicago, IL 800-722-2370
A. Battaglia Processing Company
Chicago, IL .773-523-5900
Abbott's Candy Shop
Hagerstown, IN 877-801-1200
Acme Candy Company
Arlington, TX 254-634-2825
Adirondack Maple Farms
Fonda, NY 518-853-4022
Aglamesis Brothers
Cincinnati, OH 513-531-5196
Alaska Jack's Trading Post
Anchorage, AK 888-660-2257
Alinosi French Superfine Candies
Detroit, MI 313-527-3195
All Wrapped Up
Lauderhill, FL 800-891-2194
Allen Wertz Candy
Chino, CA 800-756-2676
Alma-Leo
Buffalo Grove, IL 847-821-0411
Amano Artisan Chocolate
Orem, UT 801-655-1996
Ameri-Suisse Group
Plainfield, NJ 908-222-1001
American Candy Company
Selma, AL 334-875-1496
American Food Products
Methuen, MA 978-682-1855
American Licorice Company
La Porte, IN .800-220-2399
American Mint
New York, NY 800-401-6468
American Specialty Confections
Saint Paul, MN 800-776-2085
AmeriGift
Oxnard, CA .800-421-9039
Amour Chocolates
Albuquerque, NM 505-881-2803
Amros the Second, Inc.
Somerset, NJ 732-846-7755
Amster-Kirtz Company
Canton, OH .800-257-9338
Amurol Confections Company
Yorkville, IL .630-553-4800
Andalan Confections
Fort Oglethorpe, GA 877-263-2526
Andes Candy
Chicago, IL .773-838-3400
Andre Prost
Old Saybrook, CT 800-243-0897
Andre's Confiserie Suisse
Kansas City, MO 800-892-1234
Ann Hemyng Candy
Trumbauersville, PA 800-779-7004
Annabelle Candy Company
Hayward, CA 510-783-2900
Archibald Candy Corporation
Chicago, IL .800-333-3629
Arcor USA
Coral Gables, FL 800-572-7267
Arizona Cowboy
Phoenix, AZ .800-529-8627
Art CoCo Chocolate Company
Denver, CO .800-779-8985
Arway Confections
Chicago, IL .773-267-5770
Asher's Chocolates
Souderton, PA 800-438-8882
Ashers Chocolates
Lewistown, PA 800-343-0520
Assouline & Ting
Philadelphia, PA 800-521-4491
Asti Holdings Ltd
New Westminster, BC 604-523-6866
Athena's Silverland®Desserts
Forest Park, IL 800-737-3636
Atkinson Candies Company
Lufkin, TX 936-639-2333
Atkinson Candy Company
Lufkin, TX 800-231-1203
Atlas Biscuit Company
Verona, NJ .973-239-8300

Aunt Aggie De's Pralines
Sinton, TX 888-772-5463
Aunt Sally's Praline Shops, Inc.
New Orleans, LA 800-642-7257
Aurora Products
Stratford, CT 800-398-1048
Azar Nut Company
El Paso, TX .800-592-8103
Azar Nut Company
El Paso, TX .915-877-4079
Baker Candy Company
Seattle, WA .425-776-6622
Baker Maid Products, Inc.
New Orleans, LA 504-827-5500
Bakers Candy
Greenwood, NE 800-804-7330
Banner Candy Manufacturing Company
Brooklyn, NY 718-647-4747
Barcelona Nut Company
Baltimore, MD 800-292-6887
Bari & Gail
Walpole, MA 800-828-9318
Barricini Chocolate
Avoca, PA 570-457-6756
Bazaar
River Grove, IL 800-736-1888
Beachwood Ingredient Services
Beachwood, OH 888-427-7870
Bee International
Chula Vista, CA 800-421-6465
Beehive Botanicals, Inc.
Hayward, WI 800-233-4483
Ben Heggy's Candy Company
Canton, OH .330-455-7703
Bergen Marzipan & Chocolate
Bergenfield, NJ 201-385-8343
Betty Jane Homemade Candies
Dubuque, IA .800-642-1254
Betty Lou's Golden Smackers
McMinnville, OR 800-242-5205
Bidwell Candies
Mattoon, IL .217-234-3858
Birnn Chocolates
Highland Park, NJ 732-545-4400
Birnn Chocolates of Vermont
South Burlington, VT 800-338-3141
Biscomerica Corporation
Rialto, CA 909-877-5997
Black Hound New York
Brooklyn, NY 800-344-4417
Blanton's
Sweetwater, TN 423-337-3487
Blommer Chocolate Company
East Greenville, PA 800-825-8181
Bloomer Candy Company
Zanesville, OH 800-452-7501
Bluebird Restaurant
Logan, UT 435-752-3155
Bob's Candies
Albany, GA .800-841-3602
Boca Bons, Inc.
Coral Springs, FL 800-314-2835
Bogdon Candy Company
Kansas City, MO 800-821-6641
Bohemian Biscuit Company
South San Francisco, CA 800-443-6737
Boston America Corporation
Woburn, MA 617-923-1111
Boston Fruit Slice & Confectionery Corporation
Lawrence, MA 978-686-2699
Bourbon Ball
Louisville, KY 800-280-0888
Brach's Confections
Dallas, TX 800-999-0204
Bread & Chocolate
Wells River, VT 800-524-6715
Brechet & Richter Company
Minneapolis, MN 763-545-0201
Brittle Kettle
Lebanon, TN 615-449-6257
Brokay Products
Philadelphia, PA 215-676-4800
Buon Italia
New York, NY 212-633-9090
Burke Candy & Ingredient Corporation
Milwaukee, WI 888-287-5350

Butterfields/Sweet Concepts
Nashville, NC 800-945-5957
C. Howard Company
Bellport, NY .631-286-7940
Cadbury Trebor Allan
Granby, QC .800-387-3267
Cadbury Trebor Allan
Toronto, ON .800-565-6541
Caiazza Candy Company
New Castle, PA 800-651-1171
Callard & Bowser-Suchard
White Plains, NY 877-226-3900
Cambridge Brands
Cambridge, MA 617-491-2500
Cameo Confections
Bay Village, OH 440-871-5732
Cameron Birch Syrup & Confections
Wasilla, AK .800-962-4724
Campbell Soup Company
Camden, NJ .800-257-8443
Candy Bouquet of Elko
Elko, NV 888-855-3391
Candy Factory
Hayward, CA 800-736-6887
Canelake's
Virginia, MN 888-928-8889
Capco Enterprises
East Hanover, NJ 800-252-1011
Caprine Estates
Bellbrook, OH 937-848-7406
Caribbean Cookie Company
Virginia Beach, VA 800-326-5200
Carolina Cupboard
Hillsborough, NC 800-400-3441
Carolyn Candies
Clermont, FL 352-394-8555
Carolyn's Gourmet
Concord, MA 800-656-2940
Carrie's Chocolates
Edmonton, AB 877-778-2462
Catoris Candy
New Kensington, PA 724-335-4371
Ce De Candy Southern Inc
Union, NJ 800-341-2254
Cella's Confections
Chicago, IL .773-838-3400
Charlotte's Confections
Millbrae, CA 800-798-2427
Chase Candy Company
St Joseph, MO 800-786-1625
Cheese Straws & More
Monroe, LA .800-997-1921
Cheri's Desert Harvest
Tucson, AZ .800-743-1141
Chevalier Chocolates
Enfield, CT .860-741-3330
Chex Finer Foods
Attleboro, MA 800-322-2434
Chocoholics Divine Desserts
Clements, CA 800-760-2462
Chocolat Belge Heyez
St. Bruno, QC 450-653-5616
Chocolat Jean Talon
St. Laurent, QC 888-333-8540
Chocolate Moon
Asheville, NC 800-723-1236
Chocolate Street of Hartville
Hartville, OH 888-853-5904
Chocolate Studio
Norristown, PA 610-272-3872
Chocolaterie Stam
Des Moines, IA 877-782-6246
Chocolates by Mark
Houston, TX .713-683-3866
Chocolates by Mr. Robert
Boca Raton, FL 561-392-3007
Chocolati Handmade Chocolates
Seattle, WA .206-784-5212
Chocolatier
Exeter, NH 888-246-5528
Chris A. Papas & Son Company
Covington, KY 859-431-0499
Chris Candies
Pittsburgh, PA 412-322-9400
Chupa Chups USA
Atlanta, GA .800-843-1858

Clark Bar America
Revere, MA 781-485-4500
Clarks Joe Fund Raising Candies & Novelties
Tarentum, PA 888-459-9520
Clasen Quality Coatings
Middleton, WI. 877-459-4500
Classic Confectionery
Fort Worth, TX 800-674-4435
Classic Confections
Atlanta, GA 800-359-7351
Clear-Vu Industries
Ashland, MA. 508-881-9100
Cloud Nine
San Leandro, CA. 201-358-8588
Cloverland Sweets/Priester's Pecan Company
Fort Deposit, AL 800-523-3505
CNS Confectionery Products
Bayonne, NJ 888-823-4330
Cocoline Chocolate Company
Brooklyn, NY 718-522-4500
Colts Chocolates
Nashville, TN 615-251-0100
Columbia Empire Farms
Sherwood, OR. 503-538-2156
Confection Solutions
Sylmar, CA 800-284-2422
Confectionately Yours
Buffalo Grove, IL 800-875-6978
Consolidated Simon Distributor
Union, NJ 973-674-2124
Cowgirl Chocolates
Moscow, ID. 888-882-4098
Cranberry Sweets Company
Coos Bay, OR 541-888-9824
Creative Confections
Northbrook, IL 847-291-4128
Creme Curls Bakery
Hudsonville, MI 800-466-1219
Croft's Crackers
Monroe, WI. 608-325-1223
Crown Candy Corporation
Macon, GA 800-241-3529
CTC Manufacturing
Calgary, AB. 800-668-7677
Cummings Studio Chocolates
Salt Lake City, UT 800-537-3957
Cupid Candies
Chicago, IL 773-925-8191
Custom Brands Unlimited
Solebury, PA 215-297-9842
Custom Confections & More
Algonquin, IL 888-457-4676
Cyclone Enterprises
Houston, TX 281-872-0087
Daprano & Company
South San Francisco, CA 800-722-6333
Dare Foods
Toronto, ON 800-665-5817
Dare Foods
Kitchener, ON 800-865-8225
David Bradley Chocolatier
Windsor, ON 877-289-7933
Davidson of Dundee
Dundee, FL 800-654-0647
Day Spring Enterprises
Cheektowaga, NY 800-879-7677
Dayhoff
Pocomoke City, MD 410-957-4301
Daymar Select Fine Coffees
El Cajon, CA 800-466-7590
Dayton Nut Specialties
Dayton, OH 800-548-1304
De Bas Chocolate
Fresno, CA 888-461-1276
De Bas Chocolatier
Fresno, CA 559-294-7638
De Soto Confectionery & Nut Company
De Soto, GA 800-237-8689
DE Wolfgang Candy Company
York, PA 800-248-4273
Decko Products
Sandusky, OH 800-537-6143
Delancey Dessert Company
New York, NY 800-254-5254
Dilettante Chocolates
Kent, WA. 888-600-2462
Dillon Candy Company
Boston, GA 800-382-8338
Dipasa
Brownsville, TX 956-831-5893
Divine Delights
Petaluma, CA 800-443-2836

DNO
Columbus, OH 800-686-2366
Donaldson's Finer Chocolates
Lebanon, IN 765-482-3334
Donells' Candies
Casper, WY 877-461-2009
Dorothy Timberlake Candies
Madison, NH. 603-447-2221
Dorval Trading Company
Nanuet, NY 800-367-8252
Doscher's Candies
Cincinnati, OH 513-381-8656
Double Wrap Cup & Container
Buffalo Grove, IL 312-337-0072
Doumak
Elk Grove Vlg, IL 800-323-0318
Downeast Candies
Boothbay Harbor, ME. 207-633-5178
Dryden & Palmer Company
Branford, CT. 203-481-3725
Dundee Brandied Fruit Company
Dundee, OR. 503-537-2500
Dundee Candy Shop
Louisville, KY 502-452-9266
Dynamic Confections
Alpine, UT 800-377-4368
EcoNatural Solutions
Boulder, CO 877-684-5159
Ed & Don's Candies
Honolulu, HI 808-423-8200
Eda's Sugarfree Candies
Philadelphia, PA 215-324-3412
Edner Corporation
Hayward, CA 510-441-8504
Elegant Edibles
Houston, TX 800-227-3226
Elegant Gourmet
Kirkland, WA 425-814-2500
Ellis Foods
Chino, CA 909-613-0030
Elmer Candy Corporation
Ponchatoula, LA 800-843-9537
Emmy's Candy from Belgium
Charlotte, NC 704-588-5445
Energy Club
Pacoima, CA. 800-688-6887
Enstrom Candies
Grand Junction, CO 800-367-8766
Esther Price Candies & Gifts
Dayton, OH 800-782-0326
Euphoria Chocolate Company
Eugene, OR. 541-344-4914
Evans Creole Candy Company
New Orleans, LA 800-637-6675
Fabio Imports
Bonsall, CA. 760-726-7040
Fabulous Chocolate Confections
Valdosta, GA. 800-755-5785
Family Sweets Candy Company
Elk Grove Village, IL 800-334-1607
Fannie May Candies
Wheaton, IL 630-653-3088
Farley's & Sathers Candy Company
Round Lake, MN 800-533-0330
Farley's & Sathers CandyCompany
Round Lake, MN 507-945-8181
Faroh Candies
Cleveland, OH 440-842-4070
Farr Candy Company
Idaho Falls, ID 208-522-8215
Fastachi
Watertown, MA. 800-466-3022
Favorite Brands International
Bannockburn, IL 847-374-0900
Favorite Brands International
Lincolnshire, IL 847-405-5814
FB Washburn Candy Corporation
Brockton, MA. 508-588-0820
Fernando C Pujals & Bros
San Juan, PR 787-792-3080
Ferrara Bakery & Cafe
New York, NY 212-226-6150
Fieldbrook Farms
Dunkirk, NY 800-333-0805
Fitzkee's Candies
York, PA 717-741-1031
Flaherty
Skokie, IL 847-966-1005
Foley's Candies
Richmond, BC 888-236-5397
Forbes Candies
Virginia Beach, VA 800-626-5898

Foreign Candy Company
Hull, IA 800-831-8541
Fralinger's
Atlantic City, NJ 800-938-2339
Frankford Candy & Chocolate Company
Philadelphia, PA 800-523-9090
Freed, Teller & Freed
Burlingame, CA 800-370-7371
Frolic Candy Company
Farmingdale, NY 516-756-2255
G Scaccianoce & Company
Bronx, NY. 718-991-4462
Galloway Company
Neenah, WI 800-722-8903
Gardners Candies
Tyrone, PA 800-242-2639
Gene & Boots Candies
Perryopolis, PA 800-864-4222
Genesee Farms
Oakfield, NY 716-343-5878
Georgia Nut Company
Skokie, IL 800-621-1264
Georgia Nut Ingredients
Skokie, IL 877-674-2993
Germack Pistachio Company
Detroit, MI 800-872-4006
Ghirardelli Chocolate Company
Short Hills, NJ. 800-877-9338
Gifford's Ice Cream & Candy Co
Silver Spring, MA. 800-708-1938
Gimbal's Fine Candies
S San Francisco, CA 800-344-6225
Gimbal's Fine Candy
S San Francisco, CA 800-344-6225
GKI Foods
Brighton, MI 248-486-0055
Gladstone Candies
Cleveland, OH 888-729-1960
Glee Gum
Providence, RI 401-351-6415
GNS Food
Arlington, TX 817-795-4671
Godiva Chocolatier
New York, NY 800-946-3482
Goetze's Candy Company
Baltimore, MD 800-638-1456
Golden Apples Candy Company
Southport, CT 800-776-0393

Golden Fluff Popcorn Company
Lakewood, NJ .732-367-5448
Golf Mill Chocolate Factory
Niles, IL 847-635-1107
Goodart Candy
Lubbock, TX. .806-747-2600
Gourmet Confections
Northbrook, IL 847-498-1200
Govadinas Fitness Foods
San Diego, CA 800-900-0108
Govatos
Wilmington, DE 888-799-5252
Grandpops Lollipops
Kansas City, MO. 800-255-7873
Gray & Company
Forest Grove, OR 503-357-3141
Great Expectations Confectionery Gourmet Foods
Chicago, IL 773-525-4865
Great San Saba River Pecan Company
San Saba, TX .800-621-9121
Green County Foods
Monroe, WI. .800-233-3564
Green Mountain Chocolates
Franklin, MA .508-520-7160
Greenwell Farms
Morganfield, KY. 270-389-3289
Gregg Candy & Nut Company
Munhall, PA 412-461-0301
Grist Mill Confections
Edina, MN. 952-469-4981
Gumtech International
Phoenix, AZ 602-252-7425
Gurley's Foods
Willmar, MN. .800-426-7845
GWB Foods Corporation
Brooklyn, NY .718-686-9600
H E Williams Candy Company
Chesapeake, VA 757-545-9311
H.B. Trading
Totowa, NJ 973-812-1022
H.R. Davis Candy
Canton, OH. .330-494-0155
Haby's Alsatian Bakery
Castroville, TX 830-931-2118
Hammer Corporation
Atlanta, GA 800-423-3138
Hauser Chocolates
Bethel, CT 203-794-1861
Haven's Candies
Westbrook, ME 800-639-6309
Hawaii Candy
Honolulu, HI .808-836-8955
Hawaiian Candies & Nuts
Honolulu, HI .808-841-3344
Hawaiian Host
Honolulu, HI .888-529-4678
Hawaiian Salrose Teas
Honolulu, HI. 808-848-0500
Health Asure
Santa Cruz, CA 818-577-1100
Hebert Candies
Shrewsbury, MA 866-432-3781
Helms Candy Company
Bristol, VA 276-669-2612
Hershey
Mississauga, ON. 800-468-1714
Hershey Canada Inc
Dartmouth, NS 902-469-2470
Hershey Chocolate & Confectionery Division
Pleasanton, CA 925-460-0359
Hershey Company
Hershey, PA. .800-468-1714
Hershey Corporation
Hershey, PA. .800-468-1714
Hershey International
Weston, FL 954-385-2600
Hialeah Products Company
Hollywood, FL 800-923-3379
Hillside Candy
Hillside, NJ 800-524-1304
Holistic Products Corporation
Englewood, NJ 800-221-0308
Hospitality Mints
Boone, NC. 800-334-5181
Hospitality Mints LLC
Boone, NC. 800-334-5181
House of Spices India
Flushing, NY. 718-507-4600
Humphrey Company
Cleveland, OH 800-486-3739
Huser Paul Company
Fort Wayne, IN 260-432-0557

Hyde Candy Company
Seattle, WA 206-322-5743
Image Development
San Rafael, CA 415-626-0485
Imaginings 3
Niles, IL 847-647-1370
Imperial Nougat Company
Santa Fe Springs, CA 562-693-8423
Indianola Pecan House
Indianola, MS 800-541-6252
Intergum North America
Winston Salem, NC. 336-760-5420
International Home Foods
Milton, PA. 973-359-9920
International Leisure Activities
Springfield, OH. 800-782-7448
ISG-Avne Packaging Services
New York, NY 800-722-2863
Issimo Food Group
La Jolla, CA 619-260-1900
Jakeman's Maple Products
Beachville, ON 800-382-9795
James Candy Company
Atlantic City, NJ 800-441-1404
Jason & Son Specialty Foods
Rancho Cordova, CA 800-810-9093
Jed's Maple Products
Westfield, VT 866-478-7388
Jelly Belly Candy Company
Fairfield, CA .800-522-3267
Jerbeau Chocolate
Camarillo, CA. 800-755-3723
Jerry's Nut House
Denver, CO 888-214-0747
Jeryl's Jems
Tappan, NY. .845-359-4715
Jo Mints
Corona Del Mar, CA. 877-566-4687
Jo's Candies
Torrance, CA. 800-770-1946
John F. Davis Candy Company
Scranton, PA .570-342-7696
Joseph Schmidt Confections
San Francisco, CA 866-237-0152
Josh Early Candies
Allentown, PA. 610-395-4321
Joyva Corporation
Brooklyn, NY 718-497-0170
Judy's Cream Caramels
Sherwood, OR. 503-819-5080
K&F Select Fine Coffees
Portland, OR .800-558-7788
Kara Chocolates
Orem, UT 800-284-5272
Karl Bissinger French Confections
St Louis, MO. 800-325-8881
Kastner's Pastry Shop & Grocery
Surfside, FL .305-866-6993
Kate Latter Candy Company
Metairie, LA .800-825-5359
Kehr's Kandy Kitchen
Milwaukee, WI 414-344-4305
Kellbran Candies & Snacks
Tallmadge, OH 330-794-1448
Kellogg's
Chicago, IL. .800-323-4064
Kemach Food Products   Corporation
Brooklyn, NY 888-453-6224
Kencraft
American Fork, UT. 800-377-4368
Kennedy Candy Company
Kilgore, TX 800-657-5258
Kerr Brothers
Toronto, ON .416-252-7341
Kerry Ingredients
Beloit, WI 608-362-1651
Key III Candies
Fort Wayne, IN 800-752-2382
Kidsmania
Santa Fe Springs, CA 562-946-8822
King Nut Company
Cleveland, OH 800-860-5464
Kloss Manufacturing Company
Allentown, PA. 800-445-7100
Koeze Company
Wyoming, MI 800-555-3909
Kopper's Chocolate Specialty Company
New York, NY 800-325-0026
Kraft
Parsippany, NJ. 973-292-1755
Kraft Food Ingredients
Memphis, TN 901-381-6500

Kraft Foods
Northfield, IL 800-323-0768
Kraft Foods Biscuit Confections & Snacks
East Hanover, NJ 973-503-2000
Krema Nut Company
Columbus, OH 800-222-4132
L C Good Candy Company
Allentown, PA. 610-432-3290
L. Craven & Sons
Melrose Park, IL 800-453-4303
Lagomarcino's
Moline, IL 309-764-1814
Lake Champlain Chocolates
Burlington, VT 800-465-5909
Lammes Candies Since 1885
Austin, TX. 800-252-1885
Lanco
Hauppauge, NY 800-938-4500
Landies Candies Company
Buffalo, NY. .800-955-2634
LaRosa's Bakery
Shrewsbury, NJ 800-527-6722
Laura Paige Candy Company
Newburgh, NY 845-566-4209
Laymon Candy Company
San Bernardino, CA 909-825-4408
Leader Candies
Brooklyn, NY 718-366-6900
Len Libby's Candy Shop
Scarborough, ME 207-883-4897
Lerro Candy Company
Darby, PA 610-461-8886
Libs Candies Downtown
Evansville, IN 812-422-5119
Lieber Chocolate & Food Products
Brooklyn, NY 718-499-0888
Linette Quality Chocolates
Womelsdorf, PA 610-589-4526
Log House Foods
Plymouth, MN. 763-546-8395
Long Grove ConfectioneryCompany
Buffalo Grove, IL 800-373-3102
Longford-Hamilton Company
Beaverton, OR 503-642-5661
Loretta's Authentic Pralines
New Orleans, LA 504-944-7068
Lotte USA
Battle Creek, MI 269-963-6664
Lou-Retta's Custom Chocolates
Buffalo, NY. .716-833-7111
Lou-Rod Candy
Lewiston, ME 207-784-5822
Louis J. Rheb Candy Company
Baltimore, MD 800-514-8293
Lowery's Home Made Candies
Muncie, IN 800-541-3340
Lucille's Own Make Candies
Manahawkin, NJ 800-426-9168
Ludo LLC
Cleveland, OH 440-542-6000
Ludwick's Frozen Donuts
Grand Rapids, MI 800-366-8816
Lukas Confections
York, PA 717-843-0921
Lynard Company
Stamford, CT. 203-323-0231
MacFarms of Hawaii
Captain Cook, HI 808-328-2435
Mafco Worldwide Corporation
Camden, NJ. .856-964-8840
Magna Foods Corporation
City of Industry, CA 800-995-4394
Manhattan Chocolates
Bayonne, NJ .201-339-6886
Maple Grove Farms of Vermont
St Johnsbury, VT. 800-525-2540
Marich Confectionery Company
Hollister, CA .800-624-7055
Marie's Candies
West Liberty, OH 866-465-5781
Marin Food Specialties
Byron, CA 925-634-6126
Maris Candy
Chicago, IL 773-254-3351
Marlow Candy & Nut Company
Englewood, NJ 201-569-7606
Mars
Mc Lean, VA .703-821-4900
Mars Chocolates
Hackettstown, NJ 908-852-1000
Marshmallow Cone Company
Cincinnati, OH 800-641-8551

Marshmallow Products
Cincinnati, OH 800-641-8551
Marsyl
Cody, WY 307-527-6277
Mary of Puddin Hill
Greenville, TX 800-545-8889
Mary Sue Candies
Baltimore, MD 410-467-9338
Mary's Candy Shop
Lewiston, ME 207-783-9824
Marzipan Specialties
Nashville, TN 615-226-4800
Masterfoods USA
Hackettstown, NJ 908-852-1000
Masterson Company
Milwaukee, WI 414-647-1132
Matangos Candies
Harrisburg, PA 717-234-0882
Maxfield Candy
Salt Lake City, UT 800-288-8002
Mayfair Sales
Buffalo, NY 800-248-2881
MB Candies
Bridgeport, IL 888-MBC-ANDY
McCraw Candies
Farmersville, TX 800-551-7201
Merbs Candies
St Louis, MO 314-832-7117
Mercado Latino
City of Industry, CA 626-333-6862
Merlin Candies
Harahan, LA 800-899-1549
Michelle Chocolatiers
Colorado Springs, CO. 888-447-3654
Midwest/Northern
Minneapolis, MN 800-328-5502
Miesse Candies
Lancaster, PA. 717-392-6011
Mille Lacs MP Company
Madison, WI. 800-843-1381
Minter Weisman Company
Minneapolis, MN 800-742-5655
Miss Sophia's Old World Kits & Gingerbread
Dallas, TX. 877-446-4373
Mister Snacks
Amherst, NY. 800-333-6393
Mitch Chocolate
Melville, NY 631-777-2400
Mojave Foods Corporation
Commerce, CA 323-890-8900
Mom 'N Pops
New Windsor, NY. 866-368-6767
Monogramme Confections
St Louis, MO. 314-427-4099
Monterrey Products Company
San Antonio, TX 210-435-2872
Moon Shine Trading Company
Woodland, CA. 800-678-1226
Moore's Candies
Baltimore, MD 410-426-2705
Morris National
Azusa, CA. 626-334-5114
Mother Nature's Goodies
Yucaipa, CA 909-795-6018
Mrs. Annie's Peanut Patch
Floresville, TX 830-393-7845
Mrs. London's Confections
Swampscott, MA 781-595-8140
Multiflex Company
Wyckoff, NJ 201-447-3888
Munson's Chocolates
Bolton, CT 860-649-4332
Muth Candies
Louisville, KY 502-585-2952
Mutiflex Company
Wyckoff, NJ 201-447-3888
My Sister's Caramels
Redlands, CA 909-792-6242
Nabisco Food Group
Kendallville, IN 260-347-1300
Nabisco LifeSavers Company
Holland, MI. 616-396-1411
Naron Mary Sue Candy Company
Baltimore, MD 410-467-9338
Nassau Candy Company
Hicksville, NY 516-342-1495
National Importers
Brampton, ON. 905-791-1322
Natural Foods
Toledo, OH 800-860-0006
Natural Rush
San Francisco, CA 415-863-2503

Nature's Candy
Fredericksburg, TX. 800-729-0085
Naturex (Chart Corp)
South Hackensack, NJ 201-440-5000
Naylor Candies
Mt Wolf, PA. 717-266-2706
Neal's Chocolates
Salt Lake City, UT 801-521-6500
NECCO
Revere, MA. 800-225-5508
Nestle
Franklin Park, IL. 800-225-2270
Nestle Canada Inc
North York, ON. 800-563-7853
Nestle Food Group
Toronto, ON 416-535-2181
Nestle USA Inc
Glendale, CA 800-633-2330
New England Confectionery Company
Revere, MA. 781-485-4500
New England Natural Bakers
Greenfield, MA 800-910-2884
Newton Candy Company
Houston, TX 713-691-6969
Niagara Chocolates
Cheektowaga, NY 800-234-5750
Noble Ingredients
Pennsauken, NJ 856-486-9292
Nora's Candy Shop
Rome, NY. 888-544-8224
Northwest Candy Emporium
Everett, WA. 800-404-7266
Northwest Chocolate Factory
Salem, OR. 503-362-1340
Novartis Nutrition Corporation
Minneapolis, MN 952-848-6000
Novelty Specialties
San Jose, CA 408-927-6682
NSpired Natural Foods
Melville, NY 631-845-4689
Nutty Bavarian
Sanford, FL. 800-382-4788
Oak Leaf Confections
Scarborough, ON 800-338-3631
OH Chocolate
Calgary, AB. 403-283-4612
Oh, Sugar! LLC
Roswell, GA 866-557-8427
Old Dominion Peanut Corporation
Norfolk, VA. 800-368-6887
Old Fashioned Candy
Berwyn, IL 708-788-6669
Old Monmouth Peanut Brittle
Freehold, NJ 732-462-1311
Olde Country Confections
Gettysburg, PA 717-337-9971
Olde Tyme Food Corporation
East Longmeadow, MA 800-356-6533
Olde Tyme Mercantile
Arroyo Grande, CA. 805-489-7991
Ole Smoky Candy Kitchen
Gatlinburg, TN 865-436-4886
Olivier's Candies
Calgary, AB. 403-266-6028
OraLabs
Englewood, CO. 800-290-0577
Original Nut House Brands
El Paso, TX. 800-726-7222
Pacific Gold Marketing
Madera, CA. 559-661-6176
Palmer Candy Company
Sioux City, IA 800-831-0828
Pangburn Candy Company
Fort Worth, TX 817-332-8856
Parker Products
Fort Worth, TX 800-433-5749
Parkside Candy Company
Buffalo, NY. 716-833-7540
Paron Chocolatier
New York, NY 212-481-9234
Patsy's Candies
Colorado Springs, CO. 866-372-8797
Paul's Candy Company
Sandy, UT 801-576-2547
Paul's Candy Factory
Salt Lake City, UT 801-576-2547
Paulaur Corporation
Cranbury, NJ 888-398-8844
Peanut Patch
Courtland, VA. 866-732-6883
Pearl River Pastry & Chocolates
Pearl River, NY. 800-632-2639

Pearson Candy Company
St Paul, MN. 800-328-6507
Pease's Candy Shoppe
Springfield, IL. 217-523-3721
Pecan Deluxe Candy Company
Dallas, TX. 800-733-3589
Pegi
Santa Ana, CA 800-292-3353
Penhurst Candy Company
Pittsburgh, PA 800-545-1336
Pennsylvania Dutch Candies
Camp Hill, PA. 800-233-7082
Perfetti
Erlanger, KY. 859-283-1234
Peter Paul Manufacturing Plant
Naugatuck, CT 800-468-1714
PEZ Candy
Orange, CT 203-795-0531
Pfeil & Holing
Flushing, NY. 800-247-7955
Pfizer
Parsippany, NJ. 973-541-5900
Phillips Candies
Seaside, OR. 503-738-5402
Phillips Candies of Seas
Seaside, OR. 503-738-5402
Piedmont Candy Corporation
Lexington, NC 336-248-2477
Pine River Pre-Pack
Newton, WI. 920-726-4216
Pippin Snack Pecans
Albany, GA. 800-554-6887
Plantation Candies
Telford, PA 888-678-6468
Plyley's Candies
Lagrange, IN 260-463-3351
Popcorn Connection
North Hollywood, CA 800-852-2676
Poppers Supply Company
Portland, OR 503-239-3792
Priester Pecan Company
Fort Deposit, AL. 800-277-3226
Prifti Candy Company
Worcester, MA 800-447-7438
Primrose Candy Company
Chicago, IL 800-268-9522
Prince of Peace Enterprises
Hayward, CA 800-732-2328
Produits Alimentaire
St Lambert De Lauzon, QC 800-463-1787
Progress Candy
Winnipeg, NB 204-586-8027
Pulakos
Erie, PA 814-452-4026
Purity Candy Company
Lewisburg, PA. 800-821-4748
QA Products
Elk Grove Vlg, IL. 800-635-7907
Quality Candy Company
Julian, CA 760-765-1891
Quality Candy Shoppes/Buddy Squirrel of Wisconsin
St Francis, WI 800-972-2658
Queen Bee Gardens
Lovell, WY 800-225-7553
Queensway Foods Company
Burlingame, CA 650-697-6666
Quick's Candy
Hummelstown, PA 800-443-9036
Quigley Manufacturing
Elizabethtown, PA. 800-367-2441
Quintessential Chocolates Company
Fredericksburg, TX. 830-990-9382
R.L. Albert & Son
Greenwich, CT 203-622-8655
R.M. Palmer Company
Reading, PA 610-372-8971
Ragold Confections
Wilton Manors, FL 954-566-9092
Ralphco
Worcester, MA 800-477-2574
Randag & Associates Inc
Elmhurst, IL 630-530-2830
Rebecca Ruth Candy
Frankfort, KY 800-444-3866
Regent Confections
Orange, CA 714-348-8889
Richard Donnelly Fine Chtes
Santa Cruz, CA 888-685-1871
Richards Maple Products
Chardon, OH 800-352-4052
Richardson Brands Company
South Miami, FL. 800-839-8938

Ricos Candy Snacks & Bakery
Hialeah, FL 305-885-7392
Riddles' Sweet Impressions
Edmonton, AB 780-465-8085
Rito Mints
Trois Rivieres, QC 819-379-1449
Rivard Popcorn Products
Landisville, PA 717-898-7131
Riverdale Fine Foods
Dayton, OH .800-548-1304
Rosalind Candy Castle
New Brighton, PA 724-843-1144
Rosetti Fine Foods
Clovis, CA 559-323-6450
Ross Fine Candies
Waterford, MI 248-682-5640
Royal Wine Company
Bayonne, NJ 201-437-9131
Russell Stover Candies
Kansas City, MO. 800-477-8683
Russell Stover Candies
Marion, SC .843-423-3022
Russell Stover Candies
Cookeville, TN 931-526-8424
Ruth Hunt Candies
Mt Sterling, KY 800-927-0302
S. Zitner Company
Philadelphia, PA 215-229-4990
S.L. Kaye Company
New York, NY 212-683-5600
S.P. Enterprises
Las Vegas, NV 800-746-4774
Sacharen Brothers
Montreal, QC 514-277-8205
Sahagian & Associates
Oak Park, IL 800-327-9273
Salem Old Fashioned Candies
Salem, MA 978-744-3242
Sally Lane's Candy Farm
Paris, TN 731-642-5801
Sambets Cajun Deli
Austin, TX. .800-472-6238
Sanders Candy
Clinton Twp, MI 800-852-2253
Sayklly's Candies   & Gifts
Escanaba, MI 906-786-3092
Scharffen Berger Chocolate Maker
Berkeley, CA. 800-930-4528
Sconza Candy Company
Oakdale, CA 877-568-8137
Scott's Candy
Sun Prairie, WI 800-356-2100
Scott-Bathgate
Winnipeg, NB 204-943-8525
Scripture Candy
Adamsville, AL. 888-317-7333
Seasons' Enterprises
Addison, IL .630-628-0211
Seattle Bar Company
Seattle, WA 206-601-4301
Seattle Gourmet Foods
Kent, WA. 800-800-9490
See's Candies
Los Angeles, CA. 800-347-7337
Seeley & Son Apiaries
Brooks, OR .503-792-3523
Segovia Mexican Candy Manufacturer
San Antonio, TX. 210-225-2102
Senor Murphy Candymaker
Santa Fe, NM 877-988-4311
Shade Foods
New Century, KS 800-225-6312
Shane Candy Company
Philadelphia, PA 215-922-1048
Shari Candies
Edina, MN. .800-658-7059
Sherm Edwards Candies
Trafford, PA 800-436-5424
Sherwood Brands
Rockville, MD 301-309-6161
Shoemaker's Candies
Santa Fe Springs, CA 562-944-8811
Sifers Valomilk Candy Company
Shawnee Mission, KS. 913-722-0991
Silver Sweet Candies
Lawrence, MA 978-688-0474
Simply Lite Foods Corporation
Commack, NY 800-753-4282
Smith Enterprises
Rock Hill, SC 800-845-8311
Snackerz
Commerce, CA 888-576-2253

Sorbee International
Philadelphia, PA 800-654-3997
Source Consumer Products
Westport, CT. 203-222-3881
South Beach Novelties & Confectionery
Staten Island, NY 718-727-4500
Southern Style Nuts
Sherman, TX. 800-624-8242
Spangler Candy Company
Bryan, OH. .888-636-4221
Spokandy Wedding Mints
Spokane, WA. 509-624-1969
Squirrel Brand Company
McKinney, TX 800-624-8242
St. Laurent Brothers
Bay City, MI 800-289-7688
Standard Candy Company
Nashville, TN 800-226-4340
Star Kay White
Congers, NY 800-874-8518
Stark Candy Company
Pewaukee, WI. 800-558-2300
Stark Candy Company
Revere, WI. 800-621-1983
Startup's Candy Company
Provo, UT. .801-373-8673
Stephany's Chocolates
Grand Junction, CO 800-888-1522
Sterling Candy
Hicksville, NY 516-932-8300
Stewart Candy Company
Waycross, GA 912-283-1970
Stichler Products
Reading, PA. 610-921-0211
Stockmeyer North America
Lincoln Park, NJ 973-628-7330
Stone's Home Made Candy Shop
Oswego, NY 888-223-3928
Storck
Chicago, IL .800-621-7772
Storck Canada
Mississauga, ON. 800-305-7551
Stutz Candy Company
Hatboro, PA. 888-692-2639
Sucesores de Pedro Cortes
San Juan, PR 787-754-7040
Sun Ridge Farms
Santa Cruz, CA. 800-655-3252
Sunline Brands
Saint Louis, MO 314-638-5770
Sweenor Chocolate
Wakefield, RI 800-834-3123
Sweet Candy Company
Salt Lake City, UT 800-669-8669
Sweet City Supply
Virginia Beach, VA. 888-793-3824
Sweet Shop
La Crosse, WI 608-784-7724
Sweet Shop USA
Mt Pleasant, TX 800-222-2269
Sweet'N Low
Brooklyn, NY 718-858-4200
Sweetcraft Candies
Timonium, MD 410-252-0684
SweetWorks Inc
Buffalo, NY. 716-634-0880
Swissart Candy Company
Wyckoff, NJ 201-447-0062
Tapper Candies
Cleveland, OH 216-825-1000
Tastee Apple Inc
Newcomerstown, OH 800-262-7753
Tell Chocolate Corporation
Waretown, NJ 732-583-8188
Temo's Candy
Akron, OH. .330-376-7229
Terri Lynn
Elgin, IL 800-323-0775
Testamints
Randolph, NJ 888-879-0400
Texas Toffee
Odessa, TX 432-563-4105
Thompson Candy Company
Meriden, CT 800-648-4058
Tic Gums
Belcamp, MD 800-899-3953
Tim's Cascade Chips
Algona, WA. 800-533-8467
Todd's
Vernon, CA .800-938-6337
Toffee Company
Houston, TX 713-840-9696

Tom & Sally's Handmade Chocolates
Brattleboro, VT. 800-827-0800
Tootsie Roll Industries
Chicago, IL .800-877-7655
Topps Company
Duryea, PA .570-457-6761
Torn & Glasser
Los Angeles, CA. 800-282-6887
Totally Chocolate
Blaine, WA .800-255-5506
Toucan Chocolates
Waban, MA 617-964-8696
Trappistine Quality Candy
Wrentham, MA 508-528-1282
Traverse Bay Confections
Tukwila, WA 206-725-0099
Tremblay's Sweet Shop
Hayward, WI. 715-634-2785
Triple-C
Hamilton, ON 800-263-9105
Tropical
Charlotte, NC 800-220-1413
Tropical
Columbus, OH 800-538-3941
Tropical
Marietta, GA 800-544-3762
Tropical Nut & Fruit Company
Orlando, FL. 800-749-8869
Truan's Candies
Detroit, MI .800-584-3004
Turkey Hill Sugarbush
Waterloo, QC 450-539-4822
Twenty First Century Snacks
Ronkonkoma, NY 800-975-2883
Twin City Wholesale
Opelika, AL. 334-745-4564
Tyler Candy Company
Tyler, TX. 903-561-3046
Ultimate Nut & Candy Company
Burbank, CA. 800-767-5259
Uniconfis Corporation
Atlanta, GA. 770-481-0440
Valhrona
Los Angeles, CA. 310-277-0401
Van Leer Chocolate Corporation
Hoboken, NJ 800-826-2462
Van Otis Chocolates
Manchester, NH 800-826-6847

Vande Walle's Candies
Appleton, WI 920-738-7799
Varda Chocolatier
Elizabeth, NJ 800-448-2732
Variety Foods
Warren, MI 586-268-4900
Vatore's Italian Caramel
Salisbury, MD 877-828-6737
Vaughn-Russell Candy Kitchen
Greenville, SC 864-271-7786
Velvet Creme Popcorn Company
Westwood, KS 888-553-6708
Vigneri Confections
Rochester, NY 585-254-6160
Vitality Life Choice
Carson City, NV 800-423-8365
Vrymeer Commodities
St Charles, IL 630-584-0069
Warner-Lambert Confections
Cambridge, MA 617-491-2500
Warrell Corporation
Camp Hill, PA 800-233-7082
Washburn Candy Corporation
Brockton, MA 508-588-0820
Waymouth Farms
New Hope, MN 800-527-0094
Weaver Nut Company
Ephrata, PA 717-738-3781
Webbs Citrus Candy
Davenport, FL 863-422-1051
Wedding Cake Studio
Williamsfield, OH 440-667-1765
Westbrae Natural Foods
Garden City, NY 800-434-4246
Westdale Foods Company
Orland Park, IL 708-458-7774
Whetstone Candy Company
St Augustine, FL 904-825-1710
White-Stokes Company
Chicago, IL 800-978-6537
Whitley's Peanut Factory
Hayes, VA 800-470-2244
Widmans Candy Shop
Crookston, MN 218-281-1487
Wiggin Farms
Arbuckle, CA 530-476-2288
Wilkinson-Spitz
Yonkers, NY 914-237-5000
Williams Candy Company
Somerville, MA 617-776-0814
Williamsburg Chocolatier
Williamsburg, VA 804-966-9000
Willy Wonka Candy
Itasca, IL 888-694-2656
Willy Wonka Candy Factory
Itasca, IL 630-773-0267
Wilson Candy Company
Jeannette, PA 724-523-3151
Wilson's Fantastic Candy
Memphis, TN 901-767-1900
Winans Chocolates & Coffees
Piqua, OH 937-773-1981
Windmill Candy
Lubbock, TX 806-785-4688
Windsor Confections
Oakland, CA 800-860-0021
Winfrey Fudge & Candy
Rowley, MA 888-946-3739
Wing Candy Company
Branson, MO 417-334-3238
Wisconsin Cheese
Melrose Park, IL 708-450-0074
Wisconsin Dairyland Fudge Company
Wisconsin Dells, WI 608-254-4136
Wisteria Candy Cottage
Boulevard, CA 800-458-8246
World Confections
Brooklyn, NY 718-768-8100
World's Finest Chocolate
Campbellford, ON 888-821-8452
Wright Ice Cream
Cayuga, IN 800-686-9561
Wrigley Company
Don Mills, ON 416-449-8600
Wrigley Manufacturing Company
Flowery Branch, GA 770-967-6181
Yost Candy Company
Dalton, OH 800-750-1976
Zitner Company
Philadelphia, PA 215-229-4990

Bon Bons

Candy Factory
Hayward, CA 800-736-6887
Ferrara Bakery & Cafe
New York, NY 212-226-6150
Mona Lisa® Chocolatier
Arlington, VA 866-662-5475

Breath Tablets

Ferrero USA
Somerset, NJ 800-337-7376
Hospitality Mints
Boone, NC 800-334-5181
Jo Mints
Corona Del Mar, CA 877-566-4687
Liberty Natural Products
Portland, OR 800-289-8427
Mona Lisa® Chocolatier
Arlington, VA 866-662-5475
Nabisco LifeSavers Company
Holland, MI 616-396-1411
Pfizer
Parsippany, NJ 973-541-5900
Vitech America Corporation
Kent, WA 253-859-5985

Brittles

A.L. Bazzini Company
Bronx, NY 800-228-0172
Arway Confections
Chicago, IL 773-267-5770
B&B Pecan Processors of NC
Turkey, NC 866-328-7322
Brittle Bark Company
Mechanicsburg, PA 717-697-6950
Brittle Kettle
Lebanon, TN 615-449-6257
Charlotte's Confections
Millbrae, CA 800-798-2427
Chase Candy Company
St Joseph, MO 800-786-1625
Cheese Straws & More
Monroe, LA. 800-997-1921
Churchill's Confectionery
Fort Lauderdale, FL 954-764-8195
Claeys Candy
South Bend, IN 800-348-2239
Confection Solutions
Sylmar, CA 800-284-2422
Crickle Company
Thomasville, GA. 800-237-8689
Crown Candy Corporation
Macon, GA 800-241-3529
DE Wolfgang Candy Company
York, PA 800-248-4273
Dillon Candy Company
Boston, GA 800-382-8338
Elegant Edibles
Houston, TX 800-227-3226
Enstrom Candies
Grand Junction, CO 800-367-8766
Georgia Nut Ingredients
Skokie, IL 877-674-2993
Gilliam Candy Brands
Paducah, KY 800-445-3008
GKI Foods
Brighton, MI 248-486-0055
GNS Food
Arlington, TX 817-795-4671
Gurley's Foods
Willmar, MN 800-426-7845
Hialeah Products Company
Hollywood, FL 800-923-3379
Idaho Candy Company
Boise, ID 800-898-6986
Kay Foods Company
Ionia, MI 616-527-0120
La Piccolina
Decatur, GA 800-626-1624
Laymon Candy Company
San Bernardino, CA 909-825-4408
Marie's Candies
West Liberty, OH 866-465-5781
McCraw Candies
Farmersville, TX 800-551-7201
McCraw's Candies
Farmersville, TX 800-551-7201
Michele's Chocolate Truffles
Clackamas, OR 800-656-7112

Mrs. Annie's Peanut Patch
Floresville, TX 830-393-7845
Muth Candies
Louisville, KY 502-585-2952
Old Dominion Peanut Corporation
Norfolk, VA. 800-368-6887
Olde Country Confections
Gettysburg, PA 717-337-9971
Olde Tyme Mercantile
Arroyo Grande, CA 805-489-7991
Olivier's Candies
Calgary, AB. 403-266-6028
Palmer Candy Company
Sioux City, IA 800-831-0828
Patsy's Candies
Colorado Springs, CO. 866-372-8797
Pennsylvania Dutch Candies
Camp Hill, PA 800-233-7082
Quality Candy
Milwaukee, WI 800-972-2658
Roger's Recipe
Glover, VT 802-525-3050
Sally Lane's Candy Farm
Paris, TN 731-642-5801
Sayklly's Candies   & Gifts
Escanaba, MI 906-786-3092
Sconza Candy Company
Oakdale, CA 877-568-8137
Shari Candies
Edina, MN 800-658-7059
Shoemaker's Candies
Santa Fe Springs, CA 562-944-8811
Snackerz
Commerce, CA 888-576-2253
Squirrel Brand Company
McKinney, TX 800-624-8242
St. Jacobs Candy Company Brittles 'n More
St. Jacobs, ON 519-884-3505
Susie's South 40 Confections
Midland, TX 800-221-4442
Trophy Nut Company
Tipp City, OH 800-729-6887
Vande Walle's Candies
Appleton, WI 920-738-7799
Wing Candy Company
Branson, MO. 417-334-3238

Butterscotch

Farley's & Sathers Candy Company
Round Lake, MN 800-533-0330
H.R. Davis Candy
Canton, OH 330-494-0155
Regent Confections
Orange, CA 714-348-8889
Sayklly's Candies   & Gifts
Escanaba, MI 906-786-3092
Weaver Nut Company
Ephrata, PA 717-738-3781

Candy Bars

AmeriCandy Company
Louisville, KY 502-583-1776
Ann Hemyng Candy
Trumbauersville, PA 800-779-7004
Bohemian Biscuit Company
South San Francisco, CA 800-443-6737
Cambridge Brands
Cambridge, MA 617-491-2500
Carrie's Chocolates
Edmonton, AB 877-778-2462
Chase Candy Company
St Joseph, MO. 800-786-1625
Chocolate Street of Hartville
Hartville, OH 888-853-5904
Chris A. Papas & Son Company
Covington, KY 859-431-0499
Chris Candies
Pittsburgh, PA 412-322-9400
Clark Bar America
Revere, MA 781-485-4500
Cloud Nine
San Leandro, CA 201-358-8588
Cocoline Chocolate Company
Brooklyn, NY 718-522-4500
De Bas Chocolatier
Fresno, CA 559-294-7638
Doscher's Candies
Cincinnati, OH 513-381-8656
Eda's Sugarfree Candies
Philadelphia, PA 215-324-3412

Edner Corporation
Hayward, CA 510-441-8504
Ferrara Bakery & Cafe
New York, NY 212-226-6150
Gardners Candies
Tyrone, PA. .800-242-2639
Ghirardelli Chocolate Company
Short Hills, NJ. 800-877-9338
Hershey
Mississauga, ON 800-468-1714
Hershey Chocolate & Confectionery Division
Pleasanton, CA 925-460-0359
Joyva Corporation
Brooklyn, NY 718-497-0170
Long Grove ConfectioneryCompany
Buffalo Grove, IL 800-373-3102
Lukas Confections
York, PA 717-843-0921
Mars
Mc Lean, VA 703-821-4900
Mona Lisa® Chocolatier
Arlington, VA 866-662-5475
Mooresville Ice Cream Company
Mooresville, NC 704-664-5456
Nestle Canada Inc
North York, ON. 800-563-7853
Nestle Food Group
Toronto, ON 416-535-2181
New England Confectionery Company
Revere, MA. 781-485-4500
Niagara Chocolates
Cheektowaga, NY 800-234-5750
Peter Paul Manufacturing Plant
Naugatuck, CT 800-468-1714
Randag & Associates Inc
Elmhurst, IL 630-530-2830
Ruth Hunt Candies
Mt Sterling, KY 800-927-0302
Sucesores de Pedro Cortes
San Juan, PR 787-754-7040
Sweet Productions
Jericho, NY .631-842-0548
Universal Laboratories
New Brunswick, NJ 800-872-0101
Vande Walle's Candies
Appleton, WI 920-738-7799
Weaver Nut Company
Ephrata, PA 717-738-3781
World Confections
Brooklyn, NY 718-768-8100

Coated

Mona Lisa® Chocolatier
Arlington, VA 866-662-5475

Canes

Asher Candy
Rockville, MD 301-309-6161

Caramel

Abdallah Candies
Burnsville, MN 800-348-7328
Allen Wertz Candy
Chino, CA 800-756-2676
Bequet Confections
Bozeman, MT 877-423-7838
Bohemian Biscuit Company
South San Francisco, CA 800-443-6737
Cambridge Brands
Cambridge, MA 617-491-2500
Candy Factory
Hayward, CA 800-736-6887
Carousel Candies
Cicero, IL 888-656-1552
Charlotte's Confections
Millbrae, CA 800-798-2427
Cherrydale Farms
Allentown, PA 800-333-4525
Clark Bar America
Revere, MA. 781-485-4500
Da Vinci Gourmet
Seattle, WA 800-640-6779
DNO
Columbus, OH 800-686-2366
Farley's & Sathers Candy Company
Round Lake, IL 800-533-0330
Gene & Boots Candies
Perryopolis, PA 800-864-4222
GKI Foods
Brighton, MI 248-486-0055

Goetze's Candy Company
Baltimore, MD 800-638-1456
H.R. Davis Candy
Canton, OH 330-494-0155
Jason & Son Specialty Foods
Rancho Cordova, CA 800-810-9093
Judy's Cream Caramels
Sherwood, OR. 503-819-5080
Key III Candies
Fort Wayne, IN 800-752-2382
Leader Candies
Brooklyn, NY 718-366-6900
Lowery's Home Made Candies
Muncie, IN .800-541-3340
Lukas Confections
York, PA 717-843-0921
Matangos Candies
Harrisburg, PA 717-234-0882
Moore's Candies
Baltimore, MD 410-426-2705
Mrs. Prindable's Handmade Confections
Niles, IL 888-215-1100
Muth Candies
Louisville, KY 502-585-2952
My Sister's Caramels
Redlands, CA 909-792-6242
New England Confectionery Company
Revere, MA. 781-485-4500
Nunes Farm Almonds
Newman, CA. 209-862-3033
Progress Candy
Winnipeg, NB 204-586-8027
Randag & Associates Inc
Elmhurst, IL 630-530-2830
Sayklly's Candies   & Gifts
Escanaba, MI 906-786-3092
St. Jacobs Candy Company Brittles 'n More
St. Jacobs, ON. 519-884-3505
Stark Candy Company
Pewaukee, WI 800-558-2300
Sweet Shop
Fort Worth, TX 800-222-2269
Tastee Apple Inc
Newcomerstown, OH 800-262-7753
Tropical
Columbus, OH 800-538-3941
Vande Walle's Candies
Appleton, WI 920-738-7799
Weaver Nut Company
Ephrata, PA 717-738-3781
White-Stokes Company
Chicago, IL .800-978-6537
World Confections
Brooklyn, NY 718-768-8100
Zitner Company
Philadelphia, PA 215-229-4990

Carob

Clasen Quality Coatings
Middleton, WI. 877-459-4500
Cocoline Chocolate Company
Brooklyn, NY 718-522-4500
Famarco
Virginia Beach, VA 757-460-3573
GKI Foods
Brighton, MI 248-486-0055
Kerry Ingredients
Beloit, WI 608-362-1651
Naturex (Chart Corp)
South Hackensack, NJ 201-440-5000
NSpired Natural Foods
Melville, NY 631-845-4689
Sacharen Brothers
Montreal, QC 514-277-8205
Setton International Foods
Commack, NY 800-227-4397
Spring Tree Maple Products
Brattleboro, VT 802-254-8784

Chewing Gum

Adams USA
Parsippany, NJ. 973-385-2000
Amurol Confections Company
Yorkville, IL .630-553-4800
Arcor USA
Coral Gables, FL. 800-572-7267
Beehive Botanicals, Inc.
Hayward, WI. 800-233-4483
C. Howard Company
Bellport, NY 631-286-7940

Candyrific
Louisville, KY 502-893-3626
Concord Confections
Concord, ON. 800-267-0037
Dandy US
Hampshire, IL 847-683-2868
Dayhoff
Clearwater, FL 800-354-3372
Fernando C Pujals & Bros
San Juan, PR 787-792-3080
Ford Gum & Machine Company
Akron, NY. .800-225-5535
Foreign Candy Company
Hull, IA. 800-831-8541
Glee Gum
Providence, RI 401-351-6415
Golden Fluff Popcorn Company
Lakewood, NJ 732-367-5448
Gumtech International
Phoenix, AZ 602-252-7425
Health-Tech
Boynton Beach, FL. 800-600-2861
Hershey Company
Hershey, PA. 800-468-1714
Horriea 2000 Food Industries
Reynolds, GA 478-847-4186
Lotte USA
Battle Creek, MI 269-963-6664
Mayfair Sales
Buffalo, NY. 800-248-2881
Mona Lisa® Chocolatier
Arlington, VA 866-662-5475
Nabisco LifeSavers Company
Holland, MI. 616-396-1411
Oak Leaf Confections
Scarborough, ON 800-338-3631
Pfizer
Parsippany, NJ. 973-541-5900
SP Enterprises
Las Vegas, NV 800-746-4774
Sweet Works
St Augustine, FL. 877-261-7887
SweetWorks Inc
Buffalo, NY. 716-634-0880
Topps Company
Duryea, PA .570-457-6761
World Confections
Brooklyn, NY 718-768-8100
Worldwide Sourcing LLC
Incline Village, NV. 775-833-1480
Wrigley Company
Don Mills, ON 416-449-8600
Wrigley Company
Chicago, IL .800-824-9681
Wrigley Manufacturing Company
Flowery Branch, GA. 770-967-6181

Coconut

Chase Candy Company
St Joseph, MO. 800-786-1625
Chris A. Papas & Son Company
Covington, KY 859-431-0499
Clark Bar America
Revere, MA 781-485-4500
Crown Candy Corporation
Macon, GA .800-241-3529
David Bradley Chocolatier
Windsor, NJ 877-289-7933
Davidson of Dundee
Dundee, FL 800-654-0647
GKI Foods
Brighton, MI 248-486-0055
H.R. Davis Candy
Canton, OH 330-494-0155
Lou-Rod Candy
Lewiston, ME 207-784-5822
Maris Candy
Chicago, IL .773-254-3351
Mona Lisa® Chocolatier
Arlington, VA 866-662-5475
Olde Tyme Mercantile
Arroyo Grande, CA. 805-489-7991
Peter Paul Manufacturing Plant
Naugatuck, CT 800-468-1714
Sally Lane's Candy Farm
Paris, TN 731-642-5801
Sayklly's Candies   & Gifts
Escanaba, MI 906-786-3092
Wisconsin Cheese
Melrose Park, IL 708-450-0074

Corn

American Food Products
  Methuen, MA .978-682-1855
Blueberry Hill Foods
  El Paso, TX. .800-451-8664
El Brands
  Ozark, AL. 334-445-2828
Energy Club
  Pacoima, CA. 800-688-6887
Fernando C Pujals & Bros
  San Juan, PR 787-792-3080
Frankford Candy & Chocolate Company
  Philadelphia, PA 800-523-9090
Gurley's Foods
  Willmar, MN 800-426-7845
Harmony Foods Corporation
  Fishers, IN. .800-837-2855
Hyde & Hyde
  Cerritos, CA 562-926-9238
Jelly Belly Candy Company
  Fairfield, CA. 800-522-3267
Kellogg's
  Chicago, IL .800-323-4064
Mayfair Sales
  Buffalo, NY. 800-248-2881
Rogers' Chocolates Ltd
  Victoria, BC 800-663-2220
Seattle Bar Company
  Seattle, WA. 206-601-4301
Setton International Foods
  Commack, NY 800-227-4397
Shari Candies
  Edina, MN. .800-658-7059
Snackerz
  Commerce, CA. 888-576-2253
Sweet Candy Company
  Salt Lake City, UT 800-669-8669
Sweet City Supply
  Virginia Beach, VA. 888-793-3824
Todd's
  Vernon, CA 800-938-6337
Triple-C
  Hamilton, ON 800-263-9105
Trophy Nut Company
  Tipp City, OH 800-729-6887

Cotton

Barcelona Nut Company
  Baltimore, MD 800-292-6887
Brennan Snacks Manufacturing
  Bogalusa, LA 800-290-7486
Bruno's Cajun Foods & Snacks
  Slidell, LA. .985-726-0544
Great Western Products Company
  Assumption, IL 217-226-3241
Great Western Products Company
  Bremen, IN 217-546-4010
Great Western Products Company
  Bismarck, MO. 573-734-2210
Kloss Manufacturing Company
  Allentown, PA. 800-445-7100
Olde Tyme Food Corporation
  East Longmeadow, MA 800-356-6533
Porter's Food & Produce
  Du Quoin, IL. 618-542-2155
Taste of Nature
  Beverly Hills, CA 310-396-4433

Cremes

Brown & Haley
  Tacoma, WA 253-620-3000
Chocolates a la Carte
  Valencia, CA 800-818-2462
Dayhoff
  Clearwater, FL 800-354-3372
DeFluri's Fine Chocolates
  Martinsburg, VA 304-264-3698
Energy Club
  Pacoima, CA. 800-688-6887
Fannie May/Fanny Farmer
  Chicago, IL 800-333-3629
Fernando C Pujals & Bros
  San Juan, PR 787-792-3080
Goetze's Candy Company
  Baltimore, MD 800-638-1456
Lammes Candies Since 1885
  Austin, TX. 800-252-1885
Laymon Candy Company
  San Bernardino, CA 909-825-4408
Lowery's Home Made Candies
  Muncie, IN 800-541-3340

Maramor Chocolates
  Columbus, OH 800-843-7722
Mona Lisa® Chocolatier
  Arlington, VA 866-662-5475
Moon Shine Trading Company
  Woodland, CA. 800-678-1226
Moore's Candies
  Baltimore, MD 410-426-2705
Olde Country Confections
  Gettysburg, PA 717-337-9971
Palmer Candy Company
  Sioux City, IA 800-831-0828
Patsy's Candies
  Colorado Springs, CO. 866-372-8797
Rene Rey Chocolates Ltd
  North Vancouver, BC 888-985-0949
Sanders Candy
  Clinton Twp, MI 800-852-2253
Shari Candies
  Edina, MN. .800-658-7059
Sweet City Supply
  Virginia Beach, VA. 888-793-3824
V L Foods
  White Plains, NY 914-697-4851

Dietetic

Balanced Health Products
  New York, NY 212-794-9878
Bidwell Candies
  Mattoon, IL 217-234-3858
Bohemian Biscuit Company
  South San Francisco, CA 800-443-6737
GKI Foods
  Brighton, MI 248-486-0055
Go Lightly Candy
  Hillside, NJ 800-524-1304
Gourmet Confections
  Northbrook, IL 847-498-1200
Lowery's Home Made Candies
  Muncie, IN 800-541-3340
Lukas Confections
  York, PA 717-843-0921
Olde Tyme Mercantile
  Arroyo Grande, CA. 805-489-7991

Peerless Confection Company
Lincolnwood, IL....................773-281-6100
Sally Lane's Candy Farm
Paris, TN........................731-642-5801
Setton International Foods
Commack, NY...................800-227-4397
Wisconsin Cheese
Melrose Park, IL..................708-450-0074

Divinity
Bohemian Biscuit Company
South San Francisco, CA............800-443-6737
Ludwick's Frozen Donuts
Grand Rapids, MI.................800-366-8816
Segovia Mexican Candy Manufacturer
San Antonio, TX..................210-225-2102

Filled
American Food Products
Methuen, MA....................978-682-1855
Andre's Confiserie Suisse
Kansas City, MO.................800-892-1234
Arcor USA
Coral Gables, FL.................800-572-7267
Atkinson Candy Company
Lufkin, TX......................800-231-1203
Blueberry Hill Foods
El Paso, TX.....................800-451-8664
Brockmann Chocolates
Richmond, BC...................888-494-2270
Brown & Haley
Tacoma, WA....................253-620-3000
Cadbury Trebor Allan
Granby, QC.....................800-387-3267
Cadbury Trebor Allan
Toronto, ON....................800-565-6541
Candy Factory
Hayward, CA....................800-736-6887
Ce De Candy Southern Inc
Union, NJ.......................800-341-2254
Chocolate By Design
Ronkonkoma, NY................631-737-0082
Chocolate House
Milwaukee, WI..................800-236-2022
Chocolates a la Carte
Valencia, CA....................800-818-2462
Chocolove Premium Chocolate
Boulder, CO....................888-246-2656
Churchill's Confectionery
Fort Lauderdale, FL..............954-764-8195
Double Play Foods
New York, NY...................212-535-4224
El Brands
Ozark, AL......................334-445-2828
Empress Chocolate Company
Brooklyn, NY...................800-793-3809
Energy Club
Pacoima, CA....................800-688-6887
Fannie May/Fanny Farmer
Chicago, IL.....................800-333-3629
FB Washburn Candy Corporation
Brockton, MA...................508-588-0820
Fernando C Pujals & Bros
San Juan, PR....................787-792-3080
Ferrero USA
Somerset, NJ....................800-337-7376
Frankford Candy & Chocolate Company
Philadelphia, PA.................800-523-9090
Goetze's Candy Company
Baltimore, MD...................800-638-1456
Gold Star Chocolate
Brooklyn, NY...................718-330-0187
Hagensborg Foods
Vancouver, BC..................877-554-7763

Harbor Sweets Chocolates
Salem, MA......................800-243-2115
Horriea 2000 Food Industries
Reynolds, GA....................478-847-4186
Hospitality Mints
Boone, NC......................800-334-5181
Hyde & Hyde
Cerritos, CA.....................562-926-9238
Idaho Candy Company
Boise, ID.......................800-898-6986
Karl Bissinger French Confections
St Louis, MO....................800-325-8881
Leader Candies
Brooklyn, NY...................718-366-6900
Libs Candies Downtown
Evansville, IN...................812-422-5119
Lowery's Home Made Candies
Muncie, IN.....................800-541-3340
Mayfair Sales
Buffalo, NY.....................800-248-2881
Mona Lisa® Chocolatier
Arlington, VA...................866-662-5475
Morris National
Azusa, CA......................626-334-5114
Nature's Candy
Fredericksburg, TX...............800-729-0085
Peerless Confection Company
Lincolnwood, IL.................773-281-6100
Plantation Candies
Telford, PA.....................888-678-6468
Primrose Candy Company
Chicago, IL.....................800-268-9522
Rebecca Ruth Candy
Frankfort, KY...................800-444-3866
Richardson Brands Company
South Miami, FL.................800-839-8938
Rucker's Makin' Batch Candies
Hutsonville, IL..................888-622-2639
Setton International Foods
Commack, NY...................800-227-4397
Shari Candies
Edina, MN......................800-658-7059
Sherwood Brands
Rockville, MD...................301-309-6161
Snackerz
Commerce, CA..................888-576-2253
Sweet Candy Company
Salt Lake City, UT...............800-669-8669
Todd's
Vernon, CA.....................800-938-6337
V L Foods
White Plains, NY................914-697-4851
Warner Candy
El Paso, TX.....................847-928-7200
Webbs Citrus Candy
Davenport, FL...................863-422-1051
Wisconsin Cheese
Melrose Park, IL.................708-450-0074

Fondants
CHR Hansen
Gretna, LA......................504-367-7727

Fudge
Amcan Industries
Elmsford, NY...................914-347-4838
Bear Creek Smokehouse
Marshall, TX....................800-950-2327
Betty Lou's Golden Smackers
McMinnville, OR.................800-242-5205
BODEGA Chocolates
Costa Mesa, CA.................888-326-3342
Bohemian Biscuit Company
South San Francisco, CA..........800-443-6737
Cambridge Brands
Cambridge, MA..................617-491-2500
Charlotte's Confections
Millbrae, CA....................800-798-2427
Country Fresh Food & Confections
Oliver Springs, TN...............800-545-8782
Crown Candy Corporation
Macon, GA......................800-241-3529
Donells' Candies
Casper, WY.....................877-461-2009
Downeast Candies
Boothbay Harbor, ME.............207-633-5178
Enstrom Candies
Grand Junction, CO..............800-367-8766
Fieldbrook Farms
Dunkirk, NY....................800-333-0805

Fudge Fatale
Los Angeles, CA.................888-923-8343
Gene & Boots Candies
Perryopolis, PA..................800-864-4222
Giambri's Quality Sweets
Clementon, NJ..................856-783-1099
Golden Foods
Commerce, CA..................800-350-2462
Haven's Candies
Westbrook, ME..................800-639-6309
James Candy Company
Atlantic City, NJ................800-441-1404
Jody's Gourmet Popcorn
Virginia Beach, VA...............866-797-5639
Kelly's Candies
Pittsburgh, PA...................800-523-3051
Kennedy Candy Company
Kilgore, TX.....................800-657-5258
Laymon Candy Company
San Bernardino, CA..............909-825-4408
McJak Candy Company LLC
Medina, OH.....................800-424-2942
Nancy's Candy
Salem, VA......................540-986-0550
Olde Tyme Mercantile
Arroyo Grande, CA..............805-489-7991
Phenomenal Fudge
Shoreham, VT...................800-430-5442
Phillips Candies
Seaside, OR....................503-738-5402
Rocky Top Country
Sevierville, TN..................865-428-7311
Segovia Mexican Candy Manufacturer
San Antonio, TX.................210-225-2102
Shoemaker's Candies
Santa Fe Springs, CA.............562-944-8811
St. Jacobs Candy Company Brittles 'n More
St. Jacobs, ON...................519-884-3505
Stephany's Chocolates
Grand Junction, CO..............800-888-1522
Sweenor Chocolate
Wakefield, RI...................800-834-3123
Vande Walle's Candies
Appleton, WI...................920-738-7799
Webbs Citrus Candy
Davenport, FL...................863-422-1051
Wisconsin Cheese
Melrose Park, IL.................708-450-0074

Gums & Jellies
Albanese Confectionery Group
Merrillville, IN..................800-536-0581
Amazing Candy Craft Company
Hollis, NY......................800-429-9368
American Food Products
Methuen, MA....................978-682-1855
Arcor USA
Coral Gables, FL.................800-572-7267
Au'some Candies
Monmouth Junction, NJ...........732-951-8818
Beehive Botanicals, Inc.
Hayward, WI....................800-233-4483
Blueberry Hill Foods
El Paso, TX.....................800-451-8664
Boston Fruit Slice & Confectionery Corporation
Lawrence, MA...................978-686-2699
C. Howard Company
Bellport, NY....................631-286-7940
Cadbury Trebor Allan
Granby, QC.....................800-387-3267
Cadbury Trebor Allan
Toronto, ON....................800-565-6541
Cambridge Brands
Cambridge, MA..................617-491-2500
Dare Foods
Kitchener, ON...................800-865-8225
Dayhoff
Clearwater, FL..................800-354-3372
El Brands
Ozark, AL......................334-445-2828
Energy Club
Pacoima, CA....................800-688-6887
Extreme Creations
El Dorado Hills, CA..............916-941-0444
Fannie May Candies
Wheaton, IL....................630-653-3088
Fannie May/Fanny Farmer
Chicago, IL.....................800-333-3629
Farley's & Sathers Candy Company
Round Lake, MN.................800-533-0330

149

Fernando C Pujals & Bros
San Juan, PR 787-792-3080
Ferrara Pan Candy Company
Forest Park, IL 800-323-1168
Foreign Candy Company
Hull, IA 800-831-8541
Frankford Candy & Chocolate Company
Philadelphia, PA 800-523-9090
Ganong Bros Limited   Corporate Office
St. Stephen, NB 888-426-6647
Gene & Boots Candies
Perryopolis, PA 800-864-4222
GNS Food
Arlington, TX 817-795-4671
Golden Fluff Popcorn Company
Lakewood, NJ 732-367-5448
Grist Mill Confections
Edina, MN 952-469-4981
Gumtech International
Phoenix, AZ 602-252-7425
Gurley's Foods
Willmar, MN 800-426-7845
Haribo of America
Baltimore, MD 800-638-2327
Harmony Foods Corporation
Fishers, IN 317-567-2700
Harmony Foods Corporation
Fishers, IN 800-837-2855
Hershey Company
Hershey, PA 800-468-1714
Hershey Corporation
Hershey, PA 800-468-1714
Hyde & Hyde
Cerritos, CA 562-926-9238
Jelly Belly Candy Company
Fairfield, CA 800-522-3267
Joyva Corporation
Brooklyn, NY 718-497-0170
Judson-Atkinson Candies
San Antonio, TX 800-962-3984
Kellogg's
Chicago, IL 800-323-4064
Kolatin Real Kosher Gelatin
Lakewood, NJ 732-364-8700
Kopper's Chocolate Specialty Company
New York, NY 800-325-0026
Kraft Foods Biscuit Confections & Snacks
East Hanover, NJ 973-503-2000
Leader Candies
Brooklyn, NY 718-366-6900
Liberty Orchards Company
Cashmere, WA 800-888-5696
Little I
Blaine, WA 360-332-3258
Marketing & Sales Essentials
Blaine, WA 877-915-5191
Mayfair Sales
Buffalo, NY 800-248-2881
Mona Lisa® Chocolatier
Arlington, VA 866-662-5475
Nabisco LifeSavers Company
Holland, MI 616-396-1411
New England Confectionery Company
Revere, MA 781-485-4500
Oak Leaf Confections
Scarborough, ON 800-338-3631
Original Foods, Quebec Division, Inc.
Vanier, QC 888-440-8880
Palmer Candy Company
Sioux City, IA 800-831-0828
Regent Confections
Orange, CA 714-348-8889
Richardson Brands Company
South Miami, FL 800-839-8938
Roseville Corporation
Mountain View, CA 888-247-9338
Sacharen Brothers
Montreal, QC 514-277-8205
Shari Candies
Edina, MN 800-658-7059
Sherwood Brands
Rockville, MD 301-309-6161
Snackerz
Commerce, CA 888-576-2253
Sorbee International
Philadelphia, PA 800-654-3997
Standard Candy Company
Nashville, TN 800-226-4340
Stark Candy Company
Pewaukee, WI 800-558-2300
Suity Confection Company
Miami, FL 305-639-3300

Sunrise Confections
El Paso, TX 800-685-1475
Sweet Blessings
Malibu, CA 310-317-1172
Sweet City Supply
Virginia Beach, VA 888-793-3824
SWELL Philadelphia Chewing Gum Corporation
Havertown, PA 610-449-1700
Taste of Nature
Beverly Hills, CA 310-396-4433
Toe-Food Chocolates and Candy
Berkeley, CA 888-863-3663
Topps Company
Duryea, PA 570-457-6761
Triple-C
Hamilton, ON 800-263-9105
Trophy Nut Company
Tipp City, OH 800-729-6887
Warner Candy
El Paso, TX 847-928-7200
Weaver Nut Company
Ephrata, PA 717-738-3781
World Confections
Brooklyn, NY 718-768-8100
Worldwide Sourcing LLC
Incline Village, NV 775-833-1480
Wrigley Company
Don Mills, ON 416-449-8600
Wrigley Company
Chicago, IL 800-824-9681
Wrigley Manufacturing Company
Flowery Branch, GA 770-967-6181

Hard

A La Carte
Chicago, IL 800-722-2370
Adams & Brooks
Los Angeles, CA 800-999-9808
American Candy Company
Selma, AL 334-875-1496
American Food Products
Methuen, MA 978-682-1855
Amurol Confections Company
Yorkville, IL 630-553-4800
Anastasia Confections, Inc.
Orlando, FL 800-329-7100
Archibald Candy Corporation
Chicago, IL 800-333-3629
Arcor USA
Coral Gables, FL 800-572-7267
Artek USA
Westlake Village, CA 866-278-3501
Atkinson Candies Company
Lufkin, TX 936-639-2333
Atkinson Candy Company
Lufkin, TX 800-231-1203
Baker Candy Company
Seattle, WA 425-776-6622
Barcelona Nut Company
Baltimore, MD 800-292-6887
Bidwell Candies
Mattoon, IL 217-234-3858
Blanton's
Sweetwater, TN 423-337-3487
Blueberry Hill Foods
El Paso, TX 800-451-8664
Bob's Candies
Albany, GA 800-841-3602
Butterfields/Sweet Concepts
Nashville, NC 800-945-5957
C. Howard Company
Bellport, NY 631-286-7940
Cadbury Trebor Allan
Granby, QC 800-387-3267
Cadbury Trebor Allan
Toronto, ON 800-565-6541
Cambridge Brands
Cambridge, MA 617-491-2500
Cap Candy
Napa, CA 707-251-9321
Ce De Candy
Union, NJ 800-631-7968
Ce De Candy Southern Inc
Union, NJ 800-341-2254
Churchill's Confectionery
Fort Lauderdale, FL 954-764-8195
Claeys Candy
South Bend, IN 800-348-2239
Cloud Nine
San Leandro, CA 201-358-8588

Day Spring Enterprises
Cheektowaga, NY 800-879-7677
Dayhoff
Clearwater, FL 800-354-3372
Doscher's Candies
Cincinnati, OH 513-381-8656
Dryden & Palmer Company
Branford, CT 203-481-3725
Eda's Sugarfree Candies
Philadelphia, PA 215-324-3412
El Brands
Ozark, AL 334-445-2828
Energy Club
Pacoima, CA 800-688-6887
Enstrom Candies
Grand Junction, CO 800-367-8766
F&F Foods
Chicago, IL 800-621-0225
Fannie May Candies
Wheaton, IL 630-653-3088
Fannie May/Fanny Farmer
Chicago, IL 800-333-3629
Farley's & Sathers Candy Company
Round Lake, MN 800-533-0330
FB Washburn Candy Corporation
Brockton, MA 508-588-0820
Fernando C Pujals & Bros
San Juan, PR 787-792-3080
Ferrara Pan Candy Company
Forest Park, IL 800-323-1168
Foreign Candy Company
Hull, IA 800-831-8541
Frankford Candy & Chocolate Company
Philadelphia, PA 800-523-9090
Giambri's Quality Sweets
Clementon, NJ 856-783-1099
Gilliam Candy Brands
Paducah, KY 800-445-3008
Gimbal's Fine Candies
S San Francisco, CA 800-344-6225
Go Lightly Candy
Hillside, NJ 800-524-1304
Golden Apples Candy Company
Southport, CT 800-776-0393
Gurley's Foods
Willmar, MN 800-426-7845
H E Williams Candy Company
Chesapeake, VA 757-545-9311
Harmony Foods Corporation
Fishers, IN 800-837-2855
Hawaii Candy
Honolulu, HI 808-836-8955
Hershey Company
Hershey, PA 800-468-1714
Hillside Candy
Hillside, NJ 800-524-1304
Horriea 2000 Food Industries
Reynolds, GA 478-847-4186
Hyde & Hyde
Cerritos, CA 562-926-9238
Idaho Candy Company
Boise, ID 800-898-6986
Judson-Atkinson Candies
San Antonio, TX 800-962-3984
Kencraft
American Fork, UT 800-377-4368
Leader Candies
Brooklyn, NY 718-366-6900
Lotte USA
Battle Creek, MI 269-963-6664
Masterfoods USA
Hackettstown, NJ 908-852-1000
Mayfair Sales
Buffalo, NY 800-248-2881
Mitch Chocolate
Melville, NY 631-777-2400
Mona Lisa® Chocolatier
Arlington, VA 866-662-5475
Moore's Candies
Baltimore, MD 410-426-2705
Morris National
Azusa, CA 626-334-5114
Nabisco LifeSavers Company
Holland, MI 616-396-1411
Nassau Candy Company
Hicksville, NY 516-342-1495
Nestle USA Inc
Glendale, CA 800-633-2330
New England Confectionery Company
Revere, MA 781-485-4500
Oak Leaf Confections
Scarborough, ON 800-338-3631

Old Dominion Peanut Corporation
Norfolk, VA 800-368-6887
Olde Country Confections
Gettysburg, PA 717-337-9971
Olivier's Candies
Calgary, AB 403-266-6028
Original Foods, Quebec Division, Inc.
Vanier, QC 888-440-8880
Palmer Candy Company
Sioux City, IA 800-831-0828
Peerless Confection Company
Lincolnwood, IL 773-281-6100
PEZ Candy
Orange, CT 203-795-0531
Piedmont Candy Corporation
Lexington, NC 336-248-2477
Plantation Candies
Telford, PA 888-678-6468
Primrose Candy Company
Chicago, IL 800-268-9522
Produits Alimentaire
St Lambert De Lauzon, QC 800-463-1787
Quigley Manufacturing
Elizabethtown, PA 800-367-2441
Rainbow Pops
Cheektowaga, NY 800-879-7677
Regent Confections
Orange, CA 714-348-8889
Richardson Brands Company
South Miami, FL 800-839-8938
Ricos Candy Snacks & Bakery
Hialeah, FL 305-885-7392
Rucker's Makin' Batch Candies
Hutsonville, IL 888-622-2639
Russell Stover Candies
Cookeville, TN 931-526-8424
Salem Old Fashioned Candies
Salem, MA 978-744-3242
Sconza Candy Company
Oakdale, CA 877-568-8137
Scripture Candy
Adamsville, AL 888-317-7333
Setton International Foods
Commack, NY 800-227-4397
Shade Foods
New Century, KS 800-225-6312
Shari Candies
Edina, MN 800-658-7059
Sherwood Brands
Rockville, MD 301-309-6161
Snackerz
Commerce, CA 888-576-2253
SP Enterprises
Las Vegas, NV 800-746-4774
Spangler Candy Company
Bryan, OH 888-636-4221
St. Jacobs Candy Company Brittles 'n More
St. Jacobs, ON 519-884-3505
Stark Candy Company
Pewaukee, WI 800-558-2300
Storck
Chicago, IL 800-621-7772
Sunline Brands
Saint Louis, MO 314-638-5770
Sunrise Confections
El Paso, TX 800-685-1475
Sweenor Chocolate
Wakefield, RI 800-834-3123
Sweet Candy Company
Salt Lake City, UT 800-669-8669
Sweet City Supply
Virginia Beach, VA 888-793-3824
Sweet'N Low
Brooklyn, NY 718-858-4200
SWELL Philadelphia Chewing Gum Corporation
Havertown, PA 610-449-1700
Todd's
Vernon, CA 800-938-6337
Tootsie Roll Industries
Chicago, IL 800-877-7655
Trophy Nut Company
Tipp City, OH 800-729-6887
Turkey Hill Sugarbush
Waterloo, QC 450-539-4822
V L Foods
White Plains, NY 914-697-4851
Warner Candy
El Paso, TX 847-928-7200
Weaver Nut Company
Ephrata, PA 717-738-3781
Webbs Citrus Candy
Davenport, FL 863-422-1051

Jelly Beans

American Food Products
Methuen, MA 978-682-1855
Arcor USA
Coral Gables, FL 800-572-7267
Blueberry Hill Foods
El Paso, TX 800-451-8664
Cambridge Brands
Cambridge, MA 617-491-2500
Cap Candy
Napa, CA 707-251-9321
Dayhoff
Clearwater, FL 800-354-3372
El Brands
Ozark, AL 334-445-2828
Energy Club
Pacoima, CA 800-688-6887
Fannie May/Fanny Farmer
Chicago, IL 800-333-3629
Farley's & Sathers Candy Company
Round Lake, MN 800-533-0330
Fernando C Pujals & Bros
San Juan, PR 787-792-3080
Ganong Bros Limited   Corporate Office
St. Stephen, NB 888-426-6647
Gimbal's Fine Candies
S San Francisco, CA 800-344-6225
GNS Food
Arlington, TX 817-795-4671
Gurley's Foods
Willmar, MN 800-426-7845
Harmony Foods Corporation
Fishers, IN 800-837-2855
Jelly Belly Candy Company
Fairfield, CA 800-522-3267
Judson-Atkinson Candies
San Antonio, TX 800-962-3984
Just Born
Bethlehem, PA 800-445-5787
Kellogg's
Chicago, IL 800-323-4064
Kraft Foods Biscuit Confections & Snacks
East Hanover, NJ 973-503-2000
Leader Candies
Brooklyn, NY 718-366-6900
Masterfoods USA
Hackettstown, NJ 908-852-1000
Mayfair Sales
Buffalo, NY 800-248-2881
Palmer Candy Company
Sioux City, IA 800-831-0828
Setton International Foods
Commack, NY 800-227-4397
Shari Candies
Edina, MN 800-658-7059
Sherwood Brands
Rockville, MD 301-309-6161
Snackerz
Commerce, CA 888-576-2253
Sunrise Confections
El Paso, TX 800-685-1475
Sweet Candy Company
Salt Lake City, UT 800-669-8669
Sweet City Supply
Virginia Beach, VA 888-793-3824
Todd's
Vernon, CA 800-938-6337
Triple-C
Hamilton, ON 800-263-9105
Warner Candy
El Paso, TX 847-928-7200
Weaver Nut Company
Ephrata, PA 717-738-3781
Worldwide Sourcing LLC
Incline Village, NV 775-833-1480

Kisses

Cadbury Trebor Allan
Granby, QC 800-387-3267
Mona Lisa® Chocolatier
Arlington, VA 866-662-5475
Setton International Foods
Commack, NY 800-227-4397

Licorice

American Food Products
Methuen, MA 978-682-1855
American Licorice Company
La Porte, IN 800-220-2399

Cadbury Trebor Allan
Granby, QC 800-387-3267
Cadbury Trebor Allan
Toronto, ON 800-565-6541
Cambridge Brands
Cambridge, MA 617-491-2500
Capco Enterprises
East Hanover, NJ 800-252-1011
El Brands
Ozark, AL 334-445-2828
Energy Club
Pacoima, CA 800-688-6887
Fannie May/Fanny Farmer
Chicago, IL 800-333-3629
Farley's & Sathers Candy Company
Round Lake, MN 800-533-0330
Fiesta Candy Company
Rochester, NH 800-285-9735
Foreign Candy Company
Hull, IA .800-831-8541
G Scaccianoce & Company
Bronx, NY 718-991-4462
Ganong Bros Limited   Corporate Office
St. Stephen, NB 888-426-6647
Gimbal's Fine Candies
S San Francisco, CA 800-344-6225
Gladstone Candies
Cleveland, OH 888-729-1960
Gurley's Foods
Willmar, MN 800-426-7845
H.R. Davis Candy
Canton, OH 330-494-0155
Haribo of America
Baltimore, MD 800-638-2327
Hershey Company
Hershey, PA 800-468-1714
Jelly Belly Candy Company
Fairfield, CA 800-522-3267
Kenny's Candy Company
Perham, MN 800-782-5152
Kookaburra Liquorice Co
Monroe, WA 360-805-6858
Lucas World
Laredo, TX 888-675-8227
Mafco Worldwide Corporation
Camden, NJ 856-964-8840
Masterfoods USA
Hackettstown, NJ 908-852-1000
Mayfair Sales
Buffalo, NY 800-248-2881
Mona Lisa® Chocolatier
Arlington, VA 866-662-5475
Morre-Tec Industries
Union, NJ 908-688-9009
Naturex (Chart Corp)
South Hackensack, NJ 201-440-5000
Palmer Candy Company
Sioux City, IA 800-831-0828
Patsy's Candies
Colorado Springs, CO 866-372-8797
Quality Candy
Milwaukee, WI 800-972-2658
Sahagian & Associates
Oak Park, IL 800-327-9273
Shari Candies
Edina, MN 800-658-7059
Snackerz
Commerce, CA 888-576-2253
Sorbee International
Philadelphia, PA 800-654-3997
Sweet Candy Company
Salt Lake City, UT 800-669-8669
Sweet City Supply
Virginia Beach, VA 888-793-3824
Todd's
Vernon, CA 800-938-6337
Triple-C
Hamilton, ON 800-263-9105
Warner Candy
El Paso, TX 847-928-7200
Westbrae Natural Foods
Garden City, NY 800-434-4246

Lollypops

Adams & Brooks
Los Angeles, CA 800-999-9808
All About Lollipops
Poway, CA 866-475-6554
Amazing Candy Craft Company
Hollis, NY 800-429-9368

American Candy Company
Selma, AL 334-875-1496
American Food Products
Methuen, MA 978-682-1855
Amurol Confections Company
Yorkville, IL 630-553-4800
Ann Hemyng Candy
Trumbauersville, PA 800-779-7004
Arcor USA
Coral Gables, FL 800-572-7267
Artek USA
Westlake Village, CA 866-278-3501
Au'some Candies
Monmouth Junction, NJ 732-951-8818
Baraboo Candy Company
Baraboo, WI 800-967-1690
Blueberry Hill Foods
El Paso, TX 800-451-8664
Bob's Candies
Albany, GA 800-841-3602
Browniepops LLC
Leawood, KS. 816-797-0715
Cadbury Trebor Allan
Granby, QC 800-387-3267
Cadbury Trebor Allan
Toronto, ON 800-565-6541
Cap Candy
Napa, CA. 707-251-9321
Carrie's Chocolates
Edmonton, AB 877-778-2462
Ce De Candy
Union, NJ 800-631-7968
Ce De Candy Southern Inc
Union, NJ 800-341-2254
CTC Manufacturing
Calgary, AB 800-668-7677
David Bradley Chocolatier
Windsor, NJ. 877-289-7933
Day Spring Enterprises
Cheektowaga, NY 800-879-7677
Dayhoff
Clearwater, FL 800-354-3372
El Brands
Ozark, AL 334-445-2828
Energy Club
Pacoima, CA 800-688-6887
Extreme Creations
El Dorado Hills, CA 916-941-0444
F&F Foods
Chicago, IL 800-621-0225
Farley's & Sathers Candy Company
Round Lake, MN 800-533-0330
Fernando C Pujals & Bros
San Juan, PR 787-792-3080
Foreign Candy Company
Hull, IA 800-831-8541
Frankford Candy & Chocolate Company
Philadelphia, PA 800-523-9090
Fun Factory
Milwaukee, WI 877-894-6767
Funkandy Corporation
Corona, CA 866-386-2263
Geeef America
Compton, CA 310-944-9485
Gladstone Candies
Cleveland, OH 888-729-1960
Glennys
Freeport, NY 888-864-1243
Golden Apples Candy Company
Southport, CT 800-776-0393
Gurley's Foods
Willmar, MN 800-426-7845
Harmony Foods Corporation
Fishers, IN. 800-837-2855
Hershey Company
Hershey, PA. 800-468-1714
Impact Confections
Colorado Springs, CO. 877-770-7677
James Candy Company
Atlantic City, NJ 800-441-1404
Jed's Maple Products
Westfield, VT 866-478-7388
Kencraft
American Fork, UT. 800-377-4368
Laura Paige Candy Company
Newburgh, NY 845-566-4209
Leader Candies
Brooklyn, NY 718-366-6900
Light Vision Confections
Cincinnati, OH 513-351-9444
Linda's Lollies Company
New York, NY 800-347-1545

Lucas World
Laredo, TX 888-675-8227
Masterfoods USA
Hackettstown, NJ 908-852-1000
Mayfair Sales
Buffalo, NY. 800-248-2881
Mc Jak Candy Company
Medina, OH. 330-722-3531
McIlhenny Company
New Orleans, LA 800-634-9599
McJak Candy Company LLC
Medina, OH. 800-424-2942
Melville Candy Company
Weymouth, MA. 800-638-8063
Mitch Chocolate
Melville, NY 631-777-2400
Mom 'N Pops
New Windsor, NY 866-368-6767
Mona Lisa® Chocolatier
Arlington, VA 866-662-5475
Multiflex Company
Wyckoff, NJ 201-447-3888
Nabisco LifeSavers Company
Holland, MI. 616-396-1411
Original Foods, Quebec Division, Inc.
Vanier, QC 888-440-8880
Pioneer Confections
Chicago, IL 773-281-6100
Plymouth Lollipop Company
Carver, MA 800-777-0115
Primrose Candy Company
Chicago, IL 800-268-9522
Produits Alimentaire
St Lambert De Lauzon, QC 800-463-1787
Quick's Candy
Hummelstown, PA 800-443-9036
Rainbow Pops
Cheektowaga, NY 800-879-7677
Richardson Brands Company
South Miami, FL. 800-839-8938
Riddles' Sweet Impressions
Edmonton, AB 780-465-8085
Roseville Corporation
Mountain View, CA 888-247-9338
Salem Old Fashioned Candies
Salem, MA 978-744-3242
Scripture Candy
Adamsville, AL 888-317-7333
Setton International Foods
Commack, NY 800-227-4397
Shari Candies
Edina, MN 800-658-7059
Sherwood Brands
Rockville, MD 301-309-6161
Sorbee International
Philadelphia, PA 800-654-3997
SP Enterprises
Las Vegas, NV 800-746-4774
Spangler Candy Company
Bryan, OH 888-636-4221
Suity Confection Company
Miami, FL. 305-639-3300
Tom & Sally's Handmade Chocolates
Brattleboro, VT 800-827-0800
Tootsie Roll Industries
Chicago, IL 800-877-7655
Topps Company
New York, NY 212-376-0300
Topps Company
Duryea, PA 570-457-6761
Triple-C
Hamilton, ON 800-263-9105
Turkey Hill Sugarbush
Waterloo, QC 450-539-4822
Williamsburg Chocolatier
Williamsburg, VA 804-966-9000
World Confections
Brooklyn, NY 718-768-8100
Yost Candy Company
Dalton, OH 800-750-1976

Gourmet Flavored

Bruno's Cajun Foods & Snacks
Slidell, LA. 985-726-0544

Lozenges

Adams USA
Parsippany, NJ. 973-385-2000
BestSweet
Mooresville, NC 888-211-5530

Cadbury Trebor Allan
Granby, QC 800-387-3267
F&F Foods
Chicago, IL 800-621-0225
Ganong Bros Limited   Corporate Office
St. Stephen, NB 888-426-6647
Hillside Candy
Hillside, NJ 800-524-1304
Holistic Products Corporation
Englewood, NJ 800-221-0308
Mona Lisa® Chocolatier
Arlington, VA 866-662-5475
MYNTZ!
Seattle, WA 253-395-0401
Olde Country Confections
Gettysburg, PA 717-337-9971
Rito Mints
Trois Rivieres, QC 819-379-1449
Snackerz
Commerce, CA 888-576-2253
Sorbee International
Philadelphia, PA 800-654-3997

Maple

Butternut Mountain Farm
Morrisville, VT 800-828-2376
Jed's Maple Products
Westfield, VT 866-478-7388
Key III Candies
Fort Wayne, IN 800-752-2382
Maple Grove Farms of Vermont
St Johnsbury, VT. 800-525-2540
Nature's Candy
Fredericksburg, TX. 800-729-0085
Richards Maple Products
Chardon, OH 800-352-4052
Sugarwoods Farm
Glover, VT 800-245-3718
Swisser Sweet Maple
Castorland, NY 315-346-1034

Marshmallow

Charlotte's Confections
Millbrae, CA 800-798-2427
Clown-Gysin Brands
Northbrook, IL 800-323-5778
Doumak
Elk Grove Vlg, IL 800-323-0318
Durkee-Mower
Lynn, MA 781-593-8007
Georgia Nut Ingredients
Skokie, IL 877-674-2993
Gimbal's Fine Candies
S San Francisco, CA 800-344-6225
Glatech Productions
Lakewood, NJ 732-364-8700
Golden Fluff Popcorn Company
Lakewood, NJ 732-367-5448
Judson-Atkinson Candies
San Antonio, TX. 800-962-3984
Kolatin Real Kosher Gelatin
Lakewood, NJ 732-364-8700
Kraft Food Ingredients
Memphis, TN 901-381-6500
Philadelphia Candies
Hermitage, PA 724-981-6341
Pilgrim's Pride
Lufkin, TX 936-639-1174
Sherwood Brands
Rockville, MD 301-309-6161
Sokol & Company
Countryside, IL 800-328-7656
White-Stokes Company
Chicago, IL 800-978-6537
Zitner Company
Philadelphia, PA 215-229-4990

Marshmallow Creme

Sokol & Company
Countryside, IL. 800-328-7656

Marshmallows

Amros the Second, Inc.
Somerset, NJ 732-846-7755
Annabelle Candy Company
Hayward, CA 510-783-2900
Charlotte's Confections
Millbrae, CA 800-798-2427

Chris A. Papas & Son Company
Covington, KY 859-431-0499
David Bradley Chocolatier
Windsor, NJ 877-289-7933
Doumak
Elk Grove Vlg, IL 800-323-0318
Farley's & Sathers Candy Company
Round Lake, MN 800-533-0330
Frankford Candy & Chocolate Company
Philadelphia, PA 800-523-9090
Ganong Bros Limited   Corporate Office
St. Stephen, NB 888-426-6647
Golden Fluff Popcorn Company
Lakewood, NJ 732-367-5448
Joyva Corporation
Brooklyn, NY 718-497-0170
Judson-Atkinson Candies
San Antonio, TX 800-962-3984
Just Born
Bethlehem, PA 800-445-5787
Kraft Foods Biscuit Confections & Snacks
East Hanover, NJ 973-503-2000
Marshmallow Cone Company
Cincinnati, OH 800-641-8551
Michele's Chocolate Truffles
Clackamas, OR 800-656-7112
Patsy's Candies
Colorado Springs, CO 866-372-8797
Pennsylvania Dutch Candies
Camp Hill, PA 800-233-7082
Pilgrim's Pride
Lufkin, TX 936-639-1174
Richardson Brands Company
South Miami, FL 800-839-8938
Roseville Corporation
Mountain View, CA 888-247-9338
Sherwood Brands
Rockville, MD 301-309-6161
Spangler Candy Company
Bryan, OH 888-636-4221
Suity Confection Company
Miami, FL 305-639-3300
Sweet City Supply
Virginia Beach, VA 888-793-3824
Worldwide Sourcing LLC
Incline Village, NV 775-833-1480
Zitner Company
Philadelphia, PA 215-229-4990

Marzipan

Ambassador Foods
Van Nuys, CA 800-338-3369
American Almond Products Company
Brooklyn, NY 800-825-6663
Amoretti-Capriccio
Oxnard, CA 800-266-7388
Mayfair Sales
Buffalo, NY 800-248-2881
Mona Lisa® Chocolatier
Arlington, VA 866-662-5475
Snackerz
Commerce, CA 888-576-2253
Sweet Swiss Confections
Spokane, WA 509-838-1334

Mints

Abdallah Candies
Burnsville, MN 800-348-7328
Adams USA
Parsippany, NJ 973-385-2000
American Mint
New York, NY 800-401-6468
AmeriCandy Company
Louisville, KY 502-583-1776
Amurol Confections Company
Yorkville, IL 630-553-4800
Andes Candy
Chicago, IL 773-838-3400
Art CoCo Chocolate Company
Denver, CO 800-779-8985
Atkinson Candy Company
Lufkin, TX 800-231-1203
Big Sky Brands
Toronto, ON 416-599-5415
Blueberry Hill Foods
El Paso, TX 800-451-8664
Bob's Candies
Albany, GA 800-841-3602
Boston America Corporation
Woburn, MA 617-923-1111

Brown & Haley
Tacoma, WA 253-620-3000
Cadbury Trebor Allan
Granby, QC 800-387-3267
Caiazza Candy Company
New Castle, PA 800-651-1171
Ce De Candy Southern Inc
Union, NJ 800-341-2254
Chocolati Handmade Chocolates
Seattle, WA 206-784-5212
Clarks Joe Fund Raising Candies & Novelties
Tarentum, PA 888-459-9520
Cloud Nine
San Leandro, CA 201-358-8588
Energy Club
Pacoima, CA 800-688-6887
F&F Foods
Chicago, IL 800-621-0225
Farley's & Sathers Candy Company
Round Lake, MN 800-533-0330
Foley's Candies
Richmond, BC 888-236-5397
Ford Gum & Machine Company
Akron, NY 800-225-5535
Fun Factory
Milwaukee, WI 877-894-6767
G Scaccianoce & Company
Bronx, NY 718-991-4462
Go Lightly Candy
Hillside, NJ 800-524-1304
H.R. Davis Candy
Canton, OH 330-494-0155
Health-Tech
Boynton Beach, FL 800-600-2861
Hint Mint
Los Angeles, CA 213-622-6468
Horriea 2000 Food Industries
Reynolds, GA 478-847-4186
Hospitality Mints
Boone, NC 800-334-5181
Hospitality Mints LLC
Boone, NC 800-334-5181
Hutchins-Logue
Santa Cruz, CA 800-959-7670
IFive Brands
Seattle, WA 800-882-5615
Jelly Belly Candy Company
Fairfield, CA 800-522-3267
Jo Mints
Corona Del Mar, CA 877-566-4687
Judson-Atkinson Candies
San Antonio, TX 800-962-3984
Kopper's Chocolate Specialty Company
New York, NY 800-325-0026
Kraft Foods Biscuit Confections & Snacks
East Hanover, NJ 973-503-2000
Landies Candies Company
Buffalo, NY 800-955-2634
Little I
Blaine, WA 360-332-3258
Marich Confectionery Company
Hollister, CA 800-624-7055
Matangos Candies
Harrisburg, PA 717-234-0882
Maxfield Candy
Salt Lake City, UT 800-288-8002
Mayfair Sales
Buffalo, NY 800-248-2881
Mona Lisa® Chocolatier
Arlington, VA 866-662-5475
MYNTZ!
Seattle, WA 253-395-0401
Nabisco LifeSavers Company
Holland, MI 616-396-1411
Naylor Candies
Mt Wolf, PA 717-266-2706
Nestle Canada Inc
North York, ON 800-563-7853
New England Confectionery Company
Revere, MA 781-485-4500
Palmer Candy Company
Sioux City, IA 800-831-0828
Paramount Chocolates
Hauppauge, NY 800-842-3000
Perfetti
Erlanger, KY 859-283-1234
Pez Manufacturing Corporation
Orange, CT 203-795-0531
Pfizer
Parsippany, NJ 973-541-5900
Piedmont Candy Corporation
Lexington, NC 336-248-2477

Plantation Candies
Telford, PA 888-678-6468
Rebecca Ruth Candy
Frankfort, KY 800-444-3866
Reutter Candy & Chocolates
Baltimore, MD 800-392-0870
Rito Mints
Trois Rivieres, QC 819-379-1449
Salem Old Fashioned Candies
Salem, MA 978-744-3242
Schuster Marketing Corporation
Milwaukee, WI 888-254-8948
Scripture Candy
Adamsville, AL 888-317-7333
Sencha Naturals
Los Angeles, CA 888-473-6242
Setton International Foods
Commack, NY 800-227-4397
Shari Candies
Edina, MN 800-658-7059
SP Enterprises
Las Vegas, NV 800-746-4774
Stark Candy Company
Pewaukee, WI 800-558-2300
Sweenor Chocolate
Wakefield, RI 800-834-3123
Todd's
Vernon, CA 800-938-6337
Tootsie Roll Industries
Chicago, IL 800-877-7655
Unica
Glen Ellyn, IL 630-790-8107
Vermints
Saxtons River, VT 802-869-2233
Weaver Nut Company
Ephrata, PA 717-738-3781
Webbs Citrus Candy
Davenport, FL 863-422-1051
Worldwide Sourcing LLC
Incline Village, NV 775-833-1480

Mousse

Abel & Schafer
Ronkonkoma, NY 800-443-1260
Alati-Caserta Desserts
Montreal, QC 514-271-3013
Alexian Pates/GroezingerProvisions
Neptune, NJ 800-927-9473
Blue Ridge Farms
Chicago, IL 708-748-4405
CSP Foods
Mont-Royal, QC 514-731-7621
Dean Distributors
Burlingame, CA 800-792-0816
Desserts by David Glass
Bloomfield, CT 860-769-5570
Granowska's
Toronto, ON 416-533-7755
Groezinger Provisions
Neptune, NJ 800-927-9473
HFI Foods
Redmond, WA 425-883-1320
Hormel Foods Corporation
Austin, MN 800-523-4635
Jon Donaire Pastry
Santa Fe Springs, CA 877-366-2473
Kirkland Custom Seafoods
Kirkland, WA 800-321-3474
Les Trois Petits Cochons
New York, NY 800-537-7283
Love & Quiches Desserts
Freeport, NY 800-525-5251
Morningstar Foods
Dallas, TX 225-273-2803
Paris Pastry
Los Angeles, CA 310-474-8888
Sapar
San Mateo, CA 650-340-8840
Tova Industries
Louisville, KY 888-532-8682
W&G Flavors
Hunt Valley, MD 410-771-6606
World of Chantilly
Brooklyn, NY 718-859-1110

Nougats

Allen Wertz Candy
Chino, CA 800-756-2676
Clarks Joe Fund Raising Candies & Novelties
Tarentum, PA 888-459-9520

Farley's & Sathers Candy Company
Round Lake, MN 800-533-0330
Ferrara Bakery & Cafe
New York, NY 212-226-6150
Lukas Confections
York, PA 717-843-0921
Mona Lisa® Chocolatier
Arlington, VA 866-662-5475
New England Confectionery Company
Revere, MA 781-485-4500
Webbs Citrus Candy
Davenport, FL 863-422-1051
White-Stokes Company
Chicago, IL 800-978-6537

Novelties

Ann Hemyng Candy
Trumbauersville, PA 800-779-7004
Bohemian Biscuit Company
South San Francisco, CA 800-443-6737
Carrie's Chocolates
Edmonton, AB 877-778-2462
Ce De Candy Southern Inc
Union, NJ 800-341-2254
Cella's Confections
Chicago, IL 773-838-3400
Chocolate Street of Hartville
Hartville, OH 888-853-5904
Chocolates by Mark
Houston, TX 713-683-3866
Chris A. Papas & Son Company
Covington, KY 859-431-0499
Chris Candies
Pittsburgh, PA 412-322-9400
David Bradley Chocolatier
Windsor, NJ 877-289-7933
Doscher's Candies
Cincinnati, OH 513-381-8656
Ferrara Bakery & Cafe
New York, NY 212-226-6150
Hershey Corporation
Hershey, PA 800-468-1714
Jo Mints
Corona Del Mar, CA 877-566-4687
Laura Paige Candy Company
Newburgh, NY 845-566-4209
Leader Candies
Brooklyn, NY 718-366-6900
Long Grove ConfectioneryCompany
Buffalo Grove, IL 800-373-3102
Lucas World
Laredo, TX 888-675-8227
Maxfield Candy
Salt Lake City, UT 800-288-8002
Merbs Candies
St Louis, MO 314-832-7117
Merlin Candies
Harahan, LA 800-899-1549
Mona Lisa® Chocolatier
Arlington, VA 866-662-5475
New England Confectionery Company
Revere, MA 781-485-4500
Niagara Chocolates
Cheektowaga, NY 800-234-5750
QA Products
Elk Grove Vlg, IL 800-635-7907
Stark Candy Company
Pewaukee, WI 800-558-2300
Stichler Products
Reading, PA 610-921-0211
Sunkist Candy   c/o Jelly Belly Candy Company
Fairfield, CA 800-323-9380
Weaver Nut Company
Ephrata, PA 717-738-3781
World Confections
Brooklyn, NY 718-768-8100
Yost Candy Company
Dalton, OH 800-750-1976

Peanut Brittle

Atkinson Candies Company
Lufkin, TX 936-639-2333
Atkinson Candy Company
Lufkin, TX 800-231-1203
B&B Pecan Processors of NC
Turkey, NC 866-328-7322
Confection Solutions
Sylmar, CA 800-284-2422
DE Wolfgang Candy Company
York, PA 800-248-4273

Jer's Handmade Chocolates
Solana Beach, CA 800-540-7265
Maxwell's Gourmet Food
Raleigh, NC 800-952-6887
Moore's Candies
Baltimore, MD 410-426-2705
Muth Candies
Louisville, KY 502-585-2952
Peanut Shop of Williamsburg
Portsmouth, VA 800-637-3268
Sally Lane's Candy Farm
Paris, TN 731-642-5801
Severn Peanut Company
Severn, NC 800-642-4064

Popcorn Specialties

Cloud Nine
San Leandro, CA 201-358-8588
Eda's Sugarfree Candies
Philadelphia, PA 215-324-3412
Faroh Candies
Cleveland, OH 440-842-4070
Fun City Popcorn
Las Vegas, NV 800-423-1710
GKI Foods
Brighton, MI 248-486-0055
Heartland Gourmet Popcorn
Elkhorn, WI. 866-489-4676
Humphrey Company
Cleveland, OH 800-486-3739
Kennedy Candy Company
Kilgore, TX. 800-657-5258
Koeze Company
Wyoming, MI 800-555-3909
McCleary
South Beloit, IL 800-523-8644
Midwest/Northern
Minneapolis, MN 800-328-5502
Pilgrim's Pride
Lufkin, TX 936-639-1174
Popcorn Connection
North Hollywood, CA 800-852-2676
Poppers Supply Company
Portland, OR 503-239-3792
Randag & Associates Inc
Elmhurst, IL 630-530-2830
Rygmyr Foods
South Saint Paul, MN 800-545-3903
Vande Walle's Candies
Appleton, WI 920-738-7799
Weaver Popcorn Company
Indianapolis, IN 800-999-2365

Rock

Salem Old Fashioned Candies
Salem, MA 978-744-3242
Setton International Foods
Commack, NY 800-227-4397

Taffy

Adams & Brooks
Los Angeles, CA 800-999-9808
Alaska Jack's Trading Post
Anchorage, AK 888-660-2257
Anastasia Confections, Inc.
Orlando, FL 800-329-7100
Annabelle Candy Company
Hayward, CA 510-783-2900
Bidwell Candies
Mattoon, IL 217-234-3858
Cadbury Trebor Allan
Granby, QC 800-387-3267
Ce De Candy Southern Inc
Union, NJ 800-341-2254
Charlotte's Confections
Millbrae, CA 800-798-2427
Clark Bar America
Revere, MA. 781-485-4500
Contract Comestibles
East Troy, WI 262-642-9400
Downeast Candies
Boothbay Harbor, ME. 207-633-5178
El Brands
Ozark, AL 334-445-2828
Energy Club
Pacoima, CA 800-688-6887
Farley's & Sathers Candy Company
Round Lake, MN 800-533-0330
Forbes Candies
Virginia Beach, VA 800-626-5898

Foreign Candy Company
Hull, IA 800-831-8541
Gilliam Candy Brands
Paducah, KY 800-445-3008
Gurley's Foods
Willmar, MN 800-426-7845
Haven's Candies
Westbrook, ME 800-639-6309
Horriea 2000 Food Industries
Reynolds, GA 478-847-4186
Humphrey Company
Cleveland, OH 800-486-3739
James Candy Company
Atlantic City, NJ 800-441-1404
Jelly Belly Candy Company
Fairfield, CA 800-522-3267
Judson-Atkinson Candies
San Antonio, TX 800-962-3984
Kencraft
American Fork, UT. 800-377-4368
Lammes Candies Since 1885
Austin, TX. 800-252-1885
Laymon Candy Company
San Bernardino, CA 909-825-4408
Lowery's Home Made Candies
Muncie, IN 800-541-3340
Lukas Confections
York, PA 717-843-0921
Masterfoods USA
Hackettstown, NJ 908-852-1000
Maxfield Candy
Salt Lake City, UT 800-288-8002
Mayfair Sales
Buffalo, NY 800-248-2881
McCraw Candies
Farmersville, TX 800-551-7201
McCraw's Candies
Farmersville, TX 800-551-7201
Merbs Candies
St Louis, MO 314-832-7117
Metropolis Sambeve Specialty Foods
Lawrence, MA 978-683-2873
New England Confectionery Company
Revere, MA 781-485-4500
Original Foods, Quebec Division, Inc.
Vanier, QC 888-440-8880
Paramount Chocolates
Hauppauge, NY 800-842-3000
Patsy's Candies
Colorado Springs, CO 866-372-8797
Pennsylvania Dutch Candies
Camp Hill, PA. 800-233-7082
Phillips Candies
Seaside, OR. 503-738-5402
Pioneer Confections
Chicago, IL 773-281-6100
Primrose Candy Company
Chicago, IL. 800-268-9522
Queen Bee Gardens
Lovell, WY 800-225-7553
Sahagian & Associates
Oak Park, IL 800-327-9273
Salem Old Fashioned Candies
Salem, MA 978-744-3242
Sayklly's Candies   & Gifts
Escanaba, MI 906-786-3092
Seattle Gourmet Foods
Kent, WA. 800-800-9490
Setton International Foods
Commack, NY 800-227-4397
Shari Candies
Edina, MN 800-658-7059
Snackerz
Commerce, CA 888-576-2253
Squirrel Brand Company
McKinney, TX 800-624-8242
St. Jacobs Candy Company Brittles 'n More
St. Jacobs, ON. 519-884-3505
Stark Candy Company
Pewaukee, WI 800-558-2300
Sunline Brands
Saint Louis, MO 314-638-5770
Sweet Candy Company
Salt Lake City, UT 800-669-8669
Sweet City Supply
Virginia Beach, VA 888-793-3824
Taffy Town
Salt Lake City, UT 800-765-4770
Todd's
Vernon, CA 800-938-6337
Webbs Citrus Candy
Davenport, FL. 863-422-1051

Toffee

Bohemian Biscuit Company
South San Francisco, CA 800-443-6737
BT McElrath Chocolatier
Minneapolis, MN 612-331-8800
Cadbury Trebor Allan
Granby, QC 800-387-3267
Cary's of Oregon
Grants Pass, OR 888-822-9300
Ce De Candy Southern Inc
Union, NJ 800-341-2254
Confectionately Yours
Buffalo Grove, IL 800-875-6978
Creative Confections
Northbrook, IL 847-291-4128
Elegant Edibles
Houston, TX 800-227-3226
Elegant Gourmet
Kirkland, WA 425-814-2500
Enstrom Candies
Grand Junction, CO 800-367-8766
Fancy's Candy's
Rougemont, NC 888-403-2629
Farley's & Sathers Candy Company
Round Lake, MN 800-533-0330
Georgia Nut Ingredients
Skokie, IL 877-674-2993
Jo's Candies
Torrance, CA 800-770-1946
Kerry Ingredients
Beloit, WI 608-362-1651
Landies Candies Company
Buffalo, NY 800-955-2634
Leader Candies
Brooklyn, NY 718-366-6900
Lukas Confections
York, PA 717-843-0921
Marich Confectionery Company
Hollister, CA 800-624-7055
Marie's Candies
West Liberty, OH 866-465-5781
Mona Lisa® Chocolatier
Arlington, VA 866-662-5475
Mrs. Weinstein's Toffee
Fort Worth, TX 866-965-0422
Northern Flair Foods
Mound, MN 888-530-4453
NSpired Natural Foods
Melville, NY 631-845-4689
Nunes Farm Almonds
Newman, CA 209-862-3033
Old Dominion Peanut Corporation
Norfolk, VA 800-368-6887
Pecan Deluxe Candy Company
Dallas, TX 800-733-3589
Quigley Manufacturing
Elizabethtown, PA 800-367-2441
Regent Confections
Orange, CA 714-348-8889
Seasons' Enterprises
Addison, IL 630-628-0211
Sherwood Brands
Rockville, MD 301-309-6161
Southernfood Specialties
Atlanta, GA 800-255-5323
Stephany's Chocolates
Grand Junction, CO 800-888-1522
Sweet Productions
Jericho, NY 631-842-0548
Sweet Shop USA
Mt Pleasant, TX 800-222-2269
Tall Grass Toffee
Lenexa, KS 877-344-0442
Texas Toffee
Odessa, TX 432-563-4105
Toffee Company
Houston, TX 713-840-9696
Vande Walle's Candies
Appleton, WI 920-738-7799
Weaver Nut Company
Ephrata, PA 717-738-3781
Webbs Citrus Candy
Davenport, FL 863-422-1051
Wiggin Farms
Arbuckle, CA 530-476-2288
Wisconsin Cheese
Melrose Park, IL 708-450-0074

Truffles

Anette's Chocolate Factory
Napa, CA 707-252-4228

Birnn Chocolates of Vermont
South Burlington, VT 800-338-3141
Boca Bons, Inc.
Coral Springs, FL 800-314-2835
BODEGA Chocolates
Costa Mesa, CA 888-326-3342
BT McElrath Chocolatier
Minneapolis, MN 612-331-8800
Chocoholics Divine Desserts
Clements, CA 800-760-2462
Chocolati Handmade Chocolates
Seattle, WA 206-784-5212
De Bas Chocolatier
Fresno, CA 559-294-7638
DeFluri's Fine Chocolates
Martinsburg, VA 304-264-3698
Gift Factory/Beverly Hills
Sylmar, CA 800-365-6619
GKI Foods
Brighton, MI 248-486-0055
Mona Lisa® Chocolatier
Arlington, VA 866-662-5475
Moore's Candies
Baltimore, MD 410-426-2705
Paramount Chocolates
Hauppauge, NY 800-842-3000
Sabatino Truffles USA
Long Island City, NY 888-444-9971
Sweet Shop
Fort Worth, TX 800-222-2269
Tea Room
American Canyon, CA 866-515-8866
Urbani Truffles
Culver City, CA 310-842-8850
Veritas Chocolatier
Glenview, IL 800-555-8331
Vosges Haut-Chocolat
Chicago, IL 888-309-866

Candy Coatings

Carob

Clasen Quality Coatings
Middleton, WI 877-459-4500

Chocolate

ADM Cocoa
Milwaukee, WI 800-558-9958
Ambassador Foods
Van Nuys, CA 800-338-3369
Anette's Chocolate Factory
Napa, CA 707-252-4228
Clasen Quality Coatings
Middleton, WI 877-459-4500
Cocoline Chocolate Company
Brooklyn, NY 718-522-4500
Mona Lisa® Chocolatier
Arlington, VA 866-662-5475
Mootz Candy
Pottsville, PA 570-622-4480
Pacific Gold Marketing
Madera, CA 559-661-6176
Sucesores de Pedro Cortes
San Juan, PR 787-754-7040
US Chocolate Corporation
Brooklyn, NY 718-788-8555

Confectionery

ADM Cocoa
Milwaukee, WI 800-558-9958
Cache Creek Foods
Woodland, CA 530-662-1764

Chocolate Products

A La Carte
Chicago, IL 800-722-2370
A Southern Season
Chapel Hill, NC 800-253-5317
Abdallah Candies
Burnsville, MN 800-348-7328
Adams & Brooks
Los Angeles, CA 800-999-9808
Aglamesis Brothers
Cincinnati, OH 513-531-5196
Al Richards Chocolates
Bayonne, NJ 888-777-6964
Al-Rite Fruits & Syrups
Miami, FL 305-652-2540

Alaska Jack's Trading Post
Anchorage, AK 888-660-2257
Alinosi French Superfine Candies
Detroit, MI 313-527-3195
American Nut & Chocolate Company
Boston, MA 800-797-6887
AmeriCandy Company
Louisville, KY 502-583-1776
Ames International
Fife, WA 888-469-2637
Andes Candy
Chicago, IL 773-838-3400
Andre-Boudin Bakeries
San Francisco, CA 415-882-1849
Archibald Candy Corporation
Chicago, IL 800-333-3629
Ashers Chocolates
Lewistown, PA 800-343-0520
Baker Candy Company
Seattle, WA 425-776-6622
Barry Callebaut USA LLC
Eddystone, PA 610-872-4528
Betty Lou's Golden Smackers
McMinnville, OR 800-242-5205
Blackberry Patch
Thomasville, GA 800-853-5598
Blanton's
Sweetwater, TN 423-337-3487
Blommer Chocolate Company
East Greenville, PA 800-825-8181
Bloomsberry & Co
Salem, MA 800-745-5154
Bridge Brand Chocolate
San Francisco, CA 888-732-4626
Brighams
Arlington, MA 800-274-4426
Brix Chocolates
Youngstown, OH 866-613-2749
Campbell Soup Company
Camden, NJ 800-257-8443
Candy Cottage Company
Huntingdon Vly, PA 215-953-8288
Candy Factory
Hayward, CA 800-736-6887
Canelake's
Virginia, MN 888-928-8889
Cape Cod Provisions
Pocasset, MA 508-564-5840
Cella's Confections
Chicago, IL 773-838-3400
Central Coca-Cola Bottling Company
Richmond, VA 800-359-3759
Charles Dennery Pillsbury
New Orleans, LA 504-733-2331
Chase Candy Company
St Joseph, MO 800-786-1625
Chelsea Milling Company
Chelsea, MI 734-475-1361
Chocolate Fantasies
Burr Ridge, IL 630-572-0045
Chocolate Potpourri
Glenview, IL 847-729-8878
Chocolatique
Los Angeles, CA 310-479-3849
Chris Candies
Pittsburgh, PA 412-322-9400
Chuao Chocolatier
Carlsbad, CA 888-635-1444
Chukar Cherries
Prosser, WA 800-624-9544
Clark Bar America
Revere, MA 781-485-4500
Clarks Joe Fund Raising Candies & Novelties
Tarentum, PA 888-459-9520
Clasen Quality Coatings
Middleton, WI 877-459-4500
Classic Confections
Atlanta, GA 800-359-7351
Claudio Corallo Chocolate
Seattle, WA 206-859-3534
Clear Mountain Coffee Company
Silver Spring, MD 301-587-2233
Cloverland Sweets/Priester's Pecan Company
Fort Deposit, AL 800-523-3505
Cocoline Chocolate Company
Brooklyn, NY 718-522-4500
Cocomira Confections
Toronto, ON 866-413-9049
Confection Solutions
Sylmar, CA 800-284-2422
Crown Candy Corporation
Macon, GA 800-241-3529

Cummings Studio Chocolates
Salt Lake City, UT 800-537-3957
D'Artagnan
Newark, NJ 800-327-8246
Da Vinci Gourmet
Seattle, WA 800-640-6779
Dare Foods
Kitchener, ON 800-865-8225
Daymar Select Fine Coffees
El Cajon, CA 800-466-7590
DE Wolfgang Candy Company
York, PA 800-248-4273
Desserts by David Glass
Bloomfield, CT 860-769-5570
Dipasa
Brownsville, TX 956-831-5893
Donaldson's Finer Chocolates
Lebanon, IN 765-482-3334
East Shore Specialty Foods
Hartland, WI 800-236-1069
Eda's Sugarfree Candies
Philadelphia, PA 215-324-3412
Elmer Candy Corporation
Ponchatoula, LA 800-843-9537
Enstrom Candies
Grand Junction, CO 800-367-8766
Eskimo Pie Corporation
Ronkonkoma, NY 631-737-9700
Euro Chocolate Fountain
San Diego, CA 800-423-9303
Fabio Imports
Bonsall, CA 760-726-7040
Faroh Candies
Cleveland, OH 440-842-4070
Fastachi
Watertown, MA 800-466-3022
Figamajigs
Petaluma, CA 707-992-0023
Fine Foods Northwest
Seattle, WA 800-862-3965
Fitzkee's Candies
York, PA 717-741-1031
Fran's Chocolates
Seattle, WA 800-422-3726
G H Bent Company
Milton, MA 617-698-5945
Gardners Candies
Tyrone, PA 800-242-2639
GEM Berry Products
Sandpoint, ID 800-426-0498
Gene & Boots Candies
Perryopolis, PA 800-864-4222
Gertrude Hawk Chocolates
Dunmore, PA 800-706-6275
Ghirardelli Chocolate Company
San Leandro, CA 800-877-9338
Gloria Jean's Gourmet Coffees
Rcho Sta Marg, CA 800-354-5258
Golden Moon Tea
Herndon, VA 877-327-5473
Gorant Candies
Youngstown, OH 800-572-4139
Gourmedas Inc
Quebec, QC 418-210-3703
Govadinas Fitness Foods
San Diego, CA 800-900-0108
Gray & Company
Forest Grove, OR 503-357-3141
Green Mountain Chocolates
Franklin, MA 508-520-7160
H. Fox & Company
Brooklyn, NY 718-385-4600
H.B. Taylor Co
Chicago, IL 773-254-4805

H.R. Davis Candy
Canton, OH 330-494-0155
Haven's Candies
Westbrook, ME 800-639-6309
Hawaiian Salrose Teas
Honolulu, HI 808-848-0500
Hialeah Products Company
Hollywood, FL 800-923-3379
Home Bakery
Laramie, WY 307-742-2721
Hospitality Mints
Boone, NC 800-334-5181
Hunt Country Foods
Middleburg, VA 540-364-2622
Island Princess
Honolulu, HI 866-872-8601
Ivydaro
Putney, VT 802-387-5597
Jason & Son Specialty Foods
Rancho Cordova, CA 800-810-9093
Jer's Handmade Chocolates
Solana Beach, CA 800-540-7265
John F. Davis Candy Company
Scranton, PA 570-342-7696
John Kelly Chocolates
Los Angeles, CA 800-609-4243
Kamish Food Products
Chicago, IL 773-267-0400
Karl Bissinger French Confections
St Louis, MO 800-325-8881
Kemach Food Products   Corporation
Brooklyn, NY 888-453-6224
Kennedy Candy Company
Kilgore, TX 800-657-5258
Kerry Ingredients
Beloit, WI 608-362-1651
Key III Candies
Fort Wayne, IN 800-752-2382
Knipschildt Chocolatier
Norwalk, CT 203-838-3131
Koeze Company
Wyoming, MI 800-555-3909
Kopper's Chocolate Specialty Company
New York, NY 800-325-0026
Kozy Shack
Hicksville, NY 516-870-3000
Kraft Canada Headquarters
Don Mills, ON 800-268-7808
Landies Candies Company
Buffalo, NY 800-955-2634
Laymon Candy Company
San Bernardino, CA 909-825-4408
Lerro Candy Company
Darby, PA 610-461-8886
Liberty Richter
Saddle Brook, NJ 201-291-8749
Little Dutch Boy Bakeries
Draper, UT 801-571-3800
Log House Foods
Plymouth, MN 763-546-8395
Long Grove ConfectioneryCompany
Buffalo Grove, IL 800-373-3102
Lou-Retta's Custom Chocolates
Buffalo, NY 716-833-7111
Louis J. Rheb Candy Company
Baltimore, MD 800-514-8293
Lowery's Home Made Candies
Muncie, IN 800-541-3340
Lukas Confections
York, PA 717-843-0921
Lynch Foods
North York, QC 416-449-5464
Lyons-Magnus
Fresno, CA 559-268-5966

Mama Lee's Gourmet Hot Chocolate
Nashville, TN 888-626-2533
Masterson Company
Milwaukee, WI 414-647-1132
Matangos Candies
Harrisburg, PA 717-234-0882
Maxfield Candy
Salt Lake City, UT 800-288-8002
Merbs Candies
St Louis, MO 314-832-7117
Mille Lacs MP Company
Madison, WI 800-843-1381
Mona Lisa® Chocolatier
Arlington, VA 866-662-5475
Mont Blanc Gourmet
Denver, CO 800-877-3811
Moon Shine Trading Company
Woodland, CA 800-678-1226
Mooresville Ice Cream Company
Mooresville, NC 704-664-5456
Morse's Sauerkraut
Waldoboro, ME 866-832-5569
Munson's Chocolates
Bolton, CT 860-649-4332
Naron Mary Sue Candy Company
Baltimore, MD 410-467-9338
Nestle Food Group
Toronto, ON 416-535-2181
New England Natural Bakers
Greenfield, MA 800-910-2884
Noble Ingredients
Pennsauken, NJ 856-486-9292
Northwest Chocolate Factory
Salem, OR 503-362-1340
Northwestern Foods
St Paul, MN 800-236-4937
Novartis Nutrition Corporation
Minneapolis, MN 952-848-6000
Oak Leaf Confections
Scarborough, ON 800-338-3631
Old Fashioned Candy
Berwyn, IL 708-788-6669
Olde Tyme Mercantile
Arroyo Grande, CA 805-489-7991
Pacari Organic Chocolate
Miami, FL 561-214-4726
Paulaur Corporation
Cranbury, NJ 888-398-8844
Pecan Deluxe Candy Company
Dallas, TX 800-733-3589
PEZ Candy
Orange, CT 203-795-0531
Philadelphia Candies
Hermitage, PA 724-981-6341
Phillips Candies
Seaside, OR 503-738-5402
Phillips Syrup Corporation
Cleveland, OH 216-661-4800
Pied-Mont/Dora
Ste Anne Des Plaines, BC 800-363-8003
Plantation Candies
Telford, PA 888-678-6468
Prince of Peace Enterprises
Hayward, CA 800-732-2328
Pulakos
Erie, PA 814-452-4026
Puratos Canada
Mississauga, ON 800-668-5537
Q Bell Foods
Nyack, NY 845-358-1475
Randag & Associates Inc
Elmhurst, IL 630-530-2830
Rapunzel Pure Organics
Chatham, NY 800-207-2814

Rich Ice Cream Company
West Palm Beach, FL 561-833-7585
Roland Industries
Saint Louis, MO 800-325-1183
Rosalind Candy Castle
New Brighton, PA 724-843-1144
Royal Wine Company
Bayonne, NJ 201-437-9131
Russell Stover Candies
Cookeville, TN 931-526-8424
Sara Lee Coffee & Tea
Earth City, MO 314-731-2500
Sara Lee Corporation
Downers Grove, IL 630-598-8100
Saxon Chocolates
Toronto, ON 416-675-6363
Sayklly's Candies   & Gifts
Escanaba, MI 906-786-3092
Scharffen Berger Choclate Maker
Berkeley, CA. 510-981-4050
Scott's Candy
Sun Prairie, WI 800-356-2100
Sea Breeze Fruit Flavors
Towaco, NJ 800-732-2733
See's Candies
Los Angeles, CA. 800-347-7337
Seller Kirk & Company
Schwenksville, PA 215-480-7342
Seth Ellis Chocolatier
Boulder, CO 720-470-3257
Shade Foods
New Century, KS 800-225-6312
Shakespeare's
Davenport, IA 800-664-4114
Shane Candy Company
Philadelphia, PA 215-922-1048
Sherwood Brands
Rockville, MD 301-309-6161
Shoemaker's Candies
Santa Fe Springs, CA 562-944-8811
Shoreline Chocolates
Alburg, VT .800-310-3730
Snack Works/Metrovox Snacks
Maywood, CA 888-224-7110
Specialty Beverages
Indian Wells, CA 626-963-5536
Spice Rack Chocolates
Fredericksburg, VA. 540-847-2063
Stutz Candy Company
Hatboro, PA. 888-692-2639
Sucesores de Pedro Cortes
San Juan, PR 787-754-7040
Sweet Shop
La Crosse, WI 608-784-7724
Sweet Traders
Huntington Beach, CA 714-903-6800
Sweetbliss by Ilene C Shane
New York, NY 212-725-6970
TCHO Ventures
San Francisco, CA 415-981-0189
Terri Lynn
Elgin, IL 800-323-0775
Theo Chocolate
Seattle, WA 206-632-5100
Tonex
Wallington, NJ 973-773-5135
Tropical Nut & Fruit Company
Orlando, FL 800-749-8869
US Chocolate Corporation
Brooklyn, NY 718-788-8555
V Chocolates
Salt Lake City, UT 801-269-8444
Valley View Blueberries
Vancouver, WA 360-892-2839
Vermont Confectionery
Shaftsbury, VT 800-545-9243
Vigneri Confections
Rochester, NY 585-254-6160
Vintage Chocolate Imports
Newark, NJ 800-207-7058
Vrymeer Commodities
St Charles, IL 630-584-0069
Weaver Nut Company
Ephrata, PA 717-738-3781
Webbs Citrus Candy
Davenport, FL. 863-422-1051
Western Syrup Company
Santa Fe Springs, CA 562-921-4485
William Bounds
Torrance, CA. 800-473-0504
Wilson Candy Company
Jeannette, PA 724-523-3151

Wisconsin Cheese
Melrose Park, IL 708-450-0074
World Confections
Brooklyn, NY 718-768-8100
World's Finest Chocolate
Chicago, IL 800-366-2462
Yoo-Hoo Chocolate Beverage Company
Carlstadt, NJ 201-933-0070
Zipp Manufacturing Company
Hornerville, OH 800-521-8700
Zitner Company
Philadelphia, PA 215-229-4990

Baking Chocolate

Ghirardelli Chocolate Company
San Leandro, CA. 800-877-9338

Boxed Chocolate

Abdallah Candies
Burnsville, MN 800-348-7328
AmeriCandy Company
Louisville, KY 502-583-1776
Andes Candy
Chicago, IL 773-838-3400
Ann Hemyng Candy
Trumbauersville, PA 800-779-7004
Astor Chocolate Corporation
Lakewood, NJ 732-901-1001
Bissinger's Handcrafted Chocolatier
St Louis, MO. 800-325-8881
Boca Bons, Inc.
Coral Springs, FL 800-314-2835
Bohemian Biscuit Company
South San Francisco, CA 800-443-6737
Brockmann Chocolates
Richmond, BC 888-494-2270
Brown & Haley
Tacoma, WA 253-620-3000
Cella's Confections
Chicago, IL. 773-838-3400
Charlotte's Confections
Millbrae, CA. 800-798-2427
Chocolates a la Carte
Valencia, CA. 800-818-2462
Chocolates by Mark
Houston, TX 713-683-3866
Chocolates Turin
Plano, TX .972-731-6771
Chris A. Papas & Son Company
Covington, KY 859-431-0499
Churchill's Confectionery
Fort Lauderdale, FL 954-764-8195
Clarks Joe Fund Raising Candies & Novelties
Tarentum, PA. 888-459-9520
Claudia B Chocolates
San Antonio, TX. 210-366-0319
Cocoline Chocolate Company
Brooklyn, NY 718-522-4500
Da Vinci Gourmet
Seattle, WA 800-640-6779
David Bradley Chocolatier
Windsor, NJ. 877-289-7933
Elmer Candy Corporation
Ponchatoula, LA. 800-843-9537
Empress Chocolate Company
Brooklyn, NY 800-793-3809
Fannie May/Fanny Farmer
Chicago, IL 800-333-3629
Faroh Candies
Cleveland, OH 440-842-4070
Fenton & Lee Chocolatiers
Eugene, OR. 800-336-8661
Frankford Candy & Chocolate Company
Philadelphia, PA 800-523-9090
Functional Foods
Roseville, MI 877-372-0550
Ganong Bros Limited   Corporate Office
St. Stephen, NB. 888-426-6647
Gertrude Hawk Chocolates
Dunmore, PA. 800-822-2032
Godiva Chocolatier
New York, NY 800-946-3482
Gold Star Chocolate
Brooklyn, NY 718-330-0187
Gorant Candies
Youngstown, OH. 800-572-4139
Gray & Company
Forest Grove, OR 800-551-6009
Hagensborg Foods
Vancouver, BC 877-554-7763

Harbor Sweets Chocolates
Salem, MA 800-243-2115
Harry London Candies
North Canton, OH. 800-321-0444
Hauser Chocolate
Westerly, RI. 888-599-8231
Hawaiian King Candies
Honolulu, HI 800-570-1902
Hershey Company
Hershey, PA 800-468-1714
Hibiscus Aloha Corporation
Honolulu, HI 808-591-8826
Hillside Candy
Hillside, NJ 800-524-1304
Horriea 2000 Food Industries
Reynolds, GA 478-847-4186
Joyva Corporation
Brooklyn, NY 718-497-0170
Koeze Company
Wyoming, MI 800-555-3909
Lammes Candies Since 1885
Austin, TX. 800-252-1885
Liberty Orchards Company
Cashmere, WA 800-888-5696
Lindt & Sprungli
Stratham, NH 800-338-0839
Long Grove ConfectioneryCompany
Buffalo Grove, IL 800-373-3102
Maggie Lyon Chocolatiers
Norcross, GA 800-969-3500
Maramor Chocolates
Columbus, OH 800-843-7722
Marshmallow Cone Company
Cincinnati, OH 800-641-8551
Maxfield Candy
Salt Lake City, UT 800-288-8002
Maxim Marketing
Aliso Viejo, CA. 800-476-2257
Michele's Chocolate Truffles
Clackamas, OR 800-656-7112
Mona Lisa® Chocolatier
Arlington, VA 866-662-5475
Munson's Chocolates
Bolton, CT .860-649-4332
Naron Mary Sue Candy Company
Baltimore, MD 410-467-9338
Nestle USA Inc
Glendale, CA 800-633-2330
Niagara Chocolates
Cheektowaga, NY 800-234-5750
Olde Country Confections
Gettysburg, PA 717-337-9971
Olympia Candies
Strongville, OH. 800-574-7747
Over The Moon Chocolate Company Ltd
Vancouver, BC 800-933-2462
Patsy's Candies
Colorado Springs, CO. 866-372-8797
Peanut Patch
Yuma, AZ .800-872-7688
Piedmont Candy Corporation
Lexington, NC 336-248-2477
Pilgrim's Pride
Lufkin, TX .936-639-1174
Quality Candy
Milwaukee, WI 800-972-2658
Queen Bee Gardens
Lovell, WY .800-225-7553
R.M. Palmer Company
Reading, PA 610-372-8971
Rene Rey Chocolates Ltd
North Vancouver, BC 888-985-0949
Reutter Candy & Chocolates
Baltimore, MD 800-392-0870
RM Palmer Company
Reading, PA 610-372-8971
Rogers' Chocolates Ltd
Victoria, BC 800-663-2220
Russell Stover Candies
Kansas City, MO. 800-477-8683
Russell Stover Candies
Cookeville, TN 931-526-8424
Sanders Candy
Clinton Twp, MI 800-852-2253
Scott's Candy
Sun Prairie, WI 800-356-2100
Seattle Chocolate Company
Tukwila, WA 800-334-3600
Stutz Candy Company
Hatboro, PA. 888-692-2639
Susie's South 40 Confections
Midland, TX 800-221-4442

Sweet Blessings
  Malibu, CA 310-317-1172
Sweet Works
  St Augustine, FL 877-261-7887
Tootsie Roll Industries
  Chicago, IL 800-877-7655
Trophy Nut Company
  Tipp City, OH 800-729-6887
Vande Walle's Candies
  Appleton, WI 920-738-7799
Vrymeer Commodities
  St Charles, IL 630-584-0069
Wilson Candy Company
  Jeannette, PA 724-523-3151
Wisconsin Cheese
  Melrose Park, IL 708-450-0074
World Confections
  Brooklyn, NY 718-768-8100
Zachary Confections
  Frankfort, IN 800-445-4222
Zitner Company
  Philadelphia, PA 215-229-4990

Carob Ingredients

Naturex (Chart Corp)
  South Hackensack, NJ 201-440-5000

Chocolate Bars

Chris Candies
  Pittsburgh, PA 412-322-9400
Dina's Organic Chocolate
  Mt Kisco, NY 888-625-2008
Divine Chocolate
  Washington, DC 202-332-8913
Eda's Sugarfree Candies
  Philadelphia, PA 215-324-3412
FunkyChunky
  Edina, MN 888-473-8659
Greenwell Farms
  Morganfield, KY 270-389-3289
Malie Kai Hawaiian Chocolates
  Honolulu, HI 808-599-8600
Munson's Chocolates
  Bolton, CT 860-649-4332
New England Confectionery Company
  Revere, MA 781-485-4500
Travel Chocolate
  Middle Village, NY 718-841-7030

Chocolate Candy

Abbott's Candy Shop
  Hagerstown, IN 877-801-1200
Acme Candy Company
  Arlington, TX 254-634-2825
Aglamesis Brothers
  Cincinnati, OH 513-531-5196
Alexandra & Nicolay
  Brooklyn, NY 718-253-9400
Alinosi French Superfine Candies
  Detroit, MI 313-527-3195
All American Snacks
  Midland, TX 800-840-2455
All Wrapped Up
  Lauderhill, FL 800-891-2194
Allen Wertz Candy
  Chino, CA 800-756-2676
Alma-Leo
  Buffalo Grove, IL 847-821-0411
Ambassador Foods
  Van Nuys, CA 800-338-3369
Ameri-Suisse Group
  Plainfield, NJ 908-222-1001
American Nut & Chocolate Company
  Boston, MA 800-797-6887
AmeriGift
  Oxnard, CA 800-421-9039
Amour Chocolates
  Albuquerque, NM 505-881-2803
Amros the Second, Inc.
  Somerset, NJ 732-846-7755
Amster-Kirtz Company
  Canton, OH 800-257-9338
Andes Candy
  Chicago, IL 773-838-3400
Andre Prost
  Old Saybrook, CT 800-243-0897
Andre's Confiserie Suisse
  Kansas City, MO 800-892-1234
Ann Hemyng Candy
  Trumbauersville, PA 800-779-7004

Anthony-Thomas Candy Company
  Columbus, OH 877-226-3921
Archibald Candy Corporation
  Chicago, IL 800-333-3629
Art CoCo Chocolate Company
  Denver, CO 800-779-8985
Ashers Chocolates
  Lewistown, PA 800-343-0520
Assouline & Ting
  Philadelphia, PA 800-521-4491
Athena's Silverland®Desserts
  Forest Park, IL 800-737-3636
Aunt Sally's Praline Shops, Inc.
  New Orleans, LA 800-642-7257
B&B Pecan Processors of NC
  Turkey, NC 866-328-7322
Baker Candy Company
  Seattle, WA 425-776-6622
Baker Maid Products, Inc.
  New Orleans, LA 504-827-5500
Bakers Candy
  Greenwood, NE 800-804-7330
Banner Candy Manufacturing Company
  Brooklyn, NY 718-647-4747
Baraboo Candy Company
  Baraboo, WI 800-967-1690
Bari & Gail
  Walpole, MA 800-828-9318
Barricini Chocolate
  Avoca, PA 570-457-6756
Barry Callebaut USA LLC
  St. Albans, VT 802-524-9711
Barry Callebaut USA, LLC
  Saint Albans, VT 800-556-8845
Bee International
  Chula Vista, CA 800-421-6465
Ben Heggy's Candy Company
  Canton, OH 330-455-7703
Bergen Marzipan & Chocolate
  Bergenfield, NJ 201-385-8343
Best Chocolate In Town
  Indianapolis, IN 888-294-2378
Bidwell Candies
  Mattoon, IL 217-234-3858
Birnn Chocolates
  Highland Park, NJ 732-545-4400
Birnn Chocolates of Vermont
  South Burlington, VT 800-338-3141
Biscomerica Corporation
  Rialto, CA 909-877-5997
Black Hound New York
  Brooklyn, NY 800-344-4417
Blanton's
  Sweetwater, TN 423-337-3487
Blommer Chocolate Company
  East Greenville, PA 800-825-8181
Bloomer Candy Company
  Zanesville, OH 800-452-7501
Bluebird Restaurant
  Logan, UT 435-752-3155
Boca Bons, Inc.
  Coral Springs, FL 800-314-2835
Bogdon Candy Company
  Kansas City, MO 800-821-6641
Bohemian Biscuit Company
  South San Francisco, CA 800-443-6737
Bourbon Ball
  Louisville, KY 800-280-0888
Boyer Candy Company
  Altoona, PA 814-944-9401
Bread & Chocolate
  Wells River, VT 800-524-6715
Brechet & Richter Company
  Minneapolis, MN 763-545-0201
Brockmann Chocolates
  Richmond, BC 888-494-2270
BT McElrath Chocolatier
  Minneapolis, MN 612-331-8800
Byrne & Carlson
  Portsmouth, NH 888-559-9778
Caiazza Candy Company
  New Castle, PA 800-651-1171
Callard & Bowser-Suchard
  White Plains, NY 877-226-3900
Cambridge Brands
  Cambridge, MA 617-491-2500
Cameo Confections
  Bay Village, OH 440-871-5732
Campbell Soup Company
  Camden, NJ 800-257-8443
Candy Factory
  Hayward, CA 800-736-6887

Candy Flowers
  Mentor, OH 888-476-6467
Canelake's
  Virginia, MN 888-928-8889
Caribbean Cookie Company
  Virginia Beach, VA 800-326-5200
Carolyn Candies
  Clermont, FL 352-394-8555
Carousel Candies
  Cicero, IL 888-656-1552
Carrie's Chocolates
  Edmonton, AB 877-778-2462
Cella's Confections
  Chicago, IL 773-838-3400
Charlotte's Confections
  Millbrae, CA 800-798-2427
Chase Candy Company
  St Joseph, MO 800-786-1625
Chevalier Chocolates
  Enfield, CT 860-741-3330
Chocoholics Divine Desserts
  Clements, CA 800-760-2462
Chocolat Belge Heyez
  St. Bruno, QC 450-653-5616
Chocolat Jean Talon
  St. Laurent, QC 888-333-8540
Chocolate Creations
  Los Angeles, CA 800-229-4140
Chocolate House
  Milwaukee, WI 800-236-2022
Chocolate Moon
  Asheville, NC 800-723-1236
Chocolate Street of Hartville
  Hartville, OH 888-853-5904
Chocolate Studio
  Norristown, PA 610-272-3872
Chocolaterie Bernard Callebaut
  Calgary, AB 800-661-8367
Chocolaterie Stam
  Des Moines, IA 877-782-6246
Chocolates a la Carte
  Valencia, CA 800-818-2462
Chocolates by Mark
  Houston, TX 713-683-3866
Chocolates by Mr. Robert
  Boca Raton, FL 561-392-3007
Chocolates El Rey
  Fredericksburg, TX 830-997-2200
Chocolati Handmade Chocolates
  Seattle, WA 206-784-5212
Chocolatier
  Exeter, NH 888-246-5528
Chocolove Premium Chocolate
  Boulder, CO 888-246-2656
Chris A. Papas & Son Company
  Covington, KY 859-431-0499
Chris Candies
  Pittsburgh, PA 412-322-9400
Christopher Norman Chocolates
  New York, NY 212-402-1243
Clark Bar America
  Revere, MA 781-485-4500
Clarks Joe Fund Raising Candies & Novelties
  Tarentum, PA 888-459-9520
Clasen Quality Coatings
  Middleton, WI 877-459-4500
Classic Confectionery
  Fort Worth, TX 800-674-4435
Classic Confections
  Atlanta, GA 800-359-7351
Clear-Vu Industries
  Ashland, MA 508-881-9100
Cloud Nine
  San Leandro, CA 201-358-8588
CNS Confectionery Products
  Bayonne, NJ 888-823-4330
Colts Chocolates
  Nashville, TN 615-251-0100
Confection Solutions
  Sylmar, CA 800-284-2422
Consolidated Brands
  Altoona, PA 814-941-2200
Consolidated Simon Distributor
  Union, NJ 973-674-2124
Cora Italian Specialties
  Countryside, IL 800-696-2672
Cowgirl Chocolates
  Moscow, ID 888-882-4098
Creative Confections
  Northbrook, IL 847-291-4128
Criterion Chocolates
  Eatontown, NJ 800-804-6060

Croft's Crackers
Monroe, WI.......................608-325-1223
Crown Candy Corporation
Macon, GA.......................800-241-3529
Cummings Studio Chocolates
Salt Lake City, UT.................800-537-3957
Dairy Management
Rosemont, IL.....................800-248-8829
Daniele Imports
Rochester, NY....................800-298-9410
Daprano & Company
South San Francisco, CA...........800-722-6333
Dare Foods
Kitchener, ON....................800-865-8225
David Bradley Chocolatier
Windsor, NJ......................877-289-7933
Davidson of Dundee
Dundee, FL.......................800-654-0647
Daymar Select Fine Coffees
El Cajon, CA.....................800-466-7590
Dayton Nut Specialties
Dayton, OH.......................800-548-1304
De Bas Chocolate
Fresno, CA.......................888-461-1276
De Bas Chocolatier
Fresno, CA.......................559-294-7638
DE Wolfgang Candy Company
York, PA.........................800-248-4273
Delancey Dessert Company
New York, NY.....................800-254-5254
DGZ Chocolates
Houston, TX......................877-949-9444
Dilettante Chocolates
Kent, WA.........................888-600-2462
Dipasa
Brownsville, TX..................956-831-5893
Divine Delights
Petaluma, CA.....................800-443-2836
Dolphin Natural Chocolates
Cambria, CA......................800-236-5744
Donaldson's Finer Chocolates
Lebanon, IN......................765-482-3334
Donells' Candies
Casper, WY.......................877-461-2009
Doscher's Candies
Cincinnati, OH...................513-381-8656
Double Play Foods
New York, NY.....................212-535-4224
Dundee Brandied Fruit Company
Dundee, OR.......................503-537-2500
Dundee Candy Shop
Louisville, KY...................502-452-9266
Ed & Don's Candies
Honolulu, HI.....................808-423-8200
Eda's Sugarfree Candies
Philadelphia, PA.................215-324-3412
Elegant Gourmet
Kirkland, WA.....................425-814-2500
Ellis Foods
Chino, CA........................909-613-0030
Emmy's Candy from Belgium
Charlotte, NC....................704-588-5445
Endangered Species Chocolate
Indianapolis, IN.................800-293-0160
Esther Price Candies & Gifts
Dayton, OH.......................800-782-0326
Euphoria Chocolate Company
Eugene, OR.......................541-344-4914
Evans Creole Candy Company
New Orleans, LA..................800-637-6675
Fabulous Chocolate Confections
Valdosta, GA.....................800-755-5785
Fairytale Brownies
Phoenix, AZ......................800-324-7982
Fancy's Candy's
Rougemont, NC....................888-403-2629
Fannie May Candies
Wheaton, IL......................630-653-3088
Fantasy Chocolates
Delray Beach, FL.................800-804-4962
Farb's
San Luis Obispo, CA..............805-543-1412
Farley's & Sathers Candy Company
Round Lake, MN...................800-533-0330
Farley's & Sathers CandyCompany
Round Lake, MN...................507-945-8181
Faroh Candies
Cleveland, OH....................440-842-4070
Fauchon
New York, NY.....................877-605-0130
Favorite Brands International
Bannockburn, IL..................847-374-0900

Fenton & Lee Chocolatiers
Eugene, OR.......................800-336-8661
Ferrero USA
Somerset, NJ.....................800-337-7376
Fitzkee's Candies
York, PA.........................717-741-1031
Flaherty
Skokie, IL.......................847-966-1005
Foley's Candies
Richmond, BC.....................888-236-5397
Forbes Chocolate
Cleveland, OH....................800-433-1090
Fralinger's
Atlantic City, NJ................800-938-2339
Frankford Candy & Chocolate Company
Philadelphia, PA.................800-523-9090
Frolic Candy Company
Farmingdale, NY..................516-756-2255
Functional Foods
Roseville, MI....................877-372-0550
Ganong Bros Limited   Corporate Office
St. Stephen, NB..................888-426-6647
Gardners Candies
Tyrone, PA.......................800-242-2639
Garry Packing
Del Rey, CA......................800-248-2126
Gene & Boots Candies
Perryopolis, PA..................800-864-4222
Genesee Farms
Oakfield, NY.....................716-343-5878
Georgia Nut Ingredients
Skokie, IL.......................877-674-2993
Germack Pistachio Company
Detroit, MI......................800-872-4006
Gertrude Hawk Chocolates
Dunmore, PA......................800-822-2032
Ghirardelli Chocolate Company
Short Hills, NJ..................800-877-9338
Ghyslain Chocolatier
Union City, IN...................866-449-7524
Gift Factory/Beverly Hills
Sylmar, CA.......................800-365-6619
GKI Foods
Brighton, MI.....................248-486-0055
Godiva Chocolatier
New York, NY.....................800-946-3482
Gold Star Chocolate
Brooklyn, NY.....................718-330-0187
Goldenberg Candy Company
Philadelphia, PA.................800-727-2439
Golf Mill Chocolate Factory
Niles, IL........................847-635-1107
Gorant Candies
Youngstown, OH...................800-572-4139
Gourmet Confections
Northbrook, IL...................847-498-1200
Govatos
Wilmington, DE...................888-799-5252
Gray & Company
Forest Grove, OR.................800-551-6009
Great Expectations Confectionery Gourmet Foods
Chicago, IL......................773-525-4865
Green County Foods
Monroe, WI.......................800-233-3564
Green Mountain Chocolates
Franklin, MA.....................508-520-7160
Greenwell Farms
Morganfield, KY..................270-389-3289
Gregg Candy & Nut Company
Munhall, PA......................412-461-0301
Gurley's Foods
Willmar, MN......................800-426-7845
H E Williams Candy Company
Chesapeake, VA...................757-545-9311
H.R. Davis Candy
Canton, OH.......................330-494-0155
Hagensborg Foods
Vancouver, BC....................877-554-7763
Harbor Sweets Chocolates
Salem, MA........................800-243-2115
Hauser Chocolate
Westerly, RI.....................888-599-8231
Hauser Chocolates
Bethel, CT.......................203-794-1861
Haven's Candies
Westbrook, ME....................800-639-6309
Hawaiian Candies & Nuts
Honolulu, HI.....................808-841-3344
Hawaiian Host
Honolulu, HI.....................888-529-4678
Hawaiian King Candies
Honolulu, HI.....................800-570-1902

Hawaiian Salrose Teas
Honolulu, HI.....................808-848-0500
Health Asure
Santa Cruz, CA...................818-577-1100
Hebert Candies
Shrewsbury, MA...................866-432-3781
Helen Grace Chocolates
Compton, CA......................800-367-4240
Helms Candy Company
Bristol, VA......................276-669-2612
Hershey Canada Inc
Dartmouth, NS....................902-469-2470
Hershey Chocolate & Confectionery Division
Pleasanton, CA...................925-460-0359
Hershey Company
Hershey, PA......................800-468-1714
Hershey International
Weston, FL.......................954-385-2600
Hialeah Products Company
Hollywood, FL....................800-923-3379
Hibiscus Aloha Corporation
Honolulu, HI.....................808-591-8826
Hillside Candy
Hillside, NJ.....................800-524-1304
Horriea 2000 Food Industries
Reynolds, GA.....................478-847-4186
Hospitality Mints
Boone, NC........................800-334-5181
Huppen Bakery
Los Angeles, CA..................323-656-7501
Huser Paul Company
Fort Wayne, IN...................260-432-0557
Hyde Candy Company
Seattle, WA......................206-322-5743
Idaho Candy Company
Boise, ID........................800-898-6986
Image Development
San Rafael, CA...................415-626-0485
Imperial Nougat Company
Santa Fe Springs, CA.............562-693-8423
Intergum North America
Winston Salem, NC................336-760-5420
International Leisure Activities
Springfield, OH..................800-782-7448
Issimo Food Group
La Jolla, CA.....................619-260-1900
Jason & Son Specialty Foods
Rancho Cordova, CA...............800-810-9093
Jerbeau Chocolate
Camarillo, CA....................800-755-3723
Jeryl's Jems
Tappan, NY.......................845-359-4715
Jo's Candies
Torrance, CA.....................800-770-1946
John F. Davis Candy Company
Scranton, PA.....................570-342-7696
Joseph Schmidt Confections
San Francisco, CA................866-237-0152
Josh Early Candies
Allentown, PA....................610-395-4321
Kara Chocolates
Orem, UT.........................800-284-5272
Karl Bissinger French Confections
St Louis, MO.....................800-325-8881
Kastner's Pastry Shop & Grocery
Surfside, FL.....................305-866-6993
Kate Latter Candy Company
Metairie, LA.....................800-825-5359
Kellbran Candies & Snacks
Tallmadge, OH....................330-794-1448
Kelly's Candies
Pittsburgh, PA...................800-523-3051
Kemach Food Products   Corporation
Brooklyn, NY.....................888-453-6224
Kennedy Candy Company
Kilgore, TX......................800-657-5258
Kennedy Gourmet
Houston, TX......................800-882-6253
Kerry Ingredients
Beloit, WI.......................608-362-1651
Key III Candies
Fort Wayne, IN...................800-752-2382
Koeze Company
Wyoming, MI......................800-555-3909
Kopper's Chocolate Specialty Company
New York, NY.....................800-325-0026
Kraft Foods Biscuit Confections & Snacks
East Hanover, NJ.................973-503-2000
L C Good Candy Company
Allentown, PA....................610-432-3290
Lake Champlain Chocolates
Burlington, VT...................800-465-5909

Lanco
Hauppauge, NY 800-938-4500
Landies Candies Company
Buffalo, NY 800-955-2634
Laymon Candy Company
San Bernardino, CA 909-825-4408
Lazzaroni USA
Saddle Brook, NJ 201-368-1240
Len Libby's Candy Shop
Scarborough, ME 207-883-4897
Les Chocolats Vadeboncoeur
Montreal, QC 800-276-8504
Lieber Chocolate & Food Products
Brooklyn, NY 718-499-0888
Lindt & Sprungli
Stratham, NH 800-338-0839
Linette Quality Chocolates
Womelsdorf, PA 610-589-4526
Long Grove ConfectioneryCompany
Buffalo Grove, IL 800-373-3102
Longford-Hamilton Company
Beaverton, OR 503-642-5661
Loretta's Authentic Pralines
New Orleans, LA 504-944-7068
Lou-Retta's Custom Chocolates
Buffalo, NY 716-833-7111
Louis J. Rheb Candy Company
Baltimore, MD 800-514-8293
Lowery's Home Made Candies
Muncie, IN 800-541-3340
Lucille's Own Make Candies
Manahawkin, NJ 800-426-9168
Lukas Confections
York, PA 717-843-0921
Lynard Company
Stamford, CT 203-323-0231
Madelaine Chocolate Novelties, Inc
Far Rockaway, NY 800-322-1505
Maggie Lyon Chocolatiers
Norcross, GA 800-969-3500
Manhattan Chocolates
Bayonne, NJ 201-339-6886
Mantrose-Haeuser Company
Westport, CT 800-344-4229
Maramor Chocolates
Columbus, OH 800-843-7722
Marich Confectionery Company
Hollister, CA 800-624-7055
Marlow Candy & Nut Company
Englewood, NJ 201-569-7606
Marshmallow Products
Cincinnati, OH 800-641-8551
Marsyl
Cody, WY 307-527-6277
Mary of Puddin Hill
Greenville, TX 800-545-8889
Mary Sue Candies
Baltimore, MD 410-467-9338
Masterfoods USA
Hackettstown, NJ 908-852-1000
Masterson Company
Milwaukee, WI 414-647-1132
Maxfield Candy
Salt Lake City, UT 800-288-8002
Mayfair Sales
Buffalo, NY 800-248-2881
Merbs Candies
St Louis, MO 314-832-7117
Merlin Candies
Harahan, LA 800-899-1549
Michele's Chocolate Truffles
Clackamas, OR 800-656-7112
Michelle Chocolatiers
Colorado Springs, CO 888-447-3654
Miesse Candies
Lancaster, PA 717-392-6011
Mille Lacs MP Company
Madison, WI 800-843-1381
Minter Weisman Company
Minneapolis, MN 800-742-5655
Mom 'N Pops
New Windsor, NY 866-368-6767
Mona Lisa Food Products
Hendersonville, NC 800-982-2546
Monogramme Confections
St Louis, MO 314-427-4099
Moon Shine Trading Company
Woodland, CA 800-678-1226
Moore's Candies
Baltimore, MD 410-426-2705
Mooresville Ice Cream Company
Mooresville, NC 704-664-5456

Morris National
Azusa, CA 626-334-5114
Mrs. London's Confections
Swampscott, MA 781-595-8140
Munson's Chocolates
Bolton, CT 860-649-4332
Muth Candies
Louisville, KY 502-585-2952
Mutiflex Company
Wyckoff, NJ 201-447-3888
Nancy's Candy
Salem, VA 540-986-0550
Naron Mary Sue Candy Company
Baltimore, MD 410-467-9338
Nassau Candy Company
Hicksville, NY 516-342-1495
Natural Rush
San Francisco, CA 415-863-2503
Neal's Chocolates
Salt Lake City, UT 801-521-6500
NECCO
Revere, MA 800-225-5508
Nestle
Franklin Park, IL 800-225-2270
Nestle Canada Inc
North York, ON. 800-563-7853
Nestle Food Group
Toronto, ON 416-535-2181
Nestle USA Inc
Glendale, CA 800-633-2330
Neuchatel Chocolates
Oxford, PA 800-597-0759
New England Confectionery Company
Revere, MA 781-485-4500
New England Natural Bakers
Greenfield, MA 800-910-2884
Newton Candy Company
Houston, TX 713-691-6969
Niagara Chocolates
Cheektowaga, NY 800-234-5750
Nora's Candy Shop
Rome, NY 888-544-8224
Northern Flair Foods
Mound, MN 888-530-4453
Northwest Chocolate Factory
Salem, OR. 503-362-1340
Novelty Specialties
San Jose, CA 408-927-6682
NSpired Natural Foods
Melville, NY 631-845-4689
Nunes Farm Almonds
Newman, CA. 209-862-3033
Oak Leaf Confections
Scarborough, ON 800-338-3631
OH Chocolate
Calgary, AB. 403-283-4612
Old Dominion Peanut Corporation
Norfolk, VA. 800-368-6887
Old Fashioned Candy
Berwyn, IL 708-788-6669
Old Monmouth Peanut Brittle
Freehold, NJ 732-462-1311
Olde Country Confections
Gettysburg, PA 717-337-9971
Olde Tyme Mercantile
Arroyo Grande, CA. 805-489-7991
Olivier's Candies
Calgary, AB. 403-266-6028
Omanhene Cocoa Bean Company
Milwaukee, WI 800-588-2462
OraLabs
Englewood, CO. 800-290-0577
Over The Moon Chocolate Company Ltd
Vancouver, BC 800-933-2462
Pacific Gold Marketing
Madera, CA. 559-661-6176
Palmer Candy Company
Sioux City, IA 800-831-0828
Pangburn Candy Company
Fort Worth, TX 817-332-8856
Paramount Chocolates
Hauppauge, NY 800-842-3000
Paron Chocolatier
New York, NY 212-481-9234
Patsy's Candies
Colorado Springs, CO. 866-372-8797
Paul's Candy Factory
Salt Lake City, UT 801-576-2547
Paulaur Corporation
Cranbury, NJ 888-398-8844
Peanut Patch
Yuma, AZ 800-872-7688

Pearl River Pastry & Chocolates
Pearl River, NY 800-632-2639
Pease's Candy Shoppe
Springfield, IL 217-523-3721
Pecan Deluxe Candy Company
Dallas, TX 800-733-3589
Pegi
Santa Ana, CA 800-292-3353
Penhurst Candy Company
Pittsburgh, PA 800-545-1336
Pennsylvania Dutch Candies
Camp Hill, PA 800-233-7082
Peter Paul Manufacturing Plant
Naugatuck, CT 800-468-1714
Pfeil & Holing
Flushing, NY 800-247-7955
Phillips Candies
Seaside, OR. 503-738-5402
Pine River Pre-Pack
Newton, WI. 920-726-4216
Pippin Snack Pecans
Albany, GA 800-554-6887
Pittsburgh Snax & Nut Company
Pittsburgh, PA 800-404-6887
Plantation Candies
Telford, PA 888-678-6468
Plyley's Candies
Lagrange, IN 260-463-3351
Prifti Candy Company
Worcester, MA 800-447-7438
Prince of Peace Enterprises
Hayward, CA 800-732-2328
Pulakos
Erie, PA 814-452-4026
Purity Candy Company
Lewisburg, PA 800-821-4748
Quality Candy
Milwaukee, WI 800-972-2658
Queen Bee Gardens
Lovell, WY 800-225-7553
Quintessential Chocolates Company
Fredericksburg, TX. 830-990-9382
Qzina Specialty Foods
Las Vegas, NV 702-451-3916
R.L. Albert & Son
Greenwich, CT 203-622-8655
Ragold Confections
Wilton Manors, FL 954-566-9092
Randag & Associates Inc
Elmhurst, IL 630-530-2830
Rebecca Ruth Candy
Frankfort, KY 800-444-3866
Rene Rey Chocolates Ltd
North Vancouver, BC 888-985-0949
Reutter Candy & Chocolates
Baltimore, MD 800-392-0870
Richard Donnelly Fine Chtes
Santa Cruz, CA 888-685-1871
Riddles' Sweet Impressions
Edmonton, AB 780-465-8085
Riverdale Fine Foods
Dayton, OH 800-548-1304
RM Palmer Company
Reading, PA 610-372-8971
Rogers' Chocolates Ltd
Victoria, BC 800-663-2220
Rosalind Candy Castle
New Brighton, PA. 724-843-1144
Rosetti Fine Foods
Clovis, CA 559-323-6450
Roseville Corporation
Mountain View, CA 888-247-9338
Royal Baltic
Brooklyn, NY 718-385-8300
Royal Wine Company
Bayonne, NJ 201-437-9131
Russell Stover Candies
Cookeville, TN 931-526-8424
S. Zitner Company
Philadelphia, PA 215-229-4990
S.L. Kaye Company
New York, NY 212-683-5600
S.P. Enterprises
Las Vegas, NV 800-746-4774
Sahagian & Associates
Oak Park, IL 800-327-9273
Sanders Candy
Clinton Twp, MI 800-852-2253
Sayklly's Candies   & Gifts
Escanaba, MI 906-786-3092
Scharffen Berger Chocolate Maker
Berkeley, CA 800-930-4528

Scott's Candy
Sun Prairie, WI 800-356-2100
Seattle Bar Company
Seattle, WA 206-601-4301
Seattle Chocolate Company
Tukwila, WA 800-334-3600
Seattle Gourmet Foods
Kent, WA. .800-800-9490
Setton International Foods
Commack, NY 800-227-4397
Shakespeare's
Davenport, IA 800-664-4114
Shane Candy Company
Philadelphia, PA 215-922-1048
Sherm Edwards Candies
Trafford, PA 800-436-5424
Sherwood Brands
Rockville, MD 301-309-6161
Shoemaker's Candies
Santa Fe Springs, CA 562-944-8811
Sifers Valomilk Candy Company
Shawnee Mission, KS. 913-722-0991
Silver Sweet Candies
Lawrence, MA 978-688-0474
Simply Lite Foods Corporation
Commack, NY 800-753-4282
Smith Enterprises
Rock Hill, SC 800-845-8311
Sorbee International
Philadelphia, PA 800-654-3997
Source Consumer Products
Westport, CT 203-222-3881
South Beach Novelties & Confectionery
Staten Island, NY 718-727-4500
South Bend Chocolate
South Bend, IN 800-301-4961
SP Enterprises
Las Vegas, NV 800-746-4774
Spangler Candy Company
Bryan, OH .888-636-4221
Spokandy Wedding Mints
Spokane, WA. 509-624-1969
Sporting Colors LLC
Manhattan, KS 888-394-2292
Squirrel Brand Company
McKinney, TX 800-624-8242
St. Jacobs Candy Company Brittles 'n More
St. Jacobs, ON. 519-884-3505
Stanchfield Farms
Milo, ME 207-732-5173
Standard Candy Company
Nashville, TN 800-226-4340
Stephany's Chocolates
Grand Junction, CO 800-888-1522
Sterling Candy
Hicksville, NY 516-932-8300
Stewart Candy Company
Waycross, GA 912-283-1970
Stockmeyer North America
Lincoln Park, NJ 973-628-7330
Storck
Chicago, IL 800-621-7772
Stutz Candy Company
Hatboro, PA. 888-692-2639
Sucesores de Pedro Cortes
San Juan, PR 787-754-7040
Suity Confection Company
Miami, FL .305-639-3300
Sun Empire Foods
Kerman, CA 800-252-4786
Supreme Chocolatier
Staten Island, NY 718-761-9600
Susie's South 40 Confections
Midland, TX 800-221-4442
Sweenor Chocolate
Wakefield, RI 800-834-3123
Sweet Blessings
Malibu, CA 310-317-1172
Sweet Candy Company
Salt Lake City, UT 800-669-8669
Sweet Shop
La Crosse, WI 608-784-7724
Sweet Shop
Fort Worth, TX 800-222-2269
Sweet Shop USA
Mt Pleasant, TX 800-222-2269
Sweet Shop USA
Mt Pleasant, TX 903-575-0033
Sweet Works
St Augustine, FL 877-261-7887
Sweet'N Low
Brooklyn, NY 718-858-4200

Tapper Candies
Cleveland, OH 216-825-1000
Tell Chocolate Corporation
Waretown, NJ 732-583-8188
Testamints
Randolph, NJ 888-879-0400
Thompson Candy Company
Meriden, CT 800-648-4058
Tic Gums
Belcamp, MD 800-899-3953
Toe-Food Chocolates and Candy
Berkeley, CA. 888-863-3663
Tom & Sally's Handmade Chocolates
Brattleboro, VT 800-827-0800
Tootsie Roll Industries
Chicago, IL 800-877-7655
Totally Chocolate
Blaine, WA 800-255-5506
Toucan Chocolates
Waban, MA 617-964-8696
Trappistine Quality Candy
Wrentham, MA 508-528-1282
Tremblay's Sweet Shop
Hayward, WI. 715-634-2785
Triple-C
Hamilton, ON 800-263-9105
Trophy Nut Company
Tipp City, OH 800-729-6887
Tropical Nut & Fruit Company
Orlando, FL. 800-749-8869
Truan's Candies
Detroit, MI .800-584-3004
Turnbull Bakeries
Chattanooga, TN. 800-488-7628
Ultimate Nut & Candy Company
Burbank, CA. 800-767-5259
Uniconfis Corporation
Atlanta, GA 770-481-0440
US Chocolate Corporation
Brooklyn, NY 718-788-8555
V L Foods
White Plains, NY 914-697-4851
Valhrona
Los Angeles, CA. 310-277-0401
Van Leer Chocolate Corporation
Hoboken, NJ 800-826-2462
Van Otis Chocolates
Manchester, NH 800-826-6847
Vande Walle's Candies
Appleton, WI 920-738-7799
Varda Chocolatier
Elizabeth, NJ. 800-448-2732
Vaughn-Russell Candy Kitchen
Greenville, SC 864-271-7786
Vermont Nut Free Chocolates
Grand Isle, VT 888-468-8373
Vigneri Confections
Rochester, NY 585-254-6160
Vitality Life Choice
Carson City, NV 800-423-8365
Vrymeer Commodities
St Charles, IL 630-584-0069
Warner-Lambert Confections
Cambridge, MA 617-491-2500
Washburn Candy Corporation
Brockton, MA. 508-588-0820
Waymouth Farms
New Hope, MN. 800-527-0094
Weaver Nut Company
Ephrata, PA 717-738-3781
Webbs Citrus Candy
Davenport, FL. 863-422-1051
Westdale Foods Company
Orland Park, IL 708-458-7774
Whetstone Candy Company
St Augustine, FL 904-825-1710
Widmans Candy Shop
Crookston, MN 218-281-1487
Wilbur Chocolate Company
Lititz, PA 800-448-1063
Wilkinson-Spitz
Yonkers, NY 914-237-5000
Williams Candy Company
Somerville, MA 617-776-0814
Williamsburg Chocolatier
Williamsburg, VA 804-966-9000
Willy Wonka Candy
Itasca, IL 888-694-2656
Wilson Candy Company
Jeannette, PA 724-523-3151
Windmill Candy
Lubbock, TX. 806-785-4688

Windsor Confections
Oakland, CA 800-860-0021
Winfrey Fudge & Candy
Rowley, MA 888-946-3739
Wisconsin Cheese
Melrose Park, IL 708-450-0074
Wisconsin Dairyland Fudge Company
Wisconsin Dells, WI 608-254-4136
Wisteria Candy Cottage
Boulevard, CA 800-458-8246
World Confections
Brooklyn, NY 718-768-8100
World's Finest Chocolate
Campbellford, ON 888-821-8452
Worldwide Sourcing LLC
Incline Village, NV 775-833-1480
Yamate Chocolatier
Highland Park, NJ. 800-433-2462
Zachary Confections
Frankfort, IN 800-445-4222
Zenobia Company
Bronx, NY .866-936-6242
Zitner Company
Philadelphia, PA 215-229-4990

Chocolate Cherries

Cambridge Brands
Cambridge, MA 617-491-2500
Cella's Confections
Chicago, IL 773-838-3400
Chris A. Papas & Son Company
Covington, KY 859-431-0499
Faroh Candies
Cleveland, OH 440-842-4070
Farr Candy Company
Idaho Falls, ID 208-522-8215
GKI Foods
Brighton, MI 248-486-0055
Godiva Chocolatier
New York, NY 800-946-3482
Gray & Company
Forest Grove, OR 503-357-3141
H.R. Davis Candy
Canton, OH 330-494-0155
Hialeah Products Company
Hollywood, FL 800-923-3379
Karl Bissinger French Confections
St Louis, MO. 800-325-8881
Lerro Candy Company
Darby, PA .610-461-8886
Lowery's Home Made Candies
Muncie, IN 800-541-3340
Marich Confectionery Company
Hollister, CA 800-624-7055
Maxfield Candy
Salt Lake City, UT 800-288-8002
Moore's Candies
Baltimore, MD 410-426-2705
New England Confectionery Company
Revere, MA. 781-485-4500
Terri Lynn
Elgin, IL 800-323-0775
Truan's Candies
Detroit, MI .800-584-3004

Chocolate Chips

ADM Cocoa
Milwaukee, WI 800-558-9958
Cocoline Chocolate Company
Brooklyn, NY 718-522-4500
GPR Company
Stowe, PA .610-326-4777
Log House Foods
Plymouth, MN. 763-546-8395
Masterson Company
Milwaukee, WI 414-647-1132
Setton International Foods
Commack, NY 800-227-4397

Chocolate Chunks

ADM Cocoa
Milwaukee, WI 800-558-9958
Mootz Candy
Pottsville, PA. 570-622-4480

Cocoa & Cocoa Products

ADM Cocoa
Milwaukee, WI 800-558-9958

ADM Cocoa
Mansfield, MA 800-637-2536
ADM Cocoa
Glassboro, NJ 856-881-4000
Al-Rite Fruits & Syrups
Miami, FL 305-652-2540
Alaska Herb Tea Company
Anchorage, AK 800-654-2764
Alexander Gourmet Imports
Mississauga, ON 800-265-5081
American Health & Nutrition
Ann Arbor, MI 734-677-5572
American Key Food Products
Closter, NJ 800-767-0237
American Nut & Chocolate Company
Boston, MA 800-797-6887
American Yeast/Lallemand
Pembroke, NH 866-920-9885
Amros the Second, Inc.
Somerset, NJ 732-846-7755
Andre's Confiserie Suisse
Kansas City, MO 800-892-1234
Andre-Boudin Bakeries
San Francisco, CA 415-882-1849
Ann Hemyng Candy
Trumbauersville, PA 800-779-7004
Archer Daniels Midland Company
Decatur, IL 800-637-5843
Associated Brands, Inc.
Medina, NY 800-265-0050
Assouline & Ting
Philadelphia, PA 800-521-4491
Aunt Aggie De's Pralines
Sinton, TX 888-772-5463
BakeMark Canada
Laval, QC 800-361-4998
Barry Callebaut USA, Inc.
Pennsauken, NJ 800-836-2626
Blommer Chocolate Company
East Greenville, PA 800-825-8181
Bourbon Ball
Louisville, KY 800-280-0888
Boyd Coffee Company
Portland, OR 800-545-4077
Bread & Chocolate
Wells River, VT 800-524-6715
Brookema Company
West Chicago, IL 630-562-2290
Calico Cottage
Amityville, NY 800-645-5345
Cambridge Brands
Cambridge, MA 617-491-2500
Campbell Soup Company
Camden, NJ 800-257-8443
Caprine Estates
Bellbrook, OH 937-848-7406
Carrie's Chocolates
Edmonton, AB 877-778-2462
Cella's Confections
Chicago, IL 773-838-3400
Chadler
Swedesboro, NJ 856-467-0099
Chatz Roasting Company
Ceres, CA 800-792-6333
Chocolat Belge Heyez
St. Bruno, QC 450-653-5616
Chocolat Jean Talon
St. Laurent, QC 888-333-8540
Chocolate Street of Hartville
Hartville, OH 888-853-5904
Chocolaterie Bernard Callebaut
Calgary, AB 800-661-8367
Chocolates by Mark
Houston, TX 713-683-3866
Cloud Nine
San Leandro, CA 201-358-8588
Cocoline Chocolate Company
Brooklyn, NY 718-522-4500
Coffee Bean International
Portland, OR 800-877-0474
Compact Industries
St Charles, IL 800-513-4262
ConAgra Grocery Products
Irvine, CA 714-680-1000
Consolidated Mills
Houston, TX 713-896-4196
Creative Confections
Northbrook, IL 847-291-4128
Crown Candy Corporation
Macon, GA 800-241-3529
Cuisinary Fine Foods
Dallas, TX 888-283-5303

Dare Foods
Kitchener, ON 800-865-8225
Davidsons
Reno, NV 800-882-5888
De Bas Chocolatier
Fresno, CA 559-294-7638
Donells' Candies
Casper, WY 877-461-2009
Doscher's Candies
Cincinnati, OH 513-381-8656
Erba Food Products
Brooklyn, NY 718-272-7700
Foley's Candies
Richmond, BC 888-236-5397
Forbes Chocolates
Cleveland, OH 800-433-1090
Gel Spice Company, Inc
Bayonne, NJ 800-922-0230
Georgia Nut Ingredients
Skokie, IL 877-674-2993
Germack Pistachio Company
Detroit, MI 800-872-4006
Ghirardelli Chocolate Company
Short Hills, NJ 800-877-9338
Givaudan Flavors
Bridgeton, MO 800-422-5444
GKI Foods
Brighton, MI 248-486-0055
Godiva Chocolatier
New York, NY 800-946-3482
Golden Foods
Commerce, CA 800-350-2462
Gourmet Confections
Northbrook, IL 847-498-1200
Govatos
Wilmington, DE 888-799-5252
Hauser Chocolates
Bethel, CT 203-794-1861
Hebert Candies
Shrewsbury, MA 866-432-3781
Herb Patch of Vermont
Bellows Falls, VT 800-282-4372
Hershey
Mississauga, ON 800-468-1714
Hershey Chocolate & Confectionery Division
Pleasanton, CA 925-460-0359
Hershey Company
Hershey, PA 800-468-1714
Hershey International
Weston, FL 954-385-2600
Hialeah Products Company
Hollywood, FL 800-923-3379
Home Bakery
Laramie, WY 307-742-2721
Jason & Son Specialty Foods
Rancho Cordova, CA 800-810-9093
Jenny's Country Kitchen
Dover, MN 800-357-3497
John F. Davis Candy Company
Scranton, PA 570-342-7696
King's Cupboard
Red Lodge, MT 800-962-6555
Koeze Company
Wyoming, MI 800-555-3909
Log House Foods
Plymouth, MN 763-546-8395
Magna Foods Corporation
City of Industry, CA 800-995-4394
Marich Confectionery Company
Hollister, CA 800-624-7055
Martha Olson's Great Foods
Sutter Creek, CA 800-973-3966
McSteven's
Vancouver, WA 800-838-1056
Merlin Candies
Harahan, LA 800-899-1549
Michelle Chocolatiers
Colorado Springs, CO 888-447-3654
Mona Lisa® Chocolatier
Arlington, VA 866-662-5475
Monster Cone
Montreal, QC 800-542-9801
Nantucket Tea Traders
Nantucket, MA 508-325-0203
Natra US
Chula Vista, CA 800-262-6216
Nestle
Franklin Park, IL 800-225-2270
Nestle Canada Inc
North York, ON 800-563-7853
New England Confectionery Company
Revere, MA 781-485-4500

New England Natural Bakers
Greenfield, MA 800-910-2884
Niagara Chocolates
Cheektowaga, NY 800-234-5750
Nora's Candy Shop
Rome, NY 888-544-8224
NSpired Natural Foods
Melville, NY 631-845-4689
OH Chocolate
Calgary, AB 403-283-4612
Olivier's Candies
Calgary, AB 403-266-6028
Paulaur Corporation
Cranbury, NJ 888-398-8844
Phillips Syrup Corporation
Cleveland, OH 216-661-4800
Pine River Pre-Pack
Newton, WI 920-726-4216
Plantation Candies
Telford, PA 888-678-6468
Quality Naturally! Foods
City of Industry, CA 888-498-6986
R.M. Palmer Company
Reading, PA 610-372-8971
Rapunzel Pure Organics
Chatham, NY 800-207-2814
Riddles' Sweet Impressions
Edmonton, AB 780-465-8085
Sara Lee Coffee & Tea
Earth City, MO 314-731-2500
Sara Lee Coffee & Tea   Wholesale Coffee & Tea
Location
Minneapolis, MN 888-246-2598
Schokinag North America
Bakersfield, CA 661-322-4020
Seller Kirk & Company
Schwenksville, PA 215-480-7342
Service Packing Company
Vancouver, BC 604-681-0264
Setton International Foods
Commack, NY 800-227-4397
Shade Foods
New Century, KS 800-225-6312
Spring Tree Maple Products
Brattleboro, VT 802-254-8784
St. Charles Trading
Lake Saint Louis, MO 800-336-1333
Sturm Foods
Manawa, WI 800-347-8876
Sucesores de Pedro Cortes
San Juan, PR 787-754-7040
Sweenor Chocolate
Wakefield, RI 800-834-3123
Terri Lynn
Elgin, IL 800-323-0775
Timber Peaks Gourmet
Parker, CO 800-982-7687
Tom & Sally's Handmade Chocolates
Brattleboro, VT 800-827-0800
Top Hat Company
Wilmette, IL 847-256-6565
Tova Industries
Louisville, KY 888-532-8682
Vande Walle's Candies
Appleton, WI 920-738-7799
Varda Chocolatier
Elizabeth, NJ 800-448-2732
Vigneri Confections
Rochester, NY 585-254-6160
Vrymeer Commodities
St Charles, IL 630-584-0069
Weber Flavors
Wheeling, IL 800-558-9078
White Coffee Corporation
Long Island City, NY 800-221-0140
Wilbur Chocolate
Lititz, PA 800-233-0139
Wilbur Chocolate Company
Lititz, PA 800-448-1063
Williamsburg Chocolatier
Williamsburg, VA 804-966-9000
Wisconsin Cheese
Melrose Park, IL 708-450-0074
Wisconsin Cheeseman
Madison, WI 608-837-5166
World's Finest Chocolate
Campbellford, ON 888-821-8452

Fudge

Bakemark Ingredients Canada
Richmond, BC 800-665-9441

Herkimer Foods
Herkimer, NY 315-895-7832
Mc Jak Candy Company
Medina, OH. 330-722-3531
Sokol & Company
Countryside, IL. 800-328-7656

Confectionery

Confectioners Crunch

Cocomira Confections
Toronto, ON 866-413-9049
Island Princess
Honolulu, HI. 866-872-8601

Confectionery

A. Battaglia Processing Company
Chicago, IL 773-523-5900
A.L. Bazzini Company
Bronx, NY 800-228-0172
Advance Food Brokers
West Bloomfield, MI 248-851-9045
Affy Tapple, LLC
Niles, IL 847-588-2900
Aglamesis Brothers
Cincinnati, OH 513-531-5196
Alinosi French Superfine Candies
Detroit, MI 313-527-3195
Amcan Industries
Elmsford, NY 914-347-4838
American Almond Products Company
Brooklyn, NY 800-825-6663
American Food Products
Methuen, MA 978-682-1855
American Key Food Products
Closter, NJ. 800-767-0237
American Licorice Company
La Porte, IN. 800-220-2399
Ames International
Fife, WA 888-469-2637
Amros the Second, Inc.
Somerset, NJ 732-846-7755
Amurol Confections Company
Yorkville, IL 630-553-4800
Andre's Confiserie Suisse
Kansas City, MO. 800-892-1234
Andrews Caramel Apples
Chicago, IL 800-305-3004
Ann Hemyng Candy
Trumbauersville, PA 800-779-7004
Archibald Candy Corporation
Chicago, IL 800-333-3629
Arway Confections
Chicago, IL 773-267-5770
Ashers Chocolates
Lewistown, PA 800-343-0520
Assouline & Ting
Philadelphia, PA 800-521-4491
Atkinson Candies Company
Lufkin, TX 936-639-2333
Aunt Aggie De's Pralines
Sinton, TX. 888-772-5463
Baker Candy Company
Seattle, WA 425-776-6622
Barry Callebaut USA, Inc.
Pennsauken, NJ 800-836-2626
Baum International
Brooklyn, NY 718-376-4508
Beehive Botanicals, Inc.
Hayward, WI. 800-233-4483
BestSweet
Mooresville, NC 888-211-5530
Betty Jane Homemade Candies
Dubuque, IA 800-642-1254
Betty Lou's Golden Smackers
McMinnville, OR 800-242-5205
Blanton's
Sweetwater, TN. 423-337-3487
Blommer Chocolate Company
East Greenville, PA 800-825-8181
Boca Bons, Inc.
Coral Springs, FL 800-314-2835
BODEGA Chocolates
Costa Mesa, CA 888-326-3342
Bogdon Candy Company
Kansas City, MO. 800-821-6641
Bourbon Ball
Louisville, KY 800-280-0888
Brach's Confections
Dallas, TX. 800-999-0204

Brennan Snacks Manufacturing
Bogalusa, LA 800-290-7486
Brenntag
Reading, PA 888-926-4151
Brenntag Pacific
Santa Fe Springs, CA 562-903-9626
Brittle Kettle
Lebanon, TN 615-449-6257
Brokay Products
Philadelphia, PA 215-676-4800
Brookside Foods
Abbotsford, BC. 877-793-3866
Burke Candy & Ingredient Corporation
Milwaukee, WI. 888-287-5350
Byrne & Carlson
Portsmouth, NH 888-559-9778
C. Howard Company
Bellport, NY 631-286-7940
Cambridge Brands
Cambridge, MA 617-491-2500
Campbell Soup Company
Camden, NJ 800-257-8443
Candy Factory
Hayward, CA 800-736-6887
Canelake's
Virginia, MN 888-928-8889
Caprine Estates
Bellbrook, OH. 937-848-7406
Carrie's Chocolates
Edmonton, AB 877-778-2462
Casani Candy Company
Philadelphia, PA 215-535-0110
Catoris Candy
New Kensington, PA. 724-335-4371
Ce De Candy
Union, NJ 800-631-7968
Ce De Candy Southern Inc
Union, NJ 800-341-2254
Cedarlane Natural Foods
Carson, CA 310-886-7720
Cella's Confections
Chicago, IL 773-838-3400
Charlotte's Confections
Millbrae, CA 800-798-2427
Chase Candy Company
St Joseph, MO. 800-786-1625
Cheese Straws & More
Monroe, LA. 800-997-1921
Chefmaster
Garden Grove, CA 800-333-7443
Cherrydale Farms
Allentown, PA 800-333-4525
Chex Finer Foods
Attleboro, MA 800-322-2434
Chocolat Belge Heyez
St. Bruno, QC 450-653-5616
Chocolat Jean Talon
St. Laurent, QC 888-333-8540
Chocolate Street of Hartville
Hartville, OH 888-853-5904
Chocolates by Mark
Houston, TX 713-683-3866
Chocolati Handmade Chocolates
Seattle, WA 206-784-5212
Chris Candies
Pittsburgh, PA 412-322-9400
Christopher Norman Chocolates
New York, NY 212-402-1243
Clark Bar America
Revere, MA. 781-485-4500
Clarks Joe Fund Raising Candies & Novelties
Tarentum, PA. 888-459-9520
Clasen Quality Coatings
Middleton, WI. 877-459-4500
Classic Confections
Atlanta, GA. 800-359-7351
Cloud Nine
San Leandro, CA. 201-358-8588
Cloverland Sweets/Priester's Pecan Company
Fort Deposit, AL. 800-523-3505
Cocoline Chocolate Company
Brooklyn, NY 718-522-4500
Coffee Bean International
Portland, OR 800-877-0474
Concord Confections
Concord, ON. 800-267-0037
Concord Foods
Brockton, MA 508-580-1700
Confection Solutions
Sylmar, CA 800-284-2422
Confectionately Yours
Buffalo Grove, IL 800-875-6978

Creative Confections
Northbrook, IL 847-291-4128
Creme Curls Bakery
Hudsonville, MI 800-466-1219
Creole Delicacies Pralines
New Orleans, LA 504-523-6425
Crown Candy Corporation
Macon, GA 800-241-3529
CTC Manufacturing
Calgary, AB. 800-668-7677
Cuisinary Fine Foods
Dallas, TX. 888-283-5303
Cummings Studio Chocolates
Salt Lake City, UT 800-537-3957
Cupid Candies
Chicago, IL 773-925-8191
Custom Industries
St Louis, MO. 314-787-2828
Dangold
Flushing, NY. 718-591-5286
Dare Foods
Kitchener, ON 800-865-8225
David Bradley Chocolatier
Windsor, NJ. 877-289-7933
Day Spring Enterprises
Cheektowaga, NY. 800-879-7677
Daymar Select Fine Coffees
El Cajon, CA. 800-466-7590
De Bas Chocolatier
Fresno, CA 559-294-7638
De Soto Confectionery & Nut Company
De Soto, GA 800-237-8689
DE Wolfgang Candy Company
York, PA 800-248-4273
Decko Products
Sandusky, OH 800-537-6143
Delta Distributors
Longview, TX 800-945-1858
Dillon Candy Company
Boston, GA 800-382-8338
Dipasa
Brownsville, TX 956-831-5893
DMH Ingredients
Libertyville, IL 847-362-9977
DNO
Columbus, OH 800-686-2366
Dolphin Natural Chocolates
Cambria, CA 800-236-5744
Donaldson's Finer Chocolates
Lebanon, IN 765-482-3334
Donells' Candies
Casper, WY. 877-461-2009
Doscher's Candies
Cincinnati, OH 513-381-8656
Doumak
Elk Grove Vlg, IL 800-323-0318
Downeast Candies
Boothbay Harbor, ME. 207-633-5178
Duo Delights
Madison, WI. 800-303-4416
EcoNatural Solutions
Boulder, CO 877-684-5159
Eda's Sugarfree Candies
Philadelphia, PA 215-324-3412
Edward & Sons Trading Company
Carpinteria, CA. 805-684-8500
El Brands
Ozark, AL 334-445-2828
Elite Industries
Syosset, NY. 888-488-3458
Elmer Candy Corporation
Ponchatoula, LA 800-843-9537
Energy Club
Pacoima, CA. 800-688-6887
Enstrom Candies
Grand Junction, CO 800-367-8766
F&F Foods
Chicago, IL 800-621-0225
Fannie May Candies
Wheaton, IL 630-653-3088
Fantazzmo Fun Stuff
Schaumburg, IL. 847-413-1700
Farley's & Sathers Candy Company
Round Lake, MN 800-533-0330
Faroh Candies
Cleveland, OH 440-842-4070
Farr Candy Company
Idaho Falls, ID 208-522-8215
Favorite Brands International
Lincolnshire, IL 847-405-5814
Fernando C Pujals & Bros
San Juan, PR 787-792-3080

Ferrara Bakery & Cafe
New York, NY 212-226-6150

Fitzkee's Candies
York, PA 717-741-1031

FNI Group LLC
Sherborn, MA 508-655-8816

Forbes Candies
Virginia Beach, VA 800-626-5898

Frankford Candy & Chocolate Company
Philadelphia, PA 800-523-9090

FrutStix Company
Santa Barbara, CA 805-965-1656

Fudge Farms
South Bend, IN 800-874-0261

G Scaccianoce & Company
Bronx, NY 718-991-4462

Gardners Candies
Tyrone, PA 800-242-2639

Gene & Boots Candies
Perryopolis, PA 800-864-4222

Georgia Nut Ingredients
Skokie, IL 877-674-2993

Germack Pistachio Company
Detroit, MI 800-872-4006

Gertrude Hawk Ingredients
Orlando, FL .800-822-2032

Ghirardelli Chocolate Company
Short Hills, NJ 800-877-9338

Gift Factory/Beverly Hills
Sylmar, CA 800-365-6619

Gimbal's Fine Candies
S San Francisco, CA 800-344-6225

Gindi Gourmet
Boulder, CO .303-473-9177

GKI Foods
Brighton, MI 248-486-0055

Gladstone Candies
Cleveland, OH 888-729-1960

Go Lightly Candy
Hillside, NJ .800-524-1304

Godiva Chocolatier
New York, NY 800-946-3482

Gold Cup Farms
Clayton, CA .800-752-1341

Golden Apples Candy Company
Southport, CT 800-776-0393

Golden Fluff Popcorn Company
Lakewood, NJ 732-367-5448

Golden Foods
Commerce, CA 800-350-2462

Golden Temple
Eugene, OR .800-964-4832

Golf Mill Chocolate Factory
Niles, IL 847-635-1107

Goodart Candy
Lubbock, TX 806-747-2600

Gourmet Confections
Northbrook, IL 847-498-1200

Gourmet Ice Cream
Palmer, MA .413-283-3740

Govatos
Wilmington, DE 888-799-5252

Gray & Company
Forest Grove, OR 503-357-3141

Green Mountain Chocolates
Franklin, MA 508-520-7160

Greenwell Farms
Morganfield, KY 270-389-3289

Grist Mill Confections
Edina, MN 952-469-4981

Gumtech International
Phoenix, AZ 602-252-7425

Gurley's Foods
Willmar, MN 800-426-7845

GWB Foods Corporation
Brooklyn, NY 718-686-9600

H.B. Trading
Totowa, NJ .973-812-1022

H.R. Davis Candy
Canton, OH 330-494-0155

Haby's Alsatian Bakery
Castroville, TX 830-931-2118

Happy Hive
Dearborn Heights, MI 313-562-3707

Harlow House Company
Atlanta, GA .404-325-1270

Harold M. Lincoln Company
Toledo, OH .800-345-4911

Hauser Chocolates
Bethel, CT 203-794-1861

Haven's Candies
Westbrook, ME 800-639-6309

Hawaii Candy
Honolulu, HI 808-836-8955

Hawaiian Salrose Teas
Honolulu, HI 808-848-0500

Hebert Candies
Shrewsbury, MA 866-432-3781

Heinemann's
Milwaukee, WI 414-265-1900

Hershey
Mississauga, ON 800-468-1714

Hershey Canada Inc
Dartmouth, NS 902-469-2470

Hershey Chocolate & Confectionery Division
Pleasanton, CA 925-460-0359

Hershey Corporation
Hershey, PA 800-468-1714

Hershey International
Weston, FL .954-385-2600

Hialeah Products Company
Hollywood, FL 800-923-3379

Holistic Products Corporation
Englewood, NJ 800-221-0308

Honey Bar/Creme de la Creme
Kingston, NY 845-331-4643

Horriea 2000 Food Industries
Reynolds, GA 478-847-4186

Hospitality Mints
Boone, NC .800-334-5181

Hospitality Mints LLC
Boone, NC .800-334-5181

J.A.M.B. Low Carb Distributor
Pompano Beach, FL 800-708-6738

James Candy Company
Atlantic City, NJ 800-441-1404

Jason & Son Specialty Foods
Rancho Cordova, CA 800-810-9093

Jelly Belly Candy Company
Fairfield, CA 800-522-3267

John F. Davis Candy Company
Scranton, PA 570-342-7696

Joyva Corporation
Brooklyn, NY 718-497-0170

Judson-Atkinson Candies
San Antonio, TX 800-962-3984

Judy's Cream Caramels
Sherwood, OR 503-819-5080

Karl Bissinger French Confections
St Louis, MO 800-325-8881

Kay Foods Company
Ionia, MI 616-527-0120

Kellogg's
Chicago, IL 800-323-4064

Kemach Food Products Corporation
Brooklyn, NY 888-453-6224

Kennedy Candy Company
Kilgore, TX .800-657-5258

Kerr Brothers
Toronto, ON 416-252-7341

Kerry Ingredients
Beloit, WI .608-362-1651

Key III Candies
Fort Wayne, IN 800-752-2382

KHS-Bartelt
Sarasota, FL 800-829-9980

Kloss Manufacturing Company
Allentown, PA 800-445-7100

Koeze Company
Wyoming, MI 800-555-3909

Kolatin Real Kosher Gelatin
Lakewood, NJ 732-364-8700

Kopper's Chocolate Specialty Company
New York, NY 800-325-0026

Labrada Nutrition
Houston, TX 281-209-2137

Lanco
Hauppauge, NY 800-938-4500

Landies Candies Company
Buffalo, NY 800-955-2634

Landrin USA
Wilmington, DE 302-250-4394

Laura Paige Candy Company
Newburgh, NY 845-566-4209

Laymon Candy Company
San Bernardino, CA 909-825-4408

Leader Candies
Brooklyn, NY 718-366-6900

Lerro Candy Company
Darby, PA .610-461-8886

Libs Candies Downtown
Evansville, IN 812-422-5119

Log House Foods
Plymouth, MN 763-546-8395

Long Grove ConfectioneryCompany
Buffalo Grove, IL 800-373-3102

Lou-Retta's Custom Chocolates
Buffalo, NY 716-833-7111

Lou-Rod Candy
Lewiston, ME 207-784-5822

Louis J. Rheb Candy Company
Baltimore, MD 800-514-8293

Lowery's Home Made Candies
Muncie, IN 800-541-3340

Lukas Confections
York, PA 717-843-0921

MacFarms of Hawaii
Captain Cook, HI 808-328-2435

Magna Foods Corporation
City of Industry, CA 800-995-4394

Maple Grove Farms of Vermont
St Johnsbury, VT 800-525-2540

Marich Confectionery Company
Hollister, CA 800-624-7055

Marie's Candies
West Liberty, OH 866-465-5781

Maris Candy
Chicago, IL 773-254-3351

Mary of Puddin Hill
Greenville, TX 800-545-8889

Mary's Candy Shop
Lewiston, ME 207-783-9824

Marzipan Specialties
Nashville, TN 615-226-4800

Masterson Company
Milwaukee, WI 414-647-1132

Matangos Candies
Harrisburg, PA 717-234-0882

Maxfield Candy
Salt Lake City, UT 800-288-8002

Mayfair Sales
Buffalo, NY 800-248-2881

McCraw Candies
Farmersville, TX 800-551-7201

Merbs Candies
St Louis, MO 314-832-7117

Mercado Latino
City of Industry, CA 626-333-6862

Merlin Candies
Harahan, LA 800-899-1549

Michelle Chocolatiers
Colorado Springs, CO 888-447-3654

Midwest/Northern
Minneapolis, MN 800-328-5502

Mille Lacs MP Company
Madison, WI 800-843-1381

Milsolv Corporation
Butler, WI .800-558-8501

Milton A. Klein Company
New York, NY 800-221-0248

Mitch Chocolate
Melville, NY 631-777-2400

Mitsubishi Chemical America
White Plains, NY 914-286-3600

Moon Shine Trading Company
Woodland, CA 800-678-1226

Moore's Candies
Baltimore, MD 410-426-2705

Mootz Candy
Pottsville, PA 570-622-4480

Morris National
Azusa, CA .626-334-5114

Mrs. Annie's Peanut Patch
Floresville, TX 830-393-7845

Multiflex Company
Wyckoff, NJ 201-447-3888

Munson's Chocolates
Bolton, CT 860-649-4332

Muth Candies
Louisville, KY 502-585-2952

My Daddy's Cheesecake
Cape Girardeau, MO 800-735-6765

My Sister's Caramels
Redlands, CA 909-792-6242

MYNTZ!
Seattle, WA 253-395-0401

Nabisco Food Group
Kendallville, IN 260-347-1300

Nabisco LifeSavers Company
Holland, MI 616-396-1411

Naron Mary Sue Candy Company
Baltimore, MD 410-467-9338

Natural Quick Foods
Seattle, WA 206-365-5757

Nature's Candy
Fredericksburg, TX 800-729-0085

Naylor Candies
Mt Wolf, PA 717-266-2706
Nestle
Franklin Park, IL 800-225-2270
Nestle Canada Inc
North York, ON 800-563-7853
Nestle Food Group
Toronto, ON 416-535-2181
Nestle USA Inc
Glendale, CA 800-633-2330
New England Confectionery Company
Revere, MA 781-485-4500
New England Natural Bakers
Greenfield, MA 800-910-2884
Niagara Chocolates
Cheektowaga, NY 800-234-5750
Nomura Tofu Company
Chicago, IL 773-486-7224
Nora's Candy Shop
Rome, NY 888-544-8224
Northwest Candy Emporium
Everett, WA 800-404-7266
Northwest Chocolate Factory
Salem, OR 503-362-1340
Novartis Nutrition Corporation
Minneapolis, MN 952-848-6000
NSpired Natural Foods
Melville, NY 631-845-4689
Nunes Farm Almonds
Newman, CA 209-862-3033
Oak Leaf Confections
Scarborough, ON 800-338-3631
OCG Cacao
Whitinsville, MA 888-482-2226
OH Chocolate
Calgary, AB 403-283-4612
Old Fashioned Candy
Berwyn, IL 708-788-6669
Olde Tyme Food Corporation
East Longmeadow, MA 800-356-6533
Olde Tyme Mercantile
Arroyo Grande, CA 805-489-7991
Ole Smoky Candy Kitchen
Gatlinburg, TN 865-436-4886
Olivier's Candies
Calgary, AB 403-266-6028
Olmarc Packaging Company
Chicago, IL 708-562-2000
Original Nut House Brands
El Paso, TX 800-726-7222
Palmer Candy Company
Sioux City, IA 800-831-0828
Parker Products
Fort Worth, TX 800-433-5749
Parkside Candy Company
Buffalo, NY 716-833-7540
Paul's Candy Company
Sandy, UT 801-576-2547
Paulaur Corporation
Cranbury, NJ 888-398-8844
PB&S Chemicals
Henderson, KY 800-950-7267
Peanut Patch
Courtland, VA 866-732-6883
Pecan Deluxe Candy Company
Dallas, TX 800-733-3589
PEZ Candy
Orange, CT 203-795-0531
Pez Manufacturing Corporation
Orange, CT 203-795-0531
Pfizer
Parsippany, NJ 973-541-5900
Philadelphia Candies
Hermitage, PA 724-981-6341
Phillips Candies
Seaside, OR 503-738-5402
Pine River Pre-Pack
Newton, WI 920-726-4216
Pioneer Confections
Chicago, IL 773-281-6100
Pioneer Marketing International
Los Gatos, CA 408-356-4990
Pittsburgh Snax & Nut Company
Pittsburgh, PA 800-404-6887
Plaidberry Company
Vista, CA 760-727-5403
Plantation Candies
Telford, PA 888-678-6468
Popcorn Connection
North Hollywood, CA 800-852-2676
Poppers Supply Company
Portland, OR 503-239-3792

Priester Pecan Company
Fort Deposit, AL 800-277-3226
Prince of Peace Enterprises
Hayward, CA 800-732-2328
Produits Alimentaire
St Lambert De Lauzon, QC 800-463-1787
Progress Candy
Winnipeg, NB 204-586-8027
Pulakos
Erie, PA 814-452-4026
QA Products
Elk Grove Vlg, IL 800-635-7907
Quigley Manufacturing
Elizabethtown, PA 800-367-2441
R.M. Palmer Company
Reading, PA 610-372-8971
Randag & Associates Inc
Elmhurst, IL 630-530-2830
Rebecca Ruth Candy
Frankfort, KY 800-444-3866
Richards Maple Products
Chardon, OH 800-352-4052
Ricos Candy Snacks & Bakery
Hialeah, FL 305-885-7392
Riddles' Sweet Impressions
Edmonton, AB 780-465-8085
Rito Mints
Trois Rivieres, QC 819-379-1449
Rivard Popcorn Products
Landisville, PA 717-898-7131
Rosalind Candy Castle
New Brighton, PA 724-843-1144
Ross Fine Candies
Waterford, MI 248-682-5640
Royal Wine Company
Bayonne, NJ 201-437-9131
Russell Stover Candies
Marion, SC 843-423-3022
Russell Stover Candies
Cookeville, TN 931-526-8424
Ruth Hunt Candies
Mt Sterling, KY 800-927-0302
Sacharen Brothers
Montreal, QC 514-277-8205
Salem Old Fashioned Candies
Salem, MA 978-744-3242
Sally Lane's Candy Farm
Paris, TN 731-642-5801
Sayklly's Candies   & Gifts
Escanaba, MI 906-786-3092
Scott's Candy
Sun Prairie, WI 800-356-2100
Seasons' Enterprises
Addison, IL 630-628-0211
See's Candies
Los Angeles, CA 800-347-7337
Seeley & Son Apiaries
Brooks, OR 503-792-3523
Segovia Mexican Candy Manufacturer
San Antonio, TX 210-225-2102
Senor Murphy Candymaker
Santa Fe, NM 877-988-4311
Sensational Sweets
Lewisburg, PA 570-524-4361
Shade Foods
New Century, KS 800-225-6312
Shane Candy Company
Philadelphia, PA 215-922-1048
Shari Candies
Edina, MN 800-658-7059
Sherm Edwards Candies
Trafford, PA 800-436-5424
Sherwood Brands
Rockville, MD 301-309-6161
Shoemaker's Candies
Santa Fe Springs, CA 562-944-8811
Signature Brands
Ocala, FL 800-456-9573
Simply Gourmet Confections
Irvine, CA 714-505-3955
Snackerz
Commerce, CA 888-576-2253
Somerset Syrup & Beverage
Edison, NJ 800-526-8865
Southchem
Durham, NC 800-849-7000
Southern Style Nuts
Sherman, TX 800-624-8242
Splendid Specialties
Novato, CA 415-506-3000
Star Kay White
Congers, NY 800-874-8518

Starbucks Coffee Company
Seattle, WA 800-782-7282
Stark Candy Company
Pewaukee, WI 800-558-2300
Stark Candy Company
Revere, MA 800-621-1983
Startup's Candy Company
Provo, UT 801-373-8673
Stichler Products
Reading, PA 610-921-0211
Stone's Home Made Candy Shop
Oswego, NY 888-223-3928
Stutz Candy Company
Hatboro, PA 888-692-2639
Sucesores de Pedro Cortes
San Juan, PR 787-754-7040
Sugar Plum Farm
Plumtree, NC 888-257-0019
Sunline Brands
Saint Louis, MO 314-638-5770
Sweenor Chocolate
Wakefield, RI 800-834-3123
Sweet City Supply
Virginia Beach, VA 888-793-3824
Sweet Productions
Jericho, NY 631-842-0548
Sweet Shop
La Crosse, WI 608-784-7724
Sweet Shop
Fort Worth, TX 800-222-2269
Sweet Works
St Augustine, FL 877-261-7887
Taste of Nature
Beverly Hills, CA 310-396-4433
Taste Teasers
Dallas, TX 800-526-1840
Temo's Candy
Akron, OH 330-376-7229
Texas Toffee
Odessa, TX 432-563-4105
Tim's Cascade Chips
Algona, WA 800-533-8467
Todd's
Vernon, CA 800-938-6337
Tom & Sally's Handmade Chocolates
Brattleboro, VT 800-827-0800
Topps Company
Duryea, PA 570-457-6761
Torn & Glasser
Los Angeles, CA 800-282-6887
Torn Ranch
Novato, CA 415-506-3000
Tropical
Charlotte, NC 800-220-1413
Tropical
Columbus, OH 800-538-3941
Tropical
Marietta, GA 800-544-3762
Tropical Nut & Fruit Company
Orlando, FL 800-749-8869
Vande Walle's Candies
Appleton, WI 920-738-7799
Varda Chocolatier
Elizabeth, NJ 800-448-2732
Variety Foods
Warren, MI 586-268-4900
Vigneri Confections
Rochester, NY 585-254-6160
Vrymeer Commodities
St Charles, IL 630-584-0069
Warner Candy
El Paso, TX 847-928-7200
Warrell Corporation
Camp Hill, PA 800-233-7082
Waymouth Farms
New Hope, MN 800-527-0094
Weaver Nut Company
Ephrata, PA 717-738-3781
Weaver Popcorn Company
Indianapolis, IN 800-999-2365
Webbs Citrus Candy
Davenport, FL 863-422-1051
Wedding Cake Studio
Williamsfield, OH 440-667-1765
Westbrae Natural Foods
Garden City, NY 800-434-4246
White-Stokes Company
Chicago, IL 800-978-6537
Wiggin Farms
Arbuckle, CA 530-476-2288
Wilbur Chocolate Company
Lititz, PA 800-448-1063

Williamsburg Chocolatier
Williamsburg, VA 804-966-9000
Willy Wonka Candy Factory
Itasca, IL 630-773-0267
Wilson Candy Company
Jeannette, PA 724-523-3151
Wilson's Fantastic Candy
Memphis, TN 901-767-1900
Winans Chocolates & Coffees
Piqua, OH 937-773-1981
Wing Candy Company
Branson, MO 417-334-3238
Wisconsin Cheese
Melrose Park, IL 708-450-0074
Wisconsin Cheeseman
Madison, WI 608-837-5166
World Confections
Brooklyn, NY 718-768-8100
World's Finest Chocolate
Campbellford, ON 888-821-8452
Wright Ice Cream
Cayuga, IN 800-686-9561
Wrigley Company
Don Mills, ON 416-449-8600
Wrigley Manufacturing Company
Flowery Branch, GA 770-967-6181
Xcell International Corporation
Lemont, IL 800-722-7751
Yamate Chocolatier
Highland Park, NJ 800-433-2462
Yost Candy Company
Dalton, OH 800-750-1976
Zitner Company
Philadelphia, PA 215-229-4990

Decorations & Icings

Decorations

Baking

Chefmaster
Garden Grove, CA 800-333-7443
Nuvex Ingredients
Blue Earth, MN 507-526-4331
Signature Brands
Ocala, FL 800-456-9573

Cake

Adams Foods
Dothan, AL 334-983-4233
American Key Food Products
Closter, NJ 800-767-0237
BakeMark Canada
Laval, QC 800-361-4998
Bakery Crafts
West Chester, OH 800-543-1673
Chefmaster
Garden Grove, CA 800-333-7443
Decko Products
Sandusky, OH 800-537-6143
El Segundo Bakery
El Segundo, CA 310-322-3422
Erba Food Products
Brooklyn, NY 718-272-7700
Lucks Food Decorating Company
Tacoma, WA 800-426-9778
Multiflex Company
Wyckoff, NJ 201-447-3888
Paulaur Corporation
Cranbury, NJ 888-398-8844
Petra International
Hamilton, ON 800-261-7226
QA Products
Elk Grove Vlg, IL 800-635-7907
Signature Brands
Ocala, FL 800-456-9573
Sugar Flowers Plus
Glendale, CA 800-972-2935

Icings

ACH Food Companies, Inc.
Cordova, TN 800-691-1106
BakeMark Canada
Laval, QC 800-361-4998
Bakemark Ingredients Canada
Richmond, BC 800-665-9441
Baker & Baker, Inc.
Schaumburg, IL 800-593-5777
Best Brands Corporation
Dallas, TX 800-969-2253

Charles Dennery Pillsbury
New Orleans, LA 504-733-2331
Chefmaster
Garden Grove, CA 800-333-7443
Chelsea Milling Company
Chelsea, MI 734-475-1361
Cremes Unlimited
Matteson, IL 800-227-3637
Dawn Food Products
Louisville, KY 800-626-2542
Erba Food Products
Brooklyn, NY 718-272-7700
Frostbite
Toledo, OH 800-968-7711
H.C. Brill Company
Tucker, GA 800-241-8526
Lawrence Foods
Elk Grove Vlg, IL 800-323-7848
Louisiana Gourmet Enterprises
Houma, LA 800-328-5586
Millers Ice Cream
Houston, TX 713-861-3138
Mimac Glaze
Brampton, ON 877-990-9975
Morningstar Foods
Dallas, TX 225-273-2803
Newport Flavours & Fragrances
Orange, CA 714-628-9894
Parrish's Cake Decorating Supplies
Gardena, CA 800-736-8443
Price's Creameries
El Paso, TX 915-565-2711
Quality Naturally! Foods
City of Industry, CA 888-498-6986
RIBUS
St Louis, MO 314-727-4287
Snelgrove Ice Cream Company
Salt Lake City, UT 800-569-0005
Sokol & Company
Countryside, IL 800-328-7656
Warwick Ice Cream Company
Warwick, RI 401-821-8403
Westco-Bake Mark
Pico Rivera, CA 562-949-1054

Ready to Use

Allen Canning Company
Siloam Springs, AR 800-234-2553
H.C. Brill Company
Tucker, GA 800-241-8526
Presto Avoset Group
Claremont, CA 909-399-0062

Specialty-Packaged Candy

Bagged

American Licorice Company
La Porte, IN 800-220-2399
Ann Hemyng Candy
Trumbausville, PA 800-779-7004
Bloomer Candy Company
Zanesville, OH 800-452-7501
Bohemian Biscuit Company
South San Francisco, CA 800-443-6737
Brach's Confections
Dallas, TX 800-999-0204
Cambridge Brands
Cambridge, MA 617-491-2500
Ce De Candy Southern Inc
Union, NJ 800-341-2254
Chase Candy Company
St Joseph, MO 800-786-1625
Chris A. Papas & Son Company
Covington, KY 859-431-0499
Cocoline Chocolate Company
Brooklyn, NY 718-522-4500
Crown Candy Corporation
Macon, GA 800-241-3529
David Bradley Chocolatier
Windsor, NJ 877-289-7933
Eda's Sugarfree Candies
Philadelphia, PA 215-324-3412
GKI Foods
Brighton, MI 248-486-0055
Go Lightly Candy
Hillside, NJ 800-524-1304
Golden Apples Candy Company
Southport, CT 800-776-0393
Hialeah Products Company
Hollywood, FL 800-923-3379

Jelly Belly Candy Company
Fairfield, CA 800-522-3267
Joyva Corporation
Brooklyn, NY 718-497-0170
Judson-Atkinson Candies
San Antonio, TX 800-962-3984
Leader Candies
Brooklyn, NY 718-366-6900
Ludwick's Frozen Donuts
Grand Rapids, MI 800-366-8816
Lukas Confections
York, PA 717-843-0921
New England Confectionery Company
Revere, MA 781-485-4500
Olde Tyme Mercantile
Arroyo Grande, CA 805-489-7991
Peter Paul Manufacturing Plant
Naugatuck, CT 800-468-1714
Piedmont Candy Corporation
Lexington, NC 336-248-2477
Pilgrim's Pride
Lufkin, TX 936-639-1174
Quigley Manufacturing
Elizabethtown, PA 800-367-2441
Randag & Associates Inc
Elmhurst, IL 630-530-2830
Russell Stover Candies
Cookeville, TN 931-526-8424
Salem Old Fashioned Candies
Salem, MA 978-744-3242
Sherwood Brands
Rockville, MD 301-309-6161
Stark Candy Company
Pewaukee, WI 800-558-2300
Sunline Brands
Saint Louis, MO 314-638-5770
Weaver Nut Company
Ephrata, PA 717-738-3781
Webbs Citrus Candy
Davenport, FL 863-422-1051
World Confections
Brooklyn, NY 718-768-8100
Yost Candy Company
Dalton, OH 800-750-1976

Boxed

Anastasia Confections, Inc.
Orlando, FL 800-329-7100
Anthony-Thomas Candy Company
Columbus, OH 877-226-3921
Arcor USA
Coral Gables, FL 800-572-7267
Astor Chocolate Corporation
Lakewood, NJ 732-901-1001
Baraboo Candy Company
Baraboo, WI 800-967-1690
Best Chocolate In Town
Indianapolis, IN 888-294-2378
Blanton's
Sweetwater, TN 423-337-3487
Blommer Chocolate Company
East Greenville, PA 800-825-8181
Boyer Candy Company
Altoona, PA 814-944-9401
Chocolate House
Milwaukee, WI 800-236-2022
Ghirardelli Chocolate Company
San Leandro, CA 800-877-9338
GKI Foods
Brighton, MI 248-486-0055
Mona Lisa® Chocolatier
Arlington, VA 866-642-5475
Naron Mary Sue Candy Company
Baltimore, MD 410-467-9338
Peter Paul Manufacturing Plant
Naugatuck, CT 800-468-1714
Ruth Hunt Candies
Mt Sterling, KY 800-927-0302
Scott's Candy
Sun Prairie, WI 800-356-2100
Terri Lynn
Elgin, IL 800-323-0775

Christmas

Atkinson Candies Company
Lufkin, TX 936-639-2333
Bee International
Chula Vista, CA 800-421-6465
Blanton's
Sweetwater, TN 423-337-3487

Bohemian Biscuit Company
South San Francisco, CA 800-443-6737
Brach's Confections
Dallas, TX 800-999-0204
Ce De Candy Southern Inc
Union, NJ 800-341-2254
Charlotte's Confections
Millbrae, CA 800-798-2427
Chase Candy Company
St Joseph, MO 800-786-1625
Chocolat Jean Talon
St. Laurent, QC 888-333-8540
Chris A. Papas & Son Company
Covington, KY 859-431-0499
Clark Bar America
Revere, MA 781-485-4500
David Bradley Chocolatier
Windsor, NJ 877-289-7933
Day Spring Enterprises
Cheektowaga, NY 800-879-7677
Doscher's Candies
Cincinnati, OH 513-381-8656
Elegant Gourmet
Kirkland, WA 425-814-2500
Ferrara Bakery & Cafe
New York, NY 212-226-6150
Garry Packing
Del Rey, CA 800-248-2126
Gimbal's Fine Candies
S San Francisco, CA 800-344-6225
GKI Foods
Brighton, MI 248-486-0055
Gladstone Candies
Cleveland, OH 888-729-1960
H.R. Davis Candy
Canton, OH 330-494-0155
Haven's Candies
Westbrook, ME 800-639-6309
Jelly Belly Candy Company
Fairfield, CA 800-522-3267
John F. Davis Candy Company
Scranton, PA 570-342-7696
Judson-Atkinson Candies
San Antonio, TX 800-962-3984
Kennedy Candy Company
Kilgore, TX 800-657-5258
Landies Candies Company
Buffalo, NY 800-955-2634
Leader Candies
Brooklyn, NY 718-366-6900
Lukas Confections
York, PA 717-843-0921
Mona Lisa® Chocolatier
Arlington, VA 866-662-5475
Novartis Nutrition Corporation
Minneapolis, MN 952-848-6000
Old Dominion Peanut Corporation
Norfolk, VA. 800-368-6887
Peerless Confection Company
Lincolnwood, IL 773-281-6100
Piedmont Candy Corporation
Lexington, NC 336-248-2477
R.M. Palmer Company
Reading, PA 610-372-8971
Randag & Associates Inc
Elmhurst, IL 630-530-2830
Setton International Foods
Commack, NY 800-227-4397
Shane Candy Company
Philadelphia, PA 215-922-1048
Sherwood Brands
Rockville, MD 301-309-6161
Stark Candy Company
Pewaukee, WI 800-558-2300
Sunline Brands
Saint Louis, MO 314-638-5770
Wisconsin Cheese
Melrose Park, IL 708-450-0074
World Confections
Brooklyn, NY 718-768-8100

Easter

Bee International
Chula Vista, CA 800-421-6465
Blanton's
Sweetwater, TN. 423-337-3487
Bohemian Biscuit Company
South San Francisco, CA 800-443-6737
Ce De Candy Southern Inc
Union, NJ 800-341-2254

Charlotte's Confections
Millbrae, CA. 800-798-2427
Chase Candy Company
St Joseph, MO 800-786-1625
Chocolat Jean Talon
St. Laurent, QC 888-333-8540
Chris A. Papas & Son Company
Covington, KY 859-431-0499
Clark Bar America
Revere, MA 781-485-4500
David Bradley Chocolatier
Windsor, NJ. 877-289-7933
Day Spring Enterprises
Cheektowaga, NY. 800-879-7677
Doscher's Candies
Cincinnati, OH 513-381-8656
Elegant Gourmet
Kirkland, WA 425-814-2500
Ferrara Bakery & Cafe
New York, NY 212-226-6150
Gimbal's Fine Candies
S San Francisco, CA 800-344-6225
GKI Foods
Brighton, MI 248-486-0055
Gladstone Candies
Cleveland, OH 888-729-1960
Golden Fluff Popcorn Company
Lakewood, NJ 732-367-5448
Jelly Belly Candy Company
Fairfield, CA. 800-522-3267
Judson-Atkinson Candies
San Antonio, TX 800-962-3984
Leader Candies
Brooklyn, NY 718-366-6900
Mona Lisa® Chocolatier
Arlington, VA 866-662-5475
Multiflex Company
Wyckoff, NJ 201-447-3888
New England Confectionery Company
Revere, MA 781-485-4500
Piedmont Candy Corporation
Lexington, NC 336-248-2477
R.M. Palmer Company
Reading, PA 610-372-8971
Sayklly's Candies   & Gifts
Escanaba, MI 906-786-3092
Sherwood Brands
Rockville, MD 301-309-6161
Stark Candy Company
Pewaukee, WI 800-558-2300
Sunline Brands
Saint Louis, MO 314-638-5770
Vande Walle's Candies
Appleton, WI 920-738-7799
Variety Foods
Warren, MI 586-268-4900
Vigneri Confections
Rochester, NY 585-254-6160
Wisconsin Cheese
Melrose Park, IL 708-450-0074
World Confections
Brooklyn, NY 718-768-8100
Zitner Company
Philadelphia, PA 215-229-4990

Fund Raising

Ce De Candy Southern Inc
Union, NJ 800-341-2254
Chase Candy Company
St Joseph, MO. 800-786-1625
Chris A. Papas & Son Company
Covington, KY 859-431-0499
Clarks Joe Fund Raising Candies & Novelties
Tarentum, PA. 888-459-9520
David Bradley Chocolatier
Windsor, NJ. 877-289-7933
Go Lightly Candy
Hillside, NJ 800-524-1304
Joyva Corporation
Brooklyn, NY 718-497-0170
Koeze Company
Wyoming, MI 800-555-3909
Leader Candies
Brooklyn, NY 718-366-6900
Lukas Confections
York, PA 717-843-0921
New England Confectionery Company
Revere, MA 781-485-4500
Novartis Nutrition Corporation
Minneapolis, MN 952-848-6000

Old Dominion Peanut Corporation
Norfolk, VA. 800-368-6887
Quigley Manufacturing
Elizabethtown, PA. 800-367-2441
Randag & Associates Inc
Elmhurst, IL 630-530-2830
Sherwood Brands
Rockville, MD 301-309-6161
Sweet Productions
Jericho, NY. 631-842-0548
Terri Lynn
Elgin, IL 800-323-0775
Vande Walle's Candies
Appleton, WI 920-738-7799
Wisconsin Cheese
Melrose Park, IL 708-450-0074

Halloween

Astor Chocolate Corporation
Lakewood, NJ 732-901-1001
Atkinson Candies Company
Lufkin, TX 936-639-2333
Atkinson Candy Company
Lufkin, TX 800-231-1203
Bee International
Chula Vista, CA 800-421-6465
Blanton's
Sweetwater, TN. 423-337-3487
Bohemian Biscuit Company
South San Francisco, CA 800-443-6737
Brach's Confections
Dallas, TX. 800-999-0204
Ce De Candy Southern Inc
Union, NJ 800-341-2254
Charlotte's Confections
Millbrae, CA 800-798-2427
Chase Candy Company
St Joseph, MO. 800-786-1625
Chocolat Jean Talon
St. Laurent, QC 888-333-8540
Clark Bar America
Revere, MA 781-485-4500
David Bradley Chocolatier
Windsor, NJ. 877-289-7933
Day Spring Enterprises
Cheektowaga, NY. 800-879-7677
Elegant Gourmet
Kirkland, WA 425-814-2500
Ferrara Bakery & Cafe
New York, NY 212-226-6150
Gimbal's Fine Candies
S San Francisco, CA 800-344-6225
GKI Foods
Brighton, MI. 248-486-0055
Gladstone Candies
Cleveland, OH 888-729-1960
Jelly Belly Candy Company
Fairfield, CA 800-522-3267
Joyva Corporation
Brooklyn, NY 718-497-0170
Judson-Atkinson Candies
San Antonio, TX 800-962-3984
Leader Candies
Brooklyn, NY 718-366-6900
Lukas Confections
York, PA 717-843-0921
New England Confectionery Company
Revere, MA. 781-485-4500
Novartis Nutrition Corporation
Minneapolis, MN 952-848-6000
Peter Paul Manufacturing Plant
Naugatuck, CT 800-468-1714
Piedmont Candy Corporation
Lexington, NC 336-248-2477
R.M. Palmer Company
Reading, PA 610-372-8971
Shane Candy Company
Philadelphia, PA 215-922-1048
Sherwood Brands
Rockville, MD 301-309-6161
Sunline Brands
Saint Louis, MO 314-638-5770
World Confections
Brooklyn, NY 718-768-8100
Yost Candy Company
Dalton, OH 800-750-1976

Multi-Packs

Mona Lisa® Chocolatier
Arlington, VA 866-662-5475

New England Confectionery Company
  Revere, MA 781-485-4500
Peter Paul Manufacturing Plant
  Naugatuck, CT 800-468-1714
Sunline Brands
  Saint Louis, MO 314-638-5770
Wisconsin Cheese
  Melrose Park, IL 708-450-0074
World Confections
  Brooklyn, NY 718-768-8100

Non-Chocolate - Boxed

Go Lightly Candy
  Hillside, NJ 800-524-1304
Hershey International
  Weston, FL 954-385-2600
Leader Candies
  Brooklyn, NY 718-366-6900
Moore's Candies
  Baltimore, MD 410-426-2705
NECCO
  Revere, MA 800-225-5508
Ozone Confectioners & Bakers Supplies
  Elmwood Park, NJ 201-791-4444
Stark Candy Company
  Pewaukee, WI 800-558-2300
Webbs Citrus Candy
  Davenport, FL 863-422-1051
Willy Wonka Candy Factory
  Itasca, IL 630-773-0267

Packaged for Racks

American Licorice Company
  La Porte, IN 800-220-2399
Ce De Candy Southern Inc
  Union, NJ 800-341-2254
David Bradley Chocolatier
  Windsor, NJ 877-289-7933
Golden Apples Candy Company
  Southport, CT 800-776-0393
Jason & Son Specialty Foods
  Rancho Cordova, CA 800-810-9093
Jelly Belly Candy Company
  Fairfield, CA 800-522-3267
Jo Mints
  Corona Del Mar, CA 877-566-4687
Joyva Corporation
  Brooklyn, NY 718-497-0170
Mona Lisa® Chocolatier
  Arlington, VA 866-662-5475
New England Confectionery Company
  Revere, MA 781-485-4500
Setton International Foods
  Commack, NY 800-227-4397
Stark Candy Company
  Pewaukee, WI 800-558-2300
Sunline Brands
  Saint Louis, MO 314-638-5770
Weaver Nut Company
  Ephrata, PA 717-738-3781

Packaged for Theaters

American Licorice Company
  La Porte, IN 800-220-2399
Bruno's Cajun Foods & Snacks
  Slidell, LA 985-726-0544
Clark Bar America
  Revere, MA 781-485-4500
Joyva Corporation
  Brooklyn, NY 718-497-0170
Mona Lisa® Chocolatier
  Arlington, VA 866-662-5475
New England Confectionery Company
  Revere, MA 781-485-4500
Stark Candy Company
  Pewaukee, WI 800-558-2300
Sunline Brands
  Saint Louis, MO 314-638-5770

Valentine

Arway Confections
  Chicago, IL 773-267-5770
Astor Chocolate Corporation
  Lakewood, NJ 732-901-1001
Bee International
  Chula Vista, CA 800-421-6465
Blanton's
  Sweetwater, TN 423-337-3487

Bohemian Biscuit Company
  South San Francisco, CA 800-443-6737
Brach's Confections
  Dallas, TX 800-999-0204
Ce De Candy Southern Inc
  Union, NJ 800-341-2254
Charlotte's Confections
  Millbrae, CA 800-798-2427
Chase Candy Company
  St Joseph, MO 800-786-1625
Clark Bar America
  Revere, MA 781-485-4500
David Bradley Chocolatier
  Windsor, NJ 877-289-7933
Day Spring Enterprises
  Cheektowaga, NY 800-879-7677
Ferrara Bakery & Cafe
  New York, NY 212-226-6150
Gimbal's Fine Candies
  S San Francisco, CA 800-344-6225
Gladstone Candies
  Cleveland, OH 888-729-1960
Jelly Belly Candy Company
  Fairfield, CA 800-522-3267
Judson-Atkinson Candies
  San Antonio, TX 800-962-3984
Leader Candies
  Brooklyn, NY 718-366-6900
Mona Lisa® Chocolatier
  Arlington, VA 866-662-5475
New England Confectionery Company
  Revere, MA 781-485-4500
R.M. Palmer Company
  Reading, PA 610-372-8971
Rito Mints
  Trois Rivieres, QC 819-379-1449
Shane Candy Company
  Philadelphia, PA 215-922-1048
Sherwood Brands
  Rockville, MD 301-309-6161
Stark Candy Company
  Pewaukee, WI 800-558-2300
Sunline Brands
  Saint Louis, MO 314-638-5770
Vande Walle's Candies
  Appleton, WI 920-738-7799
Wisconsin Cheese
  Melrose Park, IL 708-450-0074
World Confections
  Brooklyn, NY 718-768-8100

Vending

Bruno's Cajun Foods & Snacks
  Slidell, LA 985-726-0544
Ce De Candy Southern Inc
  Union, NJ 800-341-2254
Chase Candy Company
  St Joseph, MO 800-786-1625
Chris A. Papas & Son Company
  Covington, KY 859-431-0499
Clark Bar America
  Revere, MA 781-485-4500
GKI Foods
  Brighton, MI 248-486-0055
Jo Mints
  Corona Del Mar, CA 877-566-4687
Joyva Corporation
  Brooklyn, NY 718-497-0170
Lukas Confections
  York, PA 717-843-0921
Mona Lisa® Chocolatier
  Arlington, VA 866-662-5475
New England Confectionery Company
  Revere, MA 781-485-4500
Peter Paul Manufacturing Plant
  Naugatuck, CT 800-468-1714
Stark Candy Company
  Pewaukee, WI 800-558-2300
Sunline Brands
  Saint Louis, MO 314-638-5770

Cereals, Grains, Rice & Flour

Alfalfa

American Health & Nutrition
Ann Arbor, MI 734-677-5572
Herb Connection
Springville, UT 801-489-4254
Naturex (Chart Corp)
South Hackensack, NJ 201-440-5000
S&E Organic Farms
Bakersfield, CA 661-325-2644
Sungarden Sprouts
Cookeville, TN 931-526-1106
Verhoff Alfalfa Mills
Toledo, OH 800-834-8563

Barley

ADM Milling Company
Shawnee Mission, KS. 800-422-1688
Agricore United
Winnipeg, MB. 204-944-5411
AgriCulver Seeds
Trumansburg, NY 800-836-3701
Archer Daniels Midland Company
Decatur, IL .800-637-5843
Chieftain Wild Rice Company
Spooner, WI 800-262-6368
ConAgra Mills
Omaha, NE .877-717-1694
Cooperative Elevator Company
Pigeon, MI .989-453-4500
Ferris Organic Farm
Eaton Rapids, MI 800-628-8736
Fizzle Flat Farm
Yale, IL 618-793-2060
Froedtert Malt
Winona, MN 507-454-1535
Froedtert Malt Corporation
Milwaukee, WI 800-493-4886
Grain Millers
Eden Prairie, MN 800-232-6287
Grain Millers Eugene
Eugene, OR .800-443-8972
Graysmarsh Farm
Sequim, WA 800-683-4367
Green Foods Corporation
Oxnard, CA .800-777-4430
Herb Connection
Springville, UT 801-489-4254
Honeyville Grain
Rancho Cucamonga, CA 888-810-3212
Minnesota Grain
Lake City, MN 800-535-7405
Minnesota Malting Company
Saint Paul, MN 507-263-3911
Natural Way Mills
Middle River, MN. 218-222-3677
Ottawa Valley Grain Products
Renfrew, ON 613-432-3614
Pines International
Lawrence, KS 800-697-4637
Prairie Malt
Biggar, SK. .306-948-3500
Quaker Oats Company
Cedar Rapids, IA. 319-362-3121
Rahr Malting Company
Shakopee, MN 952-445-1431
Raymond-Hadley Corporation
Spencer, NY 800-252-5220
T.S. Smith & Sons
Bridgeville, DE. 302-337-8271
Wallace Grain & Pea Company
Palouse, WA 509-878-1561
Weetabix Company
Clinton, MA 800-343-0590
Western Pacific Commodities
Las Vegas, NV 702-312-8080

Bran

ADM Food Ingredients
Olathe, KS. .800-255-6637
American Health & Nutrition
Ann Arbor, MI 734-677-5572
Blue Chip Group
Salt Lake City, UT 800-878-0099

Canadian Harvest
Cambridge, MN 888-689-5800
Chef Hans Gourmet Foods
Monroe, LA. 800-890-4267
Dakota Organic Products
Watertown, SD 800-243-7264
Farmers Rice Milling Company
Lake Charles, LA 337-433-5205
G S Dunn & Company
Hamilton, ON 905-522-0833
Glorybee Foods
Eugene, OR .800-456-7923
Great Grains Milling Company
Scobey, MT. 406-783-5588
Humboldt Flour Mills
Humboldt, SK. 306-682-2577
J.R. Short Canadian Mills
Toronto, ON 416-421-3463
Knappen Milling Company
Augusta, MI 800-562-7736
Ohta Wafer Factory
Honolulu, HI 808-949-2775
Pacific International Rice Mills
Woodland, CA. 800-747-4764
Raymond-Hadley Corporation
Spencer, NY 800-252-5220
Ricex Company
El Dorado Hills, CA 916-933-3000
Riviana Foods
Houston, TX
Riviana Foods
Memphis, TN 901-948-8556
SJH Enterprises
Middleton, WI. 888-745-3845
Southern Brown Rice
Weiner, AR .800-421-7423
Star of the West MillingCompany
Frankenmuth, MI 989-652-9971
Stearns & Lehman
Mansfield, OH 800-533-2722
Wall-Rogalsky Milling Company
Mc Pherson, KS 800-835-2067
Weetabix Company
Clinton, MA 800-343-0590

Mustard

G S Dunn & Company
Hamilton, ON 905-522-0833

Rice

Beaumont Rice Mills
Beaumont, TX. 409-832-2521
Farmers Rice Milling Company
Lake Charles, LA 337-433-5205
Janca's Jojoba Oil & Seed Company
Mesa, AZ. 480-497-9494
Louis Dreyfus Corporation
Wilton, CT .203-761-2000
Morningstar Foods
Gustine, CA 209-854-6461
Pacific International Rice Mills
Woodland, CA. 800-747-4764
Producers Rice Mill
Stuttgart, AR 870-673-4444
Ricex Company
El Dorado Hills, CA 916-933-3000
Riviana Foods
Houston, TX
Sahara Natural Foods
San Leandro, CA. 510-352-5111
Southern Brown Rice
Weiner, AR .800-421-7423
Suzanne's Specialties
New Brunswick, NJ 800-762-2135

Wheat

ADM Food Ingredients
Olathe, KS. .800-255-6637
American Health & Nutrition
Ann Arbor, MI 734-677-5572
Blue Chip Group
Salt Lake City, UT 800-878-0099
Canadian Harvest
Cambridge, MN 888-689-5800

Wall-Rogalsky Milling Company
Mc Pherson, KS 800-835-2067

Cereal

Amcan Industries
Elmsford, NY 914-347-4838
American Health & Nutrition
Ann Arbor, MI 734-677-5572
Barbara's Bakery
Petaluma, CA 707-765-2273
Bob's Red Mill Natural Foods
Milwaukie, OR 800-349-2173
Cambridge Food
Monterey, CA 800-433-2584
Cereal Ingredients
Kansas City, MO. 816-891-1055
Clara Foods
Clara City, MN 888-844-8518
Coach's Oats
Yorba Linda, CA. 714-692-6885
Earth Song Whole Foods
Fair Oaks, CA 877-327-8476
Festive Finer Foods
Jamaica, NY 718-341-2100
Fiddlers Green Farm
Belfast, ME. 800-729-7935
Food Ingredients
Elgin, IL 800-500-7676
Gilster Mary Lee/Jasper Foods
Jasper, MO .800-777-2168
Golden Temple
Los Angeles, CA. 310-275-9891
Golden Temple
Eugene, OR. 800-964-4832
Grain Place Foods
Marquette, NE. 402-854-3195
Grain Process Enterprises Ltd.
Scarborough, ON 800-387-5292
Harvest Innovations
Indianola, IA 515-962-5063
Inn Maid Food
Lenox, MA .413-637-2732
Kashi Company
La Jolla, CA 858-274-8870
Kellogg Company
Battle Creek, MI 800-962-1413
Kemach Food Products   Corporation
Brooklyn, NY 888-453-6224
Kraft
Parsippany, NJ. 973-292-1755
Kraft Canada Headquarters
Don Mills, ON 800-268-7808
Malt-O-Meal Company
Northfield, MN. 612-338-8551
McKee Foods Corporation
Collegedale, TN 423-238-7111
Nature's Path Foods
Delta, BC. 604-940-0505
New England Natural Bakers
Greenfield, MA. 800-910-2884
Nu-World Amaranth
Naperville, IL 630-369-6851
Prairie Mills Company
Wayzata, MN 612-473-9407
Quaker
Barrington, IL 800-333-8027
Quaker Oats Company
Cedar Rapids, IA. 319-362-3121
Raymond-Hadley Corporation
Spencer, NY 800-252-5220
Rhodia Inc
Cranbury, NJ 609-860-4000
Ryt Way Industries
Lakeville, MN. 952-469-1417
SBK Preserves
Bronx, NY. .800-773-7378
Summercorn Foods
Fayetteville, AR 888-328-9473
Sun Ridge Farms
Santa Cruz, CA 800-655-3252
Sunridge Farms
Salinas, CA. 831-755-1430
US Foods
Lincoln, NE. 402-470-2021

Watson Foods Company
West Haven, CT 800-388-3481
Wildtime Foods
Eugene, OR 800-356-4458

Bars

Flowers Bakery of Winston-Salem
Winston Salem, NC. 800-334-5260

Breakfast

Agricore United
Winnipeg, MB 204-944-5411
AlpineAire Foods
Rocklin, CA 800-322-6325
Aventine Renewable Energy
Pekin, IL 309-347-9200
Bake Crafters Food
Collegedale, TN 800-296-8935
Barbara's Bakery
Petaluma, CA 707-765-2273
Bartlett Milling Company
Coffeyville, KS 620-251-4650
Bede Inc
Haledon, NJ 866-239-6565
Birkett Mills
Penn Yan, NY 315-536-3311
Black Ranch Organic Grains
Etna, CA 530-467-3387
Blue Chip Group
Salt Lake City, UT 800-878-0099
Blue Planet Foods, Inc.
Collegedale, TN 877-396-3145
C.H. Guenther & Son
San Antonio, TX 800-531-7912
California Cereal Products
Oakland, CA 510-452-4500
Carbon's Golden Malted
South Bend, IN 800-253-0590
Carlisle Cereal Company
Bismarck, ND 800-809-6018
Central Michigan Foods
Owosso, MI. 517-723-3846
Cereal Food Processors
Mission, KS 913-890-6300
Christine & Rob's
Stayton, OR. 503-769-2993
Colorado Cereal
Fort Collins, CO 970-282-9733
Con Agra Store Brands
Edina, MN. 952-835-6900
Cook Natural Products
Oakland, CA 800-537-7589
Cook-In-The-Kitchen
White River Junction, VT 802-333-4141
Country Choice Naturals
Eden Prairie, MN 952-829-8824
Cream of the West
Harlowton, MT 800-477-2383
Eagle Agricultural Products
Huntsville, AR 501-738-2203
Edwards Mill
Point Lookout, MO. 800-222-0525
Efco Products
Poughkeepsie, NY 800-284-3326
Ener-G Foods
Seattle, WA 800-331-5222
Farmers Rice Milling Company
Lake Charles, LA 337-433-5205
Fearn Natural Foods
Mequon, WI 800-877-8935
Fry Krisp Food Products
Jackson, MI. 517-784-8531
General Mills
Minneapolis, MN 800-248-7310
GFA Brands
Paramus, NJ 201-568-9300
Gilster Mary Lee/Jasper Foods
Jasper, MO 800-777-2168
Gilster-Mary Lee Corporation
Chester, IL. 800-851-5371
GKI Foods
Brighton, MI 248-486-0055
Golden Temple, Sunshine & Yogi Tea
Los Angeles, CA. 800-225-3623
Grain Process Enterprises Ltd.
Scarborough, ON 800-387-5292
Health Valley Company
Irwindale, CA 800-334-3204
Hilltown Whole Food Company
Cummington, MA 413-634-5677

Hodgson Mill Inc
Effingham, IL 800-525-0177
Homestead Mills
Cook, MN 800-652-5233
House Autry Mills
Four Oaks, NC 800-849-0802
Indiana Grain Company
Baltimore, MD 410-685-6410
International Home Foods
Milton, PA. 973-359-9920
Kellogg Canada Inc
Mississauga, ON 888-876-3750
Kellogg Company
Omaha, NE 402-331-7717
Kellogg Company
Lancaster, PA 717-898-0161
Kellogg Company
Battle Creek, MI 800-962-1413
Kellogg Company
Memphis, TN 901-743-0250
Kellogg Ingredients Company
Battle Creek, MI 888-223-7723
Klemme Cooperative Grainery
Klemme, IA. 641-444-4262
Knappen Milling Company
Augusta, MI 800-562-7736
Lassen Foods
Santa Barbara, CA 805-683-7696
Liberty Richter
Saddle Brook, NJ 201-291-8749
Lincoln Mills
Jersey City, NJ 201-433-0070
Little Crow Foods
Warsaw, IN 800-288-2769
Louisiana Rice Company
Welsh, LA 337- 73-4 44
Luban International
Doral, FL. 305-629-8730
Lundberg Family Farm
Richvale, CA. 530-882-4551
Malt-O-Meal Company
Northfield, MN 612-338-8551
Malt-O-Meal Company
Northfield, MN 800-743-3029
Mantrose-Haeuser Company
Westport, CT. 800-344-4229
Martha Olson's Great Foods
Sutter Creek, CA. 800-973-3966
Mills Brothers International
Tukwila, WA 206-575-3000
Milner Milling
Chattanooga, TN 423-265-2313
Mixes By Danielle
Warren, OH 800-537-6499
Morrison Milling Company
Denton, TX 800-580-5487
Nabisco Dry Foods
Glenview, IL 612-331-4325
National Vinegar Company
Houston, TX 713-223-4214
Natural Way Mills
Middle River, MN. 218-222-3677
Nature's Hand
Burnsville, MN. 952-890-6033
New England Natural Bakers
Greenfield, MA 800-910-2884
New Morning
Needham, MA. 781-444-0440
Nutri Base
Phoenix, AZ 800-225-3623
Olmarc Packaging Company
Chicago, IL 708-562-2000
Organic Milling Company
San Dimas, CA 800-638-8686
Pepsi
Chicago, IL 312-821-1000
PepsiCo
Barrington, IL 847-842-4652
Prairie Sun Grains
Calgary, AB. 800-556-6807
Premier Cereals
Clyde Hill, WA 425-451-1451
Quaker
Barrington, IL 800-333-8027
Quaker Oats Company
Stockton, CA 209-982-5580
Quaker Oats Company
Danville, IL 217-443-3990
Quaker Oats Company
Cedar Rapids, IA. 319-362-3121
Quaker Oats Company
Peterborough, ON 800-267-6287

Ralcorp Holdings
St Louis, MO. 800-772-6757
Roman Meal Milling Company
Fargo, ND 877-282-9743
Sam Wylde Flour Company
Seattle, WA 206-762-5400
Senor Pinos de Santa Fe
Santa Fe, NM 505-473-3437
Silver Palate Kitchens
Cresskill, NJ 800-872-5283
Stafford County Flour Mills Company
Hudson, KS 800-530-5640
Star of the West MillingCompany
Frankenmuth, MI 989-652-9971
Sturm Foods
Manawa, WI 800-347-8876
Thymly Products
Colora, MD 410-658-4820
Trinidad Benham Company
Mineola, TX 903-569-2636
US Foods
Lincoln, NE. 402-470-2021
US Mills
Needham, MA. 800-422-1125
Wanda's Nature Farm
Lincoln, NE. 402-423-1234
Washington Quality Food Products
Ellicott City, MD. 800-735-3585
Weetabix of Canada
Cobourg, ON 905-372-5441

Corn-Based

Quaker Oats Company
Cedar Rapids, IA. 319-362-3121

Farina

Sturm Foods
Manawa, WI 800-347-8876

Instant

Malt-O-Meal Company
Northfield, MN 612-338-8551
Purity Foods
Okemos, MI 800-997-7358

Muesli

Baker
Milford, NJ 800-995-3989

Oatmeal

American Health & Nutrition
Ann Arbor, MI 734-677-5572
Sturm Foods
Manawa, WI 800-347-8876

Rice-Based

Fantastic Foods
Napa, CA. 800-288-1089
Lundberg Family Farm
Richvale, CA. 530-882-4551
Producers Rice Mill
Stuttgart, AR 870-673-4444
Quaker Oats Company
Cedar Rapids, IA. 319-362-3121

Rolled Oats

American Health & Nutrition
Ann Arbor, MI 734-677-5572

Wheat-Based

Central Michigan Foods
Owosso, MI. 517-723-3846
H. Fox & Company
Brooklyn, NY 718-385-4600
Malt-O-Meal Company
Northfield, MN 612-338-8551
Quaker Oats Company
Cedar Rapids, IA. 319-362-3121

Corn Meal

Abbitt's
Williamston, NC 252-792-3646
Adluh Flour Mill
Columbia, SC 800-692-3584

ADM Milling Company
Jackson, TN 731-424-3535
ADM Milling Company
Shawnee Mission, KS. 913-266-6300
Agricor
Marion, IN. 765-662-0606
American Key Food Products
Closter, NJ. 800-767-0237
Ashland Milling
Ashland, VA 804-798-8329
Atkinson Milling Company
Selma, NC. 800-948-5707
Bob's Red Mill Natural Foods
Milwaukie, OR 800-349-2173
California Oils Corporation
Richmond, CA 800-225-6457
Cargill Dry Corn Ingredients
Paris, IL 800-637-6481
Chieftain Wild Rice Company
Spooner, WI 800-262-6368
Chowan Milling Company
Ellicott City, MD. 252-398-4238
Eagle Agricultural Products
Huntsville, AR 501-738-2203
Hodgson Mill Inc
Effingham, IL .800-525-0177
Homestead Mills
Cook, MN 800-652-5233
Honeyville Grain
Rancho Cucamonga, CA 888-810-3212
Hoople Country Kitchens
Rockport, IN 812-649-2351
J.P. Green Milling Company
Mocksville, NC. 336-751-2126
Lakeside Mills
Rutherfordton, NC 828-286-4866
Maysville Milling Company
Maysville, NC. 910-743-3481
Midstate Mills
Newton, NC 800-222-1032
Mills Brothers International
Tukwila, WA .206-575-3000
Nustef Foods
Mississauga, ON. 905-896-3060
Scott's Auburn Mills
Auburn, KY. 800-962-7857
Shawnee Milling Company
Shawnee, OK .405-273-7000
Shenandoah Mills
Lebanon, TN .615-444-0841
SJH Enterprises
Middleton, WI. 888-745-3845
Southeastern Mills
Rome, GA. 800-334-4468
UNOI Grainmill
Seaford, DE. 302-629-4083
War Eagle Mill
Rogers, AR 479-789-5343
White Lily Foods Company
San Antonio, TX. 800-264-5459
Wilkins-Rogers
Ellicott City, MD. 410-465-5800

Crisps

Brown Rice

Nuvex Ingredients
Blue Earth, MN. 507-526-4331

Cereal

Nuvex Ingredients
Blue Earth, MN. 507-526-4331

Cocoa Rice

Nuvex Ingredients
Blue Earth, MN. 507-526-4331

Cocoa Soy

Nuvex Ingredients
Blue Earth, MN. 507-526-4331

Colored

Nuvex Ingredients
Blue Earth, MN. 507-526-4331

Crisped Bran

Nuvex Ingredients
Blue Earth, MN. 507-526-4331

Crisped Corn

Nuvex Ingredients
Blue Earth, MN. 507-526-4331

Crisped Oat

Nuvex Ingredients
Blue Earth, MN. 507-526-4331

Crisped Rice

Nuvex Ingredients
Blue Earth, MN. 507-526-4331

Crisped Soy

Nuvex Ingredients
Blue Earth, MN. 507-526-4331

Crisped Wheat

Nuvex Ingredients
Blue Earth, MN. 507-526-4331

Flax

Harvest Innovations
Indianola, IA .515-962-5063
Nuvex Ingredients
Blue Earth, MN. 507-526-4331

Oat Fiber

Nuvex Ingredients
Blue Earth, MN. 507-526-4331

Rice

Nuvex Ingredients
Blue Earth, MN. 507-526-4331

Soy

Nuvex Ingredients
Blue Earth, MN. 507-526-4331

Whey

Nuvex Ingredients
Blue Earth, MN. 507-526-4331

Fiber

ADM Corn Processing
Decatur, IL 800-553-8411
ADM Food Ingredients
Olathe, KS. 800-255-6637
Agriproducts
Coral Springs, FL 800-277-4979
Alfred L. Wolff, Inc.
Park Ridge, IL. 312-265-9889
Canadian Harvest
Cambridge, MN 888-689-5800
Cereal Ingredients
Kansas City, MO. 816-891-1055
CreaFill Fibers Corporation
Chestertown, MD 800-832-4662
Dakota Organic Products
Watertown, SD 800-243-7264
Eckhart Corporation
Novato, CA 800-200-4201
Functional Foods
Englishtown, NJ 800-442-9524
Garuda International
Lemon Cove, CA 559-594-4380
Grain Millers
Eden Prairie, MN 800-232-6287
Great Grains Milling Company
Scobey, MT. 406-783-5588
Gum Technology Corporation
Tucson, AZ. 800-369-4867
International Fiber Corporation
North Tonawanda, NY 716-693-4040
International Fiber Corporation
North Tonawanda, NY 888-698-1936
Loders Croklaan
Channahon, IL 800-621-4710
Mineral & Pigment Solutions
South Plainfield, NJ 800-732-0562

ND Labs Inc
Lynbrook, NY .888-263-5227
Omni-Pak Industries
Garden Grove, CA 714-899-3100
Organic Milling Company
San Dimas, CA 800-638-8686
Ricex Company
El Dorado Hills, CA 916-933-3000
San-Ei Gen FFI
New York, NY 212-315-7840
Southern Brown Rice
Weiner, AR 800-421-7423
Sun Opta Ingredients
Chelmsford, MA. 800-353-6782
Suzanne's Specialties
New Brunswick, NJ 800-762-2135
Tastee Apple Inc
Newcomerstown, OH 800-262-7753
TIC Gums
Belcamp, MD .800-221-3953
Unique Ingredients
Naches, WA. 509-653-1991
Vivion
San Carlos, CA 800-479-0997
Watson Foods Company
West Haven, CT 800-388-3481
World Flavors
Warminster, PA 215-672-4400
Yerba Prima
Ashland, OR 800-488-4339

Barley Bran

Roman Meal Milling Company
Tacoma, WA 253-475-0964

Cellulose

Gum Technology Corporation
Tucson, AZ. 800-369-4867

Corn Bran

Canadian Harvest
Cambridge, MN 888-689-5800

Oat Bran

American Health & Nutrition
Ann Arbor, MI 734-677-5572
Canadian Harvest
Cambridge, MN 888-689-5800

Oats

American Health & Nutrition
Ann Arbor, MI 734-677-5572
Canadian Harvest
Cambridge, MN 888-689-5800
Organic Planet
San Francisco, CA 415-765-5590
Roman Meal Milling Company
Tacoma, WA 253-475-0964

Resistant Starch

Cargill Texturizing Solutions
Cedar Rapids, IA. 877-650-7080

Soy Bran

Fibred-Maryland
Cumberland, MD 800-598-8894

Supplements

Abunda Life Laboratories
Asbury Park, NJ 732-775-4141
ADM Food Ingredients
Olathe, KS. 800-255-6637
Innovative Health Products
Largo, FL 800-654-2347
Southern Brown Rice
Weiner, AR 800-421-7423
Suzanne's Specialties
New Brunswick, NJ 800-762-2135
Tastee Apple Inc
Newcomerstown, OH 800-262-7753

Wheat Bran

Canadian Harvest
Cambridge, MN 888-689-5800

Cereal Ingredients
  Kansas City, MO..............816-891-1055

Flour

Acadian Seaplants
  Dartmouth, NS 800-575-9100
ACATRIS
  Oakville, ON................905-829-2414
Adluh Flour Mill
  Columbia, SC...............800-692-3584
ADM Food Ingredients
  Olathe, KS.................800-255-6637
ADM Milling Company
  Chicago, IL................312-666-2465
ADM Milling Company
  Carthage, MO...............417-358-2197
ADM Milling Company
  Cleveland, TN..............423-476-7551
ADM Milling Company
  Chattanooga, TN............423-756-0503
ADM Milling Company
  Spokane, WA................509-534-2636
ADM Milling Company
  Arkansas City, KS..........620-442-6200
ADM Milling Company
  Charlotte, NC..............704-332-3165
ADM Milling Company
  Abilene, KS................785-263-1631
ADM Milling Company
  Mississauga, ON............800-267-8492
ADM Milling Company
  Minneapolis, MN............800-528-7877
ADM Milling Company
  Shawnee Mission, KS........913-266-6300
AG Processing, Inc.
  Omaha, NE..................800-247-1345
Agri-Dairy Products
  Purchase, NY...............914-697-9580
Agricor
  Marion, IN.................765-662-0606
Agricore United
  Winnipeg, MB...............204-944-5411
Amendt Corporation
  Monroe, MI.................734-242-2411
American Almond Products Company
  Brooklyn, NY...............800-825-6663
American Health & Nutrition
  Ann Arbor, MI..............734-677-5572
Ashland Milling
  Ashland, VA................804-798-8329
Atlantic Seasonings
  Kinston, NC................800-433-5261
Attala Company
  Kosciusko, MS..............800-824-2691
Azteca Milling
  Irving, TX.................800-364-0040
Bay State Milling Company
  Winona, MN.................800-533-8098
Bay State Milling Company
  Quincy, MA.................800-553-5687
Beta Pure Foods
  Aptos, CA..................831-685-6565
Big J Milling & Elevator Company
  Brigham City, UT...........435-723-3459
Birkett Mills
  Penn Yan, NY...............315-536-3311
Blend Pak
  Bloomfield, KY.............502-252-8000
Blue Chip Group
  Salt Lake City, UT.........800-878-0099
Bob's Red Mill Natural Foods
  Milwaukie, OR..............800-349-2173
Bouchard Family Farm
  Fort Kent, ME..............800-239-3237
Brandt Mills
  Mifflinville, PA...........570-752-4271
Byrd Mill Company
  Ashland, VA................888-897-3336
California Cereal Products
  Oakland, CA................510-452-4500
Cargill Dry Corn Ingredients
  Paris, IL..................800-637-6481
Cargill Flour Milling
  Minneapolis, MN............800-227-4455
Centennial Mills
  Cheney, WA.................509-235-6216
Central Milling Company
  Logan, UT..................435-752-6625
Cereal Food Processors
  Cleveland, OH..............216-621-3206
Cereal Food Processors
  Salt Lake City, UT.........801-265-3855

Cereal Food Processors
  Mission, KS................913-890-6300
Champlain Valley Milling Corporation
  Westport, NY...............518-962-4711
Chr Hansen
  Elyria, OH.................800-558-0802
CHS
  Inver Grove Heights, MN....800-232-3639
Clofine Dairy & Food Products
  Linwood, NJ................800-441-1001
Community Mill & Bean
  Savannah, NY...............800-755-0554
ConAgra Flour Milling
  Commerce City, CO..........303-289-6141
ConAgra Flour Milling
  Fremont, NE................402-721-4200
ConAgra Flour Milling
  Macon, GA..................478-743-5424
ConAgra Flour Milling
  Martins Creek, PA..........610-253-9341
ConAgra Flour Milling
  Alton, IL..................618-463-4411
ConAgra Flour Milling
  Chester, IL................618-826-2371
ConAgra Flour Milling
  Red Lion, PA...............717-244-4559
ConAgra Flour Milling
  York, PA...................717-846-7773
ConAgra Flour Milling
  Omaha, NE..................800-214-0349
ConAgra Flour Milling
  Colton, CA.................800-736-2212
ConAgra Flour Milling
  Sherman, TX................903-893-8111
ConAgra Mills
  Tampa, FL..................800-582-1483
ConAgra Mills
  Omaha, NE..................800-851-9618
ConAgra Mills
  Kansas City, MO............816-942-3700
ConAgra Mills
  Omaha, NE..................877-717-1694
CSP Foods
  Mont-Royal, QC.............514-731-7621
Dakota Organic Products
  Watertown, SD..............800-243-7264
Dan's Feed Bin
  Superior, WI...............715-394-6639
Devansoy
  Carroll, IA................800-747-8605
Dillman Farm
  Bloomington, IN............800-359-1362
Dipasa
  Brownsville, TX............956-831-5893
Dover Industries Limited
  Burlington, ON.............800-387-7316
Dover Industries Limited
  Burlington, ON.............905-333-1515
Eagle Agricultural Products
  Huntsville, AR.............501-738-2203
Eden Foods Inc
  Clinton, MI................800-248-0320
El Peto Products
  Cambridge, ON..............800-387-4064
Ellison Milling Company
  Lethbridge, AB.............403-328-6622
Ener-G Foods
  Seattle, WA................800-331-5222
Erba Food Products
  Brooklyn, NY...............718-272-7700
Fairhaven Cooperative Flour Mill
  Bellingham, WA.............360-734-9947
Fastachi
  Watertown, MA..............800-466-3022
Fearn Natural Foods
  Mequon, WI.................800-877-8935
French's Ingredients
  Springfield, MO............417-837-1813
Fresh Hemp Foods
  Winnipeg, NB...............800-665-4367
G S Dunn & Company
  Hamilton, ON...............905-522-0833
General Mills
  Minneapolis, MN............800-248-7310
Gilt Edge Flour Mills
  Richmond, UT...............435-258-2425
Goldilocks Bakeshop
  S San Francisco, CA........650-873-6566
Grain Process Enterprises Ltd.
  Scarborough, ON............800-387-5292
Great Grains Milling Company
  Scobey, MT.................406-783-5588

Greenfield Mills
  Howe, IN...................260-367-2394
Halton Flour Milling
  Acton, ON..................800-608-7694
Harbar Corporation
  Canton, MA.................800-881-7040
Heartland Mill
  Marienthal, KS.............620-379-4472
Hialeah Products Company
  Hollywood, FL..............800-923-3379
Hodgson Mill Inc
  Effingham, IL..............800-525-0177
Homestead Mills
  Cook, MN...................800-652-5233
Honeyville Grain
  Rancho Cucamonga, CA.......888-810-3212
Humboldt Flour Mills
  Humboldt, SK...............306-682-2577
Idaho Pacific Corporation
  Ririe, ID..................800-238-5503
Idaho-Frank Associates
  Pleasant Hill, CA..........925-609-8458
J.P. Green Milling Company
  Mocksville, NC.............336-751-2126
J.R. Short Canadian Mills
  Toronto, ON................416-421-3463
J.R. Short Milling Company
  Kankakee, IL...............800-544-8734
Kaufman Ingredients
  Vernon Hills, IL...........847-573-0844
Kemach Food Products   Corporation
  Brooklyn, NY...............888-453-6224
King Arthur Flour
  Norwich, VT................802-649-3881
King Milling Company
  Lowell, MI.................616-897-9264
Knappen Milling Company
  Augusta, MI................800-562-7736
Lacey Milling Company
  Hanford, CA................559-584-6634
Lehi Roller Mills
  Lehi, UT...................800-660-4346
Lucas Meyer
  Decatur, IL................800-769-3660
Mennel Milling Company
  Fostoria, OH...............419-435-8151
Mennel Milling Company
  Fostoria, OH...............419-436-5130
Mennel Milling Company
  Fostoria, OH...............800-688-8151
MexAmerica Foods
  St Marys, PA...............814-781-1447
Midstate Mills
  Newton, NC.................800-222-1032
Mills Brothers International
  Tukwila, WA................206-575-3000
Minn-Dak Growers Limited
  Grand Forks, ND............701-746-7453
Montana Flour & Grain
  Fort Benton, MT............406-622-5436
Morris J. Golombeck
  Brooklyn, NY...............718-284-3505
Mother Earth Enterprises
  New York, NY...............866-436-7688
Natural Products
  Grinnell, IA...............641-236-0852
Natural Way Mills
  Middle River, MN...........218-222-3677
Naturex (Chart Corp)
  South Hackensack, NJ.......201-440-5000
New Hope Mills
  Auburn, NY.................315-252-2676
Newly Weds Foods
  Chicago, IL................800-621-7521
North Dakota Mill
  Grand Forks, ND............800-538-7721
Northwestern Foods
  St Paul, MN................800-236-4937
Nunn Milling Company
  Evansville, IN.............800-547-6866
Oak Creek Farms
  Edgar, NE..................402-224-3038
Okeene Milling
  Shawnee, OK................405-273-7000
Old Dutch Mustard Company
  Great Neck, NY.............516-466-0522
Oregon Potato Company
  Boardman, OR...............800-336-6311
Orlinda Milling Company
  Orlinda, TN................615-654-3633
Particle Control
  Albertville, MN............763-497-3075

Pendleton Flour Mills
Pendleton, OR .541-276-6511
Pillsbury
Minneapolis, MN 800-845-3103
Prairie Mills Company
Wayzata, MN 612-473-9407
Prairie Sun Grains
Calgary, AB. 800-556-6807
Premier Blending
Wichita, KS .316-267-5533
Produits Alimentaire
St Lambert De Lauzon, QC 800-463-1787
Purato's
Seattle, WA .206-762-5400
Purity Foods
Okemos, MI .800-997-7358
Quality Naturally! Foods
City of Industry, CA 888-498-6986
R&J Farms
West Salem, OH 419-846-3179
Raymond-Hadley Corporation
Spencer, NY .800-252-5220
Research Products Company
Salina, KS 800-234-7174
Roanoke City Mills
Roanoke, VA 540-343-9383
Roman Meal Milling Company
Fargo, ND 877-282-9743
Sanford Milling Company
Henderson, NC 252-438-4526
Scott's Auburn Mills
Auburn, KY. 800-962-7857
Seaboard Corporation
Shawnee Mission, KS. 913-676-8800
SFP Food Products
Conway, AR .800-654-5329
Shawnee Milling Company
Shawnee, OK 405-273-7000
Shepherdsfield Bakery
Fulton, MO .573-642-1439
Siemer Milling Company
Teutopolis, IL 800-826-1065
SJH Enterprises
Middleton, WI. 888-745-3845
Solnuts
Hudson, IA .800-648-3503
Southeastern Mills
Rome, GA 800-334-4468
Southern Brown Rice
Weiner, AR .800-421-7423
Star of the West
Kent, OH. 330-673-2941
Star of the West MillingCompany
Frankenmuth, MI 989-652-9971
Streamline Foods
West Bloomfield, MI. 248-851-2611
Teff Company
Caldwell, ID 888-822-2221
Uhlmann Company
Kansas City, MO. 800-383-8201
Wall-Rogalsky Milling Company
Mc Pherson, KS 800-835-2067
War Eagle Mill
Rogers, AR .479-789-5343
Western Pacific Commodities
Las Vegas, NV 702-312-8080
Wheat Montana Farms & Bakery
Three Forks, MT. 800-535-2798
White Lily Foods Company
San Antonio, TX 800-264-5459
Wilkins-Rogers
Ellicott City, MD. 410-465-5800

All Purpose

ConAgra Flour Milling
Colton, CA .800-736-2212
Dan's Feed Bin
Superior, WI 715-394-6639
Glorybee Foods
Eugene, OR. 800-456-7923
Orlinda Milling Company
Orlinda, TN .615-654-3633
Uhlmann Company
Kansas City, MO. 800-383-8201
UNOI Grainmill
Seaford, DE. 302-629-4083
Wall-Rogalsky Milling Company
Mc Pherson, KS 800-835-2067
White Lily Foods Company
San Antonio, TX 800-264-5459

Almond

Chieftain Wild Rice Company
Spooner, WI 800-262-6368

Amaranth

ConAgra Mills
Omaha, NE .800-851-9618

Arrowroot

American Key Food Products
Closter, NJ. .800-767-0237

Bakery Mix

Regular & Lowfat

ConAgra Mills
Kansas City, MO. 816-942-3700
General Mills
Minneapolis, MN 800-248-7310

Baking Mixes

Harvest Innovations
Indianola, IA 515-962-5063
Okeene Milling
Shawnee, OK 405-273-7000
Wall-Rogalsky Milling Company
Mc Pherson, KS 800-835-2067
White Lily Foods Company
San Antonio, TX. 800-264-5459

Barley

ADM Milling Company
Abilene, KS. 785-263-1631
American Health & Nutrition
Ann Arbor, MI 734-677-5572
CHS
Inver Grove Heights, MN. 800-232-3639
ConAgra Mills
Omaha, NE .800-851-9618
Eden Foods Inc
Clinton, MI .800-248-0320
Ettlinger Corporation
Lincolnshire, IL 847-564-5020
Grain Millers
Eden Prairie, MN 800-232-6287
Heartland Mill
Marienthal, KS 620-379-4472
Homestead Mills
Cook, MN 800-652-5233
Honeyville Grain
Rancho Cucamonga, CA 888-810-3212
SJH Enterprises
Middleton, WI. 888-745-3845

Bean

Bob's Red Mill Natural Foods
Milwaukie, OR 800-349-2173

Buckwheat

American Health & Nutrition
Ann Arbor, MI 734-677-5572
Bouchard Family Farm
Fort Kent, ME. 800-239-3237
Byrd Mill Company
Ashland, VA. 888-897-3336
Eden Foods Inc
Clinton, MI .800-248-0320
Ener-G Foods
Seattle, WA .800-331-5222
Fairhaven Cooperative Flour Mill
Bellingham, WA 360-734-9947
Greenfield Mills
Howe, IN. 260-367-2394
Homestead Mills
Cook, MN 800-652-5233
Minn-Dak Growers Limited
Grand Forks, ND. 701-746-7453
New Hope Mills
Auburn, NY. 315-252-2676
Purity Foods
Okemos, MI .800-997-7358
UNOI Grainmill
Seaford, DE. 302-629-4083
Woodland Foods
Gurnee, IL. .847-625-8600

Cake

ADM Milling Company
Chicago, IL. 312-666-2465
Byrd Mill Company
Ashland, VA. 888-897-3336
Cereal Food Processors
Mission, KS 913-890-6300
ConAgra Mills
Omaha, NE .800-851-9618
H. Nagel & Son Company
Cincinnati, OH 513-665-4550
Mennel Milling Company
Fostoria, OH 419-436-5130
Pillsbury
Minneapolis, MN 800-845-3103
Reily Foods Company
New Orleans, LA 504-524-6132

Chestnut Flower

Chieftain Wild Rice Company
Spooner, WI 800-262-6368

Corn

Adluh Flour Mill
Columbia, SC 800-692-3584
ADM Food Ingredients
Olathe, KS. .800-255-6637
Agricor
Marion, IN. .765-662-0606
Attala Company
Kosciusko, MS 800-824-2691
Azteca Milling
Irving, TX. .800-364-0040
Byrd Mill Company
Ashland, VA. 888-897-3336
Cargill Dry Corn Ingredients
Paris, IL. 800-637-6481
ConAgra Flour Milling
Colton, CA .800-736-2212
Eagle Agricultural Products
Huntsville, AR 501-738-2203
Ener-G Foods
Seattle, WA .800-331-5222
Fairhaven Cooperative Flour Mill
Bellingham, WA 360-734-9947
Harbar Corporation
Canton, MA 800-881-7040
Honeyville Grain
Rancho Cucamonga, CA 888-810-3212
J.R. Short Milling Company
Kankakee, IL. 800-544-8734
MexAmerica Foods
St Marys, PA 814-781-1447
Mills Brothers International
Tukwila, WA 206-575-3000
Randag & Associates Inc
Elmhurst, IL 630-530-2830
Shenandoah Mills
Lebanon, TN 615-444-0841
White Lily Foods Company
San Antonio, TX. 800-264-5459

Gluten

ADM Food Ingredients
Olathe, KS. .800-255-6637
Blue Chip Group
Salt Lake City, UT 800-878-0099
Clofine Dairy & Food Products
Linwood, NJ 800-441-1001
Heartland Wheat Growers
Russell, KS .785-483-5559
North Dakota Mill
Grand Forks, ND. 800-538-7721
Organic Planet
San Francisco, CA 415-765-5590
SJH Enterprises
Middleton, WI. 888-745-3845

Hazelnut

Fastachi
Watertown, MA. 800-466-3022

Instantized

AlpineAire Foods
Rocklin, CA 800-322-6325

Masa

Harbar Corporation
Canton, MA 800-881-7040

Millet

American Health & Nutrition
Ann Arbor, MI 734-677-5572
Heartland Mill
Marienthal, KS 620-379-4472
Ore-Ida Foods
Pittsburgh, PA 412-237-3450
Purity Foods
Okemos, MI 800-997-7358

Mustard

French's Ingredients
Springfield, MO 417-837-1813
G S Dunn & Company
Hamilton, ON 905-522-0833
Harvest Innovations
Indianola, IA 515-962-5063
Minn-Dak Growers Limited
Grand Forks, ND 701-746-7453
Montana Specialty Mills
Great Falls, MT 406-761-2338
Tova Industries
Louisville, KY 888-532-8682

Nut

American Almond Products Company
Brooklyn, NY 800-825-6663
Amoretti-Capriccio
Oxnard, CA 800-266-7388
Chieftain Wild Rice Company
Spooner, WI 800-262-6368
Fastachi
Watertown, MA 800-466-3022
Harvest Innovations
Indianola, IA 515-962-5063
Hialeah Products Company
Hollywood, FL 800-923-3379
Mother Earth Enterprises
New York, NY 866-436-7688
Naturex (Chart Corp)
South Hackensack, NJ 201-440-5000

Oat

American Health & Nutrition
Ann Arbor, MI 734-677-5572
Can-Oat Milling
Portage la Prairie, MB 800-663-6287
ConAgra Flour Milling
Colton, CA 800-736-2212
ConAgra Mills
Omaha, NE 877-717-1694
Dakota Organic Products
Watertown, SD 800-243-7264
Eden Foods Inc
Clinton, MI 800-248-0320
Grain Millers
Eden Prairie, MN 800-232-6287
Heartland Mill
Marienthal, KS 620-379-4472
Particle Control
Albertville, MN 763-497-3075
SJH Enterprises
Middleton, WI 888-745-3845

Pancake

ADM Milling Company
Shawnee Mission, KS 913-266-6300
Bette's Diner Products
Berkeley, CA 510-644-3230
Bouchard Family Farm
Fort Kent, ME 800-239-3237
Byrd Mill Company
Ashland, VA 888-897-3336
Carbon's Golden Malted
South Bend, IN 800-686-6258
Champlain Valley Milling Corporation
Westport, NY 518-962-4711

Crosby Molasses Company
St. John, NB 506-634-7515
Foxtail Foods
Fairfield, OH 800-323-6944
Heritage Tymes/Pancake House
Spearsville, LA 806-765-8566
Homestead Mills
Cook, MN 800-652-5233
John Gust Foods & Products Corporation
Batavia, IL 800-756-5886
Little Crow Foods
Warsaw, IN 800-288-2769
Marie Callender's Gourmet Products/Goldrush Products
San Jose, CA 800-729-5428
Martha Olson's Great Foods
Sutter Creek, CA 800-973-3966
New Hope Mills
Auburn, NY 315-252-2676
Northwestern Foods
St Paul, MN 800-236-4937
Quality Naturally! Foods
City of Industry, CA 888-498-6986
Randag & Associates Inc
Elmhurst, IL 630-530-2830
SFP Food Products
Conway, AR 800-654-5329
Shenandoah Mills
Lebanon, TN 615-444-0841
Wanda's Nature Farm
Lincoln, NE 402-423-1234
Wilsonhill Farm
Underhill, VT 802-899-2154

Pastry

ADM Milling Company
Chicago, IL 312-666-2465
American Health & Nutrition
Ann Arbor, MI 734-677-5572
Brandt Mills
Mifflinville, PA 570-752-4271
Cereal Food Processors
Mission, KS 913-890-6300
Champlain Valley Milling Corporation
Westport, NY 518-962-4711
Eden Foods Inc
Clinton, MI 800-248-0320
Ellison Milling Company
Lethbridge, AB 403-328-6622
H. Nagel & Son Company
Cincinnati, OH 513-665-4550
Mennel Milling Company
Fostoria, OH 419-436-5130
Natural Way Mills
Middle River, MN 218-222-3677
Purato's
Seattle, WA 206-762-5400
SJH Enterprises
Middleton, WI 888-745-3845
Star of the West MillingCompany
Frankenmuth, MI 989-652-9971

Peanut

Synergy Foods
West Bloomfield, MI 313-849-2900

Potato

AgraWest Foods
Prince Edward Island, NS 877-687-1400
Chr Hansen
Elyria, OH 800-558-0802
ConAgra Flour Milling
Colton, CA 800-736-2212

EMERLING INTERNATIONAL FOODS, INC.

Emerling International Foods
Buffalo, NY 716-833-7381

Ener-G Foods
Seattle, WA 800-331-5222
Ettlinger Corporation
Lincolnshire, IL 847-564-5020

Idaho Pacific Corporation
Ririe, ID 800-238-5503
Nonpareil Corporation
Blackfoot, ID 800-522-2223
Oregon Potato Company
Boardman, OR 800-336-6311

Pancake

Linda's Gourmet Latkes
Los Angeles, CA 888-452-8537

Rice

A&B Ingredients
Fairfield, NJ 973-227-1390
ADM Food Ingredients
Olathe, KS 800-255-6637
Affiliated Rice Milling
Alvin, TX 281-331-6176
California Cereal Products
Oakland, CA 510-452-4500
Chr Hansen
Elyria, OH 800-558-0802
ConAgra Flour Milling
Colton, CA 800-736-2212
Domino Specialty Ingredients
Baltimore, MD 800-446-9763
Eagle Agricultural Products
Huntsville, AR 501-738-2203
Eden Foods Inc
Clinton, MI 800-248-0320
Ener-G Foods
Seattle, WA 800-331-5222
Fearn Natural Foods
Mequon, WI 800-877-8935
Harvest Innovations
Indianola, IA 515-962-5063
Koda Farms
South Dos Palos, CA 209-392-2191
Lundberg Family Farm
Richvale, CA 530-882-4551
Sage V Foods LLC
Los Angeles, CA 310-820-4496

Rye

Bay State Milling Company
Winona, MN 800-533-8098
Champlain Valley Milling Corporation
Westport, NY 518-962-4711
ConAgra Flour Milling
Colton, CA 800-736-2212
ConAgra Mills
Omaha, NE 800-851-9618
Ellison Milling Company
Lethbridge, AB 403-328-6622
Fairhaven Cooperative Flour Mill
Bellingham, WA 360-734-9947
Heartland Mill
Marienthal, KS 620-379-4472
Homestead Mills
Cook, MN 800-652-5233
SJH Enterprises
Middleton, WI 888-745-3845

Self-Rising

Nunn Milling Company
Evansville, IN 800-547-6866
Orlinda Milling Company
Orlinda, TN 615-654-3633
Wall-Rogalsky Milling Company
Mc Pherson, KS 800-835-2067
White Lily Foods Company
San Antonio, TX 800-264-5459

Semolina

CHS
Inver Grove Heights, MN 800-232-3639
ConAgra Mills
Omaha, NE 800-851-9618
Heartland Mill
Marienthal, KS 620-379-4472
Howson & Howson Limited
Blyth, ON 519-523-4241
North Dakota Mill
Grand Forks, ND 800-538-7721
Woodland Foods
Gurnee, IL 847-625-8600

Soy Protein

Champlain Valley Milling Corporation
Westport, NY......................518-962-4711

Soybean

ACATRIS
Oakville, ON.....................905-829-2414
Acatris USA
Edina, MN.......................952-920-7700
AG Processing, Inc.
Omaha, NE......................800-247-1345
American Health & Nutrition
Ann Arbor, MI...................734-677-5572
Chr Hansen
Elyria, OH......................800-558-0802
CHS Oilseed Processing & Refining
Mankato, MN....................800-525-6237
Clofine Dairy & Food Products
Linwood, NJ....................800-441-1001
Dakota Organic Products
Watertown, SD..................800-243-7264
Devansoy
Carroll, IA....................800-747-8605
Fearn Natural Foods
Mequon, WI.....................800-877-8935
J.R. Short Milling Company
Kankakee, IL...................800-544-8734
Lucas Meyer
Decatur, IL....................800-769-3660
Modern Macaroni Company
Honolulu, HI...................808-845-6841
Solnuts
Hudson, IA.....................800-648-3503

Spelt

Heartland Mill
Marienthal, KS.................620-379-4472
Purity Foods
Okemos, MI.....................800-997-7358
Woodland Foods
Gurnee, IL.....................847-625-8600

Tapioca

Agriproducts
Coral Springs, FL..............800-277-4979
American Key Food Products
Closter, NJ....................800-767-0237
Chr Hansen
Elyria, OH.....................800-558-0802
Ener-G Foods
Seattle, WA....................800-331-5222
Kinnikinnick Foods
Edmonton, AB...................877-503-4466
Tipiak
Stamford, CT...................203-961-9117

Wheat

American Health & Nutrition
Ann Arbor, MI..................734-677-5572
ConAgra Flour Milling
Fremont, NE....................402-721-4200
ConAgra Flour Milling
Martins Creek, PA..............610-253-9341
ConAgra Flour Milling
Chester, IL....................618-826-2371
ConAgra Flour Milling
Red Lion, PA...................717-244-4559
ConAgra Flour Milling
York, PA.......................717-846-7773
ConAgra Flour Milling
Sherman, TX....................903-893-8111
ConAgra Mills
Omaha, NE......................800-851-9618
Mennel Milling Company
Fostoria, OH...................419-435-8151
Okeene Milling
Shawnee, OK....................405-273-7000

White Unbleached

Champlain Valley Milling Corporation
Westport, NY...................518-962-4711
Eagle Agricultural Products
Huntsville, AR.................501-738-2203
Ener-G Foods
Seattle, WA....................800-331-5222
Great Grains Milling Company
Scobey, MT.....................406-783-5588

Heartland Mill
Marienthal, KS.................620-379-4472
King Milling Company
Lowell, MI.....................616-897-9264
Lehi Roller Mills
Lehi, UT.......................800-660-4346
Natural Way Mills
Middle River, MN...............218-222-3677
Star of the West MillingCompany
Frankenmuth, MI................989-652-9971
Uhlmann Company
Kansas City, MO................800-383-8201
White Lily Foods Company
San Antonio, TX................800-264-5459

Whole wheat

American Health & Nutrition
Ann Arbor, MI..................734-677-5572
Brandt Mills
Mifflinville, PA...............570-752-4271
Cereal Food Processors
Mission, KS....................913-890-6300
Eagle Agricultural Products
Huntsville, AR.................501-738-2203
Great Grains Milling Company
Scobey, MT.....................406-783-5588
Homestead Mills
Cook, MN.......................800-652-5233
Keynes Brothers
Logan, OH......................740-385-6824
Montana Specialty Mills
Great Falls, MT................406-761-2338
SJH Enterprises
Middleton, WI..................888-745-3845
Terra Botanica Products
Nakusp, BC.....................888-410-9977
Uhlmann Company
Kansas City, MO................800-383-8201
War Eagle Mill
Rogers, AR.....................479-789-5343

Pastry

American Health & Nutrition
Ann Arbor, MI..................734-677-5572
Brandt Mills
Mifflinville, PA...............570-752-4271
Nuthouse Company
Mobile, AL.....................251-433-1689
SJH Enterprises
Middleton, WI..................888-745-3845

Grains

Acharice Specialties
Greenville, MS.................800-432-4901
ADM Milling Company
Chattanooga, TN................423-756-0503
ADM Milling Company
Charlotte, NC..................704-332-3165
ADM Milling Company
Abilene, KS....................785-263-1631
ADM Milling Company
Shawnee Mission, KS............913-266-6300
Agland, Inc.
Eaton, CO......................800-433-4688
Agricor
Marion, IN.....................765-662-0606
Aliments Trigone
Quebec, QC.....................877-259-7491
AlpineAire Foods
Rocklin, CA....................800-322-6325
Amaranth Marketing Group
Dearborn, MI...................313-724-0313
American Health & Nutrition
Ann Arbor, MI..................734-677-5572
Attala Company
Kosciusko, MS..................800-824-2691
Azteca Milling
Irving, TX.....................800-364-0040
Beaumont Rice Mills
Beaumont, TX...................409-832-2521
Beta Pure Foods
Aptos, CA......................831-685-6565
Big J Milling & Elevator Company
Brigham City, UT...............435-723-3459
Black Ranch Organic Grains
Etna, CA.......................530-467-3387
Blue Planet Foods, Inc.
Collegedale, TN................877-396-3145
Briess Industries
Chilton, WI....................920-849-7711

Bush Brothers & Company
Dandridge, TN..................865-509-2361
California Cereal Products
Oakland, CA....................510-452-4500
Canadian Harvest
Cambridge, MN..................888-689-5800
Canasoy Enterprises
Vancouver, BC..................800-663-1222
Cargill Dry Corn Ingredients
Paris, IL......................800-637-6481
Caribbean Food Delights
Tappan, NY.....................845-398-3000
Cayuga Grain
Cayuga, IN.....................765-492-3324
Central Milling Company
Logan, UT......................435-752-6625
Champlain Valley Milling Corporation
Westport, NY...................518-962-4711
Chef Hans Gourmet Foods
Monroe, LA.....................800-890-4267
Chieftain Wild Rice Company
Spooner, WI....................800-262-6368
China Doll Company
Saraland, AL...................251-457-7641
CHS
Inver Grove Heights, MN........800-232-3639
CHS Sunflower
Grandin, ND....................701-484-5313
Cinnabar Specialty Foods
Prescott, AZ...................866-293-6433
Coach's Oats
Yorba Linda, CA................714-692-6885
ConAgra Foods   Grain Processing
Milan, MO......................660-265-1243
ConAgra Foods Inc
Omaha, NE......................402-240-4000
ConAgra Mills
Omaha, NE......................877-717-1694
ConAgra PV Grain
Superior, WI...................715-398-3541
Conrad Rice Mill
New Iberia, LA.................800-551-3245
Continental Grain/ContiGroup Companies
New York, NY...................212-207-5930
Cooperative Elevator Company
Pigeon, MI.....................989-453-4500
Cormier Rice Milling Company
De Witt, AR....................870-946-3561
Dakota Organic Products
Watertown, SD..................800-243-7264
Deer River Wild Rice
Deer River, MN.................218-246-2713
Devansoy
Carroll, IA....................800-747-8605
DMH Ingredients
Libertyville, IL...............847-362-9977
Dover Industries Limited
Burlington, ON.................905-333-1515
Ellison Milling Company
Lethbridge, AB.................403-328-6622
Fairhaven Cooperative Flour Mill
Bellingham, WA.................360-734-9947
Falcon Rice Mill Inc
Crowley, LA....................800-738-7423
Fall River Wild Rice
Fall River Mills, CA...........800-626-4366
Farmers Grain Company
Morganfield, KY................800-339-4241
Farmers Rice Milling Company
Lake Charles, LA...............337-433-5205
Ferris Organic Farm
Eaton Rapids, MI...............800-628-8736
Fizzle Flat Farm
Yale, IL.......................618-793-2060
Food for Life Baking Company
Corona, CA.....................951-279-5090
Freeland Bean & Grain
Freeland, MI...................800-447-9131
Froedtert Malt
Winona, MN.....................507-454-1535
Froedtert Malt Corporation
Milwaukee, WI..................800-493-4886
Garber Farms
Iota, LA.......................800-824-2284
Goldilocks Bakeshop
S San Francisco, CA............650-873-6566
Good Star Foods
Reno, NV.......................775-851-2442
Grain Bin Bakers
Carmel, CA.....................831-624-3883
Grain Millers Eugene
Eugene, OR.....................800-443-8972

Grain Place Foods
Marquette, NE 402-854-3195
Grain Process Enterprises Ltd.
Scarborough, ON 800-387-5292
Great Western Malting Company
Vancouver, WA 877-770-7055
Grey Owl Foods
Grand Rapids, MN 800-527-0172
Hall Grain Company
Akron, CO. 970-345-2206
Halton Flour Milling
Acton, ON 800-608-7694
Harvest Innovations
Indianola, IA 515-962-5063
Harvest States Milling
Inver Grove Heights, MN 800-232-3639
HealthBest
San Marcos, CA 760-752-5230
Heartland Mill
Marienthal, KS 620-379-4472
Homegrown Naturals
Napa, CA 800-288-1089
Homestead Mills
Cook, MN 800-652-5233
Honeyville Grain
Salt Lake City, UT 801-972-2168
Indian Harvest
Colusa, CA 800-294-2433
Indian Harvest Specialitifoods
Bemidji, MN 800-346-7032
Inn Maid Food
Lenox, MA 413-637-2732
J&L Grain Processing
Riceville, IA 800-244-9211
J.R. Short Canadian Mills
Toronto, ON 416-421-3463
JLH European Trading
San Francisco, CA 415-626-3672
Kaufman Ingredients
Vernon Hills, IL 847-573-0844
Kimco World Trade Company
Los Angeles, CA. 323-662-5836
Knappen Milling Company
Augusta, MI 800-562-7736
LaCrosse Milling Company
Cochrane, WI 800-441-5411
Landreth Wild Rice
Norman, OK 800-333-3533
Lassen Foods
Santa Barbara, CA 805-683-7696
Leech Lake Reservation
Cass Lake, MN 218-335-8200
Life-Renewal
Garrison, MN 320-692-4498
Lone Pine Enterprises
Carlisle, AR 870-552-3217
Lowell Farms
El Campo, TX 888-484-9213
Luxor California ExportsCorporation
San Diego, CA 619-692-9330
Maple Leaf Foods International
Toronto, ON 416-480-8900
McKnight Milling Company
Hickory Ridge, AR 870-697-2504
Mid-Kansas Cooperative
Moundridge, KS 800-864-4284
Mille Lacs Wild Rice Corporation
Aitkin, MN 800-626-3809
Mills Brothers International
Tukwila, WA 206-575-3000
Minn-Dak Growers Limited
Grand Forks, ND. 701-746-7453
Minnesota Grain
Lake City, MN 800-535-7405
Minnesota Malting Company
Saint Paul, MN 507-263-3911
Minnesota Specialty Crops
McGregor, MN 800-328-6731
Montana Flour & Grain
Fort Benton, MT 406-622-5436
Montana Specialty Mills
Great Falls, MT 406-761-2338
Mosher Products
Cheyenne, WY 307-632-1492
Mustard Seed
Central, SC 877-621-2591
Natural Way Mills
Middle River, MN. 218-222-3677
Naturex (Chart Corp)
South Hackensack, NJ 201-440-5000
NorCal Wild Rice
Davis, CA 530-758-8550

Northwestern Extract Company
Brookfield, WI 800-466-3034
Oak Creek Farms
Edgar, NE 402-224-3038
Osowski Farms
Minto, ND. 701-248-3341
Ottawa Valley Grain Products
Renfrew, ON 613-432-3614
Pacific International Rice Mills
Woodland, CA 800-747-4764
Pendleton Flour Mills
Pendleton, OR. 541-276-6511
Perfect Foods
Monroe, NY 800-933-3288
Pines International
Lawrence, KS 800-697-4637
Pizzey's Milling & Baking Company
Angusville, NB 800-804-6433
Pleasant Grove Farms
Pleasant Grove, CA 916-655-3391
Purity Foods
Okemos, MI 800-997-7358
R&J Farms
West Salem, OH 419-846-3179
Raymond-Hadley Corporation
Spencer, NY 800-252-5220
Rice Hull Specialty Pro Company
Stuttgart, AR. 870-673-8507
Riceland Foods   Rice Milling Operations
Stuttgart, AR. 800-226-9522
Ricetec
Alvin, TX 281-393-3502
Riviana Foods
Houston, TX
Riviana Foods
Edison, NJ 732-225-7210
Riviana Foods
Houston, TX 800-226-9522
Riviana Foods
Memphis, TN 901-948-8556
Roberts Seed
Axtell, NE 308-743-2565
Roman Meal Milling Company
Fargo, ND 877-282-9743
S&E Organic Farms
Bakersfield, CA 661-325-2644
Sage V Farms
Los Angeles, CA. 310-820-4496
Scott's Auburn Mills
Auburn, KY. 800-962-7857
SJH Enterprises
Middleton, WI. 888-745-3845
Sorrenti Family Farms
Escalon, CA 888-435-9490
Southeastern Mills
Rome, GA 800-334-4468
Southern Brown Rice
Weiner, AR 800-421-7423
Specialty Rice Marketing
Brinkley, AR 800-467-1233
Stan-Mark Food Products
Chicago, IL 800-651-0994
Star of the West MillingCompany
Frankenmuth, MI 989-652-9971
Stengel Seed & Grain Company
Milbank, SD 605-432-6030
Sun Ridge Farms
Santa Cruz, CA 800-655-3252
Sunnyland Mills
Fresno, CA 800-501-8017
SunOpta Grains
Hope, MN 800-297-5997
Sunwest Foods
Davis, CA 530-758-8550
Super Bakes
Lincoln, NE 800-222-3276
Supreme Rice Mill
Crowley, LA 337-783-5222
Suzanne's Specialties
New Brunswick, NJ 800-762-2135
Sycamore Creek Company
Stockbridge, MI 517-851-0049
T.S. Smith & Sons
Bridgeville, DE 302-337-8271
Teff Company
Caldwell, ID 888-822-2221
Tradewinds International
Ellendale, TN 800-385-8884
Trinidad Benham Company
Denver, CO 303-220-1400
Tundra Wild Rice
Pine Falls, NB 204-367-8651

Uhlmann Company
Kansas City, MO. 800-383-8201
US Foods
Lincoln, NE. 402-470-2021
US Fresh Marketing
Virginia Beach, VA 757-481-2606
Viobin USA
Monticello, IL 217-762-2561
Vitamins
Chicago, IL 312-861-0700
Wagner Gourmet Foods
Shawnee Mission, KS 913-469-5411
Weetabix Company
Clinton, MA 800-343-0590
Weisenberger Mills
Midway, KY 800-643-8678
WG Thompson & Sons
Blenheim, ON 519-676-5411
Wheat Montana Farms & Bakery
Three Forks, MT. 800-535-2798
Wild Rice Exchange
Woodland, CA 800-223-7423
Woodland Foods
Gurnee, IL 847-625-8600
World Nutrition
Scottsdale, AZ 800-548-2710
WSI
Caldwell, ID 208-459-0777

Amaranth

Woodland Foods
Gurnee, IL. 847-625-8600

Granola

Alvarado Street Bakery
Petaluma, CA 707-283-0300
Ambrosial Granola
Brooklyn, NY 718-491-1335
Baker
Milford, NJ 800-995-3989
Barbara's Bakery
Petaluma, CA 707-765-2273
Blue Planet Foods, Inc.
Collegedale, TN 877-396-3145
Chappaqua Crunch
Marblehead, MA 781-631-8118
Con Agra Store Brands
Edina, MN. 952-835-6900
Cream of the West
Harlowton, MT 800-477-2383
Edner Corporation
Hayward, CA 510-441-8504
Energy Club
Pacoima, CA 800-688-6887
GKI Foods
Brighton, MI 248-486-0055
Grain Process Enterprises Ltd.
Scarborough, ON 800-387-5292
Grain-Free JK Gourmet
Toronto, ON 800-608-0465
Health Valley Company
Irwindale, CA 800-334-3204
Hialeah Products Company
Hollywood, FL 800-923-3379
Inn Maid Food
Lenox, MA 413-637-2732
Isabella's Healthy Bakery
Cuyahoga Falls, OH 800-476-6328
Kraft Foods
East Hanover, NJ 973-503-2000
Kraft Foods Biscuit Confections & Snacks
East Hanover, NJ 973-503-2000
Lassen Foods
Santa Barbara, CA 805-683-7696
Lehi Valley Trading Company
Mesa, AZ. 480-684-1402
Main Street Gourmet
Cuyahoga Falls, OH 800-533-6246
Masterfoods USA
Hackettstown, NJ 908-852-1000
McKee Foods Corporation
Collegedale, TN 423-238-7111
Michaelene's Gourmet Granola
Clarkston, MI 248-625-0156
Mother Nature's Goodies
Yucaipa, CA 909-795-6018
National Vinegar Company
Houston, TX 713-223-4214
Nature's Hand
Burnsville, MN 952-890-6033

New England Natural Bakers
Greenfield, MA .800-910-2884
Organic Milling Company
San Dimas, CA .800-638-8686
Partners, A Tastful Cracker
Seattle, WA 800-632-7477
Poppa's Granola
Perkinsville, VT 802-263-5342
Positively Third Street Bakery
Duluth, MN 218-724-8619
Quaker Oats Company
Danville, IL 217-443-3990
Quaker Oats Company
Chicago, IL 800-367-6287
Red Rose Trading Company
Wrightsville, PA 717-252-5500
SBK Preserves
Bronx, NY 800-773-7378
Schulze & Burch Biscuit Company
Chicago, IL 773-927-6622
Shade Foods
New Century, KS 800-225-6312
Snackerz
Commerce, CA .888-576-2253
Torn & Glasser
Los Angeles, CA. 800-282-6887
Udi's Granola
Denver, CO 303-657-6366
US Mills
Needham, MA. .800-422-1125
Well Dressed Food Company
Tupper Lake, NY 866-567-0845

Grits

ADM Milling Company
Jackson, TN 731-424-3535
Agricor
Marion, IN. 765-662-0606
Allen Canning Company
Siloam Springs, AR 800-234-2553
Cargill Dry Corn Ingredients
Paris, IL. 800-637-6481
Dakota Organic Products
Watertown, SD 800-243-7264
J.P. Green Milling Company
Mocksville, NC 336-751-2126
Minn-Dak Growers Limited
Grand Forks, ND. 701-746-7453
Minnesota Grain
Lake City, MN .800-535-7405
Natural Products
Grinnell, IA. 641-236-0852
Natural Way Mills
Middle River, MN. 218-222-3677
Quaker Oats Company
Cedar Rapids, IA. 319-362-3121
Sturm Foods
Manawa, WI 800-347-8876
White Lily Foods Company
San Antonio, TX 800-264-5459

Corn White & Yellow

Mills Brothers International
Tukwila, WA 206-575-3000

Hominy

Allen Canning Company
Siloam Springs, AR 800-234-2553
Bush Brothers & Company
Dandridge, TN 865-509-2361
Cateraid
Howell, MI 800-508-8217

Josie's Best New Mexican Foods
Santa Fe, NM .505-473-3437
Juanita's Foods
Wilmington, CA 310-834-5339
Mercado Latino
City of Industry, CA 626-333-6862

Canned

Juanita's Foods
Wilmington, CA 310-834-5339

Hops

Froedtert Malt Company
Milwaukee, WI 414-671-1166
Hop Growers of America
Moxee, WA 509-248-7043
Hops Extract Corporation of America
Yakima, WA 509-248-1530
Hopunion CBS
Yakima, WA 800-952-4873
John I. Haas
Washington, DC 202-223-0005
Naturex (Chart Corp)
South Hackensack, NJ 201-440-5000
Northwestern Extract Company
Brookfield, WI 800-466-3034
Steiner, S.S.
New York, NY .212-515-7200
Watson Nutritional Ingredients
West Haven, CT 203-932-3000

Hummus

Hommus Factory
Haverhill, MA. 508-460-0212
Quong Hop & Company
S San Francisco, CA. 650-553-9900
Tribe Mediterranean Foods Company LLC
Taunton, MA. .800-421-3474

Malt

Briess Industries
Chilton, WI 920-849-7711
Domino Specialty Ingredients
Baltimore, MD 800-446-9763
Froedtert Malt
Winona, MN 507-454-1535
Froedtert Malt Company
Milwaukee, WI 414-671-1166
Froedtert Malt Corporation
Wahpeton, ND. 800-493-4886
Great Western Malting Company
Vancouver, WA 877-770-7055
International Malting Company
Milwaukee, WI 414-671-1166
Jones Brewing Company
Smithton, PA .800-237-2337
Ladish Malting
Jefferson, WI .920-674-8500
Lake Country Foods
Oconomowoc, WI. 262-567-5521
Lion Brewery
Wilkes Barre, PA. 800-233-8327
Malt Products Corporation
Saddle Brook, NJ 800-526-0180
Minnesota Malting Company
Saint Paul, MN 507-263-3911
Northwestern Extract Company
Brookfield, WI 800-466-3034
Novartis Nutrition Corporation
Minneapolis, MN 952-848-6000

PepsiAmericas
New Orleans, LA 504-467-3774
Prairie Malt
Biggar, SK. 306-948-3500
Premier Malt Products
Warren, MI 586-443-3355
Quality Ingredients Corporation
Chester, NJ 800-843-6314
Rahr Malting Company
Shakopee, MN 952-445-1431
Schreier Malting Companypecialty Malt Division
Sheboygan, WI 800-669-6258
Suzanne's Specialties
New Brunswick, NJ 800-762-2135
United Canadian Malt
Peterborough, ON. 800-461-6400
Watson Nutritional Ingredients
West Haven, CT 203-932-3000

Dry

Oregon Specialty Company
Lakewood, WA 877-254-7494

Syrup

Briess Industries
Chilton, WI 920-849-7711
Malt-Diastase Company
Saddle Brook, NJ 800-772-0416
Schiff Food Products
North Bergen, NJ 201-861-2503
United Canadian Malt
Peterborough, ON. 800-461-6400

Millet

American Key Food Products
Closter, NJ. 800-767-0237
CHS Sunflower
Grandin, ND 701-484-5313
Dakota Organic Products
Watertown, SD 800-243-7264
Hialeah Products Company
Hollywood, FL 800-923-3379
Mills Brothers International
Tukwila, WA 206-575-3000
Natural Way Mills
Middle River, MN. 218-222-3677
Organic Planet
San Francisco, CA 415-765-5590
Red River Commodities
Fargo, ND 701-282-2600

Oats & Oat Products

ADM Milling Company
Shawnee Mission, KS. 800-422-1688
Agricore United
Winnipeg, MB. 204-944-5411
Anna's Oatcakes
Weston, VT 802-824-3535
Archer Daniels Midland Company
Decatur, IL 800-637-5843
Barbara's Bakery
Petaluma, CA .707-765-2273
Blue Planet Foods, Inc.
Collegedale, TN 877-396-3145
Can-Oat Milling
Portage la Prairie, MB 800-663-6287
ConAgra Mills
Omaha, NE 877-717-1694
ConAgra PV Grain
Superior, WI 715-398-3541

Cooperative Elevator Company
Pigeon, MI 989-453-4500
Dakota Organic Products
Watertown, SD 800-243-7264
Fizzle Flat Farm
Yale, IL 618-793-2060
Grain Millers
Eden Prairie, MN 800-232-6287
Heartland Mill
Marienthal, KS 620-379-4472
Honeyville Grain
Salt Lake City, UT 801-972-2168
Honeyville Grain
Rancho Cucamonga, CA 888-810-3212
J. Rettenmaier
Schoolcraft, MI 877-243-4661
Nuvex Ingredients
Blue Earth, MN 507-526-4331
Particle Control
Albertville, MN 763-497-3075
Roman Meal Milling Company
Tacoma, WA 253-475-0964
SJH Enterprises
Middleton, WI 888-745-3845
Weetabix Company
Clinton, MA 800-343-0590

Groats

Can-Oat Milling
Portage la Prairie, MB 800-663-6287

Oat Bran

Can-Oat Milling
Portage la Prairie, MB 800-663-6287
Foley's Candies
Richmond, BC 888-236-5397
Grain Millers
Eden Prairie, MN 800-232-6287
Natural Foods
Toledo, OH 800-860-0006
SJH Enterprises
Middleton, WI 888-745-3845

Oatmeal

Grain Millers
Eden Prairie, MN 800-232-6287
Honeyville Grain
Salt Lake City, UT 801-972-2168
Kenlake Foods
Murray, KY 800-632-6900
LaCrosse Milling Company
Cochrane, WI 800-441-5411
Pepsi
Chicago, IL 312-821-1000
PepsiCo
Barrington, IL 847-842-4652
Quaker Oats Company
Stockton, CA 209-982-5580
Silver Palate Kitchens
Cresskill, NJ 800-872-5283

Rolled

Can-Oat Milling
Portage la Prairie, MB 800-663-6287
Grain Millers
Eden Prairie, MN 800-232-6287
Heartland Mill
Marienthal, KS 620-379-4472
Honeyville Grain
Salt Lake City, UT 801-972-2168
Honeyville Grain
Rancho Cucamonga, CA 888-810-3212

Poi

Aloha Poi Factory
Wailuku, HI........................808-244-3536
Puueo Poi Factory
Hilo, HI 808-935-8435

Quinoa

Quinoa Corporation
Gardena, CA 310-217-8125
Woodland Foods
Gurnee, IL 847-625-8600

Rice

A&B Ingredients
Fairfield, NJ 973-227-1390
ACH Food Companies
Cordova, TN 800-691-1106
Acharice Specialties
Greenville, MS 800-432-4901
ADM Milling Company
Shawnee Mission, KS 800-422-1688
Affiliated Rice Milling
Alvin, TX 281-331-6176
Agrusa, Inc.
Leonia, NJ 201-592-5950
Ankeny Lakes Wild Rice
Salem, OR 800-555-5380
Baycliff Company
New York, NY 212-772-6078
Beaumont Rice Mills
Beaumont, TX......................409-832-2521
Berberian Nut Company
Stocton, CA 209-465-9181
Blue Chip Group
Salt Lake City, UT 800-878-0099
Buon Italia
New York, NY 212-633-9090
California Cereal Products
Oakland, CA 510-452-4500
California Natural Products
Lathrop, CA 209-858-2525
Caribbean Food Delights
Tappan, NY 845-398-3000
Chef Hans Gourmet Foods
Monroe, LA. 800-890-4267
Chef Merito
Encino, CA 800-637-4861
Chieftain Wild Rice Company
Spooner, WI 800-262-6368
China Doll Company
Saraland, AL 251-457-7641
Cinnabar Specialty Foods
Prescott, AZ 866-293-6433
Comet Rice
Houston, TX 281-272-8800
Commodities Marketing, Inc.
Edison, NJ. 732-516-0700
Conrad Rice Mill
New Iberia, LA....................800-551-3245
Cormier Rice Milling Company
De Witt, AR 870-946-3561
Country Cupboard
Virginia City, NV 775-847-7300
Deer River Wild Rice
Deer River, MN...................218-246-2713
Dixie Rice
Gueydan, LA. 337-536-9276
Domino Specialty Ingredients
Baltimore, MD 800-446-9763
Eagle Agricultural Products
Huntsville, AR 501-738-2203
Eden Foods Inc
Clinton, MI 800-248-0320
Falcon Rice Mill Inc
Crowley, LA 800-738-7423
Fall River Wild Rice
Fall River Mills, CA 800-626-4366
Fantastic Foods
Napa, CA. 800-288-1089
Farmers Rice Milling Company
Lake Charles, LA 337-433-5205
Farmers' Rice Cooperative
Sacramento, CA 800-326-2799
Florida Crystals
West Palm Beach, FL 877-835-2828
Garber Farms
Iota, LA. 800-824-2284
Golden Gate Foods
Dallas, TX..........................214-747-2223
Golden Grain Company
Bridgeview, IL 708-458-7020
Goya Foods
Secaucus, NJ 201-348-4900
Goya Foods of Florida
Miami, FL...........................305-592-3150
Grey Owl Foods
Grand Rapids, MN 800-527-0172
Hershey Pasta Group
Louisville, KY 800-468-1714
Hung's Noodle House
Calgary, AB........................403-250-1663
Indian Harvest
Colusa, CA 800-294-2433

Indian Harvest Specialitifoods
Bemidji, MN. 800-346-7032
Kalustyan Corporation
Union, NJ 908-688-6111
Koda Farms
South Dos Palos, CA 209-392-2191
Kraft Food Ingredients
Memphis, TN 901-381-6500
Landreth Wild Rice
Norman, OK 800-333-3533
Leech Lake Reservation
Cass Lake, MN 218-335-8200
Liberty Richter
Saddle Brook, NJ 201-291-8749
Lone Pine Enterprises
Carlisle, AR 870-552-3217
Lotus Foods
El Cerrito, CA 510-525-3137
Louis Dreyfus Corporation
Wilton, CT 203-761-2000
Louisiana Gourmet Enterprises
Houma, LA 800-328-5586
Lowell Farms
El Campo, TX 888-484-9213
Lundberg Family Farm
Richvale, CA 530-882-4551
McKnight Milling Company
Hickory Ridge, AR 870-697-2504
Mercado Latino
City of Industry, CA 626-333-6862
Mermaid Spice Corporation
Fort Myers, FL 239-693-1986
Mille Lacs Wild Rice Corporation
Aitkin, MN 800-626-3809
Mills Brothers International
Tukwila, WA 206-575-3000
Minnesota Specialty Crops
McGregor, MN 800-328-6731
Natural Way Mills
Middle River, MN.................218-222-3677
Near East Food Products
Barrington, IL......................847-842-4654
North Bay Trading Company
Brule, WI. 800-348-0164
Oak Grove Smokehouse
Prairieville, LA 225-673-6857
Pacific International Rice Mills
Woodland, CA 800-747-4764
Pleasant Grove Farms
Pleasant Grove, CA 916-655-3391
Primo Foods
Toronto, ON 800-377-6945
Producer's Rice
Stuttgart, AR 870-673-4444
Producers Rice Mill
Stuttgart, AR 870-673-4444
Raymond-Hadley Corporation
Spencer, NY 800-252-5220
Reggie Ball's Cajun Foods
Lake Charles, LA 337-436-0291
RIBUS
St Louis, MO. 314-727-4287
Rice Company
Roseville, CA 916-787-1084
Rice Deerwood & Grain Processing
Deerwood, MN 218-534-3762
Rice Foods
Mount Vernon, IL 618-242-0026
Rice Hull Specialty Pro Company
Stuttgart, AR 870-673-8507
Rice River Farms/Chieftan Wild Rice Company
Spooner, WI 800-262-6368
Rice Select
Alvin, TX 800-232-7423
Riceland Foods   Rice Milling Operations
Stuttgart, AR 800-226-9522
Ricetec
Alvin, TX 281-393-3502
Riviana Foods
Houston, TX
Riviana Foods
Abbeville, LA 337-893-2236
Riviana Foods
Edison, NJ. 732-225-7210
Riviana Foods
Houston, TX 800-226-9522
Riviana Foods
Memphis, TN 901-948-8556
Royal Caribbean Bakery
Mt Vernon, NY 888-818-0971
Sage V Foods LLC
Los Angeles, CA...................310-820-4496

Sara Lee Corporation
Downers Grove, IL.................630-598-8100
Satnam Overseas Limited
Somerset, NJ....................732-868-3141
Shah Trading Company
Toronto, ON....................416-292-6927
Shahi Food Corporation
Mississauga, ON.................905-677-4327
Sorrenti Family Farms
Escalon, CA....................888-435-9490
Southern Brown Rice
Weiner, AR.....................800-421-7423
Specialty Rice Marketing
Brinkley, AR...................800-467-1233
SPI Foods
Fremont, NE....................866-266-1304
St Mary's & Ankeny Lakes Wild Rice Company
Salem, OR......................800-555-5380
Sun West
Torrance, CA...................310-320-4000
Sunwest Foods
Davis, CA......................530-758-8550
SunWest Organics
Davis, CA......................530-758-8550
Supreme Rice Mill
Crowley, LA....................337-783-5222
Tipiak
Stamford, CT...................203-961-9117
Torn & Glasser
Los Angeles, CA................800-282-6887
Tradewinds International
Ellendale, TN..................800-385-8884
Trinidad Benham Company
Denver, CO.....................303-220-1400
Tropical
Marietta, GA...................800-544-3762
Tundra Wild Rice
Pine Falls, NB.................204-367-8651
Uncle Ben's
Houston, TX....................713-674-9484
US Foods
Lincoln, NE....................402-470-2021
Van Bennett Food Company
Reading, PA....................800-423-8897
Vigo Importing Company
Tampa, FL......................813-884-3491
Wagner Gourmet Foods
Shawnee Mission, KS............913-469-5411
Weetabix Company
Clinton, MA....................800-343-0590
Western Pacific Commodities
Las Vegas, NV..................702-312-8080
Westlam Foods
Chino, CA......................800-722-9519
Wild Rice Exchange
Woodland, CA...................800-223-7423
Willow Foods
Beaverton, OR..................800-338-3609
Woodland Foods
Gurnee, IL.....................847-625-8600
Wright Enrichment
Crowley, LA....................800-201-3096
Wysong Corporation
Midland, MI....................800-748-0188
Zatarain's
Gretna, LA.....................800-435-6639

Aborio

Chieftain Wild Rice Company
Spooner, WI....................800-262-6368
Woodland Foods
Gurnee, IL.....................847-625-8600

Basmati

American Health & Nutrition
Ann Arbor, MI..................734-677-5572
Asian Brands
Hayward, CA....................510-523-7474
Chieftain Wild Rice Company
Spooner, WI....................800-262-6368
Commodities Marketing, Inc.
Edison, NJ.....................732-516-0700
Eagle Agricultural Products
Huntsville, AR.................501-738-2203
Kalustyan Corporation
Union, NJ......................908-688-6111
Lone Pine Enterprises
Carlisle, AR...................870-552-3217
McKnight Milling Company
Hickory Ridge, AR..............870-697-2504

Rice Select
Alvin, TX......................800-232-7423
Shahi Food Corporation
Mississauga, ON................905-677-4327
Southern Brown Rice
Weiner, AR.....................800-421-7423
Specialty Rice Marketing
Brinkley, AR...................800-467-1233
Wild Rice Exchange
Woodland, CA...................800-223-7423
Woodland Foods
Gurnee, IL.....................847-625-8600

Black Puinoa

Chieftain Wild Rice Company
Spooner, WI....................800-262-6368

Black Thai

Chieftain Wild Rice Company
Spooner, WI....................800-262-6368

Brewers'

Beaumont Rice Mills
Beaumont, TX...................409-832-2521
Commodities Marketing, Inc.
Edison, NJ.....................732-516-0700
Golden Gate Foods
Dallas, TX.....................214-747-2223
Riceland Foods   Rice Milling Operations
Little Rock, AR................888-532-4844

Brown

American Health & Nutrition
Ann Arbor, MI..................734-677-5572
California Natural Products
Lathrop, CA....................209-858-2525
Chieftain Wild Rice Company
Spooner, WI....................800-262-6368
Cormier Rice Milling Company
De Witt, AR....................870-946-3561
Eagle Agricultural Products
Huntsville, AR.................501-738-2203
Lone Pine Enterprises
Carlisle, AR...................870-552-3217
McKnight Milling Company
Hickory Ridge, AR..............870-697-2504
Pacific International Rice Mills
Woodland, CA...................800-747-4764
Rice Select
Alvin, TX......................800-232-7423
Riceland Foods   Rice Milling Operations
Little Rock, AR................888-532-4844
Riviana Foods
Abbeville, LA..................337-893-2236
Riviana Foods
Edison, NJ.....................732-225-7210
Sobaya
Cowansville, QC................800-319-8808
Southern Brown Rice
Weiner, AR.....................800-421-7423
Supreme Rice Mill
Crowley, LA....................337-783-5222
Wild Rice Exchange
Woodland, CA...................800-223-7423

Chinese Black

Woodland Foods
Gurnee, IL.....................847-625-8600

Frozen

Sage V Foods LLC
Los Angeles, CA................310-820-4496

Hulls

Rice Hull Specialty Pro Company
Stuttgart, AR..................870-673-8507

IQF (Individual Quick Frozen)

EMERLING INTERNATIONAL FOODS, INC.

Emerling International Foods
Buffalo, NY....................716-833-7381

We supply food manufacturers and food service customers worldwide (since 1988) with bulk ingredients including: Fruits & Vegetables; Juice Concentrates; Herbs & Spices; Oils & Vinegars; Flavors & Colors; Honey & Molasses. We also produce PURE MAPLE SYRUP.

Sage V Foods LLC
Los Angeles, CA................310-820-4496

Instant

Riceland Foods   Rice Milling Operations
Little Rock, AR................888-532-4844
Sage V Foods LLC
Los Angeles, CA................310-820-4496

Jasmine

American Health & Nutrition
Ann Arbor, MI..................734-677-5572
Asian Brands
Hayward, CA....................510-523-7474
Chieftain Wild Rice Company
Spooner, WI....................800-262-6368
Commodities Marketing, Inc.
Edison, NJ.....................732-516-0700
KP USA Trading
Los Angeles, CA................323-881-9871
Lowell Farms
El Campo, TX...................888-484-9213
Rice Select
Alvin, TX......................800-232-7423
Woodland Foods
Gurnee, IL.....................847-625-8600

Milled

Cormier Rice Milling Company
De Witt, AR....................870-946-3561
Riceland Foods   Rice Milling Operations
Little Rock, AR................888-532-4844

Organic

Domino Specialty Ingredients
Baltimore, MD..................800-446-9763
Sage V Foods LLC
Los Angeles, CA................310-820-4496

Parboiled

Riceland Foods   Rice Milling Operations
Little Rock, AR................888-532-4844

US #1 Long Grain

McKnight Milling Company
Hickory Ridge, AR..............870-697-2504
Mercado Latino
City of Industry, CA...........626-333-6862

Pilaf

Asian Brands
Hayward, CA....................510-523-7474
Chef Hans Gourmet Foods
Monroe, LA.....................800-890-4267
Chieftain Wild Rice Company
Spooner, WI....................800-262-6368
Country Cupboard
Virginia City, NV..............775-847-7300
Geetha's Gourmet of India
Las Cruces, NM.................800-274-0475
Riceland Foods   Rice Milling Operations
Little Rock, AR................888-532-4844
Wild Rice Exchange
Woodland, CA...................800-223-7423

Precooked

Riviana Foods
Houston, TX
Sage V Foods LLC
Los Angeles, CA................310-820-4496

Protein

A&B Ingredients
Fairfield, NJ 973-227-1390

Purple Sticky

Woodland Foods
Gurnee, IL 847-625-8600

Risotto

Agrusa, Inc.
Leonia, NJ 201-592-5950
Italian Foods Corporation
Oakland, CA 510-444-9050

Spanish

Country Cupboard
Virginia City, NV 775-847-7300

Canned

Conrad Rice Mill
New Iberia, LA 800-551-3245

Wehani

Chieftain Wild Rice Company
Spooner, WI 800-262-6368

Wild

Ankeny Lakes Wild Rice
Salem, OR 800-555-5380
Chef Hans Gourmet Foods
Monroe, LA 800-890-4267
Chieftain Wild Rice Company
Spooner, WI 800-262-6368
Conrad Rice Mill
New Iberia, LA 800-551-3245
Country Cupboard
Virginia City, NV 775-847-7300
Deer River Wild Rice
Deer River, MN 218-246-2713
Fall River Wild Rice
Fall River Mills, CA 800-626-4366
Grey Owl Foods
Grand Rapids, MN 800-527-0172
Landreth Wild Rice
Norman, OK 800-333-3533
Leech Lake Reservation
Cass Lake, MN 218-335-8200
Mille Lacs Wild Rice Corporation
Aitkin, MN 800-626-3809
Minnesota Specialty Crops
McGregor, MN 800-328-6731
NorCal Wild Rice
Davis, CA 530-758-5550
North Bay Trading Company
Brule, WI. 800-348-0164
Rice Deerwood & Grain Processing
Deerwood, MN 218-534-3762
Rice River Farms/Chieftan Wild Rice Company
Spooner, WI 800-262-6368
Riceland Foods   Rice Milling Operations
Little Rock, AR 888-532-4844
Riviana Foods
Abbeville, LA 337-893-2236
Riviana Foods
Houston, TX 800-226-9522
Secret Garden
Park Rapids, MN 800-950-4409
Select Marketing Group
Huron, OH. 888-805-0800

Sorrenti Family Farms
Escalon, CA 888-435-9490
Southern Brown Rice
Weiner, AR 800-421-7423
St Mary's & Ankeny Lakes Wild Rice Company
Salem, OR. 800-555-5380
Sunwest Foods
Davis, CA 530-758-5550
Tradewinds International
Ellendale, TN 800-385-8884
Tundra Wild Rice
Pine Falls, NB 204-367-8651
US Foods
Lincoln, NE. 402-470-2021
Wild Rice Exchange
Woodland, CA. 800-223-7423
Woodland Foods
Gurnee, IL 847-625-8600

Rye

Alfred & Sam Italian Bakery
Lancaster, PA. 717-392-6311
Dakota Organic Products
Watertown, SD 800-243-7264
Fizzle Flat Farm
Yale, IL 618-793-2060
Grain Millers Eugene
Eugene, OR. 800-443-8972
Honeyville Grain
Rancho Cucamonga, CA 888-810-3212
Minnesota Grain
Lake City, MN 800-535-7405
Montana Specialty Mills
Great Falls, MT. 406-761-2338
Natural Way Mills
Middle River, MN. 218-222-3677
Naturex (Chart Corp)
South Hackensack, NJ 201-440-5000

Sorghum

ADM Milling Company
Shawnee Mission, KS 800-422-1688
Dakota Organic Products
Watertown, SD 800-243-7264
Donald McCoun
Versailles, KY 859-873-4650
Suzanne's Specialties
New Brunswick, NJ 800-762-2135
Webbpak
Trussville, AL 800-655-3500
Wing Candy Company
Branson, MO. 417-334-3238
Yoder Foods
Liberty, KY 877-702-0010

Soy Bean Meal

Bunge Corporation
Vicksburg, MS 601-638-3824
Cargill Vegetable Oils
Minneapolis, MN 612-378-0551
Clofine Dairy & Food Products
Linwood, NJ 800-441-1001
International Service Group
Alpharetta, GA 770-518-0988

Tapioca

Agriproducts
Coral Springs, FL 800-277-4979
American Key Food Products
Closter, NJ. 800-767-0237

Cargill Texturizing Solutions
Cedar Rapids, IA. 877-650-7080
Chloe Foods Corporation
Brooklyn, NY 718-827-3600
Commodities Marketing, Inc.
Edison, NJ. 732-516-0700
ConAgra Grocery Products
Irvine, CA 714-680-1000
Dean Distributors
Burlingame, CA 800-792-0816
Heartline Foods
Westport, CT. 203-222-0381
Kraft Food Ingredients
Memphis, TN 901-381-6500
Organic Planet
San Francisco, CA 415-765-5590
Primera Foods
Cameron, WI. 800-365-2409
Van Bennett Food Company
Reading, PA 800-423-8897

Cassava

Cargill Texturizing Solutions
Cedar Rapids, IA. 877-650-7080

Pearl

Granulated, Starch

Cargill Texturizing Solutions
Cedar Rapids, IA. 877-650-7080

Wheat

ADM Milling Company
Carthage, MO 417-358-2197
ADM Milling Company
Abilene, KS. 785-263-1631
ADM Milling Company
Shawnee Mission, KS 800-422-1688
Agri-Dairy Products
Purchase, NY 914-697-9580
Agricore United
Winnipeg, MB 204-944-5411
AgriCulver Seeds
Trumansburg, NY 800-836-3701
Aliments Trigone
Quebec, QC. 877-259-7491
American Health & Nutrition
Ann Arbor, MI 734-677-5572
Archer Daniels Midland Company
Decatur, IL 800-637-5843
Blue Chip Group
Salt Lake City, UT 800-878-0099
Briess Industries
Chilton, WI. 920-849-7711
Chieftain Wild Rice Company
Spooner, WI 800-262-6368
ConAgra Flour Milling
Fremont, NE 402-721-4200
ConAgra Flour Milling
Martins Creek, PA. 610-253-9341
ConAgra Flour Milling
Chester, IL. 618-826-2371
ConAgra Flour Milling
Red Lion, PA 717-244-4559
ConAgra Flour Milling
York, PA 717-846-7773
ConAgra Flour Milling
Sherman, TX 903-893-8111
ConAgra Mills
Tampa, FL. 800-582-1483

ConAgra Mills
Omaha, NE .877-717-1694
Cooperative Elevator Company
Pigeon, MI .989-453-4500
Dakota Organic Products
Watertown, SD 800-243-7264
Dover Industries Limited
Burlington, ON 905-333-1515
El Peto Products
Cambridge, ON. 800-387-4064
Ferris Organic Farm
Eaton Rapids, MI 800-628-8736
Fizzle Flat Farm
Yale, IL 618-793-2060
Florence Macaroni Manufacturing
Chicago, IL .800-647-2782
Gabriele Macaroni Company
City of Industry, CA 626-964-2324
Grain Millers Eugene
Eugene, OR. 800-443-8972
Heartland Wheat Growers
Russell, KS .785-483-5559
Honeyville Grain
Rancho Cucamonga, CA 888-810-3212
J. Rettenmaier
Schoolcraft, MI 877-243-4661
Kaufman Ingredients
Vernon Hills, IL 847-573-0844
Knappen Milling Company
Augusta, MI 800-562-7736
Knight Seed Company
Burnsville, MN 800-328-2999
Lone Pine Enterprises
Carlisle, AR 870-552-3217
Louis Dreyfus Corporation
Wilton, CT .203-761-2000
Manildra Milling Corporation
Fairway, KS. 800-323-8435
Minnesota Grain
Lake City, MN 800-535-7405
Montana Specialty Mills
Great Falls, MT 406-761-2338
Natural Way Mills
Middle River, MN. 218-222-3677
Perfect Foods
Monroe, NY 800-933-3288
Pines International
Lawrence, KS 800-697-4637
Pleasant Grove Farms
Pleasant Grove, CA 916-655-3391
Purity Foods
Okemos, MI 800-997-7358
Roberts Seed
Axtell, NE 308-743-2565
Roman Meal Milling Company
Tacoma, WA 253-475-0964
SJH Enterprises
Middleton, WI. 888-745-3845
Sunnyland Mills
Fresno, CA .800-501-8017
T.S. Smith & Sons
Bridgeville, DE 302-337-8271
Weetabix Company
Clinton, MA 800-343-0590
Western Pacific Commodities
Las Vegas, NV 702-312-8080
Wysong Corporation
Midland, MI 800-748-0188

Bread

New White Palace Bakery
Philadelphia, PA 215-324-9852
Turano Pastry Shops
Bloomingdale, IL 630-529-6161

Bulgar

ADM Milling Company
Mississauga, ON. 800-267-8492
Chieftain Wild Rice Company
Spooner, WI 800-262-6368

Flakes

ADM Milling Company
Mississauga, ON. 800-267-8492
Attala Company
Kosciusko, MS 800-824-2691

Germ

American Health & Nutrition
Ann Arbor, MI 734-677-5572
Canadian Harvest
Cambridge, MN 888-689-5800
Fearn Natural Foods
Mequon, WI 800-877-8935
Garuda International
Lemon Cove, CA 559-594-4380
Green Foods Corporation
Oxnard, CA 800-777-4430
Norac Technologies
Edmonton, AB 780-414-9595
Star of the West MillingCompany
Frankenmuth, MI 989-652-9971
VIOBIN
Monticello, IL 888-473-9645
Viobin USA
Monticello, IL 217-762-2561
Vitamins
Chicago, IL 312-861-0700

Defatted

Vitamins
Chicago, IL 312-861-0700

Gluten

ADM Food Ingredients
Olathe, KS. 800-255-6637
Blue Chip Group
Salt Lake City, UT 800-878-0099
Clofine Dairy & Food Products
Linwood, NJ 800-441-1001
El Peto Products
Cambridge, ON. 800-387-4064
Manildra Milling Corporation
Fairway, KS. 800-323-8435

Spring

ADM Milling Company
Abilene, KS. 785-263-1631

Winter

Conquest International LLC
Plainville, KS 785-434-2483
Natural Way Mills
Middle River, MN. 218-222-3677

Whey & Whey Products

ACH Food Companies
Boyceville, WI 715-643-2600
Agri-Dairy Products
Purchase, NY 914-697-9580
Alto Dairy Cooperative
Waupun, WI 920-346-2215
American Whey
Ridgewood, NJ 201-493-2662
Anderson Custom Processing
New Ulm, MN. 877-588-4950
Arla Foods Ingredients
Basking Ridge, NJ 800-243-3730
Ault Foods
Toronto, ON 416-626-1973
Berkshire Dairy & Food Products
Wyomissing, PA 888-654-8008
Blossom Farm Products
Ridgewood, NJ 800-729-1818
Bongard's Creameries
Perham, MN 218-346-4680
Brewster Dairy
Brewster, OH 800-874-0874
Calpro Ingredients
Corona, CA. 909-493-4890
Century Foods International
Sparta, WI. 800-269-1901
Clofine Dairy & Food Products
Linwood, NJ 800-441-1001
Con Yeager Spice Company
Zelienople, PA. 800-222-2460
CP Kelco
Chicago, IL 800-535-2687
Crest Foods Company
Ashton, IL 800-435-6972
Crowley Foods
Binghamton, NY 800-637-0019
Dairy Farmers of America
Smithfield, UT 800-453-2820

Dairy Farmers of America
Kansas City, MO. 816-801-6200
Darigold Inc
Seattle, WA 800-333-6455
Davisco Foods International
Eden Prairie, MN 800-757-7611
Davisco International
Eden Prairie, MN 800-757-7611
Ellsworth Cooperative Creamery
Ellsworth, WI 715-273-4311
Empire Cheese
Cuba, NY .585-968-1552
First District Association
Litchfield, MN 320-693-3236
Foremost Farms
Waukon, IA 563-568-3474
Foremost Farms
Plover, WI 715-341-0101
Foremost Farms
Baraboo, WI 800-365-9196
Foremost Farms
Appleton, WI 920-738-1555
Foremost Farms USA
Sparta, WI 608-269-3126
Friendship Dairies
Friendship, NY 585-973-3031
Grande Custom Ingredients Group
Brownsville, WI 800-772-3210
Hilmar Cheese Company
Hilmar, CA 800-577-5772
Holmes Cheese Company
Millersburg, OH 330-674-6451
Honeyville Grain
Salt Lake City, UT 801-972-2168
Honeyville Grain
Rancho Cucamonga, CA 888-810-3212
Kantner Group
Wapakoneta, OH 419-738-4060
Keebler Company
Battle Creek, MI 800-962-1413
Land O'Lakes, Inc
Arden Hills, MN 800-328-9680
Leprino Foods Company
Denver, CO 800-537-7466
Main Street Ingredients
La Crosse, WI 800-359-2345
Minerva Cheese Factory
Minerva, OH 330-868-4196
Mount Capra Cheese
Chehalis, WA 800-574-1961
Particle Control
Albertville, MN. 763-497-3075
Plainview Milk Products Cooperative
Plainview, MN 507-534-3872
Quality Ingredients Corporation
Burnsville, MN 952-898-4002
Quest International Flavors
1411 GP Naarden
Reilly Dairy & Food Company
Tampa, FL 813-839-8458
San Fernando Creamery Farmdale Creamery
San Bernardino, CA 909-889-3002
Saputo
St Leonard, QC 514-328-6662
Saputo Cheese
Fond Du Lac, WI 800-824-3373
Saputo Cheese
Lena, WI .920-829-5251
Tillamook County Creamery Association
Tillamook, OR 503-842-4481
Valley Queen Cheese Factory
Milbank, SD 605-432-4563
Westin
Omaha, NE 800-228-6098

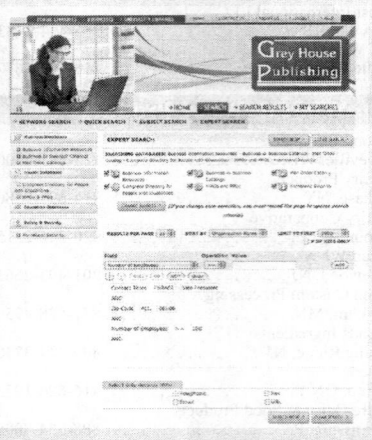
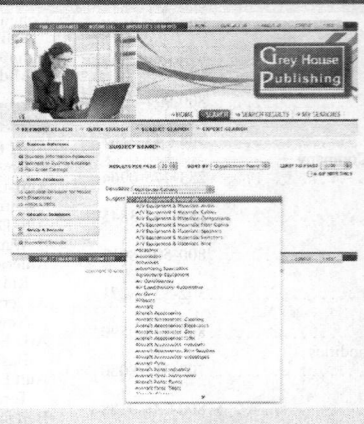

Cheese & Cheese Products

General

Agri-Mark
  Lawrence, MA 978-687-4936
Dairiconcepts
  Springfield, MO 877-596-4374
Dairyfood USA Inc
  Blue Mounds, WI 800-236-3300
Golden Valley Dairy Products
  Tulare, CA. 559-687-1188
Hormel Foods Corporation
  Austin, MN 800-523-4635
J&M Foods
  Little Rock, AR 800-264-2278
Kantner Group
  Wapakoneta, OH. 419-738-4060
Kraft Foods
  Northfield, IL 800-323-0768
Lactalis USA   Merrill Plant
  Merrill, WI 888-766-3353
Marathon Cheese
  Marathon, WI 715-443-2211
Market Day Corporation
  Itasca, IL 877-632-7753
Mozzarella Fresca   Tipton Plant
  Tipton, CA 559-752-4823
Old Tavern Food Products
  Waukesha, WI. 888-425-1788
Parmalat Canada
  Toronto, ON .800-563-1515
Sorrento Lactalis   Plant & Distribution Center
  Nampa, ID. 208-467-4424
Stanz Foodservice
  South Bend, IN 574-232-6666
Swiss Heritage Cheese
  Monticello, WI 608-938-4455
Twin County Dairy
  Kalona, IA. 319-656-2776

Cheese

ACH Food Companies
  Boyceville, WI 715-643-2600
ACH Food Companies
  Cordova, TN 800-691-1106
Aegean Cheese
  Austin, MN 507-433-1292
AFP Advanced Food Products, LLC
  Visalia, CA 559-627-2070
Agri-Dairy Products
  Purchase, NY 914-697-9580
Agri-Mark
  Lawrence, MA 978-687-4936
Agropur Cooperative Agro-Alimentaire
  Granby, QC .800-363-5686
AgSource Milk Analysis Laboratory
  Menomonie, WI 715-235-1128
Al Pete Meats
  Muncie, IN 765-288-8817
Alberta Cheese Company
  Calgary, AB. .403-279-4353
Alberto-Culver Company
  Melrose Park, IL 708-450-3000
Alpine Cheese Company
  Winesburg, OH. 330-359-6291
Alta Dena Certified Dairy
  City of Industry, CA 800-535-1369
Alto Dairy Cooperative
  Waupun, WI .920-346-2215
Amberwave Foods
  Oakmont, PA. 412-828-3040
Amboy Specialty Foods Company
  Dixon, IL. 800-892-0400
American Cheesemen
  Clear Lake, IA. 641-357-7176
American Foodservice
  Dallas, TX. 972-385-5800
Anchor Appetizer Group
  Appleton, WI 920-997-2659
Anchor Food Products/ McCain Foods
  Appleton, WI 920-734-0627
Anco Foods
  Caldwell, NJ .800-526-2596
Annie's Homegrown
  Napa, CA. 800-288-1089
Applegate Farms
  Bridgewater, NJ 908-725-2768

Ardmore Cheese Company
  Shelbyville, TN. 931-427-2191
Ariza Cheese Company
  Paramount, CA 800-762-4736
Aslanis Seafoods
  Quincy, MA. .800-876-3712
Associated Milk Producers
  Duluth, MN. .218-624-4803
Associated Milk Producers
  Paynesville, MN 320-243-3794
Associated Milk Producers
  Dawson, MN. 320-769-2994
Associated Milk Producers
  New Ulm, MN. 507-233-4600
Associated Milk Producers
  Arlington, IA. 563-933-4521
Associated Milk Producers
  Freeman, SD .605-925-4234
Associated Milk Producers
  Hoven, SD 605-948-2211
Associated Milk Producers
  Portage, WI .608-742-2114
Associated Milk Producers
  Blair, WI 608-989-2535
Associated Milk Producers
  Mason City, IA 641-424-6111
Associated Milk Producers
  Fargo, ND 701-293-6455
Associated Milk Producers
  Sanborn, IA. .712-729-3255
Associated Milk Producers
  Jim Falls, WI. 715-382-4113
Associated Milk Producers
  New Ulm, MN. 800-533-3580
Astro Dairy Products
  Etobicoke, ON. 416-622-2811
Atalanta Corporation
  Elizabeth, NJ 908-352-6517
Atwood Cheese Company
  Atwood, ON .519-356-2271
Aunt Lizzie's
  Memphis, TN 800-993-7788
Avanti Food Company
  Walnut, IL 800-243-3739
B&D Foods
  Boise, ID 208-344-1183
Baker Cheese Factory
  St Cloud, WI .920-477-7871
Baker's Coconut
  Memphis, TN 800-323-1092
Barnum-Goodfriend Farms
  Jeffersonville, NY 845-482-4123
Bass Lake Cheese Factory
  Somerset, WI. 800-368-2437
Bedford Cheese Store
  Shelbyville, TN. 800-264-1115
Bel/Kaukauna USA
  Kaukauna, WI. 800-558-3500
BelGioioso Cheese
  Denmark, WI. 877-863-2123
Belle Plaine Cheese Factory
  Shawano, WI. 866-245-5924
Bellwether Farms
  Valley Ford, CA 888-527-8606
Berger Foods
  Tucker, GA 770-934-8983
Berner Cheese Corporation
  Dakota, IL. 800-819-8199
Berner Cheese Corporation
  Rock City, IL. 815-865-5136
Berner Foods, Inc.
  Roscoe, IL. 800-819-8199
Biazzo Dairy Products
  Ridgefield, NJ 201-941-6800
Bieri's Jackson Cheese
  Jackson, WI. 262-677-3227
Biery Cheese Company
  Louisville, OH 800-243-3731
Black Diamond Cheese
  Toronto, ON 800-263-2858
Blakely Freezer Locker
  Thomasville, GA. 229-723-3622
Blaser's USA, Inc.
  Comstock, WI. 715-822-2437
Bletsoe's Cheese
  Marathon, WI 715-443-2526

Blue Ribbon Meats
  Cleveland, OH 216-631-8850
Bongard's Creameries
  Perham, MN .218-346-4680
Bongards Creameries
  Norwood, MN. 800-877-6417
Bongrain Cheese
  New Holland, PA 717-355-8500
Bongrain North America
  Mahwah, NJ .201-512-8825
Bravo Farms
  Visalia, CA 559-627-3525
Brenntag
  Reading, PA .888-926-4151
Brenntag Pacific
  Santa Fe Springs, CA 562-903-9626
Brewster Dairy
  Brewster, OH 800-874-0874
Brier Run Farm
  Birch River, WV. 304-649-2975
Broughton Foods
  Marietta, OH. 800-283-2479
Brunkow Cheese Company
  Darlington, WI 608-776-3716
Bunker Hill Cheese Company
  Millersburg, OH 800-253-6636
Buon Italia
  New York, NY 212-633-9090
Burnette Dairy Cooperative
  Grantsburg, WI 715-689-2468
Byrne Dairy
  Syracuse, NY 800-899-1535
C.E. Zuercher & Company
  Chicago, IL. .312-666-6992
CA Fortune
  Westby, WI. .608-634-2468
Cabot Creamery
  Montpelier, VT 888-792-2268
Cady Cheese Factory
  Wilson, WI 715-772-4218
Calabro Cheese Corporation
  East Haven, CT 203-469-1311
Cantare Foods
  San Diego, CA 858-578-8490
Cappiello Dairy Products
  Schenectady, NY. 518-374-5064
Caprine Estates
  Bellbrook, OH. 937-848-7406
Carr Cheese Factory/GileCheese Company
  Cuba City, WI 608-744-8455
Carr Valley Cheese Company
  La Valle, WI .800-462-7258
Cascade Cheese Company
  Cascade, WI .920-528-8221
Cass Clay
  Fargo, ND 701-232-1566
Castle Cheese
  Slippery Rock, PA. 800-252-4373
Cedar Grove Cheese
  Plain, WI. 800-200-6020
Cedar Valley Cheese
  Belgium, WI .920-994-9500
Cemac Foods Corporation
  Philadelphia, PA 800-724-0179
Chalet Cheese Cooperative
  Monroe, WI. .608-325-4343
Cheddar Box Cheese House
  Shawano, WI. 715-526-5411
Cheese Factory
  Borden, IN. .812-923-8861
Cheese Smokers
  Brooklyn, NY 718-456-0531
CheeseLand
  Seattle, WA .206-709-1220
Chianti Cheese Company
  Wapakoneta, OH. 800-220-3503
Chicago 58 Food Products
  Toronto, ON 416-603-4244
Chicopee Provision Company
  Chicopee, MA. 800-924-6328
Chloe Foods Corporation
  Brooklyn, NY 718-827-3600
Chula Vista Cheese Company
  Browntown, WI. 608-439-5211
Churny Company
  Waupaca, WI. 715-258-4040

Clofine Dairy & Food Products
Linwood, NJ 800-441-1001
Clover Leaf Cheese
Calgary, AB 888-835-0126
Cloverland Green Spring Dairy
Baltimore, MD 410-235-4477
Cloverleaf Dairy
Stanley, WI 715-669-3145
Cobb Hill Chesse
Hartland, VT 802-436-1612
Coburg Dairy
North Charleston, SC 843-554-4870
Colonna Brothers
North Bergen, NJ 201-864-1115
Commercial Creamery Company
Spokane, WA 800-541-0850
ConAgra Grocery Products
Irvine, CA 714-680-1000
ConAgra Refrigerated Foods International
Omaha, NE 800-624-4724
Conlin Food Sales
Placentia, CA 800-429-1136
Continental Culture Specialists
Glendale, CA 818-240-7400
Corfu Foods
Bensenville, IL 630-595-2510
Country Fresh
Grand Rapids, MI 800-748-0480
Cow Girl Creamery
Point Reyes Sta, CA 415-663-8153
Cream O' Weaver Dairy
Salt Lake City, UT 801-973-9922
Creamland Dairies
Albuquerque, NM 505-247-0721
Cropp Cooperative-Organic Valley
La Farge, WI 888-444-6455
Crowley Cheese
Mt Holly, VT 802-259-2340
Crowley Foods
La Fargeville, NY 800-247-6269
Crowley Foods
Binghamton, NY 800-637-0019
Cultured Specialties
Fullerton, CA 714-772-8861
Curran's Cheese Plant
Browntown, WI 608-966-3361
Cyclone Enterprises
Houston, TX 281-872-0087
D'Artagnan
Newark, NJ 800-327-8246
Dairy Concepts
Greenwood, WI 888-680-5400
Dairy Farmers of America
Smithfield, UT 800-453-2820
Dairy Farmers of America
Kansas City, MO 816-801-6200
Dairy Farmers of America
New Wilmington, PA 800-837-5214
Dairy Fresh Foods
Taylor, MI 313-295-6300
Dairy Group
Jericho, NY 516-433-0080
Dairyman's/Land O' Lakes
Tulare, CA 559-687-8287
Dakota Country Cheese
Mandan, ND 701-663-0246
Dan Carter
Richfield, WI 800-782-0741
Darigold
Seattle, WA 360-354-2151
Dave's Gourmet
San Francisco, CA 800-758-0372
DCI Cheese Company
Richfield, WI 262-677-3407
Dean Foods Company
Dallas, TX 800-431-9214
Dean Foods Company/Country Fresh
Grand Rapids, MI 616-243-0173
Decatur Dairy
Brodhead, WI 608-897-8661
Del Rey Tortilleria
Chicago, IL 800-446-1459
Delta Distributors
Longview, TX 800-945-1858
Delta Valley Farms
Delta, UT 435-864-2725
Deppeler Cheese Factory
Monroe, WI 608-325-6311
Deutsch Kase Haus
Middlebury, IN 574-825-9511
Dimock Dairy Products
Dimock, SD 605-928-3833

Dixie Dairy Company
Gary, IN 219-885-6101
Dixon Associates
Mechanicsburg, PA 717-691-0800
DPI Dairy Fresh Products Company
Ontario, CA 909-605-7300
Drangle Foods
Gilman, WI 715-447-8241
Dulce de Leche Delcampo Products
Hialeah, FL 877-472-9408
Dupont Cheese
Marion, WI 800-895-2873
Durrett Cheese Sales
Manchester, TN 800-209-6792
Eatem Foods Company
Vineland, NJ 800-683-2836
Eau Galle Cheese Factory Shop
Durand, WI 800-283-1085
Ellsworth Cooperative Creamery
Ellsworth, WI 715-273-4311
Elm City Cheese Company
Hamden, CT 203-865-5768
Emkay Trading Corporation
Elmsford, NY 914-592-9000
Empire Cheese
Cuba, NY 585-968-1552
Empire Foods
Bellmore, NY 516-679-1414
Enon Valley Cheese Compay
Enon Valley, PA 724-336-5207
Equinox Enterprises
Sherwood Park, AB 888-378-7364
Eskimo Pie Corporation
Ronkonkoma, NY 631-737-9700
Excelpro Manufacturing Corporation
Los Angeles, CA 323-268-1918
Excelsior Dairy
Hilo, HI 808-961-3608
F&A Cheese Corporation
Irvine, CA 800-634-4109
F&A Dairy Products
Dresser, WI 715-755-3485
F. Soderlund Company
Bonita Springs, FL 239-498-0600
Fairmont Products
Belleville, PA 717-935-2121
Fairview Swiss Cheese
Fredonia, PA 724-475-4154
Fanny Mason Farmstead Cheese
Walpole, NH 603-756-3300
Fantis Foods
Carlstadt, NJ 201-933-6200
Faribault Dairy Company
Faribault, MN 507-334-5260
Farmers Cooperative Dairy
Halifax, NS 902-835-3373
Father's Country Hams
Bremen, KY 270-525-3554
Favreau's Cheese
Green Island, NY 518-273-1146
Fennimore Cheese
Fennimore, WI 888-499-3778
Finlandia Cheese
Parsippany, NJ 973-316-6699
First District Association
Litchfield, MN 320-693-3236
Fleur De Lait Foods
New Holland, PA 717-355-8500
Floron Food Services
Edmonton, AB 780-438-9300
Foothills Creamery
Calgary, AB 800-661-4909
Foremost Dairies-Hawaii
Honolulu, HI 808-841-5831
Foremost Farms
Richland Center, WI 608-647-2186
Foremost Farms
Wilson, WI 715-772-4211
Foremost Farms
Clayton, WI 715-948-2166
Foremost Farms
Alma Center, WI 715-964-7411
Foremost Farms USA
Richland Center, WI 608-647-2186
Foremost Farms USA
Lancaster, WI 608-723-7681
Foster Farms Dairy
Modesto, CA 209-576-3470
Four C Foods Corporation
Brooklyn, NY 718-272-4242
Frankfort Cheese
Edgar, WI 715-352-2345

Franklin Foods
Enosburg Falls, VT 800-933-6114
Fried Provisions Company
Evans City, PA 724-538-3160
Friendship Dairies
Jericho, NY 516-719-4000
Friendship Dairies
Friendship, NY 585-973-3031
Fritsch Cheese
Cobb, WI 608-623-2205
Frog City Cheese
Plymouth Notch, VT 802-672-3650
Froma-Dar
St. Boniface, QC 819-535-3946
Fry Foods
Tiffin, OH 800-626-2294
Gad Cheese Company
Medford, WI 715-748-4273
Galaxy Dairy Products, Incorporated
Ramsey, NJ 201-818-2030
Galaxy Nutritional Foods
Orlando, FL 800-441-9419
GFA Brands
Paramus, NJ 201-568-9300
Gibbsville Cheese Company
Sheboygan Falls, WI 920-564-3242
Gile Cheese Company
Cuba City, WI 608-744-3456
Glanbia Foods
Twin Falls, ID 208-733-7555
Glanbia Foods
Twin Falls, ID 800-427-9477
Gold Cup Farms
Clayton, NY 800-752-1341
Golden Cheese Company of California
Corona, CA 951-493-4700
Golden Cheese of California
Corona, CA 800-842-0264
Gossner Food
Logan, UT 800-944-0454
GPI USA LLC.
Athens, GA 706-850-7826
Grafton Village Cheese Company
Grafton, VT 800-472-3866
Graham Cheese Corporation
Washington, IN 800-472-9178
Grande Cheese Company
Brownsville, WI 800-678-3122
Great American Appetizers
Nampa, ID 800-282-4834
Great Lakes Cheese Company
Hiram, OH 440-834-2500
Great Lakes Cheese of NY
Adams, NY 315-232-4511
Green Bay Cheese Company
Green Bay, WI 920-434-3233
Green Valley Foods
Tranquility, NJ 800-853-8399
Greenberg Cheese Company
Glendale, CA 800-301-4507
Guggisberg Cheese
Millersburg, OH 800-262-2505
H.B. Taylor Co
Chicago, IL 773-254-4805
H.E. Butt Grocery Company
San Antonio, TX 800-432-3113
H.P. Hood
Agawam, MA 413-786-7166
H.P. Hood
Chelsea, MA 800-343-6592
Hallman International
Louisville, KY 502-778-0459
Harrington's of Vermont
Richmond, VT 802-434-7500
Hazelwood Farm Bakeries
Minneapolis, MN 314-595-4150
Heidi's Cheese Products
Mundelein, IL 847-362-5971

Heluva Good Cheese
Sodus, NY 315-483-6971
Henning's Cheese
Kiel, WI. 920-894-3032
Henningsen Foods
Purchase, NY 914-701-4020
Heritage Cheese House
Heuvelton, NY 315-344-2216
Heritage Farms Dairy
Murfreesboro, TN. 615-895-2790
Heritage Foods
Santa Ana, CA 714-775-5000
Herkimer Foods
Herkimer, NY 315-895-7832
Hickory Farms
Maumee, OH. 419-893-7611
Hidden Villa Ranch
Fullerton, CA 800-326-3220
High Ridge Foods LLC
White Plains, NY 914-761-2900
Hiland Dairy Foods Company
Wichita, KS. 316-267-4221
Hiland Dairy Foods Company
Springfield, MO 417-862-9311
Hilmar Cheese Company
Hilmar, CA 800-577-5772
Hitz Cheese Company
Linwood, MI. 517-697-5932
Hollow Road Farms
Stuyvesant, NY 518-758-7214
Holmes Cheese Company
Millersburg, OH 330-674-6451
Hook's Cheese Company
Mineral Point, WI. 608-987-3259
Icco Cheese Company
Orangeburg, NY 845-398-9800
Idaho Milk Products
Jerome, ID. 208-644-2882
IMAC
Oklahoma City, OK 888-878-7827
Imperia Foods
S Plainfield, NJ. 800-526-7333
Imperial Foods
Long Island City, NY 718-784-3400
Industria Lechera de Puerto Rico
San Juan, PR. 787-765-7545
Inter-American Products
Cincinnati, OH 800-645-2233
International Cheese Company
Toronto, ON 416-769-3547
International Trading Company
Houston, TX 713-224-5901
Isaar Cheese
Seymour, WI. 920-833-6190
Ito Cariani Sausage Company
Hayward, CA 510-887-0882
Ivanhoe Cheese Inc
Madoc, ON 613-473-4269
J&G Cheese Company
Columbus, OH 614-436-1070
J.B. Sons
Yonkers, NY 914-963-5192
Janes Family Foods
Mississauga, ON. 800-565-2637
Jersey Pride
New Brunswick, NJ 406-585-0014
Jim's Cheese Pantry
Waterloo, WI. 800-345-3571
John Koller & Sons
Fredonia, PA. 724-475-4154
Jolina Foods
Hinesburg, VT. 802-434-2185
Joseph Gallo Farms
Atwater, CA 209-394-7984

Kantner Group
Wapakoneta, OH. 419-738-4060
Karoun Dairies
Los Angeles, CA. 323-666-6222
Kayem Foods
Chelsea, MA 800-426-6100
Keebler Company
Battle Creek, MI. 800-962-1413
Keller's Creamery
Harleysville, PA 800-535-5371
Kerry Ingredients
Tralee, Co. Kerry,
Key Ingredients
Harrisburg, PA 800-227-4448
Kirby & Holloway Provisions
Harrington, DE 800-995-4729
Klondike Cheese
Monroe, WI. 608-325-3021
Klondike Cheese Factory
Monroe, WI. 608-325-3021
Kolb-Lena Cheese Company
Lena, IL. 815-369-4577
Kraemer's Wisconsin Cheese
Watertown, WI 800-236-8033
Kraft Foods
Albany, MN. 320-845-2131
Kraft Foods
Springfield, MO 417-881-2701
Kraft Foods
Walton, NY. 607-865-7131
Kraft Foods
Allentown, PA. 610-398-0311
Kraft Foods
Northfield, IL 800-323-0768
Krinos Foods
Long Island City, NY 718-729-9000
Krohn Dairy Products
Luxemburg, WI. 920-845-2901
Laack Brothers Cheese Company
Greenleaf, WI 800-589-5127
Lactalis USA
New York, NY 888-766-3353
LaGrander Hillside Dairy
Stanley, WI 715-644-2275
Lake Erie Frozen Foods Company
Ashland, OH 800-766-8501
Lamagna Cheese Company
Verona, PA. 412-828-6112
Lamex Foods
Edina, MN. 952-844-0585
Land O'Lakes
St Paul, MN. 651-730-2100
Land O'Lakes
Spencer, WI. 715-659-2311
Land O'Lakes
Kiel, WI. 920-894-2204
Land O'Lakes, Inc
Arden Hills, MN 800-328-9680
Land-O-Sun Dairies
O Fallon, IL. 618-632-6381
Larsen Farms
Hamer, ID 208-662-5501
Laura Chenel's Chevre
Sonoma, CA 707-996-4477
Le Sueur Cheese
Le Sueur, MN 800-757-7611
Lebanon Cheese Company
Lebanon, NJ 908-236-2611
Lemke Cheese Company
Wausau, WI. 715-842-3214
Lengacher's Cheese House
Kinzers, PA. 717-355-6490
Leprino Foods Company
Denver, CO 800-537-7466

LeRaysville Cheese
Le Raysville, PA 800-595-5196
Level Valley Creamery
Antioch, TN 800-251-1292
LFI
Fairfield, NJ 973-882-0550
Liberty Enterprises
Stateline, NV 800-723-3690
Lifeline Food Company
Sand City, CA 831-899-5040
Lifeway Foods Inc
Morton Grove, IL 847-967-1010
Linden Cheese Factory
Linden, WI 800-660-5051
Lioni Latticini, Inc
Brooklyn, NY 718-232-1166
Lone Elm Sales
Van Dyne, WI. 800-950-8275
Los Altos Food Products
City of Industry, CA 626-330-6555
Losurdo Creamery
Heuvelton, NY 315-344-2444
Lov-It Creamery
Green Bay, WI. 800-344-0333
Lucille Farm Products
Montville, NJ 973-334-6030
Lynn Dairy
Granton, WI 715-238-7129
M-C Dairy Company
Etobicoke, ON 416-231-1491
M.H. Greenebaum
Airmont, NY. 973-538-9200
Mahoning Swiss Cheese Cooperative
Smicksburg, PA. 814-257-8884
Mancuso Cheese Company
Joliet, IL 815-722-2475
Mann Packing
Salinas, CA 831-422-7405
Maple Leaf Cheesemakers
New Glarus, WI 608-527-2000
Marathon Cheese Corporation
Booneville, MS. 662-728-6242
Marcus Dairy
Danbury, CT 800-243-2511
Marin French Cheese Company
Petaluma, CA 800-292-6001
Marketing Specialists
Fairfield, NJ 973-227-7070
Marrese Cheese Company
Lomira, WI. 920-269-4288
Marshallville Packing Company
Marshallville, OH 330-855-2871
Marva Maid Dairy
Newport News, VA 800-544-4439
Masson Cheese Corporation
Vernon, CA 800-637-7262
Masters Gallery Foods
Plymouth, WI 800-236-8431
Matador Processors
Blanchard, OK 800-847-0797
Max P.E. Radloff & Sons
Hustisford, WI 920-349-3266
Mayer Dairy
Neillsville, WI. 715-255-8456
McArthur Dairy
Miami, FL. 877-803-6565
McCadam Cheese Company
Chateaugay, NY 518-497-6644
McCain Foods
Fort Atkinson, WI. 920-563-6625
Meadow Gold Dairy
Lewiston, ID 208-746-9006
Meister Cheese Company
Muscoda, WI. 800-634-7837

Merkts Cheese Company
Bristol, WI 262-857-2316
Miceli Dairy Products Company
Cleveland, OH 800-551-7196
Michael Granese & Company
Norristown, PA 610-272-5099
Michigan Dairy
Livonia, MI 734-367-5390
Michigan Farm Cheese Dairy
Fountain, MI .231-462-3301
Mid States Dairy
Hazelwood, MO 314-731-1150
Mid-Atlantic Cheese Company
Parsippany, NJ 973-998-9000
Middlefield Cheese House
Middlefield, OH 800-327-9477
Mille Lacs Gourmet Foods
Madison, WI .800-843-1381
Mille Lacs MP Company
Madison, WI .800-843-1381
Miller's Cheese
Brooklyn, NY 718-384-5243
Milsolv Corporation
Butler, WI 800-558-8501
Minerva Cheese Factory
Minerva, OH .330-868-4196
Monroe Cheese Corporation
Monroe, WI .608-325-5161
Monterrey Provisions
San Diego, CA 800-201-1600
Morningland Dairy CheeseCompany
Mountain View, MO 417-469-3817
Morrisons Pastries/Turf Cheesecake
Harrison, NY 914-835-6629
Moscahlades Brothers
New York, NY 212-226-5410
Mossholder's Farm Cheese Factory
Appleton, WI 920-734-7575
Mozzarella Company
Dallas, TX 800-798-2954
Mozzarella Fresca   Corporate & Commercial
Headquarters
Concord, CA 800-572-6818
Murphy House
Louisburg, NC 919-496-4173
Nasonville Dairy
Marshfield, WI 715-676-2177
National Cheese Company
Concord, ON 905-669-9393
Nelson Cheese Factory
Nelson, WI .715-673-4725
Nelson Ricks Creamery
Salt Lake City, UT 801-364-3607
Nelson Ricks Creamery Company
Salt Lake City, UT 801-364-3607
Network Food Brokers
Haverford, PA 610-649-7210
Newburg Corners Cheese Factory
Bangor, WI .608-452-3636
Nodine's Smokehouse
Torrington, CT 800-222-2059
Noon Hour Food Products
Chicago, IL .800-621-6636
Nor-Tech Dairy Advisors
Sioux Falls, SD 605-338-2404
Northern Utah Manufacturing
Wellsville, UT 435-245-6014
Northern Wisconsin Cheese Company
Manitowoc, WI 920-684-4461
Oak Grove Dairy
Clintonville, WI 715-823-6226
Old Chatham Sheepherding
Old Chatham, NY 888-743-3760
Old Country Cheese
Cashton, WI .888-320-9469
Old Europe Cheese
Benton Harbor, MI 800-447-8182
Old Fashioned Foods Inc
Mayville, WI 920-387-4444
Old Wisconsin Food Products
Prospect Heights, IL 800-621-0868
Olde Tyme Food Corporation
East Longmeadow, MA 800-356-6533
Ore-Ida Foods
Pittsburgh, PA 412-237-3450
Oshkosh Cold Storage Company
Oshkosh, WI 800-580-4680
Owl's Nest Cheese
Kaukauna, WI 608-825-6818
P.J. Lisac & Associates
Oregon City, OR 503-652-1988

Pace Dairy Foods Company
Rochester, MN 507-288-6315
Pacific Cheese Company
Hayward, CA 510-784-8800
Park Cheese Company
Fond Du Lac, WI 800-752-7275
Parker Farm
Minneapolis, MN 763-780-5100
Parkers Farm
Minneapolis, MN 800-869-6685
Parmalat
Toronto, ON 416-626-1973
Pastene Companies
Canton, MA .781-830-8200
Pastorelli Food Products
Chicago, IL .800-767-2829
PB&S Chemicals
Henderson, KY 800-950-7267
Pearl Valley Cheese Company
Fresno, OH .740-545-6002
Pecoraro Dairy Products
Rome, NY 315-339-0101
Peluso Cheese Company
Los Banos, CA 209-826-3744
Pend Oreille Cheese Company
Sandpoint, ID 208-263-2030
Penn Cheese Corporation
Winfield, PA 570-524-7700
Penn Maid Crowley Foods
Philadelphia, PA 800-247-6269
Pine River Cheese & Butter Company
Ripley, ON. .800-265-1175
Pine River Pre-Pack
Newton, WI .920-726-4216
Plumrose USA
East Brunswick, NJ. 732-257-6600
Plymouth Cheese Counter
Plymouth, WI 888-607-9477
Pollio Dairy Products
Mineola, NY 516-741-8000
Polly-O Dairy Products
Mineola, NY 516-741-8000
Portion Pak
Stone Mountain, GA 770-934-3200
Prairie Farms Dairy
Carlinville, IL 217-854-2547
Prairie Farms Dairy
Carbondale, IL 618-457-4167
Prairie Farms Dairy Inc
Carlinville, IL 217-854-2547
Prima Kase
Monticello, WI 608-938-4227
Protein Palace
Hartford, WI 262-673-2698
Providence Cheese
Johnston, RI 401-421-5653
Purity Dairies
Nashville, TN 615-244-1900
Quality Ingredients Corporation
Burnsville, MN 952-898-4002
Quality Jersey Products
Seaforth, ON 519-527-1272
Queensboro Farm Products
Canastota, NY 315-697-2235
Queensboro Farm Products
Jamaica, NY 718-658-5000
Radloff's Cheese
Hustisford, WI 920-349-3266
Ragersville Swiss Cheese
Sugarcreek, OH 330-897-3055
Rahco International
St Augustine, FL 800-851-7681
Ranieri Fine Foods
Brooklyn, NY 718-599-0665
Raven Creamery Company
Portland, OR 503-288-5101
Redi-Froze
South Bend, IN 574-237-5111
Redwood Hill Farm
Sebastopol, CA 707-823-8250
Regez Cheese & Paper Supply
Monroe, WI. 608-325-3417
Reilly Dairy & Food Company
Tampa, FL. .813-839-8458
Renard's Cheese
Algoma, WI. 920-487-2825
Rey Food Company
Hoboken, NJ 201-792-1955
Rich-Seapak Corporation
St Simons Island, GA 800-654-9731
Roberto A Cheese Factory
East Canton, OH 330-488-1551

Rochester Cheese
Rochester, MN 888-288-6678
Roelli Cheese Company
Shullsburg, WI 800-575-4372
Rogue Creamery
Central Point, OR 541-665-1155
Roma
Rice, MN 800-328-8514
Ron's Wisconsin Cheese
Luxemburg, WI 920-845-5330
Rondel, Specialty Foods
Merrill, WI .800-766-3353
Roos Foods
Kenton, DE .800-343-3642
Rosenberger's Dairies
Hatfield, PA. 800-355-9074
Roth Kase
Mendham, NJ 608-328-2122
Royal Baltic
Brooklyn, NY 718-385-8300
Rumiano Cheese Company
Crescent City, CA. 707-465-1535
Safeway Dairy Products
Walnut Creek, CA 925-944-4000
Salemville Cheese Cooperative
Cambria, WI 920-394-3433
Salmans & Associates
Chicago, IL .312-226-1820
San Fernando Creamery Farmdale Creamery
San Bernardino, CA 909-889-3002
Sapudo Cheese
Lincolnshire, IL. 847-267-1100
Saputo
Montreal, QC 514-328-6662
Saputo
Big Stone City, SD 800-824-3373
Saputo Cheese
Tulare, CA 559-687-9999
Saputo Cheese
Almena, WI. 715-357-3775
Saputo Cheese
Peru, IN 765-472-1961
Saputo Cheese
Reedsburg, WI 800-824-3373
Saputo Cheese
Lena, WI 920-829-5251
Saputo Cheese
Fond Du Lac, WI 920-929-8060
Sardinia Cheese
Seymour, CT 203-735-3374
Sargento Foods Inc
Plymouth, WI 800-243-3737
Sartori Food Corporation
Plymouth, WI 800-558-5888
Sartori Foods
Plymouth, WI 800-356-5655
Saxon Creamery
Cleveland, WI. 920-547-4108
Schepps Dairy
Dallas, TX 800-428-6455
Schneider Cheese
Waldo, WI. .920-467-3351
Schneider's Dairy Holdings Inc
Pittsburgh, PA. 412-881-3525
Schobert's Cottage Cheese Corporation
Akron, OH .216-733-6876
Schreiber Foods   Plant
Logan, UT. .435-787-8490
Schreiber Foods   Plant
Clinton, MO 660-885-6133
Schreiber Foods   Plant
Shippensburg, PA 717-530-5000
Schreiber Foods   Plant/Distribution Center
Wisconsin Rapids, WI 715-422-7500
Schreiber Foods Inc
Green Bay, WI. 800-344-0333
Schwartz Meat Company
Sophia, WV. 304-683-4595
Scotsburn Dairy Group
Truro, NS 902-895-4412
Scott's of Wisconsin
Sun Prairie, WI 800-698-1721
Scray's Cheese Company
De Pere, WI. 920-336-8359
Sea Stars Goat Cheese
Santa Cruz, CA 831-423-7200
Sekan Cheese Company
Girard, KS .316-724-8827
Sequoia Specialty Cheese Company
Visalia, CA .559-752-4106
Shelburne Farms
Shelburne, VT 802-985-8686

Shenk's Foods
Lancaster, PA 717-393-4240
Sierra Cheese Manufacturing Company
Compton, CA 800-266-4270
Silani Sweet Cheese
Schomberg, ON. 905-939-2561
Simon's Specialty Cheese
Little Chute, WI 800-444-0374
Sini Fulvi U.S.A.
Long Island City, NY 718-267-8325
Sinton Dairy Foods Company
Colorado Springs, CO. 800-388-4970
Sinton Dairy Foods Company
Denver, CO .800-666-4808
Sisler's Ice & Ice Cream
Ohio, IL 888-891-3856
Smith Dairy Products Company
Orrville, OH .800-776-7076
Smith, Weber & Swinton Company
Cleveland, OH 440-248-1500
Sofo Foods
Toledo, OH .800-447-4211
Sommer Maid Creamery
Doylestown, PA 215-345-6160
Sorrento Lactalis
Buffalo, NY. 800-828-7031
Sorrento Lactalis   Corporate & Commercial
Headquarters
Buffalo, NY. 800-828-7031
Southchem
Durham, NC 800-849-7000
Southwestern Wisconsin Dairy Goat Products
Mt Sterling, WI 608-734-3151
Sparboe Companies
Los Angeles, CA. 213-626-7538
Spaulding Sales
Brighton, MI 810-229-4166
Specialty Cheese Company
Reeseville, WI 800-367-1711
Spring Grove Foods
Miamisburg, OH 937-866-4311
Springbank Cheese Company
Woodstock, ON. 800-265-1973
Springdale Cheese Factory
Richland Center, WI. 608-538-3213
St. Charles Trading
Lake Saint Louis, MO. 800-336-1333
St. Maurice Laurent
St. Bruno, QC 418-343-3655
Stallings Headcheese Company
Houston, TX 713-523-1751
Star Valley Cheese
Thayne, WY 307-883-2510
State of Maine Cheese Company
Rockport, ME 800-762-8895
Steiner Cheese
Baltic, OH 330-897-5505
Stockton Cheese
Stockton, IL. 815-947-3361
Sugarbush Farm
Woodstock, VT 800-281-1757
Sun States
Charlotte, NC 704-821-0615
Sun-Re Cheese
Sunbury, PA. 570-286-1511
Sunnyrose Cheese
Diamond City, AB 403-381-4024
Sunshine Farms
Portage, WI .608-742-2016
Sunshine Farms Dairy
Elyria, OH. .440-322-6301
Superstore Industries
Fairfield, CA. 707-864-0502
Suprema Specialties
Manteca, CA 209-858-9696
Suprema Specialties
Paterson, NJ 800-543-2479
Supreme Dairy Farms Company
Warwick, RI 401-739-8180
Swiss Colony
Monroe, WI. 608-328-8400
Swiss Valley Farms Company
Cedar Rapids, IA. 319-364-8153
Swiss Valley Farms Company
Davenport, IA 563-468-6600
Swiss Way Cheese
Berne, IN. 260-589-3531
Swiss-American
St Louis, MO. 800-325-8150
T. Sterling Associates
Jamestown, NY 716-483-0769

Taftsville Country Store
Corinth, VT. 800-854-0013
Tall Talk Dairy
Canby, OR. .503-266-1644
Tate Cheese Company
Valley City, IL. 217-833-2314
Taylor Cheese Corporation
Weyauwega, WI. 920-867-2337
Thiel Cheese & Ingredients
Hilbert, WI .920-989-1440
Thiry Daems Cheese Factory
Luxemburg, WI. 920-845-2117
Tholstrup Cheese
Muskegon, MI. 800-426-0938
Thumann's
Carlstadt, NJ 201-935-3636
Tillamook County Creamery Association
Tillamook, OR. 503-842-4481
Timber Lake Cheese Company
Timber Lake, SD. 605-865-3605
Tony's Fine Foods
Broderick, CA. 916-374-4000
Torkelson Cheese Company
Lena, IL. 815-369-4265
Trega Foods
Weyauwega, WI 920-867-2137
Tropical Cheese Industries
Perth Amboy, NJ. 800-487-7850
Turner Dairies
Covington, TN 901-476-2643
Tuscan Dairy Farms
Dallas, TX 800-526-4416
Twin County Dairy
Kalona, IA 319-656-2776
Ulfert Broockmann
Libertyville, IL 847-680-3771
Ultima Foods
Longueuil, ON 800-363-9496
Umpqua Dairy Products Company
Roseburg, OR. 541-672-2638
V&V Supremo Foods
Chicago, IL. 800-547-8773
Valley Grain Products
Madera, CA. 559-675-3400
Valley Queen Cheese Factory
Milbank, SD 605-432-4563
Valley View Cheese Company
Conewango Vly, NY. 716-296-5821
Vella Cheese
Sonoma, CA 800-848-0505
Vern's Cheese
Chilton, WI .920-849-7717
VOD Gourmet
Greenwich, CT 203-531-5172
Wapsie Valley Creamery
Independence, IA 319-334-7193
Warren Cheese Plant
Warren, IL. .815-745-2627
Weaver Brothers
Berne, IN. 219-589-2869
Welcome Dairy
Colby, WI 800-472-2315
Wells' Dairy
Le Mars, IA. 800-942-3800
Wengers Springbrook Cheese
Davis, IL 815-865-5855
West Point Dairy Products
West Point, NE 402-372-5551
Western Dairy Products
Santa Rosa, CA. 800-433-2479
Western Dairymen Corporation
Smithfield, UT 435-563-3281
WestFarm Foods
Seattle, WA 509-837-8000
Westfield Farm
Hubbardston, MA 877-777-3900
Westhill Dairy
North York, ON. 416-661-0580
Weyauwega Star Dairy
Weyauwega, WI 920-867-2870
Weyhaupt Brothers Packing
Belleville, IL. 618-233-0452
White Wave
Broomfield, CO 800-488-9283
Whitehall Specialties
Whitehall, WI 888-755-9900
Widmer's Cheese Cellars
Theresa, WI 888-878-1107
Williams Cheese Company
Linwood, MI 800-968-4462
Winder Dairy
West Valley, UT 800-946-3371

Winger Cheese
Towner, ND. 701-537-5463
Wisconsin Cheese
Melrose Park, IL 708-450-0074
Wisconsin Cheese
Westwood, MA 781-320-0288
Wisconsin Cheese Group
Monroe, WI. 800-332-6518
Wisconsin Dairy State Cheese
Rudolph, WI 715-435-3144
Wisconsin Farmers' Union Cheese Company
Montfort, WI. 608-943-6771
Wohlt Cheese Corporation
New London, WI 920-982-9000
Woolwich Dairy
Orangeville, ON 877-438-3499
World Cheese Company
Brooklyn, NY 718-965-1700
Yerba Santa Goat Dairy
Lakeport, CA 707-263-8131
Zimmerman Cheese
South Wayne, WI 608-968-3414
Zivney Cheese
Minonk, IL .800-732-3068

American

Sargento Foods Inc
Plymouth, WI 800-243-3737
Schreiber Foods   Plant
Monett, MO 417-235-6061
Schreiber Foods   Plant
Green Bay, WI. 800-344-0333

Asiago

BelGioioso Cheese
Denmark, WI. 877-863-2123
Chianti Cheese Company
Wapakoneta, OH. 800-220-3503
D'Artagnan
Newark, NJ .800-327-8246
Dairy Concepts
Greenwood, WI. 888-680-5400
Kantner Group
Wapakoneta, OH 419-738-4060
Lactalis USA
New York, NY 888-766-3353
Park Cheese Company
Fond Du Lac, WI. 800-752-7275
Sapudo Cheese
Lincolnshire, IL. 847-267-1100
Sargento Foods Inc
Plymouth, WI 800-243-3737
Sorrento Lactalis
Buffalo, NY .800-828-7031
Vella Cheese
Sonoma, CA 800-848-0505

Blend - American/Skim Milk

Sliced

Kantner Group
Wapakoneta, OH. 419-738-4060

Blue

Chianti Cheese Company
Wapakoneta, OH. 800-220-3503
Clofine Dairy & Food Products
Linwood, NJ 800-441-1001
D'Artagnan
Newark, NJ .800-327-8246
Great Hill Dairy
Marion, MA 888-748-2208
Klondike Cheese Factory
Monroe, WI. 608-325-3021
Marathon Cheese Corporation
Booneville, MS 662-728-6242
Reilly Dairy & Food Company
Tampa, FL 813-839-8458
Roth Kase
Mendham, NJ 608-328-2122
Saputo Cheese
Fond Du Lac, WI. 920-929-8060
Sargento Foods Inc
Plymouth, WI 800-243-3737
Sorrento Lactalis
Buffalo, NY. 800-828-7031

Brie

Foothills Creamery
Calgary, AB 800-661-4909
Kolb-Lena Cheese Company
Lena, IL 815-369-4577
Lactalis USA
New York, NY 888-766-3353
Marin French Cheese Company
Petaluma, CA 800-292-6001
Sorrento Lactalis
Buffalo, NY 800-828-7031
Wisconsin Cheese
Melrose Park, IL 708-450-0074
Woolwich Dairy
Orangeville, ON 877-438-3499

Camembert

Cheese Smokers
Brooklyn, NY 718-456-0531
Foothills Creamery
Calgary, AB 800-661-4909
Glanbia Foods
Twin Falls, ID 800-427-9477
Kolb-Lena Cheese Company
Lena, IL 815-369-4577
Marin French Cheese Company
Petaluma, CA 800-292-6001
Nelson Ricks Creamery
Salt Lake City, UT 801-364-3607
Swiss Valley Farms Company
Davenport, IA 563-468-6600
Wisconsin Cheese
Melrose Park, IL 708-450-0074

Cheddar

Alberta Cheese Company
Calgary, AB 403-279-4353
Alta Dena Certified Dairy
City of Industry, CA 800-535-1369
Alto Dairy Cooperative
Waupun, WI 920-346-2215
Ardmore Cheese Company
Shelbyville, TN 931-427-2191
Associated Milk Producers
Dawson, MN 320-769-2994
Associated Milk Producers
New Ulm, MN 507-233-4600
Bass Lake Cheese Factory
Somerset, WI 800-368-2437
Cady Cheese Factory
Wilson, WI 715-772-4218
Cropp Cooperative-Organic Valley
La Farge, WI 888-444-6455
Father's Country Hams
Bremen, KY 270-525-3554
Golden Cheese of California
Corona, CA 800-842-0264
Golden Valley Dairy Products
Tulare, CA 559-687-1188
Heritage Cheese House
Heuvelton, NY 315-344-2216
Hilmar Cheese Company
Hilmar, CA 800-577-5772
Kantner Group
Wapakoneta, OH 419-738-4060
Klondike Cheese Factory
Monroe, WI 608-325-3021
Nelson Cheese Factory
Nelson, WI 715-673-4725
Sargento Foods Inc
Plymouth, WI 800-243-3737
Trega Foods
Weyauwega, WI 920-867-2137
Twin County Dairy
Kalona, IA 319-656-2776
Welcome Dairy
Colby, WI 800-472-2315

Reduced Fat

Heidi's Cheese Products
Mundelein, IL 847-362-5971
Kantner Group
Wapakoneta, OH 419-738-4060

Reduced Fat - Shredded

Crowley Cheese
Mt Holly, VT 802-259-2340
Kantner Group
Wapakoneta, OH 419-738-4060

Shredded

Kantner Group
Wapakoneta, OH 419-738-4060

Colby

Alto Dairy Cooperative
Waupun, WI 920-346-2215
Associated Milk Producers
Dawson, MN 320-769-2994
Associated Milk Producers
New Ulm, MN 507-233-4600
Bass Lake Cheese Factory
Somerset, WI 800-368-2437
Belle Plaine Cheese Factory
Shawano, WI 866-245-5924
Brewster Dairy
Brewster, OH 800-874-0874
Brunkow Cheese Company
Darlington, WI 608-776-3716
Burnette Dairy Cooperative
Grantsburg, WI 715-689-2468
Cady Cheese Factory
Wilson, WI 715-772-4218
Cream O' Weaver Dairy
Salt Lake City, UT 801-973-9922
Cropp Cooperative-Organic Valley
La Farge, WI 888-444-6455
Crowley Foods
Binghamton, NY 800-637-0019
Dupont Cheese
Marion, WI 800-895-2873
Foothills Creamery
Calgary, AB 800-661-4909
Graham Cheese Corporation
Washington, IN 800-472-9178
Heluva Good Cheese
Sodus, NY 315-483-6971
Henning's Cheese
Kiel, WI 920-894-3032
Klondike Cheese Factory
Monroe, WI 608-325-3021
Knoll Creek Dairy
Harrison, NY 718-892-4500
Louis Trauth Dairy
Newport, KY 800-544-6455
M-C Dairy Company
Etobicoke, ON 416-231-1491
Marcus Dairy
Danbury, CT 800-243-2511
Nelson Cheese Factory
Nelson, WI 715-673-4725
Oak Grove Dairy
Clintonville, WI 715-823-6226
Pine River Cheese & Butter Company
Ripley, ON 800-265-1175
Reilly Dairy & Food Company
Tampa, FL 813-839-8458
Sargento Foods Inc
Plymouth, WI 800-243-3737
Scotsburn Dairy Group
Truro, NS 902-895-4412
Swiss Valley Farms Company
Davenport, IA 563-468-6600
Swiss-American
St Louis, MO 800-325-8150
Tuscan Dairy Farms
Dallas, TX 800-526-4416
Wapsie Valley Creamery
Independence, IA 319-334-7193
Welcome Dairy
Colby, WI 800-472-2315
Wells' Dairy
Le Mars, IA 800-942-3800
Widmer's Cheese Cellars
Theresa, WI 888-878-1107
Winder Dairy
West Valley, UT 800-946-3371

Cottage

Aimonetto and Sons
Seattle, WA 866-823-2777
Alta Dena Certified Dairy
City of Industry, CA 800-535-1369
Anderson Erickson Dairy
Des Moines, IA 515-265-2521
Astro Dairy Products
Etobicoke, ON 416-622-2811
Berkeley Farms
Hayward, CA 510-265-8600

Broughton Foods
Marietta, OH 800-283-2479
Byrne Dairy
Syracuse, NY 800-899-1535
Chloe Foods Corporation
Brooklyn, NY 718-827-3600
Clofine Dairy & Food Products
Linwood, NJ 800-441-1001
Cloverland Green Spring Dairy
Baltimore, MD 410-235-4477
Cloverland Green Spring Dairy
Baltimore, MD 800-876-6455
Coburg Dairy
North Charleston, SC 843-554-4870
Country Fresh
Grand Rapids, MI 800-748-0480
Cropp Cooperative-Organic Valley
La Farge, WI 888-444-6455
Crowley Foods
La Fargeville, NY 800-247-6269
Crowley Foods
Arkport, NY 800-637-0019
Cultured Specialties
Fullerton, CA 714-772-8861
Dean Foods Company
Rochester, IN 800-336-7215
Dean Foods Company
Rockford, IL 815-962-0647
Dean Foods Company/Country Fresh
Grand Rapids, MI 616-243-0173
Dixie Dairy Company
Gary, IN 219-885-6101
Eskimo Pie Corporation
Ronkonkoma, NY 631-737-9700
Fairmont Products
Belleville, PA 717-935-2121
Foster Farms Dairy
Modesto, CA 209-576-3470
Friendship Dairies
Jericho, NY 516-719-4000
Friendship Dairies
Friendship, NY 585-973-3031
Golden Cheese of California
Corona, CA 800-842-0264
H.E. Butt Grocery Company
San Antonio, TX 800-432-3113
H.P. Hood
Vernon, NY 315-829-3004
H.P. Hood
Agawam, MA 413-786-7166
Heritage Farms Dairy
Murfreesboro, TN 615-895-2790
Hiland Dairy Foods Company
Wichita, KS 316-267-4221
Kraft Foods
Walton, NY 607-865-7131
Kraft Foods
Northfield, IL 800-323-0768
Kraft Foods/Knudson Products
Visalia, CA 800-323-0768
Land O'Lakes
St Paul, MN 651-730-2100
Land-O-Sun Dairies
O Fallon, IL 618-632-6381
Marva Maid Dairy
Newport News, VA 800-544-4439
Meadow Gold Dairies
Lincoln, NE 800-742-7349
Meadow Gold Dairies
Honolulu, HI 808-949-6161
Michigan Dairy
Livonia, MI 734-367-5390
Mid States Dairy
Hazelwood, MO 314-731-1150
Oakhurst Dairy
Portland, ME 207-772-7468
Old Home Foods
St Paul, MN 800-628-8700
Prairie Farms Dairy
Quincy, IL 217-223-5530
Prairie Farms Dairy
Carlinville, IL 217-854-2547
Prairie Farms Dairy
Granite City, IL 618-451-5600
Prairie Farms Dairy
Carbondale, IL 618-457-4167
Prairie Farms Dairy Inc
Carlinville, IL 217-854-2547
Purity Dairies
Nashville, TN 615-244-1900
Queensboro Farm Products
Canastota, NY 315-697-2235

Queensboro Farm Products
 Jamaica, NY .718-658-5000
Roberts Dairy Company
 Omaha, NE .402-344-4321
Sinton Dairy Foods Company
 Colorado Springs, CO. 800-388-4970
Sinton Dairy Foods Company
 Denver, CO 800-666-4808
Sisler's Ice & Ice Cream
 Ohio, IL 888-891-3856
Smith Dairy Products Company
 Orrville, OH 800-776-7076
Springfield Creamery
 Eugene, OR 541-689-2911
Sunshine Farms Dairy
 Elyria, OH 440-322-6301
Superstore Industries
 Fairfield, CA. 707-864-0502
Swiss Valley Farms Company
 Cedar Rapids, IA. 319-364-8153
Swiss Valley Farms Company
 Davenport, IA 563-468-6600
Turner Dairies
 Covington, TN 901-476-2643
Umpqua Dairy Products Company
 Roseburg, OR 541-672-2638
WestFarm Foods
 Seattle, WA. 800-333-6544
Westhill Dairy
 North York, ON. 416-661-0580

Cream

Astro Dairy Products
 Etobicoke, ON. 416-622-2811
Clofine Dairy & Food Products
 Linwood, NJ 800-441-1001
Cloverland Green Spring Dairy
 Baltimore, MD 410-235-4477
Crowley Foods
 La Fargeville, NY 800-247-6269
Don's Food Products
 Schwenksville, PA 888-321-3667
Emkay Trading Corporation
 Elmsford, NY 914-592-9000
Franklin Foods
 Enosburg Falls, VT 800-933-6114
Herkimer Foods
 Herkimer, NY 315-895-7832
Kraft Foods
 Springfield, MO 417-881-2701
Kraft Foods
 Northfield, IL 800-323-0768
Level Valley Creamery
 Antioch, TN 800-251-1292
Level Valley Creamery
 West Bend, WI 800-558-1707
Lov-It Creamery
 Green Bay, WI 800-344-0333
M-C Dairy Company
 Etobicoke, ON 416-231-1491
Mozzarella Company
 Dallas, TX 800-798-2954
National Food Corporation
 Everett, WA. 425-349-4257
Parmalat
 St George Brant, ON. 519-448-1311
Penn Maid Crowley Foods
 Philadelphia, PA 800-247-6269
Queensboro Farm Products
 Jamaica, NY 718-658-5000
Reilly Dairy & Food Company
 Tampa, FL 813-839-8458
Schneider's Dairy Holdings Inc
 Pittsburgh, PA 412-881-3525
Schreiber Foods   Plant
 Shippensburg, PA 717-530-5000
Springfield Creamery
 Eugene, OR 541-689-2911
Springfield Smoked Fish Company
 Springfield, MA 800-327-3412
Tofutti Brands
 Cranford, NJ 908-272-2400
Woolwich Dairy
 Orangeville, ON 877-438-3499

Edam

Alto Dairy Cooperative
 Waupun, WI 920-346-2215
Lactalis USA
 New York, NY 888-766-3353

Feta

Alberta Cheese Company
 Calgary, AB. 403-279-4353
Aslanis Seafoods
 Quincy, MA. 800-876-3712
Atwood Cheese Company
 Atwood, ON 519-356-2271
Castella Imports
 Hauppauge, NY 866-227-8355
Cropp Cooperative-Organic Valley
 La Farge, WI 888-444-6455
Fage USA
 Flushing, NY. 718-204-5323
Klondike Cheese Factory
 Monroe, WI. 608-325-3021
Kolb-Lena Cheese Company
 Lena, IL. .815-369-4577
Lactalis USA
 New York, NY 888-766-3353
Lucille Farm Products
 Montville, NJ 973-334-6030
Michigan Farm Cheese Dairy
 Fountain, MI. 231-462-3301
Mount Capra Cheese
 Chehalis, WA 800-574-1961
Mozzarella Company
 Dallas, TX. 800-798-2954
Pecoraro Dairy Products
 Rome, NY. 315-339-0101
Saputo Cheese
 Hinesburg, VT. 800-824-3373
Sierra Cheese Manufacturing Company
 Compton, CA 800-266-4270
Sorrento Lactalis
 Buffalo, NY. 800-828-7031
Southwestern Wisconsin Dairy Goat Products
 Mt Sterling, WI. 608-734-3151
Trega Foods
 Weyauwega, WI 920-867-2137
Woolwich Dairy
 Orangeville, ON 877-438-3499

Fontina

Atwood Cheese Company
 Atwood, ON 519-356-2271
BelGioioso Cheese
 Denmark, WI. 877-863-2123
Lactalis USA
 New York, NY 888-766-3353
Park Cheese Company
 Fond Du Lac, WI 800-752-7275
Prima Kase
 Monticello, WI 608-938-4227
Sartori Food Corporation
 Plymouth, WI 800-558-5888
Sorrento Lactalis
 Buffalo, NY. 800-828-7031

Goat's

Alta Dena Certified Dairy
 City of Industry, CA 800-535-1369
Bass Lake Cheese Factory
 Somerset, WI. 800-368-2437
Brier Run Farm
 Birch River, WV 304-649-2975
Cypress Grove Chevre
 Arcata, CA 707-825-1100
Montchevre
 Rolling Hls Ests, CA. 310-544-0450
Mount Capra Cheese
 Chehalis, WA 800-574-1961
Mozzarella Company
 Dallas, TX. 800-798-2954
Quillisascut Cheese Company
 Rice, WA. 509-738-2011
Rollingstone Chevre
 Parma, ID 208-722-6460
Sorrento Lactalis
 Buffalo, NY. 800-828-7031
Southwestern Wisconsin Dairy Goat Products
 Mt Sterling, WI. 608-734-3151
Swiss-American
 St Louis, MO. 800-325-8150
Vermont Butter & Cheese Company
 Websterville, NY. 802-479-9371
West Field Farm
 Hubbardston, MA 877-777-3900
Westfield Farm
 Hubbardston, MA 877-777-3900

Gorgonzola

BelGioioso Cheese
 Denmark, WI. 877-863-2123
Chianti Cheese Company
 Wapakoneta, OH 800-220-3503
Pastene Companies
 Canton, MA 781-830-8200
Sapudo Cheese
 Lincolnshire, IL. 847-267-1100
Sorrento Lactalis
 Buffalo, NY. 800-828-7031

Gouda

Bass Lake Cheese Factory
 Somerset, WI. 800-368-2437
Bel/Kaukauna USA
 Kaukauna, WI. 800-558-3500
Klondike Cheese Factory
 Monroe, WI. 608-325-3021
Lactalis USA
 New York, NY 888-766-3353
Prima Kase
 Monticello, WI 608-938-4227
Winchester Cheese Company
 Winchester, CA 951-926-4239
Woolwich Dairy
 Orangeville, ON 877-438-3499

Grated

Calabro Cheese Corporation
 East Haven, CT. 203-469-1311
Chianti Cheese Company
 Wapakoneta, OH. 800-220-3503
Clofine Dairy & Food Products
 Linwood, NJ 800-441-1001
Colonna Brothers
 North Bergen, NJ 201-864-1115
Dairy Concepts
 Greenwood, WI. 888-680-5400
Elm City Cheese Company
 Hamden, CT 203-865-5768
Four C Foods Corporation
 Brooklyn, NY. 718-272-4242
Icco Cheese Company
 Orangeburg, NY 845-398-9800
Kantner Group
 Wapakoneta, OH. 419-738-4060
Lactalis USA
 New York, NY 888-766-3353
Lucy's Foods
 Latrobe, PA 724-539-1430
Mancuso Cheese Company
 Joliet, IL. 815-722-2475
Park Cheese Company
 Fond Du Lac, WI 800-752-7275
Penn Maid Crowley Foods
 Philadelphia, PA 800-247-6269
Reilly Dairy & Food Company
 Tampa, FL 813-839-8458
Sargento Foods Inc
 Plymouth, WI 800-243-3737
Sartori Food Corporation
 Plymouth, WI 800-558-5888
Sun-Re Cheese
 Sunbury, PA. 570-286-1511
Suprema Specialties
 Paterson, NJ 800-543-2479

Gruyere

Castella Imports
 Hauppauge, NY 866-227-8355

Havarti

Prima Kase
 Monticello, WI 608-938-4227
Roth Kase
 Mendham, NJ 608-328-2122
Zivney Cheese
 Minonk, IL 800-732-3068

Limburger

Klondike Cheese Factory
 Monroe, WI. 608-325-3021

Low-Fat

Cabot Creamery
 Montpelier, VT 888-792-2268

Froma-Dar
St. Boniface, QC 819-535-3946
Heidi's Cheese Products
Mundelein, IL 847-362-5971
Lactalis USA
New York, NY 888-766-3353
Le Sueur Cheese
Le Sueur, MN 800-757-7611
Sorrento Lactalis
Buffalo, NY 800-828-7031
Sorrento Lactalis   Corporate & Commercial
Headquarters
Buffalo, NY 800-828-7031

Mascarpone

BelGioioso Cheese
Denmark, WI 877-863-2123
Glanbia Foods
Twin Falls, ID 800-427-9477
Lactalis USA
New York, NY 888-766-3353
Mozzarella Company
Dallas, TX 800-798-2954
Mozzarella Fresca   Corporate & Commercial
Headquarters
Concord, CA 800-572-6818
Mozzarella Fresca   Tipton Plant
Tipton, CA 559-752-4823
Pecoraro Dairy Products
Rome, NY 315-339-0101
Sorrento Lactalis
Buffalo, NY 800-828-7031
Sorrento Lactalis   Corporate & Commercial
Headquarters
Buffalo, NY 800-828-7031
Vermont Butter & Cheese Company
Websterville, NY 802-479-9371

Monterey Jack

Alberta Cheese Company
Calgary, AB 403-279-4353
Alta Dena Certified Dairy
City of Industry, CA 800-535-1369
Associated Milk Producers
Dawson, MN 320-769-2994
Associated Milk Producers
New Ulm, MN 507-233-4600
Avanti Food Company
Walnut, IL 800-243-3739
Bass Lake Cheese Factory
Somerset, WI 800-368-2437
Belle Plaine Cheese Factory
Shawano, WI 866-245-5924
Brewster Dairy
Brewster, OH 800-874-0874
Brunkow Cheese Company
Darlington, WI 608-776-3716
Cabot Creamery
Montpelier, VT 888-792-2268
Cady Cheese Factory
Wilson, WI 715-772-4218
Cheese Smokers
Brooklyn, NY 718-456-0531
Cropp Cooperative-Organic Valley
La Farge, WI 888-444-6455
Foothills Creamery
Calgary, AB 800-661-4909
Glanbia Foods
Twin Falls, ID 208-733-7555
Golden Cheese of California
Corona, CA 800-842-0264
Henning's Cheese
Kiel, WI 920-894-3032
Hilmar Cheese Company
Hilmar, CA 800-577-5772
Klondike Cheese Factory
Monroe, WI 608-325-3021
Nelson Cheese Factory
Nelson, WI 715-673-4725
Nelson Ricks Creamery
Salt Lake City, UT 801-364-3607
Oak Grove Dairy
Clintonville, WI 715-823-6226
Pine River Cheese & Butter Company
Ripley, ON 800-265-1175
Sargento Foods Inc
Plymouth, WI 800-243-3737
Star Valley Cheese
Thayne, WY 307-883-2510
Suprema Specialties
Manteca, CA 209-858-9696

Swiss-American
St Louis, MO 800-325-8150
Vella Cheese
Sonoma, CA 800-848-0505
Wapsie Valley Creamery
Independence, IA 319-334-7193
Welcome Dairy
Colby, WI 800-472-2315

Mozzarella

Antonio Mozzarella Factory
Springfield, NJ 973-379-3738
Associated Milk Producers
Dawson, MN 320-769-2994
Associated Milk Producers
New Ulm, MN 507-233-4600
Atwood Cheese Company
Atwood, ON 519-356-2271
B&D Foods
Boise, ID 208-344-1183
BelGioioso Cheese
Denmark, WI 877-863-2123
Biazzo Dairy Products
Ridgefield, NJ 201-941-6800
Burnette Dairy Cooperative
Grantsburg, WI 715-689-2468
Cacique
City of Industry, CA 626-961-3399
Cady Cheese Factory
Wilson, WI 715-772-4218
Calabro Cheese Corporation
East Haven, CT 203-469-1311
Cappiello Dairy Products
Schenectady, NY 518-374-5064
Chianti Cheese Company
Wapakoneta, OH 800-220-3503
Clofine Dairy & Food Products
Linwood, NJ 800-441-1001
Cropp Cooperative-Organic Valley
La Farge, WI 888-444-6455
Crowley Foods
Binghamton, NY 800-637-0019
Empire Cheese
Cuba, NY 585-968-1552
F&A Cheese Corporation
Irvine, CA 800-634-4109
Floron Food Services
Edmonton, AB 780-438-9300
Foothills Creamery
Calgary, AB 800-661-4909
Foremost Farms
Richland Center, WI 608-647-2186
Foremost Farms
Wilson, WI 715-772-4211
Foremost Farms
Clayton, WI 715-948-2166
Foremost Farms
Alma Center, WI 715-964-7411
Fry Foods
Tiffin, OH 800-626-2294
Golden Cheese of California
Corona, CA 800-842-0264
Golden Valley Dairy Products
Tulare, CA 559-687-1188
Henning's Cheese
Kiel, WI 920-894-3032
J.B. Sons
Yonkers, NY 914-963-5192
Kantner Group
Wapakoneta, OH 419-738-4060
Klondike Cheese Factory
Monroe, WI 608-325-3021
Laack Brothers Cheese Company
Greenleaf, WI 800-589-5127
Lactalis USA
New York, NY 888-766-3353
Leprino Foods Company
Denver, CO 800-537-7466
Losurdo Creamery
Heuvelton, NY 315-344-2444
Lucille Farm Products
Montville, NJ 973-334-6030
Mancuso Cheese Company
Joliet, IL 815-722-2475
Marathon Cheese Corporation
Booneville, MS 662-728-6242
Michael Granese & Company
Norristown, PA 610-272-5099
Mozzarella Company
Dallas, TX 800-798-2954

Mozzarella Fresca   Corporate & Commercial
Headquarters
Concord, CA 800-572-6818
Mozzarella Fresca   Tipton Plant
Tipton, CA 559-752-4823
Nelson Ricks Creamery
Salt Lake City, UT 801-364-3607
Pecoraro Dairy Products
Rome, NY 315-339-0101
Penn Maid Crowley Foods
Philadelphia, PA 800-247-6269
Pine River Cheese & Butter Company
Ripley, ON 800-265-1175
Pollio Dairy Products
Mineola, NY 516-741-8000
Reilly Dairy & Food Company
Tampa, FL 813-839-8458
Sapudo Cheese
Lincolnshire, IL 847-267-1100
Saputo
St Leonard, QC 514-328-6662
Saputo Cheese
Reedsburg, WI 800-824-3373
Sargento Foods Inc
Plymouth, WI 800-243-3737
Sartori Food Corporation
Plymouth, WI 800-558-5888
Sierra Cheese Manufacturing Company
Compton, CA 800-266-4270
Sorrento Lactalis
Buffalo, NY 800-828-7031
Sorrento Lactalis   Corporate & Commercial
Headquarters
Buffalo, NY 800-828-7031
Sun-Re Cheese
Sunbury, PA 570-286-1511
Suprema Specialties
Manteca, CA 209-858-9696
Suprema Specialties
Paterson, NJ 800-543-2479
Supreme Dairy Farms Company
Warwick, RI 401-739-8180
Trega Foods
Weyauwega, WI 920-867-2137
Woolwich Dairy
Orangeville, ON 877-438-3499

Baby

Crowley Foods
Binghamton, NY 800-637-0019

Lite Shredded - Frozen

Kantner Group
Wapakoneta, OH 419-738-4060

Low Moisture Part Skim - U

Crowley Foods
Binghamton, NY 800-637-0019
Kantner Group
Wapakoneta, OH 419-738-4060

Low Moisture Part Skim Shredded - Frozen

Kantner Group
Wapakoneta, OH 419-738-4060

Muenster

Associated Milk Producers
Dawson, MN 320-769-2994
Associated Milk Producers
New Ulm, MN 507-233-4600
Brewster Dairy
Brewster, OH 800-874-0874
Cady Cheese Factory
Wilson, WI 715-772-4218
Cropp Cooperative-Organic Valley
La Farge, WI 888-444-6455
Heidi's Cheese Products
Mundelein, IL 847-362-5971
Heluva Good Cheese
Sodus, NY 315-483-6971
Klondike Cheese Factory
Monroe, WI 608-325-3021
Reilly Dairy & Food Company
Tampa, FL 813-839-8458
Roth Kase
Mendham, NJ 608-328-2122
Sargento Foods Inc
Plymouth, WI 800-243-3737
Springdale Cheese Factory
Richland Center, WI 608-538-3213

Torkelson Cheese Company
Lena, IL 815-369-4265
Welcome Dairy
Colby, WI 800-472-2315
Wengers Springbrook Cheese
Davis, IL 815-865-5855

No-Fat

Le Sueur Cheese
Le Sueur, MN 800-757-7611
Shenk's Foods
Lancaster, PA 717-393-4240

Parmesan

Atwood Cheese Company
Atwood, ON 519-356-2271
BelGioioso Cheese
Denmark, WI. 877-863-2123
Cass Clay
Fargo, ND 701-232-1566
Castella Imports
Hauppauge, NY 866-227-8355
Chianti Cheese Company
Wapakoneta, OH 800-220-3503
Clofine Dairy & Food Products
Linwood, NJ 800-441-1001
Colonna Brothers
North Bergen, NJ 201-864-1115
Cropp Cooperative-Organic Valley
La Farge, WI 888-444-6455
Dairy Concepts
Greenwood, WI. 888-680-5400
Icco Cheese Company
Orangeburg, NY 845-398-9800
Kantner Group
Wapakoneta, OH 419-738-4060
Klondike Cheese Factory
Monroe, WI. 608-325-3021
Lactalis USA
New York, NY 888-766-3353
Mancuso Cheese Company
Joliet, IL 815-722-2475
Park Cheese Company
Fond Du Lac, WI 800-752-7275
Parmx
Calgary, AB. 403-237-0707
Pastene Companies
Canton, MA 781-830-8200
Reilly Dairy & Food Company
Tampa, FL. 813-839-8458
Sapudo Cheese
Lincolnshire, IL. 847-267-1100
Sargento Foods Inc
Plymouth, WI 800-243-3737
Sartori Food Corporation
Plymouth, WI 800-558-5888
Sorrento Lactalis
Buffalo, NY. 800-828-7031
Suprema Specialties
Manteca, CA 209-858-9696
Suprema Specialties
Paterson, NJ 800-543-2479
Valley Grain Products
Madera, CA 559-675-3400
Wisconsin Cheese
Melrose Park, IL 708-450-0074

Pecorino

Chianti Cheese Company
Wapakoneta, OH. 800-220-3503
Kantner Group
Wapakoneta, OH. 419-738-4060
Pastene Companies
Canton, MA 781-830-8200

Process Loaves

Yellow

Kantner Group
Wapakoneta, OH. 419-738-4060
Kraft Foods
Avon, NY 585-226-4400

Process Sliced

White/Yellow

Kantner Group
Wapakoneta, OH. 419-738-4060

Processed American

Associated Milk Producers
Dawson, MN. 320-769-2994
Associated Milk Producers
New Ulm, MN. 507-233-4600
Kantner Group
Wapakoneta, OH. 419-738-4060
Reilly Dairy & Food Company
Tampa, FL 813-839-8458
Welcome Dairy
Colby, WI 800-472-2315

Processed Swiss

Cheese Smokers
Brooklyn, NY 718-456-0531
Star Valley Cheese
Thayne, WY 307-883-2510

Provolone

Alberta Cheese Company
Calgary, AB. 403-279-4353
Associated Milk Producers
Dawson, MN. 320-769-2994
Associated Milk Producers
New Ulm, MN. 507-233-4600
BelGioioso Cheese
Denmark, WI. 877-863-2123
Cady Cheese Factory
Wilson, WI 715-772-4218
Cropp Cooperative-Organic Valley
La Farge, WI 888-444-6455
Golden Valley Dairy Products
Tulare, CA. 559-687-1188
Kantner Group
Wapakoneta, OH. 419-738-4060
Klondike Cheese Factory
Monroe, WI. 608-325-3021
Losurdo Creamery
Heuvelton, NY 315-344-2444
Lucille Farm Products
Montville, NJ 973-334-6030
Mancuso Cheese Company
Joliet, IL 815-722-2475
Park Cheese Company
Fond Du Lac, WI 800-752-7275
Pastene Companies
Canton, MA 781-830-8200
Penn Maid Crowley Foods
Philadelphia, PA 800-247-6269
Reilly Dairy & Food Company
Tampa, FL 813-839-8458
Sapudo Cheese
Lincolnshire, IL. 847-267-1100
Sargento Foods Inc
Plymouth, WI 800-243-3737
Sartori Food Corporation
Plymouth, WI 800-558-5888
Sorrento Lactalis
Buffalo, NY. 800-828-7031
Sorrento Lactalis   Corporate & Commercial
Headquarters
Buffalo, NY. 800-828-7031
Trega Foods
Weyauwega, WI 920-867-2137

Ricotta

Alberta Cheese Company
Calgary, AB. 403-279-4353
BelGioioso Cheese
Denmark, WI. 877-863-2123
Biazzo Dairy Products
Ridgefield, NJ 201-941-6800
Calabro Cheese Corporation
East Haven, CT. 203-469-1311
Cappiello Dairy Products
Schenectady, NY. 518-374-5064
Castella Imports
Hauppauge, NY 866-227-8355
Chianti Cheese Company
Wapakoneta, OH. 800-220-3503
Crowley Foods
Binghamton, NY 800-637-0019
J.B. Sons
Yonkers, NY 914-963-5192
Kantner Group
Wapakoneta, OH. 419-738-4060
Lactalis USA
New York, NY 888-766-3353

Losurdo Creamery
Heuvelton, NY 315-344-2444
Losurdo Creamery
Hackensack, NJ. 800-245-6787
Mancuso Cheese Company
Joliet, IL 815-722-2475
Michael Granese & Company
Norristown, PA 610-272-5099
Mozzarella Company
Dallas, TX. 800-798-2954
Mozzarella Fresca   Corporate & Commercial
Headquarters
Concord, CA 800-572-6818
Mozzarella Fresca   Tipton Plant
Tipton, CA 559-752-4823
Pecoraro Dairy Products
Rome, NY 315-339-0101
Penn Maid Crowley Foods
Philadelphia, PA 800-247-6269
Pollio Dairy Products
Mineola, NY 516-741-8000
Sapudo Cheese
Lincolnshire, IL. 847-267-1100
Saputo Cheese
South Gate, CA. 800-824-3373
Sargento Foods Inc
Plymouth, WI 800-243-3737
Schneider's Dairy Holdings Inc
Pittsburgh, PA. 412-881-3525
Sierra Cheese Manufacturing Company
Compton, CA 800-266-4270
Sorrento Lactalis
Buffalo, NY. 800-828-7031
Sorrento Lactalis   Corporate & Commercial
Headquarters
Buffalo, NY. 800-828-7031
Sun-Re Cheese
Sunbury, PA. 570-286-1511
Suprema Specialties
Paterson, NJ 800-543-2479
Supreme Dairy Farms Company
Warwick, RI 401-739-8180

Romano

BelGioioso Cheese
Denmark, WI. 877-863-2123
Castella Imports
Hauppauge, NY 866-227-8355

Chianti Cheese Company
Wapakoneta, OH 800-220-3503
Clofine Dairy & Food Products
Linwood, NJ 800-441-1001
Colonna Brothers
North Bergen, NJ 201-864-1115
Cropp Cooperative-Organic Valley
La Farge, WI 888-444-6455
Dairy Concepts
Greenwood, WI 888-680-5400
Kantner Group
Wapakoneta, OH 419-738-4060
Mancuso Cheese Company
Joliet, IL 815-722-2475
Park Cheese Company
Fond Du Lac, WI 800-752-7275
Pastene Companies
Canton, MA 781-830-8200
Reilly Dairy & Food Company
Tampa, FL 813-839-8458
Sapudo Cheese
Lincolnshire, IL 847-267-1100
Sargento Foods Inc
Plymouth, WI 800-243-3737
Sartori Food Corporation
Plymouth, WI 800-558-5888
Suprema Specialties
Manteca, CA 209-858-9696
Suprema Specialties
Paterson, NJ 800-543-2479
Valley Grain Products
Madera, CA. 559-675-3400
Wisconsin Cheese
Melrose Park, IL 708-450-0074

Roquefort

Lactalis USA
New York, NY 888-766-3353

String

Baker Cheese Factory
St Cloud, WI 920-477-7871
Cropp Cooperative-Organic Valley
La Farge, WI. 888-444-6455
Penn Maid Crowley Foods
Philadelphia, PA 800-247-6269

Swiss

Associated Milk Producers
Dawson, MN 320-769-2994
Associated Milk Producers
New Ulm, MN. 507-233-4600
Brewster Dairy
Brewster, OH 800-874-0874
C.E. Zuercher & Company
Chicago, IL 312-666-6992
Cady Cheese Factory
Wilson, WI 715-772-4218
Clofine Dairy & Food Products
Linwood, NJ 800-441-1001
Cropp Cooperative-Organic Valley
La Farge, WI. 888-444-6455
Crowley Foods
Binghamton, NY 800-637-0019
Guggisberg Cheese
Millersburg, OH 800-262-2505
Heidi's Cheese Products
Mundelein, IL 847-362-5971
Heluva Good Cheese
Sodus, NY. 315-483-6971
Holmes Cheese Company
Millersburg, OH 330-674-6451
Klondike Cheese Factory
Monroe, WI. 608-325-3021
Kolb-Lena Cheese Company
Lena, IL 815-369-4577
Lactalis USA
New York, NY 888-766-3353
Los Altos Food Products
City of Industry, CA 626-330-6555
Marathon Cheese Corporation
Booneville, MS. 662-728-6242
Middlefield Cheese House
Middlefield, OH 800-327-9477
Penn Cheese Corporation
Winfield, PA 570-524-7700
Ragersville Swiss Cheese
Sugarcreek, OH. 330-897-3055
Reilly Dairy & Food Company
Tampa, FL. 813-839-8458

Sargento Foods Inc
Plymouth, WI 800-243-3737
Steiner Cheese
Baltic, OH. 330-897-5505
Stockton Cheese
Stockton, IL. 815-947-3361
Swiss Valley Farms Company
Davenport, IA 563-468-6600
Welcome Dairy
Colby, WI 800-472-2315
Wengers Springbrook Cheese
Davis, IL 815-865-5855
Zivney Cheese
Minonk, IL 800-732-3068

Imitation Cheeses & Substitutes

Cheese Foods & Substitutes

AFP Advanced Food Products, LLC
Visalia, CA 559-627-2070
Al Pete Meats
Muncie, IN 765-288-8817
Amberwave Foods
Oakmont, PA 412-828-3040
Anchor Food Products/ McCain Foods
Appleton, WI 920-734-0627
B&D Foods
Boise, ID 208-344-1183
Baker Cheese Factory
St Cloud, WI 920-477-7871
Bel/Kaukauna USA
Kaukauna, WI 800-558-3500
Bernardi Italian Foods Company
Bloomsburg, PA 570-389-5500
Birds Eye Foods
Berlin, PA 814-267-4641
Black Diamond Cheese
Toronto, ON 800-263-2858
Bongrain North America
Mahwah, NJ 201-512-8825
Brooks Food Group Corporate Office
Bedford, VA 800-873-4934
Carolina Cupboard
Hillsborough, NC 800-400-3441
Castle Cheese
Slippery Rock, PA. 800-252-4373
Cemac Foods Corporation
New York, NY 800-724-0179
Century Foods International
Sparta, WI 800-269-1901
Cheese Straws & More
Monroe, LA. 800-997-1921
Clofine Dairy & Food Products
Linwood, NJ 800-441-1001
Durrett Cheese Sales
Manchester, TN. 800-209-6792
Earth Island Natural Foods
Canoga Park, CA 818-725-2820
Great American Appetizers
Nampa, ID. 800-282-4834
Hormel Foods Corporation
Austin, MN 800-523-4635
Ingretec
Lebanon, PA 717-273-1360
John Wm. Macy's Cheesesticks
Elmwood Park, NJ 800-643-0573
Kantner Group
Wapakoneta, OH 419-738-4060
Laack Brothers Cheese Company
Greenleaf, WI 800-589-5127
Land O'Lakes
Spencer, WI. 715-659-2311
Liono Latticini
Union, NJ 908-686-6061
Marcus Dairy
Danbury, CT 800-243-2511
Matador Processors
Blanchard, OK 800-847-0797
Medallion Foods
Newport, AR. 870-523-3500
Mehaffie Pies
Dayton, OH. 937-253-1163
Merkts Cheese Company
Bristol, WI. 262-857-2316
Nelson Ricks Creamery Company
Salt Lake City, UT 801-364-3607
Omstead Foods Ltd
Burlington, ON 905-315-8883
Parkers Farm
Minneapolis, MN 800-869-6685

Pend Oreille Cheese Company
Sandpoint, ID 208-263-2030
Pine River Pre-Pack
Newton, WI. 920-726-4216
Pocono Cheesecake Factory
Swiftwater, PA 570-839-6844
Saputo Cheese
Peru, IN 765-472-1961
Saputo Cheese
Fond Du Lac, WI 920-929-8060
Schreiber Foods Inc
Green Bay, WI. 800-344-0333
Sierra Cheese Manufacturing Company
Compton, CA 800-266-4270
Texas Heat
San Antonio, TX 800-656-5916
Trugman-Nash
New York, NY 212-869-6910
Tulkoff Food Products
Baltimore, MD 800-638-7343
Variety Foods
Warren, MI 586-268-4900
Wynn Starr Foods of Kentucky
Louisville, KY 800-996-7827

Imitation

American

Kantner Group
Wapakoneta, OH 419-738-4060

Cheddar

Kantner Group
Wapakoneta, OH 419-738-4060

Mozzarella

Kantner Group
Wapakoneta, OH 419-738-4060

Parmesan

Kantner Group
Wapakoneta, OH 419-738-4060

Substitutes

Alberto-Culver Company
Melrose Park, IL 708-450-3000
Black Diamond Cheese
Toronto, ON 800-263-2858
Earth Island Natural Foods
Canoga Park, CA 818-725-2820
Hormel Foods Corporation
Austin, MN 800-523-4635
Kantner Group
Wapakoneta, OH 419-738-4060
Saputo Cheese
Peru, IN 765-472-1961

American

Kantner Group
Wapakoneta, OH 419-738-4060

Dairy Products

Butter

Agri-Mark
  Lawrence, MA 978-687-4936
Alberto-Culver Company
  Melrose Park, IL 708-450-3000
Allfresh Food Products
  Evanston, IL .847-869-3100
American Almond Products Company
  Brooklyn, NY 800-825-6663
Associated Milk Producers
  Dawson, MN .320-769-2994
Associated Milk Producers
  New Ulm, MN. 800-533-3580
Ault Foods
  Toronto, ON .416-626-1973
Beaver Meadow Creamery
  Du Bois, PA 800-262-3711
Bongards Creameries
  Norwood, MN. 800-877-6417
Bottineau Cooperative Creamery
  Bottineau, ND. 701-228-2216
Butterball Farms
  Grand Rapids, MI 616-243-0105
Byrne Dairy
  Syracuse, NY 800-899-1535
California Dairies
  Fresno, CA 559-233-5154
Cass Clay Creamery
  Fargo, ND 701-293-6455
Challenge Dairy Products
  Dublin, CA 800-733-2479
Cloverland Dairy
  Saint Clairsville, OH. 740-699-0509
Coburg Dairy
  North Charleston, SC 843-554-4870
Cream O'Weaver Dairy
  Salt Lake City, UT 801-973-9922
Cropp Cooperative-Organic Valley
  La Farge, WI. 888-444-6455
Dairy Farmers of America
  Franklinton, LA 800-735-2038
Dairy Farmers of America
  Sulphur Springs, TX. 903-885-6518
Dairyman's/Land O' Lakes
  Tulare, CA. 559-687-8287
Darigold Inc
  Seattle, WA .800-333-6455
Dixie Dairy Company
  Gary, IN. 219-885-6101
Ellsworth Cooperative Creamery
  Ellsworth, WI. 715-273-4311
Epicurean Butter
  Denver, CO 720-261-8175
George L. Wells Meat Company
  Philadelphia, PA 800-523-1730
Graf Creamery
  Zachow, WI. .715-758-2137
Grassland Dairy Products
  Greenwood, WI. 800-428-8837
Green River Chocolates
  Hinesburg, VT. 802-246-2652
Grouse Hunt Farms
  Tamaqua, PA. 570-467-2850
Guggisberg Cheese
  Millersburg, OH 800-262-2505
H.B. Taylor Co
  Chicago, IL 773-254-4805
Hazelwood Farm Bakeries
  Minneapolis, MN 314-595-4150
Hope Creamery
  Hope, MN. 507-451-2029
Kozlowski Farms
  Forestville, CA 800-473-2767
Kraft Foods/Knudson Products
  Visalia, CA. 800-323-0768
Land O'Lakes
  St Paul, MN. .651-730-2100
Land O'Lakes
  Carlisle, PA 717-486-7000
Land O'Lakes
  Kent, OH 800-328-9680
Land O'Lakes, Inc
  Arden Hills, MN 800-328-9680
Level Valley Creamery
  Antioch, TN .800-251-1292

Level Valley Creamery
  West Bend, WI 800-558-1707
Lost Trail Root Beer Com
  Louisburg, KS 800-748-7765
Lov-It Creamery
  Green Bay, WI. 800-344-0333
Madison Dairy Produce Company
  Madison, WI .608-256-5561
Marcus Dairy
  Danbury, CT .800-243-2511
Meadow Gold Dairy
  Lewiston, ID .208-746-9006
Milnot Company
  Neosho, MO .800-877-6455
Minerva Cheese Factory
  Minerva, OH .330-868-4196
Naterl
  St. Bruno, QC 800- 50- 115
O-At-Ka Milk Products Cooperative
  Batavia, NY. .800-828-8152
Oasis Foods Company
  Hillside, NJ 908-964-0477
Once Again Nut Butter
  Nunda, NY 888-800-8075
Parmalat
  St George Brant, ON. 519-448-1311
Penn Maid Crowley Foods
  Philadelphia, PA 800-247-6269
Plainview Milk Products Cooperative
  Plainview, MN. 507-534-3872
Prairie Farms Dairy Inc
  Carlinville, IL 217-854-2547
Purity Farms
  Sedalia, CO 800-568-4433
QA Products
  Elk Grove Vlg, IL. 800-635-7907
Queensboro Farm Products
  Canastota, NY 315-697-2235
Reilly Dairy & Food Company
  Tampa, FL. 813-839-8458
Rogue Creamery
  Central Point, OR 541-665-1155
San Fernando Creamery Farmdale Creamery
  San Bernardino, CA 909-889-3002
Saputo
  Montreal, QC 514-328-6662
Schneider's Dairy Holdings Inc
  Pittsburgh, PA 412-881-3525
Scotsburn Dairy Group
  Truro, NS 902-895-4412
Shenk's Foods
  Lancaster, PA 717-393-4240
Sinton Dairy Foods Company
  Colorado Springs, CO. 800-388-4970
Sisler's Ice & Ice Cream
  Ohio, IL. 888-891-3856
Sommer Maid Creamery
  Doylestown, PA 215-345-6160
Sparboe Companies
  Los Angeles, CA. 213-626-7538
Stone Cellar Kitchens
  Riverside, CA 951-352-5713
Turner & Pease Company
  Seattle, WA .206-282-9535
Umpqua Dairy Products Company
  Roseburg, OR 541-672-2638
United Dairymen of Arizona
  Tempe, AZ. 480-966-7211
Ventura Foods
  Ontario, CA .714-257-3700
Vrymeer Commodities
  St Charles, IL 630-584-0069
WestFarm Foods
  Seattle, WA .800-333-6544
Westin
  Omaha, NE 800-228-6098

Blends

Schreiber Foods Inc
  Green Bay, WI. 800-344-0333

Dairy

Agropur Cooperative Agro-Alimentaire
  Granby, QC 800-363-5686

Alberto-Culver Company
  Melrose Park, IL 708-450-3000
Allfresh Food Products
  Evanston, IL .847-869-3100
Alliston Creamery & Dairy
  Alliston, ON .705-435-6751
Beaver Meadow Creamery
  Du Bois, PA. .800-262-3711
Century Foods International
  Sparta, WI. 800-269-1901
Clofine Dairy & Food Products
  Linwood, NJ .800-441-1001
Crystal Cream & Butter Company
  Sacramento, CA 916-447-6455
Dairy Farmers Of America
  Kansas City, MO. 816-801-6455
Danish Maid Butter Company
  Chicago, IL 773-731-8787
Darisweet Farms
  Mountlake Terrace, WA 425-771-5007
Farmers Cooperative Creamery
  McMinnville, OR 503-227-5133
Foothills Creamery
  Calgary, AB. .403-263-7725
Grassland Dairy Products
  Greenwood, WI. 800-428-8837
Guggisberg Cheese
  Millersburg, OH 800-262-2505
Keller's Creamery
  Harleysville, PA 800-535-5371
LaRosa Bakery
  Shrewsbury, NJ 800-527-6722
Lov-It Creamery
  Green Bay, WI. 800-344-0333
Reilly Dairy & Food Company
  Tampa, FL. 813-839-8458
San Joaquin Valley Dairymen
  Los Banos, CA 209-826-4901
Scotsburn Dairy Group
  Truro, NS 902-895-4412
Southwestern Wisconsin Dairy Goat Products
  Mt Sterling, WI 608-734-3151
St. Maurice Laurent
  St. Bruno, QC 418-343-3655
Swagger Foods Corporation
  Vernon Hills, IL 847-913-1200
Tillamook County Creamery Association
  Tillamook, OR 503-842-4481
United Dairymen of Arizona
  Tempe, AZ. 480-966-7211

Low Fat

Dixie USA
  Tomball, TX .800-233-3668

Salted

Associated Milk Producers
  Dawson, MN. 320-769-2994
Cropp Cooperative-Organic Valley
  La Farge, WI. 888-444-6455
Grassland Dairy Products
  Greenwood, WI. 800-428-8837
San Joaquin Valley Dairymen
  Los Banos, CA 209-826-4901

Unsalted

Associated Milk Producers
  Dawson, MN. 320-769-2994
Cropp Cooperative-Organic Valley
  La Farge, WI. 888-444-6455
Grassland Dairy Products
  Greenwood, WI. 800-428-8837
Keller's Creamery
  Harleysville, PA 800-535-5371
Reilly Dairy & Food Company
  Tampa, FL. 813-839-8458

Buttermilk & Buttermilk Products

Buttermilk

Agri-Dairy Products
  Purchase, NY 914-697-9580

Alta Dena Certified Dairy
City of Industry, CA 800-535-1369
Barber's Dairy
Birmingham, AL 205-942-2351
Barkers Farm Dairy
Pecks Mill, WV. 304-855-4512
Bell Dairy Products
Lubbock, TX 806-293-1367
California Dairies
Fresno, CA 559-233-5154
Century Foods International
Sparta, WI 800-269-1901
Chase Brothers Dairy
Oxnard, CA 800-438-6455
Clofine Dairy & Food Products
Linwood, NJ 800-441-1001
Cloverland Dairy
Saint Clairsville, OH. 740-699-0509
Coburg Dairy
North Charleston, SC 843-554-4870
Cream O'Weaver Dairy
Salt Lake City, UT 801-973-9922
Crowley Foods
Binghamton, NY 800-637-0019
Dairy Maid Dairy
Frederick, MD 301-663-5114
Dean Foods/Land O'Lakes
Bismarck, ND 701-222-3131
Foremost Farms
Waukon, IA 563-568-3474
Foremost Farms
Waukesha, WI 800-289-7787
Friendship Dairies
Jericho, NY 516-719-4000
Graf Creamery
Zachow, WI. 715-758-2137
Hygeia Dairy Company
McAllen, TX 956-686-0511
Inland Northwest Dairies
Spokane, WA. 509-489-8600
Kerry Ingredients
Tralee, Co. Kerry,
Knoll Creek Dairy
Harrison, NY 718-892-4500
Land O'Lakes
Carlisle, PA 717-486-7000
McArthur Dairy
Miami, FL 305-576-2880
Meadow Gold Dairies
Honolulu, HI 808-949-6161
Mid States Dairy
Hazelwood, MO 314-731-1150
Mom's Bakery
Atlanta, GA 404-344-4189
Plainview Milk Products Cooperative
Plainview, MN 507-534-3872
Pleasant View Dairy
Highland, IN 219-838-0155
Quality Ingredients Corporation
Burnsville, MN 952-898-4002
Quality Jersey Products
Seaforth, ON 519-527-1272
Queensboro Farm Products
Jamaica, NY 718-658-5000
Reilly Dairy & Food Company
Tampa, FL 813-839-8458
San Joaquin Valley Dairymen
Los Banos, CA 209-826-4901
Schneider Valley Farms Dairy
Williamsport, PA. 570-326-2021
Sinton Dairy Foods Company
Colorado Springs, CO. 800-388-4970
Sunshine Farms Dairy
Elyria, OH 440-322-6301
Welsh Farms
Newark, NJ 800-221-0663
Winchester Farms Dairy
Winchester, KY 859-745-5500
Winder Dairy
West Valley, UT 800-946-3371
Yoder Dairies
Chesapeake, VA 757-497-3518

Buttermilk Products

Graf Creamery
Zachow, WI. 715-758-2137

Condensed

Graf Creamery
Zachow, WI. 715-758-2137

Dry

Foremost Farms
Waukon, IA 563-568-3474
Kantner Group
Wapakoneta, OH 419-738-4060
Kerry Ingredients
Tralee, Co. Kerry,

Dry Sweetcream

Kantner Group
Wapakoneta, OH 419-738-4060

Cream

Accra Pac Group
Elkhart, IN. 574-295-0000
Alta Dena Certified Dairy
City of Industry, CA 800-535-1369
Anastasia Confections, Inc.
Orlando, FL 800-329-7100
Arcor USA
Coral Gables, FL. 800-572-7267
Associated Milk Producers
New Ulm, MN 800-533-3580
Atlanta Flagship Dairy
Atlanta, GA 800-224-0669
Ault Foods
Toronto, ON 416-626-1973
Berkeley Farms
Hayward, CA 510-265-8600
Berkshire Dairy & Food Products
Wyomissing, PA 888-654-8008
Blue Chip Group
Salt Lake City, UT 800-878-0099
Byrne Dairy
Syracuse, NY 800-899-1535
Cass Clay Creamery
Fargo, ND 701-293-6455
Cropp Cooperative-Organic Valley
La Farge, WI 888-444-6455
Dairy Farmers of America
Sulphur Springs, TX 903-885-6518
Dietrich's Milk Products
Reading, PA 800-526-6455
Dixie Dairy Company
Gary, IN. 219-885-6101
Ellsworth Cooperative Creamery
Ellsworth, WI 715-273-4311
Fairmont Products
Belleville, PA 717-935-2121
Farmland Dairies
Wallington, NJ 973-777-2500
First District Association
Litchfield, MN 320-693-3236
Foremost Dairies-Hawaii
Honolulu, HI 808-841-5831
GPI USA LLC.
Athens, GA 706-850-7826
H.B. Taylor Co
Chicago, IL 773-254-4805
Ideal Dairy
Richfield, UT 435-896-5061
Kemps
Cedarburg, WI. 262-377-5040
Knoll Creek Dairy
Harrison, NY 718-892-4500
Land O'Lakes
St Paul, MN. 800-328-9680
Marcus Dairy
Danbury, CT 800-243-2511
Muller-Pinehurst Dairy C
Rockford, IL 815-968-0441
Oak Farms
Dallas, TX. 214-941-0302
Pepperidge Farm
Richmond, UT. 888-737-7374
Pioneer Dairy
Southwick, MA 413-569-6132
Plains Creamery
Amarillo, TX. 806-374-0385
Prairie Farms Dairy
Carlinville, IL 217-854-2547
Price's Creameries
El Paso, TX 915-565-2711
Purity Dairies
Nashville, TN 615-244-1900
Queensboro Farm Products
Jamaica, NY 718-658-5000
Reiter Dairy
Akron, OH. 800-362-0825

Reiter Dairy
Springfield, OH. 937-323-5777
Rosenberger's Dairies
Hatfield, PA. 800-355-9074
Sabatino Truffles USA
Long Island City, NY 888-444-9971
Saint Albans CooperativeCreamy
Saint Albans, VT. 800-559-0343
San Fernando Creamery Farmdale Creamery
San Bernardino, CA 909-889-3002
San Joaquin Valley Dairymen
Los Banos, CA 209-826-4901
Schneider's Dairy Holdings Inc
Pittsburgh, PA 412-881-3525
Sugarwoods Farm
Glover, VT 800-245-3718
Swiss Valley Farms Company
Cedar Rapids, IA 319-364-8153
Velda Farms
North Miami Bch, FL 800-795-4649
W.J. Stearns & Sons/Mountain Dairy
Storrs Mansfield, CT 860-423-9289
Went's Dairy
Niagara Falls, NY 716-692-6543
Westhill Dairy
North York, ON 416-661-0580
White Wave Foods
Jacksonville, FL 800-874-6765

Dried

Agri-Dairy Products
Purchase, NY 914-697-9580
Blossom Farm Products
Ridgewood, NJ 800-729-1818
Century Foods International
Sparta, WI 800-269-1901
Clofine Dairy & Food Products
Linwood, NJ 800-441-1001
Custom Food Processors International
New Hampton, IA 641-394-4802
Kantner Group
Wapakoneta, OH 419-738-4060
Kerry Ingredients
Tralee, Co. Kerry,
Parmalat
St George Brant, ON 519-448-1311
Quality Ingredients Corporation
Burnsville, MN 952-898-4002

Fresh

Agri-Dairy Products
Purchase, NY 914-697-9580
Agropur Cooperative Agro-Alimentaire
Granby, QC 800-363-5686
Auburn Dairy Products
Auburn, WA 800-950-9264
Barbe's Dairy
Westwego, LA 504-347-6201
Brum's Dairy
Pembroke, ON. 613-735-4686
Clofine Dairy & Food Products
Linwood, NJ 800-441-1001
Dean Foods Company
Dallas, TX 214-303-3400
Heritage Foods
Santa Ana, CA 714-775-5000
LaRosa Bakery
Shrewsbury, NJ 800-527-6722
LeHigh Valley Dairies
Lansdale, PA 215-855-8205
Northumberland Cooperative
Miramichi, NB 800-332-3328
O-At-Ka Milk Products Cooperative
Batavia, NY 800-828-8152
Prairie Farms Dairy
Carlinville, IL 217-854-2547
Reilly Dairy & Food Company
Tampa, FL 813-839-8458
Turner Dairies
Jackson, TN 731-427-6012

Non-Dairy

ACH Food Companies
Memphis, TN 800-691-1106
Alamance Foods/Triton Water Company
Burlington, NC 800-476-9111
Bay Valley Foods
Green Bay, WI. 800-558-4700
Instantwhip: Arizona
Phoenix, AZ 800-544-9447

Instantwhip: Texas
San Antonio, TX 800-544-9447
Sugar Foods
Sun Valley, CA 818-768-7900

Whipped

A.C. Petersen Farms
West Hartford, CT. 860-233-8483
Alamance Foods/Triton Water Company
Burlington, NC 800-476-9111
Berkeley Farms
Hayward, CA 510-265-8600
Brighams
Arlington, MA 800-274-4426
Cass Clay Creamery
Fargo, ND 701-293-6455
Caughman's Meat Plant
Lexington, SC. 803-356-0076
Charles Dennery Pillsbury
New Orleans, LA 504-733-2331
Clofine Dairy & Food Products
Linwood, NJ 800-441-1001
ConAgra Dairy Foods
Indianapolis, IN 317-329-3700
Crave Natural Foods
Northampton, MA. 413-587-7999
Cropp Cooperative-Organic Valley
La Farge, WI 888-444-6455
Dean Foods/Land O'Lakes
Bismarck, ND 701-222-3131
Erba Food Products
Brooklyn, NY 718-272-7700
Instantwhip: Texas
San Antonio, TX 800-544-9447
Land O'Lakes
St Paul, MN. 651-730-2100
Marva Maid Dairy
Newport News, VA. 800-544-4439
Mayfield Dairy Farms
Athens, TN 800-362-9546
Morningstar Foods
Gustine, CA 209-854-6461
Penn Maid Crowley Foods
Philadelphia, PA 800-247-6269
Prairie Farms Dairy Inc
Carlinville, IL 217-854-2547
Rich Products Corporation
Claremont, CA 909-621-4711
Schneider's Dairy Holdings Inc
Pittsburgh, PA. 412-881-3525
Sunshine Farms Dairy
Elyria, OH. .440-322-6301
Tiller Foods Company
Dayton, OH. 937-435-4601
Yoder Dairies
Chesapeake, VA 757-497-3518

from Milk

Auburn Dairy Products
Auburn, WA 800-950-9264

Creamers

Auburn Dairy Products
Auburn, WA 800-950-9264
Brewfresh Coffee Company
South Salt Lake, UT 888-486-3334
Broughton Foods
Marietta, OH 800-283-2479
Cropp Cooperative-Organic Valley
La Farge, WI 888-444-6455
Crowley Foods
Binghamton, NY 800-637-0019
H.B. Taylor Co
Chicago, IL 773-254-4805
Instantwhip: Texas
San Antonio, TX 800-544-9447
Kan-Pac
Arkansas City, KS 620-442-6820
Morningstar Foods
Dallas, TX. 225-273-2803
Nulaid Foods
Ripon, CA. .209-599-2121
Quality Ingredients Corporation
Burnsville, MN 952-898-4002
S.J. McCullagh
Buffalo, NY. 800-753-3473
Schneider's Dairy Holdings Inc
Pittsburgh, PA. 412-881-3525
Sinton Dairy Foods Company
Colorado Springs, CO. 800-388-4970

Tiller Foods Company
Dayton, OH. 937-435-4601
Tuscan/Lehigh Valley Dais
Lansdale, PA. 800-937-3233
W.J. Stearns & Sons/Mountain Dairy
Storrs Mansfield, CT 860-423-9289

Coffee

Agri-Dairy Products
Purchase, NY 914-697-9580

Baldwin Richardson Foods
Frankfort, IL 866-644-2732

Baldwin Richardson Foods is a liquid ingredient manufacturer specializing in signature sauces, dessert toppings, beverage/pancake syrups, specialty fruit fillings and condiments. Packaging capabilities range from portion control cups and pouches to standard retail and foodservice packs and include industrial drums and totes. Full service R&D and Quality groups dedicated to new product development, with in-house stability and analytical testing. Call for assistance.

Boston's Best Coffee Roasters
South Easton, MA. 800-323-4889
Byrne Dairy
Syracuse, NY 800-899-1535
Cloverland Green Spring Dairy
Baltimore, MD 410-235-4477
Compact Industries
St Charles, IL 800-513-4262
Cropp Cooperative-Organic Valley
La Farge, WI 888-444-6455
H.B. Taylor Co
Chicago, IL 773-254-4805
Hanan Products Company
Hicksville, NY 516-938-1000
Industrial Products
Defiance, OH 800-251-3033
Inland Northwest Dairies
Spokane, WA. 509-489-8600
Innovative Food Solutions LLC
Columbus, OH 800-884-3314
Instantwhip: Texas
San Antonio, TX. 800-544-9447
Kemps
Cedarburg, WI. 262-377-5040
Morningstar Foods
Dallas, TX. 225-273-2803
Nestle
Glendale, CA 800-368-5594
Rich Products Corporation
Claremont, CA 909-621-4711
Safeway Milk Plant
Tempe, AZ 480-894-4391
Tova Industries
Louisville, KY 888-532-8682

Non-Dairy

ACH Food Companies
Cordova, TN 800-691-1106
Bay Valley Foods
Horsham, PA. 800-236-1119
Bay Valley Foods
Green Bay, WI. 800-558-4700
Custom Food Processors International
New Hampton, IA. 641-394-4802
Dean Foods Company
Rosemont, IL. 800-323-1571
Dean Foods Company
Rockford, IL. 815-962-0647
Diehl Food Ingredients
Defiance, OH 800-251-3033
Erba Food Products
Brooklyn, NY 718-272-7700
Lake City Foods
Mississauga, ON. 905-625-8244
Morningstar Foods
Dallas, TX. 225-273-2803
Ohio Processors Company
London, OH 740-852-9243

Quality Ingredients Corporation
Burnsville, MN 952-898-4002
S.J. McCullagh
Buffalo, NY. 800-753-3473
Stickney & Poor Company
North Andover, MA 508-261-8967
Tiller Foods Company
Dayton, OH. 937-435-4601
Tonex
Wallington, NJ 973-773-5135

Custard

Artuso Pastry Shop
Bronx, NY. 718-367-2515
Bakemark Ingredients Canada
Richmond, BC 800-665-9441
Venice Spumoni/Spring Valley Ice Cream
Philadelphia, PA 800-784-0312

Dairy

Abbott Laboratories Nutritionals/Ross Products
Columbus, OH 877-946-7747
ACH Food Companies
Cordova, TN 800-691-1106
ADM Food Ingredients
Olathe, KS. 800-255-6637
Advance Food Brokers
West Bloomfield, MI 248-851-9045
AFP Advanced Food Products, LLC
Visalia, CA 559-627-2070
Aglamesis Brothers
Cincinnati, OH 513-531-5196
Agri-Dairy Products
Purchase, NY 914-697-9580
Agri-Mark
Lawrence, MA 978-687-4936
Agropur Cooperative Agro-Alimentaire
Granby, QC 800-363-5686
Akenhead's Ice Cream Company
East Palestine, OH 330-426-9553
Al Gelato Bornay
Franklin Park, IL. 847-455-5355
Al Pete Meats
Muncie, IN 765-288-8817
Al's Beverage Company
East Windsor, CT 888-257-7632
Alamance Foods/Triton Water Company
Burlington, NC 800-476-9111
Alberto-Culver Company
Melrose Park, IL 708-450-3000
Alinosi French Superfine Candies
Detroit, MI 313-527-3195
All American Foods, Inc.
Mankato, MN 800-833-2661
Allfresh Food Products
Evanston, IL 847-869-3100
Alliston Creamery & Dairy
Alliston, ON 705-435-6751
Alpenrose Dairy
Portland, OR 503-244-1133
Alta-Dena Certified Dairy
City of Industry, CA 800-535-1369
Alto Dairy Cooperative
Waupun, WI 920-346-2215
Amberwave Foods
Oakmont, PA. 412-828-3040
Amboy Specialty Foods Company
Dixon, IL. .800-892-0400
American Classic Ice Cream Company
Bay Shore, NY 631-666-1000
American Lecithin Company
Oxford, CT 800-364-4416
American Whey
Ridgewood, NJ 201-493-2662
Americana Foods
Dallas, TX. 972-709-7100

195

Anchor Food Products/ McCain Foods
Appleton, WI 920-734-0627
Anderson Dairy
Las Vegas, NV 702-642-7507
Anderson Erickson Dairy
Des Moines, IA 515-265-2521
Ariza Cheese Company
Paramount, CA 800-762-4736
Arla Foods Ingredients
Basking Ridge, NJ 800-243-3730
Aslanis Seafoods
Quincy, MA. 800-876-3712
Associated Bakers Products
Huntington, NY 631-673-3841
Associated Milk Producers
New Ulm, MN. 507-233-4600
Associated Milk Producers
New Ulm, MN. 800-533-3580
Astro Dairy Products
Etobicoke, ON. 416-622-2811
Atlanta Flagship Dairy
Atlanta, GA 800-224-0669
Atwood Cheese Company
Atwood, ON 519-356-2271
Auburn Dairy Products
Auburn, WA 800-950-9264
Avalon Foodservice, Inc.
Canal Fulton, OH 800-362-0622
Avanti Food Company
Walnut, IL 800-243-3739
Avent Luvel Dairy Products
Kosciusko, MS 800-281-1307
Avonmore Ingredients
Monroe, WI. 800-336-2183
B&D Foods
Boise, ID 208-344-1183
Baird Dairies
Clarksville, IN. 812-283-3345
Baker Cheese Factory
St Cloud, WI 920-477-7871
Ballas Egg Products Corporation
Zanesville, OH 740-453-0386
Barbe's Dairy
Westwego, LA. 504-347-6201
Barber Pure Milk Ice Cream Company
Birmingham, AL. 205-942-2351
Barber's Dairy
Birmingham, AL. 205-942-2351
Barkers Farm Dairy
Pecks Mill, WV. 304-855-4512
Barnes Ice Cream Company
Augusta, ME 207-622-0827
Bartlett Dairy & Food Service
Jamaica, NY 718-658-2299
Beaver Meadow Creamery
Du Bois, PA. 800-262-3711
Bedford Cheese Store
Shelbyville, TN 800-264-1115
Bel/Kaukauna USA
Kaukauna, WI. 800-558-3500
Bell Dairy Products
Lubbock, TX 806-293-1367
Belle Plaine Cheese Factory
Shawano, WI. 866-245-5924
Ben E. Keith DFW
Fort Worth, TX 817-654-3663
Benson Creamery
Decatur, IL 217-429-2351
Berger Foods
Tucker, GA 770-934-8983
Bergey's Dairy Farm
Chesapeake, VA 757-482-4712
Berkeley Farms
Hayward, CA 510-265-8600
Bernardi Italian Foods Company
Bloomsburg, PA 570-389-5500

Berner Cheese Corporation
Dakota, IL. 800-819-8199
Berner Cheese Corporation
Rock City, IL. 815-865-5136
Bernie's Foods
Brooklyn, NY 718-417-6677
Biazzo Dairy Products
Ridgefield, NJ 201-941-6800
Biery Cheese Company
Louisville, OH 800-243-3731
Bill Mack's Homemade Ice Cream
Dover, PA 717-292-1931
Bio-K + International
Laval, QC 450-978-2465
Birdsall Ice Cream Company
Mason City, IA 641-423-5365
Black Diamond Cheese
Toronto, ON 800-263-2858
Blake's Creamery
Manchester, NH 603-623-7242
Bliss Brothers Dairy, Inc.
Attleboro, MA. 800-622-8789
Bloomfield Bakers
Los Alamitos, CA 800-594-4111
Blossom Farm Products
Ridgewood, NJ 800-729-1818
Blue Bell Creameries
Brenham, TX. 979-836-7977
Blue Chip Group
Salt Lake City, UT 800-878-0099
Blue Ribbon Dairy
Exeter, PA 570-655-5579
Bongard's Creameries
Perham, MN 218-346-4680
Bongrain North America
Mahwah, NJ 201-512-8825
Bonnie Doon Ice Cream Corporation
Elkhart, IN. 574-264-3390
Borden
Tulsa, OK 800-733-2230
Boston's Best Coffee Roasters
South Easton, MA. 800-323-4889
Bottineau Cooperative Creamery
Bottineau, ND 701-228-2216
Braum's Inc
Oklahoma City, OK 405-478-1656
Brenntag
Reading, PA 888-926-4151
Brenntag Pacific
Santa Fe Springs, CA 562-903-9626
Brewster Dairy
Brewster, OH 800-874-0874
Brier Run Farm
Birch River, WV 304-649-2975
Brighams
Arlington, MA 800-274-4426
Brooks Food Group Corporate Office
Bedford, VA 800-873-4934
Brookside Foods
Abbotsford, BC. 877-793-3866
Broughton Foods
Marietta, OH 800-283-2479
Brown Dairy
Coalville, UT 435-336-5952
Brown Produce Company
Farina, IL. 618-245-3301
Brown's Ice Cream
Minneapolis, MN 612-378-1075
Browns Dairy
Valparaiso, IN. 219-464-4141
Browns' Ice Cream Company
Bowling Green, KY 270-843-9882
Brum's Dairy
Pembroke, ON. 613-735-4686
Brunkow Cheese Company
Darlington, WI 608-776-3716
Bubbies Homemade Ice Cream
Aiea, HI 808-487-7218
Buck's Spumoni Company
Milford, CT 203-874-2007
Bunge Beverage & Dairy Ingredients
St Louis, MO. 314-292-2000
Bunker Hill Cheese Company
Millersburg, OH 800-253-6636
Buon Italia
New York, NY 212-633-9090
Burger Dairy
Cleveland, OH 216-896-9100
Bush Boake Allen
New York, NY 212-765-5500
Bush Brothers Provision Company
West Palm Beach, FL 800-327-1345

Butterball Farms
Grand Rapids, MI 616-243-0105
Butterbuds Food Ingredients
Racine, WI. 800-426-1119
Byrne Dairy
Syracuse, NY 800-899-1535
C.E. Zuercher & Company
Chicago, IL 312-666-6992
C.F. Burger Creamery
Detroit, MI 800-229-2322
Cabot Creamery
Montpelier, VT 888-792-2268
Cal-Maine Foods
Pine Grove, LA 225-222-4148
Cal-Maine Foods
Jackson, MS 601-948-6813
Calabro Cheese Corporation
East Haven, CT 203-469-1311
California Dairies
Fresno, CA 559-233-5154
Calpro Ingredients
Corona, CA 909-493-4890
Cappiello Dairy Products
Schenectady, NY. 518-374-5064
Caprine Estates
Bellbrook, OH 937-848-7406
Carbolite Foods
Evansville, IN 888-524-3314
Carl Colteryahn Dairy
Pittsburgh, PA 412-881-1408
Cascade Fresh
Seattle, WA 800-511-0057
Casper's Ice Cream
Richmond, UT. 800-772-4182
Cass Clay
Fargo, ND 701-232-1566
Cass Clay Creamery
Fargo, ND 701-293-6455
Castle Cheese
Slippery Rock, PA. 800-252-4373
Cedar Crest Specialties
Cedarburg, WI. 800-877-8341
Cemac Foods Corporation
New York, NY 800-724-0179
Central Dairies
St Johns, NL 800-563-6455
Central Dairy Company
Jefferson City, MO. 573-635-6148
Central Valley Dairymen
Modesto, CA. 209-551-2667
Centreside Dairy
Renfrew, ON 613-432-2914
Century Foods International
Sparta, WI 800-269-1901
Challenge Dairy Products
Dublin, CA 800-733-2479
Chase Brothers Dairy
Oxnard, CA. 800-438-6455
Cheese Smokers
Brooklyn, NY 718-456-0531
Cheese Straws & More
Monroe, LA. 800-997-1921
Cheezwhse.Com
Armonk, NY 800-243-3994
Chester Dairy Company
Chester, IL. 618-826-2394
Chicago 58 Food Products
Toronto, ON 416-603-4244
Chloe Foods Corporation
Brooklyn, NY 718-827-3600
Chocolaterie Bernard Callebaut
Calgary, AB. 800-661-8367
Churny Company
Waupaca, WI. 715-258-4040
Ciao Bella Gelato Company
Irvington, NJ 800-435-2863
Circus Man Ice Cream Corporation
Farmingdale, NY 516-249-4400
Clinton Milk Company
Newark, NJ 973-642-3000
Clofine Dairy & Food Products
Linwood, NJ 800-441-1001
Clover Farms Dairy Company
Reading, PA 800-323-0123
Clover Stornetta Farms
Petaluma, CA 800-237-3315
Cloverland Dairy
Saint Clairsville, OH. 740-699-0509
Cloverland Green Spring Dairy
Baltimore, MD 410-235-4477
Cloverland Green Spring Dairy
Baltimore, MD 800-876-6455

Co-Hen Egg Farms
Kennebunk, ME 207-985-9772
Coastlog Industries
Novi, MI 248-344-9556
Coburg Dairy
North Charleston, SC 843-554-4870
Colchester Foods
Bozrah, CT 800-243-0469
Coleman Dairy
Little Rock, AR 501-748-1700
Colonna Brothers
North Bergen, NJ 201-864-1115
Compton Dairy
Shelbyville, IN 317-398-8621
ConAgra Dairy Foods
Overland, MO 314-429-3636
ConAgra Dairy Foods
Indianapolis, IN 317-329-3700
ConAgra Grocery Products
Irvine, CA 714-680-1000
Conco Food Service
Harahan, LA .800-488-3988
Consun Food Industries
Elyria, OH 440-233-7501
Continental Culture Specialists
Glendale, CA 818-240-7400
Cordon Bleu International
Anjou, QC 514-352-3000
Corfu Foods
Bensenville, IL 630-595-2510
Country Delight Farms
Nashville, TN 615-320-1440
Country Fresh
Grand Rapids, MI 800-748-0480
Country Fresh Golden Valley
Livonia, MI 734-261-7980
Cow Palace Too
Granger, WA .509-829-5777
Cream O'Weaver Dairy
Salt Lake City, UT 801-973-9922
Creamland Dairies
Albuquerque, NM 505-247-0721
Creighton Brothers
Atwood, IN 574-267-3101
Creme Glacee Gelati
St Leonard, QC 888-322-0116

Crescent Ridge Dairy
Sharon, MA .800-660-2740
Crossroad Farms Dairy
Indianapolis, IN 317-229-7600
Crowley Cheese
Mt Holly, VT .802-259-2340
Crowley Foods
Binghamton, NY 800-247-6269
Crowley Foods
Binghamton, NY 800-637-0019
Crystal Cream & Butter Company
Sacramento, CA 916-447-6455
Crystal Farms
Chestnut Mtn, GA 770-967-6152
Crystal Lake
Warsaw, IN 574-858-2514
Culture Systems
Mishawaka, IN 574-258-0602
Cultured Specialties
Fullerton, CA 714-772-8861
Cumberland Dairy
Rosenhayn, NJ 856-451-1300
Curly's Dairy
Stayton, OR .800-785-1335
Cutler Egg Products
Abbeville, AL 334-585-2268
Cyclone Enterprises
Houston, TX .281-872-0087
Czepiel Millers Dairy
Ludlow, MA .413-589-0828
Dairy Chem Inc
Fishers, IN 317-849-8400
Dairy Concepts
Greenwood, WI 888-680-5400
Dairy Farmers of America
Springfield, MO 800-243-2479
Dairy Farmers of America
Springfield, MO 800-435-7269
Dairy Farmers of America
Smithfield, UT 800-453-2820
Dairy Farmers of America
Franklinton, LA 800-735-2038
Dairy Farmers of America
Salt Lake City, UT 801-977-3000
Dairy Farmers of America
Kansas City, MO 816-801-6200

Dairy Farmers of America
Kansas City, MO 888-332-6455
Dairy Farmers of America
Sulphur Springs, TX 903-885-6518
Dairy Farmers of AmericaGoshen Plant
Goshen, IN 800-758-0269
Dairy Fresh
Winston Salem, NC 800-446-5577
Dairy Fresh Corporation
Greensboro, AL 800-239-5114
Dairy Fresh Foods
Taylor, MI 313-295-6300
Dairy Ingredients
Davisburg, MI 248-922-0900
Dairy King Milk Farms/Foodservice
Glendale, CA 818-243-6455
Dairy Land
Macon, GA 478-742-6461
Dairy Maid Dairy
Frederick, MD 301-663-5114
Dairy Queen of Georgia
Decatur, GA .404-292-3553
Dairy-Mix
St Petersburg, FL 727-525-6101
Dairyman's/Land O' Lakes
Tulare, CA 559-687-8287
Dairytown Products Ltd
Sussex, NB 800-561-5598
Daisy Brand
Dallas, TX 877-292-9830
Dakota Country Cheese
Mandan, ND .701-663-0246
Danish Creamery Association
Fresno, CA 559-233-5154
Danish Maid Butter Company
Chicago, IL 773-731-8787
Dannon Company
Fort Worth, TX 800-211-6565
Darby Plains Dairy
Plain City, OH 614-873-4574
Darifair Foods
Jacksonville, FL 904-268-8999
Darigold Inc
Seattle, WA 800-333-6455
Darisweet Farms
Mountlake Terrace, WA 425-771-5007

Dave's Gourmet
San Francisco, CA 800-758-0372
Dave's Hawaiian Ice Cream
Pearl City, HI 808-453-0500
Davisco International
Eden Prairie, MN 800-757-7611
Daybreak Foods
Long Prairie, MN 320-732-2966
Dean Dairy Products
Sharpsville, PA 800-942-8096
Dean Foods Company
Dallas, TX 214-303-3400
Dean Foods Company
Dallas, TX 800-431-9214
Dean Foods/Land O'Lakes
Bismarck, ND 701-222-3131
Dean Foods/Verifine Dairy Products
Sheboygan, WI 800-236-6455
Dean Milk Company
Louisville, KY 800-451-3326
Deb-El Foods
Elizabeth, NJ 800-421-3447
Deep Foods
Union, NJ 908-810-7500
Del Rey Tortilleria
Chicago, IL 800-446-1459
Delta Distributors
Longview, TX 800-945-1858
Deluxe Ice Cream Company
Salem, OR 800-304-7172
Deseret Dairy Products
Salt Lake City, UT 801-240-7350
Detroit City Dairy
Highland Park, MI 313-868-5511
Dietrich's Milk Products
Reading, PA 800-526-6455
Dillon Dairy Company
Denver, CO 303-388-1645
Dimock Dairy Products
Dimock, SD 605-928-3833
Division Baking Corporation
New York, NY 800-934-9238
Dixie Dairy Company
Gary, IN 219-885-6101
Dixie Egg Company
Jacksonville, FL 800-394-3447
Double B Foods
Schulenburg, TX 800-472-6661
Dreyer's Grand Ice Cream
Oakland, CA 877-437-3937
Driftwood Dairy
El Monte, CA 626-444-9591
Dunkin Brands Inc.
Canton, MA 800-458-7731
Dupont Cheese
Marion, WI 800-895-2873
Durrett Cheese Sales
Manchester, TN 800-209-6792
Eagle Family Foods
Columbus, OH 888-656-3245
Eatem Foods Company
Vineland, NJ 800-683-2836
Eberhard Creamery
Redmond, OR 541-548-5181
Echo Spring Dairy
Eugene, OR 541-342-1291
Edy's Grand Ice Cream
Rockaway, NJ 800-362-7899
Edy's Grand Ice Cream
Glendale Heights, IL 888-377-3397
Edy's Grand Ice Cream
Weston, FL 954-384-7133
Eggland's Best Foods
King of Prussia, PA 888-922-3447
Ellsworth Cooperative Creamery
Ellsworth, WI 715-273-4311
Ellsworth Ice Cream Company
Saratoga Springs, NY 518-584-1684
Elm City Cheese Company
Hamden, CT 203-865-5768
Elmwood Dairy
Newport, VT 802-334-8125
Emkay Trading Corporation
Elmsford, NY 914-592-9000
Empire Cheese
Cuba, NY 585-968-1552
Erie Foods International
Erie, IL 800-447-1887
Erivan Dairy
Oreland, PA 215-887-2009
Eskimo Pie Corporation
Ronkonkoma, NY 631-737-9700

Everything Yogurt
Washington, DC 202-842-2990
F&A Cheese Corporation
Irvine, CA 800-634-4109
F&A Dairy of California
Newman, CA 800-554-6455
Fairmont Products
Belleville, PA 717-935-2121
Fairview Swiss Cheese
Fredonia, PA 724-475-4154
Faith Dairy
Tacoma, WA 253-531-3398
Fanny Mason Farmstead Cheese
Walpole, NH 603-756-3300
Fantis Foods
Carlstadt, NJ 201-933-6200
Farbest-Tallman Foods Corporation
Montvale, NJ 201-573-4900
Farm Stores
Palmetto Bay, FL 800-726-3276
Farmdale Creamery
San Bernardino, CA 909-889-3002
Farmers Cooperative Creamery
McMinnville, OR 503-227-5133
Farmers Dairies
El Paso, TX 915-772-2736
Farmers Hen House
Kalona, IA 319-683-2206
Farmers Seafood Company
Shreveport, LA 800-874-0203
Farmland Dairies
Grand Rapids, MI 616-538-3822
Farmland Dairies
Wallington, NJ 888-727-6252
Farmland Dairies
Wallington, NJ 973-777-2500
Farr Candy Company
Idaho Falls, ID 208-522-8215
FDP
Santa Rosa, CA 707-547-1776
Feature Foods
Etobicoke, ON 416-675-7350
Fendall Ice Cream Company
Salt Lake City, UT 801-355-3583
Fieldbrook Farms
Dunkirk, NY 800-333-0805
First District Association
Litchfield, MN 320-693-3236
Flavors from Florida
Bartow, FL 863-533-0408
Fleur De Lait Foods
New Holland, PA 717-355-8500
Food Ingredients
Elgin, IL 800-500-7676
Foodmark
Wellesley, MA 781-237-7088
Foothills Creamery
Calgary, AB 403-263-7725
Foothills Creamery
Calgary, AB 800-661-4909
Foremost Dairies-Hawaii
Honolulu, HI 808-841-5831
Foremost Farms
Preston, MN 507-765-3831
Foremost Farms
Waukesha, WI 800-289-7787
Foremost Farms USA
Sparta, WI 608-269-3126
Foster Farms Dairy
Fresno, CA 800-241-0008
Four C Foods Corporation
Brooklyn, NY 718-272-4242
Freeman Industries
Tuckahoe, NY 800-666-6454
Freeze-Dry Products
Santa Rosa, CA 707-547-1776
Fresh Farm
Arvada, CO 303-429-1536
Fried Provisions Company
Evans City, PA 724-538-3160
Friendly Ice Cream Corporation
Wilbraham, MA 800-966-9970
Friendship Dairies
Jericho, NY 516-719-4000
Friendship Dairies
Friendship, NY 585-973-3031
Frog City Cheese
Plymouth Notch, VT 802-672-3650
Froma-Dar
St. Boniface, QC 819-535-3946
Frostbite
Toledo, OH 800-968-7711

Frozfruit Corporation
Gardena, CA 310-217-1034
Gad Cheese Company
Medford, WI 715-748-4273
GAF Seelig
Flushing, NY 718-899-5000
Galaxy Nutritional Foods
Orlando, FL 800-441-9419
Galliker Dairy
Johnstown, PA 800-477-6455
Gamay Flavors
New Berlin, WI 888-345-4560
Garber Ice Cream Company
Winchester, VA 800-662-5422
Garelick Farms
Lynn, MA 800-487-8700
Gelato Fresco
Toronto, ON 416-785-5415
George L. Wells Meat Company
Philadelphia, PA 800-523-1730
GFA Brands
Paramus, NJ 201-568-9300
Gibbsville Cheese Company
Sheboygan Falls, WI 920-564-3242
Gifford's Dairy
Skowhegan, ME 207-474-9821
Glanbia Foods
Twin Falls, ID 208-733-7555
Glanbia Foods
Twin Falls, ID 800-427-9477
Global Food Industries
Townville, SC 800-225-4152
Glover's Ice Cream
Frankfort, IN 800-686-5163
Gold Cup Farms
Clayton, NY 800-752-1341
Gold Star Dairy
Little Rock, AR 501-565-6125
Golden Valley Dairy Products
Tulare, CA 559-687-1188
Goldenrod Dairy Foods/ U C Milk Company
Madisonville, KY 800-462-2354
Good Humor Breyers Ice Cream Company
Hagerstown, MD 301-797-9603
Good Humor Breyers Ice Cream Company
Framingham, MA 508-620-4300
Good Humor Breyers Ice Cream Company
Henderson, NV 702-564-0020
Good Humor Breyers Ice Cream Company
Green Bay, WI 866-204-9750
Good Humor Breyers Ice Cream Company
Green Bay, WI 920-499-5151
Goshen Dairy Company
New Philadelphia, OH 330-339-1959
Gossner Food
Logan, UT 800-944-0454
Gourmet Ice Cream
Palmer, MA 413-283-3740
Grace Foods International
Astoria, NY 718-433-4789
Graf Creamery
Zachow, WI 715-758-2137
Graham Cheese Corporation
Washington, IN 800-472-9178
Grande Cheese Company
Brownsville, WI 800-678-3122
Grassland Dairy Products
Greenwood, WI 800-428-8837
Great American Appetizers
Nampa, ID 800-282-4834
Great Lakes Cheese of NY
Adams, NY 315-232-4511
Great Valley Mills
Barto, PA 800-688-6455
Grossinger's Home Bakery
New York, NY 800-479-6996
Guers Dairy
Pottsville, PA 570-277-6611
Guggisberg Cheese
Millersburg, OH 800-262-2505
Guida's Milk & Ice Cream
New Britain, CT 800-832-8929
Gustafsons Dairy
Green Cove Spgs, FL 904-284-3750
H. Meyer Dairy Company
Cincinnati, OH 800-347-6455
H.B. Taylor Co
Chicago, IL 773-254-4805
H.E. Butt Grocery Company
San Antonio, TX 800-432-3113
H.P. Hood
Agawam, MA 413-786-7166

H.P. Hood
Lynnfield, ME 800-343-6592
H.P. Hood
Barre, VT 800-622-4468
Hanover Foods Corporation
Hanover, PA 717-632-6000
Harold M. Lincoln Company
Toledo, OH 800-345-4911
Harrisburg Dairies
Harrisburg, PA 800-692-7429
Harvest Direct
Knoxville, TN 800-838-2727
Hastings Cooperative Creamery
Hastings, MN 651-437-9414
Heidi's Cheese Products
Mundelein, IL 847-362-5971
Heluva Good Cheese
Sodus, NY 315-483-6971
HempNut
Henderson, NV 707-576-7050
Henning's Cheese
Kiel, WI. .920-894-3032
Henningsen Foods
Omaha, NE 402-330-2500
Henningsen Foods
Purchase, NY 914-701-4020
Heritage Dairy Stores
West Deptford, NJ. 856-845-2855
Heritage Foods
Santa Ana, CA 714-775-5000
Herkimer Foods
Herkimer, NY 315-895-7832
Hermany Farms
Bronx, NY. 718-823-2989
Hershey Creamery Company
Harrisburg, PA 888-240-1905
Hershey International
Weston, FL 954-385-2600
High's Dairies
Jessup, MD 301-776-7727
Highland Dairies
Wichita, KS. 800-336-0765
Hiland Dairy
Wichita, KS. 800-336-0765
Hiland Dairy Foods Company
Wichita, KS. 316-267-4221
Hiland Dairy Foods Company
Springfield, MO 417-862-9311
Hiland Roberts Ice Cream Company
Norfolk, NE. 402-371-3660
Hillandale
Gettysburg, PA 717-334-1973
Hillside Dairy
Stanley, WI 715-644-2275
Holmes Cheese Company
Millersburg, OH 330-674-6451
Holton Food Products Company
La Grange, IL 708-352-5599
Homer's Ice Cream
Wilmette, IL 847-251-0477
Homestead Dairies
Massena, NY. 315-769-2456
Honeyville Grain
Salt Lake City, UT 801-972-2168
Hope Creamery
Hope, MN 507-451-2029
Hormel Foods Corporation
Austin, MN 800-523-4635
Horstmann Mix & Cream
Long Island City, NY 718-932-4735
Houlton Farms Dairy
Houlton, ME 207-532-3170
Howler Products
Philo, CA. 800-469-5377
HP Hood
Lynnfield, MA 800-343-6592
Hudsonville Creamery & Ice Cream
Holland, MI. 616-928-0793
Humble Cremery
Los Angeles, CA. 800-697-9925
Humboldt Creamery Association
Fortuna, CA 707-725-6182
Humphreys Dairy
Hot Springs National Par, AR 501-262-1820
Hunter Farms
High Point, NC 800-446-8035
Hygeia Dairy Company
Corpus Christi, TX 361-854-4561
Hygeia Dairy Company
McAllen, TX. 956-686-0511
Icco Cheese Company
Orangeburg, NY 845-398-9800

Ice Cream & Yogurt Club
Boynton Beach, FL. 561-731-3331
Ice Cream Specialties
St Louis, MO. 314-962-3935
Ice Cream Specialties
Lafayette, IN 765-474-2989
Ideal American
Holland, IN 812-424-3351
Ideal Dairy
Richfield, UT 435-896-5061
IMAC
Oklahoma City, OK 888-878-7827
Imperial Foods
Long Island City, NY 718-784-3400
Independent Dairy
Monroe, MI. 734-241-6016
Industrial Products
Defiance, OH 800-251-3033
Ingretec
Lebanon, PA 717-273-1360
Inland Northwest Dairies
Spokane, WA. 509-489-8600
Innovative Ingredients
Reisterstown, MD. 888-403-2907
Instantwhip: Arizona
Phoenix, AZ 800-544-9447
Instantwhip: Chicago
Chicago, IL 800-933-2500
Instantwhip: Florida
Tampa, FL. 813-621-3233
Instantwhip: Texas
San Antonio, TX. 800-544-9447
International Cheese Company
Toronto, ON 416-769-3547
International Farmers Market
Chamblee, GA. 770-455-1777
International Yogurt Company
Portland, OR 800-962-7326
Inverness Dairy
Cheboygan, MI 231-627-4655
ISE Farms
Galena, MD. 410-755-6300
ISE Newberry
Newberry, SC 803-276-5803
Island Farms Dairies Cooperative Association
Victoria, BC 250-360-5200
It's It Ice Cream Company
Burlingame, CA 800-345-1928
Ito Cariani Sausage Company
Hayward, CA 510-887-0882
J&J Snack Foods Corporation
Pennsauken, NJ. 856-665-9533
J.B. Sons
Yonkers, NY 914-963-5192
J.W. Haywood & Sons Dairy
Louisville, KY. 502-774-2311
Jack & Jill Ice Cream Company
Moorestown, NJ 856-813-2300
Jackson Ice Cream Company
Denver, CO. 303-534-2454
Jackson Milk & Ice CreamCompany
Hutchinson, KS. 620-663-1244
James Cowan & Sons
Worcester, MA 508-754-5385
Janes Family Foods
Mississauga, ON 800-565-2637
Jim's Cheese Pantry
Waterloo, WI. 800-345-3571
John Wm. Macy's Cheesesticks
Elmwood Park, NJ 800-643-0573
Johnson's Real Ice Cream
Columbus, OH 614-231-0014
Johnson, Nash, & Sons Farms
Rose Hill, NC 800-682-6843
Joseph Gallo Farms
Atwater, CA 209-394-7984
Josh & John's Ice Cream
Colorado Springs, CO. 800-530-2855
Juniper Valley Farms
Jamaica, NY 718-291-3333
Kalamazoo Creamery
Kalamazoo, MI 616-343-2558
Kan-Pac
Arkansas City, KS. 620-442-6820
Katrina's Tartufo
Port Jeffrsn Sta, NY 800-480-8836
Kauai Producers
Lihue, HI .808-245-4044
KDK Inc
Draper, UT 801-571-3506
Keebler Company
Battle Creek, MI 800-962-1413

Keller's Creamery
Harleysville, PA 800-535-5371
Kemp Foods
York, PA .800-233-2007
Kemps
Cedarburg, WI. 262-377-5040
Kemps
St Paul, MN. 800-322-9566
Kent Foods
Gonzales, TX 830-672-7993
Kentucky Beer Cheese
Nicholasville, KY 859-887-1645
Kerry Ingredients
Tralee, Co. Kerry,
Kerry Ingredients & Flavours
Beloit, WI. 800-248-7310
Key Ingredients
Harrisburg, PA 800-227-4448
Kirby & Holloway Provisions
Harrington, DE 800-995-4729
Kleinpeter Farms Dairy
Baton Rouge, LA 225-753-2121
Klinke Brothers Ice Cream Company
Memphis, TN 901-743-8250
Klondike Cheese
Monroe, WI. 608-325-3021
Knoll Creek Dairy
Harrison, NY 718-892-4500
Knouse Foods
Peach Glen, PA 717-677-8181
Kohler Mix Specialties
White Bear Lake, MN. 651-426-1633
Kohler Mix Specialties
Newington, CT 860-666-1511
Kokinos Purity Ice CreamCompany
Monroe, LA. 318-322-2930
Kolb-Lena Cheese Company
Lena, IL. .815-369-4577
Kraft Foods
Albany, MN. 320-845-2131
Kraft Foods
Springfield, MO 417-881-2701
Kraft Foods
Walton, NY 607-865-7131
Kraft Foods
Allentown, PA 610-398-0311
Kraft Foods
Northfield, IL 800-323-0768
Kraft Foods
East Hanover, NJ 973-503-2000
Krinos Foods
Long Island City, NY 718-729-9000
Krohn Dairy Products
Luxemburg, WI. 920-845-2901
Laack Brothers Cheese Company
Greenleaf, WI. 800-589-5127
Lactalis USA
New York, NY 888-766-3353
Lacto Milk Products Corporation
Flemington, NJ 908-788-2200
LaGrander Hillside Dairy
Stanley, WI 715-644-2205
Lake Country Foods
Oconomowoc, WI. 262-567-5521
Lake Erie Frozen Foods Company
Ashland, OH 800-766-8501
Lakeview Farms
Delphos, OH 800-755-9925
Lambrights
Lagrange, IN 260-463-2178
Lancaster Packing Company
Lancaster, PA 717-397-9727
Land O Lakes Milk
Sioux Falls, SD 605-330-9526
Land O'Lakes
St Paul, MN. 651-730-2100
Land O'Lakes
Spencer, WI. 715-659-2311
Land O'Lakes
Carlisle, PA 717-486-7000
Land O'Lakes
St Paul, MN. 800-328-9680
Land O'Lakes
Kiel, WI. .920-894-2204
Land O'Lakes Procurement
Sioux Falls, SD 605-330-9526
Land O'Lakes, Inc
Arden Hills, MN. 800-328-9680
Land-o-Sun
Johnson City, TN 800-283-5765
Land-O-Sun Dairies
O Fallon, IL. 618-632-6381

Lane's Dairy
El Paso, TX 915-772-6700
LaRosa Bakery
Shrewsbury, NJ 800-527-6722
Lee's Century Farms
Milton Freewater, OR 541-938-6532
LeHigh Valley Dairies
Lansdale, PA 215-855-8205
Leprino Foods Company
Denver, CO 800-537-7466
Level Valley Creamery
Antioch, TN 800-251-1292
Lewes Dairy
Lewes, DE 302-645-6281
Liberty Dairy
Evart, MI 800-632-5552
Lifeway Foods Inc
Morton Grove, IL 847-967-1010
London Farm Dairy
Port Huron, MI 800-284-5111
Longacres Modern Dairy
Barto, PA 610-845-7551
Losurdo Creamery
Heuvelton, NY 315-344-2444
Losurdo Foods
Hackensack, NJ 888-567-8736
Louis Trauth Dairy
Newport, KY 800-544-6455
Lov-It Creamery
Green Bay, WI 800-344-0333
Lowell-Paul Dairy
Greeley, CO 970-353-0278
Lubbers Dairy
Pella, IA .515-628-4284
Lucille Farm Products
Montville, NJ 973-334-6030
Ludwig Dairy
Dixon, IL 815-284-7791
Lyoferm & Vivolac Cultures
Indianapolis, IN 800-844-8649
M-C Dairy Company
Etobicoke, ON 416-231-1491
M-G
Weimar, TX 800-460-8581
Mack's Homemade Ice Cream
York, PA .717-741-2027
Madison Dairy Produce Company
Madison, WI 608-256-5561
Magic Valley Quality Milk Producers
Jerome, ID 208-324-7519
Main Street Ingredients
La Crosse, WI 800-359-2345
Mallorie's Dairy
Silverton, OR 503-873-5346
Mancuso Cheese Company
Joliet, IL .815-722-2475
Mann Packing
Salinas, CA 831-422-7405
Maola Milk & Ice Cream Company
New Bern, NC 252-638-1131
Maola Milk & Ice Cream Company
Summerville, SC 803-871-6311
Maple Hill Farms
Bloomfield, CT 800-842-7304
Maple Leaf Foods International
Toronto, ON 416-480-8900
Marantha Natural Foods
San Francisco, CA 800-299-0048
Marathon Cheese Corporation
Booneville, MS 662-728-6242
Marburger Farm Dairy
Evans City, PA 800-331-1295
Marcus Dairy
Danbury, CT 800-243-2511
Marin French Cheese Company
Petaluma, CA 800-292-6001
Mario's Gelati
Vancouver, BC 604-879-9411
Mars M&M
Henderson, NV 888-265-6788
Marshall Egg Products
Seymour, IN 812-497-2557
Marshallville Packing Company
Marshallville, OH 330-855-2871
Martin Brothers Distributing Company
Cedar Falls, IA 319-266-1775
Marva Maid Dairy
Newport News, VA 800-544-4439
Marwood Sales
Shawnee Mission, KS 913-722-1534
Maryland & Virginia Milk Cooperative Association
Laurel, MD 301-953-2964

Maryland & Virginia Milk Producers Cooperative
Reston, VA 703-742-7443
Master Mix
Placentia, CA 714-524-1698
Matador Processors
Blanchard, OK 800-847-0797
Matterhorn Ice Cream Company
Caldwell, ID 800-822-1635
Max P.E. Radloff & Sons
Hustisford, WI 920-349-3266
Mayfield Dairy Farms
Athens, TN 800-362-9546
Maytag Dairy Farms
Newton, IA 800-247-2458
McAnally Enterprises
Norco, CA 800-726-2002
McArthur Dairy
Fort Myers, FL 239-334-1114
McArthur Dairy
Miami, FL 305-576-2880
McArthur Dairy
Miami, FL 877-803-6565
McCadam Cheese Company
Chateaugay, NY 518-497-6644
McCain Foods
Fort Atkinson, WI 920-563-6625
McColls Dairy Products
Sacramento, CA 916-444-7200
McConnell's Fine Ice Cream
Santa Barbara, CA 805-963-2958
McDonald Dairy
Alpena, MI 800-572-5390
McDonald Dairy Company
Flint, MI .810-232-9193
ME Franks
Wayne, PA 610-989-9688
Mead Johnson Nutritional
Zeeland, MI 616-748-7100
Meadow Brook Dairy
Erie, PA .800-352-4010
Meadow Brook Farms
Pottstown, PA 610-323-3700
Meadow Gold Dairies
Lincoln, NE 800-742-7349
Meadow Gold Dairies
Orem, UT 801-225-3660
Meadow Gold Dairies
Honolulu, HI 808-949-6161
Meadow Gold Dairy
Lewiston, ID 208-746-9006
Meadowbrook Farm
Bronx, NY 718-828-6400
Medeiros Farms
Kalaheo, HI 808-332-8211
Mentone Egg Products
Mentone, IN 219-353-7691
Merkts Cheese Company
Bristol, WI 262-857-2316
Meyer Brothers Dairy
Maple Plain, MN 952-473-7343
Micalizzi Italian Ice
Bridgeport, CT 203-366-2353
Miceli Dairy Products Company
Cleveland, OH 800-551-7196
Michael Granese & Company
Norristown, PA 610-272-5099
Michele's Family Bakery
York, PA .717-741-2027
Michelle Chocolatiers
Colorado Springs, CO 888-447-3654
Michigan Dairy
Livonia, MI 734-367-5390
Michigan Farm Cheese Dairy
Fountain, MI 231-462-3301
Michigan Milk Producers Association
Ovid, MI .989-834-2221
Mid States Dairy
Hazelwood, MO 314-731-1150
Mid-States Dairy Company
St Louis, MO. 314-994-9900
Mid-Valley Dairy
Fairfield, CA 707-864-0502
Middlefield Cheese House
Middlefield, OH 800-327-9477
Midstates Dairy
Hazelwood, MO 314-731-1150
Mikawaya Bakery
Los Angeles, CA 213-628-6514
Milk Specialties Company
Carpentersville, IL 847-426-3411
Mille Lacs MP Company
Madison, WI 800-843-1381

Miller's Cheese
Brooklyn, NY 718-384-5243
Millers Ice Cream
Houston, TX 713-861-3138
Milnot Company
Neosho, MO 800-877-6455
Milsolv Corporation
Butler, WI 800-558-8501
Minerva Cheese Factory
Minerva, OH 330-868-4196
Minerva Dairy
Minerva, OH 330-868-4196
Mister Cookie Face
Lakewood, NJ 732-370-5533
Mitchel Dairies
Bronx, NY 718-324-6261
Model Dairy
Reno, NV 800-433-2030
Monument Dairy Farms
Weybridge, VT 802-545-2119
Monument Farms
Middlebury, VT 802-545-2119
Mooresville Ice Cream Company
Mooresville, NC 704-664-5456
Morning Glory/Formost Farms
Baraboo, WI 800-362-9196
Morning Star Foods
Tempe, AZ 480-966-0080
Morning Star Foods
East Brunswick, NJ. 800-237-5320
Morningland Dairy CheeseCompany
Mountain View, MO 417-469-3817
Morningstar Foods
Gustine, CA 209-854-6461
Morningstar Foods
Dallas, TX 225-273-2803
Morningstar Foods
Mt Crawford, VA 540-434-7328
Morningstar Foods
Richland Center, WI 608-647-6360
Moscahlades Brothers
New York, NY 212-226-5410
Mountain High Yogurt
Englewood, CO. 303-761-2210
Mountainside Farms Dairy
Roxbury, NY 607-326-4161
Muller-Pinehurst Dairy C
Rockford, IL 815-968-0441
Munroe Dairy
East Providence, RI 401-438-4450
Murdock Farm Dairy
Winchendon, MA 978-297-0143
Murphy House
Louisburg, NC 919-496-4173
Mystic Lake Dairy
Sammamish, WA. 425-868-2029
Nash Finch Company
Statesboro, GA 912-681-4580
Naterl
St. Bruno, QC 800- 50- 115
National Cheese Company
Concord, ON. 905-669-9393
National Egg Products Company
Social Circle, GA 770-464-2652
Natural By Nature
West Grove, PA 610-268-6962
Natural Fruit Corporation
Hialeah, FL 305-887-7525
Nature's Dairy
Roswell, NM 575-623-9640
Nelson Ricks Creamery
Salt Lake City, UT 801-364-3607
Nelson Ricks Creamery Company
Salt Lake City, UT 801-364-3607
New Morn Foods
Oakwood, GA 770-536-4561
Newburgh Egg Processing
Woodridge, NY 888-434-8115
Niagara Milk Cooperative
Niagara Falls, NY 716-692-6543
Nodine's Smokehouse
Torrington, CT 800-222-2059
Noon Hour Food Products
Chicago, IL 800-621-6636
Nor-Tech Dairy Advisors
Sioux Falls, SD 605-338-2404
Norco Ranch
Norco, CA. 951-737-6735
North Branch Dairy
North Branch, MN 651-674-4414
Northumberland Cooperative
Miramichi, NB 800-332-3328

Norwalk Dairy
Santa Fe Springs, CA 562-921-5712
Novartis Nutrition Corporation
Minneapolis, MN 952-848-6000
NZMP
Santa Rosa, CA 800-358-9096
O'Boyle's Ice Cream Company
Bristol, PA .215-788-0421
O-At-Ka Milk Products Cooperative
Batavia, NY 800-828-8152
Oak Farm's Dairy
Waco, TX 254-756-5421
Oak Farms
Dallas, TX .214-941-0302
Oak Farms
San Antonio, TX 800-292-2169
Oak Grove Dairy
Clintonville, WI 715-823-6226
Oak Grove Dairy
Saint Paul, MN 952-467-2212
Oakhurst Dairy
Portland, ME 207-772-7468
Oberweis Dairy
North Aurora, IL 888-645-5868
OCG Cacao
Whitinsville, MA 888-482-2226
Old Home Foods
St Paul, MN 800-628-8700
Olde Tyme Food Corporation
East Longmeadow, MA 800-356-6533
Omstead Foods Ltd
Burlington, ON 905-315-8883
Ore-Ida Foods
Pittsburgh, PA 412-237-3450
Oregon Hill Farms
St Helens, OR 800-243-4541
Organic Cow
Boulder, CO 800-769-9693
Oskaloosa Food Products Corporation
Oskaloosa, IA 800-477-7239
Out of a Flower
Lancaster, TX 800-743-4696
P A Menard
New Orleans, LA 504-620-2022
Pak Technologies
Milwaukee, WI 414-438-8600
Papetti's Egg Products
Elizabeth, NJ 800-524-3447
Park Cheese Company
Fond Du Lac, WI 800-752-7275
Parkers Farm
Minneapolis, MN 800-869-6685
Parmalat Canada
Toronto, ON 800-563-1515
Pascobel Inc
Longueuil, QC 450-677-2443
Pastene Companies
Canton, MA 781-830-8200
Pastorelli Food Products
Chicago, IL 800-767-2829
PB&S Chemicals
Henderson, KY 800-950-7267
Pearl Valley Cheese Company
Fresno, OH 740-545-6002
Pecoraro Dairy Products
Rome, NY .315-339-0101
Peeler's Jersey Farms
Gaffney, SC 864-487-9996
Pend Oreille Cheese Company
Sandpoint, ID 208-263-2030
Penn Cheese Corporation
Winfield, PA 570-524-7700
Penn Maid Crowley Foods
Philadelphia, PA 800-247-6269
Perham Cooperative Cream
Savannah, GA 800-551-0777
Perry's Ice Cream Company
Akron, NY .800-873-7797
Pet Dairy
Portsmouth, VA 757-397-2387
Pet Dairy
Winston Salem, NC 800-735-2050
Pet Dairy
Spartanburg, SC 864-576-6280
Pet Milk
Florence, SC 800-735-3066
Petersen Ice Cream Company
Oak Park, IL 708-386-6130
Pevely Dairy Company
St Louis, MO 314-771-4400
Pierz Cooperative Association
Pierz, MN .320-468-6655

Pine River Cheese & Butter Company
Ripley, ON 800-265-1175
Pine River Pre-Pack
Newton, WI 920-726-4216
Pine State Creamery Company
Raleigh, NC 919-828-7401
Pioneer Dairy
Southwick, MA 413-569-6132
Plains Creamery
Amarillo, TX 806-374-0385
Plains Dairy Products
Amarillo, TX 800-365-5608
Plainview Milk Products Cooperative
Plainview, MN 507-534-3872
Platte Valley Creamery
Scottsbluff, NE 308-632-4225
Pleasant View Dairy
Highland, IN 219-838-0155
Plehn's Bakery
St Matthews, KY 502-896-4438
Plumrose USA
East Brunswick, NJ 732-257-6600
Plymouth Cheese Counter
Plymouth, WI 888-607-9477
Pocono Cheesecake Factory
Swiftwater, PA 570-839-6844
Pollio Dairy Products
Mineola, NY 516-741-8000
Polly-O Dairy Products
Mineola, NY 516-741-8000
Pon Food Corporation
Ponchatoula, LA 985-386-6941
Potomac Farms
Cumberland, MD 301-722-4410
Potter Siding Creamery Company
Tripoli, IA 319-882-4444
Poudre Valley Creamery
Fort Collins, CO 970-482-8475
Powder Pak
Round Lake, IL 847-223-4683
Praire Farms Dairy
Anderson, IN 765-649-1261
Prairie Farms Dairy
Carlinville, IL 217-854-2547
Prairie Farms Dairy
O Fallon, IL 618-632-3632
Prairie Farms Dairy Inc
Carlinville, IL 217-854-2547
Preferred Milks
Addison, IL 800-621-5046
Prestige Proteins
Boca Raton, FL 561-499-6100
Price's Creameries
El Paso, TX 915-565-2711
Primer Foods Corporation
Cameron, WI 715-458-4075
Producers Dairy Company
Clarksburg, WV 304-623-1831
Producers Dairy Foods
Fresno, CA 559-264-6583
ProSource
Alexandria, MN 320-763-2470
Protient (Land O Lakes)
St Paul, MN 651-481-2068
Puritan/ATZ Ice Cream
Kendallville, IN 260-347-2700
Purity Dairies
Nashville, TN 615-244-1900
Purity Farms
Sedalia, CO 800-568-4433
Purity Ice Cream Company
Ithaca, NY 607-272-1545
Quality Chekd Dairies
Naperville, IL 630-717-1110
Quality Dairy Company
East Lansing, MI 517-319-4114
Quality Ingredients Corporation
Burnsville, MN 952-898-4002
Quality Jersey Products
Seaforth, ON 519-527-1272
Queensboro Farm Products
Canastota, NY 315-697-2235
Queensboro Farm Products
Jamaica, NY 718-658-5000
Quest International Flavors
1411 GP Naarden,
R.D. Hemond Farms
Minot, ME 207-345-5611
Radlo Foods
Watertown, MA 800-370-1439
Radway's Dairy
New Britain, CT 800-472-3929

Ragersville Swiss Cheese
Sugarcreek, OH 330-897-3055
Ramsen
Lakeville, MN 952-431-0400
Ratners Retail Foods
New York, NY 212-677-5588
Readington Farms
Whitehouse, NJ 908-534-2121
Regis Milk Company
Charleston, SC 843-723-3418
Reilly Dairy & Food Company
Tampa, FL .813-839-8458
Reinhold Ice Cream Company
Pittsburgh, PA 412-321-7600
Reiter Dairy
Akron, OH 800-362-0825
Rich Ice Cream Company
West Palm Beach, FL 561-833-7585
Rich Products Corporation
Claremont, CA 909-621-4711
Rich-Seapak Corporation
St Simons Island, GA 800-654-9731
Richfood Dairy
Richmond, VA 804-746-6206
Richman Festival Ice Cream Company
Paterson, NJ 973-684-8935
Riser Foods
Cleveland, OH 216-292-7000
Ritchey's Dairy
Martinsburg, PA 800-296-2157
Robertet Flavors
Piscataway, NJ 732-981-8300
Roberts Dairy
Kansas City, MO 800-279-1692
Roberts Dairy Company
Omaha, NE 402-344-4321
Roberts Dairy Company
Kansas City, MO 800-279-1692
Robinson Dairy
Denver, CO 800-332-6355
Rockview Farms
Downey, CA 800- 42- 247
Rocky Top Farms
Ellsworth, MI 800-862-9303
Rod's Food Products
City of Industry, CA 909-839-8925
Rogers Brothers
Galesburg, IL 309-342-2127
Rogue Creamery
Central Point, OR 541-665-1155
Roney Oatman
Aurora, IL .630-859-2800
Ronnybrook Farm Dairy
Ancramdale, NY 800-772-6455
Ronzoni Foods Canada
Etobicoke, ON 800-387-5032
Roos Foods
Kenton, DE 800-343-3642
Rosebud Creamery
Plattsburgh, NY 518-561-5160
Roselani Tropics Ice Cream
Wailuku, HI 808-244-7951
Rosenberger's Dairies
Hatfield, PA 800-355-9074
Royal Crest Dairy Company
Denver, CO 303-777-3055
Rutter Brothers Dairy
York, PA 800-840-1664
S.B. Winsor Dairy
Johnston, RI 401-231-7832
S.T. Jerrell Company
Bessemer, AL 205-426-8930
Safeway Dairy Products
Capitol Heights, MD 301-341-9555
Safeway Dairy Products
Walnut Creek, CA 925-944-4000
Safeway Inc
Durand, WI 715-672-8911
Safeway Milk Plant
Tempe, AZ 480-894-4391
Safeway Stores
Tempe, AZ 877-723-3929
Saint Albans CooperativeCreamy
Saint Albans, VT 800-559-0343
San Fernando Creamery Farmdale Creamery
San Bernardino, CA 909-889-3002
San Joaquin Valley Dairymen
Los Banos, CA 209-826-4901
Sandusky Cooperative Milk Producers Association
Castalia, OH 419-684-5812
Sani Dairy
Johnstown, PA 814-533-2500

Sani-Dairy
Johnstown, PA....................412-568-6410
Santee Dairies
City of Industry, CA 626-923-3000
Saputo
Montreal, QC 514-328-6662
Saputo
Big Stone City, SD 800-824-3373
Saputo Cheese
Tulare, CA......................559-687-9999
Saputo Cheese
Almena, WI 715-357-3775
Saputo Cheese
Peru, IN........................765-472-1961
Saputo Cheese
Lincolnshire, IL 800-558-9714
Saputo Cheese
Reedsburg, WI 800-824-3373
Saputo Cheese
Lena, WI 920-829-5251
Saputo Cheese
Fond Du Lac, WI 920-929-8060
Sara Lee Corporation
Downers Grove, IL...............630-598-8100
Sargeant's Army Marketing
Bowmanville, ON 905-623-2888
Sartori Food Corporation
Plymouth, WI 800-558-5888
Schenkel's All Star Dairy
Huntington, IN 260-356-4225
Schepps Dairy
Dallas, TX......................800-428-6455
Schneider Valley Farms Dairy
Williamsport, PA................570-326-2021
Schneider's Dairy Holdings Inc
Pittsburgh, PA 412-881-3525
Schoep's Ice Cream Company
Madison, WI 800-236-0032
Schreiber Foods   Plant
Logan, UT.......................435-787-8490
Schreiber Foods   Plant
Clinton, MO 660-885-6133
Schreiber Foods   Plant
Shippensburg, PA 717-530-5000
Schreiber Foods   Plant
Gainesville, GA 770-534-2239
Schreiber Foods   Plant/Distribution Center
Wisconsin Rapids, WI 715-422-7500
Schwartz Meat Company
Sophia, WV......................304-683-4595
Scotsburn Dairy Group
Truro, NS 902-895-4412
Seger Egg Corporation
Farina, IL......................618-245-3301
Sekan Cheese Company
Girard, KS......................316-724-8827
Seller Kirk & Company
Schwenksville, PA 215-480-7342
Sequoia Specialty Cheese Company
Visalia, CA.....................559-752-4106
Sesinco Foods
New York, NY 212-243-1306
Shamrock Foods Company
Phoenix, AZ.....................800-289-3663
Shenandoah's Pride
Springfield, VA 703-321-9500
Shenk's Foods
Lancaster, PA 717-393-4240
Siegel Egg Company
Cambridge, MA 800-593-3447
Sierra Cheese Manufacturing Company
Compton, CA.....................800-266-4270
Silani Sweet Cheese
Schomberg, ON...................905-939-2561

Sinton Dairy Foods Company
Colorado Springs, CO.............800-388-4970
Sinton Dairy Foods Company
Denver, CO......................800-666-4808
Sisler's Ice & Ice Cream
Ohio, IL........................888-891-3856
Skim Delux Mendenhall Laboratories
Paris, TN.......................800-642-9321
Skinners' Dairy
Ponte Vedra Beach, FL...........904-733-5440
Smith Dairy Products Company
Orrville, OH 800-776-7076
Smith Packing Regional Meat
Utica, NY.......................315-732-5125
Snelgrove Ice Cream Company
Salt Lake City, UT 800-569-0005
Snow Dairy
Springville, UT.................801-489-6081
Snyder's Ice Cream
Ashland, PA 570-875-3320
Sommer Maid Creamery
Doylestown, PA 215-345-6160
Sorrento Lactalis   Corporate & Commercial
Headquarters
Buffalo, NY.....................800-828-7031
Source Food Technology
Durham, NC 866-277-3849
Southchem
Durham, NC 800-849-7000
Southeast Dairy Processors
Tampa, FL.......................813-621-3233
Southern Bell Dairy
Somerset, KY 800-468-4798
Southern Ice Cream Specialties
Marietta, GA....................770-428-0452
Southwestern Wisconsin Dairy Goat Products
Mt Sterling, WI.................608-734-3151
Sparboe Companies
Los Angeles, CA.................213-626-7538
Specialty Ingredients
Buffalo Grove, IL...............847-419-9595
Spring Grove Foods
Miamisburg, OH 937-866-4311
Spring Hill Farm Dairy
Haverhill, MA...................978-373-3481
Springbank Cheese Company
Woodstock, ON 800-265-1973
Springdale Cheese Factory
Richland Center, WI.............608-538-3213
Springfield Creamery
Eugene, OR 541-689-2911
Springfield Smoked Fish Company
Springfield, MA 800-327-3412
St. Maurice Laurent
St. Bruno, QC 418-343-3655
Star Valley Cheese
Thayne, WY 307-883-2510
Starbucks Coffee Company
Seattle, WA 800-782-7282
Steese Ice Cream
Grove City, PA 724-748-4115
Steiner Cheese
Baltic, OH 330-897-5505
Stewart's Ice Cream
Saratoga Springs, NY 518-581-1000
Stockton Cheese
Stockton, IL 815-947-3361
Stone's Home Made Candy Shop
Oswego, NY 888-223-3928
Stop & Shop Manufacturing
Readville, MA...................617-361-8400
Straus Family Creamery
Marshall, CA....................800-572-7783

Sturm Foods
Manawa, WI......................800-347-8876
Sugar Creek/Eskimo Pie
Russellville, AR................800-445-2715
Suiza Dairy Corporation
Rio Piedras, PR.................787-792-7300
Sunny Fresh Foods
Monticello, MN 800-872-3447
Sunnyslope Farms Egg Ranch
Cherry Valley, CA 951-845-1131
Sunshine Dairy
Middletown, CT 860-346-6644
Sunshine Dairy Foods
Portland, OR 503-234-7526
Sunshine Farms
Portage, WI 608-742-2016
Sunshine Farms Dairy
Elyria, OH 440-322-6301
Superbrand Dairies
Miami, FL.......................305-685-8079
Superior Dairy
Canton, OH 800-683-2479
Superstore Industries
Fairfield, CA...................707-864-0502
Suprema Specialties
Paterson, NJ....................800-543-2479
Supreme Dairy Farms Company
Warwick, RI 401-739-8180
SW Red Smith
Davie, FL 954-581-1996
Swagger Foods Corporation
Vernon Hills, IL................847-913-1200
Sweet Shop
La Crosse, WI 608-784-7724
Sweety Novelty
Monterey Park, CA...............626-282-4482
Swiss Dairy
Riverside, CA...................951-898-9427
Swiss Valley Farms Company
Cedar Rapids, IA................319-364-8153
Swiss Valley Farms Company
Davenport, IA...................563-468-6600
Swiss Valley Farms Company
Dubuque, IA 800-397-9156
Swiss-American
St Louis, MO....................800-325-8150
Tamarack Farms Dairy
Newark, OH 866-221-4141
Tanglewood Farms
Warsaw, VA......................804-394-4505
Taylor All Star Dairy Foods
Ambridge, PA....................724-266-2370
Tebay Dairy Company
Parkersburg, WV.................304-863-3705
Texas Heat
San Antonio, TX.................800-656-5916
Thomas Dairy
Rutland, VT 802-773-6788
Thornton Foods Company
Eden Prairie, MN 952-944-1735
Thrifty Ice Cream
El Monte, CA 626-571-0122
Tillamook County Creamery Association
Tillamook, OR 503-842-4481
Tiller Foods Company
Dayton, OH 937-435-4601
Titusville Dairy Products
Titusville, PA 800-352-0101
Toft Dairy
Sandusky, OH 800-521-4606
Tom Davis & Sons Dairy Company
Oak Park, MI....................800-399-6970
Tom's Ice Cream Bowl
Zanesville, OH 740-452-5267

Tony's Ice Cream Company
Gastonia, NC 704-867-7085
Tropical Treets
North York, ON 888-424-8229
Trugman-Nash
New York, NY 212-869-6910
Turner & Pease Company
Seattle, WA 206-282-9535
Turner Dairies
Jackson, TN 731-427-6012
Turner Dairies
Covington, TN 901-476-2643
Turner Dairy Farms
Penn Hills, PA 800-892-1039
Tuscan Dairy Farms
Dallas, TX 800-526-4416
Tuscan/Lehigh Valley Dais
Lansdale, PA 800-937-3233
Twin County Dairy
Kalona, IA 319-656-2776
Ultima Foods
Longueuil, ON 800-363-9496
Umpqua Dairy Products Company
Roseburg, OR 541-672-2638
Unified Western Grocers
Los Angeles, CA 323-731-8223
Union Dairy Fountain
Freeport, IL 815-233-2233
United Dairy
Martins Ferry, OH 800-252-1542
United Dairy
Uniontown, PA 800-966-6455
United Dairy Farmers
Cincinnati, OH 513-396-8700
United Dairymen of Arizona
Tempe, AZ 480-966-7211
United Valley Bell Dairy
Charleston, WV 304-344-2511
Upstate Farms Cooperative
Rochester, NY 585-458-1880
Upstate Farms Cooperative
Buffalo, NY 716-892-3156
Upstate Farms Cooperative
Buffalo, NY 866-874-6455
US Food & Pharmaceuticals
Madison, WI 608-278-1293
V&V Supremo Foods
Chicago, IL 800-547-8773
Valley Dairy Fairview Dairy
Windber, PA 814-467-5537
Valley Grain Products
Madera, CA 559-675-3400
Valley Maid Ice Cream
Aurora, IL 630-851-2241
Valley Milk Products
Strasburg, VA 540-465-5113
Valley of the Rogue Dairy
Grants Pass, OR 541-476-2020
Valley Queen Cheese Factory
Milbank, SD 605-432-4563
Valley Rich Dairy
Clarksburg, WV 304-472-7899
Van Peenans Dairy
Wayne, NJ 973-694-2551
Vance's Foods
Gilmer, TX 800-497-4834
Velda Farms
Lakeland, FL 800-279-4166
Velda Farms
North Miami Bch, FL 800-795-4649
Vella Cheese
Sonoma, CA 800-848-0505
Velvet Freeze Ice Cream
St Louis, MO 800-589-5000
Velvet Ice Cream Company
Utica, OH 800-589-5000
Ventura Foods   Foodservice/Export/Custom Pack
City of Industry, CA 800-327-3906
Vita-Plus
Las Vegas, NV 702-733-8805
Vitamilk Dairy
Bellingham, WA 206-529-4128
Vitarich Ice Cream
Fortuna, CA 707-725-6182
W.J. Stearns & Sons/Mountain Dairy
Storrs Mansfield, CT 860-423-9289
Wabash Valley Produce
Dubois, IN 812-678-3131
Wallaby Yogurt Company
American Canyon, CA 707-553-1233
Wapsie Valley Creamery
Independence, IA 319-334-7193

Warwick Ice Cream Company
Warwick, RI 401-821-8403
Waugh Foods
East Peoria, IL 309-427-8000
Wawa Food Market
Media, PA 800-444-9292
Wayne Dairy Products
Richmond, IN 800-875-9294
Webco Foods
Miami, FL 305-633-0100
Weiss Provisions
Pittsburgh, PA 800-458-6328
Weldon Ice Cream Company
Millsport, OH 740-467-2400
Wells' Dairy
Le Mars, IA 800-942-3800
Welsh Farms
Newark, NJ 800-221-0663
Welsh Farms
Newark, NJ 973-642-3000
Welsh Farms
Clifton, NJ 973-772-2388
Wengers Springbrook Cheese
Davis, IL 815-865-5855
Wengert's Dairy
Lebanon, PA 800-222-2129
Wenk Foods Inc
Madison, SD 605-256-4569
Went's Dairy
Niagara Falls, NY 716-692-6543
Wessanan
Minneapolis, MN 612-331-3775
WestFarm Foods
Seattle, WA 206-286-6832
WestFarm Foods
Boise, ID 208-375-3062
WestFarm Foods
Seattle, WA 509-837-8000
WestFarm Foods
Seattle, WA 800-333-6544
Westhill Dairy
North York, ON 416-661-0580
Westin
Omaha, NE 800-228-6098
Wetta Egg Farm
Andale, KS 316-445-2231
Whitey's Ice Cream Manufacturing
Moline, IL 888-594-4839
Whitney Foods
Jamaica, NY 718-291-3333
Widmer's Cheese Cellars
Theresa, WI 888-878-1107
Winchester Farms Dairy
Winchester, KY 859-745-5500
Winder Dairy
West Valley, UT 800-946-3371
Winmix/Natural Care Products
Englewood, FL 941-475-7432
Wisconsin Cheese
Melrose Park, IL 708-450-0074
Wisconsin Cheeseman
Madison, WI 608-837-5166
Wolf Canyon Foods
Carmel, CA 831-626-1323
Woolwich Dairy
Orangeville, ON 877-438-3499
World Cheese Company
Brooklyn, NY 718-965-1700
Wright Ice Cream
Cayuga, IN 800-686-9561
Wurth Dairy
Caseyville, IL 217-271-7580
Yarnell Ice Cream Company
Searcy, AR 800-766-2414
Yoder Dairies
Chesapeake, VA 757-497-3518
Yoplait USA
Minneapolis, MN 800-967-5248
Yoplait-Colombo
Minneapolis, MN 763-540-2311
Young's Jersey Dairy
Yellow Springs, OH 937-325-0629
Ziegenfelder Company
Wheeling, WV 304-232-6360
Zivney Cheese
Minonk, IL 800-732-3068

Dehydrated

Cheeses, Buttermilk, Milk

Fleur De Lait Foods
New Holland, PA 717-355-8500
Florence Pasta & Cheese
Marshall, MN 800-533-5290

Dairy Drinks

Agri-Mark
Lawrence, MA 978-687-4936
Baskin-Robbins Flavors
Burbank, CA 800-859-5339
C.F. Burger Creamery
Detroit, MI 800-229-2322
G A Food Service
St Petersburg, FL 727-573-2211
Level Valley Creamery
Antioch, TN 800-251-1292
Maryland & Virginia Milk Producers Cooperative
Reston, VA 703-742-7443
Meadow Gold Dairies
Boise, ID 208-343-3671
Quest International Flavors
Owings Mills, MD 410-363-7200
Regis Milk Company
Charleston, SC 843-723-3418
Scotsburn Dairy Group
Truro, NS 902-895-4412

Egg Nog

Alta Dena Certified Dairy
City of Industry, CA 800-535-1369
Cass Clay Creamery
Fargo, ND 701-293-6455
Chase Brothers Dairy
Oxnard, CA 800-438-6455
Crowley Foods
Binghamton, NY 800-637-0019
Eskimo Pie Corporation
Ronkonkoma, NY 631-737-9700
H.P. Hood
Lynnfield, ME 800-343-6592
Mid States Dairy
Hazelwood, MO 314-731-1150
Sinton Dairy Foods Company
Colorado Springs, CO 800-388-4970
Yoder Dairies
Chesapeake, VA 757-497-3518

Ice Cream

A.C. Petersen Farms
West Hartford, CT 860-233-8483
Aglamesis Brothers
Cincinnati, OH 513-531-5196
Agropur Cooperative Agro-Alimentaire
Granby, QC 800-363-5686
Akenhead's Ice Cream Company
East Palestine, OH 330-426-9553
Al Gelato Bornay
Franklin Park, IL 847-455-5355
Al-Rite Fruits & Syrups
Miami, FL 305-652-2540
Albertson's Ice-Cream
Boise, ID 877-932-7948
Alinosi French Superfine Candies
Detroit, MI 313-527-3195
Alpenrose Dairy
Portland, OR 503-244-1133
American Classic Ice Cream Company
Bay Shore, NY 631-666-1000
Anderson Erickson Dairy
Des Moines, IA 515-265-2521
Arctic Ice Cream Company
Trenton, NJ 609-393-4264
Artic Ice Cream Novelties
Seattle, WA 206-324-0414
Asael Farr & Sons CompanY (Russells Ice Cream)
Salt Lake City, UT 801-484-8724
Associated Milk Producers
New Ulm, MN 800-533-3580
Atlanta Flagship Dairy
Atlanta, GA 800-224-0669
Avalon Foodservice, Inc.
Canal Fulton, OH 800-362-0622
B&M Enterprises
Charlotte, NC 704-566-9332
Barnes Ice Cream Company
Augusta, ME 207-622-0827

Bartolini Ice Cream
Bronx, NY 718-589-5151
Baskin-Robbins Flavors
Burbank, CA 800-859-5339
Bassett's
Philadelphia, PA 888-999-6314
Beck's Ice Cream
York, PA 717-848-8400
Ben & Jerry's Homemade
South Burlington, VT 802-846-1500
Benson Creamery
Decatur, IL 217-429-2351
Berkeley Farms
Hayward, CA 510-265-8600
Berkshire Ice Cream
West Stockbridge, MA 413-232-4111
Bernie's Foods
Brooklyn, NY 718-417-6677
Bill Mack's Homemade Ice Cream
Dover, PA 717-292-1931
Birdsall Ice Cream Company
Mason City, IA 641-423-5365
Blake's Creamery
Manchester, NH 603-623-7242
Blue Bell Creameries
Brenham, TX 979-836-7977
Bonnie Doon Ice Cream Corporation
Elkhart, IN 574-264-3390
Bonnie's Ice Cream
Paradise, PA 717-687-9301
Bottineau Cooperative Creamery
Bottineau, ND 701-228-2216
Briggs Ice Cream
Hyattsville, MD 301-277-8787
Brighams
Arlington, MA 800-274-4426
Brookside Foods
Abbotsford, BC 877-793-3866
Brothers International Desserts
Irvine, CA 949-655-0080
Broughton Foods
Marietta, OH 800-283-2479
Brown's Ice Cream
Minneapolis, MN 612-378-1075
Browns Dairy
Valparaiso, IN 219-464-4141
Browns' Ice Cream Company
Bowling Green, KY 270-843-9882
Bubbies Homemade Ice Cream
Aiea, HI 808-487-7218
Buck's Spumoni Company
Milford, CT 203-874-2007
Byrne Dairy
Syracuse, NY 800-899-1535
Carberry's Home Made Ice Cream
Merritt Island, FL 321-452-8900
Carbolite Foods
Evansville, IN 888-524-3314
Casper's Ice Cream
Richmond, UT 800-772-4182
Cass Clay Creamery
Fargo, ND 701-293-6455
Cedar Crest Specialties
Cedarburg, WI 800-877-8341
Celebration Foods
New Britain, CT 800-322-4848
Centreside Dairy
Renfrew, ON 613-432-2914
Chocolate Shoppe Ice Cream Company
Madison, WI 608-221-8640
Chocolaterie Bernard Callebaut
Calgary, AB 800-661-8367
Circus Man Ice Cream Corporation
Farmingdale, NY 516-249-4400
Consun Food Industries
Elyria, OH 440-233-7501
Cool Brands International
Ronkonkoma, NY 631-737-9700

Country Clubs Famous Desserts
Langhorne, PA 800-843-2253
Country Fresh
Grand Rapids, MI 800-748-0480
Country Fresh Golden Valley
Livonia, MI 734-261-7980
Crave Natural Foods
Northampton, MA 413-587-7999
Cream O'Weaver Dairy
Salt Lake City, UT 801-973-9922
Creamland Dairies
Albuquerque, NM 505-247-0721
Creme Glacee Gelati
St Leonard, QC 888-322-0116
Crystal Cream & Butter Company
Sacramento, CA 916-447-6455
Curly's Dairy
Stayton, OR 800-785-1335
Dairy Fresh Corporation
Greensboro, AL 800-239-5114
Dairy Land
Macon, GA 478-742-6461
Dairy Queen of Georgia
Decatur, GA 404-292-3553
Dairyland Ice Cream Company
Irvington, NJ 973-923-7625
Dave's Hawaiian Ice Cream
Pearl City, HI 808-453-0500
De Ciantis Ice Cream Company
West Warwick, RI 401-821-2440
Dean Foods Company
Dallas, TX 214-303-3400
Dean Foods Company
Rosemont, IL 800-323-1571
Dean Foods Company/Country Fresh
Grand Rapids, MI 616-243-0173
Deluxe Ice Cream Company
Salem, OR 800-304-7172
Dippin' Dots
Paducah, KY 270-443-8994
Double Rainbow Gourmet Ice Creams
San Francisco, CA 800-489-3580
Dreyer's Grand Ice Cream
Oakland, CA 877-437-3937
Dreyers Grand Ice Cream
Oakland, CA 510-652-8187
Dunkin Brands Inc.
Canton, MA 800-458-7731
Edy's Grand Ice Cream
Fort Wayne, IN 260-483-3102
Edy's Grand Ice Cream
Glendale Heights, IL 888-377-3397
Elgin Dairy Foods
Chicago, IL 800-786-9900
Ellsworth Ice Cream Company
Saratoga Springs, NY 518-584-1684
Eskimo Pie Corporation
Ronkonkoma, NY 631-737-9700
Faith Dairy
Tacoma, WA 253-531-3398
Farmers Cooperative Dairy
Halifax, NS 902-835-3373
Farmland Dairies
Wallington, NJ 888-727-6252
Farr Candy Company
Idaho Falls, ID 208-522-8215
Fendall Ice Cream Company
Salt Lake City, UT 801-355-3583
Fieldbrook Farms
Dunkirk, NY 800-333-0805
Flavors from Florida
Bartow, FL 863-533-0408
Foothills Creamery
Calgary, AB 403-263-7725
Fosselman's Ice Cream Company
Alhambra, CA 626-282-6533
Friendly Ice Cream Corporation
Wilbraham, MA 800-966-9970
Frostbite
Toledo, OH 800-968-7711
Frozfruit Corporation
Gardena, CA 310-217-1034
Galliker Dairy
Johnstown, PA 800-477-6455
Garber Ice Cream Company
Winchester, VA 800-662-5422
Garelick Farms
Lynn, MA 800-487-8700
Gelato Fresco
Toronto, ON 416-785-5415
Getchell Brothers
Brewer, ME 800-949-4423

Gifford's Dairy
Skowhegan, ME 207-474-9821
Gifford's Ice Cream & Candy Co
Silver Spring, MA 800-708-1938
Glover's Ice Cream
Frankfort, IN 800-686-5163
Good Humor Breyers Ice Cream Company
Hagerstown, MD 301-797-9603
Good Humor Breyers Ice Cream Company
Framingham, MA 508-620-4300
Good Humor Breyers Ice Cream Company
Henderson, NV 702-564-0020
Good Humor Breyers Ice Cream Company
Green Bay, WI 866-204-9750
Good Humor Breyers Ice Cream Company
Green Bay, WI 920-499-5151
Gourmet Ice Cream
Palmer, MA 413-283-3740
Grays Ice Cream
Tiverton, RI 401-624-4500
Green River Chocolates
Hinesburg, VT 802-246-2652
Greenwood Ice Cream Company
Chamblee, GA 770-455-6166
H.P. Hood
Agawam, MA 413-786-7166
H.P. Hood
Chelsea, MA 800-343-6592
Herrell's Ice Cream
Northampton, MA 413-586-9700
Hershey Creamery Company
Harrisburg, PA 888-240-1905
Hey Brothers Ice Cream
Dixon, IL 815-288-4242
Hiland Dairy Foods Company
Springfield, MO 417-862-9311
Hiland Roberts Ice Cream Company
Norfolk, NE 402-371-3660
Homer's Ice Cream
Wilmette, IL 847-251-0477
Honey Hut Ice Cream
Cleveland, OH 216-749-7077
House of Flavors
Ludington, MI 800-930-7740
House of Spices India
Flushing, NY 718-507-4600
HP Hood
Lynnfield, MA 800-343-6592
Hudsonville Creamery & Ice Cream
Holland, MI 616-928-0793
Humble Cremery
Los Angeles, CA 800-697-9925
Humboldt Creamery Association
Fortuna, CA 707-725-6182
Hunt-Wesson Foods
Minneapolis, MN 612-544-2761
Hunter Farms
High Point, NC 800-446-8035
Hygeia Dairy Company
McAllen, TX 956-686-0511
Ice Cream & Yogurt Club
Boynton Beach, FL 561-731-3331
Ice Cream Specialties
St Louis, MO 314-962-3935
Ice Cream Specialties
Lafayette, IN 765-474-2989
Ideal Dairy
Richfield, UT 435-896-5061
Il Gelato
Astoria, NY 718-937-3033
Imagine Foods
Melville, NY 800-333-6339
International Yogurt Company
Portland, OR 800-962-7326
It's It Ice Cream Company
Burlingame, CA 800-345-1928
J.W. Haywood & Sons Dairy
Louisville, KY 502-774-2311
Jack & Jill Ice Cream Company
Moorestown, NJ 856-813-2300
Jackson Ice Cream Company
Denver, CO 303-534-2454
Jackson Milk & Ice CreamCompany
Hutchinson, KS 620-663-1244
Jaxsons Ice Cream
Dania, FL 954-923-4445
Johnson's Real Ice Cream
Columbus, OH 614-231-0014
Josh & John's Ice Cream
Colorado Springs, CO 800-530-2855
K&B Company
Schulenburg, TX 979-743-6555

Kan-Pac
Arkansas City, KS. 620-442-6820

Katie's Korner
Girard, OH 330-539-4140

Katrina's Tartufo
Port Jeffrsn Sta, NY 800-480-8836

Kemp Foods
York, PA 800-233-2007

Klinke Brothers Ice Cream Company
Memphis, TN 901-743-8250

Knoll Creek Dairy
Harrison, NY. 718-892-4500

Kohler Mix Specialties
Newington, CT 860-666-1511

Kokinos Purity Ice CreamCompany
Monroe, LA. .318-322-2930

Leiby's Dairy
Tamaqua, PA 570-668-2399

London Farm Dairy
Port Huron, MI 800-284-5111

Lone Star Food Products
Dallas, TX. 214-946-2185

Louis Sherry
Chicago, IL 773-486-8243

Louis Trauth Dairy
Newport, KY. 800-544-6455

Lupi
Baltimore, MD 410-752-3370

M&L Gourmet Ice Cream
Baltimore, MD 410-276-4880

Mack's Homemade Ice Cream
York, PA 717-741-2027

MacKay's Cochrane Ice Cream
Cochrane, AB 403-932-2455

Mama Tish's Italian Specialties
Chicago, IL 708-929-2023

Maola Milk & Ice Cream Company
New Bern, NC. 252-638-1131

Maple Island
St Paul, MN. 800-369-1022

Mario's Gelati
Vancouver, BC 604-879-9411

Mars M&M
Henderson, NV 888-265-6788

Matterhorn Ice Cream Company
Caldwell, ID .800-822-1635

Mattus Lowfat Ice Cream
Glen Cove, NY 718-472-1232

Mayfield Dairy Farms
Athens, TN 800-362-9546

McArthur Dairy
Miami, FL 877-803-6565

McConnell's Fine Ice Cream
Santa Barbara, CA 805-963-2958

Meadow Gold Dairies
Honolulu, HI .808-949-6161

Meadow Gold Dairy
Lewiston, ID .208-746-9006

Micalizzi Italian Ice
Bridgeport, CT 203-366-2353

Michele's Family Bakery
York, PA 717-741-2027

Michelle Chocolatiers
Colorado Springs, CO. 888-447-3654

Michigan Dairy
Livonia, MI 734-367-5390

Mid States Dairy
Hazelwood, MO 314-731-1150

Mikawaya Bakery
Los Angeles, CA. 213-628-6514

Millers Ice Cream
Houston, TX .713-861-3138

Mister Cookie Face
Lakewood, NJ 732-370-5533

Model Dairy
Reno, NV 800-433-2030

Mooresville Ice Cream Company
Mooresville, NC 704-664-5456

Morningstar Foods
Dallas, TX. 225-273-2803

Mozzicato De Pasquale Bakery Pastry
Hartford, CT .860-296-0426

Muller-Pinehurst Dairy C
Rockford, IL .815-968-0441

Nafziger Ice Cream Company
Napoleon, OH 419-592-1112

Natural Fruit Corporation
Hialeah, FL 305-887-7525

Nelson's Ice Cream
Royersford, PA 610-948-1282

New Horizon Foods
Union City, CA 510-489-8600

North Star Distributing
St Louis, MO. 314-631-8171

O'Boyle's Ice Cream Company
Bristol, PA. 215-788-0421

O'Danny Boy
Miamisburg, OH 888-840-0497

Oberweis Dairy
North Aurora, IL 888-645-5868

Omanga Ice Cream Company
Bronx, NY 800-494-6477

Oregon Cherry Growers
The Dalles, OR 800-367-2536

Out of a Flower
Lancaster, TX 800-743-4696

Pal's Homemade Ice Cream
Toledo, OH 419-382-0615

Parmalat
Toronto, ON .416-626-1973

Pecan Deluxe Candy Company
Dallas, TX. 800-733-3589

Perry's Ice Cream Company
Akron, NY. 800-873-7797

Pet Dairy
Portsmouth, VA 757-397-2387

Pet Dairy
Spartanburg, SC 864-576-6280

Petersen Ice Cream Company
Oak Park, IL .708-386-6130

Pevely Dairy Company
St Louis, MO. 314-771-4400

Pierre's French Ice Cream Company
Cleveland, OH 800-837-7342

Plains Creamery
Amarillo, TX. 806-374-0385

Platte Valley Creamery
Scottsbluff, NE 308-632-4225

Plehn's Bakery
St Matthews, KY. 502-896-4438

Pony Boy Ice Cream
Acushnet, MA. 508-994-4422

Poudre Valley Creamery
Fort Collins, CO 970-482-8475

Prairie Farms Dairy
Carlinville, IL 217-854-2547

Prairie Farms Dairy
O Fallon, IL. .618-632-3632

Prairie Farms Dairy Inc
Carlinville, IL 217-854-2547

Price's Creameries
El Paso, TX 915-565-2711

Puritan Ice Cream
Kendallville, IN 260-347-2700

Puritan/ATZ Ice Cream
Kendallville, IN 260-347-2700

Purity Dairies
Nashville, TN 615-244-1900

Purity Ice Cream Company
Ithaca, NY. 607-272-1545

Reinhold Ice Cream Company
Pittsburgh, PA 412-321-7600

Reiter Dairy
Akron, OH. 800-362-0825

Rhino Foods
Burlington, VT 800-639-3350

Rich Ice Cream Company
West Palm Beach, FL 561-833-7585

Richardson's Ice Cream
Middleton, MA 978-774-5450

Richman Festival Ice Cream Company
Paterson, NJ .973-684-8935

Roberts Dairy Company
Omaha, NE 402-344-4321

Roberts Dairy Company
Kansas City, MO. 800-279-1692

Robinson Dairy
Denver, CO 800-332-6355

Ronnybrook Farm Dairy
Ancramdale, NY 800-772-6455

Roselani Tropics Ice Cream
Wailuku, HI 808-244-7951

Safeway Dairy Products
Capitol Heights, MD 301-341-9555

Safeway Stores
Tempe, AZ 877-723-3929

Saputo
Montreal, QC 514-328-6662

Sara Lee Corporation
Downers Grove, IL 630-598-8100

Schneider Valley Farms Dairy
Williamsport, PA. 570-326-2021

Schneider's Dairy Holdings Inc
Pittsburgh, PA 412-881-3525

Schoep's Ice Cream Company
Madison, WI .800-236-0032

Seaside Ice Cream
Pelham, NY. .914-636-2751

Shaner's Family Restaurant
South Paris, ME 207-743-6367

SheerBliss Ice Cream
Aventura, FL .305-692-5800

Sinton Dairy Foods Company
Colorado Springs, CO. 800-388-4970

Sisler's Ice & Ice Cream
Ohio, IL. 888-891-3856

Smith Dairy Products Company
Orrville, OH .800-776-7076

Snelgrove Ice Cream Company
Salt Lake City, UT 800-569-0005

Snow's Ice Cream Company
Greenfield, MA 413-774-7438

Snyder's Ice Cream
Ashland, PA .570-875-3320

Southern Ice Cream Specialties
Marietta, GA 770-428-0452

Springdale Ice Cream & Beverages
Cincinnati, OH 513-671-2790

St. Clair Ice Cream Company
Norwalk, CT .203-853-4774

Starbucks Coffee Company
Seattle, WA .800-782-7282

Steese Ice Cream
Grove City, PA 724-748-4115

Stewart's Ice Cream
Saratoga Springs, NY 518-581-1000

Stone's Home Made Candy Shop
Oswego, NY .888-223-3928

Sugar Creek/Eskimo Pie
Russellville, AR 800-445-2715

Sunshine Farms Dairy
Elyria, OH 440-322-6301

Superstore Industries
Fairfield, CA .707-864-0502

Sweet Mountain Magic
Chicago, IL 773-755-4539

Sweet Shop
La Crosse, WI 608-784-7724

Sweety Novelty
Monterey Park, CA. 626-282-4482

Tebay Dairy Company
Parkersburg, WV. 304-863-3705

Ted Drewes Frozen Custard
St Louis, MO. 314-481-2652

Thrifty Ice Cream
El Monte, CA 626-571-0122

Tillamook County Creamery Association
Tillamook, OR 503-842-4481

Toft Dairy
Sandusky, OH 800-521-4606

Tom's Ice Cream Bowl
Zanesville, OH 740-452-5267

Tony's Ice Cream Company
Gastonia, NC. 704-867-7085

Treat Ice Cream Company
San Jose, CA. 408-292-9321

Tropical Treets
North York, ON. 888-424-8229

Turkey Hill Dairy
Conestoga, PA. 800-693-2479

Turner Dairies
Jackson, TN .731-427-6012

Turner Dairies
Covington, TN 901-476-2643

Tuscan Dairy Farms
Dallas, TX. 800-526-4416

Umpqua Dairy Products Company
Roseburg, OR 541-672-2638

United Dairy
Martins Ferry, OH 800-252-1542

United Dairy
Uniontown, PA 800-966-6455

Valley Dairy Fairview Dairy
Windber, PA .814-467-5537

Valley Maid Ice Cream
Aurora, IL 630-851-2241

Van Dyke Ice Cream
Ridgewood, NJ 201-444-1429

Velda Farms
Lakeland, FL .800-279-4166

Velda Farms
North Miami Bch, FL 800-795-4649

Velvet Freeze Ice Cream
St Louis, MO. 800-589-5000

Velvet Ice Cream Company
Utica, OH 800-589-5000

Velvet Milk
Owensboro, KY 270-683-4561
Venice Spumoni/Spring Valley Ice Cream
Philadelphia, PA 800-784-0312
Vincent Giordano Corporation
Philadelphia, PA 215-467-6629
Vitamilk Dairy
Bellingham, WA 206-529-4128
Vitarich Ice Cream
Fortuna, CA 707-725-6182
Warwick Ice Cream Company
Warwick, RI 401-821-8403
Wayne Dairy Products
Richmond, IN 800-875-9294
Weiss Provisions
Pittsburgh, PA 800-458-6328
Weldon Ice Cream Company
Millersport, OH. 740-467-2400
Wells' Dairy
Le Mars, IA. 800-942-3800
Welsh Farms
Newark, NJ 800-221-0663
Welsh Farms
Clifton, NJ 973-772-2388
Whitey's Ice Cream Manufacturing
Moline, IL 888-594-4839
Winmix/Natural Care Products
Englewood, FL 941-475-7432
World's Greatest Ice Cream
Miami Beach, FL 305-538-0207
Wright Ice Cream
Cayuga, IN 800-686-9561
WSU Creamery
Pullman, WA .800-457-5442
Yarnell Ice Cream Company
Searcy, AR 800-766-2414
YoCream International
Portland, OR. 800-962-7326
Ziegenfelder Company
Wheeling, WV 304-232-6360

Bases

GPI USA LLC.
Athens, GA 706-850-7826
SensoryEffects Flavor Systems
Bridgeton, MO 314-291-5444
Sokol & Company
Countryside, IL 800-328-7656

Cones

Sugar

Kellogg US Snack   Division
Battlecreek, MI 269-961-2000

Fat-Free

Cedar Crest Specialties
Cedarburg, WI. 800-877-8341
Clay Center Locker Plant
Clay Center, KS 785-632-5550
Perry's Ice Cream Company
Akron, NY. 800-873-7797

Flavored

Bill Mack's Homemade Ice Cream
Dover, PA 717-292-1931
Byrne Dairy
Syracuse, NY .800-899-1535
Eskimo Pie Corporation
Ronkonkoma, NY 631-737-9700
Petersen Ice Cream Company
Oak Park, IL 708-386-6130
Velvet Freeze Ice Cream
St Louis, MO. 800-589-5000

Fudgesicles

Gourmet Ice Cream
Palmer, MA. .413-283-3740

Gelato

Casper's Ice Cream
Richmond, UT. 800-772-4182
Ciao Bella Gelato Company
Irvington, NJ 800-435-2863
Ciao Bella Gellato Company
Los Angeles, CA. 323-965-8690

Ciao Bella Gellato Company
San Francisco, CA 415-824-3000
Creme Glacee Gelati
St Leonard, QC 888-322-0116
Crowley Foods
Binghamton, NY 800-637-0019
Frostbite
Toledo, OH 800-968-7711
Gelato Giuliana LLC
Wallingford, CT 203-269-2200
J&J Snack Foods Corporation
Pennsauken, NJ 856-665-9533
Matterhorn Ice Cream Company
Caldwell, ID .800-822-1635
Millers Ice Cream
Houston, TX .713-861-3138
Mooresville Ice Cream Company
Mooresville, NC 704-664-5456
Snelgrove Ice Cream Company
Salt Lake City, UT 800-569-0005
Talenti
Dallas, TX 214-526-3600
Weldon Ice Cream Company
Millersport, OH. 740-467-2400

Granita

Creme Glacee Gelati
St Leonard, QC 888-322-0116
Folklore Foods
Toppenish, WA 509-865-4772

Ice Milk

Perry's Ice Cream Company
Akron, NY. 800-873-7797
Safeway Dairy Products
Capitol Heights, MD. 301-341-9555
Whitey's Ice Cream Manufacturing
Moline, IL. 888-594-4839

Ices

Alamance Foods/Triton Water Company
Burlington, NC 800-476-9111
Albertson's Ice-Cream
Boise, ID 877-932-7948
Cappola Foods
Toronto, ON .416-256-1084
Carbolite Foods
Evansville, IN 888-524-3314
Chill & Moore
Fort Worth, TX 800-676-3055
Edy's Grand Ice Cream
Rockaway, NJ 800-362-7899
Gelato Fresco
Toronto, ON .416-785-5415
J&J Snack Foods Corporation
Pennsauken, NJ 856-665-9533
Kemach Food Products   Corporation
Brooklyn, NY 888-453-6224
Mackie International
Commerce, CA 800-733-9762
Mar-Key Foods
Vidalia, GA 912-537-4204
Rosati Italian Water Ice
Clifton Heights, PA. 610-626-1818
Smart Ice
Fort Myers, FL 239-334-3123
Tova Industries
Louisville, KY 888-532-8682
Venice Spumoni/Spring Valley Ice Cream
Philadelphia, PA 800-784-0312

Low-Fat

Friendly Ice Cream Corporation
Wilbraham, MA 800-966-9970
Hudsonville Creamery & Ice Cream
Holland, MI. .616-928-0793
Mayfield Dairy Farms
Athens, TN 800-362-9546
Perry's Ice Cream Company
Akron, NY. 800-873-7797
Stewart's Ice Cream
Saratoga Springs, NY 518-581-1000
Vitarich Ice Cream
Fortuna, CA 707-725-6182

Non-Dairy

Low-Calorie

Innovative Food Solutions LLC
Columbus, OH 800-884-3314

Novelties

Alinosi French Superfine Candies
Detroit, MI 313-527-3195
Atlanta Flagship Dairy
Atlanta, GA 800-224-0669
Del's Lemonade & Refreshments
Cranston, RI .401-463-6190
Dreyer's Grand Ice Cream
Oakland, CA .877-437-3937
Edy's Grand Ice Cream
Rockaway, NJ 800-362-7899
Ellsworth Ice Cream Company
Saratoga Springs, NY 518-584-1684
Eskimo Pie Corporation
Ronkonkoma, NY 631-737-9700
Fieldbrook Farms
Dunkirk, NY .800-333-0805
Frozfruit Corporation
Gardena, CA .310-217-1034
Glover's Ice Cream
Frankfort, IN 800-686-5163
Good Humor Breyers Ice Cream Company
Hagerstown, MD. 301-797-9603
Good Humor Breyers Ice Cream Company
Henderson, NV 702-564-0020
Good Humor Breyers Ice Cream Company
Green Bay, WI. 866-204-9750
Good Humor Breyers Ice Cream Company
Green Bay, WI. 920-499-5151
Grossinger's Home Bakery
New York, NY 800-479-6996
Hiland Roberts Ice Cream Company
Norfolk, NE. .402-371-3660
Ice Cream Specialties
St Louis, MO. 314-962-3935
Ice Cream Specialties
Lafayette, IN .765-474-2989
It's It Ice Cream Company
Burlingame, CA 800-345-1928
Kemp Foods
York, PA 800-233-2007
Meadow Gold Dairies
Honolulu, HI. 808-949-6161
Natural Fruit Corporation
Hialeah, FL 305-887-7525
Perry's Ice Cream Company
Akron, NY. 800-873-7797
Schneider's Dairy Holdings Inc
Pittsburgh, PA 412-881-3525
Schoep's Ice Cream Company
Madison, WI .800-236-0032
Southern Ice Cream Specialties
Marietta, GA .770-428-0452
Sweety Novelty
Monterey Park, CA 626-282-4482
Valley Maid Ice Cream
Aurora, IL 630-851-2241
Venice Spumoni/Spring Valley Ice Cream
Philadelphia, PA 800-784-0312
Vitarich Ice Cream
Fortuna, CA 707-725-6182
Weldon Ice Cream Company
Millersport, OH. 740-467-2400
Whitey's Ice Cream Manufacturing
Moline, IL 888-594-4839
Wright Ice Cream
Cayuga, IN 800-686-9561
Ziegenfelder Company
Wheeling, WV 304-232-6360

Popsicles

Good Humor Breyers Ice Cream Company
Henderson, NV 702-564-0020
Hershey Corporation
Hershey, PA. .800-468-1714
Ice Cream Specialties
St Louis, MO. 314-962-3935
J&J Snack Foods Corporation
Pennsauken, NJ 856-665-9533
Leader Candies
Brooklyn, NY 718-366-6900
Mackie International
Commerce, CA 800-733-9762

Mar-Key Foods
Vidalia, GA 912-537-4204
Oak Leaf Confections
Scarborough, ON 800-338-3631
Welch's Foods Inc
Concord, MA 800-340-6870

Ribbons

Sokol & Company
Countryside, IL 800-328-7656

Roll

Creme Glacee Gelati
St Leonard, QC 888-322-0116
Dave's Hawaiian Ice Cream
Pearl City, HI 808-453-0500
Gourmet Ice Cream
Palmer, MA 413-283-3740
Grossinger's Home Bakery
New York, NY 800-479-6996

Sherbet

A.C. Petersen Farms
West Hartford, CT 860-233-8483
Alamance Foods/Triton Water Company
Burlington, NC 800-476-9111
Albertson's Ice-Cream
Boise, ID .877-932-7948
Browns Dairy
Valparaiso, IN 219-464-4141
Byrne Dairy
Syracuse, NY 800-899-1535
Cedar Crest Specialties
Cedarburg, WI 800-877-8341
Compact Industries
St Charles, IL 800-513-4262
Creme Glacee Gelati
St Leonard, QC 888-322-0116
Dave's Hawaiian Ice Cream
Pearl City, HI 808-453-0500
Dreyers Grand Ice Cream
Oakland, CA 510-652-8187
Edy's Grand Ice Cream
Fort Wayne, IN 260-483-3102
Ellsworth Ice Cream Company
Saratoga Springs, NY 518-584-1684
Eskimo Pie Corporation
Ronkonkoma, NY 631-737-9700
Fieldbrook Farms
Dunkirk, NY 800-333-0805
Flavors from Florida
Bartow, FL 863-533-0408
Gelato Fresco
Toronto, ON 416-785-5415
Hudsonville Creamery & Ice Cream
Holland, MI. 616-928-0793
Jel-Sert Company
West Chicago, IL 800-323-2592
Johnson's Real Ice Cream
Columbus, OH 614-231-0014
Mayfield Dairy Farms
Athens, TN 800-362-9546
Perry's Ice Cream Company
Akron, NY. 800-873-7797
Prairie Farms Dairy
Carlinville, IL 217-854-2547
Schneider Valley Farms Dairy
Williamsport, PA. 570-326-2021
Sunshine Farms Dairy
Elyria, OH 440-322-6301
Tova Industries
Louisville, KY 888-532-8682
Valley Maid Ice Cream
Aurora, IL .630-851-2241

Slushes

Al-Rite Fruits & Syrups
Miami, FL .305-652-2540
Fee Brothers
Rochester, NY 800-961-3337
Flavouressence Products
Mississauga, ON. 866-209-7778
Royale International   Beverage Co Inc
Davenport, IA 563-386-5222
Tropical Illusions
Trenton, MO 660-359-6849

Sorbet

Ben & Jerry's Homemade
South Burlington, VT 802-846-1500
Bernie's Foods
Brooklyn, NY 718-417-6677
Ciao Bella Gelato Company
Irvington, NJ 800-435-2863
Dreyers Grand Ice Cream
Oakland, CA 510-652-8187
Dunkin Brands Inc.
Canton, MA 800-458-7731
Eskimo Pie Corporation
Ronkonkoma, NY 631-737-9700
Fieldbrook Farms
Dunkirk, NY 800-333-0805
Gelati Celesti
Redondo Beach, CA 800-550-7550
Gelato Fresco
Toronto, ON 416-785-5415
Homer's Ice Cream
Wilmette, IL 847-251-0477
International Yogurt Company
Portland, OR 800-962-7326
MacKay's Cochrane Ice Cream
Cochrane, AB 403-932-2455
Royal Ice Cream Company
Manchester, CT 800-246-2958
Talenti
Dallas, TX 214-526-3600
Winmix/Natural Care Products
Englewood, FL 941-475-7432

Tortoni

Royal Ice Cream Company
Manchester, CT 800-246-2958

Milk & Milk Products

Kefir

Continental Culture Specialists
Glendale, CA 818-240-7400

EMERLING INTERNATIONAL FOODS, INC.

Emerling International Foods
Buffalo, NY. 716-833-7381

> **We supply food manufacturers and food service customers worldwide (since 1988) with bulk ingredients including: Fruits & Vegetables; Juice Concentrates; Herbs & Spices; Oils & Vinegars; Flavors & Colors; Honey & Molasses. We also produce PURE MAPLE SYRUP.**

Jamieson Laboratories
Toronto, QC 519-974-8482
Lifeway Foods Inc
Morton Grove, IL 847-967-1010
M-C Dairy Company
Etobicoke, ON 416-231-1491

Milk

AFP Advanced Food Products, LLC
Visalia, CA 559-627-2070
Agri-Mark
Lawrence, MA 978-687-4936
Aimonetto and Sons
Seattle, WA 866-823-2777
All American Foods, Inc.
Mankato, MN 800-833-2661
Alpenrose Dairy
Portland, OR 503-244-1133
Alta Dena Certified Dairy
City of Industry, CA 800-535-1369
Anderson Erickson Dairy
Des Moines, IA. 515-265-2521
Associated Milk Producers
New Ulm, MN. 800-533-3580
Atlanta Flagship Dairy
Atlanta, GA 800-224-0669
Ault Foods
Toronto, ON 416-626-1973
Barber's Dairy
Birmingham, AL 205-942-2351
Barkers Farm Dairy
Pecks Mill, WV. 304-855-4512
Bell Dairy Products
Lubbock, TX. 806-293-1367

Berkeley Farms
Hayward, CA 510-265-8600
Bottineau Cooperative Creamery
Bottineau, ND 701-228-2216
Broughton Foods
Marietta, OH 800-283-2479
Byrne Dairy
Syracuse, NY 800-899-1535
C.F. Burger Creamery
Detroit, MI 800-229-2322
Cass Clay Creamery
Fargo, ND 701-293-6455
Cedar Lake Foods
Cedar Lake, MI. 800-246-5039
Chase Brothers Dairy
Oxnard, CA 800-438-6455
Clinton Milk Company
Newark, NJ 973-642-3000
Coastlog Industries
Novi, MI .248-344-9556
Coburg Dairy
North Charleston, SC 843-554-4870
Consun Food Industries
Elyria, OH. 440-233-7501
Country Fresh
Grand Rapids, MI 800-748-0480
Cow Palace Too
Granger, WA 509-829-5777
Crowley Foods
Binghamton, NY. 800-637-0019
Cultured Specialties
Fullerton, CA 714-772-8861
Cumberland Dairy
Rosenhayn, NJ 856-451-1300
Dairy Fresh Corporation
Greensboro, AL. 800-239-5114
Dairy Maid Dairy
Frederick, MD 301-663-5114
DairyAmerica
Fresno, CA 800-722-3110
Dairyman's/Land O' Lakes
Tulare, CA. 559-687-8287
Dean Foods/Land O'Lakes
Bismarck, ND 701-222-3131
Dean Foods/Verifine Dairy Products
Sheboygan, WI 800-236-6455
Devansoy
Carroll, IA. 800-747-8605
Dixie Dairy Company
Gary, IN. 219-885-6101
Ellsworth Cooperative Creamery
Ellsworth, WI 715-273-4311
Farmland Dairies
Wallington, NJ 888-727-6252
Farmland Dairies
Wallington, NJ 973-777-2500
Foremost Dairies-Hawaii
Honolulu, HI 808-841-5831
Foster Farms Dairy
Modesto, CA 209-576-3470
G A Food Service
St Petersburg, FL. 727-573-2211
Galliker Dairy
Johnstown, PA. 800-477-6455
Garelick Farms
Franklin, MA 800-343-4982
Garelick Farms
Lynn, MA 800-487-8700
Golden Cheese of California
Corona, CA 800-842-0264
GPI USA LLC.
Athens, GA. 706-850-7826
H. Meyer Dairy Company
Cincinnati, OH 800-347-6455
H.E. Butt Grocery Company
San Antonio, TX 800-432-3113
H.P. Hood
Vernon, NY 315-829-3004
H.P. Hood
Agawam, MA 413-786-7166
H.P. Hood
Lynnfield, ME. 800-343-6592
H.P. Hood
Barre, VT 800-622-4468
Harrisburg Dairies
Harrisburg, PA. 800-692-7429
Hastings Cooperative Creamery
Hastings, MN 651-437-9414
Heritage Farms Dairy
Murfreesboro, TN 615-895-2790
Hiland Dairy Foods Company
Wichita, KS 316-267-4221

Hiland Dairy Foods Company
  Springfield, MO 417-862-9311
Hygeia Dairy Company
  Corpus Christi, TX 361-854-4561
Inland Northwest Dairies
  Spokane, WA. 509-489-8600
Jackson Milk & Ice CreamCompany
  Hutchinson, KS 620-663-1244
KDK Inc
  Draper, UT 801-571-3506
Keller's Creamery
  Harleysville, PA 800-535-5371
Kemp Foods
  York, PA 800-233-2007
Kemps
  Cedarburg, WI. 262-377-5040
Kohler Mix Specialties
  White Bear Lake, MN. 651-426-1633
Lafleur Dairy
  New Orleans, LA 504-464-0812
Land O Lakes Milk
  Sioux Falls, SD 605-330-9526
Land O'Lakes
  St Paul, MN. 651-730-2100
Land O'Lakes
  St Paul, MN. 800-328-9680
Land O'Lakes, Inc
  Arden Hills, MN 800-328-9680
Land-O-Sun Dairies
  O Fallon, IL. 618-632-6381
Level Valley Creamery
  Antioch, TN 800-251-1292
Liberty Dairy
  Evart, MI. 800-632-5552
Marva Maid Dairy
  Newport News, VA 800-544-4439
Maryland & Virginia Milk Producers Cooperative
  Reston, VA 703-742-7443
Matanuska Maid Dairy
  Anchorage, AK 907-561-5223
Mayfield Dairy Farms
  Athens, TN 800-362-9546
McArthur Dairy
  Miami, FL. 305-576-2880
McDonald Dairy Company
  Flint, MI .810-232-9193

Meadow Brook Dairy
  Erie, PA 800-352-4010
Meadow Gold Dairies
  Lincoln, NE. 800-742-7349
Michigan Dairy
  Livonia, MI 734-367-5390
Mid States Dairy
  Hazelwood, MO 314-731-1150
Morningstar Foods
  Mt Crawford, VA 540-434-7328
Muller-Pinehurst Dairy C
  Rockford, IL 815-968-0441
Naterl
  St. Bruno, QC 800- 50- 115
Norwalk Dairy
  Santa Fe Springs, CA 562-921-5712
Parmalat
  Toronto, ON 800-363-4393
Parmalat Canada
  Toronto, ON 800-563-1515
Pet Dairy
  Portsmouth, VA 757-397-2387
Pet Dairy
  Spartanburg, SC 864-576-6280
Pet Milk
  Florence, SC 800-735-3066
Pevely Dairy Company
  St Louis, MO. 314-771-4400
Pleasant View Dairy
  Highland, IN 219-838-0155
Prairie Farms Dairy
  Carlinville, IL 217-854-2547
Prairie Farms Dairy
  Granite City, IL. 618-451-5600
Prairie Farms Dairy Inc
  Carlinville, IL 217-854-2547
Purity Dairies
  Nashville, TN 615-244-1900
Queensboro Farm Products
  Canastota, NY 315-697-2235
Queensboro Farm Products
  Jamaica, NY 718-658-5000
Reilly Dairy & Food Company
  Tampa, FL. 813-839-8458
Reiter Dairy
  Akron, OH. 800-362-0825

Reiter Dairy
  Springfield, OH. 937-323-5777
Roberts Dairy Company
  Omaha, NE. 402-344-4321
Roberts Dairy Company
  Kansas City, MO. 800-279-1692
Robinson Dairy
  Denver, CO 800-332-6355
Roland Industries
  Saint Louis, MO 800-325-1183
Rosenberger's Dairies
  Hatfield, PA. 800-355-9074
Safeway Milk Plant
  Tempe, AZ 480-894-4391
San Joaquin Valley Dairymen
  Los Banos, CA 209-826-4901
Saputo Cheese
  Fond Du Lac, WI 800-824-3373
Schneider Valley Farms Dairy
  Williamsport, PA. 570-326-2021
Schneider's Dairy Holdings Inc
  Pittsburgh, PA 412-881-3525
Sinton Dairy Foods Company
  Colorado Springs, CO. 800-388-4970
Sinton Dairy Foods Company
  Denver, CO 800-666-4808
Smith Dairy Products Company
  Orrville, OH 800-776-7076
Stewart's Ice Cream
  Saratoga Springs, NY 518-581-1000
Stop & Shop Manufacturing
  Readville, MA. 617-361-8400
Sunshine Farms
  Portage, WI 608-742-2016
Superbrand Dairies
  Miami, FL. 305-685-8079
Superstore Industries
  Fairfield, CA 707-864-0502
Swiss Valley Farms Company
  Cedar Rapids, IA. 319-364-8153
Swissland Milk
  Berne, IN. 260-589-2761
Tamarack Farms Dairy
  Newark, OH. 866-221-4141
Toft Dairy
  Sandusky, OH 800-521-4606

Turkey Hill Dairy
Conestoga, PA 800-693-2479
Turner Dairies
Covington, TN 901-476-2643
Tuscan/Lehigh Valley Dais
Lansdale, PA 800-937-3233
Umpqua Dairy Products Company
Roseburg, OR 541-672-2638
Unified Western Grocers
Los Angeles, CA 323-731-8223
United Dairy
Martins Ferry, OH 800-252-1542
United Dairymen of Arizona
Tempe, AZ 480-966-7211
Upstate Farms Cooperative
Rochester, NY 585-458-1880
Velda Farms
North Miami Bch, FL 800-795-4649
Vitamilk Dairy
Bellingham, WA 206-529-4128
W.J. Stearns & Sons/Mountain Dairy
Storrs Mansfield, CT 860-423-9289
Wayne Dairy Products
Richmond, IN 800-875-9294
Weiss Provisions
Pittsburgh, PA 800-458-6328
Welsh Farms
Newark, NJ 800-221-0663
Wengert's Dairy
Lebanon, PA 800-222-2129
Went's Dairy
Niagara Falls, NY 716-692-6543
WestFarm Foods
Boise, ID 208-375-3062
White Wave Foods
Jacksonville, FL 800-874-6765
Winchester Farms Dairy
Winchester, KY 859-745-5500
Yoder Dairies
Chesapeake, VA 757-497-3518
Yoo-Hoo Chocolate Beverage Company
Port Chester, NY 800-966-4669

1 Percent

Alta Dena Certified Dairy
City of Industry, CA 800-535-1369
Berkeley Farms
Hayward, CA 510-265-8600
Chase Brothers Dairy
Oxnard, CA 800-438-6455
Coburg Dairy
North Charleston, SC 843-554-4870
Cream O'Weaver Dairy
Salt Lake City, UT 801-973-9922
Cropp Cooperative-Organic Valley
La Farge, WI 888-444-6455
Crowley Foods
Binghamton, NY 800-637-0019
Cumberland Dairy
Rosenhayn, NJ 856-451-1300
Dairy Farmers of America
Sulphur Springs, TX 903-885-6518
Dairy Maid Dairy
Frederick, MD 301-663-5114
Dean Foods/Verifine Dairy Products
Sheboygan, WI 800-236-6455
KDK Inc
Draper, UT 801-571-3506
Meadow Brook Dairy
Erie, PA 800-352-4010
Mid States Dairy
Hazelwood, MO 314-731-1150
Parmalat
Toronto, ON 800-363-4393
Pleasant View Dairy
Highland, IN 219-838-0155
Reiter Dairy
Springfield, OH 937-323-5777
Safeway Milk Plant
Tempe, AZ 480-894-4391
Schneider's Dairy Holdings Inc
Pittsburgh, PA 412-881-3525
Sinton Dairy Foods Company
Colorado Springs, CO 800-388-4970
Tuscan/Lehigh Valley Dais
Lansdale, PA 800-937-3233
Unified Western Grocers
Los Angeles, CA 323-731-8223
Vermont Family Farms Milk
Saint Albans, VT 800-559-0343
White Wave Foods
Jacksonville, FL 800-874-6765

Yoder Dairies
Chesapeake, VA 757-497-3518

2 Percent

Alta Dena Certified Dairy
City of Industry, CA 800-535-1369
Berkeley Farms
Hayward, CA 510-265-8600
Coburg Dairy
North Charleston, SC 843-554-4870
Cream O'Weaver Dairy
Salt Lake City, UT 801-973-9922
Cropp Cooperative-Organic Valley
La Farge, WI 888-444-6455
Crowley Foods
Binghamton, NY 800-637-0019
Cumberland Dairy
Rosenhayn, NJ 856-451-1300
Dairy Farmers of America
Sulphur Springs, TX 903-885-6518
Dairy Maid Dairy
Frederick, MD 301-663-5114
Dean Foods/Verifine Dairy Products
Sheboygan, WI 800-236-6455
KDK Inc
Draper, UT 801-571-3506
Meadow Brook Dairy
Erie, PA 800-352-4010
Mid States Dairy
Hazelwood, MO 314-731-1150
Oak Knoll Dairy
Windsor, VT 802-674-5426
Parmalat
Toronto, ON 800-363-4393
Pleasant View Dairy
Highland, IN 219-838-0155
Reiter Dairy
Springfield, OH 937-323-5777
Safeway Milk Plant
Tempe, AZ 480-894-4391
Schneider's Dairy Holdings Inc
Pittsburgh, PA 412-881-3525
Sinton Dairy Foods Company
Colorado Springs, CO 800-388-4970
Stewart's Ice Cream
Saratoga Springs, NY 518-581-1000
T.G. Lee Dairy
Orlando, FL 407-894-4941
Unified Western Grocers
Los Angeles, CA 323-731-8223
Vermont Family Farms Milk
Saint Albans, VT 800-559-0343
Wengert's Dairy
Lebanon, PA 800-222-2129
White Wave Foods
Jacksonville, FL 800-874-6765
Winchester Farms Dairy
Winchester, KY 859-745-5500

Chocolate

Alta Dena Certified Dairy
City of Industry, CA 800-535-1369
Barbe's Dairy
Westwego, LA 504-347-6201
Berkeley Farms
Hayward, CA 510-265-8600
Chase Brothers Dairy
Oxnard, CA 800-438-6455
Cloverland Green Spring Dairy
Baltimore, MD 800-876-6455
Coburg Dairy
North Charleston, SC 843-554-4870
Crowley Foods
Binghamton, NY 800-637-0019
Dean Foods Company
Dallas, TX 214-303-3400
Dean Foods/Verifine Dairy Products
Sheboygan, WI 800-236-6455
Harrisburg Dairies
Harrisburg, PA 800-692-7429
Hygeia Dairy Company
Corpus Christi, TX 361-854-4561
Hygeia Dairy Company
McAllen, TX 956-686-0511
Ideal American
Holland, IN 812-424-3351
Kemps
Cedarburg, WI 262-377-5040
McArthur Dairy
Miami, FL 305-576-2880

Naterl
St. Bruno, QC 800- 50- 115
Norwalk Dairy
Santa Fe Springs, CA 562-921-5712
Oak Knoll Dairy
Windsor, VT 802-674-5426
Parmalat
Toronto, ON 800-363-4393
Sara Lee Coffee & Tea
Earth City, MO 314-731-2500
Seller Kirk & Company
Schwenksville, PA 215-480-7342
Sinton Dairy Foods Company
Colorado Springs, CO 800-388-4970
Swiss Dairy
Riverside, CA 951-898-9427
Tuscan/Lehigh Valley Dais
Lansdale, PA 800-937-3233
Winchester Farms Dairy
Winchester, KY 859-745-5500
Yoder Dairies
Chesapeake, VA 757-497-3518
Yoo-Hoo Chocolate Beverage Company
Carlstadt, NJ 201-933-0070
Yoo-Hoo Chocolate Beverage Company
Port Chester, NY 800-966-4669

Condensed

Abbott Laboratories Nutritionals/Ross Products
Columbus, OH 877-946-7747
Agri-Mark
Lawrence, MA 978-687-4936
All American Foods, Inc.
Mankato, MN 800-833-2661
Berkshire Dairy & Food Products
Wyomissing, PA 888-654-8008
Blossom Farm Products
Ridgewood, NJ 800-729-1818
Dairy Farmers of America
Franklinton, LA 800-735-2038
Dairy Farmers of America
Kansas City, MO 816-801-6200
Dietrich's Milk Products
Reading, PA 800-526-6455
Gehl Guernsey Farms
Germantown, WI 800-434-5713
Graf Creamery
Zachow, WI 715-758-2137
Land O'Lakes
Carlisle, PA 717-486-7000
Level Valley Creamery
Antioch, TN 800-251-1292
Master Taste International
Plant City, FL 800-237-7629
O-At-Ka Milk Products Cooperative
Batavia, NY 800-828-8152
Queensboro Farm Products
Jamaica, NY 718-658-5000
Ronzoni Foods Canada
Etobicoke, ON 800-387-5032
Saint Albans CooperativeCreamy
Saint Albans, VT 800-559-0343
San Joaquin Valley Dairymen
Los Banos, CA 209-826-4901
Saputo Cheese
Lincolnshire, IL 800-558-9714

Condensed - Bulk Only

Agri-Dairy Products
Purchase, NY 914-697-9580
Clofine Dairy & Food Products
Linwood, NJ 800-441-1001

Evaporated

Abbott Laboratories Nutritionals/Ross Products
Columbus, OH 877-946-7747
Agri-Dairy Products
Purchase, NY 914-697-9580
Associated Milk Producers
Dawson, MN 320-769-2994
Associated Milk Producers
New Ulm, MN. 507-233-4600
Clofine Dairy & Food Products
Linwood, NJ 800-441-1001
Cropp Cooperative-Organic Valley
La Farge, WI 888-444-6455
Industrial Products
Defiance, OH 800-251-3033
Mead Johnson Nutritional
Zeeland, MI. 616-748-7100

MEYENBERG Goat Milk Products
Turlock, CA 800-891-4628
Milnot Company
Neosho, MO 800-877-6455

Fat-Free

Agri-Mark
Lawrence, MA 978-687-4936
Alta Dena Certified Dairy
City of Industry, CA 800-535-1369
Berkeley Farms
Hayward, CA 510-265-8600
California Dairies
Fresno, CA 559-233-5154
Chase Brothers Dairy
Oxnard, CA 800-438-6455
Clofine Dairy & Food Products
Linwood, NJ 800-441-1001
Darigold
Seattle, WA 800-333-6455
Dean Foods Company
Huntley, IL 847-669-5123
First District Association
Litchfield, MN 320-693-3236
Humboldt Creamery Association
Fortuna, CA 707-725-6182
Ideal American
Holland, IN 812-424-3351
IMAC
Oklahoma City, OK 888-878-7827
KDK Inc
Draper, UT 801-571-3506
Main Street Ingredients
La Crosse, WI 800-359-2345
Meadow Brook Dairy
Erie, PA 800-352-4010
Norwalk Dairy
Santa Fe Springs, CA 562-921-5712
Plainview Milk Products Cooperative
Plainview, MN 507-534-3872
Quality Ingredients Corporation
Burnsville, MN 952-898-4002
Ramsen
Lakeville, MN 952-431-0400
Reilly Dairy & Food Company
Tampa, FL 813-839-8458
Reiter Dairy
Springfield, OH 937-323-5777
Safeway Inc
Durand, WI 715-672-8911
Saint Albans CooperativeCreamy
Saint Albans, VT 800-559-0343
San Joaquin Valley Dairymen
Los Banos, CA 209-826-4901
Schneider's Dairy Holdings Inc
Pittsburgh, PA 412-881-3525
Sinton Dairy Foods Company
Colorado Springs, CO. 800-388-4970
Swiss Dairy
Riverside, CA 951-898-9427
Tuscan/Lehigh Valley Dais
Lansdale, PA 800-937-3233

Flavored

Berkeley Farms
Hayward, CA 510-265-8600
Chase Brothers Dairy
Oxnard, CA................. 800-438-6455
Coburg Dairy
North Charleston, SC 843-554-4870
Coco Lopez
Miramar, FL 800-341-2242
Dean Foods/Verifine Dairy Products
Sheboygan, WI 800-236-6455
Kemps
Cedarburg, WI. 262-377-5040
Norwalk Dairy
Santa Fe Springs, CA 562-921-5712
Schneider Valley Farms Dairy
Williamsport, PA 570-326-2021
Schneider's Dairy Holdings Inc
Pittsburgh, PA.............. 412-881-3525
Tuscan/Lehigh Valley Dais
Lansdale, PA 800-937-3233
Winchester Farms Dairy
Winchester, KY.............. 859-745-5500
Yoo-Hoo Chocolate Beverage Company
Port Chester, NY............ 800-966-4669

Fresh

AFP Advanced Food Products, LLC
Visalia, CA 559-627-2070
Agropur Cooperative Agro-Alimentaire
Granby, QC 800-363-5686
Al's Beverage Company
East Windsor, CT 888-257-7632
Alpenrose Dairy
Portland, OR 503-244-1133
Anderson Dairy
Las Vegas, NV 702-642-7507
Associated Milk Producers
Dawson, MN. 320-769-2994
Associated Milk Producers
New Ulm, MN. 507-233-4600
Avent Luvel Dairy Products
Kosciusko, MS 800-281-1307
Barbe's Dairy
Westwego, LA............... 504-347-6201
Bartlett Dairy & Food Service
Jamaica, NY 718-658-2299
Bell Dairy Products
Lubbock, TX. 806-293-1367
Bergey's Dairy Farm
Chesapeake, VA 757-482-4712
Berkeley Farms
Hayward, CA 510-265-8600
Bliss Brothers Dairy, Inc.
Attleboro, MA 800-622-8789
Blue Ribbon Dairy
Exeter, PA 570-655-5579
Braum's Inc
Oklahoma City, OK 405-478-1656
Broughton Foods
Marietta, OH 800-283-2479
Brown Dairy
Coalville, UT 435-336-5952
Brum's Dairy
Pembroke, ON. 613-735-4686
Burger Dairy
Cleveland, OH 216-896-9100
Caprine Estates
Bellbrook, OH. 937-848-7406
Carl Colteryahn Dairy
Pittsburgh, PA 412-881-1408
Central Dairy Company
Jefferson City, MO 573-635-6148
Chase Brothers Dairy
Oxnard, CA 800-438-6455
Chester Dairy Company
Chester, IL. 618-826-2394
Clinton Milk Company
Newark, NJ 973-642-3000
Clover Farms Dairy Company
Reading, PA 800-323-0123
Clover Stornetta Farms
Petaluma, CA 800-237-3315
Cloverland Green Spring Dairy
Baltimore, MD 800-876-6455
Coastlog Industries
Novi, MI 248-344-9556
Coburg Dairy
North Charleston, SC 843-554-4870
Compton Dairy
Shelbyville, IN 317-398-8621
Consun Food Industries
Elyria, OH 440-233-7501
Country Delight Farms
Nashville, TN 615-320-1440
Country Fresh
Grand Rapids, MI 800-748-0480
Cow Palace Too
Granger, WA 509-829-5777
Cream O'Weaver Dairy
Salt Lake City, UT 801-973-9922
Crescent Ridge Dairy
Sharon, MA 800-660-2740
Crowley Foods
Binghamton, NY 800-637-0019
Crystal Lake
Warsaw, IN 574-858-2514
Cultured Specialties
Fullerton, CA 714-772-8861
Cypress Grove Chevre
Arcata, CA 707-825-1100
Czepiel Millers Dairy
Ludlow, MA 413-589-0828
Dairy Farmers of America
Kansas City, MO............ 888-332-6455
Dairy Fresh
Winston Salem, NC. 800-446-5577

Dairy Fresh Corporation
Greensboro, AL. 800-239-5114
Dairy Management
Rosemont, IL. 800-248-8829
Dairyman's/Land O' Lakes
Tulare, CA................. 559-687-8287
Dairymen's
Cleveland, OH 216-671-2300
Danish Creamery Association
Fresno, CA 559-233-5154
Dannon Company
Minster, OH 419-628-3861
Dannon Company
White Plains, NY 877-326-6668
Darby Plains Dairy
Plain City, OH 614-873-4574
Darifair Foods
Jacksonville, FL 904-268-8999
Darigold
Seattle, WA 800-333-6455
Daybreak Foods
Long Prairie, MN 320-732-2966
Dean Dairy Products
Sharpsville, PA 800-942-8096
Dean Foods Company
Dallas, TX................. 214-303-3400
Dean Foods Company
Rosemont, IL. 800-323-1571
Dean Foods Company
Rochester, IN 800-336-7215
Dean Foods Company
Dallas, TX................. 800-431-9214
Dean Foods Company
Huntley, IL 847-669-5123
Dean Foods Company/Country Fresh
Grand Rapids, MI 616-243-0173
Dean Foods/Land O'Lakes
Bismarck, ND 701-222-3131
Dean Foods/Verifine Dairy Products
Sheboygan, WI 800-236-6455
Dean Milk Company
Louisville, KY 800-451-3326
Deseret Dairy Products
Salt Lake City, UT 801-240-7350
Detroit City Dairy
Highland Park, MI 313-868-5511
Dillon Dairy Company
Denver, CO 303-388-1645
Eagle Family Foods
Columbus, OH 888-656-3245
Eggland's Best Foods
King of Prussia, PA. 888-922-3447
Elmwood Dairy
Newport, VT 802-334-8125
Everything Yogurt
Washington, DC 202-842-2990
F&A Dairy of California
Newman, CA. 800-554-6455
Fanny Mason Farmstead Cheese
Walpole, NH 603-756-3300
Farm Stores
Palmetto Bay, FL 800-726-3276
Farmdale Creamery
San Bernardino, CA 909-889-3002
Farmers Dairies
El Paso, TX. 915-772-2736
Farmland Dairies
Wallington, NJ 888-727-6252
Farmland Dairies
Wallington, NJ 973-777-2500
Foremost Dairies-Hawaii
Honolulu, HI. 808-841-5831
Foster Farms Dairy
Fresno, CA 800-241-0008
Fresh Farm
Arvada, CO 303-429-1536
GAF Seelig
Flushing, NY. 718-899-5000
Garelick Farms
Rensselaer, NY 518-283-0820
Garelick Farms
Lynn, MA 800-487-8700
Gold Star Dairy
Little Rock, AR. 501-565-6125
Goldenrod Dairy Foods/ U C Milk Company
Madisonville, KY............ 800-462-2354
Goshen Dairy Company
New Philadelphia, OH 330-339-1959
Guers Dairy
Pottsville, PA............... 570-277-6611
H. Meyer Dairy Company
Cincinnati, OH 800-347-6455

H.E. Butt Grocery Company
San Antonio, TX 800-432-3113
H.P. Hood
Agawam, MA 413-786-7166
H.P. Hood
Lynnfield, ME. 800-343-6592
H.P. Hood
Barre, VT 800-622-4468
Harrisburg Dairies
Harrisburg, PA 800-692-7429
Hastings Cooperative Creamery
Hastings, MN 651-437-9414
Heritage Dairy Stores
West Deptford, NJ. 856-845-2855
Heritage Farms Dairy
Murfreesboro, TN 615-895-2790
Heritage Foods
Santa Ana, CA 714-775-5000
Herkimer Foods
Herkimer, NY 315-895-7832
High's Dairies
Jessup, MD 301-776-7727
Highland Dairies
Wichita, KS 800-336-0765
Hiland Dairy
Wichita, KS 800-336-0765
Hillside Dairy
Stanley, WI 715-644-2275
Homestead Dairies
Massena, NY 315-769-2456
Horstmann Mix & Cream
Long Island City, NY 718-932-4735
Houlton Farms Dairy
Houlton, ME. 207-532-3170
Humboldt Creamery Association
Fortuna, CA 707-725-6182
Humphreys Dairy
Hot Springs National Par, AR 501-262-1820
Hygeia Dairy Company
Corpus Christi, TX 361-854-4561
Ideal American
Holland, IN 812-424-3351
Independent Dairy
Monroe, MI 734-241-6016
Inland Northwest Dairies
Spokane, WA. 509-489-8600
Inverness Dairy
Cheboygan, MI 231-627-4655
Jackson Milk & Ice CreamCompany
Hutchinson, KS 620-663-1244
Juniper Valley Farms
Jamaica, NY 718-291-3333
Kalamazoo Creamery
Kalamazoo, MI 616-343-2558
KDK Inc
Draper, UT 801-571-3506
Kemps
Cedarburg, WI. 262-377-5040
Kemps
St Paul, MN. 800-322-9566
Kleinpeter Farms Dairy
Baton Rouge, LA 225-753-2121
Lakeview Farms
Delphos, OH 800-755-9925
Land O'Lakes
St Paul, MN. 651-730-2100
Land O'Lakes
St Paul, MN. 800-328-9680
Land O'Lakes Procurement
Sioux Falls, SD 605-330-9526
Land O'Lakes, Inc
Arden Hills, MN 800-328-9680
Land-O-Sun Dairies
O Fallon, IL. 618-632-6381
LeHigh Valley Dairies
Lansdale, PA 215-855-8205
Level Valley Creamery
Antioch, TN 800-251-1292
Liberty Dairy
Evart, MI 800-632-5552
Longacres Modern Dairy
Barto, PA. 610-845-7551
Losurdo Foods
Hackensack, NJ. 888-567-8736
Lowell-Paul Dairy
Greeley, CO. 970-353-0278
Lubbers Dairy
Pella, IA .515-628-4284
Ludwig Dairy
Dixon, IL. 815-284-7791
Magic Valley Quality Milk Producers
Jerome, ID. 208-324-7519

Mallorie's Dairy
Silverton, OR 503-873-5346
Maola Milk & Ice Cream Company
Summerville, SC. 803-871-6311
Maple Hill Farms
Bloomfield, CT. 800-842-7304
Marburger Farm Dairy
Evans City, PA 800-331-1295
Maryland & Virginia Milk Cooperative Association
Laurel, MD 301-953-2964
Maryland & Virginia Milk Producers Cooperative
Reston, VA 703-742-7443
Matanuska Maid Dairy
Anchorage, AK 907-561-5223
McArthur Dairy
Fort Myers, FL 239-334-1114
McArthur Dairy
Miami, FL. 305-576-2880
McArthur Dairy
Miami, FL. 877-803-6565
McColls Dairy Products
Sacramento, CA 916-444-7200
McDonald Dairy
Alpena, MI 800-572-5390
McDonald Dairy Company
Flint, MI .810-232-9193
Meadow Brook Dairy
Erie, PA. 800-352-4010
Meadow Brook Farms
Pottstown, PA 610-323-3700
Meadow Gold Dairies
Orem, UT 801-225-3660
Meadow Gold Dairies
Salt Lake City, UT 801-908-7531
Meadow Gold Dairies
Honolulu, HI 808-949-6161
Meadowbrook Farm
Bronx, NY. 718-828-6400
Mentone Egg Products
Mentone, IN 219-353-7691
MEYENBERG Goat Milk Products
Turlock, CA 800-891-4628
Meyer Brothers Dairy
Maple Plain, MN 952-473-7343
Michigan Milk Producers Association
Ovid, MI .989-834-2221
Mid States Dairy
Hazelwood, MO 314-731-1150
Mid-States Dairy Company
St Louis, MO. 314-994-9900
Mid-Valley Dairy
Fairfield, CA. 707-864-0502
Midstates Dairy
Hazelwood, MO 314-731-1150
Minerva Dairy
Minerva, OH 330-868-4196
Mitchel Dairies
Bronx, NY. 718-324-6261
Monument Dairy Farms
Weybridge, VT 802-545-2119
Monument Farms
Middlebury, VT. 802-545-2119
Morning Star Foods
Tempe, AZ 480-966-0080
Morning Star Foods
East Brunswick, NJ. 800-237-5320
Morningstar Foods
Richland Center, WI. 608-647-6360
Mountainside Farms Dairy
Roxbury, NY. 607-326-4161
Muller-Pinehurst Dairy C
Rockford, IL. 815-968-0441
Munroe Dairy
East Providence, RI 401-438-4450
Murdock Farm Dairy
Winchendon, MA 978-297-0143
Mystic Lake Dairy
Sammamish, WA. 425-868-2029
Natural By Nature
West Grove, PA. 610-268-6962
Nature's Dairy
Roswell, NM 575-623-9640
Newburgh Egg Processing
Woodridge, NY. 888-434-8115
Niagara Milk Cooperative
Niagara Falls, NY 716-692-6543
Norco Ranch
Norco, CA. 951-737-6735
North Branch Dairy
North Branch, MN 651-674-4414
Northumberland Cooperative
Miramichi, NB 800-332-3328

Norwalk Dairy
Santa Fe Springs, CA 562-921-5712
Oak Farm's Dairy
Waco, TX 254-756-5421
Oak Grove Dairy
Saint Paul, MN. 952-467-2212
Oberweis Dairy
North Aurora, IL. 888-645-5868
Organic Cow
Boulder, CO 800-769-9693
Peeler's Jersey Farms
Gaffney, SC. 864-487-9996
Perham Cooperative Cream
Savannah, GA 800-551-0777
Pet Milk
Florence, SC 800-735-3066
Pierz Cooperative Association
Pierz, MN 320-468-6655
Pine State Creamery Company
Raleigh, NC 919-828-7401
Pioneer Dairy
Southwick, MA. 413-569-6132
Plains Dairy Products
Amarillo, TX. 800-365-5608
Polly-O Dairy Products
Mineola, NY 516-741-8000
Potomac Farms
Cumberland, MD 301-722-4410
Potter Siding Creamery Company
Tripoli, IA 319-882-4444
Praire Farms Dairy
Anderson, IN 765-649-1261
Prairie Farms Dairy
Granite City, IL 618-451-5600
Primer Foods Corporation
Cameron, WI. 715-458-4075
Producers Dairy Company
Clarksburg, WV 304-623-1831
Producers Dairy Foods
Fresno, CA 559-264-6583
Purity Dairies
Nashville, TN 615-244-1900
Quality Chekd Dairies
Naperville, IL 630-717-1110
Quality Dairy Company
East Lansing, MI. 517-319-4114
Queensboro Farm Products
Jamaica, NY 718-658-5000
R.D. Hemond Farms
Minot, ME. 207-345-5611
Radway's Dairy
New Britain, CT 800-472-3929
Readington Farms
Whitehouse, NJ. 908-534-2121
Reilly Dairy & Food Company
Tampa, FL 813-839-8458
Reiter Dairy
Akron, OH. 800-362-0825
Reiter Dairy
Springfield, OH. 937-323-5777
Richardson's Ice Cream
Middleton, MA 978-774-5450
Richfood Dairy
Richmond, VA. 804-746-6206
Riser Foods
Cleveland, OH 216-292-7000
Ritchey's Dairy
Martinsburg, PA 800-296-2157
Roberts Dairy
Kansas City, MO. 800-279-1692
Roberts Dairy Company
Omaha, NE 402-344-4321
Robinson Dairy
Denver, CO. 800-332-6355
Rockview Farms
Downey, CA 800- 42- 247
Ronnybrook Farm Dairy
Ancramdale, NY. 800-772-6455
Rosebud Creamery
Plattsburgh, NY 518-561-5160
Royal Crest Dairy Company
Denver, CO. 303-777-3055
Rutter Brothers Dairy
York, PA. 800-840-1664
Ryan Milk
Murray, KY 270-753-3012
S.B. Winsor Dairy
Johnston, RI 401-231-7832
S.T. Jerrell Company
Bessemer, AL 205-426-8930
Safeway Milk Plant
Tempe, AZ 480-894-4391

Saint Albans CooperativeCreamy
Saint Albans, VT 800-559-0343
San Joaquin Valley Dairymen
Los Banos, CA 209-826-4901
Sandusky Cooperative Milk Producers Association
Castalia, OH 419-684-5812
Sani Dairy
Johnstown, PA 814-533-2500
Sani-Dairy
Johnstown, PA 412-568-6410
Saputo
Montreal, QC 514-328-6662
Schneider's Dairy Holdings Inc
Pittsburgh, PA 412-881-3525
Schreiber Foods   Plant
Gainesville, GA 770-534-2239
Seger Egg Corporation
Farina, IL 618-245-3301
Shenandoah's Pride
Springfield, VA 703-321-9500
Skinners' Dairy
Ponte Vedra Beach, FL 904-733-5440
Snow Dairy
Springville, UT 801-489-6081
Southeast Dairy Processors
Tampa, FL 813-621-3233
Southern Bell Dairy
Somerset, KY 800-468-4798
Spring Hill Farm Dairy
Haverhill, MA 978-373-3481
Stop & Shop Manufacturing
Readville, MA 617-361-8400
Sunshine Dairy
Middletown, CT 860-346-6644
Sunshine Dairy Foods
Portland, OR 503-234-7526
Superbrand Dairies
Miami, FL 305-685-8079
Superstore Industries
Fairfield, CA 707-864-0502
Swiss Dairy
Riverside, CA 951-898-9427
Swiss Valley Farms Company
Cedar Rapids, IA 319-364-8153
Swiss Valley Farms Company
Davenport, IA 563-468-6600
Tamarack Farms Dairy
Newark, OH 866-221-4141
Tanglewood Farms
Warsaw, VA 804-394-4505
Taylor All Star Dairy Foods
Ambridge, PA 724-266-2370
Thomas Dairy
Rutland, VT 802-773-6788
Toft Dairy
Sandusky, OH 800-521-4606
Tom Davis & Sons Dairy Company
Oak Park, MI 800-399-6970
Turner Dairies
Jackson, TN 731-427-6012
Turner Dairies
Covington, TN 901-476-2643
Turner Dairy Farms
Penn Hills, PA 800-892-1039
Tuscan Dairy Farms
Dallas, TX 800-526-4416
Tuscan/Lehigh Valley Dais
Lansdale, PA 800-937-3233
Umpqua Dairy Products Company
Roseburg, OR 541-672-2638
Union Dairy Fountain
Freeport, IL 815-233-2233
United Dairy
Uniontown, PA 800-966-6455
United Dairy Farmers
Cincinnati, OH 513-396-8700
United Dairymen of Arizona
Tempe, AZ 480-966-7211
United Valley Bell Dairy
Charleston, WV 304-344-2511
Upstate Farms Cooperative
Rochester, NY 585-458-1880
Valley Milk Products
Strasburg, VA 540-465-5113
Van Peenans Dairy
Wayne, NJ 973-694-2551
Velvet Freeze Ice Cream
St Louis, MO 800-589-5000
Vitamilk Dairy
Bellingham, WA 206-529-4128
W.J. Stearns & Sons/Mountain Dairy
Storrs Mansfield, CT 860-423-9289

Wallaby Yogurt Company
American Canyon, CA 707-553-1233
Wawa Food Market
Media, PA 800-444-9292
Webco Foods
Miami, FL 305-633-0100
Welsh Farms
Newark, NJ 973-642-3000
Wengert's Dairy
Lebanon, PA 800-222-2129
Wessanan
Minneapolis, MN 612-331-3775
WestFarm Foods
Seattle, WA 206-286-6832
WestFarm Foods
Boise, ID 208-375-3062
WestFarm Foods
Seattle, WA 509-837-8000
Whitney Foods
Jamaica, NY 718-291-3333
Winchester Farms Dairy
Winchester, KY 859-745-5500
Wurth Dairy
Caseyville, IL 217-271-7580
Yoo-Hoo Chocolate Beverage Company
Port Chester, NY 800-966-4669
Young's Jersey Dairy
Yellow Springs, OH 937-325-0629

Goat

Abunda Life Laboratories
Asbury Park, NJ 732-775-4141
C.F. Burger Creamery
Detroit, MI 800-229-2322
Coach Dairy Goat Farm
Pine Plains, NY 800-999-4628
Cypress Grove Chevre
Arcata, CA 707-825-1100
MEYENBERG Goat Milk Products
Turlock, CA 800-891-4628
Oak Knoll Dairy
Windsor, VT 802-674-5426
Sunshine Farms
Portage, WI 608-742-2016
Woolwich Dairy
Orangeville, ON 877-438-3499

Half & Half

Atlanta Flagship Dairy
Atlanta, GA 800-224-0669
Broughton Foods
Marietta, OH 800-283-2479
Cass Clay Creamery
Fargo, ND 701-293-6455
Chase Brothers Dairy
Oxnard, CA 800-438-6455
Cropp Cooperative-Organic Valley
La Farge, WI 888-444-6455
Inland Northwest Dairies
Spokane, WA 509-489-8600
Instantwhip: Arizona
Phoenix, AZ 800-544-9447
Kemps
Cedarburg, WI 262-377-5040
Land O'Lakes
St Paul, MN 651-730-2100
Oak Knoll Dairy
Windsor, VT 802-674-5426
Prairie Farms Dairy Inc
Carlinville, IL 217-854-2547
Roberts Dairy Company
Omaha, NE 402-344-4321
Safeway Milk Plant
Tempe, AZ 480-894-4391
Tiller Foods Company
Dayton, OH 937-435-4601
Yoder Dairies
Chesapeake, VA 757-497-3518

Lactose-Free

Cropp Cooperative-Organic Valley
La Farge, WI 888-444-6455

Low-Fat

Anderson Erickson Dairy
Des Moines, IA 515-265-2521
Berkeley Farms
Hayward, CA 510-265-8600
Chase Brothers Dairy
Oxnard, CA 800-438-6455

Cloverland Green Spring Dairy
Baltimore, MD 800-876-6455
Coburg Dairy
North Charleston, SC 843-554-4870
Country Fresh Farms
Salt Lake City, UT 800-878-0099
Cream O'Weaver Dairy
Salt Lake City, UT 801-973-9922
Dairy Maid Dairy
Frederick, MD 301-663-5114
Darigold
Seattle, WA 800-333-6455
Dean Foods Company
Huntley, IL 847-669-5123
Dean Foods/Verifine Dairy Products
Sheboygan, WI 800-236-6455
Humboldt Creamery Association
Fortuna, CA 707-725-6182
Ideal American
Holland, IN 812-424-3351
KDK Inc
Draper, UT 801-571-3506
Level Valley Creamery
Antioch, TN 800-251-1292
Marva Maid Dairy
Newport News, VA 800-544-4439
McArthur Dairy
Miami, FL 305-576-2880
Meadow Brook Dairy
Erie, PA 800-352-4010
Mid States Dairy
Hazelwood, MO 314-731-1150
Pleasant View Dairy
Highland, IN 219-838-0155
Reiter Dairy
Springfield, OH 937-323-5777
Safeway Milk Plant
Tempe, AZ 480-894-4391
San Joaquin Valley Dairymen
Los Banos, CA 209-826-4901
Schneider Valley Farms Dairy
Williamsport, PA 570-326-2021
Schneider's Dairy Holdings Inc
Pittsburgh, PA 412-881-3525
Swiss Dairy
Riverside, CA 951-898-9427
T.G. Lee Dairy
Orlando, FL 407-894-4941
Turner Dairies
Covington, TN 901-476-2643
Tuscan/Lehigh Valley Dais
Lansdale, PA 800-937-3233
Wengert's Dairy
Lebanon, PA 800-222-2129
Winchester Farms Dairy
Winchester, KY 859-745-5500
Yoder Dairies
Chesapeake, VA 757-497-3518

Reduced-Fat

Berkeley Farms
Hayward, CA 510-265-8600
Coburg Dairy
North Charleston, SC 843-554-4870
Cream O'Weaver Dairy
Salt Lake City, UT 801-973-9922
Dairy Maid Dairy
Frederick, MD 301-663-5114
Darigold
Seattle, WA 800-333-6455
Dean Foods Company
Huntley, IL 847-669-5123
Dean Foods/Verifine Dairy Products
Sheboygan, WI 800-236-6455
Humboldt Creamery Association
Fortuna, CA 707-725-6182
Ideal American
Holland, IN 812-424-3351
KDK Inc
Draper, UT 801-571-3506
Marva Maid Dairy
Newport News, VA 800-544-4439
McArthur Dairy
Miami, FL 305-576-2880
Meadow Brook Dairy
Erie, PA 800-352-4010
Mid States Dairy
Hazelwood, MO 314-731-1150
Norwalk Dairy
Santa Fe Springs, CA 562-921-5712
Pleasant View Dairy
Highland, IN 219-838-0155

Reiter Dairy
Springfield, OH. 937-323-5777
Safeway Milk Plant
Tempe, AZ 480-894-4391
San Joaquin Valley Dairymen
Los Banos, CA 209-826-4901
Schneider Valley Farms Dairy
Williamsport, PA. 570-326-2021
Schneider's Dairy Holdings Inc
Pittsburgh, PA. 412-881-3525
Swiss Dairy
Riverside, CA 951-898-9427
Tuscan/Lehigh Valley Dais
Lansdale, PA. 800-937-3233
Wengert's Dairy
Lebanon, PA .800-222-2129
Winchester Farms Dairy
Winchester, KY. 859-745-5500
Yoder Dairies
Chesapeake, VA 757-497-3518

Skim

Agri-Mark
Lawrence, MA 978-687-4936
Berkeley Farms
Hayward, CA .510-265-8600
Chase Brothers Dairy
Oxnard, CA. .800-438-6455
Cloverland Green Spring Dairy
Baltimore, MD 800-876-6455
Coburg Dairy
North Charleston, SC 843-554-4870
Country Fresh Farms
Salt Lake City, UT 800-878-0099
Cream O'Weaver Dairy
Salt Lake City, UT 801-973-9922
Cropp Cooperative-Organic Valley
La Farge, WI .888-444-6455
Crowley Foods
Binghamton, NY. 800-637-0019
Cumberland Dairy
Rosenhayn, NJ 856-451-1300
Dairy Farmers of America
Sulphur Springs, TX. 903-885-6518
Dairy Maid Dairy
Frederick, MD. 301-663-5114
IMAC
Oklahoma City, OK 888-878-7827
KDK Inc
Draper, UT 801-571-3506
Marva Maid Dairy
Newport News, VA 800-544-4439
McArthur Dairy
Miami, FL. 305-576-2880
Meadow Brook Dairy
Erie, PA. 800-352-4010
Mid States Dairy
Hazelwood, MO 314-731-1150
Pleasant View Dairy
Highland, IN .219-838-0155
Reiter Dairy
Springfield, OH. 937-323-5777
Safeway Milk Plant
Tempe, AZ 480-894-4391
Saint Albans CooperativeCreamy
Saint Albans, VT. 800-559-0343
San Joaquin Valley Dairymen
Los Banos, CA 209-826-4901
Schneider Valley Farms Dairy
Williamsport, PA. 570-326-2021
Schneider's Dairy Holdings Inc
Pittsburgh, PA. 412-881-3525
Stewart's Ice Cream
Saratoga Springs, NY 518-581-1000
Vermont Family Farms Milk
Saint Albans, VT. 800-559-0343
Wengert's Dairy
Lebanon, PA .800-222-2129
White Wave Foods
Jacksonville, FL 800-874-6765
Winchester Farms Dairy
Winchester, KY. 859-745-5500
Yoder Dairies
Chesapeake, VA 757-497-3518

Strawberry

Berkeley Farms
Hayward, CA .510-265-8600
Hygeia Dairy Company
Corpus Christi, TX 361-854-4561

Tuscan/Lehigh Valley Dais
Lansdale, PA. 800-937-3233

Sweetened

All American Foods, Inc.
Mankato, MN 800-833-2661
Gateway Food Products Company
Dupo, IL 877-220-1963
Level Valley Creamery
Antioch, TN .800-251-1292
Master Taste International
Plant City, FL 800-237-7629
Vermont Family Farms Milk
Saint Albans, VT. 800-559-0343

Sweetened & Condensed

Arnhem Group
Cranford, NJ .800-851-1052
Suprema Specialties
Manteca, CA. 209-858-9696

Whole

Barkers Farm Dairy
Pecks Mill, WV. 304-855-4512
Berkeley Farms
Hayward, CA .510-265-8600
Cloverland Green Spring Dairy
Baltimore, MD 800-876-6455
Coburg Dairy
North Charleston, SC 843-554-4870
Cream O'Weaver Dairy
Salt Lake City, UT 801-973-9922
Cropp Cooperative-Organic Valley
La Farge, WI .888-444-6455
Crowley Foods
Binghamton, NY. 800-637-0019
Cumberland Dairy
Rosenhayn, NJ 856-451-1300
Dairy Farmers of America
Sulphur Springs, TX. 903-885-6518
DairyAmerica
Fresno, CA 800-722-3110
Dairyman's/Land O' Lakes
Tulare, CA. 559-687-8287
Darigold
Seattle, WA 800-333-6455
Dean Foods Company
Huntley, IL 847-669-5123
KDK Inc
Draper, UT 801-571-3506
Level Valley Creamery
Antioch, TN .800-251-1292
Marva Maid Dairy
Newport News, VA 800-544-4439
McArthur Dairy
Miami, FL. 305-576-2880
Meadow Brook Dairy
Erie, PA. 800-352-4010
Plainview Milk Products Cooperative
Plainview, MN 507-534-3872
Pleasant View Dairy
Highland, IN .219-838-0155
Reilly Dairy & Food Company
Tampa, FL. 813-839-8458
Reiter Dairy
Springfield, OH. 937-323-5777
Safeway Milk Plant
Tempe, AZ 480-894-4391
Saint Albans CooperativeCreamy
Saint Albans, VT. 800-559-0343
San Joaquin Valley Dairymen
Los Banos, CA 209-826-4901
Schneider Valley Farms Dairy
Williamsport, PA. 570-326-2021
Schneider's Dairy Holdings Inc
Pittsburgh, PA. 412-881-3525
Stewart's Ice Cream
Saratoga Springs, NY 518-581-1000
T.G. Lee Dairy
Orlando, FL. .407-894-4941
Tuscan/Lehigh Valley Dais
Lansdale, PA. 800-937-3233
Unified Western Grocers
Los Angeles, CA. 323-731-8223
Upstate Farms Cooperative
Buffalo, NY. .866-874-6455
Winchester Farms Dairy
Winchester, KY. 859-745-5500
Yoder Dairies
Chesapeake, VA 757-497-3518

Milk Products

Milk & Milk Fat: Enzyme

Brown's Dairy
New Orleans, LA 504-529-2221
Country Delite
Nashville, TN 615-320-1440
Country Fresh
Livonia, MI. .800-968-7980
Darigold
Seattle, WA. .800-333-6455
Farmers Cooperative Dairy
Halifax, NS 902-835-3373
Garden Spot Distributors
New Holland, PA 800-829-5100
Idaho Milk Products
Jerome, ID. 208-644-2882
Maple Island
St Paul, MN. .800-369-1022
Wilcox Farm
Roy, WA 360-458-7774
Winn-Dixie Dairies
Hammond, LA 985-549-6870

Milk Proteins

Arla Foods Ingredients
Basking Ridge, NJ 800-243-3730
Austrade Food Ingredients
Palm Beach Gdns, FL. 561-586-7145
Clofine Dairy & Food Products
Linwood, NJ .800-441-1001
Erie Foods International
Erie, IL 800-447-1887
Kantner Group
Wapakoneta, OH. 419-738-4060
Luxembourg Cheese Factory
Orangeville, IL 815-789-4227
Main Street Ingredients
La Crosse, WI 800-359-2345
NZMP
Santa Rosa, CA 800-358-9096

Modified - Dry Blends

Kantner Group
Wapakoneta, OH. 419-738-4060

Milk Solids

Non-Fat

California Dairies
Fresno, CA 559-233-5154
Kantner Group
Wapakoneta, OH. 419-738-4060
Main Street Ingredients
La Crosse, WI 800-359-2345
Ramsen
Lakeville, MN. 952-431-0400

Replacers

Kantner Group
Wapakoneta, OH. 419-738-4060

Whole

Kantner Group
Wapakoneta, OH. 419-738-4060
MEYENBERG Goat Milk Products
Turlock, CA .800-891-4628
Preferred Milks
Addison, IL. .800-621-5046

Pudding

AFP Advanced Food Products, LLC
Visalia, CA 559-627-2070
Amboy Specialty Foods Company
Dixon, IL. 800-892-0400
Associated Milk Producers
Dawson, MN 320-769-2994
Associated Milk Producers
New Ulm, MN. 507-233-4600
Associated Milk Producers
New Ulm, MN. 800-533-3580
Chloe Foods Corporation
Brooklyn, NY 718-827-3600
ConAgra Grocery Products
Perrysburg, OH. 419-661-4400
ConAgra Grocery Products
Irvine, CA 714-680-1000

Dean Distributors
Burlingame, CA 800-792-0816
Dean Foods Company
Rosemont, IL. .800-323-1571
Del Monte Foods
San Francisco, CA 800-543-3090
Dufflet Pastries
Toronto, ON .416-536-1330
Echo Farms Puddings
Hinsdale, NH 866-488-3246
Furst-McNess Company/Terrapin Ridge
Freeport, IL 800-999-4052
Gehl Guernsey Farms
Germantown, WI. 800-434-5713
Good Old Days Foods
Little Rock, AR 501-565-1257
Gourmet Baker
Burnaby, BC .800-663-1972
GPI USA LLC.
Athens, GA. .706-850-7826
Grainaissance
Emeryville, CA. 800-472-4697
Hoffman Aseptic Packaging Company
Hoffman, MN 320-986-2084
Hormel Foods Corporation
Austin, MN .800-523-4635
Inter-American Products
Cincinnati, OH 800-645-2233
Kosto Food Products Company
Wauconda, IL 847-487-2600
Kozy Shack
Hicksville, NY 516-870-3000
Kraft
Parsippany, NJ. 973-292-1755
Kraft Canada Headquarters
Don Mills, ON 800-268-7808
Michigan Dessert Corporation
Oak Park, MI. 800-328-8632
NOH Foods of Hawaii
Gardena, CA 310-324-6770
Reser's Fine Foods
Salt Lake City, UT 801-972-5633
Serv-Agen Corporation
Cherry Hill, NJ 856-663-6966
Spring Glen Fresh Foods
Ephrata, PA. 800-641-2853
Van Bennett Food Company
Reading, PA 800-423-8897

Chocolate

Associated Milk Producers
Dawson, MN. 320-769-2994
Associated Milk Producers
New Ulm, MN. 507-233-4600
Knouse Foods
Peach Glen, PA 717-677-8181
Kozy Shack
Hicksville, NY 516-870-3000

Plum

Patti's Plum Puddings
Lawndale, CA. 310-376-1463

Rice

Knouse Foods
Peach Glen, PA 717-677-8181
Kozy Shack
Hicksville, NY 516-870-3000
Penn Maid Crowley Foods
Philadelphia, PA 800-247-6269
Van Bennett Food Company
Reading, PA 800-423-8897

Tapioca

Associated Milk Producers
Dawson, MN. 320-769-2994
Associated Milk Producers
New Ulm, MN. 507-233-4600
Dean Distributors
Burlingame, CA 800-792-0816
Knouse Foods
Peach Glen, PA 717-677-8181
Kozy Shack
Hicksville, NY 516-870-3000
Van Bennett Food Company
Reading, PA 800-423-8897

Vanilla

Associated Milk Producers
Dawson, MN. 320-769-2994
Associated Milk Producers
New Ulm, MN. 507-233-4600
Knouse Foods
Peach Glen, PA 717-677-8181
Kozy Shack
Hicksville, NY 516-870-3000

Sour Cream

Aimonetto and Sons
Seattle, WA .866-823-2777
Alberto-Culver Company
Melrose Park, IL. 708-450-3000
Alta Dena Certified Dairy
City of Industry, CA 800-535-1369
Anderson Erickson Dairy
Des Moines, IA 515-265-2521
Astro Dairy Products
Etobicoke, ON. 416-622-2811
Auburn Dairy Products
Auburn, WA 800-950-9264
Berkeley Farms
Hayward, CA 510-265-8600
Byrne Dairy
Syracuse, NY 800-899-1535
Campbell Soup Company
Camden, NJ. 800-257-8443
Cascade Fresh
Seattle, WA .800-511-0057
Clofine Dairy & Food Products
Linwood, NJ 800-441-1001
Cloverland Green Spring Dairy
Baltimore, MD 410-235-4477
Cloverland Green Spring Dairy
Baltimore, MD 800-876-6455
Coburg Dairy
North Charleston, SC 843-554-4870
ConAgra Grocery Products
Irvine, CA. .714-680-1000
Country Fresh
Grand Rapids, MI 800-748-0480
Creamland Dairies
Albuquerque, NM 505-247-0721
Cropp Cooperative-Organic Valley
La Farge, WI. 888-444-6455
Crowley Foods
La Fargeville, NY 800-247-6269
Crowley Foods
Binghamton, NY 800-637-0019
Dairy Fresh Corporation
Greensboro, AL. 800-239-5114
Dairy Maid Dairy
Frederick, MD. 301-663-5114
Daisy Brand
Dallas, TX. .877-292-9830
Dean Foods Company
Dallas, TX. .214-303-3400
Dean Foods Company/Country Fresh
Grand Rapids, MI 616-243-0173
Elgin Dairy Foods
Chicago, IL .800-786-9900
Fairmont Products
Belleville, PA 717-935-2121
Farmers Cooperative Dairy
Halifax, NS .902-835-3373
Friendship Dairies
Jericho, NY .516-719-4000
Golden Cheese of California
Corona, CA 800-842-0264
H.P. Hood
Vernon, NY 315-829-3004
H.P. Hood
Agawam, MA 413-786-7166
Hunter Farms
High Point, NC 800-446-8035
Inland Northwest Dairies
Spokane, WA. 509-489-8600
Instantwhip: Texas
San Antonio, TX 800-544-9447
Jackson Milk & Ice CreamCompany
Hutchinson, KS 620-663-1244
Kerry Ingredients
Tralee, Co. Kerry,
Knoll Creek Dairy
Harrison, NY 718-892-4500
Kraft Foods
Walton, NY 607-865-7131
Marcus Dairy
Danbury, CT 800-243-2511

Marquez Brothers International
Hanford, CA 559-584-0306
Marva Maid Dairy
Newport News, VA 800-544-4439
Mayfield Dairy Farms
Athens, TN 800-362-9546
Meadow Gold Dairies
Honolulu, HI 808-949-6161
Mid States Dairy
Hazelwood, MO 314-731-1150
Morning Glory/Formost Farms
Baraboo, WI 800-362-9196
Oakhurst Dairy
Portland, ME 207-772-7468
Old Home Foods
St Paul, MN. 800-628-8700
Pevely Dairy Company
St Louis, MO. 314-771-4400
Pleasant View Dairy
Highland, IN 219-838-0155
Prairie Farms Dairy
Carlinville, IL 217-854-2547
Prairie Farms Dairy
Granite City, IL 618-451-5600
Prairie Farms Dairy
Carbondale, IL 618-457-4167
Prairie Farms Dairy Inc
Carlinville, IL 217-854-2547
Purity Dairies
Nashville, TN 615-244-1900
Queensboro Farm Products
Canastota, NY 315-697-2235
Queensboro Farm Products
Jamaica, NY 718-658-5000
Reilly Dairy & Food Company
Tampa, FL .813-839-8458
Roberts Dairy Company
Omaha, NE 402-344-4321
Roberts Dairy Company
Kansas City, MO. 800-279-1692
Robinson Dairy
Denver, CO 800-332-6355
Rod's Food Products
City of Industry, CA 909-839-8925
Roos Foods
Kenton, DE 800-343-3642
Rosenberger's Dairies
Hatfield, PA. 800-355-9074
Saputo
Montreal, QC 514-328-6662
Schepps Dairy
Dallas, TX. 800-428-6455
Schneider Valley Farms Dairy
Williamsport, PA. 570-326-2021
Schreiber Foods   Plant
Shippensburg, PA 717-530-5000
Sinton Dairy Foods Company
Colorado Springs, CO. 800-388-4970
Sisler's Ice & Ice Cream
Ohio, IL. 888-891-3856
Springfield Creamery
Eugene, OR. 541-689-2911
Sterzing Food Company
Burlington, IA. 800-754-8467
Sunshine Farms Dairy
Elyria, OH. 440-322-6301
Tiller Foods Company
Dayton, OH. 937-435-4601
Tuscan Dairy Farms
Dallas, TX. 800-526-4416
Umpqua Dairy Products Company
Roseburg, OR. 541-672-2638
Upstate Farms Cooperative
Buffalo, NY. 716-892-3156
V&V Supremo Foods
Chicago, IL. 800-547-8773
Vitamilk Dairy
Bellingham, WA 206-529-4128
Wells' Dairy
Le Mars, IA. 800-942-3800
WestFarm Foods
Seattle, WA 800-333-6544
Westhill Dairy
North York, ON. 416-661-0580
Winder Dairy
West Valley, UT 800-946-3371

Yogurt

Agro Farma Inc
New Berlin, NY 877-847-6181
Aimonetto and Sons
Seattle, WA 866-823-2777

Alta Dena Certified Dairy
City of Industry, CA 800-535-1369
Anderson Erickson Dairy
Des Moines, IA 515-265-2521
Associated Milk Producers
New Ulm, MN. 800-533-3580
Astro Dairy Products
Etobicoke, ON. 416-622-2811
Atlanta Flagship Dairy
Atlanta, GA 800-224-0669
Auburn Dairy Products
Auburn, WA 800-950-9264
Ben & Jerry's Homemade
South Burlington, VT 802-846-1500
Berkeley Farms
Hayward, CA 510-265-8600
Broughton Foods
Marietta, OH 800-283-2479
Brown Cow Farm
Antioch, CA 888-429-5459
Browns Dairy
Valparaiso, IN 219-464-4141
Byrne Dairy
Syracuse, NY 800-899-1535
Cascade Fresh
Seattle, WA 800-511-0057
Cass Clay Creamery
Fargo, ND 701-293-6455
Cedar Crest Specialties
Cedarburg, WI. 800-877-8341
Clofine Dairy & Food Products
Linwood, NJ 800-441-1001
Cloverland Green Spring Dairy
Baltimore, MD 800-876-6455
Coach Dairy Goat Farm
Pine Plains, NY 800-999-4628
Continental Yogurt
Glendale, CA 818-240-7400
Country Fresh
Grand Rapids, MI 800-748-0480
Crowley Foods
Arkport, NY 800-637-0019
Dairy Maid Dairy
Frederick, MD. 301-663-5114
Dairyman's/Land O' Lakes
Tulare, CA. 559-687-8287
Dannon Company
Fort Worth, TX 800-211-6565
Dunkin Brands Inc.
Canton, MA 800-458-7731
Eskimo Pie Corporation
Ronkonkoma, NY 631-737-9700
Fage USA
Flushing, NY. 718-204-5323
Farmers Cooperative Dairy
Halifax, NS 902-835-3373
Farmland Dairies
Wallington, NJ 888-727-6252
Farmland Dairies
Wallington, NJ 973-777-2500
Fieldbrook Farms
Dunkirk, NY 800-333-0805
Friendship Dairies
Jericho, NY 516-719-4000
General Mills
Minneapolis, MN 800-248-7310
Glover's Ice Cream
Frankfort, IN 800-686-5163
GPI USA LLC.
Athens, GA 706-850-7826
Heritage Farms Dairy
Murfreesboro, TN. 615-895-2790
Hiland Dairy Foods Company
Springfield, MO 417-862-9311
Icelandic Milk and Skyr Corporation
New York, NY 212-966-6950
Imperial Foods
Long Island City, NY 718-784-3400
Innovative Food Solutions LLC
Columbus, OH 800-884-3314
J&J Snack Foods Corporation
Pennsauken, NJ 856-665-9533
Jackson Ice Cream Company
Denver, CO 303-534-2454
Jason & Son Specialty Foods
Rancho Cordova, CA 800-810-9093
Katie's Korner
Girard, OH 330-539-4140
Klinke Brothers Ice Cream Company
Memphis, TN 901-743-8250
Kraft Foods
Northfield, IL 800-323-0768

Land O'Lakes
St Paul, MN. 651-730-2100
Lifeway Foods Inc
Morton Grove, IL 847-967-1010
Lyo-San
Lachute, QC 450-562-8525
M-C Dairy Company
Etobicoke, ON 416-231-1491
Master Mix
Placentia, CA 714-524-1698
Meadow Gold Dairies
Honolulu, HI 808-949-6161
Michigan Dairy
Livonia, MI 734-367-5390
Mid States Dairy
Hazelwood, MO 314-731-1150
Mister Snacks
Amherst, NY 800-333-6393
Morningstar Foods
Dallas, TX 225-273-2803
Mountain High Yogurt
Englewood, CO 303-761-2210
Old Chatham Sheepherding
Old Chatham, NY 888-743-3760
Old Home Foods
St Paul, MN 800-628-8700
Parmalat Canada
Toronto, ON 800-563-1515
Pecoraro Dairy Products
Rome, NY 315-339-0101
Penn Maid Crowley Foods
Philadelphia, PA 800-247-6269
Pioneer Dairy
Southwick, MA 413-569-6132
Prairie Farms Dairy
Carlinville, IL 217-854-2547
Prairie Farms Dairy
Granite City, IL 618-451-5600
Prairie Farms Dairy Inc
Carlinville, IL 217-854-2547
Purity Dairies
Nashville, TN 615-244-1900
Quality Ingredients Corporation
Burnsville, MN 952-898-4002
Quality Jersey Products
Seaforth, ON 519-527-1272
Queensboro Farm Products
Jamaica, NY 718-658-5000
Reiter Dairy
Springfield, OH. 937-323-5777
Restaurant Systems International
Staten Island, NY 718-494-8888
Roberts Dairy Company
Omaha, NE 402-344-4321
Roberts Dairy Company
Kansas City, MO 800-279-1692
Robinson Dairy
Denver, CO 800-332-6355
Safeway Stores
Tempe, AZ 877-723-3929
Saputo
Montreal, QC 514-328-6662
Shade Foods
New Century, KS 800-225-6312
Sinton Dairy Foods Company
Colorado Springs, CO. 800-388-4970
Springfield Creamery
Eugene, OR. 541-689-2911
Stonyfield Farm
Londonderry, NH 603-437-4040
Superstore Industries
Fairfield, CA. 707-864-0502
Toft Dairy
Sandusky, OH 800-521-4606
Tropical Illusions
Trenton, MO 660-359-6849
Ultima Foods
Longueuil, ON 800-363-9496
WestFarm Foods
Seattle, WA 800-333-6544
Westhill Dairy
North York, ON. 416-661-0580
White Wave
Broomfield, CO 800-488-9283
Yofarm Company
Naugatuck, CT 203-720-0000
Yoplait USA
Minneapolis, MN 800-967-5248
Yoplait-Colombo
Minneapolis, MN 763-540-2311

Bases, Flavors, Stabilizers

California Custom Fruits & Flavors
Irwindale, CA 877-558-0056
Cargill Texturizing Solutions
Cedar Rapids, IA. 877-650-7080
Idaho Milk Products
Jerome, ID 208-644-2882

Frozen

Americana Foods
Dallas, TX 972-709-7100
Blake's Creamery
Manchester, NH 603-623-7242
Brighams
Arlington, MA 800-274-4426
Browns Dairy
Valparaiso, IN 219-464-4141
Byrne Dairy
Syracuse, NY 800-899-1535
Cedar Crest Specialties
Cedarburg, WI. 800-877-8341
Crowley Foods
Arkport, NY 800-637-0019
Dave's Hawaiian Ice Cream
Pearl City, HI 808-453-0500
Edy's Grand Ice Cream
Fort Wayne, IN 260-483-3102
Edy's Grand Ice Cream
Rockaway, NJ 800-362-7899
Edy's Grand Ice Cream
Glendale Heights, IL 888-377-3397
Elgin Dairy Foods
Chicago, IL 800-786-9900
Eskimo Pie Corporation
Ronkonkoma, NY 631-737-9700
Fieldbrook Farms
Dunkirk, NY 800-333-0805
Foster Farms Dairy
Modesto, CA 209-576-3470
Friendly Ice Cream Corporation
Wilbraham, MA 800-966-9970
Glover's Ice Cream
Frankfort, IN 800-686-5163
Good Humor Breyers Ice Cream Company
Framingham, MA 508-620-4300
Hudsonville Creamery & Ice Cream
Holland, MI 616-928-0793
International Yogurt Company
Portland, OR 800-962-7326
J&J Snack Foods Corporation
Pennsauken, NJ 856-665-9533
Jack & Jill Ice Cream Company
Moorestown, NJ 856-813-2300
Jackson Ice Cream Company
Denver, CO 303-534-2454
Kemp Foods
York, PA 800-233-2007
Klinke Brothers Ice Cream Company
Memphis, TN 901-743-8250
Lafleur Dairy
New Orleans, LA 504-464-0812
MacKay's Cochrane Ice Cream
Cochrane, AB 403-932-2455
Mayfield Dairy Farms
Athens, TN 800-362-9546
Morningstar Foods
Dallas, TX 225-273-2803
O'Boyle's Ice Cream Company
Bristol, PA. 215-788-0421
Parmalat
Toronto, ON 416-626-1973
Perry's Ice Cream Company
Akron, NY. 800-873-7797
Petersen Ice Cream Company
Oak Park, IL 708-386-6130
Rainbow Valley Frozen Yogurt
White Lake, MI 800-979-8669
Reinhold Ice Cream Company
Pittsburgh, PA. 412-321-7600
Restaurant Systems International
Staten Island, NY 718-494-8888
Sargeant's Army Marketing
Bowmanville, ON. 905-623-2888
Stonyfield Farm
Londonderry, NH 603-437-4040
Toft Dairy
Sandusky, OH 800-521-4606
Turkey Hill Dairy
Conestoga, PA. 800-693-2479
Vitarich Ice Cream
Fortuna, CA 707-725-6182

Welsh Farms
Clifton, NJ 973-772-2388
Whitey's Ice Cream Manufacturing
Moline, IL 888-594-4839
YoCream International
Portland, OR 800-962-7326

Low-Fat

Alta Dena Certified Dairy
City of Industry, CA 800-535-1369
Auburn Dairy Products
Auburn, WA 800-950-9264
Bunker Hill Cheese Company
Millersburg, OH 800-253-6636
Cascade Fresh
Seattle, WA 800-511-0057
Continental Culture Specialists
Glendale, CA 818-240-7400
Crowley Foods
La Fargeville, NY 800-247-6269
Natren
Thousand Oaks, CA 800-992-3323
Perry's Ice Cream Company
Akron, NY 800-873-7797
Upstate Farms Cooperative
Buffalo, NY 716-892-3156
Vitarich Ice Cream
Fortuna, CA 707-725-6182
Yoplait-Colombo
Minneapolis, MN 763-540-2311

No-Fat

Agro Farma Inc
New Berlin, NY 877-847-6181
Cascade Fresh
Seattle, WA 800-511-0057
Cedar Crest Specialties
Cedarburg, WI. 800-877-8341
Continental Culture Specialists
Glendale, CA 818-240-7400
Gifford's Dairy
Skowhegan, ME 207-474-9821
O'Boyle's Ice Cream Company
Bristol, PA 215-788-0421
Perry's Ice Cream Company
Akron, NY 800-873-7797
Vitarich Ice Cream
Fortuna, CA 707-725-6182

with Fruit

Byrne Dairy
Syracuse, NY 800-899-1535
Petersen Ice Cream Company
Oak Park, IL 708-386-6130
Stonyfield Farm
Londonderry, NH 603-437-4040
Yoplait USA
Minneapolis, MN 800-967-5248
Yoplait-Colombo
Minneapolis, MN 763-540-2311

Doughs, Mixes & Fillings

Batters

Breading

ADM Food Ingredients
Olathe, KS........................800-255-6637
Blend Pak
Bloomfield, KY 502-252-8000
Chef Merito
Encino, CA......................800-637-4861
Concord Foods
Brockton, MA....................508-580-1700
Dorothy Dawson Foods Products
Jackson, MI.....................517-788-9830
Drum Rock Specialty Company
Warwick, RI 401-737-5165
Fry Krisp Food Products
Jackson, MI.....................517-784-8531
Griffith Laboratories
Scarborough, ON 416-288-3050
Griffith Laboratories Worldwide
Alsip, IL.......................800-346-4743
Hydroblend
Nampa, ID.......................208-467-7441
McCormick & Company Inc
Sparks, MD......................410-771-7301
Mojave Foods Corporation
Commerce, CA....................323-890-8900
Newly Weds Foods
Decatur, AL.....................800-521-6189
Old Mansion Foods
Petersburg, VA..................800-476-1877
Premier Blending
Wichita, KS.....................316-267-5533
Quality Naturally! Foods
City of Industry, CA............888-498-6986
Randag & Associates Inc
Elmhurst, IL....................630-530-2830
Reggie Ball's Cajun Foods
Lake Charles, LA................337-436-0291
Richmond Baking Company
Richmond, IN....................765-962-8535
Richmond Baking Company
Alma, GA........................912-632-7213
Shenandoah Mills
Lebanon, TN.....................615-444-0841
Specialty Products
Cleveland, OH 216-362-1050
Texas Crumb & Food Products
Farmers Branch, TX..............800-522-7862
Tova Industries
Louisville, KY 888-532-8682
UFL Foods
Mississauga, ON.................905-670-7776
Wilkins-Rogers
Ellicott City, MD...............410-465-5800
World Flavors
Warminster, PA..................215-672-4400
Yorktown Baking Company
Yorktown Heights, NY............800-235-3961

Cake

Frozen

BakeMark
Schaumburg, IL..................562-949-1054

Cookie

BakeMark
Schaumburg, IL..................562-949-1054
La Francaise Bakery
Northlake, IL...................800-654-7220

Muffin

Bagelworks
New York, NY 212-744-6444
Bake'n Joy Foods
Oviedo, FL......................800-666-4937
BakeMark
Schaumburg, IL..................562-949-1054
Coby's Cookies
North York, ON..................416-633-1567
Dough Delight
Concord, ON.....................800-465-5515

France Croissant
New York, NY 212-888-1210

Pancake

Dry

Hansmann's Mills
Bainbridge, NY..................607-967-5080

Breading

Abbitt's
Williamston, NC.................252-792-3646
ADM Food Ingredients
Olathe, KS......................800-255-6637
Andy's Seasoning
St Louis, MO....................800-305-3004
Atkinson Milling Company
Selma, NC.......................800-948-5707
Blend Pak
Bloomfield, KY 502-252-8000
Blendex Company
Jeffersontown, KY 800-626-6325
Care Ingredients
Melrose Park, IL................708-450-3260
Chef Hans Gourmet Foods
Monroe, LA......................800-890-4267
Colonna Brothers
North Bergen, NJ................201-864-1115
Dorothy Dawson Foods Products
Jackson, MI.....................517-788-9830
Drum Rock Specialty Company
Warwick, RI 401-737-5165
Drusilla Seafood Packing & Processing Company
Baton Rouge, LA 800-364-8844
Griffith Laboratories Worldwide
Alsip, IL.......................800-346-4743
House-Autry Mills
Four Oaks, NC 800-849-0802
Hydroblend
Nampa, ID.......................208-467-7441
Kellogg Company
Battle Creek, MI................800-962-1413
Kraft Canada Headquarters
Don Mills, ON 800-268-7808
Lakeside Mills
Rutherfordton, NC 828-286-4866
McClancy Seasoning Company
Fort Mill, SC...................800-843-1968
Newly Weds Foods
Chicago, IL.....................800-621-7521
Oak Grove Smokehouse
Prairieville, LA................225-673-6857
Old Mansion Foods
Petersburg, VA..................800-476-1877
Praters Foods
Lubbock, TX.....................806-745-2727
Premier Blending
Wichita, KS.....................316-267-5533
Quality Bakery Products
Fort Lauderdale, FL.............954-779-3663
Randag & Associates Inc
Elmhurst, IL....................630-530-2830
Richmond Baking Company
Richmond, IN....................765-962-8535
Roland Industries
Saint Louis, MO.................800-325-1183
Shenandoah Mills
Lebanon, TN.....................615-444-0841
Southeastern Mills
Rome, GA........................800-334-4468
Specialty Products
Cleveland, OH 216-362-1050
Taste Maker Foods
Memphis, TN.....................800-467-1407
Texas Crumb & Food Products
Farmers Branch, TX..............800-522-7862
Tova Industries
Louisville, KY 888-532-8682
Wilkins-Rogers
Ellicott City, MD...............410-465-5800
World Flavors
Warminster, PA..................215-672-4400

Doughs

Athens Baking Company
Fresno, CA......................559-485-3024
Bake'n Joy Foods
Oviedo, FL......................800-666-4937
Bridgford Foods
Anaheim, CA.....................800-527-2105
Carolina Foods
Charlotte, NC...................800-234-0441
Cohen's Bakery
Buffalo, NY.....................716-892-8149
Creme Curls Bakery
Hudsonville, MI 800-466-1219
Dimitria Delights
North Grafton, MA 800-763-1113
Dufour Pastry Kitchens
New York, NY....................212-929-2800
Entenmann's-Oroweat/BestFoods
S San Francisco, CA.............650-875-3100
Gonnella Frozen Products
Schaumburg, IL..................847-884-8829
Interstate Brands
Biddeford, ME...................207-286-1200
Leon's Bakery
North Haven, CT.................800-223-6844
Northwestern Foods
St Paul, MN.....................800-236-4937
Orange Bakery
Irvine, CA......................949-863-1377
Pillsbury
McMinnville, OR 800-325-5439
Pillsbury Canada Limited
Markham, ON.....................800-745-4777
Ranaldi Bros Frozen Food Products Inc
Warwick, RI 401-738-3444
Rhodes International
Columbus, WI....................800-876-7333
Teeny Foods Corporation
Portland, OR 503-252-3006
TNT Crust
Green Bay, WI...................920-431-7240

Baking

Bridgford Foods
Anaheim, CA 800-527-2105
Clofine Dairy & Food Products
Linwood, NJ.....................800-441-1001
Creme Curls Bakery
Hudsonville, MI 800-466-1219
Dufour Pastry Kitchens
New York, NY 212-929-2800
Interstate Brands
Biddeford, ME...................207-286-1200
Mine & Mommy's Cookies
Merkel, TX......................915-928-5870
Northwestern Foods
St Paul, MN.....................800-236-4937

Frozen

Bakery Chef
Louisville, KY 800-594-0203
Best Brands Corporate Office
St Paul, MN.....................800-328-2068
Creme Curls Bakery
Hudsonville, MI 800-466-1219
Dufour Pastry Kitchens
New York, NY 212-929-2800
Interstate Brands
Biddeford, ME 207-286-1200

Bread

Baker Boy Bake Shop
Dickinson, ND 800-437-2008
Country Home Bakers
Atlanta, GA.....................800-241-6445
Lone Star Bakery
Round Rock, TX..................512-255-3629
Lora Brody Products
West Newton, MA.................617-928-1005
Pacific Ocean Produce
Santa Cruz, CA..................831-423-2654
Pyrenees French Bakery
Bakersfield, CA.................888-898-7159

Rhodes International
　Columbus, WI. 800-876-7333
Senape's Bakery
　Hazleton, PA 570-454-0839

Cookie

Austin Special Foods Company
　Austin, TX. .866-372-8663
Best Maid Cookie Company
　River Falls, WI 888-444-0322
CBC Foods Inc
　Little River, KS. 800-276-4770
Coby's Cookies
　North York, ON. 416-633-1567
David's Cookie
　Fairfield, NJ .973-808-8248
Fat Witch Bakery
　New York, NY 888-419-4824
Gladder's Gourmet Cookies
　Lockhart, TX. 888-398-4523
Lone Star Bakery
　Round Rock, TX. 512-255-3629
Michael's Cookies
　San Diego, CA 800-822-5384
Nestle
　Cleveland, OH 440-349-5757
Otis Spunkmeyer
　San Leandro, CA. 800-938-1900
Pacific Ocean Produce
　Santa Cruz, CA 831-423-2654
Touche Bakery
　London, ON .519-455-0044

Doughnuts

BakeMark Canada
　Laval, QC 800-361-4998
Baker Boy Bake Shop
　Dickinson, ND 800-437-2008
Country Home Bakers
　Atlanta, GA. .800-241-6445

Frozen

Annie's Frozen Yogurt
　Minneapolis, MN 800-969-9648
Austin Special Foods Company
　Austin, TX. .866-372-8663

Baker & Baker, Inc.
　Schaumburg, IL. 800-593-5777
Baker Boy Bake Shop
　Dickinson, ND 800-437-2008
Bakery Chef
　Louisville, KY 800-594-0203
Best Maid Cookie Company
　River Falls, WI 888-444-0322
Bridgford Foods
　Anaheim, CA 800-527-2105
Bridgford Foods Corporation
　Anaheim, CA 800-527-2105
Carolina Foods
　Charlotte, NC 800-234-0441
Chef Solutions
　North Haven, CT. 856-848-5314
City Baker
　Calgary, AB. .403-263-8578
Coby's Cookies
　North York, ON. 416-633-1567
Cookie Tree Bakeries
　Salt Lake City, UT. 800-998-0111
Country Home Bakers
　Atlanta, GA. .800-241-6445
Creme Curls Bakery
　Hudsonville, MI 800-466-1219
Dakota Brands International
　Jamestown, ND. 800-844-5073
De-Iorio's Frozen Dough
　Utica, NY 800-649-7612
Dimitria Delights
　North Grafton, MA 800-763-1113
Dough Delight
　Concord, ON. 800-465-5515
Dough-To-Go
　Santa Clara, CA 408-727-4094
Dufour Pastry Kitchens
　New York, NY 212-929-2800
English Bay Batter
　Dublin, OH .614-760-9921
Enterprises Pates et Croutes
　Boucherville, QC 450-655-7790
Famous Specialties Company
　Island Park, NY 877-273-6999
Flowers Bakery of Montgomery
　Montgomery, AL. 334-281-7030
France Croissant
　New York, NY 212-888-1210
Gonnella Frozen Products
　Schaumburg, IL. 847-884-8829
Guttenplan's Frozen Dough
　Middletown, NJ 888-422-4357
H.C. Brill Company
　Tucker, GA. .800-241-8526
Harlan Bakeries
　Avon, IN 317-272-3600
Interstate Brands
　Biddeford, ME 207-286-1200
La Cookie
　Houston, TX. 713-784-2722
La Francaise Bakery
　Northlake, IL. 800-654-7220
Leon's Bakery
　North Haven, CT. 800-223-6844
Lone Star Bakery
　Round Rock, TX. 512-255-3629
Main Street Custom Foods
　Cuyahoga Falls, OH 800-533-6246
Main Street Gourmet
　Cuyahoga Falls, OH 800-533-6246
Main Street Gourmet Fundraising
　Cuyahoga Falls, OH 800-533-6246
Main Street Muffins
　Cuyahoga Falls, OH 800-533-6246
Main Street's Cambritt Cookies
　Cuyahoga Falls, OH 800-533-6246
Mel-O-Cream Donuts International
　Springfield, IL. 217-483-7272
Michael's Cookies
　San Diego, CA 800-822-5384
Morrison Meat Pies
　West Valley, UT 801-977-0181
Nestle
　Cleveland, OH 440-349-5757
Orange Bakery
　Huntersville, NC 704-875-3003
Orange Bakery
　Irvine, CA 949-863-1377
Original Ya-hoo! Baking Company
　Sherman, TX. 800-575-9373
Otis Spunkmeyer
　San Leandro, CA. 800-938-1900

Parco Foods
　Blue Island, IL 708-371-9200
Petrofsky's Bagels
　Saint Louis, MO 314-432-4177
Pillsbury
　Atlanta, GA. .800-767-4466
Pillsbury Canada Limited
　Markham, ON. 800-745-4777
Proferas Pizza Bakery
　Scranton, PA 570-342-4181
Quality Naturally! Foods
　City of Industry, CA 888-498-6986
Ranaldi Bros Frozen Food Products Inc
　Warwick, RI .401-738-3444
Rhodes Bake-N-Serv
　Salt Lake City, UT 800-695-0122
Rhodes International
　Columbus, WI. 800-876-7333
Rich Products Corporation
　Cameron, WI. 715-458-4556
Rich Products Corporation
　Buffalo, NY. .800-356-7094
Rich Products of Canada
　Fort Erie, ON 800-263-8174
Schwans Frozen Foods
　Marshall, MN 800-533-5290
Sinbad Sweets
　Fresno, CA 800-350-7933
Tasty Mix Quality Foods
　Brooklyn, NY. 866-TAS-TYMX
TNT Crust
　Green Bay, WI. 920-431-7240
Vie de France Yamazaki
　Vernon, LA .323-582-1241

Improvers

ADM Food Ingredients
　Olathe, KS. .800-255-6637
California Blending Corpany
　El Monte, CA 626-448-1918

Pizza

Baker Boy Bake Shop
　Dickinson, ND 800-437-2008
BBU Bakeries
　Denver, CO. .303-691-6342
Cohen's Bakery
　Buffalo, NY. .716-892-8149
Entenmann's-Oroweat/BestFoods
　S San Francisco, CA. 650-875-3100
Northwestern Foods
　St Paul, MN .800-236-4937
Oroweat Baking Company
　Montebello, CA 323-721-5161
Pillsbury Canada Limited
　Markham, ON. 800-745-4777
Proferas Pizza Bakery
　Scranton, PA 570-342-4181
Senape's Bakery
　Hazleton, PA 570-454-0839
TNT Crust
　Green Bay, WI. 920-431-7240
Weisenberger Mills
　Midway, KY .800-643-8678

Frozen

Oroweat Baking Company
　Montebello, CA 323-721-5161
Proferas Pizza Bakery
　Scranton, PA 570-342-4181
TNT Crust
　Green Bay, WI. 920-431-7240

Puff Pastry

Dough Delight
　Concord, ON. 800-465-5515

Fillings

Abel & Schafer
　Ronkonkoma, NY 800-443-1260
ACH Food Companies, Inc.
　Cordova, TN 800-691-1106
Bake'n Joy Foods
　North Andover, MA 800-666-4937
Best Brands Corporate Office
　St Paul, MN. 800-328-2068
Frank Korinek & Company
　Cicero, IL 773-242-1917

Kraft Food Ingredients
Memphis, TN .901-381-6500
Lyons-Magnus
Fresno, CA 559-268-5966
Newport Flavours & Fragrances
Orange, CA 714-628-9894
Oceana Foods
Shelby, MI. 231-861-2141
Original Ya-hoo! Baking Company
Sherman, TX. .800-575-9373
Pacific Westcoast Foods
Portland, OR 800-874-9333
Patisserie Wawel
Montreal, QC .614-524-3348
Puratos Canada
Mississauga, ON 800-668-5537
Skjodt-Barrett Foods
Mississauga, ON 877-600-1200

Baking

Bear Stewart Corporation
Chicago, IL 800-697-2327
Burnette Foods
Elk Rapids, MI 231-264-8116
Burnette Foods
Hartford, MI 616-621-3181
Clements Foods Company
Oklahoma City, OK 800-654-8355
H.C. Brill Company
Tucker, GA 800-241-8526
W&G Flavors
Hunt Valley, MD 410-771-6606

Cake

Abel & Schafer
Ronkonkoma, NY. 800-443-1260
American Key Food Products
Closter, NJ. 800-767-0237
Bear Stewart Corporation
Chicago, IL 800-697-2327
Belcolade
Pennsauken, NJ. 856-661-9123
Brookside Foods
Abbotsford, BC. 877-793-3866
California Custom Fruits & Flavors
Irwindale, CA .877-558-0056
Erba Food Products
Brooklyn, NY .718-272-7700
Georgia Nut Ingredients
Skokie, IL 877-674-2993
Golden Foods
Commerce, CA 800-350-2462
Golden West Fruit Company
Commerce, CA 323-726-9419
H.C. Brill Company
Tucker, GA 800-241-8526

Lawrence Foods
Elk Grove Vlg, IL 800-323-7848
Original Ya-hoo! Baking Company
Sherman, TX. .800-575-9373
Pacific Westcoast Foods
Portland, OR 800-874-9333
Plaidberry Company
Vista, CA. 760-727-5403
QA Products
Elk Grove Vlg, IL 800-635-7907
Quality Naturally! Foods
City of Industry, CA 888-498-6986
Skjodt-Barrett Foods
Mississauga, ON 877-600-1200
Sokol & Company
Countryside, IL 800-328-7656
Westco-Bake Mark
Pico Rivera, CA 562-949-1054
Wiggin Farms
Arbuckle, CA .530-476-2288

Chocolate

Erba Food Products
Brooklyn, NY .718-272-7700

Creme

Baker & Baker
Schaumburg, IL. 800-593-5777

Dessert

Chocolate

W&G Flavors
Hunt Valley, MD 410-771-6606

Cream

Dawn Food Products
Louisville, KY 800-626-2542
Flavor Right Foods Group
Columbus, OH 888-464-3734

Custard

Artuso Pastry Foods
Mt Vernon, NY 914-663-8806

Meringue

Bear Stewart Corporation
Chicago, IL 800-697-2327
Best Brands Corporation
Dallas, TX. 800-969-2253

Doughnuts

BakeMark
Schaumburg, IL. 562-949-1054

James Cowan & Sons
Worcester, MA 508-754-5385
Pamlico Packing Company
Grantsboro, NC. 800-682-1113
Skjodt-Barrett Foods
Mississauga, ON 877-600-1200

Fruit

Baker & Baker
Schaumburg, IL. 800-593-5777

Pie

Abel & Schafer
Ronkonkoma, NY. 800-443-1260
American Almond Products Company
Brooklyn, NY .800-825-6663
American Key Food Products
Closter, NJ. 800-767-0237
BakeMark Canada
Laval, QC 800-361-4998
Bakemark Ingredients Canada
Richmond, BC 800-665-9441
Baker & Baker, Inc.
Schaumburg, IL. 800-593-5777

Baldwin Richardson Foods
Frankfort, IL 866-644-2732

Baldwin Richardson Foods is a liquid ingredient manufacturer specializing in signature sauces, dessert toppings, beverage/pancake syrups, specialty fruit fillings and condiments. Packaging capabilities range from portion control cups and pouches to standard retail and foodservice packs and include industrial drums and totes. Full service R&D and Quality groups dedicated to new product development, with in-house stability and analytical testing. Call for assistance.

Bear Stewart Corporation
Chicago, IL 800-697-2327
Brookside Foods
Abbotsford, BC. 877-793-3866
Burnette Foods
Elk Rapids, MI 231-264-8116
Burnette Foods
Hartford, MI 616-621-3181
California Custom Fruits & Flavors
Irwindale, CA .877-558-0056

Carriere Foods Inc
Montreal, QC 514-384-4281
Cherry Hill Orchards Pelham
Fenwick, ON 905-892-3782
Clements Foods Company
Oklahoma City, OK 800-654-8355
Country Cupboard
Virginia City, NV 775-847-7300
Eden Processing
Poplar Grove, IL 815-765-2000
Erba Food Products
Brooklyn, NY 718-272-7700
Frank Korinek & Company
Cicero, IL 773-242-1917
Fruit Fillings
Fresno, CA 559-237-4715
Golden Foods
Commerce, CA 800-350-2462
Golden West Fruit Company
Commerce, CA 323-726-9419
Grandma Hoerner's Foods
Alma, KS 785-765-2300
H Cantin
Beauport, QC 800-463-5268
Indian Bay Frozen Foods
Centreville, NL 709-678-2844
Karp's
Schaumburg, IL 800-593-5277
Key Lime
Smyrna, GA 770-333-0840
Knouse Foods
Peach Glen, PA 717-677-8181
Knouse Foods Cooperative
Paw Paw, MI 269-657-5524
Lawrence Foods
Elk Grove Vlg, IL 800-323-7848
Leahy Orchards
Franklin, QC 450-827-2544
Lynch Foods
North York, QC 416-449-5464
Michigan Dessert Corporation
Oak Park, MI 800-328-8632
Nationwide Canning
Cottam, ON 519-839-4831
Oceana Foods
Shelby, MI 231-861-2141
Original Ya-hoo! Baking Company
Sherman, TX 800-575-9373
Pacific Westcoast Foods
Portland, OR 800-874-9333
Pearson's Berry Farm
Bowden, AB 403-224-3011
Pied-Mont/Dora
Ste Anne Des Plaines, BC 800-363-8003
Plaidberry Company
Vista, CA 760-727-5403
QA Products
Elk Grove Vlg, IL 800-635-7907
Reinhart Foods
Markham, ON 905-754-3503
Rohtstein Corporation
Woburn, MA 781-935-8300
Schmidt Brothers
Swanton, OH 419-826-3671
Skjodt-Barrett Foods
Mississauga, ON 877-600-1200
Steel's Gourmet Foods
Bridgeport, PA 800-678-3357
Valley View Blueberries
Vancouver, WA 360-892-2839
Whipple Company
Natick, MA 800-345-2925
White-Stokes Company
Chicago, IL 800-978-6537

Mixes

Bountiful Pantry
Nantucket, MA 888-832-6466
Boyd Coffee Company
Portland, OR 800-545-4077
Bruce Foods Corporation
New Iberia, LA 800-299-9082
Noh Foods International
Honolulu, HI 808-841-0655
Ontario Foods Exports
Mississauga, ON 888-466-2372
Paradigm Food Works
Lake Oswego, OR 503-595-4360
Shawnee Canning Company
Cross Junction, VA 800-713-1414
Terry Foods Inc
Idaho Falls, ID 208-604-8143

Baking

Abbitt's
Williamston, NC 252-792-3646
Abel & Schafer
Ronkonkoma, NY 800-443-1260
ACH Food Companies, Inc.
Cordova, TN 800-691-1106
ADM Food Ingredients
Olathe, KS 800-255-6637
ADM Milling Company
Shawnee Mission, KS 913-266-6300
Adventure Foods
Whittier, NC 828-497-4113
America's Classic Foods
Cambria, CA 805-927-0745
Annie's Frozen Yogurt
Minneapolis, MN 800-969-9648
Bake'n Joy Foods
North Andover, MA 800-666-4937
Bakemark Ingredients Canada
Richmond, BC 800-665-9441
Baker & Baker
Schaumburg, IL 800-593-5777
Baker & Baker, Inc.
Schaumburg, IL 800-593-5777
Bakery Chef
Louisville, KY 800-594-0203
Bear Stewart Corporation
Chicago, IL 800-697-2327
Bernard Food Industries
Evanston, IL 800-323-3663
Best Brands Corporation
Tampa, FL 800-282-0565
Best Brands Corporation
Dallas, TX 800-969-2253
Beth's Fine Desserts
Cotati, CA 415-464-1891
Bette's Diner Products
Berkeley, CA 510-644-3230
Big Steer Enterprises
Beaumont, TX 800-421-4951
Blend Pak
Bloomfield, KY 502-252-8000
Blue Chip Group
Salt Lake City, UT 800-878-0099
Brass Ladle Products
Glen Mills, PA 800-955-2353
Brookema Company
West Chicago, IL 630-562-2290
Byrd Mill Company
Ashland, VA 888-897-3336
Cafe Du Monde
New Orleans, LA 504-587-0835
Calhoun Bend Mill
Alexandria, LA 800-519-6455
Calico Cottage
Amityville, NY 800-645-5345
Care Ingredients
Melrose Park, IL 708-450-3260
Carol Lee Products
Lawrence, KS 785-842-5489
Century Foods International
Sparta, WI 800-269-1901
Charles Dennery Pillsbury
New Orleans, LA 504-733-2331
Chefmaster
Garden Grove, CA 800-333-7443
Chelsea Milling Company
Chelsea, MI 734-475-1361
Chr Hansen
Elyria, OH 800-558-0802
Chukar Cherries
Prosser, WA 800-624-9544
Cibolo Junction Food & Spice
Albuquerque, NM 505-888-1987
Cinnabar Specialty Foods
Prescott, AZ 866-293-6433
Clabber Girl Corporation
Terre Haute, IN 812-232-9446
Commodities Marketing, Inc.
Edison, NJ 732-516-0700
Continental Mills
Seattle, WA 253-872-8400
Cook-In-The-Kitchen
White River Junction, VT 802-333-4141
Cotswold Cottage Foods
Arvada, CO 800-208-1977
Country Home Creations
Goodrich, MI 800-457-3477
Cowboy Foods
Bozeman, MT 800-759-5489

Cream of the West
Harlowton, MT 800-477-2383
Crum Creek Mills
Springfield, PA 888-607-3500
CW Resources
New Britain, CT 860-229-7700
Dawn Food Products
Jackson, MI 800-248-1144
Dawn Food Products
Louisville, KY 800-626-2542
De Coty Coffee Company
San Angelo, TX 800-588-8001
Dorothy Dawson Foods Products
Jackson, MI 517-788-9830
Dowd & Rogers
Sacramento, CA 916-451-6480
Dr. Pete's
Savannah, GA 912-233-3035
Drusilla Seafood Packing & Processing Company
Baton Rouge, LA 800-364-8844
El Peto Products
Cambridge, ON 800-387-4064
Ellison Milling Company
Lethbridge, AB 403-328-6622
Embassy Flavours Ltd.
Brampton, ON 800-334-3371
Ener-G Foods
Seattle, WA 800-331-5222
English Bay Batter
Dublin, OH 614-760-9921
Fearn Natural Foods
Mequon, WI 800-877-8935
Fiera Foods
North York, ON 416-744-1010
Food Concentrate Corporation
Oklahoma City, OK 405-840-5633
Frank Korinek & Company
Cicero, IL 773-242-1917
Fry Krisp Food Products
Jackson, MI 517-784-8531
Galloway Company
Neenah, WI 800-722-8903
General Mills
Minneapolis, MN 800-248-7310
Gilster-Mary Lee Corporation
Chester, IL 800-851-5371
Global Food Industries
Townville, SC 800-225-4152
Good Food
Honey Brook, PA 800-327-4406
Grain Millers
Eden Prairie, MN 800-232-6287
Grain Process Enterprises Ltd.
Scarborough, ON 800-387-5292
Great Grains Milling Company
Scobey, MT 406-783-5588
Great Recipes Company
Beaverton, OR 800-273-2331
Gregory's Foods
Eagan, MN 800-231-4734
H. Nagel & Son Company
Cincinnati, OH 513-665-4550
H.C. Brill Company
Tucker, GA 800-241-8526
Hansmann's Mills
Bainbridge, NY 607-967-5080
HC Brill Company
Tucker, GA 800-241-8526
Heartland Food Products
Shawnee Mission, KS 913-831-4446
Heidi's Gourmet Desserts
Tucker, GA 800-241-4166
Heritage Tymes/Pancake House
Spearsville, LA 806-765-8566
Highland Sugarworks
Websterville, VT 800-452-4012
Hodgson Mill Inc
Effingham, IL 800-525-0177
Hollman Foods
Minden, NE 888-926-2879
Homes Packaging Company
Millersburg, OH 800-401-2529
Homestead Mills
Cook, MN 800-652-5233
Honeyville Grain
Rancho Cucamonga, CA 888-810-3212
House-Autry Mills
Four Oaks, NC 800-849-0802
Ingredients, Inc.
Buffalo Grove, IL 847-419-9595
Inn Maid Food
Lenox, MA 413-637-2732

International Multifoods Corporation
Orrville, OH 800-664-2942
Iveta Gourmet
Santa Cruz, CA 831-423-5149
John Gust Foods & Products Corporation
Batavia, IL. 800-756-5886
Johnson's Food Products
Dorchester, MA. 617-265-3400
Kamish Food Products
Chicago, IL 773-267-0400
Karp's
Georgetown, MA 800-373-5277
Karp's
Schaumburg, IL. 800-593-5277
Kerry Ingredients
Evansville, IN 812-464-9151
Little Crow Foods
Warsaw, IN 800-288-2769
Louisiana Gourmet Enterprises
Houma, LA 800-328-5586
Lynch Foods
North York, QC. 416-449-5464
Maple Grove Farms of Vermont
St Johnsbury, VT. 800-525-2540
Marie Callender's Gourmet Products/Goldrush Products
San Jose, CA 800-729-5428
Martha Olson's Great Foods
Sutter Creek, CA 800-973-3966
Master Taste International
Plant City, FL 800-237-7629
Midstate Mills
Newton, NC 800-222-1032
Milani Gourmet
Melrose Park, IL 800-333-0003
Mine & Mommy's Cookies
Merkel, TX 915-928-5870
Minnesota Specialty Crops
McGregor, MN 800-328-6731
Modern Products/Fearn Natural Foods
Mequon, WI 800-877-8935
Mojave Foods Corporation
Commerce, CA 323-890-8900
Morningstar Foods
Dallas, TX 225-273-2803
Nantucket Tea Traders
Nantucket, MA 508-325-0203
New Hope Mills
Auburn, NY. 315-252-2676
No Pudge! Foods
Wolfeboro Falls, NH. 888-667-8343
Northwestern Foods
St Paul, MN. 800-236-4937
Old Country Farms
East Sandwich, MA 888-707-5558
Old Tyme Mill Company
Chicago, IL 773-521-9484
Olmarc Packaging Company
Chicago, IL 708-562-2000
Pak Technologies
Milwaukee, WI 414-438-8600
Paradise Island Foods
Nanaimo, BC. 800-889-3370
Pelican Bay
Dunedin, FL 800-826-8982
Pepsi
Chicago, IL 312-821-1000
PepsiCo
Barrington, IL. 847-842-4652
Pett Spice Products
Atlanta, GA 404-691-5235
Pillsbury
Minneapolis, MN 800-845-3103
Premier Blending
Wichita, KS. 316-267-5533
Puratos Canada
Mississauga, ON 800-668-5537
Purity Foods
Okemos, MI 800-997-7358
Quaker Oats Company
Stockton, CA 209-982-5580
Quality Naturally! Foods
City of Industry, CA 888-498-6986
R.A.B. Food Group LLC
Secaucus, NJ 201-453-5200
Randag & Associates Inc
Elmhurst, IL 630-530-2830
Real Cookies
Merrick, NY 800-822-5113
Red Rose Trading Company
Wrightsville, PA 717-252-5500
Redco Foods
Windsor, CT 800-645-1190

Reggie Ball's Cajun Foods
Lake Charles, LA 337-436-0291
Reimann Food Classics
Palatine, IL 847-991-1366
Rich Products Corporation
Hilliard, OH. 614-771-1117
Rich Products Corporation
Cameron, WI. 715-458-4556
Richmond Baking Company
Alma, GA 912-632-7213
Roland Industries
Saint Louis, MO 800-325-1183
Roman Meal Milling Company
Fargo, ND 877-282-9743
Roskam Baking Company
Grand Rapids, MI 616-574-5757
S&N Food Company
Mesquite, TX 972-222-1184
Sells Best
Mishawaka, IN 800-837-8368
SFP Food Products
Conway, AR 800-654-5329
Shenandoah Mills
Lebanon, VA 615-444-0841
SOUPerior Bean & Spice Company
Vancouver, WA 800-878-7687
Southeastern Mills
Rome, GA 800-334-4468
Spice Advice
Ankeny, IA 800-247-5251
Sticky Fingers Bakeries
Spokane Valley, WA 800-458-5826
Strossner's Bakery
Greenville, SC. 864-233-3996
Subco Foods Inc
Sheboygan, WI 800-676-5188
Sundial Gardens
Higganum, CT. 860-345-4290
Swagger Foods Corporation
Vernon Hills, IL 847-913-1200
Tait Farm Foods
Centre Hall, PA 800-787-2716
Tarazi Specialty Foods
Chino, CA 909-628-3601
Taste Maker Foods
Memphis, TN 800-467-1407
Taste of Gourmet
Indianola, MS 800-833-7731
Tastee Fare
Little Rock, AR. 501-568-7870
Tasty Mix Quality Foods
Brooklyn, NY. 866-TAS-TYMX
Tasty Selections
Concord, ON. 905-760-2353
Texas Crumb & Food Products
Farmers Branch, TX 800-522-7862
The Lollipop Tree, Inc
Portsmouth, NH 800-842-6691
Thorough Fare Gourmet
Marlboro, VT 802-257-5612
Timber Peaks Gourmet
Parker, CO. 800-982-7687
Tova Industries
Louisville, KY 888-532-8682
Valley View Blueberries
Vancouver, WA 360-892-2839
VIP Foods
Flushing, NY. 718-821-3942
Wall-Rogalsky Milling Company
Mc Pherson, KS 800-835-2067
Wanda's Nature Farm
Lincoln, NE. 402-423-1234
War Eagle Mill
Rogers, AR 479-789-5343
Weisenberger Mills
Midway, KY. 800-643-8678
West Pac
Idaho Falls, ID 800-973-7407
Westco-Bake Mark
Pico Rivera, CA 562-949-1054
White Lily Foods Company
San Antonio, TX. 800-264-5459
Wholesome Classics
Campbell, CA 408-292-2392
Wilkins-Rogers
Ellicott City, MD. 410-465-5800
Wilsonhill Farm
Underhill, VT 802-899-2154
Wisconsin Wilderness Food Products
Milwaukee, WI. 800-359-3039
World Flavors
Warminster, PA 215-672-4400

Yorktown Baking Company
Yorktown Heights, NY 800-235-3961

Brownies

Blue Chip Group
Salt Lake City, UT 800-878-0099
Chelsea Milling Company
Chelsea, MI. 734-475-1361

Beverage

Abunda Life Laboratories
Asbury Park, NJ 732-775-4141
Al-Rite Fruits & Syrups
Miami, FL. 305-652-2540
Alexander International (USA)
Brightwaters, NY 866-965-0143
Alkinco
New York, NY. 800-424-7118
American Beverage Marketers
New Albany, IN 812-944-3585
American Beverage Marketers
Shawnee Mission, KS. 913-451-8311
Associated Brands, Inc.
Medina, NY. 800-265-0050
Atlantic Seasonings
Kinston, NC 800-433-5261
Autocrat Coffee & Extracts
Lincoln, RI 800-288-6272
Bacardi Canada, Inc.
Brampton, ON. 905-451-6100
Bainbridge Festive Foods
Tunica, MS 800-545-9205

Baldwin Richardson Foods
Frankfort, IL 866-644-2732

Baldwin Richardson Foods is a liquid ingredient manufacturer specializing in signature sauces, dessert toppings, beverage/pancake syrups, specialty fruit fillings and condiments. Packaging capabilities range from portion control cups and pouches to standard retail and foodservice packs and include industrial drums and totes. Full service R&D and Quality groups dedicated to new product development, with in-house stability and analytical testing. Call for assistance.

Barber Pure Milk Ice Cream Company
Birmingham, AL 205-942-2351
Bartush-Schnitzius Foods Company
Lewisville, TX 972-219-1270
Bede Inc
Haledon, NJ 866-239-6565
Bell Buckle Country Store
Bell Buckle, TN 800-707-0483
Beverage Specialties
Fredonia, NY 800-828-8915
Blue Crab Bay Company
Melfa, VA 800-221-2722
Boissons Miami Pomor
Longueuil, QC 877-977-3744
Boyd Coffee Company
Portland, OR 800-545-4077
Breakfast at Brennan's
New Orleans, LA 800-888-9932
Brookema Company
West Chicago, IL 630-562-2290
Cactus-Creek
Dallas, TX. 800-471-7723
Calico Cottage
Amityville, NY 800-645-5345
Cappuccine
Palm Springs, CA 800-511-3127
Carbolite Foods
Evansville, IN 888-524-3314
Carbonator Rental Service
Philadelphia, PA 800-220-3556
Carolina Treet
Wilmington, NC 800-616-6344
Century Foods International
Sparta, WI 800-269-1901
Chase Brothers Dairy
Oxnard, CA 800-438-6455

Christie Food Products
Randolph, MA 800-727-2523
Citrus Service
Winter Garden, FL 407-656-4999
Cocoline Chocolate Company
Brooklyn, NY 718-522-4500
Compact Industries
St Charles, IL 800-513-4262
ConAgra Grocery Products
Irvine, CA 714-680-1000
Consolidated Mills
Houston, TX 713-896-4196
Creative Foodworks
San Antonio, TX 210-212-4761
Crosby Molasses Company
St. John, NB 506-634-7515
Crystal Foods
Brick, NJ 732-477-0073
Dairy-Mix
St Petersburg, FL 727-525-6101
Dairyman's/Land O' Lakes
Tulare, CA. 559-687-8287
Dean Distributors
Burlingame, CA 800-792-0816
Devansoy
Carroll, IA 800-747-8605
Diamond Crystal Brands
Savannah, GA 912-651-5112
Diamond Crystal Specialty Foods
Bondurant, IA 515-967-3737
Erba Food Products
Brooklyn, NY 718-272-7700
Fair Scones
Medina, WA 800-588-9160
Farmer Brothers Company
Torrance, CA. 800-735-2878
Fine Foods International
St Louis, MO. 314-842-4473
Flavor Systems International
Cincinnati, OH 800-498-2783
Flavorbank
Tampa, FL. 813-885-1797
Fountain Shakes/MS Foods
Minneapolis, MN 877-988-6940
Four C Foods Corporation
Brooklyn, NY 718-272-4242

Four Percent Company
Highland Park, MI 313-345-5880
Franco's Cocktail Mixes
Pompano Beach, FL 800-782-4508
Frank & Dean's Cocktail Mixes
Pasadena, CA 626-351-4272
G A Food Service
St Petersburg, FL. 727-573-2211
Gerhart Coffee Company
Lancaster, PA 800-536-4310
Gilly's Hot Vanilla
Lenox, MA 413-637-1515
Gilster-Mary Lee Corporation
Chester, IL. 800-851-5371
GLCC Company
Paw Paw, MI. 269-657-3167
Global Marketing Associates
Schaumburg, IL. 847-490-6481
Green Foods Corporation
Oxnard, CA. 800-777-4430
Greinoman's/Unified Industries
Cumming, GA. 770-889-8233
H. Fox & Company
Brooklyn, NY 718-385-4600
Halben Food Manufacturing Company
Overland, MO. 800-888-4855
Heinz North America
Pittsburgh, PA 412-237-5700
Hena Coffee
Brooklyn, NY 718-272-8237
Highwood Distillers
High River, AB 403-652-3202
Hygeia Dairy Company
McAllen, TX. 956-686-0511
Imagine Foods
Melville, NY 800-333-6339
Innovative Food Solutions LLC
Columbus, OH 800-884-3314
Instant Products of America
Columbus, IN 812-372-9100
J. Crow Company
New Ipswich, NH 800-878-1965
Jazzie Smoothie
Metairie, LA 504-780-8429
Jel-Sert Company
West Chicago, IL 800-323-2592

Jogue Inc
Northville, MI. 800-521-3888
Jus-Made
Dallas, TX. 800-969-3746
K&F Select Fine Coffees
Portland, OR 800-558-7788
Kemach Food Products   Corporation
Brooklyn, NY 888-453-6224
Kennedy Candy Company
Kilgore, TX 800-657-5258
Kittling Ridge Estate Wines & Spirits
Grimsby, ON. 905-945-9225
Kohler Mix Specialties
Newington, CT 860-666-1511
Kraft Food Ingredients
Memphis, TN 901-381-6500
La Paz Products
Brea, CA 714-990-0982
Lake City Foods
Mississauga, ON. 905-625-8244
Lake Country Foods
Oconomowoc, WI. 262-567-5521
Land O'Lakes
Carlisle, PA 717-486-7000
Land O'Lakes, Inc
Arden Hills, MN 800-328-9680
Lemate of New England
Sharon, MA. 781-784-7369
Lemix
Canton, OH 330-488-3072
Lynch Foods
North York, QC. 416-449-5464
Main Street Ingredients
La Crosse, WI 800-359-2345
Mar-Key Foods
Vidalia, GA. 912-537-4204
Margarita Man
San Antonio, TX 800-950-8149
Master Taste International
Plant City, FL 800-237-7629
McSteven's
Vancouver, WA 800-838-1056
Melchers Flavors of America
Indianapolis, IN 800-235-2867
Mele-Koi Farms
Newport Beach, CA 949-660-9000

Mingo Bay Beverages
Myrtle Beach, SC 843-448-5320
Minute Maid Company
Houston, TX 888-884-8952
MLO/GeniSoy Products Company
Tulas, OK 866-606-3829
Natural Formulas
Hayward, CA 510-372-1800
Naturally Fresh Foods
College Park, GA 800-765-1950
Nestle Canada Inc
North York, ON. 800-563-7853
Northwestern Foods
St Paul, MN. 800-236-4937
Novartis Nutrition Corporation
Minneapolis, MN 952-848-6000
PACA Foods
Tampa, FL. 800-388-7419
Perfection Fine Products
Maple Heights, OH. 216-475-5744
Phillips Syrup Corporation
Cleveland, OH 216-661-4800
Pied-Mont/Dora
Ste Anne Des Plaines, BC 800-363-8003
Plainview Milk Products Cooperative
Plainview, MN 507-534-3872
PR Nutrition
San Diego, CA 800-397-5556
Premier Blending
Wichita, KS. 316-267-5533
Price's Creameries
El Paso, TX 915-565-2711
Pro Form Labs
Orinda, CA 925-299-9000
Proctor & Gamble Company
Phoenix, AZ 602-269-2171
Quality Instant Teas
Morristown, NJ 888-283-8327
Quality Naturally! Foods
City of Industry, CA 888-498-6986
Reser's Fine Foods
Beaverton, OR 800-333-6431
Robertet Flavors
Piscataway, NJ 732-981-8300
Roney Oatman
Aurora, IL 630-859-2800
Roos Foods
Kenton, DE 800-343-3642
Ruffner's
Wayne, PA. 610-687-9800
S.J. McCullagh
Buffalo, NY. 800-753-3473
Sara Lee Coffee & Tea   Wholesale Coffee & Tea
Location
Minneapolis, MN 888-246-2598
Sara Lee Corporation
Downers Grove, IL. 630-598-8100
Schlotterbeck & Foss Company
Portland, ME. 800-777-4666
Sea Breeze Fruit Flavors
Towaco, NJ 800-732-2733
Seller Kirk & Company
Schwenksville, PA 215-480-7342
SimmaLoosa Company
Covington, LA 985-892-1400
Skim Delux Mendenhall Laboratories
Paris, TN 800-642-9321
Southern Gardens Citrus Processing
Clewiston, FL 863-983-3030
Steelback Brewery
Tiverton, ON. 800-879-0541
Sturm Foods
Manawa, WI 800-347-8876
Subco Foods Inc
Sheboygan, WI. 800-676-5188
Sugar Creek/Eskimo Pie
Russellville, AR 800-445-2715
Swagger Foods Corporation
Vernon Hills, IL 847-913-1200

Synergy Foods
West Bloomfield, MI 313-849-2900
Tex-Mex Gourmet
Houston, TX 888-345-8467
Thirs-Tea Corporation
Miami, FL. 305-651-4350
Toucan Enterprises
Marrero, LA 800-736-9289
Tova Industries
Louisville, KY 888-532-8682
Trader Vic's Food Products
Emeryville, CA. 877-762-4824
Tree Ripe Products
East Hanover, NJ 800-873-3747
Tropics Beverages
Elmhurst, IL 800-926-5232
Ultra Seal
New Paltz, NY 845-255-2496
Unilever Bestfoods
Englewood Cliffs, NJ 201-894-4000
United Citrus Products
Norwood, MA 800-229-7300
VIP Foods
Flushing, NY. 718-821-3942
Vita-Pakt Citrus Company
Covina, CA 626-332-1101
Vitality Foodservice
Tampa, FL. 888-863-6726
W&G Flavors
Hunt Valley, MD. 410-771-6606
Wayne Dairy Products
Richmond, IN 800-875-9294
Webbpak
Trussville, AL 800-655-3500
Wechsler Coffee Corporation
Moonachie, NJ 800-800-2633
Welsh Farms
Newark, NJ. 800-221-0663
Williamsburg Foods
Toano, VA 757-566-0930
World Flavors
Warminster, PA 215-672-4400
Yoo-Hoo Chocolate Beverage Company
Port Chester, NY. 800-966-4669

Frozen

Al-Rite Fruits & Syrups
Miami, FL. 305-652-2540
Associated Brands, Inc.
Medina, NY. 800-265-0050

Baldwin Richardson Foods
Frankfort, IL 866-644-2732

Baldwin Richardson Foods is a liquid ingredient manufacturer specializing in signature sauces, dessert toppings, beverage/pancake syrups, specialty fruit fillings and condiments. Packaging capabilities range from portion control cups and pouches to standard retail and foodservice packs and include industrial drums and totes. Full service R&D and Quality groups dedicated to new product development, with in-house stability and analytical testing. Call for assistance.

Compact Industries
St Charles, IL 800-513-4262
Diamond Crystal Specialty Foods
Bondurant, IA 515-967-3737
J. Crow Company
New Ipswich, NH 800-878-1965
Jogue Inc
Northville, MI. 800-521-3888
Novartis Nutrition Corporation
Minneapolis, MN 952-848-6000
Reser's Fine Foods
Beaverton, OR 800-333-6431
Roney Oatman
Aurora, IL 630-859-2800

Liquid

Associated Brands, Inc.
Medina, NY. 800-265-0050

Baldwin Richardson Foods
Frankfort, IL 866-644-2732

Baldwin Richardson Foods is a liquid ingredient manufacturer specializing in signature sauces, dessert toppings, beverage/pancake syrups, specialty fruit fillings and condiments. Packaging capabilities range from portion control cups and pouches to standard retail and foodservice packs and include industrial drums and totes. Full service R&D and Quality groups dedicated to new product development, with in-house stability and analytical testing. Call for assistance.

Compact Industries
St Charles, IL 800-513-4262
ConAgra Grocery Products
Irvine, CA 714-680-1000
Diamond Crystal Specialty Foods
Bondurant, IA 515-967-3737
Hummingbird Kitchens
Whitehouse, TX 800-921-9470
J. Crow Company
New Ipswich, NH 800-878-1965
Jogue Inc
Northville, MI. 800-521-3888
Novartis Nutrition Corporation
Minneapolis, MN 952-848-6000
Reser's Fine Foods
Beaverton, OR 800-333-6431
Roney Oatman
Aurora, IL 630-859-2800

Biscuit

Atkinson Milling Company
Selma, NC 800-948-5707
Baker & Baker
Schaumburg, IL. 800-593-5777
Baker & Baker, Inc.
Schaumburg, IL. 800-593-5777
Bakery Chef
Louisville, KY 800-594-0203
Blackberry Patch
Thomasville, GA. 800-853-5598
Bountiful Pantry
Nantucket, MA 888-832-6466
Bruce Foods Corporation
New Iberia, LA 800-299-9082
Byrd Mill Company
Ashland, VA 888-897-3336
Country Cupboard
Virginia City, NV 775-847-7300
Father's Country Hams
Bremen, KY 270-525-3554
Iveta Gourmet
Santa Cruz, CA 831-423-5149
Premier Blending
Wichita, KS. 316-267-5533
Weisenberger Mills
Midway, KY 800-643-8678
White Lily Foods Company
San Antonio, TX 800-264-5459

Bread

Abel & Schafer
Ronkonkoma, NY. 800-443-1260
Ambassador Foods
Van Nuys, CA 800-338-3369
Aunt Millies Bakeries
Fort Wayne, IN 260-424-8245
BakeMark
Schaumburg, IL. 562-949-1054
Best Brands Corporation
Tampa, FL. 800-282-0565
Bountiful Pantry
Nantucket, MA 888-832-6466
Byrd Mill Company
Ashland, VA 888-897-3336
Charles Dennery Pillsbury
New Orleans, LA 504-733-2331
Chester Fried
Montgomery, AL. 800-288-1555
Chr Hansen
Elyria, OH. 800-558-0802

Cibolo Junction Food & Spice
Albuquerque, NM 505-888-1987
Cotswold Cottage Foods
Arvada, CO 800-208-1977
De Coty Coffee Company
San Angelo, TX 800-588-8001
Drusilla Seafood Packing & Processing Company
Baton Rouge, LA 800-364-8844
Grain Process Enterprises Ltd.
Scarborough, ON 800-387-5292
Hollman Foods
Minden, NE. 888-926-2879
Kokopelli's Kitchen
Phoenix, AZ 888-943-9802
Old Tyme Mill Company
Chicago, IL 773-521-9484
Pamela's Products
Ukiah, CA 707-462-6605
Pett Spice Products
Atlanta, GA 404-691-5235
Puratos Canada
Mississauga, ON 800-668-5537
Purity Foods
Okemos, MI 800-997-7358
Rabbit Creek Products
Louisburg, KS 800-837-3073
Sambets Cajun Deli
Austin, TX. 800-472-6238
Sassafras Enterprises
Chicago, IL 800-537-4941
Sells Best
Mishawaka, IN 800-837-8368
SOUPerior Bean & Spice Company
Vancouver, WA 800-878-7687
Southeastern Mills
Rome, GA 800-334-4468
Strossner's Bakery
Greenville, SC 864-233-3996
The Lollipop Tree, Inc
Portsmouth, NH 800-842-6691
Timber Peaks Gourmet
Parker, CO 800-982-7687
Valley View Blueberries
Vancouver, WA 360-892-2839

Low Carb

Dixie USA
Tomball, TX 800-233-3668

Breading

Blend Pak
Bloomfield, KY 502-252-8000
Chef Hans Gourmet Foods
Monroe, LA 800-890-4267
Chr Hansen
Elyria, OH 800-558-0802
Dorothy Dawson Foods Products
Jackson, MI 517-788-9830
Griffith Laboratories Worldwide
Alsip, IL 800-346-4743
Newly Weds Foods
Chicago, IL 800-621-7521
Roland Industries
Saint Louis, MO 800-325-1183
Specialty Products
Cleveland, OH 216-362-1050
Texas Crumb & Food Products
Farmers Branch, TX 800-522-7862

Brownie

BakeMark
Schaumburg, IL 562-949-1054
Country Cupboard
Virginia City, NV 775-847-7300
Dawn Food Products
Jackson, MI 800-248-1144
No Pudge! Foods
Wolfeboro Falls, NH 888-667-8343
Pamela's Products
Ukiah, CA 707-462-6605
Rabbit Creek Products
Louisburg, KS 800-837-3073
Touche Bakery
London, ON 519-455-0044
White Lily Foods Company
San Antonio, TX 800-264-5459

Cake

Abel & Schafer
Ronkonkoma, NY 800-443-1260
ACH Food Companies, Inc.
Cordova, TN 800-691-1106
Atkinson Milling Company
Selma, NC 800-948-5707
BakeMark
Schaumburg, IL. 562-949-1054
Bakemark Ingredients Canada
Richmond, BC 800-665-9441
Baker & Baker
Schaumburg, IL. 800-593-5777
Baker & Baker, Inc.
Schaumburg, IL. 800-593-5777
Bakery Chef
Louisville, KY 800-594-0203
Bear Stewart Corporation
Chicago, IL 800-697-2327
Best Brands Corporation
Tampa, FL 800-282-0565
Beth's Fine Desserts
Cotati, CA 415-464-1891
Brass Ladle Products
Glen Mills, PA 800-955-2353
Brookema Company
West Chicago, IL 630-562-2290
Butternut Mountain Farm
Morrisville, VT. 800-828-2376
Byrd Mill Company
Ashland, VA 888-897-3336
Charles Dennery Pillsbury
New Orleans, LA 504-733-2331
Chefmaster
Garden Grove, CA 800-333-7443
Chelsea Milling Company
Chelsea, MI 734-475-1361
Country Cupboard
Virginia City, NV 775-847-7300
Cuisinary Fine Foods
Dallas, TX 888-283-5303
Dawn Food Products
Jackson, MI 800-248-1144
Embassy Flavours Ltd.
Brampton, ON 800-334-3371
Good Food
Honey Brook, PA 800-327-4406
Halladays Harvest Barn
Bellows Falls, VT 802-463-3471
Hansmann's Mills
Bainbridge, NY 607-967-5080
Honeyville Grain
Rancho Cucamonga, CA 888-810-3212
Ingredients, Inc.
Buffalo Grove, IL 847-419-9595
Little Crow Foods
Warsaw, IN 800-288-2769
Louisiana Gourmet Enterprises
Houma, LA 800-328-5586
Martha Olson's Great Foods
Sutter Creek, CA 800-973-3966
Meadowvale
Yorkville, IL 800-953-0201
Northwestern Foods
St Paul, MN 800-236-4937
Oetker Limited
Mississauga, ON 905-678-1311
Pillsbury
Minneapolis, MN 800-845-3103
Premier Blending
Wichita, KS 316-267-5533
Quality Naturally! Foods
City of Industry, CA 888-498-6986
Rich Products Corporation
Cameron, WI 715-458-4556
Royal Resources
New Orleans, LA 800-888-9932
Sells Best
Mishawaka, IN 800-837-8368
Sundial Gardens
Higganum, CT. 860-345-4290
Tasty Selections
Concord, ON 905-760-2353
Tova Industries
Louisville, KY 888-532-8682
VIP Foods
Flushing, NY 718-821-3942
Wanda's Nature Farm
Lincoln, NE. 402-423-1234
West Pac
Idaho Falls, ID 800-973-7407

Cappuccino

Brewfresh Coffee Company
South Salt Lake, UT 888-486-3334
International Food Technologies
Evansville, IN 812-853-9432
McSteven's
Vancouver, WA 800-838-1056
Mont Blanc Gourmet
Denver, CO 800-877-3811

Frozen

International Food Technologies
Evansville, IN 812-853-9432

Chili

Basic American Foods
Walnut Creek, CA. 800-227-4050
Chili Dude
Richardson, TX 972-907-0998
Fernandez Chili Company
Alamosa, CO 719-589-6043
Legumes Plus
Fairfield, WA. 800-845-1349
Mojave Foods Corporation
Commerce, CA 800-995-8906
Monterrey Products Company
San Antonio, TX 210-435-2872
Red Lion Spicy Foods Company
Red Lion, PA 717-244-0227
Reily Foods Company
New Orleans, LA 504-524-6132
T. Marzetti Company
Columbus, OH 614-846-2232
Texas Heat
San Antonio, TX 800-656-5916
Tova Industries
Louisville, KY 888-532-8682
Westfield Foods
Greenville, RI 401-949-3558

Cocktail

Al-Rite Fruits & Syrups
Miami, FL 305-652-2540
Bacardi USA
Miami, FL 800-222-2734
Byesville Aseptics
Byesville, OH 740-685-2548
Demitri's Bloody Mary Seasonings
Seattle, WA 800-627-9649
Franco's Cocktail Mixes
Pompano Beach, FL 800-782-4508
Frank & Dean's Cocktail Mixes
Pasadena, CA 626-351-4272
La Paz Products
Brea, CA 714-990-0982
Lemon-X Corporation
Huntington Sta, NY 800-220-1061
Main Squeeze
Columbia, MO 573-817-5616
Natural Fruit Corporation
Hialeah, FL 305-887-7525
Perfection Fine Products
Maple Heights, OH 216-475-5744
Ruffner's
Wayne, PA 610-687-9800
Tree Ripe Products
East Hanover, NJ 800-873-3747
Wagner Excello Food Products
Broadview, IL 708-338-4488

Cookie

BakeMark
Schaumburg, IL. 562-949-1054
Brand Castle
Beachwood, OH 216-292-7700

Dessert

Abel & Schafer
Ronkonkoma, NY 800-443-1260
ACH Food Companies, Inc.
Cordova, TN 800-691-1106
American Key Food Products
Closter, NJ 800-767-0237
Baird Dairies
Clarksville, IN 812-283-3345
Barber Pure Milk Ice Cream Company
Birmingham, AL 205-942-2351
Bear Stewart Corporation
Chicago, IL 800-697-2327
Benson Creamery
Decatur, IL 217-429-2351
Best Brands Corporation
Tampa, FL 800-282-0565
Best Brands Corporation
Dallas, TX 800-969-2253
Blend Pak
Bloomfield, KY 502-252-8000
Brass Ladle Products
Glen Mills, PA 800-955-2353
Burnette Foods
Hartford, MI 616-621-3181
Byrd Mill Company
Ashland, VA 888-897-3336
California Custom Fruits & Flavors
Irwindale, CA 877-558-0056
Carolina Foods
Charlotte, NC 800-234-0441
Charles Dennery Pillsbury
New Orleans, LA 504-733-2331
Chefmaster
Garden Grove, CA 800-333-7443
Chelsea Milling Company
Chelsea, MI 734-475-1361
Cherry Hill Orchards Pelham
Fenwick, ON 905-892-3782
Clofine Dairy & Food Products
Linwood, NJ 800-441-1001
Creme Curls Bakery
Hudsonville, MI 800-466-1219
Cuisinary Fine Foods
Dallas, TX 888-283-5303
Dairy-Mix
St Petersburg, FL 727-525-6101
Dawn Food Products
Louisville, KY 800-626-2542
Dean Distributors
Burlingame, CA 800-792-0816
Diamond Crystal
Savannah, GA 800-227-4455
Dutch Ann Foods Company
Natchez, MS 601-445-5566
Embassy Flavours Ltd.
Brampton, ON 800-334-3371
Famous Specialties Company
Island Park, NY 877-273-6999
First Foods Company
Dallas, TX 214-637-0214
Galliker Dairy
Johnstown, PA 800-477-6455
Galloway Company
Neenah, WI 800-722-8903
General Mills
Minneapolis, MN 800-248-7310
Golden Fluff Popcorn Company
Lakewood, NJ 732-367-5448
Great Recipes Company
Beaverton, OR 800-273-2331
Gumpert's Canada
Mississauga, ON 800-387-9324
Heidi's Gourmet Desserts
Tucker, GA 800-241-4166
Honeyville Grain
Rancho Cucamonga, CA 888-810-3212
Hygeia Dairy Company
McAllen, TX 956-686-0511
Ingredients, Inc.
Buffalo Grove, IL 847-419-9595
Kohler Mix Specialties
White Bear Lake, MN 651-426-1633
Kohler Mix Specialties
Newington, CT 860-666-1511
Kosto Food Products Company
Wauconda, IL 847-487-2600
Kraft
Parsippany, NJ 973-292-1755
Kraft Canada Headquarters
Don Mills, ON 800-268-7808

Kraft Food Ingredients
Memphis, TN 901-381-6500
Land O'Lakes
St Paul, MN 800-328-9680
Limpert Brothers
Vineland, NJ 800-691-1353
Lloyd's
Berwyn, PA 610-293-0516
Louisiana Gourmet Enterprises
Houma, LA 800-328-5586
Lynch Foods
North York, QC 416-449-5464
Maple Island
St Paul, MN 800-369-1022
Master Mix
Placentia, CA 714-524-1698
Master Taste International
Plant City, FL 800-237-7629
Meadow Gold Dairies
Lincoln, NE 800-742-7349
Meadowvale
Yorkville, IL 800-953-0201
Michigan Dessert Corporation
Oak Park, MI 800-328-8632
Milani Gourmet
Melrose Park, IL 800-333-0003
Nanci's Frozen Yogurt
Mesa, AZ 800-788-0808
Naterl
St. Bruno, QC 800- 50- 115
Nog Incorporated
Dunkirk, NY 800-332-2664
Northwestern Foods
St Paul, MN 800-236-4937
Pasta Factory
Northlake, IL 800-615-6951
Paulaur Corporation
Cranbury, NJ 888-398-8844
Prairie Farms Dairy
Carlinville, IL 217-854-2547
Price's Creameries
El Paso, TX 915-565-2711
Quality Naturally! Foods
City of Industry, CA 888-498-6986
Redco Foods
Windsor, CT 800-645-1190
Rich Products Corporation
Hilliard, OH 614-771-1117
Rio Syrup Company
St Louis, MO 800-325-7666
Roberts Dairy Company
Omaha, NE 402-344-4321
Roney Oatman
Aurora, IL 630-859-2800
S&N Food Company
Mesquite, TX 972-222-1184
Schneider's Dairy Holdings Inc
Pittsburgh, PA 412-881-3525
Sells Best
Mishawaka, IN 800-837-8368
Serv-Agen Corporation
Cherry Hill, NJ 856-663-6966
Sno-Shack
Salt Lake City, UT 801-466-1771
Specialty Bakers
Marysville, PA 800-233-0778
Specialty Baking Products
Dunkirk, NY 716-366-0938
Sugar Creek/Eskimo Pie
Russellville, AR 800-445-2715
Sunshine Farms Dairy
Elyria, OH 440-322-6301
Swagger Foods Corporation
Vernon Hills, IL 847-913-1200
Swiss Valley Farms Company
Davenport, IA 563-468-6600
Timber Peaks Gourmet
Parker, CO 800-982-7687
Tova Industries
Louisville, KY 888-532-8682
Tropical Illusions
Trenton, MO 660-359-6849
VIP Foods
Flushing, NY 718-821-3942
W&G Flavors
Hunt Valley, MD 410-771-6606
Welch's Foods Inc
Concord, MA 800-340-6870
Wiggin Farms
Arbuckle, CA 530-476-2288
Wisconsin Wilderness Food Products
Milwaukee, WI 800-359-3039

Low Carb

Dixie USA
Tomball, TX 800-233-3668
International Food Technologies
Evansville, IN 812-853-9432

Dip

Amberland Foods
Harvey, ND 800-950-4558
Atlantic Quality Spice &Seasonings
Edison, NJ 800-584-0422
Au Printemps Gourmet
Prevost, QC 800-663-0416
Big Steer Enterprises
Beaumont, TX 800-421-4951
Chugwater Chili Corporation
Chugwater, WY 800-972-4454
Country Home Creations
Goodrich, MI 800-457-3477
CW Resources
New Britain, CT 860-229-7700
Erba Food Products
Brooklyn, NY 718-272-7700
Fountain Valley Foods
Colorado Springs, CO 719-573-6012
Gloria's Gourmet
New Britain, CT 860-225-9196
Heluva Good Cheese
Sodus, NY 315-483-6971
Hollman Foods
Minden, NE 888-926-2879
Jodie's Kitchen
Tarpon Springs, FL 800-728-3704
Just Delicious Gourmet Foods
Seal Beach, CA 800-871-6085
Lesley Elizabeth
Lapeer, MI 800-684-3300
Limited Edition
Midland, TX 432-686-2008
Look's Gourmet Food Company
Whiting, ME 800-962-6258
Milani Gourmet
Melrose Park, IL 800-333-0003
Olde Tyme Food Corporation
East Longmeadow, MA 800-356-6533
Rabbit Creek Products
Louisburg, KS 800-837-3073
Reser's Fine Foods
Beaverton, OR 800-333-6431
Spice Hunter
San Luis Obispo, CA 800-444-3061
Swagger Foods Corporation
Vernon Hills, IL 847-913-1200

Donut

BakeMark
Schaumburg, IL 562-949-1054

Drink

American Instants
Flanders, NJ 973-584-8811
Bread & Chocolate
Wells River, VT 800-524-6715
Diamond Crystal
Savannah, GA 800-227-4455
El Paso Chile Company
El Paso, TX 888-472-5727
Frontera Foods
Chicago, IL 800-509-4441
Granny Blossom Specialty Foods
Wells, VT 802-645-0507
SECO & Golden 100
Deland, FL 386-734-3906

Dumplings

Tova Industries
Louisville, KY 888-532-8682

Frozen

Pro Form Labs
Orinda, CA 925-299-9000
Robertet Flavors
Piscataway, NJ 732-981-8300
Unilever Bestfoods
Englewood Cliffs, NJ 201-894-4000

Dessert

International Food Technologies
Evansville, IN 812-853-9432

Granita

International Food Technologies
Evansville, IN .812-853-9432
Nanci's Frozen Yogurt
Mesa, AZ. 800-788-0808

Gravy

Ailments E.D. Foods Inc.
Pointe Claire, QC 800-267-3333
Campbell Soup Company of Canada
Listowel, ON 800-575-7687
Dorothy Dawson Foods Products
Jackson, MI. .517-788-9830
Griffith Laboratories Worldwide
Alsip, IL 800-346-4743
Lawry's Foods
Monrovia, CA 800-952-9797
Morgan Food
Austin, IN 888-430-1780
RC Fine Foods
Belle Mead, NJ 800-526-3953
Spice Advice
Ankeny, IA 800-247-5251
Spice Time Foods/Julius & Joe's
Paramus, NJ .800-345-9225
White Lily Foods Company
San Antonio, TX 800-264-5459
Williams Foods Inc
Lenexa, KS 800-255-6736
Williams-West & Witt Products
Michigan City, IN 219-879-8236

Hot Chocolate

Brewfresh Coffee Company
South Salt Lake, UT 888-486-3334

Ice Cream

Agri-Dairy Products
Purchase, NY 914-697-9580
Al-Rite Fruits & Syrups
Miami, FL. 305-652-2540
America's Classic Foods
Cambria, CA .805-927-0745
American Food & Equipment
Miami, FL. 305-361-6517
Baird Dairies
Clarksville, IN. 812-283-3345
Barber Pure Milk Ice Cream Company
Birmingham, AL. 205-942-2351
Benson Creamery
Decatur, IL 217-429-2351
Blue Bell Creameries
Brenham, TX. 979-836-7977
Carbolite Foods
Evansville, IN 888-524-3314
Clofine Dairy & Food Products
Linwood, NJ .800-441-1001
Crowley Foods
Binghamton, NY. 800-637-0019
Cumberland Dairy
Rosenhayn, NJ 856-451-1300
Dairy-Mix
St Petersburg, FL 727-525-6101
Fairmont Products
Belleville, PA 717-935-2121
Galliker Dairy
Johnstown, PA. 800-477-6455
Innovative Food Solutions LLC
Columbus, OH 800-884-3314
International Food Technologies
Evansville, IN 812-853-9432
Kalva Corporation
Gurnee, IL. 800-525-8220
Kohler Mix Specialties
White Bear Lake, MN 651-426-1633
Kohler Mix Specialties
Newington, CT 860-666-1511
Kosto Food Products Company
Wauconda, IL 847-487-2600
Land O'Lakes
St Paul, MN. .800-328-9680
Leiby's Dairy
Tamaqua, PA .570-668-2399

Master Mix
Placentia, CA 714-524-1698
Naterl
St. Bruno, QC 800- 50- 115
Nog Incorporated
Dunkirk, NY .800-332-2664
Prairie Farms Dairy
Carlinville, IL 217-854-2547
Price's Creameries
El Paso, TX 915-565-2711
Quality Naturally! Foods
City of Industry, CA 888-498-6986
Queensboro Farm Products
Canastota, NY 315-697-2235
Queensboro Farm Products
Jamaica, NY .718-658-5000
Reiter Dairy
Akron, OH. 800-362-0825
Roberts Dairy Company
Omaha, NE 402-344-4321
Schneider's Dairy Holdings Inc
Pittsburgh, PA 412-881-3525
Sunshine Farms Dairy
Elyria, OH 440-322-6301
Swiss Valley Farms Company
Cedar Rapids, IA 319-364-8153
Swiss Valley Farms Company
Davenport, IA 563-468-6600
Titusville Dairy Products
Titusville, PA 800-352-0101
Tova Industries
Louisville, KY 888-532-8682
Vitarich Ice Cream
Fortuna, CA .707-725-6182

Low Carb

International Food Technologies
Evansville, IN 812-853-9432

Jambalaya

Reggie Ball's Cajun Foods
Lake Charles, LA 337-436-0291

Liquid

National Fruit Flavor Company
New Orleans, LA 800-966-1123
Pro Form Labs
Orinda, CA 925-299-9000
Robertet Flavors
Piscataway, NJ 732-981-8300
Unilever Bestfoods
Englewood Cliffs, NJ 201-894-4000

Muffin

Abel & Schafer
Ronkonkoma, NY. 800-443-1260
ACH Food Companies, Inc.
Cordova, TN .800-691-1106
ADM Milling Company
Jackson, TN .731-424-3535
Ambassador Foods
Van Nuys, CA 800-338-3369
Atkinson Milling Company
Selma, NC 800-948-5707
Aunt Millies Bakeries
Fort Wayne, IN 260-424-8245
Bake'n Joy Foods
North Andover, MA 800-666-4937
Fiera Foods
North York, ON. 416-744-1010
Food Concentrate Corporation
Oklahoma City, OK 405-840-5633
Grain Process Enterprises Ltd.
Scarborough, ON 800-387-5292
Honeyville Grain
Rancho Cucamonga, CA 888-810-3212
Iveta Gourmet
Santa Cruz, CA 831-423-5149
John Gust Foods & Products Corporation
Batavia, IL. 800-756-5886
Kokopelli's Kitchen
Phoenix, AZ .888-943-9802
Oetker Limited
Mississauga, ON 905-678-1311
Pemberton's Gourmet Foods
Gray, ME 800-255-8401
Premier Blending
Wichita, KS. .316-267-5533

Purity Foods
Okemos, MI .800-997-7358
Sarabeth's Kitchen
Bronx, NY 800-773-7378
Sells Best
Mishawaka, IN 800-837-8368
Shepherdsfield Bakery
Fulton, MO 573-642-1439
Sorrenti Family Farms
Escalon, CA .888-435-9490
White Lily Foods Company
San Antonio, TX 800-264-5459

Pancake

ACH Food Companies, Inc.
Cordova, TN .800-691-1106
Agricore United
Winnipeg, MB. 204-944-5411
Atkinson Milling Company
Selma, NC 800-948-5707
Baker & Baker
Schaumburg, IL 800-593-5777
Baker & Baker, Inc.
Schaumburg, IL 800-593-5777
Bakery Chef
Louisville, KY 800-594-0203
Bette's Diner Products
Berkeley, CA .510-644-3230
Blackberry Patch
Thomasville, GA. 800-853-5598
Brown Family Farm
Brattleboro, VT. 888-556-2753
Bruce Foods Corporation
New Iberia, LA 800-299-9082
Byrd Mill Company
Ashland, VA .888-897-3336
Country Cupboard
Virginia City, NV 775-847-7300
Cream of the West
Harlowton, MT 800-477-2383
Fearn Natural Foods
Mequon, WI .800-877-8935
Golden Malted
South Bend, IN 800-686-6258
Gormly's Orchard
South Burlington, VT 800-639-7604
Greenfield Mills
Howe, IN. 260-367-2394
Heartland Food Products
Shawnee Mission, KS 913-831-4446
Highland Sugarworks
Websterville, VT 800-452-4012
Homestead Mills
Cook, MN 800-652-5233
Inn Maid Food
Lenox, MA 413-637-2732
John Gust Foods & Products Corporation
Batavia, IL. 800-756-5886
Kamish Food Products
Chicago, IL 773-267-0400
Kokopelli's Kitchen
Phoenix, AZ .888-943-9802
Little Crow Foods
Warsaw, IN 800-288-2769
Maple Grove Farms of Vermont
St Johnsbury, VT. 800-525-2540
Minnesota Specialty Crops
McGregor, MN 800-328-6731
Morningstar Foods
Dallas, TX. 225-273-2803
Northwestern Foods
St Paul, MN. .800-236-4937
Old Tyme Mill Company
Chicago, IL 773-521-9484
Pemberton's Gourmet Foods
Gray, ME 800-255-8401
Prairie Sun Grains
Calgary, AB. .800-556-6807
Premier Blending
Wichita, KS. .316-267-5533
Purity Foods
Okemos, MI .800-997-7358
Reimann Food Classics
Palatine, IL 847-991-1366
SFP Food Products
Conway, AR .800-654-5329
Sugarwoods Farm
Glover, VT 800-245-3718
Tait Farm Foods
Centre Hall, PA 800-787-2716

Turkey Hill Sugarbush
Waterloo, QC 450-539-4822
Valley View Blueberries
Vancouver, WA 360-892-2839
Wall-Rogalsky Milling Company
Mc Pherson, KS 800-835-2067
Weisenberger Mills
Midway, KY 800-643-8678
White Lily Foods Company
San Antonio, TX 800-264-5459

Pie Crust

Country Cupboard
Virginia City, NV 775-847-7300
Hansmann's Mills
Bainbridge, NY 607-967-5080
Master Taste International
Plant City, FL 800-237-7629

Powdered

Crystal Star Herbal Nutrition
Salinas, CA 831-422-7500
Northwestern Foods
St Paul, MN 800-236-4937
Pro Form Labs
Orinda, CA 925-299-9000
Robertet Flavors
Piscataway, NJ 732-981-8300
Schiff Nutrition International
Salt Lake City, UT 801-975-5000

Punch

Associated Brands, Inc.
Medina, NY 800-265-0050
Four Percent Company
Highland Park, MI 313-345-5880
Quality Naturally! Foods
City of Industry, CA 888-498-6986
Tova Industries
Louisville, KY 888-532-8682

Rice

R.A.B. Food Group LLC
Secaucus, NJ 201-453-5200
Riceland Foods   Rice Milling Operations
Little Rock, AR 888-532-4844

Shoofly

Good Food
Honey Brook, PA 800-327-4406

Smoothie Powder

International Food Technologies
Evansville, IN 812-853-9432
Nanci's Frozen Yogurt
Mesa, AZ 800-788-0808

Soup

Ailments E.D. Foods Inc.
Pointe Claire, QC 800-267-3333
Amalgamated Produce
Bridgeport, CT 800-358-3808
Amberland Foods
Harvey, ND 800-950-4558
Associated Brands, Inc.
Medina, NY 800-265-0050
Atlantic Quality Spice &Seasonings
Edison, NJ 800-584-0422
Bernard Food Industries
Evanston, IL 800-323-3663
Boston Spice & Tea Company
Boston, VA 800-966-4372
Bountiful Pantry
Nantucket, MA 888-832-6466
Brookema Company
West Chicago, IL 630-562-2290
Campbell Soup Company
Camden, NJ 800-257-8443
Cascade Continental Foods
Woodland, CA 415-668-6194
Commodities Marketing, Inc.
Edison, NJ 732-516-0700
Cook-In-The-Kitchen
White River Junction, VT 802-333-4141
Country Home Creations
Goodrich, MI 800-457-3477

Crazy Jerry's
Roswell, GA 770-993-0651
Diamond Crystal Brands
Savannah, GA 912-651-5112
Dismat Corporation
Toledo, OH 419-531-8963
Dorothy Dawson Foods Products
Jackson, MI 517-788-9830
Edward & Sons Trading Company
Carpinteria, CA 805-684-8500
Fair Scones
Medina, WA 800-588-9160
Fearn Natural Foods
Mequon, WI 800-877-8935
Flavor House
Adelanto, CA 760-246-9131
Four C Foods Corporation
Brooklyn, NY 718-272-4242
Gloria's Gourmet
New Britain, CT 860-225-9196
Halladays Harvest Barn
Bellows Falls, VT 802-463-3471
High Country Gourmet
Orem, UT 801-426-4383
Hummingbird Kitchens
Whitehouse, TX 800-921-9470
Idaho Pacific Corporation
Ririe, ID 800-238-5503
Kemach Food Products   Corporation
Brooklyn, NY 888-453-6224
Lake City Foods
Mississauga, ON 905-625-8244
Legumes Plus
Fairfield, WA 800-845-1349
Lynch Foods
North York, QC 416-449-5464
Magic Seasoning Blends
Harahan, LA 800-457-2857
Milani Gourmet
Melrose Park, IL 800-333-0003
Nor-Cliff Farms
Port Colborne, ON 905-835-0808
North Bay Trading Company
Brule, WI 800-348-0164
Pasta Partners
Salt Lake City, UT 800-727-8284
Pasta USA
Spokane, WA 800-456-2084
Rabbit Creek Products
Louisburg, KS 800-837-3073
RC Fine Foods
Belle Mead, NJ 800-526-3953
Sheila's Select Gourmet Recipe
Heber City, UT 800-516-7286
Sorrenti Family Farms
Escalon, CA 888-435-9490
Spice Hunter
San Luis Obispo, CA 800-444-3061
Swagger Foods Corporation
Vernon Hills, IL 847-913-1200
Tova Industries
Louisville, KY 888-532-8682
Tropical
Columbus, OH 800-538-3941
Unilever Bestfoods
Englewood Cliffs, NJ 201-894-4000
Vogue Cuisine
Culver City, CA 888-236-4144
Westfield Foods
Greenville, RI 401-949-3558
White Coffee Corporation
Long Island City, NY 800-221-0140
Williams-West & Witt Products
Michigan City, IN 219-879-8236

Trail

A.L. Bazzini Company
Bronx, NY 800-228-0172
Aurora Products
Stratford, CT 800-398-1048
Chile Today - Hot Tamale
San Francisco, CA 800-758-0372
Chukar Cherries
Prosser, WA 800-624-9544
Durey-Libby Edible Nuts
Carlstadt, NJ 800-332-6887
Hialeah Products Company
Hollywood, FL 800-923-3379
Inn Maid Food
Lenox, MA 413-637-2732

Jason & Son Specialty Foods
Rancho Cordova, CA 800-810-9093
King Nut Company
Cleveland, OH 800-860-5464
Marantha Natural Foods
San Francisco, CA 800-299-0048
Midwest/Northern
Minneapolis, MN 800-328-5502
Nature Kist Snacks
Livermore, CA 925-606-4200
New England Natural Bakers
Greenfield, MA 800-910-2884
Nspired Natural Foods
Melville, NY 631-845-4689
Nut Factory
Spokane Valley, WA 888-239-5288
Pilgrim's Pride
Lufkin, TX 936-639-1174
Randag & Associates Inc
Elmhurst, IL 630-530-2830
Sonne
Wahpeton, ND 800-727-6663
Sun Ridge Farms
Santa Cruz, CA 800-655-3252
Superior Nut & Candy Company
Chicago, IL 800-843-2238
Timber Peaks Gourmet
Parker, CO 800-982-7687
Tova Industries
Louisville, KY 888-532-8682
Tropical
Charlotte, NC 800-220-1413
Valley View Blueberries
Vancouver, WA 360-892-2839
Variety Foods
Warren, MI 586-268-4900
Waymouth Farms
New Hope, MN 800-527-0094
Weaver Nut Company
Ephrata, PA 717-738-3781
Wysong Corporation
Midland, MI 800-748-0188

Waffle

Baker & Baker
Schaumburg, IL 800-593-5777
Baker & Baker, Inc.
Schaumburg, IL 800-593-5777
Bountiful Pantry
Nantucket, MA 888-832-6466
Byrd Mill Company
Ashland, VA 888-897-3336
Country Cupboard
Virginia City, NV 775-847-7300
Cream of the West
Harlowton, MT 800-477-2383
Golden Malted
South Bend, IN 800-686-6258
Great Grains Milling Company
Scobey, MT 406-783-5588
Hansmann's Mills
Bainbridge, NY 607-967-5080
Heartland Food Products
Shawnee Mission, KS 913-831-4446
Inn Maid Food
Lenox, MA 413-637-2732
John Gust Foods & Products Corporation
Batavia, IL 800-756-5886
Kamish Food Products
Chicago, IL 773-267-0400
Maple Grove Farms of Vermont
St Johnsbury, VT 800-525-2540
Morningstar Foods
Dallas, TX 225-273-2803
Old Tyme Mill Company
Chicago, IL 773-521-9484
Reimann Food Classics
Palatine, IL 847-991-1366
SFP Food Products
Conway, AR 800-654-5329
Wall-Rogalsky Milling Company
Mc Pherson, KS 800-835-2067

Yogurt Powder

International Food Technologies
Evansville, IN 812-853-9432
Kantner Group
Wapakoneta, OH 419-738-4060

Eggs & Egg Products

General

Almark Foods
Gainesville, GA 800-849-3447
Brown Produce Company
Farina, IL 618-245-3301
Burn Brae Farms
Strathroy, ON 519-245-1630
Cal-Maine Foods
Pine Grove, LA 225-222-4148
Cal-Maine Foods
Jackson, MS 601-948-6813
ConAgra Dairy Foods
Overland, MO 314-429-3636
Cordon Bleu International
Anjou, QC 514-352-3000
Creighton Brothers
Atwood, IN 574-267-3101
Cropp Cooperative-Organic Valley
La Farge, WI 888-444-6455
Cutler Egg Products
Abbeville, AL 334-585-2268
Deb-El Foods
Elizabeth, NJ 800-421-3447
Dixie Dairy Company
Gary, IN .219-885-6101
Egg Company
Gurnee, IL 847-367-8553
Farbest-Tallman Foods Corporation
Montvale, NJ 201-573-4900
Henningsen Foods
Omaha, NE 402-330-2500
Henningsen Foods
Purchase, NY 914-701-4020
Hillandale
Gettysburg, PA 717-334-1973
Hormel Foods Corporation
Austin, MN 800-523-4635
ISE Newberry
Newberry, SC 803-276-5803
Marshall Egg Products
Seymour, IN 812-497-2557
Medeiros Farms
Kalaheo, HI 808-332-8211
National Egg Products Company
Social Circle, GA 770-464-2652
Nulaid Foods
Ripon, CA 209-599-2121
Oliver Egg Products
Crewe, VA 800-525-3447
Rembrandt Foods
Rembrandt, IA 972-847-4421
Rosenberger's Dairies
Hatfield, PA 800-355-9074
Smith Packing Regional Meat
Utica, NY 315-732-5125
Wenk Foods Inc
Madison, SD 605-256-4569
Wetta Egg Farm
Andale, KS 316-445-2231
Yoder Dairies
Chesapeake, VA 757-497-3518

Boiled

Agri-Dairy Products
Purchase, NY 914-697-9580

Cooked

Egg Low Farms
Sherburne, NY 607-674-4653

Dehydrated

Associated Bakers Products
Huntington, NY 631-673-3841
Ballas Egg Products Corporation
Zanesville, OH 740-453-0386
Culinary Foods
Chicago, IL 800-621-4049
Oskaloosa Food Products Corporation
Oskaloosa, IA 800-477-7239

Dried

Associated Bakers Products
Huntington, NY 631-673-3841

Ballas Egg Products Corporation
Zanesville, OH 740-453-0386
Cutler Egg Products
Abbeville, AL 334-585-2268
Double B Foods
Schulenburg, TX 800-472-6661
Egg Company
Gurnee, IL 847-367-8553
Henningsen Foods
Omaha, NE 402-330-2500
Inovatech USA
Montreal, QC 888-388-3447
Kelly Flour Company
Addison, IL 630-678-5300
Oskaloosa Food Products Corporation
Oskaloosa, IA 800-477-7239
Papetti's Egg Products
Elizabeth, NJ 800-524-3447
Sonstegard Foods Company
Sioux Falls, SD 800-533-3184
W&G Flavors
Hunt Valley, MD 410-771-6606
Wenk Foods Inc
Madison, SD 605-256-4569

Desiccated

Agri-Dairy Products
Purchase, NY 914-697-9580
American Health & Nutrition
Ann Arbor, MI 734-677-5572
Clofine Dairy & Food Products
Linwood, NJ 800-441-1001
Henningsen Foods
Purchase, NY 914-701-4020

Fat & Cholesterol Free

Hormel Foods Corporation
Austin, MN 800-523-4635
Tofutti Brands
Cranford, NJ 908-272-2400

Fresh

Agri-Dairy Products
Purchase, NY 914-697-9580
Creighton Brothers
Atwood, IN 574-267-3101
Dixie Egg Company
Jacksonville, FL 800-394-3447
Egg Low Farms
Sherburne, NY 607-674-4653
Feature Foods
Etobicoke, ON 416-675-7350
Great Valley Mills
Barto, PA .800-688-6455
Happy Egg Dealers
Tampa, FL 813-248-2362
Hi Point Industries
Vernon, CA 800-959-7292
ISE Farms
Galena, MD 410-755-6300
Land O'Lakes
St Paul, MN 651-730-2100
New Morn Foods
Oakwood, GA 770-536-4561
Oskaloosa Food Products Corporation
Oskaloosa, IA 800-477-7239
Rose Acre Farms
Seymour, IN 800-356-3447
Siegel Egg Company
Cambridge, MA 800-593-3447
Sinton Dairy Foods Company
Colorado Springs, CO 800-388-4970
Sommer Maid Creamery
Doylestown, PA 215-345-6160
Sparboe Companies
Los Angeles, CA 213-626-7538
Sunny Fresh Foods
Monticello, MN 800-872-3447
Sunnyslope Farms Egg Ranch
Cherry Valley, CA 951-845-1131
Suter Company
Sycamore, IL 800-435-6942
Wetta Egg Farm
Andale, KS 316-445-2231

Frozen

Agri-Dairy Products
Purchase, NY 914-697-9580
Almark Foods
Gainesville, GA 800-849-3447
Ballas Egg Products Corporation
Zanesville, OH 740-453-0386
Brown Produce Company
Farina, IL 618-245-3301
Creighton Brothers
Atwood, IN 574-267-3101
Cutler Egg Products
Abbeville, AL 334-585-2268
Dixie Egg Company
Jacksonville, FL 800-394-3447
Global Egg Corporation
Etobicoke, ON 416-231-2409
Great Valley Mills
Barto, PA .800-688-6455
Hi Point Industries
Vernon, CA 800-959-7292
ISE Farms
Galena, MD 410-755-6300
Kent Foods
Gonzales, TX 830-672-7993
Land O'Lakes, Inc
Arden Hills, MN 800-328-9680
McAnally Enterprises
Norco, CA 800-726-2002
Michael Foods, Inc.
Minnetonka, MN 952-258-4000
New Morn Foods
Oakwood, GA 770-536-4561
Oliver Egg Products
Crewe, VA 800-525-3447
Oskaloosa Food Products Corporation
Oskaloosa, IA 800-477-7239
Siegel Egg Company
Cambridge, MA 800-593-3447
Sonstegard Foods Company
Sioux Falls, SD 800-533-3184
Sparboe Companies
Los Angeles, CA 213-626-7538
Sunnyslope Farms Egg Ranch
Cherry Valley, CA 951-845-1131
W&G Flavors
Hunt Valley, MD 410-771-6606
Wenk Foods Inc
Madison, SD 605-256-4569

Hard-Boiled

Almark Foods
Gainesville, GA 800-849-3447
Creighton Brothers
Atwood, IN 574-267-3101
Dixie Egg Company
Jacksonville, FL 800-394-3447
Feature Foods
Etobicoke, ON 416-675-7350
ISE Farms
Galena, MD 410-755-6300
Newburgh Egg Corporation
Brooklyn, NY 718-692-4392
Sunny Fresh Foods
Monticello, MN 800-872-3447
Sunnyslope Farms Egg Ranch
Cherry Valley, CA 951-845-1131
Suter Company
Sycamore, IL 800-435-6942
Wetta Egg Farm
Andale, KS 316-445-2231

Hatcheries

Amick Farms, LLC
Leesville, SC 800-926-4257
Hickory Baked Food
Castle Rock, CO 303-688-2633
Norfolk Hatchery
Norfolk, NE 402-371-5710
Sanderson Farms
Laurel, MS 601-765-2221

Chicks

Turkey

Hickory Baked Food
Castle Rock, CO 303-688-2633

Liquid

Ballas Egg Products Corporation
Zanesville, OH 740-453-0386
Brown Produce Company
Farina, IL. 618-245-3301
Cutler Egg Products
Abbeville, AL 334-585-2268
Eggology
Canoga Park, CA 818-610-2222
Global Egg Corporation
Etobicoke, ON 416-231-2409
Hi Point Industries
Vernon, CA .800-959-7292
Kent Foods
Gonzales, TX 830-672-7993
McAnally Enterprises
Norco, CA. .800-726-2002
Michael Foods, Inc.
Minnetonka, MN. 952-258-4000
Nulaid Foods
Ripon, CA. .209-599-2121
Oskaloosa Food Products Corporation
Oskaloosa, IA 800-477-7239
Sonstegard Foods Company
Sioux Falls, SD 800-533-3184
Sunny Fresh Foods
Monticello, MN 800-872-3447

Whites

Eggology
Canoga Park, CA 818-610-2222
Michael Foods, Inc.
Minnetonka, MN. 952-258-4000

Whole

Michael Foods, Inc.
Minnetonka, MN. 952-258-4000

Yolk

Michael Foods, Inc.
Minnetonka, MN. 952-258-4000

Mix

Oliver Egg Products
Crewe, VA. .800-525-3447
Sunny Fresh Foods
Monticello, MN 800-872-3447

Peeled

Agri-Dairy Products
Purchase, NY 914-697-9580
Dixie Egg Company
Jacksonville, FL 800-394-3447
Feature Foods
Etobicoke, ON 416-675-7350
Great Valley Mills
Barto, PA 800-688-6455
ISE Farms
Galena, MD. 410-755-6300
New Morn Foods
Oakwood, GA 770-536-4561
Newburgh Egg Corporation
Brooklyn, NY 718-692-4392
Sunnyslope Farms Egg Ranch
Cherry Valley, CA. 951-845-1131
Wetta Egg Farm
Andale, KS .316-445-2231

Prepared

Agri-Dairy Products
Purchase, NY 914-697-9580
Almark Foods
Gainesville, GA 800-849-3447
Clofine Dairy & Food Products
Linwood, NJ 800-441-1001

Quail

Squab Producers of California
Modesto, CA. 209-537-4744

Solids

Albumen

Brown Produce Company
Farina, IL. 618-245-3301
Holton Food Products Company
La Grange, IL 708-352-5599
National Egg Products Company
Social Circle, GA 770-464-2652
Newburgh Egg Corporation
Brooklyn, NY 718-692-4392
Papetti's Egg Products
Elizabeth, NJ. 800-524-3447
Wabash Valley Produce
Dubois, IN. .812-678-3131

Whole Egg

Oliver Egg Products
Crewe, VA. .800-525-3447

Substitutes

Bay Valley Foods
Green Bay, WI. 800-558-4700
Cargill Texturizing Solutions
Cedar Rapids, IA. 877-650-7080
ConAgra Dairy Foods
Overland, MO 314-429-3636
Hi Point Industries
Vernon, CA .800-959-7292
Michael Foods, Inc.
Minnetonka, MN. 952-258-4000

Frozen

Clofine Dairy & Food Products
Linwood, NJ 800-441-1001

Refrigerated

Clofine Dairy & Food Products
Linwood, NJ 800-441-1001
Michael Foods, Inc.
Minnetonka, MN. 952-258-4000

Yolk

Clofine Dairy & Food Products
Linwood, NJ 800-441-1001
Global Egg Corporation
Etobicoke, ON 416-231-2409
Henningsen Foods
Purchase, NY 914-701-4020
Hi Point Industries
Vernon, CA .800-959-7292
Michael Foods, Inc.
Minnetonka, MN. 952-258-4000
National Egg Products Company
Social Circle, GA 770-464-2652
Newburgh Egg Corporation
Brooklyn, NY 718-692-4392
Norac Technologies
Edmonton, AB 780-414-9595
Papetti's Egg Products
Elizabeth, NJ. 800-524-3447
Wabash Valley Produce
Dubois, IN. .812-678-3131

Ethnic Foods

General

Abuelita Mexican Foods
Manassas Park, VA 703-369-0232
Aina Hawaiian Tropical Products
Hilo, HI 877-961-4774
Amy's Kitchen
Petaluma, CA 707-578-5908
Bayou Cajun Foods
Monroe, LA 318-388-2383
Bayou Crab
Grand Bay, AL 251-824-2076
Belleisle Foods
Belleisle Creek, NB 506-485-2564
Blansh International
San Jose, CA 408-997-8284
Blue Marble Brands
Edison, NJ 732-650-9905

Burke Corporation
Nevada, IA 800-654-1152

> Always make it your best® with Burke fully cooked meats. We specialize in Italian sausage, beef, and pork toppings, meatballs, taco meats, shredded meats, pepperoni, bacon, Canadian-style bacon, chicken and beef strips. Additionally, we offer a variety of specialty products: Hand-Pinched Style® brand toppings, chorizo, gyro topping, andouille sausage, and breakfast patties and links.

C&J Trading
San Francisco, CA 415-822-8910
C.N.L. Trading
Alhambra, CA 626-282-1938
Cajun Bayou Distributors & Management
Baton Rouge, LA 225-356-0387
Calidad Foods
Grand Prairie, TX 972-933-4100
California Fresh Salsa
Woodland, CA 530-662-0512
Canton Noodle
Chicago, IL 312-842-4900
Caribbean Distributors
Brentwood, MD 301-403-2929
Casa Sanchez Restaurant
San Francisco, CA 415-282-2402
Chi & Hing Food Service
Phoenix, AZ 623-939-8889
Chicago Oriental Wholesale
Chicago, IL 312-842-9993
Chong Mei Trading
Atlanta, GA 404-768-3838
Cocina de Mino
Yukon, OK 405-632-0600
Con Piacere Italian Specialty
Tulalip, WA 800-204-3594
Corfu Tasty Gyros
Bensenville, IL 630-595-2510
DCL
Honolulu, HI 808-845-3834
Discovery Foods
Hayward, CA 510-293-1838
Don Jose Foods
Oceanside, CA 760-631-0243
El Aguila Food Products
Salinas, CA 800-398-2929
El Perico Charro
Garden City, KS 620-275-6454
Elena's Food Specialties
S San Francisco, CA 800-376-5368
Goya de Puerto Rico
Bayamon, PR 787-740-4900
H&W Foods
Kapolei, HI 808-682-8300
Hong Kong Supermarket
Atlanta, GA 404-325-3999

Houston Calco
Houston, TX 713-236-8668
India's Rasoa
St Louis, MO 314-727-1414
J&M Food Products Company
Deerfield, IL 847-948-1290
J.F.C. International
Norcross, GA 770-448-0070
Joseph and Sally Krusas
Rockford, IL 815-395-1330
Juanita's Foods
Wilmington, CA 310-834-5339
Jyoti Cuisine India
Berwyn, PA 610-296-4620
Kyong Hae Kim Company
Honolulu, HI 808-926-8720
La Mexicana
Seattle, WA 206-763-1488
M&M Food Distributors/Oriental Pride
Virginia Beach, VA 757-499-5676
Maria and Son Italian Products
St Louis, MO 866-481-9009
Marukai Corporation
Gardena, CA 310-660-6300
Marukan Vinegar (U.S.A.) Inc.
Paramount, CA 562-630-6060
Maya Maimal Fine Indian Food
Rhinebeck, NY 845-876-8200
Mission Food
Irving, TX 800-424-7862
National Importers
Brampton, ON 905-791-1322
Natural Quick Foods
Seattle, WA 206-365-5757
Oriental Foods
Alhambra, CA 626-293-1994
Portugalia Imports
Fall River, MA 508-679-9307
Power-Selles Imports
Woodinville, WA 425-398-9761
Preferred Brands International
Stamford, CT 800-827-8900
R.A.B. Food Group LLC
Secaucus, NJ 201-453-5200
Raja Foods
Skokie, IL 800-800-7923
Refrigerated Foods Association
Chamblee, GA 770-452-0660
Rico Foods
Paterson, NJ 973-278-0589
Rokeach Food Corporation
Newark, NJ 973-589-1472
Rothman's Foods
St Louis, MO 314-367-5448
Sanchez Distributors
San Antonio, TX 210-341-1682
Say Ying Leong Look Funn Factory
Honolulu, HI 808-537-4304
Shell Ridge Jalapeno Project
Rockport, TX 512-790-8028
Squair Food Company
Los Angeles, CA 213-749-7041
Sukhi's Gourmet Indian Food
Hayward, CA 888-478-5447
Sun Sun Food Products
Edmonton, AB 780-454-4261
Taj Gourmet Foods
Framingham, MA 508-875-6212
Tamashiro Market
Honolulu, HI 808-841-8047
Taqueria El Milagro
Chicago, IL 312-433-7620
Tekita House Foods
El Paso, TX 915-779-2181
Thai Kitchen
Berkeley, CA 800-967-8424
Trappey's Fine Foods
New Iberia, LA 337-365-8281
True World Foods of Boston
Gloucester, MA 978-283-1324
True World Foods of Chicago
Elk Grove Vlg, IL 847-718-0088
True World Foods of Hawaii
Honolulu, HI 808-836-3222
VIP Sales Company
Hayward, CA 918-252-5791

Wing Seafood Company
Chicago, IL 312-942-9930
Wing Sing Chong Company
S San Francisco, CA 415-552-1234
Yamasho
Elk Grove Village, IL 847-981-9342
Zippy's
Honolulu, HI 808-973-0877

Asian

Asian Foods
St Paul, MN 651-558-2400
House of Tsang
San Francisco, CA 415-282-9952
Long Kow Foods USA Corporation
Torrance, CA 877-566-4569
Moody Dunbar
Johnson City, TN 800-251-8202
San-J International
Richmond, VA 800-446-5500

Burritos

Appetizers And, Inc.
Chicago, IL 800-323-5472
Baja Foods
Chicago, IL 773-376-9030
Camino Real Foods
Vernon, CA 800-421-6201
Casa Sanchez Restaurant
San Francisco, CA 415-282-2402
Cedarlane Foods
Carson, CA 800-826-3322
Del Rey Tortilleria
Chicago, IL 800-446-1459
Don Miguel Mexican Foods
Orange, CA 714-634-8441
Elena's Food Specialties
S San Francisco, CA 800-376-5368
Foodbrands America
Oklahoma City, OK 405-290-4000
Hacienda De Paco
Orlando, FL 407-859-5417
La Tang Cuisine Manufacturing
Houston, TX 713-780-4876
McLane Foods
Phoenix, AZ 602-275-5509
Mexi-Frost Specialties Company
Brooklyn, NY 718-625-3324
Mission Foods
Fort Worth, TX 817-624-2123
O Chili Frozen Foods Inc
Northbrook, IL 847-562-1991
Odessa Tortilla & Tamale Factory
Odessa, TX 800-753-2445
Pepes Mexican Foods
Rexdale, ON 416-674-0882
Queen International Foods
Monterey Park, CA 800-423-4414
Ramona's Mexican Food Products
Gardena, CA 310-323-1950
Reser's Fine Foods
Beaverton, OR 800-333-6431
Reser's Fine Foods
Salt Lake City, UT 801-972-5633
Ruiz Food Products
Dinuba, CA 800-477-6474
Specialty Brands
Ontario, CA 800-782-1180
Supreme Frozen Products
Chicago, IL 773-622-3336
Sweet Earth Natural Foods
Pacific Grove, CA 800-737-3311
Tyson Prepared Foods
Fort Worth, TX 817-258-2400

Chinese

Belleisle Foods
Belleisle Creek, NB 506-485-2564
China D Food Service
Wichita, KS 316-945-2323
First Oriental Market
Decatur, GA 404-377-6950
Grantstone Supermarket
Tucson, AZ 520-628-7445

Harvest 2000
Pomona, CA 909-622-8039
Hong Kong Supermarket
Atlanta, GA. 404-325-3999
Kahiki Foods
Columbus, OH 614-237-5425
National Importers
Brampton, ON. 905-791-1322
P&S Food Trading
Chicago, IL 773-685-0088

Chop Suey

Canned

ConAgra Grocery Products
Archbold, OH 419-445-8015
Dean Distributors
Burlingame, CA 800-792-0816
Golden Gate Foods
Dallas, TX. 214-747-2223
Young's Noodle Factory
Honolulu, HI. 808-533-6478

Frozen

ConAgra Grocery Products
Archbold, OH 419-445-8015
Nanka Seimen Company
Vernon, CA .323-585-9967

Chow Chow

Golding Farms Foods
Winston Salem, NC. 336-766-6161
Lancaster Packing Company
Lancaster, PA 717-397-9727
Our Enterprises
Oklahoma City, OK 800-821-6375
United Pickle Products Corporation
Bronx, NY 718-933-6060

Chow Mein

C&J Trading
San Francisco, CA 415-822-8910
Canton Noodle
Chicago, IL .312-842-4900
ConAgra Grocery Products
Archbold, OH 419-445-8015
Willow Foods
Beaverton, OR 800-338-3609

Couscous

Chieftain Wild Rice Company
Spooner, WI 800-262-6368
Organic Planet
San Francisco, CA 415-765-5590
Setton International Foods
Commack, NY 800-227-4397
TIPIAK INC
Stamford, CT. 203-961-9117

Dim Sum

Calco of Calgary
Calgary, AB. 403-295-3578
Fine Choice Foods
Richmond, BC. 604-522-3110
Golden Gate Foods
Dallas, TX. .214-747-2223
Shine Food
Torrance, CA. 310-533-6010

Dutch

Penn Dutch Food Center
Hollywood, FL 954-921-4635

Egg Rolls

Appetizers And, Inc.
Chicago, IL .800-323-5472
Aristocrat International Corporation
Secaucus, NJ 201-866-1900
Artel
Boisbriand, QC 450-433-1322
Belleisle Foods
Belleisle Creek, NB 506-485-2564
Cathay Foods Corporation
Boston, MA. 617-427-1507
Chang Food Company
Garden Grove, CA 714-265-9990

Chinese Spaghetti Factory
Boston, MA. 617-445-7714
Chungs Gourmet Foods
Houston, TX 713-741-2118
ConAgra Grocery Products
Archbold, OH 419-445-8015
Dong Kee Company
Chicago, IL .312-225-6340
Egg Roll Fantasy
Auburn, CA 530-887-9197
Fine Choice Foods
Richmond, BC. 604-522-3110
Frozen Specialties
Archbold, OH 419-445-9015
Harvest Food Products Company
Concord, CA 925-676-8208
Health is Wealth Foods
Williamstown, NJ 856-728-1998
Kubla Khan Food Company
Portland, OR 503-234-7494
La Tang Cuisine Manufacturing
Houston, TX 713-780-4876
Luigino's
Duluth, MN. 218-727-2059
Luigino's/Michelina Brand
Duluth, MN. 800-251-7004
Matlaw's Food Products
West Haven, CT 800-934-8266
Mexi-Frost Specialties Company
Brooklyn, NY 718-625-3324
Nanka Seimen Company
Vernon, CA 323-585-9967
Peking Noodle Company
Los Angeles, CA. 323-223-2023
Prime Food Processing Corporation
Brooklyn, NY 888-639-2323
Shine Food
Torrance, CA. 310-533-6010
Valdez Food
Philadelphia, PA 215-634-6106
Wei-Chuan
Bell Gardens, CA 562-927-6681
Willow Foods
Beaverton, OR 800-338-3609
Wing Hing Noodle Company
Los Angeles, CA. 888-223-8899
Wong Wing Foods
Montreal, QC 800-361-4820
Wonton Food
Brooklyn, NY 800-776-8889

Spring Rolls

Calco of Calgary
Calgary, AB. 403-295-3578
Chang Food Company
Garden Grove, CA 714-265-9990
Clarmil Manufacturing Corporation
Hayward, CA 888-252-7645
Health is Wealth Foods
Williamstown, NJ 856-728-1998
Willow Foods
Beaverton, OR 800-338-3609

Wrappers

Delta Food Products
Edmonton, AB 780-424-3636
International Noodle Company
Madison Heights, MI 248-583-2479
Mandarin Noodle Manufacturing Company
Calgary, AB. 403-265-1383
Wing's Food Products
Toronto, ON 416-259-2662

Enchiladas

Canned & Frozen

Baja Foods
Chicago, IL .773-376-9030
Mission Foods
Fort Worth, TX 817-624-2123
New Mexico Food Distributors
Albuquerque, NM 800-637-7084
O Chili Frozen Foods Inc
Northbrook, IL 847-562-1991
Queen International Foods
Monterey Park, CA. 800-423-4414
Reser's Fine Foods
Salt Lake City, UT 801-972-5633

Frozen

Cedarlane Foods
Carson, CA 800-826-3322
Don Miguel Mexican Foods
Orange, CA 714-634-8441
Elena's Food Specialties
S San Francisco, CA 800-376-5368
Ruiz Food Products
Dinuba, CA 800-477-6474

Guacamole

Avo King International
Orange, CA 800-286-5464
Diversified Avocado Products
Mission Viejo, CA 800-879-2555
J.R. Simplot Company
Boise, ID 208-336-2110
Jalapeno Foods Company
The Woodlands, TX 800-896-2318
Sunny Avocado
Jamul, CA .800-999-2862

Halal Foods

Al Safa Halal
Niagara Falls, NY 800-268-8174

Butterball Farms
Grand Rapids, MI 616-243-0105
Global Food Industries
Townville, SC 800-225-4152
Henningsen Foods
Purchase, NY 914-701-4020
J&M Food Products Company
Deerfield, IL 847-948-1290
Midamar Corporation
Cedar Rapids, IA. 800-362-3711
Morning Glory/Formost Farms
Baraboo, WI 800-362-9196
National Fruit Flavor Company
New Orleans, LA 800-966-1123
Northwestern Foods
St Paul, MN. 800-236-4937
Somerset Industries
Spring House, PA 800-883-8728

Italian

Italian Connection
Dumont, NJ. 201-385-2226
Italian Foods
Holly Hill, FL 904-255-5200
Italian Specialty Foods
Seattle, WA 206-322-5790
Joe Fazio's Famous Italian
Charleston, WV 304-344-3071
Molto Italian Foods
Wildwood, NJ 609-522-5444
Moody Dunbar
Johnson City, TN 800-251-8202

Jambalaya

Chef Hans Gourmet Foods
Monroe, LA. 800-890-4267
Mama Amy's Quality Foods
Mississauga, ON. 905-456-0056
Reggie Ball's Cajun Foods
Lake Charles, LA 337-436-0291

Japanese

Marukai Corporation
Gardena, CA 310-660-6300

Kosher Foods

A-1 Eastern Home Made Pickle Company
Los Angeles, CA 323-223-1141
Abraham's Natural Foods
Long Branch, NJ 800-327-9903
Adrienne's Gourmet Foods
Santa Barbara, CA 800-937-7010
Al-Rite Fruits & Syrups
Miami, FL 305-652-2540
All American Foods, Inc.
Mankato, MN 800-833-2661
Alle Processing
Flushing, NY 718-894-2000
Alle Processing Corporation
Flushing, NY 800-245-5620
Allied Wine Corporation
Monticello, NY 845-796-4160
Alta Dena Certified Dairy
City of Industry, CA 800-535-1369
Americana Marketing
Newbury Park, CA 800-742-7520
Anke Kruse Organics
Guelph, ON 519-824-6161
Annie Chun's
San Rafael, CA 415-479-8272
Aristocrat International Corporation
Secaucus, NJ 201-866-1900
Atlas Preserves Company
New York, NY 212-569-5613
Aunt Gussie Cookies & Crackers
Garfield, NJ 973-340-4480
Avatar Corporation
University Park, IL 800-255-3181
Bake Crafters Food
Collegedale, TN 800-296-8935
Ballas Egg Products Corporation
Zanesville, OH 740-453-0386
Beatrice Bakery Company
Beatrice, NE 800-228-4030
Bella Viva Orchards
Denair, CA 800-552-8218
Benson's Gourmet Seasonings
Azusa, CA 800-325-5619
Biazzo Dairy Products
Ridgefield, NJ 201-941-6800
Blue Chip Group
Salt Lake City, UT 800-878-0099
Blue Planet Foods, Inc.
Collegedale, TN 877-396-3145
Boca Bons, Inc.
Coral Springs, FL 800-314-2835
Bombay Breeze Specialty Foods
Mississauga, ON 416-410-2320
Briess Industries
Chilton, WI 920-849-7711
Bruno Specialty Foods
West Sayville, NY 631-589-1700
Butterball Farms
Grand Rapids, MI 616-243-0105
Cache Creek Foods
Woodland, CA 530-662-1764
Calhoun Bend Mill
Alexandria, LA 800-519-6455
California Custom Fruits & Flavors
Irwindale, CA 877-558-0056
Campbell Soup Company
Camden, NJ 800-257-8443
Carmi Flavor & Fragrance Company
Los Angeles, CA 800-421-9647
Casa Visco Finer Food Company
Schenectady, NY 888-607-2823
Caudill Seed Company
Louisville, KY 800-626-5357
Champlain Valley Milling Corporation
Westport, NY 518-962-4711
Cheese Smokers
Brooklyn, NY 718-456-0531
Chewys Rugulach
San Diego, CA 800-241-3456
Chloe Foods Corporation
Brooklyn, NY 718-827-3600
Chris Candies
Pittsburgh, PA 412-322-9400
Claussen Pickle Company
Woodstock, IL 800-435-2817
Coach's Oats
Yorba Linda, CA 714-692-6885

Coffee Masters
Spring Grove, IL 800-334-6485
Columbus Foods Company
Des Plaines, IL 800-322-6457
Commissariat Imports
Los Angeles, CA 310-475-5628
Coombs Vermont Gourmet
Brattleboro, VT 888-266-6271
Country Choice Naturals
Eden Prairie, MN 952-829-8824
Creme Glacee Gelati
St Leonard, QC 888-322-0116
Dakota Growers Pasta Company
Carrington, ND 701-652-2855
Dean Distributors
Burlingame, CA 800-227-3112
Deer Creek Honey Farms
London, OH 740-852-0899
Dough Delight
Concord, ON 800-465-5515
Dr. Praeger's Sensible Foods
Elmwood Park, NJ 201-703-1300
Dreyer's Grand Ice Cream
Oakland, CA 877-437-3937
Dynamic Health Labs
Brooklyn, NY 800-396-2214
Eatem Foods Company
Vineland, NJ 800-683-2836
Eco-Cuisine
Boulder, CO 303-444-6634
Eggology
Canoga Park, CA 818-610-2222
Elan Chemical Company
Newark, NJ 973-344-8014
Embassy Wine Company
Brooklyn, NY 718-272-0600
Enrico's/Ventre Packing
Syracuse, NY 888-472-8237
Erba Food Products
Brooklyn, NY 718-272-7700
FNI Group LLC
Sherborn, MA 508-655-8816
Foodbrands America
Oklahoma City, OK 405-290-4000
Freeda Vitamins
Long Island City, NY 800-777-3737
Fresh Roasted Almond Company
Westland, MI 734-466-9577
Friendship Dairies
Jericho, NY 516-719-4000
Frookie
Des Plaines, IL 847-699-3200
Georgia Spice Company
Atlanta, GA 800-453-9997
Gerber Products Company
Parsippany, NJ 800-443-7237
Gimbal's Fine Candies
S San Francisco, CA 800-344-6225
GKI Foods
Brighton, MI 248-486-0055
GMI Products/Originates
Sunrise, FL 800-999-9373
Gold Pure Foods Products Company
Hempstead, NY 800-422-4681
Golden Fluff Popcorn Company
Lakewood, NJ 732-367-5448
Golden Temple
Los Angeles, CA 310-275-9891
Griffin Food Company
Muskogee, OK 800-580-6311
Hanan Products Company
Hicksville, NY 516-938-1000
Hansen's Natural
Fullerton, CA 714-870-0310
Happy & Healthy Products
Boca Raton, FL 561-367-0739
Harbar Corporation
Canton, MA 800-881-7040
Harvest Valley Bakery
La Salle, IL 815-224-9030
Hausbeck Pickle Company
Saginaw, MI 866-754-4721
Heisler Food Enterprises
Bronx, NY 718-543-0855
Herb Connection
Springville, UT 801-489-4254
Hermann Laue Spice Company
Uxbridge, ON 905-852-5100
Hermann Pickle Farm
Garrettsville, OH 800-245-2696
Hialeah Products Company
Hollywood, FL 800-923-3379

Honey Bar/Creme de la Creme
Kingston, NY 845-331-4643
HoneyRun Winery
Chico, CA 530-345-6405
Honeywood Winery
Salem, OR 800-726-4101
Hospitality Mints
Boone, NC 800-334-5181
House of Flavors
Ludington, MI 800-930-7740
I. Epstein & Sons
East Brunswick, NJ 800-237-5320
Ice Land Corporation
Pittsburgh, PA 412-441-9512
Imagine Foods
Melville, NY 800-333-6339
International Glatt Kosher
Brooklyn, NY 718-491-2756
Isabella's Healthy Bakery
Cuyahoga Falls, OH 800-476-6328
Jazzie Smoothie
Metairie, LA 504-780-8429
Joyva Corporation
Brooklyn, NY 718-497-0170
Jurgielewicz Duck Farm
Moriches, NY 800-543-8257
Kaplan & Zubrin
Camden, NJ 800-334-0002
Kellogg Company
Zanesville, OH 740-453-7782
Kemach Food Products Corporation
Brooklyn, NY 888-453-6224
Klein's Kosher Pickles
Phoenix, AZ 602-269-2072
L&S Packing Company
Farmingdale, NY 800-286-6487
Lee Kum Kee
City of Industry, CA 800-654-5082
Leiner Davis Gelatin
Jericho, NY 516-942-4940
Lenchner Bakery
Concord, ON 905-738-8811
Lifeway Foods Inc
Morton Grove, IL 847-967-1010
Loriva Culinary Oils
San Francisco, CA 866-972-6679
Losurdo Creamery
Hackensack, NJ 800-245-6787
M&L Gourmet Ice Cream
Baltimore, MD 410-276-4880
Macabee Foods
Moonachie, NJ 201-489-4343
Mada'n Kosher Foods
Dania, FL 954-925-0077
Magic Seasoning Blends
Harahan, LA 800-457-2857
Main Street Custom Foods
Cuyahoga Falls, OH 800-533-6246
Main Street Gourmet
Cuyahoga Falls, OH 800-533-6246
Main Street Gourmet Fundraising
Cuyahoga Falls, OH 800-533-6246
Main Street Muffins
Cuyahoga Falls, OH 800-533-6246
Main Street's Cambritt Cookies
Cuyahoga Falls, OH 800-533-6246
Mancini Packing Company
Zolfo Springs, FL 863-735-2000
Maple Products
Sherbrooke, QC 819-569-5161
Maplehurst Bakeries
Carrollton, GA 800-482-4810
Marie Callender's Gourmet Products/Goldrush Products
San Jose, CA 800-729-5428
Martin Farms
Patterson, CA 877-838-7369
Marukan Vinegar (U.S.A.) Inc.
Paramount, CA 562-630-6060
Meal Mart
Flushing, NY 800-245-5620
Mendocino Mustard
Fort Bragg, CA 800-964-2270
Mille Lacs Wild Rice Corporation
Aitkin, MN 800-626-3809
Miller's Cheese
Brooklyn, NY 718-384-5243
Milligan & Higgins
Johnstown, NY 518-762-4638
Milmar Food Group
Goshen, NY 845-294-5400
Mogen David Wine Corporation
Westfield, NY 716-326-7100

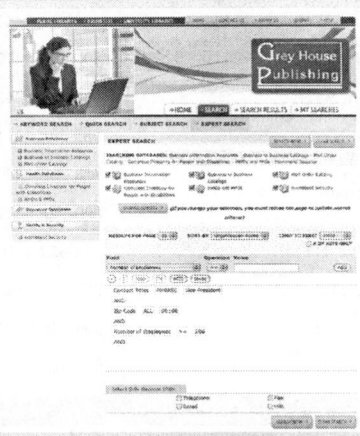
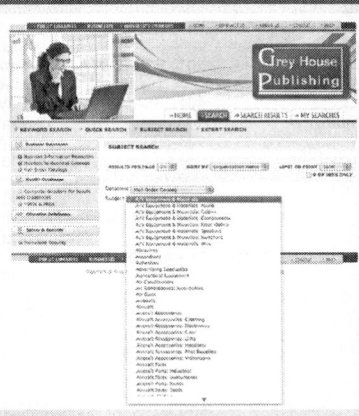
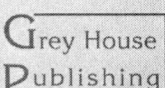

Mon Cuisine
Flushing, NY 877-666-8348
Mona Lisa Food Products
Hendersonville, NC 800-982-2546
Morning Glory/Formost Farms
Baraboo, WI 800-362-9196
Mothers Kitchen Inc
Burlington, NJ 609-387-7200
Mozzicato Depasquale Bakery & Pastry Shop
Hartford, CT 860-296-0426
Mrs. Leeper's Pasta
Kansas City, MO 800-848-5266
Mushroom Company
Cambridge, MD 410-221-8900
Musicon Deer Farm
Goshen, NY 845-294-6378
My Grandma's Coffee Cak e of New England
Hyde Park, MA 800-847-2636
National Food Corporation
Everett, WA 425-349-4257
National Fruit Flavor Company
New Orleans, LA 800-966-1123
Navarro Pecan Company
Corsicana, TX 800-333-9507
Northwestern Foods
St Paul, MN 800-236-4937
Norwalk Dairy
Santa Fe Springs, CA 562-921-5712
Nu-World Amaranth
Naperville, IL 630-369-6851
Old Fashioned Kitchen
Lakewood, NJ 732-364-4100
Pac Moore Products
Hammond, IN 219-932-2666
Pacific Salmon Company
Edmonds, WA 425-774-1315
Pak Technologies
Milwaukee, WI 414-438-8600
Palmieri Food Products
New Haven, CT 800-845-5447
Pellman Foods
New Holland, PA 717-354-8070
Preferred Brands International
Stamford, CT. 800-827-8900
Price Cold Storage & Packing Company
Yakima, WA 509-966-4110
Quality Naturally! Foods
City of Industry, CA 888-498-6986
R.A.B. Food Group LLC
Secaucus, NJ 201-453-5200
Ranaldi Bros Frozen Food Products Inc
Warwick, RI 401-738-3444
Real Kosher Sausage Company
Newark, NJ 973-690-5394
Redmond Minerals
Redmond, UT 800-367-7258
Rogers Sugar Limited
Vancouver, BC 800-661-5350
Roller Ed
Rochester, NY. 585-458-8020
Royal Palate Foods
Inglewood, CA 310-330-7701
Royal Wine Company
Bayonne, NJ 201-437-9131
Russian Chef
New York, NY 212-249-1550
Sabroso Company
Medford, OR. 509-697-7251
Sandt's Honey Company
Easton, PA 800-935-3960
Schapiro's Kosher Winery
New York, NY 212-755-5066
Schwartz Pickle Company
Chicago, IL 800-621-4273
Seabrook Brothers & Sons
Seabrook, NJ 856-455-8080
Setton International Foods
Commack, NY 800-227-4397
Shofar Kosher Foods
Linden, NJ. 888-874-6327
Sigma/Aldrich Flavors & Fragrances
Milwaukee, WI 800-227-4563
Silver Lake Cookie Company
Islip, NY .631-581-4000
Silver Spring Gardens
Eau Claire, WI 800-826-7322
Simply Divine
New York, NY 212-541-7300
Solana Gold Organics
Sebastopol, CA 800-459-1121
Somerset Industries
Spring House, PA 800-883-8728

Spilke's Baking Company
Brooklyn, NY 718-384-2150
Spring Tree Maple Products
Brattleboro, VT 802-254-8784
Springfield Smoked Fish Company
Springfield, MA 800-327-3412
Steve's Mom
Bronx, NY 800-362-4545
Strub Pickles
Brantford, ON 519-751-1717
Sun Harvest Foods
San Diego, CA 619-690-1128
Sunergia Soyfoods
Charlottesville, VA 800-693-5134
Sure Fresh Produce
Santa Maria, CA 888-423-5379
Thomas Canning/Maidstone
Maidstone, ON 519-737-1531
Todhunter Foods & Monarch Wine Company
West Palm Beach, FL 800-336-9463
Top Hat Company
Wilmette, IL 847-256-6565
Touche Bakery
London, ON 518-455-0044
Tova Industries
Louisville, KY 888-532-8682
Trebon European Specialties
South Hackensack, NJ 800-899-4332
Umanoff & Parsons
Bronx, NY 800-248-9993
US Chocolate Corporation
Brooklyn, NY 718-788-8555
Vacaville Fruit Company
Vacaville, CA 707-448-5292
Venice Spumoni/Spring Valley Ice Cream
Philadelphia, PA 800-784-0312
Ventura Foods   Foodservice/Retail/Export
Portland, OR. 503-255-5512
Vermont Country Naturals
Charlotte, VT 800-528-7021
Vic Rossano Incorporated
Montreal, QC 514-766-5252
Vienna Sausage Company
Chicago, IL 800-326-6652
Weaver Nut Company
Ephrata, PA 717-738-3781
Weinberg Foods
Kirkland, WA 800-866-3447
Weiss Homemade Kosher Bakery
Brooklyn, NY 800-498-3477
Wenner Bread Products
Bayport, NY 800-869-6262
Widmer's Wine Cellars
Naples, NY 585-374-6311
World Cheese Company
Brooklyn, NY 718-965-1700
World Harbors
Auburn, ME 800-355-6221
World of Chantilly
Brooklyn, NY 718-859-1110
World's Finest Chocolate
Chicago, IL 800-366-2462
YZ Enterprises
Maumee, OH 800-736-8779
Zapp's Potato Chips
Gramercy, LA 800-349-2447

Matzo

Erba Food Products
Brooklyn, NY 718-272-7700
R.A.B. Food Group LLC
Secaucus, NJ 201-453-5200
Streit Matzo Company
New York, NY 212-475-7000

Meal

R.A.B. Food Group LLC
Secaucus, NJ 201-453-5200

Mexican

Alamo Tamale Corporation
Houston, TX 800-252-0586
Border Foods Inc
Farmers Branch, TX 888-737-7752
Bruce Foods Corporation
New Iberia, LA 800-299-9082
Embassy of Spain Trades Commission
New York, NY 212-907-6481
Fiesta Mexican Foods
Brawley, CA 760-344-3577

Fresca Mexican Foods
Boise, ID. 208-376-6922
Garcias Mexican Foods
Duluth, GA 770-638-0881
Gardunos Mexican Food
Pomona, CA 909-469-6611
Gladstone Food Products Company
Kansas City, MO. 816-436-1255
In Ranchito
Zillah, WA 509-829-5880
Intermex Products
Grand Prairie, TX 972-660-2979
JJ's Tamales & Barbacoa
San Antonio, TX 210-737-1300
La Casita's Home Style Mexican Food
Holts Summit, MO 573-896-8306
La Chapalita
Los Angeles, CA. 323-780-7808
La Monita Mexican Food
Austin, TX. 512-524-4294
La Preferida
Chicago, IL 773-254-7200
La Reina
Monterey, CA 831-372-4003
Los Pericos Food Products
Los Angeles, CA. 323-269-5816
LPI
Chicago, IL 773-254-7200
Mission Foodservice
Oldsmar, FL 800-443-7994
Moody Dunbar
Johnson City, TN 800-251-8202
National Importers
Brampton, ON. 905-791-1322
Pancho's Mexican Foods
Memphis, TN 901-744-3900
Reser's Fine Foods
Topeka, KS 800-333-6431
T.W. Garner Food Company
Winston Salem, NC. 800-476-7383

Oriental

Hanmi
Chicago, IL 773-271-0730
Hop Kee
Chicago, IL 312-791-9111
Koha Food
Honolulu, HI 808-845-4232
M&M Food Distributors/Oriental Pride
Virginia Beach, VA 757-499-5676
Mah Chena Company
Chicago, IL 312-226-5100

Paella

Conrad Rice Mill
New Iberia, LA 800-551-3245
Cuizina Food Company
Woodinville, WA. 425-486-7000

Parve Foods

Anke Kruse Organics
Guelph, ON 519-824-6161
Bombay Breeze Specialty Foods
Mississauga, ON. 416-410-2320
Bruno Specialty Foods
West Sayville, NY 631-589-1700
Chloe Foods Corporation
Brooklyn, NY 718-827-3600
Coach's Oats
Yorba Linda, CA 714-692-6885
Country Choice Naturals
Eden Prairie, MN 952-829-8824
Dr. Praeger's Sensible Foods
Elmwood Park, NJ 201-703-1300
Dynamic Health Labs
Brooklyn, NY 800-396-2214
Eggology
Canoga Park, CA 818-610-2222
Enrico's/Ventre Packing
Syracuse, NY 888-472-8237
FNI Group LLC
Sherborn, MA 508-655-8816
Frookie
Des Plaines, IL 847-699-3200
Golden Temple
Los Angeles, CA. 310-275-9891
Hansen's Natural
Fullerton, CA 714-870-0310
Happy & Healthy Products
Boca Raton, FL 561-367-0739

Honey Bar/Creme de la Creme
  Kingston, NY 845-331-4643
HoneyRun Winery
  Chico, CA 530-345-6405
Marukan Vinegar (U.S.A.) Inc.
  Paramount, CA 562-630-6060
Mrs. Leeper's Pasta
  Kansas City, MO. 800-848-5266
New World Pasta
  Harrisburg, PA 717-526-2200
Northwestern Foods
  St Paul, MN. .800-236-4937
Touche Bakery
  London, ON .518-455-0044
US Chocolate Corporation
  Brooklyn, NY 718-788-8555
YZ Enterprises
  Maumee, OH. 800-736-8779

Shells

Chalupa

B. Martinez & Sons Company
  San Antonio, TX 210-226-6772
El Galindo
  Austin, TX. 512-478-5756
Rudy's Tortillas
  Dallas, TX. 800-878-2401

Taco

Amigos Canning Company
  San Antonio, TX. 800-580-3477
Anita's Mexican Foods Corporation
  San Bernardino, CA 800-426-4827
Artesia Tortilla Factory
  Artesia, NM. .505-746-2808
Azteca Foods
  Summit Argo, IL. 708-563-6600
B. Martinez & Sons Company
  San Antonio, TX 210-226-6772
El Galindo
  Austin, TX. 512-478-5756
El Rancho Tortilla
  San Antonio, TX 210-922-8411
Goglanian Bakeries
  Santa Ana, CA 714-444-3500
La Buena Mexican Foods Products
  Tucson, AZ 520-624-1796
La Malinche Tortilla & Tamale Factory
  Corpus Christi, TX 361-884-7883
Las Cruces Foods
  Mesilla Park, NM 575-526-2352
Li'l Guy Foods
  Kansas City, MO. 800-886-8226
Luna's Tortillas
  Dallas, TX. 214-747-2661
Mexisnax Corporation
  El Paso, TX 915-779-5709
Mission Foods
  Jefferson, GA 800-240-2447
Mission Foods
  Fort Worth, TX 817-624-2123
Mission Foodservice
  Oldsmar, FL .800-443-7994
Odessa Tortilla & TamaleFactory
  Odessa, TX. .800-753-2445
Perez Food Products
  Kansas City, MO. 816-931-8761
Pillsbury
  Hannibal, MO 800-775-4777
Pillsbury Canada Limited
  Markham, ON 800-745-4777
Puebla Foods
  Passaic, NJ 973-473-0201
Reser's Fine Foods
  Beaverton, OR 800-333-6431
Rosarita Mexican Foods Company
  Mesa, AZ. 480-964-8751
Rudy's Tortillas
  Dallas, TX. 800-878-2401
S&K Industries
  Manassas Park, VA 703-369-0232
Sams-Leon Mexican Supplies
  Omaha, NE 402-733-3809
Spanish Gardens Food Manufacturing
  Kansas City, KS 913-831-4242

Tabbouleh

Bishop Brothers
  Bristow, OK .800-859-8304

Hommus Factory
  Haverhill, MA. 508-460-0212
Tarazi Specialty Foods
  Chino, CA 909-628-3601

Tacos

Amigos Canning Company
  San Antonio, TX. 800-580-3477
Queen International Foods
  Monterey Park, CA. 800-423-4414
R&S Mexican Food Products
  Glendale, AZ. 602-272-2727
Ruiz Food Products
  Dinuba, CA 800-477-6474

Fillings

Always make it your best®

Burke Corporation
  Nevada, IA 800-654-1152

Always make it your best® with Burke fully cooked meats. We specialize in Italian sausage, beef, and pork toppings, meatballs, taco meats, shredded meats, pepperoni, bacon, Canadian-style bacon, chicken and beef strips. Additionally, we offer a variety of specialty products: Hand-Pinched Style® brand toppings, chorizo, gyro topping, andouille sausage, and breakfast patties and links.

First Original Texas Chili Company
  Fort Worth, TX 817-626-0983
Original Texas Chili Company
  Fort Worth, TX 800-507-0009
Ready Foods
  Denver, CO 303-892-5861
Tyson Prepared Foods
  Fort Worth, TX 817-258-2400

Tamales

Alamo Tamale Corporation
  Houston, TX .800-252-0586
Art's Tamales
  Metamora, IL 309-367-2850
Baja Foods
  Chicago, IL 773-376-9030
Comanche Tortilla Factory
  Fort Stockton, TX 432-336-3245
El-Rey Foods
  Ferguson, MO 314-521-3113
Grande Tortilla Factory
  Tucson, AZ 520-622-8338
Hacienda De Paco
  Orlando, FL 407-859-5417
Kelly Foods
  Jackson, TN .731-424-2255
La Buena Mexican Foods Products
  Tucson, AZ 520-624-1796
La Malinche Tortilla & Tamale Factory
  Corpus Christi, TX 361-884-7883
La Poblana Tamale Factory
  Houston, TX .713-921-4760
Leonas Foods
  Chimayo, NM 505-351-4660
Luna's Tortillas
  Dallas, TX. 214-747-2661
Mama Maria's Tortillas
  Midvale, UT .801-566-5150
Mexi-Frost Specialties Company
  Brooklyn, NY 718-625-3324
Mi Ranchito Foods
  Bayard, NM. .575-537-3868
Mr Jay's Tamales & Chili
  Lynwood, CA 310-537-3932
Odessa Tortilla & TamaleFactory
  Odessa, TX. .800-753-2445
R&S Mexican Food Products
  Glendale, AZ. 602-272-2727
Ramona's Mexican Food Products
  Gardena, CA .310-323-1950
Reser's Fine Foods
  Salt Lake City, UT 801-972-5633

Ruiz Food Products
  Dinuba, CA 800-477-6474
S&K Industries
  Manassas Park, VA 703-369-0232
Specialty Brands
  Ontario, CA 800-782-1180
Supreme Frozen Products
  Chicago, IL 773-622-3336
Supreme Frozen Products
  Chicago, IL 888-643-0405
Tom Tom Tamale Manufacturing
  Chicago, IL 773-523-5675

Frozen

Art's Tamales
  Metamora, IL 309-367-2850
Baja Foods
  Chicago, IL 773-376-9030
Edmonds Chile Company
  St Louis, MO. 314-772-1499
El-Rey Foods
  Ferguson, MO 314-521-3113
Mexi-Frost Specialties Company
  Brooklyn, NY 718-625-3324
Mi Ranchito Foods
  Bayard, NM. .575-537-3868
Ramona's Mexican Food Products
  Gardena, CA .310-323-1950
Ruiz Food Products
  Dinuba, CA 800-477-6474
Tom Tom Tamale Manufacturing
  Chicago, IL 773-523-5675

Taquitos

Queen International Foods
  Monterey Park, CA. 800-423-4414
Ruiz Food Products
  Dinuba, CA 800-477-6474
Specialty Brands
  Ontario, CA 800-782-1180

Tempeh

Twenty First Century Foods
  Jamaica Plain, MA 617-522-7595
White Wave
  Broomfield, CO 800-488-9283

Tortilla & Tortilla Products

Anita's Mexican Foods Corporation
  San Bernardino, CA 800-426-4827
Calidad Foods
  Grand Prairie, TX 972-933-4100
Comanche Tortilla Factory
  Fort Stockton, TX 432-336-3245
Cosa de Rio Foods
  Louisville, KY 502-772-2500
Del-Rey Tortilleria
  Chicago, IL 773-637-8900
El Matador Foods
  Baytown, TX. 281-838-1375
Festida Food
  Cedar Springs, MI. 616-696-0400
Fresca Mexican Foods
  Boise, ID 208-376-6922
Good Wives
  Lynn, MA 800-521-8160
Harbar Corporation
  Canton, MA .800-881-7040
La Casita's Home Style Mexican Food
  Holts Summit, MO 573-896-8306
La Mexicana Tortilla Factory
  Hayward, CA 510-889-8225
La Preferida
  Chicago, IL 773-254-7200
La Tolteca Foods
  Pueblo, CO 719-543-5733
La Tortilla Factory
  Santa Rosa, CA 800-446-1516
Los Pericos Food Products
  Los Angeles, CA. 323-269-5816
Mama Maria's Tortillas
  Midvale, UT .801-566-5150
Oh Boy Corporation
  San Fernando, CA. 818-361-1128
Rudolph's Specialty Bakery
  Toronto, ON .416-763-4315

Tortillas

Artesia Tortilla Factory
Artesia, NM............505-746-2808
Azteca Foods
Summit Argo, IL............708-563-6600
Azteca Milling
Irving, TX............800-364-0040
B. Martinez & Sons Company
San Antonio, TX............210-226-6772
Better Meat North
Bay City, MI............989-684-6271
Bien Padre Foods
Eureka, CA............707-442-4585
Bueno Food Products
Albuquerque, NM............800-888-7336
Casa Valdez
Caldwell, ID............208-459-6461
Cedarlane Foods
Carson, CA............800-826-3322
Comanche Tortilla Factory
Fort Stockton, TX............432-336-3245
Cosa de Rio Foods
Louisville, KY............502-772-2500
Custom Ingredients
New Braunfels, TX............800-457-8935
Del Rey Tortilleria
Chicago, IL............800-446-1459
Delicious Popcorn Company
Waupaca, WI............715-258-7683
El Charro Mexican Food Industries
Roswell, NM............575-622-8590
El Charro Mexican Foods
Roswell, NM............575-622-8590
El Galindo
Austin, TX............512-478-5756
El Rancho Tortilla
San Antonio, TX............210-922-8411
El-Milagro
Chicago, IL............773-847-9407
Father Sam's Syrian Bread
Buffalo, NY............800-521-6719
Fiesta Mexican Foods
Brawley, CA............760-344-3577
Flowers Baking
San Antonio, TX............210-661-2361
Food Products Corporation
Phoenix, AZ............602-273-7139
Grande Tortilla Factory
Tucson, AZ............520-622-8338
Great Western Tortilla
Denver, CO............303-298-0705
Hacienda De Paco
Orlando, FL............407-859-5417
Harbar Corporation
Canton, MA............800-881-7040
Josie's Best New Mexican Foods
Santa Fe, NM............505-473-3437
La Buena Mexican Foods Products
Tucson, AZ............520-624-1796
La Canasta Mexican Food Products
Phoenix, AZ............602-269-7721
La Chapalita
Los Angeles, CA............323-780-7808
La Chiquita Tortilla Manufacturing
Atlanta, GA............800-486-3942
La Colonial/Robles Brothers
San Jose, CA............408-436-5551
La Fronteriza
Toledo, OH............800-897-1772
La Malinche Tortilla & Tamale Factory
Corpus Christi, TX............361-884-7883
La Mexicana Tortilla Factory
Dallas, TX............214-943-7770
La Mexicana Tortilla Factory
Hayward, CA............510-889-8225
La Poblana Tamale Factory
Houston, TX............713-921-4760
La Reina
Los Angeles, CA............323-268-2791
La Tolteca Foods
Pueblo, CO............719-543-5733
La Tortilla Factory
Santa Rosa, CA............800-446-1516
Lago Tortillas International
Austin, TX............800-369-9017
Laredo Mexican Foods
Fort Wayne, IN............800-252-7336
Las Cruces Foods
Mesilla Park, NM............575-526-2352
Leonas Foods
Chimayo, NM............505-351-4660

Li'l Guy Foods
Kansas City, MO............800-886-8226
Lone Star Bakery
Round Rock, TX............512-255-3629
Los Amigos Tortilla Manufacturing
Atlanta, GA............800-969-8226
Los Arcos Tortillas
North Las Vegas, NV............702-399-3300
Luna's Tortillas
Dallas, TX............214-747-2661
Manuel's Mexican-American Fine Foods
Salt Lake City, UT............800-748-5072
Manuel's Odessa Tortillaand Tamale Factory
Odessa, TX............432-332-6676
Metzger Popcorn Company
Delphos, OH............800-819-6072
Mexi-Frost Specialties Company
Brooklyn, NY............718-625-3324
Mexican Accent
New Berlin, WI............262-784-4422
Mexican Food Products Corporation
San Francisco, CA............415-648-8550
Mexican Foods
Indianapolis, IN............317-236-1090
Mexisnax Corporation
El Paso, TX............915-779-5709
Mi Mama's Tortilla Factory
Omaha, NE............402-345-2099
Mi Ranchito Foods
Bayard, NM............575-537-3868
Mission Foods
Jefferson, GA............800-240-2447
Mission Foods Corporation
Irving, TX............800-443-7994
Mission Foods/Diane's Foods
McMinnville, OR............503-434-5534
Mission Foodservice
Oldsmar, FL............800-443-7994
New Mexico Food Distributors
Albuquerque, NM............800-637-7084
O. Malley Grain
Fairmont, NE............402-268-6001
Odessa Tortilla & TamaleFactory
Odessa, TX............800-753-2445
Ozuna Food Products Corporation
Sunnyvale, CA............408-400-0495
Pacific Ocean Produce
Santa Cruz, CA............831-423-2654
Pepes Mexican Foods
Rexdale, ON............416-674-0882
Perez Food Products
Kansas City, MO............816-931-8761
Pillsbury
Hannibal, MO............800-775-4777
Puebla Foods
Passaic, NJ............973-473-0201
R&S Mexican Food Products
Glendale, AZ............602-272-2727
Ramona's Mexican Food Products
Gardena, CA............310-323-1950
Ready Foods
Denver, CO............303-892-5861
Reser's Fine Foods
Beaverton, OR............800-333-6431
Reser's Fine Foods
Salt Lake City, UT............801-972-5633
Rudolph's Specialty Bakery
Toronto, ON............416-763-4315
Rudy's Tortillas
Dallas, TX............800-878-2401
Ruiz Food Products
Dinuba, CA............800-477-6474
Ruiz Mexican Foods
Ontario, CA............909-947-7811

S&K Industries
Manassas Park, VA............703-369-0232
Sams-Leon Mexican Supplies
Omaha, NE............402-733-3809
Sanitary Tortilla Manufacturing Company
San Antonio, TX............210-226-9209
Selecto Sausage Company
Houston, TX............713-926-1626
Severance Foods
Hartford, CT............860-724-7063
Shirley Foods
Shirley, IN............800-560-2908
Soloman Baking Company
Denver, CO............303-371-2777
Spanish Gardens Food Manufacturing
Kansas City, KS............913-831-4242
Specialty Brands
Ontario, CA............800-782-1180
Sweet Corn Products Company
Bloomfield, NE............877-628-6115
Tapatia Tortilleria
Fresno, CA............800-219-7329
Tumaro's Gourmet Tortillas & Snacks
Edison, NJ............800-777-6317

Tostadas

Del Rey Tortilleria
Chicago, IL............800-446-1459
Delicious Popcorn Company
Waupaca, WI............715-258-7683
El Rancho Tortilla
San Antonio, TX............210-922-8411
Happy's Potato Chip Company
Minneapolis, MN............612-781-3121
La Buena Mexican Foods Products
Tucson, AZ............520-624-1796
La Malinche Tortilla & Tamale Factory
Corpus Christi, TX............361-884-7883
Luna's Tortillas
Dallas, TX............214-747-2661
Manuel's Mexican-American Fine Foods
Salt Lake City, UT............800-748-5072
Mexisnax Corporation
El Paso, TX............915-779-5709
Mission Foodservice
Oldsmar, FL............800-443-7994
Reser's Fine Foods
Beaverton, OR............800-333-6431
Rosarita Mexican Foods Company
Mesa, AZ............480-964-8751
Rudy's Tortillas
Dallas, TX............800-878-2401

Wonton Chips

Maebo Noodle Factory
Hilo, HI............877-663-8667

Wontons

Chang Food Company
Garden Grove, CA............714-265-9990
Delta Food Products
Edmonton, AB............780-424-3636
Golden Gate Foods
Dallas, TX............214-747-2223
Harvest Food Products Company
Concord, CA............925-676-8208
La Tang Cuisine Manufacturing
Houston, TX............713-780-4876
Mandarin Noodle Manufacturing Company
Calgary, AB............403-265-1383
Montreal Chop Suey Company
Montreal, QC............514-522-3134
Nanka Seimen Company
Vernon, CA............323-585-9967
Peking Noodle Company
Los Angeles, CA............323-223-2023
Roxy Trading
Azusa, CA............626-610-1388
Wan Hua Foods
Seattle, WA............206-622-8417
Wing Hing Noodle Company
Los Angeles, CA............888-223-8899
Wonton Food
Brooklyn, NY............800-776-8889

Fish & Seafood

Caviar (Roe)

Angy's Food Products, Inc.
Westfield, MA 413-572-1010
Assouline & Ting
Philadelphia, PA 800-521-4491
Bens Seafood Company
Crescent, GA. 912-832-5121
Castella Imports
Hauppauge, NY 866-227-8355
Cossack Caviar
Arlington, WA. 360-435-6600
D'Artagnan
Newark, NJ 800-327-8246
Ferroclad Fishery
Batchawana Bay, ON 705-882-2295
High Liner Foods
Lunenburg, NS 902-634-9475
Kelley's Katch Caviar
Savannah, TN 888-681-8565
Liberty Richter
Saddle Brook, NJ 201-291-8749
Newell Lobsters
Yarmouth, NS 902-742-6272
Notre Dame Seafood
Comfort Cove, NL 709-244-5511
Paramount Caviar
Long Island City, NY 800-992-2842
Produits Belle Baie
Caraquet, NB 506-727-4414
Raffield Fisheries
Port St Joe, FL. 850-229-8229
Royal Caviar
Glendale, CA 818-546-5858
Russ & Daughters
New York, NY 800-787-7229
Russian Chef
New York, NY 212-249-1550
T. Marzetti Company
Columbus, OH 614-846-2232
Tribe Mediterranean Foods Company LLC
Taunton, MA 800-421-3474

Herring

Cowart Seafood Corporation
Lottsburg, VA 804-529-6101
Icicle Seafoods
Seattle, WA 206-282-0988
Sea Products Company
Watsonville, CA 831-768-2600

Salmon

Assouline & Ting
Philadelphia, PA 800-521-4491
Cossack Caviar
Arlington, WA. 360-435-6600
Crown Prince
City of Industry, CA 800-255-5063
Icicle Seafoods
Seattle, WA 206-282-0988
Johns Cove Fisheries
Yarmouth, NS 902-742-8691
Pacific Alaska Seafoods
Seattle, WA 206-587-0002

Shad

Bailey Street Bakery
Atlanta, GA 800-822-4634
Calise & Sons Bakery
Lincoln, RI .800-225-4737
Carolina Foods
Charlotte, NC 800-234-0441
Crestwood Bakery
Pleasant Prairie, WI 414-453-4790
Dare Foods
Kitchener, ON. 800-865-8225
Interstate Brands Corporation
Florence, SC 843-393-8895
Lewis Brothers Bakery
La Porte, IN. 219-362-4561
Sara Lee Bakery Group   The EarthGrains - Bakery
Jasper, TN .423-837-8856
Sarilii
Knoxville, TN 865-573-1941

Stroehmann Bakeries
Harrisburg, PA 800-220-2867
Sunbeam Baking Company
El Paso, TX 800-328-6111
Weston Bakeries
Etobicoke, ON 416-252-7323
Winder Dairy
West Valley, UT 800-946-3371

Fish

A&C Quinlin Fisheries
McGray, NS 902-745-2742
Acme Smoked Fish Corporation
Brooklyn, NY 800-221-0795
Acme Steak & Seafood Company
Youngstown, OH. 330-270-8000
Acushnet Fish Corporation
Fairhaven, MA 508-997-7482
Agger Fish
Brooklyn, NY 718-855-1717
Al Safa Halal
Niagara Falls, NY 800-268-8174
Alaska Sausage and Seafood Company
Anchorage, AK 800-798-3636
Alaska Seafood Company
Los Angeles, CA. 213-626-1212
Alaskan Gourmet Seafoods
Anchorage, AK 800-288-3740
All Alaskan Seafood
Seattle, WA. 206-285-8200
Alle Processing
Flushing, NY. 718-894-2000
Amano Fish Cake Factory
Hilo, HI 808-935-5555
Amcan Industries
Elmsford, NY 914-347-4838
American Seafoods International
New Bedford, MA 800-343-8046
Annabelle Lee
Waldoboro, ME. 207-967-4611
Appert's Foodservice
St Cloud, MN 800-225-3883
APTCO
San Francisco, CA 415-648-6688
Aquatec Seafoods Ltd.
Comox, BC 250-339-6412
Arcee Sales Company
Brooklyn, NY 718-383-0107
Arrowac Fisheries
Seattle, WA. 206-282-5655
Aslanis Seafoods
Quincy, MA. 800-876-3712
Atlantic Capes Fisheries
Cape May, NJ 609-884-3000
Atlantic Fish Specialties
Charlottetown, PE. 902-894-7005
Atlantic Sea Pride
South Boston, MA 617-269-7700
B.M. Lawrence & Company
San Francisco, CA 415-981-3650
Baensch Food
Milwaukee, WI 800-562-8234
Bakalars Brothers Sausage Company
La Crosse, WI 608-784-0384
Baker's Point Fisheries
Oyster Pond Jeddore, NS 902-845-2347
Basin Crawfish Processors
Breaux Bridge, LA 337-332-6655
Bayou Foods
Kenner, LA 800-516-8283
Bayou Land Seafood
Breaux Bridge, LA 337-667-6118
Beaver Street Fisheries
Jacksonville, FL 800-874-6426
Becker Food Company
Milwaukee, WI 414-964-5353
Bell Buoy Crab Company
Seaside, OR. 800-529-2722
Belle River Enterprises
Belle River, PE 902-962-2248
Billingsgate Fish Company
Calgary, AB. 403-571-7700
Birch Street Seafoods
Digby, NS .902-245-6551

Blalock Seafood
Orange Beach, AL 251-974-5811
Blue Lakes Trout Farm
Jerome, ID. 208-734-7151
Blue Wave Seafoods
Port Mouton, NS. 902-683-2044
BlueWater Seafoods
Lachine, QC 888-560-2539
Bolner's Fiesta Products
San Antonio, TX 210-734-6404
Bornstein Seafoods
Warrenton, OR 503-861-1233
Bos Smoked Fish Inc
Woodstock, ON. 519-537-5000
Boston Sea Farms
Somerville, MA 617-547-3474
Boutique Seafood
Atlanta, GA 404-752-8852
Breakwater Fisheries
St. John's, NL 709-754-1999
Bumble Bee Seafoods
San Diego, CA 858-715-4000
Burleigh Brothers Seafoods
Ellerslie, PE 902-831-2349
Burris Mill & Feed
Franklinton, LA 800-928-2782
Caito Fisheries
Fort Bragg, CA 707-964-6368
California Shellfish Company
Gardena, CA 310-538-4197
California Shellfish Company
San Francisco, CA 415-923-7400
Canadian Fish Exporters
Watertown, MA 800-225-4215
Canus Fisheries
Clark's Harbour, NS 902-745-2888
Captain Alex Seafood
Niles, IL. 847-803-8833
Captn's Pack Products
Columbia, MD 410-720-6668
Carrington Foods
Saraland, AL 251-675-9700
Certi-Fresh Foods
Bell Gardens, CA 562-806-1100
Charlton Deep Sea Charters
Warrenton, OR 503-338-0569
Cherokee Trout Farms
Cherokee, NC 800-732-0075
Cherry Point Products
Milbridge, ME 207-546-7056
Chicago Food Market
Chicago, IL 312-842-4361
Chicken of the Sea International
San Diego, CA 800-678-8862
Chuck's Seafoods
Charleston, OR. 541-888-5525
Clear Springs Foods
Buhl, ID. 800-635-8211
Coldwater Seafood Corporation
Norwalk, CT 203-846-8897
ConAgra Foods Inc
Omaha, NE 402-240-4000
ConFish
Isola, MS 800-228-3474
Connors Aquaculture
Eastport, ME. 207-853-6081
Consolidated Sea Products
Mobile, AL 251-433-3240
Cook Inlet Processing
Anchorage, AK 907-243-1166
Cook Inlet Processing
Nikiski, AK. 907-776-8174
Cooke Aguaculture
Blacks Harbour, NB 506-456-6600
Cossack Caviar
Arlington, WA. 360-435-6600
Cowart Seafood Corporation
Lottsburg, VA 804-529-6101
Crab King Seafood Specialties
Seattle, WA 206-283-2722
Crest International Corporation
San Diego, CA 800-548-1232
Crown Point
St John, IN 219-365-3200
Crown Prince
City of Industry, CA 800-255-5063

Cuizina Food Company
Woodinville, WA 425-486-7000
Culver's Fish Farm
Mc Pherson, KS 800-241-5205
Cushner Seafood
Baltimore, MD 410-358-5564
Daerim America
Maywood, NJ 800-635-0781
Deep Creek Custom Packing
Ninilchik, AK 800-764-0078
Delta Pride Catfish
Indianola, MS 800-421-1045
Depoe Bay Fish Company
Newport, OR 541-265-8833
Dixon's Fisheries
East Peoria, IL 309-694-6823
Dressel Collins Fish Company
Seattle, WA 206-725-0121
Dynamic Foods
Lubbock, TX 806-762-0780
Earle Brothers Fisheries
Carbonear, NL 709-596-5166
Ed Kasilof's Seafoods
Kasilof, AK 800-982-2377
Edelman Meats
Antigo, WI 715-623-7686
Emery Smith Fisheries Limited
Shag Harbour, NS 902-723-2115
Erba Food Products
Brooklyn, NY 718-272-7700
Farm Fresh Catfish Company
Hollandale, MS 800-647-8264
Feature Foods
Etobicoke, ON 416-675-7350
Ferroclad Fishery
Batchawana Bay, ON 705-882-2295
Finestkind Fish Market
York, ME 800-288-8154
First Oriental Market
Decatur, GA 404-377-6950
Fish Brothers
Blue Lake, CA 800-244-0583
Fishermens Net
Portland, ME 207-772-3565
Fishery Products International
Danvers, MA 800-374-4700
Fishking Processors
Los Angeles, CA 877-677-3329
Flavor House
Adelanto, CA 760-246-9131
Fleet Fisheries
New Bedford, MA 508-996-3742
Fresh Island Fish Company
Kahului, HI 808-871-1111
Freshwater Fish Marketing
Edmonton, AB 800-345-3113
Garden & Valley Isle Seafood
Honolulu, HI 800-689-2733
George Robberecht Seafood
Montross, VA 804-472-3556
Giovanni's Appetizing Food Products
Richmond, MI 586-727-9355
Glenn Sales Company
Atlanta, GA 770-952-9292
GMF Corporation
Gloucester, MA 978-283-0479
Gold Star Smoked Fish
Brooklyn, NY 718-522-1545
Gorton's Seafood
Gloucester, MA 978-283-3000
Goya Foods of Florida
Miami, FL 305-592-3150
Great Glacier Salmon
Prince Rupert, BC 250-627-4955
Great Northern Products
Warwick, RI 401-490-4590
Hallmark Fisheries
Charleston, OR 541-888-3253
Hamilos Brothers Inspected Meats
Madison, IL 618-451-7877

Harbor Fish Market
Portland, ME 207-775-0251
Harbor Lobster
Shelburne, NS 902-723-2500
Harbor Seafood
New Hyde Park, NY 800-585-0900
Harold Bozman Seafood
Upper Fairmount, MD 410-651-0647
Harry H. Park Company
Chicago, IL 773-478-4424
Hawaii International Seafood
Honolulu, HI 808-839-5010
Heinz Company of Canada
North York, ON 800-268-6641
HFI Foods
Redmond, WA 425-883-1320
High Liner Foods
Lunenburg, NS 902-634-9475
Hilo Fish Company
Hilo, HI 808-961-0877
Homer's Wharf Seafood Company
New Bedford, MA 508-997-0766
Hygrade Ocean Products
New Bedford, MA 508-993-5700
Icelandic USA
Newport News, VA 757-820-4000
Icicle Seafoods
Seattle, WA 206-282-0988
Idaho Trout Company
Buhl, ID 866-878-7688
Independent Packers Corporation
Seattle, WA 206-285-6000
Indian Bay Frozen Foods
Centreville, NL 709-678-2844
Indian Valley Meats
Indian, AK 907-653-7511
Inlet Salmon
Bothell, WA 425-487-0495
Inshore Fisheries
Middle West Pubnico, NS 902-762-2522
International Seafoods of Alaska
Kodiak, AK 907-486-4768
Island Marine Products
Clarks Harbour, NS 902-745-2222
J. Matassini & Sons Fish Company
Tampa, FL 813-229-0829
J. Moniz Company
Fall River, MA 508-674-8451
J. Turner Seafoods
Gloucester, MA 978-281-8535
J.S. McMillan Fisheries
Prince Rupert, BC 604-25- 519
J.S. McMillan Fisheries
Vancouver, BC 604-255-5191
James Cowan & Sons
Worcester, MA 508-754-5385
James L. Mood Fisheries
Wood's Harbour, NS 902-723-2360
Jensen Seafood Packing Company
Dulac, LA 985-563-7022
Jer-Mar Foods
Windsor, ON 519-256-3474
Jessie's Ilwaco Fish Company
Ilwaco, WA 360-642-3773
John B. Wright Fish Company
Gloucester, MA 978-283-4205
John T. Handy Company
Salisbury, MD 800-426-3977
K&N Fisheries
Shelburne, NS 902-768-2478
Key Largo Fisheries
Key Largo, FL 800-399-6970
Kirkland Custom Seafoods
Kirkland, WA 800-321-3474
Kodiak Salmon Packers
Larsen Bay, AK 907-847-2250
L&M Evans
Conyers, GA 770-918-8727
L. Isaacson
Chicago, IL 312-421-2444
Lakeside Foods
Seymour, WI 920-833-2371
Lance G. Fisher Seafood
Sanford, VA 757-824-3489
LEF McLean Brothers International
Wheatley, ON 519-825-4656
Leo G. Atkinson Fisheries
Clarks Harbor, NS 902-745-3047
Liberty Richter
Saddle Brook, NJ 201-291-8749
LLJ's Sea Products
Round Pond, ME 207-529-4224

Long Beach Seafoods
Long Beach, CA 714-995-8901
Lougheed Fisheries
Owen Sound, ON 519-376-1586
Lowland Seafood
Lowland, NC 252-745-3751
Lu-Mar Lobster & Shrimp
Brownsville, TX 956-546-5525
Lubec Packing
Lubec, ME 207-733-5572
Lund's Fisheries
Cape May, NJ 609-884-7600
Mada'n Kosher Foods
Dania, FL 954-925-0077
Marche Tramsatlantique
Montreal, QC 514-287-3530
Mariner Seafoods
Montague, PE 902-838-2481
Martin Brothers Seafood Company
Westwego, LA 504-341-2251
Mat Roland Seafood Company
Atlantic Beach, FL 904-246-9443
Maxim's Import Corporation
Miami, FL 800-331-6652
McDowell Fine Meats 2
Phoenix, AZ 602-254-6022
Menemsha Fish Market
Chilmark, MA 508-645-2282
Mercado Latino
City of Industry, CA 626-333-6862
Mersey Seafoods
Liverpool, NS 902-354-3467
Mid-South Fish Company
Aubrey, AR 870-295-5600
Mike's Fish & Seafood
Glenwood, MN 800-950-4755
Milfico Foods
Elk Grove Vlg, IL 847-427-0491
Mill Cove Lobster Pound
Boothbay Harbor, ME 207-633-3340
Millen Fish
Millen, GA 478-982-4988
Minor Fisheries
Port Colborne, ON 905-834-9232
Morey's Seafood International
Motley, MN 218-352-6345
Mutual Fish Company
Seattle, WA 206-322-4368
Nelson Crab
Tokeland, WA 800-262-0069
Neptune Foods
Vernon, CA 323-232-8300
Nodine's Smokehouse
Torrington, CT 800-222-2059
Noon Hour Food Products
Chicago, IL 800-621-6636
Nordic Group
Boston, MA 800-486-4002
North Alaska Fisheries
Anchorage, AK 907-561-2671
North Atlantic
Portland, ME 207-774-6025
North Atlantic Fish Company
Gloucester, MA 978-283-4121
North Atlantic Seafood
Stonington, ME 207-367-5099
North Pacific Ship Supply
Dutch Harbor, AK 907-581-1700
Northern Products Corporation
Seattle, WA 206-448-6677
Notre Dame Seafood
Comfort Cove, NL 709-244-5511
Ocean Beauty Seafoods
Seattle, WA 206-285-6800
Ocean Fresh Seafoods
Seattle, WA 206-285-2412
Okuhara Foods
Honolulu, HI 808-848-0581
Omstead Foods Ltd
Burlington, ON 905-315-8883
Pacific Alaska Seafoods
Seattle, WA 206-587-0002
Pacific Ocean Seafood
La Conner, WA 360-466-4455
Pacific Salmon Company
Edmonds, WA 425-774-1315
Pacific Seafoods International
Sidney, BC 250-656-0901
Pacific Shrimp Company
Newport, OR 541-265-4215
Pacific Surf Food Processors
Los Angeles, CA 800-627-5657

Pacific Trade International
  Hilo, HI 808-961-0877
Paramount Caviar
  Long Island City, NY 800-992-2842
Park 100 Foods
  Tipton, IN 800-854-6504
Pastene Companies
  Canton, MA 781-830-8200
Paul Piazza & Sons
  New Orleans, LA 504-524-6011
Pelican Marine Supply
  Belle Chasse, LA 504-392-9062
Penguin Frozen Foods
  Northbrook, IL 847-291-9400
Peter Pan Seafoods
  Seattle, WA 206-728-6000
Pine Point Fisherman's Co-Op
  Scarborough, ME 207-883-3588
Point Adams Packing Company
  Hammond, OR 503-861-2226
Port Chatham Smoked Seafood
  Everett, WA. 800-872-5666
Premier Smoked Fish Company
  Bensalem, PA 800-654-6682
Proacec USA
  Santa Monica, CA. 310-996-7770
Produits Belle Baie
  Caraquet, NB 506-727-4414
Protein Products Inc
  North Andover, MA 978-689-9083
Quinalt Pride Seafood
  Taholah, WA 360-276-4431
R.A.B. Food Group LLC
  Secaucus, NJ 201-453-5200
Raffield Fisheries
  Port St Joe, FL. 850-229-8229
Red Lake Fisheries Associates
  Redby, MN .218-679-3513
Rego Smoked Fish Company
  Flushing, NY 718-894-1400
Rivere's Seafood Processors
  Paincourtville, LA. 985-369-6055
Roman Sausage Company
  Santa Clara, CA 800-497-7462
Roy Stritmatter Company
  Hoquiam, WA 360-532-0710
Royal Seafood
  Monterey, CA 831-655-8326
Royal Wine Company
  Bayonne, NJ 800-382-8299
Russia
  Staten Island, NY 718-667-8148
Russian Chef
  New York, NY 212-249-1550
S.A.S. Foods
  Doraville, GA 770-263-9312
Sagaya Corporation
  Anchorage, AK 907-561-5173
Salmon River Smokehouse
  Gustavus, AK 907-456-3885
Salt River Lobster
  Boothbay, ME 207-633-5357
Saltspring Aqua Farms
  Salt Spring Island, BC 604-926-3261
Sau-Sea Foods
  Tarrytown, NY 914-631-1717
SC Enterprises
  Owen Sound, ON 519-371-0456
Scandia Seafood Company
  Rockland, ME. 207-596-7102
Schafer Fisheries
  Fulton, IL 815-589-3368
Sea Best Corporation
  Ipswich, MA 978-768-7475
Sea Farm & Farmfresh Importing Company
  Alhambra, CA 323-265-7075
Sea Fresh Alaska
  Kodiak, AK. .907-486-6226
Sea Fresh USA
  Portland, ME. 207-773-6799
Sea Horse Wharf
  Phippsburg, ME 207-389-2312
Sea K Fish Company
  Blaine, WA .360-332-5121
Sea Level Seafoods
  Wrangell, AK 907-874-2401
Sea Lyons
  Spanish Fort, AL. 251-626-2841
Sea Products Company
  Watsonville, CA 831-768-2600
Sea Safari
  Belhaven, NC 800-688-6174

Sea-Fresh Seafood Market
  Mobile, AL .251-478-3434
Seabear
  Anacortes, WA 800-645-3474
Seabreeze Fish
  Bakersfield, CA 661-323-7936
Seafood & Meat
  Theodore, AL 251-653-4600
Seafood Connection
  Honolulu, HI. 808-591-8550
Seafood Distributors
  Savannah, GA 912-233-6048
Seafood Express
  Brunswick, ME 207-729-0887
Seafood Hawaii
  Honolulu, HI. 808-597-1971
Seafood International
  Bayou La Batre, AL 251-824-4200
Seafood International Distributor, Inc
  Henderson, LA 337-228-7568
Seafood Packaging
  New Orleans, LA 504-522-6677
Seafood Plus Corporation
  Berwyn, IL .708-795-4820
Seafood Producers Cooperative
  Bellingham, WA 360-733-0120
Seafood Products Company
  Vancouver, BC 604-255-3141
Seafood Services
  Fairhaven, MA 508-999-1502
Seafood Specialty Sales
  Ipswich, MA 978-356-2995
Seaspan Products Corporation
  New York, NY 201-569-9234
Seaway Company
  Fairhaven, MA 508-992-1221
Service Marketing
  Dunwoody, GA 770-451-9183
Seven Seas Seafoods
  Alhambra, CA 626-570-9129
Sewell's Fish Market
  Rogersville, AL. 256-247-1378
Seymour & Sons Seafood
  Diberville, MS 228-392-4020
Sharkco Seafood International
  Venice, LA .504-534-9577
Shore Trading Company
  Alpharetta, GA 770-998-0566
Shuckman's Fish & Co. Smokery
  Louisville, KY 502-775-6478
SIF
  Shelburne, NS 902-875-2666
Silver Streak Bass Company
  Danevang, TX. 979-543-8989
SOPAKCO Foods
  Mullins, SC .800-276-9678
Sorrento Lobster
  Sorrento, ME. 207-422-9082
South Shores Seafood
  Anaheim, CA 714-956-2722
Southern Fish & Oyster Company
  Mobile, AL .251-438-2408
Southern Pride Catfish Company
  Seattle, WA 800-343-8046
Southern Star Seafood
  Fort Pierce, FL. 561-461-5787
Spence & Company
  Brockton, MA 508-427-1627
Sportsmen's Cannery & Smokehouse
  Winchester Bay, OR 541-271-3293
Sportsmen's Sea Foods
  San Diego, CA 619-224-3551
Springfield Smoked Fish Company
  Springfield, MA 800-327-3412
St. Simons Seafood
  Brunswick, GA 912-265-5225
Star Fine Foods
  Fresno, CA .559-498-2900
State Fish Company
  San Pedro, CA 888-658-3474
State Fish Distributors
  Chicago, IL .773-451-0500
Stavis Seafoods
  Boston, MA. 800-390-5103
Stinson Seafood Company
  Prospect Harbor, ME 207-963-7331
Stinson Seafood Company
  Bath, ME. 207-963-7731
Stoller Fisheries
  Spirit Lake, IA 712-336-1750
Stolt SeaFarm
  Elverta, CA .800-525-0333

Strub Pickles
  Brantford, ON 519-751-1717
Sunshine Food Sales
  Miami, FL 305-696-2885
Sunshine Seafood
  Stonington, ME. 207-367-2955
Super Snooty Sea Food Corporation
  Boston, MA. 617-426-6390
Superior Seafoods
  Tampa, FL .813-248-2749
Sweet Water Seafood Corporation
  Carlstadt, NJ 201-939-6622
SYSCO Foodservice
  Fremont, CA 650-494-7200
Taku Smokehouse
  Juneau, AK .800-582-5122
Tampa Maid Foods
  Lakeland, FL. 800-237-7637
Taylor's Frozen Foods
  Charleston, SC 843-723-1878
Tempest Fisheries Limited
  New Bedford, MA 508-997-0720
Tenth & M Seafoods
  Anchorage, AK 907-272-3474
Thompson Seafood
  Darien, GA .912-437-4649
Three Rivers Fish Company
  Simmesport, LA 318-941-2467
Tichon Seafood Corporation
  New Bedford, MA 508-999-5607
Tri-Marine InternationalInc
  San Pedro, CA. 310-732-6113
Tribe Mediterranean Foods Company LLC
  Taunton, MA 800-421-3474
Trident Seafoods Corporation
  Salem, NH. 603-893-3368
Trident Seafoods Corporation
  Seattle, WA 800-426-5490
Tropic Fish & Vegetable Center
  Honolulu, HI. 808-591-2963
Trout of Paradise
  Paradise, UT 435-245-3053
Ungars Food Products
  Elmwood Park, NJ 201-703-1300
Union Fisheries Corporation
  Chicago, IL .312-738-0448
United Fishing Agency Limited
  Honolulu, HI. 808-536-2148
United Shellfish Company
  Grasonville, MD 410-827-8171
Valdez Food
  Philadelphia, PA 215-634-6106
Van De Kamp Frozen Foods
  Erie, PA. 814-898-1500
Van de Kamp's
  Chambersburg, PA 570-263-4127
Van Dykes Chesapeake Seafood
  Cambridge, MD 410-228-9000
Viking Seafoods Inc
  Malden, MA 800-225-3020
Vinalhaven Fishermens Co-Op
  Camden, ME 207-236-0092
Virginia Trout Company
  Monterey, VA 540-468-2280
Vita Food Products
  Chicago, IL .312-738-4500
Wabash Seafood Company
  Chicago, IL .312-733-5070
Wanchese Fish Company
  Suffolk, VA .757-673-4500
Washington Crab Producers
  Westport, WA 360-268-9161
Waterfield Farms
  Amherst, MA 413-549-3558
West India Trading Company
  Petit-Cap, NB 514-849-6031
Western Alaska Fisheries
  Seattle, WA 206-447-4400
Weyand Fisheries
  Wyandotte, MI 800-521-9815
White Cap Fish Company
  Islip, NY 631-581-0125
Wrangell Fisheries
  Wrangell, AK 907-874-3346
Yamasa Fish Cake Company
  Los Angeles, CA 213-626-2211
York Beach Fish Market
  York Beach, ME 207-363-2763

Abalone

Crown Prince
   City of Industry, CA 800-255-5063
Pacific Seafood Group
   Clackamas, OR 800-388-1101
Sitka Sound Seafoods
   Sitka, AK. 907-747-6662

Amber Jack

Griffin Seafood
   Golden Meadow, LA. 985-396-2453

Anchovies

Chicken of the Sea International
   San Diego, CA 800-678-8862
Crown Prince
   City of Industry, CA 800-255-5063

Canned

Crown Prince Naturals
   Petaluma, CA 707-766-8575
Liberty Richter
   Saddle Brook, NJ 201-291-8749
Ron-Son Foods
   Swedesboro, NJ 856-241-7333

Olive Oil

Castella Imports
   Hauppauge, NY 866-227-8355

Paste

Giovanni's Appetizing Food Products
   Richmond, MI. 586-727-9355

Arctic Charr

Fumoir Grizzly
   St-Augustin, Quebec, QC 418-878-8941

Bass

Culver's Fish Farm
   Mc Pherson, KS 800-241-5205
Louisiana Seafood Exchange
   New Orleans, LA 504-283-9893
Minor Fisheries
   Port Colborne, ON 905-834-9232
Pacific Seafood Group
   Clackamas, OR 800-388-1101
Wanchese Fish Company
   Suffolk, VA 757-673-4500

Striped

Advanced Aquacultural Technologies
   Syracuse, IN 574-457-5802

Bluefish

Menemsha Fish Market
   Chilmark, MA 508-645-2282
Raffield Fisheries
   Port St Joe, FL. 850-229-8229

Bottomfish

Charlton Deep Sea Charters
   Warrenton, OR 503-338-0569
Pacific Ocean Seafood
   La Conner, WA 360-466-4455
Washington Crab Producers
   Westport, WA 360-268-9161

To advertise in the *Food & Beverage Market Place* Online Database call **(800) 562-2139** or log on to **http://gold.greyhouse.com** and click on "Advertise."

Butterfish

Atlantic Capes Fisheries
   Cape May, NJ 609-884-3000
Okuhara Foods
   Honolulu, HI 808-848-0581
Raffield Fisheries
   Port St Joe, FL. 850-229-8229

Cakes

Amano Fish Cake Factory
   Hilo, HI 808-935-5555
Cherokee Trout Farms
   Cherokee, NC 800-732-0075
Icelandic USA
   Newport News, VA 757-820-4000
LaMonica Fine Foods
   Millville, NJ 856-825-8111
Valdez Food
   Philadelphia, PA 215-634-6106
Viking Seafoods Inc
   Malden, MA 800-225-3020
Yamasa Fish Cake Company
   Los Angeles, CA 213-626-2211

Canned

Cuizina Food Company
   Woodinville, WA. 425-486-7000
LaMonica Fine Foods
   Millville, NJ 856-825-8111

Fresh

Cuizina Food Company
   Woodinville, WA. 425-486-7000
Ocean Delight Seafoods
   Vancouver, BC 604-254-8351
Valdez Food
   Philadelphia, PA 215-634-6106
Yamasa Fish Cake Company
   Los Angeles, CA 213-626-2211

Frozen

Amano Fish Cake Factory
   Hilo, HI 808-935-5555
Cuizina Food Company
   Woodinville, WA. 425-486-7000
Gorton's Seafood
   Gloucester, MA. 978-283-3000
Icelandic USA
   Newport News, VA 757-820-4000
Viking Seafoods Inc
   Malden, MA 800-225-3020
Yamasa Fish Cake Company
   Los Angeles, CA 213-626-2211

Canned

Alaskan Gourmet Seafoods
   Anchorage, AK. 800-288-3740
Amano Fish Cake Factory
   Hilo, HI 808-935-5555
B.M. Lawrence & Company
   San Francisco, CA 415-981-3650
Bornstein Seafoods
   Warrenton, OR 503-861-1233
Bumble Bee Seafoods
   San Diego, CA 858-715-4000
Chicken of the Sea International
   San Diego, CA 800-678-8862
Chuck's Seafoods
   Charleston, OR 541-888-5525
Cowart Seafood Corporation
   Lottsburg, VA 804-529-6101
Crown Point
   St John, IN 219-365-3200
Deep Creek Custom Packing
   Ninilchik, AK. 800-764-0078
Dressel Collins Fish Company
   Seattle, WA 206-725-0121
Fishhawk Fisheries
   Astoria, OR 503-325-5252
IMO Foods
   Halifax, NS 902-450-5060
Indian Valley Meats
   Indian, AK. 907-653-7511
J. Moniz Company
   Fall River, MA 508-674-8451
J. Turner Seafoods
   Gloucester, MA. 978-281-8535

J.S. McMillan Fisheries
   Prince Rupert, BC 604- 25- 519
J.S. McMillan Fisheries
   Vancouver, BC 604-255-5191
Kodiak Salmon Packers
   Larsen Bay, AK. 907-847-2250
Liberty Richter
   Saddle Brook, NJ 201-291-8749
LLJ's Sea Products
   Round Pond, ME 207-529-4224
Lubec Packing
   Lubec, ME. 207-733-5572
Mercado Latino
   City of Industry, CA 626-333-6862
Monterey Fish Company
   Salinas, CA 831-755-1923
Nelson Crab
   Tokeland, WA 800-262-0069
Noon Hour Food Products
   Chicago, IL 800-621-6636
Notre Dame Seafood
   Comfort Cove, NL 709-244-5511
Ocean Fresh Seafoods
   Seattle, WA 206-285-2412
Pacific Salmon Company
   Edmonds, WA 425-774-1315
Pastene Companies
   Canton, MA 781-830-8200
Petersburg Fisheries
   Petersburg, AK 877-772-4294
Quinalt Pride Seafood
   Taholah, WA 360-276-4431
Ron-Son Foods
   Swedesboro, NJ 856-241-7333
S&D Bait Company
   Morgan City, LA. 504-252-3500
Seafood Products Company
   Vancouver, BC 604-255-3141
Shafer-Haggart
   Vancouver, BC 888-779-7111
Sportsmen's Cannery & Smokehouse
   Winchester Bay, OR 541-271-3293
Sportsmen's Sea Foods
   San Diego, CA 619-224-3551
Tri-Marine InternationalInc
   San Pedro, CA 310-732-6113
Trout of Paradise
   Paradise, UT 435-245-3053
Ward Cove Packing Company
   Seattle, WA 206-323-3200
Wrangell Fisheries
   Wrangell, AK 907-874-3346

Carp

Culver's Fish Farm
   Mc Pherson, KS 800-241-5205
Red Lake Fisheries Associates
   Redby, MN 218-679-3513
Smoked Fish Factory
   Weston, ON. 416-745-4323
Stoller Fisheries
   Spirit Lake, IA 712-336-1750

Catfish

Alabama Catfish
   Uniontown, AL. 334-628-3474
America's Catch
   Itta Bena, MS 800-242-0041
Bolner's Fiesta Products
   San Antonio, TX 210-734-6404
Carolina Classic Catfish
   Ayden, NC. 252-746-2818
Catfish Wholesale
   Abbeville, LA 800-334-7292
CJ's Seafood
   Des Allemands, LA. 985-758-1237
Coldwater Seafood Corporation
   Norwalk, CT 203-846-8897
ConFish
   Isola, MS. 800-228-3474
Culver's Fish Farm
   Mc Pherson, KS 800-241-5205
Delta Catfish Products
   Eudora, AR 870-355-4192
Delta Pride Catfish
   Indianola, MS 800-421-1045
Farm Fresh Catfish Company
   Hollandale, MS 800-647-8264
Guidry's Catfish
   Breaux Bridge, LA 337-228-7546

Icelandic USA
Newport News, VA 757-820-4000
Inshore Fisheries
Middle West Pubnico, NS 902-762-2522
J. Matassini & Sons Fish Company
Tampa, FL 813-229-0829
Milfico Foods
Elk Grove Vlg, IL 847-427-0491
New Orleans Fish House
New Orleans, LA 800-839-3474
North Atlantic Fish Company
Gloucester, MA 978-283-4121
Pickwick Catfish Farm
Counce, TN 731-689-3805
Pond Pure Catfish
Moulton, AL 256-974-6698
Rivere's Seafood Processors
Paincourtville, LA 985-369-6055
Road Runner Seafood
Colquitt, GA 229-758-3485
Roy Dick Company
Griffin, GA 770-227-3916
Seymour & Sons Seafood
Diberville, MS 228-392-4020
Southern Farms Fish Processors
Kansas City, MO 800-264-2594
Southern Pride Catfish Company
Seattle, WA 800-343-8046
Wisner Minnow Hatchery
Wisner, LA 318-724-6133

Chowder

LaMonica Fine Foods
Millville, NJ 856-825-8111

Chub

Raffield Fisheries
Port St Joe, FL 850-229-8229
Russ & Daughters
New York, NY 800-787-7229
Smoked Fish Factory
Weston, ON 416-745-4323

Cod

All Alaskan Seafood
Seattle, WA 206-285-8200
Angy's Food Products, Inc.
Westfield, MA 413-572-1010
Arctic Seas
Little Compton, RI 401-635-4000
Arrowac Fisheries
Seattle, WA 206-282-5655
BlueWater Seafoods
Lachine, QC 888-560-2539
Bolner's Fiesta Products
San Antonio, TX 210-734-6404
Breakwater Fisheries
St. John's, NL 709-754-1999
Buns & Things Bakery
Charlottetown, PE 902-892-2600
C.L. Deveau & Son
Salmon River, NS 902-649-2812
California Shellfish Company
Gardena, CA 310-538-4197
Canadian Fish Exporters
Watertown, MA 800-225-4215
Castella Imports
Hauppauge, NY 866-227-8355
Ceilidh Fisherman's Cooperative
Inverness, NS 902-787-2666
Certi-Fresh Foods
Bell Gardens, CA 562-806-1100
Coldwater Seafood Corporation
Norwalk, CT 203-846-8897
D Waybret & Sons Fisher ies
Shelburne, NS 902-745-3477
Daerim America
Maywood, NJ 800-635-0781
Davis Strait Fisheries
Halifax, NS 902-450-5115
DB Kenney Fisheries
Westport, NS 902-839-2023
Deep Creek Custom Packing
Ninilchik, AK 800-764-0078
Depoe Bay Fish Company
Newport, OR 541-265-8833
Dorset Fisheries
St. John's, NL 709-739-7147
Felix Custom Smoking
Monroe, WA 425-485-2439

Fishery Products International
Danvers, MA 800-374-4700
Helshiron Fisheries
Grand Manan, NB 506-662-3502
High Liner Foods
Lunenburg, NS 902-634-9475
Icelandic USA
Newport News, VA 757-820-4000
Icicle Seafoods
Seattle, WA 206-282-0988
Independent Packers Corporation
Seattle, WA 206-285-6000
Inlet Salmon
Bothell, WA 425-487-0495
Inshore Fisheries
Middle West Pubnico, NS 902-762-2522
K&N Fisheries
Shelburne, NS 902-768-2478
La Have Seafoods
La Havens, NS 902-688-2773
Lund's Fisheries
Cape May, NJ 609-884-7600
M&M Fisheries
Shelburne, NS 902-723-2390
Menemsha Fish Market
Chilmark, MA 508-645-2282
Mersey Seafoods
Liverpool, NS 902-354-3467
MG Fisheries
Grand Manan, NB 506-662-3471
Mike's Fish & Seafood
Glenwood, MN 800-950-4755
Milfico Foods
Elk Grove Vlg, IL 847-427-0491
Mutual Fish Company
Seattle, WA 206-322-4368
Neptune Foods
Vernon, CA 323-232-8300
Nordic Group
Boston, MA 800-486-4002
NorQuest Seafoods
Seattle, WA 206-281-7022
North Atlantic Fish Company
Gloucester, MA 978-283-4121
Northwest Fisheries
Hubbards, NS 902-228-2232
Notre Dame Seafood
Comfort Cove, NL 709-244-5511
Ocean Pride Fisheries
Lower Wedgeport, NS 902-663-4579
Omstead Foods Ltd
Burlington, ON 905-315-8883
Pacific Ocean Seafood
La Conner, WA 360-466-4455
Pacific Seafood Group
Clackamas, OR 800-388-1101
Paul Piazza & Sons
New Orleans, LA 504-524-6011
Polar Foods International
Charlottetown, PE 902-962-3303
Produits Belle Baie
Caraquet, NB 506-727-4414
Royal Seafood
Monterey, CA 831-655-8326
Seafood Producers Cooperative
Bellingham, WA 360-733-0120
Taku Smokehouse
Juneau, AK 800-582-5122
Viking Seafoods Inc
Malden, MA 800-225-3020
Vita Food Products
Chicago, IL 312-738-4500
Washington Crab Producers
Westport, WA 360-268-9161
Western Alaska Fisheries
Seattle, WA 206-447-4400

Black

Dragnet Fisheries
Anchorage, AK 907-276-4551
Fishhawk Fisheries
Astoria, OR 503-325-5252
Inlet Salmon
Bothell, WA 425-487-0495
Pacific Ocean Seafood
La Conner, WA 360-466-4455
Pacific Salmon Company
Edmonds, WA 425-774-1315
Royal Seafood
Monterey, CA 831-655-8326
Seafood Producers Cooperative
Bellingham, WA 360-733-0120

Sitka Sound Seafoods
Sitka, AK 907-747-6662

Conch

Anchor Frozen Foods
Westbury, NY 800-566-3474
Road Runner Seafood
Colquitt, GA 229-758-3485

Croaker

Glenn Sales Company
Atlanta, GA 770-952-9292
Griffin Seafood
Golden Meadow, LA 985-396-2453
Raffield Fisheries
Port St Joe, FL 850-229-8229
Road Runner Seafood
Colquitt, GA 229-758-3485

Cusk

Canadian Fish Exporters
Watertown, MA 800-225-4215

Dogfish

Pacific Seafood Group
Clackamas, OR 800-388-1101
Seatec
Portland, ME 207-879-7199

Dolphin

Wanchese Fish Company
Suffolk, VA 757-673-4500

Eel

George Robberecht Seafood
Montross, VA 804-472-3556
Ocean Union Company
Lawrenceville, GA 770-995-1957
Pacific Seafood Group
Clackamas, OR 800-388-1101

Fillets

American Seafoods International
New Bedford, MA 800-343-8046
Arrowac Fisheries
Seattle, WA 206-282-5655
Bayou Foods
Kenner, LA 800-516-8283
Coldwater Seafood Corporation
Norwalk, CT 203-846-8897
Cozy Harbor Seafood
Portland, ME 800-225-2586
Ducktrap River Fish Farm
Belfast, ME 800-434-8727
Erba Food Products
Brooklyn, NY 718-272-7700
Good Harbor Fillet Company
Gloucester, MA 978-675-9100
Icelandic USA
Newport News, VA 757-820-4000
Jessie's Ilwaco Fish Company
Ilwaco, WA 360-642-3773
Neptune Foods
Vernon, CA 323-232-8300
Nordic Group
Boston, MA 800-486-4002
Ocean Beauty Seafoods
Seattle, WA 206-285-6800
Pacific Seafoods International
Sidney, BC 250-656-0901
Pacific Surf Food Processors
Los Angeles, CA 800-627-5657
Penguin Frozen Foods
Northbrook, IL 847-291-9400
Roman Sausage Company
Santa Clara, CA 800-497-7462
Seafood Products Company
Vancouver, BC 604-255-3141
Super Snooty Sea Food Corporation
Boston, MA 617-426-6390
Taku Smokehouse
Juneau, AK 800-582-5122
Ungars Food Products
Elmwood Park, NJ 201-703-1300
Van De Kamp Frozen Foods
Erie, PA 814-898-1500

Finfish

Arrowac Fisheries
Seattle, WA 206-282-5655
Depoe Bay Fish Company
Newport, OR 541-265-8833
Highland Fisheries
Glace Bay, NS 902-849-6016
James Cowan & Sons
Worcester, MA 508-754-5385

Flounder

Bolner's Fiesta Products
San Antonio, TX 210-734-6404
Bon Secour Fisheries
Bon Secour, AL 800-633-6854
Carrington Foods
Saraland, AL 251-675-9700
Catfish Wholesale
Abbeville, LA 800-334-7292
Depoe Bay Fish Company
Newport, OR 541-265-8833
Fishery Products International
Danvers, MA 800-374-4700
Glenn Sales Company
Atlanta, GA 770-952-9292
Gorton's Seafood
Gloucester, MA 978-283-3000
Griffin Seafood
Golden Meadow, LA 985-396-2453
Gulf City Marine Supply
Bayou La Batre, AL 251-824-4154
Inshore Fisheries
Middle West Pubnico, NS 902-762-2522
Lund's Fisheries
Cape May, NJ 609-884-7600
Menemsha Fish Market
Chilmark, MA 508-645-2282
Mersey Seafoods
Liverpool, NS 902-354-3467
Milfico Foods
Elk Grove Vlg, IL 847-427-0491
Mirasco
Atlanta, GA 770-956-1945
N.A. Boullon
Cumming, GA 770-889-2356
Pacific Seafood Group
Clackamas, OR 800-388-1101
Pamlico Packing Company
Grantsboro, NC 800-682-1113
Road Runner Seafood
Colquitt, GA 229-758-3485
Royal Seafood
Monterey, CA 831-655-8326
Tampa Maid Foods
Lakeland, FL 800-237-7637
Taylor's Frozen Foods
Charleston, SC 843-723-1878
Thompson Seafood
Darien, GA 912-437-4649
Wanchese Fish Company
Suffolk, VA 757-673-4500
Ward Cove Packing Company
Seattle, WA 206-323-3200

Fluke

Agger Fish
Brooklyn, NY 718-855-1717

Fresh

Arrowac Fisheries
Seattle, WA 206-282-5655
Aslanis Seafoods
Quincy, MA 800-876-3712
Atlantic Salmon of Maine
Belfast, ME 800-508-7861
Baker's Point Fisheries
Oyster Pond Jeddore, NS 902-845-2347
Bama Fish Atlanta
East Point, GA 404-765-9896
Bayou Land Seafood
Breaux Bridge, LA 337-667-6118
Birch Street Seafoods
Digby, NS 902-245-6551
Blue Wave Seafoods
Port Mouton, NS 902-683-2044
Bon Secour Fisheries
Bon Secour, AL 800-633-6854
Cherokee Trout Farms
Cherokee, NC 800-732-0075

Crest International Corporation
San Diego, CA 800-548-1232
DCL
Honolulu, HI 808-845-3834
Deep Creek Custom Packing
Ninilchik, AK 800-764-0078
Earle Brothers Fisheries
Carbonear, NL 709-596-5166
Ferroclad Fishery
Batchawana Bay, ON 705-882-2295
Fish Breeders of Idaho
Boise, ID 888-414-8818
Harbor Fish Market
Portland, ME 207-775-0251
Harold Bozman Seafood
Upper Fairmount, MD 410-651-0647
HFI Foods
Redmond, WA 425-883-1320
High Liner Foods
Lunenburg, NS 902-634-9475
Inshore Fisheries
Middle West Pubnico, NS 902-762-2522
International Seafoods of Alaska
Kodiak, AK 907-486-4768
Island Marine Products
Clarks Harbour, NS 902-745-2222
J. Matassini & Sons Fish Company
Tampa, FL 813-229-0829
Jessie's Ilwaco Fish Company
Ilwaco, WA 360-642-3773
Kyler Seafood
New Bedford, MA 888-859-5377
Lakeside Foods
Seymour, WI 920-833-2371
LaMonica Fine Foods
Millville, NJ 856-825-8111
Lougheed Fisheries
Owen Sound, ON 519-376-1586
MacKnight Smoked Foods
Miami, FL 305-655-0444
Marche Tramsatlantique
Montreal, QC 514-287-3530
Mariner Seafoods
Montague, PE 902-838-2481
Menemsha Fish Market
Chilmark, MA 508-645-2282
Mersey Seafoods
Liverpool, NS 902-354-3467
Minor Fisheries
Port Colborne, ON 905-834-9232
Morey's Seafood International
Motley, MN 218-352-6345
Mutual Fish Company
Seattle, WA 206-322-4368
Ocean Beauty Seafoods
Seattle, WA 206-285-6800
Ocean Fresh Seafoods
Seattle, WA 206-285-2412
Pacific Seafoods International
Sidney, BC 250-656-0901
Pacific Shrimp Company
Newport, OR 541-265-4215
Pacific Surf Food Processors
Los Angeles, CA 800-627-5657
Paul Piazza & Sons
New Orleans, LA 504-524-6011
Royal Seafood
Monterey, CA 831-655-8326
Sunshine Food Sales
Miami, FL 305-696-2885
SYSCO Foodservice
Fremont, CA 650-494-7200
Trout of Paradise
Paradise, UT 435-245-3053
Union Fisheries Corporation
Chicago, IL 312-738-0448
Virginia Trout Company
Monterey, VA 540-468-2280
Wanchese Fish Company
Suffolk, VA 757-673-4500
Washington Crab Producers
Westport, WA 360-268-9161
Weyand Fisheries
Wyandotte, MI 800-521-9815
Wrangell Fisheries
Wrangell, AK 907-874-3346
Yamasa Fish Cake Company
Los Angeles, CA 213-626-2211

Freshwater

Hamilos Brothers Inspected Meats
Madison, IL 618-451-7877

Frozen

Alaska Seafood Company
Los Angeles, CA 213-626-1212
Alaskan Gourmet Seafoods
Anchorage, AK 800-288-3740
All Alaskan Seafood
Seattle, WA 206-285-8200
Amano Fish Cake Factory
Hilo, HI 808-935-5555
American Seafoods International
New Bedford, MA 800-343-8046
Appert's Foodservice
St Cloud, MN 800-225-3883
APTCO
San Francisco, CA 415-648-6688
Arctic Seas
Little Compton, RI 401-635-4000
Arrowac Fisheries
Seattle, WA 206-282-5655
Aslanis Seafoods
Quincy, MA 800-876-3712
Baker's Point Fisheries
Oyster Pond Jeddore, NS 902-845-2347
Bama Fish Atlanta
East Point, GA 404-765-9896
Barry Group
Corner Brook, NL 709-785-7387
Bayou Land Seafood
Breaux Bridge, LA 337-667-6118
Beaver Street Fisheries
Jacksonville, FL 800-874-6426
Big Al's Seafood
Bozman, MD 410-745-3151
Birch Street Seafoods
Digby, NS 902-245-6551
Birdie Pak Products
Chicago, IL 773-247-5293
Blue Wave Seafoods
Port Mouton, NS 902-683-2044
Bolner's Fiesta Products
San Antonio, TX 210-734-6404
Bon Secour Fisheries
Bon Secour, AL 800-633-6854
Breakwater Fisheries
St. John's, NL 709-754-1999
Buedel Food Products
Chicago, IL 773-235-3637
Buns & Things Bakery
Charlottetown, PE 902-892-2600
California Shellfish Company
Gardena, CA 310-538-4197
Captn's Pack Products
Columbia, MD 410-720-6668
Carrington Foods
Saraland, AL 251-675-9700
Certi-Fresh Foods
Bell Gardens, CA 562-806-1100
Cherokee Trout Farms
Cherokee, NC 800-732-0075
Clear Springs Foods
Buhl, ID 800-635-8211
Coldwater Seafood Corporation
Norwalk, CT 203-846-8897
Cook Inlet Processing
Nikiski, AK 907-776-8174
Cozy Harbor Seafood
Portland, ME 800-225-2586
Crab King Seafood Specialties
Seattle, WA 206-283-2722
Crest International Corporation
San Diego, CA 800-548-1232
Crown Point
St John, IN 219-365-3200
Cuizina Food Company
Woodinville, WA 425-486-7000
Daerim America
Maywood, NJ 800-635-0781
DB Kenney Fisheries
Westport, NS 902-839-2023
Deep Creek Custom Packing
Ninilchik, AK 800-764-0078
Delta Pride Catfish
Indianola, MS 800-421-1045
Depoe Bay Fish Company
Newport, OR 541-265-8833
Earle Brothers Fisheries
Carbonear, NL 709-596-5166

Farm Fresh Catfish Company
  Hollandale, MS 800-647-8264
Ferroclad Fishery
  Batchawana Bay, ON 705-882-2295
Fish Breeders of Idaho
  Boise, ID 888-414-8818
Fishery Products International
  Danvers, MA 800-374-4700
Fishking Processors
  Los Angeles, CA 877-677-3329
George Robberecht Seafood
  Montross, VA 804-472-3556
Glacier Fish Company
  Seattle, WA 206-298-1200
Great Glacier Salmon
  Prince Rupert, BC 250-627-4955
Great Northern Products
  Warwick, RI 401-490-4590
Hamilos Brothers Inspected Meats
  Madison, IL 618-451-7877
Harold Bozman Seafood
  Upper Fairmount, MD 410-651-0647
HFI Foods
  Redmond, WA 425-883-1320
High Liner Foods
  Lunenburg, NS 902-634-9475
Icelandic USA
  Newport News, VA 757-820-4000
Icicle Seafoods
  Seattle, WA 206-282-0988
Independent Packers Corporation
  Seattle, WA 206-285-6000
Inlet Salmon
  Bothell, WA 425-487-0495
Inshore Fisheries
  Middle West Pubnico, NS 902-762-2522
International Seafoods of Alaska
  Kodiak, AK 907-486-4768
Island Marine Products
  Clarks Harbour, NS 902-745-2222
J. Matassini & Sons Fish Company
  Tampa, FL 813-229-0829
J.S. McMillan Fisheries
  Vancouver, BC 604-255-5191
Jer-Mar Foods
  Windsor, ON 519-256-3474
Jessie's Ilwaco Fish Company
  Ilwaco, WA 360-642-3773

John T. Handy Company
  Salisbury, MD 800-426-3977
Key Largo Fisheries
  Key Largo, FL 800-399-6970
Kodiak Salmon Packers
  Larsen Bay, AK 907-847-2250
Kyler Seafood
  New Bedford, MA 888-859-5377
Long Beach Seafoods
  Long Beach, CA 714-995-8901
Lougheed Fisheries
  Owen Sound, ON 519-376-1586
Lund's Fisheries
  Cape May, NJ 609-884-7600
Mada'n Kosher Foods
  Dania, FL 954-925-0077
Mariner Seafoods
  Montague, PE 902-838-2481
Martin Brothers Seafood Company
  Westwego, LA 504-341-2251
Menemsha Fish Market
  Chilmark, MA 508-645-2282
Mersey Seafoods
  Liverpool, NS 902-354-3467
Mike's Fish & Seafood
  Glenwood, MN 800-950-4755
Milfico Foods
  Elk Grove Vlg, IL 847-427-0491
Mill Cove Lobster Pound
  Boothbay Harbor, ME 207-633-3340
Minor Fisheries
  Port Colborne, ON 905-834-9232
Monterey Fish Company
  Salinas, CA 831-755-1923
Morey's Seafood International
  Motley, MN 218-352-6345
Mutual Fish Company
  Seattle, WA 206-322-4368
Nelson Crab
  Tokeland, WA 800-262-0069
Nordic Group
  Boston, MA 800-486-4002
North Atlantic Fish Company
  Gloucester, MA 978-283-4121
Northwest Naturals
  Olympia, WA 360-866-9661
Notre Dame Seafood
  Comfort Cove, NL 709-244-5511
Ocean Beauty Seafoods
  Seattle, WA 206-285-6800
Ocean Fresh Seafoods
  Seattle, WA 206-285-2412
Okuhara Foods
  Honolulu, HI 808-848-0581
Omstead Foods Ltd
  Burlington, ON 905-315-8883
Pacific Salmon Company
  Edmonds, WA 425-774-1315
Pacific Seafood Group
  Clackamas, OR 800-388-1101
Pacific Seafoods International
  Sidney, BC 250-656-0901
Pacific Shrimp Company
  Newport, OR 541-265-4215
Pacific Surf Food Processors
  Los Angeles, CA 800-627-5657
Pamlico Packing Company
  Grantsboro, NC 800-682-1113
Paul Piazza & Sons
  New Orleans, LA 504-524-6011
Penguin Frozen Foods
  Northbrook, IL 847-291-9400
Peter Pan Seafoods
  Seattle, WA 206-728-6000
Petersburg Fisheries
  Petersburg, AK 877-772-4294
Quinalt Pride Seafood
  Taholah, WA 360-276-4431
Roy Stritmatter Company
  Hoquiam, WA 360-532-0710
Royal Seafood
  Monterey, CA 831-655-8326
Sea Products Company
  Watsonville, CA 831-768-2600
Sea Safari
  Belhaven, NC 800-688-6174
Seafood Products Company
  Vancouver, BC 604-255-3141
Seaspan Products Corporation
  New York, NY 201-569-9234
Seymour & Sons Seafood
  Diberville, MS 228-392-4020

Stinson Seafood Company
  Prospect Harbor, ME 207-963-7331
Stolt SeaFarm
  Elverta, CA 800-525-0333
Sunshine Food Sales
  Miami, FL 305-696-2885
Super Snooty Sea Food Corporation
  Boston, MA 617-426-6390
SYSCO Foodservice
  Fremont, CA 650-494-7200
Taku Smokehouse
  Juneau, AK 800-582-5122
Tampa Maid Foods
  Lakeland, FL 800-237-7637
Taylor's Frozen Foods
  Charleston, SC 843-723-1878
Tichon Seafood Corporation
  New Bedford, MA 508-999-5607
Trident Seafoods Corporation
  Salem, NH 603-893-3368
Trident Seafoods Corporation
  Seattle, WA 800-426-5490
Union Fisheries Corporation
  Chicago, IL 312-738-0448
Van De Kamp Frozen Foods
  Erie, PA 814-898-1500
Viking Seafoods Inc
  Malden, MA 800-225-3020
Virginia Trout Company
  Monterey, VA 540-468-2280
Vita Food Products
  Chicago, IL 312-738-4500
W&W Meats
  Willoughby, OH 216-621-7846
Wanchese Fish Company
  Suffolk, VA 757-673-4500
Washington Crab Producers
  Westport, WA 360-268-9161
Western Alaska Fisheries
  Seattle, WA 206-447-4400
Weyand Fisheries
  Wyandotte, MI 800-521-9815
White Cap Fish Company
  Islip, NY 631-581-0125
Wrangell Fisheries
  Wrangell, AK 907-874-3346
Yamasa Fish Cake Company
  Los Angeles, CA 213-626-2211

Gefilte

Erba Food Products
  Brooklyn, NY 718-272-7700
R.A.B. Food Group LLC
  Secaucus, NJ 201-453-5200
Royal Wine Company
  Bayonne, NJ 800-382-8299

Grouper

Bolner's Fiesta Products
  San Antonio, TX 210-734-6404
Griffin Seafood
  Golden Meadow, LA 985-396-2453
Milfico Foods
  Elk Grove Vlg, IL 847-427-0491
Mirasco
  Atlanta, GA 770-956-1945
N.A. Boullon
  Cumming, GA 770-889-2356
Ocean Union Company
  Lawrenceville, GA 770-995-1957
Poseidon Enterprises
  Atlanta, GA 800-863-7886

Haddock

Adams Fisheries Ltd
  Shag Harbour, NS 902-723-2435
Arctic Seas
  Little Compton, RI 401-635-4000
BlueWater Seafoods
  Lachine, QC 888-560-2539
Canadian Fish Exporters
  Watertown, MA 800-225-4215
Coldwater Seafood Corporation
  Norwalk, CT 203-846-8897
Davis Strait Fisheries
  Halifax, NS 902-450-5115
DB Kenney Fisheries
  Westport, NS 902-839-2023
High Liner Foods
  Lunenburg, NS 902-634-9475

I. Deveau Fisheries
Meteghan, NS 902-645-3036
Icelandic USA
Newport News, VA 757-820-4000
Inshore Fisheries
Middle West Pubnico, NS. 902-762-2522
Island Marine Products
Clarks Harbour, NS. 902-745-2222
La Have Seafoods
La Havens, NS 902-688-2773
Leo G. Atkinson Fisheries
Clarks Harbor, NS. 902-745-3047
M&M Fisheries
Shelburne, NS 902-723-2390
Menemsha Fish Market
Chilmark, MA. 508-645-2282
Mersey Seafoods
Liverpool, NS 902-354-3467
MG Fisheries
Grand Manan, NB. 506-662-3471
Nordic Group
Boston, MA. 800-486-4002
Ocean Pride Fisheries
Lower Wedgeport, NS 902-663-4579
Omstead Foods Ltd
Burlington, ON 905-315-8883

Hake

Canadian Fish Exporters
Watertown, MA. 800-225-4215
Helshiron Fisheries
Grand Manan, NB. 506-662-3502
Mirasco
Atlanta, GA. 770-956-1945

Halibut

Alaskan Gourmet Seafoods
Anchorage, AK. 800-288-3740
All Alaskan Seafood
Seattle, WA. 206-285-8200
Angy's Food Products, Inc.
Westfield, MA. 413-572-1010
Arrowac Fisheries
Seattle, WA. 206-282-5655
Bell Buoy Crab Company
Seaside, OR. 800-529-2722
California Shellfish Company
San Francisco, CA 415-923-7400
Calkins & Burke
Vancouver, BC 604-669-3741
Certi-Fresh Foods
Bell Gardens, CA 562-806-1100
Charlton Deep Sea Charters
Warrenton, OR 503-338-0569
Chicago Steaks
Chicago, IL 800-776-4174
Cook Inlet Processing
Nikiski, AK. 907-776-8174
Crab King Seafood Specialties
Seattle, WA. 206-283-2722
D Waybret & Sons Fisher ies
Shelburne, NS. 902-745-3477
Deep Creek Custom Packing
Ninilchik, AK. 800-764-0078
Depoe Bay Fish Company
Newport, OR. 541-265-8833
Elwha Fish
Port Angeles, WA 360-457-3344
Felix Custom Smoking
Monroe, WA 425-485-2439
Fishhawk Fisheries
Astoria, OR 503-325-5252
Fjord Pacific Marine Industries
Richmond, BC 604-270-3393
High Liner Foods
Lunenburg, NS 902-634-9475
His Catch Value Added Products
Homer, AK 800-215-7110
Icicle Seafoods
Seattle, WA. 206-282-0988
Independent Packers Corporation
Seattle, WA. 206-285-6000
Indian Valley Meats
Indian, AK. 907-653-7511
Inlet Salmon
Bothell, WA. 425-487-0495
Island Marine Products
Clarks Harbour, NS. 902-745-2222
J.S. McMillan Fisheries
Vancouver, BC 604-255-5191

Long Beach Seafoods
Long Beach, CA 714-995-8901
Menemsha Fish Market
Chilmark, MA. 508-645-2282
Mersey Seafoods
Liverpool, NS 902-354-3467
Milfico Foods
Elk Grove Vlg, IL. 847-427-0491
Neptune Foods
Vernon, CA. 323-232-8300
NorQuest Seafoods
Seattle, WA. 206-281-7022
North Atlantic Fish Company
Gloucester, MA. 978-283-4121
Northwest Fisheries
Hubbards, NS 902-228-2232
Northwest Naturals
Olympia, WA 360-866-9661
Ocean Beauty Seafoods
Seattle, WA. 206-285-6800
Pacific Ocean Seafood
La Conner, WA 360-466-4455
Pacific Salmon Company
Edmonds, WA 425-774-1315
Pacific Seafood Group
Clackamas, OR 800-388-1101
Pacific Shrimp Company
Newport, OR. 541-265-4215
Petersburg Fisheries
Petersburg, AK. 877-772-4294
Sea K Fish Company
Blaine, WA 360-332-5121
Sea Products Company
Watsonville, CA. 831-768-2600
Seafood Producers Cooperative
Bellingham, WA. 360-733-0120
Seafood Products Company
Vancouver, BC 604-255-3141
Sitka Sound Seafoods
Sitka, AK. 907-747-6662
Taku Smokehouse
Juneau, AK 800-582-5122
Trident Seafoods Corporation
Seattle, WA. 800-426-5490
Viking Seafoods Inc
Malden, MA. 800-225-3020
Washington Crab Producers
Westport, WA 360-268-9161
Western Alaska Fisheries
Seattle, WA. 206-447-4400
Wrangell Fisheries
Wrangell, AK. 907-874-3346

Herring

Acme Smoked Fish Corporation
Brooklyn, NY 800-221-0795
Alimentaire Whyte's Inc
Laval, QC 800-625-1979
All Alaskan Seafood
Seattle, WA. 206-285-8200
Angy's Food Products, Inc.
Westfield, MA. 413-572-1010
Baensch Food
Milwaukee, WI 800-562-8234
Bell Buoy Crab Company
Seaside, OR. 800-529-2722
Bos Smoked Fish Inc
Woodstock, ON 519-537-5000
Breakwater Fisheries
St. John's, NL 709-754-1999
Buns & Things Bakery
Charlottetown, PE. 902-892-2600
Canadian Fish Exporters
Watertown, MA. 800-225-4215
Canadian Silver Herring
Cap-Pele, NB 506-577-6426
Castella Imports
Hauppauge, NY 866-227-8355
Chicago 58 Food Products
Toronto, ON 416-603-4244
Comeau's Sea Foods
Saulnierville, NS. 902-769-2101
Cowart Seafood Corporation
Lottsburg, VA 804-529-6101
Delta Pacific Seafoods
Delta, BC. 800-328-2547
Depoe Bay Fish Company
Newport, OR. 541-265-8833
Dragnet Fisheries
Anchorage, AK. 907-276-4551

Duguay Fish Packers
Cap-Pele, NB 506-577-2287
Feature Foods
Etobicoke, ON 416-675-7350
Ferroclad Fishery
Batchawana Bay, ON 705-882-2295
Fjord Pacific Marine Industries
Richmond, BC 604-270-3393
Flaum Appetizing
Brooklyn, NY 718-821-1970
G J Shortall
Mount Pearl, NL 709-747-0655
Gaudet & Ouellette
Cap-Pele, NB 506-577-4016
Gorman Fisheries
Conception Bay, NL 709-229-6536
Great Northern Products
Warwick, RI 401-490-4590
High Sea Foods
Glovertown, NL 709-533-2626
Icicle Seafoods
Seattle, WA. 206-282-0988
Island Marine Products
Clarks Harbour, NS. 902-745-2222
Leslie Leger & Sons
Cap-Pele, NB 506-577-4730
Lund's Fisheries
Cape May, NJ 609-884-7600
Menemsha Fish Market
Chilmark, MA. 508-645-2282
Mersey Seafoods
Liverpool, NS 902-354-3467
Mike's Fish & Seafood
Glenwood, MN 800-950-4755
Newell Lobsters
Yarmouth, NS 902-742-6272
NorQuest Seafoods
Seattle, WA. 206-281-7022
Pacific Seafood Group
Clackamas, OR 800-388-1101
Pacific Shrimp Company
Newport, OR. 541-265-4215
Petersburg Fisheries
Petersburg, AK. 877-772-4294
Polar Foods International
Charlottetown, PE. 902-962-3303
Premier Smoked Fish Company
Bensalem, PA 800-654-6682
Produits Belle Baie
Caraquet, NB 506-727-4414
Raffield Fisheries
Port St Joe, FL. 850-229-8229
Royal Seafood
Monterey, CA 831-655-8326
Russ & Daughters
New York, NY 800-787-7229
Salmolux
Federal Way, WA 253-874-6570
Sea Products Company
Watsonville, CA. 831-768-2600
Seafood Products Company
Vancouver, BC 604-255-3141
Sitka Sound Seafoods
Sitka, AK. 907-747-6662
Springfield Smoked Fish Company
Springfield, MA 800-327-3412
Stinson Seafood Company
Prospect Harbor, ME 207-963-7331
Strub Pickles
Brantford, ON 519-751-1717
Tribe Mediterranean Foods Company LLC
Taunton, MA. 800-421-3474
Vita Food Products
Chicago, IL 312-738-4500
West India Trading Company
Petit-Cap, NB 514-849-6031
Western Alaska Fisheries
Seattle, WA. 206-447-4400
Wrangell Fisheries
Wrangell, AK. 907-874-3346

Boned

Feature Foods
Etobicoke, ON 416-675-7350

Fillets

Angy's Food Products, Inc.
Westfield, MA. 413-572-1010
Seafood Products Company
Vancouver, BC 604-255-3141

Fresh

Angy's Food Products, Inc.
Westfield, MA .413-572-1010
Bella Coola Fisheries
Delta, BC 604-583-3474
Feature Foods
Etobicoke, ON 416-675-7350
Ferroclad Fishery
Batchawana Bay, ON 705-882-2295
Icicle Seafoods
Seattle, WA 206-282-0988
Mersey Seafoods
Liverpool, NS .902-354-3467
Mike's Fish & Seafood
Glenwood, MN 800-950-4755
Royal Seafood
Monterey, CA .831-655-8326
Seafood Products Company
Vancouver, BC 604-255-3141
Western Alaska Fisheries
Seattle, WA 206-447-4400
Wrangell Fisheries
Wrangell, AK .907-874-3346

Frozen

Angy's Food Products, Inc.
Westfield, MA .413-572-1010
Bella Coola Fisheries
Delta, BC 604-583-3474
Breakwater Fisheries
St. John's, NL .709-754-1999
Depoe Bay Fish Company
Newport, OR 541-265-8833
Ferroclad Fishery
Batchawana Bay, ON 705-882-2295
Great Northern Products
Warwick, RI 401-490-4590
Icicle Seafoods
Seattle, WA 206-282-0988
Island Marine Products
Clarks Harbour, NS 902-745-2222
Lund's Fisheries
Cape May, NJ .609-884-7600
Menemsha Fish Market
Chilmark, MA 508-645-2282
Mersey Seafoods
Liverpool, NS .902-354-3467
Pacific Shrimp Company
Newport, OR 541-265-4215
Peter Pan Seafoods
Seattle, WA 206-728-6000
Royal Seafood
Monterey, CA .831-655-8326
Sea Products Company
Watsonville, CA 831-768-2600
Seafood Products Company
Vancouver, BC 604-255-3141
Stinson Seafood Company
Prospect Harbor, ME 207-963-7331
Western Alaska Fisheries
Seattle, WA 206-447-4400
Wrangell Fisheries
Wrangell, AK .907-874-3346

Salted & Marinated

Feature Foods
Etobicoke, ON 416-675-7350
High Liner Foods
Lunenburg, NS 902-634-9475
Island Marine Products
Clarks Harbour, NS 902-745-2222

Spiced

Baensch Food
Milwaukee, WI 800-562-8234
Feature Foods
Etobicoke, ON 416-675-7350

Hoki

Arctic Seas
Little Compton, RI 401-635-4000
Daerim America
Maywood, NJ .800-635-0781

Imitation

Flavor House
Adelanto, CA .760-246-9131
HFI Foods
Redmond, WA 425-883-1320

Lu-Mar Lobster & Shrimp
Brownsville, TX 956-546-5525
Ocean Food Company
Scarborough, ON 416-285-6487
Peter Pan Seafoods
Seattle, WA 206-728-6000
Shining Ocean
Sumner, WA 253-826-3700
Trans-Ocean Products
Bellingham, WA 888-215-4815
Trident Seafoods Corporation
Fife, WA 253-922-5577
Trident Seafoods Corporation
Seattle, WA 800-426-5490

King Cod

Deep Creek Custom Packing
Ninilchik, AK .800-764-0078
Minor Fisheries
Port Colborne, ON 905-834-9232

Kingfish

Sunshine Food Sales
Miami, FL 305-696-2885

Lumpfish

Notre Dame Seafood
Comfort Cove, NL 709-244-5511
Russian Chef
New York, NY 212-249-1550

Mackerel

Atlantic Capes Fisheries
Cape May, NJ .609-884-3000
Atlantic Fish Specialties
Charlottetown, PE 902-894-7005
Bos Smoked Fish Inc
Woodstock, ON 519-537-5000
Breakwater Fisheries
St. John's, NL .709-754-1999
Buns & Things Bakery
Charlottetown, PE 902-892-2600
Canadian Fish Exporters
Watertown, MA 800-225-4215
Castella Imports
Hauppauge, NY 866-227-8355
Chicken of the Sea International
San Diego, CA 800-678-8862
Crown Point
St John, IN 219-365-3200
Crown Prince
City of Industry, CA 800-255-5063
Crown Prince Naturals
Petaluma, CA .707-766-8575
Ducktrap River Fish Farm
Belfast, ME 800-434-8727
Erba Food Products
Brooklyn, NY 718-272-7700
G J Shortall
Mount Pearl, NL 709-747-0655
Gorman Fisheries
Conception Bay, NL 709-229-6536
Griffin Seafood
Golden Meadow, LA 985-396-2453
Lund's Fisheries
Cape May, NJ .609-884-7600
Menemsha Fish Market
Chilmark, MA 508-645-2282
Mersey Seafoods
Liverpool, NS .902-354-3467
Notre Dame Seafood
Comfort Cove, NL 709-244-5511
Ocean Union Company
Lawrenceville, GA 770-995-1957
Pacific Seafood Group
Clackamas, OR 800-388-1101
Polar Foods International
Charlottetown, PE 902-962-3303
Royal Seafood
Monterey, CA .831-655-8326
Russ & Daughters
New York, NY 800-787-7229
Sea Products Company
Watsonville, CA 831-768-2600
Smoked Fish Factory
Weston, ON 416-745-4323
Sunshine Food Sales
Miami, FL 305-696-2885

Tri-Marine InternationalInc
San Pedro, CA 310-732-6113

Mahi-Mahi

Griffin Seafood
Golden Meadow, LA 985-396-2453
Milfico Foods
Elk Grove Vlg, IL 847-427-0491
N.A. Boullon
Cumming, GA 770-889-2356
Ocean Beauty Seafoods
Seattle, WA 206-285-6800
Omega Foods
Eugene, OR 800-200-2356

Marlin

Mid-Pacific Hawaii Fishery
Hilo, HI 808-935-6110
Sportsmen's Sea Foods
San Diego, CA 619-224-3551

Meal

Acatris USA
Edina, MN 952-920-7700

Monkfish

Agger Fish
Brooklyn, NY 718-855-1717
Atlantic Capes Fisheries
Cape May, NJ .609-884-3000
Seatec
Portland, ME .207-879-7199

Mullet

Griffin Seafood
Golden Meadow, LA 985-396-2453
Raffield Fisheries
Port St Joe, FL 850-229-8229
Road Runner Seafood
Colquitt, GA 229-758-3485

Orange Roughy

Chicago Steaks
Chicago, IL 800-776-4174
Milfico Foods
Elk Grove Vlg, IL 847-427-0491
Neptune Foods
Vernon, CA 323-232-8300

Packed

Glass

Indian Valley Meats
Indian, AK 907-653-7511
Noon Hour Food Products
Chicago, IL 800-621-6636
Petersburg Fisheries
Petersburg, AK 877-772-4294

Pouch

Indian Valley Meats
Indian, AK 907-653-7511
Noon Hour Food Products
Chicago, IL 800-621-6636
Petersburg Fisheries
Petersburg, AK 877-772-4294

Paste

Certified Savory
Countryside, IL 800-328-7656
Giovanni's Appetizing Food Products
Richmond, MI 586-727-9355
Mike's Fish & Seafood
Glenwood, MN 800-950-4755

Patties

Roman Sausage Company
Santa Clara, CA 800-497-7462

Perch

A&A Marine & Drydock Company
Blenheim, ON 519-676-2030
Coldwater Seafood Corporation
Norwalk, CT .203-846-8897

Depoe Bay Fish Company
Newport, OR .541-265-8833
Fishery Products International
Danvers, MA .800-374-4700
High Liner Foods
Lunenburg, NS 902-634-9475
Inshore Fisheries
Middle West Pubnico, NS 902-762-2522
Jer-Mar Foods
Windsor, ON .519-256-3474
Kingsville Fisherman's Company
Kingsville, ON 519-733-6534
Mersey Seafoods
Liverpool, NS 902-354-3467
Milfico Foods
Elk Grove Vlg, IL 847-427-0491
Minor Fisheries
Port Colborne, ON 905-834-9232
Mutual Fish Company
Seattle, WA 206-322-4368
Omstead Foods Ltd
Burlington, ON 905-315-8883
Pacific Seafood Group
Clackamas, OR 800-388-1101
Paul Piazza & Sons
New Orleans, LA 504-524-6011
Red Lake Fisheries Associates
Redby, MN 218-679-3513
Royal Seafood
Monterey, CA 831-655-8326
Sea Products Company
Watsonville, CA 831-768-2600
Viking Seafoods Inc
Malden, MA .800-225-3020

Ocean

DB Kenney Fisheries
Westport, NS 902-839-2023
Mill Cove Lobster Pound
Boothbay Harbor, ME 207-633-3340
Polar Foods International
Charlottetown, PE 902-962-3303

Pickerel

A&A Marine & Drydock Company
Blenheim, ON 519-676-2030
Jer-Mar Foods
Windsor, ON .519-256-3474
Kingsville Fisherman's Company
Kingsville, ON 519-733-6534
Minor Fisheries
Port Colborne, ON 905-834-9232

Pike

Milfico Foods
Elk Grove Vlg, IL 847-427-0491

Pollack

BlueWater Seafoods
Lachine, QC .888-560-2539
Bolner's Fiesta Products
San Antonio, TX 210-734-6404
Glenn Sales Company
Atlanta, GA 770-952-9292
Icelandic USA
Newport News, VA 757-820-4000
Inshore Fisheries
Middle West Pubnico, NS 902-762-2522
K&N Fisheries
Shelburne, NS 902-768-2478
Milfico Foods
Elk Grove Vlg, IL 847-427-0491
Neptune Foods
Vernon, CA 323-232-8300
Trident Seafoods Corporation
Seattle, WA 800-426-5490

Pompano

Griffin Seafood
Golden Meadow, LA 985-396-2453

Rock Fish

Deep Creek Custom Packing
Ninilchik, AK .800-764-0078

Pacific Seafood Group
Clackamas, OR 800-388-1101
Petersburg Fisheries
Petersburg, AK 877-772-4294
Seafood Producers Cooperative
Bellingham, WA 360-733-0120
Sitka Sound Seafoods
Sitka, AK 907-747-6662

Sablefish

Petersburg Fisheries
Petersburg, AK 877-772-4294
Rego Smoked Fish Company
Flushing, NY .718-894-1400
Russ & Daughters
New York, NY 800-787-7229
Smoked Fish Factory
Weston, ON .416-745-4323

Salmon

Alaskan Gourmet Seafoods
Anchorage, AK 800-288-3740
Alaskan Smoked Salmon International
Anchorage, AK 907-349-8234
Alder Springs Smoked Salmon
Sequim, WA .360-683-2829
All Alaskan Seafood
Seattle, WA 206-285-8200
American Seafoods International
New Bedford, MA 800-343-8046
Angy's Food Products, Inc.
Westfield, MA 413-572-1010
Aquatec Seafoods Ltd.
Comox, BC 250-339-6412
Arrowac Fisheries
Seattle, WA 206-282-5655
Atlantic Salmon of Maine
Belfast, ME 800-508-7861
Bell Buoy Crab Company
Seaside, OR 800-529-2722
Bella Coola Fisheries
Delta, BC 604-583-3474
Bering Sea Fisheries
Snohomish, WA 425-334-1498

Blundell Seafoods
Richmond, BC 604-270-3300
Bos Smoked Fish Inc
Woodstock, ON 519-537-5000
Bumble Bee Seafoods
San Diego, CA 858-715-4000
California Shellfish Company
San Francisco, CA 415-923-7400
Calkins & Burke
Vancouver, BC 604-669-3741
Casey Fisheries
Digby, NS 902-245-5801
Certi-Fresh Foods
Bell Gardens, CA 562-806-1100
Charlton Deep Sea Charters
Warrenton, OR 503-338-0569
Chicago Steaks
Chicago, IL 800-776-4174
Chicken of the Sea International
San Diego, CA 800-678-8862
Chuck's Seafoods
Charleston, OR 541-888-5525
Coldwater Seafood Corporation
Norwalk, CT 203-846-8897
Cook Inlet Processing
Nikiski, AK 907-776-8174
Crown Prince Naturals
Petaluma, CA 707-766-8575
Deep Creek Custom Packing
Ninilchik, AK 800-764-0078
Delta Pacific Seafoods
Delta, BC 800-328-2547
Depoe Bay Fish Company
Newport, OR 541-265-8833
Dragnet Fisheries
Anchorage, AK 907-276-4551
Dressel Collins Fish Company
Seattle, WA 206-725-0121
Ducktrap River Fish Farm
Belfast, ME 800-434-8727
Elwha Fish
Port Angeles, WA 360-457-3344
Exclusive Smoked Fish
Toronto, ON 416-766-6007
Fiddlers Green Farm
Belfast, ME 800-729-7935
Fishery Products International
Danvers, MA 800-374-4700
Fishhawk Fisheries
Astoria, OR 503-325-5252
Fjord Pacific Marine Industries
Richmond, BC 604-270-3393
Giovanni's Appetizing Food Products
Richmond, MI 586-727-9355
Great Glacier Salmon
Prince Rupert, BC 250-627-4955
Great Pacific Seafoods
Anchorage, AK 907-248-7966
Heritage Salmon Company
Richmond, BC 604-277-3093
High Liner Foods
Lunenburg, NS 902-634-9475
High Sea Foods
Glovertown, NL 709-533-2626
High Tide Seafoods
Port Angeles, WA 360-452-8488
His Catch Value Added Products
Homer, AK 800-215-7110
Icelandic USA
Newport News, VA 757-820-4000
Icicle Seafoods
Seattle, WA 206-282-0988
Independent Packers Corporation
Seattle, WA 206-285-6000
Indian Valley Meats
Indian, AK 907-653-7511
Inlet Salmon
Bothell, WA. 425-487-0495
J.S. McMillan Fisheries
Prince Rupert, BC 604- 25- 519
J.S. McMillan Fisheries
Vancouver, BC 604-255-5191
Jessie's Ilwaco Fish Company
Ilwaco, WA 360-642-3773
John T. Handy Company
Salisbury, MD 800-426-3977
Kirkland Custom Seafoods
Kirkland, WA 800-321-3474
Kodiak Salmon Packers
Larsen Bay, AK 907-847-2250
Long Beach Seafoods
Long Beach, CA 714-995-8901

Maine Coast Nordic
Beals, ME 207-497-5910
Marche Tramsatlantique
Montreal, QC 514-287-3530
Menemsha Fish Market
Chilmark, MA 508-645-2282
Mercado Latino
City of Industry, CA 626-333-6862
Milfico Foods
Elk Grove Vlg, IL 847-427-0491
Morey's Seafood International
Motley, MN 218-352-6345
Mutual Fish Company
Seattle, WA 206-322-4368
Nelson Crab
Tokeland, WA 800-262-0069
Neptune Foods
Vernon, CA 323-232-8300
Nordic Group
Boston, MA. 800-486-4002
NorQuest Seafoods
Seattle, WA 206-281-7022
Northern Products Corporation
Seattle, WA 206-448-6677
Northwest Naturals
Olympia, WA 360-866-9661
Ocean Beauty Seafoods
Seattle, WA 206-285-6800
Ocean Food Company
Scarborough, ON 416-285-6487
Ocean Garden Products
San Diego, CA 858-571-5002
Okuhara Foods
Honolulu, HI 808-848-0581
Omega Foods
Eugene, OR 800-200-2356
Pacific Ocean Seafood
La Conner, WA 360-466-4455
Pacific Salmon Company
Edmonds, WA 425-774-1315
Pacific Seafood Group
Clackamas, OR 800-388-1101
Pacific Seafoods International
Sidney, BC 250-656-0901
Pacific Shrimp Company
Newport, OR 541-265-4215
Paramount Caviar
Long Island City, NY 800-992-2842
Perona Farms Food Specialties
Andover, NJ 800-750-6190
Peter Pan Seafoods
Seattle, WA 206-728-6000
Petersburg Fisheries
Petersburg, AK 877-772-4294
Poseidon Enterprises
Atlanta, GA 800-863-7886
Premier Smoked Fish Company
Bensalem, PA 800-654-6682
Quinalt Pride Seafood
Taholah, WA 360-276-4431
Rego Smoked Fish Company
Flushing, NY 718-894-1400
Roman Sausage Company
Santa Clara, CA 800-497-7462
Roy Stritmatter Company
Hoquiam, WA 360-532-0710
Royal Seafood
Monterey, CA 831-655-8326
Russian Chef
New York, NY 212-249-1550
Salmolux
Federal Way, WA 253-874-6570
Saltspring Aqua Farms
Salt Spring Island, BC 604-926-3261
Sea Products Company
Watsonville, CA 831-768-2600
SeaBear Smokehouse
Anacortes, WA 800-454-0023
Seafood Producers Cooperative
Bellingham, WA 360-733-0120
Seafood Products Company
Vancouver, BC 604-255-3141
Shafer-Haggart
Vancouver, BC 888-779-7111
Sitka Sound Seafoods
Sitka, AK 907-747-6662
Splendid Spreads
Eagan, MN 877-632-1300
Sportsmen's Cannery & Smokehouse
Winchester Bay, OR 541-271-3293
Springfield Smoked Fish Company
Springfield, MA 800-327-3412

Stinson Seafood Company
Prospect Harbor, ME 207-963-7331
Taku Smokehouse
Juneau, AK 800-582-5122
Trident Seafoods Corporation
Seattle, WA 800-426-5490
Vita Food Products
Chicago, IL 312-738-4500
Walcan Seafood
Heroit Bay, BC 250-285-3361
Ward Cove Packing Company
Seattle, WA 206-323-3200
Woodsmoke Provisions
Atlanta, GA 404-355-5125
Wrangell Fisheries
Wrangell, AK 907-874-3346

Chum

Arctic Seas
Little Compton, RI 401-635-4000

Coho

Arctic Seas
Little Compton, RI 401-635-4000

King

Elwha Fish
Port Angeles, WA 360-457-3344

Pink

Arctic Seas
Little Compton, RI 401-635-4000
Chicken of the Sea International
San Diego, CA 800-678-8862
Crown Prince
City of Industry, CA 800-255-5063

Smoked

Alaska Bounty Seafoods & Smokery
Sitka, AK 907-966-2927
Alaska Jack's Trading Post
Anchorage, AK 888-660-2257
Alaska Seafood Company
Juneau, AK 800-451-1400
Alaska Smokehouse
Woodinville, WA. 800-422-0852
Alaskan Gourmet Seafoods
Anchorage, AK 800-288-3740
Alaskan Smoked Salmon International
Anchorage, AK 907-349-8234
Alder Springs Smoked Salmon
Sequim, WA 360-683-2829
Assouline & Ting
Philadelphia, PA 800-521-4491
California Shellfish Company
San Francisco, CA 415-923-7400
Charlie Trotter Foods
Chicago, IL 773-248-6228
Comeau's Sea Foods
Saulnierville, NS 902-769-2101
Dollar Food Manufacturing
Vancouver, BC 604-253-1422
Dressel Collins Fish Company
Seattle, WA 206-725-0121
E-Fish-Ent Fish Company
Sooke, BC 250-642-4007
Elwha Fish
Port Angeles, WA 360-457-3344
Felix Custom Smoking
Monroe, WA 425-485-2439
Fish Brothers
Blue Lake, CA 800-244-0583
Fish King Processors
Bellingham, WA 360-733-9090
Fjord Pacific Marine Industries
Richmond, BC 604-270-3393
Fumoir Grizzly
St-Augustin, Quebec, QC 418-878-8941
Giovanni's Appetizing Food Products
Richmond, MI 586-727-9355
Homarus
Atlanta, GA 404-877-1988
Imperial Salmon House
Vancouver, BC 604-251-1114
Jensen's Old Fashioned Smokehouse
Seattle, WA 206-364-5569
Kasilof Fish Company
Marysville, WA 800-322-7552
Katy's Smokehouse
Trinidad, CA 707-677-0151

248

Napa Valley Trading Company
Corte Madera, CA.................415-383-8859
Nordic Group
Boston, MA......................800-486-4002
Ocean Beauty Seafoods
Seattle, WA.....................206-285-6800
Ocean Pride Fisheries
Lower Wedgeport, NS 902-663-4579
Oceanfood Sales
Vancouver, BC...................877-255-1414
Oven Head Salmon Smokers
Bethel, NB......................877-955-2507
Pacific Seafoods International
Sidney, BC 250-656-0901
Paramount Caviar
Long Island City, NY 800-992-2842
Pickwick Catfish Farm
Counce, TN.....................731-689-3805
Port Chatham Smoked Seafood
Everett, WA.....................800-872-5666
Portier Fine Foods
Mamaroneck, NY 800-272-9463
Premier Smoked Fish Company
Bensalem, PA...................800-654-6682
Rego Smoked Fish Company
Flushing, NY....................718-894-1400
Rier Smoked Salmon
Lubec, ME......................888-733-0807
Russ & Daughters
New York, NY...................800-787-7229
Russian Chef
New York, NY 212-249-1550
Smoked Fish Factory
Weston, ON.....................416-745-4323
Southeast Alaska Smoked Salmon Company
Juneau, AK.....................907-463-4617
Sullivan Harbor Farm
Sullivan, ME....................800-422-4014
Tribe Mediterranean Foods Company LLC
Taunton, MA....................800-421-3474
Vita Food Products
Chicago, IL.....................312-738-4500

Sockeye

Alaska Smokehouse
Woodinville, WA.................800-422-0852
Arctic Seas
Little Compton, RI 401-635-4000
Elwha Fish
Port Angeles, WA...............360-457-3344
Smoked Fish Factory
Weston, ON.....................416-745-4323

Steak

Arrowac Fisheries
Seattle, WA.....................206-282-5655
Nelson Crab
Tokeland, WA...................800-262-0069
Neptune Foods
Vernon, CA.....................323-232-8300

Salted

Canadian Fish Exporters
Watertown, MA..................800-225-4215
DB Kenney Fisheries
Westport, NS....................902-839-2023
Island Marine Products
Clarks Harbour, NS...............902-745-2222
Taku Smokehouse
Juneau, AK.....................800-582-5122

Sardines

Castella Imports
Hauppauge, NY 866-227-8355
Continental Group
Huntington Beach, CA 858-391-5670
Crown Point
St John, IN 219-365-3200
Crown Prince
City of Industry, CA 800-255-5063
Erba Food Products
Brooklyn, NY...................718-272-7700
Jessie's Ilwaco Fish Company
Ilwaco, WA.....................360-642-3773
Liberty Richter
Saddle Brook, NJ 201-291-8749
Lubec Packing
Lubec, ME......................207-733-5572
Mercado Latino
City of Industry, CA 626-333-6862

Pastene Companies
Canton, MA.....................781-830-8200
Raffield Fisheries
Port St Joe, FL..................850-229-8229
Sea Products Company
Watsonville, CA.................831-768-2600
Stinson Seafood Company
Prospect Harbor, ME 207-963-7331
Stinson Seafood Company
Bath, ME.......................207-963-7331

Canned

Chicken of the Sea International
San Diego, CA 800-678-8862
Crown Point
St John, IN 219-365-3200
Crown Prince
City of Industry, CA 800-255-5063
Crown Prince Naturals
Petaluma, CA...................707-766-8575
Liberty Richter
Saddle Brook, NJ 201-291-8749
Mercado Latino
City of Industry, CA 626-333-6862
Pastene Companies
Canton, MA....................781-830-8200
Stinson Seafood Company
Prospect Harbor, ME 207-963-7331
Tri-Marine InternationalInc
San Pedro, CA..................310-732-6113

Fresh

Crown Point
St John, IN 219-365-3200
Jessie's Ilwaco Fish Company
Ilwaco, WA.....................360-642-3773

Sea Bass

Arrowac Fisheries
Seattle, WA.....................206-282-5655
Long Beach Seafoods
Long Beach, CA 714-995-8901
N.A. Boullon
Cumming, GA..................770-889-2356
Ocean Beauty Seafoods
Seattle, WA.....................206-285-6800

Sea Trout

Chicago Steaks
Chicago, IL.....................800-776-4174
Glenn Sales Company
Atlanta, GA.....................770-952-9292

Shad

Fishhawk Fisheries
Astoria, OR.....................503-325-5252
Lund's Fisheries
Cape May, NJ 609-884-7600
Nelson Crab
Tokeland, WA..................800-262-0069
Pacific Seafood Group
Clackamas, OR 800-388-1101

Shark

Agger Fish
Brooklyn, NY 718-855-1717
Arrowac Fisheries
Seattle, WA.....................206-282-5655
Bolner's Fiesta Products
San Antonio, TX.................210-734-6404
Louisiana Seafood Exchange
New Orleans, LA 504-283-9893
Mid-Pacific Hawaii Fishery
Hilo, HI.........................808-935-6110
New Orleans Fish House
New Orleans, LA 800-839-3474
Ocean Beauty Seafoods
Seattle, WA.....................206-285-6800
Pacific Salmon Company
Edmonds, WA..................425-774-1315
Pacific Seafood Group
Clackamas, OR 800-388-1101
Scandinavian Laboratories
Mt Bethel, PA...................570-897-7735

Sheephead

Griffin Seafood
Golden Meadow, LA.............985-396-2453
Stoller Fisheries
Spirit Lake, IA 712-336-1750

Smelt

Bell Buoy Crab Company
Seaside, OR....................800-529-2722
Burleigh Brothers Seafoods
Ellerslie, PE 902-831-2349
Certi-Fresh Foods
Bell Gardens, CA 562-806-1100
Fishhawk Fisheries
Astoria, OR.....................503-325-5252
Jessie's Ilwaco Fish Company
Ilwaco, WA.....................360-642-3773
Minor Fisheries
Port Colborne, ON 905-834-9232
North Atlantic Fish Company
Gloucester, MA.................978-283-4121
Omstead Foods Ltd
Burlington, ON..................905-315-8883
Pacific Salmon Company
Edmonds, WA..................425-774-1315
Pacific Seafood Group
Clackamas, OR 800-388-1101
Polar Foods International
Charlottetown, PE...............902-962-3303
Roy Stritmatter Company
Hoquiam, WA..................360-532-0710

Smoked & Cured

Acme Smoked Fish Corporation
Brooklyn, NY 800-221-0795
Alaska Jack's Trading Post
Anchorage, AK.................888-660-2257
Alaska Sausage and Seafood Company
Anchorage, AK.................800-798-3636
Alaskan Gourmet Seafoods
Anchorage, AK.................800-288-3740
Bos Smoked Fish Inc
Woodstock, ON.................519-537-5000
Buedel Food Products
Chicago, IL.....................773-235-3637
California Shellfish Company
San Francisco, CA 415-923-7400
Cherokee Trout Farms
Cherokee, NC 800-732-0075
Chuck's Seafoods
Charleston, OR 541-888-5525
Deep Creek Custom Packing
Ninilchik, AK....................800-764-0078
Dressel Collins Fish Company
Seattle, WA.....................206-725-0121
Ducktrap River Fish Farm
Belfast, ME.....................800-434-8727
Elwha Fish
Port Angeles, WA...............360-457-3344
Fish Brothers
Blue Lake, CA 800-244-0583
Fjord Pacific Marine Industries
Richmond, BC..................604-270-3393
Gold Star Smoked Fish
Brooklyn, NY 718-522-1545
High Liner Foods
Lunenburg, NS 902-634-9475
Homarus
Atlanta, GA.....................404-877-1988
J. Moniz Company
Fall River, MA...................508-674-8451
J. Turner Seafoods
Gloucester, MA.................978-281-8535
MacKnight Smoked Foods
Miami, FL.......................305-655-0444
Menemsha Fish Market
Chilmark, MA...................508-645-2282
Mersey Seafoods
Liverpool, NS...................902-354-3467
Mike's Fish & Seafood
Glenwood, MN.................800-950-4755
Mutual Fish Company
Seattle, WA.....................206-322-4368
Napa Valley Trading Company
Corte Madera, CA...............415-383-8859
Nelson Crab
Tokeland, WA..................800-262-0069
Nordic Group
Boston, MA.....................800-486-4002

Ocean Fresh Seafoods
Seattle, WA 206-285-2412
Paramount Caviar
Long Island City, NY 800-992-2842
Premier Smoked Fish Company
Bensalem, PA 800-654-6682
Quinalt Pride Seafood
Taholah, WA 360-276-4431
Rego Smoked Fish Company
Flushing, NY 718-894-1400
Russ & Daughters
New York, NY 800-787-7229
Russian Chef
New York, NY 212-249-1550
Seabear
Anacortes, WA 800-645-3474
Smoked Fish Factory
Weston, ON 416-745-4323
Stolt SeaFarm
Elverta, CA 800-525-0333
Taku Smokehouse
Juneau, AK 800-582-5122
Vita Food Products
Chicago, IL 312-738-4500
West India Trading Company
Petit-Cap, NB 514-849-6031

Snapper

Bolner's Fiesta Products
San Antonio, TX 210-734-6404
Bon Secour Fisheries
Bon Secour, AL 800-633-6854
California Shellfish Company
San Francisco, CA 415-923-7400
Griffin Seafood
Golden Meadow, LA 985-396-2453
Milfico Foods
Elk Grove Vlg, IL 847-427-0491
N.A. Boullon
Cumming, GA 770-889-2356
Ocean Union Company
Lawrenceville, GA 770-995-1957
Poseidon Enterprises
Atlanta, GA 800-863-7886

Sole

BlueWater Seafoods
Lachine, QC 888-560-2539
Daerim America
Maywood, NJ 800-635-0781
DB Kenney Fisheries
Westport, NS 902-839-2023
Gorton's Seafood
Gloucester, MA 978-283-3000
High Liner Foods
Lunenburg, NS 902-634-9475
Milfico Foods
Elk Grove Vlg, IL 847-427-0491
Pacific Seafood Group
Clackamas, OR 800-388-1101
Penguin Frozen Foods
Northbrook, IL 847-291-9400
Royal Seafood
Monterey, CA 831-655-8326
Sea Products Company
Watsonville, CA 831-768-2600
Washington Crab Producers
Westport, WA 360-268-9161

Steaks

Fjord Pacific Marine Industries
Richmond, BC 604-270-3393
Ocean Beauty Seafoods
Seattle, WA 206-285-6800

Sticks

Coldwater Seafood Corporation
Norwalk, CT 203-846-8897
High Liner Foods
Lunenburg, NS 902-634-9475
Icelandic USA
Newport News, VA 757-820-4000
Van De Kamp Frozen Foods
Erie, PA 814-898-1500
Viking Seafoods Inc
Malden, MA 800-225-3020

Sturgeon

Bell Buoy Crab Company
Seaside, OR 800-529-2722
Charlton Deep Sea Charters
Warrenton, OR 503-338-0569
Depoe Bay Fish Company
Newport, OR 541-265-8833
Fiddlers Green Farm
Belfast, ME 800-729-7935
Fish Brothers
Blue Lake, CA 800-244-0583
Fishhawk Fisheries
Astoria, OR 503-325-5252
Great Northern Products
Warwick, RI 401-490-4590
Homarus
Atlanta, GA 404-877-1988
Jessie's Ilwaco Fish Company
Ilwaco, WA 360-642-3773
Lund's Fisheries
Cape May, NJ 609-884-7600
Menemsha Fish Market
Chilmark, MA 508-645-2282
Pacific Seafood Group
Clackamas, OR 800-388-1101
Port Chatham Smoked Seafood
Everett, WA 800-872-5666
Rego Smoked Fish Company
Flushing, NY 718-894-1400
Roy Stritmatter Company
Hoquiam, WA 360-532-0710
Russ & Daughters
New York, NY 800-787-7229
Russian Chef
New York, NY 212-249-1550
Sportsmen's Cannery & Smokehouse
Winchester Bay, OR 541-271-3293
Stolt SeaFarm
Elverta, CA 800-525-0333

Swordfish

Arctic Seas
Little Compton, RI 401-635-4000
Arrowac Fisheries
Seattle, WA 206-282-5655
Caito Fisheries
Fort Bragg, CA 707-964-6368
Chicago Steaks
Chicago, IL 800-776-4174
Griffin Seafood
Golden Meadow, LA 985-396-2453
James L. Mood Fisheries
Wood's Harbour, NS 902-723-2360
Long Beach Seafoods
Long Beach, CA 714-995-8901
Menemsha Fish Market
Chilmark, MA 508-645-2282
Milfico Foods
Elk Grove Vlg, IL 847-427-0491
Ocean Beauty Seafoods
Seattle, WA 206-285-6800
Poseidon Enterprises
Atlanta, GA 800-863-7886
Ralboray
New Orleans, LA 504-524-4800

Tilapia

Bolner's Fiesta Products
San Antonio, TX 210-734-6404
Fishery Products International
Danvers, MA 800-374-4700
Icelandic USA
Newport News, VA 757-820-4000
Milfico Foods
Elk Grove Vlg, IL 847-427-0491
Pots de Creme
Lexington, KY 859-299-2254
Vince's Seafoods
Gretna, LA 504-368-1544
Waterfield Farms
Amherst, MA 413-549-3558

Trout

Alleghany's Fish Farm
Saint Philemon, QC 418-469-2823
Atlantic Fish Specialties
Charlottetown, PE 902-894-7005
Blue Lakes Trout Farm
Jerome, ID 208-734-7151

Bos Smoked Fish Inc
Woodstock, ON 519-537-5000
Burleigh Brothers Seafoods
Ellerslie, PE 902-831-2349
Catfish Wholesale
Abbeville, LA 800-334-7292
Certi-Fresh Foods
Bell Gardens, CA 562-806-1100
Cherokee Trout Farms
Cherokee, NC 800-732-0075
Culver's Fish Farm
Mc Pherson, KS 800-241-5205
Ducktrap River Fish Farm
Belfast, ME 800-434-8727
Ferroclad Fishery
Batchawana Bay, ON 705-882-2295
Fiddlers Green Farm
Belfast, ME 800-729-7935
Fish Brothers
Blue Lake, CA 800-244-0583
Fumoir Grizzly
St-Augustin, Quebec, QC 418-878-8941
Griffin Seafood
Golden Meadow, LA 985-396-2453
Homarus
Atlanta, GA 404-877-1988
Idaho Trout Company
Buhl, ID 866-878-7688
J. Matassini & Sons Fish Company
Tampa, FL 813-229-0829
Kirkland Custom Seafoods
Kirkland, WA 800-321-3474
Lenny's Bee Productions
Bearsville, NY 845-679-4514
Louisiana Seafood Exchange
New Orleans, LA 504-283-9893
Major McGill
Flowery Branch, GA 770-967-6001
Morey's Seafood International
Motley, MN 218-352-6345
Napa Valley Trading Company
Corte Madera, CA 415-383-8859
Pacific Seafood Group
Clackamas, OR 800-388-1101
Pamlico Packing Company
Grantsboro, NC 800-682-1113
Portier Fine Foods
Mamaroneck, NY 800-272-9463
Pots de Creme
Lexington, KY 859-299-2254
Rego Smoked Fish Company
Flushing, NY 718-894-1400
Russian Chef
New York, NY 212-249-1550
SC Enterprises
Owen Sound, ON 519-371-0456
Southern Star Seafood
Fort Pierce, FL 561-461-5787
Thompson Seafood
Darien, GA 912-437-4649
Vince's Seafoods
Gretna, LA 504-368-1544
Virginia Trout Company
Monterey, VA 540-468-2280
Wanchese Fish Company
Suffolk, VA 757-673-4500
Woodsmoke Provisions
Atlanta, GA 404-355-5125

Brook

Russ & Daughters
New York, NY 800-787-7229

Golden

Idaho Trout Company
Buhl, ID 866-878-7688

Rainbow

Blue Lakes Trout Farm
Jerome, ID 208-734-7151
Cherokee Trout Farms
Cherokee, NC 800-732-0075
Clear Springs Foods
Buhl, ID 800-635-8211
Idaho Trout Company
Buhl, ID 866-878-7688
Kirkland Custom Seafoods
Kirkland, WA 800-321-3474
Trout of Paradise
Paradise, UT 435-245-3053

Tuna

Bell Buoy Crab Company
Seaside, OR.....800-529-2722
Bella Luna
Sun Prairie, WI.....800-884-8884
Bolner's Fiesta Products
San Antonio, TX.....210-734-6404
Bumble Bee Seafoods
San Diego, CA.....858-715-4000
Cape Ann Tuna
Gloucester, MA.....978-283-8188
Charlton Deep Sea Charters
Warrenton, OR.....503-338-0569
Chicken of the Sea International
San Diego, CA.....800-678-8862
Chuck's Seafoods
Charleston, OR.....541-888-5525
Continental Group
Huntington Beach, CA.....858-391-5670
Crown Prince
City of Industry, CA.....800-255-5063
Depoe Bay Fish Company
Newport, OR.....541-265-8833
Elwha Fish
Port Angeles, WA.....360-457-3344
Erba Food Products
Brooklyn, NY.....718-272-7700
Great Northern Products
Warwick, RI.....401-490-4590
Griffin Seafood
Golden Meadow, LA.....985-396-2453
Hallmark Fisheries
Charleston, OR.....541-888-3253
Heinz Company of Canada
North York, ON.....800-268-6641
Homarus
Atlanta, GA.....404-877-1988
Independent Packers Corporation
Seattle, WA.....206-285-6000
Island Marine Products
Clarks Harbour, NS.....902-745-2222
James L. Mood Fisheries
Wood's Harbour, NS.....902-723-2360
Jessie's Ilwaco Fish Company
Ilwaco, WA.....360-642-3773
Kirkland Custom Seafoods
Kirkland, WA.....800-321-3474
Lund's Fisheries
Cape May, NJ.....609-884-7600
Menemsha Fish Market
Chilmark, MA.....508-645-2282
Mid-Pacific Hawaii Fishery
Hilo, HI.....808-935-6110
Milfico Foods
Elk Grove Vlg, IL.....847-427-0491
Neptune Foods
Vernon, CA.....323-232-8300
New Orleans Fish House
New Orleans, LA.....800-839-3474
Northwest Naturals
Olympia, WA.....360-866-9661
Ocean Beauty Seafoods
Seattle, WA.....206-285-6800
Ocean Union Company
Lawrenceville, GA.....770-995-1957
Omega Foods
Eugene, OR.....800-200-2356
Pacific Shrimp Company
Newport, OR.....541-265-4215
Pastene Companies
Canton, MA.....781-830-8200
Polar Foods International
Charlottetown, PE.....902-962-3303
Poseidon Enterprises
Atlanta, GA.....800-863-7886
Ralboray
New Orleans, LA.....504-524-4800
Roman Sausage Company
Santa Clara, CA.....800-497-7462
Royal Seafood
Monterey, CA.....831-655-8326
Russ & Daughters
New York, NY.....800-787-7229
Russian Chef
New York, NY.....212-249-1550
Sea Products Company
Watsonville, CA.....831-768-2600
Sportsmen's Cannery & Smokehouse
Winchester Bay, OR.....541-271-3293
Sportsmen's Sea Foods
San Diego, CA.....619-224-3551

Star-Kist Caribe
Mayaguez, PR.....787-834-2424
Stavis Seafoods
Boston, MA.....800-390-5103
Triangle Seafood
Louisville, KY.....502-561-0055
Tuna Fresh
Gretna, LA.....504-363-2744
Vince's Seafoods
Gretna, LA.....504-368-1544
Wanchese Fish Company
Suffolk, VA.....757-673-4500
White Cap Fish Company
Islip, NY.....631-581-0125

Albacore

Bumble Bee Seafoods
San Diego, CA.....858-715-4000
Chicken of the Sea International
San Diego, CA.....800-678-8862
Crown Prince
City of Industry, CA.....800-255-5063
Elwha Fish
Port Angeles, WA.....360-457-3344
Fish Brothers
Blue Lake, CA.....800-244-0583
Kirkland Custom Seafoods
Kirkland, WA.....800-321-3474
Pacific Seafood Group
Clackamas, OR.....800-388-1101
Pacific Shrimp Company
Newport, OR.....541-265-4215
Royal Seafood
Monterey, CA.....831-655-8326
Sportsmen's Sea Foods
San Diego, CA.....619-224-3551

Canned

Bumble Bee Seafoods
San Diego, CA.....858-715-4000
Chicken of the Sea International
San Diego, CA.....800-678-8862
Chuck's Seafoods
Charleston, OR.....541-888-5525
Crown Prince
City of Industry, CA.....800-255-5063
Crown Prince Naturals
Petaluma, CA.....707-766-8575
Elwha Fish
Port Angeles, WA.....360-457-3344
Hallmark Fisheries
Charleston, OR.....541-888-3253
Heinz Company of Canada
North York, ON.....800-268-6641
Scally's Imperial Importing Company Inc
Staten Island, NY.....718-983-1938
Shafer-Haggart
Vancouver, BC.....888-779-7111
Sportsmen's Cannery & Smokehouse
Winchester Bay, OR.....541-271-3293
Sportsmen's Sea Foods
San Diego, CA.....619-224-3551
Star-Kist
Pittsburgh, PA.....412-222-2200
Tri-Marine InternationalInc
San Pedro, CA.....310-732-6113

Canned - Chunk Light in Oil

Chicken of the Sea International
San Diego, CA.....800-678-8862

Canned - Chunk Light in Water

Chicken of the Sea International
San Diego, CA.....800-678-8862

Canned - Chunk Solid in Oil

Chicken of the Sea International
San Diego, CA.....800-678-8862

Canned - Chunk Solid in Water

Chicken of the Sea International
San Diego, CA.....800-678-8862

Frozen

Bell Buoy Crab Company
Seaside, OR.....800-529-2722
Bolner's Fiesta Products
San Antonio, TX.....210-734-6404

Cuizina Food Company
Woodinville, WA.....425-486-7000
Depoe Bay Fish Company
Newport, OR.....541-265-8833
Great Northern Products
Warwick, RI.....401-490-4590
Hallmark Fisheries
Charleston, OR.....541-888-3253
Independent Packers Corporation
Seattle, WA.....206-285-6000
Jessie's Ilwaco Fish Company
Ilwaco, WA.....360-642-3773
Lund's Fisheries
Cape May, NJ.....609-884-7600
Menemsha Fish Market
Chilmark, MA.....508-645-2282
Milfico Foods
Elk Grove Vlg, IL.....847-427-0491
Pacific Shrimp Company
Newport, OR.....541-265-4215
Royal Seafood
Monterey, CA.....831-655-8326
Sea Products Company
Watsonville, CA.....831-768-2600
Wanchese Fish Company
Suffolk, VA.....757-673-4500
White Cap Fish Company
Islip, NY.....631-581-0125

Pouch-Packed

Chicken of the Sea International
San Diego, CA.....800-678-8862

Yellowfin

Russ & Daughters
New York, NY.....800-787-7229

Turbot

Breakwater Fisheries
St. John's, NL.....709-754-1999
Buns & Things Bakery
Charlottetown, PE.....902-892-2600
NorQuest Seafoods
Seattle, WA.....206-281-7022
Notre Dame Seafood
Comfort Cove, NL.....709-244-5511
Penguin Frozen Foods
Northbrook, IL.....847-291-9400
Stavis Seafoods
Boston, MA.....800-390-5103

Whitefish

American Seafoods International
New Bedford, MA.....800-343-8046
Bos Smoked Fish Inc
Woodstock, ON.....519-537-5000
Ferroclad Fishery
Batchawana Bay, ON.....705-882-2295
Flaum Appetizing
Brooklyn, NY.....718-821-1970
Homarus
Atlanta, GA.....404-877-1988
Minor Fisheries
Port Colborne, ON.....905-834-9232
Rego Smoked Fish Company
Flushing, NY.....718-894-1400
Russ & Daughters
New York, NY.....800-787-7229
Russian Chef
New York, NY.....212-249-1550
Smoked Fish Factory
Weston, ON.....416-745-4323
Springfield Smoked Fish Company
Springfield, MA.....800-327-3412

Whiting

Arrowac Fisheries
Seattle, WA.....206-282-5655
Bolner's Fiesta Products
San Antonio, TX.....210-734-6404
Bon Secour Fisheries
Bon Secour, AL.....800-633-6854
Certi-Fresh Foods
Bell Gardens, CA.....562-806-1100
Depoe Bay Fish Company
Newport, OR.....541-265-8833
Glenn Sales Company
Atlanta, GA.....770-952-9292

Icelandic USA
Newport News, VA 757-820-4000
Jessie's Ilwaco Fish Company
Ilwaco, WA 360-642-3773
Milfico Foods
Elk Grove Vlg, IL 847-427-0491
Mirasco
Atlanta, GA 770-956-1945
Morey's Seafood International
Motley, MN 218-352-6345
North Atlantic Fish Company
Gloucester, MA 978-283-4121
Pacific Seafood Group
Clackamas, OR 800-388-1101
Pacific Shrimp Company
Newport, OR 541-265-4215
Pamlico Packing Company
Grantsboro, NC 800-682-1113
Seaspan Products Corporation
New York, NY 201-569-9234
Stavis Seafoods
Boston, MA 800-390-5103

Seafood

A&C Quinlin Fisheries
McGray, NS 902-745-2742
Acadian Fine Foods
New Orleans, LA 504-581-2355
Acme Steak & Seafood Company
Youngstown, OH 330-270-8000
Agger Fish
Brooklyn, NY 718-855-1717
Agri-Best Foods
Chicago, IL 773-247-5060
Ah Dor Kosher Fish Corporation
Monsey, NY 845-425-7776
Alabama Seafood Producers
Bayou La Batre, AL 251-824-4396
Alaska Aquafarms
Moose Pass, AK 907-288-3667
Alaska Fresh Seafoods
Kodiak, AK 907-486-5749
Alaska General Seafood
Kenmore, WA 425-485-7755
Alaska General Seafoods
Kenmore, WA 425-485-7755
Alaska Pacific Seafood
Kodiak, AK 907-486-3234
Alaska Sausage and Seafood Company
Anchorage, AK 800-798-3636
Alaska Sea Pack
Anchorage, AK 907-451-1400
Alaska Seafood Company
Los Angeles, CA 213-626-1212
Alaska Seafood International
Anchorage, AK 800-478-2903
Alaskan Glacier
Petersburg, AK 907-772-3333
Alaskan Gourmet Seafoods
Anchorage, AK 800-288-3740
Alaskan Leader Fisheries
Lynden, WA 360-318-1280
Aliotti Wholesale Fish Company
Monterey, CA 831-375-2881
All Alaskan Seafood
Seattle, WA 206-285-8200
Alphin Brothers
Dunn, NC 800-672-4502
Alyeska Seafoods
Seattle, WA 206-547-2100
Amcan Industries
Elmsford, NY 914-347-4838
American Canadian Fisheries
Bellingham, WA 800-344-7942
American Seafoods Group
Seattle, WA 800-275-2019
AmeriPure Processing Company
Franklin, LA 800-328-6729
Ameripure Processing Company
Kenner, LA 504-467-0474
Ampak Seafood Corporation
New Haven, CT 203-786-5121
Anchor Frozen Foods
Westbury, NY 800-566-3474
Annette Island Packing Company
Metlakatla, AK 907-886-4661
Appert's Foodservice
St Cloud, MN 800-225-3883
Appetizers And, Inc.
Chicago, IL 800-323-5472
APTCO
San Francisco, CA 415-648-6688

AquaCuisine
Eagle, ID 888-330-2782
Aquatec Seafoods Ltd.
Comox, BC 250-339-6412
Aquatech
Anchorage, AK 907-563-1387
Arcee Sales Company
Brooklyn, NY 718-383-0107
Arista Industries
Wilton, CT 800-255-6457
Arizona Sunland Foods
Tucson, AZ 520-624-7068
Arrowac Fisheries
Seattle, WA 206-282-5655
ASC Seafood
Largo, FL 800-876-3474
Aslanis Seafoods
Quincy, MA 800-876-3712
Atka Pride Seafoods
Juneau, AK 907-586-0161
Atlanta Fish Market
Atlanta, GA 404-262-3165
Atlantic Aqua Farms
Vernon Bridge, PE 902-651-2563
Atlantic Foods
Scotch Plains, NJ 800-328-7687
Atlantic Mussel Growers Corporation
Point Pleasant, PE 800-838-3106
Atlantic Queen Seafoods Limited
Lachine, QC 514-636-5114
Atlantic Sea Pride
South Boston, MA 617-269-7700
Atlantic Seacove
Boston, MA 617-442-6206
Atlantic Seafood Direct
Rockland, ME 207-596-7152
Aurora Alaska Premium Smoked Salmon & Seafood
Anchorage, AK 800-653-3474
Axelsson & Johnson Fish Company
Cape May, NJ 609-884-8426
B&C Seafood Market and Cajun Restaurant
Vacherie, LA 225-265-8356
B&J Seafood Company
New Bern, NC 252-637-0483
B&M Fisheries
Georgetown, MA 978-352-6663
B.C. Fisheries
Hancock, ME 207-422-8205
B.M. Lawrence & Company
San Francisco, CA 415-981-3650
Baensch Food
Milwaukee, WI 800-562-8234
Bailey's Basin Seafood
Morgan City, LA 985-384-4926
Bakalars Brothers Sausage Company
La Crosse, WI 608-784-0384
Bandon Bay Fisheries
Bandon, OR 541-347-4454
Banner Beef & Seafood Company
Miami, FL 305-325-0420
Basin Crawfish Processors
Breaux Bridge, LA 337-332-6655
Bay Hundred Seafood
McDaniel, MD 410-745-9329
Bay Oceans Sea Foods
Garibaldi, OR 503-322-3316
Bayley Quality Seafoods
Scarborough, ME 207-883-4581
Bayley's Lobster Pound
Scarborough, ME 800-932-6456
Bayou Crab
Grand Bay, AL 251-824-2076
Bayou Foods
Kenner, LA 800-516-8283
Bayou Gourmet
Houma, LA 504-872-4825
Bayou Land Seafood
Breaux Bridge, LA 337-667-6118
Bayou Packing
Bayou La Batre, AL 251-824-7710
Beaver Street Fisheries
Jacksonville, FL 800-874-6426
Becker Food Company
Milwaukee, WI 414-964-5353
Bell Buoy Crab Company
Seaside, OR 800-529-2722
Belle River Enterprises
Belle River, PE 902-962-2248
Benton's Seafood Center
Tifton, GA 229-382-4976
BG Smith Sons Oyster
Sharps, VA 877-483-8279

Big Island Seafood, LLC
Atlanta, GA 404-366-8667
Big River Seafood
Baton Rouge, LA 225-751-1116
Bill Lowden Seafood
Warren, ME 207-273-2162
Bill's Seafood
Baltimore, MD 410-256-9520
Billingsgate Fish Company
Calgary, AB 403-571-7700
Billy's Seafood
Bon Secour, AL 251-949-6288
Blakely Freezer Locker
Thomasville, GA 229-723-3622
Blalock Seafood
Orange Beach, AL 251-974-5811
Blau Oyster Company
Bow, WA 360-766-6171
Blount Seafood Corporation
Fall River, MA 774-888-1300
Blue Crab Bay Company
Melfa, VA 800-221-2722
Blue Ribbon Meats
Cleveland, OH 216-631-8850
BlueWater Seafoods
Lachine, QC 888-560-2539
Bodin Foods
New Iberia, LA 337-367-1344
Bohea Associates
Brooklyn, NY 718-387-6034
Bolner's Fiesta Products
San Antonio, TX 210-734-6404
Bon Secour Fisheries
Bon Secour, AL 800-633-6854
Bornstein Seafoods
Bellingham, WA 360-734-7990
Bornstein Seafoods
Warrenton, OR 503-861-1233
Boston Sea Farms
Somerville, MA 617-547-3474
Boutique Seafood
Atlanta, GA 404-752-8852
Bradye P. Todd & Son
Cambridge, MD 410-228-8633
Braun Seafood Company
Cutchogue, NY 631-734-5550
Breakwater Fisheries
St. John's, NL 709-754-1999
Breakwater Seafoods
Aberdeen, WA 360-532-5693
Brenntag
Reading, PA 888-926-4151
Brenntag Pacific
Santa Fe Springs, CA 562-903-9626
Brownsdale Meat Service
Brownsdale, MN 507-567-2211
Bullock's Country Meats
Westminster, MD 410-848-6786
Bumble Bee Seafoods
San Diego, CA 858-715-4000
Burris Mill & Feed
Franklinton, LA 800-928-2782
Byrd's Seafood
Crisfield, MD 410-968-0990
C C Conway Seafoods
Wicomico, VA 804-642-2853
C. Gould Seafoods
Scottsdale, AZ 480-314-9250
C.E. Fish Company
Jonesboro, ME 207-434-2631
C.F. Gollott & Son Seafood
Biloxi, MS 866-846-3474
Cajun Crawfish Distributors
Cottonport, LA 800-525-6813
Cajun Seafood Enterprises
Murrayville, GA 706-864-9688
Caleb Haley & Company
New York, NY 212-732-7474
California Shellfish Company
Gardena, CA 310-538-4197
California Shellfish Company
San Francisco, CA 415-923-7400
Callis Seafood
Lancaster, VA 804-462-7634
Cameron Seafood Processors
Cameron, LA 318-775-5510
Can Am Seafood
Lubec, ME 207-733-2267
Canadian Fish Exporters
Watertown, MA 800-225-4215
Cannery Row
Cordova, AK 907-424-5920

Cantrell's Seafood
 Bath, ME. 207-442-7261
Cape Ann Seafood
 Gloucester, MA. 978-282-3286
Captain Alex Seafood
 Niles, IL. .847-803-8833
Captain Collier Seafood
 Coden, AL. 251-824-4925
Captain's Choice
 Federal Way, WA. 253-941-1184
Captn's Pack Products
 Columbia, MD. 410-720-6668
Carolina Seafoods
 Mc Clellanville, SC. 843-887-3713
Carrington Foods
 Saraland, AL. 251-675-9700
Cathay Foods Corporation
 Boston, MA. 617-427-1507
Cedar Valley Fish Market
 Waterloo, IA. 319-236-2965
Centennial Food Corporation
 Calgary, AB. 403-287-2525
Central Coast Seafoods
 Atascadero, CA. 800-273-4741
Certi-Fresh Foods
 Bell Gardens, CA. 562-806-1100
Channel Fish Processing Company
 Boston, MA. 617-464-3366
Charles H. Parks & Company
 Fishing Creek, MD. 410-397-3400
Charles M. Cook
 Bailey Island, ME. 207-833-6641
Charlton Deep Sea Charters
 Warrenton, OR. 503-338-0569
Chases Lobster Pound
 Port Howe, NS. 902-243-2408
Chef Hans Gourmet Foods
 Monroe, LA. 800-890-4267
Cherbogue Fisheries
 Yarmouth, NS. 902-742-9157
Chester W. Howeth & Brother
 Crisfield, MD. 410-968-1398
Chicago Steaks
 Chicago, IL. 800-776-4174
Chicken of the Sea
 San Diego, CA. 858-558-9662
Chris Hansen Seafood
 Port Sulphur, LA. 504-564-2888
Chuck's Seafoods
 Charleston, OR. 541-888-5525
Citica
 Anaheim, CA. 714-778-8891
City Market
 Brunswick, GA. 912-265-4430
City Seafood Company of Monroe
 Monroe, LA. 318-323-3281
Claytons Crab Company
 Rockledge, FL. 321-639-0161
Clearwater Fine Foods
 Bedford, NS. 902-443-0550
Clem's Seafood & Specialties
 Buckner, KY. 502-222-7571
Coast Seafoods Company
 Bellevue, WA. 800-423-2303
Coast to Coast Seafood
 Seattle, WA. 425-889-2862
Coastal Seafood Partners
 Chicago, IL. 773-989-7788
Coastal Seafood Processors
 Harahan, LA. 504-734-9444
Cobscook Bay Seafood
 Perry, ME. 207-853-2890
Cohen's Original Tasty Coddie
 Baltimore, MD. 410-539-0111
Coldwater Fish Farms
 Lisco, NE. .800-658-4450
Coldwater Seafood Corporation
 Norwalk, CT. 203-846-8897
Coldwater Seafood Corporation
 Newport News, VA. 410-228-7500
Collier's Fisheries
 Des Allemands, LA. 985-758-7481
Collins Caviar Company
 Michigan City, IN. 219-809-8100
Comeaux's
 Lafayette, LA. 800-323-2492
ConAgra Foods Inc
 Omaha, NE. 402-240-4000
Conco Food Service
 Harahan, LA. 800-488-3988
Confish
 Isola, MS. .662-962-3101

Conroy Foods
 Pittsburgh, PA. 412-781-1446
Consolidated Factors
 Monterey, CA. 831-375-5121
Consolidated Seafood Enterprises
 Phoenix, AZ. 480-348-9548
Cook Inlet Processing
 Nikiski, AK. 907-776-8174
Country Harbor Sea Farms
 Country Harbor, NS. 902-387-2364
Cowart Seafood Corporation
 Lottsburg, VA. 804-529-6101
Cozy Harbor Seafood
 Portland, ME. 800-225-2586
Crab King Seafood Specialties
 Seattle, WA. 206-283-2722
Craby's Fish Market
 Blackwood, NJ. 856-227-9743
Cranberry Isles Fisherman's Cooperative
 Islesford, ME. 207-244-5438
Craven Crab Company
 New Bern, NC. 252-637-3562
Crescent City Seafoods
 Hilo, HI. 808-961-0877
Crest International Corporation
 San Diego, CA. 800-548-1232
Crevettes Du Nord
 Gaspe, QC. 418-368-1414
Crustaces de la Malbaie
 Gaspe, QC. 418-368-1414
Cuizina Food Company
 Woodinville, WA. 425-486-7000
Cumberland Seafood Corporation
 Cumberland, RI. 401-728-6088
Cushner Seafood
 Baltimore, MD. 410-358-5564
Custom House Seafoods
 Portland, ME. 207-773-2778
D Seafood
 Chicago, IL. 312-808-1086
D&M Seafood
 Honolulu, HI. 808-531-0687
Daerim America
 Maywood, NJ. 800-635-0781
Daniels Seafood Company
 Wanchese, NC. 252-473-5779
David Gollott Seafood
 Biloxi, MS. 228-374-2555
David's Fish Market
 Fall River, MA. 508-676-1221
Davis Street Fish Market
 Evanston, IL. 847-869-3474
DB Kenney Fisheries
 Westport, NS. 902-839-2023
Deep Creek Custom Packing
 Ninilchik, AK. 800-764-0078
Deep Sea Foods
 Bayou La Batre, AL. 251-824-7000
Deepsouth Packing Company
 New Orleans, LA. 504-488-4413
Del's Seaway Shrimp & Oyster Company
 Biloxi, MS. 228-432-2604
Delta Distributors
 Longview, TX. 800-945-1858
Demaria Seafood
 Newport News, VA. 757-930-3474
Denzer's Food Products
 Baltimore, MD. 410-889-1500
Depoe Bay Fish Company
 Newport, OR. 541-265-8833
Diamond Seafood
 Wood Dale, IL. 630-787-1100
Dick & Casey's Gourmet Seafoods
 Harbor, OR. 800-662-9494
Dicola Seafood
 Chicago, IL. 773-238-7071
Dip Seafood
 Mobile, AL. 251-479-0123
Doc Miller's Fish & Seafood Company
 Syracuse, IN. 574-457-8469
Don's Dock Seafood
 Des Plaines, IL. 847-827-1817
Door County Fish Market
 Northbrook, IL. 847-559-9229
Dorchester Crab Company
 Wingate, MD. 410-397-8103
Doug Hardy Company
 Deer Isle, ME. 207-348-6604
Dow Distribution
 Honolulu, HI. 808-836-3511
Down East Specialty Products/Cape Bald Packers
 Portland, ME. 800-369-6327

Dressel Collins Fish Company
 Seattle, WA. 206-725-0121
Drusilla Seafood Packing & Processing Company
 Baton Rouge, LA. 800-364-8844
Dubois Seafood
 Houma, LA. 985-876-2514
Ducktrap River Fish Farm
 Belfast, ME. 800-434-8727
Duxbury Mussel & Seafood Corporation
 Kingston, MA. 781-585-5517
E. Gagnon & Fils
 St Therese-De-Gaspe, QC. 418-385-3011
E.J. Green & Company
 Winterton, NL. 709-583-2670
Eagle Seafood Producers
 Brooklyn, NY. 718-963-0939
East Coast Seafood of Phoenix
 Phoenix, AZ. 602-268-3313
East Point Seafood Company
 South Bend, WA. 888-317-8459
Eastern Fish Company
 Teaneck, NJ. 800-526-9066
Eastern Quebec Sea Foods
 Matane, QC. 418-562-1273
Eastern Sea Products
 Scoudouc, NB. 800-565-6364
Eastern Seafood Company
 Chicago, IL. 312-243-2090
Eastern Shore Seafood Products
 Mappsville, VA. 800-466-8550
Eastside Seafood
 Macon, GA. 478-743-1888
Ed Kasilof's Seafoods
 Kasilof, AK. 800-982-2377
Edmonton Meat Packing Company
 Edmonton, AB. 800-361-6328
Eldorado Seafood
 Lincoln, MA. 800-416-5656
Elliott Seafood Company
 Cushing, ME. 207-354-2533
Elwha Fish
 Port Angeles, WA. 360-457-3344
Emery Smith Fisheries Limited
 Shag Harbour, NS. 902-723-2115
Errol Cajun Foods
 Pierre Part, LA. 985-252-6003
Eschete's Seafood
 Houma, LA. 985-872-4120
Eskimo Candy
 Kihei, HI. .808-879-5686
Europa Foods
 Saddle Brook, NJ. 201-368-8929
Facciola Meat
 Fremont, CA. 510-438-8600
Faidley Seafood
 Baltimore, MD. 410-727-4898
Farm 2 Market
 Roscoe, NY. 800-663-4326
Farm Fresh Catfish Company
 Hollandale, MS. 800-647-8264
Farmers Seafood Company
 Shreveport, LA. 800-874-0203
Feature Foods
 Etobicoke, ON. 416-675-7350
Ferme Ostreicole Dugas
 Caraquet, NB. 506-727-3226
Fine Line Seafood
 Newtown, PA. 215-860-1144
Fire Island Fisheries
 Bay Shore, NY. 631-666-0942
First Oriental Market
 Decatur, GA. 404-377-6950
Fish Brothers
 Blue Lake, CA. 800-244-0583
Fish Express
 Lihue, HI. .808-245-9918
Fish Market
 Louisville, KY. 502-589-6636
Fish Market
 Kansas City, MO. 816-444-3474
Fish Processors
 Hagerman, ID. 208-837-6114
Fishermens Net
 Portland, ME. 207-772-3565
Fishery Products International
 Danvers, MA. 800-374-4700
Fishhawk Fisheries
 Astoria, OR. 503-325-5252
FishKing
 Bayou La Batre, AL. 334-824-2118
Fishking
 Bayou La Batre, AL. 251-824-2118

Fishking Processors
Los Angeles, CA 877-677-3329
Fishland Market
Honolulu, HI 808-523-6902
Fishmarket Seafoods
Louisville, KY 502-587-7474
Flannery Seafood Company
San Francisco, CA 415-346-1303
Flavor House
Adelanto, CA 760-246-9131
Fleet Fisheries
New Bedford, MA 508-996-3742
Flying Seafood Incorporated
Kailua Kona, HI 808-326-7708
Fortune Seas
Gloucester, MA 978-281-6666
Frank Mattes & Sons Reliable Seafood
Bel Air, MD 410-879-5444
Frank Pagano Company
Lockport, IL 815-838-0303
French Quarter Seafood
Chalmette, LA 504-277-1679
Fresh Fish
Birmingham, AL 205-252-0344
Fresh Island Fish Company
Kahului, HI 808-871-1111
Fresh Pack Seafood
Waldoboro, ME 207-832-7720
Fresh Seafood Distributors
Daphne, AL 251-626-1106
Freshwater Farms of Ohio
Urbana, OH 800-634-7434
Friendship International
Camden, ME 207-594-1111
Frionor U.S.A.
New Bedford, MA 800-343-8046
Frozen Specialties
Archbold, OH 419-445-9015
Fulcher's Point Pride Seafood
Oriental, NC 252-249-0123
FW Thurston
Bernard, ME 207-244-3320
G&J Land and Marine Food Distributors
Morgan City, LA 800-256-9187
Galilean Seafoods
Bristol, RI 401-253-3030
Garden & Valley Isle Seafood
Honolulu, HI 800-689-2733
Gaskill Seafood
Bayboro, NC 252-745-4211
Gemini Food Industries
Fiskdale, MA 508-347-2800
George Braun Oyster Company
Cutchogue, NY 631-734-7770
George L. Wells Meat Company
Philadelphia, PA 800-523-1730
George Robberecht Seafood
Montross, VA 804-472-3556
Georgetown Fisherman's Co-Op
Georgetown, ME 207-371-2950
Georgia Seafood Wholesale
Chamblee, GA 770-936-0483
Gesco ENR
Gaspe, QC 418-368-1414
Gilmore's Seafoods
Bath, ME 800-849-9667
Giovanni's Appetizing Food Products
Richmond, MI 586-727-9355
Glacier Bay Seafood & Meat Company
Lawrence, KS 785-832-2650
Glenn Sales Company
Atlanta, GA 770-952-9292
Global Marketing Enterprises
Chicago, IL 312-733-0000
Goedens Fish Market
Madison, WI 608-256-1991
Gold Star Seafood
Chicago, IL 773-376-8080
Golden Alaska Seafoods
Seattle, WA 206-441-1990
Golden Bounty Food Processors
Bell Gardens, CA 562-806-1100
Golden Eye Seafood
Tall Timbers, MD 301-994-2274
Golden Gulf Coast Packing Company
Biloxi, MS 228-374-6121
Gollott Brothers Seafood Company
Biloxi, MS 228-432-7865
Good Harbor Fillet Company
Gloucester, MA 978-675-9100
Gorton's Seafood
Gloucester, MA 978-283-3000
Graham & Rollins
Hampton, VA 800-272-2728
Graham Fisheries
Bayou La Batre, AL 251-824-2890
Great American Seafood Company
Dewey, IL 217-352-0986
Great American Smokehouse & Seafood Company
Brookings, OR 800-828-3474
Great Glacier Salmon
Prince Rupert, BC 250-627-4955
Great Northern Products
Warwick, RI 401-490-4590
Great Plains Seafood
Shawnee, KS 913-262-6060
Great West of Hawaii
Honolulu, HI 808-593-9981
Green Turtle Cannery & Seafood
Islamorada, FL 305-664-9595
Griffin Seafood
Golden Meadow, LA 985-396-2453
Gulf Atlantic Freezers
Gretna, LA 504-392-3590
Gulf Central Seafood
Biloxi, MS 228-436-6346
Gulf City Seafoods
Pascagoula, MS 800-666-3300
Gulf Crown Seafood
Delcambre, LA 337-685-4721
Gulf Food Products Company
New Orleans, LA 504-733-1516
Gulf Island Shrimp & Seafood
Lake Charles, LA 888-626-7264
Gulf Island Shrimp & Seafood
Lake Charles, LA 985-563-4586
Gulf Marine & Industrial Supplies
New Orleans, LA 800-886-6252
Gulf Pride Enterprises
Biloxi, MS 888-689-0560
Gulf Shrimp, Inc.
Fort Myers Beach, FL 239-463-8788
H&H Fisheries Limited
Eastern Passage, NS 902-465-6330
H. Gass Seafood
Hollywood, MD 301-373-6882
H. Shenson International Export
San Francisco, CA 415-318-7000
Hallmark Fisheries
Charleston, OR 541-888-3253
Hama Hama Oyster®Company
Lilliwaup, WA 888-877-5844
Hansen Caviar Company
Kingston, NY 800-735-0441
Harbor Fish Market
Portland, ME 207-775-0251
Harbor Food Sales & Services
Alameda, CA 360-405-0677
Harbor Lobster
Shelburne, NS 902-723-2500
Haring's Pride Catfish
Wisner, LA 800-467-3474
Harlon's L.A. Fish, LLC
Kenner, LA 504-467-3809
Harold Bozman Seafood
Upper Fairmount, MD 410-651-0647
Harper Seafood Company
Kinsale, VA 804-472-3310
Harper's Seafood
Thomasville, GA 229-226-7525
Harry H. Park Company
Chicago, IL 773-478-4424
Harvard Seafood Company
Grand Bay, AL 251-865-0558
Hawaii International Seafood
Honolulu, HI 808-839-5010
Herb's Specialty Foods
Westampton, NJ 800-486-0276
Heritage Foods
Holicong, PA 215-244-0900
Heritage Salmon
Eastport, ME 207-853-6081
HFI Foods
Redmond, WA 425-883-1320
Hickory Farms
Maumee, OH 419-893-7611
Higgins Seafood
Lafitte, LA 504-689-3577
High Liner Foods
Portsmouth, NH 603-431-6865
High Liner Foods
Lunenburg, NS 902-634-9475
High Liner Foods USA
Portsmouth, NH 603-431-6865
Hillard Bloom Packing Co
Port Norris, NJ 856-785-0120
Hillman Shrimp & Oyster
Dickinson, TX 800-582-4416
Homer's Wharf Seafood Company
New Bedford, MA 508-997-0766
Hong Kong Supermarket
Atlanta, GA 404-325-3999
Honolulu Fish & Seafood Company
Honolulu, HI 808-833-1123
Horst Alaskan Seafood
Juneau, AK 877-518-4300
Hosford & Wood Fresh Seafood Providers
Tucson, AZ 520-795-1920
Huck's Seafood
Easton, MD 410-770-9211
Hue's Seafood
Baton Rouge, LA 225-383-0809
Icelandic USA
Newport News, VA 757-820-4000
Icicle Seafoods
Seattle, WA 206-282-0988
Idaho Trout Company
Buhl, ID 866-878-7688
Imaex Trading
Norcross, GA 770-825-0848
Independent Packers Corporation
Seattle, WA 206-285-6000
Indian Bay Frozen Foods
Centreville, NL 709-678-2844
Indian Ridge Shrimp Company
Chauvin, LA 985-594-5869
Indian Valley Meats
Indian, AK 907-653-7511
Inland Fresh Seafood Corporation
Atlanta, GA 404-350-5850
Inland Seafood
Milbridge, ME 207-546-7591
Inlet Salmon
Bothell, WA 425-487-0495
Inny's Wholesale
Honolulu, HI 808-841-3172
Inshore Fisheries
Middle West Pubnico, NS 902-762-2522
Inter-Ocean Seafood Traders
San Carlos, CA 650-508-0691
Interior Alaska Fish Processors
Fairbanks, AK 800-478-3885
International Oceanic Enterprises of Alabama
Bayou La Batre, AL 800-816-1832
International Seafoods of Alaska
Kodiak, AK 907-486-4768
International Seafoods of Chicago
Chicago, IL 312-243-2330
Ipswich Bay Seafoods
Ipswich, MA 978-356-9292
Ipswich Maritime Product Company
Ipswich, MA 978-356-9866
Ipswich Shellfish Company
Ipswich, MA 978-356-6941
ISF Trading
Portland, ME 207-879-1575
Island Marine Products
Clarks Harbour, NS 902-745-2222
Island Scallops
Qualicum Beach, BC 250-757-9811
Island Seafood
Eliot, ME 207-439-8508
Island Seafoods
Kodiak, AK 800-355-8575
Island Treasures Mussel Processing
Little Bay, NL 709-267-3146
J & B Seafood
Coden, AL 251-824-4512
J Bernard Seafood & Processing
Cottonport, LA 318-876-3885
J M Clayton Company
Cambridge, MD 800-652-6931
J&L Seafood
Bayou La Batre, AL 251-824-2371
J&R Fisheries
Seward, AK 907-224-5584
J&R Foods
Long Branch, NJ 732-229-4020
J. Matassini & Sons Fish Company
Tampa, FL 813-229-0829
J. Moniz Company
Fall River, MA 508-674-8451
J. Turner Seafoods
Gloucester, MA 978-281-8535
J.P. Shellfish
Eliot, ME 207-439-6018

J.R. Fish Company
Wrangell, AK 907-874-2399
J.R.'s Seafood
Oak Lawn, IL 708-422-4555
J.S. McMillan Fisheries
Prince Rupert, BC. 604- 25- 519
J.S. McMillan Fisheries
Vancouver, BC 604-255-5191
Ja-Ca Seafood Products
Boston, MA. 978-281-8848
Jack's Lobsters
Musquodoboit Harbor, NS 902-889-2771
James L. Mood Fisheries
Wood's Harbour, NS. 902-723-2360
Janes Family Foods
Mississauga, ON 800-565-2637
JBS Packing Company
Port Arthur, TX. 409-982-3216
JCW Tawes & Son
Crisfield, MD 410-968-1288
Jenport International Distributors
Coquitlam, BC 604-464-9888
Jensen Seafood Packing Company
Dulac, LA .985-563-7022
Jessie's Ilwaco Fish Company
Ilwaco, WA 360-642-3773
JF Clarke Corporation
Franklin Square, NY 800-229-7474
Jim Foley Company
Marietta, GA 770-427-0999
Joe Fazio's Famous Italian
Charleston, WV 304-344-3071
Joe Patti Seafood Company
Pensacola, FL 800-500-9929
Joel & Diane Laperyhouse Company
Chauvin, LA 504-594-9744
Joey Oysters
Amite, LA .800-748-1525
John B. Wright Fish Company
Gloucester, MA. 978-283-4205
John T. Handy Company
Salisbury, MD 800-426-3977
Johns Cove Fisheries
Yarmouth, NS 902-742-8691
Johnson Sea Products
Coden, AL. 251-824-2693
Jubilee Foods
Bayou La Batre, AL 251-824-2110
K Horton Specialty Foods
Portland, ME. 207-228-2056
K.S.M. Seafood Corporation
Baton Rouge, LA 225-383-1517
Kachemak Bay Seafood
Homer, AK 907-235-2799
Kake Tribal Corporation
Kake, AK .907-785-3465
Kalamar Seafoods
Hialeah, FL 305-822-5586
Kang's Seafood
Chicago, IL 800-269-8425
Karla's Smokehouse
Rockaway Beach, OR. 503-355-2362
Kenai Custom Seafoods
Kenai, AK .907-283-9109
Kenai Packers
Seattle, WA 206-433-6917
Kent's Wharf
Swans Island, ME 207-526-4186
Kettle Master
Hillsville, VA 276-728-7571
Key Largo Fisheries
Key Largo, FL 800-399-6970
Keyser Brothers
Lottsburg, VA 804-529-6837
Kibun Foods
Seattle, WA 206-467-6287
King & Prince Seafood Corporation
Brunswick, GA 800-841-0205
Kirkland Custom Seafoods
Kirkland, WA 800-321-3474
Kitchens Seafood
Plant City, FL 800-327-0132
Kodiak Salmon Packers
Larsen Bay, AK. 907-847-2250
Kool Ice & Seafood Company
Cambridge, MD 410-228-2300
L&C Fisheries
Kensington, PE 902-886-2770
L&M Evans
Conyers, GA 770-918-8727
L&M Frosted Food Lockers
Belt, MT 406-277-3522

L.H. Rodriguez Wholesale Seafood
Tucson, AZ 520-623-1931
L.L. Curley Packing Company
Colonial Beach, VA 804-224-7544
La Font Shrimp Company
Golden Meadow, LA. 504-475-5138
La Monegasque
Fort Lee, NJ 201-585-7877
Lady Gale Seafood
Baldwin, LA 337-923-2060
LaMonica Fine Foods
Millville, NJ 856-825-8111
Lance G. Fisher Seafood
Sanford, FL 757-824-3489
Land's End Seafood
Swanquarter, NC. 252-926-2801
Landlocked Seafoods
Carroll, IA .712-792-9599
Larry J. Williams Company
Jesup, GA .912-427-7729
Larry Towns Company
Wichita, KS. 316-265-3474
Lartigue Seafood
Daphne, AL 251-343-3404
Leblanc Seafood
Lafitte, LA. 504-689-2631
LEF McLean Brothers International
Wheatley, ON 519-825-4656
Lisbon Seafood Company
Fall River, MA 508-672-3617
Little River Seafood
Reedville, VA 804-453-3670
Livingston's Bull Bay Seafood
Mc Clellanville, SC 843-887-3519
LLJ's Sea Products
Round Pond, ME 207-529-4224
Lombardi's Seafood
Orlando, FL. 800-879-8411
Long Beach Seafoods
Long Beach, CA 714-995-8901
Long Food Industries
Fripp Island, SC 843-838-3205
Los Angeles Smoking & Curing Company
Seattle, WA 213-628-1246
Louis Kemp Seafood Company
Downers Grove, IL 218-624-3636
Louis Kemp Seafood Company
Motley, MN. 800-325-4732
Louisiana Oyster Processors
Baton Rouge, LA 225-291-6923
Louisiana Packing Company
Westwego, LA. 800-666-1293
Louisiana Premium Seafoods
Palmetto, LA. 800-222-4017
Louisiana Pride Seafood
New Orleans, LA 504-283-9893
Louisiana Royal Seafood
Henderson, LA 318-228-2988
Louisiana Royal Seafoods
Breaux Bridge, LA 318-228-7506
Lowland Seafood
Lowland, NC. 252-745-3751
Lu-Mar Lobster & Shrimp
Brownsville, TX 956-546-5525
Lucky Seafood Corporation
Morrow, GA 770-960-9889
Lumar Lobster Corporatio
Lawrence, NY 516-371-0083
Lund's Fisheries
Cape May, NJ 609-884-7600
Lusty Lobster
Portland, ME. 207-773-2829
Lyle's Seafoods
Ocean Park, WA 360-665-4666
M&M Shrimp Company
Biloxi, MS. 228-435-4915
M-G
Weimar, TX. 800-460-8581
MacGregors Meat & Seafood
Toronto, ON 800-268-5953
Machias Bay Seafood
Machias, ME. 207-255-8671
Maine Freeze
Lubec, ME 207-733-9715
Maloney Seafood Corporation
Quincy, MA. 800-566-2837
Manchac Seafood Market
Ponchatoula, LA 985-370-7070
Maple Leaf Foods International
Toronto, ON 416-480-8900
Mar-Lees Seafood
New Bedford, MA 800-836-0975

Marine MacHines
Bar Harbor, ME. 207-288-0107
Market Fisheries
Chicago, IL 773-483-3233
Marshall Smoked Fish Company
Miami, FL .305-625-5112
Martin Brothers Distributing Company
Cedar Falls, IA 319-266-1775
Martin Brothers Seafood Company
Westwego, LA. 504-341-2251
Martin Seafood Company
Jessup, MD 410-799-5822
Mat Roland Seafood Company
Atlantic Beach, FL 904-246-9443
Matlaw's Food Products
West Haven, CT 800-934-8266
Maxim's Import Corporation
Miami, FL .800-331-6652
Mazzetta Company
Highland Park, IL 847-433-1150
McCoy Matt Frontier International
Pismo Beach, CA 805-773-2994
McFarling Foods
Indianapolis, IN 317-635-2633
McLaughlin Seafood
Bangor, ME. 800-222-9107
McNasby's Seafood Market
Annapolis, MD 410-295-9022
Meat & Fish Fellas
Glendale, AZ. 623-931-6190
Menemsha Fish Market
Chilmark, MA. 508-645-2282
Mercado Latino
City of Industry, CA 626-333-6862
Meredith & Meredith
Toddville, MD. 410-397-8151
Merrill Seafood Center
Jacksonville, FL 904-744-3132
Mersey Seafoods
Liverpool, NS 902-354-3467
Metafoods, LLC
Atlanta, GA. 404-843-2400
Metompkin Bay Oyster Company
Crisfield, MD 410-968-0660
Mid-Atlantic Foods
Easton, MD 800-922-4688
Midwest Seafood
Indianapolis, IN 317-466-1027
Mike's Fish & Seafood
Glenwood, MN. 800-950-4755
Miland Seafood
New Orleans, LA 504-821-4500
Miles J H & Company
Norfolk, VA. 757-622-9264
Milfico Foods
Elk Grove Vlg, IL 847-427-0491
Mill Cove Lobster Pound
Boothbay Harbor, ME. 207-633-3340
Miller Johnson Seafood
Coden, AL. 251-873-4444
Mills Seafood
Bouctouche, NB 506-743-2444
Milsolv Corporation
Butler, WI .800-558-8501
Mino Corporation
Davenport, IA 563-388-4770
Mister Fish
Baltimore, MD 410-288-2722
Misty Islands Seafoods
Anchorage, AK 907-248-6678
Mitsubishi InternationalCorporation
Los Angeles, CA. 213-620-8652
Mobile Bay Seafood
Coden, AL. 251-973-0410
Mobile Processing
Mobile, AL 251-438-6944
Mohn's Fisheries
Harpers Ferry, IA 563-586-2269
Monarch Seafoods
Honolulu, HI 808-841-7877
Moon's Seafood Company
Melbourne, FL 800-526-5624
Morey's Seafood International
Motley, MN. 218-352-6345
Morgan Mill
Cherokee, NC 828-497-9227
Morristown
Morristown, IN 765-763-6327
Mortillaro Lobster Company
Gloucester, MA. 978-282-4621
Motivatit Seafoods
Houma, LA 985-868-7191

Mutual Fish Company
Seattle, WA 206-322-4368
N.B.J. Enterprises
Mobile, AL 251-661-2122
N.Y.K. Line (North America)
Lombard, IL 888-695-7447
Nagasako Fish
Wailuku, HI 808-242-4073
Nan Sea Enterprises of Wisconsin
Waukesha, WI 262-542-8841
Nancy's Shellfish
Falmouth, ME 207-774-3411
National Fish & Seafood
Gloucester, MA 978-282-7880
National Fisheries
Hialeah, FL 305-628-1231
National Fisheries - Marathon
Marathon, FL 305-743-5545
Nautilus Foods
Bellevue, WA 425-885-5900
Nelson Crab
Tokeland, WA 800-262-0069
Neptune Fisheries
Newport News, VA 800-545-7474
New Meadows Lobster
Portland, ME 207-775-1612
New Ocean
Doraville, GA 770-458-5235
New Orleans Gulf Seafood
New Orleans, LA 504-246-7329
New York Fish House
Elizabeth, NJ 908-351-0045
Newark Meat Supply
Newark, OH 740-345-6696
Newfound Resources
Saint John's, NL 709-579-7676
Nisbet Oyster Company
Bay Center, WA 360-875-6629
Noon Hour Food Products
Chicago, IL 800-621-6636
Nordic Group
Boston, MA 800-486-4002
Norpac Fisheries
Honolulu, HI 808-528-3474
North Alaska Fisheries
Anchorage, AK 907-561-2671
North Atlantic
Portland, ME 207-774-6025
North Atlantic Fish Company
Gloucester, MA 978-283-4121
North Atlantic Products
South Thomaston, ME 207-596-0331
North Atlantic Seafood
Stonington, ME 207-367-5099
North Pacific Enterprises
Anchorage, AK 907-243-4398
North Pacific Processors
Seattle, WA 206-726-9900
North Pacific Ship Supply
Dutch Harbor, AK 907-581-1700
Northern Discovery Seafoods
Grapeview, WA 800-843-6921
Northern Keta Caviar
Juneau, AK 907-586-6095
Northern Ocean Marine
Gloucester, MA 978-283-0222
Northern Products Corporation
Seattle, WA 206-448-6677
Northern Wind
New Bedford, MA 888-525-2525
Northwest Natural Foods
Olympia, WA 360-866-9661
Notre Dame Seafood
Comfort Cove, NL 709-244-5511
NTC Foods Corporation
Williamsville, NY 800-333-1637
O'Hara Corporation
Rockland, ME 207-594-0405
Oak Island Seafood Company
Portland, ME 207-594-9250
Ocean Beauty Seafoods
Seattle, WA 206-285-6800
Ocean Crest Seafoods
Gloucester, MA 978-281-0232
Ocean Diamond
Oakland, NJ 201-337-9515
Ocean Food Company
Scarborough, ON 416-285-6487
Ocean Foods of Astoria
Astoria, OR 503-325-2421
Ocean Fresh Seafoods
Seattle, WA 206-285-2412

Ocean King International
Alhambra, CA 626-289-9399
Ocean Select Seafood
Delcambre, LA 337-685-5315
Ocean Springs Seafood
Ocean Springs, MS 228-875-0104
Ocean Union Company
Lawrenceville, GA 770-995-1957
Oceanledge Seafoods
Rockland, ME 207-594-4955
Oceans Prome Distributi ng
Glenview, IL 847-998-5813
Off Shore Seafood Company
Point Lookout, NY 516-432-0529
Offshore Systems
Dutch Harbor, AK 907-581-1827
Ohana Seafood, LLC
Honolulu, HI 808-843-1844
Okuhara Foods
Honolulu, HI 808-848-0581
Old Salt Seafood Company
Narragansett, RI 401-783-5770
Olsen Fish Company
Minneapolis, MN 800-882-0212
Orca Bay Foods
Renton, WA 800-932-6722
Oversea Fishery & Investment Company
Honolulu, HI 808-847-2500
Oyster World
Kilmarnock, VA 804-438-5470
P&E Foods
Honolulu, HI 808-836-8821
P&J Oyster Company
New Orleans, LA 504-523-2651
P&L Seafood of Venice
Gretna, LA 504-363-2744
P. Janes & Sons
Hant's Harbor, NL 709-586-2252
P.J. Markos Seafood Company
Ipswich, MA 978-356-4347
P.J. Merrill Seafood
Portland, ME 207-773-1321
P.M. Innis Lobster Company
Biddeford Pool, ME 207-284-5000
P.T. Fish
Portland, ME 207-772-0239
Pacific Alaska Seafoods
Seattle, WA 206-587-0002
Pacific Choice Seafood
Eureka, CA 707-442-1113
Pacific Gourmet Seafood
Bakersfield, CA 661-533-1260
Pacific Ocean Producers
Honolulu, HI 808-537-2905
Pacific Ocean Seafood
La Conner, WA 360-466-4455
Pacific Salmon Company
Edmonds, WA 425-774-1315
Pacific Seafoods International
Sidney, BC 250-656-0901
Pacific Shrimp Company
Newport, OR 541-265-4215
Pacific Surf Food Processors
Los Angeles, CA 800-627-5657
Pacific Valley Foods
Bellevue, WA 425-643-1805
Pacsea Corporation
Aiea, HI 808-836-8888
Pamlico Packing Company
Grantsboro, NC 800-682-1113
Parker Fish Company
Wrightsville, GA 478-864-3406
Pastene Companies
Canton, MA 781-830-8200
Paul Piazza & Sons
New Orleans, LA 504-524-6011
PB&S Chemicals
Henderson, KY 800-950-7267
PEI Mussel King
Morrell, PE 800-673-2767
Pelican Marine Supply
Belle Chasse, LA 504-392-9062
Pemaquid Fishermen's Co-Op
New Harbor, ME 866-864-2897
Penguin Frozen Foods
Northbrook, IL 847-291-9400
Perino's Seafood
Marrero, LA 504-347-5410
Perona Farms Food Specialties
Andover, NJ 800-750-6190
Peter Pan Seafoods
Seattle, WA 206-728-6000

Petersburg Fisheries
Petersburg, AK 877-772-4294
Phillips Foods
Baltimore, MD 800-782-2722
Phillips Foods, Inc. & Seafood Restaurants
Baltimore, MD 888-234-2722
Phillips Seafood
Townsend, GA 912-832-4423
Piazza's Seafood World
St Rose, LA 504-602-5050
Pilot Meat & Sea Food Company
Galena, IL 319-556-0760
Pine Point Seafood
Scarborough, ME 207-883-4701
Pioneer Live Shrimp
Oak Brook, IL 847-718-0088
Plitt Company
Chicago, IL 773-276-2200
Point Adolphus Seafoods
Gustavus, AK 907-697-2246
Point Judith Fisherman's Company
Narragansett, RI 401-782-1500
Point Saint George Fisheries
Santa Rosa, CA 707-542-9490
Polar Foods International
Charlottetown, PE 902-962-3303
Pon Food Corporation
Ponchatoula, LA 985-386-6941
Pond Pure Catfish
Moulton, AL 256-974-6698
Pontchartrain Blue Crab
Slidell, LA 985-649-6645
Port Chatham Smoked Seafood
Everett, WA 800-872-5666
Portland Shellfish Company
South Portland, ME 207-799-9290
Portland Specialty Seafoods
Portland, ME 207-699-2989
Portsmouth Chowder Company
Portsmouth, NH 603-431-3132
Poseidon Enterprises
Atlanta, GA 800-863-7886
Poteet Seafood Company
Brunswick, GA 912-264-5340
Premier Pacific Seafoods
Seattle, WA 206-286-8584
Premiere Seafood
Lexington, KY 606-259-3474
Price Seafood
Chauvin, LA 985-594-3067
Prime Cut Meat & Seafood Company
Phoenix, AZ 602-455-8834
Produits Belle Baie
Caraquet, NB 506-727-4414
Quality Alaska Seafood
Juneau, AK 907-789-8495
Quality Crab Company
Elizabeth City, NC 888-411-4410
Quality Fisheries
Niota, IL 217-448-4241
Quality Foods from the Sea
Elizabeth City, NC 252-338-5455
Quality Meats & Seafood
West Fargo, ND 800-342-4250
Quality Seafood
Apalachicola, FL 850-653-9696
R & R Seafood
Tybee Island, GA 912-786-5504
R&J Seafoods
King Cove, AK 907-497-3060
R.A. Fayard Company
Biloxi, MS 228-436-6243
R.R. Fournier & Sons
Biloxi, MS 228-392-4293
Raffield Fisheries
Port St Joe, FL 850-229-8229
Rainbow Seafood Market
Baldwin Park, CA 626-962-6888
Rainbow Seafoods
Topsfield, MA 978-283-5103
Ralboray
New Orleans, LA 504-524-4800
Randol
Lafayette, LA 337-981-7080
RCV Seafood Corporation
Morattico, VA 804-462-5101
Red Chamber Company
Vernon, CA 323-234-9000
Red Lake Fisheries Associates
Redby, MN 218-679-3513
Registry Steaks & Seafood
Bridgeview, IL 708-458-3100

Rego Smoked Fish Company
Flushing, NY 718-894-1400

Reilly's Sea Products
South Bristol, ME 207-644-1400

Resource Trading Company
Portland, ME 207-772-2299

Rhodia Inc
Cranbury, NJ 609-860-4000

Rich-Seapak Corporation
St Simons Island, GA 800-654-9731

Rich-Seapak Corporation
Brownsville, TX 956-542-0001

Rippons Brothers Seafood
Fishing Creek, MD 410-397-3200

Rivere's Seafood Processors
Paincourtville, LA................. 985-369-6055

Road Runner Seafood
Colquitt, GA 229-758-3485

Robin & Cohn Seafood Distributors
Chalmette, LA..................... 504-277-1679

Rock Point Oyster Company
Bow, WA 360-765-3765

Rockland Boat
Rockland, ME 207-594-8181

Rockport Lobster
Gloucester, MA 978-281-0225

Rocky Point Shrimp Association
Phoenix, AZ 602-254-8041

Rogers Brothers
Galesburg, IL 309-342-2127

Rose Hill Seafood
Columbus, GA 706-322-1269

Roy Dick Company
Griffin, GA 770-227-3916

Roy Stritmatter Company
Hoquiam, WA 360-532-0710

Royal Atlantic Seafood
Gloucester, MA 978-281-6373

Royal Baltic
Brooklyn, NY 718-385-8300

Royal Lagoon Seafood
Mobile, AL 251-643-7072

Royal Pacific Fisheries
Kenai, AK 907-283-9370

Royal Seafood
Monterey, CA 831-655-8326

Royal Wine Company
Bayonne, NJ 800-382-8299

Ruark & Ashton
Woolford, MD 800-725-5032

Rubino's Seafood Company
Chicago, IL 312-258-0020

Ruggiero Seafood
Newark, NJ 800-543-2110

Russo's Seafood
Savannah, GA 912-341-8848

Rymer Seafood
Chicago, IL 312-236-3266

Sahalee of Alaska
Anchorage, AK 800-349-4151

Salamat of Seafoods
Kenai, AK 907-283-7000

Salmolux
Federal Way, WA 253-874-6570

Sanderson Farms
Bryan, TX 979-778-5730

Sanwa Foods
San Lorenzo, CA................... 510-317-8888

SC Enterprises
Owen Sound, ON 519-371-0456

Sea Garden Seafoods
Meridian, GA 912-832-4437

Sea K Fish Company
Blaine, WA 360-332-5121

Sea Nik Food Company
Ninilchik, AK 907-567-3980

Sea Pearl Seafood
Bayou La Batre, AL 800-872-8804

Sea Products Company
Astoria, OR 503-325-5023

Sea Products Company
Watsonville, CA 831-768-2600

Sea Safari
Belhaven, NC 800-688-6174

Sea Safari Limited
Belhaven, NC 800-688-6174

Sea Snack Foods
Los Angeles, CA................... 213-622-2204

Sea View Fillet Company
New Bedford, MA 508-984-1406

Sea Watch International
Easton, MD 410-822-7500

Seabear
Anacortes, WA 800-645-3474

Seafare Market Wholesale
Moody, ME 207-646-5160

Seafood Merchants
Vernon Hills, IL 847-634-0900

Seafood Producers Cooperative
Bellingham, WA 360-733-0120

Seafood Products Company
Vancouver, BC 604-255-3141

Seafood Specialties
Coden, AL......................... 251-824-2693

Seafreeze Pizza
Seattle, WA 206-767-7350

Sealaska Corporation
Juneau, AK 800-848-5921

Seapac of Idaho
Filer, ID.......................... 208-326-3100

SeaPerfect Atlantic Farms
Charleston, SC 800-728-0099

Seaspan Products Corporation
New York, NY 201-569-9234

SeaSpecialties
Miami, FL......................... 800-654-6682

Seatech Corporation
Lynnwood, WA 425-835-0312

Seatrade Corporation
Hoboken, NJ 201-963-5700

Seaview Lobster Company
Kittery, ME 800-245-4997

Seymour & Sons Seafood
Diberville, MS 228-392-4020

Shamrock Foods Company
Phoenix, AZ 800-289-3663

Shawmut Fishing Company
Anchorage, AK 709-334-2559

Shemper Seafood Company
Biloxi, MS........................ 228-435-2703

Shining Ocean
Sumner, WA 253-826-3700

Shore Seafood
Saxis, VA......................... 757-824-5517

Sigma International
St Petersburg, FL 727-822-1288

Signature Seafoods
Seattle, WA 206-285-2815

Silver Lining Seafood
Ketchikan, AK 907-225-6664

Silverston Fisheries
Superior, WI 715-392-5551

Simeus Foods International
Rocky Mount, NC 888-772-3663

Sitka Sound Seafoods
Sitka, AK......................... 907-747-6662

Sonoma Seafoods
Sonoma, CA 877-411-2123

Southchem
Durham, NC 800-849-7000

Southern Pride Catfish Company
Seattle, WA 800-343-8046

Southern Seafood Distributors
Franklinton, LA 985-839-6220

Southern Shell Fish Company
Harvey, LA 504-341-5631

Southern Shellfish
Savannah, GA 912-897-3650

Southern Star Seafood
Fort Pierce, FL 561-461-5787

Southside Seafood Company
Morrow, GA 404-366-6172

Southtowns Seafood & Meats
Blasdell, NY 716-824-4900

Spinney Creek Shellfish
Eliot, ME......................... 877-778-6727

Sportsmen's Cannery
Winchester Bay, OR 800-457-8048

Sportsmen's Cannery & Smokehouse
Winchester Bay, OR 541-271-3293

Sportsmen's Sea Foods
San Diego, CA 619-224-3551

SS Lobster Limited
Fitchburg, MA 978-342-6135

St. Ours & Company
Norwell, MA....................... 781-331-8520

St. Simons Seafood
Brunswick, GA 912-265-5225

Stacey's Famous Foods
Hayden, ID 800-782-2395

Stanley's Best Seafood
Coden, AL......................... 251-824-2801

Star Seafood
Bayou La Batre, AL 251-824-3110

Starich
Daphne, AL........................ 251-626-5037

State Fish Company
San Pedro, CA..................... 888-658-3474

Steve Connolly Seafood Company
Roxbury, MA 800-225-5595

Stewarts Seafood
Coden, AL......................... 251-824-7368

Stinson Seafood Company
Prospect Harbor, ME 207-963-7331

Stone Crabs
Miami Beach, FL 800-260-2722

Straub's
Clayton, MO 888-725-2121

Stuart Seafoods
Everett, WA....................... 425-258-2546

Sumida Fish Cake Factory
Hilo, HI.......................... 808-959-9857

Sunny's Seafood
Everett, MA....................... 617-261-7123

Sunshine Food Sales
Miami, FL......................... 305-696-2885

Sunshine Seafood
Stonington, ME 207-367-2955

Super Snooty Sea Food Corporation
Boston, MA 617-426-6390

Superior Ocean Produce
Chicago, IL 773-283-8400

Superior Seafood & Meat Company
South Bend, IN 574-289-0511

SYSCO Food Services of Northern New England
Portland, ME 800-632-4446

SYSCO Foodservice
Fremont, CA 650-494-7200

T&T Seafood
Baker, LA 225-261-5438

T. Cvitanovich
Metairie, LA 504-833-6349

T.B. Seafood
Portland, ME 207-871-2420

T.J. Kraft
Honolulu, HI 808-842-3474

Taku Smokehouse
Juneau, AK 800-582-5122

Tampa Bay Fisheries
Dover, FL 800-234-2561

Tampa Maid Foods
Lakeland, FL 800-237-7637

Taylor's Frozen Foods
Charleston, SC 843-723-1878

Tempest Fisheries Limited
New Bedford, MA 508-997-0720

Terrebonne Seafood
Dulac, LA......................... 985-563-2645

Terry Brothers
Temperanceville, VA.............. 757-824-3471

Tex-Mex Cold Storage
Brownsville, TX 956-831-9433

Tichon Seafood Corporation
New Bedford, MA 508-999-5607

Tideland Seafood Company
Dulac, LA......................... 985-563-4516

TideWays
Peaks Island, ME 207-766-0062

Toddville Seafoods
Toddville, MD..................... 410-397-8129

Tony V'S Oyster House
Amite, LA......................... 504-748-8110

Tony's Seafood
Baton Rouge, LA 225-357-9669

Trans-Ocean Products
Needham Heights, MA 508-626-0922

Tri-Cost Seafood
Baton Rouge, LA 225-757-8333

Tri-Marine InternationalInc
San Pedro, CA..................... 310-732-6113

Triangle Seafood
Louisville, KY 502-561-0055

Tribe Mediterranean Foods Company LLC
Taunton, MA...................... 800-421-3474

Trident Seafoods Corporation
Salem, NH........................ 603-893-3368

Trident Seafoods Corporation
Seattle, WA 800-426-5490

Triton Seafood Company
Medley, FL 305-805-3500

Trosclair Canning Company
Cameron, LA 337-775-5275

Tsar Nicoulai Caviar
San Francisco, CA 800-952-2842

Turk Brothers Custom Meats
Ashland, OH 800-789-1051

U. Okada & Company
Honolulu, HI 808-597-1102
Union Fisheries Corporation
Chicago, IL 312-738-0448
Union Seafoods
Phoenix, AZ 602-254-4114
United Provision Meat Company
Columbus, OH 614-252-1126
United Shellfish Company
Grasonville, MD 410-827-8171
United Universal Enterprises Corporation
Phoenix, AZ 623-842-9691
Upcountry Fisheries
Makawao, HI 808-871-8484
Val's Seafood
Mobile, AL 251-639-1103
Valdez Food
Philadelphia, PA 215-634-6106
Van De Kamp Frozen Foods
Erie, PA 814-898-1500
Van de Kamp's
Chambersburg, PA 570-263-4127
Van Dykes Chesapeake Seafood
Cambridge, MD 410-228-9000
Vantage USA
Chicago, IL 773-247-1086
Viking Seafoods Inc
Malden, MA 800-225-3020
Viking Trading
Atlanta, GA 770-455-8630
Vinalhaven Fishermens Co-Op
Camden, ME 207-236-0092
Vince's Seafoods
Gretna, LA 504-368-1544
Vincent Piazza Jr & Sons
Harahan, LA 800-259-5016
Virginia Trout Company
Monterey, VA 540-468-2280
Vision Seafood Partners
Kingston, MA 781-585-2000
Vita Food Products
Chicago, IL 312-738-4500
W. Forrest Haywood Seafood Company
Poquoson, VA 757-868-6748
W. Roberts
Annapolis, MD 410-269-5380
W.O. Sasser
Savannah, GA 912-898-9504
W.T. Ruark & Company
Fishing Creek, MD 410-397-3133
Wabash Seafood Company
Chicago, IL 312-733-5070
Wabi Fishing Company
Marysville, WA 888-536-7696
Wagner Seafood
Oak Lawn, IL 708-636-2646
Wainani Kai Seafood
Honolulu, HI 808-847-7435
Walden Foods
Winchester, VA 800-648-7688
Walker Meats Corporation
Carrollton, GA 770-834-8171
Walker's Seafood
Jonesboro, AR 870-932-0375
Wallace Fisheries
Gulf Shores, AL 251-986-7211
Wallace Plant Company
Bath, ME 207-443-2640
Walsh's Seafood
Gouldsboro, ME 207-963-2578
Waltkoch
Decatur, GA 404-378-3666
Wanchese Fish Company
Suffolk, VA 757-673-4500
Washington Crab Producers
Westport, WA 360-268-9161
Waterfront Seafood
Bayou La Batre, AL 251-824-2185
Waterfront Seafood Market
West Des Moines, IA 515-223-5106
Weems Brothers Seafood Company
Biloxi, MS 228-432-5422
West Bay Fishing
Gouldsboro, ME 207-963-2392
Western Alaska Fisheries
Seattle, WA 206-447-4400
Weyand Fisheries
Wyandotte, MI 800-521-9815
Wharton Seafood Sales
Paauilo, HI 800-352-8507
White Cap Fish Company
Islip, NY 631-581-0125

Wiegardt Brothers
Ocean Park, WA 360-665-4111
Wild Planet Foods
McKinleyville, CA 800-998-9945
William Atwood Lobster Company
Spruce Head, ME 207-596-6691
Winter Harbor Co-Op
Winter Harbor, ME 207-963-5857
WK Eckerd & Sons
Brunswick, GA 912-265-0332
Wolverton Seafood
Houlton, ME 506-276-4629
Woodfield Fish & Oyster Company
Galesville, MD 410-897-1093
World Flavors
Warminster, PA 215-672-4400
Wrangell Fisheries
Wrangell, AK 907-874-3346
Wright Brand Company
Bayou La Batre, AL 251-824-7880
Y&W Shellfish
Woodbine, GA 912-729-4814
Yarmer Boys Catfish International
Beaumont, TX 409-842-1962
Yeomen Seafoods
Gloucester, MA 978-283-7422
York Beach Fish Market
York Beach, ME 207-363-2763
Young's Shellfish Company
Belfast, ME 207-338-5032

Canned

Charles H. Parks & Company
Fishing Creek, MD 410-397-3400
Chuck's Seafoods
Charleston, OR 541-888-5525
Cowart Seafood Corporation
Lottsburg, VA 804-529-6101
Crown Prince
City of Industry, CA 800-255-5063
Crown Prince Naturals
Petaluma, CA 707-766-8575
Dressel Collins Fish Company
Seattle, WA 206-725-0121
Elwha Fish
Port Angeles, WA 360-457-3344
J. Moniz Company
Fall River, MA 508-674-8451
J. Turner Seafoods
Gloucester, MA 978-281-8535
J.S. McMillan Fisheries
Vancouver, BC 604-255-5191
Jenport International Distributors
Coquitlam, BC 604-464-9888
Kodiak Salmon Packers
Larsen Bay, AK 907-847-2250
LaMonica Fine Foods
Millville, NJ 856-825-8111
LLJ's Sea Products
Round Pond, ME 207-529-4224
Look's Gourmet Food Company
Whiting, ME 800-962-6258
Mercado Latino
City of Industry, CA 626-333-6862
Mid-Atlantic Foods
Easton, MD 800-922-4688
Noon Hour Food Products
Chicago, IL 800-621-6636
Notre Dame Seafood
Comfort Cove, NL 709-244-5511
Ocean Fresh Seafoods
Seattle, WA 206-285-2412
Sea Watch International
Easton, MD 410-822-7500
Seatech Corporation
Lynnwood, WA 425-835-0312
Southern Shell Fish Company
Harvey, LA 504-341-5631
Southern Star Seafood
Fort Pierce, FL 561-461-5787
Sportsmen's Sea Foods
San Diego, CA 619-224-3551
Stinson Seafood Company
Prospect Harbor, ME 207-963-7331
Tideland Seafood Company
Dulac, LA 985-563-4516
Wrangell Fisheries
Wrangell, AK 907-874-3346

Cocktail

Sea Snack Foods
Los Angeles, CA 213-622-2204

Freeze-Dried

Oregon Freeze Dry
Albany, OR 800-547-0245
Wolf Canyon Foods
Carmel, CA 831-626-1323

Fresh

Anderson Seafoods
Anaheim, CA 714-777-7100
Aquatec Seafoods Ltd.
Comox, BC 250-339-6412
Arrowac Fisheries
Seattle, WA 206-282-5655
Aslanis Seafoods
Quincy, MA 800-876-3712
Atlantic Capes Fisheries
Cape May, NJ 609-884-3000
Atlantic Sea Pride
South Boston, MA 617-269-7700
Bayou Land Seafood
Breaux Bridge, LA 337-667-6118
BG Smith Sons Oyster
Sharps, VA 877-483-8279
BlueWater Seafoods
Lachine, QC 888-560-2539
Bolner's Fiesta Products
San Antonio, TX 210-734-6404
Bornstein Seafoods
Warrenton, OR 503-861-1233
Briny Sea Delicacies
Tumwater, WA 360-956-1797
Brownsdale Meat Service
Brownsdale, MN 507-567-2211
Buzzards Bay Trading Company
Fairhaven, MA 508-996-0242
Caraquet Ice Company
Caraquet, NB 506-727-7211
Charles H. Parks & Company
Fishing Creek, MD 410-397-3400
Coast Seafoods Company
Bellevue, WA 800-423-2303
Cowart Seafood Corporation
Lottsburg, VA 804-529-6101
Cozy Harbor Seafood
Portland, ME 800-225-2586
Crest International Corporation
San Diego, CA 800-548-1232
DB Kenney Fisheries
Westport, NS 902-839-2023
Depoe Bay Fish Company
Newport, OR 541-265-8833
Fishery Products International
Danvers, MA 800-374-4700
French Creek Seafood
Parksville, BC 250-248-7100
Granville Gates & Sons
Hubbards, NS 902-228-2559
Great Atlantic Trading Company
Ocean Isle Beach, NC 888-268-8780
Gulf City Seafoods
Pascagoula, MS 800-666-3300
Hallmark Fisheries
Charleston, OR 541-888-3253
Harbor Fish Market
Portland, ME 207-775-0251
Harold Bozman Seafood
Upper Fairmount, MD 410-651-0647
Hillard Bloom Packing Co
Port Norris, NJ 856-785-0120
Hillman Shrimp & Oyster
Dickinson, TX 800-582-4416
Independent Packers Corporation
Seattle, WA 206-285-6000
International Seafoods of Alaska
Kodiak, AK 907-486-4768
Island Marine Products
Clarks Harbour, NS 902-745-2222
J. Matassini & Sons Fish Company
Tampa, FL 813-229-0829
Jessie's Ilwaco Fish Company
Ilwaco, WA 360-642-3773
Keyser Brothers
Lottsburg, VA 804-529-6837
LaMonica Fine Foods
Millville, NJ 856-825-8111

Little River Seafood
Reedville, VA 804-453-3670
Major McGill
Flowery Branch, GA. 770-967-6001
Menemsha Fish Market
Chilmark, MA. 508-645-2282
Mersey Seafoods
Liverpool, NS .902-354-3467
Mike's Fish & Seafood
Glenwood, MN. 800-950-4755
Minterbrook Oyster Company
Gig Harbor, WA 253-857-5251
Motivatit Seafoods
Houma, LA. 985-868-7191
National Fish & Oysters Company
Olympia, WA .360-491-5550
Nordic Group
Boston, MA. 800-486-4002
NorQuest Seafoods
Seattle, WA. 206-281-7022
Ocean Beauty Seafoods
Seattle, WA. 206-285-6800
Ocean Fresh Seafoods
Seattle, WA. 206-285-2412
Pacific Salmon Company
Edmonds, WA. 425-774-1315
Pacific Seafoods International
Sidney, BC 250-656-0901
Pacific Shrimp Company
Newport, OR. .541-265-4215
Pacific Surf Food Processors
Los Angeles, CA. 800-627-5657
Pamlico Packing Company
Grantsboro, NC. 800-682-1113
Paul Piazza & Sons
New Orleans, LA. 504-524-6011
Plitt Company
Chicago, IL. 773-276-2200
Portland Shellfish Company
South Portland, ME 207-799-9290
Quality Seafood
Apalachicola, FL. 850-653-9696
RCV Seafood Corporation
Morattico, VA. 804-462-5101
Rippons Brothers Seafood
Fishing Creek, MD. 410-397-3200

Royal Seafood
Monterey, CA .831-655-8326
Ruggiero Seafood
Newark, NJ 800-543-2110
Sea Garden Seafoods
Meridian, GA .912-832-4437
Sea K Fish Company
Blaine, WA. 360-332-5121
Sea Products Company
Watsonville, CA. 831-768-2600
Seafood Products Company
Vancouver, BC 604-255-3141
Sitka Sound Seafoods
Sitka, AK. 907-747-6662
Stone Crabs
Miami Beach, FL 800-260-2722
Sunshine Food Sales
Miami, FL. 305-696-2885
Taylor Shellfish Farms
Shelton, WA. .360-426-6178
Terry Brothers
Temperanceville, VA. 757-824-3471
Union Fisheries Corporation
Chicago, IL. 312-738-0448
United Shellfish Company
Grasonville, MD. 410-827-8171
Wanchese Fish Company
Suffolk, VA. 757-673-4500
Washington Crab Producers
Westport, WA. 360-268-9161
Western Alaska Fisheries
Seattle, WA. 206-447-4400
Weyand Fisheries
Wyandotte, MI 800-521-9815
Wiegardt Brothers
Ocean Park, WA 360-665-4111
Wrangell Fisheries
Wrangell, AK .907-874-3346

Frozen

Acme Steak & Seafood Company
Youngstown, OH. 330-270-8000
Ajinomoto Frozen Foods USA
Portland, IR. 503-734-1528

Alaska Seafood Company
Los Angeles, CA. 213-626-1212
Alaskan Gourmet Seafoods
Anchorage, AK. 800-288-3740
Aliotti Wholesale Fish Company
Monterey, CA. 831-375-2881
All Alaskan Seafood
Seattle, WA. 206-285-8200
Alphin Brothers
Dunn, NC 800-672-4502
American Seafoods Group
Seattle, WA. 800-275-2019
Anderson Seafoods
Anaheim, CA .714-777-7100
Appert's Foodservice
St Cloud, MN .800-225-3883
APTCO
San Francisco, CA 415-648-6688
Aquatec Seafoods Ltd.
Comox, BC. 250-339-6412
Arista Industries
Wilton, CT 800-255-6457
Arrowac Fisheries
Seattle, WA. 206-282-5655
ASC Seafood
Largo, FL 800-876-3474
Aslanis Seafoods
Quincy, MA. 800-876-3712
Atlantic Capes Fisheries
Cape May, NJ .609-884-3000
Atlantic Queen Seafoods Limited
Lachine, QC 514-636-5114
Azuma Foods International
Hayward, CA. 510-782-1112
Bandon Bay Fisheries
Bandon, OR 541-347-4454
Bay Oceans Sea Foods
Garibaldi, OR .503-322-3316
Bayou Land Seafood
Breaux Bridge, LA 337-667-6118
Beaver Street Fisheries
Jacksonville, FL 800-874-6426
Bell Buoy Crab Company
Seaside, OR. 800-529-2722
BG Smith Sons Oyster
Sharps, VA 877-483-8279

Blount Seafood Corporation
Fall River, MA 774-888-1300
BlueWater Seafoods
Lachine, QC 888-560-2539
Bolner's Fiesta Products
San Antonio, TX 210-734-6404
Bon Secour Fisheries
Bon Secour, AL 800-633-6854
Braun Seafood Company
Cutchogue, NY 631-734-5550
Brownsdale Meat Service
Brownsdale, MN 507-567-2211
Bullock's Country Meats
Westminster, MD 410-848-6786
Buns & Things Bakery
Charlottetown, PE 902-892-2600
Buzzards Bay Trading Company
Fairhaven, MA 508-996-0242
C.F. Gollott & Son Seafood
Biloxi, MS 866-846-3474
California Shellfish Company
Gardena, CA 310-538-4197
Callis Seafood
Lancaster, VA 804-462-7634
Captn's Pack Products
Columbia, MD 410-720-6668
Caraquet Ice Company
Caraquet, NB 506-727-7211
Carolina Atlantic Seafood Enterprises
Beaufort, NC 252-504-2663
Carrington Foods
Saraland, AL 251-675-9700
Cathay Foods Corporation
Boston, MA 617-427-1507
Certi-Fresh Foods
Bell Gardens, CA 562-806-1100
Chases Lobster Pound
Port Howe, NS 902-243-2408
Cherbogue Fisheries
Yarmouth, NS 902-742-9157
Chester W. Howeth & Brother
Crisfield, MD 410-968-1398
Clearwater Fine Foods
Bedford, NS 902-443-0550
Coldwater Seafood Corporation
Norwalk, CT 203-846-8897
Coldwater Seafood Corporation
Newport News, VA 410-228-7500
ConAgra Shrimp Companies
Tampa, FL 813-241-1501
Cook Inlet Processing
Nikiski, AK 907-776-8174
Cowart Seafood Corporation
Lottsburg, VA 804-529-6101
Cozy Harbor Seafood
Portland, ME 800-225-2586
Crab King Seafood Specialties
Seattle, WA 206-283-2722
Crest International Corporation
San Diego, CA 800-548-1232
Crevettes Du Nord
Gaspe, QC 418-368-1414
Cuizina Food Company
Woodinville, WA 425-486-7000
Czimer's Game & Sea Foods
Homer Glen, IL 708-301-0500
Daerim America
Maywood, NJ 800-635-0781
DB Kenney Fisheries
Westport, NS 902-839-2023
Deep Creek Custom Packing
Ninilchik, AK 800-764-0078
Deep Sea Foods
Bayou La Batre, AL 251-824-7000
Del's Seaway Shrimp & Oyster Company
Biloxi, MS 228-432-2604
Depoe Bay Fish Company
Newport, OR 541-265-8833
Dick & Casey's Gourmet Seafoods
Harbor, OR 800-662-9494
E. Gagnon & Fils
St Therese-De-Gaspe, QC 418-385-3011
Eastern Fish Company
Teaneck, NJ 800-526-9066
Eastern Quebec Sea Foods
Matane, QC 418-562-1273
Farm Fresh Catfish Company
Hollandale, MS 800-647-8264
Fishery Products International
Danvers, MA 800-374-4700
FishKing
Bayou La Batre, AL 334-824-2118

Fishking Processors
Los Angeles, CA 877-677-3329
Fishmarket Seafoods
Louisville, KY 502-587-7474
French Creek Seafood
Parksville, BC 250-248-7100
Frozen Specialties
Archbold, OH 419-445-9015
FW Bryce
Gloucester, MA 978-283-7080
Gemini Food Industries
Fiskdale, MA 508-347-2800
George Robberecht Seafood
Montross, VA 804-472-3556
Gesco ENR
Gaspe, QC 418-368-1414
Golden Gulf Coast Packing Company
Biloxi, MS 228-374-6121
Good Harbor Fillet Company
Gloucester, MA 978-675-9100
Gorton's Seafood
Gloucester, MA 978-283-3000
Great Atlantic Trading Company
Ocean Isle Beach, NC 888-268-8780
Great Glacier Salmon
Prince Rupert, BC 250-627-4955
Great Northern Products
Warwick, RI 401-490-4590
Gulf City Seafoods
Pascagoula, MS 800-666-3300
Gulf Pride Enterprises
Biloxi, MS 888-689-0560
H&H Fisheries Limited
Eastern Passage, NS 902-465-6330
Hallmark Fisheries
Charleston, OR 541-888-3253
Harbor Seafood
New Hyde Park, NY 800-585-0900
Harold Bozman Seafood
Upper Fairmount, MD 410-651-0647
HFI Foods
Redmond, WA 425-883-1320
Higgins Seafood
Lafitte, LA 504-689-3577
High Liner Foods
Lunenburg, NS 902-634-9475
Hillard Bloom Packing Co
Port Norris, NJ 856-785-0120
Hillman Shrimp & Oyster
Dickinson, TX 800-582-4416
Icelandic USA
Newport News, VA 757-820-4000
Icicle Seafoods
Seattle, WA 206-282-0988
Independent Packers Corporation
Seattle, WA 206-285-6000
Indian Ridge Shrimp Company
Chauvin, LA 985-594-5869
Inlet Salmon
Bothell, WA 425-487-0495
International Oceanic Enterprises of Alabama
Bayou La Batre, AL 800-816-1832
International Seafoods of Alaska
Kodiak, AK 907-486-4768
Island Marine Products
Clarks Harbour, NS 902-745-2222
Island Scallops
Qualicum Beach, BC 250-757-9811
J. Matassini & Sons Fish Company
Tampa, FL 813-229-0829
J.S. McMillan Fisheries
Vancouver, BC 604-255-5191
Jack's Lobsters
Musquodoboit Harbor, NS 902-889-2771
Janes Family Foods
Mississauga, ON 800-565-2637
JBS Packing Company
Port Arthur, TX 409-982-3216
JCW Tawes & Son
Crisfield, MD 410-968-1288
Jenport International Distributors
Coquitlam, BC 604-464-9888
Jessie's Ilwaco Fish Company
Ilwaco, WA 360-642-3773
John T. Handy Company
Salisbury, MD 800-426-3977
Jubilee Foods
Bayou La Batre, AL 251-824-2110
Key Largo Fisheries
Key Largo, FL 800-399-6970
Keyser Brothers
Lottsburg, VA 804-529-6837

Kitchens Seafood
Plant City, FL 800-327-0132
Kodiak Salmon Packers
Larsen Bay, AK 907-847-2250
L&C Fisheries
Kensington, PE 902-886-2770
Lady Gale Seafood
Baldwin, LA 337-923-2060
LaMonica Fine Foods
Millville, NJ 856-825-8111
Lombardi's Seafood
Orlando, FL 800-879-8411
Long Beach Seafoods
Long Beach, CA 714-995-8901
Louisiana Packing Company
Westwego, LA 800-666-1293
Lu-Mar Lobster & Shrimp
Brownsville, TX 956-546-5525
Lund's Fisheries
Cape May, NJ 609-884-7600
M&M Shrimp Company
Biloxi, MS 228-435-4915
Maple Leaf Foods International
Toronto, ON 416-480-8900
Martin Seafood Company
Jessup, MD 410-799-5822
Matlaw's Food Products
West Haven, CT 800-934-8266
Maxim's Import Corporation
Miami, FL 800-331-6652
Menemsha Fish Market
Chilmark, MA 508-645-2282
Mid-Atlantic Foods
Easton, MD 800-922-4688
Mike's Fish & Seafood
Glenwood, MN 800-950-4755
Miles J H & Company
Norfolk, VA 757-622-9264
Milfico Foods
Elk Grove Vlg, IL 847-427-0491
Minterbrook Oyster Company
Gig Harbor, WA 253-857-5251
Mobile Processing
Mobile, AL 251-438-6944
Morey's Seafood International
Motley, MN 218-352-6345
Motivatit Seafoods
Houma, LA 985-868-7191
Mutual Fish Company
Seattle, WA 206-322-4368
Nan Sea Enterprises of Wisconsin
Waukesha, WI 262-542-8841
National Fish & Oysters Company
Olympia, WA 360-491-5550
Nelson Crab
Tokeland, WA 800-262-0069
Neptune Fisheries
Newport News, VA 800-545-7474
Newfound Resources
Saint John's, NL 709-579-7676
Nordic Group
Boston, MA 800-486-4002
NorQuest Seafoods
Seattle, WA 206-281-7022
North Atlantic Fish Company
Gloucester, MA 978-283-4121
Northern Wind
New Bedford, MA 888-525-2525
Notre Dame Seafood
Comfort Cove, NL 709-244-5511
Ocean Beauty Seafoods
Seattle, WA 206-285-6800
Ocean Food Company
Scarborough, ON 416-285-6487
Ocean Fresh Seafoods
Seattle, WA 206-285-2412
Ocean Springs Seafood
Ocean Springs, MS 228-875-0104
Okuhara Foods
Honolulu, HI 808-848-0581
Omstead Foods Ltd
Burlington, ON 905-315-8883
P&J Oyster Company
New Orleans, LA 504-523-2651
P. Janes & Sons
Hant's Harbor, NL 709-586-2252
Pacific Alaska Seafoods
Seattle, WA 206-587-0002
Pacific Seafoods International
Sidney, BC 250-656-0901
Pacific Shrimp Company
Newport, OR 541-265-4215

Pacific Surf Food Processors
Los Angeles, CA 800-627-5657
Pacific Valley Foods
Bellevue, WA 425-643-1805
Pamlico Packing Company
Grantsboro, NC 800-682-1113
Paul Piazza & Sons
New Orleans, LA 504-524-6011
PEI Mussel King
Morrell, PE 800-673-2767
Peter Pan Seafoods
Seattle, WA 206-728-6000
Petersburg Fisheries
Petersburg, AK 877-772-4294
Plitt Company
Chicago, IL 773-276-2200
Port Chatham Smoked Seafood
Everett, WA 800-872-5666
Portland Shellfish Company
South Portland, ME 207-799-9290
Prairie Cajun Wholesale
Eunice, LA 337-546-6195
Price Seafood
Chauvin, LA 985-594-3067
Quality Seafood
Apalachicola, FL 850-653-9696
Resource Trading Company
Portland, ME 207-772-2299
Rich-Seapak Corporation
Brownsville, TX 956-542-0001
Roy Stritmatter Company
Hoquiam, WA 360-532-0710
Royal Seafood
Monterey, CA 831-655-8326
Ruggiero Seafood
Newark, NJ 800-543-2110
Sanderson Farms
Bryan, TX 979-778-5730
Sea K Fish Company
Blaine, WA 360-332-5121
Sea Pearl Seafood
Bayou La Batre, AL 800-872-8804
Sea Products Company
Watsonville, CA 831-768-2600
Sea Safari
Belhaven, NC 800-688-6174
Sea Safari Limited
Belhaven, NC 800-688-6174
Sea Snack Foods
Los Angeles, CA 213-622-2204
Sea Watch International
Easton, MD 410-822-7500
Seafood Producers Cooperative
Bellingham, WA 360-733-0120
Seafood Products Company
Vancouver, BC 604-255-3141
Seaspan Products Corporation
New York, NY 201-569-9234
Seatech Corporation
Lynnwood, WA 425-835-0312
Seymour & Sons Seafood
Diberville, MS 228-392-4020
Shawmut Fishing Company
Anchorage, AK 709-334-2559
Silver Lining Seafood
Ketchikan, AK 907-225-6664
Sitka Sound Seafoods
Sitka, AK 907-747-6662
Southern Star Seafood
Fort Pierce, FL 561-461-5787
Southtowns Seafood & Meats
Blasdell, NY 716-824-4900
St. Ours & Company
Norwell, MA 781-331-8520
Stacey's Famous Foods
Hayden, ID 800-782-2395
Stinson Seafood Company
Prospect Harbor, ME 207-963-7331
Stone Crabs
Miami Beach, FL 800-260-2722
Sunshine Food Sales
Miami, FL 305-696-2885
Super Snooty Sea Food Corporation
Boston, MA 617-426-6390
Sweet Water Seafood Corporation
Carlstadt, NJ 201-939-6622
Taku Smokehouse
Juneau, AK 800-582-5122
Tampa Bay Fisheries
Dover, FL 800-234-2561
Tampa Maid Foods
Lakeland, FL 800-237-7637

Taylor Shellfish Farms
Shelton, WA 360-426-6178
Taylor's Frozen Foods
Charleston, SC 843-723-1878
Tex-Mex Cold Storage
Brownsville, TX 956-831-9433
Tichon Seafood Corporation
New Bedford, MA 508-999-5607
Trident Seafoods Corporation
Salem, NH 603-893-3368
Trident Seafoods Corporation
Seattle, WA 800-426-5490
Triton Seafood Company
Medley, FL 305-805-3500
Union Fisheries Corporation
Chicago, IL 312-738-0448
Van De Kamp Frozen Foods
Erie, PA 814-898-1500
Viking Seafoods Inc
Malden, MA 800-225-3020
Vince's Seafoods
Gretna, LA 504-368-1544
Vincent Piazza Jr & Sons
Harahan, LA 800-259-5016
Virginia Trout Company
Monterey, VA 540-468-2280
Vita Food Products
Chicago, IL 312-738-4500
Wanchese Fish Company
Suffolk, VA 757-673-4500
Washington Crab Producers
Westport, WA 360-268-9161
Weems Brothers Seafood Company
Biloxi, MS 228-432-5422
Western Alaska Fisheries
Seattle, WA 206-447-4400
Weyand Fisheries
Wyandotte, MI 800-521-9815
White Cap Fish Company
Islip, NY 631-581-0125
Wrangell Fisheries
Wrangell, AK 907-874-3346

Smoked

Bell Buoy Crab Company
Seaside, OR 800-529-2722
Blount Seafood Corporation
Fall River, MA 774-888-1300
Cooke Aguaculture
Blacks Harbour, NB 506-456-6600
Depoe Bay Fish Company
Newport, OR 541-265-8833
Dressel Collins Fish Company
Seattle, WA 206-725-0121
Indian Valley Meats
Indian, AK 907-653-7511
NorQuest Seafoods
Seattle, WA 206-281-7022
Salmolux
Federal Way, WA 253-874-6570
Seabear
Anacortes, WA 800-645-3474

Cold

Tonex
Wallington, NJ 973-773-5135

Cured

J. Moniz Company
Fall River, MA 508-674-8451
J. Turner Seafoods
Gloucester, MA 978-281-8535
Ocean Fresh Seafoods
Seattle, WA 206-285-2412
Tideland Seafood Company
Dulac, LA 985-563-4516

Lox

Homarus
Atlanta, GA 404-877-1988

Turtle

Bayou Land Seafood
Breaux Bridge, LA 337-667-6118

Shellfish

Canned

Charles H. Parks & Company
Fishing Creek, MD 410-397-3400
Chicken of the Sea International
San Diego, CA 800-678-8862
Chuck's Seafoods
Charleston, OR 541-888-5525
Crown Prince
City of Industry, CA 800-255-5063
Cuizina Food Company
Woodinville, WA 425-486-7000
Eastern Shore Seafood Products
Mappsville, VA 800-466-8550
Elwha Fish
Port Angeles, WA 360-457-3344
Gulf City Marine Supply
Bayou La Batre, AL 251-824-4154
Hallmark Fisheries
Charleston, OR 541-888-3253
Mercado Latino
City of Industry, CA 626-333-6862
Mid-Atlantic Foods
Easton, MD 800-922-4688
Miles J H & Company
Norfolk, VA 757-622-9264
Nelson Crab
Tokeland, WA 800-262-0069
North Atlantic Fish Company
Gloucester, MA 978-283-4121
Notre Dame Seafood
Comfort Cove, NL 709-244-5511
NTC Foods Corporation
Williamsville, NY 800-333-1637
Omstead Foods Ltd
Burlington, ON 905-315-8883
Pacific Salmon Company
Edmonds, WA 425-774-1315
Peter Pan Seafoods
Seattle, WA 206-728-6000
Petersburg Fisheries
Petersburg, AK 877-772-4294
Sea Safari
Belhaven, NC 800-688-6174
Southern Shell Fish Company
Harvey, LA 504-341-5631
Southern Star Seafood
Fort Pierce, FL 561-461-5787
Stinson Seafood Company
Prospect Harbor, ME 207-963-7331
Sweet Water Seafood Corporation
Carlstadt, NJ 201-939-6622
Wrangell Fisheries
Wrangell, AK 907-874-3346

Chopped

S&M Fisheries
Kennebunkport, ME 207-985-3456

Clam

Atlantic Aqua Farms
Vernon Bridge, PE 902-651-2563
Atlantic Capes Fisheries
Cape May, NJ 609-884-3000
Bell Buoy Crab Company
Seaside, OR 800-529-2722
Big Al's Seafood
Bozman, MD 410-745-3151
Blount Seafood Corporation
Fall River, MA 774-888-1300
Bon Secour Fisheries
Bon Secour, AL 800-633-6854
Braun Seafood Company
Cutchogue, NY 631-734-5550
Bumble Bee Seafoods
San Diego, CA 858-715-4000
C.E. Fish Company
Jonesboro, ME 207-434-2631
Cajun Crawfish Distributors
Cottonport, LA 800-525-6813
Carolina Seafoods
Mc Clellanville, SC 843-887-3713
Certi-Fresh Foods
Bell Gardens, CA 562-806-1100
Chases Lobster Pound
Port Howe, NS 902-243-2408
Chester River Clam Co, Inc
Centreville, MD 410-758-3810

261

Chuck's Seafoods
Charleston, OR 541-888-5525
Clearwater Fine Foods
Bedford, NS 902-443-0550
Coast Seafoods Company
Bellevue, WA 800-423-2303
Comeaux's
Lafayette, LA 800-323-2492
Cook Inlet Processing
Nikiski, AK 907-776-8174
Crevettes Du Nord
Gaspe, QC 418-368-1414
Crown Prince
City of Industry, CA 800-255-5063
Cuizina Food Company
Woodinville, WA 425-486-7000
Del's Seaway Shrimp & Oyster Company
Biloxi, MS 228-432-2604
Dick & Casey's Gourmet Seafoods
Harbor, OR 800-662-9494
E. Gagnon & Fils
St Therese-De-Gaspe, QC 418-385-3011
Eastern Shore Seafood Products
Mappsville, VA 800-466-8550
Frozen Specialties
Archbold, OH 419-445-9015
Gesco ENR
Gaspe, QC 418-368-1414
Gulf Pride Enterprises
Biloxi, MS 888-689-0560
H&H Fisheries Limited
Eastern Passage, NS 902-465-6330
Hillard Bloom Packing Co
Port Norris, NJ 856-785-0120
Hillman Shrimp & Oyster
Dickinson, TX 800-582-4416
Huck's Seafood
Easton, MD 410-770-9211
Innovative Fishery Products
Clarks Harbour, NS 902-837-5163
International Enterprises
Herring Neck, NL 709-628-7406
Island Scallops
Qualicum Beach, BC 250-757-9811
Jack's Lobsters
Musquodoboit Harbor, NS 902-889-2771
JBS Packing Company
Port Arthur, TX 409-982-3216
Jubilee Foods
Bayou La Batre, AL 251-824-2110
L&C Fisheries
Kensington, PE 902-886-2770
L&M Evans
Conyers, GA 770-918-8727
Lady Gale Seafood
Baldwin, LA 337-923-2060
LaMonica Fine Foods
Millville, NJ 856-825-8111
Louisiana Packing Company
Westwego, LA 800-666-1293
M&M Shrimp Company
Biloxi, MS 228-435-4915
Matlaw's Food Products
West Haven, CT 800-934-8266
Menemsha Fish Market
Chilmark, MA 508-645-2282
Mercado Latino
City of Industry, CA 626-333-6862
Mid-Atlantic Foods
Easton, MD 800-922-4688
Miles J H & Company
Norfolk, VA 757-622-9264
Mill Cove Lobster Pound
Boothbay Harbor, ME 207-633-3340
Mobile Processing
Mobile, AL 251-438-6944
Mutual Fish Company
Seattle, WA 206-322-4368
N.A. Boullon
Cumming, GA 770-889-2356
Nan Sea Enterprises of Wisconsin
Waukesha, WI 262-542-8841
Newfound Resources
Saint John's, NL 709-579-7676
Northern Wind
New Bedford, MA 888-525-2525
Ocean Springs Seafood
Ocean Springs, MS 228-875-0104
Pacific Alaska Seafoods
Seattle, WA 206-587-0002
Pacific Seafood Group
Clackamas, OR 800-388-1101

PEI Mussel King
Morrell, PE 800-673-2767
Pine Point Seafood
Scarborough, ME 207-883-4701
Polar Foods International
Charlottetown, PE 902-962-3303
Price Seafood
Chauvin, LA 985-594-3067
Resource Trading Company
Portland, ME 207-772-2299
SeaPerfect Atlantic Farms
Charleston, SC 800-728-0099
Shawmut Fishing Company
Anchorage, AK 709-334-2559
St. Ours & Company
Norwell, MA 781-331-8520
Stavis Seafoods
Boston, MA 800-390-5103
Terry Brothers
Temperanceville, VA 757-824-3471
United Shellfish Company
Grasonville, MD 410-827-8171
Vincent Piazza Jr & Sons
Harahan, LA 800-259-5016
Young's Lobster Pound
Belfast, ME 207-338-1160

Breaded Strips

LaMonica Fine Foods
Millville, NJ 856-825-8111

Canned

Blount Seafood Corporation
Fall River, MA 774-888-1300
Chicken of the Sea International
San Diego, CA 800-678-8862
Chuck's Seafoods
Charleston, OR 541-888-5525
Crown Prince Naturals
Petaluma, CA 707-766-8575
Cuizina Food Company
Woodinville, WA 425-486-7000
Eastern Shore Seafood Products
Mappsville, VA 800-466-8550
Elwha Fish
Port Angeles, WA 360-457-3344
LaMonica Fine Foods
Millville, NJ 856-825-8111
Look's Gourmet Food Company
Whiting, ME 800-962-6258
Mercado Latino
City of Industry, CA 626-333-6862
Mid-Atlantic Foods
Easton, MD 800-922-4688
Mutual Fish Company
Seattle, WA 206-322-4368
Orleans Food Company
New Orleans, LA 800-628-4900
Seawatch International
Easton, MD 410-822-7500
Stavis Seafoods
Boston, MA 800-390-5103

Chopped

Eastern Shore Seafood Products
Mappsville, VA 800-466-8550
LaMonica Fine Foods
Millville, NJ 856-825-8111
Look's Gourmet Food Company
Whiting, ME 800-962-6258

Fresh

Coast Seafoods Company
Bellevue, WA 800-423-2303
Cuizina Food Company
Woodinville, WA 425-486-7000
LaMonica Fine Foods
Millville, NJ 856-825-8111
Menemsha Fish Market
Chilmark, MA 508-645-2282
Mutual Fish Company
Seattle, WA 206-322-4368
Sweet Water Seafood Corporation
Carlstadt, NJ 201-939-6622
Taylor Shellfish Farms
Shelton, WA 360-426-6178
Terry Brothers
Temperanceville, VA 757-824-3471

Frozen

Cedar Key Aquaculture Farms
Riverview, FL 888-252-6735
Certi-Fresh Foods
Bell Gardens, CA 562-806-1100
Clearwater Fine Foods
Bedford, NS 902-443-0550
ConAgra Shrimp Companies
Tampa, FL 813-241-1501
Cook Inlet Processing
Nikiski, AK 907-776-8174
Cuizina Food Company
Woodinville, WA. 425-486-7000
Eastern Shore Seafood Products
Mappsville, VA 800-466-8550
Gorton's Seafood
Gloucester, MA 978-283-3000
Hillard Bloom Packing Co
Port Norris, NJ 856-785-0120
LaMonica Fine Foods
Millville, NJ 856-825-8111
Matlaw's Food Products
West Haven, CT 800-934-8266
Menemsha Fish Market
Chilmark, MA 508-645-2282
Mid-Atlantic Foods
Easton, MD 800-922-4688
Minterbrook Oyster Company
Gig Harbor, WA 253-857-5251
Mutual Fish Company
Seattle, WA 206-322-4368
St. Ours & Company
Norwell, MA 781-331-8520
Taylor Shellfish Farms
Shelton, WA 360-426-6178

Frozen Strips

LaMonica Fine Foods
Millville, NJ 856-825-8111

Juice

Chincoteague Seafood Company
Parsonsburg, MD 443-260-4800
Crown Prince
City of Industry, CA 800-255-5063
Eastern Shore Seafood Products
Mappsville, VA 800-466-8550
Flavor House
Adelanto, CA 760-246-9131
Look's Gourmet Food Company
Whiting, ME 800-962-6258
Stinson Seafood Company
Prospect Harbor, ME 207-963-7331

Minced

Eastern Shore Seafood Products
Mappsville, VA 800-466-8550
LaMonica Fine Foods
Millville, NJ 856-825-8111

Whole

Eastern Shore Seafood Products
Mappsville, VA 800-466-8550
LaMonica Fine Foods
Millville, NJ 856-825-8111

Conch

Denzer's Food Products
Baltimore, MD 410-889-1500
LaMonica Fine Foods
Millville, NJ 856-825-8111
Sweet Water Seafood Corporation
Carlstadt, NJ 201-939-6622
Triton Seafood Company
Medley, FL 305-805-3500

Crab

All Alaskan Seafood
Seattle, WA 206-285-8200
Appetizers And, Inc.
Chicago, IL 800-323-5472
Arrowac Fisheries
Seattle, WA 206-282-5655
Atlantic Queen Seafoods Limited
Lachine, QC 514-636-5114
Bandon Bay Fisheries
Bandon, OR 541-347-4454

Bay Hundred Seafood
McDaniel, MD .410-745-9329
Bayou Foods
Kenner, LA 800-516-8283
Bayou Land Seafood
Breaux Bridge, LA 337-667-6118
Beaver Street Fisheries
Jacksonville, FL 800-874-6426
Bell Buoy Crab Company
Seaside, OR 800-529-2722
Big Al's Seafood
Bozman, MD 410-745-3151
Bolner's Fiesta Products
San Antonio, TX 210-734-6404
Bornstein Seafoods
Warrenton, OR 503-861-1233
Bradye P. Todd & Son
Cambridge, MD 410-228-8633
Bumble Bee Seafoods
San Diego, CA 858-715-4000
California Shellfish Company
San Francisco, CA 415-923-7400
Callis Seafood
Lancaster, VA .804-462-7634
Carrington Foods
Saraland, AL 251-675-9700
Catfish Wholesale
Abbeville, LA .800-334-7292
Cathay Foods Corporation
Boston, MA 617-427-1507
Ceilidh Fisherman's Cooperative
Inverness, NS .902-787-2666
Certi-Fresh Foods
Bell Gardens, CA 562-806-1100
Charles H. Parks & Company
Fishing Creek, MD 410-397-3400
Clearwater Fine Foods
Bedford, NS 902-443-0550
Cook Inlet Processing
Nikiski, AK 907-776-8174
Crab King Seafood Specialties
Seattle, WA 206-283-2722
Crab Quarters
Baltimore, MD 410-686-2222
Crescent City Crab Corporation
New Orleans, LA 504-646-6645
Crown Prince
City of Industry, CA 800-255-5063
Cuizina Food Company
Woodinville, WA 425-486-7000
Day's Crabmeat & Lobster
Yarmouth, ME 207-846-5871
Depoe Bay Fish Company
Newport, OR .541-265-8833
Dorchester Crab Company
Wingate, MD .410-397-8103
Fisherman's Market International
Halifax, NS 902-445-3474
Fishery Products International
Danvers, MA .800-374-4700
Fishhawk Fisheries
Astoria, OR 503-325-5252
Goldcoast Salads
Naples, FL 239-304-0710
Great Northern Products
Warwick, RI 401-490-4590
Gulf Stream Crab Company
Bayou La Batre, AL 251-824-4717
H. Gass Seafood
Hollywood, MD 301-373-6882
Hallmark Fisheries
Charleston, OR 541-888-3253
Huck's Seafood
Easton, MD 410-770-9211
Icicle Seafoods
Seattle, WA 206-282-0988
Independent Packers Corporation
Seattle, WA 206-285-6000
International Oceanic Enterprises of Alabama
Bayou La Batre, AL 800-816-1832
J. Matassini & Sons Fish Company
Tampa, FL 813-229-0829
JCW Tawes & Son
Crisfield, MD .410-968-1288
Jessie's Ilwaco Fish Company
Ilwaco, WA 360-642-3773
John T. Handy Company
Salisbury, MD 800-426-3977
Keyser Brothers
Lottsburg, VA 804-529-6837
Kirkland Custom Seafoods
Kirkland, WA .800-321-3474

Kitchens Seafood
Plant City, FL .800-327-0132
LaMonica Fine Foods
Millville, NJ 856-825-8111
Larry J. Williams Company
Jesup, GA 912-427-7729
Little River Seafood
Reedville, VA .804-453-3670
Look's Gourmet Food Company
Whiting, ME .800-962-6258
Lowland Seafood
Lowland, NC .252-745-3751
Martin Brothers Seafood Company
Westwego, LA 504-341-2251
McGraw Seafood
Tracadie Sheila, NB 506-395-3374
Menemsha Fish Market
Chilmark, MA 508-645-2282
Mercado Latino
City of Industry, CA 626-333-6862
Mercer Processing
Modesto, CA .209-529-0150
Milfico Foods
Elk Grove Vlg, IL 847-427-0491
Moon Enterprises
Richmond, BC 604-270-0088
Mutual Fish Company
Seattle, WA 206-322-4368
Nelson Crab
Tokeland, WA 800-262-0069
NorQuest Seafoods
Seattle, WA 206-281-7022
Notre Dame Seafood
Comfort Cove, NL 709-244-5511
Ocean Food Company
Scarborough, ON 416-285-6487
Ocean Union Company
Lawrenceville, GA 770-995-1957
Pacific Shrimp Company
Newport, OR .541-265-4215
Pamlico Packing Company
Grantsboro, NC 800-682-1113
Peter Pan Seafoods
Seattle, WA 206-728-6000
Petersburg Fisheries
Petersburg, AK 877-772-4294
Phillips Foods
Baltimore, MD 800-782-2722
Produits Belle Baie
Caraquet, NB .506-727-4414
RCV Seafood Corporation
Morattico, VA 804-462-5101
Rippons Brothers Seafood
Fishing Creek, MD 410-397-3200
Sea Garden Seafoods
Meridian, GA .912-832-4437
Sea Safari
Belhaven, NC .252-943-3091
Sea Safari
Belhaven, NC .800-688-6174
Sea Safari Limited
Belhaven, NC .800-688-6174
Sea Watch International
Easton, MD 410-822-7500
Silver Lining Seafood
Ketchikan, AK 907-225-6664
Southern Shell Fish Company
Harvey, LA 504-341-5631
St. Ours & Company
Norwell, MA .781-331-8520
Stinson Seafood Company
Prospect Harbor, ME 207-963-7331
Stone Crabs
Miami Beach, FL 800-260-2722
Sunshine Food Sales
Miami, FL 305-696-2885
Taku Smokehouse
Juneau, AK 800-582-5122
Taylor's Frozen Foods
Charleston, SC 843-723-1878
Toddville Seafoods
Toddville, MD 410-397-8129
Trident Seafoods Corporation
Seattle, WA 800-426-5490
Van Dykes Chesapeake Seafood
Cambridge, MD 410-228-9000
Vince's Seafoods
Gretna, LA 504-368-1544
W.H. Harris Seafood
Chester, MD .410-827-8104
W.T. Ruark & Company
Fishing Creek, MD 410-397-3133

Ward Cove Packing Company
Seattle, WA 206-323-3200
Washington Crab Producers
Westport, WA 360-268-9161
Waverly Crabs
Baltimore, MD 410-243-1181
Wrangell Fisheries
Wrangell, AK .907-874-3346
Young's Lobster Pound
Belfast, ME 207-338-1160

Blue

Arctic Seas
Little Compton, RI 401-635-4000
Casey's Seafood
Newport News, VA 757-928-1979
Gulf City Seafoods
Pascagoula, MS 800-666-3300
J M Clayton Company
Cambridge, MD 800-652-6931
JCW Tawes & Son
Crisfield, MD .410-968-1288
Little River Seafood
Reedville, VA .804-453-3670
Phillips Foods
Baltimore, MD 888-234-2722
RCV Seafood Corporation
Morattico, VA 804-462-5101
Sea Safari
Belhaven, NC .800-688-6174

Cakes

Appetizers And, Inc.
Chicago, IL 800-323-5472
Casey's Seafood
Newport News, VA 757-928-1979
J. Matassini & Sons Fish Company
Tampa, FL 813-229-0829
John T. Handy Company
Salisbury, MD 800-426-3977
LaMonica Fine Foods
Millville, NJ 856-825-8111
M&I Seafood Manufacturers
Essex, MD 410-780-0444
Tampa Bay Fisheries
Dover, FL 800-234-2561

Cakes Frozen

Chincoteague Seafood Company
Parsonsburg, MD 443-260-4800
Coastal Seafoods
Ridgefield, CT 203-431-0453
Cuizina Food Company
Woodinville, WA. 425-486-7000
J. Matassini & Sons Fish Company
Tampa, FL. 813-229-0829
John T. Handy Company
Salisbury, MD 800-426-3977
Phillips Foods
Baltimore, MD 888-234-2722
Tampa Bay Fisheries
Dover, FL 800-234-2561

Canned

Cathay Foods Corporation
Boston, MA. 617-427-1507
Charles H. Parks & Company
Fishing Creek, MD 410-397-3400
Chicken of the Sea International
San Diego, CA 800-678-8862
Crown Prince Naturals
Petaluma, CA 707-766-8575
Cuizina Food Company
Woodinville, WA. 425-486-7000
Elwha Fish
Port Angeles, WA 360-457-3344
Mercado Latino
City of Industry, CA 626-333-6862
Mutual Fish Company
Seattle, WA. 206-322-4368
Scally's Imperial Importing Company Inc
Staten Island, NY 718-983-1938
Sea Safari
Belhaven, NC 800-688-6174
Southern Shell Fish Company
Harvey, LA 504-341-5631
Wrangell Fisheries
Wrangell, AK 907-874-3346

Claws Stone

Atlantic Queen Seafoods Limited
Lachine, QC 514-636-5114

Cooked

Bayou Foods
Kenner, LA 800-516-8283

Dungeness

All Alaskan Seafood
Seattle, WA. 206-285-8200
Arrowac Fisheries
Seattle, WA. 206-282-5655
Bornstein Seafoods
Warrenton, OR 503-861-1233
Jessie's Ilwaco Fish Company
Ilwaco, WA 360-642-3773
Kirkland Custom Seafoods
Kirkland, WA 800-321-3474
Trident Seafoods Corporation
Seattle, WA. 800-426-5490
Washington Crab Producers
Westport, WA 360-268-9161

Fresh

Arrowac Fisheries
Seattle, WA. 206-282-5655
Bayou Land Seafood
Breaux Bridge, LA 337-667-6118
Bornstein Seafoods
Warrenton, OR 503-861-1233
Cathay Foods Corporation
Boston, MA. 617-427-1507
Charles H. Parks & Company
Fishing Creek, MD 410-397-3400
Cuizina Food Company
Woodinville, WA. 425-486-7000
Daley Brothers
St John's, NL. 709-364-8844
Depoe Bay Fish Company
Newport, OR. 541-265-8833
Fishery Products International
Danvers, MA. 800-374-4700
Icicle Seafoods
Seattle, WA. 206-282-0988
J. Matassini & Sons Fish Company
Tampa, FL. 813-229-0829

JCW Tawes & Son
Crisfield, MD 410-968-1288
Jessie's Ilwaco Fish Company
Ilwaco, WA 360-642-3773
Keyser Brothers
Lottsburg, VA 804-529-6837
Kirkland Custom Seafoods
Kirkland, WA 800-321-3474
Little River Seafood
Reedville, VA 804-453-3670
Lowland Seafood
Lowland, NC. 252-745-3751
Menemsha Fish Market
Chilmark, MA. 508-645-2282
Mutual Fish Company
Seattle, WA. 206-322-4368
Nelson Crab
Tokeland, WA 800-262-0069
Phillips Foods
Baltimore, MD 800-782-2722
Phillips Foods
Baltimore, MD 888-234-2722
Portland Shellfish Company
South Portland, ME 207-799-9290
RCV Seafood Corporation
Morattico, VA 804-462-5101
Rippons Brothers Seafood
Fishing Creek, MD 410-397-3200
Sea Garden Seafoods
Meridian, GA 912-832-4437
Sea Safari
Belhaven, NC 252-943-3091
Sea Watch International
Easton, MD 410-822-7500
Stone Crabs
Miami Beach, FL 800-260-2722
Sunshine Food Sales
Miami, FL 305-696-2885
Taylor Shellfish Farms
Shelton, WA 360-426-6178
Washington Crab Producers
Westport, WA 360-268-9161
Wrangell Fisheries
Wrangell, AK 907-874-3346

Frozen

All Alaskan Seafood
Seattle, WA. 206-285-8200
Arrowac Fisheries
Seattle, WA. 206-282-5655
Atlantic Queen Seafoods Limited
Lachine, QC 514-636-5114
Bandon Bay Fisheries
Bandon, OR 541-347-4454
Bayou Land Seafood
Breaux Bridge, LA 337-667-6118
Beaver Street Fisheries
Jacksonville, FL 800-874-6426
Bornstein Seafoods
Warrenton, OR 503-861-1233
Buns & Things Bakery
Charlottetown, PE. 902-892-2600
Callis Seafood
Lancaster, VA 804-462-7634
Carrington Foods
Saraland, AL. 251-675-9700
Cathay Foods Corporation
Boston, MA. 617-427-1507
Certi-Fresh Foods
Bell Gardens, CA 562-806-1100
Clearwater Fine Foods
Bedford, NS 902-443-0550
ConAgra Shrimp Companies
Tampa, FL. 813-241-1501
Cook Inlet Processing
Nikiski, AK 907-776-8174
Cowart Seafood Corporation
Lottsburg, VA 804-529-6101
Crab King Seafood Specialties
Seattle, WA. 206-283-2722
Cuizina Food Company
Woodinville, WA. 425-486-7000
Daley Brothers
St John's, NL. 709-364-8844
Depoe Bay Fish Company
Newport, OR. 541-265-8833
Fishery Products International
Danvers, MA. 800-374-4700
Fogo Island Cooperative Society
Seldom, NL. 709-627-3452
Great Northern Products
Warwick, RI 401-490-4590

Gulf City Seafoods
Pascagoula, MS. 800-666-3300
Higgins Seafood
Lafitte, LA 504-689-3577
Icicle Seafoods
Seattle, WA. 206-282-0988
Independent Packers Corporation
Seattle, WA. 206-285-6000
International Oceanic Enterprises of Alabama
Bayou La Batre, AL 800-816-1832
J. Matassini & Sons Fish Company
Tampa, FL. 813-229-0829
Jessie's Ilwaco Fish Company
Ilwaco, WA 360-642-3773
Keyser Brothers
Lottsburg, VA 804-529-6837
Kirkland Custom Seafoods
Kirkland, WA 800-321-3474
Kitchens Seafood
Plant City, FL 800-327-0132
Menemsha Fish Market
Chilmark, MA. 508-645-2282
Milfico Foods
Elk Grove Vlg, IL 847-427-0491
Mutual Fish Company
Seattle, WA. 206-322-4368
Notre Dame Seafood
Comfort Cove, NL 709-244-5511
Pacific Shrimp Company
Newport, OR. 541-265-4215
Pamlico Packing Company
Grantsboro, NC 800-682-1113
Portland Shellfish Company
South Portland, ME 207-799-9290
Sea Garden Seafoods
Meridian, GA 912-832-4437
Sea Safari
Belhaven, NC 800-688-6174
Sea Safari Limited
Belhaven, NC 800-688-6174
Sea Watch International
Easton, MD 410-822-7500
Silver Lining Seafood
Ketchikan, AK 907-225-6664
St. Ours & Company
Norwell, MA. 781-331-8520
Stone Crabs
Miami Beach, FL 800-260-2722
Sunshine Food Sales
Miami, FL 305-696-2885
Taku Smokehouse
Juneau, AK 800-582-5122
Taylor Shellfish Farms
Shelton, WA 360-426-6178
Taylor's Frozen Foods
Charleston, SC 843-723-1878
Trident Seafoods Corporation
Seattle, WA. 800-426-5490
Ward Cove Packing Company
Seattle, WA. 206-323-3200
Washington Crab Producers
Westport, WA 360-268-9161
Wrangell Fisheries
Wrangell, AK 907-874-3346

King

All Alaskan Seafood
Seattle, WA. 206-285-8200
Arctic Seas
Little Compton, RI 401-635-4000
Arrowac Fisheries
Seattle, WA. 206-282-5655
Bolner's Fiesta Products
San Antonio, TX 210-734-6404
Crab King Seafood Specialties
Seattle, WA. 206-283-2722
New Ocean
Doraville, GA 770-458-5235
Ocean Garden Products
San Diego, CA 858-571-5002
Sitka Sound Seafoods
Sitka, AK. 907-747-6662
Trident Seafoods Corporation
Seattle, WA. 800-426-5490

Live

Dorchester Crab Company
Wingate, MD. 410-397-8103

Meat

Atlantic Queen Seafoods Limited
  Lachine, QC 514-636-5114
Bandon Bay Fisheries
  Bandon, OR 541-347-4454
Bay Hundred Seafood
  McDaniel, MD 410-745-9329
Bayou Foods
  Kenner, LA 800-516-8283
Bayou Land Seafood
  Breaux Bridge, LA 337-667-6118
Beaver Street Fisheries
  Jacksonville, FL 800-874-6426
Blalock Seafood
  Orange Beach, AL 251-974-5811
Blue Crab Bay Company
  Melfa, VA .800-221-2722
Boja's Foods
  Bayou La Batre, AL 251-824-4186
Certi-Fresh Foods
  Bell Gardens, CA 562-806-1100
Charles H. Parks & Company
  Fishing Creek, MD 410-397-3400
Day's Crabmeat & Lobster
  Yarmouth, ME. 207-846-5871
Dorchester Crab Company
  Wingate, MD. 410-397-8103
Hallmark Fisheries
  Charleston, OR 541-888-3253
Harmon's Original Clam Cakes
  Kennebunkport, ME 207-283-1091
Keyser Brothers
  Lottsburg, VA 804-529-6837
Kirkland Custom Seafoods
  Kirkland, WA 800-321-3474
Little River Seafood
  Reedville, VA 804-453-3670
Martin Brothers Seafood Company
  Westwego, LA 504-341-2251
Mercado Latino
  City of Industry, CA 626-333-6862
Mutual Fish Company
  Seattle, WA 206-322-4368
Nelson Crab
  Tokeland, WA 800-262-0069
Pamlico Packing Company
  Grantsboro, NC. 800-682-1113
Penguin Frozen Foods
  Northbrook, IL 847-291-9400
Peter Pan Seafoods
  Seattle, WA 206-728-6000
Petersburg Fisheries
  Petersburg, AK 877-772-4294
Phillips Foods
  Baltimore, MD 800-782-2722
Phillips Foods
  Baltimore, MD 888-234-2722
Rippons Brothers Seafood
  Fishing Creek, MD 410-397-3200
Sea Garden Seafoods
  Meridian, GA 912-832-4437
Sea Safari
  Belhaven, NC 252-943-3091
Sea Safari
  Belhaven, NC 800-688-6174
Sea Safari Limited
  Belhaven, NC 800-688-6174
Sea Watch International
  Easton, MD. 410-822-7500
Seafood Network
  Brunswick, GA 912-267-0422
Southern Shell Fish Company
  Harvey, LA 504-341-5631
Toddville Seafoods
  Toddville, MD. 410-397-8129
Van Dykes Chesapeake Seafood
  Cambridge, MD 410-228-9000
Victory Seafood
  Abbeville, LA 337-893-9029
W.T. Ruark & Company
  Fishing Creek, MD 410-397-3133

Meat Canned

Bayou Land Seafood
  Breaux Bridge, LA 337-667-6118
Cathay Foods Corporation
  Boston, MA. 617-427-1507
Charles H. Parks & Company
  Fishing Creek, MD 410-397-3400
Day's Crabmeat & Lobster
  Yarmouth, ME. 207-846-5871

Martin Brothers Seafood Company
  Westwego, LA 504-341-2251
Mercado Latino
  City of Industry, CA 626-333-6862
Miami Crab Corporation
  Miami, FL .800-269-8395
Orleans Food Company
  New Orleans, LA 800-628-4900
Peter Pan Seafoods
  Seattle, WA 206-728-6000
Petersburg Fisheries
  Petersburg, AK 877-772-4294
Phillips Foods
  Baltimore, MD 800-782-2722
Sea Safari
  Belhaven, NC 800-688-6174
Southern Shell Fish Company
  Harvey, LA 504-341-5631

Meat Frozen

Atlantic Queen Seafoods Limited
  Lachine, QC 514-636-5114
Bandon Bay Fisheries
  Bandon, OR 541-347-4454
Bayou Land Seafood
  Breaux Bridge, LA 337-667-6118
Beaver Street Fisheries
  Jacksonville, FL 800-874-6426
Cathay Foods Corporation
  Boston, MA. 617-427-1507
Certi-Fresh Foods
  Bell Gardens, CA 562-806-1100
Day's Crabmeat & Lobster
  Yarmouth, ME. 207-846-5871
International Oceanic Enterprises of Alabama
  Bayou La Batre, AL 800-816-1832
Keyser Brothers
  Lottsburg, VA 804-529-6837
Martin Brothers Seafood Company
  Westwego, LA 504-341-2251
Miami Crab Corporation
  Miami, FL .800-269-8395
Nelson Crab
  Tokeland, WA 800-262-0069
Penguin Frozen Foods
  Northbrook, IL 847-291-9400
Peter Pan Seafoods
  Seattle, WA 206-728-6000
Petersburg Fisheries
  Petersburg, AK 877-772-4294
Phillips Foods
  Baltimore, MD 800-782-2722
Sea Garden Seafoods
  Meridian, GA 912-832-4437
Victory Seafood
  Abbeville, LA 337-893-9029

Snow

All Alaskan Seafood
  Seattle, WA 206-285-8200
Arctic Seas
  Little Compton, RI 401-635-4000
Arrowac Fisheries
  Seattle, WA 206-282-5655
Bolner's Fiesta Products
  San Antonio, TX 210-734-6404
Breakwater Fisheries
  St. John's, NL 709-754-1999
Buns & Things Bakery
  Charlottetown, PE 902-892-2600
Crab King Seafood Specialties
  Seattle, WA 206-283-2722
New Ocean
  Doraville, GA 770-458-5235
Polar Foods International
  Charlottetown, PE 902-962-3303
Sea Safari Limited
  Belhaven, NC 800-688-6174
Sitka Sound Seafoods
  Sitka, AK. .907-747-6662
Taku Smokehouse
  Juneau, AK 800-582-5122

Soft Shell

Bayou Foods
  Kenner, LA 800-516-8283
Bolner's Fiesta Products
  San Antonio, TX 210-734-6404
Cowart Seafood Corporation
  Lottsburg, VA 804-529-6101

John T. Handy Company
  Salisbury, MD 800-426-3977
Rippons Brothers Seafood
  Fishing Creek, MD 410-397-3200
W.T. Ruark & Company
  Fishing Creek, MD 410-397-3133

Stone

Stone Crabs
  Miami Beach, FL 800-260-2722

Stuffed

Belle River Enterprises
  Belle River, PE 902-962-2248
Bolner's Fiesta Products
  San Antonio, TX. 210-734-6404
Bon Secour Fisheries
  Bon Secour, AL. 800-633-6854
Claytons Crab Company
  Rockledge, FL. 321-639-0161
Dick & Casey's Gourmet Seafoods
  Harbor, OR 800-662-9494
E. Gagnon & Fils
  St Therese-De-Gaspe, QC. 418-385-3011
Gulf City Seafoods
  Pascagoula, MS. 800-666-3300
International Oceanic Enterprises of Alabama
  Bayou La Batre, AL 800-816-1832
John T. Handy Company
  Salisbury, MD 800-426-3977
Kirkland Custom Seafoods
  Kirkland, WA 800-321-3474
Lowland Seafood
  Lowland, NC 252-745-3751
Menemsha Fish Market
  Chilmark, MA. 508-645-2282
Nan Sea Enterprises of Wisconsin
  Waukesha, WI. 262-542-8841
Pamlico Packing Company
  Grantsboro, NC 800-682-1113
Randol
  Lafayette, LA 337-981-7080
Rippons Brothers Seafood
  Fishing Creek, MD 410-397-3200
Shawmut Fishing Company
  Anchorage, AK 709-334-2559
Ward Cove Packing Company
  Seattle, WA 206-323-3200

Crayfish

Bayou Land Seafood
  Breaux Bridge, LA 337-667-6118
Catahoula Crawfish
  St Martinville, LA. 337-394-4223
Louisiana Crawfish Company
  Natchitoches, LA 318-379-0539
Ocean Pride Seafood
  Delcambre, LA 337-685-2336
Raffield Fisheries
  Port St Joe, FL. 850-229-8229
Rivere's Seafood Processors
  Paincourtville, LA. 985-369-6055
Vince's Seafoods
  Gretna, LA 504-368-1544

Frozen

Bayou Land Seafood
  Breaux Bridge, LA 337-667-6118

Live

Belle River Enterprises
  Belle River, PE 902-962-2248
Depoe Bay Fish Company
  Newport, OR. 541-265-8833

Raw

Bayou Land Seafood
  Breaux Bridge, LA 337-667-6118

Dehydrated

Gulf City Seafoods
  Pascagoula, MS. 800-666-3300
Mercer Processing
  Modesto, CA. 209-529-0150

Fresh

Acme Steak & Seafood Company
Youngstown, OH 330-270-8000
Arrowac Fisheries
Seattle, WA 206-282-5655
Bay Oceans Sea Foods
Garibaldi, OR 503-322-3316
Bayou Land Seafood
Breaux Bridge, LA 337-667-6118
BG Smith Sons Oyster
Sharps, VA 877-483-8279
Blount Seafood Corporation
Fall River, MA 774-888-1300
BlueWater Seafoods
Lachine, QC 888-560-2539
Bolner's Fiesta Products
San Antonio, TX 210-734-6404
Bon Secour Fisheries
Bon Secour, AL. 800-633-6854
Bornstein Seafoods
Warrenton, OR 503-861-1233
C.F. Gollott & Son Seafood
Biloxi, MS. 866-846-3474
Charles H. Parks & Company
Fishing Creek, MD 410-397-3400
Coast Seafoods Company
Bellevue, WA 800-423-2303
Cowart Seafood Corporation
Lottsburg, VA 804-529-6101
Cozy Harbor Seafood
Portland, OR. 800-225-2586
Depoe Bay Fish Company
Newport, OR. 541-265-8833
Eastern Shore Seafood Products
Mappsville, VA 800-466-8550
Fishery Products International
Danvers, MA. 800-374-4700
Gulf City Marine Supply
Bayou La Batre, AL 251-824-4154
Gulf City Seafoods
Pascagoula, MS. 800-666-3300
Gulf Pride Enterprises
Biloxi, MS. 888-689-0560
Hallmark Fisheries
Charleston, OR 541-888-3253
Hillard Bloom Packing Co
Port Norris, NJ 856-785-0120
Hillman Shrimp & Oyster
Dickinson, TX. 800-582-4416
Icicle Seafoods
Seattle, WA 206-282-0988
Independent Packers Corporation
Seattle, WA 206-285-6000
Intervest Trading Company
Halifax, NS 902-425-2018
IOE Atlanta
Galena, MD. 410-755-6300
Island Marine Products
Clarks Harbour, NS. 902-745-2222
J. Matassini & Sons Fish Company
Tampa, FL. 813-229-0829
JCW Tawes & Son
Crisfield, MD 410-968-1288
Jessie's Ilwaco Fish Company
Ilwaco, WA 360-642-3773
Keyser Brothers
Lottsburg, VA 804-529-6837
LaMonica Fine Foods
Millville, NJ 856-825-8111
Little River Seafood
Reedville, VA 804-453-3670
Mersey Seafoods
Liverpool, NS 902-354-3467
Miles J H & Company
Norfolk, VA. 757-622-9264
Minterbrook Oyster Company
Gig Harbor, WA 253-857-5251
National Fish & Oysters Company
Olympia, WA 360-491-5550
Nelson Crab
Tokeland, WA 800-262-0069
North Atlantic Fish Company
Gloucester, MA. 978-283-4121
Omstead Foods Ltd
Burlington, ON 905-315-8883
P&J Oyster Company
New Orleans, LA 504-523-2651
Pacific Salmon Company
Edmonds, WA 425-774-1315
Pacific Shrimp Company
Newport, OR. 541-265-4215

Paul Piazza & Sons
New Orleans, LA 504-524-6011
Peter Pan Seafoods
Seattle, WA 206-728-6000
Petersburg Fisheries
Petersburg, AK 877-772-4294
Portland Shellfish Company
South Portland, ME 207-799-9290
Quality Seafood
Apalachicola, FL. 850-653-9696
RCV Seafood Corporation
Morattico, VA 804-462-5101
Rippons Brothers Seafood
Fishing Creek, MD 410-397-3200
Royal Seafood
Monterey, CA 831-655-8326
Ruggiero Seafood
Newark, NJ 800-543-2110
Sea Garden Seafoods
Meridian, GA 912-832-4437
Sea Products Company
Watsonville, CA 831-768-2600
Seafood Producers Cooperative
Bellingham, WA 360-733-0120
Sportsmen's Cannery & Smokehouse
Winchester Bay, OR 541-271-3293
Stone Crabs
Miami Beach, FL 800-260-2722
Sweet Water Seafood Corporation
Carlstadt, NJ 201-939-6622
Taylor Shellfish Farms
Shelton, WA 360-426-6178
Terry Brothers
Temperanceville, VA. 757-824-3471
Tichon Seafood Corporation
New Bedford, MA 508-999-5607
Wanchese Fish Company
Suffolk, VA 757-673-4500
Ward Cove Packing Company
Seattle, WA 206-323-3200
Washington Crab Producers
Westport, WA 360-268-9161
Western Alaska Fisheries
Seattle, WA 206-447-4400
Wiegardt Brothers
Ocean Park, WA 360-665-4111
Wrangell Fisheries
Wrangell, AK 907-874-3346
Young's Lobster Pound
Belfast, ME 207-338-1160

Frozen

All Alaskan Seafood
Seattle, WA 206-285-8200
Appert's Foodservice
St Cloud, MN 800-225-3883
APTCO
San Francisco, CA 415-648-6688
Arctic Seas
Little Compton, RI 401-635-4000
Arista Industries
Wilton, CT 800-255-6457
Arrowac Fisheries
Seattle, WA 206-282-5655
Atlantic Queen Seafoods Limited
Lachine, QC 514-636-5114
Bandon Bay Fisheries
Bandon, OR 541-347-4454
Bayou Land Seafood
Breaux Bridge, LA 337-667-6118
Beaver Street Fisheries
Jacksonville, FL 800-874-6426
BG Smith Sons Oyster
Sharps, VA 877-483-8279
Bon Secour Fisheries
Bon Secour, AL. 800-633-6854
Bornstein Seafoods
Warrenton, OR 503-861-1233
Breakwater Fisheries
St. John's, NL 709-754-1999
Buns & Things Bakery
Charlottetown, PE 902-892-2600
Callis Seafood
Lancaster, VA 804-462-7634
Carrington Foods
Saraland, AL 251-675-9700
Cathay Foods Corporation
Boston, MA. 617-427-1507
Caver Shellfish
Beals, ME 207-497-2629

Certi-Fresh Foods
Bell Gardens, CA 562-806-1100
Clearwater Fine Foods
Bedford, NS 902-443-0550
Coldwater Seafood Corporation
Norwalk, CT 203-846-8897
ConAgra Foods
Tampa, FL. 813-241-1500
Cook Inlet Processing
Nikiski, AK. 907-776-8174
Cowart Seafood Corporation
Lottsburg, VA 804-529-6101
Cozy Harbor Seafood
Portland, ME 800-225-2586
Crab King Seafood Specialties
Seattle, WA 206-283-2722
Cuizina Food Company
Woodinville, WA. 425-486-7000
Daerim America
Maywood, NJ 800-635-0781
Deep Sea Foods
Bayou La Batre, AL 251-824-7000
Eastern Fish Company
Teaneck, NJ 800-526-9066
Eastern Quebec Sea Foods
Matane, QC 418-562-1273
Eastern Shore Seafood Products
Mappsville, VA 800-466-8550
Fishery Products International
Danvers, MA. 800-374-4700
FishKing
Bayou La Batre, AL 334-824-2118
Florida Carib Fishery
Doral, FL. .305-696-2896
Glacier Fish Company
Seattle, WA 206-298-1200
Golden Gulf Coast Packing Company
Biloxi, MS. 228-374-6121
Great Northern Products
Warwick, RI 401-490-4590
Gulf City Marine Supply
Bayou La Batre, AL 251-824-4154
Hallmark Fisheries
Charleston, OR 541-888-3253
Hillard Bloom Packing Co
Port Norris, NJ 856-785-0120
Hillman Shrimp & Oyster
Dickinson, TX. 800-582-4416
Icelandic USA
Newport News, VA 757-820-4000
Icicle Seafoods
Seattle, WA 206-282-0988
Independent Packers Corporation
Seattle, WA 206-285-6000
Indian Ridge Shrimp Company
Chauvin, LA 985-594-5869
International Seafood Distributors
Hayes, VA 804-642-1417
Intervest Trading Company
Halifax, NS 902-425-2018
Island Marine Products
Clarks Harbour, NS. 902-745-2222
J. Matassini & Sons Fish Company
Tampa, FL. 813-229-0829
Janes Family Foods
Mississauga, ON 800-565-2637
Jessie's Ilwaco Fish Company
Ilwaco, WA 360-642-3773
John T. Handy Company
Salisbury, MD. 800-426-3977
Key Largo Fisheries
Key Largo, FL. 800-399-6970
Keyser Brothers
Lottsburg, VA 804-529-6837
Lu-Mar Lobster & Shrimp
Brownsville, TX 956-546-5525
Lund's Fisheries
Cape May, NJ 609-884-7600
Matlaw's Food Products
West Haven, CT 800-934-8266
Maxim's Import Corporation
Miami, FL. 800-331-6652
Menemsha Fish Market
Chilmark, MA. 508-645-2282
Mersey Seafoods
Liverpool, NS 902-354-3467
Mid-Atlantic Foods
Easton, MD. 800-922-4688
Miles J H & Company
Norfolk, VA. 757-622-9264
Milfico Foods
Elk Grove Vlg, IL. 847-427-0491

Minterbrook Oyster Company
Gig Harbor, WA 253-857-5251
National Fish & Oysters Company
Olympia, WA 360-491-5550
Nelson Crab
Tokeland, WA 800-262-0069
Neptune Fisheries
Newport News, VA 800-545-7474
North Atlantic Fish Company
Gloucester, MA 978-283-4121
O'Hara Corporation
Rockland, ME 207-594-0405
Okuhara Foods
Honolulu, HI 808-848-0581
Omstead Foods Ltd
Burlington, ON 905-315-8883
P&J Oyster Company
New Orleans, LA 504-523-2651
Pacific Salmon Company
Edmonds, WA 425-774-1315
Pacific Shrimp Company
Newport, OR 541-265-4215
Pacific Surf Food Processors
Los Angeles, CA 800-627-5657
Paul Piazza & Sons
New Orleans, LA 504-524-6011
Penguin Frozen Foods
Northbrook, IL 847-291-9400
Petersburg Fisheries
Petersburg, AK 877-772-4294
Pinnacle Foods Group
Cherry Hill, NJ 877-852-7424
Port Chatham Smoked Seafood
Everett, WA 800-872-5666
Portland Shellfish Company
South Portland, ME 207-799-9290
Quality Seafood
Apalachicola, FL 850-653-9696
Rich-Seapak Corporation
Brownsville, TX 956-542-0001
Royal Seafood
Monterey, CA 831-655-8326
Ruggiero Seafood
Newark, NJ 800-543-2110
Sea Garden Seafoods
Meridian, GA 912-832-4437
Sea Pearl Seafood
Bayou La Batre, AL 800-872-8804
Sea Safari Limited
Belhaven, NC 800-688-6174
Sea Snack Foods
Los Angeles, CA 213-622-2204
Seafood Producers Cooperative
Bellingham, WA 360-733-0120
Seaspan Products Corporation
New York, NY 201-569-9234
Seymour & Sons Seafood
Diberville, MS 228-392-4020
Silver Lining Seafood
Ketchikan, AK 907-225-6664
Southern Star Seafood
Fort Pierce, FL 561-461-5787
St. Ours & Company
Norwell, MA 781-331-8520
Stone Crabs
Miami Beach, FL 800-260-2722
Taku Smokehouse
Juneau, AK 800-582-5122
Tampa Bay Fisheries
Dover, FL 800-234-2561
Tampa Maid Foods
Lakeland, FL 800-237-7637
Taylor Shellfish Farms
Shelton, WA 360-426-6178
Taylor's Frozen Foods
Charleston, SC 843-723-1878
Tichon Seafood Corporation
New Bedford, MA 508-999-5607
Trident Seafoods Corporation
Seattle, WA 800-426-5490
Triton Seafood Company
Medley, FL 305-805-3500
Viking Seafoods Inc
Malden, MA 800-225-3020
Vince's Seafoods
Gretna, LA 504-368-1544
Wanchese Fish Company
Suffolk, VA 757-673-4500
Washington Crab Producers
Westport, WA 360-268-9161
Western Alaska Fisheries
Seattle, WA 206-447-4400

Wrangell Fisheries
Wrangell, AK 907-874-3346
Young's Lobster Pound
Belfast, ME 207-338-1160

Geoduck Clams

Peter Pan Seafoods
Seattle, WA 206-728-6000

Langostinos

Kitchens Seafood
Plant City, FL 800-327-0132

Live

Caver Shellfish
Beals, ME 207-497-2629

Lobster

Acme Steak & Seafood Company
Youngstown, OH 330-270-8000
Adams Fisheries Ltd
Shag Harbour, NS 902-723-2435
Arista Industries
Wilton, CT 800-255-6457
Atlantic Queen Seafoods Limited
Lachine, QC 514-636-5114
B.B.S. Lobster Company
Machiasport, ME 207-255-8888
Barry Group
Corner Brook, NL 709-785-7387
Bauhaven Lobster
York, ME 207-363-5265
Bayley's Lobster Pound
Scarborough, ME 207-883-4571
Beal's Lobster Pier
Southwest Harbor, ME 800-244-7178
Bickford Daniel Lobster Company
Vinalhaven, ME 207-863-4688
Black Duck Cove Lobster
Beals, ME 207-497-2232
Blount Seafood Corporation
Fall River, MA 774-888-1300
Bolner's Fiesta Products
San Antonio, TX 210-734-6404
Bon Secour Fisheries
Bon Secour, AL 800-633-6854
Boothbay Region Lobsterman
Boothbay Harbor, ME 207-633-4900
Boston Direct Lobster
Gretna, LA 504-834-6404
C.B.S. Lobster Company
Portland, ME 207-772-9056
Castle Hill Lobster
Ipswich, MA 978-356-3947
Ceilidh Fisherman's Cooperative
Inverness, NS 902-787-2666
Certi-Fresh Foods
Bell Gardens, CA 562-806-1100
Charles M. Cook
Bailey Island, ME 207-833-6641
Chases Lobster Pound
Port Howe, NS 902-243-2408
Clearwater Fine Foods
Bedford, NS 902-443-0550
Coastside Lobster Company
Stonington, ME 207-367-2297
Corea Lobster Cooperative
Corea, ME 207-963-7936
Cranberry Isles Fisherman's Cooperative
Islesford, ME 207-244-5438
Cummings Lobster Company
Kennebunk, ME 207-985-1677
D Waybret & Sons Fisher ies
Shelburne, NS 902-745-3477
DB Kenney Fisheries
Westport, NS 902-839-2023
Dick & Casey's Gourmet Seafoods
Harbor, OR 800-662-9494
Dorset Fisheries
St. John's, NL 709-739-7147
Dunham's Lobster Pot
Avon, ME 207-639-2815
Fisherman's Market International
Halifax, NS 902-445-3474
Florida Carib Fishery
Doral, FL 305-696-2896
FW Thurston
Bernard, ME 207-244-3320

Giovanni's Appetizing Food Products
Richmond, MI 586-727-9355
Goldcoast Salads
Naples, FL 239-304-0710
Gorman Fisheries
Conception Bay, NL 709-229-6536
Gouldsboro Enterprises
Gouldsboro, ME 207-963-4024
Graffam Brothers Lobster Company
Rockport, ME 800-535-5358
Great Northern Products
Warwick, RI 401-490-4590
Greg's Lobster Company
Harwich Port, MA 508-432-8080
Grindle Point Lobster Company
Lincolnville, ME 207-763-4142
H&H Fisheries Limited
Eastern Passage, NS 902-465-6330
Howard Turner & Son
Marie Joseph, NS 902-347-2616
I. Deveau Fisheries
Meteghan, NS 902-645-3036
Innovative Fishery Products
Clarks Harbour, NS. 902-837-5163
International Enterprises
Herring Neck, NL 709-628-7406
Island Fisheries
Matinicus, ME 207-366-3937
Island Marine Products
Clarks Harbour, NS 902-745-2222
J. Matassini & Sons Fish Company
Tampa, FL 813-229-0829
Jack's Lobsters
Musquodoboit Harbor, NS 902-889-2771
Kitchens Seafood
Plant City, FL 800-327-0132
Kittery Lobster Company
Kittery, ME 207-439-6035
Kona Cold Lobsters Ltd
Kailua Kona, HI 808-329-4332
L&C Fisheries
Kensington, PE 902-886-2770
Little River Lobster Company
East Boothbay, ME 207-633-2648
Lobster Gram International
Chicago, IL 800-548-3562
Look Lobster
Jonesport, ME 207-497-2353
Look's Gourmet Food Company
Whiting, ME 800-962-6258
Lusty Lobster
Portland, ME 207-773-2829
Maine Lobster Outlet
York, ME 207-363-4449
McGraw Seafood
Tracadie Sheila, NB 506-395-3374
Menemsha Fish Market
Chilmark, MA 508-645-2282
Milfico Products
Elk Grove Vlg, IL 847-427-0491
Mill Cove Lobster Pound
Boothbay Harbor, ME 207-633-3340
Moon Enterprises
Richmond, BC 604-270-0088
Nan Sea Enterprises of Wisconsin
Waukesha, WI 262-542-8841
New England Marketers
Boston, MA 800-688-9904
New Harbor Fisherman's Cooperative
New Harbor, ME 866-883-2922
Newell Lobsters
Yarmouth, NS 902-742-6272
North Lake Fish Cooperative
Elmira, PE 902-357-2572
Northern Wind
New Bedford, MA 888-525-2525
Notre Dame Seafood
Comfort Cove, NL 709-244-5511
P.M. Innis Lobster Company
Biddeford Pool, ME 207-284-5000
Paul Piazza & Sons
New Orleans, LA 504-524-6011
Paul Stevens Lobster
Hingham, MA 781-740-8001
Penguin Frozen Foods
Northbrook, IL 847-291-9400
Pine Point Seafood
Scarborough, ME 207-883-4701
Polar Foods International
Charlottetown, PE 902-962-3303
Port Lobster Company
Kennebunkport, ME 800-486-7029

Produits Belle Baie
Caraquet, NB 506-727-4414
Resource Trading Company
Portland, ME 207-772-2299
Rockport Lobster
Gloucester, MA.................978-281-0225
Sealand Lobster Corporation
Tenants Harbor, ME 207-372-6247
Seaspan Products Corporation
New York, NY.................201-569-9234
Seymour & Sons Seafood
Diberville, MS 228-392-4020
Southern Star Seafood
Fort Pierce, FL 561-461-5787
St. Ours & Company
Norwell, MA.................781-331-8520
Stavis Seafoods
Boston, MA.................800-390-5103
Stone Crabs
Miami Beach, FL 800-260-2722
Stonington Lobster Cooperative
Stonington, ME 207-367-2286
Straub's
Clayton, MO.................888-725-2121
Sunshine Food Sales
Miami, FL.................305-696-2885
Tampa Bay Fisheries
Dover, FL.................800-234-2561
Thomas Lobster Company
Islesford, ME 207-244-5876
Three Rivers Fish Company
Simmesport, LA.................318-941-2467
Trenton Bridge Lobster Pound
Trenton, ME 207-667-2977
United Shellfish Company
Grasonville, MD.................410-827-8171
West Brothers Lobster
Steuben, ME 207-546-3622
Young's Lobster Pound
Belfast, ME.................207-338-1160

Fresh

Captain Joe & Sons
Gloucester, MA.................978-283-1454
CB Seafoods
Inverness, NS 902-895-8181
Clearwater Fine Foods
Bedford, NS 902-443-0550
High Sea Foods
Glovertown, NL 709-533-2626
J. Matassini & Sons Fish Company
Tampa, FL.................813-229-0829
Menemsha Fish Market
Chilmark, MA.................508-645-2282
Paul Piazza & Sons
New Orleans, LA 504-524-6011
Portland Shellfish Company
South Portland, ME 207-799-9290
Poseidon Enterprises
Atlanta, GA.................800-863-7886
St. Ours & Company
Norwell, MA.................781-331-8520
Stone Crabs
Miami Beach, FL 800-260-2722
Sunshine Food Sales
Miami, FL.................305-696-2885

Frozen

Acme Steak & Seafood Company
Youngstown, OH.................330-270-8000
Arista Industries
Wilton, CT 800-255-6457
Atlantic Queen Seafoods Limited
Lachine, QC 514-636-5114
Bolner's Fiesta Products
San Antonio, TX.................210-734-6404
CB Seafoods
Inverness, NS 902-895-8181
Certi-Fresh Foods
Bell Gardens, CA 562-806-1100
Coldwater Seafood Corporation
Norwalk, CT 203-846-8897
ConAgra Shrimp Companies
Tampa, FL.................813-241-1501
Great Northern Products
Warwick, RI 401-490-4590
Island Marine Products
Clarks Harbour, NS.................902-745-2222
J. Matassini & Sons Fish Company
Tampa, FL.................813-229-0829

Kitchens Seafood
Plant City, FL 800-327-0132
Menemsha Fish Market
Chilmark, MA.................508-645-2282
Milfico Foods
Elk Grove Vlg, IL.................847-427-0491
North Bay Fisherman's Cooperative
Ballantyne's Cove, NS 902-863-4988
Notre Dame Seafood
Comfort Cove, NL 709-244-5511
Paul Piazza & Sons
New Orleans, LA 504-524-6011
Penguin Frozen Foods
Northbrook, IL 847-291-9400
Portland Shellfish Company
South Portland, ME 207-799-9290
Seaspan Products Corporation
New York, NY.................201-569-9234
Seymour & Sons Seafood
Diberville, MS 228-392-4020
Southern Star Seafood
Fort Pierce, FL 561-461-5787
Stone Crabs
Miami Beach, FL 800-260-2722
Sunshine Food Sales
Miami, FL.................305-696-2885
Tampa Bay Fisheries
Dover, FL.................800-234-2561

Live

Canus Fisheries
Clark's Harbour, NS.................902-745-2888
Chases Lobster Pound
Port Howe, NS 902-243-2408
Crustaces de la Malbaie
Gaspe, QC.................418-368-1414
DB Kenney Fisheries
Westport, NS 902-839-2023
H&H Fisheries Limited
Eastern Passage, NS 902-465-6330
Harbor Lobster
Shelburne, NS 902-723-2500
Island Marine Products
Clarks Harbour, NS.................902-745-2222
James L. Mood Fisheries
Wood's Harbour, NS.................902-723-2360
Johns Cove Fisheries
Yarmouth, NS 902-742-8691
Lumar Lobster Corporatio
Lawrence, NY 516-371-0083
Menemsha Fish Market
Chilmark, MA.................508-645-2282
New England Marketers
Boston, MA.................800-688-9904

Meat

Acme Steak & Seafood Company
Youngstown, OH.................330-270-8000
Atlantic Queen Seafoods Limited
Lachine, QC.................514-636-5114
Island Marine Products
Clarks Harbour, NS.................902-745-2222
Southern Star Seafood
Fort Pierce, FL 561-461-5787

Tails

Anchor Frozen Foods
Westbury, NY 800-566-3474
Arista Industries
Wilton, CT 800-255-6457
Coldwater Seafood Corporation
Norwalk, CT 203-846-8897
Florida Carib Fishery
Doral, FL.................305-696-2896
Icelandic USA
Newport News, VA.................757-820-4000
King & Prince Seafood Corporation
Brunswick, GA.................800-841-0205
Milfico Foods
Elk Grove Vlg, IL.................847-427-0491
Neptune Fisheries
Newport News, VA.................800-545-7474
New Ocean
Doraville, GA 770-458-5235
Ocean Garden Products
San Diego, CA 858-571-5002
Seaspan Products Corporation
New York, NY 201-569-9234
Stone Crabs
Miami Beach, FL 800-260-2722

Mussels

Atlantic Aqua Farms
Vernon Bridge, PE 902-651-2563
Atlantic Mussel Growers Corporation
Point Pleasant, PE.................800-838-3106
Blount Seafood Corporation
Fall River, MA.................774-888-1300
Country Harbor Sea Farms
Country Harbor, NS 902-387-2364
Hillman Shrimp & Oyster
Dickinson, TX.................800-582-4416
L&C Fisheries
Kensington, PE 902-886-2770
Look's Gourmet Food Company
Whiting, ME 800-962-6258
Milfico Foods
Elk Grove Vlg, IL.................847-427-0491
Minterbrook Oyster Company
Gig Harbor, WA 253-857-5251
New England Marketers
Boston, MA.................800-688-9904
PEI Mussel King
Morrell, PE 800-673-2767
Polar Foods International
Charlottetown, PE.................902-962-3303
Stavis Seafoods
Boston, MA.................800-390-5103
Sweet Water Seafood Corporation
Carlstadt, NJ 201-939-6622
Taylor Shellfish Farms
Shelton, WA.................360-426-6178

Octopus

Anchor Frozen Foods
Westbury, NY 800-566-3474
Arista Industries
Wilton, CT 800-255-6457
FishKing
Bayou La Batre, AL 334-824-2118
Miles J H & Company
Norfolk, VA.................757-622-9264

Oysters

AmeriPure Processing Company
Franklin, LA 800-328-6729
Ameripure Processing Company
Kenner, LA 504-467-0474
Aquatec Seafoods Ltd.
Comox, BC 250-339-6412
Atlantic Aqua Farms
Vernon Bridge, PE 902-651-2563
Atlantic Capes Fisheries
Cape May, NJ 609-884-3000
Bay Hundred Seafood
McDaniel, MD 410-745-9329
BG Smith Sons Oyster
Sharps, VA.................877-483-8279
Blalock Seafood
Orange Beach, AL 251-974-5811
Blau Oyster Company
Bow, WA 360-766-6171
Bolner's Fiesta Products
San Antonio, TX.................210-734-6404
Bon Secour Fisheries
Bon Secour, AL.................800-633-6854
Braun Seafood Company
Cutchogue, NY 631-734-5550
Bumble Bee Seafoods
San Diego, CA 858-715-4000
Callis Seafood
Lancaster, VA 804-462-7634
Canoe Lagoon Oyster Company
Coffman Cove, AK 907-329-2253
Carolina Seafoods
Mc Clellanville, SC 843-887-3713
Coast Seafoods Company
Bellevue, WA.................800-423-2303
Cowart Seafood Corporation
Lottsburg, VA.................804-529-6101
Crown Prince
City of Industry, CA 800-255-5063
Elwha Fish
Port Angeles, WA.................360-457-3344
Farm 2 Market
Roscoe, NY 800-663-4326
Ferme Ostreicole Dugas
Caraquet, NB 506-727-3226
Great Northern Products
Warwick, RI 401-490-4590

Gulf City Marine Supply
Bayou La Batre, AL 251-824-4154
Gulf City Seafoods
Pascagoula, MS 800-666-3300
H. Gass Seafood
Hollywood, MD 301-373-6882
Harper Seafood Company
Kinsale, VA 804-472-3310
Higgins Seafood
Lafitte, LA 504-689-3577
Hillard Bloom Packing Co
Port Norris, NJ 856-785-0120
Hillman Shrimp & Oyster
Dickinson, TX 800-582-4416
Huck's Seafood
Easton, MD 410-770-9211
J. Matassini & Sons Fish Company
Tampa, FL 813-229-0829
Joey Oysters
Amite, LA 800-748-1525
Kirkland Custom Seafoods
Kirkland, WA 800-321-3474
Louisiana Oyster Processors
Baton Rouge, LA 225-291-6923
McGraw Seafood
Tracadie Sheila, NB 506-395-3374
Mercado Latino
City of Industry, CA 626-333-6862
Milfico Foods
Elk Grove Vlg, IL 847-427-0491
Mill Cove Lobster Pound
Boothbay Harbor, ME 207-633-3340
Moon Enterprises
Richmond, BC 604-270-0088
Neptune Foods
Vernon, CA 323-232-8300
Nisbet Oyster Company
Bay Center, WA 360-875-6629
P&J Oyster Company
New Orleans, LA 504-523-2651
Pamlico Packing Company
Grantsboro, NC 800-682-1113
Pearl Reef Oyster Company
Broussard, LA 318-839-9000
PEI Mussel King
Morrell, PE 800-673-2767
Polar Foods International
Charlottetown, PE 902-962-3303
Port Chatham Smoked Seafood
Everett, WA 800-872-5666
Rich-Seapak Corporation
Brownsville, TX 956-542-0001
Rippons Brothers Seafood
Fishing Creek, MD 410-397-3200
Road Runner Seafood
Colquitt, GA 229-758-3485
Roy Dick Company
Griffin, GA 770-227-3916
Sea Pearl Seafood
Bayou La Batre, AL 800-872-8804
Southern Shell Fish Company
Harvey, LA 504-341-5631
Tampa Bay Fisheries
Dover, FL 800-234-2561
Tampa Maid Foods
Lakeland, FL 800-237-7637
Terry Brothers
Temperanceville, VA 757-824-3471
W.H. Harris Seafood
Chester, MD 410-827-8104
W.T. Ruark & Company
Fishing Creek, MD 410-397-3133
Wiegardt Brothers
Ocean Park, WA 360-665-4111
Wilson's Oysters
Houma, LA 985-857-8855

Canned

Chicken of the Sea International
San Diego, CA 800-678-8862
Crown Prince Naturals
Petaluma, CA 707-766-8575
Mercado Latino
City of Industry, CA 626-333-6862
Olympia Oyster Company
Shelton, WA 360-426-3354
Orleans Food Company
New Orleans, LA 800-628-4900
Southern Shell Fish Company
Harvey, LA 504-341-5631

Cooked

Port Chatham Smoked Seafood
Everett, WA 800-872-5666

Fresh

BG Smith Sons Oyster
Sharps, VA 877-483-8279
Blau Oyster Company
Bow, WA 360-766-6171
Boquet's Oyster House
Chauvin, LA 504-594-5574
Coast Seafoods Company
Bellevue, WA 800-423-2303
Cowart Seafood Corporation
Lottsburg, VA 804-529-6101
Great Northern Products
Warwick, RI 401-490-4590
Hillman Shrimp & Oyster
Dickinson, TX 800-582-4416
J. Matassini & Sons Fish Company
Tampa, FL 813-229-0829
Mac's Oysters
Fanny Bay, BC 250-335-2233
Minterbrook Oyster Company
Gig Harbor, WA 253-857-5251
National Fish & Oysters Company
Olympia, WA 360-491-5550
P&J Oyster Company
New Orleans, LA 504-523-2651
Port Chatham Smoked Seafood
Everett, WA 800-872-5666
Rippons Brothers Seafood
Fishing Creek, MD 410-397-3200
Taylor Shellfish Farms
Shelton, WA 360-426-6178
Terry Brothers
Temperanceville, VA 757-824-3471
Wiegardt Brothers
Ocean Park, WA 360-665-4111

Fried

J. Matassini & Sons Fish Company
Tampa, FL 813-229-0829

Frozen

BG Smith Sons Oyster
Sharps, VA 877-483-8279
Big Al's Seafood
Bozman, MD 410-745-3151
Bolner's Fiesta Products
San Antonio, TX 210-734-6404
Bon Secour Fisheries
Bon Secour, AL 800-633-6854
Boquet's Oyster House
Chauvin, LA 504-594-5574
Callis Seafood
Lancaster, VA 804-462-7634
ConAgra Shrimp Companies
Tampa, FL 813-241-1501
Cowart Seafood Corporation
Lottsburg, VA 804-529-6101
Daerim America
Maywood, NJ 800-635-0781
Great Northern Products
Warwick, RI 401-490-4590
Gulf City Seafoods
Pascagoula, MS 800-666-3300
Hillard Bloom Packing Co
Port Norris, NJ 856-785-0120
Hillman Shrimp & Oyster
Dickinson, TX 800-582-4416
Kirkland Custom Seafoods
Kirkland, WA 800-321-3474
Milfico Foods
Elk Grove Vlg, IL 847-427-0491
Minterbrook Oyster Company
Gig Harbor, WA 253-857-5251
National Fish & Oysters Company
Olympia, WA 360-491-5550
Olympia Oyster Company
Shelton, WA 360-426-3354
P&J Oyster Company
New Orleans, LA 504-523-2651
Pamlico Packing Company
Grantsboro, NC 800-682-1113
Rich-Seapak Corporation
Brownsville, TX 956-542-0001
Sea Pearl Seafood
Bayou La Batre, AL 800-872-8804

Tampa Bay Fisheries
Dover, FL 800-234-2561
Tampa Maid Foods
Lakeland, FL 800-237-7637

Prawns

NorQuest Seafoods
Seattle, WA 206-281-7022
Pots de Creme
Lexington, KY 859-299-2254

Scallops

American Seafoods International
New Bedford, MA 800-343-8046
APTCO
San Francisco, CA 415-648-6688
Arctic Seas
Little Compton, RI 401-635-4000
Arista Industries
Wilton, CT 800-255-6457
Atlantic Capes Fisheries
Cape May, NJ 609-884-3000
BlueWater Seafoods
Lachine, QC 888-560-2539
Bolner's Fiesta Products
San Antonio, TX 210-734-6404
Bon Secour Fisheries
Bon Secour, AL 800-633-6854
Braun Seafood Company
Cutchogue, NY 631-734-5550
Casey Fisheries
Digby, NS 902-245-5801
Centennial Food Corporation
Calgary, AB 403-287-2525
Certi-Fresh Foods
Bell Gardens, CA 562-806-1100
Clearwater Fine Foods
Bedford, NS 902-443-0550
Contessa Food Products
San Pedro, CA 310-832-8000
DB Kenney Fisheries
Westport, NS 902-839-2023
Ducktrap River Fish Farm
Belfast, ME 800-434-8727
Exclusive Smoked Fish
Toronto, ON 416-766-6007
Farm 2 Market
Roscoe, NY 800-663-4326
FishKing
Bayou La Batre, AL 334-824-2118
Georgia Seafood Wholesale
Chamblee, GA 770-936-0483
Great Northern Products
Warwick, RI 401-490-4590
Gulf City Seafoods
Pascagoula, MS 800-666-3300
Hillman Shrimp & Oyster
Dickinson, TX 800-582-4416
Homarus
Atlanta, GA 404-877-1988
Hygrade Ocean Products
New Bedford, MA 508-993-5700
Innovative Fishery Products
Clarks Harbour, NS 902-837-5163
Island Scallops
Qualicum Beach, BC 250-757-9811
J. Matassini & Sons Fish Company
Tampa, FL 813-229-0829
LaMonica Fine Foods
Millville, NJ 856-825-8111
Lowland Seafood
Lowland, NC 252-745-3751
Menemsha Fish Market
Chilmark, MA 508-645-2282
Milfico Foods
Elk Grove Vlg, IL 847-427-0491
Mill Cove Lobster Pound
Boothbay Harbor, ME 207-633-3340
Mills Seafood
Bouctouche, NB 506-743-2444
Neptune Fisheries
Newport News, VA 800-545-7474
Neptune Foods
Vernon, CA 323-232-8300
New Ocean
Doraville, GA 770-458-5235
North Bay Fisherman's Cooperative
Ballantyne's Cove, NS 902-863-4988
North Lake Fish Cooperative
Elmira, PE 902-357-2572

Northern Wind
New Bedford, MA 888-525-2525
O'Hara Corporation
Rockland, ME 207-594-0405
Pamlico Packing Company
Grantsboro, NC 800-682-1113
Polar Foods International
Charlottetown, PE 902-962-3303
Portier Fine Foods
Mamaroneck, NY 800-272-9463
Resource Trading Company
Portland, ME 207-772-2299
Sea Products Company
Watsonville, CA 831-768-2600
Tampa Bay Fisheries
Dover, FL 800-234-2561
Tampa Maid Foods
Lakeland, FL 800-237-7637
Taylor Shellfish Farms
Shelton, WA 360-426-6178
Taylor's Frozen Foods
Charleston, SC 843-723-1878
Tichon Seafood Corporation
New Bedford, MA 508-999-5607
United Shellfish Company
Grasonville, MD 410-827-8171
Viking Seafoods Inc
Malden, MA 800-225-3020
Wanchese Fish Company
Suffolk, VA 757-673-4500
Young's Lobster Pound
Belfast, ME 207-338-1160

Scampi

Frozen

Contessa Food Products
San Pedro, CA 310-832-8000

Shellfish

Acme Steak & Seafood Company
Youngstown, OH 330-270-8000
All Alaskan Seafood
Seattle, WA 206-285-8200
Anglo American Trading
Harvey, LA 504-341-5631
Appert's Foodservice
St Cloud, MN 800-225-3883
Appetizers And, Inc.
Chicago, IL 800-323-5472
APTCO
San Francisco, CA 415-648-6688
Aquatec Seafoods Ltd.
Comox, BC 250-339-6412
Arista Industries
Wilton, CT 800-255-6457
Arrowac Fisheries
Seattle, WA 206-282-5655
Atlantic Queen Seafoods Limited
Lachine, QC 514-636-5114
Badger Island Shell-Fish & Lobster
Kittery, ME 207-439-3820
Bandon Bay Fisheries
Bandon, OR 541-347-4454
Bay Hundred Seafood
McDaniel, MD 410-745-9329
Bay Oceans Sea Foods
Garibaldi, OR 503-322-3316
Bayou Foods
Kenner, LA 800-516-8283
Bayou Land Seafood
Breaux Bridge, LA 337-667-6118
Beaver Street Fisheries
Jacksonville, FL 800-874-6426
Bell Buoy Crab Company
Seaside, OR 800-529-2722
BG Smith Sons Oyster
Sharps, VA 877-483-8279
Blount Seafood Corporation
Fall River, MA 774-888-1300
BlueWater Seafoods
Lachine, QC 888-560-2539
Bolner's Fiesta Products
San Antonio, TX 210-734-6404
Bornstein Seafoods
Warrenton, OR 503-861-1233
Boyton Shellfish
Ellsworth, ME 207-667-8580
Bradye P. Todd & Son
Cambridge, MD 410-228-8633

Breakwater Fisheries
St. John's, NL 709-754-1999
Burris Mill & Feed
Franklinton, LA 800-928-2782
C.F. Gollott & Son Seafood
Biloxi, MS. 866-846-3474
California Shellfish Company
San Francisco, CA 415-923-7400
Callis Seafood
Lancaster, VA 804-462-7634
Carolina Seafoods
Mc Clellanville, SC 843-887-3713
Carrington Foods
Saraland, AL 251-675-9700
Cathay Foods Corporation
Boston, MA 617-427-1507
Centennial Food Corporation
Calgary, AB. 403-287-2525
Certi-Fresh Foods
Bell Gardens, CA 562-806-1100
Charles H. Parks & Company
Fishing Creek, MD 410-397-3400
Chuck's Seafoods
Charleston, OR 541-888-5525
Clearwater Fine Foods
Bedford, NS 902-443-0550
Coast Seafoods Company
Bellevue, WA 800-423-2303
Coldwater Seafood Corporation
Norwalk, CT 203-846-8897
ConAgra Frozen Foods Company
Omaha, NE 402-595-4000
Contessa Food Products
San Pedro, CA 310-832-8000
Cook Inlet Processing
Nikiski, AK. 907-776-8174
Cooke Aguaculture
Blacks Harbour, NB 506-456-6600
Cowart Seafood Corporation
Lottsburg, VA 804-529-6101
Cozy Harbor Seafood
Portland, ME 800-225-2586
Crab King Seafood Specialties
Seattle, WA 206-283-2722
Crown Prince
City of Industry, CA 800-255-5063
Cuizina Food Company
Woodinville, WA. 425-486-7000
Daerim America
Maywood, NJ 800-635-0781
DB Kenney Fisheries
Westport, NS. 902-839-2023
Deep Sea Foods
Bayou La Batre, AL 251-824-7000
Denzer's Food Products
Baltimore, MD 410-889-1500
Depoe Bay Fish Company
Newport, OR. 541-265-8833
Dorchester Crab Company
Wingate, MD. 410-397-8103
Ducktrap River Fish Farm
Belfast, ME. 800-434-8727
Eastern Fish Company
Teaneck, NJ 800-526-9066
Eastern Quebec Sea Foods
Matane, QC. 418-562-1273
Elwha Fish
Port Angeles, WA 360-457-3344
Fishery Products International
Danvers, MA. 800-374-4700
Fishhawk Fisheries
Astoria, OR 503-325-5252
FishKing
Bayou La Batre, AL 334-824-2118
Fishking Processors
Los Angeles, CA 877-677-3329
Frozen Specialties
Archbold, OH 419-445-9015
Golden Gulf Coast Packing Company
Biloxi, MS. 228-374-6121
Gollott Brothers Seafood Company
Biloxi, MS. 228-432-7865
Gorton's Seafood
Gloucester, MA. 978-283-3000
Great Northern Products
Warwick, RI 401-490-4590
Gulf City Seafoods
Pascagoula, MS. 800-666-3300
Gulf Island Shrimp & Seafood
Lake Charles, LA 985-563-4586
Gulf Pride Enterprises
Biloxi, MS. 888-689-0560

H. Gass Seafood
Hollywood, MD 301-373-6882
H.B. Dawe
Cupids, NL 709-528-4347
Henry H. Misner
Port Dover, ON 519-583-1811
Hillard Bloom Packing Co
Port Norris, NJ 856-785-0120
Hillman Shrimp & Oyster
Dickinson, TX. 800-582-4416
Hingham Shellfish
Hingham, MA 781-749-1374
His Catch Value Added Products
Homer, AK 800-215-7110
Huck's Seafood
Easton, MD 410-770-9211
Icelandic USA
Newport News, VA 757-820-4000
Icicle Seafoods
Seattle, WA 206-282-0988
Independent Packers Corporation
Seattle, WA 206-285-6000
Indian Ridge Shrimp Company
Chauvin, LA 985-594-5869
International Oceanic Enterprises of Alabama
Bayou La Batre, AL 800-816-1832
Island Marine Products
Clarks Harbour, NS. 902-745-2222
J M Clayton Company
Cambridge, MD 800-652-6931
J&R Foods
Long Branch, NJ. 732-229-4020
J. Matassini & Sons Fish Company
Tampa, FL 813-229-0829
JCW Tawes & Son
Crisfield, MD 410-968-1288
Jessie's Ilwaco Fish Company
Ilwaco, WA 360-642-3773
Joey Oysters
Amite, LA 800-748-1525
John T. Handy Company
Salisbury, MD. 800-426-3977
Key Largo Fisheries
Key Largo, FL. 800-399-6970
Keyser Brothers
Lottsburg, VA 804-529-6837
King & Prince Seafood Corporation
Brunswick, GA 800-841-0205
Kirkland Custom Seafoods
Kirkland, WA 800-321-3474
Kitchens Seafood
Plant City, FL 800-327-0132
LaMonica Fine Foods
Millville, NJ 856-825-8111
Larry Matthews Company
Dennysville, ME 207-726-0609
Little River Seafood
Reedville, VA 804-453-3670
Long Food Industries
Fripp Island, SC 843-838-3205
Lowland Seafood
Lowland, NC 252-745-3751
Lu-Mar Lobster & Shrimp
Brownsville, TX 956-546-5525
Lund's Fisheries
Cape May, NJ 609-884-7600
Maine Mahogany Shellfish
Addison, ME 207-483-2865
Martin Brothers Seafood Company
Westwego, LA. 504-341-2251
Mat Roland Seafood Company
Atlantic Beach, FL 904-246-9443
Matlaw's Food Products
West Haven, CT 800-934-8266
Maxim's Import Corporation
Miami, FL 800-331-6652
Menemsha Fish Market
Chilmark, MA. 508-645-2282
Mercado Latino
City of Industry, CA 626-333-6862
Mercer Processing
Modesto, CA. 209-529-0150
Mersey Seafoods
Liverpool, NS 902-354-3467
Mid-Atlantic Foods
Easton, MD 800-922-4688
Milfico Foods
Elk Grove Vlg, IL 847-427-0491
Nancy's Shellfish
Falmouth, ME 207-774-3411
Neptune Fisheries
Newport News, VA 800-545-7474

Notre Dame Seafood
Comfort Cove, NL 709-244-5511
NTC Foods Corporation
Williamsville, NY 800-333-1637
Okuhara Foods
Honolulu, HI 808-848-0581
Pacific Ocean Seafood
La Conner, WA 360-466-4455
Pacific Salmon Company
Edmonds, WA 425-774-1315
Pacific Shrimp Company
Newport, OR 541-265-4215
Pacific Surf Food Processors
Los Angeles, CA 800-627-5657
Pamlico Packing Company
Grantsboro, NC 800-682-1113
Paul Piazza & Sons
New Orleans, LA 504-524-6011
Penguin Frozen Foods
Northbrook, IL 847-291-9400
Phillips Foods
Baltimore, MD 888-234-2722
Produits Belle Baie
Caraquet, NB 506-727-4414
Quality Seafood
Apalachicola, FL 850-653-9696
Raffield Fisheries
Port St Joe, FL 850-229-8229
RCV Seafood Corporation
Morattico, VA 804-462-5101
Rich-Seapak Corporation
Brownsville, TX 956-542-0001
Rippons Brothers Seafood
Fishing Creek, MD 410-397-3200
Rivere's Seafood Processors
Paincourtville, LA 985-369-6055
Royal Seafood
Monterey, CA 831-655-8326
Ruggiero Seafood
Newark, NJ 800-543-2110
Sea Garden Seafoods
Meridian, GA 912-832-4437
Sea Pearl Seafood
Bayou La Batre, AL 800-872-8804
Sea Products Company
Watsonville, CA 831-768-2600
Sea Safari
Belhaven, NC 252-943-3091
Sea Safari
Belhaven, NC 800-688-6174
Sea Safari Limited
Belhaven, NC 800-688-6174
Sea Snack Foods
Los Angeles, CA 213-622-2204
SeaPerfect Atlantic Farms
Charleston, SC 800-728-0099
Seaspan Products Corporation
New York, NY 201-569-9234
Seymour & Sons Seafood
Diberville, MS 228-392-4020
Silver Lining Seafood
Ketchikan, AK 907-225-6664
Southern Shell Fish Company
Harvey, LA 504-341-5631
Southern Star Seafood
Fort Pierce, FL 561-461-5787
Sportsmen's Cannery & Smokehouse
Winchester Bay, OR 541-271-3293
St. Ours & Company
Norwell, MA 781-331-8520
State Fish Company
San Pedro, CA 888-658-3474
Stinson Seafood Company
Prospect Harbor, ME 207-963-7331
Stone Crabs
Miami Beach, FL 800-260-2722
Sunshine Food Sales
Miami, FL 305-696-2885
Sunshine Seafood
Stonington, ME 207-367-2955
Taku Smokehouse
Juneau, AK 800-582-5122
Tampa Bay Fisheries
Dover, FL 800-234-2561
Tampa Maid Foods
Lakeland, FL 800-237-7637
Taylor's Frozen Foods
Charleston, SC 843-723-1878
Terry Brothers
Temperanceville, VA 757-824-3471
Thompson Seafood
Darien, GA 912-437-4649

Toddville Seafoods
Toddville, MD 410-397-8129
Trident Seafoods Corporation
Seattle, WA 800-426-5490
Triton Seafood Company
Medley, FL 305-805-3500
Turner New Zealand
Aliso Viejo, CA 949-622-6181
United Shellfish Company
Grasonville, MD 410-827-8171
Valdez Food
Philadelphia, PA 215-634-6106
Viking Seafoods Inc
Malden, MA 800-225-3020
Vince's Seafoods
Gretna, LA 504-368-1544
W.T. Ruark & Company
Fishing Creek, MD 410-397-3133
Wanchese Fish Company
Suffolk, VA 757-673-4500
Washington Crab Producers
Westport, WA 360-268-9161
Western Alaska Fisheries
Seattle, WA 206-447-4400
Wiegardt Brothers
Ocean Park, WA 360-665-4111
Wrangell Fisheries
Wrangell, AK 907-874-3346

Shrimp

All Alaskan Seafood
Seattle, WA 206-285-8200
Anchor Frozen Foods
Westbury, NY 800-566-3474
Appert's Foodservice
St Cloud, MN 800-225-3883
APTCO
San Francisco, CA 415-648-6688
Arista Industries
Wilton, CT 800-255-6457
Atlantic Queen Seafoods Limited
Lachine, QC 514-636-5114
Bandon Bay Fisheries
Bandon, OR 541-347-4454
Bay Oceans Sea Foods
Garibaldi, OR 503-322-3316
Bayou Foods
Kenner, LA 800-516-8283
Bayou Land Seafood
Breaux Bridge, LA 337-667-6118
Beaver Street Fisheries
Jacksonville, FL 800-874-6426
Bell Buoy Crab Company
Seaside, OR 800-529-2722
Blalock Seafood
Orange Beach, AL 251-974-5811
BlueWater Seafoods
Lachine, QC 888-560-2539
Bolner's Fiesta Products
San Antonio, TX 210-734-6404
Bon Secour Fisheries
Bon Secour, AL 800-633-6854
Breakwater Fisheries
St. John's, NL 709-754-1999
Burris Mill & Feed
Franklinton, LA 800-928-2782
C.F. Gollott & Son Seafood
Biloxi, MS 866-846-3474
Callis Seafood
Lancaster, VA 804-462-7634
Carolina Seafoods
Mc Clellanville, SC 843-887-3713
Carrington Foods
Saraland, AL 251-675-9700
Catfish Wholesale
Abbeville, LA 800-334-7292
Certi-Fresh Foods
Bell Gardens, CA 562-806-1100
Chuck's Seafoods
Charleston, OR 541-888-5525
Clearwater Fine Foods
Bedford, NS 902-443-0550
Coldwater Seafood Corporation
Norwalk, CT 203-846-8897
Contessa Food Products
San Pedro, CA 310-832-8000
Cozy Harbor Seafood
Portland, ME 800-225-2586
Crevettes Du Nord
Gaspe, QC 418-368-1414

Crown Prince
City of Industry, CA 800-255-5063
D' Luke Seafood
Dulac, LA 504-563-2328
Deep Sea Foods
Bayou La Batre, AL 251-824-7000
Del's Seaway Shrimp & Oyster Company
Biloxi, MS 228-432-2604
Dick & Casey's Gourmet Seafoods
Harbor, OR 800-662-9494
Ducktrap River Fish Farm
Belfast, ME 800-434-8727
Eastern Fish Company
Teaneck, NJ 800-526-9066
Eastern Quebec Sea Foods
Matane, QC 418-562-1273
Eldorado Seafood
Lincoln, MA 800-416-5656
Elwha Fish
Port Angeles, WA 360-457-3344
Farm 2 Market
Roscoe, NY 800-663-4326
Fishery Products International
Danvers, MA 800-374-4700
Fishhawk Fisheries
Astoria, OR 503-325-5252
FishKing
Bayou La Batre, AL 334-824-2118
G & R Food Sales
Glendale, AZ 602-939-7337
Georgia Seafood Wholesale
Chamblee, GA 770-936-0483
Gesco ENR
Gaspe, QC 418-368-1414
Golden Gulf Coast Packing Company
Biloxi, MS 228-374-6121
Gollott Brothers Seafood Company
Biloxi, MS 228-432-7865
Great Northern Products
Warwick, RI 401-490-4590
Gulf City Marine Supply
Bayou La Batre, AL 251-824-4154
Gulf City Seafoods
Pascagoula, MS 800-666-3300
Gulf Island Shrimp & Seafood
Lake Charles, LA 888-626-7264
Gulf Island Shrimp & Seafood
Lake Charles, LA 985-563-4586
Gulf Pride Enterprises
Biloxi, MS 888-689-0560
Hallmark Fisheries
Charleston, OR 541-888-3253
Hi-Seas of Dulac
Dulac, LA 985-563-7155
Homarus
Atlanta, GA 404-877-1988
Imaex Trading
Norcross, GA 770-825-0848
Indian Ridge Shrimp Company
Chauvin, LA 985-594-5869
International Oceanic Enterprises of Alabama
Bayou La Batre, AL 800-816-1832
J. Matassini & Sons Fish Company
Tampa, FL 813-229-0829
JBS Packing Company
Port Arthur, TX 409-982-3216
Jessie's Ilwaco Fish Company
Ilwaco, WA 360-642-3773
Jubilee Foods
Bayou La Batre, AL 251-824-2110
King & Prince Seafood Corporation
Brunswick, GA 800-841-0205
Kirkland Custom Seafoods
Kirkland, WA 800-321-3474
Kitchens Seafood
Plant City, FL 800-327-0132
Lady Gale Seafood
Baldwin, LA 337-923-2060
LaMonica Fine Foods
Millville, NJ 856-825-8111
Larry J. Williams Company
Jesup, GA 912-427-7729
Louisiana Packing Company
Westwego, LA 800-666-1293
Louisiana Shrimp & Packing Company
New Orleans, LA 504-283-9893
Lowland Seafood
Lowland, NC 252-745-3751
Lu-Mar Lobster & Shrimp
Brownsville, TX 956-546-5525
M&I Seafood Manufacturers
Essex, MD 410-780-0444

M&M Shrimp Company
Biloxi, MS. 228-435-4915
Mat Roland Seafood Company
Atlantic Beach, FL 904-246-9443
Maxim's Import Corporation
Miami, FL. 800-331-6652
Mercado Latino
City of Industry, CA 626-333-6862
Mersey Seafoods
Liverpool, NS 902-354-3467
Milfico Foods
Elk Grove Vlg, IL 847-427-0491
Mill Cove Lobster Pound
Boothbay Harbor, ME. 207-633-3340
Mobile Processing
Mobile, AL 251-438-6944
Nelson Crab
Tokeland, WA 800-262-0069
Neptune Fisheries
Newport News, VA 800-545-7474
Neptune Foods
Vernon, CA 323-232-8300
New Ocean
Doraville, GA 770-458-5235
Newfound Resources
Saint John's, NL 709-579-7676
NorQuest Seafoods
Seattle, WA 206-281-7022
North Atlantic Fish Company
Gloucester, MA. 978-283-4121
NTC Foods Corporation
Williamsville, NY 800-333-1637
Ocean Garden Products
San Diego, CA 858-571-5002
Ocean Pride Seafood
Delcambre, LA 337-685-2336
Ocean Springs Seafood
Ocean Springs, MS 228-875-0104
Omstead Foods Ltd
Burlington, ON 905-315-8883
Ore-Cal Corporation
Los Angeles, CA 800-827-7474
Pacific Surf Food Processors
Los Angeles, CA 800-627-5657
Pamlico Packing Company
Grantsboro, NC 800-682-1113
Paul Piazza & Sons
New Orleans, LA 504-524-6011
Penguin Frozen Foods
Northbrook, IL 847-291-9400
Pioneer Live Shrimp
Oak Brook, IL 847-718-0088
Price Seafood
Chauvin, LA 985-594-3067
Produits Belle Baie
Caraquet, NB 506-727-4414
Quality Seafood
Apalachicola, FL. 850-653-9696
Randol
Lafayette, LA 337-981-7080
Resource Trading Company
Portland, ME. 207-772-2299
Rich-Seapak Corporation
St Simons Island, GA 800-654-9731
Rich-Seapak Corporation
Brownsville, TX 956-542-0001
Rocky Point Shrimp Association
Phoenix, AZ 602-254-8041
Roy Dick Company
Griffin, GA 770-227-3916
Sau-Sea Foods
Tarrytown, NY 914-631-1717
Sea Pearl Seafood
Bayou La Batre, AL 800-872-8804
Sea Snack Foods
Los Angeles, CA. 213-622-2204
Seafood Producers Cooperative
Bellingham, WA 360-733-0120
Seaspan Products Corporation
New York, NY 201-569-9234
Seatec
Portland, ME. 207-879-7199
Shrimp World
Gretna, LA 504-368-1571
Singleton Seafood
Tampa, FL. 800-553-3954
Smith & Son Seafood
Darien, GA 912-437-6471
Southern Shell Fish Company
Harvey, LA 504-341-5631
Stavis Seafoods
Boston, MA 800-390-5103

Tampa Bay Fisheries
Dover, FL 800-234-2561
Tampa Maid Foods
Lakeland, FL. 800-237-7637
Terrebonne Seafood
Dulac, LA 985-563-2645
Tex-Mex Cold Storage
Brownsville, TX 956-831-9433
Thompson Seafood
Darien, GA 912-437-4649
Tideland Seafood Company
Dulac, LA 985-563-4516
Triple T Enterprises
Chauvin, LA 985-594-5869
United Shellfish Company
Grasonville, MD 410-827-8171
Valdez Food
Philadelphia, PA 215-634-6106
Viking Seafoods Inc
Malden, MA 800-225-3020
Vincent Piazza Jr & Sons
Harahan, LA 800-259-5016
Washington Crab Producers
Westport, WA 360-268-9161
Wayne Estay Shrimp Company
Grand Isle, LA 985-787-3237
Weems Brothers Seafood Company
Biloxi, MS. 228-432-5422
Wrangell Fisheries
Wrangell, AK 907-874-3346
Young's Lobster Pound
Belfast, ME 207-338-1160

Black Tiger

Arctic Seas
Little Compton, RI 401-635-4000
Bay Oceans Sea Foods
Garibaldi, OR 503-322-3316
Bell Buoy Crab Company
Seaside, OR. 800-529-2722
BlueWater Seafoods
Lachine, QC 888-560-2539
Bolner's Fiesta Products
San Antonio, TX 210-734-6404
Crevettes Du Nord
Gaspe, QC. 418-368-1414
Del's Seaway Shrimp & Oyster Company
Biloxi, MS. 228-432-2604
Depoe Bay Fish Company
Newport, OR. 541-265-8833
Dick & Casey's Gourmet Seafoods
Harbor, OR 800-662-9494
Gesco ENR
Gaspe, QC. 418-368-1414
Gulf Pride Enterprises
Biloxi, MS. 888-689-0560
JBS Packing Company
Port Arthur, TX 409-982-3216
Jubilee Foods
Bayou La Batre, AL 251-824-2110
Lady Gale Seafood
Baldwin, LA 337-923-2060
Louisiana Packing Company
Westwego, LA 800-666-1293
M&M Shrimp Company
Biloxi, MS. 228-435-4915
Mobile Processing
Mobile, AL 251-438-6944
Newfound Resources
Saint John's, NL 709-579-7676
Ocean Springs Seafood
Ocean Springs, MS 228-875-0104
Price Seafood
Chauvin, LA 985-594-3067
Resource Trading Company
Portland, ME. 207-772-2299
Stavis Seafoods
Boston, MA. 800-390-5103
Vincent Piazza Jr & Sons
Harahan, LA 800-259-5016
Weems Brothers Seafood Company
Biloxi, MS. 228-432-5422

Breaded

Appert's Foodservice
St Cloud, MN 800-225-3883
Depoe Bay Fish Company
Newport, OR. 541-265-8833
Eldorado Seafood
Lincoln, MA 800-416-5656

Fishery Products International
Danvers, MA. 800-374-4700
FishKing
Bayou La Batre, AL 334-824-2118
Golden Gulf Coast Packing Company
Biloxi, MS. 228-374-6121
Icelandic USA
Newport News, VA 757-820-4000
J. Matassini & Sons Fish Company
Tampa, FL. 813-229-0829
King & Prince Seafood Corporation
Brunswick, GA 800-841-0205
LaMonica Fine Foods
Millville, NJ 856-825-8111
M&I Seafood Manufacturers
Essex, MD. 410-780-0444
Milfico Foods
Elk Grove Vlg, IL 847-427-0491
Neptune Foods
Vernon, CA 323-232-8300
Ocean Springs Seafood
Ocean Springs, MS 228-875-0104
Pacific Surf Food Processors
Los Angeles, CA 800-627-5657
Penguin Frozen Foods
Northbrook, IL 847-291-9400
Rich-Seapak Corporation
Brownsville, TX 956-542-0001
Sea Pearl Seafood
Bayou La Batre, AL 800-872-8804
Tampa Bay Fisheries
Dover, FL 800-234-2561
Tampa Maid Foods
Lakeland, FL. 800-237-7637

Canned

Bayou Land Seafood
Breaux Bridge, LA 337-667-6118
Chicken of the Sea International
San Diego, CA 800-678-8862
Chuck's Seafoods
Charleston, OR 541-888-5525
Elwha Fish
Port Angeles, WA 360-457-3344
Mercado Latino
City of Industry, CA 626-333-6862
Nelson Crab
Tokeland, WA 800-262-0069
North Atlantic Fish Company
Gloucester, MA. 978-283-4121
NTC Foods Corporation
Williamsville, NY 800-333-1637
Ore-Cal Corporation
Los Angeles, CA 800-827-7474
Orleans Food Company
New Orleans, LA 800-628-4900
Scally's Imperial Importing Company Inc
Staten Island, NY 718-983-1938
Seafood Producers Cooperative
Bellingham, WA 360-733-0120
Southern Shell Fish Company
Harvey, LA 504-341-5631
Wrangell Fisheries
Wrangell, AK 907-874-3346

Cocktail

Elwha Fish
Port Angeles, WA 360-457-3344

Cooked

Depoe Bay Fish Company
Newport, OR. 541-265-8833
King & Prince Seafood Corporation
Brunswick, GA 800-841-0205
Neptune Fisheries
Newport News, VA 800-545-7474
Neptune Foods
Vernon, CA 323-232-8300
Pacific Surf Food Processors
Los Angeles, CA 800-627-5657
Tampa Bay Fisheries
Dover, FL 800-234-2561

Fresh

Cozy Harbor Seafood
Portland, ME. 800-225-2586
Great Northern Products
Warwick, RI 401-490-4590
J. Matassini & Sons Fish Company
Tampa, FL. 813-229-0829

Jessie's Ilwaco Fish Company
Ilwaco, WA 360-642-3773
Nelson Crab
Tokeland, WA .800-262-0069
Paul Piazza & Sons
New Orleans, LA 504-524-6011
Quality Seafood
Apalachicola, FL. 850-653-9696
Washington Crab Producers
Westport, WA .360-268-9161
Wrangell Fisheries
Wrangell, AK .907-874-3346

Frozen

All Alaskan Seafood
Seattle, WA 206-285-8200
Appert's Foodservice
St Cloud, MN .800-225-3883
APTCO
San Francisco, CA 415-648-6688
Arista Industries
Wilton, CT 800-255-6457
Atlantic Queen Seafoods Limited
Lachine, QC 514-636-5114
Bandon Bay Fisheries
Bandon, OR 541-347-4454
Bayou Land Seafood
Breaux Bridge, LA 337-667-6118
Beaver Street Fisheries
Jacksonville, FL 800-874-6426
Bon Secour Fisheries
Bon Secour, AL. 800-633-6854
Breakwater Fisheries
St. John's, NL .709-754-1999
Buns & Things Bakery
Charlottetown, PE. 902-892-2600
C.F. Gollott & Son Seafood
Biloxi, MS. 866-846-3474
Callis Seafood
Lancaster, VA .804-462-7634
Carrington Foods
Saraland, AL. .251-675-9700
Certi-Fresh Foods
Bell Gardens, CA 562-806-1100
Clearwater Fine Foods
Bedford, NS 902-443-0550
Coldwater Seafood Corporation
Norwalk, CT 203-846-8897
ConAgra Shrimp Companies
Tampa, FL. 813-241-1501
Cozy Harbor Seafood
Portland, ME. .800-225-2586
Deep Sea Foods
Bayou La Batre, AL 251-824-7000
Depoe Bay Fish Company
Newport, OR. .541-265-8833
Eastern Fish Company
Teaneck, NJ. 800-526-9066
Eastern Quebec Sea Foods
Matane, QC. 418-562-1273
Fisherman's Reef Shrimp Company
Beaumont, TX. 409-842-9528
Fishery Products International
Danvers, MA. .800-374-4700
Golden Gulf Coast Packing Company
Biloxi, MS. 228-374-6121
Great Northern Products
Warwick, RI 401-490-4590
Gulf City Seafoods
Pascagoula, MS. 800-666-3300
Indian Ridge Shrimp Company
Chauvin, LA 985-594-5869
International Oceanic Enterprises of Alabama
Bayou La Batre, AL 800-816-1832
J. Matassini & Sons Fish Company
Tampa, FL. 813-229-0829
Jessie's Ilwaco Fish Company
Ilwaco, WA 360-642-3773
Kitchens Seafood
Plant City, FL .800-327-0132
Lu-Mar Lobster & Shrimp
Brownsville, TX 956-546-5525
Maxim's Import Corporation
Miami, FL. 800-331-6652
Mersey Seafoods
Liverpool, NS .902-354-3467
Neptune Fisheries
Newport News, VA 800-545-7474
North Atlantic Fish Company
Gloucester, MA 978-283-4121
Pacific Surf Food Processors
Los Angeles, CA. 800-627-5657

Paul Piazza & Sons
New Orleans, LA 504-524-6011
Penguin Frozen Foods
Northbrook, IL 847-291-9400
Portland Shellfish Company
South Portland, ME 207-799-9290
Quality Seafood
Apalachicola, FL. 850-653-9696
Rich-Seapak Corporation
Brownsville, TX 956-542-0001
Sea Pearl Seafood
Bayou La Batre, AL 800-872-8804
Sea Snack Foods
Los Angeles, CA. 213-622-2204
Seafood Producers Cooperative
Bellingham, WA 360-733-0120
Seaspan Products Corporation
New York, NY 201-569-9234
Suram Trading Corporation
Coral Gables, FL. 305-448-7165
Tampa Bay Fisheries
Dover, FL 800-234-2561
Tampa Maid Foods
Lakeland, FL. .800-237-7637
Tex-Mex Cold Storage
Brownsville, TX 956-831-9433
Viking Seafoods Inc
Malden, MA 800-225-3020
Washington Crab Producers
Westport, WA .360-268-9161
Weems Brothers Seafood Company
Biloxi, MS. 228-432-5422
Wrangell Fisheries
Wrangell, AK .907-874-3346

Peeled

Bayou Foods
Kenner, LA 800-516-8283
Depoe Bay Fish Company
Newport, OR. .541-265-8833
Fishery Products International
Danvers, MA. .800-374-4700
Neptune Fisheries
Newport News, VA 800-545-7474
Tampa Maid Foods
Lakeland, FL. .800-237-7637

Smoked

Menemsha Fish Market
Chilmark, MA .508-645-2282
Port Chatham Smoked Seafood
Everett, WA. 800-872-5666

Snails

S-Car-Go
Sanibel, FL 239-472-1900

Squid

Aliotti Wholesale Fish Company
Monterey, CA .831-375-2881
Anchor Frozen Foods
Westbury, NY .800-566-3474
Arctic Seas
Little Compton, RI 401-635-4000
Atlantic Capes Fisheries
Cape May, NJ .609-884-3000
Blue Gold Mussels
Newport, RI. 508-993-2635
Breakwater Fisheries
St. John's, NL .709-754-1999
Buns & Things Bakery
Charlottetown, PE. 902-892-2600
G J Shortall
Mount Pearl, NL 709-747-0655
Great Northern Products
Warwick, RI 401-490-4590
International Seafood Distributors
Hayes, VA 804-642-1417
LaMonica Fine Foods
Millville, NJ 856-825-8111
Lund's Fisheries
Cape May, NJ .609-884-7600
Menemsha Fish Market
Chilmark, MA .508-645-2282
Mutual Fish Company
Seattle, WA 206-322-4368
North Atlantic Fish Company
Gloucester, MA 978-283-4121

Notre Dame Seafood
Comfort Cove, NL 709-244-5511
Pacific Salmon Company
Edmonds, WA. 425-774-1315
Pacific Surf Food Processors
Los Angeles, CA. 800-627-5657
Royal Seafood
Monterey, CA .831-655-8326
Ruggiero Seafood
Newark, NJ. 800-543-2110
Sea Products Company
Watsonville, CA 831-768-2600
Sea Watch International
Easton, MD. 410-822-7500
Stavis Seafoods
Boston, MA. 800-390-5103
Sweet Water Seafood Corporation
Carlstadt, NJ 201-939-6622
Taylor's Frozen Foods
Charleston, SC 843-723-1878
Tichon Seafood Corporation
New Bedford, MA 508-999-5607
Tri-Marine InternationalInc
San Pedro, CA. 310-732-6113

Ink

Chieftain Wild Rice Company
Spooner, WI 800-262-6368

Sushi

Azuma Foods International
Hayward, CA. .510-782-1112
IOE Atlanta
Galena, MD 410-755-6300

Fruits & Vegetables

General

Alfred Louie
Bakersfield, CA 661-831-2520
Black's Barbecue
Lockhart, TX. 512-398-2712
Coco Lopez
Miramar, FL 800-341-2242
Del Monte Foods
Cambria, WI 920-348-5121
Graceland Fruit Inc
Frankfort, MI 800-352-7181
Oberweis Dairy
North Aurora, IL. 888-645-5868
Patsy's
New York, NY 212-247-3491
Prairie Thyme
Santa Fe, NM 800-869-0009
Seneca Foods Corporation
Marion, NY. 315-926-8100
Z&S Distributing
Fresno, CA 800-467-0788

Algae

Cell Tech International
Klamath Falls, OR 541-882-5406
Vitarich Laboratories
Naples, FL. 800-817-9999

Aloe Vera

Alfer Laboratories
Chatsworth, CA 818-709-0737
Aloe Commodities International
Carrollton, TX. 800-701-2563
Aloe Dynamics
Dallas, TX. 214-630-8808
Aloe Farms
Harlingen, TX 800-262-6771
Aloe Laboratories, Inc.
Harlingen, TX 800-258-5380
Baywood International
Scottsdale, AZ. 800-481-7169

EMERLING INTERNATIONAL FOODS, INC.

Emerling International Foods
Buffalo, NY. 716-833-7381

We supply food manufacturers and food service customers worldwide (since 1988) with bulk ingredients including: Fruits & Vegetables; Juice Concentrates; Herbs & Spices; Oils & Vinegars; Flavors & Colors; Honey & Molasses. We also produce PURE MAPLE SYRUP.

Florida Food Products
Eustis, FL 800-874-2331
Herb Connection
Springville, UT 801-489-4254
Naturex (Chart Corp)
South Hackensack, NJ 201-440-5000
Real Aloe Company
Carlsbad, CA. 800-541-7809
Russo Farms
Vineland, NJ 856-692-5942
Universal Preservachem Inc
Edison, NJ 732-777-7338
Warren Laboratories
Abbott, TX 800-421-2563
Winning Solutions
Pagosa Springs, CO 800-899-2563

Apple

A. Gagliano Company
Milwaukee, WI 800-272-1516
Agrinorthwest
Kennewick, WA 509-734-1195
AgroCepia
Miami, FL 305-704-3488
Agvest
Cleveland, OH 440-735-6900
American Health & Nutrition
Ann Arbor, MI 734-677-5572

Apple Acres
La Fayette, NY 315-677-5144
Applewood Orchards
Deerfield, MI 800-447-3854
Baker Produce Company
Kennewick, WA 800-624-7553
Ballantine Produce Company
Reedley, CA 559-637-2400
Ben B. Schwartz & Sons
Detroit, MI 313-841-8300
Bennett's Apples & Cider
Ancaster, ON. 905-648-6878
Bluebird
Peshastin, WA 509-548-1700
Boekhout Farms
Ontario, NY. 315-524-4041
Bridenbaughs Orchards
Martinsburg, PA 814-793-2364
Burnette Foods
Elk Rapids, MI 231-264-8116
Burnette Foods
Hartford, MI 616-621-3181
Cahoon Farms
Wolcott, NY 315-594-8081
Cal-Harvest Marketing
Hanford, CA 559-582-4000
Chazy Orchards
Chazy, NY. 518-846-7171
Chelan Fresh
Chelan, WA. 509-682-5133
Cherry Growers
Grawn, MI. 231-276-9241
Chief Tonasket Growers
Portland, OR. 509-486-2914
Chief Wenatchee
Wenatchee, WA. 509-662-5197
Chiquita Brands International
Cincinnati, OH 800-438-0015
Citrus Citrosuco North America
Lake Wales, FL. 800-356-4592
Clements Foods Company
Oklahoma City, OK 800-654-8355
Coloma Frozen Foods
Coloma, MI. 800-642-2723
Congdon Orchards
Yakima, WA 509-965-2886
Crane & Crane
Brewster, WA 509-689-3447
Del Mar Food Products Corporation
Watsonville, CA 831-722-3516
Diamond Fruit Growers
Odell, OR 541-354-5300
Dole Food Company
Westlake Village, CA 818-879-6600
Ever Fresh Fruit Company
Boring, OR 800-239-8026
Flippin-Seaman
Tyro, VA 434-277-5828
Franklin Reister & Sons
Conklin, MI 616-887-9689
Fruit Growers Marketing Association
Newcomerstown, OH 800-466-5171
George W Saulpaugh & Sons
Germantown, NY 518-537-6500
Golden Town Apple Products
Thornbury, ON 519-599-6300
Green Valley Apples of California
Arvin, CA 661-854-4436
H H Dobbins
Lyndonville, NY 877-362-2467
H. Naraghi Farms
Escalon, CA 209-577-5777
Harner Farms
State College, PA 814-237-7919
Hazel Creek Orchards
Mt Airy, GA 706-754-4899
Henggeler Packing Company
Fruitland, ID 208-452-4212
Hillcrest Orchard
Lake Placid, FL 865-397-5273
Indian Hollow Farms
Richland Center, WI 800-236-3944
International Home Foods
Milton, PA 973-359-9920
J. Rettenmaier
Schoolcraft, MI 877-243-4661

J.C. Watson Company
Parma, ID 208-722-5141
Kingsburg Apple Sale
Kingsburg, CA 559-897-5132
Knights Appleden Fruit
Colborne, ON 905-349-2521
Kozlowski Farms
Forestville, CA 800-473-2767
Leroux Creek Foods
Hotchkiss, CO. 877-970-5670
Love Creek Orchards
Medina, TX. 800-449-0882
Lucks Food Decorating Company
Tacoma, WA 206-674-7200
M&R Company
Lodi, CA. 209-369-2725
Manzanita Ranch
Julian, CA 760-765-0102
Mariani Packing Company
Vacaville, CA 800-672-8655
Marley Orchards Corporation
Yakima, WA 509-248-5231
Mason County Fruit Packers Cooperative
Ludington, MI. 231-845-6248
Matson Fruit Company
Selah, WA 509-697-7100
Mayer's Cider Mill
Webster, NY 800-543-0043
Mayfair Packing Company
San Jose, CA 408-280-2349
Mayfield Farms
Brampton, ON. 905-846-0506
McCain Foods USA
Grand Island, NE. 308-382-7770
Mountain Orchard Cooperative
Aspers, PA. 800-322-6867
Mrs. Prindable's Handmade Confections
Niles, IL 888-215-1100
National Fruit Product Company
Winchester, VA 540-662-3401
Natural Foods
Toledo, OH 800-860-0006
Naumes
Medford, OR. 541-772-6268
New Era Canning Company
New Era, MI 231-861-2151
New York Apples Sales
Castletn on Hdsn, NY 518-477-7200
Niagara Foods
Middleport, NY. 716-735-7722
North Bay Produce
Traverse City, MI 231-946-1941
Northern Fruit Company
Wenatchee, WA. 509-884-6651
Northern Michigan Fruit Company
Omena, MI 231-386-5142
Northern Orchard Company
Peru, NY 518-643-9718
Nuchief Sales
East Wenatchee, WA. 888-269-4638
Oceana Foods
Shelby, MI. 231-861-2141
P-R Farms
Clovis, CA 559-299-0201
Pacific Coast Fruit Company
Portland, OR. 503-234-6411
Park 100 Foods
Tipton, IN 800-854-6504
Pastor Chuck Orchards
Portland, ME. 207-773-1314
Pavero Cold Storage Corporation
Highland, NY 800-435-2994
Per-Clin Orchards
Bear Lake, MI 231-889-4289
Placerville Fruit Growers Association
Placerville, CA 530-622-2640
Premier Packing Company
Bakersfield, CA 661-393-3320
Reinhart Foods
Markham, ON 905-754-3503
Rice Fruit Company
Gardners, PA. 800-627-3359
Scotian Gold Cooperative
Coldbrook, NS 902-679-2191
Shafer Lake Fruit
Hartford, MI 269-621-3194

Shawnee Canning Company
Cross Junction, VA 800-713-1414
Smeltzer Orchard Company
Frankfort, MI 231-882-4421
Snowcrest Packer
Abbotsford, BC. 604-859-4881
Solana Gold Organics
Sebastopol, CA 800-459-1121
Stadelman Fruit
Zillah, WA. 509-829-5145
Summit Point Raceway Orchards
Summit Point, WV 800-927-7531
Sunfresh
Royal City, WA. 509-346-9438
Sunmet
Del Rey, CA 559-445-1574
Sunshine Farm & Gardens
Renick, WV. 304-497-2208
Symms Fruit Ranch
Caldwell, ID 208-459-4821
T.S. Smith & Sons
Bridgeville, DE 302-337-8271
Talbott Farms
Palisade, CO 970-464-5656
Tastee Apple Inc
Newcomerstown, OH 800-262-7753
Those Hersey Brothers
Casnovia, MI. 800-289-2767
Timber Crest Farms
Healdsburg, CA 888-374-9325
Tom Ringhausen Orchards
Hardin, IL 618-576-2311
Tony Vitrano Company
Jessup, MD 410-799-7444
Trinity Fruit Sales
Clovis, CA 559-322-7100
Triple D Orchards
Empire, MI 866-781-9410
Trout-Blue Chelan
Chelan, WA. 509-682-2591
United Apple Sales
New Paltz, NY 845-256-1500
United Fruits Corporation
Santa Monica, CA. 310-829-0261
Watermill Foods
Milton Freewater, OR. 541-938-6601
Williams Creek Farms
Williams, OR. 541-846-6481
Yakima Fruit & Cold Storage Company
Wapato, WA 509-877-0440
Zitner Company
Philadelphia, PA 215-229-4990

Canned

American Health & Nutrition
Ann Arbor, MI 734-677-5572
Burnette Foods
Elk Rapids, MI 231-264-8116
Burnette Foods
Hartford, MI 616-621-3181

EMERLING INTERNATIONAL FOODS, INC.

Emerling International Foods
Buffalo, NY. 716-833-7381

We supply food manufacturers and food service customers worldwide (since 1988) with bulk ingredients including: Fruits & Vegetables; Juice Concentrates; Herbs & Spices; Oils & Vinegars; Flavors & Colors; Honey & Molasses. We also produce PURE MAPLE SYRUP.

Independent Food Processors
Sunnyside, WA 509-837-3806
Knouse Foods Cooperative
Chambersburg, PA 717-263-9177
Knouse Foods Cooperative
Orrtanna, PA 717-642-8291
Lucks Food Decorating Company
Tacoma, WA 206-674-7200
New Era Canning Company
New Era, MI 231-861-2151
Setton International Foods
Commack, NY 800-227-4397
Terri Lynn
Elgin, IL 800-323-0775
Unique Ingredients
Naches, WA. 509-653-1991

Caramel

Affy Tapple, LLC
Niles, IL 847-588-2900
Andrews Caramel Apples
Chicago, IL 800-305-3004
B&B Caramel Apple Company
Chicago, IL 773-927-7559
Tastee Apple Inc
Newcomerstown, OH 800-262-7753
Zitner Company
Philadelphia, PA 215-229-4990

Covered

Caramel

Carousel Candies
Cicero, IL 888-656-1552
DGZ Chocolates
Houston, TX 877-949-9444
Zitner Company
Philadelphia, PA 215-229-4990

Chocolate

Ivydaro
Putney, VT 802-387-5597

Criterion

Natural Foods
Toledo, OH 800-860-0006
Weaver Nut Company
Ephrata, PA 717-738-3781

Dried

AgroCepia
Miami, FL 305-704-3488
American Health & Nutrition
Ann Arbor, MI 734-677-5572
American Importing Company
Minneapolis, MN 612-331-9226
Atwater Foods
Lyndonville, NY 585-765-2639

EMERLING INTERNATIONAL FOODS, INC.

Emerling International Foods
Buffalo, NY. 716-833-7381

We supply food manufacturers and food service customers worldwide (since 1988) with bulk ingredients including: Fruits & Vegetables; Juice Concentrates; Herbs & Spices; Oils & Vinegars; Flavors & Colors; Honey & Molasses. We also produce PURE MAPLE SYRUP.

Golden Town Apple Products
Thornbury, ON 519-599-6300
Independent Food Processors Company
Yakima, WA 800-476-5398
Just Tomatoes Company
Westley, CA. 800-537-1985
Kozlowski Farms
Forestville, CA 800-473-2767
Leroux Creek Foods
Hotchkiss, CO. 877-970-5670
Mariani Packing Company
Vacaville, CA 800-672-8655
Mayfair Packing Company
San Jose, CA 408-280-2349
Mayfield Farms
Brampton, ON. 905-846-0506
Niagara Foods
Middleport, NY 716-735-7722
Quality Brands
Deland, FL 386-738-3808
Seneca Foods Corporation
Marion, NY. 315-926-8100
Setton International Foods
Commack, NY 800-227-4397
Solana Gold Organics
Sebastopol, CA 800-459-1121
Tastee Apple Inc
Newcomerstown, OH 800-262-7753
Terri Lynn
Elgin, IL 800-323-0775
Timber Crest Farms
Healdsburg, CA 888-374-9325
Unique Ingredients
Naches, WA. 509-653-1991

Fresh

Bridenbaughs Orchards
Martinsburg, PA 814-793-2364
Ever Fresh Fruit Company
Boring, OR 800-239-8026
Golden Town Apple Products
Thornbury, ON 519-599-6300
H. Naraghi Farms
Escalon, CA 209-577-5777
Mountain Orchard Cooperative
Aspers, PA 800-322-6867
Price Cold Storage & Packing Company
Yakima, WA 509-966-4110
Summit Point Raceway Orchards
Summit Point, WV 800-927-7531
Sunmet
Del Rey, CA 559-445-1574
Unique Ingredients
Naches, WA. 509-653-1991

Frozen

Agvest
Cleveland, OH 440-735-6900
American Health & Nutrition
Ann Arbor, MI 734-677-5572
Cahoon Farms
Wolcott, NY 315-594-8081
Citrus Citrosuco North America
Lake Wales, FL 800-356-4592

EMERLING INTERNATIONAL FOODS, INC.

Emerling International Foods
Buffalo, NY. 716-833-7381

We supply food manufacturers and food service customers worldwide (since 1988) with bulk ingredients including: Fruits & Vegetables; Juice Concentrates; Herbs & Spices; Oils & Vinegars; Flavors & Colors; Honey & Molasses. We also produce PURE MAPLE SYRUP.

Ever Fresh Fruit Company
Boring, OR 800-239-8026
Mason County Fruit Packers Cooperative
Ludington, MI. 231-845-6248
Northern Michigan Fruit Company
Omena, MI 231-386-5142
Oceana Foods
Shelby, MI. 231-861-2141
Pacific Coast Fruit Company
Portland, OR 503-234-6411
Quality Brands
Deland, FL 386-738-3808
Setton International Foods
Commack, NY 800-227-4397
Sill Farms Market
Lawrence, MI 269-674-3755
Smeltzer Orchard Company
Frankfort, MI 231-882-4421
Snowcrest Packer
Abbotsford, BC. 604-859-4881
Terri Lynn
Elgin, IL 800-323-0775
Triple D Orchards
Empire, MI 866-781-9410
Unique Ingredients
Naches, WA. 509-653-1991

Granny Smith

Sunmet
Del Rey, CA 559-445-1574

Pomace

EMERLING INTERNATIONAL FOODS, INC.

Emerling International Foods
Buffalo, NY. 716-833-7381

We supply food manufacturers and food service customers worldwide (since 1988) with bulk ingredients including: Fruits & Vegetables; Juice Concentrates; Herbs & Spices; Oils & Vinegars; Flavors & Colors; Honey & Molasses. We also produce PURE MAPLE SYRUP.

Tree Top
Selah, WA 800-367-6571

Unique Ingredients
Naches, WA.....................509-653-1991

Rings

AgroCepia
Miami, FL.....................305-704-3488
Timber Crest Farms
Healdsburg, CA.....................888-374-9325

Slices

Bridenbaughs Orchards
Martinsburg, PA.....................814-793-2364
Ever Fresh Fruit Company
Boring, OR.....................800-239-8026
Golden Town Apple Products
Thornbury, ON.....................519-599-6300
Green Valley Apples of California
Arvin, CA.....................661-854-4436
H. Naraghi Farms
Escalon, CA.....................209-577-5777
Lucks Food Decorating Company
Tacoma, WA.....................206-674-7200
Mayfield Farms
Brampton, ON.....................905-846-0506
National Fruit Product Company
Winchester, VA.....................540-662-3401
New Era Canning Company
New Era, MI.....................231-861-2151
Northern Michigan Fruit Company
Omena, MI.....................231-386-5142

Canned

Lucks Food Decorating Company
Tacoma, WA.....................206-674-7200
Mayfield Farms
Brampton, ON.....................905-846-0506
New Era Canning Company
New Era, MI.....................231-861-2151

Frozen

Ever Fresh Fruit Company
Boring, OR.....................800-239-8026
Mayfield Farms
Brampton, ON.....................905-846-0506
Sill Farms Market
Lawrence, MI.....................269-674-3755

Apricot

Agrinorthwest
Kennewick, WA.....................509-734-1195
American Key Food Products
Closter, NJ.....................800-767-0237
Ballantine Produce Company
Reedley, CA.....................559-637-2400
Brandt Farms
Reedley, CA.....................559-638-6961
California Fruit
Sanger, CA.....................559-266-7117
Copper Hills Fruit Sales
Fresno, CA.....................559-277-1970
Del Mar Food Products Corporation
Watsonville, CA.....................831-722-3516
Del Monte Foods
San Francisco, CA.....................800-543-3090
Dole Food Company
Westlake Village, CA.....................818-879-6600
Fowler Packing Company
Fresno, CA.....................559-834-5911
Giumarra Companies
Reedley, CA.....................559-897-5060
HMC Marketing Group
Kingsburg, CA.....................559-897-1009
Janca's Jojoba Oil & Seed Company
Mesa, AZ.....................480-497-9494
JR Wood/Big Valley
Atwater, CA.....................209-358-5643
Kalustyan Corporation
Union, NJ.....................908-688-6111
Kings Canyon Corrin
Reedley, CA.....................559-638-3571

Mayfair Packing Company
San Jose, CA.....................408-280-2349
Meridian Nut Growers
Clovis, CA.....................559-458-7272
Miss Scarlett's
Chandler, AZ.....................800-345-6734
Muirhead Canning Company
The Dalles, OR.....................541-298-1660
Natural Foods
Toledo, OH.....................800-860-0006
P-R Farms
Clovis, CA.....................559-299-0201
Produce Edge
Reedley, CA.....................559-637-9988
Spring Tree Maple Products
Brattleboro, VT.....................802-254-8784
Stapleton-Spence PackingCompany
San Jose, CA.....................800-297-8815
Sun-Maid Growers of California
Kingsburg, CA.....................800-272-4746
Sunsweet Growers
Yuba City, CA.....................800-417-2253
Terri Lynn
Elgin, IL.....................800-323-0775
Trinity Fruit Sales
Clovis, CA.....................559-322-7100
Tufts Ranch
Winters, CA.....................530-795-4144
Unique Ingredients
Naches, WA.....................509-653-1991
United Fruits Corporation
Santa Monica, CA.....................310-829-0261
Vintage Produce Sales
Kingsburg, CA.....................559-897-1622
Wawona Packing Company
Cutler, C9.....................559-528-4000
Z&S Distributing
Fresno, CA.....................800-467-0788

Canned

EMERLING INTERNATIONAL FOODS, INC.

Emerling International Foods
Buffalo, NY.....................716-833-7381

We supply food manufacturers and food service customers worldwide (since 1988) with bulk ingredients including: Fruits & Vegetables; Juice Concentrates; Herbs & Spices; Oils & Vinegars; Flavors & Colors; Honey & Molasses. We also produce PURE MAPLE SYRUP.

Pacific Coast Producers Corporate Office
Lodi, CA.....................209-367-8800
Stapleton-Spence PackingCompany
San Jose, CA.....................800-297-8815

Dried

American Importing Company
Minneapolis, MN.....................612-331-9226
California Fruit
Sanger, CA.....................559-266-7117
Central California Raisin Packers
Del Rey, CA.....................559-888-2195
Chieftain Wild Rice Company
Spooner, WI.....................800-262-6368
Fastachi
Watertown, MA.....................800-466-3022
Kalustyan Corporation
Union, NJ.....................908-688-6111
King Nut Company
Cleveland, OH.....................800-860-5464
Mariani Packing Company
Vacaville, CA.....................800-672-8655
Natural Foods
Toledo, OH.....................800-860-0006
Purity Foods
Okemos, MI.....................800-997-7358
Setton International Foods
Commack, NY.....................800-227-4397
Spring Tree Maple Products
Brattleboro, VT.....................802-254-8784
Stapleton-Spence PackingCompany
San Jose, CA.....................800-297-8815
Sunsweet Growers
Yuba City, CA.....................800-417-2253
Timber Crest Farms
Healdsburg, CA.....................888-374-9325
Weaver Nut Company
Ephrata, PA.....................717-738-3781

Frozen

EMERLING INTERNATIONAL FOODS, INC.

Emerling International Foods
Buffalo, NY.....................716-833-7381

We supply food manufacturers and food service customers worldwide (since 1988) with bulk ingredients including: Fruits & Vegetables; Juice Concentrates; Herbs & Spices; Oils & Vinegars; Flavors & Colors; Honey & Molasses. We also produce PURE MAPLE SYRUP.

JR Wood/Big Valley
Atwater, CA.....................209-358-5643
Pacific Coast Producers Corporate Office
Lodi, CA.....................209-367-8800

Kernals

EMERLING INTERNATIONAL FOODS, INC.

Emerling International Foods
Buffalo, NY.....................716-833-7381

We supply food manufacturers and food service customers worldwide (since 1988) with bulk ingredients including: Fruits & Vegetables; Juice Concentrates; Herbs & Spices; Oils & Vinegars; Flavors & Colors; Honey & Molasses. We also produce PURE MAPLE SYRUP.

Mayfair Packing Company
San Jose, CA.....................408-280-2349
Naturex (Chart Corp)
South Hackensack, NJ.....................201-440-5000

Artichoke

A.M. Braswell Jr. Food Company
Statesboro, GA.....................800-673-9388
Fayter Farms Produce
Bradley, CA.....................831-385-8515
Ocean Mist
Castroville, CA.....................831-633-2144
Orleans Packing Company
Hyde Park, MA.....................617-361-6611
Scally's Imperial Importing Company Inc
Staten Island, NY.....................718-983-1938

SupHerb Farms
Turlock, CA.....................800-787-4372

CrEATe! Get ready-to-use fresh flavor with SupHerb Farms' all-natural fresh frozen culinary herbs, specialty vegetables, culinary herb pastes, vegetable purees and creative blends. Complete microbiological testing ensures food safety. We set the standard for outstanding customer service, inspired culinary support, collaborative customer partnerships and innovative custom products.

Vegetable Juices
Chicago, IL.....................888-776-9752

Canned

Agrocan
Toronto, ON.....................877-247-6226

EMERLING INTERNATIONAL FOODS, INC.

Emerling International Foods
Buffalo, NY.....................716-833-7381

We supply food manufacturers and food service customers worldwide (since 1988) with bulk ingredients including: Fruits & Vegetables; Juice Concentrates; Herbs & Spices; Oils & Vinegars; Flavors & Colors; Honey & Molasses. We also produce PURE MAPLE SYRUP.

Ron-Son Foods
Swedesboro, NJ 856-241-7333

Frozen

EMERLING INTERNATIONAL FOODS, INC.

Emerling International Foods
Buffalo, NY. 716-833-7381

We supply food manufacturers and food service customers worldwide (since 1988) with bulk ingredients including: Fruits & Vegetables; Juice Concentrates; Herbs & Spices; Oils & Vinegars; Flavors & Colors; Honey & Molasses. We also produce PURE MAPLE SYRUP.

SupHerb Farms
Turlock, CA 800-787-4372

CrEATe! Get ready-to-use fresh flavor with SupHerb Farms' all-natural fresh frozen culinary herbs, specialty vegetables, culinary herb pastes, vegetable purees and creative blends. Complete microbiological testing ensures food safety. We set the standard for outstanding customer service, inspired culinary support, collaborative customer partnerships and innovative custom products.

Vegetable Juices
Chicago, IL 888-776-9752

Hearts

Castella Imports
Hauppauge, NY 866-227-8355
Colonna Brothers
North Bergen, NJ 201-864-1115

SupHerb Farms
Turlock, CA 800-787-4372

CrEATe! Get ready-to-use fresh flavor with SupHerb Farms' all-natural fresh frozen culinary herbs, specialty vegetables, culinary herb pastes, vegetable purees and creative blends. Complete microbiological testing ensures food safety. We set the standard for outstanding customer service, inspired culinary support, collaborative customer partnerships and innovative custom products.

Victoria Packing Corporation
Brooklyn, NY 718-649-2180

Asparagus

A. Duda Farm Fresh Foods
Belle Glade, FL 561-996-7621
American Food & Equipment
Miami, FL 305-361-6517
Brock Seed Company
El Centro, CA 760-353-1632
Burnette Foods
Elk Rapids, MI 231-264-8116
Cal-Harvest Marketing
Hanford, CA 559-582-4000
Chase Farms
Walkerville, MI 231-873-3337
Chiquita Processed Foods
Milton Freewater, OR 541-938-4461
Coloma Frozen Foods
Coloma, MI 800-642-2723
Delta Packing Company of Lodi
Lodi, CA .209-334-0689

DiMare International
Indio, CA .760-564-3762
Dole Food Company
Westlake Village, CA 818-879-6600
Foster Family Farm
South Windsor, CT 860-648-9366
George W Saulpaugh & Sons
Germantown, NY 518-537-6500
Indian Rock Produce
Perkasie, PA 800-882-0512
Lakeside Foods
Manitowoc, WI 920-684-3356
M&R Company
Lodi, CA .209-369-2725
Metzger Specialty Brands
New York, NY 212-957-0055
Michigan Freeze Pack
Hart, MI. .231-873-2175
Miss Scarlett's
Chandler, AZ. 800-345-6734
New Era Canning Company
New Era, MI 231-861-2151
Ocean Mist
Castroville, CA 831-633-2144
Pictsweet Frozen Foods
Bells, TN .731-663-7600
Premier Packing Company
Bakersfield, CA 661-393-3320
Sedlock Farm
Lynn Center, IL 309-521-8284
Shafer Lake Fruit
Hartford, MI 269-621-3194
Smeltzer Orchard Company
Frankfort, MI 231-882-4421
Snowcrest Packer
Abbotsford, BC 604-859-4881
Sunfresh
Royal City, WA 509-346-9438
Superior Foods
Watsonville, CA 831-728-3691
T.S. Smith & Sons
Bridgeville, DE 302-337-8271
Walla Walla Gardeners' Association
Walla Walla, WA. 800-553-5014
Weil's Food Processing
Wheatley, ON 519-825-4572

Canned

Carriere Foods Inc
Montreal, QC 514-384-4281

EMERLING INTERNATIONAL FOODS, INC.

Emerling International Foods
Buffalo, NY. 716-833-7381

We supply food manufacturers and food service customers worldwide (since 1988) with bulk ingredients including: Fruits & Vegetables; Juice Concentrates; Herbs & Spices; Oils & Vinegars; Flavors & Colors; Honey & Molasses. We also produce PURE MAPLE SYRUP.

Fruit Belt Foods
Lawrence, MI 269-674-3939
Seneca Foods
Janesville, WI 608-757-6000
Seneca Foods Corporation
Marion, NY. 315-926-8100
Unique Ingredients
Naches, WA. 509-653-1991

Frozen

EMERLING INTERNATIONAL FOODS, INC.

Emerling International Foods
Buffalo, NY. 716-833-7381

We supply food manufacturers and food service customers worldwide (since 1988) with bulk ingredients including: Fruits & Vegetables; Juice Concentrates; Herbs & Spices; Oils & Vinegars; Flavors & Colors; Honey & Molasses. We also produce PURE MAPLE SYRUP.

Fruit Belt Foods
Lawrence, MI 269-674-3939
Unique Ingredients
Naches, WA. 509-653-1991

Avocado

Brooks Tropicals
Homestead, FL 800-327-4833
Calavo Foods
Santa Paula, CA 800-422-5280
Chiquita Brands International
Cincinnati, OH 800-438-0015
Del Monte Fresh Produce Company
Coral Gables, FL. 800-950-3683
Diversified Avocado Products
Mission Viejo, CA 800-879-2555

EMERLING INTERNATIONAL FOODS, INC.

Emerling International Foods
Buffalo, NY. 716-833-7381

We supply food manufacturers and food service customers worldwide (since 1988) with bulk ingredients including: Fruits & Vegetables; Juice Concentrates; Herbs & Spices; Oils & Vinegars; Flavors & Colors; Honey & Molasses. We also produce PURE MAPLE SYRUP.

Giumarra Companies
Escondido, CA 760-480-8502
J.R. Simplot Company
Boise, ID .208-336-2110
Janca's Jojoba Oil & Seed Company
Mesa, AZ. 480-497-9494
McDaniel Fruit Company
Fallbrook, CA 760-728-8438
Prime Produce
Orange, CA 714-771-0718
Reed Lang Farms
Rio Hondo, TX 956-748-2354
West Pak Avocado
Temecula, CA 800-266-4414

Avocado Products

Henry Avocado Company
Escondido, CA 760-745-6632

Bamboo Shoots

ConAgra Grocery Products
Archbold, OH 419-445-8015
Dong Kee Company
Chicago, IL 312-225-6340

EMERLING INTERNATIONAL FOODS, INC.

Emerling International Foods
Buffalo, NY. 716-833-7381

We supply food manufacturers and food service customers worldwide (since 1988) with bulk ingredients including: Fruits & Vegetables; Juice Concentrates; Herbs & Spices; Oils & Vinegars; Flavors & Colors; Honey & Molasses. We also produce PURE MAPLE SYRUP.

Lee's Food Products
Toronto, ON 416-465-2407

SupHerb Farms
Turlock, CA 800-787-4372

CrEATe! Get ready-to-use fresh flavor with SupHerb Farms' all-natural fresh frozen culinary herbs, specialty vegetables, culinary herb pastes, vegetable purees and creative blends. Complete microbiological testing ensures food safety. We set the standard for outstanding customer service, inspired culinary support, collaborative customer partnerships and innovative custom products.

Banana

A. Gagliano Company
Milwaukee, WI 800-272-1516

Chiquita Brands
  Cincinnati, OH 513-784-8000
Chiquita Brands International
  Cincinnati, OH 800-438-0015
Del Monte Fresh Produce Company
  Coral Gables, FL 800-950-3683

EMERLING INTERNATIONAL FOODS, INC.

Emerling International Foods
  Buffalo, NY. 716-833-7381

> We supply food manufacturers and food service customers worldwide (since 1988) with bulk ingredients including: Fruits & Vegetables; Juice Concentrates; Herbs & Spices; Oils & Vinegars; Flavors & Colors; Honey & Molasses. We also produce PURE MAPLE SYRUP.

Hawaiian Solar Dried Fruit
  Pahoa, HI. 808-965-8915
Papita USA
  Lancaster, PA 717-392-6376
Santanna Banana Company
  Harrisburg, PA 717-238-8321
Surface Banana Company
  Bluewell, WV 304-589-7202
Unique Ingredients
  Naches, WA. 509-653-1991
Very Best Foods
  Miami, FL .305-824-9165

Banana Products

Banana Distributing Company
  San Antonio, TX. 210-227-8285
Chiquita Brands International
  Cincinnati, OH 800-438-0015
Kozy Shack
  Hicksville, NY 516-870-3000
Spreda Group
  Prospect, KY. 502-426-9411

Dried

Chieftain Wild Rice Company
  Spooner, WI 800-262-6368
Fastachi
  Watertown, MA. 800-466-3022
Mariani Packing Company
  Vacaville, CA 800-672-8655
Setton International Foods
  Commack, NY 800-227-4397

Plantain

MIC Foods
  Miami, FL. 800-788-9335
Tantos Foods International
  Richmond Hill, ON. 905-763-9994
Very Best Foods
  Miami, FL .305-824-9165

Beans

A. Lassonde, Inc.
  Rougemont, QC 514-878-1057
Agricore United
  Winnipeg, MB. 204-944-5411
Allen Canning Company
  Siloam Springs, AR 800-234-2553
Amigos Canning Company
  San Antonio, TX. 800-580-3477
Archer Daniels Midland Company
  Decatur, IL 800-637-5843
Atlantic Quality Spice &Seasonings
  Edison, NJ. 800-584-0422
B&G Foods
  Parsippany, NJ. 973-401-6500
B&M
  Portland, ME. 207-772-8341
Basic American Foods
  Walnut Creek, CA. 800-227-4050
Beckman & Gast Company
  St Henry, OH. 419-678-4195
Buckhead Gourmet
  Atlanta, GA. 800-605-5754
Burnette Foods
  Elk Rapids, MI 231-264-8116
Bush Brothers & Company
  Dandridge, TN 865-509-2361
Bush Brothers & Company
  Knoxville, TN 865-588-7685

Buxton Foods
  Buxton, ND 800-726-8057
Cajun Boy's Louisiana Products
  Baton Rouge, LA 800-880-9575
California Fruit and Tomato Kitchens
  Riverbank, CA 209-869-9300
Camellia Beans
  New Orleans, LA 504-733-8480
Campbell Soup Company
  Camden, NJ 800-257-8443
Capco Enterprises
  East Hanover, NJ. 800-252-1011
Castella Imports
  Hauppauge, NY 866-227-8355
Chase Farms
  Walkerville, MI 231-873-3337
Chef Merito
  Encino, CA 800-637-4861
Chieftain Wild Rice Company
  Spooner, WI 800-262-6368
China Doll Company
  Saraland, AL 251-457-7641
Chiquita Processed Foods
  Milton Freewater, OR. 541-938-4461
Cobi Foods
  Hantsport, NS 800-565-8229
Coffee Bean International
  Portland, OR 800-877-0474
Colorado Bean Company/ Greeley Trading
  Greeley, CO. 888-595-2326
Cool Beans Coffee Company
  Portland, OR 503-520-0836
Cooperative Elevator
  Pigeon, MI 989-453-4500
Cooperative Elevator Company
  Pigeon, MI 989-453-4500
Country Cupboard
  Virginia City, NV 775-847-7300
Crookston Bean
  Crookston, MN 218-281-2567
Del Monte Foods
  San Francisco, CA 800-543-3090
Eckroat Seed Company
  Oklahoma City, OK 405-427-2484
Eden Foods Inc
  Clinton, MI 800-248-0320
Faribault Foods
  Minneapolis, MN 612-333-6461
Fine Foods Northwest
  Seattle, WA 800-862-3965
Foster Family Farm
  South Windsor, CT 860-648-9366
Georgia Vegetable Company
  Tifton, GA. 229-386-2374
Goya Foods
  Secaucus, NJ 201-348-4900
Goya Foods of Florida
  Miami, FL. 305-592-3150
Grandma Brown's Beans Inc
  Mexico, NY 315-963-7221
H.J. Heinz Company
  Pittsburgh, PA 412-237-5948
Hanover Foods Corporation
  Hanover, PA 717-632-6000
HealthBest
  San Marcos, CA 760-752-5230
Heartline Foods
  Westport, CT 203-222-0381
Heinz Company of Canada
  North York, ON. 800-268-6641
Hoopeston Foods
  Burnsville, MN 952-854-0903
Hormel Foods Corporation
  Austin, MN 800-523-4635
HP Schmid
  San Francisco, CA 415-765-5925
Indian Harvest
  Colusa, CA 800-294-2433
Inland Empire Foods
  Riverside, CA 888-452-3267
Inter-American Products
  Cincinnati, OH 800-645-2233
International Home Foods
  Milton, PA. 973-359-9920
Kalustyan Corporation
  Union, NJ .908-688-6111
Kelley Bean Company
  Torrington, WY. 307-532-2131
Kelley Bean Company
  Scottsbluff, NE 308-635-6438
Kennebec Bean Company
  North Vassalboro, ME 207-873-3473

Knight Seed Company
  Burnsville, MN 800-328-2999
L&S Packing Company
  Farmingdale, NY 800-286-6487
Lakeside Foods
  Plainview, MN 507-534-3141
Lakeside Foods
  Seymour, WI 920-833-2371
Les Aliments Ramico Foods
  St. Leonard, QC 514-329-1844
Louis Dreyfus Corporation
  Wilton, CT 203-761-2000
Lucks Food Decorating Company
  Tacoma, WA 206-674-7200
M&R Company
  Lodi, CA 209-369-2725
McCain Foods Canada
  Florenceville, NB 506-392-5541
Mercado Latino
  City of Industry, CA 626-333-6862
Midland Bean Company
  Cahone, CO. 970-562-4235
Mills Brothers International
  Tukwila, WA 206-575-3000
Miramar Fruit Trading Company
  Medley, FL 305-883-4774
Miyako Oriental Foods
  Baldwin Park, CA 877-788-6476
Morgan Food
  Austin, IN .888-430-1780
Moscow Seed Company
  Moscow, ID. 208-882-2324
National Frozen Foods Corporation
  Seattle, WA 206-322-8900
Nationwide Canning
  Cottam, ON 519-839-4831
Natural Foods
  Toledo, OH 800-860-0006
Naturex (Chart Corp)
  South Hackensack, NJ 201-440-5000
New Era Canning Company
  New Era, MI 231-861-2151
New Harvest Foods
  Pulaski, WI 920-822-2578
New Meridian
  Eaton, IN .765-396-3344
NORPAC Foods
  Lake Oswego, OR 503-635-9311
NORPAC Plant
  Salem, OR. 800-822-2898
North Bay Trading Company
  Brule, WI. 800-348-0164
Northern Feed & Bean Company
  Lucerne, CO 970-352-7875
Old Ranchers Canning Company
  Upland, CA 909-982-8895
Osowski Farms
  Minto, ND. 701-248-3341
Pacific Collier Fresh Company
  Immokalee, FL 800-226-7274
Paisano Food Products
  Elk Grove Village, IL 773-237-3773
Pastene Companies
  Canton, MA 781-830-8200
Pictsweet Frozen Foods
  Bells, TN .731-663-7600
Pleasant Grove Farms
  Pleasant Grove, CA 916-655-3391
Producers Cooperative
  Olathe, CO 970-323-5913
Produits Ronald
  St. Damase, QC 450-797-3303
Quetzal Company
  San Francisco, CA 888-673-8181
R&J Farms
  West Salem, OH 419-846-3179
Randall Food Products
  Cincinnati, OH 513-793-6525
Raymond-Hadley Corporation
  Spencer, NY 800-252-5220
Red River Commodities
  Fargo, ND 701-282-2600
Rice Company
  Roseville, CA 916-787-1084
Roberts Seed
  Axtell, NE .308-743-2565
Rosarita Mexican Foods Company
  Mesa, AZ. 480-964-8751
Ruskin Packaging
  Miami, FL. 305-324-1529
Sambets Cajun Deli
  Austin, TX. 800-472-6238

Scally's Imperial Importing Company Inc
Staten Island, NY 718-983-1938
Seabrook Brothers & Sons
Seabrook, NJ. 856-455-8080
Seapoint Farms
Costa Mesa, CA 888-722-7098
Seneca Foods
Marion, NY 315-926-8100
Seneca Foods
Cumberland, WI 715-822-2181
Smith Frozen Foods
Weston, OR. 541-566-3515
Smith Frozen Foods
Weston, OR. 800-547-0203
Snowcrest Packer
Abbotsford, BC. 604-859-4881
Somerset Industries
Spring House, PA 800-883-8728
SOPAKCO Foods
Mullins, SC. 800-276-9678
Spokane Seed Company
Spokane Valley, WA 509-535-3671
Sprague Foods
Belleville, ON 613-966-1200
Star of the West MillingCompany
Frankenmuth, MI 989-652-9971
Sugai Kona Coffee
Kealakekua, HI 808-322-7717
Talley Farms
Arroyo Grande, CA. 805-489-2508
Tipiak
Stamford, CT. 203-961-9117
Torn & Glasser
Los Angeles, CA. 800-282-6887
Torrefazione Barzula & Import
Mississauga, ON 905-625-6082
Trappe Packing Corporation
Trappe, MD. 410-476-3185
Trinidad Benham Company
Denver, CO 303-220-1400
Truitt Brothers Inc
Salem, OR. 800-547-8712
Twin City Foods
Stanwood, WA 206-515-2400
United Intertrade Corporation
Houston, TX 800-969-2233
US Foods
Lincoln, NE. 402-470-2021
Veronica Foods Company
Oakland, CA 800-370-5554
Weaver Nut Company
Ephrata, PA 717-738-3781
Webster Farms
Cambridge Station, NS 902-538-9492
Westlam Foods
Chino, CA .800-722-9519
WG Thompson & Sons
Blenheim, ON 519-676-5411
Wicklund Farms
Springfield, OR. 541-747-5998
Wildcat Produce
McGrew, NE 308-783-2438
Woodland Foods
Gurnee, IL. 847-625-8600
Z&S Distributing
Fresno, CA 800-467-0788
Zarda Bar-B-Q & Catering Company
Blue Springs, MO 800-776-7427

Adzuki

American Health & Nutrition
Ann Arbor, MI 734-677-5572
Chieftain Wild Rice Company
Spooner, WI 800-262-6368

EMERLING INTERNATIONAL FOODS, INC.

Emerling International Foods
Buffalo, NY. 716-833-7381

We supply food manufacturers and food service customers worldwide (since 1988) with bulk ingredients including: Fruits & Vegetables; Juice Concentrates; Herbs & Spices; Oils & Vinegars; Flavors & Colors; Honey & Molasses. We also produce PURE MAPLE SYRUP.

Organic Planet
San Francisco, CA 415-765-5590

Appaloosa

Chieftain Wild Rice Company
Spooner, WI 800-262-6368

Baked

A. Lassonde, Inc.
Rougemont, QC 514-878-1057
AlpineAire Foods
Rocklin, CA 800-322-6325
B&M
Portland, ME. 207-772-8341
Bush Brothers & Company
Augusta, WI 715-286-2211
Capco Enterprises
East Hanover, NJ. 800-252-1011
Captain Ken's Foods
St Paul, MN. 651-298-0071
Grandma Brown's Beans Inc
Mexico, NY 315-963-7221
Hanover Foods Corporation
Hanover, PA 717-632-6000
Mercado Latino
City of Industry, CA 626-333-6862
Produits Ronald
St. Damase, QC 450-797-3303
Wornick Company
Cincinnati, OH 800-860-4555
Zarda Bar-B-Q & Catering Company
Blue Springs, MO 800-776-7427

Black

Agricore United
Winnipeg, MB. 204-944-5411
Buckhead Gourmet
Atlanta, GA. 800-605-5754
Bush Brothers & Company
Augusta, WI 715-286-2211
Country Cupboard
Virginia City, NV 775-847-7300
Miyako Oriental Foods
Baldwin Park, CA. 877-788-6476

Blackeye (Cowpeas)

Bush Brothers & Company
Augusta, WI 715-286-2211
Chieftain Wild Rice Company
Spooner, WI 800-262-6368
Hanover Foods Corporation
Hanover, PA 717-632-6000
Trinidad Benham Company
Denver, CO 303-220-1400

Blue Lake

Canned

Allen Canning Company
Siloam Springs, AR 800-234-2553

EMERLING INTERNATIONAL FOODS, INC.

Emerling International Foods
Buffalo, NY. 716-833-7381

We supply food manufacturers and food service customers worldwide (since 1988) with bulk ingredients including: Fruits & Vegetables; Juice Concentrates; Herbs & Spices; Oils & Vinegars; Flavors & Colors; Honey & Molasses. We also produce PURE MAPLE SYRUP.

Faribault Foods
Minneapolis, MN 612-333-6461
Georgia Vegetable Company
Tifton, GA. 229-386-2374
Lakeside Foods
Seymour, WI 920-833-2371
McCain Foods Canada
Florenceville, NB 506-392-5541
New Era Canning Company
New Era, MI 231-861-2151
NORPAC Foods
Lake Oswego, OR. 503-635-9311
Omstead Foods Ltd
Burlington, ON 905-315-8883
Seneca Foods
Cumberland, WI 715-822-2181

Frozen

Allen Canning Company
Siloam Springs, AR 800-234-2553

EMERLING INTERNATIONAL FOODS, INC.

Emerling International Foods
Buffalo, NY. 716-833-7381

We supply food manufacturers and food service customers worldwide (since 1988) with bulk ingredients including: Fruits & Vegetables; Juice Concentrates; Herbs & Spices; Oils & Vinegars; Flavors & Colors; Honey & Molasses. We also produce PURE MAPLE SYRUP.

Faribault Foods
Minneapolis, MN 612-333-6461
Georgia Vegetable Company
Tifton, GA. 229-386-2374
Lakeside Foods
Seymour, WI 920-833-2371
McCain Foods Canada
Florenceville, NB 506-392-5541
NORPAC Foods
Lake Oswego, OR. 503-635-9311
Omstead Foods Ltd
Burlington, ON 905-315-8883
Pictsweet Frozen Foods
Bells, TN. .731-663-7600
Seabrook Brothers & Sons
Seabrook, NJ. 856-455-8080
Seneca Foods
Marion, NY 315-926-8100
Twin City Foods
Stanwood, WA 206-515-2400

Broad

Park 100 Foods
Tipton, IN .800-854-6504

Butter

Canned

EMERLING INTERNATIONAL FOODS, INC.

Emerling International Foods
Buffalo, NY. 716-833-7381

We supply food manufacturers and food service customers worldwide (since 1988) with bulk ingredients including: Fruits & Vegetables; Juice Concentrates; Herbs & Spices; Oils & Vinegars; Flavors & Colors; Honey & Molasses. We also produce PURE MAPLE SYRUP.

Frozen

EMERLING INTERNATIONAL FOODS, INC.

Emerling International Foods
Buffalo, NY. 716-833-7381

We supply food manufacturers and food service customers worldwide (since 1988) with bulk ingredients including: Fruits & Vegetables; Juice Concentrates; Herbs & Spices; Oils & Vinegars; Flavors & Colors; Honey & Molasses. We also produce PURE MAPLE SYRUP.

Canned

Carriere Foods Inc
Montreal, QC 514-384-4281
Goya of Great Lakes NewYYork
Angola, NY 716-549-0076
Seneca Foods Corporation
Marion, NY 315-926-8100

Cannellini

American Health & Nutrition
Ann Arbor, MI 734-677-5572
Bush Brothers & Company
Augusta, WI 715-286-2211
Chieftain Wild Rice Company
Spooner, WI 800-262-6368

EMERLING INTERNATIONAL FOODS, INC.

Emerling International Foods
Buffalo, NY 716-833-7381

We supply food manufacturers and food service customers worldwide (since 1988) with bulk ingredients including: Fruits & Vegetables; Juice Concentrates; Herbs & Spices; Oils & Vinegars; Flavors & Colors; Honey & Molasses. We also produce PURE MAPLE SYRUP.

Organic Planet
San Francisco, CA 415-765-5590

Chick

Agrocan
Toronto, ON 877-247-6226
American Health & Nutrition
Ann Arbor, MI 734-677-5572

EMERLING INTERNATIONAL FOODS, INC.

Emerling International Foods
Buffalo, NY 716-833-7381

We supply food manufacturers and food service customers worldwide (since 1988) with bulk ingredients including: Fruits & Vegetables; Juice Concentrates; Herbs & Spices; Oils & Vinegars; Flavors & Colors; Honey & Molasses. We also produce PURE MAPLE SYRUP.

Organic Planet
San Francisco, CA 415-765-5590

Chili

Bush Brothers & Company
Augusta, WI 715-286-2211
ConAgra Grocery Products
Irvine, CA 714-680-1000

EMERLING INTERNATIONAL FOODS, INC.

Emerling International Foods
Buffalo, NY 716-833-7381

We supply food manufacturers and food service customers worldwide (since 1988) with bulk ingredients including: Fruits & Vegetables; Juice Concentrates; Herbs & Spices; Oils & Vinegars; Flavors & Colors; Honey & Molasses. We also produce PURE MAPLE SYRUP.

Faribault Foods
Minneapolis, MN 612-333-6461
Hanover Foods Corporation
Hanover, PA 717-632-6000
Milnot Company
Litchfield, IL. 800-877-6455
Organic Planet
San Francisco, CA 415-765-5590
SOPAKCO Foods
Mullins, SC 800-276-9678

Dried

Lentil Blend

Moscow Seed Company
Moscow, ID. 208-882-2324

Dry

Adm Edible Bean Specialties
Kinde, MI 989-874-4720
Agland, Inc.
Eaton, CO 800-433-4688
Agri-Sales
Nashville, TN 800-251-1141
American Health & Nutrition
Ann Arbor, MI 734-677-5572
Basic American Foods
Blackfoot, ID 800-227-4050
Berberian Nut Company
Stocton, CA 209-465-9181
Burnette Foods
Elk Rapids, MI 231-264-8116
Bush Brothers & Company
Dandridge, TN 865-509-2361

C&F Foods
City of Industry, CA 626-723-1000
Camellia Beans
New Orleans, LA 504-733-8480
Central Bean Company
Quincy, WA 509-787-1544
Chieftain Wild Rice Company
Spooner, WI 800-262-6368
China Doll Company
Saraland, AL 251-457-7641
Colorado Bean Company/ Greeley Trading
Greeley, CO. 888-595-2326
Commodities Marketing, Inc.
Edison, NJ. 732-516-0700
ConAgra Trading and Processing
Omaha, NE 402-595-5775
Continental Grain/ContiGroup Companies
New York, NY 212-207-5930
Cooperative Elevator
Pigeon, MI 989-453-4500
Cooperative Elevator Company
Pigeon, MI 989-453-4500
Crookston Bean
Crookston, MN 218-281-2567
Eckhart Seed Company
Spreckels, CA 831-758-0925
Eckroat Seed Company
Oklahoma City, OK 405-427-2484

EMERLING INTERNATIONAL FOODS, INC.

Emerling International Foods
Buffalo, NY 716-833-7381

We supply food manufacturers and food service customers worldwide (since 1988) with bulk ingredients including: Fruits & Vegetables; Juice Concentrates; Herbs & Spices; Oils & Vinegars; Flavors & Colors; Honey & Molasses. We also produce PURE MAPLE SYRUP.

Faribault Foods
Minneapolis, MN 612-333-6461
Farmers Co-operative Grain Company
Kinde, MI 989-874-4200
Fowler Cooperative Association
Fowler, CO. 719-263-4266
Freeland Bean & Grain
Freeland, MI 800-447-9131
Greeley Elevator Company
Greeley, CO. 970-352-2575
H.K. Canning
Ventura, CA. 805-652-1392
High Country Elevators
Dove Creek, CO 970-677-2251
Hoopeston Foods
Burnsville, MN 952-854-0903
HP Schmid
San Francisco, CA 415-765-5925
Jack's Bean Company
Holyoke, CO 800-274-3702
Kalustyan Corporation
Union, NJ 908-688-6111
KBC Trading & Processing Company
Stockton, CA. 661-758-5178
Kelley Bean Company
Torrington, WY 307-532-2131
Kelley Bean Company
Scottsbluff, NE 308-635-6438
Kennebec Bean Company
North Vassalboro, ME 207-873-3473
Knight Seed Company
Burnsville, MN 800-328-2999
Lucks Food Decorating Company
Tacoma, WA 206-674-7200
Luxor California ExportsCorporation
San Diego, CA 619-692-9330
Michigan Ag Commodities
Breckenridge, MI 800-472-4629
Midland Bean Company
Cahone, CO. 970-562-4235
Mills Brothers International
Tukwila, WA 206-575-3000
Montrose Potato Growers
Montrose, CO 970-249-5623
Morrison Farms
Clearwater, NE 402-887-5335
N.K. Hurst Company
Indianapolis, IN 317-634-6425
New Meridian
Eaton, IN. 765-396-3344

Northern Feed & Bean Company
Lucerne, CO 970-352-7875
Northwest Pea & Bean Company
Spokane Valley, WA 509-534-3821
Oakland Bean Cleaning & Storage
Knights Landing, CA 530-735-6203
Organic Planet
San Francisco, CA 415-765-5590
Osowski Farms
Minto, ND. 701-248-3341
Paisano Food Products
Elk Grove Village, IL 773-237-3773
Powell Bean
Powell, WY 307-754-3121
Premier Packing Company
Bakersfield, CA 661-393-3320
Producers Cooperative
Olathe, CO 970-323-5913
Purity Foods
Okemos, MI 800-997-7358
R&J Farms
West Salem, OH 419-846-3179
Randag & Associates Inc
Elmhurst, IL 630-530-2830
Randall Food Products
Cincinnati, OH 513-793-6525
Red River Commodities
Fargo, ND 701-282-2600
Rhodes Bean & Supply Cooperative
Tracy, CA 209-835-1284
Roberts Seed
Axtell, NE 308-743-2565
Ruskin Packaging
Miami, FL. 305-324-1529
Russell E. Womack
Lubbock, TX. 877-787-3559
S&E Organic Farms
Bakersfield, CA 661-325-2644
Seed Enterprises
West Point, NE 888-440-7333
Smith Frozen Foods
Weston, OR 541-566-3515
Somerset Industries
Spring House, PA 800-883-8728
Sprague Foods
Belleville, ON 613-966-1200
Star of the West MillingCompany
Frankenmuth, MI 989-652-9971
Stockton District Kidney Bean
Tracy, CA 209-887-3420
Townsends Inc
Georgetown, DE 302-855-7100
Trinidad Bean & Elevator Company
Greeley, CO. 970-352-0346
Trinidad Benham Company
Denver, CO 303-220-1400
Trinidad Benham Company
Bridgeport, NE 308-262-1361
Trinidad/Benham Corporation
Patterson, CA 209-892-9002
Vege-Cool
Newman, CA. 209-862-2360
Webster Farms
Cambridge Station, NS 902-538-9492
Westbrae Natural Foods
Garden City, NY 800-434-4246
Westlam Foods
Chino, CA. 800-722-9519
WG Thompson & Sons
Blenheim, ON 519-676-5411
WSI
Caldwell, ID 208-459-0777

Canned

Carriere Foods Inc
Montreal, QC 514-384-4281

EMERLING INTERNATIONAL FOODS, INC.

Emerling International Foods
Buffalo, NY. 716-833-7381

We supply food manufacturers and food service customers worldwide (since 1988) with bulk ingredients including: Fruits & Vegetables; Juice Concentrates; Herbs & Spices; Oils & Vinegars; Flavors & Colors; Honey & Molasses. We also produce PURE MAPLE SYRUP.

Lucks Food Decorating Company
Tacoma, WA 206-674-7200

Edible

Agland, Inc.
Eaton, CO .800-433-4688
Russell E. Womack
Lubbock, TX. 877-787-3559
Star of the West MillingCompany
Frankenmuth, MI 989-652-9971

Fava

Chieftain Wild Rice Company
Spooner, WI 800-262-6368

EMERLING INTERNATIONAL FOODS, INC.

Emerling International Foods
Buffalo, NY. 716-833-7381

> We supply food manufacturers and food service customers worldwide (since 1988) with bulk ingredients including: Fruits & Vegetables; Juice Concentrates; Herbs & Spices; Oils & Vinegars; Flavors & Colors; Honey & Molasses. We also produce PURE MAPLE SYRUP.

Kalustyan Corporation
Union, NJ 908-688-6111
Organic Planet
San Francisco, CA 415-765-5590
Tarazi Specialty Foods
Chino, CA. .909-628-3601
Trappe Packing Corporation
Trappe, MD. 410-476-3185

Frozen

Agland, Inc.
Eaton, CO .800-433-4688
Allen Canning Company
Siloam Springs, AR 800-234-2553
Amigos Canning Company
San Antonio, TX. 800-580-3477
Buxton Foods
Buxton, ND. 800-726-8057
Campbell Soup Company
Camden, NJ. 800-257-8443
Captain Ken's Foods
St Paul, MN. 651-298-0071
Chase Farms
Walkerville, MI. 231-873-3337
Chiquita Brands
Cincinnati, OH 513-784-8000
Cobi Foods
Hantsport, NS 800-565-8229
ConAgra Grocery Products
Irvine, CA. .714-680-1000
Diversified Foods & Seasoning
Metairie, LA 504-846-5090

EMERLING INTERNATIONAL FOODS, INC.

Emerling International Foods
Buffalo, NY. 716-833-7381

> We supply food manufacturers and food service customers worldwide (since 1988) with bulk ingredients including: Fruits & Vegetables; Juice Concentrates; Herbs & Spices; Oils & Vinegars; Flavors & Colors; Honey & Molasses. We also produce PURE MAPLE SYRUP.

Faribault Foods
Minneapolis, MN 612-333-6461
Hanover Foods Corporation
Hanover, PA 717-632-6000
Lakeside Foods
Plainview, MN 507-534-3141
Lakeside Foods
Manitowoc, WI. 920-684-3356
Lakeside Foods
Seymour, WI. 920-833-2371
Lucerne Foods
Abbotsford, BC. 604-854-1191
National Frozen Foods Corporation
Seattle, WA 206-322-8900
New Meridian
Eaton, IN 765-396-3344
NORPAC Foods
Lake Oswego, OR. 503-635-9311
NORPAC Plant
Salem, OR. .800-822-2898

Omstead Foods Ltd
Burlington, ON 905-315-8883
Pictsweet Frozen Foods
Bells, TN. 731-663-7600
Randall Food Products
Tekonsha, MI 517-767-3247
Seabrook Brothers & Sons
Seabrook, NJ. 856-455-8080
Seneca Foods
Marion, NY. 315-926-8100
Smith Frozen Foods
Weston, OR. 541-566-3515
Smith Frozen Foods
Weston, OR. 800-547-0203
Snowcrest Packer
Abbotsford, BC. 604-859-4881
Trappe Packing Corporation
Trappe, MD. 410-476-3185
Twin City Foods
Stanwood, WA 206-515-2400

Garbanzo

Allen Canning Company
Siloam Springs, AR 800-234-2553
American Health & Nutrition
Ann Arbor, MI 734-677-5572
Bruce Foods Corporation
New Iberia, LA 800-299-9082
Buckhead Gourmet
Atlanta, GA. 800-605-5754
Bush Brothers & Company
Augusta, WI. 715-286-2211
California Fruit and Tomato Kitchens
Riverbank, CA 209-869-9300
Capco Enterprises
East Hanover, NJ. 800-252-1011
Chieftain Wild Rice Company
Spooner, WI 800-262-6368
Cobi Foods
Hantsport, NS 800-565-8229

EMERLING INTERNATIONAL FOODS, INC.

Emerling International Foods
Buffalo, NY. 716-833-7381

> We supply food manufacturers and food service customers worldwide (since 1988) with bulk ingredients including: Fruits & Vegetables; Juice Concentrates; Herbs & Spices; Oils & Vinegars; Flavors & Colors; Honey & Molasses. We also produce PURE MAPLE SYRUP.

Fastachi
Watertown, MA. 800-466-3022
Kalustyan Corporation
Union, NJ 908-688-6111
Northwest Pea & Bean Company
Spokane Valley, WA 509-534-3821
Organic Planet
San Francisco, CA 415-765-5590
Sprague Foods
Belleville, ON 613-966-1200

Great Northern

Agricore United
Winnipeg, MB. 204-944-5411
American Health & Nutrition
Ann Arbor, MI 734-677-5572
Bush Brothers & Company
Augusta, WI. 715-286-2211
Callaway Packing Company
Delta, CO 800-332-6932
Chieftain Wild Rice Company
Spooner, WI 800-262-6368
Culinary Standards Corporation
Louisville, KY 800-778-3434

EMERLING INTERNATIONAL FOODS, INC.

Emerling International Foods
Buffalo, NY. 716-833-7381

> We supply food manufacturers and food service customers worldwide (since 1988) with bulk ingredients including: Fruits & Vegetables; Juice Concentrates; Herbs & Spices; Oils & Vinegars; Flavors & Colors; Honey & Molasses. We also produce PURE MAPLE SYRUP.

Hanover Foods Corporation
Hanover, PA 717-632-6000
Jack's Bean Company
Holyoke, CO 800-274-3702
Kelley Bean Company
Scottsbluff, NE 308-635-6438
Lucks Food Decorating Company
Tacoma, WA 206-674-7200
Organic Planet
San Francisco, CA 415-765-5590
Randall Food Products
Cincinnati, OH 513-793-6525
Randall Food Products
Tekonsha, MI 517-767-3247

Greek

Canned

Agrocan
Toronto, ON 877-247-6226

Green

Allen Canning Company
Siloam Springs, AR 800-234-2553
Beckman & Gast Company
St Henry, OH. 419-678-4195
Burnette Foods
Elk Rapids, MI 231-264-8116
Bush Brothers & Company
Dandridge, TN 865-509-2361
Cobi Foods
Hantsport, NS 800-565-8229
Culinary Standards Corporation
Louisville, KY 800-778-3434
Faribault Foods
Minneapolis, MN 612-333-6461
Georgia Vegetable Company
Tifton, GA. .229-386-2374
Hanover Foods Corporation
Hanover, PA 717-632-6000
Lakeside Foods
Seymour, WI. 920-833-2371
Miss Scarlett's
Chandler, AZ. 800-345-6734
National Frozen Foods Corporation
Seattle, WA 206-322-8900
New Era Canning Company
New Era, MI 231-861-2151
New Harvest Foods
Pulaski, WI. 920-822-2578
NORPAC Foods
Lake Oswego, OR. 503-635-9311
NORPAC Plant
Salem, OR. .800-822-2898
Patterson Frozen Foods
Patterson, CA 209-892-2611
Pictsweet Frozen Foods
Bells, TN. 731-663-7600
Princeville Canning Company
Princeville, IL 309-385-4301
Seabrook Brothers & Sons
Seabrook, NJ. 856-455-8080
Seneca Foods
Marion, NY. 315-926-8100
Sunrise Growers
Placentia, CA 714-630-2170
Trappe Packing Corporation
Trappe, MD. 410-476-3185
Twin City Foods
Stanwood, WA 206-515-2400
Veronica Foods Company
Oakland, CA 800-370-5554
Wicklund Farms
Springfield, OR. 541-747-5998
Wildcat Produce
McGrew, NE 308-783-2438

Canned

Allen Canning Company
Siloam Springs, AR 800-234-2553
Beckman & Gast Company
St Henry, OH. 419-678-4195
Burnette Foods
Elk Rapids, MI 231-264-8116
Carriere Foods Inc
Montreal, QC 514-384-4281
Chiquita Brands
Cincinnati, OH 513-784-8000
Commodities Marketing, Inc.
Edison, NJ. 732-516-0700

EMERLING INTERNATIONAL FOODS, INC.

Emerling International Foods
Buffalo, NY. 716-833-7381

We supply food manufacturers and food service customers worldwide (since 1988) with bulk ingredients including: Fruits & Vegetables; Juice Concentrates; Herbs & Spices; Oils & Vinegars; Flavors & Colors; Honey & Molasses. We also produce PURE MAPLE SYRUP.

Faribault Foods
Minneapolis, MN 612-333-6461
Lakeside Foods
Mondovi, WI 715-926-5075
Lakeside Foods
Seymour, WI 920-833-2371
New Era Canning Company
New Era, MI 231-861-2151
New Harvest Foods
Pulaski, WI 920-822-2578
NORPAC Foods
Lake Oswego, OR. 503-635-9311
NORPAC Plant
Salem, OR. 800-822-2898
Omstead Foods Ltd
Burlington, ON 905-315-8883
Poynette Distribution Center
Poynette, WI 608-635-4396

Princeville Canning Company
Princeville, IL. 309-385-4301
Seneca Foods
Cumberland, WI 715-822-2181
Truitt Brothers Inc
Salem, OR. 800-547-8712

Frozen

Cobi Foods
Hantsport, NS 800-565-8229
Lakeside Foods
Seymour, WI 920-833-2371
National Frozen Foods Corporation
Seattle, WA 206-322-8900
NORPAC Foods
Lake Oswego, OR. 503-635-9311
NORPAC Plant
Salem, OR. 800-822-2898
Omstead Foods Ltd
Burlington, ON 905-315-8883
Pictsweet Frozen Foods
Bells, TN 731-663-7600
Seabrook Brothers & Sons
Seabrook, NJ 856-455-8080
Seneca Foods
Marion, NY 315-926-8100
Trappe Packing Corporation
Trappe, MD. 410-476-3185
Twin City Foods
Stanwood, WA 206-515-2400

Green Mung

American Health & Nutrition
Ann Arbor, MI 734-677-5572
Organic Planet
San Francisco, CA 415-765-5590

Italian

National Frozen Foods Corporation
Seattle, WA 206-322-8900
Pictsweet Frozen Foods
Bells, TN 731-663-7600

Kidney

Agland, Inc.
Eaton, CO 800-433-4688
Burnette Foods
Elk Rapids, MI 231-264-8116
Cobi Foods
Hantsport, NS 800-565-8229
ConAgra Grocery Products
Irvine, CA 714-680-1000
Cooperative Elevator Company
Pigeon, MI 989-453-4500
Cordon Bleu International
Anjou, QC 514-352-3000
Hanover Foods Corporation
Hanover, PA 717-632-6000
International Home Foods
Milton, PA. 973-359-9920
Jack's Bean Company
Holyoke, CO 800-274-3702
Look's Gourmet Food Company
Whiting, ME 800-962-6258
Lucks Food Decorating Company
Tacoma, WA 206-674-7200
Michigan Ag Commodities
Breckenridge, MI 800-472-4629
Nationwide Canning
Cottam, ON 519-839-4831
New Era Canning Company
New Era, MI 231-861-2151
Oakland Bean Cleaning & Storage
Knights Landing, CA 530-735-6203
Pleasant Grove Farms
Pleasant Grove, CA 916-655-3391
Red River Commodities
Fargo, ND 701-282-2600
Sprague Foods
Belleville, ON. 613-966-1200
WG Thompson & Sons
Blenheim, ON 519-676-5411

Canned

Burnette Foods
Elk Rapids, MI 231-264-8116
Cordon Bleu International
Anjou, QC 514-352-3000

EMERLING INTERNATIONAL FOODS, INC.

Emerling International Foods
Buffalo, NY 716-833-7381

We supply food manufacturers and food service customers worldwide (since 1988) with bulk ingredients including: Fruits & Vegetables; Juice Concentrates; Herbs & Spices; Oils & Vinegars; Flavors & Colors; Honey & Molasses. We also produce PURE MAPLE SYRUP.

International Home Foods
Milton, PA 973-359-9920
Lucks Food Decorating Company
Tacoma, WA 206-674-7200
Michigan Ag Commodities
Breckenridge, MI 800-472-4629
Nationwide Canning
Cottam, ON 519-839-4831
New Era Canning Company
New Era, MI 231-861-2151
Red River Commodities
Fargo, ND 701-282-2600
Vegetable Juices
Chicago, IL 888-776-9752

Dark Red

Agrocan
Toronto, ON 877-247-6226
Bush Brothers & Company
Augusta, WI 715-286-2211
Cobi Foods
Hantsport, NS 800-565-8229
Cordon Bleu International
Anjou, QC 514-352-3000
Red River Commodities
Fargo, ND 701-282-2600
Sprague Foods
Belleville, ON 613-966-1200

Frozen

Cobi Foods
Hantsport, NS 800-565-8229

EMERLING INTERNATIONAL FOODS, INC.

Emerling International Foods
Buffalo, NY 716-833-7381

We supply food manufacturers and food service customers worldwide (since 1988) with bulk ingredients including: Fruits & Vegetables; Juice Concentrates; Herbs & Spices; Oils & Vinegars; Flavors & Colors; Honey & Molasses. We also produce PURE MAPLE SYRUP.

Michigan Ag Commodities
Breckenridge, MI 800-472-4629
Vegetable Juices
Chicago, IL 888-776-9752

Light Red

Cobi Foods
Hantsport, NS 800-565-8229
Jack's Bean Company
Holyoke, CO 800-274-3702
Red River Commodities
Fargo, ND 701-282-2600

Lentil

Agricore United
Winnipeg, MB 204-944-5411
Allen Canning Company
Siloam Springs, AR 800-234-2553
American Health & Nutrition
Ann Arbor, MI 734-677-5572
C&F Foods
City of Industry, CA 626-723-1000
Camellia Beans
New Orleans, LA 504-733-8480
Chieftain Wild Rice Company
Spooner, WI 800-262-6368
China Doll Company
Saraland, AL 251-457-7641

EMERLING INTERNATIONAL FOODS, INC.

Emerling International Foods
Buffalo, NY 716-833-7381

We supply food manufacturers and food service customers worldwide (since 1988) with bulk ingredients including: Fruits & Vegetables; Juice Concentrates; Herbs & Spices; Oils & Vinegars; Flavors & Colors; Honey & Molasses. We also produce PURE MAPLE SYRUP.

Garden Valley Foods
Sutherlin, OR 541-459-9565
HP Schmid
San Francisco, CA 415-765-5925
Humboldt Flour Mills
Humboldt, SK 306-682-2577
Inland Empire Foods
Riverside, CA 888-452-3267
Kalustyan Corporation
Union, NJ 908-688-6111
Kennebec Bean Company
North Vassalboro, ME 207-873-3473
Mezza
Lake Forest, IL 888-206-6054
Mills Brothers International
Tukwila, WA 206-575-3000
Northwest Pea & Bean Company
Spokane Valley, WA 509-534-3821
Primo Foods
Toronto, ON 800-377-6945
Sara Lee Corporation
Downers Grove, IL 630-598-8100
Shah Trading Company
Toronto, ON 416-292-6927
Spokane Seed Company
Spokane Valley, WA 509-535-3671
United Pulse Trading
Bismarck, ND 701-751-1623
Wallace Grain & Pea Company
Palouse, WA 509-878-1561
Woodland Foods
Gurnee, IL 847-625-8600

Canned

Allen Canning Company
Siloam Springs, AR 800-234-2553
Kennebec Bean Company
North Vassalboro, ME 207-873-3473
Organic Planet
San Francisco, CA 415-765-5590

Lima

Allen Canning Company
Siloam Springs, AR 800-234-2553
California Fruit and Tomato Kitchens
Riverbank, CA 209-869-9300
Chieftain Wild Rice Company
Spooner, WI 800-262-6368
Cobi Foods
Hantsport, NS 800-565-8229
Country Cupboard
Virginia City, NV 775-847-7300
Culinary Standards Corporation
Louisville, KY 800-778-3434
Del Monte Foods
San Francisco, CA 800-543-3090
Hanover Foods Corporation
Hanover, PA 717-632-6000
Lakeside Foods
Plainview, MN 507-534-3141
Lucks Food Decorating Company
Tacoma, WA 206-674-7200
National Frozen Foods Corporation
Seattle, WA 206-322-8900
Patterson Frozen Foods
Patterson, CA 209-892-2611
Pictsweet Frozen Foods
Bells, TN 731-663-7600
Ruskin Packaging
Miami, FL 305-324-1529
Seabrook Brothers & Sons
Seabrook, NJ 856-455-8080
Smith Frozen Foods
Weston, OR 541-566-3515
Smith Frozen Foods
Weston, OR 800-547-0203
Trappe Packing Corporation
Trappe, MD 410-476-3185

Trinidad Benham Company
Denver, CO 303-220-1400
Vege-Cool
Newman, CA 209-862-2360

Canned

Allen Canning Company
Siloam Springs, AR 800-234-2553
Del Monte Foods
San Francisco, CA 800-543-3090

EMERLING INTERNATIONAL FOODS, INC.

Emerling International Foods
Buffalo, NY 716-833-7381

We supply food manufacturers and food service customers worldwide (since 1988) with bulk ingredients including: Fruits & Vegetables; Juice Concentrates; Herbs & Spices; Oils & Vinegars; Flavors & Colors; Honey & Molasses. We also produce PURE MAPLE SYRUP.

Hanover Foods Corporation
Hanover, PA 717-632-6000
Lakeside Foods
Plainview, MN 507-534-3141
Lucks Food Decorating Company
Tacoma, WA 206-674-7200

Frozen

Allen Canning Company
Siloam Springs, AR 800-234-2553
Cobi Foods
Hantsport, NS 800-565-8229
Hanover Foods Corporation
Hanover, PA 717-632-6000
National Frozen Foods Corporation
Seattle, WA 206-322-8900
Pictsweet Frozen Foods
Bells, TN 731-663-7600
Seabrook Brothers & Sons
Seabrook, NJ 856-455-8080
Smith Frozen Foods
Weston, OR 541-566-3515
Smith Frozen Foods
Weston, OR 800-547-0203

Lupini

Castella Imports
Hauppauge, NY 866-227-8355
Chieftain Wild Rice Company
Spooner, WI 800-262-6368
Cobi Foods
Hantsport, NS 800-565-8229

EMERLING INTERNATIONAL FOODS, INC.

Emerling International Foods
Buffalo, NY 716-833-7381

We supply food manufacturers and food service customers worldwide (since 1988) with bulk ingredients including: Fruits & Vegetables; Juice Concentrates; Herbs & Spices; Oils & Vinegars; Flavors & Colors; Honey & Molasses. We also produce PURE MAPLE SYRUP.

L&S Packing Company
Farmingdale, NY 800-286-6487

Mung

Green

Chieftain Wild Rice Company
Spooner, WI 800-262-6368
Cobi Foods
Hantsport, NS 800-565-8229
Commodities Marketing, Inc.
Edison, NJ 732-516-0700
Eckroat Seed Company
Oklahoma City, OK 405-427-2484

EMERLING INTERNATIONAL FOODS, INC.

Emerling International Foods
Buffalo, NY 716-833-7381

We supply food manufacturers and food service
customers worldwide (since 1988) with bulk ingredients including: Fruits & Vegetables; Juice
Concentrates; Herbs & Spices; Oils & Vinegars;
Flavors & Colors; Honey & Molasses. We also
produce PURE MAPLE SYRUP.

Jonathan's Sprouts
Rochester, MA 508-763-2577
Kalustyan Corporation
Union, NJ 908-688-6111

Navy

Central Bean Company
Quincy, WA 509-787-1544
Chieftain Wild Rice Company
Spooner, WI 800-262-6368
Cooperative Elevator Company
Pigeon, MI 989-453-4500
Jack's Bean Company
Holyoke, CO 800-274-3702
Lucks Food Decorating Company
Tacoma, WA 206-674-7200
New Era Canning Company
New Era, MI 231-861-2151
Sprague Foods
Belleville, ON 613-966-1200

Canned

EMERLING INTERNATIONAL FOODS, INC.

Emerling International Foods
Buffalo, NY 716-833-7381

We supply food manufacturers and food service
customers worldwide (since 1988) with bulk ingredients including: Fruits & Vegetables; Juice
Concentrates; Herbs & Spices; Oils & Vinegars;
Flavors & Colors; Honey & Molasses. We also
produce PURE MAPLE SYRUP.

Lucks Food Decorating Company
Tacoma, WA 206-674-7200
New Era Canning Company
New Era, MI 231-861-2151

Pink

Central Bean Company
Quincy, WA 509-787-1544
Oakland Bean Cleaning & Storage
Knights Landing, CA 530-735-6203

Pinto

Adm Edible Bean Specialties
Kinde, MI 989-874-4720
Agland, Inc.
Eaton, CO 800-433-4688
Agricore United
Winnipeg, MB 204-944-5411
American Health & Nutrition
Ann Arbor, MI 734-677-5572
Bush Brothers & Company
Augusta, WI 715-286-2211
Buxton Foods
Buxton, ND 800-726-8057
Central Bean Company
Quincy, WA 509-787-1544
Chieftain Wild Rice Company
Spooner, WI 800-262-6368
Crookston Bean
Crookston, MN 218-281-2567

To advertise in the *Food &
Beverage Market Place* Online Database
call **(800) 562-2139** or log on to
http://gold.greyhouse.com
and click on "Advertise."

EMERLING INTERNATIONAL FOODS, INC.

Emerling International Foods
Buffalo, NY 716-833-7381

We supply food manufacturers and food service
customers worldwide (since 1988) with bulk ingredients including: Fruits & Vegetables; Juice
Concentrates; Herbs & Spices; Oils & Vinegars;
Flavors & Colors; Honey & Molasses. We also
produce PURE MAPLE SYRUP.

Fowler Cooperative Association
Fowler, CO 719-263-4266
Hanover Foods Corporation
Hanover, PA 717-632-6000
International Home Foods
Milton, PA 973-359-9920
Jack's Bean Company
Holyoke, CO 800-274-3702
Kelley Bean Company
Scottsbluff, NE 308-635-6438
Lucks Food Decorating Company
Tacoma, WA 206-674-7200
Midland Bean Company
Cahone, CO 970-562-4235
Montrose Potato Growers
Montrose, CO 970-249-5623
Northern Feed & Bean Company
Lucerne, CO 970-352-7875
Organic Planet
San Francisco, CA 415-765-5590
Powell Bean
Powell, WY 307-754-3121
Premier Packing Company
Bakersfield, CA 661-393-3320
Producers Cooperative
Olathe, CO 970-323-5913
Randall Food Products
Cincinnati, OH 513-793-6525
Randall Food Products
Tekonsha, MI 517-767-3247
Russell E. Womack
Lubbock, TX 877-787-3559
Sunfresh
Royal City, WA 509-346-9438
Trinidad Benham Company
Denver, CO 303-220-1400
Vegetable Juices
Chicago, IL 888-776-9752
WSI
Caldwell, ID 208-459-0777

Refried

Allen Canning Company
Siloam Springs, AR 800-234-2553
Amigos Canning Company
San Antonio, TX 800-580-3477
Basic American Foods
Walnut Creek, CA 800-227-4050
Colorado Bean Company/ Greeley Trading
Greeley, CO 888-595-2326
Hormel Foods Corporation
Austin, MN 800-523-4635
Rosarita Mexican Foods Company
Mesa, AZ 480-964-8751
Trappe Packing Corporation
Trappe, MD 410-476-3185

Canned

Allen Canning Company
Siloam Springs, AR 800-234-2553
Amigos Canning Company
San Antonio, TX 800-580-3477
Bruce Foods Corporation
New Iberia, LA 800-299-9082
Bush Brothers & Company
Augusta, WI 715-286-2211
Morgan Food
Austin, IN 888-430-1780
Rosarita Mexican Foods Company
Mesa, AZ 480-964-8751

Dried

Colorado Bean Company/ Greeley Trading
Greeley, CO 888-595-2326

Small Red

Central Bean Company
Quincy, WA 509-787-1544

ConAgra Grocery Products
Irvine, CA 714-680-1000

Snake

Del Monte Foods
San Francisco, CA 800-543-3090

Wax

Allen Canning Company
Siloam Springs, AR 800-234-2553
Cobi Foods
Hantsport, NS 800-565-8229
Hanover Foods Corporation
Hanover, PA 717-632-6000
Lakeside Foods
Seymour, WI 920-833-2371
National Frozen Foods Corporation
Seattle, WA 206-322-8900
New Era Canning Company
New Era, MI 231-861-2151
NORPAC Foods
Lake Oswego, OR 503-635-9311
Pictsweet Frozen Foods
Bells, TN 731-663-7600
Seabrook Brothers & Sons
Seabrook, NJ 856-455-8080
Seneca Foods
Marion, NY 315-926-8100
Trappe Packing Corporation
Trappe, MD 410-476-3185
Twin City Foods
Stanwood, WA 206-515-2400

Canned

Allen Canning Company
Siloam Springs, AR 800-234-2553
Carriere Foods Inc
Montreal, QC 514-384-4281

EMERLING INTERNATIONAL FOODS, INC.

Emerling International Foods
Buffalo, NY 716-833-7381

We supply food manufacturers and food service
customers worldwide (since 1988) with bulk ingredients including: Fruits & Vegetables; Juice
Concentrates; Herbs & Spices; Oils & Vinegars;
Flavors & Colors; Honey & Molasses. We also
produce PURE MAPLE SYRUP.

Lakeside Foods
Seymour, WI 920-833-2371
New Era Canning Company
New Era, MI 231-861-2151
NORPAC Foods
Lake Oswego, OR 503-635-9311
Omstead Foods Ltd
Burlington, ON 905-315-8883
Seneca Foods
Cumberland, WI 715-822-2181

Frozen

Allen Canning Company
Siloam Springs, AR 800-234-2553
Cobi Foods
Hantsport, NS 800-565-8229

EMERLING INTERNATIONAL FOODS, INC.

Emerling International Foods
Buffalo, NY 716-833-7381

We supply food manufacturers and food service
customers worldwide (since 1988) with bulk ingredients including: Fruits & Vegetables; Juice
Concentrates; Herbs & Spices; Oils & Vinegars;
Flavors & Colors; Honey & Molasses. We also
produce PURE MAPLE SYRUP.

Lakeside Foods
Seymour, WI 920-833-2371
National Frozen Foods Corporation
Seattle, WA 206-322-8900
NORPAC Foods
Lake Oswego, OR 503-635-9311
Omstead Foods Ltd
Burlington, ON 905-315-8883

Pictsweet Frozen Foods
Bells, TN 731-663-7600
Seabrook Brothers & Sons
Seabrook, NJ. 856-455-8080
Seneca Foods
Marion, NY .315-926-8100
Trappe Packing Corporation
Trappe, MD. 410-476-3185
Twin City Foods
Stanwood, WA 206-515-2400

Beets

A. Duda Farm Fresh Foods
Belle Glade, FL. 561-996-7621
Dehydrates Inc
Hewlett, NY 800-983-4443
Frank Capurro & Son
Moss Landing, CA 831-728-3904
Ghirardelli Ranch
Petaluma, CA 707-795-7616
Gouw Quality Onions
Taber, AB 403-223-1440
Indian Rock Produce
Perkasie, PA 800-882-0512
Lakeside Foods
Seymour, WI 920-833-2371
NORPAC Plant
Salem, OR. .800-822-2898
Old Country Packers
Duryea, PA .570-655-9608
Osowski Farms
Minto, ND. .701-248-3341
S&G Products
Nicholasville, KY 800-826-7652
Schiff Food Products
North Bergen, NJ 201-861-2503
Seneca Foods
Marion, NY .315-926-8100
Vegetable Juices
Chicago, IL .888-776-9752

Canned

EMERLING INTERNATIONAL FOODS, INC.

Emerling International Foods
Buffalo, NY. 716-833-7381

We supply food manufacturers and food service customers worldwide (since 1988) with bulk ingredients including: Fruits & Vegetables; Juice Concentrates; Herbs & Spices; Oils & Vinegars; Flavors & Colors; Honey & Molasses. We also produce PURE MAPLE SYRUP.

Lakeside Foods
Seymour, WI 920-833-2371
NORPAC Plant
Salem, OR. .800-822-2898
Seneca Foods
Marion, NY .315-926-8100
Seneca Foods Corporation
Marion, NY .315-926-8100

Frozen

EMERLING INTERNATIONAL FOODS, INC.

Emerling International Foods
Buffalo, NY. 716-833-7381

We supply food manufacturers and food service customers worldwide (since 1988) with bulk ingredients including: Fruits & Vegetables; Juice Concentrates; Herbs & Spices; Oils & Vinegars; Flavors & Colors; Honey & Molasses. We also produce PURE MAPLE SYRUP.

NORPAC Plant
Salem, OR. .800-822-2898
Vegetable Juices
Chicago, IL .888-776-9752

Pickled

Seneca Foods Corporation
Marion, NY. 315-926-8100

Sugar

Agri-Dairy Products
Purchase, NY 914-697-9580
Imperial Sugar Company
Sugar Land, TX. 800-727-8427
Michigan Sugar Company
Saginaw, MI 989-799-7300
Nyssa-Nampa Beet Growers
Nyssa, OR. .541-372-2904
Osowski Farms
Minto, ND. .701-248-3341
Western Sugar Company
Scottsbluff, NE 308-632-4155
Western Sugar Cooperative
Denver, CO .303-830-3939

Berries

Abbotsford Growers Co-operative
Abbotsford, BC. 604-864-0022
Allen's Blueberry Freezer
Ellsworth, ME. 207-667-5561
Atlantic Blueberry Company
Hammonton, NJ 609-561-8600
Behm Blueberry Farms
Grand Haven, MI 616-846-1650
Blue Chip Group
Salt Lake City, UT 800-878-0099
Boekhout Farms
Ontario, NY 315-524-4041
Brady Farms
West Olive, MI 616-842-3916
Cal-Sun Produce Company
Oxnard, CA. 805-985-2262
Carolina Blueberry Association
Garland, NC. 910-588-4220
Charles Dennery Pillsbury
New Orleans, LA 504-733-2331
Cherry Central Cooperative Inc
Traverse City, MI 231-946-1860
Chieftain Wild Rice Company
Spooner, WI 800-262-6368
Coastal Classics
Duxbury, MA 508-746-6058
Columbia Empire Farms
Sherwood, OR. 503-538-2156
Cranberry Products
Eagle River, WI. 715-479-4466
Daerim America
Maywood, NJ 800-635-0781
Decas Cranberry Products
Wareham, MA 800-649-9811
Del Mar Food Products Corporation
Watsonville, CA 831-722-3516
E.W. Bowker Company
Pemberton, NJ. 609-894-9508
Eagle Eye Produce
Iona, ID 208-522-2343
Europa Foods
Saddle Brook, NJ 201-368-8929
Firestone Packing Company
Vancouver, WA 360-695-9484
From Oregon
Springfield, OR. 541-747-4222
Grove Fresh Distributors
Chicago, IL .773-288-2065
Grow-Pac
Cornelius, OR 503-357-9691
J.H. Verbridge & Son
Williamson, NY 315-589-2366
Jersey Fruit CooperativeAssociation
Glassboro, NJ 856-863-9100
JRL
Hammonton, NJ 609-561-1572
K.B. Hall Ranch
Ojai, CA 805-646-4512
Kerr Concentrates
Salem, OR. .800-910-5377
Krupka's Blueberries
Fennville, MI 269-857-4278
Leelanau Fruit Company
Suttons Bay, MI 231-271-3514
Leelanau Fruit Company
Suttons Bay, MI 800-431-0718
Macrie Brothers
Hammonton, NJ 609-561-6822
Mazzoni Brothers
Minotola, NJ 609-561-6515
Meduri Farms Inc
Dallas, OR. .503-831-1097
Midwest Blueberry Farms
Holland, MI. 616-399-2133

North American Blueberry Council
Folsom, CA. 800-824-6395
Northern Michigan Fruit Company
Omena, MI .231-386-5142
Old Country Farms
East Sandwich, MA 888-707-5558
Overlake Blueberry Farm
Bellevue, WA 425-453-8613
Oxford Frozen Foods Limited
Oxford, NS .902-447-2100
Pacific Blueberries
Rochester, WA 360-273-5405
Pamlico Packing Company
Grantsboro, NC. 800-682-1113
Pavich Family Farms
Terra Bella, CA. 661-391-1000
Plaidberry Company
Vista, CA. 760-727-5403
R M Lawton Cranberries
Middleboro, MA 508-947-7465
Ragold Confections
Wilton Manors, FL 954-566-9092
Richard Lanza
Hammonton, NJ 609-561-3984
Scenic Fruit Company
Gresham, OR. 800-554-5578
Setton International Foods
Commack, NY 800-227-4397
Smeltzer Orchard Company
Frankfort, MI 231-882-4421
Snokist Growers
Yakima, WA 509-457-8444
Snowcrest Packer
Abbotsford, BC. 604-859-4881
Stanley Orchards
Modena, NY 845-883-7351
Stilwell Foods
Stilwell, OK 918-696-8325
Sun Groves
Safety Harbor, FL 800-672-6438
Terri Lynn
Elgin, IL 800-323-0775
Timber Crest Farms
Healdsburg, CA 888-374-9325
Tom Ringhausen Orchards
Hardin, IL 618-576-2311
Tru-Blu Cooperative Associates
New Lisbon, NJ 609-894-8717
Usine de Congelation St. Bruno
St. Bruno, QC 418-343-2206
Valley View Blueberries
Vancouver, WA 360-892-2839
Vintage Produce Sales
Kingsburg, CA 559-897-1622
Violore Foods Company
Laredo, TX .956-726-3633
Well Pict Berries
Watsonville, CA 831-722-3871
Wetherby Cranberry Company
Warrens, WI 608-378-4813
Wilhelm Foods
Newberg, OR 503-538-2929
Zipp Manufacturing Company
Hornerville, OH 800-521-8700

Canned & Frozen

Abbotsford Growers Co-operative
Abbotsford, BC. 604-864-0022
Allen's Blueberry Freezer
Ellsworth, ME. 207-667-5561
Atlantic Blueberry Company
Hammonton, NJ 609-561-8600
Boekhout Farms
Ontario, NY. 315-524-4041
Brady Farms
West Olive, MI 616-842-3916
Carolina Blueberry Association
Garland, NC 910-588-4220

Cherry Central Cooperative Inc
Traverse City, MI 231-946-1860
E.W. Bowker Company
Pemberton, NJ. 609-894-9508
G M Allen & Son
Blue Hill, ME .207-469-7060
Grow-Pac
Cornelius, OR .503-357-9691
J.H. Verbridge & Son
Williamson, NY 315-589-2366
JRL
Hammonton, NJ 609-561-1572
Kerr Concentrates
Salem, OR 800-910-5377
Leelanau Fruit Company
Suttons Bay, MI 231-271-3514
Leelanau Fruit Company
Suttons Bay, MI 800-431-0718
Lucerne Foods
Abbotsford, BC. 604-854-1191
Northern Michigan Fruit Company
Omena, MI 231-386-5142
Oxford Frozen Foods Limited
Oxford, NS 902-447-2100
Pacific Blueberries
Rochester, WA .360-273-5405
Plaidberry Company
Vista, CA 760-727-5403
Rainbow Farms
Upper Rawdon, NS 902-632-2548
Scenic Fruit Company
Gresham, OR 800-554-5578
Snowcrest Packer
Abbotsford, BC 604-859-4881
Stinson Seafood Company
Prospect Harbor, ME 207-963-7331
Tru-Blu Cooperative Associates
New Lisbon, NJ 609-894-8717
Unique Ingredients
Naches, WA. 509-653-1991
Usine de Congelation St. Bruno
St. Bruno, QC .418-343-2206
Wawona Frozen Foods
Clovis, CA 559-299-2901

Blackberry

Coloma Frozen Foods
Coloma, MI 800-642-2723
Driscoll Strawberry Associates
Watsonville, CA 831-763-3050
Ever Fresh Fruit Company
Boring, OR 800-239-8026
George Richter Farm
Fife, WA 253-922-5649
Grow-Pac
Cornelius, OR .503-357-9691
Heikes Produce Company
Medford, OR. .541-772-5653
Kerr Concentrates
Salem, OR 800-910-5377
Oregon Fruit Products Company
Salem, OR 800-394-9333
Rain Sweet
Salem, OR 800-363-4293
Sand Hill Berries
Mt Pleasant, PA. 724-547-4760
Symons Frozen Foods
Centralia, WA .360-736-1321
Tom Ringhausen Orchards
Hardin, IL 618-576-2311
Townsend Farms
Fairview, OR. .503-666-1780
Unique Ingredients
Naches, WA. 509-653-1991
Venture Vineyards
Lodi, NY. 888-635-6277

Frozen

Coloma Frozen Foods
Coloma, MI. 800-642-2723

EMERLING INTERNATIONAL FOODS, INC.

Emerling International Foods
Buffalo, NY. 716-833-7381

We supply food manufacturers and food service
customers worldwide (since 1988) with bulk ingredients including: Fruits & Vegetables; Juice
Concentrates; Herbs & Spices; Oils & Vinegars;
Flavors & Colors; Honey & Molasses. We also
produce PURE MAPLE SYRUP.

Ever Fresh Fruit Company
Boring, OR. 800-239-8026
George Richter Farm
Fife, WA 253-922-5649
Grow-Pac
Cornelius, OR .503-357-9691
Heikes Produce Company
Medford, OR. .541-772-5653
Kerr Concentrates
Salem, OR 800-910-5377
Merrill's Blueberry Farms
Ellsworth, ME. 800-711-6551
Oregon Fruit Products Company
Salem, OR 800-394-9333
Overlake Foods Corporation
Olympia, WA .800-683-1078
Rain Sweet
Salem, OR 800-363-4293
Symons Frozen Foods
Centralia, WA .360-736-1321
Townsend Farms
Fairview, OR. .503-666-1780
Unique Ingredients
Naches, WA. 509-653-1991

Blueberry

Agvest
Franklin, ME. .207-565-3303
Agvest
Cleveland, OH .440-735-6900
Allen's Blueberry Freezer
Ellsworth, ME. 207-667-5561
Blueberry Store
Grand Junction, MI. 877-654-2400
Charles Dennery Pillsbury
New Orleans, LA 504-733-2331
Coloma Frozen Foods
Coloma, MI. 800-642-2723
Diamond Blueberry
Hammonton, NJ 609-561-3661
Driscoll Strawberry Associates
Watsonville, CA 831-763-3050
E.W. Bowker Company
Pemberton, NJ. 609-894-9508
Enfield Farms
Lynden, WA 360-354-3019
Ever Fresh Fruit Company
Boring, OR. 800-239-8026
G M Allen & Son
Blue Hill, ME .207-469-7060
Hawkins Farms
Pennfield, NB .506-755-6241
Heikes Produce Company
Medford, OR. .541-772-5653
Hialeah Products Company
Hollywood, FL 800-923-3379
Indian Bay Frozen Foods
Centreville, NL 709-678-2844
International Food Trade
Amherst, NS 902-667-3013
Jasper Wyman & Son
Milbridge, ME .800-341-1758
JRL
Hammonton, NJ 609-561-1572
Just Tomatoes Company
Westley, CA. 800-537-1985
Krupka's Blueberries
Fennville, MI 269-857-4278
Macrie Brothers
Hammonton, NJ 609-561-6822
Maine Wild Blueberry Company
Cherryfield, ME 800-243-4005
Meduri Farms Inc
Dallas, OR. 503-831-1097

Memba
Lynden, WA 360-354-7708
Merrill's Blueberry Farms
Ellsworth, ME. 800-711-6551
Midwest Blueberry Farms
Holland, MI 616-399-2133
New England Cranberry Company
Lynn, MA 800-410-2892
New West Foods
San Francisco, CA 701-947-2505
Niagara Foods
Middleport, NY 716-735-7722
North American Blueberry Council
Folsom, CA 800-824-6395
North Bay Produce
Traverse City, MI 231-946-1941
Northern Michigan Fruit Company
Omena, MI 231-386-5142
Oregon Fruit Products Company
Salem, OR 800-394-9333
Overlake Blueberry Farm
Bellevue, WA .425-453-8613
Pacific Blueberries
Rochester, WA .360-273-5405
Pacific Coast Fruit Company
Portland, OR 503-234-6411
Packers Canning Company
Lawton, MI 269-624-4681
Producer Marketing Overlake
Olympia, WA .360-352-7989
Quality Brands
Deland, FL 386-738-3808
Rain Sweet
Salem, OR 800-363-4293
Richard Lanza
Hammonton, NJ 609-561-3984
Royal Ridge Fruits
Royal City, WA 509-346-1520
Royalmark Services
South Haven, MI. 269-637-7450
Sill Farms Market
Lawrence, MI 269-674-3755
Smeltzer Orchard Company
Frankfort, MI 231-882-4421
Snowcrest Packer
Abbotsford, BC. 604-859-4881
Symons Frozen Foods
Centralia, WA .360-736-1321
Terri Lynn
Elgin, IL 800-323-0775
Timber Crest Farms
Healdsburg, CA 888-374-9325
Townsend Farms
Fairview, OR. .503-666-1780
Unique Ingredients
Naches, WA. 509-653-1991
Usine de Congelation St. Bruno
St. Bruno, QC .418-343-2206
Valley View Blueberries
Vancouver, WA 360-892-2839
Venture Vineyards
Lodi, NY. 888-635-6277
Vintage Produce Sales
Kingsburg, CA .559-897-1622
Wild Blueberry Companies
Kennebunkport, ME 207-967-5024

Canned

Jasper Wyman & Son
Milbridge, ME .800-341-1758
Maine Wild Blueberry Company
Cherryfield, ME 800-243-4005
Merrill's Blueberry Farms
Ellsworth, ME. 800-711-6551
Oregon Fruit Products Company
Salem, OR 800-394-9333
Packers Canning Company
Lawton, MI 269-624-4681

Dried

Atwater Foods
Lyndonville, NY 585-765-2639
Chieftain Wild Rice Company
Spooner, WI 800-262-6368
Fastachi
Watertown, MA. 800-466-3022
Setton International Foods
Commack, NY .800-227-4397

Frozen

Agvest
Cleveland, OH 440-735-6900
Allen's Blueberry Freezer
Ellsworth, ME 207-667-5561
Blueberry Store
Grand Junction, MI 877-654-2400
Diamond Blueberry
Hammonton, NJ 609-561-3661
E.W. Bowker Company
Pemberton, NJ 609-894-9508

EMERLING INTERNATIONAL FOODS, INC.

Emerling International Foods
Buffalo, NY 716-833-7381

> **We supply food manufacturers and food service customers worldwide (since 1988) with bulk ingredients including: Fruits & Vegetables; Juice Concentrates; Herbs & Spices; Oils & Vinegars; Flavors & Colors; Honey & Molasses. We also produce PURE MAPLE SYRUP.**

Enfield Farms
Lynden, WA 360-354-3019
Ever Fresh Fruit Company
Boring, OR 800-239-8026
G M Allen & Son
Blue Hill, ME 207-469-7060
Heikes Produce Company
Medford, OR 541-772-5653
International Food Trade
Amherst, NS 902-667-3013
Jasper Wyman & Son
Milbridge, ME 800-341-1758
JRL
Hammonton, NJ 609-561-1572
Lucerne Foods
Abbotsford, BC 604-854-1191
Maine Wild Blueberry Company
Cherryfield, ME 800-243-4005
Memba
Lynden, WA 360-354-7708
Northern Michigan Fruit Company
Omena, MI 231-386-5142
Oregon Fruit Products Company
Salem, OR 800-394-9333
Overlake Foods Corporation
Olympia, WA 800-683-1078
Pacific Blueberries
Rochester, WA 360-273-5405
Pacific Coast Fruit Company
Portland, OR 503-234-6411
Quality Brands
Deland, FL 386-738-3808
Rain Sweet
Salem, OR 800-363-4293
Rainbow Farms
Upper Rawdon, NS 902-632-2548
Sill Farms Market
Lawrence, MI 269-674-3755
Snowcrest Packer
Abbotsford, BC 604-859-4881
Townsend Farms
Fairview, OR 503-666-1780
Unique Ingredients
Naches, WA 509-653-1991
Usine de Congelation St. Bruno
St. Bruno, QC 418-343-2206

High Bush

Victor Packing Company
Madera, CA 559-673-5908

Boysenberry

Ever Fresh Fruit Company
Boring, OR 800-239-8026
Heikes Produce Company
Medford, OR 541-772-5653
Kerr Concentrates
Salem, OR 800-910-5377
Oregon Fruit Products Company
Salem, OR 800-394-9333
Rain Sweet
Salem, OR 800-363-4293
Townsend Farms
Fairview, OR 503-666-1780

Canned

Oregon Fruit Products Company
Salem, OR 800-394-9333

Frozen

EMERLING INTERNATIONAL FOODS, INC.

Emerling International Foods
Buffalo, NY 716-833-7381

> **We supply food manufacturers and food service customers worldwide (since 1988) with bulk ingredients including: Fruits & Vegetables; Juice Concentrates; Herbs & Spices; Oils & Vinegars; Flavors & Colors; Honey & Molasses. We also produce PURE MAPLE SYRUP.**

Ever Fresh Fruit Company
Boring, OR 800-239-8026
Heikes Produce Company
Medford, OR 541-772-5653
Kerr Concentrates
Salem, OR 800-910-5377
Oregon Fruit Products Company
Salem, OR 800-394-9333
Rain Sweet
Salem, OR 800-363-4293
Townsend Farms
Fairview, OR 503-666-1780

Canned

EMERLING INTERNATIONAL FOODS, INC.

Emerling International Foods
Buffalo, NY 716-833-7381

> **We supply food manufacturers and food service customers worldwide (since 1988) with bulk ingredients including: Fruits & Vegetables; Juice Concentrates; Herbs & Spices; Oils & Vinegars; Flavors & Colors; Honey & Molasses. We also produce PURE MAPLE SYRUP.**

George Richter Farm
Fife, WA 253-922-5649
Jasper Wyman & Son
Milbridge, ME 800-341-1758
Maine Wild Blueberry Company
Cherryfield, ME 800-243-4005
Plaidberry Company
Vista, CA 760-727-5403

Cranberry

Agvest
Franklin, ME 207-565-3303
Agvest
Cleveland, OH 440-735-6900
Coastal Classics
Duxbury, MA 508-746-6058
Cranberry Products
Eagle River, WI 715-479-4466
Decas Cranberry Products
Wareham, MA 800-649-9811
E.W. Bowker Company
Pemberton, NJ 609-894-9508
Ever Fresh Fruit Company
Boring, OR 800-239-8026
Fastachi
Watertown, MA 800-466-3022
Hialeah Products Company
Hollywood, FL 800-923-3379
Jasper Wyman & Son
Milbridge, ME 800-341-1758
Joseph J. White
Browns Mills, NJ 609-893-2332
New England Cranberry Company
Lynn, MA 800-410-2892
Niagara Foods
Middleport, NY 716-735-7722
Old Country Farms
East Sandwich, MA 888-707-5558
Pacific Coast Fruit Company
Portland, OR 503-234-6411
R M Lawton Cranberries
Middleboro, MA 508-947-7465
Setton International Foods
Commack, NY 800-227-4397

Shiloh Foods
Savannah, TN 800-795-2550
Smeltzer Orchard Company
Frankfort, MI 231-882-4421
Snowcrest Packer
Abbotsford, BC 604-859-4881
Terri Lynn
Elgin, IL .800-323-0775
Timber Crest Farms
Healdsburg, CA 888-374-9325
Unique Ingredients
Naches, WA 509-653-1991
Wetherby Cranberry Company
Warrens, WI 608-378-4813

Canned

Jasper Wyman & Son
Milbridge, ME 800-341-1758
Shiloh Foods
Savannah, TN 800-795-2550

Dried

American Importing Company
Minneapolis, MN 612-331-9226
Atwater Foods
Lyndonville, NY 585-765-2639
Mariani Packing Company
Vacaville, CA 800-672-8655
Meridian Nut Growers
Clovis, CA 559-458-7272

Frozen

Agvest
Franklin, ME 207-565-3303
Agvest
Cleveland, OH 440-735-6900
E.W. Bowker Company
Pemberton, NJ 609-894-9508
Ever Fresh Fruit Company
Boring, OR 800-239-8026
Jasper Wyman & Son
Milbridge, ME 800-341-1758
Lucerne Foods
Abbotsford, BC 604-854-1191
Niagara Foods
Middleport, NY 716-735-7722
Pacific Coast Fruit Company
Portland, OR 503-234-6411
Snowcrest Packer
Abbotsford, BC 604-859-4881

Products

EMERLING INTERNATIONAL FOODS, INC.

Emerling International Foods
Buffalo, NY 716-833-7381

> **We supply food manufacturers and food service customers worldwide (since 1988) with bulk ingredients including: Fruits & Vegetables; Juice Concentrates; Herbs & Spices; Oils & Vinegars; Flavors & Colors; Honey & Molasses. We also produce PURE MAPLE SYRUP.**

Jasper Wyman & Son
Milbridge, ME 800-341-1758
Shiloh Foods
Savannah, TN 800-795-2550
Unique Ingredients
Naches, WA 509-653-1991

Currants

Chieftain Wild Rice Company
Spooner, WI 800-262-6368

EMERLING INTERNATIONAL FOODS, INC.

Emerling International Foods
Buffalo, NY 716-833-7381

> **We supply food manufacturers and food service customers worldwide (since 1988) with bulk ingredients including: Fruits & Vegetables; Juice Concentrates; Herbs & Spices; Oils & Vinegars; Flavors & Colors; Honey & Molasses. We also produce PURE MAPLE SYRUP.**

Fastachi
Watertown, MA 800-466-3022

George Richter Farm
Fife, WA 253-922-5649
Milne Fruit Products
Prosser, WA 509-786-2611
Pacific Coast Fruit Company
Portland, OR 503-234-6411
Setton International Foods
Commack, NY 800-227-4397

Red

George Richter Farm
Fife, WA 253-922-5649
Pacific Coast Fruit Company
Portland, OR 503-234-6411

Frozen

Abbotsford Growers Co-operative
Abbotsford, BC 604-864-0022
Agvest
Franklin, ME 207-565-3303
Agvest
Cleveland, OH 440-735-6900
Cleugh's Frozen Foods
Buena Park, CA 714-521-1002
Coloma Frozen Foods
Coloma, MI 800-642-2723
Diamond Blueberry
Hammonton, NJ 609-561-3661
E.W. Bowker Company
Pemberton, NJ 609-894-9508

EMERLING INTERNATIONAL FOODS, INC.

Emerling International Foods
Buffalo, NY 716-833-7381

We supply food manufacturers and food service customers worldwide (since 1988) with bulk ingredients including: Fruits & Vegetables; Juice Concentrates; Herbs & Spices; Oils & Vinegars; Flavors & Colors; Honey & Molasses. We also produce PURE MAPLE SYRUP.

Enfield Farms
Lynden, WA 360-354-3019
Ever Fresh Fruit Company
Boring, OR 800-239-8026
Frozsun Foods
Anaheim, CA 714-630-2170
G M Allen & Son
Blue Hill, ME 207-469-7060
George Richter Farm
Fife, WA 253-922-5649
Grow-Pac
Cornelius, OR 503-357-9691
Heikes Produce Company
Medford, OR 541-772-5653
Hiscock Enterprises
Brigus, NL 709-528-4577
International Food Trade
Amherst, NS 902-667-3013
J.H. Verbridge & Son
Williamson, NY 315-589-2366
Jasper Wyman & Son
Milbridge, ME 800-341-1758
JRL
Hammonton, NJ 609-561-1572
Leelanau Fruit Company
Suttons Bay, MI 800-431-0718
Lucerne Foods
Abbotsford, BC 604-854-1191
Maine Wild Blueberry Company
Cherryfield, ME 800-243-4005
Memba
Lynden, WA 360-354-7708
New West Foods
San Francisco, CA 701-947-2505
Niagara Foods
Middleport, NY 716-735-7722
Northern Michigan Fruit Company
Omena, MI 231-386-5142
Ocean Spray Cranberries
Lakeville-Middleboro, MA 800-662-3263
Oregon Fruit Products Company
Salem, OR 800-394-9333
Overlake Foods Corporation
Olympia, WA 800-683-1078
Pacific Blueberries
Rochester, WA 360-273-5405
Pacific Coast Fruit Company
Portland, OR 503-234-6411

Quality Brands
Deland, FL 386-738-3808
Rain Sweet
Salem, OR 800-363-4293
Rainbow Farms
Upper Rawdon, NS 902-632-2548
Sill Farms Market
Lawrence, MI 269-674-3755
Snowcrest Packer
Abbotsford, BC 604-859-4881
Symons Frozen Foods
Centralia, WA 360-736-1321
Townsend Farms
Fairview, OR 503-666-1780
Webster Farms
Cambridge Station, NS 902-538-9492

Goose

Oregon Fruit Products Company
Salem, OR 800-394-9333

Juniper

Naturex (Chart Corp)
South Hackensack, NJ 201-440-5000
Schiff Food Products
North Bergen, NJ 201-861-2503

Lingonberries

Indian Bay Frozen Foods
Centreville, NL 709-678-2844

Mulberries

Kalustyan Corporation
Union, NJ 908-688-6111

Raspberries

Bridenbaughs Orchards
Martinsburg, PA 814-793-2364
Charles Dennery Pillsbury
New Orleans, LA 504-733-2331
Coloma Frozen Foods
Coloma, MI 800-642-2723
Decker Farms
Hillsboro, OR 503-628-1532
Driscoll Strawberry Associates
Watsonville, CA 831-763-3050
Enfield Farms
Lynden, WA 360-354-3019
Ever Fresh Fruit Company
Boring, OR 800-239-8026
George Richter Farm
Fife, WA 253-922-5649
Graysmarsh Farm
Sequim, WA 800-683-4367
Heikes Produce Company
Medford, OR 541-772-5653
Jasper Wyman & Son
Milbridge, ME 800-341-1758
Just Tomatoes Company
Westley, CA 800-537-1985
Kerr Concentrates
Salem, OR 800-910-5377
Oregon Fruit Products Company
Salem, OR 800-394-9333
Pacific Coast Fruit Company
Portland, OR 503-234-6411
Rain Sweet
Salem, OR 800-363-4293
Royal Ridge Fruits
Royal City, WA 509-346-1520
Sand Hill Berries
Mt Pleasant, PA 724-547-4760
Snowcrest Packer
Abbotsford, BC 604-859-4881
Strebin Farms
Troutdale, OR 503-665-8328
Symons Frozen Foods
Centralia, WA 360-736-1321
Terri Lynn
Elgin, IL 800-323-0775
Townsend Farms
Fairview, OR 503-666-1780
Unique Ingredients
Naches, WA 509-653-1991
Venture Vineyards
Lodi, NY 888-635-6277

Frozen

Abbotsford Growers Co-operative
Abbotsford, BC 604-864-0022
Coloma Frozen Foods
Coloma, MI 800-642-2723

EMERLING INTERNATIONAL FOODS, INC.

Emerling International Foods
Buffalo, NY 716-833-7381

We supply food manufacturers and food service customers worldwide (since 1988) with bulk ingredients including: Fruits & Vegetables; Juice Concentrates; Herbs & Spices; Oils & Vinegars; Flavors & Colors; Honey & Molasses. We also produce PURE MAPLE SYRUP.

Enfield Farms
Lynden, WA 360-354-3019
Ever Fresh Fruit Company
Boring, OR 800-239-8026
Heikes Produce Company
Medford, OR 541-772-5653
Jasper Wyman & Son
Milbridge, ME 800-341-1758
Kerr Concentrates
Salem, OR 800-910-5377
Oregon Fruit Products Company
Salem, OR 800-394-9333
Overlake Foods Corporation
Olympia, WA 800-683-1078
Pacific Coast Fruit Company
Portland, OR 503-234-6411
Radar Farms
Lynden, WA 360-354-6574
Rain Sweet
Salem, OR 800-363-4293
Snowcrest Packer
Abbotsford, BC 604-859-4881
Strebin Farms
Troutdale, OR 503-665-8328
Symons Frozen Foods
Centralia, WA 360-736-1321
Townsend Farms
Fairview, OR 503-666-1780
Unique Ingredients
Naches, WA 509-653-1991

Strawberry

Blue Chip Group
Salt Lake City, UT 800-878-0099
Bridenbaughs Orchards
Martinsburg, PA 814-793-2364
CAL Sun Produce Company
Oxnard, CA 805-985-2262
Cal-Sun Produce Company
Oxnard, CA 805-985-2262
Charles Dennery Pillsbury
New Orleans, LA 504-733-2331
Chieftain Wild Rice Company
Spooner, WI 800-262-6368
Cleugh's Frozen Foods
Buena Park, CA 714-521-1002
Clofine Dairy & Food Products
Linwood, NJ 800-441-1001
Coloma Frozen Foods
Coloma, MI 800-642-2723
Decker Farms
Hillsboro, OR 503-628-1532
Del Mar Food Products Corporation
Watsonville, CA 831-722-3516
Driscoll Strawberry Associates
Watsonville, CA 831-763-3050
Ever Fresh Fruit Company
Boring, OR 800-239-8026
Fastachi
Watertown, MA 800-466-3022
Frozsun Foods
Anaheim, CA 714-630-2170
Grow-Pac
Cornelius, OR 503-357-9691
Heikes Produce Company
Medford, OR 541-772-5653
Hialeah Products Company
Hollywood, FL 800-923-3379
J.H. Verbridge & Son
Williamson, NY 315-589-2366
Kerr Concentrates
Salem, OR 800-910-5377

Leelanau Fruit Company
Suttons Bay, MI 800-431-0718
New West Foods
San Francisco, CA 701-947-2505
Niagara Foods
Middleport, NY 716-735-7722
Northern Michigan Fruit Company
Omena, MI 231-386-5142
Oregon Fruit Products Company
Salem, OR 800-394-9333
Pacific Coast Fruit Company
Portland, OR 503-234-6411
Paradise
Plant City, FL 800-330-8952
Producer Marketing Overlake
Olympia, WA 360-352-7989
Rain Sweet
Salem, OR 800-363-4293
Sill Farms Market
Lawrence, MI 269-674-3755
Smeltzer Orchard Company
Frankfort, MI 231-882-4421
Snowcrest Packer
Abbotsford, BC 604-859-4881
Sunrise Growers
Placentia, CA 714-630-2170
T.S. Smith & Sons
Bridgeville, DE 302-337-8271
Terri Lynn
Elgin, IL 800-323-0775
Townsend Farms
Fairview, OR 503-666-1780
Unique Ingredients
Naches, WA 509-653-1991
Valley View Blueberries
Vancouver, WA 360-892-2839
Webster Farms
Cambridge Station, NS 902-538-9492
Well Pict Berries
Watsonville, CA 831-722-3871
Zipp Manufacturing Company
Hornerville, OH 800-521-8700

Canned

EMERLING INTERNATIONAL FOODS, INC.

Emerling International Foods
Buffalo, NY 716-833-7381

We supply food manufacturers and food service customers worldwide (since 1988) with bulk ingredients including: Fruits & Vegetables; Juice Concentrates; Herbs & Spices; Oils & Vinegars; Flavors & Colors; Honey & Molasses. We also produce PURE MAPLE SYRUP.

Oregon Fruit Products Company
Salem, OR 800-394-9333
Overlake Foods Corporation
Olympia, WA 800-683-1078
Unique Ingredients
Naches, WA 509-653-1991

Dried

Atwater Foods
Lyndonville, NY 585-765-2639

Frozen

Cleugh's Frozen Foods
Buena Park, CA 714-521-1002
Coloma Frozen Foods
Coloma, MI 800-642-2723

EMERLING INTERNATIONAL FOODS, INC.

Emerling International Foods
Buffalo, NY 716-833-7381

We supply food manufacturers and food service customers worldwide (since 1988) with bulk ingredients including: Fruits & Vegetables; Juice Concentrates; Herbs & Spices; Oils & Vinegars; Flavors & Colors; Honey & Molasses. We also produce PURE MAPLE SYRUP.

Ever Fresh Fruit Company
Boring, OR 800-239-8026
Frozsun Foods
Anaheim, CA 714-630-2170
Fruit Belt Foods
Lawrence, MI 269-674-3939
Grow-Pac
Cornelius, OR 503-357-9691
Heikes Produce Company
Medford, OR 541-772-5653
J.H. Verbridge & Son
Williamson, NY 315-589-2366
J.R. Simplot Company
Boise, ID .208-336-2110
Kerr Concentrates
Salem, OR 800-910-5377
Leelanau Fruit Company
Suttons Bay, MI 800-431-0718
New West Foods
San Francisco, CA 701-947-2505
New West Foods
Oxnard, CA 805-485-3745
Niagara Foods
Middleport, NY 716-735-7722
Northern Michigan Fruit Company
Omena, MI 231-386-5142
Oregon Fruit Products Company
Salem, OR 800-394-9333
Overlake Foods Corporation
Olympia, WA 800-683-1078
Pacific Coast Fruit Company
Portland, OR 503-234-6411
Rain Sweet
Salem, OR 800-363-4293
Sill Farms Market
Lawrence, MI 269-674-3755
Snowcrest Packer
Abbotsford, BC 604-859-4881
Townsend Farms
Fairview, OR 503-666-1780
Webster Farms
Cambridge Station, NS 902-538-9492

Brandied Fruits

Au Printemps Gourmet
Prevost, QC 800-663-0416
Dundee Brandied Fruit Company
Dundee, OR 503-537-2500
Hurd Orchards
Holley, NY 585-638-8838
Jubilee Gourmet Creations
Manchester, NH 603-625-0654
Silver Palate Kitchens
Cresskill, NJ 800-872-5283

Broccoli

A. Duda Farm Fresh Foods
Belle Glade, FL 561-996-7621
Cal-Harvest Marketing
Hanford, CA 559-582-4000
Cobi Foods
Hantsport, NS 800-565-8229
D'Arrigo Brothers Company of California
Salinas, CA 800-995-5939
Dehydrates Inc
Hewlett, NY 800-983-4443
Dole Food Company
Westlake Village, CA 818-879-6600
Dole Fresh Vegetable Company
Soledad, CA 800-333-5454
Goebbert's Home Grown Vegetables
South Barrington, IL 847-428-6727
Great American Appetizers
Nampa, ID 800-282-4834
Hanover Foods Corporation
Hanover, PA 717-632-6000
Indian Rock Produce
Perkasie, PA 800-882-0512

JR Wood/Big Valley
Atwater, CA 209-358-5643
Kuhlmann's Market Gardens & Greenhouses
Edmonton, AB 780-475-7500
Mann Packing
Salinas, CA 831-422-7405
McCain Foods Canada
Florenceville, NB 506-392-5541
Michigan Freeze Pack
Hart, MI 231-873-2175
Mills
Salinas, CA 831-758-8179
Omstead Foods Ltd
Burlington, ON 905-315-8883
Paisley Farms
Willoughby, OH 800-676-8656
Patterson Frozen Foods
Patterson, CA 209-892-2611
Pictsweet Frozen Foods
Bells, TN .731-663-7600
Silva Harvesting
Gonzales, CA 831-675-2327
Snowcrest Packer
Abbotsford, BC 604-859-4881
Sunrise Growers
Placentia, CA 714-630-2170
Superior Foods
Watsonville, CA 831-728-3691
Talley Farms
Arroyo Grande, CA 805-489-2508
Tami Great Food
Monsey, NY 718-788-4200
Tanimura & Antle
Salinas, CA 831-455-2255
Teixeira Farms
Santa Maria, CA 805-928-3801
Trappe Packing Corporation
Trappe, MD 410-476-3185
Vegetable Juices
Chicago, IL 888-776-9752

Chopped

Pictsweet Frozen Foods
Bells, TN .731-663-7600

Frozen

Cobi Foods
Hantsport, NS 800-565-8229

EMERLING INTERNATIONAL FOODS, INC.

Emerling International Foods
Buffalo, NY 716-833-7381

We supply food manufacturers and food service customers worldwide (since 1988) with bulk ingredients including: Fruits & Vegetables; Juice Concentrates; Herbs & Spices; Oils & Vinegars; Flavors & Colors; Honey & Molasses. We also produce PURE MAPLE SYRUP.

Great American Appetizers
Nampa, ID 800-282-4834
J.R. Simplot Company
Boise, ID .208-336-2110
JR Wood/Big Valley
Atwater, CA 209-358-5643
McCain Foods Canada
Florenceville, NB 506-392-5541
Omstead Foods Ltd
Burlington, ON 905-315-8883
Pictsweet Frozen Foods
Bells, TN .731-663-7600
Snowcrest Packer
Abbotsford, BC 604-859-4881
Sun Harvest Foods
San Diego, CA 619-690-1128
Superior Foods
Watsonville, CA 831-728-3691
Sure Fresh Produce
Santa Maria, CA 888-423-5379
Trappe Packing Corporation
Trappe, MD 410-476-3185
Unique Ingredients
Naches, WA 509-653-1991
Vegetable Juices
Chicago, IL 888-776-9752

Whole

Dole Fresh Vegetable Company
Soledad, CA 800-333-5454

Brussel Sprouts

Cara Mia Products
Fresno, CA 559-498-2900
Cleugh's Frozen Foods
Buena Park, CA 714-521-1002
Cobi Foods
Hantsport, NS 800-565-8229
Dole Food Company
Westlake Village, CA 818-879-6600
McCain Foods Canada
Florenceville, NB 506-392-5541
Miss Scarlett's
Chandler, AZ. 800-345-6734
Paisley Farms
Willoughby, OH 800-676-8656
Patterson Frozen Foods
Patterson, CA 209-892-2611
Pictsweet Frozen Foods
Bells, TN 731-663-7600
Snowcrest Packer
Abbotsford, BC. 604-859-4881

Frozen

Cleugh's Frozen Foods
Buena Park, CA 714-521-1002
Cobi Foods
Hantsport, NS 800-565-8229

EMERLING INTERNATIONAL FOODS, INC.

Emerling International Foods
Buffalo, NY. 716-833-7381

> **We supply food manufacturers and food service customers worldwide (since 1988) with bulk ingredients including: Fruits & Vegetables; Juice Concentrates; Herbs & Spices; Oils & Vinegars; Flavors & Colors; Honey & Molasses. We also produce PURE MAPLE SYRUP.**

Lucerne Foods
Abbotsford, BC. 604-854-1191
McCain Foods Canada
Florenceville, NB 506-392-5541
Pictsweet Frozen Foods
Bells, TN 731-663-7600
Snowcrest Packer
Abbotsford, BC. 604-859-4881

Cabbage

A. Duda Farm Fresh Foods
Belle Glade, FL. 561-996-7621
Abbott & Cobb, Inc.
Langhorne, PA. 800-345-7333
Carando Gourmet Frozen Foods
Springfield, MA 413-730-4205
Club Chef
Covington, KY 859-578-3100
Custom Cuts
Milwaukee, WI 414-483-0491
Dehydrates Inc
Hewlett, NY 800-983-4443
Eckert Cold Storage
Escalon, CA 209-838-4040
Exeter Produce & Storage Company
Exeter, ON. 519-235-0141
F&S Produce Company
Rosenhayn, NJ 800-886-3316
Georgia Vegetable Company
Tifton, GA. 229-386-2374
Goebbert's Home Grown Vegetables
South Barrington, IL 847-428-6727
H H Dobbins
Lyndonville, NY 877-362-2467
Hoson Produce
Los Angeles, CA 323-550-8695
Indian Rock Produce
Perkasie, PA 800-882-0512
Kuhlmann's Market Gardens & Greenhouses
Edmonton, AB 780-475-7500
Kurtz Produce
Ariss, ON 519-824-3279
Mills
Salinas, CA 831-758-8179

Pacific Collier Fresh Company
Immokalee, FL 800-226-7274
R.C. McEntire & Company
Columbia, SC 803-799-3388
Ruskin Packaging
Miami, FL. 305-324-1529
Russo Farms
Vineland, NJ 856-692-5942
Sales USA
Salado, TX 800-766-7344
Silva Harvesting
Gonzales, CA 831-675-2327
Sunrise Growers
Placentia, CA 714-630-2170
Sure Fresh Produce
Santa Maria, CA 888-423-5379
Teixeira Farms
Santa Maria, CA 805-928-3801
Vegetable Juices
Chicago, IL 888-776-9752
Vessey & Company
Holtville, CA. 760-352-6376

Bok Choy

Eckert Cold Storage
Escalon, CA 209-838-4040
Sure Fresh Produce
Santa Maria, CA 888-423-5379
Talley Farms
Arroyo Grande, CA 805-489-2508
Vessey & Company
Holtville, CA. 760-352-6376

Canned

EMERLING INTERNATIONAL FOODS, INC.

Emerling International Foods
Buffalo, NY. 716-833-7381

> **We supply food manufacturers and food service customers worldwide (since 1988) with bulk ingredients including: Fruits & Vegetables; Juice Concentrates; Herbs & Spices; Oils & Vinegars; Flavors & Colors; Honey & Molasses. We also produce PURE MAPLE SYRUP.**

Sure Fresh Produce
Santa Maria, CA 888-423-5379

Chinese

Pioneer Growers Cooperative
Belle Glade, FL. 561-996-5561

Frozen

Carando Gourmet Frozen Foods
Springfield, MA 413-730-4205
Eckert Cold Storage
Escalon, CA 209-838-4040

EMERLING INTERNATIONAL FOODS, INC.

Emerling International Foods
Buffalo, NY. 716-833-7381

> **We supply food manufacturers and food service customers worldwide (since 1988) with bulk ingredients including: Fruits & Vegetables; Juice Concentrates; Herbs & Spices; Oils & Vinegars; Flavors & Colors; Honey & Molasses. We also produce PURE MAPLE SYRUP.**

Ripon Pickle Company
Ripon, WI 800-324-5493
Sure Fresh Produce
Santa Maria, CA 888-423-5379
Vegetable Juices
Chicago, IL 888-776-9752

Green

Baker Produce Company
Kennewick, WA 800-624-7553
Del Monte Foods
San Francisco, CA 800-543-3090
Princeville Canning Company
Princeville, IL 309-385-4301
Vessey & Company
Holtville, CA. 760-352-6376

Red

F&S Produce Company
Rosenhayn, NJ 800-886-3316
Ruskin Packaging
Miami, FL. 305-324-1529
Vessey & Company
Holtville, CA. 760-352-6376

Cactus

D'Arrigo Brothers Company of California
Salinas, CA 800-995-5939
Naturex (Chart Corp)
South Hackensack, NJ 201-440-5000

Candied Fruits

Crystallized, Glace

American Key Food Products
Closter, NJ. 800-767-0237
California Custom Fruits & Flavors
Irwindale, CA 877-558-0056

EMERLING INTERNATIONAL FOODS, INC.

Emerling International Foods
Buffalo, NY. 716-833-7381

> **We supply food manufacturers and food service customers worldwide (since 1988) with bulk ingredients including: Fruits & Vegetables; Juice Concentrates; Herbs & Spices; Oils & Vinegars; Flavors & Colors; Honey & Molasses. We also produce PURE MAPLE SYRUP.**

Gray & Company
Forest Grove, OR 503-357-3141
Hialeah Products Company
Hollywood, FL 800-923-3379
Kerry Ingredients
Beloit, WI. 608-362-1651
Limpert Brothers
Vineland, NJ 800-691-1353
Olde Tyme Food Corporation
East Longmeadow, MA 800-356-6533
Oregon Cherry Growers
The Dalles, OR 800-367-2536
Paradise
Plant City, FL 800-330-8952
Reinhart Foods
Markham, ON 905-754-3503
Setton International Foods
Commack, NY 800-227-4397
Unique Ingredients
Naches, WA 509-653-1991
Weaver Nut Company
Ephrata, PA 717-738-3781
White Swan Fruit Products
Plant City, FL 813-752-1155

Caneberries

Rain Sweet
Salem, OR 800-363-4293

Canned Fruits

Agrocan
Toronto, ON 877-247-6226
B.M. Lawrence & Company
San Francisco, CA 415-981-3650
Bob Gordon & Associates
Chicago, IL 773-247-0588
Bowman Apple Products Company
Mt Jackson, VA 877-426-9626
Burnette Foods
Elk Rapids, MI 231-264-8116
California Farms & Canners
San Francisco, CA 415-433-3522
Cherry Growers
Grawn, MI. 231-276-9241
China Food Merchant Corporation
Fullerton, CA 877-465-2582
Coco Lopez
Miramar, FL 800-341-2242
ConAgra Grocery Products
Irvine, CA 714-680-1000
Cooperative Cosecheros de Cidra
Adjuntas, PR 787-829-2845
Curtice Burns Foods
Fennville, MI. 269-927-2111

Derco Foods
Fresno, CA 559-435-2664

EMERLING INTERNATIONAL FOODS, INC.

Emerling International Foods
Buffalo, NY .716-833-7381

> We supply food manufacturers and food service customers worldwide (since 1988) with bulk ingredients including: Fruits & Vegetables; Juice Concentrates; Herbs & Spices; Oils & Vinegars; Flavors & Colors; Honey & Molasses. We also produce PURE MAPLE SYRUP.

Florida Citrus
Tampa, FL 813-626-5580
Hurd Orchards
Holley, NY 585-638-8838
Independent Food Processors
Sunnyside, WA 509-837-3806
International Home Foods
Milton, PA 973-359-9920
Jasper Wyman & Son
Milbridge, ME 800-341-1758
Jenport International Distributors
Coquitlam, BC 604-464-9888
Kagome
Los Banos, CA 209-826-8850
Knouse Foods
Peach Glen, PA 717-677-8181
L&S Packing Company
Farmingdale, NY 800-286-6487
Lancaster Packing Company
Lancaster, PA 717-397-9727
Lucks Food Decorating Company
Tacoma, WA 206-674-7200
Maine Wild Blueberry Company
Cherryfield, ME 800-243-4005
Majestic Foods
Huntington, NY 631-424-9444
Manzana Products Company
Sebastopol, CA 707-823-5313
Maui Pineapple Company
Kahului, HI 808-877-3351
New Era Canning Company
New Era, MI 231-861-2151
NTC Foods Corporation
Williamsville, NY 800-333-1637
Oasis Foods
Planada, CA 209-382-0263
Oregon Cherry Growers
Salem, OR 800-367-2536
Oregon Fruit Products Company
Salem, OR 800-394-9333
Pacific Coast Producers
Oroville, CA 530-533-4311
Patterson Frozen Foods
Patterson, CA 209-892-2611
Plaidberry Company
Vista, CA 760-727-5403
San Benito Foods
Vancouver, WA 800-453-7832
Seneca Foods
Marion, NY 315-926-8100
Snokist Growers
Yakima, WA 800-377-2857
Stapleton-Spence PackingCompany
San Jose, CA 800-297-8815
Symms Fruit Ranch
Caldwell, ID 208-459-4821
Tri-Valley Growers
Sandy, OR 209-572-5200
Tri-Valley Growers
Langhorne, PA 215-702-8131
Triple D Orchards
Empire, MI 866-781-9410
Tropical Fruit Products Company
San German, PR 787-892-1345
Truitt Brothers Inc
Salem, OR 800-547-8712
Tupman-Thurlow Company
Deerfield Beach, FL 954-596-9989
United Universal Enterprises Corporation
Phoenix, AZ 623-842-9691
Zel R. Kahn & Sons
Corte Madera, CA. 415-924-9600

Canned Vegetables

A. Lassonde, Inc.
Rougemont, QC 514-878-1057

Anchor Food Products/ McCain Foods
Appleton, WI 920-734-0627
Appleton Produce Company
Weiser, ID 208-414-1102
B.M. Lawrence & Company
San Francisco, CA 415-981-3650
Bob Gordon & Associates
Chicago, IL 773-247-0588
Border Foods Inc
Deming, NM. 888-737-7752
Burnette Foods
Elk Rapids, MI 231-264-8116
Burnette Foods
Hartford, MI 616-621-3181
California Farms & Canners
San Francisco, CA 415-433-3522
Capitol Foods
Memphis, TN 662-781-9021
Carriere Foods Inc
Montreal, QC 514-384-4281
Chiquita Brands International
Cincinnati, OH 800-438-0015
Chiquita Processed Foods
Milton Freewater, OR 541-938-4461
Coco Lopez
Miramar, FL 800-341-2242
ConAgra Grocery Products
Perrysburg, OH 419-661-4400
ConAgra Grocery Products
Irvine, CA 714-680-1000
Conserverie Larose
Calixa-Lavallee, QC 450-583-6438
Cordon Bleu International
Anjou, QC. 514-352-3000
Crown Point
St John, IN 219-365-3200
Curtice Burns Foods
Fennville, MI 269-927-2111
Deep Foods
Union, NJ 908-810-7500
Dong Kee Company
Chicago, IL 312-225-6340
Ebro Foods
Chicago, IL 773-696-0150

EMERLING INTERNATIONAL FOODS, INC.

Emerling International Foods
Buffalo, NY. 716-833-7381

> We supply food manufacturers and food service customers worldwide (since 1988) with bulk ingredients including: Fruits & Vegetables; Juice Concentrates; Herbs & Spices; Oils & Vinegars; Flavors & Colors; Honey & Molasses. We also produce PURE MAPLE SYRUP.

Escalon Premier Brand
Escalon, CA 209-838-7341
Faribault Foods
Cokato, MN 320-286-2166
Faribault Foods
Minneapolis, MN 612-333-6461
Fiesta Canning Company
Mc Neal, AZ. 520-364-7541
Ful-Flav-R Foods
Alamo, CA 510-339-9618
G L Mezzetta
American Canyon, CA 707-648-1050
GWB Foods Corporation
Brooklyn, NY 718-686-9600
Hanover Foods Corporation
Hanover, PA 717-632-6000
Hartford City Foam Pack aging & Converting
Hartford City, IN. 765-348-2500
Hermann Pickle Farm
Garrettsville, OH. 800-245-2696
International Home Foods
Milton, PA. 973-359-9920
John N Wright Jr
Federalsburg, MD. 410-754-9044
Juanita's Foods
Wilmington, CA 310-834-5339
Kelly Pickle Company
Oconto, WI 920-834-4433
Kennebec Bean Company
North Vassalboro, ME 207-873-3473
L&S Packing Company
Farmingdale, NY 800-286-6487
Lakeside Foods
Plainview, MN 507-534-3141

Lakeside Foods
Manitowoc, WI 920-684-3356
Lakeside Foods
Seymour, WI 920-833-2371
Lakeside Foods
New Holstein, WI 920-898-5702
Lakeside Packing Company
Harrow, ON 519-738-2314
Lodi Canning Company
Lodi, WI 608-592-4236
Lucks Food Decorating Company
Tacoma, WA 206-674-7200
Majestic Foods
Huntington, NY 631-424-9444
McCall Farms
Effingham, SC. 800-277-2012
Miami Purveyors
Miami, FL 305-262-6170
Milroy Canning Company
Milroy, IN 765-629-2221
Monterey Mushrooms
Watsonville, CA 831-763-5300
Monticello Canning Company
Crossville, TN 931-484-3696
Moody Dunbar
Johnson City, TN 800-251-8202
Mr. Dell Foods
Kearney, MO 816-628-4644
Musco Olive Products
Tracy, CA 800-523-9828
Mushroom Company
Cambridge, MD 410-221-8900
Nationwide Canning
Cottam, ON 519-839-4831
New Era Canning Company
New Era, MI 231-861-2151
New Harvest Foods
Pulaski, WI 920-822-2578
New Meridian
Eaton, IN 765-396-3344
Nickabood's Company
Los Angeles, CA. 213-746-1541
NORPAC Foods
Lake Oswego, OR 503-635-9311
NORPAC Plant
Salem, OR. 800-822-2898
Oh Boy Corporation
San Fernando, CA 818-361-1128
Omstead Foods Ltd
Burlington, ON 905-315-8883
Ore-Ida Foods
Pittsburgh, PA 412-237-3450
Paisley Farms
Willoughby, OH 800-676-8656
Paradise Products Corporation
Roslyn, NY 800-826-1235
Pastene Companies
Canton, MA 781-830-8200
Patterson Frozen Foods
Patterson, CA 209-892-2611
Produits Ronald
St. Damase, QC 450-797-3303
Pure Food Ingredients
Verona, WI 800-355-9601
Ralph Sechler & Son Inc
St Joe, IN 800-332-5461
Ray Brothers & Noble Canning Company
Hobbs, IN 765-675-7451
Reckitt Benckiser
Parsippany, NJ. 800-333-3899
Red Gold
Elwood, IN 877-748-9798
Red River Commodities
Fargo, ND 701-282-2600
Ron-Son Foods
Swedesboro, NJ 856-241-7333
San Benito Foods
Hollister, CA 831-637-4434
Saticoy Foods Corporation
Ventura, CA. 805-647-5266
Seneca Foods
Marion, NY 315-926-8100
Seneca Foods
Janesville, WI 608-757-6000
Seneca Foods
Cumberland, WI 715-822-2181
SEW Friel
Queenstown, MD 410-827-8841
Simplot Food Group
Boise, ID 800-572-7783
Sopacko Packaging
Bennettsville, SC 843-479-3811

Sumida Pickle Products
Honolulu, HI 808-841-4227
Sun Harvest Foods
San Diego, CA 619-690-1128
Sun-Brite Canning
Ruthven, ON 519-326-9033
Tami Great Food
Monsey, NY 718-788-4200
Thomas Canning/Maidstone
Maidstone, ON 519-737-1531
Truitt Brothers Inc
Salem, OR 800-547-8712
Unilever Foods
Stockton, CA 209-466-9580
United Canning Corporation
North Lima, OH 330-549-9807
US Fresh Marketing
Virginia Beach, VA 757-481-2606
Van De Walle Farms
San Antonio, TX 210-436-5551
Van Drunen Farms
Momence, IL 815-472-3100
Weil's Food Processing
Wheatley, ON 519-825-4572
Western Pacific Commodities
Las Vegas, NV 702-312-8080
Wornick Company
Cincinnati, OH 800-860-4555

Carrot

A. Duda Farm Fresh Foods
Belle Glade, FL 561-996-7621
Atlantic Quality Spice &Seasonings
Edison, NJ 800-584-0422
Beck Farms
Lethbridg, AB 403-227-1020
Chase Farms
Walkerville, MI 231-873-3337
Cleugh's Frozen Foods
Buena Park, CA 714-521-1002
Cobi Foods
Hantsport, NS 800-565-8229
Columbia Foods
Quincy, WA 509-787-1585
Culinary Standards Corporation
Louisville, KY 800-778-3434
Dehydrates Inc
Hewlett, NY 800-983-4443
Del Monte Fresh Produce Company
Kankakee, IL 815-936-7400
Exeter Produce & Storage Company
Exeter, ON. 519-235-0141
F&S Produce Company
Rosenhayn, NJ 800-886-3316
Fresh Express
Franklin Park, IL 800-242-5472
Grimmway Farms
Bakersfield, CA 800-301-3101
Hanover Foods Corporation
Hanover, PA 717-632-6000
Hoson Produce
Los Angeles, CA. 323-550-8695
Indian Rock Produce
Perkasie, PA 800-882-0512
J.R. Simplot Food Group
Pasco, WA. 509-544-6700
JES Foods
Cleveland, OH 216-883-8987
Just Tomatoes Company
Westley, CA 800-537-1985
Kern Ridge Growers
Arvin, CA 661-854-3141
Kuhlmann's Market Gardens & Greenhouses
Edmonton, AB 780-475-7500
Lakeside Foods
Seymour, WI 920-833-2371
Lakeside Foods
New Holstein, WI 920-898-5702
Mar Distributing Company
Los Angeles, CA. 213-627-4006
Miss Scarlett's
Chandler, AZ. 800-345-6734
Mr. Dell Foods
Kearney, MO 816-628-4644
National Frozen Foods Corporation
Seattle, WA 206-322-8900
New Harvest Foods
Pulaski, WI 920-822-2578
NORPAC Plant
Salem, OR. 800-822-2898
Omstead Foods Ltd
Burlington, ON 905-315-8883

Paisley Farms
Willoughby, OH 800-676-8656
Patterson Frozen Foods
Patterson, CA 209-892-2611
Pictsweet Frozen Foods
Bells, TN. 731-663-7600
Pioneer Growers Cooperative
Belle Glade, FL 561-996-5561
R.C. McEntire & Company
Columbia, SC 803-799-3388
Ripon Pickle Company
Ripon, WI 800-324-5493
Rousseau Farming Company
Tolleson, AZ 623-936-7100
Ruskin Packaging
Miami, FL 305-324-1529
S. Kennedy Vegetable Lifestock Company
Clear Lake, IA 641-357-6101
Seneca Foods
Marion, NY 315-926-8100
Seneca Foods
Janesville, WI 608-757-6000
Smith Frozen Foods
Weston, OR 541-566-3515
Smith Frozen Foods
Weston, OR 800-547-0203
Strathroy Foods
Strathroy, ON 519-245-4600
Trappe Packing Corporation
Trappe, MD. 410-476-3185
Twin City Foods
Stanwood, WA 206-515-2400
Vegetable Juices
Chicago, IL 888-776-9752
William Bolthouse Farms
Bakersfield, CA 661-366-7205

Baby

Sales USA
Salado, TX 800-766-7344

Canned

Chiquita Brands International
Cincinnati, OH 877-833-5551

EMERLING INTERNATIONAL FOODS, INC.

Emerling International Foods
Buffalo, NY. 716-833-7381

We supply food manufacturers and food service customers worldwide (since 1988) with bulk ingredients including: Fruits & Vegetables; Juice Concentrates; Herbs & Spices; Oils & Vinegars; Flavors & Colors; Honey & Molasses. We also produce PURE MAPLE SYRUP.

Hanover Foods Corporation
Hanover, PA 717-632-6000
Lakeside Foods
Seymour, WI 920-833-2371
Lakeside Foods
New Holstein, WI 920-898-5702
Mr. Dell Foods
Kearney, MO 816-628-4644
New Harvest Foods
Pulaski, WI 920-822-2578
NORPAC Plant
Salem, OR. 800-822-2898
Omstead Foods Ltd
Burlington, ON 905-315-8883
Seneca Foods
Marion, NY 315-926-8100

Dehydrated

Advanced Spice & Trading
Carrollton, TX. 800-872-7811
Tova Industries
Louisville, KY 888-532-8682

Frozen

Chase Farms
Walkerville, MI 231-873-3337
Cleugh's Frozen Foods
Buena Park, CA 714-521-1002
Cobi Foods
Hantsport, NS 800-565-8229
Columbia Foods
Quincy, WA 509-787-1585

EMERLING INTERNATIONAL FOODS, INC.

Emerling International Foods
Buffalo, NY. 716-833-7381

We supply food manufacturers and food service customers worldwide (since 1988) with bulk ingredients including: Fruits & Vegetables; Juice Concentrates; Herbs & Spices; Oils & Vinegars; Flavors & Colors; Honey & Molasses. We also produce PURE MAPLE SYRUP.

Hanover Foods Corporation
Hanover, PA 717-632-6000
J.R. Simplot Company
Boise, ID 208-336-2110
Lakeside Foods
Seymour, WI 920-833-2371
Mr. Dell Foods
Kearney, MO 816-628-4644
National Frozen Foods Corporation
Seattle, WA 206-322-8900
NORPAC Plant
Salem, OR. 800-822-2898
Omstead Foods Ltd
Burlington, ON 905-315-8883
Pictsweet Frozen Foods
Bells, TN. 731-663-7600
Smith Frozen Foods
Weston, OR 541-566-3515
Smith Frozen Foods
Weston, OR 800-547-0203
Strathroy Foods
Strathroy, ON 519-245-4600
Trappe Packing Corporation
Trappe, MD. 410-476-3185
Twin City Foods
Stanwood, WA 206-515-2400
Vegetable Juices
Chicago, IL 888-776-9752

Organic

Princeville Canning Company
Princeville, IL 309-385-4301

Peeled

Rousseau Farming Company
Tolleson, AZ 623-936-7100

Cauliflower

Al Pete Meats
Muncie, IN 765-288-8817
Anchor Food Products/ McCain Foods
Appleton, WI 920-734-0627
Cobi Foods
Hantsport, NS 800-565-8229
Crown Packing Company
Salinas, CA 831-424-2067
Exeter Produce & Storage Company
Exeter, ON. 519-235-0141
F&S Produce Company
Rosenhayn, NJ 800-886-3316
Giuliano's Specialty Foods
Garden Grove, CA 714-895-9661
Great American Appetizers
Nampa, ID. 800-282-4834
Indian Rock Produce
Perkasie, PA 800-882-0512
L.I. Cauliflower Association
Riverhead, NY 631-727-2212
Lake Erie Frozen Foods Company
Ashland, OH 800-766-8501
McCain Foods
Fort Atkinson, WI. 920-563-6625
McCain Foods Canada
Florenceville, NB 506-392-5541
Mills
Salinas, CA 831-758-8179
Omstead Foods Ltd
Burlington, ON 905-315-8883
Paradise Products Corporation
Roslyn, NY 800-826-1235
Patterson Frozen Foods
Patterson, CA 209-892-2611
Pictsweet Frozen Foods
Bells, TN. 731-663-7600
RES Food Products International
Green Bay, WI. 800-255-3768
Ripon Pickle Company
Ripon, WI 800-324-5493

S&G Products
Nicholasville, KY 800-826-7652
Snowcrest Packer
Abbotsford, BC. 604-859-4881
Sunrise Growers
Placentia, CA 714-630-2170
Tanimura & Antle
Salinas, CA 831-455-2255
Teixeira Farms
Santa Maria, CA 805-928-3801
Trappe Packing Corporation
Trappe, MD. 410-476-3185
Vegetable Juices
Chicago, IL 888-776-9752

Canned

Anchor Food Products/ McCain Foods
Appleton, WI 920-734-0627
Del Monte Foods
San Francisco, CA 800-543-3090

EMERLING INTERNATIONAL FOODS, INC.

Emerling International Foods
Buffalo, NY. 716-833-7381

We supply food manufacturers and food service customers worldwide (since 1988) with bulk ingredients including: Fruits & Vegetables; Juice Concentrates; Herbs & Spices; Oils & Vinegars; Flavors & Colors; Honey & Molasses. We also produce PURE MAPLE SYRUP.

McCain Foods Canada
Florenceville, NB 506-392-5541
Omstead Foods Ltd
Burlington, ON 905-315-8883
Paradise Products Corporation
Roslyn, NY 800-826-1235
Seneca Foods
Clyman, WI. 920-696-3331

Frozen

Al Pete Meats
Muncie, IN 765-288-8817
Anchor Food Products/ McCain Foods
Appleton, WI 920-734-0627
Cobi Foods
Hantsport, NS 800-565-8229

EMERLING INTERNATIONAL FOODS, INC.

Emerling International Foods
Buffalo, NY. 716-833-7381

We supply food manufacturers and food service customers worldwide (since 1988) with bulk ingredients including: Fruits & Vegetables; Juice Concentrates; Herbs & Spices; Oils & Vinegars; Flavors & Colors; Honey & Molasses. We also produce PURE MAPLE SYRUP.

Great American Appetizers
Nampa, ID 800-282-4834
J.R. Simplot Company
Boise, ID 208-336-2110
McCain Foods
Fort Atkinson, WI. 920-563-6625
McCain Foods Canada
Florenceville, NB 506-392-5541
Omstead Foods Ltd
Burlington, ON 905-315-8883
Pictsweet Frozen Foods
Bells, TN 731-663-7600
Snowcrest Packer
Abbotsford, BC. 604-859-4881
Trappe Packing Corporation
Trappe, MD. 410-476-3185

Celery

A. Duda Farm Fresh Foods
Belle Glade, FL. 561-996-7621
Crown Packing Company
Salinas, CA 831-424-2067
Dehydrates Inc
Hewlett, NY 800-983-4443
F&S Produce Company
Rosenhayn, NJ 800-886-3316
JES Foods
Cleveland, OH 216-883-8987

Leach Foods Products
Berlin, WI 920-361-1880
Michigan Celery Promotion Cooperative
Hudsonville, MI 616-669-1250
Michigan Freeze Pack
Hart, MI. 231-873-2175
Mills
Salinas, CA 831-758-8179
Mr. Dell Foods
Kearney, MO. 816-628-4644
Nature Quality
San Martin, CA 408-683-2182
Pioneer Growers Cooperative
Belle Glade, FL 561-996-5561
R.C. McEntire & Company
Columbia, SC 803-799-3388
Ruskin Packaging
Miami, FL 305-324-1529
Silva Harvesting
Gonzales, CA 831-675-2327
Sure Fresh Produce
Santa Maria, CA 888-423-5379
Tanimura & Antle
Salinas, CA 831-455-2255
Teixeira Farms
Santa Maria, CA 805-928-3801
Tri-Counties Packing Company
Salinas, CA 831-422-7841

Canned

A. Duda Farm Fresh Foods
Belle Glade, FL. 561-996-7621
Duda Redifoods
Oviedo, FL 407-365-2189

EMERLING INTERNATIONAL FOODS, INC.

Emerling International Foods
Buffalo, NY. 716-833-7381

We supply food manufacturers and food service customers worldwide (since 1988) with bulk ingredients including: Fruits & Vegetables; Juice Concentrates; Herbs & Spices; Oils & Vinegars; Flavors & Colors; Honey & Molasses. We also produce PURE MAPLE SYRUP.

Mr. Dell Foods
Kearney, MO. 816-628-4644
Sure Fresh Produce
Santa Maria, CA 888-423-5379

Chopped

Ruskin Packaging
Miami, FL 305-324-1529

Dehydrated

Advanced Spice & Trading
Carrollton, TX. 800-872-7811

EMERLING INTERNATIONAL FOODS, INC.

Emerling International Foods
Buffalo, NY. 716-833-7381

We supply food manufacturers and food service customers worldwide (since 1988) with bulk ingredients including: Fruits & Vegetables; Juice Concentrates; Herbs & Spices; Oils & Vinegars; Flavors & Colors; Honey & Molasses. We also produce PURE MAPLE SYRUP.

Tova Industries
Louisville, KY 888-532-8682
Unique Ingredients
Naches, WA. 509-653-1991

Frozen

A. Duda Farm Fresh Foods
Belle Glade, FL. 561-996-7621
Duda Redifoods
Oviedo, FL 407-365-2189

EMERLING INTERNATIONAL FOODS, INC.

Emerling International Foods
Buffalo, NY. 716-833-7381

We supply food manufacturers and food service customers worldwide (since 1988) with bulk ingredients including: Fruits & Vegetables; Juice Concentrates; Herbs & Spices; Oils & Vinegars; Flavors & Colors; Honey & Molasses. We also produce PURE MAPLE SYRUP.

Leach Farms
Berlin, WI 920-361-1880
Mr. Dell Foods
Kearney, MO. 816-628-4644
Nature Quality
San Martin, CA 408-683-2182
Sure Fresh Produce
Santa Maria, CA 888-423-5379
Vegetable Juices
Chicago, IL 888-776-9752

Sticks

R.C. McEntire & Company
Columbia, SC 803-799-3388

Cherries

Agvest
Cleveland, OH 440-735-6900
Bob Gordon & Associates
Chicago, IL 773-247-0588
Bridenbaughs Orchards
Martinsburg, PA 814-793-2364
Burnette Foods
Elk Rapids, MI 231-264-8116
Cahoon Farms
Wolcott, NY 315-594-8081
Cal-Harvest Marketing
Hanford, CA 559-582-4000
California Fruit Processors
Stockton, CA. 209-931-1760
Castella Imports
Hauppauge, NY 866-227-8355
Charles Dennery Pillsbury
New Orleans, LA 504-733-2331
Chase Farms
Walkerville, MI 231-873-3337
Cherry Central Cooperative Inc
Traverse City, MI 231-946-1860
Cherry Growers
Grawn, MI. 231-276-9241
Cherry Growers
Grawn, MI. 800-530-9030
Cherry Hut
Traverse City, MI 888-882-4431
Cherry Lane Frozen Fruits
Vineland Station, ON 905-562-4337
Chief Tonasket Growers
Portland, OR 509-486-2914
Chief Wenatchee
Wenatchee, WA. 509-662-5197
Chieftain Wild Rice Company
Spooner, WI. 800-262-6368
Chiquita Brands International
Cincinnati, OH 800-438-0015
Chooljian Brothers Packing Company
Sanger, CA 559-875-5501
Christopher Ranch
Gilroy, CA. 408-847-1100
Chukar Cherries
Prosser, WA. 800-624-9544
Coloma Frozen Foods
Coloma, MI. 800-642-2723
Delta Packing Company of Lodi
Lodi, CA 209-334-0689
Diamond Fruit Growers
Odell, OR 541-354-5300
Diana Fruit Company
Santa Clara, CA 408-727-9631
G L Mezzetta
American Canyon, CA 707-648-1050
Gray & Company
Forest Grove, OR 503-357-3141
Harner Farms
State College, PA 814-237-7919
J.H. Verbridge & Son
Williamson, NY 315-589-2366
Just Tomatoes Company
Westley, CA. 800-537-1985

Kalustyan Corporation
  Union, NJ 908-688-6111
L&S Packing Company
  Farmingdale, NY 800-286-6487
Leelanau Fruit Company
  Suttons Bay, MI 800-431-0718
Leroux Creek Foods
  Hotchkiss, CO 877-970-5670
M&R Company
  Lodi, CA 209-369-2725
Mason County Fruit Packers Cooperative
  Ludington, MI 231-845-6248
Mayfair Packing Company
  San Jose, CA 408-280-2349
Meduri Farms Inc
  Dallas, OR 503-831-1097
Miss Scarlett's
  Chandler, AZ 800-345-6734
Natural Foods
  Toledo, OH 800-860-0006
Niagara Foods
  Middleport, NY 716-735-7722
North Bay Produce
  Traverse City, MI 231-946-1941
Northern Fruit Company
  Wenatchee, WA 509-884-6651
Northern Michigan Fruit Company
  Omena, MI 231-386-5142
Oregon Cherry Growers
  Salem, OR 800-367-2536
Oregon Fruit Products Company
  Salem, OR 800-394-9333
Packers Canning Company
  Lawton, MI 269-624-4681
Paradise
  Plant City, FL 800-330-8952
Paradise Products Corporation
  Roslyn, NY 800-826-1235
Peninsula Fruit Exchange
  Traverse City, MI 231-223-4282
Per-Clin Orchards
  Bear Lake, MI 231-889-4289
Premier Packing Company
  Bakersfield, CA 661-393-3320
Price Cold Storage & Packing Company
  Yakima, WA 509-966-4110
Purity Products
  Plainview, NY 888-769-7873
Quality Brands
  Deland, FL 386-738-3808
Reinhart Foods
  Markham, ON 905-754-3503
Shoreline Fruit
  Traverse City, MI 800-836-3972
Signature Fruit
  Stockton, CA 209-931-1531
Sill Farms Market
  Lawrence, MI 269-674-3755
Smeltzer Orchard Company
  Frankfort, MI 231-882-4421
Snowcrest Packer
  Abbotsford, BC 604-859-4881
Stadelman Fruit
  Zillah, WA 509-829-5145
Sunfresh
  Royal City, WA 509-346-9438
Terri Lynn
  Elgin, IL 800-323-0775
Timber Crest Farms
  Healdsburg, CA 888-374-9325
Trinity Fruit Sales
  Clovis, CA 559-322-7100
Triple D Orchards
  Empire, MI 866-781-9410
Unique Ingredients
  Naches, WA 509-653-1991
United Fruits Corporation
  Santa Monica, CA 310-829-0261
Watermill Foods
  Milton Freewater, OR 541-938-6601

Wiard's Orchards
  Ypsilanti, MI 734-482-7744
Yakima Fruit & Cold Storage Company
  Wapato, WA 509-877-0440

Bing

Chieftain Wild Rice Company
  Spooner, WI 800-262-6368

Canned

Bob Gordon & Associates
  Chicago, IL 773-247-0588
Burnette Foods
  Elk Rapids, MI 231-264-8116
Cherry Growers
  Grawn, MI 231-276-9241

EMERLING INTERNATIONAL FOODS, INC.

Emerling International Foods
  Buffalo, NY 716-833-7381

We supply food manufacturers and food service customers worldwide (since 1988) with bulk ingredients including: Fruits & Vegetables; Juice Concentrates; Herbs & Spices; Oils & Vinegars; Flavors & Colors; Honey & Molasses. We also produce PURE MAPLE SYRUP.

Heikes Produce Company
  Medford, OR 541-772-5653
Independent Food Processors
  Sunnyside, WA 509-837-3806
Independent Food Processors Company
  Yakima, WA 800-476-5398
L&S Packing Company
  Farmingdale, NY 800-286-6487
Northwest Packing Company
  Vancouver, WA 800-543-4356
Oregon Cherry Growers
  Salem, OR 800-367-2536
Oregon Fruit Products Company
  Salem, OR 800-394-9333
Packers Canning Company
  Lawton, MI 269-624-4681
Paradise Products Corporation
  Roslyn, NY 800-826-1235
Quality Brands
  Deland, FL 386-738-3808
San Benito Foods
  Vancouver, WA 800-453-7832
Triple D Orchards
  Empire, MI 866-781-9410
Truitt Brothers Inc
  Salem, OR 800-547-8712
Unique Ingredients
  Naches, WA 509-653-1991

Dried

American Importing Company
  Minneapolis, MN 612-331-9226
Atwater Foods
  Lyndonville, NY 585-765-2639
Chieftain Wild Rice Company
  Spooner, WI 800-262-6368
Fastachi
  Watertown, MA 800-466-3022
Royal Ridge Fruits
  Royal City, WA 509-346-1520
Setton International Foods
  Commack, NY 800-227-4397

Frozen

Agvest
  Cleveland, OH 440-735-6900
Cahoon Farms
  Wolcott, NY 315-594-8081
Chase Farms
  Walkerville, MI 231-873-3337
Cherry Growers
  Grawn, MI 231-276-9241
Cherry Growers
  Grawn, MI 800-530-9030
Cherry Hill Orchards Pelham
  Fenwick, ON 905-892-3782
Cherry Lane Frozen Fruits
  Vineland Station, ON 905-562-4337
Coloma Frozen Foods
  Coloma, MI 800-642-2723

EMERLING INTERNATIONAL FOODS, INC.

Emerling International Foods
  Buffalo, NY 716-833-7381

We supply food manufacturers and food service customers worldwide (since 1988) with bulk ingredients including: Fruits & Vegetables; Juice Concentrates; Herbs & Spices; Oils & Vinegars; Flavors & Colors; Honey & Molasses. We also produce PURE MAPLE SYRUP.

Fruithill
  Yamhill, OR 503-662-3926
Great Lakes Packing Company
  Kewadin, MI 231-264-5561
Heikes Produce Company
  Medford, OR 541-772-5653
Independent Food Processors Company
  Yakima, WA 800-476-5398
J.H. Verbridge & Son
  Williamson, NY 315-589-2366
Leelanau Fruit Company
  Suttons Bay, MI 231-271-3514
Leelanau Fruit Company
  Suttons Bay, MI 800-431-0718
Mason County Fruit Packers Cooperative
  Ludington, MI 231-845-6248
Muir-Roberts Company
  Salt Lake City, UT 801-363-5809
Niagara Foods
  Middleport, NY 716-735-7722
Norfood Cherry Growers
  Simcoe, ON 519-426-5784
Northern Michigan Fruit Company
  Omena, MI 231-386-5142
Oceana Foods
  Shelby, MI 231-861-2141
Oregon Cherry Growers
  Salem, OR 800-367-2536
Oregon Fruit Products Company
  Salem, OR 800-394-9333
Packers Canning Company
  Lawton, MI 269-624-4681
Peninsula Fruit Exchange
  Traverse City, MI 231-223-4282
Quality Brands
  Deland, FL 386-738-3808
Sill Farms Market
  Lawrence, MI 269-674-3755
Smeltzer Orchard Company
  Frankfort, MI 231-882-4421
Snowcrest Packer
  Abbotsford, BC 604-859-4881
Triple D Orchards
  Empire, MI 866-781-9410
Unique Ingredients
  Naches, WA 509-653-1991
Watermill Foods
  Milton Freewater, OR 541-938-6601
Windatt Farms
  Picton, ON 613-393-5289

IQF (Individually Quick Frozen)

Northern Michigan Fruit Company
  Omena, MI 231-386-5142

Maraschino

A. Camacho
  Plant City, FL 800-881-4534
Bob Gordon & Associates
  Chicago, IL 773-247-0588
Charles Dennery Pillsbury
  New Orleans, LA 504-733-2331
Diana Fruit Company
  Santa Clara, CA 408-727-9631
Eden Processing
  Poplar Grove, IL 815-765-2000

EMERLING INTERNATIONAL FOODS, INC.

Emerling International Foods
  Buffalo, NY 716-833-7381

We supply food manufacturers and food service customers worldwide (since 1988) with bulk ingredients including: Fruits & Vegetables; Juice Concentrates; Herbs & Spices; Oils & Vinegars; Flavors & Colors; Honey & Molasses. We also produce PURE MAPLE SYRUP.

Eola Specialty Foods
Gervais, OR.........................503-390-1425
G L Mezzetta
American Canyon, CA.............707-648-1050
Gray & Company
Forest Grove, OR.................503-357-3141
Johnson Canning Company
Sunnyside, WA....................509-837-4188
L&S Packing Company
Farmingdale, NY..................800-286-6487
Metzger Specialty Brands
New York, NY.....................212-957-0055
Oregon Cherry Growers
Salem, OR........................800-367-2536
Pacific Choice Brands
Fresno, CA.......................559-237-5583
Paradise Products Corporation
Roslyn, NY.......................800-826-1235
Purity Products
Plainview, NY....................888-769-7873
Reinhart Foods
Markham, ON......................905-754-3503
Signature Fruit
Stockton, CA.....................209-931-1531
Unique Ingredients
Naches, WA.......................509-653-1991

Sweet

Baker Produce Company
Kennewick, WA....................800-624-7553
Northern Michigan Fruit Company
Omena, MI........................231-386-5142

Tart

Baker Produce Company
Kennewick, WA....................800-624-7553
Cherry Hill Orchards Pelham
Fenwick, ON......................905-892-3782
Chieftain Wild Rice Company
Spooner, WI......................800-262-6368
Fruit Belt Foods
Lawrence, MI.....................269-674-3939
Hygeia Dairy Company
McAllen, TX......................956-686-0511
Northern Michigan Fruit Company
Omena, MI........................231-386-5142

Chicory

Whole Herb Company
Sonoma, CA.......................707-935-1077

Chives

Josie's Best New Mexican Foods
Santa Fe, NM.....................505-473-3437
Mission Foods/Diane's Foods
McMinnville, OR..................503-434-5534
Pillsbury
Hannibal, MO.....................800-775-4777

SupHerb Farms
Turlock, CA......................800-787-4372

CrEATe! Get ready-to-use fresh flavor with SupHerb Farms' all-natural fresh frozen culinary herbs, specialty vegetables, culinary herb pastes, vegetable purees and creative blends. Complete microbiological testing ensures food safety. We set the standard for outstanding customer service, inspired culinary support, collaborative customer partnerships and innovative custom products.

Vegetable Juices
Chicago, IL......................888-776-9752

Citrus Fruits

A. Duda & Sons
Oviedo, FL.......................407-365-2111
A. Duda Farm Fresh Foods
Belle Glade, FL..................561-996-7621

Armistead Citrus Company
Mesa, AZ.........................480-830-2491
Ben Hill Griffin, Inc.
Frostproof, FL...................863-635-2251
Brooks Tropicals
Homestead, FL....................800-327-4833
California Citrus Producer
Lindsay, CA......................559-562-5169
California Farms & Canners
San Francisco, CA................415-433-3522
Corona College Heights Orange & Lemon Associates
Riverside, CA....................951-688-1811
Country Pure Foods
Akron, OH........................877-995-8423
Crown Processing Company
Bellflower, CA...................562-865-0293
Davidson of Dundee
Dundee, FL.......................800-654-0647
Del Monte Foods
San Francisco, CA................800-543-3090
Dimare
Visalia, CA......................559-627-0821
DiMare International
Indio, CA........................760-564-3762
DNE World Fruit Sales
Fort Pierce, FL..................800-327-6676
Dundee Citrus Growers
Dundee, FL.......................800-447-1574
Fillmore Piru Citrus Association
Piru, CA.........................800-524-8787
Golden River Fruit Company
Vero Beach, FL...................772-562-4502
Haines City Citrus Growers Association
Haines City, FL..................800-422-4245
Heller Brothers Packing Corporation
Winter Garden, FL................407-656-4986
Hunt Brothers Cooperative
Lake Wales, FL...................863-676-9471
Leroy Smith & Sons Inc
Vero Beach, FL...................772-567-3421
Magnolia Citrus Association
Porterville, CA..................559-784-4455
Mixon Fruit Farms
Bradenton, FL....................800-608-2525
Orange Cove Sanger Citrus Association
Orange Cove, CA..................559-626-4453
P-R Farms
Clovis, CA.......................559-299-0201
Reed Lang Farms
Rio Hondo, TX....................956-748-2354
Shields Date Gardens
Indio, CA........................800-414-2555
Sun Orchard of Florida
Haines City, FL..................863-422-5062
Sunkist Growers
Stafford, TX.....................281-240-6446
Sunkist Growers
Detroit, MI......................313-843-4160
Sunkist Growers
Cary, NC.........................410-663-2967
Sunkist Growers
Pittsburgh, PA...................412-967-9801
Sunkist Growers
West Chester, OH.................513-741-9494
Sunkist Growers
Visalia, CA......................559-739-8392
Sunkist Growers
Chelsea, MA......................617-884-9750
Sunkist Growers
Buffalo, NY......................716-895-3744
Sunkist Growers
Ontario, CA......................800-798-9005
Sunkist Growers
Cherry Hill, NJ..................856-663-2343
Tony Vitrano Company
Jessup, MD.......................410-799-7444
Valley Fruit & Vegetable
McAllen, TX......................956-686-8056
Wileman Bros & Elliott, Inc
Cutler, CA.......................559-732-5321
Yokhol Valley Packing Company
Lindsay, CA......................559-562-1327

Peels

Con Yeager Spice Company
Zelienople, PA...................800-222-2460
Crown Processing Company
Bellflower, CA...................562-865-0293
Naturex (Chart Corp)
South Hackensack, NJ.............201-440-5000

Paradise
Plant City, FL...................800-330-8952
Vita-Pakt Citrus Company
Lindsay, CA......................559-562-6008

Citrus Peel Products

Eden Processing
Poplar Grove, IL.................815-765-2000
Fmali Herb
Santa Cruz, CA...................831-423-7913
Vita-Pakt Citrus Company
Lindsay, CA......................559-562-6008

Coconut & Coconut Products

AFP Advanced Food Products, LLC
Visalia, CA......................559-627-2070
American Key Food Products
Closter, NJ......................800-767-0237
Baker's Coconut
Memphis, TN......................800-323-1092
C.F. Burger Creamery
Detroit, MI......................800-229-2322
Catania-Spagna Corporation
Ayer, MA.........................800-343-5522
Charles Dennery Pillsbury
New Orleans, LA..................504-733-2331
Clark Bar America
Revere, MA.......................781-485-4500
Coco Rico
Montreal, QC.....................514-849-5554
Commodities Marketing, Inc.
Edison, NJ.......................732-516-0700
Eden Processing
Poplar Grove, IL.................815-765-2000

EMERLING INTERNATIONAL FOODS, INC.

Emerling International Foods
Buffalo, NY......................716-833-7381

We supply food manufacturers and food service customers worldwide (since 1988) with bulk ingredients including: Fruits & Vegetables; Juice Concentrates; Herbs & Spices; Oils & Vinegars; Flavors & Colors; Honey & Molasses. We also produce PURE MAPLE SYRUP.

Far Eastern Coconut Company
Central Islip, NY................631-851-8800
Hawaii Candy
Honolulu, HI.....................808-836-8955
Hialeah Products Company
Hollywood, FL....................800-923-3379
Kraft Food Ingredients
Memphis, TN......................901-381-6500
L&M Bakery
Lawrence, MA.....................978-687-7346
Marx Brothers
Birmingham, AL...................800-633-6376
Mehaffie Pies
Dayton, OH.......................937-253-1163
Mercado Latino
City of Industry, CA.............626-333-6862
Miramar Fruit Trading Company
Medley, FL.......................305-883-4774
Olde Tyme Mercantile
Arroyo Grande, CA................805-489-7991
Reinhart Foods
Markham, ON......................905-754-3503
RV Industries
Atlanta, GA......................770-729-8983
Sacharen Brothers
Montreal, QC.....................514-277-8205
Sally Lane's Candy Farm
Paris, TN........................731-642-5801
Sayklly's Candies & Gifts
Escanaba, MI.....................906-786-3092
Segovia Mexican Candy Manufacturer
San Antonio, TX..................210-225-2102
Sun Garden Growers
Bard, CA.........................800-228-4690
White-Stokes Company
Chicago, IL......................800-978-6537
Wisconsin Cheese
Melrose Park, IL.................708-450-0074

Desiccated & Shredded

Commodities Marketing, Inc.
Edison, NJ.......................732-516-0700

EMERLING INTERNATIONAL FOODS, INC.

Emerling International Foods
Buffalo, NY....................716-833-7381

> We supply food manufacturers and food service customers worldwide (since 1988) with bulk ingredients including: Fruits & Vegetables; Juice Concentrates; Herbs & Spices; Oils & Vinegars; Flavors & Colors; Honey & Molasses. We also produce PURE MAPLE SYRUP.

Far Eastern Coconut Company
Central Islip, NY.................631-851-8800
International Coconut Corporation
Elizabeth, NJ...................908-289-1555
Log House Foods
Plymouth, MN..................763-546-8395
Organic Planet
San Francisco, CA...............415-765-5590
RV Industries
Atlanta, GA....................770-729-8983
Service Packing Company
Vancouver, BC..................604-681-0264
Setton International Foods
Commack, NY...................800-227-4397

Dried

Far Eastern Coconut Company
Central Islip, NY.................631-851-8800
Hialeah Products Company
Hollywood, FL..................800-923-3379

Frozen

EMERLING INTERNATIONAL FOODS, INC.

Emerling International Foods
Buffalo, NY....................716-833-7381

> We supply food manufacturers and food service customers worldwide (since 1988) with bulk ingredients including: Fruits & Vegetables; Juice Concentrates; Herbs & Spices; Oils & Vinegars; Flavors & Colors; Honey & Molasses. We also produce PURE MAPLE SYRUP.

Milk

Epicurean International
Berkeley, CA...................800-967-7424

Processed

Far Eastern Coconut Company
Central Islip, NY.................631-851-8800
Hialeah Products Company
Hollywood, FL..................800-923-3379

Collard Greens

Abbott & Cobb, Inc.
Langhorne, PA..................800-345-7333

EMERLING INTERNATIONAL FOODS, INC.

Emerling International Foods
Buffalo, NY....................716-833-7381

> We supply food manufacturers and food service customers worldwide (since 1988) with bulk ingredients including: Fruits & Vegetables; Juice Concentrates; Herbs & Spices; Oils & Vinegars; Flavors & Colors; Honey & Molasses. We also produce PURE MAPLE SYRUP.

Frank Capurro & Son
Moss Landing, CA................831-728-3904
Lucks Food Decorating Company
Tacoma, WA....................206-674-7200
McCain Foods USA
Grand Island, NE................308-382-7770
Oxford Frozen Foods Limited
Oxford, NS....................902-447-2100
Pictsweet Frozen Foods
Bells, TN.....................731-663-7600
Ruskin Packaging
Miami, FL.....................305-324-1529
Seabrook Brothers & Sons
Seabrook, NJ...................856-455-8080

Canned & Frozen

Allen Canning Company
Siloam Springs, AR..............800-234-2553
Lucks Food Decorating Company
Tacoma, WA....................206-674-7200
Pictsweet Frozen Foods
Bells, TN.....................731-663-7600
Seabrook Brothers & Sons
Seabrook, NJ...................856-455-8080
Walter P. Rawl & Sons
Pelion, SC....................803-359-3645

Corn

A. Duda Farm Fresh Foods
Belle Glade, FL.................561-996-7621
A. Lassonde, Inc.
Rougemont, QC..................514-878-1057
ADM Growmark
Decatur, IL....................217-451-8602
ADM Milling Company
Shawnee Mission, KS.............800-422-1688
Archer Daniels Midland Company
Decatur, IL....................800-637-5843
Bush Brothers & Company
Dandridge, TN..................865-509-2361
Chiquita Processed Foods
Milton Freewater, OR............541-938-4461
Christopher Ranch
Gilroy, CA....................408-847-1100
Cobi Foods
Hantsport, NS..................800-565-8229
Columbia Foods
Quincy, WA....................509-787-1585
Conserverie Larose
Calixa-Lavallee, QC.............450-583-6438
Cooperative Elevator Company
Pigeon, MI....................989-453-4500
Coutts Specialty Foods
Boxborough, MA.................800-919-2952
Dehydrates Inc
Hewlett, NY...................800-983-4443
Del Monte Foods
Mendota, IL...................815-539-9361
F&S Produce Company
Rosenhayn, NJ..................800-886-3316
Faribault Foods
Minneapolis, MN................612-333-6461
Georgia Vegetable Company
Tifton, GA....................229-386-2374
Indian Rock Produce
Perkasie, PA...................800-882-0512
John Copes Food Products
Manheim, PA...................800-745-8211
Just Tomatoes Company
Westley, CA...................800-537-1985
Lakeside Foods
Plainview, MN..................507-534-3141
Lakeside Foods
Seymour, WI...................920-833-2371
Lucks Food Decorating Company
Tacoma, WA....................206-674-7200
McCain Foods Canada
Florenceville, NB...............506-392-5541
Miss Scarlett's
Chandler, AZ...................800-345-6734
National Frozen Foods Corporation
Seattle, WA...................206-322-8900
Natural Way Mills
Middle River, MN...............218-222-3677
Nebraska Salt & Grain Company
Gothenburg, NE.................308-537-7191
New Harvest Foods
Pulaski, WI....................920-822-2578
Omstead Foods Ltd
Burlington, ON.................905-315-8883
Paisley Farms
Willoughby, OH.................800-676-8656
Paradise Products Corporation
Roslyn, NY....................800-826-1235
Pioneer Growers Cooperative
Belle Glade, FL.................561-996-5561
Produits Ronald
St. Damase, QC.................450-797-3303
Roberts Seed
Axtell, NE....................308-743-2565
Seneca Foods
Marion, NY....................315-926-4280
Seneca Foods
Marion, NY....................315-926-8100
Seneca Foods
Arlington, MN..................507-964-2204

SEW Friel
Queenstown, MD................410-827-8841
Smith Frozen Foods
Weston, OR....................541-566-3515
Sno Pac Foods
Caledonia, MN..................800-533-2215
Snowcrest Packer
Abbotsford, BC.................604-859-4881
Sonne
Wahpeton, ND..................800-727-6663
Subco Foods Inc
Sheboygan, WI..................800-676-5188
Symons Frozen Foods
Centralia, WA..................360-736-1321
Trappe Packing Corporation
Trappe, MD....................410-476-3185
Twin City Foods
Stanwood, WA..................206-515-2400
Unique Ingredients
Naches, WA....................509-653-1991
Vegetable Juices
Chicago, IL....................888-776-9752
Veronica Foods Company
Oakland, CA...................800-370-5554
Walpex Trading Company
Coral Gables, FL................305-662-9744
Weetabix Company
Clinton, MA...................800-343-0590
Western Pacific Commodities
Las Vegas, NV..................702-312-8080
Woodland Foods
Gurnee, IL....................847-625-8600
Z&S Distributing
Fresno, CA....................800-467-0788

Canned

A. Lassonde, Inc.
Rougemont, QC..................514-878-1057
Carriere Foods Inc
Montreal, QC...................514-384-4281
Chiquita Brands International
Cincinnati, OH..................877-833-5551
Chiquita Processed Foods
Milton Freewater, OR............541-938-4461
Chiquita Processed Foods
Markesan, WI...................920-398-2386

EMERLING INTERNATIONAL FOODS, INC.

Emerling International Foods
Buffalo, NY....................716-833-7381

> We supply food manufacturers and food service customers worldwide (since 1988) with bulk ingredients including: Fruits & Vegetables; Juice Concentrates; Herbs & Spices; Oils & Vinegars; Flavors & Colors; Honey & Molasses. We also produce PURE MAPLE SYRUP.

Faribault Foods
Cokato, MN....................320-286-2166
Faribault Foods
Minneapolis, MN................612-333-6461
Lakeside Foods
Plainview, MN..................507-534-3141
Lakeside Foods
Manitowoc, WI..................920-684-3356
Lakeside Foods
Seymour, WI...................920-833-2371
Lodi Canning Company
Lodi, WI.....................608-592-4236
Lucks Food Decorating Company
Tacoma, WA....................206-674-7200
McCain Foods Canada
Florenceville, NB...............506-392-5541
New Harvest Foods
Pulaski, WI....................920-822-2578
Omstead Foods Ltd
Burlington, ON.................905-315-8883
Paradise Products Corporation
Roslyn, NY....................800-826-1235

Produits Ronald
St. Damase, QC.................450-797-3303
Seneca Foods
Buhl, ID.......................208-543-9350
Seneca Foods
Marion, NY....................315-926-8100
Seneca Foods
Montgomery, MN...............507-364-8641
Seneca Foods
Blue Earth, MN................507-526-2131
Seneca Foods
Janesville, WI.................608-757-6000
Seneca Foods
Oakfield, WI..................920-583-3161
SEW Friel
Queenstown, MD..............410-827-8841

Canned & Frozen

Princeville Canning Company
Princeville, IL.................309-385-4301

Corn-on-the-Cob

A. Lassonde, Inc.
Rougemont, QC................514-878-1057
Conserverie Larose
Calixa-Lavallee, QC............450-583-6438

EMERLING INTERNATIONAL FOODS, INC.

Emerling International Foods
Buffalo, NY....................716-833-7381

We supply food manufacturers and food service customers worldwide (since 1988) with bulk ingredients including: Fruits & Vegetables; Juice Concentrates; Herbs & Spices; Oils & Vinegars; Flavors & Colors; Honey & Molasses. We also produce PURE MAPLE SYRUP.

National Frozen Foods Corporation
Seattle, WA....................206-322-8900
Pictsweet Frozen Foods
Bells, TN......................731-663-7600
Produits Ronald
St. Damase, QC.................450-797-3303
Smith Frozen Foods
Weston, OR....................541-566-3515
Smith Frozen Foods
Weston, OR....................800-547-0203
Twin City Foods
Stanwood, WA.................206-515-2400

Frozen

Bennett's Apples & Cider
Ancaster, ON..................905-648-6878
National Frozen Foods Corporation
Seattle, WA....................206-322-8900
Ore-Ida Foods
Pittsburgh, PA.................412-237-3450
Pictsweet Frozen Foods
Bells, TN......................731-663-7600
Smith Frozen Foods
Weston, OR....................541-566-3515
Smith Frozen Foods
Weston, OR....................800-547-0203
Twin City Foods
Stanwood, WA.................206-515-2400
Vessey & Company
Holtville, CA...................760-352-6376

Frozen

Cobi Foods
Hantsport, NS..................800-565-8229
Columbia Foods
Quincy, WA....................509-787-1585
J.R. Simplot Company
Boise, ID......................208-336-2110
Lakeside Foods
Plainview, MN.................507-534-3141
Lakeside Foods
Manitowoc, WI................920-684-3356
Lakeside Foods
Seymour, WI..................920-833-2371
Lodi Canning Company
Lodi, WI......................608-592-4236
Ocean Mist
Castroville, CA.................831-633-2144
Omstead Foods Ltd
Burlington, ON.................905-315-8883

Seneca Foods
Marion, NY....................315-926-4280
Seneca Foods
Montgomery, MN...............507-364-8641
Smith Frozen Foods
Weston, OR....................541-566-3515
Snowcrest Packer
Abbotsford, BC................604-859-4881
Symons Frozen Foods
Centralia, WA.................360-736-1321
Trappe Packing Corporation
Trappe, MD....................410-476-3185
Zuccaro's Fruit & Produce Company
Minneapolis, MN...............612-333-1122

Husks

Woodland Foods
Gurnee, IL.....................847-625-8600

Stored

Acme Steak & Seafood Company
Youngstown, OH...............330-270-8000
Seneca Foods
Clyman, WI....................920-696-3331

Sweet

Abbott & Cobb, Inc.
Langhorne, PA.................800-345-7333
Christopher Ranch
Gilroy, CA.....................408-847-1100
Goebbert's Home Grown Vegetables
South Barrington, IL...........847-428-6727
J.R. Simplot Food Group
Pasco, WA.....................509-544-6700
New Harvest Foods
Pulaski, WI....................920-822-2578
T.S. Smith & Sons
Bridgeville, DE.................302-337-8271

Sweet Processed

Woodland Foods
Gurnee, IL.....................847-625-8600

Whole

Abbott & Cobb, Inc.
Langhorne, PA.................800-345-7333

Crushed

Baldwin Richardson Foods
Frankfort, IL...................866-644-2732

Baldwin Richardson Foods is a liquid ingredient manufacturer specializing in signature sauces, dessert toppings, beverage/pancake syrups, specialty fruit fillings and condiments. Packaging capabilities range from portion control cups and pouches to standard retail and foodservice packs and include industrial drums and totes. Full service R&D and Quality groups dedicated to new product development, with in-house stability and analytical testing. Call for assistance.

Clofine Dairy & Food Products
Linwood, NJ...................800-441-1001

EMERLING INTERNATIONAL FOODS, INC.

Emerling International Foods
Buffalo, NY....................716-833-7381

We supply food manufacturers and food service customers worldwide (since 1988) with bulk ingredients including: Fruits & Vegetables; Juice Concentrates; Herbs & Spices; Oils & Vinegars; Flavors & Colors; Honey & Molasses. We also produce PURE MAPLE SYRUP.

Richardson Foods Corporation
Macedon, NY..................315-986-2807

Crysanthemums

Heritage Farms Dairy
Murfreesboro, TN..............615-895-2790

Cucumber

Abbott & Cobb, Inc.
Langhorne, PA.................800-345-7333
Ben B. Schwartz & Sons
Detroit, MI....................313-841-8300
Carson City Pickle Company
Carson City, MI................989-584-3148
Cates Addis Company
Parkton, NC...................800-423-1883
F&S Produce Company
Rosenhayn, NJ.................800-886-3316
Georgia Vegetable Company
Tifton, GA.....................229-386-2374
Nash Produce Company
Nashville, NC..................800-334-3032
Pacific Collier Fresh Company
Immokalee, FL.................800-226-7274
Rene Produce Distributors
Nogales, AZ...................520-281-9014
Russo Farms
Vineland, NJ...................856-692-5942
Tony Vitrano Company
Jessup, MD....................410-799-7444
United Pickle Products Corporation
Bronx, NY.....................718-933-6060
Vegetable Juices
Chicago, IL....................888-776-9752
Wildcat Produce
McGrew, NE...................308-783-2438
Z&S Distributing
Fresno, CA....................800-467-0788

for Pickling

Bissett Produce Company
Spring Hope, NC...............800-849-5073

Dates

American Health & Nutrition
Ann Arbor, MI.................734-677-5572
American Importing Company
Minneapolis, MN...............612-331-9226
Amport Foods
Minneapolis, MN...............800-989-5665
Bard Valley Medjool Date Growers
Yuma, AZ.....................928-726-0901
Bautista Organic Dates
Mecca, CA....................760-396-2337
CalSungold
Indio, CA......................760-399-5646
Chieftain Wild Rice Company
Spooner, WI...................800-262-6368

EMERLING INTERNATIONAL FOODS, INC.

Emerling International Foods
Buffalo, NY....................716-833-7381

We supply food manufacturers and food service customers worldwide (since 1988) with bulk ingredients including: Fruits & Vegetables; Juice Concentrates; Herbs & Spices; Oils & Vinegars; Flavors & Colors; Honey & Molasses. We also produce PURE MAPLE SYRUP.

Fastachi
Watertown, MA................800-466-3022
Hadley Date Gardens
Thermal, CA...................760-399-5191
Kalustyan Corporation
Union, NJ.....................908-688-6111
Lee Andersons's Covalda Dates
Coachella, CA..................760-398-3441
Marin Food Specialties
Byron, CA.....................925-634-6126
Nut Factory
Spokane Valley, WA...........888-239-5288

Purity Foods
  Okemos, MI 800-997-7358
Reinhart Foods
  Markham, ON 905-754-3503
Royal Medjool Date Gardens
  Bard, CA 760-572-0524
Service Packing Company
  Vancouver, BC 604-681-0264
Setton International Foods
  Commack, NY 800-227-4397
Shields Date Gardens
  Indio, CA .800-414-2555
Sun Garden Growers
  Bard, CA 800-228-4690
Terri Lynn
  Elgin, IL 800-323-0775
Timber Crest Farms
  Healdsburg, CA 888-374-9325

Dehydrated

Abbotsford Growers Co-operative
  Abbotsford, BC 604-864-0022
Advanced Spice & Trading
  Carrollton, TX 800-872-7811
Agvest
  Cleveland, OH 440-735-6900
Amport Foods
  Minneapolis, MN 800-989-5665
Associated Fruit Company
  Phoenix, OR 541-535-1787
Atlantic Blueberry Company
  Hammonton, NJ 609-561-8600
Atlantic Quality Spice &Seasonings
  Edison, NJ. 800-584-0422
Baker Produce Company
  Kennewick, WA 800-624-7553
Basic American Foods
  Walnut Creek, CA. 800-227-4050
Bay Cities Produce Company
  San Leandro, CA. 510-346-4943
Boekhout Farms
  Ontario, NY. 315-524-4041
Brady Farms
  West Olive, MI 616-842-3916
California Fruit and Tomato Kitchens
  Riverbank, CA 209-869-9300
Caltex Foods
  Canoga Park, CA 800-522-5839
Carolina Blueberry Association
  Garland, NC 910-588-4220
Chazy Orchards
  Chazy, NY. 518-846-7171
Cherry Central Cooperative Inc
  Traverse City, MI 231-946-1860
Cherry Hill Orchards Pelham
  Fenwick, ON. 905-892-3782
Chooljian Brothers Packing Company
  Sanger, CA 559-875-5501
Chukar Cherries
  Prosser, WA. 800-624-9544
Congdon Orchards
  Yakima, WA 509-965-2886
Cooperative Elevator
  Pigeon, MI 989-453-4500
Crane & Crane
  Brewster, WA 509-689-3447
DeFrancesco & Sons
  Firebaugh, CA 209-364-7000
Del Monte Foods
  San Francisco, CA 800-543-3090
Del Rey Packing Company
  Del Rey, CA 559-888-2031
Fig Garden Packing
  Fresno, CA 559-271-9000

Fine Dried Foods International
  Santa Cruz, CA 831-426-1413
Gilroy Foods
  Gilroy, CA. 800-921-7502
Henry Broch & Company/APK, Inc.
  Libertyville, IL 847-816-6225
Hialeah Products Company
  Hollywood, FL 800-923-3379
Ingredients Corporation of America
  Memphis, TN 901-525-6660
Jasper Wyman & Son
  Milbridge, ME 800-341-1758
Larsen Farms
  Hamer, ID 208-662-5501
Larsen of Idaho
  Hamer, ID 208-662-5501
Made in Nature
  Fresno, CA 800-906-7426
Magic Valley Foods
  Rupert, ID 208-436-3126
Maine Wild Blueberry Company
  Cherryfield, ME 800-243-4005
Master Taste International
  Plant City, FL 800-237-7629
Mayfield Farms
  Brampton, ON. 905-846-0506
McCain Foods USA
  Grand Island, NE 308-382-7770
Mercer Processing
  Modesto, CA 209-529-0150
Oxford Frozen Foods Limited
  Oxford, NS 902-447-2100
Pack Ryt, Inc
  Thermal, CA 760-399-5026
Paisano Food Products
  Elk Grove Village, IL 773-237-3773
Quality Brands
  Deland, FL 386-738-3808
Red River Foods
  Richmond, VA. 800-443-6637
Reinhart Foods
  Markham, ON 905-754-3503
RFI Ingredients
  Blauvelt, NY 800-962-7663
Scotsburn Dairy Group
  Truro, NS 902-895-4412
Seneca Foods
  Marion, NY 315-926-8100
Serv-Agen Corporation
  Cherry Hill, NJ 856-663-6966
Shields Date Gardens
  Indio, CA. 800-414-2555
Smeltzer Orchard Company
  Frankfort, MI 231-882-4421
Solana Gold Organics
  Sebastopol, CA 800-459-1121
Stapleton-Spence PackingCompany
  San Jose, CA 800-297-8815
Sterigenics International
  Los Angeles, CA. 800-472-4508
Tastee Apple Inc
  Newcomerstown, OH 800-262-7753
Terri Lynn
  Elgin, IL .800-323-0775
Timber Crest Farms
  Healdsburg, CA 888-374-9325
Tova Industries
  Louisville, KY 888-532-8682
Tree Top
  Selah, WA 800-367-6571
Tru-Blu Cooperative Associates
  New Lisbon, NJ 609-894-8717
Ursula's Island Farms
  Seattle, WA 206-762-3113
Valley View Packing Company
  San Jose, CA 408-289-8300
Van Drunen Farms
  Momence, IL. 815-472-3100
Very Best Foods
  Miami, FL 305-824-9165
W&G Flavors
  Hunt Valley, MD. 410-771-6606
Washington Potato Company
  Warden, WA 509-349-8803
Zuccaro's Fruit & Produce Company
  Minneapolis, MN 612-333-1122

Freeze Dried

Advanced Spice & Trading
  Carrollton, TX. 800-872-7811

Master Taste International
  Plant City, FL 800-237-7629
RFI Ingredients
  Blauvelt, NY 800-962-7663
Setton International Foods
  Commack, NY 800-227-4397

SupHerb Farms
  Turlock, CA 800-787-4372

CrEATe! Get ready-to-use fresh flavor with SupHerb Farms' all-natural fresh frozen culinary herbs, specialty vegetables, culinary herb pastes, vegetable purees and creative blends. Complete microbiological testing ensures food safety. We set the standard for outstanding customer service, inspired culinary support, collaborative customer partnerships and innovative custom products.

Unique Ingredients
  Naches, WA 509-653-1991
Van Drunen Farms
  Momence, IL 815-472-3100

Dipping Fruit

Confectioners'

Baldwin Richardson Foods
  Frankfort, IL 866-644-2732

Baldwin Richardson Foods is a liquid ingredient manufacturer specializing in signature sauces, dessert toppings, beverage/pancake syrups, specialty fruit fillings and condiments. Packaging capabilities range from portion control cups and pouches to standard retail and foodservice packs and include industrial drums and totes. Full service R&D and Quality groups dedicated to new product development, with in-house stability and analytical testing. Call for assistance.

Bella Viva Orchards
  Denair, CA 800-552-8218
Terri Lynn
  Elgin, IL .800-323-0775

Dried & Dehydrated Fruits

Dehydrated Fruit

Agvest
  Cleveland, OH 440-735-6900
American Nut & Chocolate Company
  Boston, MA. 800-797-6887
Amport Foods
  Minneapolis, MN 800-989-5665
Atlantic Quality Spice &Seasonings
  Edison, NJ 800-584-0422
Basic American Foods
  Walnut Creek, CA. 800-227-4050
Casados Farms
  San Juan Pueblo, NM 505-852-2433
Cherry Central Cooperative Inc
  Traverse City, MI 231-946-1860
Chia I Foods Company
  South El Monte, CA 626-401-3038
Chukar Cherries
  Prosser, WA. 800-624-9544
Desert Valley Date
  Coachella, CA 760-398-0999
Diamond Foods
  Fishers, IN. 317-845-5534
Fig Garden Packing
  Fresno, CA 559-271-9000

Fine Dried Foods International
  Santa Cruz, CA 831-426-1413
Freeman Industries
  Tuckahoe, NY 800-666-6454
Gilroy Foods
  Gilroy, CA. 800-921-7502
Golden Town Apple Products
  Thornbury, ON 519-599-6300
Hialeah Products Company
  Hollywood, FL 800-923-3379
Hurd Orchards
  Holley, NY 585-638-8838
Kamish Food Products
  Chicago, IL 773-267-0400
Kozlowski Farms
  Forestville, CA 800-473-2767
Leroux Creek Foods
  Hotchkiss, CO. 877-970-5670
Made in Nature
  Fresno, CA 800-906-7426
Maine Wild Blueberry Company
  Cherryfield, ME 800-243-4005
Mariani Packing Company
  Vacaville, CA 800-672-8655
Mayfair Packing Company
  San Jose, CA. 408-280-2349
Mercer Processing
  Modesto, CA .209-529-0150
Mojave Foods Corporation
  Commerce, CA 323-890-8900
New England Natural Bakers
  Greenfield, MA. 800-910-2884
Niagara Foods
  Middleport, NY 716-735-7722
Organic Planet
  San Francisco, CA 415-765-5590
Ramos Orchards
  Winters, CA .530-795-4748
Red River Foods
  Richmond, VA. 800-443-6637
Seneca Foods
  Marion, NY 315-926-8100
Seneca Foods Corporation
  Marion, NY 315-926-8100
Shade Foods
  New Century, KS 800-225-6312
Shields Date Gardens
  Indio, CA. 800-414-2555
Silva International
  Momence, IL 815-472-3535
Specialty Commodities
  Fargo, ND 701-282-8222
Specialty Ingredients
  Buffalo Grove, IL 847-419-9595
Spice King Corporation
  Beverly Hills, CA 310-836-7770
Spreda Group
  Prospect, KY 502-426-9411
Sun Garden Growers
  Bard, CA 800-228-4690
Timber Crest Farms
  Healdsburg, CA 888-374-9325
Torn & Glasser
  Los Angeles, CA. 800-282-6887
Torn Ranch
  Novato, CA. .415-506-3000
Ursula's Island Farms
  Seattle, WA .206-762-3113
Valley View Packing Company
  San Jose, CA 408-289-8300
Van Drunen Farms
  Momence, IL 815-472-3100
Very Best Foods
  Miami, FL 305-824-9165
W&G Flavors
  Hunt Valley, MD 410-771-6606
World Nutrition
  Scottsdale, AZ. 800-548-2710

Desiccated Fruit

Fig Garden Packing
  Fresno, CA 559-271-9000
Gilroy Foods
  Gilroy, CA. 800-921-7502
Hialeah Products Company
  Hollywood, FL 800-923-3379
Kozlowski Farms
  Forestville, CA 800-473-2767
Leroux Creek Foods
  Hotchkiss, CO. 877-970-5670

Maine Wild Blueberry Company
  Cherryfield, ME 800-243-4005
New England Natural Bakers
  Greenfield, MA. 800-910-2884
Ramos Orchards
  Winters, CA .530-795-4748
San Joaquin Figs
  Fresno, CA 559-224-4492
Shade Foods
  New Century, KS 800-225-6312
Spreda Group
  Prospect, KY 502-426-9411
Sun Garden Growers
  Bard, CA 800-228-4690
Very Best Foods
  Miami, FL 305-824-9165

Dried Fruit

A.L. Bazzini Company
  Bronx, NY. 800-228-0172
Agrexco USA
  Jamaica, NY 718-481-8700
AlpineAire Foods
  Rocklin, CA. .800-322-6325
Amalgamated Produce
  Bridgeport, CT 800-358-3808
American Food Ingredients
  Oceanside, CA 760-967-6287
American Health & Nutrition
  Ann Arbor, MI 734-677-5572
American Importing Company
  Minneapolis, MN 612-331-9226
American Key Food Products
  Closter, NJ. .800-767-0237
American Spoon Foods
  Petoskey, MI 800-222-5886
Amport Foods
  Minneapolis, MN 800-989-5665
Ann's House of Nuts, Inc.
  Jessup, MD .301-498-4920
Atwater Foods
  Lyndonville, NY 585-765-2639
Aurora Products
  Stratford, CT. 800-398-1048
Azar Nut Company
  El Paso, TX .800-592-8103
Azar Nut Company
  El Paso, TX .915-877-4079
Bella Viva Orchards
  Denair, CA 800-552-8218
Blueberry Store
  Grand Junction, MI. 877-654-2400
Boghosian Raisin Packing Company
  Fowler, CA. .559-834-5348
Buchanan Hollow Nut Company
  Le Grand, CA 800-532-1500
California Fruit
  Sanger, CA .559-266-7117
California Fruit & Nut
  Gustine, CA .888-747-8224
California Prune Packing Company
  Live Oak, CA 530-671-4200
Casados Farms
  San Juan Pueblo, NM 505-852-2433
Chia I Foods Company
  South El Monte, CA 626-401-3038
Chieftain Wild Rice Company
  Spooner, WI 800-262-6368
Chukar Cherries
  Prosser, WA. 800-624-9544
Derco Foods
  Fresno, CA 559-435-2664
Desert Valley Date
  Coachella, CA 760-398-0999
Diamond Foods
  Fishers, IN. .317-845-5534
Energy Club
  Pacoima, CA 800-688-6887
Fannie May/Fanny Farmer
  Chicago, IL .800-333-3629
Fine Dried Foods International
  Santa Cruz, CA 831-426-1413
Ganong Bros Limited   Corporate Office
  St. Stephen, NB. 888-426-6647
Garry Packing
  Del Rey, CA .800-248-2126
Gilroy
  Hanford, CA 559-584-2711
Gilroy Foods
  Gilroy, CA. 800-921-7502

GNS Food
  Arlington, TX 817-795-4671
Gold Pure Foods Products Company
  Hempstead, NY. 800-422-4681
Golden Town Apple Products
  Thornbury, ON 519-599-6300
Hadley Date Gardens
  Thermal, CA .760-399-5191
Harmony Foods Corporation
  Fishers, IN. .317-567-2700
Harmony Foods Corporation
  Fishers, IN. .800-837-2855
HealthBest
  San Marcos, CA 760-752-5230
Healthco Canada Enterprises
  Victoria, BC .877-468-2875
Hialeah Products Company
  Hollywood, FL 800-923-3379
Hickory Harvest Foods
  Akron, OH. 330-644-6266
HP Schmid
  San Francisco, CA 415-765-5925
International Food Trade
  Amherst, NS 902-667-3013
International Harvest
  Mt Vernon, NY 914-939-1505
JF Braun & Sons Inc.
  Westbury, NY. 800-997-7177
Just Tomatoes Company
  Westley, CA. 800-537-1985
Kalustyan Corporation
  Union, NJ 908-688-6111
Kamish Food Products
  Chicago, IL .773-267-0400
King Nut Company
  Cleveland, OH 800-860-5464
Kozlowski Farms
  Forestville, CA 800-473-2767
Krispy Kernels
  Sainte Foy, QC 418-658-1515
Leroux Creek Foods
  Hotchkiss, CO. 877-970-5670
Liberty Richter
  Saddle Brook, NJ 201-291-8749
Lion Raisins
  Selma, CA. .559-834-6677
Made in Nature
  Fresno, CA 800-906-7426
Maine Wild Blueberry Company
  Cherryfield, ME 800-243-4005
Majestic Foods
  Huntington, NY 631-424-9444
Mariani Packing Company
  Vacaville, CA 800-672-8655
Marx Brothers
  Birmingham, AL. 800-633-6376
Mayfair Packing Company
  San Jose, CA. 408-280-2349
Mayfair Sales
  Buffalo, NY. .800-248-2881
Meduri Farms Inc
  Dallas, OR. .503-831-1097
Mezza
  Lake Forest, IL 888-206-6054
Midwest/Northern
  Minneapolis, MN 800-328-5502
National Food Corporation
  Medley, FL .305-884-2020
Natural Foods
  Toledo, OH .800-860-0006
New England Natural Bakers
  Greenfield, MA. 800-910-2884
Newtown Foods
  Langhorne, PA 215-579-2120
Niagara Foods
  Middleport, NY 716-735-7722

Nspired Natural Foods
Melville, NY 631-845-4689
Nut Factory
Spokane Valley, WA 888-239-5288
Oasis Foods
Planada, CA 209-382-0263
Old Country Farms
East Sandwich, MA 888-707-5558
Organically Grown Company
Eugene, OR 541-689-5320
Osage Pecan Company
Butler, MO 660-679-6137
Pacific Fruit Processors
South Gate, CA 323-774-6000
Pacific Gold Marketing
Madera, CA 559-661-6176
Patsy's Candies
Colorado Springs, CO. 866-372-8797
Peloian Packing Company
Dinuba, CA 559-591-0101
Pittsburgh Snax & Nut Company
Pittsburgh, PA 800-404-6887
Primex International Trading Corporation
Los Angeles, CA. 310-568-8855
Ramos Orchards
Winters, CA 530-795-4748
Raymond-Hadley Corporation
Spencer, NY 800-252-5220
Red River Foods
Richmond, VA. 800-443-6637
Regal Health Foods International
Chicago, IL 773-252-1044
Reinhart Foods
Markham, ON 905-754-3503
Service Packing Company
Vancouver, BC 604-681-0264
Setton International Foods
Commack, NY 800-227-4397
Shade Foods
New Century, KS 800-225-6312
Shields Date Gardens
Indio, CA 800-414-2555
Shoreline Fruit
Traverse City, MI 800-836-3972
Smeltzer Orchard Company
Frankfort, MI 231-882-4421
Snackerz
Commerce, CA 888-576-2253
Society Hill Snacks
Philadelphia, PA 800-595-0050
Solana Gold Organics
Sebastopol, CA 800-459-1121
South Exotic Foods
San Diego, CA 619-491-0438
Spreda Group
Prospect, KY 502-426-9411
Spring Tree Maple Products
Brattleboro, VT 802-254-8784
Stapleton-Spence PackingCompany
San Jose, CA 800-297-8815
Star Snacks Company
Jersey City, NJ 800-775-9909
Stretch Island Fruit
Allyn, WA 360-275-6050
Sugar Plum Farm
Plumtree, NC. 888-257-0019
Sun Empire Foods
Kerman, CA 800-252-4786
Sun Garden Growers
Bard, CA 800-228-4690
Sun Ridge Farms
Santa Cruz, CA 800-655-3252
Sunmaid Growers
Pleasanton, CA 800-752-9277
Sunridge Farms
Salinas, CA 831-755-1430
SunRise Commodities
Englewood Cliffs, NJ 201-947-1000
Sunsweet Growers
Yuba City, CA 800-417-2253
Terri Lynn
Elgin, IL 800-323-0775
Timber Crest Farms
Healdsburg, CA 888-374-9325
Todd's
Vernon, CA 800-938-6337
Torn & Glasser
Los Angeles, CA 800-282-6887
TRAINA Foods
Patterson, CA 209-892-5472
Tree Top
Selah, WA 800-367-6571

Trophy Nut Company
Tipp City, OH 800-729-6887
Tropical
Charlotte, NC 800-220-1413
Tropical
Columbus, OH 800-538-3941
Tropical
Marietta, GA 800-544-3762
Twenty First Century Snacks
Ronkonkoma, NY 800-975-2883
Unique Ingredients
Naches, WA. 509-653-1991
Unison
Hacienda Heights, CA 626-917-3668
Ursula's Island Farms
Seattle, WA 206-762-3113
Vacaville Fruit Company
Vacaville, CA 707-448-5292
Valley View Blueberries
Vancouver, WA 360-892-2839
Valley View Packing Company
San Jose, CA 408-289-8300
Van Drunen Farms
Momence, IL 815-472-3100
Very Best Foods
Miami, FL 305-824-9165
Vic Rossano Incorporated
Montreal, QC 514-766-5252
Waymouth Farms
New Hope, MN 800-527-0094
Weaver Nut Company
Ephrata, PA 717-738-3781
Woodland Foods
Gurnee, IL 847-625-8600
Z Foods Inc
Madera, CA 888-400-1015

Fig

Chieftain Wild Rice Company
Spooner, WI 800-262-6368
Fig Garden Packing
Fresno, CA 559-271-9000
Kalustyan Corporation
Union, NJ 908-688-6111
Natural Foods
Toledo, OH 800-860-0006
Nut Factory
Spokane Valley, WA 888-239-5288
San Joaquin Figs
Fresno, CA 559-224-4492
Timber Crest Farms
Healdsburg, CA 888-374-9325
Unique Ingredients
Naches, WA. 509-653-1991

Freeze Dried

Brothers International Food Corp
Batavia, NY. 888-842-7477
Crispy Green
Fairfield, NJ 866-582-5577
FDP
Santa Rosa, CA. 707-547-1776
Freeze-Dry Products
Santa Rosa, CA. 707-547-1776
St. Charles Trading
Lake Saint Louis, MO. 800-336-1333
Wolf Canyon Foods
Carmel, CA 831-626-1323

Dried & Dehydrated Vegetables

AgroCepia
Miami, FL 305-704-3488
DeFrancesco & Sons
Firebaugh, CA. 209-364-7000

EMERLING INTERNATIONAL FOODS, INC.

Emerling International Foods
Buffalo, NY. 716-833-7381

We supply food manufacturers and food service
customers worldwide (since 1988) with bulk ingredients including: Fruits & Vegetables; Juice
Concentrates; Herbs & Spices; Oils & Vinegars;
Flavors & Colors; Honey & Molasses. We also
produce PURE MAPLE SYRUP.

Gilroy
Hanford, CA 559-584-2711

Gilroy Foods
Gilroy, CA 800-921-7502
Healthco Canada Enterprises
Victoria, BC 877-468-2875
Hialeah Products Company
Hollywood, FL 800-923-3379
International Harvest
Mt Vernon, NY 914-939-1505
Just Tomatoes Company
Westley, CA. 800-537-1985
Made in Nature
Fresno, CA 800-906-7426
Mills Brothers International
Tukwila, WA 206-575-3000
Primera Foods
Cameron, WI. 800-365-2409
Quest International Flavors
Hoffman Estates, IL 847-645-7000
Randag & Associates Inc
Elmhurst, IL 630-530-2830
RFI Ingredients
Blauvelt, NY 800-962-7663
Specialty Ingredients
Buffalo Grove, IL 847-419-9595
Sun Ray International
Davis, CA 530-758-0088

SupHerb Farms
Turlock, CA 800-787-4372

CrEATe! Get ready-to-use fresh flavor with
SupHerb Farms' all-natural fresh frozen culinary
herbs, specialty vegetables, culinary herb pastes,
vegetable purees and creative blends. Complete
microbiological testing ensures food safety. We
set the standard for outstanding customer service, inspired culinary support, collaborative customer partnerships and innovative custom
products.

Unison
Hacienda Heights, CA 626-917-3668

Beet Powder

RFI Ingredients
Blauvelt, NY. 800-962-7663
Seneca Foods
Clyman, WI. 920-696-3331

Bell Peppers

Green

RFI Ingredients
Blauvelt, NY. 800-962-7663

Red

RFI Ingredients
Blauvelt, NY. 800-962-7663

Broccoli

Chopped

RFI Ingredients
Blauvelt, NY. 800-962-7663

Cabbage Flakes

RFI Ingredients
Blauvelt, NY. 800-962-7663

Celery Flakes

RFI Ingredients
Blauvelt, NY. 800-962-7663

Dehydrated Vegetables

AgroCepia
Miami, FL 305-704-3488
American Food Ingredients
Oceanside, CA 760-967-6287
Atlantic Quality Spice & Seasonings
Edison, NJ. 800-584-0422

Basic American Foods
Walnut Creek, CA 800-227-4050
Caltex Foods
Canoga Park, CA 800-522-5839
DeFrancesco & Sons
Firebaugh, CA. 209-364-7000
Dehydrates Inc
Hewlett, NY 800-983-4443
FDP
Santa Rosa, CA. 707-547-1776
Freeman Industries
Tuckahoe, NY .800-666-6454
Garden Valley Foods
Sutherlin, OR .541-459-9565
Gilroy Foods
Modesto, CA. .209-538-1071
Gilroy Foods
Gilroy, CA. 800-921-7502
Henry Broch & Company/APK, Inc.
Libertyville, IL 847-816-6225
Idahoan
Lewisville, ID .800-635-6100
Ingredients Corporation of America
Memphis, TN .901-525-6660
Inland Empire Foods
Riverside, CA .888-452-3267
Larsen Farms
Hamer, ID 208-662-5501
Larsen of Idaho
Hamer, ID 208-662-5501
Magic Valley Foods
Rupert, ID 208-436-3126
Mercer Processing
Modesto, CA. .209-529-0150
Minnesota Dehydrated Vegetables
Fosston, MN .218-435-1997
Mojave Foods Corporation
Commerce, CA 323-890-8900
New Season Foods
Forest Grove, OR 503-357-7124
Oregon Potato Company
Boardman, OR 800-336-6311
Paisano Food Products
Elk Grove Village, IL 773-237-3773
Sarant International Commodities
Centereach, NY 631-689-2845
Schiff Food Products
North Bergen, NJ 201-861-2503
Sensient Dehydrated Flavors
Turlock, CA 800-558-9892
Serv-Agen Corporation
Cherry Hill, NJ 856-663-6966
Silva International
Momence, IL. .815-472-3535
South Mill Distribution
Kennett Square, PA. 610-444-4800
Spice King Corporation
Beverly Hills, CA 310-836-7770
Sterigenics International
Los Angeles, CA. 800-472-4508
Two Guys Spice Company
Jacksonville, FL 800-874-5656
Unified Foods
San Marcos, CA 760-744-7225
Vauxhall Foods
Vauxhall, AB. .403-654-2771
Washington Potato Company
Warden, WA 509-349-8803
World Spice
Roselle, NJ 800-234-1060

Desiccated Vegetables

DeFrancesco & Sons
Firebaugh, CA. 209-364-7000
Gilroy Foods
Gilroy, CA. 800-921-7502

Dried Chives

SupHerb Farms
Turlock, CA 800-787-4372

CrEATe! Get ready-to-use fresh flavor with SupHerb Farms' all-natural fresh frozen culinary herbs, specialty vegetables, culinary herb pastes, vegetable purees and creative blends. Complete microbiological testing ensures food safety. We set the standard for outstanding customer service, inspired culinary support, collaborative customer partnerships and innovative custom products.

Eggplant

Setton International Foods
Commack, NY 800-227-4397

Freeze Dried

American Food Ingredients
Oceanside, CA 760-967-6287
DNO
Columbus, OH 800-686-2366
FDP
Santa Rosa, CA. 707-547-1776
Freeze-Dry Products
Santa Rosa, CA. 707-547-1776
Gilroy Foods
Modesto, CA. .209-538-1071
Hanover Foods Corporation
Hanover, PA 717-632-6000
Ocean Mist
Castroville, CA 831-633-2144
RFI Ingredients
Blauvelt, NY 800-962-7663

SupHerb Farms
Turlock, CA 800-787-4372

CrEATe! Get ready-to-use fresh flavor with SupHerb Farms' all-natural fresh frozen culinary herbs, specialty vegetables, culinary herb pastes, vegetable purees and creative blends. Complete microbiological testing ensures food safety. We set the standard for outstanding customer service, inspired culinary support, collaborative customer partnerships and innovative custom products.

Wolf Canyon Foods
Carmel, CA. 831-626-1323
Zuccaro's Fruit & Produce Company
Minneapolis, MN 612-333-1122

Leeks - Chopped

RFI Ingredients
Blauvelt, NY 800-962-7663

Mushrooms

Chieftain Wild Rice Company
Spooner, WI 800-262-6368
D'Artagnan
Newark, NJ. 800-327-8246
Modern Mushroom Farms
Avondale, PA .610-268-3535
North American Reishi/Nammex
Gibsons, BC 604-886-7799
South Mill Distribution
Kennett Square, PA. 610-444-4800

Black Trumpets

D'Artagnan
Newark, NJ 800-327-8246

Freeze Dried

L.K. Bowman Company
Nottingham, PA. 800-853-1919

Morels Whole

D'Artagnan
Newark, NJ 800-327-8246

Oyster

Modern Mushroom Farms
Avondale, PA .610-268-3535

Porcini

D'Artagnan
Newark, NJ 800-327-8246
Modern Mushroom Farms
Avondale, PA .610-268-3535

Wood Ears

Modern Mushroom Farms
Avondale, PA .610-268-3535

Onion

Dehydrated

Advanced Spice & Trading
Carrollton, TX. 800-872-7811
American Key Food Products
Closter, NJ. 800-767-0237
Atlantic Quality Spice &Seasonings
Edison, NJ. 800-584-0422
DeFrancesco & Sons
Firebaugh, CA. 209-364-7000

EMERLING INTERNATIONAL FOODS, INC.

Emerling International Foods
Buffalo, NY. 716-833-7381

We supply food manufacturers and food service customers worldwide (since 1988) with bulk ingredients including: Fruits & Vegetables; Juice Concentrates; Herbs & Spices; Oils & Vinegars; Flavors & Colors; Honey & Molasses. We also produce PURE MAPLE SYRUP.

Gilroy Foods
Gilroy, CA. 800-921-7502
Ingredients Corporation of America
Memphis, TN .901-525-6660
Schiff Food Products
North Bergen, NJ 201-861-2503
Swagger Foods Corporation
Vernon Hills, IL 847-913-1200

Granulated

Acme Preserve Company
Adrian, MI. 517-265-7222
Acme Steak & Seafood Company
Youngstown, OH. 330-270-8000
Allen Canning Company
Siloam Springs, AR 800-234-2553
B&M
Portland, ME. .207-772-8341
Basic American Foods
Blackfoot, ID .800-227-4050
Beckman & Gast Company
St Henry, OH. .419-678-4195
Bottomline Foods
Pembroke Pines, FL 954-843-0562
Bryant Preserving Company
Alma, AR 800-634-2413
Cut Above Foods
Carlsbad, CA. .760-931-6777
Del Monte Foods
San Francisco, CA 800-543-3090
H.K. Canning
Ventura, CA 805-652-1392
Heinz Company of Canada
North York, ON. 800-268-6641
Hye Cuisine
Del Rey, CA 559-834-3000
Lakeside Foods
Mondovi, WI. .715-926-5075

Les Aliments Livabec Foods
Sherrington, QC 450-454-7971
Lucerne Foods
Lethbridge, AB 403-328-5501
McCain Foods USA
Grand Island, NE 308-382-7770
Nor-Cliff Farms
Port Colborne, ON 905-835-0808
Oxford Frozen Foods Limited
Oxford, NS 902-447-2100
Pacific Valley Foods
Bellevue, WA 425-643-1805
Poynette Distribution Center
Poynette, WI 608-635-4396
Princeville Canning Company
Princeville, IL 309-385-4301
Seneca Foods
Clyman, WI 920-696-3331
Supreme Dairy Farms Company
Warwick, RI 401-739-8180

Minced

Chieftain Wild Rice Company
Spooner, WI 800-262-6368

for Dehydration

Ful-Flav-R Foods
Alamo, CA 510-339-9618

Peas - Air-dried

Allen Canning Company
Siloam Springs, AR 800-234-2553
Bryant Preserving Company
Alma, AR 800-634-2413
Del Monte Foods
San Francisco, CA 800-543-3090
Oxford Frozen Foods Limited
Oxford, NS 902-447-2100

Shallots - Freeze Dried

Oxford Frozen Foods Limited
Oxford, NS 902-447-2100
RFI Ingredients
Blauvelt, NY 800-962-7663

SupHerb Farms
Turlock, CA 800-787-4372

CrEATe! Get ready-to-use fresh flavor with SupHerb Farms' all-natural fresh frozen culinary herbs, specialty vegetables, culinary herb pastes, vegetable purees and creative blends. Complete microbiological testing ensures food safety. We set the standard for outstanding customer service, inspired culinary support, collaborative customer partnerships and innovative custom products.

Soup Blend

Sentry Seasonings
Elmhurst, IL 630-530-5370

The product development experts of Sentry Seasonings are eager to offer the assistance and hands-on experience to food processors of all sizes. Sentry Seasonings will ensure the consistent high quality and repeat sales of your products, whether you choose one of our many off-the-shelf Bench Mark products or a modified version to meet your preferences. Sentry Seasonings can also duplicate and/or improve your present flavor profile; formulate, blend and package specifically for your requirements.

Spinach Powder

RFI Ingredients
Blauvelt, NY 800-962-7663

Tomatoes

Halves

Bryant Preserving Company
Alma, AR 800-634-2413
De Bruyn Produce Company
Zeeland, MI 800-733-9177
Del Monte Foods
San Francisco, CA 800-543-3090
DNO
Columbus, OH 800-686-2366
Oxford Frozen Foods Limited
Oxford, NS 902-447-2100
Zuccaro's Fruit & Produce Company
Minneapolis, MN 612-333-1122

Tomato Powder

Bryant Preserving Company
Alma, AR 800-634-2413
De Bruyn Produce Company
Zeeland, MI 800-733-9177

Eggplant

Buona Vita
Bridgeton, NJ 856-453-7972
Castella Imports
Hauppauge, NY 866-227-8355
Dolce Nonna
Whitestone, NY 718-767-3501
Georgia Vegetable Company
Tifton, GA 229-386-2374
Goebbert's Home Grown Vegetables
South Barrington, IL 847-428-6727
Indian Rock Produce
Perkasie, PA 800-882-0512
L&S Packing Company
Farmingdale, NY 800-286-6487
M&R Company
Lodi, CA 209-369-2725
McCain Foods USA
Grand Island, NE 308-382-7770
Michigan Freeze Pack
Hart, MI 231-873-2175
Miss Scarlett's
Chandler, AZ 800-345-6734
Ocean Mist
Castroville, CA 831-633-2144
Rene Produce Distributors
Nogales, AZ 520-281-9014
Russo Farms
Vineland, NJ 856-692-5942
Turris Italian Foods
Roseville, MI 586-773-6010
Vegetable Juices
Chicago, IL 888-776-9752
Windsor Frozen Foods
Houston, TX 800-437-6936
Z&S Distributing
Fresno, CA 800-467-0788

Figs

American Health & Nutrition
Ann Arbor, MI 734-677-5572
Chieftain Wild Rice Company
Spooner, WI 800-262-6368
DeBenedetto Farms
Fresno, CA 559-276-3447
Fig Garden Packing
Fresno, CA 559-271-9000
Figamajigs
Petaluma, CA 707-992-0023
Hadley Date Gardens
Thermal, CA 760-399-5191
Kalashian Packing Company
Fresno, CA 559-237-4287
Kalustyan Corporation
Union, NJ 908-688-6111
Meridian Nut Growers
Clovis, CA 559-458-7272
Natural Foods
Toledo, OH 800-860-0006
Oasis Foods
Planada, CA 209-382-0263
Oregon Fruit Products Company
Salem, OR 800-394-9333

Purity Foods
Okemos, MI 800-997-7358
Service Packing Company
Vancouver, BC 604-681-0264
Setton International Foods
Commack, NY 800-227-4397
Terri Lynn
Elgin, IL 800-323-0775
Timber Crest Farms
Healdsburg, CA 888-374-9325
Valley Fig Growers
Fresno, CA 559-237-3893
Wawona Packing Company
Cutler, C9 559-528-4000

Canned

Oasis Foods
Planada, CA 209-382-0263
Oregon Fruit Products Company
Salem, OR 800-394-9333

Frozen

Oregon Fruit Products Company
Salem, OR 800-394-9333

Fire Roasted Vegetables

SupHerb Farms
Turlock, CA 800-787-4372

CrEATe! Get ready-to-use fresh flavor with SupHerb Farms' all-natural fresh frozen culinary herbs, specialty vegetables, culinary herb pastes, vegetable purees and creative blends. Complete microbiological testing ensures food safety. We set the standard for outstanding customer service, inspired culinary support, collaborative customer partnerships and innovative custom products.

Flowers - Edible

Fmali Herb
Santa Cruz, CA 831-423-7913
Generation Farms
Rice, TX 903-326-4263
Green House Fine Herbs
Encinitas, CA 760-942-5371

Fresh Fruit

Agrinorthwest
Kennewick, WA 509-734-1195
Amber Foods
Downsview, ON 416-746-2455
American Foodservice
Dallas, TX 972-385-5800
Bay Cities Produce Company
San Leandro, CA 510-346-4943
BelleHarvest Sales
Belding, MI 800-452-7753
California Farms & Canners
San Francisco, CA 415-433-3522
Del Monte Fresh Produce Company
Coral Gables, FL 800-950-3683
Diamond Blueberry
Hammonton, NJ 609-561-3661
Dole Food Company
Westlake Village, CA 818-879-6600
Driscoll Strawberry Associates
Watsonville, CA 831-763-3050
Ever Fresh Fruit Company
Boring, OR 800-239-8026
Family Tree Farms
Reedley, CA 559-591-6280
Florida Citrus
Tampa, FL 813-626-5580
G&G Marketing
Naples, FL 239-593-4564
Glacier Foods
Sanger, CA 559-875-3354
Golden Town Apple Products
Thornbury, ON 519-599-6300

Maui Pineapple Company
Kahului, HI 808-877-3351
Modoc Orchard Company
Medford, OR 541-535-1437
Muir-Roberts Company
Salt Lake City, UT 801-363-5809
Nash Finch Company
Statesboro, GA 912-681-4580
Pillsbury Canada Limited
Markham, ON 800-745-4777
Silver Creek Farms
Twin Falls, ID 208-736-0829
Snokist Growers
Yakima, WA 800-377-2857
Verdelli Farms
Harrisburg, PA 800-422-8344
W.F. Cosart Packing Company
Exeter, CA 559-592-2821
Washington Fruit & Produce Company
Yakima, WA 509-457-6177

Fresh Vegetables

American Foodservice
Dallas, TX 972-385-5800
Bay Cities Produce Company
San Leandro, CA 510-346-4943
BelleHarvest Sales
Belding, MI 800-452-7753
Boskovich Farms
Oxnard, CA 805-487-2299
California Farms & Canners
San Francisco, CA 415-433-3522
Dole Food Company
Westlake Village, CA 818-879-6600
G&G Marketing
Naples, FL 239-593-4564
Glacier Foods
Sanger, CA 559-875-3354
Hanover Foods Corporation
Hanover, PA 717-632-6000
Lakeside Foods
Seymour, WI 920-833-2371
Lennox Farm
Shelburne, ON 519-925-6444
Monterey Mushrooms
Watsonville, CA 800-333-6874
Monterey Mushrooms
Watsonville, CA 831-763-5300
Muir-Roberts Company
Salt Lake City, UT 801-363-5809
Musco Olive Products
Tracy, CA 800-523-9828
Nash Finch Company
Statesboro, GA 912-681-4580
Omstead Foods Ltd
Burlington, ON 905-315-8883
R.C. McEntire & Company
Columbia, SC 803-799-3388
Silver Creek Farms
Twin Falls, ID 208-736-0829
Sungarden Sprouts
Cookeville, TN 931-526-1106
Verdelli Farms
Harrisburg, PA 800-422-8344
Western Pacific Commodities
Las Vegas, NV 702-312-8080

Frozen Fruit

Abbotsford Growers Co-operative
Abbotsford, BC 604-864-0022
Agvest
Franklin, ME 207-565-3303
Agvest
Cleveland, OH 440-735-6900
Assouline & Ting
Philadelphia, PA 800-521-4491
Bay Cities Produce Company
San Leandro, CA 510-346-4943
Beta Pure Foods
Aptos, CA 831-685-6565
Cahoon Farms
Wolcott, NY 315-594-8081
California Farms & Canners
San Francisco, CA 415-433-3522
Carriere Foods Inc
Montreal, QC 514-384-4281
Chase Farms
Walkerville, MI 231-873-3337
Cherry Growers
Grawn, MI 231-276-9241

Cherry Growers
Grawn, MI 800-530-9030
Cherry Lane Frozen Fruits
Vineland Station, ON 905-562-4337
Chiquita Brands International
Cincinnati, OH 800-438-0015
Clermont
Hillsboro, OR 503-648-8544
Cleugh's Frozen Foods
Buena Park, CA 714-521-1002
Clofine Dairy & Food Products
Linwood, NJ 800-441-1001
Coloma Frozen Foods
Coloma, MI 800-642-2723
ConAgra Grocery Products
Irvine, CA 714-680-1000
Contessa Food Products
San Pedro, CA 310-832-8000
Decker Farms
Hillsboro, OR 503-628-1532
Diamond Blueberry
Hammonton, NJ 609-561-3661
Dole Food Company
Westlake Village, CA 818-879-6600
E.W. Bowker Company
Pemberton, NJ 609-894-9508
Eckert Cold Storage
Escalon, CA 209-838-4040

EMERLING INTERNATIONAL FOODS, INC.

Emerling International Foods
Buffalo, NY 716-833-7381

We supply food manufacturers and food service
customers worldwide (since 1988) with bulk ingredients including: Fruits & Vegetables; Juice
Concentrates; Herbs & Spices; Oils & Vinegars;
Flavors & Colors; Honey & Molasses. We also
produce PURE MAPLE SYRUP.

Enfield Farms
Lynden, WA 360-354-3019
Ever Fresh Fruit Company
Boring, OR 800-239-8026
Family Tradition Foods
Wheatley, ON 519-825-4673
Freeze-Dry Products
Santa Rosa, CA 707-547-1776
Frozfruit Corporation
Gardena, CA 310-217-1034
Frozsun Foods
Anaheim, CA 714-630-2170
Fruit Belt Foods
Lawrence, MI 269-674-3939
G A Food Service
St Petersburg, FL 727-573-2211
Glacier Foods
Sanger, CA 559-875-3354
Global Trading
Buena Park, CA 864-288-7332
Golden Town Apple Products
Thornbury, ON 519-599-6300
Grow-Pac
Cornelius, OR 503-357-9691
Hartog Rahal Foods
New York, NY 212-687-2000
Heikes Produce Company
Medford, OR 541-772-5653
Hiscock Enterprises
Brigus, NL 709-528-4577
Inn Foods
Watsonville, CA 831-724-2026
Interfrost
East Rochester, NY 585-381-0320
International Food Trade
Amherst, NS 902-667-3013
J.H. Verbridge & Son
Williamson, NY 315-589-2366
Jasper Wyman & Son
Milbridge, ME 800-341-1758
JR Wood/Big Valley
Atwater, CA 209-358-5643
JRL
Hammonton, NJ 609-561-1572
Kerr Concentrates
Salem, OR 800-910-5377
Leelanau Fruit Company
Suttons Bay, MI 800-431-0718
Lucerne Foods
Abbotsford, BC 604-854-1191

Maine Wild Blueberry Company
Cherryfield, ME 800-243-4005
Majestic Foods
Huntington, NY 631-424-9444
Mason County Fruit Packers Cooperative
Ludington, MI 231-845-6248
Midwest Frozen Foods, Inc.
Hanover Park, IL 866-784-0123
Milne Fruit Products
Prosser, WA 509-786-2611
National Frozen Foods Corporation
Seattle, WA 206-322-8900
New West Foods
San Francisco, CA 701-947-2505
Niagara Foods
Middleport, NY 716-735-7722
Northern Michigan Fruit Company
Omena, MI 231-386-5142
Oasis Foods
Planada, CA 209-382-0263
Ocean Spray Cranberries
Lakeville-Middleboro, MA 800-662-3263
Oceana Foods
Shelby, MI 231-861-2141
Olympia Frosted Foods
Olympia, WA 360-943-2210
Omstead Foods Ltd
Burlington, ON 905-315-8883
Ore-Ida Foods
Pittsburgh, PA 412-237-3450
Oregon Cherry Growers
Salem, OR 800-367-2536
Oregon Fruit Products Company
Salem, OR 800-394-9333
Overlake Foods Corporation
Olympia, WA 800-683-1078
Pacific Blueberries
Rochester, WA 360-273-5405
Pacific Coast Fruit Company
Portland, OR 503-234-6411
Paris Foods Corporation
Camden, NJ 856-964-0915
Patterson Frozen Foods
Patterson, CA 209-892-2611
Quality Brands
Deland, FL 386-738-3808
Rain Sweet
Salem, OR 800-363-4293
Ravifruit
Hackensack, NJ 201-939-5656
Seneca Foods Corporation
Marion, NY 315-926-8100
Sill Farms Market
Lawrence, MI 269-674-3755
Smeltzer Orchard Company
Frankfort, MI 231-882-4421
Snowcrest Packer
Abbotsford, BC 604-859-4881
Sparboe Companies
Los Angeles, CA 213-626-7538
Superior Foods
Watsonville, CA 831-728-3691
Symons Frozen Foods
Centralia, WA 360-736-1321
Tatangelo's Wholesale Fruit & Vegetables
Vaughan, ON 877-328-8503
Townsend Farms
Fairview, OR 503-666-1780
Tree Top
Selah, WA 800-367-6571
Triple D Orchards
Empire, MI 866-781-9410
Unique Ingredients
Naches, WA 509-653-1991
VIP Sales Company
Hayward, CA 918-252-5791
Watermill Foods
Milton Freewater, OR 541-938-6601
Webster Farms
Cambridge Station, NS 902-538-9492

Berries

Agvest
Franklin, ME 207-565-3303
Cherry Central Cooperative Inc
Traverse City, MI 231-946-1860

Frozen Vegetables

Ajinomoto Frozen Foods USA
Portland, IR 503-734-1528

Al Pete Meats
  Muncie, IN 765-288-8817
Anchor Food Products/ McCain Foods
  Appleton, WI 920-734-0627
Appleton Produce Company
  Weiser, ID 208-414-1102
Beta Pure Foods
  Aptos, CA 831-685-6565
Boskovich Farms
  Oxnard, CA 805-487-2299
Bright Harvest Sweet Potato Company
  Clarksville, AR 800-793-7440
Brooks Food Group Corporate Office
  Bedford, VA 800-873-4934
California Farms & Canners
  San Francisco, CA 415-433-3522
Carando Gourmet Frozen Foods
  Springfield, MA 413-730-4205
Carriere Foods Inc
  Montreal, QC 514-384-4281
Cavendish Farms
  Jamestown, ND 888-284-5687
Cavendish Farms
  Dieppe, NB 888-883-7437
Chase Farms
  Walkerville, MI 231-873-3337
Cleugh's Frozen Foods
  Buena Park, CA 714-521-1002
Cobi Foods
  Hantsport, NS 800-565-8229
Coloma Frozen Foods
  Coloma, MI 800-642-2723
Columbia Foods
  Snohomish, WA 360-568-0838
Columbia Foods
  Quincy, WA 509-787-1585
ConAgra Grocery Products
  Archbold, OH 419-445-8015
ConAgra Grocery Products
  Irvine, CA 714-680-1000
Contessa Food Products
  San Pedro, CA 310-832-8000
Crown Point
  St John, IN 219-365-3200
Dairy King Milk Farms/Foodservice
  Glendale, CA 818-243-6455
Deep Foods
  Union, NJ 908-810-7500
Dickinson Frozen Foods
  Fruitland, ID 208-452-5200
Eckert Cold Storage
  Escalon, CA 209-838-4040
Ever Fresh Fruit Company
  Boring, OR 800-239-8026
Family Tradition Foods
  Wheatley, ON 519-825-4673
Faribault Foods
  Cokato, MN 320-286-2166
Faribault Foods
  Minneapolis, MN 612-333-6461
Freeze-Dry Products
  Santa Rosa, CA 707-547-1776
Fresh Frozen Foods
  Jefferson, GA 800-277-9851
Fruit Belt Foods
  Lawrence, MI 269-674-3939
George L. Wells Meat Company
  Philadelphia, PA 800-523-1730
Glacier Foods
  Sanger, CA 559-875-3354
Great American Appetizers
  Nampa, ID 800-282-4834
H.J. Heinz Company
  Pittsburgh, PA 412-237-5948
Hanover Foods Corporation
  Hanover, PA 717-632-6000
Hartford City Foam Pack aging & Converting
  Hartford City, IN 765-348-2500
Hermann Pickle Farm
  Garrettsville, OH 800-245-2696
Hunt-Wesson Food Service Company
  Rochester, NY 800-633-1002
Inn Foods
  Watsonville, CA 831-724-2026
Interfrost
  East Rochester, NY 585-381-0320
J G Townsend Jr & Company
  Georgetown, DE 302-856-2525
J.R. Simplot Company
  Boise, ID 208-336-2110
J.R. Simplot Food Group
  Pasco, WA 509-544-6700

John Copes Food Products
  Manheim, PA 800-745-8211
JR Wood/Big Valley
  Atwater, CA 209-358-5643
Juanita's Foods
  Wilmington, CA 310-834-5339
Lakeside Foods
  Brooten, MN 320-346-2900
Lakeside Foods
  Plainview, MN 507-534-3141
Lakeside Foods
  Manitowoc, WI 920-684-3356
Lakeside Foods
  Seymour, WI 920-833-2371
Leach Farms
  Berlin, WI 920-361-1880
Lennox Farm
  Shelburne, ON 519-925-6444
Lodi Canning Company
  Lodi, WI 608-592-4236
Lucerne Foods
  Abbotsford, BC 604-854-1191
Magic Valley Foods
  Rupert, ID 208-436-3126
McCain Foods
  Fort Atkinson, WI 920-563-6625
Miami Purveyors
  Miami, FL 305-262-6170
Midwest Frozen Foods, Inc.
  Hanover Park, IL. 866-784-0123
Milroy Canning Company
  Milroy, IN 765-629-2221
Monterey Mushrooms
  Watsonville, CA 800-333-6874
Monticello Canning Company
  Crossville, TN. 931-484-3696
Mr. Dell Foods
  Kearney, MO 816-628-4644
Mushroom Company
  Cambridge, MD 410-221-8900
National Frozen Foods Corporation
  Seattle, WA 206-322-8900
Nature Quality
  San Martin, CA 408-683-2182
New Meridian
  Eaton, IN 765-396-3344
Niagara Foods
  Middleport, NY 716-735-7722
NORPAC Foods
  Lake Oswego, OR 503-635-9311
NORPAC Plant
  Salem, OR. 800-822-2898
Ocean Spray Cranberries
  Aberdeen, WA. 800-662-3263
Oceana Foods
  Shelby, MI 231-861-2141
Oh Boy Corporation
  San Fernando, CA 818-361-1128
Olympia Frosted Foods
  Olympia, WA 360-943-2210
Ore-Ida Foods
  Pittsburgh, PA. 412-237-3450
Oregon Potato Company
  Boardman, OR 800-336-6311
Paisley Farms
  Willoughby, OH 800-676-8656
Paris Foods Corporation
  Camden, NJ 856-964-0915
Patterson Frozen Foods
  Patterson, CA 209-892-2611
Pictsweet Frozen Foods
  Bells, TN 731-663-7600
Rain Sweet
  Salem, OR 800-363-4293
Ray Brothers & Noble Canning Company
  Hobbs, IN 765-675-7451
Red Gold
  Elwood, IN 877-748-9798
Rich-Seapak Corporation
  Brownsville, TX 956-542-0001
Roca Food Sales
  Roswell, GA 770-993-0030
Schwans Bakeries
  Stilwell, OK 918-696-8325
Seabrook Brothers & Sons
  Seabrook, NJ 856-455-8080
Seenergy Foods
  Woodbridge, ON 800-609-7674
Seneca Foods
  Marion, NY 315-926-8100
Seneca Foods Corporation
  Marion, NY 315-926-8100

Simplot Food Group
  Boise, ID 800-572-7783
Smeltzer Orchard Company
  Frankfort, MI 231-882-4421
Smith Frozen Foods
  Weston, OR 541-566-3515
Smith Frozen Foods
  Weston, OR 800-547-0203
Snowcrest Packer
  Abbotsford, BC 604-859-4881
Strathroy Foods
  Strathroy, ON 519-245-4600
Sungarden Sprouts
  Cookeville, TN 931-526-1106
Superior Foods
  Watsonville, CA 831-728-3691
Superior Frozen Vegetables
  Cornell, MI 906-384-6466

SupHerb Farms
  Turlock, CA 800-787-4372

CrEATe! Get ready-to-use fresh flavor with SupHerb Farms' all-natural fresh frozen culinary herbs, specialty vegetables, culinary herb pastes, vegetable purees and creative blends. Complete microbiological testing ensures food safety. We set the standard for outstanding customer service, inspired culinary support, collaborative customer partnerships and innovative custom products.

Symons Frozen Foods
  Centralia, WA 360-736-1321
Tatangelo's Wholesale Fruit & Vegetables
  Vaughan, ON. 877-328-8503
Trans Pecos Foods
  San Antonio, TX 210-228-0896
Trappe Packing Corporation
  Trappe, MD 410-476-3185
Twin City Foods
  Stanwood, WA 206-515-2400
Unique Ingredients
  Naches, WA. 509-653-1991
US Fresh Marketing
  Virginia Beach, VA 757-481-2606
Van De Walle Farms
  San Antonio, TX 210-436-5551
Van Drunen Farms
  Momence, IL 815-472-3100
VIP Sales Company
  Hayward, CA 918-252-5791
W&W Meats
  Willoughby, OH 216-621-7846
Washington Potato Company
  Warden, WA 509-349-8803
Washington Rhubarb Growers Association
  Sumner, WA 800-435-9911
Webster Farms
  Cambridge Station, NS 902-538-9492
Westin
  Omaha, NE 800-228-6098
Wornick Company
  Cincinnati, OH 800-860-4555

Fruit

A. Duda Farm Fresh Foods
  Belle Glade, FL 561-996-7621
A. Gagliano Company
  Milwaukee, WI 800-272-1516
Acme Preserve Company
  Adrian, MI. 517-265-7222
Adobe Creek Packing
  Kelseyville, CA. 707-279-4204
Agvest
  Cleveland, OH 440-735-6900
Alamance Foods/Triton Water Company
  Burlington, NC 800-476-9111
Amber Foods
  Downsview, ON 416-746-2455
American Food Products
  Methuen, MA 978-682-1855
American Yeast/Lallemand
  Pembroke, NH. 866-920-9885

Amport Foods
Minneapolis, MN 800-989-5665
Anastasia Confections, Inc.
Orlando, FL .800-329-7100
Applewood Orchards
Deerfield, MI 800-447-3854
Arbor Crest Wine Cellars
Spokane, WA. 509-927-8571
Arcor USA
Coral Gables, FL. 800-572-7267
Ariel Natural Foods
Bellevue, WA 425-637-3345
Atlanta Bread Company International, Inc.
Smyrna, GA .800-398-3728
Ben B. Schwartz & Sons
Detroit, MI .313-841-8300
Bilgore's Groves
Clearwater, FL 727-442-2171
Bob Gordon & Associates
Chicago, IL .773-247-0588
Bridenbaughs Orchards
Martinsburg, PA 814-793-2364
Bridenbaughs Orchards
West Sacramento, CA. 916-739-6540
Burnette Foods
Elk Rapids, MI 231-264-8116
Burnette Foods
Hartford, MI 616-621-3181
Cahoon Farms
Wolcott, NY .315-594-8081
California Citrus Producer
Lindsay, CA .559-562-5169
Casados Farms
San Juan Pueblo, NM 505-852-2433
Cascadian Farm & MUIR GLEN; Division of General
Mills
Sedro Woolley, WA. 360-855-0100
Charles Dennery Pillsbury
New Orleans, LA 504-733-2331
Chase Farms
Walkerville, MI 231-873-3337
Cherry Growers
Grawn, MI. .800-530-9030
Cherry Lane Frozen Fruits
Vineland Station, ON 905-562-4337
Chieftain Wild Rice Company
Spooner, WI 800-262-6368
Chiquita Brands
Cincinnati, OH 513-784-8000
Chiquita Brands International
Cincinnati, OH 800-438-0015
Chudleigh's
Milton, ON .800-387-4028
Chukar Cherries
Prosser, WA. 800-624-9544
Cinnabar Specialty Foods
Prescott, AZ 866-293-6433
Citrus Citrosuco North America
Lake Wales, FL. 800-356-4592
Classic Commissary
Binghamton, NY. 800-929-3486
Clements Foods Company
Oklahoma City, OK 800-654-8355
Clermont
Hillsboro, OR 503-648-8544
Cleugh's Frozen Foods
Buena Park, CA 714-521-1002
Concannon Vineyard
Livermore, CA 800-258-9866
Concord Foods
Brockton, MA 508-580-1700
Cranberry Products
Eagle River, WI 715-479-4466

Custom Brands Unlimited
Solebury, PA 215-297-9842
Decas Cranberry Products
Wareham, MA. 800-649-9811
Del Mar Food Products Corporation
Watsonville, CA 831-722-3516
Del Monte Fresh Produce Company
Coral Gables, FL. 800-950-3683
Del Monte Fresh Produce Company
Kankakee, IL. 815-936-7400
Delta Packing Company of Lodi
Lodi, CA 209-334-0691
Desert Valley Date
Coachella, CA 760-398-0999
Diamond Blueberry
Hammonton, NJ 609-561-3661
Diamond Foods
Fishers, IN. .317-845-5534
Diamond Fruit Growers
Odell, OR 541-354-5300
Diamond Nut Company
Lemont, IL .630-739-3000
Diana Fruit Company
Santa Clara, CA 408-727-9631
DMH Ingredients
Libertyville, IL 847-362-9977
Dole Food Company
Westlake Village, CA 818-879-6600
Driscoll Strawberry Associates
Watsonville, CA 831-763-3050
E. Waldo Ward & Son Corporation
Sierra Madre, CA 800-355-9273
E.D. Smith & Sons
Winona, ON 905-643-1211
E.W. Bowker Company
Pemberton, NJ. 609-894-9508
Eagle Eye Produce
Iona, ID 208-522-2343
Eckert Cold Storage
Escalon, CA .209-838-4040
El Brands
Ozark, AL 334-445-2828
Energy Club
Pacoima, CA. 800-688-6887
Enfield Farms
Lynden, WA 360-354-3019
Ever Fresh Fruit Company
Boring, OR .800-239-8026
Family Tree Farms
Reedley, CA .559-591-6280
Fannie May/Fanny Farmer
Chicago, IL .800-333-3629
Fernando C Pujals & Bros
San Juan, PR 787-792-3080
Fillmore Piru Citrus Association
Piru, CA 800-524-8787
Fine Dried Foods International
Santa Cruz, CA 831-426-1413
Fine Foods Northwest
Seattle, WA .800-862-3965
Firestone Packing Company
Vancouver, WA. 360-695-9484
Flippin-Seaman
Tyro, VA 434-277-5828
Forakers Joy Orchard
Malaga, WA 509-663-6097
Franklin Reister & Sons
Conklin, MI. 616-887-9689
Freeze-Dry Products
Santa Rosa, CA 707-547-1776
Frozfruit Corporation
Gardena, CA 310-217-1034
Frozsun Foods
Anaheim, CA 714-630-2170
Fruit Fillings
Fresno, CA .559-237-4715
G A Food Service
St Petersburg, FL. 727-573-2211
G L Mezzetta
American Canyon, CA 707-648-1050
G&G Marketing
Naples, FL. .239-593-4564
Ganong Bros Limited   Corporate Office
St. Stephen, NB. 888-426-6647
Garden State Farms
Philadelphia, PA 215-463-8000
Gene Belk Fruit Packers
Bloomington, CA 909-877-1819
Gilroy Foods
Gilroy, CA. .800-921-7502
Glacier Foods
Sanger, CA .559-875-3354

Graceland Fruit
Frankfort, MI 800-352-7181
Gray & Company
Forest Grove, OR 503-357-3141
Graysmarsh Farm
Sequim, WA 800-683-4367
Green Valley Apples of California
Arvin, CA 661-854-4436
Grouse Hunt Farms
Tamaqua, PA 570-467-2850
Grove Fresh Distributors
Chicago, IL. 773-288-2065
Grow-Pac
Cornelius, OR 503-357-9691
Gurley's Foods
Willmar, MN 800-426-7845
H H Dobbins
Lyndonville, NY 877-362-2467
H. Naraghi Farms
Escalon, CA .209-577-5777
Hallcrest Vineyards
Felton, CA. .831-335-4441
Harmony Foods Corporation
Fishers, IN. .800-837-2855
Harris Farms
Coalinga, CA 800-742-1955
Harry & David
Medford, OR. 877-322-1200
Hartog Rahal Foods
New York, NY 212-687-2000
Heikes Produce Company
Medford, OR. 541-772-5653
Heller Brothers Packing Corporation
Winter Garden, FL 407-656-4986
Henggeler Packing Company
Fruitland, ID 208-452-4212
Hialeah Products Company
Hollywood, FL 800-923-3379
Hiscock Enterprises
Brigus, NL. .709-528-4577
Indian Bay Frozen Foods
Centreville, NL 709-678-2844
Indian Hollow Farms
Richland Center, WI 800-236-3944
Indian Rock Produce
Perkasie, PA 800-882-0512
International Food Trade
Amherst, NS 902-667-3013
International Home Foods
Milton, PA. .973-359-9920
J.C. Watson Company
Parma, ID 208-722-5141
J.H. Verbridge & Son
Williamson, NY 315-589-2366
J.R. Simplot Company
Boise, ID 208-336-2110
Jasper Wyman & Son
Milbridge, ME 800-341-1758
Jersey Fruit CooperativeAssociation
Glassboro, NJ 856-863-9100
JES Foods
Cleveland, OH 216-883-8987
JF Braun & Sons Inc.
Westbury, NY 800-997-7177
Johnson Fruit Company
Sunnyside, WA 509-837-4600
Joseph J. White
Browns Mills, NJ 609-893-2332
JR Wood/Big Valley
Atwater, CA 209-358-5643
JRL
Hammonton, NJ 609-561-1572
K.B. Hall Ranch
Ojai, CA 805-646-4512
Kagome
Los Banos, CA 209-826-8850
Kalashian Packing Company
Fresno, CA .559-237-4287
Kalustyan Corporation
Union, NJ 908-688-6111
Karl Bissinger French Confections
St Louis, MO. 800-325-8881
Kettle Valley Fruits
Summerland, BC. 888-297-6944
Kiona Vineyards Winery
Benton City, WA 509-588-6716
Knights Appleden Fruit
Colborne, ON 905-349-2521
Knouse Foods
Peach Glen, PA 717-677-8181
Kozlowski Farms
Forestville, CA 800-473-2767

Krupka's Blueberries
Fennville, MI 269-857-4278
L&S Packing Company
Farmingdale, NY 800-286-6487
La Vigne Enterprises
Fallbrook, CA 760-723-9997
Lee Andersons's Covalda Dates
Coachella, CA 760-398-3441
Leelanau Fruit Company
Suttons Bay, MI 800-431-0718
Leroux Creek Foods
Hotchkiss, CO 877-970-5670
Leroy Smith & Sons Inc
Vero Beach, FL 772-567-3421
Liberty Orchards Company
Cashmere, WA 800-888-5696
Lucks Food Decorating Company
Tacoma, WA 206-674-7200
Macrie Brothers
Hammonton, NJ 609-561-6822
Made in Nature
Fresno, CA 800-906-7426
Maine Wild Blueberry Company
Cherryfield, ME 800-243-4005
Majestic Foods
Huntington, NY 631-424-9444
Manzanita Ranch
Julian, CA 760-765-0102
Mariani Packing Company
Vacaville, CA 800-672-8655
Mason County Fruit Packers Cooperative
Ludington, MI 231-845-6248
Maui Pineapple Company
Kahului, HI 808-877-3351
Maui Pineapple Company
Concord, CA 925-798-0240
Mayer's Cider Mill
Webster, NY 800-543-0043
Mayfair Sales
Buffalo, NY 800-248-2881
Mayfield Farms
Brampton, ON 905-846-0506
Mazzoni Brothers
Minotola, NJ 609-561-6515
McCartney Produce Company
Paducah, KY 800-522-2791
Melissa's/World VarietyPProduce
Vernon, CA 800-588-0151
Mercer Processing
Modesto, CA 209-529-0150
Midwest Blueberry Farms
Holland, MI. 616-399-2133
Mira International Foods
East Brunswick, NJ 800-818-6472
Miramar Fruit Trading Company
Medley, FL 305-883-4774
Modoc Orchard Company
Medford, OR 541-535-1437
Mountain Orchard Cooperative
Aspers, PA 800-322-6867
Nassau Candy Company
Hicksville, NY 516-342-1495
National Products Company
Kalamazoo, MI 269-344-3640
Natural Fruit Corporation
Hialeah, FL 305-887-7525
Naturex (Chart Corp)
South Hackensack, NJ 201-440-5000
Nekta
Lakeville, MN. 952-898-8020
New England Natural Bakers
Greenfield, MA. 800-910-2884
New Era Canning Company
New Era, MI 231-861-2151
New York Apples Sales
Castletn on Hdsn, NY 518-477-7200
North American Blueberry Council
Folsom, CA 800-824-6395
Northern Michigan Fruit Company
Omena, MI 231-386-5142
Northern Orchard Company
Peru, NY 518-643-9718
Nutri-Fruit
Sumner, WA 866-343-7848
Orange Bang
Sylmar, CA 818-833-1000
Orange Cove Sanger Citrus Association
Orange Cove, CA 559-626-4453
Oregon Cherry Growers
Salem, OR. 800-367-2536
Oregon Fruit Products Company
Salem, OR. 800-394-9333

Organically Grown Company
Eugene, OR. 541-689-5320
Overlake Blueberry Farm
Bellevue, WA 425-453-8613
Pacific Blueberries
Rochester, WA 360-273-5405
Pacific Coast Fruit Company
Portland, OR 503-234-6411
Pacific Coast Producers
Oroville, CA 530-533-4311
Pacific Coast Producers Corporate Office
Lodi, CA 209-367-8800
Pacific Trellis
Reedley, CA 559-638-5100
Pacific Westcoast Foods
Portland, OR 800-874-9333
Palmer Candy Company
Sioux City, IA 800-831-0828
Paradise Products Corporation
Roslyn, NY 800-826-1235
Pavero Cold Storage Corporation
Highland, NY 800-435-2994
Peninsula Fruit Exchange
Traverse City, MI 231-223-4282
Plaidberry Company
Vista, CA 760-727-5403
Premium Waters
Minneapolis, MN 800-243-1163
Purity Products
Plainview, NY 888-769-7873
QA Products
Elk Grove Vlg, IL 800-635-7907
Quest International Fruits & Vegetables
Silverton, OR 503-873-3600
R M Lawton Cranberries
Middleboro, MA 508-947-7465
Rain Flavor
Salem, OR. 800-363-4293
Ramos Orchards
Winters, CA 530-795-4748
Red River Foods
Richmond, VA. 800-443-6637
Reed Lang Farms
Rio Hondo, TX 956-748-2354
Regal Health Foods International
Chicago, IL 773-252-1044
Reinhart Foods
Markham, ON 905-754-3503
Reter Fruit Company
Medford, OR. 541-772-5256
Rice Fruit Company
Gardners, PA 800-627-3359
Richard Lanza
Hammonton, NJ 609-561-3984
Robert Rothschild Berry Farm
Urbana, OH 866-565-6790
Roche Fruit
Yakima, WA 509-248-7200
Royal Moonlight
Reedley, CA 559-637-7799
Russo Farms
Vineland, NJ 856-692-5942
SA Carlson
Yakima, WA 509-965-8333
Sand Hill Berries
Mt Pleasant, PA 724-547-4760
Santanna Banana Company
Harrisburg, PA 717-238-8321
Satiety
Davis, CA 530-757-2699
Schwan's Consumer Brands North America
Bloomington, MN. 952-832-4300
Scotian Gold Cooperative
Coldbrook, NS 902-679-2191
Shafer Lake Fruit
Hartford, MI 269-621-3194
Shari Candies
Edina, MN. 800-658-7059
Shields Date Gardens
Indio, CA. 800-414-2555
Signature Fruit
Stockton, CA. 209-931-1531
Signature Fruit
Bloomingdale, IL 630-980-2481
Sill Farms Market
Lawrence, MI 269-674-3755
Silver Palate Kitchens
Cresskill, NJ 800-872-5283
SimmaLoosa Company
Covington, LA 985-892-1400
SKW Flavor & Fruit Preparation
Langhorne, PA 215-702-1000

Smeltzer Orchard Company
Frankfort, MI 231-882-4421
Snackerz
Commerce, CA 888-576-2253
Snokist Growers
Yakima, WA 509-457-8444
Snowcrest Packer
Abbotsford, BC 604-859-4881
Solana Gold Organics
Sebastopol, CA 800-459-1121
SOPAKCO Foods
Mullins, SC 800-276-9678
Sparboe Companies
Los Angeles, CA. 213-626-7538
Spreda Group
Prospect, KY 502-426-9411
Spring Ledge Farms
Dundee, NY 607-678-4038
Spring Tree Maple Products
Brattleboro, VT 802-254-8784
Stanley Orchards
Modena, NY 845-883-7351
Stapleton-Spence PackingCompany
San Jose, CA 800-297-8815
Sugar Cane Industry Glades Correctional Institution
Belle Glade, FL 561-829-1400
Suity Confection Company
Miami, FL 305-639-3300
Summit Point Raceway Orchards
Summit Point, WV 800-927-7531
Sun Groves
Safety Harbor, FL 800-672-6438
Sun-Maid
Pleasanton, CA 800-246-4849
Sunsweet Growers
Yuba City, CA 800-417-2253
Superior Foods
Watsonville, CA 831-728-3691
Surface Banana Company
Bluewell, WV 304-589-7202
Sweet Candy Company
Salt Lake City, UT 800-669-8669
T.S. Smith & Sons
Bridgeville, DE 302-337-8271
Talbott Farms
Palisade, CO 970-464-5656
Tastee Apple Inc
Newcomerstown, OH 800-262-7753
Taylor Farms
Salinas, CA 831-754-0471
Tejon Ranch
Lebec, CA 661-248-3000
Tom Ringhausen Orchards
Hardin, IL 618-576-2311
Tony Vitrano Company
Jessup, MD 410-799-7444
Townsend Farms
Fairview, OR. 503-666-1780
Trailblazer Food Products
Portland, OR 800-777-7179
Traver Ranch
Kingsburg, CA 559-897-4091
Trefethen Vineyards
Napa, CA. 800-556-4847
Tri-Boro Fruit Company
Fresno, CA 559-486-4141
Triple D Orchards
Empire, MI 866-781-9410
Trophy Nut Company
Tipp City, OH 800-729-6887
Truitt Brothers Inc
Salem, OR. 800-547-8712
Tuscarora Organic Growers Cooperative
Hustontown, PA 814-448-2173

Unimark Group Inc
   Bartonville, TX.....................817-491-2992
United Fruit Growers
   Palisade, CO.......................970-464-5671
United Marketing Exchange
   Delta, CO.........................970-874-3332
Ursula's Island Farms
   Seattle, WA.......................206-762-3113
USA Fruit
   Greenwich, CT....................203-661-8280
Valley Fig Growers
   Fresno, CA........................559-237-3893
Valley Fruit & Vegetable
   McAllen, TX.......................956-686-8056
Valley View Blueberries
   Vancouver, WA....................360-892-2839
Valley View Packing Company
   San Jose, CA......................408-289-8300
Varet Street Market
   Brooklyn, NY......................718-387-5452
Verdelli Farms
   Harrisburg, PA....................800-422-8344
Very Best Foods
   Miami, FL.........................305-824-9165
Violore Foods Company
   Laredo, TX........................956-726-3633
Visalia Produce Sales Inc
   Kingsburg, CA.....................559-897-6652
Warner Candy
   El Paso, TX.......................847-928-7200
Washington Fruit & Produce Company
   Yakima, WA.......................509-457-6177
Webster Farms
   Cambridge Station, NS.............902-538-9492
Well Pict Berries
   Watsonville, CA...................831-722-3871
Wesco Foods Company
   Cincinnati, OH....................513-762-4139
Wetherby Cranberry Company
   Warrens, WI.......................608-378-4813
Wiard's Orchards
   Ypsilanti, MI......................734-482-7744
Woodland Foods
   Gurnee, IL........................847-625-8600
World Nutrition
   Scottsdale, AZ.....................800-548-2710
Yakima Fruit & Cold Storage Company
   Wapato, WA.......................509-877-0440
Yakima Valley Grape Producers
   Grandview, WA....................509-882-1223
Yokhol Valley Packing Company
   Lindsay, CA.......................559-562-1327
Zipp Manufacturing Company
   Hornerville, OH...................800-521-8700
Zitner Company
   Philadelphia, PA..................215-229-4990

Cocktail

EMERLING INTERNATIONAL FOODS, INC.

Emerling International Foods
   Buffalo, NY.......................716-833-7381

> We supply food manufacturers and food service customers worldwide (since 1988) with bulk ingredients including: Fruits & Vegetables; Juice Concentrates; Herbs & Spices; Oils & Vinegars; Flavors & Colors; Honey & Molasses. We also produce PURE MAPLE SYRUP.

Orval Kent Food Company
   Wheeling, IL......................847-459-9000
Pacific Coast Producers
   Oroville, CA.......................530-533-4311
Pacific Coast Producers Corporate Office
   Lodi, CA..........................209-367-8800
Tupman-Thurlow Company
   Deerfield Beach, FL...............954-596-9989

Jarred or Cupped

Chiquita Brands International
   Cincinnati, OH....................800-438-0015
Del Monte Foods
   Cambria, WI.......................920-348-5121

EMERLING INTERNATIONAL FOODS, INC.

Emerling International Foods
   Buffalo, NY.......................716-833-7381

> We supply food manufacturers and food service customers worldwide (since 1988) with bulk ingredients including: Fruits & Vegetables; Juice Concentrates; Herbs & Spices; Oils & Vinegars; Flavors & Colors; Honey & Molasses. We also produce PURE MAPLE SYRUP.

Orval Kent Food Company
   Wheeling, IL......................847-459-9000
Pacific Coast Producers
   Oroville, CA.......................530-533-4311
Tupman-Thurlow Company
   Deerfield Beach, FL...............954-596-9989

Salad

Amber Foods
   Downsview, ON...................416-746-2455

Galangal

Nickabood's Company
   Los Angeles, CA..................213-746-1541

Garlic

Black Garlic Inc
   Hayward, CA.......................888-811-9065
California Garlic Co
   San Diego, CA.....................951-506-8883
Christopher Ranch
   Gilroy, CA........................408-847-1100
Colonna Brothers
   North Bergen, NJ..................201-864-1115
Country Cupboard
   Virginia City, NV.................775-847-7300

EMERLING INTERNATIONAL FOODS, INC.

Emerling International Foods
   Buffalo, NY.......................716-833-7381

> We supply food manufacturers and food service customers worldwide (since 1988) with bulk ingredients including: Fruits & Vegetables; Juice Concentrates; Herbs & Spices; Oils & Vinegars; Flavors & Colors; Honey & Molasses. We also produce PURE MAPLE SYRUP.

Miss Scarlett's
   Chandler, AZ......................800-345-6734

SupHerb Farms
   Turlock, CA.......................800-787-4372

> CrEATe! Get ready-to-use fresh flavor with SupHerb Farms' all-natural fresh frozen culinary herbs, specialty vegetables, culinary herb pastes, vegetable purees and creative blends. Complete microbiological testing ensures food safety. We set the standard for outstanding customer service, inspired culinary support, collaborative customer partnerships and innovative custom products.

Vegetable Juices
   Chicago, IL.......................888-776-9752
Victoria Packing Corporation
   Brooklyn, NY......................718-649-2180

Granulated

American Key Food Products
   Closter, NJ........................800-767-0237

EMERLING INTERNATIONAL FOODS, INC.

Emerling International Foods
   Buffalo, NY.......................716-833-7381

> We supply food manufacturers and food service customers worldwide (since 1988) with bulk ingredients including: Fruits & Vegetables; Juice Concentrates; Herbs & Spices; Oils & Vinegars; Flavors & Colors; Honey & Molasses. We also produce PURE MAPLE SYRUP.

Vegetable Juices
   Chicago, IL.......................888-776-9752

Ginger

Atlantic Quality Spice &Seasonings
   Edison, NJ........................800-584-0422
Christopher Ranch
   Gilroy, CA........................408-847-1100
Con Yeager Spice Company
   Zelienople, PA....................800-222-2460
Cut Above Foods
   Carlsbad, CA......................760-931-6777

EMERLING INTERNATIONAL FOODS, INC.

Emerling International Foods
   Buffalo, NY.......................716-833-7381

> We supply food manufacturers and food service customers worldwide (since 1988) with bulk ingredients including: Fruits & Vegetables; Juice Concentrates; Herbs & Spices; Oils & Vinegars; Flavors & Colors; Honey & Molasses. We also produce PURE MAPLE SYRUP.

Fiji Ginger Company
   Santa Monica, CA.................310-452-0878
Ful-Flav-R Foods
   Alamo, CA.........................510-339-9618
Ginger People®
   Monterey, CA......................800-551-5284
Herb Connection
   Springville, UT...................801-489-4254
International Glace
   Fallbrook, CA.....................800-884-5041
Morris J. Golombeck
   Brooklyn, NY......................718-284-3505
Paradise
   Plant City, FL....................800-330-8952
Schiff Food Products
   North Bergen, NJ..................201-861-2503

SupHerb Farms
   Turlock, CA.......................800-787-4372

> CrEATe! Get ready-to-use fresh flavor with SupHerb Farms' all-natural fresh frozen culinary herbs, specialty vegetables, culinary herb pastes, vegetable purees and creative blends. Complete microbiological testing ensures food safety. We set the standard for outstanding customer service, inspired culinary support, collaborative customer partnerships and innovative custom products.

Texas Coffee Company
   Beaumont, TX.....................800-259-3400
Triple Leaf Tea
   S San Francisco, CA...............800-552-7448
Tulkoff Food Products
   Baltimore, MD.....................800-638-7343
Ungerer & Company
   Lincoln Park, NJ.................973-628-0600
Vegetable Juices
   Chicago, IL.......................888-776-9752

Crystallized

EMERLING INTERNATIONAL FOODS, INC.

Emerling International Foods
Buffalo, NY .716-833-7381

We supply food manufacturers and food service
customers worldwide (since 1988) with bulk ingredients including: Fruits & Vegetables; Juice
Concentrates; Herbs & Spices; Oils & Vinegars;
Flavors & Colors; Honey & Molasses. We also
produce PURE MAPLE SYRUP.

Fastachi
Watertown, MA 800-466-3022
Organic Planet
San Francisco, CA 415-765-5590
Setton International Foods
Commack, NY 800-227-4397

Pickled

Paradise
Plant City, FL 800-330-8952

Glace

Dixie Dew Products
Erlanger, KY 800-867-8548
Fruit Fillings
Fresno, CA .559-237-4715
International Glace
Fallbrook, CA 800-884-5041

Grape

Amber Foods
Downsview, ON 416-746-2455
Ballantine Produce Company
Reedley, CA 559-637-2400
Cal-Harvest Marketing
Hanford, CA 559-582-4000
Concannon Vineyard
Livermore, CA 800-258-9866
Dan Tudor & Sons
Delano, CA .661-792-3176
Delta Packing Company of Lodi
Lodi, CA 209-334-0689
Fowler Packing Company
Fresno, CA .559-834-5911
George W Saulpaugh & Sons
Germantown, NY 518-537-6500
Gerawan Farming
Sanger, CA .559-787-8780
H. Naraghi Farms
Escalon, CA 209-577-5777
Hallcrest Vineyards
Felton, CA .831-335-4441
Hillcrest Orchard
Lake Placid, FL 865-397-5273
Janca's Jojoba Oil & Seed Company
Mesa, AZ 480-497-9494
Jasmine Vineyards
Delano, CA .661-792-2141
M&R Company
Lodi, CA 209-369-2725
Oceana Foods
Shelby, MI .231-861-2141
Oregon Fruit Products Company
Salem, OR .800-394-9333
Pacific Trellis
Reedley, CA 559-638-5100
Peter Rabbit Farms
Coachella, CA 760-398-0151
Produce Edge
Reedley, CA 559-637-9988
Royal Moonlight
Reedley, CA 559-637-7799

Royal Vista Marketing
Visalia, CA .559-636-9198
Satiety
Davis, CA 530-757-2699
Spring Ledge Farms
Dundee, NY 607-678-4038
Sunmet
Del Rey, CA 559-445-1574
Tejon Ranch
Lebec, CA 661-248-3000
Trefethen Vineyards
Napa, CA 800-556-4847
United Fruits Corporation
Santa Monica, CA 310-829-0261
Venture Vineyards
Lodi, NY 888-635-6277
Vintage Produce Sales
Kingsburg, CA 559-897-1622
Wawona Packing Company
Cutler, C9 559-528-4000
Yakima Valley Grape Producers
Grandview, WA 509-882-1223
Z&S Distributing
Fresno, CA .800-467-0788

Leaves

Castella Imports
Hauppauge, NY 866-227-8355
Corfu Foods
Bensenville, IL 630-595-2510
Grecian Delight Foods
Elk Grove Vlg, IL 800-621-4387
Hye Cuisine
Del Rey, CA 559-834-3000
Pacific Choice Brands
Fresno, CA .559-237-5583
Setton International Foods
Commack, NY 800-227-4397
Yergat Packing Co Inc
Fresno, CA .559-276-9180

Table

Anton Caratan & Son
Delano, CA .661-725-2575
Chiquita Brands International
Cincinnati, OH 800-438-0015
Corrin Produce Sales
Reedley, CA 559-638-3970
Lindemann Produce
Los Banos, CA 209-826-2442
Lucich Farms
Delano, CA .661-725-4550
Oregon Cherry Growers
The Dalles, OR 800-367-2536
Satiety
Davis, CA 530-757-2699
Sunmet
Del Rey, CA 559-445-1574
Vincent B. Zaninovich & Son
Richgrove, CA 661-725-2497
Z&S Distributing
Fresno, CA .800-467-0788

Wine

Galleano Winery
Mira Loma, CA 951-685-5376
Kiona Vineyards Winery
Benton City, WA 509-588-6716
Satiety
Davis, CA 530-757-2699
Tejon Ranch
Lebec, CA 661-248-3000
Trefethen Vineyards
Napa, CA 800-556-4847

Grapefruit

A. Duda Farm Fresh Foods
Belle Glade, FL 561-996-7621
Agrexco USA
Jamaica, NY 718-481-8700
Amber Foods
Downsview, ON 416-746-2455
Bautista Organic Dates
Mecca, CA .760-396-2337
Ben Hill Griffin, Inc.
Frostproof, FL 863-635-2251
Corona College Heights Orange & Lemon Associates
Riverside, CA 951-688-1811

Davidson of Dundee
Dundee, FL .800-654-0647
Dimare
Visalia, CA .559-627-0821
DNE World Fruit Sales
Fort Pierce, FL 800-327-6676
Dole Food Company
Westlake Village, CA 818-879-6600
Gene's Citrus Ranch
Palmetto, FL 888-723-2006
Golden River Fruit Company
Vero Beach, FL 772-562-4502
Haines City Citrus Growers Association
Haines City, FL 800-422-4245
Hale Indian River Groves
Wabasso, FL 800-562-4502
Heller Brothers Packing Corporation
Winter Garden, FL 407-656-4986
Hunt Brothers Cooperative
Lake Wales, FL 863-676-9471
Leroy Smith & Sons Inc
Vero Beach, FL 772-567-3421
Reed Lang Farms
Rio Hondo, TX 956-748-2354
River One
Vero Beach, FL 800-288-6614
Seald Sweet Growers & Packers
Vero Beach, FL 772-569-2244
Sugar Cane Industry Glades Correctional Institution
Belle Glade, FL 561-829-1400
United Fruits Corporation
Santa Monica, CA 310-829-0261
Valley Fruit & Vegetable
McAllen, TX 956-686-8056

Pink

DNE World Fruit Sales
Fort Pierce, FL 800-327-6676

White

DNE World Fruit Sales
Fort Pierce, FL 800-327-6676

Guava

Brooks Tropicals
Homestead, FL 800-327-4833
Chieftain Wild Rice Company
Spooner, WI 800-262-6368
Unique Ingredients
Naches, WA 509-653-1991

Canned & Frozen

EMERLING INTERNATIONAL FOODS, INC.

Emerling International Foods
Buffalo, NY .716-833-7381

We supply food manufacturers and food service
customers worldwide (since 1988) with bulk ingredients including: Fruits & Vegetables; Juice
Concentrates; Herbs & Spices; Oils & Vinegars;
Flavors & Colors; Honey & Molasses. We also
produce PURE MAPLE SYRUP.

Unique Ingredients
Naches, WA 509-653-1991

Kale

Abbott & Cobb, Inc.
Langhorne, PA 800-345-7333

EMERLING INTERNATIONAL FOODS, INC.

Emerling International Foods
Buffalo, NY .716-833-7381

We supply food manufacturers and food service
customers worldwide (since 1988) with bulk ingredients including: Fruits & Vegetables; Juice
Concentrates; Herbs & Spices; Oils & Vinegars;
Flavors & Colors; Honey & Molasses. We also
produce PURE MAPLE SYRUP.

Frank Capurro & Son
Moss Landing, CA 831-728-3904
Ruskin Packaging
Miami, FL 305-324-1529

Seabrook Brothers & Sons
Seabrook, NJ 856-455-8080

Frozen

Vegetable Juices
Chicago, IL 888-776-9752

Kelp Products

Acadian Seaplants
Dartmouth, NS 800-575-9100
Atlantic Laboratories
Waldoboro, ME. 207-832-5376
Gum Technology Corporation
Tucson, AZ 800-369-4867
Naturex (Chart Corp)
South Hackensack, NJ 201-440-5000
Silver Ferm Chemical
Seattle, WA 206-282-3376

Kiwi

Chiquita Brands International
Cincinnati, OH 800-438-0015
Nekta
Lakeville, MN. 952-898-8020
Royal Vista Marketing
Visalia, CA 559-636-9198
Setton International Foods
Commack, NY 800-227-4397
Unique Ingredients
Naches, WA. 509-653-1991

Gold

Brandt Farms
Reedley, CA 559-638-6961

Kohlrabi

Abbott & Cobb, Inc.
Langhorne, PA 800-345-7333
Baker Produce Company
Kennewick, WA 800-624-7553
Del Monte Foods
San Francisco, CA 800-543-3090
Princeville Canning Company
Princeville, IL 309-385-4301

Kumquat

Paradise Products Corporation
Roslyn, NY 800-826-1235
Setton International Foods
Commack, NY 800-227-4397
West Pak Avocado
Temecula, CA 800-266-4414

Leek

California Watercress
Fillmore, CA 805-524-4808
Ghirardelli Ranch
Petaluma, CA 707-795-7616

SupHerb Farms
Turlock, CA 800-787-4372

CrEATe! Get ready-to-use fresh flavor with
SupHerb Farms' all-natural fresh frozen culinary
herbs, specialty vegetables, culinary herb pastes,
vegetable purees and creative blends. Complete
microbiological testing ensures food safety. We
set the standard for outstanding customer service, inspired culinary support, collaborative customer partnerships and innovative custom
products.

Sure Fresh Produce
Santa Maria, CA 888-423-5379
Terry Foods Inc
Idaho Falls, ID 208-604-8143
Vegetable Juices
Chicago, IL 888-776-9752

Lemon

Corona College Heights Orange & Lemon Associates
Riverside, CA 951-688-1811
Dimare
Visalia, CA 559-627-0821
DiMare International
Indio, CA. 760-564-3762
DNE World Fruit Sales
Fort Pierce, FL 800-327-6676
Dole Food Company
Westlake Village, CA 818-879-6600
Paradise
Plant City, FL 800-330-8952
Seald Sweet Growers & Packers
Vero Beach, FL 772-569-2244
United Fruits Corporation
Santa Monica, CA. 310-829-0261
Z&S Distributing
Fresno, CA 800-467-0788

Peels

Fmali Herb
Santa Cruz, CA 831-423-7913

Lettuce

A. Duda Farm Fresh Foods
Belle Glade, FL 561-996-7621
Baker Produce Company
Kennewick, WA 800-624-7553
Ben B. Schwartz & Sons
Detroit, MI 313-841-8300
Cal-Harvest Marketing
Hanford, CA 559-582-4000
Club Chef
Covington, KY 859-578-3100
Crown Packing Company
Salinas, CA 831-424-2067
Custom Cuts
Milwaukee, WI 414-483-0491
Del Monte Foods
San Francisco, CA 800-543-3090
Del Monte Fresh Produce Company
Kankakee, IL 815-936-7400
Dole Food Company
Westlake Village, CA 818-879-6600
Dole Fresh Vegetable Company
Soledad, CA 800-333-5454
F&S Produce Company
Rosenhayn, NJ 800-886-3316
Fresh Express
Franklin Park, IL. 800-242-5472
Garden State Farms
Philadelphia, PA 215-463-8000
Ghirardelli Ranch
Petaluma, CA 707-795-7616
Hari Om Farms
Eagleville, TN. 615-368-7778
Hoson Produce
Los Angeles, CA. 323-550-8695
Indian Rock Produce
Perkasie, PA 800-882-0512
Mills
Salinas, CA 831-758-8179
R.C. McEntire & Company
Columbia, SC 803-799-3388
Royal Packing Company
Salinas, CA 831-641-4450
Sales USA
Salado, TX 800-766-7344
Silva Harvesting
Gonzales, CA 831-675-2327
Sunrise Growers
Placentia, CA 714-630-2170
Talley Farms
Arroyo Grande, CA. 805-489-2508
Tanimura & Antle
Salinas, CA 831-455-2255
Teixeira Farms
Santa Maria, CA 805-928-3801
Tony Vitrano Company
Jessup, MD 410-799-7444
Vegetable Juices
Chicago, IL 888-776-9752
Williams Creek Farms
Williams, OR. 541-846-6481

Butterhead

Boston

Tanimura & Antle
Salinas, CA 831-455-2255

Looseleaf

Green

Tanimura & Antle
Salinas, CA 831-455-2255

Red

Tanimura & Antle
Salinas, CA 831-455-2255

Miners

Del Monte Foods
San Francisco, CA 800-543-3090

Romaine

Royce C. Bone Farms
Nashville, NC 252-443-3773
Talley Farms
Arroyo Grande, CA. 805-489-2508
Tanimura & Antle
Salinas, CA 831-455-2255

Lime

Agri-Dairy Products
Purchase, NY 914-697-9580
Brooks Tropicals
Homestead, FL 800-327-4833
Del Monte Foods
San Francisco, CA 800-543-3090
Dimare
Visalia, CA 559-627-0821
DNE World Fruit Sales
Fort Pierce, FL 800-327-6676
Hunt Brothers Cooperative
Lake Wales, FL 863-676-9471

Loganberries

Ever Fresh Fruit Company
Boring, OR 800-239-8026
Kerr Concentrates
Salem, OR. 800-910-5377
Townsend Farms
Fairview, OR. 503-666-1780

Mango

Brooks Tropicals
Homestead, FL 800-327-4833
Chieftain Wild Rice Company
Spooner, WI 800-262-6368
Clofine Dairy & Food Products
Linwood, NJ 800-441-1001
Commodities Marketing, Inc.
Edison, NJ. 732-516-0700
Couture Farms
Kettleman City, CA. 559-945-2226
Del Monte Fresh Produce Company
Coral Gables, FL. 800-950-3683
Dole Food Company
Westlake Village, CA 818-879-6600
Eckert Cold Storage
Escalon, CA 209-838-4040
Just Tomatoes Company
Westley, CA. 800-537-1985
Natural Foods
Toledo, OH 800-860-0006
Organic Planet
San Francisco, CA 415-765-5590
Setton International Foods
Commack, NY 800-227-4397
Unique Ingredients
Naches, WA. 509-653-1991

Dried

American Importing Company
Minneapolis, MN 612-331-9226
Mariani Packing Company
Vacaville, CA 800-672-8655

Melon

Chiquita Brands International
Cincinnati, OH 800-438-0015
Custom Cuts
Milwaukee, WI 414-483-0491
Del Monte Fresh Produce Company
Coral Gables, FL 800-950-3683

EMERLING INTERNATIONAL FOODS, INC.

Emerling International Foods
Buffalo, NY 716-833-7381

We supply food manufacturers and food service customers worldwide (since 1988) with bulk ingredients including: Fruits & Vegetables; Juice Concentrates; Herbs & Spices; Oils & Vinegars; Flavors & Colors; Honey & Molasses. We also produce PURE MAPLE SYRUP.

Balls

Frozen

EMERLING INTERNATIONAL FOODS, INC.

Emerling International Foods
Buffalo, NY 716-833-7381

We supply food manufacturers and food service customers worldwide (since 1988) with bulk ingredients including: Fruits & Vegetables; Juice Concentrates; Herbs & Spices; Oils & Vinegars; Flavors & Colors; Honey & Molasses. We also produce PURE MAPLE SYRUP.

Cantaloupe

Abbott & Cobb, Inc.
Langhorne, PA 800-345-7333
Couture Farms
Kettleman City, CA 559-945-2226
F&S Produce Company
Rosenhayn, NJ 800-886-3316
Hialeah Products Company
Hollywood, FL 800-923-3379
Lindemann Produce
Los Banos, CA 209-826-2442
Vessey & Company
Holtville, CA 760-352-6376
Zuccaro's Fruit & Produce Company
Minneapolis, MN 612-333-1122

Dried

Setton International Foods
Commack, NY 800-227-4397

Honeydew

Couture Farms
Kettleman City, CA 559-945-2226
Lindemann Produce
Los Banos, CA 209-826-2442
Rose Valley Group
Woodland, CA 530-666-7857
Turlock Fruit Company
Turlock, CA 209-634-7207
United Fruits Corporation
Santa Monica, CA 310-829-0261
Zuccaro's Fruit & Produce Company
Minneapolis, MN 612-333-1122

Watermelon

Bryant Preserving Company
Alma, AR 800-634-2413
Custom Cuts
Milwaukee, WI 414-483-0491
Del Monte Fresh Produce Company
Coral Gables, FL 800-950-3683
Eastern Marketing Service
Lakeland, FL 863-701-8214
F&S Produce Company
Rosenhayn, NJ 800-886-3316
Zuccaro's Fruit & Produce Company
Minneapolis, NJ 612-333-1122

Seedless

Bissett Produce Company
Spring Hope, NC 800-849-5073

Miso

Great Eastern Sun
Asheville, NC 800-334-5809
Miyako Oriental Foods
Baldwin Park, CA 877-788-6476
Organic Gourmet
Sherman Oaks, CA 800-400-7772

Mushrooms

Al Pete Meats
Muncie, IN 765-288-8817
Alimentaire Whyte's Inc
Laval, QC 800-625-1979
Anchor Food Products/ McCain Foods
Appleton, WI 920-734-0627
Basciani Foods
Avondale, PA 610-268-3610
Bob Gordon & Associates
Chicago, IL 773-247-0588
Buon Italia
New York, NY 212-633-9090
Cara Mia Products
Fresno, CA 559-498-2900
Chieftain Wild Rice Company
Spooner, WI 800-262-6368
Colonna Brothers
North Bergen, NJ 201-864-1115
Country Fresh Mushrooms
Avondale, PA 610-268-3033
Crazy Jerry's
Roswell, GA 770-993-0651
Creekside Mushrooms
Worthington, PA 724-297-5491
Cutone Specialty Foods
Chelsea, MA 617-889-1122
D'Artagnan
Newark, NJ 800-327-8246
Dong Kee Company
Chicago, IL 312-225-6340
Dove Mushrooms
Avondale, PA 610-441-9928

EMERLING INTERNATIONAL FOODS, INC.

Emerling International Foods
Buffalo, NY 716-833-7381

We supply food manufacturers and food service customers worldwide (since 1988) with bulk ingredients including: Fruits & Vegetables; Juice Concentrates; Herbs & Spices; Oils & Vinegars; Flavors & Colors; Honey & Molasses. We also produce PURE MAPLE SYRUP.

Epicurean Specialty
Sebastopol, CA 800-500-0065
Flavor House
Adelanto, CA 760-246-9131
Franklin Farms
North Franklin, CT 860-642-3019
FungusAmongUs Inc
Snohomish, WA 360-568-3403
Giorgio Foods
Temple, PA 800-220-2139
Giovanni's Appetizing Food Products
Richmond, MI 586-727-9355
Gourmet's Finest
Avondale, PA 610-268-6910
Great American Appetizers
Nampa, ID 800-282-4834
Great Lakes Foods
Hamilton, ON 905-560-4223
H.K. Canning
Ventura, CA 805-652-1392
Hanover Foods Corporation
Hanover, PA 717-632-6000
Health Concerns
Oakland, CA 800-233-9355
Kitchen Pride Mushroom Farms
Gonzales, TX 830-540-4516
L K Bowman & Company
Nottingham, PA 800-853-1919
L&S Packing Company
Farmingdale, NY 800-286-6487
L.F. Lambert Spawn Company
Coatesville, PA 610-384-5031
L.K. Bowman Company
Nottingham, PA 800-853-1919
Lake Erie Frozen Foods Company
Ashland, OH 800-766-8501

Lee's Food Products
Toronto, ON 416-465-2407
Les Aliments Livabec Foods
Sherrington, QC 450-454-7971
LK Bowman
Nottingham, PA 800-853-1919
Matador Processors
Blanchard, OK 800-847-0797
McCain Foods
Fort Atkinson, WI 920-563-6625
Miss Scarlett's
Chandler, AZ 800-345-6734
Modern Mushroom Farms
Avondale, PA 610-268-3535
Money's Mushrooms
Vancouver, BC 604-669-3741
Money's Mushrooms
Langley, BC 800-661-8623
Monterey Mushrooms
Watsonville, CA 800-333-6874
Monterey Mushrooms
Watsonville, CA 831-763-5300
Mushroom Company
Cambridge, MD 410-221-8900
Nationwide Canning
Cottam, ON 519-839-4831
North American Reishi/Nammex
Gibsons, BC 604-886-7799
NTC Foods Corporation
Williamsville, NY 800-333-1637
Olympic Food Products
Kokomo, IN 800-445-6923
Omstead Foods Ltd
Burlington, ON 905-315-8883
Ostrom Mushroom Farms
Lacey, WA 360-491-1410
Paisley Farms
Willoughby, OH 800-676-8656
Paradise Products Corporation
Roslyn, NY 800-826-1235
Phillips Gourmet
Kennett Square, PA 610-925-0520
Prairie Mushrooms
Sherwood Park, AB 780-467-3555
Rain Sweet
Salem, OR 800-363-4293
Ron-Son Foods
Swedesboro, NJ 856-241-7333
S.D. Mushrooms
Avondale, PA 610-268-8082
Sabatino Truffles USA
Long Island City, NY 888-444-9971
Scally's Imperial Importing Company Inc
Staten Island, NY 718-983-1938
Setton International Foods
Commack, NY 800-227-4397
South Mill Distribution
Kennett Square, PA 610-444-4800
Sunny Dell Foods
Oxford, PA 610-932-5164
Superior Mushroom Farms
Ardrossan, AB 866-687-2242

Terry Foods Inc
Idaho Falls, ID 208-604-8143
Tiger Mushroom Farm
Nanton, AB 403-646-2578
Unique Foods
Raleigh, NC 919-779-5600
United Canning Corporation
North Lima, OH 330-549-9807

Vegetable Juices
Chicago, IL 888-776-9752
Victoria Packing Corporation
Brooklyn, NY 718-649-2180
Woodland Foods
Gurnee, IL 847-625-8600

Beech

Franklin Farms
North Franklin, CT 860-642-3019

Black Trumpet

Chieftain Wild Rice Company
Spooner, WI 800-262-6368
D'Artagnan
Newark, NJ 800-327-8246
Woodland Foods
Gurnee, IL 847-625-8600

Boletes

Chieftain Wild Rice Company
Spooner, WI 800-262-6368

Canned

Agrocan
Toronto, ON 877-247-6226
Bob Gordon & Associates
Chicago, IL 773-247-0588
Dong Kee Company
Chicago, IL 312-225-6340
Giorgio Foods
Temple, PA 800-220-2139
Great Lakes Foods
Hamilton, ON 905-560-4223
L.K. Bowman Company
Nottingham, PA 800-853-1919
Lee's Food Products
Toronto, ON 416-465-2407
Money's Mushrooms
Vancouver, BC 604-669-3741
Monterey Mushrooms
Bonne Terre, MO 800-333-6874
Mushroom Company
Cambridge, MD 410-221-8900
Nationwide Canning
Cottam, ON 519-839-4831
NTC Foods Corporation
Williamsville, NY 800-333-1637
Paradise Products Corporation
Roslyn, NY 800-826-1235
Ron-Son Foods
Swedesboro, NJ 856-241-7333
Shafer-Haggart
Vancouver, BC 888-779-7111
Sunny Dell Foods
Oxford, PA 610-932-5164
Unique Foods
Raleigh, NC 919-779-5600
United Canning Corporation
North Lima, OH 330-549-9807

Chanterelle

Chieftain Wild Rice Company
Spooner, WI 800-262-6368
D'Artagnan
Newark, NJ 800-327-8246

EMERLING INTERNATIONAL FOODS, INC.

Emerling International Foods
Buffalo, NY 716-833-7381

We supply food manufacturers and food service customers worldwide (since 1988) with bulk ingredients including: Fruits & Vegetables; Juice Concentrates; Herbs & Spices; Oils & Vinegars; Flavors & Colors; Honey & Molasses. We also produce PURE MAPLE SYRUP.

Modern Mushroom Farms
Avondale, PA 610-268-3535

Cloudear

Chieftain Wild Rice Company
Spooner, WI 800-262-6368

Criminis

Creekside Mushrooms
Worthington, PA 724-297-5491
Franklin Farms
North Franklin, CT 860-642-3019
Ostrom Mushroom Farms
Lacey, WA 360-491-1410

Dehydrated

EMERLING INTERNATIONAL FOODS, INC.

Emerling International Foods
Buffalo, NY 716-833-7381

We supply food manufacturers and food service customers worldwide (since 1988) with bulk ingredients including: Fruits & Vegetables; Juice Concentrates; Herbs & Spices; Oils & Vinegars; Flavors & Colors; Honey & Molasses. We also produce PURE MAPLE SYRUP.

Nikken Foods Company
St Louis, MO 636-532-1019
South Mill Distribution
Kennett Square, PA 610-444-4800
Unique Ingredients
Naches, WA 509-653-1991

Enokis

Creekside Mushrooms
Worthington, PA 724-297-5491
Franklin Farms
North Franklin, CT 860-642-3019
Monterey Mushrooms
Watsonville, CA 800-333-6874
Ostrom Mushroom Farms
Lacey, WA 360-491-1410

Fresh

Country Fresh Mushrooms
Avondale, PA 610-268-3033
Creekside Mushrooms
Worthington, PA 724-297-5491
L.K. Bowman Company
Nottingham, PA 800-853-1919
Modern Mushroom Farms
Avondale, PA 610-268-3535
Money's Mushrooms
Langley, BC 800-661-8623
Monterey Mushrooms
Watsonville, CA 800-333-6874

Frozen

Al Pete Meats
Muncie, IN 765-288-8817
Great American Appetizers
Nampa, ID 800-282-4834
Hanover Foods Corporation
Hanover, PA 717-632-6000
L.K. Bowman Company
Nottingham, PA 800-853-1919
Lake Erie Frozen Foods Company
Ashland, OH 800-766-8501
Matador Processors
Blanchard, OK 800-847-0797
McCain Foods
Fort Atkinson, WI 920-563-6625
Monterey Mushrooms
Watsonville, CA 800-333-6874
Monterey Mushrooms
Watsonville, CA 831-763-5300
Mushroom Company
Cambridge, MD 410-221-8900
Olympic Food Products
Kokomo, IN 800-445-6923
Rain Sweet
Salem, OR 800-363-4293

Lobster

Chieftain Wild Rice Company
Spooner, WI 800-262-6368

Maitakes

D'Artagnan
Newark, NJ 800-327-8246

Franklin Farms
North Franklin, CT 860-642-3019
Hardscrabble Enterprises
Franklin, WV 304-358-2921

Morel

Chieftain Wild Rice Company
Spooner, WI 800-262-6368
D'Artagnan
Newark, NJ 800-327-8246

EMERLING INTERNATIONAL FOODS, INC.

Emerling International Foods
Buffalo, NY 716-833-7381

We supply food manufacturers and food service customers worldwide (since 1988) with bulk ingredients including: Fruits & Vegetables; Juice Concentrates; Herbs & Spices; Oils & Vinegars; Flavors & Colors; Honey & Molasses. We also produce PURE MAPLE SYRUP.

Modern Mushroom Farms
Avondale, PA 610-268-3535

Mousseron

Chieftain Wild Rice Company
Spooner, WI 800-262-6368

Oyster

Chieftain Wild Rice Company
Spooner, WI 800-262-6368
Concord Farms
Union City, CA 510-429-8855
Creekside Mushrooms
Worthington, PA 724-297-5491

EMERLING INTERNATIONAL FOODS, INC.

Emerling International Foods
Buffalo, NY 716-833-7381

We supply food manufacturers and food service customers worldwide (since 1988) with bulk ingredients including: Fruits & Vegetables; Juice Concentrates; Herbs & Spices; Oils & Vinegars; Flavors & Colors; Honey & Molasses. We also produce PURE MAPLE SYRUP.

Franklin Farms
North Franklin, CT 860-642-3019
Modern Mushroom Farms
Avondale, PA 610-268-3535
Monterey Mushrooms
Watsonville, CA 800-333-6874
Ostrom Mushroom Farms
Lacey, WA 360-491-1410

Porcini

Chieftain Wild Rice Company
Spooner, WI 800-262-6368

EMERLING INTERNATIONAL FOODS, INC.

Emerling International Foods
Buffalo, NY 716-833-7381

We supply food manufacturers and food service customers worldwide (since 1988) with bulk ingredients including: Fruits & Vegetables; Juice Concentrates; Herbs & Spices; Oils & Vinegars; Flavors & Colors; Honey & Molasses. We also produce PURE MAPLE SYRUP.

Modern Mushroom Farms
Avondale, PA 610-268-3535
Woodland Foods
Gurnee, IL 847-625-8600

Portobello

Chieftain Wild Rice Company
Spooner, WI 800-262-6368
Creekside Mushrooms
Worthington, PA 724-297-5491
Franklin Farms
North Franklin, CT 860-642-3019

Ostrom Mushroom Farms
Lacey, WA 360-491-1410
Phillips Gourmet
Kennett Square, PA 610-925-0520
Woodland Foods
Gurnee, IL 847-625-8600

Shiitake

Baycliff Company
New York, NY 212-772-6078
Chieftain Wild Rice Company
Spooner, WI 800-262-6368
Concord Farms
Union City, CA 510-429-8855
Creekside Mushrooms
Worthington, PA 724-297-5491

EMERLING INTERNATIONAL FOODS, INC.

Emerling International Foods
Buffalo, NY 716-833-7381

We supply food manufacturers and food service customers worldwide (since 1988) with bulk ingredients including: Fruits & Vegetables; Juice Concentrates; Herbs & Spices; Oils & Vinegars; Flavors & Colors; Honey & Molasses. We also produce PURE MAPLE SYRUP.

Franklin Farms
North Franklin, CT 860-642-3019
Hardscrabble Enterprises
Franklin, WV 304-358-2921
Modern Mushroom Farms
Avondale, PA 610-268-3535
Monterey Mushrooms
Watsonville, CA 800-333-6874
Ostrom Mushroom Farms
Lacey, WA 360-491-1410

SupHerb Farms
Turlock, CA 800-787-4372

CrEATe! Get ready-to-use fresh flavor with SupHerb Farms' all-natural fresh frozen culinary herbs, specialty vegetables, culinary herb pastes, vegetable purees and creative blends. Complete microbiological testing ensures food safety. We set the standard for outstanding customer service, inspired culinary support, collaborative customer partnerships and innovative custom products.

Woodland Foods
Gurnee, IL 847-625-8600

Truffles

Assouline & Ting
Philadelphia, PA 800-521-4491
Buon Italia
New York, NY 212-633-9090
Chieftain Wild Rice Company
Spooner, WI 800-262-6368
D'Artagnan
Newark, NJ 800-327-8246
Woodland Foods
Gurnee, IL 847-625-8600

Black Whole

Assouline & Ting
Philadelphia, PA 800-521-4491

WhiteWhole

Assouline & Ting
Philadelphia, PA 800-521-4491

White

Creekside Mushrooms
Worthington, PA 724-297-5491
Ostrom Mushroom Farms
Lacey, WA 360-491-1410

Wild

Grapevine Trading Company
Santa Rosa, CA 800-469-6478

Wood Ear

Chieftain Wild Rice Company
Spooner, WI 800-262-6368
Modern Mushroom Farms
Avondale, PA 610-268-3535

Mustard

A. Bauer's Mustard
Flushing, NY 718-821-3570
Arbor Hill Grapery & Winery
Naples, NY 800-554-7553
Ashman Manufacturing & Distributing Company
Virginia Beach, VA 800-641-9924
Assouline & Ting
Philadelphia, PA 800-521-4491
Baumer Foods
New Orleans, LA 504-482-5761
Beaverton Foods
Beaverton, OR 800-223-8076
Boetje Foods
Rock Island, IL 877-726-3853
Booneway Farms
Berea, KY 859-986-2636
Boston Spice & Tea Company
Boston, VA 800-966-4372
Brad's Taste of New York
Floral Park, NY 516-354-9004
Bread & Chocolate
Wells River, VT 800-524-6715
Buon Italia
New York, NY 212-633-9090
Cains Foods/Olde Cape Cod
Ayer, MA 800-225-0601
California Style Gourmet Products
San Diego, CA 800-243-5226
Casa Visco Finer Food Company
Schenectady, NY 888-607-2823
Cedarvale Food Products
Toronto, ON 416-656-6330
Cherchies
Malvern, PA 800-644-1980
Ciro Foods
Pittsburgh, PA 412-771-9018
Clements Foods Company
Oklahoma City, OK 800-654-8355
Coastal Classics
Duxbury, MA 508-746-6058
Culinary Imports
Jericho, VT 800-958-7678
Dean Distributing Inc
Green Bay, WI. 920-469-6500
Delicae Gourmet
Tarpon Springs, FL 800-942-2502
Dorina/So-Good
Union, IL. 815-923-2144
East Shore Specialty Foods
Hartland, WI 800-236-1069
Erba Food Products
Brooklyn, NY 718-272-7700
Erbrich-Sewell Products Company
Indianapolis, IN 317-925-6433
Fauchon
New York, NY 877-605-0130
Fischer & Wieser Specialty Foods
Fredericksburg, TX 800-880-8526
Food Specialties
Indianapolis, IN 317-271-0862
Ford's Fancy Fruit
Raleigh, NC 800-446-0947

Fox Hollow Farm
Hanover, NH 603-643-6002
French's Flavor Ingredients
Springfield, MO 800-437-3624
G E Barbour
Sussex, NB 506-432-2300
G S Dunn & Company
Hamilton, ON 905-522-0833
Garden Complements
Kansas City, MO. 800-966-1091
Garlic Festival Foods
Gilroy, CA 888-427-5423
Gold Pure Foods Products Company
Hempstead, NY. 800-422-4681
Golden State Foods
Irvine, CA 949-252-2000
Gormly's Orchard
South Burlington, VT 800-639-7604
Grapevine Trading Company
Santa Rosa, CA 800-469-6478
Groeb Farms
Onsted, MI 517-467-7100
Grouse Hunt Farms
Tamaqua, PA 570-467-2850
H.J. Heinz Company
Pittsburgh, PA 412-237-5948
Hawaiian Fruit Specialties
Kalaheo, HI 808-332-9333
Heinz Company of Canada
North York, ON 800-268-6641
Hot Licks Hot Sauces
Spring Valley, CA 888-766-6468
International Home Foods
Milton, PA 973-359-9920
J.M. Smucker Company
Orrville, OH 330-682-3000
J.N. Bech
Elk Rapids, MI 800-232-4583
Kari-Out Company
White Plains, NY 800-433-8799
Kathy's Gourmet Specialties
Mendocino, CA. 707-937-1383
Kelchner's Horseradish
Dublin, PA. 215-249-3439
Kelly Pickle Company
Oconto, WI 920-834-4433
Knese Enterprise
Floral Park, NY 516-354-9004
Kozlowski Farms
Forestville, CA 800-473-2767
Kraft
Parsippany, NJ. 973-292-1755
Kraft Food Ingredients
Memphis, TN 901-381-6500
Kraft Foods
Garland, TX 972-272-7511
Liberty Richter
Saddle Brook, NJ 201-291-8749
Lounsbury Foods
Toronto, ON 416-656-6330
Mad Will's Food Company
Auburn, CA. 888-275-9455
McCutcheon's Apple Products
Frederick, MD. 800-888-7537
Miceli's Specialty Foods Company
Danbury, CT 888-264-2354
Mizkam Americas
Kansas City, MO. 816-483-1700
Morehouse Foods
City of Industry, CA 626-854-1655
Mothers Mountain Mustard
Falmouth, ME 800-440-9891
Mountainbrook of Vermont
Jeffersonville, VT 802-644-1988
Mucky Duck Mustard Company
Ferndale, MI 248-544-4610
Mutchler's Dakota Gold Mustard
Spearfish, SD 605-642-7325
New Canaan Farms
Dripping Springs, TX 800-727-5267
Northeast Kingdom Mustard Company
Brownington, VT 802-754-2813
Old Cavendish Products
Cavendish, VT 800-536-7899
Olde Tyme Mercantile
Arroyo Grande, CA. 805-489-7991
Olds Products Company
Pleasant Prairie, WI 800-233-8064
Pemberton's Gourmet Foods
Gray, ME 800-255-8401
Pictsweet Frozen Foods
Bells, TN 731-663-7600

Piknik Products Company Inc
Montgomery, AL................334-265-1567
Pilgrim Foods
Greenville, NH..................603-878-2100
Plochman
Manteno, IL.....................815-468-3434
Portion Pac
Mason, OH......................800-232-4829
Purity Products
Plainview, NY...................888-769-7873
Quality Foods
San Pedro, CA..................877-833-7890
Rapazzini Winery
Gilroy, CA......................408-842-5649
Red Pelican Food Products
Detroit, MI.....................313-921-2500
Restaurant Lulu Gourmet Products
San Francisco, CA...............888-693-5800
REX Pure Foods
Gonzales, TX...................800-344-8314
Riba Foods
Houston, TX....................800-327-7422
Rising Sun Farms
Phoenix, OR....................541-535-8331
Robert Rothschild Berry Farm
Urbana, OH.....................866-565-6790
Robert Rothschild Farm
Urbana, OH.....................866-565-6790
Schlotterbeck & Foss Company
Portland, ME....................800-777-4666
Scott-Bathgate
Winnipeg, NB...................204-943-8525
Select Food Products
Toronto, ON....................800-699-8016
Silver Palate Kitchens
Cresskill, NJ....................800-872-5283
Silver Spring Gardens
Eau Claire, WI..................800-826-7322
Stello Foods
Punxsutawney, PA...............800-849-4599
Stonewall Kitchen
York, ME.......................800-207-5267
T. Marzetti Company
Columbus, OH..................614-846-2232
Tandem Enterprises
Darien, CT......................800-779-3276
Terrapin Ridge
Freeport, IL.....................800-999-4052
TexaFrance
Austin, TX......................800-776-8937
Tropical
Charlotte, NC...................800-220-1413
UFL Foods
Mississauga, ON................905-670-7776
Ultra Seal
New Paltz, NY..................845-255-2496
Uncle Dave's Kitchen
South Londonderry, VT..........802-824-3600
Uncle Fred's Fine Foods
Rockport, TX...................361-729-8320
Westport Rivers Vineyard& Winery
Westport, MA...................800-993-9695
Wild Thymes Farm
Greenville, NY..................800-724-2877
William Poll
New York, NY..................800-993-7655
Wing Nien Company
Hayward, CA...................510-487-8877
Wing's Food Products
Toronto, ON....................416-259-2662
Wisconsin Spice
Berlin, WI......................920-361-3555
Woeber Mustard Manufacturing
Springfield, OH.................800-548-2929
Wood Brothers
West Columbia, SC..............803-796-5146

Cress

Koppert Cress USA
Cutchogue, NY..................516-437-5700

Greens

Canned & Frozen

A. Bauer's Mustard
Flushing, NY....................718-821-3570
Allen Canning Company
Siloam Springs, AR..............800-234-2553
Furst-McNess Company/Terrapin Ridge
Freeport, IL.....................800-999-4052

Haus Barhyte
Pendleton, OR..................800-407-9241
Heintz & Weber Company
Buffalo, NY.....................716-852-7171
Mendocino Mustard
Fort Bragg, CA..................800-964-2270
Montana Specialty Mills
Great Falls, MT..................406-761-2338
Mrs. Dog's Products
Tampa, FL......................800-267-7364
Seabrook Brothers & Sons
Seabrook, NJ...................856-455-8080
Wisconsin Wilderness Food Products
Milwaukee, WI..................800-359-3039

Osaka Purple

Alfred L. Wolff, Inc.
Park Ridge, IL...................312-265-9889
Trade Farm
Oakland, CA....................510-836-2938

Nectar

Mira International Foods
East Brunswick, NJ...............800-818-6472
Vilore Foods Company
Laredo, TX.....................956-726-3633
WCC Honey Marketing
City of Industry, CA..............626-855-3086

Canned

Healthmate Products
Highland Park, IL................800-584-8642

Nectarines

Ballantine Produce Company
Reedley, CA....................559-637-2400
Brandt Farms
Reedley, CA....................559-638-6961
California Fruit
Sanger, CA.....................559-266-7117
Chiquita Brands International
Cincinnati, OH..................800-438-0015
Copper Hills Fruit Sales
Fresno, CA.....................559-277-1970
Corrin Produce Sales
Reedley, CA....................559-638-3970
Dole Food Company
Westlake Village, CA.............818-879-6600
Fastachi
Watertown, MA.................800-466-3022
Fowler Packing Company
Fresno, CA.....................559-834-5911
Giumarra Companies
Reedley, CA....................559-897-5060
HMC Marketing Group
Kingsburg, CA..................559-897-1009
Mountain View Fruit Sales
Reedley, CA....................559-637-9933
P-R Farms
Clovis, CA......................559-299-0201
Produce Edge
Reedley, CA....................559-637-9988
Rice Fruit Company
Gardners, PA...................800-627-3359
Stadelman Fruit
Zillah, WA......................509-829-5145
Sun Valley
Reedley, CA....................559-591-1515
Sunmet
Del Rey, CA....................559-445-1574
T.S. Smith & Sons
Bridgeville, DE..................302-337-8271
Tom Ringhausen Orchards
Hardin, IL......................618-576-2311
Trinity Fruit Sales
Clovis, CA......................559-322-7100
Unique Ingredients
Naches, WA....................509-653-1991
United Fruits Corporation
Santa Monica, CA...............310-829-0261
Vintage Produce Sales
Kingsburg, CA..................559-897-1622
Wawona Packing Company
Cutler, C9.....................559-528-4000
Z&S Distributing
Fresno, CA.....................800-467-0788

Okra

Anchor Food Products/ McCain Foods
Appleton, WI...................920-734-0627
Brooks Food Group Corporate Office
Bedford, VA....................800-873-4934
Culinary Standards Corporation
Louisville, KY...................800-778-3434
Miss Scarlett's
Chandler, AZ...................800-345-6734
Pictsweet Frozen Foods
Bells, TN.......................731-663-7600
Talk O' Texas Brands
San Angelo, TX.................325-655-6077

Canned

Anchor Food Products/ McCain Foods
Appleton, WI...................920-734-0627

EMERLING INTERNATIONAL FOODS, INC.

Emerling International Foods
Buffalo, NY.....................716-833-7381

> We supply food manufacturers and food service
> customers worldwide (since 1988) with bulk in-
> gredients including: Fruits & Vegetables; Juice
> Concentrates; Herbs & Spices; Oils & Vinegars;
> Flavors & Colors; Honey & Molasses. We also
> produce PURE MAPLE SYRUP.

Frozen

Anchor Food Products/ McCain Foods
Appleton, WI...................920-734-0627
Brooks Food Group Corporate Office
Bedford, VA....................800-873-4934

EMERLING INTERNATIONAL FOODS, INC.

Emerling International Foods
Buffalo, NY.....................716-833-7381

> We supply food manufacturers and food service
> customers worldwide (since 1988) with bulk in-
> gredients including: Fruits & Vegetables; Juice
> Concentrates; Herbs & Spices; Oils & Vinegars;
> Flavors & Colors; Honey & Molasses. We also
> produce PURE MAPLE SYRUP.

Pictsweet Frozen Foods
Bells, TN.......................731-663-7600

Olives

A. Camacho
Plant City, FL...................800-881-4534
ACH Food Companies
Memphis, TN...................800-691-1106
Adams Olive Ranch
Lindsay, CA....................888-216-5483
Agrocan
Toronto, ON....................877-247-6226
Alimentaire Whyte's Inc
Laval, QC......................800-625-1979
Bell-Carter Foods
Lafayette, CA...................800-252-3557
Bob Gordon & Associates
Chicago, IL.....................773-247-0588
Cains Foods/Olde Cape Cod
Ayer, MA......................800-225-0601
California Olive Growers
Fresno, CA.....................888-965-4837
Caltex Foods
Canoga Park, CA...............800-522-5839
Castella Imports
Hauppauge, NY................866-227-8355
Comet Rice
Houston, TX...................281-272-8800
Consumers Vinegar & Spice Company
Chicago, IL.....................773-376-4100
Conway Import Company
Franklin Park, IL................800-323-8801
Corfu Foods
Bensenville, IL..................630-595-2510
Cormier Rice Milling Company
De Witt, AR....................870-946-3561
Cosmo's Food Products
West Haven, CT................800-933-6766
Country Cupboard
Virginia City, NV................775-847-7300

Crazy Jerry's
Roswell, GA 770-993-0651
E. Waldo Ward & Son Corporation
Sierra Madre, CA 800-355-9273
Ehmann Olive Company
Oroville, CA 530-533-3303

EMERLING INTERNATIONAL FOODS, INC.

Emerling International Foods
Buffalo, NY............................716-833-7381

We supply food manufacturers and food service customers worldwide (since 1988) with bulk ingredients including: Fruits & Vegetables; Juice Concentrates; Herbs & Spices; Oils & Vinegars; Flavors & Colors; Honey & Molasses. We also produce PURE MAPLE SYRUP.

Fantis Foods
Carlstadt, NJ 201-933-6200
FoodMatch Inc
New York, NY........................800-350-3411
G L Mezzetta
American Canyon, CA 707-648-1050
Goya Foods of Florida
Miami, FL 305-592-3150
Grainaissance
Emeryville, CA 800-472-4697
Greek Gourmet Limited
Mill Valley, CA 415-480-8050
H&F Food Products Company
Buffalo, NY 716-876-4345
Heinz Company of Canada
North York, ON. 800-268-6641
HVJ International
Spring, TX. 877-730-3663
Kaiser Foods
Cincinnati, OH 888-291-0608
Krinos Foods
Long Island City, NY 718-729-9000
L&S Packing Company
Farmingdale, NY 800-286-6487
Lakeside Packing Company
Harrow, ON............................519-738-2314
Liberty Richter
Saddle Brook, NJ 201-291-8749
M&CP Farms
Orland, CA 530-865-9810
Mancuso Cheese Company
Joliet, IL 815-722-2475
Moscahlades Brothers
New York, NY 212-226-5410
Musco Olive Products
Orland, CA 530-865-4111
Musco Olive Products
Tracy, CA 800-523-9828
Nature Quality
San Martin, CA 408-683-2182
New Morning
Needham, MA........................781-444-0440
Northcenter Foodservice Corporation
Augusta, ME 207-623-8451
NTC Foods Corporation
Williamsville, NY 800-333-1637
Nuvex Ingredients
Blue Earth, MN. 507-526-4331
Olde Tyme Mercantile
Arroyo Grande, CA. 805-489-7991
Olives & Foods Inc
Hialeah, FL 305-821-3444
Orleans Packing Company
Hyde Park, MA. 617-361-6611
Pacific Choice Brands
Fresno, CA 559-237-5583
Paradise Products Corporation
Roslyn, NY 800-826-1235
Pastene Companies
Canton, MA 781-830-8200
Picklesmith
Taft, TX................................800-499-3401
Price Cold Storage & Packing Company
Yakima, WA 509-966-4110
Proacec USA
Santa Monica, CA..................310-996-7770
Pure Food Ingredients
Verona, WI 800-355-9601
Rahco International
St Augustine, FL....................800-851-7681
Ron-Son Foods
Swedesboro, NJ 856-241-7333

S&G Products
Nicholasville, KY 800-826-7652
San Marzano Foods
Nashville, TN 615-385-4398
Sandt's Honey Company
Easton, PA............................800-935-3960
Santa Barbara Olive Company
Goleta, CA 800-624-4896
Scally's Imperial Importing Company Inc
Staten Island, NY 718-983-1938
Seasons' Enterprises
Addison, IL 630-628-0211
Sieco USA Corporation
Houston, TX 800-325-9443
SilverLeaf International
Stafford, TX 800-442-7542
Spruce Foods
San Clemente, CA..................949-366-9457
Star Fine Foods
Fresno, CA 559-498-2900
Tee Pee Olives
Scarsdale, NY 800-431-1529
Tri-Valley Growers
Langhorne, PA 215-702-8131
Trotters Imports
Colrain, MA 800-863-8437
US Fresh Marketing
Virginia Beach, VA 757-481-2606
Vegetable Juices
Chicago, IL 888-776-9752
Ventura Foods
Philadelphia, PA 215-223-8700
Veronica Foods Company
Oakland, CA 800-370-5554
Victoria Packing Corporation
Brooklyn, NY 718-649-2180
Vlasic Foods
Tracy, CA 559-734-7455
West Coast Products Corporation
Orland, CA 800-382-3072
Woodlake Ranch
Woodlake, CA 559-564-2161

Black

Agrocan
Toronto, ON 877-247-6226
Bell-Carter Foods
Lafayette, CA 800-252-3557
Bob Gordon & Associates
Chicago, IL 773-247-0588

Whole

Adams Olive Ranch
Lindsay, CA 888-216-5483

Greek

A. Camacho
Plant City, FL 800-881-4534
Adams Olive Ranch
Lindsay, CA 888-216-5483
Castella Imports
Hauppauge, NY 866-227-8355

Green

Agrocan
Toronto, ON 877-247-6226
Bob Gordon & Associates
Chicago, IL............................773-247-0588
Ron-Son Foods
Swedesboro, NJ 856-241-7333
Woodlake Ranch
Woodlake, CA. 559-564-2161

with Pimiento

Bell-Carter Foods
Lafayette, CA 800-252-3557

Italian

Adams Olive Ranch
Lindsay, CA 888-216-5483
Castella Imports
Hauppauge, NY 866-227-8355

Onion

A. Duda Farm Fresh Foods
Belle Glade, FL. 561-996-7621

Agri-Pack
Pasco, WA 509-545-6181
Alsum Produce
Friesland, WI 800-236-5127
Appleton Produce Company
Weiser, ID 208-414-1102
Atlantic Quality Spice &Seasonings
Edison, NJ............................800-584-0422
Boardman Foods
Boardman, OR 541-481-3000
Bob Gordon & Associates
Chicago, IL 773-247-0588
Castella Imports
Hauppauge, NY 866-227-8355
Christopher Ranch
Gilroy, CA 408-847-1100
Club Chef
Covington, KY 859-578-3100
Custom Cuts
Milwaukee, WI 414-483-0491
DeFrancesco & Sons
Firebaugh, CA 209-364-7000
Del Monte Fresh Produce Company
Coral Gables, FL. 800-950-3683
Del Monte Fresh Produce Company
Kankakee, IL. 815-936-7400
Delta Packing Company of Lodi
Lodi, CA 209-334-0689
Diamond Nut Company
Lemont, IL 630-739-3000
Dickinson Frozen Foods
Fruitland, ID 208-452-5200
Dole Food Company
Westlake Village, CA 818-879-6600
Exeter Produce & Storage Company
Exeter, ON. 519-235-0141
F&S Produce Company
Rosenhayn, NJ 800-886-3316
Fiesta Farms
Nyssa, OR 541-372-2248
Fresh Express
Franklin Park, IL....................800-242-5472
Ful-Flav-R Foods
Alamo, CA 510-339-9618
G L Mezzetta
American Canyon, CA 707-648-1050
Gill's Onions
Oxnard, CA............................800-348-2255
Gilroy Foods
Gilroy, CA..............................800-921-7502
Giuliano's Specialty Foods
Garden Grove, CA 714-895-9661
Gouw Quality Onions
Taber, AB 403-223-1440
Haliburton International Corporation
Fontana, CA 877-980-4295
Harris Farms
Coalinga, CA 800-742-1955
Heinz North America
Pittsburgh, PA 412-237-5700
Indian Rock Produce
Perkasie, PA 800-882-0512
Ingredients Corporation of America
Memphis, TN 901-525-6660
Isadore A. Rapasadi & Son
Canastota, NY. 315-697-2216
J.C. Watson Company
Parma, ID 208-722-5141
JES Foods
Cleveland, OH 216-883-8987
Kurtz Produce
Ariss, ON 519-824-3279
L&S Packing Company
Farmingdale, NY 800-286-6487
Magic Valley Growers
Wendell, ID. 208-536-6693
McCain Foods
Fort Atkinson, WI. 920-563-6625
Miss Scarlett's
Chandler, AZ. 800-345-6734
Modern Grocery Company
Macon, GA 478-745-3381
Montrose Potato Growers
Montrose, CO 970-249-5623
Mr. Dell Foods
Kearney, MO. 816-628-4644
Muir-Roberts Company
Salt Lake City, UT 801-363-5809
Murakami Produce Company
Ontario, OR. 800-421-8814
National Frozen Foods Corporation
Seattle, WA 206-322-8900

Nature Quality
San Martin, CA .408-683-2182
Ontario Produce Company
Ontario, OR 541-889-6485
Pak-Wel Produce
Vauxhall, AB .403-654-2116
Paradise Products Corporation
Roslyn, NY 800-826-1235
Peter Rabbit Farms
Coachella, CA 760-398-0151
POG
Grand Bend, ON 519-238-5704
Premier Packing Company
Bakersfield, CA 661-393-3320
R.C. McEntire & Company
Columbia, SC 803-799-3388
Rain Sweet
Salem, OR 800-363-4293
Reckitt Benckiser
Parsippany, NJ 800-333-3899
S&G Products
Nicholasville, KY 800-826-7652
Schiff Food Products
North Bergen, NJ 201-861-2503
Seald Sweet Growers & Packers
Vero Beach, FL 772-569-2244
Smith-Coulter Company
Chittenango, NY 315-687-6510
Star Fine Foods
Fresno, CA 559-498-2900
Sunfresh
Royal City, WA 509-346-9438
Superior Nutrition Corporation
Wilmington, DE 302-655-5762

SupHerb Farms
Turlock, CA 800-787-4372

CrEATe! Get ready-to-use fresh flavor with
SupHerb Farms' all-natural fresh frozen culinary
herbs, specialty vegetables, culinary herb pastes,
vegetable purees and creative blends. Complete
microbiological testing ensures food safety. We
set the standard for outstanding customer service, inspired culinary support, collaborative customer partnerships and innovative custom
products.

Swagger Foods Corporation
Vernon Hills, IL 847-913-1200
Tanimura & Antle
Salinas, CA 831-455-2255
Tony Vitrano Company
Jessup, MD 410-799-7444
Too Goo Doo Farms/Easy Tray LLC
North Charleston, SC 843-767-0196
Trappe Packing Corporation
Trappe, MD 410-476-3185
United Marketing Exchange
Delta, CO 970-874-3332
Vegetable Juices
Chicago, IL 888-776-9752
Vessey & Company
Holtville, CA .760-352-6376
Walla Walla Gardeners' Association
Walla Walla, WA 800-553-5014
Wildcat Produce
McGrew, NE .308-783-2438
William Bolthouse Farms
Bakersfield, CA 661-366-7205
William Karas & Sons
Churchville, NY 585-757-2751
Williams Creek Farms
Williams, OR .541-846-6481
Z&S Distributing
Fresno, CA 800-467-0788

Canned

Appleton Produce Company
Weiser, ID 208-414-1102
Bob Gordon & Associates
Chicago, IL 773-247-0588
Ful-Flav-R Foods
Alamo, CA 510-339-9618

G L Mezzetta
American Canyon, CA 707-648-1050
L&S Packing Company
Farmingdale, NY 800-286-6487
Mr. Dell Foods
Kearney, MO .816-628-4644
Paradise Products Corporation
Roslyn, NY 800-826-1235
Reckitt Benckiser
Parsippany, NJ 800-333-3899

Cocktail

A. Camacho
Plant City, FL 800-881-4534
Castella Imports
Hauppauge, NY 866-227-8355
Giuliano's Specialty Foods
Garden Grove, CA 714-895-9661
H&F Food Products Company
Buffalo, NY 716-876-4345

Crushed

Schiff Food Products
North Bergen, NJ 201-861-2503

Eastern Oregon dry bulb on

Tami Great Food
Monsey, NY .718-788-4200

Frozen

Appleton Produce Company
Weiser, ID 208-414-1102
Cobi Foods
Hantsport, NS 800-565-8229
Dickinson Frozen Foods
Fruitland, ID .208-452-5200
Gilroy Foods
Gilroy, CA 800-921-7502
McCain Foods
Fort Atkinson, WI 920-563-6625
Mr. Dell Foods
Kearney, MO .816-628-4644
National Frozen Foods Corporation
Seattle, WA 206-322-8900
Nature Quality
San Martin, CA 408-683-2182
POG
Grand Bend, ON 519-238-5704
Rain Sweet
Salem, OR 800-363-4293

SupHerb Farms
Turlock, CA 800-787-4372

CrEATe! Get ready-to-use fresh flavor with
SupHerb Farms' all-natural fresh frozen culinary
herbs, specialty vegetables, culinary herb pastes,
vegetable purees and creative blends. Complete
microbiological testing ensures food safety. We
set the standard for outstanding customer service, inspired culinary support, collaborative customer partnerships and innovative custom
products.

Trappe Packing Corporation
Trappe, MD 410-476-3185

Vegetable Juices
Chicago, IL 888-776-9752

Green

DiMare International
Indio, CA 760-564-3762
Peter Rabbit Farms
Coachella, CA 760-398-0151
Russo Farms
Vineland, NJ .856-692-5942

SupHerb Farms
Turlock, CA 800-787-4372

CrEATe! Get ready-to-use fresh flavor with
SupHerb Farms' all-natural fresh frozen culinary
herbs, specialty vegetables, culinary herb pastes,
vegetable purees and creative blends. Complete
microbiological testing ensures food safety. We
set the standard for outstanding customer service, inspired culinary support, collaborative customer partnerships and innovative custom
products.

Tanimura & Antle
Salinas, CA 831-455-2255
Walter P. Rawl & Sons
Pelion, SC 803-359-3645

Minced

Swagger Foods Corporation
Vernon Hills, IL 847-913-1200

Pearl & Cocktail Onions - O

Dave Kingston Produce
Idaho Falls, ID 800-888-7783
L&S Packing Company
Farmingdale, NY 800-286-6487
Les Trois Petits Cochons
New York, NY 800-537-7283
Magic Valley Growers
Wendell, ID 208-536-6693
National Frozen Foods Corporation
Seattle, WA 206-322-8900
POG
Grand Bend, ON 519-238-5704
Weiser River Packing
Weiser, ID 208-549-0200

Red

Modern Grocery Company
Macon, GA 478-745-3381

SupHerb Farms
Turlock, CA 800-787-4372

CrEATe! Get ready-to-use fresh flavor with
SupHerb Farms' all-natural fresh frozen culinary
herbs, specialty vegetables, culinary herb pastes,
vegetable purees and creative blends. Complete
microbiological testing ensures food safety. We
set the standard for outstanding customer service, inspired culinary support, collaborative customer partnerships and innovative custom
products.

Vessey & Company
Holtville, CA .760-352-6376

Spanish

SupHerb Farms
Turlock, CA 800-787-4372

CrEATe! Get ready-to-use fresh flavor with SupHerb Farms' all-natural fresh frozen culinary herbs, specialty vegetables, culinary herb pastes, vegetable purees and creative blends. Complete microbiological testing ensures food safety. We set the standard for outstanding customer service, inspired culinary support, collaborative customer partnerships and innovative custom products.

Orange

A. Duda Farm Fresh Foods
Belle Glade, FL 561-996-7621
A. Gagliano Company
Milwaukee, WI 800-272-1516
Agrexco USA
Jamaica, NY 718-481-8700
Amber Foods
Downsview, ON 416-746-2455
Ben Hill Griffin, Inc.
Frostproof, FL 863-635-2251
Cal-Harvest Marketing
Hanford, CA 559-582-4000
California Citrus Producer
Lindsay, CA 559-562-5169
Corona College Heights Orange & Lemon Associates
Riverside, CA 951-688-1811
Davidson of Dundee
Dundee, FL 800-654-0647
Dimare
Visalia, CA 559-627-0821
DiMare International
Indio, CA 760-564-3762
DNE World Fruit Sales
Fort Pierce, FL 800-327-6676
Dole Food Company
Westlake Village, CA 818-879-6600
Fillmore Piru Citrus Association
Piru, CA 800-524-8787
Gene's Citrus Ranch
Palmetto, FL 888-723-2006
Haines City Citrus Growers Association
Haines City, FL 800-422-4245
Hale Indian River Groves
Wabasso, FL 800-562-4502
Heller Brothers Packing Corporation
Winter Garden, FL 407-656-4986
Hunt Brothers Cooperative
Lake Wales, FL 863-676-9471
J. Rettenmaier
Schoolcraft, MI 877-243-4661
Karl Bissinger French Confections
St Louis, MO. 800-325-8881
Leroy Smith & Sons Inc
Vero Beach, FL 772-567-3421
Magnolia Citrus Association
Porterville, CA 559-784-4455
Orange Cove Sanger Citrus Association
Orange Cove, CA 559-626-4453
P-R Farms
Clovis, CA 559-299-0201
Paradise
Plant City, FL 800-330-8952
Premium Waters
Minneapolis, MN 800-243-1163
Reed Lang Farms
Rio Hondo, TX 956-748-2354
River One
Vero Beach, FL 800-288-6614
Seald Sweet Growers & Packers
Vero Beach, FL 772-569-2244
Sugar Cane Industry Glades Correctional Institution
Belle Glade, FL 561-829-1400
Tony Vitrano Company
Jessup, MD 410-799-7444
Unique Ingredients
Naches, WA. 509-653-1991
United Fruits Corporation
Santa Monica, CA 310-829-0261

Valley Fruit & Vegetable
McAllen, TX 956-686-8056
Yokhol Valley Packing Company
Lindsay, CA 559-562-1327
Z&S Distributing
Fresno, CA 800-467-0788

Blood

Z&S Distributing
Fresno, CA 800-467-0788

Mandarin

Agrocan
Toronto, ON 877-247-6226
Au Printemps Gourmet
Prevost, QC 800-663-0416
DNE World Fruit Sales
Fort Pierce, FL 800-327-6676
NTC Foods Corporation
Williamsville, NY 800-333-1637

Canned

NTC Foods Corporation
Williamsville, NY 800-333-1637

Naval

DNE World Fruit Sales
Fort Pierce, FL 800-327-6676
Johnston Farms
Edison, CA 661-366-3201
Magnolia Citrus Association
Porterville, CA 559-784-4455
Z&S Distributing
Fresno, CA 800-467-0788

Peels

California Citrus Pulp Company
Lindsay, CA. 626-332-1101
Fmali Herb
Santa Cruz, CA 831-423-7913

Pieces

Agriproducts
Coral Springs, FL 800-277-4979
Citrico
Northbrook, IL 888-625-8516

Sections

Canned

Del Monte Foods
San Francisco, CA 800-543-3090

EMERLING INTERNATIONAL FOODS, INC.

Emerling International Foods
Buffalo, NY. 716-833-7381

We supply food manufacturers and food service customers worldwide (since 1988) with bulk ingredients including: Fruits & Vegetables; Juice Concentrates; Herbs & Spices; Oils & Vinegars; Flavors & Colors; Honey & Molasses. We also produce PURE MAPLE SYRUP.

Valencia

Magnolia Citrus Association
Porterville, CA 559-784-4455
Z&S Distributing
Fresno, CA 800-467-0788

Oriental Vegetables

Canned

Lee's Food Products
Toronto, ON 416-465-2407
Nikken Foods Company
St Louis, MO. 636-532-1019

Papaya

Brooks Tropicals
Homestead, FL 800-327-4833
Calavo Foods
Santa Paula, CA 800-422-5280

Chieftain Wild Rice Company
Spooner, WI 800-262-6368
Del Monte Fresh Produce Company
Coral Gables, FL 800-950-3683
Fastachi
Watertown, MA. 800-466-3022
Hawaiian Solar Dried Fruit
Pahoa, HI. 808-965-8915
Natural Foods
Toledo, OH 800-860-0006
Organic Planet
San Francisco, CA 415-765-5590
Setton International Foods
Commack, NY 800-227-4397
Timber Crest Farms
Healdsburg, CA 888-374-9325
Unique Ingredients
Naches, WA. 509-653-1991

Dried

American Importing Company
Minneapolis, MN 612-331-9226

Peach

Ballantine Produce Company
Reedley, CA 559-637-2400
Ben B. Schwartz & Sons
Detroit, MI 313-841-8300
Brandt Farms
Reedley, CA 559-638-6961
Bridenbaughs Orchards
Martinsburg, PA 814-793-2364
California Fruit
Sanger, CA 559-266-7117
Capitol Foods
Memphis, TN 662-781-9021
Central California Raisin Packers
Del Rey, CA 559-888-2195
Cherry Lane Frozen Fruits
Vineland Station, ON 905-562-4337
Chieftain Wild Rice Company
Spooner, WI 800-262-6368
Chiquita Brands International
Cincinnati, OH 800-438-0015
Clofine Dairy & Food Products
Linwood, NJ 800-441-1001
Copper Hills Fruit Sales
Fresno, CA 559-277-1970
Corrin Produce Sales
Reedley, CA 559-638-3970
Del Mar Food Products Corporation
Watsonville, CA 831-722-3516
Dole Food Company
Westlake Village, CA 818-879-6600
Garden State Farms
Philadelphia, PA 215-463-8000
Giumarra Companies
Reedley, CA 559-897-5060
H. Naraghi Farms
Escalon, CA 209-577-5777
Hialeah Products Company
Hollywood, FL 800-923-3379
HMC Marketing Group
Kingsburg, CA 559-897-1009
JR Wood/Big Valley
Atwater, CA 209-358-5643
Kings Canyon Corrin
Reedley, CA 559-638-3571
Lane Packing Company
Fort Valley, GA 478-825-3592
Livingston Farmers Association
Livingston, CA 209-394-7611
Mason County Fruit Packers Cooperative
Ludington, MI. 231-845-6248
Mayfair Packing Company
San Jose, CA 408-280-2349
Miss Scarlett's
Chandler, AZ. 800-345-6734
Mountain Orchard Cooperative
Aspers, PA 800-322-6867
Natural Foods
Toledo, OH 800-860-0006
New West Foods
San Francisco, CA 701-947-2505
North Bay Produce
Traverse City, MI 231-946-1941
Nut Factory
Spokane Valley, WA 888-239-5288
Oasis Foods
Planada, CA 209-382-0263

 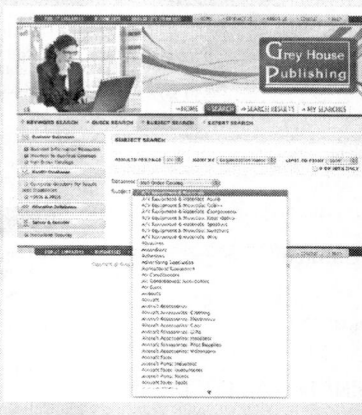

Omstead Foods Ltd
Burlington, ON 905-315-8883
Organic Planet
San Francisco, CA 415-765-5590
Overlake Foods Corporation
Olympia, WA 800-683-1078
P-R Farms
Clovis, CA 559-299-0201
Pacific Coast Producers
Oroville, CA 530-533-4311
Produce Edge
Reedley, CA 559-637-9988
Rice Fruit Company
Gardners, PA 800-627-3359
Shafer Lake Fruit
Hartford, MI 269-621-3194
Shawnee Canning Company
Cross Junction, VA 800-713-1414
Stapleton-Spence PackingCompany
San Jose, CA 800-297-8815
Sun Valley
Reedley, CA 559-591-1515
Sun-Maid Growers of California
Kingsburg, CA 800-272-4746
Sunmet
Del Rey, CA 559-445-1574
Sunsweet Growers
Yuba City, CA 800-417-2253
Symms Fruit Ranch
Caldwell, ID 208-459-4821
T.S. Smith & Sons
Bridgeville, DE 302-337-8271
Talbott Farms
Palisade, CO 970-464-5656
Taylor Orchards
Reynolds, GA 478-847-4186
Terri Lynn
Elgin, IL 800-323-0775
Those Hersey Brothers
Casnovia, MI. 800-289-2767
Timber Crest Farms
Healdsburg, CA 888-374-9325
Tom Ringhausen Orchards
Hardin, IL 618-576-2311
Trinity Fruit Sales
Clovis, CA 559-322-7100
Unique Ingredients
Naches, WA. 509-653-1991
United Fruit Growers
Palisade, CO 970-464-5671
Vintage Produce Sales
Kingsburg, CA 559-897-1622
Wawona Frozen Foods
Clovis, CA 559-299-2901
Wawona Packing Company
Cutler, C9 559-528-4000
Z&S Distributing
Fresno, CA 800-467-0788

Canned

Agrocan
Toronto, ON 877-247-6226
ConAgra Grocery Products
Irvine, CA 714-680-1000

EMERLING INTERNATIONAL FOODS, INC.

Emerling International Foods
Buffalo, NY. 716-833-7381

> We supply food manufacturers and food service customers worldwide (since 1988) with bulk ingredients including: Fruits & Vegetables; Juice Concentrates; Herbs & Spices; Oils & Vinegars; Flavors & Colors; Honey & Molasses. We also produce PURE MAPLE SYRUP.

George Noroian
Oakland, CA 510-591-7044
Oasis Foods
Planada, CA 209-382-0263
Omstead Foods Ltd
Burlington, ON 905-315-8883
Overlake Foods Corporation
Olympia, WA 800-683-1078
Pacific Coast Producers
Oroville, CA 530-533-4311
Pacific Coast Producers Corporate Office
Lodi, CA 209-367-8800
Shafer-Haggart
Vancouver, BC 888-779-7111

Shawnee Canning Company
Cross Junction, VA 800-713-1414
Stapleton-Spence PackingCompany
San Jose, CA 800-297-8815

Dried

Chieftain Wild Rice Company
Spooner, WI 800-262-6368
Fastachi
Watertown, MA. 800-466-3022

Frozen

Cherry Lane Frozen Fruits
Vineland Station, ON 905-562-4337
ConAgra Grocery Products
Irvine, CA 714-680-1000

EMERLING INTERNATIONAL FOODS, INC.

Emerling International Foods
Buffalo, NY. 716-833-7381

> We supply food manufacturers and food service customers worldwide (since 1988) with bulk ingredients including: Fruits & Vegetables; Juice Concentrates; Herbs & Spices; Oils & Vinegars; Flavors & Colors; Honey & Molasses. We also produce PURE MAPLE SYRUP.

George Noroian
Oakland, CA 510-591-7044
JR Wood/Big Valley
Atwater, CA 209-358-5643
New West Foods
San Francisco, CA 701-947-2505
Omstead Foods Ltd
Burlington, ON 905-315-8883
Overlake Foods Corporation
Olympia, WA 800-683-1078
Pacific Coast Producers Corporate Office
Lodi, CA 209-367-8800

Klingstone

Canned - Sliced & Diced

Del Monte Foods
San Francisco, CA 800-543-3090
Mountain View Fruit Sales
Reedley, CA 559-637-9933

Sliced

Producer Marketing Overlake
Olympia, WA 360-352-7989

Pear

A. Gagliano Company
Milwaukee, WI 800-272-1516
Adobe Creek Packing
Kelseyville, CA. 707-279-4204
Ben B. Schwartz & Sons
Detroit, MI 313-841-8300
Bluebird
Peshastin, WA 509-548-1700
California Fruit
Sanger, CA 559-266-7117
Chelan Fresh
Chelan, WA. 509-682-5133
Chief Tonasket Growers
Portland, OR 509-486-2914
Chief Wenatchee
Wenatchee, WA. 509-662-5197
Chieftain Wild Rice Company
Spooner, WI 800-262-6368
Chiquita Brands International
Cincinnati, OH 800-438-0015
D'Arrigo Brothers Company of California
Salinas, CA 800-995-5939
Delta Packing Company of Lodi
Lodi, CA 209-334-0689
Diamond Fruit Growers
Odell, OR 541-354-5300
Dole Food Company
Westlake Village, CA 818-879-6600
George W Saulpaugh & Sons
Germantown, NY 518-537-6500
H H Dobbins
Lyndonville, NY 877-362-2467

Hialeah Products Company
Hollywood, FL 800-923-3379
M&R Company
Lodi, CA 209-369-2725
Matson Fruit Company
Selah, WA 509-697-7100
Mayfair Packing Company
San Jose, CA 408-280-2349
Miss Scarlett's
Chandler, AZ. 800-345-6734
Mountain Orchard Cooperative
Aspers, PA. 800-322-6867
Mt. Konocti Growers
Kelseyville, CA 707-279-4213
Northern Fruit Company
Wenatchee, WA 509-884-6651
Nuchief Sales
East Wenatchee, WA. 888-269-4638
Pavero Cold Storage Corporation
Highland, NY 800-435-2994
Placerville Fruit Growers Association
Placerville, CA 530-622-2640
Reter Fruit Company
Medford, OR 541-772-5256
Rice Fruit Company
Gardners, PA 800-627-3359
Scotian Gold Cooperative
Coldbrook, NS 902-679-2191
Stadelman Fruit
Zillah, WA 509-829-5145
Sun-Maid Growers of California
Kingsburg, CA 800-272-4746
Talbott Farms
Palisade, CO 970-464-5656
Terri Lynn
Elgin, IL 800-323-0775
Timber Crest Farms
Healdsburg, CA 888-374-9325
Trinity Fruit Sales
Clovis, CA 559-322-7100
Truitt Brothers Inc
Salem, OR 800-547-8712
Unique Ingredients
Naches, WA. 509-653-1991
United Fruits Corporation
Santa Monica, CA. 310-829-0261
Yakima Fruit & Cold Storage Company
Wapato, WA 509-877-0440

Asian

Ballantine Produce Company
Reedley, CA 559-637-2400
Fowler Packing Company
Fresno, CA 559-834-5911
Naumes
Medford, OR. 541-772-6268
Price Cold Storage & Packing Company
Yakima, WA 509-966-4110

Bartlett

Adobe Creek Packing
Kelseyville, CA. 707-279-4204

Bosc

Adobe Creek Packing
Kelseyville, CA. 707-279-4204

Canned

Agrocan
Toronto, ON 877-247-6226
ConAgra Grocery Products
Irvine, CA 714-680-1000

EMERLING INTERNATIONAL FOODS, INC.

Emerling International Foods
Buffalo, NY. 716-833-7381

> We supply food manufacturers and food service customers worldwide (since 1988) with bulk ingredients including: Fruits & Vegetables; Juice Concentrates; Herbs & Spices; Oils & Vinegars; Flavors & Colors; Honey & Molasses. We also produce PURE MAPLE SYRUP.

Northwest Packing Company
Vancouver, WA 800-543-4356
Pacific Coast Producers Corporate Office
Lodi, CA 209-367-8800

Diced

Del Monte Foods
San Francisco, CA 800-543-3090

Halves

Del Monte Foods
San Francisco, CA 800-543-3090

D'Anjou/Bosc

Associated Fruit Company
Phoenix, OR 541-535-1787
Mountain Orchard Cooperative
Aspers, PA. 800-322-6867

Dried

Chieftain Wild Rice Company
Spooner, WI 800-262-6368
Fastachi
Watertown, MA. 800-466-3022

Frozen

ConAgra Grocery Products
Irvine, CA 714-680-1000

EMERLING INTERNATIONAL FOODS, INC.

Emerling International Foods
Buffalo, NY. 716-833-7381

> We supply food manufacturers and food service customers worldwide (since 1988) with bulk ingredients including: Fruits & Vegetables; Juice Concentrates; Herbs & Spices; Oils & Vinegars; Flavors & Colors; Honey & Molasses. We also produce PURE MAPLE SYRUP.

Red

Adobe Creek Packing
Kelseyville, CA. 707-279-4204

Peas

Camellia Beans
New Orleans, LA 504-733-8480
Caribbean Food Delights
Tappan, NY. 845-398-3000
Castella Imports
Hauppauge, NY 866-227-8355
Chieftain Wild Rice Company
Spooner, WI 800-262-6368
Chiquita Processed Foods
Milton Freewater, OR. 541-938-4461
Cobi Foods
Hantsport, NS 800-565-8229
Columbia Foods
Quincy, WA. 509-787-1585
Culinary Standards Corporation
Louisville, KY 800-778-3434
Del Monte Foods
Mendota, IL 815-539-9361
Faribault Foods
Minneapolis, MN 612-333-6461
Garden Valley Foods
Sutherlin, OR 541-459-9565
Hanover Foods Corporation
Hanover, PA 717-632-6000
Hong Kong Market Company
Chicago, IL 312-791-9111
Humboldt Flour Mills
Humboldt, SK 306-682-2577
International Home Foods
Milton, PA 973-359-9920
Knight Seed Company
Burnsville, MN 800-328-2999
Lakeside Foods
Plainview, MN 507-534-3141
Lakeside Foods
Seymour, WI. 920-833-2371
Lakeside Foods
New Holstein, WI. 920-898-5702
Lucks Food Decorating Company
Tacoma, WA 206-674-7200
Mezza
Lake Forest, IL 888-206-6054
Mills Brothers International
Tukwila, WA. 206-575-3000
Miramar Fruit Trading Company
Medley, FL 305-883-4774

Moscow Seed Company
Moscow, ID. 208-882-2324
National Frozen Foods Corporation
Seattle, WA 206-322-8900
New Harvest Foods
Pulaski, WI 920-822-2578
Norben Company
Willoughby, OH 888-466-7236
Omstead Foods Ltd
Burlington, ON 905-315-8883
Pictsweet Frozen Foods
Bells, TN. 731-663-7600
Pillsbury Canada Limited
Markham, ON 800-745-4777
Royal Caribbean Bakery
Mt Vernon, NY 888-818-0971
Ruskin Packaging
Miami, FL 305-324-1529
Seneca Foods
Arlington, MN 507-964-2204
Seneca Foods
Cumberland, WI 715-822-2181
Smith Frozen Foods
Weston, OR 541-566-3515
Smith Frozen Foods
Weston, OR 800-547-0203
Snowcrest Packer
Abbotsford, BC 604-859-4881
Spokane Seed Company
Spokane Valley, WA 509-535-3671
Strathroy Foods
Strathroy, ON 519-245-4600
Superior Foods
Watsonville, CA 831-728-3691
Symons Frozen Foods
Centralia, WA 360-736-1321
Talley Farms
Arroyo Grande, CA. 805-489-2508
Trappe Packing Corporation
Trappe, MD. 410-476-3185
Twin City Foods
Stanwood, WA 206-515-2400
Vege-Cool
Newman, CA. 209-862-2360
Veronica Foods Company
Oakland, CA 800-370-5554
Wallace Grain & Pea Company
Palouse, WA 509-878-1561
Woodland Foods
Gurnee, IL 847-625-8600
Z&S Distributing
Fresno, CA 800-467-0788

Black-eyed

Lucks Food Decorating Company
Tacoma, WA 206-674-7200
Pictsweet Frozen Foods
Bells, TN. 731-663-7600
Ruskin Packaging
Miami, FL 305-324-1529

Canned

EMERLING INTERNATIONAL FOODS, INC.

Emerling International Foods
Buffalo, NY. 716-833-7381

> We supply food manufacturers and food service customers worldwide (since 1988) with bulk ingredients including: Fruits & Vegetables; Juice Concentrates; Herbs & Spices; Oils & Vinegars; Flavors & Colors; Honey & Molasses. We also produce PURE MAPLE SYRUP.

Lucks Food Decorating Company
Tacoma, WA 206-674-7200

Frozen

EMERLING INTERNATIONAL FOODS, INC.

Emerling International Foods
Buffalo, NY. 716-833-7381

> We supply food manufacturers and food service customers worldwide (since 1988) with bulk ingredients including: Fruits & Vegetables; Juice Concentrates; Herbs & Spices; Oils & Vinegars; Flavors & Colors; Honey & Molasses. We also produce PURE MAPLE SYRUP.

Pictsweet Frozen Foods
Bells, TN. 731-663-7600

Canned

Blue Runner Foods
Gonzales, LA 225-647-3016
Carriere Foods Inc
Montreal, QC 514-384-4281
Chiquita Processed Foods
Milton Freewater, OR. 541-938-4461

EMERLING INTERNATIONAL FOODS, INC.

Emerling International Foods
Buffalo, NY. 716-833-7381

> We supply food manufacturers and food service customers worldwide (since 1988) with bulk ingredients including: Fruits & Vegetables; Juice Concentrates; Herbs & Spices; Oils & Vinegars; Flavors & Colors; Honey & Molasses. We also produce PURE MAPLE SYRUP.

Faribault Foods
Minneapolis, MN 612-333-6461
Hanover Foods Corporation
Hanover, PA 717-632-6000
International Home Foods
Milton, PA. 973-359-9920
Lakeside Foods
Plainview, MN 507-534-3141
Lakeside Foods
Manitowoc, WI 920-684-3356
Lakeside Foods
Seymour, WI. 920-833-2371
Lakeside Foods
New Holstein, WI. 920-898-5702
Lodi Canning Company
Lodi, WI 608-592-4236
Lucks Food Decorating Company
Tacoma, WA 206-674-7200
New Harvest Foods
Pulaski, WI 920-822-2578
Seneca Foods
Buhl, ID. 208-543-9350
Seneca Foods
Marion, NY 315-926-4280
Seneca Foods
Montgomery, MN 507-364-8641
Seneca Foods
Blue Earth, MN 507-526-2131
Seneca Foods
Janesville, WI 608-757-6000
Seneca Foods
Cumberland, WI 715-822-2181
Seneca Foods Corporation
Marion, NY. 315-926-8100

Dry

Camellia Beans
New Orleans, LA 504-733-8480
Just Tomatoes Company
Westley, CA. 800-537-1985
Mills Brothers International
Tukwila, WA. 206-575-3000
Moscow Seed Company
Moscow, ID. 208-882-2324
Spokane Seed Company
Spokane Valley, WA 509-535-3671

Fresh

Lakeside Foods
Seymour, WI. 920-833-2371

Frozen

Cavendish Farms
Burlington, MA . . . . 888-88 -7437
Cobi Foods
Hantsport, NS 800-565-8229
Columbia Foods
Quincy, WA. 509-787-1585

EMERLING INTERNATIONAL FOODS, INC.

Emerling International Foods
Buffalo, NY...........................716-833-7381

> We supply food manufacturers and food service customers worldwide (since 1988) with bulk ingredients including: Fruits & Vegetables; Juice Concentrates; Herbs & Spices; Oils & Vinegars; Flavors & Colors; Honey & Molasses. We also produce PURE MAPLE SYRUP.

Faribault Foods
Minneapolis, MN.................612-333-6461
Hanover Foods Corporation
Hanover, PA.....................717-632-6000
J.R. Simplot Company
Boise, ID.......................208-336-2110
Lakeside Foods
Plainview, MN...................507-534-3141
Lakeside Foods
Manitowoc, WI..................920-684-3356
Lakeside Foods
Seymour, WI....................920-833-2371
Lodi Canning Company
Lodi, WI.......................608-592-4236
Lucerne Foods
Abbotsford, BC.................604-854-1191
National Frozen Foods Corporation
Seattle, WA....................206-322-8900
Omstead Foods Ltd
Burlington, ON.................905-315-8883
Pictsweet Frozen Foods
Bells, TN......................731-663-7600
Seneca Foods
Marion, NY.....................315-926-4280
Seneca Foods
Montgomery, MN.................507-364-8641
Smith Frozen Foods
Weston, OR.....................541-566-3515
Smith Frozen Foods
Weston, OR.....................800-547-0203
Snowcrest Packer
Abbotsford, BC.................604-859-4881
Strathroy Foods
Strathroy, ON..................519-245-4600
Symons Frozen Foods
Centralia, WA..................360-736-1321
Trappe Packing Corporation
Trappe, MD.....................410-476-3185
Twin City Foods
Stanwood, WA...................206-515-2400

Green

Fastachi
Watertown, MA..................800-466-3022
Knight Seed Company
Burnsville, MN.................800-328-2999
Moscow Seed Company
Moscow, ID.....................208-882-2324
Pictsweet Frozen Foods
Bells, TN......................731-663-7600
Ruskin Packaging
Miami, FL......................305-324-1529
Sno Pac Foods
Caledonia, MN..................800-533-2215

Green & Yellow Split - Dried

American Health & Nutrition
Ann Arbor, MI..................734-677-5572
Chieftain Wild Rice Company
Spooner, WI....................800-262-6368
Country Cupboard
Virginia City, NV..............775-847-7300

EMERLING INTERNATIONAL FOODS, INC.

Emerling International Foods
Buffalo, NY...........................716-833-7381

> We supply food manufacturers and food service customers worldwide (since 1988) with bulk ingredients including: Fruits & Vegetables; Juice Concentrates; Herbs & Spices; Oils & Vinegars; Flavors & Colors; Honey & Molasses. We also produce PURE MAPLE SYRUP.

Organic Planet
San Francisco, CA..............415-765-5590
Spokane Seed Company
Spokane Valley, WA.............509-535-3671

Unique Ingredients
Naches, WA.....................509-653-1991
Vege-Cool
Newman, CA.....................209-862-2360

Snap

Miss Scarlett's
Chandler, AZ...................800-345-6734
National Frozen Foods Corporation
Seattle, WA....................206-322-8900
Pictsweet Frozen Foods
Bells, TN......................731-663-7600
Superior Foods
Watsonville, CA................831-728-3691

Southern

Naturex (Chart Corp)
South Hackensack, NJ...........201-440-5000
Trinidad Benham Company
Denver, CO.....................303-220-1400

Yellow Split

Knight Seed Company
Burnsville, MN.................800-328-2999
Moscow Seed Company
Moscow, ID.....................208-882-2324
United Pulse Trading
Bismarck, ND...................701-751-1623
Woodland Foods
Gurnee, IL.....................847-625-8600

Peppers

AgroCepia
Miami, FL......................305-704-3488
Anchor Food Products/ McCain Foods
Appleton, WI...................920-734-0627
Atlantic Quality Spice &Seasonings
Edison, NJ.....................800-584-0422
B&G Foods
Parsippany, NJ.................973-401-6500
Baumer Foods
New Orleans, LA................504-482-5761
Bifulco Farms
Pittsgrove, NJ.................856-692-0707
Big B Distributors
Evansville, IN.................812-425-5235
Bloch & Guggenheimer
Hurlock, MD....................800-541-2809
Bob Gordon & Associates
Chicago, IL....................773-247-0588
Border Foods Inc
Deming, NM.....................888-737-7752
Carando Gourmet Frozen Foods
Springfield, MA................413-730-4205
Cherchies
Malvern, PA....................800-644-1980
Chieftain Wild Rice Company
Spooner, WI....................800-262-6368
Christopher Ranch
Gilroy, CA.....................408-847-1100
Chugwater Chili Corporation
Chugwater, WY..................800-972-4454
Cleugh's Frozen Foods
Buena Park, CA.................714-521-1002
Cobi Foods
Hantsport, NS..................800-565-8229
Comanche Tortilla Factory
Fort Stockton, TX..............432-336-3245
Del Mar Food Products Corporation
Watsonville, CA................831-722-3516
Delta Packing Company of Lodi
Lodi, CA.......................209-334-0689
Dickinson Frozen Foods
Fruitland, ID..................208-452-5200
Dolce Nonna
Whitestone, NY.................718-767-3501
Dole Food Company
Westlake Village, CA...........818-879-6600
Dunbar Foods
Dunn, NC.......................910-892-3175
Eckert Cold Storage
Escalon, CA....................209-838-4040

EMERLING INTERNATIONAL FOODS, INC.

Emerling International Foods
Buffalo, NY...........................716-833-7381

> We supply food manufacturers and food service customers worldwide (since 1988) with bulk ingredients including: Fruits & Vegetables; Juice Concentrates; Herbs & Spices; Oils & Vinegars; Flavors & Colors; Honey & Molasses. We also produce PURE MAPLE SYRUP.

F&S Produce Company
Rosenhayn, NJ..................800-886-3316
Fiesta Canning Company
Mc Neal, AZ....................520-364-7541
Food City Pickle Company
Chicago, IL....................269-781-9135
Fountain Valley Foods
Colorado Springs, CO...........719-573-6012
Frog Ranch Foods
Glouster, OH...................800-742-2488
Ful-Flav-R Foods
Alamo, CA......................510-339-9618
G L Mezzetta
American Canyon, CA............707-648-1050
Garon Industries
Mosinee, WI....................715-693-1593
George Chiala Farms
Morgan Hill, CA................408-778-0562
Georgia Vegetable Company
Tifton, GA.....................229-386-2374
Gilroy Foods
Gilroy, CA.....................800-921-7502
Giuliano's Specialty Foods
Garden Grove, CA...............714-895-9661
GNS Spices
Walnut, CA.....................800-870-6657
Goebbert's Home Grown Vegetables
South Barrington, IL...........847-428-6727
Great American Appetizers
Nampa, ID......................800-282-4834
Greek Gourmet Limited
Mill Valley, CA................415-480-8050
GWB Foods Corporation
Brooklyn, NY...................718-686-9600
Haliburton International Corporation
Fontana, CA....................877-980-4295
Harris Farms
Coalinga, CA...................800-742-1955
Heinz
Holland, MI....................800-528-5757
Heinz North America
Pittsburgh, PA.................412-237-5700
Hermann Pickle Farm
Garrettsville, OH..............800-245-2696
Indel Food Products
El Paso, TX....................800-472-0159
Ingredients Corporation of America
Memphis, TN....................901-525-6660
Jalapeno Foods Company
The Woodlands, TX..............800-896-2318
JES Foods
Cleveland, OH..................216-883-8987
Johnston Farms
Edison, CA.....................661-366-3201
Kaiser Foods
Cincinnati, OH.................888-291-0608
Kaplan & Zubrin
Camden, NJ.....................800-334-0002
Kelly Pickle Company
Oconto, WI.....................920-834-4433
L&S Packing Company
Farmingdale, NY................800-286-6487
Lakeside Packing Company
Harrow, ON.....................519-738-2314
Landry's Pepper Company
St Martinville, LA.............337-394-6097
Mama Lil's Peppers
Seattle, WA....................206-322-8824
Matador Processors
Blanchard, OK..................800-847-0797
McCain Foods
Fort Atkinson, WI..............920-563-6625
Mercado Latino
City of Industry, CA...........626-333-6862
Michigan Freeze Pack
Hart, MI.......................231-873-2175
Miguel's Stowe Away
Stowe, VT......................800-448-6517
Mojave Foods Corporation
Commerce, CA...................323-890-8900

Monticello Canning Company
Crossville, TN 931-484-3696
Moody Dunbar
Johnson City, TN 800-251-8202
Mount Olive Pickle Company
Mt Olive, NC 800-672-5041
Mr. Dell Foods
Kearney, MO. 816-628-4644
Nature Quality
San Martin, CA. 408-683-2182
Naturex (Chart Corp)
South Hackensack, NJ 201-440-5000
Norpaco
New Britain, CT 800-252-0222
Omstead Foods Ltd
Burlington, ON 905-315-8883
Pacific Choice Brands
Fresno, CA 559-237-5583
Paisley Farms
Willoughby, OH 800-676-8656
Pastene Companies
Canton, MA 781-830-8200
Pastorelli Food Products
Chicago, IL 800-767-2829
Pepper Creek Farms
Lawton, OK. 800-526-8132
Pure Food Ingredients
Verona, WI 800-355-9601
Ralph Sechler & Son Inc
St Joe, IN. 800-332-5461
Rene Produce Distributors
Nogales, AZ 520-281-9014
RES Food Products International
Green Bay, WI. 800-255-3768
Ripon Pickle Company
Ripon, WI 800-324-5493
Ron-Son Foods
Swedesboro, NJ 856-241-7333
S&G Products
Nicholasville, KY 800-826-7652
Saticoy Foods Corporation
Ventura, CA. 805-647-5266
Scally's Imperial Importing Company Inc
Staten Island, NY 718-983-1938
Schiff Food Products
North Bergen, NJ 201-861-2503
Sedlock Farm
Lynn Center, IL. 309-521-8284
Snowcrest Packer
Abbotsford, BC. 604-859-4881
South Mill Distribution
Kennett Square, PA. 610-444-4800
Star Fine Foods
Fresno, CA 559-498-2900
Strub Pickles
Brantford, ON. 519-751-1717

SupHerb Farms
Turlock, CA 800-787-4372

CrEATe! Get ready-to-use fresh flavor with
SupHerb Farms' all-natural fresh frozen culinary
herbs, specialty vegetables, culinary herb pastes,
vegetable purees and creative blends. Complete
microbiological testing ensures food safety. We
set the standard for outstanding customer service, inspired culinary support, collaborative customer partnerships and innovative custom
products.

Too Goo Doo Farms/Easy Tray LLC
North Charleston, SC 843-767-0196
Topor's Pickle Company
Detroit, MI 313-237-0288
Trappe Packing Corporation
Trappe, MD. 410-476-3185
Tropical
Charlotte, NC 800-220-1413
US Fresh Marketing
Virginia Beach, VA. 757-481-2606
Van Drunen Farms
Momence, IL. 815-472-3100
Vega Food Industries
Cranston, RI 800-973-7737
Vegetable Juices
Chicago, IL 888-776-9752

Victoria Packing Corporation
Brooklyn, NY 718-649-2180
Vincent Formusa Company
Chicago, IL 312-421-0485
Violet Packing
Williamstown, NJ 856-629-7428
Whyte's Food Corporation
Mississauga, ON 905-624-5065
Willy's Pickle Products
Holland Landing, ON 905-836-6532
Woodland Foods
Gurnee, IL. 847-625-8600
Z&S Distributing
Fresno, CA 800-467-0788

Ancho

Chieftain Wild Rice Company
Spooner, WI 800-262-6368

Banana

A. Camacho
Plant City, FL 800-881-4534
Food City Pickle Company
Chicago, IL 269-781-9135
G L Mezzetta
American Canyon, CA 707-648-1050
Giuliano's Specialty Foods
Garden Grove, CA 714-895-9661
Indel Food Products
El Paso, TX. 800-472-0159
Kaplan & Zubrin
Camden, NJ. 800-334-0002
Topor's Pickle Company
Detroit, MI 313-237-0288

Bell

Chieftain Wild Rice Company
Spooner, WI 800-262-6368
Christopher Ranch
Gilroy, CA. 408-847-1100
Cleugh's Frozen Foods
Buena Park, CA 714-521-1002
Culinary Standards Corporation
Louisville, KY 800-778-3434
Dehydrates Inc
Hewlett, NY 800-983-4443
Dickinson Frozen Foods
Fruitland, ID 208-452-5200
Eckert Cold Storage
Escalon, CA 209-838-4040
F&S Produce Company
Rosenhayn, NJ 800-886-3316
Ful-Flav-R Foods
Alamo, CA 510-339-9618
Gel Spice Company, Inc
Bayonne, NJ 800-922-0230
George Chiala Farms
Morgan Hill, CA. 408-778-0562
Grasso Foods
Woolwich Township, NJ. 856-467-2222
Kern Ridge Growers
Arvin, CA. 661-854-3141
M&R Company
Lodi, CA 209-369-2725
Moody Dunbar
Johnson City, TN 800-251-8202
Nature Quality
San Martin, CA. 408-683-2182
Oxford Frozen Foods Limited
Oxford, NS 902-447-2100
Rene Produce Distributors
Nogales, AZ 520-281-9014
Ripon Pickle Company
Ripon, WI 800-324-5493
Saticoy Foods Corporation
Ventura, CA. 805-647-5266
Schiff Food Products
North Bergen, NJ 201-861-2503

SupHerb Farms
Turlock, CA 800-787-4372

CrEATe! Get ready-to-use fresh flavor with
SupHerb Farms' all-natural fresh frozen culinary
herbs, specialty vegetables, culinary herb pastes,
vegetable purees and creative blends. Complete
microbiological testing ensures food safety. We
set the standard for outstanding customer service, inspired culinary support, collaborative customer partnerships and innovative custom
products.

Sure Fresh Produce
Santa Maria, CA 888-423-5379
Talley Farms
Arroyo Grande, CA 805-489-2508
Tropical
Charlotte, NC 800-220-1413
Vegetable Juices
Chicago, IL 888-776-9752
Z&S Distributing
Fresno, CA 800-467-0788

Canned

Bob Gordon & Associates
Chicago, IL 773-247-0588
Colonna Brothers
North Bergen, NJ 201-864-1115

EMERLING INTERNATIONAL FOODS, INC.

Emerling International Foods
Buffalo, NY. 716-833-7381

We supply food manufacturers and food service
customers worldwide (since 1988) with bulk ingredients including: Fruits & Vegetables; Juice
Concentrates; Herbs & Spices; Oils & Vinegars;
Flavors & Colors; Honey & Molasses. We also
produce PURE MAPLE SYRUP.

Ful-Flav-R Foods
Alamo, CA 510-339-9618
L&S Packing Company
Farmingdale, NY 800-286-6487
Mancini Packing Company
Zolfo Springs, FL 863-735-2000
Moody Dunbar
Johnson City, TN 800-251-8202
Ron-Son Foods
Swedesboro, NJ 856-241-7333
Van Drunen Farms
Momence, IL. 815-472-3100
Violet Packing
Williamstown, NJ 856-629-7428

Capsicums

Advanced Spice & Trading
Carrollton, TX. 800-872-7811

EMERLING INTERNATIONAL FOODS, INC.

Emerling International Foods
Buffalo, NY. 716-833-7381

We supply food manufacturers and food service
customers worldwide (since 1988) with bulk ingredients including: Fruits & Vegetables; Juice
Concentrates; Herbs & Spices; Oils & Vinegars;
Flavors & Colors; Honey & Molasses. We also
produce PURE MAPLE SYRUP.

Gilroy Foods
Gilroy, CA. 800-921-7502
Vegetable Juices
Chicago, IL 888-776-9752

Aseptic Packed

Allen Canning Company
Siloam Springs, AR 800-234-2553

Dehydrated

Gilroy Foods
Gilroy, CA 800-921-7502
Naturex (Chart Corp)
South Hackensack, NJ 201-440-5000

Frozen

SupHerb Farms
Turlock, CA 800-787-4372

CrEATe! Get ready-to-use fresh flavor with SupHerb Farms' all-natural fresh frozen culinary herbs, specialty vegetables, culinary herb pastes, vegetable purees and creative blends. Complete microbiological testing ensures food safety. We set the standard for outstanding customer service, inspired culinary support, collaborative customer partnerships and innovative custom products.

Cascabel

Chieftain Wild Rice Company
Spooner, WI 800-262-6368

Cherry

A. Camacho
Plant City, FL 800-881-4534
B&G Foods
Parsippany, NJ 973-401-6500
F&S Produce Company
Rosenhayn, NJ 800-886-3316
Giuliano's Specialty Foods
Garden Grove, CA 714-895-9661
Kaplan & Zubrin
Camden, NJ 800-334-0002
L&S Packing Company
Farmingdale, NY 800-286-6487
Norpaco
New Britain, CT 800-252-0222

Chile

American Key Food Products
Closter, NJ 800-767-0237
Border Foods Inc
Deming, NM 888-737-7752
Chieftain Wild Rice Company
Spooner, WI 800-262-6368
Chile Today - Hot Tamale
San Francisco, CA 800-758-0372
Chili Dude
Richardson, TX 972-907-0998
Chugwater Chili Corporation
Chugwater, WY 800-972-4454

EMERLING INTERNATIONAL FOODS, INC.

Emerling International Foods
Buffalo, NY 716-833-7381

We supply food manufacturers and food service customers worldwide (since 1988) with bulk ingredients including: Fruits & Vegetables; Juice Concentrates; Herbs & Spices; Oils & Vinegars; Flavors & Colors; Honey & Molasses. We also produce PURE MAPLE SYRUP.

Fiesta Canning Company
Mc Neal, AZ 520-364-7541
Ful-Flav-R Foods
Alamo, CA 510-339-9618
G L Mezzetta
American Canyon, CA 707-648-1050
George Chiala Farms
Morgan Hill, CA 408-778-0562
Giuliano's Specialty Foods
Garden Grove, CA 714-895-9661
Indel Food Products
El Paso, TX 800-472-0159
Magic Seasoning Blends
Harahan, LA 800-457-2857

Mancini Packing Company
Zolfo Springs, FL 863-735-2000
Mercado Latino
City of Industry, CA 626-333-6862
Pepperland Farms
Denham Springs, LA 225-665-3555
Pure Food Ingredients
Verona, WI 800-355-9601

SupHerb Farms
Turlock, CA 800-787-4372

CrEATe! Get ready-to-use fresh flavor with SupHerb Farms' all-natural fresh frozen culinary herbs, specialty vegetables, culinary herb pastes, vegetable purees and creative blends. Complete microbiological testing ensures food safety. We set the standard for outstanding customer service, inspired culinary support, collaborative customer partnerships and innovative custom products.

Tropical Commodities
Miami, FL 305-471-9825
Vega Food Industries
Cranston, RI 800-973-7737
Vegetable Juices
Chicago, IL 888-776-9752
Walker Foods
Los Angeles, CA 800-966-5199
Z&S Distributing
Fresno, CA 800-467-0788

Dried Pods

American Key Food Products
Closter, NJ 800-767-0237

EMERLING INTERNATIONAL FOODS, INC.

Emerling International Foods
Buffalo, NY 716-833-7381

We supply food manufacturers and food service customers worldwide (since 1988) with bulk ingredients including: Fruits & Vegetables; Juice Concentrates; Herbs & Spices; Oils & Vinegars; Flavors & Colors; Honey & Molasses. We also produce PURE MAPLE SYRUP.

Gel Spice Company, Inc
Bayonne, NJ 800-922-0230
Gilroy Foods
Gilroy, CA 800-921-7502
Magic Seasoning Blends
Harahan, LA 800-457-2857
Mojave Foods Corporation
Commerce, CA 323-890-8900

Chipotle

Chieftain Wild Rice Company
Spooner, WI 800-262-6368

EMERLING INTERNATIONAL FOODS, INC.

Emerling International Foods
Buffalo, NY 716-833-7381

We supply food manufacturers and food service customers worldwide (since 1988) with bulk ingredients including: Fruits & Vegetables; Juice Concentrates; Herbs & Spices; Oils & Vinegars; Flavors & Colors; Honey & Molasses. We also produce PURE MAPLE SYRUP.

Jalapeno Foods Company
The Woodlands, TX 800-896-2318
Magic Seasoning Blends
Harahan, LA 800-457-2857
Ripon Pickle Company
Ripon, WI 800-324-5493
Vegetable Juices
Chicago, IL 888-776-9752
Woodland Foods
Gurnee, IL 847-625-8600

De Arbol

Chieftain Wild Rice Company
Spooner, WI 800-262-6368

Frozen

Anchor Food Products/ McCain Foods
Appleton, WI 920-734-0627
Carando Gourmet Frozen Foods
Springfield, MA 413-730-4205
Cleugh's Frozen Foods
Buena Park, CA 714-521-1002
Cobi Foods
Hantsport, NS 800-565-8229
Dickinson Frozen Foods
Fruitland, ID 208-452-5200
Eckert Cold Storage
Escalon, CA 209-838-4040

EMERLING INTERNATIONAL FOODS, INC.

Emerling International Foods
Buffalo, NY 716-833-7381

We supply food manufacturers and food service customers worldwide (since 1988) with bulk ingredients including: Fruits & Vegetables; Juice Concentrates; Herbs & Spices; Oils & Vinegars; Flavors & Colors; Honey & Molasses. We also produce PURE MAPLE SYRUP.

Great American Appetizers
Nampa, ID 800-282-4834
Hermann Pickle Farm
Garrettsville, OH 800-245-2696
Matador Processors
Blanchard, OK 800-847-0797
McCain Foods
Fort Atkinson, WI 920-563-6625
Monticello Canning Company
Crossville, TN 931-484-3696
Mr. Dell Foods
Kearney, MO 816-628-4644
Omstead Foods Ltd
Burlington, ON 905-315-8883
Rain Sweet
Salem, OR 800-363-4293
Snowcrest Packer
Abbotsford, BC 604-859-4881

SupHerb Farms
Turlock, CA 800-787-4372

CrEATe! Get ready-to-use fresh flavor with SupHerb Farms' all-natural fresh frozen culinary herbs, specialty vegetables, culinary herb pastes, vegetable purees and creative blends. Complete microbiological testing ensures food safety. We set the standard for outstanding customer service, inspired culinary support, collaborative customer partnerships and innovative custom products.

Trappe Packing Corporation
Trappe, MD 410-476-3185
Van De Walle Farms
San Antonio, TX 210-436-5551
Van Drunen Farms
Momence, IL 815-472-3100
Vegetable Juices
Chicago, IL 888-776-9752

Guajillo

Chieftain Wild Rice Company
Spooner, WI 800-262-6368

Habanero

Brooks Tropicals
Homestead, FL 800-327-4833
Chieftain Wild Rice Company
Spooner, WI 800-262-6368
Garon Industries
Mosinee, WI 715-693-1593

George Chiala Farms
Morgan Hill, CA 408-778-0562
Indel Food Products
El Paso, TX .800-472-0159
Woodland Foods
Gurnee, IL 847-625-8600

Jalapeno

A. Camacho
Plant City, FL 800-881-4534
Advanced Spice & Trading
Carrollton, TX 800-872-7811
AgroCepia
Miami, FL 305-704-3488
Anchor Food Products/ McCain Foods
Appleton, WI 920-734-0627
Border Foods Inc
Farmers Branch, TX 888-737-7752
Chieftain Wild Rice Company
Spooner, WI 800-262-6368
Dehydrates Inc
Hewlett, NY 800-983-4443
Eckert Cold Storage
Escalon, CA 209-838-4040

EMERLING INTERNATIONAL FOODS, INC.

Emerling International Foods
Buffalo, NY .716-833-7381

We supply food manufacturers and food service customers worldwide (since 1988) with bulk ingredients including: Fruits & Vegetables; Juice Concentrates; Herbs & Spices; Oils & Vinegars; Flavors & Colors; Honey & Molasses. We also produce PURE MAPLE SYRUP.

F&S Produce Company
Rosenhayn, NJ 800-886-3316
Fountain Valley Foods
Colorado Springs, CO 719-573-6012
Ful-Flav-R Foods
Alamo, CA .510-339-9618
G L Mezzetta
American Canyon, CA 707-648-1050
Garon Industries
Mosinee, WI 715-693-1593
George Chiala Farms
Morgan Hill, CA 408-778-0562
Gilroy Foods
Gilroy, CA. .800-921-7502
Giuliano's Specialty Foods
Garden Grove, CA 714-895-9661
Great American Appetizers
Nampa, ID. .800-282-4834
Ingredients Corporation of America
Memphis, TN 901-525-6660
Jalapeno Foods Company
The Woodlands, TX 800-896-2318
L&S Packing Company
Farmingdale, NY 800-286-6487
Leon's Texas Cuisine
McKinney, TX 972-529-2244
Limited Edition
Midland, TX 432-686-2008
Matador Processors
Blanchard, OK 800-847-0797
Miguel's Stowe Away
Stowe, VT .800-448-6517
Nature Quality
San Martin, CA 408-683-2182
Pepper Creek Farms
Lawton, OK. 800-526-8132
Pure Food Ingredients
Verona, WI .800-355-9601
RES Food Products International
Green Bay, WI. 800-255-3768
Strub Pickles
Brantford, ON 519-751-1717

SupHerb Farms
Turlock, CA 800-787-4372

CrEATe! Get ready-to-use fresh flavor with SupHerb Farms' all-natural fresh frozen culinary herbs, specialty vegetables, culinary herb pastes, vegetable purees and creative blends. Complete microbiological testing ensures food safety. We set the standard for outstanding customer service, inspired culinary support, collaborative customer partnerships and innovative custom products.

Van De Walle Farms
San Antonio, TX 210-436-5551
Van Drunen Farms
Momence, IL. 815-472-3100
Vegetable Juices
Chicago, IL .888-776-9752
Vilore Foods Company
Laredo, TX .956-726-3633
Walker Foods
Los Angeles, CA 800-966-5199

Jalapeno & Chiles

Gilroy Foods
Gilroy, CA. .800-921-7502
La Victoria Foods
Rosemead, CA 800-423-4450
Matador Processors
Blanchard, OK 800-847-0797
Nature Quality
San Martin, CA 408-683-2182
Pure Food Ingredients
Verona, WI .800-355-9601

SupHerb Farms
Turlock, CA 800-787-4372

CrEATe! Get ready-to-use fresh flavor with SupHerb Farms' all-natural fresh frozen culinary herbs, specialty vegetables, culinary herb pastes, vegetable purees and creative blends. Complete microbiological testing ensures food safety. We set the standard for outstanding customer service, inspired culinary support, collaborative customer partnerships and innovative custom products.

Woodland Foods
Gurnee, IL. .847-625-8600

Japones

Chieftain Wild Rice Company
Spooner, WI 800-262-6368

Mulato

Chieftain Wild Rice Company
Spooner, WI 800-262-6368

Pepperoncini

A. Camacho
Plant City, FL 800-881-4534
Agrocan
Toronto, ON 877-247-6226
Baumer Foods
New Orleans, LA 504-482-5761
Big B Distributors
Evansville, IN 812-425-5235
Bob Gordon & Associates
Chicago, IL .773-247-0588
Cains Foods/Olde Cape Cod
Ayer, MA. 800-225-0601
Castella Imports
Hauppauge, NY 866-227-8355

EMERLING INTERNATIONAL FOODS, INC.

Emerling International Foods
Buffalo, NY. 716-833-7381

We supply food manufacturers and food service customers worldwide (since 1988) with bulk ingredients including: Fruits & Vegetables; Juice Concentrates; Herbs & Spices; Oils & Vinegars; Flavors & Colors; Honey & Molasses. We also produce PURE MAPLE SYRUP.

Food City Pickle Company
Chicago, IL .269-781-9135
G L Mezzetta
American Canyon, CA 707-648-1050
Giuliano's Specialty Foods
Garden Grove, CA 714-895-9661
H&F Food Products Company
Buffalo, NY. 716-876-4345
L&S Packing Company
Farmingdale, NY 800-286-6487
Ron-Son Foods
Swedesboro, NJ 856-241-7333
Vegetable Juices
Chicago, IL .888-776-9752

Roasted

Agrocan
Toronto, ON 877-247-6226
Bloch & Guggenheimer
Hurlock, MD. 800-541-2809
Castella Imports
Hauppauge, NY 866-227-8355
Ful-Flav-R Foods
Alamo, CA .510-339-9618
Indel Food Products
El Paso, TX. 800-472-0159
Mancini Packing Company
Zolfo Springs, FL 863-735-2000
Moody Dunbar
Johnson City, TN 800-251-8202
Ron-Son Foods
Swedesboro, NJ 856-241-7333

SupHerb Farms
Turlock, CA 800-787-4372

CrEATe! Get ready-to-use fresh flavor with SupHerb Farms' all-natural fresh frozen culinary herbs, specialty vegetables, culinary herb pastes, vegetable purees and creative blends. Complete microbiological testing ensures food safety. We set the standard for outstanding customer service, inspired culinary support, collaborative customer partnerships and innovative custom products.

Serrano

Chieftain Wild Rice Company
Spooner, WI 800-262-6368

EMERLING INTERNATIONAL FOODS, INC.

Emerling International Foods
Buffalo, NY. 716-833-7381

We supply food manufacturers and food service customers worldwide (since 1988) with bulk ingredients including: Fruits & Vegetables; Juice Concentrates; Herbs & Spices; Oils & Vinegars; Flavors & Colors; Honey & Molasses. We also produce PURE MAPLE SYRUP.

F&S Produce Company
Rosenhayn, NJ 800-886-3316
Jalapeno Foods Company
The Woodlands, TX 800-896-2318
RES Food Products International
Green Bay, WI. 800-255-3768

SupHerb Farms
Turlock, CA 800-787-4372

CrEATe! Get ready-to-use fresh flavor with SupHerb Farms' all-natural fresh frozen culinary herbs, specialty vegetables, culinary herb pastes, vegetable purees and creative blends. Complete microbiological testing ensures food safety. We set the standard for outstanding customer service, inspired culinary support, collaborative customer partnerships and innovative custom products.

Van De Walle Farms
San Antonio, TX 210-436-5551

Sweet

Carando Gourmet Frozen Foods
Springfield, MA 413-730-4205
Coutts Specialty Foods
Boxborough, MA 800-919-2952
Georgia Vegetable Company
Tifton, GA 229-386-2374
Kaplan & Zubrin
Camden, NJ 800-334-0002
Mancini Packing Company
Zolfo Springs, FL 863-735-2000
Moody Dunbar
Johnson City, TN 800-251-8202
Ripon Pickle Company
Ripon, WI 800-324-5493
Willy's Pickle Products
Holland Landing, ON 905-836-6532

Persimmons

Ballantine Produce Company
Reedley, CA 559-637-2400
Copper Hills Fruit Sales
Fresno, CA 559-277-1970

EMERLING INTERNATIONAL FOODS, INC.

Emerling International Foods
Buffalo, NY 716-833-7381

We supply food manufacturers and food service customers worldwide (since 1988) with bulk ingredients including: Fruits & Vegetables; Juice Concentrates; Herbs & Spices; Oils & Vinegars; Flavors & Colors; Honey & Molasses. We also produce PURE MAPLE SYRUP.

HMC Marketing Group
Kingsburg, CA 559-897-1009
Just Tomatoes Company
Westley, CA 800-537-1985
Naumes
Medford, OR 541-772-6268
Produce Edge
Reedley, CA 559-637-9988
Tufts Ranch
Winters, CA 530-795-4144
West Pak Avocado
Temecula, CA 800-266-4414

Pimientos

EMERLING INTERNATIONAL FOODS, INC.

Emerling International Foods
Buffalo, NY 716-833-7381

We supply food manufacturers and food service customers worldwide (since 1988) with bulk ingredients including: Fruits & Vegetables; Juice Concentrates; Herbs & Spices; Oils & Vinegars; Flavors & Colors; Honey & Molasses. We also produce PURE MAPLE SYRUP.

Indel Food Products
El Paso, TX 800-472-0159
Monticello Canning Company
Crossville, TN 931-484-3696

Moody Dunbar
Johnson City, TN 800-251-8202
Paradise Products Corporation
Roslyn, NY 800-826-1235
Pastene Companies
Canton, MA 781-830-8200
Saticoy Foods Corporation
Ventura, CA 805-647-5266
Strub Pickles
Brantford, ON 519-751-1717
Victoria Packing Corporation
Brooklyn, NY 718-649-2180

Pineapple

Amber Foods
Downsview, ON 416-746-2455
Chieftain Wild Rice Company
Spooner, WI 800-262-6368
Chiquita Brands International
Cincinnati, OH 800-438-0015
Custom Cuts
Milwaukee, WI 414-483-0491
Del Monte Fresh Produce Company
Coral Gables, FL 800-950-3683
F&S Produce Company
Rosenhayn, NJ 800-886-3316
Fastachi
Watertown, MA 800-466-3022
Hawaiian Solar Dried Fruit
Pahoa, HI 808-965-8915
Hialeah Products Company
Hollywood, FL 800-923-3379
J.H. Verbridge & Son
Williamson, NY 315-589-2366
Maui Pineapple Company
Kahului, HI 808-877-3351
Maui Pineapple Company
Concord, CA 925-798-0240
NTC Foods Corporation
Williamsville, NY 800-333-1637
Nut Factory
Spokane Valley, WA 888-239-5288
Organic Planet
San Francisco, CA 415-765-5590
Pacific Coast Fruit Company
Portland, OR 503-234-6411
Paradise
Plant City, FL 800-330-8952
Setton International Foods
Commack, NY 800-227-4397
Terri Lynn
Elgin, IL 800-323-0775
Timber Crest Farms
Healdsburg, CA 888-374-9325
Unique Ingredients
Naches, WA 509-653-1991

Canned

Agrocan
Toronto, ON 877-247-6226

EMERLING INTERNATIONAL FOODS, INC.

Emerling International Foods
Buffalo, NY 716-833-7381

We supply food manufacturers and food service customers worldwide (since 1988) with bulk ingredients including: Fruits & Vegetables; Juice Concentrates; Herbs & Spices; Oils & Vinegars; Flavors & Colors; Honey & Molasses. We also produce PURE MAPLE SYRUP.

Maui Pineapple Company
Kahului, HI 808-877-3351
Maui Pineapple Company
Concord, CA 925-798-0240
NTC Foods Corporation
Williamsville, NY 800-333-1637

Dried

American Importing Company
Minneapolis, MN 612-331-9226
Mariani Packing Company
Vacaville, CA 800-672-8655

Frozen

EMERLING INTERNATIONAL FOODS, INC.

Emerling International Foods
Buffalo, NY 716-833-7381

We supply food manufacturers and food service customers worldwide (since 1988) with bulk ingredients including: Fruits & Vegetables; Juice Concentrates; Herbs & Spices; Oils & Vinegars; Flavors & Colors; Honey & Molasses. We also produce PURE MAPLE SYRUP.

J.H. Verbridge & Son
Williamson, NY 315-589-2366
Pacific Coast Fruit Company
Portland, OR 503-234-6411

Plums

Ballantine Produce Company
Reedley, CA 559-637-2400
Brandt Farms
Reedley, CA 559-638-6961
Burnette Foods
Elk Rapids, MI 231-264-8116
Chiquita Brands International
Cincinnati, OH 800-438-0015
Copper Hills Fruit Sales
Fresno, CA 559-277-1970
Corrin Produce Sales
Reedley, CA 559-638-3970
Fowler Packing Company
Fresno, CA 559-834-5911
Giumarra Companies
Reedley, CA 559-897-5060
Henggeler Packing Company
Fruitland, ID 208-452-4212
J.C. Watson Company
Parma, ID 208-722-5141
Mountain View Fruit Sales
Reedley, CA 559-637-9933
North Bay Produce
Traverse City, MI 231-946-1941
Oregon Fruit Products Company
Salem, OR 800-394-9333
Organic Planet
San Francisco, CA 415-765-5590
P-R Farms
Clovis, CA 559-299-0201
Produce Edge
Reedley, CA 559-637-9988
Shafer Lake Fruit
Hartford, MI 269-621-3194
Stadelman Fruit
Zillah, WA 509-829-5145
Sun Valley
Reedley, CA 559-591-1515
Sunmet
Del Rey, CA 559-445-1574
Symms Fruit Ranch
Caldwell, ID 208-459-4821
Terri Lynn
Elgin, IL 800-323-0775
Timber Crest Farms
Healdsburg, CA 888-374-9325
Trinity Fruit Sales
Clovis, CA 559-322-7100
Unique Ingredients
Naches, WA 509-653-1991
United Fruits Corporation
Santa Monica, CA 310-829-0261
Vintage Produce Sales
Kingsburg, CA 559-897-1622
Wawona Packing Company
Cutler, C9 559-528-4000
Z&S Distributing
Fresno, CA 800-467-0788

Canned

Burnette Foods
Elk Rapids, MI 231-264-8116

EMERLING INTERNATIONAL FOODS, INC.

Emerling International Foods
Buffalo, NY......................716-833-7381

We supply food manufacturers and food service customers worldwide (since 1988) with bulk ingredients including: Fruits & Vegetables; Juice Concentrates; Herbs & Spices; Oils & Vinegars; Flavors & Colors; Honey & Molasses. We also produce PURE MAPLE SYRUP.

Northwest Packing Company
Vancouver, WA...................800-543-4356
Oregon Fruit Products Company
Salem, OR........................800-394-9333
Packers Canning Company
Lawton, MI.......................269-624-4681
San Benito Foods
Vancouver, WA...................800-453-7832
Truitt Brothers Inc
Salem, OR........................800-547-8712

Dried

American Importing Company
Minneapolis, MN.................612-331-9226
Fastachi
Watertown, MA....................800-466-3022
Mariani Packing Company
Vacaville, CA....................800-672-8655
Setton International Foods
Commack, NY.....................800-227-4397

Frozen

Coloma Frozen Foods
Coloma, MI.......................800-642-2723

EMERLING INTERNATIONAL FOODS, INC.

Emerling International Foods
Buffalo, NY......................716-833-7381

We supply food manufacturers and food service customers worldwide (since 1988) with bulk ingredients including: Fruits & Vegetables; Juice Concentrates; Herbs & Spices; Oils & Vinegars; Flavors & Colors; Honey & Molasses. We also produce PURE MAPLE SYRUP.

Fruithill
Yamhill, OR......................503-662-3926
Oregon Fruit Products Company
Salem, OR........................800-394-9333
Watermill Foods
Milton Freewater, OR.............541-938-6601

Pomegranate

Ballantine Produce Company
Reedley, CA......................559-637-2400
Copper Hills Fruit Sales
Fresno, CA.......................559-277-1970

EMERLING INTERNATIONAL FOODS, INC.

Emerling International Foods
Buffalo, NY......................716-833-7381

We supply food manufacturers and food service customers worldwide (since 1988) with bulk ingredients including: Fruits & Vegetables; Juice Concentrates; Herbs & Spices; Oils & Vinegars; Flavors & Colors; Honey & Molasses. We also produce PURE MAPLE SYRUP.

Fowler Packing Company
Fresno, CA.......................559-834-5911
HMC Marketing Group
Kingsburg, CA....................559-897-1009
Naumes
Medford, OR......................541-772-6268

Potatoes

Au Gratin

Basic American Foods
Walnut Creek, CA.................800-227-4050
Captain Ken's Foods
St Paul, MN......................651-298-0071
Idaho Fresh-Pak/Idahoan Foods
Lewisville, ID...................800-635-6100

Frozen

Captain Ken's Foods
St Paul, MN......................651-298-0071

Baked & Stuffed

Oh Boy! Corporation
San Fernando, CA.................818-361-1128
Sun-Glo of Idaho
Sugar City, ID...................208-356-7346

Frozen

Penobscot McCrum
Belfast, ME......................800-435-4456
Sun-Glo of Idaho
Sugar City, ID...................208-356-7346

Canned

Burnette Foods
Elk Rapids, MI...................231-264-8116
Burnette Foods
Hartford, MI.....................616-621-3181
ConAgra Grocery Products
Irvine, CA.......................714-680-1000

EMERLING INTERNATIONAL FOODS, INC.

Emerling International Foods
Buffalo, NY......................716-833-7381

We supply food manufacturers and food service customers worldwide (since 1988) with bulk ingredients including: Fruits & Vegetables; Juice Concentrates; Herbs & Spices; Oils & Vinegars; Flavors & Colors; Honey & Molasses. We also produce PURE MAPLE SYRUP.

Mr. Dell Foods
Kearney, MO......................816-628-4644
Nationwide Canning
Cottam, ON.......................519-839-4831
New Harvest Foods
Pulaski, WI......................920-822-2578
Nickabood's Company
Los Angeles, CA..................213-746-1541
Oh Boy Corporation
San Fernando, CA.................818-361-1128
Omstead Foods Ltd
Burlington, ON...................905-315-8883
Ore-Ida Foods
Pittsburgh, PA...................412-237-3450
Reckitt Benckiser
Parsippany, NJ...................800-333-3899
Seneca Foods
Janesville, WI...................608-757-6000
Weil's Food Processing
Wheatley, ON.....................519-825-4572

Dehydrated

Basic American Foods
Plover, WI.......................715-341-5960
Basic American Foods
Walnut Creek, CA.................800-227-4050
Idaho Fresh-Pak/Idahoan Foods
Lewisville, ID...................800-635-6100
Specialty Ingredients
Buffalo Grove, IL................847-419-9595

Frozen

Agri-Dairy Products
Purchase, NY.....................914-697-9580

EMERLING INTERNATIONAL FOODS, INC.

Emerling International Foods
Buffalo, NY......................716-833-7381

We supply food manufacturers and food service customers worldwide (since 1988) with bulk ingredients including: Fruits & Vegetables; Juice Concentrates; Herbs & Spices; Oils & Vinegars; Flavors & Colors; Honey & Molasses. We also produce PURE MAPLE SYRUP.

Jones Produce
Quincy, WA.......................509-787-3537
Magic Valley Foods
Rupert, ID.......................208-436-3126
Oregon Potato Company
Boardman, OR.....................800-336-6311
Unique Ingredients
Naches, WA.......................509-653-1991

Fresh

Beamon Brothers
Goldsboro, NC....................919-734-4931
Del Monte Fresh Produce Company
Coral Gables, FL.................800-950-3683
Green Garden Food Products
Kent, WA.........................800-304-1033
Hanover Potato Products
Hanover, PA......................717-632-0700
Magic Valley Foods
Rupert, ID.......................208-436-3126
McKenna Brothers
Cardigan, PE.....................902-583-2951
Oregon Potato Company
Boardman, OR.....................800-336-6311
Pacific Collier Fresh Company
Immokalee, FL....................800-226-7274
Pride of Sampson
Clinton, NC......................910-592-6188
Seald Sweet Growers & Packers
Vero Beach, FL...................772-569-2244

Russet

Bottomline Foods
Pembroke Pines, FL...............954-843-0562
Del Monte Foods
San Francisco, CA................800-543-3090
Les Aliments Livabec Foods
Sherrington, QC..................450-454-7971

White

Galegher Farms
Thompson, ND.....................701-847-2151

Frozen

Burnette Foods
Hartford, MI.....................616-621-3181
Cavendish Farms
Jamestown, ND....................888-284-5687
Cavendish Farms
Burlington, MA...................888-88 -7437
Cavendish Farms
Dieppe, NB.......................888-883-7437
Cleugh's Frozen Foods
Buena Park, CA...................714-521-1002
ConAgra Grocery Products
Irvine, CA.......................714-680-1000

EMERLING INTERNATIONAL FOODS, INC.

Emerling International Foods
Buffalo, NY......................716-833-7381

We supply food manufacturers and food service customers worldwide (since 1988) with bulk ingredients including: Fruits & Vegetables; Juice Concentrates; Herbs & Spices; Oils & Vinegars; Flavors & Colors; Honey & Molasses. We also produce PURE MAPLE SYRUP.

Endico Potatoes
Mt Vernon, NY....................914-664-1151
H.J. Heinz Company
Pittsburgh, PA...................412-237-5948
Hot Potato Distributor
Chicago, IL......................312-243-0640
J.R. Simplot Company
Boise, ID........................208-336-2110

J.R. Simplot Food Group
Pasco, WA 509-544-6700
Lamb-Weston
Hermiston, OR 800-766-7783
Magic Valley Foods
Rupert, ID 208-436-3126
McCain Foods USA
Easton, ME 207-488-2561
McCain Foods USA
Lisle, IL 800-258-1098
Michael Foods, Inc.
Minnetonka, MN 952-258-4000
Mr. Dell Foods
Kearney, MO 816-628-4644
Nickabood's Company
Los Angeles, CA 213-746-1541
Oh Boy Corporation
San Fernando, CA 818-361-1128
Omstead Foods Ltd
Burlington, ON 905-315-8883
Ore-Ida Foods
Pittsburgh, PA 412-237-3450
Oregon Potato Company
Boardman, OR 800-336-6311
R.D. Offutt Company
Fargo, ND 701-237-6062
Sun-Glo of Idaho
Sugar City, ID 208-356-7346
Trappe Packing Corporation
Trappe, MD 410-476-3185
Twin City Foods
Stanwood, WA 206-515-2400
Washington Potato Company
Warden, WA 509-349-8803

Rounds

Penobscot McCrum
Belfast, ME 800-435-4456

Wedges

Penobscot McCrum
Belfast, ME 800-435-4456

Instant

Barbara's Bakery
Petaluma, CA 707-765-2273
Gilster-Mary Lee Corporation
Chester, IL. 800-851-5371
Idaho Fresh-Pak/Idahoan Foods
Lewisville, ID 800-635-6100

Oven Type

Frozen

Sun-Glo of Idaho
Sugar City, ID 208-356-7346

Potatoes

Aaland Potato Company
Hoople, ND. 701-894-6144
Alsum Produce
Friesland, WI 800-236-5127
B.M. Tibbitts & Sons
Saint Anthony, ID 208-624-3402
Basic American Foods
Walnut Creek, CA 800-227-4050
Ben B. Schwartz & Sons
Detroit, MI 313-841-8300
Bjorneby Potato Company
Minto, ND 701-248-3482

Burnette Foods
Elk Rapids, MI 231-264-8116
Burnette Foods
Hartford, MI 616-621-3181
Byrnes Packing
Hastings, FL 904-692-1643
Cavendish Farms
Jamestown, ND 888-284-5687
Cavendish Farms
Dieppe, NB 888-883-7437
Chiquita Brands International
Cincinnati, OH 800-438-0015
Cleugh's Frozen Foods
Buena Park, CA 714-521-1002
ConAgra Grocery Products
Irvine, CA 714-680-1000
Crystal Seed Potato Company
Crystal, ND 701-657-2143
Custom Cuts
Milwaukee, WI 414-483-0491
Dave Kingston Produce
Idaho Falls, ID 800-888-7783
Diamond Nut Company
Lemont, IL 630-739-3000
Edmonton Potato Growers
Edmonton, AB 780-447-1860
Galegher Farms
Thompson, ND 701-847-2151
Green Garden Food Products
Kent, WA 800-304-1033
Grower Shipper Potato Company
Monte Vista, CO 719-852-3569
Hanover Potato Products
Hanover, PA 717-632-0700
Idaho Fresh-Pak/Idahoan Foods
Lewisville, ID 800-635-6100
Idahoan
Lewisville, ID 800-635-6100
Isadore A. Rapasadi & Son
Canastota, NY 315-697-2216
J.C. Watson Company
Parma, ID 208-722-5141
Johnston Farms
Edison, CA 661-366-3201
Kiska Farms
Pasco, WA 509-547-7765
Lamb-Weston
Eagle, ID 208-938-1047
Lamb-Weston
Hermiston, OR 800-766-7783
Larsen Farms
Hamer, ID 208-662-5501
Larsen of Idaho
Hamer, ID 208-662-5501
Larson Potato
Park River, ND 701-284-6437
Lehr Brothers
Edison, CA 661-366-3244
Livingston Farmers Association
Livingston, CA 209-394-7611
Magic Valley Foods
Rupert, ID 208-436-3126
Maple Leaf Foods International
Toronto, ON 416-480-8900
Marten's Country Kitchen
Port Byron, NY 315-776-8821
McCain Foods
Easton, ME 207-488-2561
McCain Foods USA
Lisle, IL 800-258-1098
Michael Foods, Inc.
Minnetonka, MN 952-258-4000
Modern Grocery Company
Macon, GA 478-745-3381

Mr. Dell Foods
Kearney, MO 816-628-4644
Muir-Roberts Company
Salt Lake City, UT 801-363-5809
National Harvest
Kansas City, MO 816-842-9600
Nationwide Canning
Cottam, ON 519-839-4831
New Harvest Foods
Pulaski, WI 920-822-2578
Nonpareil Dehydrated Potatoes
Blackfoot, ID 800-522-2223
Northern Star Company
Minneapolis, MN 612-339-8981
Nu-Way Potato Products
Toronto, ON 416-241-9151
OC Schulz & Sons
Crystal, ND 701-657-2152
Oetker Limited
Mississauga, ON 905-678-1311
Oh Boy! Corporation
San Fernando, CA 818-361-1128
Oregon Potato Company
Boardman, OR 800-336-6311
Pak-Wel Produce
Vauxhall, AB 403-654-2116
Penobscot McCrum
Belfast, ME 800-435-4456
Potato Services of Michigan
Edmore, MI 989-427-3314
Premier Packing Company
Bakersfield, CA 661-393-3320
Reckitt Benckiser
Parsippany, NJ. 800-333-3899
Somerset Industries
Spring House, PA 800-883-8728
Sun-Glo of Idaho
Sugar City, ID 208-356-7346
Sunfresh
Royal City, WA 509-346-9438
Tami Great Food
Monsey, NY 718-788-4200
Trappe Packing Corporation
Trappe, MD 410-476-3185
Twin City Foods
Stanwood, WA 206-515-2400
Vauxhall Foods
Vauxhall, AB 403-654-2771
Vessey & Company
Holtville, CA. 760-352-6376
Washington Potato Company
Warden, WA 509-349-8803
Weil's Food Processing
Wheatley, ON 519-825-4572
Wildcat Produce
McGrew, NE 308-783-2438
William Karas & Sons
Churchville, NY 585-757-2751

Red

Kiska Farms
Pasco, WA 509-547-7765
Vessey & Company
Holtville, CA. 760-352-6376

Powdered Vegetables

Atlantic Quality Spice &Seasonings
Edison, NJ. 800-584-0422

EMERLING INTERNATIONAL FOODS, INC.

Emerling International Foods
Buffalo, NY 716-833-7381

> We supply food manufacturers and food service customers worldwide (since 1988) with bulk ingredients including: Fruits & Vegetables; Juice Concentrates; Herbs & Spices; Oils & Vinegars; Flavors & Colors; Honey & Molasses. We also produce PURE MAPLE SYRUP.

Green Foods Corporation
Oxnard, CA .800-777-4430
Idaho Supreme Potatoes
Firth, ID 208-346-6841
Master Taste International
Plant City, FL 800-237-7629
Niagara Foods
Middleport, NY 716-735-7722
Oregon Freeze Dry
Albany, OR .800-547-0245
Spreda Group
Prospect, KY 502-426-9411
Vegetable Juices
Chicago, IL .888-776-9752
Vi-Gor Cup Corporation
Bellmore, NY 516-431-7722
Weinberg Foods
Kirkland, WA 800-866-3447

Produce

A. Duda & Sons
Oviedo, FL .407-365-2111
Aaland Potato Company
Hoople, ND .701-894-6144
Abbott & Cobb, Inc.
Langhorne, PA 800-345-7333
Adobe Creek Packing
Kelseyville, CA 707-279-4204
Agrinorthwest
Kennewick, WA 509-734-1195
Alsum Produce
Friesland, WI 800-236-5127
Annapolis Produce & Restaurant Supply
Annapolis, MD 410-266-5211
Anton Caratan & Son
Delano, CA .661-725-2575
Apple Acres
La Fayette, NY 315-677-5144
Appleton Produce Company
Weiser, ID .208-414-1102
Applewood Orchards
Deerfield, MI 800-447-3854
Argee Corporation
Santee, CA .800-449-3030
Associated Fruit Company
Phoenix, OR 541-535-1787
Atlantic Blueberry Company
Hammonton, NJ 609-561-8600
Atwater Fruit Exchange
Atwater, CA 209-358-2272
Avalon Foodservice, Inc.
Canal Fulton, OH 800-362-0622
B.M. Tibbitts & Sons
Saint Anthony, ID 208-624-3402
Babe Farms
Santa Maria, CA 800-648-6772
Baker Produce Company
Kennewick, WA 800-624-7553
Ballantine Produce Company
Reedley, CA 559-637-2400
Banana Distributing Company
San Antonio, TX 210-227-8285
Bay Cities Produce Company
San Leandro, CA 510-346-4943
BelleHarvest Sales
Belding, MI .800-452-7753
Ben B. Schwartz & Sons
Detroit, MI .313-841-8300
Ben E. Keith DFW
Fort Worth, TX 817-654-3663
Ben Hill Griffin, Inc.
Frostproof, FL 863-635-2251
Ben-Bud Growers Inc.
Boca Raton, FL 954-574-4040
Bifulco Farms
Pittsgrove, NJ 856-692-0707
Bjorneby Potato Company
Minto, ND .701-248-3482
Bluebird
Peshastin, WA 509-548-1700

Bodek Kosher Produce
Brooklyn, NY 718-377-4163
Boekhout Farms
Ontario, NY 315-524-4041
Boggiatto Produce
Salinas, CA 831-424-4864
Brady Farms
West Olive, MI 616-842-3916
Brandt Farms
Reedley, CA 559-638-6961
Bridenbaughs Orchards
Martinsburg, PA 814-793-2364
Brooks Tropicals
Homestead, FL 800-327-4833
Bruce Church
Salinas, CA 800-538-2861
Byrnes Packing
Hastings, FL 904-692-1643
CAL Sun Produce Company
Oxnard, CA .805-985-2262
Cal-Harvest Marketing
Hanford, CA 559-582-4000
Calco of Calgary
Calgary, AB 403-295-3578
California Citrus Producer
Lindsay, CA 559-562-5169
California Farms & Canners
San Francisco, CA 415-433-3522
California Specialty Farms
Los Angeles, CA 800-437-2702
California Watercress
Fillmore, CA 805-524-4808
CalSungold
Indio, CA .760-399-5646
Capital Seaboard
Jessup, MD .443-755-1733
Caro Foods
Houma, LA .985-872-1483
Carolina Blueberry Association
Garland, NC 910-588-4220
Carson City Pickle Company
Carson City, MI 989-584-3148
Castellini Company
Newport, KY 800-233-8560
Cates Addis Company
Parkton, NC 800-423-1883
Chazy Orchards
Chazy, NY .518-846-7171
Chief Wenatchee
Wenatchee, WA 509-662-5197
Chiquita Brands International
Cincinnati, OH 800-438-0015
Chris' Farm Stand
Hubbardston, MA 978-928-4732
Christopher Ranch
Gilroy, CA .408-847-1100
Circle Valley Produce
Idaho Falls, ID 208-524-2628
Claussen Pickle Company
Woodstock, IL 800-435-2817
Clermont
Hillsboro, OR 503-648-8544
Cleugh's Frozen Foods
Buena Park, CA 714-521-1002
Columbia Empire Farms
Sherwood, OR 503-538-2156
ConAgra Grocery Products
Irvine, CA .714-680-1000
Concannon Vineyard
Livermore, CA 800-258-9866
Congdon Orchards
Yakima, WA 509-965-2886
Cooperative Elevator Company
Pigeon, MI .989-453-4500
Corona College Heights Orange & Lemon Associates
Riverside, CA 951-688-1811
Corrin Produce Sales
Reedley, CA 559-638-3970
Country Fresh Mushrooms
Avondale, PA 610-268-3033
Couture Farms
Kettleman City, CA 559-945-2226
Crane & Crane
Brewster, WA 509-689-3447
Creekside Mushrooms
Worthington, PA 724-297-5491
Crown Packing Company
Salinas, CA 831-424-2067
Crystal Seed Potato Company
Crystal, ND 701-657-2143
Custom Cuts
Milwaukee, WI 414-483-0491

Cut Above Foods
Carlsbad, CA 760-931-6777
D'Arrigo Brothers Company of California
Salinas, CA .800-995-5939
Dan Tudor & Sons
Delano, CA .661-792-3176
Dave Kingston Produce
Idaho Falls, ID 800-888-7783
DCL
Honolulu, HI 808-845-3834
De Bruyn Produce Company
Zeeland, MI 800-733-9177
Del Monte Foods
San Francisco, CA 800-543-3090
Delta Packing Company of Lodi
Lodi, CA 209-334-0689
Diamond Blueberry
Hammonton, NJ 609-561-3661
Diamond Fruit Growers
Odell, OR .541-354-5300
Diamond Nut Company
Lemont, IL .630-739-3000
Dimare
Visalia, CA .559-627-0821
DiMare International
Indio, CA .760-564-3762
Dimond Tager Company Products
Tampa, FL .813-238-3111
DNE World Fruit Sales
Fort Pierce, FL 800-327-6676
DNO
Columbus, OH 800-686-2366
Dole Fresh Vegetable Company
Soledad, CA 800-333-5454
Driscoll Strawberry Associates
Watsonville, CA 831-763-3050
Dundee Citrus Growers
Dundee, FL 800-447-1574
E.W. Bowker Company
Pemberton, NJ 609-894-9508
Eastern Marketing Service
Lakeland, FL 863-701-8214
Ever Fresh Fruit Company
Boring, OR .800-239-8026
Exeter Produce & Storage Company
Exeter, ON .519-235-0141
F&S Produce Company
Rosenhayn, NJ 800-886-3316
Farm Pak Products
Spring Hope, NC 252-459-3101
Federation of Southern Cooperatives
East Point, GA 404-765-0991
Ferris Organic Farm
Eaton Rapids, MI 800-628-8736
Festive Finer Foods
Jamaica, NY 718-341-2100
Fiesta Farms
Nyssa, OR .541-372-2248
Fig Garden Packing
Fresno, CA .559-271-9000
Fillmore Piru Citrus Association
Piru, CA 800-524-8787
Finer Foods
Chicago, IL .773-579-3870
Flippin-Seaman
Tyro, VA 434-277-5828
Florida Citrus
Tampa, FL .813-626-5580
Fowler Cooperative Association
Fowler, CO .719-263-4266
Frank Capurro & Son
Moss Landing, CA 831-728-3904
Franklin Reister & Sons
Conklin, MI .616-887-9689
Fresh Express
Franklin Park, IL 800-242-5472
Fruit Acres
La Crescent, MN 507-895-4750
Ful-Flav-R Foods
Alamo, CA .510-339-9618
G Cefalu & Brothers
Jessup, MD .410-799-3414
Galegher Farms
Thompson, ND 701-847-2151
Garber Farms
Iota, LA 800-824-2284
Garden State Farms
Philadelphia, PA 215-463-8000
Gentile Brothers Company
Cincinnati, OH 800-877-7954
George Chiala Farms
Morgan Hill, CA 408-778-0562

George Richter Farm
Fife, WA 253-922-5649
George W Saulpaugh & Sons
Germantown, NY 518-537-6500
Georgia Vegetable Company
Tifton, GA 229-386-2374
Gerawan Farming
Sanger, CA 559-787-8780
Ghirardelli Ranch
Petaluma, CA 707-795-7616
Gilroy
Hanford, CA 559-584-2711
Giumarra Companies
Escondido, CA 760-480-8502
Glacier Foods
Sanger, CA 559-875-3354
Godwin Produce Company
Dunn, NC 910-892-4171
Gold Seal Fruit Bouquet
Milwaukee, WI 800-558-5558
Golden River Fruit Company
Vero Beach, FL 772-562-4502
Golden Town Apple Products
Thornbury, ON 519-599-6300
Great Eastern Sun
Asheville, NC 800-334-5809
Grimmway Farms
Bakersfield, CA 800-301-3101
Grower Shipper Potato Company
Monte Vista, CO 719-852-3569
H H Dobbins
Lyndonville, NY 877-362-2467
H. Naraghi Farms
Escalon, CA 209-577-5777
Haines City Citrus Growers Association
Haines City, FL 800-422-4245
Half Moon Fruit & Produce Company
Yolo, CA 530-662-1727
Harlin Fruit Company
Monett, MO 417-235-7370
Harner Farms
State College, PA 814-237-7919
Harris Farms
Coalinga, CA 800-742-1955
Heinz North America
Pittsburgh, PA 412-237-5700
Heller Brothers Packing Corporation
Winter Garden, FL 407-656-4986
Henggeler Packing Company
Fruitland, ID 208-452-4212
Herold's Salad
Cleveland, OH 800-427-2523
Hong Kong Market Company
Chicago, IL 312-791-9111
Hopkins Food Service
Cairo, NY 229-872-3214
Horton Fruit Company
Louisville, KY 800-626-2245
Hunt Brothers Cooperative
Lake Wales, FL 863-676-9471
Indian Bay Frozen Foods
Centreville, NL 709-678-2844
Indian Hollow Farms
Richland Center, WI 800-236-3944
Inland Fruit Company
Wapato, WA 509-877-2126
International Specialty Supply
Cookeville, TN 931-526-1106
Isadore A. Rapasadi & Son
Canastota, NY 315-697-2216
J&J Produce Company
Hattiesburg, MS 601-582-1512
J.C. Watson Company
Parma, ID 208-722-5141
Jack Brown Produce
Sparta, MI 800-348-0834
Jacobs, Malcolm, & Burtt
San Francisco, CA 415-285-0400
Jalapeno Foods Company
The Woodlands, TX 800-896-2318
Jasmine Vineyards
Delano, CA 661-792-2141
Jasper Wyman & Son
Milbridge, ME 800-341-1758
JES Foods
Cleveland, OH 216-883-8987
Jonathan's Sprouts
Rochester, MA 508-763-2577
Joseph J. White
Browns Mills, NJ 609-893-2332
JRL
Hammonton, NJ 609-561-1572

Kaiser Foods
Cincinnati, OH 888-291-0608
Kelley Bean Company
Torrington, WY 307-532-2131
Kelley Bean Company
Scottsbluff, NE 308-635-6438
Kennebec Bean Company
North Vassalboro, ME 207-873-3473
Kitchen Pride Mushroom Farms
Gonzales, TX 830-540-4516
Knight Seed Company
Burnsville, MN 800-328-2999
Knights Appleden Fruit
Colborne, ON 905-349-2521
Koch
Chattanooga, TN 423-266-0351
Krugers
St Paul, MN 651-699-1356
Kurtz Produce
Ariss, ON 519-824-3279
L.F. Lambert Spawn Company
Coatesville, PA 610-384-5031
L.I. Cauliflower Association
Riverhead, NY 631-727-2212
Lagorio Enterprises
Manteca, CA 209-982-5691
Lake Helen Sprout Farm
Lake Helen, FL 386-228-2871
Lane Packing Company
Fort Valley, GA 478-825-3592
Larson Potato
Park River, ND 701-284-6437
Lehr Brothers
Edison, CA 661-366-3244
Lennox Farm
Shelburne, ON 519-925-6444
Leroy Smith & Sons Inc
Vero Beach, FL 772-567-3421
Lindemann Produce
Los Banos, CA 209-826-2442
Livingston Farmers Association
Livingston, CA 209-394-7611
Lou Pizzo Produce
Parkland, FL 954-941-8830
Lucich Farms
Delano, CA 661-725-4550
M&R Company
Lodi, CA 209-369-2725
M&S Tomato Repacking Company
Springfield, MA 800-343-0371
M.A. Patout & Son
Jeanerette, LA 337-276-4592
Magnolia Citrus Association
Porterville, CA 559-784-4455
Mancuso Cheese Company
Joliet, IL 815-722-2475
Mann Packing
Salinas, CA 831-422-7405
Manzana Products Company
Sebastopol, CA 707-823-5313
Manzanita Ranch
Julian, CA 760-765-0102
Maple Leaf Foods International
Toronto, ON 416-480-8900
Mar Distributing Company
Los Angeles, CA 213-627-4006
Marley Orchards Corporation
Yakima, WA 509-248-5231
Marten's Country Kitchen
Port Byron, NY 315-776-8821
Martin Brothers Distributing Company
Cedar Falls, IA 319-266-1775
Matson Fruit Company
Selah, WA 509-697-7100
Maui Pineapple Company
Kahului, HI 808-877-3351
Maui Pineapple Company
Concord, CA 925-798-0240
McDaniel Fruit Company
Fallbrook, CA 760-728-8438
McFarling Foods
Indianapolis, IN 317-635-2633
McKenna Brothers
Cardigan, PE 902-583-2951
Merrill's Blueberry Farms
Ellsworth, ME 800-711-6551
Michigan Celery Promotion Cooperative
Hudsonville, MI 616-669-1250
Mike & Jean's Berry Farm
Mt Vernon, WA 360-424-7220
Mills
Salinas, CA 831-758-8179

Mister Spear
Stockton, CA 800-677-7327
Mixon Fruit Farms
Bradenton, FL 800-608-2525
Modern Grocery Company
Macon, GA 478-745-3381
Modern Mushroom Farms
Avondale, PA 610-268-3535
Modoc Orchard Company
Medford, OR 541-535-1437
Money's Mushrooms
Langley, BC 800-661-8623
Monsour's
Pittsburg, KS 620-232-7600
Monterey Mushrooms
Watsonville, CA 800-333-6874
Montreal Chop Suey Company
Montreal, QC 514-522-3134
Montrose Potato Growers
Montrose, CO 970-249-5623
Moscow Seed Company
Moscow, ID 208-882-2324
Mountain Orchard Cooperative
Aspers, PA 800-322-6867
Nathan Seagall Company
Montgomery, AL 334-279-3174
National Raisin Company
Fowler, CA 559-834-5981
Nebraska Salt & Grain Company
Gothenburg, NE 308-537-7191
New West Foods
San Francisco, CA 701-947-2505
New York Apples Sales
Castletn on Hdsn, NY 518-477-7200
Newark Meat Supply
Newark, OH 740-345-6696
Nonpareil Dehydrated Potatoes
Blackfoot, ID 800-522-2223
Nor-Cliff Farms
Port Colborne, ON 905-835-0808
North Bay Produce
Traverse City, MI 231-946-1941
Northern Feed & Bean Company
Lucerne, CO 970-352-7875
Northern Fruit Company
Wenatchee, WA 509-884-6651
Northwest Pea & Bean Company
Spokane Valley, WA 509-534-3821
Nuchief Sales
East Wenatchee, WA 888-269-4638
Nunes Company
Salinas, CA 831-757-1521
Nut Factory
Spokane Valley, WA 888-239-5288
OC Schulz & Sons
Crystal, ND 701-657-2152
Ocean Mist
Castroville, CA 831-633-2144
Ocean Spray Cranberries
Lakeville-Middleboro, MA 800-662-3263
Ontario Produce Company
Ontario, OR 541-889-6485
Orange Cove Sanger Citrus Association
Orange Cove, CA 559-626-4453
Oregon Cherry Growers
The Dalles, OR 800-367-2536
Oregon Potato Company
Boardman, OR 800-336-6311
Oxford Frozen Foods Limited
Oxford, NS 902-447-2100
P-R Farms
Clovis, CA 559-299-0201
Pacific Tomato Growers
Palmetto, FL 941-722-3291
Pandol Brothers
Delano, CA 661-725-3755
Pavero Cold Storage Corporation
Highland, NY 800-435-2994
Per-Clin Orchards
Bear Lake, MI 231-889-4289
Peter Rabbit Farms
Coachella, CA 760-398-0151
Phillips Gourmet
Kennett Square, PA 610-925-0520
Pioneer Growers Cooperative
Belle Glade, FL 561-996-5561
Pitman & Sons
Jacksonville, FL 904-768-6888
Placerville Fruit Growers Association
Placerville, CA 530-622-2640
Pleasant Grove Farms
Pleasant Grove, CA 916-655-3391

Pompeian
Baltimore, MD 800-638-1224
Post Familie Vineyards
Altus, AR 800-275-8423
Potato Services of Michigan
Edmore, MI 989-427-3314
Pots de Creme
Lexington, KY 859-299-2254
Prairie Mushrooms
Sherwood Park, AB 780-467-3555
Premier Packing Company
Bakersfield, CA 661-393-3320
Price Cold Storage & Packing Company
Yakima, WA 509-966-4110
Pride of Sampson
Clinton, NC 910-592-6188
Prime Produce
Orange, CA 714-771-0718
Produce Buyers Company
Detroit, MI 313-843-0132
Producers Cooperative
Olathe, CO 970-323-5913
Quality Brands
Deland, FL 386-738-3808
Quillin Produce Company
Huntsville, AL 256-883-7374
R&S Mexican Food Products
Glendale, AZ 602-272-2727
R.C. McEntire & Company
Columbia, SC 803-799-3388
Red Hot Cooperative
Redcliff, AB 403-548-6453
Reed Lang Farms
Rio Hondo, TX 956-748-2354
Reinhart Foods
Markham, ON 905-754-3503
Rene Produce Distributors
Nogales, AZ 520-281-9014
Reter Fruit Company
Medford, OR 541-772-5256
Rice Fruit Company
Gardners, PA 800-627-3359
Rio Grande Valley Sugar Growers
Santa Rosa, TX 956-636-1411
River One
Vero Beach, FL 800-288-6614
Rogers Brothers
Galesburg, IL 309-342-2127
Royal Packing Company
Salinas, CA 831-641-4450
Royal Wine Company
Bayonne, NJ 800-382-8299
Ruskin Packaging
Miami, FL 305-324-1529
Russo Farms
Vineland, NJ 856-692-5942
S&E Organic Farms
Bakersfield, CA 661-325-2644
S. Kennedy Vegetable Lifestock Company
Clear Lake, IA. 641-357-6101
Salad Ranch/Cattle Canada
Bentley, AB......................403-748-3017
Sales USA
Salado, TX 800-766-7344
Santanna Banana Company
Harrisburg, PA 717-238-8321
Schmidt Brothers
Swanton, OH. 419-826-3671
Scotian Gold Cooperative
Coldbrook, NS 902-679-2191
Sea Products Company
Watsonville, CA 831-768-2600
Seaboard Corporation
Shawnee Mission, KS. 913-676-8800
Seald Sweet Growers & Packers
Vero Beach, FL 772-569-2244
Sedlock Farm
Lynn Center, IL 309-521-8284
Shamrock Foods Company
Phoenix, AZ 800-289-3663
Shields Date Gardens
Indio, CA. 800-414-2555
Signature Fruit
Stockton, CA.....................209-931-1531
Silva Harvesting
Gonzales, CA 831-675-2327
SKW Biosystems
Philadelphia, PA 800-223-7073
Smith Frozen Foods
Weston, OR......................800-547-0203
Smith-Coulter Company
Chittenango, NY 315-687-6510

Snokist Growers
Yakima, WA 800-377-2857
Solana Gold Organics
Sebastopol, CA 800-459-1121
South Mill Distribution
Kennett Square, PA...............610-444-4800
Spring Ledge Farms
Dundee, NY 607-678-4038
Stadelman Fruit
Zillah, WA.......................509-829-5145
Star Route Farms
Bolinas, CA......................415-868-1658
Strube Vegetable & Celery Company
Chicago, IL 312-226-6888
Sugar Cane Industry Glades Correctional Institution
Belle Glade, FL...................561-829-1400
Sun Garden Growers
Bard, CA 800-228-4690
Sun Hing Foods
S San Francisco, CA...............800-258-6669
Sun Orchard of Florida
Haines City, FL...................863-422-5062
Sun Pacific Shippers
Exeter, CA.......................559-592-7121
Sunfresh
Royal City, WA...................509-346-9438
Sungarden Sprouts
Cookeville, TN 931-526-1106
Sunkist Growers
Stafford, TX 281-240-6446
Sunkist Growers
Detroit, MI 313-843-4160
Sunkist Growers
Cary, NC 410-663-2967
Sunkist Growers
Pittsburgh, PA 412-967-9801
Sunkist Growers
West Chester, OH 513-741-9494
Sunkist Growers
Visalia, CA.......................559-739-8392
Sunkist Growers
Chelsea, MA 617-884-9750
Sunkist Growers
Buffalo, NY......................716-895-3744
Sunkist Growers
Ontario, CA......................800-798-9005
Sunkist Growers
Cherry Hill, NJ 856-663-2343
Sunmet
Del Rey, CA 559-445-1574
Sunrise Growers
Placentia, CA 714-630-2170
Superior Frozen Vegetables
Cornell, MI 906-384-6466
Superior Mushroom Farms
Ardrossan, AB 866-687-2242
Sure Fresh Produce
Santa Maria, CA 888-423-5379
Surface Banana Company
Bluewell, WV 304-589-7202
Symms Fruit Ranch
Caldwell, ID 208-459-4821
Talbott Farms
Palisade, CO 970-464-5656
Talley Farms
Arroyo Grande, CA 805-489-2508
Tanimura & Antle
Salinas, CA 831-455-2255
Taylor Farms
Salinas, CA 831-754-0471
Taylor Orchards
Reynolds, GA 478-847-4186
Teixeira Farms
Santa Maria, CA 805-928-3801
Tejon Ranch
Lebec, CA 661-248-3000
Those Hersey Brothers
Casnovia, MI. 800-289-2767
Thrifty Vegetable Company
Los Angeles, CA..................213-485-8804
Tiger Mushroom Farm
Nanton, AB 403-646-2578
Tony Vitrano Company
Jessup, MD 410-799-7444
Too Goo Doo Farms/Easy Tray LLC
North Charleston, SC 843-767-0196
Trefethen Vineyards
Napa, CA 800-556-4847
Tri-Valley Growers
Los Banos, CA 209-827-5000
Trout-Blue Chelan
Chelan, WA......................509-682-2591

Tru-Blu Cooperative Associates
New Lisbon, NJ 609-894-8717
Tucson Food Service
Tucson, AZ 520-622-4605
Tufts Ranch
Winters, CA 530-795-4144
Turlock Fruit Company
Turlock, CA 209-634-7207
United Apple Sales
New Paltz, NY 845-256-1500
United Fruit Growers
Palisade, CO 970-464-5671
United Fruits Corporation
Santa Monica, CA 310-829-0261
United Marketing Exchange
Delta, CO 970-874-3332
United Pickle Products Corporation
Bronx, NY 718-933-6060
US Fresh Marketing
Virginia Beach, VA 757-481-2606
Valley Fruit & Vegetable
McAllen, TX 956-686-8056
Van de Kamp's
Chambersburg, PA 570-263-4127
Vaughn Rue Produce
Wilson, NC 800-388-8138
Venture Vineyards
Lodi, NY 888-635-6277
Verdelli Farms
Harrisburg, PA 800-422-8344
Veronica Foods Company
Oakland, CA 800-370-5554
Vidalia Sweets Brand
Lyons, GA 912-565-8881
Vincent B. Zaninovich & Son
Richgrove, CA 661-725-2497
Vincent Formusa Company
Chicago, IL.......................312-421-0485
Walla Walla Gardeners' Association
Walla Walla, WA.................800-553-5014
Walter P. Rawl & Sons
Pelion, SC 803-359-3645
Washington Fruit & Produce Company
Yakima, WA 509-457-6177
Weiser River Packing
Weiser, ID 208-549-0200
Wesco Foods Company
Cincinnati, OH 513-762-4139
West Pak Avocado
Temecula, CA 800-266-4414
Wetherby Cranberry Company
Warrens, WI 608-378-4813
Whitney & Son SeaFoods
Pittsfield, MA 800-414-6223
Wileman Bros & Elliott, Inc
Cutler, CA 559-732-5321
William Bolthouse Farms
Bakersfield, CA 661-366-7205
William Karas & Sons
Churchville, NY 585-757-2751
Wisconsin Cheese
Melrose Park, IL 708-450-0074
Yakima Fruit & Cold Storage Company
Wapato, WA.....................509-877-0440
Yarbrough Produce Company
Birmingham, AL 205-323-8651
Yokhol Valley Packing Company
Lindsay, CA 559-562-1327
Zipp Manufacturing Company
Hornerville, OH 800-521-8700
Zuccaro's Fruit & Produce Company
Minneapolis, MN 612-333-1122

Prunes

Central California Raisin Packers
Del Rey, CA 559-888-2195
Chieftain Wild Rice Company
Spooner, WI.....................800-262-6368
George W Saulpaugh & Sons
Germantown, NY 518-537-6500
H H Dobbins
Lyndonville, NY 877-362-2467
Henggeler Packing Company
Fruitland, ID 208-452-4212
Hialeah Products Company
Hollywood, FL 800-923-3379
Kalustyan Corporation
Union, NJ 908-688-6111
Meridian Nut Growers
Clovis, CA 559-458-7272
Organic Planet
San Francisco, CA 415-765-5590

Ramos Orchards
  Winters, CA 530-795-4748
Service Packing Company
  Vancouver, BC 604-681-0264
Shoei Foods USA
  Olivehurst, CA 800-527-4712
Stadelman Fruit
  Zillah, WA 509-829-5145
Stapleton-Spence PackingCompany
  San Jose, CA 800-297-8815
Sunsweet Growers
  Yuba City, CA 800-417-2253
Taylor Packing Company
  Yuba City, CA 530-671-1505
Terri Lynn
  Elgin, IL 800-323-0775
Timber Crest Farms
  Healdsburg, CA 888-374-9325
Tufts Ranch
  Winters, CA 530-795-4144
Unique Ingredients
  Naches, WA 509-653-1991
Valley View Packing Company
  San Jose, CA 408-289-8300

Canned

EMERLING INTERNATIONAL FOODS, INC.

Emerling International Foods
  Buffalo, NY 716-833-7381

We supply food manufacturers and food service customers worldwide (since 1988) with bulk ingredients including: Fruits & Vegetables; Juice Concentrates; Herbs & Spices; Oils & Vinegars; Flavors & Colors; Honey & Molasses. We also produce PURE MAPLE SYRUP.

Oasis Foods
  Planada, CA 209-382-0263
Stapleton-Spence PackingCompany
  San Jose, CA 800-297-8815
Valley View Packing Company
  San Jose, CA 408-289-8300

Dried

Chieftain Wild Rice Company
  Spooner, WI 800-262-6368
Fastachi
  Watertown, MA 800-466-3022
Setton International Foods
  Commack, NY 800-227-4397

Frozen

EMERLING INTERNATIONAL FOODS, INC.

Emerling International Foods
  Buffalo, NY 716-833-7381

We supply food manufacturers and food service customers worldwide (since 1988) with bulk ingredients including: Fruits & Vegetables; Juice Concentrates; Herbs & Spices; Oils & Vinegars; Flavors & Colors; Honey & Molasses. We also produce PURE MAPLE SYRUP.

Packers Canning Company
  Lawton, MI 269-624-4681
Watermill Foods
  Milton Freewater, OR............ 541-938-6601

Pulps & Purees

Assouline & Ting
  Philadelphia, PA 800-521-4491
Frozsun Foods
  Anaheim, CA 714-630-2170
Haywood Enterprises
  Napa, CA........................ 707-261-5100

Pastorelli Food Products
  Chicago, IL 800-767-2829
Rain Sweet
  Salem, OR....................... 800-363-4293
RV Industries
  Atlanta, GA 770-729-8983
SK Foods
  Lemoore, CA..................... 559-924-6527

SupHerb Farms
  Turlock, CA 800-787-4372

CrEATe! Get ready-to-use fresh flavor with SupHerb Farms' all-natural fresh frozen culinary herbs, specialty vegetables, culinary herb pastes, vegetable purees and creative blends. Complete microbiological testing ensures food safety. We set the standard for outstanding customer service, inspired culinary support, collaborative customer partnerships and innovative custom products.

Tulkoff Food Products
  Baltimore, MD 800-638-7343

Citrus

Amboy Specialty Foods Company
  Dixon, IL....................... 800-892-0400
Chloe Foods Corporation
  Brooklyn, NY 718-827-3600
Del Monte Foods
  San Francisco, CA 800-543-3090

Fruit

Ravifruit
  Hackensack, NJ 201-939-5656
Sabroso Company
  Medford, OR 509-697-7251

Fruit & Vegetable

Assouline & Ting
  Philadelphia, PA 800-521-4491
Brady Farms
  West Olive, MI 616-842-3916
California Custom Fruits & Flavors
  Irwindale, CA 877-558-0056
ConAgra Grocery Products
  Irvine, CA 714-680-1000

EMERLING INTERNATIONAL FOODS, INC.

Emerling International Foods
  Buffalo, NY 716-833-7381

We supply food manufacturers and food service customers worldwide (since 1988) with bulk ingredients including: Fruits & Vegetables; Juice Concentrates; Herbs & Spices; Oils & Vinegars; Flavors & Colors; Honey & Molasses. We also produce PURE MAPLE SYRUP.

Furmano Foods
  Northumberland, PA 877-877-6032
Global Trading
  Buena Park, CA 864-288-7332
Golden Town Apple Products
  Thornbury, ON 519-599-6300
Greenwood Associates
  Highland Park, IL 847-242-7900
Hiller Cranberries
  Rochester, MA 508-763-5257
Hirzel Canning Company &Farms
  Northwood, OH 419-693-0531
Louis Dreyfus Citrus
  Winter Garden, FL 407-656-1000
Parman-Kendall Corporation
  Goulds, FL 305-258-1628
Pastorelli Food Products
  Chicago, IL 800-767-2829
Peace River Citrus Products
  Vero Beach, FL 772-467-1234
Prima Foods International
  Ocala, FL....................... 800-774-8751

Red Gold
  Elwood, IN 877-748-9798
S&E Organic Farms
  Bakersfield, CA 661-325-2644
Seneca Foods
  Clyman, WI. 920-696-3331
Vegetable Juices
  Chicago, IL 888-776-9752
Vita-Pakt Citrus Company
  Lindsay, CA 559-562-6008

Pulp

Dried Beet

EMERLING INTERNATIONAL FOODS, INC.

Emerling International Foods
  Buffalo, NY 716-833-7381

We supply food manufacturers and food service customers worldwide (since 1988) with bulk ingredients including: Fruits & Vegetables; Juice Concentrates; Herbs & Spices; Oils & Vinegars; Flavors & Colors; Honey & Molasses. We also produce PURE MAPLE SYRUP.

Fruit

Avo King International
  Orange, CA...................... 800-286-5464
Calavo Foods
  Santa Paula, CA 800-422-5280
Hiller Cranberries
  Rochester, MA 508-763-5257
Miramar Fruit Trading Company
  Medley, FL 305-883-4774
Sunny Avocado
  Jamul, CA 800-999-2862
Tantos Foods International
  Richmond Hill, ON. 905-763-9994
Three Vee Food & Syrup Company
  Brooklyn, NY 800-801-7330

Vegetable

Pastorelli Food Products
  Chicago, IL...................... 800-767-2829

Puree

Fruit

Assouline & Ting
  Philadelphia, PA 800-521-4491
Beta Pure Foods
  Aptos, CA 831-685-6565
Calavo Foods
  Santa Paula, CA 800-422-5280
Chiquita Brands International
  Cincinnati, OH 800-438-0015
Clermont
  Hillsboro, OR 503-648-8544
Frozsun Foods
  Anaheim, CA 714-630-2170
Fruithill
  Yamhill, OR 503-662-3926
Gerber Products Company
  Parsippany, NJ 800-443-7237
Global Trading
  Buena Park, CA 864-288-7332
Golden Town Apple Products
  Thornbury, ON 519-599-6300
Granny's Best Strawberry Products
  Victoria, ON 519-426-0705

Greenwood Associates
Highland Park, IL 847-242-7900
Hartog Rahal Foods
New York, NY 212-687-2000
Hiller Cranberries
Rochester, MA 508-763-5257
Johnson Concentrates
Sunnyside, WA 509-837-4600
Johnson Fruit Company
Sunnyside, WA 509-837-4600
Milne Fruit Products
Prosser, WA 509-786-2611
National Frozen Foods Corporation
Seattle, WA 206-322-8900
Northern Michigan Fruit Company
Omena, MI 231-386-5142
Ocean Spray Cranberries
Middleboro, MA 800-662-3263
Pacific Coast Fruit Company
Portland, OR 503-234-6411
Princeville Canning Company
Princeville, IL 309-385-4301
Radar Farms
Lynden, WA 360-354-6574
Rain Sweet
Salem, OR 800-363-4293
RFI Ingredients
Blauvelt, NY 800-962-7663
RV Industries
Atlanta, GA 770-729-8983
Summerland Sweets
Summerland, BC 800-577-1277
Tupman-Thurlow Company
Deerfield Beach, FL 954-596-9989
Usine de Congelation St. Bruno
St. Bruno, QC 418-343-2206

Fruit & Vegetable

Ful-Flav-R Foods
Alamo, CA 510-339-9618
National Frozen Foods Corporation
Seattle, WA 206-322-8900
Pastorelli Food Products
Chicago, IL 800-767-2829

Orange

KMC Citrus Enterprises
Winter Haven, FL 352-821-3666

Tomato

ConAgra Grocery Products
Irvine, CA 714-680-1000

EMERLING INTERNATIONAL FOODS, INC.

Emerling International Foods
Buffalo, NY 716-833-7381

We supply food manufacturers and food service customers worldwide (since 1988) with bulk ingredients including: Fruits & Vegetables; Juice Concentrates; Herbs & Spices; Oils & Vinegars; Flavors & Colors; Honey & Molasses. We also produce PURE MAPLE SYRUP.

Hirzel Canning Company &Farms
Northwood, OH 419-693-0531
Pastorelli Food Products
Chicago, IL 800-767-2829

Vegetable

Beta Pure Foods
Aptos, CA 831-685-6565
Furmano Foods
Northumberland, PA 877-877-6032
National Frozen Foods Corporation
Seattle, WA 206-322-8900
Pastorelli Food Products
Chicago, IL 800-767-2829

Tomato

Canned

Furmano Foods
Northumberland, PA 877-877-6032
Heinz Company of Canada
North York, ON 800-268-6641
Nationwide Canning
Cottam, ON 519-839-4831

Pastorelli Food Products
Chicago, IL 800-767-2829
Red Gold
Elwood, IN 877-748-9798
Seneca Foods
Clyman, WI 920-696-3331
Tip Top Canning Company
Tipp City, OH 937-667-3713
Vegetable Juices
Chicago, IL 888-776-9752
Violet Packing
Williamstown, NJ 856-629-7428

Pumpkin

Abbott & Cobb, Inc.
Langhorne, PA 800-345-7333
Bennett's Apples & Cider
Ancaster, ON 905-648-6878
Contract Comestibles
East Troy, WI 262-642-9400
Goebbert's Home Grown Vegetables
South Barrington, IL 847-428-6727
NORPAC Plant
Salem, OR 800-822-2898
Organic Planet
San Francisco, CA 415-765-5590
Schmidt Brothers
Swanton, OH 419-826-3671
Sunshine Farms
Roseboro, NC 910-564-2421
Tom Ringhausen Orchards
Hardin, IL 618-576-2311
Unique Ingredients
Naches, WA 509-653-1991
Wildcat Produce
McGrew, NE 308-783-2438

Canned

Agrocan
Toronto, ON 877-247-6226

EMERLING INTERNATIONAL FOODS, INC.

Emerling International Foods
Buffalo, NY 716-833-7381

We supply food manufacturers and food service customers worldwide (since 1988) with bulk ingredients including: Fruits & Vegetables; Juice Concentrates; Herbs & Spices; Oils & Vinegars; Flavors & Colors; Honey & Molasses. We also produce PURE MAPLE SYRUP.

Harvest-Pac Products
Chatham, ON 519-436-0446
Lakeside Foods
Manitowoc, WI 920-684-3356
NORPAC Plant
Salem, OR 800-822-2898
Seneca Foods Corporation
Marion, NY 315-926-8100

Frozen

EMERLING INTERNATIONAL FOODS, INC.

Emerling International Foods
Buffalo, NY 716-833-7381

We supply food manufacturers and food service customers worldwide (since 1988) with bulk ingredients including: Fruits & Vegetables; Juice Concentrates; Herbs & Spices; Oils & Vinegars; Flavors & Colors; Honey & Molasses. We also produce PURE MAPLE SYRUP.

Lakeside Foods
Manitowoc, WI 920-684-3356
NORPAC Plant
Salem, OR 800-822-2898

Winter Squash

NORPAC Plant
Salem, OR 800-822-2898

Quince

Hiller Cranberries
Rochester, MA 508-763-5257

Radish

A. Duda Farm Fresh Foods
Belle Glade, FL 561-996-7621
F&S Produce Company
Rosenhayn, NJ 800-886-3316
Frank Capurro & Son
Moss Landing, CA 831-728-3904
Gouw Quality Onions
Taber, AB 403-223-1440
Pioneer Growers Cooperative
Belle Glade, FL 561-996-5561
Vegetable Juices
Chicago, IL 888-776-9752
Walla Walla Gardeners' Association
Walla Walla, WA 800-553-5014

Raisins

ACH Food Companies
Boyceville, WI 715-643-2600
American Health & Nutrition
Ann Arbor, MI 734-677-5572
American Key Food Products
Closter, NJ 800-767-0237
American Raisin Packers
Selma, CA 559-896-4760
Boghosian Raisin Packing Company
Fowler, CA 559-834-5348
Central California Raisin Packers
Del Rey, CA 559-888-2195
Chieftain Wild Rice Company
Spooner, WI 800-262-6368
Chooljian Brothers Packing Company
Sanger, CA 559-875-5501
Del Rey Packing Company
Del Rey, CA 559-888-2031
Dipasa
Brownsville, TX 956-831-5893

EMERLING INTERNATIONAL FOODS, INC.

Emerling International Foods
Buffalo, NY 716-833-7381

We supply food manufacturers and food service customers worldwide (since 1988) with bulk ingredients including: Fruits & Vegetables; Juice Concentrates; Herbs & Spices; Oils & Vinegars; Flavors & Colors; Honey & Molasses. We also produce PURE MAPLE SYRUP.

Fig Garden Packing
Fresno, CA 559-271-9000
Foley's Candies
Richmond, BC 888-236-5397
Jason & Son Specialty Foods
Rancho Cordova, CA 800-810-9093
Jewel Date Company
Thermal, CA 760-399-4474
Just Tomatoes Company
Westley, CA 800-537-1985
Kalustyan Corporation
Union, NJ 908-688-6111
Lion Raisins
Selma, CA 559-834-6677
Mariani Packing Company
Vacaville, CA 800-672-8655
Meridian Nut Growers
Clovis, CA 559-458-7272
National Raisin Company
Fowler, CA 559-834-5981
NSpired Natural Foods
Melville, NY 631-845-4689
Nut Factory
Spokane Valley, WA 888-239-5288
Organic Planet
San Francisco, CA 415-765-5590
Peloian Packing Company
Dinuba, CA 559-591-0101
Reinhart Foods
Markham, ON 905-754-3503
Setton International Foods
Commack, NY 800-227-4397
Shade Foods
New Century, KS 800-225-6312
Sun-Maid Growers of California
Kingsburg, CA 800-272-4746
Terri Lynn
Elgin, IL 800-323-0775
Timber Crest Farms
Healdsburg, CA 888-374-9325

Unique Ingredients
Naches, WA. 509-653-1991
Victor Packing Company
Madera, CA. 559-673-5908
Waymouth Farms
New Hope, MN. 800-527-0094

Chocolate Coated

Shade Foods
New Century, KS 800-225-6312

Dried

ACH Food Companies
Boyceville, WI 715-643-2600
Boghosian Raisin Packing Company
Fowler, CA. 559-834-5348
Camara Raisin Packing Company
Fresno, CA .559-661-3780
Chieftain Wild Rice Company
Spooner, WI 800-262-6368
Fastachi
Watertown, MA. 800-466-3022
Fig Garden Packing
Fresno, CA .559-271-9000
Jason & Son Specialty Foods
Rancho Cordova, CA 800-810-9093
Kalustyan Corporation
Union, NJ 908-688-6111
National Raisin Company
Fowler, CA .559-834-5981
Nut Factory
Spokane Valley, WA 888-239-5288
Shade Foods
New Century, KS 800-225-6312

Yogurt Coated

Foley's Candies
Richmond, BC 888-236-5397
GKI Foods
Brighton, MI 248-486-0055
Mariani Packing Company
Vacaville, CA 800-672-8655
Setton International Foods
Commack, NY 800-227-4397
Shade Foods
New Century, KS 800-225-6312
Terri Lynn
Elgin, IL. 800-323-0775

Rhubarb

Allen Canning Company
Siloam Springs, AR 800-234-2553
Bryant Preserving Company
Alma, AR 800-634-2413
Cajun Chef Products
St Martinville, LA. 337-394-7112
Cleugh's Frozen Foods
Buena Park, CA 714-521-1002
Coloma Frozen Foods
Coloma, MI. 800-642-2723
Ever Fresh Fruit Company
Boring, OR .800-239-8026
Lennox Farm
Shelburne, ON 519-925-6444
McCain Foods USA
Grand Island, NE 308-382-7770
Snowcrest Packer
Abbotsford, BC. 604-859-4881
Washington Rhubarb Growers Association
Sumner, WA 800-435-9911
Webster Farms
Cambridge Station, NS 902-538-9492

Canned

EMERLING INTERNATIONAL FOODS, INC.

Emerling International Foods
Buffalo, NY. 716-833-7381

We supply food manufacturers and food service
customers worldwide (since 1988) with bulk ingredients including: Fruits & Vegetables; Juice
Concentrates; Herbs & Spices; Oils & Vinegars;
Flavors & Colors; Honey & Molasses. We also
produce PURE MAPLE SYRUP.

Frozen

Cleugh's Frozen Foods
Buena Park, CA 714-521-1002
Coloma Frozen Foods
Coloma, MI. 800-642-2723

EMERLING INTERNATIONAL FOODS, INC.

Emerling International Foods
Buffalo, NY. 716-833-7381

We supply food manufacturers and food service
customers worldwide (since 1988) with bulk ingredients including: Fruits & Vegetables; Juice
Concentrates; Herbs & Spices; Oils & Vinegars;
Flavors & Colors; Honey & Molasses. We also
produce PURE MAPLE SYRUP.

Ever Fresh Fruit Company
Boring, OR .800-239-8026
Lennox Farm
Shelburne, ON 519-925-6444
Radar Farms
Lynden, WA 360-354-6574
Snowcrest Packer
Abbotsford, BC. 604-859-4881
Washington Rhubarb Growers Association
Sumner, WA 800-435-9911
Webster Farms
Cambridge Station, NS 902-538-9492
Windatt Farms
Picton, ON. .613-393-5289

Roasted Vegetables

Moody Dunbar
Johnson City, TN 800-251-8202
Supermarket Productions
San Rafael, CA 415-479-0211

SupHerb Farms
Turlock, CA .800-787-4372

CrEATe! Get ready-to-use fresh flavor with
SupHerb Farms' all-natural fresh frozen culinary
herbs, specialty vegetables, culinary herb pastes,
vegetable purees and creative blends. Complete
microbiological testing ensures food safety. We
set the standard for outstanding customer service, inspired culinary support, collaborative customer partnerships and innovative custom
products.

Roots & Tubers

Allen Canning Company
Siloam Springs, AR 800-234-2553
American Botanicals
Eolia, MO 800-684-6070

EMERLING INTERNATIONAL FOODS, INC.

Emerling International Foods
Buffalo, NY. 716-833-7381

We supply food manufacturers and food service
customers worldwide (since 1988) with bulk ingredients including: Fruits & Vegetables; Juice
Concentrates; Herbs & Spices; Oils & Vinegars;
Flavors & Colors; Honey & Molasses. We also
produce PURE MAPLE SYRUP.

Penn Herb Company
Philadelphia, PA 800-523-9971
Pharmline
Florida, NY .845-651-4443
Winder Dairy
West Valley, UT 800-946-3371

Rutabaga

Exeter Produce & Storage Company
Exeter, ON. .519-235-0141
Kurtz Produce
Ariss, ON 519-824-3279

Canned

Chiquita Brands International
Cincinnati, OH 877-833-5551

EMERLING INTERNATIONAL FOODS, INC.

Emerling International Foods
Buffalo, NY. 716-833-7381

We supply food manufacturers and food service
customers worldwide (since 1988) with bulk ingredients including: Fruits & Vegetables; Juice
Concentrates; Herbs & Spices; Oils & Vinegars;
Flavors & Colors; Honey & Molasses. We also
produce PURE MAPLE SYRUP.

Frozen

EMERLING INTERNATIONAL FOODS, INC.

Emerling International Foods
Buffalo, NY. 716-833-7381

We supply food manufacturers and food service
customers worldwide (since 1988) with bulk ingredients including: Fruits & Vegetables; Juice
Concentrates; Herbs & Spices; Oils & Vinegars;
Flavors & Colors; Honey & Molasses. We also
produce PURE MAPLE SYRUP.

Salad Greens

Atlanta Bread Company International, Inc.
Smyrna, GA 800-398-3728
Del Monte Fresh Produce Company
Coral Gables, FL. 800-950-3683
Pasta USA
Spokane, WA. 800-456-2084
Victoria Packing Corporation
Brooklyn, NY 718-649-2180

Sauces

Apple

Blue Jay Orchards
Bethel, CT 203-748-0119
Bowman Apple Products Company
Mt Jackson, VA. 877-426-9626
Burnette Foods
Elk Rapids, MI 231-264-8116
Burnette Foods
Hartford, MI .616-621-3181
Cold Hollow Cider Mill
Waterbury Center, VT. 800-327-7537
Commodities Marketing, Inc.
Edison, NJ 732-516-0700
Coutts Specialty Foods
Boxborough, MA 800-919-2952
Del Mar Food Products Corporation
Watsonville, CA 831-722-3516

EMERLING INTERNATIONAL FOODS, INC.

Emerling International Foods
Buffalo, NY. 716-833-7381

We supply food manufacturers and food service
customers worldwide (since 1988) with bulk ingredients including: Fruits & Vegetables; Juice
Concentrates; Herbs & Spices; Oils & Vinegars;
Flavors & Colors; Honey & Molasses. We also
produce PURE MAPLE SYRUP.

Graves Mountain Cannery
Syria, VA 540-923-4747

Independent Food Processors Company
Yakima, WA 800-476-5398
Knouse Foods
Peach Glen, PA 717-677-8181
Knouse Foods Cooperative
Paw Paw, MI 269-657-5524
Knouse Foods Cooperative
Chambersburg, PA 717-263-9177
Knouse Foods Cooperative
Orrtanna, PA 717-642-8291
Leahy Orchards
Franklin, QC 450-827-2544
Leroux Creek Foods
Hotchkiss, CO. 877-970-5670
Let's Serve
Plattsburgh, NY. 518-293-7119
Love Creek Orchards
Medina, TX. 800-449-0882
Mott's
Port Chester, NY. 914-612-4000
Nana Mae's Organics
Sebastopol, CA 707-829-7359
National Fruit Product Company
Winchester, VA 540-662-3401
National Fruit Product Company
Lincolnton, NC 704-735-2531
New Era Canning Company
New Era, MI 231-861-2151
New Morning
Needham, MA. 781-444-0440
Solana Gold Organics
Sebastopol, CA 800-459-1121
Stone Cellar Kitchens
Riverside, CA 951-352-5713
Tree Top
Selah, WA 800-367-6571
Tree Top
Selah, WA 800-542-4055
Unique Ingredients
Naches, WA. 509-653-1991

Canned
Bowman Apple Products Company
Mt Jackson, VA. 877-426-9626
Independent Food Processors Company
Yakima, WA 800-476-5398
Leahy Orchards
Franklin, QC 450-827-2544

New Era Canning Company
New Era, MI 231-861-2151

with Other Fruit or Spices
Leahy Orchards
Franklin, QC 450-827-2544

Cranberry
Chung's Gourmet Foods
Houston, TX 800-824-8647
Coastal Classics
Duxbury, MA 508-746-6058
Columbia County Fruit Processors
Hanson, MA 508-763-5257
Delectable Gourmet LLC
Lindenhurst, NY 800-696-1350
Fireside Kitchen
Halifax, NS 902-454-7387
Golden Valley Foods
Abbotsford, BC. 888-299-8855
Johnston's Home Style Products
Charlottetown, PE. 902-629-1300
Ocean Spray Cranberries
Lakeville-Middleboro, MA 800-662-3263
Shiloh Foods
Savannah, TN 800-795-2550
Skjodt-Barrett Foods
Mississauga, ON. 877-600-1200
Steel's Gourmet Foods
Bridgeport, PA 800-678-3357

Jellied
Ocean Spray Cranberries
Lakeville-Middleboro, MA 800-662-3263

Scallions

EMERLING INTERNATIONAL FOODS, INC.

Emerling International Foods
Buffalo, NY. 716-833-7381

We supply food manufacturers and food service customers worldwide (since 1988) with bulk ingredients including: Fruits & Vegetables; Juice Concentrates; Herbs & Spices; Oils & Vinegars; Flavors & Colors; Honey & Molasses. We also produce PURE MAPLE SYRUP.

Ferris Organic Farm
Eaton Rapids, MI 800-628-8736
S&E Organic Farms
Bakersfield, CA 661-325-2644

SupHerb Farms
Turlock, CA 800-787-4372

CrEATe! Get ready-to-use fresh flavor with SupHerb Farms' all-natural fresh frozen culinary herbs, specialty vegetables, culinary herb pastes, vegetable purees and creative blends. Complete microbiological testing ensures food safety. We set the standard for outstanding customer service, inspired culinary support, collaborative customer partnerships and innovative custom products.

Tanimura & Antle
Salinas, CA. 831-455-2255

Seaweeds & Sea Vegetables
Acadian Seaplants
Dartmouth, NS 800-575-9100
Atlantic Laboratories
Waldoboro, ME. 207-832-5376
Chieftain Wild Rice Company
Spooner, WI 800-262-6368
Great Eastern Sun
Asheville, NC 800-334-5809
Maine Coast Sea Vegetables
Franklin, ME. 207-565-2907

Maine Seaweed Company
Steuben, ME 207-546-2875

Shallot
Chieftain Wild Rice Company
Spooner, WI 800-262-6368
Christopher Ranch
Gilroy, CA. 408-847-1100
Diamond Nut Company
Lemont, IL 630-739-3000
Haliburton International Corporation
Fontana, CA 877-980-4295

SupHerb Farms
Turlock, CA 800-787-4372

CrEATe! Get ready-to-use fresh flavor with SupHerb Farms' all-natural fresh frozen culinary herbs, specialty vegetables, culinary herb pastes, vegetable purees and creative blends. Complete microbiological testing ensures food safety. We set the standard for outstanding customer service, inspired culinary support, collaborative customer partnerships and innovative custom products.

Tulkoff Food Products
Baltimore, MD 800-638-7343
Van Drunen Farms
Momence, IL. 815-472-3100
Vegetable Juices
Chicago, IL 888-776-9752

Soy
Agri-Dairy Products
Purchase, NY 914-697-9580
Ajinomoto Food Ingredients LLC
Chicago, IL 773-380-7000
Avatar Corporation
University Park, IL 800-255-3181
Basic Food Flavors
North Las Vegas, NV 702-643-0043
Blue Chip Group
Salt Lake City, UT 800-878-0099
California Natural Products
Lathrop, CA 209-858-2525
Cedar Lake Foods
Cedar Lake, MI. 800-246-5039
Clofine Dairy & Food Products
Linwood, NJ 800-441-1001
Columbus Foods Company
Des Plaines, IL 800-322-6457
Cricklewood Soyfoods
Mertztown, PA 610-682-4109
Dakota Organic Products
Watertown, SD 800-243-7264
Ener-G Foods
Seattle, WA 800-331-5222
Farmers Grain Company
Morganfield, KY. 800-339-4241
Flavor House
Adelanto, CA 760-246-9131
Genisoy Food Company
Tulsa, OK 888-437-4769
Genisoy Products Company
Tulsa, OK 800-228-4656
Glennys
Freeport, NY 888-864-1243
Heartland Fields
West Des Moines, IA 515-225-1166
Heartland Fields, LLC
West Des Moines, IA 866-769-7200
Hialeah Products Company
Hollywood, FL 800-923-3379
House Foods America Corporation
Garden Grove, CA 714-901-4350
Innovative Food Solutions LLC
Columbus, OH 800-884-3314
International Service Group
Alpharetta, GA 770-518-0988
Island Spring
Vashon, WA. 206-463-9848
Lee's Food Products
Toronto, ON 416-465-2407

Lightlife Foods
Turners Falls, MA 800-274-6001
Mandarin Soy Sauce
Middletown, NY 845-343-1505
Mei Shun Tofu Products Company
Chicago, IL 312-842-7000
Microsoy Corporation
Jefferson, IA 515-386-2100
Miyako Oriental Foods
Baldwin Park, CA 877-788-6476
ND Labs Inc
Lynbrook, NY 888-263-5227
New England Natural Bakers
Greenfield, MA 800-910-2884
Northern Soy
Rochester, NY 585-235-8970
P.J. Lisac & Associates
Oregon City, OR 503-652-1988
Pokonobe Industries
Santa Monica, CA 310-392-1259
Purity Foods
Okemos, MI 800-997-7358
Red River Commodities
Fargo, ND 701-282-2600
San-Ei Gen FFI
New York, NY 212-315-7840
San-J International
Richmond, VA 800-446-5500
Solae
St. Louis, MO 800-325-7108
Solnuts
Hudson, IA 800-648-3503
Soyfoods of America
Duarte, CA 626-358-3836
SoyLife Division
Edina, MN 952-920-7700
Specialty Ingredients
Buffalo Grove, IL 847-419-9595
SunOpta Grains
Hope, MN 800-297-5997
SunRich
Hope, MN 800-297-5997
Turtle Island Foods
Hood River, OR 800-508-8100
Vincent Formusa Company
Chicago, IL 312-421-0485
Vitasoy USA
Ayer, MA 978-772-6880
Walpex Trading Company
Coral Gables, FL 305-662-9744
White Wave
Broomfield, CO 800-488-9283

Fresh

Smoke & Fire Natural Food
Great Barrington, MA 413-528-8008
Vitasoy USA
Ayer, MA 978-772-6880

Protein

Texturized

Allen Canning Company
Siloam Springs, AR 800-234-2553
Del Monte Foods
San Francisco, CA 800-543-3090
Princeville Canning Company
Princeville, IL 309-385-4301

Soy Bean

Aarhus United USA, Inc.
Newark, NJ 800-776-1338
ACATRIS
Oakville, ON 905-829-2414
ADM Nutraceuticals
Decatur, IL 800-510-2178
AG Processing, Inc.
Omaha, NE 800-247-1345
American Culinary Gardens
Springfield, MO 888-831-2433
Bellatti Soybeans-Bellatti Soynuts
Mount Pulaski, IL 217-792-5503
Bunge Corporation
Vicksburg, MS 601-638-3824
Cargill Vegetable Oils
Minneapolis, MN 612-378-0551
Continental Grain/ContiGroup Companies
New York, NY 212-207-5930
Durey-Libby Edible Nuts
Carlstadt, NJ 800-332-6887

Felbro Food Products
Los Angeles, CA 800-335-2761
Fizzle Flat Farm
Yale, IL 618-793-2060
Frontier Commodities
Byron, MN 507-775-2174
Gama Products
Medley, FL 305-883-1200
Hain Celestial Canada
Delta, BC 866-983-7834
Heartland Fields, LLC
West Des Moines, IA 866-769-7200
IMAC
Oklahoma City, OK 888-878-7827
Ingredient Innovations
Kansas City, MO 816-587-1426
Knight Seed Company
Burnsville, MN 800-328-2999
Lone Pine Enterprises
Carlisle, AR 870-552-3217
Louis Dreyfus Corporation
Wilton, CT 203-761-2000
Myron's Fine Foods
Erving, MA 800-730-2820
Producer's Rice
Stuttgart, AR 870-673-4444
ProSource
Alexandria, MN 320-763-2470
Purity Foods
Okemos, MI 800-997-7358
R&J Farms
West Salem, OH 419-846-3179
Red River Commodities
Fargo, ND 701-282-2600
Roberts Seed
Axtell, NE 308-743-2565
Seapoint Farms
Costa Mesa, CA 888-722-7098
Seed Enterprises
West Point, NE 888-440-7333
Shepherd Farms
South Beloit, IL 800-383-2676
Sno Pac Foods
Caledonia, MN 800-533-2215
Sonne
Wahpeton, ND 800-727-6663
Star of the West Milling Company
Frankenmuth, MI 989-652-9971
T.S. Smith & Sons
Bridgeville, DE 302-337-8271
The Solae Company
St Louis, MO 800-325-7108
Tofu Shop Specialty Foods
Arcata, CA 707-822-7401
Townsends Inc
Georgetown, DE 302-855-7100
Western Pacific Commodities
Las Vegas, NV 702-312-8080

Soy Milk

Agri-Dairy Products
Purchase, NY 914-697-9580
Clofine Dairy & Food Products
Linwood, NJ 800-441-1001
Commodities Marketing, Inc.
Edison, NJ 732-516-0700
Devansoy
Carroll, IA 800-747-8605
Eden Foods Inc
Clinton, MI 800-248-0320
Ener-G Foods
Seattle, WA 800-331-5222
Local Tofu
Nyack, NY 845-727-6393
Nutrisoya Foods
Saint-Hyacinthe, QC 450-796-4261
Pacific Foods of Oregon
Tualatin, OR 503-692-9666
San Diego Soy Dairy
El Cajon, CA 619-447-8638
Soyfoods of America
Duarte, CA 626-358-3836
Sunrise Markets
Vancouver, BC 604-685-8019
Tofu Shop Specialty Foods
Arcata, CA 707-822-7401
Vance's Foods
Gilmer, TX 800-497-4834
White Wave
Broomfield, CO 800-488-9283

Soy Protein

Cemac Foods Corporation
Philadelphia, PA 800-724-0179
Farbest-Tallman Foods Corporation
Montvale, NJ 201-573-4900
ND Labs Inc
Lynbrook, NY 888-263-5227
Solae Company
St Louis, MO 800-325-7108
SoyTex
West Orange, NJ 888-769-8391
The Solae Company
St Louis, MO 800-325-7108

Concentrate

The Solae Company
St Louis, MO 800-325-7108

Isolate

Solae Company
St Louis, MO 800-325-7108

Texturized

Nuvex Ingredients
Blue Earth, MN 507-526-4331
Solae Company
St Louis, MO 800-325-7108

Spinach

Avon Heights Mushrooms
Avondale, PA 610-268-2092
Chiquita Processed Foods
Milton Freewater, OR 541-938-4461
F&S Produce Company
Rosenhayn, NJ 800-886-3316
Frank Capurro & Son
Moss Landing, CA 831-728-3904
J.R. Simplot Company
Boise, ID 208-336-2110
Leach Farms
Berlin, WI 920-361-1880
McCain Foods Canada
Florenceville, NB 506-392-5541
Patterson Frozen Foods
Patterson, CA 209-892-2611
Pictsweet Frozen Foods
Bells, TN 731-663-7600
Ruskin Packaging
Miami, FL 305-324-1529
Seabrook Brothers & Sons
Seabrook, NJ 856-455-8080
Snowcrest Packer
Abbotsford, BC 604-859-4881
Tami Great Food
Monsey, NY 718-788-4200
Unique Ingredients
Naches, WA 509-653-1991
Vegetable Juices
Chicago, IL 888-776-9752
Walla Walla Gardeners' Association
Walla Walla, WA 800-553-5014

Canned

Chiquita Processed Foods
Milton Freewater, OR 541-938-4461
ConAgra Grocery Products
Irvine, CA 714-680-1000

EMERLING INTERNATIONAL FOODS, INC.

Emerling International Foods
Buffalo, NY 716-833-7381

We supply food manufacturers and food service customers worldwide (since 1988) with bulk ingredients including: Fruits & Vegetables; Juice Concentrates; Herbs & Spices; Oils & Vinegars; Flavors & Colors; Honey & Molasses. We also produce PURE MAPLE SYRUP.

McCain Foods Canada
Florenceville, NB 506-392-5541

Frozen

EMERLING INTERNATIONAL FOODS, INC.

Emerling International Foods
Buffalo, NY 716-833-7381

We supply food manufacturers and food service customers worldwide (since 1988) with bulk ingredients including: Fruits & Vegetables; Juice Concentrates; Herbs & Spices; Oils & Vinegars; Flavors & Colors; Honey & Molasses. We also produce PURE MAPLE SYRUP.

Vegetable Juices
Chicago, IL 888-776-9752

Sponge Gourd

Acme Steak & Seafood Company
Youngstown, OH. 330-270-8000
Bifulco Farms
Pittsgrove, NJ 856-692-0707
Cajun Chef Products
St Martinville, LA. 337-394-7112
McCain Foods USA
Grand Island, NE 308-382-7770

Sprouts

Amigos Canning Company
San Antonio, TX 800-580-3477
Calco of Calgary
Calgary, AB. .403-295-3578
Jonathan's Sprouts
Rochester, MA 508-763-2577
Lake Helen Sprout Farm
Lake Helen, FL 386-228-2871
Montreal Chop Suey Company
Montreal, QC .514-522-3134
Mung Dynasty
Pittsburgh, PA. 412-381-1350
Snowcrest Packer
Abbotsford, BC. 604-859-4881
Sungarden Sprouts
Cookeville, TN 931-526-1106

Alfalfa

International Specialty Supply
Cookeville, TN 931-526-1106
Jonathan's Sprouts
Rochester, MA 508-763-2577
Sungarden Sprouts
Cookeville, TN 931-526-1106

Bean

ConAgra Grocery Products
Archbold, OH 419-445-8015
ConAgra Grocery Products
Irvine, CA 714-680-1000

EMERLING INTERNATIONAL FOODS, INC.

Emerling International Foods
Buffalo, NY 716-833-7381

We supply food manufacturers and food service customers worldwide (since 1988) with bulk ingredients including: Fruits & Vegetables; Juice Concentrates; Herbs & Spices; Oils & Vinegars; Flavors & Colors; Honey & Molasses. We also produce PURE MAPLE SYRUP.

International Specialty Supply
Cookeville, TN 931-526-1106
Sungarden Sprouts
Cookeville, TN 931-526-1106

Mung Bean

Hong Kong Market Company
Chicago, IL 312-791-9111

Squash

Anchor Food Products/ McCain Foods
Appleton, WI 920-734-0627
Chase Farms
Walkerville, MI 231-873-3337
Cobi Foods
Hantsport, NS 800-565-8229

F&S Produce Company
Rosenhayn, NJ 800-886-3316
Frank Capurro & Son
Moss Landing, CA 831-728-3904
Georgia Vegetable Company
Tifton, GA. 229-386-2374
Goebbert's Home Grown Vegetables
South Barrington, IL 847-428-6727
Haliburton International Corporation
Fontana, CA .877-980-4295
Indian Rock Produce
Perkasie, PA .800-882-0512
McCain Foods Canada
Florenceville, NB 506-392-5541
Michigan Freeze Pack
Hart, MI. 231-873-2175
National Frozen Foods Corporation
Seattle, WA 206-322-8900
Organically Grown Company
Eugene, OR. .541-689-5320
Pacific Collier Fresh Company
Immokalee, FL 800-226-7274
Pictsweet Frozen Foods
Bells, TN. 731-663-7600
Rene Produce Distributors
Nogales, AZ .520-281-9014
Snowcrest Packer
Abbotsford, BC. 604-859-4881
Tom Ringhausen Orchards
Hardin, IL 618-576-2311
Tony Vitrano Company
Jessup, MD 410-799-7444
Vegetable Juices
Chicago, IL 888-776-9752
Walter P. Rawl & Sons
Pelion, SC 803-359-3645

Acorn

Georgia Vegetable Company
Tifton, GA. 229-386-2374

Canned

EMERLING INTERNATIONAL FOODS, INC.

Emerling International Foods
Buffalo, NY 716-833-7381

We supply food manufacturers and food service customers worldwide (since 1988) with bulk ingredients including: Fruits & Vegetables; Juice Concentrates; Herbs & Spices; Oils & Vinegars; Flavors & Colors; Honey & Molasses. We also produce PURE MAPLE SYRUP.

Sure Fresh Produce
Santa Maria, CA 888-423-5379

Frozen

EMERLING INTERNATIONAL FOODS, INC.

Emerling International Foods
Buffalo, NY 716-833-7381

We supply food manufacturers and food service customers worldwide (since 1988) with bulk ingredients including: Fruits & Vegetables; Juice Concentrates; Herbs & Spices; Oils & Vinegars; Flavors & Colors; Honey & Molasses. We also produce PURE MAPLE SYRUP.

Sure Fresh Produce
Santa Maria, CA 888-423-5379
Vegetable Juices
Chicago, IL 888-776-9752

Golden Scallopino

Agrinorthwest
Kennewick, WA 509-734-1195
Allen Canning Company
Siloam Springs, AR 800-234-2553
Baker Produce Company
Kennewick, WA 800-624-7553
Circle Valley Produce
Idaho Falls, ID 208-524-2628
DNO
Columbus, OH 800-686-2366

McCain Foods USA
Grand Island, NE 308-382-7770
Zuccaro's Fruit & Produce Company
Minneapolis, MN 612-333-1122

Star Fruit

Brooks Tropicals
Homestead, FL 800-327-4833

Succotash

Allen Canning Company
Siloam Springs, AR 800-234-2553

EMERLING INTERNATIONAL FOODS, INC.

Emerling International Foods
Buffalo, NY. .716-833-7381

We supply food manufacturers and food service customers worldwide (since 1988) with bulk ingredients including: Fruits & Vegetables; Juice Concentrates; Herbs & Spices; Oils & Vinegars; Flavors & Colors; Honey & Molasses. We also produce PURE MAPLE SYRUP.

McCain Foods USA
Grand Island, NE 308-382-7770
Pictsweet Frozen Foods
Bells, TN. 731-663-7600
Symons Frozen Foods
Centralia, WA 360-736-1321
Trappe Packing Corporation
Trappe, MD .410-476-3185
Twin City Foods
Stanwood, WA 206-515-2400

Canned

EMERLING INTERNATIONAL FOODS, INC.

Emerling International Foods
Buffalo, NY. .716-833-7381

We supply food manufacturers and food service customers worldwide (since 1988) with bulk ingredients including: Fruits & Vegetables; Juice Concentrates; Herbs & Spices; Oils & Vinegars; Flavors & Colors; Honey & Molasses. We also produce PURE MAPLE SYRUP.

Ore-Ida Foods
Pittsburgh, PA. 412-237-3450
Patterson Frozen Foods
Patterson, CA 209-892-2611

Frozen

EMERLING INTERNATIONAL FOODS, INC.

Emerling International Foods
Buffalo, NY. .716-833-7381

We supply food manufacturers and food service customers worldwide (since 1988) with bulk ingredients including: Fruits & Vegetables; Juice Concentrates; Herbs & Spices; Oils & Vinegars; Flavors & Colors; Honey & Molasses. We also produce PURE MAPLE SYRUP.

Ore-Ida Foods
Pittsburgh, PA 412-237-3450
Patterson Frozen Foods
Patterson, CA 209-892-2611
Pictsweet Frozen Foods
Bells, TN. 731-663-7600
Symons Frozen Foods
Centralia, WA 360-736-1321
Trappe Packing Corporation
Trappe, MD. .410-476-3185

Sun Dried Fruit

Chooljian Brothers Packing Company
Sanger, CA 559-875-5501
Del Monte Foods
San Francisco, CA 800-543-3090
Del Rey Packing Company
Del Rey, CA .559-888-2031

Sun-Maid Growers of California
Kingsburg, CA 800-272-4746

Sunflower

SunOpta Sunflower
Breckenridge, MN 800-654-4145

Sweet Potatoes

B&B Produce
Benson, NC 800-633-4902
Barnes Farming Corporation
Spring Hope, NC 252-459-9380
Best Ever Bake Shop
Mount Vernon, NY 914-665-7005
Bissett Produce Company
Spring Hope, NC 800-849-5073
Bright Harvest Sweet Potato Company
Clarksville, AR 800-793-7440
Burch Farms
Faison, NC 800-466-9668
Carolina Pride Products
Enfield, NC 252-445-3154
Dunbar Foods
Dunn, NC 910-892-3175
Godwin Produce Company
Dunn, NC 910-892-4171
Johnson Brothers Produce Company
Whitakers, NC 252-437-2111
Joseph D Teachey Produce
Wallace, NC 910-285-4502
Livingston Farmers Association
Livingston, CA 209-394-7611
Moody Dunbar
Johnson City, TN 800-251-8202
Nash Produce Company
Nashville, NC 800-334-3032
Royce C. Bone Farms
Nashville, NC 252-443-3773
Scott Farms
Lucama, NC 877-284-4030
Seneca Foods Corporation
Marion, NY 315-926-8100
Spring Acres Sales Company
Spring Hope, NC 800-849-5436
Tull Hill Farms
Kinston, NC 252-523-4406
Wayne E. Bailey Produce Company
Chadbourn, NC 800-845-6149

Frozen

Bright Harvest Sweet Potato Company
Clarksville, AR 800-793-7440

EMERLING INTERNATIONAL FOODS, INC.

Emerling International Foods
Buffalo, NY. 716-833-7381

We supply food manufacturers and food service
customers worldwide (since 1988) with bulk ingredients including: Fruits & Vegetables; Juice
Concentrates; Herbs & Spices; Oils & Vinegars;
Flavors & Colors; Honey & Molasses. We also
produce PURE MAPLE SYRUP.

Mashed

Bright Harvest Sweet Potato Company
Clarksville, AR 800-793-7440
Moody Dunbar
Johnson City, TN 800-251-8202

Frozen

Bright Harvest Sweet Potato Company
Clarksville, AR 800-793-7440

Tamarind

Cinnabar Specialty Foods
Prescott, AZ 866-293-6433

Tangelos

A. Duda Farm Fresh Foods
Belle Glade, FL. 561-996-7621
Heller Brothers Packing Corporation
Winter Garden, FL 407-656-4986

Tangerines

A. Duda Farm Fresh Foods
Belle Glade, FL. 561-996-7621
Dimare
Visalia, CA 559-627-0821
DNE World Fruit Sales
Fort Pierce, FL 800-327-6676
Haines City Citrus Growers Association
Haines City, FL. 800-422-4245
Hale Indian River Groves
Wabasso, FL 800-562-4502
Heller Brothers Packing Corporation
Winter Garden, FL 407-656-4986
Hunt Brothers Cooperative
Lake Wales, FL 863-676-9471
Seald Sweet Growers & Packers
Vero Beach, FL 772-569-2244

Taro

Sweety Novelty
Monterey Park, CA. 626-282-4482

Tartufo

Creme Glacee Gelati
St Leonard, QC 888-322-0116
Gelato Fresco
Toronto, ON 416-785-5415
Vigneri Confections
Rochester, NY 585-254-6160

Textured Vegetable Protein

Advanced Spice & Trading
Carrollton, TX 800-872-7811
American Health & Nutrition
Ann Arbor, MI 734-677-5572
CHS, Inc.
Inner Grove Heights, MN. 800-232-3639
Clofine Dairy & Food Products
Linwood, NJ 800-441-1001
DMH Ingredients
Libertyville, IL 847-362-9977
First Spice Mixing Company
Long Island City, NY 800-221-1105
The Solae Company
St Louis, MO 800-325-7108
Westin
Omaha, NE 800-228-6098

Tomatillos

EMERLING INTERNATIONAL FOODS, INC.

Emerling International Foods
Buffalo, NY. 716-833-7381

We supply food manufacturers and food service
customers worldwide (since 1988) with bulk ingredients including: Fruits & Vegetables; Juice
Concentrates; Herbs & Spices; Oils & Vinegars;
Flavors & Colors; Honey & Molasses. We also
produce PURE MAPLE SYRUP.

George Chiala Farms
Morgan Hill, CA 408-778-0562
Haliburton International Corporation
Fontana, CA 877-980-4295

Tomato

AgroCepia
Miami, FL 305-704-3488
Agrusa, Inc.
Leonia, NJ. 201-592-5950
Atlantic Quality Spice &Seasonings
Edison, NJ. 800-584-0422
Ballantine Produce Company
Reedley, CA 559-637-2400
BGS Jourdan & Sons
Darlington, MD. 410-457-4904
Char-Wil Canning Company
Hurlock, MD. 410-943-3580
Chieftain Wild Rice Company
Spooner, WI 800-262-6368
Colusa Canning Company
Williams, CA. 530-473-2871
ConAgra Grocery Products
Perrysburg, OH 419-661-4400
ConAgra Grocery Products
Irvine, CA 714-680-1000

Del Monte Fresh Produce Company
Coral Gables, FL. 800-950-3683
Dixon Canning Company
Dixon, CA 707-678-4406
Eden Foods Inc
Clinton, MI 800-248-0320
Escalon Premier Brand
Escalon, CA 209-838-7341
F&S Produce Company
Rosenhayn, NJ 800-886-3316
Fresh Express
Franklin Park, IL 800-242-5472
Garden State Farms
Philadelphia, PA 215-463-8000
George Chiala Farms
Morgan Hill, CA 408-778-0562
Goebbert's Home Grown Vegetables
South Barrington, IL 847-428-6727
Haliburton International Corporation
Fontana, CA 877-980-4295
Harris Farms
Coalinga, CA 800-742-1955
Hermann Pickle Farm
Garrettsville, OH. 800-245-2696
Indian Rock Produce
Perkasie, PA 800-882-0512
John N Wright Jr
Federalsburg, MD. 410-754-9044
Kaplan & Zubrin
Camden, NJ. 800-334-0002
Lagorio Enterprises
Manteca, CA 209-982-5691
M&S Tomato Repacking Company
Springfield, MA 800-343-0371
Mangia
Mission Viejo, CA 866-462-6442
Miramar Pickles & Food Products
Fort Lauderdale, FL 954-351-8030
Moscahlades Brothers
New York, NY 212-226-5410
Nationwide Canning
Cottam, ON 519-839-4831
Pacific Collier Fresh Company
Immokalee, FL 800-226-7274
Pacific Tomato Growers
Palmetto, FL 941-722-3291
Pastene Companies
Canton, MA 781-830-8200
Pastorelli Food Products
Chicago, IL 800-767-2829
Pure Food Ingredients
Verona, WI 800-355-9601
Rene Produce Distributors
Nogales, AZ 520-281-9014
Royce C. Bone Farms
Nashville, NC 252-443-3773
San Benito Foods
Hollister, CA 831-637-4434
SEW Friel
Queenstown, MD 410-827-8841
Signature Fruit
Stockton, CA. 209-931-1531
Somerset Industries
Spring House, PA 800-883-8728
Spreda Group
Prospect, KY 502-426-9411
Stanislaus Food Products
Modesto, CA. 800-327-7201
Sun-Brite Canning
Ruthven, ON 519-326-9033
Surface Banana Company
Bluewell, WV 304-589-7202
Talley Farms
Arroyo Grande, CA. 805-489-2508
Thomas Canning/Maidstone
Maidstone, ON 519-737-1531

Timber Crest Farms
Healdsburg, CA 888-374-9325
Tip Top Canning Company
Tipp City, OH 937-667-3713
Topor's Pickle Company
Detroit, MI 313-237-0288
Topper Food Products
East Brunswick, NJ 800-377-2823
Transa
Libertyville, IL 847-281-9582
Tri-Valley Growers
Los Banos, CA 209-827-5000
Unilever Foods
Stockton, CA 209-466-9580
Vegetable Juices
Chicago, IL 888-776-9752
Veronica Foods Company
Oakland, CA 800-370-5554
Violet Packing
Williamstown, NJ 856-629-7428
Waterfield Farms
Amherst, MA 413-549-3558
Weil's Food Processing
Wheatley, ON 519-825-4572
Wisconsin Cheese
Melrose Park, IL 708-450-0074
Woodland Foods
Gurnee, IL 847-625-8600
Z&S Distributing
Fresno, CA 800-467-0788

Canned

Agrocan
Toronto, ON 877-247-6226
Char-Wil Canning Company
Hurlock, MD 410-943-3580
ConAgra Grocery Products
Perrysburg, OH 419-661-4400
ConAgra Grocery Products
Irvine, CA 714-680-1000
Eden Foods Inc
Clinton, MI 800-248-0320
Escalon Premier Brand
Escalon, CA 209-838-7341
Hartford City Foam Pack aging & Converting
Hartford City, IN 765-348-2500
John N Wright Jr
Federalsburg, MD 410-754-9044
Milroy Canning Company
Milroy, IN 765-629-2221
Nationwide Canning
Cottam, ON 519-839-4831
Natural Value Products
Sacramento, CA 916-427-7242
Ottawa Foods
Ottawa, OH 800-837-1631
Pacific Coast Producers Corporate Office
Lodi, CA 209-367-8800
Pastene Companies
Canton, MA 781-830-8200
Pastorelli Food Products
Chicago, IL 800-767-2829
Pure Food Ingredients
Verona, WI 800-355-9601
Ray Brothers & Noble Canning Company
Hobbs, IN 765-675-7451
Red Gold
Elwood, IN 877-748-9798
Rio Valley Canning Company
Donna, TX 956-464-7843
San Benito Foods
Vancouver, WA 800-453-7832
San Benito Foods
Hollister, CA 831-637-4434
Shafer-Haggart
Vancouver, BC 888-779-7111
Stanislaus Food Products
Modesto, CA 800-327-7201
Sun-Brite Canning
Ruthven, ON 519-326-9033
Thomas Canning/Maidstone
Maidstone, ON 519-737-1531
Tip Top Canning Company
Tipp City, OH 937-667-3713
Violet Packing
Williamstown, NJ 856-629-7428
Weil's Food Processing
Wheatley, ON 519-825-4572

Crushed

Agrocan
Toronto, ON 877-247-6226
Colonna Brothers
North Bergen, NJ 201-864-1115
Hirzel Canning Company &Farms
Northwood, OH 419-693-0531
Violet Packing
Williamstown, NJ 856-629-7428

Cherry

Exeter Produce & Storage Company
Exeter, ON 519-235-0141
Talley Farms
Arroyo Grande, CA 805-489-2508

Cocktail

Miss Scarlett's
Chandler, AZ 800-345-6734
Pacific Coast Producers Corporate Office
Lodi, CA 209-367-8800
Princeville Canning Company
Princeville, IL 309-385-4301

Diced

Hirzel Canning Company &Farms
Northwood, OH 419-693-0531
Ingomar Packing Company
Los Banos, CA 209-826-9494
Tip Top Canning Company
Tipp City, OH 937-667-3713

Dried

Chieftain Wild Rice Company
Spooner, WI 800-262-6368

EMERLING INTERNATIONAL FOODS, INC.

Emerling International Foods
Buffalo, NY 716-833-7381

> We supply food manufacturers and food service customers worldwide (since 1988) with bulk ingredients including: Fruits & Vegetables; Juice Concentrates; Herbs & Spices; Oils & Vinegars; Flavors & Colors; Honey & Molasses. We also produce PURE MAPLE SYRUP.

Grapevine Trading Company
Santa Rosa, CA 800-469-6478
Just Tomatoes Company
Westley, CA 800-537-1985
Kennedy Candy Company
Kilgore, TX 800-657-5258
Rising Sun Farms
Phoenix, OR 541-535-8331
Setton International Foods
Commack, NY 800-227-4397
Terri Lynn
Elgin, IL 800-323-0775
Timber Crest Farms
Healdsburg, CA 888-374-9325
Unique Ingredients
Naches, WA 509-653-1991
Woodland Foods
Gurnee, IL 847-625-8600

Fresh

F&S Produce Company
Rosenhayn, NJ 800-886-3316
Fresh Express
Franklin Park, IL 800-242-5472
G Cefalu & Brothers
Jessup, MD 410-799-3414
Harris Farms
Coalinga, CA 800-742-1955
Lagorio Enterprises
Manteca, CA 209-982-5691
Mixon Fruit Farms
Bradenton, FL 800-608-2525
Rene Produce Distributors
Nogales, AZ 520-281-9014
Signature Fruit
Stockton, CA 209-931-1531
Talley Farms
Arroyo Grande, CA 805-489-2508

Tri-Valley Growers
Los Banos, CA 209-827-5000

Frozen

Allen Canning Company
Siloam Springs, AR 800-234-2553
ConAgra Grocery Products
Irvine, CA 714-680-1000
Del Monte Foods
San Francisco, CA 800-543-3090
Hartford City Foam Pack aging & Converting
Hartford City, IN 765-348-2500
Milroy Canning Company
Milroy, IN 765-629-2221
Ocean Mist
Castroville, CA 831-633-2144
Pacific Coast Producers Corporate Office
Lodi, CA 209-367-8800
Ray Brothers & Noble Canning Company
Hobbs, IN 765-675-7451
Red Gold
Elwood, IN 877-748-9798

SupHerb Farms
Turlock, CA 800-787-4372

> CrEATe! Get ready-to-use fresh flavor with SupHerb Farms' all-natural fresh frozen culinary herbs, specialty vegetables, culinary herb pastes, vegetable purees and creative blends. Complete microbiological testing ensures food safety. We set the standard for outstanding customer service, inspired culinary support, collaborative customer partnerships and innovative custom products.

Vegetable Juices
Chicago, IL 888-776-9752

Marinated

American Importing Company
Minneapolis, MN 612-331-9226

Plum

Kaplan & Zubrin
Camden, NJ 800-334-0002

Processed

Escalon Premier Brand
Escalon, CA 209-838-7341
Pastorelli Food Products
Chicago, IL 800-767-2829
Weil's Food Processing
Wheatley, ON 519-825-4572

Products

American Chalkis International Foods Company
Walnut, CA 909-595-5358
Burnette Foods
Hartford, MI 616-621-3181
ConAgra Grocery Products
Irvine, CA 714-680-1000
Country Pure Foods
Akron, OH 330-753-2293

EMERLING INTERNATIONAL FOODS, INC.

Emerling International Foods
Buffalo, NY 716-833-7381

> We supply food manufacturers and food service customers worldwide (since 1988) with bulk ingredients including: Fruits & Vegetables; Juice Concentrates; Herbs & Spices; Oils & Vinegars; Flavors & Colors; Honey & Molasses. We also produce PURE MAPLE SYRUP.

Escalon Premier Brand
Escalon, CA 209-838-7341
F&S Produce Company
Rosenhayn, NJ 800-886-3316

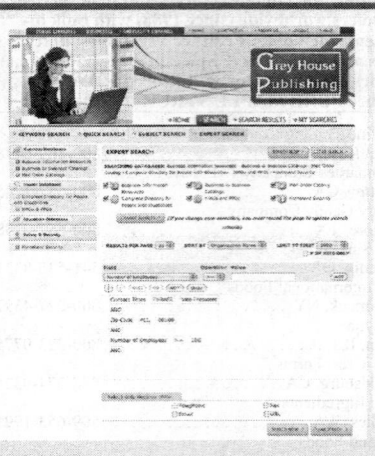
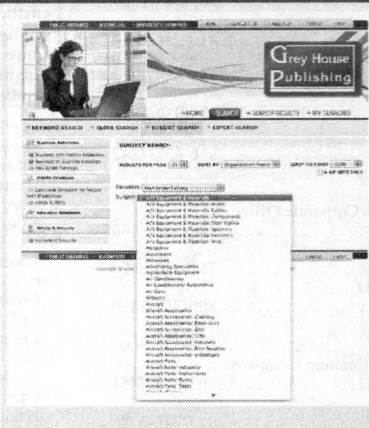

Fresh Express
Franklin Park, IL 800-242-5472
George Chiala Farms
Morgan Hill, CA 408-778-0562
Golden Valley Foods
Abbotsford, BC 888-299-8855
Heinz Company
Trevose, PA 215-639-2343
Hermann Pickle Farm
Garrettsville, OH 800-245-2696
Hunt-Wesson Foods
Rochester, NY 209-847-0321
International Home Foods
Milton, PA 973-359-9920
Kennedy Candy Company
Kilgore, TX 800-657-5258
Lagorio Enterprises
Manteca, CA 209-982-5691
Lake Packing Company
Lottsburg, VA 804-529-6101
Los Gatos Tomato Products
Huron, CA 559-945-2700
Milroy Canning Company
Milroy, IN 765-629-2221
Nationwide Canning
Cottam, ON 519-839-4831
Pacific Coast Producers
Oroville, CA 530-533-4311
Paradise Tomato Kitchens
Louisville, KY 502-637-1700
Pasta Factory
Northlake, IL 800-615-6951
Pastene Companies
Canton, MA 781-830-8200
Pastorelli Food Products
Chicago, IL 800-767-2829
Precision Foods
St Louis, MO 800-647-8170
Progresso Quality Foods
Vineland, NJ 800-200-9377
Pure Food Ingredients
Verona, WI 800-355-9601
Quest International Flavors
Hoffman Estates, IL 847-645-7000
Ray Brothers & Noble Canning Company
Hobbs, IN 765-675-7451
Red Gold
Elwood, IN 877-748-9798
San Benito Foods
Hollister, CA 831-637-4434
SEW Friel
Queenstown, MD 410-827-8841
Signature Fruit
Stockton, CA 209-931-1531
Somerset Industries
Spring House, PA 800-883-8728
Spreda Group
Prospect, KY 502-426-9411
Talley Farms
Arroyo Grande, CA 805-489-2508
Terry Foods Inc
Idaho Falls, ID 208-604-8143
Thomas Canning/Maidstone
Maidstone, ON 519-737-1531
Timber Crest Farms
Healdsburg, CA 888-374-9325
Tip Top Canning Company
Tipp City, OH 937-667-3713
Topper Food Products
East Brunswick, NJ 800-377-2823
Transa
Libertyville, IL 847-281-9582
Unilever Foods
Stockton, CA 209-466-9580
Unique Ingredients
Naches, WA 509-653-1991
Valley Tomato Products
Stockton, CA 209-982-4586
Vegetable Juices
Chicago, IL 888-776-9752
Veronica Foods Company
Oakland, CA 800-370-5554
Walker Foods
Los Angeles, CA 800-966-5199
Weil's Food Processing
Wheatley, ON 519-825-4572
Welch's Foods Inc
Concord, MA 800-340-6870
Wisconsin Cheese
Melrose Park, IL 708-450-0074

Roma (Egg)

Lagorio Enterprises
Manteca, CA 209-982-5691
McCain Foods USA
Grand Island, NE 308-382-7770

Stewed

Nationwide Canning
Cottam, ON 519-839-4831
San Benito Foods
Hollister, CA 831-637-4434
Signature Fruit
Stockton, CA 209-931-1531
Tip Top Canning Company
Tipp City, OH 937-667-3713

Sun-Dried

Agrocan
Toronto, ON 877-247-6226
American Importing Company
Minneapolis, MN 612-331-9226
Castella Imports
Hauppauge, NY 866-227-8355
Claussen Pickle Company
Woodstock, IL 800-435-2817
Martin Farms
Patterson, CA 877-838-7369
Mezza
Lake Forest, IL 888-206-6054
Mooney Farms
Chico, CA 530-899-2661
Pacific Choice Brands
Fresno, CA 559-237-5583
Quality Choice Foods
Toronto, ON 416-650-9595
Veronica Foods Company
Oakland, CA 800-370-5554
Victoria Packing Corporation
Brooklyn, NY 718-649-2180
Woodland Foods
Gurnee, IL 847-625-8600

Yellow Cherry

Acme Preserve Company
Adrian, MI 517-265-7222
Beckman & Gast Company
St Henry, OH 419-678-4195
California Fruit and Tomato Kitchens
Riverbank, CA 209-869-9300
Del Monte Foods
San Francisco, CA 800-543-3090
Supreme Dairy Farms Company
Warwick, RI 401-739-8180

Tropical & Exotic Fruit

Chieftain Wild Rice Company
Spooner, WI 800-262-6368
Diamond Nut Company
Lemont, IL 630-739-3000
Heikes Produce Company
Medford, OR 541-772-5653
New West Foods
San Francisco, CA 701-947-2505
NTC Foods Corporation
Williamsville, NY 800-333-1637
Varet Street Market
Brooklyn, NY 718-387-5452
Very Best Foods
Miami, FL 305-824-9165

Turnip

Abbott & Cobb, Inc.
Langhorne, PA 800-345-7333
Cobi Foods
Hantsport, NS 800-565-8229
Lucks Food Decorating Company
Tacoma, WA 206-674-7200
Pictsweet Frozen Foods
Bells, TN 731-663-7600
Snowcrest Packer
Abbotsford, BC 604-859-4881
Tom Ringhausen Orchards
Hardin, IL 618-576-2311
Walter P. Rawl & Sons
Pelion, SC 803-359-3645

Canned

EMERLING INTERNATIONAL FOODS, INC.

Emerling International Foods
Buffalo, NY 716-833-7381

> We supply food manufacturers and food service customers worldwide (since 1988) with bulk ingredients including: Fruits & Vegetables; Juice Concentrates; Herbs & Spices; Oils & Vinegars; Flavors & Colors; Honey & Molasses. We also produce PURE MAPLE SYRUP.

Frozen

EMERLING INTERNATIONAL FOODS, INC.

Emerling International Foods
Buffalo, NY 716-833-7381

> We supply food manufacturers and food service customers worldwide (since 1988) with bulk ingredients including: Fruits & Vegetables; Juice Concentrates; Herbs & Spices; Oils & Vinegars; Flavors & Colors; Honey & Molasses. We also produce PURE MAPLE SYRUP.

Turnip Greens: Canned

Bush Brothers & Company
Augusta, WI 715-286-2211

Vegetables

A. Duda Farm Fresh Foods
Belle Glade, FL 561-996-7621
A. Lassonde, Inc.
Rougemont, QC 514-878-1057
Aaland Potato Company
Hoople, ND 701-894-6144
Acme Preserve Company
Adrian, MI 517-265-7222
Acme Steak & Seafood Company
Youngstown, OH 330-270-8000
Affiliated Rice Milling
Alvin, TX 281-331-6176
Agri-Northwest
Kennewick, WA 509-734-1195
Agro Foods, Inc.
Key Biscayne, FL 305-361-7200
Al Pete Meats
Muncie, IN 765-288-8817
Alimentaire Whyte's Inc
Laval, QC 800-625-1979
Allen Canning Company
Siloam Springs, AR 800-234-2553
Associated Potato Growers, Inc.
Grand Forks, ND 800-437-4685
B&G Foods
Parsippany, NJ 973-401-6500
B&M
Portland, ME 207-772-8341
B.M. Lawrence & Company
San Francisco, CA 415-981-3650
Baker Produce Company
Kennewick, WA 800-624-7553
Baumer Foods
New Orleans, LA 504-482-5761
Bay Cities Produce Company
San Leandro, CA 510-346-4943
Bean Buddies
New Hyde Park, NY 516-775-3726
Ben B. Schwartz & Sons
Detroit, MI 313-841-8300
Big B Distributors
Evansville, IN 812-425-5235
Birds Eye Foods
Rochester, NY 800-999-5044
Bjorneby Potato Company
Minto, ND 701-248-3482
Blissfield Canning Company
Blissfield, MI 517-486-3815
Bob Gordon & Associates
Chicago, IL 773-247-0588
Border Foods Inc
Deming, NM 888-737-7752
Bornt Family Farms
Holtville, CA 760-356-1066
Bottomline Foods
Pembroke Pines, FL 954-843-0562

Bright Harvest Sweet Potato Company
Clarksville, AR 800-793-7440
Brooks Food Group Corporate Office
Bedford, VA 800-873-4934
Brooks Tropicals
Homestead, FL 800-327-4833
Bruce Church
Salinas, CA 800-538-2861
Bruce Foods Corporation
New Iberia, LA 337-365-8101
Bryant Preserving Company
Alma, AR 800-634-2413
Bubbles of San Francisco
Stockton, CA 209-951-6071
Burnette Foods
Elk Rapids, MI 231-264-8116
Burnette Foods
Hartford, MI 616-621-3181
Bush Brothers & Company
Dandridge, TN 865-509-2361
Byrnes Packing
Hastings, FL 904-692-1643
C.C. Graber Company
Ontario, CA 800-996-5483
Cagnon Foods Company
Brooklyn, NY 718-647-2244
Cajun Chef Products
St Martinville, LA 337-394-7112
California & Washington Company
San Francisco, CA 415-344-5200
California Farms & Canners
San Francisco, CA 415-433-3522
California Fruit and Tomato Kitchens
Riverbank, CA 209-869-9300
Caltex Foods
Canoga Park, CA 800-522-5839
Cannon Potato Company
Center, CO 719-754-3445
Cara Mia Foods
Castroville, CA 831-633-2423
Carando Gourmet Frozen Foods
Springfield, MA 413-730-4205
Caribbean Food Delights
Tappan, NY 845-398-3000
Cascade Specialties
Boardman, OR 541-481-2522
Cascadian Farm & MUIR Glen; Division of General
Mills
Sedro Woolley, WA............... 360-855-0100
Cates Addis Company
Parkton, NC 800-423-1883
Cebro Frozen Foods
Newman, CA 209-862-0150
Chase Farms
Walkerville, MI.................. 231-873-3337
Chiquita Brands
Cincinnati, OH 513-784-8000
Chiquita Brands International
Cincinnati, OH 800-438-0015
Chiquita Processed Foods
Milton Freewater, OR 541-938-4461
Christopher Ranch
Gilroy, CA 408-847-1100
Chugwater Chili Corporation
Chugwater, WY 800-972-4454
Claussen Pickle Company
Woodstock, IL 800-435-2817
Cleugh's Frozen Foods
Buena Park, CA 714-521-1002
Club Chef
Covington, KY 859-578-3100
Cobi Foods
Hantsport, NS 800-565-8229
Coloma Frozen Foods
Coloma, MI 800-642-2723
Columbia Foods
Snohomish, WA 360-568-0838
Columbia Foods
Quincy, WA 509-787-1585
ConAgra Grocery Products
Archbold, OH 419-445-8015
Conserverie Larose
Calixa-Lavallee, QC 450-583-6438
Cooperative Elevator Company
Pigeon, MI 989-453-4500
Coutts Specialty Foods
Boxborough, MA 800-919-2952
Crown Point
St John, IN 219-365-3200
Crystal Seed Potato Company
Crystal, ND 701-657-2143

Culinary Standards Corporation
Louisville, KY 800-778-3434
Cut Above Foods
Carlsbad, CA..................... 760-931-6777
D'Arrigo Brothers Company of California
Salinas, CA 800-995-5939
Dairy King Milk Farms/Foodservice
Glendale, CA 818-243-6455
Dairy Management
Rosemont, IL 800-248-8829
De Bruyn Produce Company
Zeeland, MI 800-733-9177
Deep Foods
Union, NJ 908-810-7500
DeFrancesco & Sons
Firebaugh, CA 209-364-7000
Del Mar Food Products Corporation
Watsonville, CA 831-722-3516
Del Monte Foods
San Francisco, CA 800-543-3090
Del Monte Fresh Produce Company
Coral Gables, FL................. 800-950-3683
Delicious Valley Frozen Foods
McAllen, TX 956-631-7177
Delta Packing Company of Lodi
Lodi, CA 209-334-0689
Diamond Nut Company
Lemont, IL 630-739-3000
Dickinson Frozen Foods
Fruitland, ID 208-452-5200
DMH Ingredients
Libertyville, IL 847-362-9977
DNO
Columbus, OH 800-686-2366
Dole Fresh Vegetable Company
Soledad, CA 800-333-5454
Dole Fresh Vegetables
Monterey, CA 831-422-8871
Dong Kee Company
Chicago, IL 312-225-6340
East Coast Fresh Cuts Company
Savage, MD...................... 410-799-9900
Eckert Cold Storage
Escalon, CA 209-838-4040
Eden Foods Inc
Clinton, MI 800-248-0320
Emil Lerch
Hatfield, PA 215-855-2233
Erba Food Products
Brooklyn, NY 718-272-7700
Escalon Premier Brand
Escalon, CA 209-838-7341
Ever Fresh Fruit Company
Boring, OR 800-239-8026
F&S Produce Company
Rosenhayn, NJ 800-886-3316
Faribault Foods
Minneapolis, MN 612-333-6461
Fearnow Brothers
Cape May, NJ 609-884-0440
Federation of Southern Cooperatives
East Point, GA 404-765-0991
Fiesta Canning Company
Mc Neal, AZ 520-364-7541
Florida Citrus
Tampa, FL 813-626-5580
Fort Boise Produce Company
Nyssa, OR 541-372-3837
Foster Family Farm
South Windsor, CT............... 860-648-9366
Fountain Valley Foods
Colorado Springs, CO........... 719-573-6012
Franklin Mushroom Farms
North Franklin, CT 860-642-3019
Freeze-Dry Products
Santa Rosa, CA 707-547-1776
Fresh Express
Salinas, CA 831-775-2300
Fresh Frozen Foods
Jefferson, GA 800-277-9851
Frieda's
Los Alamitos, CA 800-421-9477
Ful-Flav-R Foods
Alamo, CA 510-339-9618
Furmano Foods
Northumberland, PA............. 877-877-6032
G L Mezzetta
American Canyon, CA 707-648-1050
G S Dunn & Company
Hamilton, ON 905-522-0833
G&G Marketing
Naples, FL 239-593-4564

Galegher Farms
Thompson, ND 701-847-2151
Garber Farms
Iota, LA 800-824-2284
Garden State Farms
Philadelphia, PA 215-463-8000
Garden Valley Foods
Sutherlin, OR 541-459-9565
Garon Industries
Mosinee, WI 715-693-1593
Gene Belk Fruit Packers
Bloomington, CA 909-877-1819
George Chiala Farms
Morgan Hill, CA 408-778-0562
George L. Wells Meat Company
Philadelphia, PA 800-523-1730
Ghirardelli Ranch
Petaluma, CA 707-795-7616
Gibsonburg Canning Company
Gibsonburg, OH 419-637-2221
Gilleshammer Thiele Farms
St Thomas, ND 701-257-6634
Gilroy Foods
Gilroy, CA 800-921-7502
Giuliano's Specialty Foods
Garden Grove, CA 714-895-9661
Glacier Foods
Sanger, CA 559-875-3354
Glory Foods
Columbus, OH 614-252-2042
Godwin Produce Company
Dunn, NC 910-892-4171
Gotliebs Guacamole
Sharon, CT 860-364-0842
Grant & Janet Brians
Hollister, CA..................... 831-637-8497
Great American Appetizers
Nampa, ID. 800-282-4834
Great Lakes Kraut Company
Shortsville, NY 585-289-4414
Green Garden Food Products
Kent, WA........................ 800-304-1033
Griffin Food Company
Muskogee, OK 800-580-6311
GWB Foods Corporation
Brooklyn, NY 718-686-9600
H H Dobbins
Lyndonville, NY................. 877-362-2467
H.K. Canning
Ventura, CA...................... 805-652-1392
Haliburton International Corporation
Fontana, CA 877-980-4295
Hard-E Foods
St Louis, MO..................... 314-533-2211
Harner Farms
State College, PA 814-237-7919
Harris Farms
Coalinga, CA 800-742-1955
Harvest-Pac Products
Chatham, ON 519-436-0446
Henderson's Gardens
Berwyn, AB 780-338-2128
Henry Broch & Company/APK, Inc.
Libertyville, IL 847-816-6225
Herold's Salad
Cleveland, OH 800-427-2523
Hetty Fair Foods Company
Buffalo, NY...................... 716-876-4345
HMC Marketing Group
Kingsburg, CA 559-897-1009
Houston Calco
Houston, TX 713-236-8668
Hunt-Wesson Food Service Company
Rochester, NY.................... 800-633-1002
Indian Rock Produce
Perkasie, PA 800-882-0512
Ingredients Corporation of America
Memphis, TN 901-525-6660
Inland Empire Foods
Riverside, CA 888-452-3267
International Home Foods
Milton, PA 973-359-9920
J.C. Watson Company
Parma, ID 208-722-5141
J.R. Simplot Company
Boise, ID 208-336-2110
J.R. Simplot Food Group
Pasco, WA 509-544-6700
Jalapeno Foods Company
The Woodlands, TX 800-896-2318
JES Foods
Cleveland, OH 216-883-8987

Jimmy's Chiles
Rosemont, IL 708-429-2803
Joe's Vegetables
Hollister, CA 831-636-3224
John N Wright Jr
Federalsburg, MD 410-754-9044
JR Wood/Big Valley
Atwater, CA 209-358-5643
Jubilee-Sedgefield Salads
Greensboro, NC 336-288-6646
Jyoti Cruisine India
Berwyn, PA 610-522-2650
Kaplan & Zubrin
Camden, NJ 800-334-0002
Kelly Pickle Company
Oconto, WI 920-834-4433
Kings Processing
Middleton, NS 902-825-2188
Knight Seed Company
Burnsville, MN 800-328-2999
L&S Packing Company
Farmingdale, NY 800-286-6487
L.H. Hayward & Company
New Orleans, LA 504-733-8480
L.I. Cauliflower Association
Riverhead, NY 631-727-2212
Lagorio Enterprises
Manteca, CA 209-982-5691
Lake Helen Sprout Farm
Lake Helen, FL 386-228-2871
Lakeside Foods
Plainview, MN 507-534-3141
Lakeside Foods
Seymour, WI 920-833-2371
Lakeside Foods
New Holstein, WI 920-898-5702
Lakeside Packing Company
Harrow, ON 519-738-2314
Lamb-Weston
Hermiston, OR 800-766-7783
Larson Potato
Park River, ND 701-284-6437
LDI
Cincinnati, OH 513-421-1671
Lennox Farm
Shelburne, ON 519-925-6444
Limited Edition
Midland, TX 432-686-2008
Livingston Farmers Association
Livingston, CA 209-394-7611
Lodi Canning Company
Lodi, WI 608-592-4236
Louise Metafora Company
Medford, MA 781-871-6918
Lucks Food Decorating Company
Tacoma, WA 206-674-7200
Made in Nature
Fresno, CA 800-906-7426
Magic Valley Foods
Rupert, ID 208-436-3126
Mancini Packing Company
Zolfo Springs, FL 863-735-2000
Maple Leaf Foods International
Toronto, ON 416-480-8900
Mar Distributing Company
Los Angeles, CA 213-627-4006
Marten's Country Kitchen
Port Byron, NY 315-776-8821
Martha's Garden
Toronto, ON 866-773-2887
Maryland Fresh Tomato Company
Jessup, MD 410-799-5050
Matador Processors
Blanchard, OK 800-847-0797
McCain Foods
Fort Atkinson, WI 920-563-6625
McCain Foods USA
Grand Island, NE 308-382-7770
McCall Farms
Effingham, SC 843-662-2223
McCartney Produce Company
Paducah, KY 800-522-2791
Melissa's/World VarietyPProduce
Vernon, CA 800-588-0151
Mercado Latino
City of Industry, CA 626-333-6862
Mercer Processing
Modesto, CA 209-529-0150
Miami Purveyors
Miami, FL 305-262-6170
Michael Foods, Inc.
Minnetonka, MN 952-258-4000

Michigan Celery Promotion Cooperative
Hudsonville, MI 616-669-1250
Miguel's Stowe Away
Stowe, VT 800-448-6517
Millie's Pierogi
Chicopee Falls, MA 800-743-7641
Mills Brothers International
Tukwila, WA 206-575-3000
Milos
New York, NY 212-245-7400
Minnesota Dehydrated Vegetables
Fosston, MN 218-435-1997
Miramar Fruit Trading Company
Medley, FL 305-883-4774
Mister Spear
Stockton, CA 800-677-7327
Mitake Trading International
La Verne, CA 909-596-1981
Mixon Fruit Farms
Bradenton, FL 800-608-2525
Modern Grocery Company
Macon, GA 478-745-3381
Monterey Mushrooms
Watsonville, CA 800-333-6874
Monterey Mushrooms Inc.
Temple, PA 800-763-0700
Monticello Canning Company
Crossville, TN 931-484-3696
Montrose Potato Growers
Montrose, CO 970-249-5623
Moody Dunbar
Johnson City, TN 800-251-8202
Moscahlades Brothers
New York, NY 212-226-5410
Mother Teresa's
Clute, TX 888-265-7429
Mount Olive Pickle Company
Mt Olive, NC 800-672-5041
Mrs. Mazzula's Food Products
Edison, NJ 732-248-0555
Muir Glen Organic Tomato
Sacramento, CA 916-557-0900
Musco Olive Products
Orland, CA 530-865-4111
National Frozen Foods Corporation
Seattle, WA 206-322-8900
Nationwide Canning
Cottam, ON 519-839-4831
Natural Choice Distribution
Oakland, CA 510-653-8212
Natural Quality Company
San Martin, CA 408-683-2182
Nature Quality
San Martin, CA 408-683-2182
Naturex (Chart Corp)
South Hackensack, NJ 201-440-5000
New Era Canning Company
New Era, MI 231-861-2151
New Harvest Foods
Pulaski, WI 920-822-2578
New Meridian
Eaton, IN 765-396-3344
Nicola International
Los Angeles, CA 818-545-1515
Nonpareil Dehydrated Potatoes
Blackfoot, ID 800-522-2223
NORPAC Foods
Lake Oswego, OR 503-635-9311
NORPAC Plant
Salem, OR 800-822-2898
Northern Star Company
Minneapolis, MN 612-339-8981
Nunes Company
Salinas, CA 831-757-1521
OC Schulz & Sons
Crystal, ND 701-657-2152
Ocean Mist
Castroville, CA 831-633-2144
Oh Boy! Corporation
San Fernando, CA 818-361-1128
Ohio Mushroom Company
Lima, OH 419-221-1721
Omega Produce Company
Nogales, AZ 520-281-0410
Ontario Produce Company
Ontario, OR 541-889-6485
Oregon Potato Company
Boardman, OR 800-336-6311
Organically Grown Company
Eugene, OR 541-689-5320
Osowski Farms
Minto, ND 701-248-3341

Pacific Choice Brands
Fresno, CA 559-237-5583
Pacific Coast Producers
Lodi, CA 209-367-8800
Pacific Collier Fresh Company
Immokalee, FL 800-226-7274
Pacific Tomato Growers
Palmetto, FL 941-722-3291
Pacific Valley Foods
Bellevue, WA 425-643-1805
Paradise Products Corporation
Roslyn, NY 800-826-1235
Paris Foods Corporation
Camden, NJ 856-964-0915
Pastene Companies
Canton, MA 781-830-8200
Pastorelli Food Products
Chicago, IL 800-767-2829
Pavich Family Farms
Terra Bella, CA 661-391-1000
Pictsweet Frozen Foods
Bells, TN 731-663-7600
Pompeian
Baltimore, MD 800-638-1224
Pope Corporation
Novi, MI 248-888-8989
Potato Services of Michigan
Edmore, MI 989-427-3314
Pride Enterprises Glades
Belle Glade, FL 561-996-1091
Princeville Canning Company
Princeville, IL 309-385-4301
Proacec USA
Santa Monica, CA 310-996-7770
Produits Ronald
St. Damase, QC 450-797-3303
Pure Food Ingredients
Verona, WI 800-355-9601
Queensway Foods Company
Burlingame, CA 650-697-6666
Quest International Fruits & Vegetables
Silverton, OR 503-873-3600
R&S Mexican Food Products
Glendale, AZ 602-272-2727
R.C. McEntire & Company
Columbia, SC 803-799-3388
Rain Sweet
Salem, OR 800-363-4293
Ralph Sechler & Son
St Joe, IN 800-332-5461
Ralph Sechler & Son Inc
St Joe, IN 800-332-5461
Raymond-Hadley Corporation
Spencer, NY 800-252-5220
Ready-Pac Produce
Irwindale, CA 800-800-7822
Reckitt Benckiser
Parsippany, NJ 800-333-3899
Red River Commodities
Fargo, ND 701-282-2600
Rene Produce Distributors
Nogales, AZ 520-281-9014
Rich-Seapak Corporation
Brownsville, TX 956-542-0001
Ripon Pickle Company
Ripon, WI 800-324-5493
Ron-Son Foods
Swedesboro, NJ 856-241-7333
Ruskin Packaging
Miami, FL 305-324-1529
S&G Products
Nicholasville, KY 800-826-7652
S. Kennedy Vegetable Lifestock Company
Clear Lake, IA 641-357-6101
Salad Depot
Moonachie, NJ 201-507-1980
San Benito Foods
Hollister, CA 831-637-4434
Santa Barbara Olive Company
Goleta, CA 800-624-4896
Saticoy Foods Corporation
Ventura, CA 805-647-5266
Schiff Food Products
North Bergen, NJ 201-861-2503
Schmidt Brothers
Swanton, OH 419-826-3671
Schwans Bakeries
Stilwell, OK 918-696-8325
Scotsburn Dairy Group
Truro, NS 902-895-4412
Seabrook Brothers & Sons
Seabrook, NJ 856-455-8080

Sedlock Farm
Lynn Center, IL 309-521-8284
Seneca Foods
Marion, NY 315-926-8100
Seneca Foods
Cumberland, WI 715-822-2181
Seneca Foods
Clyman, WI 920-696-3331
Serv-Agen Corporation
Cherry Hill, NJ 856-663-6966
Seville Olive Company
Los Angeles, CA 323-261-2218
SEW Friel
Queenstown, MD 410-827-8841
Shafer Lake Fruit
Hartford, MI 269-621-3194
Signature Fruit
Stockton, CA 209-931-1531
Silva Farms
Gonzales, CA 831-675-2327
Smeltzer Orchard Company
Frankfort, MI 231-882-4421
Smith Frozen Foods
Weston, OR 541-566-3515
Smith Frozen Foods
Weston, OR 800-547-0203
Smith-Coulter Company
Chittenango, NY 315-687-6510
Snowcrest Packer
Abbotsford, BC 604-859-4881
Somerset Industries
Spring House, PA 800-883-8728
Sonne
Wahpeton, ND 800-727-6663
SOPAKCO Foods
Mullins, SC 800-276-9678
South Mill Distribution
Kennett Square, PA 610-444-4800
Spokane Seed Company
Spokane Valley, WA 509-535-3671
Spreda Group
Prospect, KY 502-426-9411
Stahlbush Island Farms
Corvallis, OR 541-753-8942
Star Fine Foods
Fresno, CA 559-498-2900
Sterigenics International
Los Angeles, CA 800-472-4508
Strathroy Foods
Strathroy, ON 519-245-4600
Strub Pickles
Brantford, ON 519-751-1717
Sumida Pickle Products
Honolulu, HI 808-841-4227
Sun-Brite Canning
Ruthven, ON 519-326-9033
Sun-Glo of Idaho
Sugar City, ID 208-356-7346
Sungarden Sprouts
Cookeville, TN 931-526-1106
Sunnyside Vegetable Packing
Millville, NJ 856-451-5077
Sunrise Growers
Placentia, CA 714-630-2170
Superior Bean & Spice Company
Brush Prairie, WA 360-694-0819
Superior Foods
Watsonville, CA 831-728-3691
Superior Frozen Vegetables
Cornell, MI 906-384-6466
Supermarket Productions
San Rafael, CA 415-479-0211

SupHerb Farms
Turlock, CA 800-787-4372

CrEATe! Get ready-to-use fresh flavor with SupHerb Farms' all-natural fresh frozen culinary herbs, specialty vegetables, culinary herb pastes, vegetable purees and creative blends. Complete microbiological testing ensures food safety. We set the standard for outstanding customer service, inspired culinary support, collaborative customer partnerships and innovative custom products.

Surface Banana Company
Bluewell, WV 304-589-7202
Sysco I&S Foodservices Inc
Edmonton, AB 780-478-3451
T.S. Smith & Sons
Bridgeville, DE 302-337-8271
Talk O'Texas Brands
San Angelo, TX 325-655-6077
Taylor Farms
Salinas, CA 831-754-0471
Teixeira Farms
Santa Maria, CA 805-928-3801
Thomas Canning/Maidstone
Maidstone, ON 519-737-1531
Timber Crest Farms
Healdsburg, CA 888-374-9325
Tom Ringhausen Orchards
Hardin, IL 618-576-2311
Tony Vitrano Company
Jessup, MD 410-799-7444
Too Goo Doo Farms/Easy Tray LLC
North Charleston, SC 843-767-0196
Topor's Pickle Company
Detroit, MI 313-237-0288
Trade Farm
Oakland, CA 510-836-2938
Trans Pecos Foods
San Antonio, TX 210-228-0896
Transa
Libertyville, IL 847-281-9582
Trappe Packing Corporation
Trappe, MD 410-476-3185
Tri-Valley Growers
Los Banos, CA 209-827-5000
Tropic Fish & Vegetable Center
Honolulu, HI 808-591-2963
Tropical
Charlotte, NC 800-220-1413
Tuscarora Organic Growers Cooperative
Hustontown, PA 814-448-2173
Twin City Foods
Stanwood, WA 206-515-2400
Unilever Foods
Stockton, CA 209-466-9580
United Marketing Exchange
Delta, CO 970-874-3332
United Natural Foods
Dayville, CT 800-877-8898
Vegetable Juices
Chicago, IL 888-776-9752
Verdelli Farms
Harrisburg, PA 800-422-8344
Veronica Foods Company
Oakland, CA 800-370-5554
Violet Packing
Williamstown, NJ 856-629-7428
Visalia Produce Sales Inc
Kingsburg, CA 559-897-6652
W&W Meats
Willoughby, OH 216-621-7846
W.F. Cosart Packing Company
Exeter, CA 559-592-2821
Wallace Grain & Pea Company
Palouse, WA 509-878-1561
Washington Potato Company
Warden, WA 509-349-8803
Washington Rhubarb Growers Association
Sumner, WA 800-435-9911
Webster Farms
Cambridge Station, NS 902-538-9492
Weil's Food Processing
Wheatley, ON 519-825-4572
Wesco Foods Company
Cincinnati, OH 513-762-4139
Westin
Omaha, NE 800-228-6098
Wildcat Produce
McGrew, NE 308-783-2438
William Bolthouse Farms
Bakersfield, CA 661-366-7205
William Karas & Sons
Churchville, NY 585-757-2751
Winslow B. Whitley
Oakley, ID 208-862-3229
Wolter Farms
Carmel, CA 831-624-8807
Zuccaro's Fruit & Produce Company
Minneapolis, MN 612-333-1122

IQF (Individual Quick Frozen)

Eckert Cold Storage
Escalon, CA 209-838-4040
LaMonica Fine Foods
Millville, NJ 856-825-8111
Rain Sweet
Salem, OR 800-363-4293

SupHerb Farms
Turlock, CA 800-787-4372

CrEATe! Get ready-to-use fresh flavor with SupHerb Farms' all-natural fresh frozen culinary herbs, specialty vegetables, culinary herb pastes, vegetable purees and creative blends. Complete microbiological testing ensures food safety. We set the standard for outstanding customer service, inspired culinary support, collaborative customer partnerships and innovative custom products.

Washington Rhubarb Growers Association
Sumner, WA 800-435-9911

Vegetables Mixed

Agrocan
Toronto, ON 877-247-6226
Birds Eye Foods
Rochester, NY 800-999-5044
Chiquita Processed Foods
Milton Freewater, OR 541-938-4461
Cobi Foods
Hantsport, NS 800-565-8229
Deep Foods
Union, NJ 908-810-7500
Del Monte Foods
San Francisco, CA 800-543-3090
Del Monte Foods
Mendota, IL 815-539-9361
DiMare International
Indio, CA 760-564-3762
H&F Food Products Company
Buffalo, NY 716-876-4345
J.R. Simplot Company
Boise, ID 208-336-2110
JR Wood/Big Valley
Atwater, CA 209-358-5643
Just Tomatoes Company
Westley, CA 800-537-1985
Lakeside Foods
Seymour, WI 920-833-2371
Lucks Food Decorating Company
Tacoma, WA 206-674-7200
McCain Foods Canada
Florenceville, NB 506-392-5541
Mills
Salinas, CA 831-758-8179
Musco Olive Products
Orland, CA 530-865-4111
New Harvest Foods
Pulaski, WI 920-822-2578
Patterson Frozen Foods
Patterson, CA 209-892-2611
Seneca Foods
Marion, NY 315-926-8100
Strathroy Foods
Strathroy, ON 519-245-4600
Trappe Packing Corporation
Trappe, MD 410-476-3185

Broccoli & Cauliflower

Cobi Foods
Hantsport, NS 800-565-8229

Broccoli, Peas & Carrots

Cobi Foods
Hantsport, NS 800-565-8229
Del Monte Foods
San Francisco, CA 800-543-3090
Faribault Foods
Minneapolis, MN 612-333-6461

Canned

Bryant Preserving Company
 Alma, AR 800-634-2413
Carriere Foods Inc
 Montreal, QC 514-384-4281
Cates Addis Company
 Parkton, NC 800-423-1883
Chiquita Processed Foods
 Milton Freewater, OR. 541-938-4461
Deep Foods
 Union, NJ 908-810-7500
Del Monte Foods
 Cambria, WI 920-348-5121

EMERLING INTERNATIONAL FOODS, INC.

Emerling International Foods
 Buffalo, NY. 716-833-7381

> **We supply food manufacturers and food service customers worldwide (since 1988) with bulk ingredients including: Fruits & Vegetables; Juice Concentrates; Herbs & Spices; Oils & Vinegars; Flavors & Colors; Honey & Molasses. We also produce PURE MAPLE SYRUP.**

Lakeside Foods
 Seymour, WI. 920-833-2371
Lucks Food Decorating Company
 Tacoma, WA 206-674-7200
McCain Foods Canada
 Florenceville, NB 506-392-5541
New Harvest Foods
 Pulaski, WI 920-822-2578
Seneca Foods
 Marion, NY 315-926-8100

Frozen

Birds Eye Foods
 Rochester, NY 800-999-5044
Cobi Foods
 Hantsport, NS 800-565-8229
Deep Foods
 Union, NJ 908-810-7500
JR Wood/Big Valley
 Atwater, CA 209-358-5643
Lakeside Foods
 Seymour, WI. 920-833-2371
McCain Foods Canada
 Florenceville, NB 506-392-5541
Strathroy Foods
 Strathroy, ON 519-245-4600
Symons Frozen Foods
 Centralia, WA 360-736-1321
Trappe Packing Corporation
 Trappe, MD. 410-476-3185

Peas & Carrots

Cates Addis Company
 Parkton, NC 800-423-1883
Chiquita Processed Foods
 Milton Freewater, OR. 541-938-4461
Cobi Foods
 Hantsport, NS 800-565-8229
Lakeside Foods
 Seymour, WI. 920-833-2371
Strathroy Foods
 Strathroy, ON 519-245-4600
Symons Frozen Foods
 Centralia, WA 360-736-1321
Twin City Foods
 Stanwood, WA 206-515-2400

Canned

Chiquita Processed Foods
 Milton Freewater, OR. 541-938-4461
Lakeside Foods
 Seymour, WI. 920-833-2371

Frozen

Cates Addis Company
 Parkton, NC 800-423-1883
Lakeside Foods
 Seymour, WI. 920-833-2371
Strathroy Foods
 Strathroy, ON 519-245-4600
Symons Frozen Foods
 Centralia, WA 360-736-1321

Twin City Foods
 Stanwood, WA 206-515-2400

Water Chestnuts

Dong Kee Company
 Chicago, IL 312-225-6340

EMERLING INTERNATIONAL FOODS, INC.

Emerling International Foods
 Buffalo, NY. 716-833-7381

> **We supply food manufacturers and food service customers worldwide (since 1988) with bulk ingredients including: Fruits & Vegetables; Juice Concentrates; Herbs & Spices; Oils & Vinegars; Flavors & Colors; Honey & Molasses. We also produce PURE MAPLE SYRUP.**

Lee's Food Products
 Toronto, ON 416-465-2407
Sona & Hollen Foods
 Los Alamitos, CA. 800-200-7662

SupHerb Farms
 Turlock, CA 800-787-4372

> **CrEATe! Get ready-to-use fresh flavor with SupHerb Farms' all-natural fresh frozen culinary herbs, specialty vegetables, culinary herb pastes, vegetable purees and creative blends. Complete microbiological testing ensures food safety. We set the standard for outstanding customer service, inspired culinary support, collaborative customer partnerships and innovative custom products.**

Watercress

California Watercress
 Fillmore, CA. 805-524-4808

Yams

Agrinorthwest
 Kennewick, WA 509-734-1195
Atwater Fruit Exchange
 Atwater, CA 209-358-2272
Baker Produce Company
 Kennewick, WA 800-624-7553
Bright Harvest Sweet Potato Company
 Clarksville, AR 800-793-7440
Cut Above Foods
 Carlsbad, CA. 760-931-6777
De Bruyn Produce Company
 Zeeland, MI. 800-733-9177
DNO
 Columbus, OH 800-686-2366
F&S Produce Company
 Rosenhayn, NJ 800-886-3316
Garber Farms
 Iota, LA 800-824-2284
Godwin Produce Company
 Dunn, NC 910-892-4171
Moody Dunbar
 Johnson City, TN 800-251-8202
Ocean Mist
 Castroville, CA. 831-633-2144
Seneca Foods
 Clyman, WI. 920-696-3331
Vaughn Rue Produce
 Wilson, NC 800-388-8138
Zuccaro's Fruit & Produce Company
 Minneapolis, MN 612-333-1122

Canned

Bruce Foods Corporation
 New Iberia, LA 800-299-9082
Moody Dunbar
 Johnson City, TN 800-251-8202

Frozen

Bright Harvest Sweet Potato Company
 Clarksville, AR 800-793-7440

Prepared

Moody Dunbar
 Johnson City, TN 800-251-8202

Zucchini

Anchor Food Products/ McCain Foods
 Appleton, WI 920-734-0627
Bifulco Farms
 Pittsgrove, NJ 856-692-0707

EMERLING INTERNATIONAL FOODS, INC.

Emerling International Foods
 Buffalo, NY. 716-833-7381

> **We supply food manufacturers and food service customers worldwide (since 1988) with bulk ingredients including: Fruits & Vegetables; Juice Concentrates; Herbs & Spices; Oils & Vinegars; Flavors & Colors; Honey & Molasses. We also produce PURE MAPLE SYRUP.**

F&S Produce Company
 Rosenhayn, NJ 800-886-3316
Ghirardelli Ranch
 Petaluma, CA 707-795-7616
Great American Appetizers
 Nampa, ID. 800-282-4834
Haliburton International Corporation
 Fontana, CA 877-980-4295
Miss Scarlett's
 Chandler, AZ. 800-345-6734
Ore-Ida Foods
 Pittsburgh, PA 412-237-3450
Pictsweet Frozen Foods
 Bells, TN. 731-663-7600
Ruskin Packaging
 Miami, FL 305-324-1529
Sure Fresh Produce
 Santa Maria, CA 888-423-5379
Talley Farms
 Arroyo Grande, CA. 805-489-2508
Tami Great Food
 Monsey, NY 718-788-4200
Vegetable Juices
 Chicago, IL 888-776-9752

Dark Green

Allen Canning Company
 Siloam Springs, AR 800-234-2553

General Grocery

General

A Gift Basket by Carmela
Longmeadow, MA 888-481-4438
A.T. Gift Company
Harpers Ferry, WV 304-876-6680
Abitec Corporation
Columbus, OH 800-555-1255
ACH Food Companies
Cordova, TN 800-691-1106
Alamo Onions
Pharr, TX 210-281-0962
Allied Food Products
Brooklyn, NY 212-230-4227
Allied Resource Corporation
Orem, UT 888-226-1096
AmeriQual Foods
Evansville, IN 812-867-1444
Apple Ledge
Holden, ME 207-989-5576
Arctic Glacier
Albany, NY 518-438-2082
Arctic Glacier
Buffalo, NY 800-688-5950
Arctic Glacier
Utica, NY 800-792-5958
Arctic Glacier
Fairport, NY 800-937-4423
Ashley Food Company, Inc.
Sudbury, MA 800-617-2823

Baldwin Richardson Foods
Frankfort, IL 866-644-2732

> **Baldwin Richardson Foods is a liquid ingredient manufacturer specializing in signature sauces, dessert toppings, beverage/pancake syrups, specialty fruit fillings and condiments. Packaging capabilities range from portion control cups and pouches to standard retail and foodservice packs and include industrial drums and totes. Full service R&D and Quality groups dedicated to new product development, with in-house stability and analytical testing. Call for assistance.**

Barnes Foods
Goldsboro, NC 919-778-7889
Basic Grain Products
Coldwater, OH 419-678-2304
Ben E. Keith DFW
Fort Worth, TX 817-654-3663
Binding Brauerei USA
Norwalk, CT 203-229-0111
Boyajian, Inc
Canton, MA 800-965-0665
Brooks Food Group, Inc
Monroe, NC 800-873-4934
Bungalow Brand Foods
Santa Barbara, CA 800-899-5267
Canyon Specialty Foods
Dallas, TX 877-815-3663
Capalbo's Gift Baskets
Nutley, NJ 800-252-6262
Cappello Foods
Hagerstown, MD 301-745-6641
Cargill Foods
Springdale, AR 479-750-6816
Caribbean Distributors
Brentwood, MD 301-403-2929
Central Grocers Cooperative
Franklin Park, IL 847-451-0660
Chicken of the Sea International
San Diego, CA 800-678-8862
Chong Mei Trading
Atlanta, GA 404-768-3838
Choyce Produce
Honolulu, HI 808-839-1502
Christmas Point Wild Rice Company
Baxter, MN 218-828-0603

Classic Foods
San Francisco, CA 800-574-8122
Colony Foods
Lawrence, MA 978-682-9677
Con Agro Food
Peru, IN 765-473-3086
ConAgra Food Store Brands
Edina, MN 952-469-4981
ConAgra Grocery Products
Omaha, NE 402-595-4000
Conco Food Service
Harahan, LA 800-488-3988
Consumer Packing Company
Lancaster, PA 717-397-6141
Cosgrove Distributors
Spring Valley, IL 815-664-4121
Creative Foods
Osceola, AR 800-643-0006
Cresinco
Overland Park, KS 913-897-4220
Culinary Farms, Inc.
Woodland, CA 888-383-2767
Custom Food Service
Phoenix, AZ 602-254-1876
Dakota Organic Products
Watertown, SD 800-243-7264
Dalton's Best Maid Products
Fort Worth, TX 800-447-3581
De Bilio Food Distributors
Anaheim, CA 714-773-9323
Derby Cone Company
Louisville, KY 502-491-1220
Dick Garber Company
Davie, FL 954-236-0456
Dillon Companies
Hutchinson, KS 620-665-5511
Double Wrap Cup & Container
Buffalo Grove, IL 312-337-0072
Ellsworth Foods
Tifton, GA 229-386-8448
Emil's Original
Philadelphia, PA 215-763-3311
Fabrique Delices
Hayward, CA 510-441-9500
Farallon Fisheries
S San Francisco, CA 650-583-3474
Fast Fixin Foods
Boaz, AL 256-593-7221
Fehr Foods
Abilene, TX 325-691-5425
Festive Foods
Virginia Beach, VA 757-490-9186
Filippo Berio Brand
Hackensack, NJ 201-525-2900
Foodmark
Wellesley, MA 781-237-7088
Formost Friedman Company
Merrick, NY 516-378-4919
Fountain Shakes/MS Foods
Minneapolis, MN 877-988-6940
French and Brawn
Camden, ME 207-236-3361
Freshmark Foods Corporation
Kent, WA 253-872-9426
Fulgenzi Foods
Leland Grove, IL 217-787-7495
G S Robins & Company
St Louis, MO 800-777-5155
Gallands Institutional Foodservice
Bakersfield, CA 661-631-5505
Giulia Specialty Food
Lodi, NJ 973-478-3111
Goya de Puerto Rico
Bayamon, PR 787-740-4900
Grantstone Supermarket
Tucson, AZ 520-628-7445
Great River Milling
Fountain City, WI 608-687-9580
Gregerson's Foods
Gadsden, AL 256-549-0644
Gulf Marine & Industrial Supplies
New Orleans, LA 800-886-6252
H&W Foods
Kapolei, HI 808-682-8300
Haile Resources
Dallas, TX 800-357-1471

Hanmi
Chicago, IL 773-271-0730
Hans Kissle Company
Haverhill, MA 978-372-2504
Harold M. Lincoln Company
Toledo, OH 800-345-4911
HBP Services
Dallas, TX 214-337-3488
HEB Foods & Drugs
San Antonio, TX 210-938-8000
Hickey Foods
Sun Valley, ID 208-788-9033
Hurd Orchards
Holley, NY 585-638-8838
I. Epstein & Sons
East Brunswick, NJ 800-237-5320
Ice House
Big Pine Key, FL 305-872-1215
Imperial Food Supply
Baton Rouge, LA 225-924-4222
Imsco Technology
North Andover, MA 978-689-2080
Inland Products
Carthage, MO 417-358-4046
International Delicacies
Emeryville, CA 510-428-9364
Ira Higdon Grocery Company
Cairo, GA 229-377-1272
Itella Foods
Los Angeles, CA 213-765-0967
J. Frasinetti & Sons
Sacramento, CA 916-383-2444
James Cowan & Sons
Worcester, MA 508-754-5385
John Morrell & Company
Cincinnati, OH 800-445-2013
Johnston County Hams
Smithfield, NC 800-543-4267
Kaladi Brothers
Anchorage, AK 907-644-7400
Karlin Foods Corporation
Northfield, IL 847-441-8330
Kashi Company
La Jolla, CA 858-274-8870
Khalsa International Trading
Los Angeles, CA 310-275-9891
Kids Cooking Club
San Diego, CA 858-539-1855
Kilauea Agronomics
Kilauea, HI 808-828-1761
Kombucha King International
Phoenix, AZ 800-896-9676
Kraft Foods
Northfield, IL 800-323-0768
Kusha
Irvine, CA 800-550-7423
La Superior Food Products
Shawnee Mission, KS 913-432-4933
Lamm Food Service
Lafayette, LA 337-896-0331
Landry Armand Company
Cottonport, LA 318-876-2716
Lemke Wholesale
Rogers, AR 501-636-3288
Life International
Naples, FL 239-592-9788
Linkmark International
Paxton, MA 508-753-2797
Little Freddy's
Clearwater, FL 727-791-1118
Loftshouse Foods
Ogden, UT 800-877-7055
Lopez Foods
Oklahoma City, OK 405-789-7500
Lotus Manufacturing Company
San Antonio, TX 210-223-1421
Lyman Jenkins
Jericho Center, VT 800-528-7021
M&L Ventures
Tucson, AZ 520-884-8232
M.J. Kellner Company
Springfield, IL 217-529-1663
Magic Valley Fresh Frozen
McAllen, TX 956-618-1251
Maher Marketing Services
Irving, TX 972-751-7700

Mallard Food Products
Modesto, CA.....................209-522-1018
Market Day Corporation
Itasca, IL......................877-632-7753
Marshakk Smoked Fish Company
Flushing, NY....................718-326-2170
Martin Brothers Distributing Company
Cedar Falls, IA.................319-266-1775
Marukan Vinegar (U.S.A.) Inc.
Paramount, CA...................562-630-6060
Mathews Packing Company
Marysville, CA..................530-743-9000
McCain Foods USA
Fort Atkinson, WI...............920-563-6625
McFarling Foods
Indianapolis, IN................317-635-2633
Merlen Foods
Saint Charles, IL...............630-513-9886
Mesa Cold Storage
Tolleson, AZ....................623-478-9392
Mickelberry's
Falls City, NE..................800-228-0037
Mid-Georgia Processing Company
Vienna, GA.....................229-268-6496
Milton A. Klein Company
New York, NY....................800-221-0248
Minh Food Corporation
Pasadena, TX....................800-344-7655
Mission Valley Foods
Middlebury, CT..................203-573-0652
Mitsui Foods
Norwood, NJ.....................800-777-2322
Moledina Commodities
Flower Mound, TX................817-490-1101
Monte Cristo Trading
Scarsdale, NY...................914-725-8025
MoonLight Kitchen
Newark, DE......................302-266-0558
Morr-Ad Foodservice
Wailuku, HI.....................808-877-2017
MPK Sonoma Company
Sonoma, CA......................707-996-3931
National Food Company
Honolulu, HI....................808-839-1118
National Importers
Brampton, ON....................905-791-1322

New City Packing Company
North Aurora, IL................630-898-1900
Nikola's Biscotti & European Specialties
Minneapolis, MN.................888-645-6527
O'Brines Pickling
Spokane, WA.....................509-534-7255
Oasis Foods
Lake Charles, LA................337-439-5262
Oscar Mayer Foods
Madison, WI.....................608-241-3311
Outerbridge Peppers
Wharton, NJ.....................800-989-7007
Pacific Resources International
Carpinteria, CA.................805-684-0624
Particle Control
Albertville, MN.................763-497-3075
Peanut Wonder Corporation
Water Mill, NY..................631-726-4433
Pinnacle Food Products
Lake Zurich, IL.................847-438-1598
Plantextrakt
Parsippany, NJ..................973-683-1411
PMC Specialties
Cincinnati, OH..................800-228-3673
Pon Food Corporation
Ponchatoula, LA.................985-386-6941
Pristine Foods
Baton Rouge, LA.................225-926-4677
Quality Foods Products
Chicago, IL.....................312-666-4559
Quantum Foods
Chicago, IL.....................630-679-2300
R.H. Bauman & Company
Chatsworth, CA..................818-709-1093
Ralcorp Holdings
Ripon, WI.......................800-445-8338
Ramsen
Lakeville, MN...................952-431-0400
Redi-Froze
South Bend, IN..................574-237-5111
Richards Natural Foods
Eagle, MI.......................517-627-7965
Roxy Trading
Azusa, CA.......................626-610-1388
Rye Sales Unlimited
Detroit, MI.....................313-838-1020

Salem Food Service
Salem, IN.......................812-883-2196
Sally Sherman Foods
Mt Vernon, NY...................914-664-6262
Sapporo
New York, NY....................800-827-8234
Select Origins
Mansfield, OH...................419-924-5447
Seven Brothers Trading
La Habra, CA....................562-697-8888
Severance Foods
Hartford, CT....................860-724-7063
Smart & Final
Los Angeles, CA.................323-869-7500
Solo Worldwide Enterprises
Falls Church, VA................703-845-7072
Stassen North America
Louisville, CO..................303-527-1700
Stilwell Foods
Stilwell, OK....................918-696-8325
Sumptuous Selections
Rocky Hill, NJ..................860-563-6390
Sun Garden Sprouts
Cookeville, TN..................931-526-1106
Sun Opta Ingredients
Chelmsford, MA..................800-353-6782
Sun World International
Bakersfield, CA.................661-392-5000
Sun-Rise
Alexandria, MN..................320-846-5720
Sunny Delight Beverage Company
Atlanta, GA.....................800-395-5849
Tase-Rite Company
Wakefield, RI...................401-783-7300
Thermice Company
Old Greenwich, CT...............203-637-4500
Thymly Products
Colora, MD......................410-658-4820
Topco
Skokie, IL......................847-676-3030
TRADE
Pittsburgh, PA..................412-366-6332
Trade Marcs Group
Brooklyn, NY....................718-387-9696
Trader's Blend
Findley Lake, NY................716-769-7720

Tradeshare Corporation
Brooklyn, NY .718-237-2295
Turnbull Bakeries
New Orleans, LA 504-523-5480
Ugo di Lullo & Sons
Westville, NJ .856-456-3700
Unicof
Sterling, VA. .703-904-0777
Unilever
New York, NY 212-888-1260
V.G. Buck California Foods DB
Kenwood, CA. 707-833-6548
Valley Sun Products of California
Newman, CA. 888-786-3743
Van Ekris & Company
New York, NY 212-898-9600
Venice Maid Foods
Vineland, NJ .800-257-7070
Volpi Italian Meats
St Louis, MO. 314-772-8550
Wallace Edwards & Sons
Surry, VA. 757-294-3121
Weathervane Foods
Woburn, MA .781-935-5458
Wendy's International
Dublin, OH 800-937-5449
Windward Trading Company
San Rafael, CA 800-858-8119
Yamamotoyama of America
Pomona, CA .909-594-7356
Zausner Foods
New Holland, PA 717-355-8505

Ingredients, Flavors & Additives

Freeze Dried Ingredients

Master Taste International
Plant City, FL 800-237-7629

SupHerb Farms
Turlock, CA 800-787-4372

CrEATe! Get ready-to-use fresh flavor with SupHerb Farms' all-natural fresh frozen culinary herbs, specialty vegetables, culinary herb pastes, vegetable purees and creative blends. Complete microbiological testing ensures food safety. We set the standard for outstanding customer service, inspired culinary support, collaborative customer partnerships and innovative custom products.

General

Ames Company
New Ringgold, PA 570-386-2131

Asiamerica Ingredients
Westwood, NJ 201-497-5531

Processor, importer, exporter and distributor of bulk vitamins, amino acids, nutraceuticals, aromatic chemicals, food additives, herbs, mineral nutrients and pharmaceuticals.

Biothera
Eagan, MN 651-675-0300
Bunge Ingredients
Seattle, WA 206-623-7740
Creative Flavors & Specialties LLP
Linden, NJ. 908-862-4678
Diversified Foods
Metairie, LA 504-831-6651
Edlong Dairy Flavors
Elk Grove Vlg, IL. 888-698-2783
Garuda International
Lemon Cove, CA 559-594-4380
Global Preservatives
Lake Charles, LA 800-256-2253
GMI Products/Originates
Sunrise, FL 800-999-9373
GTC Nutrition Company
Golden, CO 800-522-4682
Imperial Sensus
Sugar Land, TX. 281-490-9522
Infraready Products Ltd.
Saskatoon, SK. 306-242-4950
Ingredients Unlimited
Bell Gardens, CA 562-806-7560
International Flavors & Fragrances
New York, NY 212-765-5500
Jel-Sert Company
West Chicago, IL 800-323-2592
Kerry Ingredients
Woodstock, ON. 519-537-3461
Marukan Vinegar (U.S.A.) Inc.
Paramount, CA 562-630-6060
McCormick Industrial Flavor Solutions
Sparks Glencoe, MD. 800-632-5847

To advertise in the *Food & Beverage Market Place* Online Database call **(800) 562-2139** or log on to **http://gold.greyhouse.com** and click on "Advertise."

MGP Ingredients, Inc.
Atchinson, KS. 800-255-0302
Morgan Specialties
Paris, IL. 217-465-8577
Nissin Foods USA Company
Gardena, CA 310-327-8478
Old Cavendish Products
Cavendish, VT 800-536-7899
Phamous Phloyd's Barbeque Sauce
Denver, CO 303-757-3285
Pizzey's Nutritionals   A Granbia Company
Fitchburg, WI 877-804-6444
Primer Foods Corporation
Cameron, WI. 715-458-4075
R. Torre & Company
S San Francisco, CA. 800-775-1925
Reheis
Berkeley Heights, NJ 908-464-1500
Ribus
St Louis, MO. 314-727-4287
Silliker, Inc
Homewood, IL 888-957-5227
Specialty Minerals
Bethlehem, PA 800-801-1031

Acids

ADM Food Ingredients
Olathe, KS. 800-255-6637
Amerol Corporation
Farmingdale, NY 631-694-4700
Bartek Ingredients, Inc.
Stoney Creek, ON. 800-263-4165
BASF Corporation
Florham Park, NJ 800-526-1072
Cargill Corn Milling
Naperville, IL 800-344-1633
Cargill Worldwide Acidulants
Naperville, IL 800-344-1633
Gadot Biochemical Industries
Rolling Meadows, IL 888-424-1424
Henkel Corporation
Cincinnati, OH 800-543-7370
Jarchem Industries
Newark, NJ 973-578-4560
Jungbunzlauer
Newton, MA. 800-828-0062
Particle Dynamics
St Louis, MO. 800-452-4682
Pfanstiehl Laboratories
Waukegan, IL 847-623-2645
Phibro Animal Health
Ridgefield Park, NJ. 888-403-0074
PMP Fermentation Products
Peoria, IL. 800-558-1031
Protein Research Associates
Livermore, CA 800-948-1991
Roquette America
Keokuk, IA 800-553-7035
Silver Ferm Chemical
Seattle, WA 206-282-3376
Symrise
Teterboro, NJ. 201-288-3200
Trumark
Linden, NJ. 800-752-7877
Wilke International
Shawnee Mission, KS. 800-779-5545

Adipic

Silver Ferm Chemical
Seattle, WA 206-282-3376
Universal Preservachem Inc
Edison, NJ. 732-777-7338

Aminoacetic

ADH Health Products
Congers, NY 800-292-6002
Ajinomoto Food Ingredients LLC
Chicago, IL 773-380-7000
Albion Laboratories
Clearfield, UT 866-243-5283
AMT Labs
North Salt Lake, UT 801-299-1661
Anabol Naturals
Santa Cruz, CA 800-426-2265

Asiamerica Ingredients
Westwood, NJ 201-497-5531

Processor, importer, exporter and distributor of bulk vitamins, amino acids, nutraceuticals, aromatic chemicals, food additives, herbs, mineral nutrients and pharmaceuticals.

Belmont Chemicals
Clifton, NJ. 800-722-5070
DMH Ingredients
Libertyville, IL 847-362-9977
Eckhart Corporation
Novato, CA 800-200-4201
Integrated Health
Torrance, CA. 800-799-3232
Jo Mar Laboratories
Campbell, CA 800-538-4545
Kyowa Hakko
New York, NY 212-715-0572
Now Foods
Bloomingdale, IL 888-669-3663
NuNaturals
Eugene, OR. 800-753-4372
Pro-Pharm
Lake Bluff, IL 847-234-3570
Universal Preservachem Inc
Edison, NJ. 732-777-7338

Benzoic

Kalama Chemical
Seattle, WA 800-742-6147
Luyties Pharmacal Company
Saint Louis, MO 800-325-8080
Universal Preservachem Inc
Edison, NJ. 732-777-7338

Boric/Boracic

Universal Preservachem Inc
Edison, NJ. 732-777-7338

Gluconic (Gluconolactone)

Glucona America
Janesville, WI 608-752-0449
Jungbunzlauer
Newton, MA. 800-828-0062
PMP Fermentation Products
Peoria, IL. 800-558-1031
Roquette America
Keokuk, IA 800-553-7035
Universal Preservachem Inc
Edison, NJ. 732-777-7338

Glutamic

Universal Preservachem Inc
Edison, NJ. 732-777-7338
Woodland Foods
Gurnee, IL. 847-625-8600

Acidulants

Asiamerica Ingredients
Westwood, NJ 201-497-5531

Processor, importer, exporter and distributor of bulk vitamins, amino acids, nutraceuticals, aromatic chemicals, food additives, herbs, mineral nutrients and pharmaceuticals.

Marukan Vinegar (U.S.A.) Inc.
Paramount, CA 562-630-6060

Acetic

Asiamerica Ingredients
Westwood, NJ 201-497-5531

Processor, importer, exporter and distributor of bulk vitamins, amino acids, nutraceuticals, aromatic chemicals, food additives, herbs, mineral nutrients and pharmaceuticals.

Jarchem Industries
Newark, NJ 973-578-4560
Universal Preservachem Inc
Edison, NJ .732-777-7338

Citric

ADM Food Ingredients
Olathe, KS. 800-255-6637
American Key Food Products
Closter, NJ. 800-767-0237
Archer Daniels Midland Company
Decatur, IL 800-637-5843

Asiamerica Ingredients
Westwood, NJ 201-497-5531

Processor, importer, exporter and distributor of bulk vitamins, amino acids, nutraceuticals, aromatic chemicals, food additives, herbs, mineral nutrients and pharmaceuticals.

Cargill Corn Milling
Naperville, IL 800-344-1633
Cargill Worldwide Acidulants
Naperville, IL 800-344-1633
Embassy Flavours Ltd.
Brampton, ON. 800-334-3371
FBC Industries
Schaumburg, IL. 888-322-4637
Gadot Biochemical Industries
Rolling Meadows, IL 888-424-1424
Hosemen & Roche Vitamins & Fine Chemicals
Nutley, NJ .800-526-6367
International Chemical
Milltown, NJ 800-914-2436
Jungbunzlauer
Newton, MA 800-828-0062
Kimson Chemicals
Waltham, MA 781-893-6878
Luyties Pharmacal Company
Saint Louis, MO 800-325-8080
Nichem Company
Hillside, NJ 908-933-0770
Phibro Animal Health
Ridgefield Park, NJ. 888-403-0074
Shekou Chemicals
Waltham, MA 781-893-6878
Universal Preservachem Inc
Edison, NJ .732-777-7338

Fumaric

Asiamerica Ingredients
Westwood, NJ 201-497-5531

Processor, importer, exporter and distributor of bulk vitamins, amino acids, nutraceuticals, aromatic chemicals, food additives, herbs, mineral nutrients and pharmaceuticals.

Bartek Ingredients, Inc.
Stoney Creek, ON 800-263-4165
Gadot Biochemical Industries
Rolling Meadows, IL 888-424-1424
Jungbunzlauer
Newton, MA 800-828-0062
Silver Ferm Chemical
Seattle, WA 206-282-3376
Universal Preservachem Inc
Edison, NJ .732-777-7338

Lactic

ADM Food Ingredients
Olathe, KS. 800-255-6637
Archer Daniels Midland Company
Decatur, IL 800-637-5843

Asiamerica Ingredients
Westwood, NJ 201-497-5531

Processor, importer, exporter and distributor of bulk vitamins, amino acids, nutraceuticals, aromatic chemicals, food additives, herbs, mineral nutrients and pharmaceuticals.

Fleurchem
Middletown, NY 845-341-2170
Jungbunzlauer
Newton, MA 800-828-0062
Pfanstiehl Laboratories
Waukegan, IL 847-623-2645
Trumark
Linden, NJ. 800-752-7877
Universal Preservachem Inc
Edison, NJ. 732-777-7338
Varied Industries Corporation
Mason City, IA 800-654-5617
Wilke International
Shawnee Mission, KS. 800-779-5545

Malic

Asiamerica Ingredients
Westwood, NJ 201-497-5531

Processor, importer, exporter and distributor of bulk vitamins, amino acids, nutraceuticals, aromatic chemicals, food additives, herbs, mineral nutrients and pharmaceuticals.

Bartek Ingredients, Inc.
Stoney Creek, ON 800-263-4165
Jungbunzlauer
Newton, MA 800-828-0062
Universal Preservachem Inc
Edison, NJ. 732-777-7338

Phosphoric

Asiamerica Ingredients
Westwood, NJ 201-497-5531

Processor, importer, exporter and distributor of bulk vitamins, amino acids, nutraceuticals, aromatic chemicals, food additives, herbs, mineral nutrients and pharmaceuticals.

Universal Preservachem Inc
Edison, NJ. 732-777-7338

Sorbic

Amerol Corporation
Farmingdale, NY 631-694-4700

Asiamerica Ingredients
Westwood, NJ 201-497-5531

Processor, importer, exporter and distributor of bulk vitamins, amino acids, nutraceuticals, aromatic chemicals, food additives, herbs, mineral nutrients and pharmaceuticals.

Gadot Biochemical Industries
Rolling Meadows, IL 888-424-1424
International Chemical
Milltown, NJ 800-914-2436
Jungbunzlauer
Newton, MA 800-828-0062
Silver Ferm Chemical
Seattle, WA 206-282-3376
Universal Preservachem Inc
Edison, NJ. 732-777-7338

Tartaric

American Tartaric Products
Larchmont, NY 914-834-1881

Asiamerica Ingredients
Westwood, NJ 201-497-5531

Processor, importer, exporter and distributor of bulk vitamins, amino acids, nutraceuticals, aromatic chemicals, food additives, herbs, mineral nutrients and pharmaceuticals.

Bartek Ingredients, Inc.
Stoney Creek, ON 800-263-4165
H. Interdonati
Cold Spring Hbr, NY 800-367-6617
International Chemical
Milltown, NJ 800-914-2436
Jungbunzlauer
Newton, MA 800-828-0062
Universal Preservachem Inc
Edison, NJ. 732-777-7338

Additives

Anticaking

Asiamerica Ingredients
Westwood, NJ 201-497-5531

Processor, importer, exporter and distributor of bulk vitamins, amino acids, nutraceuticals, aromatic chemicals, food additives, herbs, mineral nutrients and pharmaceuticals.

Bulking

Cargill Texturizing Solutions
Cedar Rapids, IA. 877-650-7080

Enrichment & Nutrient

Single & Blended

Asiamerica Ingredients
Westwood, NJ 201-497-5531

Processor, importer, exporter and distributor of bulk vitamins, amino acids, nutraceuticals, aromatic chemicals, food additives, herbs, mineral nutrients and pharmaceuticals.

Cargill Texturizing Solutions
Cedar Rapids, IA 877-650-7080

Free Flow

Amerol Corporation
Farmingdale, NY 631-694-4700

Asiamerica Ingredients
Westwood, NJ .201-497-5531

Processor, importer, exporter and distributor of bulk vitamins, amino acids, nutraceuticals, aromatic chemicals, food additives, herbs, mineral nutrients and pharmaceuticals.

Cargill Texturizing Solutions
Cedar Rapids, IA 877-650-7080
Crompton Corporation
Greenwich, CT 800-295-2392
DMV International Nutritional
Delhi, NY 607-746-0100
Eurodrinks
Fresno, CA 559-449-9463
Garuda International
Lemon Cove, CA 559-594-4380
Hangzhou Sanhe Food Company
Walnut, CA 909-869-6016
Henkel Corporation
Countryside, IL 800-328-6199
Prolume Biolume
Lakeside, AZ .928-367-1200

Adjuncts

Brewing

Acadian Seaplants
Dartmouth, NS 800-575-9100
Boyd Coffee Company
Portland, OR .800-545-4077

Agents

Asiamerica Ingredients
Westwood, NJ .201-497-5531

Processor, importer, exporter and distributor of bulk vitamins, amino acids, nutraceuticals, aromatic chemicals, food additives, herbs, mineral nutrients and pharmaceuticals.

Crest Foods Company
Ashton, IL 800-435-6972
Gadot Biochemical Industries
Rolling Meadows, IL 888-424-1424
International Foodcraft Corporation
Linden, NJ 800-875-9393

Anticaking

Cereal Solids Hydrolyzed

Cargill Texturizing Solutions
Cedar Rapids, IA 877-650-7080

Modified Food Starch

Cargill Texturizing Solutions
Cedar Rapids, IA 877-650-7080

To advertise in the *Food & Beverage Market Place* Online Database call **(800) 562-2139** or log on to **http://gold.greyhouse.com** and click on "Advertise."

Tricalcium Phosphate

Gadot Biochemical Industries
Rolling Meadows, IL 888-424-1424

Antimicrobial

A&B Ingredients
Fairfield, NJ .973-227-1390
Inovatech USA
Montreal, QC 888-388-3447

Bulking

Cargill Texturizing Solutions
Cedar Rapids, IA 877-650-7080

Clarifying

American Laboratories, Inc.
Omaha, NE 402-339-2494

Compacting

Tabletizing

Cargill Texturizing Solutions
Cedar Rapids, IA 877-650-7080

Firming

Cargill Texturizing Solutions
Cedar Rapids, IA 877-650-7080

Foaming & Whipping

Cargill Texturizing Solutions
Cedar Rapids, IA 877-650-7080

Modifiers

Texture

Domino Specialty Ingredients
Baltimore, MD 800-446-9763

Release,Grease

Edible

Shoei Foods USA
Olivehurst, CA 800-527-4712
Spray Dynamics
St Clair, MO .800-260-7366

Thickening

Cargill Texturizing Solutions
Cedar Rapids, IA 877-650-7080
P.L. Thomas
Morristown, NJ 973-984-0900
Sno-Shack
Salt Lake City, UT 801-466-1771

Arrowroot

Advanced Spice & Trading
Carrollton, TX 800-872-7811
Schiff Food Products
North Bergen, NJ 201-861-2503

Ammonium Carbonate

ADM Food Ingredients
Olathe, KS 800-255-6637
Luyties Pharmacal Company
Saint Louis, MO 800-325-8080
Universal Preservachem Inc
Edison, NJ 732-777-7338

Analogs

Meat

Alle Processing Corporation
Flushing, NY 800-245-5620
Caribbean Food Delights
Tappan, NY .845-398-3000
Cedar Lake Foods
Cedar Lake, MI 800-246-5039
Chr Hansen
Elyria, OH 800-558-0802
CHS, Inc.
Inner Grove Heights, MN 800-232-3639

Earth Island Natural Foods
Canoga Park, CA 818-725-2820
Innovative Food Solutions LLC
Columbus, OH 800-884-3314
Ivy Foods
Phoenix, AZ .877-223-5459
Phillips Gourmet
Kennett Square, PA 610-925-0520
Pilgrim's Pride
Timberville, VA 540-896-7000
Tami Great Food
Monsey, NY .718-788-4200
Today's Traditions
Chico, CA 800-816-6873
Vitasoy USA
Ayer, MA 978-772-6880
Westin
Omaha, NE .800-228-6098
White Wave
Broomfield, CO 800-488-9283
Winmix/Natural Care Products
Englewood, FL 941-475-7432

Antioxidants

Action Labs
Park City, UT 800-669-8877
Amerol Corporation
Farmingdale, NY 631-694-4700

Asiamerica Ingredients
Westwood, NJ .201-497-5531

Processor, importer, exporter and distributor of bulk vitamins, amino acids, nutraceuticals, aromatic chemicals, food additives, herbs, mineral nutrients and pharmaceuticals.

Avatar Corporation
University Park, IL 800-255-3181
Body Breakthrough
Deer Park, NY 800-874-6299
First Spice Mixing Company
Long Island City, NY 800-221-1105
Henkel Corporation
Countryside, IL 800-328-6199
Herbal Products & Development
Aptos, CA 831-688-4200
IVC American Vitamin
Freehold, NJ 800-666-8482
Now Foods
Bloomingdale, IL 888-669-3663
P.L. Thomas
Morristown, NJ 973-984-0900
QBI
South Plainfield, NJ 908-668-0088
RFI Ingredients
Blauvelt, NY .800-962-7663
RPM Total Vitality
Yorba Linda, CA 800-234-3092
UAS Laboratories
Eden Prairie, MN 800-422-3371

Ascorbic Acid

Asiamerica Ingredients
Westwood, NJ .201-497-5531

Processor, importer, exporter and distributor of bulk vitamins, amino acids, nutraceuticals, aromatic chemicals, food additives, herbs, mineral nutrients and pharmaceuticals.

China Pharmaceutical Enterprises
Baton Rouge, LA 800-345-1658
Gadot Biochemical Industries
Rolling Meadows, IL 888-424-1424
Hermann Laue Spice Company
Uxbridge, ON 905-852-5100
International Chemical
Milltown, NJ 800-914-2436

Kimson Chemicals
Waltham, MA 781-893-6878
Shekou Chemicals
Waltham, MA 781-893-6878
Universal Preservachem Inc
Edison, NJ .732-777-7338

Aroma Chemicals

Asiamerica Ingredients
Westwood, NJ 201-497-5531

Processor, importer, exporter and distributor of bulk vitamins, amino acids, nutraceuticals, aromatic chemicals, food additives, herbs, mineral nutrients and pharmaceuticals.

Astral Extracts Ltd
Syosset, NY 516-496-2505
Firmenich
Plainsboro, NJ 800-452-1090

Aroma Chemicals & Materials

Chemicals

Asiamerica Ingredients
Westwood, NJ 201-497-5531

Processor, importer, exporter and distributor of bulk vitamins, amino acids, nutraceuticals, aromatic chemicals, food additives, herbs, mineral nutrients and pharmaceuticals.

Native Scents
Taos, NM 800-645-3471

Methyl Salicylate

Asiamerica Ingredients
Westwood, NJ 201-497-5531

Processor, importer, exporter and distributor of bulk vitamins, amino acids, nutraceuticals, aromatic chemicals, food additives, herbs, mineral nutrients and pharmaceuticals.

Fragrances

A M Todd Company
Kalamazoo, OR 269-343-2603
AFF International
Marietta, GA 800-241-7764
Agilex™ Flavors & Fragrances, Inc.
Upper Saddle River, NJ 800-542-7662
Arizona Chemical Company
Jacksonville, FL 800-526-5294
Aroma Vera
Los Angeles, CA 800-669-9514
Aromachem
Brooklyn, NY 718-497-4664

Asiamerica Ingredients
Westwood, NJ 201-497-5531

Processor, importer, exporter and distributor of bulk vitamins, amino acids, nutraceuticals, aromatic chemicals, food additives, herbs, mineral nutrients and pharmaceuticals.

Avoca
Merry Hill, NC 252-482-2133
AVRI Companies
Richmond, CA 800-883-9574
Baywood International
Scottsdale, AZ 800-481-7169
Centflor Manufacturing Company
New York, NY 212-246-8307
Classic Flavors & Fragrances
New York, NY 212-777-0004
Dolav
Totowa, NJ 800-842-5033
Dream Time
Santa Cruz, CA 831-464-6702
Elan Chemical Company
Newark, NJ 973-344-8014
Essential Products of America
Tampa, FL .800-822-9698
Fidelity Flavors & Fragrances
Goshen, NY 845-294-5356
Firmenich
Plainsboro, NJ 800-452-1090
Flavor & Fragrance Specialties
Mahwah, NJ 800-998-4337
Flavormatic Industries
Wappingers Falls, NY 845-297-9100
Fleurchem
Middletown, NY 845-341-2170
Flower Essence Services
Nevada City, CA 800-548-0075
Givaudan Access
Cincinnati, OH 866-448-2832
Givaudan-Roure
Teaneck, NJ 201-833-2300
Green Spot Packaging
Claremont, CA 800-456-3210
H&R Florasynth
Teterboro, NJ 888-473-5672
Haldin International
Closter, NJ 201-784-0044
International Flavors & Fragrances
New York, NY 212-765-5500
International Flavors & Fragrances
Dayton, NJ 800-433-3528
Janca's Jojoba Oil & Seed Company
Mesa, AZ. .480-497-9494
Jogue Inc
Northville, MI 800-521-3888
Lebermuth Company
South Bend, IN 800-648-1123
Maryland & Virginia Milk Producers Cooperative
Reston, VA 703-742-7443
Mastertaste Company
South Hackensack, NJ 201-641-6555
McCormick & Company Inc
Sparks, MD. 410-771-7301
Millennium Specialty Chemicals
Jacksonville, FL 800-231-6728
Naturex (Chart Corp)
South Hackensack, NJ 201-440-5000
Newport Flavours & Fragrances
Orange, CA 714-628-9894
Noville
Wayne, NJ .201-641-2700
Oxford Organics
Livingston, NJ 908-351-0002
PMC Specialties Group
Cincinnati, OH 800-543-2466
RCB International
Albany, OR 541-967-3814
Sigma/Aldrich Flavors & Fragrances
Milwaukee, WI 800-227-4563
SKW Nature Products
Langhorne, PA 215-702-1000
Symrise
Teterboro, NJ 201-288-3200
Synergy Flavors Inc
Wauconda, IL 847-487-1011
T Hasegawa
Cerritos, CA 714-670-1586

Technology Flavors & Fragrances
Amityville, NY 631-842-7600
Treatt USA
Lakeland, FL 800-866-7704
Ungerer & Company
Lincoln Park, NJ 973-628-0600
Universal Flavor Corporation
Indianapolis, IN 317-243-3521

Materials

Uncompounded

Accurate Ingredients
Syosset, NY 516-496-2500

Bases

Ailments E.D. Foods Inc.
Pointe Claire, QC 800-267-3333
Al-Rite Fruits & Syrups
Miami, FL .305-652-2540
American Fruits and Flavors
Los Angeles, CA 800-527-6709
American Saucery
Oak Park, MI. 800-328-8632
Atlantic Quality Spice &Seasonings
Edison, NJ .800-584-0422
Autocrat Coffee & Extracts
Lincoln, RI .800-288-6272
BakeMark Canada
Laval, QC 800-361-4998
Bakemark Ingredients Canada
Richmond, BC 800-665-9441
Bartush-Schnitzius Foods Company
Lewisville, TX 972-219-1270
Beverage Technologies
East Brunswick, NJ. 888-204-4299
Blount Seafood Corporation
Fall River, MA 774-888-1300
Cagnon Foods Company
Brooklyn, NY 718-647-2244
California Brands Flavors
Oakland, CA 800-348-0111
California Dairies
Fresno, CA .559-233-5154
Chef Hans Gourmet Foods
Monroe, LA. 800-890-4267
Citrus Citrosuco North America
Lake Wales, FL 800-356-4592
Classic Tea
Libertyville, IL 630-680-9934
Clofine Dairy & Food Products
Linwood, NJ 800-441-1001
ConAgra Food Ingredients
Omaha, NE 800-872-9236
Concord Foods
Brockton, MA 508-580-1700
Consolidated Mills
Houston, TX 713-896-4196
Crest Foods Company
Ashton, IL .800-435-6972
Crystal Foods
Brick, NJ 732-477-0073
CTL Foods
Colfax, WI. .800-962-5227
Custom Food Products
Alsip, IL 708-388-8883
Dean Distributors
Burlingame, CA 800-227-3112
Dean Distributors
Burlingame, CA 800-792-0816
Dorothy Dawson Foods Products
Jackson, MI 517-788-9830
Eatem Foods Company
Vineland, NJ 800-683-2836
Erba Food Products
Brooklyn, NY 718-272-7700
Flavor House
Adelanto, CA 760-246-9131
Flavor Innovations
South Plainfield, NJ 800-536-2030
Folklore Foods
Toppenish, WA 509-865-4772
Fuji Foods
Browns Summit, NC 336-375-3111
Givaudan Flavors
Bridgeton, MO 800-422-5444
Global Food Industries
Townville, SC 800-225-4152
GS-AFI
South Plainfield, NJ 800-345-4342

Gum Technology Corporation
Tucson, AZ 800-369-4867
Hormel Foods Corporation
Austin, MN .800-523-4635
Illes Seasonings & Flavors
Carrollton, TX. 800-683-4553
JMH International
Delafield, WI. 888-741-4564
Johnson's Food Products
Dorchester, MA. 617-265-3400
Manildra Milling Corporation
Fairway, KS. .800-323-8435
Meat-O-Mat Corporation
Brooklyn, NY 718-965-7250
Merci Spring Water
Saint Louis, MO 314-812-4812
Microsoy Corporation
Jefferson, IA .515-386-2100
Olympia Oyster Company
Shelton, WA .360-426-3354
Pacific Harvest Products
Bellevue, WA 425-401-7990
Particle Dynamics
St Louis, MO. 800-452-4682
Produits Ronald
St. Damase, QC. 450-797-3303
Roos Foods
Kenton, DE 800-343-3642
Serv-Agen Corporation
Cherry Hill, NJ 856-663-6966
SimmaLoosa Company
Covington, LA 985-892-1400
Skjodt-Barrett Foods
Mississauga, ON 877-600-1200
Spice Advice
Ankeny, IA 800-247-5251
Spice Hunter
San Luis Obispo, CA 800-444-3061
Spice Time Foods/Julius & Joe's
Paramus, NJ .800-345-9225
Stevens Tropical Plantation
West Palm Beach, FL 561-683-4701
Sweet Sue Kitchens
Athens, AL 256-216-0500
Swiss Food Products
Chicago, IL 773-394-6480
Texas Spice Company
Cedar Park, TX 800-880-8007
Tone Products Company
Melrose Park, IL 708-681-3660
Unilever
Lisle, IL. 877-995-4483
United Citrus Products
Norwood, MA 800-229-7300
V&E Kohnstamm
Brooklyn, NY 800-847-4500
Vita-Pakt Citrus Company
Lindsay, CA .559-562-6008
Vita-Pakt Citrus Company
Covina, CA 626-332-1101
Welch's Foods Inc
Concord, MA 800-340-6870
Western Syrup Company
Santa Fe Springs, CA 562-921-4485
White Coffee Corporation
Long Island City, NY 800-221-0140
Williams-West & Witt Products
Michigan City, IN 219-879-8236

Beef

Associated Brands, Inc.
Medina, NY. .800-265-0050
Castella Imports
Hauppauge, NY 866-227-8355
Golden Specialty Foods
Norwalk, CA. 562-802-2537

Broth Cubes

Gel Spice Company, Inc
Bayonne, NJ .800-922-0230

Beverage

Allen Flavors
Edison, NJ. 908-561-5995
American Health & Nutrition
Ann Arbor, MI 734-677-5572
American Purpac Technologies, LLC
Beloit, WI. 877-787-7221
Astral Extracts Ltd
Syosset, NY. .516-496-2505

Autocrat Coffee & Extracts
Lincoln, RI 800-288-6272

Baldwin Richardson Foods
Frankfort, IL .866-644-2732

Baldwin Richardson Foods is a liquid ingredient manufacturer specializing in signature sauces, dessert toppings, beverage/pancake syrups, specialty fruit fillings and condiments. Packaging capabilities range from portion control cups and pouches to standard retail and foodservice packs and include industrial drums and totes. Full service R&D and Quality groups dedicated to new product development, with in-house stability and analytical testing. Call for assistance.

Bartush-Schnitzius Foods Company
Lewisville, TX 972-219-1270
California Brands Flavors
Oakland, CA .800-348-0111
California Custom Fruits & Flavors
Irwindale, CA 877-558-0056
Carmi Flavor & Fragrance Company
Los Angeles, CA 800-421-9647
Century Foods International
Sparta, WI 800-269-1901
Classic Tea
Libertyville, IL 630-680-9934
Consolidated Mills
Houston, TX .713-896-4196
Country Pure Foods
Akron, OH. 877-995-8423
Crystal Foods
Brick, NJ 732-477-0073
CTL Foods
Colfax, WI. 800-962-5227
Delano Growers Grape Products
Delano, CA 661-725-3255
E.B. Evans Company
Saint Louis, MO 215-425-0558
Essential Flavors & Fragrances, Inc
Corona, CA. .888-333-9935
Flavor Innovations
South Plainfield, NJ 800-536-2030
Folklore Foods
Toppenish, WA 509-865-4772
Franco's Cocktail Mixes
Pompano Beach, FL 800-782-4508
Fruitcrown Products Corporation
Farmingdale, NY 800-441-3210
Georgia Sun
Newnan, GA .770-251-2500
Global Food Industries
Townville, SC 800-225-4152
H R Nicholson Company
Baltimore, MD 800-638-3514
H.P. Hood
Barre, VT 800-622-4468
Hagelin & Company
Branchburg, NJ 800-229-2112
Hig-Country Corona
Selah, WA 509-697-7950
I Rice & Company
Philadelphia, PA 800-232-6022
Innovative Food Solutions LLC
Columbus, OH 800-884-3314
J.M. Smucker Company
Grandview, WA. 509-882-1530
Kalva Corporation
Gurnee, IL. 800-525-8220
Milne Fruit Products
Prosser, WA. .509-786-2611
Nedlog Company
Wheeling, IL. 800-323-6201
Plaidberry Company
Vista, CA 760-727-5403
Precision Foods
Melrose Park, IL 800-333-0003
Quality Naturally! Foods
City of Industry, CA 888-498-6986
Rio Syrup Company
St Louis, MO. 800-325-7666
Roos Foods
Kenton, DE 800-343-3642

Schlotterbeck & Foss Company
Portland, ME. 800-777-4666
Singer Extract Laboratory
Livonia, MI. .313-345-5880
Skjodt-Barrett Foods
Mississauga, ON 877-600-1200
Stevens Tropical Plantation
West Palm Beach, FL 561-683-4701
SunPure
Lakeland, FL. 863-619-2222
Tampico Beverages
Chicago, IL 877-826-7426
Thirs-Tea Corporation
Miami, FL 305-651-4350
Tova Industries
Louisville, KY 888-532-8682
Tupman-Thurlow Company
Deerfield Beach, FL 954-596-9989
Vance's Foods
Gilmer, TX 800-497-4834
Vegetable Juices
Chicago, IL 888-776-9752
Vita-Pakt Citrus Company
Covina, CA 626-332-1101
Wechsler Coffee Corporation
Moonachie, NJ 800-800-2633
Welch's Foods Inc
Concord, MA 800-340-6870
Western Syrup Company
Santa Fe Springs, CA 562-921-4485
Winmix/Natural Care Products
Englewood, FL 941-475-7432

Bouillon

Gel Spice Company, Inc
Bayonne, NJ .800-922-0230
Hormel Foods Corporation
Austin, MN .800-523-4635
Organic Gourmet
Sherman Oaks, CA 800-400-7772
Vilore Foods Company
Laredo, TX 956-726-3633

Beef

Hormel Foods Corporation
Austin, MN .800-523-4635
Supreme Dairy Farms Company
Warwick, RI .401-739-8180

Chicken

Associated Brands, Inc.
Medina, NY. .800-265-0050
Castella Imports
Hauppauge, NY 866-227-8355
Golden Specialty Foods
Norwalk, CA. 562-802-2537

Chocolate

Seller Kirk & Company
Schwenksville, PA 215-480-7342
US Chocolate Corporation
Brooklyn, NY 718-788-8555

Dairy

ACH Food Companies
Boyceville, WI. 715-643-2600
Givaudan Flavors
Bridgeton, MO 800-422-5444
Johnson's Food Products
Dorchester, MA. 617-265-3400
Seller Kirk & Company
Schwenksville, PA 215-480-7342
WILD Flavors (Canada)
Mississauga, ON 800-263-5286

Non-Dairy & Imitation

Al-Rite Fruits & Syrups
Miami, FL 305-652-2540
American Health & Nutrition
Ann Arbor, MI 734-677-5572
Bakemark Ingredients Canada
Richmond, BC 800-665-9441
California Custom Fruits & Flavors
Irwindale, CA 877-558-0056
Century Foods International
Sparta, WI 800-269-1901
Clofine Dairy & Food Products
Linwood, NJ .800-441-1001

Forbes Chocolates
Cleveland, OH 800-433-1090
Freeman Industries
Tuckahoe, NY 800-666-6454
Galloway Company
Neenah, WI 800-722-8903
Givaudan Flavors
Bridgeton, MO 800-422-5444
Global Food Industries
Townville, SC 800-225-4152
I Rice & Company
Philadelphia, PA 800-232-6022
Johnson's Food Products
Dorchester, MA 617-265-3400
Land O'Lakes, Inc
Arden Hills, MN 800-328-9680
Limpert Brothers
Vineland, NJ 800-691-1353
Nog Incorporated
Dunkirk, NY 800-332-2664
Plaidberry Company
Vista, CA 760-727-5403
Quality Naturally! Foods
City of Industry, CA 888-498-6986
Seller Kirk & Company
Schwenksville, PA 215-480-7342
Tova Industries
Louisville, KY 888-532-8682
Welsh Farms
Newark, NJ 800-221-0663
Westin
Omaha, NE 800-228-6098

Flavor

Creative Flavors & Specialties LLP
Linden, NJ 908-862-4678
GS-AFI
South Plainfield, NJ 800-345-4342
JMH International
Delafield, WI. 888-741-4564
Pecan Deluxe Candy Company
Dallas, TX 800-733-3589
Proliant
Ankeny, IA 800-369-2672
Ventura Foods   Production Plant
Los Angeles, CA. 323-265-4300

Food

Abimco USA, Inc.
Mendham, NJ 973-543-7393
ADM Food Ingredients
Olathe, KS. 800-255-6637
American Purpac Technologies, LLC
Beloit, WI 877-787-7221
Atlantic Quality Spice &Seasonings
Edison, NJ. 800-584-0422
Clofine Dairy & Food Products
Linwood, NJ 800-441-1001
General Spice
South Plainfield, NJ 800-345-7742
GS-AFI
South Plainfield, NJ 800-345-4342
Henningsen Foods
Purchase, NY 914-701-4020
I Rice & Company
Philadelphia, PA 800-232-6022
Summit Hill Flavors
Middlesex, NJ 732-805-0335
Tova Industries
Louisville, KY 888-532-8682
Vita-Pakt Citrus Company
Lindsay, CA 559-562-6008

Fruit

American Purpac Technologies, LLC
Beloit, WI 877-787-7221
California Custom Fruits & Flavors
Irwindale, CA 877-558-0056
Fee Brothers
Rochester, NY 800-961-3337
Givaudan Flavors
Bridgeton, MO 800-422-5444
Ramsey/SIAS
Cleveland, OH 800-477-3788
SimmaLoosa Company
Covington, LA 985-892-1400
Tova Industries
Louisville, KY 888-532-8682

Gravy

Advance Food Brokers
West Bloomfield, MI 248-851-9045
Ailments E.D. Foods Inc.
Pointe Claire, QC 800-267-3333
Atlantic Quality Spice &Seasonings
Edison, NJ. 800-584-0422
Bernard Food Industries
Evanston, IL 800-323-3663
Con Yeager Spice Company
Zelienople, PA. 800-222-2460
Cordon Bleu International
Anjou, QC 514-352-3000
Custom Food Products
Alsip, IL 708-388-8883
Dean Distributors
Burlingame, CA 800-227-3112
Dean Distributors
Burlingame, CA 800-792-0816
Dorothy Dawson Foods Products
Jackson, MI 517-788-9830
Eatem Foods Company
Vineland, NJ 800-683-2836
Felbro Food Products
Los Angeles, CA. 800-335-2761
Flavor Innovations
South Plainfield, NJ 800-536-2030
Fuji Foods
Browns Summit, NC 336-375-3111
Gel Spice Company, Inc
Bayonne, NJ 800-922-0230
Geneva Ingredients
Waunakee, WI. 800-828-5924
Griffith Laboratories Worldwide
Alsip, IL 800-346-4743
Halben Food Manufacturing Company
Overland, MO 800-888-4855
Henningsen Foods
Purchase, NY 914-701-4020
Hormel Foods Corporation
Austin, MN 800-523-4635
Karlsburger Foods
Monticello, MN 800-383-6549
L.J. Minor Factory
Cleveland, OH 216-861-8350
Lawry's Foods
Monrovia, CA 800-952-9797
Magic Seasoning Blends
Harahan, LA 800-457-2857
Meat-O-Mat Corporation
Brooklyn, NY 718-965-7250
More Than Gourmet
Akron, OH. 800-860-9385
Newly Weds Foods
Memphis, TN 800-647-9314
Olympia Oyster Company
Shelton, WA 360-426-3354
Pacific Foods
Kent, WA. 800-347-9444
Premier Blending
Wichita, KS. 316-267-5533
Presco Food Seasonings
Flemington, NJ 800-526-1713
Produits Ronald
St. Damase, QC. 450-797-3303
Proliant Meat Ingredients
Ankeny, IA 800-369-2672
RL Schreiber
Pompano Beach, FL 954-972-7102
Serv-Agen Corporation
Cherry Hill, NJ 856-663-6966
Shenandoah Mills
Lebanon, TN 615-444-0841
Spice Advice
Ankeny, IA 800-247-5251
Sweet Sue Kitchens
Athens, AL 256-216-0500
Swiss Food Products
Chicago, IL 773-394-6480
Tova Industries
Louisville, KY 888-532-8682
Vanee Foods Company
Berkeley, IL. 708-449-7300
Ventura Foods
Philadelphia, PA 215-223-8700
Ventura Foods   Foodservice
Salem, OR 503-585-6423
Vogue Cuisine
Culver City, CA 888-236-4144
Williams-West & Witt Products
Michigan City, IN 219-879-8236

World Flavors
Warminster, PA 215-672-4400

Juice

Citrus Citrosuco North America
Lake Wales, FL 800-356-4592
Delano Growers Grape Products
Delano, CA 661-725-3255
Merci Spring Water
Saint Louis, MO 314-812-4812
SensoryEffects Flavor Systems
Bridgeton, MO 314-291-5444
SimmaLoosa Company
Covington, LA 985-892-1400

Sauce

Eatem Foods Company
Vineland, NJ 800-683-2836
Illes Seasonings & Flavors
Carrollton, TX 800-683-4553
JMH International
Delafield, WI. 888-741-4564
Produits Ronald
St. Damase, QC 450-797-3303
Summit Hill Flavors
Middlesex, NJ 732-805-0335
UFL Foods
Mississauga, ON 905-670-7776

Seafood

Blount Seafood Corporation
Fall River, MA 774-888-1300
Swiss Food Products
Chicago, IL. 773-394-6480

Soup

Advance Food Brokers
West Bloomfield, MI 248-851-9045
Ailments E.D. Foods Inc.
Pointe Claire, QC 800-267-3333
Atlantic Quality Spice &Seasonings
Edison, NJ. 800-584-0422
Bernard Food Industries
Evanston, IL 800-323-3663
Bestfoods Foodservice
Somerset, NJ. 732-627-8722
Blount Seafood Corporation
Fall River, MA 774-888-1300
Blue Chip Group
Salt Lake City, UT 800-878-0099
Chef Hans Gourmet Foods
Monroe, LA. 800-890-4267
Chr Hansen
Elyria, OH. 800-558-0802
Con Yeager Spice Company
Zelienople, PA. 800-222-2460
Custom Food Products
Alsip, IL 708-388-8883
Dean Distributors
Burlingame, CA 800-227-3112
Dean Distributors
Burlingame, CA 800-792-0816
Dismat Corporation
Toledo, OH 419-531-8963
Dorothy Dawson Foods Products
Jackson, MI 517-788-9830
Erba Food Products
Brooklyn, NY 718-272-7700
Five Star Food Base Company
St Paul, MN. 800-505-7827
Flavor House
Adelanto, CA 760-246-9131
Flavor Innovations
South Plainfield, NJ 800-536-2030
Fuji Foods
Browns Summit, NC 336-375-3111
Gel Spice Company, Inc
Bayonne, NJ 800-922-0230
Griffith Laboratories Worldwide
Alsip, IL 800-346-4743
Halben Food Manufacturing Company
Overland, MO. 800-888-4855
Henningsen Foods
Purchase, NY 914-701-4020
Hormel Foods Corporation
Austin, MN 800-523-4635
JMH International
Delafield, WI. 888-741-4564

Kerry Ingredients
  Tralee, Co. Kerry,
Lake City Foods
  Mississauga, ON 905-625-8244
Magic Seasoning Blends
  Harahan, LA 800-457-2857
Meat-O-Mat Corporation
  Brooklyn, NY .718-965-7250
Mermaid Spice Corporation
  Fort Myers, FL 239-693-1986
Olympia Oyster Company
  Shelton, WA 360-426-3354
Oskri Organics
  Thiensville, WI 800-628-1110
Pacific Foods
  Kent, WA. 800-347-9444
Precision Foods
  Melrose Park, IL 800-333-0003
Presco Food Seasonings
  Flemington, NJ 800-526-1713
Produits Alimentaires Berthelet
  Laval, QC 514-334-5503
Produits Ronald
  St. Damase, QC 450-797-3303
Proliant Meat Ingredients
  Ankeny, IA 800-369-2672
R.L. Schreiber
  Pompano Beach, FL 800-624-8777
R.L. Schreiber Company
  Pompano Beach, FL 800-624-8777
RC Fine Foods
  Belle Mead, NJ 800-526-3953
Sams Food Group
  Chicago, IL 800-852-0283
Senba USA
  Hayward, CA 888-922-5852
Serv-Agen Corporation
  Cherry Hill, NJ 856-663-6966
Spice Hunter
  San Luis Obispo, CA 800-444-3061
St. Ours & Company
  Norwell, MA. .781-331-8520
Summit Hill Flavors
  Middlesex, NJ. 732-805-0335
Superior Quality Foods
  Ontario, CA. 800-300-4210
Sweet Sue Kitchens
  Athens, AL 256-216-0500
Tone Products Company
  Melrose Park, IL 708-681-3660
Tova Industries
  Louisville, KY .888-532-8682
UFL Foods
  Mississauga, ON 905-670-7776
Unilever
  Lisle, IL. 877-995-4483
Vanee Foods Company
  Berkeley, IL. 708-449-7300
Ventura Foods
  Philadelphia, PA 215-223-8700
Ventura Foods   Foodservice
  Salem, OR. 503-585-6423
Ventura Foods   Production Plant
  Los Angeles, CA. 323-265-4300
Vogue Cuisine
  Culver City, CA 888-236-4144
White Coffee Corporation
  Long Island City, NY 800-221-0140
Williams-West & Witt Products
  Michigan City, IN 219-879-8236
World Flavors
  Warminster, PA 215-672-4400
Young Winfield
  Kleinburg, ON. 905-893-2536

Seafood

Blount Seafood Corporation
  Fall River, MA 774-888-1300

Vegetable

American Purpac Technologies, LLC
  Beloit, WI 877-787-7221
Associated Brands, Inc.
  Medina, NY. 800-265-0050

To advertise in the *Food &
Beverage Market Place* Online Database
call **(800) 562-2139** or log on to
http://gold.greyhouse.com
and click on "Advertise."

Cagnon Foods Company
  Brooklyn, NY .718-647-2244
California Custom Fruits & Flavors
  Irwindale, CA .877-558-0056

Yogurt

Givaudan Flavors
  Bridgeton, MO 800-422-5444
Gum Technology Corporation
  Tucson, AZ 800-369-4867
Honeyville Grain
  Rancho Cucamonga, CA 888-810-3212
Johanna Foods
  Flemington, NJ 800-727-6700
Maple Island
  St Paul, MN. 800-369-1022
Plaidberry Company
  Vista, CA. 760-727-5403

Binders

Cereal

Griffith Laboratories
  Scarborough, ON 416-288-3050

Sentry Seasonings
  Elmhurst, IL 630-530-5370

**The product development experts of Sentry Sea-
sonings are eager to offer the assistance and
hands-on experience to food processors of all
sizes. Sentry Seasonings will ensure the consistent
high quality and repeat sales of your products,
whether you choose one of our many off-the-shelf
Bench Mark products or a modified version to
meet your preferences. Sentry Seasonings can
also duplicate and/or improve your present flavor
profile; formulate, blend and package specifically
for your requirements.**

Sausage

Cargill Texturizing Solutions
  Cedar Rapids, IA. 877-650-7080
Lemix
  Canton, OH. 330-488-3072
Roland Industries
  Saint Louis, MO 800-325-1183

Sentry Seasonings
  Elmhurst, IL 630-530-5370

**The product development experts of Sentry Sea-
sonings are eager to offer the assistance and
hands-on experience to food processors of all
sizes. Sentry Seasonings will ensure the consistent
high quality and repeat sales of your products,
whether you choose one of our many off-the-shelf
Bench Mark products or a modified version to
meet your preferences. Sentry Seasonings can
also duplicate and/or improve your present flavor
profile; formulate, blend and package specifically
for your requirements.**

World Flavors
  Warminster, PA 215-672-4400
Yosemite Waters
  Los Angeles, CA. 800-427-8420

for Meat Products

Cargill Texturizing Solutions
  Cedar Rapids, IA. 877-650-7080
MGP
  Atchinson, KS. 913-367-1480

Sentry Seasonings
  Elmhurst, IL 630-530-5370

**The product development experts of Sentry Sea-
sonings are eager to offer the assistance and
hands-on experience to food processors of all
sizes. Sentry Seasonings will ensure the consistent
high quality and repeat sales of your products,
whether you choose one of our many off-the-shelf
Bench Mark products or a modified version to
meet your preferences. Sentry Seasonings can
also duplicate and/or improve your present flavor
profile; formulate, blend and package specifically
for your requirements.**

Bioflavinoids

Asiamerica Ingredients
  Westwood, NJ .201-497-5531

**Processor, importer, exporter and distributor of
bulk vitamins, amino acids, nutraceuticals, aromatic chemicals, food additives, herbs, mineral
nutrients and pharmaceuticals.**

Brewster Foods TestLab
  Reseda, CA 818-881-4268
H. Interdonati
  Cold Spring Hbr, NY 800-367-6617
Naturex (Chart Corp)
  South Hackensack, NJ 201-440-5000
P.L. Thomas
  Morristown, NJ. 973-984-0900
QBI
  South Plainfield, NJ 908-668-0088

Biopolymers

Cargill Texturizing Solutions
  Cedar Rapids, IA. 877-650-7080
CP Kelco
  Chicago, IL 800-535-2687

Bits

Baking

Erba Food Products
  Brooklyn, NY .718-272-7700
Nuvex Ingredients
  Blue Earth, MN. 507-526-4331

Colored Starch

Nuvex Ingredients
  Blue Earth, MN. 507-526-4331

Cookie

Nuvex Ingredients
  Blue Earth, MN. 507-526-4331

Flavor

Nuvex Ingredients
  Blue Earth, MN. 507-526-4331

Flavored Sugar

Nuvex Ingredients
  Blue Earth, MN. 507-526-4331
SensoryEffects Flavor Systems
  Bridgeton, MO 314-291-5444

Ham

Imitation

Gel Spice Company, Inc
  Bayonne, NJ 800-922-0230

Blends

Cheese

Cemac Foods Corporation
New York, NY 800-724-0179
Classic Tea
Libertyville, IL 630-680-9934
Leprino Foods Company
Denver, CO 800-537-7466

Sentry Seasonings
Elmhurst, IL 630-530-5370

The product development experts of Sentry Seasonings are eager to offer the assistance and hands-on experience to food processors of all sizes. Sentry Seasonings will ensure the consistent high quality and repeat sales of your products, whether you choose one of our many off-the-shelf Bench Mark products or a modified version to meet your preferences. Sentry Seasonings can also duplicate and/or improve your present flavor profile; formulate, blend and package specifically for your requirements.

Custom

Cargill Texturizing Solutions
Cedar Rapids, IA. 877-650-7080
Maple Island
St Paul, MN. 800-369-1022

Sentry Seasonings
Elmhurst, IL 630-530-5370

The product development experts of Sentry Seasonings are eager to offer the assistance and hands-on experience to food processors of all sizes. Sentry Seasonings will ensure the consistent high quality and repeat sales of your products, whether you choose one of our many off-the-shelf Bench Mark products or a modified version to meet your preferences. Sentry Seasonings can also duplicate and/or improve your present flavor profile; formulate, blend and package specifically for your requirements.

World Flavors
Warminster, PA 215-672-4400

Enrichment

Nu-Tek Products, LLC
Minnetonka, MN. 952-936-3600

Sentry Seasonings
Elmhurst, IL 630-530-5370

The product development experts of Sentry Seasonings are eager to offer the assistance and hands-on experience to food processors of all sizes. Sentry Seasonings will ensure the consistent high quality and repeat sales of your products, whether you choose one of our many off-the-shelf Bench Mark products or a modified version to meet your preferences. Sentry Seasonings can also duplicate and/or improve your present flavor profile; formulate, blend and package specifically for your requirements.

Herbs

All Purpose

Sentry Seasonings
Elmhurst, IL 630-530-5370

The product development experts of Sentry Seasonings are eager to offer the assistance and hands-on experience to food processors of all sizes. Sentry Seasonings will ensure the consistent high quality and repeat sales of your products, whether you choose one of our many off-the-shelf Bench Mark products or a modified version to meet your preferences. Sentry Seasonings can also duplicate and/or improve your present flavor profile; formulate, blend and package specifically for your requirements.

SupHerb Farms
Turlock, CA 800-787-4372

CrEATe! Get ready-to-use fresh flavor with SupHerb Farms' all-natural fresh frozen culinary herbs, specialty vegetables, culinary herb pastes, vegetable purees and creative blends. Complete microbiological testing ensures food safety. We set the standard for outstanding customer service, inspired culinary support, collaborative customer partnerships and innovative custom products.

Herbs & Spices

Asiamerica Ingredients
Westwood, NJ 201-497-5531

Processor, importer, exporter and distributor of bulk vitamins, amino acids, nutraceuticals, aromatic chemicals, food additives, herbs, mineral nutrients and pharmaceuticals.

CaJohns Fiery Foods
Columbus, OH 888-703-3473
Colorado Spice
Boulder, CO 800-677-7423
Georgia Spice Company
Atlanta, GA..................... 800-453-9997
Jodie's Kitchen
Tarpon Springs, FL 800-728-3704
La Flor Spices
Hauppauge, NY 631-885-9601
Marion-Kay Spices
Brownstown, IN 800-627-7423
Marnap Industries
Buffalo, NY..................... 716-897-1220
McCormick & Company Inc
Sparks, MD..................... 410-771-7301
North American Seasonings
Lake Oswego, OR................ 503-636-7043
Pendery's
Dallas, TX...................... 800-533-1870
Premier Blending
Wichita, KS 316-267-5533

Sentry Seasonings
Elmhurst, IL 630-530-5370

The product development experts of Sentry Seasonings are eager to offer the assistance and hands-on experience to food processors of all sizes. Sentry Seasonings will ensure the consistent high quality and repeat sales of your products, whether you choose one of our many off-the-shelf Bench Mark products or a modified version to meet your preferences. Sentry Seasonings can also duplicate and/or improve your present flavor profile; formulate, blend and package specifically for your requirements.

St. John's Botanicals
Bowie, MD 301-262-5302

SupHerb Farms
Turlock, CA 800-787-4372

CrEATe! Get ready-to-use fresh flavor with SupHerb Farms' all-natural fresh frozen culinary herbs, specialty vegetables, culinary herb pastes, vegetable purees and creative blends. Complete microbiological testing ensures food safety. We set the standard for outstanding customer service, inspired culinary support, collaborative customer partnerships and innovative custom products.

Wisconsin Spice
Berlin, WI 920-361-3555

Pepper

Sentry Seasonings
Elmhurst, IL 630-530-5370

The product development experts of Sentry Seasonings are eager to offer the assistance and hands-on experience to food processors of all sizes. Sentry Seasonings will ensure the consistent high quality and repeat sales of your products, whether you choose one of our many off-the-shelf Bench Mark products or a modified version to meet your preferences. Sentry Seasonings can also duplicate and/or improve your present flavor profile; formulate, blend and package specifically for your requirements.

Caffeine

Alcan Chemical
Stamford, CT.................... 800-736-7893

Asiamerica Ingredients
Westwood, NJ 201-497-5531

Processor, importer, exporter and distributor of bulk vitamins, amino acids, nutraceuticals, aromatic chemicals, food additives, herbs, mineral nutrients and pharmaceuticals.

Certified Processing Corporation
Hillside, NJ 973-923-5200
Jungbunzlauer
Newton, MA 800-828-0062
Natra US
Chula Vista, CA 800-262-6216

Casein & Caseinates

Agri-Dairy Products
Purchase, NY 914-697-9580
American Casein Company
Burlington, NJ 609-387-2988
Arla Foods Ingredients
Basking Ridge, NJ 800-243-3730
Blossom Farm Products
Ridgewood, NJ 800-729-1818
Crest Foods Company
Ashton, IL. .800-435-6972
Erie Foods International
Erie, IL 800-447-1887
Kantner Group
Wapakoneta, OH 419-738-4060
NZMP
Santa Rosa, CA. 800-358-9096

Casein

Austrade Food Ingredients
Palm Beach Gdns, FL. 561-586-7145
Century Foods International
Sparta, WI. .800-269-1901
Clofine Dairy & Food Products
Linwood, NJ 800-441-1001
Excelpro Manufacturing Corporation
Los Angeles, CA. 323-268-1918
International Casein Corporation
Great Neck, NY 516-466-4363
NZMP
Santa Rosa, CA. 800-358-9096
Oxford Frozen Foods Limited
Oxford, NS .902-447-2100
Prestige Proteins
Boca Raton, FL. 561-499-6100
Prestige Technology Corporation
Boca Raton, FL. 888-697-4141
Reilly Dairy & Food Company
Tampa, FL. .813-839-8458
Silver Creek Specialty Meats
Oshkosh, WI. 920-232-3581
St. Charles Trading
Lake Saint Louis, MO. 800-336-1333

Cellulose Gel

Asiamerica Ingredients
Westwood, NJ 201-497-5531

Processor, importer, exporter and distributor of bulk vitamins, amino acids, nutraceuticals, aromatic chemicals, food additives, herbs, mineral nutrients and pharmaceuticals.

J. Rettenmaier
Schoolcraft, MI. 877-243-4661
P.L. Thomas
Morristown, NJ 973-984-0900
Reed Corporation
Pompton Plains, NJ 800-820-REED

Chemicals

Natural

Arizona Chemical Company
Jacksonville, FL 800-526-5294

Asiamerica Ingredients
Westwood, NJ 201-497-5531

Processor, importer, exporter and distributor of bulk vitamins, amino acids, nutraceuticals, aromatic chemicals, food additives, herbs, mineral nutrients and pharmaceuticals.

BASF Corporation
Florham Park, NJ 800-526-1072
Cheese Smokers
Brooklyn, NY 718-456-0531
Chempacific Corporation
Baltimore, MD 410-633-5771
Crompton Corporation
Greenwich, CT 800-295-2392
Flavorchem
Downers Grove, IL. 800-323-1301
Haldin International
Closter, NJ. 201-784-0044
Specialty Industrial Products
Spartanburg, SC 800-747-9001
Symrise
Teterboro, NJ. 201-288-3200
Van Waters & Roger
Summit, IL .708-728-6830
VANCO Trading
Darien, CT. 203-656-2800

Chlorophyll

Asiamerica Ingredients
Westwood, NJ 201-497-5531

Processor, importer, exporter and distributor of bulk vitamins, amino acids, nutraceuticals, aromatic chemicals, food additives, herbs, mineral nutrients and pharmaceuticals.

DeSouza International
Beaumont, CA. 800-373-5171
H. Interdonati
Cold Spring Hbr, NY 800-367-6617
Herb Connection
Springville, UT 801-489-4254
Naturex (Chart Corp)
South Hackensack, NJ 201-440-5000
Pro-Pharm
Lake Bluff, IL 847-234-3570
World Organics Corporation
Huntington Beach, CA 714-893-0017

Chocolate Products

ADM Cocoa
Milwaukee, WI. 800-558-9958
Chefmaster
Garden Grove, CA 800-333-7443
Qzina Specialty Foods
Las Vegas, NV 702-451-3916
SensoryEffects Flavor Systems
Bridgeton, MO 314-291-5444

Chocolate Chip Compound for Ice Cream

ADM Cocoa
Milwaukee, WI. 800-558-9958

Coagulants

Dairy

Cargill Texturizing Solutions
Cedar Rapids, IA. 877-650-7080

Coatings

Compound

BASF Corporation
Florham Park, NJ 800-526-1072

CHR Hansen
Stoughton, WI. 608-877-8970

Edible

Spray Dynamics
St Clair, MO 800-260-7366

Cocoa Butter

Aarhus United USA, Inc.
Newark, NJ .800-776-1338
ADM Cocoa
Milwaukee, WI. 800-558-9958
Barry Callebaut USA LLC
St. Albans, VT. 802-524-9711
Chadler
Swedesboro, NJ 856-467-0099
Ecom Agroindustrial Corporation Ltd
New York, NY 212-248-7475
Flowers Bakeries
Thomasville, GA. 800-568-3476
Natra US
Chula Vista, CA 800-262-6216
Spring Tree Maple Products
Brattleboro, VT. 802-254-8784
Vrymeer Commodities
St Charles, IL 630-584-0069
Wilbur Chocolate
Lititz, PA. 800-233-0139

Colors

Ameri Color Corporation
Placentia, CA 800-556-0233
CHR Hansen Inc
Milwaukee, WI. 800-558-0802
Erba Food Products
Brooklyn, NY 718-272-7700
Flavorchem
Downers Grove, IL. 800-323-1301
LorAnn Oils Inc
Lansing, MI. 888-456-7266
McCormick & Company Inc
Sparks, MD 410-771-7301
Noveon
Cleveland, OH 216-447-5000
Particle Dynamics
St Louis, MO. 800-452-4682
Sensient Food Colors
Milwaukee, WI. 800-558-9892
Sensient Technologies
Milwaukee, WI. 800-558-9892
Singer Extract Laboratory
Livonia, MI. 313-345-5880
Unette Corporation
Wharton, NJ 973-328-6800
WILD Flavors
Erlanger, KY. 859-342-3600

Annatto

Burlington Bio-Medical Corporation
Farmingdale, NY 631-694-4700
Schiff Food Products
North Bergen, NJ 201-861-2503
SJH Enterprises
Middleton, WI. 888-745-3845

Burnt Sugar

D.D. Williamson & Company
Louisville, KY 866-412-6567
DD Williamson & Company
Louisville, KY 800-227-2635
Four Percent Company
Highland Park, MI 313-345-5880
Produits Alimentaire
St Lambert De Lauzon, QC 800-463-1787
RFI Ingredients
Blauvelt, NY 800-962-7663
Sethness Products Company
Chicago, IL .847-329-2080
Seydel International
Pendergrass, GA 706-693-2295

Caramel

Carmi Flavor & Fragrance Company
Los Angeles, CA. 800-421-9647
Gel Spice Company, Inc
Bayonne, NJ 800-922-0230

Butter & Cheese

Agri-Dairy Products
Purchase, NY 914-697-9580
Carmi Flavor & Fragrance Company
Los Angeles, CA 800-421-9647
Prime Ingredients
Saddle Brook, NJ 888-791-6655
SJH Enterprises
Middleton, WI................888-745-3845

Caramel

D.D. Williamson & Company
Louisville, KY 866-412-6567
Sethness Products Company
Chicago, IL 888-772-1880

Cider & Vinegar

Asiamerica Ingredients
Westwood, NJ 201-497-5531

Processor, importer, exporter and distributor of bulk vitamins, amino acids, nutraceuticals, aromatic chemicals, food additives, herbs, mineral nutrients and pharmaceuticals.

Prime Ingredients
Saddle Brook, NJ 888-791-6655

Dyes

Certified

Castella Imports
Hauppauge, NY 866-227-8355

Grape Skin Extract Color

Asiamerica Ingredients
Westwood, NJ 201-497-5531

Processor, importer, exporter and distributor of bulk vitamins, amino acids, nutraceuticals, aromatic chemicals, food additives, herbs, mineral nutrients and pharmaceuticals.

Natural

Asiamerica Ingredients
Westwood, NJ 201-497-5531

Processor, importer, exporter and distributor of bulk vitamins, amino acids, nutraceuticals, aromatic chemicals, food additives, herbs, mineral nutrients and pharmaceuticals.

CHR Hansen Inc
Milwaukee, WI 800-558-0802
LaMonde Wild Flavors
Placentia, CA 714-993-7700
P.L. Thomas
Morristown, NJ 973-984-0900

Annatto

SJH Enterprises
Middleton, WI...............888-745-3845

Anthocyanins Grape Skin

Asiamerica Ingredients
Westwood, NJ 201-497-5531

Processor, importer, exporter and distributor of bulk vitamins, amino acids, nutraceuticals, aromatic chemicals, food additives, herbs, mineral nutrients and pharmaceuticals.

RFI Ingredients
Blauvelt, NY 800-962-7663

Betaine Beet

RFI Ingredients
Blauvelt, NY 800-962-7663

Carmine

Asiamerica Ingredients
Westwood, NJ 201-497-5531

Processor, importer, exporter and distributor of bulk vitamins, amino acids, nutraceuticals, aromatic chemicals, food additives, herbs, mineral nutrients and pharmaceuticals.

RFI Ingredients
Blauvelt, NY 800-962-7663

Carotenoids

Asiamerica Ingredients
Westwood, NJ 201-497-5531

Processor, importer, exporter and distributor of bulk vitamins, amino acids, nutraceuticals, aromatic chemicals, food additives, herbs, mineral nutrients and pharmaceuticals.

RFI Ingredients
Blauvelt, NY 800-962-7663

Others

Asiamerica Ingredients
Westwood, NJ 201-497-5531

Processor, importer, exporter and distributor of bulk vitamins, amino acids, nutraceuticals, aromatic chemicals, food additives, herbs, mineral nutrients and pharmaceuticals.

Turmeric

Asiamerica Ingredients
Westwood, NJ 201-497-5531

Processor, importer, exporter and distributor of bulk vitamins, amino acids, nutraceuticals, aromatic chemicals, food additives, herbs, mineral nutrients and pharmaceuticals.

RFI Ingredients
Blauvelt, NY 800-962-7663

Vegetable

Moody Dunbar
Johnson City, TN 800-251-8202

Compounds

Cooking

Coast Packing Company
Vernon, CA 323-277-7700
Columbus Foods Company
Des Plaines, IL 800-322-6457
Mallet & Company
Carnegie, PA 800-245-2757
Prime Ingredients
Saddle Brook, NJ 888-791-6655

Tenderizing

Custom Food Products
Alsip, IL 708-388-8883
Tova Industries
Louisville, KY 888-532-8682
Turano Pastry Shops
Bloomingdale, IL 630-529-6161
World Flavors
Warminster, PA 215-672-4400

Concentrates

Fruit

Apple & Eve
Roslyn, NY 800-969-8018
Beta Pure Foods
Aptos, CA 831-685-6565
Citrus Citrosuco North America
Lake Wales, FL 800-356-4592
Coloma Frozen Foods
Coloma, MI 800-642-2723
Country Pure Foods
Akron, OH. 877-995-8423
Gerber Products Company
Parsippany, NJ. 800-443-7237
Greenwood Associates
Highland Park, IL 847-242-7900
Hiller Cranberries
Rochester, MA 508-763-5257
Johnson Concentrates
Sunnyside, WA 509-837-4600
Kerr Concentrates
Salem, OR. 800-910-5377
Miline Fruit Products
Prosser, WA. 509-786-2611
Minute Maid Company
Houston, TX 888-884-8952
Sabroso Company
Medford, OR. 509-697-7251
SimmaLoosa Company
Covington, LA 985-892-1400
Stiebs
Madera, CA. 559-661-0031
Three Vee Food & Syrup Company
Brooklyn, NY 800-801-7330
Tupman-Thurlow Company
Deerfield Beach, FL 954-596-9989

Fruit Puree

Greenwood Associates
Highland Park, IL 847-242-7900
Milne Fruit Products
Prosser, WA.................509-786-2611
RFI Ingredients
Blauvelt, NY 800-962-7663

Tomato

A&B Ingredients
Fairfield, NJ 973-227-1390

Vegetable

Beta Pure Foods
Aptos, CA 831-685-6565
Global Citrus Resources
Lakeland, FL 863-647-9020
Greenwood Associates
Highland Park, IL 847-242-7900

Whey Protein Concentrates & Isolates

Arla Foods Ingredients
Basking Ridge, NJ 800-243-3730
Bongards Creameries
Norwood, MN. 800-877-6417
Calpro Ingredients
Corona, CA 909-493-4890
Glanbia Foods
Twin Falls, ID 800-427-9477
Glanbia Nutritionals
Monroe, WI. .800-336-2183
Inovatech USA
Montreal, QC 888-388-3447
Kantner Group
Wapakoneta, OH. 419-738-4060
Main Street Ingredients
La Crosse, WI 800-359-2345
Milky Whey
Missoula, MT 800-379-6455
The Scoular Company
Omaha, NE 402-342-3500

Confectionery

Bakers' & Confectioners' Supplies

Abel & Schafer
Ronkonkoma, NY 800-443-1260
ACH Food Companies, Inc.
Cordova, TN .800-691-1106
ADM Food Ingredients
Olathe, KS 800-255-6637
ADM Milling Company
Carthage, MO 417-358-2197
ADM Milling Company
Cleveland, TN 423-476-7551
ADM Milling Company
Chattanooga, TN. 423-756-0503
ADM Milling Company
Minneapolis, MN 800-528-7877
ADM Milling Company
Shawnee Mission, KS 913-266-6300
Agricor
Marion, IN. 765-662-0606
Al-Rite Fruits & Syrups
Miami, FL 305-652-2540
American Almond Products Company
Brooklyn, NY. 800-825-6663
American Key Food Products
Closter, NJ. 800-767-0237
AnaCon Foods Company
Atchison, KS. 800-328-0291
Ann's House of Nuts, Inc.
Jessup, MD 301-498-4920
Arcor USA
Coral Gables, FL. 800-572-7267
Astor Chocolate Corporation
Lakewood, NJ. 732-901-1001
Atlantic Quality Spice &Seasonings
Edison, NJ. 800-584-0422
Baker Boy Bake Shop
Dickinson, ND 800-437-2008
Barry Callebaut USA, LLC
Saint Albans, VT. 800-556-8845
Bay State Milling Company
Winona, MN .800-533-8098
Best Brands Corporate Office
St Paul, MN. .800-328-2068
Best Brands Corporation
Tampa, FL. 800-282-0565
Best Maid Cookie Company
River Falls, WI. 888-444-0322
Bette's Diner Products
Berkeley, CA. 510-644-3230
Blend Pak
Bloomfield, KY 502-252-8000
Blommer Chocolate Company
Chicago, IL. .800-621-1606
Blue Pacific Flavors & Fragrances
City of Industry, CA 800-248-7499
Blue Planet Foods, Inc.
Collegedale, TN. 877-396-3145
Bob's Red Mill Natural Foods
Milwaukie, OR 800-349-2173
Brass Ladle Products
Glen Mills, PA 800-955-2353
Brown & Haley
Tacoma, WA. 253-620-3000
Byrd Mill Company
Ashland, VA .888-897-3336

Cadbury Trebor Allan
Toronto, ON .800-565-6541
California Brands Flavors
Oakland, CA .800-348-0111
California Independent Almond Growers
Ballico, CA 209-667-4855
Cangel
Toronto, ON .800-267-4795
Carol Lee Products
Lawrence, KS 785-842-5489
Century Foods International
Sparta, WI. 800-269-1901
Chadler
Swedesboro, NJ 856-467-0099
Charles Dennery Pillsbury
New Orleans, LA 504-733-2331
Charles H. Baldwin & Sons
West Stockbridge, MA 413-232-7785
Chase Brothers Dairy
Oxnard, CA 800-438-6455
Chef Solutions
North Haven, CT. 856-848-5314
Chefmaster
Garden Grove, CA 800-333-7443
CHS
Inver Grove Heights, MN. 800-232-3639
Classic Confections
Atlanta, GA 800-359-7351
Commodities Marketing, Inc.
Edison, NJ. 732-516-0700
Compact Industries
St Charles, IL 800-513-4262
Con Agra Store Brands
Edina, MN. 952-835-6900
ConAgra Mills
Omaha, NE 800-851-9618
ConAgra Mills
Kansas City, MO. 816-942-3700
Cream of the West
Harlowton, MT 800-477-2383
CSP Foods
Mont-Royal, QC 514-731-7621
Dakota Organic Products
Watertown, SD 800-243-7264
DD Williamson & Company
Louisville, KY 800-227-2635
De-Iorio's Frozen Dough
Utica, NY 800-649-7612
Dean Distributors
Burlingame, CA 800-792-0816
Devansoy
Carroll, IA 800-747-8605
Dorothy Dawson Foods Products
Jackson, MI. .517-788-9830
Eden Foods Inc
Clinton, MI 800-248-0320
Eden Processing
Poplar Grove, IL 815-765-2000
EFCO Products
Poughkeepsie, NY 800-284-3326
Fizzle Flat Farm
Yale, IL 618-793-2060
Florida Shortening Corporation
Miami, FL. 305-691-2992
Flowers Bakery of Montgomery
Montgomery, AL. 334-281-7030
Food Concentrate Corporation
Oklahoma City, OK 405-840-5633
France Croissant
New York, NY 212-888-1210
Frankford Candy & Chocolate Company
Philadelphia, PA 800-523-9090
Franklin Foods
Enosburg Falls, VT. 800-933-6114
Galloway Company
Neenah, WI. .800-722-8903
General Mills
Minneapolis, MN 800-248-7310
Ghirardelli Chocolate Company
San Leandro, CA 800-877-9338
Golden Fluff Popcorn Company
Lakewood, NJ. 732-367-5448
Gorant Candies
Youngstown, OH. 800-572-4139
Greenfield Mills
Howe, IN. 260-367-2394
Guittard Chocolate Company
Burlingame, CA 800-468-2462
Gurley's Foods
Willmar, MN .800-426-7845
H.B. Taylor Co
Chicago, IL 773-254-4805

Harlan Bakeries
Avon, IN 317-272-3600
Hauser Chocolate
Westerly, RI. .888-599-8231
Heartland Food Products
Shawnee Mission, KS 913-831-4446
Heidi's Gourmet Desserts
Tucker, GA 800-241-4166
Holland-American Wafer Company
Wyoming, MI. 800-253-8350
Holton Food Products Company
La Grange, IL 708-352-5599
Homestead Mills
Cook, MN 800-652-5233
Honeyville Grain
Salt Lake City, UT 801-972-2168
Horriea 2000 Food Industries
Reynolds, GA 478-847-4186
I Rice & Company
Philadelphia, PA 800-232-6022
Ingredients Corporation of America
Memphis, TN 901-525-6660
Interstate Brands
Biddeford, ME 207-286-1200
J.R. Short Canadian Mills
Toronto, ON .416-421-3463
J.R. Short Milling Company
Kankakee, IL. 800-544-8734
John Gust Foods & Products Corporation
Batavia, IL. 800-756-5886
Kalsec
Kalamazoo, MI. 800-323-9320
Kargher Corporation
Hatfield, PA. .800-355-1247
Karp's
Schaumburg, IL. 800-593-5277
Kencraft
American Fork, UT. 800-377-4368
Kerry Ingredients
Tralee, Co. Kerry,
Kimmie Candy Company
Reno, NV 888-532-1325
King Milling Company
Lowell, MI 616-897-9264
Knappen Milling Company
Augusta, MI .800-562-7736
Knouse Foods
Peach Glen, PA 717-677-8181
L&S Packing Company
Farmingdale, NY 800-286-6487
Lacey Milling Company
Hanford, CA. 559-584-6634
Lake States Yeast
Rhinelander, WI 918-535-2676
Lawrence Foods
Elk Grove Vlg, IL 800-323-7848
Leon's Bakery
North Haven, CT. 800-223-6844
Little Crow Foods
Warsaw, IN. .800-288-2769
Log House Foods
Plymouth, MN. 763-546-8395
Louisiana Gourmet Enterprises
Houma, LA 800-328-5586
Lucas Meyer
Decatur, IL 800-769-3660
Lyoferm & Vivolac Cultures
Indianapolis, IN 800-844-8649
Main Street Ingredients
La Crosse, WI 800-359-2345
Malt Products Corporation
Saddle Brook, NJ 800-526-0180
Marx Brothers
Birmingham, AL. 800-633-6376
Masterfoods USA
Hackettstown, NJ 908-852-1000
Mayfair Sales
Buffalo, NY. .800-248-2881
Mennel Milling Company
Fostoria, OH. 419-435-8151
Merlino Italian Baking Company
Seattle, WA. .800-207-2997
Mills Brothers International
Tukwila, WA .206-575-3000
Minn-Dak Yeast Company
Wahpeton, ND. 701-642-3300
Mississippi Blending Company
Keokuk, IA 800-758-4080
Moorhead & Company
Loomis, CA 877-290-2427
Morningstar Foods
Dallas, TX. 225-273-2803

Morris J. Golombeck
  Brooklyn, NY 718-284-3505
Nature's Hand
  Burnsville, MN 952-890-6033
Nestle
  Cleveland, OH 440-349-5757
Northwestern Foods
  St Paul, MN 800-236-4937
Nuvex Ingredients
  Blue Earth, MN 507-526-4331
NZMP
  Santa Rosa, CA 800-358-9096
Orange Bakery
  Irvine, CA 949-863-1377
Orlinda Milling Company
  Orlinda, TN 615-654-3633
Pacific Westcoast Foods
  Portland, OR 800-874-9333
Palmer Candy Company
  Sioux City, IA 800-831-0828
Pasta Factory
  Northlake, IL 800-615-6951
Pelican Bay
  Dunedin, FL 800-826-8982
Pied-Mont/Dora
  Ste Anne Des Plaines, BC 800-363-8003
Pillsbury Frozen Foods
  Lithonia, GA 770-482-5092
Plaidberry Company
  Vista, CA .760-727-5403
QA Products
  Elk Grove Vlg, IL 800-635-7907
Quali Tech
  Chaska, MN 800-328-5870
Quality Ingredients Corporation
  Chester, NJ 800-843-6314
Quality Naturally! Foods
  City of Industry, CA 888-498-6986
Quest International Flavors
  1411 GP Naarden,
R&J Farms
  West Salem, OH 419-846-3179
Reinhart Foods
  Markham, ON 905-754-3503
Rene Rey Chocolates Ltd
  North Vancouver, BC 888-985-0949
Rhodes International
  Columbus, WI 800-876-7333
Rich Products Corporation
  Buffalo, NY 800-356-7094
Richmond Baking Company
  Richmond, IN 765-962-8535
Roland Industries
  Saint Louis, MO 800-325-1183
Roman Meal Milling Company
  Fargo, ND 877-282-9743
Rucker's Makin' Batch Candies
  Hutsonville, IL 888-622-2639
Rumford Baking Powder Company
  Terre Haute, IN 812-232-9446
RV Industries
  Atlanta, GA 770-729-8983
Schlotterbeck & Foss Company
  Portland, ME 800-777-4666
Scott's Auburn Mills
  Auburn, KY 800-962-7857
Serv-Agen Corporation
  Cherry Hill, NJ 856-663-6966
Service Packing Company
  Vancouver, BC 604-681-0264
Setton Pistachio of Terra Bella
  Terra Bella, CA 800-227-4397
Shawnee Milling Company
  Shawnee, OK 405-273-7000
Signature Brands
  Ocala, FL .800-456-9573
Skjodt-Barrett Foods
  Mississauga, ON 877-600-1200
SOUPerior Bean & Spice Company
  Vancouver, WA 800-878-7687
Southeastern Mills
  Rome, GA 800-334-4468
Star of the West
  Kent, OH .330-673-2941
Star of the West MillingCompany
  Frankenmuth, MI 989-652-9971
Strossner's Bakery
  Greenville, SC 864-233-3996
Sucesores de Pedro Cortes
  San Juan, PR 787-754-7040
Swatt Baking Company
  Olean, NY 800-370-6656

Tara Foods
  Atlanta, GA 404-559-0605
Taste Maker Foods
  Memphis, TN 800-467-1407
Tate & Lyle North American Sugars
  Rutherford, NJ 201-842-7723
The Bama Company
  Tulsa, OK .800-756-2262
The Lollipop Tree, Inc
  Portsmouth, NH 800-842-6691
TNT Crust
  Green Bay, WI. 920-431-7240
Tova Industries
  Louisville, KY 888-532-8682
Uhlmann Company
  Kansas City, MO. 800-383-8201
Valley View Blueberries
  Vancouver, WA 360-892-2839
Vie de France Yamazaki
  Vernon, LA 323-582-1241
VIP Foods
  Flushing, NY 718-821-3942
Vrymeer Commodities
  St Charles, IL 630-584-0069
Wall-Rogalsky Milling Company
  Mc Pherson, KS 800-835-2067
Watson Foods Company
  West Haven, CT 800-388-3481
Weaver Nut Company
  Ephrata, PA 717-738-3781
West Pac
  Idaho Falls, ID 800-973-7407
Whipple Company
  Natick, MA 800-345-2925
White Swan Fruit Products
  Plant City, FL 813-752-1155
White-Stokes Company
  Chicago, IL 800-978-6537
Whittaker & Associates
  Atlanta, GA 404-266-1265
Willmark Sales Company
  West Hempstead, NY 718-388-7141
Worldwide Sourcing LLC
  Incline Village, NV 775-833-1480
Yohay Baking Company
  Lindenhurst, NY 631-225-0300
Young Winfield
  Kleinburg, ON. 905-893-2536

Cultures & Yeasts

Acidophilus Cultures

Cargill Texturizing Solutions
  Cedar Rapids, IA. 877-650-7080

Bacillus

Cargill Texturizing Solutions
  Cedar Rapids, IA. 877-650-7080

Bacteria

Buttermilk

Cargill Texturizing Solutions
  Cedar Rapids, IA. 877-650-7080

Cheese

Cargill Texturizing Solutions
  Cedar Rapids, IA. 877-650-7080

Yogurt

Cargill Texturizing Solutions
  Cedar Rapids, IA. 877-650-7080

Bacterial Cultures, Starter Media & Culture Replac

Cargill Texturizing Solutions
  Cedar Rapids, IA. 877-650-7080
Kantner Group
  Wapakoneta, OH 419-738-4060

Bacteriological

Cargill Texturizing Solutions
  Cedar Rapids, IA. 877-650-7080

Cultures

Alfer Laboratories
  Chatsworth, CA 818-709-0737
Alternative Health & Herbs
  Albany, OR 800-345-4152
Berkshire Dairy & Food Products
  Wyomissing, PA 888-654-8008
Brewster Foods TestLab
  Reseda, CA 818-881-4268
Cargill Texturizing Solutions
  Cedar Rapids, IA. 877-650-7080
CHR Hansen Inc
  Milwaukee, WI 800-558-0802
Continental Culture Specialists
  Glendale, CA 818-240-7400
Continental Custom Ingredients
  Oakville, ON 905-815-8158
Controlled Food Systems
  Oakmont, PA. 412-828-2844
Crystal Cream & Butter Company
  Sacramento, CA 916-447-6455
Fairmont Products
  Belleville, PA 717-935-2121
GEM Cultures
  Fort Bragg, CA 707-964-2922
IMAC
  Oklahoma City, OK 888-878-7827
Ingredient Innovations
  Kansas City, MO. 816-587-1426
Lallemand/American Yeast
  Addison, IL 630-932-1290
Lyoferm & Vivolac Cultures
  Indianapolis, IN 800-844-8649
Maryland & Virginia Milk Producers Cooperative
  Reston, VA 703-742-7443
Old Home Foods
  St Paul, MN 800-628-8700
Quality Ingredients Corporation
  Burnsville, MN 952-898-4002
Rhodia
  Cranbury, NJ 800-343-8324
Rosell Institute
  Rexdale, ON 514-522-2133
Sunshine Dairy Foods
  Portland, OR 503-234-7526
Vivolac Cultures Corporation
  Indianapolis, IN 317-356-8460

Lactobacillus Acidophilus

Cargill Texturizing Solutions
  Cedar Rapids, IA. 877-650-7080

Yeast

ADM Food Ingredients
  Olathe, KS 800-255-6637
Bakon Yeast
  Scottsdale, AZ. 480-595-9370
Blue Chip Group
  Salt Lake City, UT 800-878-0099
California Blending Corpany
  El Monte, CA 626-448-1918
Cardi Foods
  Fuquay Varina, NC 973-983-8818
Church & Dwight Company
  Princeton, NJ 800-221-0453
CSP Foods
  Mont-Royal, QC 514-731-7621
DSM Food Specialties
  Menomonee Falls, WI. 800-423-7906
DSM Food Specialties
  Eagleville, PA 800-662-4478
Fleischmann's Yeast
  Chesterfield, MO 800-247-7473
Kyowa Hakko
  New York, NY 212-715-0572
Lake States Yeast
  Rhinelander, WI 918-535-2676
Lallemand/American Yeast
  Addison, IL 630-932-1290
Lesaffre Yeast Corporation
  Milwaukee, WI 414-271-6755
Luxor California ExportsCorporation
  San Diego, CA 619-692-9330
Minn-Dak Yeast Company
  Wahpeton, ND 701-642-3300
Mississippi Blending Company
  Keokuk, IA 800-758-4080
Natural Foods
  Toledo, OH 800-860-0006

Norcrest Consulting
Divide, CO 719-687-7636
Organic Gourmet
Sherman Oaks, CA 800-400-7772
Pascobel Inc
Longueuil, QC 450-677-2443
RBW & Associates
Portland, OR 503-223-0843
Red Star Yeast
Milwaukee, WI 877-677-7000
SAF Products
Minneapolis, MN 800-641-4615
SAS Bakers Yeast
Headland, AL .877-677-7000
Sensient Technologies
Milwaukee, WI 800-558-9892
Southeastern Wisconsin Products Company
Milwaukee, WI 414-482-1730
Vinquiry
Windsor, CA 707-838-6312

Autolysates

Lake States Yeast
Rhinelander, WI 918-535-2676

Bakers Active

SAF Products
Minneapolis, MN 800-641-4615

Bakers'

Lallemand/American Yeast
L.I.C., NY 773-267-2223
Minn-Dak Yeast Company
Wahpeton, ND. 701-642-3300
SAS Bakers Yeast
Headland, AL .877-677-7000

Brewers Active

SAF Products
Minneapolis, MN 800-641-4615

Brewers'

Energen Products
Norwalk, CA. .800-423-8837

Froedtert Malt Company
Milwaukee, WI 414-671-1166
NPC Dehydrators
Payette, ID. 208-642-4471
Nutraceutical Corporation
Park City, UT .435-655-6000
Watson Nutritional Ingredients
West Haven, CT 203-932-3000

Extracts

Organic Gourmet
Sherman Oaks, CA 800-400-7772

Fresh

Lallemand/American Yeast
Addison, IL. 630-932-1290

Primary Dried

Lallemand/American Yeast
Addison, IL. 630-932-1290

Torula Dried

Lake States Yeast
Rhinelander, WI 918-535-2676

Wine

Americana Foods
Dallas, TX. 972-709-7100
Dave's Hawaiian Ice Cream
Pearl City, HI .808-453-0500
Lallemand
Petaluma, CA .800-423-6625

Yogurt

Cargill Texturizing Solutions
Cedar Rapids, IA. 877-650-7080
Lyo-San
Lachute, QC 450-562-8525

Curing Preparations

Meat

Cargill Texturizing Solutions
Cedar Rapids, IA. 877-650-7080
First Spice Mixing Company
Long Island City, NY 800-221-1105

Decorative Items

Petra International
Hamilton, ON .800-261-7226
Sugar Flowers Plus
Glendale, CA .800-972-2935

Digestive Aids

Arise & Shine Herbal Products
Medford, OR. .800-688-2444
Bio-K + International
Laval, QC 450-978-2465
Bionutritional Research Group
Santa Ana, CA 714-427-6990
Cargill Texturizing Solutions
Cedar Rapids, IA. 877-650-7080
Dancing Paws
Pacific Palisades, CA 888-644-7297
Earth Products
Vista, CA. 760-494-2000
Enzymatic Therapy
Green Bay, WI. 800-783-2286
Enzyme Formulations
Madison, WI 800-614-4400
National Enzyme Company
Forsyth, MO 800-825-8545
Russo Farms
Vineland, NJ 856-692-5942

Emulsifiers

ADM Food Ingredients
Olathe, KS. 800-255-6637
ADM Lecithin & Monoglycerides
Decatur, IL 800-637-5843

Asiamerica Ingredients
Westwood, NJ 201-497-5531

Processor, importer, exporter and distributor of bulk vitamins, amino acids, nutraceuticals, aromatic chemicals, food additives, herbs, mineral nutrients and pharmaceuticals.

Avatar Corporation
    University Park, IL 800-255-3181
Bunge Canada
    Oakville, ON 800-361-3043
Cargill Texturizing Solutions
    Cedar Rapids, IA 877-650-7080
Continental Custom Ingredients
    Oakville, ON 905-815-8158
Controlled Food Systems
    Oakmont, PA 412-828-2844
Enterprise Foods
    Atlanta, GA 404-351-2251
Lambent Technologies
    Skokie, IL .800-432-7187
Mallet & Company
    Carnegie, PA 800-245-2757
Mitsubishi InternationalCorporation
    New York, NY 800-442-6266
Montello
    Tulsa, OK .800-331-4628
P.L. Thomas
    Morristown, NJ 973-984-0900
Quality Ingredients Corporation
    Burnsville, MN 952-898-4002
RIBUS
    St Louis, MO 314-727-4287
Specialty Industrial Products
    Spartanburg, SC 800-747-9001
Technical Oil
    Easton, PA .610-252-8350

Lecithin

ACATRIS
    Oakville, ON 905-829-2414
Acatris USA
    Edina, MN .952-920-7700
ADM Food Ingredients
    Olathe, KS .800-255-6637
AG Processing, Inc.
    Omaha, NE 800-247-1345
American Lecithin Company
    Oxford, CT .800-364-4416

Asiamerica Ingredients
Westwood, NJ 201-497-5531

Processor, importer, exporter and distributor of bulk vitamins, amino acids, nutraceuticals, aromatic chemicals, food additives, herbs, mineral nutrients and pharmaceuticals.

Avatar Corporation
    University Park, IL 800-255-3181
Blue Chip Group
    Salt Lake City, UT 800-878-0099
CanAmera Foods
    Winnipeg, NB 204-324-6481
Cargill Texturizing Solutions
    Cedar Rapids, IA 877-650-7080
Columbus Foods Company
    Des Plaines, IL 800-322-6457
Lucas Meyer
    Decatur, IL .800-769-3660
Mid Atlantic Vegetable Shortening Company
    Kearny, NJ .800-966-1645
Natural Foods
    Toledo, OH 800-860-0006
Riceland Foods   Rice Milling Operations
    Little Rock, AR 888-532-4844
Technical Oil Products
    Boonton, NJ 973-335-0300
The Solae Company
    St Louis, MO 800-325-7108

Trophic International
    Salt Lake City, UT 801-269-6667
W.A. Cleary Products
    Somerset, NJ 800-238-7813
WA Cleary Products
    Somerset, NJ 800-238-7813
Westin
    Omaha, NE 800-228-6098

Enhancers

Apple Flavor & FragranceUSA Corp.
    Edison, NJ .732-393-0600
Blue Chip Group
    Salt Lake City, UT 800-878-0099
Cinnabar Specialty Foods
    Prescott, AZ 866-293-6433
First Spice Mixing Company
    Long Island City, NY 800-221-1105
Lora Brody Products
    West Newton, MA 617-928-1005

Enzymes

ADM Food Ingredients
    Olathe, KS .800-255-6637
Ajinomoto Food Ingredients LLC
    Chicago, IL 773-380-7000
Amano Enzyme USA Company, Ltd
    Elgin, IL 800-446-7652
American Laboratories, Inc.
    Omaha, NE 402-339-2494
American Yeast/Lallemand
    Pembroke, NH 866-920-9885

Asiamerica Ingredients
Westwood, NJ 201-497-5531

Processor, importer, exporter and distributor of bulk vitamins, amino acids, nutraceuticals, aromatic chemicals, food additives, herbs, mineral nutrients and pharmaceuticals.

Bio-Nutritional Products
    Northvale, NJ 201-784-8200
Brewster Foods TestLab
    Reseda, CA 818-881-4268
Genencor International
    Beloit, WI .608-365-1112
George A Jeffreys & Company
    Salem, VA .540-389-8220
Inovatech USA
    Montreal, QC 888-388-3447
Malabar Formulas
    Lake Arrowhead, CA 800-462-6617
Mitsubishi InternationalCorporation
    New York, NY 800-442-6266
Novozymes North America
    Franklinton, NC 800-879-6686
SKW Nature Products
    Dubuque, IA 563-588-6244
Specialty Enzymes
    Chino, CA .909-613-1660
Universal Formulas
    Portage, MI 800-342-6960
Valley Research
    South Bend, IN 800-522-8110

Additives

Cargill Texturizing Solutions
    Cedar Rapids, IA 877-650-7080

Extenders

Arboris, LLC.
    Savannah, GA 912-238-7573
Cargill Texturizing Solutions
    Cedar Rapids, IA 877-650-7080

Chicken

Valley Grain Products
    Madera, CA 559-675-3400

Coffee

I Rice & Company
    Philadelphia, PA 800-232-6022

RH Bauman & Company
    Chatsworth, CA 877-228-6263

Meat

ADM Food Ingredients
    Olathe, KS .800-255-6637
Cargill Texturizing Solutions
    Cedar Rapids, IA 877-650-7080
Flavor House
    Adelanto, CA 760-246-9131
Gum Technology Corporation
    Tucson, AZ 800-369-4867
Proliant Meat Ingredients
    Ankeny, IA .800-369-2672
Tova Industries
    Louisville, KY 888-532-8682
World Flavors
    Warminster, PA 215-672-4400

Extracts

A M Todd Company
    Kalamazoo, OR 269-343-2603
Active Organics
    Lewisville, TX 972-221-7500
Advanced Food Systems, Inc.
    Somerset, NJ 732-873-6776
Al-Rite Fruits & Syrups
    Miami, FL .305-652-2540
AM Todd Company
    Eugene, OR 800-827-4372
AM Todd Company
    Kalamazoo, MI 800-968-2603
American Instants
    Flanders, NJ 973-584-8811
American Laboratories, Inc.
    Omaha, NE 402-339-2494
American Mercantile Corporation
    Memphis, TN 901-454-1900
Aphrodisia Products
    Brooklyn, NY 877-274-3677
Apotheca Naturale
    Woodbine, IA 800-736-3130

Asiamerica Ingredients
Westwood, NJ 201-497-5531

Processor, importer, exporter and distributor of bulk vitamins, amino acids, nutraceuticals, aromatic chemicals, food additives, herbs, mineral nutrients and pharmaceuticals.

Associated Bakers Products
    Huntington, NY 631-673-3841
Autocrat Coffee & Extracts
    Lincoln, RI .800-288-6272
Bartek Ingredients, Inc.
    Stoney Creek, ON 800-263-4165
Bear Stewart Corporation
    Chicago, IL 800-697-2327
Beck Flavors
    St Louis, MO 800-851-8100
Berghausen Corporation
    Cincinnati, OH 800-648-5887
Best Brands Corporation
    Dallas, TX .800-969-2253
Beta Pure Foods
    Aptos, CA .831-685-6565
Bickford Flavors
    Cleveland, OH 800-283-8322
Blessed Herbs
    Oakham, MA. 800-489-4372
Blue California Company
    Rancho Santa Margarita, CA 949-635-1991
Blue Mountain Flavors
    Kinston, NC 800-522-1544
Briess Industries
    Chilton, WI 920-849-7711
Brucia Plant Extracts
    Shingle Springs, CA 530-676-2774
Cafe Du Monde
    New Orleans, LA 504-587-0835
Cajun Chef Products
    St Martinville, LA 337-394-7112
California Brands Flavors
    Oakland, CA 800-348-0111

Cargill Corn Milling
Naperville, IL 800-344-1633
Castella Imports
Hauppauge, NY 866-227-8355
Cellu-Con
Strathmore, CA 559-568-0190
Charles Boggini
Coventry, CT 860-742-2652
Chefmaster
Garden Grove, CA 800-333-7443
Classic Flavors & Fragrances
New York, NY 212-777-0004
Clements Foods Company
Oklahoma City, OK 800-654-8355
Coco Rico
Montreal, QC 514-849-5554
Concord Foods
Brockton, MA 508-580-1700
Consolidated Mills
Houston, TX 713-896-4196
Consumers Flavoring Extract Company
Brooklyn, NY 718-435-0201
Contact International
Skokie, IL 847-324-4411
Crestmont Enterprises
Camden, NJ 856-966-0700
Crystal Foods
Brick, NJ 732-477-0073
Dean Distributors
Burlingame, CA 800-227-3112
Dean Distributors
Burlingame, CA 800-792-0816
DSM Food Specialties
Eagleville, PA 800-662-4478
Edgar A. Weber Company
Wheeling, IL 800-558-9078
Erba Food Products
Brooklyn, NY 718-272-7700
Everfresh Food Corporation
Minneapolis, MN 612-331-6393
Flavor & Fragrance Specialties
Mahwah, NJ 800-998-4337
Flavor House
Adelanto, CA 760-246-9131
Flavor Innovations
South Plainfield, NJ 800-536-2030
Flavor Sciences
Stamford, CT. 800-535-2867
Flavorchem
Downers Grove, IL 800-323-1301
Florida Food Products
Eustis, FL 800-874-2331
FoodScience of Vermont
Essex Junction, VT. 800-874-9444
Genarom International
Cranbury, NJ 609-409-6200
Green Foods Corporation
Oxnard, CA 800-777-4430
H.B. Taylor Co
Chicago, IL 773-254-4805
Hagelin & Company
Branchburg, NJ 800-229-2112
Haldin International
Closter, NJ. 201-784-0044
Herb Connection
Springville, UT 801-489-4254
Herbs, Etc.
Santa Fe, NM 888-694-3727
Inter-American Products
Cincinnati, OH 800-645-2233
Kalsec
Kalamazoo, MI 800-323-9320
Lochhead Manufacturing Company
Fenton, MO. 888-776-2088
Mafco Natural Products
Richmond, VA. 804-222-1600
MAFCO Worldwide Corporation
Camden, NJ 856-964-8840
Malt-Diastase Company
Saddle Brook, NJ 800-772-0416
Maryland & Virginia Milk Producers Cooperative
Reston, VA 703-742-7443
McCormick & Company Inc
Sparks, MD. 410-771-7301
McCormick Ingredients
Hunt Valley, MD. 800-632-5847
MD Labs
Phoenix, AZ 602-437-0127
Metarom Corporation
Newport, VT. 888-882-5555
Mother Murphy's Labs
Greensboro, NC 800-849-1277

Natra US
Chula Vista, CA 800-262-6216
Naturex (Chart Corp)
South Hackensack, NJ 201-440-5000
Newtown Foods
Langhorne, PA 215-579-2120
Now Foods
Bloomingdale, IL 888-669-3663
Nutricepts
Burnsville, MN 800-949-9060
P.L. Thomas
Morristown, NJ. 973-984-0900
Parker Flavors, Inc
Baltimore, MD 800-336-9113
Particle Control
Albertville, MN. 763-497-3075
Particle Dynamics
St Louis, MO. 800-452-4682
Perlarom Technology
Columbia, MD 410-997-5114
Phyto-Technologies
Woodbine, IA 877-809-3404
Phytotherapy Research Laboratory
Lobelville, TN. 800-274-3727
PMC Specialties Group
Cincinnati, OH 800-543-2466
Pro-Pharm
Lake Bluff, IL 847-234-3570
Pure World Botanicals
South Hackensack, NJ 201-440-5000
QA Products
Elk Grove Vlg, IL. 800-635-7907
RC Fine Foods
Belle Mead, NJ 800-526-3953
RFI Ingredients
Blauvelt, NY. 800-962-7663
Royal Foods & Flavors
Elk Grove Vlg, IL. 847-595-9166
San-Ei Gen FFI
New York, NY 212-315-7840
Scan American Food Compampany
Everett, WA. 425-514-0500
Senba USA
Hayward, CA 888-922-5852
SimmaLoosa Company
Covington, LA 985-892-1400
Simpson Spring Company
South Easton, MA. 508-238-4472
Singer Extract Laboratory
Livonia, MI. 313-345-5880
Sivetz Coffee
Corvallis, OR 541-753-9713
SJH Enterprises
Middleton, WI. 888-745-3845
Sno-Shack
Salt Lake City, UT 801-466-1771
Spiceman
Eugene, OR. 800-725-8373
Star Kay White
Congers, NY 800-874-8518
Stearns & Lehman
Mansfield, OH 800-533-2722
Sterling Extract Company
Franklin Park, IL. 847-451-9728
Stiebs
Madera, CA. 559-661-0031
T.W. Burleson & Son
Waxahachie, TX 972-937-4810
Target Flavors
Brookfield, CT 800-538-3350
Technology Flavors & Fragrances
Amityville, NY. 631-842-7600
Texas Coffee Company
Beaumont, TX. 800-259-3400
Texas Spice Company
Cedar Park, TX. 800-880-8007
Triple K Manufacturing Company
Shenandoah, IA. 888-987-2824
United Canadian Malt
Peterborough, ON 800-461-6400

V&E Kohnstamm
Brooklyn, NY 800-847-4500
Vanlaw Food Products
Fullerton, CA 714-870-9091
Virginia Dare
Brooklyn, NY 800-847-4500
W&G Flavors
Hunt Valley, MD. 410-771-6606
Western Flavors & Fragrances
Livermore, CA 925-373-9433
Young Winfield
Kleinburg, ON. 905-893-2536

Beef

Blue Mountain Flavors
Kinston, NC 800-522-1544
David Michael & Company
Philadelphia, PA 800-363-5286
Flavor House
Adelanto, CA 760-246-9131
Geneva Ingredients
Waunakee, WI. 800-828-5924
Gold Coast Ingredients
Commerce, CA 800-352-8673
Henningsen Foods
Purchase, NY 914-701-4020
Prime Ingredients
Saddle Brook, NJ 888-791-6655
Proliant Meat Ingredients
Ankeny, IA 800-369-2672
RFI Ingredients
Blauvelt, NY 800-962-7663
Superior Quality Foods
Ontario, CA. 800-300-4210
Wynn Starr Foods of Kentucky
Louisville, KY 800-996-7827

Beverages

Mother Murphy's Labs
Greensboro, NC 800-849-1277
Virginia Dare
Brooklyn, NY 800-847-4500

Botanical

A.M. Todd Company
Kalamazoo, MI. 800-968-2603
Abkit Camocare Nature Works
New York, NY 800-226-6227
Active Organics
Lewisville, TX 972-221-7500
Alta Health Products
Boise, ID 800-423-4155
American Biosciences
Blauvelt, NY. 845-727-0800
American Fruit Processors
Pacoima, CA 818-899-9574
Apex Marketing Group
Las Vegas, NV 866-610-6165
Aphrodisia Products
Brooklyn, NY 877-274-3677
Apotheca Naturale
Woodbine, IA 800-736-3130

Asiamerica Ingredients
Westwood, NJ 201-497-5531

Processor, importer, exporter and distributor of bulk vitamins, amino acids, nutraceuticals, aromatic chemicals, food additives, herbs, mineral nutrients and pharmaceuticals.

Atlantic Quality Spice &Seasonings
Edison, NJ. 800-584-0422
Avoca
Merry Hill, NC 252-482-2133
Blue California Company
Rancho Santa Margarita, CA 949-635-1991
Botanical Products
Springville, CA 559-539-3432
Brewster Foods TestLab
Reseda, CA 818-881-4268
Brucia Plant Extracts
Shingle Springs, CA 530-676-2774
Danisco-Cultor
Ardsley, NY 914-674-6300

Dolisos America
Henderson, NV 800-365-4767
Eclectic Institute
Sandy, OR 503-668-4120

EMERLING INTERNATIONAL FOODS, INC.

Emerling International Foods
Buffalo, NY 716-833-7381

> We supply food manufacturers and food service
> customers worldwide (since 1988) with bulk in-
> gredients including: Fruits & Vegetables; Juice
> Concentrates; Herbs & Spices; Oils & Vinegars;
> Flavors & Colors; Honey & Molasses. We also
> produce PURE MAPLE SYRUP.

Energique
Woodbine, IA 800-869-8078
Extracts Plus
Vista, CA 760-597-0200
Frutarom Meer Corporation
North Bergen, NJ 800-526-7147
GCI Nutrients (USA)
Foster City, CA 650-697-4700
Geni
Noblesville, IN 888-656-4364
GMI Products/Originates
Sunrise, FL 800-999-9373
Graminex
Saginaw, MI 877-472-6469
Haldin International
Closter, NJ 201-784-0044
Health from the Sun/ArkoPharma
Bedford, MA 781-276-0505
Herb Connection
Springville, UT 801-489-4254
Herb Pharm
Williams, OR 800-348-4372
Herbalist & Alchemist
Washington, NJ 908-689-9020
Kelatron Corporation
Ogden, UT 801-394-4558
Nature's Apothecary
Boulder, CO 800-999-7422
Naturex (Chart Corp)
South Hackensack, NJ 201-440-5000
P.L. Thomas
Morristown, NJ 973-984-0900
Pharmachem Laboratories
Hackensack, NJ 201-343-3611
Pure World Botanicals
South Hackensack, NJ 201-440-5000
RFI Ingredients
Blauvelt, NY 800-962-7663
Sabinsa Corporation
Piscataway, NJ 732-777-1111
San Francisco Herb & Natural Food Company
Fremont, CA 800-227-2830
Shanks Extracts
Lancaster, PA 800-346-3135
Stevia LLC
Valley Forge, PA 888-878-3842
Terra Botanica Products
Nakusp, BC 888-410-9977
Universal Preservachem Inc
Edison, NJ 732-777-7338
VitaTech International
Tustin, CA 714-832-9700
Whole Herb Company
Sonoma, CA 707-935-1077

Chicken

Blue Mountain Flavors
Kinston, NC 800-522-1544
Flavor House
Adelanto, CA 760-246-9131
Geneva Ingredients
Waunakee, WI 800-828-5924
Prime Ingredients
Saddle Brook, NJ 888-791-6655
Wynn Starr Foods of Kentucky
Louisville, KY 800-996-7827

Coffee

Advanced Food Technology
Littleton, CO 303-980-5221
American Instants
Flanders, NJ 973-584-8811
Atlantic Manufacturing Company
Baltimore, MD 410-752-7223

Autocrat Coffee & Extracts
Lincoln, RI 800-288-6272
Beck Flavors
St Louis, MO. 800-851-8100
California Custom Fruits & Flavors
Irwindale, CA 877-558-0056
Coffee Enterprises
Burlington, VT 800-375-3398
Prime Ingredients
Saddle Brook, NJ 888-791-6655
Stearns & Lehman
Mansfield, OH 800-533-2722
Virginia Dare
Brooklyn, NY 800-847-4500
X Cafe
Princeton, MA. 877-492-2331

Crab

American Instants
Flanders, NJ 973-584-8811
Atlantic Manufacturing Company
Baltimore, MD 410-752-7223
Autocrat Coffee & Extracts
Lincoln, RI 800-288-6272
Barlean's
Ferndale, WA 360-384-0325
Blue Mountain Flavors
Kinston, NC 800-522-1544
Boyajian, Inc
Canton, MA 800-965-0665
Brewster Foods TestLab
Reseda, CA 818-881-4268
Cajun Chef Products
St Martinville, LA 337-394-7112
Chefmaster
Garden Grove, CA 800-333-7443
CJ America
Fort Lee, NJ 201-461-7407
Consolidated Mills
Houston, TX 713-896-4196
Consumers Flavoring Extract Company
Brooklyn, NY 718-435-0201
Dairy Chem Inc
Fishers, IN. 317-849-8400
Danisco USA
Lakeland, FL 863-646-0165
Delmonico's Winery
Brooklyn, NY 718-768-7020
Dragoco
Teterboro, NJ 201-288-3200
Elan Chemical Company
Newark, NJ 973-344-8014
Embassy Flavours Ltd.
Brampton, ON. 800-334-3371
Empire Spice Mills
Winnipeg, NB 204-786-1594
FBC Industries
Schaumburg, IL. 888-322-4637
Felbro Food Products
Los Angeles, CA. 800-335-2761
Fidelity Flavors & Fragrances
Goshen, NY 845-294-5356
Fis USA
Solon, OH 800-233-3133
Flavor Sciences
Stamford, CT. 800-535-2867
Flavor Systems International
Cincinnati, OH 800-498-2783
Flavorganics
Newark, NJ 973-344-8014
Flavormatic Industries
Wappingers Falls, NY 845-297-9100
Flavtek
Los Angeles, CA. 800-562-5880
Flavurence Corporation
Commerce, CA 800-717-1957
Fleurchem
Middletown, NY 845-341-2170
Four Percent Company
Highland Park, MI 313-345-5880
Geneva Ingredients
Waunakee, WI 800-828-5924
Givaudan
Cincinnati, OH 800-892-1199
Glucona America
Janesville, WI 608-752-0449
Gold Coast Ingredients
Commerce, CA 800-352-8673
GSB & Associates
Kennesaw, GA 877-472-2776

Ingredient Innovations
Kansas City, MO. 816-587-1426
International Food Solutions
Germantown, WI. 262-251-9230
John I. Haas
Washington, DC 202-223-0005
Joseph Adams Corporation
Valley City, OH 330-225-9135
Lochhead Manufacturing Company
Fenton, MO. 888-776-2088
Magic Ice Products
Stockton, CA 800-776-7923
Mane Incorporated
Milford, OH 800-595-8936
Medallion International
Pompton Plains, NJ 973-616-3401
Millennium Specialty Chemicals
Jacksonville, FL 800-231-6728
Mountain Lake Specialty Ingredients Company
Omaha, NE 402-595-7463
Naturex
South Hackensack, NJ 201-440-5000
Old 97 Manufacturing Company
Tampa, FL. 813-247-6677
Ottens Flavors
Philadelphia, PA 800-523-0767
Prime Ingredients
Saddle Brook, NJ 888-791-6655
Quest International Flavors
Owings Mills, MD 410-363-7200
Quest International Flavors
Hoffman Estates, IL 800-235-6122
RCB International
Albany, OR 541-967-3814
SKW Nature Products
Langhorne, PA 215-702-1000
Stirling Foods
Renton, WA 800-332-1714
Takasago International Corporation
Rockleigh, NJ 201-767-9001
Torre Products Company
New York, NY 212-925-8989
Triple K Manufacturing Company
Shenandoah, IA. 888-987-2824
WILD Flavors
Cincinnati, OH 888-945-3352
Wynn Starr Foods of Kentucky
Louisville, KY 800-996-7827

Flavoring

Amoretti-Capriccio
Oxnard, CA 800-266-7388
I Rice & Company
Philadelphia, PA 800-232-6022
Kikkoman International
San Francisco, CA 415-956-7750
Paradigm Food Works
Lake Oswego, OR. 503-595-4360

Fruit

Brewster Foods TestLab
Reseda, CA 818-881-4268
Chefmaster
Garden Grove, CA 800-333-7443
Contact International
Skokie, IL 847-324-4411
Ramsey/SIAS
Cleveland, OH 800-477-3788
SimmaLoosa Company
Covington, LA 985-892-1400

Root Beer

California Custom Fruits & Flavors
Irwindale, CA 877-558-0056
Flavtek
Los Angeles, CA. 800-562-5880
Four Percent Company
Highland Park, MI 313-345-5880
Gold Coast Ingredients
Commerce, CA 800-352-8673
Prime Ingredients
Saddle Brook, NJ 888-791-6655
Rio Syrup Company
St Louis, MO. 800-325-7666

Seafood

Ocean Cliff Corporation
New Bedford, MA 508-990-7900

Tea

California Custom Fruits & Flavors
Irwindale, CA 877-558-0056
Jogue Inc
Northville, MI 800-521-3888
P.L. Thomas
Morristown, NJ 973-984-0900
RFI Ingredients
Blauvelt, NY 800-962-7663
Stearns & Lehman
Mansfield, OH 800-533-2722
Virginia Dare
Brooklyn, NY 800-847-4500

Vanilla

Astral Extracts Ltd
Syosset, NY 516-496-2505
Beck Flavors
St Louis, MO. 800-851-8100
Bickford Flavors
Cleveland, OH 800-283-8322
Bush Boake Allen
New York, NY 212-765-5500
California Custom Fruits & Flavors
Irwindale, CA 877-558-0056
Carmi Flavor & Fragrance Company
Los Angeles, CA. 800-421-9647
Castella Imports
Hauppauge, NY 866-227-8355
Clements Foods Company
Oklahoma City, OK 800-654-8355
David Michael & Company
Philadelphia, PA 800-363-5286
Elan Chemical Company
Newark, NJ 973-344-8014
Embassy Flavours Ltd.
Brampton, ON. 800-334-3371

EMERLING INTERNATIONAL FOODS, INC.

Emerling International Foods
Buffalo, NY. 716-833-7381

We supply food manufacturers and food service customers worldwide (since 1988) with bulk ingredients including: Fruits & Vegetables; Juice Concentrates; Herbs & Spices; Oils & Vinegars; Flavors & Colors; Honey & Molasses. We also produce PURE MAPLE SYRUP.

Everfresh Food Corporation
Minneapolis, MN 612-331-6393
Flavorchem
Downers Grove, IL 800-323-1301
Flavorganics
Newark, NJ 973-344-8014
Flavtek
Los Angeles, CA. 800-562-5880
Four Percent Company
Highland Park, MI 313-345-5880
Gel Spice Company, Inc
Bayonne, NJ 800-922-0230
Gold Coast Ingredients
Commerce, CA 800-352-8673
Goodman Manufacturing Company
Carthage, MO 417-358-3231
Grapevine Trading Company
Santa Rosa, CA. 800-469-6478
H.B. Taylor Co
Chicago, IL 773-254-4805
Hagelin & Company
Branchburg, NJ 800-229-2112
I Rice & Company
Philadelphia, PA 800-232-6022
Jogue Inc
Northville, MI 800-521-3888
Lochhead Manufacturing Company
Fenton, MO. 888-776-2088
LorAnn Oils Inc
Lansing, MI. 888-456-7266
Nielsen-Massey Vanillas
Waukegan, IL 800-525-7873
Parker Flavors, Inc
Baltimore, MD 800-336-9113
Prime Ingredients
Saddle Brook, NJ 888-791-6655
R.R. Lochhead Manufacturing
Paso Robles, CA. 800-735-0545
Rio Syrup Company
St Louis, MO. 800-325-7666

Rodelle Vanillas
Fort Collins, CO 800-898-5457
Shanks Extracts
Lancaster, PA 800-346-3135
Sterling Extract Company
Franklin Park, IL 847-451-9728
Triple K Manufacturing Company
Shenandoah, IA 888-987-2824
V&E Kohnstamm
Brooklyn, NY 800-847-4500
Van Tone Creative Flavors Inc
Terrell, TX. 800-856-0802
Virginia Dare
Brooklyn, NY 800-847-4500
Weber Flavors
Wheeling, IL. 800-558-9078

Vegetable

Basic American Foods
Blackfoot, ID 800-227-4050
Cajun Chef Products
St Martinville, LA. 337-394-7112
Geneva Ingredients
Waunakee, WI 800-828-5924
Gold Coast Ingredients
Commerce, CA 800-352-8673
Kalsec
Kalamazoo, MI 800-323-9320
Naturex (Chart Corp)
South Hackensack, NJ 201-440-5000
Prime Ingredients
Saddle Brook, NJ 888-791-6655
Ted Shear Associates
Larchmont, NY 914-833-0017
Varied Industries Corporation
Mason City, IA 800-654-5617
Vegetable Juices
Chicago, IL 888-776-9752
Western Flavors & Fragrances
Livermore, CA 925-373-9433

Yeast

Quest International Flavors
Hoffman Estates, IL 847-645-7000
Royal Foods & Flavors
Elk Grove Vlg, IL 847-595-9166

Fatty Acids

Essential

ChildLife-Nutrition for Kids
Marina Del Rey, CA 800-993-0332
RFI Ingredients
Blauvelt, NY 800-962-7663

Fillers

Meal

Agri-Dairy Products
Purchase, NY 914-697-9580

Flakes

Banana

Agvest
Cleveland, OH 440-735-6900

EMERLING INTERNATIONAL FOODS, INC.

Emerling International Foods
Buffalo, NY. 716-833-7381

We supply food manufacturers and food service customers worldwide (since 1988) with bulk ingredients including: Fruits & Vegetables; Juice Concentrates; Herbs & Spices; Oils & Vinegars; Flavors & Colors; Honey & Molasses. We also produce PURE MAPLE SYRUP.

Gerber Products Company
Parsippany, NJ. 800-443-7237
Spreda Group
Prospect, KY 502-426-9411
Unique Ingredients
Naches, WA. 509-653-1991

Oats

LaCrosse Milling Company
Cochrane, WI 800-441-5411

Potato

AgraWest Foods
Prince Edward Island, NS. 877-687-1400
American Health & Nutrition
Ann Arbor, MI 734-677-5572

EMERLING INTERNATIONAL FOODS, INC.

Emerling International Foods
Buffalo, NY. 716-833-7381

We supply food manufacturers and food service customers worldwide (since 1988) with bulk ingredients including: Fruits & Vegetables; Juice Concentrates; Herbs & Spices; Oils & Vinegars; Flavors & Colors; Honey & Molasses. We also produce PURE MAPLE SYRUP.

Idaho Pacific Corporation
Ririe, ID 800-238-5503
Idaho Supreme Potatoes
Firth, ID. 208-346-6841
McCain Foods Canada
Florenceville, NB 506-392-5541
Nonpareil Corporation
Blackfoot, ID 800-522-2223
Oregon Potato Company
Boardman, OR 800-336-6311
Terry Foods Inc
Idaho Falls, ID 208-604-8143
Tova Industries
Louisville, KY 888-532-8682
Unique Ingredients
Naches, WA. 509-653-1991

Soy

American Health & Nutrition
Ann Arbor, MI 734-677-5572
Microsoy Corporation
Jefferson, IA 515-386-2100

Flavor Enhancers

American Fruit Processors
Pacoima, CA. 818-899-9574

Asiamerica Ingredients
Westwood, NJ 201-497-5531

Processor, importer, exporter and distributor of bulk vitamins, amino acids, nutraceuticals, aromatic chemicals, food additives, herbs, mineral nutrients and pharmaceuticals.

International Flavors & Fragrances
New York, NY 212-765-5500
LifeSpice Ingredients
Palm Beach, FL. 561-844-6334
Mixerz All Natural Cocktail Mixers
Beverly, MA 978-922-6497
Nutra Food Ingredients, LLC
Kentwood, MI 616-656-9928
QST Ingredients, Inc.
Rancho Cucamonga, CA 909-989-4343
SensoryEffects Flavor Systems
Bridgeton, MO 314-291-5444

Summit Hill Flavors
Middlesex, NJ .732-805-0335

Gluconates

![asiamerica logo]

Asiamerica Ingredients
Westwood, NJ 201-497-5531

Processor, importer, exporter and distributor of
bulk vitamins, amino acids, nutraceuticals, aromatic chemicals, food additives, herbs, mineral
nutrients and pharmaceuticals.

Lifewise Ingredients
Lake Zurich, IL 847-550-8270

Flavors

A M Todd Company
Kalamazoo, OR. 269-343-2603
ADM Food Ingredients
Olathe, KS. 800-255-6637
Advanced Food Systems, Inc.
Somerset, NJ .732-873-6776
AFF International
Marietta, GA .800-241-7764
Ajinomoto Food Ingredients LLC
Chicago, IL 773-380-7000
Al-Rite Fruits & Syrups
Miami, FL 305-652-2540
Allen Flavors
Edison, NJ 908-561-5995
AM Todd Company
Eugene, OR. 800-827-4372
American Instants
Flanders, NJ .973-584-8811
American Laboratories, Inc.
Omaha, NE 402-339-2494
Armand's Coffee Flavors
Atlanta, GA 404-696-4178
Aromor Flavors & Fragrances
Englewood Cliffs, NJ 201-503-1662

![asiamerica logo]

Asiamerica Ingredients
Westwood, NJ 201-497-5531

Processor, importer, exporter and distributor of
bulk vitamins, amino acids, nutraceuticals, aromatic chemicals, food additives, herbs, mineral
nutrients and pharmaceuticals.

Assets Health Foods
Hillsborough, NJ. 888-849-2048
Associated Bakers Products
Huntington, NY 631-673-3841
Austin Special Foods Company
Austin, TX. 866-372-8663
Autocrat Coffee & Extracts
Lincoln, RI 800-288-6272
AVRI Companies
Richmond, CA 800-883-9574
Avron Resources
Richmond, CA 800-883-9574
Baker's Coconut
Memphis, TN .800-323-1092
Bartek Ingredients, Inc.
Stoney Creek, ON 800-263-4165
Batko Flavors LLC
North Brunswick, NJ 732-991-3462
Bear Stewart Corporation
Chicago, IL 800-697-2327
Beck Flavors
St Louis, MO. .800-851-8100
Best Brands Corporation
Dallas, TX 800-969-2253
Beta Pure Foods
Aptos, CA 831-685-6565
Blendex Company
Jeffersontown, KY 800-626-6325
Blue Pacific Flavors & Fragrances
City of Industry, CA 800-248-7499

Borthwicks Flavors
Hauppauge, NY 800-255-6837
Brewster Foods TestLab
Reseda, CA 818-881-4268
Cajun Chef Products
St Martinville, LA. 337-394-7112
California Brands Flavors
Oakland, CA 800-348-0111
Capriccio
Chatsworth, CA 818-718-7620
Cargill Corn Milling
Naperville, IL .800-344-1633
CHR Hansen
Milwaukee, WI 800-343-4680
Citrop
Tampa, FL. 813-249-5955
Classic Flavors & Fragrances
New York, NY 212-777-0004
Clements Foods Company
Oklahoma City, OK 800-654-8355
Coca-Cola North America
Columbus, OH 614-491-6305
Comax Flavors
Melville, NY 800-992-0629
Commercial Creamery Company
Spokane, WA. 800-541-0850
ConAgra Food Ingredients
Omaha, NE 800-872-9236
Consolidated Mills
Houston, TX 713-896-4196
Consumers Flavoring Extract Company
Brooklyn, NY .718-435-0201
Contact International
Skokie, IL 847-324-4411
Cosco International
Chicago, IL 800-621-4549
Creative Flavors
Chagrin Falls, OH 800-848-9043
Crestmont Enterprises
Camden, NJ 856-966-0700
Crystal Foods
Brick, NJ 732-477-0073
Danisco-Cultor
Ardsley, NY 914-674-6300
Dean Distributors
Burlingame, CA 800-227-3112
Dean Distributors
Burlingame, CA 800-792-0816
DSM Food Specialties
Eagleville, PA .800-662-4478
Ecom Manufacturing Corporation
Markham, ON 905-477-2441
Edlong Dairy Flavors
Elk Grove Vlg, IL 888-698-2783
Essential Flavors & Fragrances, Inc
Corona, CA 888-333-9935
Everfresh Food Corporation
Minneapolis, MN 612-331-6393
Fee Brothers
Rochester, NY 800-961-3337
Flavor & Fragrance Specialties
Mahwah, NJ .800-998-4337
Flavor Dynamics
South Plainfield, NJ 888-271-8424
Flavor House
Adelanto, CA .760-246-9131
Flavor Innovations
South Plainfield, NJ 800-536-2030
Flavor Waves
Novato, CA. 415-899-0084
Flavorchem
Downers Grove, IL 800-323-1301
Flavors
Edwardsville, PA. 570-287-8642
Flavors of North America
Geneva, IL. 800-308-3662
Florida Food Products
Eustis, FL 800-874-2331
Food Ingredients Solutions
Blauvelt, NY 845-353-8501
Genarom International
Cranbury, NJ .609-409-6200
Givaudan
Bridgeton, MO 800-422-5444
Givaudan Access
Cincinnati, OH 866-448-2832
Givaudan Flavors
Bridgeton, MO 800-422-5444
GMI Products/Originates
Sunrise, FL 800-999-9373
Great Northern Maple Products
Saint Honor, De Shenley, QC 418-485-7777

Green Spot Packaging
Claremont, CA 800-456-3210
Greinoman's/Unified Industries
Cumming, GA. 770-889-8233
Griffith Laboratories
Scarborough, ON 416-288-3050
Griffith Laboratories Worldwide
Alsip, IL 800-346-4743
Grow Company
Ridgefield, NJ. 201-941-8777
Gum Technology Corporation
Tucson, AZ 800-369-4867
H.B. Taylor Co
Chicago, IL 773-254-4805
Hagelin & Company
Branchburg, NJ 800-229-2112
HB Taylor Company
Chicago, IL 773-254-4805
I Rice & Company
Philadelphia, PA 800-232-6022
Illes Seasonings & Flavors
Carrollton, TX. 800-683-4553
International Flavors & Fragrances
New York, NY 212-765-5500
International Flavors & Fragrances
Dayton, NJ 800-433-3528
J&K Ingredients
Paterson, NJ .973-340-8700
James Finley & Company
Florham Park, NJ 973-539-8030
Johnson's Food Products
Dorchester, MA. 617-265-3400
Kalsec
Kalamazoo, MI 800-323-9320
Kerry Ingredients & Flavours
Beloit, WI 800-248-7310
Key Essentials
Rcho Sta Marg, CA 949-635-1000
Lebermuth Company
South Bend, IN 800-648-1123
Liberty Natural Products
Portland, OR .800-289-8427
Lochhead Manufacturing Company
Fenton, MO 888-776-2088
Lorann Oils
Lansing, MI. 800-248-1302
Lucks Food Decorating Company
Tacoma, WA .800-426-9778
MAFCO Worldwide Corporation
Camden, NJ 856-964-8840
Mane Incorporated
Milford, OH 800-595-8936
Maryland & Virginia Milk Producers Cooperative
Reston, VA 703-742-7443
Master Taste International
Plant City, FL .800-237-7629
Mastertaste
Fenton, MO 636-349-0020
Mastertaste Company
South Hackensack, NJ 201-641-6555
McCormick & Company Inc
Sparks, MD. 410-771-7301
Metarom Corporation
Newport, VT. .888-882-5555
Millers Blue Ribbon Beef
Hyrum, UT 800-873-0939
Mother Murphy's Labs
Greensboro, NC 800-849-1277
Mutual Flavors
South Jordan, UT 888-343-2922
Naturex (Chart Corp)
South Hackensack, NJ 201-440-5000
Newly Weds Foods
Memphis, TN .800-647-9314
Northeastern Products Company
South Plainfield, NJ 908-561-1610
Northwestern Extract Company
Brookfield, WI 800-466-3034
Nutricepts
Burnsville, MN 800-949-9060
Ocean Cliff Corporation
New Bedford, MA 508-990-7900
OSF Flavors
Windsor, CT 800-466-6015
Ottens Flavors
Philadelphia, PA 800-523-0767
Parker Flavors, Inc
Baltimore, MD 800-336-9113
Particle Control
Albertville, MN. 763-497-3075
Particle Dynamics
St Louis, MO. .800-452-4682

Perlarom Technology
Columbia, MD 410-997-5114
PMC Specialties Group
Cincinnati, OH 800-543-2466
Progressive Flavors
Hawley, PA 805-383-2640
Pure World Botanicals
South Hackensack, NJ 201-440-5000
Richard E. Colgin Company
Dallas, TX 214-951-8687
Rio Syrup Company
St Louis, MO .800-325-7666
Rose Brand Corporation
Brooklyn, NY .800-854-5356
Royal Foods & Flavors
Elk Grove Vlg, IL 847-595-9166
San-Ei Gen FFI
New York, NY 212-315-7840
Sartori Food Corporation
Plymouth, WI 800-558-5888
Seller Kirk & Company
Schwenksville, PA 215-480-7342
Sensient Technologies
Milwaukee, WI 800-558-9892
Serv-Agen Corporation
Cherry Hill, NJ 856-663-6966
Sethness-Greenleaf
Chicago, IL 800-621-4549
Shanks Extracts
Lancaster, PA 800-346-3135
Silesia Flavors
Hoffman Estates, IL 847-645-0270
SimmaLoosa Company
Covington, LA 985-892-1400
Singer Extract Laboratory
Livonia, MI 313-345-5880
SJH Enterprises
Middleton, WI. 888-745-3845
SKW Nature Products
Dubuque, IA .563-588-6244
Sno-Shack
Salt Lake City, UT 801-466-1771
Southern Flavoring Company
Bedford, VA .800-765-8565
Spiceman
Eugene, OR. .800-725-8373
Star Kay White
Congers, NY .800-874-8518
Stearns & Lehman
Mansfield, OH 800-533-2722
Sterling Extract Company
Franklin Park, IL. 847-451-9728
Sun Pure
Lakeland, FL .863-619-2222
Symrise
Teterboro, NJ. 201-288-3200
T Hasegawa
Cerritos, CA .714-670-1586
Target Flavors
Brookfield, CT 800-538-3350
Technology Flavors & Fragrances
Amityville, NY 631-842-7600
Texas Spice Company
Cedar Park, TX 800-880-8007
TFF Seasoning Division
Milford, OH .513-248-9876
Triple K Manufacturing Company
Shenandoah, IA. 888-987-2824
Ungerer & Company
Lincoln Park, NJ 973-628-0600
Universal Flavor Corporation
Indianapolis, IN 317-243-3521
Universal Flavors
Indianapolis, IN 800-325-3826
US Chocolate Corporation
Brooklyn, NY 718-788-8555
US Ingredients
Naperville, IL 630-820-1711
V&E Kohnstamm
Brooklyn, NY 800-847-4500
Valley Grain Products
Madera, CA. .559-675-3400
Vanlab Corporation
Rochester, NY. 585-232-6647
Vanlaw Food Products
Fullerton, CA 714-870-9091
Virginia Dare
Brooklyn, NY 800-847-4500
W&G Flavors
Hunt Valley, MD. 410-771-6606
Webbpak
Trussville, AL 800-655-3500

Western Flavors & Fragrances
Livermore, CA 925-373-9433
Western Syrup Company
Santa Fe Springs, CA 562-921-4485
WILD Flavors
Erlanger, KY .859-342-3600
WILD Flavors (Canada)
Mississauga, ON. 800-263-5286
World Flavors
Warminster, PA 215-672-4400
Wynn Starr Flavors
Allendale, NJ 800-996-7827

Almond

Castella Imports
Hauppauge, NY 866-227-8355
Nielsen-Massey Vanillas
Waukegan, IL 800-525-7873
Shanks Extracts
Lancaster, PA 800-346-3135

Amaretto

Allen Flavors
Edison, NJ 908-561-5995

Anise (See also Spices/Anise Seed)

Castella Imports
Hauppauge, NY 866-227-8355

Apple

Allen Flavors
Edison, NJ. 908-561-5995

Artificial

Clarendon Flavor Engineering
Louisville, KY 502-634-9215
Domino Specialty Ingredients
Baltimore, MD 800-446-9763

Banana

Allen Flavors
Edison, NJ. 908-561-5995
Castella Imports
Hauppauge, NY 866-227-8355

Beer

Oregon Specialty Company
Lakewood, WA 877-254-7494

Beverage

Allen Flavors
Edison, NJ. 908-561-5995
Clarendon Flavor Engineering
Louisville, KY 502-634-9215
Flavor & Fragrance Specialties
Mahwah, NJ .800-998-4337
Flavors from Florida
Bartow, FL 863-533-0408
Mother Murphy's Labs
Greensboro, NC 800-849-1277
Sethness-Greenleaf
Chicago, IL 800-621-4549
Universal Flavor Corporation
Indianapolis, IN 317-243-3521

Blackberry

Allen Flavors
Edison, NJ. 908-561-5995

Blueberry

Allen Flavors
Edison, NJ. 908-561-5995

Butter

Edlong Dairy Flavors
Elk Grove Vlg, IL 888-698-2783

Pecan

Edlong Dairy Flavors
Elk Grove Vlg, IL 888-698-2783

Vanilla

Edlong Dairy Flavors
Elk Grove Vlg, IL 888-698-2783

Buttermilk

Edlong Dairy Flavors
Elk Grove Vlg, IL 888-698-2783

Butterscotch

Edlong Dairy Flavors
Elk Grove Vlg, IL 888-698-2783

Cajeta

Edlong Dairy Flavors
Elk Grove Vlg, IL 888-698-2783

Caramel

Edlong Dairy Flavors
Elk Grove Vlg, IL 888-698-2783
Mont Blanc Gourmet
Denver, CO 800-877-3811

Cheese

Dean Distributors
Burlingame, CA 800-227-3112
Edlong Dairy Flavors
Elk Grove Vlg, IL 888-698-2783
Flavor Dynamics
South Plainfield, NJ 888-271-8424
H.B. Taylor Co
Chicago, IL 773-254-4805
Ingretec
Lebanon, PA .717-273-1360
Sartori Food Corporation
Plymouth, WI 800-558-5888
Thiel Cheese & Ingredients
Hilbert, WI 920-989-1440

Cheesecake

Edlong Dairy Flavors
Elk Grove Vlg, IL 888-698-2783

Cherry

A M Todd Company
Kalamazoo, OR. 269-343-2603
Allen Flavors
Edison, NJ. 908-561-5995

Chocolate

Allen Flavors
Edison, NJ. 908-561-5995
Big Shoulders Baking
Chicago, IL 800-456-9328
H.B. Taylor Co
Chicago, IL 773-254-4805
Mont Blanc Gourmet
Denver, CO 800-877-3811
Seller Kirk & Company
Schwenksville, PA 215-480-7342
US Chocolate Corporation
Brooklyn, NY 718-788-8555

Citrus

Allen Flavors
Edison, NJ. 908-561-5995

H.B. Taylor Co
Chicago, IL 773-254-4805
Kendall Citrus Corporation
Goulds, FL 305-258-1628

Parman-Kendall Corporation
Goulds, FL 305-258-1628
Western Flavors & Fragrances
Livermore, CA 925-373-9433

Cocoa

Flavor Dynamics
South Plainfield, NJ 888-271-8424
Seller Kirk & Company
Schwenksville, PA 215-480-7342

Coconut

Castella Imports
Hauppauge, NY 866-227-8355

Coffee

Acqua Blox LLC
Santa Fe Springs, CA 562-693-9599
American Instants
Flanders, NJ 973-584-8811
Autocrat Coffee & Extracts
Lincoln, RI 800-288-6272
Beck Flavors
St Louis, MO 800-851-8100
Coffee Grounds
St Paul, MN 651-644-9959
Flavor & Fragrance Specialties
Mahwah, NJ 800-998-4337
Flavor Dynamics
South Plainfield, NJ 888-271-8424
RH Bauman & Company
Chatsworth, CA 877-228-6263
Sausalito Expresso
Sausalito, CA 415-331-5407
Tops Manufacturing Company
Darien, CT 203-655-9367
U Roast Em
Hayward, WI 715-634-6255
Universal Flavor Corporation
Indianapolis, IN 317-243-3521

Cultured

Edlong Dairy Flavors
Elk Grove Vlg, IL 888-698-2783

Dairy

Blossom Farm Products
Ridgewood, NJ 800-729-1818
Edlong Dairy Flavors
Elk Grove Vlg, IL 888-698-2783
GMI Products/Originates
Sunrise, FL 800-999-9373
H.B. Taylor Co
Chicago, IL 773-254-4805
Ingretec
Lebanon, PA 717-273-1360
Seller Kirk & Company
Schwenksville, PA 215-480-7342
Southeastern Wisconsin Products Company
Milwaukee, WI 414-482-1730
Universal Flavor Corporation
Indianapolis, IN 317-243-3521

Extract

A.M. Todd Company
Kalamazoo, MI 800-968-2603
Advanced Food Technology
Littleton, CO 303-980-5221
American Fruits and Flavors
Los Angeles, CA 800-527-6709

asiamerica

Asiamerica Ingredients
Westwood, NJ 201-497-5531

Processor, importer, exporter and distributor of bulk vitamins, amino acids, nutraceuticals, aromatic chemicals, food additives, herbs, mineral nutrients and pharmaceuticals.

Bell Flavors & Fragrances
Northbrook, IL 800-323-4387
Bickford Flavors
Cleveland, OH 800-283-8322

California Custom Fruits & Flavors
Irwindale, CA 877-558-0056
Carmi Flavor & Fragrance Company
Los Angeles, CA 800-421-9647
Charles Dennery Pillsbury
New Orleans, LA 504-733-2331
Charles H. Baldwin & Sons
West Stockbridge, MA 413-232-7785
CHR Hansen Inc
Milwaukee, WI 800-558-0802
Crest Foods Company
Ashton, IL 800-435-6972
Crestmont Enterprises
Camden, NJ 856-966-0700
David Michael & Company
Philadelphia, PA 800-363-5286
Edlong Dairy Flavors
Elk Grove Vlg, IL 888-698-2783
Ervan Guttman Company
Cincinnati, OH 800-203-9213
Eskimo Pie Corporation
Ronkonkoma, NY 631-737-9700
Freeman Industries
Tuckahoe, NY 800-666-6454
Froedtert Malt
Winona, MN 507-454-1535
Frutarom Meer Corporation
North Bergen, NJ 800-526-7147
Fuji Foods
Browns Summit, NC 336-375-3111
GLCC Company
Paw Paw, MI 269-657-3167
Goodman Manufacturing Company
Carthage, MO 417-358-3231
H.R. Nicholson Company
Sykesville, MD 800-638-3514
Hosemen & Roche Vitamins & Fine Chemicals
Nutley, NJ 800-526-6367
IMC-Agrico Company
Convent, LA 225-562-3501
International Bakers Services
South Bend, IN 800-345-7175
Jogue Inc
Northville, MI 800-521-3888
Kloss Manufacturing Company
Allentown, PA 800-445-7100
Marmap Industries
Buffalo, NY 716-897-1220
Master Mix
Placentia, CA 714-524-1698
National Products Company
Kalamazoo, MI 269-344-3640
Newly Weds Foods
Memphis, TN 800-647-9314
Newport Flavours & Fragrances
Orange, CA 714-628-9894
Nielsen-Massey Vanillas
Waukegan, IL 800-525-7873
Parman-Kendall Corporation
Goulds, FL 305-258-1628
Pecan Deluxe Candy Company
Dallas, TX 800-733-3589
Proliant
Ankeny, IA 800-369-2672
R.R. Lochhead Manufacturing
Paso Robles, CA 800-735-0545
Red Arrow Products Company LLC
Manitowoc, WI 920-769-1100
Rhodia
Cranbury, NJ 800-343-8324
Robertet Flavors
Piscataway, NJ 732-981-8300
Seller Kirk & Company
Schwenksville, PA 215-480-7342
Simpson Spring Company
South Easton, MA 508-238-4472
SnoWizard Extracts
New Orleans, LA 800-366-9766
Southeastern Wisconsin Products Company
Milwaukee, WI 414-482-1730
Southern Flavoring Company
Bedford, VA 800-765-8565
Southern Snow Manufacturing
Belle Chasse, LA 504-393-8967
Tara Foods
Atlanta, GA 404-559-0605
Tops Manufacturing Company
Darien, CT 203-655-9367
Van Tone Creative Flavors Inc
Terrell, TX 800-856-0802
Vegetable Juices
Chicago, IL 888-776-9752

Virginia Dare
Brooklyn, NY 800-847-4500
Western Flavors & Fragrances
Livermore, CA 925-373-9433
Zatarain's
Gretna, LA 800-435-6639
Zipp Manufacturing Company
Hornerville, OH 800-521-8700

Fat

Edlong Dairy Flavors
Elk Grove Vlg, IL 888-698-2783

Flavors

Dressing

Edlong Dairy Flavors
Elk Grove Vlg, IL 888-698-2783

Enhancers

Edlong Dairy Flavors
Elk Grove Vlg, IL 888-698-2783
Flavor & Fragrance Specialties
Mahwah, NJ 800-998-4337
H & A Canada, Inc.
Toronto, ON 416-412-9518
Proliant
Ankeny, IA 800-369-2672
Sensient Technologies
Milwaukee, WI 800-558-9892
WTI, Inc.
Jefferson, GA 800-827-1727

Fruit

Contact International
Skokie, IL 847-324-4411
Eskimo Pie Corporation
Ronkonkoma, NY 631-737-9700
H.B. Taylor Co
Chicago, IL 773-254-4805
Ramsey/SIAS
Cleveland, OH 800-477-3788
Universal Flavor Corporation
Indianapolis, IN 317-243-3521

Grain

GKI Foods
Brighton, MI 248-486-0055

Half & Half

Edlong Dairy Flavors
Elk Grove Vlg, IL 888-698-2783

Hazelnut

Allen Flavors
Edison, NJ 908-561-5995

Heat Stable

Edlong Dairy Flavors
Elk Grove Vlg, IL 888-698-2783

Hickory Smoke Oil

Talk O'Texas Brands
San Angelo, TX 325-655-6077

Irish Creme

Edlong Dairy Flavors
Elk Grove Vlg, IL 888-698-2783

Lemon

Allen Flavors
Edison, NJ 908-561-5995
Brewster Foods TestLab
Reseda, CA 818-881-4268
Castella Imports
Hauppauge, NY 866-227-8355
Charles H. Baldwin & Sons
West Stockbridge, MA 413-232-7785
Nielsen-Massey Vanillas
Waukegan, IL 800-525-7873
Serv-Agen Corporation
Cherry Hill, NJ 856-663-6966
Shanks Extracts
Lancaster, PA 800-346-3135

Ungerer & Company
Lincoln Park, NJ 973-628-0600

Licorice

A M Todd Company
Kalamazoo, OR. 269-343-2603

Asiamerica Ingredients
Westwood, NJ. 201-497-5531

Processor, importer, exporter and distributor of bulk vitamins, amino acids, nutraceuticals, aromatic chemicals, food additives, herbs, mineral nutrients and pharmaceuticals.

Lime

Allen Flavors
Edison, NJ 908-561-5995
Ungerer & Company
Lincoln Park, NJ 973-628-0600

Liqueur

Edgar A. Weber Company
Wheeling, IL 800-558-9078

Macadamia

Allen Flavors
Edison, NJ 908-561-5995
Buon Italia
New York, NY 212-633-9090

Maple

Allen Flavors
Edison, NJ 908-561-5995
Castella Imports
Hauppauge, NY 866-227-8355

Butter

Edlong Dairy Flavors
Elk Grove Vlg, IL. 888-698-2783

Masking

Edlong Dairy Flavors
Elk Grove Vlg, IL. 888-698-2783

Meat

Flavor & Fragrance Specialties
Mahwah, NJ 800-998-4337
Flavor House
Adelanto, CA 760-246-9131
Genarom International
Cranbury, NJ 609-409-6200
Griffith Laboratories
Scarborough, ON 416-288-3050

Microwave

Edlong Dairy Flavors
Elk Grove Vlg, IL. 888-698-2783

Milk

Edlong Dairy Flavors
Elk Grove Vlg, IL. 888-698-2783

Butter

Edlong Dairy Flavors
Elk Grove Vlg, IL. 888-698-2783

Nut

H.B. Taylor Co
Chicago, IL 773-254-4805

Orange

Allen Flavors
Edison, NJ 908-561-5995
Castella Imports
Hauppauge, NY 866-227-8355

Charles H. Baldwin & Sons
West Stockbridge, MA 413-232-7785
Nielsen-Massey Vanillas
Waukegan, IL 800-525-7873
Ungerer & Company
Lincoln Park, NJ 973-628-0600

Passion Fruit

Allen Flavors
Edison, NJ. 908-561-5995

Peach

Allen Flavors
Edison, NJ. 908-561-5995

Pear

Allen Flavors
Edison, NJ. 908-561-5995

Peppermint

A.M. Todd Company
Kalamazoo, MI 800-968-2603
Castella Imports
Hauppauge, NY 866-227-8355
Ungerer & Company
Lincoln Park, NJ 973-628-0600

Pineapple

Allen Flavors
Edison, NJ. 908-561-5995
Castella Imports
Hauppauge, NY 866-227-8355

Poultry

Flavor House
Adelanto, CA 760-246-9131

Raspberry

Allen Flavors
Edison, NJ. 908-561-5995

Root Beer

Allen Flavors
Edison, NJ. 908-561-5995

Rum

Butter Toffee

Edlong Dairy Flavors
Elk Grove Vlg, IL. 888-698-2783

Seafood

Flavor House
Adelanto, CA 760-246-9131

Smoke

Dean Distributors
Burlingame, CA 800-227-3112
Hickory Specialties
Burns, TN 800-251-2076
Red Arrow Products Company LLC
Manitowoc, WI 920-769-1100

Sour

Cream

Edlong Dairy Flavors
Elk Grove Vlg, IL. 888-698-2783

Spearmint

A.M. Todd Company
Kalamazoo, MI 800-968-2603
Ungerer & Company
Lincoln Park, NJ 973-628-0600

Strawberry

Allen Flavors
Edison, NJ. 908-561-5995
Castella Imports
Hauppauge, NY 866-227-8355

Tea

Acqua Blox LLC
Santa Fe Springs, CA 562-693-9599
Allen Flavors
Edison, NJ. 908-561-5995
Flavor & Fragrance Specialties
Mahwah, NJ 800-998-4337
Flavor Dynamics
South Plainfield, NJ 888-271-8424
Sausalito Expresso
Sausalito, CA 415-331-5407
Universal Flavor Corporation
Indianapolis, IN 317-243-3521

Vanilla

Agri-Dairy Products
Purchase, NY 914-697-9580
Allen Flavors
Edison, NJ. 908-561-5995
American Health & Nutrition
Ann Arbor, MI 734-677-5572
Beck Flavors
St Louis, MO. 800-851-8100
Carmi Flavor & Fragrance Company
Los Angeles, CA. 800-421-9647
Charles H. Baldwin & Sons
West Stockbridge, MA 413-232-7785
Clements Foods Company
Oklahoma City, OK 800-654-8355
Everfresh Food Corporation
Minneapolis, MN 612-331-6393
Goodman Manufacturing Company
Carthage, MO 417-358-3231
Hagelin & Company
Branchburg, NJ 800-229-2112
Jogue Inc
Northville, MI 800-521-3888
Serv-Agen Corporation
Cherry Hill, NJ 856-663-6966
Shanks Extracts
Lancaster, PA 800-346-3135
SnoWizard Extracts
New Orleans, LA 800-366-9766
Sterling Extract Company
Franklin Park, IL. 847-451-9728
Teawolf Industries, Ltd
Pine Brook, NJ 973-575-4600

Triple K Manufacturing Company
  Shenandoah, IA 888-987-2824
Universal Flavor Corporation
  Indianapolis, IN 317-243-3521
Webbpak
  Trussville, AL 800-655-3500
Western Flavors & Fragrances
  Livermore, CA 925-373-9433

Vanillin

A M Todd Company
  Kalamazoo, OR 269-343-2603
Agri-Dairy Products
  Purchase, NY 914-697-9580

asiamerica

Asiamerica Ingredients
  Westwood, NJ 201-497-5531

Processor, importer, exporter and distributor of bulk vitamins, amino acids, nutraceuticals, aromatic chemicals, food additives, herbs, mineral nutrients and pharmaceuticals.

Astral Extracts Ltd
  Syosset, NY 516-496-2505
California Custom Fruits & Flavors
  Irwindale, CA 877-558-0056
International Chemical
  Milltown, NJ 800-914-2436
Naturex (Chart Corp)
  South Hackensack, NJ 201-440-5000
Nichem Company
  Hillside, NJ 908-933-0770
Rhodia
  Cranbury, NJ 800-343-8324
Singer Extract Laboratory
  Livonia, MI 313-345-5880
Universal Preservachem Inc
  Edison, NJ 732-777-7338
Zink & Triest Company
  Montgomeryville, PA 800-537-5070

Variegates

Triple K Manufacturing Company
  Shenandoah, IA 888-987-2824

Vegetable

Kalsec
  Kalamazoo, MI 800-323-9320
Summit Hill Flavors
  Middlesex, NJ 732-805-0335
Western Flavors & Fragrances
  Livermore, CA 925-373-9433

Wine

Edgar A. Weber Company
  Wheeling, IL 800-558-9078
Oregon Specialty Company
  Lakewood, WA 877-254-7494

Yogurt

Edlong Dairy Flavors
  Elk Grove Vlg, IL 888-698-2783
Givaudan Flavors
  Bridgeton, MO 800-422-5444
Gum Technology Corporation
  Tucson, AZ 800-369-4867
Johanna Foods
  Flemington, NJ 800-727-6700
Plaidberry Company
  Vista, CA 760-727-5403

Glandulars

Ultra Enterprises
  Whittier, CA 800-543-0627

Grain-Based

Beaumont Rice Mills
  Beaumont, TX 409-832-2521
Nuvex Ingredients
  Blue Earth, MN 507-526-4331

Gums

A M Todd Company
  Kalamazoo, OR 269-343-2603
American Food Products
  Methuen, MA 978-682-1855

asiamerica

Asiamerica Ingredients
  Westwood, NJ 201-497-5531

Processor, importer, exporter and distributor of bulk vitamins, amino acids, nutraceuticals, aromatic chemicals, food additives, herbs, mineral nutrients and pharmaceuticals.

Associated Bakers Products
  Huntington, NY 631-673-3841
Au'some Candies
  Monmouth Junction, NJ 732-951-8818
Beehive Botanicals, Inc.
  Hayward, WI 800-233-4483
Cap Candy
  Napa, CA 707-251-9321
Cargill Texturizing Solutions
  Cedar Rapids, IA 877-650-7080
Concord Confections
  Concord, ON 800-267-0037
DMH Ingredients
  Libertyville, IL 847-362-9977
El Brands
  Ozark, AL 334-445-2828
Food Ingredients Solutions
  Blauvelt, NY 845-353-8501
Fun Factory
  Milwaukee, WI 877-894-6767
Generation Foods Too
  Woodland Hills, CA 818-887-5858
Gum Technology Corporation
  Tucson, AZ 800-369-4867
Gurley's Foods
  Willmar, MN 800-426-7845
H & A Canada, Inc.
  Toronto, ON 416-412-9518
Hercules Incorporated
  Wilmington, DE 800-345-8104
Jungbunzlauer
  Newton, MA 800-828-0062
Kolatin Real Kosher Gelatin
  Lakewood, NJ 732-364-8700
Kraft
  Parsippany, NJ 973-292-1755
LA Dreyfus
  Edison, NJ 732-549-1600
Lotte USA
  Battle Creek, MI 269-963-6664
Magic Gumball International
  Chatsworth, CA 800-576-2020
Main Street Ingredients
  La Crosse, WI 800-359-2345
Maryland & Virginia Milk Producers Cooperative
  Reston, VA 703-742-7443
Montello
  Tulsa, OK 800-331-4628
Nabisco LifeSavers Company
  Holland, MI 616-396-1411
Naturex (Chart Corp)
  South Hackensack, NJ 201-440-5000
Oak Leaf Confections
  Scarborough, ON 800-338-3631
P.L. Thomas
  Morristown, NJ 973-984-0900
Polypro International
  Minneapolis, MN 800-765-9776
Richardson Brands Company
  South Miami, FL 800-839-8938
Sahagian & Associates
  Oak Park, IL 800-327-9273
Scripture Candy
  Adamsville, AL 888-317-7333
Sherwood Brands
  Rockville, MD 301-309-6161
Snackerz
  Commerce, CA 888-576-2253
SP Enterprises
  Las Vegas, NV 800-746-4774
Sweet Works
  St Augustine, FL 877-261-7887

SWELL Philadelphia Chewing Gum Corporation
  Havertown, PA 610-449-1700
Topps Company
  New York, NY 212-376-0300
Topps Company
  Duryea, PA 570-457-6761
Triple-C
  Hamilton, ON 800-263-9105
World Confections
  Brooklyn, NY 718-768-8100
Worldwide Sourcing LLC
  Incline Village, NV 775-833-1480
Wrigley Company
  Don Mills, ON 416-449-8600
Wrigley Manufacturing Company
  Flowery Branch, GA 770-967-6181

Acacia Gum

Agriproducts
  Coral Springs, FL 800-277-4979
Alfred L. Wolff, Inc.
  Park Ridge, IL 312-265-9889
Gum Technology Corporation
  Tucson, AZ 800-369-4867
Gumix International
  Fort Lee, NJ 800-248-6492
Main Street Ingredients
  La Crosse, WI 800-359-2345
Naturex (Chart Corp)
  South Hackensack, NJ 201-440-5000
P.L. Thomas
  Morristown, NJ 973-984-0900
TIC Gums
  Belcamp, MD 800-221-3953

Agar-Agar

A M Todd Company
  Kalamazoo, OR 269-343-2603
Cargill Texturizing Solutions
  Cedar Rapids, IA 877-650-7080
Gum Technology Corporation
  Tucson, AZ 800-369-4867
Naturex (Chart Corp)
  South Hackensack, NJ 201-440-5000
P.L. Thomas
  Morristown, NJ 973-984-0900
TIC Gums
  Belcamp, MD 800-221-3953
Universal Preservachem Inc
  Edison, NJ 732-777-7338

Algin & Alginates

Associated Bakers Products
  Huntington, NY 631-673-3841
Cargill Texturizing Solutions
  Cedar Rapids, IA 877-650-7080
P.L. Thomas
  Morristown, NJ 973-984-0900

Arabic

P.L. Thomas
  Morristown, NJ 973-984-0900

Carboxymethylcellulose

P.L. Thomas
  Morristown, NJ 973-984-0900

Carrageenan

Cargill Texturizing Solutions
  Cedar Rapids, IA 877-650-7080
CP Kelco
  Chicago, IL 800-535-2687
GPI USA LLC.
  Athens, GA 706-850-7826
Hercules Incorporated
  Wilmington, DE 800-345-8104
Hermann Laue Spice Company
  Uxbridge, ON 905-852-5100
P.L. Thomas
  Morristown, NJ 973-984-0900

Gellan

CP Kelco
  Chicago, IL 800-535-2687
P.L. Thomas
  Morristown, NJ 973-984-0900

Ghatti

P.L. Thomas
Morristown, NJ.................973-984-0900

Guar Gum

Agri-Dairy Products
Purchase, NY.................914-697-9580

Asiamerica Ingredients
Westwood, NJ.................201-497-5531

Processor, importer, exporter and distributor of bulk vitamins, amino acids, nutraceuticals, aromatic chemicals, food additives, herbs, mineral nutrients and pharmaceuticals.

Associated Bakers Products
Huntington, NY.................631-673-3841
Cargill Texturizing Solutions
Cedar Rapids, IA.................877-650-7080
Commodities Marketing, Inc.
Edison, NJ.................732-516-0700
ConAgra Grocery Products
Irvine, CA.................714-680-1000
Gum Technology Corporation
Tucson, AZ.................800-369-4867
H. Fox & Company
Brooklyn, NY.................718-385-4600
P.L. Thomas
Morristown, NJ.................973-984-0900
Polypro International
Minneapolis, MN.................800-765-9776
TIC Gums
Belcamp, MD.................800-221-3953
Universal Preservachem Inc
Edison, NJ.................732-777-7338

Hydroxypropyl Methylcellulose

Asiamerica Ingredients
Westwood, NJ.................201-497-5531

Processor, importer, exporter and distributor of bulk vitamins, amino acids, nutraceuticals, aromatic chemicals, food additives, herbs, mineral nutrients and pharmaceuticals.

Hercules Incorporated
Wilmington, DE.................800-345-8104

Karaya Gum

Gum Technology Corporation
Tucson, AZ.................800-369-4867
TIC Gums
Belcamp, MD.................800-221-3953
Universal Preservachem Inc
Edison, NJ.................732-777-7338

Locust Bean Gum

Cargill Texturizing Solutions
Cedar Rapids, IA.................877-650-7080
CP Kelco
Chicago, IL.................800-535-2687
Gum Technology Corporation
Tucson, AZ.................800-369-4867
Naturex (Chart Corp)
South Hackensack, NJ.................201-440-5000
P.L. Thomas
Morristown, NJ.................973-984-0900
TIC Gums
Belcamp, MD.................800-221-3953

Methylcellulose

Hercules Incorporated
Wilmington, DE.................800-345-8104
P.L. Thomas
Morristown, NJ.................973-984-0900

Natural

Cargill Texturizing Solutions
Cedar Rapids, IA.................877-650-7080
P.L. Thomas
Morristown, NJ.................973-984-0900

Pectin

Asiamerica Ingredients
Westwood, NJ.................201-497-5531

Processor, importer, exporter and distributor of bulk vitamins, amino acids, nutraceuticals, aromatic chemicals, food additives, herbs, mineral nutrients and pharmaceuticals.

Cargill Texturizing Solutions
Cedar Rapids, IA.................877-650-7080
CP Kelco
Chicago, IL.................800-535-2687

Tara

P.L. Thomas
Morristown, NJ.................973-984-0900

Tragacanth

Gum Technology Corporation
Tucson, AZ.................800-369-4867
Naturex (Chart Corp)
South Hackensack, NJ.................201-440-5000
Universal Preservachem Inc
Edison, NJ.................732-777-7338

Vegetable Gum

Agriproducts
Coral Springs, FL.................800-277-4979
Functional Foods
Englishtown, NJ.................800-442-9524
Gum Technology Corporation
Tucson, AZ.................800-369-4867
Gumix International
Fort Lee, NJ.................800-248-6492
TIC Gums
Belcamp, MD.................800-221-3953

Xanthan Gum

A M Todd Company
Kalamazoo, OR.................269-343-2603
Archer Daniels Midland Company
Decatur, IL.................800-637-5843

Asiamerica Ingredients
Westwood, NJ.................201-497-5531

Processor, importer, exporter and distributor of bulk vitamins, amino acids, nutraceuticals, aromatic chemicals, food additives, herbs, mineral nutrients and pharmaceuticals.

Cargill Texturizing Solutions
Cedar Rapids, IA.................877-650-7080
CP Kelco
Chicago, IL.................800-535-2687
Gum Technology Corporation
Tucson, AZ.................800-369-4867

Half-Products

Nuvex Ingredients
Blue Earth, MN.................507-526-4331

Calcium & Nutritionally Fortified Pellets

Nuvex Ingredients
Blue Earth, MN.................507-526-4331

Cocoa & Rice Pellets

Nuvex Ingredients
Blue Earth, MN.................507-526-4331

Colored Pellets

Nuvex Ingredients
Blue Earth, MN.................507-526-4331

Flavored Pellets

Nuvex Ingredients
Blue Earth, MN.................507-526-4331

Organic Pellets

Nuvex Ingredients
Blue Earth, MN.................507-526-4331

Veggie & Rice Pellets

Nuvex Ingredients
Blue Earth, MN.................507-526-4331

Humectants

Cargill Texturizing Solutions
Cedar Rapids, IA.................877-650-7080
Crowley Foods
Binghamton, NY.................800-637-0019
Nutricepts
Burnsville, MN.................800-949-9060

Hydrocolloids

A&B Ingredients
Fairfield, NJ.................973-227-1390
Cargill Texturizing Solutions
Cedar Rapids, IA.................877-650-7080
P.L. Thomas
Morristown, NJ.................973-984-0900
TIC Gums
Belcamp, MD.................800-221-3953

Hydrolyzed Products

Cereal Solids

Cargill Texturizing Solutions
Cedar Rapids, IA.................877-650-7080

Milk Proteins

Arla Foods Ingredients
Basking Ridge, NJ.................800-243-3730
First Spice Mixing Company
Long Island City, NY.................800-221-1105
Kantner Group
Wapakoneta, OH.................419-738-4060

Vegetable Proteins

Arla Foods Ingredients
Basking Ridge, NJ.................800-243-3730
Flavor House
Adelanto, CA.................760-246-9131
J&B Meats Corporation
Coal Valley, IL.................309-799-7341

Inclusions

Nuvex Ingredients
Blue Earth, MN.................507-526-4331

Ingredients

Blue California Company
Rancho Santa Margarita, CA.................949-635-1991
Carolina Ingredients
Rock Hill, SC.................803-323-6550
Century Foods International
Sparta, WI.................800-269-1901
Diana Naturals
Valley Cottage, NY.................845-268-5200
Ful-Flav-R Foods
Alamo, CA.................510-339-9618
Hayashibara International Inc
Broomfield, CO.................303-650-4590
Marukan Vinegar (U.S.A.) Inc.
Paramount, CA.................562-630-6060
Newtown Foods
Langhorne, PA.................215-579-2120

P.L. Thomas
  Morristown, NJ 973-984-0900
PGP International
  Woodland, CA 800-233-0110
Quali Tech
  Chaska, MN 800-328-5870
Sabroso Company
  Medford, OR 509-697-7251
Season Harvest Foods
  Sunnyvale, CA 408-749-8018

Sentry Seasonings
  Elmhurst, IL 630-530-5370

The product development experts of Sentry Seasonings are eager to offer the assistance and hands-on experience to food processors of all sizes. Sentry Seasonings will ensure the consistent high quality and repeat sales of your products, whether you choose one of our many off-the-shelf Bench Mark products or a modified version to meet your preferences. Sentry Seasonings can also duplicate and/or improve your present flavor profile; formulate, blend and package specifically for your requirements.

Sun Ray International
  Davis, CA 530-758-0088
Taiyo
  Minneapolis, MN 763-398-3003

Bakery

American Casein Company
  Burlington, NJ 609-387-2988
Amoretti-Capriccio
  Oxnard, CA 800-266-7388
New Horizon Foods
  Union City, CA 510-489-8600

Dairy

Cargill Texturizing Solutions
  Cedar Rapids, IA 877-650-7080
Century Foods International
  Sparta, WI 800-269-1901
Kantner Group
  Wapakoneta, OH 419-738-4060
Trega Foods
  Weyauwega, WI 920-867-2137

Food

Acatris
  Edina, MN 952-835-9590
Capriccio
  Chatsworth, CA 818-718-7620
Century Foods International
  Sparta, WI 800-269-1901
Land O Frost
  Lansing, IL 800-643-5654
Mallet & Company
  Carnegie, PA 800-245-2757

P.L. Thomas
  Morristown, NJ 973-984-0900
Summit Hill Flavors
  Middlesex, NJ 732-805-0335

Lactoferrin

Glanbia Nutritionals
  Monroe, WI 800-336-2183

Leaveners

Baking Soda

Agri-Dairy Products
  Purchase, NY 914-697-9580
Bunny Bread
  Covington, LA 504-241-1206
Church & Dwight Company
  Princeton, NJ 800-221-0453
Clabber Girl Corporation
  Terre Haute, IN 812-232-9446
Natrium Products
  Cortland, NY 800-962-4203
Old Baldy Brewing Company
  Upland, CA 909-946-1750

Maltodextrin

ADM Corn Processing
  Decatur, IL 800-553-8411
ADM Food Ingredients
  Olathe, KS 800-255-6637
Agri-Dairy Products
  Purchase, NY 914-697-9580
American Health & Nutrition
  Ann Arbor, MI 734-677-5572
California Natural Products
  Lathrop, CA 209-858-2525
Cargill Texturizing Solutions
  Cedar Rapids, IA 877-650-7080
Cerestar USA
  Hammond, IN 800-348-9896
Clofine Dairy & Food Products
  Linwood, NJ 800-441-1001
Corn Products International
  Westchester, IL 708-551-2600
Grain Processing Corporation
  Muscatine, IA 800-448-4472
Malt Products Corporation
  Saddle Brook, NJ 800-526-0180
Roquette America
  Keokuk, IA 800-553-7035

Milk Calcium

Glanbia Nutritionals
  Monroe, WI 800-336-2183
Kantner Group
  Wapakoneta, OH 419-738-4060

Particulates

Nuvex Ingredients
  Blue Earth, MN 507-526-4331

Pastes

Almond

**Ingredients, Flavors &
Additives: Pastes: Almond**

EMERLING INTERNATIONAL FOODS, INC.

Emerling International Foods
  Buffalo, NY 716-833-7381

We supply food manufacturers and food service customers worldwide (since 1988) with bulk ingredients including: Fruits & Vegetables; Juice Concentrates; Herbs & Spices; Oils & Vinegars; Flavors & Colors; Honey & Molasses. We also produce PURE MAPLE SYRUP.

Fig

EMERLING INTERNATIONAL FOODS, INC.

Emerling International Foods
  Buffalo, NY 716-833-7381

We supply food manufacturers and food service customers worldwide (since 1988) with bulk ingredients including: Fruits & Vegetables; Juice Concentrates; Herbs & Spices; Oils & Vinegars; Flavors & Colors; Honey & Molasses. We also produce PURE MAPLE SYRUP.

Fig Garden Packing
  Fresno, CA 559-271-9000
Kalashian Packing Company
  Fresno, CA 559-237-4287
Unique Ingredients
  Naches, WA 509-653-1991

Fruit

Cinnabar Specialty Foods
  Prescott, AZ 866-293-6433
Citadelle Maple Syrup Produce Cooperative
  Plessisville, QC 819-362-3241

EMERLING INTERNATIONAL FOODS, INC.

Emerling International Foods
  Buffalo, NY 716-833-7381

We supply food manufacturers and food service customers worldwide (since 1988) with bulk ingredients including: Fruits & Vegetables; Juice Concentrates; Herbs & Spices; Oils & Vinegars; Flavors & Colors; Honey & Molasses. We also produce PURE MAPLE SYRUP.

Fig Garden Packing
  Fresno, CA 559-271-9000
Kapaa Poi Factory
  Kapaa, HI 808-822-5426
Lion Raisins
  Selma, CA 559-834-6677
Mayfair Packing Company
  San Jose, CA 408-280-2349
QA Products
  Elk Grove Vlg, IL 800-635-7907
Sun-Maid Growers of California
  Kingsburg, CA 800-272-4746
Unique Ingredients
  Naches, WA 509-653-1991
Vacaville Fruit Company
  Vacaville, CA 707-448-5292

Tomato

American Food & Equipment
  Miami, FL 305-361-6517
Del Monte Foods
  San Francisco, CA 800-543-3090
Dixon Canning Company
  Dixon, CA 707-678-4406

EMERLING INTERNATIONAL FOODS, INC.

Emerling International Foods
  Buffalo, NY 716-833-7381

We supply food manufacturers and food service customers worldwide (since 1988) with bulk ingredients including: Fruits & Vegetables; Juice Concentrates; Herbs & Spices; Oils & Vinegars; Flavors & Colors; Honey & Molasses. We also produce PURE MAPLE SYRUP.

Hartford City Foam Pack aging & Converting
  Hartford City, IN 765-348-2500
Heinz
  Stockton, CA 800-253-3399
Ingomar Packing Company
  Los Banos, CA 209-826-9494
International Home Foods
  Milton, PA 973-359-9920
Pacific Coast Producers
  Oroville, CA 530-533-4311
Pastene Companies
  Canton, MA 781-830-8200
San Benito Foods
  Hollister, CA 831-637-4434

Spreda Group
Prospect, KY 502-426-9411
Stanislaus Food Products
Modesto, CA 800-327-7201
Unilever Bestfoods
Merced, CA 877-995-4483
Unilever Foods
Stockton, CA 209-466-9580
Valley Tomato Products
Stockton, CA 209-982-4586

Canned & Frozen

Crown Point
St John, IN 219-365-3200
Hartford City Foam Pack aging & Converting
Hartford City, IN 765-348-2500
International Home Foods
Milton, PA 973-359-9920
Pastene Companies
Canton, MA 781-830-8200
Unilever Foods
Stockton, CA 209-466-9580
Valley Tomato Products
Stockton, CA 209-982-4586

Pectins

Apple

Asiamerica Ingredients
Westwood, NJ 201-497-5531

Processor, importer, exporter and distributor of
bulk vitamins, amino acids, nutraceuticals, aromatic chemicals, food additives, herbs, mineral
nutrients and pharmaceuticals.

Cargill Texturizing Solutions
Cedar Rapids, IA 877-650-7080
Gum Technology Corporation
Tucson, AZ 800-369-4867
Naturex (Chart Corp)
South Hackensack, NJ 201-440-5000
Spreda Group
Prospect, KY 502-426-9411
Universal Preservachem Inc
Edison, NJ 732-777-7338
W&G Flavors
Hunt Valley, MD 410-771-6606

Citrus

Asiamerica Ingredients
Westwood, NJ 201-497-5531

Processor, importer, exporter and distributor of
bulk vitamins, amino acids, nutraceuticals, aromatic chemicals, food additives, herbs, mineral
nutrients and pharmaceuticals.

Cargill Texturizing Solutions
Cedar Rapids, IA 877-650-7080
Citrico
Northbrook, IL 888-625-8516
Gum Technology Corporation
Tucson, AZ 800-369-4867
Naturex (Chart Corp)
South Hackensack, NJ 201-440-5000
Universal Preservachem Inc
Edison, NJ 732-777-7338
W&G Flavors
Hunt Valley, MD 410-771-6606

Fruit

Cargill Texturizing Solutions
Cedar Rapids, IA 877-650-7080
Hercules Incorporated
Wilmington, DE 800-345-8104

Naturex (Chart Corp)
South Hackensack, NJ 201-440-5000
Spreda Group
Prospect, KY 502-426-9411
W&G Flavors
Hunt Valley, MD 410-771-6606
Williams Foods Inc
Lenexa, KS 800-255-6736

Phosphates

Asiamerica Ingredients
Westwood, NJ 201-497-5531

Processor, importer, exporter and distributor of
bulk vitamins, amino acids, nutraceuticals, aromatic chemicals, food additives, herbs, mineral
nutrients and pharmaceuticals.

BK Giulini Corporation
Simi Valley, CA 800-526-2688
First Spice Mixing Company
Long Island City, NY 800-221-1105

Ammonium Phosphates

ADM Food Ingredients
Olathe, KS 800-255-6637
Luyties Pharmacal Company
Saint Louis, MO 800-325-8080
Universal Preservachem Inc
Edison, NJ 732-777-7338

Calcium Phosphate

Asiamerica Ingredients
Westwood, NJ 201-497-5531

Processor, importer, exporter and distributor of
bulk vitamins, amino acids, nutraceuticals, aromatic chemicals, food additives, herbs, mineral
nutrients and pharmaceuticals.

Luyties Pharmacal Company
Saint Louis, MO 800-325-8080
Natural Enrichment Industries, LLC
Sesser, IL 618-625-2112

Sodium Phosphate

Agri-Dairy Products
Purchase, NY 914-697-9580

Asiamerica Ingredients
Westwood, NJ 201-497-5531

Processor, importer, exporter and distributor of
bulk vitamins, amino acids, nutraceuticals, aromatic chemicals, food additives, herbs, mineral
nutrients and pharmaceuticals.

Luyties Pharmacal Company
Saint Louis, MO 800-325-8080
Universal Preservachem Inc
Edison, NJ 732-777-7338

Potassium Bitartrate (Cream of Tartar)

Advanced Spice & Trading
Carrollton, TX 800-872-7811
American Tartaric Products
Larchmont, NY 914-834-1881
Jungbunzlauer
Newton, MA 800-828-0062

Potassium Bromate

Morre-Tec Industries
Union, NJ 908-688-9009

Potassium Citrate

Agri-Dairy Products
Purchase, NY 914-697-9580

Asiamerica Ingredients
Westwood, NJ 201-497-5531

Processor, importer, exporter and distributor of
bulk vitamins, amino acids, nutraceuticals, aromatic chemicals, food additives, herbs, mineral
nutrients and pharmaceuticals.

Cargill Corn Milling
Naperville, IL 800-344-1633
Cargill Worldwide Acidulants
Naperville, IL 800-344-1633
Gadot Biochemical Industries
Rolling Meadows, IL 888-424-1424
Jungbunzlauer
Newton, MA 800-828-0062
Shekou Chemicals
Waltham, MA 781-893-6878
Universal Preservachem Inc
Edison, NJ 732-777-7338

Potassium Lactate

Trumark
Linden, NJ 800-752-7877

Potassium Sorbate

Agri-Dairy Products
Purchase, NY 914-697-9580
Amerol Corporation
Farmingdale, NY 631-694-4700

Asiamerica Ingredients
Westwood, NJ 201-497-5531

Processor, importer, exporter and distributor of
bulk vitamins, amino acids, nutraceuticals, aromatic chemicals, food additives, herbs, mineral
nutrients and pharmaceuticals.

Hermann Laue Spice Company
Uxbridge, ON 905-852-5100
Jungbunzlauer
Newton, MA 800-828-0062
Shekou Chemicals
Waltham, MA 781-893-6878
Silver Ferm Chemical
Seattle, WA 206-282-3376
Universal Preservachem Inc
Edison, NJ 732-777-7338

Powders

Adobo

American Key Food Products
Closter, NJ 800-767-0237
Gel Spice Company, Inc
Bayonne, NJ 800-922-0230
Magic Seasoning Blends
Harahan, LA 800-457-2857

Baking

ADM Food Ingredients
Olathe, KS. 800-255-6637
Agri-Dairy Products
Purchase, NY 914-697-9580
Allied Blending & Ingredients
Keokuk, IA 319-524-4080
American Tartaric Products
Larchmont, NY 914-834-1881
Church & Dwight Company
Princeton, NJ. 800-221-0453
Erba Food Products
Brooklyn, NY 718-272-7700
Ghirardelli Chocolate Company
Short Hills, NJ. 800-877-9338
Groeb Farms
Onsted, MI 517-467-7100
Kraft
Parsippany, NJ. 973-292-1755
Lallemand/American Yeast
Addison, IL. 630-932-1290
Lynch Foods
North York, QC. 416-449-5464
Mississippi Blending Company
Keokuk, IA 800-758-4080
Roland Industries
Saint Louis, MO 800-325-1183
Rumford Baking Powder Company
Terre Haute, IN 812-232-9446
Tasty Mix Quality Foods
Brooklyn, NY. 866-TAS-TYMX
Young Winfield
Kleinburg, ON. 905-893-2536

Beef Stock

GPR Company
Stowe, PA .610-326-4777

Beverage

Aromatech USA
Orlando, FL. 407-277-5727
Associated Brands, Inc.
Medina, NY 800-265-0050

Baldwin Richardson Foods
Frankfort, IL 866-644-2732

Baldwin Richardson Foods is a liquid ingredient
manufacturer specializing in signature sauces,
dessert toppings, beverage/pancake syrups, specialty fruit fillings and condiments. Packaging capabilities range from portion control cups and
pouches to standard retail and foodservice packs
and include industrial drums and totes. Full service R&D and Quality groups dedicated to new
product development, with in-house stability and
analytical testing. Call for assistance.

Cappuccine
Palm Springs, CA 800-511-3127
ConAgra Grocery Products
Irvine, CA 714-680-1000
Diamond Crystal Specialty Foods
Bondurant, IA 515-967-3737
GPR Company
Stowe, PA .610-326-4777
Instant Products of America
Columbus, IN 812-372-9100
J. Crow Company
New Ipswich, NH 800-878-1965

Lynch Foods
North York, QC. 416-449-5464
Mele-Koi Farms
Newport Beach, CA 949-660-9000
Natural Formulas
Hayward, CA 510-372-1800
Northwestern Foods
St Paul, MN. 800-236-4937
Novartis Nutrition Corporation
Minneapolis, MN 952-848-6000
SECO & Golden 100
Deland, FL 386-734-3906
Seller Kirk & Company
Schwenksville, PA 215-480-7342
SensoryEffects Flavor Systems
Bridgeton, MO 314-291-5444
Unilever Bestfoods
Englewood Cliffs, NJ 201-894-4000
Unilever United States
Englewood Cliffs, NJ 201-567-8000
Wechsler Coffee Corporation
Moonachie, NJ 800-800-2633

Broth

International Dehydrated Foods
Springfield, MO 800-525-7435
Proliant
Ankeny, IA 800-369-2672

Buttermilk

Diehl Food Ingredients
Defiance, OH 800-251-3033
Kantner Group
Wapakoneta, OH. 419-738-4060
San Joaquin Valley Dairymen
Los Banos, CA 209-826-4901
St. Charles Trading
Lake Saint Louis, MO. 800-336-1333

Cappuccino

International Food Technologies
Evansville, IN 812-853-9432

Carob

Spring Tree Maple Products
Brattleboro, VT 802-254-8784
Universal Preservachem Inc
Edison, NJ. 732-777-7338

Cassava

Cargill Texturizing Solutions
Cedar Rapids, IA. 877-650-7080

Celery

Advanced Spice & Trading
Carrollton, TX. 800-872-7811
American Key Food Products
Closter, NJ. 800-767-0237
Con Yeager Spice Company
Zelienople, PA. 800-222-2460

EMERLING INTERNATIONAL FOODS, INC.

Emerling International Foods
Buffalo, NY. 716-833-7381

We supply food manufacturers and food service
customers worldwide (since 1988) with bulk ingredients including: Fruits & Vegetables; Juice
Concentrates; Herbs & Spices; Oils & Vinegars;
Flavors & Colors; Honey & Molasses. We also
produce PURE MAPLE SYRUP.

Gel Spice Company, Inc
Bayonne, NJ 800-922-0230
Unique Ingredients
Naches, WA. 509-653-1991

Cheese

Anderson Custom Processing
New Ulm, MN 877-588-4950
Baker's Coconut
Memphis, TN 800-323-1092
DMH Ingredients
Libertyville, IL 847-362-9977
Kantner Group
Wapakoneta, OH. 419-738-4060

Kraft Food Ingredients
Memphis, TN 901-381-6500
Kraft Foods
Albany, MN. 320-845-2131

American

Kantner Group
Wapakoneta, OH. 419-738-4060

Bakers

Kantner Group
Wapakoneta, OH. 419-738-4060

Cheddar

Kantner Group
Wapakoneta, OH. 419-738-4060

Cream

Kantner Group
Wapakoneta, OH. 419-738-4060

Chili

Advanced Spice & Trading
Carrollton, TX. 800-872-7811
American Key Food Products
Closter, NJ. 800-767-0237
Atlantic Quality Spice &Seasonings
Edison, NJ. 800-584-0422
Bruce Foods Corporation
New Iberia, LA 800-299-9082
Bueno Food Products
Albuquerque, NM 800-888-7336
Chile Today - Hot Tamale
San Francisco, CA 800-758-0372
Fernandez Chili Company
Alamosa, CO. 719-589-6043
Gel Spice Company, Inc
Bayonne, NJ 800-922-0230
Gilroy Foods
Gilroy, CA. 800-921-7502
Monterrey Products Company
San Antonio, TX. 210-435-2872
Morris J. Golombeck
Brooklyn, NY 718-284-3505
New Mexico Food Distributors
Albuquerque, NM 800-637-7084
Reily Foods Company
New Orleans, LA 504-524-6132
Rosarita Mexican Foods Company
Mesa, AZ. .480-964-8751
Santa Cruz Chili & SpiceCompany
Tumacacori, AZ 520-398-2591
Swagger Foods Corporation
Vernon Hills, IL 847-913-1200
Texas Coffee Company
Beaumont, TX. 800-259-3400
Victoria Packing Corporation
Brooklyn, NY 718-649-2180
Whole Herb Company
Sonoma, CA 707-935-1077
Woodland Foods
Gurnee, IL. 847-625-8600

Hot

Atlantic Quality Spice &Seasonings
Edison, NJ. 800-584-0422

Regular

Atlantic Quality Spice &Seasonings
Edison, NJ. 800-584-0422

Salt-free

Atlantic Quality Spice &Seasonings
Edison, NJ. 800-584-0422

Cocoa

Ambassador Foods
Van Nuys, CA 800-338-3369
Chadler
Swedesboro, NJ 856-467-0099
Cocoline Chocolate Company
Brooklyn, NY 718-522-4500
Ecom Agroindustrial Corporation Ltd
New York, NY 212-248-7475
Gilster-Mary Lee Corporation
Chester, IL. 800-851-5371

GPR Company
  Stowe, PA 610-326-4777
Mont Blanc Gourmet
  Denver, CO 800-877-3811
Natra US
  Chula Vista, CA 800-262-6216
Northwestern Foods
  St Paul, MN. .800-236-4937
Sucesores de Pedro Cortes
  San Juan, PR .787-754-7040
Vrymeer Commodities
  St Charles, IL .630-584-0069
World's Finest Chocolate
  Chicago, IL 800-366-2462

Curry

American Key Food Products
  Closter, NJ. 800-767-0237
Atlantic Quality Spice &Seasonings
  Edison, NJ. 800-584-0422
Bo-Ling's Products
  Overland Park, KS 913-888-8223
China Bowl Trading Company
  Westport, CT. .203-222-0381
Commissariat Imports
  Los Angeles, CA. 310-475-5628
Gel Spice Company, Inc
  Bayonne, NJ 800-922-0230
Victoria Packing Corporation
  Brooklyn, NY .718-649-2180

Hot

Atlantic Quality Spice &Seasonings
  Edison, NJ. 800-584-0422
Commissariat Imports
  Los Angeles, CA. 310-475-5628

Custard

GPR Company
  Stowe, PA 610-326-4777

EchinaceaPurpurea

Asiamerica Ingredients
  Westwood, NJ. 201-497-5531

Processor, importer, exporter and distributor of
bulk vitamins, amino acids, nutraceuticals, aromatic chemicals, food additives, herbs, mineral
nutrients and pharmaceuticals.

RFI Ingredients
  Blauvelt, NY 800-962-7663

Egg

Inovatech USA
  Montreal, QC .888-388-3447

Feverfew

Asiamerica Ingredients
  Westwood, NJ. 201-497-5531

Processor, importer, exporter and distributor of
bulk vitamins, amino acids, nutraceuticals, aromatic chemicals, food additives, herbs, mineral
nutrients and pharmaceuticals.

RFI Ingredients
  Blauvelt, NY 800-962-7663

Fish

Certified Savory
  Countryside, IL. 800-328-6656

Fruit

Agvest
  Cleveland, OH 440-735-6900
Blue California Company
  Rancho Santa Margarita, CA 949-635-1991
Carmi Flavor & Fragrance Company
  Los Angeles, CA. 800-421-9647

EMERLING INTERNATIONAL FOODS, INC.

Emerling International Foods
  Buffalo, NY. 716-833-7381

We supply food manufacturers and food service
customers worldwide (since 1988) with bulk ingredients including: Fruits & Vegetables; Juice
Concentrates; Herbs & Spices; Oils & Vinegars;
Flavors & Colors; Honey & Molasses. We also
produce PURE MAPLE SYRUP.

Master Taste International
  Plant City, FL .800-237-7629
Mayfield Farms
  Brampton, ON. 905-846-0506
Niagara Foods
  Middleport, NY 716-735-7722
Prime Ingredients
  Saddle Brook, NJ 888-791-6655
QBI
  South Plainfield, NJ 908-668-0088
RFI Ingredients
  Blauvelt, NY 800-962-7663
Spreda Group
  Prospect, KY .502-426-9411
Unique Ingredients
  Naches, WA. .509-653-1991
United Citrus Products
  Norwood, MA. 800-229-7300
Valley Fig Growers
  Fresno, CA 559-237-3893

Garlic (See also Spices/Garlic Powder)

Advanced Spice & Trading
  Carrollton, TX. 800-872-7811
Alfred L. Wolff, Inc.
  Park Ridge, IL .312-265-9889
American Key Food Products
  Closter, NJ. 800-767-0237

Asiamerica Ingredients
  Westwood, NJ. 201-497-5531

Processor, importer, exporter and distributor of
bulk vitamins, amino acids, nutraceuticals, aromatic chemicals, food additives, herbs, mineral
nutrients and pharmaceuticals.

DeFrancesco & Sons
  Firebaugh, CA. 209-364-7000

EMERLING INTERNATIONAL FOODS, INC.

Emerling International Foods
  Buffalo, NY. 716-833-7381

We supply food manufacturers and food service
customers worldwide (since 1988) with bulk ingredients including: Fruits & Vegetables; Juice
Concentrates; Herbs & Spices; Oils & Vinegars;
Flavors & Colors; Honey & Molasses. We also
produce PURE MAPLE SYRUP.

Gel Spice Company, Inc
  Bayonne, NJ 800-922-0230
Gilroy Foods
  Gilroy, CA. 800-921-7502
Great Garlic Foods
  Bradley Beach, NJ 732-775-3311
Italian Rose Garlic Products
  West Palm Beach, FL 800-338-8899
RFI Ingredients
  Blauvelt, NY 800-962-7663
Texas Coffee Company
  Beaumont, TX. 800-259-3400
Vegetable Juices
  Chicago, IL 888-776-9752

Gingko

Asiamerica Ingredients
  Westwood, NJ. 201-497-5531

Processor, importer, exporter and distributor of
bulk vitamins, amino acids, nutraceuticals, aromatic chemicals, food additives, herbs, mineral
nutrients and pharmaceuticals.

RFI Ingredients
  Blauvelt, NY 800-962-7663

Ginseng

Asiamerica Ingredients
  Westwood, NJ. 201-497-5531

Processor, importer, exporter and distributor of
bulk vitamins, amino acids, nutraceuticals, aromatic chemicals, food additives, herbs, mineral
nutrients and pharmaceuticals.

RFI Ingredients
  Blauvelt, NY 800-962-7663

Gotu Kola

Asiamerica Ingredients
  Westwood, NJ. 201-497-5531

Processor, importer, exporter and distributor of
bulk vitamins, amino acids, nutraceuticals, aromatic chemicals, food additives, herbs, mineral
nutrients and pharmaceuticals.

RFI Ingredients
  Blauvelt, NY 800-962-7663

Ice Cream

Agri-Dairy Products
  Purchase, NY .914-697-9580
America's Classic Foods
  Cambria, CA .805-927-0745
Clofine Dairy & Food Products
  Linwood, NJ 800-441-1001
International Food Technologies
  Evansville, IN .812-853-9432
Quality Naturally! Foods
  City of Industry, CA 888-498-6986

Jelly

Lake City Foods
  Mississauga, ON. 905-625-8244

Meat

American Key Food Products
  Closter, NJ. 800-767-0237
Certified Savory
  Countryside, IL. 800-328-7656
Flavor House
  Adelanto, CA .760-246-9131
Henningsen Foods
  Purchase, NY .914-701-4020
QST Ingredients, Inc.
  Rancho Cucamonga, CA 909-989-4343
Summit Hill Flavors
  Middlesex, NJ .732-805-0335

Meat Stock

Aromont-USA
  Southlake, TX. 817-552-5544

Proliant Meat Ingredients
Ankeny, IA 800-369-2672

Meringue
Dean Distributors
Burlingame, CA 800-792-0816

Milk
Abunda Life Laboratories
Asbury Park, NJ 732-775-4141
Agri-Dairy Products
Purchase, NY 914-697-9580
All American Foods, Inc.
Mankato, MN 800-833-2661
Ault Foods
Toronto, ON .416-626-1973
Berkshire Dairy & Food Products
Wyomissing, PA 888-654-8008
Blossom Farm Products
Ridgewood, NJ 800-729-1818
California Dairies
Fresno, CA 559-233-5154
California Dairies
Artesia, CA 562-865-1291
Century Foods International
Sparta, WI 800-269-1901
Challenge Dairy Products
Dublin, CA 800-733-2479
Clofine Dairy & Food Products
Linwood, NJ .800-441-1001
Con Yeager Spice Company
Zelienople, PA 800-222-2460
Country Fresh Farms
Salt Lake City, UT 800-878-0099
CTL Foods
Colfax, WI 800-962-5227
Dairy Farmers of America
Springfield, MO 800-243-2479
Dairy Farmers of America
Franklinton, LA 800-735-2038
Dairy Farmers of AmericaGoshen Plant
Goshen, IN 800-758-0269
Dairyman's/Land O' Lakes
Tulare, CA 559-687-8287
Darigold Inc
Seattle, WA .800-333-6455
Dean Foods Company
Pecatonica, IL 815-239-1632
Devansoy
Carroll, IA 800-747-8605
Dietrich's Milk Products
Reading, PA .800-526-6455
Farmers Cooperative Creamery
McMinnville, OR 503-227-5133
Fearn Natural Foods
Mequon, WI .800-877-8935
First District Association
Litchfield, MN 320-693-3236
First Spice Mixing Company
Long Island City, NY 800-221-1105
G A Food Service
St Petersburg, FL 727-573-2211
GPR Company
Stowe, PA 610-326-4777
Graf Creamery
Zachow, WI .715-758-2137
Honeyville Grain
Rancho Cucamonga, CA 888-810-3212
Humboldt Creamery Association
Fortuna, CA .707-725-6182
IMAC
Oklahoma City, OK 888-878-7827
Kantner Group
Wapakoneta, OH 419-738-4060
Kelly Flour Company
Addison, IL .630-678-5300
Kerry Ingredients
Tralee, Co. Kerry,
Kraft Foods/Knudson Products
Visalia, CA 800-323-0768
Lake Country Foods
Oconomowoc, WI 262-567-5521
Land O'Lakes
Carlisle, PA .717-486-7000
Land O'Lakes, Inc
Arden Hills, MN 800-328-9680
Level Valley Creamery
Antioch, TN .800-251-1292
Main Street Ingredients
La Crosse, WI 800-359-2345

Maple Island
St Paul, MN .800-369-1022
Master Taste International
Plant City, FL 800-237-7629
MEYENBERG Goat Milk Products
Turlock, CA .800-891-4628
Parmalat
St George Brant, ON 519-448-1311
Plainview Milk Products Cooperative
Plainview, MN 507-534-3872
Preferred Milks
Addison, IL .800-621-5046
Protient (Land O Lakes)
St Paul, MN .651-481-2068
Ramsen
Lakeville, MN 952-431-0400
Reilly Dairy & Food Company
Tampa, FL 813-839-8458
RV Industries
Atlanta, GA .770-729-8983
Safeway Inc
Durand, WI .715-672-8911
Saint Albans CooperativeCreamy
Saint Albans, VT. 800-559-0343
Saputo Cheese
Lincolnshire, IL 800-558-9714
Saputo Cheese
Fond Du Lac, WI 800-824-3373
Saputo Cheese
Lena, WI 920-829-5251
Seller Kirk & Company
Schwenksville, PA 215-480-7342
Swiss Valley Farms Company
Davenport, IA 563-468-6600
The Scoular Company
Omaha, NE .402-342-3500
United Dairymen of Arizona
Tempe, AZ. .480-966-7211
Vance's Foods
Gilmer, TX .800-497-4834
Weinberg Foods
Kirkland, WA 800-866-3447
Welsh Farms
Newark, NJ .800-221-0663
Westin
Omaha, NE .800-228-6098

Molasses
Groeb Farms
Onsted, MI .517-467-7100
Rogers Sugar Limited
Vancouver, BC 800-661-5350
Smolich Brothers
Crest Hill, IL 815-727-2144

Mustard
Kathy's Gourmet Specialties
Mendocino, CA. 707-937-1383

Onion (See also Spices/Onion Powder)
Advanced Spice & Trading
Carrollton, TX. 800-872-7811
American Key Food Products
Closter, NJ. .800-767-0237
Atlantic Quality Spice &Seasonings
Edison, NJ. .800-584-0422
Con Yeager Spice Company
Zelienople, PA. 800-222-2460
DeFrancesco & Sons
Firebaugh, CA. 209-364-7000

EMERLING INTERNATIONAL FOODS, INC.

Emerling International Foods
Buffalo, NY. 716-833-7381

> We supply food manufacturers and food service
> customers worldwide (since 1988) with bulk in-
> gredients including: Fruits & Vegetables; Juice
> Concentrates; Herbs & Spices; Oils & Vinegars;
> Flavors & Colors; Honey & Molasses. We also
> produce PURE MAPLE SYRUP.

Erba Food Products
Brooklyn, NY. 718-272-7700
Gel Spice Company, Inc
Bayonne, NJ 800-922-0230
Gilroy Foods
Gilroy, CA. .800-921-7502

GPR Company
Stowe, PA 610-326-4777
Texas Coffee Company
Beaumont, TX. 800-259-3400
Vegetable Juices
Chicago, IL .888-776-9752

Pau D'Arco Bark

asiamerica

Asiamerica Ingredients
Westwood, NJ 201-497-5531

> Processor, importer, exporter and distributor of
> bulk vitamins, amino acids, nutraceuticals, aro-
> matic chemicals, food additives, herbs, mineral
> nutrients and pharmaceuticals.

RFI Ingredients
Blauvelt, NY 800-962-7663

Pregelatinized
Cargill Texturizing Solutions
Cedar Rapids, IA. 877-650-7080

Prepared for Further Processing
Akay USA, LLC.
Sayreville, NJ 732-254-7177
Olcott Plastics
St Charles, IL 888-313-5277

Protein
International Food Technologies
Evansville, IN 812-853-9432

Punch
GPR Company
Stowe, PA 610-326-4777

Rice

Milk
A&B Ingredients
Fairfield, NJ 973-227-1390

Saw Palmetto Berry

asiamerica

Asiamerica Ingredients
Westwood, NJ 201-497-5531

> Processor, importer, exporter and distributor of
> bulk vitamins, amino acids, nutraceuticals, aro-
> matic chemicals, food additives, herbs, mineral
> nutrients and pharmaceuticals.

RFI Ingredients
Blauvelt, NY 800-962-7663

Seafood
American Key Food Products
Closter, NJ. .800-767-0237
Certified Savory
Countryside, IL 800-328-7656
Flavor House
Adelanto, CA 760-246-9131
Henningsen Foods
Purchase, NY 914-701-4020

Seasoning
American Key Food Products
Closter, NJ. .800-767-0237
Gel Spice Company, Inc
Bayonne, NJ 800-922-0230

Magic Seasoning Blends
Harahan, LA .800-457-2857
Summit Hill Flavors
Middlesex, NJ 732-805-0335
Vegetable Juices
Chicago, IL .888-776-9752
Victoria Packing Corporation
Brooklyn, NY 718-649-2180

Smoothie

International Food Technologies
Evansville, IN 812-853-9432
SensoryEffects Flavor Systems
Bridgeton, MO 314-291-5444

Soy

Cargill Texturizing Solutions
Cedar Rapids, IA. 877-650-7080

Soy Milk

Cedar Lake Foods
Cedar Lake, MI 800-246-5039
Innovative Food Solutions LLC
Columbus, OH 800-884-3314

St. John's Wort

RFI Ingredients
Blauvelt, NY 800-962-7663

Tofu

Clofine Dairy & Food Products
Linwood, NJ 800-441-1001
Dixie USA
Tomball, TX 800-233-3668

Tomato

A&B Ingredients
Fairfield, NJ 973-227-1390
Transa
Libertyville, IL 847-281-9582

Valerian Root

Asiamerica Ingredients
Westwood, NJ 201-497-5531

Processor, importer, exporter and distributor of bulk vitamins, amino acids, nutraceuticals, aromatic chemicals, food additives, herbs, mineral nutrients and pharmaceuticals.

RFI Ingredients
Blauvelt, NY 800-962-7663

Vanilla

Agri-Dairy Products
Purchase, NY 914-697-9580
Carmi Flavor & Fragrance Company
Los Angeles, CA. 800-421-9647
Contract Comestibles
East Troy, WI 262-642-9400

Emerling International Foods
Buffalo, NY. 716-833-7381

We supply food manufacturers and food service customers worldwide (since 1988) with bulk ingredients including: Fruits & Vegetables; Juice Concentrates; Herbs & Spices; Oils & Vinegars; Flavors & Colors; Honey & Molasses. We also produce PURE MAPLE SYRUP.

H.B. Taylor Co
Chicago, IL 773-254-4805
Prime Ingredients
Saddle Brook, NJ 888-791-6655
Sterling Extract Company
Franklin Park, IL. 847-451-9728

Whole Herb Company
Sonoma, CA 707-935-1077

Yogurt

Associated Bakers Products
Huntington, NY 631-673-3841
Cargill Texturizing Solutions
Cedar Rapids, IA. 877-650-7080
Commercial Creamery Company
Spokane, WA. 800-541-0850
Kantner Group
Wapakoneta, OH. 419-738-4060
Maple Island
St Paul, MN. 800-369-1022
Master Mix
Placentia, CA 714-524-1698
Quality Ingredients Corporation
Burnsville, MN 952-898-4002

Frozen

Cargill Texturizing Solutions
Cedar Rapids, IA. 877-650-7080
International Food Technologies
Evansville, IN 812-853-9432

Preservatives

A&B Ingredients
Fairfield, NJ 973-227-1390
A. Camacho
Plant City, FL 800-881-4534
Batko Flavors LLC
North Brunswick, NJ 732-991-3462

Food

A.M. Braswell Jr. Food Company
Statesboro, GA 800-673-9388
Cargill Corn Milling
Naperville, IL 800-344-1633
FBC Industries
Schaumburg, IL. 888-322-4637
Hosemen & Roche Vitamins & Fine Chemicals
Nutley, NJ .800-526-6367
Hurd Orchards
Holley, NY .585-638-8838
Jarchem Industries
Newark, NJ 973-578-4560
Jungbunzlauer
Newton, MA 800-828-0062
Kalama Chemical
Seattle, WA 800-742-6147
Macco Organiques
Valleyfield, QC. 450-371-1066
Mineral & Pigment Solutions
South Plainfield, NJ 800-732-0562
Nutricepts
Burnsville, MN 800-949-9060
Parish Chemical Company
Orem, UT .801-226-2018
PMC Specialties Group
Cincinnati, OH 800-543-2466
Shekou Chemicals
Waltham, MA 781-893-6878
Silver Ferm Chemical
Seattle, WA 206-282-3376
Tasty Mix Quality Foods
Brooklyn, NY. 866-TAS-TYMX
Universal Preservachem Inc
Edison, NJ .732-777-7338
Wisconsin Wilderness Food Products
Milwaukee, WI 800-359-3039

Proteins

American Casein Company
Burlington, NJ. 609-387-2988
Cargill Texturizing Solutions
Cedar Rapids, IA. 877-650-7080
Clofine Dairy & Food Products
Linwood, NJ 800-441-1001
Kantner Group
Wapakoneta, OH. 419-738-4060

Releases

Food

Barbara's Bakery
Petaluma, CA 707-765-2273

Barlean's
Ferndale, WA 360-384-0325
Black Diamond Cheese
Toronto, ON 800-263-2858
Capri Bagel & Pizza Corporation
Brooklyn, NY 718-497-4431
Cloud Nine
San Leandro, CA. 201-358-8588
Corn Poppers
San Diego, CA 858-231-2617
Desert King International
Chula Vista, CA 800-982-2235
EcoNatural Solutions
Boulder, CO 877-684-5159
Ferris Organic Farm
Eaton Rapids, MI 800-628-8736
Flavorganics
Newark, NJ 973-344-8014
Glanbia Foods
Twin Falls, ID 800-427-9477
Ingredient Innovations
Kansas City, MO. 816-587-1426
Jazzie Smoothie
Metairie, LA 504-780-8429
Jewel Date Company
Thermal, CA 760-399-4474
Leech Lake Reservation
Cass Lake, MN 218-335-8200
Lone Pine Enterprises
Carlisle, AR 870-552-3217
Lowell Farms
El Campo, TX. 888-484-9213
Marantha Natural Foods
San Francisco, CA 800-299-0048
Martha Olson's Great Foods
Sutter Creek, CA. 800-973-3966
Montana Specialty Mills
Great Falls, MT. 406-761-2338
Nelson Ricks Creamery Company
Salt Lake City, UT 801-364-3607
Nicola Valley Apiaries
Merritt, BC 250-378-5208
NSpired Natural Foods
Melville, NY 631-845-4689
Pack Ryt, Inc
Thermal, CA 760-399-5026
S&E Organic Farms
Bakersfield, CA 661-325-2644
Schreiber Foods   Plant/Distribution Center
Wisconsin Rapids, WI 715-422-7500
Southern Brown Rice
Weiner, AR 800-421-7423
Stengel Seed & Grain Company
Milbank, SD 605-432-6030
Sunnyland Mills
Fresno, CA .800-501-8017
Tianfu China Cola
Katonah, NY. 914-232-3102
Top Hat Company
Wilmette, IL 847-256-6565
US Mills
Needham, MA 800-422-1125
Victor Packing Company
Madera, CA. 559-673-5908

Replacers

Cocoa

Associated Bakers Products
Huntington, NY 631-673-3841

Egg

Associated Bakers Products
Huntington, NY 631-673-3841
Cargill Texturizing Solutions
Cedar Rapids, IA. 877-650-7080
Inovatech USA
Montreal, QC 888-388-3447

Fat

Edlong Dairy Flavors
Elk Grove Vlg, IL. 888-698-2783
Hercules Incorporated
Wilmington, DE 800-345-8104
MD Foods Ingredients
Union, NJ .800-972-2096
Penwest Foods Company
Centennial, CO 303-649-1900
Tate & Lyle Staley Company
Decatur, IL .217-423-4411

Raisin Juice

Dry

Cajun Chef Products
St Martinville, LA.................337-394-7112

Sodium

Asiamerica Ingredients
Westwood, NJ....................201-497-5531

Processor, importer, exporter and distributor of
bulk vitamins, amino acids, nutraceuticals, aromatic chemicals, food additives, herbs, mineral
nutrients and pharmaceuticals.

Cargill Worldwide Acidulants
Naperville, IL....................800-344-1633
Erie Foods International
Erie, IL..........................800-447-1887
Gadot Biochemical Industries
Rolling Meadows, IL.............888-424-1424
Gum Technology Corporation
Tucson, AZ......................800-369-4867
Jungbunzlauer
Newton, MA.....................800-828-0062
Luxembourg Cheese Factory
Orangeville, IL..................815-789-4227
Nutricepts
Burnsville, MN..................800-949-9060
PMP Fermentation Products
Peoria, IL........................800-558-1031
Trumark
Linden, NJ.......................800-752-7877

Sodium Alginates

Asiamerica Ingredients
Westwood, NJ....................201-497-5531

Processor, importer, exporter and distributor of
bulk vitamins, amino acids, nutraceuticals, aromatic chemicals, food additives, herbs, mineral
nutrients and pharmaceuticals.

Gum Technology Corporation
Tucson, AZ......................800-369-4867
P.L. Thomas
Morristown, NJ..................973-984-0900
TIC Gums
Belcamp, MD....................800-221-3953

Sodium Benzoate

Agri-Dairy Products
Purchase, NY....................914-697-9580

Asiamerica Ingredients
Westwood, NJ....................201-497-5531

Processor, importer, exporter and distributor of
bulk vitamins, amino acids, nutraceuticals, aromatic chemicals, food additives, herbs, mineral
nutrients and pharmaceuticals.

Cargill Corn Milling
Naperville, IL....................800-344-1633
Jarchem Industries
Newark, NJ.....................973-578-4560
Jungbunzlauer
Newton, MA.....................800-828-0062
Kalama Chemical
Seattle, WA......................800-742-6147
Luyties Pharmacal Company
Saint Louis, MO.................800-325-8080

Shekou Chemicals
Waltham, MA...................781-893-6878
Silver Ferm Chemical
Seattle, WA......................206-282-3376
Singer Extract Laboratory
Livonia, MI......................313-345-5880
Universal Preservachem Inc
Edison, NJ.......................732-777-7338

Sodium Citrate

Asiamerica Ingredients
Westwood, NJ....................201-497-5531

Processor, importer, exporter and distributor of
bulk vitamins, amino acids, nutraceuticals, aromatic chemicals, food additives, herbs, mineral
nutrients and pharmaceuticals.

Cargill Corn Milling
Naperville, IL....................800-344-1633
Gadot Biochemical Industries
Rolling Meadows, IL.............888-424-1424
International Chemical
Milltown, NJ.....................800-914-2436
Jungbunzlauer
Newton, MA.....................800-828-0062
Shekou Chemicals
Waltham, MA...................781-893-6878
Universal Preservachem Inc
Edison, NJ.......................732-777-7338

Spirulina

Alternative Health & Herbs
Albany, OR......................800-345-4152

Asiamerica Ingredients
Westwood, NJ....................201-497-5531

Processor, importer, exporter and distributor of
bulk vitamins, amino acids, nutraceuticals, aromatic chemicals, food additives, herbs, mineral
nutrients and pharmaceuticals.

Cyanotech Corporation
Kailua Kona, HI..................800-395-1353
Herb Connection
Springville, UT...................801-489-4254

Stabilizers

Cargill Texturizing Solutions
Cedar Rapids, IA.................877-650-7080
Mallet & Company
Carnegie, PA.....................800-245-2757
Marukan Vinegar (U.S.A.) Inc.
Paramount, CA...................562-630-6060
P.L. Thomas
Morristown, NJ..................973-984-0900

Colloids

Custom Designed

Cargill Texturizing Solutions
Cedar Rapids, IA.................877-650-7080

Lecithinated

Agri-Dairy Products
Purchase, NY....................914-697-9580
American Health & Nutrition
Ann Arbor, MI...................734-677-5572
Arnhem Group
Cranford, NJ.....................800-851-1052
McCain Foods USA
Grand Island, NE................308-382-7770
Universal Preservachem Inc
Edison, NJ.......................732-777-7338

Yogurt

Cargill Texturizing Solutions
Cedar Rapids, IA.................877-650-7080
Johanna Foods
Flemington, NJ..................800-727-6700
Maple Island
St Paul, MN......................800-369-1022

Starches

ADM
Marshall, MN....................800-328-4150
ADM Lecithin & Monoglycerides
Decatur, IL.......................800-637-5843
Anderson Custom Processing
New Ulm, MN....................877-588-4950
Cargill Corn Milling
Naperville, IL....................800-344-1633
Cargill Texturizing Solutions
Cedar Rapids, IA.................877-650-7080
Domino Foods
Yonkers, NY.....................914-963-2400

Your Total Sweetener Solution.

Evergreen Sweeteners, Inc
Aventura, FL.....................305-931-1321

Evergreen Sweeteners is a full service sweetener
distributor serving the entire state of Florida.
From bulk liquid sweeteners to bagged sweeteners, Evergreen provides its customers with industry-leading service and unsurpassed quality.

Marsan Foods
Toronto, ON.....................416-755-9262
Mississippi Blending Company
Keokuk, IA.......................800-758-4080
National Starch & Chemical Corporate Office
Bridgewater, NJ..................800-366-4031
Norben Company
Willoughby, OH..................888-466-7236
Raymond-Hadley Corporation
Spencer, NY.....................800-252-5220

Roquette America
  Keokuk, IA 800-553-7035
Seydel International
  Pendergrass, GA 706-693-2295
St. Lawrence Starch
  Mississauga, ON 905-274-3671
TIPIAK INC
  Stamford, CT. 203-961-9117
Westin
  Omaha, NE 800-228-6098

Arrowroot
American Key Food Products
  Closter, NJ. 800-767-0237

Cassava
Cargill Texturizing Solutions
  Cedar Rapids, IA. 877-650-7080

Corn
ADM
  Marshall, MN .800-328-4150
American Health & Nutrition
  Ann Arbor, MI 734-677-5572
American Key Food Products
  Closter, NJ. 800-767-0237
Cargill Texturizing Solutions
  Cedar Rapids, IA. 877-650-7080
Cerestar USA
  Decatur, AL. 256-355-8815
Cerestar USA
  Hammond, IN .800-348-9896
Corn Products International
  Westchester, IL 708-551-2600

Evergreen Sweeteners, Inc
  Aventura, FL. .305-931-1321

Evergreen Sweeteners is a full service sweetener distributor serving the entire state of Florida. From bulk liquid sweeteners to bagged sweeteners, Evergreen provides its customers with industry-leading service and unsurpassed quality.

Grain Processing Corporation
  Muscatine, IA .800-448-4472
Meelunie America
  Farmington Hills, MI 248-473-2100
Mills Brothers International
  Tukwila, WA 206-575-3000
Nacan Products
  Brampton, ON. 905-454-4466
Reilly Dairy & Food Company
  Tampa, FL. 813-839-8458
Tate & Lyle Staley Company
  Decatur, IL 217-423-4411
Westin
  Omaha, NE 800-228-6098

Dextrin
ADM Corn Processing
  Decatur, IL 800-553-8411
Cargill Texturizing Solutions
  Cedar Rapids, IA. 877-650-7080
Cerestar USA
  Hammond, IN .800-348-9896
Penford Food Ingredients
  Centennial, CO 303-649-1900
Seydel International
  Pendergrass, GA 706-693-2295
Tate & Lyle Staley Company
  Decatur, IL 217-423-4411

Dusting
Cargill Texturizing Solutions
  Cedar Rapids, IA. 877-650-7080
Mississippi Blending Company
  Keokuk, IA 800-758-4080

High Amylose
Cargill Texturizing Solutions
  Cedar Rapids, IA. 877-650-7080

Modified
Cargill Texturizing Solutions
  Cedar Rapids, IA. 877-650-7080
Penford Food Ingredients
  Centennial, CO 303-649-1900

Molding
Cargill Texturizing Solutions
  Cedar Rapids, IA. 877-650-7080

Potato
Penford Food Ingredients
  Centennial, CO 303-649-1900
Penwest Foods Company
  Richland, WA .509-375-1261
Terry Foods Inc
  Idaho Falls, ID 208-604-8143

Pregelatinized
A&B Ingredients
  Fairfield, NJ 973-227-1390
Cargill Texturizing Solutions
  Cedar Rapids, IA. 877-650-7080
Penford Food Ingredients
  Centennial, CO 303-649-1900

Rice
A&B Ingredients
  Fairfield, NJ 973-227-1390
American Key Food Products
  Closter, NJ. 800-767-0237
AVEBE America, Inc.
  Princeton, NJ. 609-951-2030

Modified
A&B Ingredients
  Fairfield, NJ 973-227-1390

Tapioca
Cargill Texturizing Solutions
  Cedar Rapids, IA. 877-650-7080
Penford Food Ingredients
  Centennial, CO 303-649-1900

Thin Boiling
Cargill Texturizing Solutions
  Cedar Rapids, IA. 877-650-7080

Waxy
Cargill Texturizing Solutions
  Cedar Rapids, IA. 877-650-7080

Waxy Maize
Cargill Texturizing Solutions
  Cedar Rapids, IA. 877-650-7080
Penford Food Ingredients
  Centennial, CO 303-649-1900

Wheat
ADM Food Ingredients
  Olathe, KS. 800-255-6637

Starter Media

Cheese
Cargill Texturizing Solutions
  Cedar Rapids, IA. 877-650-7080
Hygeia Dairy Company
  McAllen, TX. .956-686-0511

Surfactants & Solubilizers

Solubilizers
P.L. Thomas
  Morristown, NJ 973-984-0900

Sweeteners
Agri-Dairy Products
  Purchase, NY .914-697-9580
Ajinomoto Food Ingredients, LLC
  Chicago, IL 773-714-1436

Atlantic Chemicals Trading Of North America, Inc.
  Glendale, CA .818-246-0077

Evergreen Sweeteners, Inc
  Aventura, FL. .305-931-1321

Evergreen Sweeteners is a full service sweetener distributor serving the entire state of Florida. From bulk liquid sweeteners to bagged sweeteners, Evergreen provides its customers with industry-leading service and unsurpassed quality.

GLG Life Tech Corporation
  Vancouver, BC 604-641-1368
H & A Canada, Inc.
  Toronto, ON .416-412-9518
Natur Sweeteners, Inc.
  Los Angeles, CA. 310-445-0020
Rio Naturals
  El Dorado Hills, CA 916-719-3924

Dextrose
ADM Corn Processing
  Decatur, IL 800-553-8411
ADM Food Ingredients
  Olathe, KS. 800-255-6637
Agri-Dairy Products
  Purchase, NY .914-697-9580
Cargill Corn Milling
  Naperville, IL .800-344-1633
Corn Products International
  Westchester, IL 708-551-2600
Domino Foods
  Yonkers, NY .914-963-2400

Evergreen Sweeteners, Inc
  Aventura, FL. .305-931-1321

Evergreen Sweeteners is a full service sweetener distributor serving the entire state of Florida. From bulk liquid sweeteners to bagged sweeteners, Evergreen provides its customers with industry-leading service and unsurpassed quality.

Malt Products Corporation
  Saddle Brook, NJ 800-526-0180
Roquette America
  Keokuk, IA 800-553-7035
Tate & Lyle Staley Company
  Decatur, IL 217-423-4411
Westin
  Omaha, NE 800-228-6098

Lactose
Agri-Dairy Products
  Purchase, NY .914-697-9580

![asiamerica]

Asiamerica Ingredients
  Westwood, NJ 201-497-5531

Processor, importer, exporter and distributor of bulk vitamins, amino acids, nutraceuticals, aromatic chemicals, food additives, herbs, mineral nutrients and pharmaceuticals.

Blossom Farm Products
  Ridgewood, NJ 800-729-1818
Century Foods International
  Sparta, WI 800-269-1901
Clofine Dairy & Food Products
  Linwood, NJ .800-441-1001
Davisco International
  Eden Prairie, MN 800-757-7611

First District Association
 Litchfield, MN 320-693-3236
Foremost Farms
 Baraboo, WI 800-365-9196
Glanbia Foods
 Twin Falls, ID 800-427-9477
Glanbia Nutritionals
 Monroe, WI. 800-336-2183
Grande Custom Ingredients Group
 Brownsville, WI 800-772-3210
Leprino Foods Company
 Denver, CO .800-537-7466
Main Street Ingredients
 La Crosse, WI 800-359-2345
Reilly Dairy & Food Company
 Tampa, FL. .813-839-8458
Saputo
 St Leonard, QC 514-328-6662
Universal Preservachem Inc
 Edison, NJ. .732-777-7338

Sorbitol

Agri-Dairy Products
 Purchase, NY 914-697-9580
Archer Daniels Midland Company
 Decatur, IL .800-637-5843

Asiamerica Ingredients
 Westwood, NJ 201-497-5531

Processor, importer, exporter and distributor of
bulk vitamins, amino acids, nutraceuticals, aromatic chemicals, food additives, herbs, mineral
nutrients and pharmaceuticals.

EMD Chemicals
 Gibbstown, NJ 800-364-4535
Roquette America
 Keokuk, IA .800-553-7035

Universal Preservachem Inc
 Edison, NJ. .732-777-7338

Tenderizers

A M Todd Company
 Kalamazoo, OR. 269-343-2603
ADM Food Ingredients
 Olathe, KS. .800-255-6637
Dean Distributors
 Burlingame, CA 800-227-3112
Phamous Phloyd's Barbeque Sauce
 Denver, CO .303-757-3285

Sentry Seasonings
 Elmhurst, IL .630-530-5370

The product development experts of Sentry Seasonings are eager to offer the assistance and
hands-on experience to food processors of all
sizes. Sentry Seasonings will ensure the consistent
high quality and repeat sales of your products,
whether you choose one of our many off-the-shelf
Bench Mark products or a modified version to
meet your preferences. Sentry Seasonings can
also duplicate and/or improve your present flavor
profile; formulate, blend and package specifically
for your requirements.

Three Vee Food & Syrup Company
 Brooklyn, NY 800-801-7330
WTI, Inc.
 Jefferson, GA 800-827-1727

Meat

A M Todd Company
 Kalamazoo, OR. 269-343-2603

ADM Food Ingredients
 Olathe, KS. .800-255-6637
Alltech Natural Food Division
 Nicholasville, KY 859-885-9613
American Key Food Products
 Closter, NJ. .800-767-0237
Custom Food Products
 Alsip, IL 708-388-8883
Enzyme Development Corporation
 New York, NY 212-736-1580

Sentry Seasonings
 Elmhurst, IL .630-530-5370

The product development experts of Sentry Seasonings are eager to offer the assistance and
hands-on experience to food processors of all
sizes. Sentry Seasonings will ensure the consistent
high quality and repeat sales of your products,
whether you choose one of our many off-the-shelf
Bench Mark products or a modified version to
meet your preferences. Sentry Seasonings can
also duplicate and/or improve your present flavor
profile; formulate, blend and package specifically
for your requirements.

Spiceman
 Eugene, OR. 800-725-8373
Texas Coffee Company
 Beaumont, TX. 800-259-3400
Three Vee Food & Syrup Company
 Brooklyn, NY 800-801-7330
Universal Concepts
 Lauderhill, FL 918-367-0197
Valley Research
 South Bend, IN 800-522-8110

World Flavors
Warminster, PA 215-672-4400

Thickeners

Cargill Texturizing Solutions
Cedar Rapids, IA. 877-650-7080

Gelatin

Asiamerica Ingredients
Westwood, NJ 201-497-5531

Processor, importer, exporter and distributor of bulk vitamins, amino acids, nutraceuticals, aromatic chemicals, food additives, herbs, mineral nutrients and pharmaceuticals.

Associated Brands
Toronto, ON 800-265-0050
Blue Ridge Farms
Chicago, IL 708-748-4405
Cangel
Toronto, ON 800-267-4795
Con Yeager Spice Company
Zelienople, PA. 800-222-2460
Dean Distributors
Burlingame, CA 800-792-0816
Dynagel
Calumet City, IL 888-396-2435
Erba Food Products
Brooklyn, NY 718-272-7700
First Foods Company
Dallas, TX 214-637-0214
Gelita USA
Sioux City, IA 888-456-5435
Gelita/Kind & Knox Gelatine
Sioux City, IA 888-456-5435
GMI Products
Plantation, FL 800-999-9373
GMI Products/Originates
Sunrise, FL 800-999-9373
Golden Fluff Popcorn Company
Lakewood, NJ 732-367-5448
Inter-American Products
Cincinnati, OH 800-645-2233
Kraft Canada Headquarters
Don Mills, ON 800-268-7808
Kraft Food Ingredients
Memphis, TN 901-381-6500
Kraft Foods/Atlantic Gelatin
Woburn, MA 781-933-2800
Leiner Davis Gelatin
Jericho, NY 516-942-4940

Marquez Brothers International
Hanford, CA 559-584-0306
Maryland & Virginia Milk Producers Cooperative
Reston, VA 703-742-7443
Milligan & Higgins
Johnstown, NY 518-762-4638
Nitta Gelatin NA
Rochelle Park, NJ 800-278-7680
Protein Products Inc
North Andover, MA 978-689-9083
Rousselot Gelatin
Mukwonago, WI. 262-363-2789
Shionogi Qualicaps
Whitsett, NC 800-227-7853
SKW Nature Products
Langhorne, PA 215-702-1000
Spring Glen Fresh Foods
Ephrata, PA. 800-641-2853
Synergy Foods
West Bloomfield, MI 313-849-2900
Tessenderlo Kerley
Phoenix, AZ 800-669-0559
Tova Industries
Louisville, KY 888-532-8682
Vyse Gelatin Company
Schiller Park, IL 800-533-2152
White Coffee Corporation
Long Island City, NY 800-221-0140

Toppings

Affy Tapple, LLC
Niles, IL 847-588-2900
Al-Rite Fruits & Syrups
Miami, FL. 305-652-2540
Bake'n Joy Foods
North Andover, MA 800-666-4937
Baker & Baker
Schaumburg, IL. 800-593-5777

Baldwin Richardson Foods
Frankfort, IL 866-644-2732

Baldwin Richardson Foods is a liquid ingredient manufacturer specializing in signature sauces, dessert toppings, beverage/pancake syrups, specialty fruit fillings and condiments. Packaging capabilities range from portion control cups and pouches to standard retail and foodservice packs and include industrial drums and totes. Full service R&D and Quality groups dedicated to new product development, with in-house stability and analytical testing. Call for assistance.

Berner Foods, Inc.
Roscoe, IL. 800-819-8199
C.F. Burger Creamery
Detroit, MI 800-229-2322
Consolidated Mills
Houston, TX 713-896-4196
Dark Tickle Company
Griquet, NL. 709-623-2354
Golden State Foods
Irvine, CA 949-252-2000
Gumpert's Canada
Mississauga, ON 800-387-9324
Instant Products of America
Columbus, IN 812-372-9100
Nuvex Ingredients
Blue Earth, MN. 507-526-4331
O Chili Frozen Foods Inc
Northbrook, IL 847-562-1991
Paulaur Corporation
Cranbury, NJ 888-398-8844
Phillips Syrup Corporation
Cleveland, OH 216-661-4800
Presto Avoset Group
Claremont, CA 909-399-0062
QA Products
Elk Grove Vlg, IL 800-635-7907
Richardson Foods Corporation
Macedon, NY 315-986-2807
Shine Companies
Spring, TX. 281-353-8392
Stearns & Lehman
Mansfield, OH 800-533-2722
World's Finest Chocolate
Chicago, IL 800-366-2462

Cakes & Donuts

Signature Brands
Ocala, FL. 800-456-9573

Colored Starch Bits

Nuvex Ingredients
Blue Earth, MN. 507-526-4331

Confectionery

Nuvex Ingredients
Blue Earth, MN. 507-526-4331
Paulaur Corporation
Cranbury, NJ 888-398-8844
QA Products
Elk Grove Vlg, IL 800-635-7907
Ribble Production
Warminster, PA 215-674-1706

Crisp Rice

Nuvex Ingredients
Blue Earth, MN. 507-526-4331

Crunch

American Almond Products Company
Brooklyn, NY 800-825-6663
Nature's Hand
Burnsville, MN 952-890-6033
Nuvex Ingredients
Blue Earth, MN..................... 507-526-4331
Paulaur Corporation
Cranbury, NJ 888-398-8844
QA Products
Elk Grove Vlg, IL 800-635-7907

Dessert

Al-Rite Fruits & Syrups
Miami, FL 305-652-2540
Alamance Foods/Triton Water Company
Burlington, NC 800-476-9111
American Almond Products Company
Brooklyn, NY 800-825-6663
American Classic Ice Cream Company
Bay Shore, NY 631-666-1000
Aunt Aggie De's Pralines
Sinton, TX 888-772-5463

Baldwin Richardson Foods
Frankfort, IL 866-644-2732

Baldwin Richardson Foods is a liquid ingredient manufacturer specializing in signature sauces, dessert toppings, beverage/pancake syrups, specialty fruit fillings and condiments. Packaging capabilities range from portion control cups and pouches to standard retail and foodservice packs and include industrial drums and totes. Full service R&D and Quality groups dedicated to new product development, with in-house stability and analytical testing. Call for assistance.

Bell Buckle Country Store
Bell Buckle, TN 800-707-0483
Brighams
Arlington, MA 800-274-4426
Broughton Foods
Marietta, OH 800-283-2479
C.F. Burger Creamery
Detroit, MI 800-229-2322
Calhoun Bend Mill
Alexandria, LA 800-519-6455
California Custom Fruits & Flavors
Irwindale, CA 877-558-0056
Carole's Cheesecake Company
Toronto, ON 416-256-0000
Charles Dennery Pillsbury
New Orleans, LA 504-733-2331
Chocolaterie Bernard Callebaut
Calgary, AB. 800-661-8367
ConAgra Dairy Foods
Indianapolis, IN 317-329-3700
ConAgra Grocery Products
Irvine, CA 714-680-1000
ConAgra Refrigerated Foods International
Omaha, NE 800-624-4724
Consolidated Mills
Houston, TX 713-896-4196
Country Fresh Food & Confections
Oliver Springs, TN 800-545-8782
Cremes Unlimited
Matteson, IL 800-227-3637
Cuisinary Fine Foods
Dallas, TX 888-283-5303
Dean Foods Company
Dallas, TX 214-303-3400
Durkee-Mower
Lynn, MA 781-593-8007
Felbro Food Products
Los Angeles, CA 800-335-2761
Gold Coast Ingredients
Commerce, CA 800-352-8673
Golden Foods
Commerce, CA 800-350-2462
Golden West Fruit Company
Commerce, CA 323-726-9419
Gourmet Central
Romney, WV. 800-984-3722
Great San Saba River Pecan Company
San Saba, TX 800-621-9121
H. Fox & Company
Brooklyn, NY 718-385-4600
H.C. Brill Company
Tucker, GA 800-241-8526
Hanan Products Company
Hicksville, NY 516-938-1000
Heinz Company of Canada
North York, ON. 800-268-6641
Homemade By Dorothy
Boise, ID 208-375-3720
I Rice & Company
Philadelphia, PA 800-232-6022
Industrial Products
Defiance, OH 800-251-3033
Instant Products of America
Columbus, IN 812-372-9100
Instantwhip: Arizona
Phoenix, AZ 800-544-9447
Instantwhip: Chicago
Chicago, IL 800-933-2500
Instantwhip: Texas
San Antonio, TX. 800-544-9447
J.M. Smucker Company
Orrville, OH 330-682-3000
Jogue Inc
Northville, MI. 800-521-3888
Johnson's Food Products
Dorchester, MA. 617-265-3400
Kalva Corporation
Gurnee, IL 800-525-8220
Kerry Ingredients
Beloit, WI 608-362-1651
Kraft Foods
Avon, NY 585-226-4400
Kraft Foods
Northfield, IL 800-323-0768
Kraus & Company
Commerce Twp, MI 800-662-5871
Lyons-Magnus
Fresno, CA 559-268-5966
Masterson Company
Milwaukee, WI 414-647-1132
Michigan Dessert Corporation
Oak Park, MI. 800-328-8632

Morningstar Foods
Dallas, TX. 225-273-2803
Newport Flavours & Fragrances
Orange, CA. 714-628-9894
Nuvex Ingredients
Blue Earth, MN 507-526-4331
Oak State Products
Wenona, IL 815-853-4348
Ohio Processors Company
London, OH 740-852-9243
Oregon Hill Farms
St Helens, OR 800-243-4541
Parker Products
Fort Worth, TX 800-433-5749
Paulaur Corporation
Cranbury, NJ. 888-398-8844
Pearson's Berry Farm
Bowden, AB 403-224-3011
Pecan Deluxe Candy Company
Dallas, TX. 800-733-3589
Phillips Syrup Corporation
Cleveland, OH 216-661-4800
QA Products
Elk Grove Vlg, IL 800-635-7907
Rich Products Corporation
Hilliard, OH. 614-771-1117
Rich Products Corporation
Claremont, CA 909-621-4711
Rich Products of Canada
Fort Erie, ON 800-263-8174
Rod's Food Products
City of Industry, CA 909-839-8925
Rose Brand Corporation
Brooklyn, NY 800-854-5356
Rowena's
Norfolk, VA. 800-627-8699
Sea Breeze Fruit Flavors
Towaco, NJ 800-732-2733
Spruce Mountain Blueberries
West Rockport, ME. 207-23-6 35
Steel's Gourmet Foods
Bridgeport, PA 800-678-3357
Swatt Baking Company
Olean, NY 800-370-6656
Three Vee Food & Syrup Company
Brooklyn, NY 800-801-7330
Tiller Foods Company
Dayton, OH. 937-435-4601
Tom & Sally's Handmade Chocolates
Brattleboro, VT. 800-827-0800
Tone Products Company
Melrose Park, IL 708-681-3660
Top Hat Company
Wilmette, IL 847-256-6565
Tres Classique
Ukiah, CA. 888-644-5127
Tropical
Marietta, GA 800-544-3762
Valley Grain Products
Madera, CA. 559-675-3400
Vanlaw Food Products
Fullerton, CA 714-870-9091
Vermont BS
Hinesburg, VT. 802-482-2152
Wax Orchards
Vashon Island, WA 800-634-6132
Western Syrup Company
Santa Fe Springs, CA 562-921-4485
Whipple Company
Natick, MA 800-345-2925
White-Stokes Company
Chicago, IL 800-978-6537
Williamsburg Chocolatier
Williamsburg, VA 804-966-9000

Fruit

E.D. Smith & Sons
Winona, ON 905-643-1211
Nuvex Ingredients
Blue Earth, MN..................... 507-526-4331

Graham

Nuvex Ingredients
Blue Earth, MN..................... 507-526-4331

Granola

Nuvex Ingredients
Blue Earth, MN..................... 507-526-4331

Meringue

Zuccaro's Fruit & Produce Company
Minneapolis, MN 612-333-1122

Non-Fruit

Nuvex Ingredients
Blue Earth, MN 507-526-4331
O Chili Frozen Foods Inc
Northbrook, IL 847-562-1991

Protein Clusters

Nuvex Ingredients
Blue Earth, MN 507-526-4331

Soy Crumbs

Nuvex Ingredients
Blue Earth, MN 507-526-4331

Specialty Bread Crumbs

Nuvex Ingredients
Blue Earth, MN 507-526-4331

Sprinkles

Erba Food Products
Brooklyn, NY 718-272-7700
Nuvex Ingredients
Blue Earth, MN 507-526-4331
QA Products
Elk Grove Vlg, IL 800-635-7907
Randag & Associates Inc
Elmhurst, IL 630-530-2830
Weaver Nut Company
Ephrata, PA 717-738-3781
Xcell International Corporation
Lemont, IL 800-722-7751

Whipped

Broughton Foods
Marietta, OH 800-283-2479
Bunge Canada
Oakville, ON 800-361-3043
C.F. Burger Creamery
Detroit, MI 800-229-2322
CanAmera Foods
Winnipeg, NB 204-324-6481
ConAgra Dairy Foods
Indianapolis, IN 317-329-3700
Fieldbrook Farms
Dunkirk, NY 800-333-0805
Henkel Corporation
Countryside, IL 800-328-6199
Johnson's Food Products
Dorchester, MA 617-265-3400
Kraft Foods
Avon, NY 585-226-4400
Now & Zen
Mill Valley, CA 800-335-1959
Ohio Processors Company
London, OH 740-852-9243
Rich Products of Canada
Fort Erie, ON 800-263-8174
Schneider's Dairy Holdings Inc
Pittsburgh, PA 412-881-3525
Sunshine Farms Dairy
Elyria, OH 440-322-6301
Tiller Foods Company
Dayton, OH 937-435-4601

Dairy

Brighams
Arlington, MA 800-274-4426
C.F. Burger Creamery
Detroit, MI 800-229-2322
Elgin Dairy Foods
Chicago, IL 800-786-9900
Instantwhip: Chicago
Chicago, IL 800-933-2500
Johnson's Food Products
Dorchester, MA 617-265-3400

Non-Dairy

Broughton Foods
Marietta, OH 800-283-2479
ConAgra Grocery Products
Irvine, CA 714-680-1000

Elgin Dairy Foods
Chicago, IL 800-786-9900
Instantwhip: Chicago
Chicago, IL 800-933-2500
Johnson's Food Products
Dorchester, MA 617-265-3400

Vitamins & Supplements

A

Asiamerica Ingredients
Westwood, NJ 201-497-5531

> Processor, importer, exporter and distributor of bulk vitamins, amino acids, nutraceuticals, aromatic chemicals, food additives, herbs, mineral nutrients and pharmaceuticals.

Healthwave
Santa Barbara, CA 805-899-4240
Synergy Plus
Freehold, NJ 732-308-3000

Beta Carotene

Asiamerica Ingredients
Westwood, NJ 201-497-5531

> Processor, importer, exporter and distributor of bulk vitamins, amino acids, nutraceuticals, aromatic chemicals, food additives, herbs, mineral nutrients and pharmaceuticals.

Roche Pharmaceuticals
Nutley, NJ 973-235-5000

Biotin

Asiamerica Ingredients
Westwood, NJ 201-497-5531

> Processor, importer, exporter and distributor of bulk vitamins, amino acids, nutraceuticals, aromatic chemicals, food additives, herbs, mineral nutrients and pharmaceuticals.

Roche Pharmaceuticals
Nutley, NJ 973-235-5000

C

Asiamerica Ingredients
Westwood, NJ 201-497-5531

> Processor, importer, exporter and distributor of bulk vitamins, amino acids, nutraceuticals, aromatic chemicals, food additives, herbs, mineral nutrients and pharmaceuticals.

ChildLife-Nutrition for Kids
Marina Del Rey, CA 800-993-0332
Naturally Vitamin Supplements
Phoenix, AZ 800-899-4499
Vitech America Corporation
Kent, WA 253-859-5985

Ascorbic Acid

World Ginseng Center
San Francisco, CA 800-747-8808

Calcium

Allied Custom Gypsum Company
Norman, OK 800-624-5963
American Micronutrients
Kansas City, MO 816-254-6000

Asiamerica Ingredients
Westwood, NJ 201-497-5531

> Processor, importer, exporter and distributor of bulk vitamins, amino acids, nutraceuticals, aromatic chemicals, food additives, herbs, mineral nutrients and pharmaceuticals.

Specialty Minerals
Bethlehem, PA 800-801-1031

E - Tocopherol

Asiamerica Ingredients
Westwood, NJ 201-497-5531

> Processor, importer, exporter and distributor of bulk vitamins, amino acids, nutraceuticals, aromatic chemicals, food additives, herbs, mineral nutrients and pharmaceuticals.

JR Carlson Laboratories
Arlington Hts, IL 888-234-5656
World Ginseng Center
San Francisco, CA 800-747-8808

Inositol

Asiamerica Ingredients
Westwood, NJ 201-497-5531

Processor, importer, exporter and distributor of
bulk vitamins, amino acids, nutraceuticals, aromatic chemicals, food additives, herbs, mineral
nutrients and pharmaceuticals.

Tabco Enterprises
Pomona, CA 909-623-4565

Medical Nutritionals

Alternative Health & Herbs
Albany, OR 800-345-4152
Apotheca Naturale
Woodbine, IA 800-736-3130

Asiamerica Ingredients
Westwood, NJ 201-497-5531

Processor, importer, exporter and distributor of
bulk vitamins, amino acids, nutraceuticals, aromatic chemicals, food additives, herbs, mineral
nutrients and pharmaceuticals.

Atrium Biotech
Fairfield, NJ 866-628-2355
Champion Nutrition
Sunrise, FL 800-225-4831
Chattem Chemicals
Chattanooga, TN 423-822-5000
Eatem Foods Company
Vineland, NJ 800-683-2836
Green Turtle Bay Vitamin Company
Summit, NJ 800-887-8535
Life-Renewal
Garrison, MN 320-692-4498
Mineral & Pigment Solutions
South Plainfield, NJ 800-732-0562
National Vinegar Company
Houston, TX 713-223-4214
Penta Manufacturing Company
Livingston, NJ 973-740-2300
Ross Laboratories
Sturgis, MI 269-651-0600
Tova Industries
Louisville, KY 888-532-8682
Westar Nutrition Corporation
Costa Mesa, CA 800-645-1868

Mineral Blends

Asiamerica Ingredients
Westwood, NJ 201-497-5531

Processor, importer, exporter and distributor of
bulk vitamins, amino acids, nutraceuticals, aromatic chemicals, food additives, herbs, mineral
nutrients and pharmaceuticals.

M-CAP Technologies
Wilmington, DE 800-641-2001
World Nutrition
Scottsdale, AZ 800-548-2710

Minerals

Acta Health Products
Sunnyvale, CA 408-732-6830
ADH Health Products
Congers, NY 800-292-6002
Advanced Nutritional Research, Inc.
Ellicottville, NY 800-836-0644
Alacer Corporation
Foothill Ranch, CA 800-854-0249
Albion Laboratories
Clearfield, UT 866-243-5283
Alpine Health Products
Orem, UT 800-572-5076
Alta Health Products
Idaho City, ID 800-423-4155
Ameri-Kal Inc
Wichita Falls, TX 940-322-5400
Anabol Naturals
Santa Cruz, CA 800-426-2265

Asiamerica Ingredients
Westwood, NJ 201-497-5531

Processor, importer, exporter and distributor of
bulk vitamins, amino acids, nutraceuticals, aromatic chemicals, food additives, herbs, mineral
nutrients and pharmaceuticals.

Beverly International Nutrition
Cold Spring, KY 800-888-3364
Bio-Tech Pharmacal
Fayetteville, AR 800-345-1199
Body Ammo Research Center
Hayward, CA 800-346-2303
Champion Nutrition
Sunrise, FL 800-225-4831
ChildLife-Nutrition for Kids
Marina Del Rey, CA 800-993-0332
Coating Place
Verona, WI 608-845-9521
Connection Source
Alpharetta, GA 770-667-1051
Designed Nutritional Products
Orem, UT 801-224-4518
Eidon Mineral Supplements
Poway, CA 800-700-1169
Foremost Farms
Baraboo, WI 800-365-9196
Fortitech
Schenectady, NY 800-950-5156
Grow Company
Ridgefield, NJ 201-941-8777
Healthy'N Fit Nutrition als
Croton on Hudson, NY 800-338-5200
Herbal Products & Development
Aptos, CA 831-688-4200
Jamieson Laboratories
Toronto, QC 519-974-8482
JR Carlson Laboratories
Arlington Hts, IL 888-234-5656
Jungbunzlauer
Newton, MA 800-828-0062
JWS Delavau Company
Philadelphia, PA 215-671-1400
Michael's Naturopathic
San Antonio, TX 800-525-9643
Milwhite
Brownsville, TX 956-547-1970
Mineral & Pigment Solutions
South Plainfield, NJ 800-732-0562
Naturally Vitamin Supplements
Phoenix, AZ 800-899-4499
Nature's Sunshine Products Company
Provo, UT 800-223-8225
NatureMost Laboratories
Middletown, CT 800-234-2112
NBTY
Ronkonkoma, NY 800-920-6090
Now Foods
Bloomingdale, IL 888-669-3663
Nutricepts
Burnsville, MN 800-949-9060
Nutritech Corporation
Santa Barbara, CA 800-235-5727
Nutrition 21
Purchase, NY 914-696-0505

P.L. Thomas
Morristown, NJ 973-984-0900
Paragon Laboratories
Torrance, CA 310-370-1563
Particle Dynamics
St Louis, MO 800-452-4682
Performance Labs
Calabasas, CA 800-848-2537
PMP Fermentation Products
Peoria, IL 800-558-1031
Pro Pac Labs
Ogden, UT 888-277-6722
Protein Research Associates
Livermore, CA 800-948-1991
Randal Nutritional Products
Santa Rosa, CA 800-221-1697
Seppic
Newark, NJ 877-737-7421
Universal Formulas
Portage, MI 800-342-6960
US Food & Pharmaceuticals
Madison, WI 608-278-1293
USA Laboratories
Burns, TN 800-489-4872
Vitamin Power
Freeport, NY 800-645-6567
Watson Foods Company
West Haven, CT 800-388-3481

Niacin

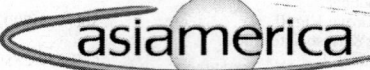

Asiamerica Ingredients
Westwood, NJ 201-497-5531

Processor, importer, exporter and distributor of
bulk vitamins, amino acids, nutraceuticals, aromatic chemicals, food additives, herbs, mineral
nutrients and pharmaceuticals.

EMD Chemicals
Gibbstown, NJ 800-364-4535
NuNaturals
Eugene, OR 800-753-4372
Roche Pharmaceuticals
Nutley, NJ 973-235-5000

Nutraceuticals

A.M. Todd Company
Kalamazoo, MI 800-968-2603
ADM Food Ingredients
Olathe, KS 800-255-6637
ADM Nutraceuticals
Decatur, IL 800-510-2178
Amcan Industries
Elmsford, NY 914-347-4838
American Supplement Technologies
Phoenix, AZ 888-469-0242
AquaTec Development
Sugar Land, TX 281-242-7771

Asiamerica Ingredients
Westwood, NJ 201-497-5531

Processor, importer, exporter and distributor of
bulk vitamins, amino acids, nutraceuticals, aromatic chemicals, food additives, herbs, mineral
nutrients and pharmaceuticals.

Assets Health Foods
Hillsborough, NJ 888-849-2048
Atlantic Quality Spice & Seasonings
Edison, NJ 800-584-0422
BASF Corporation
Florham Park, NJ 800-526-1072
Basic American Foods
Blackfoot, ID 800-227-4050
Bio-Foods
Pine Brook, NJ 973-808-5856
Bio-Tech Pharmacal
Fayetteville, AR 800-345-1199

BioTech Corporation
  Glastonbury, CT 800-880-7188
Century Foods International
  Sparta, WI 800-269-1901
Cyanotech Corporation
  Kailua Kona, HI 800-395-1353
Farbest-Tallman Foods Corporation
  Montvale, NJ 201-573-4900
Genesis Research Corporation
  Lake Bluff, IL 888-225-2201
Innovative Food Solutions LLC
  Columbus, OH 800-884-3314
Institut Rosell/Lallemand
  Montreal, QC 514-858-4627
Jarrow Industries
  Santa Fe Springs, CA 562-906-1919
Juice Guys
  Cambridge, MA 508-228-4464
Master Taste International
  Plant City, FL 800-237-7629
Mineral & Pigment Solutions
  South Plainfield, NJ 800-732-0562
Natra US
  Chula Vista, CA 800-262-6216
Naturex (Chart Corp)
  South Hackensack, NJ 201-440-5000
Nutraceutics Corporation
  Saint Louis, MO 877-664-6684
Nutranique Labs
  Santa Rosa, CA 707-545-9017
Nuvex Ingredients
  Blue Earth, MN 507-526-4331
P.L. Thomas
  Morristown, NJ 973-984-0900
Pure World Botanicals
  South Hackensack, NJ 201-440-5000
QBI
  South Plainfield, NJ 908-668-0088
Soluble Products Company
  Lakewood, NJ 732-364-8855
SoyLife Division
  Edina, MN 952-920-7700
Trans-Packers Services Corporation
  Brooklyn, NY 877-787-8837
Unique Ingredients
  Naches, WA 509-653-1991
Vitarich Laboratories
  Naples, FL 800-817-9999
Vivolac Cultures Corporation
  Indianapolis, IN 317-356-8460
Westar Nutrition Corporation
  Costa Mesa, CA 800-645-1868

Nutritional Supplements

ADH Health Products
  Congers, NY 800-292-6002
Alfer Laboratories
  Chatsworth, CA 818-709-0737
Alpine Health Products
  Orem, UT 800-572-5076
Alta Health Products
  Boise, ID 800-423-4155
Ameri-Kal Inc
  Wichita Falls, TX 940-322-5400
American Health
  Ronkonkoma, NY 800-445-7137
American Supplement Technologies
  Phoenix, AZ 888-469-0242
Amerilift Brands, Inc.
  Cromwell, CT 800-722-3476
Amrion
  Boulder, CO 800-627-7775
Anabol Naturals
  Santa Cruz, CA 800-426-2265
Arizona Natural Products
  Phoenix, AZ 602-997-6098
Arizona Nutritional Supplements
  Chandler, AZ 888-742-7675

asiamerica

Asiamerica Ingredients
  Westwood, NJ 201-497-5531

Processor, importer, exporter and distributor of
bulk vitamins, amino acids, nutraceuticals, aromatic chemicals, food additives, herbs, mineral
nutrients and pharmaceuticals.

Atrium Biotech
  Fairfield, NJ 866-628-2355
Belmont Chemicals
  Clifton, NJ 800-722-5070
Bio-Foods
  Pine Brook, NJ 973-808-5856
BioSynergy
  Boise, ID 800-554-7145
Body Ammo Research Center
  Hayward, CA 800-346-2303
Botanical Laboratories
  Ferndale, WA 800-232-4005
Bricker Labs
  Jackson, WI. 800-274-2537
Bristol Myers-Squibb Company
  New York, NY 212-546-4000
Broadmoor Labs
  Ventura, CA. 800-822-3712
Century Foods International
  Sparta, WI. 800-269-1901
Champion Nutrition
  Sunrise, FL 800-225-4831
CHR Hansen
  Stoughton, WI 608-877-8970
Cognis
  Cincinnati, OH 513-482-2100
Cyanotech Corporation
  Kailua Kona, HI 800-395-1353
Dean Distributors
  Burlingame, CA 800-227-3112
Dean Distributors
  Burlingame, CA 800-792-0816
Dr. Christopher's Original Foods
  Springville, UT 800-453-1406
Eclipse Sports Supplements
  Scranton, PA 800-320-0062
Eco Foods
  St Charles, IL 866-326-1646
Elan Nutrition
  Grand Rapids, MI 616-940-6000
Esteem Products
  Bellevue, WA 800-255-7631
Food Sciences Corporation
  Mt Laurel, NJ 800-320-7928
FoodScience of Vermont
  Essex Junction, VT 800-874-9444
Gehl Guernsey Farms
  Germantown, WI. 800-434-5713
Gulf Performance Group
  Mandeville, LA 800-562-7514
Herbal Products & Development
  Aptos, CA 831-688-4200
Impact Nutrition
  Aurora, CO 720-374-7111
Integrated Therapeutics
  Lake Oswego, OR. 800-648-4755
JSL Foods
  Los Angeles, CA. 800-745-3236
Klaire Laboratories
  Reno, NV 888-488-2488
Lewis Laboratories International
  Westport, CT 800-243-6020
Lifestar Millennium
  Novato, CA 800-858-7477
Maitake Products
  East Rutherford, NJ 800-747-7418
Matrix Health Products
  Santee, CA 888-736-5609
Mead Johnson Nutrition
  Evansville, IN 812-429-5000
Mega Pro International
  St George, UT 800-541-9469
MLO/GeniSoy Products Company
  Tulas, OK 866-606-3829
Natural Balance
  Englewood, CO. 800-624-4260
Naturally Scientific
  Leonia, NJ 888-428-0700
Nature's Best Food Supplement
  Hauppauge, NY 800-345-2378
Nature's Nutrition
  Melbourne, FL 800-242-1115
ND Labs Inc
  Lynbrook, NY 888-263-5227
Nestle USA Inc
  Glendale, CA 800-633-2330
New Horizon Foods
  Union City, CA 510-489-8600
Nurture
  Devon, PA 888-395-3300
Nutraceutical Corporation
  Park City, UT 800-669-8877

Nutri-West
  Douglas, WY. 800-443-3333
Nutritional Laboratories International
  Missoula, MT 406-273-5493
Nutritional Life Support Systems
  San Diego, CA 619-294-3954
Nutritional Specialties
  Orange, CA 800-333-6168
Nutritional Supply Corporation
  Carson City, NV 888-541-3997
O'Donnell Formula
  San Marcos, CA 800-736-1991
Odwalla
  Half Moon Bay, CA 800-639-2552
Orange Peel Enterprises
  Vero Beach, FL. 800-643-1210
P-Bee Products
  Laguna Hills, CA 800-322-5572
Pacific Nutritional
  Vancouver, WA 360-253-3197
Pacific Standard Distributors
  Sandy, OR 503-668-0057
Paragon Laboratories
  Torrance, CA 310-370-1563
Performance Labs
  Calabasas, CA. 800-848-2537
Phoenician Herbals
  Scottsdale, AZ. 800-966-8144
Phyto-Technologies
  Woodbine, IA 877-809-3404
Pioneer Nutritional Formulas
  Shelburne Falls, MA. 800-458-8483
Premier Nutrition
  Carlsbad, CA. 888-836-8972
Prosource
  Alexandria, MN 320-763-2470
Protein Research Associates
  Livermore, CA 800-948-1991
Quaker Oats Company
  Chicago, IL 800-367-6287
Randal Nutritional Products
  Santa Rosa, CA. 800-221-1697
Royal Body Care
  Irving, TX 972-893-4000
Royal Products
  Scottsdale, AZ 480-948-2509
Shaklee Corporation
  Pleasanton, CA 800-742-5533
Soft Gel Technologies
  Commerce, CA 800-360-7484
Solgar Vitamin & Herb
  Leonia, NJ 201-944-2311
Source Food Technology
  Burnsville, MN 612-890-6366
SportPharma USA
  Concord, CA 925-686-1451
St. John's Botanicals
  Bowie, MD 301-262-5302
Tabco Enterprises
  Pomona, CA 909-623-4565
Twinlab
  New York, NY 800-645-5626
UAS Laboratories
  Eden Prairie, MN 800-422-3371
Unipro/Ethical Nutrients
  San Clemente, CA 800-621-6070
USA Laboratories
  Burns, TN 800-489-4872
Valley Research
  South Bend, IN 800-522-8110
Vita-Pure
  Roselle, NJ 908-245-1212
Vitatech International
  Tustin, CA. 714-832-9700
Vitech America Corporation
  Kent, WA. 253-859-5985
Wakunaga of America
  Mission Viejo, CA 800-421-2998
WCC Honey Marketing
  City of Industry, CA 626-855-3086
Wilke International
  Shawnee Mission, KS. 800-779-5545
World Ginseng Center
  San Francisco, CA 800-747-8808
Zone Perfect Nutrition Company
  Columbus, OH 800-390-6690

Pantothenic Acid

Asiamerica Ingredients
Westwood, NJ.....................201-497-5531

> Processor, importer, exporter and distributor of
> bulk vitamins, amino acids, nutraceuticals, aro-
> matic chemicals, food additives, herbs, mineral
> nutrients and pharmaceuticals.

Roche Pharmaceuticals
Nutley, NJ.........................973-235-5000

Protein Supplements

Alkinco
New York, NY.....................800-424-7118

Asiamerica Ingredients
Westwood, NJ.....................201-497-5531

> Processor, importer, exporter and distributor of
> bulk vitamins, amino acids, nutraceuticals, aro-
> matic chemicals, food additives, herbs, mineral
> nutrients and pharmaceuticals.

Belmont Chemicals
Clifton, NJ........................800-722-5070
Bio-Foods
Pine Brook, NJ....................973-808-5856
Croda, Inc.
Edison, NJ........................732-417-0800
Energenetics International
Keokuk, IA........................217-453-2340
Flavex Protein Ingredients
Cranford, NJ......................800-851-1052
Impact Nutrition
Aurora, CO........................720-374-7111
Innovative Health Products
Largo, FL.........................800-654-2347
Mariner Neptune Fish & Seafood Company
Winnipeg, NB......................800-668-8862
World Ginseng Center
San Francisco, CA.................800-747-8808

Fortification Protein

Cargill Texturizing Solutions
Cedar Rapids, IA..................877-650-7080

Supplements

Acta Health Products
Sunnyvale, CA.....................408-732-6830
Action Labs
Park City, UT.....................800-669-8877
ADH Health Products
Congers, NY.......................800-292-6002
Advanced Nutritional Research, Inc.
Ellicottville, NY.................800-836-0644
Agger Fish
Brooklyn, NY......................718-855-1717
Albion Laboratories
Clearfield, UT....................866-243-5283
Alfer Laboratories
Chatsworth, CA....................818-709-0737
Alkinco
New York, NY......................800-424-7118
Aloe Farms
Harlingen, TX.....................800-262-6771
AMT Labs
North Salt Lake, UT...............801-299-1661
Anabol Naturals
Santa Cruz, CA....................800-426-2265
Archon Vitamin Corporation
Irvington, NJ.....................800-349-1700
Arizona Natural Products
Phoenix, AZ.......................602-997-6098

Asiamerica Ingredients
Westwood, NJ.....................201-497-5531

> Processor, importer, exporter and distributor of
> bulk vitamins, amino acids, nutraceuticals, aro-
> matic chemicals, food additives, herbs, mineral
> nutrients and pharmaceuticals.

Atlantic Laboratories
Waldoboro, ME.....................207-832-5376
Atrium Biotech
Fairfield, NJ.....................866-628-2355
Beehive Botanicals, Inc.
Hayward, WI.......................800-233-4483
Belmont Chemicals
Clifton, NJ.......................800-722-5070
BestSweet
Mooresville, NC...................888-211-5530
Bio San Laboratories/MegaFood
Derry, NH.........................800-848-5022
Body Ammo Research Center
Hayward, CA.......................800-346-2303
Brassica Protection Products
Baltimore, MD.....................877-747-1277
Cactu Life Inc
Corona Del Mar, CA................800-500-1713
Century Foods International
Sparta, WI........................800-269-1901
Champion Nutrition
Sunrise, FL.......................800-225-4831
CVC Specialties
Vernon, CA........................800-421-6175
Dean Distributors
Burlingame, CA....................800-227-3112
Dean Distributors
Burlingame, CA....................800-792-0816
Doctor's Best
San Clemente, CA..................800-333-6977
Eckhart Corporation
Novato, CA........................800-200-4201
En Garde Health Products
Van Nuys, CA......................818-901-8505
Food Reserves
Concordia, MO.....................800-944-1511
Gadot Biochemical Industries
Rolling Meadows, IL...............888-424-1424
GCI Nutrients (USA)
Foster City, CA...................650-697-4700
Global Health Laboratories
Melville, NY......................631-293-0030
Herb Connection
Springville, UT...................801-489-4254
Herbal Products & Development
Aptos, CA.........................831-688-4200
Heritage Store
Virginia Beach, VA................757-428-0110
Hillestad Pharmaceuticals
Woodruff, WI......................800-535-7742
Innovative Health Products
Largo, FL.........................800-654-2347
IVC American Vitamin
Freehold, NJ......................800-666-8482
Jo Mar Laboratories
Campbell, CA......................800-538-4545
JR Carlson Laboratories
Arlington Hts, IL.................888-234-5656
JWS Delavau Company
Philadelphia, PA..................215-671-1400
Labrada Nutrition
Houston, TX.......................281-209-2137
Laci Le Beau Corporation
Fresno, CA........................800-356-0490
National Enzyme Company
Forsyth, MO.......................800-825-8545
Natural Balance
Englewood, CO.....................800-624-4260
Nature's Herbs
American Fork, UT.................800-437-2257
Nature's Plus
Long Beach, CA....................800-525-0200
Nature's Provision Company
Olivebridge, NY...................845-657-6020
NBTY
Ronkonkoma, NY....................800-920-6090
Nutricepts
Burnsville, MN....................800-949-9060
Nutritional Counselors of America
Spencer, TN.......................931-946-3600

Nutriwest
Douglas, WY.......................800-443-3333
O'Donnell Formula
San Marcos, CA....................800-736-1991
Old Fashioned Natural Products
Santa Ana, CA.....................800-552-9045
Pharmavite Corporation
Mission Hills, CA.................800-276-2878
Pro Form Labs
Orinda, CA........................925-299-9000
Protein Research Associates
Livermore, CA.....................800-948-1991
Randal Nutritional Products
Santa Rosa, CA....................800-221-1697
Royal Body Care
Irving, TX........................972-893-4000
Source Naturals
Scotts Valley, CA.................800-815-2333
Sweet Productions
Jericho, NY.......................631-842-0548
Tova Industries
Louisville, KY....................888-532-8682
Twinlab
New York, NY......................800-645-5626
Vita-Pure
Roselle, NJ.......................908-245-1212
Vital Products
Blackwood, NJ.....................856-228-1150
Vitamer Laboratories
Irvine, CA........................800-432-8355
Vitaminerals
Glendale, CA......................818-500-8718
VitaTech International
Tustin, CA........................714-832-9700
Wakunaga of America
Mission Viejo, CA.................800-421-2998
Wilke International
Shawnee Mission, KS...............800-779-5545
World Organics Corporation
Huntington Beach, CA..............714-893-0017

Minerals

Action Labs
Park City, UT.....................800-669-8877
Advanced Nutritional Research, Inc.
Ellicottville, NY.................800-836-0644
Albion Laboratories
Clearfield, UT....................866-243-5283
AMT Labs
North Salt Lake, UT...............801-299-1661

Asiamerica Ingredients
Westwood, NJ.....................201-497-5531

> Processor, importer, exporter and distributor of
> bulk vitamins, amino acids, nutraceuticals, aro-
> matic chemicals, food additives, herbs, mineral
> nutrients and pharmaceuticals.

Baywood International
Scottsdale, AZ....................800-481-7169
Integrated Health
Torrance, CA......................800-799-3232
Jamieson Laboratories
Toronto, QC.......................519-974-8482
Matrix Health Products
Santee, CA........................888-736-5609
Nutricepts
Burnsville, MN....................800-949-9060
Protein Research Associates
Livermore, CA.....................800-948-1991
Randal Nutritional Products
Santa Rosa, CA....................800-221-1697
Watson Foods Company
West Haven, CT....................800-388-3481
York Barbell Company
York, PA..........................800-358-9675

Vitamins

Advanced Nutritional Research, Inc.
Ellicottville, NY.................800-836-0644
AHD International, LLC
Atlanta, GA.......................404-233-4022

Asiamerica Ingredients
Westwood, NJ 201-497-5531

Processor, importer, exporter and distributor of
bulk vitamins, amino acids, nutraceuticals, aromatic chemicals, food additives, herbs, mineral
nutrients and pharmaceuticals.

Bio San Laboratories/MegaFood
    Derry, NH 800-848-5022
CVC Specialties
    Vernon, CA 800-421-6175
FoodScience of Vermont
    Essex Junction, VT 800-874-9444
Freeda Vitamins
    Long Island City, NY 800-777-3737
Garcoa
    Calabasas, CA 800-831-4247
Good 'N Natural
    Ronkonkoma, NY 800-544-0095
Healthy'N Fit Nutrition als
    Croton on Hudson, NY 800-338-5200
IVC American Vitamin
    Freehold, NJ 800-666-8482
Jamieson Laboratories
    Toronto, QC 519-974-8482
Nutribiotic
    Lakeport, CA 800-225-4345
Nutrilabs
    San Francisco, CA 800-658-5343
Nutritional International Enterprises Company
    Irvine, CA 949-854-4855
Optimum Nutrition
    Walterboro, SC 800-763-3444
Protein Research Associates
    Livermore, CA 800-948-1991
Randal Nutritional Products
    Santa Rosa, CA 800-221-1697
Sandco International
    Northport, AL 800-382-2075
Scandinavian Formulas Inc
    Sellersville, PA 800-288-2844
Solgar Vitamin & Herb
    Leonia, NJ .201-944-2311
Tree of Life
    St Augustine, FL 904-940-2100
Twinlab
    New York, NY 800-645-5626
Vital Products
    Blackwood, NJ 856-228-1150
Vitatech International
    Tustin, CA .714-832-9700
Watson Foods Company
    West Haven, CT 800-388-3481
Wilke International
    Shawnee Mission, KS 800-779-5545

Vitamins

21st Century Products
    Ft. Worth, TX 817-282-8000
Abunda Life Laboratories
    Asbury Park, NJ 732-775-4141
Acatris
    Edina, MN .952-835-9590
Accucaps Industries Limited
    Windsor, ON 800-665-7210
Acta Health Products
    Sunnyvale, CA 408-732-6830
Action Labs
    Placentia, CA 800-400-5696
Action Labs
    Park City, UT 800-669-8877
ADH Health Products
    Congers, NY 800-292-6002
Advanced Nutritional Research, Inc.
    Ellicottville, NY 800-836-0644
Agumm
    Coral Springs, FL 954-344-0607
AHD International, LLC
    Atlanta, GA 404-233-4022
Alacer Corporation
    Foothill Ranch, CA 800-854-0249
Albion Laboratories
    Clearfield, UT 866-243-5283
Alfer Laboratories
    Chatsworth, CA 818-709-0737

Alpine Health Products
    Orem, UT .800-572-5076
Alternative Health & Herbs
    Albany, OR 800-345-4152
Ameri-Kal Inc
    Wichita Falls, TX 940-322-5400
American Biosciences
    Blauvelt, NY 845-727-0800
Amerilab Technologies
    Plymouth, MN 800-445-6468
Amerilift Brands, Inc.
    Cromwell, CT 800-722-3476
Anabol Naturals
    Santa Cruz, CA 800-426-2265
Anmar Nutrition
    Bridgeport, CT 203-336-8330
Anti-Aging ASAP
    Santa Monica, CA 888-334-2000
Apotheca Naturale
    Woodbine, IA 800-736-3130
Apple Valley Market
    Berrien Springs, MI 800-237-7436
Archon Vitamin Corporation
    Irvington, NJ 800-349-1700
Argee Corporation
    Santee, CA 800-449-3030

Asiamerica Ingredients
Westwood, NJ 201-497-5531

Processor, importer, exporter and distributor of
bulk vitamins, amino acids, nutraceuticals, aromatic chemicals, food additives, herbs, mineral
nutrients and pharmaceuticals.

At Last Naturals
    Valhalla, NY 800-527-8123
Atkins Nutritionals
    Melville, NY 800-628-5467
Banner Pharmacaps
    High Point, NC 336-812-3442
BASF Corporation
    Florham Park, NJ 800-526-1072
Baywood International
    Scottsdale, AZ 800-481-7169
Belmont Chemicals
    Clifton, NJ 800-722-5070
Beverly International Nutrition
    Cold Spring, KY 800-888-3364
Bio San Laboratories/MegaFood
    Derry, NH 800-848-5022
Bio-Tech Pharmacal
    Fayetteville, AR 800-345-1199
Bioforce USA
    Ghent, NY 800-641-7555
Botanical Products
    Springville, CA 559-539-3432
Capsule Works
    Bayport, NY 800-920-6090
Carlson Vitamins
    Arlington Hts, IL 888-234-5656
Carob Tree
    Arcadia, CA 626-445-0215
Champion Nutrition
    Sunrise, FL 800-225-4831
ChildLife-Nutrition for Kids
    Marina Del Rey, CA 800-993-0332
China Pharmaceutical Enterprises
    Baton Rouge, LA 800-345-1658
Coating Place
    Verona, WI 608-845-9521
Connection Source
    Alpharetta, GA 770-667-1051
Continental Vitamin Company
    Vernon, CA 800-421-6175
Country Life
    Hauppauge, NY 800-645-5768
CVC Specialties
    Vernon, CA 800-421-6175
Cyanotech Corporation
    Kailua Kona, HI 800-395-1353
Cytodyne Technologies
    Lakewood, NJ 732-942-0393
DDC
    San Clemente, CA 949-498-0030
Dean Distributors
    Burlingame, CA 800-792-0816

DeSouza International
    Beaumont, CA 800-373-5171
DMH Ingredients
    Libertyville, IL 847-362-9977
DynaPro International
    Ogden, UT 800-877-1413
Earth Science
    Corona, CA 909-371-7565
Eastman Chemical Company
    Kingsport, TN 800-327-8626
Eckhart Corporation
    Novato, CA 800-200-4201
Eclectic Institute
    Sandy, OR 503-668-4120
Edge Labs
    Trenton, NJ 866-334-3522
Edom Laboratories
    Deer Park, NY 800-723-3366
EMD Chemicals
    Gibbstown, NJ 800-364-4535
Energen Products
    Norwalk, CA 800-423-8837
Enzymatic Therapy
    Green Bay, WI 800-783-2286
ERBL
    Carlsbad, CA 800-275-3725
Esteem Products
    Bellevue, WA 800-255-7631
Europa Sports Products
    Charlotte, NC 800-447-4795
Farbest-Tallman Foods Corporation
    Montvale, NJ 201-573-4900
Figuerola Laboratories
    Santa Ynez, CA 800-219-1147
Fortitech
    Schenectady, NY 800-950-5156
Fortress Systems LLC
    Omaha, NE 888-331-6601
Freeda Vitamins
    Long Island City, NY 800-777-3737
Freeman Industries
    Tuckahoe, NY 800-666-6454
Functional Products LLC
    Atlantic Beach, FL 800-628-5908
Futurebiotics
    Hauppauge, NY 800-645-1721
Garcoa
    Calabasas, CA 800-831-4247
GCI Nutrients (USA)
    Foster City, CA 650-697-4700
Geon Technologies
    Whippany, NJ 800-467-3041
GINCO International
    Simi Valley, CA 800-284-2598
Givaudan Flavors
    Bridgeton, MO 800-422-5444
Global Nutrition Research Corporation
    Tempe, AZ 602-454-2248
GMP Laboratories
    Anaheim, CA 714-630-2467
Good 'N Natural
    Ronkonkoma, NY 800-544-0095
Graminex
    Saginaw, MI 877-472-6469
Green Foods Corporation
    Oxnard, CA 800-777-4430
Green Turtle Bay Vitamin Company
    Summit, NJ 800-887-8535
Greens Today®
    Plainview, NY 800-473-3641
Grow Company
    Ridgefield, NJ 201-941-8777
H. Reisman Corporation
    Orange, NJ 973-882-1670
Hair Fitness
    Long Beach, CA 888-348-4247
Health Products Corporation
    Yonkers, NY 914-423-2900
Healthy'N Fit Nutrition als
    Croton on Hudson, NY 800-338-5200
Helmuth Country Bakery
    Hutchinson, KS 800-567-6360
Herbal Products & Development
    Aptos, CA 831-688-4200
Heritage Store
    Virginia Beach, VA 757-428-0110
Heterochemical Corporation
    Valley Stream, NY 516-561-8225
Highland Laboratories
    Mt Angel, OR 888-717-4917
Hillestad Pharmaceuticals
    Woodruff, WI 800-535-7742

Hormel Health Labs
Austin, MN 800-866-7757
Hosemen & Roche Vitamins & Fine Chemicals
Nutley, NJ 800-526-6367
Indiana Botanic Gardens
Hobart, IN 219-947-4040
Innovative Health Products
Largo, FL 800-654-2347
Integrated Health
Torrance, CA 800-799-3232
Interhealth Nutraceuticals
Benicia, CA 800-783-4636
IVC American Vitamin
Freehold, NJ 800-666-8482
Jamieson Laboratories
Toronto, QC 519-974-8482
Jarrow Industries
Santa Fe Springs, CA 562-906-1919
JR Carlson Laboratories
Arlington Hts, IL 888-234-5656
K&K Laboratories
Carlsbad, CA. 760-434-6044
Kabco
Amityville, NY 631-842-3600
Kemin Health
Des Moines, IA.....................888-248-5040
Kid Care
Carpinteria, CA 805-566-2473
Leiner Health Products
Carson, CA 310-513-2116
Liberty Natural Products
Portland, OR 800-289-8427
Licata Enterprises/World Organics
Huntington Beach, CA 714-893-0017
Life-Renewal
Garrison, MN 320-692-4498
Luyties Pharmacal Company
Saint Louis, MO 800-325-8080
Madys Company
San Francisco, CA 415-822-2227
Mead Johnson Nutrition
Evansville, IN 812-429-5000
Mega Pro International
St George, UT.......................800-541-9469
Metabolic Nutrition
Tamarac, FL 800-541-2980
Michael's Naturopathic
San Antonio, TX 800-525-9643
Mineral & Pigment Solutions
South Plainfield, NJ 800-732-0562
Mission Pharmacal Company
San Antonio, TX 800-292-7364
Motherland International Inc
Rancho Cucamonga, CA 800-590-5407
National Enzyme Company
Forsyth, MO 800-825-8545
Natural Food Supplements
Canoga Park, CA 818-341-3375
Naturally Vitamin Supplements
Phoenix, AZ 800-899-4499
Nature's Bounty
Ronkonkoma, NY 800-433-2990
Nature's Sunshine Products Company
Provo, UT 800-223-8225
Nature's Way
Springville, UT 800-962-8873
NatureMost Laboratories
Middletown, CT 800-234-2112
Naturex
South Hackensack, NJ 201-440-5000
NBTY
Ronkonkoma, NY 800-920-6090
New Chapter
Brattleboro, VT.....................800-543-7279
Northridge Laboratories
Chatsworth, CA 818-882-5622
NOW Foods
Bloomingdale, IL 888-669-3663
Now Foods
Bloomingdale, IL 888-669-3663
NuNaturals
Eugene, OR 800-753-4372
Nutraceutical Solutions
Corpus Christi, TX 800-338-4788
Nutraceutics Corporation
Saint Louis, MO 877-664-6684
Nutri-Cell
Orange, CA..........................714-953-8307
Nutribiotic
Lakeport, CA 800-225-4345
Nutrilabs
San Francisco, CA 800-658-5343

Nutritech Corporation
Santa Barbara, CA 800-235-5727
Nutritional Counselors of America
Spencer, TN 931-946-3600
Nutritional Research Associates
South Whitley, IN 800-456-4931
Nutro Laboratories
South Plainfield, NJ 800-446-8876
O C Lugo Company
Nyack, NY 845-708-7080
O'Donnell Formula
San Marcos, CA 800-736-1991
Old Fashioned Natural Products
Santa Ana, CA 800-552-9045
Optimal Nutrients
Foster City, CA 707-528-1800
Ortho Molecular Products
Stevens Point, WI 800-332-2351
P.J. Noyes Company
Lancaster, NH 800-522-2469
Pacific Nutritional
Vancouver, WA 360-253-3197
Pak Technologies
Milwaukee, WI 414-438-8600
Paragon Laboratories
Torrance, CA 310-370-1563
Parish Chemical Company
Orem, UT 801-226-2018
Particle Dynamics
St Louis, MO 800-452-4682
Pharmachem Laboratories
Hackensack, NJ 201-343-3611
Phoenix Laboratories
Farmingdale, NY 800-236-6583
Pro Pac Labs
Ogden, UT. 888-277-6722
Pro-Pharm
Lake Bluff, IL 847-234-3570
Proper-Chem
Dix Hills, NY 631-420-8000
Protein Research Associates
Livermore, CA 800-948-1991
Pure Source
Doral, FL 800-324-6273
Randal Nutritional Products
Santa Rosa, CA......................800-221-1697
Raway Pharmacal
Accord, NY 914-626-8133
Roche Pharmaceuticals
Nutley, NJ 973-235-5000
Ross Laboratories
Columbus, OH 614-564-0019
Sadkhin Complex
Brooklyn, NY 800-723-5446
Sandco International
Northport, AL 800-382-2075
Scandinavian Formulas Inc
Sellersville, PA 800-288-2844
Select Supplements, Inc
Carlsbad, CA. 760-431-7509
Solgar Vitamin & Herb
Leonia, NJ 201-944-2311
Source Naturals
Scotts Valley, CA 800-815-2333
Sportabs International
Los Angeles, CA. 888-814-7767
St. Charles Trading
Lake Saint Louis, MO. 800-336-1333
Super Nutrition Life Extension
Fort Lauderdale, FL 800-678-8989
Tabco Enterprises
Pomona, CA 909-623-4565
Terra Botanica Products
Nakusp, BC..........................888-410-9977
Texas Coffee Company
Beaumont, TX. 800-259-3400
Thor Incorporated
Ogden, UT...........................888-846-7462
Twinlab
New York, NY 800-645-5626
Unipro/Ethical Nutrients
San Clemente, CA. 800-621-6070
Unique Vitality Products
Agoura Hills, CA 818-889-7739
Universal Laboratories
New Brunswick, NJ 800-872-0101
USA Laboratories
Burns, TN 800-489-4872
Vita-Pure
Roselle, NJ 908-245-1212
Vital Products
Blackwood, NJ 856-228-1150

Vitamer Laboratories
Irvine, CA 800-432-8355
Vitamin Power
Freeport, NY 800-645-6567
Vitaminerals
Glendale, CA 818-500-8718
Vitamins
Chicago, IL 312-861-0700
Vitarich Laboratories
Naples, FL 800-817-9999
Vivion
San Carlos, CA 800-479-0997
Wakunaga of America
Mission Viejo, CA 800-421-2998
Watson Foods Company
West Haven, CT 800-388-3481
Westar Nutrition Corporation
Costa Mesa, CA 800-645-1868
Whole Life Nutritional Supplements
North Hollywood, CA 800-748-5841
Wilke International
Shawnee Mission, KS 800-779-5545
World Ginseng Center
San Francisco, CA 800-747-8808
World Nutrition
Scottsdale, AZ......................800-548-2710
World Organics Corporation
Huntington Beach, CA 714-893-0017
World Softgel
Compton, CA 310-900-1199
Wright Enrichment
Crowley, LA 800-201-3096
Wright Group
Crowley, LA 800-201-3096
Wysong Corporation
Midland, MI 800-748-0188

Zinc Citrate

Gadot Biochemical Industries
Rolling Meadows, IL 888-424-1424

Waxes

Lanaetex Products Incorporated
Elizabeth, NJ 908-351-9700

Paraffin

Stevenson-Cooper
Philadelphia, PA 215-223-2600

Jams, Jellies & Spreads

Jams

A Taste of the Kingdom
Kingdom City, MO 888-592-5080
Alaska Herb Tea Company
Anchorage, AK 800-654-2764
Algood Food Company
Louisville, KY 502-637-3631
Ambassador Foods
Van Nuys, CA 800-338-3369
Amberland Foods
Harvey, ND 800-950-4558
Atlas Preserves Company
New York, NY 212-569-5613
Au Printemps Gourmet
Prevost, QC 800-663-0416
Bakemark Ingredients Canada
Richmond, BC 800-665-9441
Bear Meadow Farm
Colrain, MA 800-653-9241
Bella Vista Farm
Lawton, OK 866-237-8526
Benbow's Coffee Roasters
Bar Harbor, ME 207-288-5271
Brad's Organic
Haverstraw, NY 845-429-9080
Bread & Chocolate
Wells River, VT 800-524-6715
Buckhead Gourmet
Atlanta, GA 800-605-5754
Buon Italia
New York, NY 212-633-9090
California Custom Fruits & Flavors
Irwindale, CA 877-558-0056
California Style Gourmet Products
San Diego, CA 800-243-5226
Carol Hall's Hot Pepper Jelly
Fort Bragg, CA 866-737-7379
Chelsea Market Baskets
New York, NY 888-727-7887
Choice of Vermont
Destin, FL 800-444-6261
Clements Foods Company
Oklahoma City, OK 800-654-8355
Coco Lopez
Miramar, FL 800-341-2242
Colorado Mountain Jams & Jellies
Palisade, CO 970-464-0745
Cotswold Cottage Foods
Arvada, CO 800-208-1977
Daregal Gourmet
Princeton, NJ 609-375-2312
Dark Tickle Company
Griquet, NL 709-623-2354
Delicae Gourmet
Tarpon Springs, FL 800-942-2502
E.D. Smith & Sons
Winona, ON 905-643-1211
Earth & Vine Provisions
Lincoln, CA 888-723-8463
Erba Food Products
Brooklyn, NY 718-272-7700
Fruit Fillings
Fresno, CA 559-237-4715
GEM Berry Products
Sandpoint, ID 800-426-0498
Granny Annie Jams
South Londonderry, VT 802-824-6625
Griffin Food Company
Muskogee, OK 800-580-6311
Herb Bee's Products
Colchester, VT 802-864-7387
Hilltop Herb Farm & Restaurant
Cleveland, TX 832-397-4020
J.M. Smucker Company
Orrville, OH 330-682-3000
Jim's Cheese Pantry
Waterloo, WI 800-345-3571
Kitchen Kettle Foods
Intercourse, PA 800-732-3538
Kozlowski Farms
Forestville, CA 800-473-2767
Mad River Farm
Arcata, CA 707-822-0248
Mardale Specialty Foods
Waukegan, IL 847-336-4777

Mixon Fruit Farms
Bradenton, FL 800-608-2525
National Grape Cooperative
Westfield, NY 716-326-5200
New Canaan Farms
Dripping Springs, TX 800-727-5267
Oasis Foods Company
Hillside, NJ 908-964-0477
Old Country Cheese
Cashton, WI 888-320-9469
Pacific Westcoast Foods
Portland, OR 800-874-9333
Peanut Butter & Co
New York, NY 212-757-3130
Pemberton's Gourmet Foods
Gray, ME 800-255-8401
Portion Pac
Mason, OH 800-232-4829
Reid Foods
Gurnee, IL 888-295-8478
Rowena's
Norfolk, VA 800-627-8699
Sarabeth's Kitchen
Bronx, NY 800-773-7378
Sargent's Bear Necessities
North Troy, VT 802-988-2903
Scott Hams
Greenville, KY 800-318-1353
Shawnee Canning Company
Cross Junction, VA 800-713-1414
Side Hill Farm
Brattleboro, VT 802-254-2018
Spruce Mountain Blueberries
West Rockport, ME 207- 23-6 35
Stanchfield Farms
Milo, ME 207-732-5173
Steel's Gourmet Foods
Bridgeport, PA 800-678-3357
Sticky Fingers Bakeries
Spokane Valley, WA 800-458-5826
Stonewall Kitchen
York, ME 800-207-5267
Summer In Vermont Jams
Hinesburg, VT 802-453-3793
Sunfresh Foods
Seattle, WA 800-669-9625
T.J. Blackburn Syrup Works
Jefferson, TX 800-527-8630
T.W. Garner Food Company
Winston Salem, NC 800-476-7383
Valley View Blueberries
Vancouver, WA 360-892-2839
Vermont Harvest Speciality Foods
Stowe, VT 800-338-5354
Welch's Foods Inc
Concord, MA 800-340-6870

Apricot

Allied Old English
Port Reading, NJ 732-602-8955
Erba Food Products
Brooklyn, NY 718-272-7700
J.M. Smucker Company
Orrville, OH 330-682-3000

Grape

Allied Old English
Port Reading, NJ 732-602-8955
J.M. Smucker Company
Orrville, OH 330-682-3000
T.W. Garner Food Company
Winston Salem, NC 800-476-7383

Strawberry

Allied Old English
Port Reading, NJ 732-602-8955
D'Artagnan
Newark, NJ 800-327-8246
Erba Food Products
Brooklyn, NY 718-272-7700
J.M. Smucker Company
Orrville, OH 330-682-3000
New Canaan Farms
Dripping Springs, TX 800-727-5267

T.W. Garner Food Company
Winston Salem, NC 800-476-7383

Jellies

Alaska Herb Tea Company
Anchorage, AK 800-654-2764
B&B Pecan Processors of NC
Turkey, NC 866-328-7322
Bear Meadow Farm
Colrain, MA 800-653-9241
Beetroot Delights
Foothill, ON 888-842-3387
Coco Lopez
Miramar, FL 800-341-2242
Colorado Mountain Jams & Jellies
Palisade, CO 970-464-0745
Davidson of Dundee
Dundee, FL 800-654-0647
Kettle Master
Hillsville, VA 276-728-7571
Kitchen Kettle Foods
Intercourse, PA 800-732-3538
Low Country Produce
Lobeco, SC 800-935-2792
McIlhenny Company
New Orleans, LA 800-634-9599
Northeast Kingdom Mustard Company
Brownington, VT 802-754-2813
Palmetto Canning Company
Palmetto, FL 941-722-1100
Shenk's Foods
Lancaster, PA 717-393-4240

Beets

Beetroot Delights
Foothill, ON 888-842-3387

Royal

Algood Food Company
Louisville, KY 502-637-3631
Bear Stewart Corporation
Chicago, IL 800-697-2327
Campagna
Lebanon, OR 800-959-4372
CC Pollen Company
Phoenix, AZ 800-875-0096
Dawes Hill Honey Company
Nunda, NY 888-800-8075
Delicae Gourmet
Tarpon Springs, FL 800-942-2502
Fiesta Gourmet of Tejas
Canyon Lake, TX 800-585-8250
Herb Bee's Products
Colchester, VT 802-864-7387
Moon Shine Trading Company
Woodland, CA 800-678-1226
Royal Resources
New Orleans, LA 800-888-9932
Sargent's Bear Necessities
North Troy, VT 802-988-2903
Stanchfield Farms
Milo, ME 207-732-5173
Summer In Vermont Jams
Hinesburg, VT 802-453-3793
Vermont Harvest Speciality Foods
Stowe, VT 800-338-5354
WCC Honey Marketing
City of Industry, CA 626-855-3086

Marmalades & Preserves

A Perfect Pear from NapaValley
Napa, CA 800-553-5753
A.M. Braswell Jr. Food Company
Statesboro, GA 800-673-9388
Alaska Jack's Trading Post
Anchorage, AK 888-660-2257
Algood Food Company
Louisville, KY 502-637-3631
Allied Old English
Port Reading, NJ 732-602-8955
Ambassador Foods
Van Nuys, CA 800-338-3369

Amberland Foods
Harvey, ND .800-950-4558
Amcan Industries
Elmsford, NY 914-347-4838
American Spoon Foods
Petoskey, MI 800-222-5886
Anna's Unlimited, Inc
Austin, TX. 800-849-7054
Arbor Hill Grapery & Winery
Naples, NY 800-554-7553
Arizona Cowboy
Phoenix, AZ .800-529-8627
Arome Fleurs & Fruits
St-Jean-Sur-Richelie, QC 877-349-3282
Artichoke Kitchen
Hamilton, NC 252-798-2471
Atlas Preserves Company
New York, NY 212-569-5613
Au Printemps Gourmet
Prevost, QC. .800-663-0416
Bainbridge Festive Foods
Tunica, MS 800-545-9205
Bartons Fine Foods
Denniston, KY 888-810-3750
Baumer Foods
New Orleans, LA 504-482-5761
Bear Meadow Farm
Colrain, MA 800-653-9241
Bear Stewart Corporation
Chicago, IL 800-697-2327
Bell Buckle Country Store
Bell Buckle, TN 800-707-0483
Blackberry Patch
Thomasville, GA. 800-853-5598
Blueberry Store
Grand Junction, MI. 877-654-2400
Booneway Farms
Berea, KY 859-986-2636
Bottle Green Drinks
Mississauga, ON 905-273-6137
Bowman Apple Products Company
Mt Jackson, VA. 877-426-9626
Breakfast at Brennan's
New Orleans, LA 800-888-9932
California Custom Fruits & Flavors
Irwindale, CA .877-558-0056
Carolina Cupboard
Hillsborough, NC 800-400-3441
Carriage House Companies
Fredonia, NY .800-828-8915
Castella Imports
Hauppauge, NY 866-227-8355
Catamount Specialties of Vermont
Stowe, VT 800-820-8096
Cherchies
Malvern, PA 800-644-1980
Cheri's Desert Harvest
Tucson, AZ 800-743-1141
Cherith Valley Gardens
Fort Worth, TX 800-610-9813
Cherry Hut
Traverse City, MI 888-882-4431
Chris' Farm Stand
Hubbardston, MA 978-928-4732
Chugwater Chili Corporation
Chugwater, WY 800-972-4454
Chukar Cherries
Prosser, WA. .800-624-9544
Cincinnati Preserves Company
Cincinnati, OH 800-222-9966
Clements Foods Company
Oklahoma City, OK 800-654-8355
Coco Lopez
Miramar, FL 800-341-2242
Cold Hollow Cider Mill
Waterbury Center, VT 800-327-7537
Country Cupboard
Virginia City, NV 775-847-7300
Coutts Specialty Foods
Boxborough, MA 800-919-2952
CSP Foods
Mont-Royal, QC 514-731-7621
CW Resources
New Britain, CT 860-229-7700
D'Artagnan
Newark, NJ 800-327-8246
Davidson of Dundee
Dundee, FL 800-654-0647
Dawn's Foods
Portage, WI 608-742-2494
Deep South Products
Fitzgerald, GA. 229-423-1121

Deer Mountain Berry Farms
Granite Falls, WA 360-691-7586
Deneen Company
Belen, NM 505-988-1515
Dennco
Chicago, IL 708-862-0070
Dillman Farm
Bloomington, IN 800-359-1362
E. Waldo Ward & Son Corporation
Sierra Madre, CA 800-355-9273
EFCO Products
Poughkeepsie, NY 800-284-3326
Erba Food Products
Brooklyn, NY .718-272-7700
Esper Products DeLuxe
Kissimmee, FL 800-268-0892
Eva Gates Homemade Preserves
Bigfork, MT 800-682-4283
Eweberry Farms
Brownsville, OR 541-466-3470
Fiesta Gourmet of Tejas
Canyon Lake, TX 800-585-8250
Fireside Kitchen
Halifax, NS 902-454-7387
Fischer & Wieser Specialty Foods
Fredericksburg, TX 800-880-8526
Forge Mountain Foods
Hendersonville, NC 800-823-6743
Freed, Teller & Freed
Burlingame, CA 800-370-7371
Fresh Squeezed Juice Company
Sebastian, FL .561-589-0390
From Oregon
Springfield, OR 541-747-4222
Frostproof Sunkist Groves
Fort Meade, FL 863-635-4873
Gem Berry Products
Sandpoint, ID .800-426-0498
Glencourt
Napa, CA. 707-944-4444
Golden State Foods
City of Industry, CA 626-968-6431
Golden State Foods
Irvine, CA 949-252-2000
Golden Valley Foods
Abbotsford, BC 888-299-8855
Gormly's Orchard
South Burlington, VT 800-639-7604
Gourmet Central
Romney, WV .800-984-3722
Graves Mountain Cannery
Syria, VA 540-923-4747
Graysmarsh Farm
Sequim, WA 800-683-4367
Great Northern Maple Products
Saint Honor, De Shenley, QC 418-485-7777
Great San Saba River Pecan Company
San Saba, TX .800-621-9121
Greaves Jams & Marmalades
Niagara-on-the-Lake, ON 800-515-9939
Green Grown Products
Santa Monica, CA 310-828-1686
Grey Eagle Distributors
Maryland Heights, MO. 314-429-9100
Grouse Hunt Farms
Tamaqua, PA .570-467-2850
H Cantin
Beauport, QC .800-463-5268
Hawaiian Fruit Specialties
Kalaheo, HI 808-332-9333
Hillcrest Orchard
Lake Placid, FL. 865-397-5273
Hilltop Herb Farm & Restaurant
Cleveland, TX. 832-397-4020
Hollman Foods
Minden, NE 888-926-2879
Homemade By Dorothy
Boise, ID 208-375-3720
Honey Bear Fruit Basket
Denver, CO 888-330-2327
House of Webster
Rogers, AR 800-369-4641
Huckleberry Patch
Hungry Horse, MT 800-527-7340
Hurd Orchards
Holley, NY 585-638-8838
Indi-Bel
Indianola, MS .662-887-1226
Indian Bay Frozen Foods
Centreville, NL 709-678-2844
Inter-American Products
Cincinnati, OH 800-645-2233

J.M. Smucker Company
Orrville, OH 330-682-3000
Jim's Cheese Pantry
Waterloo, WI. .800-345-3571
JMS Specialty Foods
Ripon, WI 800-535-5437
John C. Meier Juice Company
Cincinnati, OH 800-346-2941
Kamish Food Products
Chicago, IL 773-267-0400
Kerr Jellies
Dana, NC 877-685-8381
King Kelly Marmalade Company
Bellflower, CA .562-865-0291
Knott's Berry Farm Foods
Placentia, CA .800-289-9927
Knouse Foods
Peach Glen, PA 717-677-8181
Korinek & Company
Cicero, IL 773-242-1917
Kozlowski Farms
Forestville, CA 800-473-2767
Kraft Foods
Northfield, IL 800-323-0768
La Caboose Specialties
Sunset, LA. 337-662-5401
Lancaster Packing Company
Lancaster, PA .717-397-9727
Lawrence Foods
Elk Grove Vlg, IL. 800-323-7848
Let's Serve
Plattsburgh, NY 518-293-7119
Love Creek Orchards
Medina, TX 800-449-0882
Lynch Foods
North York, QC. 416-449-5464
Lyons-Magnus
Fresno, CA 559-268-5966
Mad River Farm
Arcata, CA 707-822-0248
Minnesota Specialty Crops
McGregor, MN 800-328-6731
Mixon Fruit Farms
Bradenton, FL 800-608-2525
Moon Shine Trading Company
Woodland, CA. 800-678-1226
Mountainbrook of Vermont
Jeffersonville, VT 802-644-1988
Mrs. Auld's Gourmet Foods
Reno, NV 800-322-8537
New Canaan Farms
Dripping Springs, TX 800-727-5267
New England Cranberry Company
Lynn, MA 800-410-2892
Ocean Spray Cranberries
Kenosha, WI .262-694-0621
Oregon Hill Farms
St Helens, OR 800-243-4541
Our Enterprises
Oklahoma City, OK 800-821-6375
Pacific Westcoast Foods
Portland, OR .800-874-9333
Palmetto Canning Company
Palmetto, FL .941-722-1100
Pearson's Berry Farm
Bowden, AB 403-224-3011
Pepper Creek Farms
Lawton, OK. 800-526-8132
Pied-Mont/Dora
Ste Anne Des Plaines, BC 800-363-8003
Plaidberry Company
Vista, CA. 760-727-5403
Poiret International
Tamarac, FL .954-724-3261
Portion Pac
Mason, OH 800-232-4829
Post Familie Vineyards
Altus, AR 800-275-8423
Purity Factories
St.John's, NL .800-563-3411
Purity Products
Plainview, NY .888-769-7873
Quality Naturally! Foods
City of Industry, CA 888-498-6986
R.E. Kimball & Company
Amesbury, MA 978-388-1826
Rapazzini Winery
Gilroy, CA. 408-842-5649
Restaurant Lulu Gourmet Products
San Francisco, CA 888-693-5800
Robert Rothschild Berry Farm
Urbana, OH. 866-565-6790

Robert Rothschild Farm
Urbana, OH 866-565-6790
Rocky Top Farms
Ellsworth, MI 800-862-9303
Rose City Pepperheads
Portland, OR 503-226-0862
Roseland Manufacturing
Roseland, NJ 973-228-2500
Rowena's
Norfolk, VA. 800-627-8699
Sambets Cajun Deli
Austin, TX. 800-472-6238
Sand Hill Berries
Mt Pleasant, PA. 724-547-4760
Santa Barbara Gourmet
Buellton, CA. 805-686-0951
Sarabeth's Kitchen
Bronx, NY. 800-773-7378
SBK Preserves
Bronx, NY. 800-773-7378
Sedlock Farm
Lynn Center, IL. 309-521-8284
Seven Keys Company of Florida
Pompano Beach, FL 954-946-5010
Shahi Food Corporation
Mississauga, ON 905-677-4327
Shawnee Canning Company
Cross Junction, VA 800-713-1414
Shenk's Foods
Lancaster, PA 717-393-4240
Shooting Star Farms
Bartlesville, OK 888-850-8540
Silver Palate Kitchens
Cresskill, NJ 800-872-5283
Skjodt-Barrett Foods
Mississauga, ON 877-600-1200
Sona & Hollen Foods
Los Alamitos, CA 800-200-7662
St. Charles Trading
Lake Saint Louis, MO. 800-336-1333
Stickney & Poor Company
North Andover, MA 508-261-8967
Stone Cellar Kitchens
Riverside, CA 951-352-5713
Sugarman of Vermont
Hardwick, VT 800-932-7700
Summercorn Foods
Fayetteville, AR 888-328-9473
Summerland Sweets
Summerland, BC. 800-577-1277
Suzanne's Specialties
New Brunswick, NJ 800-762-2135
T.J. Blackburn Syrup Works
Jefferson, TX. 800-527-8630
T.W. Garner Food Company
Winston Salem, NC. 800-476-7383
Tait Farm Foods
Centre Hall, PA. 800-787-2716
Tandem Enterprises
Darien, CT. 800-779-3276
Terrapin Ridge
Freeport, IL 800-999-4052
Tex-Mex Gourmet
Houston, TX 888-345-8467
The Lollipop Tree, Inc
Portsmouth, NH 800-842-6691
Thomson Food
Duluth, MN 218-722-2529
Trailblazer Food Products
Portland, OR 800-777-7179
Trappist Preserves
Spencer, MA 508-885-8740
Tropical Fruit Products Company
San German, PR 787-892-1345
Tropical Preserving Company
Los Angeles, CA. 213-748-5108
Uncle Fred's Fine Foods
Rockport, TX 361-729-8320
Underground Sauce Network
Cranston, RI 888-919-6664
Valley View Blueberries
Vancouver, WA 360-892-2839
Vic Rossano Incorporated
Montreal, QC 514-766-5252
Wagner Gourmet Foods
Shawnee Mission, KS. 913-469-5411
Wax Orchards
Vashon Island, WA 800-634-6132
WCC Honey Marketing
City of Industry, CA 626-855-3086
Welch's Foods Inc
Lawton, MI 269-624-1308

Welch's Foods Inc
Kennewick, WA 509-582-2131
Welch's Foods Inc
Concord, MA 800-340-6870
Welch's Foods Inc
North East, PA. 814-725-4577
Westport Rivers Vineyard& Winery
Westport, MA. 800-993-9695
Whipple Company
Natick, MA 800-345-2925
Whispering Gardens Gourmet Foods
Pasadena, CA 626-795-7334
Wild Thyme Cottage Products
Pointe Claire, QC 514-695-3602
Wing Candy Company
Branson, MO. 417-334-3238
Yoder Foods
Liberty, KY 877-702-0010

Spreads

A. Bauer's Mustard
Flushing, NY. 718-821-3570
A.M. Braswell Jr. Food Company
Statesboro, GA 800-673-9388
Aarhus United USA, Inc.
Newark, NJ 800-776-1338
Alaska Smokehouse
Woodinville, WA. 800-422-0852
Algood Food Company
Louisville, KY 502-637-3631
Allfresh Food Products
Evanston, IL 847-869-3100
Allied Old English
Port Reading, NJ. 732-602-8955
Amcan Industries
Elmsford, NY 914-347-4838
American Almond Products Company
Brooklyn, NY 800-825-6663
American Food Traders
Miami, FL .305-670-6250
American Spoon Foods
Petoskey, MI 800-222-5886
Arbor Hill Grapery & Winery
Naples, NY 800-554-7553
Artichoke Kitchen
Hamilton, NC 252-798-2471
Assouline & Ting
Philadelphia, PA 800-521-4491
Atlas Preserves Company
New York, NY 212-569-5613
Bainbridge Festive Foods
Tunica, MS 800-545-9205
Bakemark Ingredients Canada
Richmond, BC 800-665-9441
Baumer Foods
New Orleans, LA 504-482-5761
Bear Meadow Farm
Colrain, MA 800-653-9241
Beaver Meadow Creamery
Du Bois, PA. 800-262-3711
Bel/Kaukauna USA
Kaukauna, WI. 800-558-3500
Bell Buckle Country Store
Bell Buckle, TN 800-707-0483
Berner Foods, Inc.
Roscoe, IL. 800-819-8199
Bestfoods Specialty Products
Englewood Cliffs, NJ 800-338-8831
Betty Lou's Golden Smackers
McMinnville, OR 800-242-5205
Black Bear
St Johnsbury, VT. 802-748-5888
Black Diamond Cheese
Toronto, ON 800-263-2858
Blue Jay Orchards
Bethel, CT. 203-748-0119
Bowman Apple Products Company
Mt Jackson, VA. 877-426-9626
BP Gourmet
Hauppauge, NY 631-234-5200
Bread Dip Company
Philadelphia, PA 215-563-9455
Butterball Farms
Grand Rapids, MI 616-243-0105
Butternut Mountain Farm
Morrisville, VT. 800-828-2376
California Dairies
Fresno, CA 559-233-5154
Carolina Cupboard
Hillsborough, NC 800-400-3441
Carriage House Companies
Fredonia, NY 800-828-8915

Castella Imports
Hauppauge, NY 866-227-8355
Chelsea Market Baskets
New York, NY 888-727-7887
Cheri's Desert Harvest
Tucson, AZ 800-743-1141
Cherry Hut
Traverse City, MI 888-882-4431
Chloe Foods Corporation
Brooklyn, NY 718-827-3600
Chocolaterie Bernard Callebaut
Calgary, AB. 800-661-8367
Chris' Farm Stand
Hubbardston, MA 978-928-4732
Chugwater Chili Corporation
Chugwater, WY 800-972-4454
Cinnabar Specialty Foods
Prescott, AZ 866-293-6433
Citadelle Maple Syrup Produce Cooperative
Plessisville, QC. 819-362-3241
Clements Foods Company
Oklahoma City, OK 800-654-8355
Cold Hollow Cider Mill
Waterbury Center, VT. 800-327-7537
ConAgra Dairy Foods
Indianapolis, IN 317-329-3700
ConAgra Grocery Products
Irvine, CA .714-680-1000
Consumer Guild Foods
Toledo, OH 419-726-3406
Consumers Vinegar & Spice Company
Chicago, IL. 773-376-4100
Cowboy Caviar
Berkeley, CA. 877-509-1796
Cugino's Gourmet Foods
Crystal Lake, IL 888-592-8446
Cumberland Packing Corporation
Brooklyn, NY 718-858-4200
Dairyman's/Land O' Lakes
Tulare, CA. 559-687-8287
Dawes Hill Honey Company
Nunda, NY 888-800-8075
Dean Distributing Inc
Green Bay, WI. 920-469-6500
Deer Mountain Berry Farms
Granite Falls, WA 360-691-7586
Dutch Gold Honey, Inc.
Lancaster, PA 800-338-0587
E. Waldo Ward & Son Corporation
Sierra Madre, CA 800-355-9273
East Wind Nut Butters
Tecumseh, MO 417-679-4682
Erba Food Products
Brooklyn, NY 718-272-7700
Esper Products DeLuxe
Kissimmee, FL. 800-268-0892
Eva Gates Homemade Preserves
Bigfork, MT 800-682-4283
Fireside Kitchen
Halifax, NS 902-454-7387
Flaum Appetizing
Brooklyn, NY 718-821-1970
Food Ingredients
Elgin, IL 800-500-7676
Food Specialties Company
Cincinnati, OH 513-761-1242
Forge Mountain Foods
Hendersonville, NC 800-823-6743
Fox Hollow Farm
Hanover, NH 603-643-6002
Fresh Squeezed Juice Company
Sebastian, FL 561-589-0390
From Oregon
Springfield, OR. 541-747-4222
Furst-McNess Company/Terrapin Ridge
Freeport, IL 800-999-4052
G&G Foods
Santa Rosa, CA 707-542-6300
Gardners Candies
Tyrone, PA. 800-242-2639
GEM Berry Products
Sandpoint, ID 800-426-0498
Gem Berry Products
Sandpoint, ID 800-426-0498
GFA Brands
Paramus, NJ 201-568-9300
Giovanni's Appetizing Food Products
Richmond, MI 586-727-9355
Golden Heritage Foods
Latty, OH .888-233-6446
Golden State Foods
City of Industry, CA 626-968-6431

Golden State Foods
Irvine, CA 949-252-2000
Golden Valley Foods
Abbotsford, BC............. 888-299-8855
Gourmet Central
Romney, WV................. 800-984-3722
Graham Cheese Corporation
Washington, IN 800-472-9178
Graves Mountain Cannery
Syria, VA 540-923-4747
Graysmarsh Farm
Sequim, WA 800-683-4367
Great Garlic Foods
Bradley Beach, NJ 732-775-3311
Great San Saba River Pecan Company
San Saba, TX 800-621-9121
Greaves Jams & Marmalades
Niagara-on-the-Lake, ON.......... 800-515-9939
Groeb Farms
Onsted, MI 517-467-7100
Groezinger Provisions
Neptune, NJ 800-927-9473
Grouse Hunt Farms
Tamaqua, PA 570-467-2850
H&B Packing Company
Waco, TX 254-752-2506
Halben Food Manufacturing Company
Overland, MO................. 800-888-4855
Harold Food Company
Charlotte, NC 704-588-8061
Hawaiian Fruit Specialties
Kalaheo, HI 808-332-9333
Heinz Company of Canada
North York, ON............... 800-268-6641
Herb Bee's Products
Colchester, VT 802-864-7387
Herkimer Foods
Herkimer, NY................. 315-895-7832
Hillcrest Orchard
Lake Placid, FL............... 865-397-5273
Hillside Lane Farm
Randolph, VT 802-728-0070
Hollman Foods
Minden, NE................... 888-926-2879
Homemade By Dorothy
Boise, ID 208-375-3720
Honey Bear Fruit Basket
Denver, CO 888-330-2327
Honey Butter Products Company
Manheim, PA 717-665-9323
House of Thaller
Knoxville, TN................. 865-689-5893
House of Webster
Rogers, AR 800-369-4641
Huckleberry Patch
Hungry Horse, MT 800-527-7340
Indi-Bel
Indianola, MS 662-887-1226
Indian Bay Frozen Foods
Centreville, NL 709-678-2844
Innovative Food Corporation
Mississauga, ON.............. 905-670-8878
J.M. Smucker Company
Orrville, OH 330-682-3000
JMS Specialty Foods
Ripon, WI 800-535-5437
John C. Meier Juice Company
Cincinnati, OH 800-346-2941
K&S Bakery Products
Edmonton, AB 780-481-8155
Kerr Jellies
Dana, NC 877-685-8381
Kettle Foods
Salem, OR 503-364-0399
King Kelly Marmalade Company
Bellflower, CA 562-865-0291
Knott's Berry Farm Foods
Placentia, CA 800-289-9927
Knotts Wholesale Foods
Paris, TN 731-642-1961
Knouse Foods
Peach Glen, PA............... 717-677-8181
Korinek & Company
Cicero, IL 773-242-1917
Kozlowski Farms
Forestville, CA 800-473-2767
Kraft Foods
Northfield, IL 800-323-0768
Kraft Foods
Garland, TX 972-272-7511
Kraft Foods
East Hanover, NJ 973-503-2000

Krema Nut Company
Columbus, OH 800-222-4132
Kretschmar
Don Mills, ON 800-561-4532
La Caboose Specialties
Sunset, LA................... 337-662-5401
Laack Brothers Cheese Company
Greenleaf, WI 800-589-5127
Lancaster Packing Company
Lancaster, PA 717-397-9727
Land O'Lakes
Kent, OH 800-328-9680
Land O'Lakes, Inc
Arden Hills, MN 800-328-9680
Landis Peanut Butter
Souderton, PA 215-723-9366
Lawry's Foods
Monrovia, CA 800-952-9797
Leavitt Corporation
Everett, MA................... 617-389-2600
Leroux Creek Foods
Hotchkiss, CO 877-970-5670
Let's Serve
Plattsburgh, NY............... 518-293-7119
Level Valley Creamery
Antioch, TN 800-251-1292
Look's Gourmet Food Company
Whiting, ME 800-962-6258
Lost Trail Root Beer Com
Louisburg, KS................. 800-748-7765
Lov-It Creamery
Green Bay, WI................. 800-344-0333
Love Creek Orchards
Medina, TX 800-449-0882
Lynch Foods
North York, QC................ 416-449-5464
Mad River Farm
Arcata, CA 707-822-0248
Madison Dairy Produce Company
Madison, WI 608-256-5561
Madison Foods
St Paul, MN 651-265-8212
Marantha Natural Foods
San Francisco, CA 800-299-0048
Marin Food Specialties
Byron, CA 925-634-6126
McCutcheon's Apple Products
Frederick, MD................. 800-888-7537
Merkts Cheese Company
Bristol, WI.................... 262-857-2316
Minnesota Specialty Crops
McGregor, MN 800-328-6731
Miss Scarlett's
Chandler, AZ................. 800-345-6734
Mixon Fruit Farms
Bradenton, FL 800-608-2525
Montana Mountain Smoked Fish
Montana City, MT.............. 800-649-2959
Moon Shine Trading Company
Woodland, CA................. 800-678-1226
Mountainbrook of Vermont
Jeffersonville, VT 802-644-1988
Mrs. Annie's Peanut Patch
Floresville, TX 830-393-7845
National Grape Cooperative
Westfield, NY................. 716-326-5200
New Canaan Farms
Dripping Springs, TX............ 800-727-5267
New Morning
Needham, MA................. 781-444-0440
Novartis Nutrition Corporation
Minneapolis, MN 952-848-6000
Ocean Spray Cranberries
Kenosha, WI.................. 262-694-0621
Old Country Farms
East Sandwich, MA 888-707-5558
Once Again Nut Butter
Nunda, NY.................... 888-800-8075
Oregon Hill Farms
St Helens, OR................. 800-243-4541
Organic Gourmet
Sherman Oaks, CA 800-400-7772
Original Nut House Brands
El Paso, TX................... 800-726-7222
Pak Technologies
Milwaukee, WI................ 414-438-8600
Palmetto Canning Company
Palmetto, FL 941-722-1100
Parkers Farm
Minneapolis, MN 800-869-6685
Patak Spices USA
Clearwater, FL 727-796-2126

Peaceworks
New York, NY................. 212-897-3995
Penotti USA
Westport, CT.................. 877-720-0896
Pied-Mont/Dora
Ste Anne Des Plaines, BC 800-363-8003
Pillsbury Canada Limited
Markham, ON................. 800-745-4777
Pine River Pre-Pack
Newton, WI................... 920-726-4216
Plochman
Manteno, IL 815-468-3434
Portion Pac
Mason, OH 800-232-4829
Private Harvest
Lakeport, CA 800-463-0594
Proctor & Gamble Company
Lexington, KY 859-254-5544
Producers Peanut Company
Suffolk, VA................... 800-847-5491
Protient (Land O Lakes)
St Paul, MN................... 651-481-2068
Purity Factories
St.John's, NL 800-563-3411
Purity Farms
Sedalia, CO 800-568-4433
Purity Products
Plainview, NY................. 888-769-7873
Quality Choice Foods
Toronto, ON 416-650-9595
Quong Hop & Company
S San Francisco, CA 650-553-9900
R C Bigelow
Fairfield, CT 800-243-5587
Rapazzini Winery
Gilroy, CA 408-842-5649
Rapunzel Pure Organics
Chatham, NY 800-207-2814
Regal Food Service
Houston, TX 713-222-8231
Reily Foods Company
New Orleans, LA 504-524-6132
Reily Foods/JFG Coffee Company
Knoxville, TN................. 800-535-1961
Restaurant Lulu Gourmet Products
San Francisco, CA 888-693-5800
Rocky Top Farms
Ellsworth, MI................. 800-862-9303
Roseland Manufacturing
Roseland, NJ 973-228-2500
Rowena's
Norfolk, VA.................. 800-627-8699
Sabra Blue & White Food Products
Astoria, NY 718-389-3800
Sacharen Brothers
Montreal, QC 514-277-8205
Salmolux
Federal Way, WA.............. 253-874-6570
San Joaquin Valley Dairymen
Los Banos, CA 209-826-4901
Sapar
San Mateo, CA 650-340-8840
Sarabeth's Kitchen
Bronx, NY.................... 800-773-7378
Sassafras Enterprises
Chicago, IL................... 800-537-4941
SBK Preserves
Bronx, NY.................... 800-773-7378
Schlotterbeck & Foss Company
Portland, ME................. 800-777-4666
Schreiber Foods   Plant
Shippensburg, PA 717-530-5000
Scotsburn Dairy Group
Truro, NS 902-895-4412
Scott-Bathgate
Winnipeg, NB................. 204-943-8525
Sedlock Farm
Lynn Center, IL 309-521-8284
Sessions Company
Enterprise, AL................. 334-393-0200
Shawnee Canning Company
Cross Junction, VA 800-713-1414
Shenk's Foods
Lancaster, PA 717-393-4240
Silver Palate Kitchens
Cresskill, NJ 800-872-5283
Skjodt-Barrett Foods
Mississauga, ON.............. 877-600-1200
Sommer Maid Creamery
Doylestown, PA 215-345-6160
Southern Gold Honey CompAny
Vidor, TX 808-899-2494

Southern Peanut Company
Dublin, NC 910-862-2136
Springfield Smoked Fish Company
Springfield, MA 800-327-3412
St. Laurent Brothers
Bay City, MI 800-289-7688
Stello Foods
Punxsutawney, PA. 800-849-4599
Stone Cellar Kitchens
Riverside, CA 951-352-5713
Sugarman of Vermont
Hardwick, VT 800-932-7700
Summerland Sweets
Summerland, BC. 800-577-1277
Suzanne's Specialties
New Brunswick, NJ 800-762-2135
Sweet Mele's Hawaiian Products
Kailua, HI .800-990-8441
Synergy Foods
West Bloomfield, MI 313-849-2900
T. Marzetti Company
Columbus, OH 614-846-2232
T.W. Garner Food Company
Winston Salem, NC. 800-476-7383
Tait Farm Foods
Centre Hall, PA 800-787-2716
Tara Foods
Atlanta, GA. 404-559-0605
Tarazi Specialty Foods
Chino, CA .909-628-3601
The Lollipop Tree, Inc
Portsmouth, NH 800-842-6691
Thistledew Farm
Proctor, WV 800-854-6639
Thomson Food
Duluth, MN 218-722-2529
Timber Crest Farms
Healdsburg, CA 888-374-9325
Trappist Preserves
Spencer, MA 508-885-8740
Treasure Foods
West Valley, UT. 801-974-0911
Tribe Mediterranean Foods Company LLC
Taunton, MA 800-421-3474
Tropical
Charlotte, NC 800-220-1413
Tropical Fruit Products Company
San German, PR 787-892-1345
Tropical Preserving Company
Los Angeles, CA. 213-748-5108
Valley View Blueberries
Vancouver, WA 360-892-2839
Ventura Foods
Ontario, CA. 714-257-3700
Ventura Foods
Ft Worth, TX. 817-232-5450
Ventura Foods   Foodservice
Salem, OR. 503-585-6423
Vic Rossano Incorporated
Montreal, QC 514-766-5252
Virginia & Spanish Peanut Company
Providence, RI 800-673-3562
Wagner Gourmet Foods
Shawnee Mission, KS. 913-469-5411
WCC Honey Marketing
City of Industry, CA 626-855-3086
Welch's Foods Inc
Lawton, MI 269-624-1308
Welch's Foods Inc
Kennewick, WA 509-582-2131
Welch's Foods Inc
Concord, MA 800-340-6870
Welch's Foods Inc
North East, PA. 814-725-4577
Welcome Dairy
Colby, WI .800-472-2315
Westbrae Natural Foods
Garden City, NY 800-434-4246
Whipple Company
Natick, MA 800-345-2925
Wild Thymes Farm
Greenville, NY 800-724-2877
WillowOak Farms
Woodland, CA. 888-963-2767
Wilsonhill Farm
Underhill, VT 802-899-2154
Wing Candy Company
Branson, MO. 417-334-3238
Wisconsin Wilderness Food Products
Milwaukee, WI 800-359-3039
Yoder Foods
Liberty, KY 877-702-0010

Apple Butter

A.W. Jantzi & Sons
Wellesley, ON 519-656-2400
Bear Meadow Farm
Colrain, MA 800-653-9241
Betty Lou's Golden Smackers
McMinnville, OR 800-242-5205
Blue Jay Orchards
Bethel, CT. 203-748-0119
Bowman Apple Products Company
Mt Jackson, VA. 877-426-9626
Centennial Farms
Augusta, MO. 636-228-4338
Clements Foods Company
Oklahoma City, OK 800-654-8355
Cold Hollow Cider Mill
Waterbury Center, VT. 800-327-7537
Coutts Specialty Foods
Boxborough, MA 800-919-2952
Father's Country Hams
Bremen, KY 270-525-3554
Graves Mountain Cannery
Syria, VA. .540-923-4747
Hillcrest Orchard
Lake Placid, FL. 865-397-5273
House of Webster
Rogers, AR 800-369-4641
Kimes Cider Mill
Bendersville, PA. 717-677-7539
Knouse Foods
Peach Glen, PA 717-677-8181
Let's Serve
Plattsburgh, NY. 518-293-7119
Lost Trail Root Beer Com
Louisburg, KS. 800-748-7765
Love Creek Orchards
Medina, TX. 800-449-0882
McCutcheon's Apple Products
Frederick, MD. 800-888-7537
Shawnee Canning Company
Cross Junction, VA 800-713-1414
Shenk's Foods
Lancaster, PA 717-393-4240
Stone Cellar Kitchens
Riverside, CA 951-352-5713
Summercorn Foods
Fayetteville, AR 888-328-9473
Timber Crest Farms
Healdsburg, CA 888-374-9325
Tropical Preserving Company
Los Angeles, CA. 213-748-5108
Wilsonhill Farm
Underhill, VT 802-899-2154
Yoder Foods
Liberty, KY 877-702-0010

Fruit Butter

A.M. Braswell Jr. Food Company
Statesboro, GA 800-673-9388
American Almond Products Company
Brooklyn, NY 800-825-6663
Applecreek Farms
Lexington, KY 800-747-8871
Betty Lou's Golden Smackers
McMinnville, OR 800-242-5205
Bowman Apple Products Company
Mt Jackson, VA. 877-426-9626
Clements Foods Company
Oklahoma City, OK 800-654-8355
Cold Hollow Cider Mill
Waterbury Center, VT. 800-327-7537
Dillman Farm
Bloomington, IN. 800-359-1362
Hollman Foods
Minden, NE. 888-926-2879
House of Webster
Rogers, AR 800-369-4641
J.M. Smucker Company
Orrville, OH 330-682-3000
JMS Specialty Foods
Ripon, WI .800-535-5437
Knouse Foods
Peach Glen, PA 717-677-8181
Kozlowski Farms
Forestville, CA 800-473-2767
Lancaster Packing Company
Lancaster, PA 717-397-9727
Leroux Creek Foods
Hotchkiss, CO. 877-970-5670
Lost Trail Root Beer Com
Louisburg, KS. 800-748-7765

McCutcheon's Apple Products
Frederick, MD. 800-888-7537
New Morning
Needham, MA. 781-444-0440
Oregon Hill Farms
St Helens, OR 800-243-4541
Scott Hams
Greenville, KY 800-318-1353
Shenk's Foods
Lancaster, PA 717-393-4240
Stone Cellar Kitchens
Riverside, CA 951-352-5713
Timber Crest Farms
Healdsburg, CA 888-374-9325
Tropical Preserving Company
Los Angeles, CA. 213-748-5108
Wilsonhill Farm
Underhill, VT 802-899-2154

Olive

A. Camacho
Plant City, FL 800-881-4534

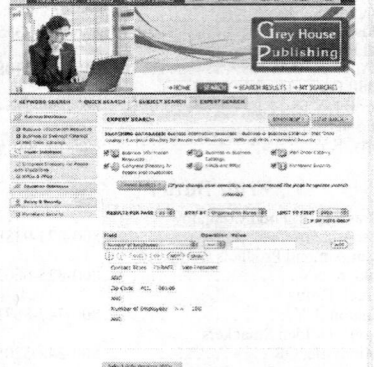
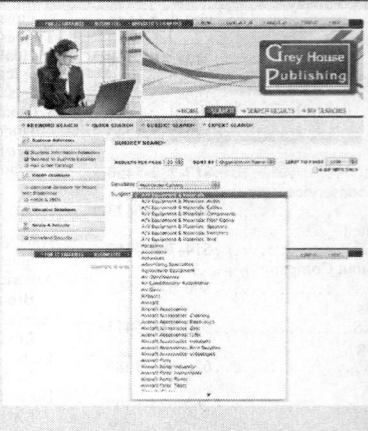

Meats & Meat Products

Canned

Broughton Cannery
   Paulding, OH 419-399-3182
Bunker Hill Foods
   Augusta, GA 706-733-7765
Calihan Pork Processing
   Peoria, IL. 309-674-9175
Campbell Soup Company
   Camden, NJ. 800-257-8443
Castleberry/Snow Brands
   Augusta, GA 800-241-3520
ConAgra Food Store Brands
   Edina, MN. 952-469-4981
ConAgra Foods Trenton Plant
   Trenton, MO 660-359-3913
ConAgra Foods/International Home Foods
   Niagara Falls, ON 905-356-2661
Cordon Bleu International
   Anjou, QC. 514-352-3000
Cumberland Gap Provision Company
   Middlesboro, KY 800-331-7154
Dorina/So-Good
   Union, IL. 815-923-2144
Fredericksburg Lockers/OPA's Smoke
   Fredericksburg, TX. 800-543-6750
Gary's Frozen Foods
   Lubbock, TX. 806-745-1933
Goya Foods of Florida
   Miami, FL 305-592-3150
Grabill Country Meats
   Grabill, IN. 866-333-6328
Hormel Foods Corporation
   Fremont, NE 402-721-2300
Hormel Foods Corporation
   Beloit, WI 608-365-9501
Hormel Foods Corporation
   Orchard Park, NY 716-675-7700
Hormel Foods Corporation
   Austin, MN 800-523-4635
Hsin Tung Yang Foods Co.
   S San Francisco, CA. 650-589-6789
J&B Sausage Company
   Waelder, TX 830-788-7511
Kelly Foods
   Jackson, TN 731-424-2255
Kraft Foodservices
   Tampa, FL 800-551-2559
Mertz Sausage Company
   San Antonio, TX. 210-433-3263
O Chili Frozen Foods Inc
   Northbrook, IL 847-562-1991
Pillsbury Canada Limited
   Markham, ON. 800-745-4777
Triple U Enterprises
   Fort Pierre, SD 605-567-3624
Vietti Foods Company Inc
   Nashville, TN .800-240-7864
Yoders
   Grantsville, MD 301-895-5121

Cooked

Burke Corporation
   Nevada, IA 800-654-1152

> Always make it your best® with Burke fully cooked meats. We specialize in Italian sausage, beef, and pork toppings, meatballs, taco meats, shredded meats, pepperoni, bacon, Canadian-style bacon, chicken and beef strips. Additionally, we offer a variety of specialty products: Hand-Pinched Style® brand toppings, chorizo, gyro topping, andouille sausage, and breakfast patties and links.

Specialty Foods Group
   Newport News, VA. 800-238-0020

Dried

Alderfer Bologna
   Harleysville, PA 877-253-6328
Armour
   Omaha, NE 402-453-3766
Breslow Deli Products
   Philadelphia, PA 215-739-4200
Citterio USA Corporation
   Freeland, PA 800-435-8888
Henningsen Foods
   Omaha, NE 402-330-2500
High Country Snack Foods
   Lincoln, MT 800-433-3916
Hoopeston Foods
   Burnsville, MN 952-854-0903
Hsin Tung Yang Foods Co.
   S San Francisco, CA. 650-589-6789
Lone Star Beef Jerky Company
   Lubbock, TX. 806-762-8833
Prime Smoked Meats
   Oakland, CA 510-832-7167
Riverview Foods
   Warsaw, KY 859-567-5211
Serv-Rite Meat Company
   Los Angeles, CA. 323-227-1911
Shelton's Poultry
   Pomona, CA 800-541-1833
Silver Star Meats
   Mc Kees Rocks, PA 412-771-5539
Sparrer Sausage Company
   Chicago, IL 800-666-3287
Tupman-Thurlow Company
   Deerfield Beach, FL 954-596-9989
Wolf Canyon Foods
   Carmel, CA 831-626-1323

Frozen

Acme Steak & Seafood Company
   Youngstown, OH. 330-270-8000
Ajinomoto Frozen Foods USA
   Portland, IR. 503-734-1528
Al Pete Meats
   Muncie, IN 765-288-8817
Alphin Brothers
   Dunn, NC 800-672-4502
APTCO
   San Francisco, CA 415-648-6688
AquaCuisine
   Eagle, ID 888-330-2782
Armbrust Meats
   Medford, WI 715-748-3102
Atlantic Meat Company
   Savannah, GA .912-964-8511
Atlantic Veal & Lamb
   Brooklyn, NY .800-221-6988
B&D Foods
   Boise, ID. 208-344-1183
Beatty Fresh Frozen Meats
   Bourbon, IN 574-342-2665
Big Apple Produce & Seafood Market
   Pocomoke City, MD 410-957-1151
Blakely Freezer Locker
   Thomasville, GA. 229-723-3622
Bosell Foods
   Cleveland, OH .216-991-7600
Bouma Meats
   Provost, AB. 780-753-2092
Broadleaf Venison USA
   Vernon, CA. 800-336-3844
Brook Locker Plant
   Brook, IN 219-275-2611

> To advertise in the *Food & Beverage Market Place* Online Database call **(800) 562-2139** or log on to **http://gold.greyhouse.com** and click on "Advertise."

Brownsdale Meat Service
   Brownsdale, MN. 507-567-2211

Burke Corporation
   Nevada, IA 800-654-1152

> Always make it your best® with Burke fully cooked meats. We specialize in Italian sausage, beef, and pork toppings, meatballs, taco meats, shredded meats, pepperoni, bacon, Canadian-style bacon, chicken and beef strips. Additionally, we offer a variety of specialty products: Hand-Pinched Style® brand toppings, chorizo, gyro topping, andouille sausage, and breakfast patties and links.

Bush Brothers Provision Company
   West Palm Beach, FL 800-327-1345
Butterfield Foods Company
   Butterfield, MN. 507-956-5103
Buzz Food Service
   Charleston, WV 304-925-4781
Calihan Pork Processing
   Peoria, IL. 309-674-9175
Carando Gourmet Frozen Foods
   Springfield, MA 413-730-4205
Cardinal Meat Specialists
   Mississauga, ON. 800-363-1439
Caribbean Food Delights
   Tappan, NY 845-398-3000
Carriage House Foods
   Ames, IA 515-232-2273
Casa Di Bertacchi
   Vineland, NJ 800-818-9261
Cedaredge Meats
   Cedaredge, CO 970-856-3517
Centennial Food Corporation
   Calgary, AB. 403-287-2525
Chef's Requested Foods
   Oklahoma City, OK 800-256-0259
Cher-Make Sausage Company
   Manitowoc, WI 800-242-7679
Cheraw Packing
   Cheraw, SC 843-537-7426
Colonial Beef Company
   Philadelphia, PA 215-289-7042
Conti Packing Company
   Rochester, NY. 585-424-2500
Culinary Foods
   Chicago, IL 800-621-4049
Culinary Standards Corporation
   Louisville, KY .800-778-3434
Curly's Foods
   Edina, MN. 612-920-3400
Davidson Meat Processing Plant
   Waynesville, OH. 513-897-2971
Davidson Meat Products
   New Bedford, MA 508-999-6293
Devault Foods
   Devault, PA. 800-426-2874
Dold Foods
   Wichita, KS. 316-838-9101
Duis Meat Processing
   Concordia, KS. 800-281-4295
Duma Meats
   Mogadore, OH 330-628-3438
El-Rey Foods
   Ferguson, MO. 314-521-3113
Florida Veal Processors
   Wimauma, FL .813-634-5545
Fuji Foods
   Denver, CO 303-377-3738
Gaucho Foods
   Westmont, IL. .630-889-4241
Gemini Food Industries
   Fiskdale, MA .508-347-2800
Glenn's Rabbit & Emu Farm
   Portland, TN 877-325-6903
Grecian Delight Foods
   Elk Grove Vlg, IL. 800-621-4387

Hall Brothers Meats
Cleveland, OH 440-235-3262
Hamm's Custom Meats
McKinney, TX 972-542-3359
Hamner Provision Company
San Antonio, TX 210-736-3117
Hanover Foods Corporation
Hanover, PA 717-632-6000
Hatfield Quality Meats
Hatfield, PA 800-523-5291
Heringer Meats
Covington, KY 859-291-2000
Holten Meats
Sauget, IL 800-851-4684
Hormel Foods Corporation
Houston, TX 281-492-1770
Hormel Foods Corporation
Columbia, MD 410-290-1855
Hormel Foods Corporation
Orchard Park, NY 716-675-7700
Hormel Foods Corporation
Austin, MN 800-523-4635
International Food Packers Corporation
Miami, FL 305-669-1662
International Packers Corporation
Watertown, MA. 508-963-8214
Italian Foods Manufacturing
Vestal, NY. 800-962-7700
J&B Meats Corporation
Coal Valley, IL 309-799-7341
J.J. Andrade's Slaughterhouse
Honokaa, HI 808-775-0741
Jacob & Sons Wholesale Meats
Martins Ferry, OH. 740-633-3091
James Cowan & Sons
Worcester, MA 508-754-5385
Jbs Packerland Inc
Green Bay, WI. 920-468-4000
John Garner Meats
Van Buren, AR 800-543-5473
John Morrell & Company
Cincinnati, OH 513-346-3540
K&K Gourmet Meats
Leetsdale, PA 724-266-8400
Kelley Foods of Alabama
Elba, AL 334-897-5761
Kenosha Beef International
Kenosha, WI. 800-541-1685
King Kold Meats
Englewood, OH 800-836-2797
Kraft Foodservices
Tampa, FL. 800-551-2559
Kutztown Bologna Company
Leola, PA. 800-723-8824
L&H Packing Company
San Antonio, TX. 210-532-3241
Ladoga Frozen Food & Retail Meat
Ladoga, IN 765-942-2225
Leo G. Fraboni Sausage Company
Hibbing, MN 218-263-5074
MacFarlane Pheasants
Janesville, WI 877-269-8957
Mada'n Kosher Foods
Dania, FL 954-925-0077
Maid-Rite Steak Company
Dunmore, PA. 800-233-4259
Maple Leaf Foods International
Toronto, ON 416-480-8900
Miami Beef Company
Hialeah, FL 305-621-3252
Morrison Lamothe
Toronto, ON 416-291-6762
Mountain City Meat Company
Denver, CO 800-937-8325
Nemecek Brothers
West, TX 254-826-5182

Newark Meat Supply
Newark, OH 740-345-6696
North Side Foods Corporation
Arnold, PA 800-486-2201
O Chili Frozen Foods Inc
Northbrook, IL 847-562-1991
Olympic Food Products
Kokomo, IN 800-445-6923
Omaha Steaks International
Omaha, NE 800-562-0500
Ottman Meat Company
New York, NY 212-879-4160
Otto & Son
West Jordan, UT 800-453-9462
P.A. Braunger Institutional Foods
Sioux City, IA 712-258-4515
Pacific Valley Foods
Bellevue, WA 425-643-1805
Paris Frozen Foods
Hillsboro, IL 217-532-3822
Party Steak Company
Springfield, MO 417-358-9091
Pel-Freez
Rogers, AR 800-223-8751
Phoenix Agro-Industrial Corporation
Westbury, NY 516-334-1194
Pierceton Foods
Pierceton, IN 574-594-2344
Pilgrim's Pride
Enterprise, AL. 800-633-0908
Pilgrim's Pride
Pittsburg, TX. 800-683-1968
Praters Foods
Lubbock, TX. 806-745-2727
Prime Smoked Meats
Oakland, CA 510-832-7167
Provimi Veal Corporation
Seymour, WI 800-833-8325
R Four Meats
Chatfield, MN 507-867-4180
Redi-Serve Food Company
Fort Atkinson, WI 920-563-6391
Republic Foods
Dallas, TX 214-826-8050
Rogers Brothers
Galesburg, IL 309-342-2127
Rymer Foods
Chicago, IL 800-247-9637
Saletts
Randolph, MA 781-961-9900
Sanderson Farms
Collins, MS 601-765-8211
Sanderson Farms
Bryan, TX 979-778-5730
Sara Lee Corporation
Downers Grove, IL 630-598-8100
Sara Lee Food Service
Haltom City, TX 800-261-4754
Scotsburn Dairy Group
Truro, NS 902-895-4412
Shelley's Prime Meats
Jersey City, NJ 201-433-3434
Smith Packing Regional Meat
Utica, NY 315-732-5125
Southeastern Meat Association
Oviedo, FL 407-365-5661
Specialty Brands
Carthage, MO 417-358-8104
Steak-Umm Company
Shillington, PA 860-928-5900
Stegall Smoked Turkey
Marshville, NC 800-851-6034
Sudlersville Frozen Food Locker
Sudlersville, MD 410-438-3106
Swissland Packing Company
Frankfort, IL 800-321-8325
SYSCO Foodservice
Fremont, CA 650-494-7200
Tenn Valley Ham Company
Paris, TN 731-642-9740
Thompson Packers
Slidell, LA. 800-989-6328
Topps Meat Company
Elizabeth, NJ 908-351-0500
Travis Meats
Powell, TN 800-247-7606
Triple U Enterprises
Fort Pierre, SD 605-567-3624
Tucker Packing Company
Orrville, OH 330-683-3311
Tupman-Thurlow Company
Deerfield Beach, FL 954-596-9989

Tyson Fresh Meats
Emporia, KS 620-343-3640
United Meat Company
San Francisco, CA 415-864-2118
Valley Meat Company
Modesto, CA. 800-222-6328
Valley Packing Company
Lansing, OH 740-635-0154
W&G Marketing Company
Ames, IA 515-233-4774
Wexler Meat Company
Skokie, IL 773-927-5656
Whitaker Foods
Evansdale, IA 800-553-7490
Windsor Frozen Foods
Houston, TX 800-437-6936
Yoders
Grantsville, MD 301-895-5121
Zartic Inc
Rome, GA. 800-241-0516

Ingredients

Burke Corporation
Nevada, IA 800-654-1152

Cargill Texturizing Solutions
Cedar Rapids, IA 877-650-7080
GPI USA LLC.
Athens, GA 706-850-7826
Proliant Meat Ingredients
Ankeny, IA 800-369-2672

Minced

Groff Meats
Elizabethtown, PA. 717-367-1246
Reinhart Foods
Markham, ON 905-754-3503
Rohtstein Corporation
Woburn, MA 781-935-8300

Packers

A.C. Kissling Company
Philadelphia, PA 800-445-1943
A.L. Duck
Zuni, VA 757-562-2387
Abattoir Aliments Asta Inc.
St Alexandre Kamouraska, QC. 418-495-2728
Agri Processors
Postville, IA 563-864-7811
AJM Meat Packing
San Juan, PR 787-787-4050
Al Safa Halal
Niagara Falls, NY 800-268-8174
Alaska Sausage and Seafood Company
Anchorage, AK 800-798-3636
Alewel's Country Meats
Warrensburg, MO 800-353-8553
Alex Froehlich Packing Company
Johnstown, PA. 814-535-7694
Alle Processing
Flushing, NY. 718-894-2000
Alle Processing Corporation
Flushing, NY. 800-245-5620
Amcan Industries
Elmsford, NY 914-347-4838
Appert's Foodservice
St Cloud, MN 800-225-3883
APTCO
San Francisco, CA 415-648-6688
Arizona Sunland Foods
Tucson, AZ 520-624-7068

Armour
Omaha, NE 402-453-3766

Arnold's Meat Food Products
Brooklyn, NY 800-633-7023

Atlantic Meat Company
Savannah, GA 912-964-8511

Atlantic Veal & Lamb
Brooklyn, NY 800-221-6988

B&D Foods
Boise, ID 208-344-1183

B&R Quality Meats
Waterloo, IA .319-232-6328

Bakalars Brothers Sausage Company
La Crosse, WI 608-784-0384

Ball Park Franks
Southfield, MI 888-317-5867

Bar-S Foods Company
Phoenix, AZ .602-264-7272

Baretta Provision
East Berlin, CT 860-828-0802

Barone Foods
Tucson, AZ 520-623-8571

Baum International
Brooklyn, NY 718-376-4508

Beatty Fresh Frozen Meats
Bourbon, IN .574-342-2665

Beef Packers, Inc.
Fresno, CA 559-268-5586

Bellville Meat Market
Bellville, TX .800-571-6328

Bierig Brothers
Vineland, NJ .856-691-9765

Big Apple Produce & Seafood Market
Pocomoke City, MD 410-957-1151

Big B Distributors
Evansville, IN 812-425-5235

Birchwood Foods
Kenosha, WI .800-541-1685

Blakely Freezer Locker
Thomasville, GA 229-723-3622

Blue Ribbon Meat Company
Sparks, NV 775-358-8116

Blue Ribbon Meats
Miami, FL 800-522-6115

Boesl Packing Company
Baltimore, MD 410-675-1071

Bowser Meat Processing
Meriden, KS .785-484-2454

Braham Food Locker Service
Braham, MN .320-396-2636

Brenntag Pacific
Santa Fe Springs, CA 562-903-9626

Breslow Deli Products
Philadelphia, PA 215-739-4200

Bridgford Foods Corporation
Anaheim, CA 800-527-2105

Broadaway Ham Company
Jonesboro, AR 870-932-6688

Broadleaf Venison USA
Vernon, CA .800-336-3844

Broken Bow Pack
Broken Bow, NE 308-872-2833

Brook Locker Plant
Brook, IN 219-275-2611

Brook Meadow Provisions Corporation
Hagerstown, MD 301-739-3107

Brooks County Sausage
Quitman, GA 800-342-4111

Brown Packing Company
Gaffney, SC .864-489-5723

Bruce Packing Company
Silverton, OR 800-899-3629

Brush Locker
Fort Morgan, CO 970-842-2660

Bryant's Meats
Taylorsville, MS 601-785-6507

Buckhead Beef Company
Atlanta, GA .800-888-5578

Burgers Smokehouse
California, MO 800-624-5426

Burnett & Son Meat Company
Monrovia, CA 626-357-2165

Busseto Foods
Fresno, CA 800-628-2633

Buzz Food Service
Charleston, WV 304-925-4781

C&C Packing Company
Stamps, AR .870-533-2251

C&S Wholesale Meat Company
Atlanta, GA .404-627-3547

C. Roy Meat Products
Brockway, MI 810-387-3957

Callaway Packing Company
Delta, CO 800-332-6932

Calumet Diversified Meat Company
Pleasant Prairie, WI 262-947-7200

Cambridge Packing Company
Boston, MA .800-722-6726

Carando Gourmet Frozen Foods
Springfield, MA 413-730-4205

Cardinal Meat Specialists
Mississauga, ON 800-363-1439

Cargill Meat Solutions
Timberville, VA 540-896-7041

Caribbean Food Delights
Tappan, NY .845-398-3000

Carl Streit & Son Company
Neptune, NJ .732-775-0803

Carl Venezia Meats
Plymouth Meeting, PA 610-239-6750

Carlton Farms
Carlton, OR .800-932-0946

Carolina By-Products Company
Winchester, VA 540-877-2590

Carolina Packers
Smithfield, NC 800-682-7675

Casa Di Bertacchi
Vineland, NJ .800-818-9261

Catelli Brothers
Camden, NJ .856-869-9293

Caughman's Meat Plant
Lexington, SC 803-356-0076

Cavens Meats
Conover, OH 937-368-3841

Caviness Packing Company
Hereford, TX 806-357-2443

Cedaredge Meats
Cedaredge, CO 970-856-3517

Centennial Food Corporation
Calgary, AB .403-287-2525

Center Locker Service Company
Center, MO .573-267-3343

Central Beef
Center Hill, FL 352-793-3671

Central Meat & Provision Company
San Diego, CA 619-239-1391

Charlie's Country Sausage
Minot, ND 701-838-6302

Charlie's Pride Meats
Los Angeles, CA 877-866-0982

Chatham Foods
Siler City, NC 919-742-2141

Chef's Requested Foods
Oklahoma City, OK 800-256-0259

Chicago 58 Food Products
Toronto, ON 416-603-4244

Chino Meat Provision Corporation
Chino, CA 909-627-1997

Chisesi Brothers Meat Packing Company
New Orleans, LA 504-822-3550

Cibao Meat Product
Bronx, NY 718-993-5072

Cifelli & Sons
South River, NJ 732-238-0090

Circle B Meat Company
Groom, TX .806-248-7332

Clay Center Locker Plant
Clay Center, KS 785-632-5550

Cloud's Meat Processing
Carthage, MO 417-358-5855

Clyde's Italian & German Sausage
Denver, CO .303-433-8744

Collbran Locker Plant
Collbran, CO 970-487-3329

Coloma Meat Products
Coloma, WI .715-228-4080

Colonial Beef Company
Philadelphia, PA 215-289-7042

Community Market & Deli
Lindstrom, MN 651-257-1128

Con Agra Foods
Omaha, NE .402-475-6700

ConAgra Beef Company
Yuma, CO 970-395-8226

ConAgra Beef Company
Greeley, CO .970-506-8000

ConAgra Foods Trenton Plant
Trenton, MO 660-359-3913

ConAgra Foods/Eckrich
Omaha, NE .800-327-4424

ConAgra Refrigerated Foods International
Omaha, NE .800-624-4724

ConAgra Refrigerated Prepared Foods
Downers Grove, IL 630-857-1000

ConAgra Snack Foods
San Jose, CA 408-436-0329

Conecuh Sausage Company
Evergreen, AL 800-726-0507

Contract Comestibles
East Troy, WI 262-642-9400

Corfu Foods
Bensenville, IL 630-595-2510

Corte Provisions
Newark, NJ .201-653-7246

Country Butcher Shop
Palmyra, MO 573-769-2257

Country Smoked Meats
Bowling Green, OH 800-321-4766

Counts Sausage Company
Prosperity, SC 803-364-2392

Crater Meat Packing Company
Medford, OR 541-772-6966

Crofton & Sons
Brandon, FL .800-878-7675

Crystal Lake
Decatur, AR .800-382-4425

Cudlin's Market
Newfield, NY 607-564-3443

Culinary Standards Corporation
Louisville, KY 800-778-3434

Culver Duck
Middlebury, IN 800-825-9225

Curly's Foods
Edina, MN 612-920-3400

Curtis Packing Company
Greensboro, NC 336-275-7684

Custom-Pak Meats
Knoxville, TN 800-457-4437

Dakota Premium Foods
South St Paul, MN 651-552-8230

Dale T. Smith & Sons Meat Packing Corporation
Draper, UT 801-571-3611

Dallas City Packing
Dallas, TX 214-948-3901

David Mosner Meat Products
Bronx, NY 718-328-5600

Davidson Meat Products
New Bedford, MA 508-999-6293

Davis Custom Meat Processing
Overbrook, KS 785-665-7713

Dean Sausage Company
Attalla, AL 800-228-0704

DeBragga & Spitler
New York, NY 212-924-1311

Dee's Cheesecake Factory/Dee's Foodservice
Albuquerque, NM 505-884-1777

Dennison Meat Locker
Dennison, MN 507-645-8734

Devine Meat Company
Devine, TX .830-663-4621

Dick's Packing Company
Columbia, MO 573-449-2995

Diggs Packing Company
Columbia, MO 573-449-2995

Dinner Bell Meat Product
Lynchburg, VA 434-847-7766

DiPasquale's
Baltimore, MD 410-276-6787

Dold Foods
Wichita, KS .316-838-9101

Dolores Canning Company
Los Angeles, CA 323-263-9155

Duis Meat Processing
Concordia, KS 800-281-4295

Dunham's Meats
Urbana, OH .937-834-2411

Dutterer's Home Food Service
Baltimore, MD 410-298-3663

E&H Packing Company
Detroit, MI .313-567-8286

E.E. Mucke & Sons
Hartford, CT 800-726-5598

E.W. Knauss & Son
Quakertown, PA 800-648-4220

East Dayton Meat & Poultry
Dayton, OH .937-253-6185

Edelman Meats
Antigo, WI 715-623-7686

Egon Binkert Meat Products
Baltimore, MD 410-687-5959

Ehresman Packing Company
Garden City, KS 620-276-3791

El Paso Meat Company
El Paso, TX .915-838-8600

El-Rey Foods
Ferguson, MO 314-521-3113

Elba Custom Meats
Elba, AL 334-897-2007
Elkhart Locker Plant
Elkhart, KS 620-697-4424
Ellsworth Locker
Ellsworth, MN 507-967-2544
Enslin & Son Packing Company
Hattiesburg, MS 800-898-4687
Excel Corporation
Wichita, KS 316-832-7500
F&Y Enterprises
Naperville, IL 630-637-8519
Fairbury Food Products
Fairbury, NE 402-729-3379
Fargo Packing & Sausage Company
West Fargo, ND 701-282-3211
Farm Boy Food Service
Evansville, IN 800-852-3976
Farmers Produce
Ashby, MN 218-747-2749
Farmington Food
Forest Park, IL 800-609-3276
Farmland Foods
Carroll, IA 712-792-1660
Farmland Foods
Denison, IA 800-831-1812
Ferko Meat Company
Milwaukee, WI 414-967-5500
Finchville Farms
Finchville, KY 800-678-1521
Fineberg Packing Company
Memphis, TN 901-458-2622
Fiorucci Foods
Colonial Heights, VA 800-524-7775
Fischer Meats
Issaquah, WA 425-392-3131
Flanders Provision Company
Waycross, GA 912-283-5191
Flint Hills Foods
Wamego, KS 785-765-3396
Florida Veal Processors
Wimauma, FL 813-634-5545
Foell Packing Company
Naperville, IL 919-776-0592
Fortenberry Ice Company
Kodak, TN 865-933-2568

Foster Farms
Demopolis, AL 800-255-7227
Frank Wardynski & Sons
Buffalo, NY 716-854-6083
Frank's Foods
Hilo, HI .808-959-9121
Freeze-Dry Products
Santa Rosa, CA 707-547-1776
Fresh Mark
Canton, OH 800-860-6777
Fricks Meat Products
Washington, MO 800-241-2209
Fuji Foods
Denver, CO 303-377-3738
Fulton Provision Company
Portland, OR 800-333-6328
G Di Lullo & Sons
Westville, NJ 856-456-3700
G E Hawthorn Meat Company
Hot Springs, AR 501-623-8111
G&G Sheep Farm
Boston, KY 502-833-4863
Gaiser's European Style Provisions
Union, NJ 908-206-9822
Garrard's Sausage Company
Durham, NC 919-383-4657
Gem Meat Packing Company
Boise, ID 208-375-9424
Gemini Food Industries
Fiskdale, MA 508-347-2800
George L. Wells Meat Company
Philadelphia, PA 800-523-1730
Gibbon Packing
Gibbon, NE 308-468-5771
Gilleshammer Thiele Farms
St Thomas, ND 701-257-6634
Glasco Locker Plant
Glasco, KS 785-568-2364
Glazier Packing Company
Malone, NY. 518-483-4990
Glen's Packing Company
Hallettsville, TX 800-368-2333
Glenn's Rabbit & Emu Farm
Portland, TN 877-325-6903
Glier's Meats
Covington, KY 800-446-3882

Global Food Industries
Townville, SC 800-225-4152
Godshall's Quality Meats
Franconia, PA 888-463-7425
Gold Cup Farms
Clayton, NY 800-752-1341
Gold Star Sausage Company
Denver, CO 800-258-7229
Golden City Meats
Golden City, MO. 417-537-8560
Golden State Foods
Irvine, CA 949-252-2000
Grabill Country Meats
Grabill, IN. 866-333-6328
Grant Park Packing
Chicago, IL 312-421-4096
Greater Omaha Packing Company
Omaha, NE 402-731-1700
Grecian Delight Foods
Elk Grove Vlg, IL. 800-621-4387
Green Valley Packing
Claysville, PA 800-522-9970
Griffin Industries
Cold Spring, KY 859-781-2010
Groezinger Provisions
Neptune, NJ 800-927-9473
Grote & Weigel
Bloomfield, CT. 860-242-8528
Gulf Packing Company
San Benito, TX 956-399-2631
Gunnoe Farms-Sausage & Salad Company
Charleston, WV 304-343-7686
Gwaltney of Smithfield
Portsmouth, VA. 757-465-0666
H&H Foods
Mercedes, TX 800-365-4632
H&K Packers Company
Winnipeg, NB 204-233-2354
H. Shenson International Export
San Francisco, CA 415-318-7000
Hahn Brothers
Westminster, MD 800-227-7675
Halal Transactions
Omaha, NE 402-572-6120
Hampton House
Langley, BC 800-665-4355

Hansen Packing Meat Company
Jerseyville, IL .618-498-3714
Harvest Direct
Knoxville, TN 800-838-2727
Hastings Meat Supply
Hastings, NE 402-463-9857
Hatfield Quality Meats
Hatfield, PA 800-523-5291
Henningsen Foods
Omaha, NE .402-330-2500
Henry J Meat Specialties
Chicago, IL .800-242-1314
Herman Falter Packing Company
Columbus, OH 800-325-6328
Herring Brothers
Dover Foxcroft, ME 207-876-2631
Hickory Valley Farm
Swiftwater, PA 570-839-6492
High Country Snack Foods
Lincoln, MT 800-433-3916
Hightower's Packing
Minden, LA 318-377-5459
Hillsboro Refrigerated Lockers
Hillsboro, KS 316-947-3781
Hilltop Meat Company
Gantt, AL 334-388-2393
Hoekstra Meat Company
Kalamazoo, MI 616-321-0797
Hoffman Sausage Company
Cincinnati, OH 513-621-4160
Holly Hill Locker Company
Holly Hill, SC 803-496-3611
Holten Meats
Sauget, IL 800-851-4684
Holton Meat Processing
Holton, KS .785-364-2331
Home Delivery Food Service
Jefferson, GA 706-367-9551
Hoopeston Foods
Burnsville, MN 952-854-0903
Hoople Country Kitchens
Rockport, IN 812-649-2351
Hormel Foods Corporation
Omaha, NE .402-493-8470
Hormel Foods Corporation
Fremont, NE 402-721-2300
Hormel Foods Corporation
Oklahoma City, OK 405-745-3471
Hormel Foods Corporation
Oklahoma City, OK 405-843-5643
Hormel Foods Corporation
Maitland, FL 407-660-0808
Hormel Foods Corporation
Columbia, MD 410-290-1855
Hormel Foods Corporation
Pittsburgh, PA 412-921-7036
Hormel Foods Corporation
West Allis, WI 414-604-0570
Hormel Foods Corporation
Franklin, MA 508-541-7112
Hormel Foods Corporation
Cincinnati, OH 513-563-0211
Hormel Foods Corporation
Urbandale, IA 515-276-8872
Hormel Foods Corporation
Phoenix, AZ 602-230-2400
Hormel Foods Corporation
Charlotte, NC 704-527-4388
Hormel Foods Corporation
Orchard Park, NY 716-675-7700
Hormel Foods Corporation
Austin, MN 800-523-4635
Hormel Foods Corporation
Lisle, IL 800-533-2000
Hormel Foods Corporation
Salt Lake City, UT 801-487-8251
Hormel Foods Corporation
Lubbock, TX 806-796-3630
Hormel Foods Corporation
Arlington, TX 817-465-4735
Hormel Foods Corporation
Cordova, TN 901-753-4282
Hormel Foods Corporation
Lebanon, NJ 908-236-7009
Hormel Foods Corporation
Shawnee Mission, KS 913-888-8744
Hormel Foods Corporation
Pleasanton, CA 925-225-9349
Hot Springs Packing Company
Hot Springs, AR 800-535-0449
Hsin Tung Yang Foods Co.
S San Francisco, CA 650-589-6789

Hubbard Farms
Pikeville, TN 501-262-1061
Hubbard Meat Company
Big Spring, TX 432-267-7781
Hughes Springs Frozen Food Center
Hughes Springs, TX 903-639-2941
Hughson Meat Company
San Marcos, TX 877-462-6328
Huisken Meat Center
Sauk Rapids, MN 320-259-0305
Humphrey Blue Ribbon Meats
Springfield, IL 800-747-6328
Hyde Meat Packing
Robert, LA .985-345-5756
IBP Foods
Troy, MI 248-588-4710
Indian Valley Meats
Indian, AK .907-653-7511
International Casing Group
Chicago, IL .800-825-5151
International Casings Group
Santa Fe Springs, CA 800-635-9518
International Food Packers Corporation
Miami, FL .305-669-1662
International Meat Company
Elmwood Park, IL. 773-622-1400
International Packers Corporation
Watertown, MA 508-963-8214
Iowa Quality Meats
Clive, IA 800-677-6868
Iowa Turkey Products
Marshall, MN 563-864-7676
Isernio Sausage Company
Seattle, WA 888-495-8674
Ito Cariani Sausage Company
Hayward, CA 510-887-0882
Ittels Meats
Howard Lake, MN 320-543-2285
J Freirich Food Products
Long Island City, NY 800-221-1315
J.J. Andrade's Slaughterhouse
Honokaa, HI 808-775-0741
J.T. Ward Meats & Provisions
Vernon, CA 323-585-9935
J.W. Treuth & Sons
Baltimore, MD 410-465-4650
Jack's Wholesale Meat Company
Trenton, TX. 903-989-2293
Jackson Brothers Food Locker
Post, TX 806-495-3245
Jackson Frozen Food Center
Hutchinson, KS. 620-662-4465
Jacobsmuhlen's Meats
Cornelius, OR 503-359-0479
Jaindl's Turkey Farms
Orefield, PA 800-475-6654
Jbs Packerland Inc
Green Bay, WI. 920-468-4000
Jemm Wholesale Meat Company
Chicago, IL 773-523-8161
Jensen Meat Company
Vista, CA 760-727-6700
Jesse's Fine Meats
Cherokee, IA. 712-225-3637
John Garner Meats
Van Buren, AR 800-543-5473
John R Morreale
Chicago, IL 312-421-3664
John R. Daily
Missoula, MT 406-721-7007
John Volpi & Company
St Louis, MO 800-288-3439
Johnson's Wholesale Meats
Opelousas, LA 337-948-4444
Johnson, Nash, & Sons Farms
Rose Hill, NC 800-682-6843
Johnsonville Food Company
Sheboygan, WI 920-459-6800
Jones Dairy Farm
Fort Atkinson, WI. 800-563-1004
Jordahl Meats
Manchester, MN 507-826-3418
Joseph Kirschner & Company
Augusta, ME 207-623-3544
Joseph Sanders
Custer, MI 800-968-5035
Keeter's Meat Company
Tulia, TX. .800-456-5019
Kelley Foods of Alabama
Elba, AL 334-897-5761
Kelly Packing Company
Torrington, WY 307-532-2210

Kenosha Beef International
Kenosha, WI 800-541-1685
Kent Quality Foods
Grand Rapids, MI 800-748-0141
Kershenstine Beef Jerky
Eupora, MS 662-258-2049
Ketters Meat Market & Locker Plant
Frazee, MN 218-334-2351
Keystone Foods Corporation
W Conshohocken, PA 610-667-6700
Kiefer Company
Louisville, KY 502-587-7474
King Meat
Los Angeles, CA 323-582-7401
King's Meat & Seafood
Houston, TX 713-923-6868
Kingsbury Country Market
Kingsbury, IN 219-393-3016
Kiolbassa Provision Company
San Antonio, TX. 800-456-5465
Koegel Meats
Flint, MI .810-238-3685
Konetzkos Market
Browerville, MN 320-594-2915
Kowalski Sausage Company
Hamtramck, MI. 800-482-2400
Kretschmar
Don Mills, ON 800-561-4532
Kruse & Son
Monrovia, CA 626-358-4536
Kruse Meat Products
Alexander, AR 501-316-1046
Kunzler & Company
Lancaster, PA 888-586-9537
Kutztown Bologna Company
Leola, PA. 800-723-8824
L&H Packing Company
San Antonio, TX 210-532-3241
L&L Packing Company
Chicago, IL 800-628-6328
L&M Frosted Food Lockers
Belt, MT .406-277-3522
Lad's Smokehouse Catering
Needville, TX 979-793-6210
Ladoga Frozen Food & Retail Meat
Ladoga, IN 765-942-2225
Lakeside Foods
Plainview, MN 507-534-3141
Lampost Meats
Grimes, IA. 515-288-6111
Land O'Frost
Searcy, AR 800-643-5654
Larsen Packers
Burwick, NS 902-538-8060
Lees Sausage Company
Orangeburg, SC 803-534-5517
Lengerich Meats
Zanesville, IN 260-638-4123
Leo G. Fraboni Sausage Company
Hibbing, MN. 218-263-5074
Lewis Smoked Meat Company
Chicago, IL 800-648-6328
Lindner Bison
Valencia, CA 866-247-8753
Lionel Lavallee Company
Haverhill, MA 800-343-8292
Livingston Provision Company
Tallahassee, FL 850-576-0153
Lombardi Brothers Meat Packers
Denver, CO 800-421-4412
Lone Star Beef Jerky Company
Lubbock, TX. 806-762-8833
Lords Sausage & Country Ham
Dexter, GA 800-342-6002
Lykes Meat Group
Plant City, FL 813-752-1102
Lynden Meat Company
Lynden, WA 360-354-2449
M K Meat Processing Plant
Burton, TX 979-289-4022
M&M Packing Company
Ballinger, TX 915-365-2227
Mac's Meats Wholesale
Las Cruces, NM 575-524-2751
MacFarlane Pheasants
Janesville, WI 877-269-8957
MacGregors Meat & Seafood
Toronto, ON 800-268-5953
Maid-Rite Steak Company
Dunmore, PA 800-233-4259
Manger Packing Company
Baltimore, MD 800-227-9262

Maple Leaf Foods International
Toronto, ON 416-480-8900
Maple Leaf Meats
Winnipeg, NB 204-233-2421
Maple Leaf Pork
Burlington, ON 905-637-2301
Marburger Foods
Peru, IN 765-689-5198
Marcel et Henri Charcuterie Francaise
S San Francisco, CA 800-227-6436
Marks Meat
Canby, OR 503-266-2048
MBM Corporation
Rocky Mount, NC 252-985-7200
McKiever Packing Company
Monticello, AR 870-367-6938
McLemore's Abattoir
Vidalia, GA 912-537-4476
Meal Mart
Flushing, NY 800-245-5620
Meat Center
Edna, TX 361-782-3776
Meat Shop
Cape Girardeau, MO 800-791-5104
Meating Place
Buffalo, NY 716-885-3623
Medeiros Farms
Kalaheo, HI 808-332-8211
Menu Meats
Huntertown, IN 800-848-2902
Merkley & Sons Packing
Jasper, IN 812-482-7020
Michael's Finer Meats & Seafoods
Columbus, OH 800-282-0518
Midway Meats
Centralia, WA 360-736-5257
Mike's Meats
Eitzen, MN 507-495-3336
Miller Brothers Packing Company
Sylvester, GA 229-776-2014
Mishler Packing Company
Lagrange, IN 260-768-4156
Mongolia Casing Corporation
Flushing, NY 800-221-4887
Moonlite Bar BQ Inn
Owensboro, KY 800-322-8989

Morrison Lamothe
Toronto, ON 416-291-6762
Morrison Meat Packers
Miami, FL 305-836-4461
Mosby Packing Company
Meridian, MS 800-844-7225
Mountain City Meat Company
Denver, CO 800-937-8325
Mountain States Rosen, LLc
Bronx, NY 800-872-5262
Moyer Packing Company
Souderton, PA 800-967-8325
Napoleon Locker
Napoleon, IN. 812-852-4333
National Beef Packing
Kansas City, MO. 800-449-2333
National By-Products
Omaha, NE 402-291-2646
National Foods
Indianapolis, IN 800-683-6565
Neithart Meats
Sylmar, CA 818-361-7141
New City Packing & Provision Company
North Aurora, IL 630-898-1900
New Generation Foods
Omaha, NE 402-733-5755
New Glarus Foods
New Glarus, WI 800-356-6685
Newark Meat Supply
Newark, OH 740-345-6696
Newburgh Packing Corporation
New Windsor, NY 845-562-1185
Nicky
Portland, OR 800-469-4162
Niemuth's Steak & Chop Shop
Waupaca, WI. 715-258-2666
North Star Foods
St Charles, MN 507-932-4831
O'Brien & Company
Bellevue, NE. 800-433-7567
O'Neill Packing Company
Omaha, NE 402-733-1200
Oh Boy! Corporation
San Fernando, CA. 818-361-1128
Ohio Packing Company
Columbus, OH 800-282-6403

Oklahoma City Meat
Oklahoma City, OK 405-235-3308
Olson Locker
Fairmont, MN 507-238-2563
Olympic Food Products
Kokomo, IN 800-445-6923
Omaha Meat Processors
Omaha, NE 402-554-1965
Omaha Steaks International
Omaha, NE 800-562-0500
On-Cor Foods Products
Northbrook, IL 847-205-1040
Original Chili Bowl
Tulsa, OK 918-628-0225
Oscars Wholesale Meats
Ogden, UT. 801-394-6472
Ossian Seafood Meats
Ossian, IN 260-622-4191
Otto & Son
West Chicago, IL 630-231-9091
Our Best Foods
Tewksbury, MA. 978-858-0077
Owens Country Sausage
Richardson, TX. 800-966-9367
Package Concepts & Materials Inc
Greenville, SC. 800-424-7264
Palmer Packing Company
Tremonton, UT 435-257-5329
Paradise Locker Company
Trimble, MO 816-370-6328
Party Steak Company
Springfield, MO 417-358-9091
Pasqualichio Brothers
Scranton, PA 800-232-6233
PB&S Chemicals
Henderson, KY 800-950-7267
Peco Foods
Tuscaloosa, AL 205-345-4711
Peerless Packing Company
Beckley, WV. 304-252-4731
Pekarna's Meat Market
Jordan, MN 952-492-6101
Pel-Freez
Rogers, AR 800-223-8751
Pender Packing Company
Rocky Point, NC 910-675-3311

Petschl's Meats
Tukwila, WA 206-575-4400
Pfeffer's Country Market
Sauk Centre, MN 320-352-3095
Phoenix Agro-Industrial Corporation
Westbury, NY 516-334-1194
Pie Piper Products
Bensenville, IL 800-621-8183
Pierceton Foods
Pierceton, IN 574-594-2344
Pierre Foods
Cincinnati, OH 513-874-8741
Pilgrim's Pride
Timberville, VA 540-896-7000
Pilgrim's Pride
Enterprise, AL. 800-633-0908
Pilgrim's Pride
Pittsburg, TX 800-683-1968
Piller Sausages & Delicatessens
Waterloo, ON 519-743-1412
Pinter's Packing Plant
Dorchester, WI 715-654-5444
Plumrose USA
Elkhart, IN .574-295-8190
Plymouth Beef
New York, NY 718-589-8600
PM Windom
Windom, MN 507-831-2761
Pork Packers International
Downs, KS .785-454-3396
Prairie Cajun Wholesale
Eunice, LA .337-546-6195
Premium Meat Company
Brigham City, UT 435-723-5944
Premium Standard Farms
Kansas City, MO. 800-994-7675
Prime Smoked Meats
Oakland, CA 510-832-7167
Promiseland Meat PackingCompany
Madill, OK .580-795-3567
Provimi Veal Corporation
Seymour, WI 800-833-8325
Pruden Packing Company
Suffolk, VA .757-539-8773
Puueo Poi Factory
Hilo, HI 808-935-8435
Quality Beef Company
Providence, RI 877-233-3462
Quality Meats & Seafood
West Fargo, ND. 800-342-4250
Quality Sausage Company
Dallas, TX. .214-634-3400
Quantum Foods LLC
Bolingbrook, IL 800-334-6328
R Four Meats
Chatfield, MN 507-867-4180
R.E. Meyer Company
Lincoln, NE. 402-474-8500
R.M. Felts Packing Company
Ivor, VA 888-300-0971
Rabbit Barn
Turlock, CA 209-632-1123
Raber Packing
Peoria, IL 309-673-0721
Raemica
Running Springs, CA 800-772-6328
Ralph Packing Company
Perkins, OK. 800-522-3979
Rancher's Lamb of Texas
San Angelo, TX 325-659-4004
Randolph Packing Corporation
Asheboro, NC 336-672-1470
Randy's Frozen Meats
Faribault, MN 800-354-7177
Ray's Sausage Company Inc
Cleveland, OH 216-921-8782
Real Kosher Sausage Company
Newark, NJ 973-690-5394
Redi-Serve Food Company
Fort Atkinson, WI. 920-563-6391
Register Meat Company
Cottondale, FL 850-352-4269
Rego's Purity Foods
Honolulu, HI. 808-947-9005
Reser's Fine Foods
Beaverton, OR 800-333-6431
Rhodia Inc
Cranbury, NJ 609-860-4000
Rinehart Meat Processing
Branson, MO. 417-334-2044
Ringhands' Meat Processing Plant
Evansville, WI 608-882-5025

Ritchie Wholesale Meats
Piketon, OH 800-628-1290
Riverton Packing
Riverton, WY 307-856-3838
Robbins Packing Company
Statesboro, GA 912-764-7503
Robinsons Sausage Company
London, KY 606-864-2914
Rock River Provision Company
Rock Falls, IL 800-685-1195
Rocky Mountain Packing Company
Havre, MT. .406-265-3401
Roman Packing Company
Norfolk, NE. 800-373-5990
Roman Sausage Company
Santa Clara, CA 800-497-7462
Roode Packing Company
Fairbury, NE 402-729-2253
Rosa Brothers
Miami, FL. .305-324-1510
Rose Packing Company
South Barrington, IL 800-323-7363
Rosen's Diversified
Fairmont, MN 800-798-2000
Royal Center Locker Plant
Royal Center, IN 574-643-3275
Royal Home Bakery
Newmarket, ON 905-715-7044
Royal Palate Foods
Inglewood, CA 310-330-7701
Rudolph's Market & Sausage Factory
Dallas, TX. .214-741-1874
Russer Foods
Buffalo, NY. 800-828-7021
Ryley Sausage
Ryley, AB 780-663-3990
Rymer Foods
Chicago, IL 800-247-9637
S.S. Logan Packing Company
Huntington, WV 800-642-3524
S.W. Meat & Provision Company
Phoenix, AZ 602-275-2000
Sadler's BBQ Sales
Henderson, TX 903-657-5581
Sahlen Packing Company
Buffalo, NY. 716-852-8677
Saletts
Randolph, MA 781-961-9900
Saluda Meat Center
Saluda, SC. 864-445-2188
Sambol Meat Company
Kansas City, KS 913-721-2817
San Angelo Packing
San Angelo, TX 325-653-6951
San Antonio Packing Company
San Antonio, TX. 210-224-5441
Sanderson Farms
Bryan, TX 979-778-5730
Sara Lee Corporation
Downers Grove, IL 630-598-8100
Sara Lee Foods
Cincinnati, OH 800-351-7111
Sara Lee Foods
Neenah, WI. 800-558-8440
Sara Lee Foods
Cordova, TN 901-756-4051
Sardinha Sausage
Somerset, MA. 800-678-0178
Saunders Provision Company
Norfolk, VA. 800-486-5611
Saval Foods
Elkridge, MD 800-527-2825
Savoie's Sausage & Food Products
Opelousas, LA. 337-948-4115
Scala Packing Company
Chicago, IL 312-944-3567
Scanga Meat Company
Salida, CO .719-539-3511
Schaefer Packing
Mundelein, IL 847-949-2820
Schaller's Packers
Cassville, NY 315-822-3924
Schleswig Specialty Meats
Schleswig, IA 712-676-3324
Schultz Provisions Company
Dracut, MA 800-932-7477
Schumacher Wholesale Meats
Golden Valley, MN 800-432-7020
Schweigert Foods
Albert Lea, MN. 507-377-2526
Seaboard Foods
Shawnee Mission, KS. 800-262-7907

Seitz Foods
Saint Joseph, MO 800-383-3128
Serv-Rite Meat Company
Los Angeles, CA. 323-227-1911
Shaker Valley Foods
Cleveland, OH 216-961-8600
Shamrock Slaughter Plant
Shamrock, TX 806-256-3241
Shapiro Packing Company
Augusta, GA 706-724-6401
Shelley's Prime Meats
Jersey City, NJ 201-433-3434
Shelton's Poultry
Pomona, CA 800-541-1833
Shofar Kosher Foods
Linden, NJ. 888-874-6327
Siena Foods
Toronto, ON 800-465-0422
Silver Creek Specialty Meats
Oshkosh, WI 920-232-3581
Silver Star Meats
Mc Kees Rocks, PA 412-771-5539
Sioux-Preme Packing Company
Sioux Center, IA 712-722-2555
Skylark Meats
Omaha, NE 800-759-5275
Smith Meat Packing
Port Huron, MI 810-985-5900
Smith Packing Regional Meat
Utica, NY .315-732-5125
Smith Provision Company
Erie, PA 800-334-9151
Smithfield Packing Company
Smithfield, VA 757-357-4321
SOPAKCO Foods
Mullins, SC. 800-276-9678
Souris Valley Processors
Melita, NB. 204-522-8210
Southchem
Durham, NC 800-849-7000
Southern Packing Corporation
Chesapeake, VA 757-421-2131
Sparrer Sausage Company
Chicago, IL 800-666-3287
Specialty Brands
Carthage, MO 417-358-8104
Specialty Steak Service
Erie, PA 814-452-2281
Spencer Packing Company
Washington, NC 252-946-4161
Spring Hill Meat Market
Spring Hill, KS 913-592-3501
Springville Meat & Cold Storage
Springville, UT 801-489-6391
Stampede Meat
Bridgeview, IL 800-353-0933
Standard Beef Company
New Haven, CT 203-787-2164
Statewide Meats & Poultry
New Haven, CT 203-777-6669
Steak-Umm Company
Shillington, PA 860-928-5900
Stewarts Market
Yelm, WA .360-458-2091
Stock Yards Packing Company
Chicago, IL 800-621-1119
Stoffle Meat Company
Topeka, KS 785-234-2683
Stone Meat Processor
Ogden, UT. 801-782-9825
Stonies Sausage Shop Inc
Perryville, MO 888-546-2540
Strasburg Provision
Strasburg, OH 800-207-6009
Striplings
Moultrie, GA. 229-985-4226
Strube Packing Company
Rowena, TX 325-442-2851
Sudlersville Frozen Food Locker
Sudlersville, MD. 410-438-3106
Sunergia Soyfoods
Charlottesville, VA 800-693-5134
Sunnydale Meats
Gaffney, SC. 864-489-6091
Superior Meat Company
Vernal, UT. 435-789-3274
Suwannee Packing Company
Live Oak, FL 904-362-1422
Suzanna's Kitchen
Duluth, GA. 800-241-2455
SW Red Smith
Davie, FL. .954-581-1996

Swanton's Packing
Fairfax, VT 802-868-4469
Swift & Company
Greeley, CO. 970-324-2180
Swiss American Sausage Corporation
Lathrop, CA .209-858-5555
Swiss-American Sausage Company
Lathrop, CA .209-858-5555
Swissland Packing Company
Frankfort, IL 800-321-8325
T O Williams
Portsmouth, VA 757-397-0771
T.L. Herring & Company
Wilson, NC 252-291-1141
Taylor Meat Company
Taylor, TX 512-352-6357
Taylor Provisions Company
Trenton, NJ .609-392-1113
Temptee Specialty Foods
Denver, CO .800-842-1233
Tenn Valley Ham Company
Paris, TN 731-642-9740
Tennessee Valley PackingCompany
Columbia, TN 931-388-2623
Theriaults Abattoir
Van Buren, ME 207-868-3344
Thomas Brothers Ham Company
Asheboro, NC 336-672-0337
Thomas Packing Company
Columbus, GA 800-729-0976
Thompson Packers
Slidell, LA. .800-989-6328
Thumann's
Carlstadt, NJ 201-935-3636
Tiger Meat Provisions
Miami, FL. 305-324-0083
Tillamook Meat Company
Tillamook, OR 503-842-4802
Tooele Valley Meat
Grantsville, UT 435-884-3837
Top Choice Meat Processing
Buffalo, WY 307-684-7741
Topps Meat Company
Elizabeth, NJ. 908-351-0500
Townsends
Pittsboro, NC 919-542-3215
Townsends Inc
Siler City, NC 919-663-2050
Travis Meats
Powell, TN .800-247-7606
Triple U Enterprises
Fort Pierre, SD 605-567-3624
Troy Pork Store
Troy, NY 518-272-8291
Tupman-Thurlow Company
Deerfield Beach, FL 954-596-9989
Turner Brothers
Nowata, OK 918-273-1858
Tyler Packing Company
Tyler, TX. 903-593-9592
Tyson Foods
Fort Smith, AR 479-783-8996
Tyson Foods
Amarillo, TX. 806-335-1531
Tyson Foods Plant
Santa Teresa, NM 800-351-8184
Tyson Fresh Meats
Dakota Dunes, SD. 605-235-2061
Tyson Fresh Meats
Emporia, KS 620-343-3640
Une-Viandi
St. Jean Sur Richelieu, NB 800-363-1955
United Meat Company
San Francisco, CA 415-864-2118
United Packing
Providence, RI 401-751-6935
United Provision Meat Company
Columbus, OH 614-252-1126
Universal Meat Products
Pikesville, MD 410-484-3900
V&V Supremo Foods
Chicago, IL .800-547-8773
V.W. Joyner & Company
Smithfield, VA 757-357-2161
Valley Institutional Foods Company
Edinburg, TX 956-687-6211
Valley Meat Company
Modesto, CA 800-222-6328
Valley Packing Company
Hartford, CT 860-522-3805
Victor Ostrowski & Son
Baltimore, MD 410-327-8935

Vienna Meat Products
Scarborough, ON 800-588-1931
Vienna Sausage Company
Chicago, IL .800-326-6652
Vietti Foods Company Inc
Nashville, TN 800-240-7864
Vollwerth & Company
Hancock, MI 800-562-7620
W&G Marketing Company
Ames, IA 515-233-4774
Waco Beef & Pork Processors
Waco, TX 254-772-4669
Wall Meat Processing
Wall, SD 605-279-2348
Wampler's Farm Sausage Company
Lenoir City, TN 800-728-7243
Wasatch Meats
Salt Lake City, UT 801-363-5747
Washington Beef
Toppenish, WA 800-289-2333
Watson's Quality Food Products
Blackwood, NJ 800-257-7870
Wayco Ham Company
Goldsboro, NC 800-962-2614
Weber-Stephen Products Company
Palatine, IL .800-446-1071
Weiss Provisions
Pittsburgh, PA 800-458-6328
West Virginia Sausage Company
New Haven, WV 304-882-3194
Western Meats
Rapid City, SD 605-342-0322
Westport Locker Service
Westport, IN 877-265-0551
White Castle System
Columbus, OH 866-272-8372
White Packing Company
Fredericksburg, VA 540-898-2029
Whittaker & Associates
Atlanta, GA. 404-266-1265
Wichita Packing Company
Chicago, IL .312-421-0606
Willcox Packing House
Willcox, AZ 520-384-2015
Williams Packing Company
Goldsboro, NC 919-735-0262
Willies Smoke House
Harrisville, PA 800-742-4184
Wimmer's Meat Products
West Point, NE 800-358-0761
Windcrest Meat Packers
Port Perry, ON. 800-750-2542
Wolff Meat Company
San Antonio, TX. 210-335-2626
Wolverine Packing
Detroit, MI .313-392-9403
Woodbine
Norfolk, VA. 757-461-2731
Wright Brand Foods
Vernon, TX .940-553-1888
XL Beef
Calgary, AB. 403-236-2424
Y&T Packing
Springfield, IL. 217-522-3345
Yates Country Hams
Asheboro, NC 336-629-1795
Yoakum Packing Company
Yoakum, TX 361-293-3541
Yoders
Grantsville, MD 301-895-5121
Zartic Inc
Rome, GA 800-241-0516
Zerna Packing
Labadie, MO 636-742-4190
Zummo Meat Company
Beaumont, TX. 409-842-1810
Zweigle's
Rochester, NY. 585-546-1740

Patties

Acme Steak & Seafood Company
Youngstown, OH. 330-270-8000
Cargill Foods
Minneapolis, MN 800-227-455
Caribbean Food Delights
Tappan, NY .845-398-3000
Chicago Meat Authority
Chicago, IL .773-254-0020
Corfu Foods
Bensenville, IL 630-595-2510

Dallas Dressed Beef
Dallas, TX. .214-638-0142
Decker & Son Company
Colorado Springs, CO. 719-634-8311
Elkhart Locker Plant
Elkhart, KS .620-697-4424
Golden State Foods
Irvine, CA 949-252-2000
Holten Meats
Sauget, IL 800-851-4684
Karn Meats
Columbus, OH 800-221-9585
Kenosha Beef International
Kenosha, WI 800-541-1685
Kutztown Bologna Company
Leola, PA. 800-723-8824
L&H Packing Company
San Antonio, TX. 210-532-3241
Laurent Meat Market
Marrero, LA 504-341-1771
Les Trois Petits Cochons 3 Little Pigs
Brooklyn, NY 212-219-1230
Meating Place
Buffalo, NY. 716-885-3623
Mosey's Inc
Bloomfield, CT. 860-243-1725
Otto & Son
West Jordan, UT 800-453-9462
Purnell's Old Folks Sausage Company
Simpsonville, KY 800-626-1512
Redi-Serve Food Company
Fort Atkinson, WI 920-563-6391
Rego's Purity Foods
Honolulu, HI 808-947-9005
Roman Sausage Company
Santa Clara, CA 800-497-7462
S.W. Meat & Provision Company
Phoenix, AZ 602-275-2000
Springville Meat & Cold Storage
Springville, UT 801-489-6391
Topps Meat Company
Elizabeth, NJ. 908-351-0500
Travis Meats
Powell, TN .800-247-7606
Valley Meat Company
Modesto, CA 800-222-6328
Wisconsin Packing Company
Butler, WI 800-558-2000
Zartic Inc
Rome, GA 800-241-0516

Frozen

Big Apple Produce & Seafood Market
Pocomoke City, MD 410-957-1151
Birchwood Foods
Kenosha, WI 800-541-1685

Burke Corporation
Nevada, IA .800-654-1152

Always make it your best® with Burke fully
cooked meats. We specialize in Italian sausage,
beef, and pork toppings, meatballs, taco meats,
shredded meats, pepperoni, bacon, Canadian-style bacon, chicken and beef strips. Additionally, we offer a variety of specialty products:
Hand-Pinched Style® brand toppings, chorizo,
gyro topping, andouille sausage, and breakfast
patties and links.

Cardinal Meat Specialists
Mississauga, ON 800-363-1439
Caribbean Food Delights
Tappan, NY .845-398-3000
Chicago Meat Authority
Chicago, IL .773-254-0020
Corfu Foods
Bensenville, IL 630-595-2510
Edmonds Chile Company
St Louis, MO. 314-772-1499
Flanders Provision Company
Waycross, GA 912-283-5191
Glenmark Food Processors
Chicago, IL .800-621-0117

Holten Meats
Sauget, IL 800-851-4684
Jemm Wholesale Meat Company
Chicago, IL 773-523-8161
Joette's Sausage
Kincaid, IL 217-789-6300
John Garner Meats
Van Buren, AR 800-543-5473
Kenosha Beef International
Kenosha, WI .800-541-1685
King Kold Meats
Englewood, OH 800-836-2797
Kutztown Bologna Company
Leola, PA 800-723-8824
Leo G. Fraboni Sausage Company
Hibbing, MN .218-263-5074
Maid-Rite Steak Company
Dunmore, PA .800-233-4259
Matlaw's Food Products
West Haven, CT 800-934-8266
Mello's North End Manufacturings
Fall River, MA 800-673-2320
New Bedford Linguica
New Bedford, MA 877-372-4616
On-Cor Foods Products
Northbrook, IL 847-205-1040
Plymouth Beef
New York, NY 718-589-8600
Redi-Serve Food Company
Fort Atkinson, WI 920-563-6391
Thompson Packers
Slidell, LA 800-989-6328
Topps Meat Company
Elizabeth, NJ .908-351-0500
Valley Meat Company
Modesto, CA .800-222-6328
Wampler Foods
Dallas, TX 717-624-2191
Wisconsin Packing Company
Butler, WI 800-558-2000
Zartic Inc
Rome, GA 800-241-0516

Portion Cuts

A to Z Portion Meats
Bluffton, OH .800-338-6328
Atlantic Veal & Lamb
Brooklyn, NY 800-221-6988
B&D Foods
Boise, ID 208-344-1183
Beef Products
North Sioux City, SD 605-217-8000
Blue Ribbon Meats
Miami, FL 800-522-6115
Boar's Head Provisions Company
Sarasota, FL .888-884-2627
Bouma Meats
Provost, AB 780-753-2092
Broadleaf Venison USA
Vernon, CA 800-336-3844
Bruss Company
Chicago, IL 800-621-3882
Bush Brothers Provision Company
West Palm Beach, FL 800-327-1345
C&S Wholesale Meat Company
Atlanta, GA 404-627-3547
Cambridge Packing Company
Boston, MA 800-722-6726
Canal Fulton Provision
Canal Fulton, OH 800-321-3502

Caribbean Food Delights
Tappan, NY 845-398-3000
Carl Streit & Son Company
Neptune, NJ .732-775-0803
Castleberry's Meats
Atlanta, GA 404-873-1804
Chicago Meat Authority
Chicago, IL 773-254-0020
Cloverdale Foods Company
Mandan, ND .800-669-9511
Corfu Foods
Bensenville, IL 630-595-2510
Dairy Fresh Foods
Taylor, MI 313-295-6300
Decker & Son Company
Colorado Springs, CO 719-634-8311
Devault Foods
Devault, PA 800-426-2874
Foodbrands America
Oklahoma City, OK 405-290-4000
Frank's Foods
Hilo, HI 808-959-9121
Greenwood Packing Plant
Greenwood, SC 864-229-5611
H. Shenson International Export
San Francisco, CA 415-318-7000
Henry J Meat Specialties
Chicago, IL 800-242-1314
Hoekstra Meat Company
Kalamazoo, MI 616-321-0797
International Packers Corporation
Watertown, MA 508-963-8214
James J. Derba Company
Boston, MA 800-732-3848
King Kold Meats
Englewood, OH 800-836-2797
Kraft Foodservices
Tampa, FL 800-551-2559
L&L Packing Company
Chicago, IL 800-628-6328
Land O'Frost
Searcy, AR 800-643-5654
Loggins Meat Company
Tyler, TX 800-527-8610
Marshallville Packing Company
Marshallville, OH 330-855-2871
National Foods
Indianapolis, IN 800-683-6565
O Chili Frozen Foods Inc
Northbrook, IL 847-562-1991
Ottman Meat Company
New York, NY 212-879-4160
Otto W Liebold & Company
Flint, MI 800-999-6328
Pacific Poultry Company
Honolulu, HI .808-841-2828
Paris Frozen Foods
Hillsboro, IL .217-532-3822
Quality Meats & Seafood
West Fargo, ND 800-342-4250
Randy's Frozen Meats
Faribault, MN 800-354-7177
Robinsons Sausage Company
London, KY 606-864-2914
Russer Foods
Buffalo, NY 800-828-7021
S.W. Meat & Provision Company
Phoenix, AZ .602-275-2000
Saletts
Randolph, MA 781-961-9900
Saunders Provision Company
Norfolk, VA 800-486-5611
SOPAKCO Foods
Mullins, SC 800-276-9678
Standard Beef Company
New Haven, CT 203-787-2164
Tenn Valley Ham Company
Paris, TN 731-642-9740
Triple U Enterprises
Fort Pierre, SD 605-567-3624
United Meat Company
San Francisco, CA 415-864-2118
Waco Beef & Pork Processors
Waco, TX 254-772-4669
Whitaker Foods
Evansdale, IA 800-553-7490
Wisconsin Packing Company
Butler, WI 800-558-2000

Prepared

Burke Corporation
Nevada, IA 800-654-1152

Always make it your best® with Burke fully
cooked meats. We specialize in Italian sausage,
beef, and pork toppings, meatballs, taco meats,
shredded meats, pepperoni, bacon, Canadian-style bacon, chicken and beef strips. Additionally, we offer a variety of specialty products:
Hand-Pinched Style® brand toppings, chorizo,
gyro topping, andouille sausage, and breakfast
patties and links.

Gutheinz Meats
Scranton, PA .570-344-1191
Specialty Foods Group
Newport News, VA 800-238-0020

Proteins

Burke Corporation
Nevada, IA 800-654-1152

Always make it your best® with Burke fully
cooked meats. We specialize in Italian sausage,
beef, and pork toppings, meatballs, taco meats,
shredded meats, pepperoni, bacon, Canadian-style bacon, chicken and beef strips. Additionally, we offer a variety of specialty products:
Hand-Pinched Style® brand toppings, chorizo,
gyro topping, andouille sausage, and breakfast
patties and links.

Proliant Meat Ingredients
Ankeny, IA 800-369-2672

General

Aala Meat Market
Honolulu, HI .808-832-6650
Acme Farms
Seattle, WA 800-542-8309
Alexian Pates/GroezingerProvisions
Neptune, NJ .800-927-9473
American Foodservice
Dallas, TX 972-385-5800
Ballard Custom Meats
Manchester, ME 207-622-9764
Baltimore Poultry & Meats
Baltimore, MD 410-783-7361
Belleville Brothers Packing
North Baltimore, OH 419-257-3529
Bering Sea Raindeer Products
Mekoryuk, AK 907-827-8940
Bernard & Sons
Bakersfield, CA 661-327-4431
Blalock Seafood
Orange Beach, AL 251-974-5811
Broadbent's B&B Foods
Kuttawa, KY .800-841-2202
Brooks Meat
Walton, KY 859-485-7104
Brown Foods
Dallas, GA 770-445-4554
Brownsdale Meat Service
Brownsdale, MN 507-567-2211
Buffalo Bob's Everything Sauce
Virginia Beach, VA 757-490-9186

Burke Corporation
Nevada, IA .800-654-1152

Always make it your best® with Burke fully cooked meats. We specialize in Italian sausage, beef, and pork toppings, meatballs, taco meats, shredded meats, pepperoni, bacon, Canadian-style bacon, chicken and beef strips. Additionally, we offer a variety of specialty products: Hand-Pinched Style® brand toppings, chorizo, gyro topping, andouille sausage, and breakfast patties and links.

C&J Tender Meat
  Anchorage, AK 907-562-2838
Casper Foodservice Company
  Chicago, IL 312-226-2265
Cher-Make Sausage Co (Smokey Valley Meat Products Co)
  Manitowoc, WI 920-683-5980
Chipper Snax
  Salt Lake City, UT 801-977-0742
Chong Mei Trading
  Atlanta, GA 404-768-3838
Cimpl Meats
  Yankton, SD 605-665-1665
CJ Vitner Company
  Chicago, IL 773-523-7900
Coleman Purely Natural Brands
  Golden, CO 877-810-8291
ConAgra Beef Company
  Garden City, KS 620-275-9661
Conco Food Service
  Harahan, LA 800-488-3988
Country - Fed - Meats Company
  Riverdale, GA 800-637-7559
Cross Creek Foods
  Fayetteville, NC 910-323-9477
Dick's Packing Plant
  New Lexington, OH 740-342-4150
Distinctive Brands
  Golden, CO 303-273-9049
Double B Distributors
  Lexington, KY 859-255-8822
Dutch Valley Veal
  South Holland, IL 800-832-8325
E-Fish-Ent Fish Company
  Sooke, BC 250-642-4007
Ellsworth Foods
  Tifton, GA 229-386-8448
Evan's Food Products
  Chicago, IL 773-254-7400
G&W Packing Company
  Chicago, IL 773-847-5400
Glenoaks Foods
  Sun Valley, CA 818-768-9091
GoodMark Foods
  Stamford, CT. 919-790-9940
Great West of Hawaii
  Honolulu, HI 808-593-9981
Grennan Meats
  Rochelle, IL 815-562-5565
Gulf Marine & Industrial Supplies
  New Orleans, LA 800-886-6252
Hammons Meat Sales
  Bakersfield, CA 661-831-9541
Harbison Wholesale Meats
  Cullman, AL 256-739-5105
Higa Meat and Pork Market Limited
  Honolulu, HI 808-531-3591
Hinojosa Bros Wholesale
  Roma, TX 800-554-4119
International Farmers Market
  Chamblee, GA. 770-455-1777
Jimmy Dean Foods
  Cincinnati, OH 800-925-3326
Kern Meat Distributing
  Brooksville, KY 606-756-2255
King Nut Company
  Cleveland, OH 800-860-5464
Kunzler & Company
  Lancaster, PA 888-586-9537
Levonian Brothers
  Troy, NY 518-274-3610

Link Snacks
  Minong, WI. 800-346-6896
Manda Fine Meats
  Baton Rouge, LA 225-344-7636
Manhattan Wholesale MeatCompany
  Manhattan, KS 785-776-9203
Market Day Corporation
  Itasca, IL 877-632-7753
McDowell Fine Meats 2
  Phoenix, AZ 602-254-6022
McFarling Foods
  Indianapolis, IN 317-635-2633
McKenzie of Vermont
  Burlington, VT 802-864-4585
McRedmond Brothers
  Nashville, TN 615-361-8997
Meat & Fish Fellas
  Glendale, AZ. 623-931-6190
Meat Corral Company
  Gainesville, GA 770-536-9188
Monsour's
  Pittsburg, KS 620-232-7600
My Favorite Jerky
  Boulder, CO 303-444-2846
Naman's Meat Company
  Mobile, AL 251-633-2700
Nash Finch Company
  Statesboro, GA 912-681-4580
National Meat & Provision Company
  New Orleans, LA 504-525-7224
New Grass Bison
  Shawnee, KS. 866-422-5888
Northern Meats
  Anchorage, AK 907-561-1729
Northwest Meat Company
  Chicago, IL 312-733-1418
Oberto Sausage Company
  Kent, WA. 877-453-7591
Oberweis Dairy
  North Aurora, IL 888-645-5868
Oscars Wholesale Meats
  Ogden, UT. 801-394-6472
Otto W Liebold & Company
  Flint, MI 800-999-6328
Park 100 Foods
  Tipton, IN 800-854-6504
Phenix Food Service
  Phenix City, AL 334-298-6288
Piggie Park Enterprises
  West Columbia, SC. 800-628-7423
Pilot Meat & Sea Food Company
  Galena, IL 319-556-0760
Pioneer Snacks
  Farmington Hills, MI 248-862-1990
Pluester's Quality Meat Company
  Hardin, IL 618-396-2224
Pon Food Corporation
  Ponchatoula, LA 985-386-6941
Porkie Company of Wisconsin
  Cudahy, WI. 800-333-2588
Porrhoff Foods Company
  Des Moines, IA 515-244-5271
Prime Cut Meat & Seafood Company
  Phoenix, AZ 602-455-8834
Primera Meat Service
  Harlingen, TX 956-423-4846
Protos Foods
  Greensburg, PA 724-836-1802
Ready Portion Meat Company
  Baton Rouge, LA 225-355-5641
Schenk Packing Company
  Mt Vernon, WA. 360-336-2128
Seafood Dimension International
  Anaheim, CA 714-692-6464
Service Foods
  Norcross, GA 770-448-5300
Shuffs Meat Company
  Thurmont, MD 301-271-2231
Smoke House
  Sagle, ID 208-263-6312
Snak King Corporation
  City of Industry, CA 626-336-7711
Southeastern Meats
  Birmingham, AL 205-785-3194
Speco
  Schiller Park, IL 800-541-5415
SRA Foods
  Birmingham, AL 205-323-7447
SSI Food Service
  Caldwell, ID 208-482-7844
Stegall Smoked Turkey
  Marshville, NC 800-851-6034

Surlean Food Solutions
  San Antonio, TX. 800-999-4370
Taylor Packing Company
  Wyalusing, PA 570-746-3000
Teddy's Tasty Meats
  Anchorage, AK 907-562-2320
Thumann's
  Carlstadt, NJ 201-935-3636
Todd's
  Vernon, CA 800-938-6337
Trail's Best Snacks
  Memphis, TN 800-852-1863
Trenton Processing
  Trenton, IL 618-224-7383
Trio Foods
  Cabot, AR 501-843-9446
Troyer Foods
  Goshen, IN 574-533-0302
Turkey Creek Snacks
  Thomaston, GA 706-647-8841
Tyson Prepared Foods
  Fort Worth, TX 817-258-2400
United Universal Enterprises Corporation
  Phoenix, AZ 623-842-9691
Utz Quality Foods
  Hanover, PA 800-367-7629
Vac Pac Manufacturing Company
  Baltimore, MD 800-368-2301
Vantage USA
  Chicago, IL 773-247-1086
Vity Meat & Provisions Company
  Phoenix, AZ 602-269-7768
W.L. Halsey Grocery Company
  Huntsville, AL 256-772-9691
YB Meats of Wichita
  Wichita, KS. 316-942-1213

Beef & Beef Products

A to Z Portion Meats
  Bluffton, OH 800-338-6328
A. Stein Meat Products
  Brooklyn, NY 718-492-0760
A. Thomas Food Service
  Louisville, KY 800-253-2020
A.C. Kissling Company
  Philadelphia, PA 800-445-1943
Abbott's Meat
  Flint, MI 810-232-7128
Abbyland Foods
  Abbotsford, WI. 800-732-5483
Abeles & Heymann GourmetKosher Provisions, Inc.
  Bronx, NY. 718-589-0100
Acme Steak & Seafood Company
  Youngstown, OH 330-270-8000
Adolf's Meats & Sausage Kitchen
  Hartford, CT 860-522-1588
Advance Food Company
  Enid, OK 888-723-8237
AFI-FlashGril'd Steak
  Salt Lake City, UT 800-382-2862
Agri-Best Foods
  Chicago, IL 773-247-5060
Al Safa Halal
  Niagara Falls, NY 800-268-8174
Alderfer Bologna
  Harleysville, PA 877-253-6328
Alle Processing
  Flushing, NY 718-894-2000
Allied Meat Service
  Hayward, CA 800-794-2554
Alphin Brothers
  Dunn, NC 800-672-4502
Alpine Cheese Company
  Winesburg, OH 330-359-6291
Alpine Meats
  Stockton, CA. 800-399-6328
American Food Traders
  Miami, FL. 305-670-6250

American Foods Group
Green Bay, WI 920-437-6330
Amity Packing Company
Chicago, IL 800-837-0270
Arena & Sons
Hopkinton, MA 508-435-3673
Arizona Sunland Foods
Tucson, AZ 520-624-7068
Arlund Meat Company
Overland Park, KS 913-321-3450
Armbrust Meats
Medford, WI 715-748-3102
Aspen Food Marketing
Denver, CO 303-320-3400
Atlantic Meat Company
Savannah, GA 912-964-8511
Atlantic Premium Brands
Northbrook, IL 847-412-6200
Aurora Packing Company
North Aurora, IL 630-897-0551
B&R Quality Meats
Waterloo, IA 319-232-6328
B3R Country Meats
Childress, TX 940-937-3668
Bakalars Brothers Sausage Company
La Crosse, WI 608-784-0384
Ball Park Franks
Southfield, MI 888-317-5867
Banner Beef & Seafood Company
Miami, FL 305-325-0420
Bar-W Meat Company
Fort Worth, TX 817-831-0051
Baretta Provision
East Berlin, CT 860-828-0802
Barney Pork House
Decatur, AL 256-350-9988
Barone Foods
Tucson, AZ 520-623-8571
Bartlow Brothers
Rushville, IL 800-252-7202
Beatty Fresh Frozen Meats
Bourbon, IN 574-342-2665
Beef Packers, Inc.
Fresno, CA 559-268-5586
Beef Products
North Sioux City, SD 605-217-8000
Bellville Meat Market
Bellville, TX 800-571-6328
Berks Packing Company, Inc.
Reading, PA 800-882-3757
Berry Processing
Watseka, IL 815-432-3264
Best Kosher Foods
Chicago, IL 888-800-0072
Best Provision Company, Inc.
Newark, NJ 800-631-4466
Big Apple Produce & Seafood Market
Pocomoke City, MD 410-957-1151
Big B Distributors
Evansville, IN 812-425-5235
Bill Holt Packing Plant
Salina, UT 435-529-7203
Binkert's Meat Products
Baltimore, MD 410-687-5959
Birchwood Foods
Kenosha, WI 800-541-1685
Blakely Freezer Locker
Thomasville, GA 229-723-3622
Blue Ribbon Meats
Cleveland, OH 216-631-8850
Blue Ribbon Meats
Miami, FL 800-522-6115
Bohrer & Moore Packing Company
Wapakoneta, OH 419-738-7719
Boones Abattoir
Bardstown, KY 502-348-3668
Border's Market
Plymouth, OH 419-687-2634
Boulder Sausage
Louisville, CO 303-665-6302
Bouma Meats
Provost, AB 780-753-2092
Bouvry Exports Calgary
Calgary, AB 403-253-0717
Boyd Sausage Company
Washington, IA 319-653-5715
Boyle Meat Company
Kansas City, MO 800-821-3626
Braham Food Locker Service
Braham, MN 320-396-2636
Breslow Deli Products
Philadelphia, PA 215-739-4200

Brockton Beef & Provisions Corporation
Brockton, MA 508-583-4703
Brook Locker Plant
Brook, IN 219-275-2611
Brook Meadow Provisions Corporation
Hagerstown, MD 301-739-3107
Brookfield Farms
Chicago, IL 773-468-1739
Brown Foods
Dallas, GA 770-445-4554
Brown Packing Company
Gaffney, SC 864-489-5723
Brown Thompson & Sons
Fancy Farm, KY 270-623-6321
Brownsdale Meat Service
Brownsdale, MN 507-567-2211
Bruce Foods Corporation
New Iberia, LA 337-365-8101
Bruss Company
Chicago, IL 800-621-3882
Bullock's Country Meats
Westminster, MD 410-848-6786
Bunker Hill Foods
Augusta, GA 706-733-7765

Burke Corporation
Nevada, IA 800-654-1152

Always make it your best® with Burke fully
cooked meats. We specialize in Italian sausage,
beef, and pork toppings, meatballs, taco meats,
shredded meats, pepperoni, bacon, Canadian-style bacon, chicken and beef strips. Additionally, we offer a variety of specialty products:
Hand-Pinched Style® brand toppings, chorizo,
gyro topping, andouille sausage, and breakfast
patties and links.

Burnett & Son Meat Company
Monrovia, CA 626-357-2165
Bush Brothers Provision Company
West Palm Beach, FL 800-327-1345
Buzz Food Service
Charleston, WV 304-925-4781
C&J Tender Meat
Anchorage, AK 907-562-2838
C&S Wholesale Meat Company
Atlanta, GA 404-627-3547
Caddo Packing Company
Marshall, TX 903-935-2211
Callaway Packing Company
Delta, CO 800-332-6932
Cambridge Slaughtering
Cambridge, IL 309-937-2455
Campbell Soup Company
Camden, NJ 800-257-8443
Campbell's Quality Cuts
Sidney, OH 937-492-2194
Camrose Packers
Camrose, AB 780-672-4887
Canal Fulton Provision
Canal Fulton, OH 800-321-3502
Candelari's Specialty Sausage
Houston, TX 800-953-5343
Capital Packers
Edmonton, AB 800-272-8868
Capolla Foods
North York, ON 416-633-0389
Carando Gourmet Frozen Foods
Springfield, MA 413-730-4205
Cargill Foods
Minneapolis, MN 800-227-455
Cargill Meats
Milwaukee, WI 800-558-4242
Caribbean Food Delights
Tappan, NY 845-398-3000
Caribbean Products
Baltimore, MD 410-235-7700
Carl Rittberger Sr.
Zanesville, OH 740-452-2767
Carl Streit & Son Company
Neptune, NJ 732-775-0803
Carmel Meat/Specialty Foods
Marina, CA 800-298-5823

Caro Foods
Houma, LA 985-872-1483
Casson & Sons
Des Moines, IA 515-266-3197
Castle Rock Meats
Denver, CO 303-292-0855
Castleberry's Meats
Atlanta, GA 404-873-1804
Castleberry/Snow Brands
Augusta, GA 800-241-3520
Cattaneo Brothers
San Luis Obispo, CA 800-243-8537
Centennial Food Corporation
Calgary, AB 403-287-2525
Center Locker Service Company
Center, MO 573-267-3343
Central Beef
Center Hill, FL 352-793-3671
Central Meat & Provision Company
San Diego, CA 619-239-1391
Chalmette Packing Company
Covington, LA 504-271-6241
Chandler Foods
Greensboro, NC 800-537-6219
Charles Smart Donair Submarine
Edmonton, AB 780-468-2099
Charlie's Pride Meats
Los Angeles, CA 877-866-0982
Chef's Requested Foods
Oklahoma City, OK 800-256-0259
Cher-Make Sausage Company
Manitowoc, WI 800-242-7679
Cheraw Packing
Cheraw, SC 843-537-7426
Chicago 58 Food Products
Toronto, ON 416-603-4244
Chicago Meat Authority
Chicago, IL 773-254-0020
Chicago Steaks
Chicago, IL 800-776-4174
Chip Steak & Provision Company
Mankato, MN 507-388-6277
Choice One Foods
Los Angeles, CA 323-231-7777
Cimpl Meats
Yankton, SD 605-665-1665
Circle V Meat Company
Spanish Fork, UT 801-798-3081
Clay Center Locker Plant
Clay Center, KS 785-632-5550
Clem's Refrigerated Foods
Lexington, KY 800-544-5571
Clover Valley Food
Pierce, NE 402-329-4025
Cloverdale Foods Company
Mandan, ND 800-669-9511
Cloverdale Packing
Parkersburg, WV 304-485-5409
Clovervale Farms
Amherst, OH 800-433-0146
Colegate Processing & Convenience Market
Marietta, OH 740-373-5699
Coleman Purely Natural Brands
Golden, CO 877-810-8291
Collbran Locker Plant
Collbran, CO 970-487-3329
Columbia Packing Company
Dallas, TX 800-460-8171
Community Market & Deli
Lindstrom, MN 651-257-1128
Comstock's Marketing
Barton, VT 802-754-2426
Con Agra Food Coperative
Montgomery, AL 334-288-8660
ConAgra Beef Company
Hyrum, UT 435-245-6456
ConAgra Beef Company
Garden City, KS 620-275-9661
ConAgra Beef Company
Yuma, CO 970-395-8226
ConAgra Foods/Eckrich
Omaha, NE 800-327-4424
ConAgra Foods/International Home Foods
Niagara Falls, ON 905-356-2661
ConAgra Refrigerated Foods International
Omaha, NE 800-624-4724
ConAgra Snack Foods
San Jose, CA 408-436-0329
Conti Packing Company
Rochester, NY 585-424-2500
Continental Deli Foods
Cherokee, IA 712-225-5161

Continental Sausage
Denver, CO 303-288-9787

Corfu Foods
Bensenville, IL 630-595-2510

Corte Provisions
Newark, NJ. 201-653-7246

Couch's Country Style Sausages
Cleveland, OH 216-587-2333

Country Butcher Shop
Palmyra, MO. .573-769-2257

Country Village Meats
Sublette, IL 815-849-5532

Covemaker Packing Company
Moline, IL 309-764-1480

Creuzebergers Meats
Duncansville, PA. 814-695-3061

Critchfield Meats
Lexington, KY .800-866-3287

Crofton & Sons
Brandon, FL 800-878-7675

Cropp Cooperative-Organic Valley
La Farge, WI. .888-444-6455

Crown Point
St John, IN 219-365-3200

Cuba Lockers
Cuba, IL 309-785-2211

Cumberland Gap Provision Company
Middlesboro, KY 800-331-7154

Curly's Custom Meats
Jackson Center, OH 937-596-6518

Curly's Foods
Edina, MN. 612-920-3400

Curtis Packing Company
Greensboro, NC 336-275-7684

Cyclone Enterprises
Houston, TX 281-872-0087

D'Artagnan
Newark, NJ. 800-327-8246

Daily Foods
Salt Lake City, UT 801-269-1998

Dakota Premium Foods
South St Paul, MN 651-552-8230

Dale T. Smith & Sons Meat Packing Corporation
Draper, UT 801-571-3611

Dallas City Packing
Dallas, TX. 214-948-3901

Dallas Dressed Beef
Dallas, TX. 214-638-0142

Daniel Weaver Company
Lebanon, PA 800-932-8377

Darling International
Omaha, NE 402-733-3010

David Berg & Company
Chicago, IL. 773-489-4711

Davidson Meat Processing Plant
Waynesville, OH 513-897-2971

Day-Lee Foods
Santa Fe Springs, CA 562-903-3020

Dearborn Sausage Company
Dearborn, MI .313-842-2375

DeBragga & Spitler
New York, NY. 212-924-1311

Dee's Cheesecake Factory/Dee's Foodservice
Albuquerque, NM 505-884-1777

Deen Meat Company
Fort Worth, TX 800-333-3953

Devault Foods
Devault, PA. 800-426-2874

Devine Meat Company
Devine, TX 830-663-4621

Dick's Packing Company
Columbia, MO 573-449-2995

Diggs Packing Company
Columbia, MO 573-449-2995

Dino's Sausage & Meat Company
Utica, NY 315-732-2661

DiPasquale's
Baltimore, MD 410-276-6787

Dom's Sausage Company
Malden, MA 781-324-1310

Donald E. Hunter Meat Company
Hillsboro, OH .937-466-2311

Dorina/So-Good
Union, IL 815-923-2144

Drier's Meats
Three Oaks, MI 269-756-3101

Dryden Provision Company
Louisville, KY .502-583-1777

Dugdale Beef Company
Indianapolis, IN 317-291-9660

Duma Meats
Mogadore, OH 330-628-3438

Dutch Packing Company
Miami, FL 305-871-3640

Dutch Valley Veal
South Holland, IL 800-832-8325

Dutterer's Home Food Service
Baltimore, MD 410-298-3663

Dynamic Foods
Lubbock, TX. .806-762-0780

E&H Packing Company
Detroit, MI 313-567-8286

E.W. Knauss & Son
Quakertown, PA. 800-648-4220

East Beauregard Meat Processing Center
Deridder, LA. .337-328-7171

East Dayton Meat & Poultry
Dayton, OH. 937-253-6185

Ed Miniat
Homewood, IL 708-957-3800

Edelman Meats
Antigo, WI 715-623-7686

Edelmann Provision Company
Fairfield, OH. .513-881-5801

Edmac Foods
Woodruff, WI .715-356-5394

Edmonton Meat Packing Company
Edmonton, AB 800-361-6328

Eickman's Processing
Seward, IL. 815-247-8451

Eiserman Meats
Slave Lake, AB. 780-849-5507

El Paso Meat Company
El Paso, TX. 915-838-8600

Elkhart Locker Plant
Elkhart, KS 620-697-4424

Ellsworth Locker
Ellsworth, MN 507-967-2544

Empire Beef Company
Rochester, NY. 800-462-6804

Empire Kosher Foods
Mifflintown, PA. 800-367-4734

Enjoy Foods International
Fontana, CA 909-823-2228

Eureka Lockers
Eureka, IL. 309-467-2731

Eurocaribe Packing Company
Rio Piedras, PR. 787-752-8181

Ezzo Sausage Company
Columbus, OH 800-558-8841

F&M Food Products
Chicago, IL. 773-862-2432

F.M. Brown Sons
Sinking Spring, PA 800-345-3344

Fabbri Sausage Manufacturing
Chicago, IL 312-829-6363

Farley Candy Company
Chicago, IL 773-254-0900

Farm Boy Food Service
Evansville, IN. 800-852-3976

Farmland Foods
Kansas City, MO. 888-327-6526

Ferko Meat Company
Milwaukee, WI 414-967-5500

First Original Texas Chili Company
Fort Worth, TX 817-626-0983

Flanders Provision Company
Waycross, GA .912-283-5191

Flint Hills Foods
Wamego, KS. .785-765-3396

Foodbrands America
Oklahoma City, OK 405-290-4000

Foster Farms
Demopolis, AL 334-289-5082

Four Star Meat Company of Louisiana
Amite, LA 800-444-5228

Fred Usinger
Milwaukee, WI 800-558-9998

Fremont Beef Company
Fremont, NE 402-727-7200

Frontier Beef Company
Huntingdon Valley, PA 215-663-2120

Fuji Foods
Denver, CO 303-377-3738

G E Hawthorn Meat Company
Hot Springs, AR 501-623-8111

Gary's Frozen Foods
Lubbock, TX. .806-745-1933

Gaucho Foods
Westmont, IL. 630-889-4241

Gelsinger Food Products
Montrose, CA .818-248-7811

Gem Meat Packing Company
Boise, ID 208-375-9424

Gemini Food Industries
Fiskdale, MA .508-347-2800

George L. Wells Meat Company
Philadelphia, PA 800-523-1730

Georgetown Farm
Free Union, VA 888-328-5326

GFI Premium Foods
Minneapolis, MN 800-669-8996

Glasco Locker Plant
Glasco, KS 785-568-2364

Glenmark Industries
Chicago, IL 773-927-4800

Godshall's Quality Meats
Franconia, PA .888-463-7425

Golden City Meats
Golden City, MO. 417-537-8560

Golden Locker Cooperative
Golden, IL. 217-696-4456

Greater Omaha Packing Company
Omaha, NE 402-731-1700

Grimm's Fine Food
Richmond, AB 780-415-4331

Grimm's Locker Service
Sherwood, OH 419-899-2655

Grinde Sausage House
Drayton Valley, AB. 866-621-1755

Groff Meats
Elizabethtown, PA. 717-367-1246

Gunsberg Corned Beef
Detroit, MI 313-894-6600

Gwinn's Foods
St Louis, MO. .314-521-8792

H&K Packers Company
Winnipeg, NB 204-233-2354
H. Shenson International Export
San Francisco, CA 415-318-7000
Hahn & Company
San Francisco, CA 415-394-6512
Hahn Brothers
Westminster, MD 800-227-7675
Halal Transactions
Omaha, NE 402-572-6120
Hall Brothers Meats
Cleveland, OH 440-235-3262
Ham I Am
Dallas, TX 800-742-6426
Hamilos Brothers Inspected Meats
Madison, IL 618-451-7877
Hamm's Custom Meats
McKinney, TX 972-542-3359
Hamner Provision Company
San Antonio, TX 210-736-3117
Happy Acres Packing Company
Petal, MS 601-584-8301
Harper's Country Hams
Clinton, KY 888-427-7377
Harris Ranch Beef Company
Selma, CA 800-742-1955
Hartford Provision Company
South Windsor, CT 860-583-3908
Harvin Choice Meats
Sumter, SC 803-775-9367
Heinke Industrial Park
Paradise, CA 530-877-7864
Henry J Meat Specialties
Chicago, IL 800-242-1314
Henson & Courtner Ham House
Butler, TN 423-369-1121
Heringer Meats
Covington, KY 859-291-2000
Hi-Point Beef Company
Ayr, NE 937-599-2115
Hickory Baked Food
Castle Rock, CO 303-688-2633
Hickory Farms
Maumee, OH 419-893-7611
High Country Snack Foods
Lincoln, MT 800-433-3916
High Valley Farm
Castle Rock, CO 303-634-2944
Hillbilly Smokehouse
Rogers, AR 479-636-1927
Hoekstra Meat Company
Kalamazoo, MI 616-321-0797
Hoff's United Foods
Brownsville, WI 920-583-3734
Holly Hill Locker Company
Holly Hill, SC 803-496-3611
Holmes Foods
Nixon, TX 830-582-1551
Holten Meats
Sauget, IL 800-851-4684
Holton Meat Processing
Holton, KS 785-364-2331
Home Market Foods
Norwood, MA 781-948-1500
Honey Baked Ham Company
Cincinnati, OH 513-583-9700
Horlacher's Fine Meats
Logan, UT 435-752-1287
Hormel Foods Corporation
Maitland, FL 407-660-0808
Hormel Foods Corporation
Beloit, WI 608-365-9501
Hormel Foods Corporation
Austin, MN 800-523-4635
Houser Meats
Rushville, IL 217-322-4994
Hsin Tung Yang Foods Co.
S San Francisco, CA 650-589-6789
Humeniuk's Meat Cutting
Ranfurly, AB 780-658-2381
Huse's Country Meats
Malone, TX 254-533-2205
Hyde Meat Packing
Robert, LA 985-345-5756
IBP Foods
Troy, MI 248-588-4710
Idaho Beverages
Lewiston, ID 208-743-6535
Independent Master Casing Company
Santa Fe Springs, CA 800-635-9518
International Food Packers Corporation
Miami, FL 305-669-1662

International Meat Company
Elmwood Park, IL 773-622-1400
Isernio Sausage Company
Seattle, WA 888-495-8674
Ito Cariani Sausage Company
Hayward, CA 510-887-0882
Ittels Meats
Howard Lake, MN 320-543-2285
J&B Meats Corporation
Coal Valley, IL 309-799-7341
J&B Wholesale Distributing
St Michael, MN 800-872-4642
J.J. Andrade's Slaughterhouse
Honokaa, HI 808-775-0741
J.M. Schneider
Saint Anselme, QC 418-885-4474
Jack's Wholesale Meat Company
Trenton, TX 903-989-2293
Jackson Brothers Food Locker
Post, TX 806-495-3245
Jacob & Sons Wholesale Meats
Martins Ferry, OH 740-633-3091
Jacobs Meats
Defiance, OH 419-782-7831
Jacobsmuhlen's Meats
Cornelius, OR 503-359-0479
Jakes Brothers Country Meats
Joelton, TN 615-876-2911
Janowski's Hamburgers
Rockville Centre, NY 516-764-9591
Jay & Boots Meats
Knoxville, TN 865-922-3213
JBS Packerland
Souderton, PA 800-967-8325
Jbs Packerland Inc
Green Bay, WI 920-468-4000
Jemm Wholesale Meat Company
Chicago, IL 773-523-8161
Jensen Meat Company
Vista, CA 760-727-6700
Jesse's Best
Suffolk, VA 757-489-8383
Jesse's Fine Meats
Cherokee, IA 712-225-3637
John Garner Meats
Van Buren, AR 800-543-5473
John Hene Specialty Meats
Indianapolis, IN 317-972-9400
John R Morreale
Chicago, IL 312-421-3664
Jones Packing Company
Harvard, IL 815-943-4488
Jordahl Meats
Manchester, MN 507-826-3418
Joseph McSweeney & Sons
Windom, MN 804-359-6024
Joseph Sanders
Custer, WY 800-968-5035
K&K Gourmet Meats
Leetsdale, PA 724-266-8400
Karl Ehmer
Flushing, NY 800-487-5275
Kayem Foods
Chelsea, MA 800-426-6100
Kelble Brothers
Berlin Heights, OH 800-247-2333
Kelley Meats
Taberg, NY 315-337-4272
Kelly Kornbeef Company
Chicago, IL 773-588-2882
Kelly Packing Company
Torrington, WY 307-532-2210
Kelly-Eisenberg Gourmet Deli Products
Chicago, IL 773-588-2882
Kenosha Beef International
Kenosha, WI 800-541-1685
Kent Meats
Grand Rapids, MI 616-459-4595
Kershenstine Beef Jerky
Eupora, MS 662-258-2049
Kessler's, Inc
Lemoyne, PA 800-382-1328
Ketters Meat Market & Locker Plant
Frazee, MN 218-334-2351
Keystone Foods Corporation
W Conshohocken, PA 610-667-6700
Keystone Foods Corporation
Huntsville, AL 800-327-6701
King Kold Meats
Englewood, OH 800-836-2797
King Meat
Los Angeles, CA 323-582-7401

King's Command Foods
Kent, WA 800-247-3138
King's Meat & Seafood
Houston, TX 713-923-6868
Kingsbury Country Market
Kingsbury, IN 219-393-3016
Kiolbassa Provision Company
San Antonio, TX 800-456-5465
Kirsco/Kay Packing
Detroit, MI 313-963-2900
Klement Sausage Company
Milwaukee, WI 800-553-6368
Korte Meat Processors
Highland, IL 618-654-3813
Kretschmar
Don Mills, ON 800-561-4532
Kroger Company
Cincinnati, OH 800-576-4377
Kulana Foods
Hilo, HI 808-959-9144
Kutztown Bologna Company
Leola, PA 800-723-8824
L&H Packing Company
San Antonio, TX 210-532-3241
L&L Packing Company
Chicago, IL 800-628-6328
L&M Frosted Food Lockers
Belt, MT 406-277-3522
L&M Slaughtering
Georgetown, IL 217-662-6841
Ladoga Frozen Food & Retail Meat
Ladoga, IN 765-942-2225
Lampasas Locker Plant
Lampasas, TX 512-556-5121
Lampost Meats
Grimes, IA 515-288-6111
Land O Frost
Lansing, IL 800-643-5654
Land O'Frost
Searcy, AR 800-643-5654
Landis Meat Company
Quakertown, PA 800-421-1565
Laxson Provision Company
San Antonio, TX 210-226-8397
Lay Packing Company
Knoxville, TN 865-922-4320
Leidy's
Souderton, PA 800-222-2319
Lena Maid Meats
Lena, IL 815-369-4522
Lengerich Meats
Zanesville, IN 260-638-4123
Leo G. Fraboni Sausage Company
Hibbing, MN 218-263-5074
Levonian Brothers
Troy, NY 518-274-3610
Lilydale Foods
Edmonton, AB 800-661-5341
Lionel Lavallee Company
Haverhill, MA 800-343-8292
Lisbon Sausage Company
New Bedford, MA 508-993-7645
Lombardi Brothers Meat Packers
Denver, CO 800-421-4412
Lone Star Beef Jerky Company
Lubbock, TX 806-762-8833
Long Food Industries
Fripp Island, SC 843-838-3205
Longview Meat & Merchandise
Longview, AB 403-558-3706
Lowell Provision Company
Lowell, MA 978-454-5603
Lykes Meat Group
Plant City, FL 813-752-1102
M K Meat Processing Plant
Burton, TX 979-289-4022
Mac's Meats Wholesale
Las Cruces, NM 575-524-2751
MacGregors Meat & Seafood
Toronto, ON 800-268-5953
Mack's Packing
Richfield, UT 435-896-4447
Mada'n Kosher Foods
Dania, FL 954-925-0077
Magnolia Beef Company
Elizabeth, NJ 908-352-9412
Magnolia Meats
Shreveport, LA 318-221-2814
Maid-Rite Steak Company
Dunmore, PA 800-233-4259
Malcolm Meat Company
Northwood, OH 800-822-6328

Manger Packing Company
Baltimore, MD 800-227-9262
Manley Meats
Decatur, IN 260-592-7313
Maple Leaf Foods & Scheider Foods
Saint Laurent, QC 800-567-1890
Marathon Enterprises
Englewood, NJ 201-935-3330
Marie F
Markham, ON 800-365-4464
Marks Meat
Canby, OR 503-266-2048
Marshallville Packing Company
Marshallville, OH 330-855-2871
Matthiesen's Deer & Custom Processing
De Witt, IA 563-659-8409
Maurice's Gourmet Barbeque
West Columbia, SC 800-628-7423
Maverick Ranch Natural Meats
Denver, CO 800-497-2624
Mayo Sausage Company
Nashville, TN 615-742-1162
McKenzie of Vermont
Burlington, VT 802-864-4585
McKiever Packing Company
Monticello, AR 870-367-6938
McLemore's Abattoir
Vidalia, GA 912-537-4476
Meatco Sales
Mirror, AB 403-788-2292
Meating Place
Buffalo, NY 716-885-3623
Meatland Packers
Medicine Hat, AB 403-528-4321
Medeiros Farms
Kalaheo, HI 808-332-8211
Menu Meats
Huntertown, IN 800-848-2902
Merkley & Sons Packing
Jasper, IN 812-482-7020
Merrill's Meat Company
Encampment, WY 307-327-5345
Metafoods, LLC
Atlanta, GA 404-843-2400
Metropolitan Sausage Manufacturing Company
Flossmoor, IL 708-331-3232
Miami Beef Company
Hialeah, FL 305-621-3252
Michael's Finer Meats & Seafoods
Columbus, OH 800-282-0518
Midway Meats
Centralia, WA 360-736-5257
Mike's Meats
Eitzen, MN 507-495-3336
Mike's Prime Cut Meats
Brigham City, UT 435-723-7333
Miko Meat
Hilo, HI 808-935-0841
Miller Brothers Packing Company
Sylvester, GA 229-776-2014
Miller's Country Hams
Dresden, TN 800-622-0606
Miller's Meat Market
Red Bud, IL 618-282-3334
Mims Meat Company
Houston, TX 713-453-0151
Mirasco
Atlanta, GA 770-956-1945
Mishler Packing Company
Lagrange, IN 260-768-4156
Montana Ranch Brand
Billings, MT 406-294-2333
Moo & Oink
Chicago, IL 773-493-2755
Mooney's Packing
Williamsfield, OH 440-293-7269
Mortimer's Fine Foods
Burlington, ON 905-336-0000
Mountain City Meat Company
Denver, CO 800-937-8325
Mountaire Farms of Delmarva
Selbyville, DE 800-441-8263
Moweaqua Packing
Moweaqua, IL 217-768-4714
Mr. Brown's Bar-B-Que
Portland, OR 503-274-0966
Munsee Meats
Muncie, IN 765-288-3645
Mutual Trading Company
Los Angeles, CA 213-626-9458
Nagel Veal
San Bernardino, CA 909-383-7075

Napoleon Locker
Napoleon, IN 812-852-4333
National Beef Packing
Kansas City, MO 800-449-2333
National Foods
Indianapolis, IN 800-683-6565
National Steak & Poultry
Owasso, OK 800-366-6772
Nature's Sungrown Foods
San Rafael, CA 415-491-4944
Nebraska Beef
Omaha, NE 402-734-6823
Nephi Packing Company
Nephi, UT 435-623-0435
Nesbitt Processing
Aledo, IL 309-582-5183
Nestle Pizza
Medford, WI 715-748-5550
New Braunfels Smokehouse
New Braunfels, TX 800-537-6932
New Zealand Lamb Company
Wilton, CT 800-438-5262
Nodine's Smokehouse
Torrington, CT 800-222-2059
Nolechek's Meats
Thorp, WI 715-669-5580
North Star Foods
St Charles, MN 507-932-4831
Northern Packing Company
Brier Hill, NY 315-375-8801
Nossack Fine Meats
Red Deer, AB 403-346-5006
Nueske's Applewood Smoked Meats
Wittenberg, WI 800-386-2266
O Chili Frozen Foods Inc
Northbrook, IL 847-562-1991
O'Neill Packing Company
Omaha, NE 402-733-1200
Old Country Meat & Sausage Company
San Diego, CA 619-297-4301
Old Kentucky Hams
Cynthiana, KY 859-234-5015
Old Neighborhood Foods
Lynn, MA 781-592-0014
Old Wisconsin Sausage Company
Sheboygan, WI 800-558-7840
Olson Locker
Fairmont, MN 507-238-2563
Omaha Meat Processors
Omaha, NE 402-554-1965
Onoway Custom Packers
Onoway, AB 780-967-2727
Ossian Seafood Meats
Ossian, IN 260-622-4191
Otto W Liebold & Company
Flint, MI 800-999-6328
P.G. Molinari & Sons
San Francisco, CA 415-822-5555
Palmer Packing Company
Tremonton, UT 435-257-5329
Palmyra Bologna
Palmyra, PA 717-838-6336
Paradise Locker Company
Trimble, MO 816-370-6328
Paris Frozen Foods
Hillsboro, IL 217-532-3822
Party Steak Company
Springfield, MO 417-358-9091
Pasco Beverage
Lake Placid, FL 863-465-4127
Pasqualichio Brothers
Scranton, PA 800-232-6233
Pat's Meat Discounter
Mills, WY 307-237-7549
Patrick Cudahy
Cudahy, WI 800-486-6900
Paul Schafer Meat Products
Baltimore, MD 410-528-1250
Payne Packing Company
Artesia, NM 575-746-2779
Pekarna's Meat Market
Jordan, MN 952-492-6101
Pekarskis Sausage
South Deerfield, MA 413-665-4537
Penthouse Meat Company
Boston, MA 570-563-1153
Petschl's Meats
Tukwila, WA 206-575-4400
Pierceton Foods
Pierceton, IN 574-594-2344
Pierre Foods
Cincinnati, OH 513-874-8741

Pilgrim's Pride
Elberton, GA 800-262-7907
Pinter's Packing Plant
Dorchester, WI 715-654-5444
Piper Processing
Andover, OH 440-293-7170
Plymouth Beef
New York, NY 718-589-8600
PM Windom
Windom, MN 507-831-2761
Poche's Smokehouse
Breaux Bridge, LA 800-376-2437
Polarica
San Francisco, CA 800-426-3872
Pork Shop of Vermont
Charlotte, VT 800-458-3441
Premium Meat Company
Brigham City, UT 435-723-5944
Prime Pak Foods
Gainesville, GA 770-536-8708
Proliant Meat Ingredients
Ankeny, IA 800-369-2672
Provost Packers
Provost, AB 780-753-2415
Quaker Maid Meats
Shillington, PA 610-376-1500
Quality Beef Company
Providence, RI 877-233-3462
Quality Sausage Company
Dallas, TX 214-634-3400
Quantum Foods LLC
Bolingbrook, IL 800-334-6328
R Four Meats
Chatfield, MN 507-867-4180
R.E. Meyer Company
Lincoln, NE 402-474-8500
R.I. Provision Company
Johnston, RI 401-831-0815
Raemica
Running Springs, CA 800-772-6328
Ralph Packing Company
Perkins, OK 800-522-3979
Ranch Oak Farm
Fort Worth, TX 800-888-0327
Randolph Packing Company
Streamwood, IL 630-830-3100
Ray's Sausage Company Inc
Cleveland, OH 216-921-8782
Real Sausage Company
Chicago, IL 312-842-5330
Red Deer Lake Meat Processing
Calgary, AB 403-256-4925
Red Hot Chicago
Chicago, IL 800-249-5226
Red Oak Farms
Red Oak, IA 712-623-9224
Red Steer Meats
Phoenix, AZ 602-272-6677
Redi-Serve Food Company
Fort Atkinson, WI 920-563-6391
Redondo's Sausage Factory
Waipahu, HI 808-671-5444
Republic Foods
Dallas, TX 214-826-8050
Rinehart Meat Processing
Branson, MO 417-334-2044
Ritchie Wholesale Meats
Piketon, OH 800-628-1290
Riverside Packers
Drumheller, AB 403-823-2595
Robbins Packing Company
Statesboro, GA 912-764-7503
Robertson's Country Meat Hams
Finchville, KY 800-678-1521
Robichaux's Meat Market
Crowley, LA 337-788-4124
Rocco Enterprises
Harrisonburg, VA 800-336-4003
Rock River Provision Company
Rock Falls, IL 800-685-1195
Rocky Mountain Meats
Rocky Mountain House, AB 403-845-3434
Rocky Mountain Natural Meats
Henderson, CO 800-327-2706
Rocky Mountain Packing Company
Havre, MT 406-265-3401
Roger Wood Foods
Savannah, GA 800-849-9272
Rolet Food Products Company
Brooklyn, NY 718-497-0476
Roman Packing Company
Norfolk, NE 800-373-5990

Romanian Kosher Sausage
Chicago, IL 773-761-4141
Ron Tankersley Farms
Los Angeles, CA. 213-622-0724
Roode Packing Company
Fairbury, NE 402-729-2253
Rosa Brothers
Miami, FL. 305-324-1510
Rose Packing Company
Chicago, IL. 800-323-7363
Rosen's Diversified
Fairmont, MN 800-798-2000
Royal Center Locker Plant
Royal Center, IN 574-643-3275
Royal Palate Foods
Inglewood, CA 310-330-7701
Rubashkin
Brooklyn, NY 718-436-5511
Rude Custom Butchering
Mt Morris, IL 815-946-3795
Ruef's Meat Market
New Glarus, WI 608-527-2554
Rymer Foods
Chicago, IL. 800-247-9637
S.W. Meat & Provision Company
Phoenix, AZ 602-275-2000
Sadler's BBQ Sales
Henderson, TX 903-657-5581
Saletts
Randolph, MA 781-961-9900
Sam Hausman Meat Packer
Corpus Christi, TX 361-883-5521
Sam Kane Beef Processors
Corpus Christi, TX 361-241-5000
Sampco
Chicago, IL. 800-767-1689
San Angelo Packing
San Angelo, TX 325-653-6951
San Francisco Sausage Company
S San Francisco, CA 650-583-4993
Sangudo Custom Meat Packers
Sangudo, AB. 888-785-3353
Sani-Dairy
Johnstown, PA. 412-568-6410
Sara Lee Foods
Neenah, WI 800-558-8440
Sara Lee Foods
Cordova, TN 901-756-4051

Saunders Provision Company
Norfolk, VA. 800-486-5611
Sausage Kitchen
Oak Grove, OR 503-656-9766
Saval Foods
Elkridge, MD 800-527-2825
Schneider Foods
Guelph, ON. 519-837-4848
Schneider Foods
Etobicoke, ON 800-268-0634
Sculli Brothers
Philadelphia, PA 215-336-1223
Seitz Foods
Saint Joseph, MO 800-383-3128
Seltzer's Smokehouse Meats
Palmyra, PA. 717-838-6336
Shapiro Packing Company
Augusta, GA 706-724-6401
Shelley's Prime Meats
Jersey City, NJ 201-433-3434
Shirer Brothers Slaughter House
Adamsville, OH 740-796-3214
Shreve Meats Processing
Shreve, OH 330-567-2142
Silver Lake Sausage Shop
Providence, RI 401-944-4081
Simeus Foods International
Mansfield, TX 888-772-3663
Sky Haven Farm
Cincinnati, OH 513-681-2303
Skylark Meats
Omaha, NE 800-759-5275
Slathars Smokehouse
Lake City, MN 507-753-2080
SMG
Crestview Hills, KY 757-952-1100
Smith Packing Regional Meat
Utica, NY .315-732-5125
Smith Provision Company
Erie, PA 800-334-9151
Smokey Denmark Sausage
Austin, TX. 512-385-0718
Souris Valley Processors
Melita, NB. 204-522-8210
Southeastern Meat Association
Oviedo, FL 407-365-5661
Southern Packing Corporation
Chesapeake, VA 757-421-2131
Southington Packing Company Inc
Southington, CT 860-628-9544
Southtowns Seafood & Meats
Blasdell, NY 716-824-4900
Specialty Foods Group
Newport News, VA. 800-238-0020
Spring Grove Foods
Miamisburg, OH 937-866-4311
Springville Meat & Cold Storage
Springville, UT 801-489-6391
Square-H Brands
Vernon, CA 323-267-4600
Stallings Headcheese Company
Houston, TX 713-523-1751
Standard Beef Company
New Haven, CT 203-787-2164
Steak Specialists
Atlanta, GA 404-874-8073
Steak-Umm Company
Shillington, PA 860-928-5900
Stehlin & Sons Company
Cincinnati, OH 513-385-6164
Steinbach Provisions Company
Chicago, IL. 773-538-1511
Sterling Pacific Meat Company
Los Angeles, CA. 310-274-7635
Stettler Meats
Stettler, AB. 403-742-1427
Stevison Ham Company
Portland, TN 800-844-4267
Stock Yards Packing Company
Chicago, IL. 800-621-1119
Stone Meat Processor
Ogden, UT. 801-782-9825
Straub's
Clayton, MO. 888-725-2121
Strauss Veal & Lamb International
Hales Corners, WI. 800-562-7775
Striplings
Moultrie, GA. 229-985-4226
Sudlersville Frozen Food Locker
Sudlersville, MD. 410-438-3106
Sugardale Foods
Canton, OH 330-455-5253

Sun-Rise
Alexandria, MN 320-846-5720
Sunnydale Meats
Gaffney, SC. 864-489-6091
Superior's Brand Meats
Massillon, OH. 330-830-0356
Supreme Beef
Dallas, TX. 214-428-1761
Suwannee Packing Company
Live Oak, FL. 904-362-1422
Suzanna's Kitchen
Duluth, GA. 800-241-2455
Swanton's Packing
Fairfax, VT 802-868-4469
Swift & Company
Greeley, CO. 970-324-2180
SYSCO Foodservice
Fremont, CA 650-494-7200
Tankersley Food Service
Van Buren, AR 800-726-6182
Tanks Meat
Elmore, OH 419-862-3312
Tarpoff Packing Company
Granite City, IL 618-452-8180
Taylor Meat Company
Taylor, TX. 512-352-6357
Taylor's Sausage Company
St Louis, MO. 314-652-3476
Tayse Meats
Cleveland, OH 216-664-1799
Temptee Specialty Foods
Denver, CO 800-842-1233
Terra's
Perham, MN 218-346-4100
Terrell Meats
Delta, UT. 435-864-2600
Teutopolis Lockers Service
Teutopolis, IL 217-857-3319
Texas Reds Steak House
Red River, NM 575-754-2964
Thompson Packers
Slidell, LA. 800-989-6328
Thomson Meats
Melfort, SK 306-752-2802
Tillamook Meat Company
Tillamook, OR 503-842-4802
Tom Clamon Foods
Palestine, TX. 903-729-3932
Tooele Valley Meat
Grantsville, UT 435-884-3837
Topper Meat Company
Belle Glade, FL. 561-996-6541
Topps Meat Company
Elizabeth, NJ 908-351-0500
Townsend-Piller Packing
Cumberland, WI 715-822-4910
Travis Meats
Powell, TN 800-247-7606
Tri-State Beef Company
Cincinnati, OH 513-579-1722
Troy Pork Store
Troy, NY 518-272-8291
Troyer Foods
Goshen, IN 574-533-0302
Tucker Packing Company
Orrville, OH 330-683-3311
Tupman-Thurlow Company
Deerfield Beach, FL. 954-596-9989
Turk Brothers Custom Meats
Ashland, OH 800-789-1051
Turner Brothers
Nowata, OK 918-273-1858
Tyler Packing Company
Tyler, TX. .903-593-9592
Tyson Foods
Amarillo, TX. 806-335-1531
Tyson Fresh Meats
Dakota Dunes, SD. 605-235-2061
Tyson Fresh Meats
Emporia, KS 620-343-3640
Uncle Charley's Sausage Company
Vandergrift, PA 724-845-3302
Une-Viandi
St. Jean Sur Richelieu, NB 800-363-1955
United Meat Company
San Francisco, CA 415-864-2118
United Provision Meat Company
Columbus, OH 614-252-1126
Universal Beef Products
Houston, TX 713-224-6043
Unruh's Quality Meats
Deridder, LA. 337-463-7688

Uvalde Meat Processing
Uvalde, TX 830-278-6247
Valley Meat Company
Modesto, CA 800-222-6328
Valley Packing Company
Lansing, OH 740-635-0154
Valley Pride Pack
Norwalk, WI 608-823-7445
Vantage USA
Chicago, IL .773-247-1086
Victoria Fancy Sausage
Edmonton, AB 780-471-2283
Vienna Beef
Chicago, IL .773-278-7800
Vienna Beef
Chicago, IL .800-621-8183
Vienna Meat Products
Scarborough, ON 800-588-1931
Vietti Foods Company Inc
Nashville, TN 800-240-7864
Voget Meats
Hubbard, OR 503-981-6271
W&G Marketing Company
Ames, IA 515-233-4774
W&W Meats
Willoughby, OH 216-621-7846
W.R. Delozier Sausage Company
Seymour, TN 865-577-5907
WA Bean & Sons
Bangor, ME .800-649-1958
Waco Beef & Pork Processors
Waco, TX 254-772-4669
Waken Meat Company
Atlanta, GA .404-627-3537
Walker Meats Corporation
Carrollton, GA 770-834-8171
Wall Meat Processing
Wall, SD 605-279-2348
Waltham Beef Company
Boston, MA .617-269-2250
Warren & Son Meat Processing
Whipple, OH 740-585-2421
Wasatch Meats
Salt Lake City, UT 801-363-5747
Washington Beef
Toppenish, WA 800-289-2333
Webster City Custom Meats
Webster City, IA 888-786-3287
Weiss Brothers Smoke House
Johnstown, PA 814-539-4085
West Liberty Foods
West Liberty, IA 888-511-4500
West Meat & Locker Company
Washington, IL 309-444-8475
Westbrook Trading Company
Calgary, AB .800-563-5785
Western Meats
Tumwater, WA 360-357-6601
Western Meats
Rapid City, SD 605-342-0322
Westport Locker Service
Westport, IN 877-265-0551
Wexler Meat Company
Skokie, IL 773-927-5656
White's Meat Processing
Peebles, OH 937-587-2930
Wildwood Natural Foods
Watsonville, CA 800-464-3915
Willcox Packing House
Willcox, AZ .520-384-2015
Wimmer's Meat Products
West Point, NE 800-358-0761
Windcrest Meat Packers
Port Perry, ON 800-750-2542
Winona Packing Company
Winona, MS 662-283-4317
Winter Sausage Manufacturing Company
Eastpointe, MI 586-777-9080
Wisconsin Packing Company
Butler, WI 800-558-2000
Wohrles Foods
Pittsfield, MA 800-628-6114
Wolff Meat Company
San Antonio, TX 210-335-2626
Wolverine Packing
Detroit, MI .313-392-9403
Woodbine
Norfolk, VA 757-461-2731
Woods Smoked Meats
Bowling Green, MO 800-458-8426
XL Beef
Calgary, AB .403-236-2424

Yewig Brothers Packing Company
Haubstadt, IN 812-768-6208
Yoakum Packing Company
Yoakum, TX 361-293-3541
Zartic Inc
Rome, GA 800-241-0516

Barbecued

Art's Tamales
Metamora, IL 309-367-2850
Bear Creek Smokehouse
Marshall, TX 800-950-2327

BURKE
Always make it your best®

Burke Corporation
Nevada, IA .800-654-1152

> Always make it your best® with Burke fully cooked meats. We specialize in Italian sausage, beef, and pork toppings, meatballs, taco meats, shredded meats, pepperoni, bacon, Canadian-style bacon, chicken and beef strips. Additionally, we offer a variety of specialty products: Hand-Pinched Style® brand toppings, chorizo, gyro topping, andouille sausage, and breakfast patties and links.

Curly's Foods
Edina, MN .612-920-3400
Dankworth Packing Company
Ballinger, TX 325-365-3552
Dorina/So-Good
Union, IL 815-923-2144
Gary's Frozen Foods
Lubbock, TX 806-745-1933
Gaucho Foods
Westmont, IL 630-889-4241
King Kold Meats
Englewood, OH 800-836-2797
Moonlite Bar BQ Inn
Owensboro, KY 800-322-8989
Sadler's BBQ Sales
Henderson, TX 903-657-5581
Travis Meats
Powell, TN .800-247-7606
W&G Marketing Company
Ames, IA 515-233-4774

Frozen

Art's Tamales
Metamora, IL 309-367-2850

BURKE
Always make it your best®

Burke Corporation
Nevada, IA .800-654-1152

> Always make it your best® with Burke fully cooked meats. We specialize in Italian sausage, beef, and pork toppings, meatballs, taco meats, shredded meats, pepperoni, bacon, Canadian-style bacon, chicken and beef strips. Additionally, we offer a variety of specialty products: Hand-Pinched Style® brand toppings, chorizo, gyro topping, andouille sausage, and breakfast patties and links.

El-Rey Foods
Ferguson, MO 314-521-3113
Gary's Frozen Foods
Lubbock, TX 806-745-1933
Gaucho Foods
Westmont, IL 630-889-4241
Hormel Foods Corporation
Austin, MN .800-523-4635
Jesse's Fine Meats
Cherokee, IA 712-225-3637
King Kold Meats
Englewood, OH 800-836-2797

Party Steak Company
Springfield, MO 417-358-9091

Brisket

Bear Creek Smokehouse
Marshall, TX 800-950-2327
Farmland Foods
Kansas City, MO 888-327-6526
Lewis Smoked Meat Company
Chicago, IL .800-648-6328
Nueces Canyon Texas Style Meat Seasoning
Brenham, TX 800-925-5058
Sara Lee Corporation
Downers Grove, IL 630-598-8100
Saval Foods
Elkridge, MD 800-527-2825

Canned with Natural Juices

Bunker Hill Foods
Augusta, GA 706-733-7765
Crown Point
St John, IN .219-365-3200
Hormel Foods Corporation
Beloit, WI 608-365-9501
International Food Packers Corporation
Miami, FL 305-669-1662
Tupman-Thurlow Company
Deerfield Beach, FL 954-596-9989

Chipped

Alderfer Bologna
Harleysville, PA 877-253-6328

Dinners

Campbell Soup Company
Camden, NJ 800-257-8443
ConAgra Foods/International Home Foods
Niagara Falls, ON 905-356-2661

Filet Mignon

Amana Meat Shop & Smokehouse
Amana, IA 800-373-6328
Boyle Meat Company
Kansas City, MO 800-821-3626
Chef's Requested Foods
Oklahoma City, OK 800-256-0259
Chicago Steaks
Chicago, IL .800-776-4174

Fresh

Amity Packing Company
Chicago, IL .800-837-0270
Beatty Fresh Frozen Meats
Bourbon, IN 574-342-2665
Brook Locker Plant
Brook, IN 219-275-2611
Brookfield Farms
Chicago, IL .773-468-1739
Brownsdale Meat Service
Brownsdale, MN 507-567-2211
Buckhead Beef Company
Atlanta, GA .800-888-5578
Cattleman's Meat Company
Detroit, MI .313-833-2700
Colorado Boxed Beef Company
Auburndale, FL 863-967-0636
Farmland Foods
Kansas City, MO 888-327-6526
International Meat Company
Elmwood Park, IL 773-622-1400
Jbs Packerland Inc
Green Bay, WI 920-468-4000
L&H Packing Company
San Antonio, TX 210-532-3241
Lengerich Meats
Zanesville, IN 260-638-4123
Mountain City Meat Company
Denver, CO .800-937-8325
National Beef Packing
Kansas City, MO 800-449-2333
Plymouth Beef
New York, NY 718-589-8600
R Four Meats
Chatfield, MN 507-867-4180
Sara Lee Foods
Neenah, WI .800-558-8440

Schneider Foods
Etobicoke, ON .416-252-5790
Shelley's Prime Meats
Jersey City, NJ 201-433-3434
Smith Packing Regional Meat
Utica, NY 315-732-5125
SYSCO Foodservice
Fremont, CA 650-494-7200
Temptee Specialty Foods
Denver, CO 800-842-1233
Thumann's
Carlstadt, NJ 201-935-3636
Topps Meat Company
Elizabeth, NJ 908-351-0500
Troy Pork Store
Troy, NY 518-272-8291
Tyson Fresh Meats
Emporia, KS 620-343-3640
Waco Beef & Pork Processors
Waco, TX 254-772-4669

Frozen

Alphin Brothers
Dunn, NC 800-672-4502
Amity Packing Company
Chicago, IL 800-837-0270
Armbrust Meats
Medford, WI 715-748-3102
Art's Tamales
Metamora, IL .309-367-2850
Atlantic Meat Company
Savannah, GA .912-964-8511
Beatty Fresh Frozen Meats
Bourbon, IN 574-342-2665
Birchwood Foods
Kenosha, WI 800-541-1685
Birdie Pak Products
Chicago, IL 773-247-5293
Blakely Freezer Locker
Thomasville, GA. 229-723-3622
Bob's Custom Cuts
Bonnyville, AB 780-826-2627
Brook Locker Plant
Brook, IN 219-275-2611
Brookfield Farms
Chicago, IL 773-468-1739
Brookview Farms
Archbold, OH .419-445-6366
Brownsdale Meat Service
Brownsdale, MN 507-567-2211
Buckhead Beef Company
Atlanta, GA 800-888-5578

Always make it your best®

Burke Corporation
Nevada, IA 800-654-1152

Always make it your best® with Burke fully
cooked meats. We specialize in Italian sausage,
beef, and pork toppings, meatballs, taco meats,
shredded meats, pepperoni, bacon, Canadian-style bacon, chicken and beef strips. Additionally, we offer a variety of specialty products:
Hand-Pinched Style® brand toppings, chorizo,
gyro topping, andouille sausage, and breakfast
patties and links.

Bush Brothers Provision Company
West Palm Beach, FL 800-327-1345
Buzz Food Service
Charleston, WV 304-925-4781
Carando Gourmet Frozen Foods
Springfield, MA 413-730-4205
Caribbean Food Delights
Tappan, NY 845-398-3000
Caribbean Products
Baltimore, MD 410-235-7700
Carl Buddig & Company
Homewood, IL 800-621-0868
Cattleman's Meat Company
Detroit, MI 313-833-2700
Chip Steak & Provision Company
Mankato, MN .507-388-6277
City Foods
Chicago, IL 773-523-1566

Colonial Beef Company
Philadelphia, PA 215-289-7042
Colorado Boxed Beef Company
Auburndale, FL 863-967-0636
Curly's Foods
Edina, MN 612-920-3400
Dallas Dressed Beef
Dallas, TX 214-638-0142
Davidson Meat Processing Plant
Waynesville, OH 513-897-2971
Devault Foods
Devault, PA 800-426-2874
Duma Meats
Mogadore, OH 330-628-3438
Dynamic Foods
Lubbock, TX 806-762-0780
Edmonds Chile Company
St Louis, MO .314-772-1499
El-Rey Foods
Ferguson, MO 314-521-3113
Farmland Foods
Kansas City, MO 888-327-6526
Fuji Foods
Denver, CO 303-377-3738
Gary's Frozen Foods
Lubbock, TX 806-745-1933
Gaucho Foods
Westmont, IL .630-889-4241
Gemini Food Industries
Fiskdale, MA .508-347-2800
Hall Brothers Meats
Cleveland, OH 440-235-3262
Hamm's Custom Meats
McKinney, TX 972-542-3359
Hamner Provision Company
San Antonio, TX 210-736-3117
Heringer Meats
Covington, KY 859-291-2000
Holten Meats
Sauget, IL 800-851-4684
Hormel Foods Corporation
Austin, MN 800-523-4635
International Food Packers Corporation
Miami, FL 305-669-1662
J.J. Andrade's Slaughterhouse
Honokaa, HI .808-775-0741
Jacob & Sons Wholesale Meats
Martins Ferry, OH 740-633-3091
Jbs Packerland Inc
Green Bay, WI. 920-468-4000
Jemm Wholesale Meat Company
Chicago, IL 773-523-8161
Jesse's Fine Meats
Cherokee, IA .712-225-3637
K&K Gourmet Meats
Leetsdale, PA .724-266-8400
King Kold Meats
Englewood, OH 800-836-2797
Kutztown Bologna Company
Leola, PA 800-723-8824
L&H Packing Company
San Antonio, TX 210-532-3241
Ladoga Frozen Food & Retail Meat
Ladoga, IN 765-942-2225
Lengerich Meats
Zanesville, IN .260-638-4123
Leo G. Fraboni Sausage Company
Hibbing, MN .218-263-5074
Loggins Meat Company
Tyler, TX 800-527-8610
Maid-Rite Steak Company
Dunmore, PA .800-233-4259
Meat-O-Mat Corporation
Brooklyn, NY .718-965-7250
Miami Beef Company
Hialeah, FL 305-621-3252
Mountain City Meat Company
Denver, CO 800-937-8325
National Beef Packing
Kansas City, MO 800-449-2333
Northern Packing Company
Brier Hill, NY .315-375-8801
Paris Frozen Foods
Hillsboro, IL 217-532-3822
Party Steak Company
Springfield, MO 417-358-9091
Phoenix Agro-Industrial Corporation
Westbury, NY 516-334-1194
Pierceton Foods
Pierceton, IN .574-594-2344
Plymouth Beef
New York, NY 718-589-8600

R Four Meats
Chatfield, MN 507-867-4180
Redi-Serve Food Company
Fort Atkinson, WI. 920-563-6391
Republic Foods
Dallas, TX 214-826-8050
Saletts
Randolph, MA 781-961-9900
Sam Hausman Meat Packer
Corpus Christi, TX 361-883-5521
Sam Kane Beef Processors
Corpus Christi, TX 361-241-5000
Scarborough Meat Packers
Scarborough, ON 416-269-7758
Schneider Foods
Etobicoke, ON 416-252-5790
Shelley's Prime Meats
Jersey City, NJ 201-433-3434
Smith Packing Regional Meat
Utica, NY 315-732-5125
Southeastern Meat Association
Oviedo, FL 407-365-5661
Steak-Umm Company
Shillington, PA 860-928-5900
Sudlersville Frozen Food Locker
Sudlersville, MD. 410-438-3106
SYSCO Foodservice
Fremont, CA 650-494-7200
Thompson Packers
Slidell, LA. 800-989-6328
Topps Meat Company
Elizabeth, NJ 908-351-0500
Travis Meats
Powell, TN 800-247-7606
Tucker Packing Company
Orrville, OH 330-683-3311
Tyson Fresh Meats
Emporia, KS 620-343-3640
United Meat Company
San Francisco, CA 415-864-2118
Valley Packing Company
Lansing, OH 740-635-0154
Wexler Meat Company
Skokie, IL 773-927-5656
Zartic Inc
Rome, GA 800-241-0516

Ground

Acme Steak & Seafood Company
Youngstown, OH. 330-270-8000
American Foods Group
Green Bay, WI. 920-437-6330
Atlantic Meat Company
Savannah, GA .912-964-8511
Blue Ribbon Meats
Miami, FL 800-522-6115
Brockton Beef & Provisions Corporation
Brockton, MA 508-583-4703
Caribbean Food Delights
Tappan, NY 845-398-3000
Centennial Food Corporation
Calgary, AB. 403-287-2525
Chicago Steaks
Chicago, IL 800-776-4174
Chip Steak & Provision Company
Mankato, MN .507-388-6277
Cropp Cooperative-Organic Valley
La Farge, WI. .888-444-6455
Devault Foods
Devault, PA 800-426-2874
Glenmark Industries
Chicago, IL 773-927-4800
J&B Corporation
Coal Valley, IL 309-799-7341
Jensen Meat Company
Vista, CA. 760-727-6700
John Garner Meats
Van Buren, AR 800-543-5473
Karn Meats
Columbus, OH 800-221-9585
Kenosha Beef International
Kenosha, WI 800-541-1685
Kessler's, Inc
Lemoyne, PA .800-382-1328
L&H Packing Company
San Antonio, TX 210-532-3241
Miami Beef Company
Hialeah, FL 305-621-3252
O Chili Frozen Foods Inc
Northbrook, IL 847-562-1991

Palmer Packing Company
Tremonton, UT 435-257-5329
Quality Beef Company
Providence, RI 877-233-3462
Rinehart Meat Processing
Branson, MO. 417-334-2044
S.W. Meat & Provision Company
Phoenix, AZ 602-275-2000
Springville Meat & Cold Storage
Springville, UT. 801-489-6391
Stanley Provision Company
Manchester, CT 888-688-6347
Stone Meat Processor
Ogden, UT. 801-782-9825
SYSCO Foodservice
Fremont, CA 650-494-7200
Thompson Packers
Slidell, LA. 800-989-6328
Valley Meat Company
Modesto, CA 800-222-6328

Coarse Frozen

Devault Foods
Devault, PA. 800-426-2874

Frozen

Acme Steak & Seafood Company
Youngstown, OH. 330-270-8000
Caribbean Food Delights
Tappan, NY. 845-398-3000
Chip Steak & Provision Company
Mankato, MN 507-388-6277
Kenosha Beef International
Kenosha, WI 800-541-1685
L&H Packing Company
San Antonio, TX. 210-532-3241
Miami Beef Company
Hialeah, FL. 305-621-3252
SYSCO Foodservice
Fremont, CA 650-494-7200
Thompson Packers
Slidell, LA. 800-989-6328

Hamburger

Acme Steak & Seafood Company
Youngstown, OH. 330-270-8000
Alphin Brothers
Dunn, NC 800-672-4502
Atlantic Meat Company
Savannah, GA 912-964-8511
Bakalars Brothers Sausage Company
La Crosse, WI 608-784-0384
Birchwood Foods
Kenosha, WI 800-541-1685
Brockton Beef & Provisions Corporation
Brockton, MA 508-583-4703

Burke Corporation
Nevada, IA 800-654-1152

Always make it your best® with Burke fully cooked meats. We specialize in Italian sausage, beef, and pork toppings, meatballs, taco meats, shredded meats, pepperoni, bacon, Canadian-style bacon, chicken and beef strips. Additionally, we offer a variety of specialty products: Hand-Pinched Style® brand toppings, chorizo, gyro topping, andouille sausage, and breakfast patties and links.

Chicago Meat Authority
Chicago, IL. 773-254-0020
Chicopee Provision Company
Chicopee, MA 800-924-6328
Crocetti Oakdale Packing
East Bridgewater, MA 508-587-0035
Devault Foods
Devault, PA. 800-426-2874
Edmonds Chile Company
St Louis, MO. 314-772-1499
Hormel Foods Corporation
Austin, MN 800-523-4635

Keystone Foods Corporation
W Conshohocken, PA. 610-667-6700
Miami Beef Company
Hialeah, FL. 305-621-3252
O Chili Frozen Foods Inc
Northbrook, IL 847-562-1991
Ossian Seafood Meats
Ossian, IN 260-622-4191
Otto & Son
West Jordan, UT 800-453-9462
Pierceton Foods
Pierceton, IN 574-594-2344
Rego's Purity Foods
Honolulu, HI 808-947-9005
Rinehart Meat Processing
Branson, MO. 417-334-2044
Rymer Foods
Chicago, IL 800-247-9637
Thompson Packers
Slidell, LA. 800-989-6328
Topps Meat Company
Elizabeth, NJ. 908-351-0500
Travis Meats
Powell, TN 800-247-7606
Valley Meat Company
Modesto, CA 800-222-6328

Cooked Frozen

Burke Corporation
Nevada, IA 800-654-1152

Always make it your best® with Burke fully cooked meats. We specialize in Italian sausage, beef, and pork toppings, meatballs, taco meats, shredded meats, pepperoni, bacon, Canadian-style bacon, chicken and beef strips. Additionally, we offer a variety of specialty products: Hand-Pinched Style® brand toppings, chorizo, gyro topping, andouille sausage, and breakfast patties and links.

Maid-Rite Steak Company
Dunmore, PA. 800-233-4259
On-Cor Foods Products
Northbrook, IL 847-205-1040

Uncooked Frozen

Al Safa Halal
Niagara Falls, NY 800-268-8174
Caribbean Food Delights
Tappan, NY. 845-398-3000
Maid-Rite Steak Company
Dunmore, PA. 800-233-4259
On-Cor Foods Products
Northbrook, IL 847-205-1040
Pierceton Foods
Pierceton, IN 574-594-2344

Italian

Burke Corporation
Nevada, IA 800-654-1152

Always make it your best® with Burke fully cooked meats. We specialize in Italian sausage, beef, and pork toppings, meatballs, taco meats, shredded meats, pepperoni, bacon, Canadian-style bacon, chicken and beef strips. Additionally, we offer a variety of specialty products: Hand-Pinched Style® brand toppings, chorizo, gyro topping, andouille sausage, and breakfast patties and links.

Liver

Caughman's Meat Plant
Lexington, SC 803-356-0076
D'Artagnan
Newark, NJ 800-327-8246
Dynamic Foods
Lubbock, TX. 806-762-0780
Giovanni's Appetizing Food Products
Richmond, MI. 586-727-9355
Lees Sausage Company
Orangeburg, SC 803-534-5517
Republic Foods
Dallas, TX 214-826-8050
Skylark Meats
Omaha, NE 800-759-5275
Stauber Performance Ingredients
Fullerton, CA 888-441-4233

London Broil

Burnett & Son Meat Company
Monrovia, CA. 626-357-2165

NY Strip Steak

Amana Meat Shop & Smokehouse
Amana, IA 800-373-6328
Chef's Requested Foods
Oklahoma City, OK 800-256-0259
Cropp Cooperative-Organic Valley
La Farge, WI 888-444-6455

Patties

Burke Corporation
Nevada, IA 800-654-1152

Always make it your best® with Burke fully cooked meats. We specialize in Italian sausage, beef, and pork toppings, meatballs, taco meats, shredded meats, pepperoni, bacon, Canadian-style bacon, chicken and beef strips. Additionally, we offer a variety of specialty products: Hand-Pinched Style® brand toppings, chorizo, gyro topping, andouille sausage, and breakfast patties and links.

Cooked Frozen

Loggins Meat Company
Tyler, TX 800-527-8610
O Chili Frozen Foods Inc
Northbrook, IL 847-562-1991

Frozen

Buzz Food Service
Charleston, WV 304-925-4781
Caribbean Food Delights
Tappan, NY. 845-398-3000
Centennial Food Corporation
Calgary, AB. 403-287-2525
Corfu Foods
Bensenville, IL 630-595-2510
Glenmark Food Processors
Chicago, IL 800-621-0117
Holten Meats
Sauget, IL 800-851-4684
John Garner Meats
Van Buren, AR 800-543-5473
Kenosha Beef International
Kenosha, WI 800-541-1685
King Kold Meats
Englewood, OH 800-836-2797
Kutztown Bologna Company
Leola, PA. 800-723-8824
Maid-Rite Steak Company
Dunmore, PA. 800-233-4259
Meat-O-Mat Corporation
Brooklyn, NY 718-965-7250
Patty Palace
Scarborough, ON 416-297-0510
Topps Meat Company
Elizabeth, NJ. 908-351-0500

Travis Meats
Powell, TN 800-247-7606
Valley Meat Company
Modesto, CA 800-222-6328
Wisconsin Packing Company
Butler, WI 800-558-2000

Jamacain

Matlaw's Food Products
West Haven, CT 800-934-8266
Royal Home Bakery
Newmarket, ON 905-715-7044

Porterhouse

Chef's Requested Foods
Oklahoma City, OK 800-256-0259
Chicago Steaks
Chicago, IL 800-776-4174

Pot Roast

Fontanini Italian Meats & Sausages
Chicago, IL 800-331-6328

Processed

Al Safa Halal
Niagara Falls, NY 800-268-8174
Alderfer Bologna
Harleysville, PA 877-253-6328
Alewel's Country Meats
Warrensburg, MO 800-353-8553
Alpine Meats
Stockton, CA. .800-399-6328
Best Provision Company, Inc.
Newark, NJ 800-631-4466
Big B Distributors
Evansville, IN .812-425-5235
Bruss Company
Chicago, IL 800-621-3882
Buckhead Beef Company
Atlanta, GA. 800-888-5578
Bunker Hill Foods
Augusta, GA 706-733-7765
Bush Brothers Provision Company
West Palm Beach, FL 800-327-1345
Caddo Packing Company
Marshall, TX. .903-935-2211
Campbell Soup Company
Camden, NJ. 800-257-8443
Carando Gourmet Frozen Foods
Springfield, MA 413-730-4205
Cargill Meats
Milwaukee, WI 800-558-4242
Caribbean Food Delights
Tappan, NY 845-398-3000
Casson & Sons
Des Moines, IA. 515-266-3197
Castleberry's Meats
Atlanta, GA 404-873-1804
Castleberry/Snow Brands
Augusta, GA 800-241-3520
Cattaneo Brothers
San Luis Obispo, CA 800-243-8537
Central Beef
Center Hill, FL 352-793-3671

Central Meat & Provision Company
San Diego, CA 619-239-1391
Chalmette Packing Company
Covington, LA 504-271-6241
Chandler Foods
Greensboro, NC 800-537-6219
Charlie's Pride Meats
Los Angeles, CA. 877-866-0982
Cher-Make Sausage Company
Manitowoc, WI. 800-242-7679
Cheraw Packing
Cheraw, SC 843-537-7426
Chip Steak & Provision Company
Mankato, MN .507-388-6277
Columbia Packing Company
Dallas, TX. 800-460-8171
ConAgra Foods/Eckrich
Omaha, NE 800-327-4424
ConAgra Foods/International Home Foods
Niagara Falls, ON 905-356-2661
Conti Packing Company
Rochester, NY 585-424-2500
Continental Deli Foods
Cherokee, IA .712-225-5161
Corfu Foods
Bensenville, IL 630-595-2510
Covemaker Packing Company
Moline, IL 309-764-1480
Darling International
Omaha, NE 402-733-3010
David Berg & Company
Chicago, IL 773-489-4711
Dutterer's Home Food Service
Baltimore, MD 410-298-3663
E.W. Knauss & Son
Quakertown, PA 800-648-4220
F&Y Enterprises
Naperville, IL .630-637-8519
Gunsberg Corned Beef
Detroit, MI 313-894-6600
Hahn Brothers
Westminster, MD 800-227-7675
Hamilton Quality Convenience Foods
Romulus, MI .734-946-1800
Hamm's Custom Meats
McKinney, TX 972-542-3359
Henry J Meat Specialties
Chicago, IL 800-242-1314
High Country Snack Foods
Lincoln, MT 800-433-3916
Horlacher's Fine Meats
Logan, UT. 435-752-1287
Hsin Tung Yang Foods Co.
S San Francisco, CA 650-589-6789
Jensen Meat Company
Vista, CA. 760-727-6700
Jesse's Fine Meats
Cherokee, IA .712-225-3637
John Garner Meats
Van Buren, AR 800-543-5473
Kershenstine Beef Jerky
Eupora, MS 662-258-2049
Keystone Foods Corporation
W Conshohocken, PA. 610-667-6700
King's Command Foods
Kent, WA. 800-247-3138
Kutztown Bologna Company
Leola, PA. 800-723-8824
Lampasas Locker Plant
Lampasas, TX. 512-556-5121
Land O'Frost
Searcy, AR 800-643-5654
Lone Star Beef Jerky Company
Lubbock, TX. .806-762-8833
Longview Meat & Merchandise
Longview, AB. 403-558-3706
Lower Foods
Richmond, UT. 435-258-2449
Moo & Oink
Chicago, IL 773-493-2755
Mosey's Inc
Bloomfield, CT. 860-243-1725
Moyer Packing Company
Souderton, PA 800-967-8325
National Beef Packing
Kansas City, MO 800-449-2333
Nebraska Beef
Omaha, NE 402-734-6823
Nestle Pizza
Medford, WI .715-748-5550
Peoples Sausage Company
Los Angeles, CA. 213-627-8633

Pierceton Foods
Pierceton, IN .574-594-2344
Plumrose USA
East Brunswick, NJ. 732-257-6600
Plymouth Beef
New York, NY 718-589-8600
Red Oak Farms
Red Oak, IA 712-623-9224
Rinehart Meat Processing
Branson, MO. 417-334-2044
Saletts
Randolph, MA 781-961-9900
Saval Foods
Elkridge, MD .800-527-2825
Smith Provision Company
Erie, PA. 800-334-9151
Southtowns Seafood & Meats
Blasdell, NY 716-824-4900
Sunset Farm Foods
Valdosta, GA .800-882-1121
Temptee Specialty Foods
Denver, CO 800-842-1233
Terrell Meats
Delta, UT. 435-864-2600
Thompson Packers
Slidell, LA 800-989-6328
Tri-State Beef Company
Cincinnati, OH 513-579-1722
Tupman-Thurlow Company
Deerfield Beach, FL 954-596-9989
Tyson Fresh Meats
Emporia, KS 620-343-3640
Valley Meat Company
Modesto, CA. .800-222-6328
Weaver Nut Company
Ephrata, PA 717-738-3781
Weiss Provisions
Pittsburgh, PA 800-458-6328
Wexler Meat Company
Skokie, IL 773-927-5656
Wimmer's Meat Products
West Point, NE 800-358-0761
Wisconsin Packing Company
Butler, WI 800-558-2000
Woods Smoked Meats
Bowling Green, MO 800-458-8426

Products

A. Stein Meat Products
Brooklyn, NY 718-492-0760
Alderfer Bologna
Harleysville, PA 877-253-6328
Alewel's Country Meats
Warrensburg, MO 800-353-8553
Bakalars Brothers Sausage Company
La Crosse, WI .608-784-0384
Big B Distributors
Evansville, IN .812-425-5235
Birchwood Foods
Kenosha, WI 800-541-1685
Bruss Company
Chicago, IL 800-621-3882
Buona Vita
Bridgeton, NJ 856-453-7972
Bush Brothers Provision Company
West Palm Beach, FL 800-327-1345
Caddo Packing Company
Marshall, TX .903-935-2211
Campbell Soup Company
Camden, NJ. 800-257-8443
Caribbean Food Delights
Tappan, NY 845-398-3000
Carl Buddig & Company
Homewood, IL 800-621-0868
Casson & Sons
Des Moines, IA. 515-266-3197
Castleberry/Snow Brands
Augusta, GA 800-241-3520
Chicago Meat Authority
Chicago, IL 773-254-0020
Columbia Packing Company
Dallas, TX. 800-460-8171
ConAgra Snack Foods
San Jose, CA 408-436-0329
Counts Sausage Company
Prosperity, SC 803-364-2392
David Berg & Company
Chicago, IL 773-489-4711
Dino's Sausage & Meat Company
Utica, NY 315-732-2661

Dutterer's Home Food Service
Baltimore, MD 410-298-3663
E.W. Knauss & Son
Quakertown, PA 800-648-4220
Edmonds Chile Company
St Louis, MO 314-772-1499
El-Rey Foods
Ferguson, MO 314-521-3113
Elkhart Locker Plant
Elkhart, KS .620-697-4424
Elmwood Lockers
Elmwood, IL 309-742-8929
F&Y Enterprises
Naperville, IL 630-637-8519
Flint Hills Foods
Wamego, KS 785-765-3396
Foodbrands America
Oklahoma City, OK 405-290-4000
G Di Lullo & Sons
Westville, NJ 856-456-3700
Glenmark Food Processors
Chicago, IL .800-621-0117
Groff Meats
Elizabethtown, PA. 717-367-1246
Gunsberg Corned Beef
Detroit, MI .313-894-6600
Hahn Brothers
Westminster, MD 800-227-7675
Harris Ranch Beef Company
Selma, CA 800-742-1955
Hazle Park Packing Company
West Hazleton, PA 800-238-4331
Henry J Meat Specialties
Chicago, IL .800-242-1314
Holly Hill Locker Company
Holly Hill, SC 803-496-3611
Holten Meats
Sauget, IL 800-851-4684
Hormel Foods Corporation
Austin, MN .800-523-4635
Ito Cariani Sausage Company
Hayward, CA 510-887-0882
Ittels Meats
Howard Lake, MN 320-543-2285
John Garner Meats
Van Buren, AR 800-543-5473
Joseph Sanders
Custer, MI 800-968-5035
K&K Gourmet Meats
Leetsdale, PA 724-266-8400
Karn Meats
Columbus, OH 800-221-9585
Kelly Kornbeef Company
Chicago, IL .773-588-2882
Kenosha Beef International
Kenosha, WI 800-541-1685
Kershenstine Beef Jerky
Eupora, MS .662-258-2049
Keystone Foods Corporation
W Conshohocken, PA 610-667-6700
Kutztown Bologna Company
Leola, PA 800-723-8824
L&H Packing Company
San Antonio, TX 210-532-3241
Leo G. Fraboni Sausage Company
Hibbing, MN 218-263-5074
Lower Foods
Richmond, UT 435-258-2449
Maid-Rite Steak Company
Dunmore, PA 800-233-4259
Marathon Enterprises
Englewood, NJ 201-935-3330
Meating Place
Buffalo, NY. 716-885-3623
Moo & Oink
Chicago, IL .773-493-2755
National Foods
Indianapolis, IN 800-683-6565
Nestle Pizza
Medford, WI 715-748-5550
Peer Foods Inc
Chicago, IL .800-365-5644
Penn Valley Farms
Gainesville, GA 773-685-9929
Peoples Sausage Company
Los Angeles, CA 213-627-8633
Pinter's Packing Plant
Dorchester, WI 715-654-5444
Plumrose USA
East Brunswick, NJ 732-257-6600
Plymouth Beef
New York, NY 718-589-8600

R-K Sausage Company
Cleveland, OH 216-341-1251
Redi-Serve Food Company
Fort Atkinson, WI. 920-563-6391
Rinehart Meat Processing
Branson, MO 417-334-2044
Rudolph Foods
Dallas, TX. .214-638-2204
Rymer Foods
Chicago, IL .800-247-9637
S.W. Meat & Provision Company
Phoenix, AZ 602-275-2000
Sadler's BBQ Sales
Henderson, TX 903-657-5581
Sara Lee Corporation
Downers Grove, IL 630-598-8100
Sara Lee Foods
Zeeland, MI 616-875-8131
Sara Lee Foods
Neenah, WI 800-558-8440
Saval Foods
Elkridge, MD 800-527-2825
Sheinman Provision Company
Philadelphia, PA 215-473-7065
Steak-Umm Company
Shillington, PA 860-928-5900
Striplings
Moultrie, GA. 229-985-4226
Temptee Specialty Foods
Denver, CO .800-842-1233
Terrell Meats
Delta, UT. 435-864-2600
Tyson Fresh Meats
Emporia, KS 620-343-3640
Une-Viandi
St. Jean Sur Richelieu, NB 800-363-1955
Vienna Meat Products
Scarborough, ON 800-588-1931
Weaver Nut Company
Ephrata, PA .717-738-3781
Wisconsin Packing Company
Butler, WI. .800-558-2000
Woods Smoked Meats
Bowling Green, MO 800-458-8426
XL Beef
Calgary, AB .403-236-2424

Raw

Caribbean Food Delights
Tappan, NY .845-398-3000
Maid-Rite Steak Company
Dunmore, PA 800-233-4259

Rib Eye Roast

Cropp Cooperative-Organic Valley
La Farge, WI 888-444-6455

Rib Eye Steak

Amana Meat Shop & Smokehouse
Amana, IA. .800-373-6328
Boyle Meat Company
Kansas City, MO. 800-821-3626
Chef's Requested Foods
Oklahoma City, OK 800-256-0259
Chicago Steaks
Chicago, IL .800-776-4174
Cropp Cooperative-Organic Valley
La Farge, WI 888-444-6455
Father's Country Hams
Bremen, KY 270-525-3554
Woods Smoked Meats
Bowling Green, MO 800-458-8426

Rib Steak

Chicago Steaks
Chicago, IL .800-776-4174

Roast Beef

Alderfer Bologna
Harleysville, PA 877-253-6328
Applegate Farms
Bridgewater, NJ 908-725-2768
Berks Packing Company, Inc.
Reading, PA 800-882-3757
Burnett & Son Meat Company
Monrovia, CA 626-357-2165
Carando Gourmet Frozen Foods
Springfield, MA 413-730-4205

Charlie's Pride Meats
Los Angeles, CA 877-866-0982
Chip Steak & Provision Company
Mankato, MN 507-388-6277
Cold Springs Farm
Thamesford, ON 800-265-1978
Curly's Foods
Edina, MN. .612-920-3400
David Berg & Company
Chicago, IL .773-489-4711
Dorina/So-Good
Union, IL. 815-923-2144
Dutterer's Home Food Service
Baltimore, MD 410-298-3663
El-Rey Foods
Ferguson, MO 314-521-3113
Four Star Meat Company of Louisiana
Amite, LA 800-444-5228
Gunsberg Corned Beef
Detroit, MI .313-894-6600
Hahn Brothers
Westminster, MD 800-227-7675
Henry J Meat Specialties
Chicago, IL .800-242-1314
Hormel Foods Corporation
Austin, MN .800-523-4635
Ito Cariani Sausage Company
Hayward, CA 510-887-0882
Lower Foods
Richmond, UT 435-258-2449
Miami Beef Company
Hialeah, FL .305-621-3252
Mosey's Inc
Bloomfield, CT 860-243-1725
Ottman Meat Company
New York, NY 212-879-4160
Sara Lee Corporation
Downers Grove, IL 630-598-8100
Saval Foods
Elkridge, MD 800-527-2825
Sheinman Provision Company
Philadelphia, PA 215-473-7065
Upstate Farms Cooperative
Buffalo, NY. 716-892-3156
Vienna Meat Products
Scarborough, ON 800-588-1931

Rolls - Frozen

Alphin Brothers
Dunn, NC 800-672-4502
Columbia Packing Company
Dallas, TX. .800-460-8171
Party Steak Company
Springfield, MO 417-358-9091
Travis Meats
Powell, TN .800-247-7606

Sirloin Cubes

Chicago Steaks
Chicago, IL .800-776-4174
Cropp Cooperative-Organic Valley
La Farge, WI 888-444-6455
Farmland Foods
Kansas City, MO. 888-327-6526

Sliced

E.W. Knauss & Son
Quakertown, PA 800-648-4220
Gemini Food Industries
Fiskdale, MA 508-347-2800
Plymouth Beef
New York, NY 718-589-8600
Republic Foods
Dallas, TX. .214-826-8050

Dried

Alderfer Bologna
Harleysville, PA 877-253-6328
E.W. Knauss & Son
Quakertown, PA 800-648-4220
Palmyra Bologna
Palmyra, PA. 717-838-6336
Red Oak Farms
Red Oak, IA 712-623-9224

Food & Beverage Market Place

now available for subscription on

G.O.L.D.

Grey House OnLine Databases

Immediate Access to the US Food & Beverage Industry!

- Easy-To-Use Keyword & Quick Searches
- Organization Type & Subject Searches
- Cross-Database Searching
- Search by Area Code or Zip Code Ranges
- Search by Company Size & Geographic Area
- Search by Contact Name or Title

- Hotlinks to Websites & Email Addresses
- Combine Multiple Search Criteria with our Expert Search Page
- Sort Search Results by City, Company Name, Area Code & more
- Save Searches for Quick Lookups
- Create & Save Your Own Search Results Lists
- Download Search Results in TXT, CSV or DOC Formats

Quick Search

Expert Search

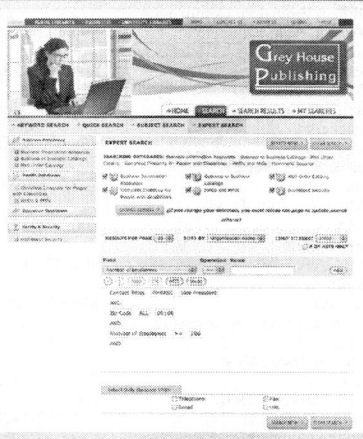

Subject Search

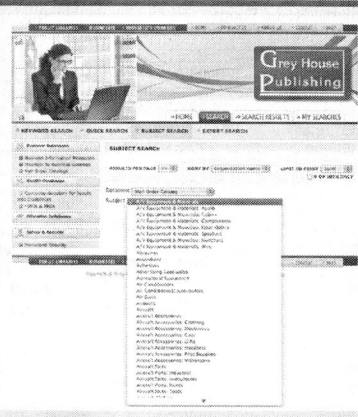

Call (800) 562-2139 for a free trial of the new G.O.L.D. OnLine Database Platform or visit http://gold.greyhouse.com for more information!

Grey House Publishing

PO Box 56 | 4919 Route 22 | Amenia, NY 12501
(800) 562-2139 | (518) 789-8700 | FAX (845) 373-6360
www.greyhouse.com | e-mail: books@greyhouse.com

Frozen

Burke Corporation
Nevada, IA 800-654-1152

Always make it your best® with Burke fully
cooked meats. We specialize in Italian sausage,
beef, and pork toppings, meatballs, taco meats,
shredded meats, pepperoni, bacon, Canadian-style bacon, chicken and beef strips. Additionally, we offer a variety of specialty products:
Hand-Pinched Style® brand toppings, chorizo,
gyro topping, andouille sausage, and breakfast
patties and links.

Gemini Food Industries
Fiskdale, MA 508-347-2800

Special Trim

Buckhead Beef Company
Atlanta, GA 800-888-5578

Steak

Alaskan Gourmet Seafoods
Anchorage, AK 800-288-3740
Bakalars Brothers Sausage Company
La Crosse, WI 608-784-0384
Bear Creek Smokehouse
Marshall, TX 800-950-2327
Blue Ribbon Meats
Miami, FL 800-522-6115
Burnett & Son Meat Company
Monrovia, CA 626-357-2165
Campbell Soup Company
Camden, NJ 800-257-8443
Castleberry/Snow Brands
Augusta, GA 800-241-3520
ConAgra Foods/International Home Foods
Niagara Falls, ON 905-356-2661
Elkhart Locker Plant
Elkhart, KS 620-697-4424
Flint Hills Foods
Wamego, KS 785-765-3396
Jemm Wholesale Meat Company
Chicago, IL 773-523-8161
Joe Fazio's Famous Italian
Charleston, WV 304-344-3071
Karn Meats
Columbus, OH 800-221-9585
Kutztown Bologna Company
Leola, PA 800-723-8824
Loggins Meat Company
Tyler, TX 800-527-8610
Pine Point Seafood
Scarborough, ME 207-883-4701
Pinter's Packing Plant
Dorchester, WI 715-654-5444
Rymer Foods
Chicago, IL 800-247-9637
Steak-Umm Company
Shillington, PA 860-928-5900
Woods Smoked Meats
Bowling Green, MO 800-458-8426

Stew

Burnett & Son Meat Company
Monrovia, CA 626-357-2165
Campbell Soup Company
Camden, NJ 800-257-8443
Castleberry/Snow Brands
Augusta, GA 800-241-3520
ConAgra Foods/International Home Foods
Niagara Falls, ON 905-356-2661
Johnston's Home Style Products
Charlottetown, PE 902-629-1300
Plymouth Beef
New York, NY 718-589-8600

Frozen

Edmonds Chile Company
St Louis, MO 314-772-1499

Tongue

A. Stein Meat Products
Brooklyn, NY 718-492-0760
Marathon Enterprises
Englewood, NJ 201-935-3330
Sara Lee Corporation
Downers Grove, IL 630-598-8100
Saval Foods
Elkridge, MD 800-527-2825

Veal

A to Z Portion Meats
Bluffton, OH 800-338-6328
A. Stein Meat Products
Brooklyn, NY 718-492-0760
A. Thomas Food Service
Louisville, KY 800-253-2020
A.C. Kissling Company
Philadelphia, PA 800-445-1943
Adolf's Meats & Sausage Kitchen
Hartford, CT 860-522-1588
Alphin Brothers
Dunn, NC 800-672-4502
Arena & Sons
Hopkinton, MA 508-435-3673
Atlantic Veal
Olyphant, PA 570-489-4781
Atlantic Veal & Lamb
Brooklyn, NY 800-221-6988
B&R Quality Meats
Waterloo, IA 319-232-6328
Baretta Provision
East Berlin, CT 860-828-0802
Big Apple Produce & Seafood Market
Pocomoke City, MD 410-957-1151
Border's Market
Plymouth, OH 419-687-2634
Brook Locker Plant
Brook, IN 219-275-2611
Brown Packing Company
South Holland, IL 800-832-8325
Bruss Company
Chicago, IL 800-621-3882
Buckhead Beef Company
Atlanta, GA 800-888-5578
Bush Brothers Provision Company
West Palm Beach, FL 800-327-1345
Buzz Food Service
Charleston, WV 304-925-4781
Canada West Foods
Innisfail, AB 403-227-3386
Capital Packers
Edmonton, AB 800-272-8868
Carl Streit & Son Company
Neptune, NJ 732-775-0803
Carmel Meat/Specialty Foods
Marina, CA 800-298-5823
Castleberry's Meats
Atlanta, GA 404-873-1804
Catelli Brothers
Camden, NJ 856-869-9293
Central Meat & Provision Company
San Diego, CA 619-239-1391
Chiappetti Wholesale Meat
Chicago, IL 773-927-9476
Community Market & Deli
Lindstrom, MN 651-257-1128
Conti Packing Company
Rochester, NY 585-424-2500
Country Village Meats
Sublette, IL 815-849-5532
Culinary Foods
Chicago, IL 800-621-4049
Cusack Wholesale Meat Company
Oklahoma City, OK 800-241-6328
D'Artagnan
Newark, NJ 800-327-8246
David Mosner Meat Products
Bronx, NY 718-328-5600
DeBragga & Spitler
New York, NY 212-924-1311
Empire Beef Company
Rochester, NY 800-462-6804
Ferko Meat Company
Milwaukee, WI 414-967-5500
Florida Veal Processors
Wimauma, FL 813-634-5545
George L. Wells Meat Company
Philadelphia, PA 800-523-1730
Glenmark Food Processors
Chicago, IL 800-621-0117

Godshall's Quality Meats
Franconia, PA 888-463-7425
H. Shenson International Export
San Francisco, CA 415-318-7000
Hamilton Provision Company
Hamilton, OH 800-328-9979
Heringer Meats
Covington, KY 859-291-2000
Holten Meats
Sauget, IL 800-851-4684
IBP Foods
Troy, MI 248-588-4710
International Meat Company
Elmwood Park, IL 773-622-1400
J&B Meats Corporation
Coal Valley, IL 309-799-7341
Jordahl Meats
Manchester, MN 507-826-3418
Joseph McSweeney & Sons
Windom, MN 804-359-6024
Kelley Meats
Taberg, NY 315-337-4272
King Kold Meats
Englewood, OH 800-836-2797
King's Command Foods
Kent, WA 800-247-3138
L&L Packing Company
Chicago, IL 800-628-6328
L&M Slaughtering
Georgetown, IL 217-662-6841
Lay Packing Company
Knoxville, TN 865-922-4320
Lionel Lavallee Company
Haverhill, MA 800-343-8292
Lombardi Brothers Meat Packers
Denver, CO 800-421-4412
Lowell Provision Company
Lowell, MA 978-454-5603
Magnolia Beef Company
Elizabeth, NJ 908-352-9412
Maid-Rite Steak Company
Dunmore, PA 800-233-4259
Marcho Farms Veal
Harleysville, PA 215-721-7131
Meat-O-Mat Corporation
Brooklyn, NY 718-965-7250
Michael's Finer Meats & Seafoods
Columbus, OH 800-282-0518
Mosey's Inc
Bloomfield, CT 860-243-1725
Mountain City Meat Company
Denver, CO 800-937-8325
Mountain States Rosen, LLc
Bronx, NY 800-872-5262
Nagel Veal
San Bernardino, CA 909-383-7075
O Chili Frozen Foods Inc
Northbrook, IL 847-562-1991
Otto W Liebold & Company
Flint, MI 800-999-6328
Pasqualichio Brothers
Scranton, PA 800-232-6233
Penn Valley Farms
Gainesville, GA 773-685-9929
Petschl's Meats
Tukwila, WA 206-575-4400
Provimi Veal Corporation
Seymour, WI 800-833-8325
Quaker Maid Meats
Shillington, PA 610-376-1500
Rainbow Slaughtering
Creston, OH 330-435-4351
Rancher's Lamb of Texas
San Angelo, TX 325-659-4004
Redi-Serve Food Company
Fort Atkinson, WI 920-563-6391
Rendulic Packing
McKeesport, PA 412-678-9541
Saletts
Randolph, MA 781-961-9900
Saunders Provision Company
Norfolk, VA. 800-486-5611
Sculli Brothers
Philadelphia, PA 215-336-1223
Shelley's Prime Meats
Jersey City, NJ 201-433-3434
Smith Packing Regional Meat
Utica, NY 315-732-5125
Southeastern Meat Association
Oviedo, FL 407-365-5661
Southern Packing Corporation
Chesapeake, VA 757-421-2131

Southtowns Seafood & Meats
Blasdell, NY 716-824-4900
Standard Beef Company
New Haven, CT 203-787-2164
Stock Yards Packing Company
Chicago, IL 800-621-1119
Superior Farms
Davis, CA 800-228-5262
Suzanna's Kitchen
Duluth, GA .800-241-2455
Swanton's Packing
Fairfax, VT .802-868-4469
Swissland Packing Company
Frankfort, IL 800-321-8325
Thompson Packers
Slidell, LA. .800-989-6328
Tooele Valley Meat
Grantsville, UT 435-884-3837
Travis Meats
Powell, TN .800-247-7606
Tyler Packing Company
Tyler, TX. 903-593-9592
Une-Viandi
St. Jean Sur Richelieu, NB 800-363-1955
United Meat Company
San Francisco, CA 415-864-2118
United Provision Meat Company
Columbus, OH 614-252-1126
Valley Packing Company
Lansing, OH 740-635-0154
Vantage USA
Chicago, IL 773-247-1086
W&W Meats
Willoughby, OH 216-621-7846
Wasatch Meats
Salt Lake City, UT 801-363-5747
Windcrest Meat Packers
Port Perry, ON. 800-750-2542
Wolverine Packing
Detroit, MI 313-392-9403

Breaded Frozen

Holten Meats
Sauget, IL. .800-851-4684
J&B Meats Corporation
Coal Valley, IL 309-799-7341
King's Command Foods
Kent, WA. .800-247-3138
Meat-O-Mat Corporation
Brooklyn, NY 718-965-7250
O Chili Frozen Foods Inc
Northbrook, IL 847-562-1991
Olympic Food Products
Kokomo, IN 800-445-6923
Ottman Meat Company
New York, NY 212-879-4160
Redi-Serve Food Company
Fort Atkinson, WI. 920-563-6391
W&W Meats
Willoughby, OH 216-621-7846

Burgers

Meat-O-Mat Corporation
Brooklyn, NY 718-965-7250

Cutlet

Redi-Serve Food Company
Fort Atkinson, WI. 920-563-6391

Fresh

Colorado Boxed Beef Company
Auburndale, FL. 863-967-0636
Florida Veal Processors
Wimauma, FL 813-634-5545
Jesse's Best
Suffolk, VA 757-489-8383
Provimi Veal Corporation
Seymour, WI 800-833-8325
Shelley's Prime Meats
Jersey City, NJ 201-433-3434
Smith Packing Regional Meat
Utica, NY .315-732-5125
Swissland Packing Company
Frankfort, IL 800-321-8325

Frozen

Atlantic Veal & Lamb
Brooklyn, NY 800-221-6988
Brook Locker Plant
Brook, IN .219-275-2611

Buckhead Beef Company
Atlanta, GA 800-888-5578
Bush Brothers Provision Company
West Palm Beach, FL 800-327-1345
Buzz Food Service
Charleston, WV 304-925-4781
Colorado Boxed Beef Company
Auburndale, FL. 863-967-0636
Empire Beef Company
Rochester, NY. 800-462-6804
Florida Veal Processors
Wimauma, FL 813-634-5545
Glenmark Food Processors
Chicago, IL 800-621-0117
Heringer Meats
Covington, KY 859-291-2000
Holten Meats
Sauget, IL .800-851-4684
Jesse's Best
Suffolk, VA 757-489-8383
King Kold Meats
Englewood, OH 800-836-2797
Maid-Rite Steak Company
Dunmore, PA 800-233-4259
Meat-O-Mat Corporation
Brooklyn, NY 718-965-7250
Montage Foods
Scranton, PA 800-521-8325
Mountain City Meat Company
Denver, CO 800-937-8325
O Chili Frozen Foods Inc
Northbrook, IL 847-562-1991
Omaha Steaks International
Omaha, NE 800-562-0500
Provimi Veal Corporation
Seymour, WI 800-833-8325
Redi-Serve Food Company
Fort Atkinson, WI 920-563-6391
Saletts
Randolph, MA 781-961-9900
Shelley's Prime Meats
Jersey City, NJ 201-433-3434
Smith Packing Regional Meat
Utica, NY .315-732-5125
Southeastern Meat Association
Oviedo, FL 407-365-5661
Swissland Packing Company
Frankfort, IL 800-321-8325
Thompson Packers
Slidell, LA .800-989-6328
Travis Meats
Powell, TN 800-247-7606
United Meat Company
San Francisco, CA 415-864-2118
Valley Packing Company
Lansing, OH 740-635-0154

Ground

Colonial Beef Company
Philadelphia, PA 215-289-7042
Dutch Valley Veal
South Holland, IL 800-832-8325

Loin Chop

Chicago Steaks
Chicago, IL 800-776-4174

Rib Chop

Chicago Steaks
Chicago, IL 800-776-4174

Frankfurters

Al Pete Meats
Muncie, IN 765-288-8817
Alle Processing Corporation
Flushing, NY. 800-245-5620
Appetizers And, Inc.
Chicago, IL 800-323-5472
Applegate Farms
Bridgewater, NJ 908-725-2768
AquaCuisine
Eagle, ID. .888-330-2782
Aristocrat International Corporation
Secaucus, NJ. 201-866-1900
Ball Park Franks
Southfield, MI 888-317-5867
Bar-S Foods Company
Phoenix, AZ 602-264-7272
Best Provision Company, Inc.
Newark, NJ 800-631-4466

Big City Reds
Omaha, NE 800-850-8003
Boesl Packing Company
Baltimore, MD 410-675-1071
Carolina Packers
Smithfield, NC 800-682-7675
Chicago 58 Food Products
Toronto, ON 416-603-4244
Chicago Steaks
Chicago, IL 800-776-4174
Chicopee Provision Company
Chicopee, MA 800-924-6328
Chisesi Brothers Meat Packing Company
New Orleans, LA 504-822-3550
Cloverdale Foods Company
Mandan, ND 800-669-9511
ConAgra Foods Inc
Omaha, NE 402-240-4000
ConAgra Poultry Company
Duluth, GA 800-609-6050
Continental Deli Foods
Cherokee, IA 712-225-5161
Corte Provisions
Newark, NJ 201-653-7246
Country Village Meats
Sublette, IL 815-849-5532
Curtis Packing Company
Greensboro, NC 336-275-7684
David Berg & Company
Chicago, IL 773-489-4711
Dennison Meat Locker
Dennison, MN. 507-645-8734
Dietz & Watson
Philadelphia, PA 800-333-1974
Double B Foods
Schulenburg, TX. 800-472-6661
Dutterer's Home Food Service
Baltimore, MD 410-298-3663
Farmland Foods
Kansas City, MO. 888-327-6526
Foodbrands America
Oklahoma City, OK 405-290-4000
Foster Farms
Corvallis, OR 541-754-6211
Foster Farms
Livingston, CA 800-255-7227
Frank's Foods
Hilo, HI. 808-959-9121
Gary's Frozen Foods
Lubbock, TX 806-745-1933
Georges Chicken
Edinburg, VA 540-984-4121
Glazier Packing Company
Malone, NY. 518-483-4990
Gold Star Sausage Company
Denver, CO 800-258-7229
Grote & Weigel
Bloomfield, CT. 860-242-8528
Gwaltney of Smithfield
Portsmouth, VA 757-465-0666
Gwaltney of Smithfield
Smithfield, VA 800-888-7521
Hatfield Quality Meats
Hatfield, PA. 800-523-5291
Hazle Park Packing Company
West Hazleton, PA 800-238-4331
Health is Wealth Foods
Williamstown, NJ 856-728-1998
Hormel Foods Corporation
Fremont, NE 402-721-2300
Hormel Foods Corporation
Austin, MN 800-523-4635
Hummel Brothers
New Haven, CT 800-828-8978
IBP Foods
Troy, MI 248-588-4710
IBP Foods
Grand Rapids, MI 616-774-0711
Kayem Foods
Chelsea, MA 800-426-6100
Kelly Kornbeef Company
Chicago, IL. 773-588-2882
Kent Quality Foods
Grand Rapids, MI 800-748-0141
Kessler's, Inc
Lemoyne, PA. 800-382-1328
Kilgus Meats
Toledo, OH 419-472-9721
Koegel Meats
Flint, MI 810-238-3685
Levonian Brothers
Troy, NY 518-274-3610

Little Rhody Brand Frankfurts
Johnston, RI 401-831-0815
Lykes Meat Group
Plant City, FL 813-752-1102
Marathon Enterprises
Englewood, NJ 201-935-3330
Martin Rosol's
New Britain, CT 860-223-2707
Matthiesen's Deer & Custom Processing
De Witt, IA 563-659-8409
Miller's Stratford Provision Company
Southport, CT 203-375-1598
Milling Sausage Company
Milwaukee, WI 414-645-2677
National Foods
Indianapolis, IN 800-683-6565
O'Brien & Company
Bellevue, NE 800-433-7567
Ohio Packing Company
Columbus, OH 800-282-6403
P & L Poultry
Spokane Valley, WA 509-892-1242
Pfeffer's Country Market
Sauk Centre, MN 320-352-3095
Pie Piper Products
Bensenville, IL 800-621-8183
Pilgrim's Pride
Timberville, VA 540-896-7000
Porter's Food & Produce
Du Quoin, IL 618-542-2155
Quong Hop & Company
S San Francisco, CA 650-553-9900
R-K Sausage Company
Cleveland, OH 216-341-1251
R.L. Zeigler Company
Tuscaloosa, AL 800-392-6328
Raemica
Running Springs, CA 800-772-6328
Rego's Purity Foods
Honolulu, HI 808-947-9005
Saag's Products
San Leandro, CA 800-352-7224
Sahlen Packing Company
Buffalo, NY 716-852-8677
Sara Lee Corporation
Downers Grove, IL 630-598-8100
Sara Lee Food Service
Haltom City, TX 800-261-4754

Sara Lee Foods
Zeeland, MI 616-875-8131
Sara Lee Foods
Cincinnati, OH 800-351-7111
Saugy
Providence, RI 866-467-2849
Schaller's Packers
Cassville, NY 315-822-3924
Schneider Foods
Kitchener, ON 519-741-5000
Sechrist Brothers
Dallastown, PA 717-244-2975
Seitz Foods
Saint Joseph, MO 800-383-3128
Shelton's Poultry
Pomona, CA 800-541-1833
Simeus Foods International
Rocky Mount, NC 888-772-3663
Smith Packing Regional Meat
Utica, NY 315-732-5125
Smith Provision Company
Erie, PA 800-334-9151
Stawnichy Holdings
Mundare, AB 888-764-7646
Stevens Sausage Company
Smithfield, NC 800-338-0561
Sunnydale Meats
Gaffney, SC 864-489-6091
Tennessee Valley PackingCompany
Columbia, TN 931-388-2623
Thomas Packing Company
Columbus, GA 800-729-0976
Thumann's
Carlstadt, NJ 201-935-3636
Troy Frozen Food
Troy, IL 618-667-6332
Vitasoy USA
Ayer, MA 978-772-6880
Wimmer's Meat Products
West Point, NE 800-358-0761

Beef

Berks Packing Company, Inc.
Reading, PA 800-882-3757
Big City Reds
Omaha, NE 800-850-8003
Chicago Steaks
Chicago, IL 800-776-4174
D'Artagnan
Newark, NJ 800-327-8246
Farmland Foods
Kansas City, MO 888-327-6526
Grote & Weigel
Bloomfield, CT 860-242-8528
Health is Wealth Foods
Williamstown, NJ 856-728-1998
Hormel Foods Corporation
Austin, MN 800-523-4635
Kelly Kornbeef Company
Chicago, IL 773-588-2882
National Foods
Indianapolis, IN 800-683-6565
Pie Piper Products
Bensenville, IL 800-621-8183
Red Hot Chicago
Chicago, IL 800-249-5226
Wimmer's Meat Products
West Point, NE 800-358-0761

Chicken

Applegate Farms
Bridgewater, NJ 908-725-2768
ConAgra Poultry Company
Duluth, GA 800-609-6050
Foster Farms
Corvallis, OR 541-754-6211
Foster Farms
Livingston, CA 800-255-7227
Georges Chicken
Edinburg, VA 540-984-4121
P & L Poultry
Spokane Valley, WA 509-892-1242
Pilgrim's Pride
Timberville, VA 540-896-7000
Tyson Foods
Springdale, AR 800-643-3410
Zacky Farms
South El Monte, CA 800-888-0235

Corn Dogs

Al Pete Meats
Muncie, IN 765-288-8817
Foster Farms
Livingston, CA 800-255-7227
Hormel Foods Corporation
Austin, MN 800-523-4635
Olympic Food Products
Kokomo, IN 800-445-6923
Porter's Food & Produce
Du Quoin, IL 618-542-2155
Sara Lee Foods
Cincinnati, OH 800-351-7111
Seitz Foods
Saint Joseph, MO 800-383-3128
Suzanna's Kitchen
Duluth, GA 800-241-2455

Hot Dogs

Specialty Foods Group
Newport News, VA 800-238-0020

Kosher

Aristocrat International Corporation
Secaucus, NJ 201-866-1900

Mini

Grote & Weigel
Bloomfield, CT 860-242-8528
Hormel Foods Corporation
Austin, MN 800-523-4635

Pork

Hormel Foods Corporation
Fremont, NE 402-721-2300
Levonian Brothers
Troy, NY 518-274-3610

Soy

Lightlife Foods
Turners Falls, MA 800-274-6001
Quong Hop & Company
S San Francisco, CA 650-553-9900

Turkey

Applegate Farms
Bridgewater, NJ 908-725-2768
Foster Farms
Livingston, CA 800-255-7227
Georges Chicken
Edinburg, VA 540-984-4121
Longmont Foods
Longmont, CO 303-776-4803
P & L Poultry
Spokane Valley, WA 509-892-1242
Pilgrim's Pride
Timberville, VA 540-896-7000
Sardinha Sausage
Somerset, MA 800-678-0178
Zacky Farms
South El Monte, CA 800-888-0235

Game

Alewel's Country Meats
Warrensburg, MO 800-353-8553
Bayou Land Seafood
Breaux Bridge, LA 337-667-6118
Bob's Custom Cuts
Bonnyville, AB 780-826-2627
Bolner's Fiesta Products
San Antonio, TX 210-734-6404
Boyd Sausage Company
Washington, IA 319-653-5715
Broadleaf Venison USA
Vernon, CA 800-336-3844
Brome Lake Ducks Ltd
Knowlton, QC 888-956-1977
Bryant Preserving Company
Alma, AR 800-634-2413
Burgers Smokehouse
California, MO 800-624-5426
Burris Mill & Feed
Franklinton, LA 800-928-2782
Camrose Packers
Camrose, AB 780-672-4887

Carolina Blueberry Association
Garland, NC 910-588-4220
Clay Center Locker Plant
Clay Center, KS 785-632-5550
Collbran Locker Plant
Collbran, CO.....................970-487-3329
Community Market & Deli
Lindstrom, MN 651-257-1128
D'Artagnan
Newark, NJ 800-327-8246
Dick's Packing Company
Columbia, MO 573-449-2995
Eickman's Processing
Seward, IL........................815-247-8451
Eiserman Meats
Slave Lake, AB 780-849-5507
Ellsworth Locker
Ellsworth, MN 507-967-2544
Farmers Meat Market
Viking, AB 780-336-3193
Fossil Farms
Oakland, NJ.....................201-651-1190
Georgetown Farm
Free Union, VA...................888-328-5326
Golden City Meats
Golden City, MO..................417-537-8560
Goodheart Brand Specialty Foods
San Antonio, TX 888-466-3992
Grinde Sausage House
Drayton Valley, AB 866-621-1755
Hickory Baked Food
Castle Rock, CO 303-688-2633
Humeniuk's Meat Cutting
Ranfurly, AB.....................780-658-2381
Indian Valley Meats
Indian, AK.......................907-653-7511
Jewel Date Company
Thermal, CA 760-399-4474
Ketters Meat Market & Locker Plant
Frazee, MN 218-334-2351
MacFarlane Pheasants
Janesville, WI 877-269-8957
Mahantongo Game Farms
Dalmatia, PA.....................570-758-6284
Matthiesen's Deer & Custom Processing
De Witt, IA......................563-659-8409
McLane's Meats
Wetaskiwin, AB 780-352-4321
Meat-O-Mat Corporation
Brooklyn, NY 718-965-7250
Meatco Sales
Mirror, AB 403-788-2292
Michael's Finer Meats & Seafoods
Columbus, OH 800-282-0518
Miller's Meat Market
Red Bud, IL......................618-282-3334
Musicon Deer Farm
Goshen, NY......................845-294-6378
Nicky
Portland, OR.....................800-469-4162
Onoway Custom Packers
Onoway, AB 780-967-2727
Oxford Frozen Foods Limited
Oxford, NS 902-447-2100
Palmetto Pigeon Plant
Sumter, SC 803-775-1204
Payne Packing Company
Artesia, NM......................575-746-2779
Pekarna's Meat Market
Jordan, MN 952-492-6101
Pinter's Packing Plant
Dorchester, WI 715-654-5444
Prairie Cajun Wholesale
Eunice, LA 337-546-6195
R Four Meats
Chatfield, MN 507-867-4180
Rabbit Barn
Turlock, CA......................209-632-1123
Rocky Mountain Meats
Rocky Mountain House, AB 403-845-3434

Springville Meat & Cold Storage
Springville, UT 801-489-6391
Squab Producers of California
Modesto, CA.....................209-537-4744
Stonies Sausage Shop Inc
Perryville, MO 888-546-2540
Thornbury Grandview Farms
Thornbury, ON 519-599-2225
Tofield Packers
Tofield, AB 780-662-4842
United Meat Company
San Francisco, CA 415-864-2118
Uvalde Meat Processing
Uvalde, TX 830-278-6247
Vantage USA
Chicago, IL......................773-247-1086
Venison America
Hudson, WI......................715-386-6628
Victoria Fancy Sausage
Edmonton, AB 780-471-2283
Wall Meat Processing
Wall, SD 605-279-2348
Western Meats
Rapid City, SD 605-342-0322

Alligator

Acadian Ostrich Ranch
Clinton, LA......................800-350-0167
Bayou Land Seafood
Breaux Bridge, LA 337-667-6118
Bolner's Fiesta Products
San Antonio, TX..................210-734-6404
Burris Mill & Feed
Franklinton, LA 800-928-2782
Fish Breeders of Idaho
Boise, ID........................888-414-8818
Nicky
Portland, OR.....................800-469-4162
Prairie Cajun Wholesale
Eunice, LA 337-546-6195

Boar

Broadleaf Venison USA
Vernon, CA 800-336-3844
D'Artagnan
Newark, NJ 800-327-8246
Nicky
Portland, OR.....................800-469-4162
Thornbury Grandview Farms
Thornbury, ON 519-599-2225

Buffalo

Alewel's Country Meats
Warrensburg, MO 800-353-8553
Broadleaf Venison USA
Vernon, CA 800-336-3844
Clay Center Locker Plant
Clay Center, KS 785-632-5550
D'Artagnan
Newark, NJ 800-327-8246
Miller's Meat Market
Red Bud, IL......................618-282-3334
Nicky
Portland, OR.....................800-469-4162
Pinter's Packing Plant
Dorchester, WI 715-654-5444
Rocky Mountain Natural Meats
Henderson, CO 800-327-2706
Springville Meat & Cold Storage
Springville, UT 801-489-6391
Superior Farms
Davis, CA 800-228-5262
Triple U Enterprises
Fort Pierre, SD 605-567-3624
Vantage USA
Chicago, IL......................773-247-1086
Wall Meat Processing
Wall, SD 605-279-2348
Western Meats
Rapid City, SD 605-342-0322
YB Meats of Wichita
Wichita, KS......................316-942-1213

Caribou

Thornbury Grandview Farms
Thornbury, ON 519-599-2225

Emu

Dino-Meat Company
White House, TN 877-557-6493
Glenn's Rabbit & Emu Farm
Portland, TN 877-325-6903
Thornbury Grandview Farms
Thornbury, ON 519-599-2225
YB Meats of Wichita
Wichita, KS......................316-942-1213

Farm-Raised

Burris Mill & Feed
Franklinton, LA 800-928-2782
Clay Center Locker Plant
Clay Center, KS 785-632-5550
D'Artagnan
Newark, NJ 800-327-8246
Golden City Meats
Golden City, MO..................417-537-8560
Triple U Enterprises
Fort Pierre, SD 605-567-3624
Wall Meat Processing
Wall, SD 605-279-2348
Western Meats
Rapid City, SD 605-342-0322

Guinea Hen

D'Artagnan
Newark, NJ 800-327-8246

Meat & Poultry

Becker Food Company
Milwaukee, WI 414-964-5353
Bolner's Fiesta Products
San Antonio, TX..................210-734-6404
Bon Secour Fisheries
Bon Secour, AL...................800-633-6854
Broadleaf Venison USA
Vernon, CA 800-336-3844
Burris Mill & Feed
Franklinton, LA 800-928-2782
Clay Center Locker Plant
Clay Center, KS 785-632-5550
Community Market & Deli
Lindstrom, MN 651-257-1128
Crescent Duck Farm
Aquebogue, NY 631-722-8700
Culinary Foods
Chicago, IL......................800-621-4049
Czimer's Game & Sea Foods
Homer Glen, IL...................708-301-0500
D'Artagnan
Newark, NJ 800-327-8246
Dick's Packing Company
Columbia, MO 573-449-2995
Eickman's Processing
Seward, IL........................815-247-8451
Ellsworth Locker
Ellsworth, MN 507-967-2544
Fox Deluxe Foods
Chicago, IL......................312-421-3737
Frontier Game Company
Fort Worth, TX...................888-432-1581
Glenn's Rabbit & Emu Farm
Portland, TN 877-325-6903
Golden City Meats
Golden City, MO..................417-537-8560
Grimaud Farms
Stockton, CA.....................800-466-9955
Hickory Baked Food
Castle Rock, CO 303-688-2633
Indian Valley Meats
Indian, AK.......................907-653-7511
Ketters Meat Market & Locker Plant
Frazee, MN 218-334-2351
Lindner Bison
Valencia, CA 866-247-8753
MacFarlane Pheasants
Janesville, WI 877-269-8957
Metzer Farms
Gonzales, CA 800-424-7755
Miller Brothers Packing Company
Sylvester, GA 229-776-2014
Musicon Deer Farm
Goshen, NY......................845-294-6378
Palmetto Pigeon Plant
Sumter, SC 803-775-1204
Pekarna's Meat Market
Jordan, MN 952-492-6101

Pel-Freez
Rogers, AR 800-223-8751
Pinter's Packing Plant
Dorchester, WI 715-654-5444
R Four Meats
Chatfield, MN 507-867-4180
Schiltz Foods
Sisseton, SD 877-872-4458
Springville Meat & Cold Storage
Springville, UT 801-489-6391
Squab Producers of California
Modesto, CA 209-537-4744
Stonies Sausage Shop Inc
Perryville, MO 888-546-2540
Thornbury Grandview Farms
Thornbury, ON 519-599-2225
Triple U Enterprises
Fort Pierre, SD 605-567-3624
United Meat Company
San Francisco, CA 415-864-2118
Uvalde Meat Processing
Uvalde, TX 830-278-6247
Wall Meat Processing
Wall, SD 605-279-2348
Wapsie Produce
Decorah, IA 563-382-4271
Western Meats
Rapid City, SD 605-342-0322

Muscovy Duck

D'Artagnan
Newark, NJ 800-327-8246

Muskox

Thornbury Grandview Farms
Thornbury, ON 519-599-2225

Ostrich

Acadian Ostrich Ranch
Clinton, LA 800-350-0167
Broadleaf Venison USA
Vernon, CA 800-336-3844
Clay Center Locker Plant
Clay Center, KS 785-632-5550
Community Market & Deli
Lindstrom, MN 651-257-1128
D'Artagnan
Newark, NJ 800-327-8246
Golden City Meats
Golden City, MO 417-537-8560
Kingsbury Country Market
Kingsbury, IN 219-393-3016
Meat-O-Mat Corporation
Brooklyn, NY 718-965-7250
Nicky
Portland, OR 800-469-4162
Pokanoket Ostrich Farm
South Dartmouth, MA 508-992-6188
Prime Ostrich International
Morinville, AB 800-340-2311
Protos Foods
Greensburg, PA 724-836-1802
Struthious Ostrich Farm
Allentown, NJ 609-208-0702
Thornbury Grandview Farms
Thornbury, ON 519-599-2225
YB Meats of Wichita
Wichita, KS 316-942-1213

Partridge

D'Artagnan
Newark, NJ 800-327-8246

Peking Duck

D'Artagnan
Newark, NJ 800-327-8246

Pheasant

Burgers Smokehouse
California, MO 800-624-5426
D'Artagnan
Newark, NJ 800-327-8246
Hickory Baked Food
Castle Rock, CO 303-688-2633
MacFarlane Pheasants
Janesville, WI 877-269-8957
Mahantongo Game Farms
Dalmatia, PA 570-758-6284
Nicky
Portland, OR 800-469-4162
Squab Producers of California
Modesto, CA 209-537-4744

Quail (See also Eggs: Quail)

Burgers Smokehouse
California, MO 800-624-5426
D'Artagnan
Newark, NJ 800-327-8246
Manchester Farms
Dalzell, SC 800-845-0421
Nicky
Portland, OR 800-469-4162
Nueces Canyon Texas Style Meat Seasoning
Brenham, TX 800-925-5058
Squab Producers of California
Modesto, CA 209-537-4744

Rabbit

D'Artagnan
Newark, NJ 800-327-8246
Glenn's Rabbit & Emu Farm
Portland, TN 877-325-6903
Nicky
Portland, OR 800-469-4162
Rabbit Barn
Turlock, CA 209-632-1123

Frozen

Glenn's Rabbit & Emu Farm
Portland, TN 877-325-6903

Fryer

Mahantongo Game Farms
Dalmatia, PA 570-758-6284
Squab Producers of California
Modesto, CA 209-537-4744
Tarazi Specialty Foods
Chino, CA 909-628-3601

Squab

Carmel Meat/Specialty Foods
Marina, CA 800-298-5823
D'Artagnan
Newark, NJ 800-327-8246
Palmetto Pigeon Plant
Sumter, SC 803-775-1204
Squab Producers of California
Modesto, CA 209-537-4744

Venison

Alewel's Country Meats
Warrensburg, MO 800-353-8553
Bellville Meat Market
Bellville, TX 800-571-6328
Blakely Freezer Locker
Thomasville, GA 229-723-3622
Boyd Sausage Company
Washington, IA 319-653-5715
Broadleaf Venison USA
Vernon, CA 800-336-3844
Brookview Farms
Archbold, OH 419-445-6366
Collbran Locker Plant
Collbran, CO 970-487-3329
Community Market & Deli
Lindstrom, MN 651-257-1128
D'Artagnan
Newark, NJ 800-327-8246
Dick's Packing Company
Columbia, MO 573-449-2995

Ellsworth Locker
Ellsworth, MN 507-967-2544
Houser Meats
Rushville, IL 217-322-4994
Indian Valley Meats
Indian, AK 907-653-7511
Jackson Brothers Food Locker
Post, TX 806-495-3245
Ketters Meat Market & Locker Plant
Frazee, MN 218-334-2351
Lena Maid Meats
Lena, IL 815-369-4522
MacGregors Meat & Seafood
Toronto, ON 800-268-5953
Matthiesen's Deer & Custom Processing
De Witt, IA 563-659-8409
Musicon Deer Farm
Goshen, NY 845-294-6378
Nesbitt Processing
Aledo, IL 309-582-5183
New Zealand Lamb Company
Wilton, CT 800-438-5262
Nicky
Portland, OR 800-469-4162
R Four Meats
Chatfield, MN 507-867-4180
Smokey Denmark Sausage
Austin, TX 512-385-0718
Stonies Sausage Shop Inc
Perryville, MO 888-546-2540
Superior Farms
Davis, CA 800-228-5262
Thornbury Grandview Farms
Thornbury, ON 519-599-2225
Turner New Zealand
Aliso Viejo, CA 949-622-6181
United Meat Company
San Francisco, CA 415-864-2118
Uvalde Meat Processing
Uvalde, TX 830-278-6247
Venison America
Hudson, WI 715-386-6628
YB Meats of Wichita
Wichita, KS 316-942-1213

Canned

Indian Valley Meats
Indian, AK 907-653-7511

Frozen

Broadleaf Venison USA
Vernon, CA 800-336-3844
Brookview Farms
Archbold, OH 419-445-6366
Indian Valley Meats
Indian, AK 907-653-7511
R Four Meats
Chatfield, MN 507-867-4180
United Meat Company
San Francisco, CA 415-864-2118

Wild

Clay Center Locker Plant
Clay Center, KS 785-632-5550
D'Artagnan
Newark, NJ 800-327-8246
Eickman's Processing
Seward, IL 815-247-8451
Triple U Enterprises
Fort Pierre, SD 605-567-3624
Wall Meat Processing
Wall, SD 605-279-2348
Western Meats
Rapid City, SD 605-342-0322

Wood Pigeon

D'Artagnan
Newark, NJ 800-327-8246

Goat

Braham Food Locker Service
Braham, MN 320-396-2636
Caribbean Food Delights
Tappan, NY 845-398-3000
Community Market & Deli
Lindstrom, MN 651-257-1128
D'Artagnan
Newark, NJ 800-327-8246

East Beauregard Meat Processing Center
Deridder, LA 337-328-7171
Halsted Packing House
Chicago, IL 312-421-5147
Jones Packing Company
Harvard, IL 815-943-4488
Nesbitt Processing
Aledo, IL. 309-582-5183
Rancher's Lamb of Texas
San Angelo, TX 325-659-4004
Red Deer Lake Meat Processing
Calgary, AB 403-256-4925
Southington Packing Company Inc
Southington, CT 860-628-9544
Strube Packing Company
Rowena, TX 325-442-2851
Windcrest Meat Packers
Port Perry, ON. 800-750-2542

Horse

Bouvry Exports Calgary
Calgary, AB. 403-253-0717
Phoenix Agro-Industrial Corporation
Westbury, NY 516-334-1194

Lamb

A. Thomas Food Service
Louisville, KY 800-253-2020
A.C. Kissling Company
Philadelphia, PA 800-445-1943
Acme Steak & Seafood Company
Youngstown, OH. 330-270-8000
Agri-Best Foods
Chicago, IL 773-247-5060
Alpine Meats
Stockton, CA. 800-399-6328
Big Apple Produce & Seafood Market
Pocomoke City, MD 410-957-1151
Blakely Freezer Locker
Thomasville, GA. 229-723-3622
Border's Market
Plymouth, OH 419-687-2634
Brookview Farms
Archbold, OH 419-445-6366
Bruss Company
Chicago, IL 800-621-3882
Bush Brothers Provision Company
West Palm Beach, FL 800-327-1345
Buzz Food Service
Charleston, WV 304-925-4781
Callaway Packing Company
Delta, CO 800-332-6932
Cambridge Slaughtering
Cambridge, IL. 309-937-2455
Campbell's Quality Cuts
Sidney, OH 937-492-2194
Canada West Foods
Innisfail, AB 403-227-3386
Canal Fulton Provision
Canal Fulton, OH 800-321-3502
Carl Streit & Son Company
Neptune, NJ 732-775-0803
Carmel Meat/Specialty Foods
Marina, CA 800-298-5823
Castleberry's Meats
Atlanta, GA 404-873-1804
Catelli Brothers
Camden, NJ. 856-869-9293
Center Locker Service Company
Center, MO 573-267-3343
Chiappetti Wholesale Meat
Chicago, IL. 773-927-9476
Chicago Steaks
Chicago, IL. 800-776-4174
Clay Center Locker Plant
Clay Center, KS 785-632-5550
Coleman Purely Natural Brands
Golden, CO 877-810-8291
Community Market & Deli
Lindstrom, MN 651-257-1128
ConAgra Beef Company
Yuma, CO 970-395-8226
Conti Packing Company
Rochester, NY. 585-424-2500
Country Butcher Shop
Palmyra, MO. 573-769-2257
Country Village Meats
Sublette, IL 815-849-5532
Cusack Wholesale Meat Company
Oklahoma City, OK 800-241-6328

D'Artagnan
Newark, NJ 800-327-8246
Dale T. Smith & Sons Meat Packing Corporation
Draper, UT 801-571-3611
David Mosner Meat Products
Bronx, NY 718-328-5600
Davidson Meat Processing Plant
Waynesville, OH. 513-897-2971
DeBragga & Spitler
New York, NY 212-924-1311
Dino's Sausage & Meat Company
Utica, NY 315-732-2661
Duma Meats
Mogadore, OH 330-628-3438
Eickman's Processing
Seward, IL 815-247-8451
Eiserman Meats
Slave Lake, AB 780-849-5507
Empire Beef Company
Rochester, NY 800-462-6804
Eureka Lockers
Eureka, IL 309-467-2731
Ferko Meat Company
Milwaukee, WI 414-967-5500
G&G Sheep Farm
Boston, KY 502-833-4863
Glasco Locker Plant
Glasco, KS 785-568-2364
Godshall's Quality Meats
Franconia, PA 888-463-7425
H. Shenson International Export
San Francisco, CA 415-318-7000
Halal Transactions
Omaha, NE 402-572-6120
Halsted Packing House
Chicago, IL 312-421-5147
Hamilton Provision Company
Hamilton, OH 800-328-9979
Heringer Meats
Covington, KY 859-291-2000
Houser Meats
Rushville, IL 217-322-4994
International Meat Company
Elmwood Park, IL 773-622-1400
Isernio Sausage Company
Seattle, WA 888-495-8674
J.J. Andrade's Slaughterhouse
Honokaa, HI 808-775-0741
Jones Packing Company
Harvard, IL 815-943-4488
Jordahl Meats
Manchester, MN 507-826-3418
Joseph McSweeney & Sons
Windom, MN 804-359-6024
Kelble Brothers
Berlin Heights, OH 800-247-2333
Kelly Packing Company
Torrington, WY. 307-532-2210
L&L Packing Company
Chicago, IL 800-628-6328
L&M Slaughtering
Georgetown, IL 217-662-6841
Lay Packing Company
Knoxville, TN. 865-922-4320
Lena Maid Meats
Lena, IL .815-369-4522
Lionel Lavallee Company
Haverhill, MA 800-343-8292
Lombardi Brothers Meat Packers
Denver, CO 800-421-4412
Lowell Provision Company
Lowell, MA. 978-454-5603
Mack's Packing
Richfield, UT 435-896-4447
Magnolia Beef Company
Elizabeth, NJ. 908-352-9412
Maid-Rite Steak Company
Dunmore, PA. 800-233-4259
Manger Packing Company
Baltimore, MD 800-227-9262
Marks Meat
Canby, OR. 503-266-2048
Matthiesen's Deer & Custom Processing
De Witt, IA 563-659-8409
Meatland Packers
Medicine Hat, AB 403-528-4321
Miami Beef Company
Hialeah, FL 305-621-3252
Mike's Prime Cut Meats
Brigham City, UT 435-723-7333
Miller Brothers Packing Company
Sylvester, GA 229-776-2014

Mountain City Meat Company
Denver, CO 800-937-8325
Mountain States Rosen, LLc
Bronx, NY 800-872-5262
Nagel Veal
San Bernardino, CA 909-383-7075
Nephi Packing Company
Nephi, UT. 435-623-0435
Nesbitt Processing
Aledo, IL. 309-582-5183
New Zealand Lamb Company
Wilton, CT 800-438-5262
Old Neighborhood Foods
Lynn, MA 781-592-0014
Onoway Custom Packers
Onoway, AB 780-967-2727
Otto W Liebold & Company
Flint, MI .800-999-6328
Pasqualichio Brothers
Scranton, PA 800-232-6233
Petschl's Meats
Tukwila, WA 206-575-4400
Premium Meat Company
Brigham City, UT 435-723-5944
R Four Meats
Chatfield, MN 507-867-4180
Ralph Packing Company
Perkins, OK. 800-522-3979
Rancher's Lamb of Texas
San Angelo, TX 325-659-4004
Red Deer Lake Meat Processing
Calgary, AB. 403-256-4925
Rendulic Packing
McKeesport, PA 412-678-9541
Rocky Mountain Meats
Rocky Mountain House, AB 403-845-3434
Royal Center Locker Plant
Royal Center, IN 574-643-3275
Saletts
Randolph, MA 781-961-9900
Saunders Provision Company
Norfolk, VA. 800-486-5611
Shelley's Prime Meats
Jersey City, NJ 201-433-3434
Smith Packing Regional Meat
Utica, NY 315-732-5125
Southington Packing Company Inc
Southington, CT 860-628-9544
Southtowns Seafood & Meats
Blasdell, NY 716-824-4900
Springville Meat & Cold Storage
Springville, UT. 801-489-6391
Standard Beef Company
New Haven, CT 203-787-2164
Sterling Pacific Meat Company
Los Angeles, CA 310-274-7635
Stock Yards Packing Company
Chicago, IL 800-621-1119
Strube Packing Company
Rowena, TX 325-442-2851
Superior Farms
Davis, CA 800-228-5262
Superior Packing Company
Ellensburg, WA. 509-925-1495
Terrell Meats
Delta, UT 435-864-2600
Thompson Packers
Slidell, LA 800-989-6328
Tillamook Meat Company
Tillamook, OR 503-842-4802
Tooele Valley Meat
Grantsville, UT 435-884-3837
Tucker Packing Company
Orrville, OH 330-683-3311
Turk Brothers Custom Meats
Ashland, OH 800-789-1051
Une-Viandi
St. Jean Sur Richelieu, NB 800-363-1955
United Meat Company
San Francisco, CA 415-864-2118
United Provision Meat Company
Columbus, OH 614-252-1126
Unruh's Quality Meats
Deridder, LA. 337-463-7688
Uvalde Meat Processing
Uvalde, TX 830-278-6247
Valley Packing Company
Lansing, OH 740-635-0154
Vantage USA
Chicago, IL 773-247-1086
Victoria Fancy Sausage
Edmonton, AB 780-471-2283

W&W Meats
Willoughby, OH 216-621-7846
Wall Meat Processing
Wall, SD 605-279-2348
Warren & Son Meat Processing
Whipple, OH 740-585-2421
Wasatch Meats
Salt Lake City, UT 801-363-5747
Westport Locker Service
Westport, IN 877-265-0551
White's Meat Processing
Peebles, OH 937-587-2930
Willcox Packing House
Willcox, AZ 520-384-2015
Windcrest Meat Packers
Port Perry, ON 800-750-2542
Wolverine Packing
Detroit, MI 313-392-9403
YB Meats of Wichita
Wichita, KS 316-942-1213

Fresh

Mountain City Meat Company
Denver, CO 800-937-8325
R Four Meats
Chatfield, MN 507-867-4180
Shelley's Prime Meats
Jersey City, NJ 201-433-3434
Smith Packing Regional Meat
Utica, NY 315-732-5125

Frozen

Buzz Food Service
Charleston, WV 304-925-4781
J.J. Andrade's Slaughterhouse
Honokaa, HI 808-775-0741
Maid-Rite Steak Company
Dunmore, PA 800-233-4259
Montage Foods
Scranton, PA 800-521-8325
Mountain City Meat Company
Denver, CO 800-937-8325
Phoenix Agro-Industrial Corporation
Westbury, NY 516-334-1194
R Four Meats
Chatfield, MN 507-867-4180
Saletts
Randolph, MA 781-961-9900
Shelley's Prime Meats
Jersey City, NJ 201-433-3434
Smith Packing Regional Meat
Utica, NY 315-732-5125
Thompson Packers
Slidell, LA 800-989-6328
United Meat Company
San Francisco, CA 415-864-2118

Leg of

Chicago Steaks
Chicago, IL 800-776-4174

Loin Chop

Chicago Steaks
Chicago, IL 800-776-4174

Rib Chop

Chicago Steaks
Chicago, IL 800-776-4174

Meat Meal

Carolina By-Products Company
Winchester, VA 540-877-2590
McRedmond Brothers
Nashville, TN 615-361-8997

Mutton

Center Locker Service Company
Center, MO 573-267-3343

Packaged

Burke Corporation
Nevada, IA 800-654-1152

Always make it your best® with Burke fully cooked meats. We specialize in Italian sausage, beef, and pork toppings, meatballs, taco meats, shredded meats, pepperoni, bacon, Canadian-style bacon, chicken and beef strips. Additionally, we offer a variety of specialty products: Hand-Pinched Style® brand toppings, chorizo, gyro topping, andouille sausage, and breakfast patties and links.

Sara Lee Foods
Cincinnati, OH 800-351-7111

Pates & Fois Gras

Foie Gras

Assouline & Ting
Philadelphia, PA 800-521-4491
D'Artagnan
Newark, NJ 800-327-8246
DeChoix Specialty Foods
Woodside, NY 800-332-4649
Sapar
San Mateo, CA 650-340-8840

Pates

Alexian Pates/GroezingerProvisions
Neptune, NJ 800-927-9473
Caughman's Meat Plant
Lexington, SC 803-356-0076
Cordon Bleu International
Anjou, QC 514-352-3000
D'Artagnan
Newark, NJ 800-327-8246
Ducktrap River Fish Farm
Belfast, ME 800-434-8727
Giovanni's Appetizing Food Products
Richmond, MI 586-727-9355
Groezinger Provisions
Neptune, NJ 800-927-9473
Hickory Baked Food
Castle Rock, CO 303-688-2633
International Trading Company
Houston, TX 713-224-5901
Kirkland Custom Seafoods
Kirkland, WA 800-321-3474
Kretschmar
Don Mills, ON 800-561-4532
Les Trois Petits Cochons
New York, NY 800-537-7283
Marcel et Henri Charcuterie Francaise
S San Francisco, CA 800-227-6436
Michel's Magnifique
New York, NY 212-431-1070
Organic Gourmet
Sherman Oaks, CA 800-400-7772
Phoenicia Patisserie
Arlington, TX 817-261-2898
Salmolux
Federal Way, WA 253-874-6570
Sapar
San Mateo, CA 650-340-8840
Sunset Farm Foods
Valdosta, GA 800-882-1121
Taste of Gourmet
Indianola, MS 800-833-7731

Pork & Pork Products

A to Z Portion Meats
Bluffton, OH 800-338-6328
A. Stein Meat Products
Brooklyn, NY 718-492-0760
A. Thomas Food Service
Louisville, KY 800-253-2020
Abattoir Aliments Asta Inc.
St Alexandre Kamouraska, QC 418-495-2728

Alaska Sausage and Seafood Company
Anchorage, AK 800-798-3636
Alderfer Bologna
Harleysville, PA 877-253-6328
Alphin Brothers
Dunn, NC 800-672-4502
Amana Meat Shop & Smokehouse
Amana, IA 800-373-6328
American Foods Group
Green Bay, WI 920-437-6330
Armbrust Meats
Medford, WI 715-748-3102
Armour
Omaha, NE 402-453-3766
Aspen Food Marketing
Denver, CO 303-320-3400
Atlantic Pork & Provisions
Brooklyn, NY 800-245-3536
B&D Foods
Boise, ID 208-344-1183
Banner Beef & Seafood Company
Miami, FL 305-325-0420
Bartlow Brothers
Rushville, IL 800-252-7202
Bear Creek Smokehouse
Marshall, TX 800-950-2327
Big Apple Produce & Seafood Market
Pocomoke City, MD 410-957-1151
Big B Distributors
Evansville, IN 812-425-5235
Bob Evans Farms
Hillsdale, MI 517-437-3349
Bodin Foods
New Iberia, LA 337-367-1344
Boones Abattoir
Bardstown, KY 502-348-3668
Bristol Pork Company
Bristol, PA 215-788-3356
Bruss Company
Chicago, IL 800-621-3882
Burgers Smokehouse
California, MO 800-624-5426

Burke Corporation
Nevada, IA 800-654-1152

Always make it your best® with Burke fully cooked meats. We specialize in Italian sausage, beef, and pork toppings, meatballs, taco meats, shredded meats, pepperoni, bacon, Canadian-style bacon, chicken and beef strips. Additionally, we offer a variety of specialty products: Hand-Pinched Style® brand toppings, chorizo, gyro topping, andouille sausage, and breakfast patties and links.

Burnett & Son Meat Company
Monrovia, CA 626-357-2165
Bush Brothers Provision Company
West Palm Beach, FL 800-327-1345
C. Roy Meat Products
Brockway, MI 810-387-3957
Caddo Packing Company
Marshall, TX 903-935-2211
Calihan Pork Processing
Peoria, IL 309-674-9175
Caribbean Products
Baltimore, MD 410-235-7700
Carmelita Provisions Company
Monterey Park, CA 323-262-6751
Casson & Sons
Des Moines, IA 515-266-3197
Castleberry's Meats
Atlanta, GA 404-873-1804
Castleberry/Snow Brands
Augusta, GA 800-241-3520
Caughman's Meat Plant
Lexington, SC 803-356-0076
Central Meat & Provision Company
San Diego, CA 619-239-1391
Chalmette Packing Company
Covington, LA 504-271-6241
Chandler Foods
Greensboro, NC 800-537-6219

Product Categories / Meats & Meat Products: Pork & Pork Products

Chef's Requested Foods
Oklahoma City, OK 800-256-0259
Cheraw Packing
Cheraw, SC .843-537-7426
Chicago Steaks
Chicago, IL .800-776-4174
Chip Steak & Provision Company
Mankato, MN 507-388-6277
Chisesi Brothers Meat Packing Company
New Orleans, LA 504-822-3550
Cimpl Meats
Yankton, SD .605-665-1665
Circle V Meat Company
Spanish Fork, UT 801-798-3081
Clem Becker
Two Rivers, WI 920-793-1391
Clougherty Packing Company
Los Angeles, CA 323-583-4621
Cloverdale Foods Company
Mandan, ND .800-669-9511
Coloma Meat Products
Coloma, WI 715-228-4080
Columbia Packing Company
Dallas, TX 800-460-8171
Community Market & Deli
Lindstrom, MN 651-257-1128
ConAgra Foods/Eckrich
Omaha, NE 800-327-4424
Conti Packing Company
Rochester, NY 585-424-2500
Continental Deli Foods
Cherokee, IA .712-225-5161
Cordon Bleu International
Anjou, QC 514-352-3000
Corte Provisions
Newark, NJ 201-653-7246
Country Butcher Shop
Palmyra, MO .573-769-2257
Country Smoked Meats
Bowling Green, OH 800-321-4766
Country Village Meats
Sublette, IL 815-849-5532
Counts Sausage Company
Prosperity, SC 803-364-2392
Covemaker Packing Company
Moline, IL 309-764-1480
Crawford Sausage Company
Chicago, IL 866-653-2479
Crofton & Sons
Brandon, FL .800-878-7675
Cropp Cooperative-Organic Valley
La Farge, WI .888-444-6455
Curtis Packing Company
Greensboro, NC 336-275-7684
Cusack Wholesale Meat Company
Oklahoma City, OK 800-241-6328
D'Artagnan
Newark, NJ 800-327-8246
Dietz & Watson
Philadelphia, PA 800-333-1974
Dohar Meats
Cleveland, OH 216-241-4197
Dolores Canning Company
Los Angeles, CA 323-263-9155
Dreymiller & Kray
Hampshire, IL 847-683-2271
Duma Meats
Mogadore, OH 330-628-3438
Dutch Valley Veal
South Holland, IL 800-832-8325
Edmonds Chile Company
St Louis, MO. 314-772-1499
Fabbri Sausage Manufacturing
Chicago, IL 312-829-6363
Family Brand International
Lenoir City, TN 865-986-8005
Fanestil Packing Company
Emporia, KS .620-342-6354
Fletcher's Fine Foods
Red Deer, AB 403-343-8700
Foodbrands America
Oklahoma City, OK 405-290-4000
Fortenberry Ice Company
Kodak, TN. 865-933-2568
Four Star Meat Company of Louisiana
Amite, LA 800-444-5228
Fricks Meat Products
Washington, MO 800-241-2209
Glazier Packing Company
Potsdam, NY .315-265-2500
Greenwood Packing Plant
Greenwood, SC 864-229-5611

Groff Meats
Elizabethtown, PA 717-367-1246
Gulf Marine & Industrial Supplies
New Orleans, LA 800-886-6252
Gunsberg Corned Beef
Detroit, MI 313-894-6600
Gwaltney Food Service
Spartanburg, SC 864-587-7761
Hahn Brothers
Westminster, MD 800-227-7675
Hamm's Custom Meats
McKinney, TX 972-542-3359
Hancock's Old Fashioned
Franklinville, NC 336-824-2145
Hansel 'N Gretel
Flushing, NY .718-326-0041
Hatfield Quality Meats
Hatfield, PA 800-523-5291
Hazle Park Packing Company
West Hazleton, PA 800-238-4331
Hickory Baked Food
Castle Rock, CO 303-688-2633
Higa Meat and Pork Market Limited
Honolulu, HI .808-531-3591
Hillbilly Smokehouse
Rogers, AR 479-636-1927
Hillsboro Refrigerated Lockers
Hillsboro, KS 316-947-3781
Holly Hill Locker Company
Holly Hill, SC 803-496-3611
Hoople Country Kitchens
Rockport, IN .812-649-2351
Hormel Foods Corporation
Fremont, NE .402-721-2300
Hormel Foods Corporation
Austin, MN 800-523-4635
Hormel Foods Pork Division
Tucker, GA 770-908-4000
Humphrey Blue Ribbon Meats
Springfield, IL 800-747-6328
IBP Foods
Troy, MI 248-588-4710
Iowa Quality Meats
Clive, IA 800-677-6868
J&B Meats Corporation
Coal Valley, IL 309-799-7341
John Hofmeister & Son
Chicago, IL 800-923-4267
Johnsonville Food Company
Sheboygan, WI 920-459-6800
Joseph Sanders
Custer, MI 800-968-5035
Karn Meats
Columbus, OH 800-221-9585
Kelley Foods of Alabama
Elba, AL 334-897-5761
Kelley Meats
Taberg, NY 315-337-4272
Kessler's, Inc
Lemoyne, PA 800-382-1328
Kilgus Meats
Toledo, OH 419-472-9721
Kowalski Sausage Company
Hamtramck, MI 800-482-2400
Kubla Khan Food Company
Portland, OR 503-234-7494
Kunzler/Juniata Packing Company
Tyrone, PA 814-684-2270
Kutztown Bologna Company
Leola, PA 800-723-8824
Lampasas Locker Plant
Lampasas, TX 512-556-5121
Land O'Frost
Searcy, AR 800-643-5654
Lay Packing Company
Knoxville, TN 865-922-4320
Lees Sausage Company
Orangeburg, SC 803-534-5517
Leo G. Fraboni Sausage Company
Hibbing, MN .218-263-5074
Leona Meat Plant
Troy, PA 570-297-3574
Levonian Brothers
Troy, NY 518-274-3610
Lewis Smoked Meat Company
Chicago, IL 800-648-6328
Locustdale Meat Packing
Locustdale, PA 570-875-1270
Lords Sausage & Country Ham
Dexter, GA 800-342-6002
Lowell Packing Company
Fitzgerald, GA 800-342-0313

Maple Leaf Foods
Winnipeg, NB 800-564-6253
Marathon Enterprises
Englewood, NJ 201-935-3330
Marshallville Packing Company
Marshallville, OH 330-855-2871
McKenzie of Vermont
Burlington, VT 802-864-4585
Meating Place
Buffalo, NY. .716-885-3623
Mello's North End Manufacturings
Fall River, MA 800-673-2320
Metafoods, LLC
Atlanta, GA 404-843-2400
Miller's Stratford Provision Company
Southport, CT 203-375-1598
Mirasco
Atlanta, GA 770-956-1945
Mitchell Foods
Barbourville, KY 888-202-9745
Montana Ranch Brand
Billings, MT 406-294-2333
Moo & Oink
Chicago, IL 773-493-2755
Morse's Sauerkraut
Waldoboro, ME. 866-832-5569
Mosby Packing Company
Meridian, MS 800-844-7225
National Steak & Poultry
Owasso, OK .800-366-6772
New Braunfels Smokehouse
New Braunfels, TX 800-537-6932
Niemuth's Steak & Chop Shop
Waupaca, WI 715-258-2666
O Chili Frozen Foods Inc
Northbrook, IL 847-562-1991
Olympic Food Products
Kokomo, IN .800-445-6923
Ossian Seafood Meats
Ossian, IN 260-622-4191
Owens Country Sausage
Richardson, TX 800-966-9367
Parma Sausage Products
Pittsburgh, PA 877-294-4207
Pasqualichio Brothers
Scranton, PA 800-232-6233
Payne Packing Company
Artesia, NM. .575-746-2779
Peer Foods Inc
Chicago, IL 800-365-5644
Penn Valley Farms
Gainesville, GA 773-685-9929
Pierceton Foods
Pierceton, IN 574-594-2344
Pioneer Packing Company
Bowling Green, OH 419-352-5283
Plumrose
East Brunswick, NJ. 800-526-4909
Plumrose USA
East Brunswick, NJ. 732-257-6600
Premium Standard Farms
Kansas City, MO. 816-472-7675
Proliant Meat Ingredients
Ankeny, IA 800-369-2672
R-K Sausage Company
Cleveland, OH 216-341-1251
R.L. Zeigler Company
Tuscaloosa, AL 800-392-6328
R.M. Felts Packing Company
Ivor, VA 888-300-0971
Ray's Sausage Company Inc
Cleveland, OH 216-921-8782
Register Meat Company
Cottondale, FL 850-352-4269
Rego's Purity Foods
Honolulu, HI .808-947-9005
Rendulic Packing
McKeesport, PA 412-678-9541
Rinehart Meat Processing
Branson, MO. 417-334-2044
Robertson's Country Meat Hams
Finchville, KY 800-678-1521
Rose Packing Company
South Barrington, IL 800-323-7363
Rudolph Foods
Dallas, TX 214-638-2204
Sadler's BBQ Sales
Henderson, TX 903-657-5581
Salaison Levesque
Montreal, QC 514-273-1702
Saletts
Randolph, MA 781-961-9900

Sara Lee Corporation
Downers Grove, IL 630-598-8100
Sara Lee Foods
Cincinnati, OH 800-351-7111
Sara Lee Foods
Neenah, WI 800-558-8440
Sausage Shoppe
Cleveland, OH 216-351-5213
Saval Foods
Elkridge, MD 800-527-2825
Savoie's Sausage & Food Products
Opelousas, LA 337-948-4115
Schaller & Weber
Long Island City, NY 800-847-4115
Schweigert Foods
Albert Lea, MN 507-377-2526
Sculli Brothers
Philadelphia, PA 215-336-1223
Seaboard Foods
Shawnee Mission, KS 800-262-7907
Sechrist Brothers
Dallastown, PA 717-244-2975
Sheinman Provision Company
Philadelphia, PA 215-473-7065
Simeus Foods Internatio nal
Mansfield, TX 888-772-3663
Smithfield Foods
Smithfield, VA 888-366-6767
Smithfield Foods
Clinton, NC 910-592-2104
Smolich Brothers
Crest Hill, IL 815-727-2144
Southtowns Seafood & Meats
Blasdell, NY 716-824-4900
Stevens Sausage Company
Smithfield, NC 800-338-0561
Stonies Sausage Shop Inc
Perryville, MO 888-546-2540
Striplings
Moultrie, GA 229-985-4226
Sugar Creek Packing
Washington Ct Hs, OH 800-848-8205
Suncrest Farms
Totowa, NJ 973-595-0214
Sunnydale Meats
Gaffney, SC 864-489-6091
SW Red Smith
Davie, FL 954-581-1996
Swift & Company
Greeley, CO 970-324-2180
T&J Meat Packing
Chicago Heights, IL 708-758-6748
Thomas Packing Company
Columbus, GA 800-729-0976
Tomahawk Farms Meat Packers
Dunn, NC 910-892-3155
Tomasinos Sausage
Canton, OH 330-454-4171
Troy Frozen Food
Troy, IL 618-667-6332
Troyers Trail Bologna
Dundee, OH 877-893-2414
Tupman-Thurlow Company
Deerfield Beach, FL 954-596-9989
Unruh's Quality Meats
Deridder, LA 337-463-7688
V&V Supremo Foods
Chicago, IL 800-547-8773
V.W. Joyner & Company
Smithfield, VA 757-357-2161
Vantage USA
Chicago, IL 773-247-1086
Vollwerth & Company
Hancock, MI 800-562-7620
WA Bean & Sons
Bangor, ME 800-649-1958
Waco Beef & Pork Processors
Waco, TX 254-772-4669
Waken Meat Company
Atlanta, GA 404-627-3537
Wayco Ham Company
Goldsboro, NC 800-962-2614
Weyhaupt Brothers Packing
Belleville, IL 618-233-0452
Whitaker Foods
Evansdale, IA 800-553-7490
William's Pork
Lumberton, NC 910-608-2226
Willies Smoke House
Harrisville, PA 800-742-4184
WSMP
Claremont, NC 828-459-7626

YB Meats of Wichita
Wichita, KS 316-942-1213

Barbecued

Big B Distributors
Evansville, IN 812-425-5235
Calumet Diversified Meat Company
Pleasant Prairie, WI 262-947-7200
Chandler Foods
Greensboro, NC 800-537-6219
Dankworth Packing Company
Ballinger, TX 325-365-3552
Dorina/So-Good
Union, IL 815-923-2144
Moonlite Bar BQ Inn
Owensboro, KY 800-322-8989
Piggie Park Enterprises
West Columbia, SC 800-628-7423
Sadler's BBQ Sales
Henderson, TX 903-657-5581
W&G Marketing Company
Ames, IA 515-233-4774
Woods Smoked Meats
Bowling Green, MO 800-458-8426
Zoll Foods Corporation
South Holland, IL 708-333-3900

Frozen

Always make it your best®

Burke Corporation
Nevada, IA 800-654-1152

> Always make it your best® with Burke fully cooked meats. We specialize in Italian sausage, beef, and pork toppings, meatballs, taco meats, shredded meats, pepperoni, bacon, Canadian-style bacon, chicken and beef strips. Additionally, we offer a variety of specialty products: Hand-Pinched Style® brand toppings, chorizo, gyro topping, andouille sausage, and breakfast patties and links.

Tenn Valley Ham Company
Paris, TN 731-642-9740

Breaded

J&B Meats Corporation
Coal Valley, IL 309-799-7341
King's Command Foods
Kent, WA 800-247-3138
Simeus Foods International
Mansfield, TX 888-772-3663
W&W Meats
Willoughby, OH 216-621-7846

Canned with Natural Juices

Hormel Foods Corporation
Beloit, WI 608-365-9501

Fresh

Abattoir A. Trahan Company
Yamachiche, QC 819-296-3791
Aliments Jolibec
St Jacques De Montcalm, QC 514-861-6082
Amity Packing Company
Chicago, IL 800-837-0270
Aspen Food Marketing
Denver, CO 303-320-3400
Beatty Fresh Frozen Meats
Bourbon, IN 574-342-2665
Botsford Fisheries
Petit-Cap, NB 506-577-4327
Brook Locker Plant
Brook, IN 219-275-2611
Brownsdale Meat Service
Brownsdale, MN 507-567-2211
Buckhead Beef Company
Atlanta, GA 800-888-5578
Camrose Packers
Camrose, AB 780-672-4887
Charcuterie LaTour Eiffel
Vanier, QC 418-687-2840

Colorado Boxed Beef Company
Auburndale, FL 863-967-0636
Devro, Inc.
Columbus, SC
Farmland Foods
Kansas City, MO 888-327-6526
IBP Foods
Troy, MI 248-588-4710
J&M Meats
Warburg, AB 780-848-7598
John Morrell & Company
Cincinnati, OH 513-346-3540
John Morrell & Company
Sioux City, IA 712-279-7360
John Morrell & Company
Cincinnati, OH 800-345-0743
Les Salaisons Brochu
St. Henri De Levis, QC 418-882-2282
Les Viandes Or-Fil
Laval, QC 450-687-5664
Maple Leaf Pork
Lethbridge, AB 403-328-1756
Mountain City Meat Company
Denver, CO 800-937-8325
Ontario Pork
Guelph, ON 877-668-7675
Quality Meat Packers
Toronto, ON 416-703-7675
R Four Meats
Chatfield, MN 507-867-4180
Sara Lee Foods
Neenah, WI 800-558-8440
Schwab & Company
Oklahoma City, OK 800-888-8668
Shelley's Prime Meats
Jersey City, NJ 201-433-3434
Smith Packing Regional Meat
Utica, NY 315-732-5125
Thomson Meats
Melfort, SK 306-752-2802
Trochu Meat Processors
Trochu, AB 403-442-4202
Troy Pork Store
Troy, NY 518-272-8291

Frozen

Abattoir A. Trahan Company
Yamachiche, QC 819-296-3791
Alcester Meats
Alcester, SD 605-934-2540
Aliments Jolibec
St Jacques De Montcalm, QC 514-861-6082
Amity Packing Company
Chicago, IL 800-837-0270
Aspen Food Marketing
Denver, CO 303-320-3400
B&D Foods
Boise, ID 208-344-1183
Beatty Fresh Frozen Meats
Bourbon, IN 574-342-2665
Blakely Freezer Locker
Thomasville, GA 229-723-3622
Bob's Custom Cuts
Bonnyville, AB 780-826-2627
Botsford Fisheries
Petit-Cap, NB 506-577-4327
Brook Locker Plant
Brook, IN 219-275-2611
Brookfield Farms
Chicago, IL 773-468-1739
Brownsdale Meat Service
Brownsdale, MN 507-567-2211
Buckhead Beef Company
Atlanta, GA 800-888-5578

Burke Corporation
Nevada, IA 800-654-1152

Always make it your best® with Burke fully cooked meats. We specialize in Italian sausage, beef, and pork toppings, meatballs, taco meats, shredded meats, pepperoni, bacon, Canadian-style bacon, chicken and beef strips. Additionally, we offer a variety of specialty products: Hand-Pinched Style® brand toppings, chorizo, gyro topping, andouille sausage, and breakfast patties and links.

Buzz Food Service
Charleston, WV 304-925-4781
Charcuterie LaTour Eiffel
Vanier, QC 418-687-2840
Colonial Beef Company
Philadelphia, PA 215-289-7042
Colorado Boxed Beef Company
Auburndale, FL. 863-967-0636
Curly's Foods
Edina, MN. 612-920-3400
Edmonds Chile Company
St Louis, MO. 314-772-1499
El-Rey Foods
Ferguson, MO 314-521-3113
Farmland Foods
Kansas City, MO. 888-327-6526
Fuji Foods
Denver, CO 303-377-3738
Gwaltney Food Service
Spartanburg, SC 864-587-7761
Hatfield Quality Meats
Hatfield, PA. 800-523-5291
Holten Meats
Sauget, IL .800-851-4684
J&M Meats
Warburg, AB. 780-848-7598
J.J. Andrade's Slaughterhouse
Honokaa, HI 808-775-0741
John Morrell & Company
Cincinnati, OH 513-346-3540
John Morrell & Company
Sioux City, IA 712-279-7360
John Morrell & Company
Cincinnati, OH 800-345-0743
Kutztown Bologna Company
Leola, PA. .800-723-8824
Ladoga Frozen Food & Retail Meat
Ladoga, IN 765-942-2225
Lengerich Meats
Zanesville, IN 260-638-4123
Les Salaisons Brochu
St. Henri De Levis, QC 418-882-2282
Les Viandes du Breton
Riviere-Du-Lup,, QC 418-899-6711
Les Viandes Or-Fil
Laval, QC .450-687-5664
Maid-Rite Steak Company
Dunmore, PA. 800-233-4259
Maple Leaf Pork
Lethbridge, AB 403-328-1756
Mountain City Meat Company
Denver, CO 800-937-8325
Olympic Food Products
Kokomo, IN 800-445-6923
Phoenix Agro-Industrial Corporation
Westbury, NY 516-334-1194
Pierceton Foods
Pierceton, IN 574-594-2344
Quality Meat Packers
Toronto, ON 416-703-7675
R Four Meats
Chatfield, MN 507-867-4180
Saletts
Randolph, MA 781-961-9900
Scarborough Meat Packers
Scarborough, ON 416-269-7758
Schwab & Company
Oklahoma City, OK 800-888-8668
Shelley's Prime Meats
Jersey City, NJ 201-433-3434
Smith Packing Regional Meat
Utica, NY .315-732-5125

Springhill Farms
Neepawa, NB 204-476-3393
Steak-Umm Company
Shillington, PA 860-928-5900
Sudlersville Frozen Food Locker
Sudlersville, MD. 410-438-3106
Tenn Valley Ham Company
Paris, TN .731-642-9740
Thompson Packers
Slidell, LA. 800-989-6328
Thomson Meats
Melfort, SK 306-752-2802
Travis Meats
Powell, TN 800-247-7606

Loin Chop

Amana Meat Shop & Smokehouse
Amana, IA. 800-373-6328
Chicago Steaks
Chicago, IL 800-776-4174

Loins

Bear Creek Smokehouse
Marshall, TX. 800-950-2327
Black's Barbecue
Lockhart, TX. 512-398-2712
Calumet Diversified Meat Company
Pleasant Prairie, WI 262-947-7200
Chicago Steaks
Chicago, IL 800-776-4174
Country Smoked Meats
Bowling Green, OH 800-321-4766
Farmland Foods
Kansas City, MO. 888-327-6526
Father's Country Hams
Bremen, KY 270-525-3554
IBP Foods
Troy, MI 248-588-4710
Pasqualichio Brothers
Scranton, PA 800-232-6233
Saval Foods
Elkridge, MD 800-527-2825

Pigs' Feet

Canned

Peer Foods Inc
Chicago, IL 800-365-5644
SW Red Smith
Davie, FL .954-581-1996

Prepared

Frozen

Advance Food Company
Enid, OK .888-723-8237
Brookview Farms
Archbold, OH 419-445-6366
Buckhead Beef Company
Atlanta, GA. 800-888-5578

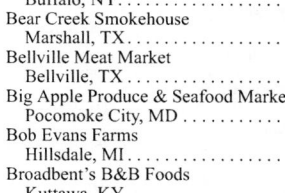

Burke Corporation
Nevada, IA 800-654-1152

Always make it your best® with Burke fully cooked meats. We specialize in Italian sausage, beef, and pork toppings, meatballs, taco meats, shredded meats, pepperoni, bacon, Canadian-style bacon, chicken and beef strips. Additionally, we offer a variety of specialty products: Hand-Pinched Style® brand toppings, chorizo, gyro topping, andouille sausage, and breakfast patties and links.

Chicago Meat Authority
Chicago, IL 773-254-0020
Dallas Dressed Beef
Dallas, TX. 214-638-0142
Davidson Meat Processing Plant
Waynesville, OH 513-897-2971

Empire Beef Company
Rochester, NY. 800-462-6804
Hall Brothers Meats
Cleveland, OH 440-235-3262
Hamm's Custom Meats
McKinney, TX 972-542-3359
Holten Meats
Sauget, IL .800-851-4684
Jacob & Sons Wholesale Meats
Martins Ferry, OH. 740-633-3091
Jesse's Fine Meats
Cherokee, IA 712-225-3637
King Kold Meats
Englewood, OH 800-836-2797
Land O'Frost
Searcy, AR 800-643-5654
Larsen Packers
Burwick, NS 902-538-8060
Miami Beef Company
Hialeah, FL 305-621-3252
O Chili Frozen Foods Inc
Northbrook, IL 847-562-1991
Olympic Food Products
Kokomo, IN 800-445-6923
Paris Frozen Foods
Hillsboro, IL 217-532-3822
Party Steak Company
Springfield, MO 417-358-9091
Pierceton Foods
Pierceton, IN 574-594-2344
Puueo Poi Factory
Hilo, HI 808-935-8435
Saletts
Randolph, MA 781-961-9900
Tucker Packing Company
Orrville, OH 330-683-3311
Valley Packing Company
Lansing, OH 740-635-0154
Whitaker Foods
Evansdale, IA 800-553-7490

Raw

Duma Meats
Mogadore, OH 330-628-3438

Rib Center Cut

Bear Creek Smokehouse
Marshall, TX. 800-950-2327
Chicago Steaks
Chicago, IL 800-776-4174

Sausage

Alaska Sausage and Seafood Company
Anchorage, AK 800-798-3636
Armour
Omaha, NE 402-453-3766
Battistoni Italana Specialty Meats
Buffalo, NY. 800-248-2705
Bear Creek Smokehouse
Marshall, TX. 800-950-2327
Bellville Meat Market
Bellville, TX. 800-571-6328
Big Apple Produce & Seafood Market
Pocomoke City, MD 410-957-1151
Bob Evans Farms
Hillsdale, MI 517-437-3349
Broadbent's B&B Foods
Kuttawa, KY 800-841-2202

Burke Corporation
Nevada, IA 800-654-1152

Always make it your best® with Burke fully cooked meats. We specialize in Italian sausage, beef, and pork toppings, meatballs, taco meats, shredded meats, pepperoni, bacon, Canadian-style bacon, chicken and beef strips. Additionally, we offer a variety of specialty products: Hand-Pinched Style® brand toppings, chorizo, gyro topping, andouille sausage, and breakfast patties and links.

Caughman's Meat Plant
Lexington, SC 803-356-0076
Chisesi Brothers Meat Packing Company
New Orleans, LA 504-822-3550
Cimpl Meats
Yankton, SD 605-665-1665
Clougherty Packing Company
Los Angeles, CA 323-583-4621
Coloma Meat Products
Coloma, WI 715-228-4080
ConAgra Foods/Eckrich
Omaha, NE 800-327-4424
Crofton & Sons
Brandon, FL 800-878-7675
Dutch Valley Veal
South Holland, IL 800-832-8325
Ebro Foods
Chicago, IL 773-696-0150
Fortenberry Ice Company
Kodak, TN 865-933-2568
Hahn Brothers
Westminster, MD 800-227-7675
Hillsboro Refrigerated Lockers
Hillsboro, KS 316-947-3781
Hoople Country Kitchens
Rockport, IN 812-649-2351
Hormel Foods Corporation
Fremont, NE 402-721-2300
Humphrey Blue Ribbon Meats
Springfield, IL 800-747-6328
IBP Foods
Troy, MI 248-588-4710
Johnsonville Food Company
Sheboygan, WI 920-459-6800
Kowalski Sausage Company
Hamtramck, MI 800-482-2400
Kramarczuk Sausage Company
Minneapolis, MN 612-379-3018
Kubisch Sausage Company
Shelby Twp, MI 586-566-4661
Lees Sausage Company
Orangeburg, SC 803-534-5517
Leo G. Fraboni Sausage Company
Hibbing, MN 218-263-5074
Lords Sausage & Country Ham
Dexter, GA 800-342-6002
Magic Seasoning Blends
Harahan, LA 800-457-2857
Meating Place
Buffalo, NY 716-885-3623
Morse's Sauerkraut
Waldoboro, ME 866-832-5569
New Braunfels Smokehouse
New Braunfels, TX 800-537-6932
Niemuth's Steak & Chop Shop
Waupaca, WI 715-258-2666
Nodine's Smokehouse
Torrington, CT 800-222-2059
Owens Country Sausage
Richardson, TX 800-966-9367
Purnell Sausage Company
Simpsonville, KY 800-626-1512
R.M. Felts Packing Company
Ivor, VA 888-300-0971
Ray's Sausage Company Inc
Cleveland, OH 216-921-8782
Register Meat Company
Cottondale, FL 850-352-4269
Rego's Purity Foods
Honolulu, HI 808-947-9005
Rinehart Meat Processing
Branson, MO 417-334-2044
Rose Packing Company
South Barrington, IL 800-323-7363
Sara Lee Corporation
Downers Grove, IL 630-598-8100
Sara Lee Foods
Cincinnati, OH 800-351-7111
Sara Lee Foods
Neenah, WI 800-558-8440
Savoie's Sausage & Food Products
Opelousas, LA 337-948-4115
Schweigert Foods
Albert Lea, MN 507-377-2526
Smith Provision Company
Erie, PA 800-334-9151
Specialty Foods Group
Newport News, VA 800-238-0020
Stonies Sausage Shop Inc
Perryville, MO 888-546-2540
Striplings
Moultrie, GA 229-985-4226

Sunnydale Meats
Gaffney, SC 864-489-6091
Sunset Farm Foods
Valdosta, GA 800-882-1121
SW Red Smith
Davie, FL 954-581-1996
Thomas Packing Company
Columbus, GA 800-729-0976
Tupman-Thurlow Company
Deerfield Beach, FL 954-596-9989
V&V Supremo Foods
Chicago, IL 800-547-8773
Vollwerth & Company
Hancock, MI 800-562-7620
Waco Beef & Pork Processors
Waco, TX 254-772-4669
William's Pork
Lumberton, NC 910-608-2226
Windsor Frozen Foods
Houston, TX 800-437-6936
YB Meats of Wichita
Wichita, KS 316-942-1213

Ardouille

Burke Corporation
Nevada, IA 800-654-1152

Always make it your best® with Burke fully cooked meats. We specialize in Italian sausage, beef, and pork toppings, meatballs, taco meats, shredded meats, pepperoni, bacon, Canadian-style bacon, chicken and beef strips. Additionally, we offer a variety of specialty products: Hand-Pinched Style® brand toppings, chorizo, gyro topping, andouille sausage, and breakfast patties and links.

Magic Seasoning Blends
Harahan, LA 800-457-2857
Sunset Farm Foods
Valdosta, GA 800-882-1121

Scrapple

Kirby & Holloway Provisions
Harrington, DE 800-995-4729

Spareribs

Farmland Foods
Kansas City, MO 888-327-6526
RJ Balson and Sons Inc
Fayetteville, AR 321-281-9473

Tenderloin Roast

Amana Meat Shop & Smokehouse
Amana, IA 800-373-6328
Bear Creek Smokehouse
Marshall, TX 800-950-2327
New Braunfels Smokehouse
New Braunfels, TX 800-537-6932

Poultry

50th State Poultry Processors
Honolulu, HI 808-845-5902
A. Thomas Food Service
Louisville, KY 800-253-2020
Acme Farms
Seattle, WA 800-542-8309
Adolf's Meats & Sausage Kitchen
Hartford, CT 860-522-1588
AFC Enterprises
Atlanta, GA 800-222-5857
AJM Meat Packing
San Juan, PR 787-787-4050
Al Safa Halal
Niagara Falls, NY 800-268-8174
Alderfer Bologna
Harleysville, PA 877-253-6328
All-States Quality Foods
Charles City, IA 800-247-4195

Allen Family Foods
Seaford, DE 302-629-9163
American Egg Products
Blackshear, GA 912-449-5700
Amick Farms, LLC
Leesville, SC 800-926-4257
Applegate Farms
Bridgewater, NJ 908-725-2768
Arizona Sunland Foods
Tucson, AZ 520-624-7068
Armbrust Meats
Medford, WI 715-748-3102
Aspen Foods
Park Ridge, IL 847-384-5940
Atlantic Premium Brands
Northbrook, IL 847-412-6200
B&B Poultry Company
Norma, NJ 856-692-8893
B&D Foods
Boise, ID 208-344-1183
B&R Quality Meats
Waterloo, IA 319-232-6328
Baltimore Poultry & Meats
Baltimore, MD 410-783-7361
Banner Beef & Seafood Company
Miami, FL 305-325-0420
Barber Foods
Portland, ME 800-577-2595
Bear Creek Smokehouse
Marshall, TX 800-950-2327
Becker Food Company
Milwaukee, WI 414-964-5353
Bell & Evans
Fredericksburg, PA 717-865-6626
Bird-In-Hand Farms, Inc.
Lancaster, PA 717-291-5855
Birdie Pak Products
Chicago, IL 773-247-5293
Black's Barbecue
Lockhart, TX 512-398-2712
Blakely Freezer Locker
Thomasville, GA 229-723-3622
Blue Grass Dairy Foods
Glasgow, KY 270-651-2146
Blue Ridge Poultry
Athens, GA 706-546-6767
Bon Ton Products
Wheeling, IL 847-520-3102
Bowman & Landes Turkeys
New Carlisle, OH 937-845-9466
Brakebush Brothers
Westfield, WI 800-933-2121
Brook Locker Plant
Brook, IN 219-275-2611
Brown Foods
Dallas, GA 770-445-4554
Brownsdale Meat Service
Brownsdale, MN 507-567-2211
Bryant's Meats
Taylorsville, MS 601-785-6507
Bullock's Country Meats
Westminster, MD 410-848-6786
Burgers Smokehouse
California, MO 800-624-5426

Burke Corporation
Nevada, IA 800-654-1152

Always make it your best® with Burke fully cooked meats. We specialize in Italian sausage, beef, and pork toppings, meatballs, taco meats, shredded meats, pepperoni, bacon, Canadian-style bacon, chicken and beef strips. Additionally, we offer a variety of specialty products: Hand-Pinched Style® brand toppings, chorizo, gyro topping, andouille sausage, and breakfast patties and links.

Bush Brothers Provision Company
West Palm Beach, FL 800-327-1345
Butterball Turkey Company
Carthage, MO 800-641-4228
Butterfield Foods Company
Butterfield, MN 507-956-5103

Buzz Food Service
Charleston, WV 304-925-4781
Cadick Poultry Company
Grandview, IN. 812-649-4491
Cagle's
Collinsville, AL 256-524-2147
Cagle's Inc
Atlanta, GA. 800-476-2820
Campbell Soup Company
Camden, NJ. 800-257-8443
Canal Fulton Provision
Canal Fulton, OH 800-321-3502
Cargill Foods
Springdale, AR 479-750-6816
Cargill Meat Solutions
Timberville, VA 540-896-7041
Caribbean Food Delights
Tappan, NY. 845-398-3000
Carl Streit & Son Company
Neptune, NJ 732-775-0803
Carmel Meat/Specialty Foods
Marina, CA .800-298-5823
Carolina By-Products Company
Winchester, VA 540-877-2590
Carolina Culinary
West Columbia, SC. 803-739-8920
Case Farms of Ohio
Winesburg, OH 330-359-7141
Casson & Sons
Des Moines, IA. 515-266-3197
Castleberry/Snow Brands
Augusta, GA. 800-241-3520
Chandler Foods
Greensboro, NC 800-537-6219
Charles Poultry Company
Lancaster, PA 717-872-7621
Chef Hans Gourmet Foods
Monroe, LA. 800-890-4267
Chef's Requested Foods
Oklahoma City, OK 800-256-0259
Chester Fried
Montgomery, AL. 800-288-1555
Chestertown Foods
Chestertown, MD 410-778-3131
Chick-Fil-A
Atlanta, GA. 800-232-2677

Chisesi Brothers Meat Packing Company
New Orleans, LA 504-822-3550
Chloe Foods Corporation
Brooklyn, NY 718-827-3600
Choctaw Maid Farms
Carthage, MS 601-298-5300
Cold Springs Farm
Thamesford, ON 800-265-1978
College Hill Poultry
Fredericksburg, PA 800-533-3361
Colorado Boxed Beef Company
Auburndale, FL. 863-967-0636
Community Market & Deli
Lindstrom, MN 651-257-1128
ConAgra Broiler Company
Dalton, GA. 706-278-3212
ConAgra Frozen Foods Company
Omaha, NE .402-595-4000
ConAgra Frozen Foods Company
Clinton, AR. 501-745-2416
ConAgra Frozen Foods Company
Macon, MO. 660-385-3184
ConAgra Frozen Foods Company
Marshall, MO 660-886-3301
ConAgra Poultry Company
Chattanooga, TN. 423-756-2471
ConAgra Poultry Company
Duluth, GA .800-609-6050
ConAgra Refrigerated Foods International
Omaha, NE .800-624-4724
Contigroup Companies
Oakwood, GA. 770-538-2120
Cordon Bleu International
Anjou, QC. .514-352-3000
Corfu Foods
Bensenville, IL 630-595-2510
Couch's Country Style Sausages
Cleveland, OH 216-587-2333
Country Smoked Meats
Bowling Green, OH 800-321-4766
Crescent Duck Farm
Aquebogue, NY 631-722-8700
Crystal Lake
Decatur, AR 800-382-4425
Culinary Foods
Chicago, IL .800-621-4049

Culver Duck
Middlebury, IN 800-825-9225
Cusack Wholesale Meat Company
Oklahoma City, OK 800-241-6328
Custom Food Service
Phoenix, AZ 602-254-1876
Danny's Poultry
Hamilton, OH 513-737-7780
David Elliott Poultry Farms
Scranton, PA 570-344-6348
Deb-El Foods
Elizabeth, NJ. 800-421-3447
Delphos Poultry Products
Delphos, OH 419-692-5816
Dietz & Watson
Philadelphia, PA 800-333-1974
DiPasquale's
Baltimore, MD 410-276-6787
DNO
Columbus, OH 800-686-2366
Double B Foods
Schulenburg, TX. 800-472-6661
Draper Valley Farms
Mt Vernon, WA. 360-424-7947
Drohan Company
Woodside, NY. 718-898-9672
Dutterer's Home Food Service
Baltimore, MD 410-298-3663
E&G Food
Brooklyn, NY 888-525-8855
E.C. Phillips & Son
Ketchikan, AK 907-225-3121
East Dayton Meat & Poultry
Dayton, OH. 937-253-6185
East Poultry Company
Austin, TX. .512-476-5367
Eberly Poultry
Stevens, PA .717-336-6440
Edelman Meats
Antigo, WI .715-623-7686
Egg Company
Gurnee, IL. .847-367-8553
Elwell Farms
South Gate, CA. 714-546-9280
Empire Beef Company
Rochester, NY 800-462-6804

Empire Kosher Foods
  Mifflintown, PA 800-367-4734
Equity Group
  Reidsville, NC. 336-342-6601
Exceldor Cooperative
  St. Anselme, QC 418-885-4451
Fair Oaks Farms
  Pleasant Prairie, WI 262-947-0320
Farbest Foods
  Huntingburg, IN 812-683-4200
Farm T Market Company
  Somerville, TN 901-465-2844
Farmers Produce
  Ashby, MN .218-747-2749
Fieldale Farms
  Gainesville, GA 800-241-5400
Fieldale Farms Corporation
  Baldwin, GA 800-241-5400
Forest Packing Company
  Forest, MS. 601-469-3321
Foster Farms
  Livingston, CA 800-255-7227
Freezer Queen Foods
  Buffalo, NY. 800-828-8383
Fried Provisions Company
  Evans City, PA 724-538-3160
Galco Food Products
  Brampton, ON. 888-793-5291
Gemini Food Industries
  Fiskdale, MA 508-347-2800
Gentry's Poultry Company
  Ward, SC 800-926-2161
George L. Wells Meat Company
  Philadelphia, PA 800-523-1730
George's
  Springdale, AR 877-855-3447
George's Chicken
  Edinburg, VA 540-984-4121
Georges Chicken
  Edinburg, VA 540-984-4121
Gerbers Poultry
  Kidron, OH 800-362-7381
Giovanni's Appetizing Food Products
  Richmond, MI 586-727-9355
Glenmark Industries
  Chicago, IL 773-927-4800
Godshall's Quality Meats
  Franconia, PA 888-463-7425
Gold'n Plump Poultry
  St Cloud, MN 800-328-2838
Golden City Meats
  Golden City, MO. 417-537-8560
Golden Platter Foods
  Newark, NJ 973-242-0291
Golden Rod Broilers
  Cullman, AL 256-734-0941
Grabill Country Meats
  Grabill, IN. 866-333-6328
Gress Poultry
  Scranton, PA 570-561-0150
Grimaud Farms
  Stockton, CA. 800-466-9955
Gunsberg Corned Beef
  Detroit, MI 313-894-6600
H. Shenson International Export
  San Francisco, CA 415-318-7000
Hahn Brothers
  Westminster, MD 800-227-7675
Halal Transactions
  Omaha, NE 402-572-6120
Hall Brothers Meats
  Cleveland, OH 440-235-3262
Hamilos Brothers Inspected Meats
  Madison, IL. 618-451-7877
Hampton House
  Langley, BC 800-665-4355
Hanover Foods Corporation
  Hanover, PA 717-632-6000
Harrison Poultry
  Bethlehem, GA 770-867-9105
Health is Wealth Foods
  Williamstown, NJ 856-728-1998
Heinkel's Packing Company
  Decatur, IL 800-594-2738
Henningsen Foods
  Purchase, NY 914-701-4020
Herb's Specialty Foods
  Westampton, NJ 800-486-0276
Hickory Baked Food
  Castle Rock, CO 303-688-2633
Hillbilly Smokehouse
  Rogers, AR 479-636-1927

Hollman Foods
  Minden, NE. 888-926-2879
Hormel Foods Corporation
  Beloit, WI .608-365-9501
Hormel Foods Corporation
  Austin, MN 800-523-4635
House of Raeford Farms
  Raeford, NC 800-888-7539
Hubbard Farms
  Pikeville, TN. 501-262-1061
IBP Foods
  Troy, MI 248-588-4710
Indian Springs Fresh Poultry
  Columbus, OH 614-443-7473
Indian Valley Meats
  Indian, AK. 907-653-7511
International Home Foods
  Milton, PA 973-359-9920
International Meat Company
  Elmwood Park, IL. 773-622-1400
Iowa Turkey Products
  Marshall, MN 563-864-7676
J&G Poultry
  Gainesville, GA 770-536-5540
J.R. Poultry
  Fults, IL. 618-476-7342
Jacob & Sons Wholesale Meats
  Martins Ferry, OH. 740-633-3091
Jacobs Meats
  Defiance, OH 419-782-7831
Jaindl's Turkey Farms
  Orefield, PA 800-475-6654
James Cowan & Sons
  Worcester, MA 508-754-5385
James J. Derba Company
  Boston, MA. 800-732-3848
Janes Family Foods
  Mississauga, ON 800-565-2637
Jay Poultry Corporation
  Voorhees, NJ 856-435-0900
Jennie-O Turkey Store
  Willmar, MN 320-235-2622
Jitney Jungle Stores of America
  Jackson, MS 800-647-2364
John Garner Meats
  Van Buren, AR 800-543-5473
Johnson, Nash, & Sons Farms
  Rose Hill, NC 800-682-6843
Joseph McSweeney & Sons
  Windom, MN 804-359-6024
Jurgielewicz Duck Farm
  Moriches, NY 800-543-8257
K&K Gourmet Meats
  Leetsdale, PA 724-266-8400
Kauffman Turkey Farms
  Waterman, IL 815-264-3470
Kelly Gourmet Foods
  San Francisco, CA 415-648-9200
Keystone Foods
  Camilla, GA 229-336-5211
Keystone Foods Corporation
  W Conshohocken, PA. 610-667-6700
Keystone Foods Corporation
  Huntsville, AL 800-327-6701
King Cole Ducks Limited
  Aurora, ON 800-363-3825
King's Command Foods
  Kent, WA. 800-247-3138
King's Meat & Seafood
  Houston, TX 713-923-6868
Kings Delight
  Gainesville, GA 770-532-2395
Kirsco/Kay Packing
  Detroit, MI 313-963-2900
Koch Food
  Chattanooga, TN 423-266-0351
Koch Foods
  Morristown, TN 423-586-5722
Koch Foods
  Park Ridge, IL. 800-837-2778
Kretschmar
  Don Mills, ON 800-561-4532
L&L Packing Company
  Chicago, IL 800-628-6328
L. East Poultry Company
  Austin, TX. 512-476-5367
Lake Charles Poultry
  Lake Charles, LA 337-433-6818
Lamb-Weston
  Pasco, WA. 800-766-7783
Land O Frost
  Lansing, IL 800-643-5654

Land O'Frost
  Searcy, AR 800-643-5654
Lendy's
  Virginia Beach, VA 757-491-3511
Leon's Sausage Company
  Chicago, IL 312-829-2250
Lewis Smoked Meat Company
  Chicago, IL 800-648-6328
Lilydale Foods
  Edmonton, AB 800-661-5341
Lionel Lavallee Company
  Haverhill, MA 800-343-8292
Locustdale Meat Packing
  Locustdale, PA 570-875-1270
Loggins Meat Company
  Tyler, TX. 800-527-8610
London Pantry Foods
  Mt Pleasant, SC 888-208-7787
Long Food Industries
  Fripp Island, SC 843-838-3205
Longmont Foods
  Longmont, CO 303-776-4803
Lowell Provision Company
  Lowell, MA. 978-454-5603
LSK Smoked Turkey Products
  Bronx, NY 718-792-1300
Lucks Food Decorating Company
  Tacoma, WA 206-674-7200
M-G
  Weimar, TX 800-460-8581
MacFarlane Pheasants
  Janesville, WI 877-269-8957
MacGregors Meat & Seafood
  Toronto, ON 800-268-5953
Mada'n Kosher Foods
  Dania, FL 954-925-0077
Mahantongo Game Farms
  Dalmatia, PA 570-758-6284
Maid-Rite Steak Company
  Dunmore, PA. 800-233-4259
Manchester Farms
  Dalzell, SC 800-845-0421
Manger Packing Company
  Baltimore, MD 800-227-9262
Manley Meats
  Decatur, IN 260-592-7313
Maple Leaf Farms
  Milford, IN 800-384-2812
Mar-Jac Poultry
  Gainesville, GA 800-226-0561
Marathon Enterprises
  Englewood, NJ 201-935-3330
Marshall Durbin Industries
  Irondale, AL 205-956-3505
Marshall Durbin Poultry Company
  Birmingham, AL 205-841-7315
Marshall Egg Products
  Seymour, IN 812-497-2557
Marshallville Packing Company
  Marshallville, OH 330-855-2871
McCain Foods USA
  Othello, WA 800-541-4808
McFarland Foods
  Riverton, UT. 209-869-6611
McFarland Foods
  Riverton, UT. 800-441-9596
Meat-O-Mat Corporation
  Brooklyn, NY 718-965-7250
Medeiros Farms
  Kalaheo, HI 808-332-8211
Metafoods, LLC
  Atlanta, GA. 404-843-2400
Miller Brothers Packing Company
  Sylvester, GA 229-776-2014
Miller's Stratford Provision Company
  Southport, CT. 203-375-1598
Mirasco
  Atlanta, GA. 770-956-1945
Molbert Brothers Poultry & Egg Company
  Lake Charles, LA 337-439-2579
Montana Legacy Premium Ostrich Products
  Billings, MT 406-656-6444
Moretti's Poultry
  Columbus, OH 614-486-2333
Moroni Feed Company
  West Liberty, IA 435-436-8221
Motz Poultry
  Batavia, OH. 513-732-1381
Mountain Valley Poultry
  Springdale, AR 479-751-7266
Mountaire Corporation
  North Little Rock, AR 501-372-6524

Mountaire Farms of Delmarva
Selbyville, DE 800-441-8263
Mountaire Farms of North Carolina
Lumber Bridge, NC 910-843-5942
Murray's Chicken
South Fallsburg, NY 800-770-6347
Mutual Trading Company
Los Angeles, CA 213-626-9458
National Egg Products Company
Social Circle, GA 770-464-2652
New Braunfels Smokehouse
New Braunfels, TX 800-537-6932
Nodine's Smokehouse
Torrington, CT 800-222-2059
North Star Foods
St Charles, MN 507-932-4831
O Chili Frozen Foods Inc
Northbrook, IL 847-562-1991
O.K. Industries
Fort Smith, AR 800-635-9441
Oak Valley Farm
Voorhees, NJ 856-435-0900
Oak Valley Farms
Watertown, SD 605-886-8025
Olson Locker
Fairmont, MN 507-238-2563
Olymel
Iberville, QC 450-347-1900
Omaha Steaks International
Omaha, NE 800-562-0500
Oregon Freeze Dry
Albany, OR 800-547-0245
Ottman Meat Company
New York, NY 212-879-4160
P & L Poultry
Spokane Valley, WA 509-892-1242
Pacific Poultry Company
Honolulu, HI 808-841-2828
Paisano Food Products
Elk Grove Village, IL 773-237-3773
Palmetto Pigeon Plant
Sumter, SC 803-775-1204
Park Farms
Canton, OH 800-683-6511
Pasqualichio Brothers
Scranton, PA 800-232-6233
Peco Foods
Tuscaloosa, AL 205-345-4711
Peco Foods
Canton, MS 601-407-1699
Peco Foods
Sebastopol, MS 601-625-7432
Penn Valley Farms
Gainesville, GA 773-685-9929
Pennfield Corporation
Lancaster, PA 717-299-2561
Pennfield Farms
Lancaster, PA 717-865-2153
Perdue Farms
Bridgewater, VA 540-828-2581
Perdue Farms
Thorntown, IN 765-436-7990
Perdue Farms
Horsham, PA 800-473-7383
Perdue Farms
Defuniak Springs, FL 850-951-6107
Perdue Farms
Rockingham, NC 910-997-8600
Petaluma Poultry Processors
Petaluma, CA 800-556-6789
Peterson Farms
Decatur, AR 800-382-4425
Petschl's Meats
Tukwila, WA 206-575-4400
Pfeffer's Country Market
Sauk Centre, MN 320-352-3095
Pierre Foods
Cincinnati, OH 513-874-8741
Pilgrim's Pride
Boaz, AL 256-593-4223
Pilgrim's Pride
Timberville, VA 540-896-7000
Pilgrim's Pride
Elberton, GA 706-283-3821
Pilgrim's Pride
Athens, GA 706-548-5641
Pilgrim's Pride
Moorefield, WV 800-336-9876
Pilgrim's Pride
Athens, GA 800-476-6702
Pilgrim's Pride
Enterprise, AL 800-633-0908

Pilgrim's Pride
Pittsburg, TX 800-683-1968
Pilgrim's Pride
Athens, GA 800-824-1159
Pilgrim's Pride
Lufkin, TX 936-639-1174
Pinty's Premium Foods
St. Catharines, ON 800-263-7223
Pintys Delicious Foods
Port Colborne, ON 800-263-9710
Plantation Foods
Waco, TX 800-733-0900
Pocono Foods
Mt Bethel, PA 570-897-5000
Poultry Foods Industry
Fort Smith, AR 479-783-8996
Prime Pak Foods
Gainesville, GA 770-536-8708
Puueo Poi Factory
Hilo, HI 808-935-8435
Radlo Foods
Watertown, MA 800-370-1439
Randall Foods
Huntington Park, CA 800-372-6581
Ray's Sausage Company Inc
Cleveland, OH 216-921-8782
Redi-Serve Food Company
Fort Atkinson, WI 920-563-6391
Registry Steaks & Seafood
Bridgeview, IL 708-458-3100
Rhodia Inc
Cranbury, NJ 609-860-4000
Rocco Enterprises
Harrisonburg, VA 800-336-4003
Roman Sausage Company
Santa Clara, CA 800-497-7462
Rooster Brand Kosher Poultry
Gardena, CA 310-719-2390
Rose Hill Distributors
Branford, CT 203-488-7231
Rosebud Farms
Chicago, IL 773-928-5331
RusDun Farms
Collierville, TN 901-853-0931
Rymer Foods
Chicago, IL 800-247-9637
Sadler's BBQ Sales
Henderson, TX 903-657-5581
Sanderson Farms
Collins, MS 601-765-8211
Sanderson Farms
Hazlehurst, MS 601-894-3721
Sanderson Farms
Bryan, TX 979-778-5730
Sara Lee Foods
Zeeland, MI 616-875-8131
Sara Lee Foods
Cordova, TN 901-756-4051
Saunders Provision Company
Norfolk, VA 800-486-5611
Scanga Meat Company
Salida, CO 719-539-3511
Schaller & Weber
Long Island City, NY 800-847-4115
Schiltz Foods
Sisseton, SD 877-872-4458
Schneider Foods
Kitchener, ON 519-741-5000
Schneider Foods
Saint Marys, ON 800-567-1890
Schweigert Foods
Albert Lea, MN 507-377-2526
Scotsburn Dairy Group
Truro, NS 902-895-4412
Seaboard Corporation
Shawnee Mission, KS 913-676-8800
Seaboard Farms
Chattanooga, TN 423-756-2471
Selwoods Farm Hunting Preserve
Alpine, AL 256-362-7595
Serenade Foods
Milford, IN 574-658-4121
Seven K Feather Farm
Taylorsville, IN 812-526-2651
Shelley's Prime Meats
Jersey City, NJ 201-433-3434
Shelton's Poultry
Pomona, CA 800-541-1833
Simeus Foods Internatio nal
Mansfield, TX 888-772-3663
Simeus Foods International
Rocky Mount, NC 888-772-3663

Simmons Foods
South West City, MO 417-762-3271
Simmons Foods
Siloam Springs, AR 479-524-8151
SJH Enterprises
Middleton, WI 888-745-3845
Smith Packing Regional Meat
Utica, NY 315-732-5125
Snow Ball Foods
Fredericksburg, PA 800-360-7669
Somerset Industries
Spring House, PA 800-883-8728
SOPAKCO Foods
Mullins, SC 800-276-9678
Southeastern Meat Association
Oviedo, FL 407-365-5661
Southeastern Sales
Hixson, TN 423-877-3781
Southtowns Seafood & Meats
Blasdell, NY 716-824-4900
Springville Meat & Cold Storage
Springville, UT 801-489-6391
Squab Producers of California
Modesto, CA 209-537-4744
Standard Beef Company
New Haven, CT 203-787-2164
Starkel Poultry
Puyallup, WA 253-845-2876
Steak-Umm Company
Shillington, PA 860-928-5900
Stegall Smoked Turkey
Marshville, NC 800-851-6034
Sunnydale Meats
Gaffney, SC 864-489-6091
Sunshine Farms Poultry
West Palm Beach, FL 561-881-4500
Suzanna's Kitchen
Duluth, GA 800-241-2455
Sweet Sue Kitchens
Athens, AL 256-216-0500
Sylvest Farms Inc
Montgomery, AL 334-281-0482
Tampa Farm Services
Dover, FL 813-659-0605
Taylor's Poultry Place
Lexington, SC 803-356-3431
Tenn Valley Ham Company
Paris, TN 731-642-9740
Thomas Packing Company
Columbus, GA 800-729-0976
Tillamook Meat Company
Tillamook, OR 503-842-4802
Tip Top Poultry
Marietta, GA 770-973-8070
Townsend Culinary
Millsboro, DE 302-777-6650
Townsends
Pittsboro, NC 919-542-3215
Townsends Inc
Georgetown, DE 302-855-7100
Townsends Inc
Siler City, NC 919-663-2050
Troyer Foods
Goshen, IN 574-533-0302
Turkey Store Company
Faribault, MN 507-334-2050
Tyson Foods
Springdale, AR 479-290-4000
Tyson Foods
Fort Smith, AR 479-783-8996
Tyson Foods
Bloomfield, MO 573-568-2153
Tyson Foods
Jackson, MS 601-372-7441
Tyson Foods
Forest, MS 601-469-1712
Tyson Foods
Corydon, IN 800-223-3719
Tyson Foods
Springdale, AR 800-643-3410
Tyson Foods
Berryville, AR 870-423-2164
Tyson Foods
Hope, AR 870-777-8646
United Poultry Company
Los Angeles, CA 213-620-9948
United Provision Meat Company
Columbus, OH 614-252-1126
Universal Poultry Company
Athens, GA 706-546-6767
Vantage USA
Chicago, IL 773-247-1086

Vienna Meat Products
Scarborough, ON 800-588-1931
Vitale Poultry Company
Columbus, OH 614-267-1874
W&G Marketing Company
Ames, IA 515-233-4774
Waco Beef & Pork Processors
Waco, TX .254-772-4669
Walden Foods
Winchester, VA 800-648-7688
Walker Meats Corporation
Carrollton, GA 770-834-8171
Walt Koch
Decatur, GA 404-378-3666
Waltkoch
Decatur, GA 404-378-3666
Wampler Foods
Dallas, TX .717-624-2191
Wapsie Produce
Decorah, IA 563-382-4271
Wasatch Meats
Salt Lake City, UT 801-363-5747
Watson's Quality Food Products
Blackwood, NJ 800-257-7870
Wayco Ham Company
Goldsboro, NC 800-962-2614
Wayne Farms, LLC
Union Springs, AL 334-738-2930
Wayne Farms, LLC
Jack, AL 334-897-3435
Wayne Farms, LLC
Laurel, MS .601-425-4721
Wayne Farms, LLC
Oakwood, GA 678-989-3900
Wayne Farms, LLC
Pendergrass, GA 706-693-2271
Wayne Farms, LLC
Oakwood, GA 800-392-0844
West Central Turkeys
Pelican Rapids, MN 218-863-6800
White Fence Farm Chicken
Romeoville, IL 630-739-1720
Whittaker & Associates
Atlanta, GA 404-266-1265
Will Poultry Company
Buffalo, NY 716-853-2000
Willies Smoke House
Harrisville, PA 800-742-4184
Willow Tree Poultry Farm
Attleboro, MA 508-222-2479
Willowbrook Foods
Wichita, KS 800-423-2362
Wimmer's Meat Products
West Point, NE 800-358-0761
Wong Wing Foods
Montreal, QC 800-361-4820
Woods Smoked Meats
Bowling Green, MO 800-458-8426
World Flavors
Warminster, PA 215-672-4400
Wornick Company
Cincinnati, OH 800-860-4555
Yoakum Packing Company
Yoakum, TX 361-293-3541
Young's Farm
Paulina, OR 928-632-7272
Zacky Farms
Fresno, CA .800-888-0235
Zartic Inc
Rome, GA .800-241-0516

Chicken

50th State Poultry Processors
Honolulu, HI 808-845-5902
A. Stein Meat Products
Brooklyn, NY 718-492-0760
Al Safa Halal
Niagara Falls, NY 800-268-8174
All-States Quality Foods
Charles City, IA 800-247-4195
Atlantic Premium Brands
Northbrook, IL 847-412-6200
B&D Foods
Boise, ID 208-344-1183
Bear Creek Smokehouse
Marshall, TX 800-950-2327
Black's Barbecue
Lockhart, TX 512-398-2712
Blakely Freezer Locker
Thomasville, GA 229-723-3622

Brakebush Brothers
Westfield, WI 800-933-2121
Brook Locker Plant
Brook, IN 219-275-2611
Bryant's Meats
Taylorsville, MS 601-785-6507
Bullock's Country Meats
Westminster, MD 410-848-6786
Burgers Smokehouse
California, MO 800-624-5426

BURKE

Always make it your best®

Burke Corporation
Nevada, IA .800-654-1152

Always make it your best® with Burke fully
cooked meats. We specialize in Italian sausage,
beef, and pork toppings, meatballs, taco meats,
shredded meats, pepperoni, bacon, Canadian-style bacon, chicken and beef strips. Additionally, we offer a variety of specialty products:
Hand-Pinched Style® brand toppings, chorizo,
gyro topping, andouille sausage, and breakfast
patties and links.

Buzz Food Service
Charleston, WV 304-925-4781
Cargill Meat Solutions
Timberville, VA 540-896-7041
Caribbean Food Delights
Tappan, NY 845-398-3000
Caribbean Products
Baltimore, MD 410-235-7700
Case Farms of North Carolina
Morganton, NC 828-438-6900
Cericola Farms
Bradford, ON 877-939-4449
Charles Poultry Company
Lancaster, PA 717-872-7621
Chef Hans Gourmet Foods
Monroe, LA 800-890-4267
Chester Fried
Montgomery, AL 800-288-1555
Chicago Steaks
Chicago, IL 800-776-4174
Chick-Fil-A
Atlanta, GA 800-232-2677
Chisesi Brothers Meat Packing Company
New Orleans, LA 504-822-3550
Choctaw Maid Farms
Carthage, MS 601-298-5300
ConAgra Broiler Company
Dalton, GA 706-278-3212
ConAgra Foods Inc
Omaha, NE 402-240-4000
ConAgra Frozen Foods Company
Omaha, NE 402-595-4000
ConAgra Frozen Foods Company
Macon, MO 660-385-3184
ConAgra Frozen Foods Company
Marshall, MO 660-886-3301
ConAgra Poultry Company
Duluth, GA 800-609-6050
Cordon Bleu International
Anjou, QC .514-352-3000
Corfu Foods
Bensenville, IL 630-595-2510
Crystal Lake
Decatur, AR 800-382-4425
Culver Duck
Middlebury, IN 800-825-9225
D'Artagnan
Newark, NJ 800-327-8246
Delphos Poultry Products
Delphos, OH 419-692-5816
Double B Foods
Schulenburg, TX 800-472-6661
E&G Food
Brooklyn, NY 888-525-8855
East Poultry Company
Austin, TX .512-476-5367
Egg Company
Gurnee, IL .847-367-8553
Equity Group
Reidsville, NC 336-342-6601

Exceldor Cooperative
St. Anselme, QC 418-885-4451
Farmers Produce
Ashby, MN .218-747-2749
Ferko Meat Company
Milwaukee, WI 414-967-5500
Fieldale Farms
Gainesville, GA 800-241-5400
Fieldale Farms Corporation
Baldwin, GA 706-778-5100
Fieldale Farms Corporation
Baldwin, GA 800-241-5400
Foster Farms
Corvallis, OR 541-754-6211
Foster Farms
Livingston, CA 800-255-7227
Freezer Queen Foods
Buffalo, NY 800-828-8383
Galco Food Products
Brampton, ON 888-793-5291
Gemini Food Industries
Fiskdale, MA 508-347-2800
George L. Wells Meat Company
Philadelphia, PA 800-523-1730
Georges Chicken
Edinburg, VA 540-984-4121
Gress Poultry
Scranton, PA 570-561-0150
Hampton House
Langley, BC 800-665-4355
Health is Wealth Foods
Williamstown, NJ 856-728-1998
Henningsen Foods
Purchase, NY 914-701-4020
Home Delivery Food Service
Jefferson, GA 706-367-9551
Horizon Poultry
Toronto, ON 519-364-3200
Hormel Foods Corporation
Houston, TX 281-492-1770
Hormel Foods Corporation
Oklahoma City, OK 405-745-3471
Hormel Foods Corporation
Oklahoma City, OK 405-843-5643
Hormel Foods Corporation
Columbia, MD 410-290-1855
Hormel Foods Corporation
West Allis, WI 414-604-0570
Hormel Foods Corporation
Cincinnati, OH 513-563-0211
Hormel Foods Corporation
Phoenix, AZ 602-230-2400
Hormel Foods Corporation
Beloit, WI .608-365-9501
Hormel Foods Corporation
Charlotte, NC 704-527-4388
Hormel Foods Corporation
Orchard Park, NY 716-675-7700
Hormel Foods Corporation
Austin, MN 800-523-4635
Hormel Foods Corporation
Lisle, IL 800-533-2000
Hormel Foods Corporation
Salt Lake City, UT 801-487-8251
Hormel Foods Corporation
Lubbock, TX 806-796-3630
Hormel Foods Corporation
Lebanon, NJ 908-236-7009
Hormel Foods Corporation
Shawnee Mission, KS 913-888-8744
Hormel Foods Corporation
Pleasanton, CA 925-225-9349
House of Raeford Farms
Raeford, NC 800-888-7539
Hubbard Farms
Pikeville, TN 501-262-1061
Hunter Food Inc
Anaheim, CA 714-666-1888
International Home Foods
Milton, PA .973-359-9920
Janes Family Foods
Mississauga, ON 800-565-2637
Jesse's Fine Meats
Cherokee, IA 712-225-3637
K&K Gourmet Meats
Leetsdale, PA 724-266-8400
Karn Meats
Columbus, OH 800-221-9585
Kelly Gourmet Foods
San Francisco, CA 415-648-9200
Keystone Foods Corporation
W Conshohocken, PA 610-667-6700

Keystone Foods Corporation
Huntsville, AL 800-327-6701
King's Command Foods
Kent, WA. .800-247-3138
King's Meat & Seafood
Houston, TX 713-923-6868
Koch Foods
Park Ridge, IL. 800-837-2778
Koch Poultry
Chicago, IL 800-837-2778
La Nova Wings
Buffalo, NY. 800-652-6682
Land O Frost
Lansing, IL 800-643-5654
Land O'Frost
Searcy, AR 800-643-5654
Lionel Lavallee Company
Haverhill, MA. 800-343-8292
Locustdale Meat Packing
Locustdale, PA 570-875-1270
Loggins Meat Company
Tyler, TX .800-527-8610
Lucks Food Decorating Company
Tacoma, WA 206-674-7200
Magnolia Meats
Shreveport, LA 318-221-2814
Manger Packing Company
Baltimore, MD 800-227-9262
Maple Leaf Farms
Milford, IN 800-384-2812
Mar-Jac Poultry
Gainesville, GA 800-226-0561
McFarland Foods
Riverton, UT 209-869-6611
Meat-O-Mat Corporation
Brooklyn, NY 718-965-7250
Mexi-Frost Specialties Company
Brooklyn, NY 718-625-3324
Mitchell Foods
Barbourville, KY 888-202-9745
Moretti's Poultry
Columbus, OH 614-486-2333
Mountaire Farms of North Carolina
Lumber Bridge, NC 910-843-5942
North Star Foods
St Charles, MN 507-932-4831
O.K. Industries
Fort Smith, AR 800-635-9441
P & L Poultry
Spokane Valley, WA 509-892-1242
Paisano Food Products
Elk Grove Village, IL 773-237-3773
Palmetto Pigeon Plant
Sumter, SC 803-775-1204
Park Farms
Canton, OH 800-683-6511
Penn Valley Farms
Gainesville, GA 773-685-9929
Pennfield Corporation
Lancaster, PA 717-299-2561
Perdue Farms
Pantego, NC 252-943-3061
Perdue Farms
Bridgewater, VA 540-828-2581
Perdue Farms
Statesville, NC 800-457-3738
Perdue Farms
Horsham, PA 800-473-7383
Perdue Farms
Rockingham, NC 910-997-8600
Petaluma Poultry Processors
Petaluma, CA 800-556-6789
Petschl's Meats
Tukwila, WA 206-575-4400
Pilgrim's Pride
Timberville, VA 540-896-7000
Pilgrim's Pride
Elberton, GA. 706-283-3821
Pilgrim's Pride
Athens, GA 706-548-5641
Pilgrim's Pride
Moorefield, WV 800-336-9876
Pilgrim's Pride
Enterprise, AL 800-633-0908
Pilgrim's Pride
Pittsburg, TX 800-683-1968
Pilgrim's Pride
Lufkin, TX 936-639-1174
Pinty's Premium Foods
St. Catharines, ON 800-263-7223
Plantation Foods
Waco, TX .800-733-0900

Prime Pak Foods
Gainesville, GA 770-536-8708
Proliant Meat Ingredients
Ankeny, IA 800-369-2672
Puueo Poi Factory
Hilo, HI 808-935-8435
Readyfoods
Winnipeg, NB 204-661-6955
Redi-Serve Food Company
Fort Atkinson, WI. 920-563-6391
Roman Sausage Company
Santa Clara, CA 800-497-7462
Roy Dick Company
Griffin, GA 770-227-3916
Royal Palate Foods
Inglewood, CA 310-330-7701
Rymer Foods
Chicago, IL 800-247-9637
Sanderson Farms
Hazlehurst, MS 601-894-3721
Sanderson Farms
Bryan, TX .979-778-5730
Saunders Provision Company
Norfolk, VA 800-486-5611
Scarborough Meat Packers
Scarborough, ON 416-269-7758
Schneider Foods
Guelph, ON. 519-837-4848
Schweigert Foods
Albert Lea, MN. 507-377-2526
Simeus Foods Internatio nal
Mansfield, TX. 888-772-3663
Simeus Foods International
Rocky Mount, NC. 888-772-3663
Simmons Foods
Siloam Springs, AR 479-524-8151
SJH Enterprises
Middleton, WI. 888-745-3845
Smith Packing Regional Meat
Utica, NY .315-732-5125
Snow Ball Foods
Fredericksburg, PA 800-360-7669
SOPAKCO Foods
Mullins, SC 800-276-9678
Southeastern Sales
Hixson, TN 423-877-3781
Steak-Umm Company
Shillington, PA 860-928-5900
Sterling Pacific Meat Company
Los Angeles, CA. 310-274-7635
Sunnydale Meats
Gaffney, SC 864-489-6091
Suzanna's Kitchen
Duluth, GA 800-241-2455
Sweet Sue Kitchens
Athens, AL 256-216-0500
Thomson Meats
Melfort, SK 306-752-2802
Tony Downs Foods Company
Madelia, MN. 507-642-3203
Townsends
Pittsboro, NC 919-542-3215
Townsends Inc
Siler City, NC 919-663-2050
Tyson Foods
Wilkesboro, NC 336-838-2171
Tyson Foods
Bloomfield, MO 573-568-2153
Tyson Foods
Dexter, MO 573-624-4551
Tyson Foods
Jackson, MS 601-372-7441
Tyson Foods
Star City, AR 800-351-8184
Tyson Foods
Springdale, AR 800-643-3410
Tyson Foods
Hope, AR .870-777-8646
United Poultry Company
Los Angeles, CA. 213-620-9948
Vantage USA
Chicago, IL 773-247-1086
Waco Beef & Pork Processors
Waco, TX .254-772-4669
Waken Meat Company
Atlanta, GA. 404-627-3537
Wasatch Meats
Salt Lake City, UT 801-363-5747
Wayne Farms, LLC
Union Springs, AL 334-738-2930
Wayne Farms, LLC
Laurel, MS 601-425-4721

Wayne Farms, LLC
Oakwood, GA. 678-989-3900
Wayne Farms, LLC
Pendergrass, GA 706-693-2271
Wayne Farms, LLC
Oakwood, GA. 800-392-0844
West Liberty Foods
West Liberty, IA 888-511-4500
Wong Wing Foods
Montreal, QC 800-361-4820
Wornick Company
Cincinnati, OH 800-860-4555
Zartic Inc
Rome, GA. 800-241-0516

Barbecued

Black's Barbecue
Lockhart, TX. 512-398-2712
Woods Smoked Meats
Bowling Green, MO 800-458-8426

Barbecued Frozen

Burke Corporation
Nevada, IA 800-654-1152

Always make it your best® with Burke fully cooked meats. We specialize in Italian sausage, beef, and pork toppings, meatballs, taco meats, shredded meats, pepperoni, bacon, Canadian-style bacon, chicken and beef strips. Additionally, we offer a variety of specialty products: Hand-Pinched Style® brand toppings, chorizo, gyro topping, andouille sausage, and breakfast patties and links.

Breaded

Delphos Poultry Products
Delphos, OH 419-692-5816
Gemini Food Industries
Fiskdale, MA 508-347-2800
Janes Family Foods
Mississauga, ON 800-565-2637
Meat-O-Mat Corporation
Brooklyn, NY 718-965-7250
Pilgrim's Pride
Pittsburg, TX. 800-683-1968
Schneider Foods
Ayr, ON 519-632-7416

Broilers

Grand River Poultry Farm
Paris, ON. .800-853-5454
Koala Moa Char Broiled Chicken
Waipahu, HI 808-677-0126

Bulk - Leg Quarters - Legs - T

ConAgra Frozen Foods Company
Clinton, AR. 501-745-2416
Pennfield Farms
Lancaster, PA 717-865-2153

Canned Boned

Criders Poultry
Stillmore, GA 800-342-3851
International Home Foods
Milton, PA. 973-359-9920
Lucks Food Decorating Company
Tacoma, WA 206-674-7200

Capon

D'Artagnan
Newark, NJ 800-327-8246
Wayne Farms, LLC
Jack, AL 334-897-3435
Wayne Farms, LLC
Laurel, MS 601-425-4721

Cooked - Breaded - Frozen

Advance Food Company
Enid, OK .888-723-8237

Bear Creek Smokehouse
Marshall, TX 800-950-2327
Loggins Meat Company
Tyler, TX 800-527-8610

Cut-Up Frozen

Park Farms
Canton, OH 800-683-6511
Wayne Farms, LLC
Jack, AL 334-897-3435
Wayne Farms, LLC
Laurel, MS 601-425-4721
Wayne Farms, LLC
Oakwood, GA 800-392-0844

Cut-Up IQF (Individually Quick Frozen)

Bell & Evans
Fredericksburg, PA 717-865-6626
Pilgrim's Pride
Pittsburg, TX 800-683-1968
Wayne Farms, LLC
Laurel, MS 601-425-4721

Diced Frozen

Burke Corporation
Nevada, IA 800-654-1152

Always make it your best® with Burke fully
cooked meats. We specialize in Italian sausage,
beef, and pork toppings, meatballs, taco meats,
shredded meats, pepperoni, bacon, Canadian-style bacon, chicken and beef strips. Additionally, we offer a variety of specialty products:
Hand-Pinched Style® brand toppings, chorizo,
gyro topping, andouille sausage, and breakfast
patties and links.

Fajita Strips

Burke Corporation
Nevada, IA 800-654-1152

Always make it your best® with Burke fully
cooked meats. We specialize in Italian sausage,
beef, and pork toppings, meatballs, taco meats,
shredded meats, pepperoni, bacon, Canadian-style bacon, chicken and beef strips. Additionally, we offer a variety of specialty products:
Hand-Pinched Style® brand toppings, chorizo,
gyro topping, andouille sausage, and breakfast
patties and links.

Chef's Requested Foods
Oklahoma City, OK 800-256-0259

Fillets

Delphos Poultry Products
Delphos, OH 419-692-5816
Grand River Poultry Farm
Paris, ON 800-853-5454
Simeus Foods Internatio nal
Mansfield, TX 888-772-3663

Fresh

Becker Food Company
Milwaukee, WI 414-964-5353
Bell & Evans
Fredericksburg, PA 717-865-6626
Brook Locker Plant
Brook, IN 219-275-2611
Choctaw Maid Farms
Carthage, MS 601-298-5300
Exceldor Cooperative
St. Anselme, QC 418-885-4451

Fieldale Farms
Gainesville, GA 800-241-5400
Fieldale Farms Corporation
Baldwin, GA 800-241-5400
Foster Farms
Creswell, OR. 541-895-2161
Galco Food Products
Brampton, ON. 888-793-5291
Georges Chicken
Edinburg, VA 540-984-4121
Keystone Foods
Camilla, GA 229-336-5211
Perdue Farms
Nashville, NC 252-459-9763
Perdue Farms
Plymouth, NC 252-793-9119
Perdue Farms
Candor, NC 410-543-3000
Perdue Farms
Bridgewater, VA 540-828-2581
Perdue Farms
Salisbury, MD 800-473-7383
Perdue Farms
Georgetown, DE 888-737-3832
Perdue Farms
Rockingham, NC 910-997-8600
Perdue Farms
Kenly, NC 919-284-2033
Petaluma Poultry Processors
Petaluma, CA 800-556-6789
Pilgrim's Pride
Timberville, VA 540-896-7000
Pilgrim's Pride
Dallas, TX 800-824-1159
Pilgrim's Pride
Nacogdoches, TX 936-564-6145
Smith Packing Regional Meat
Utica, NY 315-732-5125
Tyson Foods
Hope, AR 870-777-8646
Wayne Farms, LLC
Union Springs, AL 334-738-2930
Wayne Farms, LLC
Jack, AL 334-897-3435
Wayne Farms, LLC
Laurel, MS 601-425-4721
Wayne Farms, LLC
Oakwood, GA 678-989-3900
Wayne Farms, LLC
Pendergrass, GA 706-693-2271
Wayne Farms, LLC
Oakwood, GA 800-392-0844

Frozen

B&D Foods
Boise, ID 208-344-1183
Blakely Freezer Locker
Thomasville, GA. 229-723-3622
Brakebush Brothers
Westfield, WI 800-933-2121
Brook Locker Plant
Brook, IN 219-275-2611

Burke Corporation
Nevada, IA 800-654-1152

Always make it your best® with Burke fully
cooked meats. We specialize in Italian sausage,
beef, and pork toppings, meatballs, taco meats,
shredded meats, pepperoni, bacon, Canadian-style bacon, chicken and beef strips. Additionally, we offer a variety of specialty products:
Hand-Pinched Style® brand toppings, chorizo,
gyro topping, andouille sausage, and breakfast
patties and links.

Buzz Food Service
Charleston, WV 304-925-4781
Caribbean Food Delights
Tappan, NY 845-398-3000
Caribbean Products
Baltimore, MD 410-235-7700
Choctaw Maid Farms
Carthage, MS 601-298-5300

ConAgra Broiler Company
Dalton, GA 706-278-3212
ConAgra Frozen Foods Company
Macon, MO 660-385-3184
ConAgra Frozen Foods Company
Marshall, MO 660-886-3301
ConAgra Poultry Company
Duluth, GA 800-609-6050
Draper Valley Farms
Mt Vernon, WA 360-424-7947
Equity Group
Reidsville, NC 336-342-6601
Exceldor Cooperative
St. Anselme, QC 418-885-4451
Fieldale Farms
Gainesville, GA 800-241-5400
Fieldale Farms Corporation
Baldwin, GA 706-778-5100
Fieldale Farms Corporation
Baldwin, GA 800-241-5400
Foster Farms
Creswell, OR. 541-895-2161
Galco Food Products
Brampton, ON. 888-793-5291
Gemini Food Industries
Fiskdale, MA 508-347-2800
Georges Chicken
Edinburg, VA 540-984-4121
Gress Poultry
Scranton, PA 570-561-0150
Health is Wealth Foods
Williamstown, NJ 856-728-1998
House of Raeford Farms
Raeford, NC 800-888-7539
Janes Family Foods
Mississauga, ON 800-565-2637
K&K Gourmet Meats
Leetsdale, PA 724-266-8400
Keystone Foods
Camilla, GA 229-336-5211
Koch Foods
Park Ridge, IL 800-837-2778
Manchester Farms
Dalzell, SC 800-845-0421
Maple Leaf Farms
Milford, IN 800-384-2812
Mar-Jac Poultry
Gainesville, GA 800-226-0561
Mexi-Frost Specialties Company
Brooklyn, NY 718-625-3324
Mountaire Farms of Delmarva
Selbyville, DE. 800-441-8263
Paisano Food Products
Elk Grove Village, IL 773-237-3773
Palmetto Pigeon Plant
Sumter, SC 803-775-1204
Park Farms
Canton, OH 800-683-6511
Pennfield Corporation
Lancaster, PA 717-299-2561
Perdue Farms
Nashville, NC 252-459-9763
Perdue Farms
Plymouth, NC 252-793-9119
Perdue Farms
Candor, NC 410-543-3000
Perdue Farms
Bridgewater, VA 540-828-2581
Perdue Farms
Salisbury, MD 800-473-7383
Perdue Farms
Rockingham, NC 910-997-8600
Perdue Farms
Kenly, NC 919-284-2033
Phoenix Agro-Industrial Corporation
Westbury, NY 516-334-1194
Pilgrim's Pride
Broadway, VA 540-896-0607
Pilgrim's Pride
Timberville, VA 540-896-7000
Pilgrim's Pride
Elberton, GA. 706-283-3821
Pilgrim's Pride
Moorefield, WV 800-336-9876
Pilgrim's Pride
Pittsburg, TX 800-683-1968
Pilgrim's Pride
Dallas, TX 800-824-1159
Pilgrim's Pride
Nacogdoches, TX 936-564-6145
Pilgrim's Pride
Lufkin, TX 936-639-1174

Redi-Serve Food Company
Fort Atkinson, WI. 920-563-6391
Rymer Foods
Chicago, IL 800-247-9637
Sanderson Farms
Hazlehurst, MS 601-894-3721
Sanderson Farms
Bryan, TX 979-778-5730
Simmons Foods
Siloam Springs, AR 479-524-8151
SJH Enterprises
Middleton, WI. 888-745-3845
Smith Packing Regional Meat
Utica, NY 315-732-5125
Snow Ball Foods
Fredericksburg, PA 800-360-7669
Southeastern Meat Association
Oviedo, FL 407-365-5661
Southeastern Sales
Hixson, TN 423-877-3781
Steak-Umm Company
Shillington, PA 860-928-5900
Tony Downs Foods Company
Madelia, MN 507-642-3203
Tyson Foods
Bloomfield, MO 573-568-2153
Tyson Foods
Springdale, AR 800-643-3410
Tyson Foods
Hope, AR 870-777-8646
Wayne Farms, LLC
Union Springs, AL 334-738-2930
Wayne Farms, LLC
Jack, AL 334-897-3435
Wayne Farms, LLC
Laurel, MS 601-425-4721
Wayne Farms, LLC
Oakwood, GA 678-989-3900
Wayne Farms, LLC
Pendergrass, GA 706-693-2271
Wayne Farms, LLC
Oakwood, GA 800-392-0844
Wong Wing Foods
Montreal, QC 800-361-4820
Zartic Inc
Rome, GA 800-241-0516

Grilled Patties

Chloe Foods Corporation
Brooklyn, NY 718-827-3600

Nuggets

Barber Foods
Portland, ME. 800-577-2595
Bell & Evans
Fredericksburg, PA 717-865-6626
Equity Group
Reidsville, NC. 336-342-6601
Hampton House
Langley, BC 800-665-4355
Health is Wealth Foods
Williamstown, NJ 856-728-1998
Pinty's Premium Foods
St. Catharines, ON 800-263-7223
Redi-Serve Food Company
Fort Atkinson, WI. 920-563-6391
Snow Ball Foods
Fredericksburg, PA 800-360-7669

Patties

Caribbean Food Delights
Tappan, NY 845-398-3000
Grand River Poultry Farm
Paris, ON. 800-853-5454
Royal Caribbean Bakery
Mt Vernon, NY 888-818-0971

Patties Breaded

Meat-O-Mat Corporation
Brooklyn, NY 718-965-7250

Prepared

Cargill Meat Solutions
Timberville, VA 540-896-7041
Caribbean Food Delights
Tappan, NY 845-398-3000
Delphos Poultry Products
Delphos, OH 419-692-5816
Equity Group
Reidsville, NC 336-342-6601

House of Raeford Farms
Raeford, NC 800-888-7539
Lucks Food Decorating Company
Tacoma, WA 206-674-7200
Pasqualichio Brothers
Scranton, PA 800-232-6233
Pilgrim's Pride
Pittsburg, TX. 800-683-1968
Pocono Foods
Mt Bethel, PA 570-897-5000
Snow Ball Foods
Fredericksburg, PA 800-360-7669

Prepared Frozen

Burke Corporation
Nevada, IA 800-654-1152

> Always make it your best® with Burke fully cooked meats. We specialize in Italian sausage, beef, and pork toppings, meatballs, taco meats, shredded meats, pepperoni, bacon, Canadian-style bacon, chicken and beef strips. Additionally, we offer a variety of specialty products: Hand-Pinched Style® brand toppings, chorizo, gyro topping, andouille sausage, and breakfast patties and links.

Caribbean Food Delights
Tappan, NY 845-398-3000
Chang Food Company
Garden Grove, CA 714-265-9990
Chef Hans Gourmet Foods
Monroe, LA. 800-890-4267
ConAgra Frozen Foods Company
Marshall, MO 660-886-3301
ConAgra Poultry Company
Duluth, GA 800-609-6050
Equity Group
Reidsville, NC. 336-342-6601
Gemini Food Industries
Fiskdale, MA 508-347-2800
Hormel Foods Corporation
Austin, MN 800-523-4635
House of Raeford Farms
Raeford, NC 800-888-7539
Meat-O-Mat Corporation
Brooklyn, NY 718-965-7250
Morrison Lamothe
Toronto, ON 416-291-6762
Paisano Food Products
Elk Grove Village, IL 773-237-3773
Perdue Farms
Georgetown, DE 888-737-3832
Pilgrim's Pride
Timberville, VA 540-896-7000
Pilgrim's Pride
Lufkin, TX 936-639-1174
SJH Enterprises
Middleton, WI. 888-745-3845
Snow Ball Foods
Fredericksburg, PA 800-360-7669
Tyson Foods
Springdale, AR 800-643-3410
Wong Wing Foods
Montreal, QC 800-361-4820

Raw

Caribbean Food Delights
Tappan, NY 845-398-3000
Kelly Gourmet Foods
San Francisco, CA 415-648-9200

Cornish Game Hens

Chicago Steaks
Chicago, IL 800-776-4174
Culinary Foods
Chicago, IL 800-621-4049
Tyson Foods
Springdale, AR 800-643-3410
Woods Smoked Meats
Bowling Green, MO 800-458-8426

Duck

Bear Creek Smokehouse
Marshall, TX. 800-950-2327
Chicago Steaks
Chicago, IL 800-776-4174
Crescent Duck Farm
Aquebogue, NY 631-722-8700
Culver Duck
Middlebury, IN 800-825-9225
Maple Leaf Farms
Franksville, WI 262-878-1234

Goose

Schiltz Foods
Sisseton, SD 877-872-4458
Wenk Foods Inc
Madison, SD 605-256-4569

Turkey

Alderfer Bologna
Harleysville, PA 877-253-6328
Amana Meat Shop & Smokehouse
Amana, IA 800-373-6328
Applegate Farms
Bridgewater, NJ 908-725-2768
Bear Creek Smokehouse
Marshall, TX. 800-950-2327
Becker Food Company
Milwaukee, WI 414-964-5353
Boyle Meat Company
Kansas City, MO. 800-821-3626
Bullock's Country Meats
Westminster, MD 410-848-6786
Burgers Smokehouse
California, MO 800-624-5426

Burke Corporation
Nevada, IA 800-654-1152

> Always make it your best® with Burke fully cooked meats. We specialize in Italian sausage, beef, and pork toppings, meatballs, taco meats, shredded meats, pepperoni, bacon, Canadian-style bacon, chicken and beef strips. Additionally, we offer a variety of specialty products: Hand-Pinched Style® brand toppings, chorizo, gyro topping, andouille sausage, and breakfast patties and links.

Buzz Food Service
Charleston, WV 304-925-4781
Campbell Soup Company
Camden, NJ. 800-257-8443
Cargill Meat Solutions
Timberville, VA 540-896-7041
Carl Buddig & Company
Homewood, IL 800-621-0868
Carolina Turkeys
Mt Olive, NC 800-523-4559
Cericola Farms
Bradford, ON 877-939-4449
Charles Poultry Company
Lancaster, PA 717-872-7621
Chef's Requested Foods
Oklahoma City, OK 800-256-0259
Chicago Steaks
Chicago, IL 800-776-4174
Cold Springs Farm
Thamesford, ON 800-265-1978
Couch's Country Style Sausages
Cleveland, OH 216-587-2333
Country Smoked Meats
Bowling Green, OH 800-321-4766
Culinary Foods
Chicago, IL 800-621-4049
Dietz & Watson
Philadelphia, PA 800-333-1974
Draper Valley Farms
Mt Vernon, WA 360-424-7947
E&G Food
Brooklyn, NY 888-525-8855
Farbest Foods
Huntingburg, IN 812-683-4200

Foster Farms
Livingston, CA 800-255-7227
Freezer Queen Foods
Buffalo, NY 800-828-8383
Georges Chicken
Edinburg, VA 540-984-4121
Grabill Country Meats
Grabill, IN 866-333-6328
Gunsberg Corned Beef
Detroit, MI 313-894-6600
Heinkel's Packing Company
Decatur, IL 800-594-2738
Hickory Baked Food
Castle Rock, CO 303-688-2633
Hillbilly Smokehouse
Rogers, AR 479-636-1927
Hollman Foods
Minden, NE 888-926-2879
Hormel Foods Corporation
Beloit, WI 608-365-9501
Hormel Foods Corporation
Austin, MN 800-523-4635
House of Raeford Farms
Raeford, NC 800-888-7539
IBP Foods
Troy, MI 248-588-4710
Iowa Ham Canning
Independence, IA 319-334-7134
Iowa Turkey Products
Marshall, MN 563-864-7676
Jaindl's Turkey Farms
Orefield, PA 800-475-6654
Jennie-O Turkey Store
Willmar, MN 320-235-2622
Kauffman Turkey Farms
Waterman, IL 815-264-3470
Kraft Foodservices
Tampa, FL 800-551-2559
Land O'Frost
Searcy, AR 800-643-5654
Lewis Smoked Meat Company
Chicago, IL 800-648-6328
Lindner Bison
Valencia, CA 866-247-8753
Lionel Lavallee Company
Haverhill, MA 800-343-8292
Locustdale Meat Packing
Locustdale, PA 570-875-1270
Longmont Foods
Longmont, CO 303-776-4803
Mada'n Kosher Foods
Dania, FL 954-925-0077
Marathon Enterprises
Englewood, NJ 201-935-3330
McFarland Foods
Riverton, UT 209-869-6611
Meat-O-Mat Corporation
Brooklyn, NY 718-965-7250
Moretti's Poultry
Columbus, OH 614-486-2333
Moroni Feed Company
West Liberty, IA 435-436-8221
New Braunfels Smokehouse
New Braunfels, TX 800-537-6932
Norbest
Midvale, UT 800-453-5327
North Star Foods
St Charles, MN 507-932-4831
Oak Valley Farm
Voorhees, NJ 856-435-0900
Oak Valley Farms
Watertown, SD 605-886-8025
P & L Poultry
Spokane Valley, WA 509-892-1242
Pasqualichio Brothers
Scranton, PA 800-232-6233
Perdue Farms
Salisbury, MD 800-473-7383
Piggie Park Enterprises
West Columbia, SC 800-628-7423
Pilgrim's Pride
Timberville, VA 540-896-7000
Plainville Farms
Memphis, NY 800-724-0206
Plantation Foods
Waco, TX 800-733-0900
Proliant Meat Ingredients
Ankeny, IA 800-369-2672
Raemica
Running Springs, CA 800-772-6328
Ray's Sausage Company Inc
Cleveland, OH 216-921-8782

Readyfoods
Winnipeg, NB 204-661-6955
Riverside Packers
Drumheller, AB 403-823-2595
Roman Sausage Company
Santa Clara, CA 800-497-7462
Sahlen Packing Company
Buffalo, NY 716-852-8677
Sara Lee Foods
Zeeland, MI 616-875-8131
Schweigert Foods
Albert Lea, MN 507-377-2526
Selwoods Farm Hunting Preserve
Alpine, AL 256-362-7595
Smith Packing Regional Meat
Utica, NY 315-732-5125
Snow Ball Foods
Fredericksburg, PA 800-360-7669
Southeastern Sales
Hixson, TN 423-877-3781
Specialty Foods Group
Newport News, VA 800-238-0020
Standard Beef Company
New Haven, CT 203-787-2164
Sunnydale Meats
Gaffney, SC 864-489-6091
Suzanna's Kitchen
Duluth, GA 800-241-2455
Sweet Sue Kitchens
Athens, AL 256-216-0500
Talisman Foods
Salt Lake City, UT 801-487-6409
Tenn Valley Ham Company
Paris, TN 731-642-9740
Thomas Packing Company
Columbus, GA 800-729-0976
Turkey Store Company
Faribault, MN 507-334-2050
Vantage USA
Chicago, IL 773-247-1086
Vienna Meat Products
Scarborough, ON 800-588-1931
W&G Marketing Company
Ames, IA 515-233-4774
Wampler Foods
Dallas, TX 717-624-2191
Wayco Ham Company
Goldsboro, NC 800-962-2614
West Central Turkeys
Pelican Rapids, MN 218-863-6800
West Liberty Foods
West Liberty, IA 888-511-4500
Wimmer's Meat Products
West Point, NE 800-358-0761
Woods Smoked Meats
Bowling Green, MO 800-458-8426
Zacky Farms
Fresno, CA 800-888-0235

Breast

Alderfer Bologna
Harleysville, PA 877-253-6328
Amana Meat Shop & Smokehouse
Amana, IA 800-373-6328
Berks Packing Company, Inc.
Reading, PA 800-882-3757
Chicago Steaks
Chicago, IL 800-776-4174
Dietz & Watson
Philadelphia, PA 800-333-1974
Grote & Weigel
Bloomfield, CT 860-242-8528
Hickory Baked Food
Castle Rock, CO 303-688-2633
IBP Foods
Troy, MI 248-588-4710
Rose Packing Company
South Barrington, IL 800-323-7363
Smith Packing Regional Meat
Utica, NY 315-732-5125
Wampler Foods
Dallas, TX 717-624-2191
Woods Smoked Meats
Bowling Green, MO 800-458-8426

Canned

Grabill Country Meats
Grabill, IN 866-333-6328
Hormel Foods Corporation
Beloit, WI 608-365-9501

Sweet Sue Kitchens
Athens, AL 256-216-0500

Fillets

Carolina Turkeys
Mt Olive, NC 800-523-4559

Fresh

Becker Food Company
Milwaukee, WI 414-964-5353
Blue Ridge Poultry
Athens, GA 706-546-6767
Carolina Turkeys
Mt Olive, NC 800-523-4559
Cooper Farms
Van Wert, OH 419-238-4056
Georges Chicken
Edinburg, VA 540-984-4121
Moroni Feed Company
West Liberty, IA 435-436-8221
Perdue Farms
Plymouth, NC 252-793-9119
Perdue Farms
Bridgewater, VA 540-828-2581
Perdue Farms
Salisbury, MD 800-473-7383
Perdue Farms
Washington, IN 800-654-6972
Perdue Farms
Kenly, NC 919-284-2033
Pilgrim's Pride
Broadway, VA 540-896-0607
Smith Packing Regional Meat
Utica, NY 315-732-5125
Turkey Store Company
Faribault, MN 507-334-2050

Frozen

Burke Corporation
Nevada, IA 800-654-1152

Always make it your best® with Burke fully
cooked meats. We specialize in Italian sausage,
beef, and pork toppings, meatballs, taco meats,
shredded meats, pepperoni, bacon, Canadian-style bacon, chicken and beef strips. Additionally, we offer a variety of specialty products:
Hand-Pinched Style® brand toppings, chorizo,
gyro topping, andouille sausage, and breakfast
patties and links.

North Side Foods Corporation
Arnold, PA 800-486-2201

Ground

Carolina Turkeys
Mt Olive, NC 800-523-4559

Leg

Karn Meats
Columbus, OH 800-221-9585
Wampler Foods
Dallas, TX 717-624-2191

Raw

Carl Buddig & Company
Homewood, IL 800-621-0868
Foster Farms
Creswell, OR 541-895-2161
Wayne Farms, LLC
Jack, AL 334-897-3435

Sausage

Golden Platter Foods
Newark, NJ 973-242-0291
Hahn Brothers
Westminster, MD 800-227-7675
Miller's Stratford Provision Company
Southport, CT 203-375-1598

Whole Frozen

Hickory Baked Food
Castle Rock, CO 303-688-2633
Wampler Foods
Dallas, TX. 717-624-2191

Smoked, Cured & Deli Meats

Alphin Brothers
Dunn, NC 800-672-4502
Applegate Farms
Bridgewater, NJ 908-725-2768
Blue Grass Quality Meat
Covington, KY 859-331-7100
Boones Abattoir
Bardstown, KY 502-348-3668
Boyd Sausage Company
Washington, IA 319-653-5715
Braham Food Locker Service
Braham, MN 320-396-2636

Burke Corporation
Nevada, IA 800-654-1152

Always make it your best® with Burke fully cooked meats. We specialize in Italian sausage, beef, and pork toppings, meatballs, taco meats, shredded meats, pepperoni, bacon, Canadian-style bacon, chicken and beef strips. Additionally, we offer a variety of specialty products: Hand-Pinched Style® brand toppings, chorizo, gyro topping, andouille sausage, and breakfast patties and links.

Caddo Packing Company
Marshall, TX. 903-935-2211
Campbell Soup Company
Camden, NJ .800-257-8443
Castleberry's Meats
Atlanta, GA. .404-873-1804
Castleberry/Snow Brands
Augusta, GA .800-241-3520
Chicopee Provision Company
Chicopee, MA. 800-924-6328
Chip Steak & Provision Company
Mankato, MN 507-388-6277
Circle V Meat Company
Spanish Fork, UT 801-798-3081
Cloverdale Foods Company
Mandan, ND .800-669-9511
Columbia Packing Company
Dallas, TX. 800-460-8171
ConAgra Beef Company
Hyrum, UT 435-245-6456
Continental Deli Foods
Cherokee, IA. 712-225-5161
Covemaker Packing Company
Moline, IL 309-764-1480
Crawford Sausage Company
Chicago, IL 866-653-2479
Curtis Packing Company
Greensboro, NC 336-275-7684
Cusack Wholesale Meat Company
Oklahoma City, OK 800-241-6328
Dallas Dressed Beef
Dallas, TX. 214-638-0142
Dankworth Packing Company
Ballinger, TX 325-365-3552
David Berg & Company
Chicago, IL 773-489-4711
Double Wrap Cup & Container
Buffalo Grove, IL 312-337-0072
Fredericksburg Lockers/OPA's Smoke
Fredericksburg, TX. 800-543-6750
Fricks Meat Products
Washington, MO. 800-241-2209
Gary's Frozen Foods
Lubbock, TX. 806-745-1933
Gunsberg Corned Beef
Detroit, MI 313-894-6600
H&B Packing Company
Waco, TX 254-752-2506
Harrington's of Vermont
Richmond, VT. 802-434-7500

Heringer Meats
Covington, KY 859-291-2000
Humboldt Sausage Company
Humboldt, IA 515-332-4121
Hummel Brothers
New Haven, CT 800-828-8978
Independent Meat Company
Twin Falls, ID. 208-733-0980
J&B Sausage Company
Waelder, TX .830-788-7511
Kretschmar
Don Mills, ON 800-561-4532
Lampasas Locker Plant
Lampasas, TX 512-556-5121
Lay Packing Company
Knoxville, TN. 865-922-4320
Little Rhody Brand Frankfurts
Johnston, RI .401-831-0815
Lords Sausage & Country Ham
Dexter, GA 800-342-6002
Mada'n Kosher Foods
Dania, FL 954-925-0077
Matthiesen's Deer & Custom Processing
De Witt, IA 563-659-8409
Meat Shop
Cape Girardeau, MO. 800-791-5104
Mertz Sausage Company
San Antonio, TX. 210-433-3263
Mike's Prime Cut Meats
Brigham City, UT 435-723-7333
Miller's Meat Market
Red Bud, IL .618-282-3334
Miller's Stratford Provision Company
Southport, CT 203-375-1598
Moo & Oink
Chicago, IL 773-493-2755
Murphy House
Louisburg, NC 919-496-4173
Neese Country Sausage
Greensboro, NC 800-632-1010
New Packing Company
Chicago, IL 312-666-1314
Patrick Cudahy
Cudahy, WI. .800-486-6900
Peer Foods Inc
Chicago, IL 800-365-5644
Plumrose
East Brunswick, NJ. 800-526-4909
Plumrose USA
East Brunswick, NJ. 732-257-6600
R.M. Felts Packing Company
Ivor, VA 888-300-0971
S. Abuin Packing
Elizabeth, NJ. 908-354-2674
Sara Lee Corporation
Downers Grove, IL 630-598-8100
Sara Lee Foods
Neenah, WI. .800-558-8440
Smithfield Foods
Clinton, NC .910-592-2104
Stevens Sausage Company
Smithfield, NC 800-338-0561
Stonies Sausage Shop Inc
Perryville, MO 888-546-2540
Terrell Meats
Delta, UT. 435-864-2600
Thomas Packing Company
Columbus, GA 800-729-0976
Thumann's
Carlstadt, NJ 201-935-3636
Tomahawk Farms Meat Packers
Dunn, NC 910-892-3155
Troy Frozen Food
Troy, IL 618-667-6332
Vermilion Packers
Vermilion, AB. 780-853-4622
Vienna Sausage Company
Chicago, IL 800-326-6652
Webster City Custom Meats
Webster City, IA 888-786-3287
Yoakum Packing Company
Yoakum, TX .361-293-3541

Bacon

Alderfer Bologna
Harleysville, PA 877-253-6328
Aliments Prince Foods
Anjou, QC. 800-361-3898
Amana Meat Shop & Smokehouse
Amana, IA. 800-373-6328

American Foods Group
Green Bay, WI. 920-437-6330
Applegate Farms
Bridgewater, NJ 908-725-2768
Bacon America
Drummondville, QC. 819-475-3030
Bear Creek Smokehouse
Marshall, TX 800-950-2327
Big Apple Produce & Seafood Market
Pocomoke City, MD 410-957-1151
Blakely Freezer Locker
Thomasville, GA. 229-723-3622
Broadbent's B&B Foods
Kuttawa, KY 800-841-2202

Burke Corporation
Nevada, IA 800-654-1152

Always make it your best® with Burke fully cooked meats. We specialize in Italian sausage, beef, and pork toppings, meatballs, taco meats, shredded meats, pepperoni, bacon, Canadian-style bacon, chicken and beef strips. Additionally, we offer a variety of specialty products: Hand-Pinched Style® brand toppings, chorizo, gyro topping, andouille sausage, and breakfast patties and links.

Chef's Requested Foods
Oklahoma City, OK 800-256-0259
Chisesi Brothers Meat Packing Company
New Orleans, LA 504-822-3550
Cloverdale Foods Company
Mandan, ND .800-669-9511
Community Market & Deli
Lindstrom, MN 651-257-1128
Cropp Cooperative-Organic Valley
La Farge, WI. 888-444-6455
D'Artagnan
Newark, NJ .800-327-8246
Farmland Foods
Kansas City, MO. 888-327-6526
Father's Country Hams
Bremen, KY .270-525-3554
Hahn Brothers
Westminster, MD 800-227-7675
Hickory Baked Food
Castle Rock, CO 303-688-2633
Hormel Foods Corporation
Fremont, NE .402-721-2300
Maple Leaf Consumer Foods
Fair Oaks, CA 800-999-7603
Niemuth's Steak & Chop Shop
Waupaca, WI. 715-258-2666
Patrick Cudahy
Cudahy, WI. .800-486-6900
R.L. Zeigler Company
Tuscaloosa, AL 800-392-6328
Rinehart Meat Processing
Branson, MO. 417-334-2044
Rose Packing Company
South Barrington, IL. 800-323-7363
Sara Lee Foods
Neenah, WI. .800-558-8440
Scott Hams
Greenville, KY 800-318-1353
Seaboard Foods
Shawnee Mission, KS. 800-262-7907
Simeus Foods Internatio nal
Mansfield, TX. 888-772-3663
Sugar Creek Packing
Washington Ct Hs, OH 800-848-8205
Sunnydale Meats
Gaffney, SC. .864-489-6091
Sunset Farm Foods
Valdosta, GA 800-882-1121
Thomas Packing Company
Columbus, GA 800-729-0976
V.W. Joyner & Company
Smithfield, VA 757-357-2161
Woods Smoked Meats
Bowling Green, MO 800-458-8426

Bits Imitation

American Key Food Products
Closter, NJ 800-767-0237
Chr Hansen
Elyria, OH 800-558-0802
CHS, Inc.
Inner Grove Heights, MN 800-232-3639
Con Yeager Spice Company
Zelienople, PA 800-222-2460
Fairbury Food Products
Fairbury, NE 402-729-3379
Feaster Foods
Omaha, NE 800-228-6098
Schiff Food Products
North Bergen, NJ 201-861-2503
Tova Industries
Louisville, KY 888-532-8682
Westin
Omaha, NE 800-228-6098

Bits Real

Burke Corporation
Nevada, IA 800-654-1152

Always make it your best® with Burke fully
cooked meats. We specialize in Italian sausage,
beef, and pork toppings, meatballs, taco meats,
shredded meats, pepperoni, bacon, Canadian-style bacon, chicken and beef strips. Additionally, we offer a variety of specialty products:
Hand-Pinched Style® brand toppings, chorizo,
gyro topping, andouille sausage, and breakfast
patties and links.

Con Yeager Spice Company
Zelienople, PA 800-222-2460
Sugar Creek Packing
Washington Ct Hs, OH 800-848-8205
Tova Industries
Louisville, KY 888-532-8682

Canadian Style

Al & John's Glen Rock Ham
Paterson, NJ 800-969-4990
Burgers Smokehouse
California, MO 800-624-5426

Burke Corporation
Nevada, IA 800-654-1152

Always make it your best® with Burke fully
cooked meats. We specialize in Italian sausage,
beef, and pork toppings, meatballs, taco meats,
shredded meats, pepperoni, bacon, Canadian-style bacon, chicken and beef strips. Additionally, we offer a variety of specialty products:
Hand-Pinched Style® brand toppings, chorizo,
gyro topping, andouille sausage, and breakfast
patties and links.

Calihan Pork Processing
Peoria, IL 309-674-9175
Country Smoked Meats
Bowling Green, OH 800-321-4766
Foodbrands America
Oklahoma City, OK 405-290-4000
Hickory Baked Food
Castle Rock, CO 303-688-2633
Hormel Foods Corporation
Austin, MN 800-523-4635
Peer Foods Inc
Chicago, IL 800-365-5644
Pioneer Packing Company
Bowling Green, OH 419-352-5283

Rose Packing Company
South Barrington, IL 800-323-7363

Slices

ConAgra Foods/Eckrich
Omaha, NE 800-327-4424
Country Smoked Meats
Bowling Green, OH 800-321-4766
Greenwood Packing Plant
Greenwood, SC 864-229-5611
IBP Foods
Troy, MI 248-588-4710
Kunzler/Juniata Packing Company
Tyrone, PA 814-684-2270
Webster City Custom Meats
Webster City, IA 888-786-3287

Slices Thick

Healthy Oven
Croton on Hudson, NY 914-271-5458
Westbrae Natural Foods
Garden City, NY 800-434-4246

Beef Jerky

Alderfer Bologna
Harleysville, PA 877-253-6328
Alewel's Country Meats
Warrensburg, MO 800-353-8553
Amana Meat Shop & Smokehouse
Amana, IA 800-373-6328
Baier's Sausage & Meats
Red Deer, AB 403-346-1535
Big Chief Meat Snacks
Calgary, AB 403-264-2641
Boyd Sausage Company
Washington, IA 319-653-5715
Cattaneo Brothers
San Luis Obispo, CA 800-243-8537
Chickasaw Trading Company
Denver City, TX 800-848-3515
ConAgra Snack Foods
San Jose, CA 408-436-0329
David Berg & Company
Chicago, IL 773-489-4711
Debbie D's Jerky & Sausage
Tillamook, OR 503-842-2622
E.W. Knauss & Son
Quakertown, PA 800-648-4220
Eastside Deli Supply
Lansing, MI 800-349-6694
Eiserman Meats
Slave Lake, AB 780-849-5507
Enjoy Foods International
Fontana, CA 909-823-2228
F&Y Enterprises
Naperville, IL 630-637-8519
High Country Snack Foods
Lincoln, MT 800-433-3916
Hsin Tung Yang Foods Co.
S San Francisco, CA 650-589-6789
Ittels Meats
Howard Lake, MN 320-543-2285
J&B Sausage Company
Waelder, TX 830-788-7511
Kershenstine Beef Jerky
Eupora, MS 662-258-2049
King B Meat Snacks
Minong, WI 800-346-6896
King Nut Company
Cleveland, OH 800-860-5464
Lone Star Beef Jerky Company
Lubbock, TX 806-762-8833
Longview Meat & Merchandise
Longview, AB 403-558-3706
Mike's Meats
Eitzen, MN 507-495-3336
Nestle Pizza
Medford, WI 715-748-5550
New Braunfels Smokehouse
New Braunfels, TX 800-537-6932
Norpaco
New Britain, CT 800-252-0222
Palmer Packing Company
Tremonton, UT 435-257-5329
Peoples Sausage Company
Los Angeles, CA 213-627-8633
Red Oak Farms
Red Oak, IA 712-623-9224
Rinehart Meat Processing
Branson, MO 417-334-2044

Rudolph Foods
Dallas, TX 214-638-2204
Schaller's Packers
Cassville, NY 315-822-3924
Smokey Farm Meats
Carbon, AB 403-272-6587
Terrell Meats
Delta, UT 435-864-2600
Toxic Tommy's Beef Jerky & Spices
Wadsworth, OH 866-448-6942
WA Bean & Sons
Bangor, ME 800-649-1958
Weaver Nut Company
Ephrata, PA 717-738-3781
Western Beef Jerky
Edmonton, AB 780-469-4817
Wild Bill's Foods
Lancaster, PA 800-848-3236
Willies Smoke House
Harrisville, PA 800-742-4184
Wimmer's Meat Products
West Point, NE 800-358-0761
Woods Smoked Meats
Bowling Green, MO 800-458-8426

Bologna

Alderfer Bologna
Harleysville, PA 877-253-6328
Atlantic Pork & Provisions
Brooklyn, NY 800-245-3536
Boeckman JJ Wholesale Meats
Dayton, OH 937-222-4679
Boesl Packing Company
Baltimore, MD 410-675-1071
Boyd Sausage Company
Washington, IA 319-653-5715
C. Roy Meat Products
Brockway, MI 810-387-3957
Cargill Meat Solutions
Timberville, VA 540-896-7041
Carolina Packers
Smithfield, NC 800-682-7675
Chisesi Brothers Meat Packing Company
New Orleans, LA 504-822-3550
Curtis Packing Company
Greensboro, NC 336-275-7684
Farmland Foods
Kansas City, MO 888-327-6526
Foodbrands America
Oklahoma City, OK 405-290-4000
Frank Wardynski & Sons
Buffalo, NY 716-854-6083
Greenwood Packing Plant
Greenwood, SC 864-229-5611
Groff Meats
Elizabethtown, PA 717-367-1246
Grote & Weigel
Bloomfield, CT 860-242-8528
Hazle Park Packing Company
West Hazleton, PA 800-238-4331
Heritage Cheese House
Heuvelton, NY 315-344-2216
Hofmann Sausage Company
Syracuse, NY 800-724-8410
Ito Cariani Sausage Company
Hayward, CA 510-887-0882
Kayem Foods
Chelsea, MA 800-426-6100
Kessler's, Inc
Lemoyne, PA 800-382-1328
Kilgus Meats
Toledo, OH 419-472-9721
Kitts Meat Processing
Dedham, IA 712-683-5622
Larsen Packers
Burwick, NS 902-538-8060
Locustdale Meat Packing
Locustdale, PA 570-875-1270
Miller's Stratford Provision Company
Southport, CT 203-375-1598
Palmyra Bologna
Palmyra, PA 717-838-6336
Pfeffer's Country Market
Sauk Centre, MN 320-352-3095
Raemica
Running Springs, CA 800-772-6328
Rego's Purity Foods
Honolulu, HI 808-947-9005
Rendulic Packing
McKeesport, PA 412-678-9541

Sara Lee Corporation
Downers Grove, IL 630-598-8100
Schaller's Packers
Cassville, NY 315-822-3924
Sechrist Brothers
Dallastown, PA 717-244-2975
Sheinman Provision Company
Philadelphia, PA 215-473-7065
Silver Star Meats
Mc Kees Rocks, PA 412-771-5539
Spring Grove Foods
Miamisburg, OH 937-866-4311
Stawnichy Holdings
Mundare, AB 888-764-7646
Storer Meat Company
Cleveland, OH 800-355-7537
Sunset Farm Foods
Valdosta, GA 800-882-1121
Tennessee Valley PackingCompany
Columbia, TN 931-388-2623
Thumann's
Carlstadt, NJ 201-935-3636
Troy Frozen Food
Troy, IL .618-667-6332
Troyers Trail Bologna
Dundee, OH 877-893-2414
Wampler Foods
Dallas, TX 717-624-2191
Weyhaupt Brothers Packing
Belleville, IL 618-233-0452
Wimmer's Meat Products
West Point, NE 800-358-0761

Bratwurst

Bob Evans Farms
Hillsdale, MI 517-437-3349
Country Smoked Meats
Bowling Green, OH 800-321-4766
David Berg & Company
Chicago, IL 773-489-4711
Elmwood Lockers
Elmwood, IL 309-742-8929
Fontanini Italian Meats & Sausages
Chicago, IL 800-331-6328
Kilgus Meats
Toledo, OH 419-472-9721
Koegel Meats
Flint, MI 810-238-3685
Miller's Stratford Provision Company
Southport, CT 203-375-1598
Penn Valley Farms
Gainesville, GA 773-685-9929
Purnell's Old Folks Sausage Company
Simpsonville, KY 800-626-1512
Raemica
Running Springs, CA 800-772-6328
S.W. Meat & Provision Company
Phoenix, AZ 602-275-2000
Saugy
Providence, RI 866-467-2849
Schaller's Packers
Cassville, NY 315-822-3924
Silver Star Meats
Mc Kees Rocks, PA 412-771-5539
Smolich Brothers
Crest Hill, IL 815-727-2144
Sunset Farm Foods
Valdosta, GA 800-882-1121
Waco Beef & Pork Processors
Waco, TX 254-772-4669
Wimmer's Meat Products
West Point, NE 800-358-0761
Woods Smoked Meats
Bowling Green, MO 800-458-8426

Corned Beef

Alderfer Bologna
Harleysville, PA 877-253-6328
American Food Traders
Miami, FL 305-670-6250
Art's Tamales
Metamora, IL 309-367-2850
Best Provision Company, Inc.
Newark, NJ 800-631-4466
Burnett & Son Meat Company
Monrovia, CA 626-357-2165
Carando Gourmet Frozen Foods
Springfield, MA 413-730-4205
Charlie's Pride Meats
Los Angeles, CA. 877-866-0982

Chicopee Provision Company
Chicopee, MA 800-924-6328
Curly's Foods
Edina, MN 612-920-3400
D'Artagnan
Newark, NJ 800-327-8246
David Berg & Company
Chicago, IL 773-489-4711
Dutterer's Home Food Service
Baltimore, MD 410-298-3663
Gunsberg Corned Beef
Detroit, MI 313-894-6600
Hahn Brothers
Westminster, MD 800-227-7675
Henry J Meat Specialties
Chicago, IL 800-242-1314
Hormel Foods Corporation
Austin, MN 800-523-4635
International Food Packers Corporation
Miami, FL 305-669-1662
Kelly Foods
Jackson, TN 731-424-2255
Kelly Kornbeef Company
Chicago, IL 773-588-2882
Levonian Brothers
Troy, NY 518-274-3610
Lower Foods
Richmond, UT. 435-258-2449
Marathon Enterprises
Englewood, NJ 201-935-3330
Mosey's Inc
Bloomfield, CT. 860-243-1725
Nossack Fine Meats
Red Deer, AB 403-346-5006
Otto W Liebold & Company
Flint, MI 800-999-6328
Peer Foods Inc
Chicago, IL 800-365-5644
Plumrose USA
East Brunswick, NJ. 732-257-6600
Sara Lee Corporation
Downers Grove, IL. 630-598-8100
Saval Foods
Elkridge, MD 800-527-2825
Sheinman Provision Company
Philadelphia, PA 215-473-7065
Stawnichy Holdings
Mundare, AB 888-764-7646
Thompson Packers
Slidell, LA. 800-989-6328
Tupman-Thurlow Company
Deerfield Beach, FL 954-596-9989
Vienna Meat Products
Scarborough, ON 800-588-1931

Deli Foods

Advance Food Brokers
West Bloomfield, MI 248-851-9045
American Food Traders
Miami, FL 305-670-6250
ASK Foods
Palmyra, PA. 800-879-4275
Bagels By Bell
Brooklyn, NY 718-272-2780
Billingsgate Fish Company
Calgary, AB. 403-571-7700
Bloomfield Bakers
Los Alamitos, CA 800-594-4111
Boeckman JJ Wholesale Meats
Dayton, OH. 937-222-4679
Bottomline Foods
Pembroke Pines, FL 954-843-0562
Bouma Meats
Provost, AB. 780-753-2092
Boyd Sausage Company
Washington, IA 319-653-5715
Bridgford Foods Corpora tion
Anaheim, CA 800-527-2105
Carl Buddig & Company
Homewood, IL 800-621-0868
Carolina Packers
Smithfield, NC 800-682-7675
Chalmette Packing Company
Covington, LA 504-271-6241
Charlie's Pride Meats
Los Angeles, CA 877-866-0982
Chicago 58 Food Products
Toronto, ON 416-603-4244
Chloe Foods Corporation
Brooklyn, NY 718-827-3600

Cibao Meat Product
Bronx, NY. 718-993-5072
Continental Deli Foods
Cherokee, IA. 712-225-5161
Corfu Foods
Bensenville, IL 630-595-2510
Cumberland Gap Provision Company
Middlesboro, KY 800-331-7154
Curtis Packing Company
Greensboro, NC 336-275-7684
Czimer's Game & Sea Foods
Homer Glen, IL 708-301-0500
Dairy Fresh Foods
Taylor, MI 313-295-6300
Dan's Prize
Gainesville, GA 800-233-5845
Danner Salads
Peoria, IL. 309-691-0289
David Berg & Company
Chicago, IL 773-489-4711
DNO
Columbus, OH 800-686-2366
Donut Tree & Deli
Anchorage, AK 907-274-6969
Durrett Cheese Sales
Manchester, TN. 800-209-6792
Earth Island Natural Foods
Canoga Park, CA 818-725-2820
Eastside Deli Supply
Lansing, MI. 800-349-6694
Farmland Foods
Carroll, IA 712-792-1660
Foodmark
Wellesley, MA. 781-237-7088
Freda Quality Meats
Philadelphia, PA 800-443-7332
Gilardi Foods
Sidney, OH 937-498-4511
Global Food Industries
Townville, SC 800-225-4152
Gwaltney of Smithfield
Portsmouth, VA. 757-465-0666
Gwaltney of Smithfield
Smithfield, VA 800-888-7521
Harold M. Lincoln Company
Toledo, OH 800-345-4911
Heinkel's Packing Company
Decatur, IL 800-594-2738
HFI Foods
Redmond, WA. 425-883-1320
Hoekstra Meat Company
Kalamazoo, MI 616-321-0797
Home Made Brand Foods Company
Newburyport, MA. 978-462-3663
Homestyle Foods Company
Hamtramck, MI 313-874-3250
Hormel Foods Corporation
Houston, TX 281-492-1770
Hormel Foods Corporation
Oklahoma City, OK 405-843-5643
Hormel Foods Corporation
Columbia, MD 410-290-1855
Hormel Foods Corporation
Urbandale, IA 515-276-8872
Hormel Foods Corporation
Charlotte, NC 704-527-4388
Hormel Foods Corporation
Austin, MN 800-523-4635
Hormel Foods Corporation
Lisle, IL. 800-533-2000
Hormel Foods Corporation
Lubbock, TX. 806-796-3630
Hormel Foods Corporation
Cordova, TN 901-753-4282
Hormel Foods Corporation
Lebanon, NJ 908-236-7009
Hormel Foods Corporation
Pleasanton, CA 925-225-9349
Humboldt Sausage Company
Humboldt, IA 515-332-4121
Hummel Brothers
New Haven, CT 800-828-8978
IBP Foods
Grand Rapids, MI 616-774-0711
Kay Foods Company
Ionia, MI 616-527-0120
Kayem Foods
Chelsea, MA 800-426-6100
Kelly Foods
Jackson, TN 731-424-2255
Kelly Kornbeef Company
Chicago, IL 773-588-2882

Kitts Meat Processing
Dedham, IA 712-683-5622
Klein's Kosher Pickles
Phoenix, AZ 602-269-2072
Landshire
Belleville, IL 618-398-8122
Lower Foods
Richmond, UT 435-258-2449
Manda Fine Meats
Baton Rouge, LA 225-344-7636
Marshallville Packing Company
Marshallville, OH 330-855-2871
McClane Distribution Center
Fredericksburg, VA 540-374-2000
Meadows Country Products
Hollidaysburg, PA 888-499-1001
Miller's Stratford Provision Company
Southport, CT 203-375-1598
Murphy House
Louisburg, NC 919-496-4173
Norbest
Midvale, UT 800-453-5327
Ohio Packing Company
Columbus, OH 800-282-6403
Orval Kent Food Company
Wheeling, IL 847-459-9000
Palmyra Bologna
Palmyra, PA 717-838-6336
Plumrose USA
East Brunswick, NJ 732-257-6600
Promiseland Meat PackingCompany
Madill, OK 580-795-3567
Randy's Frozen Meats
Faribault, MN 800-354-7177
Real Kosher Sausage Company
Newark, NJ 973-690-5394
Ruskin Packaging
Miami, FL 305-324-1529
Russer Foods
Buffalo, NY. 800-828-7021
Schneider Foods
Kitchener, ON 519-741-5000
Seneca Foods
Clyman, WI. 920-696-3331
Siena Foods
Toronto, ON 800-465-0422
Silver Star Meats
Mc Kees Rocks, PA 412-771-5539
SMG
Crestview Hills, KY 757-952-1100
Smith Provision Company
Erie, PA 800-334-9151
Smithfield Foods
Clinton, NC 910-592-2104
Spring Glen Fresh Foods
Ephrata, PA 800-641-2853
Spring Grove Foods
Miamisburg, OH 937-866-4311
Springfield Smoked Fish Company
Springfield, MA 800-327-3412
Stevens Sausage Company
Smithfield, NC 800-338-0561
Swift & Company
Greeley, CO. 970-324-2180
Temptee Specialty Foods
Denver, CO 800-842-1233
Trebon European Specialties
South Hackensack, NJ 800-899-4332
Vegi-Deli
San Rafael, CA 888-473-3667
Weiss Provisions
Pittsburgh, PA 800-458-6328
Weyhaupt Brothers Packing
Belleville, IL. 618-233-0452

Deli Meats

Alderfer Bologna
Harleysville, PA 877-253-6328
Alle Processing Corporation
Flushing, NY. 800-245-5620
American Food Traders
Miami, FL. 305-670-6250
Armour
Omaha, NE 402-453-3766
Atlantic Pork & Provisions
Brooklyn, NY 800-245-3536
Atlantic Premium Brands
Northbrook, IL 847-412-6200
Bar-S Foods Company
Phoenix, AZ 602-264-7272

Berks Packing Company, Inc.
Reading, PA 800-882-3757
Boar's Head Provisions Company
Sarasota, FL 888-884-2627
Boeckman JJ Wholesale Meats
Dayton, OH 937-222-4679
Boesl Packing Company
Baltimore, MD 410-675-1071
Bridgford Foods Corpora tion
Anaheim, CA 800-527-2105
Broadaway Ham Company
Jonesboro, AR. 870-932-6688

Burke Corporation
Nevada, IA 800-654-1152

Always make it your best® with Burke fully cooked meats. We specialize in Italian sausage, beef, and pork toppings, meatballs, taco meats, shredded meats, pepperoni, bacon, Canadian-style bacon, chicken and beef strips. Additionally, we offer a variety of specialty products: Hand-Pinched Style® brand toppings, chorizo, gyro topping, andouille sausage, and breakfast patties and links.

C. Roy Meat Products
Brockway, MI 810-387-3957
Cargill Meat Solutions
Timberville, VA 540-896-7041
Carl Buddig & Company
Homewood, IL 800-621-0868
Carolina Packers
Smithfield, NC 800-682-7675
Chalmette Packing Company
Covington, LA 504-271-6241
Charlie's Country Sausage
Minot, ND 701-838-6302
Charlie's Pride Meats
Los Angeles, CA. 877-866-0982
Citterio USA Corporation
Freeland, PA 800-435-8888
ConAgra Foods Inc
Omaha, NE 402-240-4000
Continental Deli Foods
Cherokee, IA 712-225-5161
Country Smoked Meats
Bowling Green, OH 800-321-4766
Curtis Packing Company
Greensboro, NC 336-275-7684
David Berg & Company
Chicago, IL 773-489-4711
Dietz & Watson
Philadelphia, PA 800-333-1974
Dohar Meats
Cleveland, OH 216-241-4197
Dutterer's Home Food Service
Baltimore, MD 410-298-3663
Egon Binkert Meat Products
Baltimore, MD 410-687-5959
Farmland Foods
Carroll, IA 712-792-1660
Foodbrands America
Oklahoma City, OK 405-290-4000
Frank Wardynski & Sons
Buffalo, NY. 716-854-6083
Freda Quality Meats
Philadelphia, PA 800-443-7332
Fried Provisions Company
Evans City, PA 724-538-3160
Gaiser's European Style Provisions
Union, NJ 908-206-9822
Galileo Foods
San Lorenzo, CA. 510-276-1300
Greenwood Packing Plant
Greenwood, SC 864-229-5611
Groff Meats
Elizabethtown, PA. 717-367-1246
Gunsberg Corned Beef
Detroit, MI 313-894-6600
Hansel 'N Gretel
Flushing, NY. 718-326-0041
Hazle Park Packing Company
West Hazleton, PA 800-238-4331

Heinkel's Packing Company
Decatur, IL 800-594-2738
Henry J Meat Specialties
Chicago, IL 800-242-1314
Humboldt Sausage Company
Humboldt, IA 515-332-4121
Hummel Brothers
New Haven, CT 800-828-8978
IBP Foods
Troy, MI 248-588-4710
Kelly Foods
Jackson, TN 731-424-2255
Kelly Kornbeef Company
Chicago, IL 773-588-2882
Kessler's, Inc
Lemoyne, PA. 800-382-1328
Kilgus Meats
Toledo, OH 419-472-9721
Kitts Meat Processing
Dedham, IA. 712-683-5622
Kunzler/Juniata Packing Company
Tyrone, PA. 814-684-2270
Land O'Frost
Searcy, AR 800-643-5654
Lengerich Meats
Zanesville, IN 260-638-4123
Leona Meat Plant
Troy, PA. 570-297-3574
Levonian Brothers
Troy, NY 518-274-3610
Locustdale Meat Packing
Locustdale, PA 570-875-1270
Lowell Provision Company
Lowell, MA. 978-454-5603
Lower Foods
Richmond, UT. 435-258-2449
Lykes Meat Group
Plant City, FL 813-752-1102
Manda Fine Meats
Baton Rouge, LA 225-344-7636
Marathon Enterprises
Englewood, NJ 201-935-3330
Marshallville Packing Company
Marshallville, OH 330-855-2871
Martin Rosol's
New Britain, CT 860-223-2707
Miller's Stratford Provision Company
Southport, CT 203-375-1598
Mishler Packing Company
Lagrange, IN 260-768-4156
Mosey's Inc
Bloomfield, CT 860-243-1725
Murphy House
Louisburg, NC 919-496-4173
O'Brien & Company
Bellevue, NE 800-433-7567
Otto W Liebold & Company
Flint, MI 800-999-6328
Parma Sausage Products
Pittsburgh, PA 877-294-4207
Penn Valley Farms
Gainesville, GA 773-685-9929
Pfeffer's Country Market
Sauk Centre, MN 320-352-3095
Pilgrim's Pride
Timberville, VA 540-896-7000
Plumrose
East Brunswick, NJ 800-526-4909
Plumrose USA
East Brunswick, NJ. 732-257-6600
Queen City Sausage
Cincinnati, OH 877-544-5588
R.L. Zeigler Company
Tuscaloosa, AL. 800-392-6328
Raemica
Running Springs, CA 800-772-6328
Rego's Purity Foods
Honolulu, HI 808-947-9005
Rendulic Packing
McKeesport, PA 412-678-9541
Robinsons Sausage Company
London, KY 606-864-2914
Roman Packing Company
Norfolk, NE. 800-373-5990
Russer Foods
Buffalo, NY. 800-828-7021
Ryley Sausage
Ryley, AB 780-663-3990
Saag's Products
San Leandro, CA. 800-352-7224
Sara Lee Corporation
Downers Grove, IL 630-598-8100

Sara Lee Foods
Zeeland, MI .616-875-8131
Sara Lee Foods
Cincinnati, OH 800-351-7111
Sausage Shoppe
Cleveland, OH 216-351-5213
Saval Foods
Elkridge, MD 800-527-2825
Schaller & Weber
Long Island City, NY 800-847-4115
Schaller's Packers
Cassville, NY 315-822-3924
Sculli Brothers
Philadelphia, PA 215-336-1223
Sechrist Brothers
Dallastown, PA 717-244-2975
Seitz Foods
Saint Joseph, MO 800-383-3128
Sheinman Provision Company
Philadelphia, PA 215-473-7065
Shofar Kosher Foods
Linden, NJ. .888-874-6327
Smith Packing Regional Meat
Utica, NY 315-732-5125
Smith Provision Company
Erie, PA. 800-334-9151
Smithfield Foods
Clinton, NC .910-592-2104
Snow Ball Foods
Fredericksburg, PA 800-360-7669
Spring Grove Foods
Miamisburg, OH 937-866-4311
Standard Beef Company
New Haven, CT 203-787-2164
Stawnichy Holdings
Mundare, AB 888-764-7646
Stevens Sausage Company
Smithfield, NC 800-338-0561
Stonies Sausage Shop Inc
Perryville, MO 888-546-2540
Storer Meat Company
Cleveland, OH 800-355-7537
Swift & Company
Greeley, CO. 970-324-2180
Temptee Specialty Foods
Denver, CO. .800-842-1233
Tennessee Valley PackingCompany
Columbia, TN 931-388-2623
Troy Frozen Food
Troy, IL 618-667-6332
Troyers Trail Bologna
Dundee, OH .877-893-2414
Tupman-Thurlow Company
Deerfield Beach, FL 954-596-9989
United Provision Meat Company
Columbus, OH 614-252-1126
Upstate Farms Cooperative
Buffalo, NY. 716-892-3156
V.W. Joyner & Company
Smithfield, VA 757-357-2161
Vienna Meat Products
Scarborough, ON 800-588-1931
Wampler Foods
Dallas, TX 717-624-2191
Warren & Son Meat Processing
Whipple, OH. 740-585-2421
Weyhaupt Brothers Packing
Belleville, IL. 618-233-0452
Wimmer's Meat Products
West Point, NE 800-358-0761

Ham

Aliments Prince Foods
Anjou, QC. .800-361-3898
American Foods Group
Green Bay, WI. 920-437-6330
Ashland Sausage Company
Carol Stream, IL 630-690-2600
Big Apple Produce & Seafood Market
Pocomoke City, MD 410-957-1151
Broadbent's B&B Foods
Kuttawa, KY. 800-841-2202
Chicago Steaks
Chicago, IL. 800-776-4174
Chisesi Brothers Meat Packing Company
New Orleans, LA 504-822-3550
Cloverdale Foods Company
Mandan, ND 800-669-9511
Community Market & Deli
Lindstrom, MN 651-257-1128

ConAgra Foods/Eckrich
Omaha, NE .800-327-4424
D'Artagnan
Newark, NJ .800-327-8246
Farmland Foods
Kansas City, MO. 888-327-6526
Father's Country Hams
Bremen, KY .270-525-3554
Fricks Meat Products
Washington, MO. 800-241-2209
Grote & Weigel
Bloomfield, CT. 860-242-8528
Hancock's Old Fashioned
Franklinville, NC 336-824-2145
Hickory Baked Food
Castle Rock, CO 303-688-2633
Holly Hill Locker Company
Holly Hill, SC 803-496-3611
Hormel Foods Corporation
Fremont, NE 402-721-2300
Humphrey Blue Ribbon Meats
Springfield, IL. 800-747-6328
Maple Leaf Consumer Foods
Fair Oaks, CA 800-999-7603
Niemuth's Steak & Chop Shop
Waupaca, WI. 715-258-2666
Patrick Cudahy
Cudahy, WI. 800-486-6900
Rinehart Meat Processing
Branson, MO. 417-334-2044
Rose Packing Company
South Barrington, IL. 800-323-7363
Scott Hams
Greenville, KY 800-318-1353
Silver Star Meats
Mc Kees Rocks, PA 412-771-5539
Specialty Foods Group
Newport News, VA. 800-238-0020
Stonies Sausage Shop Inc
Perryville, MO 888-546-2540
Thomas Packing Company
Columbus, GA 800-729-0976
Thumann's
Carlstadt, NJ 201-935-3636
Tupman-Thurlow Company
Deerfield Beach, FL 954-596-9989
V.W. Joyner & Company
Smithfield, VA 757-357-2161
Wayco Ham Company
Goldsboro, NC 800-962-2614

Canned

Badger Gourmet Ham
Milwaukee, WI 414-645-1756
Calihan Pork Processing
Peoria, IL. 309-674-9175
ConAgra Foods/Eckrich
Omaha, NE .800-327-4424
Dold Foods
Wichita, KS. 316-838-9101
Farmland Foods
Carroll, IA. .712-792-1660
Hickory Baked Food
Castle Rock, CO 303-688-2633
Horlacher's Fine Meats
Logan, UT. .435-752-1287
Hormel Foods Corporation
Fremont, NE 402-721-2300
International Trading Company
Houston, TX 713-224-5901
Levonian Brothers
Troy, NY 518-274-3610
S. Wallace Edward & Sons
Surry, VA. .800-290-9213
Sara Lee Corporation
Downers Grove, IL 630-598-8100
Smithfield Packing Company
Smithfield, VA 757-357-4321
Stegall Smoked Turkey
Marshville, NC 800-851-6034
Tenn Valley Ham Company
Paris, TN 731-642-9740
Tupman-Thurlow Company
Deerfield Beach, FL 954-596-9989
Wayco Ham Company
Goldsboro, NC 800-962-2614
WSMP
Claremont, NC 828-459-7626

Cooked - Water-added Chilled

Madrange
Millington, NJ. 908-647-6485

Fresh

Amana Meat Shop & Smokehouse
Amana, IA. .800-373-6328
Gwaltney of Smithfield
Smithfield, VA 800-888-7521
Smith Provision Company
Erie, PA. 800-334-9151

Frozen

Burke Corporation
Nevada, IA .800-654-1152

> Always make it your best® with Burke fully cooked meats. We specialize in Italian sausage, beef, and pork toppings, meatballs, taco meats, shredded meats, pepperoni, bacon, Canadian-style bacon, chicken and beef strips. Additionally, we offer a variety of specialty products: Hand-Pinched Style® brand toppings, chorizo, gyro topping, andouille sausage, and breakfast patties and links.

Smoked

Alderfer Bologna
Harleysville, PA 877-253-6328
Badger Gourmet Ham
Milwaukee, WI. 414-645-1756
Bear Creek Smokehouse
Marshall, TX. 800-950-2327
Big Apple Produce & Seafood Market
Pocomoke City, MD 410-957-1151
Blakely Freezer Locker
Thomasville, GA. 229-723-3622
Boyle Meat Company
Kansas City, MO. 800-821-3626
Carolina Packers
Smithfield, NC 800-682-7675
Con Agra Foods
Omaha, NE .402-475-6700
Continental Deli Foods
Cherokee, IA. 712-225-5161
Cumberland Gap Provision Company
Middlesboro, KY 800-331-7154
Finchville Farms
Finchville, KY 800-678-1521
Fresh Mark
Canton, OH .800-860-6777
Fricks Meat Products
Washington, MO. 800-241-2209
Gaiser's European Style Provisions
Union, NJ 908-206-9822
Groff Meats
Elizabethtown, PA. 717-367-1246
Gunsberg Corned Beef
Detroit, MI .313-894-6600
Hillbilly Smokehouse
Rogers, AR .479-636-1927
Honeyville Grain
Rancho Cucamonga, CA 888-810-3212
Hormel Foods Corporation
Fremont, NE 402-721-2300
Humphrey Blue Ribbon Meats
Springfield, IL. 800-747-6328
J&B Sausage Company
Waelder, TX 830-788-7511
John Hofmeister & Son
Chicago, IL. 800-923-4267
Kelley Meats
Taberg, NY .315-337-4272
Kessler's, Inc
Lemoyne, PA. 800-382-1328
Levonian Brothers
Troy, NY 518-274-3610
Manger Packing Company
Baltimore, MD 800-227-9262
Nueske's Applewood Smoked Meats
Wittenberg, WI. 800-386-2266

Ohio Packing Company
Columbus, OH 800-282-6403
Parma Sausage Products
Pittsburgh, PA 877-294-4207
Peer Foods Inc
Chicago, IL 800-365-5644
Quality Meats & Seafood
West Fargo, ND. 800-342-4250
R.M. Felts Packing Company
Ivor, VA 888-300-0971
Rinehart Meat Processing
Branson, MO. 417-334-2044
Rose Packing Company
South Barrington, IL. 800-323-7363
S. Wallace Edward & Sons
Surry, VA 800-290-9213
Sahlen Packing Company
Buffalo, NY. 716-852-8677
Sara Lee Foods
Zeeland, MI. 616-875-8131
Sechrist Brothers
Dallastown, PA 717-244-2975
Selwoods Farm Hunting Preserve
Alpine, AL 256-362-7595
Serv-Rite Meat Company
Los Angeles, CA. 323-227-1911
Smith Provision Company
Erie, PA 800-334-9151
Swiss-American Sausage Company
Lathrop, CA 209-858-5555
Thomas Packing Company
Columbus, GA 800-729-0976
Tomahawk Farms Meat Packers
Dunn, NC 910-892-3155
Troy Frozen Food
Troy, IL 618-667-6332
Tupman-Thurlow Company
Deerfield Beach, FL 954-596-9989
V.W. Joyner & Company
Smithfield, VA 757-357-2161
Wampler Foods
Dallas, TX 717-624-2191
Webster City Custom Meats
Webster City, IA 888-786-3287
Willies Smoke House
Harrisville, PA 800-742-4184

Steak

Grote & Weigel
Bloomfield, CT. 860-242-8528

Head Cheese

Ashland Sausage Company
Carol Stream, IL. 630-690-2600
Chicopee Provision Company
Chicopee, MA. 800-924-6328
Savoie's Sausage & Food Products
Opelousas, LA. 337-948-4115
Sweet Traders
Huntington Beach, CA 714-903-6800
Weyhaupt Brothers Packing
Belleville, IL. 618-233-0452
Wimmer's Meat Products
West Point, NE 800-358-0761

Knockwurst

Boesl Packing Company
Baltimore, MD 410-675-1071
Chicopee Provision Company
Chicopee, MA 800-924-6328
Country Smoked Meats
Bowling Green, OH 800-321-4766
David Berg & Company
Chicago, IL 773-489-4711
Matthiesen's Deer & Custom Processing
De Witt, IA 563-659-8409
Miller's Stratford Provision Company
Southport, CT 203-375-1598
Raemica
Running Springs, CA 800-772-6328
Rego's Purity Foods
Honolulu, HI. 808-947-9005
Sunset Farm Foods
Valdosta, GA. 800-882-1121

Liverwurst

Atlantic Pork & Provisions
Brooklyn, NY. 800-245-3536

Chicopee Provision Company
Chicopee, MA. 800-924-6328
Gaiser's European Style Provisions
Union, NJ 908-206-9822
Grote & Weigel
Bloomfield, CT. 860-242-8528
Schaller's Packers
Cassville, NY 315-822-3924
Silver Star Meats
Mc Kees Rocks, PA 412-771-5539
Sunset Farm Foods
Valdosta, GA 800-882-1121

Luncheon Meat

Alderfer Bologna
Harleysville, PA 877-253-6328
Alle Processing Corporation
Flushing, NY 800-245-5620
Armour
Omaha, NE 402-453-3766
Aspen Food Marketing
Denver, CO 303-320-3400
Atlantic Pork & Provisions
Brooklyn, NY. 800-245-3536
Atlantic Premium Brands
Northbrook, IL 847-412-6200
Bar-S Foods Company
Phoenix, AZ 602-264-7272
Berks Packing Company, Inc.
Reading, PA 800-882-3757
Birchwood Foods
Kenosha, WI 800-541-1685
Boar's Head Provisions Company
Sarasota, FL 888-884-2627
Boeckman JJ Wholesale Meats
Dayton, OH 937-222-4679
Boesl Packing Company
Baltimore, MD 410-675-1071
Boyd Sausage Company
Washington, IA 319-653-5715
Broadaway Ham Company
Jonesboro, AR. 870-932-6688
C. Roy Meat Products
Brockway, MI 810-387-3957
Cargill Meat Solutions
Timberville, VA 540-896-7041
Carl Buddig & Company
Homewood, IL 800-621-0868
Carolina Packers
Smithfield, NC 800-682-7675
Chalmette Packing Company
Covington, LA 504-271-6241
Charlie's Country Sausage
Minot, ND. 701-838-6302
Charlie's Pride Meats
Los Angeles, CA. 877-866-0982
Chicopee Provision Company
Chicopee, MA. 800-924-6328
Chisesi Brothers Meat Packing Company
New Orleans, LA 504-822-3550
Cibao Meat Product
Bronx, NY. 718-993-5072
Citterio USA Corporation
Freeland, PA 800-435-8888
Country Smoked Meats
Bowling Green, OH 800-321-4766
Curtis Packing Company
Greensboro, NC 336-275-7684
David Berg & Company
Chicago, IL 773-489-4711
Dietz & Watson
Philadelphia, PA 800-333-1974
Dutterer's Home Food Service
Baltimore, MD 410-298-3663
Egon Binkert Meat Products
Baltimore, MD 410-687-5959
Evergood Sausage Company
San Francisco, CA 800-253-6733
Farmland Foods
Carroll, IA. 712-792-1660
Foodbrands America
Oklahoma City, OK 405-290-4000
Frank Wardynski & Sons
Buffalo, NY. 716-854-6083
Fried Provisions Company
Evans City, PA 724-538-3160
Greenwood Packing Plant
Greenwood, SC 864-229-5611
Groff Meats
Elizabethtown, PA. 717-367-1246

Gunsberg Corned Beef
Detroit, MI 313-894-6600
Gwaltney of Smithfield
Portsmouth, VA. 757-465-0666
Hansel 'N Gretel
Flushing, NY 718-326-0041
Hazle Park Packing Company
West Hazleton, PA 800-238-4331
Henry J Meat Specialties
Chicago, IL 800-242-1314
Hoekstra Meat Company
Kalamazoo, MI 616-321-0797
Hoffman Sausage Company
Cincinnati, OH 513-621-4160
Hormel Foods Corporation
Austin, MN 800-523-4635
Humboldt Sausage Company
Humboldt, IA 515-332-4121
Hummel Brothers
New Haven, CT 800-828-8978
IBP Foods
Troy, MI 248-588-4710
Ito Cariani Sausage Company
Hayward, CA. 510-887-0882
John Volpi & Company
St Louis, MO. 800-288-3439
Kayem Foods
Chelsea, MA 800-426-6100
Kelly Kornbeef Company
Chicago, IL 773-588-2882
Kessler's, Inc
Lemoyne, PA. 800-382-1328
Kilgus Meats
Toledo, OH 419-472-9721
Kitts Meat Processing
Dedham, IA. 712-683-5622
Kunzler/Juniata Packing Company
Tyrone, PA. 814-684-2270
Land O Frost
Lansing, IL 800-643-5654
Land O'Frost
Searcy, AR. 800-643-5654
Larsen Packers
Burwick, NS 902-538-8060
Lengerich Meats
Zanesville, IN. 260-638-4123
Leona Meat Plant
Troy, PA. 570-297-3574
Levonian Brothers
Troy, NY. 518-274-3610
Locustdale Meat Packing
Locustdale, PA. 570-875-1270
Lower Foods
Richmond, UT. 435-258-2449
Lykes Meat Group
Plant City, FL 813-752-1102
Manda Fine Meats
Baton Rouge, LA 225-344-7636
Marshallville Packing Company
Marshallville, OH 330-855-2871
Martin Rosol's
New Britain, CT 860-223-2707
Milan Salami Company
Oakland, CA 510-654-7055
Miller's Stratford Provision Company
Southport, CT 203-375-1598
Mishler Packing Company
Lagrange, IN. 260-768-4156
Mosey's Inc
Bloomfield, CT. 860-243-1725
Murphy House
Louisburg, NC 919-496-4173
Norbest
Midvale, UT. 800-453-5327
O'Brien & Company
Bellevue, NE. 800-433-7567
Ohio Packing Company
Columbus, OH 800-282-6403
Otto W Liebold & Company
Flint, MI. 800-999-6328
Palmyra Bologna
Palmyra, PA. 717-838-6336
Parma Sausage Products
Pittsburgh, PA. 877-294-4207
Patrick Cudahy
Cudahy, WI. 800-486-6900
Penn Valley Farms
Gainesville, GA 773-685-9929
Pfeffer's Country Market
Sauk Centre, MN 320-352-3095
Pilgrim's Pride
Timberville, VA 540-896-7000

Plumrose
East Brunswick, NJ. 800-526-4909
Plumrose USA
East Brunswick, NJ. 732-257-6600
Promiseland Meat PackingCompany
Madill, OK .580-795-3567
R.L. Zeigler Company
Tuscaloosa, AL 800-392-6328
Raemica
Running Springs, CA 800-772-6328
Rego's Purity Foods
Honolulu, HI. 808-947-9005
Rendulic Packing
McKeesport, PA 412-678-9541
Robinsons Sausage Company
London, KY 606-864-2914
Roman Packing Company
Norfolk, NE. 800-373-5990
Russer Foods
Buffalo, NY. 800-828-7021
Ryley Sausage
Ryley, AB 780-663-3990
Saag's Products
San Leandro, CA. 800-352-7224
Sara Lee Corporation
Downers Grove, IL 630-598-8100
Sara Lee Foods
Zeeland, MI. 616-875-8131
Sara Lee Foods
Cincinnati, OH 800-351-7111
Sausage Shoppe
Cleveland, OH 216-351-5213
Saval Foods
Elkridge, MD 800-527-2825
Schaller & Weber
Long Island City, NY 800-847-4115
Schaller's Packers
Cassville, NY 315-822-3924
Sculli Brothers
Philadelphia, PA 215-336-1223
Sechrist Brothers
Dallastown, PA 717-244-2975
Seitz Foods
Saint Joseph, MO 800-383-3128
Sheinman Provision Company
Philadelphia, PA 215-473-7065
Shofar Kosher Foods
Linden, NJ. .888-874-6327
Siena Foods
Toronto, ON 800-465-0422
Smith Packing Regional Meat
Utica, NY 315-732-5125
Smith Provision Company
Erie, PA. 800-334-9151
Smithfield Foods
Clinton, NC 910-592-2104
Snow Ball Foods
Fredericksburg, PA 800-360-7669
Spring Grove Foods
Miamisburg, OH 937-866-4311
Standard Beef Company
New Haven, CT 203-787-2164
Stevens Sausage Company
Smithfield, NC 800-338-0561
Stonies Sausage Shop Inc
Perryville, MO 888-546-2540
Storer Meat Company
Cleveland, OH 800-355-7537
Sunset Farm Foods
Valdosta, GA. 800-882-1121
Superior's Brand Meats
Massillon, OH. 330-830-0356
Swift & Company
Greeley, CO. 970-324-2180
Tennessee Valley PackingCompany
Columbia, TN 931-388-2623
Thumann's
Carlstadt, NJ 201-935-3636
Troy Frozen Food
Troy, IL 618-667-6332
Troyers Trail Bologna
Dundee, OH 877-893-2414
Tupman-Thurlow Company
Deerfield Beach, FL 954-596-9989
United Provision Meat Company
Columbus, OH 614-252-1126
Upstate Farms Cooperative
Buffalo, NY. 716-892-3156
V.W. Joyner & Company
Smithfield, VA 757-357-2161
Vienna Meat Products
Scarborough, ON 800-588-1931

Wampler Foods
Dallas, TX. .717-624-2191
Warren & Son Meat Processing
Whipple, OH. 740-585-2421
Weyhaupt Brothers Packing
Belleville, IL 618-233-0452
Wimmer's Meat Products
West Point, NE 800-358-0761

Canned

Continental Deli Foods
Cherokee, IA. 712-225-5161
Lowell Provision Company
Lowell, MA. 978-454-5603

Olive Loaf

Allen Canning Company
Siloam Springs, AR 800-234-2553
Bryant Preserving Company
Alma, AR 800-634-2413
Cajun Chef Products
St Martinville, LA. 337-394-7112
Farmland Foods
Kansas City, MO. 888-327-6526
Grain Millers Eugene
Eugene, OR. 800-443-8972
McCain Foods USA
Grand Island, NE 308-382-7770
Wimmer's Meat Products
West Point, NE 800-358-0761

Pastrami

A. Stein Meat Products
Brooklyn, NY 718-492-0760
Alderfer Bologna
Harleysville, PA 877-253-6328
Best Provision Company, Inc.
Newark, NJ 800-631-4466
Bottomline Foods
Pembroke Pines, FL 954-843-0562
Carando Gourmet Frozen Foods
Springfield, MA 413-730-4205
Carl Buddig & Company
Homewood, IL 800-621-0868
Charlie's Pride Meats
Los Angeles, CA. 877-866-0982
Chicago 58 Food Products
Toronto, ON 416-603-4244
Curly's Foods
Edina, MN. .612-920-3400
David Berg & Company
Chicago, IL 773-489-4711
Dutterer's Home Food Service
Baltimore, MD 410-298-3663
Evergood Sausage Company
San Francisco, CA 800-253-6733
Gunsberg Corned Beef
Detroit, MI .313-894-6600
Henry J Meat Specialties
Chicago, IL 800-242-1314
Hoekstra Meat Company
Kalamazoo, MI. 616-321-0797
Kelly Kornbeef Company
Chicago, IL 773-588-2882
Levonian Brothers
Troy, NY 518-274-3610
Lower Foods
Richmond, UT. 435-258-2449
Marathon Enterprises
Englewood, NJ 201-935-3330
Mosey's Inc
Bloomfield, CT. 860-243-1725
Nossack Fine Meats
Red Deer, AB 403-346-5006
Otto W Liebold & Company
Flint, MI 800-999-6328
Sara Lee Corporation
Downers Grove, IL. 630-598-8100
Sara Lee Foods
Zeeland, MI. 616-875-8131
Saval Foods
Elkridge, MD 800-527-2825
Snow Ball Foods
Fredericksburg, PA 800-360-7669
Vienna Meat Products
Scarborough, ON 800-588-1931

Pepperoni

Armour
Omaha, NE .402-453-3766
Big Chief Meat Snacks
Calgary, AB. 403-264-2641

Always make it your best®

Burke Corporation
Nevada, IA .800-654-1152

Always make it your best® with Burke fully cooked meats. We specialize in Italian sausage, beef, and pork toppings, meatballs, taco meats, shredded meats, pepperoni, bacon, Canadian-style bacon, chicken and beef strips. Additionally, we offer a variety of specialty products: Hand-Pinched Style® brand toppings, chorizo, gyro topping, andouille sausage, and breakfast patties and links.

Busseto Foods
Fresno, CA .800-628-2633
Cattaneo Brothers
San Luis Obispo, CA 800-243-8537
Country Smoked Meats
Bowling Green, OH 800-321-4766
Farmland Foods
Kansas City, MO. 888-327-6526
Fiorucci Foods
Colonial Heights, VA 800-524-7775
Foodbrands America
Oklahoma City, OK 405-290-4000
Hormel Foods Corporation
Algona, IA. .515-295-2477
Hormel Foods Corporation
Austin, MN. 800-523-4635
Humboldt Sausage Company
Humboldt, IA 515-332-4121
Ito Cariani Sausage Company
Hayward, CA 510-887-0882
Joette's Sausage
Kincaid, IL .217-789-6300
Larsen Packers
Burwick, NS 902-538-8060
Milan Salami Company
Oakland, CA 510-654-7055
Quality Sausage Company
Dallas, TX. .214-634-3400
Sangudo Custom Meat Packers
Sangudo, AB. 888-785-3353
Sara Lee Corporation
Downers Grove, IL 630-598-8100
Schaller's Packers
Cassville, NY 315-822-3924
Smokey Farm Meats
Carbon, AB. 403-272-6587
Spring Grove Foods
Miamisburg, OH 937-866-4311
Stawnichy Holdings
Mundare, AB 888-764-7646
Swift & Company
Greeley, CO. 970-324-2180
Swiss American Sausage Corporation
Lathrop, CA 209-858-5555

Swiss-American Sausage Company
Lathrop, CA 209-858-5555
Upstate Farms Cooperative
Buffalo, NY..................716-892-3156
Viau Foods
Montreal, QC 800-663-5492

Prosciutto

Armour
Omaha, NE 402-453-3766
Fiorucci Foods
Colonial Heights, VA 800-524-7775
Hormel Foods Corporation
Austin, MN 800-523-4635
Parma Sausage Products
Pittsburgh, PA 877-294-4207
Santa Maria Foods
Branpton, ON 416-434-9559
Siena Foods
Toronto, ON 800-465-0422

Salami

Applegate Farms
Bridgewater, NJ 908-725-2768
Armour
Omaha, NE 402-453-3766
Baier's Sausage & Meats
Red Deer, AB 403-346-1535
Boesl Packing Company
Baltimore, MD 410-675-1071

Burke Corporation
Nevada, IA 800-654-1152

Busseto Foods
Fresno, CA 800-628-2633
Cargill Meat Solutions
Timberville, VA 540-896-7041
Charlie's Country Sausage
Minot, ND 701-838-6302
Chicago 58 Food Products
Toronto, ON 416-603-4244
Chicopee Provision Company
Chicopee, MA 800-924-6328
Chisesi Brothers Meat Packing Company
New Orleans, LA 504-822-3550
Cibao Meat Product
Bronx, NY 718-993-5072
Farmland Foods
Kansas City, MO 888-327-6526
Fiorucci Foods
Colonial Heights, VA 800-524-7775
Foodbrands America
Oklahoma City, OK 405-290-4000
Grinde Sausage House
Drayton Valley, AB 866-621-1755
Hormel Foods Corporation
Austin, MN 800-523-4635
Humboldt Sausage Company
Humboldt, IA 515-332-4121
Ito Cariani Sausage Company
Hayward, CA 510-887-0882
John Volpi & Company
St Louis, MO.................800-288-3439
Kessler's, Inc
Lemoyne, PA 800-382-1328
Larsen Packers
Burwick, NS 902-538-8060
Milan Salami Company
Oakland, CA 510-654-7055
Parma Sausage Products
Pittsburgh, PA 877-294-4207
Patrick Cudahy
Cudahy, WI 800-486-6900

Plumrose USA
East Brunswick, NJ 732-257-6600
Raemica
Running Springs, CA 800-772-6328
Santa Maria Foods
Branpton, ON 416-434-9559
Sara Lee Corporation
Downers Grove, IL 630-598-8100
Schaller & Weber
Long Island City, NY 800-847-4115
Schaller's Packers
Cassville, NY 315-822-3924
Sculli Brothers
Philadelphia, PA 215-336-1223
Siena Foods
Toronto, ON 800-465-0422
Spring Grove Foods
Miamisburg, OH 937-866-4311
Stawnichy Holdings
Mundare, AB 888-764-7646
Swift & Company
Greeley, CO 970-324-2180
Swiss American Sausage Corporation
Lathrop, CA 209-858-5555
Swiss-American Sausage Company
Lathrop, CA 209-858-5555
Upstate Farms Cooperative
Buffalo, NY..................716-892-3156

Sausages

A.L. Duck
Zuni, VA 757-562-2387
Abbyland Foods
Abbotsford, WI...............800-732-5483
Adolf's Meats & Sausage Kitchen
Hartford, CT 860-522-1588
Aidell's Sausage Company
San Leandro, CA..............800-546-5795
Alaska Sausage and Seafood Company
Anchorage, AK 800-798-3636
Alewel's Country Meats
Warrensburg, MO 800-353-8553
Alexian Pates/GroezingerProvisions
Neptune, NJ 800-927-9473
Aliments Prince Foods
Anjou, QC 800-361-3898
Alpine Meats
Stockton, CA.................800-399-6328
Applegate Farms
Bridgewater, NJ 908-725-2768
AquaCuisine
Eagle, ID 888-330-2782
Aries Prepared Beef
Burbank, CA 818-526-4855
Armbrust Meats
Medford, WI 715-748-3102
Armour
Omaha, NE 402-453-3766
Arnold's Meat Food Products
Brooklyn, NY 800-633-7023
Ashland Sausage Company
Carol Stream, IL 630-690-2600
Atlantic Premium Brands
Northbrook, IL 847-412-6200
Baier's Sausage & Meats
Red Deer, AB 403-346-1535
Baja Foods
Chicago, IL 773-376-9030
Bakalars Brothers Sausage Company
La Crosse, WI 608-784-0384
Bar-S Foods Company
Phoenix, AZ 602-264-7272
Berks Packing Company, Inc.
Reading, PA 800-882-3757
Big City Reds
Omaha, NE 800-850-8003
Black's Barbecue
Lockhart, TX.................512-398-2712
Blue Grass Quality Meat
Covington, KY 859-331-7100

Boesl Packing Company
Baltimore, MD 410-675-1071
Bouma Meats
Provost, AB 780-753-2092
Bowser Meat Processing
Meriden, KS 785-484-2454
Boyd Sausage Company
Washington, IA 319-653-5715
Braham Food Locker Service
Braham, MN 320-396-2636
Bridgford Foods
Anaheim, CA 800-527-2105
Bridgford Foods Corporation
Anaheim, CA 800-527-2105
Broadleaf Venison USA
Vernon, CA 800-336-3844
Brockton Beef & Provisions Corporation
Brockton, MA 508-583-4703
Brook Meadow Provisions Corporation
Hagerstown, MD. 301-739-3107
Bryan Foods
West Point, MS 662-494-3741
Bryant's Meats
Taylorsville, MS 601-785-6507
Burgers Smokehouse
California, MO 800-624-5426

Burke Corporation
Nevada, IA 800-654-1152

Butcher Shop
Beaverlodge, AB 780-354-8600
Camellia General Provision
Buffalo, NY 716-893-5352
Capitol Wholesale MeatsCCompany
Mc Cook, IL 800-331-6328
Caribbean Food Delights
Tappan, NY 845-398-3000
Carl Buddig & Company
Homewood, IL 800-621-0868
Carl Streit & Son Company
Neptune, NJ 732-775-0803
Carolina Packers
Smithfield, NC 800-682-7675
Casa Di Bertacchi
Vineland, NJ 800-818-9261
Casa di Carfagna
Columbus, OH 614-846-6340
Casual Gourmet Foods
Clearwater, FL 727-298-8307
Cattaneo Brothers
San Luis Obispo, CA 800-243-8537
Caughman's Meat Plant
Lexington, SC.................803-356-0076
Cedaredge Meats
Cedaredge, CO 970-856-3517
Center Locker Service Company
Center, MO 573-267-3343
Charlie's Country Sausage
Minot, ND 701-838-6302
Chatham Foods
Siler City, NC 919-742-2141
Cher-Make Sausage Company
Manitowoc, WI...............800-242-7679
Chicopee Provision Company
Chicopee, MA 800-924-6328
Chisesi Brothers Meat Packing Company
New Orleans, LA 504-822-3550
Cibao Meat Product
Bronx, NY...................718-993-5072
Cifelli & Sons
South River, NJ 732-238-0090
Cimpl Meats
Yankton, SD 605-665-1665

Cloverdale Foods Company
Mandan, ND 800-669-9511

Clyde's Italian & German Sausage
Denver, CO 303-433-8744

Coloma Meat Products
Coloma, WI 715-228-4080

Community Market & Deli
Lindstrom, MN 651-257-1128

ConAgra Foods Inc
Omaha, NE 402-240-4000

ConAgra Foods/Eckrich
Omaha, NE 800-327-4424

Conecuh Sausage Company
Evergreen, AL 800-726-0507

Conti Packing Company
Rochester, NY 585-424-2500

Corte Provisions
Newark, NJ 201-653-7246

Couch's Country Style Sausages
Cleveland, OH 216-587-2333

Country Pies
Coombs, BC 250-248-6415

Country Smoked Meats
Bowling Green, OH 800-321-4766

Counts Sausage Company
Prosperity, SC 803-364-2392

Crawford Sausage Company
Chicago, IL 866-653-2479

Crocetti Oakdale Packing
East Bridgewater, MA 508-587-0035

Crofton & Sons
Brandon, FL 800-878-7675

Cropp Cooperative-Organic Valley
La Farge, WI 888-444-6455

Culver Duck
Middlebury, IN 800-825-9225

Cumberland Gap Provision Company
Middlesboro, KY 800-331-7154

D'Artagnan
Newark, NJ 800-327-8246

Dallas City Packing
Dallas, TX 214-948-3901

Dankworth Packing Company
Ballinger, TX 325-365-3552

David Berg & Company
Chicago, IL 773-489-4711

Dean Sausage Company
Attalla, AL 800-228-0704

Debbie D's Jerky & Sausage
Tillamook, OR 503-842-2622

Decker & Son Company
Colorado Springs, CO 719-634-8311

Del Rey Tortilleria
Chicago, IL 800-446-1459

Dennison Meat Locker
Dennison, MN 507-645-8734

Diggs Packing Company
Columbia, MO 573-449-2995

DiGregorio Food Products
St Louis, MO 314-776-1062

Dinner Bell Meat Product
Lynchburg, VA 434-847-7766

Dino's Sausage & Meat Company
Utica, NY 315-732-2661

Dohar Meats
Cleveland, OH 216-241-4197

Dreymiller & Kray
Hampshire, IL 847-683-2271

Duis Meat Processing
Concordia, KS 800-281-4295

Dutch Packing Company
Miami, FL 305-871-3640

E.W. Knauss & Son
Quakertown, PA 800-648-4220

Edmonton Meat Packing Company
Edmonton, AB 800-361-6328

Egon Binkert Meat Products
Baltimore, MD 410-687-5959

Ellsworth Locker
Ellsworth, MN 507-967-2544

Elmwood Lockers
Elmwood, IL 309-742-8929

Elore Enterprises
Miami, FL 305-477-1650

Enslin & Son Packing Company
Hattiesburg, MS 800-898-4687

European Egg Noodle Manufacturing
Edmonton, AB 780-453-6767

Evergood Sausage Company
San Francisco, CA 800-253-6733

F&Y Enterprises
Naperville, IL 630-637-8519

Fabbri Sausage Manufacturing
Chicago, IL 312-829-6363

Fanestil Packing Company
Emporia, KS 620-342-6354

Fargo Packing & Sausage Company
West Fargo, ND 701-282-3211

Farmland Foods
Kansas City, MO 888-327-6526

Ferris Stahl-Meyer Packing Corporation
Bronx, NY 718-328-0059

Foell Packing Company
Naperville, IL 919-776-0592

Fontanini Italian Meats & Sausages
Chicago, IL 800-331-6328

Foodbrands America
Oklahoma City, OK 405-290-4000

Fortenberry Ice Company
Kodak, TN 865-933-2568

Foster Farms
Demopolis, AL 800-255-7227

Frank Wardynski & Sons
Buffalo, NY 716-854-6083

Frank's Foods
Hilo, HI .808-959-9121

Fred Busch Foods
Evanston, IL 773-545-2650

Fredericksburg Lockers/OPA's Smoke
Fredericksburg, TX 800-543-6750

Fresh Mark
Canton, OH 800-860-6777

Fricks Meat Products
Washington, MO 800-241-2209

Fried Provisions Company
Evans City, PA 724-538-3160

Gaiser's European Style Provisions
Union, NJ 908-206-9822

Galileo Foods
San Lorenzo, CA 510-276-1300

Gaspar's Sausage Company
North Dartmouth, MA 800-542-2038

Gem Meat Packing Company
Boise, ID 208-375-9424

Gerhard's Napa Valley Sausage
Napa, CA 707-252-4116

Glazier Packing Company
Potsdam, NY 315-265-2500

Glazier Packing Company
Malone, NY 518-483-4990

Glier's Meats
Covington, KY 800-446-3882

Gold Star Sausage Company
Denver, CO 800-258-7229

Grimm's Fine Food
Richmond, AB 780-415-4331

Grote & Weigel
Bloomfield, CT 860-242-8528

Gunnoe Farms-Sausage & Salad Company
Charleston, WV 304-343-7686

Gwaltney of Smithfield
Portsmouth, VA 757-465-0666

H&B Packing Company
Waco, TX 254-752-2506

Hahn Brothers
Westminster, MD 800-227-7675

Hansel 'N Gretel
Flushing, NY 718-326-0041

Hatfield Quality Meats
Hatfield, PA 800-523-5291

Hazle Park Packing Company
West Hazleton, PA 800-238-4331

Heinkel's Packing Company
Decatur, IL 800-594-2738

Hillbilly Smokehouse
Rogers, AR 479-636-1927

Hillsboro Refrigerated Lockers
Hillsboro, KS 316-947-3781

Hoffman Sausage Company
Cincinnati, OH 513-621-4160

Hofmann Sausage Company
Syracuse, NY 800-724-8410

Hoople Country Kitchens
Rockport, IN 812-649-2351

Hormel Foods
Rochelle, IL 800-523-4635

Hormel Foods Corporation
Fremont, NE 402-721-2300

Hormel Foods Corporation
Maitland, FL 407-660-0808

Hormel Foods Corporation
Austin, MN 800-523-4635

Hot Springs Packing Company
Hot Springs, AR 800-535-0449

Humboldt Sausage Company
Humboldt, IA 515-332-4121

Hummel Brothers
New Haven, CT 800-828-8978

Humphrey Blue Ribbon Meats
Springfield, IL 800-747-6328

Huse's Country Meats
Malone, TX 254-533-2205

IBP Foods
Troy, MI .248-588-4710

IBP Foods
Grand Rapids, MI 616-774-0711

Independent Meat Company
Twin Falls, ID 208-733-0980

Indian Valley Meats
Indian, AK 907-653-7511

International Packers Corporation
Watertown, MA 508-963-8214

Isernio Sausage Company
Seattle, WA 888-495-8674

Italian Foods Manufacturing
Vestal, NY 800-962-7700

Ito Cariani Sausage Company
Hayward, CA 510-887-0882

Ittels Meats
Howard Lake, MN 320-543-2285

J&B Sausage Company
Waelder, TX 830-788-7511

Jody Maroni's Sausage Kingdom
Venice, CA 310-822-5639

Joette's Sausage
Kincaid, IL 217-789-6300

John Morrell & Company
Cincinnati, OH 800-345-0743

Johnsonville Food Company
Sheboygan, WI 920-459-6800

Jones Dairy Farm
Fort Atkinson, WI 800-563-1004

Kayem Foods
Chelsea, MA 800-426-6100

Kelley Foods of Alabama
Elba, AL .334-897-5761

Kelley Meats
Taberg, NY 315-337-4272

Kent Quality Foods
Grand Rapids, MI 800-748-0141

Kessler's, Inc
Lemoyne, PA 800-382-1328

Kilgus Meats
Toledo, OH 419-472-9721

Kiolbassa Provision Company
San Antonio, TX 800-456-5465

Kirby & Holloway Provisions
Harrington, DE 800-995-4729

Koegel Meats
Flint, MI .810-238-3685

Konetzkos Market
Browerville, MN 320-594-2915

Kowalski Sausage Company
Hamtramck, MI 800-482-2400

Kunzler/Juniata Packing Company
Tyrone, PA 814-684-2270

La Poblana Tamale Factory
Houston, TX 713-921-4760

Lad's Smokehouse Catering
Needville, TX 979-793-6210

Larry's Sausage Corporation
Fayetteville, NC 910-483-5148

Larsen Packers
Burwick, NS 902-538-8060

Laurent Meat Market
Marrero, LA 504-341-1771

Le Pique-Nique
Oakland, CA 800-400-6454

Lebermuth Company
South Bend, IN 800-648-1123

Lee Kum Kee
Brooklyn, NY 800-346-7562

Lees Sausage Company
Orangeburg, SC 803-534-5517

Leon's Sausage Company
Chicago, IL 312-829-2250

Leona Meat Plant
Troy, PA .570-297-3574

Leone Provision Company
Cape Coral, FL 941-574-3355

Levonian Brothers
Troy, NY 518-274-3610

Lewis Sausage Corporation
Burgaw, NC 910-259-2642

Lionel Lavallee Company
Haverhill, MA 800-343-8292

Little Rhody Brand Frankfurts
Johnston, RI 401-831-0815

Locustdale Meat Packing
Locustdale, PA 570-875-1270

London Pantry Foods
Mt Pleasant, SC 888-208-7787

Lords Sausage & Country Ham
Dexter, GA 800-342-6002

Lowell Packing Company
Fitzgerald, GA 800-342-0313

Lykes Meat Group
Plant City, FL 813-752-1102

M K Meat Processing Plant
Burton, TX 979-289-4022

M&M Packing Company
Ballinger, TX 915-365-2227

Mac's Farms Sausage Company
Newton Grove, NC 910-594-0095

Manda Fine Meats
Baton Rouge, LA 225-344-7636

Marcel et Henri Charcuterie Francaise
S San Francisco, CA 800-227-6436

Marshallville Packing Company
Marshallville, OH 330-855-2871

McKenzie of Vermont
Burlington, VT 802-864-4585

McLane's Meats
Wetaskiwin, AB 780-352-4321

Meat Shop
Cape Girardeau, MO 800-791-5104

Meating Place
Buffalo, NY 716-885-3623

Medeiros Farms
Kalaheo, HI 808-332-8211

Mello's North End Manufacturings
Fall River, MA 800-673-2320

Menu Meats
Huntertown, IN 800-848-2902

Mertz Sausage Company
San Antonio, TX 210-433-3263

Michael's Provision Company
Fall River, MA 508-672-0982

Michel's Magnifique
New York, NY 212-431-1070

Mike's Meats
Eitzen, MN 507-495-3336

Milan Provision Company
Flushing, NY 718-899-7678

Milan Salami Company
Oakland, CA 510-654-7055

Miller Brothers Packing Company
Sylvester, GA 229-776-2014

Miller's Meat Market
Red Bud, IL 618-282-3334

Miller's Stratford Provision Company
Southport, CT 203-375-1598

Milling Sausage Company
Milwaukee, WI 414-645-2677

Momence Packing Company
Momence, IL 815-472-6485

Neese Country Sausage
Greensboro, NC 800-632-1010

Nemecek Brothers
West, TX 254-826-5182

Neto Sausage Company
Santa Clara, CA 888-482-6386

New Bedford Linguica
New Bedford, MA 877-372-4616

New Glarus Foods
New Glarus, WI 800-356-6685

New Packing Company
Chicago, IL 312-666-1314

Niemuth's Steak & Chop Shop
Waupaca, WI 715-258-2666

Norpaco
New Britain, CT 800-252-0222

North Side Foods Corporation
Arnold, PA 800-486-2201

Nossack Fine Meats
Red Deer, AB 403-346-5006

Nueske's Applewood Smoked Meats
Wittenberg, WI 800-386-2266

O'Brien & Company
Bellevue, NE 800-433-7567

Odom's Tennessee Pride Sausage Company
Madison, TN 800-327-6269

Ohio Packing Company
Columbus, OH 800-282-6403

Omaha Steaks International
Omaha, NE 800-562-0500

Ossian Seafood Meats
Ossian, IN 260-622-4191

Otto W Liebold & Company
Flint, MI 800-999-6328

Owens Country Sausage
Richardson, TX 800-966-9367

Paris Frozen Foods
Hillsboro, IL 217-532-3822

Parma Sausage Products
Pittsburgh, PA 877-294-4207

Patrick Cudahy
Cudahy, WI 800-486-6900

Peer Foods Inc
Chicago, IL 800-365-5644

Pekarna's Meat Market
Jordan, MN 952-492-6101

Penn Valley Farms
Gainesville, GA 773-685-9929

Pfeffer's Country Market
Sauk Centre, MN 320-352-3095

Piller Sausages & Delicatessens
Waterloo, ON 519-743-1412

Pinter's Packing Plant
Dorchester, WI 715-654-5444

Pioneer Packing Company
Bowling Green, OH 419-352-5283

Pokanoket Ostrich Farm
South Dartmouth, MA 508-992-6188

Polka Home Style Sausage
Chicago, IL 773-221-0395

Premier Casing Company
Shrewsbury, NJ 800-933-9766

Purnell's Old Folks Sausage Company
Simpsonville, KY 800-626-1512

Quality Meats & Seafood
West Fargo, ND 800-342-4250

Queen City Sausage
Cincinnati, OH 877-544-5588

R & D Sausage Company
Cleveland, OH 216-692-1832

R-K Sausage Company
Cleveland, OH 216-341-1251

Raemica
Running Springs, CA 800-772-6328

Ray's Sausage Company Inc
Cleveland, OH 216-921-8782

Real Kosher Sausage Company
Newark, NJ 973-690-5394

Register Meat Company
Cottondale, FL 850-352-4269

Rego's Purity Foods
Honolulu, HI 808-947-9005

Rinehart Meat Processing
Branson, MO 417-334-2044

Riverside Packers
Drumheller, AB 403-823-2595

Robbins Packing Company
Statesboro, GA 912-764-7503

Robinsons Sausage Company
London, KY 606-864-2914

Roma Packing Company
Chicago, IL 773-927-7371

Roman Packing Company
Norfolk, NE. 800-373-5990

Roman Sausage Company
Santa Clara, CA 800-497-7462

Roode Packing Company
Fairbury, NE 402-729-2253

Rudolph's Market & Sausage Factory
Dallas, TX .214-741-1874

Ryley Sausage
Ryley, AB .780-663-3990

S. Wallace Edward & Sons
Surry, VA .800-290-9213

S.W. Meat & Provision Company
Phoenix, AZ 602-275-2000

Saag's Products
San Leandro, CA 800-352-7224

Sahlen Packing Company
Buffalo, NY 716-852-8677

Sangudo Custom Meat Packers
Sangudo, AB 888-785-3353

Sapar
San Mateo, CA 650-340-8840

Sara Lee Corporation
Downers Grove, IL 630-598-8100

Sara Lee Food Service
Haltom City, TX 800-261-4754

Sara Lee Foods
Zeeland, MI 616-875-8131

Sara Lee Foods
Cincinnati, OH 800-351-7111

Sara Lee Foods
Neenah, WI 800-558-8440

Sardinha Sausage
Somerset, MA 800-678-0178

Sausage Shoppe
Cleveland, OH 216-351-5213

Sausages by Amy
Chicago, IL 312-666-6989

Savoie's Sausage & Food Products
Opelousas, LA. 337-948-4115

Schaller & Weber
Long Island City, NY 800-847-4115

Schaller's Packers
Cassville, NY 315-822-3924

Schneider Foods
Surrey, BC .604-576-1191

Schweigert Foods
Albert Lea, MN 507-377-2526

Scott Hams
Greenville, KY 800-318-1353

Sculli Brothers
Philadelphia, PA 215-336-1223

Sechrist Brothers
Dallastown, PA 717-244-2975

Selecto Sausage Company
Houston, TX 713-926-1626

Serv-Rite Meat Company
Los Angeles, CA 323-227-1911

Sheinman Provision Company
Philadelphia, PA 215-473-7065

Siena Foods
Toronto, ON 800-465-0422

Silver Creek Specialty Meats
Oshkosh, WI 920-232-3581

Silver Star Meats
Mc Kees Rocks, PA 412-771-5539

Simeus Foods Internatio nal
Mansfield, TX 888-772-3663

Smith Packing Regional Meat
Utica, NY .315-732-5125

Smith Provision Company
Erie, PA 800-334-9151

Smokey Denmark Sausage
Austin, TX. 512-385-0718

Smokey Farm Meats
Carbon, AB 403-272-6587

Smolich Brothers
Crest Hill, IL 815-727-2144

Sparrer Sausage Company
Chicago, IL 800-666-3287

Spring Grove Foods
Miamisburg, OH 937-866-4311

Stanley Provision Company
Manchester, CT. 888-688-6347

Stauber Performance Ingredients
Fullerton, CA 888-441-4233

Stawnichy Holdings
Mundare, AB 888-764-7646

Stevens Sausage Company
Smithfield, NC 800-338-0561

Stewarts Market
Yelm, WA .360-458-2091

Stonies Sausage Shop Inc
Perryville, MO 888-546-2540

Strasburg Provision
Strasburg, OH 800-207-6009

Striplings
Moultrie, GA 229-985-4226

Sunergia Soyfoods
Charlottesville, VA 800-693-5134

Sunnydale Meats
Gaffney, SC 864-489-6091

SW Red Smith
Davie, FL .954-581-1996

Swiss American Sausage Corporation
Lathrop, CA 209-858-5555

Swiss-American Sausage Company
Lathrop, CA 209-858-5555

T.L. Herring & Company
Wilson, NC 252-291-1141

Tennessee Valley PackingCompany
Columbia, TN 931-388-2623

Texas Sausage Company
Austin, TX. 512-472-6707

Thomas Packing Company
Columbus, GA 800-729-0976

Tofield Packers
Tofield, AB 780-662-4842

Tomasinos Sausage
Canton, OH 330-454-4171

Troy Frozen Food
Troy, IL 618-667-6332

Tupman-Thurlow Company
Deerfield Beach, FL 954-596-9989

United Packing
Providence, RI .401-751-6935
Unruh's Quality Meats
Deridder, LA .337-463-7688
Upstate Farms Cooperative
Buffalo, NY. 716-892-3156
Uvalde Meat Processing
Uvalde, TX. 830-278-6247
V&V Supremo Foods
Chicago, IL. 800-547-8773
Valenie Packers
Colinton, AB. 780-675-5881
Vermilion Packers
Vermilion, AB. 780-853-4622
Viau Foods
Montreal, QC 800-663-5492
Victor Ostrowski & Son
Baltimore, MD 410-327-8935
Vienna Meat Products
Scarborough, ON 800-588-1931
Vienna Sausage Company
Chicago, IL .800-326-6652
Vollwerth & Company
Hancock, MI. 800-562-7620
WA Bean & Sons
Bangor, ME. 800-649-1958
Waco Beef & Pork Processors
Waco, TX. .254-772-4669
Wampler's Farm Sausage Company
Lenoir City, TN. 800-728-7243
Warren & Son Meat Processing
Whipple, OH. 740-585-2421
West Virginia Sausage Company
New Haven, WV. 304-882-3194
Weyhaupt Brothers Packing
Belleville, IL. 618-233-0452
Whitaker Foods
Evansdale, IA 800-553-7490
Williams Packing Company
Goldsboro, NC 919-735-0262
Willies Smoke House
Harrisville, PA. 800-742-4184
Wimmer's Meat Products
West Point, NE 800-358-0761
Wolfson Casing Corporation
Mt Vernon, NY 800-221-8042
Woods Smoked Meats
Bowling Green, MO 800-458-8426
Zummo Meat Company
Beaumont, TX. 409-842-1810

Andouille

Applegate Farms
Bridgewater, NJ 908-725-2768

Burke Corporation
Nevada, IA .800-654-1152

Always make it your best® with Burke fully cooked meats. We specialize in Italian sausage, beef, and pork toppings, meatballs, taco meats, shredded meats, pepperoni, bacon, Canadian-style bacon, chicken and beef strips. Additionally, we offer a variety of specialty products: Hand-Pinched Style® brand toppings, chorizo, gyro topping, andouille sausage, and breakfast patties and links.

D'Artagnan
Newark, NJ. 800-327-8246
Grote & Weigel
Bloomfield, CT. 860-242-8528
Laurent Meat Market
Marrero, LA 504-341-1771

Parma Sausage Products
Pittsburgh, PA 877-294-4207
Savoie's Sausage & Food Products
Opelousas, LA. 337-948-4115
Thomas Packing Company
Columbus, GA 800-729-0976

Blood

Bavarian Meat Products
Seattle, WA 206-448-3540
Chicopee Provision Company
Chicopee, MA. 800-924-6328
Rego's Purity Foods
Honolulu, HI 808-947-9005
Weyhaupt Brothers Packing
Belleville, IL. 618-233-0452

Bockwurst

Chicopee Provision Company
Chicopee, MA. 800-924-6328
Country Smoked Meats
Bowling Green, OH 800-321-4766
Koegel Meats
Flint, MI 810-238-3685
Schaller's Packers
Cassville, NY 315-822-3924

Boudin

Comeaux's
Lafayette, LA 800-323-2492
Marcel et Henri Charcuterie Francaise
S San Francisco, CA. 800-227-6436
Savoie's Sausage & Food Products
Opelousas, LA. 337-948-4115
Stallings Headcheese Company
Houston, TX 713-523-1751
Sunset Farm Foods
Valdosta, GA 800-882-1121
Woods Smoked Meats
Bowling Green, MO 800-458-8426
Zummo Meat Company
Beaumont, TX. 409-842-1810

Bratwurst

Chicopee Provision Company
Chicopee, MA. 800-924-6328
Country Smoked Meats
Bowling Green, OH 800-321-4766
Cropp Cooperative-Organic Valley
La Farge, WI. 888-444-6455
Elmwood Lockers
Elmwood, IL. 309-742-8929
Grote & Weigel
Bloomfield, CT. 860-242-8528
Kilgus Meats
Toledo, OH 419-472-9721
Koegel Meats
Flint, MI 810-238-3685
New Braunfels Smokehouse
New Braunfels, TX. 800-537-6932
Penn Valley Farms
Gainesville, GA 773-685-9929
Purnell Sausage Company
Simpsonville, KY 800-626-1512
Raemica
Running Springs, CA 800-772-6328
S.W. Meat & Provision Company
Phoenix, AZ 602-275-2000
Schaller's Packers
Cassville, NY 315-822-3924
Smolich Brothers
Crest Hill, IL 815-727-2144
Waco Beef & Pork Processors
Waco, TX. .254-772-4669
Wimmer's Meat Products
West Point, NE 800-358-0761

Braunschweiger

Farmland Foods
Kansas City, MO. 888-327-6526
Weyhaupt Brothers Packing
Belleville, IL. 618-233-0452

Cajun

Fontanini Italian Meats & Sausages
Chicago, IL 800-331-6328

Casings: Sausage, Pork, Beef

Austrade Food Ingredients
Palm Beach Gdns, FL. 561-586-7145
Con Yeager Spice Company
Zelienople, PA. 800-222-2460
Dewied International
San Antonio, TX. 800-992-5600
Hofmann Sausage Company
Syracuse, NY 800-724-8410
International Casing Group
Chicago, IL 800-825-5151
International Casings Group
Santa Fe Springs, CA. 800-635-9518
International Casings Group
Chicago, IL 800-825-5151
Koegel Meats
Flint, MI 810-238-3685
Marie F
Markham, ON 800-365-4464
Mongolia Casing Corporation
Flushing, NY. 800-221-4887
Nitta Casings
Somerville, NJ 908-218-4400
Package Concepts & Materials Inc
Greenville, SC. 800-424-7264
Premier Casing Company
Shrewsbury, NJ 800-933-9766
Syracuse Casing Company
Syracuse, NY 315-475-0309

Chicken

Bell & Evans
Fredericksburg, PA. 717-865-6626
Penn Valley Farms
Gainesville, GA 773-685-9929
WA Bean & Sons
Bangor, ME. 800-649-1958

Chorizo

Burke Corporation
Nevada, IA .800-654-1152

Always make it your best® with Burke fully cooked meats. We specialize in Italian sausage, beef, and pork toppings, meatballs, taco meats, shredded meats, pepperoni, bacon, Canadian-style bacon, chicken and beef strips. Additionally, we offer a variety of specialty products: Hand-Pinched Style® brand toppings, chorizo, gyro topping, andouille sausage, and breakfast patties and links.

Carmelita Provisions Company
Monterey Park, CA. 323-262-6751
Corte Provisions
Newark, NJ. 201-653-7246
Country Smoked Meats
Bowling Green, OH 800-321-4766
D'Artagnan
Newark, NJ. 800-327-8246
Del Rey Tortilleria
Chicago, IL 800-446-1459
Parma Sausage Products
Pittsburgh, PA 877-294-4207
Purnell Sausage Company
Simpsonville, KY 800-626-1512
Sunset Farm Foods
Valdosta, GA 800-882-1121
V&V Supremo Foods
Chicago, IL 800-547-8773
Waco Beef & Pork Processors
Waco, TX. .254-772-4669
Weyhaupt Brothers Packing
Belleville, IL. 618-233-0452

Chourico

Mertz Sausage Company
San Antonio, TX. 210-433-3263
Odessa Tortilla & TamaleFactory
Odessa, TX 800-753-2445
Sardinha Sausage
Somerset, MA 800-678-0178

Hot

Boesl Packing Company
Baltimore, MD 410-675-1071
Chicopee Provision Company
Chicopee, MA 800-924-6328
D'Artagnan
Newark, NJ 800-327-8246
E.W. Knauss & Son
Quakertown, PA 800-648-4220
Farmland Foods
Kansas City, MO. 888-327-6526
Gecko Gary's
Scottsdale, AZ. 602-765-3756
H&B Packing Company
Waco, TX 254-752-2506
Hofmann Sausage Company
Syracuse, NY 800-724-8410
Hormel Foods Corporation
Austin, MN 800-523-4635
Ray's Sausage Company Inc
Cleveland, OH 216-921-8782
Sheinman Provision Company
Philadelphia, PA 215-473-7065
Siena Foods
Toronto, ON 800-465-0422
Wy's Wings
Strasburg, VA 800-997-9464

Hot Italian

Atlantic Quality Spice &Seasonings
Edison, NJ. 800-584-0422
Decker & Son Company
Colorado Springs, CO. 719-634-8311
Eagle Rock Food Company
Albuquerque, NM 505-323-1183
Grote & Weigel
Bloomfield, CT. 860-242-8528
Purnell Sausage Company
Simpsonville, KY 800-626-1512
Siena Foods
Toronto, ON 800-465-0422

Kielbasa

Atlantic Quality Spice &Seasonings
Edison, NJ. 800-584-0422
Berks Packing Company, Inc.
Reading, PA 800-882-3757
Boesl Packing Company
Baltimore, MD 410-675-1071
Chicopee Provision Company
Chicopee, MA 800-924-6328
Country Smoked Meats
Bowling Green, OH 800-321-4766
Frank Wardynski & Sons
Buffalo, NY. 716-854-6083
Grote & Weigel
Bloomfield, CT. 860-242-8528
Hot Springs Packing Company
Hot Springs, AR 800-535-0449
Leo G. Fraboni Sausage Company
Hibbing, MN 218-263-5074
Locustdale Meat Packing
Locustdale, PA 570-875-1270
Martin Rosol's
New Britain, CT 860-223-2707
Norpaco
New Britain, CT 800-252-0222
Otto W Liebold & Company
Flint, MI 800-999-6328
Parma Sausage Products
Pittsburgh, PA 877-294-4207
Raemica
Running Springs, CA 800-772-6328
Roma Packing Company
Chicago, IL. 773-927-7371
Sardinha Sausage
Somerset, MA. 800-678-0178
Schaller's Packers
Cassville, NY 315-822-3924
Silver Star Meats
Mc Kees Rocks, PA 412-771-5539
Smith Packing Regional Meat
Utica, NY. 315-732-5125
Stanley Provision Company
Manchester, CT. 888-688-6347
Storer Meat Company
Cleveland, OH 800-355-7537
Victor Ostrowski & Son
Baltimore, MD 410-327-8935
Weyhaupt Brothers Packing
Belleville, IL 618-233-0452

Wimmer's Meat Products
West Point, NE 800-358-0761

Knockwurst

Boesl Packing Company
Baltimore, MD 410-675-1071
Country Smoked Meats
Bowling Green, OH 800-321-4766
D'Artagnan
Newark, NJ 800-327-8246
Grote & Weigel
Bloomfield, CT. 860-242-8528
Raemica
Running Springs, CA 800-772-6328
Rego's Purity Foods
Honolulu, HI 808-947-9005

Linguica

BURKE
Always make it your best®

Burke Corporation
Nevada, IA 800-654-1152

> Always make it your best® with Burke fully cooked meats. We specialize in Italian sausage, beef, and pork toppings, meatballs, taco meats, shredded meats, pepperoni, bacon, Canadian-style bacon, chicken and beef strips. Additionally, we offer a variety of specialty products: Hand-Pinched Style® brand toppings, chorizo, gyro topping, andouille sausage, and breakfast patties and links.

Swiss-American Sausage Company
Lathrop, CA 209-858-5555

Link

Bakalars Brothers Sausage Company
La Crosse, WI. 608-784-0384
Bellville Meat Market
Bellville, TX 800-571-6328

BURKE
Always make it your best®

Burke Corporation
Nevada, IA 800-654-1152

> Always make it your best® with Burke fully cooked meats. We specialize in Italian sausage, beef, and pork toppings, meatballs, taco meats, shredded meats, pepperoni, bacon, Canadian-style bacon, chicken and beef strips. Additionally, we offer a variety of specialty products: Hand-Pinched Style® brand toppings, chorizo, gyro topping, andouille sausage, and breakfast patties and links.

Country Smoked Meats
Bowling Green, OH 800-321-4766
Father's Country Hams
Bremen, KY 270-525-3554
Fontanini Italian Meats & Sausages
Chicago, IL. 800-331-6328
Fredericksburg Lockers/OPA's Smoke
Fredericksburg, TX. 800-543-6750
H&B Packing Company
Waco, TX 254-752-2506
Hormel Foods Corporation
Austin, MN 800-523-4635
Mello's North End Manufacturings
Fall River, MA 800-673-2320
Purnell Sausage Company
Simpsonville, KY 800-626-1512
Purnell's Old Folks Sausage Company
Simpsonville, KY 800-626-1512
Ray's Sausage Company Inc
Cleveland, OH 216-921-8782
Upstate Farms Cooperative
Buffalo, NY. 716-892-3156

Mortadella

Fiorucci Foods
Colonial Heights, VA 800-524-7775
John Volpi & Company
St Louis, MO. 800-288-3439
Parma Sausage Products
Pittsburgh, PA 877-294-4207
Siena Foods
Toronto, ON 800-465-0422
Swift & Company
Greeley, CO 970-324-2180

Patti

Farmland Foods
Kansas City, MO. 888-327-6526
Father's Country Hams
Bremen, KY 270-525-3554
Fontanini Italian Meats & Sausages
Chicago, IL. 800-331-6328
Hormel Foods Corporation
Austin, MN 800-523-4635
Italian Foods Manufacturing
Vestal, NY 800-962-7700
Joette's Sausage
Kincaid, IL 217-789-6300
Mello's North End Manufacturings
Fall River, MA 800-673-2320
New Bedford Linguica
New Bedford, MA 877-372-4616
Purnell Sausage Company
Simpsonville, KY 800-626-1512
Purnell's Old Folks Sausage Company
Simpsonville, KY 800-626-1512
Ray's Sausage Company Inc
Cleveland, OH 216-921-8782
Roman Sausage Company
Santa Clara, CA 800-497-7462

Polish

Fontanini Italian Meats & Sausages
Chicago, IL. 800-331-6328

Pork

Farmland Foods
Kansas City, MO. 888-327-6526
Grote & Weigel
Bloomfield, CT. 860-242-8528

Salmon

Aquatec Seafoods Ltd.
Comox, BC 250-339-6412

Sicilian Style (with Cheese)

Atlantic Quality Spice &Seasonings
Edison, NJ. 800-584-0422

Sweet

Chicopee Provision Company
Chicopee, MA 800-924-6328
Farmland Foods
Kansas City, MO. 888-327-6526

Sweet Italian

Atlantic Quality Spice &Seasonings
Edison, NJ. 800-584-0422
Grote & Weigel
Bloomfield, CT. 860-242-8528

Turkey

Couch's Country Style Sausages
Cleveland, OH 216-587-2333
Eagle Rock Food Company
Albuquerque, NM 505-323-1183

Veal

Penn Valley Farms
Gainesville, GA 773-685-9929

Venison

Broadleaf Venison USA
Vernon, CA 800-336-3844

Smoked Meat

Alewel's Country Meats
Warrensburg, MO 800-353-8553

Alpine Meats
Stockton, CA......................800-399-6328
Applegate Farms
Bridgewater, NJ 908-725-2768
Arnold's Meat Food Products
Brooklyn, NY 800-633-7023
Bellville Meat Market
Bellville, TX 800-571-6328
Berks Packing Company, Inc.
Reading, PA 800-882-3757
Big Apple Produce & Seafood Market
Pocomoke City, MD 410-957-1151
Boesl Packing Company
Baltimore, MD 410-675-1071
Braham Food Locker Service
Braham, MN 320-396-2636
Brook Meadow Provisions Corporation
Hagerstown, MD....................301-739-3107
Burgers Smokehouse
California, MO 800-624-5426
Cedaredge Meats
Cedaredge, CO 970-856-3517
Chicago 58 Food Products
Toronto, ON 416-603-4244
Cloud's Meat Processing
Carthage, MO 417-358-5855
Community Market & Deli
Lindstrom, MN 651-257-1128
ConAgra Snack Foods
San Jose, CA......................408-436-0329
Country Smoked Meats
Bowling Green, OH 800-321-4766
Crofton & Sons
Brandon, FL 800-878-7675
Duis Meat Processing
Concordia, KS.....................800-281-4295
E.W. Knauss & Son
Quakertown, PA 800-648-4220
F&Y Enterprises
Naperville, IL 630-637-8519
Fairbury Food Products
Fairbury, NE 402-729-3379
Fiorucci Foods
Colonial Heights, VA 800-524-7775
Fresh Mark
Canton, OH 800-860-6777

Fricks Meat Products
Washington, MO....................800-241-2209
Gaiser's European Style Provisions
Union, NJ 908-206-9822
Greenwood Packing Plant
Greenwood, SC.....................864-229-5611
Hickory Baked Food
Castle Rock, CO 303-688-2633
Hollman Foods
Minden, NE........................888-926-2879
Hormel Foods Corporation
Fremont, NE 402-721-2300
Hormel Foods Corporation
Austin, MN 800-523-4635
Humphrey Blue Ribbon Meats
Springfield, IL...................800-747-6328
IBP Foods
Troy, MI 248-588-4710
Ittels Meats
Howard Lake, MN 320-543-2285
John Hofmeister & Son
Chicago, IL 800-923-4267
John Volpi & Company
St Louis, MO......................800-288-3439
Kelley Meats
Taberg, NY 315-337-4272
Kessler's, Inc
Lemoyne, PA.......................800-382-1328
Koegel Meats
Flint, MI 810-238-3685
Konetzkos Market
Browerville, MN...................320-594-2915
Laurent Meat Market
Marrero, LA 504-341-1771
Leo G. Fraboni Sausage Company
Hibbing, MN.......................218-263-5074
Lords Sausage & Country Ham
Dexter, GA 800-342-6002
Manger Packing Company
Baltimore, MD 800-227-9262
McKenzie of Vermont
Burlington, VT 802-864-4585
Meat Shop
Cape Girardeau, MO................800-791-5104
Mike's Meats
Eitzen, MN........................507-495-3336

Mountain City Meat Company
Denver, CO 800-937-8325
Nestle Pizza
Medford, WI.......................715-748-5550
Nodine's Smokehouse
Torrington, CT 800-222-2059
Nueces Canyon Texas Style Meat Seasoning
Brenham, TX.......................800-925-5058
Original Chili Bowl
Tulsa, OK 918-628-0225
Penn Valley Farms
Gainesville, GA 773-685-9929
Peoples Sausage Company
Los Angeles, CA...................213-627-8633
Pioneer Packing Company
Bowling Green, OH 419-352-5283
Quality Meats & Seafood
West Fargo, ND....................800-342-4250
R-K Sausage Company
Cleveland, OH 216-341-1251
R.M. Felts Packing Company
Ivor, VA..........................888-300-0971
Raemica
Running Springs, CA 800-772-6328
Rinehart Meat Processing
Branson, MO.......................417-334-2044
Robbins Packing Company
Statesboro, GA 912-764-7503
Rose Packing Company
South Barrington, IL 800-323-7363
Saag's Products
San Leandro, CA...................800-352-7224
Sahlen Packing Company
Buffalo, NY.......................716-852-8677
Sara Lee Corporation
Downers Grove, IL.................630-598-8100
Sara Lee Foods
Zeeland, MI.......................616-875-8131
Sara Lee Foods
Cincinnati, OH 800-351-7111
Sara Lee Foods
Neenah, WI........................800-558-8440
Sardinha Sausage
Somerset, MA......................800-678-0178
Savoie's Sausage & Food Products
Opelousas, LA.....................337-948-4115

Schaller & Weber
  Long Island City, NY 800-847-4115
Sechrist Brothers
  Dallastown, PA 717-244-2975
Smith Meat Packing
  Port Huron, MI 810-985-5900
Stonies Sausage Shop Inc
  Perryville, MO 888-546-2540
Storer Meat Company
  Cleveland, OH 800-355-7537
Striplings
  Moultrie, GA 229-985-4226
Superior's Brand Meats
  Massillon, OH 330-830-0356
Swiss-American Sausage Company
  Lathrop, CA 209-858-5555
Thomas Packing Company
  Columbus, GA 800-729-0976
Tomasinos Sausage
  Canton, OH 330-454-4171
Triple U Enterprises
  Fort Pierre, SD 605-567-3624
Troy Pork Store
  Troy, NY 518-272-8291
Tupman-Thurlow Company
  Deerfield Beach, FL 954-596-9989
V.W. Joyner & Company
  Smithfield, VA 757-357-2161
Warren & Son Meat Processing
  Whipple, OH 740-585-2421
Wayco Ham Company
  Goldsboro, NC 800-962-2614
Willies Smoke House
  Harrisville, PA 800-742-4184
Wimmer's Meat Products
  West Point, NE 800-358-0761
Woods Smoked Meats
  Bowling Green, MO 800-458-8426
Yoakum Packing Company
  Yoakum, TX 361-293-3541
Yoders
  Grantsville, MD 301-895-5121
Zerna Packing
  Labadie, MO 636-742-4190

Poultry & Game
Selwoods Farm Hunting Preserve
  Alpine, AL 256-362-7595

Tasso
Comeaux's
  Lafayette, LA 800-323-2492
Savoie's Sausage & Food Products
  Opelousas, LA 337-948-4115

Turkey

Deli Breast - Fresh
Carolina Turkeys
  Mt Olive, NC 800-523-4559
Farmland Foods
  Kansas City, MO 888-327-6526
Norbest
  Midvale, UT 800-453-5327
Wimmer's Meat Products
  West Point, NE 800-358-0761

Deli Breast - Frozen
Norbest
  Midvale, UT 800-453-5327

Deli Breast - Smoked
Applegate Farms
  Bridgewater, NJ 908-725-2768

Smoked
Applegate Farms
  Bridgewater, NJ 908-725-2768
Burgers Smokehouse
  California, MO 800-624-5426
Chickasaw Trading Company
  Denver City, TX 800-848-3515
Crofton & Sons
  Brandon, FL 800-878-7675
Hollman Foods
  Minden, NE 888-926-2879
Ranch Oak Farm
  Fort Worth, TX 800-888-0327

Sara Lee Foods
  Zeeland, MI 616-875-8131
Selwoods Farm Hunting Preserve
  Alpine, AL 256-362-7595
Thomas Packing Company
  Columbus, GA 800-729-0976
Wampler Foods
  Dallas, TX 717-624-2191
Wayco Ham Company
  Goldsboro, NC 800-962-2614

Steaks
B&D Foods
  Boise, ID 208-344-1183
Bakalars Brothers Sausage Company
  La Crosse, WI 608-784-0384
Blue Ribbon Meats
  Miami, FL 800-522-6115
Burnett & Son Meat Company
  Monrovia, CA 626-357-2165
Buzz Food Service
  Charleston, WV 304-925-4781
Cambridge Packing Company
  Boston, MA 800-722-6726
Centennial Food Corporation
  Calgary, AB 403-287-2525
Devault Foods
  Devault, PA 800-426-2874
Dynamic Foods
  Lubbock, TX 806-762-0780
Elkhart Locker Plant
  Elkhart, KS 620-697-4424
Flint Hills Foods
  Wamego, KS 785-765-3396
Glenmark Food Processors
  Chicago, IL 800-621-0117
Hoekstra Meat Company
  Kalamazoo, MI 616-321-0797
International Packers Corporation
  Watertown, MA 508-963-8214
J&B Meats Corporation
  Coal Valley, IL 309-799-7341
Kutztown Bologna Company
  Leola, PA 800-723-8824
Ossian Seafood Meats
  Ossian, IN 260-622-4191
Pierceton Foods
  Pierceton, IN 574-594-2344
Pinter's Packing Plant
  Dorchester, WI 715-654-5444
Rymer Foods
  Chicago, IL 800-247-9637
S.W. Meat & Provision Company
  Phoenix, AZ 602-275-2000
Stampede Meat
  Bridgeview, IL 800-353-0933
Steak-Umm Company
  Shillington, PA 860-928-5900

Tripe
Bradshaw's Food Products
  Dighton, MA 508-669-6088

Nuts & Nut Butters

Nut Butters

American Almond Products Company
Brooklyn, NY 800-825-6663
Amoretti-Capriccio
Oxnard, CA 800-266-7388
Brost International Trading Company
Chicago, IL 312-861-7100
Cache Creek Foods
Woodland, CA. 530-662-1764
East Wind Nut Butters
Tecumseh, MO 417-679-4682
Fastachi
Watertown, MA. 800-466-3022
Food Mill
Oakland, CA 510-482-3848
Fresh Hemp Foods
Winnipeg, NB 800-665-4367
Justin's Nut Butter
Boulder, CO 303-449-9559
Marin Food Specialties
Byron, CA 925-634-6126
Moon Shine Trading Company
Woodland, CA. 800-678-1226
Once Again Nut Butter
Nunda, NY .888-800-8075
QA Products
Elk Grove Vlg, IL. 800-635-7907
Seabrook Ingredients
Peachtree City, GA 770-487-1230
Sokol & Company
Countryside, IL. 800-328-7656
Sungold Foods
Fargo, ND 866-798-4786

Almond

Fastachi
Watertown, MA. 800-466-3022
Marin Food Specialties
Byron, CA. .925-634-6126
Wiggin Farms
Arbuckle, CA 530-476-2288

Hazelnut

Fastachi
Watertown, MA. 800-466-3022

Peanut Butter

Algood Food Company
Louisville, KY 502-637-3631
American Almond Products Company
Brooklyn, NY 800-825-6663
American Food Traders
Miami, FL. .305-670-6250
Azar Nut Company
El Paso, TX .800-592-8103
Azar Nut Company
El Paso, TX .915-877-4079
Bella Vista Farm
Lawton, OK. 866-237-8526
Carriage House Companies
Fredonia, NY 800-828-8915
Clements Foods Company
Oklahoma City, OK 800-654-8355
ConAgra Grocery Products
Irvine, CA 714-680-1000
E.F. Lane & Son
Oakland, CA 510-569-8980
East Wind Nut Butters
Tecumseh, MO 417-679-4682
Fastachi
Watertown, MA. 800-466-3022
Food Ingredients
Elgin, IL 800-500-7676
Gardners Candies
Tyrone, PA. .800-242-2639
Golden Foods
Commerce, CA 800-350-2462
Griffin Food Company
Muskogee, OK 800-580-6311
Groeb Farms
Onsted, MI .517-467-7100
Hershey Company
Hershey, PA. 800-468-1714

Innovative Food Corporation
Mississauga, ON 905-670-8878
J.M. Smucker Company
Orrville, OH 888-550-9555
JMS Specialty Foods
Ripon, WI 800-535-5437
Krema Nut Company
Columbus, OH 800-222-4132
Landis Peanut Butter
Souderton, PA 215-723-9366
Leavitt Corporation
Everett, MA. 617-389-2600
Lynch Foods
North York, QC. 416-449-5464
Marantha Natural Foods
San Francisco, CA 800-299-0048
Mrs. Annie's Peanut Patch
Floresville, TX 830-393-7845
Once Again Nut Butter
Nunda, NY .888-800-8075
Peanut Butter & Co
New York, NY 212-757-3130
Proctor & Gamble Company
Lexington, KY 859-254-5544
Producers Peanut Company
Suffolk, VA .800-847-5491
Ralcorp Holdings
St Louis, MO. 800-772-6757
Reily Foods Company
New Orleans, LA 504-524-6132
Reily Foods/JFG Coffee Company
Knoxville, TN 800-535-1961
Scott-Bathgate
Winnipeg, NB 204-943-8525
Sessions Company
Enterprise, AL. 334-393-0200
Simple Foods
Tonawanda, NY 800-234-8850
Southern Peanut Company
Dublin, NC .910-862-2136
St. Laurent Brothers
Bay City, MI 800-289-7688
Sunland Inc/Peanut Better
Portales, NM. 575-356-6638
Synergy Foods
West Bloomfield, MI 313-849-2900
Tara Foods
Atlanta, GA. 404-559-0605
Vic Rossano Incorporated
Montreal, QC 514-766-5252
Virginia & Spanish Peanut Company
Providence, RI 800-673-3562

Crunchy

Griffin Food Company
Muskogee, OK 800-580-6311
Groeb Farms
Onsted, MI .517-467-7100

No Additives

Groeb Farms
Onsted, MI .517-467-7100

Smooth

Griffin Food Company
Muskogee, OK 800-580-6311
Groeb Farms
Onsted, MI .517-467-7100

Nut Pastes

American Almond Products Company
Brooklyn, NY 800-825-6663
Amoretti-Capriccio
Oxnard, CA 800-266-7388
Georgia Nut Ingredients
Skokie, IL 877-674-2993
QA Products
Elk Grove Vlg, IL. 800-635-7907
Sokol & Company
Countryside, IL. 800-328-7656
Wiggin Farms
Arbuckle, CA 530-476-2288

Almond

Bear Stewart Corporation
Chicago, IL 800-697-2327
Georgia Nut Ingredients
Skokie, IL 877-674-2993
Heinz North America
Pittsburgh, PA 412-237-5700
Putney Pasta Company
Chester, VT 800-253-3683
QA Products
Elk Grove Vlg, IL. 800-635-7907
Wiggin Farms
Arbuckle, CA 530-476-2288

Nuts

A La Carte
Chicago, IL 800-722-2370
A Southern Season
Chapel Hill, NC 800-253-5317
A. Battaglia Processing Company
Chicago, IL 773-523-5900
A.L. Bazzini Company
Bronx, NY .800-228-0172
Adams & Brooks
Los Angeles, CA. 800-999-9808
Adkin & Son Associated Food Products
South Haven, MI. 269-637-7450
Albanese Confectionery Group
Merrillville, IN 800-536-0581
All Wrapped Up
Lauderhill, FL 800-891-2194
Alldrin Brothers
Ballico, CA 209-667-1600
American Almond Products Company
Brooklyn, NY 800-825-6663
American Health & Nutrition
Ann Arbor, MI 734-677-5572
American Key Food Products
Closter, NJ. 800-767-0237
American Nut & Chocolate Company
Boston, MA. 800-797-6887
American Yeast/Lallemand
Pembroke, NH. 866-920-9885
Ames International
Fife, WA 888-469-2637
AnaCon Foods Company
Atchison, KS. 800-328-0291
Anderson Peanuts
Opp, AL 334-493-4591
Ann's House of Nuts, Inc.
Jessup, MD 301-498-4920
ARA Food Corporation
Miami, FL. 800-533-8831
Archibald Candy Corporation
Chicago, IL 800-333-3629
Arizona Cowboy
Phoenix, AZ 800-529-8627
Arizona Pistachio Company
Tulare, CA. 800-333-8575
Arway Confections
Chicago, IL 773-267-5770
Atwater Fruit Exchange
Atwater, CA. 209-358-2272
Aunt Aggie De's Pralines
Sinton, TX. 888-772-5463
Aurora Products
Stratford, CT. 800-398-1048
Azar Nut Company
El Paso, TX 800-592-8103
Azar Nut Company
El Paso, TX 915-877-4079
Baldwin-Minkler Farms
Orland, CA 530-865-8080
Balsu
Miami Beach, FL 617-539-0880
Barcelona Nut Company
Baltimore, MD 800-292-6887
Bavarian Nut Company
Stockton, CA. 209-465-9181
Beard's Quality Nut Company
Empire, CA 209-526-3590
Beer Nuts
Bloomington, IL 800-233-7688
Bened Food Corporation
Bronx, NY. 718-842-8644

Berberian Nut Company
Stocton, CA 209-465-9181
Beta Pure Foods
Aptos, CA 831-685-6565
Birdsong Corporation
Suffolk, VA 757-539-3456
Birdsong Peanut Company
Gorman, TX 254-734-3153
Blue Diamond Growers
Sacramento, CA 916-442-0771
Brans Nut Company
Wauconda, IL 800-238-0400
Brooks Peanut Company
Samson, AL 334-898-7194
Buchanan Hollow Nut Company
Le Grand, CA 800-532-1500
Byrd's Pecans
Butler, MO 866-679-5583
Cache Creek Foods
Woodland, CA 530-662-1764
Cajun Creole Products
New Iberia, LA 800-946-8688
Cal-Grown Nut Company
Hughson, CA 209-883-4081
California Almond Packers
Corning, CA 530-824-3836
California Fruit & Nut
Gustine, CA 888-747-8224
California Independent Almond Growers
Ballico, CA 209-667-4855
California Wholesale Nut Company
Chico, CA 530-895-0512
Capay Canyon Ranch
Esparto, CA 530-662-2372
Capco Enterprises
East Hanover, NJ 800-252-1011
Carolina Cracker
Garner, NC 919-779-6899
Cascade Continental Foods
Woodland, CA 415-668-6194
Casey's Food Products
Blakely, GA 229-723-3411
Cheese Straws & More
Monroe, LA 800-997-1921
Cherrydale Farms
Allentown, PA 800-333-4525
Chico Nut Company
Chico, CA 530-891-1493
Chieftain Wild Rice Company
Spooner, WI 800-262-6368
China Doll Company
Saraland, AL 251-457-7641
CHS
Inver Grove Heights, MN 800-232-3639
Churchill's Confectionery
Fort Lauderdale, FL 954-764-8195
CJ Dannemiller Company
Norton, OH 800-624-8671
Cloverland Sweets/Priester's Pecan Company
Fort Deposit, AL 800-523-3505
Columbia Empire Farms
Sherwood, OR 503-538-2156
Commodities Marketing, Inc.
Edison, NJ 732-516-0700
ConAgra Grocery Products
Irvine, CA 714-680-1000
Crain Ranch
Los Molinos, CA 530-527-1077
Crown Point
St John, IN 219-365-3200
D Steengrafe & Company
Pleasant Valley, NY 845-635-4067
Dakota Gourmet
Wahpeton, ND 800-727-6663
Dave's Gourmet
San Francisco, CA 800-758-0372
Del Rio Nut Company
Livingston, CA 209-394-7945
Derco Foods
Fresno, CA 559-435-2664
Diamond Foods
Fishers, IN 317-845-5534
Diamond Foods Inc
Stockton, CA 209-467-6000
Diamond Nut Company
Lemont, IL 630-739-3000
Diamond of California
Stockton, CA 925-251-3816
Durey-Libby Edible Nuts
Carlstadt, NJ 800-332-6887
E.F. Lane & Son
Oakland, CA 510-569-8980

E.J. Cox Company/Sachs Nut Company
Clarkton, NC 800-732-6933
El Brands
Ozark, AL 334-445-2828
El Paso Chile Company
El Paso, TX 888-472-5727
Elegant Edibles
Houston, TX 800-227-3226
Energy Club
Pacoima, CA 800-688-6887
Fastachi
Watertown, MA 800-466-3022
Fine Foods Northwest
Seattle, WA 800-862-3965
Flanigan Farms
Culver City, CA 800-525-0228
Foley's Candies
Richmond, BC 888-236-5397
Ford's Fancy Fruit
Raleigh, NC 800-446-0947
Fran's Gifts to Go
Charlotte, NC 800-476-6887
Frazier Nut Farms
Waterford, CA 209-522-1406
Fresh Roasted Almond Company
Westland, MI 734-466-9577
Frito-Lay
Dallas, TX 800-352-4477
Fun Factory
Milwaukee, WI 877-894-6767
G Scaccianoce & Company
Bronx, NY 718-991-4462
Garry Packing
Del Rey, CA 800-248-2126
Germack Pistachio Company
Detroit, MI 800-872-4006
Gillam Brothers Peanut Sheller
Windsor, NC 252-794-3435
Glennys
Freeport, NY 888-864-1243
GNS Food
Arlington, TX 817-795-4671
Golden Kernel Pecan Company
Cameron, SC 800-845-2448
Golden Peanut Company
Ashburn, GA 229-567-3311
Golden Peanut Company
Aulander, NC 252-345-1661
Golden Peanut Company
Alpharetta, GA 770-752-8205
Golden West Nuts
Ripon, CA 209-599-6193
Goodart Candy
Lubbock, TX 806-747-2600
Govadinas Fitness Foods
San Diego, CA 800-900-0108
Granite State Potato Chip Company
Salem, NH 603-898-2171
Great Northern Maple Products
Saint Honor, De Shenley, QC 418-485-7777
Green Valley Pecan Company
Sahuarita, AZ 800-533-5269
Guerra Nut Shelling Company
Hollister, CA 831-637-4471
Gurley's Foods
Willmar, MN 800-426-7845
H&S Edible Products Corporation
Mount Vernon, NY 800-253-3364
H. Naraghi Farms
Escalon, CA 209-577-5777
Hammons Products Company
Stockton, MO 888-429-6887
Hampton Farms
Severn, NC 800-313-2748
Hancock Peanut Company
Courtland, VA 757-653-9351
Harmony Foods Corporation
Fishers, IN 800-837-2855
Harrell Pecan Company
Camilla, GA 800-526-8770
Harris Farms
Coalinga, CA 800-742-1955
Haven's Candies
Westbrook, ME 800-639-6309
Hawaiian King Candies
Honolulu, HI 800-570-1902
Hazelnut Growers of Oregon
Premium, OR 800-273-4676
HempNut
Henderson, NV 707-576-7050
Herkimer Foods
Herkimer, NY 315-895-7832

Hershey
Mississauga, ON 800-468-1714
Hialeah Products Company
Hollywood, FL 800-923-3379
Hickory Harvest Foods
Akron, OH 330-644-6266
Honey Bar/Creme de la Creme
Kingston, NY 845-331-4643
Horriea 2000 Food Industries
Reynolds, GA 478-847-4186
HP Schmid
San Francisco, CA 415-765-5925
Hubbard Peanut Company
Sedley, VA 800-889-7688
Idaho Candy Company
Boise, ID .800-898-6986
International Harvest
Mt Vernon, NY 914-939-1505
International Service Group
Alpharetta, GA 770-518-0988
Jardine Organic Ranch Co
Paso Robles, CA 866-833-5050
Jason & Son Specialty Foods
Rancho Cordova, CA 800-810-9093
Jerry's Nut House
Denver, CO 888-214-0747
Jewel Date Company
Thermal, CA 760-399-4474
JF Braun & Sons Inc.
Westbury, NY 800-997-7177
Jimbo's Jumbos
Edenton, NC 800-334-4771
John B Sanfilippo & Son
Garysburg, NC 252-536-5111
John B Sanfilippo & Son
Gustine, CA 800-218-3077
John B Sanfilippo & Son
Selma, TX 800-423-6546
John B Sanfilippo & Son
Elgin, IL .847-289-1800
John B Sanfilippo & Sons
Selma, TX 800-423-6546
Kalustyan Corporation
Union, NJ 908-688-6111
Karl Bissinger French Confections
St Louis, MO 800-325-8881
Kenlake Foods
Murray, KY 800-632-6900
Kerry Ingredients
Beloit, WI 608-362-1651
Kettle Foods
Salem, OR 503-364-0399
King Nut Company
Cleveland, OH 800-860-5464
Koeze Company
Wyoming, MI 800-555-3909
Kraft
Parsippany, NJ 973-292-1755
Kraft Foods Biscuit Confections & Snacks
East Hanover, NJ 973-503-2000
Kraft Foods North America
Suffolk, VA 757-925-3000
Krema Nut Company
Columbus, OH 800-222-4132
Krispy Kernels
Sainte Foy, QC 418-658-1515
L&S Packing Company
Farmingdale, NY 800-286-6487
LA Wholesale Produce Market
Los Angeles, CA 888-454-6887
Leavitt Corporation
Everett, MA 617-389-2600
Lee Seed Company
Inwood, IA 800-736-6530
Lewis Smoked Meat Company
Chicago, IL 800-648-6328
Livingston Farmers Association
Livingston, CA 209-394-7611
Lodi Nut Company
Lodi, CA .800-234-6887
Lou-Retta's Custom Chocolates
Buffalo, NY 716-833-7111
Lowery's Home Made Candies
Muncie, IN 800-541-3340
MacFarms of Hawaii
Captain Cook, HI 808-328-2435
Majestic Foods
Huntington, NY 631-424-9444
Malatchie Farms Pecans
Fort Valley, GA 912-982-5199
Marantha Natural Foods
San Francisco, CA 800-299-0048

Mareblu Naturals
Anaheim, CA 714-238-1192
Mariani Nut Company
Winters, CA. 530-795-3311
Masterson Company
Milwaukee, WI 414-647-1132
Mayfair Packing Company
San Jose, CA. 408-280-2349
Mayfair Sales
Buffalo, NY 800-248-2881
McCleskey Mills
Smithville, GA. 229-846-4110
Meridian Nut Growers
Clovis, CA .559-458-7272
Merritt Pecan Company
Weston, GA. 800-762-9152
Mezza
Lake Forest, IL 888-206-6054
Midwest/Northern
Minneapolis, MN 800-328-5502
Mon Santo
St Louis, MO. 314-694-1000
Monte Vista Farming Company
Denair, CA 209-874-1866
Mound City Shelled Nut Company
St Louis, MO. 800-647-6887
Mrs May's Naturals
Carson, CA 877-677-6297
Mrs. Dog's Products
Tampa, FL 800-267-7364
Natural Foods
Toledo, OH 800-860-0006
Nature's Candy
Fredericksburg, TX. 800-729-0085
Nature's Select
Grand Rapids, MI 888-715-4321
Navarro Pecan Company
Corsicana, TX. 800-333-9507
Naylor Candies
Mt Wolf, PA 717-266-2706
New England Natural Bakers
Greenfield, MA. 800-910-2884
Northwest Chocolate Factory
Salem, OR 503-362-1340
Northwest Hazelnut Company
Hubbard, OR. 503-982-8030
NSpired Natural Foods
Melville, NY 631-845-4689
Nspired Natural Foods
Melville, NY 631-845-4689
Nutorious
Green Bay, WI. 877-688-6746
Nutsco Inc
Camden, NJ. 856-966-6400
Nuttery Farms
Saint Helena, CA 707-963-1101
Nutty Bavarian
Sanford, FL 800-382-4788
Old Dominion Peanut Corporation
Norfolk, VA. 800-368-6887
Once Again Nut Butter
Nunda, NY 888-800-8075
Orangeburg Pecan Company
Orangeburg, SC 800-845-6970
Organic Planet
San Francisco, CA 415-765-5590
Original Nut House Brands
Portales, NM 575-356-6691
Original Nut House Brands
El Paso, TX. 800-726-7222
Osage Pecan Company
Butler, MO 660-679-6137
P-R Farms
Clovis, CA .559-299-0201
Pacific Gold Marketing
Madera, CA. 559-661-6176
Panoche Creek Packing
Fresno, CA 559-449-1721
Pape's Pecan Company
Seguin, TX 888-688-7273
Paramount Farms
Los Angeles, CA 877-450-9493
Patsy's Candies
Colorado Springs, CO. 866-372-8797
Peanut Patch
Courtland, VA. 866-732-6883
Peanut Roaster
Henderson, NC 800-445-1404
Pear's Coffee
Omaha, NE 800-317-1773
Pease's Candy Shoppe
Springfield, IL. 217-523-3721

Peavey Company
Ama, LA 225-869-4405
Pecan Deluxe Candy Company
Dallas, TX. 800-733-3589
Pennsylvania Dutch Candies
Camp Hill, PA 800-233-7082
Picard Peanuts
Windham Centre, ON 888-244-7688
Pippin Snack Pecans
Albany, GA 800-554-6887
Pippin Snack Pecans Incorporated
Albany, GA 229-432-9316
Pittsburgh Snax & Nut Company
Pittsburgh, PA 800-404-6887
Planters LifeSavers Com pany
Fort Smith, AR 479-648-0100
Pleasant Grove Farms
Pleasant Grove, CA 916-655-3391
Porkie Company of Wisconsin
Cudahy, WI. 800-333-2588
Priester Pecan Company
Fort Deposit, AL 800-277-3226
Prince of Peace Enterprises
Hayward, CA 800-732-2328
Producers Peanut Company
Suffolk, VA 800-847-5491
Punch's Nut Company
Medina, NY 585-798-3890
QA Products
Elk Grove Vlg, IL 800-635-7907
Quality Candy
Milwaukee, WI 800-972-2658
Ramos Orchards
Winters, CA 530-795-4748
Red River Foods
Richmond, VA. 800-443-6637
Reed Lang Farms
Rio Hondo, TX 956-748-2354
Regal Health Foods International
Chicago, IL 773-252-1044
Richard Green Company
Indianapolis, IN 317-972-0941
Roberts Ferry Nut Company
Waterford, CA 209-874-3247
Ross-Smith Pecan Company
Thomasville, GA. 800-841-5503
Royal Wine Company
Bayonne, NJ 201-437-9131
Ryan-Parreira Almond Company
Los Banos, CA 209-826-0272
Sambets Cajun Deli
Austin, TX. 800-472-6238
Santa Clara Nut Company
San Jose, CA. 408-298-2425
Sara Lee Corporation
Downers Grove, IL 630-598-8100
Segovia Mexican Candy Manufacturer
San Antonio, TX. 210-225-2102
Service Packing Company
Vancouver, BC 604-681-0264
Setton International Foods
Commack, NY 800-227-4397
Severn Peanut Company
Severn, NC 800-642-4064
Shade Foods
New Century, KS 800-225-6312
Shields Date Gardens
Indio, CA. .800-414-2555
Sivetz Coffee
Corvallis, OR 541-753-9713
Snackerz
Commerce, CA 888-576-2253
Society Hill Snacks
Philadelphia, PA 800-595-0050
Solnuts
Hudson, IA 800-648-3503
South Georgia Pecan
Valdosta, GA. 800-627-6630
South Georgia Pecan Company
Valdosta, GA. 800-627-6630
South Valley Farms
Wasco, CA 661-391-9000
Southern Peanut Company
Dublin, NC 910-862-2136
Southern Style Nuts
Sherman, TX. 800-624-8242
Spice World
Orlando, FL. 800-433-4979
Spring Tree Maple Products
Brattleboro, VT. 802-254-8784
Sprucewood Handmade Cookie Company
Warkworth, ON. 877-632-1300

Squirrel Brand Company
McKinney, TX 800-624-8242
St. Laurent Brothers
Bay City, MI 800-289-7688
Stahmann Farms
La Mesa, NM 575-526-2453
Stapleton-Spence PackingCompany
San Jose, CA. 800-297-8815
Star Snacks Company
Jersey City, NJ 800-775-9909
Stone Mountain Pecan Company
Monroe, GA. 800-633-6887
Sugai Kona Coffee
Kealakekua, HI 808-322-7717
Sun Empire Foods
Kerman, CA 800-252-4786
Sun Garden Growers
Bard, CA. .800-228-4690
Sun Ridge Farms
Santa Cruz, CA 800-655-3252
Sunny South Pecan Company
Statesboro, GA. 800-764-3687
Sunnyland Farms
Albany, GA 800-999-2488
SunOpta Sunflower
Breckenridge, MN 800-654-4145
Sunray Food Products Corporation
Bronx, NY .718-548-2255
Sunridge Farms
Salinas, CA 831-755-1430
SunRise Commodities
Englewood Cliffs, NJ 201-947-1000
Sunwest Foods
Davis, CA .530-758-8550
Superior Nut & Candy Company
Chicago, IL 800-843-2238
Superior Nut Company
Cambridge, MA. 800-251-6060
Superior Pecan
Eufaula, AL 800-628-2350
Synergy Foods
West Bloomfield, MI 313-849-2900
T.M. Duche Company
Orland, CA 530-865-5511
Tejon Ranch
Lebec, CA .661-248-3000
Terri Lynn
Elgin, IL 800-323-0775
Timber Crest Farms
Healdsburg, CA 888-374-9325
Todd's
Vernon, CA 800-938-6337
Torn & Glasser
Los Angeles, CA. 800-282-6887
Torn Ranch
Novato, CA 415-506-3000
Tracy-Luckey Company
Harlem, GA. 800-476-4796
Treehouse Farms
Earlimart, CA 559-757-4100
Trophy Nut Company
Tipp City, OH 800-729-6887
Tropical
Charlotte, NC 800-220-1413
Tropical
Marietta, GA. 800-544-3762
Tropical Nut & Fruit Company
Orlando, FL. 800-749-8869
Tucker Pecan Company
Montgomery, AL. 800-239-4470
Twenty First Century Snacks
Ronkonkoma, NY 800-975-2883
Utz Quality Foods
Hanover, PA 800-367-7629
Vanco Products Company
Houston, TX. 800-231-9564
Variety Foods
Warren, MI 586-268-4900
Vic Rossano Incorporated
Montreal, QC 514-766-5252
Virginia & Spanish Peanut Company
Providence, RI 800-673-3562
Warner Candy
El Paso, TX. 847-928-7200
Waymouth Farms
New Hope, MN. 800-527-0094
Weaver Nut Company
Ephrata, PA 717-738-3781
Westnut
Cornelius, OR 503-538-2161
Whaley Pecan Company
Troy, AL 800-824-6827

Whitley's Peanut Factory
Hayes, VA 800-470-2244
Wiggin Farms
Arbuckle, CA 530-476-2288
Willamette Valley Walnuts
McMinnville, OR 503-472-3215
Williamette Filbert Growers
Newberg, OR 503-538-9256
Williamsburg Foods
Toano, VA 757-566-0930
Willmar Cookie & Nut Company
Willmar, MN 320-235-0600
Wise Foods
Kennesaw, GA 770-426-5821
Wolfies Roasted Nuts
Findlay, OH 866-889-6887
Woodland Foods
Gurnee, IL 847-625-8600
Young Pecan
Las Cruces, NM 575-524-4321
Young Pecan Company
Florence, SC 800-829-6864
Zenobia Company
Bronx, NY 866-936-6242

Almonds

Alldrin Brothers
Ballico, CA 209-667-1600
Almond Board of California
Modesto, CA 209-549-8262
American Almond Products Company
Brooklyn, NY 800-825-6663
American Key Food Products
Closter, NJ 800-767-0237
Atwater Fruit Exchange
Atwater, CA 209-358-2272
Baldwin-Minkler Farms
Orland, CA 530-865-8080
Buchanan Hollow Nut Company
Le Grand, CA 800-532-1500
Cache Creek Foods
Woodland, CA 530-662-1764
Cal-Grown Nut Company
Hughson, CA 209-883-4081
California Almond Packers
Corning, CA 530-824-3836
California Independent Almond Growers
Ballico, CA 209-667-4855
Capco Enterprises
East Hanover, NJ 800-252-1011
Charles H. Baldwin & Sons
West Stockbridge, MA 413-232-7785
Chico Nut Company
Chico, CA 530-891-1493
Chieftain Wild Rice Company
Spooner, WI 800-262-6368
Chocolate Moon
Asheville, NC 800-723-1236
Commodities Marketing, Inc.
Edison, NJ 732-516-0700
Del Rio Nut Company
Livingston, CA 209-394-7945
Diamond Foods Inc
Stockton, CA 209-467-6000
Diamond Nut Company
Lemont, IL 630-739-3000
Durey-Libby Edible Nuts
Carlstadt, NJ 800-332-6887
Erba Food Products
Brooklyn, NY 718-272-7700
Fastachi
Watertown, MA 800-466-3022
Foley's Candies
Richmond, BC 888-236-5397
Frazier Nut Farms
Waterford, CA 209-522-1406
Fresh Roasted Almond Company
Westland, MI 734-466-9577
G Scaccianoce & Company
Bronx, NY 718-991-4462
Golden West Nuts
Ripon, CA 209-599-6193
H. Naraghi Farms
Escalon, CA 209-577-5777
Harris Farms
Coalinga, CA 800-742-1955
Hershey
Mississauga, ON 800-468-1714
Hialeah Products Company
Hollywood, FL 800-923-3379

Hughson Nut Company
Hughson, CA 209-883-0403
Jardine Organic Ranch Co
Paso Robles, CA 866-833-5050
Jasmine Vineyards
Delano, CA 661-792-2141
John B Sanfilippo & Son
Gustine, CA 800-218-3077
John B Sanfilippo & Son
Selma, TX 800-423-6546
John B Sanfilippo & Sons
Selma, TX 800-423-6546
Krema Nut Company
Columbus, OH 800-222-4132
Livingston Farmers Association
Livingston, CA 209-394-7611
Lodi Nut Company
Lodi, CA 800-234-6887
Lou-Retta's Custom Chocolates
Buffalo, NY 716-833-7111
Mapled Nut Company
Montgomery, VT 800-726-4661
Mariani Nut Company
Winters, CA 530-795-3311
Masterson Company
Milwaukee, WI 414-647-1132
Meridian Nut Growers
Clovis, CA 559-458-7272
Monte Vista Farming Company
Denair, CA 209-874-1866
Nunes Farm Almonds
Newman, CA 209-862-3033
Nut Factory
Spokane Valley, WA 888-239-5288
Nutty Bavarian
Sanford, FL 800-382-4788
OMEGA Nutrition
Bellingham, WA 800-661-3529
Organic Planet
San Francisco, CA 415-765-5590
Original Nut House Brands
El Paso, TX 800-726-7222
P-R Farms
Clovis, CA 559-299-0201
Pacific Gold Marketing
Madera, CA 559-661-6176
Panoche Creek Packing
Fresno, CA 559-449-1721
Paramount Farms
Los Angeles, CA 800-246-6887
Paramount Farms
Los Angeles, CA 877-450-9493
Pilgrim's Pride
Lufkin, TX 936-639-1174
Planters LifeSavers Com pany
Fort Smith, AR 479-648-0100
Pleasant Grove Farms
Pleasant Grove, CA 916-655-3391
QA Products
Elk Grove Vlg, IL 800-635-7907
Ramos Orchards
Winters, CA 530-795-4748
Roberts Ferry Nut Company
Waterford, CA 209-874-3247
Rotteveel Orchards
Dixon, CA 707-678-1495
Ryan-Parreira Almond Company
Los Banos, CA 209-826-0272
Service Packing Company
Vancouver, BC 604-681-0264
Setton International Foods
Commack, NY 800-227-4397
Simple Foods
Tonawanda, NY 800-234-8850
South Valley Farms
Wasco, CA 661-391-9000
Southern Style Nuts
Sherman, TX 800-624-8242
Spring Tree Maple Products
Brattleboro, VT 802-254-8784
Stapleton-Spence PackingCompany
San Jose, CA 800-297-8815
Sun Garden Growers
Bard, CA 800-228-4690
Sunwest Foods
Davis, CA 530-758-8550
T.M. Duche Company
Orland, CA 530-865-5511
Tejon Ranch
Lebec, CA 661-248-3000
Terri Lynn
Elgin, IL 800-323-0775

Timber Crest Farms
Healdsburg, CA 888-374-9325
Treehouse Farms
Earlimart, CA 559-757-4100
Unique Ingredients
Naches, WA 509-653-1991
Virginia Diner
Wakefield, VA 888-823-4637
Weaver Nut Company
Ephrata, PA 717-738-3781
Whitley's Peanut Factory
Hayes, VA 800-470-2244
Wiggin Farms
Arbuckle, CA 530-476-2288
Wolfies Roasted Nuts
Findlay, OH 866-889-6887

Salted

Cache Creek Foods
Woodland, CA 530-662-1764
Golden West Nuts
Ripon, CA 209-599-6193
Hialeah Products Company
Hollywood, FL 800-923-3379
Setton International Foods
Commack, NY 800-227-4397
Terri Lynn
Elgin, IL 800-323-0775
Wiggin Farms
Arbuckle, CA 530-476-2288

Brazil

American Almond Products Company
Brooklyn, NY 800-825-6663
Cache Creek Foods
Woodland, CA 530-662-1764
Chieftain Wild Rice Company
Spooner, WI 800-262-6368
Diamond Foods
Fishers, IN 317-845-5534
Diamond Foods Inc
Stockton, CA 209-467-6000
Diamond Nut Company
Lemont, IL 630-739-3000
Durey-Libby Edible Nuts
Carlstadt, NJ 800-332-6887
Fastachi
Watertown, MA 800-466-3022
Hialeah Products Company
Hollywood, FL 800-923-3379
John B Sanfilippo & Sons
Selma, TX 800-423-6546
LA Wholesale Produce Market
Los Angeles, CA 888-454-6887
Pilgrim's Pride
Lufkin, TX 936-639-1174
Setton International Foods
Commack, NY 800-227-4397
Stapleton-Spence PackingCompany
San Jose, CA 800-297-8815
Terri Lynn
Elgin, IL 800-323-0775
Weaver Nut Company
Ephrata, PA 717-738-3781
Woodland Foods
Gurnee, IL 847-625-8600

Cashews

American Almond Products Company
Brooklyn, NY 800-825-6663
American Health & Nutrition
Ann Arbor, MI 734-677-5572
American Key Food Products
Closter, NJ 800-767-0237
Cache Creek Foods
Woodland, CA 530-662-1764
California Fruit & Nut
Gustine, CA 888-747-8224
Casey's Food Products
Blakely, GA 229-723-3411
Chieftain Wild Rice Company
Spooner, WI 800-262-6368
Commodities Marketing, Inc.
Edison, NJ 732-516-0700
Diamond Foods
Fishers, IN 317-845-5534
Durey-Libby Edible Nuts
Carlstadt, NJ 800-332-6887
Fastachi
Watertown, MA 800-466-3022

Fresh Roasted Almond Company
Westland, MI.....................734-466-9577
Germack Pistachio Company
Detroit, MI 800-872-4006
Hialeah Products Company
Hollywood, FL....................800-923-3379
John B Sanfilippo & Son
Selma, TX........................800-423-6546
John B Sanfilippo & Sons
Selma, TX........................800-423-6546
Koeze Company
Wyoming, MI......................800-555-3909
Krema Nut Company
Columbus, OH 800-222-4132
LA Wholesale Produce Market
Los Angeles, CA..................888-454-6887
Landies Candies Company
Buffalo, NY......................800-955-2634
Lou-Retta's Custom Chocolates
Buffalo, NY......................716-833-7111
Mapled Nut Company
Montgomery, VT...................800-726-4661
Marantha Natural Foods
San Francisco, CA................800-299-0048
Maxwell's Gourmet Food
Raleigh, NC 800-952-6887
Meridian Nut Growers
Clovis, CA 559-458-7272
Naylor Candies
Mt Wolf, PA 717-266-2706
Nut Factory
Spokane Valley, WA...............888-239-5288
Nuts & Stems
Rosharon, TX 281-464-6887
Nutsco Inc
Camden, NJ.......................856-966-6400
Nutty Bavarian
Sanford, FL......................800-382-4788
Organic Planet
San Francisco, CA................415-765-5590
Pacific Gold Marketing
Madera, CA.......................559-661-6176
Pilgrim's Pride
Lufkin, TX 936-639-1174
Planters LifeSavers Company
Fort Smith, AR...................479-648-0100
Setton International Foods
Commack, NY 800-227-4397
Southern Style Nuts
Sherman, TX......................800-624-8242
Spring Tree Maple Products
Brattleboro, VT..................802-254-8784
Stapleton-Spence PackingCompany
San Jose, CA.....................800-297-8815
Sunray Food Products Corporation
Bronx, NY........................718-548-2255
Terri Lynn
Elgin, IL 800-323-0775
Tropical
Marietta, GA.....................800-544-3762
Virginia Diner
Wakefield, VA....................888-823-4637
Weaver Nut Company
Ephrata, PA 717-738-3781
Wolfies Roasted Nuts
Findlay, OH......................866-889-6887
Woodland Foods
Gurnee, IL.......................847-625-8600

Chestnuts

Adkin & Son Associated Food Products
South Haven, MI..................269-637-7450
Chieftain Wild Rice Company
Spooner, WI 800-262-6368

Coated

Chocolate

A.L. Bazzini Company
Bronx, NY........................800-228-0172
Karl Bissinger French Confections
St Louis, MO.....................800-325-8881
Kerry Ingredients
Beloit, WI.......................608-362-1651
Lowery's Home Made Candies
Muncie, IN.......................800-541-3340
Weaver Nut Company
Ephrata, PA 717-738-3781

Yogurt

GKI Foods
Brighton, MI.....................248-486-0055
Setton International Foods
Commack, NY 800-227-4397
Terri Lynn
Elgin, IL 800-323-0775

Filberts

American Almond Products Company
Brooklyn, NY.....................800-825-6663
Cache Creek Foods
Woodland, CA.....................530-662-1764
Commodities Marketing, Inc.
Edison, NJ.......................732-516-0700
Diamond Foods
Fishers, IN......................317-845-5534
Diamond Nut Company
Lemont, IL.......................630-739-3000
Durey-Libby Edible Nuts
Carlstadt, NJ....................800-332-6887
Erba Food Products
Brooklyn, NY 718-272-7700
Germack Pistachio Company
Detroit, MI 800-872-4006
Hialeah Products Company
Hollywood, FL....................800-923-3379
Krema Nut Company
Columbus, OH 800-222-4132
Nut Factory
Spokane Valley, WA...............888-239-5288
Organic Planet
San Francisco, CA................415-765-5590
Pilgrim's Pride
Lufkin, TX 936-639-1174
Setton International Foods
Commack, NY 800-227-4397
Stapleton-Spence PackingCompany
San Jose, CA.....................800-297-8815
Terri Lynn
Elgin, IL 800-323-0775
Weaver Nut Company
Ephrata, PA 717-738-3781

Glazed & Coated

A.L. Bazzini Company
Bronx, NY........................800-228-0172
Archibald Candy Corporation
Chicago, IL 800-333-3629
Arway Confections
Chicago, IL......................773-267-5770
Atkinson Candies Company
Lufkin, TX 936-639-2333
Betty Lou's Golden Smackers
McMinnville, OR..................800-242-5205
Cache Creek Foods
Woodland, CA.....................530-662-1764
Candy Factory
Hayward, CA 800-736-6887
Cheese Straws & More
Monroe, LA.......................800-997-1921
Chocolate Moon
Asheville, NC 800-723-1236
Cloverland Sweets/Priester's Pecan Company
Fort Deposit, AL.................800-523-3505
Columbia Empire Farms
Sherwood, OR.....................503-538-2156
Crown Candy Corporation
Macon, GA 800-241-3529
Dillon Candy Company
Boston, GA.......................800-382-8338
Farr Candy Company
Idaho Falls, ID..................208-522-8215
Foley's Candies
Richmond, BC 888-236-5397
G Scaccianoce & Company
Bronx, NY........................718-991-4462
GKI Foods
Brighton, MI.....................248-486-0055
Goodart Candy
Lubbock, TX......................806-747-2600
Haven's Candies
Westbrook, ME 800-639-6309
Hershey
Mississauga, ON..................800-468-1714
Jason & Son Specialty Foods
Rancho Cordova, CA...............800-810-9093
Karl Bissinger French Confections
St Louis, MO.....................800-325-8881

Kay Foods Company
Ionia, MI........................616-527-0120
Kerry Ingredients
Beloit, WI 608-362-1651
King Nut Company
Cleveland, OH 800-860-5464
Laymon Candy Company
San Bernardino, CA...............909-825-4408
Libs Candies Downtown
Evansville, IN...................812-422-5119
Lowery's Home Made Candies
Muncie, IN.......................800-541-3340
MacFarms of Hawaii
Captain Cook, HI.................808-328-2435
Marich Confectionery Company
Hollister, CA....................800-624-7055
Matangos Candies
Harrisburg, PA 717-234-0882
McCraw Candies
Farmersville, TX 800-551-7201
Midwest/Northern
Minneapolis, MN 800-328-5502
Moore's Candies
Baltimore, MD....................410-426-2705
Mrs. Annie's Peanut Patch
Floresville, TX 830-393-7845
Muth Candies
Louisville, KY...................502-585-2952
Nature's Candy
Fredericksburg, TX...............800-729-0085
Naylor Candies
Mt Wolf, PA 717-266-2706
New England Confectionery Company
Revere, MA.......................781-485-4500
Northwest Chocolate Factory
Salem, OR........................503-362-1340
Novartis Nutrition Corporation
Minneapolis, MN 952-848-6000
NSpired Natural Foods
Melville, NY.....................631-845-4689
Nutty Bavarian
Sanford, FL......................800-382-4788
Old Dominion Peanut Corporation
Norfolk, VA......................800-368-6887
Original Nut House Brands
El Paso, TX......................800-726-7222
Pippin Snack Pecans
Albany, GA.......................800-554-6887
Popcorn Connection
North Hollywood, CA..............800-852-2676
Priester Pecan Company
Fort Deposit, AL.................800-277-3226
Prince of Peace Enterprises
Hayward, CA 800-732-2328
Randag & Associates Inc
Elmhurst, IL.....................630-530-2830
Segovia Mexican Candy Manufacturer
San Antonio, TX..................210-225-2102
Setton International Foods
Commack, NY 800-227-4397
Shade Foods
New Century, KS 800-225-6312
Southern Style Nuts
Sherman, TX......................800-624-8242
St. Laurent Brothers
Bay City, MI 800-289-7688
Superior Nut & Candy Company
Chicago, IL 800-843-2238
Terri Lynn
Elgin, IL 800-323-0775
Tom & Sally's Handmade Chocolates
Brattleboro, VT..................800-827-0800
Tonex
Wallington, NJ 973-773-5135
Tropical
Columbus, OH 800-538-3941
Warrell Corporation
Camp Hill, PA 800-233-7082
Waymouth Farms
New Hope, MN.....................800-527-0094
Weaver Nut Company
Ephrata, PA 717-738-3781
Webbs Citrus Candy
Davenport, FL....................863-422-1051
Whitley's Peanut Factory
Hayes, VA 800-470-2244

Hazelnuts

Balsu
Miami Beach, FL 617-539-0880

Cache Creek Foods
  Woodland, CA. 530-662-1764
Chieftain Wild Rice Company
  Spooner, WI 800-262-6368
Columbia Empire Farms
  Sherwood, OR. 503-538-2156
Commodities Marketing, Inc.
  Edison, NJ. .732-516-0700
Fancy's Candy's
  Rougemont, NC 888-403-2629
Fastachi
  Watertown, MA. 800-466-3022
Hazelnut Growers of Oregon
  Premium, OR 800-273-4676
Hazy Grove Nuts
  Lake Oswego, OR. 800-574-6887
Hialeah Products Company
  Hollywood, FL 800-923-3379
Krema Nut Company
  Columbus, OH 800-222-4132
LA Wholesale Produce Market
  Los Angeles, CA. 888-454-6887
Meridian Nut Growers
  Clovis, CA 559-458-7272
Northwest Chocolate Factory
  Salem, OR. .503-362-1340
Northwest Hazelnut Company
  Hubbard, OR. 503-982-8030
OMEGA Nutrition
  Bellingham, WA 800-661-3529
Organic Planet
  San Francisco, CA 415-765-5590
Pilgrim's Pride
  Lufkin, TX .936-639-1174
Purity Foods
  Okemos, MI 800-997-7358
Setton International Foods
  Commack, NY 800-227-4397
Terri Lynn
  Elgin, IL 800-323-0775
Westnut
  Cornelius, OR 503-538-2161
Williamette Filbert Growers
  Newberg, OR 503-538-9256

Macadamia

American Key Food Products
  Closter, NJ. .800-767-0237
Cache Creek Foods
  Woodland, CA 530-662-1764
Chieftain Wild Rice Company
  Spooner, WI 800-262-6368
Diamond Foods
  Fishers, IN. .317-845-5534
Durey-Libby Edible Nuts
  Carlstadt, NJ 800-332-6887
Fastachi
  Watertown, MA. 800-466-3022
Hawaiian Sun Products
  Honolulu, HI 808-845-3211
Hialeah Products Company
  Hollywood, FL 800-923-3379
Island Princess
  Honolulu, HI 866-872-8601
John B Sanfilippo & Sons
  Selma, TX. .800-423-6546
Koeze Company
  Wyoming, MI 800-555-3909
Lodi Nut Company
  Lodi, CA. 800-234-6887
MacFarms of Hawaii
  Captain Cook, HI 808-328-2435
Mauana Loa Macadamia Nut Corporation
  Florence, SC 843-629-1685
Meridian Nut Growers
  Clovis, CA 559-458-7272
Organic Planet
  San Francisco, CA 415-765-5590
Pilgrim's Pride
  Lufkin, TX .936-639-1174
Prince of Peace Enterprises
  Hayward, CA 800-732-2328
Setton International Foods
  Commack, NY 800-227-4397
Stapleton-Spence PackingCompany
  San Jose, CA. 800-297-8815
Sugai Kona Coffee
  Kealakekua, HI 808-322-7717
Terri Lynn
  Elgin, IL 800-323-0775

Woodland Foods
  Gurnee, IL. .847-625-8600

Mixed Nuts

Crazy Jerry's
  Roswell, GA 770-993-0651
Mapled Nut Company
  Montgomery, VT. 800-726-4661

Nut Meats

American Almond Products Company
  Brooklyn, NY 800-825-6663
Baldwin-Minkler Farms
  Orland, CA .530-865-8080
Cache Creek Foods
  Woodland, CA 530-662-1764
Durey-Libby Edible Nuts
  Carlstadt, NJ 800-332-6887
Hammons Products Company
  Stockton, MO 888-429-6887
Jerry's Nut House
  Denver, CO 888-214-0747
King Nut Company
  Cleveland, OH 800-860-5464
Mid-Valley Nut Company
  Hughson, CA 209-883-4491
Mother Earth Enterprises
  New York, NY 866-436-7688
Nuttery Farms
  Saint Helena, CA 707-963-1101
QA Products
  Elk Grove Vlg, IL 800-635-7907
Service Packing Company
  Vancouver, BC 604-681-0264
Setton International Foods
  Commack, NY 800-227-4397
South Georgia Pecan Company
  Valdosta, GA 800-627-6630
Superior Nut & Candy Company
  Chicago, IL. 800-843-2238
Superior Pecan
  Eufaula, AL 800-628-2350
Terri Lynn
  Elgin, IL 800-323-0775
Waymouth Farms
  New Hope, MN 800-527-0094
Whaley Pecan Company
  Troy, AL 800-824-6827
Willamette Valley Walnuts
  McMinnville, OR 503-472-3215
Young Pecan Company
  Florence, SC 800-829-6864

Peanuts

American Health & Nutrition
  Ann Arbor, MI 734-677-5572
Anderson Peanuts
  Opp, AL 334-493-4591
Belmont Peanuts of Southampton Inc
  Capron, VA 800-648-4613
E.F. Lane & Son
  Oakland, CA 510-569-8980
Fastachi
  Watertown, MA. 800-466-3022
Golden Peanuts Company
  Alpharetta, GA 770-752-8160
Hardy Farms Peanuts
  Hawkinsville, GA 888-368-6887
Koeze Company
  Wyoming, MI 800-555-3909
Krema Nut Company
  Columbus, OH 800-222-4132
Peanut Corporation of America
  Lynchburg, VA 434-384-7098
Peanut Processors
  Dublin, NC 910-862-2136
Peanut Shop of Williamsburg
  Portsmouth, VA 800-637-3268
Queensway Foods Company
  Burlingame, CA 650-697-6666
Richfield Foods
  Cairo, GA .229-377-2102
Royal Oak Peanuts
  Drewryville, VA 800-608-4590
Setton International Foods
  Commack, NY 800-227-4397
Southern Peanut Company
  Dublin, NC 910-862-2136
Terri Lynn
  Elgin, IL 800-323-0775

Virginia Diner
  Wakefield, VA 888-823-4637

Granulated

American Almond Products Company
  Brooklyn, NY 800-825-6663
American Key Food Products
  Closter, NJ .800-767-0237
Cajun Creole Products
  New Iberia, LA 800-946-8688
Hialeah Products Company
  Hollywood, FL 800-923-3379
Pilgrim's Pride
  Lufkin, TX .936-639-1174
Producers Peanut Company
  Suffolk, VA 800-847-5491
Seabrook Ingredients
  Peachtree City, GA 770-487-1230
Terri Lynn
  Elgin, IL 800-323-0775

Raw

American Almond Products Company
  Brooklyn, NY 800-825-6663
Birdsong Corporation
  Suffolk, VA 757-539-3456
Birdsong Peanut Company
  Gorman, TX 254-734-3153
Cajun Creole Products
  New Iberia, LA 800-946-8688
Hialeah Products Company
  Hollywood, FL 800-923-3379
John B Sanfilippo & Son
  Elgin, IL 847-289-1800
Krema Nut Company
  Columbus, OH 800-222-4132
LA Wholesale Produce Market
  Los Angeles, CA. 888-454-6887
Original Nut House Brands
  El Paso, TX. 800-726-7222
St. Laurent Brothers
  Bay City, MI 800-289-7688

Raw & Shelled

American Health & Nutrition
  Ann Arbor, MI 734-677-5572
American Key Food Products
  Closter, NJ .800-767-0237
Cajun Creole Products
  New Iberia, LA 800-946-8688
E.J. Cox Company/Sachs Nut Company
  Clarkton, NC 800-732-6933
Golden Peanut Company
  Ashburn, GA 229-567-3311
Hialeah Products Company
  Hollywood, FL 800-923-3379
King Nut Company
  Cleveland, OH 800-860-5464
McCleskey Mills
  Smithville, GA 229-846-4110
Pilgrim's Pride
  Lufkin, TX .936-639-1174
Royal Oak Peanuts
  Drewryville, VA 800-608-4590
Seabrook Ingredients
  Peachtree City, GA 770-487-1230
Setton International Foods
  Commack, NY 800-227-4397
Southern Peanut Company
  Dublin, NC 910-862-2136
Terri Lynn
  Elgin, IL 800-323-0775

Roasted

American Almond Products Company
  Brooklyn, NY 800-825-6663
Cajun Creole Products
  New Iberia, LA 800-946-8688
Casey's Food Products
  Blakely, GA. 229-723-3411
CJ Dannemiller Company
  Norton, OH 800-624-8671
E.F. Lane & Son
  Oakland, CA 510-569-8980
John B Sanfilippo & Son
  Elgin, IL 847-289-1800
King Nut Company
  Cleveland, OH 800-860-5464
Naylor Candies
  Mt Wolf, PA 717-266-2706

Queensway Foods Company
Burlingame, CA 650-697-6666
Southern Peanut Company
Dublin, NC 910-862-2136
St. Laurent Brothers
Bay City, MI 800-289-7688
Synergy Foods
West Bloomfield, MI 313-849-2900

Salted

American Health & Nutrition
Ann Arbor, MI 734-677-5572
Cajun Creole Products
New Iberia, LA 800-946-8688
Durey-Libby Edible Nuts
Carlstadt, NJ 800-332-6887
Hialeah Products Company
Hollywood, FL 800-923-3379
Koeze Company
Wyoming, MI 800-555-3909
LA Wholesale Produce Market
Los Angeles, CA 888-454-6887
Pilgrim's Pride
Lufkin, TX 936-639-1174
Seabrook Ingredients
Peachtree City, GA 770-487-1230
Setton International Foods
Commack, NY 800-227-4397
Southern Peanut Company
Dublin, NC 910-862-2136
St. Laurent Brothers
Bay City, MI 800-289-7688
Terri Lynn
Elgin, IL 800-323-0775
Virginia & Spanish Peanut Company
Providence, RI 800-673-3562

Pecan

American Health & Nutrition
Ann Arbor, MI 734-677-5572
American Key Food Products
Closter, NJ 800-767-0237
Aunt Aggie De's Pralines
Sinton, TX 888-772-5463
Cache Creek Foods
Woodland, CA 530-662-1764
Carolina Cracker
Garner, NC 919-779-6899
Carolyn's Gourmet
Concord, MA 800-656-2940
Cheese Straws & More
Monroe, LA. 800-997-1921
Chieftain Wild Rice Company
Spooner, WI 800-262-6368
Claxton Bakery
Claxton, GA 800-841-4211
Cloverland Sweets/Priester's Pecan Company
Fort Deposit, AL 800-523-3505
Columbus Gourmet
Columbus, GA 800-356-1858
Diamond Foods Inc
Stockton, CA. 209-467-6000
Diamond Nut Company
Lemont, IL 630-739-3000
Durey-Libby Edible Nuts
Carlstadt, NJ 800-332-6887
Elegant Edibles
Houston, TX 800-227-3206
Fancy's Candy's
Rougemont, NC 888-403-2629
Fastachi
Watertown, MA. 800-466-3022
Fresh Roasted Almond Company
Westland, MI 734-466-9577
Golden Harvest Pecans
Cairo, GA 800-597-0968
Golden Kernel Pecan Company
Cameron, SC 800-845-2448
Hialeah Products Company
Hollywood, FL 800-923-3379
Indianola Pecan House
Indianola, MS 800-541-6252
Jewel Date Company
Thermal, CA 760-399-4474
John B Sanfilippo & Son
Selma, TX 800-423-6546
John B Sanfilippo & Sons
Selma, TX 800-423-6546
Koeze Company
Wyoming, MI 800-555-3909

Krema Nut Company
Columbus, OH 800-222-4132
Landies Candies Company
Buffalo, NY....................800-955-2634
Lane Packing Company
Fort Valley, GA 478-825-3592
Lou-Retta's Custom Chocolates
Buffalo, NY....................716-833-7111
Mapled Nut Company
Montgomery, VT. 800-726-4661
Maxwell's Gourmet Food
Raleigh, NC 800-952-6887
Meridian Nut Growers
Clovis, CA 559-458-7272
Merritt Pecan Company
Weston, GA 800-762-9152
Mingo River Pecan Company
Florence, SC 800-440-6442
Mountain States Pecan
Roswell, NM...................505-623-2216
Navarro Pecan Company
Corsicana, TX 800-333-9507
Nuthouse Company
Mobile, AL 251-433-1689
Nutty Bavarian
Sanford, FL 800-382-4788
Orangeburg Pecan Company
Orangeburg, SC 800-845-6970
Original Nut House Brands
El Paso, TX....................800-726-7222
Pape's Pecan Company
Seguin, TX 888-688-7273
Pilgrim's Pride
Lufkin, TX 936-639-1174
Pippin Snack Pecans
Albany, GA 800-554-6887
Pippin Snack Pecans Incorporated
Albany, GA 229-432-9316
Planters LifeSavers Com pany
Fort Smith, AR 479-648-0100
Priester Pecan Company
Fort Deposit, AL................800-277-3226
Reed Lang Farms
Rio Hondo, TX 956-748-2354
Ross-Smith Pecan Company
Thomasville, GA. 800-841-5503
San Saba Pecan
San Saba, TX 800-683-2101
Santa Cruz Valley Pecan
Sahuarita, AZ 800-533-5269
Setton International Foods
Commack, NY 800-227-4397
South Georgia Pecan
Valdosta, GA 800-627-6630
South Georgia Pecan Company
Valdosta, GA 800-627-6630
Southern Style Nuts
Sherman, TX...................800-624-8242
Southwest Nut Company
Fabens, TX 915-764-4949
Stahmann Farms
La Mesa, NM 575-526-2453
Stapleton-Spence PackingCompany
San Jose, CA...................800-297-8815
Stone Mountain Pecan Company
Monroe, GA 800-633-6887
Sunny South Pecan Company
Statesboro, GA 800-764-3687
Sunnyland Farms
Albany, GA 800-999-2488
Sunshine Farms
Roseboro, NC 910-564-2421
Sunwest Foods
Davis, CA 530-758-8550
Superior Pecan
Eufaula, AL 800-628-2350
Terri Lynn
Elgin, IL 800-323-0775
Tracy-Luckey Company
Harlem, GA 800-476-4796
Tucker Pecan Company
Montgomery, AL................800-239-4470
Weaver Nut Company
Ephrata, PA 717-738-3781
Whaley Pecan Company
Troy, AL 800-824-6827
Whitley's Peanut Factory
Hayes, VA 800-470-2244
Young Pecan
Las Cruces, NM 575-524-4321
Young Pecan Company
Florence, SC 800-829-6864

Salted

Stahmann Farms
La Mesa, NM 575-526-2453

Pignolias

Castella Imports
Hauppauge, NY 866-227-8355
L&S Packing Company
Farmingdale, NY 800-286-6487

Pine

American Importing Company
Minneapolis, MN 612-331-9226
American Key Food Products
Closter, NJ 800-767-0237
Chieftain Wild Rice Company
Spooner, WI 800-262-6368
Diamond Foods
Fishers, IN.....................317-845-5534
Diamond Foods Inc
Stockton, CA 209-467-6000
Durey-Libby Edible Nuts
Carlstadt, NJ 800-332-6887
Fastachi
Watertown, MA. 800-466-3022
Grapevine Trading Company
Santa Rosa, CA 800-469-6478
Hialeah Products Company
Hollywood, FL 800-923-3379
John B Sanfilippo & Sons
Selma, TX 800-423-6546
Pilgrim's Pride
Lufkin, TX 936-639-1174
Setton International Foods
Commack, NY 800-227-4397
Spring Tree Maple Products
Brattleboro, VT 802-254-8784
Stapleton-Spence PackingCompany
San Jose, CA...................800-297-8815
Terri Lynn
Elgin, IL 800-323-0775
Woodland Foods
Gurnee, IL 847-625-8600

Pistachio

Arizona Pistachio Company
Tulare, CA 800-333-8575
Buchanan Hollow Nut Company
Le Grand, CA 800-532-1500
Cache Creek Foods
Woodland, CA. 530-662-1764
California Fruit & Nut
Gustine, CA 888-747-8224
Capco Enterprises
East Hanover, NJ. 800-252-1011
Chieftain Wild Rice Company
Spooner, WI 800-262-6368
Commodities Marketing, Inc.
Edison, NJ.....................732-516-0700
Diamond Foods
Fishers, IN.....................317-845-5534
Durey-Libby Edible Nuts
Carlstadt, NJ 800-332-6887
Fastachi
Watertown, MA. 800-466-3022
Germack Pistachio Company
Detroit, MI 800-872-4006
H. Naraghi Farms
Escalon, CA 209-577-5777
Hialeah Products Company
Hollywood, FL 800-923-3379
Jardine Organic Ranch Co
Paso Robles, CA 866-833-5050
John B Sanfilippo & Sons
Selma, TX 800-423-6546
Kalustyan Corporation
Union, NJ 908-688-6111
Keenan Farms
Avenal, CA 559-945-1400
Koeze Company
Wyoming, MI 800-555-3909
Krema Nut Company
Columbus, OH 800-222-4132
LA Wholesale Produce Market
Los Angeles, CA................888-454-6887
Meridian Nut Growers
Clovis, CA 559-458-7272
Mrs. Dog's Products
Tampa, FL.....................800-267-7364

Nunes Farm Almonds
Newman, CA. 209-862-3033
Nuts & Stems
Rosharon, TX 281-464-6887
OMEGA Nutrition
Bellingham, WA 800-661-3529
Organic Planet
San Francisco, CA 415-765-5590
Pacific Gold Marketing
Madera, CA 559-661-6176
Paramount Farms
Los Angeles, CA. 800-246-6887
Paramount Farms
Los Angeles, CA. 877-450-9493
Pilgrim's Pride
Lufkin, TX 936-639-1174
Planters LifeSavers Com pany
Fort Smith, AR 479-648-0100
Primex International Trading Corporation
Los Angeles, CA 310-568-8855
Santa Barbara Pistachio Company
Santa Barbara, CA 800-896-1044
Setton International Foods
Commack, NY 800-227-4397
South Valley Farms
Wasco, CA 661-391-9000
Spring Tree Maple Products
Brattleboro, VT 802-254-8784
Stapleton-Spence PackingCompany
San Jose, CA 800-297-8815
Sunray Food Products Corporation
Bronx, NY 718-548-2255
Sunwest Foods
Davis, CA 530-758-8550
Tejon Ranch
Lebec, CA 661-248-3000
Terri Lynn
Elgin, IL 800-323-0775
Timber Crest Farms
Healdsburg, CA 888-374-9325
Weaver Nut Company
Ephrata, PA 717-738-3781
Woodland Foods
Gurnee, IL 847-625-8600

Pralines (See also Confectionery)

Aunt Aggie De's Pralines
Sinton, TX. 888-772-5463
B&B Pecan Processors of NC
Turkey, NC 866-328-7322
Blueberry Store
Grand Junction, MI. 877-654-2400
Creole Delicacies Pralines
New Orleans, LA 504-523-6425
Landies Candies Company
Buffalo, NY. 800-955-2634
Pecan Deluxe Candy Company
Dallas, TX. 800-733-3589
Wing Candy Company
Branson, MO. 417-334-3238

Roasted

Adkin & Son Associated Food Products
South Haven, MI. 269-637-7450
American Almond Products Company
Brooklyn, NY 800-825-6663
Baker Candy Company
Seattle, WA 425-776-6622
Brans Nut Company
Wauconda, IL 800-238-0400
Bruno's Cajun Foods & Snacks
Slidell, LA. 985-726-0544
CJ Dannemiller Company
Norton, OH 800-624-8671
Dakota Gourmet
Wahpeton, ND. 800-727-6663
Osage Pecan Company
Butler, MO 660-679-6137
Solnuts
Hudson, IA 800-648-3503
Superior Nut & Candy Company
Chicago, IL 800-843-2238
Tropical
Charlotte, NC 800-220-1413
Tropical Nut & Fruit Company
Orlando, FL. 800-749-8869
Wiggin Farms
Arbuckle, CA 530-476-2288
Williamette Filbert Growers
Newberg, OR 503-538-9256

Willmar Cookie & Nut Company
Willmar, MN. 320-235-0600
Wolfies Gourmet Nuts
Findlay, OH 866-889-6887

Shelled

A. Battaglia Processing Company
Chicago, IL 773-523-5900
Alldrin Brothers
Ballico, CA 209-667-1600
Bruno's Cajun Foods & Snacks
Slidell, LA. 985-726-0544
Frazier Nut Farms
Waterford, CA. 209-522-1406
Jerry's Nut House
Denver, CO 888-214-0747
Pippin Snack Pecans
Albany, GA 800-554-6887
Ross-Smith Pecan Company
Thomasville, GA. 800-841-5503
Santa Clara Nut Company
San Jose, CA 408-298-2425
Tracy-Luckey Company
Harlem, GA 800-476-4796
Whaley Pecan Company
Troy, AL 800-824-6827
Williamette Filbert Growers
Newberg, OR 503-538-9256

Soy

American Health & Nutrition
Ann Arbor, MI 734-677-5572
American Importing Company
Minneapolis, MN 612-331-9226
Bellatti Soybeans-Bellatti Soynuts
Mount Pulaski, IL 217-792-5503
Fastachi
Watertown, MA. 800-466-3022
Hialeah Products Company
Hollywood, FL 800-923-3379
Just Tomatoes Company
Westley, CA. 800-537-1985
Lee Seed Company
Inwood, IA 800-736-6530
Nature's Select
Grand Rapids, MI 888-715-4321
Pilgrim's Pride
Lufkin, TX 936-639-1174
Solnuts
Hudson, IA 800-648-3503

Walnuts

American Almond Products Company
Brooklyn, NY 800-825-6663
American Health & Nutrition
Ann Arbor, MI 734-677-5572
Beard's Quality Nut Company
Empire, CA 209-526-3590
Berberian Nut Company
Stocton, CA 209-465-9181
Byrd's Pecans
Butler, MO 866-679-5583
Chieftain Wild Rice Company
Spooner, WI 800-262-6368
Crain Ranch
Los Molinos, CA 530-527-1077
Diamond Foods
Fishers, IN. 317-845-5534
Diamond Foods Inc
Stockton, CA. 209-467-6000
Diamond Nut Company
Lemont, IL 630-739-3000
Durey-Libby Edible Nuts
Carlstadt, NJ 800-332-6887
Erba Food Products
Brooklyn, NY 718-272-7700
Fastachi
Watertown, MA. 800-466-3022
Frazier Nut Farms
Waterford, CA. 209-522-1406
Fresh Roasted Almond Company
Westland, MI. 734-466-9577
Guerra Nut Shelling Company
Hollister, CA 831-637-4471
H. Naraghi Farms
Escalon, CA 209-577-5777
Hammons Products Company
Stockton, MO 888-429-6887
Hialeah Products Company
Hollywood, FL 800-923-3379

John B Sanfilippo & Son
Gustine, CA 800-218-3077
John B Sanfilippo & Son
Selma, TX. 800-423-6546
Lodi Nut Company
Lodi, CA 800-234-6887
Mapled Nut Company
Montgomery, VT 800-726-4661
Mariani Nut Company
Winters, CA 530-795-3311
Meridian Nut Growers
Clovis, CA 559-458-7272
Mid-Valley Nut Company
Hughson, CA 209-883-4491
Nut Factory
Spokane Valley, WA 888-239-5288
Pilgrim's Pride
Lufkin, TX 936-639-1174
Planters LifeSavers Com pany
Fort Smith, AR 479-648-0100
Ramos Orchards
Winters, CA 530-795-4748
Santa Clara Nut Company
San Jose, CA 408-298-2425
Service Packing Company
Vancouver, BC 604-681-0264
Specialty Commodities
Fargo, ND 701-282-8222
Spring Tree Maple Products
Brattleboro, VT 802-254-8784
Stapleton-Spence PackingCompany
San Jose, CA 800-297-8815
Sunwest Foods
Davis, CA 530-758-8550
Tejon Ranch
Lebec, CA 661-248-3000
Weaver Nut Company
Ephrata, PA 717-738-3781
Willamette Valley Walnuts
McMinnville, OR 503-472-3215
Woodland Foods
Gurnee, IL 847-625-8600

Black

American Health & Nutrition
Ann Arbor, MI 734-677-5572
American Key Food Products
Closter, NJ 800-767-0237
Cache Creek Foods
Woodland, CA. 530-662-1764
Frazier Nut Farms
Waterford, CA. 209-522-1406
Guerra Nut Shelling Company
Hollister, CA 831-637-4471
Hammons Products Company
Stockton, MO 888-429-6887
Hialeah Products Company
Hollywood, FL 800-923-3379
John B Sanfilippo & Son
Selma, TX. 800-423-6546
Lodi Nut Company
Lodi, CA 800-234-6887
Mayfair Packing Company
San Jose, CA 408-280-2349
Organic Planet
San Francisco, CA 415-765-5590
Pilgrim's Pride
Lufkin, TX 936-639-1174
Setton International Foods
Commack, NY 800-227-4397
Terri Lynn
Elgin, IL 800-323-0775
Unique Ingredients
Naches, WA. 509-653-1991

Oils, Shortening & Fats

General

ACH Food Companies
Cordova, TN 800-691-1106
CHS
Inver Grove Heights, MN 800-232-3639
Oasis Foods Company
Hillside, NJ 908-964-0477
Patrick Cudahy
Cudahy, WI 800-486-6900
Ventura Foods
Philadelphia, PA 215-223-8700

Fats & Lard

Chicken

All-States Quality Foods
Charles City, IA 800-247-4195

Dried

Agri-Dairy Products
Purchase, NY 914-697-9580

Frozen

Clofine Dairy & Food Products
Linwood, NJ 800-441-1001
Henningsen Foods
Purchase, NY 914-701-4020
Proliant Meat Ingredients
Ankeny, IA 800-369-2672

Liquid

Agri-Dairy Products
Purchase, NY 914-697-9580
Clofine Dairy & Food Products
Linwood, NJ 800-441-1001
Henningsen Foods
Purchase, NY 914-701-4020

Powdered

Clofine Dairy & Food Products
Linwood, NJ 800-441-1001
Henningsen Foods
Purchase, NY 914-701-4020

Hydrogenated

AG Processing, Inc.
Omaha, NE 800-247-1345
Agri-Dairy Products
Purchase, NY 914-697-9580
Baker Commodities
Vernon, CA 323-268-2883
Blossom Farm Products
Ridgewood, NJ 800-729-1818
CBP Resources
Gastonia, NC. 704-868-4573
Columbus Foods Company
Des Plaines, IL 800-322-6457
Griffin Industries
Starke, FL 904-964-8083
Loders Croklaan
Channahon, IL 800-621-4710
Mallet & Company
Carnegie, PA 800-245-2757
National Starch & Chemical Corporate Office
Bridgewater, NJ 800-366-4031
Theriaults Abattoir
Van Buren, ME 207-868-3344
Werling & Sons Slaughterhouse
Burkettsville, OH 419-375-4186

Lard

CanAmera Foods
Winnipeg, NB 204-324-6481
Columbus Foods Company
Des Plaines, IL 800-322-6457
Hillsboro Refrigerated Lockers
Hillsboro, KS 316-947-3781
Stella Baking Company
Rockford, IL 815-398-5191

Cooking Compounds

Columbus Foods Company
Des Plaines, IL 800-322-6457
WWS
Spring Park, MN 952-541-9001

Margarine

ACH Food Companies
Cordova, TN 800-691-1106
ADM Refined Oils
Decatur, IL 800-637-5866
Allfresh Food Products
Evanston, IL 847-869-3100
Beaver Meadow Creamery
Du Bois, PA. 800-262-3711
Bunge Canada
Oakville, ON. 800-361-3043
Bunge North America
St Louis, MO. 314-569-1339
Butterball Farms
Grand Rapids, MI 616-243-0105
CanAmera Foods
Winnipeg, NB 204-324-6481
CHS
Inver Grove Heights, MN 800-232-3639
ConAgra Dairy Foods
Indianapolis, IN 317-329-3700
Darisweet Farms
Mountlake Terrace, WA 425-771-5007
Florida Shortening Corporation
Miami, FL. 305-691-2992
GFA Brands
Paramus, NJ 201-568-9300
Innovative Food Corporation
Mississauga, ON. 905-670-8878
JE Bergeron & Sons
Bromptonville, QC 800-567-2798
Keller's Creamery
Harleysville, PA 800-535-5371
Land O'Lakes
Kent, OH. 800-328-9680
Land O'Lakes, Inc
Arden Hills, MN 800-328-9680
Lov-It Creamery
Green Bay, WI. 800-344-0333
Madison Dairy Produce Company
Madison, WI 608-256-5561
Madison Foods
St Paul, MN 651-265-8212
Oasis Foods Company
Hillside, NJ 908-964-0477
Parmalat Canada
Toronto, ON 800-563-1515
Protient (Land O Lakes)
St Paul, MN. 651-481-2068
Schneider's Dairy Holdings Inc
Pittsburgh, PA 412-881-3525
Sommer Maid Creamery
Doylestown, PA 215-345-6160
Spring Tree Maple Products
Brattleboro, VT. 802-254-8784
Ventura Foods
Ontario, CA. 714-257-3700
Ventura Foods
Ft Worth, TX. 817-232-5450
Ventura Foods   Foodservice
Salem, OR. 503-585-6423
Ventura Foods   Foodservice/Export/Custom Pack
City of Industry, CA 800-327-3906
Ventura Foods   Foodservice/Retail/Export
Portland, OR. 503-255-5512
Ventura Foods   Production Plant
Los Angeles, CA. 323-265-4300

Oils

A M Todd Company
Kalamazoo, OR. 269-343-2603
ACH Food Companies
Jacksonville, IL. 217-245-4131
ACH Food Companies
Cordova, TN 800-691-1106
ACH Food Companies
New Milford, CT 860-355-9421

ACH Food Companies, Inc.
Cordova, TN 800-691-1106
ADM Packaged Oils
Decatur, IL 800-637-1550
Agrusa, Inc.
Leonia, NJ. 201-592-5950
Alexander International (USA)
Brightwaters, NY 866-965-0143
American Mercantile Corporation
Memphis, TN 901-454-1900
American Yeast/Lallemand
Pembroke, NH. 866-920-9885
Aphrodisia Products
Brooklyn, NY 877-274-3677
Arista Industries
Wilton, CT 800-255-6457
Aroma Vera
Los Angeles, CA. 800-669-9514
Aroma-Life
Encino, CA 818-905-7761
ARRO Corporation
Hodgkins, IL. 708-352-8200
Astral Extracts Ltd
Syosset, NY. 516-496-2505
Atlas Preserves Company
New York, NY 212-569-5613
Au Printemps Gourmet
Prevost, QC 800-663-0416
Avatar Corporation
University Park, IL 800-255-3181
Best Brands Corporation
Dallas, TX. 800-969-2253
Beta Pure Foods
Aptos, CA 831-685-6565
Birdsong Peanut Company
Gorman, TX 254-734-3153
Bittersweet Herb Farm
Shelburne Falls, MA 800-456-1599
Brand Aromatics International
Holmdel, NJ 732-706-3411
Bunge North America
St Louis, MO. 314-569-1339
Bungy Oils
Pawtucket, RI 401-724-3800
Buon Italia
New York, NY 212-633-9090
C.F. Sauer Company
Richmond, VA. 800-688-5676
California Olive Oil Corporation
Salem, MA 800-386-6457
CanAmera Foods
Winnipeg, NB 204-324-6481
Cargill Refined Oils
Minneapolis, MN 800-323-6232
Cargill Vegetable Oils
Minneapolis, MN 612-378-0551
Carothers Research Laboratories
Flint, MI .810-235-2055
Cascade Continental Foods
Woodland, CA. 415-668-6194
Catania-Spagna Corporation
Ayer, MA. 800-343-5522
Centflor Manufacturing Company
New York, NY 212-246-8307
Central Soya
Pawtucket, RI 800-556-6777
China Bowl Trading Company
Westport, CT. 203-222-0381
Chr Hansen
Elyria, OH. 800-558-0802
CHS
Inver Grove Heights, MN. 800-232-3639
Classic Flavors & Fragrances
New York, NY 212-777-0004
Clic International Inc
Laval, QC 450-669-2663
Coast Packing Company
Vernon, CA 323-277-7700
Colonna Brothers
North Bergen, NJ 201-864-1115
Columbus Foods Company
Des Plaines, IL 800-322-6457
Columbus Vegetable Oils
Des Plaines, IL 800-322-6457
Consumer Guild Foods
Toledo, OH 419-726-3406

Consumers Vinegar & Spice Company
Chicago, IL 773-376-4100
Conway Import Company
Franklin Park, IL 800-323-8801
Corn Products International
Westchester, IL 708-551-2600
Critelli Olive Oil
Napa, CA 800-865-4836
CW Resources
New Britain, CT 860-229-7700
Darling International
Omaha, NE 402-733-3010
Delicae Gourmet
Tarpon Springs, FL 800-942-2502
East Coast Olive Oil
Utica, NY 315-797-3151
Ed Miniat
Homewood, IL 708-957-3800
Erba Food Products
Brooklyn, NY 718-272-7700
Fauchon
New York, NY 877-605-0130
Flavorchem
Downers Grove, IL 800-323-1301
Flora Manufacturing & Distributing
Burnaby, BC 888-436-6697
Florida Shortening Corporation
Miami, FL 305-691-2992
Follmer Development/Americana
Newbury Park, CA 805-498-4531
Food Ingredients
Elgin, IL 800-500-7676
Freed, Teller & Freed
Burlingame, CA 800-370-7371
GFA Brands
Paramus, NJ 201-568-9300
Golden Brands
Louisville, KY 800-622-3055
Golden Eagle Olive Products
Porterville, CA 559-784-3468
Golden Whisk
South San Francisco, CA 800-660-5222
Good Food
Honey Brook, PA 800-327-4406
Grapevine Trading Company
Santa Rosa, CA 800-469-6478
Hartsville Oil Mill
Darlington, SC 843-393-2855
Herbal Products & Development
Aptos, CA 831-688-4200
HVJ International
Spring, TX 877-730-3663
Hybco USA
Los Angeles, CA 323-269-3111
II Sisters
Moss Beach, CA 800-282-7058
Ingredients Corporation of America
Memphis, TN 901-525-6660
International Home Foods
Milton, PA 973-359-9920
Kalsec
Kalamazoo, MI 800-323-9320
Kalustyan Corporation
Union, NJ 908-688-6111
Kendall Citrus Corporation
Goulds, FL 305-258-1628
Krinos Foods
Long Island City, NY 718-729-9000
La Tourangelle
Richmond, CA 866-688-6457
Lesley Elizabeth
Lapeer, MI 800-684-3300
Liberty Natural Products
Portland, OR 800-289-8427
Liberty Vegetable Oil Company
Santa Fe Springs, CA 562-921-3567
Lorann Oils
Lansing, MI 800-248-1302
Loriva Culinary Oils
San Francisco, CA 866-972-6679
Lou Ana Foods
Opelousas, LA 337-948-6561
Lubriplate Lubricants
Newark, NJ 800-733-4755
Lucini Italia Company
San Francisco, CA 888-558-2464
M. Brown & Sons
Bremen, IN 800-258-7450
Mallet & Company
Carnegie, PA 800-245-2757
Marathon Packing Corporation
San Leandro, CA 510-895-2000

Marnap Industries
Buffalo, NY 716-897-1220
Mastertaste Company
South Hackensack, NJ 201-641-6555
McLaughlin Oil Company
Columbus, OH 614-231-2518
Medallion International
Pompton Plains, NJ 973-616-3401
Mercado Latino
City of Industry, CA 626-333-6862
Minute Maid Company
Houston, TX 888-884-8952
Monini North America
Norwalk, CT 203-750-0531
Mott's
Port Chester, NY 914-612-4000
Mountainbrook of Vermont
Jeffersonville, VT 802-644-1988
Napa Valley Kitchens
Napa, CA 800-288-1089
National Products Company
Kalamazoo, MI 269-344-3640
Natural Value Products
Sacramento, CA 916-427-7242
NatureMost Laboratories
Middletown, CT 800-234-2112
Naturex (Chart Corp)
South Hackensack, NJ 201-440-5000
Newport Flavours & Fragrances
Orange, CA 714-628-9894
North American Enterprises
Tucson, AZ 800-817-8666
O Olive Oil
Petaluma, CA 888-827-7148
Oil-Dri Corporation of America
Chicago, IL 800-233-9802
Omega Nutrition
Bellingham, WA 800-661-3529
Omega Protein
Houston, TX 877-866-3423
Pacifica Culinaria
Temecula, CA 800-622-8880
Pak Technologies
Milwaukee, WI 414-438-8600
Paradise Products Corporation
Roslyn, NY 800-826-1235
Pastorelli Food Products
Chicago, IL 800-767-2829
Patsy's
New York, NY 212-247-3491
Perdue Farms
Salisbury, MD 800-473-7383
Pompeian
Baltimore, MD 800-638-1224
Prairie Thyme
Santa Fe, NM 800-869-0009
Proacec USA
Santa Monica, CA 310-996-7770
Purity Products
Plainview, NY 888-769-7873
RCB International
Albany, OR 541-967-3814
Rising Sun Farms
Phoenix, OR 541-535-8331
Ron-Son Foods
Swedesboro, NJ 856-241-7333
Rose Brier
Albany, OR 888-926-4378
Salute Sante! Food & Wine
Napa, CA 707-251-3900
Santini Foods
San Lorenzo, CA 800-835-6888
Sieco USA Corporation
Houston, TX 800-325-9443
Silver Palate Kitchens
Cresskill, NJ 800-872-5283
Solae Company
St Louis, MO 800-325-7108
Sona & Hollen Foods
Los Alamitos, CA 800-200-7662
Source Food Technology
Durham, NC 866-277-3849
Sovena USA
Rome, NY 315-797-7070
Sparboe Companies
Los Angeles, CA 213-626-7538
Spectrum Organic Products
Petaluma, CA 800-995-2705
Star Fine Foods
Fresno, CA 559-498-2900
Steiner, S.S.
New York, NY 212-515-7200

Tait Farm Foods
Centre Hall, PA 800-787-2716
Technical Oil
Easton, PA 610-252-8350
Tee Pee Olives
Scarsdale, NY 800-431-1529
The Solae Company
St Louis, MO 800-325-7108
Tres Classique
Ukiah, CA 888-644-5127
Tropical
Charlotte, NC 800-220-1413
Trotters Imports
Colrain, MA 800-863-8437
Unilever Bertolli USA, Inc.
Englewood Cliffs, NJ 201-894-4000
Ventura Foods   Foodservice/Retail/Export
Portland, OR 503-255-5512
Ventura Foods   Production Plant
Los Angeles, CA 323-265-4300
Veronica Foods Company
Oakland, CA 800-370-5554
Vitamins
Chicago, IL 312-861-0700
Welch, Home & Clark Company
Newark, NJ 973-465-1200
Wild Things
Beverly Hills, CA 310-412-4139
Wine Country Kitchens
Napa, CA 707-252-9463
Wing Nien Company
Hayward, CA 510-487-8877
Wisconsin Cheese
Melrose Park, IL 708-450-0074
WWS
Spring Park, MN 952-541-9001

Almond

AG Processing, Inc.
Omaha, NE 800-247-1345
Aroma-Life
Encino, CA 818-905-7761
Astral Extracts Ltd
Syosset, NY 516-496-2505
Embassy Flavours Ltd.
Brampton, ON 800-334-3371

EMERLING INTERNATIONAL FOODS, INC.

Emerling International Foods
Buffalo, NY 716-833-7381

We supply food manufacturers and food service customers worldwide (since 1988) with bulk ingredients including: Fruits & Vegetables; Juice Concentrates; Herbs & Spices; Oils & Vinegars; Flavors & Colors; Honey & Molasses. We also produce PURE MAPLE SYRUP.

Flavtek
Los Angeles, CA 800-562-5880
Flora
Lynden, WA 800-446-2110
Gold Coast Ingredients
Commerce, CA 800-352-8673
Janca's Jojoba Oil & Seed Company
Mesa, AZ 480-497-9494
K.L. Keller Imports
Oakland, CA 510-839-7890
Naturex (Chart Corp)
South Hackensack, NJ 201-440-5000
Pokonobe Industries
Santa Monica, CA 310-392-1259
Pure Extracts Inc
Ronkonkoma, NY 631-588-9727
Universal Preservachem Inc
Edison, NJ 732-777-7338
Welch, Home & Clark Company
Newark, NJ 973-465-1200

Anise or Aniseed

Astral Extracts Ltd
Syosset, NY 516-496-2505
Embassy Flavours Ltd.
Brampton, ON 800-334-3371

EMERLING INTERNATIONAL FOODS, INC.

Emerling International Foods
Buffalo, NY.......................716-833-7381

We supply food manufacturers and food service customers worldwide (since 1988) with bulk ingredients including: Fruits & Vegetables; Juice Concentrates; Herbs & Spices; Oils & Vinegars; Flavors & Colors; Honey & Molasses. We also produce PURE MAPLE SYRUP.

Medallion International
Pompton Plains, NJ.................973-616-3401
Naturex (Chart Corp)
South Hackensack, NJ 201-440-5000
Pure Extracts Inc
Ronkonkoma, NY 631-588-9727

Avocado

Arista Industries
Wilton, CT 800-255-6457

Bean

ADM Refined Oils
Decatur, IL 800-637-5866
Avatar Corporation
University Park, IL 800-255-3181
Irving R. Boody & Company
New York, NY 212-947-8300
Pure Extracts Inc
Ronkonkoma, NY 631-588-9727

Black Pepper

Medallion International
Pompton Plains, NJ.................973-616-3401
Naturex (Chart Corp)
South Hackensack, NJ 201-440-5000
Pure Extracts Inc
Ronkonkoma, NY 631-588-9727

Borage

OMEGA Nutrition
Bellingham, WA 800-661-3529

Canola

ACH Food Companies
Cordova, TN 800-691-1106
ACH Food Companies
New Milford, CT 860-355-9421
ADM Food Oils
Decatur, IL 800-637-5866
ADM Refined Oils
Decatur, IL 800-637-5866
AG Processing, Inc.
Omaha, NE 800-247-1345
American Health & Nutrition
Ann Arbor, MI 734-677-5572
Avatar Corporation
University Park, IL 800-255-3181
Bunge Canada
Oakville, ON 800-361-3043
California Olive Oil Corporation
Salem, MA 800-386-6457
Cargill Refined Oils
Minneapolis, MN 800-323-6232
Catania-Spagna Corporation
Ayer, MA 800-343-5522
Central Soya
Pawtucket, RI 800-556-6777

EMERLING INTERNATIONAL FOODS, INC.

Emerling International Foods
Buffalo, NY.......................716-833-7381

We supply food manufacturers and food service customers worldwide (since 1988) with bulk ingredients including: Fruits & Vegetables; Juice Concentrates; Herbs & Spices; Oils & Vinegars; Flavors & Colors; Honey & Molasses. We also produce PURE MAPLE SYRUP.

Flora
Lynden, WA........................800-446-2110
Gama Products
Medley, FL 305-883-1200

Good Food
Honey Brook, PA 800-327-4406
Heartland Gourmet Popcorn
Elk Grove Village, IL 866-489-4676
Intermountain Canola Cargill
Idaho Falls, ID 800-822-6652
Janca's Jojoba Oil & Seed Company
Mesa, AZ..........................480-497-9494
Loriva Culinary Oils
San Francisco, CA 866-972-6679
Montana Specialty Mills
Great Falls, MT 406-761-2338
OMEGA Nutrition
Bellingham, WA 800-661-3529
Pokonobe Industries
Santa Monica, CA.................310-392-1259
Pure Extracts Inc
Ronkonkoma, NY 631-588-9727
Spring Tree Maple Products
Brattleboro, VT....................802-254-8784
Universal Preservachem Inc
Edison, NJ.........................732-777-7338
Ventura Foods
Opelousas, LA 337-948-6561

Caraway

EMERLING INTERNATIONAL FOODS, INC.

Emerling International Foods
Buffalo, NY.......................716-833-7381

We supply food manufacturers and food service customers worldwide (since 1988) with bulk ingredients including: Fruits & Vegetables; Juice Concentrates; Herbs & Spices; Oils & Vinegars; Flavors & Colors; Honey & Molasses. We also produce PURE MAPLE SYRUP.

Medallion International
Pompton Plains, NJ.................973-616-3401
Naturex (Chart Corp)
South Hackensack, NJ 201-440-5000
Pure Extracts Inc
Ronkonkoma, NY 631-588-9727

Cardamom

Medallion International
Pompton Plains, NJ.................973-616-3401
Naturex (Chart Corp)
South Hackensack, NJ 201-440-5000
Pure Extracts Inc
Ronkonkoma, NY 631-588-9727

Cassia

Embassy Flavours Ltd.
Brampton, ON.....................800-334-3371
Naturex (Chart Corp)
South Hackensack, NJ 201-440-5000
Pure Extracts Inc
Ronkonkoma, NY 631-588-9727

Castor

Arista Industries
Wilton, CT 800-255-6457
Avatar Corporation
University Park, IL 800-255-3181
Heritage Store
Virginia Beach, VA 757-428-0110
Leatex Chemical Company
Philadelphia, PA 215-739-2000
Pure Extracts Inc
Ronkonkoma, NY 631-588-9727
Salem Oil & Grease Company
Salem, MA 978-745-0585

Celery

Naturex (Chart Corp)
South Hackensack, NJ 201-440-5000
Pure Extracts Inc
Ronkonkoma, NY 631-588-9727

Cinnamon - Leaf & Bark

Flavtek
Los Angeles, CA...................800-562-5880
Medallion International
Pompton Plains, NJ.................973-616-3401

Pure Extracts Inc
Ronkonkoma, NY 631-588-9727

Citrus

Astral Extracts Ltd
Syosset, NY........................516-496-2505
Boyajian, Inc
Canton, MA 800-965-0665
California Olive Oil Corporation
Salem, MA 800-386-6457
Diana's Specialty Foods
Pingree Grove, IL 847-683-1200
Embassy Flavours Ltd.
Brampton, ON.....................800-334-3371

EMERLING INTERNATIONAL FOODS, INC.

Emerling International Foods
Buffalo, NY.......................716-833-7381

We supply food manufacturers and food service customers worldwide (since 1988) with bulk ingredients including: Fruits & Vegetables; Juice Concentrates; Herbs & Spices; Oils & Vinegars; Flavors & Colors; Honey & Molasses. We also produce PURE MAPLE SYRUP.

Flavtek
Los Angeles, CA...................800-562-5880
Gold Coast Ingredients
Commerce, CA 800-352-8673
Kendall Citrus Corporation
Goulds, FL 305-258-1628
Louis Dreyfus Citrus
Winter Garden, FL 407-656-1000
Medallion International
Pompton Plains, NJ.................973-616-3401
Minute Maid Company
Houston, TX 888-884-8952
O Olive Oil
Petaluma, CA 888-827-7148
Peace River Citrus Products
Vero Beach, FL 772-467-1234
Prime Ingredients
Saddle Brook, NJ 888-791-6655
Pure Extracts Inc
Ronkonkoma, NY 631-588-9727
Robertet Flavors
Piscataway, NJ 732-981-8300
Ungerer & Company
Lincoln Park, NJ 973-628-0600

Clove

Pure Extracts Inc
Ronkonkoma, NY 631-588-9727

Coconut

Aarhus United USA, Inc.
Newark, NJ 800-776-1338
ADM Food Oils
Decatur, IL 800-637-5866
ADM Refined Oils
Decatur, IL 800-637-5866
AG Processing, Inc.
Omaha, NE 800-247-1345
Avatar Corporation
University Park, IL 800-255-3181
Catania-Spagna Corporation
Ayer, MA 800-343-5522
Central Soya
Pawtucket, RI 800-556-6777
Clofine Dairy & Food Products
Linwood, NJ 800-441-1001

EMERLING INTERNATIONAL FOODS, INC.

Emerling International Foods
Buffalo, NY.......................716-833-7381

We supply food manufacturers and food service customers worldwide (since 1988) with bulk ingredients including: Fruits & Vegetables; Juice Concentrates; Herbs & Spices; Oils & Vinegars; Flavors & Colors; Honey & Molasses. We also produce PURE MAPLE SYRUP.

Flavtek
Los Angeles, CA...................800-562-5880

Gold Coast Ingredients
Commerce, CA 800-352-8673
Good Food
Honey Brook, PA 800-327-4406
Janca's Jojoba Oil & Seed Company
Mesa, AZ. 480-497-9494
Pokonobe Industries
Santa Monica, CA 310-392-1259
Pure Extracts Inc
Ronkonkoma, NY 631-588-9727
Ventura Foods
Opelousas, LA 337-948-6561
Welch, Home & Clark Company
Newark, NJ 973-465-1200

Cod Liver

Irving R. Boody & Company
New York, NY 212-947-8300
Jamieson Laboratories
Toronto, QC 519-974-8482
JR Carlson Laboratories
Arlington Hts, IL 888-234-5656

Cooking

ACATRIS
Oakville, ON 905-829-2414
ACH Food Companies
Memphis, TN 800-691-1106
ACH Food Companies
New Milford, CT 860-355-9421
ADM
Decatur, IL 800-637-5843
Agrusa, Inc.
Leonia, NJ 201-592-5950
Alberto-Culver Company
Melrose Park, IL 708-450-3000
Allfresh Food Products
Evanston, IL 847-869-3100
Americana Marketing
Newbury Park, CA 800-742-7520
Arista Industries
Wilton, CT 800-255-6457
ARRO Corporation
Hodgkins, IL 708-352-8200
Atlas Preserves Company
New York, NY 212-569-5613
Avatar Corporation
University Park, IL 800-255-3181
Butterbuds Food Ingredients
Racine, WI. 800-426-1119
C&T Refinery
Richmond, VA. 800-284-6457
California Oils Corporation
Richmond, CA 800-225-6457
California Olive Oil Corporation
Salem, MA 800-386-6457
Capital City Processors
Oklahoma City, OK 800-473-2731
Cargill Refined Oils
Minneapolis, MN 800-323-6232
Cargill Specialty Oils
Minneapolis, MN 800-851-8331
Cargill Vegetable Oils
Minneapolis, MN 612-378-0551
Casey's Food Products
Blakely, GA. 229-723-3411
Catania-Spagna Corporation
Ayer, MA. 800-343-5522
Central Soya
Pawtucket, RI 800-556-6777
Coast Packing Company
Vernon, CA 323-277-7700
Colonna Brothers
North Bergen, NJ 201-864-1115
ConAgra Grocery Products
Irvine, CA 714-680-1000
Deep South Products
Fitzgerald, GA. 229-423-1121
Diana's Specialty Foods
Pingree Grove, IL 847-683-1200
Dipasa
Brownsville, TX 956-831-5893
Embassy Flavours Ltd.
Brampton, ON. 800-334-3371

EMERLING INTERNATIONAL FOODS, INC.

Emerling International Foods
Buffalo, NY. 716-833-7381

We supply food manufacturers and food service customers worldwide (since 1988) with bulk ingredients including: Fruits & Vegetables; Juice Concentrates; Herbs & Spices; Oils & Vinegars; Flavors & Colors; Honey & Molasses. We also produce PURE MAPLE SYRUP.

Flora
Lynden, WA. 800-446-2110
Follmer Development/Americana
Newbury Park, CA 805-498-4531
Gateway Food Products Company
Dupo, IL 877-220-1963
Good Food
Honey Brook, PA 800-327-4406
Intermountain Canola Cargill
Idaho Falls, ID 800-822-6652
Janca's Jojoba Oil & Seed Company
Mesa, AZ. 480-497-9494
Liberty Vegetable Oil Company
Santa Fe Springs, CA 562-921-3567
Loriva Culinary Oils
San Francisco, CA 866-972-6679
Louis Dreyfus Citrus
Winter Garden, FL 407-656-1000
Mallet & Company
Carnegie, PA 800-245-2757
Marathon Packing Corporation
San Leandro, CA 510-895-2000
Mercado Latino
City of Industry, CA 626-333-6862
Milnot Company
Neosho, MO 800-877-6455
Morris J. Golombeck
Brooklyn, NY 718-284-3505
Mother Earth Enterprises
New York, NY 866-436-7688
Mott's
Port Chester, NY 914-612-4000
Natural Oils International
Simi Valley, CA. 805-433-0160
Nick Sciabica & Sons
Modesto, CA. 800-551-9612
North American Enterprises
Tucson, AZ 800-817-8666
Orland Olive Oil Company
Orland, CA 530-865-4040
Our Thyme Garden
Cleburne, TX 800-482-4372
Par-Way Tryson
Saint Clair, MO 800-844-4554
Pastorelli Food Products
Chicago, IL 800-767-2829
Pokonobe Industries
Santa Monica, CA. 310-392-1259
Producers Cooperative Oil Mill
Oklahoma City, OK 405-232-7555
Progresso Quality Foods
Vineland, NJ 800-200-9377
Pure Extracts Inc
Ronkonkoma, NY 631-588-9727
Purity Products
Plainview, NY. 888-769-7873
Ron-Son Foods
Swedesboro, NJ 856-241-7333
Rose Brier
Albany, OR 888-926-4378
Solae Company
St Louis, MO 800-325-7108
Sona & Hollen Foods
Los Alamitos, CA 800-200-7662
Sovena USA
Rome, NY 315-797-7070
Ventura Foods
Opelousas, LA 337-948-6561
Ventura Foods   Foodservice
Salem, OR. 503-585-6423
Viobin USA
Monticello, IL. 217-762-2561
Welch, Home & Clark Company
Newark, NJ 973-465-1200
Western Pacific Commodities
Las Vegas, NV 702-312-8080

Spray

ACH Food Companies
New Milford, CT 860-355-9421

Butterbuds Food Ingredients
Racine, WI. 800-426-1119
Follmer Development/Americana
Newbury Park, CA 805-498-4531
International Home Foods
Milton, PA 973-359-9920

Coriander Seed

Pure Extracts Inc
Ronkonkoma, NY 631-588-9727

Corn

ACH Food Companies
Cordova, TN 800-691-1106
ACH Food Companies
New Milford, CT 860-355-9421
ADM Food Oils
Decatur, IL 800-637-5866
ADM Refined Oils
Decatur, IL 800-637-5866
AG Processing, Inc.
Omaha, NE 800-247-1345
ARRO Corporation
Hodgkins, IL 708-352-8200
Avatar Corporation
University Park, IL 800-255-3181
Cargill Dry Corn Ingredients
Paris, IL. 800-637-6481
Cargill Refined Oils
Minneapolis, MN 800-323-6232
Catania-Spagna Corporation
Ayer, MA. 800-343-5522
Central Soya
Pawtucket, RI 800-556-6777
Corn Products International
Westchester, IL 708-551-2600
Erba Food Products
Brooklyn, NY 718-272-7700
Gama Products
Medley, FL 305-883-1200
Good Food
Honey Brook, PA 800-327-4406
Mallet & Company
Carnegie, PA 800-245-2757
Mercado Latino
City of Industry, CA 626-333-6862
Olde Tyme Food Corporation
East Longmeadow, MA 800-356-6533
Pastorelli Food Products
Chicago, IL 800-767-2829
Pokonobe Industries
Santa Monica, CA. 310-392-1259
Pure Extracts Inc
Ronkonkoma, NY 631-588-9727
Purity Products
Plainview, NY. 888-769-7873
Sovena USA
Rome, NY 315-797-7070
Universal Preservachem Inc
Edison, NJ. 732-777-7338
Ventura Foods
Opelousas, LA 337-948-6561
Welch, Home & Clark Company
Newark, NJ 973-465-1200

Cottonseed

Aarhus United USA, Inc.
Newark, NJ. 800-776-1338
ADM Food Oils
Decatur, IL 800-637-5866
ADM Refined Oils
Decatur, IL 800-637-5866
AG Processing, Inc.
Omaha, NE 800-247-1345
Cargill Refined Oils
Minneapolis, MN 800-323-6232
Catania-Spagna Corporation
Ayer, MA. 800-343-5522
Central Soya
Pawtucket, RI 800-556-6777

EMERLING INTERNATIONAL FOODS, INC.

Emerling International Foods
Buffalo, NY 716-833-7381

> We supply food manufacturers and food service
> customers worldwide (since 1988) with bulk in-
> gredients including: Fruits & Vegetables; Juice
> Concentrates; Herbs & Spices; Oils & Vinegars;
> Flavors & Colors; Honey & Molasses. We also
> produce PURE MAPLE SYRUP.

Golden Brands
    Louisville, KY 800-622-3055
Good Food
    Honey Brook, PA 800-327-4406
Lamesa Cotton Oil Mill
    Chandler, AZ. 806-872-2166
Lubbock Cotton Oil Company
    Lubbock, TX. 806-763-4371
Plains Cooperative Oil Mill
    Lubbock, TX. 806-747-3434
Producers Cooperative Oil Mill
    Oklahoma City, OK 405-232-7555
Pure Extracts Inc
    Ronkonkoma, NY. 631-588-9727
Pyco Industries
    Lubbock, TX. 800-289-7266
Stevenson-Cooper
    Philadelphia, PA 215-223-2600
Ventura Foods
    Opelousas, LA 337-948-6561
Welch, Home & Clark Company
    Newark, NJ .973-465-1200

Dillweed

Pure Extracts Inc
    Ronkonkoma, NY. 631-588-9727
RCB International
    Albany, OR .541-967-3814

Edible

Aarhus United USA, Inc.
    Newark, NJ .800-776-1338
ABITEC Corporation
    Janesville, WI 800-457-1977
Abitec Corporation
    Columbus, OH 800-555-1255
ACATRIS
    Oakville, ON 905-829-2414
ACH Food Companies
    Cordova, TN 800-691-1106
ACH Food Companies
    New Milford, CT 860-355-9421
ADM
    Decatur, IL .800-637-5843
ADM Refined Oils
    Decatur, IL .800-637-5866
AG Processing, Inc.
    Omaha, NE .800-247-1345
Agri-Dairy Products
    Purchase, NY 914-697-9580
Agrusa, Inc.
    Leonia, NJ. .201-592-5950
Alberto-Culver Company
    Melrose Park, IL 708-450-3000
Allfresh Food Products
    Evanston, IL 847-869-3100
American Health & Nutrition
    Ann Arbor, MI 734-677-5572
Americana Marketing
    Newbury Park, CA 800-742-7520
Arista Industries
    Wilton, CT .800-255-6457
ARRO Corporation
    Hodgkins, IL. 708-352-8200
Atlas Preserves Company
    New York, NY 212-569-5613
Avatar Corporation
    University Park, IL 800-255-3181
Barlean's
    Ferndale, WA 360-384-0325
Boyajian, Inc
    Canton, MA 800-965-0665
Bungy Oils
    Pawtucket, RI 401-724-3800
Butterbuds Food Ingredients
    Racine, WI. .800-426-1119
California Oils Corporation
    Richmond, CA 800-225-6457

California Olive Oil Corporation
    Salem, MA .800-386-6457
Capital City Processors
    Oklahoma City, OK 800-473-2731
Capitol Foods
    Memphis, TN 662-781-9021
Cargill Dry Corn Ingredients
    Paris, IL 800-637-6481
Cargill Vegetable Oils
    Minneapolis, MN 612-378-0551
Casey's Food Products
    Blakely, GA .229-723-3411
Catania-Spagna Corporation
    Ayer, MA. 800-343-5522
Central Soya
    Pawtucket, RI 800-556-6777
China Bowl Trading Company
    Westport, CT 203-222-0381
Colavita
    Linden, NJ. .908-862-5454
Colonna Brothers
    North Bergen, NJ 201-864-1115
ConAgra Grocery Products
    Irvine, CA 714-680-1000
Consumer Guild Foods
    Toledo, OH .419-726-3406
CP Vegetable Oil
    Brampton, ON. 905-792-2309
Darling International
    Omaha, NE .402-733-3010
Dipasa
    Brownsville, TX 956-831-5893
Embassy Flavours Ltd.
    Brampton, ON. 800-334-3371

EMERLING INTERNATIONAL FOODS, INC.

Emerling International Foods
Buffalo, NY 716-833-7381

> We supply food manufacturers and food service
> customers worldwide (since 1988) with bulk in-
> gredients including: Fruits & Vegetables; Juice
> Concentrates; Herbs & Spices; Oils & Vinegars;
> Flavors & Colors; Honey & Molasses. We also
> produce PURE MAPLE SYRUP.

Energen Products
    Norwalk, CA 800-423-8837
Erba Food Products
    Brooklyn, NY 718-272-7700
Flora
    Lynden, WA. 800-446-2110
Gama Products
    Medley, FL .305-883-1200
Gateway Food Products Company
    Dupo, IL 877-220-1963
Golden Whisk
    South San Francisco, CA 800-660-5222
Good Food
    Honey Brook, PA 800-327-4406
Grassland Dairy Products
    Greenwood, WI. 800-428-8837
Herbal Products & Development
    Aptos, CA 831-688-4200
Intermountain Canola Cargill
    Idaho Falls, ID 800-822-6652
Irving R. Boody & Company
    New York, NY 212-947-8300
Janca's Jojoba Oil & Seed Company
    Mesa, AZ. 480-497-9494
John I. Haas
    Washington, DC 202-223-0005
JR Carlson Laboratories
    Arlington Hts, IL 888-234-5656
Krinos Foods
    Long Island City, NY 718-729-9000
Liberty Vegetable Oil Company
    Santa Fe Springs, CA 562-921-3567
Loders Croklaan
    Channahon, IL 800-621-4710
Loriva Culinary Oils
    San Francisco, CA 866-972-6679
Lou Ana Foods
    Opelousas, LA 337-948-6561
Louis Dreyfus Citrus
    Winter Garden, FL 407-656-1000
Marina Foods
    Dania, FL 954-929-9047
Medallion International
    Pompton Plains, NJ. 973-616-3401

Mercado Latino
    City of Industry, CA 626-333-6862
Milnot Company
    Neosho, MO 800-877-6455
Morris J. Golombeck
    Brooklyn, NY 718-284-3505
Mother Earth Enterprises
    New York, NY 866-436-7688
Natural Oils International
    Simi Valley, CA. 805-433-0160
Nick Sciabica & Sons
    Modesto, CA 800-551-9612
North American Enterprises
    Tucson, AZ .800-817-8666
Oils of Aloha
    Waialua, HI. 800-367-6010
Ottens Flavors
    Philadelphia, PA 800-523-0767
Our Thyme Garden
    Cleburne, TX 800-482-4372
Paradise Products Corporation
    Roslyn, NY .800-826-1235
Pastorelli Food Products
    Chicago, IL .800-767-2829
Perdue Farms
    Salisbury, MD 800-473-7383
Pokonobe Industries
    Santa Monica, CA 310-392-1259
Pompeian
    Baltimore, MD 800-638-1224
Progresso Quality Foods
    Vineland, NJ. 800-200-9377
Pure Extracts Inc
    Ronkonkoma, NY. 631-588-9727
Purity Products
    Plainview, NY. 888-769-7873
Riceland Foods   Rice Milling Operations
    Little Rock, AR. 888-532-4844
Ron-Son Foods
    Swedesboro, NJ 856-241-7333
Scally's Imperial Importing Company Inc
    Staten Island, NY 718-983-1938
Sessions Company
    Enterprise, AL 334-393-0200
Silver Palate Kitchens
    Cresskill, NJ 800-872-5283
Solae Company
    St Louis, MO. 800-325-7108
Sona & Hollen Foods
    Los Alamitos, CA 800-200-7662
Sovena USA
    Rome, NY 315-797-7070
Stuart Hale Company
    Chicago, IL .773-638-1800
Tropical
    Charlotte, NC 800-220-1413
Unilever Bertolli USA, Inc.
    Englewood Cliffs, NJ 201-894-4000
Universal Preservachem Inc
    Edison, NJ. .732-777-7338
Ventura Foods
    Opelousas, LA 337-948-6561
Ventura Foods   Foodservice
    Salem, OR. .503-585-6423
Veronica Foods Company
    Oakland, CA 800-370-5554
Vincent Formusa Company
    Chicago, IL .312-421-0485
Viobin USA
    Monticello, IL. 217-762-2561
Vogel Popcorn
    Hamburg, IA 800-831-5818
Welch, Home & Clark Company
    Newark, NJ .973-465-1200
Wisconsin Cheese
    Melrose Park, IL 708-450-0074

Essential

A M Todd Company
    Kalamazoo, OR. 269-343-2603
A.M. Todd Company
    Kalamazoo, MI 800-968-2603
American Mercantile Corporation
    Memphis, TN 901-454-1900
Aphrodisia Products
    Brooklyn, NY 877-274-3677
Aroma Vera
    Los Angeles, CA. 800-669-9514
Aroma-Life
    Encino, CA .818-905-7761

Aromachem
Brooklyn, NY 718-497-4664
AVRI Companies
Richmond, CA 800-883-9574
Blue California Company
Rancho Santa Margarita, CA 949-635-1991
Britannia Natural Products
New Windsor, NY 845-534-1335
Cargill Juice Products
Frostproof, FL 800-227-4455
Centflor Manufacturing Company
New York, NY 212-246-8307
Classic Flavors & Fragrances
New York, NY 212-777-0004
Colin Ingram
Comptche, CA 707-937-1824
Consumers Flavoring Extract Company
Brooklyn, NY 718-435-0201
Embassy Flavours Ltd.
Brampton, ON 800-334-3371

EMERLING INTERNATIONAL FOODS, INC.

Emerling International Foods
Buffalo, NY 716-833-7381

We supply food manufacturers and food service customers worldwide (since 1988) with bulk ingredients including: Fruits & Vegetables; Juice Concentrates; Herbs & Spices; Oils & Vinegars; Flavors & Colors; Honey & Molasses. We also produce PURE MAPLE SYRUP.

Essential Products of America
Tampa, FL 800-822-9698
Flavor Sciences
Stamford, CT 800-535-2867
Flavorchem
Downers Grove, IL 800-323-1301
Flavormatic Industries
Wappingers Falls, NY 845-297-9100
Flavtek
Los Angeles, CA 800-562-5880
Global Botanical
Barrie, ON 705-733-2117
Green Turtle Bay Vitamin Company
Summit, NJ 800-887-8535
Greenwood Associates
Highland Park, IL 847-242-7900
H.B. Taylor Co
Chicago, IL 773-254-4805
Heritage Store
Virginia Beach, VA 757-428-0110
Hi-Country Corona
Selah, WA 909-272-2600
Ingredients Corporation of America
Memphis, TN 901-525-6660
Irving R. Boody & Company
New York, NY 212-947-8300
Joseph Adams Corporation
Valley City, OH 330-225-9135
Kalsec
Kalamazoo, MI 800-323-9320
Lebermuth Company
South Bend, IN 800-648-1123
Leeward Resources
Baltimore, MD 410-837-9003
Loriva Culinary Oils
San Francisco, CA 866-972-6679
M. Brown & Sons
Bremen, IN 800-258-7450
Mane Incorporated
Milford, OH 800-595-8936
Maple Ridge Farms
Prince Albert, SK 306-922-8056
Marnap Industries
Buffalo, NY 716-897-1220
Mastertaste
Teterboro, NJ 888-547-8844
Mastertaste Company
South Hackensack, NJ 201-641-6555
Medallion International
Pompton Plains, NJ 973-616-3401
Millennium Specialty Chemicals
Jacksonville, FL 800-231-6728
Mother Earth Enterprises
New York, NY 866-436-7688
Native Scents
Taos, NM 800-645-3471
Naturex
South Hackensack, NJ 201-440-5000

Noville
Wayne, NJ 201-641-2700
Now Foods
Bloomingdale, IL 888-669-3663
Pure Extracts Inc
Ronkonkoma, NY 631-588-9727
Robertet Flavors
Piscataway, NJ 732-981-8300
Starwest Botanicals
Rancho Cordova, CA 888-273-4372
SunPure
Lakeland, FL 863-619-2222
Torre Products Company
New York, NY 212-925-8989
Treatt USA
Lakeland, FL 800-866-7704
Ungerer & Company
Lincoln Park, NJ 973-628-0600
Whole Herb Company
Sonoma, CA 707-935-1077

Fish

Daybrook Fisheries
Empire, LA 985-657-9711
Eckhart Corporation
Novato, CA 800-200-4201
Irving R. Boody & Company
New York, NY 212-947-8300
Jamieson Laboratories
Toronto, QC 519-974-8482
Jedwards International
Quincy, MA 617-472-9300
JR Carlson Laboratories
Arlington Hts, IL 888-234-5656
Nutraceutical Corporation
Park City, UT 435-655-6000
Scandinavian Laboratories
Mt Bethel, PA 570-897-7735
Tabco Enterprises
Pomona, CA 909-623-4565

Fruit

Arista Industries
Wilton, CT 800-255-6457

Garlic

Astral Extracts Ltd
Syosset, NY 516-496-2505
California Olive Oil Corporation
Salem, MA 800-386-6457
Diana's Specialty Foods
Pingree Grove, IL 847-683-1200

EMERLING INTERNATIONAL FOODS, INC.

Emerling International Foods
Buffalo, NY 716-833-7381

We supply food manufacturers and food service customers worldwide (since 1988) with bulk ingredients including: Fruits & Vegetables; Juice Concentrates; Herbs & Spices; Oils & Vinegars; Flavors & Colors; Honey & Molasses. We also produce PURE MAPLE SYRUP.

Halladays Harvest Barn
Bellows Falls, VT 802-463-3471
Lebermuth Company
South Bend, IN 800-648-1123
Loriva Culinary Oils
San Francisco, CA 866-972-6679
Nutraceutical Corporation
Park City, UT 435-655-6000
Our Thyme Garden
Cleburne, TX 800-482-4372
Prime Ingredients
Saddle Brook, NJ 888-791-6655
Pure Extracts Inc
Ronkonkoma, NY 631-588-9727
Vegetable Juices
Chicago, IL 888-776-9752

Ginger

Astral Extracts Ltd
Syosset, NY 516-496-2505
Pure Extracts Inc
Ronkonkoma, NY 631-588-9727
Ungerer & Company
Lincoln Park, NJ 973-628-0600

Grapefruit

Astral Extracts Ltd
Syosset, NY 516-496-2505

EMERLING INTERNATIONAL FOODS, INC.

Emerling International Foods
Buffalo, NY 716-833-7381

We supply food manufacturers and food service customers worldwide (since 1988) with bulk ingredients including: Fruits & Vegetables; Juice Concentrates; Herbs & Spices; Oils & Vinegars; Flavors & Colors; Honey & Molasses. We also produce PURE MAPLE SYRUP.

Flavtek
Los Angeles, CA 800-562-5880
Gold Coast Ingredients
Commerce, CA 800-352-8673
Pure Extracts Inc
Ronkonkoma, NY 631-588-9727
SunPure
Lakeland, FL 863-619-2222

Grapeseed

AG Processing, Inc.
Omaha, NE 800-247-1345
Ameri-Kal Inc
Wichita Falls, TX 940-322-5400
Arista Industries
Wilton, CT 800-255-6457
Cuisine Perel
Richmond, CA 800-887-3735
Diana's Specialty Foods
Pingree Grove, IL 847-683-1200

EMERLING INTERNATIONAL FOODS, INC.

Emerling International Foods
Buffalo, NY 716-833-7381

We supply food manufacturers and food service customers worldwide (since 1988) with bulk ingredients including: Fruits & Vegetables; Juice Concentrates; Herbs & Spices; Oils & Vinegars; Flavors & Colors; Honey & Molasses. We also produce PURE MAPLE SYRUP.

Food & Vine
Napa, CA 707-251-3900
Hormel Foods Corporation
Austin, MN 507-437-5611
Lifestar Millennium
Novato, CA 800-858-7477
Pokonobe Industries
Santa Monica, CA 310-392-1259
Pure Extracts Inc
Ronkonkoma, NY 631-588-9727
Queensway Foods Company
Burlingame, CA 650-697-6666
Salute Sante! Food & Wine
Napa, CA 707-251-3900
Tabco Enterprises
Pomona, CA 909-623-4565

Hazelnut

K.L. Keller Imports
Oakland, CA 510-839-7890
Loriva Culinary Oils
San Francisco, CA 866-972-6679
Pure Extracts Inc
Ronkonkoma, NY 631-588-9727

Hemp Nut

Herbal Products & Development
Aptos, CA 831-688-4200
Mother Earth Enterprises
New York, NY 866-436-7688
Pure Extracts Inc
Ronkonkoma, NY 631-588-9727

Lemon

AG Processing, Inc.
Omaha, NE 800-247-1345
Astral Extracts Ltd
Syosset, NY 516-496-2505

Boyajian, Inc
  Canton, MA 800-965-0665
Diana's Specialty Foods
  Pingree Grove, IL 847-683-1200
Embassy Flavours Ltd.
  Brampton, ON. 800-334-3371

EMERLING INTERNATIONAL FOODS, INC.

Emerling International Foods
  Buffalo, NY. 716-833-7381

We supply food manufacturers and food service customers worldwide (since 1988) with bulk ingredients including: Fruits & Vegetables; Juice Concentrates; Herbs & Spices; Oils & Vinegars; Flavors & Colors; Honey & Molasses. We also produce PURE MAPLE SYRUP.

Flavtek
  Los Angeles, CA 800-562-5880
Gold Coast Ingredients
  Commerce, CA 800-352-8673
Prime Ingredients
  Saddle Brook, NJ 888-791-6655
Pure Extracts Inc
  Ronkonkoma, NY 631-588-9727
SunPure
  Lakeland, FL. 863-619-2222
Ungerer & Company
  Lincoln Park, NJ 973-628-0600

Lemon Grass

EMERLING INTERNATIONAL FOODS, INC.

Emerling International Foods
  Buffalo, NY. 716-833-7381

We supply food manufacturers and food service customers worldwide (since 1988) with bulk ingredients including: Fruits & Vegetables; Juice Concentrates; Herbs & Spices; Oils & Vinegars; Flavors & Colors; Honey & Molasses. We also produce PURE MAPLE SYRUP.

Pure Extracts Inc
  Ronkonkoma, NY 631-588-9727

Lime

Astral Extracts Ltd
  Syosset, NY. 516-496-2505
Boyajian, Inc
  Canton, MA 800-965-0665

EMERLING INTERNATIONAL FOODS, INC.

Emerling International Foods
  Buffalo, NY. 716-833-7381

We supply food manufacturers and food service customers worldwide (since 1988) with bulk ingredients including: Fruits & Vegetables; Juice Concentrates; Herbs & Spices; Oils & Vinegars; Flavors & Colors; Honey & Molasses. We also produce PURE MAPLE SYRUP.

Flavtek
  Los Angeles, CA 800-562-5880
Gold Coast Ingredients
  Commerce, CA 800-352-8673
Pure Extracts Inc
  Ronkonkoma, NY 631-588-9727
Ungerer & Company
  Lincoln Park, NJ 973-628-0600

Mustard

China Bowl Trading Company
  Westport, CT. 203-222-0381

EMERLING INTERNATIONAL FOODS, INC.

Emerling International Foods
  Buffalo, NY. 716-833-7381

We supply food manufacturers and food service customers worldwide (since 1988) with bulk ingredients including: Fruits & Vegetables; Juice Concentrates; Herbs & Spices; Oils & Vinegars; Flavors & Colors; Honey & Molasses. We also produce PURE MAPLE SYRUP.

Hemisphere Associated
  Huntington, NY 631-673-3840
Montana Specialty Mills
  Great Falls, MT. 406-761-2338
Pure Extracts Inc
  Ronkonkoma, NY 631-588-9727

Nutmeg

EMERLING INTERNATIONAL FOODS, INC.

Emerling International Foods
  Buffalo, NY. 716-833-7381

We supply food manufacturers and food service customers worldwide (since 1988) with bulk ingredients including: Fruits & Vegetables; Juice Concentrates; Herbs & Spices; Oils & Vinegars; Flavors & Colors; Honey & Molasses. We also produce PURE MAPLE SYRUP.

Pure Extracts Inc
  Ronkonkoma, NY 631-588-9727
Whole Herb Company
  Sonoma, CA 707-935-1077

Olive

A Southern Season
  Chapel Hill, NC 800-253-5317
A. Camacho
  Plant City, FL 800-881-4534
ACH Food Companies
  New Milford, CT 860-355-9421
AG Processing, Inc.
  Omaha, NE 800-247-1345
Agrocan
  Toronto, ON 877-247-6226
Agrusa, Inc.
  Leonia, NJ. 201-592-5950
Arista Industries
  Wilton, CT 800-255-6457
Ariston Specialties
  Bloomfield, CT. 860-224-7184
Arnabal International
  Tustin, CA. 714-665-9477
Assouline & Ting
  Philadelphia, PA 800-521-4491
Avatar Corporation
  University Park, IL 800-255-3181
B.R. Cohn Olive Oil
  Glen Ellen, CA 877-933-9675
Bella Cucina Artful Food
  Atlanta, GA. 800-671-3136
Bella Vista Farm
  Lawton, OK. 866-237-8526
BR Cohn Winery
  Glen Ellen, CA 707-938-4064
California Olive Growers
  Fresno, CA 888-965-4837
California Olive Oil Corporation
  Salem, MA 800-386-6457
Calio Groves
  Berkeley, CA. 800-865-4836
Castella Imports
  Hauppauge, NY 866-227-8355
Catania-Spagna Corporation
  Ayer, MA. 800-343-5522
Colavita
  Linden, NJ. 908-862-5454
Colonna Brothers
  North Bergen, NJ 201-864-1115
Continental Group
  Huntington Beach, CA 858-391-5670

CreAgri
  Hayward, CA 510-732-6478
Critelli Olive Oil
  Napa, CA. 800-865-4836
Diana's Specialty Foods
  Pingree Grove, IL 847-683-1200
East Coast Olive Oil
  Utica, NY 315-797-3151

EMERLING INTERNATIONAL FOODS, INC.

Emerling International Foods
  Buffalo, NY. 716-833-7381

We supply food manufacturers and food service customers worldwide (since 1988) with bulk ingredients including: Fruits & Vegetables; Juice Concentrates; Herbs & Spices; Oils & Vinegars; Flavors & Colors; Honey & Molasses. We also produce PURE MAPLE SYRUP.

Erba Food Products
  Brooklyn, NY 718-272-7700
Fantis Foods
  Carlstadt, NJ 201-933-6200
G B Ratto & Company International
  Oakland, CA. 800-325-3483
Golden Eagle Olive Products
  Porterville, CA 559-784-3468
Golden Whisk
  South San Francisco, CA 800-660-5222
Good Food
  Honey Brook, PA 800-327-4406
Good Health Natural Foods
  Northport, NY 631-261-2111
Gourmet Food Mall
  Kenner, LA 800-903-7553
Goya Foods of Florida
  Miami, FL. 305-592-3150
Grapevine Trading Company
  Santa Rosa, CA 800-469-6478
Greek Gourmet Limited
  Mill Valley, CA. 415-480-8050
Hormel Foods Corporation
  Oklahoma City, OK 405-843-5643
Hormel Foods Corporation
  Austin, MN 507-437-5611
HVJ International
  Spring, TX. 877-730-3663
Krinos Foods
  Long Island City, NY 718-729-9000
La Piccolina
  Decatur, GA 800-626-1624
Live Food Products
  Santa Barbara, CA 800-446-1990
Loriva Culinary Oils
  San Francisco, CA 866-972-6679
Lucero Olive Oil
  Corning, CA 916-625-4360
Lucini Italia Company
  San Francisco, CA 888-558-2464
Mancini Packing Company
  Zolfo Springs, FL 863-735-2000
Mancuso Cheese Company
  Joliet, IL 815-722-2475
Mid-Western Enterprises Limited
  Palos Hills, IL. 800-222-3032
MNH Erickson Ranch
  Orland, CA 530-865-9587
Moscahlades Brothers
  New York, NY 212-226-5410
Mountainbrook of Vermont
  Jeffersonville, VT 802-644-1988
Napa Valley Trading Company
  Corte Madera, CA. 415-383-8859
Nick Sciabica & Sons
  Modesto, CA. 800-551-9612
North American Enterprises
  Tucson, AZ 800-817-8666
Olive Oil Factory
  Watertown, CT 860-945-9549
Organic Planet
  San Francisco, CA 415-765-5590
Orland Olive Oil Company
  Orland, CA 530-865-4040
Our Thyme Garden
  Cleburne, TX 800-482-4372
Paradise Products Corporation
  Roslyn, NY 800-826-1235
Pastorelli Food Products
  Chicago, IL. 800-767-2829

Pokonobe Industries
Santa Monica, CA 310-392-1259
Pompeian
Baltimore, MD 800-638-1224
Proacec USA
Santa Monica, CA. 310-996-7770
Pure Extracts Inc
Ronkonkoma, NY 631-588-9727
Purity Products
Plainview, NY. 888-769-7873
Queensway Foods Company
Burlingame, CA 650-697-6666
Ron-Son Foods
Swedesboro, NJ 856-241-7333
Rose Brier
Albany, OR 888-926-4378
SilverLeaf International
Stafford, TX 800-442-7542
Sovena USA
Rome, NY. 315-797-7070
Sun Olive Oil Company
Templeton, CA 805-434-0626
Sweet Corn Products Company
Bloomfield, NE. 877-628-6115
Tee Pee Olives
Scarsdale, NY 800-431-1529
Trotters Imports
Colrain, MA 800-863-8437
Tutto Sicilia
Hartford, CT 860-986-7377
Unilever Bertolli USA, Inc.
Englewood Cliffs, NJ 201-894-4000
Valley Grain Products
Madera, CA. 559-675-3400
Veronica Foods Company
Oakland, CA 800-370-5554
Victoria Packing Corporation
Brooklyn, NY 718-649-2180
Wild Things
Beverly Hills, CA 310-412-4139

Extra Virgin

A. Camacho
Plant City, FL 800-881-4534
Adams Olive Ranch
Lindsay, CA 888-216-5483
Agrocan
Toronto, ON 877-247-6226
Agrusa, Inc.
Leonia, NJ. 201-592-5950
Arnabal International
Tustin, CA. 714-665-9477
Assouline & Ting
Philadelphia, PA 800-521-4491
Calio Groves
Berkeley, CA. 800-865-4836
Castella Imports
Hauppauge, NY 866-227-8355
Colonna Brothers
North Bergen, NJ 201-864-1115
Critelli Olive Oil
Napa, CA. 800-865-4836
Golden Eagle Olive Products
Porterville, CA 559-784-3468
K.L. Keller Imports
Oakland, CA 510-839-7890
Lucini Italia Company
San Francisco, CA 888-558-2464
O Olive Oil
Petaluma, CA 888-827-7148
Paesana Products
East Farmingdale, NY. 631-845-1717

Paradise Products Corporation
Roslyn, NY 800-826-1235
Pastorelli Food Products
Chicago, IL 800-767-2829
Pepper Mill Imports
Carmel, CA 800-928-1744
Proacec USA
Santa Monica, CA. 310-996-7770
Queensway Foods Company
Burlingame, CA 650-697-6666
Robert Rothschild Berry Farm
Urbana, OH 866-565-6790
Ron-Son Foods
Swedesboro, NJ 856-241-7333
Sabatino Truffles USA
Long Island City, NY 888-444-9971
Sieco USA Corporation
Houston, TX 800-325-9443
Specialty Foods International
Atlanta, GA 404-816-8268
Spruce Foods
San Clemente, CA. 949-366-9457
Veronica Foods Company
Oakland, CA 800-370-5554

Pomace

A. Camacho
Plant City, FL 800-881-4534
Agrocan
Toronto, ON 877-247-6226

Onion

Astral Extracts Ltd
Syosset, NY. 516-496-2505
Naturex (Chart Corp)
South Hackensack, NJ 201-440-5000
Pure Extracts Inc
Ronkonkoma, NY 631-588-9727
Vegetable Juices
Chicago, IL 888-776-9752
Whole Herb Company
Sonoma, CA 707-935-1077

Orange

Astral Extracts Ltd
Syosset, NY. 516-496-2505
Boyajian, Inc
Canton, MA 800-965-0665
Diana's Specialty Foods
Pingree Grove, IL 847-683-1200
Embassy Flavours Ltd.
Brampton, ON. 800-334-3371

EMERLING INTERNATIONAL FOODS, INC.

Emerling International Foods
Buffalo, NY. 716-833-7381

We supply food manufacturers and food service customers worldwide (since 1988) with bulk ingredients including: Fruits & Vegetables; Juice Concentrates; Herbs & Spices; Oils & Vinegars; Flavors & Colors; Honey & Molasses. We also produce PURE MAPLE SYRUP.

Flavtek
Los Angeles, CA. 800-562-5880
Gold Coast Ingredients
Commerce, CA 800-352-8673
Naturex (Chart Corp)
South Hackensack, NJ 201-440-5000

Pure Extracts Inc
Ronkonkoma, NY 631-588-9727
SunPure
Lakeland, FL 863-619-2222
Ungerer & Company
Lincoln Park, NJ 973-628-0600
V&E Kohnstamm
Brooklyn, NY 800-847-4500
Whole Herb Company
Sonoma, CA 707-935-1077

Palm

Aarhus United USA, Inc.
Newark, NJ 800-776-1338
ADM Food Oils
Decatur, IL 800-637-5866
ADM Refined Oils
Decatur, IL 800-637-5866
AG Processing, Inc.
Omaha, NE 800-247-1345

EMERLING INTERNATIONAL FOODS, INC.

Emerling International Foods
Buffalo, NY. 716-833-7381

We supply food manufacturers and food service customers worldwide (since 1988) with bulk ingredients including: Fruits & Vegetables; Juice Concentrates; Herbs & Spices; Oils & Vinegars; Flavors & Colors; Honey & Molasses. We also produce PURE MAPLE SYRUP.

Pokonobe Industries
Santa Monica, CA 310-392-1259
Pure Extracts Inc
Ronkonkoma, NY 631-588-9727
Stevenson-Cooper
Philadelphia, PA 215-223-2600
Ventura Foods
Opelousas, LA 337-948-6561
Welch, Home & Clark Company
Newark, NJ 973-465-1200

Kernel

ADM Food Oils
Decatur, IL 800-637-5866

Peanut

ADM Food Oils
Decatur, IL 800-637-5866
ADM Refined Oils
Decatur, IL 800-637-5866
AG Processing, Inc.
Omaha, NE 800-247-1345
ARRO Corporation
Hodgkins, IL 708-352-8200
Avatar Corporation
University Park, IL 800-255-3181
Birdsong Peanut Company
Gorman, TX 254-734-3153
California Olive Oil Corporation
Salem, MA 800-386-6457
Cargill Refined Oils
Minneapolis, MN 800-323-6232
Casey's Food Products
Blakely, GA 229-723-3411
Catania-Spagna Corporation
Ayer, MA. 800-343-5522
Central Soya
Pawtucket, RI 800-556-6777

Good Food
  Honey Brook, PA 800-327-4406
K.L. Keller Imports
  Oakland, CA 510-839-7890
Loriva Culinary Oils
  San Francisco, CA 866-972-6679
Mallet & Company
  Carnegie, PA 800-245-2757
Pastorelli Food Products
  Chicago, IL 800-767-2829
Pokonobe Industries
  Santa Monica, CA 310-392-1259
Pure Extracts Inc
  Ronkonkoma, NY 631-588-9727
Purity Products
  Plainview, NY 888-769-7873
Sessions Company
  Enterprise, AL 334-393-0200
Sovena USA
  Rome, NY 315-797-7070
Synergy Foods
  West Bloomfield, MI 313-849-2900
Ventura Foods
  Opelousas, LA 337-948-6561

Pepper

Pure Extracts Inc
  Ronkonkoma, NY 631-588-9727
Whole Herb Company
  Sonoma, CA 707-935-1077

Peppermint

A.M. Todd Company
  Kalamazoo, MI 800-968-2603

EMERLING INTERNATIONAL FOODS, INC.

Emerling International Foods
  Buffalo, NY 716-833-7381

We supply food manufacturers and food service
customers worldwide (since 1988) with bulk ingredients including: Fruits & Vegetables; Juice
Concentrates; Herbs & Spices; Oils & Vinegars;
Flavors & Colors; Honey & Molasses. We also
produce PURE MAPLE SYRUP.

Gold Coast Ingredients
  Commerce, CA 800-352-8673
Lebermuth Company
  South Bend, IN 800-648-1123
Medallion International
  Pompton Plains, NJ 973-616-3401
Naturex (Chart Corp)
  South Hackensack, NJ 201-440-5000
Pure Extracts Inc
  Ronkonkoma, NY 631-588-9727
Ungerer & Company
  Lincoln Park, NJ 973-628-0600

Pimiento

Naturex (Chart Corp)
  South Hackensack, NJ 201-440-5000
Pure Extracts Inc
  Ronkonkoma, NY 631-588-9727

Popping Corn

Acatris USA
  Edina, MN 952-920-7700
ADM Refined Oils
  Decatur, IL 800-637-5866
Avatar Corporation
  University Park, IL 800-255-3181
Central Soya
  Pawtucket, RI 800-556-6777
Delicious Popcorn Company
  Waupaca, WI 715-258-7683
Great Western Products Company
  Assumption, IL 217-226-3241

Great Western Products Company
  Bremen, IN 217-546-4010
Great Western Products Company
  Bismarck, MO 573-734-2210
Pure Extracts Inc
  Ronkonkoma, NY 631-588-9727
Vogel Popcorn
  Hamburg, IA 800-831-5818

Poppy Seed

Herbal Products & Development
  Aptos, CA 831-688-4200
Pure Extracts Inc
  Ronkonkoma, NY 631-588-9727
Whole Herb Company
  Sonoma, CA 707-935-1077

Pumpkin Seed

Arista Industries
  Wilton, CT 800-255-6457

Rice Bran

Arista Industries
  Wilton, CT 800-255-6457

Safflower

AG Processing, Inc.
  Omaha, NE 800-247-1345
American Health & Nutrition
  Ann Arbor, MI 734-677-5572
Arista Industries
  Wilton, CT 800-255-6457
California Oils Corporation
  Richmond, CA 800-225-6457
Flora
  Lynden, WA 800-446-2110
Loriva Culinary Oils
  San Francisco, CA 866-972-6679
Pokonobe Industries
  Santa Monica, CA 310-392-1259
Pure Extracts Inc
  Ronkonkoma, NY 631-588-9727
Sona & Hollen Foods
  Los Alamitos, CA 800-200-7662
Welch, Home & Clark Company
  Newark, NJ 973-465-1200

Sage

Astral Extracts Ltd
  Syosset, NY 516-496-2505

EMERLING INTERNATIONAL FOODS, INC.

Emerling International Foods
  Buffalo, NY 716-833-7381

We supply food manufacturers and food service
customers worldwide (since 1988) with bulk ingredients including: Fruits & Vegetables; Juice
Concentrates; Herbs & Spices; Oils & Vinegars;
Flavors & Colors; Honey & Molasses. We also
produce PURE MAPLE SYRUP.

Naturex (Chart Corp)
  South Hackensack, NJ 201-440-5000
Pure Extracts Inc
  Ronkonkoma, NY 631-588-9727
Southeastern Wisconsin Products Company
  Milwaukee, WI 414-482-1730
Whole Herb Company
  Sonoma, CA 707-935-1077

Salad

ADM Refined Oils
  Decatur, IL 800-637-5866
Arista Industries
  Wilton, CT 800-255-6457
ARRO Corporation
  Hodgkins, IL 708-352-8200
Avatar Corporation
  University Park, IL 800-255-3181
Cargill Refined Oils
  Minneapolis, MN 800-323-6232
Consumer Guild Foods
  Toledo, OH 419-726-3406

EMERLING INTERNATIONAL FOODS, INC.

Emerling International Foods
  Buffalo, NY 716-833-7381

We supply food manufacturers and food service
customers worldwide (since 1988) with bulk ingredients including: Fruits & Vegetables; Juice
Concentrates; Herbs & Spices; Oils & Vinegars;
Flavors & Colors; Honey & Molasses. We also
produce PURE MAPLE SYRUP.

Pure Extracts Inc
  Ronkonkoma, NY 631-588-9727
Sovena USA
  Rome, NY 315-797-7070
Ventura Foods
  Ontario, CA 714-257-3700
Ventura Foods   Foodservice/Export/Custom Pack
  City of Industry, CA 800-327-3906

Sassafras

Astral Extracts Ltd
  Syosset, NY 516-496-2505
Pure Extracts Inc
  Ronkonkoma, NY 631-588-9727
Whole Herb Company
  Sonoma, CA 707-935-1077

Sesame

AG Processing, Inc.
  Omaha, NE 800-247-1345
Arista Industries
  Wilton, CT 800-255-6457
Avatar Corporation
  University Park, IL 800-255-3181
California Olive Oil Corporation
  Salem, MA 800-386-6457
China Bowl Trading Company
  Westport, CT 203-222-0381
Columbus Foods Company
  Des Plaines, IL 800-322-6457
Dipasa
  Brownsville, TX 956-831-5893

EMERLING INTERNATIONAL FOODS, INC.

Emerling International Foods
  Buffalo, NY 716-833-7381

We supply food manufacturers and food service
customers worldwide (since 1988) with bulk ingredients including: Fruits & Vegetables; Juice
Concentrates; Herbs & Spices; Oils & Vinegars;
Flavors & Colors; Honey & Molasses. We also
produce PURE MAPLE SYRUP.

Flora
  Lynden, WA 800-446-2110
Golden Gate Foods
  Dallas, TX 214-747-2223
Loriva Culinary Oils
  San Francisco, CA 866-972-6679
Organic Planet
  San Francisco, CA 415-765-5590
Pokonobe Industries
  Santa Monica, CA 310-392-1259
Pure Extracts Inc
  Ronkonkoma, NY 631-588-9727
Sona & Hollen Foods
  Los Alamitos, CA 800-200-7662
Universal Preservachem Inc
  Edison, NJ 732-777-7338

Soybean

Aarhus United USA, Inc.
  Newark, NJ 800-776-1338
ADM Food Oils
  Decatur, IL 800-637-5866
ADM Refined Oils
  Decatur, IL 800-637-5866
AG Processing, Inc.
  Omaha, NE 800-247-1345
Agri-Dairy Products
  Purchase, NY 914-697-9580
American Health & Nutrition
  Ann Arbor, MI 734-677-5572
ARRO Corporation
  Hodgkins, IL 708-352-8200

Avatar Corporation
 University Park, IL 800-255-3181
Bunge Corporation
 Vicksburg, MS 601-638-3824
Bunge Ingredients
 Seattle, WA 206-623-7740
California Olive Oil Corporation
 Salem, MA 800-386-6457
Cargill Refined Oils
 Minneapolis, MN 800-323-6232
Cargill Vegetable Oils
 Minneapolis, MN 612-378-0551
Catania-Spagna Corporation
 Ayer, MA 800-343-5522
Central Soya
 Pawtucket, RI 800-556-6777
CHS
 Inver Grove Heights, MN 800-232-3639
Clofine Dairy & Food Products
 Linwood, NJ 800-441-1001
Columbus Foods Company
 Des Plaines, IL 800-322-6457
Dixie USA
 Tomball, TX 800-233-3668

EMERLING INTERNATIONAL FOODS, INC.

Emerling International Foods
 Buffalo, NY 716-833-7381

We supply food manufacturers and food service
customers worldwide (since 1988) with bulk ingredients including: Fruits & Vegetables; Juice
Concentrates; Herbs & Spices; Oils & Vinegars;
Flavors & Colors; Honey & Molasses. We also
produce PURE MAPLE SYRUP.

Gama Products
 Medley, FL 305-883-1200
Golden Brands
 Louisville, KY 800-622-3055
Mallet & Company
 Carnegie, PA 800-245-2757
Organic Planet
 San Francisco, CA 415-765-5590
Owensboro Grain Edible Oils
 Owensboro, KY 270-273-5443
Pastorelli Food Products
 Chicago, IL 800-767-2829
Pokonobe Industries
 Santa Monica, CA 310-392-1259
Pure Extracts Inc
 Ronkonkoma, NY 631-588-9727
Purity Products
 Plainview, NY 888-769-7873
Solae Company
 St Louis, MO 800-325-7108
Sovena USA
 Rome, NY 315-797-7070
Universal Preservachem Inc
 Edison, NJ 732-777-7338
Ventura Foods
 Opelousas, LA 337-948-6561
Vincent Formusa Company
 Chicago, IL 312-421-0485
Welch, Home & Clark Company
 Newark, NJ 973-465-1200

Sunflower

Aarhus United USA, Inc.
 Newark, NJ 800-776-1338
ACATRIS
 Oakville, ON 905-829-2414
ACH Food Companies
 New Milford, CT 860-355-9421
ADM Food Oils
 Decatur, IL 800-637-5866
ADM Refined Oils
 Decatur, IL 800-637-5866
AG Processing, Inc.
 Omaha, NE 800-247-1345
American Health & Nutrition
 Ann Arbor, MI 734-677-5572

Columbus Foods Company
 Des Plaines, IL 800-322-6457

EMERLING INTERNATIONAL FOODS, INC.

Emerling International Foods
 Buffalo, NY 716-833-7381

We supply food manufacturers and food service
customers worldwide (since 1988) with bulk ingredients including: Fruits & Vegetables; Juice
Concentrates; Herbs & Spices; Oils & Vinegars;
Flavors & Colors; Honey & Molasses. We also
produce PURE MAPLE SYRUP.

Flora
 Lynden, WA 800-446-2110
Loriva Culinary Oils
 San Francisco, CA 866-972-6679
Pokonobe Industries
 Santa Monica, CA 310-392-1259
Pure Extracts Inc
 Ronkonkoma, NY 631-588-9727
Solae Company
 St Louis, MO 800-325-7108
Welch, Home & Clark Company
 Newark, NJ 973-465-1200

Tangerine

Astral Extracts Ltd
 Syosset, NY 516-496-2505

EMERLING INTERNATIONAL FOODS, INC.

Emerling International Foods
 Buffalo, NY 716-833-7381

We supply food manufacturers and food service
customers worldwide (since 1988) with bulk ingredients including: Fruits & Vegetables; Juice
Concentrates; Herbs & Spices; Oils & Vinegars;
Flavors & Colors; Honey & Molasses. We also
produce PURE MAPLE SYRUP.

Gold Coast Ingredients
 Commerce, CA 800-352-8673
Pure Extracts Inc
 Ronkonkoma, NY 631-588-9727

Thyme

Astral Extracts Ltd
 Syosset, NY 516-496-2505

EMERLING INTERNATIONAL FOODS, INC.

Emerling International Foods
 Buffalo, NY 716-833-7381

We supply food manufacturers and food service
customers worldwide (since 1988) with bulk ingredients including: Fruits & Vegetables; Juice
Concentrates; Herbs & Spices; Oils & Vinegars;
Flavors & Colors; Honey & Molasses. We also
produce PURE MAPLE SYRUP.

Naturex (Chart Corp)
 South Hackensack, NJ 201-440-5000
Pure Extracts Inc
 Ronkonkoma, NY 631-588-9727
Whole Herb Company
 Sonoma, CA 707-935-1077

Vegetable

Aarhus United USA, Inc.
 Newark, NJ 800-776-1338
Abitec Corporation
 Columbus, OH 800-555-1255
ACATRIS
 Oakville, ON 905-829-2414
ACH Food Companies
 Cordova, TN 800-691-1106
ACH Food Companies
 New Milford, CT 860-355-9421
Adams Vegetable Oils
 Arbuckle, CA 530-668-2000
ADM
 Decatur, IL 800-637-5843
ADM Refined Oils
 Decatur, IL 800-637-5866

AG Processing, Inc.
 Omaha, NE 800-247-1345
Allfresh Food Products
 Evanston, IL 847-869-3100
American Chemical Service
 Griffith, IN 219-924-4370
ARC Diversified
 Cookeville, TN 800-239-9029
Arista Industries
 Wilton, CT 800-255-6457
ARRO Corporation
 Hodgkins, IL 708-352-8200
Atlas Preserves Company
 New York, NY 212-569-5613
Avatar Corporation
 University Park, IL 800-255-3181
Blue California Company
 Rancho Santa Margarita, CA 949-635-1991
Bunge Canada
 Oakville, ON 800-361-3043
Bungy Oils
 Pawtucket, RI 401-724-3800
C&T Refinery
 Richmond, VA 800-284-6457
California Oils Corporation
 Richmond, CA 800-225-6457
Cargill Specialty Oils
 Minneapolis, MN 800-851-8331
Cargill Vegetable Oils
 Minneapolis, MN 612-378-0551
Catania-Spagna Corporation
 Ayer, MA 800-343-5522
CBS Food Products Corporation
 Brooklyn, NY 718-452-2500
Central Soya
 Pawtucket, RI 800-556-6777
CHS
 Inver Grove Heights, MN 800-232-3639
Columbus Foods Company
 Des Plaines, IL 800-322-6457
ConAgra Grocery Products
 Irvine, CA 714-680-1000
CP Vegetable Oil
 Brampton, ON 905-792-2309

EMERLING INTERNATIONAL FOODS, INC.

Emerling International Foods
 Buffalo, NY 716-833-7381

We supply food manufacturers and food service
customers worldwide (since 1988) with bulk ingredients including: Fruits & Vegetables; Juice
Concentrates; Herbs & Spices; Oils & Vinegars;
Flavors & Colors; Honey & Molasses. We also
produce PURE MAPLE SYRUP.

Follmer Development/Americana
 Newbury Park, CA 805-498-4531
Fuji Vegetable Oil
 White Plains, NY 914-761-7900
Gateway Food Products Company
 Dupo, IL 877-220-1963
Good Food
 Honey Brook, PA 800-327-4406
Hybco USA
 Los Angeles, CA 323-269-3111
Janca's Jojoba Oil & Seed Company
 Mesa, AZ 480-497-9494
Liberty Vegetable Oil Company
 Santa Fe Springs, CA 562-921-3567
Loriva Culinary Oils
 San Francisco, CA 866-972-6679
Mallet & Company
 Carnegie, PA 800-245-2757
Mercado Latino
 City of Industry, CA 626-333-6862
Milnot Company
 Neosho, MO 800-877-6455
Montana Specialty Mills
 Great Falls, MT 406-761-2338
Natural Oils International
 Simi Valley, CA 805-433-0160
Oasis Foods Company
 Hillside, NJ 908-964-0477
Ottens Flavors
 Philadelphia, PA 800-523-0767
Pokonobe Industries
 Santa Monica, CA 310-392-1259
Pure Extracts Inc
 Ronkonkoma, NY 631-588-9727

Food & Beverage Market Place

now available for subscription on

G.O.L.D.

Grey House OnLine Databases

Immediate Access to the US Food & Beverage Industry!

- Easy-To-Use Keyword & Quick Searches
- Organization Type & Subject Searches
- Cross-Database Searching
- Search by Area Code or Zip Code Ranges
- Search by Company Size & Geographic Area
- Search by Contact Name or Title

- Hotlinks to Websites & Email Addresses
- Combine Multiple Search Criteria with our Expert Search Page
- Sort Search Results by City, Company Name, Area Code & more
- Save Searches for Quick Lookups
- Create & Save Your Own Search Results Lists
- Download Search Results in TXT, CSV or DOC Formats

Quick Search

Expert Search

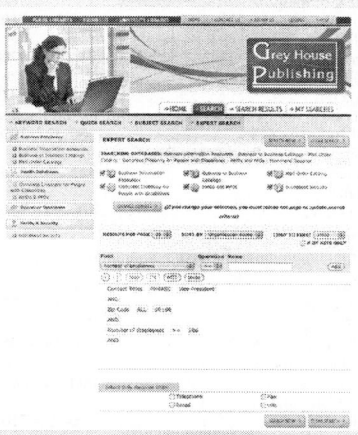

Subject Search

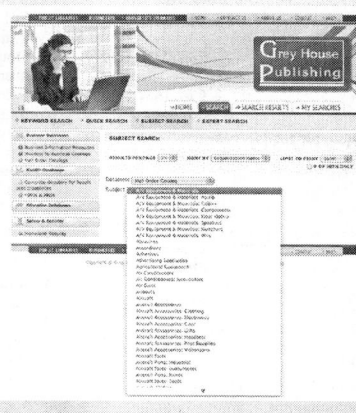

Call (800) 562-2139 for a free trial of the new G.O.L.D. OnLine Database Platform or visit http://gold.greyhouse.com for more information!

Grey House Publishing

PO Box 56 | 4919 Route 22 | Amenia, NY 12501
(800) 562-2139 | (518) 789-8700 | FAX (845) 373-6360
www.greyhouse.com | e-mail: books@greyhouse.com

Purity Products
Plainview, NY 888-769-7873
Riceland Foods   Rice Milling Operations
Little Rock, AR 888-532-4844
Solae Company
St Louis, MO 800-325-7108
Sona & Hollen Foods
Los Alamitos, CA 800-200-7662
Spruce Foods
San Clemente, CA 949-366-9457
Starwest Botanicals
Rancho Cordova, CA 888-273-4372
Stepan Company
Maywood, NJ 800-523-3614
Technical Oil Products
Boonton, NJ 973-335-0300
The Solae Company
St Louis, MO 800-325-7108
Universal Preservachem Inc
Edison, NJ 732-777-7338
Ventura Foods   Foodservice
Salem, OR 503-585-6423
Welch, Home & Clark Company
Newark, NJ 973-465-1200

Fortified Refined

ABITEC Corporation
Janesville, WI 800-457-1977

Vitamin

Arista Industries
Wilton, CT 800-255-6457
Columbus Foods Company
Des Plaines, IL 800-322-6457
Green Turtle Bay Vitamin Company
Summit, NJ 800-887-8535
P.J. Noyes Company
Lancaster, NH 800-522-2469
Pure Extracts Inc
Ronkonkoma, NY 631-588-9727
Universal Preservachem Inc
Edison, NJ 732-777-7338

Walnut

K.L. Keller Imports
Oakland, CA 510-839-7890
Loriva Culinary Oils
San Francisco, CA 866-972-6679
Welch, Home & Clark Company
Newark, NJ 973-465-1200

Wheat Germ

Arista Industries
Wilton, CT 800-255-6457
Avatar Corporation
University Park, IL 800-255-3181
Energen Products
Norwalk, CA 800-423-8837
Pokonobe Industries
Santa Monica, CA 310-392-1259
Pure Extracts Inc
Ronkonkoma, NY 631-588-9727
Universal Preservachem Inc
Edison, NJ 732-777-7338
VIOBIN
Monticello, IL 888-473-9645
Viobin USA
Monticello, IL 217-762-2561
Vitamins
Chicago, IL 312-861-0700

Pan Coatings & Sprays

Americana Marketing
Newbury Park, CA 800-742-7520
Technical Oil
Easton, PA 610-252-8350
Ventura Foods   Production Plant
Los Angeles, CA 323-265-4300

Shortening

ACH Food Companies
Cordova, TN 800-691-1106
ACH Food Companies
New Milford, CT 860-355-9421
ADM Refined Oils
Decatur, IL 800-637-5866
Allfresh Food Products
Evanston, IL 847-869-3100

Atlas Preserves Company
New York, NY 212-569-5613
Brand Aromatics International
Holmdel, NJ 732-706-3411
Bunge North America
St Louis, MO 314-569-1339
Bungy Oils
Pawtucket, RI 401-724-3800
C.F. Sauer Company
Richmond, VA 800-688-5676
C.W. Brown & Company
Mount Royal, NJ 856-423-3700
CanAmera Foods
Winnipeg, NB 204-324-6481
Cargill Refined Oils
Minneapolis, MN 800-323-6232
Central Soya
Pawtucket, RI 800-556-6777
Clofine Dairy & Food Products
Linwood, NJ 800-441-1001
Coast Packing Company
Vernon, CA 323-277-7700
Columbus Foods Company
Des Plaines, IL 800-322-6457
Florida Shortening Corporation
Miami, FL 305-691-2992
Golden Brands
Louisville, KY 800-622-3055
JE Bergeron & Sons
Bromptonville, QC 800-567-2798
Mallet & Company
Carnegie, PA 800-245-2757
Mercado Latino
City of Industry, CA 626-333-6862
Mid Atlantic Vegetable Shortening Company
Kearny, NJ 800-966-1645
Pak Technologies
Milwaukee, WI 414-438-8600
Pastorelli Food Products
Chicago, IL 800-767-2829
Price's Creameries
El Paso, TX 915-565-2711
Riceland Foods   Rice Milling Operations
Little Rock, AR 888-532-4844
Source Food Technology
Durham, NC 866-277-3849
The Solae Company
St Louis, MO 800-325-7108
Ventura Foods
Ontario, CA 714-257-3700
Ventura Foods   Foodservice
Salem, OR 503-585-6423
Ventura Foods   Foodservice/Export/Custom Pack
City of Industry, CA 800-327-3906
Ventura Foods   Production Plant
Los Angeles, CA 323-265-4300
Wells' Dairy
Le Mars, IA 800-942-3800

Fluid

Central Soya
Pawtucket, RI 800-556-6777
Mercado Latino
City of Industry, CA 626-333-6862
Pastorelli Food Products
Chicago, IL 800-767-2829
The Solae Company
St Louis, MO 800-325-7108

Vegetable

Atlas Preserves Company
New York, NY 212-569-5613
Bunge Canada
Oakville, ON 800-361-3043
Central Soya
Pawtucket, RI 800-556-6777
Gateway Food Products Company
Dupo, IL 877-220-1963
JE Bergeron & Sons
Bromptonville, QC 800-567-2798
Mercado Latino
City of Industry, CA 626-333-6862
Pastorelli Food Products
Chicago, IL 800-767-2829
The Solae Company
St Louis, MO 800-325-7108

Liquid

Central Soya
Pawtucket, RI 800-556-6777

Mallet & Company
Carnegie, PA 800-245-2757
Mercado Latino
City of Industry, CA 626-333-6862
Pastorelli Food Products
Chicago, IL 800-767-2829
The Solae Company
St Louis, MO 800-325-7108

Pasta & Noodles

General

A Zerega's Sons, Inc.
Fair Lawn, NJ 201-797-1400
AGNESI USA
New York, NY 212-619-3255
Agrusa, Inc.
Leonia, NJ. 201-592-5950
Al Dente
Whitmore Lake, MI 800-536-7278
Alaska Pasta Company
Anchorage, AK. 907-276-2632
Alaska Smokehouse
Woodinville, WA. 800-422-0852
American Italian Pasta Company
Columbia, SC 803-695-7300
American Italian Pasta Company
Kansas City, MO. 816-584-5000
Archer Daniels Midland Company
Lincoln, NE. 800-228-4060
Armanino Foods of Distinction
Hayward, CA 510-441-9300
Arrowhead Mills
Hereford, TX. 800-749-0730
Associated Brands, Inc.
Medina, NY. 800-265-0050
Atlanta Bread Company International, Inc.
Smyrna, GA 800-398-3728
Belletieri Company
Allentown, PA. 800-708-7280
Bernie's Foods
Brooklyn, NY 718-417-6677
Better Baked Foods
North East, PA. 814-725-8778
Biagio's Banquets
Chicago, IL 800-392-2837
Borden Foods
Columbus, OH 614-233-3759
Borinquen Macaroni Corporation
Yauco, PR 787-856-1450
Boudreaux's Foods
New Orleans, LA 504-733-8440
Bruno Specialty Foods
West Sayville, NY. 631-589-1700
Buon Italia
New York, NY 212-633-9090
Buona Vita
Bridgeton, NJ 856-453-7972
Burnette Foods
Elk Rapids, MI 231-264-8116
Caesar's Pasta Products
Blackwood, NJ 856-227-2585
Cafferata
San Anselmo, CA 800-626-8115
Canasoy Enterprises
Vancouver, BC 800-663-1222
Canton Noodle Corporation
New York, NY 212-226-3276
Capone Foods
Somerville, MA 617-629-2296
Carando Gourmet Frozen Foods
Springfield, MA 413-730-4205
Carla's Pasta
South Windsor, CT 800-957-2782
Castella Imports
Hauppauge, NY 866-227-8355
Cedarlane Foods
Carson, CA 800-826-3322
China Bowl Trading Company
Westport, CT. 203-222-0381
Codino's Italian Foods
Scotia, NY. 800-246-8908
Comet Rice
Houston, TX 281-272-8800
ConAgra Frozen Foods Company
Omaha, NE 402-595-4000
ConAgra Frozen Foods Company
Marshall, MO 660-886-3301
ConAgra Grocery Products
Irvine, CA 714-680-1000
Conte Luna Foods
Warminster, PA 215-441-5220
Conte Luna Foods
Philadelphia, PA 215-923-3141
Continental Group
Huntington Beach, CA 858-391-5670

Corsetti's Pasta Products
Woodbury, NJ 800-989-1188
Costa's Pasta
Kennesaw, GA 770-514-8814
Cottage Street Pasta
Barre, VT. 802-476-4024
Country Foods
Polson, MT 406-883-4384
Cuizina Food Company
Woodinville, WA. 425-486-7000
Cumberland Pasta
Cumberland, MD 800-572-7821
D'Orazio Foods
Bellmawr, NJ. 888-328-7287
Dairy Maid Ravioli Manufacturing Corporation
Brooklyn, NY 718-449-2620
Dakota Growers Pasta Company
Carrington, ND 701-652-2855
De Cio Pasta Primo
Cave Creek, AZ 800-397-0770
Difiore Pasta Company
Hartford, CT 860-296-1077
Double Wrap Cup & Container
Buffalo Grove, IL 312-337-0072
Downeast Pasta
Portland, ME. 800-587-2782
Drakes Fresh Pasta Company
High Point, NC 336-861-5454
E.D. Smith & Sons
Winona, ON 905-643-1211
Eden Foods Inc
Clinton, MI 800-248-0320
Eden Organic Pasta Company
Detroit, MI 800-248-0320
El Peto Products
Cambridge, ON. 800-387-4064
Elena's
Auburn Hills, MI 800-723-5362
Ener-G Foods
Seattle, WA 800-331-5222
Epicurean International
Berkeley, CA. 800-967-7424
Ethnic Gourmet Foods
West Chester, PA. 610-692-7575
European Egg Noodle Manufacturing
Edmonton, AB 780-453-6767
Faribault Foods
Minneapolis, MN 612-333-6461
Fiori-Bruna Pasta Products
Hialeah, FL 305-621-0074
Florence Macaroni Manufacturing
Los Angeles, CA. 323-232-7269
Florence Macaroni Manufacturing
Chicago, IL 800-647-2782
Florence Pasta & Cheese
Marshall, MN 800-533-5290
Florentyna's Fresh Pasta Factory
Vernon, CA 800-747-2782
Fontana's Casa De La Pasta
Vandergrift, PA 724-567-2782
Food City USA
Arvada, CO. 303-321-4447
Food Source
McKinney, TX 972-548-9001
Foulds
Libertyville, IL 847-362-3062
Fresh Market Pasta Company
Portland, ME. 207-773-7146
Fun Foods
East Rutherford, NJ 800-507-2782
Gabriele Macaroni Company
City of Industry, CA 626-964-2324
Gaston Dupre
Excelsior Springs, MO 817-629-6275
Geetha's Gourmet of India
Las Cruces, NM 800-274-0475
Gentilini's Italian Products
Sunriver, OR 541-593-5053
German Village Products
Wauseon, OH 419-335-1515
Gilardi Foods
Sidney, OH 937-498-4511
Gilster-Mary Lee Corporation
Chester, IL. 800-851-5371
Golden Grain
Pleasanton, CA 925-734-8800

Golden Grain Company
Bridgeview, IL 708-458-7020
Golden Whisk
South San Francisco, CA 800-660-5222
Good Old Dad Food Products
Sault Ste. Marie, ON. 800-267-7426
Gourmets Fresh Pasta
Pasadena, CA 626-798-0841
Great Eastern Sun
Asheville, NC 800-334-5809
Greenfield Noodle & Specialty Company
Detroit, MI 313-873-2212
H.J. Heinz Company
Pittsburgh, PA 412-237-5948
Haypress Gourmet Pasta
Haverstraw, NY 845-947-4580
Heartline Foods
Westport, CT. 203-222-0381
Hershey Pasta Group
Louisville, KY 800-468-1714
HFI Foods
Redmond, WA. 425-883-1320
Hodgson Mill Inc
Effingham, IL 800-525-0177
Hong Tou Noodle Company
Los Angeles, CA. 323-256-3843
Hung's Noodle House
Calgary, AB. 403-250-1663
Hunt-Wesson Food Service Company
Rochester, NY. 800-633-1002
Iltaco Food Products
Chicago, IL. 800-244-8935
International Harvest
Mt Vernon, NY 914-939-1505
International Home Foods
Milton, PA. 973-359-9920
International Noodle Company
Madison Heights, MI 248-583-2479
Ital Florida Foods
Weston, FL 305-769-0799
Italia Foods
Schaumburg, IL. 800-747-1109
Italian Gourmet Foods Canada
Calgary, AB. 403-263-6996

Itarca
  Inglewood, CA 800-747-2782
J-N-D Company
  Fort Wayne, IN 260-459-6206
J.B. Sons
  Yonkers, NY 914-963-5192
Joseph's Gourmet Pasta & Sauces
  Haverhill, MA 800-863-8998
Joseph's Pasta Company
  Ward Hill, MA 888-327-2782
JSL Foods
  Los Angeles, CA. 800-745-3236
Juno Chef's
  Brooklyn, NY 718-492-1300
Kay Foods Company
  Ionia, MI 616-527-0120
Kemach Food Products   Corporation
  Brooklyn, NY 888-453-6224
Koyo Foods
  Richmond, CA 510-527-7066
Kozlowski Farms
  Forestville, CA 800-473-2767
Kraft
  Parsippany, NJ. 973-292-1755
Kraft Foods
  Springfield, MO 417-881-2701
Kraft Foods
  Northfield, IL 847-646-2000
Krinos Foods
  Long Island City, NY 718-729-9000
La Piccolina
  Decatur, GA 800-626-1624
La Romagnola
  Orlando, FL. 800-843-8359
La Spiga D'Oro Fresh Pasta Co
  San Rafael, CA 800-847-2782
Ladson Homemade Pasta Company
  Phoenix, AZ 480-353-0874
LaMonica Fine Foods
  Millville, NJ 856-825-8111
Landolfi Food Products
  Trenton, NJ 609-392-1830
Lapasta
  Silver Spring, MD 301-588-1111
Liberty Richter
  Saddle Brook, NJ 201-291-8749
Lombardo's Ravioli Kitchen
  New Britain, CT 860-223-7800
Lotsa Pasta
  San Diego, CA. 858-581-6777
Louis Severino Pasta
  Westmont, NJ 856-854-7666
Louisa Food Products
  St Louis, MO. 314-868-3000
Luigino's
  Duluth, MN 218-727-2059
Mama Del's Macaroni
  East Haven, CT. 203-469-6255
Mama Mucci's Pasta
  Canton, MI 734-453-4555
Mama Rosie's Ravioli Company
  Charlestown, MA 888-246-4300
Mamma Lina Ravioli Company
  San Diego, CA. 858-535-0620
Marsan Foods
  Toronto, ON 416-755-9262
Maruchan
  Irvine, CA 949-789-2300
McCain Foods USA
  Lisle, IL 630-955-0400
Michael Angelo's Gourmet Foods
  Austin, TX. .877-482-5486
Midwest Foods
  Owatonna, MN 507-451-7670
Modern Macaroni Company
  Honolulu, HI 808-845-6841
Montreal Chop Suey Company
  Montreal, QC 514-522-3134
Morrison Lamothe
  Toronto, ON 416-291-6762
Mount Rose Ravioli & Macaroni Company
  Farmingdale, NY 516-694-6940
Mrs. Leeper's Pasta
  Kansas City, MO. 800-848-5266
Muruchan
  Irvine, CA 949-789-2300
Mutual Trading Company
  Los Angeles, CA. 213-626-9458
Napoli Pasta Manufacturers
  Miami, FL. .305-666-1942
Natural Value Products
  Sacramento, CA 916-427-7242

Nestle
  Cleveland, OH 440-349-5757
New World Pasta Company 7
  Harrisburg, PA 800-730-5957
Nino's Enterprises
  Melrose Park, IL 708-344-8082
Nissin Foods USA Company
  Gardena, CA 310-327-8478
Nissin Foods USA Company
  Lancaster, PA 717-291-5901
Noodles by Leonardo
  Cando, ND 701-968-4464
North American Enterprises
  Tucson, AZ 800-817-8666
Oakland Noodle Company
  Oakland, IL 217-346-2322
OB Macaroni Company
  Fort Worth, TX 800-555-4336
Oh Boy! Corporation
  San Fernando, CA. 818-361-1128
Okahara Saimin Factory
  Honolulu, HI 808-949-0588
Olmarc Packaging Company
  Chicago, IL 708-562-2000
On-Cor Foods Products
  Northbrook, IL 847-205-1040
Ore-Ida Foods
  Pittsburgh, PA 412-237-3450
Original Italian Pasta Poducts Company
  Chelsea, MA 800-999-9603
P&S Ravioli Company
  Philadelphia, PA 215-465-8888
Pak Technologies
  Milwaukee, WI 414-438-8600
Pappardelle's Pasta Company
  Denver, CO 800-607-2782
Pascucci Family Pasta
  San Diego, CA 619-285-8000
Pasta Del Mondo
  Carmel, NY 800-392-8887
Pasta Factory
  Northlake, IL. 800-615-6951
Pasta International
  Mississauga, ON 888-607-2782
Pasta Italiana
  Massapequa, NY 800-536-5611
Pasta Mami
  Smyrna, GA 770-438-6022
Pasta Mill
  Edmonton, AB 780-454-8665
Pasta Montana
  Great Falls, MT. 406-761-1516
Pasta Partners
  Salt Lake City, UT 800-727-8284
Pasta Quistini
  Woodbridge, ON 905-851-2030
Pasta Shoppe
  Nashville, TN 800-247-0188
Pasta Sonoma
  Rohnert Park, CA 707-584-0800
Pasta USA
  Spokane, WA. 800-456-2084
Pastorelli Food Products
  Chicago, IL 800-767-2829
PaStreeta Fresca
  Dublin, OH 800-343-5266
Peace Village Organic Foods
  Berkeley, CA. 510-524-4420
Pede Brothers
  Schenectady, NY 518-356-3042
Peking Noodle Company
  Los Angeles, CA 323-223-2023
Pennsylvania Macaroni Company
  Pittsburgh, PA 800-223-5928
Philadelphia Macaroni Company
  Philadelphia, PA 215-923-3141
Pierino Frozen Foods
  Lincoln Park, MI. 313-928-0950
Porinos Gourmet Food
  Central Falls, RI 800-826-3938
Primo Foods
  North York, ON. 800-377-6945
Primo Piatto
  Minneapolis, MN 763-531-9194
Pulgini Pasta Products
  Fort Lauderdale, FL 954-973-7458
Pure Sales
  Costa Mesa, CA 714-540-5455
Purity Foods
  Okemos, MI 800-997-7358
Quality Choice Foods
  Toronto, ON 416-650-9595

Queen Ann Ravioli & Macaroni Company
  Brooklyn, NY 718-256-1061
Quinoa Corporation
  Gardena, CA 310-217-8125
Raffetto's Corporation
  New York, NY 212-727-8222
Rahco International
  St Augustine, FL 800-851-7681
Randag & Associates Inc
  Elmhurst, IL 630-530-2830
Ravioli Store
  New York, NY 212-925-1737
Rice Innovations
  Norval, ON 905-451-7423
Riviera Ravioli Company
  Bronx, NY .718-823-0260
Roccas Italian Foods
  New Castle, PA 724-654-3344
Ron-Son Foods
  Swedesboro, NJ 856-241-7333
Ronzoni Foods Canada
  Etobicoke, ON 800-387-5032
Rosa Food Products Co Inc
  Philadelphia, PA 215-467-2214
Roses Ravioli
  Oglesby, IL .815-883-8011
Rossi Pasta
  Marietta, OH 800-227-6774
S.T. Specialty Foods Inc
  Brooklyn Park, MN. 763-493-9600
Sabatino Truffles USA
  Long Island City, NY 888-444-9971
Salt Lake Macaroni & Noodle Company
  Salt Lake City, UT 801-969-9855
Savoia Foods
  Chicago Heights, IL 800-867-2782
Sedlock Farm
  Lynn Center, IL 309-521-8284
Sfoglia Fine Pastas & Gourmet
  Freeland, WA 360-331-4080
Shanghai Company
  Portland, OR 503-235-2527
Shreveport Macaroni Company
  Shreveport, LA 318-222-6857
Silver Palate Kitchens
  Cresskill, NJ 800-872-5283
Silver State Foods
  Denver, CO 800-423-3351
Somerset Industries
  Spring House, PA 800-883-8728
SOPAKCO Foods
  Mullins, SC 800-276-9678
SOUPerior Bean & Spice Company
  Vancouver, WA 800-878-7687
Specialty Brands
  Carthage, MO 417-358-8104
Specialty Brands
  Ontario, CA. 800-782-1180
SPI Foods
  Fremont, NE 866-266-1304
Spring Glen Fresh Foods
  Ephrata, PA 800-641-2853
Spruce Foods
  San Clemente, CA. 949-366-9457
ST Specialty Foods
  Brooklyn Park, MN 763-493-9600
Star Ravioli Manufacturing Company
  Moonachie, NJ 201-933-6427
Strom Products Ltd
  Bannockburn, IL 800-862-3311
Sun Ridge Farms
  Santa Cruz, CA 800-655-3252
Suns Noodle Company
  Atlanta, GA 770-448-7799
Swiss Colony
  Monroe, WI 608-328-8400
TAIF
  Folcroft, PA 610-631-5544
Taif Foods
  Norristown, PA 610-631-5544
Tasty Mix Quality Foods
  Brooklyn, NY 866-TAS-TYMX
TexaFrance
  Austin, TX. .800-776-8937
Tomasso Corporation
  Baie D'Urfe, QC 514-325-3000
Tommaso's Fresh Pasta
  Dallas, TX .972-869-1111
Tropical
  Charlotte, NC 800-220-1413
Tsue Chong Noodle Company
  Seattle, WA 206-623-0801

Turris Italian Foods
Roseville, MI 586-773-6010
Twin Marquis
Brooklyn, NY 800-367-6868
Unilever
Harrisburg, PA 717-234-6215
Union
Irvine, CA.......................800-854-7292
United Noodle Manufacturing Company
Salt Lake City, UT 801-485-0951
US Durum Products
Lancaster, PA 866-268-7268
Vantage USA
Chicago, IL......................773-247-1086
Varco Brothers
Chicago, IL......................312-642-4740
Viamar Foods
Glen Cove, NY 516-759-0652
Vitasoy USA
Ayer, MA........................978-772-6880
Wan Hua Foods
Seattle, WA......................206-622-8417
Weiss Noodle Company
Solon, OH 440-248-4550
Willow Foods
Beaverton, OR 800-338-3609
Wine Country Pasta
Sonoma, CA 707-935-1366
Wing's Food Products
Toronto, ON 416-259-2662
Wisconsin Cheese
Melrose Park, IL..................708-450-0074
Wisconsin Whey International
Juda, WI 608-233-5101
WMFB
Beaver Dam, WI...................920-887-1771
Wonton Food
Brooklyn, NY 800-776-8889
Woodland Foods
Gurnee, IL.......................847-625-8600
Wornick Company
Cincinnati, OH 800-860-4555
Young's Noodle Factory
Honolulu, HI.....................808-533-6478

Agnolotti

Agrusa, Inc.
Leonia, NJ.......................201-592-5950
Caesar's Pasta Products
Blackwood, NJ 856-227-2585
ConAgra Foods/International Home Foods
Niagara Falls, ON.................905-356-2661
Pasta Factory
Northlake, IL.....................800-615-6951
Putney Pasta Company
Chester, VT......................800-253-3683
Queen Ann Ravioli & Macaroni Company
Brooklyn, NY 718-256-1061
Supreme Dairy Farms Company
Warwick, RI......................401-739-8180
Wisconsin Whey International
Juda, WI 608-233-5101

Angel Hair

Al Dente
Whitmore Lake, MI 800-536-7278
Caesar's Pasta Products
Blackwood, NJ 856-227-2585
Cipriani's Spaghetti & Sauce Company
Chicago Heights, IL 708-755-6212
Costa Macaroni Manufacturing
Los Angeles, CA..................800-433-7785

Food City USA
Arvada, CO.......................303-321-4447
La Romagnola
Orlando, FL......................800-843-8359
Mrs. Leeper's Pasta
Kansas City, MO..................800-848-5266
Pascucci Family Pasta
San Diego, CA 619-285-8000
Pasta By Valente
Charlottesville, VA 888-575-7670
Pasta Factory
Northlake, IL.....................800-615-6951
Pasta USA
Spokane, WA.....................800-456-2084
Putney Pasta Company
Chester, VT......................800-253-3683

Canned

Canton Noodle Corporation
New York, NY 212-226-3276
ConAgra Foods/International Home Foods
Niagara Falls, ON.................905-356-2661
ConAgra Grocery Products
Irvine, CA.......................714-680-1000
Heinz Company of Canada
North York, ON..................800-268-6641
International Home Foods
Milton, PA.......................973-359-9920
Midwest Foods
Owatonna, MN 507-451-7670
Natural Value Products
Sacramento, CA 916-427-7242
Pulgini Pasta Products
Fort Lauderdale, FL 954-973-7458
Seneca Foods
Clyman, WI......................920-696-3331
Shanghai Company
Portland, OR 503-235-2527

Cannelloni

Food Source
McKinney, TX 972-548-9001
Louisa Food Products
St Louis, MO.....................314-868-3000
Marsan Foods
Toronto, ON 416-755-9262
Pasta Factory
Northlake, IL.....................800-615-6951
Pasta International
Mississauga, ON..................888-607-2782
Riviera Ravioli Company
Bronx, NY.......................718-823-0260
Star Ravioli Manufacturing Company
Moonachie, NJ 201-933-6427
Tomasso Corporation
Baie D'Urfe, QC..................514-325-3000
Turris Italian Foods
Roseville, MI 586-773-6010
Windsor Frozen Foods
Houston, TX 800-437-6936

Cavatappi

Costa Macaroni Manufacturing
Los Angeles, CA..................800-433-7785

Cavatelli

Alfredo's Italian Foods Manufacturing Company
Quincy, MA......................617-479-6360
Caesar's Pasta Products
Blackwood, NJ 856-227-2585

Fiori-Bruna Pasta Products
Hialeah, FL......................305-621-0074
Italian Village Ravioli & Pasta Products
Portsmouth, NH 603-431-6865
J.B. Sons
Yonkers, NY 914-963-5192
Landolfi Food Products
Trenton, NJ......................609-392-1830
Lombardo's Ravioli Kitchen
New Britain, CT 860-223-7800
Lucy's Foods
Latrobe, PA......................724-539-1430
Pasta Del Mondo
Carmel, NY 800-392-8887
Pasta Factory
Northlake, IL.....................800-615-6951
Pasta USA
Spokane, WA.....................800-456-2084
Queen Ann Ravioli & Macaroni Company
Brooklyn, NY 718-256-1061
Riviera Ravioli Company
Bronx, NY.......................718-823-0260
Star Ravioli Manufacturing Company
Moonachie, NJ 201-933-6427
Wisconsin Whey International
Juda, WI 608-233-5101

Elbow Macaroni

A Zerega's Sons, Inc.
Fair Lawn, NJ 201-797-1400
Archer Daniels Midland Company
Lincoln, NE......................800-228-4060
Borinquen Macaroni Corporation
Yauco, PR 787-856-1450
Costa Macaroni Manufacturing
Los Angeles, CA..................800-433-7785
Cuizina Food Company
Woodinville, WA..................425-486-7000
Pascucci Family Pasta
San Diego, CA 619-285-8000
Pasta USA
Spokane, WA.....................800-456-2084
Superior Pasta Company
Philadelphia, PA 215-922-7278

Farfalle

Costa Macaroni Manufacturing
Los Angeles, CA..................800-433-7785
Italia Foods
Schaumburg, IL...................800-747-1109
Pasta USA
Spokane, WA.....................800-456-2084

Fettuccine

Pasta By Valente
Charlottesville, VA 888-575-7670

Gnocchi

Agrusa, Inc.
Leonia, NJ.......................201-592-5950
Dixie USA
Tomball, TX 800-233-3668
Italian Foods Corporation
Oakland, CA.....................510-444-9050
Lucy's Foods
Latrobe, PA......................724-539-1430
Queen Ann Ravioli & Macaroni Company
Brooklyn, NY 718-256-1061

Frozen

Queen Ann Ravioli & Macaroni Company
Brooklyn, NY 718-256-1061
Turris Italian Foods
Roseville, MI 586-773-6010

Lasagna

Lucy's Foods
Latrobe, PA 724-539-1430

Frozen

Alfredo's Italian Foods Manufacturing Company
Quincy, MA. 617-479-6360
Bruno Specialty Foods
West Sayville, NY 631-589-1700
Caesar's Pasta Products
Blackwood, NJ 856-227-2585
Cedarlane Foods
Carson, CA 800-826-3322
Codino's Italian Foods
Scotia, NY 800-246-8908
D'Orazio Foods
Bellmawr, NJ. 888-328-7287
Food Source
McKinney, TX 972-548-9001
Foodbrands America
Oklahoma City, OK 405-290-4000
Gilardi Foods
Sidney, OH 937-498-4511
Italia Foods
Schaumburg, IL. 800-747-1109
LaMonica Fine Foods
Millville, NJ 856-825-8111
Landolfi Food Products
Trenton, NJ 609-392-1830
Lombardo's Ravioli Kitchen
New Britain, CT 860-223-7800
Mamma Lina Ravioli Company
San Diego, CA 858-535-0620
Marcetti Frozen Pasta
Altoona, IA 515-967-4254
Marsan Foods
Toronto, ON 416-755-9262
McCain Foods Canada
Florenceville, NB 506-392-5541
Molinaro's Fine Italian Foods
Mississauga, ON 800-268-4959
Pasta Factory
Northlake, IL. 800-615-6951
Pasta International
Mississauga, ON. 888-607-2782
Riviera Ravioli Company
Bronx, NY 718-823-0260
Specialty Brands
Carthage, MO 417-358-8104
Tomasso Corporation
Baie D'Urfe, QC 514-325-3000
Windsor Frozen Foods
Houston, TX 800-437-6936
Wisconsin Whey International
Juda, WI 608-233-5101

Noodles

A Zerega's Sons, Inc.
Fair Lawn, NJ 201-797-1400
Archer Daniels Midland Company
Lincoln, NE. 800-228-4060
Borinquen Macaroni Corporation
Yauco, PR 787-856-1450
Costa Macaroni Manufacturing
Los Angeles, CA. 800-433-7785
Pasta USA
Spokane, WA. 800-456-2084

Canned

Canton Noodle Corporation
New York, NY 212-226-3276
ConAgra Grocery Products
Irvine, CA 714-680-1000
National Noodle Company
San Francisco, CA 415-781-5143
Pulgini Pasta Products
Fort Lauderdale, FL 954-973-7458
Shanghai Company
Portland, OR 503-235-2527
United Noodle Manufacturing Company
Salt Lake City, UT 801-485-0951

Chow Mein

Everfresh Food Corporation
Minneapolis, MN 612-331-6393
Nanka Seimen Company
Vernon, CA 323-585-9967
National Noodle Company
San Francisco, CA 415-781-5143
Tsue Chong Noodle Company
Seattle, WA 206-623-0801
Valdez Food
Philadelphia, PA 215-634-6106
Wan Hua Foods
Seattle, WA 206-622-8417
Willow Foods
Beaverton, OR 800-338-3609
Wing Hing Noodle Company
Los Angeles, CA. 888-223-8899
Wonton Food
Brooklyn, NY 800-776-8889

Egg

A Zerega's Sons, Inc.
Fair Lawn, NJ 201-797-1400
Costa Macaroni Manufacturing
Los Angeles, CA. 800-433-7785
Cumberland Pasta
Cumberland, MD 800-572-7821
Eden Organic Pasta Company
Detroit, MI 800-248-0320
Foulds
Libertyville, IL 847-362-3062
Hershey Pasta Group
Louisville, KY 800-468-1714
Nanka Seimen Company
Vernon, CA 323-585-9967
R.A.B. Food Group LLC
Secaucus, NJ 201-453-5200
Reames Foods
Columbus, OH 614-846-2232
Silver State Foods
Denver, CO 800-423-3351
Strom Products Ltd
Bannockburn, IL. 800-862-3311
Tsue Chong Noodle Company
Seattle, WA 206-623-0801

Mung Bean

China Bowl Trading Company
Westport, CT. 203-222-0381

Oriental

Allied Old English
Port Reading, NJ. 732-602-8955
Annie Chun's
San Rafael, CA 415-479-8272
Chieftain Wild Rice Company
Spooner, WI 800-262-6368
China Bowl Trading Company
Westport, CT 203-222-0381
Uni-President
La Puente, CA 626-961-1671
Union
Irvine, CA 800-854-7292
Vitasoy USA
Ayer, MA. 978-772-6880
Wonton Food
Brooklyn, NY 800-776-8889
Woodland Foods
Gurnee, IL. 847-625-8600

Ramen

Maruchan
Irvine, CA 949-789-2300
Union
Irvine, CA 800-854-7292

Pasta

Borinquen Macaroni Corporation
Yauco, PR 787-856-1450
Caesar's Pasta Products
Blackwood, NJ 856-227-2585
Canada Bread
North Bay, ON 800-461-6122
Conte's Pasta Company
Vineland, NJ 800-211-6607
Costa Macaroni Manufacturing
Los Angeles, CA. 800-433-7785

Cuizina Food Company
Woodinville, WA. 425-486-7000
Faribault Foods
Minneapolis, MN 612-333-6461
Gia Russa
Coitsville, OH 800-527-8772
La Romagnola
Orlando, FL 800-843-8359
Lapasta
Silver Spring, MD 301-588-1111
Lombardo's Ravioli Kitchen
New Britain, CT 860-223-7800
Lucy's Foods
Latrobe, PA 724-539-1430
Mezza
Lake Forest, IL 888-206-6054
Park 100 Foods
Tipton, IN 800-854-6504
Philadelphia Macaroni Company
Warminster, PA 215-441-5220
Plentiful Pantry
Salt Lake City, UT 800-727-8284
Queen Ann Ravioli & Macaroni Company
Brooklyn, NY 718-256-1061
Ragozzino Food
Meriden, CT 800-348-1240
Reid Foods
Gurnee, IL 888-295-8478
Royal Angelus Macaroni
Chino, CA 909-627-7312
Superior Pasta Company
Philadelphia, PA 215-922-7278
Turris Italian Foods
Roseville, MI 586-773-6010
Viamar Foods
Glen Cove, NY 516-759-0652
Wisconsin Whey International
Juda, WI 608-233-5101

Frozen

Homestead Ravioli Company
S San Francisco, CA 650-615-0750
LaMonica Fine Foods
Millville, NJ 856-825-8111
Lapasta
Silver Spring, MD 301-588-1111
Lucca Foods
Sparks, NV 775-356-8611

Orzo

Chieftain Wild Rice Company
Spooner, WI 800-262-6368
Woodland Foods
Gurnee, IL 847-625-8600

Polenta

Chieftain Wild Rice Company
Spooner, WI 800-262-6368
Woodland Foods
Gurnee, IL 847-625-8600

Penne

A Zerega's Sons, Inc.
Fair Lawn, NJ 201-797-1400
Costa Macaroni Manufacturing
Los Angeles, CA. 800-433-7785
Cuizina Food Company
Woodinville, WA. 425-486-7000
Pasta USA
Spokane, WA. 800-456-2084
Turris Italian Foods
Roseville, MI 586-773-6010

Ravioli

Agrusa, Inc.
Leonia, NJ. 201-592-5950
Alfonso Gourmet Pasta
Pompano Beach, FL 800-370-7278
Alfredo's Italian Foods Manufacturing Company
Quincy, MA. 617-479-6360
Antoni Ravioli
North Massapequa, NY 800-783-0350
Armanino Foods of Distinction
Hayward, CA 510-441-9300
Bella Ravioli
Medford, MA 781-396-0875
Borgattis Ravioli
Bronx, NY. 718-367-3799

Bruno Specialty Foods
West Sayville, NY 631-589-1700
Caesar's Pasta Products
Blackwood, NJ 856-227-2585
Campbell Soup Company
Camden, NJ 800-257-8443
Celentano Brothers
Verona, NJ 973-239-2557
Chinese Spaghetti Factory
Boston, MA 617-445-7714
Codino's Italian Foods
Scotia, NY 800-246-8908
ConAgra Foods/International Home Foods
Niagara Falls, ON 905-356-2661
Cottage Street Pasta
Barre, VT 802-476-4024
Cuizina Food Company
Woodinville, WA 425-486-7000
D'Orazio Foods
Bellmawr, NJ 888-328-7287
Dairy Maid Ravioli Manufacturing Corporation
Brooklyn, NY 718-449-2620
Fiori-Bruna Pasta Products
Hialeah, FL 305-621-0074
Fontana's Casa De La Pasta
Vandergrift, PA 724-567-2782
Food Source
McKinney, TX 972-548-9001
International Home Foods
Milton, PA 973-359-9920
Italia Foods
Schaumburg, IL 800-747-1109
J.B. Sons
Yonkers, NY 914-963-5192
La Romagnola
Orlando, FL 800-843-8359
Landolfi Food Products
Trenton, NJ 609-392-1830
Lombardo's Ravioli Kitchen
New Britain, CT 860-223-7800
Louisa Food Products
St Louis, MO 314-868-3000
Lucy's Foods
Latrobe, PA 724-539-1430
Mamma Lina Ravioli Company
San Diego, CA 858-535-0620
Maria and Son Italian Products
St Louis, MO 866-481-9009
Mount Rose Ravioli & Macaroni Company
Farmingdale, NY 516-694-6940
New York Ravioli & Pasta Company
New Hyde Park, NY 888-588-7287
Nuovo Pasta Productions
Stratford, CT 800-803-0033
O Chili Frozen Foods Inc
Northbrook, IL 847-562-1991
Pasta Del Mondo
Carmel, NY 800-392-8887
Pasta Factory
Northlake, IL 800-615-6951
Pasta International
Mississauga, ON 888-607-2782
Pasta Italiana
Massapequa, NY 800-536-5611
Pasta Mill
Edmonton, AB 780-454-8665
Pulgini Pasta Products
Fort Lauderdale, FL 954-973-7458
Queen Ann Ravioli & Macaroni Company
Brooklyn, NY 718-256-1061
Raffetto's Corporation
New York, NY 212-727-8222
Roses Ravioli
Oglesby, IL 815-883-8011

Specialty Brands
Carthage, MO 417-358-8104
Star Ravioli Manufacturing Company
Moonachie, NJ 201-933-6427
Tomasso Corporation
Baie D'Urfe, QC 514-325-3000
Viamar Foods
Glen Cove, NY 516-759-0652
Wisconsin Whey International
Juda, WI 608-233-5101

Canned

Alfredo's Italian Foods Manufacturing Company
Quincy, MA 617-479-6360
Campbell Soup Company
Camden, NJ 800-257-8443
Celentano Brothers
Verona, NJ 973-239-2557
ConAgra Foods/International Home Foods
Niagara Falls, ON 905-356-2661
Cuizina Food Company
Woodinville, WA 425-486-7000
International Home Foods
Milton, PA 973-359-9920
Lombardo's Ravioli Kitchen
New Britain, CT 860-223-7800
Pulgini Pasta Products
Fort Lauderdale, FL 954-973-7458
Specialty Brands
Carthage, MO 417-358-8104

Cheese

Alfredo's Italian Foods Manufacturing Company
Quincy, MA 617-479-6360
Fiori-Bruna Pasta Products
Hialeah, FL 305-621-0074
La Romagnola
Orlando, FL 800-843-8359
Louisa Food Products
St Louis, MO 314-868-3000
Queen Ann Ravioli & Macaroni Company
Brooklyn, NY 718-256-1061

Frozen

Alfredo's Italian Foods Manufacturing Company
Quincy, MA 617-479-6360
Bruno Specialty Foods
West Sayville, NY 631-589-1700
Caesar's Pasta Products
Blackwood, NJ 856-227-2585
Codino's Italian Foods
Scotia, NY 800-246-8908
Cuizina Food Company
Woodinville, WA 425-486-7000
D'Orazio Foods
Bellmawr, NJ 888-328-7287
Fiori-Bruna Pasta Products
Hialeah, FL 305-621-0074
Food Source
McKinney, TX 972-548-9001
Homestead Ravioli Company
S San Francisco, CA 650-615-0750
Italia Foods
Schaumburg, IL 800-747-1109
Italian Village Ravioli & Pasta Products
Portsmouth, NH 603-431-6865
J.B. Sons
Yonkers, NY 914-963-5192
LaMonica Fine Foods
Millville, NJ 856-825-8111
Landolfi Food Products
Trenton, NJ 609-392-1830

Lombardo's Ravioli Kitchen
New Britain, CT 860-223-7800
Louisa Food Products
St Louis, MO 314-868-3000
Mount Rose Ravioli & Macaroni Company
Farmingdale, NY 516-694-6940
Pascucci Family Pasta
San Diego, CA 619-285-8000
Pasta Del Mondo
Carmel, NY 800-392-8887
Pasta Factory
Northlake, IL 800-615-6951
Pasta International
Mississauga, ON 888-607-2782
Pasta Italiana
Massapequa, NY 800-536-5611
Pulgini Pasta Products
Fort Lauderdale, FL 954-973-7458
Specialty Brands
Carthage, MO 417-358-8104
Star Ravioli Manufacturing Company
Moonachie, NJ 201-933-6427
Tomasso Corporation
Baie D'Urfe, QC 514-325-3000
Turris Italian Foods
Roseville, MI 586-773-6010
Viamar Foods
Glen Cove, NY 516-759-0652
Windsor Frozen Foods
Houston, TX 800-437-6936
Wisconsin Whey International
Juda, WI 608-233-5101

Meat

La Romagnola
Orlando, FL 800-843-8359
Queen Ann Ravioli & Macaroni Company
Brooklyn, NY 718-256-1061

Seafood

La Romagnola
Orlando, FL 800-843-8359
Queen Ann Ravioli & Macaroni Company
Brooklyn, NY 718-256-1061

Vegetable

La Romagnola
Orlando, FL 800-843-8359
Queen Ann Ravioli & Macaroni Company
Brooklyn, NY 718-256-1061

Rigatoni

Al Dente
Whitmore Lake, MI 800-536-7278
Codino's Italian Foods
Scotia, NY 800-246-8908
Landolfi Food Products
Trenton, NJ 609-392-1830
Lucy's Foods
Latrobe, PA 724-539-1430
Pascucci Family Pasta
San Diego, CA 619-285-8000
Pasta Factory
Northlake, IL 800-615-6951
Pasta USA
Spokane, WA 800-456-2084

Rotelle

Cuizina Food Company
Woodinville, WA 425-486-7000

Pascucci Family Pasta
San Diego, CA 619-285-8000
Pasta USA
Spokane, WA 800-456-2084

Rotini

A Zerega's Sons, Inc.
Fair Lawn, NJ 201-797-1400
Al Dente
Whitmore Lake, MI 800-536-7278
Archer Daniels Midland Company
Lincoln, NE 800-228-4060
Pascucci Family Pasta
San Diego, CA 619-285-8000
Pasta USA
Spokane, WA 800-456-2084
Turris Italian Foods
Roseville, MI 586-773-6010
Windsor Frozen Foods
Houston, TX 800-437-6936

Semolina

D. Merlino & Sons
Oakland, CA 510-568-2151
Florence Macaroni Manufacturing
Chicago, IL 800-647-2782
Gabriele Macaroni Company
City of Industry, CA 626-964-2324
Pasta USA
Spokane, WA 800-456-2084

Shells

A Zerega's Sons, Inc.
Fair Lawn, NJ 201-797-1400
Borinquen Macaroni Corporation
Yauco, PR 787-856-1450
Costa Macaroni Manufacturing
Los Angeles, CA 800-433-7785
LaMonica Fine Foods
Millville, NJ 856-825-8111
Windsor Frozen Foods
Houston, TX 800-437-6936

Spaghetti

Archer Daniels Midland Company
Lincoln, NE 800-228-4060
Borinquen Macaroni Corporation
Yauco, PR 787-856-1450
Caesar's Pasta Products
Blackwood, NJ 856-227-2585
Campbell Soup Company
Camden, NJ 800-257-8443
ConAgra Foods/International Home Foods
Niagara Falls, ON 905-356-2661
Costa Macaroni Manufacturing
Los Angeles, CA 800-433-7785
Country Cupboard
Virginia City, NV 775-847-7300
De Cio Pasta Primo
Cave Creek, AZ 800-397-0770
Foulds
Libertyville, IL 847-362-3062
Heinz Company of Canada
North York, ON 800-268-6641
Heinz North America
Pittsburgh, PA 412-237-5700
Hershey Pasta Group
Louisville, KY 800-468-1714
International Home Foods
Milton, PA 973-359-9920
Iwamoto Natto Factory
Paia, HI 808-579-9933
La Romagnola
Orlando, FL 800-843-8359
Ladson Homemade Pasta Company
Phoenix, AZ 480-353-0874
Landolfi Food Products
Trenton, NJ 609-392-1830
Marcetti Frozen Pasta
Altoona, IA 515-967-4254
Noodles by Leonardo
Cando, ND 701-968-4464
O Chili Frozen Foods Inc
Northbrook, IL 847-562-1991
Pasta Factory
Northlake, IL 800-615-6951
Pasta International
Mississauga, ON 888-607-2782

Shreveport Macaroni Company
Shreveport, LA 318-222-6857
Superior Pasta Company
Philadelphia, PA 215-922-7278
Taif Foods
Norristown, PA 610-631-5544
Varco Brothers
Chicago, IL 312-642-4740
Wisconsin Whey International
Juda, WI 608-233-5101

Canned

ConAgra Foods/International Home Foods
Niagara Falls, ON 905-356-2661
Heinz Company of Canada
North York, ON 800-268-6641
Heinz North America
Pittsburgh, PA 412-237-5700
International Home Foods
Milton, PA 973-359-9920
O Chili Frozen Foods Inc
Northbrook, IL 847-562-1991
Seneca Foods
Clyman, WI 920-696-3331

Frozen

Caesar's Pasta Products
Blackwood, NJ 856-227-2585
Heinz North America
Pittsburgh, PA 412-237-5700
Landolfi Food Products
Trenton, NJ 609-392-1830
Marcetti Frozen Pasta
Altoona, IA 515-967-4254
Pasta International
Mississauga, ON 888-607-2782

Spelt

A Zerega's Sons, Inc.
Fair Lawn, NJ 201-797-1400
Costa Macaroni Manufacturing
Los Angeles, CA 800-433-7785
Purity Foods
Okemos, MI 800-997-7358

Spinach

Cipriani's Spaghetti & Sauce Company
Chicago Heights, IL 708-755-6212
La Romagnola
Orlando, FL 800-843-8359
Marsan Foods
Toronto, ON 416-755-9262
Pascucci Family Pasta
San Diego, CA 619-285-8000
Pasta USA
Spokane, WA 800-456-2084
Wonton Food
Brooklyn, NY 800-776-8889

Stuffed Shells

Armanino Foods of Distinction
Hayward, CA 510-441-9300
Lucy's Foods
Latrobe, PA 724-539-1430
Pasta USA
Spokane, WA 800-456-2084
Queen Ann Ravioli & Macaroni Company
Brooklyn, NY 718-256-1061
Turris Italian Foods
Roseville, MI 586-773-6010

Tagliatelle

Costa Macaroni Manufacturing
Los Angeles, CA 800-433-7785
Pasta USA
Spokane, WA 800-456-2084

Tortellini

Agrusa, Inc.
Leonia, NJ 201-592-5950
Alfredo's Italian Foods Manufacturing Company
Quincy, MA 617-479-6360
Armanino Foods of Distinction
Hayward, CA 510-441-9300
Bruno Specialty Foods
West Sayville, NY 631-589-1700

Costa Macaroni Manufacturing
Los Angeles, CA 800-433-7785
Cuizina Food Company
Woodinville, WA 425-486-7000
Dairy Maid Ravioli Manufacturing Corporation
Brooklyn, NY 718-449-2620
Fiori-Bruna Pasta Products
Hialeah, FL 305-621-0074
Italia Foods
Schaumburg, IL 800-747-1109
LaMonica Fine Foods
Millville, NJ 856-825-8111
Landolfi Food Products
Trenton, NJ 609-392-1830
Mount Rose Ravioli & Macaroni Company
Farmingdale, NY 516-694-6940
Nestle
Cleveland, OH 440-349-5757
New York Ravioli & Pasta Company
New Hyde Park, NY 888-588-7287
Pascucci Family Pasta
San Diego, CA 619-285-8000
Pasta Del Mondo
Carmel, NY 800-392-8887
Pasta Factory
Northlake, IL 800-615-6951
Pasta International
Mississauga, ON 888-607-2782
Pasta Mill
Edmonton, AB 780-454-8665
Pasta USA
Spokane, WA 800-456-2084
Putney Pasta Company
Chester, VT 800-253-3683
Queen Ann Ravioli & Macaroni Company
Brooklyn, NY 718-256-1061
Raffetto's Corporation
New York, NY 212-727-8222
Riviera Ravioli Company
Bronx, NY 718-823-0260
Roses Ravioli
Oglesby, IL 815-883-8011
Taif Foods
Norristown, PA 610-631-5544
Turris Italian Foods
Roseville, MI 586-773-6010
Viamar Foods
Glen Cove, NY 516-759-0652
Windsor Frozen Foods
Houston, TX 800-437-6936

Vermicelli

Archer Daniels Midland Company
Lincoln, NE 800-228-4060
Cipriani's Spaghetti & Sauce Company
Chicago Heights, IL 708-755-6212
Costa Macaroni Manufacturing
Los Angeles, CA 800-433-7785
Iwamoto Natto Factory
Paia, HI 808-579-9933
Pasta USA
Spokane, WA 800-456-2084
Superior Pasta Company
Philadelphia, PA 215-922-7278

Prepared Foods

Battered

Simeus Foods International
Mansfield, TX 888-772-3663

Refrigerated

Alderfer Bologna
Harleysville, PA 877-253-6328
AquaCuisine
Eagle, ID 888-330-2782
Armour
Omaha, NE 402-453-3766
Atlantic Pork & Provisions
Brooklyn, NY .800-245-3536
Avon Heights Mushrooms
Avondale, PA .610-268-2092
Boesl Packing Company
Baltimore, MD 410-675-1071
Bosell Foods
Cleveland, OH 216-991-7600
Boudreaux's Foods
New Orleans, LA 504-733-8440
Bridgford Foods Corpora tion
Anaheim, CA .800-527-2105
C. Roy Meat Products
Brockway, MI .810-387-3957
Charlie's Country Sausage
Minot, ND 701-838-6302
Chicago 58 Food Products
Toronto, ON 416-603-4244
Chisesi Brothers Meat Packing Company
New Orleans, LA 504-822-3550
Citterio USA Corporation
Freeland, PA 800-435-8888
Corfu Foods
Bensenville, IL 630-595-2510
Country Maid
Milwaukee, WI 800-628-4354
Dairy Fresh Foods
Taylor, MI 313-295-6300
Danner Salads
Peoria, IL 309-691-0289
Dietz & Watson
Philadelphia, PA 800-333-1974
Dohar Meats
Cleveland, OH 216-241-4197
Dole Fresh Vegetable Company
Soledad, CA 800-333-5454
Egon Binkert Meat Products
Baltimore, MD 410-687-5959
F&S Produce Company
Rosenhayn, NJ 800-886-3316
Foodbrands America
Oklahoma City, OK 405-290-4000
Frank Wardynski & Sons
Buffalo, NY 716-854-6083
Fried Provisions Company
Evans City, PA 724-538-3160
Gilardi Foods
Sidney, OH 937-498-4511
Green Garden Food Products
Kent, WA 800-304-1033
Groff Meats
Elizabethtown, PA 717-367-1246
Gunsberg Corned Beef
Detroit, MI 313-894-6600
Hansel 'N Gretel
Flushing, NY 718-326-0041
Hazle Park Packing Company
West Hazleton, PA 800-238-4331
Helens Pure Foods
Cheltenham, PA 215-379-6433
Henry J Meat Specialties
Chicago, IL 800-242-1314
Herold's Salad
Cleveland, OH 800-427-2523
HFI Foods
Redmond, WA 425-883-1320
Hoople Country Kitchens
Rockport, IN 812-649-2351
House of Thaller
Knoxville, TN .865-689-5893
IBP Foods
Troy, MI 248-588-4710
IBP Foods
Grand Rapids, MI 616-774-0711

Ito Cariani Sausage Company
Hayward, CA .510-887-0882
John Volpi & Company
St Louis, MO .800-288-3439
Kayem Foods
Chelsea, MA 800-426-6100
Kelly Kornbeef Company
Chicago, IL 773-588-2882
Kessler's, Inc
Lemoyne, PA .800-382-1328
Kilgus Meats
Toledo, OH 419-472-9721
Knotts Wholesale Foods
Paris, TN 731-642-1961
Kunzler/Juniata Packing Company
Tyrone, PA 814-684-2270
Lakeside Foods
Manitowoc, WI 920-684-3356
Land O'Frost
Searcy, AR 800-643-5654
Lengerich Meats
Zanesville, IN .260-638-4123
Leona Meat Plant
Troy, PA 570-297-3574
Levonian Brothers
Troy, NY 518-274-3610
Litehouse
Sandpoint, ID .208-263-2030
Locustdale Meat Packing
Locustdale, PA 570-875-1270
Lowell Provision Company
Lowell, MA 978-454-5603
Marathon Enterprises
Englewood, NJ 201-935-3330
Marshallville Packing Company
Marshallville, OH 330-855-2871
Martin Rosol's
New Britain, CT 860-223-2707
McClane Distribution Center
Fredericksburg, VA 540-374-2000
Meadows Country Products
Hollidaysburg, PA 888-499-1001
Milan Salami Company
Oakland, CA 510-654-7055
Mishler Packing Company
Lagrange, IN .260-768-4156
Mosey's Inc
Bloomfield, CT 860-243-1725
Mrs. Grissom's Salad
Nashville, TN .800-255-0571
Mrs. Minnick's Salads
Baltimore, MD 410-235-6748
Newhart Foods
Allentown, PA .610-437-5539
Northern Star Company
Minneapolis, MN 612-339-8981
O'Brien & Company
Bellevue, NE 800-433-7567
Ohio Packing Company
Columbus, OH 800-282-6403
Orval Kent Food Company
Wheeling, IL 847-459-9000
Otto W Liebold & Company
Flint, MI 800-999-6328
Parma Sausage Products
Pittsburgh, PA 877-294-4207
Penn Valley Farms
Gainesville, GA 773-685-9929
Pfeffer's Country Market
Sauk Centre, MN 320-352-3095
Phillips Gourmet
Kennett Square, PA 610-925-0520
Pilgrim's Pride
Timberville, VA 540-896-7000
Promiseland Meat PackingCompany
Madill, OK 580-795-3567
Queen City Sausage
Cincinnati, OH 877-544-5588
R.C. McEntire & Company
Columbia, SC .803-799-3388
Real Kosher Sausage Company
Newark, NJ 973-690-5394
Rego's Purity Foods
Honolulu, HI .808-947-9005
Rendulic Packing
McKeesport, PA 412-678-9541

Reser's Fine Foods
Salt Lake City, UT 801-972-5633
Roman Packing Company
Norfolk, NE 800-373-5990
Ruskin Packaging
Miami, FL 305-324-1529
Ryley Sausage
Ryley, AB 780-663-3990
Saag's Products
San Leandro, CA 800-352-7224
Sandridge Food Corporation
Medina, OH 330-725-2348
Sara Lee Corporation
Downers Grove, IL 630-598-8100
Sara Lee Foods
Zeeland, MI 616-875-8131
Sara Lee Foods
Cincinnati, OH 800-351-7111
Sausage Shoppe
Cleveland, OH 216-351-5213
Saval Foods
Elkridge, MD .800-527-2825
Schaller & Weber
Long Island City, NY 800-847-4115
Schaller's Packers
Cassville, NY .315-822-3924
Sculli Brothers
Philadelphia, PA 215-336-1223
Sechrist Brothers
Dallastown, PA 717-244-2975
Seitz Foods
Saint Joseph, MO 800-383-3128
Sheinman Provision Company
Philadelphia, PA 215-473-7065
Smith Packing Regional Meat
Utica, NY 315-732-5125
Snow Ball Foods
Fredericksburg, PA 800-360-7669
Spring Glen Fresh Foods
Ephrata, PA 800-641-2853
Spring Grove Foods
Miamisburg, OH 937-866-4311
Springfield Smoked Fish Company
Springfield, MA 800-327-3412
Standard Beef Company
New Haven, CT 203-787-2164
Stawnichy Holdings
Mundare, AB .888-764-7646
Stonies Sausage Shop Inc
Perryville, MO 888-546-2540
Storer Meat Company
Cleveland, OH 800-355-7537
Suter Company
Sycamore, IL .800-435-6942
Swift & Company
Greeley, CO 970-324-2180
Tennessee Valley PackingCompany
Columbia, TN 931-388-2623
Teti Bakery
Etobicoke, ON 800-465-0123
Troy Frozen Food
Troy, IL 618-667-6332
Troyers Trail Bologna
Dundee, OH 877-893-2414
Tupman-Thurlow Company
Deerfield Beach, FL 954-596-9989
United Provision Meat Company
Columbus, OH 614-252-1126
Upstate Farms Cooperative
Buffalo, NY 716-892-3156
Van Bennett Food Company
Reading, PA 800-423-8897
Vienna Meat Products
Scarborough, ON 800-588-1931
Wampler Foods
Dallas, TX 717-624-2191
Warren & Son Meat Processing
Whipple, OH .740-585-2421
Weyhaupt Brothers Packing
Belleville, IL 618-233-0452
Wimmer's Meat Products
West Point, NE 800-358-0761
Wornick Company
Cincinnati, OH 800-860-4555
Yarbrough Produce Company
Birmingham, AL 205-323-8651

General

1-2-3 Gluten Inc
Pittsburgh, PA 843-768-7231
A Gift Basket by Carmela
Longmeadow, MA 888-481-4438
A.C. Petersen Farms
West Hartford, CT. 860-233-8483
AccuLift
Alexandria, MN 320-763-6587
Acme Steak & Seafood Company
Youngstown, OH......................330-270-8000
Advance Food Company
Enid, OK 888-723-8237
Agrusa, Inc.
Leonia, NJ.............................201-592-5950
Al Pete Meats
Muncie, IN.............................765-288-8817
Alderfer Bologna
Harleysville, PA 877-253-6328
Alfonso Gourmet Pasta
Pompano Beach, FL 800-370-7278
Alfonso Gourmet Pasta
Pompano Beach, FL 800-370-7278
Alfonso Gourmet Pasta
Pompano Beach, FL 800-370-7278
Alfredo's Italian Foods Manufacturing Company
Quincy, MA............................617-479-6360
Amberwave Foods
Oakmont, PA..........................412-828-3040
Aristocrat International Corporation
Secaucus, NJ 201-866-1900
Armanino Foods of Distinction
Hayward, CA 510-441-9300
Armour
Omaha, NE 402-453-3766
Artel
Boisbriand, QC 450-433-1322
Atlantic Pork & Provisions
Brooklyn, NY 800-245-3536
Avalon Gourmet
Phoenix, AZ 602-253-0343
Avon Heights Mushrooms
Avondale, PA..........................610-268-2092
Bake Crafters Food
Collegedale, TN 800-296-8935
Barber Foods
Portland, ME..........................800-577-2595
Battaglia Distributing Corporation
Chicago, IL 312-738-1111
Bay Cities Produce Company
San Leandro, CA......................510-346-4943
Beaver Street Fisheries
Jacksonville, FL 800-874-6426
Bellisio Foods, Inc.
Lakeville, MN..........................800-368-7337
Bernardi Italian Foods Company
Bloomsburg, PA 570-389-5500
Better Baked Foods
North East, PA.........................814-725-8778
Biagio's Banquets
Chicago, IL 800-392-2837
Biagio's Banquets
Chicago, IL 800-392-2837
Big B Distributors
Evansville, IN..........................812-425-5235
Bill Grubb Sales
Saint Simons Island, GA............912-638-5777
Blue Ridge Farms
Brooklyn, NY 718-827-9000
BlueWater Seafoods
Lachine, QC 888-560-2539
Boeckman JJ Wholesale Meats
Dayton, OH............................937-222-4679
Boesl Packing Company
Baltimore, MD 410-675-1071
Bosell Foods
Cleveland, OH 216-991-7600
Bouma Meats
Provost, AB............................780-753-2092
Boyd Sausage Company
Washington, IA 319-653-5715
Boyle Meat Company
Kansas City, MO......................800-821-3626
Bridgford Foods Corpora tion
Anaheim, CA 800-527-2105
Bruno Specialty Foods
West Sayville, NY 631-589-1700
Buxton Foods
Buxton, ND 800-726-8057
C. Roy Meat Products
Brockway, MI 810-387-3957

Cafferata
San Anselmo, CA 800-626-8115
Cafferata
San Anselmo, CA 800-626-8115
Cajun Chef Products
St Martinville, LA 337-394-7112
Camino Real Foods
Vernon, CA 800-421-6201
Campbell Soup Company
Camden, NJ............................800-257-8443
Campbell Soup Company
Camden, NJ............................800-257-8443
Canada Bread
Etobicoke, ON 416-622-2040
Caribbean Food Delights
Tappan, NY 845-398-3000
Carl Buddig & Company
Homewood, IL 800-621-0868
Carolina Packers
Smithfield, NC 800-682-7675
Carrington Foods
Saraland, AL...........................251-675-9700
Casa Di Bertacchi
Vineland, NJ...........................800-818-9261
Castleberry/Snow Brands
Augusta, GA 800-241-3520
Cedar Lake Foods
Cedar Lake, MI 800-246-5039
Cedarlane Foods
Carson, CA 800-826-3322
Celentano Brothers
Verona, NJ.............................973-239-2557
Chalmette Packing Company
Covington, LA 504-271-6241
Chang Food Company
Garden Grove, CA 714-265-9990
Charlie's Country Sausage
Minot, ND 701-838-6302
Chateau Food Products
Cicero, IL 708-863-4207
Chef America
Chatsworth, CA........................818-718-8111
Chef America East
Mount Sterling, KY 859-498-4300
Chef Hans Gourmet Foods
Monroe, LA. 800-890-4267
Chicago 58 Food Products
Toronto, ON 416-603-4244
Chicago Meat Authority
Chicago, IL.............................773-254-0020
Chincoteague Seafood Company
Parsonsburg, MD 443-260-4800
Chisesi Brothers Meat Packing Company
New Orleans, LA 504-822-3550
Chloe Foods Corporation
Brooklyn, NY 718-827-3600
Chungs Gourmet Foods
Houston, TX 713-741-2118
Citterio USA Corporation
Freeland, PA 800-435-8888
Cobi Foods
Hantsport, NS 800-565-8229
ConAgra Foods Inc
Omaha, NE 402-240-4000
ConAgra Frozen Foods Company
Marshall, MO 660-886-3301
ConAgra Mexican Foods
Compton, CA 310-223-1499
Continental Deli Foods
Cherokee, IA 712-225-5161
Continental Mills
Seattle, WA 253-872-8400
Contract Comestibles
East Troy, WI 262-642-9400
Corfu Foods
Bensenville, IL 630-595-2510
Country Pies
Coombs, BC 250-248-6415
County Gourmet Foods, LLC
Sewickley, PA 412-741-8902
Cuisine Solutions
Alexandria, VA 888-285-4679
Culinary Foods
Chicago, IL 800-621-4049
Culinary Standards Corporation
Louisville, KY 800-778-3434
Cumberland Gap Provision Company
Middlesboro, KY 800-331-7154
Curtis Packing Company
Greensboro, NC 336-275-7684
D'Orazio Foods
Bellmawr, NJ...........................888-328-7287

Dairy Fresh Foods
Taylor, MI 313-295-6300
Danner Salads
Peoria, IL. 309-691-0289
David Berg & Company
Chicago, IL 773-489-4711
De Bilio Food Distributors
Anaheim, CA 714-773-9323
Deep Foods
Union, NJ 908-810-7500
Depoe Bay Fish Company
Newport, OR 541-265-8833
Depoe Bay Fish Company
Newport, OR 541-265-8833
Devault Foods
Devault, PA 800-426-2874
Dietz & Watson
Philadelphia, PA 800-333-1974
Dippy Foods
Cypress, CA 800-819-8551
DNO
Columbus, OH 800-686-2366
Doerle Food Services
New Iberia, LA 337-367-8551
Dohar Meats
Cleveland, OH 216-241-4197
Dole Fresh Vegetable Company
Soledad, CA 800-333-5454
DPI Midwest
Arlington Hts, IL 847-364-9704
Earth Island Natural Foods
Canoga Park, CA 818-725-2820
Earth Island Natural Foods
Canoga Park, CA 818-725-2820
Egon Binkert Meat Products
Baltimore, MD 410-687-5959
El Aguila Food Products
Salinas, CA 800-398-2929

EMERLING INTERNATIONAL FOODS, INC.

Emerling International Foods
Buffalo, NY. 716-833-7381

> We supply food manufacturers and food service customers worldwide (since 1988) with bulk ingredients including: Fruits & Vegetables; Juice Concentrates; Herbs & Spices; Oils & Vinegars; Flavors & Colors; Honey & Molasses. We also produce **PURE MAPLE SYRUP.**

Enjoy Foods International
Fontana, CA 909-823-2228
Equity Group
Reidsville, NC 336-342-6601
Euro Source Gourmet
Cedar Grove, NJ 973-857-6000
F&S Produce Company
Rosenhayn, NJ 800-886-3316
F&S Produce Company
Rosenhayn, NJ 800-886-3316
Fast Food Merchandisers
Rocky Mount, NC......................252-450-4000
Fine Choice Foods
Richmond, BC 604-522-3110
Fisher Rex Sandwiches
Raleigh, NC 919-832-6494
Flavor Right Foods Group
Columbus, OH 888-464-3734
Food Source
McKinney, TX 972-548-9001
Foodbrands America
Oklahoma City, OK 405-290-4000
Four Star Meat Company of Louisiana
Amite, LA 800-444-5228
Frank Wardynski & Sons
Buffalo, NY. 716-854-6083
Fried Provisions Company
Evans City, PA 724-538-3160
G A Food Service
St Petersburg, FL. 727-573-2211
George L. Wells Meat Company
Philadelphia, PA 800-523-1730
Gilardi Foods
Sidney, OH 937-498-4511
Glendora Quiche Company
San Dimas, CA 909-394-1777
Golden Gulf Coast Packing Company
Biloxi, MS 228-374-6121
Gonard Foods
Calgary, AB 403-277-0991

Great West of Hawaii
  Honolulu, HI 808-593-9981
Grecian Delight Foods
  Elk Grove Vlg, IL 800-621-4387
Green Garden Food Products
  Kent, WA. 800-304-1033
Green Garden Food Products
  Kent, WA. 800-304-1033
Groff Meats
  Elizabethtown, PA. 717-367-1246
Guiltless Gourmet®
  Secaucus, NJ 512-389-0770
Gunsberg Corned Beef
  Detroit, MI 313-894-6600
Gutheinz Meats
  Scranton, PA 570-344-1191
Hamilton Quality Convenience Foods
  Romulus, MI 734-946-1800
Hamilton Quality Convenience Foods
  Romulus, MI 734-946-1800
Hansel 'N Gretel
  Flushing, NY. 718-326-0041
Harold Food Company
  Charlotte, NC 704-588-8061
Hartselle Frozen Foods
  Hartselle, AL. 256-773-7261
Harvest Time Foods
  Ayden, NC. 252-746-6675
Hazle Park Packing Company
  West Hazleton, PA 800-238-4331
Heinkel's Packing Company
  Decatur, IL 800-594-2738
Heinz Company of Canada
  North York, ON. 800-268-6641
Heinz Company of Canada
  North York, ON. 800-268-6641
Helens Pure Foods
  Cheltenham, PA 215-379-6433
Henry J Meat Specialties
  Chicago, IL 800-242-1314
Herold's Salad
  Cleveland, OH 800-427-2523
HFI Foods
  Redmond, WA. 425-883-1320
HFI Foods
  Redmond, WA. 425-883-1320
Holland American International Specialties
  Bellflower, CA 562-867-7589
Homestead Fine Foods
  S San Francisco, CA 650-615-0750
Homestead Fine Foods
  S San Francisco, CA 650-615-0750
Hoople Country Kitchens
  Rockport, IN 812-649-2351
Hormel Foods Corporation
  Algona, IA. 515-295-2477
Hot Potato Distributor
  Chicago, IL 312-243-0640
House of Raeford Farms
  Raeford, NC 800-888-7539
House of Thaller
  Knoxville, TN. 865-689-5893
House of Webster
  Rogers, AR 800-369-4641
Humboldt Sausage Company
  Humboldt, IA 515-332-4121
Hummel Brothers
  New Haven, CT 800-828-8978
Hunt-Wesson Food Service Company
  Rochester, NY. 800-633-1002
I & K Distributors
  Delphos, OH 800-869-6337
Ians Natural Foods
  Revere, MA. 781-284-1999
IBP Foods
  Troy, MI 248-588-4710
IBP Foods
  Grand Rapids, MI 616-774-0711
Independent Packers Corporation
  Seattle, WA 206-285-6000
Independent Packers Corporation
  Seattle, WA 206-285-6000
ISE Farms
  Galena, MD. 410-755-6300
ISE Farms
  Galena, MD. 410-755-6300
Italian Foods Manufacturing
  Vestal, NY. 800-962-7700
Ito Cariani Sausage Company
  Hayward, CA 510-887-0882
Jesse's Fine Meats
  Cherokee, IA 712-225-3637

Jimm's Pizza
  Racine, WI 262-634-2164
John Volpi & Company
  St Louis, MO. 800-288-3439
Kanai Tofu Factory
  Honolulu, HI 808-591-8205
Karam Elsaha Baking Company
  Manlius, NY 315-682-2780
Kay Foods Company
  Ionia, MI 616-527-0120
Kayem Foods
  Chelsea, MA 800-426-6100
Kelly Foods
  Jackson, TN 731-424-2255
Kelly Kornbeef Company
  Chicago, IL 773-588-2882
Kessler's, Inc
  Lemoyne, PA 800-382-1328
Key Ingredients
  Harrisburg, PA 800-227-4448
Kilgus Meats
  Toledo, OH 419-472-9721
King Kold Meats
  Englewood, OH 800-836-2797
Kitts Meat Processing
  Dedham, IA 712-683-5622
Knotts Wholesale Foods
  Paris, TN 731-642-1961
Kronos Products
  Chicago, IL 800-621-0099
Kubla Khan Food Company
  Portland, OR 503-234-7494
Kunzler/Juniata Packing Company
  Tyrone, PA. 814-684-2270
Lafitte Frozen Foods Corporation
  Lafitte, LA. 504-689-2041
Lakeside Foods
  Manitowoc, WI 920-684-3356
Land O'Frost
  Searcy, AR 800-643-5654
Landolfi Food Products
  Trenton, NJ 609-392-1830
Lengerich Meats
  Zanesville, IN 260-638-4123
Leona Meat Plant
  Troy, PA. 570-297-3574
Levonian Brothers
  Troy, NY 518-274-3610
Levonian Brothers
  Troy, NY 518-274-3610
Locustdale Meat Packing
  Locustdale, PA 570-875-1270
Loggins Meat Company
  Tyler, TX. 800-527-8610
Lombardo's Ravioli Kitchen
  New Britain, CT 860-223-7800
Louisiana Packing Company
  Westwego, LA. 800-666-1293
Love & Quiches Desserts
  Freeport, NY. 800-525-5251
Lowell Provision Company
  Lowell, MA. 978-454-5603
Lowell Provision Company
  Lowell, MA. 978-454-5603
Lower Foods
  Richmond, UT. 435-258-2449
Lucks Food Decorating Company
  Tacoma, WA 206-674-7200
Macabee Foods
  Moonachie, NJ 201-489-4343
Made Rite Foods
  Burlington, NC 336-288-6646
Mah Chena Company
  Chicago, IL 312-226-5100
Manda Fine Meats
  Baton Rouge, LA 225-344-7636
Manda Fine Meats
  Baton Rouge, LA 225-344-7636
Manda Fine Meats
  Baton Rouge, LA 225-344-7636
Marathon Enterprises
  Englewood, NJ 201-935-3330
Maria and Son Italian Products
  St Louis, MO. 866-481-9009
Market Fare Foods
  Phoenix, AZ 800-782-9136
Marsan Foods
  Toronto, ON 416-755-9262
Marshallville Packing Company
  Marshallville, OH 330-855-2871
Martin Rosol's
  New Britain, CT 860-223-2707

Martin Rosol's
  New Britain, CT 860-223-2707
Martin Seafood Company
  Jessup, MD 410-799-5822
McCain Foods
  Lodi, NJ 800-258-1098
McClane Distribution Center
  Fredericksburg, VA. 540-374-2000
McClane Distribution Center
  Fredericksburg, VA. 540-374-2000
McFarling Foods
  Indianapolis, IN 317-635-2633
McGrath's Frozen Foods
  Streator, IL 815-672-2654
McLane Foods
  Phoenix, AZ 602-275-5509
Meadows Country Products
  Hollidaysburg, PA. 888-499-1001
Menemsha Fish Market
  Chilmark, MA. 508-645-2282
Metafoods, LLC
  Atlanta, GA. 404-843-2400
Mexi-Frost Specialties Company
  Brooklyn, NY 718-625-3324
Michael Foods, Inc.
  Minnetonka, MN. 952-258-4000
Michael Foods, Inc.
  Minnetonka, MN. 952-258-4000
Milan Salami Company
  Oakland, CA 510-654-7055
Miller's Stratford Provision Company
  Southport, CT 203-375-1598
Mishler Packing Company
  Lagrange, IN 260-768-4156
Molinaro's Fine Italian Foods
  Mississauga, ON. 800-268-4959
Molinaro's Fine Italian Foods
  Mississauga, ON. 800-268-4959
Monsour's
  Pittsburg, KS 620-232-7600
Mosey's Inc
  Bloomfield, CT. 860-243-1725
Mosey's Inc
  Bloomfield, CT. 860-243-1725
Mrs. Grissom's Salad
  Nashville, TN 800-255-0571
Mrs. Minnick's Salads
  Baltimore, MD 410-235-6748
Murphy House
  Louisburg, NC 919-496-4173
Naleway Foods
  Winnipeg, MB. 800-665-7448
Naleway Foods
  Winnipeg, MB. 800-665-7448
Nash Finch Company
  Statesboro, GA 912-681-4580
Nestle
  Cleveland, OH 440-349-5757
Nestle Canada Inc
  North York, ON. 800-563-7853
Nestle Pizza
  Medford, WI 715-748-5550
Nestle USA Inc
  Glendale, CA 800-633-2330
Newhart Foods
  Allentown, PA. 610-437-5539
Night Hawk Frozen Foods
  Buda, TX. 800-580-4166
North Atlantic Fish Company
  Gloucester, MA. 978-283-4121
Northern Star Company
  Minneapolis, MN 612-339-8981
O Chili Frozen Foods Inc
  Northbrook, IL 847-562-1991
O'Brien & Company
  Bellevue, NE 800-433-7567
Ohio Packing Company
  Columbus, OH 800-282-6403
Old Fashioned Kitchen
  Lakewood, NJ. 732-364-4100
Olympic Food Products
  Kokomo, IN 800-445-6923
On-Cor Foods Products
  Northbrook, IL 847-205-1040
Orval Kent Food Company
  Wheeling, IL 847-459-9000
Otto W Liebold & Company
  Flint, MI 800-999-6328
P.A. Braunger Institutional Foods
  Sioux City, IA 712-258-4515
Parma Sausage Products
  Pittsburgh, PA. 877-294-4207

Pasta Factory
Northlake, IL..............800-615-6951
Pasta USA
Spokane, WA..............800-456-2084
Penguin Natural Foods
Commerce, CA..............800-600-8448
Penn Valley Farms
Gainesville, GA 773-685-9929
Pfeffer's Country Market
Sauk Centre, MN..............320-352-3095
Phillips Gourmet
Kennett Square, PA..............610-925-0520
Pictsweet Frozen Foods
Bells, TN..............731-663-7600
Pilgrim's Pride
Timberville, VA..............540-896-7000
Pilgrim's Pride
Timberville, VA..............540-896-7000
Pilgrim's Pride
Lufkin, TX 936-639-1174
Pillsbury
Allentown, PA..............610-797-5947
Pinnacle Foods Group
Cherry Hill, NJ..............877-852-7424
Plumrose
East Brunswick, NJ..............800-526-4909
Plumrose USA
East Brunswick, NJ..............732-257-6600
Pocino Foods
City of Industry, CA..............800-345-0150
Pon Food Corporation
Ponchatoula, LA..............985-386-6941
Preferred Meal Systems
Scranton, PA..............570-457-8311
Promiseland Meat PackingCompany
Madill, OK..............580-795-3567
Queen International Foods
Monterey Park, CA..............800-423-4414
R.C. McEntire & Company
Columbia, SC..............803-799-3388
R.L. Zeigler Company
Tuscaloosa, AL..............800-392-6328
Ramona's Mexican Food Products
Gardena, CA..............310-323-1950
Ready Portion Meat Company
Baton Rouge, LA..............225-355-5641
Real Kosher Sausage Company
Newark, NJ..............973-690-5394
Redi-Serve Food Company
Fort Atkinson, WI..............920-563-6391
Regal Food Service
Houston, TX..............713-222-8231
Rego's Purity Foods
Honolulu, HI..............808-947-9005
Rendulic Packing
McKeesport, PA..............412-678-9541
Request Foods
Holland, MI..............800-748-0378
Reser's Fine Foods
Salt Lake City, UT..............801-972-5633
Reser's Fine Foods
Salt Lake City, UT..............801-972-5633
Roman Packing Company
Norfolk, NE..............800-373-5990
Ruiz Food Products
Dinuba, CA..............800-477-6474
Ruskin Packaging
Miami, FL..............305-324-1529
Ryley Sausage
Ryley, AB..............780-663-3990
S-Car-Go
Sanibel, FL..............239-472-1900
Saag's Products
San Leandro, CA..............800-352-7224
Salad-De-Lites
Bronx, NY..............718-828-1200
Salem Food Service
Salem, IN..............812-883-2196
Sales Associates of Alaska
Fairbanks, AK..............907-458-0000
Salvage Sale
Houston, TX..............800-856-7445
Samjin America
Vernon, CA..............213-622-5111
Sana Foods
Bainbridge Island, WA..............206-842-4741
Sanderson Farms
Bryan, TX..............979-778-5730
Sandridge Food Corporation
Medina, OH..............330-725-2348
Sara Lee Corporation
Downers Grove, IL..............630-598-8100

Sara Lee Foods
Cincinnati, OH 800-351-7111
Sausage Shoppe
Cleveland, OH 216-351-5213
Saval Foods
Elkridge, MD..............800-527-2825
Schaller & Weber
Long Island City, NY 800-847-4115
Schaller's Packers
Cassville, NY..............315-822-3924
Sculli Brothers
Philadelphia, PA 215-336-1223
Sechrist Brothers
Dallastown, PA..............717-244-2975
Seitz Foods
Saint Joseph, MO 800-383-3128
Seneca Foods
Clyman, WI..............920-696-3331
Sheinman Provision Company
Philadelphia, PA..............215-473-7065
Shiloh Foods
Savannah, TN 800-795-2550
Shiloh Foods
Savannah, TN 800-795-2550
Simco Foods
Los Angeles, CA..............310-284-9050
Simeus Foods International
Mansfield, TX..............888-772-3663
Sims Wholesale
Batesville, AR..............870-793-1109
Smith Packing Regional Meat
Utica, NY..............315-732-5125
Smithfield Foods
Clinton, NC..............910-592-2104
Snow Ball Foods
Fredericksburg, PA..............800-360-7669
Somerset Food Service
Somerset, KY..............606-274-4858
Somerset Industries
Spring House, PA..............800-883-8728
Sonoco Wholesale Grocers
Houma, LA..............985-851-0727
Specialty Brands
Carthage, MO..............417-358-8104
Specialty Brands
Ontario, CA..............800-782-1180
Spring Glen Fresh Foods
Ephrata, PA..............800-641-2853
Spring Grove Foods
Miamisburg, OH 937-866-4311
Springfield Smoked Fish Company
Springfield, MA 800-327-3412
Standard Beef Company
New Haven, CT 203-787-2164
Star Ravioli Manufacturing Company
Moonachie, NJ 201-933-6427
Stawnichy Holdings
Mundare, AB 888-764-7646
Steak-Umm Company
Shillington, PA..............860-928-5900
Stefano Gourmet A Taste of Italy
Rural Ridge, PA 888-781-4104
Stevens Sausage Company
Smithfield, NC 800-338-0561
Stonies Sausage Shop Inc
Perryville, MO 888-546-2540
Storer Meat Company
Cleveland, OH 800-355-7537
Storheim's
Green Bay, WI..............920-498-2343
Su Bee's Discount Foods
Portland, OR 503-234-2000
Sunburst Foods
Goldsboro, NC 919-778-2151
Sunset Specialty Foods
Sunset Beach, CA 562-592-4976
Sunset Wholesale
Lebanon, PA..............800-876-2123
Sunstates Refrigerated
Moultrie, GA..............912-985-8918
Swift & Company
Greeley, CO..............970-324-2180
Swiss Colony
Monroe, WI..............608-328-8400
Symphony Foods
Berkeley, CA..............510-845-8275
Tampa Maid Foods
Lakeland, FL..............800-237-7637
Tasty Mix Quality Foods
Brooklyn, NY..............866-TAS-TYMX
Taylor's Frozen Foods
Charleston, SC 843-723-1878

Tennessee Valley PackingCompany
Columbia, TN..............931-388-2623
Teti Bakery
Etobicoke, ON 800-465-0123
Theoworld
Fairfield, OH 773-268-2800
Tomasso Corporation
Baie D'Urfe, QC..............514-325-3000
Too Goo Doo Farms/Easy Tray LLC
North Charleston, SC..............843-767-0196
Tree Tavern Products
Paterson, NJ 973-279-1617
Trident Seafoods Corporation
Seattle, WA 800-426-5490
Troy Frozen Food
Troy, IL..............618-667-6332
Troyers Trail Bologna
Dundee, OH 877-893-2414
Tupman-Thurlow Company
Deerfield Beach, FL..............954-596-9989
Turrentine Salvage Company
Nashville, TN 615-832-3018
Tyson Foods
Springdale, AR..............800-643-3410
United Provision Meat Company
Columbus, OH 614-252-1126
Upstate Farms Cooperative
Buffalo, NY..............716-892-3156
Van Bennett Food Company
Reading, PA 800-423-8897
Vantage USA
Chicago, IL..............773-247-1086
Vienna Meat Products
Scarborough, ON 800-588-1931
Viking Seafoods Inc
Malden, MA 800-225-3020
WA Bean & Sons
Bangor, ME..............800-649-1958
Wampler Foods
Dallas, TX..............717-624-2191
Warren & Son Meat Processing
Whipple, OH..............740-585-2421
Wawona Frozen Foods
Clovis, CA..............559-299-2901
Webster Distributing Company
Chattanooga, TN..............423-622-1428
Weyhaupt Brothers Packing
Belleville, IL..............618-233-0452
William E. Caudle Company
Idaho Falls, ID 208-523-6637
Wimmer's Meat Products
West Point, NE..............800-358-0761
Winkler
Winkler, MB 812-937-2044
Wong Wing Foods
Montreal, QC 800-361-4820
Woods Fabricators
Taylorsville, GA..............770-684-5377
Wornick Company
Cincinnati, OH 800-860-4555
Wornick Company
Cincinnati, OH 800-860-4555
Wornick Company
Cincinnati, OH 800-860-4555
Yarbrough Produce Company
Birmingham, AL..............205-323-8651
Zartic Inc
Rome, GA..............800-241-0516
Zuccaro's Fruit & Produce Company
Minneapolis, MN 612-333-1122

Antipasto

Victoria Packing Corporation
Brooklyn, NY..............718-649-2180

Appetizers

Anchor Appetizer Group
Appleton, WI 920-997-2659
Anchor Food Products/ McCain Foods
Appleton, WI 920-734-0627
Appetizers And
Chicago, IL..............800-323-5472
Appetizers And, Inc.
Chicago, IL..............800-323-5472
Aristocrat International Corporation
Secaucus, NJ 201-866-1900
B&D Foods
Boise, ID 208-344-1183
Barber Foods
Portland, ME..............800-577-2595

Belle River Enterprises
Belle River, PE 902-962-2248
Biagio's Banquets
Chicago, IL 800-392-2837
Bocconcino Food Products
Moonachie, NJ 201-933-7474
Caribbean Food Delights
Tappan, NY 845-398-3000
Cateraid
Howell, MI 800-508-8217
Cathay Foods Corporation
Boston, MA 617-427-1507
Chang Food Company
Garden Grove, CA 714-265-9990
Chateau Food Products
Cicero, IL 708-863-4207
Chinese Spaghetti Factory
Boston, MA 617-445-7714
Chungs Gourmet Foods
Houston, TX 713-741-2118
ConAgra Grocery Products
Irvine, CA 714-680-1000
ConAgra Mexican Foods
Compton, CA 310-223-1499
Cordon Bleu International
Anjou, QC 514-352-3000
Culinary Foods
Chicago, IL 800-621-4049
Dominex
St Augustine, FL 800-282-1030
Dufour Pastry Kitchens
New York, NY 212-929-2800
Egg Roll Fantasy
Auburn, CA 530-887-9197
Excelline Foods
Chatsworth, CA 818-701-7710
Fillo Factory
Dumont, NJ 800-653-4556
Fine Choice Foods
Richmond, BC 604-522-3110
Fishking Processors
Los Angeles, CA 877-677-3329
Foodbrands America
Oklahoma City, OK 405-290-4000
Frozen Specialties
Archbold, OH 419-445-9015
Fry Foods
Tiffin, OH 800-626-2294
Glendora Quiche Company
San Dimas, CA 909-394-1777
Golden Gate Foods
Dallas, TX 214-747-2223
Great American Appetizers
Nampa, ID 800-282-4834
Harvest Food Products Company
Concord, CA 925-676-8208
Health is Wealth Foods
Williamstown, NJ 856-728-1998
Heinz North America
Fort Myers, FL 239-694-3663
Hors D'Oeuvres Unlimited
North Bergen, NJ 800-648-3787
Kretschmar
Don Mills, ON 800-561-4532
L&S Packing Company
Farmingdale, NY 800-286-6487
La Tang Cuisine Manufacturing
Houston, TX 713-780-4876
Lamb-Weston
Pasco, WA 800-766-7783
LaMonica Fine Foods
Millville, NJ 856-825-8111
Lees Sausage Company
Orangeburg, SC 803-534-5517
Mama Amy's Quality Foods
Mississauga, ON 905-456-0056
Matador Processors
Blanchard, OK 800-847-0797
Matlaw's Food Products
West Haven, CT 800-934-8266
McCain Foods
Fort Atkinson, WI 920-563-6625
McCain Foods USA
Lisle, IL 800-258-1098
Mt. Olympus Specialty Foods
Buffalo, NY 716-874-0771
Musco Olive Products
Tracy, CA 800-523-9828
Nancy's Specialty Foods
Newark, CA 510-494-1100
Omstead Foods Ltd
Burlington, ON 905-315-8883

Pastene Companies
Canton, MA 781-830-8200
Perfect Bite Company
Glendale, CA 818-507-1527
Phillips Gourmet
Kennett Square, PA 610-925-0520
Pie Piper Products
Bensenville, IL 800-621-8183
Produits Belle Baie
Caraquet, NB 506-727-4414
Rubschlager Baking Corporation
Chicago, IL 773-826-1245
Sable & Rosenfeld Foods
Toronto, ON 416-929-4214
Sabra Blue & White Food Products
Astoria, NY 718-389-3800
Seckinger-Lee Company
Savannah, GA 800-291-2973
Shonna's Gourmet Goodies
West Bridgewater, MA 888-312-7868
Simeus Foods Internatio nal
Mansfield, TX 888-772-3663
Simeus Foods International
Mansfield, TX 888-772-3663
Sinbad Sweets
Fresno, CA 800-350-7933
Specialty Brands
Ontario, CA 800-782-1180
Steak-Umm Company
Shillington, PA 860-928-5900
Tampa Maid Foods
Lakeland, FL 800-237-7637
Thyme & Truffles Hors D'oeuvres
Toronto, ON 877-489-8636
Tipiak
Stamford, CT 203-961-9117
Tribe Mediterranean Foods Company LLC
Taunton, MA 800-421-3474
Valdez Food
Philadelphia, PA 215-634-6106
Van-Lang Foods
Lombard, IL 630-268-1953
Wayne Farms, LLC
Pendergrass, GA 706-693-2271
William Poll
New York, NY 800-993-7655
Willow Foods
Beaverton, OR 800-338-3609
Windsor Foods
Houston, TX 713-843-5200
Wonton Food
Brooklyn, NY 800-776-8889

Fresh, Canned & Frozen

Anchor Food Products/ McCain Foods
Appleton, WI 920-734-0627
Appetizers And, Inc.
Chicago, IL 800-323-5472
Aristocrat International Corporation
Secaucus, NJ 201-866-1900
Barber Foods
Portland, ME 800-577-2595
Belle River Enterprises
Belle River, PE 902-962-2248
Biagio's Banquets
Chicago, IL 800-392-2837
Caribbean Food Delights
Tappan, NY 845-398-3000
Cateraid
Howell, MI 800-508-8217
Cathay Foods Corporation
Boston, MA 617-427-1507
Caughman's Meat Plant
Lexington, SC 803-356-0076
Cedar Key Aquaculture Farms
Riverview, FL 888-252-6735
Chang Food Company
Garden Grove, CA 714-265-9990
Chateau Food Products
Cicero, IL 708-863-4207
Chinese Spaghetti Factory
Boston, MA 617-445-7714
Chungs Gourmet Foods
Houston, TX 713-741-2118
Cordon Bleu International
Anjou, QC 514-352-3000
Culinary Foods
Chicago, IL 800-621-4049
Dufour Pastry Kitchens
New York, NY 212-929-2800

Fine Choice Foods
Richmond, BC 604-522-3110
Fishking Processors
Los Angeles, CA 877-677-3329
Foodbrands America
Oklahoma City, OK 405-290-4000
Frozen Specialties
Archbold, OH 419-445-9015
Glendora Quiche Company
San Dimas, CA 909-394-1777
Golden Gate Foods
Dallas, TX 214-747-2223
Good Wives
Lynn, MA 800-521-8160
Gourmet Foods
Compton, CA 310-632-3300
Great American Appetizers
Nampa, ID 800-282-4834
Hors D'Oeuvres Unlimited
North Bergen, NJ 800-648-3787
Kabob's
Morrow, GA 800-732-9484
Kretschmar
Don Mills, ON 800-561-4532
La Tang Cuisine Manufacturing
Houston, TX 713-780-4876
LaMonica Fine Foods
Millville, NJ 856-825-8111
Lees Sausage Company
Orangeburg, SC 803-534-5517
Matador Processors
Blanchard, OK 800-847-0797
Matlaw's Food Products
West Haven, CT 800-934-8266
McCain Foods
Fort Atkinson, WI 920-563-6625
Musco Olive Products
Tracy, CA 800-523-9828
Nancy's Specialty Foods
Newark, CA 510-494-1100
Phillips Gourmet
Kennett Square, PA 610-925-0520
Pie Piper Products
Bensenville, IL 800-621-8183
Produits Belle Baie
Caraquet, NB 506-727-4414
Royal Palate Foods
Inglewood, CA 310-330-7701
Seckinger-Lee Company
Savannah, GA 800-291-2973
Shonna's Gourmet Goodies
West Bridgewater, MA 888-312-7868
SilverLeaf International
Stafford, TX 800-442-7542
Steak-Umm Company
Shillington, PA 860-928-5900
Tampa Maid Foods
Lakeland, FL 800-237-7637
Thyme & Truffles Hors D'oeuvres
Toronto, ON 877-489-8636
Tipiak
Stamford, CT 203-961-9117
Van-Lang Foods
Lombard, IL 630-268-1953
Victoria Packing Corporation
Brooklyn, NY 718-649-2180
VLR Food Corporation
Concord, ON 800-387-7437
Windsor Foods
Houston, TX 713-843-5200

Frozen

Appetizers And
Chicago, IL 800-323-5472
Aristocrat International Corporation
Secaucus, NJ 201-866-1900
B&D Foods
Boise, ID 208-344-1183
Barber Foods
Portland, ME 800-577-2595
Bocconcino Food Products
Moonachie, NJ 201-933-7474
Caribbean Food Delights
Tappan, NY 845-398-3000
Cathay Foods Corporation
Boston, MA 617-427-1507
Chang Food Company
Garden Grove, CA 714-265-9990
Chateau Food Products
Cicero, IL 708-863-4207

Clear Springs Foods
Cherry Hill, NJ .800-635-8211
Coastal Seafoods
Ridgefield, CT 203-431-0453
ConAgra Mexican Foods
Compton, CA 310-223-1499
Cordon Bleu International
Anjou, QC .514-352-3000
Dufour Pastry Kitchens
New York, NY 212-929-2800
Foodbrands America
Oklahoma City, OK 405-290-4000
Good Wives
Lynn, MA 800-521-8160
Great American Appetizers
Nampa, ID. .800-282-4834
Health is Wealth Foods
Williamstown, NJ 856-728-1998
Heinz North America
Fort Myers, FL 239-694-3663
Hors D'Oeuvres Unlimited
North Bergen, NJ 800-648-3787
LaMonica Fine Foods
Millville, NJ .856-825-8111
Matador Processors
Blanchard, OK 800-847-0797
Matlaw's Food Products
West Haven, CT 800-934-8266
McCain Foods
Fort Atkinson, WI. 920-563-6625
McCain Foods USA
Lisle, IL. 800-258-1098
Specialty Brands
Ontario, CA 800-782-1180
Stacey's Famous Foods
Hayden, ID .800-782-2395
Steak-Umm Company
Shillington, PA 860-928-5900
Tampa Maid Foods
Lakeland, FL. 800-237-7637
Thyme & Truffles Hors D'oeuvres
Toronto, ON 877-489-8636
Tipiak
Stamford, CT. 203-961-9117
William Poll
New York, NY 800-993-7655

Refrigerated

Cyclone Enterprises
Houston, TX 281-872-0087
Larsen Packers
Burwick, NS 902-538-8060
Reser's Fine Foods
Beaverton, OR 800-333-6431

Baked Beans (see also Pork & Beans)

Canned

Agland, Inc.
Eaton, CO .800-433-4688
Allen Canning Company
Siloam Springs, AR 800-234-2553
AlpineAire Foods
Rocklin, CA 800-322-6325
Amigos Canning Company
San Antonio, TX. 800-580-3477
B&M
Portland, ME. 207-772-8341
Beckman & Gast Company
St Henry, OH. 419-678-4195
Blue Runner Foods
Gonzales, LA 225-647-3016
Burnette Foods
Elk Rapids, MI 231-264-8116

Bush Brothers & Company
Augusta, WI 715-286-2211
California Fruit and Tomato Kitchens
Riverbank, CA 209-869-9300
Campbell Soup Company
Camden, NJ 800-257-8443
Carriere Foods Inc
Montreal, QC 514-384-4281
Chiquita Brands
Cincinnati, OH 513-784-8000
Chiquita Processed Foods
Milton Freewater, OR 541-938-4461
ConAgra Grocery Products
Irvine, CA 714-680-1000
Cordon Bleu International
Anjou, QC .514-352-3000
Del Monte Foods
San Francisco, CA 800-543-3090
Eden Foods Inc
Clinton, MI .800-248-0320
Faribault Foods
Minneapolis, MN 612-333-6461
Grandma Brown's Beans Inc
Mexico, NY. 315-963-7221
H.K. Canning
Ventura, CA. 805-652-1392
Hanover Foods Corporation
Hanover, PA 717-632-6000
Heinz Company of Canada
North York, ON. 800-268-6641
Hoopeston Foods
Burnsville, MN 952-854-0903
International Home Foods
Milton, PA. .973-359-9920
Kennebec Bean Company
North Vassalboro, ME 207-873-3473
L&S Packing Company
Farmingdale, NY 800-286-6487
Lakeside Foods
Plainview, MN 507-534-3141
Lakeside Foods
Mondovi, WI. 715-926-5075
Lakeside Foods
Manitowoc, WI 920-684-3356
Lakeside Foods
Seymour, WI 920-833-2371
Lucks Food Decorating Company
Tacoma, WA 206-674-7200
McCall Farms
Effingham, SC. 800-277-2012
Mercado Latino
City of Industry, CA 626-333-6862
Miyako Oriental Foods
Baldwin Park, CA 877-788-6476
Morgan Food
Austin, IN 888-430-1780
Nationwide Canning
Cottam, ON. 519-839-4831
Natural Value Products
Sacramento, CA 916-427-7242
New Era Canning Company
New Era, MI 231-861-2151
New Harvest Foods
Pulaski, WI .920-822-2578
New Meridian
Eaton, IN 765-396-3344
NORPAC Foods
Lake Oswego, OR 503-635-9311
NORPAC Plant
Salem, OR .800-822-2898
Old Ranchers Canning Company
Upland, CA .909-982-8895
Omstead Foods Ltd
Burlington, ON 905-315-8883
Pillsbury Canada Limited
Markham, ON 800-745-4777
Poynette Distribution Center
Poynette, WI 608-635-4396
Princeville Canning Company
Princeville, IL 309-385-4301
Randall Food Products
Tekonsha, MI 517-767-3247
Red River Commodities
Fargo, ND .701-282-2600
Rio Valley Canning Company
Donna, TX. 956-464-7843
Rosarita Mexican Foods Company
Mesa, AZ. .480-964-8751
Seneca Foods
Cumberland, WI 715-822-2181
Sunrise Growers
Placentia, CA 714-630-2170

Truitt Brothers Inc
Salem, OR .800-547-8712
United Intertrade Corporation
Houston, TX 800-969-2233
Wornick Company
Cincinnati, OH 800-860-4555

Breaded Vegetables

Al Pete Meats
Muncie, IN .765-288-8817
Anchor Food Products/ McCain Foods
Appleton, WI 920-734-0627
Brooks Food Group Corporate Office
Bedford, VA 800-873-4934
Great American Appetizers
Nampa, ID. .800-282-4834
Lake Erie Frozen Foods Company
Ashland, OH 800-766-8501
Omstead Foods Ltd
Burlington, ON 905-315-8883
Ore-Ida Foods
Pittsburgh, PA 412-237-3450
Phillips Gourmet
Kennett Square, PA 610-925-0520
Pictsweet Frozen Foods
Bells, TN. 731-663-7600
Schwans Bakeries
Stilwell, OK 918-696-8325
Trans Pecos Foods
San Antonio, TX. 210-228-0896
Westin
Omaha, NE 800-228-6098

Breakfast Foods: Instant

Agricore United
Winnipeg, MB. 204-944-5411
Bake Crafters Food
Collegedale, TN 800-296-8935
Bede Inc
Haledon, NJ 866-239-6565
California Cereal Products
Oakland, CA 510-452-4500
Campbell Soup Company
Camden, NJ. 800-257-8443
Con Agra Store Brands
Edina, MN. .952-835-6900
ConAgra Snack Foods Group/Act II Popcorn
Edina, MN. .800-328-6286
Continental Mills
Seattle, WA 253-872-8400
Country Smoked Meats
Bowling Green, OH 800-321-4766
Cream of the West
Harlowton, MT 800-477-2383
GFA Brands
Paramus, NJ 201-568-9300
Gilster Mary Lee/Jasper Foods
Jasper, MO 800-777-2168
GPR Company
Stowe, PA .610-326-4777
Hodgson Mill Inc
Effingham, IL 800-525-0177
Homestead Mills
Cook, MN 800-652-5233
International Home Foods
Milton, PA. .973-359-9920
Kellogg Canada Inc
Mississauga, ON 888-876-3750
Kellogg Company
Omaha, NE 402-331-7717
Kellogg Company
San Jose, CA 408-295-8656
Kellogg Company
Hammonton, NJ 609-567-2300
Kellogg Company
Lancaster, PA 717-898-0161
Kellogg Company
Battle Creek, MI 800-962-1413
Kellogg Company
Memphis, TN 901-743-0250
Little Crow Foods
Warsaw, IN 800-288-2769
Nabisco Dry Foods
Glenview, IL 612-331-4325
Nestle' Handheld Foods Group
Englewood, CO. 800-225-2270
New England Natural Bakers
Greenfield, MA. 800-910-2884
Northern Star Company
Minneapolis, MN 612-339-8981

Pillsbury
Allentown, PA 610-797-5947
Purity Foods
Okemos, MI .800-997-7358
Quaker Oats Company
Peterborough, ON 800-267-6287
Real Food Marketing
Kansas City, MO 816-221-4100
Rhodes Bake-N-Serv
Salt Lake City, UT 800-695-0122
Rich-Seapak Corporation
St Simons Island, GA 800-654-9731
Sara Lee Food Service
Haltom City, TX 800-261-4754
Sturm Foods
Manawa, WI .800-347-8876
Tami Great Food
Monsey, NY .718-788-4200
Tova Industries
Louisville, KY 888-532-8682
US Mills
Needham, MA 800-422-1125

Broth

Canned,Frozen,Powdered

Blount Seafood Corporation
Fall River, MA 774-888-1300
Clofine Dairy & Food Products
Linwood, NJ .800-441-1001
Cordon Bleu International
Anjou, QC 514-352-3000
Fuji Foods
Browns Summit, NC 336-375-3111
Hormel Foods Corporation
Austin, MN .800-523-4635
International Dehydrated Foods
Springfield, MO 800-525-7435
International Dehydreated Foods
Springfield, MO 800-641-6509
Old Ranchers Canning Company
Upland, CA 909-982-8895
Organic Gourmet
Sherman Oaks, CA 800-400-7772

Sentry Seasonings
Elmhurst, IL .630-530-5370

The product development experts of Sentry Seasonings are eager to offer the assistance and hands-on experience to food processors of all sizes. Sentry Seasonings will ensure the consistent high quality and repeat sales of your products, whether you choose one of our many off-the-shelf Bench Mark products or a modified version to meet your preferences. Sentry Seasonings can also duplicate and/or improve your present flavor profile; formulate, blend and package specifically for your requirements.

SOUPerior Bean & Spice Company
Vancouver, WA 800-878-7687
St. Ours & Company
Norwell, MA .781-331-8520
Sweet Sue Kitchens
Athens, AL .256-216-0500
Tova Industries
Louisville, KY 888-532-8682

Chicken

All-States Quality Foods
Charles City, IA 800-247-4195
Clofine Dairy & Food Products
Linwood, NJ .800-441-1001
Kerry Ingredients
Tralee, Co. Kerry,

Sentry Seasonings
Elmhurst, IL .630-530-5370

The product development experts of Sentry Seasonings are eager to offer the assistance and hands-on experience to food processors of all sizes. Sentry Seasonings will ensure the consistent high quality and repeat sales of your products, whether you choose one of our many off-the-shelf Bench Mark products or a modified version to meet your preferences. Sentry Seasonings can also duplicate and/or improve your present flavor profile; formulate, blend and package specifically for your requirements.

Sweet Sue Kitchens
Athens, AL .256-216-0500

Frozen

Proliant Meat Ingredients
Ankeny, IA .800-369-2672

Powdered

Proliant Meat Ingredients
Ankeny, IA .800-369-2672

Chili

Baja Foods
Chicago, IL .773-376-9030
Bear Creek Kitchens
Marshall, TX 888-300-7687
Big B Distributors
Evansville, IN 812-425-5235
Bunker Hill Foods
Augusta, GA 706-733-7765
Burnett & Son Meat Company
Monrovia, CA 626-357-2165
Bush Brothers & Company
Augusta, WI 715-286-2211
Buxton Foods
Buxton, ND .800-726-8057
Campbell Soup Company
Camden, NJ .800-257-8443
Castleberry/Snow Brands
Augusta, GA 800-241-3520
Chandler Foods
Greensboro, NC 800-537-6219
Cherchies
Malvern, PA .800-644-1980
Culinary Standards Corporation
Louisville, KY 800-778-3434
Detroit Chili Company
Southfield, MI 248-440-5933
Edmonds Chile Company
St Louis, MO 314-772-1499
El-Rey Foods
Ferguson, MO 314-521-3113
Faribault Foods
Minneapolis, MN 612-333-6461
Harold Food Company
Charlotte, NC 704-588-8061
Health Valley Company
Irwindale, CA 800-334-3204
Heinz North America
Pittsburgh, PA 412-237-5700
Hoopeston Foods
Burnsville, MN 952-854-0903
International Home Foods
Milton, PA 973-359-9920
Josie's Best New Mexican Foods
Santa Fe, NM 505-473-3437
Kelly Foods
Jackson, TN 731-424-2255
Lees Sausage Company
Orangeburg, SC 803-534-5517
M&M Packing Company
Ballinger, TX 915-365-2227
Mexisnax Corporation
El Paso, TX .915-779-5709
Mi Ranchito Foods
Bayard, NM .575-537-3868

Milnot Company
Litchfield, IL 800-877-6455
Moonlite Bar BQ Inn
Owensboro, KY 800-322-8989
Mr Jay's Tamales & Chili
Lynwood, CA 310-537-3932
North of the Border
Tesuque, NM 800-860-0681
O Chili Frozen Foods Inc
Northbrook, IL 847-562-1991
Original Chili Bowl
Tulsa, OK 918-628-0225
Peppi Chili
Norcross, GA 770-449-6149
Pokanoket Ostrich Farm
South Dartmouth, MA 508-992-6188
Reser's Fine Foods
Salt Lake City, UT 801-972-5633
Seitz Foods
Saint Joseph, MO 800-383-3128
Stockpot
Woodinville, WA 800-468-1611
Supreme Frozen Products
Chicago, IL .773-622-3336
T.L. Herring & Company
Wilson, NC .252-291-1141
Taylor's Mexican Chili
Carlinville, IL 800-382-4454
Terra Sol Chile Company
Austin, TX 512-836-3525
Todd's Enterprises
Irvine, CA 949-250-4080
Torn & Glasser
Los Angeles, CA 800-282-6887
Tyson Prepared Foods
Fort Worth, TX 817-258-2400
Wisconsin Packing Company
Butler, WI 800-558-2000
Yankee Specialty Foods
Boston, MA .617-951-9904

Canned

Blue Ribbon Meats
Cleveland, OH 216-631-8850
Milnot Company
Litchfield, IL 800-877-6455
Peco Foods
Canton, MS .601-407-1699
Pure Food Ingredients
Verona, WI .800-355-9601

Canned & Frozen

Baja Foods
Chicago, IL .773-376-9030
Big B Distributors
Evansville, IN 812-425-5235
Bunker Hill Foods
Augusta, GA 706-733-7765
Campbell Company of Canada
Toronto, ON 800-575-7687
Castleberry/Snow Brands
Augusta, GA 800-241-3520
Caughman's Meat Plant
Lexington, SC 803-356-0076
Chandler Foods
Greensboro, NC 800-537-6219
Culinary Standards Corporation
Louisville, KY 800-778-3434
Don Miguel Mexican Foods
Orange, CA .714-634-8441
Edmonds Chile Company
St Louis, MO 314-772-1499
First Original Texas Chili Company
Fort Worth, TX 817-626-0983
G Di Lullo & Sons
Westville, NJ 856-456-3700
H.J. Heinz Company
Pittsburgh, PA 412-237-5948
Heinz North America
Pittsburgh, PA 412-237-5700
Kelly Foods
Jackson, TN 731-424-2255
M&M Packing Company
Ballinger, TX 915-365-2227
Marsan Foods
Toronto, ON 416-755-9262
Mi Ranchito Foods
Bayard, NM .575-537-3868
Milnot Company
Litchfield, IL 800-877-6455

North of the Border
Tesuque, NM 800-860-0681
O Chili Frozen Foods Inc
Northbrook, IL 847-562-1991
Old Ranchers Canning Company
Upland, CA 909-982-8895
SOPAKCO Foods
Mullins, SC 800-276-9678
Stauber Performance Ingredients
Fullerton, CA 888-441-4233
Todd's Enterprises
Irvine, CA 949-250-4080
Vietti Foods Company Inc
Nashville, TN 800-240-7864
Westbrae Natural Foods
Garden City, NY 800-434-4246
Worthmore Food Product
Cincinnati, OH 513-559-1473

Frozen

Bueno Food Products
Albuquerque, NM 800-888-7336
Original Texas Chili Company
Fort Worth, TX 800-507-0009

with Cheese

Mexisnax Corporation
El Paso, TX 915-779-5709

Chowder

Blount Seafood Corporation
Fall River, MA 774-888-1300
Bunker Hill Foods
Augusta, GA 706-733-7765
Campbell Company of Canada
Toronto, ON 800-575-7687
Campbell Soup Company
Camden, NJ 800-257-8443
Cherchies
Malvern, PA 800-644-1980
Denzer's Food Products
Baltimore, MD 410-889-1500
Fish Hopper
Monterey, CA 831-372-8543
LaMonica Fine Foods
Millville, NJ 856-825-8111
Mid-Atlantic Foods
Easton, MD 800-922-4688
New England Marketers
Boston, MA 800-688-9904
Ronzoni Foods Canada
Etobicoke, ON 800-387-5032
Specialty Brands of America
Westbury, NY 516-997-6969
Triton Seafood Company
Medley, FL 305-805-3500
Valdez Food
Philadelphia, PA 215-634-6106
Yankee Specialty Foods
Boston, MA 617-951-9904

Clam & Fish

Blount Seafood Corporation
Fall River, MA 774-888-1300
Bunker Hill Foods
Augusta, GA 706-733-7765
Campbell Company of Canada
Toronto, ON 800-575-7687
Campbell Soup Company
Camden, NJ 800-257-8443
Chincoteague Seafood Company
Parsonsburg, MD 443-260-4800
Fish Hopper
Monterey, CA 831-372-8543
Kettle Cuisine
Chelsea, MA 877-302-7687
LaMonica Fine Foods
Millville, NJ 856-825-8111
Mid-Atlantic Foods
Easton, MD 800-922-4688
New England Marketers
Boston, MA 800-688-9904
Sea Watch International
Easton, MD 410-822-7500

Chutney

A Perfect Pear from NapaValley
Napa, CA 800-553-5753

Blue Jay Orchards
Bethel, CT 203-748-0119
Blueberry Store
Grand Junction, MI 877-654-2400
Bottle Green Drinks
Mississauga, ON 905-273-6137
Chelsea Market Baskets
New York, NY 888-727-7887
Chicama Vineyards
West Tisbury, MA 888-244-2262
Cinnabar Specialty Foods
Prescott, AZ 866-293-6433
Coastal Classics
Duxbury, MA 508-746-6058
Commissariat Imports
Los Angeles, CA 310-475-5628
Creative Foodworks
San Antonio, TX 210-212-4761
Cuizina Food Company
Woodinville, WA 425-486-7000
Curry King Corporation
Waldwick, NJ 800-287-7987
Delicae Gourmet
Tarpon Springs, FL 800-942-2502
Earth & Vine Provisions
Lincoln, CA 888-723-8463
Graves Mountain Cannery
Syria, VA 540-923-4747
Hawaiian Fruit Specialties
Kalaheo, HI 808-332-9333
Jay Shah Foods
Mississauga, ON 905-696-0172
Kozlowski Farms
Forestville, CA 800-473-2767
Nulhegan Brands
Canaan, VT 802-524-0768
Outback Kitchens LLC
Huntington, VT 802-434-5262
Patak Spices USA
Clearwater, FL 727-796-2126
Shahi Food Corporation
Mississauga, ON 905-677-4327
Silver Palate Kitchens
Cresskill, NJ 800-872-5283
Sokol & Company
Countryside, IL 800-328-7656
Spruce Mountain Blueberries
West Rockport, ME 207- 23-6 35
Steel's Gourmet Foods
Bridgeport, PA 800-678-3357
Tait Farm Foods
Centre Hall, PA 800-787-2716
Terrapin Ridge
Freeport, IL 800-999-4052
Vermont Harvest Speciality Foods
Stowe, VT 800-338-5354
Wild Thymes Farm
Greenville, NY 800-724-2877
Wisconsin Wilderness Food Products
Milwaukee, WI 800-359-3039

Convenience Food

Ailments E.D. Foods Inc.
Pointe Claire, QC 800-267-3333
American Food Distributors
Harvey, IL 708-331-1982
American Wholesale Grocery
Mobile, AL 251-433-2500
Andalusia Distributing Company
Andalusia, AL 334-222-3671
Anmar Foods
Chicago, IL 312-733-6160
Arizona Institutional Foods
Tucson, AZ 520-624-8667
Bar NA, Inc.
Champaign, IL 217-687-4810
Biagio's Banquets
Chicago, IL 800-392-2837
Big B Distributors
Evansville, IN 812-425-5235
Camino Real Foods
Vernon, CA 800-421-6201
ConAgra Grocery Products
Fullerton, CA 800-736-2212
Crum Creek Mills
Springfield, PA 888-607-3500
Dorothy Dawson Foods Products
Jackson, MI 517-788-9830
Fantastic Foods
Napa, CA 800-288-1089
Frookie
Des Plaines, IL 847-699-3200

General Mills
Minneapolis, MN 800-248-7310
Gilroy Foods
Gilroy, CA 800-921-7502
Grecian Delight Foods
Elk Grove Vlg, IL 800-621-4387
Hamilton Quality Convenience Foods
Romulus, MI 734-946-1800
J&J Wholesale
Junction City, KS 785-238-4721
Kellogg Company
Hammonton, NJ 609-567-2300
Kelly Foods
Jackson, TN 731-424-2255
Kraft Canada Headquarters
Don Mills, ON 800-268-7808
Kraft Foods
Northfield, IL 800-323-0768
Lacassagne's
Metairie, LA 504-834-0900
LD Foods
Annapolis, MD 410-216-9300
Lender's Bagel Bakery
West Seneca, NY 716-668-6761
Lucks Food Decorating Company
Tacoma, WA 206-674-7200
McCain Foods Canada
Florenceville, NB 506-392-5541
McClane Distribution Center
Fredericksburg, VA 540-374-2000
Michael Foods, Inc.
Minnetonka, MN 952-258-4000
Movie Breads Food
Chateauguay, QC 450-692-7606
Naleway Foods
Winnipeg, MB 800-665-7448
Nancy's Specialty Foods
Newark, CA 510-494-1100
Natural Quick Foods
Seattle, WA 206-365-5757
Pasta USA
Spokane, WA 800-456-2084
Sunburst Foods
Goldsboro, NC 919-778-2151
Suzanna's Kitchen
Duluth, GA 800-241-2455
U.S. Foodservice
Norcross, GA 800-554-8050
US Foods
Lincoln, NE 402-470-2021

Frozen

Advance Food Company
Enid, OK 888-723-8237
Agrusa, Inc.
Leonia, NJ 201-592-5950
Al Pete Meats
Muncie, IN 765-288-8817
American Seafoods International
New Bedford, MA 800-343-8046
Applegate Farms
Bridgewater, NJ 908-725-2768
Barber Foods
Portland, ME 800-577-2595
Bernardi Italian Foods Company
Bloomsburg, PA 570-389-5500
Better Baked Foods
North East, PA. 814-725-8778
Biagio's Banquets
Chicago, IL 800-392-2837
Bocconcino Food Products
Moonachie, NJ 201-933-7474
Buxton Foods
Buxton, ND 800-726-8057
Camino Real Foods
Vernon, CA 800-421-6201
Campbell Soup Company
Camden, NJ 800-257-8443
Canada Bread
Etobicoke, ON 416-622-2040
Cedar Lake Foods
Cedar Lake, MI 800-246-5039
Cedarlane Foods
Carson, CA 800-826-3322
Chloe Foods Corporation
Brooklyn, NY 718-827-3600
Chungs Gourmet Foods
Houston, TX 713-741-2118
ConAgra Foods   Lamb Weston Plant
Richland, WA 509-375-4181

ConAgra Frozen Foods Company
Marshall, MO 660-886-3301
ConAgra Snack Foods Group/Act II Popcorn
Edina, MN. 800-328-6286
Culinary Standards Corporation
Louisville, KY 800-778-3434
Don Miguel Mexican Foods
Orange, CA. .714-634-8441
Endico Potatoes
Mt Vernon, NY 914-664-1151
English Bay Batter
Dublin, OH 614-760-9921
Fine Choice Foods
Richmond, BC. 604-522-3110
Food Source
McKinney, TX 972-548-9001
Foodbrands America
Oklahoma City, OK 405-290-4000
Forte Stromboli Company
Philadelphia, PA 215-463-6336
Gemini Food Industries
Fiskdale, MA .508-347-2800
Gilardi Foods
Sidney, OH 937-498-4511
Gilroy Foods
Gilroy, CA. 800-921-7502
Gonard Foods
Calgary, AB. .403-277-0991
H.J. Heinz Company
Pittsburgh, PA 412-237-5948
Hamilton Quality Convenience Foods
Romulus, MI .734-946-1800
Harvest Time Foods
Ayden, NC 252-746-6675
Heinz Company of Canada
North York, ON. 800-268-6641
High Liner Foods
Lunenburg, NS 902-634-9475
Hormel Foods Corporation
Austin, MN 800-523-4635
House of Raeford Farms
Raeford, NC .800-888-7539
Ice Land Corporation
Pittsburgh, PA 412-441-9512
Juno Chef's
Brooklyn, NY 718-492-1300
Kellogg Canada Inc
Mississauga, ON 888-876-3750
Kellogg Company
San Jose, CA. 408-295-8656
Kellogg Company
Hammonton, NJ 609-567-2300
Kellogg Company
Battle Creek, MI 800-962-1413
Kraft Pizza Company
Little Chute, WI 920-788-0605
Lamb-Weston
Pasco, WA. 800-766-7783
Landolfi Food Products
Trenton, NJ .609-392-1830
Lender's Bagel Bakery
West Seneca, NY 716-668-6761
Little Lady Foods
Elk Grove, IL 800-439-1440
Love & Quiches Desserts
Freeport, NY .800-525-5251
Luigino's/Michelina Brand
Duluth, MN. .800-251-7004
Macabee Foods
Moonachie, NJ 201-489-4343
Made Rite Foods
Burlington, NC 336-288-6646
Maple Leaf Farms
Milford, IN 800-384-2812
Market Fare Foods
Phoenix, AZ .800-782-9136
Marsan Foods
Toronto, ON .416-755-9262
Martin Seafood Company
Jessup, MD 410-799-5822
McCain Foods
Lodi, NJ. 800-258-1098
McCain Foods USA
Easton, ME 207-488-2561
McCain Foods USA
Othello, WA .800-541-4808
McClane Distribution Center
Fredericksburg, VA. 540-374-2000
McLane Foods
Phoenix, AZ .602-275-5509
Michael Foods, Inc.
Minnetonka, MN. 952-258-4000

Milnot Company
Litchfield, IL. 800-877-6455
Morrison Lamothe
Toronto, ON .416-291-6762
Mrs. Smith's Bakeries
Spartanburg, SC 864-503-9588
Naleway Foods
Winnipeg, MB. 800-665-7448
Nestle Canada Inc
North York, ON. 800-563-7853
Nestle Pizza
Medford, WI. 715-748-5550
Nestle' Handheld Foods Group
Englewood, CO. 800-225-2270
Nickabood's Company
Los Angeles, CA. 213-746-1541
Night Hawk Frozen Foods
Buda, TX. 800-580-4166
O Chili Frozen Foods Inc
Northbrook, IL 847-562-1991
Old Fashioned Kitchen
Lakewood, NJ. 732-364-4100
Olympic Food Products
Kokomo, IN .800-445-6923
Omstead Foods Ltd
Burlington, ON 905-315-8883
Ore-Ida Foods
Pittsburgh, PA 412-237-3450
Pasta Factory
Northlake, IL. 800-615-6951
Petrofsky's Bagels
Saint Louis, MO 314-432-4177
Pilgrim's Pride
Timberville, VA 540-896-7000
Pillsbury
Allentown, PA. 610-797-5947
Praters Foods
Lubbock, TX. 806-745-2727
Proferas Pizza Bakery
Scranton, PA. 570-342-4181
Queen International Foods
Monterey Park, CA. 800-423-4414
Ragozzino Foods
Meriden, CT .800-348-1240
Ramona's Mexican Food Products
Gardena, CA. 310-323-1950
Randy's Frozen Meats
Faribault, MN 800-354-7177
Redi-Serve Food Company
Fort Atkinson, WI. 920-563-6391
Request Foods
Holland, MI .800-748-0378
Reser's Fine Foods
Salt Lake City, UT 801-972-5633
Ruiz Food Products
Dinuba, CA. .800-477-6474
Sara Lee Food Service
Haltom City, TX 800-261-4754
Specialty Brands
Carthage, MO 417-358-8104
Specialty Brands
Ontario, CA. .800-782-1180
Steak-Umm Company
Shillington, PA 860-928-5900
Sunset Specialty Foods
Sunset Beach, CA 562-592-4976
Tami Great Food
Monsey, NY .718-788-4200
Thyme & Truffles Hors D'oeuvres
Toronto, ON .877-489-8636
Tomasso Corporation
Baie D'Urfe, QC. 514-325-3000
Turris Italian Foods
Roseville, MI 586-773-6010
Van De Kamp Frozen Foods
Erie, PA. 814-898-1500
Wawona Frozen Foods
Clovis, CA. 559-299-2901
Worthington Foods
Zanesville, OH 800-535-5644
Zartic Inc
Rome, GA 800-241-0516

Crepes

Culinary Foods
Chicago, IL 800-621-4049
Echo Lake Farm Produce Company
Burlington, WI 262-763-9551
Old Fashioned Kitchen
Lakewood, NJ. 732-364-4100
Table de France
Ontario, CA. .909-923-5205

Croquettes

Hanover Foods Corporation
Hanover, PA .717-632-6000
Heinz Company of Canada
North York, ON. 800-268-6641

French Fries

Cavendish Farms
Jamestown, ND. 888-284-5687
Cavendish Farms
Dieppe, NB. .888-883-7437
ConAgra Foods   Lamb Weston Plant
Richland, WA 509-375-4181
ConAgra Foods   Lamb Weston® Headquarters
Kennewick, WA 509-736-0456
Endico Potatoes
Mt Vernon, NY 914-664-1151
H.J. Heinz Company
Pittsburgh, PA 412-237-5948
Hanover Potato Products
Hanover, PA .717-632-0700
J.R. Simplot Company
Boise, ID 208-336-2110
J.R. Simplot Company
Grand Forks, ND. 701-746-6431
Lamb-Weston
Hermiston, OR 800-766-7783
McCain Foods
Easton, ME 207-488-2561
McCain Foods Canada
Florenceville, NB 506-392-5541
McCain Foods USA
Easton, ME 207-488-2561
McCain Foods USA
Lisle, IL. 800-258-1098
Paris Foods Corporation
Camden, NJ .856-964-0915
Qualifresh Michel St. Arneault
St. Hubert, QC. 800-565-0550
Terry Foods Inc
Idaho Falls, ID 208-604-8143
Twin City Foods
Stanwood, WA 206-515-2400
Yum Yum Potato Chips
Warwick, QC. 800-567-5792

Canned

EMERLING INTERNATIONAL FOODS, INC.

Emerling International Foods
Buffalo, NY. .716-833-7381

McCain Foods Canada
Florenceville, NB 506-392-5541

Frozen

Cavendish Farms
Laval, QC 450-973-1952

ConAgra Foods   Lamb Weston Plant
Richland, WA 509-375-4181
ConAgra Foods   Lamb Weston® Headquarters
Kennewick, WA 509-736-0456

EMERLING INTERNATIONAL FOODS, INC.

Emerling International Foods
Buffalo, NY 716-833-7381

We supply food manufacturers and food service customers worldwide (since 1988) with bulk ingredients including: Fruits & Vegetables; Juice Concentrates; Herbs & Spices; Oils & Vinegars; Flavors & Colors; Honey & Molasses. We also produce PURE MAPLE SYRUP.

Endico Potatoes
Mt Vernon, NY 914-664-1151
H.J. Heinz Company
Pittsburgh, PA 412-237-5948
J.R. Simplot Company
Grand Forks, ND. 701-746-6431
Lamb-Weston
Hermiston, OR 800-766-7783
Maple Leaf Potatoes
Lethbridge, AB 800-268-3708
McCain Foods Canada
Florenceville, NB 506-392-5541
McCain Foods Canada
Toronto, ON 800-363-8516
Ore-Ida Foods
Pittsburgh, PA 412-237-3450
Qualifresh Michel St. Arneault
St. Hubert, QC. 800-565-0550
Twin City Foods
Stanwood, WA 206-515-2400

Shoestring

EMERLING INTERNATIONAL FOODS, INC.

Emerling International Foods
Buffalo, NY. 716-833-7381

We supply food manufacturers and food service customers worldwide (since 1988) with bulk ingredients including: Fruits & Vegetables; Juice Concentrates; Herbs & Spices; Oils & Vinegars; Flavors & Colors; Honey & Molasses. We also produce PURE MAPLE SYRUP.

H.J. Heinz Company
Pittsburgh, PA 412-237-5948
Lamb-Weston
Hermiston, OR 800-766-7783
McCain Foods Canada
Florenceville, NB 506-392-5541
Ore-Ida Foods
Pittsburgh, PA 412-237-3450

Tater Tots

Cavendish Farms
Jamestown, ND 888-284-5687

French Toast

Brooks Food Group Corporate Office
Bedford, VA 800-873-4934
Continental Mills
Seattle, WA 253-872-8400
Rich-Seapak Corporation
St Simons Island, GA 800-654-9731
Tami Great Food
Monsey, NY 718-788-4200

Frozen

Bake Crafters Food
Collegedale, TN 800-296-8935
Brooks Food Group Corporate Office
Bedford, VA 800-873-4934
Continental Mills
Seattle, WA 253-872-8400
Tami Great Food
Monsey, NY 718-788-4200

Fresh

American Foodservice
Dallas, TX 972-385-5800

Frozen

American Foodservice
Dallas, TX. 972-385-5800
Bridgford Foods Corpora tion
Anaheim, CA 800-527-2105

BURKE
Always make it your best®

Burke Corporation
Nevada, IA 800-654-1152

Always make it your best® with Burke fully cooked meats. We specialize in Italian sausage, beef, and pork toppings, meatballs, taco meats, shredded meats, pepperoni, bacon, Canadian-style bacon, chicken and beef strips. Additionally, we offer a variety of specialty products: Hand-Pinched Style® brand toppings, chorizo, gyro topping, andouille sausage, and breakfast patties and links.

Charles Rockel & Son
Cincinnati, OH 513-631-3009

EMERLING INTERNATIONAL FOODS, INC.

Emerling International Foods
Buffalo, NY. 716-833-7381

We supply food manufacturers and food service customers worldwide (since 1988) with bulk ingredients including: Fruits & Vegetables; Juice Concentrates; Herbs & Spices; Oils & Vinegars; Flavors & Colors; Honey & Molasses. We also produce PURE MAPLE SYRUP.

H.J. Heinz Company
Pittsburgh, PA 800-872-2229
Old Fashioned Kitchen
Newport Beach, CA 800-833-4635

Giardiniera

A. Camacho
Plant City, FL 800-881-4534
Castella Imports
Hauppauge, NY 866-227-8355
Colonna Brothers
North Bergen, NJ 201-864-1115
Fontanini Italian Meats & Sausages
Chicago, IL 800-331-6328
Giuliano's Specialty Foods
Garden Grove, CA 714-895-9661
L&S Packing Company
Farmingdale, NY 800-286-6487
Orleans Packing Company
Hyde Park, MA 617-361-6611
Victoria Packing Corporation
Brooklyn, NY 718-649-2180

Hash

Canned & Frozen

Bunker Hill Foods
Augusta, GA 706-733-7765
Castleberry/Snow Brands
Augusta, GA 800-241-3520
Caughman's Meat Plant
Lexington, SC 803-356-0076
Hormel Foods Corporation
Austin, MN 800-523-4635
Kelly Foods
Jackson, TN 731-424-2255
Lees Sausage Company
Orangeburg, SC 803-534-5517
Ninety Six Canning Company
Ninety Six, SC 864-543-2700
SOPAKCO Foods
Mullins, SC 800-276-9678

Hush Puppies

Abbitt's
Williamston, NC 252-792-3646

Atkinson Milling Company
Selma, NC. 800-948-5707
Delta Pride Catfish
Indianola, MS 800-421-1045
Fry Krisp Food Products
Jackson, MI 517-784-8531
Lakeside Mills
Rutherfordton, NC 828-286-4866
Lone Star Consolidated Foods
Dallas, TX. 800-658-5637
Shenandoah Mills
Lebanon, TN 615-444-0841
Shiloh Foods
Savannah, TN 800-795-2550
Triton Seafood Company
Medley, FL 305-805-3500

Frozen & Mixes

Lone Star Consolidated Foods
Dallas, TX. 800-658-5637
Premier Blending
Wichita, KS 316-267-5533
Shiloh Foods
Savannah, TN 800-795-2550
Tova Industries
Louisville, KY 888-532-8682
Triton Seafood Company
Medley, FL 305-805-3500
Weisenberger Mills
Midway, KY 800-643-8678

Individual Packets

Foodservice

Baldwin Richardson Foods
Frankfort, IL 866-644-2732

Baldwin Richardson Foods is a liquid ingredient manufacturer specializing in signature sauces, dessert toppings, beverage/pancake syrups, specialty fruit fillings and condiments. Packaging capabilities range from portion control cups and pouches to standard retail and foodservice packs and include industrial drums and totes. Full service R&D and Quality groups dedicated to new product development, with in-house stability and analytical testing. Call for assistance.

Magic Seasoning Blends
Harahan, LA 800-457-2857
Portion Pac
Mason, OH 800-232-4829
Star Packaging Corporation
Atlanta, GA. 404-763-2800
Sugar Foods
Lawrenceville, GA 770-339-0184

Individual Quick Frozen Food

Applegate Farms
Bridgewater, NJ 908-725-2768
Appleton Produce Company
Weiser, ID 208-414-1102
Bandon Bay Fisheries
Bandon, OR 541-347-4454
Beef Products
North Sioux City, SD 605-217-8000
Boardman Foods
Boardman, OR 541-481-3000

Burke Corporation
Nevada, IA .800-654-1152

Always make it your best® with Burke fully cooked meats. We specialize in Italian sausage, beef, and pork toppings, meatballs, taco meats, shredded meats, pepperoni, bacon, Canadian-style bacon, chicken and beef strips. Additionally, we offer a variety of specialty products: Hand-Pinched Style® brand toppings, chorizo, gyro topping, andouille sausage, and breakfast patties and links.

Cherryfield Foods
Cherryfield, ME 207-255-8364
Cuizina Food Company
Woodinville, WA. 425-486-7000
Cut Above Foods
Carlsbad, CA. 760-931-6777
Eckert Cold Storage
Escalon, CA .209-838-4040

EMERLING INTERNATIONAL FOODS, INC.

Emerling International Foods
Buffalo, NY. .716-833-7381

We supply food manufacturers and food service customers worldwide (since 1988) with bulk ingredients including: Fruits & Vegetables; Juice Concentrates; Herbs & Spices; Oils & Vinegars; Flavors & Colors; Honey & Molasses. We also produce PURE MAPLE SYRUP.

FishKing
Bayou La Batre, AL 334-824-2118
Freezer Queen Foods
Buffalo, NY. .800-828-8383
Gay's Wild Maine Blueberries
Cherryfield, ME 978-649-3256
Guptill's Farms
Machias, ME. 207-255-8536
GYMA IQF Herbs, Garlic & Mushrooms & Vegetables
Stroudsburg, PA 888-496-2872
High Liner Foods
Lunenburg, NS 902-634-9475
Hillman Shrimp & Oyster
Dickinson, TX. 800-582-4416
Icelandic USA
Newport News, VA 757-820-4000
International Food Trade
Amherst, NS .902-667-3013
International Oceanic Enterprises of Alabama
Bayou La Batre, AL 800-816-1832
International Packers Corporation
Watertown, MA. 508-963-8214
Jasper Wyman & Son
Milbridge, ME 800-341-1758
Jasper Wyman & Son Canada
Morell, PE. 902-961-3330
LaMonica Fine Foods
Millville, NJ .856-825-8111
Leach Foods Products
Berlin, WI 920-361-1880
Lef Bleuges Marinor Incorporated
St-Felicien, QC 418-679-4577
Louisiana Packing Company
Westwego, LA. 800-666-1293
Mega Blue A Blue
Tracadie-Sheila, NB 506-358-6366
Merkel McDonald
Austin, TX. 800-356-0229
Merrill's Blueberry Farms
Ellsworth, ME. 800-711-6551
Mon Cuisine
Flushing, NY. 877-666-8348
Mr. Dell Foods
Kearney, MO. 816-628-4644
My Grandma's of New England®
Hyde Park, MA 800-847-2636
Nature Quality
San Martin, CA 408-683-2182
Nestle
Cleveland, OH 440-349-5757

New West Foods
San Francisco, CA 701-947-2505
NorSun Food Group
West Chester, OH 800-886-4326
Northern Michigan Fruit Company
Omena, MI 231-386-5142
Ore-Cal Corporation
Los Angeles, CA. 800-827-7474
Pilgrim's Pride
Timberville, VA 540-896-7000
Rain Sweet
Salem, OR. 800-363-4293
Randag & Associates Inc
Elmhurst, IL .630-530-2830
Sea Snack Foods
Los Angeles, CA. 213-622-2204
Stahlbush Island Farms
Corvallis, OR 541-753-8942
Sun Harvest Foods
San Diego, CA 619-690-1128
Sun-Glo of Idaho
Sugar City, ID 208-356-7346
Supermarket Productions
San Rafael, CA 415-479-0211
Sure Fresh Produce
Santa Maria, CA 888-423-5379
Unique Ingredients
Naches, WA. .509-653-1991
Washington Rhubarb Growers Association
Sumner, WA .800-435-9911
Winder Dairy
West Valley, UT 800-946-3371

Knishes

Chloe Foods Corporation
Brooklyn, NY 718-827-3600
Gabilas Knishes
Brooklyn, NY 718-387-0750
Miller's Stratford Provision Company
Southport, CT 203-375-1598
Oceanside Knish Factory
Oceanside, NY 516-766-4445

Meat Balls

Aristocrat International Corporation
Secaucus, NJ. 201-866-1900
Armanino Foods of Distinction
Hayward, CA 510-441-9300
Buona Vita
Bridgeton, NJ 856-453-7972
Capitol Wholesale MeatsCCompany
Mc Cook, IL .800-331-6328
Carando Gourmet Frozen Foods
Springfield, MA 413-730-4205
Casa Di Bertacchi
Vineland, NJ .800-818-9261
Cordon Bleu International
Anjou, QC. 514-352-3000
Devault Foods
Devault, PA. .800-426-2874
Fontanini Italian Meats & Sausages
Chicago, IL 800-331-6328
G Di Lullo & Sons
Westville, NJ .856-456-3700
King's Command Foods
Kent, WA. 800-247-3138
Maid-Rite Steak Company
Dunmore, PA. 800-233-4259
Marcho Farms Veal
Harleysville, PA 215-721-7131
Oh Boy! Corporation
San Fernando, CA. 818-361-1128
Quality Sausage Company
Dallas, TX. 214-634-3400
Redi-Serve Food Company
Fort Atkinson, WI. 920-563-6391
Specialty Brands
Carthage, MO 417-358-8104
Tupman-Thurlow Company
Deerfield Beach, FL 954-596-9989
Tyson Foods Plant
Santa Teresa, NM 800-351-8184

Canned

Acme Steak & Seafood Company
Youngstown, OH. 330-270-8000
Campbell Soup Company
Camden, NJ. .800-257-8443
Cordon Bleu International
Anjou, QC. 514-352-3000

Italian Foods Manufacturing
Vestal, NY. 800-962-7700
Leone Provision Company
Cape Coral, FL 941-574-3355
O Chili Frozen Foods Inc
Northbrook, IL 847-562-1991
On-Cor Foods Products
Northbrook, IL 847-205-1040
Specialty Brands
Carthage, MO 417-358-8104

Frozen

Aristocrat International Corporation
Secaucus, NJ. 201-866-1900

Burke Corporation
Nevada, IA .800-654-1152

Always make it your best® with Burke fully cooked meats. We specialize in Italian sausage, beef, and pork toppings, meatballs, taco meats, shredded meats, pepperoni, bacon, Canadian-style bacon, chicken and beef strips. Additionally, we offer a variety of specialty products: Hand-Pinched Style® brand toppings, chorizo, gyro topping, andouille sausage, and breakfast patties and links.

Carando Gourmet Frozen Foods
Springfield, MA 413-730-4205
Carolina Turkeys
Mt Olive, NC 800-523-4559
Casa Di Bertacchi
Vineland, NJ .800-818-9261
Devault Foods
Devault, PA. .800-426-2874
Lucy's Foods
Latrobe, PA .724-539-1430
Maid-Rite Steak Company
Dunmore, PA. 800-233-4259
On-Cor Foods Products
Northbrook, IL 847-205-1040
Redi-Serve Food Company
Fort Atkinson, WI. 920-563-6391
Specialty Brands
Carthage, MO 417-358-8104
Turris Italian Foods
Roseville, MI 586-773-6010
West Liberty Foods
West Liberty, IA 888-511-4500
Windsor Frozen Foods
Houston, TX .800-437-6936

Swedish

Burke Corporation
Nevada, IA .800-654-1152

Always make it your best® with Burke fully cooked meats. We specialize in Italian sausage, beef, and pork toppings, meatballs, taco meats, shredded meats, pepperoni, bacon, Canadian-style bacon, chicken and beef strips. Additionally, we offer a variety of specialty products: Hand-Pinched Style® brand toppings, chorizo, gyro topping, andouille sausage, and breakfast patties and links.

Rose Packing Company
South Barrington, IL. 800-323-7363

Meat Loaf

Buona Vita
Bridgeton, NJ 856-453-7972
Burnett & Son Meat Company
Monrovia, CA 626-357-2165

Capitol Wholesale MeatsCCompany
Mc Cook, IL 800-331-6328
Corfu Foods
Bensenville, IL 630-595-2510
Fontanini Italian Meats & Sausages
Chicago, IL 800-331-6328
King's Command Foods
Kent, WA 800-247-3138
Marcho Farms Veal
Harleysville, PA 215-721-7131
Mitchell Foods
Barbourville, KY 888-202-9745
Ryley Sausage
Ryley, AB 780-663-3990
Rymer Foods
Chicago, IL 800-247-9637
Sandridge Food Corporation
Medina, OH. 330-725-2348
Sunset Farm Foods
Valdosta, GA 800-882-1121

Onion Rings

Agri-Pack
Pasco, WA 509-545-6181
Brooks Food Group Corporate Office
Bedford, VA 800-873-4934
Great American Appetizers
Nampa, ID. 800-282-4834
Matador Processors
Blanchard, OK 800-847-0797
McCain Foods
Fort Atkinson, WI. 920-563-6625
McCain Foods USA
Grand Island, NE 308-382-7770
Olympic Food Products
Kokomo, IN 800-445-6923
Oxford Frozen Foods Limited
Oxford, NS 902-447-2100
Westin
Omaha, NE 800-228-6098
Yum Yum Potato Chips
Warwick, QC. 800-567-5792

Frozen

Brooks Food Group Corporate Office
Bedford, VA 800-873-4934

EMERLING INTERNATIONAL FOODS, INC.

Emerling International Foods
Buffalo, NY. 716-833-7381

We supply food manufacturers and food service
customers worldwide (since 1988) with bulk ingredients including: Fruits & Vegetables; Juice
Concentrates; Herbs & Spices; Oils & Vinegars;
Flavors & Colors; Honey & Molasses. We also
produce PURE MAPLE SYRUP.

Fry Foods
Tiffin, OH 800-626-2294
Great American Appetizers
Nampa, ID. 800-282-4834
H.J. Heinz Company
Pittsburgh, PA. 412-237-5948
Matador Processors
Blanchard, OK 800-847-0797
McCain Foods
Fort Atkinson, WI. 920-563-6625
Olympic Food Products
Kokomo, IN 800-445-6923
Oxford Frozen Foods Limited
Oxford, NS 902-447-2100
Westin
Omaha, NE 800-228-6098

Pancakes

ConAgra Snack Foods Group/Act II Popcorn
Edina, MN. 800-328-6286
Continental Mills
Seattle, WA 253-872-8400
Cook-In-The-Kitchen
White River Junction, VT. 802-333-4141
Flapjacks
Santa Barbara, CA 805-964-4743
Old Fashioned Kitchen
Lakewood, NJ 732-364-4100
Pamela's Products
Ukiah, CA 707-462-6605

Pillsbury
Allentown, PA. 610-797-5947
Red Rose Trading Company
Wrightsville, PA 717-252-5500
Ungars Food Products
Elmwood Park, NJ 201-703-1300
Wagner Excello Food Products
Broadview, IL 708-338-4488

Frozen

Adm Edible Bean Specialties
Kinde, MI 989-874-4720
Bake Crafters Food
Collegedale, TN 800-296-8935
ConAgra Snack Foods Group/Act II Popcorn
Edina, MN. 800-328-6286
Continental Mills
Seattle, WA 253-872-8400
Crosby Molasses Company
St. John, NB 506-634-7515
Old Fashioned Kitchen
Lakewood, NJ 732-364-4100
Pillsbury
Allentown, PA. 610-797-5947
Tami Great Food
Monsey, NY 718-788-4200
Thomas Brothers Ham Company
Asheboro, NC 336-672-0337

Refrigerated

Echo Lake Farm Produce Company
Burlington, WI. 262-763-9551
Sara Lee Food Service
Haltom City, TX 800-261-4754

with Fruit

Continental Mills
Seattle, WA 253-872-8400

Pierogies

Aristocrat International Corporation
Secaucus, NJ 201-866-1900
Aunt Kathy's Homestyle Products
Waldheim, SK 306-945-2181
Babci's Specialty Foods
Holyoke, MA 800-225-2023
Brom Food Group
St. Laurent, QC 514-744-5152
Giorgio Foods
Temple, PA 800-220-2139
Heritage Foods
Edmonton, AB 780-454-7383
Millie's Pierogi
Chicopee Falls, MA 800-743-7641
Mrs. T's Pierogies
Shenandoah, PA 800-233-3170
Naleway Foods
Winnipeg, MB. 800-665-7448
Old Fashioned Kitchen
Lakewood, NJ 732-364-4100
Old Fashioned Kitchen
Newport Beach, CA 800-833-4635
Pierogi Place
Mears, MI 231- 87-3 53

Pizelle

Del Monte Foods
San Francisco, CA 800-543-3090

Pizza & Pizza Products

Al Safa Halal
Niagara Falls, NY 800-268-8174
Amberwave Foods
Oakmont, PA 412-828-3040
Andre-Boudin Bakeries
San Francisco, CA 415-882-1849
Armour
Omaha, NE 402-453-3766
Artel
Boisbriand, QC 450-433-1322
Avanti Food Company
Walnut, IL 800-243-3739
Baja Foods
Chicago, IL 773-376-9030
BBU Bakeries
Denver, CO 303-691-6342
Bertucci's
Northborough, MA 508-351-2500

Better Baked Foods
North East, PA. 814-725-8778
Biagio's Banquets
Chicago, IL 800-392-2837
Blue Planet Foods, Inc.
Collegedale, TN 877-396-3145
Bocconcino Food Products
Moonachie, NJ 201-933-7474
Brownie Products Company
Gardner, IL 815-237-2163

BURKE
Always make it your best®

Burke Corporation
Nevada, IA 800-654-1152

Always make it your best® with Burke fully
cooked meats. We specialize in Italian sausage,
beef, and pork toppings, meatballs, taco meats,
shredded meats, pepperoni, bacon, Canadian-style bacon, chicken and beef strips. Additionally, we offer a variety of specialty products:
Hand-Pinched Style® brand toppings, chorizo,
gyro topping, andouille sausage, and breakfast
patties and links.

California Blending Corpany
El Monte, CA 626-448-1918
Calise & Sons Bakery
Lincoln, RI 800-225-4737
Canada Bread
Etobicoke, ON 416-622-2040
Capri Bagel & Pizza Corporation
Brooklyn, NY 718-497-4431
Chelsea Milling Company
Chelsea, MI 734-475-1361
Chr Hansen
Elyria, OH 800-558-0802
Continental Food Products
Flushing, NY. 718-358-7894
Del Grosso Foods
Tipton, PA 800-521-5880
Del Monte Foods
San Francisco, CA 800-543-3090
Dorothy Dawson Foods Products
Jackson, MI. 517-788-9830
Entenmann's-Oroweat/BestFoods
S San Francisco, CA 650-875-3100
F&A Cheese Corporation
Irvine, CA 800-634-4109
Foodbrands America
Oklahoma City, OK 405-290-4000
Fresh Mark
Canton, OH 800-860-6777
Frozen Specialties
Archbold, OH 419-445-9015
Furmano Foods
Northumberland, PA 877-877-6032
George Weston Bakeries
Bay Shore, NY 800-356-3314
Gold Standard Baking
Chicago, IL 800-648-7904
H.J. Heinz Company
Pittsburgh, PA. 412-237-5948
Hamilton Quality Convenience Foods
Romulus, MI 734-946-1800
Harbar Corporation
Canton, MA 800-881-7040

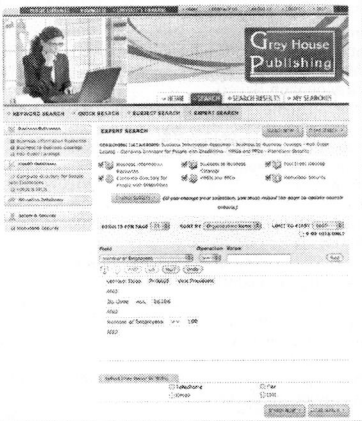
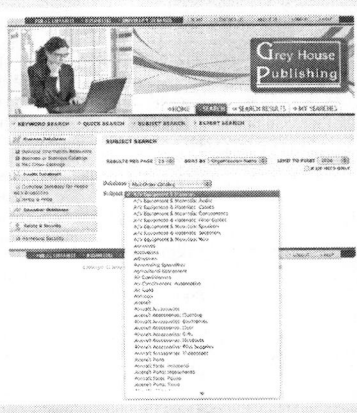

Heinz Company of Canada
North York, ON. 800-268-6641
Heinz North America
Fort Myers, FL 239-694-3663
Home Run Inn Frozen Foods
Woodridge, IL 800-636-9696
I & K Distributors
Delphos, OH 800-869-6337
Ice Land Corporation
Pittsburgh, PA 412-441-9512
Indian Foods Company
Minneapolis, MN 763-593-3000
Italian Baking Company
Youngstown, OH. 330-782-1358
Kamish Food Products
Chicago, IL .773-267-0400
Kosto Food Products Company
Wauconda, IL 847-487-2600
Kraft Pizza Company
Little Chute, WI 920-788-0605
L&S Packing Company
Farmingdale, NY 800-286-6487
Lamb-Weston
Weston, OR. 800-766-7783
Lamonaca Bakery
Windber, PA 814-467-4909
Leprino Foods Company
Denver, CO. 800-537-7466
Little Lady Foods
Elk Grove, IL 800-439-1440
Livermore Falls Baking Company
Livermore Falls, ME. 207-897-3442
Longo's Bakery
Hazleton, PA 570-454-5825
Luigino's
Duluth, MN 218-727-2059
Luigino's/Michelina Brand
Duluth, MN 800-251-7004
Magic Seasoning Blends
Harahan, LA 800-457-2857
Mama Amy's Quality Foods
Mississauga, ON 905-456-0056
Matlaw's Food Products
West Haven, CT 800-934-8266
McCain Foods
Lodi, NJ 800-258-1098
McCain Foods Canada
Florenceville, NB 506-392-5541
McClane Distribution Center
Fredericksburg, VA. 540-374-2000
Molinaro's Fine Italian Foods
Mississauga, ON 800-268-4959
Nardone Brothers Baking Pizza Company
Hanover Twp, PA 800-822-5320
Nation Pizza Products
Schaumburg, IL. 847-397-3320
Nationwide Canning
Cottam, ON 519-839-4831
Nestle Pizza
Medford, WI 715-748-5550
Northwestern Foods
St Paul, MN. 800-236-4937
O Chili Frozen Foods Inc
Northbrook, IL 847-562-1991
O'Neal's Fresh Frozen Pizza Crust
Springfield, OH. 937-323-0050
Ore-Ida Foods
Pittsburgh, PA 412-237-3450
Oroweat Baking Company
Montebello, CA 323-721-5161
Palmieri Food Products
New Haven, CT 800-845-5447
Pecoraro Dairy Products
Rome, NY. .315-339-0101
Penn Valley Farms
Gainesville, GA 773-685-9929
Piqua Pizza Supply Company
Piqua, OH .800-521-4442
Pizzas of Eight
St Louis, MO. 800-422-2901
Proferas Pizza Bakery
Scranton, PA 570-342-4181
Quality Sausage Company
Dallas, TX .214-634-3400
Red Gold
Elwood, IN 877-748-9798
Rosina Food Products
Buffalo, NY. 888-767-4621
Salvatore's Pizza Shells
Utica, NY .315-735-7919
Schwartz Meat Company
Sophia, WV 304-683-4595

Stella Baking Company
Rockford, IL 815-398-5191
Sterling Foods
San Antonio, TX 210-490-1669
Sunset Farm Foods
Valdosta, GA 800-882-1121
Supreme Dairy Farms Company
Warwick, RI 401-739-8180
Swiss-American Sausage Company
Lathrop, CA 209-858-5555
Teeny Foods Corporation
Portland, OR. 503-252-3006
Teti Bakery
Etobicoke, ON 800-465-0123
Tip Top Canning Company
Tipp City, OH 937-667-3713
TNT Crust
Green Bay, WI. 920-431-7240
Tomanetti Food Products
Oakmont, PA 800-875-3040
Tomaro's Bakery
Clarksburg, WV 304-622-0691
Triple K Manufacturing Company
Shenandoah, IA. 888-987-2824
Tyson Prepared Foods
Fort Worth, TX 817-258-2400
Valdez Food
Philadelphia, PA 215-634-6106
Violet Packing
Williamstown, NJ 856-629-7428
Wanda's Nature Farm
Lincoln, NE 402-423-1234
Weisenberger Mills
Midway, KY 800-643-8678
Welcome Dairy
Colby, WI .800-472-2315
Worthmore Food Product
Cincinnati, OH 513-559-1473

Pizza

Amy's Kitchen
Petaluma, CA 707-578-5908
Andre-Boudin Bakeries
San Francisco, CA 415-882-1849
Art's Tamales
Metamora, IL 309-367-2850
Atlanta Bread Company International, Inc.
Smyrna, GA 800-398-3728
Aunt Kathy's Homestyle Products
Waldheim, SK 306-945-2181
Berkshire Mountain Bakery
Housatonic, MA 866-274-6124
Biagio's Banquets
Chicago, IL 800-392-2837
Bocconcino Food Products
Moonachie, NJ 201-933-7474
Cafe Moak
Rockford, MI 800-757-8776
Cedarlane Foods
Carson, CA 800-826-3322
Chelsea Milling Company
Chelsea, MI. 734-475-1361
Chicago Pizza & Brewery
Huntington Beach, CA 714-848-3747
Colors Gourmet Pizza
Carlsbad, CA. 760-431-2203
Continental Food Products
Flushing, NY. 718-358-7894
Dorothy Dawson Foods Products
Jackson, MI. 517-788-9830
European Egg Noodle Manufacturing
Edmonton, AB 780-453-6767
Frozen Specialties
Archbold, OH 419-445-9015
George Weston Bakeries
Bay Shore, NY 800-356-3314
Gilardi Foods
Sidney, OH 937-498-4511
Ice Land Corporation
Pittsburgh, PA 412-441-9512
Italian Baking Company
Youngstown, OH. 330-782-1358
Jimm's Pizza
Racine, WI 262-634-2164
Joe Corbis' Wholesale Pizza
Baltimore, MD 888-526-7247
Kraft Pizza & Foodservice
Medford, WI 800-323-0768
Lamb-Weston
Pasco, WA 800-766-7783

Lucia's Pizza Company
St Louis, MO. 314-843-2553
Macabee Foods
Moonachie, NJ 201-489-4343
McCain Foods Canada
Florenceville, NB 506-392-5541
McCain Foods Canada
Toronto, ON 800-363-8516
McClane Distribution Center
Fredericksburg, VA. 540-374-2000
Molinaro's Fine Italian Foods
Mississauga, ON 800-268-4959
Mozzicato De Pasquale Bakery Pastry
Hartford, CT 860-296-0426
Nardone Brothers Baking Pizza Company
Hanover Twp, PA 800-822-5320
Nestle Pizza
Medford, WI 715-748-5550
New York Pizza
Daytona Beach, FL 386-257-2050
Oh Boy! Corporation
San Fernando, CA 818-361-1128
Proferas Pizza Bakery
Scranton, PA 570-342-4181
Randy's Frozen Meats
Faribault, MN 800-354-7177
Sunset Specialty Foods
Sunset Beach, CA 562-592-4976
Superbrand Dairies
Montgomery, AL. 334-277-6010
Teeny Foods Corporation
Portland, OR. 503-252-3006
Teti Bakery
Etobicoke, ON 800-465-0123
Wholesale Pizza Company
Nashville, TN 615-242-1655

Cheese

Amberwave Foods
Oakmont, PA 412-828-3040
Avanti Food Company
Walnut, IL 800-243-3739
F&A Cheese Corporation
Irvine, CA .800-634-4109
Jimm's Pizza
Racine, WI 262-634-2164
Leprino Foods Company
Denver, CO. 800-537-7466
Pecoraro Dairy Products
Rome, NY. 315-339-0101
Schwartz Meat Company
Sophia, WV 304-683-4595
Sun-Re Cheese
Sunbury, PA. 570-286-1511

Crust

Amberwave Foods
Oakmont, PA 412-828-3040
Baker & Baker, Inc.
Schaumburg, IL. 800-593-5777
Berkshire Mountain Bakery
Housatonic, MA 866-274-6124
Boboli International Inc
Stockton, CA. 209-473-3507
Brownie Products Company
Gardner, IL 815-237-2163
Calise & Sons Bakery
Lincoln, RI 800-225-4737
Chelsea Milling Company
Chelsea, MI. 734-475-1361
Colors Gourmet Pizza
Carlsbad, CA. 760-431-2203
Dorothy Dawson Foods Products
Jackson, MI. 517-788-9830
Flamin' Red's Woodfired
Pawlet, VT 802-325-3641
Goglanian Bakeries
Santa Ana, CA 714-444-3500
H.J. Heinz Company
Pittsburgh, PA 412-237-5948
Kraft Foods
East Hanover, NJ 973-503-2000
Livermore Falls Baking Company
Livermore Falls, ME. 207-897-3442
Lone Star Bakery
Round Rock, TX 512-255-3629
Molinaro's Fine Italian Foods
Mississauga, ON 800-268-4959
Northwestern Foods
St Paul, MN. 800-236-4937

Pacific Ocean Produce
Santa Cruz, CA 831-423-2654
Pascucci Family Pasta
San Diego, CA 619-285-8000
Piqua Pizza Supply Company
Piqua, OH 800-521-4442
Teeny Foods Corporation
Portland, OR 503-252-3006
Teti Bakery
Etobicoke, ON 800-465-0123
TNT Crust
Green Bay, WI. 920-431-7240
Tomaro's Bakery
Clarksburg, WV 304-622-0691

Frozen

Aristocrat International Corporation
Secaucus, NJ 201-866-1900
Badger Best Pizzas
Green Bay, WI. 920-336-6464
Better Baked Foods
North East, PA. 814-725-8778
Biagio's Banquets
Chicago, IL 800-392-2837
Bocconcino Food Products
Moonachie, NJ 201-933-7474
Calise & Sons Bakery
Lincoln, RI 800-225-4737
Cedarlane Foods
Carson, CA 800-826-3322
Chelsea Milling Company
Chelsea, MI. 734-475-1361
Continental Food Products
Flushing, NY 718-358-7894
Gilardi Foods
Sidney, OH 937-498-4511
H.J. Heinz Company
Pittsburgh, PA 412-237-5948
Hamilton Quality Convenience Foods
Romulus, MI 734-946-1800
I & K Distributors
Delphos, OH 800-869-6337
Ice Land Corporation
Pittsburgh, PA 412-441-9512
Iltaco Food Products
Chicago, IL 800-244-8935
Lucca Foods
Sparks, NV 775-356-8611
Lucia's Pizza Company
St Louis, MO. 314-843-2553
Macabee Foods
Moonachie, NJ 201-489-4343
McCain Foods
Lodi, NJ. 800-258-1098
Molinaro's Fine Italian Foods
Mississauga, ON 800-268-4959
Nestle Pizza
Medford, WI 715-748-5550
Oh Boy Corporation
San Fernando, CA. 818-361-1128
Pride of Italy
Kenosha, WI 262-634-2164
Proferas Pizza Bakery
Scranton, PA 570-342-4181
Randy's Frozen Meats
Faribault, MN 800-354-7177
Schwan's Sales Enterprises
Marshall, MN 800-533-5290

Schwartz Meat Company
Sophia, WV 304-683-4595
Sunset Specialty Foods
Sunset Beach, CA 562-592-4976
Superbrand Dairies
Montgomery, AL. 334-277-6010

Pizza Bagels

Heinz North America
Fort Myers, FL 239-694-3663

Pizza Toppings

Armour
Omaha, NE 402-453-3766
Avanti Food Company
Walnut, IL 800-243-3739
Baja Foods
Chicago, IL 773-376-9030
Buona Vita
Bridgeton, NJ 856-453-7972

Always make it your best®

Burke Corporation
Nevada, IA 800-654-1152

Always make it your best® with Burke fully
cooked meats. We specialize in Italian sausage,
beef, and pork toppings, meatballs, taco meats,
shredded meats, pepperoni, bacon, Canadian-style bacon, chicken and beef strips. Additionally, we offer a variety of specialty products:
Hand-Pinched Style® brand toppings, chorizo,
gyro topping, andouille sausage, and breakfast
patties and links.

Fontanini Italian Meats & Sausages
Chicago, IL 800-331-6328
Fresh Mark
Canton, OH 800-860-6777
Moody Dunbar
Johnson City, TN 800-251-8202
O Chili Frozen Foods Inc
Northbrook, IL 847-562-1991
Patrick Cudahy
Cudahy, WI 800-486-6900
Penn Valley Farms
Gainesville, GA 773-685-9929
Quality Sausage Company
Dallas, TX. 214-634-3400
Schwartz Meat Company
Sophia, WV 304-683-4595
Swiss-American Sausage Company
Lathrop, CA 209-858-5555
Tyson Prepared Foods
Fort Worth, TX 817-258-2400

Shells

Bowness Bakery
Calgary, AB. 403-250-9760
Lamonaca Bakery
Windber, PA 814-467-4909

Livermore Falls Baking Company
Livermore Falls, ME. 207-897-3442
Longo's Bakery
Hazleton, PA 570-454-5825
Proferas Pizza Bakery
Scranton, PA 570-342-4181
Stella Baking Company
Rockford, IL 815-398-5191

Frozen

Proferas Pizza Bakery
Scranton, PA 570-342-4181

Pork & Beans (see also Baked Beans)

ConAgra Grocery Products
Irvine, CA 714-680-1000
International Home Foods
Milton, PA. 973-359-9920
Morgan Food
Austin, IN 888-430-1780

Canned

Allen Canning Company
Siloam Springs, AR 800-234-2553
Bush Brothers & Company
Augusta, WI 715-286-2211
Dankworth Packing Company
Ballinger, TX 325-365-3552
Grandma Brown's Beans Inc
Mexico, NY. 315-963-7221
International Home Foods
Milton, PA. 973-359-9920

Porkskins

Fried

Cajun

Bruno's Cajun Foods & Snacks
Slidell, LA. 985-726-0544

Portion Contol & Packaged Foods

A to Z Portion Meats
Bluffton, OH. 800-338-6328
Acme Steak & Seafood Company
Youngstown, OH. 330-270-8000
Advance Food Company
Enid, OK. 888-723-8237
Al Pete Meats
Muncie, IN 765-288-8817
AlpineAire Foods
Rocklin, CA 800-322-6325
Arizona Sunland Foods
Tucson, AZ 520-624-7068
ASC Seafood
Largo, FL 800-876-3474
Associated Brands, Inc.
Medina, NY. 800-265-0050

Baldwin Richardson Foods
Frankfort, IL 866-644-2732

Baldwin Richardson Foods is a liquid ingredient manufacturer specializing in signature sauces, dessert toppings, beverage/pancake syrups, specialty fruit fillings and condiments. Packaging capabilities range from portion control cups and pouches to standard retail and foodservice packs and include industrial drums and totes. Full service R&D and Quality groups dedicated to new product development, with in-house stability and analytical testing. Call for assistance.

Beaver Meadow Creamery
Du Bois, PA 800-262-3711
Black Diamond Cheese
Toronto, ON .800-263-2858
Blue Ribbon Meats
Miami, FL 800-522-6115
Bouma Meats
Provost, AB 780-753-2092
Broadleaf Venison USA
Vernon, CA 800-336-3844
Bruno Specialty Foods
West Sayville, NY 631-589-1700
Bruno's Cajun Foods & Snacks
Slidell, LA 985-726-0544
Bruss Company
Chicago, IL 800-621-3882
Bush Brothers Provision Company
West Palm Beach, FL 800-327-1345
C&S Wholesale Meat Company
Atlanta, GA 404-627-3547
Cal-Tex Citrus Juice
Houston, TX 800-231-0133
Cambridge Packing Company
Boston, MA 800-722-6726
Canal Fulton Provision
Canal Fulton, OH 800-321-3502
Cardinal Meat Specialists
Mississauga, ON 800-363-1439
Carl Streit & Son Company
Neptune, NJ 732-775-0803
Cloverdale Foods Company
Mandan, ND 800-669-9511
Cloverland Dairy
Saint Clairsville, OH 740-699-0509
Coldwater Seafood Corporation
Norwalk, CT 203-846-8897
Colonial Beef Company
Philadelphia, PA 215-289-7042
Compact Industries
St Charles, IL .800-513-4262
Country Pure Foods
Akron, OH 330-753-2293
Country Pure Foods
Akron, OH 877-995-8423
Cuizina Food Company
Woodinville, WA 425-486-7000
Danish Baking Company
Van Nuys, CA .800-777-4970
Darisweet Farms
Mountlake Terrace, WA 425-771-5007
Devault Foods
Devault, PA 800-426-2874
Dynamic Foods
Lubbock, TX 806-762-0780
Elkhart Locker Plant
Elkhart, KS 620-697-4424
Elwood International
Copiague, NY .631-842-6600
Fancy Farms Popcorn
Bernie, MO 800-833-8154
Flint Hills Foods
Wamego, KS 785-765-3396
Glenmark Food Processors
Chicago, IL 800-621-0117
Golden State Foods
City of Industry, CA 626-968-6431
Golden State Foods
Irvine, CA 949-252-2000
Good Old Days Foods
Little Rock, AR 501-565-1257

Gregory Packaging
Newark, NJ 973-465-1113
H. Shenson International Export
San Francisco, CA 415-318-7000
H.J. Heinz Company
Pittsburgh, PA 412-237-5948
Heinz Company of Canada
North York, ON 800-268-6641
Henry J Meat Specialties
Chicago, IL 800-242-1314
Hoekstra Meat Company
Kalamazoo, MI 616-321-0797
Holten Meats
Sauget, IL 800-851-4684
Instantwhip: Arizona
Phoenix, AZ 800-544-9447
International Packers Corporation
Watertown, MA 508-963-8214
Iowa Quality Meats
Clive, IA 800-677-6868
Italia Foods
Schaumburg, IL 800-747-1109
Jemm Wholesale Meat Company
Chicago, IL 773-523-8161
John Garner Meats
Van Buren, AR 800-543-5473
Kenosha Beef International
Kenosha, WI .800-541-1685
Kessler's, Inc
Lemoyne, PA .800-382-1328
King Kold Meats
Englewood, OH 800-836-2797
King's Command Foods
Kent, WA 800-247-3138
Knouse Foods
Peach Glen, PA 717-677-8181
Koch Foods
Park Ridge, IL 800-837-2778
Kraft Foods
Avon, NY 585-226-4400
Kutik's Honey Farm
Norwich, NY .607-336-4105
Kutztown Bologna Company
Leola, PA 800-723-8824
L&L Packing Company
Chicago, IL 800-628-6328
Lamb-Weston
Pasco, WA 800-766-7783
Land O'Frost
Searcy, AR 800-643-5654
Leahy Orchards
Franklin, QC .450-827-2544
Litehouse
Sandpoint, ID 208-263-2030
Love & Quiches Desserts
Freeport, NY .800-525-5251
Lynch Foods
North York, QC 416-449-5464
Maid-Rite Steak Company
Dunmore, PA .800-233-4259
Marcho Farms Veal
Harleysville, PA 215-721-7131
Mardale Specialty Foods
Waukegan, IL .847-336-4777
Maxim's Import Corporation
Miami, FL 800-331-6652
McCain Foods Canada
Florenceville, NB 506-392-5541
Meat-O-Mat Corporation
Brooklyn, NY .718-965-7250
Menu Meats
Huntertown, IN 800-848-2902
Miami Beef Company
Hialeah, FL 305-621-3252
Mosey's Inc
Bloomfield, CT 860-243-1725
National Foods
Indianapolis, IN 800-683-6565
Nestle
Cleveland, OH 440-349-5757
New Generation Foods
Omaha, NE 402-733-5755
North Side Foods Corporation
Arnold, PA 800-486-2201
O Chili Frozen Foods Inc
Northbrook, IL 847-562-1991
Ocean Beauty Seafoods
Seattle, WA 206-285-6800
Okuhara Foods
Honolulu, HI .808-848-0581
Omaha Steaks International
Omaha, NE 800-562-0500

Ossian Seafood Meats
Ossian, IN 260-622-4191
Ottman Meat Company
New York, NY 212-879-4160
Otto & Son
West Jordan, UT 800-453-9462
Otto W Liebold & Company
Flint, MI 800-999-6328
Pacific Poultry Company
Honolulu, HI .808-841-2828
Paris Frozen Foods
Hillsboro, IL .217-532-3822
Pascucci Family Pasta
San Diego, CA 619-285-8000
Peggy Lawton Kitchens
East Walpole, MA 800-843-7325
Pierceton Foods
Pierceton, IN .574-594-2344
Pierre Foods
Cincinnati, OH 513-874-8741
Pilgrim's Pride
Timberville, VA 540-896-7000
Pillsbury
Allentown, PA 610-797-5947
Plymouth Beef
New York, NY 718-589-8600
Pokanoket Ostrich Farm
South Dartmouth, MA 508-992-6188
Portion Pac
Mason, OH 800-232-4829
Preferred Meal Systems
Scranton, PA .570-457-8311
Premier Meats
Calgary, AB 403-287-3550
Prime Ostrich International
Morinville, AB 800-340-2311
Quality Croutons
Chicago, IL 800-334-2796
Quality Meats & Seafood
West Fargo, ND 800-342-4250
Quality Naturally! Foods
City of Industry, CA 888-498-6986
Randy's Frozen Meats
Faribault, MN 800-354-7177
Ready Portion Meat Company
Baton Rouge, LA 225-355-5641
Redi-Serve Food Company
Fort Atkinson, WI 920-563-6391
Rego's Purity Foods
Honolulu, HI .808-947-9005
Russer Foods
Buffalo, NY 800-828-7021
Saletts
Randolph, MA 781-961-9900
Saunders Provision Company
Norfolk, VA 800-486-5611
Savannah Foods Industrial
Port Wentworth, GA 912-964-1361
Schneider's Dairy Holdings Inc
Pittsburgh, PA 412-881-3525
Serv-Rite Meat Company
Los Angeles, CA 323-227-1911
Skylark Meats
Omaha, NE 800-759-5275
Smith Packing Regional Meat
Utica, NY 315-732-5125
Somerset Industries
Spring House, PA 800-883-8728
Sona & Hollen Foods
Los Alamitos, CA 800-200-7662
Southeastern Meat Association
Oviedo, FL 407-365-5661
Spilke's Baking Company
Brooklyn, NY .718-384-2150
Stampede Meat
Bridgeview, IL 800-353-0933
Stickney & Poor Company
North Andover, MA 508-261-8967
Sugar Foods
Lawrenceville, GA 770-339-0184
Swiss Colony
Monroe, WI 608-328-8400
Taku Smokehouse
Juneau, AK 800-582-5122
Temptee Specialty Foods
Denver, CO 800-842-1233
Tiller Foods Company
Dayton, OH 937-435-4601
Travis Meats
Powell, TN 800-247-7606
Trident Seafoods Corporation
Salem, NH 603-893-3368

Triple U Enterprises
Fort Pierre, SD 605-567-3624
Tyson Foods
Springdale, AR 800-643-3410
Ultra Seal
New Paltz, NY 845-255-2496
United Meat Company
San Francisco, CA 415-864-2118
United Provision Meat Company
Columbus, OH 614-252-1126
Valley Meat Company
Modesto, CA .800-222-6328
Waco Beef & Pork Processors
Waco, TX 254-772-4669
Wawona Frozen Foods
Clovis, CA 559-299-2901
Wayne Farms, LLC
Pendergrass, GA 706-693-2271
Wing Nien Company
Hayward, CA .510-487-8877
Wing's Food Products
Toronto, ON .416-259-2662
Wolverine Packing
Detroit, MI 313-392-9403
Yarbrough Produce Company
Birmingham, AL 205-323-8651

Pot Pies

Cedarlane Foods
Carson, CA 800-826-3322
Morrison Lamothe
Toronto, ON .416-291-6762
Real Food Marketing
Kansas City, MO 816-221-4100
Stacey's Famous Foods
Hayden, ID 800-782-2395
Twin Hens
Princeton, NJ 908-281-9911

Pot Stickers

Chang Food Company
Garden Grove, CA 714-265-9990
Golden Gate Foods
Dallas, TX 214-747-2223
Harvest Food Products Company
Concord, CA .925-676-8208
Health is Wealth Foods
Williamstown, NJ 856-728-1998
Kubla Khan Food Company
Portland, OR .503-234-7494
Peking Noodle Company
Los Angeles, CA 323-223-2023
Shine Food
Torrance, CA .310-533-6010
Wan Hua Foods
Seattle, WA 206-622-8417

Potato Products

Alexia Foods
Long Island City, NY 718-937-0100
Allen Canning Company
Siloam Springs, AR 800-234-2553
Bob Evans Farms
Hillsdale, MI .517-437-3349
Chloe Foods Corporation
Brooklyn, NY .718-827-3600
ConAgra Foods   Lamb Weston Plant
Richland, WA .509-375-4181
ConAgra Foods   Lamb Weston® Headquarters
Kennewick, WA 509-736-0456
Del Monte Foods
San Francisco, CA 800-543-3090
Frito-Lay
Jeffersontown, KY 502-491-9616
Idaho Fresh-Pak/Idahoan Foods
Lewisville, ID .800-635-6100
Lamb-Weston
Pasco, WA 800-766-7783
Maple Leaf Foods International
Toronto, ON .416-480-8900
McCain Foods
Easton, ME 207-488-2561
McCain Foods USA
Grand Island, NE 308-382-7770
McCain Foods USA
Othello, WA 800-541-4808
Pacific Valley Foods
Bellevue, WA .425-643-1805
Rices Potato Chips
Biloxi, MS 228-396-5775

Seneca Foods
Clyman, WI. .920-696-3331
Somerset Industries
Spring House, PA 800-883-8728
Sturm Foods
Manawa, WI .800-347-8876

Hash Browned Potatoes

Basic American Foods
Plover, WI 715-341-5960
Basic American Foods
Walnut Creek, CA. 800-227-4050
Basin Frozen Foods
Warden, WA .509-349-2210
Bob Evans Farms
Hillsdale, MI .517-437-3349
Cavendish Farms
Jamestown, ND 888-284-5687

EMERLING INTERNATIONAL FOODS, INC.

Emerling International Foods
Buffalo, NY 716-833-7381

> We supply food manufacturers and food service customers worldwide (since 1988) with bulk ingredients including: Fruits & Vegetables; Juice Concentrates; Herbs & Spices; Oils & Vinegars; Flavors & Colors; Honey & Molasses. We also produce PURE MAPLE SYRUP.

Idaho Fresh-Pak/Idahoan Foods
Lewisville, ID .800-635-6100
J.R. Simplot Company
Boise, ID 208-336-2110
McCain Foods Canada
Florenceville, NB 506-392-5541
McCain Foods USA
Easton, ME 207-488-2561
Michael Foods, Inc.
Minnetonka, MN. 952-258-4000
Mr. Dell Foods
Kearney, MO .816-628-4644
Northern Star Company
Minneapolis, MN 612-339-8981
Sun-Glo of Idaho
Sugar City, ID 208-356-7346

Puffs - Frozen

Lamb-Weston
Pasco, WA. 800-766-7783
McCain Foods USA
Easton, ME 207-488-2561
McCain Foods USA
Othello, WA .800-541-4808

Prepared Meals

Amigos Canning Company
San Antonio, TX 800-580-3477
Barber Foods
Portland, ME. 800-577-2595
BlueWater Seafoods
Lachine, QC .888-560-2539
Bunker Hill Foods
Augusta, GA .706-733-7765
Cafferata
San Anselmo, CA 800-626-8115
Castleberry/Snow Brands
Augusta, GA .800-241-3520
Celentano Brothers
Verona, NJ 973-239-2557
Chandler Foods
Greensboro, NC 800-537-6219
Chef Hans Gourmet Foods
Monroe, LA. .800-890-4267
Chloe Foods Corporation
Brooklyn, NY .718-827-3600
Cobi Foods
Hantsport, NS 800-565-8229
ConAgra Foods/International Home Foods
Niagara Falls, ON 905-356-2661
Culinary Foods
Chicago, IL 800-621-4049
Foodbrands America
Oklahoma City, OK 405-290-4000
Heinz Company of Canada
North York, ON. 800-268-6641
J.B. Sons
Yonkers, NY .914-963-5192

La Tolteca Foods
Pueblo, CO 719-543-5733
Molinaro's Fine Italian Foods
Mississauga, ON. 800-268-4959
Nestle Canada Inc
North York, ON. 800-563-7853
O Chili Frozen Foods Inc
Northbrook, IL 847-562-1991
Pasta USA
Spokane, WA. 800-456-2084
Seneca Foods
Clyman, WI. .920-696-3331

Beef Dinner

Big B Distributors
Evansville, IN .812-425-5235
Bob Evans Farms
Hillsdale, MI. 517-437-3349
Kelly Foods
Jackson, TN .731-424-2255
Noodles by Leonardo
Cando, ND 701-968-4464
Simeus Foods International
Mansfield, TX 888-772-3663

Breakfast

Bob Evans Farms
Hillsdale, MI .517-437-3349
Gilster Mary Lee/Jasper Foods
Jasper, MO 800-777-2168
ISE Farms
Galena, MD 410-755-6300
Michael Foods, Inc.
Minnetonka, MN. 952-258-4000

Burritos

Chimichangas

Camino Real Foods
Vernon, CA 800-421-6201
Queen International Foods
Monterey Park, CA 800-423-4414

Canned

Kelly Foods
Jackson, TN .731-424-2255
Lucks Food Decorating Company
Tacoma, WA .206-674-7200

Casseroles

Dynamic Foods
Lubbock, TX .806-762-0780
Good Old Days Foods
Little Rock, AR. 501-565-1257
Marsan Foods
Toronto, ON .416-755-9262
Shiloh Foods
Savannah, TN 800-795-2550

Chicken

Kiev

Tyson Foods
Springdale, AR 800-643-3410

Convenience

Chef Hans Gourmet Foods
Monroe, LA. .800-890-4267
ConAgra Frozen Foods Company
Marshall, MO .660-886-3301
Contessa Food Products
San Pedro, CA. 310-832-8000
Gemini Food Industries
Fiskdale, MA .508-347-2800
Homegrown Naturals
Napa, CA. 800-288-1089
Lucks Food Decorating Company
Tacoma, WA .206-674-7200

Corn Fritters

Tami Great Food
Monsey, NY .718-788-4200
Triton Seafood Company
Medley, FL 305-805-3500

Crab

Hancock Lobster Gourmet Company
Cundys Harbor, ME 800-552-0142

Frozen

Taylor's Frozen Foods
Charleston, SC 843-723-1878

Stuffed

Boja's Foods
Bayou La Batre, AL 251-824-4186
Taylor's Frozen Foods
Charleston, SC 843-723-1878

Eggplant Parmigiana

Bruno Specialty Foods
West Sayville, NY. 631-589-1700
Pasta Factory
Northlake, IL 800-615-6951

Eggs

Dixie Egg Company
Jacksonville, FL 800-394-3447
Great Valley Mills
Barto, PA 800-688-6455
ISE Farms
Galena, MD. 410-755-6300
Michael Foods, Inc.
Minnetonka, MN. 952-258-4000
New Morn Foods
Oakwood, GA. 770-536-4561
Sunnyslope Farms Egg Ranch
Cherry Valley, CA. 951-845-1131

Entrees

Atlantic Premium Brands
Northbrook, IL 847-412-6200
Bellisio Foods, Inc.
Lakeville, MN. 800-368-7337
Bernardi Italian Foods Company
Bloomsburg, PA 570-389-5500
Bestfoods Foodservice
Somerset, NJ 732-627-8722
Blue Runner Foods
Gonzales, LA 225-647-3016
Boudreaux's Foods
New Orleans, LA 504-733-8440
Burnett & Son Meat Company
Monrovia, CA 626-357-2165
Carando Gourmet Frozen Foods
Springfield, MA 413-730-4205
ConAgra Foods Inc
Omaha, NE 402-240-4000
Culinary Revolution
La Jolla, CA 323-939-1099
Culinary Standards Corporation
Louisville, KY 800-778-3434
Deep Foods
Union, NJ 908-810-7500
Don Miguel Mexican Foods
Orange, CA. 714-634-8441
Earth Mother Foods Company
Arcata, CA 707-825-6723
Ethnic Gourmet Foods
West Chester, PA 610-692-7575
Heinz Company
Trevose, PA 215-639-2343
HFI Foods
Redmond, WA. 425-883-1320
Home Made Brand Foods Company
Newburyport, MA. 978-462-3663
Hormel Foods Corporation
Houston, TX 281-492-1770
Hormel Foods Corporation
Omaha, NE 402-493-8470
Hormel Foods Corporation
Oklahoma City, OK 405-843-5643
Hormel Foods Corporation
Pittsburgh, PA. 412-921-7036
Hormel Foods Corporation
West Allis, WI. 414-604-0570
Hormel Foods Corporation
Franklin, MA. 508-541-7112
Hormel Foods Corporation
Cincinnati, OH 513-563-0211
Hormel Foods Corporation
Urbandale, IA 515-276-8872

Hormel Foods Corporation
Phoenix, AZ 602-230-2400
Hormel Foods Corporation
Charlotte, NC 704-527-4388
Hormel Foods Corporation
Lisle, IL 800-533-2000
Hormel Foods Corporation
Salt Lake City, UT 801-487-8251
Hormel Foods Corporation
Lubbock, TX 806-796-3630
Hormel Foods Corporation
Arlington, TX 817-465-4735
Hormel Foods Corporation
Cordova, TN 901-753-4282
Hormel Foods Corporation
Lebanon, NJ 908-236-7009
Hormel Foods Corporation
Shawnee Mission, KS 913-888-8744
Hormel Foods Corporation
Pleasanton, CA 925-225-9349
Hunt-Wesson Food Service Company
Rochester, NY 800-633-1002
JTM Food Group
Harrison, OH. 800-626-2308
Kellogg Company
Zanesville, OH 740-453-7782
King Kold Meats
Englewood, OH 800-836-2797
Major McGill
Flowery Branch, GA. 770-967-6001
Mann's International Meat Specialties
Omaha, NE 800-228-2170
Marsan Foods
Toronto, ON 416-755-9262
McCain Foods Canada
Toronto, ON 800-363-8516
Natural Quick Foods
Seattle, WA 206-365-5757
Oh Boy! Corporation
San Fernando, CA. 818-361-1128
Olympic Food Products
Kokomo, IN 800-445-6923
Pasta USA
Spokane, WA. 800-456-2084
Pilgrim's Pride
Timberville, VA 540-896-7000
Pinnacle Foods Group
Cherry Hill, NJ 877-852-7424
Quality Chef Foods
Cedar Rapids, IA 800-356-8307
Ragozzino Food
Meriden, CT 800-348-1240
Reser's Fine Foods
Beaverton, OR 800-333-6431
Ruggiero Seafood
Newark, NJ 800-543-2110
Sanderson Farms
Laurel, MS 800-844-4030
Spring Glen Fresh Foods
Ephrata, PA 800-641-2853
Steak-Umm Company
Shillington, PA 860-928-5900
Sugar Foods
Sun Valley, CA 818-768-7900
Tamarind Tree
Neshanic Station, NJ 800-432-8733
Thyme & Truffles Hors D'oeuvres
Toronto, ON 877-489-8636
Truesoups
Kent, WA. 253-872-0403
Vanee Foods Company
Berkeley, IL. 708-449-7300
Wong Wing Foods
Montreal, QC 800-361-4820

Frozen

Alfredo's Italian Foods Manufacturing Company
Quincy, MA. 617-479-6360
Amy's Kitchen
Petaluma, CA 707-578-5908
Atlantic Premium Brands
Northbrook, IL 847-412-6200
Bellisio Foods, Inc.
Lakeville, MN. 800-368-7337
Bernardi Italian Foods Company
Bloomsburg, PA 570-389-5500
Campbell Soup Company of Canada
Listowel, ON. 800-575-7687
Carando Gourmet Frozen Foods
Springfield, MA 413-730-4205
Cedarlane Natural Foods
Carson, CA 310-886-7720

ConAgra Mexican Foods
Compton, CA 310-223-1499
Contessa Food Products
San Pedro, CA 310-832-8000
Culinary Standards Corporation
Louisville, KY 800-778-3434
Deep Foods
Union, NJ 908-810-7500
Don Miguel Mexican Foods
Orange, CA. 714-634-8441
Dynamic Foods
Lubbock, TX 806-762-0780
Fairfield Farm Kitchens
Tamworth, NH 508-584-9300
HFI Foods
Redmond, WA. 425-883-1320
Hunt-Wesson Food Service Company
Rochester, NY 800-633-1002
Kelly Gourmet Foods
San Francisco, CA 415-648-9200
King Kold Meats
Englewood, OH 800-836-2797
Lenchner Bakery
Concord, ON 905-738-8811
Marsan Foods
Toronto, ON 416-755-9262
Milmar Food Group
Goshen, NY 845-294-5400
Morningstar Foods
Dallas, TX. 214-303-3400
Olympic Food Products
Kokomo, IN 800-445-6923
Oven Poppers
Manchester, NH 603-644-3773
Pasta USA
Spokane, WA. 800-456-2084
Reser's Fine Foods
Beaverton, OR 800-333-6431
Royal Palate Foods
Inglewood, CA 310-330-7701
Ruggiero Seafood
Newark, NJ 800-543-2110
Sanderson Farms
Laurel, MS 800-844-4030
Simeus Foods Internaı nal
Mansfield, TX. 888-772-3663
Steak-Umm Company
Shillington, PA 860-928-5900
Thyme & Truffles Hors D'oeuvres
Toronto, ON 877-489-8636
Wong Wing Foods
Montreal, QC 800-361-4820

Microwavable

Alle Processing Corporation
Flushing, NY. 800-245-5620
Atlantic Premium Brands
Northbrook, IL 847-412-6200

Shelf Stable

Associated Brands, Inc.
Medina, NY. 800-265-0050
California Creative Foods
Oceanside, CA 760-757-2622
Cordon Bleu International
Anjou, QC 514-352-3000
Dorina/So-Good
Union, IL 815-923-2144
Food Reserves
Concordia, MO 800-944-1511
Global Marketing Associates
Schaumburg, IL. 847-490-6481
Hanover Foods Corporation
Hanover, PA 717-632-6000
Health Valley Company
Irwindale, CA 800-334-3204
Heinz North America
Pittsburgh, PA. 412-237-5700
Hormel Foods Corporation
Orchard Park, NY 716-675-7700
Hormel Foods Corporation
Austin, MN 800-523-4635
J&M Food Products Company
Deerfield, IL 847-948-1290
Kraft Foods
Avon, NY 585-226-4400
Lundberg Family Farm
Richvale, CA 530-882-4551
Morningstar Foods
Dallas, TX. 214-303-3400

Mr Jay's Tamales & Chili
Lynwood, CA .310-537-3932
Noodles by Leonardo
Cando, ND .701-968-4464
Oregon Freeze Dry
Albany, OR .800-547-0245
Pillsbury Canada Limited
Markham, ON .800-745-4777
SOPAKCO Foods
Mullins, SC .800-276-9678
Spring Glen Fresh Foods
Ephrata, PA .800-641-2853
Sugar Foods
Sun Valley, CA .818-768-7900
Truitt Brothers Inc
Salem, OR .800-547-8712
Vigo Importing Company
Tampa, FL .813-884-3491

Escargot

S-Car-Go
Sanibel, FL .239-472-1900

Etoufee

Chef Hans Gourmet Foods
Monroe, LA. 800-890-4267

Fish

American Seafoods International
New Bedford, MA 800-343-8046
Carrington Foods
Saraland, AL. 251-675-9700
Cuizina Food Company
Woodinville, WA. 425-486-7000
Icelandic USA
Newport News, VA 757-820-4000
Janes Family Foods
Mississauga, ON. 800-565-2637
Menemsha Fish Market
Chilmark, MA .508-645-2282
Omstead Foods Ltd
Burlington, ON 905-315-8883
Quinalt Pride Seafood
Taholah, WA .360-276-4431
Stacey's Famous Foods
Hayden, ID .800-782-2395
Trident Seafoods Corporation
Seattle, WA .800-426-5490

Stuffed

Anchor Frozen Foods
Westbury, NY .800-566-3474
Beaver Street Fisheries
Jacksonville, FL 800-874-6426
King & Prince Seafood Corporation
Brunswick, GA 800-841-0205
Sweet Water Seafood Corporation
Carlstadt, NJ .201-939-6622
Tampa Maid Foods
Lakeland, FL. 800-237-7637

Fish & Chips

Viking Seafoods Inc
Malden, MA .800-225-3020

Fish Patties

Northwest Naturals
Olympia, WA .360-866-9661
Pacific Salmon Company
Edmonds, WA. 425-774-1315
Viking Seafoods Inc
Malden, MA .800-225-3020

Fish Sticks

Coldwater Seafood Corporation
Norwalk, CT .203-846-8897
Icelandic USA
Newport News, VA 757-820-4000
North Atlantic Fish Company
Gloucester, MA 978-283-4121
Ungars Food Products
Elmwood Park, NJ 201-703-1300
Van De Kamp Frozen Foods
Erie, PA .814-898-1500
Viking Seafoods Inc
Malden, MA .800-225-3020

Frozen

Al Safa Halal
Niagara Falls, NY 800-268-8174
Coldwater Seafood Corporation
Norwalk, CT .203-846-8897
Tichon Seafood Corporation
New Bedford, MA 508-999-5607
Van De Kamp Frozen Foods
Erie, PA .814-898-1500
Viking Seafoods Inc
Malden, MA .800-225-3020

Fried Rice

Willow Foods
Beaverton, OR .800-338-3609
Wong Wing Foods
Montreal, QC .800-361-4820

Frozen

Bake Crafters Food
Collegedale, TN 800-296-8935
Biagio's Banquets
Chicago, IL .800-392-2837
Birds Eye Foods
Rochester, NY. 800-999-5044
ConAgra Frozen Foods Company
Marshall, MO .660-886-3301
Cuizina Food Company
Woodinville, WA. 425-486-7000
Food Source
McKinney, TX .972-548-9001
Foodbrands America
Oklahoma City, OK 405-290-4000
Hamilton Quality Convenience Foods
Romulus, MI .734-946-1800
Heinkel's Packing Company
Decatur, IL .800-594-2738
High Liner Foods
Lunenburg, NS 902-634-9475
House of Spices
Flushing, NY. 718-507-4900
Kraft Pizza & Foodservice
Medford, WI .800-323-0768
McCain Foods Canada
Florenceville, NB 506-392-5541
McClane Distribution Center
Fredericksburg, VA. 540-374-2000
Pasta USA
Spokane, WA. 800-456-2084
Philadelphia Cheese Steak Company
Philadelphia, PA 800-342-9771
Reser's Fine Foods
Beaverton, OR .800-333-6431

Gyros

Corfu Foods
Bensenville, IL .630-595-2510
Corfu Tasty Gyros
Bensenville, IL .630-595-2510

Lasagna

Alfredo's Italian Foods Manufacturing Company
Quincy, MA. 617-479-6360
Foodbrands America
Oklahoma City, OK 405-290-4000
Homestead Fine Foods
S San Francisco, CA. 650-615-0750
Luigino's
Duluth, MN. 218-727-2059
McCain Foods Canada
Florenceville, NB 506-392-5541
Reames Foods
Columbus, OH .614-846-2232

Macaroni

Campbell Soup Company
Camden, NJ. 800-257-8443
ConAgra Foods/International Home Foods
Niagara Falls, ON 905-356-2661
Gilster-Mary Lee Corporation
Chester, IL. 800-851-5371
Molinaro's Fine Italian Foods
Mississauga, ON. 800-268-4959
Pasta USA
Spokane, WA. 800-456-2084
Strom Products Ltd
Bannockburn, IL. 800-862-3311

Mozzarella Sticks

Giorgio Foods
Temple, PA .800-220-2139
Matador Processors
Blanchard, OK .800-847-0797

Pasta & Noodle Dishes

Agrusa, Inc.
Leonia, NJ. 201-592-5950
Alfredo's Italian Foods Manufacturing Company
Quincy, MA. 617-479-6360
Antoni Ravioli
North Massapequa, NY 800-783-0350
Bernardi Italian Foods Company
Bloomsburg, PA 570-389-5500
Bruno Specialty Foods
West Sayville, NY. 631-589-1700
Carando Gourmet Frozen Foods
Springfield, MA 413-730-4205
Casa Di Bertacchi
Vineland, NJ .800-818-9261
ConAgra Frozen Foods Company
Marshall, MO .660-886-3301
Cuizina Food Company
Woodinville, WA. 425-486-7000
D'Orazio Foods
Bellmawr, NJ. 888-328-7287
Dabruzzi's Italian Foods
Hudson, WI. 715-386-3653
Food City USA
Arvada, CO. 303-321-4447
Global Marketing Associates
Schaumburg, IL. 847-490-6481
Kraft Foods
Springfield, MO 417-881-2701
Kraft Foods
Northfield, IL .800-323-0768
Landolfi Food Products
Trenton, NJ .609-392-1830
Lombardo's Ravioli Kitchen
New Britain, CT 860-223-7800
Lucy's Foods
Latrobe, PA .724-539-1430
Noodles by Leonardo
Cando, ND .701-968-4464
Pasta USA
Spokane, WA. 800-456-2084
Penn Valley Farms
Gainesville, GA 773-685-9929
Ragozzino Food
Meriden, CT .800-348-1240
Sandridge Food Corporation
Medina, OH. 330-725-2348
Specialty Brands
Carthage, MO .417-358-8104
ST Specialty Foods
Brooklyn Park, MN. 763-493-9600
Star Ravioli Manufacturing Company
Moonachie, NJ .201-933-6427

Rice

Amalgamated Produce
Bridgeport, CT .800-358-3808
Tony Chachere's Creole Foods
Opelousas, LA .800-551-9066

Salad

Classic Commissary
Binghamton, NY 800-929-3486
Club Chef
Covington, KY .859-578-3100
Dole Fresh Vegetable Company
Soledad, CA .800-333-5454
Earth Island Natural Foods
Canoga Park, CA 818-725-2820
F&S Produce Company
Rosenhayn, NJ .800-886-3316
Lakeside Foods
Manitowoc, WI .920-684-3356
Paisley Farms
Willoughby, OH 800-676-8656
Phillips Gourmet
Kennett Square, PA 610-925-0520
R.C. McEntire & Company
Columbia, SC .803-799-3388
Ready-Pac Produce
Florence, NJ .609-499-1900
Reser's Fine Foods
Salt Lake City, UT 801-972-5633

Sandridge Food Corporation
Medina, OH. 330-725-2348
Suter Company
Sycamore, IL 800-435-6942
Van Bennett Food Company
Reading, PA 800-423-8897

Sandwiches

B-S Foods Company
Oklahoma City, OK 405-949-9797
Bake Crafters Food
Collegedale, TN 800-296-8935
Black's Barbecue
Lockhart, TX. 512-398-2712
Bridgford Foods
Anaheim, CA 800-527-2105
Bridgford Foods Corporation
Anaheim, CA 800-527-2105
Camino Real Foods
Vernon, CA 800-421-6201
Classic Delight
St Marys, OH 800-274-9828
Corfu Foods
Bensenville, IL 630-595-2510
Country Smoked Meats
Bowling Green, OH 800-321-4766
D&A Foodservice
Dartmouth, NS 902-468-4715
Deli Express/EA Sween Company
Eden Prairie, MN 800-328-8184
Eastside Deli Supply
Lansing, MI. 800-349-6694
Food Factory
Honolulu, HI 808-593-2633
G A Food Service
St Petersburg, FL. 727-573-2211
Gilardi Foods
Sidney, OH 937-498-4511
Hamilton Quality Convenience Foods
Romulus, MI 734-946-1800
Helens Pure Foods
Cheltenham, PA 215-379-6433
Honeybake Farms
Kansas City, KS 913-371-7777
Hormel Foods Corporation
Austin, MN 800-523-4635
Knotts Wholesale Foods
Paris, TN. 731-642-1961
Landshire
Belleville, IL 618-398-8122
Lilydale Foods
Edmonton, AB 800-661-5341
Made-Rite Sandwich Company
Ooltewah, TN 800-343-1327
Market Fare Foods
Phoenix, AZ 800-782-9136
Maui Bagel
Kahului, HI 808-270-7561
McClane Distribution Center
Fredericksburg, VA. 540-374-2000
McLane Foods
Phoenix, AZ 602-275-5509
Oh Boy! Corporation
San Fernando, CA. 818-361-1128
Piemonte's Bakery
Rockford, IL 815-962-4833
Pierre Foods
Cincinnati, OH 513-874-8741
Randy's Frozen Meats
Faribault, MN 800-354-7177
Royal Touch Foods
Etobicoke, ON 416-213-1077
Southern Belle Sandwich Company
Baton Rouge, LA 800-344-4670
Steak-Umm Company
Shillington, PA 860-928-5900
Sunburst Foods
Goldsboro, NC 919-778-2151
Zartic Inc
Rome, GA 800-241-0516

Pocket

Applegate Farms
Bridgewater, NJ 908-725-2768
Hamilton Quality Convenience Foods
Romulus, MI 734-946-1800
Ore-Ida Foods
Pittsburgh, PA 412-237-3450

Scampi

Shrimp Frozen

Contessa Food Products
San Pedro, CA. 310-832-8000

Seafood

AquaCuisine
Eagle, ID 888-330-2782
Carnival Brands
New Orleans, LA 800-925-2774
Carrington Foods
Saraland, AL 251-675-9700
Chincoteague Seafood Company
Parsonsburg, MD 443-260-4800
Contessa Food Products
San Pedro, CA. 310-832-8000
Cuizina Food Company
Woodinville, WA. 425-486-7000
FishKing
Bayou La Batre, AL 334-824-2118
Gemini Food Industries
Fiskdale, MA 508-347-2800
Gulf City Marine Supply
Bayou La Batre, AL 251-824-4154
Icelandic USA
Newport News, VA 757-820-4000
International Oceanic Enterprises of Alabama
Bayou La Batre, AL 800-816-1832
King & Prince Seafood Corporation
Brunswick, GA 800-841-0205
Menemsha Fish Market
Chilmark, MA 508-645-2282
Neptune Fisheries
Newport News, VA 800-545-7474
North Atlantic Fish Company
Gloucester, MA. 978-283-4121
Oven Poppers
Manchester, NH 603-644-3773
Ruggiero Seafood
Newark, NJ 800-543-2110
Sanderson Farms
Bryan, TX. 979-778-5730
Sea Pearl Seafood
Bayou La Batre, AL 800-872-8804
Tex-Mex Cold Storage
Brownsville, TX 956-831-9433
Triton Seafood Company
Medley, FL 305-805-3500
Weyand Fisheries
Wyandotte, MI 800-521-9815

Spaghetti

Matlaw's Food Products
West Haven, CT 800-934-8266

Canned

Campbell Soup Company
Camden, NJ. 800-257-8443
Castleberry/Snow Brands
Augusta, GA 800-241-3520
ConAgra Foods/International Home Foods
Niagara Falls, ON 905-356-2661
Heinz Company of Canada
North York, ON. 800-268-6641
Hormel Foods Corporation
Austin, MN 800-523-4635
Seneca Foods
Clyman, WI. 920-696-3331

with Meatballs

Burnett & Son Meat Company
Monrovia, CA. 626-357-2165

Stuffed Cabbage

Aristocrat International Corporation
Secaucus, NJ 201-866-1900
Morrison Lamothe
Toronto, ON 416-291-6762
Olympic Food Products
Kokomo, IN 800-445-6923

Frozen

Aristocrat International Corporation
Secaucus, NJ 201-866-1900
Olympic Food Products
Kokomo, IN 800-445-6923

Stuffed Peppers

L&S Packing Company
Farmingdale, NY 800-286-6487
Matador Processors
Blanchard, OK 800-847-0797
Norpaco
New Britain, CT 800-252-0222
Olympic Food Products
Kokomo, IN 800-445-6923
Vega Food Industries
Cranston, RI 800-973-7737

Stuffed Shells

Antoni Ravioli
North Massapequa, NY 800-783-0350
Bruno Specialty Foods
West Sayville, NY. 631-589-1700
Caesar's Pasta Products
Blackwood, NJ 856-227-2585
Codino's Italian Foods
Scotia, NY. 800-246-8908
D'Orazio Foods
Bellmawr, NJ. 888-328-7287
J.B. Sons
Yonkers, NY 914-963-5192
Landolfi Food Products
Trenton, NJ 609-392-1830
Lombardo's Ravioli Kitchen
New Britain, CT 860-223-7800
Pasta Del Mondo
Carmel, NY 800-392-8887
Pasta Factory
Northlake, IL 800-615-6951
Star Ravioli Manufacturing Company
Moonachie, NJ 201-933-6427
Windsor Frozen Foods
Houston, TX 800-437-6936
Wisconsin Whey International
Juda, WI 608-233-5101

Turkey Dinner

Morrison Lamothe
Toronto, ON 416-291-6762

Vegetarian

Alle Processing
Flushing, NY 718-894-2000
Alle Processing Corporation
Flushing, NY 800-245-5620
Dixie USA
Tomball, TX 800-233-3668
F&S Produce Company
Rosenhayn, NJ 800-886-3316
Health Valley Company
Irwindale, CA 800-334-3204
Mortimer's Fine Foods
Burlington, ON 905-336-0000
Tamarind Tree
Neshanic Station, NJ. 800-432-8733

Prepared Salads

Avon Heights Mushrooms
Avondale, PA 610-268-2092
Bay Cities Produce Company
San Leandro, CA 510-346-4943
Black's Barbecue
Lockhart, TX. 512-398-2712
Blue Ridge Farms
Brooklyn, NY 718-827-9000
Bosell Foods
Cleveland, OH 216-991-7600
Chef Solutions
Baxter Springs, KS 620-856-2203
Chiquita Brands International
Cincinnati, OH 800-438-0015
Chloe Foods Corporation
Brooklyn, NY 718-827-3600
Danner Salads
Peoria, IL. 309-691-0289
Delsa Foods Processors
Delisle, SK 306-493-2400
Giovanni's Appetizing Food Products
Richmond, MI. 586-727-9355
Hanover Foods Corporation
Hanover, PA 717-632-6000
Harold Food Company
Charlotte, NC 704-588-8061

Helens Pure Foods
 Cheltenham, PA 215-379-6433
Herold's Salad
 Cleveland, OH 800-427-2523
HFI Foods
 Redmond, WA. 425-883-1320
Homestyle Foods Company
 Hamtramck, MI. 313-874-3250
Honeybake Farms
 Kansas City, KS 913-371-7777
Hoople Country Kitchens
 Rockport, IN 812-649-2351
House of Thaller
 Knoxville, TN 865-689-5893
Kay Foods Company
 Ionia, MI 616-527-0120
Kings Processing
 Middleton, NS. 902-825-2188
L&S Packing Company
 Farmingdale, NY 800-286-6487
Meadows Country Products
 Hollidaysburg, PA 888-499-1001
Mrs. Grissom's Salad
 Nashville, TN 800-255-0571
Mrs. Minnick's Salads
 Baltimore, MD 410-235-6748
Mrs. Stratton's Salads
 Birmingham, AL. 205-940-9640
Orval Kent Food Company
 Wheeling, IL. 847-459-9000
Pastene Companies
 Canton, MA .781-830-8200
Pilgrim's Pride
 Timberville, VA 540-896-7000
PowerBar
 Berkeley, CA. 800-587-6937
Reser's Fine Foods
 Salt Lake City, UT 801-972-5633
Ruskin Packaging
 Miami, FL. .305-324-1529
Salad-De-Lites
 Bronx, NY. .718-828-1200
Sandridge Food Corporation
 Medina, OH. 330-725-2348
Sara Lee Corporation
 Downers Grove, IL. 630-598-8100
Spring Glen Fresh Foods
 Ephrata, PA .800-641-2853
Thumann's
 Carlstadt, NJ 201-935-3636
Vega Food Industries
 Cranston, RI 800-973-7737
Yarbrough Produce Company
 Birmingham, AL. 205-323-8651
Zuccaro's Fruit & Produce Company
 Minneapolis, MN 612-333-1122

Antipasto

Giovanni's Appetizing Food Products
 Richmond, MI. 586-727-9355
L&S Packing Company
 Farmingdale, NY 800-286-6487
Pastene Companies
 Canton, MA .781-830-8200

Chicken

Burnette Foods
 Hartford, MI 616-621-3181
Mrs. Stratton's Salads
 Birmingham, AL. 205-940-9640
Old Dutch Mustard Company
 Great Neck, NY 516-466-0522
Orval Kent Food Company
 Wheeling, IL. 847-459-9000
Quality Brands
 Deland, FL .386-738-3808
Sara Lee Corporation
 Downers Grove, IL. 630-598-8100

Cole Slaw

Avon Heights Mushrooms
 Avondale, PA 610-268-2092
Black's Barbecue
 Lockhart, TX. 512-398-2712
Chef Solutions
 Baxter Springs, KS 620-856-2203
Flaum Appetizing
 Brooklyn, NY 718-821-1970
Kay Foods Company
 Ionia, MI 616-527-0120

Mrs. Minnick's Salads
 Baltimore, MD 410-235-6748
Mrs. Stratton's Salads
 Birmingham, AL. 205-940-9640
Orval Kent Food Company
 Wheeling, IL. 847-459-9000
Ruskin Packaging
 Miami, FL. .305-324-1529
Spring Glen Fresh Foods
 Ephrata, PA .800-641-2853
Yarbrough Produce Company
 Birmingham, AL. 205-323-8651

Iceberg Lettuce Based

Bay Cities Produce Company
 San Leandro, CA. 510-346-4943
Chloe Foods Corporation
 Brooklyn, NY 718-827-3600
Zuccaro's Fruit & Produce Company
 Minneapolis, MN 612-333-1122

Macaroni

Black's Barbecue
 Lockhart, TX. 512-398-2712
Chef Solutions
 Baxter Springs, KS 620-856-2203
Hanover Foods Corporation
 Hanover, PA .717-632-6000
Mrs. Minnick's Salads
 Baltimore, MD 410-235-6748
Spring Glen Fresh Foods
 Ephrata, PA .800-641-2853

Pasta

Chloe Foods Corporation
 Brooklyn, NY 718-827-3600
Herold's Salad
 Cleveland, OH 800-427-2523
HFI Foods
 Redmond, WA. 425-883-1320
Homestyle Foods Company
 Hamtramck, MI. 313-874-3250
Kay Foods Company
 Ionia, MI 616-527-0120
Kraft Foods
 Northfield, IL 800-323-0768
Mrs. Minnick's Salads
 Baltimore, MD 410-235-6748
Sandridge Food Corporation
 Medina, OH. 330-725-2348
Spring Glen Fresh Foods
 Ephrata, PA .800-641-2853

Potato

Black's Barbecue
 Lockhart, TX. 512-398-2712
Chef Solutions
 Baxter Springs, KS 620-856-2203
Danner Salads
 Peoria, IL. .309-691-0289
Hanover Foods Corporation
 Hanover, PA .717-632-6000
Herold's Salad
 Cleveland, OH 800-427-2523
Kay Foods Company
 Ionia, MI 616-527-0120
Mrs. Minnick's Salads
 Baltimore, MD 410-235-6748
Mrs. Stratton's Salads
 Birmingham, AL. 205-940-9640
Orval Kent Food Company
 Wheeling, IL. 847-459-9000
Sandridge Food Corporation
 Medina, OH. 330-725-2348
Spring Glen Fresh Foods
 Ephrata, PA .800-641-2853

Salmon

Springfield Smoked Fish Company
 Springfield, MA 800-327-3412

Seafood

Springfield Smoked Fish Company
 Springfield, MA 800-327-3412

Tuna

Bumble Bee Seafoods
 San Diego, CA 858-715-4000
Flaum Appetizing
 Brooklyn, NY 718-821-1970
Mrs. Stratton's Salads
 Birmingham, AL. 205-940-9640
Orval Kent Food Company
 Wheeling, IL. 847-459-9000
Sara Lee Corporation
 Downers Grove, IL. 630-598-8100

Turkey

Sara Lee Corporation
 Downers Grove, IL. 630-598-8100

Quiche

Cobi Foods
 Hantsport, NS 800-565-8229
Culinary Foods
 Chicago, IL. .800-621-4049
Glendora Quiche Company
 San Dimas, CA 909-394-1777
Love & Quiches Desserts
 Freeport, NY .800-525-5251
Nancy's Specialty Foods
 Newark, CA .510-494-1100
Naturally Fresh Foods
 College Park, GA 800-765-1950
Pie Piper Products
 Bensenville, IL 800-621-8183
Quelle Quiche
 Brentwood, MO 314-961-6554
Quiche & Tell
 Flushing, NY. 718-381-7562
Renaissance Foods
 Saint Louis, MO 314-961-6554
Stacey's Famous Foods
 Hayden, ID .800-782-2395

Soups & Stews

Abbey Road Farms
 Tallahassee, FL 850-878-7677
Advance Food Brokers
 West Bloomfield, MI 248-851-9045
AFP Advanced Food Products, LLC
 Visalia, CA .559-627-2070
Ailments E.D. Foods Inc.
 Pointe Claire, QC 800-267-3333
Alaska Smokehouse
 Woodinville, WA. 800-422-0852
All American Foods, Inc.
 Mankato, MN 800-833-2661
Andersen's Pea Soup
 Buellton, CA .805-688-5581
Anke Kruse Organics
 Guelph, ON .519-824-6161
Annie Chun's
 San Rafael, CA 415-479-8272
Associated Brands, Inc.
 Medina, NY. 800-265-0050
Atlanta Bread Company International, Inc.
 Smyrna, GA .800-398-3728
Automot
 Odessa, FL .813-920-1000
Barbara Lyn Foods
 Elyria, OH .440-324-5445
Baycliff Company
 New York, NY 212-772-6078
Bear Creek Country Kitchens
 Heber City, UT 800-516-7286
Bear Creek Kitchens
 Marshall, TX 888-300-7687
Belleisle Foods
 Belleisle Creek, NB 506-485-2564
Bellisio Foods, Inc.
 Lakeville, MN. 800-368-7337
Blount Seafood Corporation
 Fall River, MA 774-888-1300
Blue Crab Bay Company
 Melfa, VA 800-221-2722
Bombay Breeze Specialty Foods
 Mississauga, ON 416-410-2320
Bonjour
 Pacheco, CA 800-266-5687
Boston Chowda Company
 Lowell, MA. 800-992-0054
Boudreaux's Foods
 New Orleans, LA 504-733-8440

Brinkley Dryer and Storage
Brinkley, AR 870-734-1616

Bunker Hill Foods
Augusta, GA 706-733-7765

Cagnon Foods Company
Brooklyn, NY 718-647-2244

Cajun Fry Company
Pierre Part, LA 888-272-2586

California Natural Products
Lathrop, CA 209-858-2525

California Wild Rice Growers
Fall River Mills, CA 800-626-4366

Caltex Foods
Canoga Park, CA 800-522-5839

Cambridge Food
Monterey, CA 800-433-2584

Campbell Company of Canada
Toronto, ON 800-575-7687

Campbell Soup Company
Camden, NJ 800-257-8443

Campbell Soup Company of Canada
Listowel, ON 800-575-7687

Cape Cod Chowders
Hyannis, MA 508-771-0040

Chef Francisco of Pennsylvania
King of Prussia, PA 610-265-7400

Chef Hans Gourmet Foods
Monroe, LA 800-890-4267

Cherchies
Malvern, PA 800-644-1980

Chicopee Provision Company
Chicopee, MA 800-924-6328

Chincoteague Seafood Company
Parsonsburg, MD 443-260-4800

Christie Food Products
Randolph, MA 800-727-2523

Cibolo Junction Food & Spice
Albuquerque, NM 505-888-1987

Clarmil Manufacturing Corporation
Hayward, CA 888-252-7645

Colonna Brothers
North Bergen, NJ 201-864-1115

Comfort Foods
Tijeras, NM 800-460-5803

ConAgra Grocery Products
Fullerton, CA 800-736-2212

Conifer Specialties Inc
Woodinville, WA 800-588-9160

Cooke Tavern Ltd
Spring Mills, PA 866-422-7687

Country Cupboard
Virginia City, NV 775-847-7300

Cugino's Gourmet Foods
Crystal Lake, IL 888-592-8446

Culinary Standards Corporation
Louisville, KY 800-778-3434

Custom Food Products
Alsip, IL 708-388-8883

Daily Soup
New York, NY 888-393-7687

Daniel Webster Hearth N Kettle
Hyannis, MA 888-774-5511

David Berg & Company
Chicago, IL 773-489-4711

Delsa Foods Processors
Delisle, SK 306-493-2400

Denzer's Food Products
Baltimore, MD 410-889-1500

Diversified Foods & Seasoning
Metairie, LA 504-846-5090

Dorothy Dawson Foods Products
Jackson, MI 517-788-9830

Dr McDougall's Right Foods
South San Francisco, CA 650-583-4993

Eatem Foods Company
Vineland, NJ 800-683-2836

Edmonds Chile Company
St Louis, MO 314-772-1499

El Peto Products
Cambridge, ON 800-387-4064

Epicurean International
Berkeley, CA 800-967-7424

Erba Food Products
Brooklyn, NY 718-272-7700

Fair Scones
Medina, WA 800-588-9160

Fantastic Foods
Napa, CA 800-288-1089

Fish Hopper
Monterey, CA 831-372-8543

Flavor House
Adelanto, CA 760-246-9131

Food Source
McKinney, TX 972-548-9001

Foodbrands America
Oklahoma City, OK 405-290-4000

Fresh Express
Salinas, CA 831-775-2300

Gemini Food Industries
Fiskdale, MA 508-347-2800

George F Brocke & Sons
Kendrick, ID 208-289-4231

Global Express Gourmet
Bozeman, MT 406-587-5571

Grace Foods International
Astoria, NY 718-433-4789

Grandma Brown's Beans Inc
Mexico, NY 315-963-7221

Grandma Pat's Products
Albin, WY 307-631-0801

Great Eastern Sun
Asheville, NC 800-334-5809

Griffith Laboratories Worldwide
Alsip, IL 800-346-4743

H.J. Heinz Company
Pittsburgh, PA 412-237-5948

H.K. Canning
Ventura, CA 805-652-1392

Hains Celestial Group
Melville, NY 877-612-4246

Hale & Hearty Soups/Chelsea Markets
New York, NY 888-727-7887

Hanover Foods Corporation
Hanover, PA 717-632-6000

Health Valley Company
Irwindale, CA 800-334-3204

Heartline Foods
Westport, CT 203-222-0381

Hega Food Products
Cranbury, NJ 800-345-7742

Heinz Company
Trevose, PA 215-639-2343

Heinz Company of Canada
North York, ON 800-268-6641

Heinz North America
Pittsburgh, PA 412-237-5700

Hirzel Canning Company &Farms
Northwood, OH 419-693-0531

Home Made Brand Foods Company
Newburyport, MA 978-462-3663

Hoopeston Foods
Burnsville, MN 952-854-0903

Hormel Foods Corporation
Houston, TX 281-492-1770

Hormel Foods Corporation
Oklahoma City, OK 405-745-3471

Hormel Foods Corporation
Oklahoma City, OK 405-843-5643

Hormel Foods Corporation
Pittsburgh, PA 412-921-7036

Hormel Foods Corporation
West Allis, WI 414-604-0570

Hormel Foods Corporation
Cincinnati, OH 513-563-0211

Hormel Foods Corporation
Urbandale, IA 515-276-8872

Hormel Foods Corporation
Phoenix, AZ 602-230-2400

Hormel Foods Corporation
Charlotte, NC 704-527-4388

Hormel Foods Corporation
Orchard Park, NY 716-675-7700

Hormel Foods Corporation
Austin, MN 800-523-4635

Hormel Foods Corporation
Lisle, IL 800-533-2000

Hormel Foods Corporation
Salt Lake City, UT 801-487-8251

Hormel Foods Corporation
Lubbock, TX 806-796-3630

Hormel Foods Corporation
Arlington, TX 817-465-4735

Hormel Foods Corporation
Cordova, TN 901-753-4282

Hormel Foods Corporation
Lebanon, NJ 908-236-7009

Hormel Foods Corporation
Shawnee Mission, KS 913-888-8744

Idaho Pacific Corporation
Ririe, ID 800-238-5503

Indian Harvest
Colusa, CA 800-294-2433

Jager Foods
Long Prairie, MN 800-358-7251

JC World Foods
Brooklyn, NY 347-386-1130

Juanita's Foods
Wilmington, CA 310-834-5339

Just Delicious Gourmet Foods
Seal Beach, CA 800-871-6085

Jyoti Cruisine India
Berwyn, PA 610-522-2650

K&S Riddle
Buzzards Bay, MA 508-563-7333

K.B. Specialty Foods
Greensburg, IN 812-663-8184

Karlsburger Foods
Monticello, MN 800-383-6549

Kay Brown Company
Ionia, MI 616-527-0120

Kettle Cooked Food
Fort Worth, TX 817-615-4500

Kettle Cuisine
Chelsea, MA 877-302-7687

Leonard Mountain Trading
Leonard, OK 800-822-7700

Les Aliments Ramico Foods
St. Leonard, QC 514-329-1844

Liberty Richter
Saddle Brook, NJ 201-291-8749

Locus Foods
Findlay, OH 419-425-1118

Loffredo Produce
Rock Island, IL 800-397-2096

Long Kow Foods USA Corporation
Torrance, CA 877-566-4569

Manor Hill Food Corporation
Baltimore, MD 410-355-1014

Marburger Foods
Peru, IN 765-689-5198

Marsan Foods
Toronto, ON 416-755-9262

Meat-O-Mat Corporation
Brooklyn, NY 718-965-7250

Mercer Processing
Modesto, CA 209-529-0150

Mid-Atlantic Foods
Easton, MD 800-922-4688

Montana Soup Company
Whitefish, MT 800-862-7687

Moonlite Bar BQ Inn
Owensboro, KY 800-322-8989

Morgan Food
Austin, IN 888-430-1780

Near East Food Products
Leominster, MA 800-822-7423

New Covent Garden Soup Company
San Francisco, CA 415-536-0333

New England Marketers
Boston, MA 800-688-9904

Nissin Foods USA Company
Lancaster, PA 717-291-5901

North Aire Market
Shakopee, MN 800-662-3781

North of the Border
Tesuque, NM 800-860-0681

Old Ranchers Canning Company
Upland, CA 909-982-8895

Organic Gourmet
Sherman Oaks, CA 800-400-7772

Overhill Farms
Vernon, CA 800-859-6406

Park 100 Foods
Tipton, IN 800-854-6504

Pasta USA
Spokane, WA 800-456-2084

Perez Food Products
Kansas City, MO 816-931-8761

Phillips Foods
Baltimore, MD 888-234-2722

Pillsbury
Hannibal, MO 800-775-4777

Pioneer Foods Industries
Eudora, AR 870-355-2506

Progresso Quality Foods
Vineland, NJ 800-200-9377

Quality Chef Foods
Cedar Rapids, IA 800-356-8307

R.A.B. Food Group LLC
Secaucus, NJ 201-453-5200

R.L. Schreiber Company
Pompano Beach, FL 800-624-8777

Ragozzino Food
Meriden, CT 800-348-1240

Rapunzel Pure Organics
Chatham, NY 800-207-2814

Reily Foods Company
New Orleans, LA 504-524-6132
RL Schreiber
Pompano Beach, FL 954-972-7102
Ronzoni Foods Canada
Etobicoke, ON 800-387-5032
Royal Palate Foods
Inglewood, CA 310-330-7701
Sallock International Foods
Millbury, OH .419-838-7223
Sams Food Group
Chicago, IL .800-852-0283
San-J International
Richmond, VA 800-446-5500
Sanderson Farms
Laurel, MS 800-844-4030
Sandridge Food Corporation
Medina, OH .330-725-2348
Sea Watch International
Easton, MD .410-822-7500
Shelton's Poultry
Pomona, CA .800-541-1833
Simeus Foods Internacio nal
Mansfield, TX 888-772-3663
Simeus Foods International
Mansfield, TX 888-772-3663
SOUPerior Bean & Spice Company
Vancouver, WA 800-878-7687
Spice Hunter
San Luis Obispo, CA 800-444-3061
Sprague Foods
Belleville, ON 613-966-1200
Spring Glen Fresh Foods
Ephrata, PA .800-641-2853
St. Ours & Company
Norwell, MA .781-331-8520
Stinson Seafood Company
Prospect Harbor, ME 207-963-7331
Stockpot
Woodinville, WA 800-468-1611
Stokes Canning Company
Englewood, CO 303-790-0623
Sudbury Soups and Salads
Sudbury, MA 888-783-7687
Sweet Earth Natural Foods
Pacific Grove, CA 800-737-3311
Sweet Sue Kitchens
Athens, AL 256-216-0500
Swiss Food Products
Chicago, IL .773-394-6480
Tabatchnick's Fine Foods
Somerset, NJ 732-247-6668
Techni-Brew International
Portland, OR 800-454-4077
Tex-Mex Gourmet
Houston, TX 888-345-8467
Thumann's
Carlstadt, NJ 201-935-3636
Timber Peaks Gourmet
Parker, CO .800-982-7687
Truesoups
Kent, WA 253-872-0403
Turtle Island Foods
Hood River, OR 800-508-8100
Twin Marquis
Brooklyn, NY 800-367-6868
Tyson Prepared Foods
Fort Worth, TX 817-258-2400
Uni-President
La Puente, CA 626-961-1671
Unilever
Lisle, IL 877-995-4483
Unilever Canada
Toronto, ON 416-964-1857
Ventura Foods
Philadelphia, PA 215-223-8700
Vermont Sprout House
Bristol, VT 802-453-3098
Vienna Sausage Company
Chicago, IL .800-326-6652
Vigor Cup Corp
Long Beach, NY 516-785-6352
Vince's Seafoods
Gretna, LA .504-368-1544
VIP Foods
Flushing, NY 718-821-3942
Westbrae Natural Foods
Garden City, NY 800-434-4246
White Coffee Corporation
Long Island City, NY 800-221-0140
William Poll
New York, NY 800-993-7655

Williams-West & Witt Products
Michigan City, IN 219-879-8236
Worthmore Food Product
Cincinnati, OH 513-559-1473
Yankee Specialty Foods
Boston, MA .617-951-9904

Beef Soup

Country Cupboard
Virginia City, NV 775-847-7300
Culinary Standards Corporation
Louisville, KY 800-778-3434
Erba Food Products
Brooklyn, NY 718-272-7700
Williams-West & Witt Products
Michigan City, IN 219-879-8236

Beef Stew

Bunker Hill Foods
Augusta, GA .706-733-7765
Caltex Foods
Canoga Park, CA 800-522-5839
Campbell Company of Canada
Toronto, ON 800-575-7687
Castleberry/Snow Brands
Augusta, GA .800-241-3520
Cibolo Junction Food & Spice
Albuquerque, NM 505-888-1987
Cleugh's Frozen Foods
Buena Park, CA 714-521-1002
ConAgra Foods/International Home Foods
Niagara Falls, ON 905-356-2661
H.J. Heinz Company
Pittsburgh, PA 412-237-5948
Heinz Company of Canada
North York, ON 800-268-6641
Hoopeston Foods
Burnsville, MN 952-854-0903
Kelly Foods
Jackson, TN 731-424-2255
Marsan Foods
Toronto, ON 416-755-9262
Midwest Foods
Owatonna, MN 507-451-7670
Old Ranchers Canning Company
Upland, CA .909-982-8895
Sanderson Farms
Bryan, TX 979-778-5730
Spring Glen Fresh Foods
Ephrata, PA .800-641-2853
Sweet Sue Kitchens
Athens, AL 256-216-0500

Borscht

Gold Pure Foods Products Company
Hempstead, NY 800-422-4681

Canned Soup

Amy's Kitchen
Petaluma, CA 707-578-5908
Caltex Foods
Canoga Park, CA 800-522-5839
Campbell Sales Company
Schaumburg, IL 847-297-0900
Campbell Soup Company
Camden, NJ .800-257-8443
Carriere Foods Inc
Montreal, QC 514-384-4281
Chef Hans Gourmet Foods
Monroe, LA .800-890-4267
Chincoteague Seafood Company
Parsonsburg, MD 443-260-4800
Colonna Brothers
North Bergen, NJ 201-864-1115
Dynamic Foods
Lubbock, TX 806-762-0780
Faribault Foods
Minneapolis, MN 612-333-6461
Heinz
Muscatine, IA 563-263-5711
Heinz North America
Pittsburgh, PA 412-237-5700
Hoopeston Foods
Burnsville, MN 952-854-0903
Look's Gourmet Food Company
Whiting, ME 800-962-6258
Marburger Foods
Peru, IN 765-689-5198

Mid-Atlantic Foods
Easton, MD .800-922-4688
Old Ranchers Canning Company
Upland, CA .909-982-8895
Overhill Farms
Vernon, CA .800-859-6406
Progresso Quality Foods
Vineland, NJ 800-200-9377
Sea Watch International
Easton, MD .410-822-7500
Shelton's Poultry
Pomona, CA .800-541-1833
Stinson Seafood Company
Prospect Harbor, ME 207-963-7331
Sweet Sue Kitchens
Athens, AL 256-216-0500
Unilever
Lisle, IL 877-995-4483
Worthmore Food Product
Cincinnati, OH 513-559-1473

Canned Stew

Bunker Hill Foods
Augusta, GA .706-733-7765
Caltex Foods
Canoga Park, CA 800-522-5839
Campbell Company of Canada
Toronto, ON 800-575-7687
Campbell Soup Company
Camden, NJ .800-257-8443
Castleberry/Snow Brands
Augusta, GA .800-241-3520
ConAgra Foods/International Home Foods
Niagara Falls, ON 905-356-2661
Cordon Bleu International
Anjou, QC 514-352-3000
Faribault Foods
Minneapolis, MN 612-333-6461
Glenmark Food Processors
Chicago, IL .800-621-0117
Hoopeston Foods
Burnsville, MN 952-854-0903
Kelly Foods
Jackson, TN 731-424-2255
Midwest Foods
Owatonna, MN 507-451-7670
Old Ranchers Canning Company
Upland, CA .909-982-8895
On-Cor Foods Products
Northbrook, IL 847-205-1040
Sweet Sue Kitchens
Athens, AL 256-216-0500
Vietti Foods Company Inc
Nashville, TN 800-240-7864

Chicken & Dumplings

Culinary Standards Corporation
Louisville, KY 800-778-3434

Chicken & Noodles

Aunt Kathy's Homestyle Products
Waldheim, SK 306-945-2181
Country Cupboard
Virginia City, NV 775-847-7300
Culinary Standards Corporation
Louisville, KY 800-778-3434
Shelton's Poultry
Pomona, CA .800-541-1833
Swagger Foods Corporation
Vernon Hills, IL 847-913-1200

Chowder

Culinary Standards Corporation
Louisville, KY 800-778-3434
Fish Hopper
Monterey, CA 831-372-8543
LaMonica Fine Foods
Millville, NJ 856-825-8111
Look's Gourmet Food Company
Whiting, ME 800-962-6258
Mid-Atlantic Foods
Easton, MD .800-922-4688
Phillips Foods
Baltimore, MD 888-234-2722
Ronzoni Foods Canada
Etobicoke, ON 800-387-5032
Sea Watch International
Easton, MD .410-822-7500

Yankee Specialty Foods
Boston, MA.....................617-951-9904

Manhattan

Culinary Standards Corporation
Louisville, KY...................800-778-3434
LaMonica Fine Foods
Millville, NJ....................856-825-8111

New England

Advance Food Brokers
West Bloomfield, MI.............248-851-9045
Cagnon Foods Company
Brooklyn, NY...................718-647-2244
Campbell Company of Canada
Toronto, ON...................800-575-7687
Culinary Standards Corporation
Louisville, KY...................800-778-3434
Custom Food Products
Alsip, IL......................708-388-8883
Hormel Foods Corporation
Austin, MN....................800-523-4635
LaMonica Fine Foods
Millville, NJ....................856-825-8111

Cream of Broccoli

Culinary Standards Corporation
Louisville, KY...................800-778-3434

Cream of Mushroom

Culinary Standards Corporation
Louisville, KY...................800-778-3434

Cream of Potato

Culinary Standards Corporation
Louisville, KY...................800-778-3434

Dehydrated Soup

Associated Brands, Inc.
Medina, NY....................800-265-0050
Atlantic Quality Spice &Seasonings
Edison, NJ.....................800-584-0422
Borden Foods
Columbus, OH..................614-233-3759
Chef Merito
Encino, CA.....................800-637-4861
Dorothy Dawson Foods Products
Jackson, MI....................517-788-9830
Flavor House
Adelanto, CA...................760-246-9131
Frontier Soups
Waukegan, IL...................800-300-7867
Henningsen Foods
Purchase, NY...................914-701-4020
Maruchan
Irvine, CA.....................949-789-2300
Mayacamas Fine Foods
Sonoma, CA....................800-826-9621
Northwestern Foods
St Paul, MN...................800-236-4937

Sentry Seasonings
Elmhurst, IL....................630-530-5370

The product development experts of Sentry Seasonings are eager to offer the assistance and
hands-on experience to food processors of all
sizes. Sentry Seasonings will ensure the consistent
high quality and repeat sales of your products,
whether you choose one of our many off-the-shelf
Bench Mark products or a modified version to
meet your preferences. Sentry Seasonings can
also duplicate and/or improve your present flavor
profile; formulate, blend and package specifically
for your requirements.

Serv-Agen Corporation
Cherry Hill, NJ...................856-663-6966
SOUPerior Bean & Spice Company
Vancouver, WA..................800-878-7687

Tropical
Columbus, OH..................800-538-3941
VIP Foods
Flushing, NY...................718-821-3942
Vogue Cuisine
Culver City, CA.................888-236-4144
Williams-West & Witt Products
Michigan City, IN...............219-879-8236

Egg Drop Soup

Bestfoods Foodservice
Somerset, NJ...................732-627-8722

Fresh Stew

Heinz Company of Canada
North York, ON.................800-268-6641
Midwest Foods
Owatonna, MN.................507-451-7670
On-Cor Foods Products
Northbrook, IL.................847-205-1040
Vietti Foods Company Inc
Nashville, TN..................800-240-7864

Frozen Soup

Ajinomoto Frozen Foods USA
Portland, IR....................503-734-1528
Bellisio Foods, Inc.
Lakeville, MN..................800-368-7337
Campbell Soup Company of Canada
Listowel, ON...................800-575-7687
Chef Francisco of Pennsylvania
King of Prussia, PA..............610-265-7400
Chincoteague Seafood Company
Parsonsburg, MD...............443-260-4800
Culinary Standards Corporation
Louisville, KY...................800-778-3434
Dorothy Dawson Foods Products
Jackson, MI....................517-788-9830
Edmonds Chile Company
St Louis, MO...................314-772-1499
Fairfield Farm Kitchens
Tamworth, NH..................508-584-9300
Food Source
McKinney, TX..................972-548-9001
Gemini Food Industries
Fiskdale, MA...................508-347-2800
Heinz North America
Pittsburgh, PA..................412-237-5700
Mann's International Meat Specialties
Omaha, NE....................800-228-2170
Marburger Foods
Peru, IN......................765-689-5198
Marsan Foods
Toronto, ON...................416-755-9262
Progressa Quality Foods
Vineland, NJ...................800-200-9377
Shelton's Poultry
Pomona, CA...................800-541-1833
Truesoups
Kent, WA.....................253-872-0403
William Poll
New York, NY..................800-993-7655

Frozen Stew

Ajinomoto Frozen Foods USA
Portland, IR....................503-734-1528
Campbell Soup Company
Camden, NJ....................800-257-8443
Cleugh's Frozen Foods
Buena Park, CA.................714-521-1002
Edmonds Chile Company
St Louis, MO...................314-772-1499
Glenmark Food Processors
Chicago, IL....................800-621-0117
Heinz Company of Canada
North York, ON.................800-268-6641
Marsan Foods
Toronto, ON...................416-755-9262
Midwest Foods
Owatonna, MN.................507-451-7670
On-Cor Foods Products
Northbrook, IL.................847-205-1040
Sanderson Farms
Bryan, TX.....................979-778-5730

Gumbo

Bear Creek Kitchens
Marshall, TX...................888-300-7687

Cajun Crawfish Distributors
Cottonport, LA.................800-525-6813
Cajun Fry Company
Pierre Part, LA.................888-272-2586
Chef Hans Gourmet Foods
Monroe, LA....................800-890-4267
Cuizina Food Company
Woodinville, WA...............425-486-7000
Gazin's
New Orleans, LA...............800-262-6410
Kajun Kettle Foods
New Orleans, LA...............504-733-8800
Louisiana Gourmet Enterprises
Houma, LA....................800-328-5586
Vince's Seafoods
Gretna, LA....................504-368-1544
Yankee Specialty Foods
Boston, MA...................617-951-9904

Lentil Soup

Colonna Brothers
North Bergen, NJ...............201-864-1115
Country Cupboard
Virginia City, NV...............775-847-7300

Wonton Soup

Maruchan
Irvine, CA.....................949-789-2300
Wong Wing Foods
Montreal, QC..................800-361-4820

Stuffing

Meat

Texas Crumb & Food Products
Farmers Branch, TX.............800-522-7862
World Flavors
Warminster, PA.................215-672-4400

Relishes & Pickled Products

Pickled Products

A-1 Eastern Home Made   Pickle Company
Los Angeles, CA 323-223-1141
A.M. Braswell Jr. Food Company
Statesboro, GA 800-673-9388
Baensch Food
Milwaukee, WI 800-562-8234
Big B Distributors
Evansville, IN 812-425-5235
Bob Gordon & Associates
Chicago, IL 773-247-0588
Bryant Preserving Company
Alma, AR 800-634-2413
Cajun Chef Products
St Martinville, LA 337-394-7112
Campbell Soup Company
Camden, NJ 800-257-8443
Carson City Pickle Company
Carson City, MI 989-584-3148
Chloe Foods Corporation
Brooklyn, NY 718-827-3600
Commissariat Imports
Los Angeles, CA 310-475-5628
Cordon Bleu International
Anjou, QC 514-352-3000
Corsair Pepper Sauce
Gulfport, MS 228-452-9238
David Berg & Company
Chicago, IL 773-489-4711
Del Monte Foods
San Francisco, CA 800-543-3090
Dolores Canning Company
Los Angeles, CA 323-263-9155
F&S Produce Company
Rosenhayn, NJ 800-886-3316
Feature Foods
Etobicoke, ON 416-675-7350
Fjord Pacific Marine Industries
Richmond, BC 604-270-3393
Food City Pickle Company
Chicago, IL 269-781-9135
Foster Family Farm
South Windsor, CT 860-648-9366
Freestone Pickle Company
Bangor, MI 877-874-2553
G L Mezzetta
American Canyon, CA 707-648-1050
Giovanni's Appetizing Food Products
Richmond, MI 586-727-9355
Granny Blossom Specialty Foods
Wells, VT 802-645-0507
Great Lakes Kraut Company
Bear Creek, WI 715-752-4105
Hell on the Red
Telephone, TX 903-664-2573
Hermann Pickle Farm
Garrettsville, OH 800-245-2696
HVJ International
Spring, TX 877-730-3663
J.L. DeGraffenried & Sons
Springfield, MO 417-862-9411
L&S Packing Company
Farmingdale, NY 800-286-6487
Lakeside Packing Company
Harrow, ON 519-738-2314
Lancaster Packing Company
Lancaster, PA 717-397-9727
McCutcheon's Apple Products
Frederick, MD 800-888-7537
Mike's Fish & Seafood
Glenwood, MN 800-950-4755
Money's Mushrooms
Vancouver, BC 604-669-3741
Musco Olive Products
Orland, CA 530-865-4111
Ocean Beauty Seafoods
Seattle, WA 206-285-6800
Papetti's Egg Products
Elizabeth, NJ 800-524-3447
Paradise Products Corporation
Roslyn, NY 800-826-1235
Peer Foods Inc
Chicago, IL 800-365-5644
Pepperland Farms
Denham Springs, LA 225-665-3555

Porinos Gourmet Food
Central Falls, RI 800-826-3938
S&G Products
Nicholasville, KY 800-826-7652
Sara Lee Corporation
Downers Grove, IL 630-598-8100
Seneca Foods
Clyman, WI 920-696-3331
Sona & Hollen Foods
Los Alamitos, CA 800-200-7662
Springfield Smoked Fish Company
Springfield, MA 800-327-3412
Stanchfield Farms
Milo, ME 207-732-5173
Star Fine Foods
Fresno, CA 559-498-2900
Sumida Pickle Products
Honolulu, HI 808-841-4227
SW Red Smith
Davie, FL 954-581-1996
Talk O'Texas Brands
San Angelo, TX 325-655-6077
Tribe Mediterranean Foods Company LLC
Taunton, MA 800-421-3474
Troy Pork Store
Troy, NY 518-272-8291
Tucker Cellars
Sunnyside, WA 509-837-8701
United Pickle Products Corporation
Bronx, NY 718-933-6060
Wetta Egg Farm
Andale, KS 316-445-2231
Yergat Packing Co Inc
Fresno, CA 559-276-9180

Cauliflower

Bloch & Guggenheimer
Hurlock, MD 800-541-2809
S&G Products
Nicholasville, KY 800-826-7652

Eggs

Cordon Bleu International
Anjou, QC 514-352-3000
Feature Foods
Etobicoke, ON 416-675-7350
Papetti's Egg Products
Elizabeth, NJ 800-524-3447
SW Red Smith
Davie, FL 954-581-1996
Wetta Egg Farm
Andale, KS 316-445-2231

Meats

Sara Lee Corporation
Downers Grove, IL 630-598-8100
Troy Pork Store
Troy, NY 518-272-8291

Peppers

Apecka
Rockwall, TX 972-772-2654
Bay Valley Foods
Horsham, PA 800-236-1119
Bloch & Guggenheimer
Hurlock, MD 800-541-2809
F&S Produce Company
Rosenhayn, NJ 800-886-3316
G L Mezzetta
American Canyon, CA 707-648-1050
Porinos Gourmet Food
Central Falls, RI 800-826-3938
S&G Products
Nicholasville, KY 800-826-7652
Star Fine Foods
Fresno, CA 559-498-2900

Pickles

A-1 Eastern Home Made   Pickle Company
Los Angeles, CA 323-223-1141
A.M. Braswell Jr. Food Company
Statesboro, GA 800-673-9388

Alimentaire Whyte's Inc
Laval, QC 800-625-1979
Allen's Pickle Works
Glen Cove, NY 516-676-0640
Artichoke Kitchen
Hamilton, NC 252-798-2471
B&G Foods
Parsippany, NJ 973-401-6500
Bainbridge Festive Foods
Tunica, MS 800-545-9205
Batampte Pickle Foods, Inc.
Brooklyn, NY 718-251-2100
Bay Valley Foods
Horsham, PA 800-236-1119
Bay Valley Foods
Green Bay, WI 800-558-4700
Bessinger Pickle Company
Au Gres, MI 989-876-8008
Bick's Pickles
Dunnville, ON 905-774-7447
Blazzin Pickle Company
McAllen, TX 956-630-0733
Bloch & Guggenheimer
Hurlock, MD 800-541-2809
Blue Ridge Farms
Brooklyn, NY 718-827-9000
Cains Foods/Olde Cape Cod
Ayer, MA 800-225-0601
Caltex Foods
Canoga Park, CA 800-522-5839
Campbell Soup Company
Camden, NJ 800-257-8443
Carson City Pickle Company
Carson City, MI 989-584-3148
Cates & Sons
Faison, NC 910-267-4711
Chloe Foods Corporation
Brooklyn, NY 718-827-3600
Claussen Pickle Company
Woodstock, IL 800-435-2817
Clic International Inc
Laval, QC 450-669-2663
Commissariat Imports
Los Angeles, CA 310-475-5628
Country Cupboard
Virginia City, NV 775-847-7300
Dalton's Best Maid Products
Fort Worth, TX 817-335-5494
David Berg & Company
Chicago, IL 773-489-4711
Dean Distributing Inc
Green Bay, WI 920-469-6500
Dean Foods Company
Rosemont, IL 800-323-1571
Del Monte Foods
San Francisco, CA 800-543-3090
Erba Food Products
Brooklyn, NY 718-272-7700
Flaum Appetizing
Brooklyn, NY 718-821-1970
Florida Deli Pickle
Fort Lauderdale, FL 954-463-0222
Forge Mountain Foods
Hendersonville, NC 800-823-6743
GFA Brands
Paramus, NJ 201-568-9300
Gielow Pickles
Lexington, MI 810-359-7680
GWB Foods Corporation
Brooklyn, NY 718-686-9600
H.J. Heinz Company
Pittsburgh, PA 412-237-5948
Hausbeck Pickle Company
Saginaw, MI 866-754-4721
Heinz
Holland, MI 800-528-5757
Heinz Company
Trevose, PA 215-639-2343
Heinz Company of Canada
North York, ON 800-268-6641
Hermann Pickle Farm
Garrettsville, OH 800-245-2696
Hilltop Herb Farm & Restaurant
Cleveland, TX 832-397-4020
House of Spices India
Flushing, NY 718-507-4600

Howard Foods
Danvers, MA 978-774-6207
Hurd Orchards
Holley, NY 585-638-8838
Island Spring
Vashon, WA...................206-463-9848
J G Van Holten & Son
Waterloo, WI..................800-256-0619
J.L. DeGraffenried & Sons
Springfield, MO 417-862-9411
Jane Specialty Foods
Green Bay, WI.................800-558-4700
Kaiser Foods
Cincinnati, OH 888-291-0608
Kaplan & Zubrin
Camden, NJ...................800-334-0002
Kelly Pickle Company
Oconto, WI...................920-834-4433
Klein's Kosher Pickles
Phoenix, AZ 602-269-2072
Kruger Foods
Hayward, CA 510-782-2636
L&S Packing Company
Farmingdale, NY 800-286-6487
Lakeside Packing Company
Harrow, ON 519-738-2314
Lancaster Packing Company
Lancaster, PA 717-397-9727
Liberty Richter
Saddle Brook, NJ 201-291-8749
Limited Edition
Midland, TX 432-686-2008
Maine Coast Sea Vegetables
Franklin, ME 207-565-2907
Miramar Pickles & Food Products
Fort Lauderdale, FL 954-351-8030
Miss Ginny's Orginal Vermont Pickle Works
Northfield, VT 802-485-3057
Mixon Fruit Farms
Bradenton, FL 800-608-2525
Mount Olive Pickle Company
Mt Olive, NC 800-672-5041
Mr. Pickle
Brooklyn, NY 718-251-2500
Mt. Olive Pickle Company
Mt Olive, NC 800-672-5041
New Morning
Needham, MA 781-444-0440
Ocean Spray Cranberries
Aberdeen, WA.................800-662-3263
Olde Tyme Mercantile
Arroyo Grande, CA.............805-489-7991
Our Enterprises
Oklahoma City, OK 800-821-6375
Paisley Farms
Willoughby, OH 800-676-8656
Paradise Products Corporation
Roslyn, NY 800-826-1235
Patak Spices USA
Clearwater, FL 727-796-2126
Pemberton's Gourmet Foods
Gray, ME.....................800-255-8401
Picklesmith
Taft, TX 800-499-3401
Pinnacle Foods Group
Cherry Hill, NJ 877-852-7424
Porter's Pick-A-Dilly
Stowe, VT 802-253-6338
Precision Foods
St Louis, MO 800-647-8170
Pudlo Food Products Company
Chicago, IL 312-421-4862
Purity Products
Plainview, NY.................888-769-7873
Ralph Sechler & Son Inc
St Joe, IN....................800-332-5461
Regal Crown Foods
Worcester, MA 508-752-2679
Ripon Pickle Company
Ripon, WI 800-324-5493
Robert & Joseph
Redgranite, WI 920-566-2333
S&G Products
Nicholasville, KY 800-826-7652
Sambets Cajun Deli
Austin, TX....................800-472-6238
Sargent's Bear Necessities
North Troy, VT 802-988-2903
Schwartz Pickle Company
Chicago, IL 800-621-4273
Shawnee Canning Company
Cross Junction, VA.............800-713-1414

Stan-Mark Food Products
Chicago, IL 800-651-0994
Strub Pickles
Brantford, ON.................519-751-1717
Sumida Pickle Products
Honolulu, HI 808-841-4227
Sunshine Fresh
Totowa, NJ 973-812-4777
Texas Sassy Foods
Austin, TX....................512-215-4022
Tony Packo Food Company
Toledo, OH 866-472-2567
Topor's Pickle Company
Detroit, MI 313-237-0288
United Pickle Products Corporation
Bronx, NY 718-933-6060
Vaughn Rue Produce
Wilson, NC 800-388-8138
Vienna Sausage Company
Chicago, IL 800-326-6652
Whyte's Food Corporation
Mississauga, ON...............905-624-5065
William Harrison Vineyar
St Helena, CA.................800-913-9463
Willy's Pickle Products
Holland Landing, ON 905-836-6532

Dill

Allen's Pickle Works
Glen Cove, NY 516-676-0640
Bessinger Pickle Company
Au Gres, MI 989-876-8008
Food City Pickle Company
Chicago, IL 269-781-9135
Hausbeck Pickle Company
Saginaw, MI 866-754-4721
Hermann Pickle Farm
Garrettsville, OH...............800-245-2696
Schwartz Pickle Company
Chicago, IL 800-621-4273
Strub Pickles
Brantford, ON.................519-751-1717
United Pickle Products Corporation
Bronx, NY 718-933-6060

Gherkins

Paradise Products Corporation
Roslyn, NY 800-826-1235
S&G Products
Nicholasville, KY 800-826-7652

Kosher

Kaplan & Zubrin
Camden, NJ...................800-334-0002
Willy's Pickle Products
Holland Landing, ON 905-836-6532

Sweet

Food City Pickle Company
Chicago, IL 269-781-9135
Hausbeck Pickle Company
Saginaw, MI 866-754-4721
Schwartz Pickle Company
Chicago, IL 800-621-4273
United Pickle Products Corporation
Bronx, NY 718-933-6060
Willy's Pickle Products
Holland Landing, ON 905-836-6532

Vegetables

Apecka
Rockwall, TX 972-772-2654
Bloch & Guggenheimer
Hurlock, MD..................800-541-2809
Bob Gordon & Associates
Chicago, IL 773-247-0588
Carson City Pickle Company
Carson City, MI................989-584-3148
F&S Produce Company
Rosenhayn, NJ 800-886-3316
Foster Family Farm
South Windsor, CT 860-648-9366
G L Mezzetta
American Canyon, CA...........707-648-1050
Hell on the Red
Telephone, TX.................903-664-2573
Hermann Pickle Farm
Garrettsville, OH...............800-245-2696
HVJ International
Spring, TX....................877-730-3663

Johnson Canning Company
Sunnyside, WA................509-837-4188
L&S Packing Company
Farmingdale, NY 800-286-6487
Lancaster Packing Company
Lancaster, PA 717-397-9727
Landry's Pepper Company
St Martinville, LA...............337-394-6097
Miramar Pickles & Food Products
Fort Lauderdale, FL 954-351-8030
Money's Mushrooms
Vancouver, BC 604-669-3741
Musco Olive Products
Orland, CA 530-865-4111
Paradise Products Corporation
Roslyn, NY 800-826-1235
Pepperland Farms
Denham Springs, LA 225-665-3555
RES Food Products International
Green Bay, WI.................800-255-3768
Star Fine Foods
Fresno, CA 559-498-2900
Sumida Pickle Products
Honolulu, HI 808-841-4227
Talk O'Texas Brands
San Angelo, TX................325-655-6077
Tucker Cellars
Sunnyside, WA................509-837-8701
Yergat Packing Co Inc
Fresno, CA 559-276-9180

Relishes

A. Bauer's Mustard
Flushing, NY..................718-821-3570
A.M. Braswell Jr. Food Company
Statesboro, GA 800-673-9388
Adams
Fargo, ND 800-342-4748
Alimentaire Whyte's Inc
Laval, QC 800-625-1979
Aloha from Oregon
Eugene, OR 800-241-0300
Alto Rey Food Corporation
Studio City, CA................323-969-0178
American Culinary Gardens
Springfield, MO 888-831-2433
American Fine Food Corporation
Doral, FL.....................305-392-5000
Amigos Canning Company
San Antonio, TX...............800-580-3477
Arizona Pepper Products
Mesa, AZ....................800-359-3912
Aromont/USA
Paoli, PA.....................610-296-3748
Artichoke Kitchen
Hamilton, NC 252-798-2471
Assouline & Ting
Philadelphia, PA 800-521-4491
Au Printemps Gourmet
Prevost, QC...................800-663-0416
Authentic Specialty Foods
Chino, CA....................909-631-2000

Baldwin Richardson Foods
Frankfort, IL 866-644-2732

Baldwin Richardson Foods is a liquid ingredient manufacturer specializing in signature sauces, dessert toppings, beverage/pancake syrups, specialty fruit fillings and condiments. Packaging capabilities range from portion control cups and pouches to standard retail and foodservice packs and include industrial drums and totes. Full service R&D and Quality groups dedicated to new product development, with in-house stability and analytical testing. Call for assistance.

Bay Valley Foods
Horsham, PA 800-236-1119
Bay Valley Foods
Green Bay, WI.................800-558-4700
BBQ Bunch
Kansas City, MO..............816-941-6789

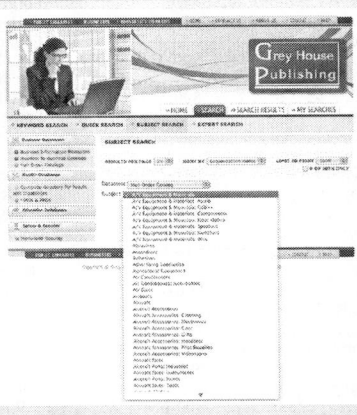

Best Provision Company, Inc.
Newark, NJ 800-631-4466
Big B Distributors
Evansville, IN 812-425-5235
Blue Jay Orchards
Bethel, CT 203-748-0119
Blue Ridge Farms
Brooklyn, NY 718-827-9000
Boca Grande Foods
Duluth, GA 800-788-8026
Boetje Foods
Rock Island, IL 877-726-3853
Bogland
Pembroke, MA 781-829-9549
Bottle Green Drinks
Mississauga, ON 905-273-6137
Brede
Detroit, MI 313-273-1079
Brockles Foods Company
Garland, TX 972-272-5593
Bryant Preserving Company
Alma, AR 800-634-2413
Burleson's
Waxahachie, TX 972-937-4810
C&E Canners
Hammonton, NJ 609-561-1078
C.F. Sauer Company
Richmond, VA 800-688-5676
Cafe Terra Cotta
Tucson, AZ 800-492-4454
Cains Foods/Olde Cape Cod
Ayer, MA 800-225-0601
Cajun Chef Products
St Martinville, LA 337-394-7112
California Fruit Packing Company
Yuba City, CA 530-822-9020
Califrance
Los Angeles, CA 310-440-0729
Campbell Soup Company
Camden, NJ 800-257-8443
Carolina Treet
Wilmington, NC 800-616-6344
Carolyn's Caribbean Heat
Malvern, PA 610-647-0336
Castleberry/Snow Brands
Augusta, GA 800-241-3520
Cates & Sons
Faison, NC 910-267-4711
Catskill Mountain Specialties
Saugerties, NY 800-311-3473
Chandler Foods
Greensboro, NC 800-537-6219
Cherith Valley Gardens
Fort Worth, TX 800-610-9813
Chicago Sweeteners
Des Plaines, IL 847-299-1999
Chipotle Chile Company
Milford, MI 248-496-8308
Chloe Foods Corporation
Brooklyn, NY 718-827-3600
Christie Food Products
Randolph, MA 800-727-2523
Cinnabar Specialty Foods
Prescott, AZ 866-293-6433
Claussen Pickle Company
Woodstock, IL 800-435-2817
Clements Foods Company
Oklahoma City, OK 800-654-8355
Commissariat Imports
Los Angeles, CA 310-475-5628
ConAgra Grocery Products
Irvine, CA 714-680-1000
Conroy Foods
Pittsburgh, PA 412-781-1446
Consumer Guild Foods
Toledo, OH 419-726-3406
Consumers Vinegar & Spice Company
Chicago, IL 773-376-4100
Corfu Foods
Bensenville, IL 630-595-2510
Cosmopolitan Foods
Glen Ridge, NJ 973-680-4560
Country Cupboard
Virginia City, NV 775-847-7300
Culinary Imports
Jericho, VT 800-958-7678
Curry King Corporation
Waldwick, NJ 800-287-7987
Cyclone Enterprises
Houston, TX 281-872-0087
Daisy Brand
Dallas, TX 877-292-9830

Danisco USA
Lakeland, FL 863-646-0165
Darling International
Cleveland, OH 216-651-9300
Davis Food Company
Plantation, FL 954-791-5868
Dean Distributing Inc
Green Bay, WI. 920-469-6500
Del Grosso Foods
Tipton, PA 800-521-5880
Del Monte Foods
San Francisco, CA 800-543-3090
Delallo Italian Foods
Jeannette, PA 724-523-5000
Dhidow Enterprises
Oxford, PA 610-932-7868
Dickson's Pure Honey
San Angelo, TX 915-655-9233
E. Waldo Ward & Son Corporation
Sierra Madre, CA 800-355-9273
Earth Island Natural Foods
Canoga Park, CA 818-725-2820
Ehmann Olive Company
Oroville, CA 530-533-3303
Elwood International
Copiague, NY 631-842-6600
Embasa Foods
Chino, CA 888-236-2272
Europa Foods
Saddle Brook, NJ 201-368-8929
Firth Maple Products
Spartansburg, PA 814-654-2435
Flamm Pickle & Packing Company
Eau Claire, MI 269-461-6916
Flavormatic Industries
Wappingers Falls, NY 845-297-9100
Flavors of the Heartland
Rocheport, MO 800-269-3210
Fliinko
South Dartmouth, MA 508-996-9609
Florasynth
New York, NY 212-371-7700
Florida Deli Pickle
Fort Lauderdale, FL 954-463-0222
Food City Pickle Company
Chicago, IL 269-781-9135
Forge Mountain Foods
Hendersonville, NC 800-823-6743
Fountain Valley Foods
Colorado Springs, CO. 719-573-6012
Fox Hollow Farm
Hanover, NH 603-643-6002
French's Ingredients
Springfield, MO 417-837-1813
Furst-McNess Company/Terrapin Ridge
Freeport, IL 800-999-4052
Garden Row Foods
St Charles, IL 800-505-9999
Garden Row Foods
Franklin Park, IL 800-555-9798
Gerkens Cacao   Wilbur Chocolate Company
Lititz, PA. 800-233-0139
Gil's Gourmet Gallery
Sand City, CA 800-438-7480
Glen Rose Meat Company
Vernon, IL 323-589-3393
Golding Farms Foods
Winston Salem, NC. 336-766-6161
Graves Mountain Cannery
Syria, VA 540-923-4747
Green Garden Food Products
Kent, WA. 800-304-1033
Groeb Farms
Onsted, MI 517-467-7100
Grouse Hunt Farms
Tamaqua, PA 570-467-2850
Growth Products
Racine, WI 262-637-9287
H.J. Heinz Company
Pittsburgh, PA 412-237-5948
Half Moon Bay Trading Company
Atlantic Beach, FL 888-447-2823
Halifax Group
Doraville, GA 770-452-8828
Hanson Thompson Honey Farms
Redfield, SD 605-472-0474
Hartford City Foam Pack aging & Converting
Hartford City, IN. 765-348-2500
Haus Barhyte
Pendleton, OR. 800-407-9241
Hausbeck Pickle Company
Saginaw, MI 866-754-4721

Heintz & Weber Company
Buffalo, NY. 716-852-7171
Heinz
Fremont, OH 419-332-7357
Heinz Company of Canada
North York, ON 800-268-6641
Heinz North America
Pittsburgh, PA 412-237-5700
Heller Seasonings
Chicago, IL 800-323-2726
Heluva Good Cheese
Sodus, NY 315-483-6971
Hendon & David
Millbrook, NY 845-677-9696
Herlocher Foods
State College, PA 800-437-5624
Hilltop Herb Farm & Restaurant
Cleveland, TX 832-397-4020
Honey Acres
Ashippun, WI 800-558-7745
Honeypot Treats
Camden, NY 800-223-1024
Howard Foods
Danvers, MA 978-774-6207
Hudson Valley Homestead
Craryville, NY 518-851-7336
Hume Specialties
Winston Salem, NC 802-875-3117
IMEX Enterprises
Hatboro, PA 215-672-2887
Imus Ranch Foods
Holtsville, NY 888-284-4687
Isabel's Country Mustard
Columbia, MO 877-441-9188
J G Van Holten & Son
Waterloo, WI. 800-256-0619
J.L. DeGraffenried & Sons
Springfield, MO 417-862-9411
J.N. Bech
Elk Rapids, MI 800-232-4583
J.W. Raye & Company
Eastport, ME 800-853-1903
Jalapeno Foods Company
Brea, CA 800-863-9198
Jalapeno Foods Company
The Woodlands, TX 800-896-2318
Jardine Foods
Buda, TX. 800-544-1880
Jay Shah Foods
Mississauga, ON 905-696-0172
Joe Hutson Foods
Jacksonville, FL 904-731-9065
Joseph Bertman Foods
Cleveland, OH 216-431-4460
Kaiser Foods
Cincinnati, OH 888-291-0608
Kaplan & Zubrin
Camden, NJ. 800-334-0002
Keller's Creamery
Harleysville, PA 800-535-5371
Kelly Pickle Company
Oconto, WI 920-834-4433
Khatsa & Company
Bellevue, WA 888-542-8728
Kid's Pantry
Grants Pass, OR 800-452-9551
Kitchen Kettle Foods
Intercourse, PA 800-732-3538
Klein Pickle Company
Phoenix, AZ 602-269-2072
Klein's Kosher Pickles
Phoenix, AZ 602-269-2072
Kozlowski Farms
Forestville, CA 800-473-2767
Kruger Foods
Hayward, CA 510-782-2636
La Vencedora Products
Los Angeles, CA. 800-327-2572
Lakeside Packing Company
Harrow, ON 519-738-2314
Lancaster Packing Company
Lancaster, PA 717-397-9727
Landry's Pepper Company
St Martinville, LA. 337-394-6097
Laredo Mexican Foods
Fort Wayne, IN 800-252-7336
Letraw Manufacturing Company
Rockford, IL 815-987-9670
Lochhead Manufacturing Company
Fenton, MO 888-776-2088
Lounsbury Foods
Toronto, ON 416-656-6330

M&G Honey Farms
Bushton, KS .316-562-3643
M.A. Hatt & Sons
Lunenburg, NS 902-634-8407
M.W. Milton & Company
Louisville, KY 502-587-5016
MacDonald Honey Company
Sauquoit, NY 315-737-5662
Marburger Foods
Peru, IN 765-689-5198
Mardale Specialty Foods
Waukegan, IL 847-336-4777
McCutcheon's Apple Products
Frederick, MD 800-888-7537
Mendocino Mustard
Fort Bragg, CA 800-964-2270
Mo Hotta-Mo Betta
San Luis Obispo, CA 800-462-3220
Monticello Canning Company
Crossville, TN 931-484-3696
Mount Olive Pickle Company
Mt Olive, NC 800-672-5041
Mrs. Dog's Products
Tampa, FL .800-267-7364
National Vinegar Company
Houston, TX 713-223-4214
Nature Quality
San Martin, CA 408-683-2182
Nestelles's
Tangent, OR 503-393-7056
New Canaan Farms
Dripping Springs, TX 800-727-5267
New England Natural Bakers
Greenfield, MA 800-910-2884
Newman's Own
Westport, CT 203-222-0136
Novartis Nutrition Corporation
Minneapolis, MN 952-848-6000
NPC Dehydrators
Eden, NC 336-635-5190
NutraSweet Company
Chicago, IL 800-535-2656
O'Garvey Sauces
New Braunfels, TX 830-620-6127
Oasis Foods Company
Hillside, NJ 908-964-0477
Ocean Spray Cranberries
Kenosha, WI 262-694-0621
Ocean Spray Cranberries
Lakeville-Middleboro, MA 800-662-3263
Ojai Cook
Los Angeles, CA 886-571-1551
Old Dutch Mustard Company
Great Neck, NY 516-466-0522
Olds Products Company
Pleasant Prairie, WI 800-233-8064
Olives & Foods Inc
Hialeah, FL 305-821-3444
Orleans Packing Company
Hyde Park, MA 617-361-6611
Paisley Farms
Willoughby, OH 800-676-8656
Palmieri Food Products
New Haven, CT 800-845-5447
Patak Spices USA
Clearwater, FL 727-796-2126
Peaceworks
New York, NY 212-897-3995
Pepper Creek Farms
Lawton, OK 800-526-8132
Peter's Mustards
Sharon, CT 860-364-0842
Plochman
Manteno, IL 815-468-3434
PM AG Products
Homewood, IL 800-323-2663
Precise Food Ingredients
Carrollton, TX 972-323-4951
Quaker Sugar Company
Brooklyn, NY 718-387-6500
R.B. Morriss Company
Diamond Bar, CA 909-861-8671
R.E. Kimball & Company
Amesbury, MA 978-388-1826
Ragsdale-Overton Food Traditions
Smithfield, NC 888-424-8863
Red Gold
Elwood, IN 877-748-9798
Red Pelican Food Products
Detroit, MI 313-921-2500
Refined Sugars
Yonkers, NY 800-431-1020

Reily Foods Company
New Orleans, LA 504-524-6132
Reily Foods/JFG Coffee Company
Knoxville, TN 800-535-1961
Renfro Foods
Fort Worth, TX 817-336-3849
Rex Wine Vinegar Company
Newark, NJ 973-589-6911
Ripon Pickle Company
Ripon, WI .800-324-5493
Robert & James Brands
Birmingham, MI 248-646-0578
Ruby Apiaries
Milnor, ND 701-427-5263
Sal's Caesar Dressing
Novato, CA 415-897-0605
Salad Oils International Corporation
Chicago, IL 773-261-0500
Seminole Foods
Springfield, OH 800-881-1177
Seneca Foods
Clyman, WI 920-696-3331
Sensient Technologies
Milwaukee, WI 800-558-9892
Shenk's Foods
Lancaster, PA 717-393-4240
Shiloh Foods
Savannah, TN 800-795-2550
Smiling Fox Pepper Company
North Aurora, IL 630-337-3734
Snowizard Extracts
New Orleans, LA 800-366-9766
Somerset Industries
Spring House, PA 800-883-8728
Sona & Hollen Foods
Los Alamitos, CA 800-200-7662
Sperry Apiaries
Kindred, ND 701-428-3000
St. Martin Sugar Cooperative
St Martinville, LA 337-394-3255
St. Mary Sugar Cooperative
Jeanerette, LA 337-276-6761
Stage Coach Sauces
Palatka, FL 386-328-6330
Stan-Mark Food Products
Chicago, IL 800-651-0994
Stickney & Poor Company
North Andover, MA 508-261-8967
Strub Pickles
Brantford, ON 519-751-1717
Sun Valley Mustard
Hailey, ID .800-628-7124
Sunshine Fresh
Totowa, NJ 973-812-4777
Sweet Baby Ray's
Marlboro, MA 877-729-2229
T Hasegawa Flavors USA
Cerritos, CA 714-670-1586
T. Marzetti Company
Columbus, OH 614-846-2232
Tapatio Hot Sauce
Vernon, CA 323-587-8933
Target Flavors
Brookfield, CT 800-538-3350
Terrapin Ridge
Freeport, IL 800-999-4052
Thistledew Farm
Proctor, WV 800-854-6639
Tipp Distributors
El Paso, TX 888-668-2639
Tony Packo Food Company
Toledo, OH 866-472-2567
Topper Food Products
East Brunswick, NJ 800-377-2823
Ultimate Gourmet
Belle Mead, NJ 908-359-4050
United Pickle Products Corporation
Bronx, NY .718-933-6060
Van De Walle Farms
San Antonio, TX 210-436-5551
Ventura Foods
Philadelphia, PA 215-223-8700
Ventura Foods
Ft Worth, TX 817-232-5450
Vi-Gor Cup Corporation
Bellmore, NY 516-431-7722
Vidalia Sweets Brand
Lyons, GA .912-565-8881
Welch's Foods Inc
Kennewick, WA 509-582-2131
Whipple Company
Natick, MA 800-345-2925

Wild Thyme Cottage Products
Pointe Claire, QC 514-695-3602
Wing Candy Company
Branson, MO 417-334-3238
Wing's Food Products
Toronto, ON 416-259-2662
Wing-Time
Steamboat Spgs, CO 970-871-1198
Wisconsin Wilderness Food Products
Milwaukee, WI 800-359-3039
Yangtze Agribusiness Group
Great Neck, NY 516-466-1996
Ye Olde Pepper Company
Salem, MA 866-393-6533

Beets

Beetroot Delights
Foothill, ON 888-842-3387

Relishes & Condiments

Baldwin Richardson Foods
Frankfort, IL 866-644-2732

Baldwin Richardson Foods is a liquid ingredient manufacturer specializing in signature sauces, dessert toppings, beverage/pancake syrups, specialty fruit fillings and condiments. Packaging capabilities range from portion control cups and pouches to standard retail and foodservice packs and include industrial drums and totes. Full service R&D and Quality groups dedicated to new product development, with in-house stability and analytical testing. Call for assistance.

Grandma Hoerner's Foods
Alma, KS .785-765-2300
Howard Foods
Danvers, MA 978-774-6207
Shawnee Canning Company
Cross Junction, VA 800-713-1414

Texas Sassy Foods
Austin, TX 512-215-4022
Virginia Chutney Company
Washington, VA 540-675-1984

Sauerkraut

A.C. Kissling Company
Philadelphia, PA 800-445-1943
Alimentaire Whyte's Inc
Laval, QC 800-625-1979
Bick's Pickles
Dunnville, ON 905-774-7447
Bush Brothers & Company
Shiocton, WI 920-986-3816
Del Monte Foods
San Francisco, CA 800-543-3090
Dietz & Watson
Philadelphia, PA 800-333-1974

EMERLING INTERNATIONAL FOODS, INC.

Emerling International Foods
Buffalo, NY 716-833-7381

We supply food manufacturers and food service
customers worldwide (since 1988) with bulk ingredients including: Fruits & Vegetables; Juice
Concentrates; Herbs & Spices; Oils & Vinegars;
Flavors & Colors; Honey & Molasses. We also
produce PURE MAPLE SYRUP.

Flaum Appetizing
Brooklyn, NY 718-821-1970
Fremont Company
Fremont, OH 419-334-8995
Great Lakes Kraut Company
Bear Creek, WI 715-752-4105
Hirzel Canning Company &Farms
Northwood, OH 419-693-0531
Kaiser Foods
Cincinnati, OH 888-291-0608
Kruger Foods
Hayward, CA 510-782-2636
Lakeside Foods
Seymour, WI 920-833-2371
Lakeside Packing Company
Harrow, ON 519-738-2314
Miramar Pickles & Food Products
Fort Lauderdale, FL 954-351-8030
New Harvest Foods
Pulaski, WI 920-822-2578
New Morning
Needham, MA 781-444-0440
Rea-D-Pak Foodservices
North Norwich, NY 800-255-7288
Red Pelican Food Products
Detroit, MI 313-921-2500
Ripon Pickle Company
Ripon, WI 800-324-5493
Schwartz Pickle Company
Chicago, IL 800-621-4273
Strub Pickles
Brantford, ON 519-751-1717
United Pickle Products Corporation
Bronx, NY 718-933-6060
Victor Preserving Company
Ontario, NY 315-524-2711
Willy's Pickle Products
Holland Landing, ON 905-836-6532

Juice

Claussen Pickle Company
Woodstock, IL 800-435-2817
Del Monte Foods
San Francisco, CA 800-543-3090
Fremont Company
Fremont, OH 419-334-8995
Gwaltney of Smithfield
Smithfield, VA 800-888-7521
Hirzel Canning Company &Farms
Northwood, OH 419-693-0531
Kaiser Foods
Cincinnati, OH 888-291-0608
Leo G. Fraboni Sausage Company
Hibbing, MN 218-263-5074
M.A. Hatt & Sons
Lunenburg, NS 902-634-8407

Sauces, Dips & Dressings

Condiments

A Taste of the Kingdom
Kingdom City, MO 888-592-5080
A.M. Braswell Jr. Food Company
Statesboro, GA 800-673-9388
Alimentaire Whyte's Inc
Laval, QC 800-625-1979
Allied Old English
Port Reading, NJ 732-602-8955
American Spoon Foods
Petoskey, MI 800-222-5886
Appledore Cove LLC
North Berwick, ME. 888-849-1787
Ashman Manufacturing & Distributing Company
Virginia Beach, VA. 800-641-9924
Atlantic Quality Spice &Seasonings
Edison, NJ 800-584-0422
Au Printemps Gourmet
Prevost, QC 800-663-0416
Bartush-Schnitzius Foods Company
Lewisville, TX 972-219-1270
Baumer Foods
New Orleans, LA 504-482-5761
Bear Meadow Farm
Colrain, MA 800-653-9241
Beetroot Delights
Foothill, ON 888-842-3387
Bel/Kaukauna USA
Kaukauna, WI. 800-558-3500
Bessinger Pickle Company
Au Gres, MI 989-876-8008
Betty Lou's Golden Smackers
McMinnville, OR 800-242-5205
Bick's Pickles
Dunnville, ON. 905-774-7447
Big B Distributors
Evansville, IN 812-425-5235
Blue Ridge Farms
Brooklyn, NY 718-827-9000
Bob Gordon & Associates
Chicago, IL 773-247-0588
Boetje Foods
Rock Island, IL 877-726-3853
Border Foods Inc
Deming, NM 888-737-7752
Bottle Green Drinks
Mississauga, ON. 905-273-6137
Brad's Taste of New York
Floral Park, NY 516-354-9004
Brede
Detroit, MI 313-273-1079
Bryant Preserving Company
Alma, AR 800-634-2413
Bush Brothers & Company
Shiocton, WI. 920-986-3816
C&E Canners
Hammonton, NJ 609-561-1078
C.F. Sauer Company
Mauldin, SC 800-688-5676
Cains Foods
Ayer, MA. 978-772-0300
CaJohns Fiery Foods
Columbus, OH 888-703-3473
Cajun Chef Products
St Martinville, LA. 337-394-7112
California Creative Foods
Oceanside, CA 760-757-2622
Caltex Foods
Canoga Park, CA 800-522-5839
Carol Hall's Hot Pepper Jelly
Fort Bragg, CA 866-737-7379
Carolina Treet
Wilmington, NC 800-616-6344
Carolyn's Caribbean Heat
Malvern, PA 610-647-0336
Carriage House Companies
Fredonia, NY 800-828-8915
Casa Visco Finer Food Company
Schenectady, NY. 888-607-2823
Castleberry/Snow Brands
Augusta, GA 800-241-3520
Cedarvale Food Products
Toronto, ON 416-656-6330
Chandler Foods
Greensboro, NC 800-537-6219

Chicago 58 Food Products
Toronto, ON 416-603-4244
Chloe Foods Corporation
Brooklyn, NY 718-827-3600
Christie Food Products
Randolph, MA 800-727-2523
Christopher Ranch
Gilroy, CA. 408-847-1100
CHS, Inc.
Inner Grove Heights, MN 800-232-3639
Cinnabar Specialty Foods
Prescott, AZ 866-293-6433
Clements Foods Company
Oklahoma City, OK 800-654-8355
Cold Hollow Cider Mill
Waterbury Center, VT 800-327-7537
Commissariat Imports
Los Angeles, CA. 310-475-5628
Consumers Vinegar & Spice Company
Chicago, IL 773-376-4100
Corfu Foods
Bensenville, IL 630-595-2510
Creative Foodworks
San Antonio, TX 210-212-4761
Creole Fermentation Industries
Abbeville, LA 337-898-9377
Cuizina Food Company
Woodinville, WA. 425-486-7000
Cumberland Packing Corporation
Brooklyn, NY 718-858-4200
Dalton's Best Maid Products
Fort Worth, TX 817-335-5494
Dave's Gourmet
San Francisco, CA 800-758-0372
Deer Mountain Berry Farms
Granite Falls, WA 360-691-7586
Del Monte Foods
San Francisco, CA 800-543-3090
Del Monte Foods
Cambria, WI. 920-348-5121
Diamond Crystal
Savannah, GA 800-227-4455
Diamond Crystal Brands
Savannah, GA 912-651-5112
Dorina/So-Good
Union, IL 815-923-2144
Earth Island Natural Foods
Canoga Park, CA 818-725-2820
Edward & Sons Trading Company
Carpinteria, CA 805-684-8500
El Paso Chile Company
El Paso, TX 888-472-5727
El Toro Food Products
Watsonville, CA 831-728-9266
Elwood International
Copiague, NY 631-842-6600
Enrico's/Ventre Packing
Syracuse, NY 888-472-8237
Erba Food Products
Brooklyn, NY 718-272-7700
Erbrich-Sewell Products Company
Indianapolis, IN 317-925-6433
Famous Chili
Fort Smith, AR 479-782-0096
Fernandez Chili Company
Alamosa, CO. 719-589-6043
Fireside Kitchen
Halifax, NS 902-454-7387
Ford's Fancy Fruit
Raleigh, NC 800-446-0947
Fountain Valley Foods
Colorado Springs, CO 719-573-6012
Freda Quality Meats
Philadelphia, PA 800-443-7332
Fremont Company
Fremont, OH. 419-334-8995
French's Flavor Ingredients
Springfield, MO 800-437-3624
G E Barbour
Sussex, NB 506-432-2300
Garden Complements
Kansas City, MO. 800-966-1091
GFA Brands
Paramus, NJ 201-568-9300
GFF
City of Industry, CA 323-232-6255

Gibbons Bee Farm
Ballwin, MO. 877-736-8607
Girard's Food Service Dressings
City of Industry, CA 888-327-8442
Golden Gate Foods
Dallas, TX 214-747-2223
Golden Specialty Foods
Norwalk, CA 562-802-2537
Golden State Foods
City of Industry, CA 626-968-6431
Golden State Foods
Irvine, CA 949-252-2000
Golden Valley Foods
Abbotsford, BC. 888-299-8855
Golden Whisk
South San Francisco, CA 800-660-5222
Gourmet Central
Romney, WV. 800-984-3722
Gourmet Foods
Knoxville, TN 865-970-2982
Goya Foods
Secaucus, NJ 201-348-4900
Graysmarsh Farm
Sequim, WA 800-683-4367
Greaves Jams & Marmalades
Niagara-on-the-Lake, ON. 800-515-9939
Green Garden Food Products
Kent, WA. 800-304-1033
Griffin Food Company
Muskogee, OK 800-580-6311
GWB Foods Corporation
Brooklyn, NY 718-686-9600
H&F Food Products Company
Buffalo, NY. 716-876-4345
H.J. Heinz Company
Pittsburgh, PA 800-872-2229
Halben Food Manufacturing Company
Overland, MO 800-888-4855
Harpo's
Honolulu, HI 808-537-3439
Hawaiian Fruit Specialties
Kalaheo, HI. 808-332-9333
Heinz Company
Trevose, PA 215-639-2343
Heinz Company of Canada
North York, ON. 800-268-6641
Hell on the Red
Telephone, TX. 903-664-2573
Hombres Foods
Cedar Creek, TX 877-446-6273
Homegrown Naturals
Napa, CA. 800-288-1089
Hoople Country Kitchens
Rockport, IN 812-649-2351
Hormel Foods Corporation
Austin, MN 800-523-4635
House of Spices India
Flushing, NY. 718-507-4600
House of Webster
Rogers, AR 800-369-4641
Howjax
Pembroke Pines, FL 954-441-2491
HVJ International
Spring, TX. 877-730-3663
Hyde & Hyde
Cerritos, CA 562-926-9238
Instantwhip: Florida
Tampa, FL. 813-621-3233
International Food Products Corporation
Saint Louis, MO 800-227-8427
International Home Foods
Milton, PA. 973-359-9920
J.L. DeGraffenried & Sons
Springfield, MO 417-862-9411
J.N. Bech
Elk Rapids, MI 800-232-4583
Jalapeno Foods Company
The Woodlands, TX 800-896-2318
Jasmine & Bread
S Royalton, VT 802-763-7115
JMS Specialty Foods
Ripon, WI 800-535-5437
John Volpi & Company
St Louis, MO. 800-288-3439
Junuis Food Products
Palatine, IL 847-359-4300

Kamish Food Products
Chicago, IL 773-267-0400
Kari-Out Company
White Plains, NY 800-433-8799
Kathy's Gourmet Specialties
Mendocino, CA 707-937-1383
Ken's Foods
Marlborough, MA 800-633-5800
Kitchen Kettle Foods
Intercourse, PA 800-732-3538
Knese Enterprise
Floral Park, NY 516-354-9004
Korinek & Company
Cicero, IL 773-242-1917
Kozlowski Farms
Forestville, CA 800-473-2767
Kraft
Parsippany, NJ 973-292-1755
Kraft Foods
Garland, TX 972-272-7511
Krinos Foods
Long Island City, NY 718-729-9000
Kruger Foods
Hayward, CA 510-782-2636
L&S Packing Company
Farmingdale, NY 800-286-6487
Lakeside Foods
Seymour, WI 920-833-2371
Lakeside Packing Company
Harrow, ON 519-738-2314
Landry's Pepper Company
St Martinville, LA 337-394-6097
Lea & Perrins
Fair Lawn, NJ 800-289-5797
Lee Kum Kee
Brooklyn, NY 800-346-7562
Li'l Guy Foods
Kansas City, MO 800-886-8226
Liberty Richter
Saddle Brook, NJ 201-291-8749
Litehouse Foods
Sandpoint, ID 800-669-3169
Lounsbury Foods
Toronto, ON 416-656-6330
M.A. Gedney
Chaska, MN 952-448-2612
Mad Will's Food Company
Auburn, CA 888-275-9455
Mardale Specialty Foods
Waukegan, IL 847-336-4777
Marsa Specialty Products
Vernon, CA 800-628-0500
Marukan Vinegar (U.S.A.) Inc.
Paramount, CA 562-630-6060
McIlhenny Company
New Orleans, LA 800-634-9599
Miguel's Stowe Away
Stowe, VT 800-448-6517
Mizkam Americas
Kansas City, MO 816-483-1700
Modern Packaging
Duluth, GA 770-622-1500
Morgan Food
Austin, IN 888-430-1780
Morse's Sauerkraut
Waldoboro, ME 866-832-5569
Mullins Food Products
Broadview, IL 708-344-3224
Musco Olive Products
Orland, CA 530-865-4111
Nature Quality
San Martin, CA 408-683-2182
New Canaan Farms
Dripping Springs, TX 800-727-5267
New England Natural Bakers
Greenfield, MA 800-910-2884
New Morning
Needham, MA 781-444-0440
Oasis Foods Company
Hillside, NJ 908-964-0477
Oberweis Dairy
North Aurora, IL 888-645-5868
Olde Tyme Mercantile
Arroyo Grande, CA 805-489-7991
Olympia International
Belvidere, IL 815-547-5972
Once Again Nut Butter
Nunda, NY 888-800-8075
Original Juan
Kansas City, KS 800-568-8468
Pacific Choice Brands
Fresno, CA 559-237-5583

Palmieri Food Products
New Haven, CT 800-845-5447
Paradise Products Corporation
Roslyn, NY 800-826-1235
Pastene Companies
Canton, MA 781-830-8200
Phamous Phloyd's Barbeque Sauce
Denver, CO 303-757-3285
Piknik Products Company Inc
Montgomery, AL 334-265-1567
Pilgrim Foods
Greenville, NH 603-878-2100
Porinos Gourmet Food
Central Falls, RI 800-826-3938
Portion Pac
Mason, OH 800-232-4829
Prairie Thyme
Santa Fe, NM 800-869-0009
Progress Industries
Mansfield, OH 419-756-0044
Pudlo Food Products Company
Chicago, IL 312-421-4862
Purity Farms
Sedalia, CO 800-568-4433
Purity Products
Plainview, NY 888-769-7873
Ralph Sechler & Son Inc
St Joe, IN 800-332-5461
Rapazzini Winery
Gilroy, CA 408-842-5649
Rea-D-Pak Foodservices
North Norwich, NY 800-255-7288
Ready Foods
Denver, CO 303-892-5861
Reser's Fine Foods
Salt Lake City, UT 801-972-5633
Restaurant Lulu Gourmet Products
San Francisco, CA 888-693-5800
REX Pure Foods
Gonzales, TX 800-344-8314
Richardson Foods Corporation
Macedon, NY 315-986-2807
River Run
Burlington, VT 802-863-0499
Rod's Food Products
City of Industry, CA 909-839-8925
Roller Ed
Rochester, NY 585-458-8020
Rosarita Mexican Foods Company
Mesa, AZ 480-964-8751
Rowena's
Norfolk, VA 800-627-8699
Royal Food Products
Indianapolis, IN 317-782-2660
S&G Products
Nicholasville, KY 800-826-7652
Sambets Cajun Deli
Austin, TX 800-472-6238
San Benito Foods
Hollister, CA 831-637-4434
Santa Barbara Olive Company
Goleta, CA 800-624-4896
Sara Lee Coffee & Tea   Wholesale Coffee & Tea
Location
Minneapolis, MN 888-246-2598
Savoie's Sausage & Food Products
Opelousas, LA 337-948-4115
Schlotterbeck & Foss Company
Portland, ME 800-777-4666
Schwartz Pickle Company
Chicago, IL 800-621-4273
Scott-Bathgate
Winnipeg, NB 204-943-8525
Seneca Foods
Clyman, WI 920-696-3331
Shenk's Foods
Lancaster, PA 717-393-4240
Shiloh Foods
Savannah, TN 800-795-2550
Signature Fruit
Stockton, CA 209-931-1531
Silver Palate Kitchens
Cresskill, NJ 800-872-5283
Silver Spring Gardens
Eau Claire, WI 800-826-7322
Sioux Honey Association/Sue Bee
Sioux City, IA 712-258-0638
Sisler's Ice & Ice Cream
Ohio, IL 888-891-3856
Skjodt-Barrett Foods
Mississauga, ON 877-600-1200

Somerset Industries
Spring House, PA 800-883-8728
Sona & Hollen Foods
Los Alamitos, CA 800-200-7662
Spanish Gardens Food Manufacturing
Kansas City, KS 913-831-4242
Spectrum Organic Products
Petaluma, CA 800-995-2705
Sprague Foods
Belleville, ON 613-966-1200
Steel's Gourmet Foods
Bridgeport, PA 800-678-3357
Stickney & Poor Company
North Andover, MA 508-261-8967
Stone Cellar Kitchens
Riverside, CA 951-352-5713
Stonewall Kitchen
York, ME 800-207-5267
Strub Pickles
Brantford, ON 519-751-1717
Sumida Pickle Products
Honolulu, HI 808-841-4227
Sweet Sides
Mission Hills, CA 818-832-0174
T. Marzetti Company
Columbus, OH 614-846-2232
Tamarind Tree
Neshanic Station, NJ 800-432-8733
Target Flavors
Brookfield, CT 800-538-3350
Taste Teasers
Dallas, TX 800-526-1840
Terrell's Potato Chip Company
Seattle, WA 800-331-5222
Texas Heat
San Antonio, TX 800-656-5916
The Lollipop Tree, Inc
Portsmouth, NH 800-842-6691
Thompson's Fine Foods
Shoreview, MN 800-807-0025
Thor-Shackel HorseradishCompany
Burr Ridge, IL 630-986-1333
Thumann's
Carlstadt, NJ 201-935-3636
Trappist Preserves
Spencer, MA 508-885-8740
Tribe Mediterranean Foods Company LLC
Taunton, MA 800-421-3474
Tropical
Charlotte, NC 800-220-1413
Tulkoff Food Products
Baltimore, MD 800-638-7343
Tutto Sicilia
Hartford, CT 860-986-7377
Twang
San Antonio, TX 800-950-8095
Two Chefs on a Roll
Carson, CA 800-842-3025
Ultra Seal
New Paltz, NY 845-255-2496
Uncle Dave's Kitchen
South Londonderry, VT 802-824-3600
Unette Corporation
Wharton, NJ 973-328-6800
Unilever United States
Englewood Cliffs, NJ 201-567-8000
V&V Supremo Foods
Chicago, IL 800-547-8773
Ventura Foods
Ontario, CA 714-257-3700
Ventura Foods   Foodservice
Salem, OR 503-585-6423
Vienna Sausage Company
Chicago, IL 800-326-6652
Village Imports
Brisbane, CA 888-865-8714
Vlasic Foods
Tracy, CA 559-734-7455
Wagner Gourmet Foods
Shawnee Mission, KS 913-469-5411
Walker Foods
Los Angeles, CA 800-966-5199
Wei-Chuan
Bell Gardens, CA 562-927-6681
Welch's Foods Inc
Lawton, MI 269-624-1308
Welch's Foods Inc
Concord, MA 800-340-6870
Welch's Foods Inc
North East, PA 814-725-4577
Westbrae Natural Foods
Garden City, NY 800-434-4246

Westin
Omaha, NE 800-228-6098
Westport Rivers Vineyard& Winery
Westport, MA .800-993-9695
Wild Thymes Farm
Greenville, NY .800-724-2877
Willy's Pickle Products
Holland Landing, ON 905-836-6532
Wing Nien Company
Hayward, CA 510-487-8877
Wings Foods of Alberta
Edmonton, AB .780-433-6406
Wisconsin Spice
Berlin, WI 920-361-3555
Woeber Mustard Manufacturing
Springfield, OH. 800-548-2929
Wood Brothers
West Columbia, SC. 803-796-5146
Woodlake Ranch
Woodlake, CA. .559-564-2161
Woody's Bar-B-Q Sauce Company
Waldenburg, AR 870-579-2251
World Harbors
Auburn, ME 800-355-6221
York Mountain Winery
Paso Robles, CA 805-238-3925
Zatarain's
Gretna, LA 800-435-6639

Dips

A.M. Braswell Jr. Food Company
Statesboro, GA .800-673-9388
Abraham's Natural Foods
Long Branch, NJ 800-327-9903
Amigos Canning Company
San Antonio, TX 800-580-3477
Anderson Erickson Dairy
Des Moines, IA .515-265-2521
Appledore Cove LLC
North Berwick, ME. 888-849-1787
Arbor Hill Grapery & Winery
Naples, NY 800-554-7553
Ashman Manufacturing & Distributing Company
Virginia Beach, VA. 800-641-9924
ASK Foods
Palmyra, PA. 800-879-4275
Au Printemps Gourmet
Prevost, QC 800-663-0416
Baptista's Bakery
Franklin, WI 877-261-3157
Barber's Dairy
Birmingham, AL. 205-942-2351
Bear Creek Country Kitchens
Heber City, UT .800-516-7286
Bear Creek Kitchens
Marshall, TX. 888-300-7687
Bel/Kaukauna USA
Kaukauna, WI .800-558-3500
Border Foods Inc
Farmers Branch, TX 888-737-7752
Bread Dip Company
Philadelphia, PA 215-563-9455
Bruno's Cajun Foods & Snacks
Slidell, LA. 985-726-0544
Byrne Dairy
Syracuse, NY 800-899-1535
Cass Clay Creamery
Fargo, ND 701-293-6455
Chelten House Products
Bridgeport, NJ. 856-467-1600
Country Cupboard
Virginia City, NV 775-847-7300
Crazy Jerry's
Roswell, GA 770-993-0651
Creamland Dairies
Albuquerque, NM. 505-247-0721
Creative Foodworks
San Antonio, TX. 210-212-4761
Crowley Foods
Binghamton, NY. 800-637-0019
Culinary Standards Corporation
Louisville, KY .800-778-3434
Custom Ingredients
New Braunfels, TX. 800-457-8935
Dairy Fresh Corporation
Greensboro, AL. 800-239-5114
DCI Cheese Company
Richfield, WI 262-677-3407
Dean Foods Company
Rosemont, IL. .800-323-1571
Dean Foods Company
Rochester, IN 800-336-7215

Dean Foods Company
Rockford, IL 815-962-0647
Dixie Dew Products
Erlanger, KY. .800-867-8548
Dorina/So-Good
Union, IL. 815-923-2144
El Toro Food Products
Watsonville, CA 831-728-9266
Flamous Brands
Pasadena, CA 626-799-7909
Fountain Valley Foods
Colorado Springs, CO. 719-573-6012
Franklin Foods
Enosburg Falls, VT. 800-933-6114
Frito-Lay
Arlington, TX. .817-385-5834
Garden Complements
Kansas City, MO. 800-966-1091
Golden Specialty Foods
Norwalk, CA. 562-802-2537
Goldwater's Food of Arizona
Fredericksburg, TX. 800-488-4932
Gourmet Village
Morin Heights, QC 800-668-2314
Guiltless Gourmet
Secaucus, NJ. 201-453-5200
Halladays Harvest Barn
Bellows Falls, VT. 802-463-3471
Havana's Limited
Titusville, FL. .321-267-0513
Havoc Maker Products
Guilford, CT 800-681-3909
Helens Pure Foods
Cheltenham, PA 215-379-6433
Heluva Good Cheese
Sodus, NY. 315-483-6971
Herb Patch of Vermont
Bellows Falls, VT. 800-282-4372
Herkimer Foods
Herkimer, NY. .315-895-7832
Herlocher Foods
State College, PA 800-437-5624
Hiland Dairy Foods Company
Springfield, MO 417-862-9311
Hirzel Canning Company & Farms
Northwood, OH 419-693-0531
Hombres Foods
Cedar Creek, TX. 877-446-6273
Innovative Ingredients
Reisterstown, MD. 888-403-2907
Intercorp Excelle Foods
Toronto, ON 888-476-2124
Jalapeno Foods Company
The Woodlands, TX 800-896-2318
Kentucky Beer Cheese
Nicholasville, KY. 859-887-1645
Knese Enterprise
Floral Park, NY 516-354-9004
Kraft Foods
Walton, NY 607-865-7131
Leigh Olivers
Tyler, TX 903-245-9183
Litehouse
Sandpoint, ID .208-263-2030
Litehouse Foods
Sandpoint, ID .800-669-3169
Look's Gourmet Food Company
Whiting, ME 800-962-6258
Lost Trail Root Beer Com
Louisburg, KS .800-748-7765
Low Country Produce
Lobeco, SC 800-935-2792
Mayfield Dairy Farms
Athens, TN 800-362-9546
Mid States Dairy
Hazelwood, MO 314-731-1150
Mixon Fruit Farms
Bradenton, FL. .800-608-2525
Naturally Fresh Foods
College Park, GA 800-765-1950
New Canaan Farms
Dripping Springs, TX 800-727-5267
Penn Maid Crowley Foods
Philadelphia, PA 800-247-6269
Phillips Foods
Baltimore, MD .888-234-2722
Pied-Mont/Dora
Ste Anne Des Plaines, BC 800-363-8003
Prairie Farms Dairy
Carlinville, IL 217-854-2547
Prairie Farms Dairy
Carbondale, IL .618-457-4167

Prairie Farms Dairy Inc
Carlinville, IL 217-854-2547
Quality Foods
San Pedro, CA. .877-833-7890
Refrigerated Foods Association
Chamblee, GA. .770-452-0660
Renfro Foods
Fort Worth, TX. 817-336-3849
Reser's Fine Foods
Beaverton, OR .800-333-6431
Road's End Organics
Morrisville, VT. 877-247-3373
Robert Rothschild Berry Farm
Urbana, OH. 866-565-6790
Roberts Dairy Company
Omaha, NE 402-344-4321
Rod's Food Products
City of Industry, CA 909-839-8925
Sabra Blue & White Food Products
Astoria, NY. 718-389-3800
Sabra-Go Mediterranean
Farmingdale, NY 631-694-9500
Sambets Cajun Deli
Austin, TX. 800-472-6238
Schneider Valley Farms Dairy
Williamsport, PA. 570-326-2021
Sea Gold Seafood Products
New Bedford, MA 508-993-3060

Sentry Seasonings
Elmhurst, IL 630-530-5370

The product development experts of Sentry Seasonings are eager to offer the assistance and hands-on experience to food processors of all sizes. Sentry Seasonings will ensure the consistent high quality and repeat sales of your products, whether you choose one of our many off-the-shelf Bench Mark products or a modified version to meet your preferences. Sentry Seasonings can also duplicate and/or improve your present flavor profile; formulate, blend and package specifically for your requirements.

Sheila's Select Gourmet Recipe
Heber City, UT 800-516-7286
Shine Companies
Spring, TX. 281-353-8392
Shooting Star Farms
Bartlesville, OK 888-850-8540
Simeus Foods International
Mansfield, TX. .888-772-3663
Sinton Dairy Foods Company
Colorado Springs, CO. 800-388-4970
Sterzing Food Company
Burlington, IA. .800-754-8467
Sunshine Farms Dairy
Elyria, OH. 440-322-6301
Texas Heat
San Antonio, TX. 800-656-5916
Thompson's Fine Foods
Shoreview, MN 800-807-0025
Tova Industries
Louisville, KY .888-532-8682
Tribe Mediterranean Foods Company LLC
Taunton, MA 800-421-3474
Two Chefs on a Roll
Carson, CA 800-842-3025
US Chocolate Corporation
Brooklyn, NY 718-788-8555
Ventre Packing Company
Syracuse, NY 315-463-2384
Victoria Packing Corporation
Brooklyn, NY 718-649-2180
Wells' Dairy
Le Mars, IA. 800-942-3800
Wild West Spices
Cody, WY 888-587-8887
William Poll
New York, NY .800-993-7655

Bean

Garden Complements
Kansas City, MO. 800-966-1091
Hormel Foods Corporation
Austin, MN 800-523-4635

Sentry Seasonings
Elmhurst, IL 630-530-5370

The product development experts of Sentry Seasonings are eager to offer the assistance and hands-on experience to food processors of all sizes. Sentry Seasonings will ensure the consistent high quality and repeat sales of your products, whether you choose one of our many off-the-shelf Bench Mark products or a modified version to meet your preferences. Sentry Seasonings can also duplicate and/or improve your present flavor profile; formulate, blend and package specifically for your requirements.

Valley of Mexico
Norwalk, CT. 203-348-0402
Ventre Packing Company
Syracuse, NY 315-463-2384

Cheese

Hell on the Red
Telephone, TX. 903-664-2573
Hormel Foods Corporation
Austin, MN 800-523-4635
Kentucky Beer Cheese
Nicholasville, KY 859-887-1645

Sentry Seasonings
Elmhurst, IL 630-530-5370

The product development experts of Sentry Seasonings are eager to offer the assistance and hands-on experience to food processors of all sizes. Sentry Seasonings will ensure the consistent high quality and repeat sales of your products, whether you choose one of our many off-the-shelf Bench Mark products or a modified version to meet your preferences. Sentry Seasonings can also duplicate and/or improve your present flavor profile; formulate, blend and package specifically for your requirements.

Southernfood Specialties
Atlanta, GA. 800-255-5323
Texas Heat
San Antonio, TX. 800-656-5916
Ventre Packing Company
Syracuse, NY 315-463-2384

Chili

Food Processor of New Mexico
Albuquerque, NM. 877-634-3772
Golden Specialty Foods
Norwalk, CA. 562-802-2537

Sentry Seasonings
Elmhurst, IL 630-530-5370

The product development experts of Sentry Seasonings are eager to offer the assistance and hands-on experience to food processors of all sizes. Sentry Seasonings will ensure the consistent high quality and repeat sales of your products, whether you choose one of our many off-the-shelf Bench Mark products or a modified version to meet your preferences. Sentry Seasonings can also duplicate and/or improve your present flavor profile; formulate, blend and package specifically for your requirements.

Chip

Amigos Canning Company
San Antonio, TX. 800-580-3477
Dorina/So-Good
Union, IL. 815-923-2144
Frito-Lay
Arlington, TX 817-385-5834
Rod's Food Products
City of Industry, CA 909-839-8925

Sentry Seasonings
Elmhurst, IL 630-530-5370

The product development experts of Sentry Seasonings are eager to offer the assistance and hands-on experience to food processors of all sizes. Sentry Seasonings will ensure the consistent high quality and repeat sales of your products, whether you choose one of our many off-the-shelf Bench Mark products or a modified version to meet your preferences. Sentry Seasonings can also duplicate and/or improve your present flavor profile; formulate, blend and package specifically for your requirements.

Sunshine Farms Dairy
Elyria, OH. 440-322-6301

Guacamole

Jalapeno Foods Company
The Woodlands, TX 800-896-2318

Sentry Seasonings
Elmhurst, IL 630-530-5370

The product development experts of Sentry Seasonings are eager to offer the assistance and hands-on experience to food processors of all sizes. Sentry Seasonings will ensure the consistent high quality and repeat sales of your products, whether you choose one of our many off-the-shelf Bench Mark products or a modified version to meet your preferences. Sentry Seasonings can also duplicate and/or improve your present flavor profile; formulate, blend and package specifically for your requirements.

Salsa

Allied Old English
Port Reading, NJ. 732-602-8955
Arizona Beverage Company
New Hyde Park, NY. 800-832-3775
Bachman Company
Reading, PA 800-523-8253
Bel/Kaukauna USA
Kaukauna, WI. 800-558-3500
Border Foods Inc
Deming, NM. 888-737-7752
Casa Visco Finer Food Company
Schenectady, NY. 888-607-2823
Choice of Vermont
Destin, FL 800-444-6261
Colorado Salsa Company
Littleton, CO. 303-932-2617
El Paso Chile Company
El Paso, TX. 888-472-5727
Fountain Valley Foods
Colorado Springs, CO. 719-573-6012
Franklin Foods
Enosburg Falls, VT. 800-933-6114
Frontera Foods
Chicago, IL 800-509-4441
Golden Specialty Foods
Norwalk, CA. 562-802-2537
Golden Valley Foods
Abbotsford, BC. 888-299-8855
Granny Blossom Specialty Foods
Wells, VT 802-645-0507
Green Mountain Gringo
Winston Salem, NC. 802-875-3117
Herlocher Foods
State College, PA 800-437-5624
Jalapeno Foods Company
The Woodlands, TX. 800-896-2318
Li'l Guy Foods
Kansas City, MO. 800-886-8226
Maggie's Salsa
Charleston, WV 304-550-5460
Miceli's Specialty Foods Company
Danbury, CT 888-264-2354
Native South Services
Fredericksburg, TX. 800-236-2848
New Canaan Farms
Dripping Springs, TX 800-727-5267
North of the Border
Tesuque, NM. 800-860-0681
Old Home Foods
St Paul, MN. 800-628-8700

Original Juan
   Kansas City, KS 800-568-8468
Pacific Choice Brands
   Fresno, CA 559-237-5583
Quality Foods
   San Pedro, CA .877-833-7890
Ready Foods
   Denver, CO 303-892-5861
Royal Resources
   New Orleans, LA 800-888-9932

Sentry Seasonings
   Elmhurst, IL 630-530-5370

The product development experts of Sentry Seasonings are eager to offer the assistance and hands-on experience to food processors of all sizes. Sentry Seasonings will ensure the consistent high quality and repeat sales of your products, whether you choose one of our many off-the-shelf Bench Mark products or a modified version to meet your preferences. Sentry Seasonings can also duplicate and/or improve your present flavor profile; formulate, blend and package specifically for your requirements.

Shooting Star Farms
   Bartlesville, OK 888-850-8540
Sona & Hollen Foods
   Los Alamitos, CA 800-200-7662
T.W. Garner Food Company
   Winston Salem, NC. 800-476-7383
Terrell's Potato Chip Company
   Seattle, WA 800-331-5222
Ventre Packing Company
   Syracuse, NY .315-463-2384

Glazes

A Taste of the Kingdom
   Kingdom City, MO 888-592-5080
Abel & Schafer
   Ronkonkoma, NY 800-443-1260
Ashman Manufacturing & Distributing Company
   Virginia Beach, VA 800-641-9924
Bakemark Ingredients Canada
   Richmond, BC 800-665-9441
Baker & Baker, Inc.
   Schaumburg, IL. 800-593-5777
Genarom International
   Cranbury, NJ .609-409-6200
Gracious Gourmet
   Bridgewater, CT 860-350-1213
Howard Foods
   Danvers, MA. .978-774-6207
Newly Weds Foods
   Chicago, IL 800-621-7521
Newport Flavours & Fragrances
   Orange, CA 714-628-9894
Puratos Canada
   Mississauga, ON 800-668-5537

Sentry Seasonings
   Elmhurst, IL 630-530-5370

The product development experts of Sentry Seasonings are eager to offer the assistance and hands-on experience to food processors of all sizes. Sentry Seasonings will ensure the consistent high quality and repeat sales of your products, whether you choose one of our many off-the-shelf Bench Mark products or a modified version to meet your preferences. Sentry Seasonings can also duplicate and/or improve your present flavor profile; formulate, blend and package specifically for your requirements.

Tandem Enterprises
   Darien, CT. 800-779-3276
Valley View Blueberries
   Vancouver, WA 360-892-2839

Gravy

Ailments E.D. Foods Inc.
   Pointe Claire, QC 800-267-3333
Atlantic Seasonings
   Kinston, NC 800-433-5261
Bestfoods Foodservice
   Somerset, NJ .732-627-8722
Bunker Hill Foods
   Augusta, GA 706-733-7765
Cagnon Foods Company
   Brooklyn, NY .718-647-2244
Campbell Soup Company
   Camden, NJ. 800-257-8443
Castleberry/Snow Brands
   Augusta, GA 800-241-3520
Cordon Bleu International
   Anjou, QC 514-352-3000
Custom Food Products
   Alsip, IL 708-388-8883
Diversified Foods & Seasoning
   Metairie, LA 504-846-5090
Edmonds Chile Company
   St Louis, MO. .314-772-1499
Griffith Laboratories Worldwide
   Alsip, IL 800-346-4743
Heinz
   Muscatine, IA .563-263-5711
Mayacamas Fine Foods
   Sonoma, CA 800-826-9621
O Chili Frozen Foods Inc
   Northbrook, IL 847-562-1991
Praters Foods
   Lubbock, TX. .806-745-2727
Purnell's Old Folks Sausage Company
   Simpsonville, KY 800-626-1512
R.L. Schreiber
   Pompano Beach, FL 800-624-8777
R.L. Schreiber Company
   Pompano Beach, FL 800-624-8777
Sambets Cajun Deli
   Austin, TX. 800-472-6238
Schlotterbeck & Foss Company
   Portland, ME. .800-777-4666
Select Food Products
   Toronto, ON 800-699-8016

Sentry Seasonings
   Elmhurst, IL 630-530-5370

The product development experts of Sentry Seasonings are eager to offer the assistance and hands-on experience to food processors of all sizes. Sentry Seasonings will ensure the consistent high quality and repeat sales of your products, whether you choose one of our many off-the-shelf Bench Mark products or a modified version to meet your preferences. Sentry Seasonings can also duplicate and/or improve your present flavor profile; formulate, blend and package specifically for your requirements.

Shiloh Foods
   Savannah, TN .800-795-2550
Spice Time Foods/Julius & Joe's
   Paramus, NJ 800-345-9225
Stockpot
   Woodinville, WA. 800-468-1611
Taste Maker Foods
   Memphis, TN .800-467-1407
Techni-Brew International
   Portland, OR 800-454-4077
Vanee Foods Company
   Berkeley, IL. 708-449-7300

Prepared

Ailments E.D. Foods Inc.
   Pointe Claire, QC 800-267-3333

Bunker Hill Foods
   Augusta, GA 706-733-7765
Campbell Soup Company
   Camden, NJ. 800-257-8443
Castleberry/Snow Brands
   Augusta, GA 800-241-3520
Cordon Bleu International
   Anjou, QC 514-352-3000
Custom Food Products
   Alsip, IL 708-388-8883
Lawry's Foods
   Monrovia, CA .800-952-9797
Mayacamas Fine Foods
   Sonoma, CA 800-826-9621
O Chili Frozen Foods Inc
   Northbrook, IL 847-562-1991
Praters Foods
   Lubbock, TX. .806-745-2727

Sentry Seasonings
   Elmhurst, IL 630-530-5370

The product development experts of Sentry Seasonings are eager to offer the assistance and hands-on experience to food processors of all sizes. Sentry Seasonings will ensure the consistent high quality and repeat sales of your products, whether you choose one of our many off-the-shelf Bench Mark products or a modified version to meet your preferences. Sentry Seasonings can also duplicate and/or improve your present flavor profile; formulate, blend and package specifically for your requirements.

Shiloh Foods
   Savannah, TN .800-795-2550
Spice Time Foods/Julius & Joe's
   Paramus, NJ 800-345-9225
Williams Foods Inc
   Lenexa, KS 800-255-6736

Ketchup

Alimentaire Whyte's Inc
   Laval, QC 800-625-1979

Baldwin Richardson Foods
   Frankfort, IL 866-644-2732

Baldwin Richardson Foods is a liquid ingredient manufacturer specializing in signature sauces, dessert toppings, beverage/pancake syrups, specialty fruit fillings and condiments. Packaging capabilities range from portion control cups and pouches to standard retail and foodservice packs and include industrial drums and totes. Full service R&D and Quality groups dedicated to new product development, with in-house stability and analytical testing. Call for assistance.

Brown Family Farm
   Brattleboro, VT. 888-556-2753
C&E Canners
   Hammonton, NJ 609-561-1078
Carriage House Companies
   Fredonia, NY .800-828-8915
Deep South Products
   Fitzgerald, GA. 229-423-1121
E.D. Smith & Sons
   Winona, ON 905-643-1211
Erba Food Products
   Brooklyn, NY .718-272-7700
Fremont Special Brands
   Fremont, OH .419-334-8995
Golden State Foods
   City of Industry, CA 626-968-6431
Golden State Foods
   Irvine, CA 949-252-2000

H.J. Heinz Company
Pittsburgh, PA 412-237-5948
Heinz
Fremont, OH .419-332-7357
Heinz
Muscatine, IA 563-263-5711
Heinz Company of Canada
North York, ON 800-268-6641
Kari-Out Company
White Plains, NY 800-433-8799
Kelly Pickle Company
Oconto, WI 920-834-4433
Mountain Fire Foods
Huntington, VT 802-434-2685
Mucky Duck Mustard Company
Ferndale, MI .248-544-4610
New Business Corporation
East Chicago, IN 800-742-8435
Portion Pac
Mason, OH 800-232-4829
San Benito Foods
Hollister, CA .831-637-4434
Signature Fruit
Stockton, CA .209-931-1531
Somerset Industries
Spring House, PA 800-883-8728
Sona & Hollen Foods
Los Alamitos, CA 800-200-7662
Stickney & Poor Company
North Andover, MA 508-261-8967
Ultra Seal
New Paltz, NY 845-255-2496
Uncle Dave's Kitchen
South Londonderry, VT 802-824-3600
Westport Rivers Vineyard& Winery
Westport, MA 800-993-9695
Wing's Food Products
Toronto, ON .416-259-2662
World's Best
Norwood, MA 888-690-8766

Marinades

A Perfect Pear from NapaValley
Napa, CA 800-553-5753
A. Lassonde, Inc.
Rougemont, QC 514-878-1057
Allegro Fine Foods
Paris, TN 731-642-6113
Annie's Naturals
East Calais, VT 800-434-1234
Applecreek Farms
Lexington, KY 800-747-8871
Appledore Cove LLC
North Berwick, ME. 888-849-1787
Ashman Manufacturing & Distributing Company
Virginia Beach, VA. 800-641-9924
Atlantic Quality Spice &Seasonings
Edison, NJ. 800-584-0422
B&G Foods
Parsippany, NJ. 973-401-6500
Barhyte Specialty Foods Inc
Pendleton, OR 800-227-4983
Bea & B Foods
San Diego, CA 800-952-2117
Blendex Company
Jeffersontown, KY 800-626-6325
Blue Smoke Salsa
Ansted, WV. .888-725-7298
CaJohns Fiery Foods
Columbus, OH 888-703-3473
Cajun Injector
Clinton, LA 800-221-8060
CHS
Inver Grove Heights, MN. 800-232-3639
Cinnabar Specialty Foods
Prescott, AZ .866-293-6433
Colonna Brothers
North Bergen, NJ 201-864-1115
Con Yeager Spice Company
Zelienople, PA. 800-222-2460
Creative Foodworks
San Antonio, TX. 210-212-4761
Cugino's Gourmet Foods
Crystal Lake, IL 888-592-8446
Cuizina Food Company
Woodinville, WA. 425-486-7000
Delta BBQ Sauce Company
Stockton, CA. 209-472-9284
Dixie Trail Farms
Wilmington, NC 800-665-3968
Don Tango Foods
Sterling, VA. .877-406-4064

Dorothy Dawson Foods Products
Jackson, MI. .517-788-9830
Dr Pete's
Savannah, GA 888-599-0047
Dr. Pete's
Savannah, GA 912-233-3035
Fords Gourmet Foods
Raleigh, NC .800-446-0947
Fox Hollow Farm
Hanover, NH 603-643-6002
FunniBonz
West Windsor, NJ 877-300-2669
Garden Complements
Kansas City, MO. 800-966-1091
Geetha's Gourmet of India
Las Cruces, NM 800-274-0475
Gemini Food Industries
Fiskdale, MA 508-347-2800
Genarom International
Cranbury, NJ 609-409-6200
General Spice
South Plainfield, NJ 800-345-7742
GFF
City of Industry, CA 323-232-6255
Girard's Food Service Dressings
City of Industry, CA 888-327-8442
Golden West Specialty Foods
Brisbane, CA. 800-584-4481
Havana's Limited
Titusville, FL. 321-267-0513
Intercorp Excelle Foods
Toronto, ON 888-476-2124
J.T. Pappy's Sauce
Los Angeles, CA. 323-969-9605
Judicial Flavors
Auburn, CA. .530-885-1298
L&S Packing Company
Farmingdale, NY 800-286-6487
L.J. Minor Factory
Cleveland, OH 216-861-8350
Lawry's Foods
Monrovia, CA 800-952-9797
Love'n Herbs
Waterbury, CT 203-756-4932
M.W. Milton & Company
Louisville, KY 502-587-5016
Mad Will's Food Company
Auburn, CA. .888-275-9455
Magic Seasoning Blends
Harahan, LA 800-457-2857
Maple Grove Farms of Vermont
St Johnsbury, VT. 800-525-2540
Marin Food Specialties
Byron, CA. 925-634-6126
McCormick & Company
Sparks, MD .800-632-5847
McIlhenny Company
New Orleans, LA 800-634-9599
Montebello Kitchens
Gordonsville, VA 800-743-7687
Mountain Fire Foods
Huntington, VT. 802-434-2685
Mt. Olympus Specialty Foods
Buffalo, NY. .716-874-0771
Nantucket Off-Shore Seasoning
Nantucket, MA 508-994-1300
Napa Valley Kitchens
Napa, CA. 800-288-1089
Newly Weds Foods
Decatur, AL .800-521-6189
Newly Weds Foods
Chicago, IL .800-621-7521
Newly Weds Foods
Memphis, TN 800-647-9314
North Coast Processing
North East, PA. 814-725-9617
Old Mansion Foods
Petersburg, VA 800-476-1877
Original Cajun Injector
Clinton, LA .800-221-8060
Parthenon Food Products
Ann Arbor, MI 734-994-1012
Phamous Phloyd's Barbeque Sauce
Denver, CO .303-757-3285
Porinos Gourmet Food
Central Falls, RI 800-826-3938
Produits Ronald
St. Damase, QC. 450-797-3303
Quality Foods
San Pedro, CA. 877-833-7890
Red Creek Marinade Company
Amarillo, TX. 800-687-9114

Restaurant Lulu Gourmet Products
San Francisco, CA 888-693-5800
Rivertown Foods
St Louis, MO. 800-844-3210
Rosmarino Foods/R.Z. Humbert Company
Odessa, FL .888-926-9053
Sambets Cajun Deli
Austin, TX. .800-472-6238
Santa Barbara Salsa/California Creative
Oceanside, CA 800-748-5523

Sentry Seasonings
Elmhurst, IL .630-530-5370

The product development experts of Sentry Seasonings are eager to offer the assistance and hands-on experience to food processors of all sizes. Sentry Seasonings will ensure the consistent high quality and repeat sales of your products, whether you choose one of our many off-the-shelf Bench Mark products or a modified version to meet your preferences. Sentry Seasonings can also duplicate and/or improve your present flavor profile; formulate, blend and package specifically for your requirements.

Southern Ray's Foods
Miami Beach, FL 800-972-8237
Soy Vay Enterprises
Felton, CA 800-600-2077
Surlean Food Solutions
San Antonio, TX 800-999-4370
Swagger Foods Corporation
Vernon Hills, IL 847-913-1200
Sweetwater Spice Company
Austin, TX. .800-531-6079
T. Marzetti Company
Columbus, OH 614-846-2232
Thorough Fare Gourmet
Marlboro, VT 802-257-5612
Tillie's Gourmet
Doylestown, PA 215-272-8326
Tova Industries
Louisville, KY 888-532-8682
Trailblazer Food Products
Portland, OR 800-777-7179
Ultimate Gourmet
Belle Mead, NJ 908-359-4050
Uncle Bum's Gourmet Foods
Riverside, CA 800-486-2867
Vita Specialty Foods
Inwood, WV 800-974-4778
Wicker's Food Products
Hornersville, MO 800-847-0032
Wild Thymes Farm
Greenville, NY 800-724-2877
Wine Country Chef LLC
Hidden Valley Lake, CA. 707-322-0406

Beef

Lawry's Foods
Monrovia, CA 800-952-9797
Mosey's Inc
Bloomfield, CT. 860-243-1725

Sentry Seasonings
Elmhurst, IL .630-530-5370

The product development experts of Sentry Seasonings are eager to offer the assistance and hands-on experience to food processors of all sizes. Sentry Seasonings will ensure the consistent high quality and repeat sales of your products, whether you choose one of our many off-the-shelf Bench Mark products or a modified version to meet your preferences. Sentry Seasonings can also duplicate and/or improve your present flavor profile; formulate, blend and package specifically for your requirements.

Chicken

Delphos Poultry Products
Delphos, OH 419-692-5816
Gemini Food Industries
Fiskdale, MA 508-347-2800

Sentry Seasonings
Elmhurst, IL 630-530-5370

> The product development experts of Sentry Seasonings are eager to offer the assistance and hands-on experience to food processors of all sizes. Sentry Seasonings will ensure the consistent high quality and repeat sales of your products, whether you choose one of our many off-the-shelf Bench Mark products or a modified version to meet your preferences. Sentry Seasonings can also duplicate and/or improve your present flavor profile; formulate, blend and package specifically for your requirements.

Sunchef Farms
Vernon, CA 323-588-5800

Fajita

Magic Seasoning Blends
Harahan, LA 800-457-2857

Sentry Seasonings
Elmhurst, IL 630-530-5370

> The product development experts of Sentry Seasonings are eager to offer the assistance and hands-on experience to food processors of all sizes. Sentry Seasonings will ensure the consistent high quality and repeat sales of your products, whether you choose one of our many off-the-shelf Bench Mark products or a modified version to meet your preferences. Sentry Seasonings can also duplicate and/or improve your present flavor profile; formulate, blend and package specifically for your requirements.

Tova Industries
Louisville, KY 888-532-8682
Van De Walle Farms
San Antonio, TX 210-436-5551

Lamb

Sentry Seasonings
Elmhurst, IL 630-530-5370

> The product development experts of Sentry Seasonings are eager to offer the assistance and hands-on experience to food processors of all sizes. Sentry Seasonings will ensure the consistent high quality and repeat sales of your products, whether you choose one of our many off-the-shelf Bench Mark products or a modified version to meet your preferences. Sentry Seasonings can also duplicate and/or improve your present flavor profile; formulate, blend and package specifically for your requirements.

Meat

A. Lassonde, Inc.
Rougemont, QC 514-878-1057
Allegro Fine Foods
Paris, TN 731-642-6113
American Culinary Gardens
Springfield, MO 888-831-2433
Atlantic Quality Spice &Seasonings
Edison, NJ 800-584-0422
Booneway Farms
Berea, KY 859-986-2636
Centennial Food Corporation
Calgary, AB 403-287-2525
Cinnabar Specialty Foods
Prescott, AZ 866-293-6433
Con Yeager Spice Company
Zelienople, PA 800-222-2460
D & D Foods
Columbus, GA 706-322-4507
Delta BBQ Sauce Company
Stockton, CA 209-472-9284
Favorite Foods
Burnaby, BC 604-420-5100
Fuji Foods
Denver, CO 303-377-3738
Genarom International
Cranbury, NJ 609-409-6200
L&S Packing Company
Farmingdale, NY 800-286-6487
L.J. Minor Factory
Cleveland, OH 216-861-8350
Lawry's Foods
Monrovia, CA 800-952-9797
M.W. Milton & Company
Louisville, KY 502-587-5016
Magic Seasoning Blends
Harahan, LA 800-457-2857
Mrs. Dog's Products
Tampa, FL 800-267-7364
Newly Weds Foods
Chicago, IL 800-621-7521
Newly Weds Foods
Memphis, TN 800-647-9314
Original Cajun Injector
Clinton, LA 800-221-8060
Parthenon Food Products
Ann Arbor, MI 734-994-1012
Passetti's Pride
Hayward, CA 800-521-4659
Produits Ronald
St. Damase, QC 450-797-3303
Red Creek Marinade Company
Amarillo, TX 800-687-9114
Rob Salamida Company
Johnson City, NY 607-770-7046

Sentry Seasonings
Elmhurst, IL 630-530-5370

> The product development experts of Sentry Seasonings are eager to offer the assistance and hands-on experience to food processors of all sizes. Sentry Seasonings will ensure the consistent high quality and repeat sales of your products, whether you choose one of our many off-the-shelf Bench Mark products or a modified version to meet your preferences. Sentry Seasonings can also duplicate and/or improve your present flavor profile; formulate, blend and package specifically for your requirements.

Southern Ray's Foods
Miami Beach, FL 800-972-8237
Stanchfield Farms
Milo, ME 207-732-5173
Tova Industries
Louisville, KY 888-532-8682
Van De Walle Farms
San Antonio, TX 210-436-5551

Mayonaise

Bestfoods Specialty Products
Englewood Cliffs, NJ 800-338-8831

C.F. Sauer Company
Mauldin, SC 800-688-5676
Cains Foods/Olde Cape Cod
Ayer, MA 800-225-0601
Carriage House Companies
Fredonia, NY 800-828-8915
Clements Foods Company
Oklahoma City, OK 800-654-8355
Consumer Guild Foods
Toledo, OH 419-726-3406
Consumers Vinegar & Spice Company
Chicago, IL 773-376-4100
Conway Import Company
Franklin Park, IL 800-323-8801
Cuisine Perel
Richmond, CA 800-887-3735
Dave's Gourmet
San Francisco, CA 800-758-0372
Deep South Products
Fitzgerald, GA 229-423-1121
Earth Island Natural Foods
Canoga Park, CA 818-725-2820
Erba Food Products
Brooklyn, NY 718-272-7700
Food Specialties
Indianapolis, IN 317-271-0862
Food Specialties Company
Cincinnati, OH 513-761-1242
GFA Brands
Paramus, NJ 201-568-9300
GFF
City of Industry, CA 323-232-6255
Girard's Food Service Dressings
City of Industry, CA 888-327-8442
Green Garden Food Products
Kent, WA 800-304-1033
H.J. Heinz Company
Pittsburgh, PA 412-237-5948
Heinz Company of Canada
North York, ON 800-268-6641
Independent French Manufacturers
New York, NY 212-229-1633
Innovative Food Corporation
Mississauga, ON 905-670-8878
J.M. Smucker Company
Orrville, OH 330-682-3000
Kraft Food Ingredients
Memphis, TN 901-381-6500
Kraft Foods
Northfield, IL 800-323-0768
Kraft Foods
Garland, TX 972-272-7511
Litehouse Foods
Sandpoint, ID 800-669-3169
Mardale Specialty Foods
Waukegan, IL 847-336-4777

Mrs. Clark's Foods
Ankeny, IA 800-736-5674

> **Juices, salad dressings and sauces.**

Novartis Nutrition Corporation
Minneapolis, MN 952-848-6000
Oasis Foods Company
Hillside, NJ 908-964-0477
Olde Tyme Mercantile
Arroyo Grande, CA 805-489-7991
Piknik Products Company Inc
Montgomery, AL 334-265-1567
Portion Pac
Mason, OH 800-232-4829
Purity Products
Plainview, NY 888-769-7873
Rapazzini Winery
Gilroy, CA 408-842-5649
Reily Foods Company
New Orleans, LA 504-524-6132
Reily Foods/JFG Coffee Company
Knoxville, TN 800-535-1961
Restaurant Lulu Gourmet Products
San Francisco, CA 888-693-5800
Royal Food Products
Indianapolis, IN 317-782-2660
San Gennaro Foods
Kent, WA 800-462-1916

Stickney & Poor Company
North Andover, MA 508-261-8967
T. Marzetti Company
Columbus, OH 614-846-2232
Ventura Foods
Ontario, CA 714-257-3700
Ventura Foods
Ft Worth, TX 817-232-5450
Ventura Foods   Foodservice
Salem, OR 503-585-6423
Wood Brothers
West Columbia, SC. 803-796-5146

Mustard

Brown

Groeb Farms
Onsted, MI 517-467-7100
Stickney & Poor Company
North Andover, MA 508-261-8967

Oriental

G S Dunn & Company
Hamilton, ON 905-522-0833

Yellow

Bestfoods Specialty Products
Englewood Cliffs, NJ 800-338-8831
Country Cupboard
Virginia City, NV 775-847-7300
G S Dunn & Company
Hamilton, ON 905-522-0833
Griffin Food Company
Muskogee, OK 800-580-6311
Groeb Farms
Onsted, MI 517-467-7100
Stickney & Poor Company
North Andover, MA 508-261-8967

Salad Dressings

A Perfect Pear from NapaValley
Napa, CA. 800-553-5753
Allied Old English
Port Reading, NJ 732-602-8955
American Spoon Foods
Petoskey, MI 800-222-5886
Annie's Naturals
East Calais, VT 800-434-1234
Arbor Hill Grapery & Winery
Naples, NY 800-554-7553
Argee Corporation
Santee, CA 800-449-3030
Argo Century
Charlotte, NC 800-446-7131
Arizona Sunland Foods
Tucson, AZ 520-624-7068
Ashman Manufacturing & Distributing Company
Virginia Beach, VA 800-641-9924
Atlantic Seasonings
Kinston, NC 800-433-5261
B&G Foods
Parsippany, NJ. 973-401-6500

Baldwin Richardson Foods
Frankfort, IL 866-644-2732

Baldwin Richardson Foods is a liquid ingredient manufacturer specializing in signature sauces, dessert toppings, beverage/pancake syrups, specialty fruit fillings and condiments. Packaging capabilities range from portion control cups and pouches to standard retail and foodservice packs and include industrial drums and totes. Full service R&D and Quality groups dedicated to new product development, with in-house stability and analytical testing. Call for assistance.

Bartush-Schnitzius Foods Company
Lewisville, TX 972-219-1270
Baycliff Company
New York, NY 212-772-6078

Bear Meadow Farm
Colrain, MA 800-653-9241
Bell Buckle Country Store
Bell Buckle, TN 800-707-0483
Betty Lou's Golden Smackers
McMinnville, OR 800-242-5205
Boudreaux's Foods
New Orleans, LA 504-733-8440
BP Gourmet
Hauppauge, NY 631-234-5200
Brown Family Farm
Brattleboro, VT 888-556-2753
Buckhead Gourmet
Atlanta, GA 800-605-5754
C.F. Sauer Company
Mauldin, SC 800-688-5676
Cains Foods
Ayer, MA. 978-772-0300
Cains Foods/Olde Cape Cod
Ayer, MA. 800-225-0601
California Style Gourmet Products
San Diego, CA 800-243-5226
Carole's Cheesecake Company
Toronto, ON 416-256-0000
Carriage House Companies
Fredonia, NY 800-828-8915
Chelten House Products
Bridgeport, NJ 856-467-1600
Chicama Vineyards
West Tisbury, MA 888-244-2262
Christie Food Products
Randolph, MA 800-727-2523
CHS
Inver Grove Heights, MN 800-232-3639
CHS, Inc.
Inner Grove Heights, MN. 800-232-3639
Clements Foods Company
Oklahoma City, OK 800-654-8355
Columbus Foods Company
Des Plaines, IL 800-322-6457
Consumer Guild Foods
Toledo, OH 419-726-3406
Conway Import Company
Franklin Park, IL. 800-323-8801
Corsair Pepper Sauce
Gulfport, MS 228-452-9238
Country Fresh Food & Confections
Oliver Springs, TN 800-545-8782
Creative Foodworks
San Antonio, TX 210-212-4761
Cuisine Perel
Richmond, CA 800-887-3735
CW Resources
New Britain, CT 860-229-7700
D & D Foods
Columbus, GA 706-322-4507
Dalton's Best Maid Products
Fort Worth, TX 817-335-5494
Dave's Gourmet
San Francisco, CA 800-758-0372
Del Sol Food Company
Brenham, TX. 979-836-5978
Delicae Gourmet
Tarpon Springs, FL 800-942-2502
Dorina/So-Good
Union, IL. 815-923-2144
Drusilla Seafood Packing & Processing Company
Baton Rouge, LA 800-364-8844
Dynamic Foods
Lubbock, TX. 806-762-0780
Earth Island Natural Foods
Canoga Park, CA 818-725-2820
Food Source Company
Mississauga, ON 905-625-8404
Food Specialties
Indianapolis, IN 317-271-0862
Food Specialties Company
Cincinnati, OH 513-761-1242
GFA Brands
Paramus, NJ 201-568-9300
GFF
City of Industry, CA 323-232-6255
Girard's Food Service Dressings
City of Industry, CA 888-327-8442
Gold Pure Foods Products Company
Hempstead, NY 800-422-4681
Golden Specialty Foods
Norwalk, CA 562-802-2537
Golden State Foods
Irvine, CA 949-252-2000
Gourmet Central
Romney, WV 800-984-3722

Gracie's Gourmet Shop
Stowe, VT 888-472-2437
Greek Gourmet Limited
Mill Valley, CA 415-480-8050
Green Garden Food Products
Kent, WA 800-304-1033
Griffith Laboratories Worldwide
Alsip, IL 800-346-4743
Grouse Hunt Farms
Tamaqua, PA 570-467-2850
Hagerty Foods
Orange, CA 714-628-1230
Halben Food Manufacturing Company
Overland, MO 800-888-4855
Harpo's
Honolulu, HI 808-537-3439
Heinz Company of Canada
North York, ON 800-268-6641
Hell on the Red
Telephone, TX. 903-664-2573
HVJ International
Spring, TX. 877-730-3663
Independent French Manufacturers
New York, NY 212-229-1633
Innovative Food Corporation
Mississauga, ON 905-670-8878
Instantwhip: Florida
Tampa, FL 813-621-3233
Instantwhip: Texas
San Antonio, TX 800-544-9447
International Food Products Corporation
Saint Louis, MO 800-227-8427
J.D. Mullen Company
Palestine, IL 618-586-2727
Jed's Maple Products
Westfield, VT 866-478-7388
Kauai Organic Farms
Kilauea, HI 808-651-8843
Ken's Foods
Marlborough, MA 800-633-5800
Key Ingredients
Harrisburg, PA 800-227-4448
Knott's Berry Farm Foods
Placentia, CA 800-289-9927
Kosto Food Products Company
Wauconda, IL 847-487-2600
Kozlowski Farms
Forestville, CA 800-473-2767
Kraft Foods
Allentown, PA 610-398-0311
Kraft Foods
Northfield, IL 800-323-0768
Kraft Foods
Garland, TX 972-272-7511
L&S Packing Company
Farmingdale, NY 800-286-6487
Litehouse
Sandpoint, ID 208-263-2030
Litehouse Foods
Sandpoint, ID 800-669-3169
Live A Little Gourmet Foods
Newark, CA 888-744-2300
Love'n Herbs
Waterbury, CT 203-756-4932
Lynch Foods
North York, QC 416-449-5464
M.A. Gedney
Chaska, MN 952-448-2612
Mad Will's Food Company
Auburn, CA 888-275-9455
Maple Grove Farms of Vermont
St Johnsbury, VT 800-525-2540
Mardale Specialty Foods
Waukegan, IL 847-336-4777
Marie's Quality Foods
Woodland, CA 800-544-9516
Marie's Refrigerated Dressings
Thornton, IL 800-441-3321
Marukan Vinegar (U.S.A.) Inc.
Paramount, CA 562-630-6060
Mayacamas Fine Foods
Sonoma, CA 800-826-9621
McCutcheon's Apple Products
Frederick, MD 800-888-7537
Mermaid Spice Corporation
Fort Myers, FL 239-693-1986
Milo's Whole World Gourmet
Athens, OH 866-589-6456
Mixon Fruit Farms
Bradenton, FL. 800-608-2525
Mother Teresa's
Clute, TX. 888-265-7429

Authentic Taste - Since 1926

(800) 736-5674
Ankeny, IA
Hendersonville, NC

Juices, Mayonnaise,
Salad Dressings,
Marinades &
Barbecue Sauces

WWW.MRSCLARKS.COM

Mrs. Clark's Foods
Ankeny, IA 800-736-5674

Juices, salad dressings and sauces.

Mucky Duck Mustard Company
Ferndale, MI 248-544-4610
Mullins Food Products
Broadview, IL 708-344-3224
Napa Valley Kitchens
Napa, CA. 800-288-1089
Naturally Fresh Foods
College Park, GA 800-765-1950
Newman's Own
Westport, CT 203-222-0136
North American Enterprises
Tucson, AZ .800-817-8666
North Coast Processing
North East, PA. 814-725-9617
O'Brian Brothers Food
Cincinnati, OH 513-791-9909
Oasis Foods Company
Hillside, NJ. 908-964-0477
Ocean Spray Cranberries
Lakeville-Middleboro, MA 800-662-3263
Olde Tyme Mercantile
Arroyo Grande, CA. 805-489-7991
Ott Food Products
Carthage, MO 800-866-2585
Pacific Harvest Products
Bellevue, WA 425-401-7990
Pacific Westcoast Foods
Portland, OR 800-874-9333
Parthenon Food Products
Ann Arbor, MI 734-994-1012
Pearlco of Boston
Canton, MA 781-821-1010
Pfeiffer's Foods
Wilson, NY .716-751-9371
Piknik Products Company Inc
Montgomery, AL. 334-265-1567
Porinos Gourmet Food
Central Falls, RI 800-826-3938
Precision Foods
Melrose Park, IL 800-333-0003
Purity Products
Plainview, NY 888-769-7873
Quality Foods
San Pedro, CA. 877-833-7890
Quong Hop & Company
S San Francisco, CA 650-553-9900
Reily Foods Company
New Orleans, LA 504-524-6132
Rivertown Foods
St Louis, MO. 800-844-3210
Robert Rothschild Berry Farm
Urbana, OH 866-565-6790
Rod's Food Products
City of Industry, CA 909-839-8925
Rosmarino Foods/R.Z. Humbert Company
Odessa, FL 888-926-9053
Royal Food Products
Indianapolis, IN 317-782-2660

Royal Kedem Food & Wine Company
Bayonne, NJ 201-437-9131
Royal Resources
New Orleans, LA 800-888-9932
Sal's Caesar Dressing
Novato, CA. 415-897-0605
Sallock International Foods
Millbury, OH. 419-838-7223
San Diego Soy Dairy
El Cajon, CA 619-447-8638
San Fernando Creamery Farmdale Creamery
San Bernardino, CA 909-889-3002
San Gennaro Foods
Kent, WA. .800-462-1916
San-J International
Richmond, VA. 800-446-5500
Schlotterbeck & Foss Company
Portland, ME. 800-777-4666
Seaforth Creamery
Seaforth, ON 519-527-0610
Select Food Products
Toronto, ON 800-699-8016
Sentry Seasonings
Elmhurst, IL 630-530-5370
Shawnee Canning Company
Cross Junction, VA 800-713-1414
Silver Palate Kitchens
Cresskill, NJ 800-872-5283
Sona & Hollen Foods
Los Alamitos, CA 800-200-7662
Sprague Foods
Belleville, ON 613-966-1200
Stearns & Lehman
Mansfield, OH 800-533-2722
Stickney & Poor Company
North Andover, MA 508-261-8967
Stubb's Legendary Kitchen
Austin, TX. .800-883-3238
Swagger Foods Corporation
Vernon Hills, IL 847-913-1200
Sweet Earth Natural Foods
Pacific Grove, CA. 800-737-3311
T. Marzetti Company
Columbus, OH 614-846-2232
Tasty-Toppings
Columbus, NE. 800-228-4148
Tex-Mex Gourmet
Houston, TX 888-345-8467
TexaFrance
Austin, TX. .800-776-8937
The Lollipop Tree, Inc
Portsmouth, NH 800-842-6691
Thistledew Farm
Proctor, WV 800-854-6639
Thorough Fare Gourmet
Marlboro, VT 802-257-5612
Tillie's Gourmet
Doylestown, PA 215-272-8326
Trader Vic's Food Products
Emeryville, CA 877-762-4824
Tulocay & Company
Napa, CA. .888-627-2859
Unilever Bertolli USA, Inc.
Englewood Cliffs, NJ 201-894-4000
Unilever Bestfoods
Englewood Cliffs, NJ 201-894-4000
Unilever United States
Englewood Cliffs, NJ 201-567-8000
Valley Grain Products
Madera, CA. 559-675-3400
Vanlaw Food Products
Fullerton, CA 714-870-9091

Ventura Foods
Philadelphia, PA 215-223-8700
Ventura Foods
Opelousas, LA 337-948-6561
Ventura Foods
Ontario, CA. 714-257-3700
Ventura Foods
Ft Worth, TX. 817-232-5450
Ventura Foods   Foodservice
Salem, OR. 503-585-6423
Ventura Foods   Foodservice/Export/Custom Pack
City of Industry, CA 800-327-3906
Ventura Foods   Foodservice/Retail/Export
Portland, OR 503-255-5512
Ventura Foods   Production Plant
Los Angeles, CA. 323-265-4300
Vincent Formusa Company
Chicago, IL 312-421-0485
Virginia Honey Company
Inwood, WV 800-974-4778
Vita Specialty Foods
Inwood, WV 800-974-4778
Vitasoy USA
Ayer, MA. .978-772-6880
Walden Farms
Linden, NJ. 800-229-1706
Westin
Omaha, NE 800-228-6098
Wild Thymes Farm
Greenville, NY 800-724-2877
WillowOak Farms
Woodland, CA. 888-963-2767
Wine Country Kitchens
Napa, CA. .707-252-9463
Wizards Cauldron, LTD
Yanceyville, NC 336-694-5333
Wood Brothers
West Columbia, SC. 803-796-5146
World Flavors
Warminster, PA 215-672-4400
York Mountain Winery
Paso Robles, CA 805-238-3925

Balsamic Vinegar

Adams Olive Ranch
Lindsay, CA 888-216-5483
Atlantic Quality Spice &Seasonings
Edison, NJ. 800-584-0422
Buckhead Gourmet
Atlanta, GA. 800-605-5754
Colonna Brothers
North Bergen, NJ 201-864-1115

Blue Cheese

Wood Brothers
West Columbia, SC. 803-796-5146

Ceasar

Knott's Berry Farm Foods
Placentia, CA 800-289-9927
Newman's Own
Westport, CT 203-222-0136
Sal's Caesar Dressing
Novato, CA. 415-897-0605

French

Heinz Company of Canada
North York, ON. 800-268-6641

O'Brian Brothers Food
Cincinnati, OH 513-791-9909
Ott Food Products
Carthage, MO 800-866-2585
Wood Brothers
West Columbia, SC 803-796-5146

Gourmet

Betty Lou's Golden Smackers
McMinnville, OR 800-242-5205
Olde Tyme Mercantile
Arroyo Grande, CA. 805-489-7991

Italian Style

O'Brian Brothers Food
Cincinnati, OH 513-791-9909
Olde Tyme Mercantile
Arroyo Grande, CA. 805-489-7991
Ott Food Products
Carthage, MO 800-866-2585
Wood Brothers
West Columbia, SC 803-796-5146

Mixes

Atlantic Quality Spice & Seasonings
Edison, NJ 800-584-0422
CHS
Inver Grove Heights, MN 800-232-3639
House of Thaller
Knoxville, TN 865-689-5893
Kokopelli's Kitchen
Phoenix, AZ 888-943-9802
RC Fine Foods
Belle Mead, NJ 800-526-3953

Blue Cheese

Atlantic Quality Spice & Seasonings
Edison, NJ 800-584-0422

Ceasar

Atlantic Quality Spice & Seasonings
Edison, NJ 800-584-0422

Creamy Dijon

Atlantic Quality Spice & Seasonings
Edison, NJ 800-584-0422

Dijon

Atlantic Quality Spice & Seasonings
Edison, NJ 800-584-0422

French

Atlantic Quality Spice & Seasonings
Edison, NJ 800-584-0422

Italian Style

Atlantic Quality Spice & Seasonings
Edison, NJ 800-584-0422

Oil & Vinegar

Atlantic Quality Spice & Seasonings
Edison, NJ 800-584-0422
Marukan Vinegar (U.S.A.) Inc.
Paramount, CA 562-630-6060

Parmesan

Atlantic Quality Spice & Seasonings
Edison, NJ 800-584-0422

Peppercorn

Atlantic Quality Spice & Seasonings
Edison, NJ 800-584-0422

Ranch

Atlantic Quality Spice & Seasonings
Edison, NJ 800-584-0422

Ott Food Products
Carthage, MO 800-866-2585

Raspberry Vinegrette

Atlantic Quality Spice & Seasonings
Edison, NJ. 800-584-0422

Reduced-Calorie

Atlantic Quality Spice & Seasonings
Edison, NJ. 800-584-0422

Thousand Island

Atlantic Quality Spice & Seasonings
Edison, NJ. 800-584-0422

Non-Fat

Betty Lou's Golden Smackers
McMinnville, OR 800-242-5205
Marukan Vinegar (U.S.A.) Inc.
Paramount, CA 562-630-6060
Naturally Fresh Foods
College Park, GA 800-765-1950
Walden Farms
Linden, NJ 800-229-1706

Oil & Vinegar

Au Printemps Gourmet
Prevost, QC 800-663-0416
Gourme' Mist
Coral Springs, FL 866-502-8472
Marukan Vinegar (U.S.A.) Inc.
Paramount, CA 562-630-6060
Newman's Own
Westport, CT 203-222-0136
Ventura Foods
Philadelphia, PA 215-223-8700

Ranch

Newman's Own
Westport, CT 203-222-0136
O'Brian Brothers Food
Cincinnati, OH 513-791-9909

Raspberry Vinegrette

Knott's Berry Farm Foods
Placentia, CA 800-289-9927
Rising Sun Farms
Phoenix, OR 541-535-8331

Thousand Island

Heinz Company of Canada
North York, ON 800-268-6641
Wood Brothers
West Columbia, SC 803-796-5146

Salsa

Alimentaire Whyte's Inc
Laval, QC 800-625-1979
Alimentos Naturales Sabrosa, SA de CV
San Antonio, TX 210-545-1792
Allied Old English
Port Reading, NJ 732-602-8955
American Spoon Foods
Petoskey, MI 800-222-5886
Amigos Canning Company
San Antonio, TX 800-580-3477
Anna's Unlimited, Inc
Austin, TX. 800-849-7054
Appledore Cove LLC
North Berwick, ME. 888-849-1787
Arizona Cowboy
Phoenix, AZ 800-529-8627
Ashman Manufacturing & Distributing Company
Virginia Beach, VA 800-641-9924
ATA International
Belton, TX. 816-221-0660
Authentic Specialty Foods
Chino, CA 909-631-2000
B&G Foods
Parsippany, NJ. 973-401-6500
Bartush-Schnitzius Foods Company
Lewisville, TX 972-219-1270
BBQ Bunch
Kansas City, MO. 816-941-6789
Bear Creek Kitchens
Marshall, TX 888-300-7687

Bel/Kaukauna USA
Kaukauna, WI 800-558-3500
Bell Buckle Country Store
Bell Buckle, TN 800-707-0483
Bien Padre Foods
Eureka, CA 707-442-4585
Big B Distributors
Evansville, IN 812-425-5235
Blueberry Store
Grand Junction, MI 877-654-2400
Border Foods Inc
Deming, NM 888-737-7752
CaJohns Fiery Foods
Columbus, OH 888-703-3473
California Creative Foods
Oceanside, CA 760-757-2622
California Fresh Salsa
Woodland, CA. 530-662-0512
California Style Gourmet Products
San Diego, CA 800-243-5226
California-Antilles Trading Consortium
San Diego, CA 800-330-6450
Casa Visco Finer Food Company
Schenectady, NY. 888-607-2823
Catamount Specialties of Vermont
Stowe, VT 800-820-8096
Cervantes Foods Products
Albuquerque, NM 877-982-4453
Charlie Beigg's Sauce Company
Windham, ME 888-502-8595
Chelten House Products
Bridgeport, NJ 856-467-1600
Chile Today - Hot Tamale
San Francisco, CA 800-758-0372
Choice of Vermont
Destin, FL 800-444-6261
Cibolo Junction Food & Spice
Albuquerque, NM 505-888-1987
Cinnabar Specialty Foods
Prescott, AZ 866-293-6433
Circle R Ranch Gourmet Foods
Flower Mound, TX 800-247-3077
Ciro Foods
Pittsburgh, PA 412-771-9018
Colorado Salsa Company
Littleton, CO 303-932-2617
Country Cupboard
Virginia City, NV 775-847-7300
Cowgirl Chocolates
Moscow, ID. 888-882-4098
Creative Foodworks
San Antonio, TX 210-212-4761
Cuizina Food Company
Woodinville, WA. 425-486-7000
Custom Food Solutions
Louisville, KY 800-767-2993
CW Resources
New Britain, CT 860-229-7700
Dave's Gourmet
San Francisco, CA 800-758-0372
Del Grosso Foods
Tipton, PA 800-521-5880
Deneen Company
Belen, NM. 505-988-1515
Dockside Market
Key Largo, FL. 800-813-2253
Dorina/So-Good
Union, IL. 815-923-2144
E.D. Smith & Sons
Winona, ON 905-643-1211
El Paso Chile Company
El Paso, TX. 888-472-5727
El Toro Food Products
Watsonville, CA 831-728-9266
Famous Chili
Fort Smith, AR 479-782-0096
Fiesta Gourmet of Tejas
Canyon Lake, TX 800-585-8250
Fischer & Wieser Specialty Foods
Fredericksburg, TX. 800-880-8526
Food Processor of New Mexico
Albuquerque, NM 877-634-3772
Food Specialties Company
Cincinnati, OH 513-761-1242
Ford's Fancy Fruit
Raleigh, NC 800-446-0947
Forge Mountain Foods
Hendersonville, NC 800-823-6743
Fountain Valley Foods
Colorado Springs, CO. 719-573-6012
Fremont Company
Fremont, OH 419-334-8995

 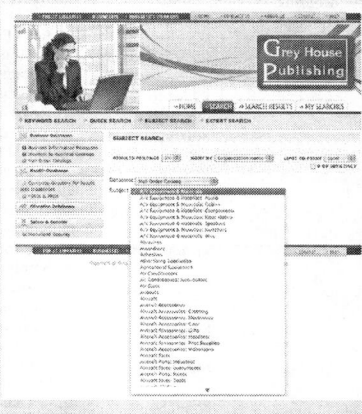

Frog Ranch Foods
Glouster, OH 800-742-2488
Galena Canning Company
Chicago, IL 773-645-9388
Garden Complements
Kansas City, MO 800-966-1091
Garden Fresh Salsa
Ferndale, MI 866-725-7239
Geetha's Gourmet of India
Las Cruces, NM 800-274-0475
Gingro Corp
Manchester Center, VT 802-362-0836
Gold Pure Foods Products Company
Hempstead, NY 800-422-4681
Golden Specialty Foods
Norwalk, CA 562-802-2537
Golden Valley Foods
Abbotsford, BC 888-299-8855
Gourmet Central
Romney, WV 800-984-3722
Green Mountain Gringo
Winston Salem, NC 336-661-1550
Green Mountain Gringo
Winston Salem, NC 802-875-3117
Groeb Farms
Onsted, MI 517-467-7100
Guiltless Gourmet
Secaucus, NJ 201-453-5200
Gumpert's Canada
Mississauga, ON 800-387-9324
Hagerty Foods
Orange, CA 714-628-1230
Hains Celestial Group
Melville, NY 877-612-4246
Hartford City Foam Pack aging & Converting
Hartford City, IN 765-348-2500
Havana's Limited
Titusville, FL 321-267-0513
Hirzel Canning Company &Farms
Northwood, OH 419-693-0531
Holy Mole
Austin, TX 877-310-8453
Hombres Foods
Cedar Creek, TX 877-446-6273
Hormel Foods Corporation
Austin, MN 800-523-4635
Hot Licks Hot Sauces
Spring Valley, CA 888-766-6468
Hot Wachula's
Lakeland, FL 877-883-8700
House of Webster
Rogers, AR 800-369-4641
Hume Specialties
Winston Salem, NC 802-875-3117
HVJ International
Spring, TX 877-730-3663
Iguana Tom's
Fremont, CA 888-827-2572
Imus Ranch Foods
Holtsville, NY 888-284-4687
Indel Food Products
El Paso, TX 800-472-0159
Jalapeno Foods Company
The Woodlands, TX 800-896-2318
JC's Midnite Salsa
Tucson, AZ 800-817-2572
Jillipepper
Albuquerque, NM 505-344-2804
Joe Hutson Foods
Jacksonville, FL 904-731-9065
Kettle Master
Hillsville, VA 276-728-7571
Kozlowski Farms
Forestville, CA 800-473-2767
La Vencedora Products
Los Angeles, CA 800-327-2572
La Victoria Foods
Rosemead, CA 800-423-4450
Laredo Mexican Foods
Fort Wayne, IN 800-252-7336
Leigh Olivers
Tyler, TX .903-245-9183
Li'l Guy Foods
Kansas City, MO 800-886-8226

Lisa's Salsa Company
St Paul, MN 651-644-4381
Los Chileros de Nuevo Mexico
Santa Fe, NM 505-768-1100
M.A. Gedney
Chaska, MN 952-448-2612
M.W. Milton & Company
Louisville, KY 502-587-5016
Mad Will's Food Company
Auburn, CA 888-275-9455
Mexisnax Corporation
El Paso, TX 915-779-5709
Miguel's Stowe Away
Stowe, VT 800-448-6517
Mixon Fruit Farms
Bradenton, FL 800-608-2525
Mojave Foods Corporation
Commerce, CA 323-890-8900
Native Kjalii Foods
San Francisco, CA 415-522-5580
Newman's Own
Westport, CT 203-222-0136
O'Garvey Sauces
New Braunfels, TX 830-620-6127
Ocean Spray Cranberries
Lakeville-Middleboro, MA 800-662-3263
Our Enterprises
Oklahoma City, OK 800-821-6375
Paisley Farms
Willoughby, OH 800-676-8656
Palmieri Food Products
New Haven, CT 800-845-5447
Paradise Products Corporation
Roslyn, NY 800-826-1235
Pepper Creek Farms
Lawton, OK 800-526-8132
Plocky's Fine Snacks
Hinsdale, IL 630-323-8888
Quality Foods
San Pedro, CA 877-833-7890
Rapazzini Winery
Gilroy, CA 408-842-5649
Ready Foods
Denver, CO 303-892-5861
Red Gold
Elwood, IN 877-748-9798
Reser's Fine Foods
Salt Lake City, UT 801-972-5633
Riba Foods
Houston, TX 800-327-7422
Robert Rothschild Berry Farm
Urbana, OH 866-565-6790
Rosarita Mexican Foods Company
Mesa, AZ 480-964-8751
Royal Resources
New Orleans, LA 800-888-9932
Ruffner's
Wayne, PA 610-687-9800
Sabra-Go Mediterranean
Farmingdale, NY 631-694-9500
Sambets Cajun Deli
Austin, TX 800-472-6238
San Angel Mexican Foods
Stowe, VT 800-598-6448
Santa Barbara Olive Company
Goleta, CA 800-624-4896
Santa Barbara Salsa/California Creative
Oceanside, CA 800-748-5523
Select Food Products
Toronto, ON 800-699-8016
Shawnee Canning Company
Cross Junction, VA 800-713-1414
Smiling Fox Pepper Company
North Aurora, IL 630-337-3734
Sona & Hollen Foods
Los Alamitos, CA 800-200-7662
Southern Bar-B-Que
Jennings, LA 866-612-2586
Southwest Spirit
Socorro, NM 800-838-0773
Soylent Brand
Irving, TX 972-255-4747
Spruce Foods
San Clemente, CA 949-366-9457
Steel's Gourmet Foods
Bridgeport, PA 800-678-3357
Stello Foods
Punxsutawney, PA 800-849-4599
Summercorn Foods
Fayetteville, AR 888-328-9473
Sun Harvest Foods
San Diego, CA 619-690-1128

T.W. Garner Food Company
Winston Salem, NC 800-476-7383
Terrell's Potato Chip Company
Seattle, WA 800-331-5222
Texas Heat
San Antonio, TX 800-656-5916
Thomson Food
Duluth, MN 218-722-2529
Timber Peaks Gourmet
Parker, CO 800-982-7687
Topper Food Products
East Brunswick, NJ 800-377-2823
Uncle Bum's Gourmet Foods
Riverside, CA 800-486-2867
Uncle Fred's Fine Foods
Rockport, TX 361-729-8320
Underground Sauce Network
Cranston, RI 888-919-6664
Valley of Mexico
Norwalk, CT 203-348-0402
Van De Walle Farms
San Antonio, TX 210-436-5551
Vegetable Juices
Chicago, IL 888-776-9752
Victoria Packing Corporation
Brooklyn, NY 718-649-2180
Vita Specialty Foods
Inwood, WV 800-974-4778
Walker Foods
Los Angeles, CA 800-966-5199
Wing Nien Company
Hayward, CA 510-487-8877
Xochitl
Dallas, TX 214-800-3551
Ynrico's Food Products Company
Syracuse, NY 888-472-8237
Zuni Foods
San Antonio, TX 800-906-3876

Canned

Hartford City Foam Pack aging & Converting
Hartford City, IN 765-348-2500
Kozlowski Farms
Forestville, CA 800-473-2767
Palmieri Food Products
New Haven, CT 800-845-5447
T.W. Garner Food Company
Winston Salem, NC 800-476-7383

Chunky

T.W. Garner Food Company
Winston Salem, NC 800-476-7383

Mild

California Creative Foods
Oceanside, CA 760-757-2622
Garden Fresh Salsa
Ferndale, MI 866-725-7239
Hot Wachula's
Lakeland, FL 877-883-8700
Iguana Tom's
Fremont, CA 888-827-2572
JC's Midnite Salsa
Tucson, AZ 800-817-2572
Lisa's Salsa Company
St Paul, MN 651-644-4381
Newman's Own
Westport, CT 203-222-0136
T.W. Garner Food Company
Winston Salem, NC 800-476-7383

Picante

Bartush-Schnitzius Foods Company
Lewisville, TX 972-219-1270
Garden Fresh Salsa
Ferndale, MI 866-725-7239
Hormel Foods Corporation
Austin, MN 800-523-4635
Hot Wachula's
Lakeland, FL 877-883-8700
Iguana Tom's
Fremont, CA 888-827-2572
JC's Midnite Salsa
Tucson, AZ 800-817-2572
Lisa's Salsa Company
St Paul, MN 651-644-4381
T.W. Garner Food Company
Winston Salem, NC 800-476-7383

Texas Heat
  San Antonio, TX 800-656-5916

with Cheese

Amigos Canning Company
  San Antonio, TX 800-580-3477
Cactus-Creek
  Dallas, TX 800-471-7723
Del Grosso Foods
  Tipton, PA 800-521-5880
Del Rey Tortilleria
  Chicago, IL 800-446-1459
Groeb Farms
  Onsted, MI 517-467-7100

Sauces

A.M. Braswell Jr. Food Company
  Statesboro, GA 800-673-9388
Adams
  Fargo, ND 800-342-4748
AFP Advanced Food Products, LLC
  Visalia, CA 559-627-2070
Ajinomoto Food Ingredients LLC
  Chicago, IL 773-380-7000
Al Dente
  Whitmore Lake, MI 800-536-7278
Alimentaire Whyte's Inc
  Laval, QC 800-625-1979
Allegro Fine Foods
  Paris, TN 731-642-6113
Allied Old English
  Port Reading, NJ 732-602-8955
Amboy Specialty Foods Company
  Dixon, IL 800-892-0400
American Culinary Gardens
  Springfield, MO 888-831-2433
American Saucery
  Oak Park, MI 800-328-8632
American Spoon Foods
  Petoskey, MI 800-222-5886
Amigos Canning Company
  San Antonio, TX 800-580-3477

Amy's Kitchen
  Petaluma, CA 707-578-5908
Anke Kruse Organics
  Guelph, ON 519-824-6161
Ankle Deep Foods
  Norfolk, NE 402-371-2991
Annie Chun's
  San Rafael, CA 415-479-8272
Annie's Naturals
  East Calais, VT 800-434-1234
Apecka
  Rockwall, TX 972-772-2654
Archie Moore's Foods Products
  Milford, CT 203-876-5088
Argo Century
  Charlotte, NC 800-446-7131
Armanino Foods of Distinction
  Hayward, CA 510-441-9300
Aromont-USA
  Southlake, TX 817-552-5544
Artel
  Boisbriand, QC 450-433-1322
Ashley Foods
  Sudbury, MA 800-617-2823
Ashman Manufacturing & Distributing Company
  Virginia Beach, VA 800-641-9924
ASK Foods
  Palmyra, PA 800-879-4275
Athena Oil
  Long Island City, NY 718-956-8893
Atlanta Burning
  Newnan, GA 800-665-5611
Atlantic Seasonings
  Kinston, NC 800-433-5261
Au Printemps Gourmet
  Prevost, QC 800-663-0416
Aunt Aggie De's Pralines
  Sinton, TX 888-772-5463
Aunt Jenny's Sauces/Melba Foods
  Brooklyn, NY 718-383-3192
Austin Slow Burn
  Austin, TX 877-513-3192
Authentic Specialty Foods
  Chino, CA 909-631-2000

B&B Pecan Processors of NC
  Turkey, NC 866-328-7322
B&G Foods
  Parsippany, NJ 973-401-6500
Bainbridge Festive Foods
  Tunica, MS 800-545-9205

Baldwin Richardson Foods
  Frankfort, IL 866-644-2732

Baldwin Richardson Foods is a liquid ingredient manufacturer specializing in signature sauces, dessert toppings, beverage/pancake syrups, specialty fruit fillings and condiments. Packaging capabilities range from portion control cups and pouches to standard retail and foodservice packs and include industrial drums and totes. Full service R&D and Quality groups dedicated to new product development, with in-house stability and analytical testing. Call for assistance.

Barefoot Contessa Pantry
  York, ME 207-351-2713
Barhyte Specialty Foods Inc
  Pendleton, OR 800-227-4983
Bartush-Schnitzius Foods Company
  Lewisville, TX 972-219-1270
Basic Food Flavors
  North Las Vegas, NV 702-643-0043
Baumer Foods
  New Orleans, LA 504-482-5761
Bay Valley Foods
  Horsham, PA 800-236-1119
Bay Valley Foods
  Green Bay, WI 800-558-4700

Baycliff Company
New York, NY 212-772-6078

BBQ Bunch
Kansas City, MO. 816-941-6789

BBQ Shack
Paola, KS. .913-294-5908

BBQ'n Fools
Bend, OR. .800-671-8652

Beaverton Foods
Beaverton, OR. 800-223-8076

Bel/Kaukauna USA
Kaukauna, WI. 800-558-3500

Bellisio Foods, Inc.
Lakeville, MN. 800-368-7337

Berner Cheese Corporation
Dakota, IL. 800-819-8199

Bestfoods Foodservice
Somerset, NJ. 732-627-8722

Bien Padre Foods
Eureka, CA. 707-442-4585

Big B Distributors
Evansville, IN. 812-425-5235

Bittersweet Herb Farm
Shelburne Falls, MA. 800-456-1599

Blackberry Patch
Thomasville, GA. 800-853-5598

Blair's Death Sauces & Snacks
Highlands, NJ. 732-872-0755

Blue Jay Orchards
Bethel, CT. 203-748-0119

Blue Smoke Salsa
Ansted, WV. 888-725-7298

Bodin Foods
New Iberia, LA. 337-367-1344

Borden Foods
Columbus, OH. 614-233-3759

Border Foods Inc
Deming, NM. 888-737-7752

Bottle Green Drinks
Mississauga, ON. 905-273-6137

Bove's of Vermont
Burlington, VT. 888-545-2321

Bowman Apple Products Company
Mt Jackson, VA. 877-426-9626

Brateka Enterprises
Ocala, FL. .877-549-3227

Brede
Detroit, MI. 313-273-1079

Brockles Foods Company
Garland, TX. 972-272-5593

Brother Bru Bru's Produce
Venice, CA. 310-396-9033

Brown Family Farm
Brattleboro, VT. 866-254-8718

Brown Family Farm
Brattleboro, VT. 888-556-2753

Bruno Specialty Foods
West Sayville, NY. 631-589-1700

Buckhead Gourmet
Atlanta, GA. 800-605-5754

Buddy's
Pocatello, ID. 208-233-1172

Buffalo Bob's Everything Sauce
Virginia Beach, VA. 757-490-9186

Buffalo Wild Wings
Minneapolis, MN. 763-546-1891

Burnette Foods
Hartford, MI. 616-621-3181

C&E Canners
Hammonton, NJ. 609-561-1078

C.F. Sauer Company
Richmond, VA. 800-688-5676

Cafe Chilku
Colchester, VT. 802-878-4645

Cafe Tequila
San Francisco, CA. 415-264-0106

Cafferata
San Anselmo, CA. 800-626-8115

Cains Foods
Ayer, MA. 978-772-0300

CaJohns Fiery Foods
Columbus, OH. 888-703-3473

Cajun Chef Products
St Martinville, LA. 337-394-7112

California Creative Foods
Oceanside, CA. 760-757-2622

Campagna
Lebanon, OR. 800-959-4372

Campbell Soup Company
Camden, NJ. 800-257-8443

Canada Bread
Etobicoke, ON. 416-622-2040

Canada Bread
North Bay, ON. 800-461-6122

Cantisano Foods
Fairport, NY. 585-377-9151

Capone Foods
Somerville, MA. 617-629-2296

Captain Bob's Jet Fuel
Fort Wayne, IN. 877-486-6468

Carando Gourmet Frozen Foods
Springfield, MA. 413-730-4205

Caribbean Food Products
Jacksonville Beach, FL. 904-246-0149

Carmela's Gourmet
Monterey, CA. 831-373-6291

Carol's Country Cuisine
Glen Ellen, CA. 707-996-1124

Carole's Cheesecake Company
Toronto, ON. 416-256-0000

Carolina Cupboard
Hillsborough, NC. 800-400-3441

Carolina Treet
Wilmington, NC. 800-616-6344

Carolyn's Caribbean Heat
Malvern, PA. 610-647-0336

Carriage Charles
Fredonia, NY. 800-828-8915

Carriage House Companies
Fredonia, NY. 800-828-8915

Carriere Foods Inc
Montreal, QC. 514-384-4281

Cary Randall's Sauces & Dressings
Highlands, NJ. 732-872-6353

Casa di Carfagna
Columbus, OH. 614-846-6340

Casa DiLisio Products
Mt Kisco, NY. 800-247-4199

Casa Visco Finer Food Company
Schenectady, NY. 888-607-2823

Castleberry/Snow Brands
Augusta, GA. 800-241-3520

Catamount Specialties of Vermont
Stowe, VT. 800-820-8096

Catskill Mountain Specialties
Saugerties, NY. 800-311-3473

Cattle Boyz Foods
Calgary, AB. 888-662-9366

Cedarvale Food Products
Toronto, ON. 416-656-6330

Certified Savory
Countryside, IL. 800-328-7656

Cervantes Foods Products
Albuquerque, NM. 877-982-4453

Charlie Palmer Group
New York, NY. 888-287-3653

Charlie Trotter Foods
Chicago, IL. 773-248-6228

Chef Merito
Encino, CA. 800-637-4861

Chef Shells Catering & Roadside Cafe
Port Huron, MI. 810-966-8371

Chef-A-Roni
East Greenwich, RI. 401-884-8798

Chelten House Products
Bridgeport, NJ. 856-467-1600

Cherchies
Malvern, PA. 800-644-1980

Cherry Hut
Traverse City, MI. 888-882-4431

China Bowl Trading Company
Westport, CT. 203-222-0381

Chincoteague Seafood Company
Parsonsburg, MD. 443-260-4800

Chocolaterie Bernard Callebaut
Calgary, AB. 800-661-8367

Chocolatique
Los Angeles, CA. 310-479-3849

Christie Food Products
Randolph, MA. 800-727-2523

Christopher Ranch
Gilroy, CA. 408-847-1100

CHS, Inc.
Inner Grove Heights, MN. 800-232-3639

Chukar Cherries
Prosser, WA. 800-624-9544

Cinnabar Specialty Foods
Prescott, AZ. 866-293-6433

Cipriani's Spaghetti & Sauce Company
Chicago Heights, IL. 708-755-6212

Ciro Foods
Pittsburgh, PA. 412-771-9018

Clarmil Manufacturing Corporation
Hayward, CA. 888-252-7645

Classy Delites
Austin, TX. 800-440-2648

Clement Pappas & Company
Seabrook, NJ. 800-257-7019

Clements Foods Company
Oklahoma City, OK. 800-654-8355

Clofine Dairy & Food Products
Linwood, NJ. 800-441-1001

Cold Hollow Cider Mill
Waterbury Center, VT. 800-327-7537

Colgin Companies
Dallas, TX. 888-226-5446

Colonna Brothers
North Bergen, NJ. 201-864-1115

Colorado Salsa Company
Littleton, CO. 303-932-2617

ConAgra Grocery Products
Archbold, OH. 419-445-8015

ConAgra Grocery Products
Irvine, CA. 714-680-1000

Consumers Vinegar & Spice Company
Chicago, IL. 773-376-4100

Continental Seasoning
Teaneck, NJ. 800-631-1564

Conway Import Company
Franklin Park, IL. 800-323-8801

Cookies Food Products
Wall Lake, IA. 800-331-4995

Cordon Bleu International
Anjou, QC. 514-352-3000

Corfu Foods
Bensenville, IL. 630-595-2510

Corsair Pepper Sauce
Gulfport, MS. 228-452-9238

Costa Deano's Gourmet Foods
Canton, OH. 800-337-2823

Couch's Original Sauce
Jonesboro, AR. 800-264-7535

Country Bob's
Centralia, IL. 800-373-2140

Country Fresh Food & Confections
Oliver Springs, TN. 800-545-8782

Country Village Meats
Sublette, IL. 815-849-5532

Cowboy Foods
Bozeman, MT. 800-759-5489

Crave Natural Foods
Northampton, MA. 413-587-7999

Crazy Jerry's
Roswell, GA. 770-993-0651

Creative Foodworks
San Antonio, TX. 210-212-4761

Crustacean Foods
Los Angeles, CA. 866-263-2625

Cucina Antica Foods Corporation
Bedford Hills, NY. 877-728-2462

Cugino's Gourmet Foods
Crystal Lake, IL. 888-592-8446

Cuizina Food Company
Woodinville, WA. 425-486-7000

Culinary Foods
Chicago, IL. 800-621-4049

Culinary Standards Corporation
Louisville, KY. 800-778-3434

Curry King Corporation
Waldwick, NJ. 800-287-7987

Custom Food Products
Alsip, IL. .708-388-8883

Custom Food Solutions
Louisville, KY. 800-767-2993

Custom Ingredients
New Braunfels, TX. 800-457-8935

Cyclone Enterprises
Houston, TX. 281-872-0087

D & D Foods
Columbus, GA. 706-322-4507

D'Oni Enterprises
Sherman Oaks, CA. 888-997-7423

Dabruzzi's Italian Foods
Hudson, WI. 715-386-3653

Dahm's Foods
Skokie, IL. 847-673-0653

Dalton's Best Maid Products
Fort Worth, TX. 817-335-5494

Daregal Gourmet
Princeton, NJ. 609-375-2312

Dean Distributors
Burlingame, CA. 800-227-3112

Dean Distributors
Burlingame, CA. 800-792-0816

Deep South Products
Fitzgerald, GA. 229-423-1121

Del Grosso Foods
Tipton, PA 800-521-5880
Del Mar Food Products Corporation
Watsonville, CA 831-722-3516
Del Monte Foods
San Francisco, CA 800-543-3090
Del Monte Foods
Cambria, WI 920-348-5121
Del Rey Tortilleria
Chicago, IL 800-446-1459
Dell'Amore Enterprises
Colchester, VT 800-962-6673
Delta BBQ Sauce Company
Stockton, CA 209-472-9284
Dhidow Enterprises
Oxford, PA 610-932-7868
Diamond Crystal
Savannah, GA 800-227-4455
DiGregorio Food Products
St Louis, MO. 314-776-1062
Dillard's Bar-B-Q Sauce
Durham, NC 919-544-1587
Dipasa
Brownsville, TX 956-831-5893
Diversified Foods & Seasoning
Metairie, LA 504-846-5090
Dixie Trail Farms
Wilmington, NC 800-665-3968
Dolefam Corporation
Arlington Hts, IL 847-577-2122
Dorina/So-Good
Union, IL. 815-923-2144
Dorothy Dawson Foods Products
Jackson, MI. 517-788-9830
Dr Pete's
Savannah, GA. 888-599-0047
Drake's Ducks Woodstream Specialty Foods
Keene, NH. 603-357-5858
Dressed in Style/Chase
Atlanta, GA. 888-368-2698
Drew's
Brattleboro, VT. 800-228-2980
Drew's All Natural
Chester, VT. 800-228-2980
E. Waldo Ward & Son Corporation
Sierra Madre, CA 800-355-9273
E.D. Smith & Sons
Winona, ON 905-643-1211
Earth & Vine Provisions
Lincoln, CA 888-723-8463
East & West Gourmet
Honolulu, HI. 800-378-6978
East Wind Nut Butters
Tecumseh, MO 417-679-4682
Eastern Food Industries
East Greenwich, RI. 401-884-8798
Eastern Foods Naturally Fresh
College Park, GA 404-765-9000

Eatem Foods Company
Vineland, NJ 800-683-2836
Eden Foods Inc
Clinton, MI 800-248-0320
Edmonds Chile Company
St Louis, MO. 314-772-1499
El Charro Mexican Food Industries
Roswell, NM. 575-622-8590
El Paso Chile Company
El Paso, TX. 888-472-5727
El Rancho Tortilla
San Antonio, TX. 210-922-8411
El Toro Food Products
Watsonville, CA 831-728-9266
El-Rey Foods
Ferguson, MO 314-521-3113
Epicurean International
Berkeley, CA. 800-967-7424
Erevia Products
Brighton, MI 810-225-0460
Escalon Premier Brand
Escalon, CA 209-838-7341
Essen Nutrition
Romeoville, IL 630-739-6700
Ethnic Gourmet Foods
West Chester, PA. 610-692-7575
Europa Foods
Saddle Brook, NJ 201-368-8929
Excalibur Seasoning Company
Pekin, IL 800-444-2169
Famous Chili
Fort Smith, AR 479-782-0096
Farmacopia
Saratoga, CA. 888-827-3623
Father's Country Hams
Bremen, KY 270-525-3554
Favorite Foods
Burnaby, BC 604-420-5100
Felbro Food Products
Los Angeles, CA. 800-335-2761
Fernandez Chili Company
Alamosa, CO. 719-589-6043
Festive Foods
Virginia Beach, VA. 757-490-9186
Fiesta Canning Company
Mc Neal, AZ. 520-364-7541
Figaro Company
Mesquite, TX 972-288-3587
Fireside Kitchen
Halifax, NS 902-454-7387
Fischer & Wieser Specialty Foods
Fredericksburg, TX. 800-880-8526
Flavor House
Adelanto, CA 760-246-9131
Fontina Foods
Port Saint Lucie, FL 800-966-7107
Food Concentrate Corporation
Oklahoma City, OK 405-840-5633

Food Masters
Griffin, GA 888-715-4394
Food Source
McKinney, TX 972-548-9001
Food Source Company
Mississauga, ON. 905-625-8404
Foodbrands America
Oklahoma City, OK 405-290-4000
Fool Proof Gourmet Products
Grapevine, TX 817-329-1839
Ford's Fancy Fruit
Raleigh, NC 800-446-0947
Fords Gourmet Foods
Raleigh, NC 800-446-0947
Fountain Valley Foods
Colorado Springs, CO. 719-573-6012
Fox Hollow Farm
Hanover, NH. 603-643-6002
Freedom Gourmet Sauce
Nashville, TN 615-333-9063
Fremont Company
Fremont, OH 419-334-8995
French's Flavor Ingredients
Springfield, MO 800-437-3624
French's Ingredients
Springfield, MO 417-837-1813
Frontera Foods
Chicago, IL. 800-509-4441
Furmano Foods
Northumberland, PA. 877-877-6032
Fusion Gourmet
Gardena, CA. 310-532-8938
Fuzzy's Wholesale Bar-B-Q
Madison, NC. 336-548-2283
G Di Lullo & Sons
Westville, NJ. 856-456-3700
Galena Canning Company
Chicago, IL. 773-645-9388
Garden Complements
Kansas City, MO. 800-966-1091
Garden Herbs
Redlands, CA 800-388-9397
Garden Row Foods
Franklin Park, IL. 800-555-9798
Garlic Festival Foods
Gilroy, CA. 888-427-5423
Garlic Survival Company
San Juan Cpstrno, CA. 800-342-7542
Gator Hammock
Felda, FL. 800-664-2867
Gayle's Sweet 'N Sassy Foods
Beverly Hills, CA 310-246-1792
Geetha's Gourmet of India
Las Cruces, NM 800-274-0475
Gehl Guernsey Farms
Germantown, WI. 800-434-5713
Gemini Food Industries
Fiskdale, MA 508-347-2800

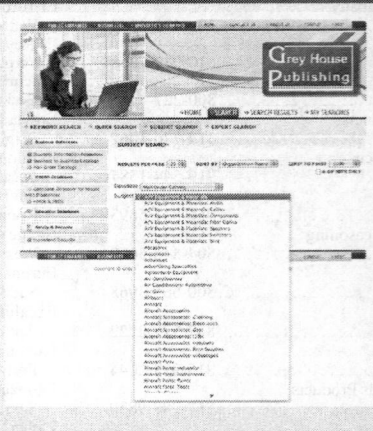

Genarom International
Cranbury, NJ .609-409-6200
Geneva Ingredients
Waunakee, WI. 800-828-5924
Gentilini's Italian Products
Sunriver, OR .541-593-5053
GFF
City of Industry, CA 323-232-6255
Gia Russa
Coitsville, OH 800-527-8772
Gingro Corp
Manchester Center, VT. 802-362-0836
Giovanni Food Company
Oswego, NY .315-342-3451
Girard's Food Service Dressings
City of Industry, CA 888-327-8442
Glencourt
Napa, CA. 707-944-4444
GMB Specialty Foods
San Juan Cpstrno, CA. 800-809-8098
Gold Dollar Products
Memphis, TN 800-971-8964
Gold Pure Foods Products Company
Hempstead, NY. 800-422-4681
Golden Specialty Foods
Norwalk, CA. 562-802-2537
Golden State Goods
City of Industry, CA 626-968-6431
Golden State Foods
Irvine, CA 949-252-2000
Golden Valley Foods
Abbotsford, BC. 888-299-8855
Golden West Specialty Foods
Brisbane, CA. 800-584-4481
Golden Whisk
South San Francisco, CA 800-660-5222
Goldrush Sourdough
San Jose, CA. 408-288-4090
Goldwater's Food of Arizona
Fredericksburg, TX. 800-488-4932
Gourmet Central
Romney, WV. 800-984-3722
Gourmet Conveniences Ltd
Litchfield, CT 866-793-3801
Gourmet Foods
Knoxville, TN 865-970-2982
Gourmet's Secret
North Highlands, CA 916-334-6161
Gracie's Gourmet Shop
Stowe, VT. 888-472-2437
Grain Processing Corporation
Muscatine, IA 800-448-4472
Gravymaster, Inc
Branford, CT. 203-481-2276
Great American Barbecue Company
Weimar, TX. .510-865-3133
Green Garden Food Products
Kent, WA. 800-304-1033
Griffin Food Company
Muskogee, OK 800-580-6311
Griffith Laboratories Worldwide
Alsip, IL 800-346-4743
Groeb Farms
Onsted, MI 517-467-7100
Grouse Hunt Farms
Tamaqua, PA 570-467-2850
Guido's International Foods
Pasadena, CA 877-994-8436
Gumpert's Canada
Mississauga, ON. 800-387-9324
H.J. Heinz Company
Pittsburgh, PA 412-237-5948
H.J. Heinz Company
Pittsburgh, PA 800-872-2229
Habby Habanero's Food Products
Jacksonville, FL 904-333-9758
Hagerty Foods
Orange, CA 714-628-1230
Hains Celestial Group
Melville, NY .877-612-4246
Halben Food Manufacturing Company
Overland, MO. 800-888-4855
Halifax Group
Doraville, GA 770-452-8828
Hampton Chutney Company
Amagansett, NY 631-267-3131
Hanan Products Company
Hicksville, NY 516-938-1000
Hanover Foods Corporation
Hanover, PA .717-632-6000
Harry's Cafe
Mount Holly, VT. 802-259-2996

Hartford City Foam Pack aging & Converting
Hartford City, IN. 765-348-2500
Hartville Kitchen
Hartville, OH 330-877-9353
Hartville Locker
Hartville, OH 330-877-9547
Harvest-Pac Products
Chatham, ON 519-436-0446
Haus Barhyte
Pendleton, OR. 800-407-9241
Havana's Limited
Titusville, FL. 321-267-0513
Havoc Maker Products
Guilford, CT .800-681-3909
Hawaiian Fruit Specialties
Kalaheo, HI .808-332-9333
Heartline Foods
Westport, CT 203-222-0381
Heintz & Weber Company
Buffalo, NY. .716-852-7171
Heinz
Fremont, OH 419-332-7357
Heinz Company of Canada
North York, ON. 800-268-6641
Heinz North America
Pittsburgh, PA 412-237-5700
Heluva Good Cheese
Sodus, NY. 315-483-6971
Heritage Family Specialty Foods Inc
Grand Prairie, TX. 972-660-6511
Heronwood Farm
Kent, WA. 877-203-5908
Hillside Lane Farm
Randolph, VT. 802-728-0070
Hirzel Canning Company &Farms
Northwood, OH 419-693-0531
Hoffman Aseptic Packaging Company
Hoffman, MN 320-986-2084
Hogtowne B-B-Q Sauce Company
Gainesville, FL 352-375-6969
Hollman Foods
Minden, NE. .888-926-2879
Homestead Fine Foods
S San Francisco, CA 650-615-0750
Honey Bear Fruit Basket
Denver, CO 888-330-2327
Honeydrop Foods
Bridgewater, NJ 908-203-1577
HongryHawg Products
Prairieville, LA 888-772-4294
Hoopeston Foods
Burnsville, MN 952-854-0903
Hopkins Inn
Warren, CT 860-868-7295
Hormel Foods Corporation
Columbia, MD 410-290-1855
Hormel Foods Corporation
Charlotte, NC 704-527-4388
Hormel Foods Corporation
Orchard Park, NY 716-675-7700
Hormel Foods Corporation
Austin, MN 800-523-4635
Hormel Foods Corporation
Lisle, IL. 800-533-2000
House of Webster
Rogers, AR 800-369-4641
Howjax
Pembroke Pines, FL 954-441-2491
Hume Specialties
Winston Salem, NC. 802-875-3117
Hunt-Wesson Food Service Company
Rochester, NY 800-633-1002
Hunt-Wesson Foods
Rochester, NY. 209-847-0321
HVJ International
Spring, TX. 877-730-3663
HVR Company
Oakland, CA .800-537-2823
Illes Seasonings & Flavors
Carrollton, TX. 800-683-4553
Imus Ranch Foods
Holtsville, NY 888-284-4687
Ingredients Corporation of America
Memphis, TN 901-525-6660
Inter-State Cider & Vinegar Company
Baltimore, MD 410-947-1529
Intercorp Excelle Foods
Toronto, ON .888-476-2124
International Bar-B-Que
Unionville, IN 812-988-6150
International Diverse Foods
Nashville, TN 615-889-8345

International Food Products Corporation
Saint Louis, MO 800-227-8427
International Foods & Confections
Alpharetta, GA 770-887-0201
International Home Foods
Milton, PA 973-359-9920
Island Spices
Asbury Park, NJ 877-229-2900
Italia Foods
Schaumburg, IL. 800-747-1109
Ittella Foods
Los Angeles, CA 213-746-6201
J&R Foods
Long Branch, NJ 732-229-4020
J.A.M.B. Low Carb Distributor
Pompano Beach, FL 800-708-6738
J.D. Mullen Company
Palestine, IL .618-586-2727
J.M. Smucker Company
Orrville, OH .330-682-3000
J.N. Bech
Elk Rapids, MI 800-232-4583
J.T. Pappy's Sauce
Los Angeles, CA 323-969-9605
J.W. Raye & Company
Eastport, ME. 800-853-1903
J.W. Raye & Company
Mira Loma, CA 909-428-8630
Jack Miller's Food Products
Ville Platte, LA 800-646-1541
Jalapeno Foods Company
The Woodlands, TX 800-896-2318
Jet's Le Frois Foods Corporation
Brockport, NY 585-637-5003
Jillipepper
Albuquerque, NM 505-344-2804
Jimtown Store
Healdsburg, CA 707-433-1212
JMS Specialty Foods
Ripon, WI 800-535-5437
Joe Hutson Foods
Jacksonville, FL 904-731-9065
Johnny Harris Famous Barbecue Sauce
Savannah, GA 912-354-8828
Joseph's Pasta Company
Ward Hill, MA 888-327-2782
Juanita's Foods
Wilmington, CA 310-834-5339
Judyth's Mountain
Spokane, WA. 509-484-5000
Jyoti Cuisine India
Berwyn, PA 610-296-4620
Kagome
Los Banos, CA 209-826-8850
Kajun Kettle Foods
New Orleans, LA 504-733-8800
Kari-Out Company
White Plains, NY 800-433-8799
Kathy's Gourmet Specialties
Mendocino, CA. 707-937-1383
Kelchner's Horseradish
Dublin, PA 215-249-3439
Kemach Food Products   Corporation
Brooklyn, NY 888-453-6224
Ken's Foods
Marlborough, MA 800-633-5800
Kentucky Bourbon
Westport, KY 866-472-7797
Kettle Cooked Food
Fort Worth, TX 817-615-4500
Kettle Master
Hillsville, VA 276-728-7571
Key Ingredients
Harrisburg, PA 800-227-4448
Kikkoman International
San Francisco, CA 415-956-7750
Kilwons Foods
Santa Cruz, CA 831-426-9670
King's Cupboard
Red Lodge, MT. 800-962-6555
Kings Food Products
Belleville, IL. 618-233-0400
Kitchen Products
Gloucester, MA. 978-283-1384
Knott's Berry Farm Foods
Placentia, CA 800-289-9927
Knouse Foods
Peach Glen, PA 717-677-8181
Knudsen's Candy
Hayward, CA 800-736-6887
Kozlowski Farms
Forestville, CA. 800-473-2767

Kraft
Parsippany, NJ.............973-292-1755
Kraft Food Ingredients
Memphis, TN.............901-381-6500
Kraus & Company
Commerce Twp, MI.........800-662-5871
Kroger Company
Cincinnati, OH...........800-576-4377
L & S Packing Company
Farmingdale, NY..........877-879-6453
L&S Packing Company
Farmingdale, NY..........800-286-6487
La Piccolina
Decatur, GA.............800-626-1624
La Vencedora Products
Los Angeles, CA..........800-327-2572
LaMonica Fine Foods
Millville, NJ............856-825-8111
Lang Naturals
Middletown, RI...........401-848-7700
Laredo Mexican Foods
Fort Wayne, IN...........800-252-7336
Le Frois Foods Corporation
Brockport, NY............585-637-5003
Lea & Perrins
Fair Lawn, NJ............800-289-5797
Leams
Hutchinson, KS...........316-662-4287
Lee Kum Kee
City of Industry, CA......800-654-5082
Lees Sausage Company
Orangeburg, SC...........803-534-5517
Lemmes Company
Coventry, RI............401-821-2575
Lendy's
Virginia Beach, VA.......757-491-3511
Leroux Creek Foods
Hotchkiss, CO...........877-970-5670
Les Aliments Livabec Foods
Sherrington, QC..........450-454-7971
Li'l Guy Foods
Kansas City, MO..........800-886-8226
Litehouse Foods
Sandpoint, ID...........800-669-3169
Lloyd's Barbeque Company
Mendota Heights, MN......651-688-6000
Lombardo's Ravioli Kitchen
New Britain, CT..........860-223-7800
Longmeadow
Longmeadow, MA...........413-565-4153
Louis Maull Company
St Louis, MO............314-241-8410
Louisa Food Products
St Louis, MO............314-868-3000
Louisiana Gourmet Enterprises
Houma, LA..............800-328-5586
Lounsbury Foods
Toronto, ON............416-656-6330
Luigino's
Duluth, MN.............218-727-2059
Lynch Foods
North York, QC..........416-449-5464
Lyons-Magnus
Fresno, CA.............559-268-5966
M.A. Gedney
Chaska, MN.............952-448-2612
M.W. Milton & Company
Louisville, KY..........502-587-5016
Mad Chef Enterprise
Mentor, OH.............800-951-2433
Mad Will's Food Company
Auburn, CA.............888-275-9455
Madison Foods
St Paul, MN............651-265-8212
Maggie Gin's
San Francisco, CA........415-221-6080
Magic Seasoning Blends
Harahan, LA............800-457-2857
Mandarin Soy Sauce
Middletown, NY..........845-343-1505
Mansmith's Barbecue
San Jn Bautista, CA......800-626-7648
Maple Grove Farms of Vermont
St Johnsbury, VT.........800-525-2540
Mar-K Anchor Bar Hot Sauces
Buffalo, NY............716-853-1791
Marsan Foods
Toronto, ON............416-755-9262
Martha Olson's Great Foods
Sutter Creek, CA.........800-973-3966
Mayacamas Fine Foods
Sonoma, CA.............800-826-9621

McCutcheon's Apple Products
Frederick, MD...........800-888-7537
McLane Foods
Phoenix, AZ............602-275-5509
McIlhenny Company
New Orleans, LA.........504-523-7370
Meditalia
New York, NY...........212-616-3006
Mercado Latino
City of Industry, CA......626-333-6862
Mexisnax Corporation
El Paso, TX............915-779-5709
Miceli's Specialty Foods Company
Danbury, CT............888-264-2354
Michele's Original Gourmet Tofu Products
Philadelphia, PA........215-922-2588
Mid-Atlantic Foods
Easton, MD.............800-922-4688
Miguel's Stowe Away
Stowe, VT..............800-448-6517
Millflow Spice Corporation
Valley Stream, NY........800-229-6122
Minnesota Specialty Crops
McGregor, MN...........800-328-6731
Mix-A-Lota Stuff LLC
Fort Pierce, FL.........561-468-4688
Miyako Oriental Foods
Baldwin Park, CA.........877-788-6476
Mizkam Americas
Kansas City, MO.........816-483-1700
Mo Hotta-Mo Betta
San Luis Obispo, CA......800-462-3220
Mojave Foods Corporation
Commerce, CA...........323-890-8900
Molinaro's Fine Italian Foods
Mississauga, ON.........800-268-4959
Mom's Barbeque Sauce
Stow, OH..............330-929-7290
Montebello Kitchens
Gordonsville, VA.........800-743-7687
Monterrey Products Company
San Antonio, TX.........210-435-2872
Monterrey Products Company
San Antonio, TX.........800-872-1652
Moonlite Bar BQ Inn
Owensboro, KY...........800-322-8989
More Than Gourmet
Akron, OH.............800-860-9385
Morgan Food
Austin, IN.............888-430-1780
Morning Star Packing Company
Los Banos, CA...........209-826-8000
Mother Teresa's
Clute, TX.............888-265-7429
Mott's
Port Chester, NY........914-612-4000
MPK Sonama Corporation
Sonoma, CA.............707-996-3931

Mrs. Clark's Foods
Ankeny, IA.............800-736-5674

| Juices, salad dressings and sauces. |

Mrs. Dog's Products
Tampa, FL..............800-267-7364
Mullins Food Products
Broadview, IL...........708-344-3224
Multi Foods
Portland, OR............800-666-8998
Mushroom Company
Cambridge, MD...........410-221-8900
Myron's Fine Foods
Erving, MA.............800-730-2820
Nana Mae's Organics
Sebastopol, CA..........707-829-7359
National Fruit Product Company
Lincolnton, NC..........704-735-2531
Nationwide Canning
Cottam, ON.............519-839-4831
Native Kjalii Foods
San Francisco, CA........415-522-5580
Naturally Fresh Foods
College Park, GA.........800-765-1950
Nestle
Cleveland, OH...........440-349-5757

New Business Corporation
East Chicago, IN.........800-742-8435
New Canaan Farms
Dripping Springs, TX......800-727-5267
New England Natural Bakers
Greenfield, MA..........800-910-2884
New Era Canning Company
New Era, MI............231-861-2151
New Morning
Needham, MA............781-444-0440
Newly Weds Foods
Memphis, TN............800-647-9314
Newman's Own
Westport, CT............203-222-0136
Nog Incorporated
Dunkirk, NY............800-332-2664
Noh Foods International
Honolulu, HI............808-841-0655
North American Enterprises
Tucson, AZ.............800-817-8666
North Coast Processing
North East, PA..........814-725-9617
Nuovo Pasta Productions
Stratford, CT...........800-803-0033
O'Brian Brothers Food
Cincinnati, OH..........513-791-9909
O'Garvey Sauces
New Braunfels, TX........830-620-6127
Ocean Spray Cranberries
Kenosha, WI............262-694-0621
Ocean Spray Cranberries
Lakeville-Middleboro, MA...800-662-3263
Ojai Cook
Los Angeles, CA.........886-571-1551
Old Mansion Foods
Petersburg, VA..........800-476-1877
Old World Spices & Seasonings
Kansas City, MO.........800-241-0070
On the Verandah
Highlands, NC...........828-526-2338
Original Italian Pasta Poducts Company
Chelsea, MA............800-999-9603
Original Juan
Kansas City, KS.........800-568-8468
Ott Food Products
Carthage, MO...........800-866-2585
Our Enterprises
Oklahoma City, OK........800-821-6375
Overhill Farms
Vernon, CA.............800-859-6406
Pacific Choice Brands
Fresno, CA.............559-237-5583
Pacific Harvest Products
Bellevue, WA...........425-401-7990
Pacific Poultry Company
Honolulu, HI............808-841-2828
Pak Technologies
Milwaukee, WI...........414-438-8600
Palmieri Food Products
New Haven, CT...........800-845-5447
Pandol Brothers
Delano, CA.............661-725-3755
Papa Leone Food Enterprises
Beverly Hills, CA........818-858-0074
Paradise Products Corporation
Roslyn, NY.............800-826-1235
Park 100 Foods
Tipton, IN.............800-854-6504
Parthenon Food Products
Ann Arbor, MI...........734-994-1012
Passetti's Pride
Hayward, CA............800-521-4659
Pasta Factory
Northlake, IL...........800-615-6951
Pasta Partners
Salt Lake City, UT.......800-727-8284
Pastor Chuck Orchards
Portland, ME............207-773-1314
Pastorelli Food Products
Chicago, IL............800-767-2829
PaStreeta Fresca
Dublin, OH.............800-343-5266
Patak Spices USA
Clearwater, FL..........727-796-2126
Peaceworks
New York, NY...........212-897-3995
Peaceworks
New York, NY...........800-732-2321
Pearlco of Boston
Canton, MA.............781-821-1010
Pearson's Homestyle
Bowden, AB.............877-224-3339

Pecan Deluxe Candy Company
Dallas, TX 800-733-3589
Pemberton's Gourmet Foods
Gray, ME 800-255-8401
Pepper Creek Farms
Lawton, OK 800-526-8132
Pepper Town
Van Nuys, CA .800-973-7738
Peppers
Rehoboth Beach, DE 302-644-6900
Pett Spice Products
Atlanta, GA 404-691-5235
Pierino Frozen Foods
Lincoln Park, MI 313-928-0950
Piggie Park Enterprises
West Columbia, SC 800-628-7423
Pillsbury
Hannibal, MO .800-775-4777
Pino's Pasta Veloce
Staten Island, NY 718-273-6660
Plentiful Pantry
Salt Lake City, UT 800-727-8284
Poison Pepper Company
Floral City, FL .888-539-5540
Pomodoro Fresca Foods
Millburn, NJ 973-467-6609
Porinos Gourmet Food
Central Falls, RI 800-826-3938
Porky's Gourmet
Gallatin, TN 800-767-5911
Portion Pac
Mason, OH 800-232-4829
Prairie Thyme
Santa Fe, NM 800-869-0009
Presco Food Seasonings
Flemington, NJ 800-526-1713
Pride of White River Valley
Gaysville, VT 802-234-9115
Private Harvest
Lakeport, CA 800-463-0594
Private Harvest Gourmet Specialities
Lakeport, CA 800-463-0594
Private Label Foods
Rochester, NY .585-254-9205
Produits Ronald
St. Damase, QC 450-797-3303
Progresso Quality Foods
Vineland, NJ 800-200-9377
Purity Products
Plainview, NY .888-769-7873
Quality Assured Packing
Stockton, CA 209-931-6700
Quality Chef Foods
Cedar Rapids, IA 800-356-8307
Quality Foods
San Pedro, CA .877-833-7890
R&R Homestead Kitchen
Oneida, WI 888-779-8245
R.L. Schreiber
Pompano Beach, FL 800-624-8777
R.L. Schreiber Company
Pompano Beach, FL 800-624-8777
R.W. Knudsen
Chico, CA 530-899-5000
Raggy-O Chutney
Smithfield, NC .888-424-8863
Ragozzino Food
Meriden, CT 800-348-1240
Ragsdale-Overton Food Traditions
Smithfield, NC .888-424-8863

Rahco International
St Augustine, FL 800-851-7681
Rancho's
Memphis, TN 901-276-8820
Randag & Associates Inc
Elmhurst, IL 630-530-2830
Rao's Specialty Foods
New York, NY .212-269-0151
Ray's Sausage Company Inc
Cleveland, OH .216-921-8782
Red Lion Spicy Foods Company
Red Lion, PA 717-244-0227
Reily Foods Company
New Orleans, LA 504-524-6132
Renfro Foods
Fort Worth, TX 817-336-3849
Restaurant Lulu Gourmet Products
San Francisco, CA 888-693-5800
REX Pure Foods
Gonzales, TX 800-344-8314
Reynolds Sugar Bush
Aniwa, WI 715-449-2057
Riba Foods
Houston, TX 800-327-7422
Richardson Foods Corporation
Macedon, NY .315-986-2807
Richelieu Foods
Randolph, MA .781-961-1537
Rio Valley Canning Company
Donna, TX 956-464-7843
River Run
Burlington, VT .802-863-0499
Rivertown Foods
St Louis, MO 800-844-3210
Robert Rothschild Farm
Urbana, OH 866-565-6790
Robinson Barbecue SauceCCompany
Oak Park, IL 800-836-6750
Robinson's Barbecue Sauce Company
Oak Park, IL 708-383-8452
Ronzoni Foods Canada
Etobicoke, ON .800-387-5032
Rosarita Mexican Foods Company
Mesa, AZ 480-964-8751
Roses Ravioli
Oglesby, IL 815-883-8011
Rosmarino Foods/R.Z. Humbert Company
Odessa, FL 888-926-9053
Rossi Pasta
Marietta, OH 800-227-6774
Rowena's
Norfolk, VA 800-627-8699
Royal Baltic
Brooklyn, NY 718-385-8300
Royal Food Products
Indianapolis, IN 317-782-2660
Ruskin Redneck Trading Company
Ruskin, FL 813-645-7710
S.D. Mushrooms
Avondale, PA 610-268-8082
Sabatino Truffles USA
Long Island City, NY 888-444-9971
Sable & Rosenfeld Foods
Toronto, ON 416-929-4214
Sadler's BBQ Sales
Henderson, TX 903-657-5581
Sambets Cajun Deli
Austin, TX 800-472-6238
San Benito Foods
Hollister, CA 831-637-4434
Santa Barbara Gourmet
Buellton, CA 805-686-0951
Santa Barbara Olive Company
Goleta, CA 800-624-4896
Santa Barbara Salsa/California Creative
Oceanside, CA .800-748-5523
Santa Cruz Chili & SpiceCompany
Tumacacori, AZ 520-398-2591
Sau-Sea Foods
Tarrytown, NY .914-631-1717
Sauces 'n Love
Lynn, MA 866-772-8237
Savoie's Sausage & Food Products
Opelousas, LA .337-948-4115
Schiavone's Casa Mia
Middletown, OH 513-422-8650
Schlotterbeck & Foss Company
Portland, ME 800-777-4666
Scott's Sauce Company
Goldsboro, NC .800-734-7282
Seeds of Change
Santa Fe, NM 888-762-7333

Select Food Products
Toronto, ON 800-699-8016
Seminole Foods
Springfield, OH 800-881-1177
Senba USA
Hayward, CA 888-922-5852
Seneca Foods
Clyman, WI 920-696-3331

Sentry Seasonings
Elmhurst, IL 630-530-5370

The product development experts of Sentry Seasonings are eager to offer the assistance and hands-on experience to food processors of all sizes. Sentry Seasonings will ensure the consistent high quality and repeat sales of your products, whether you choose one of our many off-the-shelf Bench Mark products or a modified version to meet your preferences. Sentry Seasonings can also duplicate and/or improve your present flavor profile; formulate, blend and package specifically for your requirements.

Shahi Food Corporation
Mississauga, ON 905-677-4327
Shiloh Foods
Savannah, TN .800-795-2550
Sieco USA Corporation
Houston, TX 800-325-9443
Silver Palate Kitchens
Cresskill, NJ 800-872-5283
Silver Spring Gardens
Eau Claire, WI .800-826-7322
Silver State Foods
Denver, CO 800-423-3351
Simeus Foods Internatio nal
Mansfield, TX .888-772-3663
Simeus Foods International
Mansfield, TX .888-772-3663
Simply Delicious
Cedar Grove, NC 919-732-5294
SK Foods
Lemoore, CA 559-924-6527
Skjodt-Barrett Foods
Mississauga, ON 877-600-1200
Sokol & Company
Countryside, IL 800-328-7656
Solana Gold Organics
Sebastopol, CA 800-459-1121
Sona & Hollen Foods
Los Alamitos, CA 800-200-7662
SOPAKCO Foods
Mullins, SC 800-276-9678
Sopakco Foods
Mullins, SC 843-464-7851
Sophia's Sauce Works
Carson City, NV 800-718-7769
South Ceasar Dressing Company
Novato, CA 415-897-0605
Southern Delight Gourmet Foods
Bowling Green, KY 866-782-9943
Southern Ray's Foods
Miami Beach, FL 800-972-8237
Southwest Specialty Food
Goodyear, AZ .800-536-3131
Soy Vay Enterprises
Felton, CA 800-600-2077
Spanarkel Company
Neptune City, NJ 732-775-4144
Spanish Gardens Food Manufacturing
Kansas City, KS 913-831-4242
Specialty Brands
Carthage, MO .417-358-8104
Spice Time Foods/Julius & Joe's
Paramus, NJ 800-345-9225
Spring Tree Maple Products
Brattleboro, VT 802-254-8784
Stage Coach Sauces
Palatka, FL 386-328-6330
Stanislaus Food Products
Modesto, CA 800-327-7201
Starport Foods
San Francisco, CA 866-206-9343

Stello Foods
Punxsutawney, PA 800-849-4599
Stickney & Poor Company
North Andover, MA 508-261-8967
Stone Cellar Kitchens
Riverside, CA 951-352-5713
Stonewall Kitchen
York, ME 800-207-5267
Stubb's Legendary Kitchen
Austin, TX 800-227-2283
Summercorn Foods
Fayetteville, AR 888-328-9473
Sun Harvest Foods
San Diego, CA 619-690-1128
Super Smokers BBQ
O Fallon, IL 618-624-6742
Surlean Food Solutions
San Antonio, TX 800-999-4370
Swatt Baking Company
Olean, NY 800-370-6656
Sweet Baby Ray's
Marlboro, MA 877-729-2229
Sweet Sides
Mission Hills, CA 818-832-0174
Sweetwater Spice Company
Austin, TX 800-531-6079
Swift & Company
Greeley, CO 970-324-2180
Swiss Food Products
Chicago, IL 773-394-6480
T. Marzetti Company
Columbus, OH 614-846-2232
T.W. Garner Food Company
Winston Salem, NC 800-476-7383
Tait Farm Foods
Centre Hall, PA 800-787-2716
Tandem Enterprises
Darien, CT 800-779-3276
Tantos Foods International
Richmond Hill, ON 905-763-9994
Tapatio Hot Sauce
Vernon, CA 323-587-8933
Tasty Tomato
San Antonio, TX 210-822-2443
Tate & Lyle Staley Company
Decatur, IL 217-423-4411
Techni-Brew International
Portland, OR 800-454-4077
Tex-Mex Gourmet
Houston, TX 888-345-8467
Texas Heat
San Antonio, TX 800-656-5916
Thistledew Farm
Proctor, WV 800-854-6639
Thomas Gourmet Foods
Greensboro, NC 800-867-2823
Thompson's Fine Foods
Shoreview, MN 800-807-0025
Thomson Food
Duluth, MN 218-722-2529
Thor-Shackel HorseradishCompany
Burr Ridge, IL 630-986-1333
Thornton Foods Company
Eden Prairie, MN 952-944-1735
Timber Crest Farms
Healdsburg, CA 888-374-9325
Timeless Traditions
Pittsford, VT 802-483-6024
Tip Top Canning Company
Tipp City, OH 937-667-3713
Todd's
Des Moines, IA 800-247-5363
Tomasso Corporation
Baie D'Urfe, QC 514-325-3000
Tommaso's Fresh Pasta
Dallas, TX 972-869-1111
Top Hat Company
Wilmette, IL 847-256-6565
Topper Food Products
East Brunswick, NJ 800-377-2823
Touch of South
Inglewood, CA 310-672-0700
Trader Vic's Food Products
Emeryville, CA 877-762-4824
Trappey's Fine Foods
New Iberia, LA 337-365-8281
Tree Top
Selah, WA 800-367-6571
Tree Top
Selah, WA 800-542-4055
Tres Classique
Ukiah, CA 888-644-5127

Triple H Food Processors
Riverside, CA 951-352-5700
Triple K Manufacturing Company
Shenandoah, IA 888-987-2824
Truesoups
Kent, WA 253-872-0403
Tulkoff Food Products
Baltimore, MD 800-638-7343
Twin Marquis
Brooklyn, NY 800-367-6868
Two Chefs on a Roll
Carson, CA 800-842-3025
Tyson Prepared Foods
Fort Worth, TX 817-258-2400
Ultimate Gourmet
Belle Mead, NJ 908-359-4050
Uncle Bum's Gourmet Foods
Riverside, CA 800-486-2867
Underground Sauce Network
Cranston, RI 888-919-6664
Unilever
New York, NY 212-888-1260
US Fresh Marketing
Virginia Beach, VA 757-481-2606
Valley Grain Products
Madera, CA 559-675-3400
Vanlaw Food Products
Fullerton, CA 714-870-9091
Vegetable Juices
Chicago, IL 888-776-9752
Ventre Packing Company
Syracuse, NY 315-463-2384
Ventura Foods
Philadelphia, PA 215-223-8700
Ventura Foods   Production Plant
Los Angeles, CA 323-265-4300
Vermont BS
Hinesburg, VT 802-482-2152
Victoria Packing Corporation
Brooklyn, NY 718-649-2180
Vidalia Brands
Reidsville, GA 800-752-0206
Vidalia Sweets Brand
Lyons, GA 912-565-8881
Vietti Foods Company Inc
Nashville, TN 800-240-7864
Village Imports
Brisbane, CA 888-865-8714
Vincent's Food Corporation
West Hempstead, NY 516-481-3544
Violet Packing
Williamstown, NJ 856-629-7428
Vivienne Dressings
St Louis, MO 800-827-0778
Wagner Gourmet Foods
Shawnee Mission, KS 913-469-5411
Walker Foods
Los Angeles, CA 800-966-5199
Webbpak
Trussville, AL 800-655-3500
Wei-Chuan
Bell Gardens, CA 562-927-6681
Weir Sauces
Napa, CA 415-884-5849
Welcome Dairy
Colby, WI 800-472-2315
Well Dressed Food Company
Tupper Lake, NY 866-567-0845
West Pac
Idaho Falls, ID 800-973-7407
Westbrae Natural Foods
Garden City, NY 800-434-4246
Western Dressing
Grundy Center, IA 319-824-3304
Westin
Omaha, NE 800-228-6098
WFI
Linden, NJ 908-925-9494
Whole in the Wall
Binghamton, NY 607-722-5138
Whyte's Food Corporation
Mississauga, ON 905-624-5065
Wicker's Food Products
Hornersville, MO 800-847-0032
Widow's Mite Vinegar Company
Washington, DC 877-678-5854
WILD Flavors (Canada)
Mississauga, ON 800-263-5286
Wild Thymes Farm
Greenville, NY 800-724-2877
William B. Reily & Company
Baltimore, MD 410-675-9550

William Poll
New York, NY 800-993-7655
Williams Foods Inc
Lenexa, KS 800-255-6736
Williams-West & Witt Products
Michigan City, IN 219-879-8236
Williamsburg Chocolatier
Williamsburg, VA 804-966-9000
WillowOak Farms
Woodland, CA 888-963-2767
Wing It
Falmouth, MA 508-540-9860
Wing Nien Company
Hayward, CA 510-487-8877
Wing-Time
Steamboat Spgs, CO 970-871-1198
Wizards Cauldron, LTD
Yanceyville, NC 336-694-5333
Woeber Mustard Manufacturing
Springfield, OH 800-548-2929
Wong Wing Foods
Montreal, QC 800-361-4820
Wood Brothers
West Columbia, SC 803-796-5146
World Flavors
Warminster, PA 215-672-4400
World Harbors
Auburn, ME 800-355-6221
World Herbs Gourmet Company
Hadlyme, CT 860-526-1908
Worthmore Food Product
Cincinnati, OH 513-559-1473
Wy's Wings
Strasburg, VA 800-997-9464
Y Not Foods
Madison, WI 608-222-2860
Yair Scones/Canterbury Cuisine
Medina, WA 800-588-9160
Yamasa Corporation
Torrance, CA 310-944-3883
Yellow Emperor Pepper Sauce Company
Los Angeles, CA 608-238-2991
Ynrico's Food Products Company
Syracuse, NY 888-472-8237
Yoshida Food International
Portland, OR 888-243-8371
Zarda Bar-B-Q & Catering Company
Blue Springs, MO 800-776-7427

Alfredo

Al Dente
Whitmore Lake, MI 800-536-7278
Casa DiLisio Products
Mt Kisco, NY 800-247-4199
Classy Delites
Austin, TX 800-440-2648
Cuizina Food Company
Woodinville, WA 425-486-7000
Genarom International
Cranbury, NJ 609-409-6200
Marsan Foods
Toronto, ON 416-755-9262
Nestle
Cleveland, OH 440-349-5757
Pasta Factory
Northlake, IL 800-615-6951
Sargento Foods Inc
Plymouth, WI 800-243-3737
Tomasso Corporation
Baie D'Urfe, QC 514-325-3000
Topper Food Products
East Brunswick, NJ 800-377-2823
Williams Foods Inc
Lenexa, KS 800-255-6736

Barbecue

A. Camacho
Plant City, FL 800-881-4534
A. Lassonde, Inc.
Rougemont, QC 514-878-1057
Allied Old English
Port Reading, NJ 732-602-8955
Annie's Naturals
East Calais, VT 800-434-1234
Arbor Hill Grapery & Winery
Naples, NY 800-554-7553
Ashley Foods
Sudbury, MA 800-617-2823
Ashman Manufacturing & Distributing Company
Virginia Beach, VA 800-641-9924

Baker's Rib
Dallas, TX 214-748-5433

Baldwin Richardson Foods
Frankfort, IL 866-644-2732

Baldwin Richardson Foods is a liquid ingredient manufacturer specializing in signature sauces, dessert toppings, beverage/pancake syrups, specialty fruit fillings and condiments. Packaging capabilities range from portion control cups and pouches to standard retail and foodservice packs and include industrial drums and totes. Full service R&D and Quality groups dedicated to new product development, with in-house stability and analytical testing. Call for assistance.

Bartush-Schnitzius Foods Company
Lewisville, TX 972-219-1270
Baumer Foods
New Orleans, LA 504-482-5761
BBQ Bunch
Kansas City, MO. 816-941-6789
BBQ'n Fools
Bend, OR. 800-671-8652
BBS Bodacious BBQ Company
Coral Springs, FL 800-537-5928
Bear Creek Kitchens
Marshall, TX. 888-300-7687
Big B Distributors
Evansville, IN 812-425-5235
Blueberry Store
Grand Junction, MI. 877-654-2400
Bottle Green Drinks
Mississauga, ON. 905-273-6137
Buffalo Wild Wings
Minneapolis, MN 763-546-1891
Cafe Chilku
Colchester, VT 802-878-4645
Cafe Tequila
San Francisco, CA 415-264-0106
CaJohns Fiery Foods
Columbus, OH 888-703-3473
California-Antilles Trading Consortium
San Diego, CA 800-330-6450
Captain Bob's Jet Fuel
Fort Wayne, IN 877-486-6468
Carolina Cupboard
Hillsborough, NC 800-400-3441
Carolina Treet
Wilmington, NC 800-616-6344
Casa Visco Finer Food Company
Schenectady, NY. 888-607-2823
Castleberry/Snow Brands
Augusta, GA 800-241-3520
Catamount Specialties of Vermont
Stowe, VT 800-820-8096
Catskill Mountain Specialties
Saugerties, NY 800-311-3473
Charlie Beigg's Sauce Company
Windham, ME 888-502-8595
China Bowl Trading Company
Westport, CT 203-222-0381
CHS
Inver Grove Heights, MN. 800-232-3639
CHS, Inc.
Inner Grove Heights, MN. 800-232-3639
Cinnabar Specialty Foods
Prescott, AZ 866-293-6433
Clements Foods Company
Oklahoma City, OK 800-654-8355
Colgin Companies
Dallas, TX 888-226-5446
Cookies Food Products
Wall Lake, IA 800-331-4995
Cookshack
Ponca City, OK. 800-423-0698
Couch's Original Sauce
Jonesboro, AR. 800-264-7535
Country Bob's
Centralia, IL 800-373-2140
Country Cupboard
Virginia City, NV 775-847-7300
Crazy Mary's
Tacoma, WA 253-536-8690

Creative Foodworks
San Antonio, TX. 210-212-4761
Cugino's Gourmet Foods
Crystal Lake, IL 888-592-8446
Cuisine Perel
Richmond, CA 800-887-3735
Cuizina Food Company
Woodinville, WA. 425-486-7000
Culver Duck
Middlebury, IN 800-825-9225
D & D Foods
Columbus, GA 706-322-4507
Delta BBQ Sauce Company
Stockton, CA 209-472-9284
Dillard's Bar-B-Q Sauce
Durham, NC 919-544-1587
Dorina/So-Good
Union, IL 815-923-2144
Douglas Cross Enterprises
Seattle, WA 206-448-1193
Dynamic Foods
Lubbock, TX 806-762-0780
E.D. Smith & Sons
Winona, ON 905-643-1211
El Paso Chile Company
El Paso, TX. 888-472-5727
El-Rey Foods
Ferguson, MO. 314-521-3113
Favorite Foods
Burnaby, BC 604-420-5100
Felbro Food Products
Los Angeles, CA. 800-335-2761
Fiesta Gourmet of Tejas
Canyon Lake, TX 800-585-8250
Figaro Company
Mesquite, TX 972-288-3587
Food Concentrate Corporation
Oklahoma City, OK 405-840-5633
Food Ingredients Solutions
Blauvelt, NY 845-353-8501
Food Processor of New Mexico
Albuquerque, NM 877-634-3772
Food Specialties
Indianapolis, IN 317-271-0862
Fremont Company
Fremont, OH 419-334-8995
Fremont Special Brands
Fremont, OH 419-334-8995
French's Flavor Ingredients
Springfield, MO 800-437-3624
French's Ingredients
Springfield, MO 417-837-1813
FunniBonz
West Windsor, NJ 877-300-2669
Garden Complements
Kansas City, MO. 800-966-1091
Gayle's Sweet 'N Sassy Foods
Beverly Hills, CA 310-246-1792
Golden Specialty Foods
Norwalk, CA 562-802-2537
Golden West Specialty Foods
Brisbane, CA 800-584-4481
Golden Whisk
South San Francisco, CA 800-660-5222
Golding Farms Foods
Winston Salem, NC. 336-766-6161
Gormly's Orchard
South Burlington, VT 800-639-7604
Gumpert's Canada
Mississauga, ON 800-387-9324
H.J. Heinz Company
Pittsburgh, PA 412-237-5948
Havana's Limited
Titusville, FL. 321-267-0513
Head Country Food Products
Ponca City, OK 888-762-1227
Heartland Farms
Fort Wayne, IN 888-747-7423
Heinz
Fremont, OH 419-332-7357
Heinz Company of Canada
North York, ON. 800-268-6641
Heinz North America
Pittsburgh, PA 412-237-5700
Hollman Foods
Minden, NE. 888-926-2879
Hormel Foods Corporation
Austin, MN .800-523-4635
Hot Licks Hot Sauces
Spring Valley, CA 888-766-6468
Hot Wachula's
Lakeland, FL. 877-883-8700

House of Webster
Rogers, AR .800-369-4641
J K Marley's LLC
Machesney Park, IL 815-636-7712
J.N. Bech
Elk Rapids, MI 800-232-4583
JMS Specialty Foods
Ripon, WI 800-535-5437
Johnny Harris Famous Barbecue Sauce
Savannah, GA 912-354-8828
Judicial Flavors
Auburn, CA 530-885-1298
Kings Food Products
Belleville, IL 618-233-0400
Kozlowski Farms
Forestville, CA 800-473-2767
Kraft Food Ingredients
Memphis, TN 901-381-6500
Kraft Foods
Northfield, IL 800-323-0768
Kraft Foods
Garland, TX 972-272-7511
L&S Packing Company
Farmingdale, NY 800-286-6487
Lang Naturals
Middletown, RI. 401-848-7700
Lea & Perrins
Fair Lawn, NJ 800-289-5797
Lees Sausage Company
Orangeburg, SC 803-534-5517
Lendy's
Virginia Beach, VA 757-491-3511
Lounsbury Foods
Toronto, ON 416-656-6330
M.A. Gedney
Chaska, MN 952-448-2612
Mad Will's Food Company
Auburn, CA. 888-275-9455
Mansmith's Barbecue
San Jn Bautista, CA 800-626-7648
Mar-K Anchor Bar Hot Sauces
Buffalo, NY. 716-853-1791
McCutcheon's Apple Products
Frederick, MD. 800-888-7537
Miceli's Specialty Foods Company
Danbury, CT 888-264-2354
Millflow Spice Corporation
Valley Stream, NY 800-229-6122

Mrs. Clark's Foods
Ankeny, IA .800-736-5674

Juices, salad dressings and sauces.

Mucky Duck Mustard Company
Ferndale, MI 248-544-4610
Nantucket Off-Shore Seasoning
Nantucket, MA 508-994-1300
New Business Corporation
East Chicago, IN 800-742-8435
Newly Weds Foods
Memphis, TN 800-647-9314
Noh Foods International
Honolulu, HI 808-841-0655
North of the Border
Tesuque, NM 800-860-0681
O'Brian Brothers Food
Cincinnati, OH 513-791-9909
Old Mansion Foods
Petersburg, VA 800-476-1877
Original Juan
Kansas City, KS 800-568-8468
Ott Food Products
Carthage, MO 800-866-2585
Pacific Choice Brands
Fresno, CA .559-237-5583
Pacific Poultry Company
Honolulu, HI. 808-841-2828
Palmetto Canning Company
Palmetto, FL 941-722-1100
Palmieri Food Products
New Haven, CT 800-845-5447
Paradise Products Corporation
Roslyn, NY .800-826-1235
Passetti's Pride
Hayward, CA 800-521-4659

Piggie Park Enterprises
West Columbia, SC...............800-628-7423
Porinos Gourmet Food
Central Falls, RI................800-826-3938
PorkRubbers BBQ Specialty Products
Lombard, IL....................630-424-8200
Portion Pac
Mason, OH.....................800-232-4829
Private Harvest Gourmet Specialities
Lakeport, CA...................800-463-0594
Produits Ronald
St. Damase, QC.................450-797-3303
Randag & Associates Inc
Elmhurst, IL...................630-530-2830
Red Gold
Elwood, IN....................877-748-9798
Rivertown Foods
St Louis, MO..................800-844-3210
Rob Salamida Company
Johnson City, NY...............607-770-7046
Robbie's Natural Products
Altadena, CA..................626-798-9944
Robinson's Barbecue Sauce Company
Oak Park, IL...................708-383-8452
Rosmarino Foods/R.Z. Humbert Company
Odessa, FL....................888-926-9053
Sadler's BBQ Sales
Henderson, TX.................903-657-5581
Sambets Cajun Deli
Austin, TX....................800-472-6238
San Gennaro Foods
Kent, WA.....................800-462-1916
Savoie's Sausage & Food Products
Opelousas, LA.................337-948-4115
Schlotterbeck & Foss Company
Portland, ME..................800-777-4666
Scott's Sauce Company
Goldsboro, NC.................800-734-7282
Sona & Hollen Foods
Los Alamitos, CA...............800-200-7662
Southern Bar-B-Que
Jennings, LA..................866-612-2586
Southern Delight Gourmet Foods
Bowling Green, KY..............866-782-9943
Southern Ray's Foods
Miami Beach, FL...............800-972-8237
Stanchfield Farms
Milo, ME.....................207-732-5173
Steel's Gourmet Foods
Bridgeport, PA.................800-678-3357
Subco Foods Inc
Sheboygan, WI................800-676-5188
Sweet Baby Ray's
Marlboro, MA.................877-729-2229
T. Marzetti Company
Columbus, OH.................614-846-2232
T.W. Garner Food Company
Winston Salem, NC..............800-476-7383
Thompson's Fine Foods
Shoreview, MN................800-807-0025
Todd's
Des Moines, IA................800-247-5363
Triple H Food Processors
Riverside, CA..................951-352-5700
Valley Grain Products
Madera, CA...................559-675-3400
Ventre Packing Company
Syracuse, NY..................315-463-2384
Ventura Foods
Philadelphia, PA...............215-223-8700
Vidalia Sweets Brand
Lyons, GA....................912-565-8881
Vietti Foods Company Inc
Nashville, TN..................800-240-7864
Vita Specialty Foods
Inwood, WV...................800-974-4778
VT Made Richard's Sauces
Saint Albans, VT................802-524-3196
Webbpak
Trussville, AL..................800-655-3500
Wei-Chuan
Bell Gardens, CA...............562-927-6681
West Pac
Idaho Falls, ID.................800-973-7407
Westin
Omaha, NE...................800-228-6098
Wine Country Chef LLC
Hidden Valley Lake, CA...........707-322-0406
Wing Nien Company
Hayward, CA..................510-487-8877
Wing-Time
Steamboat Spgs, CO.............970-871-1198

Wizards Cauldron, LTD
Yanceyville, NC................336-694-5333
Wood Brothers
West Columbia, SC.............803-796-5146
World Flavors
Warminster, PA................215-672-4400
Zarda Bar-B-Q & Catering Company
Blue Springs, MO..............800-776-7427

Black Bean

Favorite Foods
Burnaby, BC..................604-420-5100
Lee Kum Kee
City of Industry, CA.............800-654-5082

Cheese

AFP Advanced Food Products, LLC
Visalia, CA....................559-627-2070
Amboy Specialty Foods Company
Dixon, IL.....................800-892-0400
Berner Cheese Corporation
Dakota, IL....................800-819-8199
Berner Foods, Inc.
Roscoe, IL....................800-819-8199
Clofine Dairy & Food Products
Linwood, NJ..................800-441-1001
Cuizina Food Company
Woodinville, WA...............425-486-7000
Dean Foods Company
Rosemont, IL..................800-323-1571
Fountain Valley Foods
Colorado Springs, CO...........719-573-6012
Gehl Guernsey Farms
Germantown, WI...............800-434-5713
Genarom International
Cranbury, NJ..................609-409-6200
Knouse Foods
Peach Glen, PA................717-677-8181
Mann Packing
Salinas, CA...................831-422-7405
Marsan Foods
Toronto, ON..................416-755-9262
Sargento Foods Inc
Plymouth, WI.................800-243-3737
Thornton Foods Company
Eden Prairie, MN...............952-944-1735
Tulkoff Food Products
Baltimore, MD................800-638-7343

Nacho

Associated Milk Producers
New Ulm, MN.................507-233-4600
Bel/Kaukauna USA
Kaukauna, WI.................800-558-3500
Del Rey Tortilleria
Chicago, IL...................800-446-1459
Knouse Foods
Peach Glen, PA................717-677-8181
Olde Tyme Food Corporation
East Longmeadow, MA...........800-356-6533
Tulkoff Food Products
Baltimore, MD................800-638-7343

Chili

Baldwin Richardson Foods
Frankfort, IL...................866-644-2732

Baldwin Richardson Foods is a liquid ingredient manufacturer specializing in signature sauces, dessert toppings, beverage/pancake syrups, specialty fruit fillings and condiments. Packaging capabilities range from portion control cups and pouches to standard retail and foodservice packs and include industrial drums and totes. Full service R&D and Quality groups dedicated to new product development, with in-house stability and analytical testing. Call for assistance.

Big B Distributors
Evansville, IN..................812-425-5235

Cervantes Foods Products
Albuquerque, NM..............877-982-4453
Commodities Marketing, Inc.
Edison, NJ....................732-516-0700
Del Monte Foods
San Francisco, CA..............800-543-3090
El Charro Mexican Food Industries
Roswell, NM..................575-622-8590
Fernandez Chili Company
Alamosa, CO..................719-589-6043
Fiesta Canning Company
Mc Neal, AZ..................520-364-7541
First Original Texas Chili Company
Fort Worth, TX................817-626-0983
H.J. Heinz Company
Pittsburgh, PA.................412-237-5948
Heinz
Fremont, OH..................419-332-7357
Hurd Orchards
Holley, NY....................585-638-8838
Ingleby Farms
Dublin, PA....................877-728-7277
Lee Kum Kee
Brooklyn, NY.................800-346-7562
Lee Kum Kee
City of Industry, CA.............800-654-5082
Mexisnax Corporation
El Paso, TX...................915-779-5709
Miguel's Stowe Away
Stowe, VT....................800-448-6517
Mrs. Auld's Gourmet Foods
Reno, NV....................800-322-8537
North of the Border
Tesuque, NM.................800-860-0681
Old Mansion Foods
Petersburg, VA................800-476-1877
Red Gold
Elwood, IN...................877-748-9798
Santa Cruz Chili & SpiceCompany
Tumacacori, AZ...............520-398-2591
Sona & Hollen Foods
Los Alamitos, CA...............800-200-7662
T.W. Garner Food Company
Winston Salem, NC.............800-476-7383

Clam

Casa DiLisio Products
Mt Kisco, NY.................800-247-4199
Chincoteague Seafood Company
Parsonsburg, MD..............443-260-4800
Colonna Brothers
North Bergen, NJ..............201-864-1115
Cuizina Food Company
Woodinville, WA...............425-486-7000
Look's Gourmet Food Company
Whiting, ME..................800-962-6258
Mid-Atlantic Foods
Easton, MD...................800-922-4688
Pasta Factory
Northlake, IL..................800-615-6951
Topper Food Products
East Brunswick, NJ.............800-377-2823

Cocktail

Baldwin Richardson Foods
Frankfort, IL...................866-644-2732

Baldwin Richardson Foods is a liquid ingredient manufacturer specializing in signature sauces, dessert toppings, beverage/pancake syrups, specialty fruit fillings and condiments. Packaging capabilities range from portion control cups and pouches to standard retail and foodservice packs and include industrial drums and totes. Full service R&D and Quality groups dedicated to new product development, with in-house stability and analytical testing. Call for assistance.

Cedarvale Food Products
Toronto, ON..................416-656-6330
Clements Foods Company
Oklahoma City, OK.............800-654-8355

ConAgra Grocery Products
Irvine, CA 714-680-1000
Cuizina Food Company
Woodinville, WA 425-486-7000
Del Monte Foods
San Francisco, CA 800-543-3090
E. Waldo Ward & Son Corporation
Sierra Madre, CA 800-355-9273
Golden West Specialty Foods
Brisbane, CA 800-584-4481
Golding Farms Foods
Winston Salem, NC 336-766-6161
Joe Hutson Foods
Jacksonville, FL 904-731-9065
Kelchner's Horseradish
Dublin, PA 215-249-3439
Lounsbury Foods
Toronto, ON 416-656-6330
Palmieri Food Products
New Haven, CT 800-845-5447
Paradise Products Corporation
Roslyn, NY 800-826-1235
Roller Ed
Rochester, NY 585-458-8020
Sau-Sea Foods
Tarrytown, NY 914-631-1717
Silver Spring Gardens
Eau Claire, WI 800-826-7322
T. Marzetti Company
Columbus, OH 614-846-2232
T.W. Garner Food Company
Winston Salem, NC 800-476-7383
Thor-Shackel HorseradishCompany
Burr Ridge, IL 630-986-1333
Tulkoff Food Products
Baltimore, MD 800-638-7343
Vegetable Juices
Chicago, IL 888-776-9752

Curry

Baldwin Richardson Foods
Frankfort, IL 866-644-2732

Baldwin Richardson Foods is a liquid ingredient manufacturer specializing in signature sauces, dessert toppings, beverage/pancake syrups, specialty fruit fillings and condiments. Packaging capabilities range from portion control cups and pouches to standard retail and foodservice packs and include industrial drums and totes. Full service R&D and Quality groups dedicated to new product development, with in-house stability and analytical testing. Call for assistance.

Bo-Ling's Products
Overland Park, KS 913-888-8223
Curry King Corporation
Waldwick, NJ 800-287-7987
Lang Naturals
Middletown, RI 401-848-7700
Patak Spices USA
Clearwater, FL 727-796-2126

Dessert

Amoretti-Capriccio
Oxnard, CA 800-266-7388
Applecreek Farms
Lexington, KY 800-747-8871

Duck

Allied Old English
Port Reading, NJ 732-602-8955
Kari-Out Company
White Plains, NY 800-433-8799
L&S Packing Company
Farmingdale, NY 800-286-6487

Fish

Certified Savory
Countryside, IL 800-328-7656

Stacey's Famous Foods
Hayden, ID 800-782-2395

Fra Diavolo

Cuizina Food Company
Woodinville, WA 425-486-7000
L&S Packing Company
Farmingdale, NY 800-286-6487
Newman's Own
Westport, CT 203-222-0136
Palmieri Food Products
New Haven, CT 800-845-5447
Papa Leone Food Enterprises
Beverly Hills, CA 818-858-0074

Frozen

Bellisio Foods, Inc.
Lakeville, MN 800-368-7337
Campbell Soup Company of Canada
Listowel, ON 800-575-7687
Carando Gourmet Frozen Foods
Springfield, MA 413-730-4205
Casa DiLisio Products
Mt Kisco, NY 800-247-4199
ConAgra Grocery Products
Archbold, OH 419-445-8015
Cuizina Food Company
Woodinville, WA 425-486-7000
Culinary Standards Corporation
Louisville, KY 800-778-3434
Dynamic Foods
Lubbock, TX 806-762-0780
Food Source
McKinney, TX 972-548-9001
Gemini Food Industries
Fiskdale, MA 508-347-2800
Hunt-Wesson Food Service Company
Rochester, NY 800-633-1002
Louisa Food Products
St Louis, MO 314-868-3000
Luigino's
Duluth, MN 218-727-2059
Marsan Foods
Toronto, ON 416-755-9262
McLane Foods
Phoenix, AZ 602-275-5509
Original Italian Pasta Poducts Company
Chelsea, MA 800-999-9603
Overhill Farms
Vernon, CA 800-859-6406
Pierino Frozen Foods
Lincoln Park, MI 313-928-0950
Specialty Brands
Carthage, MO 417-358-8104
Tomasso Corporation
Baie D'Urfe, QC 514-325-3000
Topper Food Products
East Brunswick, NJ 800-377-2823
Two Chefs on a Roll
Carson, CA 800-842-3025
Vegetable Juices
Chicago, IL 888-776-9752

Fudge

Paradigm Food Works
Lake Oswego, OR 503-595-4360

Garlic

Baldwin Richardson Foods
Frankfort, IL 866-644-2732

Baldwin Richardson Foods is a liquid ingredient manufacturer specializing in signature sauces, dessert toppings, beverage/pancake syrups, specialty fruit fillings and condiments. Packaging capabilities range from portion control cups and pouches to standard retail and foodservice packs and include industrial drums and totes. Full service R&D and Quality groups dedicated to new product development, with in-house stability and analytical testing. Call for assistance.

Captain Bob's Jet Fuel
Fort Wayne, IN 877-486-6468
CHS
Inver Grove Heights, MN 800-232-3639
Cuizina Food Company
Woodinville, WA 425-486-7000
Garlic Survival Company
San Juan Cpstrno, CA 800-342-7542
Golden Whisk
South San Francisco, CA 800-660-5222
L&S Packing Company
Farmingdale, NY 800-286-6487
Lang Naturals
Middletown, RI 401-848-7700
Lee Kum Kee
City of Industry, CA 800-654-5082
Marsan Foods
Toronto, ON 416-755-9262
Pasta Factory
Northlake, IL 800-615-6951
Robbie's Natural Products
Altadena, CA 626-798-9944
Silver Spring Gardens
Eau Claire, WI 800-826-7322
Southern Ray's Foods
Miami Beach, FL 800-972-8237
Soy Vay Enterprises
Felton, CA 800-600-2077
Vegetable Juices
Chicago, IL 888-776-9752

Ginger

Baldwin Richardson Foods
Frankfort, IL 866-644-2732

Baldwin Richardson Foods is a liquid ingredient manufacturer specializing in signature sauces, dessert toppings, beverage/pancake syrups, specialty fruit fillings and condiments. Packaging capabilities range from portion control cups and pouches to standard retail and foodservice packs and include industrial drums and totes. Full service R&D and Quality groups dedicated to new product development, with in-house stability and analytical testing. Call for assistance.

Cuizina Food Company
Woodinville, WA 425-486-7000
Lang Naturals
Middletown, RI 401-848-7700
Southern Ray's Foods
Miami Beach, FL 800-972-8237
Vegetable Juices
Chicago, IL 888-776-9752

Gourmet

Wildly Delicious
Toronto, ON 888-545-9995

Habanero

Baldwin Richardson Foods
Frankfort, IL 866-644-2732

Baldwin Richardson Foods is a liquid ingredient manufacturer specializing in signature sauces, dessert toppings, beverage/pancake syrups, specialty fruit fillings and condiments. Packaging capabilities range from portion control cups and pouches to standard retail and foodservice packs and include industrial drums and totes. Full service R&D and Quality groups dedicated to new product development, with in-house stability and analytical testing. Call for assistance.

Captain Bob's Jet Fuel
Fort Wayne, IN 877-486-6468
Catskill Mountain Specialties
Saugerties, NY 800-311-3473
Chili Dude
Richardson, TX 972-907-0998
Havana's Limited
Titusville, FL 321-267-0513
Lendy's
Virginia Beach, VA 757-491-3511
Mo Hotta-Mo Betta
San Luis Obispo, CA 800-462-3220
Mrs. Dog's Products
Tampa, FL 800-267-7364
New Canaan Farms
Dripping Springs, TX 800-727-5267
Porky's Gourmet
Gallatin, TN 800-767-5911
Tex-Mex Gourmet
Houston, TX 888-345-8467
Vegetable Juices
Chicago, IL 888-776-9752
Wing-Time
Steamboat Spgs, CO 970-871-1198

Hoisin

Baldwin Richardson Foods
Frankfort, IL 866-644-2732

Baldwin Richardson Foods is a liquid ingredient manufacturer specializing in signature sauces, dessert toppings, beverage/pancake syrups, specialty fruit fillings and condiments. Packaging capabilities range from portion control cups and pouches to standard retail and foodservice packs and include industrial drums and totes. Full service R&D and Quality groups dedicated to new product development, with in-house stability and analytical testing. Call for assistance.

China Bowl Trading Company
Westport, CT 203-222-0381
Cuizina Food Company
Woodinville, WA 425-486-7000
Hormel Foods Corporation
Austin, MN 800-523-4635
Lee Kum Kee
City of Industry, CA 800-654-5082
Miyako Oriental Foods
Baldwin Park, CA 877-788-6476
Soy Vay Enterprises
Felton, CA 800-600-2077
Wei-Chuan
Bell Gardens, CA 562-927-6681

Hollandaise

Cuizina Food Company
Woodinville, WA 425-486-7000
W&G Flavors
Hunt Valley, MD 410-771-6606

Horseradish

Bartush-Schnitzius Foods Company
Lewisville, TX 972-219-1270
Beaverton Foods
Beaverton, OR 800-223-8076
Bick's Pickles
Dunnville, ON 905-774-7447
Cedarvale Food Products
Toronto, ON 416-656-6330
Chicopee Provision Company
Chicopee, MA 800-924-6328
Grouse Hunt Farms
Tamaqua, PA 570-467-2850
Hoople Country Kitchens
Rockport, IN 812-649-2351
Kelchner's Horseradish
Dublin, PA 215-249-3439
Lounsbury Foods
Toronto, ON 416-656-6330
Mothers Mountain Mustard
Falmouth, ME 800-440-9891

Mrs. Clark's Foods
Ankeny, IA 800-736-5674

Juices, salad dressings and sauces.

Penn Maid Crowley Foods
Philadelphia, PA 800-247-6269
Roller Ed
Rochester, NY 585-458-8020
Sau-Sea Foods
Tarrytown, NY 914-631-1717

Seminole Foods
Springfield, OH 800-881-1177
Silver Spring Gardens
Eau Claire, WI 800-826-7322
Southwest Specialty Food
Goodyear, AZ 800-536-3131
Strub Pickles
Brantford, ON 519-751-1717
T. Marzetti Company
Columbus, OH 614-846-2232
Thor-Shackel HorseradishCompany
Burr Ridge, IL 630-986-1333
Tulkoff Food Products
Baltimore, MD 800-638-7343
Ventura Foods
Philadelphia, PA 215-223-8700
Westin
Omaha, NE 800-228-6098
Woeber Mustard Manufacturing
Springfield, OH 800-548-2929

Hot

Adams
Fargo, ND 800-342-4748
Archie Moore's Foods Products
Milford, CT 203-876-5088
Arizona Cowboy
Phoenix, AZ 800-529-8627
Ashley Foods
Sudbury, MA 800-617-2823
Ashman Manufacturing & Distributing Company
Virginia Beach, VA 800-641-9924
B&G Foods
Parsippany, NJ 973-401-6500

Baldwin Richardson Foods
Frankfort, IL 866-644-2732

Baldwin Richardson Foods is a liquid ingredient manufacturer specializing in signature sauces, dessert toppings, beverage/pancake syrups, specialty fruit fillings and condiments. Packaging capabilities range from portion control cups and pouches to standard retail and foodservice packs and include industrial drums and totes. Full service R&D and Quality groups dedicated to new product development, with in-house stability and analytical testing. Call for assistance.

Baumer Foods
New Orleans, LA 504-482-5761
BBQ'n Fools
Bend, OR 800-671-8652
Boston Spice & Tea Company
Boston, VA 800-966-4372
Bruce Foods Corporation
New Iberia, LA 800-299-9082
Buds Kitchen
New Castle, PA 724-654-9216
Buffalo Wild Wings
Minneapolis, MN 763-546-1891
Cafe Tequila
San Francisco, CA 415-264-0106
CaJohns Fiery Foods
Columbus, OH 888-703-3473

Cajun Chef Products
St Martinville, LA 337-394-7112
California Creative Foods
Oceanside, CA 760-757-2622
California-Antilles Trading Consortium
San Diego, CA 800-330-6450
Cannon's Sweets Hots
Albuquerque, NM 877-630-7026
Captain Bob's Jet Fuel
Fort Wayne, IN 877-486-6468
Carolyn's Caribbean Heat
Malvern, PA 610-647-0336
Carriere Foods Inc
Montreal, QC 514-384-4281
Chile Today - Hot Tamale
San Francisco, CA 800-758-0372
Colorado Salsa Company
Littleton, CO 303-932-2617
ConAgra Grocery Products
Archbold, OH 419-445-8015
Country Bob's
Centralia, IL 800-373-2140
Cyclone Enterprises
Houston, TX 281-872-0087
Dave's Gourmet
San Francisco, CA 800-758-0372
Dhidow Enterprises
Oxford, PA 610-932-7868
Dockside Market
Key Largo, FL 800-813-2253
Favorite Foods
Burnaby, BC 604-420-5100
Festive Foods
Virginia Beach, VA 757-490-9186
Forge Mountain Foods
Hendersonville, NC 800-823-6743
French's Flavor Ingredients
Springfield, MO 800-437-3624
French's Ingredients
Springfield, MO 417-837-1813
Garden Complements
Kansas City, MO 800-966-1091
Garden Row Foods
Franklin Park, IL 800-555-9798
Gourmet Foods
Knoxville, TN 865-970-2982
H.J. Heinz Company
Pittsburgh, PA 412-237-5948
Hartford City Foam Pack aging & Converting
Hartford City, IN 765-348-2500
Havana's Limited
Titusville, FL 321-267-0513
Heintz & Weber Company
Buffalo, NY 716-852-7171
Hormel Foods Corporation
Austin, MN 800-523-4635
Hot Licks Hot Sauces
Spring Valley, CA 888-766-6468
Hot Wachula's
Lakeland, FL 877-883-8700
HVJ International
Spring, TX 877-730-3663
Ingleby Farms
Dublin, PA 877-728-7277
Joe Hutson Foods
Jacksonville, FL 904-731-9065
Juanita's Foods
Wilmington, CA 310-834-5339
Judicial Flavors
Auburn, CA 530-885-1298
Kari-Out Company
White Plains, NY 800-433-8799
L&S Packing Company
Farmingdale, NY 800-286-6487
Lang Naturals
Middletown, RI 401-848-7700
Lendy's
Virginia Beach, VA 757-491-3511
Lounsbury Foods
Toronto, ON 416-656-6330
M.W. Milton & Company
Louisville, KY 502-587-5016
Mad Will's Food Company
Auburn, CA 888-275-9455
Magic Seasoning Blends
Harahan, LA 800-457-2857
MAK Enterprises
Palmdale, CA 661-272-1867
Maple Grove Farms of Vermont
St Johnsbury, VT 800-525-2540
Mar-K Anchor Bar Hot Sauces
Buffalo, NY 716-853-1791

McIlhenny Company
New Orleans, LA 504-523-7370
Mexisnax Corporation
El Paso, TX 915-779-5709
Millflow Spice Corporation
Valley Stream, NY 800-229-6122
Mizkam Americas
Kansas City, MO. 816-483-1700
Mo Hotta-Mo Betta
San Luis Obispo, CA 800-462-3220
Mrs. Dog's Products
Tampa, FL. 800-267-7364
Native Kjalii Foods
San Francisco, CA 415-522-5580
Natural Value Products
Sacramento, CA 916-427-7242
North of the Border
Tesuque, NM. 800-860-0681
O'Garvey Sauces
New Braunfels, TX. 830-620-6127
Paradise Products Corporation
Roslyn, NY 800-826-1235
Pepper Creek Farms
Lawton, OK. 800-526-8132
Pepper Island Beach
Lawrence, PA 724-746-2401
Peppered Palette
Bellingham, WA 866-829-7101
Peppers
Rehoboth Beach, DE 302-644-6900
Porky's Gourmet
Gallatin, TN 800-767-5911
Quality Foods
San Pedro, CA. 877-833-7890
Ray's Sausage Company Inc
Cleveland, OH 216-921-8782
Red Hot Foods
Ventura, CA. 805-659-1614
Reily Foods Company
New Orleans, LA 504-524-6132
Robinson's Barbecue Sauce Company
Oak Park, IL 708-383-8452
Rosarita Mexican Foods Company
Mesa, AZ. 480-964-8751
Royal Resources
New Orleans, LA 800-888-9932
Sambets Cajun Deli
Austin, TX. 800-472-6238
Sams-Leon Mexican Supplies
Omaha, NE 402-733-3809

Simmons Hot Gourmet Products
Lethbridge, AB 403-327-9087
Sona & Hollen Foods
Los Alamitos, CA 800-200-7662
Southwest Specialty Food
Goodyear, AZ 800-536-3131
Spice House International Specialties
Hicksville, NY 516-942-7248
Sweet Baby Ray's
Marlboro, MA. 877-729-2229
T.W. Garner Food Company
Winston Salem, NC. 800-476-7383
Tantos Foods International
Richmond Hill, ON. 905-763-9994
Tapatio Hot Sauce
Vernon, CA 323-587-8933
Thistledew Farm
Proctor, WV 800-854-6639
Thompson's Fine Foods
Shoreview, MN 800-807-0025
Tomorrow Enterprise
New Iberia, LA 337-783-2666
Topper Food Products
East Brunswick, NJ. 800-377-2823
Ukuva Africa
Kirkland, WA 888-280-1003
Uncle Bum's Gourmet Foods
Riverside, CA 800-486-2867
Underground Sauce Network
Cranston, RI 888-919-6664
US Fresh Marketing
Virginia Beach, VA. 757-481-2606
Van De Walle Farms
San Antonio, TX. 210-436-5551
Vegetable Juices
Chicago, IL 888-776-9752
Whitfield Foods
Montgomery, AL. 800-633-8790
Wing It
Falmouth, MA. 508-540-9860
Wing-Time
Steamboat Spgs, CO 970-871-1198
Wizards Cauldron, LTD
Yanceyville, NC 336-694-5333

Jerk

Baldwin Richardson Foods
Frankfort, IL 866-644-2732

> **Baldwin Richardson Foods is a liquid ingredient manufacturer specializing in signature sauces, dessert toppings, beverage/pancake syrups, specialty fruit fillings and condiments. Packaging capabilities range from portion control cups and pouches to standard retail and foodservice packs and include industrial drums and totes. Full service R&D and Quality groups dedicated to new product development, with in-house stability and analytical testing. Call for assistance.**

Buffalo Wild Wings
Minneapolis, MN 763-546-1891
Catskill Mountain Specialties
Saugerties, NY 800-311-3473
Chieftain Wild Rice Company
Spooner, WI 800-262-6368
Cinnabar Specialty Foods
Prescott, AZ 866-293-6433
Cuizina Food Company
Woodinville, WA. 425-486-7000
Mix-A-Lota Stuff LLC
Fort Pierce, FL 561-468-4688
Ventura Foods
Philadelphia, PA 215-223-8700

Lemon

Baldwin Richardson Foods
Frankfort, IL 866-644-2732

> **Baldwin Richardson Foods is a liquid ingredient manufacturer specializing in signature sauces, dessert toppings, beverage/pancake syrups, specialty fruit fillings and condiments. Packaging capabilities range from portion control cups and pouches to standard retail and foodservice packs and include industrial drums and totes. Full service R&D and Quality groups dedicated to new product development, with in-house stability and analytical testing. Call for assistance.**

Gaspar's Sausage Company
North Dartmouth, MA 800-542-2038
Genarom International
Cranbury, NJ. 609-409-6200
Wei-Chuan
Bell Gardens, CA 562-927-6681

Marinara

Artel
Boisbriand, QC 450-433-1322

Baldwin Richardson Foods
Frankfort, IL 866-644-2732

> **Baldwin Richardson Foods is a liquid ingredient manufacturer specializing in signature sauces, dessert toppings, beverage/pancake syrups, specialty fruit fillings and condiments. Packaging capabilities range from portion control cups and pouches to standard retail and foodservice packs and include industrial drums and totes. Full service R&D and Quality groups dedicated to new product development, with in-house stability and analytical testing. Call for assistance.**

Campbell Soup Company
Camden, NJ. 800-257-8443
Casa DiLisio Products
Mt Kisco, NY 800-247-4199
CHS
Inver Grove Heights, MN. 800-232-3639
Colonna Brothers
North Bergen, NJ. 201-864-1115
Cowboy Caviar
Berkeley, CA. 877-509-1796
Cuizina Food Company
Woodinville, WA. 425-486-7000
Dell'Amore Enterprises
Colchester, VT 800-962-6673
Hartford City Foam Pack aging & Converting
Hartford City, IN. 765-348-2500
Hot Wachula's
Lakeland, FL. 877-883-8700
J&R Foods
Long Branch, NJ. 732-229-4020
Kozlowski Farms
Forestville, CA 800-473-2767
L&S Packing Company
Farmingdale, NY 800-286-6487
Mad Will's Food Company
Auburn, CA. 888-275-9455
Mamma Lombardi's All Natural Sauces
Holbrook, NY 631-471-6609
Marsan Foods
Toronto, ON 416-755-9262
Molinaro's Fine Italian Foods
Mississauga, ON 800-268-4959
Nestle
Cleveland, OH 440-349-5757

Newman's Own
  Westport, CT 203-222-0136
Palmieri Food Products
  New Haven, CT 800-845-5447
Pasta By Valente
  Charlottesville, VA 888-575-7670
Pasta Factory
  Northlake, IL 800-615-6951
Pastorelli Food Products
  Chicago, IL 800-767-2829
Red Gold
  Elwood, IN 877-748-9798
Sargento Foods Inc
  Plymouth, WI 800-243-3737
Stanislaus Food Products
  Modesto, CA 800-327-7201
T. Marzetti Company
  Columbus, OH 614-846-2232
Topper Food Products
  East Brunswick, NJ 800-377-2823
Ventre Packing Company
  Syracuse, NY 315-463-2384
Violet Packing
  Williamstown, NJ 856-629-7428
Webbpak
  Trussville, AL 800-655-3500
Windsor Frozen Foods
  Houston, TX 800-437-6936

Meat

Buffalo Bob's Everything Sauce
  Virginia Beach, VA 757-490-9186
Victoria Packing Corporation
  Brooklyn, NY 718-649-2180
Woods Smoked Meats
  Bowling Green, MO 800-458-8426

Mediterranean

Baldwin Richardson Foods
  Frankfort, IL 866-644-2732

Baldwin Richardson Foods is a liquid ingredient manufacturer specializing in signature sauces, dessert toppings, beverage/pancake syrups, specialty fruit fillings and condiments. Packaging capabilities range from portion control cups and pouches to standard retail and foodservice packs and include industrial drums and totes. Full service R&D and Quality groups dedicated to new product development, with in-house stability and analytical testing. Call for assistance.

Cookies Food Products
  Wall Lake, IA 800-331-4995
Cuizina Food Company
  Woodinville, WA 425-486-7000
L&S Packing Company
  Farmingdale, NY 800-286-6487
Papa Leone Food Enterprises
  Beverly Hills, CA 818-858-0074
Parthenon Food Products
  Ann Arbor, MI 734-994-1012

Mexican Food

Authentic Specialty Foods
  Chino, CA 909-631-2000
B&G Foods
  Parsippany, NJ 973-401-6500
Big B Distributors
  Evansville, IN 812-425-5235
Border Foods Inc
  Deming, NM 888-737-7752
Bruce Foods Corporation
  New Iberia, LA 800-299-9082
Casa Visco Finer Food Company
  Schenectady, NY 888-607-2823
ConAgra Grocery Products
  Irvine, CA 714-680-1000
Fernandez Chili Company
  Alamosa, CO 719-589-6043
Garden Complements
  Kansas City, MO 800-966-1091

Golden Specialty Foods
  Norwalk, CA 562-802-2537
Golding Farms Foods
  Winston Salem, NC 336-766-6161
Heluva Good Cheese
  Sodus, NY 315-483-6971
Jalapeno Foods Company
  The Woodlands, TX 800-896-2318
New Canaan Farms
  Dripping Springs, TX 800-727-5267
Palmieri Food Products
  New Haven, CT 800-845-5447
Pepper Creek Farms
  Lawton, OK.....................800-526-8132
Rosarita Mexican Foods Company
  Mesa, AZ 480-964-8751
Sona & Hollen Foods
  Los Alamitos, CA 800-200-7662
Subco Foods Inc
  Sheboygan, WI 800-676-5188
Topper Food Products
  East Brunswick, NJ 800-377-2823
Ventura Foods
  Philadelphia, PA 215-223-8700
Walker Foods
  Los Angeles, CA.................800-966-5199

Mint

Baldwin Richardson Foods
  Frankfort, IL 866-644-2732

Baldwin Richardson Foods is a liquid ingredient manufacturer specializing in signature sauces, dessert toppings, beverage/pancake syrups, specialty fruit fillings and condiments. Packaging capabilities range from portion control cups and pouches to standard retail and foodservice packs and include industrial drums and totes. Full service R&D and Quality groups dedicated to new product development, with in-house stability and analytical testing. Call for assistance.

Cedarvale Food Products
  Toronto, ON 416-656-6330
Lounsbury Foods
  Toronto, ON 416-656-6330
Top Hat Company
  Wilmette, IL 847-256-6565

Mixes

Breakfast at Brennan's
  New Orleans, LA 800-888-9932
CHS
  Inver Grove Heights, MN 800-232-3639
Lawry's Foods
  Monrovia, CA 800-952-9797
Premier Blending
  Wichita, KS 316-267-5533
Produits Alimentaires Berthelet
  Laval, QC 514-334-5503
RC Fine Foods
  Belle Mead, NJ 800-526-3953
Serv-Agen Corporation
  Cherry Hill, NJ 856-663-6966
Spice Advice
  Ankeny, IA 800-247-5251
Superior Quality Foods
  Ontario, CA 800-300-4210
UFL Foods
  Mississauga, ON 905-670-7776
W&G Flavors
  Hunt Valley, MD 410-771-6606

Mole

Juanita's Foods
  Wilmington, CA 310-834-5339

Mushroom

Cipriani's Spaghetti & Sauce Company
  Chicago Heights, IL 708-755-6212

Cuizina Food Company
  Woodinville, WA 425-486-7000
H.J. Heinz Company
  Pittsburgh, PA 412-237-5948
Vegetable Juices
  Chicago, IL 888-776-9752
Worthmore Food Product
  Cincinnati, OH 513-559-1473

Orange

Papa Leone Food Enterprises
  Beverly Hills, CA 818-858-0074
Southern Ray's Foods
  Miami Beach, FL 800-972-8237

Organic

Clement Pappas & Company
  Seabrook, NJ 800-257-7019

Oyster

China Bowl Trading Company
  Westport, CT 203-222-0381
Favorite Foods
  Burnaby, BC 604-420-5100
Lee Kum Kee
  City of Industry, CA 800-654-5082
Wei-Chuan
  Bell Gardens, CA 562-927-6681

Pasta

Milo's Whole World Gourmet
  Athens, OH 866-589-6456
Mondiv/Division of Lassonde Inc
  Boisbriand, QC 450-979-0717
Pacific Choice Brands
  Fresno, CA 559-237-5583
Paesana Products
  East Farmingdale, NY............631-845-1717
Patsy's Brands
  New York, NY 212-247-3491

Peanut

Golden Whisk
  South San Francisco, CA 800-660-5222
Lang Naturals
  Middletown, RI..................401-848-7700
Rowena's
  Norfolk, VA.....................800-627-8699

Pepper

Bruce Foods Corporation
  New Iberia, LA 800-299-9082
Colibri Pepper Company LLC
  Elmer, LA 316-730-6528
Genarom International
  Cranbury, NJ 609-409-6200
Judicial Flavors
  Auburn, CA 530-885-1298
Landry's Pepper Company
  St Martinville, LA................337-394-6097
McIlhenny Company
  New Orleans, LA 504-523-7370
Pepper Source
  Rogers, AR 479-246-1030
Pepper Source
  Van Buren, AR 479-474-5178
Pepper Source
  Metairie, LA 504-885-3223
Porky's Gourmet
  Gallatin, TN 800-767-5911
T.W. Garner Food Company
  Winston Salem, NC..............800-476-7383
Vermont Pepper Works
  Fairfax, VT 802-888-5311

Hot

Gourmet Foods
  Knoxville, TN....................865-970-2982
Mothers Mountain Mustard
  Falmouth, ME...................800-440-9891
Porky's Gourmet
  Gallatin, TN 800-767-5911

Pesto

Al Dente
  Whitmore Lake, MI 800-536-7278

Armanino Foods of Distinction
Hayward, CA 510-441-9300
Bella Cucina Artful Food
Atlanta, GA. 800-671-3136
Cafferata
San Anselmo, CA 800-626-8115
Casa DiLisio Products
Mt Kisco, NY 800-247-4199
Christopher Ranch
Gilroy, CA. .408-847-1100
Cuizina Food Company
Woodinville, WA. 425-486-7000
Delectable Gourmet LLC
Lindenhurst, NY 800-696-1350
Drake's Ducks Woodstream Specialty Foods
Keene, NH. .603-357-5858
Fontina Foods
Port Saint Lucie, FL 800-966-7107
Golden Specialty Foods
Norwalk, CA 562-802-2537
Golden West Specialty Foods
Brisbane, CA. 800-584-4481
Gracious Gourmet
Bridgewater, CT 860-350-1213
Great Garlic Foods
Bradley Beach, NJ 732-775-3311
Les Aliments Livabec Foods
Sherrington, QC 450-454-7971
Maison Le Grand
St Joseph du Lac, QC 450-623-3000
Millflow Spice Corporation
Valley Stream, NY 800-229-6122
Mondiv/Division of Lassonde Inc
Boisbriand, QC 450-979-0717
Nestle
Cleveland, OH 440-349-5757
North American Enterprises
Tucson, AZ .800-817-8666
Pasta Factory
Northlake, IL. 800-615-6951
Peaceworks
New York, NY 212-897-3995
Peaceworks
New York, NY 800-732-2321
Pestos with Panache by Lauren
Brooklyn, NY 917-656-3082
Red Gold
Elwood, IN .877-748-9798
Rising Sun Farms
Phoenix, OR 541-535-8331
Sauces 'n Love
Lynn, MA 866-772-8237
TexaFrance
Austin, TX. .800-776-8937
Topper Food Products
East Brunswick, NJ. 800-377-2823
Tulkoff Food Products
Baltimore, MD 800-638-7343
Waterfield Farms
Amherst, MA 413-549-3558

Pizza

Alimentaire Whyte's Inc
Laval, QC 800-625-1979

Baldwin Richardson Foods
Frankfort, IL 866-644-2732

Baldwin Richardson Foods is a liquid ingredient manufacturer specializing in signature sauces, dessert toppings, beverage/pancake syrups, specialty fruit fillings and condiments. Packaging capabilities range from portion control cups and pouches to standard retail and foodservice packs and include industrial drums and totes. Full service R&D and Quality groups dedicated to new product development, with in-house stability and analytical testing. Call for assistance.

Big B Distributors
Evansville, IN 812-425-5235
Canada Bread
Etobicoke, ON 416-622-2040

Cuizina Food Company
Woodinville, WA. 425-486-7000
Del Grosso Foods
Tipton, PA .800-521-5880
Del Monte Foods
San Francisco, CA 800-543-3090
Dorothy Dawson Foods Products
Jackson, MI. 517-788-9830
Furmano Foods
Northumberland, PA 877-877-6032
Hartford City Foam Pack aging & Converting
Hartford City, IN. 765-348-2500
Heinz Company of Canada
North York, ON. 800-268-6641
Hirzel Canning Company &Farms
Northwood, OH 419-693-0531
Lucy's Foods
Latrobe, PA .724-539-1430
Nationwide Canning
Cottam, ON 519-839-4831
Old Mansion Foods
Petersburg, VA 800-476-1877
Palmieri Food Products
New Haven, CT 800-845-5447
Paradise Tomato Kitchens
Louisville, KY 502-637-1700
Pastorelli Food Products
Chicago, IL .800-767-2829
Sargento Foods Inc
Plymouth, WI 800-243-3737
Sassafras Enterprises
Chicago, IL .800-537-4941
Stanislaus Food Products
Modesto, CA 800-327-7201
Tip Top Canning Company
Tipp City, OH 937-667-3713
Triple K Manufacturing Company
Shenandoah, IA. 888-987-2824
Violet Packing
Williamstown, NJ 856-629-7428
Worthmore Food Product
Cincinnati, OH 513-559-1473

Plum

Baldwin Richardson Foods
Frankfort, IL 866-644-2732

Baldwin Richardson Foods is a liquid ingredient manufacturer specializing in signature sauces, dessert toppings, beverage/pancake syrups, specialty fruit fillings and condiments. Packaging capabilities range from portion control cups and pouches to standard retail and foodservice packs and include industrial drums and totes. Full service R&D and Quality groups dedicated to new product development, with in-house stability and analytical testing. Call for assistance.

Cuizina Food Company
Woodinville, WA. 425-486-7000
Favorite Foods
Burnaby, BC 604-420-5100
Lee Kum Kee
City of Industry, CA 800-654-5082
Nestle
Cleveland, OH 440-349-5757
Wei-Chuan
Bell Gardens, CA 562-927-6681
Wing's Food Products
Toronto, ON 416-259-2662
Wong Wing Foods
Montreal, QC 800-361-4820

Primavera

Cuizina Food Company
Woodinville, WA. 425-486-7000
L&S Packing Company
Farmingdale, NY 800-286-6487
Topper Food Products
East Brunswick, NJ. 800-377-2823

Puttanesca

Baldwin Richardson Foods
Frankfort, IL 866-644-2732

Baldwin Richardson Foods is a liquid ingredient manufacturer specializing in signature sauces, dessert toppings, beverage/pancake syrups, specialty fruit fillings and condiments. Packaging capabilities range from portion control cups and pouches to standard retail and foodservice packs and include industrial drums and totes. Full service R&D and Quality groups dedicated to new product development, with in-house stability and analytical testing. Call for assistance.

Casa DiLisio Products
Mt Kisco, NY 800-247-4199
Cuizina Food Company
Woodinville, WA. 425-486-7000
L&S Packing Company
Farmingdale, NY 800-286-6487
Papa Leone Food Enterprises
Beverly Hills, CA 818-858-0074

Seafood

Blue Crab Bay Company
Melfa, VA 800-221-2722
Chincoteague Seafood Company
Parsonsburg, MD 443-260-4800
Clements Foods Company
Oklahoma City, OK 800-654-8355
Cuizina Food Company
Woodinville, WA. 425-486-7000
E. Waldo Ward & Son Corporation
Sierra Madre, CA 800-355-9273
Gourmet Foods
Knoxville, TN 865-970-2982
H.J. Heinz Company
Pittsburgh, PA 412-237-5948
Look's Gourmet Food Company
Whiting, ME 800-962-6258
Lounsbury Foods
Toronto, ON 416-656-6330
Mid-Atlantic Foods
Easton, MD 800-922-4688
Myron's Fine Foods
Erving, MA .800-730-2820
New Business Corporation
East Chicago, IN 800-742-8435
New Canaan Farms
Dripping Springs, TX 800-727-5267
Palmieri Food Products
New Haven, CT 800-845-5447
Paradise Products Corporation
Roslyn, NY .800-826-1235
Portion Pac
Mason, OH .800-232-4829
Red Gold
Elwood, IN .877-748-9798
Rosmarino Foods/R.Z. Humbert Company
Odessa, FL .888-926-9053
T. Marzetti Company
Columbus, OH 614-846-2232
T.W. Garner Food Company
Winston Salem, NC. 800-476-7383
Woeber Mustard Manufacturing
Springfield, OH. 800-548-2929

Soy

Ajinomoto Food Ingredients LLC
Chicago, IL .773-380-7000
Alimentaire Whyte's Inc
Laval, QC 800-625-1979
American Culinary Gardens
Springfield, MO 888-831-2433

Baldwin Richardson Foods
Frankfort, IL 866-644-2732

> Baldwin Richardson Foods is a liquid ingredient manufacturer specializing in signature sauces, dessert toppings, beverage/pancake syrups, specialty fruit fillings and condiments. Packaging capabilities range from portion control cups and pouches to standard retail and foodservice packs and include industrial drums and totes. Full service R&D and Quality groups dedicated to new product development, with in-house stability and analytical testing. Call for assistance.

Bartush-Schnitzius Foods Company
Lewisville, TX 972-219-1270
Basic Food Flavors
North Las Vegas, NV 702-643-0043
Baumer Foods
New Orleans, LA 504-482-5761
Baycliff Company
New York, NY 212-772-6078
Castella Imports
Hauppauge, NY 866-227-8355
Clements Foods Company
Oklahoma City, OK 800-654-8355
Commodities Marketing, Inc.
Edison, NJ 732-516-0700
ConAgra Grocery Products
Archbold, OH 419-445-8015
Dean Distributors
Burlingame, CA 800-792-0816
Dixie USA
Tomball, TX 800-233-3668
Edward & Sons Trading Company
Carpinteria, CA 805-684-8500
Favorite Foods
Burnaby, BC 604-420-5100
Felbro Food Products
Los Angeles, CA 800-335-2761
Flavor House
Adelanto, CA 760-246-9131
Golden Gate Foods
Dallas, TX 214-747-2223
Hormel Foods Corporation
Austin, MN 800-523-4635
Inter-American Products
Cincinnati, OH 800-645-2233
Kari-Out Company
White Plains, NY 800-433-8799
Kikkoman International
San Francisco, CA 415-956-7750
Kikkoman International
Oakbrook Terrace, IL 630-954-1244
Kikkoman International
Tucker, GA 770-496-0605
Kikkoman International
Plano, TX 972-516-4207
Lee Kum Kee
City of Industry, CA 800-654-5082
Lee's Food Products
Toronto, ON 416-465-2407
Mandarin Soy Sauce
Middletown, NY 845-343-1505
McIlhenny Company
New Orleans, LA 800-634-9599
McIlhenny Company
New Orleans, LA 504-523-7370
Millflow Spice Corporation
Valley Stream, NY 800-229-6122
Myron's Fine Foods
Erving, MA 800-730-2820
Nikken Foods Company
St Louis, MO. 636-532-1019
Randag & Associates Inc
Elmhurst, IL 630-530-2830
San-J International
Richmond, VA....................800-446-5500
Serv-Agen Corporation
Cherry Hill, NJ 856-663-6966
Sobaya
Cowansville, QC 800-319-8808
Sona & Hollen Foods
Los Alamitos, CA 800-200-7662

Tate & Lyle Staley Company
Decatur, IL 217-423-4411
Tomasso Corporation
Baie D'Urfe, QC...................514-325-3000
Wei-Chuan
Bell Gardens, CA 562-927-6681
Wing Nien Company
Hayward, CA 510-487-8877
Wing's Food Products
Toronto, ON 416-259-2662
Wizards Cauldron, LTD
Yanceyville, NC 336-694-5333
Yamasa Corporation
Torrance, CA.....................310-944-3883

Spaghetti

Alimentaire Whyte's Inc
Laval, QC 800-625-1979
Artel
Boisbriand, QC 450-433-1322

Baldwin Richardson Foods
Frankfort, IL 866-644-2732

> Baldwin Richardson Foods is a liquid ingredient manufacturer specializing in signature sauces, dessert toppings, beverage/pancake syrups, specialty fruit fillings and condiments. Packaging capabilities range from portion control cups and pouches to standard retail and foodservice packs and include industrial drums and totes. Full service R&D and Quality groups dedicated to new product development, with in-house stability and analytical testing. Call for assistance.

Campbell Soup Company
Camden, NJ 800-257-8443
Casa Visco Finer Food Company
Schenectady, NY..................888-607-2823
Chef-A-Roni
East Greenwich, RI................401-884-8798
Cipriani's Spaghetti & Sauce Company
Chicago Heights, IL 708-755-6212
Cuizina Food Company
Woodinville, WA..................425-486-7000
Del Grosso Foods
Tipton, PA.......................800-521-5880
Del Monte Foods
San Francisco, CA 800-543-3090
Eden Foods Inc
Clinton, MI 800-248-0320
G Di Lullo & Sons
Westville, NJ 856-456-3700
Gumpert's Canada
Mississauga, ON 800-387-9324
Hagerty Foods
Orange, CA.......................714-628-1230
Hanover Foods Corporation
Hanover, PA 717-632-6000
Heinz Company of Canada
North York, ON...................800-268-6641
Hirzel Canning Company &Farms
Northwood, OH 419-693-0531
Key Ingredients
Harrisburg, PA 800-227-4448
Knott's Berry Farm Foods
Placentia, CA 800-289-9927
L&S Packing Company
Farmingdale, NY 800-286-6487
Lombardo's Ravioli Kitchen
New Britain, CT 860-223-7800
Lucy's Foods
Latrobe, PA 724-539-1430
Marsan Foods
Toronto, ON 416-755-9262
Molinaro's Fine Italian Foods
Mississauga, ON 800-268-4959
Nationwide Canning
Cottam, ON......................519-839-4831
Nestle
Cleveland, OH 440-349-5757
Nicola Pizza
Rehoboth Beach, DE 302-226-2654

Palmieri Food Products
New Haven, CT 800-845-5447
Peaceworks
New York, NY 212-897-3995
Pino's Pasta Veloce
Staten Island, NY 718-273-6660
Porinos Gourmet Food
Central Falls, RI 800-826-3938
Progresso Quality Foods
Vineland, NJ 800-200-9377
Ragozzino Food
Meriden, CT 800-348-1240
Red Gold
Elwood, IN 877-748-9798
Seneca Foods
Clyman, WI. 920-696-3331
Silver State Foods
Denver, CO 800-423-3351
Specialty Brands
Carthage, MO 417-358-8104
Thomson Food
Duluth, MN 218-722-2529
Todd's
Des Moines, IA 800-247-5363
Vietti Foods Company Inc
Nashville, TN 800-240-7864
Violet Packing
Williamstown, NJ 856-629-7428
Westin
Omaha, NE 800-228-6098
Williams Foods Inc
Lenexa, KS 800-255-6736
Windsor Frozen Foods
Houston, TX 800-437-6936
Worthmore Food Product
Cincinnati, OH 513-559-1473
Ynrico's Food Products Company
Syracuse, NY.....................888-472-8237

Meat

Artel
Boisbriand, QC 450-433-1322
Campbell Soup Company
Camden, NJ. 800-257-8443
Chef-A-Roni
East Greenwich, RI................401-884-8798
Cipriani's Spaghetti & Sauce Company
Chicago Heights, IL 708-755-6212
Del Monte Foods
San Francisco, CA 800-543-3090
Gaucho Foods
Westmont, IL.....................630-889-4241
Lombardo's Ravioli Kitchen
New Britain, CT 860-223-7800

Meatless

Campbell Soup Company
Camden, NJ. 800-257-8443
Chef-A-Roni
East Greenwich, RI................401-884-8798
Del Monte Foods
San Francisco, CA 800-543-3090
Molinaro's Fine Italian Foods
Mississauga, ON...................800-268-4959

Steak

Ashman Manufacturing & Distributing Company
Virginia Beach, VA................800-641-9924
Baumer Foods
New Orleans, LA 504-482-5761
Creative Foodworks
San Antonio, TX..................210-212-4761
Golding Farms Foods
Winston Salem, NC................336-766-6161
Gourmet Foods
Knoxville, TN.....................865-970-2982
H.J. Heinz Company
Pittsburgh, PA....................412-237-5948
Inter-State Cider & Vinegar Company
Baltimore, MD....................410-947-1529
Joe Hutson Foods
Jacksonville, FL 904-731-9065
Kozlowski Farms
Forestville, CA 800-473-2767
Kraft Food Ingredients
Memphis, TN.....................901-381-6500
L&S Packing Company
Farmingdale, NY 800-286-6487
Lea & Perrins
Fair Lawn, NJ 800-289-5797

Magic Seasoning Blends
Harahan, LA 800-457-2857
McIlhenny Company
New Orleans, LA 504-523-7370
Myron's Fine Foods
Erving, MA 800-730-2820
Paradise Products Corporation
Roslyn, NY 800-826-1235
Private Harvest Gourmet Specialties
Lakeport, CA 800-463-0594
Quality Foods
San Pedro, CA 877-833-7890
Webbpak
Trussville, AL 800-655-3500
Wine Country Chef LLC
Hidden Valley Lake, CA 707-322-0406
Wizards Cauldron, LTD
Yanceyville, NC 336-694-5333

Stir-Fry

Baldwin Richardson Foods
Frankfort, IL 866-644-2732

Baldwin Richardson Foods is a liquid ingredient manufacturer specializing in signature sauces, dessert toppings, beverage/pancake syrups, specialty fruit fillings and condiments. Packaging capabilities range from portion control cups and pouches to standard retail and foodservice packs and include industrial drums and totes. Full service R&D and Quality groups dedicated to new product development, with in-house stability and analytical testing. Call for assistance.

Cuizina Food Company
Woodinville, WA 425-486-7000
Flavor House
Adelanto, CA 760-246-9131
Hormel Foods Corporation
Austin, MN 800-523-4635
L&S Packing Company
Farmingdale, NY 800-286-6487
Mandarin Soy Sauce
Middletown, NY 845-343-1505
Myron's Fine Foods
Erving, MA 800-730-2820
Wei-Chuan
Bell Gardens, CA 562-927-6681
Wing Nien Company
Hayward, CA 510-487-8877
Wizards Cauldron, LTD
Yanceyville, NC 336-694-5333

Sweet & Sour

Baldwin Richardson Foods
Frankfort, IL 866-644-2732

Baldwin Richardson Foods is a liquid ingredient manufacturer specializing in signature sauces, dessert toppings, beverage/pancake syrups, specialty fruit fillings and condiments. Packaging capabilities range from portion control cups and pouches to standard retail and foodservice packs and include industrial drums and totes. Full service R&D and Quality groups dedicated to new product development, with in-house stability and analytical testing. Call for assistance.

Big B Distributors
Evansville, IN 812-425-5235
China Bowl Trading Company
Westport, CT 203-222-0381
ConAgra Grocery Products
Archbold, OH 419-445-8015

Cuizina Food Company
Woodinville, WA 425-486-7000
Garden Complements
Kansas City, MO 800-966-1091
Gumpert's Canada
Mississauga, ON 800-387-9324
Kari-Out Company
White Plains, NY 800-433-8799
L&S Packing Company
Farmingdale, NY 800-286-6487
Lang Naturals
Middletown, RI 401-848-7700
Lee Kum Kee
City of Industry, CA 800-654-5082
Robbie's Natural Products
Altadena, CA 626-798-9944
Sona & Hollen Foods
Los Alamitos, CA 800-200-7662
Wei-Chuan
Bell Gardens, CA 562-927-6681
Wing Nien Company
Hayward, CA 510-487-8877

Szechuan

Baldwin Richardson Foods
Frankfort, IL 866-644-2732

Baldwin Richardson Foods is a liquid ingredient manufacturer specializing in signature sauces, dessert toppings, beverage/pancake syrups, specialty fruit fillings and condiments. Packaging capabilities range from portion control cups and pouches to standard retail and foodservice packs and include industrial drums and totes. Full service R&D and Quality groups dedicated to new product development, with in-house stability and analytical testing. Call for assistance.

Favorite Foods
Burnaby, BC 604-420-5100
Myron's Fine Foods
Erving, MA 800-730-2820

Taco

Amigos Canning Company
San Antonio, TX 800-580-3477
Authentic Specialty Foods
Chino, CA 909-631-2000

Baldwin Richardson Foods
Frankfort, IL 866-644-2732

Baldwin Richardson Foods is a liquid ingredient manufacturer specializing in signature sauces, dessert toppings, beverage/pancake syrups, specialty fruit fillings and condiments. Packaging capabilities range from portion control cups and pouches to standard retail and foodservice packs and include industrial drums and totes. Full service R&D and Quality groups dedicated to new product development, with in-house stability and analytical testing. Call for assistance.

Bartush-Schnitzius Foods Company
Lewisville, TX 972-219-1270
Bien Padre Foods
Eureka, CA 707-442-4585
Big B Distributors
Evansville, IN 812-425-5235
ConAgra Grocery Products
Irvine, CA 714-680-1000
Cookies Food Products
Wall Lake, IA 800-331-4995
El Rancho Tortilla
San Antonio, TX 210-922-8411

Famous Chili
Fort Smith, AR 479-782-0096
Fernandez Chili Company
Alamosa, CO 719-589-6043
Golden Specialty Foods
Norwalk, CA 562-802-2537
Golding Farms Foods
Winston Salem, NC 336-766-6161
Hagerty Foods
Orange, CA 714-628-1230
Heluva Good Cheese
Sodus, NY 315-483-6971
Hirzel Canning Company &Farms
Northwood, OH 419-693-0531
Hormel Foods Corporation
Austin, MN 800-523-4635
Hume Specialties
Winston Salem, NC 802-875-3117
Imus Ranch Foods
Holtsville, NY 888-284-4687
Jalapeno Foods Company
The Woodlands, TX 800-896-2318
Judicial Flavors
Auburn, CA 530-885-1298
La Vencedora Products
Los Angeles, CA 800-327-2572
La Victoria Foods
Rosemead, CA 800-423-4450
Laredo Mexican Foods
Fort Wayne, IN 800-252-7336
Li'l Guy Foods
Kansas City, MO 800-886-8226
M.W. Milton & Company
Louisville, KY 502-587-5016
New Canaan Farms
Dripping Springs, TX 800-727-5267
Palmieri Food Products
New Haven, CT 800-845-5447
Pepper Creek Farms
Lawton, OK 800-526-8132
Pillsbury
Hannibal, MO 800-775-4777
Red Gold
Elwood, IN 877-748-9798
Rosarita Mexican Foods Company
Mesa, AZ 480-964-8751
Sona & Hollen Foods
Los Alamitos, CA 800-200-7662
Spanish Gardens Food Manufacturing
Kansas City, KS 913-831-4242
Topper Food Products
East Brunswick, NJ 800-377-2823
Ventura Foods
Philadelphia, PA 215-223-8700

Tahini

Dipasa
Brownsville, TX 956-831-5893
East Wind Nut Butters
Tecumseh, MO 417-679-4682
Hommus Factory
Haverhill, MA 508-460-0212
Vic Rossano Incorporated
Montreal, QC 514-766-5252

Tartar

Baldwin Richardson Foods
Frankfort, IL 866-644-2732

Baldwin Richardson Foods is a liquid ingredient manufacturer specializing in signature sauces, dessert toppings, beverage/pancake syrups, specialty fruit fillings and condiments. Packaging capabilities range from portion control cups and pouches to standard retail and foodservice packs and include industrial drums and totes. Full service R&D and Quality groups dedicated to new product development, with in-house stability and analytical testing. Call for assistance.

Bestfoods Specialty Products
Englewood Cliffs, NJ 800-338-8831

Cedarvale Food Products
Toronto, ON 416-656-6330
Cuizina Food Company
Woodinville, WA 425-486-7000
Food Specialties Company
Cincinnati, OH 513-761-1242
Golding Farms Foods
Winston Salem, NC 336-766-6161
H.J. Heinz Company
Pittsburgh, PA 412-237-5948
Kelchner's Horseradish
Dublin, PA 215-249-3439
Lounsbury Foods
Toronto, ON 416-656-6330

Mrs. Clark's Foods
Ankeny, IA 800-736-5674

Juices, salad dressings and sauces.

Portion Pac
Mason, OH 800-232-4829
Private Harvest Gourmet Specialities
Lakeport, CA 800-463-0594
Sau-Sea Foods
Tarrytown, NY 914-631-1717
Schlotterbeck & Foss Company
Portland, ME 800-777-4666
Silver Spring Gardens
Eau Claire, WI 800-826-7322
Sona & Hollen Foods
Los Alamitos, CA 800-200-7662
T. Marzetti Company
Columbus, OH 614-846-2232
Ventura Foods
Philadelphia, PA 215-223-8700
Westin
Omaha, NE 800-228-6098
Wood Brothers
West Columbia, SC 803-796-5146

Teriyaki

Argo Century
Charlotte, NC 800-446-7131

Baldwin Richardson Foods
Frankfort, IL 866-644-2732

Baldwin Richardson Foods is a liquid ingredient manufacturer specializing in signature sauces, dessert toppings, beverage/pancake syrups, specialty fruit fillings and condiments. Packaging capabilities range from portion control cups and pouches to standard retail and foodservice packs and include industrial drums and totes. Full service R&D and Quality groups dedicated to new product development, with in-house stability and analytical testing. Call for assistance.

Baycliff Company
New York, NY 212-772-6078
BBQ'n Fools
Bend, OR. 800-671-8652
Buffalo Wild Wings
Minneapolis, MN 763-546-1891
Cuizina Food Company
Woodinville, WA 425-486-7000
Dean Distributors
Burlingame, CA 800-792-0816
Dynamic Foods
Lubbock, TX 806-762-0780
Favorite Foods
Burnaby, BC 604-420-5100
Golden Specialty Foods
Norwalk, CA 562-802-2537
Hormel Foods Corporation
Austin, MN 800-523-4635

Kikkoman International
San Francisco, CA 415-956-7750
Kikkoman International
Oakbrook Terrace, IL 630-954-1244
Kikkoman International
Tucker, GA 770-496-0605
Kikkoman International
Plano, TX 972-516-4207
L&S Packing Company
Farmingdale, NY 800-286-6487
Mandarin Soy Sauce
Middletown, NY 845-343-1505
Miyako Oriental Foods
Baldwin Park, CA 877-788-6476
Myron's Fine Foods
Erving, MA 800-730-2820
Passetti's Pride
Hayward, CA 800-521-4659
Sagawa's Savory Sauces
Tualatin, OR 503-692-4334
San-J International
Richmond, VA. 800-446-5500
Sona & Hollen Foods
Los Alamitos, CA 800-200-7662
T. Marzetti Company
Columbus, OH 614-846-2232
Valley Grain Products
Madera, CA 559-675-3400
Vanlaw Food Products
Fullerton, CA 714-870-9091
Wong Wing Foods
Montreal, QC 800-361-4820
World Flavors
Warminster, PA 215-672-4400
Yamasa Corporation
Torrance, CA 310-944-3883

Tomato

Mamma Lombardi's All Natural Sauces
Holbrook, NY 631-471-6609

Canned

Bartush-Schnitzius Foods Company
Lewisville, TX 972-219-1270
Bruno Specialty Foods
West Sayville, NY 631-589-1700
Cafferata
San Anselmo, CA 800-626-8115
Cajun Chef Products
St Martinville, LA 337-394-7112
Casa DiLisio Products
Mt Kisco, NY 800-247-4199
Casa Visco Finer Food Company
Schenectady, NY 888-607-2823
Colonna Brothers
North Bergen, NJ 201-864-1115
Costa Deano's Gourmet Foods
Canton, OH 800-337-2823
Cucina Antica Foods Corporation
Bedford Hills, NY 877-728-2462
Cuizina Food Company
Woodinville, WA 425-486-7000
Del Monte Foods
San Francisco, CA 800-543-3090
Escalon Premier Brand
Escalon, CA 209-838-7341
Golden Valley Foods
Abbotsford, BC. 888-299-8855
Gumpert's Canada
Mississauga, ON 800-387-9324
H.J. Heinz Company
Pittsburgh, PA 412-237-5948
Hanover Foods Corporation
Hanover, PA 717-632-6000
Hartford City Foam Pack aging & Converting
Hartford City, IN. 765-348-2500
Heinz Company of Canada
North York, ON. 800-268-6641
Hirzel Canning Company &Farms
Northwood, OH 419-693-0531
Hunt-Wesson Foods
Rochester, NY 209-847-0321
International Home Foods
Milton, PA. 973-359-9920
J&R Foods
Long Branch, NJ 732-229-4020
Kozlowski Farms
Forestville, CA 800-473-2767
L&S Packing Company
Farmingdale, NY 800-286-6487

Molinaro's Fine Italian Foods
Mississauga, ON 800-268-4959
Nationwide Canning
Cottam, ON 519-839-4831
Nestle
Cleveland, OH 440-349-5757
Palmieri Food Products
New Haven, CT 800-845-5447
Papa Leone Food Enterprises
Beverly Hills, CA 818-858-0074
Pasta Factory
Northlake, IL. 800-615-6951
Pastorelli Food Products
Chicago, IL 800-767-2829
Progresso Quality Foods
Vineland, NJ 800-200-9377
San Benito Foods
Hollister, CA 831-637-4434
Seneca Foods
Clyman, WI. 920-696-3331
Specialty Brands
Carthage, MO 417-358-8104
Tip Top Canning Company
Tipp City, OH 937-667-3713
Tomasso Corporation
Baie D'Urfe, QC 514-325-3000
Topper Food Products
East Brunswick, NJ. 800-377-2823
Walker Foods
Los Angeles, CA. 800-966-5199
Williams Foods Inc
Lenexa, KS 800-255-6736

Frozen

Cajun Chef Products
St Martinville, LA. 337-394-7112
Casa DiLisio Products
Mt Kisco, NY 800-247-4199
Cuizina Food Company
Woodinville, WA 425-486-7000
Del Monte Foods
San Francisco, CA 800-543-3090
Hanover Foods Corporation
Hanover, PA 717-632-6000
Marsan Foods
Toronto, ON 416-755-9262
Molinaro's Fine Italian Foods
Mississauga, ON 800-268-4959
Nestle
Cleveland, OH 440-349-5757
Progresso Quality Foods
Vineland, NJ 800-200-9377
Seneca Foods
Clyman, WI 920-696-3331
Specialty Brands
Carthage, MO 417-358-8104
Topper Food Products
East Brunswick, NJ. 800-377-2823

with Spices

Heinz Company of Canada
North York, ON. 800-268-6641
Palmieri Food Products
New Haven, CT 800-845-5447
Patsy's
New York, NY 212-247-3491

Worcestershire

A. Lassonde, Inc.
Rougemont, QC 514-878-1057
Annie's Naturals
East Calais, VT 800-434-1234

Baldwin Richardson Foods
Frankfort, IL 866-644-2732

> Baldwin Richardson Foods is a liquid ingredient manufacturer specializing in signature sauces, dessert toppings, beverage/pancake syrups, specialty fruit fillings and condiments. Packaging capabilities range from portion control cups and pouches to standard retail and foodservice packs and include industrial drums and totes. Full service R&D and Quality groups dedicated to new product development, with in-house stability and analytical testing. Call for assistance.

Baumer Foods
New Orleans, LA 504-482-5761
Big B Distributors
Evansville, IN 812-425-5235
Cajun Chef Products
St Martinville, LA 337-394-7112
Clements Foods Company
Oklahoma City, OK 800-654-8355
Dean Distributors
Burlingame, CA 800-792-0816
Felbro Food Products
Los Angeles, CA. 800-335-2761
French's Ingredients
Springfield, MO 417-837-1813
Gold Coast Ingredients
Commerce, CA 800-352-8673
Gourmet Foods
Knoxville, TN 865-970-2982
H.J. Heinz Company
Pittsburgh, PA 412-237-5948
Illes Seasonings & Flavors
Carrollton, TX 800-683-4553
Inter-American Products
Cincinnati, OH 800-645-2233
Inter-State Cider & Vinegar Company
Baltimore, MD 410-947-1529
Lea & Perrins
Fair Lawn, NJ 800-289-5797
McIlhenny Company
New Orleans, LA 800-634-9599
Millflow Spice Corporation
Valley Stream, NY 800-229-6122
New Business Corporation
East Chicago, IN 800-742-8435
Robbie's Natural Products
Altadena, CA 626-798-9944
Serv-Agen Corporation
Cherry Hill, NJ 856-663-6966
T.W. Garner Food Company
Winston Salem, NC 800-476-7383
Uncle Ben's
Greenville, MS 800-548-6253
Vegetable Juices
Chicago, IL 888-776-9752

Vinegar

A Perfect Pear from Napa Valley
Napa, CA. 800-553-5753
A Southern Season
Chapel Hill, NC 800-253-5317
Agrusa, Inc.
Leonia, NJ 201-592-5950
American Culinary Gardens
Springfield, MO 888-831-2433
Arbor Hill Grapery & Winery
Naples, NY 800-554-7553
Arnabal International
Tustin, CA. 714-665-9477
Assouline & Ting
Philadelphia, PA 800-521-4491
Au Printemps Gourmet
Prevost, QC 800-663-0416
B.R. Cohn Olive Oil
Glen Ellen, CA 877-933-9675
Baycliff Company
New York, NY 212-772-6078
Belton Foods
Dayton, OH 800-443-2266
Big B Distributors
Evansville, IN 812-425-5235

Bittersweet Herb Farm
Shelburne Falls, MA 800-456-1599
Blueberry Store
Grand Junction, MI 877-654-2400
Boston Spice & Tea Company
Boston, VA 800-966-4372
Boyajian, Inc
Canton, MA 800-965-0665
BR Cohn Winery
Glen Ellen, CA 707-938-4064
Buon Italia
New York, NY 212-633-9090
California Olive Oil Corporation
Salem, MA 800-386-6457
Castella Imports
Hauppauge, NY 866-227-8355
Chicama Vineyards
West Tisbury, MA 888-244-2262
China Bowl Trading Company
Westport, CT 203-222-0381
Clements Foods Company
Oklahoma City, OK 800-654-8355
Colonna Brothers
North Bergen, NJ 201-864-1115
Consumers Vinegar & Spice Company
Chicago, IL 773-376-4100
Creole Fermentation Industries
Abbeville, LA 337-898-9377
Culinary Imports
Jericho, VT 800-958-7678
CW Resources
New Britain, CT 860-229-7700
Dalton's Best Maid Products
Fort Worth, TX 817-335-5494
Dark Tickle Company
Griquet, NL 709-623-2354
Delicae Gourmet
Tarpon Springs, FL 800-942-2502
Eden Foods Inc
Clinton, MI 800-248-0320

EMERLING INTERNATIONAL FOODS, INC.

Emerling International Foods
Buffalo, NY 716-833-7381

> We supply food manufacturers and food service customers worldwide (since 1988) with bulk ingredients including: Fruits & Vegetables; Juice Concentrates; Herbs & Spices; Oils & Vinegars; Flavors & Colors; Honey & Molasses. We also produce PURE MAPLE SYRUP.

Erbrich-Sewell Products Company
Indianapolis, IN 317-925-6433
Fleischmann's Vinegar
Cerritos, CA 800-443-1067
Fleischmann's Yeast
Chesterfield, MO 800-247-7473
Fleischmanns Vinegar
Cerritos, CA 800-443-1067
Four Chimneys Farm Winery Trust
Himrod, NY 607-243-7502
Fredericksburg Herb Farm
Fredericksburg, TX 800-259-4372
Gold Pure Foods Products Company
Hempstead, NY 800-422-4681
Golden Whisk
South San Francisco, CA 800-660-5222
Grapevine Trading Company
Santa Rosa, CA 800-469-6478
Gregory-Robinson Speas
Dallas, TX 214-352-1761
Halladays Harvest Barn
Bellows Falls, VT 802-463-3471
Heinz
Holland, MI 800-528-5757
Heinz Company of Canada
North York, ON 800-268-6641
Heinz North America
Pittsburgh, PA 412-237-5700
Herb Bee's Products
Colchester, VT 802-864-7387
Hinzerling Winery
Prosser, WA. 800-722-6702
Hormel Foods Corporation
Austin, MN 507-437-5611
Hudson Valley Fruit Juice
Highland, NY 845-691-8061
Hurd Orchards
Holley, NY 585-638-8838

II Sisters
Moss Beach, CA 800-282-7058
Inter-State Cider & Vinegar Company
Baltimore, MD 410-947-1529
K.L. Keller Imports
Oakland, CA 510-839-7890
Kari-Out Company
White Plains, NY 800-433-8799
Ken's Foods
Marlborough, MA. 800-633-5800
Kennedy Candy Company
Kilgore, TX 800-657-5258
Knouse Foods
Peach Glen, PA 717-677-8181
Knouse Foods Cooperative
Paw Paw, MI 269-657-5524
Kozlowski Farms
Forestville, CA 800-473-2767
Lesley Elizabeth
Lapeer, MI 800-684-3300
Lounsbury Foods
Toronto, ON 416-656-6330
M.A. Gedney
Chaska, MN 952-448-2612
Mandarin Soy Sauce
Middletown, NY 845-343-1505
Marukan Vinegar (U.S.A.) Inc.
Paramount, CA 562-630-6060
Mizkam Americas
Kansas City, MO 816-483-1700
Morehouse Foods
City of Industry, CA 626-854-1655
Myron's Fine Foods
Erving, MA 800-730-2820
Nakano Foods
Mt Prospect, IL 847-290-0730
National Fruit Product Company
Winchester, VA 540-662-3401
National Fruit Product Company
Lincolnton, NC 704-735-2531
National Vinegar Company
Saint Louis, MO 314-842-2822
National Vinegar Company
Alton, IL 618-465-6532
National Vinegar Company
Houston, TX 713-223-4214
North American Enterprises
Tucson, AZ 800-817-8666
O Olive Oil
Petaluma, CA 888-827-7148
Oasis Foods Company
Hillside, NJ 908-964-0477
Old Dutch Mustard Company
Great Neck, NY 516-466-0522
Olds Products Company
Pleasant Prairie, WI 800-233-8064
Our Thyme Garden
Cleburne, TX 800-482-4372
Pastorelli Food Products
Chicago, IL 800-767-2829
Patsy's
New York, NY 212-247-3491
Pilgrim Foods
Greenville, NH 603-878-2100
Pompeian
Baltimore, MD 800-638-1224
Prairie Thyme
Santa Fe, NM 800-869-0009
Proacec USA
Santa Monica, CA. 310-996-7770
Purity Products
Plainview, NY 888-769-7873
Rahco International
St Augustine, FL. 800-851-7681
Red Pelican Food Products
Detroit, MI 313-921-2500
Reinhart Foods
Markham, ON 905-754-3503
Restaurant Lulu Gourmet Products
San Francisco, CA 888-693-5800
REX Pure Foods
Gonzales, TX 800-344-8314
Rex Wine Vinegar Company
Newark, NJ 973-589-6911
Roanoke Apple Products
Salem, VA 540-375-7341
Robert Rothschild Berry Farm
Urbana, OH 866-565-6790
Robert Rothschild Farm
Urbana, OH 866-565-6790
Rose Brier
Albany, OR 888-926-4378

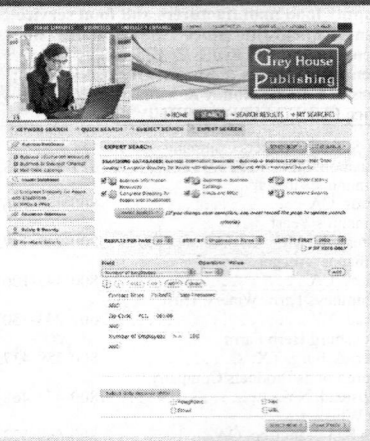
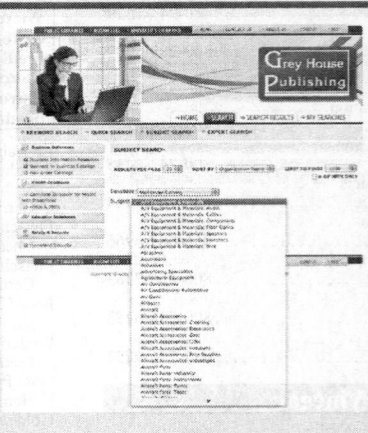

S&G Products
Nicholasville, KY 800-826-7652
Santa Barbara Olive Company
Goleta, CA 800-624-4896
Satiety
Davis, CA 530-757-2699
Sedlock Farm
Lynn Center, IL 309-521-8284
Sherrill Orchards
Arvin, CA 661-858-2035
Sieco USA Corporation
Houston, TX 800-325-9443
Silver Palate Kitchens
Cresskill, NJ 800-872-5283
Sister's Kitchen
Rutland, VT 802-775-2457
Solana Gold Organics
Sebastopol, CA 800-459-1121
Spruce Mountain Blueberries
West Rockport, ME 207- 23-6 35
Star Fine Foods
Fresno, CA 559-498-2900
Stickney & Poor Company
North Andover, MA 508-261-8967
Thistledew Farm
Proctor, WV 800-854-6639
Todhunter Foods
Lake Alfred, FL. 863-956-1116
Todhunter International
West Palm Beach, FL 561-655-8977
Tres Classique
Ukiah, CA 888-644-5127
Tropical
Charlotte, NC 800-220-1413
Unilever Bertolli USA, Inc.
Englewood Cliffs, NJ 201-894-4000
Victoria Packing Corporation
Brooklyn, NY 718-649-2180
Village Imports
Brisbane, CA 888-865-8714
Walker Foods
Los Angeles, CA. 800-966-5199
Webbpak
Trussville, AL 800-655-3500
Widow's Mite Vinegar Company
Washington, DC 877-678-5854
Wild Things
Beverly Hills, CA 310-412-4139
Wild Thymes Farm
Greenville, NY 800-724-2877
Wing's Food Products
Toronto, ON 416-259-2662
Wisconsin Cheese
Melrose Park, IL 708-450-0074
Woeber Mustard Manufacturing
Springfield, OH. 800-548-2929

Apple Cider

Eden Foods Inc
Clinton, MI 800-248-0320

EMERLING INTERNATIONAL FOODS, INC.

Emerling International Foods
Buffalo, NY. 716-833-7381

> We supply food manufacturers and food service
> customers worldwide (since 1988) with bulk in-
> gredients including: Fruits & Vegetables; Juice
> Concentrates; Herbs & Spices; Oils & Vinegars;
> Flavors & Colors; Honey & Molasses. We also
> produce PURE MAPLE SYRUP.

Erbrich-Sewell Products Company
Indianapolis, IN 317-925-6433
Fleischmanns Vinegar
Cerritos, CA 800-443-1067
Gregory-Robinson Speas
Dallas, TX. 214-352-1761
Knouse Foods
Peach Glen, PA 717-677-8181
Live Food Products
Santa Barbara, CA 800-446-1990
Mizkam Americas
Kansas City, MO. 816-483-1700
Nana Mae's Organics
Sebastopol, CA 707-829-7359
National Fruit Product Company
Winchester, VA 540-662-3401
National Fruit Product Company
Lincolnton, NC 704-735-2531

National Vinegar Company
Saint Louis, MO 314-842-2822
Pastorelli Food Products
Chicago, IL 800-767-2829
Reinhart Foods
Markham, ON 905-754-3503
Roanoke Apple Products
Salem, VA 540-375-7341
Sieco USA Corporation
Houston, TX 800-325-9443
Solana Gold Organics
Sebastopol, CA 800-459-1121
Walker Foods
Los Angeles, CA. 800-966-5199
Webbpak
Trussville, AL. 800-655-3500
Widow's Mite Vinegar Company
Washington, DC 877-678-5854

Balsamic

Agrusa, Inc.
Leonia, NJ 201-592-5950
California Olive Oil Corporation
Salem, MA 800-386-6457

EMERLING INTERNATIONAL FOODS, INC.

Emerling International Foods
Buffalo, NY. 716-833-7381

> We supply food manufacturers and food service
> customers worldwide (since 1988) with bulk in-
> gredients including: Fruits & Vegetables; Juice
> Concentrates; Herbs & Spices; Oils & Vinegars;
> Flavors & Colors; Honey & Molasses. We also
> produce PURE MAPLE SYRUP.

Fleischmanns Vinegar
Cerritos, CA 800-443-1067
Golden Whisk
South San Francisco, CA 800-660-5222
Kennedy Candy Company
Kilgore, TX. 800-657-5258
North American Enterprises
Tucson, AZ 800-817-8666
Olive Oil Factory
Watertown, CT 860-945-9549
Organic Planet
San Francisco, CA 415-765-5590
Pastorelli Food Products
Chicago, IL 800-767-2829
Proacec USA
Santa Monica, CA 310-996-7770
Reinhart Foods
Markham, ON 905-754-3503
Restaurant Lulu Gourmet Products
San Francisco, CA 888-693-5800
Rex Wine Vinegar Company
Newark, NJ 973-589-6911
Sieco USA Corporation
Houston, TX 800-325-9443
Unilever Bertolli USA, Inc.
Englewood Cliffs, NJ 201-894-4000
Valley Grain Products
Madera, CA. 559-675-3400
Victoria Packing Corporation
Brooklyn, NY 718-649-2180
Vincent Formusa Company
Chicago, IL 312-421-0485
Wild Thymes Farm
Greenville, NY 800-724-2877

Liquid

Assouline & Ting
Philadelphia, PA 800-521-4491
Clements Foods Company
Oklahoma City, OK 800-654-8355
Colonna Brothers
North Bergen, NJ 201-864-1115

Flavored

Assouline & Ting
Philadelphia, PA 800-521-4491

Malt

Eden Foods Inc
Clinton, MI 800-248-0320
Fleischmanns Vinegar
Cerritos, CA 800-443-1067

Reinhart Foods
Markham, ON 905-754-3503

Raspberry

Reinhart Foods
Markham, ON 905-754-3503
Thistledew Farm
Proctor, WV 800-854-6639

Sherry

National Vinegar Company
Saint Louis, MO 314-842-2822

White Distilled

Big B Distributors
Evansville, IN 812-425-5235
Creole Fermentation Industries
Abbeville, LA 337-898-9377

EMERLING INTERNATIONAL FOODS, INC.

Emerling International Foods
Buffalo, NY. 716-833-7381

> We supply food manufacturers and food service
> customers worldwide (since 1988) with bulk in-
> gredients including: Fruits & Vegetables; Juice
> Concentrates; Herbs & Spices; Oils & Vinegars;
> Flavors & Colors; Honey & Molasses. We also
> produce PURE MAPLE SYRUP.

Fleischmanns Vinegar
Cerritos, CA 800-443-1067
Gregory-Robinson Speas
Dallas, TX. 214-352-1761
Knouse Foods
Peach Glen, PA 717-677-8181
Mizkam Americas
Kansas City, MO. 816-483-1700
National Fruit Product Company
Winchester, VA 540-662-3401
National Fruit Product Company
Lincolnton, NC 704-735-2531
National Vinegar Company
Saint Louis, MO 314-842-2822
National Vinegar Company
Alton, IL 618-465-6532
Pastorelli Food Products
Chicago, IL 800-767-2829
Reinhart Foods
Markham, ON 905-754-3503
Roanoke Apple Products
Salem, VA 540-375-7341
Walker Foods
Los Angeles, CA. 800-966-5199
Webbpak
Trussville, AL 800-655-3500
Wisconsin Cheese
Melrose Park, IL 708-450-0074

Wine

B&G Foods
Parsippany, NJ. 973-401-6500
Eden Foods Inc
Clinton, MI 800-248-0320
Erbrich-Sewell Products Company
Indianapolis, IN 317-925-6433
Fleischmanns Vinegar
Cerritos, CA 800-443-1067
Gregory-Robinson Speas
Dallas, TX. 214-352-1761
Hansen's Juices
Azusa, CA. 626-812-6022
Knouse Foods
Peach Glen, PA 717-677-8181
Mizkan Americas
Mt Prospect, IL 800-323-4358
National Vinegar Company
Saint Louis, MO 314-842-2822
Pastorelli Food Products
Chicago, IL 800-767-2829
Pompeian
Baltimore, MD 800-638-1224
Reinhart Foods
Markham, ON 905-754-3503
Roanoke Apple Products
Salem, VA 540-375-7341
Satiety
Davis, CA 530-757-2699

Sieco USA Corporation
Houston, TX 800-325-9443
Star Fine Foods
Fresno, CA 559-498-2900
Tres Classique
Ukiah, CA 888-644-5127
Victoria Packing Corporation
Brooklyn, NY 718-649-2180
Vincent Formusa Company
Chicago, IL 312-421-0485
Wine Country Kitchens
Napa, CA. 707-252-9463

Snack Foods

General

34 Degrees
Denver, CO 303-861-4818
American Importing Company
Minneapolis, MN 612-331-9226
Bake Crafters Food
Collegedale, TN 800-296-8935
Barbara's Bakery
Petaluma, CA 707-765-2273
Bazaar
River Grove, IL 800-736-1888
Betsy's Cheese Straws
Millbrook, AL 877-902-3141
Big Steer Enterprises
Beaumont, TX 800-421-4951
Blue Crab Bay Company
Melfa, VA 800-221-2722
Brothers International Food Corp
Batavia, NY 888-842-7477
CGI Desserts
Sugar Land, TX 281-240-1200
ConAgra Food Store Brands
Edina, MN 952-469-4981
DCL
Honolulu, HI 808-845-3834
Divvies
South Salem, NY 914-533-0333
Double B Distributors
Lexington, KY 859-255-8822
East Kentucky Foods
Winchester, KY 859-744-2218
Eat Your Heart Out
New York, NY 212-989-8303
Excelline Foods
Chatsworth, CA 818-701-7710
Frito-Lay
Beloit, WI 608-365-7112
GKI Foods
Brighton, MI 248-486-0055
Govadinas Fitness Foods
San Diego, CA 800-900-0108
H.J. Heinz Company
Pittsburgh, PA 800-872-2229
Happy Herberts Food Company
Jersey City, NJ 800-764-2779
Husman Snack Food Company
Cincinnati, OH 859-282-7490
Ideal Snacks
Liberty, NY 845-292-7000
Kellogg Company
Battle Creek, MI 800-962-1413
Kettle Foods
Salem, OR 503-364-0399
King Nut Company
Cleveland, OH 800-860-5464
Kraft Foods
Northfield, IL 800-323-0768
Krema Nut Company
Columbus, OH 800-222-4132
L. Craven & Sons
Melrose Park, IL 800-453-4303
Lance Inc
Charlotte, NC 800-438-1880
Late July Organic Snacks
Barnstable, MA 508-362-5859
LesserEvil Snacks
Tuckahoe, NY 914-779-3000
Lost Trail Root Beer Com
Louisburg, KS 800-748-7765
LRM Packaging
South Hackensack, NJ 201-342-2530
Lynard Company
Stamford, CT 203-323-0231
McIlhenny Company
New Orleans, LA 800-634-9599
Mezza
Lake Forest, IL 888-206-6054
Mister Bee Potato Chip Company
Parkersburg, WV 304-428-6133
Nebraska Popcorn
Clearwater, NE 800-253-6502
Nu-World Amaranth
Naperville, IL 630-369-6851
Ozark Mountain Trading
Westfield, NJ 908-232-6365

Papa Dean's Popcorn
San Antonio, TX 210-822-3625
Peeled Snacks
Brooklyn, NY 212-706-2001
Pippin Snack Pecans
Albany, GA 800-554-6887
Poore Brothers
Boulder, CO 303-546-9939
R.A.B. Food Group LLC
Secaucus, NJ 201-453-5200
Ramsey Popcorn Company
Ramsey, IN 800-624-2060
Rudolph Foods Company
Lima, OH 419-648-3611
Ryt Way Industries
Lakeville, MN 952-469-1417
Sargento Foods Inc
Plymouth, WI 800-243-3737
Seapoint Farms
Costa Mesa, CA 888-722-7098
Setton International Foods
Commack, NY 800-227-4397
Seyfert Foods
Fort Wayne, IN 219-483-9521
Snack King Corporation
City of Industry, CA 800-748-5566
Snack Works/Metrovox Snacks
Maywood, CA 888-224-7110
Snyder's of Hanover
Hanover, PA 717-632-4477
Squire Boone Village
New Albany, IN 888-934-1804
Sugar Foods Corporation
New York, NY 212-753-6900
Sunridge Farms
Salinas, CA 831-755-1430
Terrell's Potato Chip Company
Seattle, WA 800-331-5222
Terri Lynn
Elgin, IL 800-323-0775
Thatcher's Special Popcorn
San Francisco, CA 800-926-2676
Touche Bakery
London, ON 518-455-0044
Tri-Sum Potato Chip Company
Leominster, MA 978-537-4088
Wyandot Inc
Marion, OH 800-992-6368

Cheese Curls

Barbara's Bakery
Petaluma, CA 707-765-2273
Better Meat North
Bay City, MI 989-684-6271
Cheeze Kurls
Grand Rapids, MI 616-784-6095
Cross & Peters Company
Detroit, MI 313-925-4774
Elmer's Fine Foods
New Orleans, LA 504-949-2716
Golden Flake Snack Foods
Birmingham, AL 205-323-6161
Happy's Potato Chip Company
Minneapolis, MN 612-781-3121
Hostess Frito-Lay Company
Cambridge, ON 519-653-5721
McCleary
South Beloit, IL 800-523-8644
Medallion Foods
Newport, AR 870-523-3500
Tri-Sum Potato Chip Company
Leominster, MA 978-537-4088
Variety Foods
Warren, MI 586-268-4900
Wyandot Inc
Marion, OH 800-992-6368

Cheese Twists

Aileen Quirk & Sons
Kansas City, MO 816-471-4580
Alamo Masa Company
Uvalde, TX 800-568-9651
Allen Canning Company
Siloam Springs, AR 800-234-2553

American Blanching Company
Fitzgerald, GA 229-423-4098
American Nut & Chocolate Company
Boston, MA 800-797-6887
American Skin LLC
Burgaw, NC 800-248-7463
Amsnack
Stockton, CA 209-982-5545
Archie Moore's Foods Products
Milford, CT 203-876-5088
Arizona Brands
Phoenix, AZ 602-273-7139
Arizona Pistachio Company
Tulare, CA 800-333-8575
Art's Mexican Products
Kansas City, KS 913-371-2163
Artel
Boisbriand, QC 450-433-1322
Ateeco
Shenandoah, PA 800-233-3170
Austinuts
Austin, TX 877-329-6887
B. Lloyd's Pecans
Barnesville, GA 800-322-6887
Bachman Company
Reading, PA 800-523-8253
Backer's Potato Chip Company
Fulton, MO 573-642-2833
Baldwin-Minkler Farms
Orland, CA 530-865-8080
Ballreich's Potato Chips
Tiffin, OH 800-323-2447
Barrel O'Fun Snacks Foods Company
Perham, MN 218-346-7000
Berberian Nut Company
Stocton, CA 209-465-9181
Bickels Snacks
York, PA 717-843-0738
Bimbo Bakeries
Horsham, PA 800-984-0989
Birds Eye Foods
Berlin, PA 814-267-4641
Birmhall Foods Company
Memphis, TN 901-377-9016
Black Jewell®Popcorn
St Francisville, IL 800-948-2302
Bob's Texas Style Potato Chip
Goodyear, AZ 623-932-6200
Boyd Sausage Company
Washington, IA 319-653-5715
Brandmeyer Popcorn Company
Ankeny, IA 800-568-8276
Bremner Biscuit Company
Denver, CO 800-722-1871
Brennan Snacks Manufacturing
Bogalusa, LA 800-290-7486
Browns' Ice Cream Company
Bowling Green, KY 270-843-9882
Buffalo Bill's Snack Foods
Denver, CO 303-298-0705
C.J. Distributing
Cpu Surf City, NC 800-990-2366
Cafe Fanny
Berkeley, CA 800-441-5413
Calbee America
N. Sebastopol, CA 310-370-2500
California Fruit & Nut
Gustine, CA 888-747-8224
California Garden Products
Lake Forest, CA 949-215-0000
California Snack Foods
South El Monte, CA 626-444-4508
Capri Bagel & Pizza Corporation
Brooklyn, NY 718-497-4431
Carolina Fine Snack Foods
Greensboro, NC 336-605-0773
Cattaneo Brothers
San Luis Obispo, CA 800-243-8537
Central Snacks
Carthage, MS 601-267-3112
Chappaqua Crunch
Marblehead, MA 781-631-8118
Charles' Chips
Calhoun, KY 270-273-3282
Cheese Straws & More
Monroe, LA 800-997-1921

Chelsea Milling Company
Chelsea, MI 734-475-1361
Cher-Make Sausage Company
Manitowoc, WI 800-242-7679
Chickasaw Foods
Memphis, TN 901-323-5467
Chocolate Potpourri
Glenview, IL 888-680-1600
Chooljian Brothers Packing Company
Sanger, CA 559-875-5501
City Farm/Rocky Peanut Company
Detroit, MI 800-437-6825
Cloud Nine
San Leandro, CA............201-358-8588
Colorado Cereal
Fort Collins, CO 970-282-9733
Colorado Popcorn Company
Sterling, CO 800-238-2676
Columbia Empire Farms
Sherwood, OR...............503-554-9060
Columbia Snacks
Columbia, SC 803-776-0133
Commonwealth Brands
Bowling Green, KY 270-781-9100
Community Orchard
Fort Dodge, IA 515-573-8212
Conn's Potato Chip Company
Zanesville, OH 866-486-4615
Consolidated Biscuit Company
Michigan City, IN 219-873-1880
Corbin Foods-Edibowls
Santa Ana, CA 800-695-5655
Corn Poppers
San Diego, CA 858-231-2617
Country Estate Pecans
Sahuarita, AZ 800-473-2267
Cuisinary Fine Foods
Dallas, TX 888-283-5303
Dan-Dee Pretzel & Chip Company
Cleveland, OH 216-341-1764
Dare Foods
Marblehead, MA..............781-639-1808
Dare Foods
Kitchener, ON 800-865-8225
Dellaco Classic Confections
Burlington, WI 262-537-2656
Dieffenbach Potato Chips
Womelsdorf, PA 610-589-2385
Dole Nut Company
Orland, CA 530-865-5511
Door Country Potato Chips
Milwaukee, WI 414-964-1428
Durey-Libby Edible Nuts
Carlstadt, NJ 800-332-6887
Durham/Ellis Pecan Country Store
Comanche, TX 325-356-5291
Eddy's Bakery
Boise, ID 208-377-8100
El Galindo
Austin, TX...................512-478-5756
El Grano De Oro
Pacifica, CA 650-355-8417
Elegant Edibles
Houston, TX 800-227-3226
Ellis Popcorn Company
Murray, KY 800-654-3358
Europa Foods
Saddle Brook, NJ 201-368-8929
Evans Food Products Com pany
Chicago, IL 866-254-7400
Exquisita Tortillas
Edinburg, TX 956-383-6712
Fairchester Snacks Corporation
White Plains, NY 914-761-9430
Fairmont Snacks Group
Cleveland, OH 216-573-2777
Farmers Investment Company
Sahuarita, AZ 520-791-2852
Fastachi
Watertown, MA...............800-466-3022
Fisher's Popcorn
Ocean City, MD 888-395-0335
Foley's Candies
Richmond, BC 888-236-5397
Fontazzi/Metrovox Snacks
Maywood, CA.................800-428-0522
Food Products Corporation
Phoenix, AZ 602-273-7139
Fortella Fortune Cookies
Chicago, IL 312-567-9000
Fresh Roasted Almond Company
Westland, MI.................734-466-9577

Frito-Lay
Jeffersontown, KY 502-491-9616
Frito-Lay
Underwood, IA 712-322-5561
Frito-Lay
Arlington, TX 817-385-5834
Frito-Lay
Irving, TX 972-579-2111
Fun City Popcorn
Las Vegas, NV 800-423-1710
Furukawa Potato Chip Factory
Captain Cook, HI 808-323-3785
G H Bent Company
Milton, MA..................617-698-5945
Garrett Popcorn Shops
Chicago, IL 888-476-7267
Germack Pistachio Company
Detroit, MI 800-872-4006
Gilda Industries
Hialeah, FL 305-887-8286
Glacial Ridge Foods
Redford, MI 612-239-2215
Golden Peanut Company
Apharetta, GA 770-752-8205
Govatos
Wilmington, DE 888-799-5252
Great Western Products Company
Assumption, IL 217-226-3241
Great Western Products Company
Bremen, IN 217-546-4010
Great Western Products Company
Bismarck, MO................573-734-2210
Gulf Pecan Company
Theodore, AL 334-661-2931
Guy's Food
Liberty, MO..................800-821-2405
Guylian USA
Englewood Cliffs, NJ 800-803-4123
Haby's Alsatian Bakery
Castroville, TX 830-931-2118
Hammond's Candies
Denver, CO..................888-226-3999
Happy Herberts Food Company
Jersey City, NJ 800-764-2779
Hazelnut Growers of Oregon
Premium, OR 800-273-4676
Hillson Nut Company
Cleveland, OH 800-333-2818
Hirsch Brothers & Company
Holland, MI..................616-335-5806
Hoody Corporation
Newark, MD 410-632-1766
Hume Specialties
Winston Salem, NC 802-875-3117
Humphrey Company
Cleveland, OH 800-486-3739
Hungry Sultan
Lake Forest, CA 949-215-0000
Imus Ranch Foods
Holtsville, NY 888-284-4687
Ira Middleswarth & Son
Middleburg, PA..............570-837-1431
J&B Sausage Company
Waelder, TX 830-788-7511
J.R. Short Milling Company
Kankakee, IL 800-457-3547
J.W. Haywood & Sons Dairy
Louisville, KY................502-774-2311
Jack Link Snack Foods
Minong, WI..................715-466-2234
Jay Shah Foods
Mississauga, ON 905-696-0172
Jenkins Foods
Detroit, MI 800-800-3286
Jerrell Packaging
Bessemer, AL 205-426-8930
JMS Specialty Foods
Ripon, WI 800-535-5437
Joel Harvey Distributing
Brooklyn, NY 718-629-2690
John B Sanfilippo & Son
Gustine, CA 800-218-3077
John Wm. Macy's Cheesesticks
Elmwood Park, NJ 800-643-0573
Judy's Cream Caramels
Sherwood, OR...............503-819-5080
Kendrick Gourmet Products
Columbus, GA 800-356-1858
Kettle Foods
Salem, OR...................503-364-0399
Kevton Gourmet Tea
Streetman, TX 888-538-8668

Kid's Kookie Company
San Clemente, CA............800-350-7577
Kitty Clover Snacktime Company
Omaha, NE 402-342-7342
Koehler Bakery Company
North Little Rock, AR 800-262-5900
Kraft Foods North America
Suffolk, VA 757-925-3000
La Fronteriza
Toledo, OH 800-897-1772
La Poblana Tamale Factory
Houston, TX 713-921-4760
La Vencedora Products
Los Angeles, CA..............800-327-2572
Lamb-Weston
Pasco, WA...................800-766-7783
Laredo Mexican Foods
Fort Wayne, IN 800-252-7336
LaRosa Bakery
Shrewsbury, NJ 800-527-6722
Longleaf Plantation
Lumberton, MS...............800-421-7370
Longview Meat & Merchandise
Longview, AB.................403-558-3706
Los Angeles Nut House Brands
Los Angeles, CA..............213-481-0134
Louis Trauth Dairy
Newport, KY 800-544-6455
Louise's
Shelbyville, KY 502-633-9700
Ludwick's Frozen Donuts
Grand Rapids, MI.............800-366-8816
Mac's Snacks
Arlington, TX 817-640-5626
MacFarms of Hawaii
Captain Cook, HI 808-328-2435
Madhouse Munchies
Colchester, VT 888-623-4687
Mama Amy's Quality Foods
Mississauga, ON 905-456-0056
Marantha Natural Foods
San Francisco, CA 800-299-0048
Mars M&M
Henderson, NV 888-265-6788
Martin's Potato Chips
Thomasville, PA 800-272-4477
Mauna Loa Macadamia Nut Corporation
Keaau, HI 800-832-9993
Maxin Marketing Corporation
Aliso Viejo, CA...............949-362-1177
Meadow Gold Dairy
Lewiston, ID 208-746-9006
Mental Processes
Atlanta, GA 800-431-4018
Mexican Accent
New Berlin, WI...............262-784-4422
Mexisnax Corporation
El Paso, TX 915-779-5709
Mission Foods/Diane's Foods
McMinnville, OR 503-434-5534
Mitchum Potato Chips
Charlotte, NC 704-372-6744
Molinaro's Fine Italian Foods
Mississauga, ON..............800-268-4959
Mrs. Dog's Products
Tampa, FL 800-267-7364
Mrs. Rio's Corn Products
San Angelo, TX 325-653-5640
Natchez Pecan Shelling Company
Taylorsville, MS 601-785-4333
National Foods
Bronx, NY 800-683-6565
Nichols Pistachio
Hanford, CA 559-688-9463
Nips Potato Chips
Honolulu, HI 808-593-8549
Noah's Potato Chip Company
Alexandria, LA 318-445-0283
Noble Popcorn Farms
Sac City, IA 800-537-9554
Northwest Candy Emporium
Everett, WA..................800-404-7266
Nustef Foods
Mississauga, ON 905-896-3060
Nut House
Mobile, AL 800-633-1306
Nutty Bavarian
Sanford, FL 800-382-4788
Oasis Mediterranean Cuisine
Toledo, OH 419-269-1516
Odessa Tortilla & TamaleFactory
Odessa, TX 800-753-2445

Old Dutch Foods
Roseville, MN 800-989-2447
Old Sacramento Popcorn Company
Sacramento, CA 916-446-1980
Original Nut House Brands
Portales, NM 575-356-6691
Original Nut House Brands
El Paso, TX 800-726-7222
Our Thyme Garden
Cleburne, TX 800-482-4372
Packaged Products Division
Largo, FL 888-833-2247
Paddack Enterprises
Escalon, CA 209-838-1536
Pape's Pecan Company
Seguin, TX 888-688-7273
Pepes Mexican Foods
Rexdale, ON 416-674-0882
Pepperidge Farm
Richmond, UT. 888-737-7374
Perfections by Allan
Owings Mills, MD 800-581-8670
Peterson's Ventures
Salt Lake City, UT 801-359-8880
Picard Peanuts
Windham Centre, ON 888-244-7688
Pickle Cottage
Bucklin, KS. 316-826-3502
Pioneer Snacks
Mankato, MN 507-388-1661
Pizza Products
Farmington Hills, MI 800-600-7482
Plantation Pecan Company
Waterproof, LA 800-477-3226
Plehn's Bakery
St Matthews, KY. 502-896-4438
Pond Brothers Peanut Company
Suffolk, VA 757-539-2356
Poore Brothers
Bluffton, IN. 219-824-9933
Poore Brothers
Phoenix, AZ 800-279-2250
Popcorner
Swansea, IL 618-277-2676
Poppee's Popcorn Company
Elyria, OH. 440-327-0775
Poppin Popcorn
Naples, FL 941-262-1691
Premiere Packing Company
Spokane Valley, WA 888-239-5288
Quality Snack Foods
Alsip, IL 773-548-6140
RDO Foods Company
Grand Forks, ND. 701-746-0611
Reed's Original Beverage Corporation
Los Angeles, CA. 800-997-3337
Rices Potato Chips
Biloxi, MS. 228-396-5775
Ricos Candy Snacks & Bakery
Hialeah, FL 305-885-7392
Ripensa A/S
Lehigh Acres, FL 941-561-5882
Ritts-Chavelle Snack Company
North Hills, CA. 818-830-3305
Rolet Food Products Company
Brooklyn, NY 718-497-0476
Ronald Meyer Popcorn Company
Carnarvon, IA 712-664-2331
Rudy's Tortillas
Dallas, TX. 800-878-2401
Rupari Food Service
Deerfield Beach, FL 800-578-7274
Rural Route 1 Popcorn
Livingston, WI 800-828-8115
Rygmyr Foods
South Saint Paul, MN 800-545-3903
Sachs Nut Company
Clarkton, NC 910-647-4711
Saint Amour/Powerline Foods
Stanton, CA 714-827-5366
San Saba Pecan
San Saba, TX 800-683-2101
Sanarak Paper & Popcorn Supplies
Buffalo, NY. 716-874-5662
Sara Lee
Saint Louis, MO 847-956-7575
Sara Lee Food Service
Haltom City, TX 800-261-4754
Savory Foods
Portsmouth, OH 740-354-6655
Schwans Frozen Foods
Marshall, MN 800-533-5290

Scotsburn Dairy Group
Truro, NS 902-895-4412
Sesaco Corporation
San Antonio, TX. 800-737-2260
Severance Foods
Hartford, CT. 860-724-7063
Shallowford Farms
Yadkinville, NC 800-892-9539
Shearer's Foods
Brewster, OH 800-428-6843
SLB Snacks
Lynn, MA 781-593-4422
Snack Factory
Princeton, NJ 888-683-5400
SnackMasters
Ceres, CA 800-597-9770
Snappy Popcorn Company
Breda, IA. 800-742-0228
Snelgrove Ice Cream Company
Salt Lake City, UT 800-569-0005
Sommer's Food Products
Salisbury, MO 660-388-5511
South Georgia Pecan Company
Valdosta, GA 800-627-6630
Southern Popcorn Company
Memphis, TN 901-362-5238
Southern Roasted Nuts
Fitzgerald, GA 912-423-5616
Sparta Foods
New Brighton, MN 800-700-0809
Spilke's Baking Company
Brooklyn, NY 718-384-2150
Stateline Boyd
Lynn, MA 781-593-4422
Story's Popcorn Company
Charleston, MO. 573-649-2727
Sunnyside Farms
Neligh, NE 402-791-2210
Tabard Farm Potato Chips
Middletown, VA 800-294-7783
Texas Ladies Composite Organization
Stephenville, TX. 888-968-2161
Texas Tito's
San Antonio, TX. 830-626-1123
Tim's Cascade Chips
Algona, WA. 800-533-8467
Tom Sturgis Pretzels
Reading, PA 800-817-3834
Tom's Foods
Corsicana, TX 903-874-6553
Trinidad Benham Company
Denver, CO 303-220-1400
Tuscan Bakery
Portland, OR 800-887-2261
Twin Valley Products
Greenleaf, KS 800-748-7416
Uncle Ralph's Cookie Company
Frederick, MD. 800-422-0626
Uncle Ray's Potato Chips
Detroit, MI 313-834-0800
Universal Blanchers
Blakely, GA. 229-723-4181
Van-Lang Foods
Lombard, IL 630-268-1953
Vande Walle's Candies
Appleton, WI 920-738-7799
Variety Foods
Warren, MI 586-268-4900
Vic's Gourmet Popping Corn Company
Omaha, NE 402-331-2822
Vogel Popcorn
Hamburg, IA 800-831-5818
Wabash Valley Farms
Monon, IN. 800-270-2705
Warden Peanut Company
Portales, NM 575-356-6691
Weaver Popcorn Company
Indianapolis, IN 800-999-2365
Wells' Dairy
Le Mars, IA. 800-942-3800
Wise Foods
Carlstadt, NJ 201-507-0015
Wise Foods
Berwick, PA 570-759-4000
Wise Foods
Bristol, TN 864-585-9011
Wynnewood Pecan Company
Wynnewood, OK. 800-892-4985
Yarnell Ice Cream Company
Searcy, AR 800-766-2414
Yick Lung Company
Honolulu, HI 808-841-3611

Young Pecan
Las Cruces, NM 575-524-4321
Young Pecan Company
Florence, SC 800-829-6864
Zapp's Chips
Gramercy, LA 800-349-2447
Zapp's Potato Chips
Gramercy, LA 800-349-2447

Chips

Bagel Chips

Harlan Bakeries
Avon, IN 317-272-3600
Royal Court Cookie Company
North Hollywood, CA 800-730-2545
Soloman Baking Company
Denver, CO 303-371-2777
Weaver Nut Company
Ephrata, PA 717-738-3781

Baked

Artesia Tortilla Factory
Artesia, NM. 505-746-2808
Azteca Foods
Summit Argo, IL 708-563-6600
C.J. Vitner Company
Chicago, IL 773-523-7900
Frito-Lay
San Antonio, TX. 210-662-2100
Frito-Lay
Rosenberg, TX 281-232-2363
Frito-Lay
Dearborn, MI 313-271-3000
Frito-Lay
Wooster, OH 330-262-0387
Frito-Lay
Orlando, FL 407-295-1810
Frito-Lay
Casa Grande, AZ. 520-836-2363
Frito-Lay
Williamsport, PA 570-326-4136
Frito-Lay
Bakersfield, CA 661-328-6000
Frito-Lay
Charlotte, NC 704-588-2840
Frito-Lay
Frankfort, IN 765-659-1831
Frito-Lay
Topeka, KS 785-266-2439
Frito-Lay
Rancho Cucamonga, CA 909-948-3600
Frito-Lay
Irving, TX 972-579-2111
Golden Flake Snack Foods
Ocala, FL. 800-239-2447
Golden Fluff Popcorn Company
Lakewood, NJ 732-367-5448
Harlan Bakeries
Avon, IN. 317-272-3600
Hostess Frito-Lay Company
Cambridge, ON. 519-653-5721
Humpty Dumpty Snack Foods
Lachine, QC 800-361-6440
Imus Ranch Foods
Holtsville, NY 888-284-4687
Interstate Brands Corporation/Wonder Bread Bakery
St Louis, MO. 314-385-1600
Kettle Foods
Salem, OR. 503-364-0399
La Canasta Mexican Food Products
Phoenix, AZ 602-269-7721
La Fronteriza
Toledo, OH 800-897-1772
La Mexicana
Chicago, IL 773-247-5443
Laredo Mexican Foods
Fort Wayne, IN 800-252-7336
Li'l Guy Foods
Kansas City, MO 800-886-8226
Luna's Tortillas
Dallas, TX. 214-747-2661
Medallion Foods
Newport, AR 870-523-3500
Mexican Accent
New Berlin, WI 262-784-4422
Mexican Foods
Indianapolis, IN 317-236-1090
Mission Foods
Jefferson, GA 800-240-2447

Olde Tyme Food Corporation
East Longmeadow, MA 800-356-6533
Ozuna Food Products Corporation
Sunnyvale, CA 408-400-0495
Pepes Mexican Foods
Rexdale, ON .416-674-0882
Puebla Foods
Passaic, NJ 973-473-0201
R&J Farms
West Salem, OH 419-846-3179
Rubschlager Baking Corporation
Chicago, IL 773-826-1245
Rudy's Tortillas
Dallas, TX .800-878-2401
S&K Industries
Manassas Park, VA 703-369-0232
Severance Foods
Hartford, CT 860-724-7063
Shallowford Farms
Yadkinville, NC 800-892-9539
Spanish Gardens Food Manufacturing
Kansas City, KS 913-831-4242
Tom's Foods
Corsicana, TX 903-874-6553
Tom's Snacks Company
Charlotte, NC 800-995-2623
Troyer Farms
Waterford, PA 724-746-1162
Weaver Potato Chip Company
Lincoln, NE. 402-423-6625
Westbrae Natural Foods
Garden City, NY 800-434-4246
Wyandot
Marion, OH. 800-992-6368

Banana

American Importing Company
Minneapolis, MN 612-331-9226
National Food Corporation
Medley, FL 305-884-2020

Cassava

National Food Corporation
Medley, FL 305-884-2020
Tantos Foods International
Richmond Hill, ON. 905-763-9994

Chocolate

Ghirardelli Chocolate Company
Short Hills, NJ. 800-877-9338
NSpired Natural Foods
Melville, NY 631-845-4689
Sheryl's Chocolate Creations
Hicksville, NY 888-882-2462
St. Charles Trading
Lake Saint Louis, MO. 800-336-1333
Wilbur Chocolate
Lititz, PA 800-233-0139

Corn

C.J. Vitner Company
Chicago, IL 773-523-7900
Delicious Popcorn Company
Waupaca, WI 715-258-7683
Frito-Lay
San Antonio, TX 210-662-2100
Frito-Lay
Rosenberg, TX 281-232-2363
Frito-Lay
Dearborn, MI 313-271-3000
Frito-Lay
Wooster, OH 330-262-0387
Frito-Lay
Orlando, FL. 407-295-1810
Frito-Lay
Casa Grande, AZ. 520-836-2363
Frito-Lay
Williamsport, PA. 570-326-4136
Frito-Lay
Beloit, WI 608-365-7112
Frito-Lay
Charlotte, NC 704-588-2840
Frito-Lay
Frankfort, IN 765-659-1831
Frito-Lay
Topeka, KS 785-266-2439
Golden Flake Snack Foods
Birmingham, AL. 205-323-6161

Hostess Frito-Lay Company
Cambridge, ON. 519-653-5721
La Mexicana
Chicago, IL 773-247-5443
Martin's Famous Pastries
Chambersburg, PA 717-263-9580
McCleary
South Beloit, IL 800-523-8644
Oak Creek Farms
Edgar, NE 402-224-3038
Pippin Snack Pecans
Albany, GA 800-554-6887
S&K Industries
Manassas Park, VA 703-369-0232
Tom's Snacks Company
Charlotte, NC 800-995-2623
Weaver Potato Chip Company
Lincoln, NE. 402-423-6625
Wyandot
Marion, OH. 800-992-6368
Xochitl
Dallas, TX 214-800-3551

Fried

Archie Moore's Foods Products
Milford, CT. 203-876-5088
Better Meat North
Bay City, MI 989-684-6271
Bickel's Potato Chip Company
Manheim, PA 717-665-2002
Birds Eye Foods
Berlin, PA 814-267-4641
C.J. Vitner Company
Chicago, IL 773-523-7900
Calbee America
N. Sebastopol, CA 310-370-2500
Cross & Peters Company
Detroit, MI 313-925-4774
Del Rey Tortilleria
Chicago, IL 800-446-1459
Delicious Popcorn Company
Waupaca, WI 715-258-7683
El Galindo
Austin, TX. 512-478-5756
El-Milagro
Chicago, IL 773-847-9407
Elmer's Fine Foods
New Orleans, LA 504-949-2716
Frito-Lay
San Antonio, TX 210-662-2100
Frito-Lay
Rosenberg, TX 281-232-2363
Frito-Lay
Dearborn, MI 313-271-3000
Frito-Lay
Wooster, OH 330-262-0387
Frito-Lay
Orlando, FL. 407-295-1810
Frito-Lay
Casa Grande, AZ. 520-836-2363
Frito-Lay
Williamsport, PA. 570-326-4136
Frito-Lay
Beloit, WI 608-365-7112
Frito-Lay
Bakersfield, CA 661-328-6000
Frito-Lay
Charlotte, NC 704-588-2840
Frito-Lay
Frankfort, IN 765-659-1831
Frito-Lay
Topeka, KS 785-266-2439
Frito-Lay
Rancho Cucamonga, CA 909-948-3600
Frito-Lay
Irving, TX. 972-579-2111
Golden Flake Snack Foods
Ocala, FL. 800-239-2447
Granite State Potato Chip Company
Salem, NH. 603-898-2171
Happy's Potato Chip Company
Minneapolis, MN 612-781-3121
Hartley's Potato Chip Company
Lewistown, PA 717-248-0526
Hostess Frito-Lay Company
Cambridge, ON. 519-653-5721
Humpty Dumpty Snack Foods
Lachine, QC 800-361-6440
Jays Foods
Chicago, IL 773-731-8400

Jones Potato Chip Company
Mansfield, OH 800-466-9424
Kettle Foods
Salem, OR 503-364-0399
Kitch'n Cook'd Potato Chip Company
Staunton, VA 800-752-1535
La Fronteriza
Toledo, OH 800-897-1772
La Mexicana
Chicago, IL 773-247-5443
La Vencedora Products
Los Angeles, CA 800-327-2572
Laredo Mexican Foods
Fort Wayne, IN 800-252-7336
Martin's Famous Pastries
Chambersburg, PA 717-263-9580
Maui Potato Chips
Kahului, HI 808-877-3652
Medallion Foods
Newport, AR 870-523-3500
Mexican Accent
New Berlin, WI 262-784-4422
Mexican Foods
Indianapolis, IN 317-236-1090
Middleswarth Potato Chips
Middleburg, PA 570-837-1431
Miguel's Stowe Away
Stowe, VT 800-448-6517
Mrs. Fisher's
Rockford, IL 815-964-9114
National Food Corporation
Medley, FL 305-884-2020
Olde Tyme Food Corporation
East Longmeadow, MA 800-356-6533
Ozuna Food Products Corporation
Sunnyvale, CA 408-400-0495
Peerless Potato Chips
Gary, IN. 219-885-6843
Pepes Mexican Foods
Rexdale, ON 416-674-0882
Pillsbury
Hannibal, MO 800-775-4777
Puebla Foods
Passaic, NJ 973-473-0201
Randag & Associates Inc
Elmhurst, IL 630-530-2830
Revonah Pretzel Bakery
Hanover, PA 717-630-2883
Rubschlager Baking Corporation
Chicago, IL 773-826-1245
S&K Industries
Manassas Park, VA 703-369-0232
Seasons' Enterprises
Addison, IL 630-628-0211
Severance Foods
Hartford, CT 860-724-7063
Shearer's Foods
Brewster, OH 800-428-6843
Spanish Gardens Food Manufacturing
Kansas City, KS 913-831-4242
Sun Pac Foods
Brampton, ON. 905-792-2700
Tabard Farm Potato Chips
Middletown, VA 800-294-7783
Terrell's Potato Chip Company
Seattle, WA 800-331-5222
Tim's Cascade Chips
Algona, WA. 800-533-8467
Tom's Foods
Columbus, GA 706-323-2721
Tom's Snacks Company
Charlotte, NC 800-995-2623
Troyer Farms
Waterford, PA 724-746-1162
Vincent Potato Chip Company
Marblehead, MA 978-745-1505
Wachusett Potato Chip Company
Fitchburg, MA 978-342-6038
Weaver Potato Chip Company
Lincoln, NE. 402-423-6625
Westbrae Natural Foods
Garden City, NY 800-434-4246
Wyandot
Marion, OH. 800-992-6368
Yum Yum Potato Chips
Warwick, QC 800-567-5792

Nacho

Arizona Beverage Company
New Hyde Park, NY 800-832-3775

Luna's Tortillas
Dallas, TX 214-747-2661
Mexican Foods
Indianapolis, IN 317-236-1090
Olde Tyme Food Corporation
East Longmeadow, MA 800-356-6533
Ozuna Food Products Corporation
Sunnyvale, CA 408-400-0495

Pita

Argo Fine Foods
Saint James, NY 631-703-0443
Regco Corporation
Haverhill, MA. 978-521-4370
Regenie's All Natural and Organic Snacks
Haverhill, MA. 978-521-4370
Sensible Portions
Wayne, NJ 973-283-9220
Soloman Baking Company
Denver, CO .303-371-2777

Plantain

National Food Corporation
Medley, FL 305-884-2020

Potato

All American Snacks
Midland, TX .800-840-2455
ARA Food Corporation
Miami, FL 800-533-8831
Bachman Company
Reading, PA .800-523-8253
Barbara's Bakery
Petaluma, CA 707-765-2273
Better Meat North
Bay City, MI .989-684-6271
Bickel's of York Snack Foods
York, PA 800-233-1933
Bickel's Potato Chip Company
Manheim, PA 717-665-2002
Birds Eye Foods
Berlin, PA 814-267-4641
Brad's Taste of New York
Floral Park, NY 516-354-9004
Cactus-Creek
Dallas, TX 800-471-7723
Covered Bridge Potato Chip Company
Waterville, NB 506-375-2447
Cross & Peters Company
Detroit, MI 313-925-4774
Deep River Snacks
Old Lyme, CT 860-434-7347
Delicious Popcorn Company
Waupaca, WI. 715-258-7683
Eli's Bread
New York, NY 212-831-4800
Elmer's Fine Foods
New Orleans, LA 504-949-2716
Frito-Lay
Rosenberg, TX 281-232-2363
Frito-Lay
Dearborn, MI 313-271-3000
Frito-Lay
Wooster, OH 330-262-0387
Frito-Lay
Orlando, FL. 407-295-1810
Frito-Lay
Casa Grande, AZ. 520-836-2363
Frito-Lay
Beloit, WI 608-365-7112
Frito-Lay
Charlotte, NC 704-588-2840
Frito-Lay
Frankfort, IN 765-659-1831
Frito-Lay
Topeka, KS .785-266-2439
Go-Rachel.com
Minneapolis, MN 952-884-2305
Golden Flake Snack Foods
Birmingham, AL 205-323-6161
Golden Flake Snack Foods
Ocala, FL. 800-239-2447
Grippo's Food Products
Cincinnati, OH 513-923-1900
H.E. Butt Grocery Company
San Antonio, TX. 800-432-3113
Hanover Foods Corporation
Hanover, PA 717-632-6000
Happy's Potato Chip Company
Minneapolis, MN 612-781-3121

Hartley's Potato Chip Company
Lewistown, PA 717-248-0526
Herr's Foods
Nottingham, PA. 800-344-3777
Hostess Frito-Lay Company
Cambridge, ON 519-653-5721
Humpty Dumpty Snack Foods
Scarborough, ME 800-274-2447
Husman Snack Food Company
Cincinnati, OH 859-282-7490
Jays Foods
Chicago, IL .773-731-8400
Jones Potato Chip Company
Mansfield, OH 800-466-9424
Kitch'n Cook'd Potato Chip Company
Staunton, VA. 800-752-1535
Knese Enterprise
Floral Park, NY 516-354-9004
Kraft Foods
East Hanover, NJ 973-503-2000
Lance Inc
Charlotte, NC 800-438-1880
Martin's Famous Pastries
Chambersburg, PA 717-263-9580
Maui Potato Chips
Kahului, HI .808-877-3652
McCleary
South Beloit, IL 800-523-8644
Middleswarth Potato Chips
Middleburg, PA. 570-837-1431
Mike-Sell's Potato Chip Company
Dayton, OH. 800-853-9437
Mister Bee Potato Chip Company
Parkersburg, WV. 304-428-6133
Mrs. Fisher's
Rockford, IL 815-964-9114
Ole Salty's of Rockford
Rockford, IL 815-963-3355
OSEM USA
Englewood Cliffs, NJ 201-871-4433
Pippin Snack Pecans
Albany, GA .800-554-6887
Poore Brothers
Boulder, CO 303-546-9939
Popchips
San Francisco, CA 866-217-9327
Proctor & Gamble Company
Cincinnati, OH 513-983-1100
Randag & Associates Inc
Elmhurst, IL 630-530-2830
Revonah Pretzel Bakery
Hanover, PA 717-630-2883
Rock-N-Roll Gourmet
Marina Del Ray, CA 424-228-4901
Route 11 Potato Chips
Mt Jackson, VA. 800-294-7783
Snak King Corporation
City of Industry, CA 626-336-7711
Snyder's of Hanover
Hanover, PA 717-632-4477
Sterzing Food Company
Burlington, IA. 800-754-8467
Terrell's Potato Chip Company
Seattle, WA 800-331-5222
Thomasson's Potato Chip Company
Mansfield, OH 800-466-9424
Tom's Foods
Columbus, GA 706-323-2721
Tom's Snacks Company
Charlotte, NC 800-995-2623
Tri-Sum Potato Chip Company
Leominster, MA 978-537-4088
Troyer Farms
Waterford, PA 724-746-1162
Troyer Potato Products
Waterford, PA 814-796-2611
Utz Quality Foods
Hanover, PA 800-367-7629
Vincent Potato Chip Company
Marblehead, MA. 978-745-1505
Wachusett Potato Chip Company
Fitchburg, MA 978-342-6038
Weaver Potato Chip Company
Lincoln, NE. 402-423-6625
Westbrae Natural Foods
Garden City, NY 800-434-4246
Wise Foods
Kennesaw, GA 770-426-5821
Wyandot
Marion, OH. 800-992-6368
Wysong Corporation
Midland, MI 800-748-0188

Yum Yum Potato Chips
Warwick, QC. 800-567-5792

Baked

Wyandot Inc
Marion, OH 800-992-6368

Barbecue

Mister Bee Potato Chip Company
Parkersburg, WV. 304-428-6133

Low-Fat

Snack Appeal
Fairfax, VA .540-383-0561

No Salt

Wachusett Potato Chip Company
Fitchburg, MA 978-342-6038

Salted

International Trading Company
Houston, TX 713-224-5901

Sour Cream & Onion

Mister Bee Potato Chip Company
Parkersburg, WV. 304-428-6133

Taco

Li'l Guy Foods
Kansas City, MO. 800-886-8226

Tortilla

ARA Food Corporation
Miami, FL 800-533-8831
Arizona Cowboy
Phoenix, AZ 800-529-8627
Azteca Foods
Summit Argo, IL. 708-563-6600
Bachman Company
Reading, PA 800-523-8253
Bake Crafters Food
Collegedale, TN 800-296-8935
C.J. Vitner Company
Chicago, IL .773-523-7900
Cactus-Creek
Dallas, TX 800-471-7723
Del Rey Tortilleria
Chicago, IL .800-446-1459
El Matador Foods
Baytown, TX 281-838-1375
El-Milagro
Chicago, IL .773-847-9407
Festida Food
Cedar Springs, MI. 616-696-0400
Food Should Taste Good
Needham Heights, MA 781-455-8500
Frito-Lay
Rosenberg, TX 281-232-2363
Frito-Lay
Dearborn, MI 313-271-3000
Frito-Lay
Wooster, OH 330-262-0387
Frito-Lay
Orlando, FL. 407-295-1810
Frito-Lay
Casa Grande, AZ. 520-836-2363
Frito-Lay
Williamsport, PA. 570-326-4136
Frito-Lay
Frankfort, IN 765-659-1831
Frito-Lay
Topeka, KS .785-266-2439
Frog Ranch Foods
Glouster, OH. 800-742-2488
Golden Flake Snack Foods
Birmingham, AL 205-323-6161
Golden Flake Snack Foods
Ocala, FL. 800-239-2447
Golden Fluff Popcorn Company
Lakewood, NJ 732-367-5448
Herr's Foods
Nottingham, PA. 800-344-3777
Hostess Frito-Lay Company
Cambridge, ON 519-653-5721
Husman Snack Food Company
Cincinnati, OH 859-282-7490
Jays Foods
Chicago, IL .773-731-8400

Kraft Foods
  East Hanover, NJ 973-503-2000
La Canasta Mexican Food Products
  Phoenix, AZ 602-269-7721
La Mexicana
  Chicago, IL 773-247-5443
Lance Inc
  Charlotte, NC 800-438-1880
Los Amigos Tortilla Manufacturing
  Atlanta, GA 800-969-8226
Martin's Famous Pastries
  Chambersburg, PA 717-263-9580
McCleary
  South Beloit, IL 800-523-8644
Medallion Foods
  Newport, AR....................870-523-3500
Mexi-Snax
  Addison, IL 800-974-7629
Mexican Food Products Corporation
  San Francisco, CA 415-648-8550
Mexican Foods
  Indianapolis, IN 317-236-1090
Miguel's Stowe Away
  Stowe, VT 800-448-6517
Mike-Sell's Potato Chip Company
  Dayton, OH.....................800-853-9437
Mission Foods
  Jefferson, GA 800-240-2447
Mission Foodservice
  Oldsmar, FL 800-443-7994
Nature Star Foods
  Hinsdale, IL 630-323-8888
Ozuna Food Products Corporation
  Sunnyvale, CA 408-400-0495
Plocky's Fine Snacks
  Hinsdale, IL 630-323-8888
Puebla Foods
  Passaic, NJ 973-473-0201
RW Garcia Company
  San Jose, CA....................408-287-4616
S&K Industries
  Manassas Park, VA..............703-369-0232
Snak King Corporation
  City of Industry, CA 626-336-7711
Snyder's of Hanover
  Hanover, PA 717-632-4477
Spanish Gardens Food Manufacturing
  Kansas City, KS 913-831-4242
Sun Pac Foods
  Brampton, ON...................905-792-2700
T.W. Garner Food Company
  Winston Salem, NC..............800-476-7383
Tom's Snacks Company
  Charlotte, NC 800-995-2623
Troyer Farms
  Waterford, PA 724-746-1162
Tumaro's Gourmet Tortillas & Snacks
  Edison, NJ 800-777-6317
Utz Quality Foods
  Hanover, PA 800-367-7629
Valley of Mexico
  Norwalk, CT 203-348-0402
Variety Foods
  Warren, MI 586-268-4900
Weaver Potato Chip Company
  Lincoln, NE.....................402-423-6625
Westbrae Natural Foods
  Garden City, NY 800-434-4246
Wise Foods
  Kennesaw, GA 770-426-5821
Wyandot
  Marion, OH.....................800-992-6368
Wyandot Inc
  Marion, OH.....................800-992-6368

Corn Nuts

California Nuggets
  Ripon, CA.......................209-599-7131
Dakota Gourmet
  Wahpeton, ND....................800-727-6663
Hialeah Products Company
  Hollywood, FL...................800-923-3379
Pilgrim's Pride
  Lufkin, TX 936-639-1174
Setton International Foods
  Commack, NY 800-227-4397

Popcorn

A La Carte
  Chicago, IL 800-722-2370
American Pop Corn Company
  Sioux City, IA...................712-239-1232
Angelic Gourmet Inc
  Naples, NY 585-374-9783
Bachman Company
  Reading, PA 800-523-8253
Better Meat North
  Bay City, MI 989-684-6271
Birds Eye Foods
  Berlin, PA 814-267-4641
Black Jewell Popcorn
  St Francisville, IL 618-948-2303
Black Jewell®Popcorn
  St Francisville, IL 800-948-2302
Black Shield
  Albuquerque, NM................800-653-9357
Brandmeyer Popcorn Company
  Ankeny, IA 800-568-8276
C&F Foods
  City of Industry, CA 626-723-1000
C.J. Vitner Company
  Chicago, IL.....................773-523-7900
Cape Cod Potato Chip Company
  Hyannis, MA....................508-775-3917
Carmadhy's Foods
  Waterloo, ON 519-746-0551
Casa De Oro Foods
  Omaha, NE 402-339-7740
Cheeze Kurls
  Grand Rapids, MI...............616-784-6095
Chester Inc.
  Valparaiso, IN 800-778-1131
China Doll Company
  Saraland, AL....................251-457-7641
CJ Dannemiller Company
  Norton, OH.....................800-624-8671
CJ Vitner Company
  Chicago, IL.....................773-523-7900
Cloud Nine
  San Leandro, CA.................201-358-8588
Clutter Farms
  Gambier, OH....................740-427-3515
Colorado Cereal
  Fort Collins, CO 970-282-9733
Colorado Popcorn Company
  Sterling, CO 800-238-2676
ConAgra Foods/International Home Foods
  Niagara Falls, ON...............905-356-2661
ConAgra Snack Foods Group/Act II Popcorn
  Edina, MN......................800-328-6286
Convenience Food Suppliers
  Durham, NC 800-922-1586
Corn Poppers
  San Diego, CA...................858-231-2617
Crickle Company
  Thomasville, GA.................800-237-8689

Cross & Peters Company
  Detroit, MI 313-925-4774
Deep River Snacks
  Old Lyme, CT 860-434-7347
Delicious Popcorn Company
  Waupaca, WI....................715-258-7683
Ellis Popcorn Company
  Murray, KY 800-654-3358
Elmer's Fine Foods
  New Orleans, LA 504-949-2716
Fancy Farms Popcorn
  Bernie, MO.....................800-833-8154
Fernando C Pujals & Bros
  San Juan, PR....................787-792-3080
Fireworks Popcorn Company
  Belgium, WI 877-668-4800
Fizzle Flat Farm
  Yale, IL.........................618-793-2060
Frankford Candy & Chocolate Company
  Philadelphia, PA 800-523-9090
Frito-Lay
  Dallas, TX......................800-352-4477
Fun City Popcorn
  Las Vegas, NV 800-423-1710
FunkyChunky
  Edina, MN......................888-473-8659
Gaslamp Popcorn Company
  Riverside, CA....................877-237-8276
General Mills
  Minneapolis, MN 800-248-7310
Gilster Mary Lee/Jasper Foods
  Jasper, MO 800-777-2168
Gilster-Mary Lee Corporation
  Chester, IL......................800-851-5371
Golden Fluff Popcorn Company
  Lakewood, NJ...................732-367-5448
Good Health Natural Foods
  Northport, NY...................631-261-2111
Granite State Potato Chip Company
  Salem, NH......................603-898-2171
Great American Popcorn Works of Pennsylvania
  Telford, PA 800-542-2676
Great Western Products Company
  Assumption, IL..................217-226-3241
Great Western Products Company
  Bremen, IN.....................217-546-4010
Great Western Products Company
  Bismarck, MO...................573-734-2210
Hain Celestial Group
  Melville, NY.....................800-434-4246
Happy Herberts Food Company
  Jersey City, NJ..................800-764-2779
Happy's Potato Chip Company
  Minneapolis, MN 612-781-3121
Heartland Gourmet Popcorn
  Elk Grove Village, IL 866-489-4676
Herr's Foods
  Nottingham, PA.................800-344-3777
Hostess Frito-Lay Company
  Cambridge, ON..................519-653-5721
Houston Harvest
  Franklin Park, IL................800-548-5896
Howards of Colorado
  Denver, CO.....................970-332-5662
Humpty Dumpty Snack Foods
  Scarborough, ME 800-274-2447
Humpty Dumpty Snack Foods
  Lachine, QC 800-361-6440
International Home Foods
  Milton, PA......................973-359-9920
International Service Group
  Alpharetta, GA 770-518-0988
Jays Foods
  Chicago, IL 773-731-8400

Jerry's Nut House
Denver, CO 888-214-0747
Jess Jones Farms
Dixon, CA. .707-678-3839
John J. Nissen Baking Company
Portland, ME. 207-775-3460
Kettle Foods
Salem, OR. .503-364-0399
Keystone Food Products
Easton, PA. 800-523-9426
Kloss Manufacturing Company
Allentown, PA. 800-445-7100
Koeze Company
Wyoming, MI 800-555-3909
Kornfections
Chantilly, VA. 800-469-8886
Krispy Kernels
Sainte Foy, QC 418-658-1515
Lance Inc
Charlotte, NC 800-438-1880
Lincoln Snacks Company
Stamford, CT. 800-872-7622
Lucks Food Decorating Company
Tacoma, WA 206-674-7200
Metzger Popcorn Company
Delphos, OH 800-819-6072
Michele's Chocolate Truffles
Clackamas, OR 800-656-7112
Midwest/Northern
Minneapolis, MN 800-328-5502
Mike-Sell's Potato Chip Company
Dayton, OH. 800-853-9437
Mills Brothers International
Tukwila, WA 206-575-3000
Mormac Corporation
North Loup, NE 800-445-2868
Morrison Farms
Clearwater, NE 402-887-5335
Nebraska Popcorn
Clearwater, NE 800-253-6502
Newman's Own
Westport, CT. 203-222-0136
Noble Popcorn Farms
Sac City, IA 800-537-9554
Nutra Nuts
Commerce, CA 323-260-7457
Old Sacramento Popcorn Company
Sacramento, CA 916-446-1980
Olson Livestock & Seed
Haigler, NE 308-297-3283
Oogie's Snacks LLC
Denver, CO .303-455-2107
Organic Planet
San Francisco, CA 415-765-5590
Papa Dean's Popcorn
San Antonio, TX. 210-822-3625
Patsy's Candies
Colorado Springs, CO. 866-372-8797
Pleasant Grove Farms
Pleasant Grove, CA 916-655-3391
Popcorn Connection
North Hollywood, CA 800-852-2676
Popcorn World
Kansas City, MO. 800-443-8226
Popcorner
Swansea, IL. 618-277-2676
Poppers Supply Company
Portland, OR 503-239-3792
Preston Farms
Palmyra, IN. 866-767-7464
Purity Foods
Okemos, MI 800-997-7358
Quality Candy
Milwaukee, WI 800-972-2658
R&J Farms
West Salem, OH 419-846-3179
Ramsey Popcorn Company
Ramsey, IN .800-624-2060
Randag & Associates Inc
Elmhurst, IL 630-530-2830
Reist Popcorn Company
Mt Joy, PA. .717-653-8078
Richard Green Company
Indianapolis, IN 317-972-0941
Rivard Popcorn Products
Landisville, PA 717-898-7131
Roberts Ferry Nut Company
Waterford, CA 209-874-3247
Rock-N-Roll Gourmet
Marina Del Ray, CA 424-228-4901
Rocky Mountain Popcorn Company
Wheat Ridge, CO 303-278-4352

Rygmyr Foods
South Saint Paul, MN 800-545-3903
Sahagian & Associates
Oak Park, IL 800-327-9273
Shallowford Farms
Yadkinville, NC 800-892-9539
Shepherd Farms
South Beloit, IL 800-383-2676
Sheryl's Chocolate Creations
Hicksville, NY 888-882-2462
Snack Works/Metrovox Snacks
Maywood, CA 888-224-7110
Snak King Corporation
City of Industry, CA 626-336-7711
Snappy Popcorn Company
Breda, IA. 800-742-0228
Stock Popcorn Company
Lake View, IA 712-657-2811
Sugar Plum
Kingston, PA. 800-447-8427
Tee Lee Popcorn Corp
Shannon, IL. 800-578-2363
Todd's
Vernon, CA .800-938-6337
Treier Popcorn Farms
Bloomdale, OH 419-454-2811
Tri-Sum Potato Chip Company
Leominster, MA 978-537-4088
Trinidad Benham Company
Denver, CO .303-220-1400
Troyer Farms
Waterford, PA 724-746-1162
Utz Quality Foods
Hanover, PA 800-367-7629
Vande Walle's Candies
Appleton, WI 920-738-7799
Variety Foods
Warren, MI .586-268-4900
Velvet Creme Popcorn Company
Westwood, KS. 888-553-6708
Ventura Foods   Production Plant
Los Angeles, CA. 323-265-4300
Vogel Popcorn
Lake View, IA 712-657-8561
Vogel Popcorn
Hamburg, IA 800-831-5818
Wabash Valley Farms
Monon, IN. .800-270-2705
Weaver Popcorn Company
Indianapolis, IN 800-999-2365
Weaver Potato Chip Company
Lincoln, NE 402-423-6625
Westbrae Natural Foods
Garden City, NY 800-434-4246
Westlam Foods
Chino, CA 800-722-9519
Widman Popcorn Company
Chapman, NE 308-986-2293
Worldwide Sourcing LLC
Incline Village, NV 775-833-1480
Yaya's
Corona Del Mar, CA 949-675-7708

Coated

Black Shield
Albuquerque, NM 800-653-9357
Bruno's Cajun Foods & Snacks
Slidell, LA. .985-726-0544
Golden Fluff Popcorn Company
Lakewood, NJ 732-367-5448
Kennedy Candy Company
Kilgore, TX. 800-657-5258
Lou-Retta's Custom Chocolates
Buffalo, NY. 716-833-7111

Flavored

Black Shield
Albuquerque, NM 800-653-9357
Dale and Thomas Popcorn
Englewood, NJ 800-767-4444
DGZ Chocolates
Houston, TX. 877-949-9444
Eda's Sugarfree Candies
Philadelphia, PA 215-324-3412
Golden Fluff Popcorn Company
Lakewood, NJ 732-367-5448
Happy's Potato Chip Company
Minneapolis, MN 612-781-3121
Jody's Gourmet Popcorn
Virginia Beach, VA 866-797-5639

Midwest/Northern
Minneapolis, MN 800-328-5502
Oogie's Snacks LLC
Denver, CO .303-455-2107
Popcorn World
Kansas City, MO. 800-443-8226
Rivard Popcorn Products
Landisville, PA 717-898-7131
Tri-Sum Potato Chip Company
Leominster, MA 978-537-4088
Troyer Potato Products
Waterford, PA 814-796-2611
Velvet Creme Popcorn Company
Westwood, KS. 888-553-6708
Victoria's Catered Traditions
Manteca, CA 877-272-5208
Yaya's
Corona Del Mar, CA 949-675-7708

Pork Rinds

Better Meat North
Bay City, MI 989-684-6271
Bruno's Cajun Foods & Snacks
Slidell, LA. .985-726-0544
Golden Flake Snack Foods
Birmingham, AL. 205-323-6161
National Food Corporation
Medley, FL .305-884-2020
Rudolph Foods
Dallas, TX. .214-638-2204
Rudolph Foods Company
Lima, OH. 419-648-3611
Sau-Sea Foods
Tarrytown, NY 914-631-1717
Tom's Snacks Company
Charlotte, NC 800-995-2623

Bacon

Rudolph Foods Company
Lima, OH. 419-648-3611

Potato Sticks

Golden Fluff Popcorn Company
Lakewood, NJ 732-367-5448

Pretzels

All American Snacks
Midland, TX 800-840-2455
All Wrapped Up
Lauderhill, FL. 800-891-2194
Amoroso's Baking Company
Philadelphia, PA 800-377-6557
Anderson Bakery Company
Lancaster, PA 800-732-0089
Angelic Gourmet Inc
Naples, FL .585-374-9783
Bachman Company
Reading, PA 800-523-8253
Bake Crafters Food
Collegedale, TN 800-296-8935
Benzel's Pretzel Bakery
Altoona, PA. 800-344-4438
Brad's Taste of New York
Floral Park, NY 516-354-9004
Buckeye Pretzel Company
Williamsport, PA. 800-257-6029
California Pretzel Company
Visalia, CA .559-651-0600
Candy Cottage Company
Huntingdon Vly, PA 215-953-8288
Cape Cod Potato Chip Company
Hyannis, MA 508-775-3917
Chile Today - Hot Tamale
San Francisco, CA 800-758-0372
CJ Vitner Company
Chicago, IL 773-523-7900
Clara Foods
Clara City, MN 888-844-8518
Dream Confectioners
Teaneck, NJ 201-836-9000
Frito-Lay
Bakersfield, CA 661-328-6000
Frito-Lay
Dallas, TX. .800-352-4477
GKI Foods
Brighton, MI 248-486-0055
Golden Flake Snack Food
Birmingham, AL 205-323-6161

Good Health Natural Foods
Northport, NY 631-261-2111
GWB Foods Corporation
Brooklyn, NY 718-686-9600
Happy Herberts Food Company
Jersey City, NJ 800-764-2779
Herr's Foods
Nottingham, PA 800-344-3777
Hialeah Products Company
Hollywood, FL 800-923-3379
J&J Snack Foods Corporation
Pennsauken, NJ 856-665-9533
Julius Sturgis Pretzel House
Lititz, PA 717-626-4354
K&R Pretzel Bakery
Dayton, OH 937-299-2231
Karl Bissinger French Confections
St Louis, MO. 800-325-8881
Kennedy Candy Company
Kilgore, TX. 800-657-5258
Key III Candies
Fort Wayne, IN 800-752-2382
Keystone Food Products
Easton, PA 800-523-9426
Keystone Pretzel Bakery
Lititz, PA 888-572-4500
Knese Enterprise
Floral Park, NY 516-354-9004
Kraft Foods
East Hanover, NJ 973-503-2000
Krispy Kernels
Sainte Foy, QC 418-658-1515
Legacy Soft Gourmet Pretzels
San Diego, CA 800-916-3260
Maxim Marketing
Aliso Viejo, CA. 800-476-2257
McCleary
South Beloit, IL 800-523-8644
Mike-Sell's Potato Chip Company
Dayton, OH 800-853-9437
Palmer Candy Company
Sioux City, IA 800-831-0828
Porkie Company of Wisconsin
Cudahy, WI. 800-333-2588
Pretzels
Bluffton, IN. 800-456-4838
Quality Candy
Milwaukee, WI. 800-972-2658
Quinlan Pretzels
Denver, PA 717-336-7571
R&J Farms
West Salem, OH 419-846-3179
SB Global Foods
Lansdale, PA 877-857-1727
Sheryl's Chocolate Creations
Hicksville, NY 888-882-2462
Shultz Company
Hanover, PA 717-633-4585
Snack Works/Metrovox Snacks
Maywood, CA. 888-224-7110
Snak King Corporation
City of Industry, CA 626-336-7711
Snyder's of Hanover
Hanover, PA 717-632-4477
Sporting Colors LLC
Manhattan, KS 888-394-2292
Sturgis Pretzel House
Lititz, PA 717-626-4354
Sweet City Supply
Virginia Beach, VA. 888-793-3824
Tell City Pretzel Company
Tell City, IN. 812-547-4631
Todd's
Vernon, CA 800-938-6337
Triple-C
Hamilton, ON 800-263-9105
Utz Quality Foods
Hanover, PA 800-367-7629
Vermont Pretzel
Bellows Falls, VT. 888-671-4774
Weaver Nut Company
Ephrata, PA. 717-738-3781
Wege Pretzel Company
Hanover, PA 717-843-0738
Westbrae Natural Foods
Garden City, NY 800-434-4246
Wise Foods
Kennesaw, GA 770-426-5821

Flavored

California Pretzel Company
Visalia, CA 559-651-0600
Grippo's Food Products
Cincinnati, OH 513-923-1900
Sunflower Food and Spice Company
Riverside, MO. 800-377-4693

Soft

Bakers' Best Snack Food Corporation
Hatfield, PA. 215-822-3511
Federal Pretzel Baking Company
Philadelphia, PA 215-467-0505
Hammond Pretzel Bakery
Lancaster, PA 717-392-7532
J&J Snack Foods Corporation
Pennsauken, NJ 856-665-9533
Legacy Soft Gourmet Pretzels
San Diego, CA 800-916-3260
New York Pretzel
Brooklyn, NY 718-366-9800
Vermont Pretzel
Bellows Falls, VT 888-671-4774

Sticks or Rods

Confectionately Yours
Buffalo Grove, IL 800-875-6978
Handy Pax
Randolph, MA 781-963-8300
Herr Foods
Chillicothe, OH. 800-523-8468
McCleary
South Beloit, IL 800-523-8644
Sheryl's Chocolate Creations
Hicksville, NY 888-882-2462

Twists

Herr Foods
Chillicothe, OH. 800-523-8468
Sheryl's Chocolate Creations
Hicksville, NY 888-882-2462

Rice Cakes

GWB Foods Corporation
Brooklyn, NY 718-686-9600
Hawaii Candy
Honolulu, HI 808-836-8955
Lundberg Family Farm
Richvale, CA. 530-882-4551
Ohta Wafer Factory
Honolulu, HI. 808-949-2775
Quaker
Barrington, IL 800-333-8027
Westbrae Natural Foods
Garden City, NY 800-434-4246

Snack Pellets

Preformed

Nuvex Ingredients
Blue Earth, MN. 507-526-4331
Rudolph Foods Company
Lima, OH. 419-648-3611

Trail Mix

American Importing Company
Minneapolis, MN 612-331-9226
Big Steer Enterprises
Beaumont, TX. 800-421-4951
C.J. Vitner Company
Chicago, IL 773-523-7900
East Kentucky Foods
Winchester, KY. 859-744-2218
El Paso Chile Company
El Paso, TX. 888-472-5727
Inn Maid Food
Lenox, MA 413-637-2732
King Nut Company
Cleveland, OH 800-860-5464
Lehi Valley Trading Company
Mesa, AZ. 480-684-1402
Marin Food Specialties
Byron, CA 925-634-6126
Midwest/Northern
Minneapolis, MN 800-328-5502

Mister Snacks
Amherst, NY. 800-333-6393
Nature Kist Snacks
Livermore, CA 925-606-4200
New England Natural Bakers
Greenfield, MA 800-910-2884
Nspired Natural Foods
Melville, NY 631-845-4689
Nut Factory
Spokane Valley, WA 888-239-5288
Pittsburgh Snax & Nut Company
Pittsburgh, PA 800-404-6887
Randag & Associates Inc
Elmhurst, IL 630-530-2830
Setton International Foods
Commack, NY 800-227-4397
Sonne
Wahpeton, ND. 800-727-6663
Sun Ridge Farms
Santa Cruz, CA 800-655-3252
Sunridge Farms
Salinas, CA 831-755-1430
Superior Nut & Candy Company
Chicago, IL 800-843-2238
Terri Lynn
Elgin, IL 800-323-0775
Timber Peaks Gourmet
Parker, CO. 800-982-7687
Tropical
Charlotte, NC 800-220-1413
Valley View Blueberries
Vancouver, WA 360-892-2839
Variety Foods
Warren, MI 586-268-4900
Weaver Nut Company
Ephrata, PA. 717-738-3781
Wysong Corporation
Midland, MI 800-748-0188

Specialty & Organic Foods

Aquaculture

Bayou Land Seafood
  Breaux Bridge, LA 337-667-6118
Bays English Muffin Corporation
  Chicago, IL 800-367-2297
Burris Mill & Feed
  Franklinton, LA 800-928-2782
Farm Fresh Catfish Company
  Hollandale, MS 800-647-8264
Idaho Trout Company
  Buhl, ID 866-878-7688
Island Aquaculture Company
  Bernard, ME 207-526-4144
Red Lake Fisheries Associates
  Redby, MN 218-679-3513
Silver Streak Bass Company
  Danevang, TX .979-543-8989
Southern Pride Catfish Company
  Seattle, WA 800-343-8046
Treats Island Fisheries
  Scaly Mountain, NC 207-733-4580

Baby Foods

Formula

Bay Valley Foods
  Green Bay, WI .800-558-4700
Bristol Myers-Squibb Company
  New York, NY .212-546-4000

Organic

Beech-Nut Nutrition Corporation
  Saint Louis, MO 800-233-2468

Dietary Products

Alfred L. Wolff, Inc.
  Park Ridge, IL .312-265-9889
Personal Edge Nutrition
  Ballwin, MO 877-982-3343

Diet & Weight Loss Aids

Action Labs
  Park City, UT .800-669-8877
Alkinco
  New York, NY .800-424-7118
American Supplement Technologies
  Phoenix, AZ 888-469-0242
Body Ammo Research Center
  Hayward, CA 800-346-2303
Body Breakthrough
  Deer Park, NY .800-874-6299
Eckhart Corporation
  Novato, CA 800-200-4201
Himalayan Heritage
  Fredonia, WI 888-414-9500
Innovative Food Solutions LLC
  Columbus, OH 800-884-3314
Natural Balance
  Englewood, CO 800-624-4260
Nature's Plus
  Long Beach, CA 800-525-0200
Nellson Candies
  Baldwin Park, CA 626-334-4508
Pro Form Labs
  Orinda, CA 925-299-9000
Russo Farms
  Vineland, NJ 856-692-5942
Soluble Products Company
  Lakewood, NJ .732-364-8855
Tova Industries
  Louisville, KY .888-532-8682
USA Laboratories
  Burns, TN 800-489-4872

Dietary Supplements

Acta Health Products
  Sunnyvale, CA 408-732-6830
Alacer Corporation
  Foothill Ranch, CA 800-854-0249
Archon Vitamin Corporation
  Irvington, NJ 800-349-1700

Balanced Health Products
  New York, NY 212-794-9878
BetaStatin Nutritional Rsearch
  Toms River, NJ 800-660-9570
Cargill Texturizing Solutions
  Cedar Rapids, IA 877-650-7080
Century Foods International
  Sparta, WI 800-269-1901
Edom Laboratories
  Deer Park, NY 800-723-3366
ImmuDyne
  Florence, KY 888-246-6839
Integrated Therapeutics
  Lake Oswego, OR 800-648-4755
Kabco
  Amityville, NY 631-842-3600
Lichtwer Pharma
  New York, NY 800-226-6227
Maat Nutritionals
  Los Angeles, CA 888-818-6228
Montana Naturals by HealthRite
  Park City, UT 800-872-7218
Nature's Herbs
  American Fork, UT 800-437-2257
North West Marketing Company
  Brea, CA .714-529-0980
Now Foods
  Bloomingdale, IL 888-669-3663
Omni-Pak Industries
  Garden Grove, CA 714-899-3100
Paragon Laboratories
  Torrance, CA 310-370-1563
QBI
  South Plainfield, NJ 908-668-0088
Rainbow Light Nutritional Systems
  Santa Cruz, CA 800-635-1233
Schiff Nutrition International
  Salt Lake City, UT 801-975-5000
Source Naturals
  Scotts Valley, CA 800-815-2333
Trace Mineral Research
  Roy, UT .800-624-7145
Twinlab
  New York, NY 800-645-5626
Valentine Enterprises
  Lawrenceville, GA 770-995-0661
Vita-Pure
  Roselle, NJ 908-245-1212
Vitamer Laboratories
  Irvine, CA 800-432-8355
Wilke International
  Shawnee Mission, KS 800-779-5545

Health Products

Abita Brewing Company
  Abita Springs, LA 800-737-2311
Abunda Life Laboratories
  Asbury Park, NJ 732-775-4141
Acta Health Products
  Sunnyvale, CA 408-732-6830
Action Labs
  Placentia, CA 800-400-5696
Action Labs
  Park City, UT 800-669-8877
Adee Honey Farm
  Bruce, SD 605-627-5621
ADH Health Products
  Congers, NY 800-292-6002
Advanced Nutritional Research, Inc.
  Ellicottville, NY 800-836-0644
Agger Fish
  Brooklyn, NY 718-855-1717
Alacer Corporation
  Foothill Ranch, CA 800-854-0249
Alamance Foods/Triton Water Company
  Burlington, NC 800-476-9111
Albion Laboratories
  Clearfield, UT 866-243-5283
Alfer Laboratories
  Chatsworth, CA 818-709-0737
Alkinco
  New York, NY 800-424-7118
Aloe Farms
  Harlingen, TX 800-262-6771

Aloe Laboratories, Inc.
  Harlingen, TX 800-258-5380
AlpineAire Foods
  Rocklin, CA 800-322-6325
Alternative Health & Herbs
  Albany, OR 800-345-4152
Amberwave Foods
  Oakmont, PA 412-828-3040
Amcan Industries
  Elmsford, NY 914-347-4838
American Almond Products Company
  Brooklyn, NY 800-825-6663
American Spoon Foods
  Petoskey, MI 800-222-5886
Americana Foods
  Dallas, TX 972-709-7100
Amerifit Nutrition
  Bloomfield, CT 800-722-3476
Amerilift Brands, Inc.
  Cromwell, CT 800-722-3476
Anabol Naturals
  Santa Cruz, CA 800-426-2265
Annie's Naturals
  East Calais, VT 800-434-1234
Apotheca Naturale
  Woodbine, IA 800-736-3130
Archon Vitamin Corporation
  Irvington, NJ 800-349-1700
Arizona Natural Products
  Phoenix, AZ 602-997-6098
ARRO Corporation
  Hodgkins, IL 708-352-8200
Atkins Nutritionals
  Melville, NY 800-628-5467
Atlanta Flagship Dairy
  Atlanta, GA 800-224-0669
Atlantic Laboratories
  Waldoboro, ME 207-832-5376
Atrium Biotech
  Fairfield, NJ 866-628-2355
Bake'n Joy Foods
  North Andover, MA 800-666-4937
Bay State Milling Company
  Winona, MN 800-533-8098
BBS Bodacious BBQ Company
  Coral Springs, FL 800-537-5928
Bede Inc
  Haledon, NJ 866-239-6565
Beehive Botanicals, Inc.
  Hayward, WI 800-233-4483
Bel/Kaukauna USA
  Kaukauna, WI 800-558-3500
Betty Lou's Golden Smackers
  McMinnville, OR 800-242-5205
Bevco
  Surrey, BC 800-663-0090
Beverly International Nutrition
  Cold Spring, KY 800-888-3364
Bio San Laboratories/MegaFood
  Derry, NH 800-848-5022
Bio-Foods
  Pine Brook, NJ 973-808-5856
Black Ranch Organic Grains
  Etna, CA 530-467-3387
Blessed Herbs
  Oakham, MA. 800-489-4372
Blue Planet Foods, Inc.
  Collegedale, TN 877-396-3145
Blue Sky Natural Beverage Company
  Santa Fe, NM 505-995-9761
Body Ammo Research Center
  Hayward, CA 800-346-2303
Botanical Products
  Springville, CA 559-539-3432
Bragg-Live Food Products
  Santa Barbara, CA 800-446-1990
Broughton Foods
  Marietta, OH 800-283-2479
Browns Dairy
  Valparaiso, IN 219-464-4141
Brucia Plant Extracts
  Shingle Springs, CA 530-676-2774
Buckhead Gourmet
  Atlanta, GA 800-605-5754
Bunker Hill Cheese Company
  Millersburg, OH 800-253-6636

Butterbuds Food Ingredients
Racine, WI...................800-426-1119

Cactu Life Inc
Corona Del Mar, CA..............800-500-1713

California Fruit
Sanger, CA...................559-266-7117

California Natural Products
Lathrop, CA..................209-858-2525

California Olive Oil Corporation
Salem, MA...................800-386-6457

Caltex Foods
Canoga Park, CA...............800-522-5839

Canada Dry Bottling Company
Flushing, NY.................718-661-4265

Canasoy Enterprises
Vancouver, BC................800-663-1222

Carbolite Foods
Evansville, IN................888-524-3314

Carole's Cheesecake Company
Toronto, ON 416-256-0000

Carriage House Companies
Fredonia, NY.................800-828-8915

Cascade Fresh
Seattle, WA..................800-511-0057

Cedar Crest Specialties
Cedarburg, WI.................800-877-8341

Cedar Lake Foods
Cedar Lake, MI................800-246-5039

Cedarlane Foods
Carson, CA...................800-826-3322

Cemac Foods Corporation
New York, NY.................800-724-0179

Central Coca-Cola Bottling Company
Richmond, VA.................800-359-3759

Champlain Valley Milling Corporation
Westport, NY.................518-962-4711

Chase Brothers Dairy
Oxnard, CA...................800-438-6455

China Mist Tea Company
Scottsdale, AZ................800-242-8807

Christopher Ranch
Gilroy, CA...................408-847-1100

CHS, Inc.
Inner Grove Heights, MN.........800-232-3639

Cliff Bar
Berkeley, CA.................800-884-5254

Coating Place
Verona, WI..................608-845-9521

Coburg Dairy
North Charleston, SC...........843-554-4870

Coca-Cola Bottling Company
Honolulu, HI.................808-839-6711

Coffee Bean International
Portland, OR.................800-877-0474

Con Agra Foods
Holly Ridge, NC...............910-329-9061

Con Agra Store Brands
Edina, MN...................952-835-6900

ConAgra Grocery Products
Irvine, CA...................714-680-1000

Contact International
Skokie, IL...................847-324-4411

Continental Culture Specialists
Glendale, CA 818-240-7400

Cookie Tree Bakeries
Salt Lake City, UT.............800-998-0111

Country Pure Foods
Akron, OH...................877-995-8423

Creme Glacee Gelati
St Leonard, QC................888-322-0116

Crowley Foods
La Fargeville, NY..............800-247-6269

Crowley Foods
Arkport, NY 800-637-0019

Crystal Geyser Roxanne LLC
Pensacola, FL.................850-476-8844

CVC Specialties
Vernon, CT...................800-421-6175

Cyanotech Corporation
Kailua Kona, HI...............800-395-1353

Dahlgren & Company
Crookston, MN................800-346-6050

Dairy Farmers of America
Franklinton, LA 800-735-2038

Dairy Farmers of AmericaGoshen Plant
Goshen, IN..................800-758-0269

Dairy Maid Dairy
Frederick, MD................301-663-5114

Dairyman's/Land O' Lakes
Tulare, CA...................559-687-8287

Dannon Company
Fort Worth, TX................800-211-6565

Dave's Hawaiian Ice Cream
Pearl City, HI 808-453-0500

Dean Distributors
Burlingame, CA................800-227-3112

Dean Distributors
Burlingame, CA................800-792-0816

Dean Foods Company
Huntley, IL..................847-669-5123

Dean Foods/Verifine Dairy Products
Sheboygan, WI................800-236-6455

Devansoy
Carroll, IA..................800-747-8605

Diamond Crystal Brands
Savannah, GA.................912-651-5112

Dolphin Natural Chocolates
Cambria, CA.................800-236-5744

Dorothy Dawson Foods Products
Jackson, MI..................517-788-9830

Drake's Ducks Woodstream Specialty Foods
Keene, NH...................603-357-5858

Dulce de Leche Delcampo Products
Hialeah, FL..................877-472-9408

Earth Island Natural Foods
Canoga Park, CA...............818-725-2820

Eda's Sugarfree Candies
Philadelphia, PA 215-324-3412

Edner Corporation
Hayward, CA.................510-441-8504

Elwood International
Copiague, NY.................631-842-6600

Emkay Trading Corporation
Elmsford, NY.................914-592-9000

Ener-G Foods
Seattle, WA..................800-331-5222

Energen Products
Norwalk, CA.................800-423-8837

Eskimo Pie Corporation
Ronkonkoma, NY..............631-737-9700

Essential Nutrients
Cerritos, CA.................800-767-8585

Faber Foods and Aeronautics
Evergreen, CO................800-237-3255

Fairmont Products
Belleville, PA.................717-935-2121

Falcone's Cookieland
Brooklyn, NY 718-236-4200

Farm to You
Carmel, CA..................408-626-8357

Fieldbrook Farms
Dunkirk, NY.................800-333-0805

First District Association
Litchfield, MN................320-693-3236

Food Reserves/Good For You America
Concordia, MO...............800-944-1511

Fortitech
Schenectady, NY..............800-950-5156

Freeda Vitamins
Long Island City, NY...........800-777-3737

FW Witt & Company
Yorkville, IL.................630-553-6366

G&J Pepsi-Cola Bottlers
Columbus, OH................614-253-8771

Gabriele Macaroni Company
City of Industry, CA............626-964-2324

Garratt & Gunn
Santa Rosa, CA...............707-578-8192

Garuda International
Lemon Cove, CA...............559-594-4380

George Weston Bakeries
Bay Shore, NY................800-356-3314

George Weston Bakeries
Albany, NY..................800-531-4002

Germack Pistachio Company
Detroit, MI..................800-872-4006

Gertrude & Bronner's Magic Alpsnack
Escondido, CA................760-743-2211

Gifford's Dairy
Skowhegan, ME...............207-474-9821

Ginseng Up Corporation
New York, NY................212-696-1930

Global Health Laboratories
Melville, NY.................631-293-0030

Glover's Ice Cream
Frankfort, IN.................800-686-5163

Go Lightly Candy
Hillside, NJ..................800-524-1304

Gourmet Confections
Northbrook, IL................847-498-1200

Govadinas Fitness Foods
San Diego, CA................800-900-0108

Great Circles
Bellows Falls, VT 877-877-2120

Green Foods Corporation
Oxnard, CA..................800-777-4430

Green Options
San Rafael, CA................888-473-3667

Grow Company
Ridgefield, NJ................201-941-8777

GWB Foods Corporation
Brooklyn, NY.................718-686-9600

H&K Products-Pappy's Sassafras Teas
Columbus Grove, OH............877-659-5110

H. Fox & Company
Brooklyn, NY.................718-385-4600

H. Reisman Corporation
Orange, NJ..................973-882-1670

Hagelin & Company
Branchburg, NJ...............800-229-2112

Harvest Valley Bakery
La Salle, IL..................815-224-9030

Haydenergy Health
New York, NY................800-255-1660

Health Enhancers
Flint, MI...................810-635-9899

Health Valley Company
Irwindale, CA................800-334-3204

Healthy Grain Foods
Northbrook, IL................847-272-5576

Healthy Oven
Croton on Hudson, NY..........914-271-5458

Healthy Times
Poway, CA..................858-513-1550

Heart to Heart Foods
Logan, UT..................435-753-9602

Heavenly Hemp Foods
Nederland, CO................888-328-4367

Heidi's Cheese Products
Mundelein, IL................847-362-5971

Heinz North America
Pittsburgh, PA................412-237-5700

Herb Connection
Springville, UT................801-489-4254

Herbal Products & Development
Aptos, CA...................831-688-4200

Heritage Farms Dairy
Murfreesboro, TN..............615-895-2790

Heritage Store
Virginia Beach, VA.............757-428-0110

Heterochemical Corporation
Valley Stream, NY 516-561-8225

HFI Foods
Redmond, WA................425-883-1320

Hillestad Pharmaceuticals
Woodruff, WI................800-535-7742

Hinckley Springs Water Company
Chicago, IL..................773-586-8600

Holistic Products Corporation
Englewood, NJ................800-221-0308

Home Baked Group
Boca Raton, FL................561-995-0767

Homestead Mills
Cook, MN...................800-652-5233

Hormel Foods Corporation
Austin, MN..................800-523-4635

Hormel Health Labs
Quakertown, PA...............800-887-1553

Hospitality Mints
Boone, NC..................800-334-5181

House Foods America Corporation
Garden Grove, CA..............714-901-4350

Howard Foods
Danvers, MA.................978-774-6207

Hsu's Ginseng Enterprises
Wausau, WI.................800-826-1577

Humco
Texarkana, TX................800-662-3435

Increda-Meal
Cato, NY...................315-626-2111

Innovative Food Solutions LLC
Columbus, OH................800-884-3314

Innovative Health Products
Largo, FL...................800-654-2347

Interbake Foods Corporate Office
Richmond, VA................804-755-7107

InterHealth
Benicia, CA..................800-783-4636

International Casings Group
Chicago, IL..................800-825-5151

International Packers Corporation
Watertown, MA................508-963-8214

Interstate Brands Corporation
Peoria, IL...................309-674-9221

Interstate Brands Corporation/Wonder Bread Bakery
St Louis, MO.................314-385-1600

Isabella's Healthy Bakery
Cuyahoga Falls, OH 800-476-6328
Island Spring
Vashon, WA. 206-463-9848
IVC American Vitamin
Freehold, NJ 800-666-8482
J&J Snack Foods Corporation
Vernon, CA 800-486-7622
J&J Snack Foods Corporation
Pennsauken, NJ. 856-665-9533
J.N. Bech
Elk Rapids, MI 800-232-4583
Jackson Ice Cream Company
Denver, CO 303-534-2454
Jamieson Laboratories
Toronto, QC 519-974-8482
Janet's Own Home Sweet Home
Austin, TX. 512-385-4708
Jason & Son Specialty Foods
Rancho Cordova, CA 800-810-9093
Jason Pharmaceuticals
Owings Mills, MD 800-638-7867
JMS Specialty Foods
Ripon, WI 800-535-5437
John Gust Foods & Products Corporation
Batavia, IL. 800-756-5886
Jonathan's Sprouts
Rochester, MA 508-763-2577
JR Carlson Laboratories
Arlington Hts, IL 888-234-5656
JWS Delavau Company
Philadelphia, PA 215-671-1400
Kapaa Poi Factory
Kapaa, HI 808-822-5426
KDK Inc
Draper, UT 801-571-3506
Kemach Food Products   Corporation
Brooklyn, NY 888-453-6224
Kemp Foods
York, PA 800-233-2007
Keto Foods
Neptune, NJ 732-922-0009
Klinke Brothers Ice Cream Company
Memphis, TN 901-743-8250
Knott's Berry Farm Foods
Placentia, CA 800-289-9927
Knouse Foods
Peach Glen, PA 717-677-8181
Kolb-Lena Cheese Company
Lena, IL 815-369-4577
Kozlowski Farms
Forestville, CA 800-473-2767
Kraft Foods
Walton, NY 607-865-7131
Laci Le Beau Corporation
Fresno, CA 800-356-0490
Land-O-Sun Dairies
O Fallon, IL. 618-632-6381
Lassen Foods
Santa Barbara, CA 805-683-7696
Le Bleu Corporation
Advance, NC 800-854-4471
Life Extension Foods
Fort Lauderdale, FL 800-678-8989
Life-Renewal
Garrison, MN 320-692-4498
Lifeway Foods Inc
Morton Grove, IL 847-967-1010
Lifewise Ingredients
Lake Zurich, IL. 847-550-8270
Living Farms
Tracy, MN 507-629-4431
Lucas Meyer
Decatur, IL 800-769-3660
Lukas Confections
York, PA 717-843-0921
Mafco Natural Products
Richmond, VA. 804-222-1600
Magnetic Springs Water Company
Columbus, OH 800-572-2990
Main Street Gourmet
Cuyahoga Falls, OH 800-533-6246
Main Street Muffins
Cuyahoga Falls, OH 800-533-6246
Maple Grove Farms of Vermont
St Johnsbury, VT. 800-525-2540
Marsa Specialty Products
Vernon, CA 800-628-0500
Marsan Foods
Toronto, ON 416-755-9262
Masala Chai Company
Santa Cruz, CA 831-475-8881

Master Mix
Placentia, CA 714-524-1698
Master Peace Food Imports
Pleasantville, NY 914-769-7148
Master Taste International
Plant City, FL 800-237-7629
Mayfair Packing Company
San Jose, CA 408-280-2349
Mayway Corporation
Oakland, CA 800-262-9929
McCutcheon's Apple Products
Frederick, MD 800-888-7537
Meadow Brook Dairy
Erie, PA 800-352-4010
Meadow Gold Dairies
Lincoln, NE. 800-742-7349
Mei Shun Tofu Products Company
Chicago, IL. 312-842-7000
Merlino Italian Baking Company
Seattle, WA 800-207-2997
Michigan Dairy
Livonia, MI 734-367-5390
Michigan Dessert Corporation
Oak Park, MI 800-328-8632
Microsoy Corporation
Jefferson, IA 515-386-2100
Mid States Dairy
Hazelwood, MO 314-731-1150
Midwest/Northern
Minneapolis, MN 800-328-5502
Mills Brothers International
Tukwila, WA 206-575-3000
Modoc Orchard Company
Medford, OR 541-535-1437
Monarch Beverage Company
Atlanta, GA. 800-241-3732
Morinaga Nutritional Foods
Torrance, CA 310-787-0200
Morningland Dairy CheeseCompany
Mountain View, MO 417-469-3817
Morningstar Foods
Dallas, TX. 225-273-2803
Mountain High Yogurt
Englewood, CO. 303-761-2210
Mrs. Leeper's Pasta
Kansas City, MO. 800-848-5266
Mrs. Malibu Foods
Malibu, CA 800-677-6254
Murray Cider Company
Roanoke, VA 540-977-9000
Mustard Seed
Central, SC 877-621-2591
Nabisco LifeSavers Company
Holland, MI. 616-396-1411
National Enzyme Company
Forsyth, MO 800-825-8545
National Food Corporation
Medley, FL 305-884-2020
National Vinegar Company
Houston, TX 713-223-4214
Natural Balance
Englewood, CO. 800-624-4260
Natural Company
Baltimore, MD 410-628-1262
Natural Food Supplements
Canoga Park, CA 818-341-3375
Natural Food World
Culver City, CA 310-836-7770
Naturally Fresh Foods
College Park, GA 800-765-1950
Nature's Herbs
American Fork, UT. 800-437-2257
Nature's Plus
Long Beach, CA 800-525-0200
NBTY
Ronkonkoma, NY 800-920-6090
Nellson Candies
Baldwin Park, CA 626-334-4508
Nestle Pizza
Medford, WI 715-748-5550
New England Country Bakers
Watertown, CT 800-225-3779
New England Natural Bakers
Greenfield, MA. 800-910-2884
New Morning
Needham, MA. 781-444-0440
Newman's Own
Westport, CT 203-222-0136
Nomolas Corp-Jarret Specialties
Woodbridge, NJ 732-634-5565
Nomura Tofu Company
Chicago, IL 773-486-7224

Norimoor Company
Astoria, NY. 718-721-6667
North Country Natural Spring Water
Port Kent, NY 518-834-9400
North Peace Apiaries
Fort St. John, BC 250-785-4808
Novartis Nutrition Corporation
Minneapolis, MN 952-848-6000
Now & Zen
Mill Valley, CA 800-335-1959
Now Foods
Bloomingdale, IL 888-669-3663
Nut Factory
Spokane Valley, WA 888-239-5288
Nutrilabs
San Francisco, CA 800-658-5343
Nutritional International Enterprises Company
Irvine, CA. 949-854-4855
Nutriwest
Douglas, WY. 800-443-3333
Nuttery Farms
Saint Helena, CA 707-963-1101
O'Boyle's Ice Cream Company
Bristol, PA. 215-788-0421
O'Donnell Formula
San Marcos, CA 800-736-1991
Old Fashioned Natural Products
Santa Ana, CA 800-552-9045
Olde Tyme Mercantile
Arroyo Grande, CA. 805-489-7991
Once Again Nut Butter
Nunda, NY 888-800-8075
Oorganik
Houston, TX 281-240-7992
Optimum Nutrition
Walterboro, SC 800-763-3444
Organic Gourmet
Sherman Oaks, CA 800-400-7772
Organic Milling Company
San Dimas, CA. 800-638-8686
Oroweat Baking Company
Montebello, CA 323-721-5161
Orval Kent Food Company
Wheeling, IL. 847-459-9000
Ota Tofu Company
Portland, OR 503-232-8947
P.J. Noyes Company
Lancaster, NH 800-522-2469
Palm Apiaries
Fort Myers, FL 239-334-6001
Particle Dynamics
St Louis, MO. 800-452-4682
Pasta USA
Spokane, WA. 800-456-2084
Pecan Deluxe Candy Company
Dallas, TX. 800-733-3589
Pechters Baking
Harrison, NJ 800-525-5779
Pecoraro Dairy Products
Rome, NY 315-339-0101
Peggy Lawton Kitchens
East Walpole, MA. 800-843-7325
Penta Manufacturing Company
Livingston, NJ. 973-740-2300
Pepsi Bottling Group
Fort Smith, AR 479-646-7881
Pepsi Bottling Group
Redding, CA 530-245-2100
Pepsi Bottling Group
Tulsa, OK 800-963-2424
Pepsi-Cola Bottling Company
St Louis, MO. 314-679-7000
Perfect Foods
Monroe, NY 800-933-3288
Perry's Ice Cream Company
Akron, NY. 800-873-7797
Phillips Gourmet
Kennett Square, PA. 610-925-0520
Phillips Syrup Corporation
Cleveland, OH 216-661-4800
Pied-Mont/Dora
Ste Anne Des Plaines, BC 800-363-8003
Pines International
Lawrence, KS 800-697-4637
Plainview Milk Products Cooperative
Plainview, MN 507-534-3872
Pleasant View Dairy
Highland, IN 219-838-0155
Pleasoning Gourment Seasonings
La Crosse, WI 800-279-1614
Poland Spring Water
Brea, CA 800-950-9396

Prairie Farms Dairy
Carlinville, IL 217-854-2547
Prairie Farms Dairy
Carbondale, IL 618-457-4167
Premium Water
Orange Springs, FL............800-243-1163
Pro Form Labs
Orinda, CA 925-299-9000
Pro Portion Food
Sayville, NY 631-567-4494
Progenix Corporation
Wausau, WI 800-233-3356
Proper-Chem
Dix Hills, NY 631-420-8000
Protein Research Associates
Livermore, CA 800-948-1991
Protient
Roseville, MN 651-638-2600
Pure World Botanicals
South Hackensack, NJ 201-440-5000
Purity Dairies
Nashville, TN 615-244-1900
Purity Foods
Okemos, MI 800-997-7358
Quaker Oats Company
Danville, IL 217-443-3990
Quaker Oats Company
Mountain Top, PA 800-367-6287
Quality Naturally! Foods
City of Industry, CA 888-498-6986
Quong Hop & Company
S San Francisco, CA 650-553-9900
R.J. Corr Naturals
Posen, IL 708-389-4200
Ramos Orchards
Winters, CA 530-795-4748
Ramsen
Lakeville, MN................952-431-0400
Randag & Associates Inc
Elmhurst, IL 630-530-2830
Randal Nutritional Products
Santa Rosa, CA...............800-221-1697
Raway Pharmacal
Accord, NY 914-626-8133
Red Willow Natural Foods
River Falls, WI 715-425-1489
Regal Health Foods International
Chicago, IL 773-252-1044
Reilly Dairy & Food Company
Tampa, FL 813-839-8458
Reiter Dairy
Springfield, OH...............937-323-5777
Rinehart Meat Processing
Branson, MO.................417-334-2044
Rio Syrup Company
St Louis, MO.................800-325-7666
Roberts Dairy Company
Kansas City, MO..............800-279-1692
Roquette America
Keokuk, IA 800-553-7035
Ross Laboratories
Sturgis, MI..................269-651-0600
Royal Body Care
Irving, TX 972-893-4000
Royal Products
Scottsdale, AZ................480-948-2509
Russo Farms
Vineland, NJ 856-692-5942
Sacharen Brothers
Montreal, QC 514-277-8205
Safeway Inc
Durand, WI 715-672-8911
Sahadi Fine Foods
Brooklyn, NY 800-724-2341
Sally Lane's Candy Farm
Paris, TN 731-642-5801
San Joaquin Valley Dairymen
Los Banos, CA 209-826-4901
San-J International
Richmond, VA................800-446-5500
Saratoga Beverage Group
Saratoga Springs, NY..........888-426-8642
Schiff Nutrition International
Salt Lake City, UT 801-975-5000
Schneider's Dairy Holdings Inc
Pittsburgh, PA...............412-881-3525
Schreiber Foods   Plant
Shippensburg, PA.............717-530-5000
Schulze & Burch Biscuit Company
Chicago, IL 773-927-6622
Seaforth Creamery
Seaforth, ON 519-527-0610

Seasons' Enterprises
Addison, IL 630-628-0211
Sells Best
Mishawaka, IN 800-837-8368
Setton International Foods
Commack, NY 800-227-4397
Shenk's Foods
Lancaster, PA 717-393-4240
Sisler's Ice & Ice Cream
Ohio, IL 888-891-3856
Smith Dairy Products Company
Orrville, OH 800-776-7076
Solana Gold Organics
Sebastopol, CA 800-459-1121
Solnuts
Hudson, IA 800-648-3503
Source Naturals
Scotts Valley, CA 800-815-2333
Southwestern Wisconsin Dairy Goat Products
Mt Sterling, WI 608-734-3151
Sovena USA
Rome, NY 315-797-7070
SPI Nutritional
Covina, CA 626-915-1151
Spring Tree Maple Products
Brattleboro, VT 802-254-8784
Staff of Life Natural Foods
Santa Cruz, CA 831-423-8632
Stapleton-Spence PackingCompany
San Jose, CA 800-297-8815
Star of the West MillingCompany
Frankenmuth, MI 989-652-9971
Stevia LLC
Valley Forge, PA 888-878-3842
Strom Products Ltd
Bannockburn, IL 800-862-3311
Subco Foods Inc
Sheboygan, WI 800-676-5188
Sunergia Soyfoods
Charlottesville, VA 800-693-5134
Sunray Food Products Corporation
Bronx, NY...................718-548-2255
Sunshine Farms Dairy
Elyria, OH...................440-322-6301
Sunsweet Growers
Yuba City, CA 800-417-2253
Superior Trading Company
San Francisco, CA 415-982-8722
Superstore Industries
Fairfield, CA 707-864-0502
Suzanne's Specialties
New Brunswick, NJ 800-762-2135
Swagger Foods Corporation
Vernon Hills, IL 847-913-1200
Sweet Productions
Jericho, NY 631-842-0548
Swiss Valley Farms Company
Cedar Rapids, IA...............319-364-8153
Tastee Apple Inc
Newcomerstown, OH 800-262-7753
Thornton Foods Company
Eden Prairie, MN 952-944-1735
Timber Crest Farms
Healdsburg, CA 888-374-9325
Toft Dairy
Sandusky, OH 800-521-4606
Tova Industries
Louisville, KY 888-532-8682
Tree of Life
St Augustine, FL 904-940-2100
Tree of Life North Bergen
North Bergen, NJ 800-735-5175
Trophic International
Salt Lake City, UT 801-269-6667
Tropical
Charlotte, NC 800-220-1413
Tropical
Marietta, GA 800-544-3762
Tulkoff Food Products
Baltimore, MD 800-638-7343
Turner Dairies
Covington, TN 901-476-2643
Turtle Mountain
Eugene, OR..................541-338-9400
Twinlab
New York, NY 800-645-5626
Unique Ingredients
Naches, WA..................509-653-1991
Upstate Farms Cooperative
Buffalo, NY..................716-892-3156
Valley View Blueberries
Vancouver, WA 360-892-2839

Vance's Foods
Gilmer, TX 800-497-4834
Varni Brothers/7-Up Bottling
Modesto, CA 209-521-1777
Vaxa International
Tampa, FL 800-248-8292
Ventre Packing Company
Syracuse, NY 315-463-2384
Venus Wafers
Hingham, MA................800-545-4538
Vermont Bread Company
Brattleboro, VT 802-254-4600
Vi-Gor Cup Corporation
Bellmore, NY 516-431-7722
VIP Foods
Flushing, NY 718-821-3942
Vitamer Laboratories
Irvine, CA 800-432-8355
Vitamins
Chicago, IL 312-861-0700
Vitasoy USA
Ayer, MA 978-772-6880
VitaTech International
Tustin, CA 714-832-9700
Vitatech International
Tustin, CA 714-832-9700
Vogue Cuisine
Culver City, CA 888-236-4144
Wachusett Potato Chip Company
Fitchburg, MA 978-342-6038
Wah Yet Group
Hayward, CA 800-229-3392
Walden Farms
Linden, NJ 800-229-1706
Wax Orchards
Vashon Island, WA 800-634-6132
Wellington Foods
Long Beach, CA 562-989-0111
Wengert's Dairy
Lebanon, PA 800-222-2129
Wesco Foods Company
Cincinnati, OH 513-762-4139
Westin
Omaha, NE 800-228-6098
White Rock Products Corporation
Whitestone, NY 800-969-7625
White Wave
Broomfield, CO 800-488-9283
Whitey's Ice Cream Manufacturing
Moline, IL 888-594-4839
Whole Herb Company
Sonoma, CA 707-935-1077
Wilke International
Shawnee Mission, KS 800-779-5545
Williams-West & Witt Products
Michigan City, IN 219-879-8236
Wilson's Fantastic Candy
Memphis, TN 901-767-1900
Wing Nien Company
Hayward, CA 510-487-8877
Winmix/Natural Care Products
Englewood, FL 941-475-7432
World Flavors
Warminster, PA 215-672-4400
World Ginseng Center
San Francisco, CA 800-747-8808
World Organics Corporation
Huntington Beach, CA 714-893-0017
Yoplait USA
Minneapolis, MN 800-967-5248
Yoshida Food International
Portland, OR 888-243-8371
YZ Enterprises
Maumee, OH.................800-736-8779

Low-Calorie Desserts

T. Marzetti Company
Columbus, OH 614-846-2232

Sugar-Free Foods

Allen Wertz Candy
Chino, CA 800-756-2676
American Instants
Flanders, NJ 973-584-8811
Aunt Gussie Cookies & Crackers
Garfield, NJ..................973-340-4480
Bissinger's Handcrafted Chocolatier
St Louis, MO.................800-325-8881
California Custom Fruits & Flavors
Irwindale, CA 877-558-0056

Dresden Stollen Company
Albertson, NY ... 516-746-5802
Eda's Sugarfree Candies
Philadelphia, PA ... 215-324-3412
GKI Foods
Brighton, MI ... 248-486-0055
Golden Apples Candy Company
Southport, CT ... 800-776-0393
Home Baked Group
Boca Raton, FL ... 561-995-0767
Howard Foods
Danvers, MA ... 978-774-6207
Inn Maid Food
Lenox, MA ... 413-637-2732
International Brownie
Weymouth, MA ... 800-230-1588
Isabella's Healthy Bakery
Cuyahoga Falls, OH ... 800-476-6328
John Gust Foods & Products Corporation
Batavia, IL ... 800-756-5886
Kinnikinnick Foods
Edmonton, AB ... 877-503-4466
Main Street Gourmet
Cuyahoga Falls, OH ... 800-533-6246
Maple Grove Farms of Vermont
St Johnsbury, VT ... 800-525-2540
McCutcheon's Apple Products
Frederick, MD ... 800-888-7537
Michigan Dessert Corporation
Oak Park, MI ... 800-328-8632
Mrs. Leeper's Pasta
Kansas City, MO ... 800-848-5266
Nabisco LifeSavers Company
Holland, MI ... 616-396-1411
Nancy's Pies
Rock Island, IL ... 800-480-0055
Olde Tyme Mercantile
Arroyo Grande, CA ... 805-489-7991
Perry's Ice Cream Company
Akron, NY ... 800-873-7797
Sacharen Brothers
Montreal, QC ... 514-277-8205
Sally Lane's Candy Farm
Paris, TN ... 731-642-5801
Sells Best
Mishawaka, IN ... 800-837-8368
Setton International Foods
Commack, NY ... 800-227-4397
Shenk's Foods
Lancaster, PA ... 717-393-4240
Silver Tray Cookies
Fort Lauderdale, FL ... 305-883-0800
Spring Tree Maple Products
Brattleboro, VT ... 802-254-8784
Tova Industries
Louisville, KY ... 888-532-8682

Gourmet & Specialty Foods

Gourmet & Specialty Foods

A Natural Harvest Restaurant
Chicago, IL ... 773-363-3939
A Southern Season
Chapel Hill, NC ... 800-253-5317
A.M. Braswell Jr. Food Company
Statesboro, GA ... 800-673-9388
Adrian's Bakery
Edmonton, AB ... 800-668-3533
AgriCulver Seeds
Trumansburg, NY ... 800-836-3701
Ailments E.D. Foods Inc.
Pointe Claire, QC ... 800-267-3333
Al Safa Halal
Niagara Falls, NY ... 800-268-8174
Alfonso Gourmet Pasta
Pompano Beach, FL ... 800-370-7278
Allen's Naturally
Farmington, MI ... 800-352-8971
Amaranth Resources
Albert Lea, MN ... 800-842-6689
Amberwave Foods
Oakmont, PA ... 412-828-3040
American Lecithin Company
Oxford, CT ... 800-364-4416
American Marketplace Foods
Paterson, NJ ... 800-683-3464
Ames International
Fife, WA ... 888-469-2637
Ancora Coffee Roasters
Madison, WI ... 800-260-0217

Andre-Boudin Bakeries
San Francisco, CA ... 415-882-1849
Annie's Homegrown
Napa, CA ... 800-288-1089
Appetizers And, Inc.
Chicago, IL ... 800-323-5472
Applecreek Farms
Lexington, KY ... 800-747-8871
Arbor Hill Grapery & Winery
Naples, NY ... 800-554-7553
Arbuckle Coffee
Pittsburgh, PA ... 800-533-8278
Art CoCo Chocolate Company
Denver, CO ... 800-779-8985
Artel
Boisbriand, QC ... 450-433-1322
Ashland Plantation Gourmet
Bunkie, LA ... 318-346-6600
Ashley Foods
Sudbury, MA ... 800-617-2823
Ashman Manufacturing & Distributing Company
Virginia Beach, VA ... 800-641-9924
Asian Brands
Hayward, CA ... 510-523-7474
Aspen Foods
Park Ridge, IL ... 847-384-5940
Assouline & Ting
Philadelphia, PA ... 800-521-4491
Atlas Preserves Company
New York, NY ... 212-569-5613
Autocrat Coffee & Extracts
Lincoln, RI ... 800-288-6272
Avary Farms
Odessa, TX ... 432-332-4139
Babe Farms
Santa Maria, CA ... 800-648-6772
Baker's Choice
Birmingham, MI ... 248-827-7500
Barn Stream Natural Foods
Walpole, NH ... 800-654-2882
Barrie House Gourmet Coffee
Yonkers, NY ... 800-876-2233
Basketfull
New York, NY ... 800-645-4438
Bella Cucina Artful Food
Atlanta, GA ... 800-671-3136
Berardi's Fresh Roast
Cleveland, OH ... 800-876-9109
Biagio's Banquets
Chicago, IL ... 800-392-2837
Big Steer Enterprises
Beaumont, TX ... 800-421-4951
Blue Crab Bay Company
Melfa, VA ... 800-221-2722
Blue Ridge Farms
Brooklyn, NY ... 718-827-9000
Boetje Foods
Rock Island, IL ... 877-726-3853
Bombay Breeze Specialty Foods
Mississauga, ON ... 416-410-2320
Bon Appetit Gourmet Foods
Boise, ID ... 208-345-0475
Boston's Best Coffee Roasters
South Easton, MA ... 800-323-4889
Bottle Green Drinks
Mississauga, ON ... 905-273-6137
Boyd Coffee Company
Portland, OR ... 800-545-4077
Brad's Taste of New York
Floral Park, NY ... 516-354-9004
Brandmeyer Popcorn Company
Ankeny, IA ... 800-568-8276
Brass Ladle Products
Glen Mills, PA ... 800-955-2353
Brateka Enterprises
Ocala, FL ... 877-549-3227
Brazos Legends/Texas Tamale Co
Houston, TX ... 800-882-6253
Bread Dip Company
Friday Harbor, WA ... 360-378-6070
Breaktime Snacks
Paramount, CA ... 800-677-1868
Bremner Biscuit Company
Denver, CO ... 800-722-1871
Brier Run Farm
Birch River, WV ... 304-649-2975
British American Tea & Coffee
Durham, NC ... 919-471-1357
Brutocao Cellars
Hopland, CA ... 800-433-3689
BTS Company/Hail Caesar Dressings
Nashville, TN ... 800-617-8899

Bubbles Baking Company
Van Nuys, CA ... 800-777-4970
Buckmaster Coffee
Hillsboro, OR ... 800-962-9148
Buona Vita
Bridgeton, NJ ... 856-453-7972
Busseto Foods
Fresno, CA ... 800-628-2633
Buxton Foods
Buxton, ND ... 800-726-8057
Buzzn Bee Farms
West Palm Beach, FL ... 561-881-1551
Byrd Cookie Company
Savannah, GA ... 800-291-2973
Cafe Sark's Gourmet Coffee
Yorba Linda, CA ... 626-579-6000
Cafe Terra Cotta
Tucson, AZ ... 800-492-4454
Caffe D'Oro
Chino, CA ... 800-200-5005
Cal Trading Company
Burlingame, CA ... 650-697-4615
California Oils Corporation
Richmond, CA ... 800-225-6457
California Orchards
Danville, CA ... 925-648-1500
California Specialty Farms
Los Angeles, CA ... 800-437-2702
California Treats
South El Monte, CA ... 800-966-5501
Calistoga Food Company
New York, NY ... 212-879-4940
Caltex Foods
Canoga Park, CA ... 800-522-5839
Candy Factory
Hayward, CA ... 800-736-6887
Cape Cod Specialty FoodsIncorporated
Sagamore, MA ... 508-888-7099
Cappuccine
Palm Springs, CA ... 800-511-3127
Carando Gourmet Frozen Foods
Springfield, MA ... 413-730-4205
Carbon's Golden Malted Pancake & Waffle Flour Mix
Buchanan, MI ... 800-253-0590
Carl Buddig & Company
Homewood, IL ... 800-621-0868
Carolyn's Gourmet
Concord, MA ... 800-656-2940
Cateraid
Howell, MI ... 800-508-8217
Cedarlane Foods
Carson, CA ... 800-826-3322
Champignon North America
Englewood Cliffs, NJ ... 201-871-7211
Chatz Roasting Company
Ceres, CA ... 800-792-6333
Chef Hans Gourmet Foods
Monroe, LA ... 800-890-4267
Chef Zachary's Gourmet Blended Spices
Detroit, MI ... 313-226-0000
Cherchies
Malvern, PA ... 800-644-1980
Cheryl & Company
Westerville, OH ... 614-891-8822
Chewys Rugulach
San Diego, CA ... 800-241-3456
Chex Finer Foods
Attleboro, MA ... 800-322-2434
Chieftain Wild Rice Company
Spooner, WI ... 800-262-6368
Chile Today - Hot Tamale
San Francisco, CA ... 800-758-0372
Chocolate Street of Hartville
Hartville, OH ... 888-853-5904
Chocolates by Mark
Houston, TX ... 713-683-3866
Choice of Vermont
Destin, FL ... 800-444-6261
Christie Food Products
Randolph, MA ... 800-727-2523
Christopher Ranch
Gilroy, CA ... 408-847-1100
Citterio USA Corporation
Freeland, PA ... 800-435-8888
Clem's Seafood & Specialties
Buckner, KY ... 502-222-7571
Clements Pastry Shop
Hyattsville, MD ... 800-444-7428
Cloud Nine
San Leandro, CA ... 201-358-8588
Coffee Masters
Spring Grove, IL ... 800-334-6485

Cold Fusion Foods
  West Hollywood, CA 310-287-3244
Colorado Popcorn Company
  Sterling, CO .800-238-2676
Colors Gourmet Pizza
  Carlsbad, CA 760-431-2203
Coltsfoot/Golden Eagle Herb
  Grants Pass, OR 800-736-8749
Columbus Foods Company
  Des Plaines, IL 800-322-6457
Commerce Foods
  New York, NY 212-398-0991
Cook's Gourmet Foods
  Riverside, CA 951-352-5700
Cookie Tree Bakeries
  Salt Lake City, UT. 800-998-0111
Cordon Bleu International
  Anjou, QC 514-352-3000
Corfu Foods
  Bensenville, IL 630-595-2510
Corn Poppers
  San Diego, CA 858-231-2617
Cosentino Winery
  Yountville, CA 800-764-1220
Cossack Caviar
  Arlington, WA. 360-435-6600
Costa Deano's Gourmet Foods
  Canton, OH .800-337-2823
Costadeanos Gourmet Foods
  Canton, OH .330-453-1555
Cottonwood Canyon Winery
  Santa Maria, CA 805-937-8463
Cowboy Caviar
  Berkeley, CA. 877-509-1796
Creative Confections
  Northbrook, IL 847-291-4128
Creole Delicacies Pralines
  New Orleans, LA 504-523-6425
Crown Pacific Fine Foods
  Kent, WA. 425-251-8750
Crustacean Foods
  Los Angeles, CA. 866-263-2625
CTC Manufacturing
  Calgary, AB. 800-668-7677
Cugino's Gourmet Foods
  Crystal Lake, IL 888-592-8446
Cuisinary Fine Foods
  Dallas, TX. .888-283-5303
Culinary Foods
  Chicago, IL .800-621-4049
Culinary Masters Corporation
  Alpharetta, GA 800-261-5261
Custom Brands Unlimited
  Solebury, PA 215-297-9842
Custom House Coffee Roasters
  Miami, FL 888-563-5282
CW Resources
  New Britain, CT 860-229-7700
Cyclone Enterprises
  Houston, TX 281-872-0087
D. Merlino & Sons
  Oakland, CA 510-568-2151
Davis Bakery & Delicatessen
  Cleveland, OH 216-464-5599
Dean & Deluca
  New York, NY 800-999-0306
Dean Distributors
  Burlingame, CA 800-227-3112
Dean Distributors
  Burlingame, CA 800-792-0816
DeChoix Specialty Foods
  Woodside, NY. 800-332-4649
Dee's All Natural Baking Company
  Bettendorf, IA 800-358-8099
Deep Foods
  Union, NJ 908-810-7500
Delftree Farm
  North Adams, MA 800-243-3742
DeMedici Imports
  Elizabeth, NJ. 845-651-4400
Deneen Foods
  Pueblo, CO .800-264-5535
Desserts by David Glass
  Bloomfield, CT 860-769-5570
Diana's Specialty Foods
  Pingree Grove, IL 847-683-1200
Dinkel's Bakery
  Chicago, IL .800-822-8817
Dobake
  Oakland, CA 800-834-3134
Dole & Bailey
  Woburn, MA 781-935-1234

Dolores Canning Company
  Los Angeles, CA. 323-263-9155
Don Alfonso Foods
  Austin, TX. .800-456-6100
Don Francisco Coffee Traders
  Los Angeles, CA. 800-697-5282
Dorina/So-Good
  Union, IL 815-923-2144
Dowd & Rogers
  Sacramento, CA 916-451-6480
Downeast Pasta
  Portland, ME. 800-587-2782
Dr. Tima Natural Products
  Los Angeles, CA. 310-472-2181
Dufour Pastry Kitchens
  New York, NY 212-929-2800
Dummbee Gourmet Foods
  Albany, GA .800-569-1657
Dunford Bakers
  Fayetteville, AR 479-521-3000
Dutchie Sales Corporation
  Hanover, PA 717-632-9343
E. Waldo Ward & Son Corporation
  Sierra Madre, CA 800-355-9273
Eagle Coffee Company
  Baltimore, MD 800-545-4015
Earth & Vine Provisions
  Lincoln, CA .888-723-8463
East Indies Coffee & Tea Company
  Lebanon, PA 800-220-2326
East Shore Specialty Foods
  Hartland, WI. 800-236-1069
Eat This
  Breckenridge, CO 970-389-1853
Egg Roll Fantasy
  Auburn, CA. 530-887-9197
Eilenberger Bakery
  Palestine, TX. 800-831-2544
Elegant Gourmet
  Kirkland, WA 425-814-2500
Emerald Valley Kitchen
  Eugene, OR. 541-688-3297
Emkay Trading Corporation
  Elmsford, NY 914-592-9000
Endangered Species Chocolate
  Indianapolis, IN 800-293-0160
Epicurean Specialty
  Sebastopol, CA 800-500-0065
Ethical Specialty Products
  Pleasanton, CA 925-462-3824
Europa Foods
  Saddle Brook, NJ 201-368-8929
Eweberry Farms
  Brownsville, OR 541-466-3470
Fabe's Natural Gourmet
  Reseda, CA .818-562-1804
Fairwinds Gourmet Coffee
  Auburn, NH. 800-645-4515
Fantasy Chocolates
  Delray Beach, FL 800-804-4962
Fife Vineyards
  Redwood Valley, CA 707-485-0323
Fillo Factory
  Dumont, NJ. 800-653-4556
Fiorucci Foods
  Colonial Heights, VA 800-524-7775
First District Association
  Litchfield, MN 320-693-3236
Fliinko
  South Dartmouth, MA 508-996-9609
Food Merchants
  Westminster, CO 303-466-5574
Foodbrands America
  Oklahoma City, OK 405-290-4000
Fox Hollow Farm
  Hanover, NH. 603-643-6002
Fox Meadow Farm
  Chester Springs, PA 610-827-9731
Fox's Fine Foods
  Laguna Beach, CA 888-522-3697
France Delices
  Montreal, QC 514-259-2291
Fratello Coffee
  Calgary, AB. 800-465-7227
Frontera Foods
  Chicago, IL .800-509-4441
Fun Foods
  East Rutherford, NJ 800-507-2782
Future Bakery & Cafe
  Etobicoke, ON 416-231-1491
Gadsden Coffee/Caffe
  Arivaca, AZ. 888-514-5282

Galileo Foods
  San Lorenzo, CA. 510-276-1300
Garry Packing
  Del Rey, CA 800-248-2126
General Mills
  Federalsburg, MD 410-479-4800
Geneva Foods
  Sanford, FL .800-240-2326
George Weston Bakeries
  Hollywood, FL 800-356-3314
Gerhard's Napa Valley Sausage
  Napa, CA. .707-252-4116
Germain-Robin/Alambic
  Ukiah, CA 707-462-0314
Gift Basket Supply World
  Jacksonville, FL 800-786-4438
Gillies Coffee Company
  Brooklyn, NY 800-344-5526
Gindi Gourmet
  Boulder, CO 303-473-9177
Giovanni's Appetizing Food Products
  Richmond, MI. 586-727-9355
Giusto's Specialty Foods
  S San Francisco, CA. 650-873-6566
GKI Foods
  Brighton, MI 248-486-0055
Glacial Ridge Foods
  Redford, MI 612-239-2215
Global Express Gourmet
  Bozeman, MT 406-587-5571
Gold Seal Fruit Bouquet
  Milwaukee, WI 800-558-5558
Golden Moon Tea
  Herndon, VA 877-327-5473
Golden West Specialty Foods
  Brisbane, CA. 800-584-4481
Golden Whisk
  South San Francisco, CA 800-660-5222
Gondwanaland
  Corrales, NM 505-899-5660
Good Fortunes & Edible Art
  Canoga Park, CA 800-644-9474
Good Health Natural Foods
  Northport, NY 631-261-2111
Gourmet Concepts International
  Suwanee, GA 800-241-4166
Gourmet Food Mall
  Kenner, LA .800-903-7553
Gourmet Foods Market
  Knoxville, TN. 865-584-8739
Gourmet Products
  Thomaston, CT 860-283-5147
Goya Foods
  Secaucus, NJ 201-348-4900
Grace Tea Company
  New York, NY 212-678-2008
Grande Cheese Company
  Brownsville, WI 800-678-3122
Granowska's
  Toronto, ON 416-533-7755
Great American Popcorn Works of Pennsylvania
  Telford, PA .800-542-2676
Greater Galilee Gourmet
  Santa Monica, CA. 800-290-1391
Green Mountain Gringo
  Winston Salem, NC 802-875-3117
Greenwell Farms
  Morganfield, KY. 270-389-3289
Grey Owl Foods
  Grand Rapids, MN 800-527-0172
Groezinger Provisions
  Neptune, NJ 800-927-9473
Grounds for Thought
  Bowling Green, OH 419-354-2326
GWB Foods Corporation
  Brooklyn, NY 718-686-9600
Habby Habanero's Food Products
  Jacksonville, FL 904-333-9758
Happy & Healthy Products
  Boca Raton, FL. 561-367-0739
Harbar Corporation
  Canton, MA 800-881-7040
Harrington's of Vermont
  Richmond, VT. 802-434-7500
Harrison Napa Valley
  Saint Helena, CA 800-913-9463
Haus Barhyte
  Pendleton, OR. 800-407-9241
Hawthorne Valley Farm
  Ghent, NY. .518-672-7500
Haypress Gourmet Pasta
  Haverstraw, NY. 845-947-4580

Hazelwood Farm Bakeries
Minneapolis, MN 314-595-4150
Hearthstone Whole Grain Bakery
Bozeman, MT 800-757-7919
Hendricks Apiaries
Englewood, CO. 303-789-3209
Heritage Fancy Foods Marketing
Erlanger, KY 859-282-3782
Hialeah Products Company
Hollywood, FL 800-923-3379
Hickory Baked Food
Castle Rock, CO 303-688-2633
High Liner Foods
Lunenburg, NS 902-634-9475
Hollman Foods
Minden, NE. 888-926-2879
Homestead Baking Company
Rumford, RI 800-556-7216
Hommus Factory
Haverhill, MA. 508-460-0212
Honeybake Farms
Kansas City, KS 913-371-7777
Hongar Farm Gourmet Foods
Tucker, GA .888-296-7191
Hop Kee
Chicago, IL .312-791-9111
Hospitality Mints
Boone, NC. .800-334-5181
House of Coffee Beans
Houston, TX 800-422-1799
Howards of Colorado
Denver, CO. 970-332-5662
Humphrey Blue Ribbon Meats
Springfield, IL. 800-747-6328
Hunt Country Foods
Middleburg, VA 540-364-2622
Hye Cuisine
Del Rey, CA 559-834-3000
Hye Quality Bakery
Fresno, CA .877-445-1778
I. Epstein & Sons
East Brunswick, NJ. 800-237-5320
Impromtu Gourmet
New York, NY 212-475-4640
Indian Foods Company
Minneapolis, MN 763-593-3000
Indigo Coffee Roasters
Florence, MA 800-447-5450
Intermountain Canola Cargill
Idaho Falls, ID 800-822-6652
International Brownie
Weymouth, MA. 800-230-1588
International Trading Company
Houston, TX 713-224-5901
Internova
St Lambert-De-Levis, QC. 418-889-9929
Isabella's Healthy Bakery
Cuyahoga Falls, OH 800-476-6328
Ivy Foods
Phoenix, AZ 877-223-5459
J.A.M.B. Low Carb Distributor
Pompano Beach, FL 800-708-6738
J.B. Peel Coffee Roasters
Red Hook, NY 800-231-7372
J.N. Bech
Elk Rapids, MI 800-232-4583
Jalapeno Foods Company
The Woodlands, TX 800-896-2318
James Frasinetti & Sons
Sacramento, CA 916-383-2444
Jason & Son Specialty Foods
Rancho Cordova, CA 800-810-9093
Jay Shah Foods
Mississauga, ON. 905-696-0172
Jeremiah's Pick Coffee Company
San Francisco, CA 800-537-3642
Jesse's Fine Meats
Cherokee, IA 712-225-3637
Jim's Cheese Pantry
Waterloo, WI. 800-345-3571
Jones Bakeries
Winston Salem, NC. 800-849-5663
Joy's Specialty Foods
Mancos, CO 800-831-5697
Joyva Corporation
Brooklyn, NY 718-497-0170
Just Desserts
San Francisco, CA. 415-602-9245
Karen's Fabulous Biscotti
White Plains, NY 914-682-2165
Karen's Wine Country Cafe
Sonoita, AZ. 800-453-5650

Kay Foods Company
Ionia, MI 616-527-0120
Kelly Gourmet Foods
San Francisco, CA 415-648-9200
Kemoo Farm Foods
Wahiawa, HI 808-622-8004
Kennedy Gourmet
Houston, TX 800-882-6253
Kevton Gourmet Tea
Streetman, TX. 888-538-8668
Keystone Coffee Company
San Jose, CA 408-998-2221
Kid's Kookie Company
San Clemente, CA 800-350-7577
King David's All NaturalFood
Syracuse, NY 315-471-5000
Knese Enterprise
Floral Park, NY. 516-354-9004
Knott's Berry Farm Foods
Placentia, CA 800-289-9927
Knox Mountain Farm
Franklin, NH 800-943-2822
Koch Foods
Park Ridge, IL 800-837-2778
Koegel Meats
Flint, MI 810-238-3685
Kokopelli's Kitchen
Phoenix, AZ 888-943-9802
Kolb-Lena Cheese Company
Lena, IL. 815-369-4577
Kornfections
Chantilly, VA. 800-469-8886
L&S Packing Company
Farmingdale, NY 800-286-6487
L'Esprit de Campagne
Winchester, VA 800-692-8008
La Cookie
Houston, TX 713-784-2722
La Rosa
Addison, IL. 630-916-9552
La Vigne Enterprises
Fallbrook, CA 760-723-9997
LaRosa Bakery
Shrewsbury, NJ 800-527-6722
Laska Stuff
Rochester, MI 248-652-8473
Lay's Fine Foods
Knoxville, TN 800-251-9636
Leech Lake Wild Rice
Deer River, MN. 877-246-0620
Legumes Plus
Fairfield, WA. 800-845-1349
Leon's Sausage Company
Chicago, IL .312-829-2250
Les Trois Petits Cochons
New York, NY 800-537-7283
Lesley Elizabeth
Lapeer, MI. .800-684-3300
Let's Serve
Plattsburgh, NY. 518-293-7119
Liberty Richter
Saddle Brook, NJ 201-291-8749
Lindsay Farms
Cave Spring, GA. 706-777-9797
Little Lady Foods
Elk Grove, IL 800-439-1440
Live A Little Gourmet Foods
Newark, CA 888-744-2300
Lodi Nut Company
Lodi, CA 800-234-6887
Longmeadow Foods
Gray, ME 800-255-8401
Lotus Brands
Silver Lake, WI. 800-824-6396
Louisiana Fish Fry Products
Baton Rouge, LA 800-356-2905
Louisiana Gourmet Enterprises
Houma, LA .800-328-5586
Love Creek Orchards
Medina, TX. 800-449-0882
Lucile's Creole Foods
Boulder, CO 303-442-4743
Lusitania Bakery
Blandon, PA 610-926-1311
M&L Gourmet Ice Cream
Baltimore, MD 410-276-4880
M. Marion & Company
Santa Rosa, CA 707-836-0551
M.W. Milton & Company
Louisville, KY 502-587-5016
Mad Chef Enterprise
Mentor, OH 800-951-2433

Mad Will's Food Company
Auburn, CA. 888-275-9455
Madhava Honey
Longmont, CO 800-530-2900
Maggie Gin's
San Francisco, CA 415-221-6080
Magic Ice Products
Stockton, CA. 800-776-7923
Magnum Coffee Roastery
Nunica, MI .888-937-5282
Main Street Custom Foods
Cuyahoga Falls, OH 800-533-6246
Main Street Gourmet
Cuyahoga Falls, OH 800-533-6246
Main Street Gourmet Fundraising
Cuyahoga Falls, OH 800-533-6246
Main Street Muffins
Cuyahoga Falls, OH 800-533-6246
Main Street's Cambritt Cookies
Cuyahoga Falls, OH 800-533-6246
Maitake Products
East Rutherford, NJ 800-747-7418
Mama Lee's Gourmet Hot Chocolate
Nashville, TN 888-626-2533
Mama Rose's Gourmet Foods
Phoenix, AZ 877-325-4477
Mama Vida
Randallstown, MD 877-521-0742
Mancini Packing Company
Zolfo Springs, FL 863-735-2000
Manitok Food & Gifts
Callaway, MN 800-726-1863
Maple Leaf Foods International
Toronto, ON 416-480-8900
Marantha Natural Foods
San Francisco, CA 800-299-0048
Marcel et Henri Charcuterie Francaise
S San Francisco, CA. 800-227-6436
Mardi Gras
Verona, NJ. .973-857-3777
Marich Confectionery Company
Hollister, CA. 800-624-7055
Marin Food Specialties
Byron, CA. .925-634-6126
Market Square Food Company
Highland Park, IL 800-232-2299
Marukai Corporation
Gardena, CA 310-660-6300
Meat-O-Mat Corporation
Brooklyn, NY 718-965-7250
Mendocino Mustard
Fort Bragg, CA 800-964-2270
Mercado Latino
City of Industry, CA 626-333-6862
Merlino Italian Baking Company
Seattle, WA 800-207-2997
Metropolis Sambeve Specialty Foods
Lawrence, MA 978-683-2873
Milina's Finest Organic Food Products
Freedom, CA 831-685-6575
Mille Lacs MP Company
Madison, WI 800-843-1381
Mills Brothers International
Tukwila, WA 206-575-3000
Minnestalgia
McGregor, MN 800-328-6731
Modern Baked Products
Oakdale, NY 877-727-2253
Moody Dunbar
Johnson City, TN 800-251-8202
Moon Shine Trading Company
Woodland, CA. 800-678-1226
Morningland Dairy CheeseCompany
Mountain View, MO 417-469-3817
Mother Earth Enterprises
New York, NY 866-436-7688
Mrs. Auld's Gourmet Foods
Reno, NV 800-322-8537
Mrs. Leeper's Pasta
Kansas City, MO 800-848-5266
MSRF
Chicago, IL .773-227-1115
Mt. Olympus Specialty Foods
Buffalo, NY 716-874-0771
Murvest Fine Foods
Fort Lauderdale, FL 954-772-6440
Mustard Seed
Central, SC .877-621-2591
My Sister's Caramels
Redlands, CA 909-792-6242
Nancy's Specialty Foods
Newark, CA 510-494-1100

551

Naron Mary Sue Candy Company
  Baltimore, MD 410-467-9338
National Foods
  Liberal, KS 620-624-1851
National Importers
  Brampton, ON. 905-791-1322
Natural Exotic Tropicals
  Pompano Beach, FL 800-756-5267
Natural Quick Foods
  Seattle, WA 206-365-5757
Nature's Finest Products
  Dallas, TX 800-237-5205
Neilsen-Massey Vanillas
  Waukegan, IL 800-525-7873
Nell Baking Company
  Kenedy, TX 800-215-9190
Neshaminy Valley Natural Foods
  Philadelphia, PA 215-745-3773
Nest Eggs
  Chicago, IL 773-525-4952
New Canaan Farms
  Dripping Springs, TX 800-727-5267
New England Marketers
  Boston, MA 800-688-9904
New Glarus Foods
  New Glarus, WI 800-356-6685
Newmarket Foods
  Petaluma, CA 707-778-3400
Niche Import Company
  Cedar Knolls, NJ 800-548-6882
Nina's Gourmet Dip
  Mc Lean, VA 703-356-1667
NorCal Wild Rice
  Davis, CA 530-758-8550
North American Enterprises
  Tucson, AZ 800-817-8666
North Country Smokehouse
  Claremont, NH 800-258-4304
Northern Flair Foods
  Mound, MN 888-530-4453
Northwest Candy Emporium
  Everett, WA. 800-404-7266
Nostalgic Specialty Foods
  Coral Springs, FL 800-881-2824
Nueske's Applewood Smoked Meats
  Wittenberg, WI 800-386-2266
Nutty Bavarian
  Sanford, FL 800-382-4788
OH Chocolate
  Calgary, AB. 403-283-4612
Olde Tyme Mercantile
  Arroyo Grande, CA. 805-489-7991
Olympic Specialty Foods
  Buffalo, NY. 716-874-0771
Oregon Hill Farms
  St Helens, OR 800-243-4541
Oregon Pride
  The Dalles, OR 888-697-4767
Organic By Nature
  Long Beach, CA 800-452-6884
Organic Gourmet
  Sherman Oaks, CA 800-400-7772
Orleans Packing Company
  Hyde Park, MA. 617-361-6611
Osman's Pies
  Stow, OH 330-655-2919
P & M Staiger Vineyard
  Boulder Creek, CA 831-338-0172
Pacific Ocean Producers
  Honolulu, HI 808-537-2905
Pacific Westcoast Foods
  Portland, OR 800-874-9333
Palmetto Pigeon Plant
  Sumter, SC 803-775-1204
Palmieri Food Products
  New Haven, CT 800-845-5447
Panola Pepper Corporation
  Lake Providence, LA 800-256-3013
Papa Dean's Popcorn
  San Antonio, TX 210-822-3625
Paradise Products Corporation
  Roslyn, NY 800-826-1235
Parma Sausage Products
  Pittsburgh, PA 877-294-4207
Pastene Companies
  Canton, MA 781-830-8200
PaStreeta Fresca
  Dublin, OH 800-343-5266
Pastry Chef
  Pawtucket, RI 800-639-8606
Patak Spices USA
  Clearwater, FL 727-796-2126

Pati-Petite Cookies
  Bridgeville, PA 800-253-5805
Paulaur Corporation
  Cranbury, NJ 888-398-8844
Peanut Patch
  Courtland, VA 866-732-6883
Pearl Coffee Company
  Akron, OH 800-822-5282
Peerless Coffee Company
  Oakland, CA 800-310-5662
Pelican Bay
  Dunedin, FL 800-826-8982
Phipps Desserts
  Toronto, ON 416-481-9111
Piantedosi Baking Company
  Malden, MA 800-339-0080
Picard Peanuts
  Windham Centre, ON 888-244-7688
Pickwick Catfish Farm
  Counce, TN. 731-689-3805
Pidy Gourmet Pastry Shells
  Inwood, NY. 800-231-7439
PJ's Coffee & Tea
  New Orleans, LA 800-527-1055
Plaidberry Company
  Vista, CA. 760-727-5403
Plaza de Espana Gourmet
  Sunny Isles Beach, FL 305-971-3468
Pontiac Coffee Break
  Pontiac, MI 248-332-9403
Popcorn Connection
  North Hollywood, CA 800-852-2676
Popcorner
  Swansea, IL 618-277-2676
Porinos Gourmet Food
  Central Falls, RI 800-826-3938
Power-Selles Imports
  Woodinville, WA. 425-398-9761
Prairie Thyme
  Santa Fe, NM 800-869-0009
Premium Brands
  Bardstown, KY 502-348-0081
Prince of Peace Enterprises
  Hayward, CA 800-732-2328
Private Harvest
  Lakeport, CA 800-463-0594
Pulgini Pasta Products
  Fort Lauderdale, FL 954-973-7458
Purely American
  Norfolk, VA. 800-359-7873
Purity Farms
  Sedalia, CO 800-568-4433
R.L. Schreiber
  Pompano Beach, FL 800-624-8777
Rabbit Barn
  Turlock, CA. 209-632-1123
Rainbow Valley Frozen Yogurt
  White Lake, MI. 800-979-8669
Rainforest Company
  Maryland Heights, MO. 314-344-1000
Rao's Specialty Foods
  New York, NY 212-269-0151
Raymond-Hadley Corporation
  Spencer, NY 800-252-5220
RC Fine Foods
  Belle Mead, NJ 800-526-3953
Reading Coffee Roasters
  Birdsboro, PA 800-331-6713
Regency Coffee & VendingCompany
  Olathe, KS 913-829-1994
Restaurant Lulu Gourmet Products
  San Francisco, CA 888-693-5800
Rich Products of Canada
  Fort Erie, ON 800-263-8174
Righetti Specialties
  Santa Maria, CA. 800-268-1041
Rio Trading Company
  Baltimore, MD 443-384-2500
Robert Rothschild Farm
  Urbana, OH 866-565-6790
Ron-Son Foods
  Swedesboro, NJ 856-241-7333
Rosmarino Foods/R.Z. Humbert Company
  Odessa, FL 888-926-9053
Rossi Pasta
  Marietta, OH 800-227-6774
Rowena's
  Norfolk, VA. 800-627-8699
Royal Baltic
  Brooklyn, NY 718-385-8300
Royal Coffee & Tea Company
  Mississauga, ON 800-667-6226

Royal Palm Popcorn Company
  Edison, NJ 800-526-8865
Royal Wine Company
  Bayonne, NJ 201-437-9131
Rubschlager Baking Corporation
  Chicago, IL 773-826-1245
Rudolph's Specialty Bakery
  Toronto, ON 416-763-4315
Russ & Daughters
  New York, NY 800-787-7229
Russian Chef
  New York, NY 212-249-1550
Saguaro Food Products
  Tucson, AZ 800-732-2447
Sambets Cajun Deli
  Austin, TX. 800-472-6238
San Francisco Popcorn Works
  San Francisco, CA 800-777-2676
San Gennaro Foods
  Kent, WA 800-462-1916
Sandridge Food Corporation
  Medina, OH 330-725-2348
Santa Barbara Olive Company
  Goleta, CA 800-624-4896
Santa Barbara Salsa
  Oceanside, CA 800-748-5523
Santa Fe Seasons
  Belen, NM 800-264-5535
Sapar
  San Mateo, CA 650-340-8840
Sara Lee Coffee & Tea
  Earth City, MO 314-731-2500
Sara Lee Coffee & Tea
  Houston, TX 888-246-2598
Sara Lee Corporation
  Downers Grove, IL 630-598-8100
Sardinha Sausage
  Somerset, MA 800-678-0178
Sassafras Enterprises
  Chicago, IL 800-537-4941
Savannah Cinnamon & Cookie Company
  Savannah, GA 800-288-0854
Schwan's Consumer Brands North America
  Bloomington, MN. 952-832-4300
Schwans Food Company
  Norcross, GA 800-241-0559
Scooty's Wholesome Foods
  Boulder, CO 303-440-4025
Seawind Trading International
  Carlsbad, CA. 760-438-5600
Seckinger-Lee Company
  Savannah, GA 800-291-2973
Selma's Cookies
  Apopka, FL 800-922-6654
Senor Felix's Gourmet Mexican
  Baldwin Park, CA 626-960-2800
Serranos Salsa
  Austin, TX. 512-328-9200
Sfoglia Fine Pastas & Gourmet
  Freeland, WA 360-331-4080
Shady Grove Orchards
  Onalaska, WA 360-985-7033
Sheila's Select Gourmet Recipe
  Heber City, UT 800-516-7286
Shine Food
  Torrance, CA. 310-533-6010
Shonfeld's
  South Hackensack, NJ 800-462-3464
Signature Foods
  Miami, FL 305-264-8768
Silver Palate Kitchens
  Cresskill, NJ 800-872-5283
Simply Divine
  New York, NY 212-541-7300
Simpson & Vail
  Brookfield, CT 800-282-8327
Sonoma Gourmet
  Cotati, CA. 707-792-7613
Southern Gold Honey CompAny
  Vidor, TX 808-899-2494
Southern Heritage Coffee Company
  Indianapolis, IN 800-486-1198
Southern Style Nuts
  Sherman, TX. 800-624-8242
Spanarkel Company
  Neptune City, NJ 732-775-4144
Spartan Imports
  Endicott, NY 607-748-7557
Specialty Coffee Roasters
  Miami, FL 800-253-9363
Specialty Foods South
  Charleston, SC 800-538-0003

Spring Creek Natural Foods
Spencer, WV....................304-927-3780
Sprout House
Ramona, CA......................800-777-6887
Star of the West MillingCompany
Frankenmuth, MI................989-652-9971
Star Ravioli Manufacturing Company
Moonachie, NJ...................201-933-6427
Stearns & Lehman
Mansfield, OH...................800-533-2722
Steel's Gourmet Foods
Bridgeport, PA..................800-678-3357
Sticky Fingers Bakeries
Spokane Valley, WA..............800-458-5826
Stirling Foods
Renton, WA......................800-332-1714
Sugar Plum Farm
Plumtree, NC....................888-257-0019
Summerfield Farm Products
Orange, VA......................800-898-3276
Sunset Specialty Foods
Sunset Beach, CA................562-592-4976
Sweet Shop
Fort Worth, TX..................800-222-2269
Sweety Novelty
Monterey Park, CA...............626-282-4482
Swiss Chalet Fine Foods
Doral, FL.......................800-347-9477
Swiss Colony
Monroe, WI......................608-328-8400
Swiss-American
St Louis, MO....................800-325-8150
SYSCO Foodservice
Fremont, CA.....................650-494-7200
T&A Gourmet
Somerset, NJ....................732-828-9565
T.W. Garner Food Company
Winston Salem, NC...............800-476-7383
Table de France
Ontario, CA.....................909-923-5205
Tabor Hill/CHI Company
Buchanan, MI....................269-422-1165
Taft Street Winery
Sebastopol, CA..................707-823-2049
Tait Farm Foods
Centre Hall, PA.................800-787-2716
Takara Sake
Berkeley, CA....................510-540-8250
Tarzai Specialty Foods
Chino, CA.......................909-628-3601
Teeccino Caffe
Santa Barbara, CA...............800-498-3434
Texas Traditions
Georgetown, TX..................800-547-7062
Thackery & Company
Bolinas, CA.....................415-868-1781
Thistledew Farm
Proctor, WV.....................800-854-6639
Tipiak
Stamford, CT....................203-961-9117
Tokunaga Farms
Selma, CA.......................559-896-0949
Tom & Sally's Handmade Chocolates
Brattleboro, VT.................800-827-0800
Too Good Gourmet
San Lorenzo, CA.................877-850-4663
Topolos at Russian River Vine
Forestville, CA.................707-887-1575
Torn Ranch
Novato, CA......................415-506-3000
Torrefazione Italia
Seattle, WA.....................800-827-2333
Tostino Coffee Roasters
Tucson, AZ......................800-678-3519
Tova Industries
Louisville, KY..................888-532-8682
Town & Country Foods
Greene, ME......................207-946-5489
Trader Joe's Company
Monrovia, CA....................626-358-8884
Treat Ice Cream Company
San Jose, CA....................408-292-9321
Tree of Life
St Augustine, FL................904-940-2100
Tres Classique
Ukiah, CA.......................888-644-5127
Trinity Spice
Midland, TX.....................800-460-1149
Tropical
Charlotte, NC...................800-220-1413
Tropical
Marietta, GA....................800-544-3762

Tropical Nut & Fruit Company
Orlando, FL.....................800-749-8869
Tuscan Hills
El Dorado Hills, CA.............916-939-3814
Tuterri's/Gaston Dupre
Poway, CA.......................800-848-5266
Two Chefs on a Roll
Carson, CA......................800-842-3025
Uncle Grant's Foods
San Francisco, CA...............415-752-5462
Uncle Ralph's Cookie Company
Frederick, MD...................800-422-0626
Unibroue/Unibrew
Chambly, QC.....................450-658-7658
Unique Foods
Raleigh, NC.....................919-779-5600
United Natural Foods
Chesterfield, NH................800-451-2525
Valley View Blueberries
Vancouver, WA...................360-892-2839
Van-Lang Foods
Lombard, IL.....................630-268-1953
Vega Food Industries
Cranston, RI....................800-973-7737
Ventura Foods   Foodservice
Salem, OR.......................503-585-6423
Venus Wafers
Hingham, MA.....................800-545-4538
Vermont Country Store
Manchester Center, VT...........802-362-8460
Vermont Food Experience
Shelburne, VT...................802-985-8101
Vermont Natural Company
Jacksonville, VT................802-368-2231
Vigneri Confections
Rochester, NY...................585-254-6160
Vine Village
Napa, CA........................707-255-4099
Viola's Gourmet Goodies
Los Angeles, CA.................323-731-5277
Volcano Island Honey Company
Honokaa, HI.....................888-663-6639
W.J. Clark & Co
Chicago, IL.....................312-329-0830
W.S. Wells & Sons
Wilton, ME......................207-645-3393
Wagner Gourmet Foods
Shawnee Mission, KS.............913-469-5411
Walden Foods
Winchester, VA..................800-648-7688
Warren & Son Meat Processing
Whipple, OH.....................740-585-2421
Weaver Nut Company
Ephrata, PA.....................717-738-3781
Wechsler Coffee Corporation
Moonachie, NJ...................800-800-2633
Wenner Bread Products
Bayport, NY.....................800-869-6262
Westbrae Natural Foods
Garden City, NY.................800-434-4246
Western Pacific Commodities
Las Vegas, NV...................702-312-8080
White Wave Foods
Jacksonville, FL................800-874-6765
Wild Rice Exchange
Woodland, CA....................800-223-7423
Wildwood Natural Foods
Watsonville, CA.................800-464-3915
Will-Pak Foods
Ontario, CA.....................800-874-0883
Wish List/Good Fortunes
Canoga Park, CA.................800-644-9474
Woeber Mustard Manufacturing
Springfield, OH.................800-548-2929
Wong Wing Foods
Montreal, QC....................800-361-4820
Woodstock Whole Earth Foods
Saugerties, NY..................914-247-0777
World of Coffee, World of Tea
Stirling, NJ....................908-647-1218
Yair Scones/Canterbury Cuisine
Medina, WA......................800-588-9160
Yankee Specialty Foods
Boston, MA......................617-951-9904
Yayin Corporation
Valley Village, CA..............707-829-5686
Yorktown Baking Company
Yorktown Heights, NY............800-235-3961
Yvonne's Gourmet Sensations
Marlton, NJ.....................856-985-7677
Zitos Specialty Foods
Port Charlotte, FL..............941-625-0806

Health & Dietary

Energy Bars

Eat Your Heart Out
New York, NY....................212-989-8303
Gertrude & Bronner's Magic Alpsnack
Escondido, CA...................760-743-2211
Kettle Valley Fruits
Summerland, BC..................888-297-6944
Optimum Nutrition
Walterboro, SC..................800-763-3444

Organic Foods

Abunda Life Laboratories
Asbury Park, NJ.................732-775-4141
Adrienne's Gourmet Foods
Santa Barbara, CA...............800-937-7010
AgriCulver Seeds
Trumansburg, NY.................800-836-3701
Alliston Creamery & Dairy
Alliston, ON....................705-435-6751
Alta Dena Certified Dairy
City of Industry, CA............800-535-1369
Amberwave Foods
Oakmont, PA.....................412-828-3040
American Health & Nutrition
Ann Arbor, MI...................734-677-5572
American Natural & Organic Spices
Union City, CA..................510-477-4787
Amy's Kitchen
Petaluma, CA....................707-578-5908
Andre-Boudin Bakeries
San Francisco, CA...............415-882-1849
Ankeny Lakes Wild Rice
Salem, OR.......................800-555-5380
Annie's Naturals
East Calais, VT.................800-434-1234
Applegate Farms
Bridgewater, NJ.................908-725-2768
Atlantic Quality Spice &Seasonings
Edison, NJ......................800-584-0422
Avalon Organic Coffees
Albuquerque, NM.................800-662-2575
Barrows Tea Company
New Bedford, MA.................800-832-5024
Bedrock Farm Certified Organic Medicinal Herbs
Wakefield, RI...................401-789-9943
Bel/Kaukauna USA
Kaukauna, WI....................800-558-3500
Belgravia Imports
Portsmouth, RI..................800-848-1127
Bella Vista Farm
Lawton, OK......................866-237-8526
Berardi's Fresh Roast
Cleveland, OH...................800-876-9109
Beta Pure Foods
Aptos, CA.......................831-685-6565
Beth's Fine Desserts
Cotati, CA......................415-464-1891
Blessed Herbs
Oakham, MA......................800-489-4372
Blue Marble Brands
Edison, NJ......................732-650-9905
Boehringer Ingelheim
Saint Charles, IL...............630-377-5150
Bombay Breeze Specialty Foods
Mississauga, ON.................416-410-2320
Brad's Organic
Haverstraw, NY..................845-429-9080
Brans Nut Company
Wauconda, IL....................800-238-0400
Brass Ladle Products
Glen Mills, PA..................800-955-2353
Bread Alone Bakery
Shokan, NY......................800-769-3328
Brewster Dairy
Brewster, OH....................800-874-0874
Brier Run Farm
Birch River, WV.................304-649-2975
Buchanan Hollow Nut Company
Le Grand, CA....................800-532-1500

Bunker Hill Cheese Company
Millersburg, OH 800-253-6636
Buns & Roses Organic Wholegrain Bakery
Edmonton, AB 780-438-0098
Butterbuds Food Ingredients
Racine, WI. 800-426-1119
BuyWell Coffee
Colorado Springs, CO 719-598-7870
C&H Sugar Company
Crockett, CA 800-729-4840
C.F. Burger Creamery
Detroit, MI 800-229-2322
Cafe Society Coffee Company
Dallas, TX 800-717-6000
California Custom Fruits & Flavors
Irwindale, CA 877-558-0056
California Independent Almond Growers
Ballico, CA 209-667-4855
California Olive Oil Corporation
Salem, MA 800-386-6457
Candone Fine Natural Foods
Atlanta, GA 404-469-2348
Carob Tree
Arcadia, CA 626-445-0215
Cascadian Farm & MUIR Glen; Division of General
Mills
Sedro Woolley, WA. 360-855-0100
Caudill Seed Company
Louisville, KY 800-626-5357
Cedarlane Foods
Carson, CA 800-826-3322
Century Foods International
Sparta, WI 800-269-1901
Champlain Valley Milling Corporation
Westport, NY 518-962-4711
Chartrand Imports
Rockland, ME 800-473-7307
Chelten House Products
Bridgeport, NJ. 856-467-1600
Cherith Valley Gardens
Fort Worth, TX 800-610-9813
Chino Valley Ranchers
Arcadia, CA 800-354-4503
Chris' Farm Stand
Hubbardston, MA 978-928-4732
Christopher Ranch
Gilroy, CA. 408-847-1100
Citrus Service
Winter Garden, FL 407-656-4999
Clean Foods
Santa Paula, CA 800-526-8328
Clear Mountain Coffee Company
Silver Spring, MD. 301-587-2233
Coleman Purely Natural Brands
Golden, CO. 877-810-8291
College Hill Poultry
Fredericksburg, PA 800-533-3361
Columbus Foods Company
Des Plaines, IL 800-322-6457
Con Agra Store Brands
Edina, MN. 952-835-6900
Contact International
Skokie, IL 847-324-4411
Country Choice Naturals
Eden Prairie, MN 952-829-8824
Crystal Geyser Roxanne LLC
Pensacola, FL 850-476-8844
Cuizina Food Company
Woodinville, WA. 425-486-7000
Cyanotech Corporation
Kailua Kona, HI 800-395-1353
D. Merlino & Sons
Oakland, CA 510-568-2151
Dagoba Organic Chocolate
Ashland, OR 800-482-5661
Dakota Growers Pasta Company
Carrington, ND 701-652-2855
Dakota Organic Products
Watertown, SD 800-243-7264
Dakota Prairie Organic Flour Company
Harvey, ND 701-324-4330
Dancing Paws
Pacific Palisades, CA 888-644-7297
Daymar Select Fine Coffees
El Cajon, CA. 800-466-7590
Dorothy Dawson Foods Products
Jackson, MI. 517-788-9830
Dr Kracker
Dallas, TX 214-503-1971
Driscoll Strawberry Associates
Watsonville, CA 831-763-3050

Earth Fire Products
Viroqua, WI. 608-735-4711
East Wind Nut Butters
Tecumseh, MO 417-679-4682
Eatem Foods Company
Vineland, NJ 800-683-2836
Eberly Poultry
Stevens, PA 717-336-6440
Eco-Cuisine
Boulder, CO 303-444-6634
Eden Foods Inc
Clinton, MI 800-248-0320
Eden Organic Pasta Company
Detroit, MI 800-248-0320
Eggology
Canoga Park, CA 818-610-2222
Fairhaven Cooperative Flour Mill
Bellingham, WA 360-734-9947
FarmGro Organic Foods
Regina, SK 306-522-0092
Fearn Natural Foods
Mequon, WI 800-877-8935
Fine Dried Foods International
Santa Cruz, CA 831-426-1413
Fireside Kitchen
Halifax, NS 902-454-7387
Florence Macaroni Manufacturing
Chicago, IL 800-647-2782
Florida Food Products
Eustis, FL 800-874-2331
Food Reserves/Good For You America
Concordia, MO 800-944-1511
Franklin Farms
North Franklin, CT 860-642-3019
French Meadow Bakery
Minneapolis, MN 877-669-3278
Frontier Ingredients
Norway, IA 800-669-3275
FungusAmongUs Inc
Snohomish, WA. 360-568-3403
Gabriele Macaroni Company
City of Industry, CA 626-964-2324
Gelato Fresco
Toronto, ON 416-785-5415
George Chiala Farms
Morgan Hill, CA 408-778-0562
Gerber Products Company
Parsippany, NJ. 800-443-7237
Ginseng Up Corporation
New York, NY 212-696-1930
Golden Harvest Pecans
Cairo, GA 800-597-0968
Great Eastern Sun
Asheville, NC 800-334-5809
Guayaki Sustainable Rainforest Products
Sebastopol, CA 888-482-9254
H&K Products-Pappy's Sassafras Teas
Columbus Grove, OH 877-659-5110
Hallcrest Vineyards
Felton, CA. 831-335-4441
Harbar Corporation
Canton, MA 800-881-7040
Hawkhaven Greenhouse International
Whitefish Bay, WI 800-745-4295
Health Valley Company
Irwindale, CA 800-334-3204
HempNut
Henderson, NV 707-576-7050
Herbal Magic
Forest Knolls, CA 800-684-3722
Heritage Shortbread
Hilton Head Island, SC 843-342-7268
Highland Sugarworks
Websterville, VT. 800-452-4012
Homestead Mills
Cook, MN 800-652-5233
Howards of Colorado
Denver, CO 970-332-5662
Howler Products
Philo, CA. 800-469-5377
HP Schmid
San Francisco, CA 415-765-5925
Humboldt Flour Mills
Humboldt, SK 306-682-2577
Indigo Coffee Roasters
Florence, MA 800-447-5450
Ineeka Inc
Chicago, IL 312-661-1550
International Casing Group
Chicago, IL 800-825-5151
International Foods
Paramus, NJ 201-909-0808

Island Spring
Vashon, WA. 206-463-9848
Johnson Fruit Company
Sunnyside, WA 509-837-4600
Kellogg Company
Battle Creek, MI 800-962-1413
Kopali Organics
Miami, FL 305-751-7341
Kozlowski Farms
Forestville, CA 800-473-2767
Kraft Foods
Springfield, MO 417-881-2701
La Brea Bakery
Van Nuys, CA 818-742-4242
Laci Le Beau Corporation
Fresno, CA 800-356-0490
Lakeview Bakery
Calgary, AB. 403-246-6127
Late July Organic Snacks
Barnstable, MA. 508-362-5859
Lifeway Foods Inc
Morton Grove, IL 847-967-1010
Lowell Farms
El Campo, TX 888-484-9213
Lundberg Family Farm
Richvale, CA. 530-882-4551
Made in Nature
Fresno, CA 800-906-7426
Magnum Coffee Roastery
Nunica, MI 888-937-5282
Mandarin Soy Sauce
Middletown, NY 845-343-1505
McFadden Farm
Potter Valley, CA 800-544-8230
Mercantile Food Company
Philmont, NY 518-672-0190
Merlino Italian Baking Company
Seattle, WA 800-207-2997
Middlefield Cheese House
Middlefield, OH 800-327-9477
Mills Brothers International
Tukwila, WA 206-575-3000
Minnesota Grain
Lake City, MN 800-535-7405
Minnesota Specialty Crops
McGregor, MN 800-328-6731
Miyako Oriental Foods
Baldwin Park, CA 877-788-6476
Mongolia Casing Corporation
Flushing, NY 800-221-4887
Mountain Sun Organic & Natural Juices
Dolores, CO 970-882-2283
Mr. Espresso
Oakland, CA 510-287-5200
Mrs. Leeper's Pasta
Kansas City, MO. 800-848-5266
Mushroom Company
Cambridge, MD 410-221-8900
Mustard Seed
Central, SC 877-621-2591
Napa Valley Trading Company
Corte Madera, CA. 415-383-8859
Natural Way Mills
Middle River, MN. 218-222-3677
Nature's Candy
Fredericksburg, TX 800-729-0085
Nature's Hand
Burnsville, MN 952-890-6033
Nature's Nutrition
Melbourne, FL 800-242-1115
Nature's Sungrown Foods
San Rafael, CA 415-491-4944
Naturel
Rancho Cucamonga, CA 877-242-8344
New England Natural Bakers
Greenfield, MA 800-910-2884
New Morning
Needham, MA. 781-444-0440
Newman's Own
Westport, CT 203-222-0136
Nomura Tofu Company
Chicago, IL 773-486-7224
North American Seasonings
Lake Oswego, OR. 503-636-7043
North Bay Trading Company
Brule, WI. 800-348-0164
North Country Natural Spring Water
Port Kent, NY 518-834-9400
NSpired Natural Foods
Melville, NY 631-845-4689
Nutra Nuts
Commerce, CA 323-260-7457

Nutrex Hawaii, Inc
Kailua Kona, HI 800-453-1187
Nuvex Ingredients
Blue Earth, MN. 507-526-4331
O Olive Oil
Petaluma, CA 888-827-7148
Omega Nutrition
Bellingham, WA 800-661-3529
Once Again Nut Butter
Nunda, NY 888-800-8075
Organic Gourmet
Sherman Oaks, CA 800-400-7772
Organic Valley
La Farge, WI. 608-625-2602
Organic Wine Company
San Francisco, CA 888-326-9463
Oskri Organics
Thiensville, WI 800-628-1110
Pacari Organic Chocolate
Miami, FL. 561-214-4726
Pack Ryt, Inc
Thermal, CA. 760-399-5026
Pak Technologies
Milwaukee, WI 414-438-8600
Palmieri Food Products
New Haven, CT 800-845-5447
Panos Brands
Saddle Brook, NJ 201-843-8900
Parthenon Food Products
Ann Arbor, MI 734-994-1012
Pasta USA
Spokane, WA. 800-456-2084
Peace Mountain Natural Beverages Corporation
Springfield, MA 413-567-4942
Peace Village Organic Foods
Berkeley, CA. 510-524-4420
Pearl Valley Cheese Company
Fresno, OH 740-545-6002
Personal Edge Nutrition
Ballwin, MO 877-982-3343
Pleasant Grove Farms
Pleasant Grove, CA 916-655-3391
Prairie Mills Company
Wayzata, MN 612-473-9407
Prairie Sun Grains
Calgary, AB. 800-556-6807
Progenix Corporation
Wausau, WI. 800-233-3356
Purity Farms
Sedalia, CO 800-568-4433
Purity Foods
Okemos, MI 800-997-7358
R&J Farms
West Salem, OH 419-846-3179
R.J. Corr Naturals
Posen, IL 708-389-4200
Rapunzel Pure Organics
Chatham, NY 800-207-2814
Ravioli Store
New York, NY 212-925-1737
Red River Commodities
Fargo, ND 701-282-2600
Regenie's All Natural and Organic Snacks
Haverhill, MA. 978-521-4370
Rocky Mountain Honey Company
Salt Lake City, UT 801-355-2054
Run-A-Ton Group
Morristown, NJ 800-247-6580
SafeTrek Foods
Bozeman, MT 406-586-4840
Shariann's Organics
Garden City, NY 800-434-4246
Sierra Madre Organic Coffee
Denver, CO 303-446-0050
Silver Creek Specialty Meats
Oshkosh, WI 920-232-3581
SimmaLoosa Company
Covington, LA 985-892-1400
SJH Enterprises
Middleton, WI. 888-745-3845
Slim Fast Foods Company
West Palm Beach, FL 561-833-9920
Solana Gold Organics
Sebastopol, CA 800-459-1121
Solnuts
Hudson, IA 800-648-3503
Sophia's Sauce Works
Carson City, NV 800-718-7769
Spring Tree Maple Products
Brattleboro, VT. 802-254-8784
Springfield Creamery
Eugene, OR 541-689-2911

Stevia LLC
Valley Forge, PA 888-878-3842
Straus Family Creamery
Marshall, CA. 800-572-7783
Sun Garden Growers
Bard, CA. 800-228-4690
Sun Ridge Farms
Santa Cruz, CA 800-655-3252
Sunergia Soyfoods
Charlottesville, VA 800-693-5134
Sunridge Farms
Salinas, CA 831-755-1430
Sunwest Foods
Davis, CA 530-758-8550
Sustainable Sourcing
Great Barrington, MA. 413-528-5141
Suzanne's Specialties
New Brunswick, NJ 800-762-2135
Tastybaby
Malibu, CA 866-588-8278
Tea Room
American Canyon, CA 866-515-8866
Tea-n-Crumpets
San Rafael, CA 415-457-2495
Templar Food Products
New Providence, NJ 800-883-6752
Thomas Canning/Maidstone
Maidstone, ON 519-737-1531
Tova Industries
Louisville, KY 888-532-8682
Travel Chocolate
Middle Village, NY 718-841-7030
Tree of Life
St Augustine, FL 904-940-2100
Treehouse Farms
Earlimart, CA 559-757-4100
Triple Springs Spring Water
Meriden, CT 203-235-8374
Tripper
Malibu, CA 888-336-8747
True Organic Products International
Miami, FL. 800-487-0379
Twin Marquis
Brooklyn, NY 800-367-6868
Vegetable Juices
Chicago, IL 888-776-9752
Venice Spumoni/Spring Valley Ice Cream
Philadelphia, PA 800-784-0312
Ventre Packing Company
Syracuse, NY 315-463-2384
Vermont Bread Company
Brattleboro, VT. 802-254-4600
Vic Rossano Incorporated
Montreal, QC 514-766-5252
Vienna Bakery
Edmonton, AB 780-436-8211
Vogue Cuisine
Culver City, CA 888-236-4144
WCC Honey Marketing
City of Industry, CA 626-855-3086
Westbrae Natural Foods
Garden City, NY 800-434-4246
Wholesome Sweeteners
Savannah, GA 800-680-1896
Wild Rice Exchange
Woodland, CA 800-223-7423
Wing Nien Company
Hayward, CA 510-487-8877
Wizards Cauldron, LTD
Yanceyville, NC 336-694-5333
Xochitl
Dallas, TX. 214-800-3551
YZ Enterprises
Maumee, OH. 800-736-8779
Zambezi Organic Forest Honey
Oxford, OH 513-523-9209
Zhena's Gypsy Tea
Ojai, CA 800-448-0803

Certified

American Health & Nutrition
Ann Arbor, MI 734-677-5572
American Purpac Technologies, LLC
Beloit, WI 877-787-7221
Brier Run Farm
Birch River, WV 304-649-2975
Briess Industries
Chilton, WI. 920-849-7711
California Custom Fruits & Flavors
Irwindale, CA 877-558-0056

Clofine Dairy & Food Products
Linwood, NJ 800-441-1001

EMERLING INTERNATIONAL FOODS, INC.

Emerling International Foods
Buffalo, NY. 716-833-7381

> We supply food manufacturers and food service customers worldwide (since 1988) with bulk ingredients including: Fruits & Vegetables; Juice Concentrates; Herbs & Spices; Oils & Vinegars; Flavors & Colors; Honey & Molasses. We also produce PURE MAPLE SYRUP.

Frontier Natural Co-op
Norway, IA 303-449-8137
Gilroy
Hanford, CA 559-584-2711
Hains Celestial Group
Melville, NY 877-612-4246
Hoyt's Honey Farm
Baytown, TX 281-576-5383
Innovative Food Solutions LLC
Columbus, OH 800-884-3314
J.W. Raye & Company
Eastport, ME. 800-853-1903
Jonathan's Sprouts
Rochester, MA 508-763-2577
Kozlowski Farms
Forestville, CA 800-473-2767
Lily of the Desert
Denton, TX 800-229-5459
Marukan Vinegar (U.S.A.) Inc.
Paramount, CA 562-630-6060
Mediterranean Delights
Bellows Falls, VT 800-347-5850
Minnesota Grain
Lake City, MN 800-535-7405
National Vinegar Company
Houston, TX 713-223-4214
New Morning
Needham, MA. 781-444-0440
Nu-World Amaranth
Naperville, IL 630-369-6851
Once Again Nut Butter
Nunda, NY 888-800-8075
Organic Gourmet
Sherman Oaks, CA 800-400-7772
Organic Planet
San Francisco, CA 415-765-5590
RFI Ingredients
Blauvelt, NY 800-962-7663
Roberts Seed
Axtell, NE. 308-743-2565
Royal Angelus Macaroni
Chino, CA 909-627-7312
St Mary's & Ankeny Lakes Wild Rice Company
Salem, OR. 800-555-5380
Sun Garden Growers
Bard, CA. 800-228-4690
Sure Fresh Produce
Santa Maria, CA 888-423-5379
Tuscarora Organic Growers Cooperative
Hustontown, PA 814-448-2173
Wood's Sugar Bush
Spring Valley, WI 715-772-4656

Beef

Sunnyside Organics
Washington, VA 540-675-2627

Fruit

Kozlowski Farms
Forestville, CA 800-473-2767
Sun Garden Growers
Bard, CA. 800-228-4690

Poultry

Horizon Organic Dairy
Boulder, CO 888-494-3020

Produce

Argee Corporation
Santee, CA 800-449-3030
Pack Ryt, Inc
Thermal, CA. 760-399-5026
Price Cold Storage & Packing Company
Yakima, WA 509-966-4110

Fruits

Atwater Foods
Lyndonville, NY 585-765-2639
California Custom Fruits & Flavors
Irwindale, CA 877-558-0056

EMERLING INTERNATIONAL FOODS, INC.

Emerling International Foods
Buffalo, NY 716-833-7381

We supply food manufacturers and food service customers worldwide (since 1988) with bulk ingredients including: Fruits & Vegetables; Juice Concentrates; Herbs & Spices; Oils & Vinegars; Flavors & Colors; Honey & Molasses. We also produce PURE MAPLE SYRUP.

Fine Dried Foods International
Santa Cruz, CA 831-426-1413
Golden Town Apple Products
Thornbury, ON 519-599-6300
Hallcrest Vineyards
Felton, CA 831-335-4441
Hialeah Products Company
Hollywood, FL 800-923-3379
Made in Nature
Fresno, CA 800-906-7426
Organic Planet
San Francisco, CA 415-765-5590
Price Cold Storage & Packing Company
Yakima, WA 509-966-4110
Setton International Foods
Commack, NY 800-227-4397
Solana Gold Organics
Sebastopol, CA 800-459-1121
South Exotic Foods
San Diego, CA 619-491-0438
Sunshine Farm & Gardens
Renick, WV 304-497-2208
Unique Ingredients
Naches, WA 509-653-1991

Ingredients

Harten Corporation
Fairfield, NJ 866-642-7836
SK Foods International
Fargo, ND 701-356-4106

Natural

American Health & Nutrition
Ann Arbor, MI 734-677-5572
Baker
Milford, NJ 800-995-3989
Cache Creek Foods
Woodland, CA 530-662-1764
California Custom Fruits & Flavors
Irwindale, CA 877-558-0056
Clofine Dairy & Food Products
Linwood, NJ 800-441-1001
Earthrise Nutritionals
Petaluma, CA 707-778-9078
GKI Foods
Brighton, MI 248-486-0055
Innovative Food Solutions LLC
Columbus, OH 800-884-3314
Internatural Foods
Paramus, NJ 201-909-0808
Larabar
Denver, CO 800-543-2147
Main Street Gourmet
Cuyahoga Falls, OH 800-533-6246
Main Street Muffins
Cuyahoga Falls, OH 800-533-6246
Organic Planet
San Francisco, CA 415-765-5590
Quality Naturally! Foods
City of Industry, CA 888-498-6986

Sure Fresh Produce
Santa Maria, CA 888-423-5379
Unique Ingredients
Naches, WA 509-653-1991
Vegetable Juices
Chicago, IL 888-776-9752
Wine Country Chef LLC
Hidden Valley Lake, CA 707-322-0406

Antioxidants

A&B Ingredients
Fairfield, NJ 973-227-1390

Rice Starch

A&B Ingredients
Fairfield, NJ 973-227-1390

Flour

A&B Ingredients
Fairfield, NJ 973-227-1390
Domino Specialty Ingredients
Baltimore, MD 800-446-9763

Vegetables

EMERLING INTERNATIONAL FOODS, INC.

Emerling International Foods
Buffalo, NY 716-833-7381

We supply food manufacturers and food service customers worldwide (since 1988) with bulk ingredients including: Fruits & Vegetables; Juice Concentrates; Herbs & Spices; Oils & Vinegars; Flavors & Colors; Honey & Molasses. We also produce PURE MAPLE SYRUP.

Made in Nature
Fresno, CA 800-906-7426
Organic Valley
La Farge, WI 608-625-2602
Pleasant Grove Farms
Pleasant Grove, CA 916-655-3391
R&J Farms
West Salem, OH 419-846-3179
Sno Pac Foods
Caledonia, MN 800-533-2215
Vegetable Juices
Chicago, IL 888-776-9752

Survival Foods

AlpineAire Foods
Rocklin, CA 800-322-6325
Food Reserves
Concordia, MO 800-944-1511
Hialeah Products Company
Hollywood, FL 800-923-3379
Oregon Freeze Dry
Albany, OR 800-547-0245

Vegetarian Products

Adventist Book & Food
Trenton, NJ 800-765-6955
Believe
Dallas, TX 800-428-7437
Caribbean Food Delights
Tappan, NY 845-398-3000
CHS
Inver Grove Heights, MN 800-232-3639
Cricklewood Soyfoods
Mertztown, PA 610-682-4109
Dixie USA
Tomball, TX 800-233-3668
Earth Island Natural Foods
Canoga Park, CA 818-725-2820
Eco-Cuisine
Boulder, CO 303-444-6634
Franklin Farms
North Franklin, CT 860-642-3019
Innovative Food Solutions LLC
Columbus, OH 800-884-3314
Jyoti Cruisine India
Berwyn, PA 610-522-2650
Local Tofu
Nyack, NY 845-727-6393
Mon Cuisine
Flushing, NY 877-666-8348

ND Labs Inc
Lynbrook, NY 888-263-5227
Pasta USA
Spokane, WA 800-456-2084
Phillips Gourmet
Kennett Square, PA 610-925-0520
Salvati Foods
Hicksville, NY 516-932-8300
Shiloh Foods
Savannah, TN 800-795-2550
Sweet Earth Natural Foods
Pacific Grove, CA 800-737-3311
Today's Traditions
Chico, CA 800-816-6873
Turtle Island Foods
Hood River, OR 800-508-8100
Unique Ingredients
Naches, WA 509-653-1991
Vegetable Juices
Chicago, IL 888-776-9752
VeggieLand
Parsippany, NJ 888-808-5540
Vegi-Deli
San Rafael, CA 888-473-3667
Vitasoy USA
Ayer, MA 978-772-6880
Wine Country Chef LLC
Hidden Valley Lake, CA 707-322-0406
Worthington Foods
Zanesville, OH 800-535-5644

Burgers

Dixie USA
Tomball, TX 800-233-3668
Quaker Maid Meats
Shillington, PA 610-376-1500
Sunshine Burger Company
Fort Atkinson, WI 845-647-2700
Ungars Food Products
Elmwood Park, NJ 201-703-1300
Vitasoy USA
Ayer, MA 978-772-6880

Patties

Caribbean Food Delights
Tappan, NY 845-398-3000
ConAgra Beef Company
Hyrum, UT 435-245-6456
Gardenburger
Clearfield, UT 801-773-8855
Hampton House
Langley, BC 800-665-4355
Innovative Food Solutions LLC
Columbus, OH 800-884-3314
Mack's Packing
Richfield, UT 435-896-4447
Neese Country Sausage
Greensboro, NC 800-632-1010
Nephi Packing Company
Nephi, UT 435-623-0435
Phillips Gourmet
Kennett Square, PA 610-925-0520
Tami Great Food
Monsey, NY 718-788-4200
Vitasoy USA
Ayer, MA 978-772-6880

Specialty Processed Foods

Barbecue Products (See also Specific Foods)

A. Lassonde, Inc.
Rougemont, QC 514-878-1057
Allied Old English
Port Reading, NJ. 732-602-8955
Arbor Hill Grapery & Winery
Naples, NY 800-554-7553
Art's Tamales
Metamora, IL 309-367-2850
Baker's Rib
Dallas, TX. 214-748-5433
Bartush-Schnitzius Foods Company
Lewisville, TX 972-219-1270
Baumer Foods
New Orleans, LA 504-482-5761
BBQ Bunch
Kansas City, MO. 816-941-6789
Big B Distributors
Evansville, IN 812-425-5235
Black's Barbecue
Lockhart, TX. 512-398-2712
Bottle Green Drinks
Mississauga, ON 905-273-6137
Broadaway Ham Company
Jonesboro, AR. 870-932-6688
Bunker Hill Foods
Augusta, GA 706-733-7765
Cafe Tequila
San Francisco, CA 415-264-0106
California-Antilles Trading Consortium
San Diego, CA 800-330-6450
Calumet Diversified Meat Company
Pleasant Prairie, WI 262-947-7200
Captain Bob's Jet Fuel
Fort Wayne, IN 877-486-6468
Carolina Cupboard
Hillsborough, NC 800-400-3441
Carolina Treet
Wilmington, NC 800-616-6344
Casa Visco Finer Food Company
Schenectady, NY. 888-607-2823
Castleberry/Snow Brands
Augusta, GA 800-241-3520
Catskill Mountain Specialties
Saugerties, NY 800-311-3473
Caughman's Meat Plant
Lexington, SC. 803-356-0076
Chandler Foods
Greensboro, NC 800-537-6219
China Bowl Trading Company
Westport, CT 203-222-0381
CHS, Inc.
Inner Grove Heights, MN 800-232-3639
Cinnabar Specialty Foods
Prescott, AZ 866-293-6433
Clements Foods Company
Oklahoma City, OK 800-654-8355
Colgin Companies
Dallas, TX. 888-226-5446
Consumers Vinegar & Spice Company
Chicago, IL 773-376-4100
Cookies Food Products
Wall Lake, IA 800-331-4995
Corky's Bar-B-Q
Memphis, TN 800-926-7597
Couch's Original Sauce
Jonesboro, AR. 800-264-7535
Creative Foodworks
San Antonio, TX. 210-212-4761
Culinary Standards Corporation
Louisville, KY 800-778-3434
Curly's Foods
Edina, MN. 612-920-3400
D & D Foods
Columbus, GA 706-322-4507
Dankworth Packing Company
Ballinger, TX 325-365-3552
Delta BBQ Sauce Company
Stockton, CA. 209-472-9284
Dillard's Bar-B-Q Sauce
Durham, NC 919-544-1587
Dorina/So-Good
Union, IL. 815-923-2144

Dorothy Dawson Foods Products
Jackson, MI. 517-788-9830
El-Rey Foods
Ferguson, MO 314-521-3113
Favorite Foods
Burnaby, BC 604-420-5100
Felbro Food Products
Los Angeles, CA. 800-335-2761
Figaro Company
Mesquite, TX 972-288-3587
Food Concentrate Corporation
Oklahoma City, OK 405-840-5633
Food Specialties
Indianapolis, IN 317-271-0862
Fremont Company
Fremont, OH 419-334-8995
French's Flavor Ingredients
Springfield, MO 800-437-3624
French's Ingredients
Springfield, MO 417-837-1813
Fry Krisp Food Products
Jackson, MI. 517-784-8531
Garden Complements
Kansas City, MO. 800-966-1091
Gary's Frozen Foods
Lubbock, TX 806-745-1933
Gaucho Foods
Westmont, IL. 630-889-4241
Gayle's Sweet 'N Sassy Foods
Beverly Hills, CA 310-246-1792
Golden Specialty Foods
Norwalk, CA. 562-802-2537
Golden Whisk
South San Francisco, CA 800-660-5222
Golding Farms Foods
Winston Salem, NC. 336-766-6161
Gumpert's Canada
Mississauga, ON 800-387-9324
Hampton House
Langley, BC 800-665-4355
Harold Food Company
Charlotte, NC 704-588-8061
Head Country Food Products
Ponca City, OK 888-762-1227
Heinz
Fremont, OH 419-332-7357
Heinz North America
Pittsburgh, PA 412-237-5700
Hollman Foods
Minden, NE. 888-926-2879
Hormel Foods Corporation
Austin, MN 800-523-4635
House of Webster
Rogers, AR 800-369-4641
J&B Sausage Company
Waelder, TX 830-788-7511
J.D. Mullen Company
Palestine, IL 618-586-2727
J.N. Bech
Elk Rapids, MI 800-232-4583
JMS Specialty Foods
Ripon, WI 800-535-5437
Johnny Harris Famous Barbecue Sauce
Savannah, GA 912-354-8828
King Kold Meats
Englewood, OH 800-836-2797
Kings Food Products
Belleville, IL. 618-233-0400
Kozlowski Farms
Forestville, CA 800-473-2767
Kraft Foods
Northfield, IL 800-323-0768
Kraft Foods
Garland, TX 972-272-7511
Kubla Khan Food Company
Portland, OR 503-234-7494
L&S Packing Company
Farmingdale, NY 800-286-6487
Lea & Perrins
Fair Lawn, NJ 800-289-5797
Lees Sausage Company
Orangeburg, SC 803-534-5517
Lendy's
Virginia Beach, VA 757-491-3511
Lounsbury Foods
Toronto, ON 416-656-6330

M.A. Gedney
Chaska, MN 952-448-2612
Mad Will's Food Company
Auburn, CA. 888-275-9455
Magic Seasoning Blends
Harahan, LA 800-457-2857
Mansmith's Barbecue
San Jn Bautista, CA 800-626-7648
Mar-K Anchor Bar Hot Sauces
Buffalo, NY. 716-853-1791
McCutcheon's Apple Products
Frederick, MD. 800-888-7537
Mitchell Foods
Barbourville, KY 888-202-9745
Moonlite Bar BQ Inn
Owensboro, KY 800-322-8989

Mrs. Clark's Foods
Ankeny, IA 800-736-5674

Juices, salad dressings and sauces.

New Business Corporation
East Chicago, IN. 800-742-8435
Newly Weds Foods
Memphis, TN 800-647-9314
Ninety Six Canning Company
Ninety Six, SC 864-543-2700
O'Brian Brothers Food
Cincinnati, OH 513-791-9909
Original Chili Bowl
Tulsa, OK 918-628-0225
Ott Food Products
Carthage, MO 800-866-2585
Ottman Meat Company
New York, NY 212-879-4160
Pacific Poultry Company
Honolulu, HI 808-841-2828
Palmieri Food Products
New Haven, CT 800-845-5447
Paradise Products Corporation
Roslyn, NY 800-826-1235
Party Steak Company
Springfield, MO 417-358-9091
Piggie Park Enterprises
West Columbia, SC. 800-628-7423
Porinos Gourmet Food
Central Falls, RI 800-826-3938
Portion Pac
Mason, OH 800-232-4829
Produits Ronald
St. Damase, QC 450-797-3303
Randag & Associates Inc
Elmhurst, IL 630-530-2830
Red Gold
Elwood, IN 877-748-9798
Rivertown Foods
St Louis, MO. 800-844-3210
Riverview Foods
Warsaw, KY 859-567-5211
Robinson's Barbecue Sauce Company
Oak Park, IL 708-383-8452
Roos Foods
Kenton, DE 800-343-3642
Rosmarino Foods/R.Z. Humbert Company
Odessa, FL 888-926-9053
Sadler's BBQ Sales
Henderson, TX 903-657-5581
Savoie's Sausage & Food Products
Opelousas, LA. 337-948-4115
Schiff Food Products
North Bergen, NJ 201-861-2503
Schlotterbeck & Foss Company
Portland, ME. 800-777-4666
Scott's Sauce Company
Goldsboro, NC 800-734-7282
Sona & Hollen Foods
Los Alamitos, CA. 800-200-7662
Southern Ray's Foods
Miami Beach, FL 800-972-8237

557

Steel's Gourmet Foods
Bridgeport, PA 800-678-3357
Suzanna's Kitchen
Duluth, GA 800-241-2455
Sweet Baby Ray's
Marlboro, MA 877-729-2229
T. Marzetti Company
Columbus, OH 614-846-2232
T.W. Garner Food Company
Winston Salem, NC. 800-476-7383
Tenn Valley Ham Company
Paris, TN 731-642-9740
Thompson's Fine Foods
Shoreview, MN 800-807-0025
Todd's
Des Moines, IA 800-247-5363
Travis Meats
Powell, TN 800-247-7606
Triple H Food Processors
Riverside, CA 951-352-5700
Triple K Manufacturing Company
Shenandoah, IA 888-987-2824
Triple U Enterprises
Fort Pierre, SD 605-567-3624
Tyson Foods Plant
Santa Teresa, NM 800-351-8184
Valley Grain Products
Madera, CA. 559-675-3400
Vanlaw Food Products
Fullerton, CA 714-870-9091
Ventura Foods
Philadelphia, PA 215-223-8700
Vidalia Sweets Brand
Lyons, GA 912-565-8881
Vietti Foods Company Inc
Nashville, TN 800-240-7864
W&G Marketing Company
Ames, IA 515-233-4774
Webbpak
Trussville, AL 800-655-3500
Wei-Chuan
Bell Gardens, CA 562-927-6681
West Pac
Idaho Falls, ID 800-973-7407
Westin
Omaha, NE 800-228-6098
Wing Nien Company
Hayward, CA 510-487-8877
Wood Brothers
West Columbia, SC. 803-796-5146
Woods Smoked Meats
Bowling Green, MO 800-458-8426
Zarda Bar-B-Q & Catering Company
Blue Springs, MO 800-776-7427
Zoll Foods Corporation
South Holland, IL 708-333-3900

Dehydrated Food (See also Specific Foods)

Agvest
Cleveland, OH 440-735-6900
Ailments E.D. Foods Inc.
Pointe Claire, QC 800-267-3333
Alkinco
New York, NY. 800-424-7118
American Nut & Chocolate Company
Boston, MA. 800-797-6887
American Whey
Ridgewood, NJ 201-493-2662
Amport Foods
Minneapolis, MN 800-989-5665
Anderson Custom Processing
New Ulm, MN. 877-588-4950
Associated Brands, Inc.
Medina, NY. 800-265-0050
Atlantic Quality Spice &Seasonings
Edison, NJ. 800-584-0422
Atrium Biotech
Fairfield, NJ 866-628-2355
Basic American Foods
Walnut Creek, CA. 800-227-4050
Blossom Farm Products
Ridgewood, NJ 800-729-1818
Boghosian Raisin Packing Company
Fowler, CA. 559-834-5348
Bridgford Foods Corporation
Anaheim, CA 800-527-2105
Cagnon Foods Company
Brooklyn, NY 718-647-2244
California Fruit
Sanger, CA 559-266-7117

Caltex Foods
Canoga Park, CA 800-522-5839
Casados Farms
San Juan Pueblo, NM 505-852-2433
Challenge Dairy Products
Dublin, CA 800-733-2479
Chef Merito
Encino, CA 800-637-4861
Chia I Foods Company
South El Monte, CA 626-401-3038
Chooljian Brothers Packing Company
Sanger, CA 559-875-5501
Chukar Cherries
Prosser, WA. 800-624-9544
Clofine Dairy & Food Products
Linwood, NJ 800-441-1001
Colorado Bean Company/ Greeley Trading
Greeley, CO. 888-595-2326
Commercial Creamery Company
Spokane, WA. 800-541-0850
Consumers Vinegar & Spice Company
Chicago, IL 773-376-4100
Country Cupboard
Virginia City, NV 775-847-7300
Crystal Foods
Brick, NJ. 732-477-0073
Dairy Farmers of America
Franklinton, LA 800-735-2038
Dairy Farmers of AmericaGoshen Plant
Goshen, IN 800-758-0269
Dairy King Milk Farms/Foodservice
Glendale, CA 818-243-6455
Dairy-Mix
St Petersburg, FL 727-525-6101
Dairyman's/Land O' Lakes
Tulare, CA. 559-687-8287
DeFrancesco & Sons
Firebaugh, CA 209-364-7000
Del Monte Foods
San Francisco, CA 800-543-3090
Del Rey Packing Company
Del Rey, CA 559-888-2031
Desert Valley Date
Coachella, CA. 760-398-0999
Devansoy
Carroll, IA 800-747-8605
Diamond Crystal Specialty Foods
Bondurant, IA 515-967-3737
Diamond Foods
Fishers, IN. 317-845-5534
Dietrich's Milk Products
Reading, PA 800-526-6455
Dismat Corporation
Toledo, OH 419-531-8963

EMERLING INTERNATIONAL FOODS, INC.

Emerling International Foods
Buffalo, NY. 716-833-7381

We supply food manufacturers and food service customers worldwide (since 1988) with bulk ingredients including: **Fruits & Vegetables; Juice Concentrates; Herbs & Spices; Oils & Vinegars; Flavors & Colors; Honey & Molasses**. We also produce **PURE MAPLE SYRUP**.

Fig Garden Packing
Fresno, CA 559-271-9000
Fine Dried Foods International
Santa Cruz, CA 831-426-1413
First District Association
Litchfield, MN 320-693-3236
Food Reserves
Concordia, MO 800-944-1511
Foremost Farms
Preston, MN 507-765-3831
Freeman Industries
Tuckahoe, NY 800-666-6454
Fuji Foods
Browns Summit, NC. 336-375-3111
Garden Valley Foods
Sutherlin, OR 541-459-9565
Gilroy Foods
Gilroy, CA. 800-921-7502
Global Food Industries
Townville, SC 800-225-4152
Golden Town Apple Products
Thornbury, ON 519-599-6300
Graf Creamery
Zachow, WI. 715-758-2137

Green House Fine Herbs
Encinitas, CA 760-942-5371
Henningsen Foods
Omaha, NE 402-330-2500
Henningsen Foods
Purchase, NY. 914-701-4020
Henry Broch & Company/APK, Inc.
Libertyville, IL 847-816-6225
Hialeah Products Company
Hollywood, FL 800-923-3379
Honeyville Grain
Salt Lake City, UT 801-972-2168
Humco
Texarkana, TX. 800-662-3435
Idaho Pacific Corporation
Ririe, ID 800-238-5503
Idaho Supreme Potatoes
Firth, ID. 208-346-6841
Ingredients Corporation of America
Memphis, TN 901-525-6660
Ittels Meats
Howard Lake, MN 320-543-2285
Jasper Wyman & Son
Milbridge, ME 800-341-1758
Jones Produce
Quincy, WA. 509-787-3537
Kamish Food Products
Chicago, IL 773-267-0400
Kelley Bean Company
Scottsbluff, NE 308-635-6438
Kennedy Candy Company
Kilgore, TX. 800-657-5258
Kerry Ingredients
Tralee, Co. Kerry,
Kozlowski Farms
Forestville, CA 800-473-2767
Kraft Foods
Albany, MN. 320-845-2131
Land O'Lakes, Inc
Arden Hills, MN 800-328-9680
Larsen Farms
Hamer, ID 208-662-5501
Larsen of Idaho
Hamer, ID 208-662-5501
Leroux Creek Foods
Hotchkiss, CO. 877-970-5670
Lone Star Beef Jerky Company
Lubbock, TX. 806-762-8833
Made in Nature
Fresno, CA 800-906-7426
Magic Valley Foods
Rupert, ID 208-436-3126
Main Street Ingredients
La Crosse, WI. 800-359-2345
Maine Wild Blueberry Company
Cherryfield, ME 800-243-4005
Maruchan
Irvine, CA. 949-789-2300
Master Mix
Placentia, CA. 714-524-1698
Mayacamas Fine Foods
Sonoma, CA 800-826-9621
Mercer Processing
Modesto, CA. 209-529-0150
Mojave Foods Corporation
Commerce, CA 323-890-8900
Morris J. Golombeck
Brooklyn, NY 718-284-3505
Niagara Foods
Middleport, NY. 716-735-7722
North Bay Trading Company
Brule, WI. 800-348-0164
Northern Feed & Bean Company
Lucerne, CO 970-352-7875
Nuttery Farms
Saint Helena, CA 707-963-1101
Oakland Bean Cleaning & Storage
Knights Landing, CA 530-735-6203
Ontario Foods Exports
Mississauga, ON 888-466-2372
Oregon Potato Company
Boardman, OR 800-336-6311
Pack Ryt, Inc
Thermal, CA 760-399-5026
Paisano Food Products
Elk Grove Village, IL 773-237-3773
Pasta USA
Spokane, WA. 800-456-2084
Pines International
Lawrence, KS 800-697-4637
Plainview Milk Products Cooperative
Plainview, MN 507-534-3872

Pro Form Labs
Orinda, CA 925-299-9000
Producers Cooperative
Olathe, CO 970-323-5913
Produits Alimentaires Berthelet
Laval, QC 514-334-5503
Protient (Land O Lakes)
St Paul, MN. 651-481-2068
Quality Brands
Deland, FL 386-738-3808
Quality Ingredients Corporation
Burnsville, MN 952-898-4002
Ramos Orchards
Winters, CA 530-795-4748
Ramsen
Lakeville, MN. .952-431-0400
Red River Foods
Richmond, VA. 800-443-6637
Reinhart Foods
Markham, ON .905-754-3503
Rinehart Meat Processing
Branson, MO. .417-334-2044
Russell E. Womack
Lubbock, TX 877-787-3559
San Joaquin Valley Dairymen
Los Banos, CA .209-826-4901
Schiff Food Products
North Bergen, NJ 201-861-2503
Seller Kirk & Company
Schwenksville, PA 215-480-7342
Seneca Foods
Marion, NY. 315-926-8100
Serv-Agen Corporation
Cherry Hill, NJ 856-663-6966
Shields Date Gardens
Indio, CA. 800-414-2555
Smeltzer Orchard Company
Frankfort, MI 231-882-4421
Smuggler's Kitchen
Dundee, FL. 800-604-6793
Solana Gold Organics
Sebastopol, CA 800-459-1121
Somerset Industries
Spring House, PA 800-883-8728
SOUPerior Bean & Spice Company
Vancouver, WA. 800-878-7687
South Mill Distribution
Kennett Square, PA. 610-444-4800
Spice Hunter
San Luis Obispo, CA 800-444-3061
Spreda Group
Prospect, KY 502-426-9411
St. Ours & Company
Norwell, MA. 781-331-8520
Stapleton-Spence PackingCompany
San Jose, CA 800-297-8815
Sterigenics International
Los Angeles, CA. 800-472-4508
Sugar Foods
Sun Valley, CA 818-768-7900
Tastee Apple Inc
Newcomerstown, OH 800-262-7753
Total Ultimate Foods
Columbus, OH 800-333-0732
Tova Industries
Louisville, KY .888-532-8682
Trinidad Benham Company
Denver, CO 303-220-1400
Trinidad/Benham Corporation
Patterson, CA .209-892-9002
Triple U Enterprises
Fort Pierre, SD 605-567-3624
Tropical
Charlotte, NC .800-220-1413
Tropical
Columbus, OH 800-538-3941
Tropical
Marietta, GA 800-544-3762
Unique Ingredients
Naches, WA. 509-653-1991
United Dairymen of Arizona
Tempe, AZ. 480-966-7211
Ursula's Island Farms
Seattle, WA 206-762-3113
US Foods
Lincoln, NE. 402-470-2021
US Fresh Marketing
Virginia Beach, VA. 757-481-2606
Valley View Packing Company
San Jose, CA 408-289-8300
Van Drunen Farms
Momence, IL. .815-472-3100

Verhoff Alfalfa Mills
Toledo, OH 800-834-8563
Very Best Foods
Miami, FL. 305-824-9165
Vi-Gor Cup Corporation
Bellmore, NY .516-431-7722
VIP Foods
Flushing, NY. .718-821-3942
Vogue Cuisine
Culver City, CA 888-236-4144
Vrymeer Commodities
St Charles, IL .630-584-0069
W&G Flavors
Hunt Valley, MD. 410-771-6606
WA Bean & Sons
Bangor, ME. 800-649-1958
Washington Potato Company
Warden, WA 509-349-8803
Welsh Farms
Newark, NJ 800-221-0663
Westin
Omaha, NE 800-228-6098
Westlam Foods
Chino, CA. 800-722-9519

Fermented Products (See also Specific Foods)

Roland Industries
Saint Louis, MO 800-325-1183

Freeze Dried Food (See also Specific Foods)

Bethel Eckert Enterprises
Collinsville, IL 618-345-1138

EMERLING INTERNATIONAL FOODS, INC.

Emerling International Foods
Buffalo, NY. 716-833-7381

> We supply food manufacturers and food service customers worldwide (since 1988) with bulk ingredients including: Fruits & Vegetables; Juice Concentrates; Herbs & Spices; Oils & Vinegars; Flavors & Colors; Honey & Molasses. We also produce PURE MAPLE SYRUP.

Food Reserves
Concordia, MO 800-944-1511
Freeze-Dry Products
Santa Rosa, CA. 707-547-1776
Hanover Foods Corporation
Hanover, PA 717-632-6000
L.K. Bowman Company
Nottingham, PA. 800-853-1919
Mark-Lynn Foods
Bremen, GA 800-327-0162
Master Taste International
Plant City, FL .800-237-7629
Oregon Freeze Dry
Albany, OR 800-547-0245
SafeTrek Foods
Bozeman, MT .406-586-4840
Unique Ingredients
Naches, WA. 509-653-1991
Van Drunen Farms
Momence, IL. .815-472-3100
Vivolac Cultures Corporation
Indianapolis, IN 317-356-8460

Frozen Foods (See also Specific Foods)

A Natural Harvest Restaurant
Chicago, IL 773-363-3939
A&G Food & Liquors
Chicago, IL 773-994-1541
A.C. Petersen Farms
West Hartford, CT. 860-233-8483
Abbotsford Growers Co-operative
Abbotsford, BC. 604-864-0022
Ace Food
Bayou La Batre, AL 800-884-0741
Acme Steak & Seafood Company
Youngstown, OH. 330-270-8000
Aglamesis Brothers
Cincinnati, OH 513-531-5196
Agland, Inc.
Eaton, CO 800-433-4688

Agripac
Denver, CO. 503-363-9255
Agropur Cooperative Agro-Alimentaire
Granby, QC 800-363-5686
Agvest
Franklin, ME. .207-565-3303
Agvest
Cleveland, OH 440-735-6900
Ajinomato Frozen Foods USA
Portland, OR 503-286-5869
Ajinomoto Frozen Foods USA
Portland, IR. 503-734-1528
Akenhead's Ice Cream Company
East Palestine, OH 330-426-9553
Al Gelato Bornay
Franklin Park, IL. 847-455-5355
Al Pete Meats
Muncie, IN 765-288-8817
Al-Rite Fruits & Syrups
Miami, FL. 305-652-2540
Aladdin Bakers
Brooklyn, NY .718-499-1818
Alamance Foods/Triton Water Company
Burlington, NC 800-476-9111
Alaska Seafood Company
Los Angeles, CA. 213-626-1212
Alaskan Gourmet Seafoods
Anchorage, AK 800-288-3740
Alati-Caserta Desserts
Montreal, QC .514-271-3013
Albertson's Ice-Cream
Boise, ID 877-932-7948
Alexia Foods
Long Island City, NY 718-937-0100
Alfredo's Italian Foods Manufacturing Company
Quincy, MA. 617-479-6360
Alinosi French Superfine Candies
Detroit, MI 313-527-3195
Aliotti Wholesale Fish Company
Monterey, CA .831-375-2881
All Alaskan Seafood
Seattle, WA 206-285-8200
All Round Foods
Westbury, NY .516-338-1888
Alle Processing Corporation
Flushing, NY. .800-245-5620
Allen Canning Company
Siloam Springs, AR 800-234-2553
Allen Family Foods
Seaford, DE. 302-629-9163
Allen's Blueberry Freezer
Ellsworth, ME. 207-667-5561
Alpenrose Dairy
Portland, OR 503-244-1133
Alphin Brothers
Dunn, NC 800-672-4502
Alyeska Seafoods
Seattle, WA 206-547-2100
Amano Fish Cake Factory
Hilo, HI 808-935-5555
Amberwave Foods
Oakmont, PA. .412-828-3040
American Classic Ice Cream Company
Bay Shore, NY 631-666-1000
American Seafoods Group
Seattle, WA 800-275-2019
American Seafoods International
New Bedford, MA 800-343-8046
Americana Foods
Dallas, TX. 972-709-7100
Anchor Food Products/ McCain Foods
Appleton, WI .920-734-0627
Andrew & Williamson Sales Company
San Diego, CA 619-661-6004
Angy's Food Products, Inc.
Westfield, MA. 413-572-1010
Annie's Frozen Yogurt
Minneapolis, MN 800-969-9648
Appert's Foodservice
St Cloud, MN .800-225-3883
Appleton Produce Company
Weiser, ID 208-414-1102
APTCO
San Francisco, CA 415-648-6688
AquaCuisine
Eagle, ID 888-330-2782
Arista Industries
Wilton, CT 800-255-6457
Aristocrat International Corporation
Secaucus, NJ .201-866-1900
Arkansas Poly
N Little Rock, AR 800-364-5036

Arkansas Refrigerated Services
Fort Smith, AR 479-783-1006
Armbrust Meats
Medford, WI 715-748-3102
Arrowac Fisheries
Seattle, WA 206-282-5655
Art's Tamales
Metamora, IL 309-367-2850
Artel
Boisbriand, QC 450-433-1322
Artuso Pastry Foods
Mt Vernon, NY 914-663-8806
Artuso Pastry Shop
Bronx, NY 718-367-2515
ASC Seafood
Largo, FL 800-876-3474
Aslanis Seafoods
Quincy, MA 800-876-3712
Aspen Foods
Park Ridge, IL 847-384-5940
Assouline & Ting
Philadelphia, PA 800-521-4491
Athens Pastries & Frozen Foods
Cleveland, OH 800-837-5683
Atkinson Milling Company
Selma, NC .800-948-5707
Atlanta Flagship Dairy
Atlanta, GA 800-224-0669
Atlantic Blueberry Company
Hammonton, NJ 609-561-8600
Atlantic Meat Company
Savannah, GA 912-964-8511
Atlantic Premium Brands
Northbrook, IL 847-412-6200
Atlantic Queen Seafoods Limited
Lachine, QC 514-636-5114
Atlantic Veal & Lamb
Brooklyn, NY 800-221-6988
Aurora Frozen Foods Division
Saint Louis, MO 314-801-2300
Austin Packaging Company
Austin, MN 507-433-6623
Austin Special Foods Company
Austin, TX .866-372-8663
Avalon Foodservice, Inc.
Canal Fulton, OH 800-362-0622

Avanti Food Company
Walnut, IL .800-243-3739
Avo King International
Orange, CA 800-286-5464
Awrey Bakeries
Livonia, MI 800-950-2253
B&D Foods
Boise, ID 208-344-1183
Badger Best Pizzas
Green Bay, WI. 920-336-6464
Baja Foods
Chicago, IL 773-376-9030
Baker Boy Bake Shop
Dickinson, ND 800-437-2008
Baker Boys
Calgary, AB. 877-246-6036
Baker's Point Fisheries
Oyster Pond Jeddore, NS 902-845-2347
Bakery Chef
Louisville, KY 800-594-0203
Balboa Dessert Company
Santa Ana, CA 800-974-9699
Ballas Egg Products Corporation
Zanesville, OH 740-453-0386
Bama Frozen Dough
Tulsa, OK .800-756-2262
Bandon Bay Fisheries
Bandon, OR 541-347-4454
Barber Foods
Portland, ME 800-577-2595
Barnes Ice Cream Company
Augusta, ME 207-622-0827
Barnum & Bagel Frozen Soup
Skokie, IL .847-676-4466
Basic American Foods
Blackfoot, ID 800-227-4050
Bavarian Specialty Foods
Sun Valley, CA 310-212-6199
Bay Oceans Sea Foods
Garibaldi, OR 503-322-3316
Bayou Land Seafood
Breaux Bridge, LA 337-667-6118
Beatty Fresh Frozen Meats
Bourbon, IN 574-342-2665
Beaver Street Fisheries
Jacksonville, FL 800-874-6426

Beck's Waffles of Oklahoma
Shawnee, OK 800-646-6254
Becker Food Company
Milwaukee, WI 414-964-5353
Behm Blueberry Farms
Grand Haven, MI 616-846-1650
Bell Buoy Crab Company
Seaside, OR. 800-529-2722
Bellisio Foods, Inc.
Lakeville, MN. 800-368-7337
Ben E. Keith DFW
Fort Worth, TX 817-654-3663
Benson Creamery
Decatur, IL 217-429-2351
Benson's Bakery
Bogart, GA 800-888-6059
Berkshire Cold Storage
Chicago, IL 773-254-2424
Bernardi Italian Foods Company
Bloomsburg, PA 570-389-5500
Bernie's Foods
Brooklyn, NY 718-417-6677
Best Maid Cookie Company
River Falls, WI 888-444-0322
Beta Pure Foods
Aptos, CA .831-685-6565
Bethel Eckert Enterprises
Collinsville, IL 618-345-1138
Better Baked Foods
North East, PA. 814-725-8778
BG Smith Sons Oyster
Sharps, VA 877-483-8279
Biagio's Banquets
Chicago, IL 800-392-2837
Big Apple Produce & Seafood Market
Pocomoke City, MD 410-957-1151
Bill Mack's Homemade Ice Cream
Dover, PA .717-292-1931
Birch Street Seafoods
Digby, NS .902-245-6551
Birchwood Foods
Kenosha, WI 800-541-1685
Birdie Pak Products
Chicago, IL 773-247-5293
Birdsall Ice Cream Company
Mason City, IA 641-423-5365

Blakely Freezer Locker
Thomasville, GA....................229-723-3622
Bland Farms
Reidsville, GA 800-752-0206
Blend Pak
Bloomfield, KY 502-252-8000
Blount Seafood Corporation
Fall River, MA 774-888-1300
Blue Ridge Farms
Brooklyn, NY 718-827-9000
Blue Ridge Poultry
Athens, GA 706-546-6767
Blue Wave Seafoods
Port Mouton, NS...................902-683-2044
BlueWater Seafoods
Lachine, QC 888-560-2539
Bob's Custom Cuts
Bonnyville, AB.....................780-826-2627
Boboli International Inc
Stockton, CA.......................209-473-3507
Bocconcino Food Products
Moonachie, NJ.....................201-933-7474
Bodin Foods
New Iberia, LA.....................337-367-1344
Boekhout Farms
Ontario, NY........................315-524-4041
Bolner's Fiesta Products
San Antonio, TX...................210-734-6404
Bon Secour Fisheries
Bon Secour, AL....................800-633-6854
Bonnie Doon Ice Cream Corporation
Elkhart, IN........................574-264-3390
Bornstein Seafoods
Warrenton, OR.....................503-861-1233
Bosell Foods
Cleveland, OH 216-991-7600
Boston Chowda Company
Lowell, MA.........................800-992-0054
Bottineau Cooperative Creamery
Bottineau, ND......................701-228-2216
Boyle Meat Company
Kansas City, MO...................800-821-3626
Brady Farms
West Olive, MI.....................616-842-3916
Brakebush Brothers
Westfield, WI......................800-933-2121
Braun Seafood Company
Cutchogue, NY.....................631-734-5550
Breakfast at Brennan's
New Orleans, LA...................800-888-9932
Bridgford Foods
Anaheim, CA.......................800-527-2105
Bridgford Foods Corporation
Anaheim, CA.......................800-527-2105
Bridgford Foods Corporation Superior Foods Division
Anaheim, CA.......................800-527-2105
Brighams
Arlington, MA 800-274-4426
Bright Harvest Sweet Potato Company
Clarksville, AR.....................800-793-7440
Brightwood Baking Company
Cicero, IN.........................317-356-2449
Broadleaf Venison USA
Vernon, CA........................800-336-3844
Brom Food Group
St. Laurent, QC....................514-744-5152
Brook Locker Plant
Brook, IN..........................219-275-2611
Brooklyn Bagel Company
Staten Island, NY 800-349-3055
Brooks Food Group Corporate Office
Bedford, VA 800-873-4934
Brookview Farms
Archbold, OH 419-445-6366
Broughton Foods
Marietta, OH 800-283-2479
Brown Produce Company
Farina, IL.........................618-245-3301
Brown's Ice Cream
Minneapolis, MN...................612-378-1075
Brownie Products Company
Gardner, IL........................815-237-2163
Browns Dairy
Valparaiso, IN.....................219-464-4141
Browns' Ice Cream Company
Bowling Green, KY 270-843-9882
Brownsdale Meat Service
Brownsdale, MN....................507-567-2211
Bruno Specialty Foods
West Sayville, NY..................631-589-1700
Bubbies Homemade Ice Cream
Aiea, HI...........................808-487-7218

Buck's Spumoni Company
Milford, CT........................203-874-2007
Bueno Food Products
Albuquerque, NM..................800-888-7336
Bullock's Country Meats
Westminster, MD..................410-848-6786
Buns & Things Bakery
Charlottetown, PE.................902-892-2600

Always make it your best®

Burke Corporation
Nevada, IA 800-654-1152

Always make it your best® with Burke fully cooked meats. We specialize in Italian sausage, beef, and pork toppings, meatballs, taco meats, shredded meats, pepperoni, bacon, Canadian-style bacon, chicken and beef strips. Additionally, we offer a variety of specialty products: Hand-Pinched Style® brand toppings, chorizo, gyro topping, andouille sausage, and breakfast patties and links.

Bush Brothers Provision Company
West Palm Beach, FL 800-327-1345
Butterfield Foods Company
Butterfield, MN....................507-956-5103
Buxton Foods
Buxton, ND........................800-726-8057
Buzz Food Service
Charleston, WV....................304-925-4781
C.F. Gollott & Son Seafood
Biloxi, MS.........................866-846-3474
Caesar's Pasta Products
Blackwood, NJ.....................856-227-2585
Cafferata
San Anselmo, CA..................800-626-8115
Cahoon Farms
Wolcott, NY 315-594-8081
California Brands Flavors
Oakland, CA.......................800-348-0111
California Farms & Canners
San Francisco, CA 415-433-3522
California Shellfish Company
Gardena, CA.......................310-538-4197
Callis Seafood
Lancaster, VA......................804-462-7634
Camino Real Foods
Vernon, CA........................800-421-6201
Campbell Soup Company
Camden, NJ.......................800-257-8443
Campbell Soup Company of Canada
Listowel, ON.......................800-575-7687
Caps Italian Foods
Saint Anne, IL.....................815-427-6522
Captain Ken's Foods
St Paul, MN........................651-298-0071
Captain Ottis Seafood
Morehead City, NC.................252-247-3569
Carando Gourmet Frozen Foods
Springfield, MA 413-730-4205
Carbolite Foods
Evansville, IN......................888-524-3314
Caribbean Food Delights
Tappan, NY........................845-398-3000
Caribbean Products
Baltimore, MD.....................410-235-7700
Carla's Pasta
South Windsor, CT.................800-957-2782
Carolina Blueberry Association
Garland, NC 910-588-4220
Carolina Foods
Charlotte, NC......................800-234-0441
Carousel Cakes
Nanuet, NY 800-659-2253
Carriere Foods Inc
Montreal, QC......................514-384-4281
Carrington Foods
Saraland, AL.......................251-675-9700
Casa Di Bertacchi
Vineland, NJ.......................800-818-9261
Casa di Carfagna
Columbus, OH.....................614-846-6340
Casa DiLisio Products
Mt Kisco, NY 800-247-4199

Castleberry/Snow Brands
Augusta, GA 800-241-3520
Cateraid
Howell, MI 800-508-8217
Cathay Foods Corporation
Boston, MA........................617-427-1507
Cavendish Farms
Jamestown, ND....................888-284-5687
Cavendish Farms
Dieppe, NB........................888-883-7437
CBC Foods Inc
Little River, KS....................800-276-4770
Cedar Crest Specialties
Cedarburg, WI.....................800-877-8341
Cedar Key Aquaculture Farms
Riverview, FL......................888-252-6735
Cedar Lake Foods
Cedar Lake, MI....................800-246-5039
Cedaredge Meats
Cedaredge, CO....................970-856-3517
Cedarlane Foods
Carson, CA........................800-826-3322
Celentano Brothers
Verona, NJ.........................973-239-2557
Centreside Dairy
Renfrew, ON.......................613-432-2914
Chalet Desserts
Union City, CA.....................510-783-8300
Challenge Dairy Products
Dublin, CA.........................800-733-2479
Chandler Foods
Greensboro, NC 800-537-6219
Chang Food Company
Garden Grove, CA.................714-265-9990
Chase Farms
Walkerville, MI.....................231-873-3337
Chases Lobster Pound
Port Howe, NS.....................902-243-2408
Chateau Food Products
Cicero, IL..........................708-863-4207
Chef America
Chatsworth, CA....................818-718-8111
Chef America East
Mount Sterling, KY.................859-498-4300
Chef Francisco of Pennsylvania
King of Prussia, PA.................610-265-7400
Chef Hans Gourmet Foods
Monroe, LA........................800-890-4267
Chef Solutions
North Haven, CT...................856-848-5314
Cher-Make Sausage Company
Manitowoc, WI.....................800-242-7679
Cherbogue Fisheries
Yarmouth, NS......................902-742-9157
Cherry Growers
Grawn, MI.........................231-276-9241
Cherry Growers
Grawn, MI.........................800-530-9030
Cherry Hill Orchards Pelham
Fenwick, ON.......................905-892-3782
Cherry Lane Frozen Fruits
Vineland Station, ON...............905-562-4337
Chester W. Howeth & Brother
Crisfield, MD 410-968-1398
Chewys Rugulach
San Diego, CA.....................800-241-3456
Chicago Meat Authority
Chicago, IL.........................773-254-0020
Chill & Moore
Fort Worth, TX 800-676-3055
Chincoteague Seafood Company
Parsonsburg, MD..................443-260-4800
Chloe Foods Corporation
Brooklyn, NY 718-827-3600
Chocolate Shoppe Ice Cream Company
Madison, WI.......................608-221-8640
Chocolaterie Bernard Callebaut
Calgary, AB........................800-661-8367
Choctaw Maid Farms
Carthage, MS 601-298-5300
CHR Foods
Watsonville, CA....................831-728-0157
Christie Cookie Company
Nashville, TN 615-242-3817
Chungs Gourmet Foods
Houston, TX 713-741-2118
Ciao Bella Gelato Company
Irvington, NY.......................800-435-2863
Cinderella Cheese Cake Company
Riverside, NJ.......................856-461-6302
Citrico
Northbrook, IL......................888-625-8516

Citrus Citrosuco North America
Lake Wales, FL 800-356-4592
Citrus Service
Winter Garden, FL 407-656-4999
Clark Foodservice
Elk Grove Vlg, IL 800-504-3663
Clark Foodservice
Elk Grove Vlg, IL 847-956-1730
Classic Delight
St Marys, OH 800-274-9828
Claxton Cold Storage
Claxton, GA 912-739-9800
Clear Springs Foods
Buhl, ID 800-635-8211
Clearwater Fine Foods
Bedford, NS 902-443-0550
Cleugh's Frozen Foods
Buena Park, CA 714-521-1002
Clydes Delicious Donuts
Addison, IL 630-628-6555
Coastal Seafoods
Ridgefield, CT 203-431-0453
Cobi Foods
Hantsport, NS 800-565-8229
Codino's Italian Foods
Scotia, NY 800-246-8908
Cohen's Bakery
Buffalo, NY 716-892-8149
Cold Springs Farm
Thamesford, ON 800-265-1978
Colder Products Company
St Paul, MN 800-444-2474
Coldwater Seafood Corporation
Norwalk, CT 203-846-8897
Coldwater Seafood Corporation
Newport News, VA 410-228-7500
Cole's Quality Foods
Muskegon, MI 231-722-1651
Coloma Frozen Foods
Coloma, MI 800-642-2723
Colonial Beef Company
Philadelphia, PA 215-289-7042
Columbia Foods
Snohomish, WA 360-568-0838
Columbia Foods
Quincy, WA 509-787-1585
Con Agra Foods
Holly Ridge, NC 910-329-9061
ConAgra Broiler Company
Dalton, GA 706-278-3212
ConAgra Foods
Sidney, OH 800-736-2212
ConAgra Foods   Lamb Weston Plant
Richland, WA 509-375-4181
ConAgra Foods   Lamb Weston® Headquarters
Kennewick, WA 509-736-0456
ConAgra Foods/Eckrich
Omaha, NE 800-327-4424
ConAgra Frozen Foods Company
Omaha, NE 402-595-4000
ConAgra Frozen Foods Company
Macon, MO 660-385-3184
ConAgra Frozen Foods Company
Marshall, MO 660-886-3301
ConAgra Grocery Products
Archbold, OH 419-445-8015
ConAgra Mexican Foods
Compton, CA 310-223-1499
ConAgra Poultry Company
Duluth, GA 800-609-6050
ConAgra Snack Foods Group/Act II Popcorn
Edina, MN 800-328-6286
Consolidated Mills
Houston, TX 713-896-4196

Consun Food Industries
Elyria, OH 440-233-7501
Contact International
Skokie, IL 847-324-4411
Contessa Food Products
San Pedro, CA 310-832-8000
Continental Food Products
Flushing, NY 718-358-7894
Continental Mills
Seattle, WA 253-872-8400
Contract Comestibles
East Troy, WI 262-642-9400
Cook Inlet Processing
Nikiski, AK 907-776-8174
Cookie Tree Bakeries
Salt Lake City, UT 800-998-0111
Corky's Bar-B-Q
Memphis, TN 800-926-7597
Country Fresh
Grand Rapids, MI 800-748-0480
Country Fresh Golden Valley
Livonia, MI 734-261-7980
Country Pies
Coombs, BC 250-248-6415
Country Pure Foods
Akron, OH 330-753-2293
Cozy Harbor Seafood
Portland, ME 800-225-2586
Crab King Seafood Specialties
Seattle, WA 206-283-2722
Cream O'Weaver Dairy
Salt Lake City, UT 801-973-9922
Creighton Brothers
Atwood, IN 574-267-3101
Creme Curls Bakery
Hudsonville, MI 800-466-1219
Creme D'Lite
Dallas, TX 214-637-1010
Creme Glacee Gelati
St Leonard, QC 888-322-0116
Crescent Duck Farm
Aquebogue, NY 631-722-8700
Crest International Corporation
San Diego, CA 800-548-1232
Crestar Crusts
Washington Ct Hs, OH 740-335-4813
Crevettes Du Nord
Gaspe, QC 418-368-1414
Crowley Foods
Binghamton, NY 800-637-0019
Crown Point
St John, IN 219-365-3200
Crystal Cream & Butter Company
Sacramento, CA 916-447-6455
CSV Sales
Plymouth, MI 734-453-4544
Cuisine Solutions
Alexandria, VA 888-285-4679
Cuizina Food Company
Woodinville, WA 425-486-7000
Culinary Foods
Chicago, IL 800-621-4049
Culinary Standards Corporation
Louisville, KY 800-778-3434
Culver Duck
Middlebury, IN 800-825-9225
Curly's Dairy
Stayton, OR 800-785-1335
Curly's Foods
Edina, MN 612-920-3400
Cut Above Foods
Carlsbad, CA 760-931-6777
Cutie Pie Corporation
Salt Lake City, UT 800-453-4575

Cutler Egg Products
Abbeville, AL 334-585-2268
Cyclone Enterprises
Houston, TX 281-872-0087
D'Orazio Foods
Bellmawr, NJ 888-328-7287
Daerim America
Maywood, NJ 800-635-0781
Dairy Fresh Corporation
Greensboro, AL. 800-239-5114
Dairy Fresh Foods
Taylor, MI 313-295-6300
Dairy King Milk Farms/Foodservice
Glendale, CA 818-243-6455
Dairy Land
Macon, GA 478-742-6461
Dairy Queen of Georgia
Decatur, GA 404-292-3553
Dakota Brands International
Jamestown, ND. 800-844-5073
Dallas Dressed Beef
Dallas, TX. 214-638-0142
Danish Baking Company
Van Nuys, CA 800-777-4970
Dave's Hawaiian Ice Cream
Pearl City, HI 808-453-0500
Davidson Meat Processing Plant
Waynesville, OH 513-897-2971
Dawn Food Products
Louisville, KY 800-626-2542
De-Iorio's Frozen Dough
Utica, NY 800-649-7612
Dean Foods
Dallas, TX. 214-303-3400
Dean Foods Company
Dallas, TX. 214-303-3400
DeConna Ice Cream
Orange Lake, FL 800-824-8254
Dee's Cheesecake Factory/Dee's Foodservice
Albuquerque, NM 505-884-1777
Deep Creek Custom Packing
Ninilchik, AK 800-764-0078
Deep Foods
Union, NJ 908-810-7500
Deep Sea Foods
Bayou La Batre, AL 251-824-7000
Del Campo Baking Company
Wilmington, DE 302-656-6676
Del Rey Tortilleria
Chicago, IL 800-446-1459
Del's Lemonade & Refreshments
Cranston, RI 401-463-6190
Del's Seaway Shrimp & Oyster Company
Biloxi, MS 228-432-2604
Delta Pride Catfish
Indianola, MS 800-421-1045
Deluxe Ice Cream Company
Salem, OR. 800-304-7172
Depoe Bay Fish Company
Newport, OR. 541-265-8833
Desserts of Distinction
Milwaukie, OR 503-654-8370
Detroit Chili Company
Southfield, MI. 248-440-5933
Devault Foods
Devault, PA. 800-426-2874
Devine Foods
Media, PA 888-338-4631
Diamond Blueberry
Hammonton, NJ 609-561-3661
Dick & Casey's Gourmet Seafoods
Harbor, OR 800-662-9494
Dickinson Frozen Foods
Fruitland, ID 208-452-5200

Dillman Farm
Bloomington, IN 800-359-1362
Dimitria Delights
North Grafton, MA 800-763-1113
Diversified Avocado Products
Mission Viejo, CA 800-879-2555
Divine Ice Cream Company
Arlington Heights, IL 847-398-0095
Division Baking Corporation
New York, NY 800-934-9238
Dol Cice Italian Frozen Treats
Yardley, PA 215-493-9000
Dold Foods
Wichita, KS 316-838-9101
Don Miguel Mexican Foods
Orange, CA 714-634-8441
Dorothy Dawson Foods Products
Jackson, MI 517-788-9830
Dough Delight
Concord, ON 800-465-5515
Dr. Praeger's Sensible Foods
Elmwood Park, NJ 201-703-1300
Draper Valley Farms
Mt Vernon, WA 360-424-7947
Dreyer's Grand Ice Cream
Oakland, CA 877-437-3937
Drohan Company
Woodside, NY 718-898-9672
Dufour Pastry Kitchens
New York, NY 212-929-2800
Duma Meats
Mogadore, OH 330-628-3438
Dunham Hill Bakery
Woodstock, VT 800-218-3121
Dunkin Brands Inc.
Canton, MA 800-458-7731
Dutch Ann Foods Company
Natchez, MS 601-445-5566
Dwayne Keith Brooks Company
Orangevale, CA 916-988-1030
Dynamic Foods
Lubbock, TX 806-762-0780
E. Gagnon & Fils
St Therese-De-Gaspe, QC 418-385-3011
E.W. Bowker Company
Pemberton, NJ 609-894-9508
Earle Brothers Fisheries
Carbonear, NL 709-596-5166
Eastern Fish Company
Teaneck, NJ 800-526-9066
Eastern Quebec Sea Foods
Matane, QC 418-562-1273
Eastern Shore Seafood Products
Mappsville, VA 800-466-8550
Eberhard Creamery
Redmond, OR 541-548-5181
Eckert Cold Storage
Escalon, CA 209-838-4040
Edmonds Chile Company
St Louis, MO. 314-772-1499
Edner Corporation
Hayward, CA 510-441-8504
Edwards Baking Company
Atlanta, GA 800-241-0559
Edy's Grand Ice Cream
Rockaway, NJ 800-362-7899
Edy's Grand Ice Cream
Glendale Heights, IL 888-377-3397
El Paso Meat Company
El Paso, TX 915-838-8600
El-Rey Foods
Ferguson, MO 314-521-3113
Elena's Food Specialties
S San Francisco, CA 800-376-5368
Eli's Cheesecake Company
Chicago, IL 800-999-8300
Empire Beef Company
Rochester, NY 800-462-6804
Endico Potatoes
Mt Vernon, NY 914-664-1151
Enfield Farms
Lynden, WA 360-354-3019
English Bay Batter
Dublin, OH 614-760-9921
Entenmann's-Oroweat/BestFoods
S San Francisco, CA 650-875-3100
Enterprises Pates et Croutes
Boucherville, QC 450-655-7790
Enway/Northwood
Clackamas, OR 503-657-9334
Equity Group
Reidsville, NC. 336-342-6601

Eskimo Pie Corporation
Ronkonkoma, NY 631-737-9700
Evans Bakery
Cozad, NE 800-222-5641
Evans Properties
Dade City, FL 352-567-5662
Ever Fresh Fruit Company
Boring, OR 800-239-8026
Exceldor Cooperative
St. Anselme, QC 418-885-4451
Fairmont Foods of Minnesota
Fairmont, MN 507-238-9001
Faith Dairy
Tacoma, WA 253-531-3398
Fantasia
Sedalia, MO 660-827-1172
Fantis Foods
Carlstadt, NJ 201-933-6200
Farm Fresh Catfish Company
Hollandale, MS 800-647-8264
Farm Fresh Frozen
Americus, GA 912-928-5600
Farr Candy Company
Idaho Falls, ID 208-522-8215
Fendall Ice Cream Company
Salt Lake City, UT 801-355-3583
Ferroclad Fishery
Batchawana Bay, ON 705-882-2295
Field's
Pauls Valley, OK 405-238-7381
Fieldale Farms
Gainesville, GA 800-241-5400
Fieldale Farms Corporation
Baldwin, GA 706-778-5100
Fieldale Farms Corporation
Baldwin, GA 800-241-5400
Fieldbrook Farms
Dunkirk, NY 800-333-0805
Fiera Foods
North York, ON 416-744-1010
Fine Choice Foods
Richmond, BC. 604-522-3110
Fiori-Bruna Pasta Products
Hialeah, FL 305-621-0074
First Original Texas Chili Company
Fort Worth, TX 817-626-0983
Fishery Products International
Danvers, MA. 800-374-4700
Fishery Products International
Seattle, WA 800-374-4770
FishKing
Bayou La Batre, AL 334-824-2118
Fishking Processors
Los Angeles, CA. 877-677-3329
Fishmarket Seafoods
Louisville, KY 502-587-7474
Flavors from Florida
Bartow, FL 863-533-0408
Fleischer's Bagels
Macedon, NY 315-986-9999
Florentyna's Fresh Pasta Factory
Vernon, CA 800-747-2782
Florida Veal Processors
Wimauma, FL 813-634-5545
Florida's Natural Brand
Lake Wales, FL 888-657-6600
Flowers Bakery of Montgomery
Montgomery, AL. 334-281-7030
Food City USA
Arvada, CO. 303-321-4447
Food Source
McKinney, TX 972-548-9001
Foodbrands America
Oklahoma City, OK 405-290-4000
Foodmark
Wellesley, MA. 781-237-7088
Foothills Creamery
Calgary, AB. 403-263-7725
Forte Stromboli Company
Philadelphia, PA 215-463-6336
Fran's Healthy Helpings
Burlingame, CA 650-652-5772
France Croissant
New York, NY 212-888-1210
France Delices
Montreal, QC 514-259-2291
Freeze-Dry Products
Santa Rosa, CA 707-547-1776
Freezer Queen Foods
Buffalo, NY. 800-828-8383
French Gourmet
Honolulu, HI 808-524-4000

Fresh Frozen Foods
Jefferson, GA 800-277-9851
Fresh Juice Company
Newark, NJ 973-465-7100
Friendly Ice Cream Corporation
Wilbraham, MA 800-966-9970
Frio Foods
San Antonio, TX 210-278-4525
Friuli Sorbet
New York, NY 212-966-3073
Frostbite
Toledo, OH 800-968-7711
Frozen Specialties
Archbold, OH 419-445-9015
Frozfruit Corporation
Gardena, CA 310-217-1034
Frozsun Foods
Anaheim, CA 714-630-2170
Fruit A Freeze
Norwalk, CA. 562-407-2881
Fruit Belt Foods
Lawrence, MI 269-674-3939
Fruithill
Yamhill, OR 503-662-3926
Fry Foods
Tiffin, OH 800-626-2294
FSI/MFP
West Haven, CT 203-934-5233
Fuji Foods
Denver, CO 303-377-3738
G A Food Service
St Petersburg, FL. 727-573-2211
G M Allen & Son
Blue Hill, ME 207-469-7060
Gabilas Knishes
Brooklyn, NY 718-387-0750
Gad Cheese Company
Medford, WI 715-748-4273
Galco Food Products
Brampton, ON. 888-793-5291
Galliker Dairy
Johnstown, PA. 800-477-6455
Galloway Company
Neenah, WI 800-722-8903
Garber Ice Cream Company
Winchester, VA 800-662-5422
Garden Herbs
Redlands, CA 800-388-9397
Gardenburger
Clearfield, UT 801-773-8855
Gardner Pie Company
Akron, OH. 330-245-2030
Garelick Farms
Lynn, MA 800-487-8700
Gary's Frozen Foods
Lubbock, TX 806-745-1933
Gaucho Foods
Westmont, IL 630-889-4241
Gelato Fresco
Toronto, ON 416-785-5415
Gemini Food Industries
Fiskdale, MA 508-347-2800
General Mills
Chelsea, MA 800-370-7834
George Chiala Farms
Morgan Hill, CA 408-778-0562
George L. Wells Meat Company
Philadelphia, PA 800-523-1730
George Robberecht Seafood
Montross, VA 804-472-3556
Georges Chicken
Edinburg, VA 540-984-4121
Georgia Sun
Newnan, GA 770-251-2500
Gesco ENR
Gaspe, QC. 418-368-1414
Gifford's Dairy
Skowhegan, ME 207-474-9821
Gilardi Foods
Sidney, OH 937-498-4511
Gilroy Foods
Gilroy, CA. 800-921-7502
Glacier Foods
Sanger, CA 559-875-3354
Glazier Packing Company
Potsdam, NY 315-265-2500
Glendora Quiche Company
San Dimas, CA 909-394-1777
Glenmark Food Processors
Chicago, IL 800-621-0117
Glenn's Rabbit & Emu Farm
Portland, TN 877-325-6903

Global Citrus Resources
Lakeland, FL 863-647-9020
Global Trading
Buena Park, CA 864-288-7332
Glover's Ice Cream
Frankfort, IN 800-686-5163
Gold Standard Baking
Chicago, IL 800-648-7904
Golden Gulf Coast Packing Company
Biloxi, MS. 228-374-6121
Golden Platter Foods
Newark, NJ 973-242-0291
Golden Town Apple Products
Thornbury, ON 519-599-6300
Gomax Foods
Dimmitt, TX 806-647-3504
Gonard Foods
Calgary, AB. 403-277-0991
Gonnella Baking Company
Chicago, IL. 312-733-2020
Gonnella Frozen Products
Schaumburg, IL. 847-884-8829
Good Harbor Fillet Company
Gloucester, MA. 978-675-9100
Good Humor Breyers Ice Cream Company
Hagerstown, MD. 301-797-9603
Good Humor Breyers Ice Cream Company
Framingham, MA 508-620-4300
Good Humor Breyers Ice Cream Company
Henderson, NV 702-564-0020
Good Humor Breyers Ice Cream Company
Green Bay, WI. 866-204-9750
Good Humor Breyers Ice Cream Company
Green Bay, WI. 920-499-5151
Good Old Days Foods
Little Rock, AR. 501-565-1257
Good Wives
Lynn, MA .800-521-8160
Gordon Food Service
Grand Rapids, MI 888-437-3663
Gorton's Seafood
Gloucester, MA. 978-283-3000
Gourmet Croissant
Brooklyn, NY 718-499-4911
Gourmet Ice Cream
Palmer, MA. 413-283-3740
Gourmet Organics
Waynesville, NC 828-452-7700
Goya Foods
Secaucus, NJ 201-348-4900
Goya Foods of Florida
Miami, FL .305-592-3150
Granny's Kitchens
Frankfort, NY 315-735-5000
Great American Appetizers
Nampa, ID. 800-282-4834
Great American Foods Commissary
Ore City, TX 903-968-8630
Great Northern Baking Company
Minneapolis, MN 612-331-1043
Great Northern Products
Warwick, RI 401-490-4590
Great Valley Mills
Barto, PA .800-688-6455
Grecian Delight Foods
Elk Grove Vlg, IL 800-621-4387
Gregory Packaging
Newark, NJ 973-465-1113
Gregory's Foods
Eagan, MN 800-231-4734
Gress Poultry
Scranton, PA 570-561-0150
Grimaud Farms
Stockton, CA. 800-466-9955
Grimmway Frozen Foods
Bakersfield, CA 661-845-2296
Grossinger's Home Bakery
New York, NY 800-479-6996
Grosso Foods
Woolwich Township, NJ. 856-467-2222
Grow-Pac
Cornelius, OR 503-357-9691
Gulf Pride Enterprises
Biloxi, MS. 888-689-0560
Guttenplan's Frozen Dough
Middletown, NJ 888-422-4357
GWB Foods Corporation
Brooklyn, NY 718-686-9600
Gyma
East Stroudsburg, PA 570-422-6311
H&H Bagels
New York, NY 800-692-2435

H&H Fisheries Limited
Eastern Passage, NS 902-465-6330
H.C. Brill Company
Tucker, GA 800-241-8526
H.J. Heinz Company
Pittsburgh, PA 412-237-5948
H.P. Hood
Agawam, MA 413-786-7166
Haas Baking Company
St Louis, MO. 800-325-3171
Hall Brothers Meats
Cleveland, OH 440-235-3262
Hallmark Fisheries
Charleston, OR 541-888-3253
Hamilton Quality Convenience Foods
Romulus, MI. 734-946-1800
Hamm's Custom Meats
McKinney, TX 972-542-3359
Hamner Provision Company
San Antonio, TX 210-736-3117
Hanover Foods Corporation
Hanover, PA 717-632-6000
Happy Refrigerated Services
Fairport, NY 585-388-0080
Harker's Distribution
Le Mars, IA 800-798-7700
Harlan Bakeries
Avon, IN 317-272-3600
Harold Food Company
Charlotte, NC 704-588-8061
Harold M. Lincoln Company
Toledo, OH 800-345-4911
Harrisburg Dairies
Harrisburg, PA 800-692-7429
Hartog Rahal Foods
New York, NY 212-687-2000
Harvest Time Foods
Ayden, NC. 252-746-6675
Hatfield Quality Meats
Hatfield, PA. 800-523-5291
Hawaii Coffee Company
Honolulu, HI 800-338-8353
Hazelwood Farms Bakery
Rochester, NY 585-424-1240
Health is Wealth Foods
Williamstown, NJ 856-728-1998
Heidi's Gourmet Desserts
Tucker, GA 800-241-4166
Heikes Produce Company
Medford, OR. 541-772-5653
Heinz Company of Canada
North York, ON. 800-268-6641
Heinz North America
Fort Myers, FL 239-694-3663
Heinz North America
Pittsburgh, PA 412-237-5700
Henry J's Hashtime
Chicago, IL 800-242-1313
Herbs Seafood
Westampton, NJ 800-486-0276
Heringer Meats
Covington, KY 859-291-2000
Hermann Pickle Farm
Garrettsville, OH. 800-245-2696
Hershey Creamery Company
Harrisburg, PA 888-240-1905
HFI Foods
Redmond, WA. 425-883-1320
Hi Point Industries
Vernon, CA 800-959-7292
Hi-Country Corona
Selah, WA .909-272-2600
Higgins Seafood
Lafitte, LA 504-689-3577
High Liner Foods USA
Portsmouth, NH 603-431-6865
Hiland Roberts Ice Cream Company
Norfolk, NE. 402-371-3660
Hillard Bloom Packing Co
Port Norris, NJ 856-785-0120
Hillman Shrimp & Oyster
Dickinson, TX. 800-582-4416
Hiscock Enterprises
Brigus, NL. 709-528-4577
Holten Meats
Sauget, IL .800-851-4684
Holton Food Products Company
La Grange, IL 708-352-5599
Home Delivery Food Service
Jefferson, GA 706-367-9551
Home Run Inn Frozen Foods
Woodridge, IL 800-636-9696

Homer's Ice Cream
Wilmette, IL 847-251-0477
Honeybake Farms
Kansas City, KS 913-371-7777
Hormel Foods Corporation
Houston, TX. 281-492-1770
Hormel Foods Corporation
Omaha, NE 402-493-8470
Hormel Foods Corporation
Oklahoma City, OK 405-843-5643
Hormel Foods Corporation
Columbia, MD 410-290-1855
Hormel Foods Corporation
Franklin, MA 508-541-7112
Hormel Foods Corporation
Cincinnati, OH 513-563-0211
Hormel Foods Corporation
Urbandale, IA 515-276-8872
Hormel Foods Corporation
Phoenix, AZ 602-230-2400
Hormel Foods Corporation
Charlotte, NC 704-527-4388
Hormel Foods Corporation
Austin, MN 800-523-4635
Hormel Foods Corporation
Lisle, IL 800-533-2000
Hormel Foods Corporation
Salt Lake City, UT 801-487-8251
Hormel Foods Corporation
Lubbock, TX. 806-796-3630
Hormel Foods Corporation
Arlington, TX 817-465-4735
Hormel Foods Corporation
Cordova, TN 901-753-4282
Hormel Foods Corporation
Lebanon, NJ 908-236-7009
Hormel Foods Corporation
Shawnee Mission, KS. 913-888-8744
Hors D'Oeuvres Unlimited
North Bergen, NJ 800-648-3787
Horst Alaskan Seafood
Juneau, AK 877-518-4300
Houdini
Fullerton, CA 714-525-0325
House of Flavors
Ludington, MI. 800-930-7740
House of Raeford Farms
Raeford, NC 800-888-7539
House of Spices India
Flushing, NY 718-507-4600
HP Hood
Lynnfield, MA 800-343-6592
Hudsonville Creamery & Ice Cream
Holland, MI. 616-928-0793
Humble Cremery
Los Angeles, CA. 800-697-9925
Humboldt Creamery Association
Fortuna, CA 707-725-6182
Hunt-Wesson Food Service Company
Rochester, NY 800-633-1002
Hunter Farms
High Point, NC 800-446-8035
I & K Distributors
Delphos, OH 800-869-6337
Ice Cream & Yogurt Club
Boynton Beach, FL. 561-731-3331
Ice Cream Specialties
St Louis, MO. 314-962-3935
Ice Cream Specialties
Lafayette, IN 765-474-2989
Ice Land Corporation
Pittsburgh, PA. 412-441-9512
Icelandic USA
Newport News, VA 757-820-4000
Icicle Seafoods
Seattle, WA 206-282-0988
Icy Bird
Sparta, TN 931-738-3557
Ideal Dairy
Richfield, UT 435-896-5061
Il Gelato
Astoria, NY 718-937-3033
Imagine Foods
Melville, NY 800-333-6339
Incredible Cheesecake Company
San Diego, CA 619-563-9722
Independent Packers Corporation
Seattle, WA 206-285-6000
Indian Ridge Shrimp Company
Chauvin, LA 985-594-5869
Indian River Foods
Fort Pierce, FL 561-462-2222

Indian Valley Meats
Indian, AK.........................907-653-7511
Inlet Salmon
Bothell, WA.......................425-487-0495
Inn Foods
Watsonville, CA..................831-724-2026
Inshore Fisheries
Middle West Pubnico, NS..........902-762-2522
International Cuisine
East Palatka, FL.................904-325-0002
International Food Packers Corporation
Miami, FL........................305-669-1662
International Food Trade
Amherst, NS......................902-667-3013
International Multifoods Corporation
Orrville, OH.....................800-664-2942
International Oceanic Enterprises of Alabama
Bayou La Batre, AL...............800-816-1832
International Packers Corporation
Watertown, MA....................508-963-8214
International Yogurt Company
Portland, OR.....................800-962-7326
Interstate Brands
Biddeford, ME....................207-286-1200
Isabella's Healthy Bakery
Cuyahoga Falls, OH...............800-476-6328
Island Marine Products
Clarks Harbour, NS...............902-745-2222
Island Oasis Frozen Cocktail Company
Walpole, MA......................800-777-4752
Island Scallops
Qualicum Beach, BC...............250-757-9811
It's It Ice Cream Company
Burlingame, CA...................800-345-1928
Italia Foods
Schaumburg, IL...................800-747-1109
Italian Foods Manufacturing
Vestal, NY.......................800-962-7700
Itarca
Inglewood, CA....................800-747-2782
J&B Meats Corporation
Coal Valley, IL..................309-799-7341
J&J Snack Foods Corporation
Pennsauken, NJ...................856-665-9533
J&J Wall Baking Company
Sacramento, CA...................916-381-1410
J. Matassini & Sons Fish Company
Tampa, FL........................813-229-0829
J.B. Sons
Yonkers, NY......................914-963-5192
J.H. Verbridge & Son
Williamson, NY...................315-589-2366
J.J. Andrade's Slaughterhouse
Honokaa, HI......................808-775-0741
J.R. Simplot Company
Boise, ID........................208-336-2110
J.R. Simplot Company
Grand Forks, ND..................701-746-6431
J.R. Simplot Food Group
Pasco, WA........................509-544-6700
J.S. McMillan Fisheries
Vancouver, BC....................604-255-5191
J.W. Haywood & Sons Dairy
Louisville, KY...................502-774-2311
Jack & Jill Ice Cream Company
Moorestown, NJ...................856-813-2300
Jack's Lobsters
Musquodoboit Harbor, NS..........902-889-2771
Jackson Ice Cream Company
Denver, CO.......................303-534-2454
Jackson Milk & Ice CreamCompany
Hutchinson, KS...................620-663-1244
Jacob & Sons Wholesale Meats
Martins Ferry, OH................740-633-3091
James Cowan & Sons
Worcester, MA....................508-754-5385
James Skinner Company
Omaha, NE........................800-358-7428
Janca's Jojoba Oil & Seed Company
Mesa, AZ.........................480-497-9494
Janes Family Foods
Mississauga, ON..................800-565-2637
Jasper Wyman & Son
Milbridge, ME....................800-341-1758
Jay Hoyt of California
Petaluma, CA.....................707-762-1881
Jazz Fine Foods
Montreal, QC.....................514-255-0110
Jbs Packerland Inc
Green Bay, WI....................920-468-4000
JBS Packing Company
Port Arthur, TX..................409-982-3216

Jecky's Best
Santa Clarita, CA................888-532-5972
Jel-Sert Company
West Chicago, IL.................800-323-2592
Jemm Wholesale Meat Company
Chicago, IL......................773-523-8161
Jenport International Distributors
Coquitlam, BC....................604-464-9888
Jesse's Fine Meats
Cherokee, IA.....................712-225-3637
Jessie's Ilwaco Fish Company
Ilwaco, WA.......................360-642-3773
Jimm's Pizza
Racine, WI.......................262-634-2164
John Garner Meats
Van Buren, AR....................800-543-5473
John Morrell & Company
Sioux City, IA...................712-279-7360
John T. Handy Company
Salisbury, MD....................800-426-3977
Johnson's Real Ice Cream
Columbus, OH.....................614-231-0014
Joseph Foodservice
Valdosta, GA.....................800-333-2261
Josh & John's Ice Cream
Colorado Springs, CO.............800-530-2855
JR Wood/Big Valley
Atwater, CA......................209-358-5643
JRL
Hammonton, NJ....................609-561-1572
Jubilee Foods
Bayou La Batre, AL...............251-824-2110
Juno Chef's
Brooklyn, NY.....................718-492-1300
Junuis Food Products
Palatine, IL.....................847-359-4300
Jurgielewicz Duck Farm
Moriches, NY.....................800-543-8257
K&K Gourmet Meats
Leetsdale, PA....................724-266-8400
Kan-Pac
Arkansas City, KS................620-442-6820
Karn Meats
Columbus, OH.....................800-221-9585
Karp's
Georgetown, MA...................800-373-5277
Karp's
Schaumburg, IL...................800-593-5277
Katrina's Tartufo
Port Jeffrsn Sta, NY.............800-480-8836
Kelley Foods of Alabama
Elba, AL.........................334-897-5761
Kellogg Canada Inc
Mississauga, ON..................888-876-3750
Kellogg Company
San Jose, CA.....................408-295-8656
Kellogg Company
Hammonton, NJ....................609-567-2300
Kellogg Company
Battle Creek, MI.................800-962-1413
Kemp Foods
York, PA.........................800-233-2007
Kenosha Beef International
Kenosha, WI......................800-541-1685
Kent Foods
Gonzales, TX.....................830-672-7993
Key Largo Fisheries
Key Largo, FL....................800-399-6970
Keyser Brothers
Lottsburg, VA....................804-529-6837
Keystone Foods
Camilla, GA......................229-336-5211
King Cole Ducks Limited
Aurora, ON.......................800-363-3825
King Kold
Chicago, IL......................773-278-7711
King Kold Meats
Englewood, OH....................800-836-2797
Kitchens Seafood
Plant City, FL...................800-327-0132
Klinke Brothers Ice Cream Company
Memphis, TN......................901-743-8250
Koch Foods
Park Ridge, IL...................800-837-2778
Kodiak Salmon Packers
Larsen Bay, AK...................907-847-2250
Koehler Bakery Company
North Little Rock, AR............800-262-5900
Kohler Mix Specialties
White Bear Lake, MN..............651-426-1633
Kohler Mix Specialties
Newington, CT....................860-666-1511

Kokinos Purity Ice CreamCompany
Monroe, LA.......................318-322-2930
Kona Cold Lobsters Ltd
Kailua Kona, HI..................808-329-4332
Konto's Foods
Paterson, NJ.....................973-278-2800
Kraft Foods
Avon, NY.........................585-226-4400
Kraft Pizza Company
Little Chute, WI.................920-788-0605
KT's Kitchen
Carson, CA.......................310-764-0850
Kubla Khan Food Company
Portland, OR.....................503-234-7494
Kutztown Bologna Company
Leola, PA........................800-723-8824
Kyger Bakery Products
Lafayette, IN....................765-447-1252
L&C Fisheries
Kensington, PE...................902-886-2770
L&H Packing Company
San Antonio, TX..................210-532-3241
L.K. Bowman Company
Nottingham, PA...................800-853-1919
La Cookie
Houston, TX......................713-784-2722
La Francaise Bakery
Northlake, IL....................800-654-7220
La Nova Wings
Buffalo, NY......................800-652-6682
La Tolteca Foods
Pueblo, CO.......................719-543-5733
Ladoga Frozen Food & Retail Meat
Ladoga, IN.......................765-942-2225
Lady Gale Seafood
Baldwin, LA......................337-923-2060
Lafitte Frozen Foods Corporation
Lafitte, LA......................504-689-2041
Lake Packing Company
Lottsburg, VA....................804-529-6101
Lake Shore Frozen Foods
Lake City, PA....................877-774-3668
Lakeside Foods
Brooten, MN......................320-346-2900
Lakeside Foods
Plainview, MN....................507-534-3141
Lakeside Foods
Seymour, WI......................920-833-2371
Lamb-Weston
Hermiston, OR....................800-766-7783
LaMonica Fine Foods
Millville, NJ....................856-825-8111
Land O'Lakes, Inc
Arden Hills, MN..................800-328-9680
Landolfi Food Products
Trenton, NJ......................609-392-1830
LBA
Seatac, WA.......................800-522-1185
Le Notre, Alain & Marie Baker
Houston, TX......................800-536-6873
Leach Farms
Berlin, WI.......................920-361-1880
Leader Candies
Brooklyn, NY.....................718-366-6900
Leelanau Fruit Company
Suttons Bay, MI..................231-271-3514
Leelanau Fruit Company
Suttons Bay, MI..................800-431-0718
Leidenheimer Baking Company
New Orleans, LA..................504-525-1575
Lenchner Bakery
Concord, ON......................905-738-8811
Lender's Bagel Bakery
Mattoon, IL......................217-235-3181
Lender's Bagel Bakery
West Seneca, NY..................716-668-6761
Lengerich Meats
Zanesville, IN...................260-638-4123
Lennox Farm
Shelburne, ON....................519-925-6444
Leon's Bakery
North Haven, CT..................800-223-6844
Leonetti's Frozen Food
Philadelphia, PA.................215-729-4200
Lewis Brothers Bakeries
Vincennes, IN....................812-886-6533
Lewis Packing Company
Sandy, OR........................503-668-8122
Little Lady Foods
Elk Grove, IL....................800-439-1440
Lombardi's Seafood
Orlando, FL......................800-879-8411

Lombardo's Ravioli Kitchen
New Britain, CT .860-223-7800
London Farm Dairy
Port Huron, MI 800-284-5111
Lone Star Bakery
Round Rock, TX 512-255-3629
Lone Star Consolidated Foods
Dallas, TX 800-658-5637
Long Beach Seafoods
Long Beach, CA 714-995-8901
Longmont Foods
Longmont, CO .303-776-4803
Lougheed Fisheries
Owen Sound, ON 519-376-1586
Louis Dreyfus Citrus
Winter Garden, FL 407-656-1000
Louis Trauth Dairy
Newport, KY 800-544-6455
Louisa Food Products
St Louis, MO 314-868-3000
Louisiana Packing Company
Westwego, LA .800-666-1293
Love & Quiches Desserts
Freeport, NY 800-525-5251
Lu-Mar Lobster & Shrimp
Brownsville, TX 956-546-5525
Lucerne Foods
Lethbridge, AB 403-328-5501
Lucerne Foods
Abbotsford, BC 604-854-1191
Lucia's Pizza Company
St Louis, MO 314-843-2553
Lucy's Foods
Latrobe, PA 724-539-1430
Ludwick's Frozen Donuts
Grand Rapids, MI 800-366-8816
Ludwig Fish & Produce Company
La Porte, IN 219-362-2608
Luigino's
Duluth, MN 218-727-2059
M&L Gourmet Ice Cream
Baltimore, MD 410-276-4880
M&M Shrimp Company
Biloxi, MS 228-435-4915
M-G
Weimar, TX 800-460-8581
M.A. Johnson Frozen Foods
Marion, IN 800-899-1406
Macabee Foods
Moonachie, NJ 201-489-4343
MacFarlane Pheasants
Janesville, WI .877-269-8957
Mack's Homemade Ice Cream
York, PA 717-741-2027
Mackie International
Commerce, CA 800-733-9762
Mada'n Kosher Foods
Dania, FL 954-925-0077
Magic Valley Foods
Rupert, ID 208-436-3126
Maid-Rite Steak Company
Dunmore, PA .800-233-4259
Main Street Custom Foods
Cuyahoga Falls, OH 800-533-6246
Main Street Gourmet
Cuyahoga Falls, OH 800-533-6246
Main Street Gourmet Fundraising
Cuyahoga Falls, OH 800-533-6246
Main Street Muffins
Cuyahoga Falls, OH 800-533-6246

Main Street's Cambritt Cookies
Cuyahoga Falls, OH 800-533-6246
Maine Wild Blueberry Company
Cherryfield, ME 800-243-4005
Majestic Foods
Huntington, NY 631-424-9444
Mama Rosie's Ravioli Company
Charlestown, MA 888-246-4300
Mamma Lina Ravioli Company
San Diego, CA 858-535-0620
Manchester Farms
Dalzell, SC 800-845-0421
Mancuso Cheese Company
Joliet, IL 815-722-2475
Mannhardt Inc
Sheboygan Falls, WI 920-467-1027
Maola Milk & Ice Cream Company
New Bern, NC .252-638-1131
Maple Leaf Farms
Milford, IN 800-384-2812
Maple Leaf Foods International
Toronto, ON 416-480-8900
Maplehurst Bakeries
Brownsburg, IN 317-858-9000
Mar-Jac Poultry
Gainesville, GA 800-226-0561
Mar-Key Foods
Vidalia, GA 912-537-4204
Marburger Foods
Peru, IN 765-689-5198
Marcetti Frozen Pasta
Altoona, IA 515-967-4254
Marche Tramsatlantique
Montreal, QC .514-287-3530
Mardi Gras
Verona, NJ 973-857-3777
Mariner Seafoods
Montague, PE .902-838-2481
Mario's Gelati
Vancouver, BC 604-879-9411
Market Fare Foods
Phoenix, AZ 800-782-9136
Mars M&M
Henderson, NV 888-265-6788
Marsan Foods
Toronto, ON 416-755-9262
Martin Brothers Distributing Company
Cedar Falls, IA 319-266-1775
Martin Brothers Seafood Company
Westwego, LA .504-341-2251
Martin Seafood Company
Jessup, MD 410-799-5822
MAS Sales
Northlake, IL 800-615-6951
Mason County Fruit Packers Cooperative
Ludington, MI .231-845-6248
Matador Processors
Blanchard, OK 800-847-0797
Matlaw's Food Products
West Haven, CT 800-934-8266
Matterhorn Ice Cream Company
Caldwell, ID 800-822-1635
Maui Pineapple Company
Concord, CA 925-798-0240
Maxim's Import Corporation
Miami, FL 800-331-6652
Mayfield Farms
Brampton, ON 905-846-0506
McArthur Dairy
Miami, FL 877-803-6565
McCain Foods
Lodi, NJ 800-258-1098
McCain Foods
Fort Atkinson, WI 920-563-6625
McCain Foods Canada
Florenceville, NB 506-392-5541
McCain Foods USA
Easton, ME 207-488-2561
McCain Foods USA
Grand Island, NE 308-382-7770
McCain Foods USA
Lisle, IL 800-258-1098
McCain Foods USA
Othello, WA 800-541-4808
McClane Distribution Center
Fredericksburg, VA 540-374-2000
McConnell's Fine Ice Cream
Santa Barbara, CA 805-963-2958
McLane Foods
Phoenix, AZ 602-275-5509
Meadow Gold Dairy
Lewiston, ID 208-746-9006

Meat-O-Mat Corporation
Brooklyn, NY .718-965-7250
Mehaffie Pies
Dayton, OH 937-253-1163
Meleddy Cherry Plant
Sturgeon Bay, WI 920-856-6770
Menemsha Fish Market
Chilmark, MA .508-645-2282
Merrill's Blueberry Farms
Ellsworth, ME 800-711-6551
Mersey Seafoods
Liverpool, NS .902-354-3467
Mexi-Frost Specialties Company
Brooklyn, NY .718-625-3324
Meyer's Bakeries
Hope, AR 800-643-1542
Mi Ranchito Foods
Bayard, NM 575-537-3868
Mia Products
Scranton, PA .570-457-7431
Miami Beef Company
Hialeah, FL 305-621-3252
Michael Foods, Inc.
Minnetonka, MN 952-258-4000
Michael's Cookies
San Diego, CA 800-822-5384
Michele's Family Bakery
York, PA 717-741-2027
Michelle Chocolatiers
Colorado Springs, CO 888-447-3654
Michigan Dairy
Livonia, MI 734-367-5390
Mid States Dairy
Hazelwood, MO 314-731-1150
Mid-Atlantic Foods
Easton, MD 800-922-4688
Middlesex Sales Company
North Chelmsford, MA 978-459-7776
Mikawaya Bakery
Los Angeles, CA 213-628-6514
Mike & Jean's Berry Farm
Mt Vernon, WA 360-424-7220
Mike's Fish & Seafood
Glenwood, MN 800-950-4755
Miles J H & Company
Norfolk, VA 757-622-9264
Milfico Foods
Elk Grove Vlg, IL 847-427-0491
Mill Cove Lobster Pound
Boothbay Harbor, ME 207-633-3340
Millers Ice Cream
Houston, TX 713-861-3138
Milmar Food Group
Goshen, NY 845-294-5400
Milne Fruit Products
Prosser, WA 509-786-2611
Minh Food Corporation
Pasadena, TX .800-344-7655
Minor Fisheries
Port Colborne, ON 905-834-9232
Minterbrook Oyster Company
Gig Harbor, WA 253-857-5251
Minute Maid Company
Bombay, BC 800-438-2653
Minute Maid Company
Houston, TX 888-884-8952
Mister Cookie Face
Lakewood, NJ .732-370-5533
Mobile Processing
Mobile, AL 251-438-6944
Model Dairy
Reno, NV 800-433-2030
Model Diary
Dallas, TX 775-788-7900
Molinaro's Fine Italian Foods
Mississauga, ON 800-268-4959
Momence Packing Company
Momence, IL 815-472-6485
Monterey Mushrooms
Watsonville, CA 800-333-6874
Mooresville Ice Cream Company
Mooresville, NC 704-664-5456
Morey's Seafood International
Motley, MN 218-352-6345
Morgan Food
Austin, IN 888-430-1780
Morningstar Foods
Dallas, TX 225-273-2803
Moroni Feed Company
West Liberty, IA 435-436-8221
Morrison Lamothe
Toronto, ON 416-291-6762

Morrison Meat Pies
West Valley, UT 801-977-0181
Morrison Milling Company
Denton, TX 800-580-5487
Mortimer's Fine Foods
Burlington, ON 905-336-0000
Mother's Kitchen
Burlington, NJ 800-566-8437
Mothers Kitchen Inc
Burlington, NJ 609-387-7200
Motivatit Seafoods
Houma, LA 985-868-7191
Mount Baker Vineyards
Everson, WA 800-441-8263
Mount Rose Ravioli & Macaroni Company
Farmingdale, NY 516-694-6940
Mountain City Meat Company
Denver, CO 800-937-8325
Mountaire Farms of North Carolina
Lumber Bridge, NC 910-843-5942
Mozzicato De Pasquale Bakery Pastry
Hartford, CT 860-296-0426
Mushroom Company
Cambridge, MD 410-221-8900
Mutual Fish Company
Seattle, WA 206-322-4368
Myers Frozen Food Provisions
St Paul, IN 765-525-6304
Naleway Foods
Winnipeg, MB 800-665-7448
Nan Sea Enterprises of Wisconsin
Waukesha, WI 262-542-8841
Nancy's Specialty Foods
Newark, CA 510-494-1100
National Beef Packing
Kansas City, MO 800-449-2333
National Fish & Oysters Company
Olympia, WA 360-491-5550
National Frozen Foods Corporation
Seattle, WA 206-322-8900
Natural Feast Corporation
Dover, MA 508-984-4230
Natural Fruit Corporation
Hialeah, FL 305-887-7525
Natural Wonder Foods
Brooklyn, NY 718-436-6811
Nature Quality
San Martin, CA 408-683-2182
Nelson Crab
Tokeland, WA 800-262-0069
Nelson's Ice Cream
Royersford, PA 610-948-1282
Nemecek Brothers
West, TX 254-826-5182
Neptune Fisheries
Newport News, VA 800-545-7474
Nestle
Cleveland, OH 440-349-5757
Nestle Canada Inc
North York, ON 800-563-7853
Nestle Pizza
Medford, WI 715-748-5550
Nestle' Handheld Foods Group
Englewood, CO 800-225-2270
New England Muffin Company
Fall River, MA 508-675-2833
New West Foods
San Francisco, CA 701-947-2505
New York Bagel Boys
West Sacramento, CA 916-739-6540
New York Frozen Foods
Cleveland, OH 216-292-5655
Newark Meat Supply
Newark, OH 740-345-6696
Newfound Resources
Saint John's, NL 709-579-7676
Niagara Foods
Middleport, NY 716-735-7722
Nickabood's Company
Los Angeles, CA 213-746-1541
Night Hawk Frozen Foods
Buda, TX 800-580-4166
Nino's Enterprises
Melrose Park, IL 708-344-8082

Nor-Cliff Farms
Port Colborne, ON 905-835-0808
Norbest
Midvale, UT 800-453-5327
Nordic Group
Boston, MA 800-486-4002
Norfood Cherry Growers
Simcoe, ON 519-426-5784
NORPAC Foods
Lake Oswego, OR 503-635-9311
NORPAC Plant
Salem, OR 800-822-2898
North Atlantic Fish Company
Gloucester, MA 978-283-4121
North Star Foods
St Charles, MN 507-932-4831
Northern Michigan Fruit Company
Omena, MI 231-386-5142
Northern Products Corporation
Seattle, WA 206-448-6677
Northern Wind
New Bedford, MA 888-525-2525
Northland Frozen Foods
Sugar City, ID 888-667-7837
Notre Dame Seafood
Comfort Cove, NL 709-244-5511
O Chili Frozen Foods Inc
Northbrook, IL 847-562-1991
O'Boyle's Ice Cream Company
Bristol, PA 215-788-0421
O'Hara Corporation
Rockland, ME 207-594-0405
Oak Leaf Confections
Scarborough, ON 800-338-3631
Oasis Foods
Planada, CA 209-382-0263
Ocean Beauty Seafoods
Seattle, WA 206-285-6800
Ocean Beauty Seafoods
Monroe, WA 425-482-2923
Ocean Food Company
Scarborough, ON 416-285-6487
Ocean Spray Cranberries
Lakeville-Middleboro, MA 800-662-3263
Ocean Springs Seafood
Ocean Springs, MS 228-875-0104
Oceana Foods
Shelby, MI 231-861-2141
Oh Boy Corporation
San Fernando, CA 818-361-1128
Okuhara Foods
Honolulu, HI 808-848-0581
Old Fashioned Kitchen
Lakewood, NJ 732-364-4100
Old Fashioned Kitchen
Newport Beach, CA 800-833-4635
Olymel
Iberville, QC 450-347-1900
Olympia Frosted Foods
Olympia, WA 360-943-2210
Olympic Food Products
Kokomo, IN 800-445-6923
Omaha Steaks International
Omaha, NE 800-562-0500
Omstead Foods Ltd
Burlington, ON 905-315-8883
On-Cor Foods Products
Northbrook, IL 847-205-1040
Orange Bakery
Huntersville, NC 704-875-3003
Orange Bakery
Irvine, CA 949-863-1377
Ore-Ida Foods
Pittsburgh, PA 412-237-3450
Oregon Cherry Growers
Salem, OR 800-367-2536
Oregon Fruit Products Company
Salem, OR 800-394-9333
Oregon Potato Company
Boardman, OR 800-336-6311
Original Italian Pasta Poducts Company
Chelsea, MA 800-999-9603
Original Ya-hoo! Baking Company
Sherman, TX 800-575-9373
Oroweat Baking Company
Montebello, CA 323-721-5161
Otis Spunkmeyer
San Leandro, CA 800-938-1900
Otter Valley Foods
Tillsonburg, ON 800-265-5731
Ottman Meat Company
New York, NY 212-879-4160

Otto & Son
West Jordan, UT 800-453-9462
Out of a Flower
Lancaster, TX 800-743-4696
Oven Poppers
Manchester, NH 603-644-3773
Overhill Farms
Vernon, CA 800-859-6406
Overlake Foods Corporation
Olympia, WA 800-683-1078
Oxford Frozen Foods Limited
Oxford, NS 902-447-2100
P&J Oyster Company
New Orleans, LA 504-523-2651
P. Janes & Sons
Hant's Harbor, NL 709-586-2252
Pacific Alaska Seafoods
Seattle, WA 206-587-0002
Pacific Blueberries
Rochester, WA 360-273-5405
Pacific Coast Fruit Company
Portland, OR 503-234-6411
Pacific Ocean Produce
Santa Cruz, CA 831-423-2654
Pacific Salmon Company
Edmonds, WA 425-774-1315
Pacific Seafood Group
Clackamas, OR 800-388-1101
Pacific Seafoods International
Sidney, BC 250-656-0901
Pacific Shrimp Company
Newport, OR 541-265-4215
Pacific Surf Food Processors
Los Angeles, CA 800-627-5657
Pacific Valley Foods
Bellevue, WA 425-643-1805
Paisano Food Products
Elk Grove Village, IL 773-237-3773
Palermo's Frozen Pizza
Milwaukee, WI 414-643-0919
Palmetto Pigeon Plant
Sumter, SC 803-775-1204
Pamlico Packing Company
Grantsboro, NC 800-682-1113
Paradise Island Foods
Nanaimo, BC 800-889-3370
Parco Foods
Blue Island, IL 708-371-9200
Paris Foods Corporation
Camden, NJ 856-964-0915
Paris Frozen Foods
Hillsboro, IL 217-532-3822
Park Farms
Canton, OH 800-683-6511
Party Steak Company
Springfield, MO 417-358-9091
Pascucci Family Pasta
San Diego, CA 619-285-8000
Pasta Del Mondo
Carmel, NY 800-392-8887
Pasta Factory
Northlake, IL 800-615-6951
Pasta International
Mississauga, ON 888-607-2782
Pasta Italiana
Massapequa, NY 800-536-5611
Pastry Chef
Pawtucket, RI 800-639-8606
Patterson Frozen Foods
Patterson, CA 209-892-2611
Paul Piazza & Sons
New Orleans, LA 504-524-6011
Peco Foods
Canton, MS 601-407-1699
Pede Brothers
Schenectady, NY 518-356-3042
PEI Mussel King
Morrell, PE 800-673-2767
Pel-Freez
Rogers, AR 800-223-8751
Pellman Foods
New Holland, PA 717-354-8070
Penguin Frozen Foods
Northbrook, IL 847-291-9400
Peninsula Fruit Exchange
Traverse City, MI 231-223-4282
Pennfield Corporation
Lancaster, PA 717-299-2561
Penobscot McCrum
Belfast, ME 800-435-4456
Pepe's Mexican Restaurants
Chicago, IL 312-733-2500

Pepes Mexican Foods
Rexdale, ON 416-674-0882
Pepperidge Farm
Downingtown, PA. 610-269-2500
Perdue Farms
Pantego, NC 252-943-3061
Perdue Farms
Bridgewater, VA 540-828-2581
Perdue Farms
Salisbury, MD 800-473-7383
Perdue Farms
Rockingham, NC 910-997-8600
Perfect Addition
Newport Beach, CA 949-640-0220
Perfect Foods
Monroe, NY .800-933-3288
Perry's Ice Cream Company
Akron, NY. 800-873-7797
Pet Dairy
Portsmouth, VA. 757-397-2387
Pet Dairy
Spartanburg, SC 864-576-6280
Peter Pan Seafoods
Seattle, WA .206-728-6000
Petersburg Fisheries
Petersburg, AK 877-772-4294
Petersen Ice Cream Company
Oak Park, IL .708-386-6130
Petrofsky's Bagels
Saint Louis, MO 314-432-4177
Pevely Dairy Company
St Louis, MO. 314-771-4400
Pfeffers Country Market
Sauk Centre, MN 320-352-6490
Phillips Foods
Baltimore, MD 800-782-2722
Phillips Foods
Baltimore, MD 888-234-2722
Phoenix Agro-Industrial Corporation
Westbury, NY 516-334-1194
Phranil Foods
Spokane, WA 509-534-7770
Pictsweet Frozen Foods
Bells, TN. 731-663-7600
Piemonte Foods
Greenville, SC. 864-242-0424
Pierceton Foods
Pierceton, IN. 574-594-2344
Pierino Frozen Foods
Lincoln Park, MI. 313-928-0950
Pilgrim's Pride
Boaz, AL 256-593-4223
Pilgrim's Pride
Broadway, VA 540-896-0607
Pilgrim's Pride
Timberville, VA 540-896-7000
Pilgrim's Pride
Elberton, GA. 706-283-3821
Pilgrim's Pride
Athens, GA. 706-548-5641
Pilgrim's Pride
Moorefield, WV 800-336-9876
Pilgrim's Pride
Enterprise, AL. 800-633-0908
Pilgrim's Pride
Lufkin, TX 936-639-1174
Pillsbury
Allentown, PA. 610-797-5947
Pillsbury
Atlanta, GA. 800-767-4466
Pillsbury Bakeries & Food Services
Sherwood Park, AB 780-464-1544
Pillsbury Canada Limited
Markham, ON 800-745-4777
Pinocchio Italian Ice Cream Company
Edmonton, AB 780-455-1905
Piqua Pizza Supply Company
Piqua, OH 800-521-4442
Plains Creamery
Amarillo, TX. 806-374-0385
Platte Valley Creamery
Scottsbluff, NE 308-632-4225
Plehn's Bakery
St Matthews, KY. 502-896-4438
Plymouth Beef
New York, NY 718-589-8600
POG
Grand Bend, ON 519-238-5704
Port Chatham Smoked Seafood
Everett, WA. 800-872-5666
Portland Shellfish Company
South Portland, ME 207-799-9290

Positively Third Street Bakery
Duluth, MN. 218-724-8619
Poudre Valley Creamery
Fort Collins, CO 970-482-8475
Prairie Cajun Wholesale
Eunice, LA 337-546-6195
Prairie Farms Dairy
Carlinville, IL 217-854-2547
Prairie Farms Dairy
O Fallon, IL. 618-632-3632
Prairie Farms Dairy Inc
Carlinville, IL 217-854-2547
Praters Foods
Lubbock, TX. 806-745-2727
Preferred Meal Systems
Scranton, PA 570-457-8311
Price Seafood
Chauvin, LA 985-594-3067
Price's Creameries
El Paso, TX .915-565-2711
Prime Pastry
Brooklyn, NY 888-771-2464
Prime Smoked Meats
Oakland, CA 510-832-7167
Proferas Pizza Bakery
Scranton, PA 570-342-4181
Provimi Veal Corporation
Seymour, WI 800-833-8325
Puritan/ATZ Ice Cream
Kendallville, IN 260-347-2700
Purity Dairies
Nashville, TN 615-244-1900
Purity Ice Cream Company
Ithaca, NY. .607-272-1545
Quality Brands
Deland, FL 386-738-3808
Quality Chef Foods
Cedar Rapids, IA. 800-356-8307
Quality Foods Products
Chicago, IL .312-666-4559
Quality Seafood
Apalachicola, FL. 850-653-9696
Queen International Foods
Monterey Park, CA 800-423-4414
Quelle Quiche
Brentwood, MO 314-961-6554
R Four Meats
Chatfield, MN. 507-867-4180
Radar Farms
Lynden, WA 360-354-6574
Ragozzino Food
Meriden, CT 800-348-1240
Rain Sweet
Salem, OR. .800-363-4293
Rainbow Farms
Upper Rawdon, NS 902-632-2548
Ralph's Italian Ices
Staten Island, NY 718-351-8133
Ramona's Mexican Food Products
Gardena, CA 310-323-1950
Ranaldi Bros Frozen Food Products Inc
Warwick, RI .401-738-3444
Randag & Associates Inc
Elmhurst, IL 630-530-2830
Randy's Frozen Meats
Faribault, MN. 800-354-7177
Ready Bake Foods
Mississauga, ON 905-567-0660
Ready Foods
Denver, CO .303-892-5861
Reames Foods
Columbus, OH 614-846-2232
Reames Foods
Altoona, IA .800-247-4194
Redi-Serve Food Company
Fort Atkinson, WI. 920-563-6391
Reinhold Ice Cream Company
Pittsburgh, PA 412-321-7600
Reiter Dairy
Akron, OH. .800-362-0825
Republic Foods
Dallas, TX 214-826-8050
Request Foods
Holland, MI 800-748-0378
Reser's Fine Foods
Beaverton, OR 800-333-6431
Reser's Fine Foods
Salt Lake City, UT 801-972-5633
Resource Trading Company
Portland, ME. 207-772-2299
Restaurant Systems International
Staten Island, NY 718-494-8888

Rhodes Bake-N-Serv
Salt Lake City, UT 800-695-0122
Rhodes International
Salt Lake City, UT 800-695-0122
Rhodes International
Columbus, WI 800-876-7333
Rich Ice Cream Company
West Palm Beach, FL 561-833-7585
Rich Products Corporation
Winchester, VA 540-667-1955
Rich Products Corporation
Fresno, CA .559-486-7380
Rich Products Corporation
Hilliard, OH. 614-771-1117
Rich Products Corporation
Cameron, WI. 715-458-4556
Rich Products Corporation
Buffalo, NY. 800-356-7094
Rich Products Corporation
Buffalo, NY. 800-828-2021
Rich Products of Canada
Fort Erie, ON 800-263-8174
Rich-Seapak Corporation
Brownsville, TX 956-542-0001
Richman Festival Ice Cream Company
Paterson, NJ 973-684-8935
Riviera Ravioli Company
Bronx, NY 718-823-0260
Roberts Dairy Company
Kansas City, MO. 800-279-1692
Robinson Cold Storage
Ridgefield, WA 360-887-3501
Robinson Dairy
Denver, CO .800-332-6355
Rosati Italian Water Ice
Clifton Heights, PA. 610-626-1818
Rose Frozen Shrimp
Los Angeles, CA 213-626-8251
Roselani Tropics Ice Cream
Wailuku, HI .808-244-7951
Rowena's
Norfolk, VA. 800-627-8699
Roy Stritmatter Company
Hoquiam, WA 360-532-0710
Royal Harvest Foods
Springfield, MA 413-737-8392
Royal Madera
Madera, CA 559-486-6666
Royal Seafood
Monterey, CA 831-655-8326
Rubschlager Baking Corporation
Chicago, IL .773-826-1245
Ruggiero Seafood
Newark, NJ .800-543-2110
Ruiz Food Products
Dinuba, CA .800-477-6474
Rymer Foods
Chicago, IL .800-247-9637
S&E Organic Farms
Bakersfield, CA 661-325-2644
S.D. Mushrooms
Avondale, PA 610-268-8082
Safeway Dairy Products
Capitol Heights, MD. 301-341-9555
Safeway Stores
Tempe, AZ .877-723-3929
Sahadi Fine Foods
Brooklyn, NY 800-724-2341
Sal-Serve
Mobile, AL .251-438-6944
Saletts
Randolph, MA 781-961-9900
Sam's Homemade Cheesecake
San Diego, CA 858-578-3460
Sanderson Farms
Collins, MS .601-765-8211
Sanderson Farms
Hazlehurst, MS 601-894-3721
Sanderson Farms
Laurel, MS .800-844-4030
Sanderson Farms
Bryan, TX 979-778-5730
Sara Lee Bakery Group
Earth City, MO 314-291-5480
Sara Lee Bakery Group
Greenville, SC 864-299-0604
Sara Lee Bakery Group The EarthGrains - Bakery
Traverse City, MI 231-922-3296
Sara Lee Bakery Group The EarthGrains - Bakery
Corpus Christi, TX 361-884-6311
Sara Lee Bakery Group The EarthGrains - Bakery
Beaumont, TX. 409-842-9150

Sara Lee Corporation
Downers Grove, IL 630-598-8100
Sara Lee Food Service
Haltom City, TX 800-261-4754
Sargeant's Army Marketing
Bowmanville, ON 905-623-2888
Savino's Italian Ices
Deerfield Beach, FL 954-426-4119
Saxby Foods
Edmonton, AB 780-440-4177
Scenic Fruit Company
Gresham, OR. 800-554-5578
Schneider Foods
Saint Marys, ON 800-567-1890
Schneider Valley Farms Dairy
Williamsport, PA 570-326-2021
Schneider's Dairy Holdings Inc
Pittsburgh, PA 412-881-3525
Schoep's Ice Cream Company
Madison, WI 800-236-0032
Schwans Bakeries
Stilwell, OK 918-696-8325
Schwans Food Company
Norcross, GA 800-241-0559
Schwans Frozen Foods
Marshall, MN 800-533-5290
Schwartz Meat Company
Sophia, WV 304-683-4595
Scotsburn Dairy Group
Truro, NS 902-895-4412
Sea Pearl Seafood
Bayou La Batre, AL 800-872-8804
Sea Products Company
Watsonville, CA 831-768-2600
Sea Safari
Belhaven, NC 800-688-6174
Sea Safari Limited
Belhaven, NC 800-688-6174
Sea Snack Foods
Los Angeles, CA. 213-622-2204
Sea Watch International
Easton, MD 410-822-7500
Seaberghs Frozen Foods
White Plains, NY 914-948-6377
Seabrook Brothers & Sons
Seabrook, NJ 856-455-8080
Seafood Producers Cooperative
Bellingham, WA 360-733-0120
Seafood Products Company
Vancouver, BC 604-255-3141
Seapoint Farms
Costa Mesa, CA 888-722-7098
Seaspan Products Corporation
New York, NY 201-569-9234
Seatech Corporation
Lynnwood, WA 425-835-0312
Seitz Foods
Saint Joseph, MO 800-383-3128
Seneca Foods
Marion, NY. 315-926-8100
Serendipity 3
New York, NY 800-805-5493
Sesinco Foods
New York, NY 212-243-1306
Seviroli Foods
Garden City, NY 516-222-6220
Seymour & Sons Seafood
Diberville, MS 228-392-4020
Shamrock Foods Company
Phoenix, AZ 800-289-3663
Shaw's Southern Belle Frozen
Jacksonville, FL 904-765-4487
Shawmut Fishing Company
Anchorage, AK 709-334-2559
Shelley's Prime Meats
Jersey City, NJ 201-433-3434
Shiloh Foods
Savannah, TN 800-795-2550
Shonna's Gourmet Goodies
West Bridgewater, MA 888-312-7868
Sidari's Italian Foods
Cleveland, OH 216-431-3344
Sill Farms Market
Lawrence, MI 269-674-3755
Silver Lining Seafood
Ketchikan, AK 907-225-6664
Silver State Foods
Denver, CO 800-423-3351
Simeus Foods International
Rocky Mount, NC 888-772-3663
Simmons Foods
Siloam Springs, AR 479-524-8151

Sisler's Ice & Ice Cream
Ohio, IL. 888-891-3856
Sitka Sound Seafoods
Sitka, AK. 907-747-6662
Smart Ice
Fort Myers, FL 239-334-3123
Smeltzer Orchard Company
Frankfort, MI 231-882-4421
Smith Dairy Products Company
Orrville, OH 800-776-7076
Smith Frozen Foods
Weston, OR 541-566-3515
Smith Frozen Foods
Weston, OR 800-547-0203
Smith Packing Regional Meat
Utica, NY 315-732-5125
Snelgrove Ice Cream Company
Salt Lake City, UT 800-569-0005
Sno-Co Berry Pak
Marysville, WA. 360-659-3555
Snow Ball Foods
Fredericksburg, PA 800-360-7669
Snowbear Frozen Custard
Lafayette, IN 765-743-8024
Snowcrest Packer
Abbotsford, BC. 604-859-4881
Snyder's Ice Cream
Ashland, PA 570-875-3320
Somerset Industries
Spring House, PA 800-883-8728
Sonstegard Foods Company
Sioux Falls, SD 800-533-3184
Southeastern Meat Association
Oviedo, FL 407-365-5661
Southeastern Sales
Hixson, TN 423-877-3781
Southern Ice Cream Specialties
Marietta, GA 770-428-0452
Southern Star Seafood
Fort Pierce, FL 561-461-5787
Southtowns Seafood & Meats
Blasdell, NY 716-824-4900
Sparboe Companies
Los Angeles, CA. 213-626-7538
Specialty Brands
Carthage, MO 417-358-8104
Squab Producers of California
Modesto, CA. 209-537-4744
St. Ours & Company
Norwell, MA 781-331-8520
Star Foods
Cleveland, OH 800-837-0992
Star Ravioli Manufacturing Company
Moonachie, NJ 201-933-6427
Starbucks Coffee Company
Seattle, WA 800-782-7282
Starkel Poultry
Puyallup, WA 253-845-2876
Steak-Umm Company
Shillington, PA 860-928-5900
Steese Ice Cream
Grove City, PA 724-748-4115
Stegall Smoked Turkey
Marshville, NC 800-851-6034
Stewart's Ice Cream
Saratoga Springs, NY 518-581-1000
Stinson Seafood Company
Prospect Harbor, ME 207-963-7331
Stolt SeaFarm
Elverta, CA 800-525-0333
Stone Crabs
Miami Beach, FL 800-260-2722
Stone's Home Made Candy Shop
Oswego, NY 888-223-3928
Strathroy Foods
Strathroy, ON 519-245-4600
Strebin Farms
Troutdale, OR 503-665-8328
Sudlersville Frozen Food Locker
Sudlersville, MD. 410-438-3106
Sugar Creek/Eskimo Pie
Russellville, AR 800-445-2715
Sun-Glo of Idaho
Sugar City, ID 208-356-7346
Sungarden Sprouts
Cookeville, TN 931-526-1106
Sunny Avocado
Jamul, CA 800-999-2862
Sunnyslope Farms Egg Ranch
Cherry Valley, CA 951-845-1131
Sunset Specialty Foods
Sunset Beach, CA 562-592-4976

Sunshine Dairy Foods
Portland, OR 503-234-7526
Sunshine Farms Dairy
Elyria, OH 440-322-6301
Sunshine Food Sales
Miami, FL 305-696-2885
Super Snooty Sea Food Corporation
Boston, MA. 617-426-6390
Superbrand Dairies
Montgomery, AL. 334-277-6010
Superior Foods
Watsonville, CA 831-728-3691
Superior Frozen Vegetables
Cornell, MI 906-384-6466
Supermarket Productions
San Rafael, CA 415-479-0211
Superstore Industries
Fairfield, CA 707-864-0502
Supreme Frozen Products
Chicago, IL 773-622-3336
Sutherland's Foodservice
Forest Park, GA 404-366-8550
Suzanna's Kitchen
Duluth, GA 800-241-2455
Sweet Fortunes of America
Woodstock, NY. 845-679-7327
Sweet Shop
La Crosse, WI. 608-784-7724
Sweet Water Seafood Corporation
Carlstadt, NJ 201-939-6622
Sweety Novelty
Monterey Park, CA. 626-282-4482
Swissland Packing Company
Frankfort, IL 800-321-8325
Switzer's
East St Louis, IL 618-271-6336
Symons Frozen Foods
Centralia, WA 360-736-1321
Sysco Food Services of Chicago
Des Plaines, IL 847-699-5400
Sysco Food Services of Indiana
Indianapolis, IN 317-291-2020
SYSCO Foodservice
Fremont, CA 650-494-7200
Sysco/Louisville Food Service
Louisville, KY 800-669-1236
T. Marzetti Company
Columbus, OH 614-846-2232
Table de France
Ontario, CA. 909-923-5205
TAIF
Folcroft, PA 610-631-5544
Taku Smokehouse
Juneau, AK 800-582-5122
Tami Great Food
Monsey, NY 718-788-4200
Tampa Bay Fisheries
Dover, FL 800-234-2561
Tampa Maid Foods
Lakeland, FL 800-237-7637
Tantos Foods International
Richmond Hill, ON 905-763-9994
Tasty Mix Quality Foods
Brooklyn, NY. 866-TAS-TYMX
Tasty Selections
Concord, ON 905-760-2353
Taylor Shellfish Farms
Shelton, WA 360-426-6178
Tebay Dairy Company
Parkersburg, WV. 304-863-3705
Tech Pak Solutions
Westbrook, ME 207-878-6667
Tenn Valley Ham Company
Paris, TN 731-642-9740
Tex-Mex Cold Storage
Brownsville, TX 956-831-9433
The Bama Company
Tulsa, OK 800-756-2262
Thompson Packers
Slidell, LA. 800-989-6328
Thoms-Proestler Company
Rock Island, IL 309-787-1234
Threshold RehabilitationServices
Reading, PA 610-777-7691
Thrifty Ice Cream
El Monte, CA 626-571-0122
Thyme & Truffles Hors D'oeuvres
Toronto, ON 877-489-8636
Tichon Seafood Corporation
New Bedford, MA 508-999-5607
Tillamook County Creamery Association
Tillamook, OR 503-842-4481

 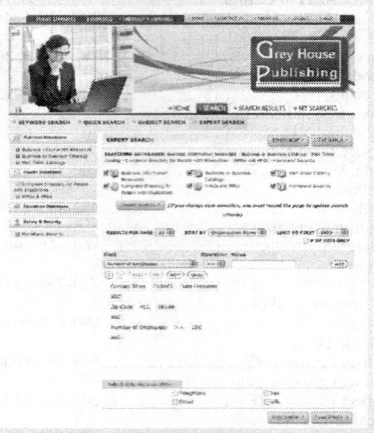 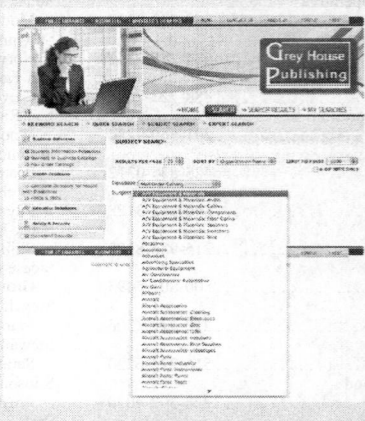

Tipiak
Stamford, CT.........................203-961-9117

TNT Crust
Green Bay, WI......................920-431-7240

Toft Dairy
Sandusky, OH......................800-521-4606

Tom's Ice Cream Bowl
Zanesville, OH.....................740-452-5267

Tomasso Corporation
Baie D'Urfe, QC....................514-325-3000

Tony Downs Foods Company
St James, MN.......................507-375-3111

Tony's Ice Cream Company
Gastonia, NC.......................704-867-7085

Topper Food Products
East Brunswick, NJ................800-377-2823

Topps Meat Company
Elizabeth, NJ......................908-351-0500

Totino's
Minneapolis, MN...................612-492-7018

Townsend Farms
Fairview, OR.......................503-666-1780

Townsends Inc
Georgetown, DE....................302-855-7100

Trade Winds Pizza
Green Bay, WI......................920-336-7810

Trans Pecos Foods
San Antonio, TX...................210-228-0896

Trappe Packing Corporation
Trappe, MD.........................410-476-3185

Travis Meats
Powell, TN.........................800-247-7606

Tree Top
Selah, WA..........................800-367-6571

Tri-State Processing Company
Kokomo, IN.........................317-452-4008

Trident Seafoods Corporation
Salem, NH..........................603-893-3368

Trident Seafoods Corporation
Seattle, WA........................800-426-5490

Triple D Orchards
Empire, MI.........................866-781-9410

Triple U Enterprises
Fort Pierre, SD....................605-567-3624

Tripp Bakers
Wheeling, IL.......................800-621-3702

Triton Seafood Company
Medley, FL.........................305-805-3500

Tropical Illusions
Trenton, MO........................660-359-6849

Tropical Treets
North York, ON.....................888-424-8229

Tropicana
Bradenton, FL......................800-828-2102

Tropics Beverages
Elmhurst, IL.......................800-926-5232

Tru-Blu Cooperative Associates
New Lisbon, NJ.....................609-894-8717

Tucson Frozen Storage
Tucson, AZ.........................520-623-0660

Tupman-Thurlow Company
Deerfield Beach, FL................954-596-9989

Turano Pasty Shops
Berwyn, IL.........................708-788-5320

Turk Brothers Custom Meats
Ashland, OH........................800-789-1051

Turkey Store Company
Faribault, MN......................507-334-2050

Turner Dairies
Jackson, TN........................731-427-6012

Turner Dairies
Covington, TN......................901-476-2643

Turris Italian Foods
Roseville, MI......................586-773-6010

Turtle Mountain
Eugene, OR.........................541-338-9400

Twin City Foods
Stanwood, WA.......................206-515-2400

Two Chefs on a Roll
Carson, CA.........................800-842-3025

Tyson Foods
Wilkesboro, NC.....................336-838-2171

Tyson Foods
Bloomfield, MO.....................573-568-2153

Tyson Foods
Dexter, MO.........................573-624-4551

Tyson Foods
Jackson, MS........................601-372-7441

Tyson Foods
Springdale, AR.....................800-643-3410

Tyson Foods
Berryville, AR.....................870-423-2164

Tyson Foods
Hope, AR...........................870-777-8646

Tyson Foods Plant
Santa Teresa, NM...................800-351-8184

Tyson Fresh Meats
Emporia, KS........................620-343-3640

Umpqua Dairy Products Company
Roseburg, OR.......................541-672-2638

Uncle Ralph's Cookie Company
Frederick, MD......................800-422-0626

Unilever
Lisle, IL..........................877-995-4483

Unique Bakery Company
Toronto, ON........................416-751-8200

Unique Ingredients
Naches, WA.........................509-653-1991

United Dairy
Martins Ferry, OH..................800-252-1542

United Dairy
Uniontown, PA......................800-966-6455

United Meat Company
San Francisco, CA..................415-864-2118

United Shellfish Company
Grasonville, MD....................410-827-8171

Universal Flavor Corporation
Indianapolis, IN...................317-243-3521

US Fresh Marketing
Virginia Beach, VA.................757-481-2606

Usine de Congelation St. Bruno
St. Bruno, QC......................418-343-2206

Valley Dairy Fairview Dairy
Windber, PA........................814-467-5537

Valley Maid Ice Cream
Aurora, IL.........................630-851-2241

Valley Meat Company
Modesto, CA........................800-222-6328

Valley Packing Company
Lansing, OH........................740-635-0154

Van De Kamp Frozen Foods
Erie, PA...........................814-898-1500

Van Drunen Farms
Momence, IL........................815-472-3100

Van Oriental Foods
Dallas, TX.........................214-630-0333

Van-Lang Foods
Lombard, IL........................630-268-1953

Velda Farms
Lakeland, FL.......................800-279-4166

Velda Farms
North Miami Bch, FL................800-795-4649

Velvet Ice Cream Company
Utica, OH..........................800-589-5000

Venice Spumoni/Spring Valley Ice Cream
Philadelphia, PA...................800-784-0312

Venison America
Hudson, WI.........................715-386-6628

Very Best Foods
Miami, FL..........................305-824-9165

Vie de France Yamazaki
Vernon, LA.........................323-582-1241

Viking Seafoods Inc
Malden, MA.........................800-225-3020

Vince's Seafoods
Gretna, LA.........................504-368-1544

Vincent Piazza Jr & Sons
Harahan, LA........................800-259-5016

Virginia Trout Company
Monterey, VA.......................540-468-2280

Vita Food Products
Chicago, IL........................312-738-4500

Vita-Pakt Citrus Company
Covina, CA.........................626-332-1101

Vitality Foodservice
Barrie, ON.........................800-668-5463

Vitamilk Dairy
Bellingham, WA.....................206-529-4128

Vivolac Cultures Corporation
Indianapolis, IN...................317-356-8460

VMI Corporation
Omaha, NE..........................800-228-2248

W&G Marketing Company
Ames, IA...........................515-233-4774

W&W Meats
Willoughby, OH.....................216-621-7846

W.L. Petrey Wholesale Company
Luverne, AL........................334-335-6582

Walt Koch
Decatur, GA........................404-378-3666

Waltkoch
Decatur, GA........................404-378-3666

Wanchese Fish Company
Suffolk, VA........................757-673-4500

Wapsie Produce
Decorah, IA........................563-382-4271

Ward Cove Packing Company
Seattle, WA........................206-323-3200

Warwick Ice Cream Company
Warwick, RI........................401-821-8403

Washington Crab Producers
Westport, WA.......................360-268-9161

Washington Potato Company
Warden, WA.........................509-349-8803

Washington Rhubarb Growers Association
Sumner, WA.........................800-435-9911

Watermill Foods
Milton Freewater, OR...............541-938-6601

Waugh Foods
East Peoria, IL....................309-427-8000

Wawona Frozen Foods
Clovis, CA.........................559-299-2901

Wayfield Foods
Atlanta, GA........................404-559-3200

Wayne Dairy Products
Richmond, IN.......................800-875-9294

Wayne Farms, LLC
Jack, AL...........................334-897-3435

Wayne Farms, LLC
Oakwood, GA........................678-989-3900

Webster Farms
Cambridge Station, NS..............902-538-9492

Weems Brothers Seafood Company
Biloxi, MS.........................228-432-5422

Weiss Provisions
Pittsburgh, PA.....................800-458-6328

Welch's Foods Inc
Lawton, MI.........................269-624-1308

Welch's Foods Inc
Concord, MA........................800-340-6870

Welch's Foods Inc
North East, PA.....................814-725-4577

Weldon Ice Cream Company
Millersport, OH....................740-467-2400

Wells' Dairy
Le Mars, IA........................800-942-3800

Welsh Farms
Newark, NJ.........................800-221-0663

Welsh Farms
Clifton, NJ........................973-772-2388

Wenk Foods Inc
Madison, SD........................605-256-4569

Wenner Bread Products
Bayport, NY........................800-869-6262

Westco-Bake Mark
Pico Rivera, CA....................562-949-1054

Western Alaska Fisheries
Seattle, WA........................206-447-4400

Western Foods
Little Rock, AR....................501-562-4646

Westin
Omaha, NE..........................800-228-6098

Wexler Meat Company
Skokie, IL.........................773-927-5656

Weyand Fisheries
Wyandotte, MI......................800-521-9815

Wham Food & Beverage
Hollywood, FL......................954-920-7857

Whitaker Foods
Evansdale, IA......................800-553-7490

White Cap Fish Company
Islip, NY..........................631-581-0125

White Toque
Perth Amboy, NJ....................800-237-6936

Whitey's Ice Cream Manufacturing
Moline, IL.........................888-594-4839

Wick's Pies
Winchester, IN.....................800-642-5880

Wild Rice Exchange
Woodland, CA.......................800-223-7423

Williams Institutional Foods
Douglas, GA........................912-384-5270

Willowbrook Foods
Wichita, KS........................800-423-2362

Windatt Farms
Picton, ON.........................613-393-5289

Winder Dairy
West Valley, UT....................800-946-3371

Windsor Foods
Houston, TX........................713-843-5200

Windsor Frozen Foods
Houston, TX........................800-437-6936

Winmix/Natural Care Products
Englewood, FL......................941-475-7432

Winter Garden Citrus
Winter Garden, FL..................407-656-4423

Wolferman's
   Medford, OR 913-888-4499
Wolfgang Puck Food Company
   Santa Monica, CA 310-432-1350
Wong Wing Foods
   Montreal, QC 800-361-4820
Wornick Company
   Cincinnati, OH 800-860-4555
Wrangell Fisheries
   Wrangell, AK 907-874-3346
Wright Ice Cream
   Cayuga, IN 800-686-9561
Yamasa Fish Cake Company
   Los Angeles, CA 213-626-2211
Yarnell Ice Cream Company
   Searcy, AR 800-766-2414
Yoders
   Grantsville, MD 301-895-5121
Yorktown Baking Company
   Yorktown Heights, NY 800-235-3961
Zartic Inc
   Rome, GA 800-241-0516
Ziegenfelder Company
   Wheeling, WV 304-232-6360

Spices, Seasonings & Seeds

Herbs

A M Todd Company
Kalamazoo, OR.....................269-343-2603
Agrexco USA
Jamaica, NY......................718-481-8700
Agrinom LLC
Hakalau, HI.......................808-963-6771
Allen & Cowley SpecialtyFoods
Phoenix, AZ......................800-279-1634
Alpine Health Products
Orem, UT........................800-572-5076
American Botanicals
Eolia, MO........................800-684-6070
American Mercantile Corporation
Memphis, TN.....................901-454-1900
Anna's Unlimited, Inc
Austin, TX.......................800-849-7054
Aphrodisia Products
Brooklyn, NY.....................877-274-3677
Ashland Sausage Company
Carol Stream, IL..................630-690-2600
Assets Health Foods
Hillsborough, NJ..................888-849-2048
Atlantic Quality Spice &Seasonings
Edison, NJ.......................800-584-0422
Badia Spices
Miami, FL........................305-629-8000
BDS Natural Products, Inc.
Carson, CA.......................310-518-2227
Belmont Chemicals
Clifton, NJ.......................800-722-5070
Beta Pure Foods
Aptos, CA........................831-685-6565
Better Living Products
Princeton, TX.....................972-736-6691
Bijols
Miami, FL........................305-634-9030
Bolner's Fiesta Products
San Antonio, TX..................210-734-6404
Brewster Foods TestLab
Reseda, CA.......................818-881-4268
Castella Imports
Hauppauge, NY...................866-227-8355
Cinnabar Specialty Foods
Prescott, AZ......................866-293-6433
Colorado Spice
Boulder, CO......................800-677-7423
Connection Source
Alpharetta, GA....................770-667-1051
Crystal Star Herbal Nutrition
Salinas, CA.......................831-422-7500
Cyclone Enterprises
Houston, TX......................281-872-0087
Daregal Gourmet
Princeton, NJ.....................609-375-2312
DynaPro International
Ogden, UT.......................800-877-1413
Eckhart Corporation
Novato, CA.......................800-200-4201
Epicurean Specialty
Sebastopol, CA....................800-500-0065
FDP
Santa Rosa, CA...................707-547-1776
Fontina Foods
Port Saint Lucie, FL...............800-966-7107
Freed, Teller & Freed
Burlingame, CA...................800-370-7371
Frontier Cooperative Herbs
Boulder, CO......................800-669-3275
Garden Herbs
Redlands, CA.....................800-388-9397
Georgia Spice Company
Atlanta, GA.......................800-453-9997
Gloria's Gourmet
New Britain, CT...................860-225-9196
Great Spice Company
San Marcos, CA...................800-730-3575
Green House
San Luis Rey, CA..................760-439-6515
Green House Fine Herbs
Encinitas, CA.....................760-942-5371
Guayaki Sustainable Rainforest Products
Sebastopol, CA....................888-482-9254
Hari Om Farms
Eagleville, TN.....................615-368-7778

Health Concerns
Oakland, CA......................800-233-9355
Health Products Corporation
Yonkers, NY......................914-423-2900
HealthBest
San Marcos, CA...................760-752-5230
Herb Connection
Springville, UT....................801-489-4254
Herb Patch of Vermont
Bellows Falls, VT..................800-282-4372
Herbs, Etc.
Santa Fe, NM.....................888-694-3727
Ingredients Corporation of America
Memphis, TN.....................901-525-6660
Jodie's Kitchen
Tarpon Springs, FL................800-728-3704
Kalustyan Corporation
Union, NJ........................908-688-6111
La Flor Spices
Hauppauge, NY...................631-885-9601
Leeward Resources
Baltimore, MD....................410-837-9003
M. Brown & Sons
Bremen, IN.......................800-258-7450
McCormick & Company Inc
Sparks, MD.......................410-771-7301
Mermaid Spice Corporation
Fort Myers, FL....................239-693-1986
Mezza
Lake Forest, IL....................888-206-6054
Mojave Foods Corporation
Commerce, CA....................323-890-8900
Morris J. Golombeck
Brooklyn, NY.....................718-284-3505
Nature's Sunshine Products Company
Provo, UT........................800-223-8225
Nature's Way
Springville, UT....................800-962-8873
Now Foods
Bloomingdale, IL..................888-669-3663
Pacific Spice Company
Commerce, CA....................800-281-0614
Pereg Gourmet Spices
Flushing, NY......................718-261-6767
Phamous Phloyd's Barbeque Sauce
Denver, CO.......................303-757-3285
Pots de Creme
Lexington, KY.....................859-299-2254
Prince of Peace Enterprises
Hayward, CA......................800-732-2328
QBI
South Plainfield, NJ...............908-668-0088
Republic of Tea
Novato, CA.......................800-354-5530
Rodelle Vanillas
Fort Collins, CO...................800-898-5457
Sampac Enterprises
S San Francisco, CA...............650-876-0808
San Francisco Herb & Natural Food Company
Fremont, CA......................800-227-2830
San Francisco Urban Naturals
Fremont, CA......................510-770-1215

Sentry Seasonings
Elmhurst, IL......................630-530-5370

The product development experts of Sentry Seasonings are eager to offer the assistance and hands-on experience to food processors of all sizes. Sentry Seasonings will ensure the consistent high quality and repeat sales of your products, whether you choose one of our many off-the-shelf Bench Mark products or a modified version to meet your preferences. Sentry Seasonings can also duplicate and/or improve your present flavor profile; formulate, blend and package specifically for your requirements.

Specialty Food America
Hopkinsville, KY..................888-881-1633
Spice House International Specialties
Hicksville, NY....................516-942-7248
Spice Time Foods/Julius & Joe's
Paramus, NJ......................800-345-9225
Spice World
Orlando, FL......................800-433-4979
Sunshine Farm & Gardens
Renick, WV.......................304-497-2208
Superior Trading Company
San Francisco, CA.................415-982-8722

SupHerb Farms
Turlock, CA.......................800-787-4372

CrEATe! Get ready-to-use fresh flavor with SupHerb Farms' all-natural fresh frozen culinary herbs, specialty vegetables, culinary herb pastes, vegetable purees and creative blends. Complete microbiological testing ensures food safety. We set the standard for outstanding customer service, inspired culinary support, collaborative customer partnerships and innovative custom products.

Universal Formulas
Portage, MI......................800-342-6960
Vantage USA
Chicago, IL.......................773-247-1086
Wagner Gourmet Foods
Shawnee Mission, KS..............913-469-5411
Whole Herb Company
Sonoma, CA......................707-935-1077
Wisdom Natural Brands
Gilbert, AZ.......................800-899-9908
Woodland Foods
Gurnee, IL........................847-625-8600
World Spice
Roselle, NJ.......................800-234-1060
Xcell International Corporation
Lemont, IL.......................800-722-7751
Yellow Emperor
Eugene, OR.......................877-485-6664
Young Winfield
Kleinburg, ON.....................905-893-2536

Herbal Supplements

A M Todd Company
Kalamazoo, OR...................269-343-2603
Abunda Life Laboratories
Asbury Park, NJ...................732-775-4141
Acta Health Products
Sunnyvale, CA....................408-732-6830
ADH Health Products
Congers, NY......................800-292-6002
Advanced Spice & Trading
Carrollton, TX.....................800-872-7811
Agriproducts
Coral Springs, FL..................800-277-4979
Agumm
Coral Springs, FL..................954-344-0607
Alfred L. Wolff, Inc.
Park Ridge, IL....................312-265-9889
Allen & Cowley SpecialtyFoods
Phoenix, AZ......................800-279-1634
Alpine Health Products
Orem, UT........................800-572-5076
Alta Health Products
Idaho City, ID....................800-423-4155
Alternative Health & Herbs
Albany, OR.......................800-345-4152
AM Todd Company
Kalamazoo, MI....................800-968-2603
Amazing Herbs Nutraceuticals
Stone Mountain, GA...............800-241-9138
Ameri-Kal Inc
Wichita Falls, TX..................940-322-5400

American Biosciences
Blauvelt, NY.....................845-727-0800
Aphrodisia Products
Brooklyn, NY...................877-274-3677
Arise & Shine Herbal Products
Medford, OR...................800-688-2444

asiamerica

Asiamerica Ingredients
Westwood, NJ..................201-497-5531

Processor, importer, exporter and distributor of bulk vitamins, amino acids, nutraceuticals, aromatic chemicals, food additives, herbs, mineral nutrients and pharmaceuticals.

Auroma International, Inc.
Silver Lake, WI................262-889-8569
Bedrock Farm Certified Organic Medicinal Herbs
Wakefield, RI..................401-789-9943
Bionutritional Research Group
Santa Ana, CA.................714-427-6990
Blessed Herbs
Oakham, MA....................800-489-4372
Bodyonics Limited
Farmingdale, NY...............516-822-1230
Botanical Products
Springville, CA................559-539-3432
Botanicals International Extracts
Denver, CO....................303-322-3859
Brewster Foods TestLab
Reseda, CA....................818-881-4268
Brucia Plant Extracts
Shingle Springs, CA...........530-676-2774
Cinnabar Specialty Foods
Prescott, AZ..................866-293-6433
Country Life
Hauppauge, NY.................800-645-5768
Cyanotech Corporation
Kailua Kona, HI...............800-395-1353
Dr. Christopher's Original Foods
Springville, UT...............800-453-1406
Dreamous Corporation
Torrance, CA..................800-251-7543
EB Botanicals
Montclair, NJ.................973-655-9585
Eclectic Institute
Sandy, OR.....................503-668-4120
Edge Labs
Trenton, NJ...................866-334-3522

EMERLING INTERNATIONAL FOODS, INC.

Emerling International Foods
Buffalo, NY...................716-833-7381

We supply food manufacturers and food service customers worldwide (since 1988) with bulk ingredients including: Fruits & Vegetables; Juice Concentrates; Herbs & Spices; Oils & Vinegars; Flavors & Colors; Honey & Molasses. We also produce PURE MAPLE SYRUP.

Empire Spice Mills
Winnipeg, NB..................204-786-1594
En Garde Health Products
Van Nuys, CA..................818-901-8505
Essaic Canada International
Lake Worth, FL................561-585-7111
Essential Flavors & Fragrances, Inc
Corona, CA....................888-333-9935
Flavorbank
Tampa, FL.....................813-885-1797
Fmali Herb
Santa Cruz, CA................831-423-7913
Fontina Foods
Port Saint Lucie, FL..........800-966-7107
Frank Capurro & Son
Moss Landing, CA..............831-728-3904
Freeman Industries
Tuckahoe, NY..................800-666-6454
Functional Products LLC
Atlantic Beach, FL............800-628-5908
Fungi Perfecti
Olympia, WA...................800-780-9126
Gaia Herbs
Brevard, NC...................800-831-7780

GCI Nutrients (USA)
Foster City, CA...............650-697-4700
Generation Farms
Rice, TX......................903-326-4263
Geni
Noblesville, IN...............888-656-4364
Ginco International
Simi Valley, CA...............800-423-5176
Ginkgoton
Gardena, CA...................310-538-8383
Global Botanical
Barrie, ON....................705-733-2117
Global Express Gourmet
Bozeman, MT...................406-587-5571
Global Health Laboratories
Melville, NY..................631-293-0030
Graminex
Saginaw, MI...................877-472-6469
Green Gold Group
Marathon, WI..................888-533-7288
Green Grown Products
Santa Monica, CA..............310-828-1686
Green Turtle Bay Vitamin Company
Summit, NJ....................800-887-8535
H. Reisman Corporation
Orange, NJ....................973-882-1670
Health & Nutrition Systems International
Boynton Beach, FL.............561-433-0733
Health Plus
Chino, CA.....................800-822-6225
Health Products Corporation
Yonkers, NY...................914-423-2900
Heart Foods Company
Minneapolis, MN...............800-229-3663
Herb Connection
Springville, UT...............801-489-4254
Herbal Magic
Forest Knolls, CA.............800-684-3722
Herbal Products & Development
Aptos, CA.....................831-688-4200
Herbalist & Alchemist
Washington, NJ................908-689-9020
HerbaSway Laboratories
Wallingford, CT...............800-672-7322
Herbco International
Duvall, WA....................425-788-7903
Herbs from China
Chicago, IL...................866-823-4372
Herbs, Etc.
Santa Fe, NM..................888-433-1212
Hill Nutritional Products
Cherry Hill, NJ...............856-857-0811
Himalaya
Houston, TX...................713-863-1622
Himalayan Heritage
Fredonia, WI..................888-414-9500
Honso USA
Phoenix, AZ...................888-461-5808
Humco
Texarkana, TX.................800-662-3435
IL HWA American Corporation
Belleville, NJ................800-446-7364
Indena USA
Seattle, WA...................206-340-6140
Indiana Botanic Gardens
Hobart, IN....................219-947-4040
IVC American Vitamin
Freehold, NJ..................800-666-8482
Jaguar Yerba Company
Ashland, OR...................800-839-0775
Janca's Jojoba Oil & Seed Company
Mesa, AZ......................480-497-9494
Jarrow Industries
Santa Fe Springs, CA..........562-906-1919
JBS Natural Products
Dallas, PA....................800-565-6207
JR Laboratories
Honesdale, PA.................570-253-5826
Kalustyan Corporation
Union, NJ.....................908-688-6111
Kid Care
Carpinteria, CA...............805-566-2473
Kimco World Trade Company
Los Angeles, CA...............323-662-5836
Kingchem
Allendale, NJ.................800-211-4330
Kombucha Wonder Drink
Portland, OR..................877-224-7331
Life-Renewal
Garrison, MN..................320-692-4498
LifeTime Nutritional Specialties
Orange, CA....................714-634-9340

Local Tofu
Nyack, NY.....................845-727-6393
Mafco Natural Products
Richmond, VA..................804-222-1600
Maharishi Ayurveda Products International
Colorado Springs, CO..........800-255-8332
Mayway Corporation
Oakland, CA...................800-262-9929
McCormick & Company
Sparks, MD....................800-632-5847
McCormick & Company Inc
Sparks, MD....................410-771-7301
McFadden Farm
Potter Valley, CA.............800-544-8230
Meridian Trading
Boulder, CO...................303-442-8683
Michael's Naturopathic
San Antonio, TX...............800-525-9643
Mincing Overseas Spice Company
Dayton, NJ....................732-355-9944
Mix Industries
Richton Park, IL..............708-339-6692
Motherland International Inc
Rancho Cucamonga, CA..........800-590-5407
Nature's Herbs
American Fork, UT.............800-437-2257
NatureMost Laboratories
Middletown, CT................800-234-2112
NBTY
Ronkonkoma, NY................800-920-6090
NorSun Food Group
West Chester, OH..............800-886-4326
North West Marketing Company
Brea, CA......................714-529-0980
Northridge Laboratories
Chatsworth, CA................818-882-5622
Nutritional Life Support Systems
San Diego, CA.................619-294-3954
Paragon Laboratories
Torrance, CA..................310-370-1563
Pendery's
Dallas, TX....................800-533-1870
Pharmline
Florida, NY...................845-651-4443
Phyto-Technologies
Woodbine, IA..................877-809-3404
Prairie Sun Grains
Calgary, AB...................800-556-6807
Prince of Peace Enterprises
Hayward, CA...................800-732-2328
Pro Form Labs
Orinda, CA....................925-299-9000
Pro Pac Labs
Ogden, UT.....................888-277-6722
Pro-Pharm
Lake Bluff, IL................847-234-3570
Progenix Corporation
Wausau, WI....................800-233-3356
Rainbow Light Nutritional Systems
Santa Cruz, CA................800-635-1233
Restaurant Lulu Gourmet Products
San Francisco, CA.............888-693-5800
Sadkhin Complex
Brooklyn, NY..................800-723-5446
San Francisco Herb & Natural Food Company
Fremont, CA...................800-227-2830
Sandbar Trading Corporation
Louisville, CO................303-499-7480
Schiff Food Products
North Bergen, NJ..............201-861-2503
Schiff Nutrition International
Salt Lake City, UT............801-975-5000
Silva International
Momence, IL...................815-472-3535
Soft Gel Technologies
Commerce, CA..................800-360-7484
Soolim
Buffalo Grove, IL.............847-357-8515
Spice Time Foods/Julius & Joe's
Paramus, NJ...................800-345-9225
Spice World
Orlando, FL...................800-433-4979
Starwest Botanicals
Rancho Cordova, CA............888-273-4372
Stevia LLC
Valley Forge, PA..............888-878-3842
Sundial Gardens
Higganum, CT..................860-345-4290
Superior Trading Company
San Francisco, CA.............415-982-8722
Swagger Foods Corporation
Vernon Hills, IL..............847-913-1200

Tova Industries
   Louisville, KY 888-532-8682
Tri-Sun International
   Santa Ana, CA 800-387-4786
Turtle Island Herbs
   Boulder, CO .800-684-4060
Tusitala
   Grand Bay, AL 251-865-6240
United Society of Shakers
   New Gloucester, ME. 888-624-6345
Van Drunen Farms
   Momence, IL. 815-472-3100
Vitamer Laboratories
   Irvine, CA 800-432-8355
Vitarich Laboratories
   Naples, FL 800-817-9999
VitaTech International
   Tustin, CA. 714-832-9700
Whole Herb Company
   Sonoma, CA .707-935-1077
World Ginseng Center
   San Francisco, CA 800-747-8808
World Organics Corporation
   Huntington Beach, CA 714-893-0017
Yerba Prima
   Ashland, OR .800-488-4339

for Beef

Sentry Seasonings
   Elmhurst, IL .630-530-5370

The product development experts of Sentry Seasonings are eager to offer the assistance and
hands-on experience to food processors of all
sizes. Sentry Seasonings will ensure the consistent
high quality and repeat sales of your products,
whether you choose one of our many off-the-shelf
Bench Mark products or a modified version to
meet your preferences. Sentry Seasonings can
also duplicate and/or improve your present flavor
profile; formulate, blend and package specifically
for your requirements.

for Pork

Sentry Seasonings
   Elmhurst, IL. .630-530-5370

The product development experts of Sentry Seasonings are eager to offer the assistance and
hands-on experience to food processors of all
sizes. Sentry Seasonings will ensure the consistent
high quality and repeat sales of your products,
whether you choose one of our many off-the-shelf
Bench Mark products or a modified version to
meet your preferences. Sentry Seasonings can
also duplicate and/or improve your present flavor
profile; formulate, blend and package specifically
for your requirements.

for Poultry

Sentry Seasonings
   Elmhurst, IL .630-530-5370

The product development experts of Sentry Seasonings are eager to offer the assistance and
hands-on experience to food processors of all
sizes. Sentry Seasonings will ensure the consistent
high quality and repeat sales of your products,
whether you choose one of our many off-the-shelf
Bench Mark products or a modified version to
meet your preferences. Sentry Seasonings can
also duplicate and/or improve your present flavor
profile; formulate, blend and package specifically
for your requirements.

for Seafood

Hsu's Ginseng Enterprises
   Wausau, WI. .800-826-1577

Sentry Seasonings
   Elmhurst, IL .630-530-5370

The product development experts of Sentry Seasonings are eager to offer the assistance and
hands-on experience to food processors of all
sizes. Sentry Seasonings will ensure the consistent
high quality and repeat sales of your products,
whether you choose one of our many off-the-shelf
Bench Mark products or a modified version to
meet your preferences. Sentry Seasonings can
also duplicate and/or improve your present flavor
profile; formulate, blend and package specifically
for your requirements.

Salt

Adluh Flour Mill
   Columbia, SC 800-692-3584
Agri-Dairy Products
   Purchase, NY 914-697-9580
Ajinomoto Food Ingredients LLC
   Chicago, IL. .773-380-7000
Atlantic Quality Spice &Seasonings
   Edison, NJ. 800-584-0422
Blue Chip Group
   Salt Lake City, UT 800-878-0099
Cabo Rojo Enterprises
   Boqueron, PR 787-254-0015
Canadian Salt Company Limited
   Pointe Claire, QC 514-630-0900
Chr Hansen
   Elyria, OH 800-558-0802
Con Yeager Spice Company
   Zelienople, PA. 800-222-2460
Franco's Cocktail Mixes
   Pompano Beach, FL 800-782-4508
Ingredients Corporation of America
   Memphis, TN 901-525-6660
Java-Gourmet/Keuka Lake Coffee Roaster
   Penn Yan, NY 888-478-2739
Jungbunzlauer
   Newton, MA .800-828-0062
Lawry's Foods
   Monrovia, CA 800-952-9797
Morton Salt
   Chicago, IL. .800-789-7258
Morton Salt Company
   Chicago, IL. .312-807-2000
North American Salt Company
   Overland Park, KS 913-344-9100
Nutricepts
   Burnsville, MN 800-949-9060
Portion Pac
   Mason, OH 800-232-4829

Rapunzel Pure Organics
   Chatham, NY 800-207-2814
Redi-Froze
   South Bend, IN 574-237-5111
Spiceman
   Eugene, OR. .800-725-8373
Stickney & Poor Company
   North Andover, MA 508-261-8967
Swagger Foods Corporation
   Vernon Hills, IL 847-913-1200
Tate & Lyle North American Sugars
   Rutherford, NJ 201-842-7723
Twang
   San Antonio, TX. 800-950-8095
United Salt Corporation
   Houston, TX .800-554-8658

Active

Particle Dynamics
   St Louis, MO. 800-452-4682

Celery

American Key Food Products
   Closter, NJ. 800-767-0237
Gel Spice Company, Inc
   Bayonne, NJ .800-922-0230

Garlic

American Key Food Products
   Closter, NJ. 800-767-0237
Gel Spice Company, Inc
   Bayonne, NJ .800-922-0230

MSG & Salt Mixture

American Food Ingredients
   Oceanside, CA 760-967-6287
Compass Minerals
   Overland Park, KS 877-462-7258
DeSouza International
   Beaumont, CA. 800-373-5171

Onion

American Key Food Products
   Closter, NJ. 800-767-0237
Atlantic Quality Spice &Seasonings
   Edison, NJ. 800-584-0422
Gel Spice Company, Inc
   Bayonne, NJ .800-922-0230

Rock

Morton Salt Company
   Chicago, IL. .312-807-2000

Sea

Blue Crab Bay Company
   Melfa, VA 800-221-2722
Chieftain Wild Rice Company
   Spooner, WI .800-262-6368
D'Artagnan
   Newark, NJ 800-327-8246
Heartland Gourmet Popcorn
   Elk Grove Village, IL 866-489-4676
Redmond Minerals
   Redmond, UT 800-367-7258

Substitutes

Ajinomoto Food Ingredients LLC
   Chicago, IL. .773-380-7000
Mermaid Spice Corporation
   Fort Myers, FL 239-693-1986
Morre-Tec Industries
   Union, NJ 908-688-9009
Morton Salt
   Chicago, IL. .800-789-7258
Spice Hunter
   San Luis Obispo, CA 800-444-3061

Seasonings

A M Todd Company
   Kalamazoo, OR. 269-343-2603
A.C. Legg Inc
   Calera, AL. 205-324-3451
AC Legg
   Calera, AL. 800-422-5344

Adluh Flour Mill
Columbia, SC 800-692-3584
Advanced Food Systems, Inc.
Somerset, NJ 732-873-6776
Ailments E.D. Foods Inc.
Pointe Claire, QC 800-267-3333
Alberto-Culver Company
Melrose Park, IL 708-450-3000
All American Seasonings
Denver, CO 303-623-2320
Alpine Touch Spices
Choteau, MT 877-755-2525
American Food Ingredients
Oceanside, CA 760-967-6287
American Key Food Products
Closter, NJ 800-767-0237
Ampacco
Hunt Valley, MD 800-632-5847
Andy's Seasoning
St Louis, MO 800-305-3004
Aphrodisia Products
Brooklyn, NY 877-274-3677
Ariake USA, Inc.
Harrisonburg, VA 888-201-5885
Arizona Natural Products
Phoenix, AZ 602-997-6098
Atlantic Quality Spice &Seasonings
Edison, NJ 800-584-0422
Atlantic Seasonings
Kinston, NC 800-433-5261
Au Printemps Gourmet
Prevost, QC 800-663-0416
Autin's Cajun Cookery
Covington, LA 800-877-7290
Badia Spices
Miami, FL 305-629-8000
Baker's Rib
Dallas, TX 214-748-5433
Bakon Yeast
Scottsdale, AZ 480-595-9370
Barataria Spice Company
Barataria, LA 800-793-7650
BBQ'n Fools
Bend, OR 800-671-8652
Bell Flavors & Fragrances
Northbrook, IL 800-323-4387
Benson's Gourmet Seasonings
Azusa, CA 800-325-5619
Bittersweet Herb Farm
Shelburne Falls, MA 800-456-1599
BKW Seasonings Inc
Knoxville, TN 865-466-8365
Blend Pak
Bloomfield, KY 502-252-8000
Blendex Company
Jeffersontown, KY 800-626-6325
Blue Crab Bay Company
Melfa, VA 800-221-2722
Boston Spice & Tea Company
Boston, VA 800-966-4372
Braswell Food Company
Statesboro, GA 912-764-6191
Bruce Foods Corporation
New Iberia, LA 800-299-9082
C.F. Sauer Company
Richmond, VA 800-688-5676
Cabo Rojo Enterprises
Boqueron, PR 787-254-0015
Cajun Boy's Louisiana Products
Baton Rouge, LA 800-880-9575
Cajun Chef Products
St Martinville, LA 337-394-7112
California Blending Corpany
El Monte, CA 626-448-1918
Canadian Salt Company Limited
Pointe Claire, QC 514-630-0900
Caribbean Food Delights
Tappan, NY 845-398-3000
Catamount Specialties ofVermont
Stowe, VT 800-820-8096
Char Crust
Chicago, IL 800-311-9884
Chef Hans Gourmet Foods
Monroe, LA 800-890-4267
Chef Merito
Encino, CA 800-637-4861
Chef Paul Prudhomme's Magic Seasonings Blends
Harahan, LA 800-457-2857
Chef Shells Catering & Roadside Cafe
Port Huron, MI 810-966-8371
Cherchies
Malvern, PA 800-644-1980
Chester Fried
Montgomery, AL 800-288-1555
Chieftain Wild Rice Company
Spooner, WI 800-262-6368
CHR Hansen
Gainesville, FL 352-332-9455
CHR Hansen
Elyria, OH 440-324-6060
CHR Hansen
Milwaukee, WI 800-343-4680
Chr Hansen
Elyria, OH 800-558-0802
Christie Food Products
Randolph, MA 800-727-2523
Christopher Ranch
Gilroy, CA 408-847-1100
Chugwater Chili Corporation
Chugwater, WY 800-972-4454
Cibolo Junction Food & Spice
Albuquerque, NM 505-888-1987
Colonna Brothers
North Bergen, NJ 201-864-1115
Colorado Spice
Boulder, CO 800-677-7423
Commercial Creamery Company
Spokane, WA 800-541-0850
Common Folk Farm
Naples, ME 207-787-2764
Con Yeager Spice Company
Zelienople, PA 800-222-2460
ConAgra Food Ingredients
Omaha, NE 800-872-9236
ConAgra Grocery Products
Irvine, CA 714-680-1000
Continental Seasoning
Teaneck, NJ 800-631-1564
Creative Seasonings
Wakefield, MA 617-246-1461
Crest Foods Company
Ashton, IL 800-435-6972
Custom Food Products
Alsip, IL 708-388-8883
Dean Distributors
Burlingame, CA 800-227-3112
Dean Distributors
Burlingame, CA 800-792-0816
DeFrancesco & Sons
Firebaugh, CA 209-364-7000
Demitri's Bloody Mary Seasonings
Seattle, WA 800-627-9649
Dismat Corporation
Toledo, OH 419-531-8963
Dona Yiya Foods
San Sebastian, PR 787-896-4007
Dorothy Dawson Foods Products
Jackson, MI 517-788-9830
Earthen Vessels Herb Company
Hockessin, DE 302-234-7667
Elite Spice
Jessup, MD 800-232-3531
Enrico's/Ventre Packing
Syracuse, NY 888-472-8237
Erba Food Products
Brooklyn, NY 718-272-7700
Everglades Foods
Labelle, FL 800-689-2221
Everson Spice Company
Long Beach, CA 800-421-3753
Excalibur Seasoning Company
Pekin, IL 800-444-2169
Fernandez Chili Company
Alamosa, CO 719-589-6043
First Spice Mixing Company
Long Island City, NY 800-221-1105
Five Star Food Base Company
St Paul, MN 800-505-7827
Flavor Dynamics
South Plainfield, NJ 888-271-8424
Flavorbank Company
Tucson, AZ 800-835-7603
Fmali Herb
Santa Cruz, CA 831-423-7913
Fontina Foods
Port Saint Lucie, FL 800-966-7107
Food Concentrate Corporation
Oklahoma City, OK 405-840-5633
Food Ingredients Solutions
Blauvelt, NY 845-353-8501
Foran Spice Company
Oak Creek, WI 800-558-6030
Fox Meadow Farm of Vermont
Rutland, VT 888-754-4204
FW Witt & Company
Yorkville, IL 630-553-6366
Garden of the Gods Seasonings
Colorado Springs, CO 877-229-1548
Georgia Spice Company
Atlanta, GA 800-453-9997
Gilroy Foods
Gilroy, CA 800-921-7502
Golden Specialty Foods
Norwalk, CA 562-802-2537
Gourmet Foods
Knoxville, TN 865-970-2982
Gravymaster, Inc
Branford, CT 203-481-2276
Green Mountain Gringo
Winston Salem, NC 802-875-3117
Griffith Laboratories
Scarborough, ON 416-288-3050
Grouse Hunt Farms
Tamaqua, PA 570-467-2850
Guapo Spices Company
Los Angeles, CA 213-322-8900
Guido's International Foods
Pasadena, CA 877-994-8436
Halladays Harvest Barn
Bellows Falls, VT 802-463-3471
Harris Farms
Coalinga, CA 800-742-1955
Head Country Food Products
Ponca City, OK 888-762-1227
Heartline Foods
Westport, CT 203-222-0381
Herb Society of America
Willoughby, OH 440-256-0514
Hollman Foods
Minden, NE 888-926-2879
Homegrown Naturals
Napa, CA 800-288-1089
Howards of Colorado
Denver, CO 970-332-5662
Illes Seasonings & Flavors
Carrollton, TX 800-683-4553
Ingredients Corporation of America
Memphis, TN 888-242-2669
Ingredients Corporation of America
Memphis, TN 901-525-6660
International Food
Germantown, WI 800-558-8696
J. Dickerson
Irondale, AL 205-956-0881
Jagulana Herbal Products
Badger, CA 559-337-2188
Jensen Luhr & Sons
Hood River, OR 541-386-3811
JM All Purpose Seasoning
Lincoln, NE 402-421-8326
Kikkoman International
San Francisco, CA 415-956-7750
Kraft Food Ingredients
Memphis, TN 901-381-6500
Kraft Foods
Northfield, IL 847-646-2000
La Flor Spices
Hauppauge, NY 631-885-9601
Lawry's Foods
Monrovia, CA 800-952-9797
Louisiana Gourmet Enterprises
Houma, LA 800-328-5586
Lucile's Famous Creole Seasonings
Boulder, CO 800-727-3653
Lynch Supply
Lenexa, KS 913-492-8500
Mad Chef Enterprise
Mentor, OH 800-951-2433
Magic Seasoning Blends
Harahan, LA 800-457-2857
Maharishi Ayurveda Products International
Colorado Springs, CO 800-255-8332
Mane Incorporated
Milford, OH 800-595-8936
Mansmith Enterprises
San Jn Bautista, CA 800-626-7648
Mansmith's Barbecue
San Jn Bautista, CA 800-626-7648
Marin Food Specialties
Byron, CA 925-634-6126
Marion-Kay Spices
Brownstown, IN 800-627-7423
Marnap Industries
Buffalo, NY 716-897-1220
Mayacamas Fine Foods
Sonoma, CA 800-826-9621

McClancy Seasoning Company
Fort Mill, SC 800-843-1968
McCormick & Company
Sparks, MD 800-632-5847
McCormick & Company Inc
Sparks, MD 410-771-7301
MD Foods Ingredients
Union, NJ 800-972-2096
Meat-O-Mat Corporation
Brooklyn, NY 718-965-7250
Mermaid Spice Corporation
Fort Myers, FL 239-693-1986
Metarom Corporation
Newport, VT 888-882-5555
Mild Bill's Spices
Bulverde, TX 830-980-4124
Misty
Lincoln, NE 402-466-8424
Modern Products/Fearn Natural Foods
Mequon, WI 800-877-8935
Moderncuts
Mequon, WI 262-242-2400
Mojave Foods Corporation
Commerce, CA 323-890-8900
Morris J. Golombeck
Brooklyn, NY 718-284-3505
Morton Salt
Chicago, IL 800-789-7258
Morton Salt Company
Chicago, IL 312-807-2000
Mrs. McGarrigle's Fine Foods
Merrickville, ON 877-768-7827
Mulligan Sales
City of Industry, CA 626-968-9621
Newly Weds Foods
Decatur, AL 800-521-6189
Newly Weds Foods
Chicago, IL 800-621-7521
Newly Weds Foods
Memphis, TN 800-647-9314
North Coast Processing
North East, PA. 814-725-9617
Nu Products Seasoning Company
South Hackensack, NJ 800-836-7692
Old Mansion Foods
Petersburg, VA 800-476-1877
Old World Spices & Seasonings
Kansas City, MO. 800-241-0070
One Source
Concord, MA 800-554-5501

Oregon Flavor Rack Spice
Eugene, OR. 800-725-8373
Oregon Spice Company
Portland, OR 800-565-1599
Organic Gourmet
Sherman Oaks, CA 800-400-7772
Original Cajun Injector
Clinton, LA 800-221-8060
Original Juan
Kansas City, KS 800-568-8468
Pacific Foods
Kent, WA. 800-347-9444
Pappy Meat Company
Fresno, CA 559-291-0218
Pearson's Homestyle
Bowden, AB 877-224-3339
Pelican Bay
Dunedin, FL 800-826-8982
Pemberton's Gourmet Foods
Gray, ME. 800-255-8401
Penwest Foods Company
Centennial, CO 303-649-1900
Peppi Chili
Norcross, GA 770-449-6149
Pillsbury Canada Limited
Markham, ON. 800-745-4777
Pleasoning Gourmet Seasonings
La Crosse, WI 800-279-1614
Precise Food Ingredients
Carrollton, TX. 972-323-4951
Presco Food Seasonings
Flemington, NJ 800-526-1713
Produits Alimentaires Berthelet
Laval, QC 514-334-5503
Quest International Flavors
Hoffman Estates, IL 847-645-7000
RC Fine Foods
Belle Mead, NJ 800-526-3953
Rector Foods
Brampton, ON. 888-314-7834
Red Lion Spicy Foods Company
Red Lion, PA. 717-244-0227
Reggie Ball's Cajun Foods
Lake Charles, LA 337-436-0291
Restaurant Lulu Gourmet Products
San Francisco, CA 888-693-5800
REX Pure Foods
Gonzales, TX 800-344-8314
Rezolex
Las Cruces, NM 575-527-1730
Robinson's Barbecue Sauce Company
Oak Park, IL 708-383-8452
Royal Foods & Flavors
Elk Grove Vlg, IL 847-595-9166
S&B International Corporation
Torrance, CA. 310-257-0177
Salmolux
Federal Way, WA 253-874-6570
San Francisco Herb & Natural Food Company
Fremont, CA 800-227-2830
San-J International
Richmond, VA. 800-446-5500
Saratoga Food Specialties
Elmhurst, IL 800-451-0407
Schiff Food Products
North Bergen, NJ 201-861-2503
Secret Garden
Park Rapids, MN. 800-950-4409

Sentry Seasonings
Elmhurst, IL 630-530-5370

The product development experts of Sentry Seasonings are eager to offer the assistance and hands-on experience to food processors of all sizes. Sentry Seasonings will ensure the consistent high quality and repeat sales of your products, whether you choose one of our many off-the-shelf Bench Mark products or a modified version to meet your preferences. Sentry Seasonings can also duplicate and/or improve your present flavor profile; formulate, blend and package specifically for your requirements.

Shine Companies
Spring, TX. 281-353-8392
Silver Palate Kitchens
Cresskill, NJ 800-872-5283
Soteria
Fairburn, GA. 404-768-5161
SOUPerior Bean & Spice Company
Vancouver, WA 800-878-7687
Southern Delight Gourmet Foods
Bowling Green, KY 866-782-9943
Spice Advice
Ankeny, IA 800-247-5251
Spice Hunter
San Luis Obispo, CA 800-444-3061
Spice King Corporation
Beverly Hills, CA 310-836-7770
Spice Time Foods/Julius & Joe's
Paramus, NJ 800-345-9225
Spice World
Orlando, FL. 800-433-4979
Spiceman
Eugene, OR. 800-725-8373
St Charles Trading
Batavia, IL. 630-377-0608
Sterigenics International
Los Angeles, CA. 800-472-4508
Sun-Rype Products
Kelowna, BC 888-786-7973
Superior Quality Foods
Ontario, CA. 800-300-4210
Swagger Foods Corporation
Vernon Hills, IL 847-913-1200
T Hasegawa
Cerritos, CA 714-670-1586
Tampico Spice Company
Los Angeles, CA. 323-235-3154
Taste Maker Foods
Memphis, TN 800-467-1407
Texas Coffee Company
Beaumont, TX. 800-259-3400
Texas Crumb & Food Products
Farmers Branch, TX 800-522-7862
Texas Traditions
Georgetown, TX 800-547-7062
TFF Seasoning Division
Milford, OH 513-248-9876
Todd's
Des Moines, IA. 800-247-5363
Tommy Tang's Thai Seasonings
Los Angeles, CA. 323-937-5733
Tony Chachere's Creole Foods
Opelousas, LA 800-551-9066
Trader Vic's Food Products
Emeryville, CA. 877-762-4824
Tri-State Specialties
Chicago, IL 773-247-0160
Triple H
Riverside, CA 951-352-5700
Tropical
Charlotte, NC 800-220-1413
UFL Foods
Mississauga, ON 905-670-7776
Unilever United States
Englewood Cliffs, NJ 201-567-8000
US Ingredients
Naperville, IL 630-820-1711
Vanns Spices
Baltimore, MD 800-583-1693
Victoria Gourmet
Woburn, MA 866-972-6879
Victoria Packing Corporation
Brooklyn, NY 718-649-2180
Wagner Gourmet Foods
Shawnee Mission, KS 913-469-5411
West Pac
Idaho Falls, ID 800-973-7407
Whole Herb Company
Sonoma, CA 707-935-1077
WILD Flavors (Canada)
Mississauga, ON 800-263-5286
Wildly Delicious
Toronto, ON 888-545-9995
William E. Martin & Sons Company
Jamaica, NY 718-291-1300
Williams Foods Inc
Lenexa, KS 800-255-6736
Williams-West & Witt Products
Michigan City, IN 219-879-8236
Wixon/Fontarome
St Francis, WI 414-769-3000
Woodland Foods
Gurnee, IL. 847-625-8600

Woody's Bar-B-Q Sauce Company
Waldenburg, AR 870-579-2251
World Flavors
Warminster, PA 215-672-4400
World Harbors
Auburn, ME 800-355-6221
Wynn Starr Flavors
Allendale, NJ 800-996-7827
Xcell International Corporation
Lemont, IL 800-722-7751
Young Winfield
Kleinburg, ON 905-893-2536
Zatarain's
Gretna, LA 800-435-6639

Baking

Atlantic Quality Spice & Seasonings
Edison, NJ 800-584-0422

Sentry Seasonings
Elmhurst, IL 630-530-5370

The product development experts of Sentry Seasonings are eager to offer the assistance and
hands-on experience to food processors of all
sizes. Sentry Seasonings will ensure the consistent
high quality and repeat sales of your products,
whether you choose one of our many off-the-shelf
Bench Mark products or a modified version to
meet your preferences. Sentry Seasonings can
also duplicate and/or improve your present flavor
profile; formulate, blend and package specifically
for your requirements.

World Spice
Roselle, NJ 800-234-1060

Barbecue

Applecreek Farms
Lexington, KY 800-747-8871
Mansmith's Barbecue
San Jn Bautista, CA 800-626-7648

Sentry Seasonings
Elmhurst, IL 630-530-5370

The product development experts of Sentry Seasonings are eager to offer the assistance and
hands-on experience to food processors of all
sizes. Sentry Seasonings will ensure the consistent
high quality and repeat sales of your products,
whether you choose one of our many off-the-shelf
Bench Mark products or a modified version to
meet your preferences. Sentry Seasonings can
also duplicate and/or improve your present flavor
profile; formulate, blend and package specifically
for your requirements.

Blackening

Atlantic Quality Spice & Seasonings
Edison, NJ 800-584-0422

Sentry Seasonings
Elmhurst, IL 630-530-5370

The product development experts of Sentry Seasonings are eager to offer the assistance and
hands-on experience to food processors of all
sizes. Sentry Seasonings will ensure the consistent
high quality and repeat sales of your products,
whether you choose one of our many off-the-shelf
Bench Mark products or a modified version to
meet your preferences. Sentry Seasonings can
also duplicate and/or improve your present flavor
profile; formulate, blend and package specifically
for your requirements.

Cajun Style

Atlantic Quality Spice & Seasonings
Edison, NJ 800-584-0422
Bruce Foods Corporation
New Iberia, LA 800-299-9082
Cajun Creole Products
New Iberia, LA 800-946-8688
Reggie Ball's Cajun Foods
Lake Charles, LA 337-436-0291

Sentry Seasonings
Elmhurst, IL 630-530-5370

The product development experts of Sentry Seasonings are eager to offer the assistance and
hands-on experience to food processors of all
sizes. Sentry Seasonings will ensure the consistent
high quality and repeat sales of your products,
whether you choose one of our many off-the-shelf
Bench Mark products or a modified version to
meet your preferences. Sentry Seasonings can
also duplicate and/or improve your present flavor
profile; formulate, blend and package specifically
for your requirements.

Slap Ya Mama Cajun Seasoning
Ville Platte, LA 337-363-6904

Cheese

Atlantic Quality Spice & Seasonings
Edison, NJ 800-584-0422

Sentry Seasonings
Elmhurst, IL 630-530-5370

The product development experts of Sentry Seasonings are eager to offer the assistance and
hands-on experience to food processors of all
sizes. Sentry Seasonings will ensure the consistent
high quality and repeat sales of your products,
whether you choose one of our many off-the-shelf
Bench Mark products or a modified version to
meet your preferences. Sentry Seasonings can
also duplicate and/or improve your present flavor
profile; formulate, blend and package specifically
for your requirements.

Chinese Style

Atlantic Quality Spice & Seasonings
Edison, NJ 800-584-0422
San Francisco Herb & Natural Food Company
Fremont, CA 800-227-2830

Sentry Seasonings
Elmhurst, IL 630-530-5370

The product development experts of Sentry Seasonings are eager to offer the assistance and
hands-on experience to food processors of all
sizes. Sentry Seasonings will ensure the consistent
high quality and repeat sales of your products,
whether you choose one of our many off-the-shelf
Bench Mark products or a modified version to
meet your preferences. Sentry Seasonings can
also duplicate and/or improve your present flavor
profile; formulate, blend and package specifically
for your requirements.

Curd

Atlantic Quality Spice & Seasonings
Edison, NJ 800-584-0422

Sentry Seasonings
Elmhurst, IL 630-530-5370

The product development experts of Sentry Seasonings are eager to offer the assistance and
hands-on experience to food processors of all
sizes. Sentry Seasonings will ensure the consistent
high quality and repeat sales of your products,
whether you choose one of our many off-the-shelf
Bench Mark products or a modified version to
meet your preferences. Sentry Seasonings can
also duplicate and/or improve your present flavor
profile; formulate, blend and package specifically
for your requirements.

Dairy Products

Atlantic Quality Spice & Seasonings
Edison, NJ 800-584-0422

Sentry Seasonings
Elmhurst, IL 630-530-5370

The product development experts of Sentry Seasonings are eager to offer the assistance and
hands-on experience to food processors of all
sizes. Sentry Seasonings will ensure the consistent
high quality and repeat sales of your products,
whether you choose one of our many off-the-shelf
Bench Mark products or a modified version to
meet your preferences. Sentry Seasonings can
also duplicate and/or improve your present flavor
profile; formulate, blend and package specifically
for your requirements.

Fajita

Atlantic Quality Spice & Seasonings
Edison, NJ 800-584-0422
Bruce Foods Corporation
New Iberia, LA 800-299-9082

Sentry Seasonings
Elmhurst, IL .630-530-5370

The product development experts of Sentry Seasonings are eager to offer the assistance and hands-on experience to food processors of all sizes. Sentry Seasonings will ensure the consistent high quality and repeat sales of your products, whether you choose one of our many off-the-shelf Bench Mark products or a modified version to meet your preferences. Sentry Seasonings can also duplicate and/or improve your present flavor profile; formulate, blend and package specifically for your requirements.

Fried Rice

Atlantic Quality Spice &Seasonings
Edison, NJ 800-584-0422

Sentry Seasonings
Elmhurst, IL .630-530-5370

The product development experts of Sentry Seasonings are eager to offer the assistance and hands-on experience to food processors of all sizes. Sentry Seasonings will ensure the consistent high quality and repeat sales of your products, whether you choose one of our many off-the-shelf Bench Mark products or a modified version to meet your preferences. Sentry Seasonings can also duplicate and/or improve your present flavor profile; formulate, blend and package specifically for your requirements.

Greek Style

Atlantic Quality Spice &Seasonings
Edison, NJ 800-584-0422

Sentry Seasonings
Elmhurst, IL .630-530-5370

The product development experts of Sentry Seasonings are eager to offer the assistance and hands-on experience to food processors of all sizes. Sentry Seasonings will ensure the consistent high quality and repeat sales of your products, whether you choose one of our many off-the-shelf Bench Mark products or a modified version to meet your preferences. Sentry Seasonings can also duplicate and/or improve your present flavor profile; formulate, blend and package specifically for your requirements.

Italian Herbs

Atlantic Quality Spice &Seasonings
Edison, NJ 800-584-0422

Sentry Seasonings
Elmhurst, IL .630-530-5370

The product development experts of Sentry Seasonings are eager to offer the assistance and hands-on experience to food processors of all sizes. Sentry Seasonings will ensure the consistent high quality and repeat sales of your products, whether you choose one of our many off-the-shelf Bench Mark products or a modified version to meet your preferences. Sentry Seasonings can also duplicate and/or improve your present flavor profile; formulate, blend and package specifically for your requirements.

Italian Style

Atlantic Quality Spice &Seasonings
Edison, NJ 800-584-0422
Schiff Food Products
North Bergen, NJ 201-861-2503

Sentry Seasonings
Elmhurst, IL .630-530-5370

The product development experts of Sentry Seasonings are eager to offer the assistance and hands-on experience to food processors of all sizes. Sentry Seasonings will ensure the consistent high quality and repeat sales of your products, whether you choose one of our many off-the-shelf Bench Mark products or a modified version to meet your preferences. Sentry Seasonings can also duplicate and/or improve your present flavor profile; formulate, blend and package specifically for your requirements.

Lemon & Basil

Atlantic Quality Spice &Seasonings
Edison, NJ 800-584-0422

Sentry Seasonings
Elmhurst, IL .630-530-5370

The product development experts of Sentry Seasonings are eager to offer the assistance and hands-on experience to food processors of all sizes. Sentry Seasonings will ensure the consistent high quality and repeat sales of your products, whether you choose one of our many off-the-shelf Bench Mark products or a modified version to meet your preferences. Sentry Seasonings can also duplicate and/or improve your present flavor profile; formulate, blend and package specifically for your requirements.

Lemon & Dill

Atlantic Quality Spice &Seasonings
Edison, NJ 800-584-0422

Sentry Seasonings
Elmhurst, IL .630-530-5370

The product development experts of Sentry Seasonings are eager to offer the assistance and hands-on experience to food processors of all sizes. Sentry Seasonings will ensure the consistent high quality and repeat sales of your products, whether you choose one of our many off-the-shelf Bench Mark products or a modified version to meet your preferences. Sentry Seasonings can also duplicate and/or improve your present flavor profile; formulate, blend and package specifically for your requirements.

Lemon Pepper

Atlantic Quality Spice &Seasonings
Edison, NJ 800-584-0422
Chieftain Wild Rice Company
Spooner, WI 800-262-6368

Sentry Seasonings
Elmhurst, IL .630-530-5370

The product development experts of Sentry Seasonings are eager to offer the assistance and hands-on experience to food processors of all sizes. Sentry Seasonings will ensure the consistent high quality and repeat sales of your products, whether you choose one of our many off-the-shelf Bench Mark products or a modified version to meet your preferences. Sentry Seasonings can also duplicate and/or improve your present flavor profile; formulate, blend and package specifically for your requirements.

Meat Products

AC Legg
Calera, AL........................800-422-5344
All American Seasonings
Denver, CO......................303-623-2320
Atlantic Quality Spice &Seasonings
Edison, NJ.......................800-584-0422
Gourmet Foods
Knoxville, TN...................865-970-2982
JM All Purpose Seasoning
Lincoln, NE.....................402-421-8326
Lynch Supply
Lenexa, KS......................913-492-8500
Nueces Canyon Texas Style Meat Seasoning
Brenham, TX.....................800-925-5058
Rector Foods
Brampton, ON....................888-314-7834
Robinson's Barbecue Sauce Company
Oak Park, IL....................708-383-8452

Sentry Seasonings
Elmhurst, IL....................630-530-5370

> The product development experts of Sentry Seasonings are eager to offer the assistance and hands-on experience to food processors of all sizes. Sentry Seasonings will ensure the consistent high quality and repeat sales of your products, whether you choose one of our many off-the-shelf Bench Mark products or a modified version to meet your preferences. Sentry Seasonings can also duplicate and/or improve your present flavor profile; formulate, blend and package specifically for your requirements.

Spice of Life
Merritt Island, FL..............321-453-5727
Wixon/Fontarome
St Francis, WI..................414-769-3000
World Flavors
Warminster, PA..................215-672-4400

Mexican Style

Atlantic Quality Spice &Seasonings
Edison, NJ.......................800-584-0422
Bea & B Foods
San Diego, CA...................800-952-2117
Bruce Foods Corporation
New Iberia, LA..................800-299-9082
El Ranchito
Portland, OR....................503-665-4919
Golden Specialty Foods
Norwalk, CA.....................562-802-2537
Schiff Food Products
North Bergen, NJ................201-861-2503

Sentry Seasonings
Elmhurst, IL....................630-530-5370

> The product development experts of Sentry Seasonings are eager to offer the assistance and hands-on experience to food processors of all sizes. Sentry Seasonings will ensure the consistent high quality and repeat sales of your products, whether you choose one of our many off-the-shelf Bench Mark products or a modified version to meet your preferences. Sentry Seasonings can also duplicate and/or improve your present flavor profile; formulate, blend and package specifically for your requirements.

Pizza

Atlantic Quality Spice &Seasonings
Edison, NJ.......................800-584-0422

California Blending Corpany
El Monte, CA....................626-448-1918
Chr Hansen
Elyria, OH......................800-558-0802
Dorothy Dawson Foods Products
Jackson, MI.....................517-788-9830

Sentry Seasonings
Elmhurst, IL....................630-530-5370

> The product development experts of Sentry Seasonings are eager to offer the assistance and hands-on experience to food processors of all sizes. Sentry Seasonings will ensure the consistent high quality and repeat sales of your products, whether you choose one of our many off-the-shelf Bench Mark products or a modified version to meet your preferences. Sentry Seasonings can also duplicate and/or improve your present flavor profile; formulate, blend and package specifically for your requirements.

Rib Rub

Atlantic Quality Spice &Seasonings
Edison, NJ.......................800-584-0422

Sentry Seasonings
Elmhurst, IL....................630-530-5370

> The product development experts of Sentry Seasonings are eager to offer the assistance and hands-on experience to food processors of all sizes. Sentry Seasonings will ensure the consistent high quality and repeat sales of your products, whether you choose one of our many off-the-shelf Bench Mark products or a modified version to meet your preferences. Sentry Seasonings can also duplicate and/or improve your present flavor profile; formulate, blend and package specifically for your requirements.

Swagger Foods Corporation
Vernon Hills, IL................847-913-1200

Sausage

Sentry Seasonings
Elmhurst, IL....................630-530-5370

> The product development experts of Sentry Seasonings are eager to offer the assistance and hands-on experience to food processors of all sizes. Sentry Seasonings will ensure the consistent high quality and repeat sales of your products, whether you choose one of our many off-the-shelf Bench Mark products or a modified version to meet your preferences. Sentry Seasonings can also duplicate and/or improve your present flavor profile; formulate, blend and package specifically for your requirements.

Andouille

Sentry Seasonings
Elmhurst, IL....................630-530-5370

> The product development experts of Sentry Seasonings are eager to offer the assistance and hands-on experience to food processors of all sizes. Sentry Seasonings will ensure the consistent high quality and repeat sales of your products, whether you choose one of our many off-the-shelf Bench Mark products or a modified version to meet your preferences. Sentry Seasonings can also duplicate and/or improve your present flavor profile; formulate, blend and package specifically for your requirements.

Hot Italian

Sentry Seasonings
Elmhurst, IL....................630-530-5370

> The product development experts of Sentry Seasonings are eager to offer the assistance and hands-on experience to food processors of all sizes. Sentry Seasonings will ensure the consistent high quality and repeat sales of your products, whether you choose one of our many off-the-shelf Bench Mark products or a modified version to meet your preferences. Sentry Seasonings can also duplicate and/or improve your present flavor profile; formulate, blend and package specifically for your requirements.

Kielbasa

Sentry Seasonings
Elmhurst, IL....................630-530-5370

> The product development experts of Sentry Seasonings are eager to offer the assistance and hands-on experience to food processors of all sizes. Sentry Seasonings will ensure the consistent high quality and repeat sales of your products, whether you choose one of our many off-the-shelf Bench Mark products or a modified version to meet your preferences. Sentry Seasonings can also duplicate and/or improve your present flavor profile; formulate, blend and package specifically for your requirements.

Sweet Italian

Sentry Seasonings
Elmhurst, IL .630-530-5370

The product development experts of Sentry Seasonings are eager to offer the assistance and hands-on experience to food processors of all sizes. Sentry Seasonings will ensure the consistent high quality and repeat sales of your products, whether you choose one of our many off-the-shelf Bench Mark products or a modified version to meet your preferences. Sentry Seasonings can also duplicate and/or improve your present flavor profile; formulate, blend and package specifically for your requirements.

Snack

Butter

Atlantic Quality Spice &Seasonings
Edison, NJ. .800-584-0422

Sentry Seasonings
Elmhurst, IL .630-530-5370

The product development experts of Sentry Seasonings are eager to offer the assistance and hands-on experience to food processors of all sizes. Sentry Seasonings will ensure the consistent high quality and repeat sales of your products, whether you choose one of our many off-the-shelf Bench Mark products or a modified version to meet your preferences. Sentry Seasonings can also duplicate and/or improve your present flavor profile; formulate, blend and package specifically for your requirements.

Cajun Spice

Atlantic Quality Spice &Seasonings
Edison, NJ. .800-584-0422

Sentry Seasonings
Elmhurst, IL .630-530-5370

The product development experts of Sentry Seasonings are eager to offer the assistance and hands-on experience to food processors of all sizes. Sentry Seasonings will ensure the consistent high quality and repeat sales of your products, whether you choose one of our many off-the-shelf Bench Mark products or a modified version to meet your preferences. Sentry Seasonings can also duplicate and/or improve your present flavor profile; formulate, blend and package specifically for your requirements.

Cheddar

Atlantic Quality Spice &Seasonings
Edison, NJ. .800-584-0422

Sentry Seasonings
Elmhurst, IL .630-530-5370

The product development experts of Sentry Seasonings are eager to offer the assistance and hands-on experience to food processors of all sizes. Sentry Seasonings will ensure the consistent high quality and repeat sales of your products, whether you choose one of our many off-the-shelf Bench Mark products or a modified version to meet your preferences. Sentry Seasonings can also duplicate and/or improve your present flavor profile; formulate, blend and package specifically for your requirements.

Cinnamon Toast

Atlantic Quality Spice &Seasonings
Edison, NJ. .800-584-0422

Sentry Seasonings
Elmhurst, IL .630-530-5370

The product development experts of Sentry Seasonings are eager to offer the assistance and hands-on experience to food processors of all sizes. Sentry Seasonings will ensure the consistent high quality and repeat sales of your products, whether you choose one of our many off-the-shelf Bench Mark products or a modified version to meet your preferences. Sentry Seasonings can also duplicate and/or improve your present flavor profile; formulate, blend and package specifically for your requirements.

Mesquite BBQ

Atlantic Quality Spice &Seasonings
Edison, NJ. .800-584-0422
Bickel's of York Snack Foods
York, PA 800-233-1933
Middleswarth Potato Chips
Middleburg, PA. 570-837-1431
Mrs. Fisher's
Rockford, IL .815-964-9114

Sentry Seasonings
Elmhurst, IL .630-530-5370

The product development experts of Sentry Seasonings are eager to offer the assistance and hands-on experience to food processors of all sizes. Sentry Seasonings will ensure the consistent high quality and repeat sales of your products, whether you choose one of our many off-the-shelf Bench Mark products or a modified version to meet your preferences. Sentry Seasonings can also duplicate and/or improve your present flavor profile; formulate, blend and package specifically for your requirements.

Nacho Cheese

Atlantic Quality Spice &Seasonings
Edison, NJ. .800-584-0422

Sentry Seasonings
Elmhurst, IL .630-530-5370

The product development experts of Sentry Seasonings are eager to offer the assistance and hands-on experience to food processors of all sizes. Sentry Seasonings will ensure the consistent high quality and repeat sales of your products, whether you choose one of our many off-the-shelf Bench Mark products or a modified version to meet your preferences. Sentry Seasonings can also duplicate and/or improve your present flavor profile; formulate, blend and package specifically for your requirements.

Ranch

Atlantic Quality Spice &Seasonings
Edison, NJ. .800-584-0422

Sentry Seasonings
Elmhurst, IL .630-530-5370

The product development experts of Sentry Seasonings are eager to offer the assistance and hands-on experience to food processors of all sizes. Sentry Seasonings will ensure the consistent high quality and repeat sales of your products, whether you choose one of our many off-the-shelf Bench Mark products or a modified version to meet your preferences. Sentry Seasonings can also duplicate and/or improve your present flavor profile; formulate, blend and package specifically for your requirements.

Sour Cream & Onion

Atlantic Quality Spice &Seasonings
Edison, NJ. .800-584-0422
Bickel's of York Snack Foods
York, PA 800-233-1933
Middleswarth Potato Chips
Middleburg, PA. 570-837-1431
Mrs. Fisher's
Rockford, IL .815-964-9114

Sentry Seasonings
Elmhurst, IL .630-530-5370

The product development experts of Sentry Seasonings are eager to offer the assistance and hands-on experience to food processors of all sizes. Sentry Seasonings will ensure the consistent high quality and repeat sales of your products, whether you choose one of our many off-the-shelf Bench Mark products or a modified version to meet your preferences. Sentry Seasonings can also duplicate and/or improve your present flavor profile; formulate, blend and package specifically for your requirements.

Southwest

Atlantic Quality Spice &Seasonings
Edison, NJ. .800-584-0422

Sentry Seasonings
Elmhurst, IL 630-530-5370

The product development experts of Sentry Seasonings are eager to offer the assistance and hands-on experience to food processors of all sizes. Sentry Seasonings will ensure the consistent high quality and repeat sales of your products, whether you choose one of our many off-the-shelf Bench Mark products or a modified version to meet your preferences. Sentry Seasonings can also duplicate and/or improve your present flavor profile; formulate, blend and package specifically for your requirements.

Tomato Pesto

Atlantic Quality Spice & Seasonings
Edison, NJ 800-584-0422

Sentry Seasonings
Elmhurst, IL 630-530-5370

The product development experts of Sentry Seasonings are eager to offer the assistance and hands-on experience to food processors of all sizes. Sentry Seasonings will ensure the consistent high quality and repeat sales of your products, whether you choose one of our many off-the-shelf Bench Mark products or a modified version to meet your preferences. Sentry Seasonings can also duplicate and/or improve your present flavor profile; formulate, blend and package specifically for your requirements.

for Corned Beef

Atlantic Quality Spice & Seasonings
Edison, NJ 800-584-0422

Sentry Seasonings
Elmhurst, IL 630-530-5370

The product development experts of Sentry Seasonings are eager to offer the assistance and hands-on experience to food processors of all sizes. Sentry Seasonings will ensure the consistent high quality and repeat sales of your products, whether you choose one of our many off-the-shelf Bench Mark products or a modified version to meet your preferences. Sentry Seasonings can also duplicate and/or improve your present flavor profile; formulate, blend and package specifically for your requirements.

for Tacos

Atlantic Quality Spice & Seasonings
Edison, NJ 800-584-0422
Badia Spices
Miami, FL 305-629-8000

Sentry Seasonings
Elmhurst, IL 630-530-5370

The product development experts of Sentry Seasonings are eager to offer the assistance and hands-on experience to food processors of all sizes. Sentry Seasonings will ensure the consistent high quality and repeat sales of your products, whether you choose one of our many off-the-shelf Bench Mark products or a modified version to meet your preferences. Sentry Seasonings can also duplicate and/or improve your present flavor profile; formulate, blend and package specifically for your requirements.

Seeds

AgriCulver Seeds
Trumansburg, NY 800-836-3701
American Mercantile Corporation
Memphis, TN 901-454-1900
Ann's House of Nuts, Inc.
Jessup, MD 301-498-4920
Atlantic Quality Spice & Seasonings
Edison, NJ 800-584-0422
Birdsong Peanut Company
Gorman, TX .254-734-3153
Brock Seed Company
El Centro, CA 760-353-1632
CHS Sunflower
Grandin, ND 701-484-5313
Con Yeager Spice Company
Zelienople, PA 800-222-2460
Diamond Foods
Fishers, IN 317-845-5534
Dipasa
Brownsville, TX 956-831-5893
Eden Foods Inc
Clinton, MI .800-248-0320
El Brands
Ozark, AL 334-445-2828
Energy Club
Pacoima, CA 800-688-6887
Fernando C Pujals & Bros
San Juan, PR 787-792-3080
Fresh Hemp Foods
Winnipeg, NB 800-665-4367
Frito-Lay
Dallas, TX 800-352-4477
Golden Valley Seed
El Centro, CA 760-337-3100
Govadinas Fitness Foods
San Diego, CA 800-900-0108
Gurley's Foods
Willmar, MN 800-426-7845
H.B. Taylor Co
Chicago, IL .773-254-4805
Harmony Foods Corporation
Fishers, IN 800-837-2855
HempNut
Henderson, NV 707-576-7050
Hialeah Products Company
Hollywood, FL 800-923-3379
Hinojosa Bros Wholesale
Roma, TX 800-554-4119
Honey Bar/Creme de la Creme
Kingston, NY 845-331-4643
HP Schmid
San Francisco, CA 415-765-5925
Ingredients Corporation of America
Memphis, TN 901-525-6660
International Harvest
Mt Vernon, NY 914-939-1505
Interstate Seed Company
West Fargo, ND 800-437-4120
Kalustyan Corporation
Union, NJ 908-688-6111
King Nut Company
Cleveland, OH 800-860-5464
Krispy Kernels
Sainte Foy, QC 418-658-1515
Mayfair Sales
Buffalo, NY .800-248-2881
Mezza
Lake Forest, IL 888-206-6054

Midwest/Northern
Minneapolis, MN 800-328-5502
Mincing Overseas Spice Company
Dayton, NJ .732-355-9944
Minn-Dak Growers Limited
Grand Forks, ND 701-746-7453
Natural Foods
Toledo, OH .800-860-0006
Nature's Candy
Fredericksburg, TX 800-729-0085
Nature's Select
Grand Rapids, MI 888-715-4321
Nestle USA Inc
Glendale, CA 800-633-2330
Nu-World Amaranth
Naperville, IL 630-369-6851
Occidental International Foods
Chester, NJ .908-879-2942
Osage Pecan Company
Butler, MO .660-679-6137
Patsy's Candies
Colorado Springs, CO 866-372-8797
Plantation Products
Norton, MA 508-285-5800
Pyco Industries
Lubbock, TX 800-289-7266
Quality Candy
Milwaukee, WI 800-972-2658
R&J Farms
West Salem, OH 419-846-3179
Red River Commodities
Fargo, ND 701-282-2600
Schiff Food Products
North Bergen, NJ 201-861-2503
Scott-Bathgate
Winnipeg, NB 204-943-8525
Snackerz
Commerce, CA 888-576-2253
Sonne
Wahpeton, ND 800-727-6663
Specialty Commodities
Fargo, ND 701-282-8222
Spitz USA
Loveland, CO 970-613-9319
Stapleton-Spence Packing Company
San Jose, CA 800-297-8815
Sun Ridge Farms
Santa Cruz, CA 800-655-3252
Sunray Food Products Corporation
Bronx, NY 718-548-2255
Sunshine Farm & Gardens
Renick, WV .304-497-2208
Tantos Foods International
Richmond Hill, ON 905-763-9994
Tasty Seeds Ltd
Winkler, NB 888-632-6906
Texas Coffee Company
Beaumont, TX 800-259-3400
Todd's
Vernon, CA .800-938-6337
Torn & Glasser
Los Angeles, CA 800-282-6887
Trophy Nut Company
Tipp City, OH 800-729-6887
Tropical
Charlotte, NC 800-220-1413
Tropical
Marietta, GA 800-544-3762
Tropical Nut & Fruit Company
Orlando, FL .800-749-8869
US Foods
Lincoln, NE .402-470-2021
Weaver Nut Company
Ephrata, PA .717-738-3781
Westin
Omaha, NE .800-228-6098
Whole Herb Company
Sonoma, CA 707-935-1077
Willmar Cookie & Nut Company
Willmar, MN 320-235-0600
Woodland Foods
Gurnee, IL 847-625-8600
Zenobia Company
Bronx, NY 866-936-6242

Alfalfa

Woodland Foods
Gurnee, IL 847-625-8600

Anise or Aniseed

Chesapeake Spice Company
Baltimore, MD 410-391-2100
Chieftain Wild Rice Company
Spooner, WI 800-262-6368
Commodities Marketing, Inc.
Edison, NJ .732-516-0700
Morris J. Golombeck
Brooklyn, NY 718-284-3505

Annatto

Chieftain Wild Rice Company
Spooner, WI 800-262-6368
Gel Spice Company, Inc
Bayonne, NJ 800-922-0230
Morris J. Golombeck
Brooklyn, NY 718-284-3505
Organic Planet
San Francisco, CA 415-765-5590
Schiff Food Products
North Bergen, NJ 201-861-2503

Cabbage

Abbott & Cobb, Inc.
Langhorne, PA 800-345-7333

Caraway

Chesapeake Spice Company
Baltimore, MD 410-391-2100
Chieftain Wild Rice Company
Spooner, WI 800-262-6368
Organic Planet
San Francisco, CA 415-765-5590

Cardamom

Advanced Spice & Trading
Carrollton, TX 800-872-7811
American Key Food Products
Closter, NJ .800-767-0237
Atlantic Quality Spice & Seasonings
Edison, NJ .800-584-0422
Con Yeager Spice Company
Zelienople, PA 800-222-2460
Organic Planet
San Francisco, CA 415-765-5590
Schiff Food Products
North Bergen, NJ 201-861-2503

Celery

Advanced Spice & Trading
Carrollton, TX 800-872-7811
American Key Food Products
Closter, NJ .800-767-0237
Atlantic Quality Spice & Seasonings
Edison, NJ .800-584-0422
Chieftain Wild Rice Company
Spooner, WI 800-262-6368
Con Yeager Spice Company
Zelienople, PA 800-222-2460
Schiff Food Products
North Bergen, NJ 201-861-2503
Unique Ingredients
Naches, WA 509-653-1991
Whole Herb Company
Sonoma, CA 707-935-1077

Ground

Chesapeake Spice Company
Baltimore, MD 410-391-2100

Coriander

Naturex (Chart Corp)
South Hackensack, NJ 201-440-5000

Cumin

Con Yeager Spice Company
Zelienople, PA 800-222-2460

Dill

Advanced Spice & Trading
Carrollton, TX 800-872-7811
Con Yeager Spice Company
Zelienople, PA 800-222-2460
Organic Planet
San Francisco, CA 415-765-5590
Schiff Food Products
North Bergen, NJ 201-861-2503
Vegetable Juices
Chicago, IL 888-776-9752

Fennel

Acatris USA
Edina, MN .952-920-7700
Advanced Spice & Trading
Carrollton, TX 800-872-7811
American Key Food Products
Closter, NJ .800-767-0237
Atlantic Quality Spice & Seasonings
Edison, NJ .800-584-0422
Commodities Marketing, Inc.
Edison, NJ .732-516-0700
Con Yeager Spice Company
Zelienople, PA 800-222-2460
Organic Planet
San Francisco, CA 415-765-5590
Schiff Food Products
North Bergen, NJ 201-861-2503

Fenugreek

Acatris USA
Edina, MN .952-920-7700
Naturex (Chart Corp)
South Hackensack, NJ 201-440-5000

Flax

American Health & Nutrition
Ann Arbor, MI 734-677-5572
Dixie USA
Tomball, TX 800-233-3668
Gel Spice Company, Inc
Bayonne, NJ 800-922-0230
Hialeah Products Company
Hollywood, FL 800-923-3379
Minn-Dak Growers Limited
Grand Forks, ND 701-746-7453
Montana Specialty Mills
Great Falls, MT 406-761-2338
Natural Way Mills
Middle River, MN 218-222-3677
Organic Planet
San Francisco, CA 415-765-5590
Pizzey's Milling & Baking Company
Angusville, NB 800-804-6433
Red River Commodities
Fargo, ND .701-282-2600
Woodland Foods
Gurnee, IL .847-625-8600

Mustard

American Health & Nutrition
Ann Arbor, MI 734-677-5572
American Key Food Products
Closter, NJ .800-767-0237
Commodities Marketing, Inc.
Edison, NJ .732-516-0700
Con Yeager Spice Company
Zelienople, PA 800-222-2460
Demeter Agro
Lethbridge, AB 800-661-1450
Phamous Phloyd's Barbeque Sauce
Denver, CO 303-757-3285

Peanut

Adkin & Son Associated Food Products
South Haven, MI 269-637-7450
Birdsong Peanut Company
Gorman, TX 254-734-3153

Poppy

Advanced Spice & Trading
Carrollton, TX 800-872-7811
American Health & Nutrition
Ann Arbor, MI 734-677-5572
American Key Food Products
Closter, NJ .800-767-0237
Atlantic Quality Spice & Seasonings
Edison, NJ .800-584-0422
Chieftain Wild Rice Company
Spooner, WI 800-262-6368
Con Yeager Spice Company
Zelienople, PA 800-222-2460
HP Schmid
San Francisco, CA 415-765-5925
Ingredients Corporation of America
Memphis, TN 901-525-6660
Organic Planet
San Francisco, CA 415-765-5590
Patisserie Wawel
Montreal, QC 614-524-3348
Schiff Food Products
North Bergen, NJ 201-861-2503
Texas Coffee Company
Beaumont, TX 800-259-3400

Pumpkin

Advanced Spice & Trading
Carrollton, TX 800-872-7811
American Health & Nutrition
Ann Arbor, MI 734-677-5572
American Key Food Products
Closter, NJ .800-767-0237
Atlantic Quality Spice & Seasonings
Edison, NJ .800-584-0422
Cache Creek Foods
Woodland, CA 530-662-1764
Chieftain Wild Rice Company
Spooner, WI 800-262-6368
Diamond Foods
Fishers, IN .317-845-5534
Durey-Libby Edible Nuts
Carlstadt, NJ 800-332-6887

EMERLING INTERNATIONAL FOODS, INC.

Emerling International Foods
Buffalo, NY 716-833-7381

We supply food manufacturers and food service customers worldwide (since 1988) with bulk ingredients including: Fruits & Vegetables; Juice Concentrates; Herbs & Spices; Oils & Vinegars; Flavors & Colors; Honey & Molasses. We also produce PURE MAPLE SYRUP.

Fastachi
Watertown, MA 800-466-3022
Hialeah Products Company
Hollywood, FL 800-923-3379
Mental Processes
Atlanta, GA 800-431-4018
Midwest/Northern
Minneapolis, MN 800-328-5502
Organic Planet
San Francisco, CA 415-765-5590
Sunray Food Products Corporation
Bronx, NY .718-548-2255
Woodland Foods
Gurnee, IL .847-625-8600

Rape

American Health & Nutrition
Ann Arbor, MI 734-677-5572
American Key Food Products
Closter, NJ .800-767-0237
Continental Grain/ContiGroup Companies
New York, NY 212-207-5930

Sesame

American Health & Nutrition
Ann Arbor, MI 734-677-5572
American Key Food Products
Closter, NJ .800-767-0237
Chesapeake Spice Company
Baltimore, MD 410-391-2100
Chieftain Wild Rice Company
Spooner, WI 800-262-6368

Organic Planet
  San Francisco, CA 415-765-5590
Setton International Foods
  Commack, NY 800-227-4397
Spice & Spice
  Rolling Hls Ests, CA.............866-729-7742
Woodland Foods
  Gurnee, IL.......................847-625-8600

Black

Atlantic Quality Spice &Seasonings
  Edison, NJ.......................800-584-0422

White

Atlantic Quality Spice &Seasonings
  Edison, NJ.......................800-584-0422
Spice & Spice
  Rolling Hls Ests, CA.............866-729-7742

Spice

Advanced Spice & Trading
  Carrollton, TX...................800-872-7811
American Key Food Products
  Closter, NJ......................800-767-0237
Atlantic Quality Spice &Seasonings
  Edison, NJ.......................800-584-0422
Ingredients Corporation of America
  Memphis, TN 901-525-6660
Stan-Mark Food Products
  Chicago, IL......................800-651-0994

Sunflower

American Health & Nutrition
  Ann Arbor, MI....................734-677-5572
American Importing Company
  Minneapolis, MN 612-331-9226
American Key Food Products
  Closter, NJ......................800-767-0237
Cache Creek Foods
  Woodland, CA.....................530-662-1764
Chieftain Wild Rice Company
  Spooner, WI......................800-262-6368
CHS Sunflower
  Grandin, ND......................701-484-5313
Commodities Marketing, Inc.
  Edison, NJ.......................732-516-0700
ConAgra Foods Inc
  Omaha, NE........................402-240-4000
Dahlgren & Company
  Crookston, MN....................800-346-6050
Diamond Foods
  Fishers, IN......................317-845-5534
Durey-Libby Edible Nuts
  Carlstadt, NJ....................800-332-6887
Eden Foods Inc
  Clinton, MI......................800-248-0320
Fastachi
  Watertown, MA....................800-466-3022
Franklin Supply Company
  Rushville, IN....................765-932-3928
Heartland Mill
  Marienthal, KS 620-379-4472
Hialeah Products Company
  Hollywood, FL....................800-923-3379
HP Schmid
  San Francisco, CA 415-765-5925
Inn Maid Food
  Lenox, MA........................413-637-2732
Marantha Natural Foods
  San Francisco, CA 800-299-0048

Midwest/Northern
  Minneapolis, MN 800-328-5502
Minn-Dak Growers Limited
  Grand Forks, ND..................701-746-7453
Organic Planet
  San Francisco, CA 415-765-5590
Purity Foods
  Okemos, MI.......................800-997-7358
R&J Farms
  West Salem, OH...................419-846-3179
Red River Commodities
  Fargo, ND........................701-282-2600
Scott-Bathgate
  Winnipeg, NB.....................204-943-8525
Setton International Foods
  Commack, NY 800-227-4397
Sonne
  Wahpeton, ND.....................800-727-6663
Sunray Food Products Corporation
  Bronx, NY........................718-548-2255
Trinidad/Benham Corporation
  Patterson, CA....................209-892-9002
Westin
  Omaha, NE........................800-228-6098

Vegetable

Abbott & Cobb, Inc.
  Langhorne, PA....................800-345-7333
Atlantic Quality Spice &Seasonings
  Edison, NJ.......................800-584-0422
Golden Valley Seed
  El Centro, CA....................760-337-3100
Harris Moran Seed Company
  Modesto, CA......................209-579-7333
McKenna Brothers
  Cardigan, PE.....................902-583-2951
Plantation Products
  Norton, MA.......................508-285-5800
Seminis Vegetable Seeds
  Oxnard, CA.......................805-351-0106

Spices

A M Todd Company
  Kalamazoo, OR....................269-343-2603
Abunda Life Laboratories
  Asbury Park, NJ..................732-775-4141
AC Legg
  Calera, AL.......................800-422-5344
Advance Food Brokers
  West Bloomfield, MI..............248-851-9045
Adventure Foods
  Whittier, NC.....................828-497-4113
Alberto-Culver Company
  Melrose Park, IL.................708-450-3000
All American Seasonings
  Denver, CO.......................303-623-2320
Allen & Cowley SpecialtyFoods
  Phoenix, AZ......................800-279-1634
American Food Ingredients
  Oceanside, CA 760-967-6287
American Key Food Products
  Closter, NJ......................800-767-0237
American Mercantile Corporation
  Memphis, TN 901-454-1900
American Natural & Organic Spices
  Union City, CA...................510-477-4787
Amfit Spices
  Orlando, FL......................407-352-5290
Ampacco
  Hunt Valley, MD..................800-632-5847
Aphrodisia Products
  Brooklyn, NY 877-274-3677

Arizona Natural Products
  Phoenix, AZ......................602-997-6098
Ashley Foods
  Sudbury, MA......................800-617-2823
Astor Products
  Jacksonville, FL.................904-783-5000
Atlantic Quality Spice &Seasonings
  Edison, NJ.......................800-584-0422
Au Printemps Gourmet
  Prevost, QC......................800-663-0416
Badia Spices
  Miami, FL........................305-629-8000
Banner Wholesale Grocers
  Chicago, IL......................312-421-2650
Barataria Spice Company
  Barataria, LA....................800-793-7650
Bell Flavors & Fragrances
  Northbrook, IL...................800-323-4387
BI Nutraceuticals
  Long Beach, CA...................310-669-2100
Big B Distributors
  Evansville, IN...................812-425-5235
Bijols
  Miami, FL........................305-634-9030
Bloch & Guggenheimer
  Hurlock, MD......................800-541-2809
Boston Spice & Tea Company
  Boston, VA.......................800-966-4372
Boyd Coffee Company
  Portland, OR.....................800-545-4077
Bruno's Cajun Foods & Snacks
  Slidell, LA......................985-726-0544
Bueno Food Products
  Albuquerque, NM..................800-888-7336
C.F. Sauer Company
  Richmond, VA.....................800-688-5676
California Blending Corpany
  El Monte, CA.....................626-448-1918
Canadian Salt Company Limited
  Pointe Claire, QC................514-630-0900
Castella Imports
  Hauppauge, NY....................866-227-8355
Chef Hans Gourmet Foods
  Monroe, LA.......................800-890-4267
Chef Merito
  Encino, CA.......................800-637-4861
Chef Paul Prudhomme's Magic Seasonings Blends
  Harahan, LA......................800-457-2857
Chef Zachary's Gourmet Blended Spices
  Detroit, MI 313-226-0000
Chesapeake Spice Company
  Baltimore, MD....................410-391-2100
Chia I Foods Company
  South El Monte, CA...............626-401-3038
Chieftain Wild Rice Company
  Spooner, WI......................800-262-6368
China Bowl Trading Company
  Westport, CT.....................203-222-0381
CHR Hansen
  Elyria, OH.......................440-324-6060
Christopher Ranch
  Gilroy, CA.......................408-847-1100
Chugwater Chili Corporation
  Chugwater, WY....................800-972-4454
Cibolo Junction Food & Spice
  Albuquerque, NM..................505-888-1987
Colonna Brothers
  North Bergen, NJ.................201-864-1115
Colorado Spice
  Boulder, CO......................800-677-7423
Commodities Marketing, Inc.
  Edison, NJ.......................732-516-0700
Con Yeager Spice Company
  Zelienople, PA...................800-222-2460

ConAgra Foods Inc
Omaha, NE 402-240-4000
Consolidated Mills
Houston, TX 713-896-4196
Consumers Vinegar & Spice Company
Chicago, IL 773-376-4100
Continental Seasoning
Teaneck, NJ 800-631-1564
Creole Delicacies Pralines
New Orleans, LA 504-523-6425
Cut Above Foods
Carlsbad, CA 760-931-6777
Cyclone Enterprises
Houston, TX 281-872-0087
D Steengrafe & Company
Pleasant Valley, NY 845-635-4067
Davidsons
Reno, NV 800-882-5888
De Coty Coffee Company
San Angelo, TX 800-588-8001
DeFrancesco & Sons
Firebaugh, CA 209-364-7000
Delicae Gourmet
Tarpon Springs, FL 800-942-2502
Devlin Trading Company
Wayzata, MN 952-475-0259
Dona Yiya Foods
San Sebastian, PR 787-896-4007
Drusilla Seafood Packing & Processing Company
Baton Rouge, LA 800-364-8844
Earthen Vessels Herb Company
Hockessin, DE 302-234-7667
Ecom Manufacturing Corporation
Markham, ON 905-477-2441
El Paso Chile Company
El Paso, TX 888-472-5727
El Ranchito
Portland, OR 503-665-4919
Elite Spice
Jessup, MD 800-232-3531

EMERLING INTERNATIONAL FOODS, INC.

Emerling International Foods
Buffalo, NY 716-833-7381

> **We supply food manufacturers and food service customers worldwide (since 1988) with bulk ingredients including: Fruits & Vegetables; Juice Concentrates; Herbs & Spices; Oils & Vinegars; Flavors & Colors; Honey & Molasses. We also produce PURE MAPLE SYRUP.**

Empire Spice Mills
Winnipeg, NB 204-786-1594
Enrico's/Ventre Packing
Syracuse, NY 888-472-8237
Epicurean Specialty
Sebastopol, CA 800-500-0065
Erba Food Products
Brooklyn, NY 718-272-7700
Excalibur Seasoning Company
Pekin, IL 800-444-2169
Farmer Brothers Company
Torrance, CA 800-735-2878
FDP
Santa Rosa, CA 707-547-1776
Feature Foods
Etobicoke, ON 416-675-7350
Fernandez Chili Company
Alamosa, CO 719-589-6043
First Spice Mixing Company
Long Island City, NY 800-221-1105

First You Make A Roux
Brattleboro, VT 802-257-9336
Flavorbank
Tampa, FL 813-885-1797
Flavorbank Company
Tucson, AZ 800-835-7603
Florida Shortening Corporation
Miami, FL 305-691-2992
Fmali Herb
Santa Cruz, CA 831-423-7913
Fontina Foods
Port Saint Lucie, FL 800-966-7107
Food Ingredients Solutions
Blauvelt, NY 845-353-8501
Fool Proof Gourmet Products
Grapevine, TX 817-329-1839
Foran Spice Company
Oak Creek, WI 800-558-6030
Fox Meadow Farm of Vermont
Rutland, VT 888-754-4204
Freed, Teller & Freed
Burlingame, CA 800-370-7371
Frontier Cooperative Herbs
Boulder, CO 800-669-3275
Frontier Ingredients
Norway, IA 800-669-3275
Ful-Flav-R Foods
Alamo, CA 510-339-9618
FW Witt & Company
Yorkville, IL 630-553-6366
G B Ratto & Company International
Oakland, CA 800-325-3483
G S Dunn & Company
Hamilton, ON 905-522-0833
Garlic Survival Company
San Juan Cpstrno, CA 800-342-7542
George Chiala Farms
Morgan Hill, CA 408-778-0562
Georgia Spice Company
Atlanta, GA 800-453-9997
Gilroy Foods
Gilroy, CA 800-921-7502
Global Botanical
Barrie, ON 705-733-2117
Gloria's Gourmet
New Britain, CT 860-225-9196
Golden Whisk
South San Francisco, CA 800-660-5222
Gourmantra Foods
Markham, ON 416-225-6711
Gourmet Food Mall
Kenner, LA 800-903-7553
Great Lakes Tea & Spice Company
Glen Arbor, MI 877-645-9363
Great Spice Company
San Marcos, CA 800-730-3575
Green Mountain Gringo
Winston Salem, NC 802-875-3117
Griffith Laboratories
Scarborough, ON 416-288-3050
Griffith Laboratories Worldwide
Alsip, IL 800-346-4743
Guapo Spices Company
Los Angeles, CA 213-322-8900
Harbor Spice Company
Forest Hill, MD 410-893-9500
Harris Farms
Coalinga, CA 800-742-1955
HealthBest
San Marcos, CA 760-752-5230
Henry Broch & Company/APK, Inc.
Libertyville, IL 847-816-6225
Herb Connection
Springville, UT 801-489-4254

Herb Society of America
Willoughby, OH 440-256-0514
Hermann Laue Spice Company
Uxbridge, ON 905-852-5100
Hollman Foods
Minden, NE 888-926-2879
Homegrown Naturals
Napa, CA 800-288-1089
House of Spices
Flushing, NY 718-507-4900
Ingredients Corporation of America
Memphis, TN 901-525-6660
Ingretec
Lebanon, PA 717-273-1360
Instant Products of America
Columbus, IN 812-372-9100
Italian Rose Garlic Products
West Palm Beach, FL 800-338-8899
Jagulana Herbal Products
Badger, CA 559-337-2188
Jodie's Kitchen
Tarpon Springs, FL 800-728-3704
Kalsec
Kalamazoo, MI 800-323-9320
Kalustyan Corporation
Union, NJ 908-688-6111
Kayem Foods
Chelsea, MA 800-426-6100
La Flor Spices
Hauppauge, NY 631-885-9601
La Flor Spices Company
Hauppauge, NY 631-851-9601
Lakeside Mills
Rutherfordton, NC 828-286-4866
Lawry's Foods
Monrovia, CA 800-952-9797
Lebermuth Company
South Bend, IN 800-648-1123
Leeward Resources
Baltimore, MD 410-837-9003
Li'l Guy Foods
Kansas City, MO 800-886-8226
Lost Trail Root Beer Com
Louisburg, KS 800-748-7765
Lucerne Foods
Taber, AB 403-223-3546
Magic Seasoning Blends
Harahan, LA 800-457-2857
Mansmith Enterprises
San Jn Bautista, CA 800-626-7648
Mansmith's Barbecue
San Jn Bautista, CA 800-626-7648
Maple Grove Farms of Vermont
St Johnsbury, VT 800-525-2540
Marin Food Specialties
Byron, CA 925-634-6126
Marion-Kay Spices
Brownstown, IN 800-627-7423
Marnap Industries
Buffalo, NY 716-897-1220
McClancy Seasoning Company
Fort Mill, SC 800-843-1968
McCormick & Company Inc
Sparks, MD 410-771-7301
McCormick Ingredients
Hunt Valley, MD 800-632-5847
Mercado Latino
City of Industry, CA 626-333-6862
Mermaid Spice Corporation
Fort Myers, FL 239-693-1986
Mezza
Lake Forest, IL 888-206-6054
Mild Bill's Spices
Bulverde, TX 830-980-4124

Milton A. Klein Company
New York, NY 800-221-0248
Mincing Overseas Spice Company
Dayton, NJ 732-355-9944
Modern Products/Fearn Natural Foods
Mequon, WI 800-877-8935
Moderncuts
Mequon, WI 262-242-2400
Mojave Foods Corporation
Commerce, CA 323-890-8900
Mojave Foods Corporation
Commerce, CA 800-995-8906
Monterrey Products Company
San Antonio, TX 210-435-2872
Morris J. Golombeck
Brooklyn, NY 718-284-3505
Morton & Bassett Spices
Novato, CA 866-972-6879
Morton Salt Company
Chicago, IL 312-807-2000
Natural Foods
Toledo, OH 800-860-0006
Nature Quality
San Martin, CA 408-683-2182
Naturex (Chart Corp)
South Hackensack, NJ 201-440-5000
Newly Weds Foods
Memphis, TN 800-647-9314
Noh Foods International
Torrance, CA 310-618-2092
North American Seasonings
Lake Oswego, OR 503-636-7043
Northwestern Coffee Mills
La Pointe, WI 800-243-5283
Oak Grove Smokehouse
Prairieville, LA 225-673-6857
Occidental International Foods
Chester, NJ 908-879-2942
Ocean Cliff Corporation
New Bedford, MA 508-990-7900
Old Mansion Foods
Petersburg, VA 800-476-1877
Old World Spices & Seasonings
Kansas City, MO 800-241-0070
One Source
Concord, MA 800-554-5501
Oregon Flavor Rack Spice
Eugene, OR 800-725-8373
Oregon Spice Company
Portland, OR 800-565-1599
Organic Planet
San Francisco, CA 415-765-5590
Ottens Flavors
Philadelphia, PA 800-523-0767
PACA Foods
Tampa, FL 800-388-7419
Pacific Spice Company
Commerce, CA 800-281-0614
Pak Technologies
Milwaukee, WI 414-438-8600
Palmieri Food Products
New Haven, CT 800-845-5447
Pappy Meat Company
Fresno, CA 559-291-0218
Papy's Foods
McHenry, IL 815-385-3313
Particle Dynamics
St Louis, MO 800-452-4682
Patak Spices USA
Clearwater, FL 727-796-2126
Pearson's Homestyle
Bowden, AB 877-224-3339
Peavey Company
Ama, LA 225-869-4405
Pecos Valley Spice Company
New York, NY 212-628-5374
Pelican Bay
Dunedin, FL 800-826-8982
Pemberton's Gourmet Foods
Gray, ME 800-255-8401

Pendery's
Dallas, TX 800-533-1870
Pereg Gourmet Spices
Flushing, NY 718-261-6767
Pett Spice Products
Atlanta, GA 404-691-5235
Precise Food Ingredients
Carrollton, TX 972-323-4951
Precision Blends
Baldwin Park, CA 800-836-9979
Premier Blending
Wichita, KS 316-267-5533
Presco Food Seasonings
Flemington, NJ 800-526-1713
Proacec USA
Santa Monica, CA 310-996-7770
R&S Mexican Food Products
Glendale, AZ 602-272-2727
R.L. Schreiber
Pompano Beach, FL 800-624-8777
R.L. Schreiber Company
Pompano Beach, FL 800-624-8777
Randag & Associates Inc
Elmhurst, IL 630-530-2830
Rapazzini Winery
Gilroy, CA 408-842-5649
Raymond-Hadley Corporation
Spencer, NY 800-252-5220
RC Fine Foods
Belle Mead, NJ 800-526-3953
Red Lion Spicy Foods Company
Red Lion, PA 717-244-0227
Reggie Ball's Cajun Foods
Lake Charles, LA 337-436-0291
REX Pure Foods
Gonzales, TX 800-344-8314
RL Schreiber
Pompano Beach, FL 954-972-7102
Sambets Cajun Deli
Austin, TX 800-472-6238
San Francisco Herb & Natural Food Company
Fremont, CA 800-227-2830
Sandbar Trading Corporation
Louisville, CO 303-499-7480
Santa Cruz Chili & SpiceCompany
Tumacacori, AZ 520-398-2591
Sara Lee Foodservice
Rolling Meadows, IL 800-261-4754
Saratoga Food Specialties
Elmhurst, IL 800-451-0407
Schiff Food Products
North Bergen, NJ 201-861-2503
Selecto Sausage Company
Houston, TX 713-926-1626

Sentry Seasonings
Elmhurst, IL 630-530-5370

Serv-Agen Corporation
Cherry Hill, NJ 856-663-6966
Shanks Extracts
Lancaster, PA 800-346-3135
SJH Enterprises
Middleton, WI 888-745-3845
Somerset Industries
Spring House, PA 800-883-8728
SOUPerior Bean & Spice Company
Vancouver, WA 800-878-7687
South Texas Spice Company
San Antonio, TX 210-436-2280
Spanish Gardens Food Manufacturing
Kansas City, KS 913-831-4242

Specialty Food America
Hopkinsville, KY 888-881-1633
Spice & Spice
Rolling Hls Ests, CA 866-729-7742
Spice Advice
Ankeny, IA 800-247-5251
Spice Hunter
San Luis Obispo, CA 800-444-3061
Spice O' Life
Seattle, WA 206-789-4195
Spice Time Foods/Julius & Joe's
Paramus, NJ 800-345-9225
Spiceco
Avenel, NJ 732-499-9070
Spiceland
Chicago, IL 800-352-8671
Spiceman
Eugene, OR 800-725-8373
St Charles Trading
Batavia, IL 630-377-0608
St. John's Botanicals
Bowie, MD 301-262-5302
Stan-Mark Food Products
Chicago, IL 800-651-0994
Starwest Botanicals
Rancho Cordova, CA 888-273-4372
Sterigenics International
Los Angeles, CA 800-472-4508
Stickney & Poor Company
North Andover, MA 508-261-8967
Sundial Gardens
Higganum, CT 860-345-4290
Sunflower Restaurant Supply
Salina, KS 785-823-6394

SupHerb Farms
Turlock, CA 800-787-4372

Sustainable Sourcing
Great Barrington, MA 413-528-5141
Swagger Foods Corporation
Vernon Hills, IL 847-913-1200
Tampico Spice Company
Los Angeles, CA 323-235-3154
Taste Maker Foods
Memphis, TN 800-467-1407
Texas Coffee Company
Beaumont, TX 800-259-3400
Texas Traditions
Georgetown, TX 800-547-7062
To Market-To Market
West Linn, OR 503-657-9192
Tommy Tang's Thai Seasonings
Los Angeles, CA 323-937-5733
Trader Vic's Food Products
Emeryville, CA 877-762-4824
Transa
Libertyville, IL 847-281-9582
Tri-State Specialties
Chicago, IL 773-247-0160
Trinity Spice
Midland, TX 800-460-1149
Triple H
Riverside, CA 951-352-5700
Tripper
Malibu, CA 888-336-8747
Tropical
Charlotte, NC 800-220-1413
Tropical Nut & Fruit Company
Orlando, FL 800-749-8869
Two Guys Spice Company
Jacksonville, FL 800-874-5656
Uncle Fred's Fine Foods
Rockport, TX 361-729-8320

Urban Accents
Chicago, IL 877-872-7742
US Spice Mills
Chicago, IL 773-378-6800
Van Roy Coffee
Cleveland, OH 877-826-7669
Vanco Products Company
Houston, TX 800-231-9564
Vanns Spices
Baltimore, MD 800-583-1693
Vegetable Juices
Chicago, IL 888-776-9752
Victoria Packing Corporation
Brooklyn, NY 718-649-2180
W&G Flavors
Hunt Valley, MD 410-771-6606
Wabash Heritage Spices
Vincennes, IN 812-895-0059
Wagner Gourmet Foods
Shawnee Mission, KS 913-469-5411
Weaver Nut Company
Ephrata, PA 717-738-3781
West Pac
Idaho Falls, ID 800-973-7407
Wheeling Coffee & Spice Company
Wheeling, WV 800-500-0141
Whole Herb Company
Sonoma, CA 707-935-1077
Wild West Spices
Cody, WY 888-587-8887
William Bounds
Torrance, CA 800-473-0504
William E. Martin & Sons Company
Jamaica, NY 718-291-1300
Wine Country Chef LLC
Hidden Valley Lake, CA 707-322-0406
Wisconsin Cheese
Melrose Park, IL 708-450-0074
Wisconsin Spice
Berlin, WI 920-361-3555
Wixon/Fontarome
St Francis, WI 414-769-3000
World Flavors
Warminster, PA 215-672-4400
World Harbors
Auburn, ME 800-355-6221
World of Spices
Stirling, NJ 908-647-1218
World Spice
Roselle, NJ 800-234-1060
Xcell International Corporation
Lemont, IL 800-722-7751
Young Winfield
Kleinburg, ON 905-893-2536
Zatarain's
Gretna, LA 800-435-6639

Allspice

Atlantic Quality Spice &Seasonings
Edison, NJ 800-584-0422
Chesapeake Spice Company
Baltimore, MD 410-391-2100
Chieftain Wild Rice Company
Spooner, WI 800-262-6368
Commodities Marketing, Inc.
Edison, NJ 732-516-0700
Ecom Manufacturing Corporation
Markham, ON 905-477-2441

EMERLING INTERNATIONAL FOODS, INC.

Emerling International Foods
Buffalo, NY 716-833-7381

We supply food manufacturers and food service
customers worldwide (since 1988) with bulk ingredients including: Fruits & Vegetables; Juice
Concentrates; Herbs & Spices; Oils & Vinegars;
Flavors & Colors; Honey & Molasses. We also
produce PURE MAPLE SYRUP.

Erba Food Products
Brooklyn, NY 718-272-7700
Gel Spice Company, Inc
Bayonne, NJ 800-922-0230
Ingredients Corporation of America
Memphis, TN 901-525-6660
Morris J. Golombeck
Brooklyn, NY 718-284-3505
Organic Planet
San Francisco, CA 415-765-5590

Schiff Food Products
North Bergen, NJ 201-861-2503
Texas Coffee Company
Beaumont, TX 800-259-3400
Tova Industries
Louisville, KY 888-532-8682
Victoria Packing Corporation
Brooklyn, NY 718-649-2180
Whole Herb Company
Sonoma, CA 707-935-1077

Ground

Con Yeager Spice Company
Zelienople, PA 800-222-2460
Schiff Food Products
North Bergen, NJ 201-861-2503
Wabash Heritage Spices
Vincennes, IN 812-895-0059
Whole Herb Company
Sonoma, CA 707-935-1077

Whole

Con Yeager Spice Company
Zelienople, PA 800-222-2460
Whole Herb Company
Sonoma, CA 707-935-1077

Anise - Star

Ground

Chesapeake Spice Company
Baltimore, MD 410-391-2100

Basil

Advanced Spice & Trading
Carrollton, TX 800-872-7811
American Key Food Products
Closter, NJ 800-767-0237
Atlantic Quality Spice &Seasonings
Edison, NJ 800-584-0422
Chesapeake Spice Company
Baltimore, MD 410-391-2100
Chieftain Wild Rice Company
Spooner, WI 800-262-6368
Con Yeager Spice Company
Zelienople, PA 800-222-2460

EMERLING INTERNATIONAL FOODS, INC.

Emerling International Foods
Buffalo, NY 716-833-7381

We supply food manufacturers and food service
customers worldwide (since 1988) with bulk ingredients including: Fruits & Vegetables; Juice
Concentrates; Herbs & Spices; Oils & Vinegars;
Flavors & Colors; Honey & Molasses. We also
produce PURE MAPLE SYRUP.

Garden Herbs
Redlands, CA 800-388-9397
Gel Spice Company, Inc
Bayonne, NJ 800-922-0230
Green House Fine Herbs
Encinitas, CA 760-942-5371
Lebermuth Company
South Bend, IN 800-648-1123
Morris J. Golombeck
Brooklyn, NY 718-284-3505
Schiff Food Products
North Bergen, NJ 201-861-2503
Specialty Food America
Hopkinsville, KY 888-881-1633

Spiceco
Avenel, NJ 732-499-9070

SupHerb Farms
Turlock, CA 800-787-4372

CrEATe! Get ready-to-use fresh flavor with
SupHerb Farms' all-natural fresh frozen culinary
herbs, specialty vegetables, culinary herb pastes,
vegetable purees and creative blends. Complete
microbiological testing ensures food safety. We
set the standard for outstanding customer service, inspired culinary support, collaborative customer partnerships and innovative custom
products.

Tova Industries
Louisville, KY 888-532-8682
Van Drunen Farms
Momence, IL 815-472-3100
Vegetable Juices
Chicago, IL 888-776-9752
Victoria Packing Corporation
Brooklyn, NY 718-649-2180
Waterfield Farms
Amherst, MA 413-549-3558
Whole Herb Company
Sonoma, CA 707-935-1077

Basil Leaf

Morris J. Golombeck
Brooklyn, NY 718-284-3505
Schiff Food Products
North Bergen, NJ 201-861-2503

Bay Leaves

Advanced Spice & Trading
Carrollton, TX 800-872-7811
American Key Food Products
Closter, NJ 800-767-0237
Atlantic Quality Spice &Seasonings
Edison, NJ 800-584-0422
Chesapeake Spice Company
Baltimore, MD 410-391-2100
Chieftain Wild Rice Company
Spooner, WI 800-262-6368
Con Yeager Spice Company
Zelienople, PA 800-222-2460
Gel Spice Company, Inc
Bayonne, NJ 800-922-0230
Ingredients Corporation of America
Memphis, TN 901-525-6660
Pendery's
Dallas, TX 800-533-1870
Spiceco
Avenel, NJ 732-499-9070
Tova Industries
Louisville, KY 888-532-8682
Vegetable Juices
Chicago, IL 888-776-9752
Victoria Packing Corporation
Brooklyn, NY 718-649-2180
Wabash Heritage Spices
Vincennes, IN 812-895-0059
Whole Herb Company
Sonoma, CA 707-935-1077

Ground

EMERLING INTERNATIONAL FOODS, INC.

Emerling International Foods
Buffalo, NY 716-833-7381

We supply food manufacturers and food service
customers worldwide (since 1988) with bulk ingredients including: Fruits & Vegetables; Juice
Concentrates; Herbs & Spices; Oils & Vinegars;
Flavors & Colors; Honey & Molasses. We also
produce PURE MAPLE SYRUP.

Black Pepper - Ground

Chesapeake Spice Company
Baltimore, MD 410-391-2100
Spice & Spice
Rolling Hls Ests, CA. 866-729-7742
Swagger Foods Corporation
Vernon Hills, IL 847-913-1200

Capers

Alimentaire Whyte's Inc
Laval, QC 800-625-1979
Castella Imports
Hauppauge, NY 866-227-8355

EMERLING INTERNATIONAL FOODS, INC.

Emerling International Foods
Buffalo, NY. 716-833-7381

We supply food manufacturers and food service customers worldwide (since 1988) with bulk ingredients including: Fruits & Vegetables; Juice Concentrates; Herbs & Spices; Oils & Vinegars; Flavors & Colors; Honey & Molasses. We also produce PURE MAPLE SYRUP.

G L Mezzetta
American Canyon, CA 707-648-1050
L&S Packing Company
Farmingdale, NY 800-286-6487
Les Trois Petits Cochons
New York, NY 800-537-7283
Orleans Packing Company
Hyde Park, MA 617-361-6611
Paradise Products Corporation
Roslyn, NY 800-826-1235
Proacec USA
Santa Monica, CA 310-996-7770
Ron-Son Foods
Swedesboro, NJ 856-241-7333
Star Fine Foods
Fresno, CA 559-498-2900
Vegetable Juices
Chicago, IL 888-776-9752
Victoria Packing Corporation
Brooklyn, NY 718-649-2180

Cardamom

Boulder Bar
San Diego, CA 858-274-1049
Fiesta Gourmet of Tejas
Canyon Lake, TX 800-585-8250
Flavouressence Products
Mississauga, ON 866-209-7778
Goodnature Products
Orchard Park, NY 800-875-3381
Legacy Soft Gourmet Pretzels
San Diego, CA 800-916-3260
Lombardo's Ravioli Kitchen
New Britain, CT 860-223-7800
Min Tong Herbs
Oakland, CA 800-562-5777
Sill Farms Market
Lawrence, MI 269-674-3755
Sunja's Oriental Foods
Waterbury, VT 802-244-7644

Ground

Chesapeake Spice Company
Baltimore, MD 410-391-2100
Chieftain Wild Rice Company
Spooner, WI 800-262-6368
Wabash Heritage Spices
Vincennes, IN 812-895-0059

Carob Powder

American Key Food Products
Closter, NJ. 800-767-0237
Gel Spice Company, Inc
Bayonne, NJ 800-922-0230

Cassia (Cinnamon)

American Key Food Products
Closter, NJ. 800-767-0237
Commodities Marketing, Inc.
Edison, NJ. 732-516-0700
Naturex (Chart Corp)
South Hackensack, NJ 201-440-5000

Cayenne

Chesapeake Spice Company
Baltimore, MD 410-391-2100
Chieftain Wild Rice Company
Spooner, WI 800-262-6368
Vegetable Juices
Chicago, IL 888-776-9752
Victoria Packing Corporation
Brooklyn, NY 718-649-2180

Cayenne Pepper

American Key Food Products
Closter, NJ. 800-767-0237
Atlantic Quality Spice & Seasonings
Edison, NJ. 800-584-0422
El Ranchito
Portland, OR 503-665-4919
Herb Connection
Springville, UT 801-489-4254
Morris J. Golombeck
Brooklyn, NY 718-284-3505
Naturex (Chart Corp)
South Hackensack, NJ 201-440-5000
Pepper Creek Farms
Lawton, OK. 800-526-8132
Tova Industries
Louisville, KY 888-532-8682
Wabash Heritage Spices
Vincennes, IN 812-895-0059

Dried

Naturex (Chart Corp)
South Hackensack, NJ 201-440-5000

Ground

Naturex (Chart Corp)
South Hackensack, NJ 201-440-5000

Whole

Texas Coffee Company
Beaumont, TX. 800-259-3400

Celery Flakes

Swagger Foods Corporation
Vernon Hills, IL 847-913-1200

Chervil

American Key Food Products
Closter, NJ. 800-767-0237
Chieftain Wild Rice Company
Spooner, WI 800-262-6368
Muirhead Canning Company
The Dalles, OR 541-298-1660

SupHerb Farms
Turlock, CA 800-787-4372

CrEATe! Get ready-to-use fresh flavor with SupHerb Farms' all-natural fresh frozen culinary herbs, specialty vegetables, culinary herb pastes, vegetable purees and creative blends. Complete microbiological testing ensures food safety. We set the standard for outstanding customer service, inspired culinary support, collaborative customer partnerships and innovative custom products.

Chile Pepper

Chesapeake Spice Company
Baltimore, MD 410-391-2100
Chieftain Wild Rice Company
Spooner, WI 800-262-6368
China Bowl Trading Company
Westport, CT. 203-222-0381
Chugwater Chili Corporation
Chugwater, WY 800-972-4454
Pendery's
Dallas, TX 800-533-1870

Chili Crush

Spice & Spice
Rolling Hls Ests, CA. 866-729-7742

Chili Pods

Whole & Dried

Spice & Spice
Rolling Hls Ests, CA. 866-729-7742

Chili Powder

Mezza
Lake Forest, IL 888-206-6054
Spice & Spice
Rolling Hls Ests, CA. 866-729-7742

Chinese

Harvest 2000
Pomona, CA 909-622-8039
San Francisco Herb & Natural Food Company
Fremont, CA 800-227-2830

Chives

Advanced Spice & Trading
Carrollton, TX. 800-872-7811
American Key Food Products
Closter, NJ. 800-767-0237
Atlantic Quality Spice & Seasonings
Edison, NJ. 800-584-0422
Chesapeake Spice Company
Baltimore, MD 410-391-2100
Chieftain Wild Rice Company
Spooner, WI 800-262-6368
Gel Spice Company, Inc
Bayonne, NJ 800-922-0230
Green House Fine Herbs
Encinitas, CA 760-942-5371
Schiff Food Products
North Bergen, NJ 201-861-2503

SupHerb Farms
Turlock, CA 800-787-4372

CrEATe! Get ready-to-use fresh flavor with SupHerb Farms' all-natural fresh frozen culinary herbs, specialty vegetables, culinary herb pastes, vegetable purees and creative blends. Complete microbiological testing ensures food safety. We set the standard for outstanding customer service, inspired culinary support, collaborative customer partnerships and innovative custom products.

Van Drunen Farms
Momence, IL. 815-472-3100

Cinnamon

Advanced Spice & Trading
Carrollton, TX. 800-872-7811
American Key Food Products
Closter, NJ. 800-767-0237
Atlantic Quality Spice & Seasonings
Edison, NJ. 800-584-0422
Chesapeake Spice Company
Baltimore, MD 410-391-2100
Chieftain Wild Rice Company
Spooner, WI 800-262-6368
Con Yeager Spice Company
Zelienople, PA. 800-222-2460

EMERLING INTERNATIONAL FOODS, INC.

Emerling International Foods
Buffalo, NY. 716-833-7381

We supply food manufacturers and food service customers worldwide (since 1988) with bulk ingredients including: Fruits & Vegetables; Juice Concentrates; Herbs & Spices; Oils & Vinegars; Flavors & Colors; Honey & Molasses. We also produce PURE MAPLE SYRUP.

Erba Food Products
Brooklyn, NY 718-272-7700
Ingredients Corporation of America
Memphis, TN 901-525-6660
Kennedy Candy Company
Kilgore, TX 800-657-5258
Lebermuth Company
South Bend, IN 800-648-1123
Morris J. Golombeck
Brooklyn, NY 718-284-3505
Organic Planet
San Francisco, CA 415-765-5590
Pendery's
Dallas, TX 800-533-1870
Schiff Food Products
North Bergen, NJ 201-861-2503
Spice & Spice
Rolling Hls Ests, CA 866-729-7742
Spice Market
Fairfield, NJ 800-223-3502
Swagger Foods Corporation
Vernon Hills, IL 847-913-1200
Texas Coffee Company
Beaumont, TX 800-259-3400
Tova Industries
Louisville, KY 888-532-8682
Tripper
Malibu, CA 888-336-8747
Victoria Packing Corporation
Brooklyn, NY 718-649-2180

Cassia

Advanced Spice & Trading
Carrollton, TX 800-872-7811
Atlantic Quality Spice &Seasonings
Edison, NJ 800-584-0422
Morris J. Golombeck
Brooklyn, NY 718-284-3505
Schiff Food Products
North Bergen, NJ 201-861-2503
Tova Industries
Louisville, KY 888-532-8682

Ground

Con Yeager Spice Company
Zelienople, PA 800-222-2460
Wabash Heritage Spices
Vincennes, IN 812-895-0059

Whole

Spice & Spice
Rolling Hls Ests, CA 866-729-7742

Citron

Cooperative Cosecheros de Cidra
Adjuntas, PR 787-829-2845

EMERLING INTERNATIONAL FOODS, INC.

Emerling International Foods
Buffalo, NY 716-833-7381

> We supply food manufacturers and food service customers worldwide (since 1988) with bulk ingredients including: Fruits & Vegetables; Juice Concentrates; Herbs & Spices; Oils & Vinegars; Flavors & Colors; Honey & Molasses. We also produce PURE MAPLE SYRUP.

River One
Vero Beach, FL 800-288-6614
Seald Sweet Growers & Packers
Vero Beach, FL 772-569-2244
Victoria Packing Corporation
Brooklyn, NY 718-649-2180

Cloves

Atlantic Quality Spice &Seasonings
Edison, NJ 800-584-0422
Chesapeake Spice Company
Baltimore, MD 410-391-2100
Chieftain Wild Rice Company
Spooner, WI 800-262-6368
Con Yeager Spice Company
Zelienople, PA 800-222-2460

EMERLING INTERNATIONAL FOODS, INC.

Emerling International Foods
Buffalo, NY 716-833-7381

> We supply food manufacturers and food service customers worldwide (since 1988) with bulk ingredients including: Fruits & Vegetables; Juice Concentrates; Herbs & Spices; Oils & Vinegars; Flavors & Colors; Honey & Molasses. We also produce PURE MAPLE SYRUP.

Schiff Food Products
North Bergen, NJ 201-861-2503
Tova Industries
Louisville, KY 888-532-8682
Victoria Packing Corporation
Brooklyn, NY 718-649-2180

Ground

Con Yeager Spice Company
Zelienople, PA 800-222-2460
Schiff Food Products
North Bergen, NJ 201-861-2503
Texas Coffee Company
Beaumont, TX 800-259-3400
Wabash Heritage Spices
Vincennes, IN 812-895-0059

Coriander (Cilantro)

Advanced Spice & Trading
Carrollton, TX 800-872-7811
Atlantic Quality Spice &Seasonings
Edison, NJ 800-584-0422
Chesapeake Spice Company
Baltimore, MD 410-391-2100
Chieftain Wild Rice Company
Spooner, WI 800-262-6368
Con Yeager Spice Company
Zelienople, PA 800-222-2460
El Ranchito
Portland, OR 503-665-4919
Garden Herbs
Redlands, CA 800-388-9397
Gel Spice Company, Inc
Bayonne, NJ 800-922-0230
Morris J. Golombeck
Brooklyn, NY 718-284-3505
Naturex (Chart Corp)
South Hackensack, NJ 201-440-5000
Schiff Food Products
North Bergen, NJ 201-861-2503
Spice & Spice
Rolling Hls Ests, CA 866-729-7742
Tova Industries
Louisville, KY 888-532-8682

Cumin

Advanced Spice & Trading
Carrollton, TX 800-872-7811
American Key Food Products
Closter, NJ 800-767-0237
Atlantic Quality Spice &Seasonings
Edison, NJ 800-584-0422
Chesapeake Spice Company
Baltimore, MD 410-391-2100
Chieftain Wild Rice Company
Spooner, WI 800-262-6368
Commodities Marketing, Inc.
Edison, NJ 732-516-0700
Con Yeager Spice Company
Zelienople, PA 800-222-2460

EMERLING INTERNATIONAL FOODS, INC.

Emerling International Foods
Buffalo, NY 716-833-7381

> We supply food manufacturers and food service customers worldwide (since 1988) with bulk ingredients including: Fruits & Vegetables; Juice Concentrates; Herbs & Spices; Oils & Vinegars; Flavors & Colors; Honey & Molasses. We also produce PURE MAPLE SYRUP.

Famarco
Virginia Beach, VA 757-460-3573
Gel Spice Company, Inc
Bayonne, NJ 800-922-0230

Spice & Spice
Rolling Hls Ests, CA 866-729-7742
Tova Industries
Louisville, KY 888-532-8682
Victoria Packing Corporation
Brooklyn, NY 718-649-2180
Wabash Heritage Spices
Vincennes, IN 812-895-0059

Curry Powder

Chieftain Wild Rice Company
Spooner, WI 800-262-6368
China Bowl Trading Company
Westport, CT 203-222-0381
Texas Coffee Company
Beaumont, TX 800-259-3400

Dill

Atlantic Quality Spice &Seasonings
Edison, NJ 800-584-0422
Chesapeake Spice Company
Baltimore, MD 410-391-2100
Chieftain Wild Rice Company
Spooner, WI 800-262-6368
Con Yeager Spice Company
Zelienople, PA 800-222-2460
Garden Herbs
Redlands, CA 800-388-9397
Gel Spice Company, Inc
Bayonne, NJ 800-922-0230
Green House Fine Herbs
Encinitas, CA 760-942-5371

SupHerb Farms
Turlock, CA 800-787-4372

> CrEATe! Get ready-to-use fresh flavor with SupHerb Farms' all-natural fresh frozen culinary herbs, specialty vegetables, culinary herb pastes, vegetable purees and creative blends. Complete microbiological testing ensures food safety. We set the standard for outstanding customer service, inspired culinary support, collaborative customer partnerships and innovative custom products.

Tova Industries
Louisville, KY 888-532-8682
Van Drunen Farms
Momence, IL 815-472-3100
Victoria Packing Corporation
Brooklyn, NY 718-649-2180

Dill Weed

Con Yeager Spice Company

[SupHerb Farms logo]

Zelienople, PA 800-222-2460
SupHerb Farms
Turlock, CA 800-787-4372

> CrEATe! Get ready-to-use fresh flavor with SupHerb Farms' all-natural fresh frozen culinary herbs, specialty vegetables, culinary herb pastes, vegetable purees and creative blends. Complete microbiological testing ensures food safety. We set the standard for outstanding customer service, inspired culinary support, collaborative customer partnerships and innovative custom products.

Dried

Island Spices
Asbury Park, NJ 877-229-2900
Van Drunen Farms
Momence, IL 815-472-3100

Endive

Frank Capurro & Son
Moss Landing, CA 831-728-3904

Epazote Herb

Chieftain Wild Rice Company
Spooner, WI .800-262-6368

Escarole

Frank Capurro & Son
Moss Landing, CA 831-728-3904

Extracts

Norac Technologies
Edmonton, AB .780-414-9595

Fennel

Chesapeake Spice Company
Baltimore, MD 410-391-2100
Chieftain Wild Rice Company
Spooner, WI .800-262-6368

SupHerb FARMS®

SupHerb Farms
Turlock, CA .800-787-4372

Wabash Heritage Spices
Vincennes, IN 812-895-0059

Fenugreek

Advanced Spice & Trading
Carrollton, TX. 800-872-7811
Chesapeake Spice Company
Baltimore, MD 410-391-2100
Chieftain Wild Rice Company
Spooner, WI .800-262-6368
Gel Spice Company, Inc
Bayonne, NJ .800-922-0230

Garlic

Arizona Natural Products
Phoenix, AZ .602-997-6098
Atlantic Quality Spice &Seasonings
Edison, NJ .800-584-0422
Badia Spices
Miami, FL. .305-629-8000
Beaverton Foods
Beaverton, OR 800-223-8076
Bio-Nutritional Products
Northvale, NJ 201-784-8200
Chieftain Wild Rice Company
Spooner, WI .800-262-6368
Christopher Ranch
Gilroy, CA. .408-847-1100
Con Yeager Spice Company
Zelienople, PA. 800-222-2460
DeFrancesco & Sons
Firebaugh, CA. 209-364-7000
Derlea Foods
Pickering, ON 888-430-7777
Ecom Manufacturing Corporation
Markham, ON 905-477-2441
Florida Shortening Corporation
Miami, FL. .305-691-2992
Freeda Vitamins
Long Island City, NY 800-777-3737
Ful-Flav-R Foods
Alamo, CA .510-339-9618
Garlic Company
Bakersfield, CA 661-393-4212

Garlic Valley Farms Inc
Glendale, CA 800-424-7990
George Chiala Farms
Morgan Hill, CA 408-778-0562
Gilroy Foods
Gilroy, CA. .800-921-7502
Golden Whisk
South San Francisco, CA 800-660-5222
Haliburton International Corporation
Fontana, CA 877-980-4295
Harris Farms
Coalinga, CA 800-742-1955
Herb Connection
Springville, UT 801-489-4254
Ingredients Corporation of America
Memphis, TN 901-525-6660
Kimball Enterprise International
Hacienda Heights, CA 213-276-8898
L&S Packing Company
Farmingdale, NY 800-286-6487
Lawry's Foods
Monrovia, CA 800-952-9797
Lebermuth Company
South Bend, IN 800-648-1123
Marin Food Specialties
Byron, CA. .925-634-6126
Morris J. Golombeck
Brooklyn, NY 718-284-3505
Nature Quality
San Martin, CA. 408-683-2182
Naturex (Chart Corp)
South Hackensack, NJ 201-440-5000
NuNaturals
Eugene, OR. 800-753-4372
Nutraceutical Corporation
Park City, UT 435-655-6000
Pacific Choice Brands
Fresno, CA .559-237-5583
Peavey Company
Ama, LA 225-869-4405
Pendery's
Dallas, TX .800-533-1870
Pikled Garlik Company
Sand City, CA 800-775-9788
Rapazzini Winery
Gilroy, CA. .408-842-5649
San Francisco Herb & Natural Food Company
Fremont, CA 800-227-2830
Schiff Food Products
North Bergen, NJ 201-861-2503
Specialty Food America
Hopkinsville, KY 888-881-1633
Spice World
Orlando, FL. 800-433-4979
Spiceco
Avenel, NJ. .732-499-9070
Spiceworld
Miramar, FL 800-433-4980

SupHerb FARMS®

SupHerb Farms
Turlock, CA .800-787-4372

Swagger Foods Corporation
Vernon Hills, IL 847-913-1200

Texas Coffee Company
Beaumont, TX 800-259-3400
Three Springs Farm
Prospect, VA 804-574-2314
Tova Industries
Louisville, KY 888-532-8682
Trout Lake Farm
Trout Lake, WA. 509-395-2025
Tulkoff Food Products
Baltimore, MD 800-638-7343
Vanco Products Company
Houston, TX. 800-231-9564
Vessey & Company
Holtville, CA. 760-352-6376

Chopped

Ful-Flav-R Foods
Alamo, CA .510-339-9618
L&S Packing Company
Farmingdale, NY 800-286-6487
San Francisco Herb & Natural Food Company
Fremont, CA 800-227-2830
Spice World
Orlando, FL. 800-433-4979
Spiceworld
Miramar, FL 800-433-4980
Tulkoff Food Products
Baltimore, MD 800-638-7343

Granulated

Advanced Spice & Trading
Carrollton, TX. 800-872-7811
Gel Spice Company, Inc
Bayonne, NJ 800-922-0230
Naturex (Chart Corp)
South Hackensack, NJ 201-440-5000
San Francisco Herb & Natural Food Company
Fremont, CA 800-227-2830
Spice & Spice
Rolling Hls Ests, CA 866-729-7742
Tova Industries
Louisville, KY 888-532-8682
Wabash Heritage Spices
Vincennes, IN 812-895-0059

Minced

Con Yeager Spice Company
Zelienople, PA. 800-222-2460
Peavey Company
Ama, LA 225-869-4405
San Francisco Herb & Natural Food Company
Fremont, CA 800-227-2830
Spice World
Orlando, FL. 800-433-4979
Spiceworld
Miramar, FL 800-433-4980
Wabash Heritage Spices
Vincennes, IN 812-895-0059

Powdered

Con Yeager Spice Company
Zelienople, PA. 800-222-2460
Erba Food Products
Brooklyn, NY 718-272-7700
San Francisco Herb & Natural Food Company
Fremont, CA 800-227-2830
Texas Coffee Company
Beaumont, TX. 800-259-3400
Victoria Packing Corporation
Brooklyn, NY 718-649-2180
Whole Herb Company
Sonoma, CA 707-935-1077

Garlic Salt

San Francisco Herb & Natural Food Company
Fremont, CA 800-227-2830
Texas Coffee Company
Beaumont, TX. 800-259-3400

Ginger

Advanced Spice & Trading
Carrollton, TX. 800-872-7811
American Key Food Products
Closter, NJ. 800-767-0237
Atlantic Quality Spice &Seasonings
Edison, NJ .800-584-0422
Chesapeake Spice Company
Baltimore, MD 410-391-2100

Chieftain Wild Rice Company
Spooner, WI 800-262-6368
Christopher Ranch
Gilroy, CA 408-847-1100
Con Yeager Spice Company
Zelienople, PA. 800-222-2460
D Steengrafe & Company
Pleasant Valley, NY 845-635-4067
Erba Food Products
Brooklyn, NY 718-272-7700
Gel Spice Company, Inc
Bayonne, NJ 800-922-0230
Herb Connection
Springville, UT 801-489-4254
Hialeah Products Company
Hollywood, FL 800-923-3379
Morris J. Golombeck
Brooklyn, NY 718-284-3505
Naturex (Chart Corp)
South Hackensack, NJ 201-440-5000
Pendery's
Dallas, TX 800-533-1870
Royal Pacific Foods/The Ginger People
Marina, CA 800-551-5284
Specialty Food America
Hopkinsville, KY 888-881-1633

SupHerb Farms
Turlock, CA 800-787-4372

CrEATe! Get ready-to-use fresh flavor with SupHerb Farms' all-natural fresh frozen culinary herbs, specialty vegetables, culinary herb pastes, vegetable purees and creative blends. Complete microbiological testing ensures food safety. We set the standard for outstanding customer service, inspired culinary support, collaborative customer partnerships and innovative custom products.

Texas Coffee Company
Beaumont, TX 800-259-3400
Tova Industries
Louisville, KY 888-532-8682
Wabash Heritage Spices
Vincennes, IN 812-895-0059

Crystallized

Hialeah Products Company
Hollywood, FL 800-923-3379

Ground

Con Yeager Spice Company
Zelienople, PA. 800-222-2460

Pieces

Ful-Flav-R Foods
Alamo, CA 510-339-9618

Ginseng

Alternative Health & Herbs
Albany, OR 800-345-4152
Atkins Ginseng Farms
Waterford, ON. 800-265-0239
Fmali Herb
Santa Cruz, CA 831-423-7913
Ginco International
Simi Valley, CA. 800-423-5176
Ginseng America
Roxbury, NY 607-326-3123
Heise's Wausau Farms
Wausau, WI. 800-764-1010
IL HWA American Corporation
Belleville, NJ 800-446-7364
Lichtwer Pharma
New York, NY 800-226-6227
Madys Company
San Francisco, CA 415-822-2227
Master Mix
Placentia, CA 714-524-1698
Naturex (Chart Corp)
South Hackensack, NJ 201-440-5000

Penn Herb Company
Philadelphia, PA 800-523-9971
Prince of Peace Enterprises
Hayward, CA 800-732-2328
Pro-Pharm
Lake Bluff, IL 847-234-3570
Progenix Corporation
Wausau, WI. 800-233-3356
San Francisco Herb & Natural Food Company
Fremont, CA 800-227-2830
Specialty Beverages
Indian Wells, CA. 626-963-5536
St. John's Botanicals
Bowie, MD 301-262-5302
Sun Wellness/Sun Chlorel
Torrance, CA. 800-829-2828
Superior Trading Company
San Francisco, CA 415-982-8722
Triple Leaf Tea
S San Francisco, CA. 800-552-7448
Yellow Emperor
Eugene, OR 877-485-6664

Heather

Chieftain Wild Rice Company
Spooner, WI 800-262-6368

Herbes de Provence

Chieftain Wild Rice Company
Spooner, WI 800-262-6368

SupHerb Farms
Turlock, CA 800-787-4372

CrEATe! Get ready-to-use fresh flavor with SupHerb Farms' all-natural fresh frozen culinary herbs, specialty vegetables, culinary herb pastes, vegetable purees and creative blends. Complete microbiological testing ensures food safety. We set the standard for outstanding customer service, inspired culinary support, collaborative customer partnerships and innovative custom products.

Horseradish

Bick's Pickles
Dunnville, ON. 905-774-7447
Buedel Food Products
Chicago, IL 773-235-3637
Feature Foods
Etobicoke, ON 416-675-7350
Gold Pure Foods Products Company
Hempstead, NY. 800-422-4681
Heintz & Weber Company
Buffalo, NY. 716-852-7171
Junuis Food Products
Palatine, IL 847-359-4300
Palmieri Food Products
New Haven, CT 800-845-5447
Red Pelican Food Products
Detroit, MI 313-921-2500
Strub Pickles
Brantford, ON 519-751-1717
Thor-Shackel HorseradishCompany
Burr Ridge, IL. 630-986-1333
United Pickle Products Corporation
Bronx, NY 718-933-6060

Juniper Berries

Chieftain Wild Rice Company
Spooner, WI 800-262-6368

Lavender

Chieftain Wild Rice Company
Spooner, WI 800-262-6368

Lavender Flowers

Wabash Heritage Spices
Vincennes, IN 812-895-0059

Lemon Grass

SupHerb Farms
Turlock, CA 800-787-4372

CrEATe! Get ready-to-use fresh flavor with SupHerb Farms' all-natural fresh frozen culinary herbs, specialty vegetables, culinary herb pastes, vegetable purees and creative blends. Complete microbiological testing ensures food safety. We set the standard for outstanding customer service, inspired culinary support, collaborative customer partnerships and innovative custom products.

Lemon Peel

Chieftain Wild Rice Company
Spooner, WI 800-262-6368

Liquid

EMERLING INTERNATIONAL FOODS, INC.

Emerling International Foods
Buffalo, NY. 716-833-7381

We supply food manufacturers and food service customers worldwide (since 1988) with bulk ingredients including: Fruits & Vegetables; Juice Concentrates; Herbs & Spices; Oils & Vinegars; Flavors & Colors; Honey & Molasses. We also produce PURE MAPLE SYRUP.

Jogue Inc
Northville, MI 800-521-3888

Sentry Seasonings
Elmhurst, IL 630-530-5370

The product development experts of Sentry Seasonings are eager to offer the assistance and hands-on experience to food processors of all sizes. Sentry Seasonings will ensure the consistent high quality and repeat sales of your products, whether you choose one of our many off-the-shelf Bench Mark products or a modified version to meet your preferences. Sentry Seasonings can also duplicate and/or improve your present flavor profile; formulate, blend and package specifically for your requirements.

Vegetable Juices
Chicago, IL 888-776-9752
World Flavors
Warminster, PA 215-672-4400

Mace (See also Nutmeg)

Advanced Spice & Trading
Carrollton, TX. 800-872-7811
American Key Food Products
Closter, NJ. 800-767-0237
Chesapeake Spice Company
Baltimore, MD 410-391-2100
Chieftain Wild Rice Company
Spooner, WI 800-262-6368
Con Yeager Spice Company
Zelienople, PA. 800-222-2460

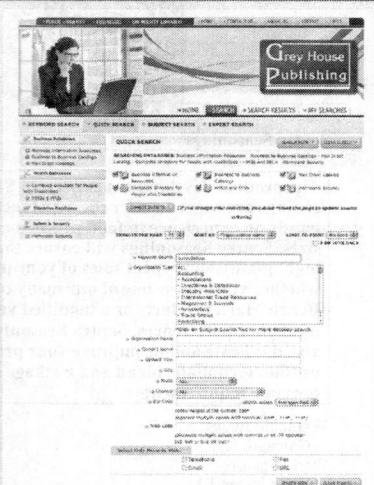
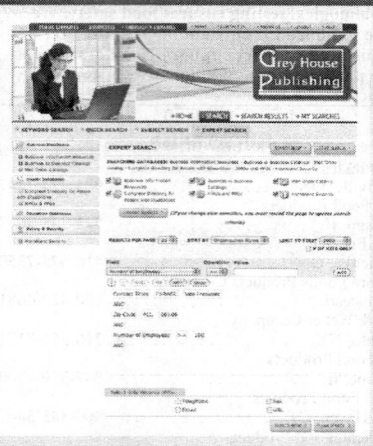
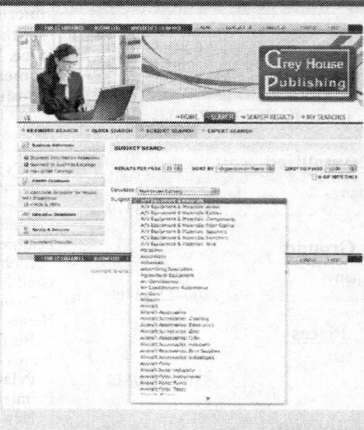

EMERLING INTERNATIONAL FOODS, INC.

Emerling International Foods
Buffalo, NY 716-833-7381

We supply food manufacturers and food service customers worldwide (since 1988) with bulk ingredients including: Fruits & Vegetables; Juice Concentrates; Herbs & Spices; Oils & Vinegars; Flavors & Colors; Honey & Molasses. We also produce PURE MAPLE SYRUP.

Gel Spice Company, Inc
Bayonne, NJ .800-922-0230
Specialty Food America
Hopkinsville, KY 888-881-1633
Tova Industries
Louisville, KY 888-532-8682

Ground

Con Yeager Spice Company
Zelienople, PA. 800-222-2460

Marjoram

American Key Food Products
Closter, NJ. 800-767-0237
Chieftain Wild Rice Company
Spooner, WI .800-262-6368
Con Yeager Spice Company
Zelienople, PA. 800-222-2460

EMERLING INTERNATIONAL FOODS, INC.

Emerling International Foods
Buffalo, NY. .716-833-7381

We supply food manufacturers and food service customers worldwide (since 1988) with bulk ingredients including: Fruits & Vegetables; Juice Concentrates; Herbs & Spices; Oils & Vinegars; Flavors & Colors; Honey & Molasses. We also produce PURE MAPLE SYRUP.

Gel Spice Company, Inc
Bayonne, NJ .800-922-0230
Naturex (Chart Corp)
South Hackensack, NJ 201-440-5000

SupHerb Farms
Turlock, CA 800-787-4372

CrEATe! Get ready-to-use fresh flavor with SupHerb Farms' all-natural fresh frozen culinary herbs, specialty vegetables, culinary herb pastes, vegetable purees and creative blends. Complete microbiological testing ensures food safety. We set the standard for outstanding customer service, inspired culinary support, collaborative customer partnerships and innovative custom products.

Tova Industries
Louisville, KY 888-532-8682
Van Drunen Farms
Momence, IL. 815-472-3100
Victoria Packing Corporation
Brooklyn, NY 718-649-2180
Wabash Heritage Spices
Vincennes, IN 812-895-0059

Mint

Whole Herb Company
Sonoma, CA .707-935-1077

Mint Leaves

Advanced Spice & Trading
Carrollton, TX. 800-872-7811
Atlantic Quality Spice &Seasonings
Edison, NJ. 800-584-0422
Charles H. Baldwin & Sons
West Stockbridge, MA 413-232-7785

EMERLING INTERNATIONAL FOODS, INC.

Emerling International Foods
Buffalo, NY 716-833-7381

We supply food manufacturers and food service customers worldwide (since 1988) with bulk ingredients including: Fruits & Vegetables; Juice Concentrates; Herbs & Spices; Oils & Vinegars; Flavors & Colors; Honey & Molasses. We also produce PURE MAPLE SYRUP.

Victoria Packing Corporation
Brooklyn, NY 718-649-2180

Spearmint

Gel Spice Company, Inc
Bayonne, NJ .800-922-0230

SupHerb Farms
Turlock, CA 800-787-4372

CrEATe! Get ready-to-use fresh flavor with SupHerb Farms' all-natural fresh frozen culinary herbs, specialty vegetables, culinary herb pastes, vegetable purees and creative blends. Complete microbiological testing ensures food safety. We set the standard for outstanding customer service, inspired culinary support, collaborative customer partnerships and innovative custom products.

Mulled Wine Spice

Chieftain Wild Rice Company
Spooner, WI .800-262-6368

Mulling

Aspen Mulling Company Inc.
Aspen, CO. 800-622-7736

Mustard

Dry - Prepared

American Key Food Products
Closter, NJ. 800-767-0237
Assouline & Ting
Philadelphia, PA 800-521-4491
Au Printemps Gourmet
Prevost, QC. .800-663-0416

Baldwin Richardson Foods
Frankfort, IL. 866-644-2732

Baldwin Richardson Foods is a liquid ingredient manufacturer specializing in signature sauces, dessert toppings, beverage/pancake syrups, specialty fruit fillings and condiments. Packaging capabilities range from portion control cups and pouches to standard retail and foodservice packs and include industrial drums and totes. Full service R&D and Quality groups dedicated to new product development, with in-house stability and analytical testing. Call for assistance.

Catamount Specialties ofVermont
Stowe, VT. 800-820-8096
Food Specialties
Indianapolis, IN 317-271-0862
G S Dunn & Company
Hamilton, ON 905-522-0833
Groeb Farms
Onsted, MI 517-467-7100
Heinz North America
Pittsburgh, PA 412-237-5700

Herlocher Foods
State College, PA 800-437-5624
Honey Acres
Ashippun, WI 800-558-7745
J.N. Bech
Elk Rapids, MI 800-232-4583
J.W. Raye & Company
Eastport, ME. 800-853-1903
Kozlowski Farms
Forestville, CA 800-473-2767
Minn-Dak Growers Limited
Grand Forks, ND. 701-746-7453
New Canaan Farms
Dripping Springs, TX. 800-727-5267
Pepper Creek Farms
Lawton, OK. .800-526-8132
T. Marzetti Company
Columbus, OH 614-846-2232
Victoria Packing Corporation
Brooklyn, NY 718-649-2180

Prepared

Walker Foods
Los Angeles, CA. 800-966-5199

Mustard Powder

Wabash Heritage Spices
Vincennes, IN 812-895-0059

Mustards

Chesapeake Spice Company
Baltimore, MD 410-391-2100
Con Yeager Spice Company
Zelienople, PA. 800-222-2460

Natural Flavorings

Spice King Corporation
Beverly Hills, CA 310-836-7770

Nutmeg (See also Mace)

Advanced Spice & Trading
Carrollton, TX. 800-872-7811
American Key Food Products
Closter, NJ. 800-767-0237
Atlantic Quality Spice &Seasonings
Edison, NJ. 800-584-0422
Commodities Marketing, Inc.
Edison, NJ. 732-516-0700
Con Yeager Spice Company
Zelienople, PA. 800-222-2460

EMERLING INTERNATIONAL FOODS, INC.

Emerling International Foods
Buffalo, NY. .716-833-7381

We supply food manufacturers and food service customers worldwide (since 1988) with bulk ingredients including: Fruits & Vegetables; Juice Concentrates; Herbs & Spices; Oils & Vinegars; Flavors & Colors; Honey & Molasses. We also produce PURE MAPLE SYRUP.

Gel Spice Company, Inc
Bayonne, NJ .800-922-0230
Schiff Food Products
North Bergen, NJ 201-861-2503
Spice & Spice
Rolling Hls Ests, CA. 866-729-7742
Texas Coffee Company
Beaumont, TX. 800-259-3400
Tripper
Malibu, CA 888-336-8747
Victoria Packing Corporation
Brooklyn, NY 718-649-2180

Ground

Con Yeager Spice Company
Zelienople, PA. 800-222-2460

Whole

Con Yeager Spice Company
Zelienople, PA. 800-222-2460

Onion

Con Yeager Spice Company
Zelienople, PA. 800-222-2460

Ful-Flav-R Foods
Alamo, CA 510-339-9618
Gel Spice Company, Inc
Bayonne, NJ 800-922-0230
Marin Food Specialties
Byron, CA 925-634-6126
Texas Coffee Company
Beaumont, TX 800-259-3400

Chopped

Con Yeager Spice Company
Zelienople, PA 800-222-2460
Ful-Flav-R Foods
Alamo, CA 510-339-9618

Granulated

Con Yeager Spice Company
Zelienople, PA 800-222-2460
Victoria Packing Corporation
Brooklyn, NY 718-649-2180
Wabash Heritage Spices
Vincennes, IN 812-895-0059

Minced

Con Yeager Spice Company
Zelienople, PA 800-222-2460
Erba Food Products
Brooklyn, NY 718-272-7700

Oregano

Advanced Spice & Trading
Carrollton, TX 800-872-7811
Atlantic Quality Spice &Seasonings
Edison, NJ 800-584-0422
Castella Imports
Hauppauge, NY 866-227-8355
Chesapeake Spice Company
Baltimore, MD 410-391-2100
Chieftain Wild Rice Company
Spooner, WI 800-262-6368
Con Yeager Spice Company
Zelienople, PA 800-222-2460

EMERLING INTERNATIONAL FOODS, INC.

Emerling International Foods
Buffalo, NY 716-833-7381

> We supply food manufacturers and food service customers worldwide (since 1988) with bulk ingredients including: Fruits & Vegetables; Juice Concentrates; Herbs & Spices; Oils & Vinegars; Flavors & Colors; Honey & Molasses. We also produce PURE MAPLE SYRUP.

Garden Herbs
Redlands, CA 800-388-9397
Morris J. Golombeck
Brooklyn, NY 718-284-3505
Schiff Food Products
North Bergen, NJ 201-861-2503
Specialty Food America
Hopkinsville, KY 888-881-1633
Spiceco
Avenel, NJ 732-499-9070

SupHerb Farms
Turlock, CA 800-787-4372

> CrEATe! Get ready-to-use fresh flavor with SupHerb Farms' all-natural fresh frozen culinary herbs, specialty vegetables, culinary herb pastes, vegetable purees and creative blends. Complete microbiological testing ensures food safety. We set the standard for outstanding customer service, inspired culinary support, collaborative customer partnerships and innovative custom products.

Texas Coffee Company
Beaumont, TX 800-259-3400
Trout Lake Farm
Trout Lake, WA 509-395-2025

Van Drunen Farms
Momence, IL 815-472-3100
Vegetable Juices
Chicago, IL 888-776-9752
Victoria Packing Corporation
Brooklyn, NY 718-649-2180
Whole Herb Company
Sonoma, CA 707-935-1077

Greek

Agrocan
Toronto, ON 877-247-6226

Mexican

Wabash Heritage Spices
Vincennes, IN 812-895-0059

Paprika

Advanced Spice & Trading
Carrollton, TX 800-872-7811
American Key Food Products
Closter, NJ 800-767-0237
Atlantic Quality Spice &Seasonings
Edison, NJ 800-584-0422
Chesapeake Spice Company
Baltimore, MD 410-391-2100
Chieftain Wild Rice Company
Spooner, WI 800-262-6368
Con Yeager Spice Company
Zelienople, PA 800-222-2460

EMERLING INTERNATIONAL FOODS, INC.

Emerling International Foods
Buffalo, NY 716-833-7381

> We supply food manufacturers and food service customers worldwide (since 1988) with bulk ingredients including: Fruits & Vegetables; Juice Concentrates; Herbs & Spices; Oils & Vinegars; Flavors & Colors; Honey & Molasses. We also produce PURE MAPLE SYRUP.

Erba Food Products
Brooklyn, NY 718-272-7700
Gel Spice Company, Inc
Bayonne, NJ 800-922-0230
Gilroy Foods
Gilroy, CA 800-921-7502
Heartline Foods
Westport, CT 203-222-0381
Morris J. Golombeck
Brooklyn, NY 718-284-3505
Naturex (Chart Corp)
South Hackensack, NJ 201-440-5000
Pendery's
Dallas, TX 800-533-1870
Schiff Food Products
North Bergen, NJ 201-861-2503
SJH Enterprises
Middleton, WI 888-745-3845
Spice & Spice
Rolling Hls Ests, CA 866-729-7742
Spiceco
Avenel, NJ 732-499-9070
Swagger Foods Corporation
Vernon Hills, IL 847-913-1200
Victoria Packing Corporation
Brooklyn, NY 718-649-2180
Wabash Heritage Spices
Vincennes, IN 812-895-0059

Parsley

Bifulco Farms
Pittsgrove, NJ 856-692-0707
Chesapeake Spice Company
Baltimore, MD 410-391-2100
Chieftain Wild Rice Company
Spooner, WI 800-262-6368
Frank Capurro & Son
Moss Landing, CA 831-728-3904
Specialty Food America
Hopkinsville, KY 888-881-1633

SupHerb Farms
Turlock, CA 800-787-4372

> CrEATe! Get ready-to-use fresh flavor with SupHerb Farms' all-natural fresh frozen culinary herbs, specialty vegetables, culinary herb pastes, vegetable purees and creative blends. Complete microbiological testing ensures food safety. We set the standard for outstanding customer service, inspired culinary support, collaborative customer partnerships and innovative custom products.

Dehydrated

Alfred L. Wolff, Inc.
Park Ridge, IL 312-265-9889
American Key Food Products
Closter, NJ 800-767-0237

EMERLING INTERNATIONAL FOODS, INC.

Emerling International Foods
Buffalo, NY 716-833-7381

> We supply food manufacturers and food service customers worldwide (since 1988) with bulk ingredients including: Fruits & Vegetables; Juice Concentrates; Herbs & Spices; Oils & Vinegars; Flavors & Colors; Honey & Molasses. We also produce PURE MAPLE SYRUP.

Gel Spice Company, Inc
Bayonne, NJ 800-922-0230
Unique Ingredients
Naches, WA 509-653-1991

Pepper

Advanced Spice & Trading
Carrollton, TX 800-872-7811
American Key Food Products
Closter, NJ 800-767-0237
Con Yeager Spice Company
Zelienople, PA 800-222-2460
Eatem Foods Company
Vineland, NJ 800-683-2836
Lawry's Foods
Monrovia, CA 800-952-9797
Morris J. Golombeck
Brooklyn, NY 718-284-3505
Pepper Mill Imports
Carmel, CA 800-928-1744
Schiff Food Products
North Bergen, NJ 201-861-2503
Spice & Spice
Rolling Hls Ests, CA 866-729-7742
Swagger Foods Corporation
Vernon Hills, IL 847-913-1200
Texas Coffee Company
Beaumont, TX 800-259-3400
Tripper
Malibu, CA 888-336-8747
Victoria Packing Corporation
Brooklyn, NY 718-649-2180
Walker Foods
Los Angeles, CA 800-966-5199
Wine Country Chef LLC
Hidden Valley Lake, CA 707-322-0406

Black - White - Red

Spice & Spice
Rolling Hls Ests, CA 866-729-7742

White Ground

Chesapeake Spice Company
Baltimore, MD 410-391-2100
Chieftain Wild Rice Company
Spooner, WI 800-262-6368

Pepper Mash

EMERLING INTERNATIONAL FOODS, INC.

Emerling International Foods
Buffalo, NY 716-833-7381

We supply food manufacturers and food service
customers worldwide (since 1988) with bulk ingredients including: Fruits & Vegetables; Juice
Concentrates; Herbs & Spices; Oils & Vinegars;
Flavors & Colors; Honey & Molasses. We also
produce PURE MAPLE SYRUP.

Vegetable Juices
Chicago, IL 888-776-9752

Peppercorns

Wabash Heritage Spices
Vincennes, IN 812-895-0059

Peppermint

Trout Lake Farm
Trout Lake, WA 509-395-2025

Pickling Spices

Texas Coffee Company
Beaumont, TX 800-259-3400

Red Pepper

Crushed

Swagger Foods Corporation
Vernon Hills, IL 847-913-1200
Victoria Packing Corporation
Brooklyn, NY .718-649-2180

Rosemary

Advanced Spice & Trading
Carrollton, TX 800-872-7811
American Key Food Products
Closter, NJ 800-767-0237
Atlantic Quality Spice &Seasonings
Edison, NJ 800-584-0422
Chesapeake Spice Company
Baltimore, MD 410-391-2100
Chieftain Wild Rice Company
Spooner, WI 800-262-6368
Con Yeager Spice Company
Zelienople, PA 800-222-2460

EMERLING INTERNATIONAL FOODS, INC.

Emerling International Foods
Buffalo, NY 716-833-7381

We supply food manufacturers and food service
customers worldwide (since 1988) with bulk ingredients including: Fruits & Vegetables; Juice
Concentrates; Herbs & Spices; Oils & Vinegars;
Flavors & Colors; Honey & Molasses. We also
produce PURE MAPLE SYRUP.

Garden Herbs
Redlands, CA .800-388-9397
Gel Spice Company, Inc
Bayonne, NJ 800-922-0230
Morris J. Golombeck
Brooklyn, NY .718-284-3505
Naturex (Chart Corp)
South Hackensack, NJ 201-440-5000
RFI Ingredients
Blauvelt, NY 800-962-7663
Schiff Food Products
North Bergen, NJ 201-861-2503

SupHerb Farms
Turlock, CA 800-787-4372

**CrEATe! Get ready-to-use fresh flavor with
SupHerb Farms' all-natural fresh frozen culinary
herbs, specialty vegetables, culinary herb pastes,
vegetable purees and creative blends. Complete
microbiological testing ensures food safety. We
set the standard for outstanding customer service, inspired culinary support, collaborative customer partnerships and innovative custom
products.**

Universal Preservachem Inc
Edison, NJ 732-777-7338
Victoria Packing Corporation
Brooklyn, NY .718-649-2180
Wabash Heritage Spices
Vincennes, IN 812-895-0059

Cut

RFI Ingredients
Blauvelt, NY 800-962-7663

Ground

Con Yeager Spice Company
Zelienople, PA 800-222-2460
RFI Ingredients
Blauvelt, NY 800-962-7663
Schiff Food Products
North Bergen, NJ 201-861-2503

Saffron

Advanced Spice & Trading
Carrollton, TX 800-872-7811
American Key Food Products
Closter, NJ 800-767-0237
Atlantic Quality Spice &Seasonings
Edison, NJ 800-584-0422
Chesapeake Spice Company
Baltimore, MD 410-391-2100
Chieftain Wild Rice Company
Spooner, WI 800-262-6368

EMERLING INTERNATIONAL FOODS, INC.

Emerling International Foods
Buffalo, NY 716-833-7381

We supply food manufacturers and food service
customers worldwide (since 1988) with bulk ingredients including: Fruits & Vegetables; Juice
Concentrates; Herbs & Spices; Oils & Vinegars;
Flavors & Colors; Honey & Molasses. We also
produce PURE MAPLE SYRUP.

Epicurean Specialty
Sebastopol, CA 800-500-0065
Gel Spice Company, Inc
Bayonne, NJ 800-922-0230
Naturex (Chart Corp)
South Hackensack, NJ 201-440-5000
Schiff Food Products
North Bergen, NJ 201-861-2503
Shanks Extracts
Lancaster, PA .800-346-3135
Whole Herb Company
Sonoma, CA 707-935-1077

Whole Threads

Chieftain Wild Rice Company
Spooner, WI 800-262-6368

Sage

Castella Imports
Hauppauge, NY 866-227-8355
Chesapeake Spice Company
Baltimore, MD 410-391-2100
Chieftain Wild Rice Company
Spooner, WI 800-262-6368
Con Yeager Spice Company
Zelienople, PA 800-222-2460

SupHerb Farms
Turlock, CA 800-787-4372

**CrEATe! Get ready-to-use fresh flavor with
SupHerb Farms' all-natural fresh frozen culinary
herbs, specialty vegetables, culinary herb pastes,
vegetable purees and creative blends. Complete
microbiological testing ensures food safety. We
set the standard for outstanding customer service, inspired culinary support, collaborative customer partnerships and innovative custom
products.**

Leaves

Advanced Spice & Trading
Carrollton, TX 800-872-7811
Atlantic Quality Spice &Seasonings
Edison, NJ 800-584-0422
Con Yeager Spice Company
Zelienople, PA 800-222-2460

EMERLING INTERNATIONAL FOODS, INC.

Emerling International Foods
Buffalo, NY 716-833-7381

We supply food manufacturers and food service
customers worldwide (since 1988) with bulk ingredients including: Fruits & Vegetables; Juice
Concentrates; Herbs & Spices; Oils & Vinegars;
Flavors & Colors; Honey & Molasses. We also
produce PURE MAPLE SYRUP.

Gel Spice Company, Inc
Bayonne, NJ 800-922-0230
Ingredients Corporation of America
Memphis, TN 901-525-6660

SupHerb Farms
Turlock, CA 800-787-4372

**CrEATe! Get ready-to-use fresh flavor with
SupHerb Farms' all-natural fresh frozen culinary
herbs, specialty vegetables, culinary herb pastes,
vegetable purees and creative blends. Complete
microbiological testing ensures food safety. We
set the standard for outstanding customer service, inspired culinary support, collaborative customer partnerships and innovative custom
products.**

Rubbed

Con Yeager Spice Company
Zelienople, PA 800-222-2460

Savory

All American Foods, Inc.
Mankato, MN 800-833-2661
American Key Food Products
Closter, NJ 800-767-0237
Certified Savory
Countryside, IL 800-328-7656
Chieftain Wild Rice Company
Spooner, WI 800-262-6368
David Michael & Company
Philadelphia, PA 800-363-5286
Flavor House
Adelanto, CA .760-246-9131
Mane Incorporated
Milford, OH 800-595-8936
Silver Palate Kitchens
Cresskill, NJ 800-872-5283
Swagger Foods Corporation
Vernon Hills, IL 847-913-1200

  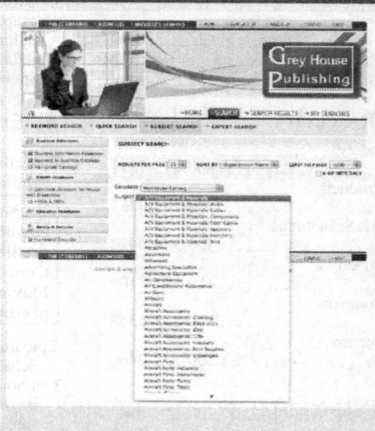

Shallots

SupHerb Farms
Turlock, CA 800-787-4372

CrEATe! Get ready-to-use fresh flavor with SupHerb Farms' all-natural fresh frozen culinary herbs, specialty vegetables, culinary herb pastes, vegetable purees and creative blends. Complete microbiological testing ensures food safety. We set the standard for outstanding customer service, inspired culinary support, collaborative customer partnerships and innovative custom products.

Sorrel

SupHerb Farms
Turlock, CA 800-787-4372

CrEATe! Get ready-to-use fresh flavor with SupHerb Farms' all-natural fresh frozen culinary herbs, specialty vegetables, culinary herb pastes, vegetable purees and creative blends. Complete microbiological testing ensures food safety. We set the standard for outstanding customer service, inspired culinary support, collaborative customer partnerships and innovative custom products.

Spearmint

SupHerb Farms
Turlock, CA 800-787-4372

CrEATe! Get ready-to-use fresh flavor with SupHerb Farms' all-natural fresh frozen culinary herbs, specialty vegetables, culinary herb pastes, vegetable purees and creative blends. Complete microbiological testing ensures food safety. We set the standard for outstanding customer service, inspired culinary support, collaborative customer partnerships and innovative custom products.

Trout Lake Farm
Trout Lake, WA 509-395-2025

Star Anise

Chesapeake Spice Company
Baltimore, MD 410-391-2100

Sumac Berries

Chieftain Wild Rice Company
Spooner, WI 800-262-6368

Tandoori

Chieftain Wild Rice Company
Spooner, WI 800-262-6368

Tarragon

Advanced Spice & Trading
Carrollton, TX 800-872-7811
Atlantic Quality Spice &Seasonings
Edison, NJ 800-584-0422
Chesapeake Spice Company
Baltimore, MD 410-391-2100
Con Yeager Spice Company
Zelienople, PA 800-222-2460
Schiff Food Products
North Bergen, NJ 201-861-2503
Specialty Food America
Hopkinsville, KY 888-881-1633

SupHerb Farms
Turlock, CA 800-787-4372

CrEATe! Get ready-to-use fresh flavor with SupHerb Farms' all-natural fresh frozen culinary herbs, specialty vegetables, culinary herb pastes, vegetable purees and creative blends. Complete microbiological testing ensures food safety. We set the standard for outstanding customer service, inspired culinary support, collaborative customer partnerships and innovative custom products.

Wabash Heritage Spices
Vincennes, IN 812-895-0059

Tartar

Cream

Chieftain Wild Rice Company
Spooner, WI 800-262-6368
Universal Preservachem Inc
Edison, NJ 732-777-7338

Teas

Castella Imports
Hauppauge, NY 866-227-8355
O'Neill Coffee Company
West Middlesex, PA 724-528-9281

Thyme

Advanced Spice & Trading
Carrollton, TX 800-872-7811

American Key Food Products
Closter, NJ 800-767-0237
Atlantic Quality Spice &Seasonings
Edison, NJ 800-584-0422
Chesapeake Spice Company
Baltimore, MD 410-391-2100
Chieftain Wild Rice Company
Spooner, WI 800-262-6368
Con Yeager Spice Company
Zelienople, PA 800-222-2460

EMERLING INTERNATIONAL FOODS, INC.

Emerling International Foods
Buffalo, NY 716-833-7381

We supply food manufacturers and food service customers worldwide (since 1988) with bulk ingredients including: Fruits & Vegetables; Juice Concentrates; Herbs & Spices; Oils & Vinegars; Flavors & Colors; Honey & Molasses. We also produce PURE MAPLE SYRUP.

Garden Herbs
Redlands, CA 800-388-9397
Morris J. Golombeck
Brooklyn, NY 718-284-3505
Schiff Food Products
North Bergen, NJ 201-861-2503
Specialty Food America
Hopkinsville, KY 888-881-1633

SupHerb Farms
Turlock, CA 800-787-4372

CrEATe! Get ready-to-use fresh flavor with SupHerb Farms' all-natural fresh frozen culinary herbs, specialty vegetables, culinary herb pastes, vegetable purees and creative blends. Complete microbiological testing ensures food safety. We set the standard for outstanding customer service, inspired culinary support, collaborative customer partnerships and innovative custom products.

Ground

Schiff Food Products
North Bergen, NJ 201-861-2503
Wabash Heritage Spices
Vincennes, IN 812-895-0059

Turmeric

Agri-Dairy Products
Purchase, NY 914-697-9580
American Key Food Products
Closter, NJ 800-767-0237
Atlantic Quality Spice &Seasonings
Edison, NJ 800-584-0422
Chieftain Wild Rice Company
Spooner, WI 800-262-6368
Con Yeager Spice Company
Zelienople, PA 800-222-2460

EMERLING INTERNATIONAL FOODS, INC.

Emerling International Foods
Buffalo, NY.....................716-833-7381

> We supply food manufacturers and food service customers worldwide (since 1988) with bulk ingredients including: Fruits & Vegetables; Juice Concentrates; Herbs & Spices; Oils & Vinegars; Flavors & Colors; Honey & Molasses. We also produce PURE MAPLE SYRUP.

Schiff Food Products
North Bergen, NJ 201-861-2503
SJH Enterprises
Middleton, WI.....................888-745-3845

Ground

Schiff Food Products
North Bergen, NJ 201-861-2503
Wabash Heritage Spices
Vincennes, IN 812-895-0059

Vanilla

Agri-Dairy Products
Purchase, NY.....................914-697-9580
Chieftain Wild Rice Company
Spooner, WI 800-262-6368
Epicurean Specialty
Sebastopol, CA...................800-500-0065
Naturex (Chart Corp)
South Hackensack, NJ 201-440-5000
Nielsen-Massey Vanillas
Waukegan, IL 800-525-7873
Spice Market
Fairfield, NJ 800-223-3502
Texas Coffee Company
Beaumont, TX.....................800-259-3400
Triple H
Riverside, CA 951-352-5700
Tripper
Malibu, CA 888-336-8747
Wabash Heritage Spices
Vincennes, IN 812-895-0059

Vanilla Beans

Ambassador Foods
Van Nuys, CA.....................800-338-3369
Atlantic Quality Spice &Seasonings
Edison, NJ.......................800-584-0422

EMERLING INTERNATIONAL FOODS, INC.

Emerling International Foods
Buffalo, NY.....................716-833-7381

> We supply food manufacturers and food service customers worldwide (since 1988) with bulk ingredients including: Fruits & Vegetables; Juice Concentrates; Herbs & Spices; Oils & Vinegars; Flavors & Colors; Honey & Molasses. We also produce PURE MAPLE SYRUP.

Naturex (Chart Corp)
South Hackensack, NJ 201-440-5000
Zink & Triest Company
Montgomeryville, PA 800-537-5070

Wasabi

Chieftain Wild Rice Company
Spooner, WI 800-262-6368

White Pepper

Ground

Spice & Spice
Rolling Hls Ests, CA.............866-729-7742

Sugars, Syrups & Sweeteners

General

ADM Food Ingredients
Olathe, KS. .800-255-6637
Bear Stewart Corporation
Chicago, IL .800-697-2327
Best Brands Corporation
Dallas, TX 800-969-2253
Cocoline Chocolate Company
Brooklyn, NY 718-522-4500
Colorado Sweet Gold
Lakewood, CO 303-384-1101
Crosby Molasses Company
St. John, NB 506-634-7515
Deer Creek Honey Farms
London, OH 740-852-0899
Diamond Crystal
Savannah, GA 800-227-4455
E.B. Evans Company
Saint Louis, MO 215-425-0558
E.F. Lane & Son
Oakland, CA 510-569-8980

Evergreen Sweeteners, Inc
Aventura, FL 305-931-1321

> Evergreen Sweeteners is a full service sweetener
> distributor serving the entire state of Florida.
> From bulk liquid sweeteners to bagged sweeten-
> ers, Evergreen provides its customers with indus-
> try-leading service and unsurpassed quality.

Glorybee Natural Sweeteners
Eugene, OR .800-456-7923
Hoyt's Honey Farm
Baytown, TX 281-576-5383
Indiana Sugar
Burr Ridge, IL 630-986-9150
JK SucraLose Inc
Edison, NJ 732-512-0886
Maple Products
Sherbrooke, QC 819-569-5161
Nuvex Ingredients
Blue Earth, MN 507-526-4331
Particle Control
Albertville, MN 763-497-3075
Paulaur Corporation
Cranbury, NJ 888-398-8844
Rogers Sugar
Montreal, QC 514-527-8686
Savannah Foods & Industries
Port Wentworth, GA 800-241-3785
Stearns & Lehman
Mansfield, OH 800-533-2722
T.W. Burleson & Son
Waxahachie, TX 972-937-4810
Unilever
Lisle, IL 877-995-4483
W&G Flavors
Hunt Valley, MD 410-771-6606
Western New York Syrup Corporation
Lakeville, NY 585-346-2311
Whitfield Foods
Montgomery, AL 800-633-8790
Wholesome Sweeteners
Savannah, GA 800-680-1896

Artificial

Silver Ferm Chemical
Seattle, WA .206-282-3376
Universal Preservachem Inc
Edison, NJ 732-777-7338
US Sugar Company
Buffalo, NY .716-828-1170

Fructose

ADM Corn Processing
Decatur, IL .800-553-8411

Agri-Dairy Products
Purchase, NY 914-697-9580
Brady Farms
West Olive, MI 616-842-3916
Cargill Corn Milling
Naperville, IL 800-344-1633

EVERGREEN sweeteners
Your Total Sweetener Solution.

Evergreen Sweeteners, Inc
Aventura, FL 305-931-1321

> Evergreen Sweeteners is a full service sweetener
> distributor serving the entire state of Florida.
> From bulk liquid sweeteners to bagged sweeten-
> ers, Evergreen provides its customers with indus-
> try-leading service and unsurpassed quality.

H. Interdonati
Cold Spring Hbr, NY 800-367-6617
Hunter Farms
High Point, NC 800-446-8035
Malt Products Corporation
Saddle Brook, NJ 800-526-0180
Oxford Frozen Foods Limited
Oxford, NS .902-447-2100
Scenic Fruit Company
Gresham, OR. 800-554-5578
St. Lawrence Starch
Mississauga, ON 905-274-3671
Wells' Dairy
Le Mars, IA .800-942-3800

Crystalline

Farbest-Tallman Foods Corporation
Montvale, NJ. 201-573-4900

Honey

Alaska Herb Tea Company
Anchorage, AK 800-654-2764
Ambrosia Honey
Parachute, CO. 970-625-0555
Babe's Honey Farm
Victoria, BC 250-658-8319
Barkman Honey Company
Hillsboro, KS 800-530-5827
Bee-Raw Honey
New York, NY 212-941-1932
Bella Vista Farm
Lawton, OK. 866-237-8526
Castella Imports
Hauppauge, NY 866-227-8355
Country Cupboard
Virginia City, NV 775-847-7300
Davidson of Dundee
Dundee, FL .800-654-0647
Domino Specialty Ingredients
Baltimore, MD 800-446-9763
Ed's Honey Company
Dickinson, ND 701-225-9223

EMERLING INTERNATIONAL FOODS, INC.

Emerling International Foods
Buffalo, NY. 716-833-7381

> We supply food manufacturers and food service
> customers worldwide (since 1988) with bulk in-
> gredients including: Fruits & Vegetables; Juice
> Concentrates; Herbs & Spices; Oils & Vinegars;
> Flavors & Colors; Honey & Molasses. We also
> produce PURE MAPLE SYRUP.

Fisher Honey Company
Lewistown, PA 717-242-4373
Glorybee Natural Sweeteners
Eugene, OR .800-456-7923
Gold Sweet Company
Fort Myers, FL 239-997-7656

Golden Heritage Food
Latty, OH. 888-233-6446
Govadinas Fitness Foods
San Diego, CA 800-900-0108
Hanna's Honey
Salem, OR. .503-393-2945
Heritage Cheese House
Heuvelton, NY 315-344-2216
Honey Bee Company
Alpharetta, GA 800-572-8838
Honeytree
Adrian, MI. .888-682-1256
Hoyt's Honey Farm
Baytown, TX. 281-576-5383
Island of the Moon Apiaries
Esparto, CA. 530-787-3993
John Paton
Doylestown, PA 215-348-7050
Klein Foods
Marshall, MN 800-657-0174
Laney Family Honey Company
North Liberty, IN 574-656-8701
Life Force Winery
Moscow, ID. 208-882-9158
Merrimack Valley Apiaries
Billerica, MA 978-667-5380
Miller's Honey Company
Colton, CA .909-825-1722
Mixon Fruit Farms
Bradenton, FL 800-608-2525
Round Rock Honey Co, LLC
Round Rock, TX 512-828-5416
Savannah Bee Company
Savannah, GA 912-234-0688
Scott Hams
Greenville, KY 800-318-1353
Shawnee Canning Company
Cross Junction, VA 800-713-1414
Sutton Honey Farms
Lancaster, KY 859-792-4277
Tropical Blossom Honey Company
Edgewater, FL. 386-428-9027
Virginia Honey Company
Inwood, WV 800-974-4778
Vita Specialty Foods
Inwood, WV 800-974-4778
Zambezi Organic Forest Honey
Oxford, OH .513-523-9209

Bee Pollen & Propolis

Alfred L. Wolff, Inc.
Park Ridge, IL 312-265-9889
Babe's Honey Farm
Victoria, BC 250-658-8319
CC Pollen Company
Phoenix, AZ 800-875-0096
Green Grown Products
Santa Monica, CA. 310-828-1686
Hsu's Ginseng Enterprises
Wausau, WI. 800-826-1577
Island of the Moon Apiaries
Esparto, CA. 530-787-3993
Lenny's Bee Productions
Bearsville, NY 845-679-4514
Madhava Honey
Longmont, CO 800-530-2900
Miller's Honey Company
Colton, CA .800-233-5463
Moon Shine Trading Company
Woodland, CA. 800-678-1226
Natural Foods
Toledo, OH .800-860-0006
Nature Cure Northwest
Poulsbo, WA 800-957-8048
Naturex (Chart Corp)
South Hackensack, NJ 201-440-5000
Nicola Valley Apiaries
Merritt, BC .250-378-5208
North Peace Apiaries
Fort St. John, BC. 250-785-4808
Paradis Honey
Girouxville, AB 780-323-4283
Penauta Products
Stouffville, ON 905-640-1564

Pro-Pharm
Lake Bluff, IL .847-234-3570
QBI
South Plainfield, NJ 908-668-0088
Rocky Mountain Honey Company
Salt Lake City, UT 801-355-2054
Southern Gold Honey CompAny
Vidor, TX 808-899-2494
Thistledew Farm
Proctor, WV .800-854-6639

Bees Wax

Adee Honey Farm
Bruce, SD 605-627-5621
Babe's Honey Farm
Victoria, BC .250-658-8319
D Steengrafe & Company
Pleasant Valley, NY 845-635-4067
Madhava Honey
Longmont, CO 800-530-2900
Miller's Honey Company
Colton, CA 800-233-5463
Moon Shine Trading Company
Woodland, CA. 800-678-1226
Paradis Honey
Girouxville, AB 780-323-4283
Pure Food Ingredients
Verona, WI 800-355-9601
Rocky Mountain Honey Company
Salt Lake City, UT 801-355-2054
Silverbow Honey Company
Moses Lake, WA. 866-444-6639
Southern Gold Honey CompAny
Vidor, TX 808-899-2494
Thistledew Farm
Proctor, WV .800-854-6639
Wixson Honey
Dundee, NY .607-243-8583

Butter

Davidson of Dundee
Dundee, FL .800-654-0647
Honey Butter Products Company
Manheim, PA 717-665-9323
Limited Edition
Midland, TX .432-686-2008
Treasure Foods
West Valley, UT. 801-974-0911

Dried

Domino Specialty Ingredients
Baltimore, MD 800-446-9763

Granules

Natural

ADM Food Ingredients
Olathe, KS. 800-255-6637
Groeb Farms
Onsted, MI 517-467-7100

Liquid

ADM Food Ingredients
Olathe, KS. 800-255-6637
Atlas Preserves Company
New York, NY 212-569-5613
Bessonet Bee Company
Donaldsonville, LA. 225-473-9428
Champlain Valley Apiaries Company
Middlebury, VT. 800-841-7334
Deer Creek Honey Farms
London, OH .740-852-0899
Delicious Food Products Company
Chicago, IL 773-763-5553
E.F. Lane & Son
Oakland, CA .510-569-8980
Groeb Farms
Onsted, MI 517-467-7100
Hoyt's Honey Farm
Baytown, TX 281-576-5383
T.W. Burleson & Son
Waxahachie, TX 972-937-4810
Western New York Syrup Corporation
Lakeville, NY 585-346-2311

Molasses

ACH Food Companies
Boyceville, WI 715-643-2600
ADM Food Ingredients
Olathe, KS. 800-255-6637
Alexander & Baldwin
Honolulu, HI 808-525-6611
Alma Plantation
Lakeland, LA 225-627-6666
Amalgamated Sugar Company
Boise, ID 208-383-6500
American Health & Nutrition
Ann Arbor, MI 734-677-5572
B&G Foods
Parsippany, NJ. 973-401-6500

Baldwin Richardson Foods
Frankfort, IL .866-644-2732

> Baldwin Richardson Foods is a liquid ingredient manufacturer specializing in signature sauces, dessert toppings, beverage/pancake syrups, specialty fruit fillings and condiments. Packaging capabilities range from portion control cups and pouches to standard retail and foodservice packs and include industrial drums and totes. Full service R&D and Quality groups dedicated to new product development, with in-house stability and analytical testing. Call for assistance.

C&H Sugar Company
Crockett, CA. 510-787-2121
C.S. Steen's Syrup Mill
Abbeville, LA 800-725-1654
CHR Hansen
Gretna, LA 504-367-7727
CHR Hansen
Chicago, IL 773-646-2203
Consumers Vinegar & Spice Company
Chicago, IL 773-376-4100
Cora-Texas Manufacturing Company
White Castle, LA 225-545-3679
Crosby Molasses Company
St. John, NB .506-634-7515
Dean Distributors
Burlingame, CA 800-792-0816
Deer Creek Honey Farms
London, OH .740-852-0899
Domino Foods
Yonkers, NY .914-963-2400
Domino Specialty Ingredients
Baltimore, MD 800-446-9763
Domino Sugar Corporation
Baltimore, MD 410-752-6150

EMERLING INTERNATIONAL FOODS, INC.

Emerling International Foods
Buffalo, NY. .716-833-7381

> We supply food manufacturers and food service customers worldwide (since 1988) with bulk ingredients including: Fruits & Vegetables; Juice Concentrates; Herbs & Spices; Oils & Vinegars; Flavors & Colors; Honey & Molasses. We also produce PURE MAPLE SYRUP.

Evan Hall Sugar Cooperative
Donaldsonville, LA. 225-473-8241
Glorybee Foods
Eugene, OR. .800-456-7923
Golding Farms Foods
Winston Salem, NC. 336-766-6161
Groeb Farms
Onsted, MI 517-467-7100
Honeytree
Adrian, MI. .888-682-1256
Imperial Sugar Company
Sugar Land, TX 800-727-8427
Jones Dairy Farm
Fort Atkinson, WI 800-563-1004
Lafourche Sugar Corporation
Thibodaux, LA 985-447-3210

Louisiana Sugar Cane Cooperation
St Martinville, LA. 337-394-3255
Louisiana Sugar Cane Cooperative
St Martinville, LA. 337-394-3255
Malt Products Corporation
Saddle Brook, NJ 800-526-0180
Malt-Diastase Company
Saddle Brook, NJ 800-772-0416
Michigan Dessert Corporation
Oak Park, MI. 800-328-8632
Michigan Sugar Company
Saginaw, MI .989-799-7300
Mid-Eastern Molasses Company
Oceanport, NJ 732-462-1868
Mott's
Port Chester, NY 914-612-4000
Osceola Farms
Pahokee, FL .561-924-4400
Pacific Westcoast Foods
Portland, OR 800-874-9333
Pure Foods
Sultan, WA 360-793-2241
Pure Sweet Honey Farm
Verona, WI 800-355-9601
Raceland Raw Sugar Corporation
Raceland, LA 985-537-3533
Rogers Sugar Limited
Vancouver, BC 800-661-5350
Savoie Industries
Belle Rose, LA 225-473-9293
Scott Hams
Greenville, KY 800-318-1353
Southern Minnesota Beet Sugar Cooperative
Renville, MN 320-329-8305
St. James Sugar Cooperative
Saint James, LA 225-265-4056
Stanley Drying Company
Stanley, WI .715-644-5827
Sugar Cane Growers Cooperative of Florida
Belle Glade, FL. 561-996-5556
Suzanne's Specialties
New Brunswick, NJ 800-762-2135
Tate & Lyle North American Sugars
Toronto, ON 800-267-1517
Tova Industries
Louisville, KY 888-532-8682
WCC Honey Marketing
City of Industry, CA 626-855-3086
Westway Trading Corporation
Mapleton, ND 701-282-5010
Whitfield Foods
Montgomery, AL. 800-633-8790
Wholesome Sweeteners
Savannah, GA. 800-680-1896

Dried

Domino Specialty Ingredients
Baltimore, MD 800-446-9763

Natural Sweeteners

Abunda Life Laboratories
Asbury Park, NJ 732-775-4141
Adee Honey Farm
Bruce, SD 605-627-5621
ADM
Marshall, MN 800-328-4150
ADM Corn Processing
Decatur, IL 800-553-8411
ADM Food Ingredients
Olathe, KS. 800-255-6637
Alfred L. Wolff, Inc.
Park Ridge, IL. 312-265-9889
Alma Plantation
Lakeland, LA 225-627-6666
Amalgamated Sugar Company
Boise, ID 208-383-6500
American Crystal Sugar Company
Moorhead, MN 218-236-4400
American Health & Nutrition
Ann Arbor, MI 734-677-5572
Artesian Honey Producers
Artesian, SD .605-527-2423
Atlantic Sugar Association
Belle Glade, FL. 877-835-2828
Atlas Preserves Company
New York, NY 212-569-5613
Babe's Honey Farm
Victoria, BC .250-658-8319
Barkman Honey Company
Hillsboro, KS 800-530-5827

Bessonet Bee Company
Donaldsonville, LA................225-473-9428
Briess Industries
Chilton, WI......................920-849-7711
C&H Sugar Company
Crockett, CA....................800-729-4840
C&H Sugar/Sweetener Products
Newport Beach, CA...............714-475-2665
C.S. Steen's Syrup Mill
Abbeville, LA...................800-725-1654
California Natural Products
Lathrop, CA.....................209-858-2525
Cargill Corn Milling
Naperville, IL..................800-344-1633
Cerestar USA
Decatur, AL.....................256-355-8815
Cerestar USA
Hammond, IN.....................800-348-9896
Champlain Valley Apiaries Company
Middlebury, VT..................800-841-7334
CHR Hansen
Gretna, LA......................504-367-7727
CHR Hansen
Chicago, IL.....................773-646-2203
Chr Hansen
Elyria, OH......................800-558-0802
Cleveland Syrup Corporation
Cleveland, OH...................216-883-1845
Clover Blossom Honey
La Fontaine, IN.................765-981-4443
Consumers Vinegar & Spice Company
Chicago, IL.....................773-376-4100
Cora-Texas Manufacturing Company
White Castle, LA................225-545-3679
Corn Products International
Westchester, IL.................708-551-2600
Crockett-Stewart Honey Company
Tempe, AZ.......................480-731-3936
Crosby Molasses Company
St. John, NB....................506-634-7515
Dakota Organic Products
Watertown, SD...................800-243-7264
Dawes Hill Honey Company
Nunda, NY.......................888-800-8075
Deer Creek Honey Farms
London, OH......................740-852-0899
Delicious Food Products Company
Chicago, IL.....................773-763-5553
Diamond Crystal
Savannah, GA....................800-227-4455
Dixie USA
Tomball, TX.....................800-233-3668
Domino Foods
Yonkers, NY.....................914-963-2400
Domino Specialty Ingredients
Baltimore, MD...................800-446-9763
Domino Sugar Corporation
Baltimore, MD...................410-752-6150
Donald McCoun
Versailles, KY..................859-873-4650
Doyon & Doyon
Toronto, ON.....................888-851-3110
Dutch Gold Honey, Inc.
Lancaster, PA...................800-338-0587
E.F. Lane & Son
Oakland, CA.....................510-569-8980
Eastman Chemical Company
Kingsport, TN...................800-327-8626
Eden Foods Inc
Clinton, MI.....................800-248-0320
Ethical Specialty Products
Pleasanton, CA..................925-462-3824
Evan Hall Sugar Cooperative
Donaldsonville, LA..............225-473-8241

EVERGREEN sweeteners
Your Total Sweetener Solution.

Evergreen Sweeteners, Inc
Aventura, FL....................305-931-1321

Evergreen Sweeteners is a full service sweetener distributor serving the entire state of Florida. From bulk liquid sweeteners to bagged sweeteners, Evergreen provides its customers with industry-leading service and unsurpassed quality.

Farbest-Tallman Foods Corporation
Montvale, NJ....................201-573-4900

Fischer Honey Company
N Little Rock, AR...............501-758-1123
Garuda International
Lemon Cove, CA..................559-594-4380
Gateway Food Products Company
Dupo, IL........................877-220-1963
GlobeTrends
Morris Plains, NJ...............800-416-8327
Golden Heritage Foods
Latty, OH.......................888-233-6446
Golding Farms Foods
Winston Salem, NC...............336-766-6161
Grain Processing Corporation
Muscatine, IA...................800-448-4472
Great Eastern Sun
Asheville, NC...................800-334-5809
Greenwood Associates
Highland Park, IL...............847-242-7900
Groeb Farms
Onsted, MI......................517-467-7100
H. Interdonati
Cold Spring Hbr, NY.............800-367-6617
Hanna's Honey
Salem, OR.......................503-393-2945
Hendricks Apiaries
Englewood, CO...................303-789-3209
Honey Acres
Ashippun, WI....................800-558-7745
Honey World
Parker, SD......................605-297-4188
Hoyt's Honey Farm
Baytown, TX.....................281-576-5383
Iberia Sugar Cooperative
New Iberia, LA..................337-367-9991
Imperial Sugar
Ludlow, KY......................859-261-1920
Indiana Sugar
Burr Ridge, IL..................630-986-9150
Jeanerette Sugar Company
Jeanerette, LA..................337-276-4238
Jogue Inc
Northville, MI..................800-521-3888
Kutik's Honey Farm
Norwich, NY.....................607-336-4105
Lafourche Sugar Corporation
Thibodaux, LA...................985-447-3210
Leighton's Honey
Haines City, FL.................863-422-1773
Leprino Foods Company
Denver, CO......................800-537-7466
Les Industries Bernard Et Fils
St. Victor, QC..................418-588-6109
Louisiana Sugar Cane Cooperation
St Martinville, LA..............337-394-3255
Louisiana Sugar Cane Cooperative
St Martinville, LA..............337-394-3255
M.A. Patout & Son
Jeanerette, LA..................337-276-4592
Madhava Honey
Longmont, CO....................800-530-2900
Malt Products Corporation
Saddle Brook, NJ................800-526-0180
Maple Products
Sherbrooke, QC..................819-569-5161
Michele's Foods
Oak Lawn, IL....................708-598-6600
Michigan Sugar Company
Saginaw, MI.....................989-799-7300
Miller's Honey Company
Colton, CA......................800-233-5463
Minn-Dak Farmers Cooperative
Wahpeton, ND....................701-642-8411
Minnesota Specialty Crops
McGregor, MN....................800-328-6731
Mississippi Blending Company
Keokuk, IA......................800-758-4080
Moon Shine Trading Company
Woodland, CA....................800-678-1226
Nickabood's Company
Los Angeles, CA.................213-746-1541
Nicola Valley Apiaries
Merritt, BC.....................250-378-5208
Norris Brothers Syrup Company
West Monroe, LA.................318-396-1960
North Peace Apiaries
Fort St. John, BC...............250-785-4808
Nu-Tek Foods
Wapakoneta, OH..................800-837-0160
Once Again Nut Butter
Nunda, NY.......................888-800-8075
Organic Planet
San Francisco, CA...............415-765-5590

Osceola Farms
Pahokee, FL.....................561-924-4400
Palm Apiaries
Fort Myers, FL..................239-334-6001
Particle Control
Albertville, MN.................763-497-3075
Paulaur Corporation
Cranbury, NJ....................888-398-8844
Pied-Mont/Dora
Ste Anne Des Plaines, BC........800-363-8003
Portion Pac
Mason, OH.......................800-232-4829
Pot O'Gold Honey Company
Hemingway, SC...................843-558-9598
Pure Food Ingredients
Verona, WI......................800-355-9601
Pure Foods
Sultan, WA......................360-793-2241
Pure Sweet Honey Farm
Verona, WI......................800-355-9601
Raceland Raw Sugar Corporation
Raceland, LA....................985-537-3533
Rio Grande Valley Sugar Growers
Santa Rosa, TX..................956-636-1411
Rocky Mountain Honey Company
Salt Lake City, UT..............801-355-2054
Rogers Sugar
Montreal, QC....................514-527-8686
Roquette America
Keokuk, IA......................800-553-7035
Royal Wine Company
Bayonne, NJ.....................800-382-8299
Sandt's Honey Company
Easton, PA......................800-935-3960
Savannah Foods & Industries
Port Wentworth, GA..............800-241-3785
Savannah Foods Industrial
Port Wentworth, GA..............912-964-1361
Savoie Industries
Belle Rose, LA..................225-473-9293
Shady Maple Farm
Mississauga, ON.................905-206-1455
Silverbow Honey Company
Moses Lake, WA..................866-444-6639
Sioux Honey Association/Sue Bee
Sioux City, IA..................712-258-0638
Sioux Honey Association/Sue Bee
Anaheim, CA.....................714-776-4112
Sno-Shack
Salt Lake City, UT..............801-466-1771
Southern Minnesota Beet Sugar Cooperative
Renville, MN....................320-329-8305
Specialty Ingredients
Watertown, WI...................920-261-4229
Spring Creek Apiaries
Beulah, ND......................701-873-4450
St. James Sugar Cooperative
Saint James, LA.................225-265-4056
St. John Levert
St Martinville, LA..............337-394-9694
Stanley Drying Company
Stanley, WI.....................715-644-5827
Stearns & Lehman
Mansfield, OH...................800-533-2722
Stickney & Poor Company
North Andover, MA...............508-261-8967
Sugar Cane Growers Cooperative of Florida
Belle Glade, FL.................561-996-5556
Sugar Cane Industry Glades Correctional Institution
Belle Glade, FL.................561-829-1400
Sugar Foods
Lawrenceville, GA...............770-339-0184
Suzanne's Specialties
New Brunswick, NJ...............800-762-2135
T.W. Burleson & Son
Waxahachie, TX..................972-937-4810
Tate & Lyle North American Sugars
Rutherford, NJ..................201-842-7723
Tate & Lyle North American Sugars
Toronto, ON.....................800-267-1517
Tate & Lyle North American Sugars
Toronto, ON.....................800-361-1657
Thistledew Farm
Proctor, WV.....................800-854-6639
Tropical Blossom Honey Company
Edgewater, FL...................800-324-8843
Unilever
Lisle, IL.......................877-995-4483
Unique Ingredients
Naches, WA......................509-653-1991
United Canadian Malt
Peterborough, ON................800-461-6400

601

Universal Preservachem Inc
  Edison, NJ 732-777-7338
Valentine Sugars
  Lockport, LA 985-532-2541
Valley View Blueberries
  Vancouver, WA 360-892-2839
VIP Foods
  Flushing, NY 718-821-3942
WCC Honey Marketing
  City of Industry, CA 626-855-3086
Weaver R. Apiaries
  Navasota, TX 936-825-2333
Western New York Syrup Corporation
  Lakeville, NY 585-346-2311
Westway Trading Corporation
  Mapleton, ND 701-282-5010
Whitfield Foods
  Montgomery, AL. 800-633-8790
Wholesome Sweeteners
  Savannah, GA 800-680-1896
Wixson Honey
  Dundee, NY 607-243-8583
Woodworth Honey Company
  Halliday, ND 701-938-4647

Sucrose

Evergreen Sweeteners, Inc
  Aventura, FL. 305-931-1321

Evergreen Sweeteners is a full service sweetener distributor serving the entire state of Florida. From bulk liquid sweeteners to bagged sweeteners, Evergreen provides its customers with industry-leading service and unsurpassed quality.

Rogers Sugar Limited
  Vancouver, BC 800-661-5350
Universal Preservachem Inc
  Edison, NJ 732-777-7338

Sugar

Adirondack Maple Farms
  Fonda, NY. 518-853-4022
ADM Food Ingredients
  Olathe, KS. 800-255-6637
Agri-Dairy Products
  Purchase, NY 914-697-9580
Alexander & Baldwin
  Honolulu, HI 808-525-6611
Alma Plantation
  Lakeland, LA 225-627-6666
Amalgamated Sugar Company
  Boise, ID. 208-383-6500
Atlantic Sugar Association
  Belle Glade, FL. 877-835-2828
Bateman Products
  Rigby, ID. 208-745-9033
Beneo Palatinit
  Morris Plains, NJ 800-476-6258
C&H Sugar Company
  Crockett, CA. 510-787-2121
C&H Sugar Company
  Crockett, CA. 800-729-4840
Caravan Products Company
  Totowa, NJ 800-526-5261
Cleveland Syrup Corporation
  Cleveland, OH 216-883-1845
Cora-Texas Manufacturing Company
  White Castle, LA 225-545-3679
Diamond Crystal
  Savannah, GA 800-227-4455
Domino Foods
  Yonkers, NY 914-963-2400
Domino Specialty Ingredients
  Baltimore, MD 800-446-9763
Domino Sugar Corporation
  Baltimore, MD 410-752-6150
EpicCure Princess of Yum
  San Luis Obispo, CA 805-466-3655
Erba Food Products
  Brooklyn, NY 718-272-7700
Evan Hall Sugar Cooperative
  Donaldsonville, LA. 225-473-8241

Evergreen Sweeteners, Inc
  Aventura, FL 305-931-1321

Evergreen Sweeteners is a full service sweetener distributor serving the entire state of Florida. From bulk liquid sweeteners to bagged sweeteners, Evergreen provides its customers with industry-leading service and unsurpassed quality.

Franco's Cocktail Mixes
  Pompano Beach, FL 800-782-4508
Gay & Robinson
  Kaumakani, HI 808-335-3133
Greenwell Farms
  Morganfield, KY. 270-389-3289
Honey Ridge Farms
  Brush Prairie, WA. 360-256-0086
Iberia Sugar Cooperative
  New Iberia, LA 337-367-9991
Imperial Sugar
  Ludlow, KY. 859-261-1920
Imperial Sugar Company
  Sugar Land, TX. 800-727-8427
Indiana Sugar
  Burr Ridge, IL. 630-986-9150
Jakeman's Maple Products
  Beachville, ON 800-382-9795
Lafourche Sugar Corporation
  Thibodaux, LA 985-447-3210
Lantic Sugar
  Montreal, QC 514-527-8686
Louisiana Sugar Cane Cooperation
  St Martinville, LA. 337-394-3255
Louisiana Sugar Cane Cooperative
  St Martinville, LA. 337-394-3255
M.A. Patout & Son
  Jeanerette, LA. 337-276-4592
Maple Products
  Sherbrooke, QC 819-569-5161

Michigan Sugar Company
Saginaw, MI 989-799-7300
Minn-Dak Farmers Cooperative
Wahpeton, ND 701-642-8411
Organic Planet
San Francisco, CA 415-765-5590
Osceola Farms
Pahokee, FL 561-924-4400
Particle Control
Albertville, MN 763-497-3075
Paulaur Corporation
Cranbury, NJ 888-398-8844
Penta Manufacturing Company
Livingston, NJ 973-740-2300
Portion Pac
Mason, OH 800-232-4829
QA Products
Elk Grove Vlg, IL 800-635-7907
Quaker Sugar Company
Brooklyn, NY 718-387-6500
Raceland Raw Sugar Corporation
Raceland, LA 985-537-3533
Rapunzel Pure Organics
Chatham, NY 800-207-2814
Refined Sugars
Yonkers, NY 800-431-1020
Rice Company
Roseville, CA 916-787-1084
Rio Grande Valley Sugar Growers
Santa Rosa, TX 956-636-1411
Rogers Sugar
Montreal, QC 514-527-8686
Rogers Sugar Limited
Vancouver, BC 800-661-5350
Savannah Foods & Industries
Port Wentworth, GA 800-241-3785
Savannah Foods Industrial
Port Wentworth, GA 912-964-1361
Savoie Industries
Belle Rose, LA 225-473-9293
Shady Maple Farm
Mississauga, ON 905-206-1455
South Louisiana Sugars
Saint James, LA 225-265-4056
Southern Minnesota Beet Sugar Cooperative
Renville, MN 320-329-8305
Specialty Ingredients
Watertown, WI 920-261-4229
St. James Sugar Cooperative
Saint James, LA 225-265-4056
Stearns & Lehman
Mansfield, OH 800-533-2722
Sugar Foods
Lawrenceville, GA 770-339-0184
Sugar Foods
Sun Valley, CA 818-768-7900
Suzanne's Specialties
New Brunswick, NJ 800-762-2135
Tate & Lyle North American Sugars
Rutherford, NJ 201-842-7723
Tate & Lyle North American Sugars
Toronto, ON 800-267-1517
Tate & Lyle North American Sugars
Toronto, ON 800-361-1657
US Sugar Company
Buffalo, NY 716-828-1170
Valentine Sugars
Lockport, LA 985-532-2541
Walpex Trading Company
Coral Gables, FL 305-662-9744
Western Pacific Commodities
Las Vegas, NV 702-312-8080
Western Sugar Company
Scottsbluff, NE 308-632-4155
Western Sugar Cooperative
Denver, CO 303-830-3939
Westin
Omaha, NE 800-228-6098
William Bounds
Torrance, CA 800-473-0504

Brown

Agri-Dairy Products
Purchase, NY 914-697-9580
C&H Sugar Company
Crockett, CA 510-787-2121
C&H Sugar Company
Crockett, CA 800-729-4840
Diamond Crystal
Savannah, GA 800-227-4455

Domino Foods
Yonkers, NY 914-963-2400
Domino Specialty Ingredients
Baltimore, MD 800-446-9763
Domino Sugar Corporation
Baltimore, MD 410-752-6150

Evergreen Sweeteners, Inc
Aventura, FL 305-931-1321

Evergreen Sweeteners is a full service sweetener distributor serving the entire state of Florida. From bulk liquid sweeteners to bagged sweeteners, Evergreen provides its customers with industry-leading service and unsurpassed quality.

Savannah Foods Industrial
Port Wentworth, GA 912-964-1361
Tate & Lyle North American Sugars
Toronto, ON 800-267-1517
US Sugar Company
Buffalo, NY 716-828-1170
Westin
Omaha, NE 800-228-6098

Cane

A. Duda Farm Fresh Foods
Belle Glade, FL 561-996-7621
Agri-Dairy Products
Purchase, NY 914-697-9580
American Health & Nutrition
Ann Arbor, MI 734-677-5572
Atlantic Sugar Association
Belle Glade, FL 877-835-2828
C&H Sugar Company
Crockett, CA 510-787-2121
C&H Sugar Company
Crockett, CA 800-729-4840
Domino Specialty Ingredients
Baltimore, MD 800-446-9763

Evergreen Sweeteners, Inc
Aventura, FL 305-931-1321

Evergreen Sweeteners is a full service sweetener distributor serving the entire state of Florida. From bulk liquid sweeteners to bagged sweeteners, Evergreen provides its customers with industry-leading service and unsurpassed quality.

Florida Crystals
West Palm Beach, FL 877-835-2828
Imperial Sugar Company
Sugar Land, TX 800-727-8427
M.A. Patout & Son
Jeanerette, LA 337-276-4592
Organic Planet
San Francisco, CA 415-765-5590
Rio Grande Valley Sugar Growers
Santa Rosa, TX 956-636-1411
Rogers Sugar
Montreal, QC 514-527-8686
St. John Levert
St Martinville, LA 337-394-9694
Sugar Cane Industry Glades Correctional Institution
Belle Glade, FL 561-829-1400
Wholesome Sweeteners
Savannah, GA 800-680-1896

Fondant

Domino Specialty Ingredients
Baltimore, MD 800-446-9763

Granulated

Amalgamated Sugar Company
Boise, ID 208-383-6500
American Crystal Sugar Company
Moorhead, MN 218-236-4400

C&H Sugar Company
Crockett, CA 800-729-4840
Diamond Crystal
Savannah, GA 800-227-4455
Domino Foods
Yonkers, NY 914-963-2400
Domino Sugar Corporation
Baltimore, MD 410-752-6150

Evergreen Sweeteners, Inc
Aventura, FL 305-931-1321

Evergreen Sweeteners is a full service sweetener distributor serving the entire state of Florida. From bulk liquid sweeteners to bagged sweeteners, Evergreen provides its customers with industry-leading service and unsurpassed quality.

Michigan Sugar Company
Saginaw, MI 989-799-7300
Paulaur Corporation
Cranbury, NJ 888-398-8844
Rogers Sugar Limited
Vancouver, BC 800-661-5350
US Sugar Company
Buffalo, NY 716-828-1170
Westin
Omaha, NE 800-228-6098

Icing

BakeMark
Schaumburg, IL 562-949-1054
Baker & Baker
Schaumburg, IL 800-593-5777
Domino Specialty Ingredients
Baltimore, MD 800-446-9763
Lantic Sugar
Montreal, QC 514-527-8686
Signature Brands
Ocala, FL 800-456-9573

Invert

Agri-Dairy Products
Purchase, NY 914-697-9580
Domino Foods
Yonkers, NY 914-963-2400
Domino Specialty Ingredients
Baltimore, MD 800-446-9763

Evergreen Sweeteners, Inc
Aventura, FL 305-931-1321

Evergreen Sweeteners is a full service sweetener distributor serving the entire state of Florida. From bulk liquid sweeteners to bagged sweeteners, Evergreen provides its customers with industry-leading service and unsurpassed quality.

Malt Products Corporation
Saddle Brook, NJ 800-526-0180
Paulaur Corporation
Cranbury, NJ 888-398-8844
Tate & Lyle North American Sugars
Toronto, ON 800-267-1517

Liquid

Amalgamated Sugar Company
Boise, ID 208-383-6500
American Crystal Sugar Company
Moorhead, MN 218-236-4400
C&H Sugar Company
Crockett, CA 800-729-4840
Domino Foods
Yonkers, NY 914-963-2400

Your Total Sweetener Solution.

Evergreen Sweeteners, Inc
Aventura, FL 305-931-1321

Evergreen Sweeteners is a full service sweetener distributor serving the entire state of Florida. From bulk liquid sweeteners to bagged sweeteners, Evergreen provides its customers with industry-leading service and unsurpassed quality.

Flavouressence Products
Mississauga, ON 866-209-7778
Lantic Sugar
Montreal, QC 514-527-8686
Paulaur Corporation
Cranbury, NJ 888-398-8844
Tate & Lyle North American Sugars
Toronto, ON 800-267-1517

Liquid & Granulated

Agri-Dairy Products
Purchase, NY 914-697-9580
Amalgamated Sugar Company
Boise, ID 208-383-6500
American Crystal Sugar Company
Moorhead, MN 218-236-4400
C&H Sugar Company
Crockett, CA 510-787-2121
C&H Sugar Company
Crockett, CA 800-729-4840
Diamond Crystal
Savannah, GA 800-227-4455

Your Total Sweetener Solution.

Evergreen Sweeteners, Inc
Aventura, FL 305-931-1321

Evergreen Sweeteners is a full service sweetener distributor serving the entire state of Florida. From bulk liquid sweeteners to bagged sweeteners, Evergreen provides its customers with industry-leading service and unsurpassed quality.

Lantic Sugar
Montreal, QC 514-527-8686
Michigan Sugar Company
Saginaw, MI 989-799-7300
Rogers Sugar
Montreal, QC 514-527-8686
Savannah Foods Industrial
Port Wentworth, GA 912-964-1361
South Louisiana Sugars
Saint James, LA 225-265-4056
Specialty Ingredients
Watertown, WI 920-261-4229

Maple

Brown Family Farm
Alstead, NH. 866-254-8718
Butternut Mountain Farm
Morrisville, VT. 800-828-2376
Citadelle Maple Syrup Produce Cooperative
Plessisville, QC. 819-362-3241

EMERLING INTERNATIONAL FOODS, INC.

Emerling International Foods
Buffalo, NY. 716-833-7381

We supply food manufacturers and food service customers worldwide (since 1988) with bulk ingredients including: Fruits & Vegetables; Juice Concentrates; Herbs & Spices; Oils & Vinegars; Flavors & Colors; Honey & Molasses. We also produce PURE MAPLE SYRUP.

Maple Hollow
Merrill, WI 715-536-7251
Maple Products
Sherbrooke, QC 819-569-5161

Richards Maple Products
Chardon, OH. 800-352-4052
Shady Maple Farm
Mississauga, ON 905-206-1455
Vermont Country Naturals
Charlotte, VT 800-528-7021
Whitfield Foods
Montgomery, AL. 800-633-8790

Butter

Butternut Mountain Farm
Morrisville, VT 800-828-2376
Choice of Vermont
Destin, FL .800-444-6261
Whitfield Foods
Montgomery, AL. 800-633-8790

Organic

Domino Specialty Ingredients
Baltimore, MD 800-446-9763

Powdered

Agri-Dairy Products
Purchase, NY 914-697-9580
C&H Sugar Company
Crockett, CA 510-787-2121
C&H Sugar Company
Crockett, CA 800-729-4840
Cleveland Syrup Corporation
Cleveland, OH 216-883-1845
Domino Foods
Yonkers, NY 914-963-2400

Your Total Sweetener Solution.

Evergreen Sweeteners, Inc
Aventura, FL 305-931-1321

Evergreen Sweeteners is a full service sweetener distributor serving the entire state of Florida. From bulk liquid sweeteners to bagged sweeteners, Evergreen provides its customers with industry-leading service and unsurpassed quality.

Flavouressence Products
Mississauga, ON 866-209-7778
Michigan Sugar Company
Saginaw, MI 989-799-7300
Savannah Foods Industrial
Port Wentworth, GA 912-964-1361
US Sugar Company
Buffalo, NY. 716-828-1170
Vermont Country Naturals
Charlotte, VT 800-528-7021
Westin
Omaha, NE 800-228-6098

Sugar Substitutes

Abunda Life Laboratories
Asbury Park, NJ 732-775-4141
Agri-Dairy Products
Purchase, NY 914-697-9580
Amcan Industries
Elmsford, NY 914-347-4838
Associated Brands, Inc.
Medina, NY. 800-265-0050
Cumberland Packing Corporation
Brooklyn, NY 718-858-4200
Diamond Crystal
Savannah, GA 800-227-4455
Eastman Chemical Company
Kingsport, TN. 800-327-8626
EMD Chemicals
Gibbstown, NJ 800-364-4535
Fasweet Company
Jonesboro, AR. 870-932-1562
Franco's Cocktail Mixes
Pompano Beach, FL 800-782-4508
Great Eastern Sun
Asheville, NC 800-334-5809
H. Interdonati
Cold Spring Hbr, NY 800-367-6617
Hoechst Food Ingredients
Edison, NJ. 800-344-5807
Jungbunzlauer
Newton, MA 800-828-0062

M. Licht & Son
Knoxville, TN 865-523-5593
Malt Products Corporation
Saddle Brook, NJ 800-526-0180
McNeil Specialty Products Company
New Brunswick, NJ 732-524-3799
Miller's Honey Company
Colton, CA 800-233-5463
Minnesota Specialty Crops
McGregor, MN 800-328-6731
Nickabood's Company
Los Angeles, CA 213-746-1541
North Peace Apiaries
Fort St. John, BC. 250-785-4808
Once Again Nut Butter
Nunda, NY 888-800-8075
Paulaur Corporation
Cranbury, NJ 888-398-8844
PMC Specialties Group
Cincinnati, OH 800-543-2466
Rit-Chem Company
Pleasantville, NY 203-769-9110
Rocky Mountain Honey Company
Salt Lake City, UT 801-355-2054
Roquette America
Keokuk, IA 800-553-7035
Savannah Foods & Industries
Port Wentworth, GA 800-241-3785
Spring Tree Maple Products
Brattleboro, VT 802-254-8784
St. Lawrence Starch
Mississauga, ON 905-274-3671
Stickney & Poor Company
North Andover, MA 508-261-8967
Sugar Foods
Lawrenceville, GA 770-339-0184
Sugar Foods
Sun Valley, CA 818-768-7900
Suzanne's Specialties
New Brunswick, NJ 800-762-2135
Sweet Green Field LLC
Bellingham, WA 360-483-4555
Tate & Lyle North American Sugars
Rutherford, NJ 201-842-7723
Universal Preservachem Inc
Edison, NJ. 732-777-7338
VIP Foods
Flushing, NY. 718-821-3942
WCC Honey Marketing
City of Industry, CA 626-855-3086
Westin
Omaha, NE 800-228-6098
Wholesome Sweeteners
Savannah, GA. 800-680-1896

Aspartame

Ajinomoto Food Ingredients LLC
Chicago, IL 773-380-7000
Holland Sweeteners N A
Atlanta, GA. 800-757-9468

Saccharin

Diamond Crystal
Savannah, GA 800-227-4455
Jungbunzlauer
Newton, MA 800-828-0062
PMC Specialties Group
Cincinnati, OH 800-543-2466
Roquette America
Keokuk, IA 800-553-7035
Tate & Lyle North American Sugars
Rutherford, NJ 201-842-7723

Sugar Alternatives

Consumers Vinegar & Spice Company
Chicago, IL 773-376-4100
Diamond Crystal
Savannah, GA 800-227-4455

Syrups

A.C. Calderoni & Company
Brisbane, CA 866-468-1897
A.W. Jantzi & Sons
Wellesley, ON 519-656-2400
Abunda Life Laboratories
Asbury Park, NJ 732-775-4141
ADM
Marshall, MN 800-328-4150
Advanced Ingredients, Inc.
Capitola, CA 888-238-4647
Al-Rite Fruits & Syrups
Miami, FL 305-652-2540
Alaska Herb Tea Company
Anchorage, AK 800-654-2764
Alimentaire Whyte's Inc
Laval, QC 800-625-1979
Amalgamated Sugar Company
Boise, ID 208-383-6500
American Health & Nutrition
Ann Arbor, MI 734-677-5572
Aunt Aggie De's Pralines
Sinton, TX 888-772-5463
Autocrat Coffee & Extracts
Lincoln, RI 800-288-6272

Baldwin Richardson Foods
Frankfort, IL 866-644-2732

Baldwin Richardson Foods is a liquid ingredient manufacturer specializing in signature sauces, dessert toppings, beverage/pancake syrups, specialty fruit fillings and condiments. Packaging capabilities range from portion control cups and pouches to standard retail and foodservice packs and include industrial drums and totes. Full service R&D and Quality groups dedicated to new product development, with in-house stability and analytical testing. Call for assistance.

Bay Valley Foods
Horsham, PA 800-236-1119
Bay Valley Foods
Green Bay, WI 800-558-4700
Belton Foods
Dayton, OH 800-443-2266
Blueberry Store
Grand Junction, MI 877-654-2400
Bosco Products
Towaco, NJ 800-438-2672

Boyd Coffee Company
Portland, OR 800-545-4077
Braswell Food Company
Statesboro, GA 912-764-6191
Briess Industries
Chilton, WI 920-849-7711
C.S. Steen's Syrup Mill
Abbeville, LA 800-725-1654
California Natural Products
Lathrop, CA 209-858-2525
Cameron Birch Syrup & Confections
Wasilla, AK 800-962-4724
Carbonator Rental Service
Philadelphia, PA 800-220-3556
Cargill Corn Milling
Naperville, IL 800-344-1633
Carolina Beverage Corporation
Salisbury, NC 704-637-5881
Carolina Treet
Wilmington, NC 800-616-6344
Carriage House Companies
Fredonia, NY 800-828-8915
Castella Imports
Hauppauge, NY 866-227-8355
Cerestar USA
Decatur, AL 256-355-8815
Cerestar USA
Hammond, IN 800-348-9896
Charles Dennery Pillsbury
New Orleans, LA 504-733-2331
Cheri's Desert Harvest
Tucson, AZ 800-743-1141
Citadelle Maple Syrup Produce Cooperative
Plessisville, QC 819-362-3241
Classic Tea
Libertyville, IL 630-680-9934
Clear Mountain Coffee Company
Silver Spring, MD 301-587-2233
Clements Foods Company
Oklahoma City, OK 800-654-8355
Cleveland Syrup Corporation
Cleveland, OH 216-883-1845
Coca-Cola Bottling Company
Kapolei, HI 800-682-5778
Coca-Cola Bottling Company
Honolulu, HI 808-839-6711
Coca-Cola North America
Columbus, OH 614-491-6305
Coffee Bean International
Portland, OR 800-877-0474
Coffee Concepts
Dallas, TX 214-363-9331
Cold Hollow Cider Mill
Waterbury Center, VT 800-327-7537
Con Yeager Spice Company
Zelienople, PA 800-222-2460
Confectionery Treasures
Cumberland, MD 301-478-2245

Consolidated Mills
Houston, TX 713-896-4196
Consumers Vinegar & Spice Company
Chicago, IL 773-376-4100
Conway Import Company
Franklin Park, IL 800-323-8801
Cora Italian Specialties
Countryside, IL 800-696-2672
Cora-Texas Manufacturing Company
White Castle, LA 225-545-3679
Corn Products International
Westchester, IL 708-551-2600
Crosby Molasses Company
St. John, NB 506-634-7515
Da Vinci Gourmet
Seattle, WA 800-640-6779
Daily Juice Products
Verona, PA 800-245-2929
Daymar Select Fine Coffees
El Cajon, CA 800-466-7590
Dean Distributors
Burlingame, CA 800-227-3112
Dean Distributors
Burlingame, CA 800-792-0816
Deer Creek Honey Farms
London, OH 740-852-0899
Delicious Food Products Company
Chicago, IL 773-763-5553
Domino Sugar Corporation
Baltimore, MD 410-752-6150
Donald McCoun
Versailles, KY 859-873-4650
E.D. Smith & Sons
Winona, ON 905-643-1211

EMERLING INTERNATIONAL FOODS, INC.

Emerling International Foods
Buffalo, NY 716-833-7381

We supply food manufacturers and food service customers worldwide (since 1988) with bulk ingredients including: Fruits & Vegetables; Juice Concentrates; Herbs & Spices; Oils & Vinegars; Flavors & Colors; Honey & Molasses. We also produce PURE MAPLE SYRUP.

Entner-Stuart Premium Syrups
Albany, OR 800-377-9787
Ethical Specialty Products
Pleasanton, CA 925-462-3824
Eva Gates Homemade Preserves
Bigfork, MT 800-682-4283
Evan Hall Sugar Cooperative
Donaldsonville, LA 225-473-8241

Evergreen Sweeteners, Inc
Aventura, FL 305-931-1321

Evergreen Sweeteners is a full service sweetener distributor serving the entire state of Florida. From bulk liquid sweeteners to bagged sweeteners, Evergreen provides its customers with industry-leading service and unsurpassed quality.

Eweberry Farms
Brownsville, OR 541-466-3470
Felbro Food Products
Los Angeles, CA 800-335-2761
Ferrara Bakery & Cafe
New York, NY 212-226-6150
Flavor Consortium
Los Angeles, CA 323-724-1010
Flavors from Florida
Bartow, FL 863-533-0408
Flavors of Hawaii
Honolulu, HI .808-597-1727
Flavouressence Products
Mississauga, ON 866-209-7778
Florida Citrus
Tampa, FL 813-626-5580
Folklore Foods
Toppenish, WA 509-865-4772
Forge Mountain Foods
Hendersonville, NC 800-823-6743
Foxtail Foods
Fairfield, OH .800-323-6944
Gateway Food Products Company
Dupo, IL 877-220-1963
GEM Berry Products
Sandpoint, ID 800-426-0498
Gem Berry Products
Sandpoint, ID 800-426-0498
Golden Cheese Company of California
Corona, CA 951-493-4700
Golden Eagle Syrup Manufacturing Company
Fayette, AL 205-932-5294
Golden Foods
Commerce, CA 800-350-2462
Golden State Foods
Irvine, CA 949-252-2000
Great Valley Mills
Barto, PA 800-688-6455
Great Western Products Company
Assumption, IL 217-226-3241
Great Western Products Company
Bremen, IN 217-546-4010
Great Western Products Company
Bismarck, MO 573-734-2210
Groeb Farms
Onsted, MI 517-467-7100
H&H Products Company
Orlando, FL 407-299-5410
H. Fox & Company
Brooklyn, NY 718-385-4600
Hawaiian Fruit Specialties
Kalaheo, HI 808-332-9333
Henry & Henry
Lancaster, NY 800-828-7130
Hershey
Mississauga, ON 800-468-1714
Hershey Company
Hershey, PA .800-468-1714
Highland Sugarworks
Websterville, VT 800-452-4012
Homemade By Dorothy
Boise, ID 208-375-3720
HoneyRun Winery
Chico, CA 530-345-6405
Howard Foods
Danvers, MA .978-774-6207
Huckleberry Patch
Hungry Horse, MT 800-527-7340
I Rice & Company
Philadelphia, PA 800-232-6022
Instant Products of America
Columbus, IN 812-372-9100
International Food Products Corporation
Saint Louis, MO 800-227-8427
J.M. Smucker Company
Orrville, OH .330-682-3000

Jakeman's Maple Products
Beachville, ON 800-382-9795
JMS Specialty Foods
Ripon, WI 800-535-5437
Jogue Inc
Northville, MI 800-521-3888
John Gust Foods & Products Corporation
Batavia, IL 800-756-5886
Josef Aaron Syrup Company
Redmond, WA 425-820-7221
Jus-Made
Dallas, TX 800-969-3746
Kalva Corporation
Gurnee, IL 800-525-8220
Kemach Food Products   Corporation
Brooklyn, NY 888-453-6224
Kerry Ingredients
Beloit, WI 608-362-1651
Kloss Manufacturing Company
Allentown, PA 800-445-7100
Knott's Berry Farm Foods
Placentia, CA 800-289-9927
Kozlowski Farms
Forestville, CA 800-473-2767
Kraft Food Ingredients
Memphis, TN 901-381-6500
Lafourche Sugar Corporation
Thibodaux, LA 985-447-3210
Lancaster Packing Company
Lancaster, PA 717-397-9727
Les Industries Bernard Et Fils
St. Victor, QC 418-588-6109
Limpert Brothers
Vineland, NJ .800-691-1353
Lost Trail Root Beer Com
Louisburg, KS 800-748-7765
Louisiana Sugar Cane Cooperation
St Martinville, LA. 337-394-3255
Louisiana Sugar Cane Cooperative
St Martinville, LA. 337-394-3255
Lowery's Premium Roast Coffee
Snohomish, WA 800-767-1783
Lynch Foods
North York, QC. 416-449-5464
Lyons-Magnus
Fresno, CA 559-268-5966
M.A. Gedney
Chaska, MN .952-448-2612
Magic Ice Products
Stockton, CA. 800-776-7923
Malt-Diastase Company
Saddle Brook, NJ 800-772-0416
Maple Grove Farms of Vermont
St Johnsbury, VT. 800-525-2540
Maple Products
Sherbrooke, QC 819-569-5161
Mardale Specialty Foods
Waukegan, IL 847-336-4777
Marsa Specialty Products
Vernon, CA .800-628-0500
Masterson Company
Milwaukee, WI 414-647-1132
Melchers Flavors of America
Indianapolis, IN 800-235-2867
Michele's Foods
Oak Lawn, IL 708-598-6600
Michigan Sugar Company
Saginaw, MI .989-799-7300
Minnesota Specialty Crops
McGregor, MN 800-328-6731
Monin
Clearwater, FL 800-966-5225
National Fruit Flavor Company
New Orleans, LA 800-966-1123
National Products Company
Kalamazoo, MI 269-344-3640
Naturally Fresh Foods
College Park, GA 800-765-1950
Naturel
Rancho Cucamonga, CA 877-242-8344
New Chapter
Brattleboro, VT. 800-543-7279
Newport Flavours & Fragrances
Orange, CA .714-628-9894
Nog Incorporated
Dunkirk, NY .800-332-2664
Northwestern Extract Company
Brookfield, WI 800-466-3034
NSpired Natural Foods
Melville, NY .631-845-4689
Orange Bang
Sylmar, CA 818-833-1000

Oregon Hill Farms
St Helens, OR 800-243-4541
Osceola Farms
Pahokee, FL .561-924-4400
Pacific Westcoast Foods
Portland, OR 800-874-9333
Paradigm Food Works
Lake Oswego, OR 503-595-4360
Paulaur Corporation
Cranbury, NJ 888-398-8844
PepsiCo
Urbandale, IA 515-270-1332
Perfection Fine Products
Maple Heights, OH 216-475-5744
Phillips Syrup Corporation
Cleveland, OH 216-661-4800
Pied-Mont/Dora
Ste Anne Des Plaines, BC 800-363-8003
Pinnacle Foods Group
Cherry Hill, NJ 877-852-7424
Poppers Supply Company
Portland, OR 503-239-3792
Portion Pac
Mason, OH 800-232-4829
Pride of Dixie Syrup Company
Jonesboro, AR. 800-530-7654
Prima Foods International
Ocala, FL. 800-774-8751
Pure Foods
Sultan, WA 360-793-2241
Purity Factories
St.John's, NL. 800-563-3411
Quaker Oats Company
Cedar Rapids, IA. 319-362-3121
Raceland Raw Sugar Corporation
Raceland, LA 985-537-3533
Richards Maple Products
Chardon, OH 800-352-4052
Richfield Foods
Cairo, GA 229-377-2102
Rio Syrup Company
St Louis, MO. 800-325-7666
Rogers Sugar
Montreal, QC 514-527-8686
Roquette America
Keokuk, IA 800-553-7035
Routin America
New York, NY 800-367-1883

Routin America
Basking Ridge, NJ 908-630-0338
Royal Crown Bottling Company
Bowling Green, KY 270-842-8106
Royal Wine Company
Bayonne, NJ 201-437-9131
Royal Wine Company
Bayonne, NJ 800-382-8299
Santini Foods
San Lorenzo, CA 800-835-6888
Savoie Industries
Belle Rose, LA 225-473-9293
SBK Preserves
Bronx, NY .800-773-7378
Sea Breeze Fruit Flavors
Towaco, NJ 800-732-2733
Seller Kirk & Company
Schwenksville, PA 215-480-7342
Sethness Products Company
Chicago, IL 847-329-2080
Shady Maple Farm
Mississauga, ON 905-206-1455
Shahi Food Corporation
Mississauga, ON 905-677-4327
Shanks Extracts
Lancaster, PA 800-346-3135
Shawnee Canning Company
Cross Junction, VA 800-713-1414
Singer Extract Laboratory
Livonia, MI 313-345-5880
Skjodt-Barrett Foods
Mississauga, ON 877-600-1200
Somerset Syrup & Beverage
Edison, NJ 800-526-8865
Southern Minnesota Beet Sugar Cooperative
Renville, MN 320-329-8305
Spring Tree Maple Products
Brattleboro, VT 802-254-8784
St. James Sugar Cooperative
Saint James, LA 225-265-4056
Stanley Drying Company
Stanley, WI 715-644-5827
Star Kay White
Congers, NY 800-874-8518
Stasero International
Seattle, WA 888-929-2378
Stearns & Lehman
Mansfield, OH 800-533-2722
Steel's Gourmet Foods
Bridgeport, PA 800-678-3357
Stevens Tropical Plantation
West Palm Beach, FL 561-683-4701
Stirling Foods
Renton, WA 800-332-1714
Stone Cellar Kitchens
Riverside, CA 951-352-5713
Sugar Cane Growers Cooperative of Florida
Belle Glade, FL 561-996-5556
Sugar Plum Farm
Plumtree, NC 888-257-0019
Sugarman of Vermont
Hardwick, VT 800-932-7700
Superior Trading Company
San Francisco, CA 415-982-8722
Suzanne's Specialties
New Brunswick, NJ 800-762-2135
Suzuki's Ice Castle
Honolulu, HI 808-533-1166
T. Marzetti Company
Columbus, OH 614-846-2232
T.J. Blackburn Syrup Works
Jefferson, TX. 800-527-8630
Tate & Lyle North American Sugars
Toronto, ON 800-267-1517
Thomson Food
Duluth, MN. 218-722-2529
Tone Products Company
Melrose Park, IL 708-681-3660
Torani Syrups
S San Francisco, CA. 800-775-1925
Tova Industries
Louisville, KY 888-532-8682
Trader Vic's Food Products
Emeryville, CA 877-762-4824
Trailblazer Food Products
Portland, OR 800-777-7179
Triple H Food Processors
Riverside, CA 951-352-5700
Tulkoff Food Products
Baltimore, MD 800-638-7343
Turtle Island Herbs
Boulder, CO 800-684-4060

Uncle Bum's Gourmet Foods
Riverside, CA 800-486-2867
United Canadian Malt
Peterborough, ON 800-461-6400
Valley Grain Products
Madera, CA 559-675-3400
Valley View Blueberries
Vancouver, BC 360-892-2839
Van Tone Creative Flavors Inc
Terrell, TX. 800-856-0802
Vanlaw Food Products
Fullerton, CA 714-870-9091
Ventura Foods
Ontario, CA 714-257-3700
Wagner Excello Food Products
Broadview, IL 708-338-4488
WCC Honey Marketing
City of Industry, CA 626-855-3086
Webbpak
Trussville, AL 800-655-3500
Western Syrup Company
Santa Fe Springs, CA 562-921-4485
Westin
Omaha, NE 800-228-6098
Westway Trading Corporation
Mapleton, ND 701-282-5010
Whipple Company
Natick, MA 800-345-2925
White-Stokes Company
Chicago, IL 800-978-6537
Whitfield Foods
Montgomery, AL. 800-633-8790
Wing Nien Company
Hayward, CA 510-487-8877
Zipp Manufacturing Company
Hornerville, OH 800-521-8700
Zumbro
Hayfield, MN 800-365-2409

Bar

Da Vinci Gourmet
Seattle, WA 800-640-6779

Beverages

Andresen Ryan Coffee Com
Superior, WI 715-395-3793
Coca-Cola North America
Columbus, OH 614-491-6305
Da Vinci Gourmet
Seattle, WA 800-640-6779
Dean Distributors
Burlingame, CA 800-792-0816
Flavouressence Products
Mississauga, ON 866-209-7778
Folklore Foods
Toppenish, WA 509-865-4772
Lenox-Martell
Jamaica Plain, MA 617-442-7777
Perfection Fine Products
Maple Heights, OH. 216-475-5744
Rio Syrup Company
St Louis, MO. 800-325-7666
Skjodt-Barrett Foods
Mississauga, ON 877-600-1200
Van Tone Creative Flavors Inc
Terrell, TX. 800-856-0802

Cane

Agri-Dairy Products
Purchase, NY 914-697-9580
American Health & Nutrition
Ann Arbor, MI 734-677-5572

Your Total Sweetener Solution.

Evergreen Sweeteners, Inc
Aventura, FL 305-931-1321

Evergreen Sweeteners is a full service sweetener distributor serving the entire state of Florida. From bulk liquid sweeteners to bagged sweeteners, Evergreen provides its customers with industry-leading service and unsurpassed quality.

Malt Products Corporation
Saddle Brook, NJ 800-526-0180
Norris Brothers Syrup Company
West Monroe, LA 318-396-1960
Rogers Sugar
Montreal, QC 514-527-8686
Seller Kirk & Company
Schwenksville, PA 215-480-7342
Suzanne's Specialties
New Brunswick, NJ 800-762-2135
Webbpak
Trussville, AL 800-655-3500

Corn

Your Total Sweetener Solution.

Evergreen Sweeteners, Inc
Aventura, FL 305-931-1321

Evergreen Sweeteners is a full service sweetener distributor serving the entire state of Florida. From bulk liquid sweeteners to bagged sweeteners, Evergreen provides its customers with industry-leading service and unsurpassed quality.

Quaker Oats Company
Cedar Rapids, IA 319-362-3121
Whitfield Foods
Montgomery, AL. 800-633-8790

Blends

Your Total Sweetener Solution.

Evergreen Sweeteners, Inc
Aventura, FL 305-931-1321

Evergreen Sweeteners is a full service sweetener distributor serving the entire state of Florida. From bulk liquid sweeteners to bagged sweeteners, Evergreen provides its customers with industry-leading service and unsurpassed quality.

Dextrose

Evergreen Sweeteners, Inc
Aventura, FL 305-931-1321

Evergreen Sweeteners is a full service sweetener distributor serving the entire state of Florida. From bulk liquid sweeteners to bagged sweeteners, Evergreen provides its customers with industry-leading service and unsurpassed quality.

Glucose - Etc.

ADM
Marshall, MN 800-328-4150
ADM Corn Processing
Decatur, IL 800-553-8411
American Health & Nutrition
Ann Arbor, MI 734-677-5572

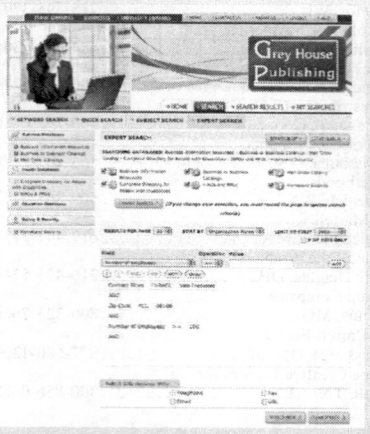
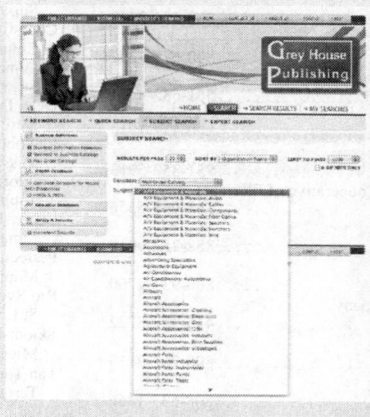

Baldwin Richardson Foods
Frankfort, IL 866-644-2732

Baldwin Richardson Foods is a liquid ingredient manufacturer specializing in signature sauces, dessert toppings, beverage/pancake syrups, specialty fruit fillings and condiments. Packaging capabilities range from portion control cups and pouches to standard retail and foodservice packs and include industrial drums and totes. Full service R&D and Quality groups dedicated to new product development, with in-house stability and analytical testing. Call for assistance.

Cargill Corn Milling
Naperville, IL 800-344-1633
Cargill Sweeteners
Minneapolis, MN 800-227-4455
Cerestar USA
Decatur, AL. 256-355-8815
Cerestar USA
Hammond, IN 800-348-9896
Con Yeager Spice Company
Zelienople, PA. 800-222-2460
Corn Products International
Westchester, IL 708-551-2600

Your Total Sweetener Solution.

Evergreen Sweeteners, Inc
Aventura, FL. 305-931-1321

Evergreen Sweeteners is a full service sweetener distributor serving the entire state of Florida. From bulk liquid sweeteners to bagged sweeteners, Evergreen provides its customers with industry-leading service and unsurpassed quality.

Gateway Food Products Company
Dupo, IL 877-220-1963
Malt Products Corporation
Saddle Brook, NJ 800-526-0180
Paulaur Corporation
Cranbury, NJ. 888-398-8844
Pepsi
Chicago, IL 312-821-1000
PepsiCo
Barrington, IL. 847-842-4652
Reilly Dairy & Food Company
Tampa, FL. 813-839-8458
Roquette America
Keokuk, IA 800-553-7035
Tate & Lyle Staley Company
Decatur, IL 217-423-4411
WCC Honey Marketing
City of Industry, CA 626-855-3086
Westin
Omaha, NE 800-228-6098

High Fructose

Corn Products International
Westchester, IL 708-551-2600

Your Total Sweetener Solution.

Evergreen Sweeteners, Inc
Aventura, FL. 305-931-1321

Evergreen Sweeteners is a full service sweetener distributor serving the entire state of Florida. From bulk liquid sweeteners to bagged sweeteners, Evergreen provides its customers with industry-leading service and unsurpassed quality.

Fruit

Al-Rite Fruits & Syrups
Miami, FL. 305-652-2540
Baker & Baker, Inc.
Schaumburg, IL. 800-593-5777

Baldwin Richardson Foods
Frankfort, IL 866-644-2732

Baldwin Richardson Foods is a liquid ingredient manufacturer specializing in signature sauces, dessert toppings, beverage/pancake syrups, specialty fruit fillings and condiments. Packaging capabilities range from portion control cups and pouches to standard retail and foodservice packs and include industrial drums and totes. Full service R&D and Quality groups dedicated to new product development, with in-house stability and analytical testing. Call for assistance.

Blackberry Patch
Thomasville, GA. 800-853-5598
California Custom Fruits & Flavors
Irwindale, CA 877-558-0056
Cold Hollow Cider Mill
Waterbury Center, VT. 800-327-7537
ConAgra Grocery Products
Irvine, CA 714-680-1000
Da Vinci Gourmet
Seattle, WA 800-640-6779
Dean Distributors
Burlingame, CA 800-792-0816
Eva Gates Homemade Preserves
Bigfork, MT 800-682-4283
GEM Berry Products
Sandpoint, ID 800-426-0498
Great Valley Mills
Barto, PA 800-688-6455
H&H Products Company
Orlando, FL. 407-299-5410
H. Fox & Company
Brooklyn, NY 718-385-4600
Hawaiian Fruit Specialties
Kalaheo, HI. 808-332-9333
Hershey
Mississauga, ON 800-468-1714
Hungerford J Smith Company
Humboldt, TN. 731-784-3461
I Rice & Company
Philadelphia, PA 800-232-6022

Inn Maid Food
Lenox, MA 413-637-2732
J.M. Smucker Company
Orrville, OH 330-682-3000
Jogue Inc
Northville, MI. 800-521-3888
Kerry Ingredients
Beloit, WI 608-362-1651
Knott's Berry Farm Foods
Placentia, CA 800-289-9927
Maple Grove Farms of Vermont
St Johnsbury, VT. 800-525-2540
Minnesota Specialty Crops
McGregor, MN 800-328-6731
Orange Bang
Sylmar, CA 818-833-1000
Pacific Westcoast Foods
Portland, OR 800-874-9333
Phillips Syrup Corporation
Cleveland, OH 216-661-4800
Purity Factories
St.John's, NL. 800-563-3411
Royal Wine Company
Bayonne, NJ 201-437-9131
Sea Breeze Fruit Flavors
Towaco, NJ 800-732-2733
Sugar Plum Farm
Plumtree, NC. 888-257-0019
Summerland Sweets
Summerland, BC. 800-577-1277
Three Vee Food & Syrup Company
Brooklyn, NY 800-801-7330
Valley View Blueberries
Vancouver, WA 360-892-2839
Van Tone Creative Flavors Inc
Terrell, TX. 800-856-0802
Vermont Specialty Food Association
Randolph, VT 802-728-0070
Western Syrup Company
Santa Fe Springs, CA 562-921-4485

Malt Extract

Briess Industries
Chilton, WI 920-849-7711
CHR Hansen
Gretna, LA 504-367-7727
CHR Hansen
Chicago, IL 773-646-2203
Froedtert Malt
Winona, MN 507-454-1535
Grounds for Thought
Bowling Green, OH 419-354-2326
Lake Country Foods
Oconomowoc, WI. 262-567-5521
Malt Products Corporation
Saddle Brook, NJ 800-526-0180
Minnesota Malting Company
Saint Paul, MN 507-263-3911
Novartis Nutrition Corporation
Minneapolis, MN 952-848-6000
Premier Malt Products
Warren, MI 586-443-3355
Roquette America
Keokuk, IA 800-553-7035
Suzanne's Specialties
New Brunswick, NJ 800-762-2135
United Canadian Malt
Peterborough, ON. 800-461-6400

Maple

A Perfect Pear from NapaValley
Napa, CA. 800-553-5753

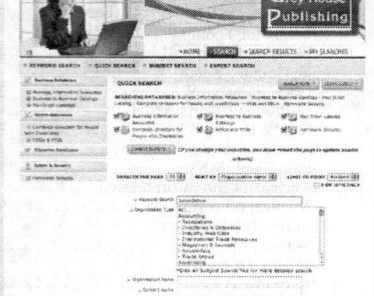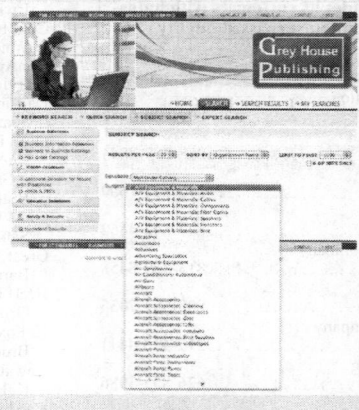

Adirondack Maple Farms
Fonda, NY......................518-853-4022
B&G Foods
Parsippany, NJ..................973-401-6500

Baldwin Richardson Foods
Frankfort, IL.....................866-644-2732

Baldwin Richardson Foods is a liquid ingredient manufacturer specializing in signature sauces, dessert toppings, beverage/pancake syrups, specialty fruit fillings and condiments. Packaging capabilities range from portion control cups and pouches to standard retail and foodservice packs and include industrial drums and totes. Full service R&D and Quality groups dedicated to new product development, with in-house stability and analytical testing. Call for assistance.

Brown Family Farm
Alstead, NH......................866-254-8718
Brown Family Farm
Brattleboro, VT.................888-556-2753
Butternut Mountain Farm
Morrisville, VT..................800-828-2376
Citadelle Maple Syrup Produce Cooperative
Plessisville, QC................819-362-3241
Citadelle Maple Syrup Producers Cooperative
Plessisville, CN................819-362-2830
Confectionery Treasures
Cumberland, MD................301-478-2245
Conway Import Company
Franklin Park, IL................800-323-8801
Coombs Vermont Gourmet
Brattleboro, VT.................888-266-6271
Couture's Maple Shop
Westfield, VT....................800-845-2733
Dean Distributors
Burlingame, CA.................800-792-0816
Dole Pond Maple Products
Jackman, ME....................418-653-5322

EMERLING INTERNATIONAL FOODS, INC.

Emerling International Foods
Buffalo, NY.....................716-833-7381

We supply food manufacturers and food service customers worldwide (since 1988) with bulk ingredients including: Fruits & Vegetables; Juice Concentrates; Herbs & Spices; Oils & Vinegars; Flavors & Colors; Honey & Molasses. We also produce PURE MAPLE SYRUP.

Glorybee Foods
Eugene, OR......................800-456-7923
Green River Chocolates
Hinesburg, VT..................802-246-2652
Heritage Cheese House
Heuvelton, NY..................315-344-2216
Highland Sugarworks
Websterville, VT................800-452-4012
Hillside Lane Farm
Randolph, VT....................802-728-0070
Howard Foods
Danvers, MA....................978-774-6207

Jed's Maple Products
Westfield, VT...................866-478-7388
JMS Specialty Foods
Ripon, WI.......................800-535-5437
Kraft Food Ingredients
Memphis, TN....................901-381-6500
Les Industries Bernard Et Fils
St. Victor, QC..................418-588-6109
Maple Acres
Kewadin, MI.....................231-264-9265
Maple Grove Farms of Vermont
St Johnsbury, VT...............800-525-2540
Maple Hollow
Merrill, WI......................715-536-7251
Maple Mark
Scott-Junction, QC.............800-261-2881
Maple Products
Sherbrooke, QC.................819-569-5161
Mclure's Honey & Maple Products
Littleton, NH...................603-444-6246
Minnesota Specialty Crops
McGregor, MN...................800-328-6731
Moosewood Hollow LLC
Plainfield, VT...................866-463-8733
Phillips Syrup Corporation
Cleveland, OH..................216-661-4800
Pride of Dixie Syrup Company
Jonesboro, AR...................800-530-7654
Richards Maple Products
Chardon, OH....................800-352-4052
Sea Breeze Fruit Flavors
Towaco, NJ......................800-732-2733
Shady Maple Farm
Mississauga, ON................905-206-1455
Spring Tree Maple Products
Brattleboro, VT.................802-254-8784
Subco Foods Inc
Sheboygan, WI..................800-676-5188
Sugarman of Vermont
Hardwick, VT....................800-932-7700
Sugarwoods Farm
Glover, VT.......................800-245-3718
Suzanne's Specialties
New Brunswick, NJ..............800-762-2135
Swisser Sweet Maple
Castorland, NY..................315-346-1034
Turkey Hill Sugarbush
Waterloo, QC....................450-539-4822
Vermont Specialty Food Association
Randolph, VT....................802-728-0070
Wagner Excello Food Products
Broadview, IL...................708-338-4488
Webbpak
Trussville, AL..................800-655-3500

Pancake

Dean Distributors
Burlingame, CA.................800-792-0816
Golden Eagle Syrup Manufacturing Company
Fayette, AL......................205-932-5294
John Gust Foods & Products Corporation
Batavia, IL......................800-756-5886
Knott's Berry Farm Foods
Placentia, CA...................800-289-9927
Pride of Dixie Syrup Company
Jonesboro, AR...................800-530-7654
Royal Crown Bottling Company
Bowling Green, KY..............270-842-8106
Sea Breeze Fruit Flavors
Towaco, NJ......................800-732-2733
Spring Tree Maple Products
Brattleboro, VT.................802-254-8784
T. Marzetti Company
Columbus, OH...................614-846-2232

Tone Products Company
Melrose Park, IL................708-681-3660
Vanlaw Food Products
Fullerton, CA...................714-870-9091
Vermont Country Naturals
Charlotte, VT...................800-528-7021
Whipple Company
Natick, MA......................800-345-2925
Whitfield Foods
Montgomery, AL.................800-633-8790

Toppings

Sundae

California Custom Fruits & Flavors
Irwindale, CA...................877-558-0056
Hungerford J Smith Company
Humboldt, TN...................731-784-3461
I Rice & Company
Philadelphia, PA................800-232-6022

Waffle

Golden Eagle Syrup Manufacturing Company
Fayette, AL......................205-932-5294
Pride of Dixie Syrup Company
Jonesboro, AR...................800-530-7654
Royal Crown Bottling Company
Bowling Green, KY..............270-842-8106
T. Marzetti Company
Columbus, OH...................614-846-2232

Food & Beverage Manufacturers, including Ingredients

A to Z Profiles

1 ## 1-2-3 Gluten Inc
5145 Penton Road
Pittsburgh, PA 15213   843-768-7231
Fax: 843-768-1817   info@123glutengfree.com
www.123glutenfree.com
Gluten-free, wheat-free, nut-free, peanut-free,
dairy-free baking mixes.

2 ## 21st Century Products
PO Box 820606
Ft. Worth, TX 76182   817-282-8000
Fax: 817-581-5883
Processor and exporter of vitamins; also, mineral
and weight loss drinks
    National Sales Director: Richard Fabose
Estimated Sales: $ 1 - 3 Million
Number Employees: 1-4
Type of Packaging: Consumer, Food Service, Private Label, Bulk

3 ## 34 Degrees
3457 Ringsby Ct
Ste 2
Denver, CO 80216   303-861-4818
Fax: 303-484-4664   sales@34-degrees.com
www.34-degrees.com
Lightier, crispier, all-natural crackers.
    Western Regional Sales Manager: Robert
    Harrison
    Public Relations Director: Jennifer Strailey
    General Manager: Jennifer Margoles

4 ## 3M Security Systems Division/Industrial Food Service Solutions
3 M Ctr
St Paul, MN 55144-0001   651-575-1326
Fax: 651-733-2181   dmsayers@mmm.com
www.mmm.com
Safety, maintenance and productivity services and
products for the food and beverage industry.
    Chairman/President/CEO: George Buckley
    SVP/Chief Financial Officer: Patrick Campbell
    CEO: James Mc Nerney Jr
    EVP/Research and Development: Frederick
    Palensky
    EVP/Industrial and Transportation: Hak Cheol
    Shin
    Marketing Development Supervisor: David
    Sayers
    SVP/Marketing and Sales: Robert MacDonald
    SVP/Legal Affairs and General Counsel: Richard
    Ziegler
    EVP/International Operations: Inge Thulin
    EVP/Consumer and Office Business: Moe Nozari
    SVP/Corporate Supply Chain Operations: John
    Woodworth

5 ## 4C Foods Corporation
580 Fountain Ave
Brooklyn, NY 11208-6002   718-272-4242
Fax: 718-272-2899   inthekitchen@4c.com
www.4c.com
Manufacturer and exporter of a variety of food products including iced tea, soft drink mix; imported
cheese; bread crumbs and soup mix.
    Founder and President: John Celauro
    SVP Operations: Wayne Celauro
Number Employees: 100-249
Sq. footage: 210000
Type of Packaging: Food Service, Private Label

6 ## 50th State Poultry Processors
P.O.Box 29490
Honolulu, HI 96820-1890   808-845-5902
Fax: 808-847-7040
Processor of poultry
    President: Darryl Uezu
    VP: Linda Uezu
Estimated Sales: $ 10 - 20 Million
Number Employees: 20-49
Type of Packaging: Consumer, Food Service

7 ## A & M Cookie Company Canada
135 Otonabee Drive
Kitchener, ON N2C 1L7
Canada   519-893-6400
Fax: 519-893-9223   800-265-6508
www.parmalat.ca
Processor of cookies
    President, Bakery Division: Ray Kingdon
    President: John Stephens
    Senior VP Finance Bakery Division: Brian Paluch

    VP Sales: Richard Bordwell
    VP Sales/Marketing: Ted Clarke
Number Employees: 500-999
Parent Co: Parmalat Bakery Group North America
Type of Packaging: Consumer
Brands:
    A & M Cookie

8 ## A Gift Basket by Carmela
64 Magnolia Cir
Longmeadow, MA 01106-2525   413-733-3999
Fax: 413-746-1441   888-481-4438
info@agiftbasketbycarmela.com
www.flowersbycarmela.com
Manufacturer of customized gift baskets; importer of
plum tomatoes, olive oil, balsamic vinegar, coffee,
cookies, cakes, artichokes and gourmet foods from
Italy
    President: Carmela Daniele
    Vice President: Frank Daniele
    Sales/Marketing Executive: David Yzevrre
Estimated Sales: Less than $500,000
Number Employees: 1-4
Sq. footage: 8200
Brands:
    Gift Baskets By Carmela

9 ## A La Carte
5610 W Bloomingdale Ave
Chicago, IL 60639-4110   773-237-3000
Fax: 773-237-3075   800-722-2370
service@alacarteline.com   www.alacarteline.com
Custom promotional products including hard candy
and popcorn in decorative tins, jars, boxes, etc.
    President: Michael Shulkin
    CEO: Adam Robins
    Sales Director: James Janowski
    Purchasing: Marly Robins
Estimated Sales: $ 10 - 20 Million
Number Employees: 50-99
Parent Co: David Scott Industries
Type of Packaging: Food Service, Private Label,
Bulk

10 ## A M Todd Company
1717 Douglas Avenue
Kalamazoo, OR 97402-5623   800-968-2603
Fax: 269-343-3399   269-343-2603
info@amtodd.com   www.amtodd.com
Processor and exporter of natural flavor extracts including alfalfa, black walnut hulls, wild cherry bark,
dandelion, spice, oleoresins, xanthan gum, agar agar,
fruit aromas (essences), essential oils, ethyl vanillin,
papain, coffeeechinacea and ginseng
    President: Bob King
    R&D: John Finley
    Quality Control: Dean Bautz
    Sales: Kyle Griffiths
Estimated Sales: $ 50 - 100 Million
Number Employees: 50-99
Type of Packaging: Bulk
Brands:
    Foenugreek
    Mountain Maple
    Peeled Chinese Ginger
    St. John's Bread

11 ## A Natural Harvest Restaurant
7122 S Jeffery Blvd
Chicago, IL 60649-2426   773-363-3939
Fax: 773-363-7101
Frozen foods with soy products
    General Manager: Cheryl Simms
Estimated Sales: Less than $500,000
Number Employees: 5-9
Type of Packaging: Private Label
Brands:
    Natural Harvest
    Vegetarian Cornmeal
    Vegetarian Tamale

12 ## A Perfect Pear from NapaValley
1283 Monticello Road
Napa, CA 94558-2019   707-251-8532
Fax: 707-257-6830   800-553-5753
info@aperfectpear.net   www.aperfectpear.net
All natural pear products to include vinegars, preserves, jellies, chutneys, marinades, salad dressings
and maple syrup

13 ## A Southern Season
201 S Estes Dr
Chapel Hill, NC 27514-6118   919-929-7133
Fax: 919-942-9274   800-253-5317
customerservice@southernseason.com
www.southernseason.com
Chocolates, preserves, relishes, hams, cookware
    Owner: Michael Cooper Barefoot
    VP Public Relations: Jay White
Estimated Sales: $131 Million
Number Employees: 250-499
Sq. footage: 59000
Other Locations:
    A Southern Season
    Hillsborough NC
Brands:
    A SOUTHERN SEASON
    ALASKA SMOKED SALMON
    ASHBY'S
    BARBERA FRANTIOIA
    CALIFORNIA HARVEST
    CAROLINA CUPBOARD
    CROOK'S
    FRESCOBALDI LAUDEMIO
    GODIVA
    JOHNSTON COUNTY HAMS
    LINDT
    MCEVOY RANCH
    MY GRANDMA'S OF NEW ENGLAND
    NUNEZ DE PRADO
    SPARROW LANE
    TERRE D'OLIVIER

14 ## A Taste of the Kingdom
3773 County Road 210
Kingdom City, MO 65262-2018
USA   573-592-7373
Fax: 573-592-4946   888-592-5080
hotstuff@tasteofkingdom.com
www.tasteofkingdom.com
Natural, kosher condiments and glazes
Estimated Sales: $ 3 - 5 Million
Number Employees: 5-9

15 ## A Zerega's Sons, Inc.
PO Box 241
Fair Lawn, NJ 07410   201-797-1400
Fax: 201-797-0148   sales@zerega.com
www.zerega.com
Dry pasta
    President: John Vermylen
    VP: Rob Vermylen
    Quality Assurance: Gary Rivers
    Assistant Production Manager: P Lee
    Purchasing Manager: Gus Deocampo
Estimated Sales: $100 Million
Number Employees: 225
Sq. footage: 130000
Type of Packaging: Consumer, Food Service, Private Label, Bulk
Brands:
    ANTOINE'S
    COLUMBIA

16 ## A to Z Portion Meats
201 N Main St
Bluffton, OH 45817-1283   419-358-2926
Fax: 419-358-8876   800-338-6328
toddb@atozmeats.com   www.atozmeats.com
Processor of beef, veal and pork including portion
cut.
    President/CEO: Lee Ann Kagy
    Product Specialist: Lois Bender
    VP/Plant Operations: Terry Strahm
    Production Manager: Ed Bucher
    Shipping & Receiving: Chris Sterling
Estimated Sales: $20-50 Million
Number Employees: 20-49
Type of Packaging: Consumer, Food Service, Private Label, Bulk

17 ## A&A Marine & Drydock Company
PO Box 1236
Blenheim, ON N0P 1A0
Canada   519-676-2030
Fax: 519-676-4343   aamarine@kent.net
Manufacturer and exporter of fresh water fish and
fresh, frozen perch and pickerel
    President: George Anderson

Number Employees: 22
Type of Packaging: Consumer, Food Service

18 A&B Ingredients
24 Spielman Rd
Fairfield, NJ 07004-3412   973-227-1390
    Fax: 973-227-0172 gbakal@abingredients.com
        www.abic-consulting.com
Supplier of technical ingredients including rice based starches for the food industry. A&B focus is to deliver unique ingredients that enable its customers to create value added products.
    President: Gill Bakal
    VP: Jim Smith
    Operations Manager: Gil Bakal
Estimated Sales: $10-20 Million
Number Employees: 10-19
Sq. footage: 20000
Type of Packaging: Bulk
Brands:
    GRS
    MIRENAT
    ORIGANOX
    REMY
    REMYLINE
    TOMESSENCE

19 A&C Quinlin Fisheries
1220 Highway 330
McGray, NS B0W 2G0
Canada
                          902-745-2742
                    Fax: 902-745-1788
Processor of salted fish and seafood
    President: Aaron Quinlin
Estimated Sales: $5-10 Million
Number Employees: 20
Type of Packaging: Consumer, Food Service
Brands:
    A&C
    CHELSEA

20 A&G Food & Liquors
6945 S State St
Chicago, IL 60637-4528   773-994-1541
                        Fax: 773-994-9623
Manufacturer of frozen foods and liquor
    President: Louis Kocsis
Estimated Sales: $ 3 - 5 Million
Number Employees: 5-9

21 A-1 Eastern Home MadePickle Company
1832 Johnston St
Los Angeles, CA 90031-3447   323-223-1141
                        Fax: 323-227-8951
Processor of kosher pickles and assorted pickle products
    President: Martin Morhar
    Sales Manager: Gary Sherlin
    Plant Manager: Hector Flores, Jr.
Estimated Sales: $10-20 Million
Number Employees: 20-49
Type of Packaging: Food Service
Brands:
    A-1 Pickle

22 A-Treat Bottling Company
2001 Union Blvd
Allentown, PA 18109-1631   610-434-6139
        Fax: 610-434-5511 800-220-1531
                www.a-treat.com
Soft drinks
    President: Joseph D Garvey Sr
    VP: Curt Thomas
Estimated Sales: $20-50 Million
Number Employees: 50-99
Brands:
    A-TREAT
    BIG BLUE
    GREEN SPOT
    TREAT-UP

23 A. Battaglia ProcessingCompany
3048 W 48th Place
Chicago, IL 60632-2000   773-523-5900
        Fax: 773-523-6469 augbatt@aol.com
            www.beatricepeanuts.com
Processor and exporter of in-shell and shelled peanuts; processor of fresh caramel apples and garlic; importer of Brazil nuts
    President: Joseph Battaglia
    Marketing: John Roschie
    Sales Director: August Battaglia
    Production Manager: H Singh

Estimated Sales: $20-50 Million
Number Employees: 20-49
Type of Packaging: Consumer, Food Service, Private Label, Bulk
Brands:
    Battaglia
    Beatrice
    Eatable Nuts & Snacks

24 A. Bauer's Mustard
5340 Metropolitan Ave
Flushing, NY 11385-1218   718-821-3570
    Fax: 718-366-3055 bart@abauersmustard.com
            www.abauersmustard.com
Processor of prepared mustard and mustard with horseradish
    President: Bart Druery
Number Employees: 1-4
Type of Packaging: Consumer, Food Service
Brands:
    A. BAUER'S

25 A. Camacho
2502 Walden Woods Dr
Plant City, FL 33566-7167   813-305-4534
        Fax: 813-305-4546 800-881-4534
            www.acamacho-usa.com
Manufacturer of olives
    CEO: Bret Milligan
    VP of Sales: John Nordquist
Estimated Sales: $ 10 - 20 Million
Number Employees: 20-49
Parent Co: Angel Camacho Group
Other Locations:
    Plant City FL
    Erlanger KY
    Chicago IL
    Antioch TN
    Atlanta GA
    Fond Du Lac WI
    Preston MD
    City of Commerce CA
    Houston TX
    Garland TX
    Portland OR
    Dayton NJ
    Manteca CA
Brands:
    BULERIAS
    CHRISTOS
    FRAGATA
    PRIDE OF SPAIN
    THE JUG

26 A. Duda & Sons
3975 20th St # K
Vero Beach, FL 32960-2493   772-978-5700
        Fax: 772-978-5705 800-248-3832
            les@duda.com www.duda.com
Citrus and juice.
    Manager: Betsy Sumner
    Sales Manager: Les Crocker
Parent Co: A. Duda & Sons

27 A. Duda & Sons
PO Box 620257
Oviedo, FL 32762   407-365-2111
            Fax: 407-365-2010 www.duda.com
Fruits and vegetables
    President/COO: Dan Duda
    VP Customer Development: Mark Bassetti
    Category R&D Director: John Castro
    VP Operations: Dean Diefenthaler
Estimated Sales: $500 Million to $1 Billion
Number Employees: 500-999

28 A. Duda & Sons
P.O.Box 2386
Salinas, CA 93902-2386   831-424-6408
            Fax: 831-424-1863 gdo@duda.com
                        www.duda.com
Vegetables; foodservice and export.
    President: Bob Gray
    Sales Manager: Grant Oswalt
Estimated Sales: $ 20 - 50 Million
Number Employees: 20-49
Parent Co: A. Duda & Sons

29 (HQ)A. Duda & Sons
P.O.Box 620257
Oviedo, FL 32762-0257   407-365-2111
            Fax: 407-365-2010 acd@duda.com
                        www.duda.com

Celery: diced, canned, frozen. Grower, shipper, marketer and exporter of citrus, vegetables, fruit, sugarcane and cattle.
    President/CEO: Joseph Duda
    VP: Richard Hanas
    Industrial Sales Manager: Amy Duda
Estimated Sales: $ 50 - 100 Million
Number Employees: 1,000-4,999
Parent Co: A. Duda & Sons
Type of Packaging: Consumer, Food Service

30 A. Duda & Sons
6000 State Road 29 S
Labelle, FL 33935-9555
            Fax: 863-675-0231 800-440-3265
                sjk@duda.com www.duda.com
Citrus nurseries and groves, frozen citrus juice concentrate plant, vegetables.
    President/CEO: Joseph Duda
    Plant Manager: Henry Hiesler
Estimated Sales: $ 10 - 20 Million
Number Employees: 100-249
Parent Co: A Duda & Sons
Brands:
    A.P. Duda
    Dandy

31 A. Duda Farm Fresh Foods
P.O.Box 2015
Belle Glade, FL 33430-7015   561-996-7621
            Fax: 561-996-1354 info@duda.com
                        www.duda.com
Manufacturer, marketer and exporter of fresh and processed vegetables and citrus, as well as sugarcane
    President: Ferdinand Duda
    VP: Ed Hamilton
    Sales Manager: Les Crocker
Estimated Sales: $2.5-5 Million
Number Employees: 100-249
Type of Packaging: Consumer, Food Service, Private Label, Bulk
Brands:
    DANDY

32 A. Gagliano Company
P.O.Box 511382
300 N Jefferson St
Milwaukee, WI 53202-5920   414-272-1515
            Fax: 414-272-7215 800-272-1516
    info@agagliano.com www.agagliano.com
Ripener, packer and importer of fresh fruits and vegetables. Warehouse providing cold storage
    President: Tony Gagliano
    VP: Mike Gagliano
    Warehouse Manager: Rick Alsum
Estimated Sales: $20 Million
Number Employees: 20-49
Number of Brands: 1
Number of Products: 500
Sq. footage: 200000
Type of Packaging: Consumer, Food Service, Private Label, Bulk
Brands:
    A. GAGLIANO

33 A. Lassonde, Inc.
170 5th Avenue
Rougemont, QC J0L 1M0
Canada
                          514-878-1057
        Fax: 514-861-9280 info@a-lassonde.com

www.lassonde.com/a_lassonde/en/adult/0_0/0_e.asp

Manufactures and processes fruit juices and drinks.
    President/Chief Executive Officer: Jean Gattuso
    Deputy CEO Management & Administration: Luc Provencher
    VP/Finance & Treasurer: Jean Tessier
    VP/Information Technologies: Pierre Brault
    Deputy CEO Research & Development/QC: Yves Dumont
    Executive VP Sales & Marketing: Peter Mattson
    Public Relations Director: Mario Allaire
    VP/General Manager Operations: Sylvain Mayrand
    Deputy CEO/HR/Communications/IT: Michel Simard
    VP Purchasing: Mario Boulay
Number Employees: 500
Type of Packaging: Food Service
Brands:
    Allen's
    Bright's

Fruite
Graves
Martins
Mont Rouge Nature's Best
Oasis Classic
Oasis Collection Premium
Oasis Del Sol
Rich n' Ready
Rougemont
Sun-Maid
SunLike
Sunkist
Tetley
Tropical Grove
Tropical Oasis

34 A. Nonini Winery
2640 N Dickenson Ave
Fresno, CA 93723-9644   559-275-1936
        Fax: 209-241-7119 www.noiniwinery.com
Wine
    President: James Jordan
    Sales Representative: James Jordan
    GM: Thomas Nonini
Estimated Sales: $1-2.5 Million
Number Employees: 1-4
Type of Packaging: Private Label
Brands:
    A NONINI

35 A. Rafanelli Winery
4685 W Dry Creek Rd
Healdsburg, CA 95448-8124   707-433-1385
        Fax: 707-433-3836 www.arafanelliwinery.com
Manufacturer of wines which include; Zinfandel,
Cabernet Sauvignon and Merlot
    Owner: David Rafanelli
Estimated Sales: $500,000-$1 Million
Number Employees: 5-9
Number of Brands: 1
Number of Products: 1
Type of Packaging: Private Label
Brands:
    A. Rafanelli

36 A. Smith Bowman Distillery
1 Bowman Dr # 100
Fredericksburg, VA 22408-7350   540-373-4555
    Fax: 540-371-2236 Bowmansales@sazerac.com
                www.bowmanco.com
Processor and exporter of bourbon, scotch, rum, te-
quila, whiskey, gin and vodka
    CEO: Mark Brown
Estimated Sales: $20-50 Million
Number Employees: 20-49
Number of Brands: 2
Number of Products: 9
Brands:
    BOWMAN'S
    VIRGINIA GENTLEMAN

37 A. Stein Meat Products
5600 1st Ave # 22
Brooklyn, NY 11220-2551   718-492-0760
        Fax: 718-439-0065 www.steinmeat.com
Processor of beef, veal, tongue, pastrami, chicken
and pork.
    President: Abraham Mora
    VP: Howard Mora
    VP: Alan Buxbaum
    Purchasing: Alan Buxbaum
Estimated Sales: $20-50 Million
Number Employees: 20-49
Type of Packaging: Consumer

38 A. Thomas Food Service
2055 Nelson Miller Pkwy
Louisville, KY 40223-2185   502-253-2000
        Fax: 502-253-2020 800-253-2020
        jathomas@athomasfoodservice.com
        www.athomasfoodservice.com
Supplier of the finest butcher shop quality meats
    President: Anthony Thomas
Estimated Sales: $100+ Million
Number Employees: 50-99
Sq. footage: 82000
Type of Packaging: Food Service

39 A.C. Calderoni & Company
P.O.Box 486
Brisbane, CA 94005-0486   415-468-2282
        Fax: 415-468-5967 866-468-1897
        calderoni@value.net www.accalderoni.com

Juices, juice concentrates, and cocktail mixes
    President: Bob Baciocco
    Purchasing: Scott Hawley
Estimated Sales: $2.5-5 Million
Number Employees: 1-4
Brands:
    A.C. CALDERONI

40 A.C. Kissling Company
161 E Allen St
Philadelphia, PA 19125-4194   215-423-4700
    Fax: 215-425-0525 800-445-1943
Manufacturer and wholesaler/distributor of sauer-
kraut
    President: R W Kissling Jr
Estimated Sales: $2 Million
Number Employees: 10-19
Type of Packaging: Consumer
Brands:
    Kissling

41 A.C. Legg Inc
PO Box 709
Calera, AL 35040   205-324-3451
        Fax: 205-668-7835 sales@aclegg.com
                www.aclegg.com
Seasonings.
    Owner/President/CEO: James Purvis
    Public Relations: Dennis Hulsey
Estimated Sales: $25.6 Million
Number Employees: 130
Sq. footage: 131500
Type of Packaging: Food Service, Bulk

42 A.C. Petersen Farms
240 Park Rd
West Hartford, CT 06119-2040   860-233-8483
    Fax: 860-233-8483 cadenton@comcast.net
                www.whchamber.com/acpetersen
Processor of ice cream
    Owner: Catherine Denton
    President: Allen Petersen
    Executive VP: Raymond Petersen
Estimated Sales: $20-50 Million
Number Employees: 10-19
Type of Packaging: Consumer, Food Service, Pri-
vate Label, Bulk

43 (HQ)A.L. Bazzini Company
200 Food Center Dr
Bronx, NY 10474-7030   718-842-8644
    Fax: 718-842-8582 800-228-0172
    bazzininut@aol.com www.bazzinionline.com
Nuts, seed, dried fruit and chocolates
    Owner/President: Rocco Damato
    VP: JoAnn Marino
Estimated Sales: $45 Million
Number Employees: 200
Sq. footage: 70000
Other Locations:
    Allentown PA
Brands:
    Bazzini
    Candy Club
    House of Bazzini
    Natures Club
    Nut Club

44 A.L. Duck
26231 River Run Trail
Zuni, VA 23898-3215   757-562-2387
Manufacturer of smoked sausages
    President: Brenda Redd
Estimated Sales: $1-2.5 Million
Number Employees: 5-9
Type of Packaging: Consumer, Food Service

45 (HQ)A.M. Braswell Jr. Food Company
P.O.Box 485
Statesboro, GA 30459-0485   912-764-6191
    Fax: 912-489-1572 800-673-9388
    customerservice@braswells.com
                www.braswells.com
Manufacturer of pear and fig preserves, fruit butter,
artichoke pickles and relish and dipping sauces
    Owner: Vinny Kochotta
    President: Andrew Oliver
    CFO: Vincent Kochetta
    VP: Stuart Saussy
    Production: Frank Farr
    Purchasing: Penny Willams
Estimated Sales: $20-50 Million
Number Employees: 50-99

Number of Brands: 4
Number of Products: 200
Sq. footage: 50000
Type of Packaging: Consumer, Food Service, Pri-
vate Label
Brands:
    BRASWELL'S
    CITRUS CREATIONS
    SOUTHERN TRADITIONS
    THE GIFT OF FLORIDA

46 A.M. Todd Company
1717 Douglas Ave
Kalamazoo, MI 49007-1600   269-343-2603
        Fax: 269-343-3399 800-968-2603
        info@amtodd.com www.amtodd.com
Manufacturer of peppermint, spearmint and lime oils
    Chairman/CEO/President: Henry Todd
    CFO/COO: Catherine Miller
    CEO: Henry W Todd Sr
    VP Marketing/Sales/Business Development: Tony
    Willard
Estimated Sales: $100+ Million
Number Employees: 50-99
Parent Co: Frutarom USA
Other Locations:
    Eugene OR
    Montgomeryville PA
    Mill Valley CA
Brands:
    Crystal White
    Rose Mitcham

47 A.T. Gift Company
RR 3
Box 802
Harpers Ferry, WV 25425-9310   304-876-6680
                Fax: 304-876-2757
Manufacturer of wine related products
    President: Angela Gift
    Sales Manager: Frank Gift
Estimated Sales: Less than $500,000
Number Employees: 2

48 A.W. Jantzi & Sons
PO Box 27
Wellesley, ON N0B 2T0
Canada   519-656-2400
    Fax: 519-656-3370 info@wellappleproducts.com
                www.wellappleproducts.com
Manufacturer of apple cider and apple butter
    President: Steve Jantzi
    Operations Manager: Kevin Jantzi
Number Employees: 15
Sq. footage: 10000
Type of Packaging: Consumer, Bulk
Brands:
    Wellesley

49 ABC Tea House
14520 Arrow Hwy
Baldwin Park, CA 91706-1732   626-813-1333
        Fax: 626-813-1338 888-220-3988
        info@teaone.com www.teaone.com
Tea and teabags
    President: Thomas Shu
    Vice President: Thomas Shu
    Production Manager: West Huang
Estimated Sales: $ 5-10 Million
Number Employees: 5-9
Brands:
    Abc Tea (A Better Choice)

50 ABITEC Corporation
P.O.Box 1759
Janesville, WI 53547-1759   608-752-9007
        Fax: 608-755-9842 800-457-1977
        wi.logistics@abiteccorp.com
                www.abiteccorp.com
Manufacturer and exporter of surfactants and vege-
table oils
    Eastern Regional Sales Manager: Anish Parker
    VP Sales/Food Director: Larry Werner
    Plant Manager: Ed Becerra
Estimated Sales: $10-20 Million
Number Employees: 20-49
Parent Co: Associated British Foods
Other Locations:
    Janesville IL
    Wisconsin IL
    Paris IL
Brands:
    Acconon
    Accoquet
    Caplube

Capmul
Caprol

51 AC Gunter
790 Welltown Road
Clear Brook, VA 22624-1720   540-662-5484
Sport and other beverages
Estimated Sales: Less than $500,000
Number Employees: 1-4

52 AC Legg
P.O.Box 709
Calera, AL 35040-0709   205-324-3451
          Fax: 205-668-7835   800-422-5344
          sales@ACLegg.com   www.aclegg.com
Processor of custom-blended seasonings for meat,
poultry, seafood and snack foods
     President: James Purvis
     CEO: James Purvis
     VP: Sandra Purvis
Estimated Sales: $20-50 Million
Number Employees: 100-249
Sq. footage: 130000
Type of Packaging: Food Service, Private Label,
Bulk
Brands:
     Legg's Old Plantation

53 ACATRIS
2770 Portland Drive
Oakville, ON N0E 1L0
Canada   905-829-2414
     Fax: 905-829-8097   sales@ca.acatris.com
          www.acatris.com
Blended dough conditioners, antioxidants and anti-
oxidant solutions, release agents, lubricants, soy
flour, isoflavones, vitamin/mineral enrichment
blends, vegetable oils, etc
     President: Vern Wilson
     CFO: Frank Hollingworth
     Sales: Rob Le Guillou
     Production: Alan Edney
     Purchasing: Paul St. Pierre
Estimated Sales: $35 Million
Sq. footage: 44000
Parent Co: Royal Schouten Group
Type of Packaging: Private Label
Brands:
     ALUBE
     DADEX
     DAEDOL
     DAMINET
     DEVONINCIDE
     EXTOL
     LESOY
     PROMASE
     SOYLIFE

54 ACH Food Companies
P.O.Box 34232
Memphis, TN 38184-0232   901-377-9016
          Fax: 901-377-0476   800-691-1106
               www.brimsnacks.com
New product development; rice side dishes, shorten-
ing, cooking oils, regular and flavored nondairy
creamers, cooking spray, balsamic vinegar, aerosol
cheese products
     Owner: Terry Brimhall
Parent Co: Associated British Foods

55 ACH Food Companies
7171 Goodlett Farms Pkwy
Cordova, TN 38016-4909   901-381-3000
          Fax: 901-381-2968   800-691-1106
          information@achfood.com
          www.achfood.com/index2.htm
Premier manufacturer of sophisticated oil-based
products
     President/CEO: Daniel Antonelli
     VP Finance: Daryl Vrbas
     Chief Financial Officer: Jeffrey Atkins
     VP Strategy/Development: Jack Straton
     VP Product Development/Quality: Pete Friedman
     Chief Information Officer: Donnie Steward
     VP Operations: Bill Wells
     VP/GM Consumer Brands Group: Chris Mings
Number Employees: 1,000-4,999
Parent Co: Associates British Foods, PLC
Brands:
     ACCOLAD
     APEX
     ASTRAL
     CAPLITE
     HUMKOTE

LIGUIMIX
NUTRILIPIAS
TRISUN
VICTORY

56 ACH Food Companies
87 Pickett District Rd
New Milford, CT 06776-4412   860-355-9421
     Fax: 860-354-9672 www.achfood.com/index2.htm
Manufacturer and packaging of shortening and
nonaerosol cooking sprays and oils including cano-
la, corn, olive, sunflower and vegetable; importer of
olive oil
     Manager: Marlene Bialecki
     General Manager: Steve Hunt
Estimated Sales: $ 20 - 50 Million
Number Employees: 20-49
Sq. footage: 70000
Parent Co: Associated British Foods
Type of Packaging: Consumer, Food Service, Pri-
vate Label

57 ACH Food Companies
7171 Goodlett Farms Pkwy
Cordova, TN 38016-4909   901-381-3000
          Fax: 901-381-2968   800-691-1106
               information@achfood.com
               www.achfood.com/index2.htm
Manufacturer of edible oils and specialty grocery
products
     President/CEO: Daniel Antonelli
     CFO: Jeffrey Atkins
     VP Operations: Bill Wells
Estimated Sales: $100-500 Million
Number Employees: 1,000-4,999
Sq. footage: 340000
Type of Packaging: Consumer, Food Service, Pri-
vate Label, Bulk
Brands:
     ARGO
     FRYMAX
     KARO
     MAZOLA
     SWEETEX
     WHIRL

58 ACH Food Companies
7171 Goodlett Farms Pkwy
Cordova, TN 38016   901-381-3000
          Fax: 901-381-2968   800-691-1106
     contact@achfood.com   www.achfood.com
Oils, spices, seasonings and sauces, baking enhance-
ments
     CEO: Richard Rankin
     EVP/CFO: Jeff Atkins
     VP: Carmen Sciackitano
     EVP/Chief Marketing Officer: Charlie Martin
     VP Human Resources: Sarah Blankenship
     VP Manufacturing: Bill Wells
Estimated Sales: $ 5 Billion
Number Employees: 1,000-4,999
Parent Co: Associated British Foods
Brands:
     ARGO
     DURKEE
     FLEISCHMANN'S
     FRENCH'S
     KARO
     KINGSFORD'S
     MAZOLA
     PATAK'S
     SPICE ISLAND'S
     TONE'S
     WEBER SEASONINS

59 ACH Food Companies
1115 Tiffany St
Boyceville, WI 54725-9594   715-643-2600
          Fax: 715-643-2221 www.ohly.com
Food and nutrition facility and custom drying opera-
tion. Spray drying, roll drying and blending capabili-
ties. Dried honey, vinegar, Worcestershire, mustards,
soy sauce, cheese products, specialty creamers and
beverage bases; food and non-food toll services.
     Manager: Brian Wolff
     General Manager: Dan Schneider
     Purchasing Manager: Brian Wolff
Estimated Sales: $20-50 Million
Number Employees: 5-9
Sq. footage: 37000
Parent Co: Associated British Foods

60 ACH Food Companies
7171 Goodlett Farms Pkwy
Cordova, TN 38016-4909   901-381-3000
          Fax: 901-381-2968   800-691-1106
               www.achfood.com/index2.htm
Two plants: One produces vegetable, corn and cano-
la oils and is distribution center for rice, pan sprays,
non-dairy creamers and baking mixes. The second
plant processes high quality fats and oils.
     President: Dan Antonelli
     Vice President: Peter Jackson
     Marketing Director: Nelson Wurth
     Operations Manager: Rick Wade
     Production Manager: Patrick Roy
     Plant Manager: Perry Willingham
Number Employees: 1,000-4,999
Sq. footage: 70000
Parent Co: Associated British Foods
Type of Packaging: Private Label

61 ACH Food Companies
1201 E Morton Ave
Jacksonville, IL 62650-2988   217-245-4131
     Fax: 217-243-4757 www.achfood.com/index2.htm
Manufacturer of oil-based products and specialty
products
     Manager: Tim Weston
     CFO: Jeffrey Atkins
     Senior VP: Carmen Sciackitano
Estimated Sales: $100+ Million
Number Employees: 250-499
Sq. footage: 417000
Parent Co: Associated British Foods

62 ACH Food Companies
7171 Goodlett Farms Pkwy
Cordova, TN 38016-4909   901-381-3000
          Fax: 901-381-2968   800-691-1106
               www.achfood.com/index2.htm
Processed cheese: sliced, loaf, bulk and shredded.
     President: Dan Antonelli
     Vice President: Peter Jackson
     Marketing Director: Nelson Wurth
     Operations Manager: Rick Wade
     Production Manager: Patrick Roy
     Plant Manager: Perry Willingham
Estimated Sales: $ 50 - 100 Million
Number Employees: 1,000-4,999
Sq. footage: 114000
Parent Co: Associated British Foods
Type of Packaging: Private Label

63 ACH Food Companies, Inc.
7171 Goodlett Farms Pkwy
Cordova, TN 38016-4909   901-381-3000
          Fax: 901-381-2968   800-691-1106
               information@achfood.com
               www.achfood.com/index2.htm
Cake, baking and bread mixes, icings, fruit fillings
and extended shelf life enzymes.
     President/CEO: Daniel Antonelli
     Senior VP/General Counsel: Carmen Sciackitano
     Chief Financial Officer: Jeffrey Atkins
     VP: James House
     Marketing Manager: Suzanne Brock
     VP, Human Resources: Deborah Murdock
     VP Operations: Joe Sharp
     President/Commercial Products Group: Gary
     Harmon
Number Employees: 1,000-4,999
Parent Co: Associated British Foods
Type of Packaging: Food Service, Private Label,
Bulk

64 (HQ)ADH Health Products
215 N Route 303
Congers, NY 10920-1726   845-268-0027
          Fax: 845-268-2988   800-292-6002
     info@adhhealth.com   www.adhhealth.com
Processor and exporter of amino acids, vitamins,
minerals, herbs and nutritional supplements. Private
label manufacturer of vitamins and dietary
supplement
     CEO: Balram Advani
     CEO: Balram Advani
Estimated Sales: $5-10 Million
Number Employees: 50-99
Sq. footage: 30000
Type of Packaging: Private Label
Brands:
     Centra-Vit
     Daily Multiple S/C
     One Daily Essential With Iron
     Prenatal Formula

Stress Formula With Zinc
Thera-M Multiple

65 ADM
4666 Faries Pkwy
Decatur, IL 62525   217-424-5200
        Fax: 217-424-6196 800-637-5843
                www.admworld.com
Manufacturer of vegetable oil
    Chairman/President/CEO: Patricia Woertz
    EVP/CFO: Steven Mills
*Estimated Sales:*K
Number Employees: 28,200
Parent Co: Archer Daniels Midland Company
Type of Packaging: Bulk

66 ADM
400 W Erie Road
Marshall, MN 56258-2736   507-537-2676
        Fax: 507-537-2643 800-328-4150
                www.admworld.com
Manufacturer of unmodified corn starch and unmodified and high fructose corn syrup
    Chairman/CEO: G Allen Andreas
    President/COO: Paul Mulhollem
    Purchasing Agent: Brad Mortland
Number Employees: 200
Type of Packaging: Bulk

67 (HQ)ADM Cocoa
12500 W Carmen Ave
Milwaukee, WI 53225-6199   414-358-5700
        Fax: 414-358-5880 800-558-9958
                www.adm.com
Manufacturer and exporter of ingredient chocolate and cocoa products
    President: Mark Bemis
    VP: Dennis Whalen
    Sales: Anthony Sepich
    Plant Manager: Dave Pollock
Estimated Sales: $50-100 Million
Parent Co: Archer Daniels Midland Company
Type of Packaging: Consumer, Private Label, Bulk
Brands:
    Ambrosia
    De Zaan
    Merckens

68 ADM Cocoa
12500 W Carmen Ave
Milwaukee, WI 53225-6199   414-358-5700
        Fax: 414-358-5880 800-558-9958
    admcocoa@admworld.com www.admworld.com
Product line includes a full range of natural and dutched powders, chocolate and compound chips and chunks, as well as chocolate and confectionery coatings
    VP: Dennis Whalen
    Confectionary Sales/Marketing: John Zima
    Sales: Anthony Sepich
    Purchasing Agent: Bob Redman
Estimated Sales: Below $500,000
Number Employees: 250-499
Parent Co: Archer Daniels Midland Company
Type of Packaging: Private Label, Bulk
Brands:
    Ambrosia
    De Zaan
    Merckens

69 ADM Cocoa
150 Oakland St
Mansfield, MA 02048-1512   508-339-8921
        Fax: 508-261-8921 800-637-2536
                www.admworld.com
    Plant Manager: Frank O'Korn
Estimated Sales: $ 50 - 100 Million
Number Employees: 50-99
Parent Co: Archer Daniels Midland Company
Brands:
    AMBROSIA
    MERCKENS

70 ADM Cocoa
600 Ellis St
Glassboro, NJ 08028-2435   856-881-4000
        Fax: 856-881-0462 www.admworld.com
Manufacturers of chocolate liquor in powdered form for use in wet or dry mix; natural and alkalized cocoa powder in all fat ranges
    Plant Manager: Allison Piers
Estimated Sales: $20-50 Million
Number Employees: 50-99
Parent Co: Archer Daniels Midland Company

Type of Packaging: Bulk

71 ADM Corn Processing
P.O.Box 1470
Decatur, IL 62525-1820   217-424-5200
        Fax: 217-424-2572 800-553-8411
    info@admworld.com www.admworld.com
Manufacturer of dextrose, crystalline fructose, maltodextrins, corn syrups, high fructose corn syrups, corn starches, alcohol food grade(190 proofs)
    Chairman/President/CEO: Patricia Woertz
    EVP/CFO: Steven Mills
    VP: Daniel Larson
Estimated Sales: $1.1 Billion
Number Employees: 10,000+
Parent Co: Archer Daniels Midland Company
Type of Packaging: Bulk
Brands:
    Clintose
    Cornsweet

72 ADM Ethanol Sales
4666 E Faries Parkway
Decatur, IL 62526-5666   217-424-2565
                www.admworld.com
Provide grain neutral spirits (GNS) to the food industry. These alcohols are 192 proof and are further processed by alcohol bottling companies to meet their specifications
    President: Terry Myers
Parent Co: Archer Daniels Midland Company
Type of Packaging: Bulk

73 ADM Food Ingredients
100 S Paniplus Roadway
Olathe, KS 66061   913-782-8800
        Fax: 913-782-8801 800-255-6637
    bcriss@admworld.com www.admworld.com
Food ingredients: dough conditioners, cake and donut conditioners, yeast foods, milk replacers, emulsifiers, diglycerides, enzymes, release agents, leavening agents, stabilizers, flavors/colors, mixes/bases/concentrates, and enrichmentproducts. Also produces wheat glutens, wheat starches, liquid honey, liquid molasses, and dry honeys.
    President: Terry Myers
Estimated Sales: $ 20 - 50 Million
Number Employees: 50-99
Parent Co: Archer Daniels Midland Company
Type of Packaging: Bulk

74 ADM Food Oils
4666 E Faries Parkway
Decatur, IL 62526-5666   217-424-5467
        Fax: 217-424-5467 800-637-5866
                www.admworld.com
Producer of vegetable oils and shortenings made from soybean, canola, corn, cottonseed, sunflower, peanut, coconut, palm kernel and palm oil
    President: Terry Myers

75 ADM Growmark
4666 E Faries Parkway
Decatur, IL 62526-5666   217-451-8602
        Fax: 217-424-5580 www.admworld.com
Manufacturer of corn and soybean products
    President: Brian Burke
Parent Co: Archer Daniels Midland Company
Type of Packaging: Bulk

76 ADM Lecithin & Monoglycerides
4666 E Faries Parkway
Decatur, IL 62526-5666   217-451-4119
        Fax: 217-451-4119 800-637-5843
    lechithinsales@admworld.com
                www.admworld.com
Product line includes standard, complexed, modified and deoiled lecithins, and is anchored by Ultralec, an innovative deoiled lecithin that offers bland flavor and clean smell. Our destilled monoglycerides are widely used in foodapplications as an emulsifier or starch complexing agent
    President: Terry Myers

77 (HQ)ADM Milling Company
P.O.Box 7007
Shawnee Mission, KS 66207-0007 913-266-6300
        Fax: 913-491-0035 www.admworld.com
Manufacturer and exporter of pancake mixes, hard wheat flour, Canadian wheat flour, specialty wheat flours, specialty products, and corn meal, including yellow and white
    President: Craig Fisher
    VP Sales: Loren Urqhart

Estimated Sales: $50-100 Million
Number Employees: 1,000-4,999
Parent Co: Archer Daniels Midland Company
Type of Packaging: Consumer, Food Service, Private Label, Bulk
Brands:
    Pillsbury Flour

78 ADM Milling Company
P.O.Box 609
Jackson, TN 38302-0609   731-424-3535
    Fax: 731-423-1652 c_coughlin@admworld.com
                www.admworld.com
Manufacturer of corn
    Telecommunications: Myles Grant
    Production Manager: David Maness
    Plant Manager: Chip Coughlin
    Purchasing Manager: Mike Sadler
Estimated Sales: $100-500 Million
Number Employees: 100-249
Number of Brands: 9
Number of Products: 25
Sq. footage: 150000
Parent Co: Archer Daniels Midland Company
Type of Packaging: Consumer, Food Service, Private Label, Bulk

79 ADM Milling Company
1200 S Mill Rd
Arkansas City, KS 67005-3764   620-442-6200
        Fax: 620-442-2309 www.admworld.com
Manufacturer and exporter of wheat flour
    President: Doug Goff
    Plant Manager: Doug Goff
    Purchasing Agent: Chris Taylor
Estimated Sales: $20-50 Million
Number Employees: 50-99
Parent Co: Archer Daniels Midland Company
Type of Packaging: Food Service, Bulk

80 ADM Milling Company
1120 King St # 1
Chattanooga, TN 37403-4305   423-756-0503
        Fax: 423-265-6745 www.admworld.com
Manufacturer of bakery flour
    GM: Lawrence Guenther
    Human Resources: Shannon Hayes
    Sales/Marketing Executive: Jack McMenus
Estimated Sales: $50-100 Million
Number Employees: 50-99
Parent Co: Archer Daniels Midland Company
Type of Packaging: Bulk

81 ADM Milling Company
P.O.Box 3268
Cleveland, TN 37320-3268   423-476-7551
        Fax: 423-478-2023 www.admworld.com
Manufacturer of flour
    Office/Lab Manager: Darrell Cooper
    Plant Manager: Brett Poland
Estimated Sales: $10-20 Million
Number Employees: 10-19
Parent Co: Archer Daniels Midland Company
Type of Packaging: Consumer, Food Service

82 ADM Milling Company
3501 Hiawatha Ave
Minneapolis, MN 55406-2526   612-729-2301
        Fax: 612-729-9321 800-528-7877
                www.admworld.com
Manufacturer of wheat flour
    Chairman: Jeffrey Skiba
    Plant Manager: Larry Glerum
Estimated Sales: $20-50 Million
Number Employees: 20-49
Sq. footage: 36000
Parent Co: Archer Daniels Midland Company
Type of Packaging: Food Service

83 ADM Milling Company
P.O.Box 427
Carthage, MO 64836-0427   417-358-2197
        Fax: 417-358-6632 www.admworld.com
Manufacturer of wheat flour
    Owner/President: Craig Hamlin
    Operations Manager: Steve Peterson
    Plant Manager: Jeremy Rupp
Estimated Sales: $ 20 - 50 Million
Number Employees: 20-49
Parent Co: Archer Daniels Midland Company
Type of Packaging: Bulk

84 ADM Milling Company
P.O.Box 7007
Shawnee Mission, KS 66207-0007   913-266-6300
          Fax: 913-491-0035 www.admworld.com
Processor and exporter of flour
     President: Craig Fisher
     Plant Manager: Les Voth
Number Employees: 1,000-4,999
Parent Co: Archer Daniels Midland Company
Type of Packaging: Consumer, Bulk

85 ADM Milling Company
7585 Danbro Crescent
Mississauga, ON L5N 6P9
Canada
          905-819-7001
     Fax: 905-819-9768 800-267-8492
          www.admworld.com
Manufacturer of flour including hard and soft wheat,
also mix products
     Director: Dave Newhook
     Quality Control: Sheliagh Arney
     Sales: Robin Beatty
Number Employees: 22
Parent Co: Archer Daniels Midland Company

86 ADM Milling Company
P.O.Box 31155
Charlotte, NC 28231-1155   704-332-3165
          Fax: 704-333-1926 www.admworld.com
Manufacturer of soft and hard wheat flour
     Commercial Manager: Dennis Tucker
     Plant Manager: Brandon Cornwell
Estimated Sales:$20-50 Million
Number Employees: 20-49
Parent Co: Archer Daniels Midland Company
Type of Packaging: Bulk

87 ADM Milling Company
P.O.Box 338
Abilene, KS 67410-0338   785-263-1631
          Fax: 785-263-7583 www.admworld.com
Processor and exporter of bulgur wheat and malted
barley flour
     Manager: Brenda Frey
     General Manager: Brenda Fry
     Plant Superintendent: Ken Huston
Estimated Sales:$20-50 Million
Number Employees: 20-49
Parent Co: Archer Daniels Midland Company
Type of Packaging: Consumer, Private Label, Bulk

88 ADM Milling Company
2301 E Trent Ave
Spokane, WA 99202-3867   509-534-2636
          Fax: 509-534-1040 www.admworld.com
Processor and exporter of flour
     Manager: Shawn Lindhorst
     Plant Supervisor: Terry Jones
     Purchasing Agent: Bill Parr
Estimated Sales:$20-50 Million
Number Employees: 50-99
Parent Co: Archer Daniels Midland Company
Type of Packaging: Consumer, Food Service, Bulk

89 ADM Milling Company
1300 W Carroll Ave # 2
Chicago, IL 60607-1165   312-666-2465
          Fax: 312-666-4277 www.admworld.com
Processor of flour including cookie, pastry, cake and
bread
     President: Jim Gill
     Sales/Marketing Executive: Stephanie Karau
     General Manager: Jim Gill
Estimated Sales:$20-50 Million
Number Employees: 20-49
Parent Co: Archer Daniels Midland Company
Type of Packaging: Bulk

90 ADM Milling Company
P.O.Box 7007
Shawnee Mission, KS 66207-0007   913-266-6300
          Fax: 913-491-0035 800-422-1688
          jim-brainard@admworld.com
Processes enough wheat, oats, rice, barley, corn and
sorghum to produce more than 400 ingredients, primarily for the baking and food industries. Mills
wheat flour for breads, cakes, pasta, cookies, and
crackers. Mills specialty cornflours including masa
that is used in tortillas and other Mexican specialty
foods
     President: Craig Fisher
     CFO: Steven Mills
     Executive VP: David Smith

Number Employees: 1,000-4,999
Parent Co: Archer Daniels Midland Company
Type of Packaging: Bulk

91 ADM Nutraceuticals
4666 E Faries Parkway
Decatur, IL 62526-5666   217-451-4112
          Fax: 217-451-4510 800-510-2178
nutrition@admworld.com www.novasoy.com
Nutraceutical products derived from all-natural
sources
     President: Molly Wilson
Parent Co: Archer Daniels Midland Company
Brands:
     Cardioaid
     Natural-Source Vitamin E
     Novasoy

92 ADM Packaged Oils
4666 E Faries Parkway
Decatur, IL 62526-5666   217-451-6112
          Fax: 217-451-2689 800-637-1550
info@admworld.com www.admworld.com
Packaged oils
     President: Todd Saathoff
     R&D: Tom Tiffany
     Quality Control: Kelly Singelton
*Estimated Sales:*Below $ 5 Million
Number Employees: 25
Parent Co: Archer Daniels Midland Company
Type of Packaging: Consumer, Food Service, Bulk
Brands:
     Gold' N Flavor
     Golden Chef
     Superb
     Superb Select
     Tastee Pop

93 ADM Refined Oils
PO Box 1470
Decatur, IL 62525-1820   217-424-5463
          Fax: 217-424-5467 800-637-5866
info@admworld.com www.admworld.com
Food grade oils for the food industry. Grains used
and oil types include corn, soy, peanut, canola, sun-
flower, cottonseed, palm and coconut
     CEO: Paul Mulhollem
     Technical Service Manager: Frank Friend
Parent Co: Archer Daniels Midland Company
Type of Packaging: Bulk

94 AFC Enterprises
5555 Glenridge Connector NE
Atlanta, GA 30342-4759   404-459-4450
          Fax: 404-459-4530 800-222-5857
popeyescommunications@popeyes.com
          www.afce.com
Restaurant,beverages,coffee roast
     Chairman: Frank J Belatti
     CFO: Frederick B Beilstein
     Executive VP/CFO: Gerald Wilkins
     CEO: Cheryl A Bachelder
     Public Relations: Sherrie Rabford
     Plant Manager: Mary Townsend-Smith
*Estimated Sales:*I
Number Employees: 1,000-4,999
Brands:
     Church's Chicken
     Cinnabon
     Popeyes
     Torrefazione Italia

95 AFF International
1265 Kennestone Circle
Marietta, GA 30066-6037   770-427-8177
          Fax: 770-427-0964 800-241-7764
          www.affintl.com
Processor and exporter of aromatic flavors and fra-
grances
     President/Owner: Richard Neill
     Perfumer: Keith Pierson
Estimated Sales:$10-20 Million
Number Employees: 20-49
Type of Packaging: Bulk

96 AFI-FlashGril'd Steak
780 Layton Ave
Salt Lake City, UT 84104-1727   801-972-0055
          Fax: 801-972-2050 800-382-2862
          afisteak@aol.com
Frozen sandwich steaks
     Manager: Goran Cvetkovic
     CFO: Eugene Hill
     VP, Marketing: Noel Working

Estimated Sales:$5-10 Million
Number Employees: 20-49
Brands:
     FlashGril'd

**97 AFP Advanced Food Products,
LLC**
P.O.Box 1551
Visalia, CA 93279-1551   559-627-2070
          Fax: 559-627-2196 www.afpllc.com
Milk, cheese sauce, coconut juice, soup, pudding
and dessert bases
     President: Miroslav Hosek
Estimated Sales:$ 20 - 50 Million
Number Employees: 100-249
Sq. footage: 98000
Parent Co: Zausner Food
Type of Packaging: Consumer, Food Service, Pri-
vate Label

98 AG Processing, Inc.
P.O.Box 2047
Omaha, NE 68103-2047   402-496-7809
          Fax: 402-492-7721 800-247-1345
info@agp.com www.agp.com
Processor and exporter of emulsifiers, lecithin, vege-
table fats, soybean flours, soy proteins and oils in-
cluding vegetable, almond, amaranth, avocado,
canola, coconut, corn, cottonseed, grapeseed, lemon,
olive, palm, peanut, rapeseedrice, safflower, etc.
     CEO: Martin Reagan
     CFO: J Keith Spackler
     CEO: Martin P Reagan
Estimated Sales:$20 Million
Number Employees: 1,000-4,999
Parent Co: AGP
Other Locations:
     AG Processing Plant
     Eagle Grove IA
     AG Processing Plant
     Emmetsburg IA
     AG Processing Plant
     Manning IA
     AG Processing Plant
     Mason City IA
     AG Processing Plant
     Sergeant Bluff IA
     AG Processing Plant
     Sheldon IA
     AG Processing Plant
     Dawson MN
     AG Processing Plant
     St. Joseph MO
     AG Processing Plant
     Hastings NE
Brands:
     AEP
     AGP GRAIN LTD
     AGP GRAIN MARKETING
     AMINOPLUS
     MASTERFEEDS
     SOYGOLD

99 AGNESI USA
111 John St # 2405
New York, NY 10038-3108   212-619-3255
          Fax: 212-619-3417
Estimated Sales:$ 5 - 10 Million
Number Employees: 5-9

100 AHD International, LLC
3340 Peachtree Rd NE
Suite 1685
Atlanta, GA 30326-1143   404-233-4022
          Fax: 404-233-4041 info@ahdintl.com
          www.ahdintl.com
Contract manufacturer of vitamins and nutritional
products; Importer and exporter of nutritional raw
materials and oils
     President: John Alkire
Estimated Sales:$ 10 - 20 Million
Number Employees: 10-19
Type of Packaging: Bulk

101 AIYA
60 E 42nd St
New York, NY 10165-0006   212-499-0610
          Fax: 212-661-7811 takeo@aiya-america.com
          www.aiya-america.com
Japanese green tea
     Sales Division Manager: Takeo Sugita

102 AIYA America, Inc.
2291 W. 205th Street
Unit 104
Torrance, CA 90501   310-212-1395
         Fax: 310-212-1386 info@aiya-america.com
                www.aiya-america.com
Wholesaler and distributor of matcha green tea and
premium leaf teas used in many types of food and
beverage applications.

103 AJM Meat Packing
PO Box 13922
San Juan, PR 00908-3922   787-787-4050
         Fax: 787-787-2445
Manufactures approved USDA, FDA, and AMS
meat and poultry for the industry which processes
products for the school lunch program
    VP of Operations: Sabah Yassin

104 (HQ)AM Todd Company
1717 Douglas Ave
Kalamazoo, MI 49007-1600   269-343-2603
         Fax: 269-343-3399 800-968-2603
         info@amtodd.com www.amtodd.com
Natural peppermint and spearmint oils and botanical
extracts, serving the food, beverage, confection, fla-
vor, dietary supplement and personal care product
industry.
    President/CEO: Robert King
    CEO: Henry W Todd Sr
    VP Sales/Marketing: Ross Sheldon
Estimated Sales:$100+ Million
Number Employees: 50-99
Sq. footage: 35000
Other Locations:
    AM Todd Botanical Therapeutics
    Logan UT
    AM Todd - EMEA
    Paris, France
    AM Todd - SEA
    Churchgate, Mumbai India

105 AM Todd Company
P.O.Box 2802
Eugene, OR 97402-0304   541-687-0155
         Fax: 541-485-7347 800-827-4372
         info@amtodd.com www.amt botanicals.com
Botanical extracts and flavors
    Manager: Lloyd Mangun
Estimated Sales:$20-50 Million
Number Employees: 50-99

106 AMK Specialty Gourmet Products
PO Box 202
De Pere, WI 54115-0202   920-336-7873
                888-317-2649
         aliciaamk@usxchange.net
Dessert and sauce medleys in five scrumptious fla-
vors
    President: Alicia Dargon-Kroner
Brands:
    Alicia's Elegant Dessert Sauce
    Alimentitalia Lapian
    Alimentitalia Oleari
    Alimentitalia Sole M
    Alimentitalia Zanini
    Beau Jacques
    D.S. Dotson
    Le Jardinet
    Louis Dupre
    Moulin De La Bidiere
    Peche D'Elysee
    Robert Ledoux
    Robert Ledoux
    Sheraton
    Telephone Bar & Gril
    Whispering Peak Vine
    Wyndham

107 AMT Labs
P.O.Box 540234
North Salt Lake, UT 84054-0234   801-299-1661
    Fax: 801-299-0220 customercare@amtlabs.net
                www.amtlabs.net
Processor and exporter of food supplements includ-
ing mineral supplements, amino acid chelates,
ascorbates, citrates, etc.; processor of energy food
bars and mineral beverage mixes
    President: Bing Fang
    VP/Research & Development: Dr Oliver Fang
Estimated Sales:$20-50 Million
Number Employees: 50-99
Sq. footage: 100000
Type of Packaging: Private Label, Bulk

108 ANKOM Technology
2052 O'Neill Road
Macedon, NY 14502   315-986-8090
         Fax: 315-986-8091 info@ankom.com
                www.ankom.com
Manufacturer of instrumentation for the meat processing and food manufacturing industry.

**109 AOI Tea Company -
NorthAmerica Office**
16651 Gothard Street
Unit M
Huntington Beach, CA 92647   714-841-2716
                877-264-0877
         consumer@AOItea.com www.aoitea.com
Manufacturer and distributor of matcha green tea.
    Madam President: Ayano Honda

110 APTCO
2300 Cesar Chavez
San Francisco, CA 94124-1004   415-648-6688
Processor, exporter and importer of frozen fish, scal-
lops, shrimp and meat; wholesaler/distributor of
frozen foods, groceries, general merchandise, meats
and seafood
    CEO: Gilbert Oei
    CFO: Meike Wibowo
    Purchasing Manager: Anne Wong
Estimated Sales:$30 Million
Number Employees: 20-49
Sq. footage: 45000
Type of Packaging: Food Service
Other Locations:
    APTCO
    Taipei
Brands:
    Ocean Gourmet

111 ARA Food Corporation
8025 NW 60th St
Miami, FL 33166-3412   305-592-9966
         Fax: 305-599-1385 800-533-8831
         salesdep@arafood.com www.arafood.com
Plantain, taro and cassava tropical chips
    President: Alberto Abrante
    VP: Alberto Abrante Jr
    Sales Manager: Michael Loriga
Estimated Sales:$10-20 Million
Number Employees: 1-4
Type of Packaging: Private Label
Brands:
    ARA
    BANANITAS
    DONITA
    MARIQUITAS
    REAL
    TROPICAL CHIPS

112 ARC Diversified
455 Universal Dr
Cookeville, TN 38506-4603   931-432-5981
         Fax: 931-432-5987 800-239-9029
         thearc@arcmis.com www.arcmis.com/arcd.htm
Vegetable oils
    President: Terri McRai
Number Employees: 100-249
Brands:
    ARC

113 AREL Group
1279 Collier Road NW
Atlanta, GA 30318-2308   404-355-3001
         Fax: 404-355-0770 800-737-3094
    President: John Freebairn
    Public Relations: Elviana Candoni De Zan
Estimated Sales:$10-20 Million
Number Employees: 20-49
Brands:
    Arel

114 ARRO Corporation
7440 Santa Fe Dr
Hodgkins, IL 60525-5022   708-352-8200
         Fax: 708-352-5293 arroliquid@aol.com
                www.arro.com
Processor of corn, peanut, salad, soybean and vege-
table oils; warehouse providing dry storage for food
and food related products. Rail siding available
    Owner: Pat Gaughn
Estimated Sales:$500,000-1 Million
Number Employees: 1 to 4
Type of Packaging: Food Service, Private Label,
    Bulk

Other Locations:
    Chicago IL
    Hodgkins IL

115 ASC Seafood
6340 118th Ave
Largo, FL 33773-3728   727-541-6896
         Fax: 727-545-1532 800-876-3474
                www.ascseafood.com
Manufacturer of quality seafood products
    Owner: Steve Annas
    VP Sales/Marketing: Nick Bouth
Estimated Sales:$10-20 Million
Number Employees: 20-49
Brands:
    Gulf-Maid

116 ASK Foods
P.O.Box 388
Palmyra, PA 17078-0388   717-838-6356
         Fax: 717-838-7458 800-879-4275
         wdimatteo@askfoods.com www.askfoods.com
Processor of desserts, dips, deli salads, sauces, soups
and entrees
    CEO: Wendie DiMatteo Holsinger
    CEO: Wendi Di Matteo
Estimated Sales:$10-20 Million
Number Employees: 100-249
Sq. footage: 200
Type of Packaging: Consumer, Food Service, Pri-
    vate Label, Bulk
Brands:
    Ask Foods
    Homestyle

117 ASV Wines
1998 Road 152
Delano, CA 93215-9437   661-792-3159
         Fax: 661-792-3995 sales@asvwines.com
                www.asvwines.com
Wines
    President: Marko Zaninovich
    VP: William Nakata
Estimated Sales:$5-10 Million
Number Employees: 20-49
Type of Packaging: Food Service, Private Label,
    Bulk
Other Locations:
    Marketing & Sales
    Napa CA
    San Martin Winery
    San Martin CA
Brands:
    CANYON OAKS
    CROW CANYON
    MUIRWOOD
    STEEL CREEK

118 ATA International
RR 4
Box 4048g
Belton, TX 76513-9408   254-939-2695
         Fax: 254-939-2695 816-221-0660
                logic7777@aol.com
    Chairman: Herb Hardwick
    General Manager: Mark Huffer

119 AVC Industries Inc
1131 N Garey Ave
Pomona, CA 91767-3803   909-868-6986
         Fax: 909-629-3388 info@avcfilms.com OR
                billpan@avcfilms.com
                www.avcfilms.com
Manufacturer of POF Shrink Film and Cross Linked
POF Film applications and uses of which include
that of the food and beverage industry.
    Owner: Bill Pan
    Vice President Sales: Bill Pan

120 AVEBE America, Inc.
305 College Road E
Princeton, NJ 08540   609-951-2030
         brains@avebe.com
                www.avebe.com
Producer and marketer of starch specialties to food
industry: improving texture, stability and appear-
ance.
    Research/Development Manager: Dale Bertrand
Estimated Sales:$20-50 Million
Number Employees: 20-49
Parent Co: AVEBE Group

121 AVRI Companies
1080 Essex Avenue
Richmond, CA 94801-2113   510-223-0633
Fax: 510-233-0636   800-883-9574
avrico@avrico.com
Flavoring supplies, flavors, fragrances, essential oils
President: Charles W Skamser
CEO: Tim Connolly
Number Employees: 10-19
Brands:
AVRI Companies

122 Aala Meat Market
751 Waiakamilo Rd
Honolulu, HI 96817-4312   808-832-6650
Fax: 808-832-6659
President: Donald Chong
Estimated Sales: $ 1 - 3 Million
Number Employees: 10-19

123 Aaland Potato Company
P.O.Box 304
Hoople, ND 58243-0304   701-894-6144
Fax: 701-894-6423
Manufacturer of potatoes
Manager: Jim Bailey
Estimated Sales: $2.5-5 Million
Number Employees: 10-19
Type of Packaging: Consumer
Brands:
AALAND

124 Aarhus United USA, Inc.
131 Marsh St
Newark, NJ 07114-3238   973-344-1300
Fax: 973-344-9049   800-776-1338
us.sales@aarhusunited.com   www.aarhususa.com
Processor and importer of cocoa butter substitutes
and oils including coconut, cottonseed, palm, soy-
bean, sunflower, vegetable, etc.; exporter of lauric
oil products
Sales Manager: Ed Wilson
Estimated Sales: $50-100 Million
Number Employees: 20-49
Parent Co: Aarhus Oliefabrik
Type of Packaging: Bulk

125 Abattoir A. Trahan Company
860 Chemin Des Acadiens
Yamachiche, QC G0X 3L0
Canada   819-296-3791
Fax: 819-296-3364
Processor of fresh and frozen pork
President: Rene Trahan
Marketing Director: Dennis Trahan
Number Employees: 50-99
Type of Packaging: Consumer, Food Service, Pri-
vate Label, Bulk

126 Abattoir Aliments AstaInc.
511 Av De La Gare
St Alexandre Kamouraska, QC G0L 2G0
Canada   418-495-2728
Fax: 418-495-2879
Manufacturer of pork. Slaughtering services avail-
able
President: Jacques Poitras
Number Employees: 405
Type of Packaging: Bulk

127 Abbey Road Farms
1 Abbey Road
Tallahassee, FL 32309-9276   850-878-7677
President: Lucia Maxwell
Plant Manager: Chad Armstrong
Estimated Sales: $2.5-5 Million
Number Employees: 5-9
Brands:
Abbey

128 Abbitt's
P.O.Box 1071
Williamston, NC 27892-1071   252-792-3646
Fax: 252-792-0795   info@abbitts.com
www.abbitts.com
Processor of self-rising corn meal, hush puppy mix
and chicken and seafood breading
Operations Manager: Robert Griesedieck
Plant Manager: Nathan Hyman
Estimated Sales: $10-20 Million
Number Employees: 5-9
Sq. footage: 100000
Type of Packaging: Consumer, Bulk

Brands:
Abbitt's
Pride of Halifax

129 Abbotsford Growers Co-operative
31825 Marshall Road
Abbotsford, BC V2T 5Z8
Canada   604-864-0022
Fax: 604-864-0020   info@abbotsfordgrowers.com
www.abbotsfordgrowers.com
Growers and processors of raspberries used in
sauces, desserts, jams, yogurts, pie filings, muffins
and many other products.
Quality Assurance Supervisor: Dan Sigfusson
General Manager of Sales: Doug Edgar
Operations Manager: Bill Sandhu
Plant Superintendent: Roger Moody
Estimated Sales: $15 Million
Number Employees: 1-4
Sq. footage: 25000
Type of Packaging: Bulk
Brands:
ABBOTSFORD GROWERS CO-OP

130 (HQ)Abbott & Cobb, Inc.
4151 E Street Rd
Langhorne, PA 19053-4960   215-245-6666
Fax: 215-245-9043   800-345-7333
acseed@abbottcobb.com   www.abbottcobb.com
Processor and exporter of vegetable seeds
Owner: Art Abbott
Estimated Sales: $ 10 - 20 Million
Number Employees: 20-49
Other Locations:
Bakersfield CA
Brawley CA
Caldwell ID
Valdosta GA
Immokalee FL
West Palm Beach FL
Nogales AZ
McAllen TX
Brands:
SUMMER
SUMMER SWEET

**131 Abbott Laboratories
Nutritionals/Ross Products**
625 Cleveland Ave
Columbus, OH 43215-1754   614-564-0019
Fax: 614-624-7155   877-946-7747
www.abbott.com
Offers a variety of pediatric and adult nutritional
products, pharmaceuticals and enteral feeding prod-
ucts. Processor of evaporated and condensed milk.
Chairman/CEO: Miles White
CFO: Thomas Freyman
Senior VP: Gary McCullough
Director Public Affairs: Tracy Noe
Number Employees: 1,000-4,999
Parent Co: Abbott Laboratories
Type of Packaging: Consumer
Brands:
Similac Toddler's Best

132 Abbott's Candy Shop
48 E Walnut St
Hagerstown, IN 47346-1542   765-489-4442
Fax: 765-489-5501   877-801-1200
abbottscandy@abbottscandy.com
www.abbottscandy.com
Gourmet chocolates and caramels
President: Suanna Goodnight
Estimated Sales: $5-10 Million
Number Employees: 20-49
Sq. footage: 7
Type of Packaging: Private Label
Brands:
Abbott's Candy

133 Abbott's Meat
3623 Blackington Ave
Flint, MI 48532-3874   810-232-7128
Fax: 810-232-7960
Beef and beef products
President: Edward P Abbott
Estimated Sales: $5-10 Million
Number Employees: 10-19
Brands:
Abbotts Meat

134 (HQ)Abbyland Foods
P.O.Box 69
Abbotsford, WI 54405-0069   715-223-6386
Fax: 715-223-6388   800-732-5483
abbyland@abbyland.com   www.abbyland.com
Meat, sausage and boneless beef
President: Harland Schraufnagel
CFO: Paul Hess
Sales Representative: Patricia Patterson
Estimated Sales: $50-100 Million
Number Employees: 250-499
Sq. footage: 122000
Type of Packaging: Food Service, Private Label,
Bulk
Brands:
ABBULAND
LONDON CLASSIC BROIL
TAILGATE

135 Abdallah Candies
3501 County Road 42 W
Burnsville, MN 55306-3805   952-890-0859
Fax: 952-890-3664   800-348-7328
service@abdallahcandies.com
www.abdallahcandies.com
Confectionery products including boxed chocolates.
President: Steven Hegedus Jr
Sales: MaDonna Schmitz
Estimated Sales: $2.5-5 Million
Number Employees: 20-49
Sq. footage: 6500
Type of Packaging: Consumer, Food Service, Pri-
vate Label, Bulk
Brands:
Alligators
Bare Paws
Chocolate Angel Mint
Downtowner Assortment
TOFFEE-ETTES

136 Abel & Schafer
20 Alexander Ct
Ronkonkoma, NY 11779-6573   631-737-2220
Fax: 631-737-2335   800-443-1260
info@kompletusa.com   www.abelandschafer.com
Processor of mixes including bread, cake, muffin,
dough conditioners, glazes and fillings
President: Martin Schafer
VP: Frank Triedman
QA: Christopher Gaumet
Production Manager: Christopher Weber
Estimated Sales: $ 20 - 25 Million
Number Employees: 50-99
Parent Co: Abel & Schafer Group
Type of Packaging: Private Label
Other Locations:
Abel & Schafer
VoLklingen, Germany
KOMPLET Berlin
Berlin
KOMPLET Italia
Grassobbio, Italy
KOMPLET Mantler
Rosenburg
Ste COMPLET
Forbach, France
KOMPLET Iberica
Barcelona, Spain
Abel & Schafer
Coulsdon, Surrey UK
Quality Bakery Products
Houston TX
KOMPLET Benelux
Luxembourg, Belium
KOMPLET Polska
Suchy Las, Poland

**137 Abeles & Heymann
GourmetKosher Provisions, Inc.**
3498 3rd Ave
Bronx, NY 10456   718-589-0100
Fax: 718-589-0102   sleav16311@aol.com
www.abeles-heymann.com
Producer of salami, pastrami, corned beef, brisket,
hot dogs, beef fry, smoked turkey, and knockwurst.
President: Seth Leavitt
Estimated Sales: $5-10 Million
Number Employees: 5-9

138 Abimco USA, Inc.
43 Hampshire Drive
Mendham, NJ 07945-2003   973-543-7393
Fax: 973-543-2948   abimcous@ix.netcom.com
www.home.netcom.com/~ambicous

Processor of fruit juice concentrates; importer and exporter of dried and frozen fruits and vegetables; Importer of juice concentrates, honey and tomato paste; exporter of fresh mushrooms
President: Paulette Krelman
General Manager: Arthur Kupperman
Number Employees: 1-4
Type of Packaging: Bulk

139 Abingdon Vineyard & Winery
20308 Alvarado Rd
Abingdon, VA 24211-6337   276-623-1255
Fax: 276-623-0125 info@abingdonwinery.com
www.abingdonwinery.com
Wines
Owner: Bob Carlson
Co-Owner: Bob Carlson
Vineyard Manager: Kevin Sutherland
Estimated Sales: $ .5 - 1 million
Number Employees: 1-4

140 Abita Brewing Company
P.O.Box 1510
Abita Springs, LA 70420-1510   985-893-3143
Fax: 985-898-3546 800-737-2311
info@abita.com www.abita.com
Lager and ale and caffeine-free root beer.
President: David Blossman
Estimated Sales: $20-50 Million
Number Employees: 10-19
Sq. footage: 14000
Type of Packaging: Consumer, Private Label
Brands:
Abita
Golden
Purple Haze
Turbodog

141 Abita Springs Water Company
P.O.Box 867
Metairie, LA 70004-0867   504-828-2500
Fax: 504-828-2520 abitman@abitasprings.com
www.abitasprings.com
Spring water
Chairman: Bill Roohi
CEO: George Mayer
Estimated Sales: $12,700,000
Number Employees: 100-249
Brands:
ABITA GOLDEN
ABITA PURPLE
ABITA ROOT BEER
ABITA SEASMALS
ABITA TURBODAY

142 (HQ)Abitec Corporation
501 West 1st Avenue
PO Box 569
Columbus, OH 43215   614-429-6464
Fax: 614-421-7996 800-555-1255
www.abiteccorp.com
Vegetable oil refining and processing
CEO: Jeff Walton
CFO: Susan Tayloe
Vice President: Frank Detrano
Research & Development: Jim Williams
VP Sales: Larry Warner
Plant Manager: Jeff Fulton
Purchasing Manager: Rick Laws
Estimated Sales: $50-100 Million
Number Employees: 50-99
Other Locations:
Abitec Corporation
Janesville WI
Abitec Corporation
Paris IL
Brands:
Abitec

143 Abkit Camocare Nature Works
61 Broadway
Room 1310
New York, NY 10006-2722   212-292-1550
Fax: 212-292-1542 800-226-6227
info@abkit.com www.abkit.com
Natural products, vitamins, etc
President: Claus Ghringer
Director International Sales: Alison Carley
Estimated Sales: $ 3 - 5 Million
Number Employees: 10-19
Brands:
Catuama
Kwai
Nature Works

144 Abraham's Natural Foods
P.O.Box 89
Long Branch, NJ 07740-0089   732-229-5799
Fax: 732-571-0890 800-327-9903
hummos1985@verizon.net
www.abrahamsnatural.com
Processor of natural gourmet dips, salads and cookies, and kosher and Middle Eastern foods
President: Louis Fellman
Estimated Sales: $5-10 Million
Number Employees: 5-9
Brands:
Baba Ghannouj
Hummos

145 (HQ)Absopure Water Company
P.O.Box 701248
Plymouth, MI 48170-0961   734-451-2000
Fax: 734-451-0055 800-422-7678
www.absopure.com
Manufacturer of bottled water.
President: William Young
Estimated Sales: $20-50 Million
Number Employees: 100-249
Type of Packaging: Consumer, Food Service
Brands:
ABSOPURE ARTESIAN SPRING WATER
ABSOPURE DRINKING WATER
ABSOPURE SPARKLING SPRING WATER
ABSOPURE STEAM DISTILLED WATER
CAP 10 MINERAL WATER (ALL FLAVORS)

146 Absopure Water Company
3201 W Clark Rd
Champaign, IL 61822-2825   217-443-8439
Fax: 734-451-0055 800-422-7678
service@absopure.com www.absopure.com
Processor of bottled water including deionized natural and distilled.
Manager: Bo Wagner
Estimated Sales: $1-2.5 Million
Number Employees: 20-49
Brands:
Greensbriar Farms
Mountain Valley
Quality

147 Absopure Water Company
425 36th St SW
Grand Rapids, MI 49548-2161   616-455-5700
Fax: 734-451-0055 800-422-7678
service@absopure.com www.absopure.com
Manufacturer of bottled water.
President/CEO: William Young
Estimated Sales: $22.9 Million
Number Employees: 50-99
Type of Packaging: Consumer, Bulk

148 Absopure Water Company -Pine Valley
1206 Jaclyn Dr
O Fallon, IL 62269-1755   618-624-6730
Fax: 618-624-8648 800-422-7678
service@absopure.com www.absopure.com
Processor of bottled water.
Plant Manager: Ken Barnhill
Estimated Sales: $ 1 - 3 Million
Number Employees: 20-49
Type of Packaging: Consumer, Food Service

149 Abuelita Mexican Foods
9209 Enterprise Ct # C
Manassas Park, VA 20111-4809   703-369-0232
Fax: 703-369-0875 office@abuelita.com
www.abuelita.com
Mexican corn and flour tortillas, flavored wraps
President: Eugene F Suarez Sr Sr.
VP/Plant Manager: Eugene Suarez Jr.
VP Marketing: Steven Dill
General Manager: Peggy Suarez
Production Manager: Paul Hammond
Estimated Sales: $1-2.5 Million
Number Employees: 50-99
Sq. footage: 36000
Type of Packaging: Private Label
Brands:
Abuelita
Casa De Carmen
Nana's Cocina

150 (HQ)Abunda Life Laboratories
208 3rd Ave
Asbury Park, NJ 07712-6016   732-775-4141
Fax: 732-502-0899 naturaldoc@abundalife.com
www.abundalife.com/labs.asp
Manufacturer exporter of natural health products including vitamins, goat milk powder, fiber supplements, herbal spices, herbal teas, rice bran syrups and sweeteners including: banana, grape, pineapple and orange
Founder: Dr Robert Sorge
Estimated Sales: $300,000-500,000
Number Employees: 1-4
Sq. footage: 4200
Type of Packaging: Consumer, Private Label
Brands:
24 Super Amino Acids
Abunda Body
Blood Building Broth
Blood Building Powder
Brain Invigoration Powder
Cholesterol Solve
Cram For Students
Dieters Tea
Energy Powder
Essaic Formula
Fruit Fiber
Live Plant Juice
Liver Detox Formula
Parasite Annihilation Powder
Royal Pollen Complex
Super Bowl Cleanse
Super C Active
Super Detox
Super Green
Super Salad Oil
Super Tonic

151 Acacia Vineyard
2750 Las Amigas Rd
Napa, CA 94559-9715   707-226-9991
Fax: 707-226-1685
acacia.info@acaciawinery.com
www.diageo.com
Manufacturer of wines
Owner: Matthew Glynn
Estimated Sales: $ 10 - 20 Million
Number Employees: 20-49
Parent Co: Chalone Wine Group
Brands:
Acacia

152 Acadian Fine Foods
228 Saint Charles Ave # 1323
New Orleans, LA 70130-2646   504-581-2355
Fax: 504-525-9841
Frozen stuffed chicken, seafood pies, canned blue crabmeat, frozen crabs, crawfish
President: Charles Williams
VP: Russell Raelston
Estimated Sales: $ .5 - 1 million
Number Employees: 5-9

153 Acadian Ostrich Ranch
9010 Highway 961
Clinton, LA 70722-4217   225-683-9988
Fax: 225-683-9988 800-350-0167
acadianostrichrh@cs.com
www.acadianostrich.com
Manufacturer of ostrich and alligator meats
President: Marco Dermody

154 (HQ)Acadian Seaplants
30 Brown Avenue
Dartmouth, NS B3B 1X8
Canada   902-468-2840
Fax: 902-468-3474 800-575-9100
info@acadian.ca www.acadianseaplants.com
Manufacturer and exporter of natural, specialty fertilizers, feed, food, food ingredients and brewery supplies
President: Louis Deveau
CFO: Perry Bevin
Vice President: Jean-Paul Deveau
Research & Development: Franklin Evans
Quality Control: Barry Galbraith
Marketing Director: John Sewuster
VP Sales: Patrick Bennett
Marketing/Communications Manager: Linda Theriault
Production Manager: Paul Empey
Purchasing Manager: Ian Rennie
Estimated Sales: $5-$10 Million
Number Employees: 130

Type of Packaging: Private Label, Bulk
Brands:
Drewclar
Hana-Nori
Nutramer

155 Acatris
3300 Edinborough Way # 300
Edina, MN 55435-5959   952-835-9590
    Fax: 952-835-9063   info@us.acatris.com
           www.great-expectations.net
Leading supplier of special health ingredients including SoyLife, FenuLife and LinumLife
    Manager: Joni Johnson
    Sales Manager: Cherie Jones
Estimated Sales: $ 5 - 10 Million
Number Employees: 20-49
Number of Brands: 3
Number of Products: 3
Parent Co: Royal Schouten Group
Type of Packaging: Bulk
Brands:
FENULIFE
LINUMLIFE
SOYLIFE

156 Acatris USA
3300 Edinborough Way # 712
Edina, MN 55435-5963   952-920-7700
    Fax: 952-920-7704   info@us.acatris.com
           www.frutarom.com
Blended dough conditioners, antioxidant solutions, release agents and lubricants; wholesaler/distributor of soy flour, vitamin/mineral blends and oils including soybean and canola
    President: Laurent Leduc
Estimated Sales: $5 Million
Number Employees: 5-9
Sq. footage: 16000
Parent Co: Royal Schouten Group
Type of Packaging: Bulk
Brands:
ALUBE
DADEX
DAEDOL
DAEJEL
DAELUBE
DAMINAIDE
DAMINCO
DAMINET
EXTOL
FENULIFE
LESOY
LINUMLIFE
MYVACET
MYVEROL
SOYLIFE

157 (HQ)Accra Pac Group
P.O.Box 2988
Elkhart, IN 46515-2988   574-295-0000
    Fax: 574-296-1710   bromak@accrapac.com
           www.accrapac.com
Aerosols, liquids and creams packaging
    Manager: Geoff Ladue
    VP, Sales: Drew Hoffman
    VP, Sales: Mike Garretson
    Inside Sales Manager: Blake Romak
Estimated Sales: $105 Million
Number Employees: 5-9
Sq. footage: 1000000
Type of Packaging: Consumer
Other Locations:
Accra Pacinc
Elkhart IN

158 AccuLift
3404 Iowa St
Alexandria, MN 56308-3399   320-763-6587
    Fax: 320-763-5754   info@douglas-machine.com
           www.douglas-machine.com
    CEO: Vern Anderson
    CEO: Vernon Anderson
Estimated Sales: $100+ Million
Number Employees: 500-999
Brands:
Apexo Servo
Axiomo
Contouro S-Series
Spectrumo Series Multipackers

159 Accucaps Industries Limited
2125 Ambassador Drive
Windsor, ON N9C 3R5
Canada   514-323-9184
    Fax: 514-323-3015   800-665-7210
    info@accucaps.com   www.accucaps.com
    President: Dwight Goraham
    Marketing Director: Peter Wares
    CFO: Ed Kanters
Brands:
Accucaps

160 Accuplace
1800 NW 69th Ave # 102
Plantation, FL 33313-4583   954-791-1500
    Fax: 954-791-1501   www.accuplace.com
    Owner: Jamie Schlinkmann
Estimated Sales: $ 10 - 20 Million
Number Employees: 50-99

161 Accurate Ingredients
160 Eileen Way
Syosset, NY 11791-5300   516-496-2500
    Fax: 516-496-2516   www.acing-iri.com
Manufacturer, Importer/Exporter of food ingredients
    Owner: Jack Sollazzo
    Executive Sales Manager: Frank Wells
Estimated Sales: $10-20 Million
Number Employees: 20-49
Other Locations:
Accurate Ingredients
Santa Ana CA

162 Ace Baking Company
PO Box 535
Wadsworth, IL 60083-0535   920-497-1893
    Fax: 920-497-1893   800-879-2231
Ice cream cones including waffle, sugar and cake, and waffle bowls
Number Employees: 250-499

163 Ace Development
31194 State Highway 51
Bruneau, ID 83604-5076   208-845-2487
    Fax: 208-845-2274   copakarobert@hotmail.com
    Presiden: Robert Williams
Estimated Sales: $800,000
Number Employees: 1-4

164 Ace Food
P.O.Box 962
Bayou La Batre, AL 36509-0962   251-824-4367
    Fax: 251-824-7950   800-884-0741
    Owner: Russell Collier
Estimated Sales: $ .5 - 1 million
Number Employees: 1-4
Brands:
Ace Seafood

165 Acharice Specialties
PO Box 690
Greenville, MS 38702-0690   800-432-4901
    Fax: 901-381-3287   www.achafood.com
Rice and grain products
    President/CEO: Jack Stratol
    Research & Development: Bill Land
    Sales/Marketing: Nelson Wurth
    Operations/Production: Mike Well
    Plant Manager: Pat Roy
Number Employees: 500-999
Type of Packaging: Private Label

166 Achem Industry America,Inc.
938 Hatcher Avenue
Los Angeles, CA 91748-1035   562-802-0998
    Fax: 562-802-5069   800-442-8273
    jonyeh@achem.com   www.achem-usa.com
Polyvinyl Chloride (PVC) and double-sided Pressure Sensitive Tapes
Estimated Sales: $ 50 - 100 Million
Number Employees: 50-100
Other Locations:
ANCHEM Industry America
Chicago IL
ANCHEM Industry America
Charlotte NC
ANCHEM
China
ANCHEM
Taiwan
ANCHEM
South Asia
ANCHEM
Europe

167 Ackerman Winery
4406 220th Trl
Amana, IA 52203-8035   319-622-3379
    Fax: 319-622-6513   sales@ackermanwinery.com
           www.ackermanwinery.com
Wine
    President: Les Ackerman
Estimated Sales: $1-2.5 Million
Number Employees: 10-19
Type of Packaging: Bulk

168 Ackerman Winery
PO Box 108
Amana, IA 52234   319-622-6513
    Fax: 319-622-6513   sales@ackermanwinery.com
           www.ackermanwinery.com
Wine and cheese
    President: Les Ackerman
Estimated Sales: $1-2.5 Million
Number Employees: 1-4

169 Acme Candy Company
2109 E Division Street
Arlington, TX 76011-7817   254-634-2825
    President: Malcolm Cohen

170 Acme Farms
P.O.Box 3065
Seattle, WA 98114-3065   206-323-4300
    Fax: 206-235-1910   800-542-8309
Manufacturer of Chicken, turkey and other poultry products.
    Manager: Tom Perry
    VP/Sales: Edward Shane
    Marketing Manager: Jerry Ryder
Estimated Sales: $40 Million
Number Employees: 5-9
Parent Co: Acme Poultry Company
Type of Packaging: Consumer, Food Service, Private Label, Bulk
Brands:
ACME
MT PARK
PEAK QUALITY
PILGRIM
SILVER BEAUTY

171 Acme Preserve Company
946 College Ave.
Adrian, MI 49221-2541   517-265-7222
    Fax: 517-263-7478   acmeprsv@c4systm.com
Canner of whole and diced tomatoes and tomato pulp
    President: J Chambers
    Executive VP: M Chambers
    VP Sales: Mark Chambers
Sq. footage: 25000
Type of Packaging: Food Service, Private Label
Brands:
BUYERS LABEL
MATCHLESS
WHITE A

172 Acme Smoked Fish Corporation
30 Gem St
Brooklyn, NY 11222-2804   718-383-8585
    Fax: 718-383-9115   800-221-0795
    acmefish@aol.com   www.acmesmokedfish.com
Processor and importer of smoked fish and herring
    President: Eric Caslow
    Controller: Nathan Sudakoff
    VP, Operations: Robert Caslow
    Marketing Director: Richard Schiff
Estimated Sales: $20-50 Million
Number Employees: 100-249
Type of Packaging: Consumer, Food Service, Private Label, Bulk
Brands:
ACME
BLUE HILL BAY

173 Acme Steak & Seafood Company
P.O.Box 688
Youngstown, OH 44501-0688   330-270-8000
           Fax: 330-270-8006
Importer and processor of sausage, hamburgers and portion controlled meat
    Owner: Michael Mike Iii III
    Marketing/National Accounts: Michael Mike III
    Sales Manager: Michael Mike III
    Secretary/Treasurer: M Charlotte Mike

Estimated Sales:$20-50 Million
Number Employees: 10-19
Sq. footage: 68000
Type of Packaging: Consumer, Food Service, Private Label

174 Acqua Blox LLC
12000 Slauson Ave # 3
Santa Fe Springs, CA 90670-8663   562-693-9599
        Fax: 562-945-3133 info@aquablox.com
                    www.aquablox.com
Purified and bacteria free water products specifically designed for emergency preparedness, first responders, and disaster victims
    Manager: Mike Harris
*Estimated Sales:*Below $ 5 Million
Number Employees: 1-4
Type of Packaging: Consumer, Bulk
Brands:
    Aqua Blox®

175 Acta Health Products
380 N Pastoria Avenue
Sunnyvale, CA 94085-4108   408-732-6830
        Fax: 408-732-0208 davidc@actaproducts.com
                    www.actaproducts.com
Processor and exporter of vitamins, minerals, herbal extracts and other dietary supplements; importer of raw materials
    President: David Chang
    VP: K Y Chang
    Director Quality Control: Michael Chang
    Director Marketing/Sales: Cal Bewicke
    Director Purchasing: Leo Liu
Estimated Sales:$10-20 Million
Number Employees: 28
Sq. footage: 31000
Type of Packaging: Private Label, Bulk

176 Action Labs
1400 Kearns Blvd # 2
Park City, UT 84060-7228   435-655-6106
        Fax: 800-767-8514 800-669-8877
            info@nutrceutical.com
    www.thomasregister.com/olc/actionlabs
Manufacturer and exporter of vitamins, minerals and nutritional supplements
    President: Bruce Hough
    CEO/Director/Chairman: Frank Gay II
    CFO/Senior VP Finance: Leslie Brown Jr
    CEO: Bill Gay
    VP Marketing/Sales: Christopher Neuberger
    COO/Director/Executive VP: Jeffrey Hinrichs
Estimated Sales:$500,000-$1 Million
Number Employees: 5-9
Type of Packaging: Consumer, Private Label, Bulk
Brands:
    Fentinel
    Keep
    Natural Health
    Un-Soap

177 Action Labs
P.O.Box 1090
Placentia, CA 92871-1090   714-630-5941
        Fax: 714-630-8221 800-400-5696
            actionvit@aol.com www.actionlab.com
Specialty Supplements for men, women, diet, energy, and specialty.
    President: James R Bailey
    Marketing: Mandy Ray
    Sales: John Russo
Brands:
    GINSENG 4X
    MADE FOR MEN
    SUPER FAT BURNER
    YOHIMBE ACTION
    YOHIMBE FOR MEN

178 Active Organics
1097 Yates St
Lewisville, TX 75057-4829   972-221-7500
        Fax: 972-221-3324 info@activeorganics.com
                    www.activeorganics.com
Manufacturer of botanical extracts
    President: Michael Bishop
    VP: Bill Hynes
    VP: Jim Bortzfield
Estimated Sales:$ 10 - 20 Million
Number Employees: 100-249

179 Acushnet Fish Corporation
46 Middle Street
Fairhaven, MA 02719-3086   508-997-7482
                    Fax: 508-999-6697
    President: Ralph Parsons

180 Adair Vineyards
52 Alhusen Rd
New Paltz, NY 12561-4217   845-255-1377
            adairwines@aol.com
                    www.adairwine.com
Wines
    Owner: Mark Stopkie
Estimated Sales:$500,000-$1 Million
Number Employees: 1-4
Type of Packaging: Private Label

181 Adam Matthews, Inc.
2104 Plantside Dr
Jeffersontown, KY 40299-1924   502-499-1244
    Fax: 502-499-8331 patriciat@adammatthews.com
                    www.adammatthews.com
Processor of bakery products including cheesecakes, Festival Pie and other miscellaneous desserts
    President: Adam Burckle
    VP Operations: Cathy Fleig
Estimated Sales:$10-20 Million
Number Employees: 20-49
Sq. footage: 20000
Brands:
    Adam Matthews

182 Adam Puchta Winery
1947 Frene Creek Rd
Hermann, MO 65041-4103   573-486-5596
    Fax: 573-486-2361 apuchta@centurytel.net
                www.adampuchtawine.com
Wines
    President: Timothy Puchta
Estimated Sales:$1-2.5 Million
Number Employees: 1-4
Type of Packaging: Private Label

183 Adams
P.O.Box 2048
Fargo, ND 58107-2048   701-277-9422
        Fax: 701-277-9411 800-342-4748
    info@adamsfargo.com www.adamsfargo.com
A leading maufacturers representative for hundreds of material handling and storage products.
    Owner: Al Hager
    Manager: Al Hager
Estimated Sales:$2.5-5 Million
Number Employees: 5-9
Sq. footage: 6000
Type of Packaging: Consumer, Food Service, Private Label

184 Adams & Brooks
P.O.Box 227303
Los Angeles, CA 90022-7303   213-749-3226
        Fax: 213-746-7614 800-999-9808
            info@adams-brooks.com
                www.adams-brooks.com
Processor and exporter of bagged candy including: chocolate cups, candy bars, lollypops, novelty, nut, caramel and taffy. Also vending, fund raising and theatre packaging
    President: John Brooks Sr
    Business Development Manager: John Brooks Jr
    Human Resources Manager/Corp. Secretary: Tempe Brooks
    Product Manager: Cindy Brooks
Estimated Sales:$10-20 Million
Number Employees: 50-99
Type of Packaging: Consumer, Private Label, Bulk
Brands:
    ADAMS & BROOKS
    COFFEE RIO
    COMIC ANIMAL
    CUP-O-GOLD
    FAIRTIME
    P-NUTTLES
    P-NUTTLES BUTTER TOFFEE PEANUTS
    PSYCHO POPS
    PSYCHO PSOURS
    UNICORN POPS

185 Adams County Winery
251 Peach Tree Rd
Orrtanna, PA 17353-9753   717-334-4631
                    Fax: 717-334-4026
    vintner@adamscountywinery.com
    www.adamscountywinery.com

Wines
    Owner: John Kramb
Estimated Sales:$1-2.5 Million
Number Employees: 1-4

186 Adams Fisheries Ltd
Prospect Street
PO Box 36
Shag Harbour, NS B0W 3B0
Canada   902-723-2435
        Fax: 902-723-2325 adamfish@auracom.com
Processor, importer and exporter of salted cod, pollack and haddock and live lobster
    President: Donald Adams
Number Employees: 10-19
Sq. footage: 8500

187 Adams Foods
RR 6
Box 143a
Dothan, AL 36303-9237   334-983-4233
                    Fax: 334-983-5596
Manufacturer of cakes including pound, sheet and decorated
    President: Ted Adams
    Manager: Larry Nowkaiski
    Manager: Joy Pettis
Estimated Sales:$5-10 Million
Number Employees: 5-9
Parent Co: Adams Milling Company
Type of Packaging: Consumer, Food Service, Private Label, Bulk
Brands:
    Adams
    Avery
    Baker's Best
    Home Style
    Mother's

188 Adams Olive Ranch
1200 S Aster Ave
Lindsay, CA 93247   559-562-2882
        Fax: 559-562-2272 888-216-5483
            adamsolives@ocsnet.net
                www.adamsoliveranch.com
Manufacturer of olives
    Owner: Denis Bonfilio
    Manager: David Adams
*Estimated Sales:*Less than $500,000
Number Employees: 10-19
Sq. footage: 6000
Type of Packaging: Consumer, Private Label
Brands:
    Adam's Ranch
    RAW EARTH ORGANICS
    Smith Home Cured

189 Adams USA
400 Interpace Parkway
Building B
Parsippany, NJ 07054-1120   973-385-2000
            Fax: 800-946-4102 www.pfizer.com
Health products

190 Adams Vegetable Oils
P.O.Box 956
Arbuckle, CA 95912-0956   530-668-2000
        Fax: 530-668-2006 info@adamsgrp.com
                    www.adamsgrp.com
Processor of specialty vegetable oils, cotton
    President: Mike Adams
    Sales Manager: David Hoffsten
Estimated Sales:$100+ Million
Number Employees: 50-99
Parent Co: Adams Group
Type of Packaging: Bulk

191 Adee Honey Farm
P.O.Box 368
Bruce, SD 57220-0368   605-627-5621
        Fax: 605-627-5622 sales@adeehoneyfarms.com
                www.adeehoneyfarms.com
Processor of honey and beeswax. Pollination services also available
    Owner: Richard Adee
    Owner: Kelvin Adee
    Owner: Bret Adee
Estimated Sales:$ 20 - 50 Million
Number Employees: 50-99
Type of Packaging: Bulk
Other Locations:
    Bakersfield CA
    Cedar Rapids NE
    Roscoe SD
    Woodville MS

192 Adelaida Cellars
5805 Adelaida Rd
Paso Robles, CA 93446-9783   805-239-8980
    Fax: 805-239-4671 800-676-1232
    wines@adelaida.com   www.adelaida.com
Wines
    Owner: Elizabeth Vansteenwyk
    National Sales: Paul Sowerby
    Production: Lalo Escalante
Estimated Sales: $1-2.5 Million
Number Employees: 10-19

193 Adelsheim Vineyard
16800 NE Calkins Ln
Newberg, OR 97132-6572   503-538-5222
Fax: 503-538-2248 info@adelsheimvineyard.com
                    www.adelsheim.com
Wines
    Owner: David Adelsheim
    CFO: Kathi Neal
    Quality Control: Erik Kramer
    Marketing: Leah Jorgensen
    National Sales: Michael Adelsheim
    Vineyard Manager: Andy Hemphrey
Estimated Sales: $10-20 Million
Number Employees: 20-49
Brands:
    Adelsheim Vineyard

194 Adirondack Beverages
701 Corporation Park
Scotia, NY 12302-1065   518-370-3621
    Fax: 518-370-3762 800-316-6096
            contact@adkbev.com
        www.adirondackbeverages.com
Processor of carbonated and noncarbonated beverages including cola, ginger ale, tonic, fruit drink, seltzer and sparkling and still water
    CEO/Owner: Ralph Crowley Jr.
    CFO: Michael Mulrain
    VP: Doug Martin
    Quality Control Manager: Garrett Rockwell
    Sales: Kent Sellner
    Operations Manager: Tom Carmichael
    Production/Plant Manager: Dan Dubovik
Estimated Sales: $65 Million
Number Employees: 200+
Sq. footage: 750000
Parent Co: Polar Corporation
Type of Packaging: Consumer, Food Service, Private Label
Brands:
    Adironack
    Clear 'n' Natural
    Waist Watcher

195 Adirondack Maple Farms
490 Persse Rd
Fonda, NY 12068-5716   518-853-4022
                    Fax: 518-853-3791
Processor and packer of pure maple syrup, sugar and candy
    Owner: Robert Roblee
Estimated Sales: Less than $100,000
Number Employees: 1-4
Type of Packaging: Private Label
Brands:
    ADIRONDACK MAPLE FARMS

196 Adkin & Son Associated Food Products
6645 107th Ave
South Haven, MI 49090-9366   269-637-7450
                    Fax: 269-637-2636
Manufacturer of edible fresh chestnut; chestnut tree production
    President: Roy Adkin
    National Accounts: L Adkin
    Research & Development: Shelly Newton
    Marketing Director: K Johnson
    Production/Quality Control: Harold Bennett
Estimated Sales: $15 Million
Number Employees: 5-9
Sq. footage: 22000
Type of Packaging: Food Service, Bulk
Brands:
    Adkin's
    Adkin's Royal Blue

197 Adler Fels Vineyards & Winery
980 Airway Ct # D
Santa Rosa, CA 95403-2000   707-569-1493
    Fax: 707-569-8301 info@adlerfels.com
                    www.adlerfels.com
Wines
    Manager: Steve Lindsey
    GM: Steve Lindsay
Estimated Sales: $20 Million
Number Employees: 20-49
Parent Co: Adams Wine Group

198 (HQ)Adluh Flour Mill
P.O.Box 1437
Columbia, SC 29202-1437   803-779-2460
    Fax: 803-252-0014 800-692-3584
        info@adluh.com   www.adluh.com
Manufacturer of flour and corn meal
    President: Jack Edgerton Jr
Estimated Sales: $5 Million
Number Employees: 10-19
Type of Packaging: Food Service
Brands:
    ADLUH
    CAROLINA GEM
    EATMOR
    GOLD BOND

199 Adm Edible Bean Specialties
P.O.Box 236
Kinde, MI 48445-0236   989-874-4720
                    Fax: 989-874-4720
Manufacturer of dried beans including, pinto, lima and black turtle
    Manager: John Schmidt
Estimated Sales: $20-50 Million
Number Employees: 1-4
Type of Packaging: Private Label, Bulk

200 Admiral Beverages
P.O.Box 726
Worland, WY 82401-0726   307-347-4201
    Fax: 307-347-3571 www.admiralbeverage.com
Manufacturer of soft drinks
    President: F Clay
    VP Operations: Kelly Clay
Estimated Sales: $ 20 - 50 Million
Number Employees: 50-99
Parent Co: Pepsi Company
Type of Packaging: Consumer, Food Service

201 Admiral Wine Merchants
603 S 21st Street
Irvington, NJ 07111-4201   973-371-2211
    Fax: 973-371-8521 800-582-9463
                www.admiralwine.com
Wines
    President: Michael Zeiger
    CFO: Jack Aizenman
    VP: Chet Zeiger
    VP, Marketing: Frank Johnson
    Sales Director: Frank Johnson
    Sales Manager: Lee Sherwood
Estimated Sales: $10-20 Million
Number Employees: 20-49
Brands:
    Alain Jungueovet ions
    Arden Woods
    Bodegas Gurpegui
    Casa De Pancas
    Castillo Perlada
    Cattani
    Caves Dom Teodosio
    Cerca Aguardente
    Chateau Haut Brisson
    Chatonet
    Conde De Amarante
    Dantello
    Dantello
    Donte Riveth
    Hopler
    J.P. Vinhos
    Lanson Champagne
    Le Ginestre
    Marble Crest
    Societe Donatien Bahaud
    Star Hill
    Staton Hill
    Tamega
    Teobar
    Valdamaror
    Velhissima
    Villa Dante - Italy

202 Adobe Creek Packing
P.O.Box 335
Kelseyville, CA 95451-0335   707-279-4204
    Fax: 707-279-0366 shirleyacp@aol.com
                www.adobecreekpacking.com
Manufacturer and exporter of Bartlett pears
    President/CEO: Kenneth Barr
    Controller: Shirley Campbell
    Shipping Manager: Floyd Saderlund
    Office Manager: Lisa Fronsman
Estimated Sales: $2.7 Million
Number Employees: 250-499
Type of Packaging: Consumer, Food Service, Bulk
Brands:
    BLAZING STAR

203 Adobe Springs
PO Box 1417
Patterson, CA 95363-1417   408-897-3023
    Fax: 408-897-3028 magnesum@ix.netcom.com
                    www.mgwater.com
Bulk magnesium rich mineral water
    President: Paul Mason
    Co-Owner: Janet Mason
Brands:
    Hi0Spring
    Noah's Spring Water
    Seven-Up

204 (HQ)Adolf's Meats & SausageKitchen
35 New Britain Ave
Hartford, CT 06106-3398   860-522-1588
Manufacturer and importer of beef, pork, veal, sausage and chicken
    President: Joseph Gorski
Estimated Sales: Less than $500,000
Number Employees: 1-4
Type of Packaging: Consumer, Food Service, Bulk
Other Locations:
    Adolf's Meat & Sausage
    Norwalk CT

205 Adrian's Bakery
9850 62nd Avenue NW
Edmonton, AB T6E 0E3
Canada   780-435-2240
    Fax: 780-435-3556 800-668-3533
Manufacturer and wholesaler/distributor of par-baked baked goods including specialty rye bread and rolls and bread sticks
    Sales Manager: Larry Dunham
Number Employees: 80
Sq. footage: 12000
Parent Co: Canada Bread
Brands:
    Adrian's

206 Adrienne's Gourmet Foods
849 Ward Dr
Santa Barbara, CA 93111-2920   805-964-6848
    Fax: 805-964-8698 800-937-7010
                www.adriennes.com
Manufacturer, importer and exporter of the finest organic and kosher cookies, crackers and high protein pastas
    President: John O'Donnell
    Vice President: Adrienne O'Donnell
    Sales/Marketing Executive: Jim Shankin
Estimated Sales: $5-10 Million
Number Employees: 20-49
Type of Packaging: Consumer, Food Service, Private Label, Bulk
Brands:
    Appeteasers
    California Crisps
    Courtney's
    Courtney's Organic Water Crackers
    Darcia's Organic Crostini
    Lavosh Hawaii
    Lavosh-Hawaii
    Papadina Pasta
    Papadini Hi-Protein

207 Advance Food Brokers
3230 Bloomfield Shore Drive
West Bloomfield, MI 48323-3300   248-851-9045
                Fax: 248-851-6756 moirssteak@aol.com

Processor of steak salt and soup bases; Export, import and domestic broker of alcoholic beverages, confectionery and dairy/deli items, groceries and spices
President: M Shanker
CEO: J Gell
Number Employees: 3
Number of Brands: 1
Number of Products: 10
Sq. footage: 2000
Type of Packaging: Consumer, Food Service
Brands:
  MOIR'S

208 Advance Food Company
301 W Broadway Ave
Enid, OK 73701-3837   580-237-6656
    Fax: 580-231-4587   888-723-8237
        tmclaughlin@advancefoodcompany.com
                www.advance-food.com
Manufacturer or breaded pre-portion, ready-to-cook, fully cooked beef, pork, veal, chicken and turkey
President/CEO: Greg Allen
Co-Founder: David McLaughlin
Co-Founder: Paul Allen
SVP Sales: Mark Allen
VP/Corporate Accounts: Tim McLaughlin
VP/Product Management: Rob McLaughlin
Estimated Sales: $194 Million
Number Employees: 50-99
Type of Packaging: Consumer, Food Service, Private Label
Other Locations:
  Advance Food Company
  Caryville TN
  Advance Food Company
  Scanton PA
  Advance Food Company - Sales
  Oklahoma City OK
Brands:
  54TH STREET DELI
  CERTIFIED ANGUS BEEF
  CHEESEBURGER FRIES
  EASY BEGINNINGS
  FAST FIXON
  KITCHEN SENSATIONS
  SHORTY'S
  SMART SERVE
  STEAK EZE
  VINCELLO LAMB AND VEAL

209 Advanced Aquacultural Technologies
14792 Cr 52
Syracuse, IN 46567   574-457-5802
                Fax: 219-457-5887
Hybrid striped bass
President: Gary Miller

210 Advanced Food Services
9807 Lackman Rd
Shawnee Mission, KS 66219-1209   913-888-8088
    Fax: 913-888-8075 info@advancedfood.com
                www.advancedfood.com
President: Raju Shah

211 (HQ)Advanced Food Systems, Inc.
21 Roosevelt Ave
Somerset, NJ 08873-5030   732-873-6776
    Fax: 732-873-4177 info@afsnj.com
                www.afsnj.com
Processor of food stabilizers, texture systems and flavor/seasoning systems; importer of raw materials; exporter of texture and flavor systems
President: Yongkeun Joh
VP: Sunny Joh
Estimated Sales: $5-10 Million
Number Employees: 20-49
Sq. footage: 60000

212 Advanced Food Technology
11252 W Cooper Dr
Littleton, CO 80127-5845   303-980-5221
                Fax: 303-799-1262
Coffee extract (concentrate), coffee filters, flavors

213 Advanced Ingredients, Inc.
331 Capitola Ave # F
Capitola, CA 95010-3251   831-464-9891
    Fax: 831-464-9895 888-238-4647
        info@advancedingredients.com
                www.advancedingredients.com
Processor and exporter of specialty ingredients
President: Fred Greenland

Estimated Sales: $ 1 - 3 Million
Number Employees: 5-9
Brands:
  BAKESMART®
  ENERGYSMART®
  ENERGYSOURCE®
  FRUITRIM®
  FRUITSAVR®
  FRUITSOURCE®
  MOISTURLOK®
  PLUS AND MOISTURIOK®

214 Advanced Nutritional Research, Inc.
PO Box 807
Ellicottville, NY 14731-0807   716-699-2020
    Fax: 716-699-2036 800-836-0644
        info@advancednutritionalresearch.com
                www.anrminerals.com
Processor of vitamin and mineral supplements
President: Nancy Jemison
Estimated Sales: $1-2.5 Million
Number Employees: 1-4
Type of Packaging: Consumer, Private Label

215 Advanced Spice & Trading
1808 Monetary Ln # 100
Carrollton, TX 75006-7027   972-242-8580
    Fax: 972-242-6920 800-872-7811
        sales@advancedspice.com
                www.advancedspice.com
Importer, processor and full line distributor of spices and manufacturing ingredients used in the food industry.
Owner: Greg Hank
CEO: Greg Hanks
Estimated Sales: $30-50 Million
Number Employees: 10-19
Sq. footage: 67200
Type of Packaging: Consumer, Food Service, Private Label, Bulk
Brands:
  Santaka Chili Pods
  Supper Topper

216 Advent Machine Company
6815 E Washington Blvd
Commerce, CA 90040-1905   323-728-5367
    Fax: 323-728-2443 800-846-7716
        info@adventmachine.net
                www.adventmachine.net
Manufacturer of pressure-sensitive or plain paper labels
Owner: Richard G Ealy
Estimated Sales: $ 1 - 3 Million
Number Employees: 5-9

217 Adventist Book & Food
2160 Us Highway 1
Trenton, NJ 08648-4447   609-392-8010
    Fax: 609-392-4477 800-765-6955
njabc@erols.com   www.adventistbookcenter.com
Vegetarian meat substitutes
Manager: Herb Shiroma
CFO: Herb Shiroma
Owner: New Jersey
Estimated Sales: $ .5 - 1 million
Number Employees: 1-4

218 Adventure Foods
481 Banjo Lane
Whittier, NC 28789-7999   828-497-4113
                Fax: 828-497-7529
    CustomerService@adventurefoods.com
                www.adventurefoods.com
Manufacturer a complete line of freeze-dried, dehydrated, shelf stable foods and instant food items for the food service, food storage programs, health food markets and the outdoor market. Also offered are baking mixes, bulk spices andingredients, specialty foods and special packing for vegetarian, diabetics, gluten intolerance and for other food or health restrictions
President: Jean Spangenberg
CEO: Sam Spangenberg
Number Employees: 5-9
Parent Co: Jean's Garden Greats
Type of Packaging: Consumer, Food Service, Private Label, Bulk
Brands:
  ADVENTURE FOODS
  BAKE PACKERS
  GSI
  HEARTTLINE

  LUMEN
  OPEN COUNTRY
  WELL SEASONED TRAVELER

219 Aegean Cheese
2606 W Oakland Avenue
Austin, MN 55912   507-433-1292
                Fax: 507-433-1909
Cheese
President: Roger Enstad
VP Marketing: Steve Enstad
Estimated Sales: $20-50 Million
Number Employees: 20-49

220 Aetna Springs Cellars
7227 Pope Valley Rd
Pope Valley, CA 94567-9441   707-965-2675
    Fax: 707-965-2675 skimsey@napanet.net
                www.aetnaspringscellars.com
Wines
General Partner: Sally Kimsey
Partner: Jim Watson
Partner: Margaret Ann Watson
Winemaker/Partner: Paul Kimsey
Estimated Sales: $500,000-$1 Million
Number Employees: 1-4
Brands:
  AETNA SPRINGS CELLARS

221 Affiliated Rice Milling
715 N 2nd St
Alvin, TX 77511-3674   281-331-6176
                Fax: 281-585-0336
Processor and exporter of rice and rice flour
Manager: Johnny Dunham
VP, Operations: Johnny Dunham
Estimated Sales: $20-50 Million
Number Employees: 10-19
Sq. footage: 130000
Parent Co: Rice Belt Warehouse
Brands:
  Eminence

222 Affy Tapple, LLC
6300 W Gross Point Rd
Niles, IL 60714-3916   847-588-2900
    Fax: 847-588-0392 mrs_p@affytapple.com
                www.affytapple.com
Handmade confections. Gourmet Caramel apples with a variety of toppings
Owner: Stuart Sorkin
Estimated Sales: $10-20 Million
Number Employees: 100-249

223 After-the-Fall Products
340 Old Bay Ln
Havre De Grace, MD 21078-4013   410-939-1403
    Fax: 410-939-6263 www.jmsmucker.com
Fruit juices
Manager: Doug Arington
Estimated Sales: $ 20 - 50 Million
Number Employees: 20-49

224 Afton Mountain Vineyards
234 Vineyard Ln
Afton, VA 22920-3702   540-456-8667
                Fax: 540-456-8002
    finewines@aftonmountainvineyards.com
        www.aftonmountainvineyards.com
Wines
President: Tom Corpora
VP: Shinko Corpora
Estimated Sales: $1-2.5 Million
Number Employees: 5-9
Type of Packaging: Private Label

225 AgSource Milk Analysis Laboratory
403 Cedar Ave W
Menomonie, WI 54751-1300   715-235-1128
    Fax: 715-235-8680 menomlab@agsource.com
                www.agsource.com
Co-Owner: Don Niles
Co-Owner: John Pagel
VP: Joel Amdall
Personnel Manager: Bruce Cornish
General Manager: C Smith
Estimated Sales: $ 1 - 3 Million
Number Employees: 20-49
Brands:
  Ag Co-Op

226 Agger Fish
63 Flushing Ave # 313
Brooklyn, NY 11205-1081   718-855-1717
Fax: 718-855-4545 marcagger@gmail.com
www.monkfish.net
Manufacturer and importer and exporter of
monkfish, fluke, monkfish liver and shark fins,
bones and cartilage for food supplements and ingre-
dients
    President: Mark Agger
Estimated Sales:$500,000-$1 Million
Number Employees: 500-999
Sq. footage: 3000
Type of Packaging: Bulk

227 (HQ)Agilex™ Flavors & Fragrances, Inc.
10 Mountainview Road
North Atrium
Upper Saddle River, NJ 07458   201-236-8150
    Fax: 201-236-8154 800-542-7662
info@agilexfandf.com www.aromatec.com
Manufacturer of Flavors and Fragrances
    President/CEO: Carlo Colesanti
    Senior VP/CFO: Richard Green Jr.
Estimated Sales:$5-10 Million
Number Employees: 50-99
Other Locations:
    Flavor Division Headquarters
    Rancho Santa Margarita CA
    Fragrance Division Headquarters
    Piscataway NJ

228 Aglamesis Brothers
3046 Madison Rd
Cincinnati, OH 45209-1797   513-531-5196
    Fax: 513-531-5403 www.aglamesis.com
Processor of ice cream and confectionery products
    President: James Aglamesis
Estimated Sales:$2.5-5 Million
Number Employees: 10-19
Type of Packaging: Consumer, Food Service

229 Agland, Inc.
P.O.Box 338
Eaton, CO 80615-0338   970-454-4000
    Fax: 970-454-2144 800-433-4688
www.aglandinc.com
Processor of pinto beans and grain
    President: William McKay
    CEO: Mitch Anderson
    CFO: Rob Lyons
    CEO: Mitch Anderson
Estimated Sales:$10-20 Million
Number Employees: 100-249
Type of Packaging: Consumer
Brands:
    RED BIRD

230 AgraWest Foods
PO Box 760
Souris
Prince Edward Island, NS C0A 2B0
Canada   902-687-1400
    Fax: 902-687-1401 877-687-1400
agrawest@agrawest.com www.agrawest.com
Manufacturer and exporter of dehydrated potato
granules
    President: Richard Zirkelback
    CEO: Richard Nickel
    VP/GM: Todd Sutton
    Quality Assurance Manager: Kendra Deagle
    Sales Manager: Mary Croucher
    Production Manager: Jamie Trainor
Parent Co: Idaho Pacific Corporation
Type of Packaging: Food Service, Bulk
Brands:
    Chef Master

231 Agrexco USA
15012 132nd Ave
Jamaica, NY 11434-3596   718-481-8700
    Fax: 718-481-8710 amoso@agrexco.com
www.agrexco.com
Processor and importer of fruits including dried
dates, grapefruits and oranges as well as fresh cut
herbs
    President: Yoram Shalev
    CFO/VP, Quality Control: Jack Aschkeigi
Estimated Sales:$20-50 Million
Number Employees: 20-49
Brands:
    Alesia
    Carmel

232 Agri Processors
P.O.Box 920
Postville, IA 52162-0920   563-864-7811
    Fax: 563-864-7890
Processor of kosher meat
    Owner: Aaron Rubashkin
    CEO: Bernard Feldman
    Manager: Donald Hunt
Estimated Sales:$50-100 Million
Number Employees: 500-999

233 Agri-Best Foods
4430 S Tripp Ave
Chicago, IL 60632-4321   773-247-5060
    Fax: 773-247-7247
    President: Bill Koulch
Estimated Sales:$100+ Million
Number Employees: 100-249

234 Agri-Dairy Products
3020 Westchester Ave # 308
Purchase, NY 10577-2525   914-697-9580
    Fax: 914-697-9517 frankjr@agridairy.com
www.agridairy.com
A full service manufacturer distributor of dairy and
food ingredients including protein powders, cheese,
butter, soy ingredients, low carb ingredients and
sweeteners
    Owner: Frank Reeves
    VP: Steve Bronfield
    Sales: Frank Reeves
Estimated Sales:$30+ Million
Number Employees: 10-19
Number of Products: 50+
Type of Packaging: Bulk

235 Agri-Mark
P.O.Box 5800
Lawrence, MA 01842-5800   978-687-4936
    Fax: 978-794-8304 information@agrimark.net
www.agrimark.net
Manufacturer of dairy products including butter and
nonfat, skim and condensed milk; exporter of butter
powder
    President: Paul P Johnston
    CEO: Paul Johnston
    Director Communications: Douglas DiMento
Estimated Sales:$521 Million
Number Employees: 100-249
Type of Packaging: Private Label, Bulk
Other Locations:
    Agri-Mark Manufacturing Plant
    West Springfield MA
    Agri-Mark Manufacturing Plant
    Middlebury VT
    Agri-Mark Manufacturing Plant
    Cabot VT
    Agri-Mark Manufacturing Plant
    Chateaugay NY
Brands:
    Cabot
    McCADAM

236 (HQ)Agri-Mark
P.O.Box 5800
Lawrence, MA 01842-5800   978-687-4936
    Fax: 978-794-8304 info@agrimark.net
www.agrimark.net
Milk, cream and butter
    President: Paul P Johnston
    CEO: Paul Johnston
    Senior VP: Robert Wellington
    VP/Marketing: John Burke
    Plant Manager: Gary Carlow
Estimated Sales:$20-50 Million
Number Employees: 50-99
Other Locations:
    Agri-Mark
    Middlebury VT
    Agri-Mark
    Cabot VT
    Agri-Mark
    Chateaugay NY

237 Agri-Mark
P.O.Box 5800
Lawrence, MA 01842-5800   978-687-4936
    Fax: 978-794-8304 ddimento@agrimark.net
www.agrimark.net
Dairy products
    President: Paul P Johnston
    CEO: Paul Johnston
    Executive VP/COO: Dr. Richard Stammer
    Director Communications: Douglas DiMento

Estimated Sales:$1-500 Million
Number Employees: 100-249
Parent Co: Agri-Mark
Brands:
    CABOT DAIRIES
    McCADAM

238 (HQ)Agri-Northwest
7404 W Hood Pl
Kennewick, WA 99336-6718   509-734-1195
    Fax: 509-734-1092
Potatoes
    President: Don Sleight
    CFO: R Thomas Mackay
Estimated Sales:$65 Million
Number Employees: 10-19

239 Agri-Pack
P.O.Box 2086
Pasco, WA 99302-2086   509-545-6181
    Fax: 509-545-5748 steve@agri-pack.com
Processor of onions including whole, rings, diced
and strips
    Manager: Tim Sessions
    Account Executive: Jon Josephson
    Director Sales/Marketing: Steve Shepard
    Plant Manager: Todd Daniko
Estimated Sales:$2.5-5 Million
Number Employees: 20-49
Sq. footage: 150000
Parent Co: Agri Pack
Type of Packaging: Food Service, Bulk

240 Agri-Sales
209 Louise Ave
Nashville, TN 37203-1811   615-329-1141
    Fax: 615-329-2770 800-251-1141
info@agri-sales.com www.agri-sales.com
Manufacturer's Representative Group
    President/Founder: Jerry Bellar
    VP: Phillip Ferrell
*Estimated Sales:*Less than $500,000
Number Employees: 20-49

241 AgriCulver Seeds
2059 State Route 96
Trumansburg, NY 14886-9129   607-387-5788
    Fax: 607-387-5789 800-836-3701
info@agriculverseeds.com
www.agriculverseeds.com
Manufacturer, packager, exporter and whole-
saler/distributor of specialty organic grains includ-
ing wheat, spelt, barley, buckwheat and alfalfa
    Manager: Wayne Brown
    GM: Rod Porter
    Office Manager/Customer Service: Nancy
    Fraboni
Estimated Sales:$2.5-5 Million
Number Employees: 10-19
Sq. footage: 32000
Brands:
    DAIRY BANQUET

242 Agricor
P.O.Box 807
Marion, IN 46952-0807   765-662-0606
    Fax: 765-662-7189 sales@agricor.org
www.agricor.info
Processor and exporter of corn grits, flour and meal
    President: Steve Wickes
    Sales Coordinator: Duane Hudson
    Operations Manager: Bill Cramer
    Plant Manager: Jack Jones
Estimated Sales:$20-50 Million
Number Employees: 20-49
Type of Packaging: Bulk
Brands:
    Agricor

243 Agricore United
CanWest Global Place 201 Portage Avenue
PO Box 6600
Winnipeg, MB R3C 3A7
Canada   204-944-5411
    Fax: 204-944-5454
infomaster@agricoreunited.com
www.agricoreunited.com

Manufacturer and exporter of wheat, barley, oats, 3-grain and instant cereals, pancake mix, organic flour and herb food bars and beans including; pinto, black, Great Northern and lentil
    CEO: Brian Hayward
    CFO: David Carefoot
    Senior VP: Ronald Enns
    VP Human Resources: Gerald Valois
    VP Operations: S MacKay
Type of Packaging: Consumer, Food Service, Bulk
Other Locations:
    Manitoba
    Saskatchewan
    Alberta
    British Columbia

244 Agrinom LLC
P.O.Box 174
Hakalau, HI 96710-0174   808-963-6771
    Fax: 808-963-6143   mail@agrinom.com
                        www.agrinom.com
    President: Jay Ram
    Marketing: Jay Ram
Brands:
    Agrinom

245 (HQ)Agrinorthwest
7404 W Hood Pl
Kennewick, WA 99336-6718   509-734-1195
                        Fax: 509-734-1092
Manufacturer and packer of produce including apples, potatoes, onions, etc.
    President: Don Sleight
    CFO: R Thomas MacKay
Estimated Sales: $65 Million
Number Employees: 10-19
Type of Packaging: Consumer, Food Service, Private Label, Bulk

246 Agripac
PO Box 5110
Denver, CO 80217-5110   503-363-9255
    Fax: 503-371-5682   consultas@agripac.com.ar
                        www.agripac.com.ar
Frozen red raspberries, strawberries, marionberries, rhubarb, snap beans, broccoli, cauliflower, corn, whole onions, peas and carrots, squash, mixed vegetables, prepared vegetables
    Director: Pablo Adreani
    Senior VP: Patrick Monaghan
    Senior VP, Operations: Russ Grubb
Brands:
    Agripac

247 Agriproducts
3111 N University Drive
Coral Springs, FL 33065-5086   954-345-1717
            Fax: 954-345-7043   800-277-4979
    agrimatt@aol.com   www.agriproducts.com
Manufacturer, exporter and importer of gum arabic
    VP: Matthew Rutter
    Operations: Ruth Porro
Estimated Sales: $1-2.5 Million
Number Employees: 1-4
Parent Co: Agrisales

248 Agro Farma Inc
669 County Rd 25
New Berlin, NY 13411   607-847-6181
    Fax: 607-847-8847   877-847-6181
                        www.chobani.com
    Greek Yogurt
    Chairman: Hamdi Ulukaya
    Controller: Besnik Fetoski
Estimated Sales: $15.8 Million
Number Employees: 60

249 Agro Foods, Inc.
256 W Mashta Dr
Key Biscayne, FL 33149-2420   305-361-7200
    Fax: 305-361-7639   agro@agrofoods.com
                        www.agrofoods.com
Manufacturer, packer, wholesaler/distributor, importer and exporter of Spanish olives
    Manager: Isa Knight
Estimated Sales: $1-2.5 Million
Number Employees: 5-9
Sq. footage: 131500
Parent Co: Agro Aceitunera SA
Type of Packaging: Consumer, Food Service, Private Label, Bulk
Brands:
    Candelita
    Exporsevilla
    Lola

250 AgroCepia
9703 Dixie Highway
Suite 3
Miami, FL 33156   305-704-3488
    Fax: 305-666-6930   acusa_us@bellsouth.net
                        www.agrocepia.cl
Low moisture colored apple flakes and nuggets, evaporated apple dices, grinds, rings and wedges, low moisture powders, dehydrated tomato, green bell pepper, red bell pepper and jalapeno pepper dices and granules
    Sales Director: Mike Zobel
Estimated Sales: $ 3 - 5 Million
Number Employees: 1-4

251 (HQ)Agrocan
93 Front Sreet E
Toronto, ON M5E 1C3
Canada   514-272-2512
    Fax: 514-270-6370   877-247-6226
info@agrocanfoods.com   www.agrocanfoods.com
Manufacturer and exporter of fruit, olives, oil, vegetables and miscellaneous products
    President: John Karellis
Number Employees: 3
Type of Packaging: Private Label
Other Locations:
    Agrocan
    Aeginion, N. Pierias
Brands:
    SUNMED

252 Agrocomplex
1100 E. Main Cross
Suite 23
Findlay, OH 45840   419-420-1800
    Fax: 419-420-1800   bill@agrocomplex.us
                        www.agrocomplex.us
Supplier of dairy products such as milk powder & milk powder blends, whey blends, casein and caseinates and butter.

253 (HQ)Agropur Cooperative Agro-Alimentaire
510 Rue Principale
Granby, QC J2G 2X2
Canada   450-375-1991
    Fax: 450-375-7160   800-363-5686
                        jarollan@agropur.com
Manufacturer, importer and exporter of milk, cream, ice cream, butter, cheese and yogurt
    Chairman: Jacques Cartier
    CEO: Claude Menard
    Secretary: Andre Gauthier
Number Employees: 2,700
Type of Packaging: Consumer, Food Service
Other Locations:
    Agropur Coop. Agro-Alimentair
    Markham ON

254 Agrusa, Inc.
PO Box 267
Leonia, NJ 07605-7244   201-592-5950
    Fax: 201-585-7244   agrusa@agrusainc.com
                        www.agritalia.com
Manufacturer and importer of Italian foods, both conventional and organic including: pasta, olive oil, balsamic vinegar, tomatoes, risotto, rice and frozen pizza.
    President: Jill Bush
Number Employees: 5
Sq. footage: 2000
Type of Packaging: Consumer, Food Service, Private Label, Bulk
Brands:
    Bella Italia
    Celio
    Don Peppe
    Private Label

255 Agumm
10636 NW 49th Street
Coral Springs, FL 33076-2702   954-344-0607
    Fax: 305-341-6667   bfjelde@corpcomm.net
Baked products, batters, breading, confectionery, dry mixes
    President: Matthew Rutter

256 Agvest
7 Winter Rd
Franklin, ME 04634-3400   207-565-3303
    Fax: 207-565-3303   www.agvest.com

Processor and exporter of frozen blueberries and cranberries; also, sugar-infused blueberries.
    Operations Manager: Robert Neuman
    Plant Manager: Anthony Kelley
Estimated Sales: $20-50 Million
Number Employees: 20-49
Parent Co: Agvest
Type of Packaging: Consumer, Food Service
Brands:
    North Eastern

257 (HQ)Agvest
7589 First Pl
Cleveland, OH 44146-6711   440-735-6900
    Fax: 440-735-1680   www.agvest.com
Processor and exporter of frozen apples, elderberries, bilberries, sugar infused blueberries, cranberries and cherries, and fruit flakes and powders.
    President/CEO: Barry Schneider
    CFO: Steve Hamilton
Estimated Sales: $1-2.5 Million
Number Employees: 5-9
Type of Packaging: Food Service
Brands:
    North Eastern
    Quality

258 Ah Dor Kosher Fish Corporation
25 Main St
Monsey, NY 10952-3707   845-425-7776
Fish
    President: Joseph Neuman
Estimated Sales: Less than $500,000
Number Employees: 1-4
Type of Packaging: Private Label

259 Ahlgren Vineyard
20320 Highway 9
Boulder Creek, CA 95006-9008   831-338-6071
            Fax: 831-338-9111   800-338-6071
    ahlgren@cruzio.com   www.ahlgrenvineyard.com
Processor of wines
    Co-Owner: Valerie Ahlgren
    Co-Owner/CEO/Winemaker: Dexter Ahlgren
Estimated Sales: $1-2.5 Million
Number Employees: 1-4
Type of Packaging: Food Service, Private Label
Brands:
    AHLGREN VINEYARD
    TRE VINI ROSSI

260 Ahmad Tea
PO Box 876
Deer Park, TX 77536-0876   281-478-0957
            Fax: 281-479-0521   800-637-7704
    info@ahmadteausa.com   www.ahmadtea.com
Tea and tea gift producer

261 Aidell's Sausage Company
1625 Alvarado St
San Leandro, CA 94577-2636   510-614-5450
            Fax: 510-614-2287   800-546-5795
    info@aidells.com   www.aidells.com
Manufacturer of sausage products
    Founder: Chef Bruce Aidells
    CEO: Bob Mc Henry
Number Employees: 20-49
Type of Packaging: Consumer, Food Service, Bulk
Brands:
    Aidell's

262 Aileen Quirk & Sons
235 W 12th Ave
Kansas City, MO 64116-4178   816-471-4580
                        Fax: 816-842-8063
Founded in 1947, packages a wide variety of dried edible beans and sell them to wholesalers and grocery stores.
    President: Larry Quirk
    CEO: Larry Quirk
    VP Operations: Kelly Quirk
Estimated Sales: $5.8 Million
Number Employees: 10-19
Type of Packaging: Food Service, Private Label, Bulk
Brands:
    Pdq Puncher Dry Edible Bean

263 Ailments E.D. Foods Inc.
6200 Trans Canada Highway
Pointe Claire, QC H9R 1B9
Canada   514-695-3333
    Fax: 514-695-0281   800-267-3333
    leslie@ed.ca   www.ed-foods.com

Manufacturer and exporter of dehydrated soup and gravy bases, specialty seasonings and dehydrated mixes including soup, gravy and side dishes; also, consultant specializing in research, development and processing of custom recipes
President: V Eiser
VP: R Eiser
Director Marketing: M Jasmin
Number Employees: 50-99
Sq. footage: 50000
Type of Packaging: Consumer, Food Service, Private Label, Bulk
Brands:
Easily Done
Inspiration
Luda
Top & Toss

264 Aimonetto and Sons
6725 E Marginal Way S
Seattle, WA 98108-3406   206-767-2777
Fax: 206-762-6792   866-823-2777
Manufacturer of milk, juice, cottage cheese, sour cream and yogurt; wholesaler/distributor of dairy products; serving the food service market
Owner: Jim Aimonetto
Estimated Sales: $17 Million
Number Employees: 10-19
Type of Packaging: Consumer, Food Service

265 (HQ)Aina Hawaiian Tropical Products
175 E Kawailani St
Hilo, HI 96720-5606   808-981-0771
Fax: 808-981-2644   877-961-4774
trinag@alohablooms.com
www.hawaiitropicals.com
Ethnic foods
Owner: Steven Parente
Manager: Steven Parente
Estimated Sales: $ .5 - 1 million
Number Employees: 5-9
Brands:
Hawaii Gourmet
Kona Coffee

266 Airlie Winery
15305 Dunn Forest Rd
Monmouth, OR 97361-9570   503-838-6013
Fax: 503-838-6279   airlie@airliewinery.com
www.airliewinery.com
Wines
Owner: Mary Olson
Marketing/Sales VP: Barry Glassman
Winemaker: Elizabeth Ogg
Estimated Sales: $500,000-$1 Million
Number Employees: 1-4
Type of Packaging: Private Label
Brands:
Airlie

267 Airlite Plastics Company
P.O.Box 8400
Omaha, NE 68108-0400   402-341-7300
Fax: 402-346-2509   800-228-9545
mosler@airliteplastics.com
www.airliteplastics.com
Plastic injection molding and printing manufacturer product line of which includes drink cups, polystyrene coolers, ICF (Insulating Concrete Form) building blocks, and customized plastic products. Additional options include in-moldlabeling (IML), shrink sleeving and offset printing.
President: Brad Crosby
CFO: Pat Kenealy
VP Sales & Marketing: Michael Corrigan
Regional Sales Manager: Mark Osler
Estimated Sales: $100-125 Million
Number Employees: 500-999
Sq. footage: 820000

268 Ajinomato Frozen Foods USA
7124 N Marine Dr
Portland, OR 97203-6480   503-286-5869
Fax: 503-286-7089   yoshimineh@ajiusa.com
www.ajinomato-usa.com
Frozen vegetables
President/CEO: Yoshio Ishii
Director Research: T Arima
Production Manager: Bruce Jenson
Plant Manager: Dan Trainer
Estimated Sales: $20-50 Million
Number Employees: 100-249

269 Ajinomoto Food Ingredients, LLC
8430 W. Bryn Mawr Avenue
Suite 635
Chicago, IL 60631   773-714-1436
Fax: 773-714-1431 www.ajiusafood.com
Manufacturer and supplier of flavor seasonings, sauces, enzymes, and sweeteners.

270 Ajinomoto Food Ingredients LLC
8430 W Bryn Mawr Ave
Chicago, IL 60631-3473   773-380-7000
Fax: 773-380-7006   naultyb@ajiusa.com
www.lysine.com
Processor of flavorings including aspartame, enzymes, monosodium glutamate, nucleotides, glutamic salts, soy oligosaccharides and amino acids. Also liquid and dry sauces, including soy sauce, sesame oil
President: Tommy Teshima
Director Sales: David Barbour
Estimated Sales: $ 600,000
Number Employees: 5
Parent Co: Ajinomoto Company
Type of Packaging: Bulk
Brands:
ACTIVA TG
KOJI-AJI
TRANSGLUTAMINASE

271 Ajinomoto Frozen FoodsUSA
7124 N Marine Drive
Portland, IR 97203-6480   503-734-1528
info@ajifrozenusa.com
www.ajifrozenusa.com
Manufacturer and exporter of frozen foods including sauteed and fried (tempura) meats, vegetables and seafood, soups, fried rice and pilafs, stews, roux, chowders and Oriental dishes; importer of noodles and spices
President, Ajinomoto Frozen Foods USA: Haruo Kurata
CIO: Brandon Sullivan
Sales Director: David Barbour
General Manager: Tomo Shiojima
Estimated Sales: $ 24 Million
Number Employees: 150
Sq. footage: 264000
Parent Co: Ajinomoto Company
Type of Packaging: Consumer, Food Service, Private Label
Other Locations:
Los Angeles CA
Portland OR
Honolulu HI
Brands:
Ajinomoto

272 (HQ)Ajinomoto USA
One Parker Plaza
400 Kelby Street
Fort Lee, NJ 07024   201-292-3200
Fax: 201-261-7343 www.ajinomoto-usa.com
Provides consumer foods, amino acids, and food ingredients.
President/CEO: shinichi Suzuki
SVP/Secretary/Treasurer: Hideki Nagano
Estimated Sales: $ 12 Billion
Number Employees: 400
Sq. footage: 264000
Parent Co: Ajinomoto Company
Type of Packaging: Consumer, Food Service, Private Label

273 Ak-Mak Bakeries
89 Academy Ave
Sanger, CA 93657-2104   559-264-4145
Fax: 559-875-2472
Armenian cracker bread
President: Manoog Soojian
VP: Hagop Soojian
Estimated Sales: $20-50 Million
Number Employees: 20-49
Brands:
Ak Mak
Country Style
Round Cracker Bread

274 Akay USA, LLC.
500 Hartle Street
Suite E
Sayreville, NJ 08872   732-254-7177
Fax: 732-254-7178   akayusallc@gmail.com
www.akay-group.com

Manufacturer and supplier of paprika and spices.

275 Akenhead's Ice Cream Company
598 Park Avenue
East Palestine, OH 44413-1571   330-426-9553
Processor of ice cream and frozen dessert
Owner: James V Akenhead
Estimated Sales: $1-2.5 Million
Number Employees: 5-9
Type of Packaging: Consumer, Food Service, Bulk

276 Al & John's Glen Rock Ham
444 Marshall St
Paterson, NJ 07503-2909   973-742-4990
Fax: 973-742-5141   800-969-4990
Processor of Canadian bacon and fresh ham including cooked, ready-to-eat, fat-free, semi-boneless, smoked boneless, honey, Virginia, maple, apple cinnamon, black forest, etc.
President/CEO: Alex Oldja
VP: Jennifer Oldja
Plant Manager: Alex Oldja, Jr.
Estimated Sales: $20-50 Million
Number Employees: 100-249

277 Al Dente
9815 Main St
Whitmore Lake, MI 48189-9438   734-449-8522
Fax: 734-449-8511   800-536-7278
info@aldentepasta.com   www.aldentepasta.com
Processor of specialty flavored pasta: linguine, fettuccine, angel hair, rigatoni, penne, fusilli, farfalle and rotini. Sauces: pesto and alfredo
President: Monique Deschaine
VP: Dennis Deschaine
Production Manager: Nanette Carson
Estimated Sales: $5-10 Million
Number Employees: 10-19
Brands:
Al Dente
Al Dente Pasta Selecta
Al Dente Sure Success
Monique's Pasta Sauces

278 Al Gelato Bornay
9133 Belden Ave
Franklin Park, IL 60131-3505   847-455-5355
Fax: 847-455-7553 www.algelato.com
Importer, exporter and processor of ice cream, sorbet, spumoni, natural fruit sorbets, and frozen desserts
President: Paula DiNardo
VP: Paula Di Nardo
Plant Manager: Sal Felix
Estimated Sales: $1-10 Million
Number Employees: 5-9
Sq. footage: 5000
Type of Packaging: Food Service, Private Label, Bulk
Brands:
Al Gelato

279 (HQ)Al Pete Meats
P.O.Box 2786
Muncie, IN 47307-0786   765-288-8817
Fax: 765-281-2759
Processor of frozen portion control foods; including corn dogs, breaded meat and cheese, raw and cooked breaded mushrooms and cauliflower; Exporter of frozen portion controlled breaded meat products
President: Arlin Mann
CEO: John Hartmeyer
CEO: John Hartmeyer
Purchasing Manager: Paul Whitechair
Estimated Sales: $10-20 Million
Number Employees: 20-49
Sq. footage: 150000
Type of Packaging: Consumer, Food Service, Private Label
Brands:
Al Pete
Pete's Pride

280 Al Richards Chocolates
851 Broadway
Bayonne, NJ 07002-3018   201-436-0915
Fax: 201-436-0485   888-777-6964
www.alrichardschocolates.com
Chocolates and ceramics
Estimated Sales: $300,000-500,000
Number Employees: 1-4

281 Al Safa Halal
PO Box 1076
Niagara Falls, NY 14303-0376   519-654-9989
            Fax: 519-654-9245   800-268-8174
info@alsafahalal.com   www.alsafahalal.com
Processor and exporter of halal processed foods including pizza, beef burgers, chicken nuggets, fish sticks, etc.
    President: David Muller
    VP: Steve Hahn
Number Employees: 10-19
Number of Brands: 40
Parent Co: Al Safa Halal
Type of Packaging: Consumer, Food Service
Other Locations:
    Al Safa Halal
    Cambridge, Ontario
Brands:
    Al Safa Halal

282 Al's Beverage Company
3 Revay Rd
East Windsor, CT 06088-9688   860-627-7003
        Fax: 860-627-8067   888-257-7632
mfeldman@alsbeverage.com
www.alsbeverage.com
Fountain soft drinks
    Owner: Marjorie Feldman
    Sr. VP Sales: John Martin
    VP: William Melcher
    Marketing Consultant: Todd Lemieux
    Sales Director: Art Gallegos
    Operations Manager: Michael McCarthy
Estimated Sales: $3-5 Million
Number Employees: 50-99
Type of Packaging: Private Label
Brands:
    Al's
    Barrel Head
    Canada Dry
    RC
    Stewarts
    Sunkist

283 Al-Rite Fruits & Syrups
18524 NE 2nd Ave
Miami, FL 33179-4427   305-652-2540
        Fax: 305-652-4478   800-652-2540
            www.al-rite.com
Processor and exporter of kosher products including isotonic iced tea, fountain and slush beverage, ice cream and nondairy bases. Also fudge and chocolate syrups, toppings, frozen cocktail/bar mixes and extracts and flavors forbeverages and desserts
    Manager: Alfredo Faubel
Estimated Sales: $5-10 Million
Number Employees: 10-19
Type of Packaging: Consumer, Food Service, Private Label, Bulk
Brands:
    Al-Rite
    Iso-Sport
    Tropical

284 Alabama Catfish
P.O. Box 769
Uniontown, AL 36786-0769   334-628-3474
    Fax: 334-628-2122 www.harvestselect.com
Catfish
    President: Jerry Whittington
    President: George Smelley
Estimated Sales: $ 20 - 50 Million
Number Employees: 250-499

285 Alabama Seafood Producers
P.O. Box 858
Bayou La Batre, AL 36509-0858   251-824-4396
            Fax: 251-824-7579
        http://www.alabamaseafood.org
    President: Richard Gazzier
    Vice President: Donna Gazzier
Estimated Sales: $ 5 - 10 Million
Number Employees: 10-19

286 Alacer Corporation
80 Icon
Foothill Ranch, CA 92610-3000   949-916-5698
        Fax: 949-951-7235   800-854-0249
    asolorzano@alacer.com   www.alacercorp.com
Processor and exporter of dietary supplements, mineral ascorbates, vitamins and distilled water
    President: Ron Fugate
    Director Marketing: Bruce Sweyd
    Executive Administration: Vernon Peck

Estimated Sales: $20-50 Million
Number Employees: 50-99
Sq. footage: 57000
Type of Packaging: Consumer
Brands:
    Emer'gen-C
    Miracle

287 Aladdin Bakers
240 25th St
Brooklyn, NY 11232-1338   718-499-1818
            Fax: 718-788-5174
    kasindorf@aladdinbakers.com
        www.aladdinbakers.com
Baker of sandwich wraps and gourmet flour tortillas, pita, panini and specialty breads, bagels, bread sticks, toast, croutons, and flatbreads
    President: Joseph Ayoub
    CFO/GM: Donald Guzzi
    VP Sales/Marketing: Paul Kasindorf
    Production Manager: Ed Curran
    Plant Manager: Arkadi Karachun
Estimated Sales: $20-50 Million
Number Employees: 100-249
Sq. footage: 100000
Type of Packaging: Consumer, Food Service, Private Label, Bulk
Brands:
    Aladdin

288 Alakef Coffee Roasters
1330 E Superior St
Duluth, MN 55805-3854   218-724-6849
        Fax: 218-724-7727   800-438-9228
        info@alakef.com   www.alakef.com
Roasted coffee
    President: Nessim Bohbot
    VP: Deborah Bohbot
Estimated Sales: $5-10 Million
Number Employees: 10-19
Type of Packaging: Private Label

289 Alamance Foods/Triton Water Company
P.O. Box 2690
Burlington, NC 27216-2690   336-226-6392
        Fax: 336-229-9768   800-476-9111
            info@alamancefoods.com
            www.alamancefoods.com
Processor of spring and distilled water, whipped cream, fruit drinks, freeze pops and nondairy whipped toppings.
    President: Bill Scott, Jr
    CEO/Chairman: Bill Scott, Sr
    CEO: Bill Scott Sr
    VP Sales and Marketing: Jeff Parker
    Sales Manager East: David Shearn
    Sales Manager West: Larry Allumbauth
    VP Operations: Roger Bates
Estimated Sales: $20-50 Million
Number Employees: 100-249

290 Alamo Masa Company
318 E Nopal Street
Uvalde, TX 78801-5331   210-732-9651
        Fax: 210-735-5236   800-568-9651
Tortillas
    President: Joe Martinez III
Estimated Sales: $10-20 Million
Number Employees: 10-19

291 Alamo Onions
PO Box 1126
Pharr, TX 78577-1621   210-281-0962
Refrigerated whole peeled onions
    President: Chris Torres
    VP: Manuel Rodriguez
Estimated Sales: $5-10 Million
Number Employees: 20-49

292 (HQ)Alamo Tamale Corporation
3713 Jensen Dr
Houston, TX 77026-3215   713-228-6446
        Fax: 713-228-7513   800-252-0586
    alamotam@texas.net   www.alamotamale.com
Manufacturer of tamales
    President: Louis Webster
    VP: Shirleen Webster
Estimated Sales: $10-20 Million
Number Employees: 50-99
Sq. footage: 25000
Type of Packaging: Consumer, Food Service, Private Label

Brands:
    Alamo

293 Alaska Aquafarms
P.O.Box 7
Moose Pass, AK 99631-0007   907-288-3667
        Fax: 907-288-3667   jjh@seward.net
            www.ternlakeinn.com
Shellfish culture gear
    Owner: James Hetrick
    President/CEO: Willard Fehr
Estimated Sales: $300,000-500,000
Number Employees: 1-4

294 Alaska Bounty Seafoods & Smokery
110 Jarvis Street
Sitka, AK 99835-9806   907-966-2927
Processor of smoked salmon
    Partner: Carol Petraborg
    Partner: Gerold Brager
Estimated Sales: $1-2.5 Million
Number Employees: 5-9
Type of Packaging: Consumer, Food Service, Bulk

295 Alaska Coffee Company
6436 Homer Dr # A
Anchorage, AK 99518-1900   907-333-3626
        Fax: 907-333-3690   coffcats@alaska.net
            www.espressoconsultants.com
Coffee
    Owner: Lori Brewer
Estimated Sales: $280,000
Number Employees: 10-19

296 Alaska Fresh Seafoods
105 E Marine Way
Kodiak, AK 99615   907-486-5749
            Fax: 907-486-6417
Seafood
    Owner: Dave Woodruff
    Treasurer: Gary Painter
    Vice President: David Woodruff
Estimated Sales: $ 20 - 50 Million
Number Employees: 50-99

297 Alaska General Seafood
6425 NE 175th St
Kenmore, WA 98028-4808   425-485-7755
        Fax: 425-485-5172 www.akgen.com
Frozen fish and seafood
    CEO: Mike Lee
    VP: Gordon Linquist
Estimated Sales: $ 20 - 50 Million
Number Employees: 10-19
Parent Co: Alaska General Seafood
Brands:
    Gold Seal

298 Alaska General Seafoods
6425 NE 175th St
Kenmore, WA 98028-4808   425-485-7755
        Fax: 425-485-5172   kenmore@akgen.com
            www.akgen.com
Frozen herring, canned and frozen salmon
    VP: Gordon Linquist
Estimated Sales: $20-50 Million
Number Employees: 10-19
Parent Co: Jim Pattison Group
Other Locations:
    Kenmore Warehouse
    Kenmore WA
    Naknek Plant
    Naknek AK
    Ketchikan Plant
    Ketchikan AK
    Egegik Office
    Egegik AK
    Ferndale Shop
    Ferndale WA

299 Alaska Herb Tea Company
6710 Weimer Dr
Anchorage, AK 99502-2054   907-245-3499
        Fax: 907-245-3499   800-654-2764
    herbtea@alaska.net   www.alaskaherbtea.com
Manufacturer of tea, honey, syrups, jams and jellies, cocoa, vinegars
    President: Charles Walsh
    VP: Sandra Fongemie
    Operations Manager: Ann Stewart
    Production Manager: Maria Salizar
Estimated Sales: Less than $500,000
Number Employees: 1-4
Sq. footage: 1

Type of Packaging: Private Label
Brands:
ALASKA WILD TEAS
ALASKAN BOREAL BOUQUET
ALASKAN FIREWEED
ALASKAN GOLD
COCOALASKA

300 Alaska Jack's Trading Post
6251 Tuttle Pl # 102
Anchorage, AK 99507-2099   907-248-9999
     Fax: 907-243-2044 888-660-2257
jack@alaskajack.com www.alaskajacks.com
Smoked salmon, chocolate, taffy, jams and jellies,
salmon, gold crunch, chikoot chews, klondike krisp,
sourdough starters, earthquake bar
     President: Starr Horton
     Sales Manager: Dave Berry
Estimated Sales: $5-10 Million
Number Employees: 20-49
Brands:
Alaska Jack's
Alaska Tea Traders

301 Alaska Pacific Seafood
627 Shelikof St
Kodiak, AK 99615-6050   907-486-3234
     Fax: 907-486-5164
www.northpacificseafoods.com
President: Bob Mickinovich
Plant Manager: Matthew Moir
Estimated Sales: $ 50 - 100 Million
Number Employees: 100-249
Brands:
Alaska Pacific Seafood

302 Alaska Pasta Company
511 W 41st Ave # A
Anchorage, AK 99503-6643   907-276-2632
     Fax: 907-276-2632
Pasta
     Owner: Hope Nelson
Estimated Sales: $1-2.5 Million
Number Employees: 5-9

303 Alaska Pride Baking Company
9431 Emerald Street
Anchorage, AK 99502-1364   907-278-2867
     Fax: 907-278-2867
Estimated Sales: $50-100 Million
Number Employees: 50-99

**304 Alaska Sausage and Seafood
Company**
2914 Arctic Blvd
Anchorage, AK 99503-3811   907-562-3636
     Fax: 907-562-7343 800-798-3636
aks@ak.net www.alaskasausage.com
Processor of sausage, processed meats and smoked
fish; exporter of smoked salmon
     Manager: Elaine Cox
     Quality Control Manager: Martin Eckmann
Estimated Sales: $10-20 Million
Number Employees: 20-49
Sq. footage: 10000
Type of Packaging: Consumer, Food Service, Pri-
vate Label, Bulk
Brands:
Alaskan

305 Alaska Sea Pack
1020 M Street
Anchorage, AK 99501-3317   907-451-1400
     Fax: 907-780-5140
Seafood
     President: Dennis Winfree
     Vice President: Bill Nix

306 Alaska Seafood Company
441 Gladys Ave
Los Angeles, CA 90013-1728   213-626-1212
     Fax: 213-626-0924
Processor and wholesaler/distributor of frozen fish
     President: J Joseph
Estimated Sales: $5-10 Million
Number Employees: 10-19

307 Alaska Seafood Company
5731 Concrete Way
Juneau, AK 99801-9543   907-780-5111
     Fax: 907-780-5140 800-451-1400
info@alaskaseafoodcompany.com
www.alaskaseafoodcompany.com

Manufacturer, wholesale co=pack, smoking, can-
ning, retort pouches, jars
     President: James Hand
     Plant Manager: Jason Wiard
Estimated Sales: $1 Million
Number Employees: 10-19
Sq. footage: 10000
Type of Packaging: Consumer, Private Label
Brands:
Alaska Cannery & Smokehouse
Alaska Gold
North Pass

308 Alaska Seafood International
111 W 16th Ave # 200
Anchorage, AK 99501-6206   907-770-8300
     Fax: 907-770-8374 800-478-2903
info@alaska-seafood.com
www.alaska-seafood.com
Organization that generically markets Alaska sea-
food globally
     Manager: Willie Redemaker
     CFO: Naresh Shrestha
     Director Food Service: Claudia Hogue
     Director Retail Marketing: Wain Jackson
     Director Public Relations: Laura Fleming
Number Employees: 20-49
Type of Packaging: Private Label
Brands:
Alaska Seafood Products

309 Alaska Smokehouse
21616 87th Ave SE
Woodinville, WA 98072-8017   360-668-9404
     Fax: 360-668-1005 800-422-0852
jackp@alaskasmokehouse.com
www.alaskasmokehouse.com
Manufacturer of shelf stable smoked salmon,
spreads, jerky, cookies, fruit purees and coffee.
     President/CEO: Jack Praino
Estimated Sales: $5-10 Million
Number Employees: 1-4
Sq. footage: 15000
Type of Packaging: Consumer, Private Label
Brands:
Alaska Smokehouse
SLEEPLESS IN SEATTLE COFFEE
THE FAMOUS PACIFIC DESSERT COMPANY

310 Alaskan Brewing Company
5429 Shaune Dr
Juneau, AK 99801-9540   907-780-5866
     Fax: 907-780-4514 info@alaskanbeer.com
www.alaskanbeer.com
Beer
     President: Geoff Larson
     Public Relations Manager: Ashkley Johnston
     General Manager: Linda Thomas
     Plant Manager: Curtis Holmes
Estimated Sales: $20-50 Million
Number Employees: 50-99
Type of Packaging: Private Label
Brands:
ALASKAN AMBER
ALASKAN IPA
ALASKAN PALE
ALASKAN SMOKED PORTER
ALASKAN STOUT
ALASKAN SUMMER ALE
ALASKAN WINTER ALE

311 Alaskan Glacier
P.O.Box 209
Petersburg, AK 99833-0209   907-772-3333
     Fax: 907-772-3330 www.norquest.com
     Plant Manager: Dave Ohmer
Estimated Sales: $ 50 - 100 Million
Number Employees: 100-249

312 Alaskan Gourmet Seafoods
1020 W International Airport Road
Anchorage, AK 99518-1005   907-563-3752
     Fax: 907-563-2592 800-288-3740
akfoods@alaska.net www.alaska.net/~akfoods
Manufacturer and exporter of frozen and canned
smoked halibut and salmon
     President: Paul Schilling
     Public Relations: John Brace
Estimated Sales: $5-10 Million
Number Employees: 18
Sq. footage: 10000
Brands:
Alaskan Gourmet

313 Alaskan Leader Fisheries
8874 Bender Rd # 201
Lynden, WA 98264-8550   360-318-1280
     Fax: 306-318-1440
www.alaskanleaderfisheries.com
Owner: Rob Wurm
Partner: Kevin O'Leary
Partner: Richard Thummel
Estimated Sales: $ .5 - 1 million
Number Employees: 1-4
Brands:
Alaskan Leader Fisheries

**314 Alaskan Smoked Salmon
International**
8430 Laviento Dr
Anchorage, AK 99515-1914   907-349-8234
     Fax: 907-344-7666 fis.com/alaskansmoked
Manufacturer of smoked salmon
     President: Chris Rosauer
Estimated Sales: $500,000-$1 Million
Number Employees: 5-9
Type of Packaging: Consumer, Food Service

315 Alati-Caserta Desserts
277 Rue Dante
Montreal, QC H2S 1K3
Canada   514-271-3013
     Fax: 514-277-5860 info@alaticaserta.com
www.alaticaserta.com
Processor and exporter of desserts including almond
cakes, cannoli ricotta and chocolate mousse
     Co-Owner: Vittorio Caldarone
     Co-Owner: Marco Caldarone
Type of Packaging: Food Service
Brands:
Alati-Casertta

316 Alba Vineyard
269 Route 627
Milford, NJ 08848-1771   908-995-7800
     Fax: 908-995-7155 albavineyard@enter.net
www.albavineyard.com
Wines
     President/Owner: Thomas Sharko
     Partner: Rudy Marchesi
Estimated Sales: $2.5-5 Million
Number Employees: 5-9
Type of Packaging: Private Label, Bulk
Brands:
ALBA

317 Albanese Confectionery Group
1910 W Us 30
Merrillville, IN 46410   219-757-6600
     Fax: 219-769-6897 800-536-0581
sales@albaneseconfectionery.com
www.albaneseconfectionery.com
Chocolate covered nut candies and gummi's
     President: Scott Albanese
     Purchasing: Alan Levinson
Estimated Sales: $5-10 Million
Number Employees: 10-19
Other Locations:
Hobart Manufacturing Facility
Hobart IN

318 Alberta Cheese Company
8420 26th Street SE
Calgary, AB T2C 1C7
Canada   403-279-4353
     Fax: 403-279-4795
Manufacturer of cheese including specialty, mozza-
rella, ricotta, cheddar, feta, provolone and monterey
jack
     President: Frank Talarico
     Sales Manager/GM: Michael Talarico
Number Employees: 20
Type of Packaging: Consumer, Food Service
Brands:
Franco's
Sorento

319 (HQ)Alberto-Culver Company
2525 Armitage Ave
Melrose Park, IL 60160-1163   708-450-3000
     Fax: 708-450-3409 crelations@alberto.com
www.alberto.com

Manufacturer and packager of spices, seasonings, cooking spray, butter, sour cream, cheese and sugar substitutes.
President/CEO/Director: V James Marino
EVP/CFO: Ralph Nicoletti
SVP/General Counsel: Gary Schmidt
Estimated Sales: $1.5 Billion
Number Employees: 2,700
Number of Brands: 5
Type of Packaging: Consumer
Brands:
BAKER'S JOY
MOLLY MCBUTTER
MRS DASH
SUGAR TWIN

320 Albertson's Bakery
42095 Washington St
Palm Desert, CA 92211-8017   760-360-6322
Fax: 760-345-6842 www.albertsons.com
Manager: Andrea Balmer
Member: Virginia Surrell
Estimated Sales: $ 20 - 50 Million
Number Employees: 100-249
Brands:
Albertson's

321 Albertson's Ice-Cream
P.O.Box 20
Boise, ID 83726-0020   208-395-6200
Fax: 208-395-6349 877-932-7948
www.albertsons.com
Manufacturer of ice cream and frozen desserts including ices and sherbets
CEO: Jeffrey Noddle
Plant Manager: James McClelland
Estimated Sales: $107 Million
Number Employees: 100-249
Type of Packaging: Consumer
Brands:
Albertson's
Janet Lee
Wild Harvest

322 Albion Laboratories
101 N Main St
Clearfield, UT 84015-2243   801-773-4631
Fax: 801-773-4633 866-243-5283
albionlabs@aol.com www.albionlabs.com
Manufacturer and exporter of nutritional mineral supplements including amino acid chelates, vitamin complexes, etc.
President: Duane Ashmead
CFO: Charles Whiting
Sales/Marketing: Ronald Wheelwright
Purchasing Manager: Brett Ashmead
Number Employees: 20-49
Type of Packaging: Consumer, Bulk
Brands:
Albion
Chela-Zone
Chelavite
Chelazome
Metalosate

323 Alca Trading Company
5301 Blue Lagoon Drive #570
Miami, FL 33126-2097   305-265-8331
Supplier of banana juices and mango purees.

324 Alcan Chemical
333 Ludlow St # 6
Stamford, CT 06902-6991   203-532-2900
Fax: 203-541-9191 800-736-7893
chemicals@alcan.com www.alcan.com
Processor and exporter of Chemical Products, Active Pharmaceutical Ingredients (APIs), to the Pharmaceutical, Personal Care, Cosmetic, Nutritional and Industrial markets
VP: Hugo Galletta
Estimated Sales: $ 10 - 20 Million
Number Employees: 100-249
Parent Co: Alcan International Network USA

325 Alcan Packaging
8770 W Bryn Mawr Ave
Chicago, IL 60631-3515   773-399-8000
Fax: 773-399-8648 joyce.musgrave@alcan.com
www.alcanpackaging.com/

Manufacturer of flexible food packaging, product range includes a large portfolio of packaging based on plastic aluminum, paper, carton and other materials: plain and converted barrier foils and films, high barrier materials, containerstrips and containers, capsules and closures, labels, pouches, steel cans and decorated tins. Foils and films are available for technical and industrial applications.
President: Mike Schmitt
Product Manager Flexible Packaging: John Reiff
Marketing Manager: Joyce Musgrave
Estimated Sales: $118 Million
Number Employees: 10,000+
Type of Packaging: Food Service, Bulk

326 Alcester Meats
PO Box 472
Alcester, SD 57001-0472   605-934-2540
Fax: 605-934-2616 qualitypork@acsnet.com
Fresh and frozen pork products
President/Owner: Doug Thompson
General Sales Manager: Doug Jensen
Accounts Manager: Gloria Thompson
Estimated Sales: $20-50 Million
Number Employees: 50-99
Number of Brands: 1

327 Alder Springs Smoked Salmon
PO Box 97
Sequim, WA 98382-0097   360-683-2829
Fax: 360-683-5359 alder@olypen.com
Manufacturer of smoked salmon, salmon jerky, oysters, cod and trout
Owner: Robert Bearden
Estimated Sales: Less than $500,000
Number Employees: 1-4
Type of Packaging: Private Label
Brands:
Alder Springs

328 Alderfer Bologna
P.O.Box 2
Harleysville, PA 19438-0002   215-256-8818
Fax: 215-256-6120 877-253-6328
sales@alderfermeats.com
www.alderfermeats.com
Processor of roast and dried beef, ham, bacon, bologna and cured turkey breasts, sliced and bulk. Exporter of dried beef
President: Earl Manhold
VP: Sherry Russel
Quality Control: Craig Chapman
Production: Brent Shoemaker
Plant Manager: Brent Shoemaker
Purchasing: Ray Keller
Estimated Sales: $12 Million
Number Employees: 50-99
Number of Brands: 1
Number of Products: 300
Sq. footage: 24000
Type of Packaging: Consumer, Food Service, Private Label, Bulk
Brands:
Alderfer

329 AleSmith Brewing Company
9368 Cabot Dr
San Diego, CA 92126-4311   858-549-9888
Fax: 858-549-1052 peter@alesmith.com
www.alesmith.com
Manufacturer of ale including seasonal
Owner: Peter Zien
Estimated Sales: $ 3 - 5 Million
Number Employees: 1-4
Sq. footage: 3200
Type of Packaging: Food Service, Bulk

330 Alessi Bakery
2909 W Cypress St
Tampa, FL 33609-1630   813-879-4544
Fax: 813-872-9103 www.alessibakeries.com
Manufacturer of tortes, pastry desserts, cakes, cookies
President: Phil Alessi
Estimated Sales: $5-10 Million
Number Employees: 50-99
Sq. footage: 15000
Type of Packaging: Consumer, Food Service
Brands:
Alessi Bakery

331 Alewel's Country Meats
911 N Simpson Dr
Warrensburg, MO 64093-9277   660-747-8261
Fax: 660-747-1857 800-353-8553
alewels@sprintmail.com
www.country-meats.com
Manufacturer of dry, shelf stable, game and summer sausage, and game jerky including deer and buffalo. Cured meat mail order operation, custom processing and catering-whole hog specialties available
President: Roger Alewel
Estimated Sales: $2.5-5 Million
Number Employees: 5-9
Sq. footage: 5000
Type of Packaging: Consumer, Food Service, Private Label, Bulk
Brands:
Alewel's Country Meats
Grandpa A'S

332 Alex Froehlich Packing Company
77 D Street Ext
Johnstown, PA 15906-2908   814-535-7694
Fax: 814-535-7695
Livestock processor
Owner: David Froehlich
VP: Vincetta Froehlich
Estimated Sales: $5-10 Million
Number Employees: 10-19
Type of Packaging: Bulk
Other Locations:
Alex Froelich Packing Company
Johnstown PA

333 (HQ)Alexander & Baldwin
822 Bishop Street
Honolulu, HI 96813-3924   808-525-6611
Fax: 808-525-6652 www.alexanderbaldwin.com
Manufacturer of molasses, raw sugar and coffee
Chairman/CEO: Allen Doane
Sr VP/CFO: Christopher Benjamin
Estimated Sales: $1.8 Billion
Number Employees: 2,160
Type of Packaging: Consumer, Food Service, Bulk
Brands:
Kauai Coffee
Maui Sugar

334 Alexander Gourmet Imports
5630 Timberlea Boulevard
Mississauga, ON L4W 4M6
Canada   905-282-0556
Fax: 905-282-0601 800-265-5081
agiltd@attcanada.ca www.alexanderstea.com
Full range of tea production: flavouring, blending, tea bagging, loose tea packaging and gift selections. Experienced in packing flavoured, estate, herbal, medicinal and organic teas.
President: Dave Elliott
Estimated Sales: $3.5 Million
Number Employees: 60+
Number of Brands: 6
Sq. footage: 30000
Type of Packaging: Consumer, Food Service, Private Label, Bulk
Brands:
Alexander's Gourmet Tea
Cocoa Creations
Herbal Teazers

335 Alexander International(USA)
132 Concourse East
Brightwaters, NY 11718   866-965-0143
service@alexander-usa.com
www.alexander-usa.com
drink mixes, herbs and spices, olive and other oils

336 Alexander Johnson's Valley Wines
8333 Highway 128
Healdsburg, CA 95448-9639   707-433-2319
Fax: 707-433-5302 800-888-5532
johnsons@funvacation.net
www.johnsonsavwines.com
Wines
President: Ellen Johnson
Estimated Sales: $1-2.5 Million
Number Employees: 1-4
Brands:
Johnson's Alexander Valley

337 Alexandra & Nicolay
2607 Nostrand Ave # 2
Brooklyn, NY 11210-4695   718-253-9400
Fax: 718-331-4986
info@alexandraandnicolay.com
www.alexandraandnicolay.com
Manufacturer of chocolates in milk, white and dark
Founder: Alexandra Mazhirov
Founder: Nicolay Mazhirov
Estimated Sales: $300,000-500,000
Number Employees: 5-9

338 Alexia Foods
5102 21st St # 3b
Long Island City, NY 11101-5838 718-937-0100
Fax: 718-937-0110 info@alexiafoods.com
www.alexiafoods.com
Manufacturer of frozen potato products including ar-
tisan breads, oven blends, onion rings, organic prod-
ucts, mashed potatoes, oven fries and oven reds,
julienne fries, and appetizers.
President: Alex Dzieduszycki
CEO: Alex Dzieduscycki
Estimated Sales: G
Type of Packaging: Food Service

**339 Alexian
Pates/GroezingerProvisions**
1200 7th Ave
Neptune, NJ 07753-5190   732-775-3220
Fax: 732-775-3223 800-927-9473
informationrequest@alexianpate.com
www.alexianpate.com
Specialty meats and sausages. All natural preserva-
tive free pates and mousses; pork, poultry, vegetar-
ian and vegan pates.
President: Laurie Groezinger
Estimated Sales: $10-20 Million
Number Employees: 10-19
Type of Packaging: Private Label

340 Alexis Bailly Vineyard
18200 Kirby Ave S
Hastings, MN 55033-9340   651-437-1413
www.abvwines.com
Wines
Founder: David Bailly
Owner/CEO: Nan Bailly
Master Winemaker: Nan Bailly
Estimated Sales: $500,000-$1 Million
Number Employees: 1-4
Type of Packaging: Consumer, Private Label
Brands:
ALEXIS BAILLY

341 Alfer Laboratories
9566 Vassar Ave
Chatsworth, CA 91311-4141   818-709-0737
Fax: 818-709-5360
Processor of nutritional supplements and vitamins
including liquid cal-mag, acidophilus cultures and
aloe vera gels/juices
President: Ines Gutierrez
Purchasing Manager: Ines Gutierrez
Estimated Sales: $2.5-5 Million
Number Employees: 5-9
Type of Packaging: Private Label

342 Alfonso Gourmet Pasta
2211 NW 30th Pl
Pompano Beach, FL 33069-1026   954-960-1010
Fax: 954-974-2773 800-370-7278
customerservice@alfonsogourmetpasta.com
www.alfonsogourmetpasta.com
Manufacturer and exporter of gourmet ravioli and
prepared foods including fresh, frozen and processed
President: David Ruiz
Sales: John Giogianni
Purchasing: Mike Mullen
Estimated Sales: $5-10 Million
Number Employees: 5-9
Sq. footage: 12000
Type of Packaging: Food Service
Brands:
ALFONSO GOURMET PASTA

343 Alfred & Sam Italian Bakery
17 Fairview Ave
Lancaster, PA 17603-5594   717-392-6311
Fax: 717-392-6311
Manufacturer of rolls, breads, cannolis and cookies
President: Salvatore Borsellino
Owner: Sam Borsellino

Estimated Sales: $500,000-$1 Million
Number Employees: 10-19
Type of Packaging: Consumer
Brands:
Alfred & Sam's

344 Alfred L. Wolff, Inc.
1440 N Northwest Highway
230
Park Ridge, IL 60068-1431   312-265-9889
Fax: 312-265-9888 tmwolffus@sbcglobal.net
www.alwolff.com
Importer of dehydrated vegetables, herbs, honey and
other bee products including royal jelly, bee pollen
and propolis; also, gum arabic, acidulating agents
and nutritional fiber
General Manager: Magnus von Buddenbrock
Estimated Sales: $5 Million
Number Employees: 3
Parent Co: Alfred L. Wolff GmbH
Type of Packaging: Bulk
Brands:
BIG ONION
FINEST HONEY ORGANIC
FINEST HONEY SELECTION
QSLIC
QUICK ACID
QUICK CHEW
QUICK COAT
QUICK FIBRE
QUICK GLANZ
QUICK GUM
QUICK LAC
QUICK OIL
QUICK SHINE
SHELLAC

345 Alfred Louie
4501 Shepard Street
Bakersfield, CA 93313-2310   661-831-2520
Fax: 805-833-9197
Fruits and vegetables, pasta, and Chinese canned
goods and vegetables.
President: Susan Louie
Estimated Sales: $5,115,628
Number Employees: 12

**346 Alfredo's Italian
FoodsManufacturing Company**
122 Water St
Quincy, MA 02169-6661   617-479-6360
Fax: 617-773-3342 www.aapasta.com
Processor of fresh lasagna, ravioli, cavatelli,
tortellini, fettuccini
President: Peter Aiello
Operations Manager: Lino Aiello
Purchasing Manager: John Lucca
Estimated Sales: $5-10 Million
Number Employees: 20-49
Type of Packaging: Consumer, Food Service, Pri-
vate Label, Bulk
Brands:
ALFREDO

347 Alfresh Beverages Canada
95 Vulcan Street
Rexdale, ON M9W 1L4
Canada   416-244-4224
Fax: 416-244-1757 800-465-1516
info@alfreshbeverages.com
www.alfreshbeverages.com
Manufacturer and exporter of fruit juice drinks, bev-
erages and cocktails
President/CEO: James Biltekoff
COO: Larry Bushey
Other Locations:
Toronto, Canada

348 Algood Food Company
7401 Trade Port Dr
Louisville, KY 40258-1896   502-637-3631
Fax: 502-637-1502 wphilpot@algoodfood.com
www.algoodfood.com
Processor and exporter of peanut butter, jams, jellies
and preserves
President: Cecil Barnett
VP: Kathy Powell
CEO: Kathy Powell
VP: Nicolas Melhuish
Quality/Technical Service: Dan Schmidt
VP Sales: Melhuish
VP Sales: Nick Melhuish
Plant Manager: David Temple
Purchasing Manager: David Frantz

Estimated Sales: $100+ Million
Number Employees: 100-249
Sq. footage: 100000
Brands:
ALGOOD BLUE LABEL
ALGOOD JELLY
ALGOOD MARMALADE
ALGOOD OLD FASHIONED
ALGOOD PRESERVES
ALGOOD RED LABEL
CAP 'N KID

349 Alimentaire Whyte's Inc
1540 Des Patriotes Rue
Laval, QC H7L 2N6
Canada   450-625-1976
Fax: 450-625-9295 800-625-1979
Manufacturer, importer and exporter of pickles, her-
rings, sauerkraut, horseradish, onions, capers, pan-
cake syrup, ketchup, tomato juice, salsa, soy, pizza
and spaghetti sauces, olives, peppers, mushrooms
and crushed tomatoes; exporterof olives, peppers,
and salad dressings.
President: Beth Kawaja
Estimated Sales: $50-70 Million
Number Employees: 100
Sq. footage: 250000

**350 Alimentos Naturales Sabrosa, SA
de CV**
2935 Thousand Oaks Drive
Suite 6-142
San Antonio, TX 78247-3312   210-545-1792
Fax: 210-545-1792 foodtek@satx.rr.com
www.lasabrosa.com

351 Aliments Jolibec
149 Montee Allard
St Jacques De Montcalm, QC J0K 2R0
Canada   514-861-6082
jolibec@megacom.net
Manufacturer of fresh and frozen pork
President: Roger Ethier
Number Employees: 43
Type of Packaging: Bulk

352 Aliments Lexus Foods
1215 Grande Caroline
Rougemont, QC J0L 1M0
Canada   450-469-0522
Fax: 450-469-0524 800-227-4891
Manufacturer and exporter of beverage mixes,
non-alcoholic, juices and soda
President: R Landry
Research & Development: Sebastien Quellet
Quality Control: Sebastien Quellet
Sales Director: Robert Leblanc
Plant Manager: Yves Beauregard
Purchasing Manager: R Landry
Estimated Sales: $15 Million
Number Employees: 20-49
Sq. footage: 95000
Type of Packaging: Consumer, Food Service, Pri-
vate Label
Brands:
ABOARDANZE
BERZI
ELIXIR
LEXUS
SWEET RIPE

353 Aliments Prince Foods
11053 Louis H Lafontaine
Anjou, QC H1S 2Z4
Canada   450-771-0400
Fax: 450-771-4872 800-361-3898
princef@odyssee.net www.princefoods.com
Manufacturer of bacon, ham and sausages
President: Marcel Heroux
GM: Alain Heroux
Director Sales: Sylvain Blais
Number Employees: 800
Type of Packaging: Consumer, Food Service, Pri-
vate Label

354 Aliments Trigone
Saint-Francois De Montmagny
Quebec, QC G1N 2Z8
Canada   418-259-7414
Fax: 418-259-2417 877-259-7491
bio@alimentstrigone.com
www.alimentstrigone.com
Manufacturer of buckwheat and shelled hempseeds.
President: Jacques Cote

355 Alinosi French Superfine Candies
12748 E McNichols Rd
Detroit, MI 48205-3397   313-527-3195
Fax: 313-527-8141   info@alinosi.com
www.alinosi.com
Manufacturer of confectionery
Owner: Steve Di Maggio
Design/Production Manager: David Tessman
Estimated Sales: $1-2.5 Million
Number Employees: 5-9
Type of Packaging: Consumer

356 Aliotti Wholesale Fish Company
PO Box 3325
Monterey, CA 93942-3325   831-375-2881
Fax: 831-375-4285
Processor and exporter of frozen squid
Sales Operation Manager: Joe Aliotti
Purchasing: Joe Aliotti
Estimated Sales: $5-10 Million
Number Employees: 10-19
Type of Packaging: Food Service
Brands:
PRIMA QUALITY

357 Alkinco
129 W 29th St # 5
New York, NY 10001-5105   212-719-3070
Fax: 212-764-7804   800-424-7118
custer@alkincohair.com   www.alkincohair.com
Processor of beverage mixes including sugared, chocolate and weight control; also, protein supplements
President: Julius Klugman
VP: Stewart Hoffman
Estimated Sales: $5-10 Million
Number Employees: 20-49
Sq. footage: 50000
Type of Packaging: Consumer, Private Label
Brands:
Alkinco

358 All About Lollipops
12155 Kirkham Road
Poway, CA 92064-6870   208-333-9896
Fax: 208-333-9938   866-475-6554
Candy
Owner: Robert Maire
Sales Manager: Lannie Davis
Plant Manager: Bill Cole
Number Employees: 25
Brands:
BIG BUNNY POP
BIG FAT TOAD POP
BIG HEART POP
BIG LIPS POP
BIG PUMPKIN POP
BIG SKULL POP
DOUBLE DIP POP
HAND MADE BALL POP
JOLLY SANTA POP
LUCKY POP
SOUR BALL POP
SOUR BRAINS POP

359 All Alaskan Seafood
2629 NW 54th St
Seattle, WA 98107-4157   206-285-8200
Fax: 206-285-2313
Manufacturer of frozen seafood including crab, salmon, herring, shrimp, halibut and cod
Manager: Lloyd Cannon
Estimated Sales: $ .5 - 1 million
Number Employees: 1-4
Type of Packaging: Consumer, Food Service
Brands:
Pioneer

360 All American Foods, Inc.
121 Mohr Drive
Box 8242
Mankato, MN 56002-8242   507-387-6480
Fax: 507-387-6111   800-833-2661
info@aafoods.com   www.aafoods.com
One-for-one replacements for dairy commodities, dairy blends, nondairy blends, kosher parve, milk replacers and dry dairy ingredients
President: Keith Brekke
CEO: Jeff Thom
CFO: Kevin Olson
CEO: Jeff Thom
QA Director: Shawn Schlueter
Market Development Director: Rod Mitchell
National Sales Manager: Chad Anderson
Operations Director: Connie Stokman
Estimated Sales: $20 Million
Number Employees: 100-249
Number of Brands: 1
Number of Products: 150
Sq. footage: 80000
Parent Co: All American Foods
Type of Packaging: Private Label, Bulk

361 All American Seasonings
10600 E. 54th Ave.
Denver, CO 80202-1784   303-623-2320
Fax: 303-623-1920
info@allamericanseasonings.com
www.allamericanseasonings.com
Manufacturer of custom blended seasonings and spices
Manager: Eric Willy
Marketing Director: Joseph Gallagher
Estimated Sales: $12 Million
Number Employees: 20-49
Sq. footage: 40000
Type of Packaging: Consumer, Food Service, Private Label, Bulk
Brands:
ALL AMERICAN

362 All American Snacks
PO Box 3
Midland, TX 79702-0003   432-687-6666
Fax: 915-699-2305   800-840-2455
www.allamericansnacks.com
White chocolate hand-stirred into crisp cereals, pretzels and pecan halves
Owner/Public Relations: Lexie Grafa Kauffman
Co-Owner/Manager: Sheri Brockett
Sales Director: Kimberlea Orson Bryand
Estimated Sales: $5-10 Million
Number Employees: 20-49
Brands:
All American Afternoon Delight
All American Precious Stones
All American White Trash

363 All Goode Organics
PO Box 61256
Santa Barbara, CA 93160-1256   805-683-3370
Fax: 805-683-7669   k-everard@home.com
www.allgoodorganics.com
Organic foods, herbal teas

364 All Juice Food & Beverage
352 Jet St
Hendersonville, NC 28792-8004   828-685-8821
Fax: 828-685-8495   800-736-5674
www.mrsclarks.com
Beverages, apple juice
President: Ron Kahrer
Plant Manager: John Weber
Estimated Sales: $ 20 - 50 Million
Number Employees: 20-49

365 All Round Foods
437 Railroad Ave
Westbury, NY 11590-4314   516-338-1888
Fax: 516-939-2338
Processor and exporter of frozen doughnuts including plain, glazed, sugar, cinnamon, jelly, etc.
Owner: Glen Wolther
Executive VP: Robert Glasser
VP: Glenn Wolther
Purchasing: Steven Finkelstein
Estimated Sales: $ 3 - 5 Million
Number Employees: 1-4
Sq. footage: 84000
Type of Packaging: Food Service
Brands:
ALL ROUND FOODS

366 All Seasons International Distributors
4427 Poplar Level Road
Louisville, KY 40213-1952   502-473-1709
Fax: 502-473-1801

President: Michael Tao

367 All Wrapped Up
3714 NW 16th St
Lauderhill, FL 33311-4132   954-587-2111
Fax: 954-587-2144   800-891-2194
info@allwrappedup-gifts.com
www.allwrappedup-gifts.com
Candies, cookies, chocolates, nuts, and pretzels, professionally wrapped
President/CEO: Pam Schwimmer
VP: Donna Merill
VP Marketing: Donna Merill
Operations Manager: Pam Schwimmer
Estimated Sales: Less than $500,000
Number Employees: 5-9
Type of Packaging: Consumer, Private Label

368 All-States Quality Foods
901 N Main Street
Charles City, IA 50616-0365   641-228-5023
Fax: 641-228-2624   800-247-4195
dmorris@netconx.net
Processor of chicken products including broth, rendered fat, diced cooked meat and turkey and chicken quesadillas
President: Elliot Jones
Quality Control: Wendy Ungs
Marketing Director: Steve Tenney
Sales Director: Deanna Morris
Public Relations: Tim Prenevost
Plant Manager: Dan Andregg
Purchasing Manager: Steve Tenney
Estimated Sales: $20-50 Million
Number Employees: 250-499
Number of Products: 10
Type of Packaging: Consumer, Food Service, Private Label, Bulk

369 Allann Brothers Coffee Company
1852 Fescue St SE
Albany, OR 97322-7075   541-812-8000
Fax: 541-812-8010   800-926-6886
info@allannbroscoffee.com
www.allannbroscoffee.com
Coffee and teas
President: A Stuart
Sales Director: Michael Harris
Estimated Sales: Less than $500,000
Number Employees: 10-19
Type of Packaging: Consumer, Food Service, Private Label, Bulk

370 Alldrin Brothers
P.O.Box 10
Ballico, CA 95303-0010   209-667-1600
Fax: 209-667-0463   sales@almondcafe.com
www.almondcafe.com
Processor and exporter of almonds
President: Gary Alldrin
Purchasing Manager: Gary Alldrin
Estimated Sales: $1-2.5 Million
Number Employees: 50-99
Type of Packaging: Bulk
Brands:
ALLDRIN

371 (HQ)Alle Processing
5620 59th St
Flushing, NY 11378-2314   718-894-2000
Fax: 718-326-4642   www.alleprocessing.com
Processor of kosher fresh and frozen beef, lamb, veal and poultry, fish, vegetables and frozen vegetarian entrees; importer of puff pastry products; exporter of kosher frozen vegetable entrees. Private label and co-packing services available
VP Sales/Marketing: Shlomi Pilo
Estimated Sales: $ 20 - 50 Million
Number Employees: 50-99
Sq. footage: 150000
Type of Packaging: Consumer, Food Service, Private Label, Bulk
Other Locations:
Alle Processing
Maspeth NY
Brands:
GLATT KOSHER
MEAL MART
MON CUISINE
NEW YORK KOSHER DELI
PASSOVER
SCHREIBER

Brands:
Trigone

372 Alle Processing Corporation
5620 59th St
Flushing, NY 11378-2314   718-894-2000
Fax: 718-326-4642 800-245-5620
ezs@alleprocessing.com
www.alleprocessing.com
Processor and exporter of kosher food products in-cluding meat analogs, luncheon meats, frankfurters and microwaveable vegetarian meals. Also kosher frozen products, frozen vegetarian products, plate meals and provisions
President: Albert WeinStreetock
CEO: Sam Hollander
Vice President: Shlomi Pilo
Operations Manager: Ivan Talevera
Plant Manager: Iran Talavera
Purchasing Manager: Zeeer Weinstock
Estimated Sales:$41100000
Number Employees: 50-99
Sq. footage: 150000
Parent Co: Alle Processing
Type of Packaging: Food Service
Brands:
Meal Mart
New York Kosher Deli
Schrieber Meatless Meats

373 Alleghany's Fish Farm
2755 Route 281
Saint Philemon, QC G0R 4A0
Canada   418-469-2823
Fax: 418-469-2872 alleghan@globetrotter.net
Manufacturer of live trout eggs
GM: Yves Boulanger
Estimated Sales:$1-5 Million
Number Employees: 22
Type of Packaging: Consumer, Food Service
Brands:
Alleghanys

374 Allegria
233 E Weddell Dr # I
Sunnyvale, CA 94089-1659   408-734-4300
Fax: 408-734-2444 800-467-8648
Bakers of traditional ethnic specialties since 1984.
President: G Giurlani
CFO: Claire Baxter
Marketing Director: R Giurlani
Plant Manager: G Portida
Purchasing Manager: G Giurlani
Estimated Sales:$ 5 - 10 Million
Number Employees: 10-19
Type of Packaging: Consumer, Food Service, Pri-vate Label, Bulk

375 Allegro Coffee Company
12799 Claude Ct # B
Thornton, CO 80241-3828   303-444-4844
Fax: 303-920-5468 800-666-4869
prodinfo@allegro-coffee.com
www.allegrocoffee.com
Manufacturer, importer and wholesaler/distributor of roasted specialty coffees; importer of green coffee beans
Chairman: Jeffrey Cohn
President/Marketing Manager: Terry Tierney
CFO: Clarence Peterson
CEO: Jeff Teter
Operations Manager: Kevin Knox
*Estimated Sales:*F
Number Employees: 50-99
Brands:
Allegro Coffee
Allegro Tea
Organic Coffee

376 Allegro Fine Foods
P.O.Box 1262
Paris, TN 38242-1262   731-642-6113
Fax: 731-642-6116 info@allegromarinade.com
www.allegromarinade.com
Processor and exporter of meat and vegetable mari-nades
President: John Fuqua
Research & Development: Lisa Downey
VP Marketing: Tim Phifer
VP Operations: Stan Nelms
Plant Manager: Al Luigs
Estimated Sales:$5-10 Million
Number Employees: 20-49
Sq. footage: 10000
Type of Packaging: Consumer, Food Service, Pri-vate Label, Bulk

Brands:
ALLEGRO

377 Allegro Vineyards
3475 Sechrist Rd
Brogue, PA 17309-9415   717-927-9148
Fax: 717-927-1521 info@allegrowines.com
www.allegrowines.com
Wines
Owner: Kris Miller
Owner: Carl Helrich
Estimated Sales:$500,000-$1 Million
Number Employees: 1-4
Sq. footage: 4000
Brands:
ALLEGRO

378 Allen & Cowley SpecialtyFoods
4053 E Washington St
Phoenix, AZ 85034-1819   602-275-9211
Fax: 602-275-9600 800-279-1634
info@allen-cowley.com www.allen-cowley.com
Crackers, croutons, herbs, spices and spreads.
Owner: Allen Sweat
Vice President: Michael Cowley
Sales Manager: Lindsey Wescott
Production Manager: JT Howard
Purchasing Manager: Lee Allen
Estimated Sales:$500,000-$1 Million
Number Employees: 20-49
Type of Packaging: Consumer, Food Service
Brands:
DUST
STARR RIDGE

379 Allen Canning Company
305 E. Main Street
Siloam Springs, AR 72761   479-524-6431
Fax: 479-524-3291 800-234-2553
www.allencanning.com
Processor and exporter of canned beans, carrots, peas, greens, hominy, kale, lentils, okra, potatoes, spinach, squash, turnips and snack foods
President: Rick Allen, Jr.
Chairman/CEO: Rick Allen
Executive Vice President: Nick Allen
Executive Vice President: Josh Allen
Quality Control: Earl Wells
Senior VP Sales/Marketing: Mike Hubbard
Government Relations: Robert Stephenson
COO: Jim Robason
Estimated Sales:$50-100 Million
Number Employees: 1,000-4,999
Number of Brands: 13
Type of Packaging: Consumer, Food Service, Pri-vate Label, Bulk
Brands:
ALLENS
ALLENS ITALIAN GREEN BEANS
BUTTERFIELD
EAST TEXAS FAIR
FRESHLIKE
POPEYE
PRINCELLA
ROYAL PRINCE
SUGARY SAM
SUNSHINE
TRAPPEYS
VEG-ALL
WAGON MASTER

380 (HQ)Allen Family Foods
126 N Shipley St
Seaford, DE 19973-3100   302-629-9163
Fax: 302-629-5081
affeob@allenfamilyfoods.com
www.allenfamilyfoods.com
Processor of poultry products including frozen parts and whole birds; exporter of frozen poultry items
President: Charles C Allen Iii III
Chairman/CEO: Charles Allen
Quality Control: Sharen Nowak
VP Sales/Marketing: Chuck Kucharik
Plant Manager (Cordova, MD): Terry Nichols
Plant Manager (Harbeson, DE): Buck Korneman
Purchasing Agent: Gary Lacher
Estimated Sales:$400 Million
Number Employees: 100-249
Type of Packaging: Consumer, Food Service, Pri-vate Label, Bulk
Other Locations:
Allen Family Foods
Delmar DE
Allen Family Foods

Hurlock MD
Allen Family Foods
Linkwood MD
Brands:
ALLENS

381 (HQ)Allen Flavors
23 Progress St
Edison, NJ 08820-1102   908-561-5995
Fax: 908-561-4164 info@allenflavors.com
www.allenflavors.com
Tea Essences, Instant Teas, Instant Coffees and Cof-fee Extracts.
President: Joseph Allen
VP: Michele Allen
Research Director: Harvey Krohn
Quality Control Director: Dr Donald Mull
VP Sales: Joe Moran
VP Operations: Al Handel
Plant Manager: Tony Parada
Estimated Sales:$10-20 Million
Number Employees: 20-49
Sq. footage: 4000
Brands:
ALLEN

382 Allen Wertz Candy
5051 Edison Avenue
Chino, CA 91710-5716   909-613-0030
Fax: 909-613-0031 800-756-2676
Sugar free: caramels, nougats, assorted fruit chews, assorted gourmet chocolates, peanut butter cups;
Sales Director: Diane Flowe
Purchasing Agent: Lynn Felan
Estimated Sales:$20-50 Million
Number Employees: 100-249
Brands:
ALLEN WERTZ GOURMET CHOCOLATES
ALLEN WERTZ HEALTHIER ALTERNA-TIVES
ALLEN WERTZ NOUGAT FLUFFS
ALLEN WERTZ SIMPLY SUGAR FREE

383 Allen's Blueberry Freezer
P.O.Box 536
Ellsworth, ME 04605-0536   207-667-5561
Fax: 207-667-8315 www.allensblueberries.com
Frozen wild blueberries.
President: Roy Allen II
Sales: Kim Allen-Wadman
Estimated Sales:$ 10 - 20 Million
Number Employees: 10-19
Type of Packaging: Consumer, Food Service
Brands:
ALLEN'S

384 Allen's Blueberry Freezer
P.O.Box 536
Ellsworth, ME 04605-0536   207-667-5561
Fax: 207-667-8315 info@allensblueberries.com
www.allensblueberries.com
Frozen blueberries
President/CEO: George Allen
CEO/Plant Manager: Roy Allen
Purchasing Agent: Roy Allen
Estimated Sales:$10-20 Million
Number Employees: 10-19
Type of Packaging: Private Label
Brands:
ALLEN'S

385 Allen's Naturally
PO Box 514
Farmington, MI 48332-0514
Fax: 248-449-7709 800-352-8971
info@allensnaturally.com
www.allensnaturally.com
Biodegradable dishwashing liquid
Purchasing Manager: W Allen Conlon
Estimated Sales:$2.5-5 Million
Number Employees: 1-4
Brands:
ALLENS NATURALLY

386 Allen's Pickle Works
36 Garvies Point Rd
Glen Cove, NY 11542-2821   516-676-0640
Fax: 516-759-5780 bgpickl@aol.com
Processor of cold packed sour dill and half sour pickles including whole, spears and chips
President: Ronald Horman
Purchasing: Ronald Horman

Estimated Sales: $2.5-5 Million
Number Employees: 10-19
Sq. footage: 18000
Type of Packaging: Private Label
Brands:
　ALLENS
　ALMA
　BUTTERFIELD
　CLEAR SAILING

387　Alley Kat Brewing Company
9929-60th Avenue NW
Edmonton, AB　T6E 0C7
Canada　　　　　　　　　　　780-436-8922
　　Fax: 780-430-7363　thekats@alleykatbeer.com
　　　　　　www.alleykatbeer.com
Manufacturer of beer, ale, lager and stout
　Co-Owner: Neil Herbst
　Co-Owner: Lavonne Herbst
　Sales Director: Christopher Ducharme
Number Employees: 8
Sq. footage: 3750
Type of Packaging: Consumer, Food Service
Brands:
　Alley Kat Amber
　Aprikat
　CHARLIE FLINT'S ORIGINAL LAGER
　EIN PROSIT!
　FULL MOON PALE ALE
　OLDE DEUTERONOMY
　RAZZYKAT
　SMOKED PORTER
　ST. PADDY'S
　WEIHNACHTSKATZE

388　Allfresh Food Products
2156 Green Bay Rd
Evanston, IL　60201-3046
　　　　　　　　　　　847-869-3100
　　　　　　　　　　　Fax: 847-869-3103
Processor of butter blends, margarine, shortening
and vegetable oil
　President: Gulshan Wadhwa
　VP: Anil Wadhwa
　Purchasing Manager: Gulshan Wadhwa
Estimated Sales: $5-10 Million
Number Employees: 5-9
Parent Co: Food Corporation of America
Type of Packaging: Consumer, Food Service
Brands:
　ALL FRESH
　BIG BOY
　BUCKSON
　FARMER BROTHERS
　TOP NOTCH

389　Allied Blending & Ingredients
121 Royal Road
Keokuk, IA　52632　　　　　319-524-4080
　　Fax: 319-524-4092　www.alliedblending.com
Anti-caking agents, food stabilizers, preservative &
shelf life extenders, specialty starches and tortilla
blends and concentrates.
　President: Randy Schmelzel
　Vice President Technical Services: John Fannon,
　PhD
　Vice President, Operations: Matt Stelzer
　Vice President], Purchasing: Stephanie Slattery

390　(HQ)Allied Custom Gypsum Company
708 24th Ave NW
Norman, OK　73069-6232　　　405-366-9500
　　Fax: 405-366-9515　800-624-5963
customerservice@alliedcustomgypsum.com
　　　　　www.alliedcustomgypsum.com
Food and pharmaceutical grade calcium sul-
fate-odorless, tasteless white powder from a select
high purity gypsum deposit. Used as a calcium
fortificant, dough conditioner, yeast food, water con-
ditioner, brewing aid, in specialty mixesand dry
blended products, tofu, milk replacers, and dietary
supplements.
　Manager: Tracy Shirley
　CFO: Tracy Shirley III
　Executive VP: Dan Northcutt
　VP Operations: Kris Kinder
Estimated Sales: $1-5 Million
Number Employees: 10-19
Number of Products: 1
Sq. footage: 50000
Parent Co: Harrison Gypsum
Type of Packaging: Food Service
Brands:
　ACG

ACG BROADCAST GYPSUM
TERRA ALBA
VALU-FIL

391　Allied Food Products
251 Saint Marks Ave
Brooklyn, NY　11238-3503　　　212-230-4227
　　　　　　www.alliedfoodproducts.com
　Manager: Ernest Stern
Estimated Sales: $1-2.5 Million
Number Employees: 5-9
Brands:
　E&S Vanilla Sugar

392　Allied Meat Service
25447 Industrial Blvd
Hayward, CA　94545-2931　　　510-351-6677
　　Fax: 510-481-7877　800-794-2554
　　tremington@alliedmeatservice.com
　　　　www.alliedmeatservice.com
Beef and beef products
　President: Greg Nigro
　Marketing Director: Akane Nigro
　CEO: Greg Nigro
Estimated Sales: $20-50 Million
Number Employees: 20-49
Brands:
　Aidells
　Farmland
　Millers
　Saralee
　Silva
　Simplot

393　Allied Old English
100 Markley St
Port Reading, NJ　07064-1897　　732-602-8955
　　Fax: 732-636-2538　info@alliedoldenglish.com
　　　　　www.alliedoldenglish.com
Processor and exporter of Oriental prepared foods
including noodles and sauces; also, pancake syrup,
molasses, salad dressings, jams, jellies, preserves,
salsa and barbecue sauce
　President/Owner/CEO: Fred Ross
　CFO: Frank Gatti
　Director of Quality Control: Josie Alves
　National Sales Manager: Dale Allen
　Human Resources Manager: JoAnn Tedesco
　COO: Steve Owen
　Production Supervisor: Eddie Richardson
　Plant Engineer: Rick McGlynn
　VP Purchasing: Bobbi James
Estimated Sales: $10-20 Million
Number Employees: 50-99
Type of Packaging: Consumer, Food Service, Pri-
vate Label, Bulk
Brands:
　Ah-So
　China Pride
　Dai Dairy
　Mee Tu
　Plantation
　Polynesian
　Rio Grande
　Saucy Susan

394　Allied Resource Corporation
PO Box 1416
Orem, UT　84059-1416　　　888-226-1096
　　　　　　　　　　　Fax: 801-492-6598
　President: Maria Gum
Estimated Sales: $2.5-5 Million
Number Employees: 5-9

395　Allied Wine Corporation
2 Fairground Rd
Monticello, NY　12701-4212　　845-796-4160
　　Fax: 845-796-4161　armonwine@verizon.net
　　　　　　　http://www.verizon.net
Processor, importer and exporter of kosher wines
and spirits
　Manager: David Fieldman
　VP: Herman Schwartz
Estimated Sales: $500,000-$1 Million
Number Employees: 1-4
Type of Packaging: Food Service, Private Label
Brands:
　Armon

396　Alliston Creamery & Dairy
26 Dominion Street
Alliston, ON　L9R 1L5
Canada　　　　　　　　　705-435-6751
　　　　　　　　　　　Fax: 705-435-6797

Manufacturer of butter; organic butter, whey butter
and occassionally goat butter
　Office Manager: Laurie Anne Kennedy
　Plant Manager: David Kennedy
Number Employees: 9
Sq. footage: 15000
Type of Packaging: Consumer, Food Service, Pri-
vate Label, Bulk
Brands:
　Golden Dawn

397　(HQ)Alljuice
352 Jet St
Hendersonville, NC　28792-8004　　828-685-8821
　　Fax: 828-685-8495　800-736-5674
　　　　　　www.mrsclarks.com
Processor of shelf-stable juices, salad dressings, and
sauces
　President: Ron Kahrer
　QC: Ned Williams
　Plant Manager: John Weber
　Purchasing: Ron Mathis
Estimated Sales: $20-50 Million
Number Employees: 20-49
Number of Brands: 12
Number of Products: 50
Sq. footage: 60000
Parent Co: AGRI Industries
Type of Packaging: Consumer, Food Service, Pri-
vate Label
Brands:
　ALLJUICE
　NATURE'S CHOICE

398　Alltech Natural Food Division
3031 Catnip Hill Rd
Nicholasville, KY　40356-9765　　859-885-9613
　　Fax: 859-887-3223　info@alltech.com
　　　　　　www.alltech.com
Meat tenderizers, gelating agents, flavor bases and
sequestrants
　President: T Pearse Lyons
　Marketing Manager: Clare Flannery
Estimated Sales: $ 20 - 50 Million
Number Employees: 250-499

399　Alma Plantation
4612 Alma Rd
Lakeland, LA　70752-3203　　225-627-6666
　　Fax: 225-627-5138　DavidStewart@Bellsouth.net
Blackstrap molasses and sugar.
　President: David Stewart
　Purchasing Agent: Stuart Carter
Estimated Sales: $20-50 Million
Number Employees: 50-99
Type of Packaging: Bulk

400　Alma-Leo
485 E Half Day Rd
Buffalo Grove, IL　60089-8806　　847-821-0411
　　　　　　　　　　　Fax: 847-291-1541
Brands:
　Alma Leo
　Count Duckula
　Slime Slurps
　Treasure Trolls
　World Wrestling Fede

401　Almark Foods
2118 Centennial Dr
Gainesville, GA　30504-5757　　770-536-4520
　　Fax: 770-536-4793　800-849-3447
almarkfoods@msn.com　www.almarkeggs.com
Processor of egg products
　President: Don Stoner
　Marketing Director: Steve Tufts
　Sales Director: David Cathey
　Operations Manager: Paul Heard
　Purchasing: Kena Seay
Estimated Sales: $5-10 Million
Number Employees: 20-49
Sq. footage: 15000
Type of Packaging: Food Service
Brands:
　ALMARK

402　Almarla Vineyards & Winery
Highway 510
Shubuta, MS　39360　　　601-687-5548
Wines
　President: Timothy Dunbar
Brands:
　Almarla Black Lightning
　Almarla Soul Train

Sautene
Thunder McCloud

403 Almond Board of California
1150 Ninth Street
Suite 1500
Modesto, CA 95354-0845   209-549-8262
    Fax: 209-549-8267 staff@almondboard.com
              www.almondboard.com
Almonds
    CEO: Richard Waycott
    Assoc. Director/N American Global Mktg.:
    Stacey Humble
Number Employees: 10-19

404 Almondina®/YZ Enterprises, Inc.
1930 Indian Wood Cir
Maumee, OH 43537-4053   419-893-8777
      Fax: 419-893-8825 800-736-8779
    yz@glasscity.net www.almondina.com
Cookies, biscuits. No artificial colors, flavors or
preservatives
    President/CEO: Yuval Zaliouk
    Public Relations: Linda Semer
Estimated Sales:$5-10 Million
Number Employees: 10-19
Type of Packaging: Consumer, Food Service, Private Label
Brands:
    ALMONDINA BISCUITS

405 Aloe Commodities International
1270 Champion Circle
Suite 100
Carrollton, TX 75006-8333   972-241-4251
    Fax: 972-241-4376 800-701-2563
    flauterbach@acinatural.com
              www.aloeonline.com
Processor and exporter of aloe vera products, cosmetics and dietary supplement drinks
    President: Mark McKnight
    CEO: L Scott McKnight
    CFO: Richard Ellis
    General Manager: Fred Lauterbach
Estimated Sales:$ 20 - 50 Million
Number Employees: 20-49
Number of Brands: 20
Number of Products: 100
Sq. footage: 64000
Type of Packaging: Consumer, Private Label
Brands:
    AVERA SPORT
    CARBMATE
    EL TORO LOCO
    KATAHNA
    NATURALLY ALOE

406 Aloe Dynamics
8120 Chancellor Row
Dallas, TX 75247-5512   214-630-8808
    Fax: 214-630-8008 creves@alodynamics.com
              www.aloedynamics.com
Custom formulation and contract packaging. All
types of skin and hair products, liquid supplements
    President: James Abanaka
    Purchasing Agent: Julie Ike
Estimated Sales:$2.5-5 Million
Number Employees: 20-49
Sq. footage: 15000
Type of Packaging: Private Label
Brands:
    ALOE DYNAMICS

407 Aloe Farms
3102 Wilson Rd
Harlingen, TX 78552-5011   956-425-1289
    Fax: 956-425-3390 800-262-6771
    aloefarms@earthlink.net
              www.aloeverafarms.com
Manufacturer and supplier of aloe vera juice, gel and
capsules.
    President: M Elliot Berry
Estimated Sales:$5-10 Million
Number Employees: 5-9
Sq. footage: 12000
Type of Packaging: Consumer, Private Label, Bulk
Brands:
    Aloe Farms

408 Aloe Laboratories, Inc.
P.O. Box 831
Harlingen, TX 78551-0831   956-428-8416
    Fax: 956-428-8482 800-258-5380
    lrodriguez@aloelabs.com www.aloelabs.com

Manufacturer and exporter of organic and conventional aloe vera gel, juice, concentrates and powder.
    President: Luis Rodriguez
    CEO: Hide Aragaki
    Operations and Logistics: Mike Hernandez
Estimated Sales:$3-5 Million
Number Employees: 50-99
Sq. footage: 40000
Brands:
    Aloe Burst
    Aloe Labs

409 Aloe Life
PO Box 710759
San Diego, CA 92171-0759   619-258-0145
    Fax: 619-258-1373 800-414-2563
    info@aloelife.com www.aloelife.com
Aloe products
    President: Karen Masterson

410 Aloe'Ha Drink Products
1908 Augusta Drive
Suite 2
Houston, TX 77057-3717   713-978-6359
    Fax: 713-978-6858 info@aloeha.com
              www.aloeha.com
Manufacturer and exporter of carbonated fruit drinks
including rasberry, kiwi-strawberry, peach,
lemon-lime, etc.
    Operations Manager: Doyle Gaskamp
Number Employees: 5
Type of Packaging: Consumer, Food Service
Brands:
    Aloe'ha

411 Aloha Distillers
5 Sand Island Access Rd # 118
Honolulu, HI 96819-4907   808-841-5787
              Fax: 808-847-2903
    alohadistillers@gyello.com/site/
Processor and exporter of liqueurs including coffee,
chocolate-coconut and chi-chi
    President: Dave Fazendin
    Marketing: Ann Fazendin
    Purchasing Manager: Dave Fazendin
Estimated Sales:$1-2.5 Million
Number Employees: 1-4
Number of Brands: 1
Number of Products: 1
Type of Packaging: Consumer
Brands:
    COFFEE
    GOLD
    KONA
    LIQUEUR

412 Aloha Poi Factory
800 Lower Main St
Wailuku, HI 96793-1417   808-244-3536
              Fax: 808-244-1914
Processor of poi
    President: Les Nakama
Estimated Sales:$2.5-5 Million
Number Employees: 10-19
Type of Packaging: Consumer, Food Service

413 Aloha from Oregon
P.O. Box 42077
Eugene, OR 97404-0571   541-343-5519
    Fax: 541-343-5499 800-241-0300
    office@alohafromoregon.com
              www.alohafromoregon.com
Pepper jellies, chutneys, and other specialty items.
    President: Judi Dodson
Estimated Sales:$ 5 - 10 Million
Number Employees: 5-9
Type of Packaging: Consumer, Food Service, Private Label

414 Alois J. Binder Bakery
940 Frenchmen St
New Orleans, LA 70116-1683   504-947-1111
              Fax: 504-947-1122
Manufacturer of bread and other bakery products
    Owner: Alois Binder Jr Jr.
    Treasurer: Joseph Binder
Estimated Sales:$4 Million
Number Employees: 50-99
Type of Packaging: Consumer, Food Service, Private Label, Bulk

415 Alpen Cellars
Hc 2 Box 3966
Trinity Center, CA 96091-9500   530-266-9513
    Fax: 530-266-3363 winemaker@alpencellars.com
              www.alpencellars.com
Wine
    Owner: Mark Groves
    Winemaker: Keith Grooves
*Estimated Sales:*Less than $500,000
Number Employees: 10-19
Brands:
    Alpen Cellars

416 Alpen Sierra Coffee Company
2222 Park Pl
Minden, NV 89423-8660   775-783-7263
    Fax: 775-783-7293 800-531-1405
    coffeentea@alpensierra.com
              www.alpensierra.com
Roast and manufactures coffee and tea
    President: Christian Waskiewicz
    Marketing: Megan Waskiewicz
Estimated Sales:$1-2.5 Million
Number Employees: 5-9
Brands:
    ALPEN SIERRA

417 Alpenrose Dairy
P.O. Box 25030
Portland, OR 97298-0030   503-244-1133
    Fax: 503-452-2139 alpenrose@alpenrose.com
              www.alpenrose.com
Processor of ice cream and milk
    President: Carl Cadanau Iii
Estimated Sales:$20-50 Million
Number Employees: 100-249
Type of Packaging: Consumer, Food Service
Brands:
    ALPENROSE

418 Alpha Baking Company
5001 W Polk St
Chicago, IL 60644-5249   773-261-6000
    Fax: 773-489-2711 ebickhem@alphabaking.com
              www.alphabaking.com
Processor of baked goods including fresh bread.
    Chairman/CEO: Michael Marcucci
    CFO: Mark Zawicki
    CEO: Michael L Marcucci
    VP/Sales & Marketing: Gary Narcisi
    VP/Sales: Mark Marcucci
    Operations: David Granger
    Production: George Pohelos
    Plant Manager: Steve Rosen
    Purchasing: Bill Harp
Estimated Sales:$170 Million
Number Employees: 1,000-4,999
Number of Products: 300
Sq. footage: 135000
Type of Packaging: Consumer, Food Service, Private Label, Bulk
Brands:
    CABLE CAR
    CASTLE
    GOLDEN HEARTH
    KREAMO
    MARYANN
    NATIONAL
    S. ROSEN

419 Alpha Baking Company
5001 W Polk St
Chicago, IL 60644-5249   773-261-6000
    Fax: 773-489-2711 tgill@alphabaking.com
              www.alphabaking.com
Processor of bread and rolls
    President: Michael Marcucci
    EVP Operations: Robert Cruice
    Controller: Sheryl Smith
Estimated Sales:$17.3 Million
Number Employees: 1,000-4,999
Parent Co: Alpha Baking Company
Brands:
    CABLE CAR
    CASTLE
    GOLDEN HEARTH
    KREAMO
    MARYANN
    NATIONAL
    S. ROSEN

420 Alpha Baking Company
360 N Fail Rd
La Porte, IN 46350-7051   219-324-7440
Fax: 219-324-9863 contact@alphabaking.com
www.alphabaking.com
Processor of bread and buns
President: Michael Marcucci
EVP Operations: Robert Cruice
Controller: Sheryl Smith
Plant Manager: Dirk Peterson
Estimated Sales:$100+ Million
Number Employees: 100-249
Parent Co: Alpha Baking Company
Type of Packaging: Consumer, Food Service, Private Label

421 Alpha Baking Company
4545 W Lyndale Ave
Chicago, IL 60639-3492   773-489-5400
Fax: 773-489-2711 www.alphabaking.com
Manufacturer of bakery products
CEO: Michael Marucci
Sales Manager: Eddy Nosalik
Estimated Sales:$39 Million
Number Employees: 250-499
Parent Co: Alpha Baking Company
Type of Packaging: Food Service
Brands:
Maryann
Rosen's

422 Alphin Brothers
2302 Us Highway 301 S
Dunn, NC 28334-6165   910-892-8751
Fax: 910-892-2709 800-672-4502
alphin@alphinbrothers.com
www.alphinbrothers.com
Wholesaler/distributor of frozen seafood, beef and pork.
President: Jesse Alphin Jr
VP/Financial Officer: Ernest Alphin
Production Manager: John Hyland
Estimated Sales:$20-50 Million
Number Employees: 50-99
Type of Packaging: Consumer, Food Service

423 Alpine Cheese Company
P.O.Box 181
Winesburg, OH 44690-0181   330-359-6291
Fax: 330-359-0035
Dairy products, natural cheeses and deli
President: Robert Ramseyer
Marketing Director: Donald Fudge
Plant Manager: Brian Barbey
Purchasing Manager: Donald Fudge
Estimated Sales:$10-20 Million
Number Employees: 20-49
Type of Packaging: Private Label

424 Alpine Coffee Roasters
894 Us Highway 2
Leavenworth, WA 98826-1340   509-548-3313
Fax: 509-548-4251 800-246-2761
java@alpinecoffeeroasters.com
www.alpinecoffeeroasters.com
Coffee
Co-Owner: Dale Harrison
Co-Owner: Veronica Harrison
Roastmaster: Bill Harrison
Estimated Sales:$2.5-5 Million
Number Employees: 5-9
Brands:
Alpine Coffee

425 Alpine Health Products
1525 W Business Park Dr
Orem, UT 84058-2221   801-225-5525
Fax: 801-225-0956 800-572-5076
gbriggs@alpinehp.com www.alpinehi.com
Manufacturer of vitamins, minerals, nutritional supplements and herbal products
President: Greg Pulido
VP, Sales/Marketing: Gaylen Briggs
General Manager: Scott Jenkins
Purchasing Manager: Kelly Colby
Estimated Sales:$17.9 Million
Number Employees: 50-99
Sq. footage: 50000
Parent Co: Alpine Health Industries
Type of Packaging: Consumer, Private Label, Bulk

426 Alpine Meats
9900 Lower Sacramento Rd
Stockton, CA 95210-3912   209-477-2691
Fax: 209-477-1994 800-399-6328
info@alpinemeats.com
www.alpinepackingco.com
Manufacturer of Frankfurters, sausages and hams, private brands.
President: Jerry Singer
Quality Control: James Sturgeon
Controller: Cecil McKie
Production: Dennis Saragoza
Purchasing: Robby Jaynes
Estimated Sales:$8 Million
Number Employees: 50-99
Sq. footage: 49000
Type of Packaging: Consumer, Food Service, Private Label, Bulk
Brands:
ALPINE

427 Alpine Pure USA
PO Box 503
Accord, MA 02018-0503   617-548-8301
Fax: 888-311-6541 866-832-7997
info@teaspree.com www.teaspree.com
Teas

428 Alpine Touch Spices
P.O.Box 864
Choteau, MT 59422-0864   406-466-2063
Fax: 406-466-2076 877-755-2525
sales@alpinetouch.com www.alpinetouch.com
Seasonings
President: Mark Southard
Co-Owner: Vicki Southard
Estimated Sales:$500,000-$1 Million
Number Employees: 1-4

429 Alpine Valley Water
16900 Lathrop Ave
Harvey, IL 60426-6033   708-333-3910
Fax: 708-333-3921
sales@AlpineValleyWater.com
www.alpinevalleywater.com
A manufacturer of distilled and bottled water
Owner: Tim Rausch
*Estimated Sales:*Less than $500,000
Number Employees: 1-4
Sq. footage: 10000
Type of Packaging: Food Service
Brands:
Alpine Valley

430 Alpine Vineyards
25904 Green Peak Rd
Monroe, OR 97456-9773   541-424-5851
Fax: 541-424-5891
www.oregonwine.org/wine/alpine
Wines
Owner: Daniel Jepsen
Winemaker: Daniel Jepsen
Estimated Sales:$1-2.5 Million
Number Employees: 1-4

431 AlpineAire Foods
PO Box 1799
Rocklin, CA 95677-7799   916-624-6050
Fax: 916-624-1604 800-322-6325
info@aa-foods.com www.aa-foods.com
Manufacturer and exporter of health, backpacking, self-heating and emergency prepared foods, freeze-dried and no cooking required foods including; pre-packed beans, cereals, desserts, dried fruits and vegetables, grains and meatsubstitutes
President: Don Gearing
Sq. footage: 50000
Parent Co: TyRy, Inc
Type of Packaging: Consumer, Private Label, Bulk
Brands:
Alpineaire
Gourmet Reserves

432 (HQ)Alsum Produce
P.O.Box 188
Friesland, WI 53935-0188   920-348-5127
Fax: 920-348-5174 800-236-5127
larry.alsum@alsum.com www.alsum.com
Processor, importer, exporter and packer of potatoes and onions; wholesaler/distributor of fresh fruits and vegetables
President/CEO: Larry Alsum
CFO: Jan Braaksma
Quality Control: Dave Breiwa
Sales: Dave Katsma
Public Relations: Randy Quade
Production: Randy Fischer
Plant Manager: Steve Tillema
Purchasing Manager: Larry Alsum
Estimated Sales:$23 Million
Number Employees: 100-249
Sq. footage: 112000
Parent Co: Alsum Farms
Type of Packaging: Consumer, Food Service, Private Label, Bulk
Brands:
WINDMILL
WOODEN SHOE

433 Alta Dena Certified Dairy
17637 Valley Blvd
City of Industry, CA 91744-5796   626-964-6401
Fax: 626-913-9062 800-535-1369
Mary_Larrowe@deanfoods.com
www.altadenadairy.com
Manufacturer of dairy products including butter, cheese, ice cream, kefir, yogurt, frozen yogurt, milk, eggnog and yogurt drinkables
Manager: John Keith
CFO: Keith Anderson
Vice President: Bob Pettigrew
Quality Control: Steve Okada
Sales Director: Mike Dobbs
Plant Manager: Stuart Saito
Estimated Sales:$100-500 Million
Number Employees: 500-999
Parent Co: Dean Foods Company
Brands:
ALTA DENA CLASSIC
CARIBBEAN CHILL
CRAZY COW
DAIRY MART
DECADENT TEMPTATIONS
LE YOUNGHURT
OLD TYME

434 Alta Health Products
2137 E Summersweet Dr
Boise, ID 83716-6697   208-344-0852
Fax: 208-367-0089 800-423-4155
altavpdebbie@aol.com
www.altahealthproducts.com
Herbal supplements
Owner/CEO: Judy Haswell
Estimated Sales:$ 1 - 3 Million
Number Employees: 1-4
Brands:
Alta Health

435 Alta Health Products
P.O.Box 990
Idaho City, ID 83631-0990   208-392-4170
Fax: 208-392-4185 800-423-4155
altavpdebbie@aol.com
www.altahealthproducts.com
Processor of herbal supplements, teas and minerals
President: Judy Haswell
Founder: Richard Barmakian
Vice President: Deborah Saw Kims
Product Promotion: Kelli Fischer
Estimated Sales:$3-5 Million
Number Employees: 1-4
Brands:
Alta

436 Alta Vineyard Cellar
PO Box 980
Calistoga, CA 94515-0980   707-942-6708
Fax: 707-942-5065
Wines
President: Benjamin Falk
Estimated Sales:$500,000-$1 Million
Number Employees: 1-4
Brands:
Alta

437 Alta-Dena Certified Dairy
17637 Valley Blvd
City of Industry, CA 91744-5796   626-964-6401
Fax: 626-913-9062 800-535-1369
Mary_Larrowe@deanfoods.com
www.altadenadairy.com

Manager: John Keith
Number Employees: 500-999
Brands:
Alta Dena

438 Altamura Vineyards & Winery
P.O.Box 3209
Napa, CA 94558-0320   707-253-2000
  Fax: 707-255-3937 altamurawinery@aol.com
              www.altamura.com
Wines
  President: Frank C Altamura
Estimated Sales:$ 3 - 5 Million
Number Employees: 5-9
Number of Brands: 1
Number of Products: 2

439 Alternative Health & Herbs
425 Jackson St SE
Albany, OR 97321-2844   541-791-8400
  Fax: 541-791-8401 800-345-4152
  healthinfo@healthherbs.com
          www.healthherbs.com
Processor of liquid herbal formulations and herbal teas and vitamins; wholesaler/distributor of air and water filters, herbs and vitamins; exporter of herbs and herbal tinctures; importer of herbs. Custom formulations available
  Owner: Truman Berst
*Estimated Sales:*Less than $500,000
Number Employees: 1-4
Sq. footage: 3000
Type of Packaging: Consumer, Private Label, Bulk
Brands:
  AMERICAN HEALTH & HERBS MINISTRY
  American Naturals
  Truman's

440 Alto Dairy Cooperative
N3545 County Road Ee
Waupun, WI 53963-9423   920-346-2215
  Fax: 920-346-2377 www.altodairy.com
Manufacturer of natural cheese products. Manufacturer and exporter of whey.
  CEO: Rich Scheuerman
  CFO: Greg Pollesch
  Executive: Kurt Sonnleitner
  Director Quality Control: Theresa Hurd
  Marketing: Rachel Bradley
  VP Sales: Dennis Kasuboski
  Piblic Relations: Karen Endres
  Director Operations: John Smedema
  Director Engineering: Hans Horetzki
  Plant Manager: David Schmidt
  Purchasing: Pam Ferch
Estimated Sales:$430 Million
Number Employees: 250-499
Number of Brands: 3
Number of Products: 12
Sq. footage: 270000
Type of Packaging: Food Service, Bulk

441 Alto Dairy Cooperative
307 N Clark Street
Black Creek, WI 54106-9719   920-346-2215
  Fax: 920-346-2377 www.altodairy.com
Cheese and cheese products, dry whey
  President: Rich Scheuerman
  CEO: Rich Scheuerman
  VP: Larry Lemmenes
  VP Sales: Dennis Kasuboski
*Estimated Sales:*Under $500,000
Number Employees: 50-99
Brands:
  Black Creek Classic

442 Alto Rey Food Corporation
11468 Dona Teresa Dr
Studio City, CA 91604-4271   323-969-0178
                Fax: 323-969-0197
Condiments, dips, salsas, dressings
  President: David Ufberg
Estimated Sales:$1-2.5 Million
Number Employees: 5-9
Brands:
  Alto Rey

443 Alto Vineyards
P.O.Box 51
Alto Pass, IL 62905-0051   618-893-4898
  Fax: 618-893-4935 altovin@midwest.net
          www.altovineyards.net
Producers of red, white and port wines.
  Owner: Paul Renzaglia

Estimated Sales:$5-10 Million
Number Employees: 5-9
Type of Packaging: Bulk
Other Locations:
  Alto Vineyards
  Champaign IL

444 Alum-A-Lift
7909 Bankhead Hwy
Winston, GA 30187-1433   770-489-0328
  Fax: 770-489-7247 applications@alum-a-lift.com
            www.alum-a-lift.com
Manufacture custom egronomic lifting solutions.
  President: Stanley Bressner
  CFO: Niels Bressner
  Vice President: Eric Bressner
  Marketing Director: Cheri Pounds
Number Employees: 50-99
Number of Brands: 4

445 Alvarado Street Bakery
2225 S McDowell Boulevard Ext
Petaluma, CA 94954-5661   707-283-0300
                Fax: 707-283-0350
  info@alvaradostreetbakery.com
  www.alvaradostreetbakery.com
Processor of organic goods including sprouted wheat bread, kosher bagels, tortillas and whole grain and oil-free granola; exporter of frozen organic wheat bread and kosher bagels
  President: Michael Girkout
  CEO: Joseph Tuck
  Plant Manager: Bryan Long
Estimated Sales:$10-20 Million
Number Employees: 100-249
Number of Brands: 2
Number of Products: 27
Sq. footage: 30000
Type of Packaging: Consumer, Private Label
Brands:
  ALVARADO STREET BAKERY

446 Alyeska Seafoods
P.O.Box 31359
Seattle, WA 98103-1359   206-547-2100
                Fax: 206-547-1808
Fresh and frozen seafoods
  President: Ken Tippett
  VP: Murry Simpson
  Purchasing Agent: Cynthia Swazo
Estimated Sales:$50-100 Million
Number Employees: 5-9

447 AmRhein Wine Cellars
9243 Patterson Dr
Bent Mountain, VA 24059-2215   540-929-4632
  Fax: 540-929-4632 info@roanokewine.com
            www.roanokewine.com
Wines
  Owner: Russel Amrhein
Estimated Sales:$ 1 - 3 Million
Number Employees: 1-4

448 Amador Foothill Winery
12500 Steiner Rd
Plymouth, CA 95669-9510   209-245-6307
  Fax: 209-245-3580 800-778-9463
  info@amadorfoothill.com
  www.amadorfoothill.com
Wines
  Owner/President: Ben Zeitman
  Owner/Winemaker: Katie Quinn
Estimated Sales:$1-$2.5 Million
Number Employees: 1-4
Type of Packaging: Private Label
Brands:
  Amador Foothill

449 Amalfitano's Italian Bakery
29 E Commons Blvd # 700
New Castle, DE 19720-1740   302-324-9005
                Fax: 302-324-9008
Bakery products
  Owner: Ralph Jacobs
Estimated Sales:$2.5-5 Million
Number Employees: 20-49

450 Amalgamated Produce
P.O.Box 2196
Bridgeport, CT 06608-0196   203-366-6919
  Fax: 203-339-3773 800-358-3808

Processor of bean soup mixes, dried fruits, stuffings, sprout products and wild rice dishes
  CEO/President: Richard Blackwell
  Vice President: Adriana Alvarez
Estimated Sales:$ 10 - 20 Million
Number Employees: 20-49
Sq. footage: 12000
Brands:
  SPECIALTY FARMS

451 Amalgamated Sugar Company
1951 S Saturn Way
Stuie 100
Boise, ID 83709   208-383-6500
  Fax: 208-383-6688 www.amalgamatedsugar.com
Manufacturer of liquid and granulated sugar, molasses and livestock feed products.
  President/CEO: Victor Jaro
  VP Finance: Wayne Neeley
  VP Marketing: Bill Smith
  VP Operations: Joe Huff
  Purchasing Agent: Nasser Shoaee
Estimated Sales:$656 Million
Number Employees: 1,500
Parent Co: Snake River Sugar Company
Type of Packaging: Consumer, Food Service, Private Label, Bulk
Brands:
  WHITE SATIN

452 Amalthea Cellars Farm Winery
267 Hayes Mill Road
Apt A
Atco, NJ 08004-2475   856-768-8585
  Winery@amaltheacellars.com
            www.amaltheacellars.com
Wines
  Owner: Louis Caracciolo
  Manager: Virginia Caracciolo
Estimated Sales:$1-2.5 Million
Number Employees: 5-9

453 Amana Meat Shop & Smokehouse
P.O.Box 158
Amana, IA 52203-0158   319-622-7586
  Fax: 319-622-6245 800-373-6328
  info@amanameatshop.com
  www.amanameatshop.com
Manufacturer and wholesaler/distributor of hickory-smoked meats including sausage, ham, bacon, pork tenderloin and bratwurst
  Manager: Greg Hergert
  Director: Mike Shoup
*Estimated Sales:*Less than $500,000
Number Employees: 20-49
Parent Co: Amana Society Corporation
Type of Packaging: Consumer, Food Service
Brands:
  Amana Meats

454 Amanda Hills Spring Water
431 W Broad St
Pataskala, OH 43062-8137   740-927-3422
        Fax: 740-927-1856 800-375-0885
  info@amandahills.com www.amandahills.com
Manufacturer of spring water
  Owner: David Betts
Estimated Sales:$300,000-500,000
Number Employees: 1-4
Number of Brands: 1
Sq. footage: 10000
Type of Packaging: Private Label
Brands:
  Amanda Hills

455 Amano Artisan Chocolate
496 S 1325 W
Orem, UT 84058   801-655-1996
  amano@amanochocolate.com
          www.amanochocolate.com
Chocolate bars
  President: Arthur Pollard
  VP: Clark Goble
  Sales Director: Rick Raile

456 Amano Enzyme USA Company, Ltd
2150 Point Boulevard
Suite 100
Elgin, IL 60123-7888   847-649-0101
  Fax: 847-649-0205 800-446-7652
  sales@amanoenzymeusa.com
  www-amano-enzyme.co.jp

Supplies the North and South American markets with non—animal and non-GMO enzymes for the dietary supplement, nutraceutical, food, diagnostic and pharmaceutical industries.
President: Motoyuki Amano
VP Science/Technology: James Jolly
Estimated Sales: $15 Million
Number Employees: 440
Sq. footage: 25000
Parent Co: Amano Enzyme

457 Amano Fish Cake Factory
30 Holomua St
Hilo, HI 96720-5102   808-935-5555
                    Fax: 808-961-2154
Processor of frozen and canned fish cakes
Owner: Hiroshi Mathubara
Purchasing Manager: Hiroshi Matsubara
Estimated Sales: $1-2.5 Million
Number Employees: 5-9
Type of Packaging: Consumer
Brands:
AMANO

458 Amaranth Marketing Group
PO Box 2458
Dearborn, MI 48123-2458   313-724-0313
                    Fax: 313-724-0323
Manager: Steve Boese

459 Amaranth Resources
139 E William Street
Suite 325
Albert Lea, MN 56007-2535   310-370-2500
    Fax: 507-373-4753 800-842-6689
        edward@dm.deskmedia.com
        http://www.dm.deskmedia.com
Grains, cereals, spices, seasonings, condiments, allergy free products
President: Edward Hubbard
CEO: Edward Hubbard
Vice President: R Merrell
Estimated Sales: $2.5-5 Million
Brands:
Ambake
Amban
Amburst
Amgrain
Best of Health

460 Amazing Candy Craft Company
18408 Jamaica Avenue
Hollis, NY 11423-2431   718-264-3031
    Fax: 718-264-8437 800-429-9368
                www.axxent.net
Candy
President: Frank Salacuse
VP: Catherine Salacuse
VP Marketing/Sales: Brad Demsky
Brands:
CANDY ACTIVITY
MAKE YOUR OWN GUMMIES

461 Amazing Herbs Nutraceuticals
1960 Parker Ct # F
Stone Mountain, GA 30087-3450   770-982-4780
                    800-241-9138
        info@amazingherbs.com
        www.amazingherbs.com
Manufacturers of nutritional supplements and natural products made from herbs and botanicals from around the globe.
Owner: Tony Goreja
Brands:
AMAZING HERBS
THERAMUNE NUTRITIONALS

462 Ambassador Foods
16625 Saticoy St
Van Nuys, CA 91406-2837   818-787-2000
    Fax: 818-778-6464 800-338-3369
        info@ambassadorfoods.com
        www.ambassadorfoods.com
A national distributor of premium imported and domestic products for the pastry and bakery trade. We supply the finest chocolate from Belgium and Switzerland, mousse cake bases and dessert pastes from Germany, jams and glazes fromBelgium, domestic fruit fillings, delicate chocolate cups and decorations from Holland, marzipan from Germany, all part of our exciting and innovative line of ingredients
Owner: Peter Seeger

Estimated Sales: $ 50 - 100 Million
Number Employees: 20-49
Parent Co: Qzina Specialty Foods
Type of Packaging: Consumer, Bulk
Other Locations:
Clifton NJ
Chicago IL
Miami FL
San Francisco CA
Vancouver BC
Toronto ON
Brands:
Ambassador

463 Amber Foods
130 Oakdale Road
Downsview, ON M3N 1V9
Canada   416-746-2455
    Fax: 416-748-8701 ambrinfo@amberfoods.com
                www.amberfoods.com
Manufacturer, importer and exporter of fresh cut fruit including grapefruit, grapes, melons, oranges and pineapples
President: William Bernstein
VP Sales: Paul Barrett
Number Employees: 20
Sq. footage: 12000
Type of Packaging: Consumer, Food Service
Other Locations:
Toronto ON
Dinuba CA
Brands:
Amber

464 Amberg Wine Cellars
2412 Seneca Castle Orleans Rd
Clifton Springs, NY 14432-9319   315-462-3455
    Fax: 315-462-6512 info@ambergwine.com
                www.ambergwine.com
Wines
Owner: Ute Amberg
President: Herman Amberg
CFO: Eric Amberg
Marketing Manager: Debbie Amberg
Plant Manager: Eric Amberg
Estimated Sales: $500,000-$1 Million
Number Employees: 1-4
Type of Packaging: Private Label
Brands:
Amberg Wine Cellars

465 Amberland Foods
P.O.Box 185
Harvey, ND 58341-0185   701-324-4804
    Fax: 701-324-4805 800-950-4558
        amberlandfoods@gondto.com
        www.dakotaseasonings.com
Processor of dehydrated soup mixes, scone and dip mixes, jams, jellies, seasonings, syrups and toppings
Owner/Manager: Susan K Schwarz
Operations Manager: Elreen Olson
Estimated Sales: $1-2.5 Million
Number Employees: 10-19
Number of Brands: 1
Number of Products: 50
Sq. footage: 4000
Type of Packaging: Consumer, Private Label
Brands:
DAKOTA SEASONINGS

466 Amberwave Foods
625 Allegheny Avenue
Oakmont, PA 15139-2003   412-828-3040
                    Fax: 412-828-2282
Processor of gourmet pizza products including cheese analogs, crusts and focaccia; also, whole wheat pizzas
Purchasing Manager: Tammy Carroll
Estimated Sales: $ 10 - 20 Million
Number Employees: 20-49
Parent Co: Tomanetti Foods
Type of Packaging: Consumer, Food Service, Private Label, Bulk
Brands:
GRAINDANCE
SOYDANCE

467 Ambootia Tea Estate
PO Box 11696
Chicago, IL 60611-0696   312-661-1550
    Fax: 312-661-1523 goels@worldnet.att.net
                www.teareport.com
Beverages
Chairman: Shashank Goel
Director: Shashank Goel

Estimated Sales: Less than $500,000
Number Employees: 5-9
Brands:
Ambootia

468 Amboy Specialty Foods Company
P.O.Box 529
Dixon, IL 61021-0529   815-288-4097
    Fax: 815-288-5022 800-892-0400
                www.bayvalleyfoods.com
Processor of canned ready-made cheese sauces and puddings
President: Randy Smith
VP of Sales: Robert Doeseckle
Plant Manager: Jerry Petrasko
Estimated Sales: $25-50 Million
Number Employees: 100-249
Parent Co: Dean Foods Company
Type of Packaging: Consumer, Food Service, Private Label, Bulk

469 Ambrosia Honey
6565 309 Road
Parachute, CO 81635   970-625-0555
                    Fax: 970-625-3382
Honey
President: Craig Gerbore
Estimated Sales: $ 1-2.5 Million
Number Employees: 3
Type of Packaging: Private Label
Brands:
Ambrosia Honey

470 Ambrosial Granola
8124 7th Avenue
Brooklyn, NY 11228   718-491-1335
    Fax: 718-425-9932 info@ambrosialgranola.com
                www.ambrosialgranola.com
Granola cereals
President: Hariclia Makoulis

471 Amcan Industries
570 Taxter Road
Elmsford, NY 10523-2356   914-347-4838
    Fax: 914-347-4960 salesus@amcan-online.com
                www.amcan-online.com
Meat, jam, jelly, preserves, health food, nutriceuticals, confectionery, fish, seafood, dairy, beverage and juices, bakery and cereal, natural and artificial sweeteners
President: Bowes Dempsey
VP: Chris Aioorenzo
Estimated Sales: $5-10 Million
Number Employees: 5-9

472 Amelia Bay Beverage Systems
11800 Wills Rd
Suite 120
Alpharetta, GA 30004   770-772-6360
    Fax: 770-772-4766 800-650-8327
    info@ameliabay.com www.ameliabay.com
Manufacture and formulate high fold liquid concentrates for coffees, teas, cappucinos, chais, and other ready - to- drink products, as well as custom formulations
President: John Crandall
Sales Manager: Ralph Lane
Estimated Sales: $ 5 - 10 Million
Number Employees: 5-9
Type of Packaging: Food Service

473 Amendt Corporation
PO Box 722
Monroe, MI 48161-0722   734-242-2411
    Fax: 734-242-9407 amendtcorp@teleweb.net
                www.amendt.com
Flour, frosting, cake and donut mixes
Estimated Sales: $5-10 Million
Number Employees: 20-49

474 Ameri Color Corporation
341 S Melrose St # C
Placentia, CA 92870-5974   714-996-1820
    Fax: 714-996-7422 800-556-0233
        info@americolorcorp.com
        www.americolorcorp.com
Manufacturer of food colors for the bakery industry
President: Ernie Molina
CFO: Fay Molina
Estimated Sales: $500,000-$1 Million
Number Employees: 1-4
Brands:
Ameri Color

475 Ameri-Kal Inc
1426 Sibley Street
Wichita Falls, TX 76301   940-322-5400
sales@amerikal.com
www.amerikal.com
Processor and exporter domestic of nutritional supplements, vitamins, minerals, herbal formulations, sports nutrition products, herb flavored grapeseed oil, capsules, tablets, bulk powder, liquids, soft gel, etc.; also, packaging, Q/Aand R/D labs and custom formulation
    CEO: Tom Soejoto
    Director/Of Marketing: Ron Soejoto
    Purchasing Agent: Ron Soejoto
Number Employees: 18
Sq. footage: 35500
Type of Packaging: Private Label, Bulk

476 Ameri-Suisse Group
1348 South Ave
Plainfield, NJ 07062-1900   908-222-1001
                                 Fax: 732-222-1929
Novelty candies
    Owner: Lew Demeter

477 AmeriCandy Company
3618 Saint Germaine Ct
Louisville, KY 40207-3722   502-583-1776
    Fax: 502-583-6627   americandy@aol.com
                         www.americandybar.com
Manufacturer and exporter of gourmet chocolates and spring water
    Owner: Omar Patum
Estimated Sales: $300,000-$500,000
Number Employees: 1-4
Sq. footage: 1000
Type of Packaging: Consumer, Private Label, Bulk
Brands:
    Americandy
    Asher
    Jim Candy
    Rooster Run

478 AmeriGift
P.O.Box 5767
Oxnard, CA 93031-5767   805-988-0350
    Fax: 805-988-4668   800-421-9039
    dneff@ameri-gift.com   www.ameri-gift.com
Candy gift items
    Owner: Lionel Meff
Estimated Sales: $2.5-5 Million
Number Employees: 50-99
Brands:
    AMERIGIFT SWEET TOOTH ORIGINALS
    GHIRARDELLI

479 AmeriPure Processing Company
803 Willow St
Franklin, LA 70538-6030   337-413-8000
    Fax: 337-413-8003   800-328-6729
    staff@ameripure.com   www.ameripure.com
Processor of raw in-shell and shucked, vibrio-free oysters
    CEO: John Tesvich
Estimated Sales: $2.5 Million
Number Employees: 50-99
Type of Packaging: Consumer, Food Service, Private Label
Brands:
    Ameripure

480 AmeriQual Foods
18200 Highway 41 N
Evansville, IN 47725-9300   812-867-1444
    Fax: 812-867-0278   info@ameriqual.com
                         www.ameriqual.com
Supplier of pre-made food items and manufacturer of heat-sealed microwavable bowls, trays and flexible pouches
    Controller: Sandy Rasche
    CEO: Dan Hermman
    Consultant: Mike Billig
Estimated Sales: $50-100 Million
Number Employees: 100-249

481 America's Best BeverageCompany
1720 Whitestone Expy
Whitestone, NY 11357-3000   800-736-7338
                                 Fax: 718-746-6282
Premium ready-to-drink flavored iced coffees and chocolate drinks
    President: Zwi Preminger

482 (HQ)America's Catch
P.O.Box 584
Itta Bena, MS 38941-0584   662-254-7200
    Fax: 662-254-9776   800-242-0041
    solons@catfish.com   www.catfish.com
Processor of fresh and frozen farm-raised catfish
    President: Solon Scott
    VP Sales: John Nelms
    Plant Manager: Bill Martin
Estimated Sales: $20-50 Million
Number Employees: 250-499
Type of Packaging: Consumer, Food Service, Private Label, Bulk
Brands:
    AMERICA'S CATCH

483 America's Classic Foods
1298 Warren Rd
Cambria, CA 93428-4642   805-927-0745
    Fax: 805-927-2280   mgr@amcf.com
                         www.amcf.com
Manufacturer and exporter of powdered ice cream mix, ice cream freezers, processor and exporter of mixes including ice cream, baking, doughnut, etc. Custom design services available
    President: Monty Rice
Estimated Sales: $1 Million
Sq. footage: 30000
Type of Packaging: Food Service, Private Label, Bulk
Brands:
    AMERICA'S CLASSIC FOODS
    AMERICAN CREAMERY
    EMPOWER
    MOMMY'S CHOICE
    SMOOTH & CREAMY

484 American Almond Products Company
103 Walworth St
Brooklyn, NY 11205-2898   718-875-8310
    Fax: 718-935-1505   800-825-6663
    info@americanalmond.com
                         www.americanalmond.com
Processed nuts, natural nut butters & pastes, specialty pastes, marzipan, lekvar, poppy butter, piping gelee, crunch toppings and coconut macaroon mix.
    President: Victor Frumolt
    Customer Service: Priscilla Morales
Estimated Sales: $5-10 Million
Number Employees: 20-49
Sq. footage: 40000
Type of Packaging: Consumer, Food Service, Private Label, Bulk
Brands:
    AMERICA ALMOND
    AMERICAN ALMOND

485 (HQ)American Beverage Marketers
810 Progress Blvd
New Albany, IN 47150-2257   812-944-3585
    Fax: 812-949-7344   www.finestcall.com
Processor and exporter of nonalcoholic cocktail mixes including margarita, pina colada, strawberry daiquiri, bloody mary, etc.
    President: George Wagner
    Purchasing Agent: Mike Shafer
Estimated Sales: $ 20 - 50 Million
Number Employees: 50-99
Type of Packaging: Consumer, Food Service, Private Label
Other Locations:
    American Beverage Marketers
    Overland Park KS
Brands:
    FINEST CALL
    MASTER OF MIXES

486 American Beverage Marketers
6900 College Blvd # 440
Shawnee Mission, KS 66211-1596   913-451-8311
                                      Fax: 913-451-8655
    finestcallinfo@abmcocktails.com
                         www.abmcocktails.com
Manufacturer of cocktail mixes including margarita, Bloody Mary and whiskey sour
    Manager: Joe Armanees
    Sr. VP: Joe Armaneef
Estimated Sales: $3-5 Million
Number Employees: 1-4

Type of Packaging: Food Service
Brands:
    Finest Call
    Master of Mix

487 American Biosciences
560 Bradley Pkwy # 4
Blauvelt, NY 10913   845-727-0800
    info@americanbiosciences.com
                         www.americanbiosciences.com
Herbs and supplements.
    President: David Wales
Estimated Sales: $ 5 - 10 Million
Number Employees: 5-9
Type of Packaging: Consumer

488 American Blanching Company
155 Rip Wiley Road
Fitzgerald, GA 31750-8932   229-423-4098
                                 Fax: 229-423-3842
    sales@americanblanching.com
Blanched peanuts
    President: Allen A Conger
    CEO: Allen A Conger
    Marketing Director: David J Conger

489 American Botanicals
P.O.Box 158
Eolia, MO 63344-0158   573-485-2400
    Fax: 573-485-3801   800-684-6070
    info@americanbotanicals.com
                         www.americanbotanicals.com
Manufacturer and exporter of whole, cut, powder, kosher, organic, and wild crafted American herbs.
    President: Allen Lockard
    Quality Control: Denise Kunzweiler
    Shipping Supervisor: Chris Zumwalt
    Production Manager: Ron Kunzweiler
    Purchasing Agent: Bob Mayfield
    Purchasing Agent: Walter Link
Estimated Sales: $10 Million
Number Employees: 10-19
Number of Products: 200
Sq. footage: 35000
Type of Packaging: Bulk

490 American Bottling & Beverage
1756 Industrial Road
Walterboro, SC 29488-9368   843-538-7709
                                 Fax: 801-975-7185
Sport beverages

491 American Brittle
1034 Hancock St
Sandusky, OH 44870-3616   419-626-8080
    Fax: 419-626-8330   800-274-8853
Candy
    Specialty Sales: John Cayten
Estimated Sales: $ 10 - 20 Million
Number Employees: 20-49

492 American Canadian Fisheries
6069 Hannegan Rd
Bellingham, WA 98226-7433   360-398-1117
    Fax: 360-398-8801   800-344-7942
Fresh salmon, red snapper, true cod, halibut, a variety of frozen seafood, shellfish and salmon and gift boxes made
    President: Andy Vitaljic
Estimated Sales: $500,000-$1 Million
Number Employees: 1-4
Brands:
    Hannegan Seafoods

493 (HQ)American Candy Company
Highway 41
Selma, AL 36701   334-875-1496
                       Fax: 334-418-1150
    customerservice@american-candy.com
                         www.american-candy.com
Hard candy, lollipops, jellies, gummies, wax
    President/CEO: Gaylon Warrington
Estimated Sales: $100+ Million
Number Employees: 250-499
Type of Packaging: Private Label
Brands:
    American
    Bradley
    Disney
    Warner Brothers

494 American Casein Company
109 Elbow Ln
Burlington, NJ 08016-4123   609-387-2988
Fax: 609-387-7204   sales@109elbow.com
www.americancustomdrying.com
Manufacturer of powdered protein ingredients for the food, beverage, and nutraceutical industries. Product line includes sodium caseinate, calcium caseinate, micellar casein, acid casein, hydrolyzed whey protein concentrate, milkprotein concentrate, milk protein isolate,Complete Milk Protein, ingredients for emulsification and stabilization, binders, extenders and acid-stable protein. Outsource blending services for powder ingredients, private label ingredients, andcertified kosher ingredients
President: Michael Geiger
General Sales Manager: Clifford Lang Jr
Estimated Sales: $ 50 - 100 Million
Number Employees: 50-99
Sq. footage: 40000
Type of Packaging: Bulk

495 American Chalkis International Foods Company
20120 Paseo Del Prada
Suite A
Walnut, CA 91789   909-595-5358
Fax: 909-992-3334   info@chalkistomato.us
www.chalkistomato.us
Supplier of tomato products & tomato paste, apricot puree, pomegranate, apple & grape concentrates.

496 American Cheesemen
PO Box 261
Clear Lake, IA 50428-0261   641-357-7176
Fax: 641-357-7177
Cheese
President: Paul Austin
Estimated Sales: $5-10 Million
Number Employees: 1-4
Brands:
American Cheesemen
Choppin N Block
E-Z Keep

497 American Chemical Service
P.O.Box 190
Griffith, IN 46319-0190   219-924-4370
Fax: 219-924-5298 www.acs-chem.com
Bromainated vegetable oil
President: James Tarpo
Estimated Sales: $10-20 Million
Number Employees: 20-49

498 American Classic Ice Cream Company
1565 5th Industrial Ct # D
Bay Shore, NY 11706-3434   631-666-1000
Fax: 631-666-1319
Manufacturer of ice cream and novelties including sandwiches, cups, pies, etc.; also, toppings
Owner: Edgar Williams
General Manager: Theresa Bellizzi
Estimated Sales: $10-20 Million
Number Employees: 50-99
Type of Packaging: Consumer, Food Service

499 American Coffee Company
P.O.Box 52018
New Orleans, LA 70152-2018   504-581-7234
Fax: 504-581-7518 800-554-7234
info@frenchmarketcoffee.com
www.frenchmarketcoffee.com
Manufacturer and packer of coffee
President: Fraser Bartlett
Estimated Sales: $2.5-5 Million
Number Employees: 20-49
Type of Packaging: Consumer
Brands:
FRENCH MARKET

500 American Copak Corporation
9175 Eton Ave
Chatsworth, CA 91311-5806   818-576-1000
Fax: 818-882-1637   info@americancopak.com
www.americancopak.com
Manufacturer of bakers' and confectioners' supplies, beverages, candy, cereals, snack foods, condiments, dairy products, spreads, kosher foods, mixes, pasta, sauces, soups, sugar, syrups, etc.
President: Steven Brooker
Business Development: Wanda Walk

Estimated Sales: $ 5 - 10 Million
Number Employees: 50-99
Sq. footage: 100000

501 (HQ)American Crystal Sugar Company
101 N Third Street
Moorhead, MN 56560   218-236-4400
Fax: 218-236-4422 www.crystalsugar.com
Largest producer of beet sugar
President/CEO: David Berg
VP Finance/CFO: Thomas Astrup
COO: Joseph Talley
Estimated Sales: $1.2 Billion
Number Employees: 1369
Type of Packaging: Consumer, Private Label, Bulk
Other Locations:
Crookston MN
Drayton ND
East Grand Forks MN
Hillsboro ND
Moorhead MN
Brands:
ALBERTSON
Crystal

502 American Culinary Gardens
3508 E Division Street
Springfield, MO 65802-2499   417-831-9797
Fax: 417-831-9933 888-831-2433
www.acgardens.com
Processor and exporter of balsamic vinegar and soy sauce and also dessert glazes and burgundy soy marinade
Sales Director: Gary Anderson
Order Desk: Lisa Clifford
Estimated Sales: $2.5-5 Million
Number Employees: 1-4
Type of Packaging: Consumer, Food Service
Brands:
American Culinary Gardens
Teatro

503 (HQ)American Dehydrated Food, Inc.
P.O.Box 4087
Springfield, MO 65808-4087   417-881-7755
Fax: 417-881-4963 800-456-3447
info@adf.com   www.adfinc.com
Dehydrated foods.
VP Engineering/Process Design: Mike Gerke
Plant Manager: Mike Scabarozi
Estimated Sales: $ 20 - 50 Million
Number Employees: 20-49

504 American Egg Products
P.O.Box 408
Blackshear, GA 31516-0408   912-449-5700
Fax: 912-449-2438
Egg products
President: James D Hull
CEO: Ken Looper
Estimated Sales: $5-10 Million
Number Employees: 50-99

505 American Fine Food Corporation
3600 NW 114th Ave
Doral, FL 33178-1842   305-392-5000
Fax: 305-392-5400 affco@affcointl.com
Processor and exporter of fine foods
President: Sam Amoudi
Marketing/Export Manager: Fadi Ladki
Estimated Sales: $5-10 Million
Number Employees: 5-9

506 American Flatbread
46 Lareau Rd
Waitsfield, VT 05673   802-496-8856
Fax: 802-496-8886
flatbread@americanflatbread.com
www.americaflatbread.com
Flatbreads
President: George Schenk
VP: Camilla Behn
Marketing Director: Jennifer Moffroid
Manager: Paul Krcmar
Purchasing: Amy Troiano
Estimated Sales: $13.9 Million
Number Employees: 100

507 American Food & Equipment
7059 SW 115th Place
Miami, FL 33173-1874   305-361-6517
Fax: 305-595-1167 linares_susan@hotmail.com

Manufacturer of coolers, freezers, ice machines, tomato paste, asparagus, ice cream mixes, wheat gluten, veggie burgers, frozen fruit, coffee, etc.; importer of tomato paste, asparagus, etc.; exporter of ice cream mix and powderedwhole and fat-free milk
President: Susana Linares
Number Employees: 1-4
Type of Packaging: Consumer, Private Label, Bulk

508 American Food Distributors
374 E 167th St
Harvey, IL 60426-6102   708-331-1982
Fax: 708-331-1876
www.americanfooddistributors.com
President: Gerry Michalak
Estimated Sales: $100+ Million
Number Employees: 20-49

509 American Food Ingredients
4021 Avenida De La Plata
Suite 501
Oceanside, CA 92056-5849   760-967-6287
Fax: 760-967-1952 amerfood@aol.com
www.americanfoodingredients.com
Dehydrated fruits and vegetables, mushrooms, truffles, non GMO ingredients, salt and salt mixtures, seasonings, spices and herbs
Owner: Karen Koppenhaver
CEO: Karen Koppenhaver
Estimated Sales: $5-10 Million
Number Employees: 5-9
Brands:
American Food

510 American Food Products
983 Riverside Dr
Methuen, MA 01844-6703   978-682-1855
Fax: 978-687-0476
Repackage candy for other companies.
President: Tom Reilly
Estimated Sales: $ 50 - 100 Million
Number Employees: 50-99
Type of Packaging: Private Label, Bulk

511 American Food Traders
10525 SW 112th Avenue
Apt 313
Miami, FL 33176-8230   305-670-6250
Fax: 305-670-6468
customerservice@americanfoodtraders.com
www.americanfoodtraders.com
Wholesaler/distributor, importer and exporter of corned beef, peanut butter, juices, foam, plastic and paper disposable goods and sodas
President: Freddy Olcese
Number Employees: 1-4
Type of Packaging: Consumer, Food Service, Private Label, Bulk

512 American Foods Group
500 S Washington St
Green Bay, WI 54301-4219   920-437-6330
Fax: 920-436-6510 www.americanfoodsgroup.com
Manufacturer of hams; both boneless and bone-in, bacon for food service and retail applications. Rosen's Diversified has merged with the company but will operate as American Foods Group
President/CEO: Carl Kuehne
Co-Chairman/Co-CEO: Thomas Rosen
CFO: Doug Hagen
Estimated Sales: $500 Million to $1 Billion
Number Employees: 1,000-4,999
Type of Packaging: Food Service, Private Label

513 (HQ)American Foods Group
500s Washington St
Green Bay, WI 54301-4219   920-437-6330
Fax: 920-436-6510 rpreska@american-foods.com
www.americanfoodsgroup.com
Manufacturer and exporter of beef products. Rosen's Diversified has merged with American Foods and will operate as American Foods Group
COO: Carl Kuehne
CEO: Carl W Kuehne
Estimated Sales: $500 Million-$1 Billion
Number Employees: 4000
Type of Packaging: Consumer, Food Service
Other Locations:
Mitchell SD
Sharonville OH
Brands:
AMERICAN FOODS
AMERICAN FOODS SPECIALTIES
BLACK ANGUS RESERVE

DAKOTA SUPREME
GREEN BAY DRESSED BEEF

514 American Foodservice
4721 Simonton Rd
Dallas, TX 75244-5399   972-385-5800
Fax: 972-385-5809 www.americanfoodservice.com
Manufacturer and importer of fresh produce, frozen
and grocery products, fresh meats and cheeses
    President: Lucian LaBarba
    CEO: Lucian M Labarba
    VP Sales: Carl LaBarba
    Operations: Derek Palmieri
Estimated Sales: $100+ Million
Number Employees: 100-249
Type of Packaging: Food Service
Brands:
    Homestyle
    Regal

515 (HQ)American Fruit Processors
10725 Sutter Ave
Pacoima, CA 91331-2553   818-899-9574
    Fax: 818-899-6042 sales@americanfruit.com
                www.americanfruits-flavors.com
Manufacturer and exporter of fruit juice and custom
blended concentrates and natural fruit sweeteners
    President: Fred Farago
    VP Marketing: Richard Linn
    Purchasing Manager: Jack Haddad
Estimated Sales: $50-100 Million
Number Employees: 50-99
Sq. footage: 40000
Parent Co: American Fruit & Flavors
Type of Packaging: Bulk
Other Locations:
    American Fruit Processors
        Los Angeles CA
Brands:
    Juicy Moo
    Moose Juice
    Phytoceuticals
    Pound-4-Pound Powdered

516 (HQ)American Fruits and Flavors
1547 North Knowles Ave
Los Angeles, CA 90063   818-899-9574
    Fax: 818-899-6042 800-527-6709
                sales@americanfruit.com
        www.americanfruits-flavors.com
Processor of natural and artificial flavoring ingredi-
ents, bases and emulsions; also, spray dried flavors
    President: Fred Farago
    Senior VP: Charles Wallasch
Estimated Sales: $13700000
Number Employees: 100
Sq. footage: 20000

517 American Health
2100 Smithtown Ave
Ronkonkoma, NY 11779-7347   631-244-2021
    Fax: 631-244-1777 800-445-7137
                infi@americanhealthus.com
            www.americanhealthus.com
American Health is the largest American-owned
prime manufacturer of quality vitamins, minerals,
food supplements, health and beauty aids.
    President/CEO: Dorie Greenblatt
    Vice President: Robert Silverman
Estimated Sales: $ 3 - 5 Million
Number Employees: 5-9
Type of Packaging: Consumer

518 American Health & Nutrition
3990 Varsity Dr
Ann Arbor, MI 48108-2226   734-677-5572
    Fax: 734-677-5572 info@organicharvest.com
            www.organicharvest.com
Organic Ingredient Supplier-grains, sweetners, oils,
soy powders
    President: Dennis Singsank
    VP: David Singsank
    Purchasing: Dennis Singsank
Estimated Sales: $10 Million
Number Employees: 20-49
Number of Brands: 3
Number of Products: 100
Sq. footage: 25000
Type of Packaging: Bulk
Other Locations:
    American Health & Nutrition
    Eaton Rapids MI
Brands:
    ORGANIC GARDEN

ORGANIC HARVEST
SOY-N-ERGY SOY POWDERS

519 American Health & Nutrition
3990 Varsity Dr
Ann Arbor, MI 48108-2226   734-677-5572
    Fax: 734-677-5572 sales@organictrading.com
            www.organicharvest.com
Organic soy snacks and cereals
    President: Dennis Singsank
    Account Manager: Kevin Lockwood
    CFO: Martha Carlton
    International Trade Representative: Catherine
    Peckham
    Public Relations: Cindy Maynard
Estimated Sales: $ 10 Million
Number Employees: 20-49
Brands:
    Organic Garden

520 American Importing Company
550 Kasota Ave SE
Minneapolis, MN 55414-2811   612-331-9226
    Fax: 612-331-1122 customers@amportfoods.com
                www.amportfoods.com
Manufacturer and an importer/exporter of dates, full
line of extruded dried fruit based bits
    President: Andrew Stillman
    CEO: Ralph Stillman
    VP Marketing: Jeff Vogel
Estimated Sales: $20-50 Million
Number Employees: 20-49
Number of Brands: 2
Number of Products: 50
Sq. footage: 65000
Type of Packaging: Consumer, Private Label, Bulk
Brands:
    AMPORT FOODS
    DESSERT JEWELL
    SALAD EXPRESSIONS

521 American Instants
P.O.Box 817
Flanders, NJ 07836-0817   973-584-8811
    Fax: 973-584-0444 sales@americaninstants.com
                www.americaninstants.com
A private label packer of instant coffee and tea. Also
a full line manufacturer of cappuccino, granita, chai,
fresh brew tea, hot chocolate, drink mixes and liquid
coffee extract.
    President: Marty Wagner
    CEO: Christopher Roche
    CEO: Chris Roche
    Research and Development: Henry Spanier
    Quality Control: Mary Short
Estimated Sales: $15 Million
Number Employees: 50-99
Sq. footage: 72000
Type of Packaging: Food Service, Private Label
Brands:
    CAPPUCCINO SUPREME
    DEEP RICH
    HOT CHOCOLATE SUPREME

522 American Italian Pasta Company
2000 American Italian Way
Columbia, SC 29209-5084   803-695-7300
    Fax: 803-695-7400 tmcbride@aipc.com
                www.aipc.com
Pasta
    Marketing Director: Robin Venn
    Plant Manager: Mike Willhoite
Estimated Sales: $20-50 Million
Number Employees: 100-249
Parent Co: American Italian Pasta Company

523 (HQ)American Italian Pasta Company
4100 N Mulberry Dr # 20
Kansas City, MO 64116-1787   816-584-5000
    Fax: 816-584-5100 consumeraffairs@aipc.com
                www.aipc.com
Manufacturer, importer and exporter of dry pasta
    President/CEO: Jim Fogarty
    VP Finance: Jeffrey Johnson
    CEO: John P Kelly
    VP Quality/Research & Development: Jayne
    Hoover
    VP Marketing: Drew Lericos
    VP Information Systems: Chrystal Johnson
    EVP/Operations & Supply Chain: Wayne George
Estimated Sales: $20-50 Million
Number Employees: 1,000-4,999
Sq. footage: 300000

Type of Packaging: Consumer, Food Service, Pri-
vate Label, Bulk
Other Locations:
    Exeisior Springs MO
    Columbia SC
    Kenosha WI
Brands:
    AMERICAN ITALIAN
    ANTHONY'S
    CALABRIA
    GLOBE A-1
    LUXURY
    MONTALCINO
    MRS. GRASS
    MUELLER'S
    PASTA AMERICAN ITALIAN
    PASTA LABELLA
    PENNYSYLVANIA DUTCH NOODLES
    R&F
    RONCO

524 American Key Food Products
1 Reuten Dr
Closter, NJ 07624-2115   201-767-8022
        Fax: 201-767-9124 800-767-0237
    www.akfponline.com www.akfponline.com
American Key Food products supplies bulk quantity
starches, spices and ingredients to a variety of food
industries such as baking, snacks, soup, spices,
meats and dairy. We have an extensive product list
which can be seen on ourwebsite
www.AmericanKeyFood.com along with product
specification sheets and Kosher Certificates.
    Manager: Luis Mansueto Jr
    VP: Ivan Sarda
    Sales: Mel Festejo
    Operations: Edwin Pacia
    Purchasing: Connie Ponce de Leon
Number Employees: 20-49
Type of Packaging: Bulk
Brands:
    EMSLAND
    KING LION

525 American Laboratories, Inc.
4410 S 102nd St
Omaha, NE 68127-1094   402-339-2494
            Fax: 402-339-0801
    sales@americanlaboratories.com
        www.americanlaboratories.com
American Laboratories Inc has more than 35 years
of expertise in manufacturing pancreatin and pepsin
enzymes as well as more than 200 biologically derived products, and are now a leading supplier of
fungal and plant enzymes for thefoid, human nutritional, pharmaceutical, veterinary, and disgnostic industries. a combination of versatile facilities,
continuous expansion, and strict adherence to
FDA/USDA regulations ensures quality products
and service.
    President/CEO: Jeff Jackson
    VP Sales: Rod Schake
    Chief Operating Officer: Kenny Soejoto
    Purchasing Manager: Tom Hall
Number Employees: 50-99
Number of Products: 960
Type of Packaging: Bulk

526 American Lecithin Company
115 Hurley Rd # 2b
Oxford, CT 06478-1047   203-262-7100
        Fax: 203-262-7101 800-364-4416
    customerservice@americanlecithin.com
        www.americanlecithin.com
Manufacturer and exporter of lecithin products and
specialty phospholipids; importer of lecithin
    President: Randall Zigmont
    CEO: Matthias Rebmann
Estimated Sales: $ .5 - 1 million
Number Employees: 5-9
Sq. footage: 7000
Type of Packaging: Consumer, Bulk
Brands:
    ALCOLEC

527 (HQ)American Licorice Company
2796 NW Clearwater Dr
Bend, OR 97701-7008   541-617-0800
        Fax: 541-617-0224 800-220-2399
                www.americanlicorice.com
Licorice candy
    CEO: John Kretchman
    CEO: John Kretchmer
    VP Sales: Michael MacDonald

Type of Packaging: Consumer
Brands:
Red Vines
Snaps
Sour Punch
Super Ropes

528 American Licorice Company
1900 Whirlpool Dr
La Porte, IN 46350-2708   219-362-5790
Fax: 219-979-2055   800-220-2399
info@redvines.com   www.americanlicorice.com
Manufacturer of licorice and licorice candy products
CEO: John Kretchmer
National Sales Manager: Michael MacDonald
Corporate Procurement Director: Ed Gerdow
Estimated Sales: $100 Million
Number Employees: 250-499
Type of Packaging: Consumer, Food Service, Private Label, Bulk
Brands:
AMERICAN
BLACK LICORICE VINES
LICORICE ROPES
RED ROPES
RED VINES
SNAPS
SOUR PUNCH
SUGAR FREE VINES
SUPER ROPES
TWISTY PUNCH

529 American Licorice Company
P.O.Box 826
Union City, CA 94587-0826   510-487-5500
Fax: 510-487-2517   800-220-2399
info@americanlicorice.com
www.americanlicorice.com
Manufacturer and exporter of licorice confections
President: James L Kretchmer
Estimated Sales: $50-100 Million
Number Employees: 250-499
Type of Packaging: Consumer, Private Label, Bulk
Brands:
RED VINES
SNAPS
SOUR PUNCH
SUPER ROPES
TWISTY

530 American Marketplace Foods
359 McLean Boulevard
Paterson, NJ 07513-1039   201-278-9060
Fax: 201-684-0174   800-683-3464
www.biscottithins.com
President: Jack Galione
Executive VP: Thomas Morgan
VP, Retail Sales: Elisabeth Hill
Sales Director: Chuck Flemballa
Operations Manager: Robert Bauet
Estimated Sales: $2.5-5 Million
Number Employees: 10-19
Brands:
Biscotti Thins
Cool Cakes
Our Daily Muffin

531 American Mercantile Corporation
PO Box 548
Groveland, FL 34736-0548   901-454-1900
Fax: 901-454-0207   dsa@memphi.net
www.americanmercantile.net
Manufacturer of citrus juice including orange, grapefruit, tangerine, etc
President/Marketing Director: Damon Arney
VP Operations: Tom Resler
Estimated Sales: $1-2.5 Million
Number Employees: 20-49
Type of Packaging: Consumer, Food Service, Bulk

532 American Mercantile Corporation
1310 Farmville Rd
Memphis, TN 38122-1001   901-454-1900
Fax: 901-454-0207   amc@memphi.net
www.americanmercantile.net
Spices, seeds, herbs, botanicals, extracts, essential oils and related natural products
President: Damond Arney
Marketing Director: Damond Arney

533 American Micronutrients
PO Box 7129
Kansas City, MO 64113-0129   816-254-6000
Fax: 816-254-6004   impdavison@worldnet.att.net

Manufacturer of chelated calcium
President: Mike Davison
Brands:
American Micronutrients

534 American Mint
727 Avenue of the Americas
New York, NY 10010-2731   212-929-1410
Fax: 212-929-1235   800-401-6468
www.theamericanmint.com
Processor of natural mints
Owner: Sam Hamirani
Estimated Sales: Less than $500,000
Number Employees: 1-4
Type of Packaging: Private Label, Bulk

535 American Natural & Organic Spices
30508 Union City Blvd
Union City, CA 94587   510-477-4787
Fax: 510-477-0807   iofo@spicely.com
www.spicely.com
organic spices
CEO: Bijan Chansari
Estimated Sales: $1.2 Million
Number Employees: 9

536 American Nut & Chocolate Company
121 Newmarket Sq
Boston, MA 02118-2603   617-268-0075
Fax: 617-268-0076   800-797-6887
Manufacturer of dried fruits, trail mixes, candy and nuts including salted, unsalted and chopped. Gift baskets available
Manager: Robert Novack
Estimated Sales: $1-2.5 Million
Number Employees: 1-4
Sq. footage: 16000
Type of Packaging: Food Service, Bulk
Brands:
HARVARD

537 American Pop Corn Company
P.O.Box 178
Sioux City, IA 51102-0178   712-239-1232
Fax: 712-239-1268   email@jollytime.com
www.jollytime.com
Manufacturer of popcorn
Founder: Cloid Smith
President: Garrett Smith
VP Marketing: Tom Elsen
VP Sales: Steve Huisenga
Facilities Manager: Damon Lohry
Purchasing Manager: Brett Hegarty
Estimated Sales: $ 20 - 50 Million
Number Employees: 100-249
Type of Packaging: Consumer, Bulk
Brands:
JOLLY TIME

538 American Purpac Technologies, LLC
2924 Wyetta Dr
Beloit, WI 53511-3964   608-362-5012
Fax: 608-362-5028   877-787-7221
www.purpac.com
American Purpac Technologies (APT) is a leading aseptic/hot fill contract manufacturer providing bulk blending, ingredient processing an dfilling for the food and beverage industries. Through the use of the latest in aseptic processing(HTST) and packaging technologies we process perishable high acid liquid ingredients into ready to use concentrates for the food and beverage industries.
Manager: Tony Rebello
CEO: D Scott Eckman
CFO: John Saladino
VP: Dan Lang
Quality Control: Dave Flora
Sales: Kevin Farrell
Plant Manager: David Devine
Purchasing: Luke Seibert
Number Employees: 50-99
Sq. footage: 65000
Type of Packaging: Consumer, Food Service, Private Label, Bulk

539 American Raisin Packers
P.O.Box 30
Selma, CA 93662-0030   559-896-4760
Fax: 559-896-8942   americanraisin@sbcglobal.net

Packers of raisins
Owner: John Paboojian
Estimated Sales: $20-50 Million
Number Employees: 20-49
Type of Packaging: Consumer, Bulk
Brands:
American Raisin Packers

540 American Saucery
10750 Capital St
Oak Park, MI 48237-3134   248-544-9485
Fax: 248-544-4384   800-328-8632
americansaucery@midasfoods.com
www.americansaucery.com
Processor of dry mix foods and bases including gravies, sauces, cheese sauce, soup bases, batter products
Owner: Richard Elias
Number Employees: 5-9
Sq. footage: 45000
Parent Co: MiDAS Foods International
Type of Packaging: Food Service, Bulk
Brands:
American Saucery

541 (HQ)American Seafoods Group
2025 1st Ave # 900
Seattle, WA 98121-2154   206-448-0300
Fax: 206-448-0505   800-275-2019
info@americanseafoods.com
www.americanseafoods.com
Manufacturer and exporter of frozen seafood
President: Inge Andreassen
President: John Cummings
CFO: Brad Bodenman
Estimated Sales: $10-20 Million
Number Employees: 50-99
Type of Packaging: Bulk
Other Locations:
Seattle WA
Dutch Harbor AK
New Bedford MA
Greensboro AL

542 American Seafoods International
P.O.Box 2087
New Bedford, MA 02741-2087   508-997-0031
Fax: 508-991-6432   800-343-8046
john.cummings@americanprideseafoods.com
www.americanprideseafoods.com
Manufacturer of the Frionor brand; prepared seafood products. Battered, breaded, precooked, coated, glazed, marinated groundfish portions, and natural fillets
President: John Cummings
VP Finance/Administration: Bob Myatt
VP Retail Sales: Robert Hatcher
Estimated Sales: $ 20 - 50 Million
Number Employees: 100-249
Number of Brands: 5
Number of Products: 500+
Sq. footage: 240000
Parent Co: American Seafoods Group
Type of Packaging: Consumer, Food Service, Private Label, Bulk
Brands:
FRIONOR USA
SOUTHERN PRIDE CATFISH LLC

543 American Skin LLC
140 Industrial Dr
Burgaw, NC 28425   910-259-2232
Fax: 910-259-2535   800-248-7463
americanskinllc@bellsouth.net
www.pork-rinds.com
Processor of pork rings and pork rinds
Manager: Wes Blake
Estimated Sales: $300,000-500,000
Number Employees: 1-4

544 American Soy Products
1474 Woodland Dr
Saline, MI 48176-1282   734-429-2310
Fax: 734-429-2112   infoasp@ameicansoy.com
www.americansoy.com
Aseptic packer of juices, teas and soy products
President: Ron Roller
Estimated Sales: $2.5-5 Million
Number Employees: 20-49
Sq. footage: 65000
Type of Packaging: Consumer, Private Label

545 American Specialty Confections
888 County Road D W
Suite 100
Saint Paul, MN 55112-8502   651-251-7000
        Fax: 651-251-7070   800-776-2085
Candy
    President: Jeff Haynes
    Marketing Director: Chris Dusk
    Sales Manager: Mike Gardener
Number Employees: 100

546 American Spoon Foods
1668 Clarion Avenue
PO Box 566
Petoskey, MI 49770-0566   231-347-9030
    Fax: 800-647-2512   800-222-5886
    information@spoon.com   www.spoon.com
Processor of preserves, dried fruit, vinaigrettes,
sauces, salsas and condiments.
    President: Justin Rashid
    Sales Manager: Dorothy Felton
    Public Relations: Noah Marshall-Rashid
    General Manager: John Kafer
Estimated Sales: $10-20 Million
Number Employees: 50-99
Type of Packaging: Consumer, Food Service
Other Locations:
    American Spoon Foods
    Petosky MI
    American Spoon Foods
    Charlevoix MI
    American Spoon Foods
    Traverse City MI
    American Spoon Foods
    Harbor Springs MI
    American Spoon Foods
    Saugatuck MI
    American Spoon Foods
    Northville MI
    American Spoon Foods
    Ann Arbor MI
Brands:
    American Chef Larry Forgione's
    American Fruit Butters
    American Fruit Toppings
    American Salad Dazzlers
    American Spoon Foods
    American Spoon Fruits
    Salad Dazzlers
    Spoon Fruit
    Spoon Toppers

**547 American Supplement
Technologies**
3312 E Broadway Rd
Phoenix, AZ 85040-2830   480-921-8277
    Fax: 480-921-9588   888-469-0242
    info@americansupplement.com
    www.americansupplement.com
Manufacturer of nutritional supplements in capsule
and tablet form. Contract manufacturing and private
labeling available
    President: Bradley Grossman
Estimated Sales: $ 50 - 100 Million
Number Employees: 50-99
Type of Packaging: Private Label, Bulk

548 American Tartaric Products
1865 Palmer Ave # 207
Larchmont, NY 10538-3037   914-834-1881
    Fax: 914-834-4611   atp@americantartaric.com
    www.americantartaric.com
Processor of tartaric acid, cream of tartar and baking
powder
    President: Luca Zanin
Estimated Sales: $5-10 Million
Number Employees: 5-9
Other Locations:
    American Tartaric Products
    Windsor CA

549 American Ultraviolet Company
212 S Mount Zion Rd
Lebanon, IN 46052-9479   765-483-9514
    Fax: 765-483-9525   800-288-9288
    mstines@auvco.com
    www.americanultraviolet.com

Founded in 1960, American Ultraviolet Company is
a manufacturer of UV curing and UV disinfection
systems that includes indoor air quality, water purification, liquid sugar/syrup storage and germicidal
sterilization.
    CEO: Meredith Stines
    Germicidal HVAC/International: Jeffrey Stines
    UV Curing/International: Rafael Hernandez
    UV Curing & Germicidal HVAC: Sam Guzman
    Germicidal HVAC: Donna Wieder

550 American Vintage Wine Biscuits
4003 27th St
Long Island City, NY 11101-3814   718-361-1003
    Fax: 718-361-0204   info@americanvintage.com
        www.americanvintage.com
Manufacturer of cracker/snack made with wine and
pepper
    President: Mary-Lynn Mondich
Estimated Sales: Less than $500,000
Number Employees: 1-4
Type of Packaging: Consumer

551 American Whey
545 State Route 17
Suite 2003
Ridgewood, NJ 07450-2035   201-493-2662
        Fax: 201-493-2666
Manufacturer and exporter of milk, cream
    President: Paul Podell
    Operations Manager: Kathy Oviedo
Number Employees: 28
Type of Packaging: Bulk
Brands:
    Amtek

552 American Wholesale Grocery
131 New Jersey Street
Mobile, AL 36603-2111   251-433-2500
        Fax: 251-432-7982
    President: Harold Owens
    Secretary/Treasurer: James Statter
    Vice President: John Carpenter

553 American Yeast/Lallemand
319 Commerce Way # 2
Pembroke, NH 03275-3718   603-228-8454
    Fax: 603-228-6745   866-920-9885
    asbe@asbe.org   www.lallemand.com
Baking enzymes, baking ingredients, dough condi-
tioners, such as bromate replacers, chocolate, cocoa,
eggs, fruit, nuts, oils, oxidizers, raisisns, spices,
sweetners, yeast foods
    Manager: Bud Spooner
    First Vice Chairwoman: Theresa S Cogswell
    VP: Christine Merenova
    Second Vice-Chairman: Eddie Perrou
Estimated Sales: $5-10 Million
Number Employees: 20-49
Brands:
    Essential
    Fermaid

554 Americana Foods
3333 Dan Morton Drive
Dallas, TX 75236-1099   972-709-7100
    Fax: 972-709-6625   gfoy@americanafoods.com
        www.americanafoods.com
Manufacturer of soft serve frozen yogurt
    Senior VP: Bill Armstrong
    VP Custom Sales: Gary Foy
Estimated Sales: $100+ Million
Number Employees: 100-249
Sq. footage: 220000
Parent Co: TCBY
Type of Packaging: Consumer

555 Americana Marketing
850 Tourmaline Dr
Newbury Park, CA 91320-1205   805-499-0451
    Fax: 805-499-4668   800-742-7520
    ami@follmerdevelopment.com
        www.follmerdevelopment.com
Manufacturer of aerosol nonstick cooking, baking
and flavor sprays
    President/CEO: Garrett Follmer
    Sales/Marketing VP: David McKenzie
Number Employees: 50-99
Type of Packaging: Consumer, Food Service, Pri-
vate Label
Brands:
    NATURAL LITE
    PURE & SIMPLE

556 Americana Vineyards
4367 E Covert Rd
Interlaken, NY 14847-9720   607-387-6801
    Fax: 607-387-3852   wineinny@aol.com
        www.americanavineyards.com
Wines
    President: Joseph Gober
Estimated Sales: $840,000
Number Employees: 10-19
Brands:
    Americana

557 Amerifit Nutrition
166 Highland Park Drive
Bloomfield, CT 06002-5306   860-242-3476
        Fax: 860-243-9400   800-722-3476
        www.Amerifit.com
Health foods
    Chairman/President: Cyrill Siewert
    Sr. VP Marketing: David D Belaga
Estimated Sales: $ 10-100 Million
Number Employees: 99
Parent Co: Amerifit/Strength Systems
Brands:
    Estroven
    Vitazll

558 Amerilab Technologies
2765 Niagara Ln N
Plymouth, MN 55447-4844   763-525-1262
        Fax: 763-525-1285   800-445-6468
    sales@amerilabtech.com   www.amerilabtech.com
Amerilab Technologies is a private label and contract manufacturer who specializes in the development and production of effervescent tablets. We
manufacture products for a large number of industries including both domestic andinternational markets. Amerilab Technologies, Inc. is a leader in the
development, manufacturing and packing of
effervescent tablets and powders.
    President: Fred Wehling
    CFO: Wes Peterson
    Research & Development: Mary Aldritt
    Quality Control: Terry Wehling
    Operations Manager: Dawn Poellinger
Estimated Sales: 8,000,000
Number Employees: 20-49
Type of Packaging: Private Label

559 (HQ)Amerilift Brands, Inc.
55 Sebethe Dr
Cromwell, CT 06416-1016   860-242-3476
    Fax: 860-243-9400   800-722-3476
    martyherman@amerifit.com   www.amerifit.com
Processor and exporter of vitamins, supplements and
health food
    CEO: Cyrill Siewert
    CFO: Victor Emerson Jr.
    CEO: Cyrill Siewert
    Executive VP Sales/Marketing: Doug Meyer
    VP Operations: Ernesto Martinez
Estimated Sales: $1.5 Million
Number Employees: 50-99
Sq. footage: 50000
Other Locations:
    Amerifit/Strength Systems USA
    Bloomfield CT
Brands:
    AZO
    CULTURELLE
    DHEA
    ESTROVEN
    FLEX ABLE
    SOOTHERBS
    VITABALL

560 Ameripec
6916 Aragon Cir
Buena Park, CA 90620-1118   714-690-9191
    Fax: 714-562-0849   sltwang@yahoo.com
        www.ameripecinc.com
Contract packing of PET bottles and glass bottles of
juices, juice drink, flavored drink and water at acidi-
fied pH
    President: Ping Wu
    Quality Assurance: Sam Wang
Estimated Sales: $20-50 Million
Number Employees: 1-4
Sq. footage: 130000
Type of Packaging: Private Label

561 Ameripure Processing Company
PO Box 308
Kenner, LA 70063-0308
504-467-0474
Fax: 504-467-0450
President: John Tesvich

562 Amerivacs
3800 Main St # 9
Chula Vista, CA 91911-6245
619-498-8227
Fax: 619-498-8227
info@amerivacs.com
www.amerivacs.com
President: Peter Tadlock
Estimated Sales: $800,000
Number Employees: 1-4
Brands:
Amerivacs

563 Amerol Corporation
71 Carolyn Blvd
Farmingdale, NY 11735-1527
631-694-4700
Fax: 631-694-9177
cmonteleone@amerolcorp.com
www.amerolcorp.com
Manufacturer and custom blender of synthetic and natural antioxidants such as BHA, BHT, TBHQ, propyl gallate and mixed tocopherols
President: C J Monteleone
CEO: D Sartorio
CFO: A Diaz
R&D: Y Liang
Marketing: S Jean Charles
Operations: F Monteleone
Production: D Ghiglieri
Purchasing Director: D Raleigh
Estimated Sales: $10 Million
Number Employees: 1-4
Sq. footage: 23000
Type of Packaging: Private Label, Bulk

564 (HQ)Amerol Corporation
71 Carolyn Blvd
Farmingdale, NY 11735-1527
631-694-4700
Fax: 631-694-9177
info@amerolcorp.com
www.amerolcorp.com
Manufacturer and exporter of antioxidants and antioxidant blends including potassium sorbate and sorbic acid
CFO: Tony Diaz
EVP: Charles Monteleone
Director New Product Development: Ora Roitberg
Estimated Sales: $300,000-500,000
Number Employees: 1-4
Sq. footage: 18000
Type of Packaging: Private Label
Brands:
Amerol

565 (HQ)Ames Company
PO Box 46
New Ringgold, PA 17960-0046
570-386-2131
Fax: 413-604-0541
info@amescompany.com
www.amescompany.com
Contract manufacturer, exporter and importer of vegetarian meat analogs and dry mixes; broker of soy concentrates, phosphates, flavors, hydrolyzed protein, autolyzed and torula yeast; consultant specializing in product development fordry and frozen foods
Owner: Joseph Ames, Sr.
Number Employees: 5-9

566 Ames International
4401 Industry Dr E # A
Fife, WA 98424-1832
253-946-4779
Fax: 253-926-4127 888-469-2637
info@amesinternational.com
www.emilyschocolates.com
Processor and exporter of nut products, and gourmet chocolates and cookies
President: George Paulose
VP: Susan Paulose
Marketing: Amy Paulose
Plant Manager: Matthew Kurian
Purchasing: Paul Van Key
Estimated Sales: $5-10 Million
Number Employees: 50-99
Sq. footage: 55000
Type of Packaging: Private Label, Bulk
Brands:
Amy's
EcoSnax
Emily's
Orchard Hills

Santa Cruz
Seven Seas

567 Amfit Spices
7380 W Sand Lake Rd # 500
Orlando, FL 32819-5257
407-352-5290
Fax: 407-351-1901
Spices
Estimated Sales: Less than $500,000
Number Employees: 1-4

568 Amick Farms, LLC
P.O.Box 2309
Leesville, SC 29070-0309
803-532-1400
Fax: 803-532-1492 800-926-4257
www.amickfarms.com
Manufacturer and exporter of poultry
President/CEO: Ben Harrison
CFO: Marcus Miller
VP: Fred West
VP Sales/Marketing: Steve Kernen
VP Operations: Fred West
Estimated Sales: $200 Million
Number Employees: 1,000-4,999
Type of Packaging: Consumer, Food Service, Private Label, Bulk
Brands:
AMICK FARMS

569 Amigos Canning Company
600 Carswell St
San Antonio, TX 78226-1888
210-798-1516
Fax: 210-798-5365 800-580-3477
osaenz@amigoscanning.com
www.amigosfoods.com
Manufactures Mexican snack food, salsa, canned refried beans, and taco shells.
Manager: Clint Mc New
Controller: Ivan Kerr
Sales Manager: Tom Murrin
COO: Gene Welka
Plant Manager: Carlos Menchaca
Estimated Sales: $16 Million
Number Employees: 20-49
Sq. footage: 39000
Parent Co: Durrset Amigos
Type of Packaging: Consumer, Private Label
Brands:
Amigos
Firehouse

570 Amity Packing Company
210 N Green St
Chicago, IL 60607-1702
312-942-0270
Fax: 312-942-0413 800-837-0270
info@amitypacking.com
www.amitypacking.com
Manufacturer of fresh and frozen pork and beef products.
President: Richard T Samuel
Vice President: Matt Buol
VP Sales/Marketing: Tom Laplant
Operations Manager: Jim Stamm
Estimated Sales: $20-50 Million
Number Employees: 100-249

571 Amity Vineyards
18150 SE Amity Vineyards Rd
Amity, OR 97101-9603
503-835-2362
Fax: 503-835-6451 888-264-8966
amity@amityvineyards.com
www.amityvineyards.com
Wines
President: Myron Redford
CFO: Jean Mead
Sales/Manager: Matt Gibson
Plant Manager: Neil Svarverud
Estimated Sales: $5-10 Million
Number Employees: 10-19
Sq. footage: 15

572 Amizetta Vineyards
1099 Greenfield Rd
St Helena, CA 94574-9625
707-963-1460
Fax: 707-963-1460 cab@amizetta.com
www.amizetta.com
Wines
President: Spencer Clark
Operations/Winemaker: Robert Egelhoff
Estimated Sales: $1-2.5 Million
Number Employees: 1-4

573 (HQ)Amoretti-Capriccio
451 Lombard St
Oxnard, CA 93030-5143
805-983-2903
Fax: 805-718-0204 800-266-7388
info@amoretti.com
www.amoretti.com
Manufacturer and exporter of nut flour, paste and butter; also, marzipan, ganache, fruit extracts and dessert sauces
Owner: Jack Barsoumian
CEO: Jack Barsoumian
Marketing President: Maral Barsoumian
Manufacturing President: Ara Barsoumian
Estimated Sales: $20+ Million
Number Employees: 1-4
Type of Packaging: Food Service, Bulk
Brands:
Amoretti
Baristella
Capriccio

574 Amoroso's Baking Company
845 S 55th St
Philadelphia, PA 19143-3142
215-471-4740
Fax: 215-472-5299 800-377-6557
info@amorosobaking.com
www.amorosobaking.com
Manufacturer of rolls, breads, bagels, jewish bread and pretzels
VP: Leonard Amoroso
Sales Director: Len Constantino
Estimated Sales: $50-100 Million
Number Employees: 250-499
Type of Packaging: Consumer, Food Service, Private Label
Brands:
AMOROSO

575 Amour Chocolates
2416 San Mateo Pl NE
Albuquerque, NM 87110-4057
505-881-2803
Fax: 505-884-8189
amourchocolates@comcast.net
www.amourchocolates.com
Chocolates
President: Lori Swanson

576 Ampac Packaging, LLC
12025 Tricon Road
Cincinnati, OH 45246
513-671-1777
Fax: 513-671-2920 800-543-7030
www.ampaconline.com
Manufacturer of flexible packaging and bags
Brands:
AB SEALERS
ALL PACKAGING MACHINERY
CHANTLAND
FISCHBEIN BAG CLOSING
FUJY
HIGHLIGHT STRETCH RAPPERS
LIFT PRODUCTS
NEW LONDON ENG
VACULET USA

577 Ampacco
211 Schilling Cir
Hunt Valley, MD 21031-1102
410-527-6283
Fax: 410-527-6337 800-632-5847
www.mccormick.com
Spices, extracts, seasonings, dry seasoning mixes
President: Robert Davey
Executive VP: Barry H Beracha
Vice President: Bob Lawless
Managing Director: James Brady
Brands:
McCormick

578 Ampak Seafood Corporation
315 Whitney Ave
New Haven, CT 06511-3715
203-786-5121
Fax: 203-786-5120
Seafood
President: Michael Gourlay
Estimated Sales: $2.5-5 Million
Number Employees: 1-4
Type of Packaging: Private Label

579 Amport Foods
560 Kasota Avenue SE
Minneapolis, MN 55414-2811
612-331-7000
Fax: 612-331-1122 800-989-5665
jamport@msn.com www.amportfoods.com

Dates, dried fruits whole and pressed
President: Andrew Stillman
Vice President: Jeff Vogel
Production Manager: Mike McIvor
Estimated Sales: $ 20 - 50 Million
Number Employees: 20-49
Type of Packaging: Bulk

580 Amrion
6565 Odell Place
Boulder, CO 80301-3306 303-530-4554
Fax: 303-530-2592 800-627-7775
Manufacturer of nutritional supplements including capsules, powders and softgels
CEO: Mark Crossen
Sales Manager: Tom Weaver
Estimated Sales: $68 Million
Number Employees: 250-499
Sq. footage: 400000
Parent Co: WholeFoods Market
Type of Packaging: Consumer

581 Amros the Second, Inc.
69 Veronica Ave # 69
Somerset, NJ 08873-3467 732-846-7755
Fax: 732-846-4956
Processor of Russian-style chocolate and marshmallow candy; importer of European food products including packaged grains, beans and kasha
Owner: Leom Mogilezer
Estimated Sales: $20-50 Million
Number Employees: 20-49
Type of Packaging: Consumer, Food Service
Brands:
Amros

582 Amsnack
7770 Longe Street
Stockton, CA 95206-3925 209-982-5545
Fax: 209-982-4955
Rice crackers, cookies crackers and chips
President: Satoshi Yamada
Shipping Coordinator: Karen Valterza
Estimated Sales: $5-9.9 Million
Number Employees: 20-49

583 Amstell Holding
209 Theodore Rice Boulevard
New Bedford, MA 02745-1213 508-995-6100
Fax: 508-995-2912
Provides state-of-the-art, Grade A Dairy, FDA- and LACF -approved processing of shelf-stable nonrefrigerated milk, nutritional supplements, juices, teas, and drink beverages. Provides Tetra Brik packs with pull tab or strawapplication
Director Operations: Cindy Aldrich

584 Amster-Kirtz Company
2830 Cleveland Ave NW
Canton, OH 44709-3204 330-535-6021
Fax: 330-437-2015 800-257-9338
www.amsterkirtzco.net
Candy and confectionery
President: Joe Bauer
Estimated Sales: $50-100 Million
Number Employees: 50-99

585 Amsterdam Brewing Company
21 Bathurst Street
Toronto, ON M5V 2N6
Canada
416-504-1040
Fax: 416-504-1043 info@amsterdambeer.com
www.amsterdambeer.com
Manufacturer of beer, lager and ale including stout
President: Jeff Carefoote
Number Employees: 12
Type of Packaging: Consumer, Food Service

586 Amurol Confections Company
2800 State Route 47
Yorkville, IL 60560-9441 630-553-4800
Fax: 630-553-4801 www.confections.com
Bubble gum, suckers and candy
Executive Director: Lupe Alvarez
CEO: A G Atwater Jr
VP Marketing: Bruce Thompson
VP Sales: Steve Howard
Estimated Sales: $50-100 Million
Number Employees: 10-19
Brands:
BIG LEAGUE CHEW
BLASTERS
BUBBLE BEEPER
BUBBLE CANE

BUBBLE JUG
BUBBLE TAPE
BUBBLE TAPE HOLIDAY STRIPE
BUBBLE TAPE MEGA ROLL
BUG CITY
BUNGEE
CANDY MOUSE
CARAMEL APPLE BUBBLE GUM
CLUCKERS
EVEREST
FRESH SQUEEZED
NEON BEACH
OUCH!
REED'S
RUGRATS BUBBLE GUM BABIES
RUGRATS COMIC BOOK
RUGRATS COOKIE JAR
RUGRATS TOY BAG
SANTA DISPENSER
SANTA'S COAL
SQUEEZE POP
SQUEEZE POP LAVA LICK
SQUEEZE POP SPORTS BOTTLE
SUGARFREE BUBBLE TAPE
TAPE SPARKLERS
TAPE TWISTERS
THUMB SUCKERS
ZING ZANG

587 Amwell Valley Vineyard
80 Old York Rd
Ringoes, NJ 08551-1309 908-788-5852
Fax: 908-788-1030
jefferyfisher@amwellvalleyvineyard.com
www.amwellvalleyvineyard.com
Wines
Owner: Jeff Fischer
VP: Jeffrey Fisher
Operations Manager: Scott Gares
Estimated Sales: $1-2.5 Million
Number Employees: 1-4
Number of Brands: 1
Number of Products: 20
Type of Packaging: Consumer
Brands:
Amwell Valley Vineyard

588 Amy's Kitchen
P.O.Box 449
Petaluma, CA 94953-0449 707-578-5908
Fax: 707-578-7995 amy@amyskitchen.net
www.amyskitchen.com
Manufacturer and exporter of frozen organic meals and entrees; also, canned soups and bottled pasta sauces.
Co-Owner: Rachel Berliner
Co-Owner: Andy Berliner
Estimated Sales: $250 Million
Number Employees: 20-49
Number of Brands: 1
Number of Products: 146
Sq. footage: 105000
Type of Packaging: Consumer, Food Service
Brands:
AMYS KITCHEN

589 AnaCon Foods Company
P.O.Box 651
Atchison, KS 66002-0651 913-367-2885
Fax: 913-367-1794 800-328-0291
anacon@journey.com www.wheatnuts.com
Processor and exporter of simulated nut and fruit particulates and analogs
Executive Director: Tom Miller
VP Sales/Marketing: Jane Hallas
Director Operations: Marvin Mikkelson
Estimated Sales: $2.5-5 Million
Number Employees: 20-49
Brands:
Bits'N'Pops
Bowlby's Bits
Mix-Ups
Nuts'N'Pops
Wheat Nuts

590 Anabol Naturals
1550 Mansfield St
Santa Cruz, CA 95062-1720 831-479-1403
Fax: 831-479-1406 800-426-2265
service@anabol.com www.anabol.com

Manufacturer and exporter of sports nutrition supplements including free-form amino acids, GH releasers, muscle octane, muscle mass and fat burner kits and life extension nutrients
President: Roger Prince
Estimated Sales: $500,000-$1 Million
Number Employees: 5-9
Sq. footage: 5000
Brands:
Anabol Naturals

591 Anastasia Confections, Inc.
1815 Cypress Lake Dr
Orlando, FL 32837-8457 407-816-9944
Fax: 407-816-9901 800-329-7100
sales@anastasiaconfections.com
www.anastasiaconfections.com
Specialty Candy
President: Mike Constantine
Purchasing Director: Mike Constantine
Estimated Sales: $2 Million
Number Employees: 20-49

592 Anchor Appetizer Group
PO Box 2518
Appleton, WI 54912-2518 920-997-2659
Fax: 920-997-7600 www.anchorfoods.com
Appetizers
Parent Co: McCain Foods USA/H.J. Heinz Company
Type of Packaging: Consumer, Food Service
Brands:
BREW CITY
CHEESE SENASATIONS
GOLDEN CRISP
GOLDEN CRISP
MOORE'S
MOZZALUNA
MOZZAMIA
OLIVENOS
POPPERS
PRIMASAMO CUBES
PROVAGO WHEELS
QUESO TRIANGULOS
WRAPPETIZERS

593 Anchor Brewing Company
1705 Mariposa St
San Francisco, CA 94107-2334 415-863-8350
Fax: 415-552-7094 info@anchorbrewing.com
www.anchorbrewing.com
Processor and exporter of beer and ale, products of which include Anchor Steam; Liberty Ale; Anchor Porter; Summer Beer; Old Foghorn; Anchor Small, and Christmas Ale.
President/Brewmaster: Fritz Maytag
Office Manager: Linda Rowe
Head Brewer: Mike Lee
Bottling Superintendent: Chris Solomon
Assistant Brewer: Mark Carpenter
General Manager: Gordon MacDermott
Estimated Sales: $20-50 Million
Number Employees: 50-99
Type of Packaging: Consumer, Private Label

594 (HQ)Anchor Food Products/ McCain Foods
555 N Hickory Farm Lane
Appleton, WI 54914-3037 920-734-0627
mberg@anchorfoods.com
www.mccainusa.com
Processor and exporter of frozen breaded appetizers including cauliflower, mushrooms, okra, squash, zucchini, cheese, onion rings and stuffed jalapenos.
Chairman: Allison McCain
President/CEO: Dale Morrison
VP/CFO: Thomas Tranetzki
COO: Greg Brook
Purchasing Director: Janet Evans
Chairman: Mack Follett
VP Procurement: Brian Follett
Plant Manager: Steven Hesseling
Estimated Sales: $10-100 Million
Number Employees: 250-499
Parent Co: McCain Foods
Type of Packaging: Food Service, Private Label, Bulk
Other Locations:
Anchor Food Products
Pecos TX
Brands:
All Kitchens
Anchor
Comsource

Nugget
Pocahontas
Poppers
Sysco
WRAPPETIZERS

595 Anchor Frozen Foods
32 Urban Ave
Westbury, NY 11590-4822   516-333-6344
    Fax: 516-997-1823   800-566-3474
    info@anchorfrozenfoods.com
    www.anchorfrozenfoods.com
Manufacturer of seafood including stuffed sole,
conch, shrimp, lobster tails, octopus, calamari and
king crab legs.
    President: Roy Tuccillo
    Controller: Adrienne Pacifico
    Director: Milan Politzer
Estimated Sales: $ 5 - 10 Million
Number Employees: 10-19
Type of Packaging: Consumer, Food Service, Bulk

596 Anco Foods
P.O.Box 2010
Caldwell, NJ 07007-2010   973-808-7148
    Fax: 973-575-5010   800-526-2596
    www.ancofinecheese.com
Cheese
    President: Alain Boss
Estimated Sales: $2.5-5 Million
Number Employees: 5-9
Type of Packaging: Bulk

597 Ancora Coffee Roasters
3701 Orin Rd
Madison, WI 53704-3642   608-255-2900
    Fax: 608-255-2901   800-260-0217
    service@ancoracoffee.com
    www.ancoracoffee.com
Specialty coffees, espresso coffee, whole bean and
ground, loose leaf teas including black, green, oo-
long, herbal and decaffinated
    President/CEO: George Krug
    Quality Control/Production: Rob Jeffries
    Marketing: Christy Gibbs
Estimated Sales: $1-5 Million
Number Employees: 10-19
Sq. footage: 15000
Type of Packaging: Consumer, Food Service, Bulk
Brands:
    ANCORA COFFEE
    ANCORA D'ORO
    ANCORA ESPRESSO

598 Andalan Confections
PO Box 2149
Fort Oglethorpe, GA 30742-0149   706-858-4640
    Fax: 706-858-4642   877-263-2526
    www.andalan.com
    President: Anita Loizeaux
Brands:
    EDO

599 Andalusia Distributing Company
Allen Avenue
Andalusia, AL 36420   334-222-3671
    Fax: 334-222-6575
    President: Michael Jones
    Vice President: Richard Jones
Estimated Sales: $ 50 - 100 Million
Number Employees: 50-99

600 Andersen's Pea Soup
376 Avenue of the Flags
Buellton, CA 93427   805-688-5581
    Fax: 805-686-5670   info@peasoupandersens.net
    www.peasoupandersens.net
Gourmet canned split pea soup
    Manager: Tony Picard
    Purchasing Director: Brinda Wolf
Estimated Sales: $2.5-5 Million
Number Employees: 50-99

601 Anderson Bakery Company
2060 Old Philadelphia Pike
Lancaster, PA 17602-3497   717-299-2321
    Fax: 717-393-3511   800-732-0089
    www.andersonpretzel.com

Processor and exporter of pretzels including salted
and no-salt, gems, logs, twists, peanut butter filled,
bread sticks and snack mixes
    Manager: Joe Baciotti
    Executive VP: Norman Randall
    Research & Development: Michael Bockman
    Quality Control: Michael Bockman
    Sales Director: Dan Walker
    Purchasing Manager: Ed Fischer
Estimated Sales: $20-50 Million
Number Employees: 250-499
Sq. footage: 175000
Type of Packaging: Consumer, Food Service, Pri-
vate Label, Bulk
Brands:
    ANDERSON
    NATIONAL

602 Anderson Custom Processing
105 1/2 N Minnesota St
New Ulm, MN 56073   507-233-2800
    Fax: 507-233-2806   877-588-4950
    acpi@newulmtel.net
    www.andersonprocessing.com
Custom manufacturer of spray-dried food products
including whey, starches, cheese and cream powders
    President: Brian Anderson
    Production Manager: Jerome Braun
Estimated Sales: $ 3 - 5 Million
Number Employees: 1-4
Type of Packaging: Bulk
Other Locations:
    Sleepy Eye MN
    Little Falls WI
    Belleville WI

603 Anderson Dairy
801 Searles Ave
Las Vegas, NV 89101-1131   702-642-7507
    Fax: 702-642-3480   andersondairy@earthlink.net
    www.andersondairy.com
Milk, dairy products
    President: Harold Bellanger
    President: Harold Bellanger
    Marketing Manager: Kim Webscer
    VP, Sales: Dave Coon
Estimated Sales: $20-50 Million
Number Employees: 100-249
Brands:
    Anderson Dairy

604 (HQ)Anderson Erickson Dairy
2420 E University Ave
Des Moines, IA 50317-6501   515-265-2521
    Fax: 515-263-6301   aedairy@aedairy.com
    www.aedairy.com
Processing and bottling dairy products
    CEO: Jim Erickson
    CEO: Miriam Erickson Brown
Estimated Sales: $100+ Million
Number Employees: 250-499
Type of Packaging: Food Service

605 Anderson Peanuts
P.O.Box 810
Opp, AL 36467-0810   334-493-4591
    Fax: 334-493-7767   andpeanut@alaweb.com
    www.alaweb.com
Manufacturer of peanuts
    Division Manager: Dennis Finch
Estimated Sales: $1-2.5 Million
Number Employees: 5-9
Type of Packaging: Bulk

606 Anderson Seafoods
P.O.Box 17636
Anaheim, CA 92817-7636   714-777-7100
    Fax: 714-777-7116   www.andersonseafoods.com
Manufacturer and wholesaler/distributor of fresh and
frozen seafood; serving the food service market and
supermarkets
    President: Dennis Anderson
    Secretary/Treasurer: Leean Anderson
    Vice President: Todd Anderson
Estimated Sales: $20-50 Million
Number Employees: 20-49
Sq. footage: 20000

607 Anderson Valley Brewing
P.O.Box 505
Boonville, CA 95415-0505   707-895-2337
    Fax: 707-895-2353   avbc@pacific.net
    www.avbc.com

Processor of seasonal beer, ale, porter, stout, lager
and pilsner
    President/CEO: Kenneth Allen
    Plant Manager: Graydon Brown
Estimated Sales: $5-10 Million
Number Employees: 50-99
Sq. footage: 20000
Type of Packaging: Consumer
Brands:
    Barney Flats Oatmeal Stout
    Beik's Esb
    Boont Amber
    High Rollers Wheat
    Hop Ottin' Ipa
    Poleeko Gold
    Winter Solstice

608 Anderson's Conn Valley Vineyards
680 Rossi Rd
St Helena, CA 94574-9646   707-963-8600
    Fax: 707-963-7818   800-946-3497
    cvvinfo@connvalleyvineyards.com
    www.connvalleyvineyards.com
Wines
    President: Todd Anderson
    Operations: Mac Sawyer
Estimated Sales: $2.5-5 Million
Number Employees: 5-9

609 (HQ)Andes Candy
7401 S Cicero Ave
Chicago, IL 60629-5885   773-838-3400
    Fax: 773-838-3435   www.tootsie.com
Manufacturer and exporter of chocolate mints
    Chairman/CEO: Melvin Gordon
    President/COO/Director: Ellen Gordon
Estimated Sales: $420 Million
Number Employees: 1,000-4,999
Type of Packaging: Consumer, Food Service, Bulk
Brands:
    ANDES

610 Andre French Bakery Retail
12901 McGregor Blvd
Fort Myers, FL 33919-4587   239-482-2011
    Fax: 941-482-1178
Bakery products
Estimated Sales: $300,000-500,000
Number Employees: 5-9

611 Andre Prost
680 Middlesex Tpke
Old Saybrook, CT 06475-1343   860-388-0838
    Fax: 860-388-0830   800-243-0897
    prostinc@andreprost.com   www.andreprost.com
Candy, confectionery, seasonings and spices.
    Owner: Frank Landrey
Estimated Sales: $10-20 Million
Number Employees: 10-19
Brands:
    A TASTE OF CHINA
    A TASTE OF INDIA
    A TASTE OF THAI
    GINGER SNAPS
    HONEES
    NOTTA PASTA
    ODENSE
    ZOTZ

612 Andre's Confiserie Suisse
5018 Main St
Kansas City, MO 64112-2755   816-561-3440
    Fax: 816-561-2922   800-892-1234
    customer service@andreschocolates.com
    www.andreschocolates.com
Processor of Swiss style chocolate candies
    President: Macel Bollier
    CEO: Rene Bollier
    CFO: Connie Bollier
Estimated Sales: $2.5-5 Million
Number Employees: 50-99
Type of Packaging: Consumer
Other Locations:
    Andre's Confiserie Suisse
    Overland Park KS
    Andre's Confiserie Suisse
    Denver CO

613 Andre-Boudin Bakeries
221 Main St # 1230
San Francisco, CA 94105-1929   415-882-1849
    Fax: 415-913-1818   boudin@boudinbakery.com
    www.boudinbakery.com

Manufacturer of sourdough bread, specialty breads, and sweet goods
Owner: Sharon Duvall
VP Sales/Marketing: Terry Wight
Plant Manager: Rick Rodrick
Estimated Sales: $300,000-500,000
Number Employees: 1,000-4,999
Type of Packaging: Private Label, Bulk
Other Locations:
Boudin Cafe
San Francisco CA
Boudin Cafe
San Mateo CA
Boudin Cafe
Santa Clara CA
Boudin Cafe
Palo Alto CA
Boudin Cafe
Corte Madera CA
Boudin Cafe
Walnut Creek CA
Boudin Cafe
Costa Mesa CA
Boudin Cafe
San Diego CA
Boudin Cafe
Escondido CA
Brands:
Boudin

614 Andresen Ryan Coffee Com
2206 Winter St
Superior, WI 54880-1437   715-395-3793
Fax: 715-392-4776 ruby@superior-wi.com
www.arcocoffee.com
Processor of coffee and coffee syrups
Owner: John Andresen
President: B Fleming
Director Manufacturing: Vern Suby
Estimated Sales: Less than $500,000
Number Employees: 1-4
Type of Packaging: Consumer, Food Service
Brands:
Arco

615 Andrew & Williamson Sales Company
9940 Marconi Dr
San Diego, CA 92154-7270   619-661-6004
Fax: 619-661-6007
accounting@andrew-williamson.com
www.andrew-williamson.com
Frozen strawberries
President: Fred Williamson
Estimated Sales: $2.5-5 Million
Number Employees: 20-49
Brands:
A&W

616 Andrew Peller Limited
697 S Service Road
Grimsby, ON L3M 4E8
Canada   905-643-4131
Fax: 905-643-4944 info@andreswines.com
www.andreswines.com
Leading producer and marketer of quality wines in Canada with wineries in British Columbia, Ontario and Nova Scotia. Products include award winning premium VQA wines, table wines, sparkling wines, Icewine, and premium craft beers.7
President Winexpert Inc./Vineco Intl.: Robert Van Wely
President/CEO: John Peller
Key Account Director: Steve Azzopardi
VP Marketing: Shari Niles
VP Sales: Chris Zarafonitis
Estimated Sales: 211.8 Million
Number Employees: 1,400
Type of Packaging: Consumer, Food Service, Bulk
Brands:
CALONA VINEYARDS
GRANVILLE ISLAND
HILLEBRAND
PELLER ESTATES
RED ROOSTER
SANDHILL
THIRTY BENCH
TRIUS
VINECO
WINEXPERT

617 Andrew's Brewing
353 High St
Lincolnville, ME 04849-5846   207-763-3305

Beer
Owner: Andrew Hazen
Estimated Sales: $500,000-$1 Million
Number Employees: 1-4
Brands:
Brown Ale
English Pale Ale
St. Nicks Poter
Summer Golden Ale

618 Andrews Caramel Apples
5001 W Belmont Ave
Chicago, IL 60641-4236   773-286-2224
Fax: 773-286-2258 800-305-3004
Info@AndysSeasoning.com
www.andysseasoning.com
Processor of caramel apples
President: Daniel De Marco
Treasurer: Sylvia Schuman
Purchasing: Rick Walker
Estimated Sales: $2.5-5 Million
Number Employees: 10-19
Type of Packaging: Consumer
Brands:
Andrews
Ms. Kays

619 Andy's Seasoning
2829 Chouteau Ave
St Louis, MO 63103-3016   314-664-2149
Fax: 314-664-2149 800-305-3004
Info@AndysSeasoning.com
www.andysseasoning.com
Seasoned salt, breadings for fish and chicken
President: Katherine Anderson
Estimated Sales: $20-50 Million
Number Employees: 1-4
Sq. footage: 27000
Type of Packaging: Consumer, Food Service, Private Label, Bulk
Brands:
Andy's Custom Blended Breading
Andy's Hot Spicey Chicken Breading
Andy's Mild Chicken Breading
Andy's Red Fish Breading
Andy's Seasoned Salt
Andy's Yellow Fish Breading

620 Anette's Chocolate Factory
1321 First Street
Napa, CA 94559   707-252-4228
Fax: 707-252-8074 www.anettes.com
Truffles, creams, brittles, chews, chocolate sauces, caramel sauces, traditional and unique seasonal specialties.
President: Anette Madsen
VP: Brent Madsen
Number Employees: 15

621 Angel's Bakeries
29 Norman Avenue
Brooklyn, NY 11222   718-389-1400
Fax: 718-389-3928 joe@angelsbakery.com
www.angelsbakery.com
Cookies, muffin tops, muffins, florentines, cakes and cake slices.
President: Joseph Angel
Marketing Director: Bill McNamee
Production Manager: Eloy Rojas
Estimated Sales: $4.1 Million
Number Employees: 45

622 Angelic Gourmet Inc
8629 State Route 21 S
PO Box 127
Naples, NY 14512   585-374-9783
Fax: 585-374-9753 www.angelicgourmet.com
Chocolate dipped pretzels and chocolate drizzled popcorn.
President: Sher Kemp
Estimated Sales: $1.8 Million
Number Employees: 20

623 Anglo American Trading
P.O.Box 97
Harvey, LA 70059-0097   504-341-5631
Fax: 504-341-5635
Manager: Dennis Skrmetta
CEO: Eric Skrmetta

624 Angy's Food Products, Inc.
77 Servistar Industrial Way
Westfield, MA 01085-5601   413-572-1010
Fax: 413-572-4785 angyfoods@msn.com
www.angysfood.com
Processor of frozen tortellini, gnocchi, cavatelli, stuffed shells, manicotti and ravioli. Also plain, seafood and Japanese and Italian flavored bread crumbs, seafood stuffing mix and golden crumb topping
President: Jack Fu
CFO: Liz Campanini
VP: Steve Campanini
R&D: Susan Tarlsey
VP/Sales: Sal Capaldo
Plant Manager: Steve Campanini
Estimated Sales: $5-10 Million
Number Employees: 20-49
Sq. footage: 23000
Type of Packaging: Consumer, Food Service, Private Label, Bulk
Brands:
Angy's
Big Y
Finast
Introvigne's
Shaw's

625 Anheuser-Busch
15800 Roscoe Blvd
Van Nuys, CA 91406-1350   818-989-5300
Fax: 818-908-5685 www.anheuser-busch.com
Manufacturer of beer including light.
Manager: Gary Lee IV
VP/Chief Legal Officer: Mark Bobak
VP/Chief Financial Officer: W Randolph Baker
Manager/Quality Assurance: Tanya Towns
VP/Communications & Consumer Affairs: Francine Katz
VP/Chief Information Officer: Joseph Castellano
VP/Corporate Human Resources: John Farrell
Plant Manager: Gary Lee
Estimated Sales: $500 Million-$1 Billion
Number Employees: 1,000-4,999
Parent Co: Anheuser-Busch Companies
Type of Packaging: Consumer, Food Service, Bulk

626 Anheuser-Busch
775 Gellhorn Dr
Houston, TX 77029-1496   713-675-2311
Fax: 713-670-1690 www.anheuser-busch.com
Manufacturer, bottler, canner and exporter of beer including light and nonalcoholic.
President/CEO: Augusta Busch IV
VP/Chief Legal Officer: Mark Bobak
VP/Chief Financial Officer: W Randolph Baker
CIO: Steve Edler
VP/Communications & Consumer Affairs: Francine Katz
VP Human Resources: Robert Alvarez
COO/General Manager/Plant Manager: Steve Ghiglieri
Estimated Sales: $500 Million-$1 Billion
Number Employees: 1,000-4,999
Parent Co: Anheuser-Busch Companies
Type of Packaging: Consumer, Food Service, Bulk

627 Anheuser-Busch
2885 Belgium Rd
Baldwinsville, NY 13027-2706   315-635-4000
Fax: 315-635-4404 www.anheuser-busch.com
Manufacturer of bottled regular and light beer.
President/Owner: Rus Adams
VP/Chief Legal Officer: Mark Bobak
VP/Chief Financial Officer: W Randolph Baker
VP/Communications & Consumer Affairs: Francine Katz
Public Relations: Larry Harmon
Plant Manager: Brian McNelis
Estimated Sales: $500 Million-$1 Billion
Number Employees: 1,000-4,999
Parent Co: Anheuser-Busch Companies
Type of Packaging: Consumer

628 Anheuser-Busch
700 Schrock Rd
Columbus, OH 43229-1123   614-888-6644
Fax: 614-847-6497 www.anheuserbusch.com

Manufacturer of bottled and canned beer, ale, malt liquor and lager.
- President: David Peacock
- VP Finance: David Almeida
- VP/Communications & Consumer Affairs: Franice Katz
- VP/Chief Information Officer: Joseph Castellano
- VP/Corporate Human Resources: John Farrell

Estimated Sales: $500 Million-$1 Billion
Number Employees: 500
Parent Co: Anheuser-Busch Companies
Type of Packaging: Consumer

629 Anheuser-Busch
P.O.Box 200248
Cartersville, GA 30120-9029   770-386-2000
      Fax: 770-606-3111 www.anheuser-busch.com
Manufacturer of canned and bottled beer.
- President/CEO: Augusta Busch IV
- VP/Chief Legal Officer: Mark Bobak
- VP/Chief Financial Officer: W Randolph Baker
- VP/Communications & Consumer Affairs: Francine Katz
- VP/Chief Information Officer: Joseph Castellano
- VP/Corporate Human Resources: John Farrell
- Plant Manager: Greg Kellerman

Estimated Sales: $2.5-5 Million
Number Employees: 10-19
Parent Co: Anheuser-Busch Companies
Type of Packaging: Consumer, Food Service, Bulk

630 Anheuser-Busch
P.O.Box Ab
Fairfield, CA 94534   707-429-2000
      Fax: 707-429-7517 www.anheuser-busch.com
Manufacturer of canned and bottled beer.
- Manager: Kevin Finger IV
- VP/Chief Legal Officer: Mark Bobak
- VP/Chief Financial Officer: W Randolph Baker
- VP/Communications & Consumer Affairs: Francine Katz
- VP/Chief Information Officer: Joseph Castellano
- VP/Corporate Human Resources: John Farrell

Estimated Sales: $100-500 Million
Number Employees: 250-499
Parent Co: Anheuser-Busch Companies
Type of Packaging: Bulk

631 Anheuser-Busch
111 Busch Dr
Jacksonville, FL 32218-5595   904-751-0700
      Fax: 904-751-8120 www.buschjobs.com
Manufacturer of canned and bottled beer.
- President/CEO: Augusta Busch IV
- VP/Chief Legal Officer: Mark Bobak
- VP/Chief Financial Officer: W Randolph Baker
- VP/Communications & Consumer Affairs: Francine Katz
- VP/Chief Information Officer: Joseph Castellano
- VP/Corporate Human Resources: John Farrell
- Plant Manager: Syl Robinson

Estimated Sales: $100-500 Million
Number Employees: 500-999
Parent Co: Anheuser-Busch Companies
Type of Packaging: Bulk

632 Anheuser-Busch
200 US Highway 1
Newark, NJ 07114-2200   973-645-7700
      Fax: 973-645-7950 www.anheuser-busch.com
Manufacturer and exporter of canned and bottled beer.
- President/CEO: Augusta Busch IV
- VP/Chief Legal Officer: Mark Bobak
- VP/Chief Financial Officer: W Randolph Baker
- VP/Communications & Consumer Affairs: Francine Katz
- VP/Chief Information Officer: Joseph Castellano
- VP/Corporate Human Resources: John Farrell
- Plant Manager: Bob Rogers

Estimated Sales: $500 Million-$1 Billion
Number Employees: 500-999
Parent Co: Anheuser-Busch Companies
Type of Packaging: Bulk

633 (HQ)Anheuser-Busch Companies
1 Busch Pl
St Louis, MO 63118-1852   314-577-2000
      Fax: 314-577-2900 800-342-5283
            www.abcorpaffairs.com

Processor, bottler, canner and exporter of beer including light and non-alcoholic.
- President: August A Busch Iv
- VP Finance: David Almeida
- VP Information/Business Services: Odilon Queiroz

Estimated Sales: K
Number Employees: 10,000+
Type of Packaging: Consumer
Brands:
- 180
- BACARDI SILVER
- BUD ICE
- BUD ICE LIGHT
- BUD LIGHT
- BUDWEISER
- BUSCH
- BUSCH ICE
- BUSCH LIGHT
- BUSCH NA
- DOC OTIS HARD LEMON MALT BEVERAGE
- HURRICANE MATL LIQUOR
- KILLARNEYRED LAGER
- KING COBRA
- MICHELOB
- MICHELOB AMBER BOCK
- MICHELOB BLACK & TAN
- MICHELOB GOLDEN DRAFT
- MICHELOB GOLDEN DRAFT LIGHT
- MICHELOB HONEY LAGER
- MICHELOB LIGHT
- NATURAL ICE
- NATURAL LIGHT
- O'DOULS
- O'DOULS AMBER
- PACIFIC RIDGE
- RED WOLF
- REDHOOK ALE
- TEQUIZA
- WIDMER BROTHERS
- ZIEGENBOCK

634 (HQ)Anheuser-Busch Inc
1 Busch Pl
St Louis, MO 63118-1852   314-577-2000
      Fax: 314-577-2900 800-342-5283
      douglas.muhleman@anheuser-busch.com
            www.anheuser-busch.com/ABInc.html
Beer, adventure park entertainment and packaging; also interests in aluminum beverage container recycling, malt production, rice milling, real estate, turf farming, creative services, metalized paper label printing and transportation.Processor, importer and exporter of beer, malt liquor, ales, lagers and non-alcoholic brews.
- President: August A Busch Iv IV
- CEO/President International Operations: Stephen Burrows
- VP Finance: David Almeida
- VP/Communications & Community Affairs: Francine Katz
- EVP/Global Industry Development: Robert Lachky
- VP/Chief Legal Officer: Mark Bobak
- VP/Business Operations: David Peacock
- VP/Global Media & Sports Marketing: Anthony Ponturo
- VP/Chief Information Officer: Joseph Castellano
- Vice President Operations & Technology: Douglas Muhleman
- VP/Corporate Human Resources: John Farrell

Estimated Sales: $2.81 Billion
Number Employees: 30,236
Type of Packaging: Consumer, Food Service, Bulk
Other Locations:
- Baldwinsville NY
- Cartersville GA
- Columbus OH
- Fairfield CA
- Fort Collins CO
- Houston TX
- Jacksonville FL
- Los Angeles CA
- Merrimack NH
- St. Louis MO
- Williamsburg VA
- Newark NJ

Brands:
- 180
- Anheuser World Select
- BE
- Bacardi Silver
- Bacardi Silver Limon
- Bacardi Silver Low Carb BlackCherry
- Bacardi Silver O3

- Bacardi Silver Raz
- Bare Knuckle Stout
- Bud Dry
- Bud Ice
- Bud Ice Light
- Bud Light
- Budweiser
- Busch
- Busch Ice
- Busch Light
- Busch NA
- Hurricane Ice
- Hurricane Malt Liquor
- King Cobra
- Michelob
- Michelob Amber Bock
- Michelob Golden Draft
- Michelob Golden Draft Light
- Michelob Hefeweizen
- Michelob Honey Lager
- Michelob Light
- Michelob Ultra
- Natural Ice
- Natural Light
- O'Douls
- O'Douls Amber
- Redhook Ale
- Tequiza
- Tilt
- Widmer Brothers
- ZiegenLight

635 Anita's Mexican Foods Corporation
1390 W 4th St
San Bernardino, CA 92411-2600   909-884-8706
      Fax: 909-383-0936   800-426-4827
            www.anitafoods.com
Manufacturer and exporter of Mexican foods including tortilla chips and taco and tostada shells, plus organic snacks, chips and popcorn.
- President: Jose Gomez
- Plant Manager: Frank Coser

Estimated Sales: $20-50 Million
Number Employees: 100-249
Sq. footage: 30000
Parent Co: La Reina
Type of Packaging: Consumer, Food Service, Private Label, Bulk
Brands:
- ANITA'S
- GO-MEX
- LA REINA
- OLD PUEBLO RANCH

636 Anke Kruse Organics
#9-685 Speedvale Avenue W
Guelph, ON N1K 1E6
Canada   519-824-6161
      Fax: 519-853-5155 info@ankekruseorganics.ca
            www.ankekruseorganics.ca
- President: Anke Kruse

Brands:
- Anke Kruse Organics

637 Ankeny Lakes Wild Rice
9594 Sidney Rd S
Salem, OR 97306-9448   503-363-3241
      Fax: 503-371-9080 800-555-5380
      info@wildriceonline.com
            www.wildriceonline.com
Grower, processor, packer and importer of certified organic wild rice and nonorganic and wild rice blends
- Co-Owner: Larry Payne
- Co-Owner: Sharon Jenkins-Payne
- Sales Director: Larry Payne
- Purchasing Manager: Larry Payne

Estimated Sales: $500,000
Number Employees: 1-4
Sq. footage: 3000
Type of Packaging: Consumer, Food Service, Private Label, Bulk
Brands:
- Canadian Jumbo Lake
- Idaho Lake Wild Rice
- Oregon
- Wild & Ricey

638 Ankle Deep Foods
912 W Omaha Avenue
Norfolk, NE 68701-5842   402-371-2991
      wings@buffalomaid.com
            www.buffalomaid.com

Manufacturer of hot suaces and marinades
Brands:
    Buffalo Maid

639 Anmar Foods
2150 W Carroll Ave
Chicago, IL 60612-1604   312-733-6160
    Fax: 312-421-2829 www.anmarfoods.com
    Owner: Bob Martinelli
Estimated Sales:$ 20 - 50 Million
Number Employees: 20-49

640 Anmar Nutrition
P.O.Box 2343
Bridgeport, CT 06608-0343   203-336-8330
    Fax: 203-336-5508 blancoanmar@snet.net
            www.anmarinternational.com
A distributor and contract manufacturer specializing
in vitamins, nutritional products, excipients,
non-prescription pharmaceutical products, herbs,
and amino acids. We offer expertise in sourcing
granulations, triturations, millingand custom blends
    President: John Blanco
    VP: Hongbing Deng
    Sales Director: Allan Pollard
    Production Manager: John Blanco
Estimated Sales:$ 10 - 20 Million
Number Employees: 10-19
Number of Products: 100+
Sq. footage: 15000
Type of Packaging: Bulk

641 Ann Hemyng Candy
P.O.Box 567
Trumbauersville, PA 18970-0567   215-536-7004
    Fax: 215-536-6848 800-779-7004
    chocolat@fast.net   www.chocolateshop.com
Manufacturer of molded chocolate including
lollypops, novelties in chocolates, custom corporate
logos
    President/Owner: Louise Spindler
Estimated Sales:$ .5 - 1 million
Number Employees: 5-9

642 Ann's House of Nuts, Inc.
8221 Preston Court
Jessup, MD 20794-8613   301-498-4920
                Fax: 301-317-6248
Processor of various nuts, dried fruits, and mixes
    President: Edward Zinke
    VP Sales: Chuck Haynsworth
    Purhcasing Director: Ike Rain
Estimated Sales:$2.5-5 Million
Number Employees: 50-99
Sq. footage: 200000
Type of Packaging: Consumer, Food Service, Pri-
    vate Label

643 Anna's Oatcakes
988 Route 100
Weston, VT 05161-5414
            802-824-3535
    abjordan@vermontel.net
        www.snackvermont.com

Oatcakes

644 Anna's Unlimited, Inc
PO Box 141154
Austin, TX 78714-1154   512-837-2203
    Fax: 512-837-0003 800-849-7054
    jim.u@anasfoods.com   www.anasfoods.com
Ana's Foods is a gourmet food product development
and marketing company. It sells Anna's salsa, a
fresh, refrigerated salsa picante, and Ana's herbs, a
dry blend of eight spices.
    President: Anna Olvera - Ullrich
    COO/VP: Jim Ullrich
    VP: James A Ullrich
    Marketing: James Ullrich Jr
Estimated Sales:$500,000
Number Employees: 1-4
Number of Brands: 3
Number of Products: 8
Type of Packaging: Consumer, Food Service, Bulk
Brands:
    Ana's

645 Annabelle Candy Company
P.O.Box 3665
Hayward, CA 94540-3665   510-783-2900
    Fax: 510-785-7675 info@annabelle-candy.com
            www.annabelle-candy.com

Processor of confectionery products including choc-
olate truffles, candy bars, nougats and taffy
    President/CEO: Susan Gamson Karl
    Director of Finance: Shelley Craft
    CEO: Susan G Karl
    VP Quality Control/Production/Purchasing:
    Carlos Osorio
    Direcotr of Sales/Marketing: David Klabunde
Estimated Sales:$20-50 Million
Number Employees: 50-99
Type of Packaging: Consumer, Bulk
Brands:
    Abba-Zaba
    Big Hunk
    Look!
    Rocky Road
    U-No

646 Annabelle Lee
PO Box 1009
Waldoboro, ME 04572-1009   207-967-4611
                Fax: 207-832-7795
    President: Frank Minio

**647 Annapolis Produce & Restaurant
Supply**
15 Lee St
Annapolis, MD 21401-3980   410-266-5211
                Fax: 410-266-0568
    President: Timothy Campbell
Estimated Sales:$ 50 - 100 Million
Number Employees: 50-99

648 Annapolis Winery
26055 Soda Springs Rd
Annapolis, CA 95412-9728   707-886-5460
                Fax: 707-886-5460
    annapoliswinery@starband.net
        www.annapoliswinery.com
Wines
    President: Basil Scalabrini
Estimated Sales:$2.5-5 Million
Number Employees: 5-9

649 Annette Island Packing Company
P.O.Box 10
Metlakatla, AK 99926-0010   907-886-4661
    Fax: 907-886-4660 info@metlakatlaseafood.com
            www.metlakatlaseafood.com
Salmon and cured seafood
    Manager: Freeman Mc Gilton
Estimated Sales:$50-100 Million
Number Employees: 100-249

650 Annie Chun's
P.O.Box 2418
San Rafael, CA 94912-2418   415-479-8272
    Fax: 415-479-8274 info@anniechun.com
            www.anniechun.com
All natural Pan-Asian soup bowls, noodle bowls,
noodle express, rice express and organic noodles
and sauce kits.
    Owner: Annie Chun
*Estimated Sales:*Less than $500,000
Number Employees: 5-9

651 Annie's Frozen Yogurt
5200 W 74th St
Minneapolis, MN 55439-2223   952-838-2110
    Fax: 952-835-2378 800-969-9648
            www.anniesyogurt.com
Processor of frozen yogurt - many delicious flavors
    President: Lawrence Serf
Estimated Sales:$500,000-$1 Million
Number Employees: 5-9

652 Annie's Homegrown
564 Gateway Dr
Napa, CA 94558-7517   707-254-3700
    Fax: 781-224-9728 800-288-1089
    bernie@annies.com   www.annies.com
Gourmet foods
    President: John Foraker
    CEO: John Foraker
    CFO: Steven Jackson
    VP Research/Development: Bob Kaake
    VP Marketing: Sarah Bird
    Senior VP Sales: Mark Mortimer
Estimated Sales:$2.5-5 Million
Number Employees: 5-9
Type of Packaging: Private Label
Brands:
    Annie's Macaroni & Cheese
    Tamarind Tree

653 Annie's Naturals
792 Foster Hill Rd
East Calais, VT 05650-8070   802-456-8866
    Fax: 802-456-8865 800-434-1234
    info@anniesnaturals.com
        www.anniesnaturals.com
Manufacturer and exporter of natural dressings and
vinigrettes, BBQ sauces, marinades and worcester-
shire sauce
    Owner/Production Development: Annie
    Christopher
    Owner/Sales/Marketing: Peter Backman
Number Employees: 10-19
Type of Packaging: Consumer, Food Service, Pri-
    vate Label
Brands:
    Annie's Naturals
    Annie's Naturals Magic Sauces
    Annie's Naturals Salad Dressings

654 Antelope Valley Winery
42041 20th St W
Lancaster, CA 93534-6912   661-722-0145
    Fax: 661-722-6035 800-282-8332
    wines@avwinery.com   www.avwinery.com
Wines
    Owner: Cyndee Donato
    Winemaker: Cecil McLester
Estimated Sales:$2.5-5 Million
Number Employees: 5-9
Type of Packaging: Private Label
Brands:
    Antelope Valley

655 Anthony & Sons Italian Bakery
1275 Bloomfield Ave
Fairfield, NJ 07004-2708   973-244-9669
    Fax: 973-244-1298 anthonyandsons@aol.com
Bread
    Owner: Anthony Pio Costa
    Plant Manager: Robert Tobia
*Estimated Sales:*Less than $500,000
Number Employees: 5-9

656 Anthony Road Wine Company
1020 Anthony Rd
Penn Yan, NY 14527-9632   315-536-2182
    Fax: 315-536-5851 800-559-2182
            info@anthonyroadwine.com
            www.anthonyroadwine.com
Wines
    President: John Martini
    VP: Ann Martini
    Operations Manager: Peter Martini
    Production Manager: Johannes Reinhardt
Estimated Sales:$2.5-5 Million
Number Employees: 10-19

**657 Anthony-Thomas Candy
Company**
1777 Arlingate Ln
Columbus, OH 43228-4114   614-274-8405
    Fax: 614-274-0019 877-226-3921
            www.anthony-thomas.com
Manufacturer of gourmet-style chocolate in prepack-
aged boxes including truffles, real butter creams,
cordial cherries, creams, peanut butter cups, pecans
and English Toffee
    President: Joseph Zanetos
Estimated Sales:$10-20 Million
Number Employees: 100-249
Sq. footage: 152000
Type of Packaging: Consumer
Brands:
    ANTHONY-THOMAS CHOCOLATES

658 Anti-Aging ASAP
2633 Lincoln Boulevard
Suite 435
Santa Monica, CA 90405-4619   310-306-3489
    Fax: 310-306-3489 888-334-2000
            info@antiagingasap.com
            www.antiagingasap.com
    Owner: Lynn Stuart

659 Anton Caratan & Son
1625 Road 160
Delano, CA 93215-9436   661-725-2575
                Fax: 661-725-5829 www.acaratan.com
Processor and exporter of table grapes
    President: Anton Caratan
    Sales Manager: George Ann Caratan

Estimated Sales: $10-20 Million
Number Employees: 250-499
Type of Packaging: Consumer
Brands:
Good Times
Prosperity

660 Antoni Ravioli
879 N Broadway
North Massapequa, NY 11758-2353   516-799-0350
Fax: 516-799-0357   800-783-0350
www.antoniravioli.com
Manufacturer of stuffed macaroni, ravioli, manicotti, stuffed shells, etc.
President: Gene Saucci
Estimated Sales: $5-10 Million
Number Employees: 10-19
Sq. footage: 8400
Type of Packaging: Food Service, Private Label, Bulk
Brands:
Antoni Ravioli

661 Antonio Mozzarella Factory
71 Springfield Avenue
Springfield, NJ 07081   973-379-3738
Fax: 973-379-0438 www.antoniomozzarella.com
Fresh mozzarella
Presdient: Tom Pugliese
Estimated Sales: $7.1 Million
Number Employees: 25

662 Antonio's Bakery
9616 Atlantic Avenue
Ozone Park, NY 11416-1619   718-322-1314
Fax: 718-322-1475
President: Peter Backman
Estimated Sales: $20-50 Million
Number Employees: 20-49

663 Anzu Technology
3180 Imjin Rd # 149
Marina, CA 93933-5111   831-582-9718
Fax: 831-855-0220 twhite@anzutech.com
www.anzutech.com
Products and services include equipment for food processing, inspection and packaging.
Executive Director: Susa Barich
Vice President: Frank Giglio
Marketing Manager: Brian Ettkin
Sales Manager: Martin Salzmann

664 Apani Southwest
5401 N 1st St
Abilene, TX 79603-6424   325-690-1550
Fax: 325-690-1412 drinkapak@sbcglobal.net
www.apanisw.com
Premium purified drinking water
Owner/President: Jay Pickens
VP: Glenda Pickens
Estimated Sales: $2 Million
Number Employees: 1-4
Type of Packaging: Private Label

665 Apecka
371 Stevens Road
Rockwall, TX 75032-6754   972-772-2654
Fax: 973-772-2655 apecka1@aol.com
Peppered pickles, pickled okra and garlic, green chile sauce
President: Sharon Eisenbraun
Estimated Sales: Less than $500,000
Number Employees: 1-4

666 Apex Marketing Group
7835 S Rainbow Blvd
Las Vegas, NV 89139   805-375-4308
Fax: 805-499-4204   866-610-6165
apexmktg@earthlink.net   www.hairnomore.com
manufacturer of natural products for personal care in the food industry
President/CEO: Mel Landyn
Vice President: Carole Landyn
Marketing Director: Mark Landyn
Operations Manager: Armen Grigorian Jr.
Product Manager: Mel Landyn
Estimated Sales: $5 Million
Number Employees: 25
Number of Brands: 2
Number of Products: 6
Sq. footage: 16000
Parent Co: Health Tec Labs
Type of Packaging: Consumer, Private Label, Bulk

Other Locations:
Apex Marketing Group
Newbury Park CA

667 Aphrodisia Products
62 Kent St
Brooklyn, NY 11222-1517   718-383-3677
Fax: 718-383-6618   877-274-3677
info@aphrodisaproducts.com
www.aphrodisaproducts.com
Manufacturer and exporter of bulk herbs, spices, botanical extracts and essential oils
President: James Adelson
Estimated Sales: $2.5-5 Million
Number Employees: 1-4
Sq. footage: 40000
Type of Packaging: Bulk

668 Apotheca Naturale
313 Lowrey Drive
Woodbine, IA 51579-1505   712-647-3133
Fax: 712-647-2573   800-736-3130
shane@apothecanaturale.com
www.apothecanaturale.com
Manufacturer of homeopathics, botanical extracts, capsules, tablets and sports nutritionals
President: Shane Hinze
Estimated Sales: $10-20 Million
Number Employees: 20-49

669 Appert's Foodservice
900 Highway 10 S
St Cloud, MN 56304-1807   320-251-3200
Fax: 320-259-0747   800-225-3883
info@apperts.com   www.apperts.com
Processor of meat, fish and seafood, canned and dry groceries, chemicals; wholesaler/distributor of fresh and frozen produce and general line items
President: Joe Omann
President: Tim Appert
Owner: Chris Appert
Quality Control: Duane Du Monceaux
Production Manager: Adrian Seguin
Purchasing Director: Wayne Harrison
Estimated Sales: $20-50 Million
Number Employees: 100-249
Sq. footage: 93000
Type of Packaging: Consumer, Food Service, Bulk

670 Appetizers And
2555 N Elston Ave
Chicago, IL 60647-2003   773-227-0400
Fax: 773-227-0448   800-323-5472
emailus@appetizersandinc.com
www.appetizersandinc.com
Manufacturer of frozen hors d'oeuvres
President/CEO/Co-Owner: George King
EVP/Co-Owner: Patricia Domanik
CFO: Scott Forester
SVP Operations/COO: Kristine Holtz
VP Manufacturing: John Trellicoso
Number Employees: 250-499
Type of Packaging: Consumer, Food Service

671 (HQ)Appetizers And, Inc.
2555 N Elston Avenue
Chicago, IL 60647-2040   773-227-0448   800-323-5472
emailus@appetizersandinc.com
www.appetizersandinc.com
Processor of appetizers including crab cakes, burritos, franks-in-a-blanket and egg rolls
President/CEO: George King
VP: Patricia Domanik
VP Production: John Trellicoso
Estimated Sales: $20-50 Million
Number Employees: 100-249

672 Apple & Eve
P.O.Box K
Roslyn, NY 11576-0410   516-621-1122
Fax: 516-621-2164   800-969-8018
info@appleandeve.com   www.appleandeve.com
Manufacturer and exporter 100% pure and natural juices and juice blends; importer of fruit concentrates
Founder/CEO: Gordon Crane
VP Sales/Marketing: Cary Crane
Operations Manager: John Donlon
Estimated Sales: $90+ Million
Number Employees: 1-4
Sq. footage: 6000
Type of Packaging: Consumer

Brands:
Apple & Eve
Made in the Shade
Sesame Street
Tribal

673 Apple Acres
Hitchings Rd & Route 20
La Fayette, NY 13084   315-677-5144
Fax: 315-677-5143
Grower, packer and exporter of apples.
Owner: Walter Blackler
CEO: Walter Blackler
Estimated Sales: $4 Million
Number Employees: 20-49
Sq. footage: 32000
Type of Packaging: Consumer

674 Apple Flavor & FragranceUSA Corp.
55 Carter Drive
Suite 103
Edison, NJ 08820   732-393-0600
Fax: 732-393-1933
Flavor ingredients and enhancers.

675 Apple Ledge
170 South Road
Holden, ME 04429-7535   207-989-5576
appleledge@aol.com
Powdered leavening agent
Brands:
Bakewell Cream

676 Apple Valley Market
9067 Us Highway 31 # A
Berrien Springs, MI 49103-1806   269-471-3234
Fax: 269-471-6035   800-237-7436
avnf@avnf.com   www.avnf.com
Vitamins and vegetarian groceries
Manager: George Schmidt
CEO: Frank Williams
Marketing Director: Frank Williams
Estimated Sales: $ 5 - 10 Million
Number Employees: 100-249
Sq. footage: 50000

677 Applecreek Farms
5751 Briar Hill Rd
Lexington, KY 40516-9721   859-293-3562
Fax: 859-293-3555   800-747-8871
bhall@mis.net   www.applecreek.net
Preserves, fruit butters, marinade, salsa, relish, caramel and chocolate fidge dessert sauces, dressings, BBQ seasonings and homemade candies.
Owner: Buddy Hall
Operations Manager: Lynn Abshear
Estimated Sales: $ 1 - 3 Million
Number Employees: 1-4
Brands:
Applecreek Orchards

678 Appledore Cove LLC
19 Buffum Road
North Berwick, ME 03906   888-849-1787
Fax: 207-636-8100   info@appledorecove.com
www.appledorecove.com
Salsas, condiments & dips, sauces & marinades, preserves & dessert sauces
President: Jeff Garstka

679 Applegate Farms
750 Us Highway 202 # 300
Bridgewater, NJ 08807-5530   908-725-2768
Fax: 908-725-3383   help@applegatefarms.com
www.applegatefarms.com
Manufacturer and distributor natural (ABF) and organic meat including beef, chicken, turkey and pork. Also cheese, sausage and hotdogs.
Owner: Seven McDonald
Co-Founder: Chris Ely
Number Employees: 50-99
Sq. footage: 7000
Type of Packaging: Consumer, Food Service, Private Label, Bulk
Brands:
APPLEGATE FARMS
GREAT ORGANIC HOTDOG
JOY STICK

680 Appleton Produce Company
P.O.Box 110
Weiser, ID 83672-0110   208-414-1102
                Fax: 208-414-3933
onions@appletonproduce.com
www.appletonproduce.com
Packer and Shipper of fresh onions.
    President: C. Robert Woods
    VP: Rob Woods
    Marketing/Sales Manager: Steve Walker
Estimated Sales:$12 Million
Number Employees: 50-99
Type of Packaging: Consumer, Food Service, Private Label, Bulk
Brands:
    APCO
    Appleton
    Gold Nugget

681 Applewood Orchards
2998 Rodesiler Hwy
Deerfield, MI 49238-9789   517-447-3002
        Fax: 517-447-3006   800-447-3854
scottaoi@cass.net   www.applewoodapples.com
Processor and exporter of apples
    President: Jim Swindeman
    VP: Scott Swindeman
    Director Operations: Steve Swindeman
Estimated Sales:$5-10 Million
Number Employees: 20-49
Type of Packaging: Consumer

682 April Hill
190 28th St SE
Grand Rapids, MI 49548   616-245-0595
                Fax: 616-245-2368
Breads, rolls
    Plant Manager: William MacKenzie
Estimated Sales:$2.5-5 Million
Number Employees: 10-19

683 Aqua Clara Bottling & Distribution
1315 Cleveland Street
Clearwater, FL 33755-5102   727-446-2999
        Fax: 727-446-3999   info@aquaclara.com
                www.aquaclara.com
Bottles and distributes oxygen-enriched premium drinking water 0-2 parts total dissolved solids, bottled with over 55 parts pure oxygen
    Chairman: E Douglas Cifers
    President: Jack Plunkett
    CEO: Jack Plunkett
Number Employees: 5-9
Brands:
    Aqua Clara

684 Aqua Vie Beverage Corporation
PO Box 6759
Ketchum, ID 83340-6759   208-622-7792
        Fax: 208-622-8829   800-744-7500
contact@aquavie.com   www.aquavie.com
Natural falvored water without carbonation, low-calorie and exotic flavors
    President: Thomas Gillespie
Estimated Sales:$1-2.5 Million
Number Employees: 20-49
Type of Packaging: Bulk
Brands:
    Avalanche

685 (HQ)AquaCuisine
1065 E Winding Creek Dr
Eagle, ID 83616-7243   208-323-2782
        Fax: 208-323-4730   888-330-2782
twallace@aquacuisine.com
www.aquacuisine.com
Processor of value added seafood products including fresh and frozen burgers, franks and refrigerated seafood entrees
    President: Mark Goforth
Estimated Sales:$5 Million
Number Employees: 1-4
Number of Products: 7
Sq. footage: 5000
Type of Packaging: Consumer
Brands:
    AQUACUISINE

686 AquaTec Development
1543 Locke Lane
Sugar Land, TX 77478-3917   281-242-7771
    Fax: 281-242-7771   stern4@alltel.net

Bulk production of algae and nutraceutical extracts and concentrates. Algae food supplements and food fortificial bulk only
    President: Howard Stern
Number Employees: 1-4
Type of Packaging: Bulk

687 Aquafina
101 W 48th St S
Wichita, KS 67217-4937   316-522-4100
    Fax: 316-529-9706   willard.walker@pepsi.com
www.aquafina.com OR www.pepsico.com
Manufacturer of bottled water
    Chairman/Chief Executive Officer: Indra Nooyi
    Chief Financial Officer: Richard Goodman
    VP: Joe Schuler
    SVP/Corporate Strategy & Development: Wahid Hamid
    SVP/Corporate Communications: Tod MacKenzie

    EVP/Operations: Hugh Johnston
    General Manager: Bill Mikulka
Estimated Sales:$100 Million
Number Employees: 250-499
Parent Co: PepsiCo North America
Type of Packaging: Consumer, Food Service
Brands:
    Aquafina
    Aquafina Alive
    Aquafina FlavorSplash
    Aquafina Sparkling

688 Aquatec Seafoods Ltd.
820 Shamrock Place
Comox, BC V9M 4G4
Canada   250-339-6412
    Fax: 250-339-4951   info@aquatec.bc.ca
                www.aquatec.bc.ca
Manufacturer of fresh and frozen salmon and oysters
    President: Paul Vroom
Number Employees: 50
Sq. footage: 7000
Type of Packaging: Consumer, Food Service, Private Label, Bulk

689 Aquatech
6221 Petersburg St
Anchorage, AK 99507-2006   907-563-1387
                Fax: 907-563-1852
    Partner: Miki Ballard
    Partner: Lamar Ballard
    General Manager: Sarah Ballard
Estimated Sales:$ 3 - 5 Million
Number Employees: 1-4

690 Aralia Olive Oils
1105 Massachusetts Avenue
Suite 2E
Cambridge, MA 02138   617-354-8556
        Fax: 617-249-1855   877-585-9510
                www.araliaoliveoils.com
Olive Oils
    President: Emmanuel Daskalakis
Number Employees: 2

691 Arbor Crest Wine Cellars
4705 N Fruit Hill Rd
Spokane, WA 99217-9562   509-927-8571
        Fax: 509-927-0574   info@arborcrest.com
                www.arborcrest.com
Wine
    Manager: Jim Van Loven Sels
    Marketing Director: Joe Algeo
    General Manager: James van Loben Sels
    Production Manager: Kristine Mielke-van Loben Sels
Estimated Sales:$1.25 Million
Number Employees: 10-19
Type of Packaging: Private Label
Brands:
    Arbor Crest

692 Arbor Crest Wine Cellars
4705 N Fruit Hill Rd
Spokane, WA 99217-9562   509-927-8571
        Fax: 509-927-0574   info@arborcrest.com
                www.arborcrest.com
Wines
    Manager: Jim Van Loven Sels
    General Manager: Jim van Loben Sels
    Marketing Director: Joe Algeo
Estimated Sales:$ 5 - 10 Million
Number Employees: 10-19

693 Arbor Hill Grapery & Winery
6461 State Route 64
Naples, NY 14512-9726   585-374-2870
    Fax: 585-374-9198   800-554-7553
js@thegrapery.com   www.thegrapery.com
Gourmet wines, grape and fruit based products, fruit preservatives, wine jellies, dressings, vinegars, barbeque sauces, mustard, spreadable sauce and dips, pretzel dips, wine sauces and tea concentrates
    President: John Brahm III
    VP: Katie Brahm
    Public Relations: Sherry Brahm-Orlando
*Estimated Sales:*Less than $5 Million
Number Employees: 5-9
Type of Packaging: Consumer, Private Label
Brands:
    Arbor Hill Wine
    Brahm's Wine Country
    Mrs. Brahms

694 Arbor Mist Winery
116 Buffalo Street
Canandaigua, NY 14424-1012   866-396-7394
                www.arbormist.com
Fruit flavored wines

695 (HQ)Arbor Springs Water Company
950 Orchard St
Ferndale, MI 48220-1439   248-543-7151
        Fax: 248-543-0488   800-343-7003
sales@aswaterco.com   www.aswaterco.com
Bottled Spring and Purified water.
Estimated Sales:$5-10 Million
Number Employees: 10-19
Other Locations:
    Arbor Springs Water Company
    Ann Arbor MI
Brands:
    Arbor Springs Drinking Water
    Arbor Springs Purified Water
    Arbor Springs Spring Water

696 Arboris, LLC.
1101 West Lathrop Avenue
Savannah, GA 31415   912-238-7573
        Fax: 912-238-7454   www.arboris-us.com
Supplier of sterols used in yogurt, milks, juices and breads.
    Vice President/General Manager: Peter Acton
    Sales: Peter Acton
    Purchasing: Jeanne Anderson

697 Arbuckle Coffee
275 Curry Hollow Road
Pittsburgh, PA 15236-4631   412-653-8878
                800-533-8278
                www.arbucklecoffee.com
Specialty coffee and tea.
    President: Denney Willis
    VP: Josh Willis
Estimated Sales:$500,000-$1 Million
Number Employees: 5-9
Brands:
    Arbuckle

698 Arcadia Dairy Farms
P.O.Box 631
Arden, NC 28704-0631   828-684-3556
    Fax: 828-684-7988   info@arcadiadairyfarms.com
                www.arcadiadairyfarms.com
Processor of juices including orange, apple, strawberry and grape; also, water
    President: J N Arthur Iii
Estimated Sales:$10-20 Million
Number Employees: 20-49
Type of Packaging: Consumer
Brands:
    Arcadia
    Sunrise

699 Arcadian Estate Winery
4184 State Route 14
Rock Stream, NY 14878-9612   607-535-2068
        Fax: 607-535-4692   800-298-1346
info@arcadianwine.com   www.arcadianwine.com
Manufacturer of red, white and fruit wines.
    Owner: John Dalonzo
Number Employees: 10-19
Type of Packaging: Consumer

700   **Arcee Sales Company**
30 Gem St
Brooklyn, NY 11222-2804   718-383-0107
                               Fax: 718-383-9115
Processor of fresh fish
   Controller: Leo Sumera
   Manager: Eric Caslow
Estimated Sales: $20-50 Million
Number Employees: 100-249
Type of Packaging: Consumer, Food Service

701   **(HQ)Archer Daniels Midland Company**
4666 Faries Parkway
P.O.Box 1470
Decatur, IL 62526
Usa   217-424-5200
   Fax: 217-424-2572 800-637-5843
   info@admworld.com   www.admworld.com
Procuring, transporting, storing, processing, and
marketing agricultural products. Processes oilseeds,
corn, wheat, cocoa beans, milo, oats, barley, and
peanuts. These operations and processes produce
products which have primarily twoend uses, either
food or feed ingredients
   President/CEO: Patricia Woertz
   CFO and Executive VP: Steven Mills
   Executive VP: David Smith
Estimated Sales: K
Number Employees: 10,000+
Type of Packaging: Consumer, Food Service, Pri-
   vate Label, Bulk
Brands:
   Arcon
   Ardex
   Beakin
   Capsulec
   Clintose
   Cornsweet
   Gold' N Flavor
   Golden Chef
   Novasoy
   Nutrisoy
   Performix
   Pro-Fam
   Soy7soy Enriched Pasta
   Soylec
   Superb
   Superb Select
   TLV
   TVC
   Tastee Pop
   Thermolec
   Ultralec
   Yelkin

702   **(HQ)Archer Daniels Midland Company**
4666 Faries Pkwy
Decatur, IL 62525   217-424-5200
   Fax: 217-424-6196 800-637-5843
   info@admworld.com   www.admworld.com
Processors of soybeans, corn, wheat and cocoa
   Chairman/President/CEO: Paticia woertz
   EVP/CFO: Steven Mills
Estimated Sales: $69 Billion
Number Employees: 28,200
Type of Packaging: Bulk
Other Locations:
   ADM
   Canada
   ADM do Brasil Ltda
   Sao Paulo, Brasil
   ADM Paraguay S.A.E.C.A
   Mingua Guaz£, Paraguay
   ADM SAO S.A. Bolivia
   Santa Cruz de la Sierra
   ADM
   Europe
   ADM
   Middle East
   ADM
   Africa
   ADM Australia
   Sydney, Australia
   ADM Hong Kong
   Wanchai, Hong Long
   ADM Trading Company Ltd
   Shanghai, China
   ADM Tianjin
   Tianjin, China
   ADM Dalian
   Dalian, China
   ADM Far East
   Bunkyo-Ku Tokyo, Japan

Brands:
   AMRBOSIA®
   ARCON®
   BEAKIN
   CAPSULEC
   CLINTOSER
   CORNSWEET®
   DE ZAAN®
   FIBERSOL-2™
   MERCKENS®
   NOVALIPID™
   NOVASOY®
   NOVAXAN™
   NUSUN®
   NUTRISOY®
   NUTRIsOY® NEXT™
   OPTIXAN™
   PFL™
   PRO-FAM®
   SUPERB®
   THERMOLEC
   ULTRALEC®
   YELKIN®

703   **Archer Daniels Midland Company**
P.O.Box 29268
Lincoln, NE 68529-0268   402-464-9131
   Fax: 402-464-5956 800-228-4060
Processor of flour and pancake mix
   President: John Baumgartner
   Plant Manager: Jeramy Fisher
Estimated Sales: $100+ Million
Number Employees: 100-249
Parent Co: Archer Daniels Midland Company
Type of Packaging: Consumer, Food Service, Pri-
   vate Label, Bulk
Brands:
   Budget
   Larosa
   Martha Gooch
   Russo
   Soy7 Soy Enriched Pasta

704   **Archibald Candy Corporation**
8850 W Bryn Mawr Avenue
Chicago, IL 60631   312-243-2700
   Fax: 312-243-3921 800-333-3629
   customerservice@archibaldcandy.com
                  www.fanniemaycandies.com
Manufacturer and exporter of confectionery prod-
ucts including chocolates, hard candy and nuts
   President: Ted Shepherd
Number Employees: 1-4
Parent Co: Fannie May
Type of Packaging: Consumer, Food Service, Pri-
   vate Label, Bulk
Brands:
   Fannie May
   Fanny Farmer
   Laura Secord
   Sweet Factory

705   **Archie Moore's Foods Products**
15 Factory Ln
Milford, CT 06460-3306   203-876-5088
   Fax: 203-876-0525 www.archiemoores.com
Manufacturer and exporter of buffalo wing sauce
and flavored potato chips
   President: Todd Ressler
Estimated Sales: $ .5 - 1 million
Number Employees: 20-49
Sq. footage: 2500
Parent Co: Archie Moore's Bar & Restaurant
Type of Packaging: Consumer, Food Service, Pri-
   vate Label, Bulk
Brands:
   Archie Moore's

706   **Archon Vitamin Corporation**
209 40th St
Irvington, NJ 07111-1154   973-371-1700
   Fax: 973-371-1277 800-349-1700
   archonvit@aol.com   www.archonvitamin.com
Established manufacturer of vitamins, minerals,
herbs, and other nutritionals.
   President: Tom Pugsley
   VP Products Division: Paul Stevens
   Technical Director: Dr. Abdoulaye Dieng
   National Sales Manager: Rick McNall
Estimated Sales: $ 5 - 10 Million
Number Employees: 50-99
Number of Brands: 1
Sq. footage: 50000
Type of Packaging: Consumer, Private Label, Bulk

Brands:
   BIONUTRIENT

707   **Archway & Mother's Cookie Company**
810 81st Avenue
Oakland, CA 94621-2583   510-569-2323
   Fax: 510-569-6604 800-369-3997
                  www.archway
Manufacturer of cookies and crackers
   Plant Manager: Terry Goodman
Estimated Sales: $250 Million
Number Employees: 200
Parent Co: Catterton Partners
Type of Packaging: Consumer, Food Service, Bulk

708   **Archway Cookies**
2041 Claremont Ave
Ashland, OH 44805-3545   419-289-0787
   Fax: 419-289-1289 888-427-2492
                  www.archwaycookies.com
Processor of cookies
   President: John Stevens
   VP Operations: Tom Seddon
   Plant Manager: Jeremy Bowman
   Purchasing Manager: Brenda Marker
Estimated Sales: $ 50 - 100 Million
Number Employees: 500-999
Sq. footage: 170000
Parent Co: Parmalat Bakery Group North America
Type of Packaging: Consumer

709   **(HQ)Archway Cookies**
87 Michigan Avenue W
Suite 608
Battle Creek, MI 49017-3605   269-962-6205
   Fax: 616-962-8149 888-427-2492
   archie@archwaycookies.com
                  www.archwaycookies.com
Manufacturer of cookies
   President: Patrick O'Dey
   CFO: Nicola Melillo
   Marketing: William Klump
   Sales: Mark O'Toole
   Public Relations: Dan Keefe
   Operations: Peter Lowes
Number Employees: 20-49
Parent Co: Parmalat Bakery Group North America
Type of Packaging: Private Label
Brands:
   ARCHWAY

710   **Arcobasso Foods Inc**
8014 N Broadway
St Louis, MO 63147-2417   314-381-8083
   Fax: 314-381-4522 800-284-0620
   pat@arcobasso.com   www.arcobasso.com
Arcobasso Foods is a full-service custom manufac-
turer and bottler of salad dressings, sauces and mari-
nades.
   President: Tom Newsham
   Vice President: Pat Newsham
Type of Packaging: Food Service

711   **Arcor USA**
550 Biltmore Way # 2a
Coral Gables, FL 33134-5721   305-592-1080
   Fax: 305-592-1081 800-572-7267
                  www.arcor.com.ar
Candies
   President: Sergio Limonti
   National Sales Manager: Michael Figueras
   Product Manager: Damian Cordova
Estimated Sales: $ 10 - 20 Million
Number Employees: 20-49
Type of Packaging: Private Label
Brands:
   ARCOR PREMIUM HARD FILLED CANDIES
   ARCOR VALUE LINE HARD CANDIES
   ROCKLETS
   WHISPER CHOCOLATE BON BONS

712   **(HQ)Arctic Beverages**
PO Box 39
Flin Flon, MB R8A 1M6
Canada   204-687-7517
   Fax: 204-687-7940 flintlon@arcticbev.com
                  www.pepsi.com
Wholesaler/distributor and bottler of soft drinks and
juices for vending, fountains and coolers; also, in-
stallation services available
   General Manager: Daniel Leoward
   CEO: Allan McLeod
   Marketing: T Brown

Number Employees: 35
Sq. footage: 17000
Parent Co: Pepsi
Other Locations:
Arctic Beverages Ltd.
The Pas MB
Arctic Beverages Ltd.
Thompson MB
Arctic Beverages Ltd.
Winnipeg MB

713 Arctic Glacier
900 Turk Hill Rd
Fairport, NY 14450-8747   585-388-0080
Fax: 585-388-0185   800-937-4423
info@arcticglacierinc.com
www.arcticglacierinc.com
Manufacturer of ice
President/CEO: Keith McMahon
Chief Financial Officer: Douglas Bailey
Manager: Sharon Douglass
Equipment Sales/Leasing: Jeff Hendler
Estimated Sales: $2.5-5 Million
Number Employees: 20-49
Parent Co: Arctic Glacier

714 Arctic Glacier
5 Sonwil Dr
Buffalo, NY 14225-2424   716-683-5950
Fax: 716-683-8995   800-688-5950
info@arcticglacierinc.com
www.arcticglacierinc.com
Manufacture ice
Manager: James Boundy
Chief Financial Officer: Douglas Bailey
Manager: Sharon Douglass
Equipment Sales/Leasing: Jeff Hendler
Estimated Sales: $ 10 - 20 Million
Number Employees: 20-49
Parent Co: Arctic Glacier
Other Locations:
Happy Ice
Buffalo NY

715 Arctic Glacier
20 Wells Ave
Utica, NY 13502-2520   315-732-4148
Fax: 315-793-8851   800-792-5958
info@arcticglacierinc.com
www.arcticglacierinc.com
Manufactures ice
Owner: Dave Dubiel
Chief Financial Officer: Douglas Bailey
Manager: Sharon Douglass
Equipment Sales/Leasing: Jeff Hendler
Estimated Sales: $ 3 - 5 Million
Number Employees: 1-4
Parent Co: Arctic Glacier
Other Locations:
Happy Ice
Utica NY

716 Arctic Glacier
234 Barker Street
Corning, NY 14830   607-936-4511
800-937-4423
info@arcticglacierinc.com
www.arcticglacierinc.com
Manufactures ice
President/CEO: Keith McMahon
Chief Financial Officer: Dougals Bailey
Manager: Sharon Douglass
Equipment Sales/Leasing: Jeff Hendler
Estimated Sales: $ 1 - 3 Million
Number Employees: 1-4
Parent Co: Arctic Glacier
Other Locations:
Happy Ice
Corning NY

717 Arctic Glacier
2 Commerce Avenue
Albany, NY 12206-2016   518-438-2070
518-438-2082
info@arcticglacierinc.com
www.arcticglacierinc.com
Manufactures ice
President/CEO: Keith McMahon
Chief Financial Officer: Douglas Bailey
Manager: Sharon Douglass
Equipment Sales/Leasing: Jeff Hendler
Estimated Sales: $ 10 - 20 Million
Number Employees: 20-49
Parent Co: Arctic Glacier

Other Locations:
Happy Ice
Albany NY

718 Arctic Ice Cream Company
22 Arctic Parkway
Trenton, NJ 08638-3093   609-393-4264
Fax: 609-392-3663   astephens@chartermi.net
www.acticicecreamco.com
Ice cream
President: Thomas Green
Estimated Sales: $5-10 Million
Number Employees: 10-19

719 Arctic Seas
21 Burchard Avenue
Little Compton, RI 02837-1602   401-635-4000
Fax: 401-635-9158   brian@arcticseas.com
www.arcticseas.com
Manufacturer of frozen fish and seafood including
whitefish, crab meat, scallops, shrimp, squid and
surimi
President: Brian Eliason
Estimated Sales: $40-50 Million
Number Employees: 1-4
Type of Packaging: Consumer, Food Service, Pri-
vate Label
Brands:
Arctic Iceland
Arctic Seas
Arctic Sprays

720 Ardmore Cheese Company
P.O.Box 888
Shelbyville, TN 37162-0888   931-427-2191
Fax: 931-427-4116
Manufacturer of cheddar cheese including sliced,
diced and shredded
Manager: Abby Woods
VP: Joe Madeo
Plant Manager: Brad Jackson
Estimated Sales: $500-1 Million appx.
Number Employees: 1-4
Sq. footage: 10000
Type of Packaging: Consumer, Private Label
Brands:
Ardmore
Avalon

721 Arena & Sons
159 Ash St
Hopkinton, MA 01748-1903   508-435-3673
Fax: 508-435-2457
Manufacturer of veal and beef
President: Frank Arena
Estimated Sales: $2.5-5 Million
Number Employees: 5-9
Type of Packaging: Bulk

722 Argee Corporation
9550 Pathway St
Santee, CA 92071-4169   619-449-5050
Fax: 619-449-8392   800-449-3030
argee@tsn.net   www.argeecorp.com
CEO: Robert Oldman
Marketing Director: Ruth Oldman
CEO: Robert Goldman
President: Robert Oldman
Estimated Sales: $ 10 - 20 Million
Number Employees: 50-99

723 Argo Century
4913 Chastain Ave
Charlotte, NC 28217-3116   704-525-6180
Fax: 704-525-6280   800-446-7131
info@tontonsauce.com   www.tontonsauce.com
Manufacturer of ginger dressing, teriyaki sauce and
vinaigrettes.
President: Yoshi Shioda
Estimated Sales: $ 1 - 3 Million
Number Employees: 1-4
Type of Packaging: Consumer

724 Argo Fine Foods
PO Box 2077
Saint James, NY 11780   631-703-0443
cdeblasio@argofinefoods.com
www.argofinefoods.com
Tzatziki (yogurt sauce), pita snacks
President/Owner: Christel DeBlasio-Pavlidis

725 Argonaut Winery
13825 Willow Creek Rd
Ione, CA 95640-9716   209-245-5567
Fax: 209-245-5567   argonautwnry@cdepot.net

Wines
Owner: Mark McMaster
CEO: Debe Fake
Vice President: Steve Fale
Marketing Director: Jennifer Marston
Operations Manager: Brian Marston
Estimated Sales: $1-2.5 Million
Number Employees: 1-4

726 (HQ)Argyle Wines
P.O.Box 280
Dundee, OR 97115-0280   503-538-8520
Fax: 503-538-2055   888-427-4953
tastingroom@argylewinery.com
www.argylewinery.com
Wines
President: Rollin Soles
General Manager: Allen Holstein
Estimated Sales: $20-50 Million
Number Employees: 50-99
Type of Packaging: Private Label
Brands:
Argyle Brut
Nuthouse Pinot Noir

727 (HQ)Ariake USA, Inc.
1711 N Liberty St
Harrisonburg, VA 22802-4518   540-432-6550
Fax: 540-432-6549   888-201-5885
polansky@ariake.com   www.ariakeusa.com
Manufacturer of Stocks, Broths, Bases, Seasonings,
Flavor Systems
Manager: Kyle Wellsford
Marketing/Sales Manager: Aaron Robinson
Sales Manager: Joe Brisby
Estimated Sales: $10-20 Million
Number Employees: 20-49
Sq. footage: 58000
Other Locations:
Ariake USA
China
Ariake USA
Japan
Ariake USA
France
Ariake USA
Belgium

728 Ariel Natural Foods
13400 N 20th St
Suite 32
Bellevue, WA 98005   425-637-3345
Fax: 425-637-8655   contactus@arielfoods.com
www.arielfoods.com
Sugar-free, dairy-free and gluten-free premium
freeze dried snacks.

729 Ariel Vineyards
P.O.Box 3437
Napa, CA 94558-0343   707-258-8050
Fax: 707-258-8052   800-456-9472
craig@arielvineyards.com
www.arielvineyards.com
Processors and exporter of nonalcoholic wine
Manager: Craig Rosser
VP Operations: Jeff Meier
Estimated Sales: $5-10 Million
Number Employees: 1-4
Sq. footage: 64000
Parent Co: J. Lohr Vineyards & Wines
Brands:
Ariel
Ariel Blanc
Ariel Brut Cuve
Ariel Cabernet
Ariel Chardonnay
Ariel Merlot
Ariel Rouge
Ariel White Zinfandel

730 Aries Prepared Beef
17 W Magnolia Blvd
Burbank, CA 91502-1719   818-526-4855
Fax: 818-845-3041
Processor of cooked and smoked beef and sausage
Owner: Fred Scholder
Sales Manager: Fred Weiss
Estimated Sales: $50-100 Million
Number Employees: 20-49
Type of Packaging: Consumer, Food Service

731 Arise & Shine Herbal Products
PO Box 400
Medford, OR 97501-0027   541-282-0894
Fax: 541-773-8866   800-688-2444
admin@ariseandshine.com
www.ariseandshine.com
Processor and exporter of digestive aids and herbal
supplements for complete body detoxification and
follow-up nourishment
Founder: Dr. Richard Anderson
CEO: Avona L'Carttier
Brands:
Chomper
Flora Grow
Herbal Nutrition
Super Antioxidant Blend
Ultimate Food Complex

732 Arista Industries
557 Danbury Rd
Wilton, CT 06897-2218   203-761-1009
Fax: 203-761-4980   800-255-6457
info@aristaindustries.com
www.aristaindustries.com
Processor, exporter and wholesaler/distributor of
oils, frozen shrimp, lobster tails and octopus; serv-
ing the food service market; importer of octopus,
shrimp, squid, lobster tails, oils and surimi products
President: Charles Hillyer
CEO: Stephen Weitzer
Sales Manager: Nick Collins
Estimated Sales: $2.5-5 Million
Number Employees: 20-49
Type of Packaging: Consumer, Food Service
Brands:
Arista
Pacific Treasures
Sea Devils

733 (HQ)Aristocrat International Corporation
20 Enterprise Ave N # 9
Secaucus, NJ 07094-2519   201-866-1900
Fax: 201-866-8338
Processor and exporter of frozen kosher and
nonkosher hors d'oeuvres including potato and sau-
sage pizza puffs, Chinese egg rolls, potato pierogies,
kreplach, meatballs, pizza straws, stuffed cabbage,
franks-in-blankets and empanadas
President: Steven Tillim
Production Manager: Ricardo Mino
Purchasing Director: Steven Tillman
Estimated Sales: $10-20 Million
Number Employees: 50-99
Type of Packaging: Consumer, Food Service, Pri-
vate Label, Bulk
Brands:
AC
Aristocrat
The Hors D'Oeuvre Factory
Unique

734 Ariston Specialties
PO Box 306
Bloomfield, CT 06002   860-224-7184
Fax: 860-726-1263   info@aristonoliveoil.com
www.aristonoliveoil.com
Olive Oils
Owner: Thomas Doukas

735 Ariza Cheese Company
7602 Jackson St
Paramount, CA 90723-4912   562-630-4144
Fax: 562-630-4174   800-762-4736
www.mexicancheese.com
Processor of Mexican cheese
Owner: Ausencio Ariza Sr
Manager: Blake Johnson
Estimated Sales: $20-50 Million
Number Employees: 20-49
Type of Packaging: Consumer, Food Service

736 Arizona Beverage Company
5 Dakota Dr
New Hyde Park, NY 11042-1109   516-812-0300
Fax: 516-326-4988   800-832-3775
info@arizonabev.com   www.arizonabev.com
Manufacturer of flavored beverages including teas,
juices and iced coffees
President: John Ferolito
VP Business Development: John Balboni
VP National Sales: Paul O'Donnell
Estimated Sales: $ 5 - 10 Million
Number Employees: 500-999

Brands:
Arizona
Ferolito, Vultaggio & Sons
Rx Extreme Energy Shot

737 Arizona Brands
3121 E Washington St
Phoenix, AZ 85034-1519   602-273-7139
Fax: 602-275-9429
Prepared Foods and Specialties
President: Ken Charbonneau
Sales Manager: Bob Stephens
VP Operations: Mike Depinto
Plant Manager: Joaquin Amaro
Estimated Sales: $20-50 Million
Number Employees: 50-99

738 (HQ)Arizona Chemical Company
P.O.Box 550850
Jacksonville, FL 32255-0850   904-928-8700
Fax: 904-928-8779   800-526-5294
www.arizonachemical.com
Manufacturer of pine chemicals
CEO: Cornelis Verhaar
Number Employees: 1,000-4,999
Other Locations:
Dover OH
Panama City FL
Pensacola FL
Port St. Joe FL
Savannah GA
Valdosta GA
Miami FL

739 (HQ)Arizona Cowboy
11049 N 23rd Dr
Phoenix, AZ 85029-4749   602-278-1427
Fax: 602-484-9482   800-529-8627
amelio@cactuscandy.com
www.arizonacowboy.net
Processor and exporter of salsa, jellies, hot sauces,
tortilla chips, honey, candy and nuts
President: Amelio Casciato
Estimated Sales: $ .5 - 1 million
Number Employees: 5-9
Sq. footage: 1650
Type of Packaging: Consumer, Food Service, Pri-
vate Label

740 Arizona Institutional Foods
1922 E 18th St
Tucson, AZ 85719-6910   520-624-8667
Fax: 520-629-4377 www.shamrockfoods.com
Manager: Paul Sedon
Estimated Sales: $ 20 - 50 Million
Number Employees: 20-49

741 Arizona Natural Products
12815 N Cave Creek Road
Phoenix, AZ 85022-5834   602-997-6098
Fax: 602-288-8331   info@arizonanatural.com
www.arizonanatural.com
Processor and exporter of herbal and vitamin supple-
ments
President: Michael Hanna
Estimated Sales: $1-2.5 Million
Number Employees: 5-9
Sq. footage: 10000
Brands:
Allirich

742 Arizona Nutritional Supplements
210 S Beck Ave
Chandler, AZ 85226-3311   480-966-9630
Fax: 480-966-9640   888-742-7675
www.aznutritional.com
Contract manufacturer and packer, custom nutri-
tional and dietary supplements
Owner: Jonathan Pinkus
Estimated Sales: $ 10 - 20 Million
Number Employees: 100-249
Sq. footage: 50000

743 Arizona Pepper Products
P.O.Box 40605
Mesa, AZ 85274-0605   480-833-1908
Fax: 480-833-0309   800-359-3912
info@azgunslinger.com   www.azgunslinger.com
Hot sauces, olives, spices and pistachios
President: Bill Marko
Purchasing Director: William Marco
Estimated Sales: $2.5-5 Million
Number Employees: 5-9

744 Arizona Pistachio Company
26487 N Highway 99
Tulare, CA 93274-9317   520-746-0880
Fax: 520-741-9797   800-333-8575
salesapc@azpistachio.com   www.azpistachio.com
Grower and processor of pistachios
President: Henry Mollner
Estimated Sales: $2.5-5 Million
Number Employees: 5-9
Type of Packaging: Consumer, Food Service, Bulk

745 Arizona Sunland Foods
3752 S Broadmont Dr
Tucson, AZ 85713-5256   520-624-7068
info@sunlandfoods.com
www.sunlandfoods.com
Processor of portion-controlled salad dressings,
chicken, beef and shrimp
Owner: Arnie L Jacobsen
VP: Josh Jacobson
Estimated Sales: $20-50 Million
Number Employees: 20-49
Type of Packaging: Food Service

746 Arizona Sunland Foods
3752 S Broadmont Dr
Tucson, AZ 85713-5256   520-624-7068
info@sunlandfoods.com
www.azsunlandfoods.com
Beef, poultry and seafood products manufactured to
customer specifications, as well as custom sauce and
dressing portion control.
Owner: Arnie L Jacobsen
CFO/VP: Tony Jacobson
Estimated Sales: $ 20-50 Million
Number Employees: 20-49
Number of Brands: 1
Number of Products: 30
Type of Packaging: Food Service

747 Arizona Vineyards
1830 E Patagonia Hwy
Nogales, AZ 85621-1226   520-287-7972
Fax: 520-287-7597
Wines
Owner/President: Arthur Ocheltree
Owner/CEO: Tino Ocheltree
Estimated Sales: Less than $150,000
Number Employees: 1-4
Brands:
Arizona Vineyards

748 Arjo Wiggins
10901 Westlake Drive
Charlotte, NC 28273
Fax: 859-448-9799   800-765-9278
chris.pelle@arjoexamerica.com
www.polyart.com
Product and services are tag and label applications
suitable for a variety of uses including that of: food
labels; slaughterhouse meat tags; bar-coded labels,
and self-adhesive labels.
Sales Representative: Chris Pelle

749 Arkansas Poly
309 Phillips Rd
N Little Rock, AR 72117-4105   501-945-5763
Fax: 501-945-0276   800-364-5036
sales@arkpoly.com   www.allampoly.com
Manager: Jim Wilson
VP Sales/Marketing: Kip Johnson
Controller: Dave Robertson
Estimated Sales: $ 20 - 50 Million
Number Employees: 50-99
Brands:
Arkansas Poly

750 Arkansas Refrigerated Services
P.O.Box 2554
Fort Smith, AR 72902-2554   479-783-1006
Fax: 479-783-1008
info@arkansasrefrigeratedservices.com
www.arkansasrefrigerated.com
Warehouse providing frozen storage for food prod-
ucts; also, rail siding available
President: Mike Group
Number Employees: 50-99

751 Arla Foods Ingredients
645 Martinsville Road
PO Box 624
Basking Ridge, NJ 07920   908-604-8551
          Fax: 908-604-9310   800-243-3730
          peter.hassing@arlafoods.com
          www.arlafoodsingredients.com
Processor and importer of caseinates, whey protein
concentrates, functional milk proteins and specialty
hydrolysates including milk/vegetable proteins; also,
encapsulated flavor delivery systems; custom blends
available
    President: Peter Hassing
    VP: Joyce Stefan
Estimated Sales:$5-10 Million
Number Employees: 5-9
Parent Co: Arla Foods Ingredients AMBA
Type of Packaging: Bulk
Brands:
    CAPOLAC®
    DANO®
    LACPRODAN®
    MILEX®
    MIPRODAN®
    MULTILAC®
    NUTRILAC®
    PERLAC®
    PIPTIGEN®
    VARIOLAC®

752 Arlington City Market
301 Burnside Street
Annapolis, MD 21403-2471   703-527-7100
          Fax: 703-527-7101
    Owner: Leif Klasson

753 Arlund Meat Company
PO Box 23443
Overland Park, KS 66283-0443   913-321-3450
          Fax: 913-321-5029
Beef, beef products
    President: Charles Arlund
Estimated Sales:$10-20 Million
Number Employees: 5-9

754 Armand's Coffee Flavors
3765 Atlanta Industrial Dr NW
Atlanta, GA 30331-1031   404-696-4178
          Fax: 404-696-4003
Flavoring supplies and flavors
    Owner: Armand Hammer
Estimated Sales:$500,000-$1 Million
Number Employees: 50-99

755 Armanino Foods of Distinction
30588 San Antonio St
Hayward, CA 94544-7102   510-441-9300
          Fax: 510-441-0101
          customerservice@armanino.biz
          www.armaninofoods.com
Manufacturer and exporter of Italian foods including
sauces, pasta, meat balls and bread; importer of Ital-
ian cheeses
    President/CEO: William Armanino
    Secretary/Treasurer/COO: Edmond Pera
    CEO: Edmond J Pera
    Controller: Edgar Estonina
    Director of Sales: Deborah Armanino
    Operations Manager: Georgianne Stephen
*Estimated Sales:*F
Number Employees: 20-49
Type of Packaging: Consumer, Food Service
Brands:
    Armanino

756 Armbrust Meats
224 S Main St
Medford, WI 54451-1843   715-748-3102
          Fax: 715-748-6399
Processor of fresh and frozen sausage, beef, pork
and poultry
    President: Thomas Armbrust
Estimated Sales:$500,000-$1 Million
Sq. footage: 33000
Type of Packaging: Consumer, Bulk

757 (HQ)Armenia Coffee Corporation
2975 Westchester Ave # 210
Purchase, NY 10577-2521   914-694-6100
          Fax: 914-694-5622   agcofy@aol.com
Coffee
    President: Joseph Apuzzo Jr.
Estimated Sales:$10-20 Million
Number Employees: 10-19

758 Armeno Coffee Roasters
75 Otis St
Northborough, MA 01532-2412   508-393-2821
          Fax: 508-393-2818   beans@armeno.com
          www.armeno.com
Coffee
    Owner: Chuck Koffman
    Co-Owner: John Parks
*Estimated Sales:*Under $1 Million
Number Employees: 5-9
Sq. footage: 5000
Type of Packaging: Consumer, Private Label
Brands:
    Armeno

759 Armistead Citrus Company
1057 N Greenfield Road
Mesa, AZ 85205-5105   480-830-2491
Processing citrus
    Owner: Ken Armistead
*Estimated Sales:*Under $500,000
Number Employees: 1-4
Brands:
    Armistead Citrus Products

760 Armour
PO Box 3768
Omaha, NE 68103-0768   402-453-3766
          Fax: 402-595-5304
Processor and exporter of prosciutto, Genoa and
hard salami, pepperoni and sausage; also, meat pizza
toppings including sausage and pepperoni
    Purchasing Manager: Craig Kingston
Estimated Sales:$300,000-500,000
Number Employees: 250
Parent Co: ConAgra Refigerated Prepared Foods
Type of Packaging: Consumer, Food Service, Pri-
vate Label, Bulk

761 Arnabal International
13459 Savanna
Tustin, CA 92782-9168   714-665-9477
          Fax: 714-665-9477   armen@arnabel.com
          www.arnabal.com
Oils and vinegars
    Owner: Nairy Balian
Estimated Sales:$ .5 - 1 million
Number Employees: 1-4

762 Arnhem Group
25 Commerce Dr
Cranford, NJ 07016-3605   908-709-4045
          Fax: 908-709-4045   800-851-1052
          info@arnhemgroup.com OR
          Sylva@arnhemgroup.com
          www.arnhemgroup.com
Products include binders and extenders, fat replacers, flavor enhancers, milk products, stabilizers.
Arnhem's Flavonoid technology division features
natural botanical powdered extracts, bioflavonoids,
and isolated flavonoids for thenutraceutical,
wellness, food, pharmaceutical and cosmetics
industries.
    President, Chairman, CEO: Michael Bonner
    National Accounts Manager: Sandra Lyna
Estimated Sales:$1-2.5 Million
Number Employees: 1-4

763 Arnold Foods Company
10 Hamilton Ave
Greenwich, CT 06830-6102   203-531-2000
          Fax: 203-531-2170 www.gwbakeries.com
Manufactures baked goods
    President: Gary Prince
    Executive VP Marketing: Christeen Halpin
Estimated Sales:$50-99.9 Million
Number Employees: 500-999
Brands:
    Beck's
    Beck's Dark
    Beck's For Oktoberfest
    Haake Beck Non-Alcoholic

764 Arnold's Meat Food Products
274 Heyward St
Brooklyn, NY 11206-2945   718-963-1400
          Fax: 718-963-2303   800-633-7023
          sales@arnolds-sausage.com
          www.arnolds-sausage.com
Processor and exporter of smoked sausage
    President: Shelly Dosik
    Vice President: Jacson Judd

Estimated Sales:$20-25 Million
Number Employees: 50-99
Type of Packaging: Consumer, Food Service, Pri-
vate Label, Bulk
Brands:
    Arnold's
    Arnold's Brands
    Caroline
    Caroline Brands
    El Cerdito
    El Cerdito Brands

765 Arns Winery
PO Box 652
Saint Helena, CA 94574   707-963-3429
          Fax: 707-963-5780   arnswine@napanet.net
          www.arnswinery.com
A 1000cs production of high end mountain fruit
grown organic methods. Arns Estate grown 100%
Cabernet Sauvignon and Arns Napa Valley Cabernet
Sauvignon.
    President: John Arns
    CEO/Winemaker: Sandi Belcher
    Marketing: Sandi Belcher
    Sales: Kathi Belcher
Estimated Sales:$100,000
Number Employees: 2
Number of Brands: 1
Number of Products: 1
Sq. footage: 1200
Type of Packaging: Consumer
Brands:
    Arns

766 Aroma Coffee Company
7650 Industrial Dr
Forest Park, IL 60130-2518   708-488-8340
          Fax: 708-488-8366
Manufacturer and packager of roasted whole bean
coffee in french and chicory and demitasse coffee,
also teas
    President: Gust Papanicholas
Estimated Sales:$5-10 Million
Number Employees: 5-9
Type of Packaging: Consumer, Food Service, Pri-
vate Label, Bulk
Brands:
    AROMA CUISINER'S CHOICE
    AROMA SOUTHERN MAISON
    AROMA TURKISH
    CUISINIERS CHOICE

767 Aroma Coffee Roasters
1601 Madison St
Hoboken, NJ 07030-2313   201-792-1730
          Fax: 201-659-1883
Coffee
    Manager: Ruth Santuccio
    Purchasing Director: Ruth Santuccio
Estimated Sales:$1-2.5 Million
Number Employees: 20-49

768 Aroma Ridge
1831 West Oak Parkway
Suite C
Marietta, GA 30062   770-421-9600
          Fax: 770-421-9116   800-528-2123
          contact@aromaridge.com www.aromaridge.com
coffee

769 Aroma Vera
5310 Beethoven St
Los Angeles, CA 90066-7015   310-204-3392
          Fax: 310-306-5873   800-669-9514
          cservice@aromavera.com www.aromavera.com
Processor, importer and exporter of essential oils
    President: Marcel Lavabre
    CEO: Klee Irwin
Estimated Sales:$5-10 Million
Number Employees: 5-9
Sq. footage: 50000
Brands:
    Aroma Vera

770 Aroma-Life
16161 Ventura Boulevard
Encino, CA 91436-2522   818-905-7761
          Fax: 818-905-0292   mzwan@aol.com
Processor, importer and exporter of essential, al-
mond and macadamia oils
    President: Moshe Zwang
    CEO: Diana Zwang
Estimated Sales:$300,000-500,000
Number Employees: 1-4

Number of Brands: 18
Number of Products: 16
Sq. footage: 27500
Type of Packaging: Private Label, Bulk
Brands:
Aroma-Life

771 Aromachem
599 Johnson Ave # 2
Brooklyn, NY 11237-1311   718-497-4664
   Fax: 718-419-4507
Processor, importer and exporter of flavors, essential oils and fragrances
   CEO: Andrew Levine
Estimated Sales: $10-20 Million
Number Employees: 10-19
Sq. footage: 25000
Type of Packaging: Bulk

772 Aromatech USA
5770 Hoffner Avenue
Suite 103
Orlando, FL 32822   407-277-5727
   Fax: 407-277-5725 www.aromatech.fr
manufacturer of flavorings for beverages, candies, baking, snacks and pastries

773 Arome Fleurs & Fruits
850 Pierre-Caisse
Suite 400
St-Jean-Sur-Richelie, QC J3B 7YS
Canada   450-349-3282
   Fax: 450-348-3518   877-349-3282
   info@floralfood.com   www.floralfood.com
Floral products incorporated into spreads, jellies and syrups.

774 Aromi d'Italia
5 N Calhoun St
Baltimore, MD 21223-1814   410-761-5215
   Fax: 410-761-5216   877-435-2869
   ashworth@ashworth.com   www.aromiditalia.com
Manufacturer and provider of the highest quality gelato products originating from Italy.
   Owner: Boris Ghazarian
Estimated Sales: $200,000
Number Employees: 5-9
Brands:
Aromi d'Italia

775 Aromont-USA
1800 E Highway 114 # 102
Southlake, TX 76092-6529   817-552-5544
   Fax: 817-552-5539 aromont@aromontusa.com
   www.texasepicenter.com
Naturally processed stocks and concentrated sauces
   Manager: Whitney Otto
Estimated Sales: $10-20 Million
Number Employees: 1-4

776 Aromont/USA
1666 Valley Greene Road
Paoli, PA 19301-1042   610-296-3748
   Fax: 610-296-7079 Aromont@aromontusa.com
   www.aromontusa.com
Demi glace
   Managing Director: Terry Wight
Number Employees: 1-4
Type of Packaging: Private Label
Brands:
Demi-Glaces

777 Aromor Flavors & Fragrances
560 Sylvan Ave # 60
Englewood Cliffs, NJ 07632-3104   201-503-1662
   Fax: 201-503-1663 sales@aromorinc.com
   www.aromor.com
Supplier of Flavors and Fragrances, Raw Materials
   Manager: Carol Feldman
   General Manager: Gary Romans
Number Employees: 50-99

778 (HQ)Arrowac Fisheries
4039 21st Ave W # 200
Seattle, WA 98199-1252   206-282-5655
   Fax: 206-282-9329 info@arrowac-merco.com
   www.arrowac-merco.com

Hholesaler, trader, processor, importer and exporter of fresh and frozen seafood including seabass, swordfish, shark, cod, crab, halibut, salmon, whiting and finfish
   President: Frank Mercker
   Vice President: Waltraut Brookes
   International Sales: Terence Tengan
   North American Sales: Brian Bell
   VP Production: R Anthony Blore
   Plant Manager: R Anthony Blore
Estimated Sales: $25 Million
Number Employees: 5-9
Number of Brands: 3
Number of Products: 15
Sq. footage: 20000
Type of Packaging: Consumer, Food Service, Private Label, Bulk
Brands:
Arrow
Merco
Ocean Dawn

779 (HQ)Arrowhead Mills
110 S Lawton Ave
Hereford, TX 79045-5802   806-364-0730
   Fax: 806-364-8242   800-749-0730
   www.arrowheadmills.com
Pasta
   President/CEO: Irwin Simon
   Operations: Gary Schultz
   Purchasing: Dale Hollingswoth
Number Employees: 50-99
Parent Co: Hain Food Group

780 Arrowood Vineyards & Winery
P.O.Box 1240
Glen Ellen, CA 95442-1240   707-935-2600
   Fax: 707-938-5947   800-938-5170
   hospitality@arrowoodvineyards.com
   www.arrowoodvineyards.com
Wines
   Manager: Patty Mullins
   VP: Alis Demers Arrowood
   Retail Operations Manager: Claudia DiClemente
Estimated Sales: $10-20 Million
Number Employees: 20-49
Type of Packaging: Private Label
Brands:
ARROWOOD
GRAND ARCHER

781 Art CoCo Chocolate Company
2660 Walnut St
Denver, CO 80205-2231   303-292-6364
   Fax: 303-292-6365   800-779-8985
   mbonick@artcoco.com   www.artcoco.com
Chocolate boxes, hand foiled chocolate novelties, specialty molded chocolates
   President: Kenneth Wolf
   VP: Gail Zucker
   National Retail Sales Director: Michele Bonnick
   Production Manager: Charles Martinez
Estimated Sales: $5-9.9 Million
Number Employees: 5-9
Parent Co: Silvestri Sweets, Inc.
Type of Packaging: Private Label
Brands:
Art Coco
Art Fidos Cookies
Art Topo

782 Art CoCo Chocolate Company
2660 Walnut St
Denver, CO 80205-2231   303-292-6364
   Fax: 303-292-6365   800-779-8985
   mbonick@artcoco.com   www.artcoco.com
Manufactures chocolate candy
   President: Markcall Callhan
Estimated Sales: $ 1-5 Million
Number Employees: 5-9
Number of Products: 300+

783 Art's Fisheries
305 E Buchanan Street
Phoenix, AZ 85004-2520   602-252-9550
   Fax: 602-340-0335
   President: E Steven Ansel
Estimated Sales: $ 10 - 20 Million
Number Employees: 20-49

784 Art's Mexican Products
615 Kansas Ave
Kansas City, KS 66105-1311   913-371-2163
   Fax: 913-371-2052 www.artsmexican.com

Mexican food specialties
   President: Bob Gutierrez
   President: Robert Gutierrez
Estimated Sales: $10-20 Million
Number Employees: 10-19

785 Art's Tamales
1453 Hickory Point Rd
Metamora, IL 61548-7803   309-367-2850
Processor of meat products including frozen hot tamales and beef barbecue; also, pizza; importer of corned and cubed beef
   President: David Chinuge
   Production Manager: Ruby Dirks
Estimated Sales: $300,000-500,000
Number Employees: 5-9
Sq. footage: 4000
Type of Packaging: Consumer
Brands:
Art's Tamales
Party Time

786 Artek USA
5700 Corsa Avenue
Suite 202f
Westlake Village, CA 91362-7332   626-333-3939
   Fax: 626-333-3308   866-278-3501
   President: Larry Jones
Estimated Sales: $ .5 - 1 million
Number Employees: 5

787 Artel
570 Boul Cure Boivin
Boisbriand, QC J7G 2A7
Canada   450-433-1322
   Fax: 450-433-9276 artel@sympatica.org
Processor and exporter of frozen foods including cooked frankfurters, spring roll, doughnuts, pizza buns and Italian meat sauce
   President: John Geminari
   VP: Anthony Parent
   Marketing Manager: William Wong
Number Employees: 250
Type of Packaging: Consumer, Food Service, Private Label, Bulk
Brands:
ARTEL
CUISIEXPRESS
FINE TABLE
POGO
QUICK MEALS
YIN YANG

788 Artesa Vineyards & Winery
1345 Henry Rd
Napa, CA 94559-9705   707-224-1668
   Fax: 707-224-1672 Info@artesawinery.com
   www.artesawinery.com
Wines
   President: Michael Kenton
   CFO: Tim O'Leary
   VP Production: Dave Dobson
Estimated Sales: $20-50 Million
Number Employees: 50-99
Type of Packaging: Private Label

789 Artesia Tortilla Factory
212 N 1st Street
Artesia, NM 88210-2104   505-746-2808
Manfuacturer of Mexican products including tortillas, chips and taco shells
   President: Raul Juarez
Estimated Sales: $2-5 Million
Number Employees: 1-4
Type of Packaging: Consumer

790 Artesian Honey Producers
P.O.Box 6
Artesian, SD 57314-0006   605-527-2423
Processor of honey
   Owner: John Zen
Estimated Sales: $1-2.5 Million
Number Employees: 5-9
Type of Packaging: Bulk

791 Artic Ice Cream Novelties
1901 23rd Avenue S
Seattle, WA 98144-4615   206-324-0414
   Fax: 206-323-0259 paddy@articicecream.com
Ice cream
   President/CEO: Bill Dinsmore
   Sales Manager: Jerry Gregory
   General Manager: S Paddy Narayan

Estimated Sales:$20-50 Million
Number Employees: 50-99
Type of Packaging: Private Label

792 Artichoke Kitchen
P.O.Box 159
Hamilton, NC 27840-0159   252-798-2471
Pickles, relish, jams, jellies
    President: Ellen Jackson
Estimated Sales:$570,000
Number Employees: 5-9

793 Artist Coffee
51 Harvey Road
Londonderry, NH 03053-7414   603-434-9385
        Fax: 603-216-8029   866-440-4511
dan@artistcoffee.com   www.artistcoffee.com
Producer of gourmet coffee, tea and candy for promotional trade. Specializing in Custom Labeling with very special products.
    President: Tom Rushton
    Marketing Director: Dan Sewell
Estimated Sales:$ 3 - 5 Million
Number Employees: 1-4
Type of Packaging: Consumer, Private Label
Other Locations:
    Lambent Technologies
    Gurnee IL
Brands:
    Cirashine
    Erucical
    Hodag
    Lamchem
    Lumisolve
    Lumisorb
    Lumulse
    Oleocal
    Polycal

794 Arturo's Bakery
53 Interstate Ln
Waterbury, CT 06705-2658   203-754-3056
Cookies
    President: Fred Napolitano
Estimated Sales:$1-2.5 Million appx.
Number Employees: 5-9

795 Artuso Pastry Foods
158 S 12th Ave
Mt Vernon, NY 10550-2915   914-663-8806
    Fax: 914-663-8815   sales@artusopastry.com
                www.artusopastry.com
Cannoli shells and cream, lobster tails, custards and pastry shells. Italian pastries.
    CEO: Anthony Artuso Jr
    CEO: Anthony Artuso Jr
Estimated Sales:$ 10 - 20 Million
Number Employees: 20-49
Brands:
    ARTUSO

796 Artuso Pastry Shop
670 E 187th St
Bronx, NY 10458-6802   718-367-2515
    Fax: 718-367-2553   sales@artusopastry.com
                www.artusopastry.com
Italian pastry ingredients, fresh and frozen
    Owner: Anthony Artuso Sr
    CEO: Anthony Artuso Jr
Estimated Sales:$1-2.5 Million
Number Employees: 20-49
Brands:
    ARTUSO

797 Arway Confections
3425 N Kimball Ave
Chicago, IL 60618-5505   773-267-5770
    Fax: 773-267-0610 www.arwayconfections.com
Manufacturer of candy including brittles, butter toffee, panned and enrobed products, sponge candy and glazed nuts
    President/Owner: James Resnick
    Sales Manager: Craig Leva
    Purchasing: Craig Leva
Estimated Sales:$5-10 Million
Number Employees: 20-49
Type of Packaging: Bulk

798 Asael Farr & Sons CompanY (Russells Ice Cream)
P.O.Box 651250
Salt Lake City, UT 84165-1250   801-484-8724
                Fax: 801-484-8768
michael.farr@farrsicecream.com
        www.farrsicecream.com
Processor of ice creams, yogurts, sorbets, ice cream and yogurt mixes, specialty foods, etc
    President: Dexter Farr
    CEO: Michael Farr
Estimated Sales:$ .5 - 1 million
Number Employees: 1-4
Brands:
    Farr
    Russell's

799 Aseltine Cider Company
533 Lamoreaux Dr NW
Comstock Park, MI 49321-9204   616-784-7676
                Fax: 616-784-7676
Bottled apple products
    Owner: John Klamt
    General Manager: John Klant
Estimated Sales:$2.5-5 Million
Number Employees: 10-19

800 Asher Candy
1803 Research Blvd # 201
Rockville, MD 20850-6106   301-309-6161
    Fax: 301-309-6162   sales@sherwoodbrands.com
                www.sherwoodbrands.com
Flavored candy canes
    President: Uziel Frydman
*Estimated Sales:*G
Number Employees: 50-99
Brands:
    ASHER

801 Asher's Chocolates
80 Wambold Rd
Souderton, PA 18964   215-721-3276
        Fax: 215-721-3209   800-438-8882
        info@ashers.com   www.ashers.com
chocolate and confections, including chocolate-covered pretzels potato chips, and graham crackers. The company also produces boxed assortments (including truffles, chews, nuts, cordials, and creams) and gift baskets, fudgepecan-caramel patties, almond bark, and sugar-free and low-carb assortments.
    President/CEO: David Asher
    CFO: Charles Clark
    VP Sales/Marketing: Jeff Asher
    VP Operations: Steve Marcanello
Estimated Sales:$17.7 Million
Number Employees: 120

802 Ashers Chocolates
19 Susquehanna Ave
Lewistown, PA 17044-2332   717-248-8613
        Fax: 717-248-8637   800-343-0520
Processor and exporter of chocolates
    President: John Asher
Estimated Sales:$10-24.9 Million
Number Employees: 50-99
Sq. footage: 46000
Type of Packaging: Consumer, Food Service, Private Label, Bulk

803 Ashland Milling
P.O.Box 1775
Ashland, VA 23005-4775   804-798-8329
        Fax: 804-798-9357   amc@ashlandmilling.com
                www.byrdmill.com
Manufacturer of flour, cornmeal and mixes
    President: Todd Attkisson
    General Manager: Lynwood Atkinson
Estimated Sales:$ 10 - 20 Million
Number Employees: 20-49
Brands:
    BLUE BARN
    DIAMOND
    EUKANUBA
    HYLAND
    KALMBACH
    PURINA

804 Ashland Plantation Gourmet
133 Highway 1177
Bunkie, LA 71322-9773   318-346-6600
                Fax: 318-346-4666
    President: Kim White
*Estimated Sales:*Less than $500,000
Number Employees: 1-4

805 Ashland Sausage Company
280 S Westgate Dr
Carol Stream, IL 60188-2243   630-690-2600
                Fax: 630-690-2612
Processor of sausage
    President: Stanley Podgorski
    Purchasing: Stanley Podgorski
Estimated Sales:$1-2.5 Million
Number Employees: 10-19
Type of Packaging: Consumer, Food Service
Brands:
    ASHLAND

806 Ashland Vineyards
2775 E Main St
Ashland, OR 97520-9781   541-488-0088
        Fax: 541-488-5857 www.winenet.com
Wines
    Owner/President: Philip Kodak
    Owner/CEO: Kathleen Kodak
*Estimated Sales:*Less than $400,000
Number Employees: 1-4
Brands:
    Ashland

807 Ashley Food Company, Inc.
P.O.Box 912
Sudbury, MA 01776-0912   978-579-8988
        Fax: 978-579-8989   800-617-2823
maddog@ashleyfood.com   www.ashleyfood.com
    President: David Ashley
Estimated Sales:$1-2.5 Million
Number Employees: 1-4
Brands:
    JOE PERRY'S
    MAD CAT
    MAD DOG
    WEIR'S

808 Ashley Foods
P.O.Box 912
Sudbury, MA 01776-0912   978-579-8988
        Fax: 978-579-8989   800-617-2823
maddog@ashleyfood.com   www.ashleyfood.com
Sauces
    President: David Ashley
    Marketing Director: David Ashley
    New Product Development: David Ashley
Estimated Sales:$5-10 Million
Number Employees: 5-9
Type of Packaging: Consumer, Private Label
Brands:
    Madcat
    Maddog

809 Ashman Manufacturing & Distributing Company
P.O.Box 1068
Virginia Beach, VA 23451-0068   757-428-6734
        Fax: 757-437-0398   800-641-9924
admin@ashmanco.com   www.ashmanco.com
Manufacturer of a wide variety of gourmet sauces, salsas, hot sauces, dry blends, marinades, dessert sauces and drink mixes
    President: Tim Ashman
    Sales Manager: Joel Lutchin
Estimated Sales:$5-10 million
Number Employees: 10-19
Type of Packaging: Consumer, Private Label
Brands:
    Ashman Armbruster's
    Ashman Bodean's
    Ashman Boli's
    Ashman Boulevard Cafe
    Ashman Chili Peppers
    Ashman Coastal Cactus
    Ashman Deathwish
    Ashman Edwards Surry Sopping Sauce
    Ashman Four Corners
    Ashman Fuller's
    Ashman George's
    Ashman Hog Heaven Sooee Sauce
    Ashman Hog Wild Bbq Sauce
    Ashman Hot Wing Sauce
    Ashman House
    Ashman House London Broil Sauce
    Ashman Jimmy Sauce
    Ashman Joni's
    Ashman King Street Blues
    Ashman Little Red Raspberry Dijon
    Ashman London House
    Ashman Magnolia
    Ashman Mini Malbon's Bbq Sauce

Ashman Nana's
Ashman Old Hickory Grille & Dip
Ashman Pass Out
Ashman Pigman's
Ashman Red Hot Rooster Sauce
Ashman Rockland's Bbq Sauce
Ashman St. Ann's Bay Jamaican Jerk
Ashman Tailgate
Ashman Tuscan Gardens Caponata
Ashman Virginia Gentleman
Ashman Whitley's
Ashman an Original Marinade
Ashman the Jewish Mother

810 Asiamerica Ingredients

245 Old Hook Rd # 3
Westwood, NJ 07675-3174   201-497-5993
Fax: 201-497-5994   201-497-5531
info@asiamericaingredients.com
www.asiamericaingredients.com

Processor, importer, exporter and distributor of bulk vitamins, amino acids, nutraceuticals, aromatic chemicals, food additives, herbs, mineral nutrients and pharmaceuticals.

President: Mark Zhang
Estimated Sales: $5-10 Million
Number Employees: 5
Type of Packaging: Bulk

811 Asian Brands

2733 McCone Avenue
Hayward, CA 94545-1614   510-523-7474
Fax: 510-523-4817   info@asianbrands.com
www.asianbrands.com
Processor, importer and exporter of natural gourmet rice pilafs, Indian basmati and Thai jasmine rice; importer of spices and botanical herbs
President: Alok Mohan
Estimated Sales: $2.5-5 Million
Number Employees: 5-9
Sq. footage: 14000
Type of Packaging: Consumer, Food Service, Private Label, Bulk
Brands:
  BAHAAR
  GOURMET GURU
  GOURMET GURU ALL NATURALL SPECIALTY
  Gourmet Guru
  Gourmet Guru All-Natural Specialty
  SEVEN STAR
  Seven Star
  TOHFA

812 Asian Foods

1300 L Orient St
St Paul, MN 55117-3995   651-558-2400
Fax: 651-558-2404   afiinfo@asianfoods.com
www.asianfoods.com
Supplier of Asian products
President: Mitch Berg
CEO: Frank Hamel
Sales Manager: Paul Hamel
Estimated Sales: $67 Million
Number Employees: 100-249
Type of Packaging: Food Service, Private Label
Other Locations:
  Kansas City MO
  Hampshire IL
Brands:
  Heartland

813 Askinosie Chocolate

514 E Commercial St
Springfield, MO 65803   417-862-9900
Fax: 417-862-9904   kesha@askinosie.com
www.askinosie.com

Chocolate/cocoa products
Operations Manager: Jill Tilman
Number Employees: 6

814 Aslanis Seafoods

10 Granite Street
Suite 300
Quincy, MA 02169-5021   781-740-0002
Fax: 781-871-8806   800-876-3712
asi@aslanis.com   www.aslanis.com
Processor and wholesaler/distributor of fresh and frozen fish and seafood.
Chairman/CEO: Patricia Aslanis
Purchasing: John MacCartny
Estimated Sales: $50-100 Million
Number Employees: 50-99
Type of Packaging: Consumer, Food Service, Private Label, Bulk
Brands:
  CAPTAIN NICK
  GLORIA
  HARBOR POINT
  PIER 12
  SIGNATURE SERIES

815 Aspen Food Marketing

4500 Cherry Creek Drive S
Suite 970
Denver, CO 80246   303-320-3400
Fax: 303-320-0226
unfo@aspenfoodmarketing.com
A Colorado based brokerage firm, specializing in sales and marketing to the retailers in the trading area.
President: John Olson
Estimated Sales: $30 Million
Number Employees: 14
Type of Packaging: Consumer, Food Service

816 Aspen Foods

1300 Higgins Rd # 100
Park Ridge, IL 60068-5766   847-384-5940
Fax: 847-384-5961 www.kochfoods.com
Manufacturer and exporter of gourmet frozen poultry products
President: Michael Fields
CEO: Joseph C Grendys
National Sales Manager: Mike Fields
Director Plant Operation: Ken Springer
Estimated Sales: $20-50 Million
Number Employees: 20-49
Sq. footage: 45000
Parent Co: Koch Foods
Type of Packaging: Consumer, Food Service, Private Label
Brands:
  ANTIOCH FARMS
  Chef Maxlotte

817 Aspen Mulling CompanyInc.

302 Aabc
Aspen, CO 81611-2540   970-925-5027
Fax: 970-925-5408   800-622-7736
info@aspenspices.com   www.aspenspices.com
Manufacturer and exporter of mulling spices
Manager: Leo Varade
Estimated Sales: Under $5 Million
Number Employees: 5-9
Type of Packaging: Consumer, Food Service

818 Assets Grille & Southwest Brewing Company

6910 Montgomery Boulevard NE
Albuquerque, NM 87109-1406   505-889-6400
Fax: 505-889-0264
Brewer of beer, ale and stout
Owner: Mark Devesti
Estimated Sales: $2.5-5 Million
Number Employees: 50-99
Parent Co: Assets Brewing Company
Type of Packaging: Consumer, Food Service, Bulk

819 Assets Health Foods

909 Merritt Drive
Apt C
Hillsborough, NJ 08844-5310   908-874-8004
Fax: 908-874-8668   888-849-2048
frisinanatfoods@rcn.com
Natural flavors, herbs, botanicals, nutraceuticals, soya products, product development
Estimated Sales: $3 Million
Number Employees: 5-9

820 Associated Bakers Products

7 High St # 208
Huntington, NY 11743-3417   631-673-3841
Fax: 631-673-3870
Manufactures dried replacement supply fruit juice blends to bakeries.
Owner: Louis Mayoka
VP: Louis Mayoka
Estimated Sales: $ 5 - 10 Million
Number Employees: 5-9
Sq. footage: 10000
Type of Packaging: Bulk
Brands:
  ALBUMIX
  NO-TEG
  OVO-TEG
  VITEG

821 Associated Brands

335 Judson Street
Toronto, ON M8Z 1B2
Canada   416-259-4317
Fax: 416-259-4317   800-265-0050
Supplier snack mix, puffed cereal, hot cocoa, dry soup mix, low calorie and concentrate fruit drinks crystals, plastic food wrap, gelatin, desserts, packaged side dishes, pie filling mixes, plastic food bags

822 Associated Brands, Inc.

P.O.Box 788
Medina, NY 14103-0788   585-798-3475
Fax: 585-798-1931   800-265-0050
info@associatedbrands.com
www.associatedbrands.com
Processor and exporter of dehydrated and packaged food mixes including instant tea, meals in a cup, soup, bouillon, hot cocoa, noodles and sauce, artificial sweeteners and fruit drinks; importer of sugar; also, dry food packagingavailable
Plant Manager: Jim Dimatteo
Estimated Sales: $ 50 - 100 Million
Number Employees: 100-249
Sq. footage: 393000
Parent Co: Associated Brands, Inc.
Type of Packaging: Consumer, Food Service, Private Label, Bulk
Brands:
  COOKS
  GOLDEN KETTLE
  NELSON
  PRO-SEAL
  SADANO'S
  SWEET * 10
  SWEET SPRINKLES
  THIRST QUENCH'R

823 Associated Fruit Company

3721 Colver Rd
Phoenix, OR 97535-9705   541-535-1787
Fax: 541-535-6936
Manufacturer and exporter of fresh fruit including plums and pears
President: David Lowry
Purchasing: Scott Martinez
Estimated Sales: $1-2.5 Million
Number Employees: 5-9
Type of Packaging: Bulk

824 (HQ)Associated Milk Producers

315 North Broadway
PO Box 455
New Ulm, MN 56073   507-354-8295
Fax: 507-359-8651   800-533-3580
www.ampi.com
Manufacturer of cheese and dairy products
President/CEO: Ed Welch
Estimated Sales: $1.7 Billion
Number Employees: 1,800
Type of Packaging: Consumer, Food Service, Private Label
Brands:
  CASS-CLAY®

825 Associated Milk Producers

1864 311th Avenue
P.O. Box 1013
Dawson, MN 56232   320-769-2994
Fax: 320-769-4692 www.ampi.com
Dairy
Manager: Joe Vaske
Production Manager: Richard Johnson
Estimated Sales: I
Number Employees: 100
Parent Co: Associated Milk Producers

Brands:
CASS-CLAY®

826 Associated Milk Producers
3281 40th Street
Arlington, IA 50606 563-933-4521
www.ampi.com
Dairy
Manager: Gary Johnson
Estimated Sales: I
Number Employees: 71
Parent Co: Associated Milk Producers
Brands:
CASS-CLAY®

827 Associated Milk Producers
220 East Center
P.O. Box 6
Blair, WI 54616 608-989-2535
www.ampi.com
Dairy
Manager: Mark Frederexion
Estimated Sales: I
Number Employees: 80
Parent Co: Associated Milk Producers
Brands:
CASS-CLAY®

828 Associated Milk Producers
4107 W Michigan Street
P.O. Box 16387
Duluth, MN 55816 218-624-4803
www.ampi.com
Dairy
Manager: Matt Quade
Estimated Sales: I
Number Employees: 5
Parent Co: Associated Milk Producers
Brands:
CASS-CLAY®

829 Associated Milk Producers
200 20th Street North
P.O. Box 3126
Fargo, ND 58108-3126 701-293-6455
www.ampi.com
Dairy
Estimated Sales: I
Number Employees: 5-9
Parent Co: Associated Milk Producers
Brands:
CASS-CLAY®

830 Associated Milk Producers
136 East Railway
P.O. Box 430
Freeman, SD 57029 605-925-4234
www.ampi.com
Dairy
Manager: Sandy Hilbret
Estimated Sales: I
Number Employees: 38
Parent Co: Associated Milk Producers
Brands:
CASS-CLAY®

831 Associated Milk Producers
127 Commercial Avenue West
P.O. Box 825
Hoven, SD 57450 605-948-2211
www.ampi.com
Dairy
Estimated Sales: I
Number Employees: 38
Parent Co: Associated Milk Producers
Brands:
CASS-CLAY®

832 Associated Milk Producers
14193 County Highway South
Jim Falls, WI 54748 715-382-4113
www.ampi.com
Dairy
Manager: John Breene
Estimated Sales: I
Number Employees: 150
Parent Co: Associated Milk Producers
Brands:
CASS-CLAY®

833 Associated Milk Producers
1305 19th SW
Mason City, IA 50401 641-424-6111
www.ampi.com

Dairy
Manager: Sylvia Brainard
Marketing Manager: Jim Walsh
Estimated Sales: I
Number Employees: 58
Parent Co: Associated Milk Producers
Brands:
CASS-CLAY®

834 Associated Milk Producers
200 Railroad Street
P.O. Box 205
Paynesville, MN 56362 320-243-3794
www.ampi.com
Dairy
Manager: Matt Quade
Estimated Sales: I
Number Employees: 78
Parent Co: Associated Milk Producers
Brands:
CASS-CLAY®

835 Associated Milk Producers
301 Brooks Street
Portage, WI 53901 608-742-2114
www.ampi.com
Dairy
Manager: Don Weideman
Estimated Sales: I
Number Employees: 50-99
Parent Co: Associated Milk Producers
Brands:
CASS-CLAY®

836 Associated Milk Producers
101 West First Street
Sanborn, IA 51248 712-729-3255
www.ampi.com
Dairy
Manager: Ed Welch
Estimated Sales: I
Number Employees: 70
Parent Co: Associated Milk Producers
Brands:
CASS-CLAY®

837 Associated Milk Producers
312 Center Street
P.O. Box 98
New Ulm, MN 56073 507-233-4600
www.ampi.com
Line of dairy products
Plant Manager: William Swan
Director, Purchasing: John Russell
Estimated Sales: H
Number Employees: 50
Parent Co: Associated Milk Producers
Brands:
CASS-CLAY®

838 (HQ)Associated Potato Growers, Inc.
2001 N 6th St
Grand Forks, ND 58203-1584 701-775-4614
Fax: 701-746-5767 800-437-4685
apgi@gfherald.infi.net www.apgspud.com
Potatoes and potato products
Manager: Paul Dolan
Sales Representative: Steve Johnson
Estimated Sales: $50-100 Million
Number Employees: 50-99
Other Locations:
Associated Potato Growers
Grafton ND
Associated Potato Growers
Drayton ND
Brands:
APG
Dole
Holsom
Natives Pride
Nodark
Potato Mity Red

839 Assouline & Ting
2050 Richmond St # A
Philadelphia, PA 19125-4323 215-627-3000
Fax: 215-627-3517 800-521-4491
info@caviar.com www.assoulineandting.com

Processor, wholesaler/distributor, importer and exporter of gourmet foods including snails, mustard, chocolate, caviar, frozen fruits and purees, flavored vinegar, etc
President: Joel Assouline
Operations Manager: S Schwartz
Estimated Sales: $10-20 Million
Number Employees: 1-4
Sq. footage: 45000
Other Locations:
Caviar Assouline
Philadelphia PA
Brands:
ABASA
AMPHORA
CAVIAR ASSOULINE
CORICELLI
MAXIM'S
ROMEO Y GUILIETA
VALRHONA
VILLA VITTORIA
VOSS

840 Asti Holdings Ltd
320 Stewardson Way
Unit 2-3
New Westminster, BC V3M 6C3
Canada 604-523-6866
Fax: 604-523-6880 www.goldenbonbon.com
Candy
President: Ricardo Mazzucco
Estimated Sales: $1.7 Million
Number Employees: 20

841 Astor Chocolate Corporation
651 New Hampshire Ave
Lakewood, NJ 08701-5452 732-901-1001
Fax: 732-901-1003 info@astorchocolates.com
www.astorchocolates.com
Manufacturer, importer and exporter of chocolate including fund raising, foiled novelties, bars, truffles, mints, shells and boxed.
President: Erwin Grunhut
VP: David Sanborn
Estimated Sales: $10-20 Million
Number Employees: 100-249
Sq. footage: 100000
Type of Packaging: Consumer, Food Service, Private Label, Bulk
Brands:
AFTER DARK
LE BELGE CHOCOLATIER
PARTY FAVORS BY ASTOR
PASTRY ESSENTIALS
SQUARE ONE

842 Astor Products
5244 Edgewood Court
Jacksonville, FL 32254-3601 904-783-5000
Fax: 904-783-5294
Manufactures teas, coffees and spices.
President: James Kufeldt
Vice President: JH Childers
Manager: Denny Courson
Estimated Sales: $ 26 Million
Number Employees: 204
Parent Co: Winn-Dixie Stores
Type of Packaging: Consumer
Brands:
DIXIE
FISHER

843 Astral Extracts Ltd
160 Eileen Way
Syosset, NY 11791-5300 516-496-2505
Fax: 516-496-4248 info@astralextracts.com
www.astralextracts.com
Processor, wholesaler, distributor, importer and exporter of fruit juice concentrates, essential oils and citrus products
President: Cynthia Astrack
General Manager: Joan Pace
Estimated Sales: $5-10 Million
Sq. footage: 30000
Type of Packaging: Food Service, Private Label, Bulk

844 Astro Dairy Products
25 Rakely Court
Etobicoke, ON M9C 5G2
Canada 416-622-2811
Fax: 416-622-4180 www.astro.ca
/www.parmalat.ca

Manufacturer of dairy products including yogurt, cottage cheese, sour cream and cream cheese
President: James Biltekoff
COO: Larry Bushey
CFO: Michael McFadden
Number Employees: 200
Parent Co: Parmalat Canada
Type of Packaging: Consumer, Food Service, Private Label, Bulk
Brands:
Astro
Biobest

845 At Last Naturals
401 Columbus Ave
Valhalla, NY 10595-1325   914-747-3599
          Fax: 914-747-3791   800-527-8123
info@atlastnaturals.com   www.atlastnaturals.com
Manufacturer and exporter of laxative tea and natural herbal health products.
VP: Fred Rosen
Estimated Sales: $ 1 - 3 Million
Number Employees: 5-9
Sq. footage: 37000
Type of Packaging: Consumer
Brands:
DHEA
INNERCLEAN
SUL-RAY
VALERIAN

846 Atalanta Corporation
1 Atalanta Plz
Elizabeth, NJ 07206-2120   908-352-6517
          Fax: 908-351-1978 www.atalanta1.com
Chesse, seafood, meats, giftware
President: Jackie Foltf
CFO: Charles Stough
VP Marketing: Sal Mazzella
Sales Director: Jim Marsh
Estimated Sales: $100-$500 Million
Number Employees: 100-249
Other Locations:
Atalanta Corporation
Dawsonville GA
Atalanta Corporation
Lexington MA
Atalanta Corporation
Bartlett IL
Atalanta Corporation
Arlington TX
Atalanta Corporation
Kingwood TX
Atalanta Corporation
Rockford MI
Atalanta Corporation
Jacksonville FL
Atalanta Corporation
Los Angeles CA
Atalanta Corporation
Miami FL
Atalanta Corporation
Elizabeth NJ
Atalanta Corporation
Union City CA
Atalanta Corporation
Sewell NJ
Brands:
Atalanta
Calypso
Casa Diva
Del Destino
Greenleaf
Ham Nik
International Choice
Le Conchon D'Oro
Marshall's
Martel
Mill Dance Brand
Nordic Pride
Polonaise
Royal Danube
Royal Kerry
Royal Manhout
Shaeen
Tivoli

847 (HQ)Ateeco
P.O.Box 606
Shenandoah, PA 17976-0606   570-462-2745
          Fax: 570-462-1392   800-233-3170
ConsumerContact@pierogies.com
          www.pierogies.com

Frozen pierogies, specialty foods, pasta, potatoes
President: Thomas Twardzik
VP: Tim Twardzik
Executive VP: Tim Twardzik
Director Operations: Ray Stasulli
Sales Director: John Putney
Public Relations: Wayne Holben
Director Operations: Ed Kerins
Estimated Sales: $20-50 Million
Number Employees: 100-249
Sq. footage: 350
Type of Packaging: Private Label

848 Athena Oil
3082 36th St
Long Island City, NY 11103-4705   718-956-8893
          Fax: 718-956-5813   m.scoullis@att.net
                    www.athenaoil.com
Olive oil
President: Moschos Scoullis
Estimated Sales: $1.2 Million
Number Employees: 10-19

849 Athena's Silverland®Desserts
439 Des Plaines Ave
Forest Park, IL 60130-1763   708-488-0800
      Fax: 708-488-0894   800-737-3636
                peter@silverlanddesserts.com
                www.silverlanddesserts.com
Tortes, dessert bars, brownies, cookies, cakes
fat-free and low-fat brownies
President/Owner: Athena Uslander
Sales: Peter Wodek
Operations: Chris Ogden
Estimated Sales: $2.5-5 Million
Number Employees: 10-19
Number of Brands: 1
Type of Packaging: Consumer, Food Service, Private Label
Brands:
Silverland

850 Athens Baking Company
3630 E Wawona Ave # 101
Fresno, CA 93725-9028   559-485-3024
          Fax: 559-485-4156 www.athensbaking.com
Manufacturer of filo dough and filo products
Owner: Dave Smart
Estimated Sales: $10-20 Million
Type of Packaging: Consumer, Food Service, Private Label
Brands:
ATHENS

851 Athens Pastries & Frozen Foods
13600 Snow Rd
Cleveland, OH 44142-2546   216-676-8500
          Fax: 216-676-0609   800-837-5683
                    www.athens.com
Processor of pastries, frozen strudel and pita bread
CFO: Bob Tansing
VP Sales/Marketing: Bill Buckingham
VP Operations: Jeff Swint
Plant Manager: Jeff Swint
Estimated Sales: $10-24.9 Million
Number Employees: 100-249
Number of Brands: 2
Number of Products: 200
Sq. footage: 120000
Type of Packaging: Consumer, Food Service, Private Label, Bulk
Brands:
APOLLO
ATHENS

852 Atka Pride Seafoods
234 Gold St
Juneau, AK 99801-1211   907-586-0161
          Fax: 907-586-0165 www.apicda.com
Chairman: George Dirks
CEO: Larry Cotter
Number Employees: 1-4

853 Atkins Elegant Desserts
11852 Allisonville Rd
Fishers, IN 46038-2312   317-570-1850
          Fax: 317-773-3766   800-887-8808
                latkins@atkins-intl-foods.com
          www.atkins-intl-foods.com/home.html

Processor of frozen cheesecakes, pies, cakes and pastries.
Manager: Debbie Llewellyn
CEO: Tom Atkins Jr
CFO: Tom Atkins
R&D: Darrell Bell
Quality Control: John Parent
Canadian National Manager: Wayne Barefoot
VP Sales & Marketing: Bob Barry
National Accounts Manager: Lisa Atkins Miller
Operations: Bill Beglin
Production: Jeff Fascko
Plant Manager: Terry Graves
Purchasing: Denise Miller
Estimated Sales: $12-13 Million
Number Employees: 50-99
Sq. footage: 35000
Type of Packaging: Consumer, Food Service, Private Label
Brands:
ATKINS

854 Atkins Ginseng Farms
RR 1
Waterford, ON NOE 1Y0
Canada   519-443-4433
          Fax: 519-443-4565   800-265-0239
                info@atkinsginseng.com
Manufacturer, importer and exporter of ginseng products including capsules, also grower of american ginseng
Owner/President: Micheal Atkins
Number Employees: 5-9
Sq. footage: 1500
Type of Packaging: Consumer, Private Label, Bulk
Brands:
Atkins
Gin Ultimate
Golden Dreams
Golden Grower
Northern Serenitea
Northern Spirit

855 Atkins Nutritionals
105 Maxess Road
Melville, NY 11747-3854   631-953-4000
                              800-628-5467
                          www.atkins.com
Atkins diet food, candy and nutritional bars.
CEO: Christopher Smith
Senior VP/CFO: Joel Shiff
VP Sales: Jason Shiver
Estimated Sales: $ 5 - 10 Million
Number Employees: 50-99
Type of Packaging: Consumer, Food Service
Brands:
ATKINS
ATKINS ADVANTAGE
ATKINS BAKERY
ATKINS ENDULGE
ATKINS KITCHEN

856 Atkinson Candies Company
P.O.Box 150220
Lufkin, TX 75915-0220   936-639-2333
          Fax: 936-639-2337 www.atkinsoncandy.com
Manufacturer of candy
President: Eric Atkinson
Estimated Sales: $2.5-5 Million
Number Employees: 100-249
Sq. footage: 100000
Type of Packaging: Consumer, Food Service

857 Atkinson Candy Company
P.O.Box 150220
Lufkin, TX 75915-0220   936-639-2333
          Fax: 936-639-2337   800-231-1203
                www.atkinsoncandy.com
Manufacturer and exporter of candy, including peanut butter and peppermint candies
President: Eric Atkinson
Estimated Sales: $25-49.9 Million
Number Employees: 100-249
Sq. footage: 100000
Type of Packaging: Consumer, Bulk
Brands:
CHICK-O-STICK
COCONUT LONGBOYS
CRUNCHY PEANUT BUTTER BARS
MINT TWISTS
PECO BRITTLE
RAINBOW COCONUT
RAINBOW STICKS

858 Atkinson Milling Company
95 Atkinson Mill Rd
Selma, NC 27576-9067   919-965-3547
        Fax: 919-202-0523 800-948-5707
        information@atkinsonmilling.com
                www.atkinsonmilling.com
Processor of: corn meal, hushpuppy mixes, breaders,
biscuit mixes, frozen hushpuppies, cornbread sticks,
chicken dumplings
        President: Glenn Wheeler
        CEO: Ray Wheeler
        VP: Ben Wheeler
Estimated Sales: $5 Million
Number Employees: 20-49
Type of Packaging: Consumer, Food Service, Pri-
vate Label, Bulk
Brands:
        ATKINSON'S
        BODDIE
        CATTAIL
        ELLIS DAVIS

**859 (HQ)Atlanta Bread Company
International, Inc.**
1955 Lake Park Dr SE # 400
Smyrna, GA 30080-8855   770-432-0933
        Fax: 770-444-1991 800-398-3728
                www.atlantabread.com
Processor of bread, pastries, bagels, rolls,muf-
fins,sandwiches,salads and desserts. Also featuring
expanded coffee selection
        President/CEO: Jerry Couvaras
        CFO: Alan Sack
Estimated Sales: $1-2.5 Million
Number Employees: 50-99
Type of Packaging: Consumer, Food Service
Brands:
        ATLANTA BREAD

860 Atlanta Brewing Company
15 Knox Rd
Bar Harbor, ME 04609-7770   207-288-2337
        Fax: 207-288-2589 800-475-5417
                realale@atlanticbrewing.com
                www.atlantabrewing.com
Processor of seasonal beer, ale, stout, lager and
pilsner
        Owner: Douglas Maffucci
        CEO: Robet Budd
Estimated Sales: $10-20 Million
Number Employees: 10-19
Type of Packaging: Consumer, Food Service
Brands:
        RED BRICK

861 Atlanta Burning
3781 Happy Valley Cir
Newnan, GA 30263-4098   770-253-8100
        Fax: 770-253-9941 800-665-5611
                information@atlantaburning.com
                www.atlantaburning.com
Manufacturer of hot sauces, BBQ sauce. Supplier of
food related products
        Owner: Marilyn Witt
Estimated Sales: $500,000-$1,000,000
Number Employees: 1-4
Type of Packaging: Consumer, Bulk
Brands:
        Atlanta Burning

862 Atlanta Coffee & Tea Company
5400 Truman Dr
Decatur, GA 30035-3912   770-981-6774
        Fax: 770-981-6697 800-426-4781
                sales@atlantacoffeeandtea.com
                www.atlantacoffeeandtea.com
Processor and importer of coffee and tea; coffee
roaster and tea packer, private label packaging avail-
able
        President: Beth Black
        VP: Harris Carver
Estimated Sales: $5-9.9 Million
Number Employees: 10-19
Type of Packaging: Food Service, Private Label

863 Atlanta Coffee Roasters
2205 Lavista Rd NE
Atlanta, GA 30329-3917   404-636-1038
        Fax: 404-255-1189 800-252-8211
                info@atlantacoffeeroasters.com
                www.atlantacoffeeroasters.com

Coffee
        Owner: William Letbetter
        CFO: Stephen Burress
Estimated Sales: $910,000
Number Employees: 5-9
Brands:
        Brazil Celebes
        Celebes
        Columbian
        Costa rica
        Jamaica Bluemountain
        Laminita

864 Atlanta Fish Market
245 Pharr Rd NE
Atlanta, GA 30305-2200   404-262-3165
                        Fax: 404-240-6665
Seafood
        Manager: Jason Zaleski
Estimated Sales: $ 5 - 10 Million
Number Employees: 100-249

865 Atlanta Flagship Dairy
777 Memorial Dr SE
Atlanta, GA 30316-1186   404-688-2671
                Fax: 404-581-9650 800-224-0669
Manufacturer of orange juice, citrus punch, teas,
fruit juice drinks, milk, half and half, cream, yogurt
and ice cream including novelties; importer of pasta,
sauces and filled cookies
        Plant Manager: Rudy Terrizzi
Estimated Sales: $14.7 Million
Number Employees: 220
Sq. footage: 78000
Type of Packaging: Consumer, Food Service, Pri-
vate Label
Brands:
        PARAMLAT/NEW ATLANTA DAIRIES
        PARMALAT/FARM BEST

866 Atlantic
17 State St
New York, NY 10004-1501   212-480-2255
                        Fax: 212-248-4102
Coffee
        President: Henry Dunlop
        CFO: David Hermanns
        Purchasing: Henry Dunlop
Estimated Sales: $10-20 Million
Number Employees: 20-49

867 Atlantic Aqua Farms
RR 2
Vernon Bridge, PE C0A 2E0
Canada   902-651-2563
                        Fax: 902-651-2513
Manufacturer and exporter of fresh mussels, oysters
and clams-hardshell
        GM: Brian Fortune
Number Employees: 50
Type of Packaging: Consumer, Food Service, Pri-
vate Label, Bulk

868 Atlantic Baking Company
6425 Penn Ave
Pittsburgh, PA 15206-4037   412-361-2516
        Fax: 412-365-9356 www.atlanticbaking.com
Baking products
        President: Dale Killmeyer
        Executive VP Marketing: William Baxter
        Executive VP Sales: William Baxter
Number Employees: 250-499

869 Atlantic Blueberry Company
7201 Weymouth Rd
Hammonton, NJ 08037-3414   609-561-8600
        Fax: 609-561-5033 art@atlanticblueberry.com
                www.atlanticblueberry.com
Processor and exporter of fresh and frozen blueber-
ries
        President/CEO: Arthur Galletta
        VP: Paul Galletta
        Sales: Art Galletta
        Operations: Bob Galletta
        Plant Manager: Denny Doyle
        Purchasing: Art Galletta
Estimated Sales: $8-9.5 Million Appx.
Number Employees: 1,000-4,999
Number of Brands: 1
Number of Products: 1
Sq. footage: 80000
Type of Packaging: Private Label
Brands:
        ATLANTIC BLUEBERRY

870 (HQ)Atlantic Capes Fisheries
P.O.Box 555
Cape May, NJ 08204-0555   609-884-3000
        Fax: 609-884-3261 jtirello@atlanticcapes.com
                www.atlanticcapes.com
Processor of fresh and frozen scallops, fish, clams,
mackerel, squid and monkfish; importer of scallops;
exporter of fresh and frozen scallops, squid,
butterfish and mackerel
        President: Daniel Cohen
        VP Sales/Marketing: Jeff Bolton
        Sales Manager: Peter Hughes
        General Manager: John Tirello
        Plant Manager: Bob Bondurant
Estimated Sales: $15 Million
Number Employees: 20-49
Sq. footage: 20000
Other Locations:
        ACF Production Facility
        Point Pleasant Beach NJ
        ACF Sales/Marketing Office
        New Bedford MA
Brands:
        ATLANTIC CAPES
        CAPE MAY SALT

**871 Atlantic Chemicals Trading Of
North America, Inc.**
116 N. Maryland Avenue #210
Glendale, CA 91206   818-246-0077
                Fax: 818-246-0079 www.act.de
Manufacturer and distributor of flavors such as peppermint & menthol, sweeteners, acidifiers and preservatives.

872 Atlantic Fish Specialties
17 Walker Drive
Charlottetown, PE C1A 8S5
Canada   902-894-7005
                        Fax: 902-566-3546
Manufacturer and exporter of smoked salmon,
mackerel and trout
        President: Glenn Cooke
        GM: Doug Galen
Number Employees: 75
Type of Packaging: Consumer, Food Service, Pri-
vate Label, Bulk

873 (HQ)Atlantic Foods
2560 US Highway 22
307
Scotch Plains, NJ 07076-1529   800-328-7687
        Fax: 909-322-9993 www.atlanticfds.com
Manufacturer of seafood
        President: Derek Ivey
Estimated Sales: $3 Million
Number Employees: 40
Type of Packaging: Consumer, Food Service, Pri-
vate Label, Bulk

874 Atlantic Laboratories
41 Cross St
Waldoboro, ME 04572-5634   207-832-5376
        Fax: 207-832-6905 nak@noamkelp.com
                www.noamkelp.com
Processor and exporter of kelp meal and powder
        President: Robert Morse
        Sales: Foster Stroup
Estimated Sales: $ 3 - 5 Million
Number Employees: 5-9
Number of Brands: 1
Number of Products: 4
Sq. footage: 15000
Type of Packaging: Bulk
Brands:
        SEA LIFE

875 Atlantic Manufacturing Company
917 S Hanover St
Baltimore, MD 21230-3979   410-752-7223
                        Fax: 410-429-4224
Manufacturer of flavoring extracts for sno-cones,
syrups, coffees and bakery products
        Owner: Gloria Beyer
        Co-Owner: Jack Beyer
Estimated Sales: $ .5 - 1 million
Number Employees: 1-4
Brands:
        Atco

876 Atlantic Meat Company
2600 Louisville Road
Savannah, GA 31416-2845   912-964-8511
                              Fax: 912-964-6831
Processor, importer and exporter of fresh and frozen
ground beef, including hamburger patties
    President/CEO: Lee Javetz
    Sales Manager: James Rourke
    Purchasing Agent: Marc Javetz
Estimated Sales: $20-50 Million
Number Employees: 50
Sq. footage: 30000
Type of Packaging: Consumer, Food Service, Pri-
    vate Label, Bulk
Brands:
    Atlantic Meat
    Circle a Brands Beef Patties
    Circlea Beef Patties

**877 Atlantic Mussel
GrowersCorporation**
PO Box 70
Point Pleasant, PE C0A 1W0
Canada   902-962-3089
        Fax: 902-962-3741   800-838-3106
        www.atlanticmusselgrowers.pe.ca
Manufacturer and exporter of fresh mussels
    President: Wayne Sonerr
    Marketing Manager: Rollie McInnis
    Manager: Marjorie Henderson
Number Employees: 25
Type of Packaging: Consumer, Food Service, Pri-
    vate Label, Bulk

878 Atlantic Pork & Provisions
1014 Stanley Avenue
Brooklyn, NY 11208-5234   718-272-9550
        Fax: 718-272-9630   800-245-3536
Manufacturer of fresh hams; also, bologna and liver-
wurst loaves
    President: Jack Antinori
Number Employees: 50
Type of Packaging: Consumer
Brands:
    Atlantic
    Eidelweiss
    Laurel Hill
    Lifeline

879 Atlantic Premium Brands
1033 Skokie Blvd # 600
Northbrook, IL 60062-4101   847-412-6200
                              Fax: 847-412-9766
    info@atlanticpremiumbrands.com
    www.atlanticpremiumbrands.com
Manufacturer of bacon, sausage, luncheon meats,
boxed beef, pork and chicken and entrees including
barbecue, cooked, microwaveable, frozen and Cajun
    President/CEO: Thomas Dalton
    CFO: Michael Lambright
    Human Resources Corporate Manager: Jennifer
    Farwell
Estimated Sales: l
Number Employees: 250-499
Type of Packaging: Consumer, Private Label
Brands:
    BLUE RIBBON
    CARLTON
    JC POTTER
    RICHARD'S

**880 Atlantic Quality Spice
&Seasonings**
200 Raritan Center Parkway
Edison, NJ 08837-3612   732-574-3200
        Fax: 732-574-3344   800-584-0422
    info@aqspice.com   www.aqspice.com
Imports, processes and packs conventional and or-
ganic spices and blends thousands of seasoning for-
mulations.
    President: Stanley Gorski
    COO: Robert Ferguson
    Quality Control: Bob Machemer
    Sales: Tom Schmidt
    Plant Manager: Hector Herrera
    Purchasing: Hector Herrera
Estimated Sales: $25 Million
Number Employees: 100
Sq. footage: 150000
Type of Packaging: Consumer, Food Service, Pri-
    vate Label, Bulk
Brands:
    KINGRED

        ROSERED
        SUNRED
        Saigon Select

881 Atlantic Queen SeafoodsLimited
9960 Cote De Liesse
Suite 200
Lachine, QC H8T 1A1
Canada   514-636-5114
        Fax: 514-636-8045 www.luxurycrab.com
Manufacturer and exporter of frozen crab and crab
claws
    President: Paul-Aurele Chiasson
    Operations Manager: Andre Roger
Other Locations:
    Toronto ON
    Winnipeg MB
    Calgary AB
    Vancouver BC
    Danvers MA
    Seattle WA
Brands:
    Atlantic Queen
    Classic
    Luxury

882 Atlantic Salmon of Maine
57 Little River Drive
Belfast, ME 04915-6035   207-338-9028
        Fax: 207-338-6288   800-508-7861
    sales@us.fjord.com   www.majesticsalmon.com
Manufacturer of fresh salmon
    GM: David Peterson
    CFO: John Thibodeau
    Sales Manager: Mary Warner
    Receptionist: Becky Darres
Number Employees: 200
Type of Packaging: Food Service
Other Locations:
    Atlantic Salmon of Maine
    Swan Island ME

883 Atlantic Sea Pride
400 Dorchester Ave
South Boston, MA 02127-2407   617-269-7700
                              Fax: 617-269-7766
Processor and wholesaler/distributor of fresh fish
and fillets; serving the food service market
    President: Anthony Corenti
Estimated Sales: $ 20 - 50 Million
Number Employees: 20-49
Type of Packaging: Consumer, Food Service, Bulk

884 Atlantic Seacove
20 Newmarket Sq
Boston, MA 02118-2601   617-442-6206
    Fax: 617-442-6258   info@atlanticseacove.com
                              www.atlanticseacove.com
Wholesale dealers in fresh and frozen fish
    Manager: Al Nickerson
Estimated Sales: $ 10 - 20 Million
Number Employees: 10-19

885 Atlantic Seafood Direct
PO Box 1128
Rockland, ME 04841-1128   207-596-7152
                              Fax: 207-594-4042
Seafood

886 Atlantic Seasonings
417 E Vernon Avenue
Kinston, NC 28503-1436   252-522-1515
                              800-433-5261
Processor of salad dressing and drink mixes, gravies,
seasoning and flour blends and sauces; custom
blending available
    President: Jay Neuhoff
    VP Marketing: Ken Neuhoff
Estimated Sales: $2.5-5 Million
Number Employees: 10-19
Sq. footage: 18000
Type of Packaging: Food Service, Private Label,
    Bulk
Brands:
    ATLANTIC SEASONINGS

887 Atlantic Sugar Association
26400 State Road 80
Belle Glade, FL 33430   561-996-6541
        Fax: 561-336-5158   877-835-2828
                www.floridacrystals.com
Manufacturer of sugar cane
    President: Donald Carson

Estimated Sales: $50-100 Million
Number Employees: 100-249
Parent Co: Florida Crystals
Type of Packaging: Consumer, Bulk

888 Atlantic Veal
218 Hull Ave
Olyphant, PA 18447-1418   570-489-4781
                              Fax: 570-489-2544
Processor and exporter of veal
    Plant Manager: Ken Thomas
Estimated Sales: $2.5-5 Million
Number Employees: 20-49
Type of Packaging: Consumer
Brands:
    ATLANTIC VEAL

889 Atlantic Veal & Lamb
275 Morgan Ave
Brooklyn, NY 11211-2713   718-599-6400
        Fax: 718-599-6400   800-221-6988
Processor and exporter of individually vacuumed
frozen veal including portion controlled, hand
sliced, leg cutlets, roasts and cubed
    Owner: Phillip Peerless
Estimated Sales: $20-50 Million
Number Employees: 50-99
Type of Packaging: Consumer, Food Service
Brands:
    ATLANTIC VEAL

890 Atlas Biscuit Company
155 Pompton Ave # 107
Verona, NJ 07044-2942   973-239-8300
                              Fax: 973-239-8301
Cookies and candies
    President: Steve Koplin
Estimated Sales: 750,000
Number Employees: 5-9
Type of Packaging: Private Label, Bulk
Brands:
    Stephans

891 Atlas Cold Storage
1680 Candler Rd
Gainesville, GA 30507-8425   770-531-9800
        Fax: 770-531-1720 www.atlascold.com
An innovative provider of warehousing and distribution services to the refrigerated food industry. Products mostly consist of chicken in this region. Second
largest cold storage in America.
    President/CEO: David Williamson
    Chief Financial Officer: Kevin Glass
    VP: Steve Gibson
    Sales/Marketing/Georgia: Stan Chatien
    Director Human Resources: Randy Wagner
    General Manager/Gainesville: Steve Gibson
Estimated Sales: $ 5 - 10 Million
Number Employees: 100-249

892 Atlas Peak Vineyards
PO Box 182
Sonoma, CA 95476
                Fax: 707-226-2306   866-522-9463
    wineclub@atlaspeak.com   www.atlaspeak.com
Red and white wines
    CFO: Chris Stenzel
    VP Operations: Darren Procsal
    VP Production: Tony Fernandez
Estimated Sales: $5-10 Million
Number Employees: 20-49
Type of Packaging: Consumer, Food Service
Brands:
    ATLAS PEAK
    CONSENSO

893 Atlas Preserves Company
10 Fort George Hill
New York, NY 10040-2558   212-569-5613
        Fax: 718-327-8378   atlaspre@juno.com
Manufactures certified kosher jams, jellies, honey
and vegetable cooking spray; also, sugar-free
spreads
    President: H Oppenheim
Estimated Sales: $5-9.9 Million
Number Employees: 5
Sq. footage: 5000
Type of Packaging: Consumer, Food Service, Pri-
    vate Label, Bulk
Brands:
    ATLAS

894 Atoka Cranberries, Inc.
3025, Route 218
Manseau, Quebec, CN G0X 1VO
Canada   819-356-2001
Fax: 819-356-2111 www.atoka.qc.ca
Distributor of fresh and dried cranberries, and cran-
berry juice concentrate for industrial applications.

895 (HQ)Atrium Biotech
9 Commerce Road
Fairfield, NJ 07004-1601   866-628-2355
Fax: 866-628-6661 info@biotherapies.com
                              www.atrium-bio.com
Processor, importer and exporter of shark cartilage,
nutritional supplements and powders
    President: Richard Bordeleau
    CEO: Luc Dupont
    Vice President: Jocelyn Harvey
    Development: Serge Yelle
    Sales: Johan Aerts
    Purchasing: Rene Augstburger
Estimated Sales: $1.5 Million
Number Employees: 20
Number of Brands: 3
Number of Products: 20
Sq. footage: 100000
Brands:
    2-MIX
    BIOMEGA
    CARTCELT
    CARTILADE
    DERMANEX
    GENISTA
    NATCELT
    PEPOGEST
    PHYTO-EST
    PROSTACARE
    PROSTAVITE

896 Attala Company
P.O.Box 9
Kosciusko, MS 39090-0009   662-289-6641
Fax: 662-289-2733 800-824-2691
Processor of corn flour meal and blended wheat
flour
    Manager: David Bain
    Purchasing: Joe Cain
Estimated Sales: $20-50 Million
Number Employees: 20-49
Type of Packaging: Consumer, Private Label
Brands:
    MAGNOLIA

897 Atwater Block Brewing Company
237 Joseph Campau St
Detroit, MI 48207-4107   313-877-9205
Fax: 313-877-9241 atwater@atwaterbeer.com
                              www.atwaterbeer.com
Processor of German-style lager, ale and beer; im-
porter of malt and hops
    President: Mark Rieth
Estimated Sales: $ .5 - 1 million
Number Employees: 10-19
Sq. footage: 20000
Type of Packaging: Consumer, Food Service, Pri-
    vate Label
Brands:
    ATWATER
    STONEY

898 Atwater Foods
10182 Roosevelt Hwy
Lyndonville, NY 14098-9785   585-765-2639
Fax: 585-765-9443 sales@atwaterfoods.com
                              www.atwaterfoods.com
Manufacturer, exporter and wholesaler of many
kinds of dried fruit, including apples, cherries, cran-
berries, blueberries and strawberries. Star-K Kosher.
Our customer service support is responsive to
timelines and responsible forkeeping everything on
track
    Manager: Randy Atwater
    Quality Control: Chris Fraser
    Sales/Marketing: Jim Palmer
    GM: Randall Atwater
    Plant Manager: Steve Mohr
    Purchasing Manager: Pat Glidden
Estimated Sales: 15-20 Million
Number Employees: 50-99
Number of Products: 50+
Sq. footage: 90000
Type of Packaging: Private Label, Bulk
Brands:
    ATWATER

    ATWATER DRIED FRUITS
    SHORELINE FRUIT

899 Atwater Fruit Exchange
PO Box 754
Atwater, CA 95301-0754   209-358-2272
Processor of sweet potatoes and almonds
    President: Walt Weirner
Estimated Sales: $ .5 - 1 million
Number Employees: 1-4
Type of Packaging: Consumer

900 Atwood Cheese Company
Rural Route 1
Atwood, ON N0G 1B0
Canada   519-356-2271
Fax: 519-356-2170
Manufacturer of cheeses including mozzarella, feta,
fontina, emmental and parmesan
    Manager: Samuel Cadeddo
Number Employees: 19
Sq. footage: 30000
Type of Packaging: Bulk

901 Au Bon Climat Winery
P.O.Box 440
Los Olivos, CA 93441-0440   805-937-9801
Fax: 805-937-2539 info@aubonclimat.com
                              www.qupe.com
Wines
    Owner: Robert Lindquist
Estimated Sales: $ .5 - 1 million
Number Employees: 1-4
Type of Packaging: Private Label

902 Au Printemps Gourmet
CP 388
Prevost, QC J0R 1T0
Canada   450-224-8221
Fax: 450-224-7943 800-663-0416
news@printempsgourmet.com
www.printempsgourmet.com
Manufacturer of vinegars, jams, jelly seasonings and
gift sets
    Co-Owner: H Weisbord
    Co-Owner: A O'Grady
    GM: M O'Connell
Brands:
    Au Printemps Gourmet

903 (HQ)Au'some Candies
2031 US Highway 130
Suite E, Building A
Monmouth Junction, NJ 08852-3014 732-951-8818
Fax: 732-951-8828 info@ausomecandy.com
                              www.ausomecandy.com
Candy
    President: Carlos Yeung
    CEO: David Tsu
    VP Operations: Rose Downey
Estimated Sales: $ 5 - 10 Million
Number Employees: 10-19
Other Locations:
    Au'some Candies
    Mission Viejo CA
    Au'some Candies
    Coppell TX
    Au'Some Candies
    Mississauga, Ontario
    Au'Some Candies Europe S.L.
    Sitges, Spain
    Au'Some Candy Asia
    Kowloon, Hong Kong
Brands:
    CANDY YO-YO
    GUMMI ALIEN INVADERS
    POP MAGIC
    SUPER SUCKER

904 Auburn Dairy Products
702 W Main St
Auburn, WA 98001-5299   253-833-3400
Fax: 253-833-3751 800-950-9264
customerservice@yamiyogurt.com
www.yamiyogurt.com
Processor of sour cream, half and half and yogurt in-
cluding plain, orange, cherry, strawberry, blueberry
and lemon.
    Manager: Jerry Dinsmore
    Executive Director: Martin Lavine
    Plant Manager: Marv Query
    Purchasing: Marv Query
Estimated Sales: $10-20 Million
Number Employees: 20-49
Parent Co: Instantwhip Foods

Type of Packaging: Consumer, Food Service
Brands:
    AUBURN
    YAMI

905 Audubon Cellars
600 Addison Street
Berkeley, CA 94710-1920   510-540-5384
Fax: 510-540-0839
Wines
    President/CEO: Dieter Tede
    Vice President: Barry Grushkowitz
    Marketing Director: Craig Napp
    Purchasing: Dieter Tede
Estimated Sales: $1-2.5 Million
Number Employees: 5-9
Type of Packaging: Private Label
Brands:
    AUDUBON CELLARS
    AUDUBON COLLECTION
    CONOMA MISSION

906 August Food Limited
4820 Avenue Q
Lubbock, TX 79412-2210   806-744-1918
Fax: 806-744-4934
Fried pies
    President: August Moeller
Estimated Sales: $750
Number Employees: 17
Sq. footage: 3600
Brands:
    AUGUST'S FRIED

907 August Foods
4820 Avenue Q
Lubbock, TX 79412-2210   806-744-1918
Fax: 806-744-4934 www.augustpies.com
Manufacturer of fresh pies
    Partner: August Moeller
    Purchasing: Ken Moeller
Estimated Sales: $10-20 Million
Number Employees: 10-19
Sq. footage: 2600
Parent Co: Excel
Type of Packaging: Consumer, Food Service
Brands:
    AUGUST'S FRIED

908 August Schell Brewing Company
P.O.Box 128
New Ulm, MN 56073-0128   507-354-5528
Fax: 507-359-9119 800-770-5020
schells@schellsbrewery.com www.grainbelt.com
Manufacturer of beer, ale and lager.
    President: Ted Marti
    Marketing Director: Bob Andersen
    Operations/Plant Manager: Jeremy Kral
Estimated Sales: $21 Million
Number Employees: 20-49
Type of Packaging: Consumer, Private Label
Brands:
    GRAIN BELT
    SCHELL'S

909 Augusta Winery
P.O.Box 8
Augusta, MO 63332-0008   636-228-4301
Fax: 636-228-4683 888-667-9463
info@augustawinery.com
www.augustawinery.com
Wines
    President: Tony Kooyumjian
Estimated Sales: $2.5-5 Million
Number Employees: 5-9
Type of Packaging: Bulk

910 Augustin's Waffles
51 Glen Ridge Drive
Long Valley, NJ 07853   908-684-0830
Fax: 908-684-4878 info@augustinswaffles.com
                              info@augustinswaffles.com
Waffles

911 Ault Foods
405 The West Mall
Toronto, ON M9C 5J1
Canada   416-626-1973
Fax: 416-620-3123 www.parmalat-ingredients.com

Manufacturer, importer and exporter of bulking agents, fat/oil substitutes, hydrolyzed animal proteins, nonfat and nonfat hydrolyzed milk solids, proteins, sweeteners, whey and whey products
Chairman: D E Loadman
President/CEO: G P M Freeman
CFO: J J Hamilton
Treasurer: P C Quintiliani
Secretary: P L Ferraro
Parent Co: Parmalat Finanziaria SpA.
Brands:
Ault-Pro
Prestige
Protelac

912 Aunt Aggie De's Pralines
311 W Sinton St
Sinton, TX 78387-2556   361-364-2711
Fax: 361-692-2971   888-772-5463
sales@auntaggiede.com   www.auntaggiede.com
Processor of original, chocolate and chewy pecan pralines and hot fudge, and pecan praline sauces
President: Eleanor Harren
Estimated Sales: $5-10 Million
Number Employees: 20-49
Sq. footage: 2200
Brands:
AUNT AGGIE DE'S PRALINES

913 Aunt Bea Bakery
3637 Scarlet Oak Boulevard
Saint Louis, MO 63122-6605   636-225-8808
Fax: 636-825-4514
Processor of brownies, cakes, corn bread, crunchmellow and prepared sandwiches
Account/System Manager: Kathy Lovett
Plant Manager: John Van Cleave
Purchasing Supervisor: Therese Heidmann
Estimated Sales: $10-20 Million
Number Employees: 50-99
Sq. footage: 21368
Type of Packaging: Consumer, Private Label, Bulk
Brands:
AUNT BEA'S

914 Aunt Gussie Cookies & Crackers
141 Lanza Ave # 8e
Garfield, NJ 07026-3538   973-340-4480
Fax: 973-340-3501   info@auntgussies.com
www.auntgussies.com
Processor of cookies and crackers including sugar-free
President: David Caine
VP: Marilyn Caine
Estimated Sales: $2.5-5 Million
Number Employees: 5-9
Number of Brands: 1
Number of Products: 45
Sq. footage: 15000
Type of Packaging: Consumer, Private Label, Bulk
Brands:
AUNT GUSSIE'S COOKIES & CRACKERS

915 Aunt Heddy's Bakery
234 N 9th Street
Brooklyn, NY 11211-2012   718-782-0582
Fax: 718-782-5583
Breads, babka
President: Richards Habrarki
Purchasing: Rich Zablocki
Estimated Sales: $10-20 Million
Number Employees: 10-19

916 Aunt Jenny's Sauces/Melba Foods
186 Huron St
Brooklyn, NY 11222-1706   718-383-3192
Fax: 718-383-3191   admin@melbafoods.com
http://www.melbafoods.com
Sauces, melba foods
President: Marie Cuoco
Estimated Sales: $2.5-5 Million
Number Employees: 10-19
Type of Packaging: Private Label

917 Aunt Kathy's Homestyle Products
PO Box 279
Waldheim, SK S0K 4R0
Canada   306-945-2181
Fax: 306-945-2043
Manufacturer of cabbage rolls, filled perogies, pizza, borscht and chicken noodle soup
Owner: Kathy Fehr
Owner: Gerald Fehr

Estimated Sales: $300M-$500M
Number Employees: 5-9
Sq. footage: 7560
Type of Packaging: Consumer, Bulk

918 Aunt Lizzie's
1531 Overton Park Ave
Memphis, TN 38112-5138   901-274-2966
Fax: 901-274-2902   800-993-7788
www.auntlizzie.com
Different flavored cheese straws and other products
President: Ginna Kelley
Co-Owner: Ginna Kelly
Founder: Elizabeth Harwell
Estimated Sales: Under $500,000
Number Employees: 5-9
Type of Packaging: Private Label
Brands:
Aunt Lizzie's
Lemon Shortbread
Libby's Pecan Cookies
Sharp Cheddar Cheese
Sun-Dried Tomato Str
Wind & Willow Key Lime Cheeseball

919 (HQ)Aunt Millies Bakeries
350 Pearl St
Fort Wayne, IN 46802-1508   260-424-8245
Fax: 260-424-5047   www.auntmillies.com
Manufacturer of breads, buns, English muffins, rolls, as well as bread and muffin mixes
President: John Popp
VP Finance: Jay Miller
Estimated Sales: $10-15 Million
Number Employees: 1,000-4,999
Type of Packaging: Consumer, Food Service
Other Locations:
Brands:
Aunt Millie's
Sumbeam

920 Aunt Sally's Praline Shops, Inc.
2831 Chartres St
New Orleans, LA 70117-7315   504-944-6090
Fax: 504-944-5925   800-642-7257
ceo@auntsallys.com   www.auntsallys.com
Manufacturer of New Orleans style creamy praline candies in four flavors, and other specialty food items.
Manager: Bethany Gex
CEO: Frank Simoncioni
Sales: Becky Hebert
Sales: Cherie Cunningham
Director Of Operations: Karl Schmidt
Materials Management: Bethany Gex
Estimated Sales: $5 Million+
Number Employees: 20-49
Sq. footage: 10000
Type of Packaging: Consumer, Food Service, Private Label, Bulk
Brands:
AUNT SALLY'S CREAMY PRALINES
AUNT SALLY'S GOURMET

921 Auroma International, Inc.
P.O.Box 1008
Silver Lake, WI 53170-1008   262-889-8569
Fax: 262-889-2461   auroma@lotuspress.com
www.auromaintl.com
Dietary supplements, herbs and herbal formulas.
CEO: Santosh Krinsky

922 Aurora Alaska Premium Smoked Salmon & Seafood
PO Box 211376
Anchorage, AK 99521-1376   800-653-3474
Fax: 907-338-2228
Seafood products
Owner: Bill Dornberger
Owner: Gloria Dornberger

923 Aurora Frozen Foods Division
11432 Lackland Road
Suite 300
Saint Louis, MO 63146-3516   314-801-2300
Fax: 314-801-2550   mourdla@vdkff.com
www.aurorafoods.com
Frozen sea food, pizza and breakfast products, including waffles, french toast
Chairman: Dale F Morrison
COO: Eric D Brenk
CFO: William R McManaman
Number Employees: 5-9

Brands:
Aunt Jemima
Celeste
Duncan Hines
Lender's
Log Cabin
Mrs Butterworth's
Mrs Paul's
Van de Kamp's

924 Aurora Packing Company
P.O.Box 209
North Aurora, IL 60542-0209   630-897-0551
Fax: 630-897-0647
Processor and exporter of beef.
President/CEO: Marvin Fagel
Plant Manager: Marty Gilbert
Estimated Sales: $50-100 Million
Number Employees: 100-249
Type of Packaging: Consumer, Food Service, Private Label

925 Aurora Products
400 Long Beach Boulevard
Stratford, CT 06615-7180   203-375-9956
Fax: 203-375-9734   800-398-1048
orders@auroraproduct.com
www.auroraproduct.com
Manufacturer of trail mixes, nuts, dried fruits and candy
Owner: Stephanie Blackwell
Estimated Sales: $ 30 - 40 Million
Number Employees: 100+

926 Austin Chase Coffee
4001 21st Ave W
Seattle, WA 98199-1201   206-282-7045
Fax: 206-282-5218   888-502-2333
www.austinchasecoffee.com
Coffee
President: Phil Sancken
VP of Sales/Marketing: Tucker McHugh
Estimated Sales: $5-10 Million
Number Employees: 50-99
Type of Packaging: Private Label

927 Austin Packaging Company
1118 N Main St
Austin, MN 55912-3359   507-433-6623
Fax: 507-433-9717   mail@austinpackaging.com
www.austinpackaging.com
Contract packager of meal kits, meat pouches, frozen liquid sauces, pizza and portion control products; exporter of frozen liquid sauces
President: Jim Heimark
VP Sales: Paul Nafzger
Estimated Sales: $10-20 Million
Number Employees: 100-249
Sq. footage: 125000
Type of Packaging: Consumer, Food Service, Private Label

928 Austin Slow Burn
P.O.Box 150042
Austin, TX 78715-0042   512-282-7140
Fax: 512-282-7140   877-513-3192
austinslowburn@austin.rr.com
www.austinslowburn.com
Marinades, jams, jellies, hot pepper sauce, red sauce, green sauce and special variety sauces.
President: Jill Lewis
VP: Kevin Lewis
Estimated Sales: $300,000-500,000
Number Employees: 1-4

929 Austin Special Foods Company
11400 Burnet Rd # 200
Austin, TX 78758-3406   512-652-2600
Fax: 512-652-2699   866-372-8663
austinspec@aol.com   www.convio.com
All natural and kosher dairy biscotti, cookies and frozen cookie dough. Many biscotti flavors
Owner: Laura Logan
CEO: Gene Austin
Estimated Sales: $ 10 - 20 Million
Number Employees: 250-499

930 Austinuts
2900 W Anderson Ln # 19b
Austin, TX 78757-1364   512-323-6887
Fax: 512-323-6889   877-329-6887
info@austinuts.com   www.austinuts.com

Dry Roasted Gourmet Nuts and Seeds, Dried Fruits, Chocolates, Candy, Trail Mixes, Gourmet Food, Go Texan Products, Gift Baskets & Corporate Gifts.
President: Cipi Ilai
Estimated Sales: $650,000
Number Employees: 5-9
Sq. footage: 2
Type of Packaging: Private Label
Brands:
Austinuts

931 Austrade Food Ingredients
3309 Northlake Blvd # 201
Palm Beach Gdns, FL 33403-1705   561-586-7145
Fax: 561-585-7164 office@austradeinc.com
www.austradeinc.com
The leader in importing fine chemicals and food products.
President: Garry Bartl
Marketing: Joseph Schantl
Sales: Sandra Bartl
Operations: Gayle Byham
Estimated Sales: $ 1 - 3 Million
Number Employees: 1-4

932 Authentic Marotti Biscotti
749 Red Wing Dr
Lewisville, TX 75067-5865   972-221-7295
Fax: 972-436-4547 biscotti@mbiscotti.com
www.mbiscotti.com
Processor of gourmet biscotti, brownies and bar cookies.
Owner: Joann Mancini
VP: Glenn Mancini
Estimated Sales: $2.5-5 Million
Number Employees: 1-4
Type of Packaging: Consumer, Private Label, Bulk
Brands:
MAROTTI BISCOTTI

933 Authentic Specialty Foods
4340 Eucalyptus Ave
Chino, CA 91710-9705   909-631-2000
Fax: 909-631-2100 www.asf-inc.com
Manufacturer of salsa; importer and exporter of Mexican foods including beans, jalapeno peppers, spices, seasonings, sauces and meats
President: Ted Gardner
CEO: Ignacio Hernandez
CFO: Rafael Beverido
Sr. VP: Peter Cowles
Estimated Sales: $197 Million
Brands:
EMBASA
LA VICTORIA

934 Autin's Cajun Cookery
804 W 8th Ave
Covington, LA 70433-2306   985-871-1199
Fax: 985-871-7290 800-877-7290
autinskjun@aol.com
www.autinscajuncookery.com
Manufacturer of Cajun dinner mixes and seasonings including jambalaya, etouffee, dirty rice, chili, gumbo, etc
President: Gibson Autin II
Estimated Sales: $500,000-$1 Million
Number Employees: 1-4
Type of Packaging: Consumer, Food Service, Private Label, Bulk
Brands:
Autin's

935 Autocrat Coffee & Extracts
10 Blackstone Valley Pl
Lincoln, RI 02865-1145   401-333-3300
Fax: 401-334-5972 800-288-6272
info@autocrat.com
Roaster and extractor of gourmet coffee; also, coffee extracts, syrups, concentrates, iced cappuccino, iced coffee, espresso and smoothies available; services include retail, distributor, OCS, food service and food ingredients
President: Richard M Field Jr
VP/Owner: Cynthia Wall
Director Technical Services: Susan Maiocchi
Director Food Ingredient Sales: Noreen Carroll
Marketing Director: Kimberly Cipriano
Plant Manager: Scott Tittle
Number Employees: 100-249
Sq. footage: 45000
Type of Packaging: Consumer, Food Service, Private Label

Brands:
AUTOCRAT
ECLIPSE
NEWPORT COFFEE TRADERS

936 Automatic Rolls of New Jersey
1 Gourmet Ln
Edison, NJ 08837-2902   732-549-2243
Fax: 732-494-4980
Manufacturer of soft hamburger rolls; serving McDonalds chains
Manager: John Lyons
Plant Manager: John Lyons
Estimated Sales: $50-100 Million
Number Employees: 50-99
Parent Co: Northeast Foods
Type of Packaging: Food Service

937 Automot
1806 Gunn Highway
Odessa, FL 33556-3524   813-920-1000
President: Gary Knudsen
Estimated Sales: $300,000-500,000
Number Employees: 1-4

938 Autumn Hill Vineyards/Blue Ridge Wine
State Route 603
Stanardsville, VA 22973   434-985-6100
autumnhill@mindspring.com
www.autumnhillwine.com
Wine
Owner: Avra Schwab
Owner: Ed Schwab
Estimated Sales: $ 1 - 3 Million
Number Employees: 1-4

939 Autumn Wind Vineyard
15225 NE North Valley Road
Newberg, OR 97132-6596   503-538-6931
Fax: 503-538-6931
chat@autumnwindwinery.com
Wines
Estimated Sales: $500,000-$1 Million
Number Employees: 1-4
Sq. footage: 3
Type of Packaging: Private Label
Brands:
Patricia Green Cellars

940 Avalon Foodservice, Inc.
P.O.Box 536
Canal Fulton, OH 44614-0536   330-854-4551
Fax: 330-854-7108 800-362-0622
marketing@avalonfoods.com
www.avalonfoods.com
Fresh and frozen foods, dry and canned goods, produce, juices, ice cream, fresh dairy products, coffee and beverage programs, fresh and custom cut meats.
President: Andy Schroer

941 Avalon Gourmet
1051 E Broadway Rd
Phoenix, AZ 85040-2301   602-253-0343
Fax: 480-253-0432
President: Richard Du Pree
VP: Dolores DuPree
Estimated Sales: $ 5 - 10 Million
Number Employees: 5-9

942 Avalon Organic Coffees
8308 Corona Loop NE
Albuquerque, NM 87113-1665   505-856-5588
Fax: 505-856-5588 800-662-2575
e-mail@avalonorganic.com
www.avalonorganic.com
Organic coffee

943 Avanti Food Company
P.O.Box 243
Walnut, IL 61376-0243   815-379-2155
Fax: 815-379-9357 800-243-3739
info@avantifoods.com www.avantifoods.com
Processor of frozen pizza ingredients including cheese.
President: Tony Zueger
Secretary/Treasurer: Robert Linley
Executive VP: Mike LePine
Marketing Director: Robert Linley
Estimated Sales: $20-50 Million
Number Employees: 50-99
Type of Packaging: Consumer, Food Service, Private Label, Bulk

Brands:
GINO'S
SWISS PARTY
WALNUT CHEESE

944 Avary Farms
S Highway 385
Odessa, TX 79761   432-332-4139
Fax: 915-332-4130
Owner: Bob Avary
Sales/Marketing Manager: Angela Avery
Estimated Sales: $300,000-500,000
Number Employees: 1-4

945 Avatar Corporation
500 Central Ave
University Park, IL 60466-3147   708-534-5511
Fax: 708-534-0123 800-255-3181
inquiries@avatarcorp.com www.avatarcorp.com
Manufacturer and Distributor of edible oils including bean, canola, castor, coconut, corn, kosher, etc.; exporter of edible oils, emulsifiers, release agents, glycerin and lecithin, propylene glycol, mineral oil.
President/CEO: Mike Shamie
VP Marketing: David Darwin
Chief Operating Officer: Phil Ternes
Estimated Sales: $10-20 Million
Number Employees: 10-19
Sq. footage: 40000
Type of Packaging: Private Label, Bulk
Brands:
AROL
AROX
AVOX
Avagel
Avapol
Avatar
Avatech
Brown 'n' Serve
Citation
DPO
LSC
PROTROLLEY
Paneze
Pankote
Pinnacle
Probio
Prochill
Procon
Prokote
Prophos
Prosyn
Protech
SNOW WHITE
SOFT WHITE
TROKOTE
WINTREX

946 Avent Luvel Dairy Products
P.O.Box 1229
Kosciusko, MS 39090-1229   662-289-2511
Fax: 662-289-2572 800-281-1307
luvelsales@hypercon.net www.luvel.com
Dairy products
Owner: Jimmy Biscoe
COO: Larry Crockett
Vice President: Richard Briscoe
Controller: Charles Terry
Quality Control: Rodney Smith
South Sales Manager: Ance Cascio
North Sales Manager: Paul Ables
General Sales Manager: G Tucker Arrington
Estimated Sales: $5-10 Million
Number Employees: 10-19

947 Aventine Renewable Energy
120 N Parkway
PO Box 1800
Pekin, IL 61555-1800   309-347-9200
Fax: 309-346-0742 www.aventinerei.com/
Beverage alcohol, food grade yeast
CEO/COO: Thomas Manuel
CFO/Secretary: John Castle
VP Human Resources: Ray Godbout
Estimated Sales: $ 500 Million
Number Employees: 100-249

948 Avery Brewing Company
5763 Arapahoe Ave # E
Boulder, CO 80303-1350   303-440-4324
Fax: 303-786-8790 877-844-5679
info@averybrewing.com
www.averybrewing.com

Beers
President: Adam Avery
CEO/CFO: Larry Avery
Quality Control Manager: Matt Thrall
Marketing Director: C V Howe
Colorado Sales: Ted Whitney
Operations Manager: Steve Breezley
Plant Manager: Steve Wadzinski
Estimated Sales:$5-10 Million
Number Employees: 5-9
Brands:
14'ER ESB
AVERY
ELLIE'S BROWN
HOG HEAVEN
OUT OF BOUNDS
REDPOINT
SALVATION
THE REVEREND
WHITE RASCAL

949   Avo King International
2140 W Chapman Ave # 240
Orange, CA 92868-2332   714-937-1551
          Fax: 714-937-1974   800-286-5464
information@avoking.com   www.avo-king.com
Processor and importer of frozen guacamole and avocado pulp
Owner: Guido Doddoli
Estimated Sales:$10-20 Million
Number Employees: 1-4
Parent Co: Doddoli Hermanos Group
Brands:
AVO-KING

950   Avoca
P.O.Box 129
Merry Hill, NC 27957-0129   252-482-2133
          Fax: 252-482-8622 www.avocainc.com
Manufacturer and exporter of flavors and fragrances
President: David Peele
COO: Danny White
Research & Development: Richard Teague
Marketing Director: Shannon Sloan
Plant Manager: Danny White
Number Employees: 50-99

951   Avon Heights Mushrooms
P.O.Box 485
Avondale, PA 19311-0485   610-268-2092
          Fax: 610-268-8706
Manufacturer of coleslaw and salad mixes; also, packer of spinach
Owner: Philip Pusey Jr Jr
Estimated Sales:$ 20 - 50 Million
Number Employees: 20-49

952   Avonmore Ingredients
523 6th St
Monroe, WI 53566-1065   608-329-2800
          Fax: 608-329-2828   800-336-2183
ingredients@avonmoreusa.com
          www.glanbianutritionals.com
Manufacturers of dairy ingredients
President: Jerry O'Dea
General Manager/VP: Jerry O'Dea
Marketing Manager: Fiona O'Keeffe
Number Employees: 10-19
Type of Packaging: Bulk
Brands:
Avonmore Ingredients

953   Avron Resources
1080 Essex Ave
Richmond, CA 94801-2113   510-233-0633
          Fax: 510-233-0636   800-883-9574
          avron@avron.com
Flavors
President: Carl Arvold
Estimated Sales:$5-10 Million
Number Employees: 5-9
Type of Packaging: Private Label

954   Award Baking International
206 State Ave S
New Germany, MN 55367-9521   952-353-2533
          Fax: 952-353-8066 awardbaking@oblaten.com
          www.oblaten.com
Manufacturer of biscottis
Co-Owner: Tim Kraft
Co-Owner: Ken Barron
Estimated Sales:$1-2.5 Million
Number Employees: 10-19

Sq. footage: 10000
Parent Co: Kenny B's Cookie
Brands:
Auer
Award Auer/Blaschke
Award Crunchy Dunkers
Biscotti Di Roma
Carlsbad Oblaten

955   Awrey Bakeries
12301 Farmington Rd
Livonia, MI 48150-1747   734-522-1100
          Fax: 734-513-0394   800-950-2253
personnel@awrey.com   www.awrey.com
Manufacturer of frozen baked goods including cakes, sweet rolls, bagels, muffins, doughnuts, danish, croissants, biscuits, rolls, english muffins, browniesand marquise desserts
President: Tom Awrey
CEO: Alden Knowles
Public Relations: Betty Jean Awrey
Plant Manager: Belanger
Estimated Sales:$75 Million
Number Employees: 250-499
Number of Brands: 4
Number of Products: 200
Sq. footage: 280000
Type of Packaging: Consumer, Food Service, Private Label
Brands:
Awrey's Maestro
Grande
Marquise

956   Axelsson & Johnson FishCompany
PO Box 180
Cape May, NJ 08204-0180   609-884-8426
          Fax: 609-898-0221
Seafood
Manager: Andrew Axelsson
Estimated Sales:$5-10 Million
Number Employees: 10-19

957   Axia Distribution Corporation
247-2628 Granville Street
Vancouver, BC V6H 4B4
Canada   778-371-9885
          Fax: 778-371-9000 info@axiadistribution.com
          www.axiadistribution.com
Distributor & Manufacutuer of High Quality Rubber Mats. The Mats are molded with virgin rubber that offers durability, less odor, stability and anti-fatigue properties
Type of Packaging: Food Service

958   Azar Nut Company
1800 Northwestern Drive
El Paso, TX 79912   915-877-4079
          Fax: 915-877-1153 www.azarnutco.com
Nuts, candy, snack mixes, coconut, peanut butter, dried fruit, and sprinkles.
VP Sales/Marketing: Gary Stewart
National Sales Manager: Barbara Powell

959   Azar Nut Company
1800 Northwestern
El Paso, TX 79912   915-877-4079
          Fax: 915-877-1186 www.azarnutco.com
Nuts, candy, snack mixes, coconut, peanut butter, dried fruit, and sprinkles
Marketing Director: Beth Podol
VP Sales/Marketing: Gary Stewart
Operations Manager: James Jamison
Type of Packaging: Food Service, Private Label, Bulk

960   Azar Nut Company
1800 Northwestern Dr
El Paso, TX 79912-1125   915-877-4079
          Fax: 915-877-1186 800-592-8103
info@nutshop.com   www.azarnutco.com
Processor of peanuts, almonds, pecans, walnuts, pine and mixed nuts, dried fruit, candy and snack mixes
CEO: Richard Condie
VP Sales/Marketing: Gary Stewart
Operations Manager: James Jamison
Estimated Sales:$50-100 Million
Number Employees: 100-249
Other Locations:
Sunlight Plant
Juarez, Mexico

961   Azteca Foods
P.O.Box 427
Summit Argo, IL 60501-0427   708-563-6600
          Fax: 708-563-0331
arthur.velasquez@aztecafoods.com
          www.aztecafoods.com
Manufacturer of Mexican food products including salad shells, tortilla chips and tortillas
President: Arthur R Velasquez
Estimated Sales:$50 Million
Number Employees: 100-249
Type of Packaging: Consumer, Food Service

962   Azteca Milling
1159 Cottonwood Ln # 130
Irving, TX 75038-6118   972-232-5300
          Fax: 972-232-5370 800-364-0040
maseca_sales@aztecamilling.com
          www.aztecamilling.com
Manufacturer of corn tortilla flours; snack flours; retail flours, and speciality flours.
President: Ignacio Hernandez
Vice President: Don Schleppegrell
Corporate Sales Manager: Rick Norton
Snack Manager Sales: Alan Davis
Estimated Sales:$40 Million
Number Employees: 100-249
Parent Co: Gruma Corporation
Type of Packaging: Bulk
Brands:
MASA MIXTA
MASECA

963   (HQ)Azuma Foods International
1787 Sabre St
Hayward, CA 94545-1015   510-782-1112
          Fax: 510-782-1188 www.azumafoods.com
Processor, exporter and importer of frozen seafood, caviar and ready-made sushi
President: Takahiro Tamura
CEO: Toshinobu Azuma
Estimated Sales:$5-10 Million
Number Employees: 50-99
Other Locations:
New York Branch
East Rutherford NJ
Hawaii Sales Office
Honolulu HI
West Coast American Division Sales
Novato CA
East Coast American Division Sales
Boston MA
Brands:
ICHIBAN DELIGHT®
MY-DOL®
SEA SALAD
TAKOHACHI
TASTE OF ISLAND LEGENDS
TOBIKKO®

964   B&A Bakery
1820 Ellesmere Road
Scarborough, ON M1H 2V5
Canada   416-289-9600
          Fax: 416-752-0950 800-263-2878
Processor of homestyle sandwich bread and rolls including hamburger, submarine, hot dog, dinner and kaiser
Persident/General Manager: Sadrudin Sunderji
Assistant Manager: Ariff Sunderji
Number Employees: 20-49
Sq. footage: 12000
Type of Packaging: Food Service

965   B&B Caramel Apple Company
2151 W 21st Street
Chicago, IL 60608-2607   773-927-7559
          Fax: 773-927-7446
Processor of caramel apples
President: John Ramondi
Estimated Sales:$1-2.5 Million
Number Employees: 5-9
Type of Packaging: Consumer, Food Service
Brands:
B&B

966   B&B Food Distributors
724 S 13th St
Terre Haute, IN 47807-4914   812-238-1438
          Fax: 812-232-0670 800-264-1438
          www.bandbfoods.net
Manufacturer of general merchandise and foodservice equipment
President: R Scott Isles

Estimated Sales:$ 10 - 20 Million
Number Employees: 50-99

967 B&B Pecan Processors ofNC
P.O.Box 421
Turkey, NC 28393-0421   910-533-2229
          Fax: 910-553-4610   866-328-7322
                info@elizabethspecans.com
                www.elizabethspecans.com
Manufacturer of pecan praline, brittle, chocolate
covered pecans, butter-roasted pecans and BBQ
sauce
     Owner: Alan Bundy
Estimated Sales:$ .5 - 1 million
Number Employees: 5-9
Brands:
     ELIZABETH'S

968 B&B Poultry Company
P.O.Box 307
Norma, NJ 08347-0307   856-692-8893
     Fax: 856-455-7681 www.bandbpoultry.com
Refrigerated chickens, whole and parts
     VP: Louis Rothman
Estimated Sales:$20-50 Million
Number Employees: 100-249

969 B&B Produce
2778 Nc Highway 50 S
Benson, NC 27504-8108   919-894-2527
          Fax: 919-894-2127   800-633-4902
     info@bbproduce.com   www.bbproduce.com
Processor of sweet potatoes
     President: Bob Bassetti
Estimated Sales:$20-50 Million
Number Employees: 50-99
Brands:
     Sun Beauty

**970 B&C Seafood Market and Cajun
Restaurant**
2155 Highway 18
Vacherie, LA 70090   225-265-8356
     Fax: 225-265-9960 info@bandcseafood.com
                www.bandcseafood.com
Processor of vacuum packed, fresh and frozen alli-
gator and seafood including catfish, flounder, mullet
and trout; also, plain and boiled, Cajun crawfish and
crab
Estimated Sales:$5-10 Million
Number Employees: 5-9
Type of Packaging: Consumer, Food Service

971 B&D Food Corporation
575 Madison Ave # 1006
New York, NY 10022-8511   212-937-8456
     Fax: 212-412-9034 info@bdfcorp.com
                www.bdfcorp.com
Manufacturer of roasted, ground coffee; chocolate
beverages and cappaccinos; and spray dried agglom-
erated soluble coffee and powdered tea.
     Chief Executive Officer/Board Directors: Yaron
     Arbell
     Chief Financial Officer/Board Directors: Yossi
     Haras
     CEO: Daniel Ollech
     Board of Directors: Daniel Ollech
Number Employees: 1-4
Type of Packaging: Food Service

972 B&D Foods
3275 Federal Way
Boise, ID 83705-5215   208-344-1183
     Fax: 208-344-6825   sales@banddfoods.net
                www.banddfoods.net
Processor of frozen finger steaks, pork and chicken
strips and battered mozzarella cheese sticks
Estimated Sales:$10-20 Million
Number Employees: 5-9
Sq. footage: 12000
Type of Packaging: Food Service, Private Label

973 B&G Foods
4 Gatehall Dr # 110
Parsippany, NJ 07054-4522   973-401-6500
     Fax: 973-630-6522 www.bgfoods.com

Manufactures, sells and distributes a diversified
portfolio of high quality, shelf stable foods across
the U.S., Canada and Puerto Rico. Products include;
Mexican-style sauces, pickles and peppers, hot
sauces, wine vinegar, maplesyrup, molasses, fruit
spreads, pasta sauces, beans, salad dressings, etc.
     Chairman of the Board: Stephen Sherrill
     President/CEO/Director: David Wennerr
     EVP/Chief Financial Officer/Director: Robert
     Cantwell
     CEO: David L Wenner
     EVP/ Marketing & Strategic Planning: Albert
     Soricelli
     Executive Vice President Sales: Vanessa Maskal
     VP General Counsel & Secretary: Scott Lerner
     Executive Vice President/Manufacturing: James
     Brown
Estimated Sales:$20-50 Million
Number Employees: 500-999
Sq. footage: 200000
Type of Packaging: Consumer, Food Service
Brands:
     AC'CENT
     AC'CENT SA-SON
     B&G
     B&M
     BRER RABBIT
     EMERIL'S
     JOAN OF ARC
     LAS PALMAS
     MAPLE GROVE FARMS OF VERMONT
     ORTEGA
     POLANER
     RED DEVIL
     REGINA
     SAN DEL
     TRAPPERY'S
     UNDERWOOD
     UP COUNTRY ORGANICS
     VERMONT MAID
     WRIGHT'S

974 B&J Seafood Company
P.O.Box 3321
New Bern, NC 28564-3321   252-637-0483
                Fax: 252-633-0775
Canned, frozen and refrigerated blue crabmeat,
frozen and refrigerated flounder fillets
     President: Brent Fulcher
Estimated Sales:$20-50 Million
Number Employees: 100-249
Type of Packaging: Private Label
Brands:
     Upper Bay

975 B&M
P.O.Box 1871
Portland, ME 04104-1871   207-772-8341
     Fax: 207-772-7043 info@bmbeans.com
                www.bmbeans.com
Manufacturer of canned baked beans and brown
bread
     Human Resources: Kelly Gagnon
Estimated Sales:$100+ Million
Number Employees: 100-249
Parent Co: B&G Foods
Type of Packaging: Consumer
Brands:
     B&M BAKED BEANS

976 B&M Enterprises
9111 Brocklehurst Lane
Charlotte, NC 28215-8705   704-566-9332
                Fax: 704-566-9332
     Owner: Marson Berry
*Estimated Sales:*Under $500,000
Number Employees: 5-9

977 B&M Fisheries
15 Pingree Farm Road
Georgetown, MA 01833-2522   978-352-6663
                Fax: 978-352-7565

978 B&R Quality Meats
200 Park Rd
Waterloo, IA 50703-3642   319-232-6328
                Fax: 319-232-8623
Processor and wholesaler/distributor of meat including beef, pork, veal and poultry; serving the
foodservice market
     President: Mark Ratkovich
     VP: Dennis Brennan

Estimated Sales:$5-10 Million
Number Employees: 5-9
Sq. footage: 6000
Type of Packaging: Consumer, Food Service, Bulk

979 B-S Foods Company
1000 Cornell Pkwy # 600
Oklahoma City, OK 73108-1800   405-949-9797
                Fax: 405-949-9802
Processor of pre-packaged luncheon meats and sand-
wiches
     Owner: Sandra Henager
     Sales Manager: Dave Heinecke
Estimated Sales:$2.5-5 Million
Number Employees: 5-9
Parent Co: B-S Foods Company
Type of Packaging: Consumer

980 B. Lloyd's Pecans
PO Box 70
Barnesville, GA 30204-0070   770-358-0782
          Fax: 770-358-4346   800-322-6887
                blloyds@gowebway.com
                www.business-atlanta.com/pecan
Pecans and pecan confections
     President: Bobby Fowler
     Executive Secretary: Janice Fowler
Estimated Sales:$500-1 Million appx.
Number Employees: 10-19
Type of Packaging: Food Service

981 B. Martinez & Sons Company
623 S Leona St
San Antonio, TX 78207-5016   210-226-6772
                Fax: 210-226-5262
Processor of corn tortillas, nacho chips and chalupa
and taco shells
     Owner: Ariel Berrueto
Estimated Sales:$20-50 Million
Number Employees: 20-49

982 B.B. Bean Coffee
583 County Line Rd
Monument, CO 80132   719-481-1170
          Fax: 719-488-2001 bbcoffee@aol.com
Coffee
     President: Elizabeth Kawczynski
     CEO: Elizabeth Kawczynski
     Marketing Director: Elizabeth Kawczynski
     Roastmaster: Bob Polito
Brands:
     Bean Coffee

983 B.B.S. Lobster Company
141 Smalls Point Rd
Machiasport, ME 04655-3231   207-255-8888
                Fax: 207-255-3987
Fish and seafoods.
     President: Susan West
Estimated Sales:$1,600,000
Number Employees: 5-9

984 B.C. Fisheries
P.O.Box 334
Hancock, ME 04640-0334   207-422-8205
                Fax: 207-422-8206
Seafood
     Manager: Pete Daley

985 B.K. Coffee
P.O.Box 1238
Oneonta, NY 13820-5238   607-432-1499
          Fax: 607-432-1592   800-432-1499
                www.bkcoffee.com
Coffee
     Owner: Paul Karabins
Estimated Sales:$10-24.9 Million
Number Employees: 20-49
Type of Packaging: Private Label
Brands:
     B.K. COFFEE

986 (HQ)B.M. Lawrence & Company
601 Montgomery St # 1115
San Francisco, CA 94111-2614   415-981-3650
     Fax: 415-981-2926 info@bmlawrence.com
Processor and exporter of soft drinks, nonalcoholic
beer, canned fruits, vegetables, juices and fish
     President: B Lawrence
     Purchasing Agent: Hugh Ditzler
Estimated Sales:$5-10 Million
Number Employees: 5-9
Sq. footage: 2000

Brands:
CALIFORNIA FARMS
GRAPEFRUIT
LEMON-LIME
US COLA
US SELECT

987 B.M. Tibbitts & Sons
383 N 1600 E
Saint Anthony, ID 83445-5116   208-624-3402
Fax: 208-624-4672

Manufacturer of potatoes
President: Evan Tibbitts
Estimated Sales: $ 10 - 20 Million
Number Employees: 32
Type of Packaging: Consumer, Food Service, Bulk

988 B.N.W. Industries
7930 N 700 E
Tippecanoe, IN 46570-9613   574-353-7855
Fax: 574-353-8152   sales@belt-o-matic.com
www.belt-o-matic.com
Manufacturer of dryers, roasters, and coolers for the
food industry.
President: Dan Norris
Founder/Consultant: Lee Norris
Regional Sale Engineer: Dick Garner
Export Department: Les Haspl
Vice President Sales: Aaron Norris
Estimated Sales: $ 1 - 3 Million
Number Employees: 5-9

989 B.R. Cohn Olive Oil
1500 Sonoma Highway
Glen Ellen, CA 95442   707-931-7931
Fax: 707-938-4585   877-933-9675
lezette@brcohn.com   www.brcohnoliveoil.com
Olive oils and vinegars

990 B3R Country Meats
PO Box 374
Childress, TX 79201-0374   940-937-3668
Fax: 940-937-6657

All natural beef
President: Mary Lou Bradley
General Manager: James Henderson
Purchasing: Kathleen Lewis
Estimated Sales: $20-50 Million
Number Employees: 50-99
Type of Packaging: Consumer, Food Service
Brands:
B 3 R
B C NATURAL

991 (HQ)BASF Corporation
100 Campus Dr # 301
Florham Park, NJ 07932-1089   973-245-6000
Fax: 973-895-8002   800-526-1072
www.basf.com
Manufacturer of vitamins including A, B, C, D, E,
K, Omega-3 and pre-mixed liquid blends
Chairman/CEO: Klaus Peter Lobbe
EVP/CFO: Hans Engel Dr.
CEO: Kurt Bock
Estimated Sales: 100+ Million
Number Employees: 10,000+
Other Locations:
Geismar LA
Shreveport LA
Livonia MI
Wyandotte MI
Sparks GA
Aberdeen MI
Palmyra MO
Belvidere NJ
Jamesburg NJ
Washington NJ
Enka NC
Morganton NC
Wilmington NC

992 BBQ Bunch
13100 Woodland Avenue
Kansas City, MO 64146-1801   816-941-6789
Fax: 816-941-0263   lewieb@aol.com
Processor of BBQ and mustard sauce; also,
three-bean salsa; wholesaler/distributor of BBQ
products; serving the BBQ industry
Owner: Lewis Bunch
Estimated Sales: $500,000-$1 Million
Number Employees: 1-4
Type of Packaging: Food Service, Private Label,
Bulk
Brands:
Jazzy Barbecue Sauce

993 BBQ Shack
1613 E Peoria St
Paola, KS 66071-1893   913-294-5908
pitmaster@thebbqshack.com
www.thebbqshack.com
Barbacue meats
Owner: Rick Schoenberger
Director Marketing/Sales: Debbie McCrackin
Brands:
BBQ Shack

994 BBQ'n Fools
61535 S Highway 97
9-367
Bend, OR 97702-2154   714-569-1310
Fax: 800-671-8652   800-671-8652
tom@bbqnfools.com   www.bbqnfools.com
Owner: Tom Brohamer
Co-Owner: Kurt Weidmann
Brands:
BBQ'n Fools
Papa Dan's World Famous Jerky

995 BBS Bodacious BBQ Company
8411 Forest Hills Dr # 303
Coral Springs, FL 33065-5405   954-752-0909
Fax: 954-345-3482   800-537-5928
bbsbbq@aol.com   www.800jerky2u.com
Processor of natural and fat-free barbecue sauces,
spicy jellies and steak, turkey jerky
President/CEO: Susan Sheldon
Estimated Sales: $500,000-$1 Million
Number Employees: 10-19
Brands:
AUNT JAYNE'S
BBS BODACIOUS
SAMMYE'S SUMPTUOUS

996 BBU Bakeries
5050 E Evans Ave
Denver, CO 80222-5218   303-691-6342
Fax: 303-757-4332
Manufacturer of cakes, pies, muffins, doughnuts,
breads, pizza dough and bagels
Plant Manager: Ron Schulthies
Estimated Sales: $300,000-500,000
Number Employees: 5-9
Type of Packaging: Consumer

997 BDS Natural Products, Inc.
2779 El Presidio Street
Carson, CA 90810   310-518-2227
Fax: 310-518-2577   swalker@bdsnatural.com
www.bdsnatural.com
Manufacturer and distributor of spices and season-
ing blends.
Co-Founder: Steve Brennis
Director Of Sales: Shauna Walker
Director Of Operations: Kevin Witt

998 BG Smith Sons Oyster
P.O.Box 69
Sharps, VA 22548-0069   804-394-2721
Fax: 804-394-2741   877-483-8279
Manufacturer and exporter of fresh and frozen oys-
ters; processor and packager of ice
President/CEO: B Smith Jr
Estimated Sales: $2.5-5 Million
Number Employees: 10-19
Number of Brands: 3
Number of Products: 1
Sq. footage: 100000
Type of Packaging: Consumer, Food Service, Pri-
vate Label
Brands:
Chesapeake Bay Ice
Chesapeake Pride
Ocean Spray
Perch Creek

999 BGS Jourdan & Sons
1415 Stafford Rd
Darlington, MD 21034-1801   410-457-4904
Processor of canned whole tomatoes
Owner: Scott Reezes
Estimated Sales: Less than $120,000
Number Employees: 1-4
Type of Packaging: Consumer, Private Label
Brands:
Point Pleasant

1000 BI Nutraceuticals
2550 El Presidio Street
Long Beach, CA 90810-1193   310-669-2100
Fax: 310-637-3644   www.binutraceuticals.com
Manufacturer and distributor of water soluable ex-
tracts, pre-mixes, herb powders and teas.

1001 BK Giulini Corporation
3695 Alamo St # 203
Simi Valley, CA 93063-2188   805-581-1979
Fax: 805-581-2139   800-526-2688
mail@bkgiulinicorp.com
www.bkgiulinicorp.com
Producer of specialty food phosphates and phos-
phates based food ingredients
President: Horst Wendt
CEO: Sandy Stone
Estimated Sales: $ 5 - 10 Million
Number Employees: 10-19

1002 BK Giulini Corporation
3695 Alamo St # 203
Simi Valley, CA 93063-2188   805-581-1979
Fax: 805-581-2139   800-526-2688
mail@bkgiulinicorp.com
www.bkgiulinicorp.com
Manufacturer of Phosphate-based food ingredients
for further processed meat, poultry, dairy and
seafood.
CEO: Sandy Stone
VP Sales: Sandy Stone
Estimated Sales: $2.5-5 Million
Number Employees: 10-19
Parent Co: BK Giulini GmbH
Brands:
BEKAPLUS®
BRIFISOL®
JOHR®
TURRISIN®

1003 BKW Seasonings Inc
Knoxville, TN 37932   865-466-8365
Fax: 865-966-6963   matt@bkwseasonings.com
www.bkwseasonings.com
Various types of seasonings

1004 BN Soda
19 Spruce Street
Watertown, MA 02472-1902   617-731-6720
Fax: 240-536-3079
tommy@tommysnakedsoda.com
www.tommysnakedsoda.com
Manufacturer of soda made of natural flavors and
cane sugar, also caffeine-free
Founder: Tom Bleier

1005 BODEGA Chocolates
3198 Airport Loop Drive
Suite A
Costa Mesa, CA 92626-3407   714-432-0708
Fax: 714-432-1537   888-326-3342
customerinfo@bodegachocolates.com
www.bodegachocolates.com
Manufacturer of fudge truffle bars and confections.
Also a frozen and refrigerated line of European
cakes and pastries. All products are kosher
Co-Owner: Jene Paz
Co-Owner: Martucci Angiano
Co-Owner: Pat Brotman
Estimated Sales: $ 5 - 10 Million
Number Employees: 15
Type of Packaging: Consumer, Food Service
Brands:
Fudgescotti

1006 BP Gourmet
135 Ricefield Ln
Hauppauge, NY 11788-2046   631-234-5200
Fax: 631-234-8200   info@bpgourmet.com
www.bpgourmet.com
Fat-free and organic cookies, sugar free cookies,
fruit spreads and salad dressing. Also produces
bread sticks and croutons
President: Florence Boris
Estimated Sales: $2.5-5 Million
Number Employees: 20-49
Brands:
Bp Gourmet
Freida's Kitchen
Monte Carlo Bake Shop
Sweet Nothings

1007 BR Cohn Winery
15000 Sonoma Hwy
Glen Ellen, CA 95442-9454   707-938-4064
Fax: 707-938-4585 stephanie@brcohn.com
www.brcohn.com
Wine, olive oils, vinegars
  Owner: Bruce Cohn
  President: Greg Reisinger
  VP Sales/Marketing: Deborah Mazzaferro
  Purchasing: Bruce Cohn
Estimated Sales: $2.5-5 Million
Number Employees: 10-19
Type of Packaging: Private Label
Brands:
  BALSAMIC AND HERB DIPPING OIL
  BALSAMIC VINEGAR OF MODENA
  CABERNET VINEGAR
  CARNEROS CHARDONNAY
  CHAMPAGNE VINEGAR
  CHARDONNAY VINEGAR
  MENDOCINO CTY. SAUVIGNON BLANC
  OLIVE HILL CABERNET SAUVIGNON
  OLIVE HILL CABERNET SAUVIGNON
  OLIVE HILL PINOT NOIR
  ORGANIC EXTRA VIRGIN OLIVE OIL
  RASPBERRY CHAMPAGNE VINEGAR
  RESERVE CARNEROS CHARDONNAY
  SILVER LABEL CABERNET SAUVIGNO
  SONOMA EXTRA VIRGIN OLIVE OIL
  SONOMA VALLEY MERLOT
  SONOMA VALLEY ZINFANDEL

1008 BT McElrath Chocolatier
2010 E Hennepin Ave # 78
Minneapolis, MN 55413-1890   612-331-8800
Fax: 612-331-2881 info@btmcelrath.com
www.btmcelrath.com
Manufacturer of chocolates
  President: Brian T Mc Elrath
  Partner/Chief Taster: Christine McElrath
Estimated Sales: $ 3 - 5 Million
Number Employees: 5-9

1009 BTS Company/Hail CaesarDressings
PO Box 218015
Nashville, TN 37221-8015   615-226-6868
Fax: 615-226-6867 800-617-8899
hail.caesar@home.com
www.hailcaesardressings.com
Gourmet dressings, pasta sauces, marinades. Available in Original, Low-Fat and Fat Free, Wide variety of flavors & sizes.
  Owner: Bunny Sundock
Estimated Sales: $ 1 - 3 Million
Number Employees: 1-4

1010 Babci's Specialty Foods
115 Clemente Street
Holyoke, MA 01040-5644   413-594-7111
Fax: 413-594-7111 800-225-2023
at@a-tsurgical.com   www.a-tsurgical.com
Bahcis pierogies, kapusta, chrust
  President: Eugene Kirejczyk
Type of Packaging: Food Service, Private Label

1011 Babcock Winery & Vineyards
P.O.Box 637
Lompoc, CA 93438-0637   805-736-1455
Fax: 805-736-3886 info@babcockwinery.com
www.babcockwinery.com
Producers of red and white wines.
  Owner: Bryan Babcock
Estimated Sales: $5-10 Million
Number Employees: 20-49
Type of Packaging: Private Label

1012 Babe Farms
1485 N Blosser Rd
Santa Maria, CA 93458-2043   805-925-4144
Fax: 805-922-3950 800-648-6772
babefarm@silcom.com   www.babefarms.com
Processor and exporter of specialty and baby produce items including peeled carrots and root vegetables; also, specialty salads and stir fry blends; importer of squash and beans
  CEO: Judy Lundberg
  Marketing Director: Judy Landberg
  Director Sales: Loren Hiltner
Estimated Sales: $ 20 - 50 Million
Number Employees: 100-249
Type of Packaging: Food Service, Private Label
Brands:
  Babe Farms

1013 Babe's Honey Farm
334 Walton Place
Victoria, BC V9E 2A4
Canada   250-658-8319
Manufacturer of fireweed and wild flower honey; also, beeswax
  Partner: Alison Warren
Estimated Sales: $100,000-$200,000
Number Employees: 10
Sq. footage: 12000
Type of Packaging: Food Service
Brands:
  Babe's

1014 Baby's Coffee
3178 Overseas Hwy
Key West, FL 33040-6124   305-744-9866
Fax: 305-744-9843 800-523-2326
info@babyscoffee.com   www.babyscoffee.com
Processor of coffee
  Manager: Mary Browman
  Co-Owner: Olga Teplitsky
  Marketing Manager: Alfonse Manosalvas
Estimated Sales: Less than $500,000
Number Employees: 1-4
Type of Packaging: Private Label
Brands:
  Baby's Breakfast Roast
  Baby's Private Buzz
  Baby's Wrelker's Roa
  Hemingway's Hair of
  Killer Joe
  Old Town Roast
  Sexpresso

1015 Bacardi Canada, Inc.
1000 Steeles Avenue E
Brampton, ON L6T 1A1
Canada   905-451-6100
Fax: 905-451-6753 www.bacardi.com
Manufacturer and importer of premium alcoholic beverages including rum, vodka, scotch, gin, vermouth, carbonated low proof beverages, and liqueurs.
  Executive Manager: Manuel Diaz
  CEO: Mr. Paul Beggan
Number Employees: 175
Parent Co: Bacardi Limited
Type of Packaging: Consumer, Food Service
Brands:
  1873 RUM
  BACARDI 151 RUM
  BACARDI 8 RUM
  BACARDI BIG APPLE RUM
  BACARDI BLACK RUM
  BACARDI BREEZER
  BACARDI COCO RUM
  BACARDI GOLD RUM
  BACARDI LIMON
  BACARDI RAZZ
  BACARDI SUPERIOR RUM
  BOMBAY GIN
  GREY GOOSE VODKA
  MARTINI & ROSSI ASTI
  MARTINI & ROSSI VERMOUTHS
  RUSSIAN PRINCE VODKA

1016 (HQ)Bacardi USA
2100 Biscayne Blvd
Miami, FL 33137-5014   305-573-8511
Fax: 305-573-0756 800-222-2734
hrbmusa@bacardi.com   www.bacardi.com
Processor and importer of tropical drink flavored coolers, rum, vodka, prepared mixed drinks
  President/CEO: Eduardo Sardina
  CEO: John P Esposito
  VP/Director Public Relations: Jose Bacardi
Estimated Sales: $650 Million
Number Employees: 250-499
Parent Co: Bacardi International
Type of Packaging: Consumer, Food Service
Brands:
  Anejo
  B&B/Benedictine
  Bacardi Breezers
  Bacardi Limon
  Bacardi Rum
  Bacardi Spice
  Bombay
  Castillo Rums
  Dewar's Scotch
  Hatuey Beers
  Martini & Rossi Asti
  Martini & Rossi Vermouth
  O
  Pommeroy

1017 Bachman Company
P.O.Box 15053
Reading, PA 19612-5053   610-320-7800
Fax: 610-320-7897 800-523-8253
inquiries@thebachmanco.com
www.bachmanco.com
Manufacturer of snack foods including potato chips, pretzels, cheese twists and puffs, popcorn and tortilla chips
  Owner: Joseph F Welch
  VP Sales: Frank Kunkel
Estimated Sales: $10-20 Million
Number Employees: 5-9
Sq. footage: 20000
Type of Packaging: Consumer, Food Service
Brands:
  Bachman
  KIDZELS
  TREAT
  VALLEY MAID

1018 Back Bay Trading
11800 Wills Rd # 120
Alpharetta, GA 30009-2080   770-772-6360
Fax: 770-772-4766 800-650-8327
ralph@ameliabay.com   www.ameliabay.com
Liquid tea and Coffee Bag-N-box
  President/CEO: John Crandall
  CFO: Sherry Harder
  Vice President: Jason Crandall
  Sales Director: Marshall Cartmill
  Public Relations: Jackie Hewitt
  Operations Manager: Dudley Blizzard
Estimated Sales: $ 5 - 10 Million
Number Employees: 5-9
Type of Packaging: Private Label
Brands:
  AMELIA BAY
  PRIVATE LABEL

1019 Backer's Potato Chip Company
P.O.Box 128
Fulton, MO 65251-0128   573-642-2833
Fax: 573-642-7617
Processors of potato chips.
  President/Purchasing: Vicki McDaniel
  Chairman: William Backer
Estimated Sales: $10-20 Million
Number Employees: 50-99

1020 Bacon America
255 Rue Rocheleau
Drummondville, QC J2C 7G2
Canada   819-475-3030
Fax: 819-475-3031
Processor, importer and exporter of bacon
  President: Marcel Heroux
Number Employees: 500-999
Parent Co: J.M. Schneider
Type of Packaging: Consumer, Food Service, Private Label

1021 Bad Frog Brewing
1093 A1A Beach Blvd
Suite 346
Saint Augustine, FL 32080
Fax: 734-629-1777 888-223-3764
badfrog@badfrog.com   www.badfrog.com
Beers
  President: Jim Wauldron
Estimated Sales: $2.5-5 Million
Number Employees: 20-49
Type of Packaging: Private Label
Brands:
  BAD FROG AMBER LAGER
  BAD FROG BAD LIGHT
  BAD FROG MICRO MALT

1022 Badger Best Pizzas
1548 Deckner Avenue
Green Bay, WI 54302-2618   920-336-6464
Frozen pizza
  President: Herm Fredericks
  Plant Manager: Peggy Seefeldt
Estimated Sales: $2.5-5 Million
Number Employees: 5-9

1023 Badger Gourmet Ham
3521 W Lincoln Ave
Milwaukee, WI 53215-2394   414-645-1756
   Fax: 414-645-5189 www.badgergourmetham.com
Processors of ham.
   President: Mark Schwellinger
Estimated Sales: $10-20 Million
Number Employees: 20-49

1024 Badger Island Shell-Fish & Lobster
2 Badgers Is W
Kittery, ME 03904-1601   207-439-3820
                Fax: 207-439-7080
Seafood, shellfish, lobster
   Owner: Ed Gokey
Estimated Sales: $ .5 - 1 million
Number Employees: 1-4

1025 Badia Spices
P.O.Box 226497
Miami, FL 33222-6497   305-629-8000
   Fax: 305-629-8100 info@badiaspices.com
                www.badiaspices.com
Manufacturer and exporter of herbs, spices and seasonings including garlic, buboric, jalapeno, lindo and taco flavoring
   President: Joseph Badia
Estimated Sales: $50-100 Million
Number Employees: 100-249
Type of Packaging: Consumer, Food Service, Private Label, Bulk
Brands:
   Arrowroot
   Chili Powder
   Cinnamon Korintje Ground
   Pepper Black Butcher
   Seasoning Complete

1026 Baensch Food
1025 E Locust St
Milwaukee, WI 53212-2637   414-562-4643
   Fax: 414-562-5525 800-562-8234
   order@mabaensch.com www.mabaensch.com
Manufacturer of herring in glass and bulk containers
   President: Kim Wall
   GM: David Jackson
Estimated Sales: $1-2.5 Million
Number Employees: 10-19
Sq. footage: 30000
Type of Packaging: Consumer, Food Service, Private Label, Bulk
Brands:
   MA BAENSCH
   MA BAENSCH HERRING

1027 Bagai Tea Company
PO Box 1046
San Marcos, CA 92079-1046   760-591-3084
   Fax: 760-510-1904 sales.chaya@juno.com
                www.chaya.com
Tea
   President: Arun Bagai
   CFO: Sanjay Bagai
   VP: Vik Bagai
   Production Manager: Maria Bagai
   Purchasing Manager: Arun Bagai
Estimated Sales: $1-5 Million
Number Employees: 5-9
Type of Packaging: Private Label
Brands:
   Chaya
   Emerald Green
   Golden Amber

1028 Bagel Factory
3640 Woodvale Road
Birmingham, AL 35223-1442   205-969-0000
Bagel manufacturers
   CEO: Jay Epstein
Estimated Sales: $500,000-$1 Million
Number Employees: 10-19
Sq. footage: 2500

1029 Bagel Guys
102 Willoughby Street
Brooklyn, NY 11201-5318   718-222-4561
   Fax: 718-222-4362 bagelguyscorp@AOL.com
                www.bagelguys.com
Processor of bagels
   President: David Abrams
Estimated Sales: Less than $500,000
Number Employees: 5-9

1030 Bagel King
1686 Locust Street
Walnut Creek, CA 94596-4136   925-938-5464
                Fax: 925-938-5468
   Treasurer: Naomi Litvin
   General Manager: Joseph Litvin

1031 Bagel Works
7200 Lombardy Street
Boynton Beach, FL 33437-7349   704-553-8822
                Fax: 704-553-0222
Processor and exporter of bagels
   President: Sadiah Hinnawi
   VP: Steven Goldstein
Estimated Sales: $500,000 appx.
Number Employees: 5-9

1032 Bagels By Bell
10013 Foster Ave
Brooklyn, NY 11236-2117   718-272-2780
        Fax: 718-272-2789 info@bialy.com
                www.bialy.com
Bakery and deli specializing in bagels and bialy
   President: Warren Bell
Estimated Sales: $1 Million
Number Employees: 10-19
Type of Packaging: Private Label
Brands:
   Bell Bialy
   Bell Mini Bagel
   bagel by bell

1033 (HQ)Bagelworks
1229 1st Ave
New York, NY 10065-6314   212-744-6444
                Fax: 718-358-3076
Processor of muffins and bagels including oat bran, sesame, poppy, cinnamon raisin, sundried tomato, chocolate, sourdough, spinach, herb, wholewheat, cheese, broccoli, rye, peanut butter, etc. including fat free
   President: Saadiah Hinnawi
   CEO: Aliyeh Hinnawi
   CFO: Joseph Hinnawi
   VP: Ramsey Hinnawi
Estimated Sales: $720,000
Number Employees: 5-9
Sq. footage: 850
Other Locations:
   Bagelworks
   New York NY

1034 Baier's Sausage & Meats
6022 67a Street
Red Deer, AB T4P 3E8
Canada   403-346-1535
                Fax: 403-346-1773
Processor of ham, sausage, beef jerky, bacon and salami
   President: Keith Baires
   CEO: Keith Baires
   Marketing: Keith Baires
Type of Packaging: Consumer, Food Service, Bulk
Brands:
   Baier's

1035 Bailey Street Bakery
165 Bailey Street SW
Atlanta, GA 30314-4801   404-584-9540
   Fax: 404-584-9526 800-822-4634
                www.flowersfoods.com
Processor of baked goods including breads and buns.
   President/COO Bakeries Group: Gene D Lord
   Chairman: George Deese
   SVP/Chief Financial Officer: R Steve Kinsey
   VP/Communications: Mary Krier
   SVP/Supply Chain: Michael Beaty
Estimated Sales: $100+ Million
Number Employees: 100
Sq. footage: 5000
Parent Co: Flowers Baking Company
Type of Packaging: Consumer

1036 Bailey's Basin Seafood
1683 Front Street
Morgan City, LA 70381-3523   985-384-4926
                Fax: 985-384-4928
Prepared, packaged fish and seafood
   President: Nolton Bailey Sr
Estimated Sales: $2.6 Million
Number Employees: 30
Type of Packaging: Consumer, Food Service

1037 Baily Vineyard & Winery
33440 La Serena Way
Temecula, CA 92591-5104   951-676-9463
   Fax: 951-676-1276 contact@bailywinery.com
                www.bailywinery.com
Wines
   Owner: Phillip Baily
   Owner: Carol Baily
Estimated Sales: $2,800,000
Number Employees: 1-4
Brands:
   Baily

1038 Bainbridge Festive Foods
PO Box 305
Tunica, MS 38676-0305   662-363-9891
   Fax: 662-363-9895 800-545-9205
                bainbridge@tecinfo.com
Jellies, pickles, preserves, spice tea mix, and parsley mustard sauce
   President: Bobbie Hood
Estimated Sales: $150,000
Number Employees: 1-4
Number of Products: 12
Sq. footage: 3500
Type of Packaging: Private Label

1039 Baird Dairies
110 N Randolph Ave
Clarksville, IN 47129-2761   812-283-3345
                Fax: 812-283-8701
Processor of ice cream mixes
   Owner: Randall Baird
Estimated Sales: $500,000-$1 Million
Number Employees: 1-4
Type of Packaging: Consumer

1040 Baja Foods
636 W Root St
Chicago, IL 60609-2630   773-376-9030
   Fax: 773-376-9245 www.bajafoodsllc.com
Processor and exporter of frozen tamales, quesadillas, chimichangas, burritos, enchiladas, taco meat and chili; processor of pizza toppings and meat crumbles
   Owner: Art Velasquez
   Sales/Marketing: Jeff Rothschild
   General Manager: Timothy Poisson
   Purchasing Manager: Cheryl Canning
Estimated Sales: $ 10 - 20 Million
Number Employees: 20-49
Sq. footage: 30000
Type of Packaging: Consumer, Food Service, Private Label, Bulk
Brands:
   AMIGO
   CAFE AMIGO
   LA MARCA
   TANGO

1041 Bakalars Brothers Sausage Company
P.O.Box 1943
La Crosse, WI 54602-1943   608-784-0384
   Fax: 608-784-8361 www.bakalarssausage.com
Manufacturer of sausage, beef, fish, pork, hamburger meat, steak, etc
   President: Michael Bakalars
   Purchasing Manager: Mike Bakalars

Estimated Sales: $15 Million
Number Employees: 20-49

Type of Packaging: Consumer, Food Service, Private Label, Bulk
Brands:
   BAKALARS

1042 Bake Crafters Food
P.O.Box 489
Collegedale, TN 37315-0489   423-396-3392
      Fax: 423-396-9604   800-296-8935
         support@bakecrafters.com
         www.bakecrafters.com
Bake Crafters is a wholesaler baking company servicing the continental Unite States with fully baked, par baked, and frozen dough products. Currently we make a wonderful line of donuts, muffins, cookies, croissants, Danish, wrapsEnglish muffins, breadsticks, Tortillas and many other baked goods. Want to develop a new product? We specialize in custom product development and would be happy to work with you to develop a signature product
   President: Michael Byrd
   Sales Manager: Bob Richmand
   General Manager: Michael Byrd
Estimated Sales:$20 Million
Number Employees: 1-4
Number of Brands: 1
Type of Packaging: Consumer, Food Service, Private Label, Bulk
Brands:
   BAKE CRAFTERS

1043 Bake Mark
7351 Crider Ave
Pico Rivera, CA 90660-3705   562-949-1054
   Fax: 562-948-2655   ibie-mgr@bakemarkwest.com
         www.bakemark.com
   VP: Bruce Reynolds
Estimated Sales:$ 20 - 50 Million
Number Employees: 250-499

1044 Bake Masters of Atlanta
3814 Oakcliff Industrial Court
Doraville, GA 30340-3407   770-447-6823
      Fax: 770-263-6098
Bread and bakery products
   VP Sales: Edward Holgate
   VP Production: Timothy Holgate
   Purchasing Agent: Robert Holgate
Estimated Sales:$50-100 Million
Number Employees: 50-99
Type of Packaging: Private Label
Brands:
   SPECIALTY

1045 Bake Rite Rolls
2945 Samuel Dr
Bensalem, PA 19020-7305   215-638-2400
      Fax: 215-638-1662
Manufacturer of soft sandwich rolls, english muffins, hamburger and hot dog rolls.
   Manager: Bob Cranmer
   Plant Manager: Bob Cranmer
Estimated Sales:$20-50 Million
Number Employees: 100-249
Parent Co: Northeast Foods
Type of Packaging: Private Label

1046 (HQ)Bake'n Joy Foods
995 Westwood Square
Suite A
Oviedo, FL 32765-9049   407-359-0713
      Fax: 978-683-1713   800-666-4937
productinfo@bakenjoy.com   www.bakenjoy.com/
Manufacturer of premixed bases, batters, icings, dough and dough conditioners for the baking industry.
   Chairman: Gerald Ogan
   President/CEO: Robert Ogan
   VP Finance: Alice Shepherd
   Public Relations: George Fregone
*Estimated Sales:*Less than $500,000
Number Employees: 5-9
Type of Packaging: Food Service, Bulk

1047 Bake'n Joy Foods
351 Willow St S
North Andover, MA 01845-5973   978-683-1414
      Fax: 978-683-1713   800-666-4937
productinfo@bakenjoy.com   www.bakenjoy.com
Processor of low-fat, fat-free and frozen batters, bakery mixes, fillings, toppings, icings and ready-to-bake items
   President/CEO: Robert Ogan
   Marketing Coordinator: Teri Larcom
Estimated Sales:$20-50 Million
Number Employees: 100-249
Type of Packaging: Food Service, Bulk
Other Locations:
   Bake'n Joy Foods
   Chuluota FL
Brands:
   FRESHBAKES
   STRAWBERRY COLADA FROZEN BATTER
   TRIPLE BERRY BLAST FROZEN BATTER

1048 BakeMark
1933 N Meacham Road
Suite 530
Schaumburg, IL 60173-4342   562-949-1054
      Fax: 562-949-1257 www.bakemark.com
Manufacturer of bakery products
   President/CEO: Robert Wallace
   CFO: Herman Brons
Estimated Sales:$4 Million
Type of Packaging: Private Label
Other Locations:
   Phoenix AZ
   Burlington NJ
   Pico Rivera CA
   North Las Vegas NV
   Rancho Cordova CA
   Reno NV
   Union City CA
   Buffalo NY
   Denver CO
   Saratoga Springs NY
   Altanta GA
   Fairfield OH
   Carol Stream IL
Brands:
   CAHOKIA FLOUR
   FEDERAL BAKERS
   KARP'S
   KIRKLAND & ROSE
   WESTCO

1049 BakeMark Canada
2345 Francis-Hughes Avenue
Laval, QC H7S 1N5
Canada   450-667-8888
      Fax: 450-667-3342   800-361-4998
         www.bakemarkcanada.com
Processor and exporter of bakers' and confectioners' supplies including fondants, cocoa chips and pieces, apricot and strawberry glazes, rainbow and chocolate sprinkles and fruit pie fillings
   President: Larry Sullivan
Number Employees: 10-19
Sq. footage: 70000
Parent Co: CSM Bakery Supplies North America
Type of Packaging: Food Service, Private Label
Brands:
   GOLDEN
   LAFAVE

1050 Bakehouse
834 W Hallandale Beach Blvd
Hallandale Beach, FL 33009-5239   954-458-1600
      Fax: 954-458-0126   bakehouse@mailcity.com
Processor of dough, yeasts and breads including pumpernickel, kalamata olive, focaccia, challah, wholewheat, chocolate cherry, sesame semolina, etc
   President: Ed Robertson
   Purchasing: Harris Ross
Estimated Sales:$10-20 Million
Number Employees: 10-19

1051 Bakemark Ingredients Canada
2480 Viking Way
Richmond, BC V6V 1N2
Canada   604-303-1700
      Fax: 604-303-1705   800-665-9441
         sales@bakemarkcanada.com
         www.bakemarkcanada.com

Bakemark Canada; manufacturers and suppliers of fine bakery and food ingredients
   President: Larry Sullivan
   Marketing: Linda McKenzie-Low
   Sales Manager: Jeff Bligh
   General Manager: Rick Barnes
   Purchasing: Linda McKenzie-Low
Estimated Sales:$50-100 Million
Number Employees: 300
Number of Brands: 12
Number of Products: 2000
Type of Packaging: Private Label, Bulk
Brands:
   BAKEMARK
   BIB ULMER SPATZ
   BRILL
   CARAVAN
   DEGOEDE
   DIAMALT
   DREIDOPPEL
   MARQUERITE
   MEISTERMARKEN

1052 Baker
P.O.Box 528
Milford, NJ 08848-0528   908-995-4040
      Fax: 908-995-9669   800-995-3989
         sales@the-baker.com   www.the-baker.com
Manufacturer of breads and rolls, organic breads, pita, cereals and grains such as wheat, oats, corn, rice, barley, rye, millet and buckwheat.
Estimated Sales:$1-3 Million
Number Employees: 20-49
Brands:
   THE BAKER

1053 Baker & Baker
1933 N Meacham Rd # 530
Schaumburg, IL 60173-4342   847-925-5170
      Fax: 847-925-5171   800-593-5777
         www.csm.nl/index3.html
Manufacturer and exporter of mixes, frozen dough and fruit fillings
   President/CEO: Paul Barron
Estimated Sales:$100+ Million
Number Employees: 100-249
Sq. footage: 100000
Parent Co: CSM
Type of Packaging: Food Service, Private Label, Bulk
Brands:
   KARP'S

1054 Baker & Baker, Inc.
1933 N Meacham Rd # 530
Schaumburg, IL 60173-4342   847-925-5170
      Fax: 847-925-5171   800-593-5777
         www.csm.nl/index3.html
Frozen muffin batters, cookies, puff pastries, pie fillings, cobblers, icings, and glazes
   Purchasing: Carmella Vasquez
Estimated Sales:$100-500 Million
Number Employees: 100-249
Brands:
   BAKER & BAKER
   BESTOVALL
   KARP'S
   ORTH
   SCOOP-N-BAKE

1055 Baker Boy Bake Shop
170 Gta Dr
Dickinson, ND 58601-7200   701-225-4444
      Fax: 701-225-7981   800-437-2008
info@bakerboy.com   www.bakerboy.com
Processor of frozen dough products; wholesaler/distributor of bakery supplies including flour, sugar, etc.; serving the foodservice market
   President/CEO: Guy Moos
Estimated Sales:$22 Million
Number Employees: 250-499
Sq. footage: 85000
Type of Packaging: Consumer, Food Service, Private Label
Brands:
   BAKER BOY

1056 Baker Boys
2140 Pegasus Road NE
Calgary, AB T2E 8G8
Canada   403-255-4556
      Fax: 403-259-5124   877-246-6036
info@bakerboys.net   www.bakerboys.net

Processor of cinnamon rolls including thaw and serve, pre-proofed and frozen
President: Berry Walton
VP of Sales: Barry Wolton
Number Employees: 20-49
Type of Packaging: Consumer, Food Service
Brands:
Baker Boys

1057 Baker Candy Company
12534 Lake City Way NE
Seattle, WA 98125-4425   425-776-6622
                    Fax: 206-361-7009
Manufacturer of roasted nuts, chocolates and hard candy
Owner: Randy Spoo
VP: Ronald Prevele
Treasurer: Ronald Prevele
VP: Lee Prevele
Estimated Sales: $5-10 Million
Number Employees: 10-19
Sq. footage: 15000
Type of Packaging: Consumer, Bulk

1058 Baker Cheese Factory
N5279 County Road G
St Cloud, WI 53079-1644   920-477-7871
    Fax: 920-477-2404 dick@bakercheese.com
                    www.bakercheese.com
Manufacturer of string cheese
President: Richard Baker
Operations Manager: Brian Baker
Purchasing: Richard Baker
Estimated Sales: $25-50 Million
Number Employees: 100-249
Type of Packaging: Consumer, Private Label
Brands:
BAKER

1059 (HQ)Baker Commodities
4020 Bandini Blvd
Vernon, CA 90058-4274   323-268-2883
                    Fax: 323-268-5166
    dluckey@bakercommodities.com
                    www.bakercommodities.com
Manufacturer of protein meal and feeding fats
President: Jim Andreoli
CFO: Jim Reynolds
Executive VP: Dennis Luckey
VP Operations: Bill Sikes
Estimated Sales: $10-20 Million
Number Employees: 500-999
Type of Packaging: Bulk
Other Locations:
Seattle WA
Spokane WA
Kerman CA
Phoenix AZ
Rochester NY
North Billerica MA

1060 Baker Maid Products, Inc.
P.O.Box 50424
New Orleans, LA 70150-0424   504-827-5500
    Fax: 504-827-5400 bakermaid@bellsouth.net
Sliced, individually-wrapped dark brandied fruit cake, chunky chocolate cookies including almond toffee crunch, pecan praline and double chocolate raspberry
President: Darryl Sorrensen
CEO: Darell Sorensen
Estimated Sales: $1-2.5 Million
Number Employees: 20-49

1061 Baker Produce Company
P.O.Box 6757
Kennewick, WA 99336-0515   509-586-6174
    Fax: 509-582-3694 800-624-7553
    pbeamer@bakerproduce.com
                    www.bakerproduce.com
Grower and exporter of produce including apples, asparagus, cherries, onions, potatoes and sweet corn.
Manager: Pam Beamer
Sales Manager: Pam Beamer
Sales Representative: Diana Hawkins
Sales Representative: Tyler Saunders
Shipping: Savannah Davis
Estimated Sales: $100-500 Million
Number Employees: 250-499
Type of Packaging: Consumer, Food Service, Bulk
Brands:
BAKER SUPREME
BAKERS BEAUTIES
RED CHIP
YOU LIKE MORE

1062 Baker's Choice
PO Box 1296
Birmingham, MI 48012-1296   248-827-7500
    Fax: 248-827-7505 info@thebakerschoice.com
                    www.thebakerschoice.com
Manufacturer and wholesaler of baked goods including muffins, cookies, danish, bread and fruit loaves, tea biscuits, brownies, specialty cakes and buns including hamburger, hot dog, submarine and hot cross
Number Employees: 3
Sq. footage: 1275
Type of Packaging: Consumer, Food Service, Bulk

1063 Baker's Coconut
8000 Horizon Center Blvd
Memphis, TN 38133-5197   901-381-6500
    Fax: 901-381-6524 800-323-1092
                    www.kraftfoodscompany.com
Processor and exporter of cheese, coconut, flavors and cheese powders
Marketing/Sales Executive: Mike Malone
National Sales Manager: Greg Leininger
Number Employees: 100-249
Parent Co: Kraft Foods
Type of Packaging: Bulk

1064 Baker's Dozen
225 E State St
Herkimer, NY 13350   315-866-6770
Manufacturer of baked goods including bread, rolls and doughnuts
Owner: Tom Watkins
Manager: Tony Durso
Estimated Sales: $ 1 - 3 Million
Number Employees: 10-19

1065 Baker's Point Fisheries

Oyster Pond Jeddore, NS B0J 1W0
Canada   902-845-2347
                    Fax: 902-845-2770
Processor and exporter of fresh and frozen haddock, cod, pollack, hake and cusk
Co-Owner: Janette Faulkner
Co-Owner: Wyman Baker
Number Employees: 50-99
Type of Packaging: Bulk

1066 Baker's Rib
2724 Commerce St
Dallas, TX 75226-1404   214-748-5433
    Fax: 214-748-8544 www.bakersribs.com
Processor of BBQ sauces and seasonings
Manager: Julie Richter
Estimated Sales: Less than $500,000
Number Employees: 5-9
Type of Packaging: Consumer, Food Service
Brands:
Baker's Rib Inc

1067 Bakerhaus Veit Limited
70 Whitmore Road
Woodbridge, ON L4L 7Z4
Canada   905-850-9229
    Fax: 905-850-9292 800-387-8860
    info@backerhausveit.com
                    www.backerhausveit.com
President/CEO: Sabine C Veit
CEO: Karen Reissmann
Brands:
Bakerhaus Veit

1068 Bakers Breakfast Cookie
4208 Meridian St
Bellingham, WA 98226-5513   360-714-9585
    Fax: 360-715-8011 877-889-1090
    info@bbcookies.com www.bbcookies.com
Manufacturer of all natural cookies
Owner: Erin Baker
Estimated Sales: $ 5 - 10 Million
Number Employees: 20-49
Sq. footage: 4000

1069 Bakers Candy
P.O.Box 88
Greenwood, NE 68366-0088   402-789-2700
    Fax: 402-789-2013 800-804-7330
Manufacturer of fine chocolates, including our chocolate meltaways in seven flavors
Owner: Kevin Baker
VP: Patty Baker
Sales Manager: Todd Baker

Estimated Sales: $ 3 - 5 Million
Number Employees: 5-9
Type of Packaging: Consumer

1070 Bakers of Paris
99 Park Ln
Brisbane, CA 94005-1309   415-468-9100
                    Fax: 415-468-4320
    customer-service@bakersofparis.com
                    www.bakersofparis.com
Manufacturer of all natural French bread and French pastries
Owner: Lionel Robbe-Jeadu
VP: Gilles Wicker
Estimated Sales: $5-10 Million
Number Employees: 50-99

1071 Bakers' Best Snack FoodCorporation
1880 N Penn Rd
Hatfield, PA 19440-1950   215-822-3511
    Fax: 215-997-2049 www.jj snacks.com
Processor of soft pretzels
Manager: Wayne Childs
VP: Bob Radano
Marketing Manager: Michael Karaban
G.M.: Wayne Childs
Number Employees: 50-99
Parent Co: J&J Snack Foods Company
Type of Packaging: Consumer
Brands:
Chill Smooth Ice
Pretzel Fillers
Super Pretzel

1072 Bakery Chef
4501 W Fullerton Ave
Chicago, IL 60639-1933   773-384-1900
    Fax: 773-384-3661 www.ralcorpfrozen.com
Processor and co-packer of baked goods including muffins, pound and crumb cakes.
Executive Director: Laura Rivera
VP Sales: Larry Gordon
General Manager: Ronald Krass
Estimated Sales: $9-14 Million
Number Employees: 1-4
Type of Packaging: Consumer, Food Service, Private Label, Bulk

1073 Bakery Chef
12650 Westport Rd
Louisville, KY 40245-1945   502-423-8944
    Fax: 502-423-9348 800-594-0203
    information@bakerychef.com
                    www.bakerychef.com
Processor of frozen ready to serve biscuits, breads, muffins, pancakes, french toast and waffles.
Customer Development VP: Terry Rice
Director Operations: David Jerome
Manager: John Bischoff
Purchasing Agent: Jim Jupin
Estimated Sales: $100-500 Million
Number Employees: 250-499
Sq. footage: 320000
Parent Co: Ralcorp Holdings
Type of Packaging: Food Service, Private Label
Brands:
CHEF SUPREME
KRUSTEAZ
WAFFLE STICKS

1074 Bakery Corp
15625 NW 15th Ave
Miami, FL 33169-5601   305-623-3838
    Fax: 305-626-9189 800-521-4345
    info@bakerycorp.com www.bakerycorp.com
Manufacturers of breads and cakes
President: Luis Lacal
Estimated Sales: $10-20 Million
Number Employees: 10-19

1075 Bakery Crafts
P.O.Box 37
West Chester, OH 45071-0037   513-942-0862
    Fax: 513-942-3835 800-543-1673
    info@BakeryCrafts.com www.bakerycrafts.com
Manufacturer, wholesaler, importer and exporter of cake decoration supplies
President: Sam Guttman
VP Marketing: Laura Guder
Estimated Sales: $ 20 - 50 Million
Number Employees: 100-249
Sq. footage: 150000
Parent Co: Jack Guttman

Type of Packaging: Bulk
Brands:
Bakery CraftS
Copy Confection

1076 Bakery Europa
500 Alakawa Street
Honolulu, HI 96817-4593   808-845-5011
Fax: 808-847-6263   europa1@gte.net
Processor of breads, croissants, pastries and desserts
President: Dennis Dolim
Cntllr.: Stuart Kimura
CFO: Walter Lum
Quality Control: Eric Gotz
Operations Manager: Glenn Wong
Plant Manager: Melvin Ishikawa
Purchasing Manager: Donna Tatupa
Estimated Sales: $50-100 Million
Number Employees: 100-249
Sq. footage: 18000
Parent Co: Global Operations Pacific
Type of Packaging: Consumer, Food Service, Private Label, Bulk
Brands:
Bakery Europa
Bakery Iwilei
Bakery Weilei
Coach House Bakeries
Old Vienna Bake Shop

1077 Bakery Management Corporation
15625 NW 15th Ave
Miami, FL 33169-5601   305-623-3838
Fax: 305-626-9189   info@bakerycorp.com
www.bakerycorp.com
Baked goods including danish, muffins, croissant, cakes, bagels, rolls, bread and buns.
President: Luis Lacal
Estimated Sales: $ 5 - 10 Million
Number Employees: 10-19

1078 Bakon Yeast
33415 N 64th Place
Scottsdale, AZ 85266-7363   480-595-9370
Fax: 480-595-9371   bakonyeast@aol.com
bakonyeast.samsbiz.com
Processor of vegetable derived bacon flavored seasonings and hickory smoked torula yeast; exporter of hickory smoked torula yeast
President: Phyl Ray
VP: Larry Ray
Plant Manager: Rebecca Schaefer
Estimated Sales: $1-2.5 Million
Number Employees: 1-4
Sq. footage: 10000
Parent Co: Bakon Yeast
Type of Packaging: Consumer, Food Service, Bulk
Brands:
Bakon Seasonings
Bakon Yeast

1079 Balagna Winery Company
223 Rio Bravo Drive
Los Alamos, NM 87544-3848   505-672-3678
Fax: 505-672-1482
Wines
Proprietor: John Balagna
Operations Manager: John Balagna
Estimated Sales: $ .5 - 1 million
Number Employees: 20
Brands:
Balagna Winery

1080 Balanced Health Products
215 E 68th St # 33a
New York, NY 10065-5736   212-794-9878
Fax: 212-794-5108   nikkistar@worldnet.att.net
www.starcaps.com
Processor of dietetic candy and supplements
President: Nikki Haskell
Estimated Sales: $790,000
Number Employees: 1-4
Sq. footage: 1000
Brands:
Nikki Bars
Star Blend
Star Caps
Star Sucker Sour
Star Suckers

1081 Balboa Dessert Company
1760 E Wilshire Avenue
Santa Ana, CA 92705-4615
Fax: 714-972-0605   800-974-9699
www.balboadessert.com
Processor and exporter of desserts including frozen cakes, cheesecakes and tortes
Estimated Sales: $20-50 Million
Number Employees: 50-99
Type of Packaging: Food Service

1082 Baldinger Bakery
215 Eva St
St Paul, MN 55107-1697   651-224-5761
Fax: 651-224-9047
Processor of baked goods including bread, rolls and buns.
President: Robert Baldinger
VP Sales: Jim Gottreich
VP/Operations: Steve Baldinger
Estimated Sales: $20-50 Million
Number Employees: 100-249
Type of Packaging: Consumer, Food Service
Brands:
Old World

1083 Baldwin Richardson Foods
20201 S Lagrange Rd # 20
Frankfort, IL 60423-1372   815-464-9994
Fax: 815-464-9995   866-644-2732
www.brfoods.com

Baldwin Richardson Foods is a liquid ingredient manufacturer specializing in signature sauces, dessert toppings, beverage/pancake syrups, specialty fruit fillings and condiments. Packaging capabilities range from portion control cupsand pouches to standard retail and foodservice packs and include industrial drums and totes. Full service R&D and Quality groups dedicated to new product development, with in-house stability and analytical testing. Call for assistance.

CEO: Eric G Johnson
Purchasing: Paula Bell
Estimated Sales: $ 5 - 10 Million
Number Employees: 5-9
Sq. footage: 900000
Type of Packaging: Consumer, Food Service, Private Label, Bulk
Brands:
Baldwin Ice Cream
Mrs Richardson Toppings
Nance's Mustards
Nance's Wing Sauce & Condiments

1084 Baldwin Vineyards
176 Hardenburg Rd
Pine Bush, NY 12566-5720   845-744-2226
Fax: 845-744-6321
baldwin_Vineyards@frontiernet.net
www.baldwinvineyards.com
Processor of wines
Owner/CEO: Patricia Baldwin
Owner/President: Jack Baldwin
VP: John Baldwin
Estimated Sales: $500,000-$1 Million
Number Employees: 1-4
Brands:
Baldwin

1085 Baldwin-Minkler Farms
320 E South St
Orland, CA 95963-9111   530-865-8080
Fax: 530-865-8085   djsoetaert@aol.com
Processor of almonds
Owner: Roderick Minkler
General Manager: Bill Minkler
Estimated Sales: $20-50 Million
Number Employees: 50-99
Type of Packaging: Bulk

1086 Balic Winery
6623 Harding Hwy
Mays Landing, NJ 08330-1022   609-625-1903
Fax: 609-625-1904   www.balicwinery.com
Wine
Owner: Bojan Boskodich
Estimated Sales: Less than $200,000
Number Employees: 5-9

1087 Ball Park Franks
21701 W 11 Mile Rd # 4
Southfield, MI 48076-3713   248-355-1100
Fax: 248-355-3436   888-317-5867
www.ballparkfranks.com
Hot dogs, packaged meat products, kosher hot dogs, kosher packaged meat products
Manager: Lucretia High
CFO: Larry Breen
VP Advertising: Margaret Reilly
Director Technical Service: Robert Jester
Estimated Sales: $100-500 Million
Number Employees: 1-4
Parent Co: Sara Lee Corporation
Brands:
Ball Park Fat Free Franks
Ball Park Franks

1088 (HQ)Ballantine Produce Company
P.O.Box 756
Reedley, CA 93654-0756   559-637-2400
Fax: 559-637-2159   info@ballantineproduce.com
www.ballantineproduce.com
Manufacturer and processor of over 200 varieties of plums, peaches, nectarines, pluots, white flesh, apricots, grapes, Asian pears, quince, pomegranates, persimmons and apples.
President: Virgil Rasmussen
CFO: Richard Graham
Plant Manager: Ron Frauenheim
Estimated Sales: $12.8 Million
Number Employees: 100-249
Type of Packaging: Consumer, Food Service
Other Locations:
Reedley Sales Office
Reedley CA
Brands:
Ballantine

1089 Ballard Custom Meats
55 Myrtle St
Manchester, ME 04351-3251   207-622-9764
Fax: 207-621-0242
Meats
President: Kenneth Ballard Jr
Estimated Sales: $2,000,000
Number Employees: 10-19

1090 Ballas Egg Products Corporation
P.O.Box 2217
Zanesville, OH 43702-2217   740-453-0386
Fax: 740-453-0491
Manufacturer of frozen, dried and liquid eggs; exporter of frozen and dried eggs.
President: Leonard Ballas
CEO: J Saliba
VP: Craig Ballas
Estimated Sales: $25 Million
Number Employees: 100-249
Sq. footage: 100000
Brands:
BALLAS

1091 Ballreich's Potato Chips
P.O.Box 186
Tiffin, OH 44883-0186   419-447-1814
Fax: 419-447-5635   800-323-2447
chips@ballreich.com   www.ballreich.com
Snacks including potato chips; flavors include BBQ, sour cream and onion, southwestern BBQ, salt and vinegar, no salt added, and marcelled
President: Brian Reis
VP: Linda Reis

Estimated Sales: $10-20 Million
Number Employees: 20-49
Number of Brands: 1
Number of Products: 52
Sq. footage: 50000
Type of Packaging: Private Label
Brands:
Ballreich
Ballreich's Caramel Corn
Ballreich's Cheese Curls
Ballreich's Cheese Popcorn
Ballreich's Party Mix
Ballreich's Pork Rinds
Ballreich's Pretzels
Ballreich's Tortilla Chips
Ballreich's Triple Mix

1092 Balsu
P.O.Box 545838
Miami Beach, FL 33154-5838   617-539-0880
Fax: 617-539-0879 balsusa@aol.com
www.balsusa.com
Processor and importer of hazelnuts
President: Cuneyd Zapsu
Sales Director: Karim Azzaoui
Estimated Sales: $300,000-500,000
Number Employees: 15
Type of Packaging: Bulk

1093 Baltic Bakery
4627 S Hermitage Avenue
Chicago, IL 60609-3887   773-523-1510
Fax: 773-523-7377
Processor of bread
President: Al Ankus
Vice President: John Ankus
Estimated Sales: $1-2.5 Million
Number Employees: 20-49
Type of Packaging: Consumer

1094 Baltimore Bakery
1140 Kingwood Ave
Norfolk, VA 23502-5603   757-855-4731
Fax: 757-855-2568 www.mamakayersbakery.com
Baked goods
President: Jason Mathis
COO: Robert Fall
Estimated Sales: $10-20 Million
Number Employees: 50-99

1095 Baltimore Brewing Company
104 Albemarle Street
Baltimore, MD 21202-4463   410-837-5000
Fax: 410-837-5024 theo@degroens.com
Processor of seasonal beer and lager
President: Theo De Groen
Estimated Sales: $20-50 Million
Number Employees: 20-49
Brands:
De Groen's

1096 Baltimore Coffee & Tea Company
9 W Aylesbury Rd
Timonium, MD 21093-4121   410-561-1080
Fax: 410-561-4816 800-823-1408
orders@baltcoffee.com
www.baltimorecoffee.com
Manufacturer of coffee and tea
President: Stanley Constantine
VP: Norman Loverde
Estimated Sales: $2.5-5 Million
Number Employees: 50-99
Type of Packaging: Private Label
Brands:
Easten Shore Tea

1097 Baltimore Poultry & Meats
1552 Ridgely Street
Baltimore, MD 21230-2013   410-783-7361
Fax: 410-783-7740
Manufacturer of poultry and meats
President: Hong Kim

1098 Bama Fish Atlanta
3113 Main Street
East Point, GA 30344-4802   404-765-9896
Fax: 404-765-9874
Fresh and frozen fish

1099 Bama Frozen Dough
2745 East 11th Street
Tulsa, OK 74104   918-732-2600
Fax: 918-592-7499 800-756-2262
dwilson@bama.com www.bama.com
Manufacturer of frozen pizza, yeast, pastry sheet
dough
CEO: Paula Marshall-Chapman
VP Operations: Ted Easton
Estimated Sales: $20-50 Million
Number Employees: 100-249
Parent Co: Bama Companies
Other Locations:
Bama Companies
Tulsa OK
Bama Foods Ltd.
Tulsa OK
Beijing Bama Food Processing Co.
Daxing County, Beijing

1100 Banana Distributing Company
1500 S Zarzamora St # 401
San Antonio, TX 78207-7375   210-227-8285
Fax: 210-227-8287 mj@banana-distributing.com
www.banana-distributing.com
Manufacturer and wholesaler/distributor of bananas
and plantains
GM: Jim Scarsdale
Sales Manager: Augie Aguilar
Operations Manager: Leo Aguilar
Estimated Sales: $ 5 - 10 Million
Number Employees: 10-19
Parent Co: Barshop Enterprises
Type of Packaging: Consumer, Food Service, Bulk

1101 Bandiera Winery
155 Cherry Creek Road
Cloverdale, CA 95425-3807   707-894-4295
Fax: 707-894-2563 info@bandiera.com
www.bandiera.com
Wines
President: Cathy Delfava
Estimated Sales: $10-20 Million
Number Employees: 20-49
Parent Co: California Winery

1102 Bandon Bay Fisheries
PO Box 485
Bandon, OR 97411-0485   541-347-4454
Fax: 541-347-4313
Processor of IQF shrimp meat and crab meat
Manager: Graydon Stinnett
Number Employees: 50-99
Sq. footage: 10000
Parent Co: S&S Seafood
Type of Packaging: Private Label

1103 Banfi Vintners
1111 Cedar Swamp Rd
Glen Head, NY 11545-2109   516-626-9200
Fax: 516-626-9218 800-645-6511
info@banfivintners.com www.banfivintners.com
Manufactuer and importer of italian wines
President: James Mariani
CEO: Cristina Mariani-May
Marketing Director: Gary Clayton
VP Public Relations: Lars Leicht
Estimated Sales: $100-500 Million
Number Employees: 50-99
Parent Co: Banfi Products Corporation
Brands:
BORGOGNO
CASTELLO BANFI
CECCHI
CONCHAY TORO
GARY MOLAGHAN
OLD BROOKVILLE
PLACIDO
RIUNITE
SARTORI
STONEHAVEN
STONES
TRIVENTO
VIGNE REGALI/PRINCIPESSA GAVIA
WALNET CREST

1104 Banfi Vintners
1111 Cedar Swamp Rd
Glen Head, NY 11545-2109   516-626-9200
Fax: 516-626-9218 800-645-6511
www.banfivintners.com
Manufacturer of Wines
Chairman/CEO: John Mariani
President/COO: Harry Mariani
EVP Global Marketing Castello Banfi: Cristina
Mariani-May
EVP Sales/Marketing Banfi Import Ops: James
Mariani
Estimated Sales: $ 100-500 Million
Number Employees: 100-249

Brands:
ALMAVIVA
BELL' AGIO
BORGOGNO
CECCHI
CONCHA Y TORO
CONO SUR
COSTELLO BANFI
ENTREE
FLORIO
OLD BROOKVILLE
PLACIDO
RIUNITE
SARTORI
SINCERITY
STONE HAVEN
STONE HAVEN
STONE'S
SUNRISE
VIGNE REGALI
WALNUT CREST
WISDOM & WARTER

1105 Banner Beef & Seafood Company
PO Box 420186
Miami, FL 33242-0186   305-325-0420
Fax: 305-324-1943
Manufacturer of beef, pork, chicken and seafood
COO: Jon Lasko
Estimated Sales: $6 Million
Number Employees: 92
Sq. footage: 50000
Parent Co: Terrace Holdings

1106 Banner Candy Manufacturing Company
700 Liberty Avenue
Brooklyn, NY 11208-2197   718-647-4747
Fax: 718-647-7192
Candy
President: Michael Smith
Plant Manager: Rose Grunther
Estimated Sales: $10-20 Million
Number Employees: 50-99
Type of Packaging: Bulk

1107 (HQ)Banner Pharmacaps
4100 Mendenhall Oaks Pkwy
High Point, NC 27265-8074   336-812-3442
Fax: 336-812-7030 globalinfo@banpharm.com
www.banpharm.com
Manufacturer and exporter of soft gel and vitamins
President/CEO: Roger Gordon PhD
CFO Banner: Robert Gretton
Global VP/R&D/Operations: Aqeel Fatmi
Global VP/Legal/Human Resources: Charles Cain

Global VP/Commercial Operations: Timothy
Doran
Estimated Sales: $114 Million
Number Employees: 250-499
Sq. footage: 250000
Parent Co: Sobel-Holland
Other Locations:
Banner Pharmacaps
Chatsworth CA
Banner Pharmacaps
Alberta, Canada
Gelcaps Exportadora De Mexico
Naucalpan, Edo. de Mexico
Banner Pharmacaps Europe BV
Tilburg, The Netherlands
Banner Pharmacaps India Pvt. Ltd.
Bangalore, India
Brands:
BANNER SOFLET

1108 Banner Wholesale Grocers
3000 S Ashland Ave # 30
Chicago, IL 60608-5348   312-421-2650
Fax: 312-421-5175 www.bannerwholesale.com
Wholesaler/distributor of groceries, general mer-
chandise, frozen and Hispanic foods; serving the
food service market
President: Richard Saltzman
Sales: Mario Gomez
Operations: Irwin Friedman
Plant Manager: Aurelio Frutos
Purchasing: Scott Hilligoss
Estimated Sales: $20-50 Million
Number Employees: 50-99
Sq. footage: 88000

1109 Banquet Schuster Bakery
115 E Abriendo Ave
Pueblo, CO 81004-4201   719-544-1062
Manufacturer of baked goods including bread, pies, cakes, pastries, etc.
President: Janet Monack
Estimated Sales:$1-2.5 Million
Number Employees: 10-19
Type of Packaging: Consumer

1110 Baptista's Bakery
P.O.Box 321010
Franklin, WI 53132-6161   414-409-2000
     Fax: 414-423-4375 877-261-3157
          mdavis@baptistas.com
Manufacturer of bread products and dipping sauces
President: Thomas Howe
CEO: Nannette Gardetto
Estimated Sales:$ 10 - 20 Million
Number Employees: 50-99
Brands:
  BAPTISTA'S
  GARDETTO'S

1111 Bar Harbor Brewing Company
8 Mount Desert St
Bar Harbor, ME 04609-1717   207-288-4592
     orders@barharborbrewing.com
          www.barharborbrewing.com

Brewers
President: Andre Lozano
Operations: Tod Foster
Estimated Sales:$1-2.5 Million
Number Employees: 1-4
Brands:
  BAR HARBOR GINGER ALE
  BAR HARBOR PEACH ALE
  CADILLAC MOUNTAIN STOUT
  HARBOR LIGHTHOUSE ALE
  THUNDER HOLE ALE
  TRUE BLUE

1112 Bar NA, Inc.
P.O.Box 6599
Champaign, IL 61826-6599   217-687-4810
     Fax: 217-687-4830 rboodram@baraninc.com
          www.baraninc.com
Manufacturer, distribution and installation of small to medium capacity equipment for soy foods and vegetable oilseeds production and processing
President: Ramlakhan Boodram
Estimated Sales:$1-2.5 Million
Number Employees: 10-19

1113 (HQ)Bar-S Foods Company
P.O.Box 29049
Phoenix, AZ 85038-9049   602-264-7272
     Fax: 602-285-5252 www.bar-s.com
Refrigerated frankfurters, bacon, hams, luncheon meats and sausages
CEO: Timothy T Day
VP Sales/Marketing: Linda Boodman
General Manager: Max Pyron
Estimated Sales:$400 Million
Number Employees: 1,000-4,999
Type of Packaging: Consumer, Food Service, Private Label, Bulk
Other Locations:
  Bar-S
  Clinton OK
  Bar-S
  Altus OK
  Bar-S
  Lawton OK
  Bar-S
  Elk City OK
Brands:
  BAR-S BRANDS
  BIGGIES
  CHUNKWAGON
  CORONADO
  EXTRA LEAN
  LITE
  PRESIDENT'S PRIDE
  REX
  THRIFTY
  VIRGINIA REEL

1114 Bar-W Meat Company
P.O.Box 7832
Fort Worth, TX 76111-0832   817-831-0051
          Fax: 817-834-6766
Meat
President: John Wehba

Estimated Sales:$50-100 Million
Number Employees: 50-99

1115 Baraboo Candy Company
P.O.Box 63
Baraboo, WI 53913-0063   608-356-7425
     Fax: 608-356-1815 800-967-1690
          sales@baraboocandy.com
          www.baraboocandy.com
Chocolate candy sugar free, dark, milk and white chocolate
Manager: Derek Smith
Estimated Sales:$10-20 Million
Number Employees: 10-19
Type of Packaging: Private Label, Bulk
Brands:
  CHEWY GOOEY PRETZEL STICKS
  COW LICK
  COW PIE
  GREEN BAY PUDDLES
  LICK-A-PIG
  MOO CHEW
  UPPER FINGERS
  WALLY WALLEYE

1116 Barataria Spice Company
2317 Privateer Blvd
Barataria, LA 70036-5715   504-689-7650
          800-793-7650
          www.seasoningspice.com
Spices
Co-Owner/President: Mike Hymel
Co-Owner/CEO: Cynthia Hymel
*Estimated Sales:*Less than $500,000
Number Employees: 1-4
Type of Packaging: Consumer, Food Service
Brands:
  Captain Mike's

1117 Barbara Lyn Foods
41889 Helen Street
Elyria, OH 44035-1145   440-324-5445
Estimated Sales:$1-2.5 Million
Number Employees: 5-9

1118 Barbara's Bakery
3900 Cypress Dr
Petaluma, CA 94954-5694   707-765-2273
     Fax: 707-765-2927 info@barbarabakery.com
          www.barbarasbakery.com
Manufacturer of organic and natural cereals. crackers, cookies, bars, puffs and chips.
President: Barabara Jaffe
Executive VP: Chuck Marble
Quality Control: Erik Smitt
Director/Marketing: Kent Spalding
Director/Sales: Linda Gerwig
Purchasing: Laura Barberio
Estimated Sales:$20-50 Million
Number Employees: 50-99
Sq. footage: 102500
Parent Co: Weetabix
Type of Packaging: Consumer, Private Label
Other Locations:
  Barbara's Bakery
  Sacramento CA
Brands:
  BARBARA'S BAKERY
  NATURE'S CHOICE
  WEETABIX

1119 Barbe's Dairy
1420 Fourth Street
PO Box 186
Westwego, LA 70094   504-347-6201
          Fax: 504-347-6201
Processor of orange juice, ice mix, fruit drinks and dairy products including fresh cream and regular and chocolate milk
General Manager: Laurent Barbe Jr
Estimated Sales:$50-100 Million
Number Employees: 100-249
Parent Co: Suiza Dairy Group
Type of Packaging: Consumer, Food Service, Private Label, Bulk

1120 Barber Foods
56 Milliken St
Portland, ME 04103-1530   207-482-5500
     Fax: 207-797-0286 800-577-2595
     Customer_relations@barberfoods.com
          www.barberfoods.com

Manufacturer and exporter of frozen chicken including stuffed breasts, entrees, appetizers, chicken fingers, nuggets, fillets and patties
CEO: Bruce Wagner
CFO: Vicki Manner
Vice President: David Barber
Estimated Sales:$ 3 - 5 Million
Sq. footage: 150000
Type of Packaging: Consumer, Food Service
Other Locations:
  Barber Foods Production Plant
  Portland ME
Brands:
  BARBER FOODS

1121 Barber Pure Milk Ice Cream Company
36 Barber Ct
Birmingham, AL 35209-6435   205-942-2351
          Fax: 205-943-0296
     edmonia_anderson@deanfoods.com
          www.barbersdairy.com
Manufacturer of dairy products, such as; egg nog, Mexican coffee, coffee parfaits
General Manager/VP: P Flagg
Plant Manager: Valerie Meyers
Estimated Sales:$5-10 Million
Number Employees: 100-249
Parent Co: Dean Foods Company
Type of Packaging: Consumer, Food Service, Private Label, Bulk

1122 Barber's Dairy
36 Barber Ct
Birmingham, AL 35209-6435   205-942-2351
     Fax: 205-943-0296 www.barbersdairy.com
Manufacturer of dairy products including ice cream and milk
VP of Sales/Marketing: Bruce Williamson
Plant Manager: Valerie Meyers
Number Employees: 100-249
Parent Co: Dean Foods Company
Type of Packaging: Consumer, Food Service, Private Label

1123 Barbero Bakery, Inc.
61 Conrad St
Trenton, NJ 08611-1011   609-394-5122
     Fax: 609-394-5567 info@barberobakery.com
          www.barberobakery.com
Manufacturer of specialty cakes, pastries, italian cookies, deserts, deli breads and rolls
President: Gerardo Barbero
Estimated Sales:$2.5-5 Million
Number Employees: 20-49

1124 Barboursville Vineyards
P.O.Box 136
Barboursville, VA 22923-0136   540-832-3824
Fax: 540-832-7572 bvvy@barboursvillewine.com
          www.barboursvillecellar.com
Manufacturer of wines
Manager: Luca Paschina
Number Employees: 20-49

1125 Barca Wine Cellars
PO Box 1150
Roseville, CA 95678   916-967-0770
     Fax: 916-784-7575 earthwine@earthlink.net
          barcawines.net
Wines
General Manager: Gino Barca
Estimated Sales:$ 3 - 5 Million
Number Employees: 5-9
Brands:
  Barbousville Vineyards

1126 Barcelona Nut Company
502 S Mount St
Baltimore, MD 21223-3495   410-233-5252
     Fax: 410-233-6555 800-292-6887
sales@barcelonanut.com www.barcelonanut.com
Over 150 different snack food items including packaged nuts, trail mixes, snack mixes, 2 for $1.00 candy and cotton candy.
President/CEO: Tony Tsonis
VP & Director Of Sales: Mike Adams
Estimated Sales:$20-50 Million
Number Employees: 100-249
Sq. footage: 50000
Type of Packaging: Consumer, Food Service, Private Label, Bulk
Brands:
  BARCELONA

CANDYMAN LANE
HEALTHNUT
SNACKNUT

1127 Barcoding Inc
2220 Boston St
Baltimore, MD 21231-3058   410-385-8559
     Fax: 410-385-8559   888-412-7226
info@barcoding.com   www.barcoding.com
Barcoding Inc works with companies within the
Food and Beverage Industry to streamline their op-
erations through the implementation of barcode and
RFID systems.
     CEO: Jay Steinmetz
     Media/Public Relations: Jon Stroz
Type of Packaging: Consumer

1128 Bard Valley Medjool Date Growers
2575 E 23rd Lane
Yuma, AZ 85365   928-726-0901
     Fax: 928-726-9413   info@datepac.com
          www.datepac.com
Medjool date packing and marketing
     President of Sales Operations: Dave Nelson
     Production Manager: Camen Wilson
     General Manager: Glen Vandervoort

1129 Barefoot Contessa Pantry
2 Stonewall Lane
York, ME 03909   207-351-2713
     Fax: 207-351-2714
kbouchie@stonewallkitchen.com
     www.stonewallkitchen.com
French citrus, dessert baking mixes, breakfast baking mixes, dessert toppings, sauces and marinades,
pancakes and syrups, preserves and lemon curd, coffee and hot chocolate
     President/Owner: Jonathan King
     CEO: James Stott

1130 Baretta Provision
P.O.Box 344
East Berlin, CT 06023-0344   860-828-0802
          Fax: 860-828-8699
Manufacturer and packer of meats including beef,
pork and veal
     President: William Baretta
     VP: Daniel Baretta
Estimated Sales:$3-5 Million
Number Employees: 10-19
Type of Packaging: Food Service
Brands:
     LENORA

1131 Bargetto's Winery
3535 N Main St
Soquel, CA 95073-2530   831-475-2258
     Fax: 831-475-2664   800-422-7438
     customerservice@bargetto.com
          www.bargetto.com
Wines
     President: Martin Bargetto
     Operations: Michael Sones
Estimated Sales:$5-9.9 Million
Number Employees: 20-49
Type of Packaging: Private Label
Brands:
     BARGETTO
     CHAUCERS
     LAVITA

1132 Barhyte Specialty FoodsInc
912 Airport Rd
PO Box 1499
Pendleton, OR 97801   800-227-4983
     Fax: 541-276-0317   guestservices@barhyte.com
          www.barhyte.com
Sauces, dressings, marinades, mustards
     President/Owner: Susan Barhyte
     CEO: Chris Barhyte
     CFO: Irene Barhyte
Estimated Sales:$5.7
Number Employees: 43

1133 Bari & Gail
24 Walpole Park S
Walpole, MA 02081-2541   508-668-5629
     Fax: 508-850-9555   800-828-9318
     info@bariandgail.com   bariandgail.com
Chocolates
     President: Joseph Sesnovich
     Owner: Barrie Steinberg
     Vice President: Lisa Gail Sesnovich

Estimated Sales:$2.5-5 Million
Number Employees: 5-9
Type of Packaging: Bulk

1134 Barilla America Inc
1200 Lakeside Dr
Bannockburn, IL 60015-1243   847-405-7500
          Fax: 847-948-8791
Catherine.Franklin@edelman.com OR
consumerrelations@barilla-usa.com
          www.barilla-usa.com
Manufacturer of pasta, pasta sauces, biscuits, toasts,
snacks, and soft breads, short pastry, cakes and
crispbread.
     President: Kirk Trofholz
     CEO: Gianluca Bolla
     Product Development Manager: Judy Glass
     VP Marketing: Sergio Pereira
     Public Relations: Catherine Franklin
*Estimated Sales:*113,400,000
Number Employees: 1,000-4,999
Type of Packaging: Food Service

1135 Barker System Bakery
209 S Oak St
Mt Carmel, PA 17851-2147   570-339-3380
     President: Cathy Saukatis
*Estimated Sales:*Less than $500,000
Number Employees: 1-4

1136 Barkers Farm Dairy
PO Box 127
Pecks Mill, WV 25547-0127   304-855-4512
Manufacturer of dairy products including whole
milk and buttermilk
     Owner: Sidney Barker
     Owner: Mack Barker
     Owner: Carroll Barker
Estimated Sales:$ .5 - 1 million
Number Employees: 12
Type of Packaging: Consumer

1137 Barkman Honey Company
120 Santa Fe St
Hillsboro, KS 67063-9688   620-947-3173
     Fax: 620-947-3640   800-530-5827
          www.ghfllc.com
Manufacturer of pure and clear honey featuring dis-
tinctive flavors, including clover honey, wildflower
honey, orange blossom honey, and honey spread
     President: Dwight Stroller
     CEO: Brent Barkman
     CEO: Dwight Stoller
Estimated Sales:$20-50 Million
Number Employees: 50-99
Type of Packaging: Consumer, Food Service
Other Locations:
     Latty OH

1138 Barlean's
4936 Lake Terrell Rd
Ferndale, WA 98248-9014   360-384-0325
     Fax: 360-384-1746   orders@barleans.com
          www.barleansfishery.com
Produces the world's finest and freshest organic
flaxseed oil, fish oil, green food supplement and
other premium essential fatty acid products.
     Owner: Cindy Smith
     CEO: Jane Beutler
     Marketing Director: Andreas Koch
Number Employees: 1-4

1139 Barn Stream Natural Foods
PO Box 896
Walpole, NH 03608-0896   800-654-2882
          Fax: 603-756-9000
Gourmet food
     Owner: Nicholas Raynor
Estimated Sales:$10-20 Million
Number Employees: 10-19
Brands:
     Zapit-Za Bread

1140 Barnes & Watson Fine Teas
270 S Hanford St # 211
Seattle, WA 98134-1941   206-625-9435
     Fax: 206-625-0345   800-447-8832
     tea@barnesandwatson.com
          www.barnesandwatson.com
Whole leaf tea bags
     Owner: Ken Rudee
Estimated Sales:$1-2.5 Million
Number Employees: 1-4
Number of Products: 50+

Type of Packaging: Consumer, Food Service, Bulk
Brands:
     Barnes
     Watson Fine Teas

1141 Barnes Farming Corporation
7840 Old Bailey Hwy
Spring Hope, NC 27882-8393   252-459-9380
     Fax: 252-459-9020   information@farmpak.com
          www.farmpak.com
     President: Carson Barnes
     VP: John Barnes
     Packhouse Manager: Frank Salinas
Estimated Sales:$100-500 Million
Number Employees: 500-999
Brands:
     Farm Pak
     Heart of Carolina
     Queen Ann

1142 Barnes Foods
401 Gateway Dr
Goldsboro, NC 27534-7058   919-778-7889
          Fax: 919-751-2398
Refrigerated flavor tortillas
     President: Don Barnes, Jr.
     Plant Manager: Scott Shafer
Estimated Sales:$20-50 Million
Number Employees: 100-249
Parent Co: Mission Foods

1143 Barnes Ice Cream Company
41 Sewall St
Augusta, ME 04330-7313   207-622-0827
Manufacturer of ice cream
     Owner: Richard Barnes
     Owner: Carl Barnes
Estimated Sales:$500,000-$1 Million
Number Employees: 1-4
Type of Packaging: Consumer

1144 Barney Pork House
433 Johnston St SE
Decatur, AL 35601-3007   256-350-9988
          Fax: 256-350-9940
Sausage
     Partner: Billy C Burney Ii
Estimated Sales:$ .5 - 1 million
Number Employees: 5-9

1145 Barnie's Coffee & Tea Company
2126 W Landstreet Rd # 300
Orlando, FL 32809-8249   407-854-6600
     Fax: 407-854-6601   800-284-1416
     customerservice@barniescoffee.com
          www.barniescoffee.com
Coffee and tea
     President: Phillip Jones Jr.
Estimated Sales:$10-100 Million
Number Employees: 50-99

1146 Barnum & Bagel Frozen Soup
4700 Dempster Street
Skokie, IL 60076-2045   847-676-4466
          Fax: 847-676-4546
Restaurant
     President: George Mellos
Estimated Sales:$1-2.5 Million
Number Employees: 50-99

1147 Barnum-Goodfriend Farms
4938 State Route 52
Jeffersonville, NY 12748-5620   845-482-4123
     Fax: 845-482-4124   jgoodfriend@zelacom.com
     Owner: Mike Barber
Number Employees: 20-49

1148 Baron Vineyards
PO Box 624
Paso Robles, CA 93447-0624   805-239-3313
     Fax: 805-239-2789   tombaron@webtv.net
Wines
     Owner: Tom Baron
     Co-Owner: Sharon Baron
Number Employees: 20-49
Brands:
     Baron

1149 Barone Foods
345 S Kino Pkwy
Tucson, AZ 85719-6228   520-623-8571
          Fax: 520-622-1599

Manufacturer of cooked and processed meats including sausage
General Manager: Tim Barone
Estimated Sales:$ 5 - 10 Million
Number Employees: 10-19
Parent Co: City Meat
Type of Packaging: Consumer, Food Service, Private Label, Bulk

1150 Barone Foods
345 S Kino Pkwy
Tucson, AZ 85719-6228 520-623-8571
Fax: 520-622-1599
Beef, beef products, sausage, deli products, meat packing
General Manager: Tim Barone
Estimated Sales:$ 5 - 10 Million
Number Employees: 20-49

1151 Baronet Coffee
P.O.Box 987
Hartford, CT 06143-0987 860-527-7253
Fax: 860-524-9130 800-227-6638
baronet@cyberusa.net www.baronetcoffee.com
Manufacturer and importer of coffee
President: Bruce Goldsmith
Estimated Sales:$10-20 Million
Number Employees: 10-19
Brands:
Baronet Coffees

1152 Barq's Beverages of Baton Rouge
7403 Rue Henri
Baton Rouge, LA 70806-7525 225-928-3971
Fax: 225-928-3973
Processor of soft drinks
Owner: Don Bourque
CEO/Executive VP: S Harlan
VP/General Manager: C Harlan
Estimated Sales:$10-20 Million
Number Employees: 1-4
Sq. footage: 8000
Type of Packaging: Consumer, Food Service, Private Label
Brands:
Barq's Rootbeer

1153 Barrel O'Fun Snacks Foods Company
P.O.Box 230
Perham, MN 56573-0230 218-346-7000
Fax: 218-346-7003 www.redtwist.com
Dry snack foods, potato chips, popcorn
President: Ken Nelson
VP/COO: Mike Holper
VP Sales/Marketing: Randy Johnson
Production: Mike Bormann
Estimated Sales:$20-50 Million
Number Employees: 250-499
Parent Co: KLN Enterprises, Inc
Type of Packaging: Private Label

1154 Barricini Chocolate
P.O.Box 5189
Avoca, PA 18641-0189 570-457-6756
Fax: 570-457-8276
customerservice@barricini.com
www.barricini.com
Manufacturer of dark and milk chocolates with hazelnuts, cashews, peanut butter confections and more.
Manager: Barnett Tessler
Estimated Sales:$20-50 Million
Number Employees: 50-99
Brands:
BARRICINI
BARRICINI CHATEAU
BARRICINI DREAM
BARRICINI EDDY LEON
BARRICINI HOLIDAY
BARRICINI ROYAL

1155 Barrie House Gourmet Coffee
945 Nepperhan Ave
Yonkers, NY 10703-1727 914-423-8252
Fax: 914-423-8499 800-876-2233
sales@barriehouse.com www.barriehouse.com
Complete selection of coffees, teas, accesories and equipment, to serve the specialty coffee and tea industry
Owner: Edward Goldstein
Estimated Sales:$20-50 Million
Number Employees: 20-49
Number of Products: 200

Type of Packaging: Food Service, Private Label, Bulk
Brands:
BARRIE HOUSE
CAFE BODEGA
CAFE EXCELLENCE
DONUT SHOP

1156 Barrington Coffee Roasting Company
165 Quarry Hill Rd
Lee, MA 01238-9623 413-243-3008
Fax: 413-528-0614 800-528-0998
coffee@barringtoncoffee.com
www.barringtoncoffee.com
Coffee
Owner: Barth Anderson
VP: Barth Anderson
Estimated Sales:$2.5-5 Million
Number Employees: 1-4
Type of Packaging: Private Label
Brands:
BARRINGTON ESTATE
BARRINGTON GOLD
DARK ROAST
LIMITED EDITION
ORGANIC/FAIR TRADE
SINGLE ORIGIN

1157 Barrington Nutritionals
500 Mamaroneck Ave # 201
Harrison, NY 10528-1636 914-381-3500
Fax: 914-381-2232 800-684-2436
info@barringtonchem.com
www.barringtonchem.com
Barrington Nutritionals offers custom granulation, blending and particle size reduction of products for the Vitamin/Nutrition, and Pharmaceutical industries.
Owner: Stuart Gelbard
National Sales Manager: Nelson Fretwell

1158 (HQ)Barrows Tea Company
PO Box 40278
New Bedford, MA 02744-0003 774-488-8684
Fax: 508-990-2760 800-832-5024
madhatter@barrowstea.com
www.barrowstea.com
Processor and importer of round unbleached tea bags and natural and organic teas
President: Sam Barrows
Estimated Sales:$1-2.5 Million
Number Employees: 1-4
Number of Brands: 1
Number of Products: 15
Type of Packaging: Consumer, Food Service
Brands:
Barrows

1159 Barry Callebaut USA LLC
903 Industrial Highway
Eddystone, PA 19022 610-872-4528
Fax: 610-872-4527 www.barry-callebaut.com
Manufacturer and supplier of chocolate, cocoa powders, ready to use fillings, coatings and decorations.

1160 (HQ)Barry Callebaut USA LLC
400 Industrial Park Road
St. Albans, VT 05478-1857 802-524-9711
Fax: 802-524-5148 stablans@barry-callebaut.com
www.barry-callebaut.com
Producer of cocoa and chocolate products
President: Gean Michel Melis
Estimated Sales:$116.5 Million
Number Employees: 197
Brands:
Cacaobarry
Carma
Cenleer
Kalibert

1161 Barry Callebaut USA, Inc.
1500 Suckle Hwy
Pennsauken, NJ 08110 856-663-2260
Fax: 856-665-0474 800-836-2626
pennsauken@barry-callebaut.com
www.barry-callebaut.com
Manufacturer of cocoa and chocolate products
Owner: Ted Bertran
Manager: Michelle Trembley
Estimated Sales:$4.9 Billion
Number Employees: 7,500
Parent Co: Barry Callebaut

1162 Barry Callebaut USA, LLC
400 Industrial Park Road
Saint Albans, VT 05478-1875 802-524-9711
Fax: 802-524-5148 800-556-8845
stalbans@barry-callebaut.com
www.barry-callebaut.com
High quality Belgium chocolate ingredients
Director Sales: Joe Lucas
Estimated Sales:$50-100 Million
Number Employees: 250-499
Parent Co: Barry Callebaut
Brands:
BARRY CALLEBAUT
BENSDORP
CACAO BARRY
CALLEBAUT
CARMA
VAN HOUTEN
VAN LEER

1163 Barry Group
415 Griffin Drive
Corner Brook, NL A2H 7T2
Canada 709-785-7387
Fax: 709-785-5365 bgi@seafreez.com
Processor and exporter of frozen fish and seafood including lobster, coldwater shrimp, opilio crab, red fish, Greenland turbot, cod, hat-fish, crab sections, herring, mackerel and capelan, frozen imitation crab meat and sticks. Alsoimporter of frozen grenadier fillets
Director Marketing: David Middleton
Estimated Sales:$300 Million
Number Employees: 5,000-9,999
Type of Packaging: Consumer, Food Service, Private Label, Bulk
Brands:
Icelandic
Ocean Leader
Pacific
Seafreez
Seafreez/Shawmut

1164 Bartek Ingredients, Inc.
421 Seaman Street
Stoney Creek, ON L8E 3J4
Canada 905-662-1127
Fax: 905-662-8849 800-263-4165
sales@bartek.ca www.bartek.ca
Manufacturer and exporter of acidulants including malic and fumaric acid; also, FCC-NF
President: S den Baars
USA Sales Manager: David Tapajna
Sales Manager: C Johnson
General Manager: A Douglas
Number Employees: 100-249
Sq. footage: 40000

1165 Bartlett Dairy & Food Service
10503 150th St
Jamaica, NY 11435-5017 718-658-2299
Fax: 718-725-2527 www.bartlettny.com
Distributor of dairy products and other perishable foods for grocery and foodservice.
President: Thomas Malave Jr.
VP Sales: Jimmy Malave
Estimated Sales:$75 Million
Number Employees: 20-49

1166 Bartlett Milling Company
1307 Maple St
Coffeyville, KS 67337-5233 620-251-4650
Fax: 620-251-4390
Flour milling
Manager: Mark Bastian
Plant Manager: Gene Horton
Estimated Sales:$20-50 Million
Number Employees: 50-99

1167 Bartlow Brothers
P.O.Box 207
Rushville, IL 62681-0207 217-322-3365
Fax: 217-322-2560 800-252-7202
http://agj3240.cafnr.missouri.edu/w06/reynoldsk/mp/index.htm
Manufacturer of beef and pork products including: sliced lunchmeats; sliced bacon; deli meats; dinner sausages; bone-in hams; hot dogs and sausages; BBQ specialty meats.
President: Dan Reynolds
Manager: Jim Foster
Manager: Bob Black

Estimated Sales:$50-100 Million
Number Employees: 50-99
Type of Packaging: Food Service
Brands:
  KORNTOP

1168 Bartolini Ice Cream
967 E 167th St
Bronx, NY 10459-1951   718-589-5151
                    Fax: 718-893-3171

Distributers of ice cream
  Owner: Michael Bartolini
Estimated Sales:$10-20 Million
Number Employees: 10-19

1169 Barton Brands
1 S Dearborn St # 1700
Chicago, IL 60603-2308   312-346-9200
        Fax: 312-855-1220 800-598-6352
                    www.bartoninc.com
Manufacturer and exporter of bourbon, scotch, whis-
key, gin and vodka; importer of scotch
  President/CEO: Alexander Berk
  CFO: Troy Christensen
  CEO: Alexander Berke
  EVP/Marketing Barton Brands: Ed Gaultieri
Estimated Sales:$158 Million
Number Employees: 100-249
Parent Co: Constellation Brands
Brands:
  99 SCHNAPPS
  BARTON
  BLACK VELVET
  CANADIAN LTD
  CHI-CHI'S
  FLEISCHMANN'S
  MONTE ALBAN
  MONTEZUMA
  MR BOSTON
  NORTHERN LIGHT CANADIAN
  THOR'S HAMMER
  di AMORE

1170 Bartons Fine Foods
Highway 460
Denniston, KY 40316   606-768-3750
        Fax: 606-768-3737 888-810-3750
Processor of jellies, jams, mustards, barbecue
sauces, molasses and relishes
  President: Bryan Allphin
  Operations Director: Phil Madrio
Estimated Sales:$2.5-5 Million
Number Employees: 5-9
Sq. footage: 6000
Type of Packaging: Consumer, Food Service, Pri-
vate Label

1171 (HQ)Bartush-Schnitzius Foods Company
P.O.Box 396
Lewisville, TX 75067-0396   972-219-1270
        Fax: 972-436-5719 sales@bartushfoods.com
                    www.bartushfoods.com
Processor of bar mixes, salad dressing and sauces in-
cluding horseradish, salsa, barbecue, taco, picante
and tomato and sugar based
  President/CEO: John Rubi
Estimated Sales:$12 Million
Number Employees: 50-99
Number of Products: 200+
Sq. footage: 50000
Type of Packaging: Consumer, Food Service, Pri-
vate Label
Brands:
  BAR-SNITZ
  FAIRWAY
  MELCER
  SCHNITZIUS
  TEXAS

1172 Basciani Foods
8876 Gap Newport Pike
Avondale, PA 19311-9749   610-268-3610
Fax: 610-268-2186 michael@bascianifoods.com
                    www.bascianifoods.com
Fresh mushrooms
  President: Mario Basciani Sr
Estimated Sales:$ 20 - 50 Million
Number Employees: 100-249

1173 Basic American Foods
2999 Oak Rd
Walnut Creek, CA 94597-2066   925-472-4000
        Fax: 925-472-4360 800-227-4050
        jmikesell@baf.com www.baf.com
Manufacturer and exporter of dehydrated potato
products including; au gratin, hash brown, mashed,
scalloped, dehydrated refried and black beans and
chili mixes
  Chairman: George Hume
  President: Jack Parks
  CFO: John Argent
  CEO: Loren Kimura
Estimated Sales:$161 Million
Number Employees: 1,000-4,999
Sq. footage: 500000
Type of Packaging: Food Service
Brands:
  CLASSIC CASSEROLE
  GOLDEN GRILL
  NATURE'S OWN
  POTATO PEARLS
  REDI-SHRED

1174 Basic American Foods
415 W Collins Rd
Blackfoot, ID 83221-5642   208-785-3200
        Fax: 208-785-8776 800-227-4050
        rgansie@baf.com www.baf.com
Manufacturer and exporter of dehydrated potatoes
and beans, canned and frozen green chiles and vege-
table extracts/nutraceuticals
  Manager: Nelson Rovig
  Director Procurement: Steve Henricksman
  Director Raw Materials: Mark Klompien
Estimated Sales:$100-500 Million
Number Employees: 500-999
Parent Co: Basic American
Type of Packaging: Consumer, Food Service, Pri-
vate Label, Bulk
Brands:
  CLASSIC CASSEROLES
  GOLDEN GRILL
  NATURE'S OWN
  POTATO PEARLS
  POTATO PEARLS EXCEL
  QUIK START
  REDI SHRED
  REGIONAL RECIPE
  SANTIAGO

1175 (HQ)Basic American Foods
2999 Oak Rd
Walnut Creek, CA 94597-2066   925-472-4000
        Fax: 925-472-4360 800-227-4050
                    www.baf.com
Processor of dehydrated potatoes
  President/CEO: Loren Kimura
  VP/CFO: John Argent
  Plant Manager: Mark Klompien
Estimated Sales:$160 Million
Number Employees: 1,000-4,999
Type of Packaging: Consumer, Food Service, Pri-
vate Label, Bulk
Brands:
  CLASSIC CASSEROLE®
  GOLDEN GRILL RUSSET™
  GOLDEN GRILL®
  NATURALLY POTATOES®
  NATURE'S OWN®
  POTATO PEARLS EXCEL®
  POTATO PEARLS®
  QUICK-START®
  REDI-SHRED®
  SANTIAGO®
  WHIPP®

1176 Basic American Foods
P.O.Box 68
Plover, WI 54467-0068   715-341-5960
        Fax: 715-341-5966 www.baf.com
Processor of dehydrated potatoes, hash browns and
beans
  Manager: Paul Landon
  Plant Manager: Dick Wood
Estimated Sales:$100+ Million
Number Employees: 100-249
Type of Packaging: Food Service, Private Label
Brands:
  CLASSIC CASSEROLE
  GOLDEN GRILL
  NATURE'S OWN
  POTATO PEARLS
  QUICK START

  REDI SHRED
  REGIONAL RECIPE
  SANTIAGO

1177 Basic Food Flavors
3950 E Craig Rd
North Las Vegas, NV 89030-7504   702-643-0043
                    Fax: 702-643-6149
        dwood@basicfoodflavors.com
                    www.basicfoodflavors.com
Manufacturer and exporter of industrial ingredients
including hydrolyzed vegetable proteins, processed
flavors, soy sauce and soy bases
  President: Kanu Patel
  Director Sales: David Wood
Estimated Sales:$10-20 Million
Number Employees: 50-99
Sq. footage: 45000
Type of Packaging: Food Service, Bulk

1178 Basic Grain Products
300 E Vine St
Coldwater, OH 45828-1399   419-678-2304
        Fax: 419-678-4647 info@tastemorr.com
                    www.tastemorr.com
Dry rice cakes
  President: Carol Knapke
Estimated Sales:$ 20 - 50 Million
Number Employees: 100-249
Brands:
  Taste More Snacks

1179 Basignani Winery
15722 Falls Rd
Sparks Glencoe, MD 21152-9582   410-472-0703
        Fax: 410-472-2536 basignaniwinery.com
Wines
  President: Bertero Basignani
  CEO: Lynn Basignani
*Estimated Sales:*Less than $300,000
Number Employees: 5-9

1180 Basin Crawfish Processors
P.O.Box 25
Breaux Bridge, LA 70517-0025   337-332-6655
        Fax: 337-332-5917 www.bbcrawfest.com
Crawfish, seafood
  President: Brayon Blanchard
Estimated Sales:$300,000-500,000
Number Employees: 1-4

1181 Basin Frozen Foods
1203 Basin St
Warden, WA 98857-9475   509-349-2210
        Fax: 509-349-2375 www.ochoa-ag.com
Processor of frozen hash browns
  Plant Manager: Don Wilson
  Process Manager: Don Wilson
  Operations: Jack Calder
Estimated Sales:$ 50 - 100 Million
Number Employees: 100-249
Type of Packaging: Food Service, Private Label,
Bulk
Brands:
  Basin Frozen Foods
  Quincy Gold

1182 Basketfull
276 5th Ave
New York, NY 10001-4509   212-686-2175
        Fax: 212-255-9019 800-645-4438
        basketfull@aol.com, info@basketfullinc.com
                    www.basketfullinc.com
Manufacturer and exporter of gourmet food and fruit
baskets
  President: Nancy Forest
*Estimated Sales:*Less than $500,000
Number Employees: 5-9

1183 Baskin-Robbins Flavors
109 E Alameda Ave
Burbank, CA 91502-2004   818-558-4000
        Fax: 818-558-1844 800-859-5339
                    www.baskinrobbins.com
High quality premium ice cream, specialty frozen
desserts, bases for dairy beverages, nondairy; flavors
  Manager: Alex Lee
  CFO: Kate Lavelle
Estimated Sales:$50 Million
Number Employees: 10-19
Parent Co: Dunkin' Brands, Inc.
Type of Packaging: Consumer, Food Service

1184 Basque French Bakery
2625 Inyo St
Fresno, CA 93721-2787   559-268-7088
       Fax: 559-268-0510
Baked goods, breads and rolls
   President: Al Lewis
   Vice President: Rita Ingmire
   Production Manager: Ed Kwiecien
Estimated Sales:$2.5-5 Million
Number Employees: 20-49

1185 Bass Lake Cheese Factory
598 Valley View Trl
Somerset, WI 54025-6800   715-247-5586
    Fax: 715-549-6617   800-368-2437
   blcheese@blcheese.com   www.blcheese.com
Manufacturer of cheese including colby, cheddar,
cheddar curds, jack, goat's and sheep's milk
   Co-Owner: Scott Erickson
   Co-Owner: Julie Erickson
Estimated Sales:$5-9.9 Million
Number Employees: 5-9
Type of Packaging: Consumer
Brands:
   MASTER'S MARK

1186 (HQ)Bassett's
1211 Chestnut St # 410
Philadelphia, PA 19107-4114   215-864-2771
    Fax: 215-864-2766   888-999-6314
   bassettsic@aol.com   www.bassettsicecream.com
Premium ice cream, yogurt, sorbet
   President: Michael Strange
   CEO: Ann Bassett
Estimated Sales:$5-10 Million
Number Employees: 5-9
Other Locations:
   Bassetts Ice Cream
   Philadelphia PA

1187 Batampte Pickle Foods, Inc.
77 Brooklyn Terminal Market
Brooklyn, NY 11236-1511   718-251-2100
       Fax: 718-531-9212
Manufacturers of pickles.
   President/CEO: Barry Silberstein
   Vice President: Scott Silberstein
Estimated Sales:$20-50 Million
Number Employees: 50-99

1188 Batavia Wine Cellars
235 N Bloomfield Road
Canandaigua, NY 14424-1059   800-879-9463
       Fax: 716-344-2675
Processor, bottler and exporter of wine, salted cook-
ing wine and sparkling fruit juices, plus bulk wines
for the food industry
   President: Tim Richenberg
Number Employees: 100-249
Parent Co: Canandaigua Wine Company
Type of Packaging: Consumer, Food Service, Pri-
vate Label, Bulk
Brands:
   CAPRI
   HENRI MERCHANT
   VINTER'S CHOICE

1189 Batdorf and Bronson Roasters
200 Market St NE
Olympia, WA 98501-6965   360-754-5282
    Fax: 360-754-5283   800-955-5282
   javatalk@batdorf.com   www.batdorf.com
Coffee roaster, mail order & wholesale
   President: Larry Challain
   CFO: Dave Wasson
   Vice President: Scott Merle
   Quality Control: Michael Elvin
   Marketing Director: Jen Boelts
   Sales Director: Stefany Dybeck
   Public Relations: Lois Maffeo
   Operations Manager: Heather Ringwood
   Production Manager: Brian Meyers
   Plant Manager: Bob Benck
   Purchasing Manager: Dave Wasson
Estimated Sales:$5-10 Million
Number Employees: 50-99
Type of Packaging: Consumer, Food Service, Pri-
vate Label, Bulk

1190 Bateman Products
251 W Main Street
Rigby, ID 83442-1351   208-745-9033
    Fax: 208-357-5317   www.mrsbateman.com

Fat products and sugar and egg replacements in the
food and health industry
   Owner: Mrs Bateman
Estimated Sales:$ .5 - 1 million
Number Employees: 5-9

1191 Batko Flavors LLC
772 Cranbury Crossroad
North Brunswick, NJ 08092   732-991-3462
   Fax: 732-932-9441   daphnahf@baktoflavors.com
       www.baktoflavors.com
Production, commercialization and distribution of
natural products, such as flavors, fragrances and pre-
servatives.
   President: Prof Chaim Frenkel
   VP/R&D Director: Dr Daphna Havkin Frenkel
Number Employees: 7

1192 Battaglia Distributing Corporation
2500 S Ashland Ave
Chicago, IL 60608-5321   312-738-1111
   Fax: 312-738-4030   www.battagliafoods.com
   President: Frank Battaglia
Estimated Sales:$100+ Million
Number Employees: 100-249

1193 Battistoni Italina Specialty Meats
81 Dingens St
Buffalo, NY 14206-2307   716-826-2700
    Fax: 716-826-0603   800-248-2705
       www.battistonibrand.com
Manufacturer of Italian Meat products including sa-
lami, pepperoni, capocollo, chorizo
   President: Alvino Battistoni Jr.
   Executive VP: Tina Battistoni
Estimated Sales:$10-24.9 Million
Number Employees: 20-49
Parent Co: Rich Products
Brands:
   RICH PRODUCTS

1194 Bauducco Foods Inc
1728 NW 82nd Avenue
Miami, FL 33126   305-477-9270
   Fax: 305-477-4703   sales@bauduccofoods.com
       www.bauduccofoods.com
bars, bite-sized cookies, butter cookies, cakes, cookies, corn flour cookies, cream-filled cookies, finger
cakes, food service, grissini, savory biscuits, toast,
wafer
   President/Owner: Djalma Oliveria
Estimated Sales:$5 Million
Number Employees: 10

1195 Bauhaven Lobster
280 Chases Pond Rd
York, ME 03909   207-363-5265
       Fax: 907-486-6417
Lobster
   Partner: Randy Small
Estimated Sales:$ 1 - 3 Million
Number Employees: 5-9

1196 Baum International
1933 E 12th Street
Brooklyn, NY 11229-2703   718-376-4508
    Fax: 718-376-6084   baumintlus@aol.com
Wholesaler/distributor of confectionery products,
canned foods, meats, juices, vodka, etc
   President: Harold Baum
   Advertising/Sales: B Chouquet
   VP of Purchasing: Setty Setton
Number Employees: 10-19

1197 (HQ)Baumer Foods
P.O.Box 19166
New Orleans, LA 70179-0166   504-482-5761
   Fax: 504-483-2425   info@baumerfoods.com
       www.baumerfoods.com
Manfacturer and exporter of sauces including hot,
steak, soy and barbecue; also, mustard, preserves
and peppers including tabasco and cortido
   Chairman/President/CEO: Alvin Baumer Jr
   EVP/COO: Terry Hanes
   CFO: Ronald Wendel
   R&D/Quality Control: Javed Rashid
   VP Operations: Doug Wakefield
Estimated Sales:$50 Million
Number Employees: 250-499
Number of Brands: 1
Number of Products: 11
Sq. footage: 220000

Type of Packaging: Consumer, Food Service, Pri-
vate Label
Brands:
   AB
   BAUMER
   CRYSTAL
   FIREY
   FLAME

1198 Bautista Organic Dates
P.O.Box 726
Mecca, CA 92254-0726   760-396-2337
Dates and grapefruits
   Owner: Enrique Bautista
Estimated Sales:$500,000 appx.
Number Employees: 1-4

1199 Bavaria Corporation
515 Cooper Commerce Dr # 100
Apopka, FL 32703-6222   407-880-0322
   Fax: 407-880-1932   bavaria@fdn.com
       www.bavariacorp.com
Manufacturer of specialty blends, the injection, mar-
inades, and dips for better color, yields and shelf-life
in beef, pork, poultry, and seafood
   President/CEO: Peter Schaeflein
   VP: Dennis Koo
Estimated Sales:$5-$10 Million
Number Employees: 10-19
Type of Packaging: Food Service, Bulk
Brands:
   BAFOS

1200 Bavarian Meat Products
2934 Western Ave
Seattle, WA 98121-1021   206-448-3540
       Fax: 206-956-0526
Processor of sausage
   President: Manny Dupper
   Co-Owner: Robert Hofstatter
   Vice President: Lynn Stewart
Estimated Sales:$2.5-5 Million
Number Employees: 10-19
Type of Packaging: Consumer, Food Service

1201 Bavarian Nut Company
1503 S Fresno Avenue
Stockton, CA 95206-1179   209-465-9181
       Fax: 360-465-6008
Dry walnuts
   Manager: Rex Lewis
   Plant Manager: Ben Fairbanks
Estimated Sales:$ 20 - 50 Million
Number Employees: 50-99

1202 Bavarian Specialty Foods
11450 Sheldon Street
Sun Valley, CA 91352-1121   310-212-6199
       Fax: 310-781-9149
Frozen baked goods
   President: Richard Tan
   CFO: Les Starnes
   General Manager: Jack Samaras
   Production Manager: Paul Trujillo
   Plant Manager: Mike Engel
Estimated Sales:$10-24.9 Million
Number Employees: 100-249
Type of Packaging: Private Label

1203 Baxter's Vineyard
P.O.Box 342
Nauvoo, IL 62354-0342   217-453-2528
    Fax: 217-453-6600   800-854-1396
   baxters@nauvoo.net   www.nauvoowinery.com
Wines
   Owner/President: Kelly Logan
   Owner/CEO: Brenda Logan
Estimated Sales:$500,000-$1 Million
Number Employees: 1-4
Brands:
   Baxters Old Nauvoo

1204 Bay Brewery Company
2283 Camel Road
Benicia, CA 94510-2346   707-747-6961
       Fax: 707-747-1664
Beer
   President: Mark Feinberg
Estimated Sales:$2.5-5,000,000
Number Employees: 5-9
Brands:
   Devil Mountain Winter Warmer
   Devil's Brew Porter
   Diablo Golden Ale

Dm Oktoberfest
Dm Wheat
Railroad Ale

1205 (HQ)Bay Cities Produce Company
2109 Williams St
San Leandro, CA 94577-3224 510-346-4943
Fax: 510-832-1509 www.baycitiesproduce.com
Manufacturer and wholesaler/distributor of fresh,
frozen and prepared fruits and vegetables
Owner: Al Del Matso
SVP: Steve Del Masso
Secretary/Treasurer: Diana Del Masso
Vice President: Steve Del Masso
GM: Rick Onstad
Sales Manager: Tony D'Amato
Estimated Sales:$20-50 Million
Number Employees: 20-49
Sq. footage: 55000
Type of Packaging: Food Service

1206 Bay Hawk Ales
2000 Main St
Irvine, CA 92614-7202 949-442-7565
Fax: 949-442-7566 info@bayhawkales.com
www.bayhawkales.com
Processor of seasonal beer, ale, lager and porter
Manager: Carl Zappa
Sales: Robert Fischer
General Manager: Karl Zappa
Estimated Sales:$2.5-5 Million
Number Employees: 5-9
Type of Packaging: Consumer, Food Service, Private Label
Brands:
AMBER ALE
BAYHAWK IPA
BAYHAWK STOUT
BEACH BLONDE
CALIFORNIA PALE ALE (CPA)
CHOCOLATE PORTER
HEFE WEIZEN
HONEY BLONDE
O.C. LAGER

1207 Bay Hundred Seafood
P.O.Box 10
McDaniel, MD 21647-0010 410-745-9329
Fax: 410-745-9176
Processor and packer of oysters and crabs including
soft and meat
President: Joseph Spurry
VP: Joseph Spurry, Jr.
Estimated Sales:$10-20 Million
Number Employees: 10-19
Type of Packaging: Consumer
Brands:
Miles River

1208 Bay Oceans Sea Foods
P.O.Box 348
Garibaldi, OR 97118-0348 503-322-3316
Fax: 503-322-0049
customerservice@bayoceanseafood.com
www.bayoceanseafood.com
Products include gourmet albacore tuna, chinook
salmon, dungeness crab and shrimp, as well as
canned tuna and salmon.
Owner: Jeff Princehouse
Estimated Sales:$10 - 20 Million
Number Employees: 20-49
Type of Packaging: Consumer, Food Service

1209 Bay Pac Beverages
1150 Civic Drive
Suite 300
Walnut Creek, CA 94596-8221 925-279-0800
Fax: 925-279-0804 baypac@pacbell.net
www.sportsenergy.com/baypaccorp
Sports drink beverages
President: Jackson Bays
Manager of Export Sales: Alan Wirsig
Estimated Sales:$2.5-5 Million
Number Employees: 5-9
Type of Packaging: Bulk

1210 Bay Star Baking Company
1222 Lincoln Ave
Alameda, CA 94501-2326 510-523-4202
Fax: 925-449-1224
Bread, rolls
Estimated Sales:$10-20 Million
Number Employees: 100-249

1211 (HQ)Bay State Milling Company
100 Congress St # 2
Quincy, MA 02169-0948 617-328-4423
Fax: 617-479-8910 800-553-5687
info@bsm.com www.bsm.com
Manufacturer of flour
Chairman: Bernard Rothwell
President: Brian Rothwell
Estimated Sales:$100+ Million
Number Employees: 20-49
Type of Packaging: Consumer, Food Service, Private Label, Bulk
Other Locations:
Tolleson AZ
Platteville CO
Minneapolis MN
Winona MN
Indiantown FL
Mooresville NC
Clifton NJ

1212 Bay State Milling Company
55 Franklin St
Winona, MN 55987-3736 507-452-1770
Fax: 507-452-1776 800-533-8098
larryo.wn@bsm.com www.bsm.com
Miller of wheat and rye flour
Manager: Tony Wasinger
Sales Manager: Larry Overhaug
Plant Manager: Tony Wasinger
Estimated Sales:$50-100 Million
Number Employees: 50-99
Parent Co: Bay State Milling Company
Type of Packaging: Consumer, Food Service, Private Label, Bulk

1213 Bay Valley Foods
857 897 School Place
Green Bay, WI 54303
Fax: 920-497-7131 800-558-4700
www.bayvalleyfoods.com
Manufacturer of shelf stable pickles, relish, peppers,
syrups, powdered non-dairy coffee creamers, liquid
non-dairy coffee creamers, egg substitutes, cheese
sauces, puddings, special sauces, soups, broths, gravies and infant foods.
President: Joe Coning
VP Finance: Greg Lewandowski
Sr. VP Retail Sales/Marketing: Kevin Holden
VP Bulk Ingredients/International Sales: Mike Cooney
VP Foodservice Sales/Marketing: Gary Schachter
Sr. VP Operations/Supply Chain: George Jurkovich
Estimated Sales:$94 Million
Number Employees: 1,000
Parent Co: TreeHouse Foods
Type of Packaging: Consumer, Food Service, Private Label, Bulk
Brands:
BENNETT'S
CREMORA
FARMANS
GRACIAS
HEIFETZ
HOFFMAN HOUSE
MOCHA MIX
NALLEY
NATURE'S GOODNESS
NORTHWOODS
PETER PIPER
PRIVATE LABEL
SECOND NATURE
STEINFELD'S
THANK YOU

1214 (HQ)Bay Valley Foods
PO Box 763
Horsham, PA 19044-0763
800-236-1119
www.bigvalleyfoods.com
Pickles, relish, non-dairy coffee creamers, salad
dressings, marinades and bbq sauces, cheese sauces,
puddings, soups, salsa and picante, egg substitutes,
and special sauces.
Estimated Sales:$800 Million
Number Employees: 20-49
Parent Co: TreeHouse Foods
Type of Packaging: Private Label
Other Locations:
Dean Specialty Foods Group
Portland OR
Dean Specialty Foods Group
New Hampton IA
Dean Specialty Foods Group
Pecatonica IL
Dean Specialty Foods Group
Chicago IL
Dean Specialty Foods Group
Benton Harbor MI
Dean Specialty Foods Group
Dixon IL
Dean Specialty Foods Group
Wayland MI

1215 Bay View Farm
P.O.Box 680
Honaunau, HI 96726-0680 808-328-9658
Fax: 808-328-8693 800-662-5880
bayview@aloha.net
www.bayviewfarmcoffees.com
Coffees, Flavored Coffees and gourmet foods
President: Andrew Roy
VP: Roslyn Roy
Estimated Sales:$5-10 Million
Number Employees: 10-19

1216 Baycliff Company
242 E 72nd St
New York, NY 10021-4574 212-772-6078
Fax: 212-472-8980
Processor, exporter and importer of Japanese food
products including rice vinegar, soy sauces, soy
salad dressing, teriyaki sauce, rice, rice cracker mix,
green tea, and soups
President: Helen Chandler
VP: Alan Johnson
Estimated Sales:$20-50 Million
Number Employees: 20-49
Type of Packaging: Consumer, Food Service
Brands:
Sushi Chef

1217 Bayley Quality Seafoods
21 Snow Canning Rd
Scarborough, ME 04074-5001 207-883-4581
Fax: 207-883-2872
Seafood
President/Treasurer: Stanley Bayley
CEO: Nancy Bayley
Vice President: Nancy Bayley
Estimated Sales:$1.5 Million
Number Employees: 5-9

1218 Bayley's Lobster Pound
9 Avenue Six
Scarborough, ME 04074 207-883-4571
Fax: 207-883-2528
Lobster
Manager: Sue Bayley
Estimated Sales:$1 - 3 Million
Number Employees: 10-19

1219 Bayley's Lobster Pound
9 Avenue Six
Scarborough, ME 04074 207-883-4571
Fax: 207-883-4797 800-932-6456
bayleys@bayleys.com www.bayleys.com
Fresh and frozen shrimp and clams
President/Treasurer: Stanley Bayley
Estimated Sales:$1,500,000
Number Employees: 5-9

1220 Bayou Cajun Foods
PO Box 8460
Monroe, LA 71211-8460 318-388-2383
Fax: 318-361-5036
Cajun foods
President: Vicki Roark

1221 Bayou Crab
10380 Foots Rd
Grand Bay, AL 36541-6491 251-824-2076
Fax: 251-824-2615
Cajun foods
Owner: Dan Viravong
Estimated Sales:$3 - 5 Million
Number Employees: 10-19

1222 Bayou Foods
949 Industry Rd
Kenner, LA 70062-6848 504-469-1745
Fax: 504-469-1852 800-516-8283
bayoufoods@hughes.com

Fillet fish, crabs and peeled and headless shrimp; importer of shrimp; wholesaler/distributor of frozen foods, provisions, beef, pork, poultry and sea-food;serving the food service market
President/Owner: Miu Lin Kong
CEO: Arthur Mitchell
Estimated Sales: $5-10 Million
Number Employees: 10-19
Sq. footage: 13600
Type of Packaging: Food Service

1223 Bayou Gourmet
412 Palm Avenue
Houma, LA 70364-3400 504-872-4825
Fax: 504-868-7472
President: Ernest Voisin

1224 Bayou Land Seafood
1108 Vincent Berard Rd
Breaux Bridge, LA 70517 337-667-6118
Fax: 337-667-6059 bayoulandseafood@aol.com
www.bayoulandseafood.com
Processor and wholesaler/distributor of seafood in-cluding fresh and frozen crawfish, fish, crabs and shrimp; also, alligator and turtle
President: Adam Johnson
Plant Manager: Jeff Guidry
Estimated Sales: $5-9.9 Million
Number Employees: 50-99
Number of Products: 100
Sq. footage: 10320
Type of Packaging: Consumer, Food Service, Bulk
Brands:
Bayou Land Seafood

1225 Bayou Packing
PO Box 515
Bayou La Batre, AL 36509-0515 251-824-7710
Fax: 251-824-4061
Owner: Richard Roush

1226 Bays English Muffin Corporation
PO Box 1455
Chicago, IL 60690-1455 312-346-5757
Fax: 316-226-3435 800-367-2297
www.bays.com
Aqua culture
President: George Bay
Estimated Sales: $1-2.5 Million
Number Employees: 20-49

1227 Baywood Cellars
5573 W Woodbridge Road
Lodi, CA 95242-9497 209-334-0445
Fax: 209-334-0132 800-214-0445
mail@baywood-cellars.com
www.baywood-cellars.com
Wines
Founder: Joe Cotta Jr
President: John Cotta
Co-Owner: James Cotta
Estimated Sales: Under $500,000
Number Employees: 1-4
Brands:
Baywood Cellars

1228 Baywood International
P.O.Box 14256
Scottsdale, AZ 85267-4256 480-951-3956
Fax: 480-483-2168 800-481-7169
www.bywd.com
Manufacturer, importer and exporter of mineral/pol-len supplements, pollen tablets, sports nutrition vita-mins, fragrances, freeze-dried aloe vera products and water purification systems
President/CEO: Neil Reithinger
CFO: Robert Geiges Jr.
CEO: Eric Skae
Director Marketing: Gerard McIntee
National Sales Director: John Staley
Estimated Sales: F
Number Employees: 20-49
Sq. footage: 10000
Brands:
BAYWOOD PURECHOICE®
BAYWOOD SOLUTIONS®
COMPLETE LA FEMME®
LIFETIME®
MAMAJUANA ENERGY™

1229 Bazaar
1900 5th Ave
River Grove, IL 60171-1931 708-583-1800
Fax: 708-583-9782 800-736-1888

Supplier of closeout packaged foods including candy, snacks and spices
Owner/President: Rob Nardick
Buyer: Gene Wishiewaki
Sales Manager: Arnie Fishbain
Estimated Sales: $20-50 Million
Number Employees: 20-49
Sq. footage: 290000

1230 Be-Bop Biscotti
601 NE 1st
Suite B
Bend, OR 97701 541-388-8164
Fax: 541-389-6185 888-545-7487
mlee@be-bop.net www.be-bop.net
biscotti
President/Owner: Robert Golden
Number Employees: 99

1231 Bea & B Foods
1771 Bervy Street
San Diego, CA 92110-3545 619-276-6534
Fax: 619-276-9254 800-952-2117
pilarcitas@aol.com www.pilarcitas.com
Mexican seasonings and marinades
President: Bea Knapp
Estimated Sales: $ 3 - 5 Million
Number Employees: 1-4
Brands:
Pilarcitas

1232 Beach Bagel Bakeries
915 NW 72nd Street
Miami, FL 33150-3616 305-691-3514
Fax: 305-836-0959
Bagels and bakery products
President: Harold Greenblatt
Vice President: David Greenblatt
Estimated Sales: $20-50 Million
Number Employees: 20-49

1233 Beachaven Vineyards & Winery
1100 Dunlop Ln
Clarksville, TN 37040-9319 931-645-8867
Fax: 931-645-3522
thefolks@beachavenwinery.com
www.beachavenwinery.com
Wines
President/Owner: Louisa Cooke
VP: Edward Cooke
Estimated Sales: $2.5-5 Million
Number Employees: 10-19

1234 Beachwood Ingredient Services
23219 Greenlawn Avenue
Beachwood, OH 44122-1421 216-291-3229
Fax: 216-291-4037 888-427-7870
www.datasweet.de/supply/foam.htm
Chocolate and candy ingredients
President: Dan Dermer
Estimated Sales: $500,000-$1 Million
Number Employees: 1-4
Brands:
Beachwood

1235 Beacon Drive In
255 John B White Sr Blvd
Spartanburg, SC 29306-6047 864-585-9387
Fax: 864-585-2888 www.beacondriveinn.com
Iced Tea
Manager: Kenny Church
CEO: Steve McManus
Estimated Sales: $ 3 - 5 Million
Number Employees: 50-99
Sq. footage: 5000
Type of Packaging: Food Service, Private Label
Brands:
Beacon Drive-In Iced Tea

1236 Beal's Lobster Pier
P.O.Box 225
Southwest Harbor, ME 04679-0225 207-244-3202
Fax: 207-244-9479 800-244-7178
beals@arcadia.net www.bealslobster.com
Lobster, all types of seafood
President: Elmer Beal
Estimated Sales: $ 1 - 3 Million
Number Employees: 10-19

1237 Beam Global Spirits &Wine
510 Lake Cook Road
Deerfield, IL 60015-4964 847-948-8888
Fax: 847-948-8610 www.beamglobal.com

Cognac, bourbon and bourbon mixes, whisky, rum, and tequila.
President & CEO: Matthew Shattock
CFO: Robert Probst
President Beam Global Spirits & Wine USA:
William Newlands
SVP & Global CMO: A Rory Finlay
SVP Operations & Supply Chain: Ian Gourlay
Estimated Sales: $2.5 Billion
Number Employees: 140
Parent Co: Fortune Brands
Type of Packaging: Consumer, Food Service
Other Locations:
Jim Beam Brands Co.
Geyserville CA
Brands:
ANIS CASTELLANA
ARDMORE
BAKER'S
BASIL HAYDEN'S
BOOKER'S
CALVERT EXTRA
CALVERT GIN
CANADIAN CLUB
COURVOISIER
CRUZAN
D-Y-C
DEKUYPER
FUNDADOR
GILBY'S
JIM BEAM
KAMCHATKA
KAMORA
KESSLER
KNOB CREEK
LAPHROAIG
LORD CALVERT
MAKER'S MARK
OLD CROW
OLD GRAND DAD WHISKY
OLD OVERHOLT
RED STAG
RI
SAUZA
SOURZ APPLE
TANGLE RIDGE
TEACHER'S
TERRY CENTENARIO
TOSORO
VOX VODKA
WINDSOR CANADIAN
WOLFSCHMIDT VODKA

1238 Beamon Brothers
3392 Us Highway 117 N
Goldsboro, NC 27530-8075 919-734-4931
Fax: 919-736-1849
Fresh potatoes
Co-Owner: Edwin Beamon
Co-Owner: Samuel Beamon
Mgr.: Gail Beamon Crawford
Estimated Sales: $10-20 Million
Number Employees: 100-249
Brands:
Mount Herman
Stoney Hill

1239 Bean Buddies
1804 Plaza Avenue
New Hyde Park, NY 11040-4937 516-775-3726
Fax: 516-775-3706
Chocolate, coffee candy
President: Nina Cole
Estimated Sales: $2.5-5 Million
Number Employees: 5-9

1240 Bean Forge
171 S Broadway
Coos Bay, OR 97420-1614 541-267-4894
Fax: 541-267-5191 888-292-1632
sales@thebeanforge.com www.thebeanforge.com
Manager: Adam Hinkle
Owner: David Herold
Estimated Sales: $500,000-$1 Million
Number Employees: 5-9
Brands:
Bean Forge
Guido & Sals Old Chicago
Kenya AA
Lighthouse
Menehune Magic
Tanzanian Peaberry
Whiskey Run

1241 Bear Brewing Company
965 McGill Place
Kamloops, BC V2C 6N9
Canada   250-851-2543
           Fax: 250-851-9953 www.bearbeer.com
Beer
    President: David Beardsell
    CFO: George Tetreau
    Sales/Marketing: Brian Keast
    General Manager: Eric Spence
Estimated Sales: $2.5 Million
Number Employees: 10-19
Number of Brands: 18
Number of Products: 18
Sq. footage: 10000
Type of Packaging: Consumer, Food Service
Brands:
    ALBINO RHINO ALE
    BLACK BEAR ALE
    BROWN BEAR ALE
    BROWN ISLAND BITTER
    HEMP CREAM ALE
    JOW STIFF'S SPIKED ROOTBEER
    POLAR BEAR ALE
    RETHINK BEER

1242 Bear Creek Country Kitchens
325 W 600 S
Heber City, UT 84032-2230   435-654-2660
      Fax: 435-654-4525 800-516-7286
           brianb@bearcreekfoods.com
                www.bearcreekfoods.com
Manufacturer of powdered dips and soups
    Owner: Donald White
    President/CEO: Kevin Ruda
    CFO: Al Van Leeuwen
    Director R&D: Brian Brinkerhoff
    VP Sales/Marketing: Stephen White
    VP Operations: Kevin Kowalski
    Purchasing Manager: Mark Hartman
Estimated Sales: $40 Million
Number Employees: 100-249
Sq. footage: 180000
Parent Co: American Capital Strategies
Type of Packaging: Consumer, Food Service
Brands:
    Bear Creek Country Kitchens
    Sheila's Select Gourmet Recipes

1243 Bear Creek Kitchens
10857 State Highway 154
Marshall, TX 75670-8105   903-935-0253
      Fax: 903-935-5560 888-300-7687
           twostep@internetwork.net
Bottled soup mix in six flavors, seasonings, BBQ
mixes
    Owner: Robbie Shoults
    CFO: Robert Ryberg
Estimated Sales: $5-10 Million
Number Employees: 5-9
Brands:
    Bear Creek Pandhandler Pasta
    Bear Creek Panhandler Brand
    Bear Creek the Texas Two Step

1244 Bear Creek Smokehouse
10857 State Highway 154
Marshall, TX 75670-8105   903-935-5217
      Fax: 903-935-2871 800-950-2327
           info@bearcreeksmokehouse.com
                www.bearcreeksmokehouse.com
Manufacturer of smoked chicken, turkey and turkey
products, smoked and cured ham, salted pork, soup
mixes, smoked bacon, sausages, pork ribs and des-
serts
    President: Charles Shoults
    VP: Robbie Shoults
    Secretary/Treasurer: Brenda Shoults
Estimated Sales: $10-20 Million
Number Employees: 20-49
Sq. footage: 20000
Type of Packaging: Consumer
Brands:
    Bear Creek Brand

1245 Bear Creek Winery
6220 Caves Hwy
Cave Junction, OR 97523-9714   541-592-3977
           Fax: 541-592-2127 www.sv-wine.com/
Wines
    President: Rene Eichmann
    CEO: Rene Eichmann
    Marketing: Lorie Eichmann

Estimated Sales: $1-2.5 Million
Number Employees: 1-4
Brands:
    Dijon Clone
    Rogue Valley

1246 Bear Meadow Farm
248 Greenfield Rd
Colrain, MA 01340-9637   413-624-0291
      Fax: 413-664-8373 800-653-9241
           retail.info@bearmeadowfarm.com
                www.bearmeadowfarm.com
Manufacturer of quality food condiments such as;
jellies, preserves, jams, salad dressings
    Principal Owner/GM: Matt Shearer
Estimated Sales: $1-2.5 Million
Number Employees: 1-4
Sq. footage: 3000
Type of Packaging: Consumer, Food Service, Pri-
vate Label
Brands:
    Bear Meadow Farm
    Rt 66 Foods

1247 Bear Stewart Corporation
1011 N Damen Ave
Chicago, IL 60622-3637   773-276-0400
      Fax: 773-276-3512 800-697-2327
           info@bearstewart.com www.bearstore.com
Processor and exporter of ingredients for bakers and
confectioners including flavoring extracts, dry and
meringue cake/pie fillings, cake mix, jellies and
almond paste.
    Owner: Clifford Brooks
    Executive VP: Cliff Brooks
    VP of Sales: Michael Hoffman
Estimated Sales: $5-10 Million
Number Employees: 20-49
Sq. footage: 50000
Type of Packaging: Food Service

1248 Bear's Distributing Company
303 Swan Ave # A
Centralia, IL 62801-6128   618-532-1901
                              Fax: 618-532-6034
    Owner: Mike Donnewald
Estimated Sales: $ 20 - 50 Million
Number Employees: 20-49

1249 Beard's Quality Nut Company
3006 Yosemite Blvd
Empire, CA 95319   209-526-3590
                              Fax: 209-526-8110
Processor of in-shell and shelled walnuts
    Owner: Rodney Beard
Estimated Sales: $ 1 - 3 Million
Number Employees: 10-19
Type of Packaging: Consumer, Food Service

1250 Beatrice Bakery Company
201 S 5th St
Beatrice, NE 68310-4408   402-223-2358
      Fax: 402-223-4465 800-228-4030
           ron@beatricebakery.com
                www.beatricebakery.com
Processor and exporter of dessert cakes, fruit cakes,
and liqueur-filled cakes
    President: Rick Curlett
    VP: Greg Leech
    Quality Control: Robin Dickinson
    Sales Director: Sue Kennedy
    Public Relations: Brooklyn Soft
    Operations Manager: Greg Leech
    Production Manager: Robin Dickinson
    Plant Manager: Greg Leech
    Purchasing Manager: Greg Leech
Estimated Sales: $ 5-10 Million
Number Employees: 20-49
Number of Brands: 10
Number of Products: 125
Sq. footage: 50000
Type of Packaging: Private Label
Brands:
    GRANDMA'S BAKE SHOPPE
    GRANDMA'S FRUIT CAKE
    INNKEEPER'S OWN
    YE OLDE ENGLISH

**1251 (HQ)Beatrice Bakery
Company/Grandma's Bake
Shoppe**
201 S 5th Street
PO Box 457
Beatrice, NE 68310-0457
      Fax: 402-223-4465 800-228-4030
                www.beatricebakery.com
Manufacturer of fruit and nut cake, baked goods
    President: Greg Leech
Estimated Sales: $ 20 - 50 Million
Number Employees: 20-34

1252 Beatty Fresh Frozen Meats
9842 State Road 331
Bourbon, IN 46504-9676   574-342-2665
Manufacturer of fresh and frozen beef and pork;
slaughtering services available
    Owner: Terry Beatty
Estimated Sales: $10-20 Million
Number Employees: 5-9
Type of Packaging: Consumer, Bulk

1253 Beaucanon Estate Wines
1006 Monticello Rd
Napa, CA 94558-2032   707-254-1460
      Fax: 707-254-1462 800-660-3520
                www.beaucanonestate.com
Wines
    President: Louis De Coninck
Estimated Sales: $2.5-5 Million
Number Employees: 10-19

1254 Beaulieu Vineyard
1960 Saint Helena Hwy
Rutherford, CA 94573   707-967-5233
      Fax: 707-967-1066 800-264-6918
           bvinfo@bvwines.com www.bvwines.com
Processor of wines
    Executive Director: Armond Rist
    Vice President Winemaking: Joel Aiken
    Winemaker: Robert Masvczek
    Purchasing Manager: Marisa Licata
Estimated Sales: $50-100 Million
Number Employees: 100-249
Parent Co: International Distillers
Type of Packaging: Bulk
Brands:
    BV BEAUTOUR
    BV CAMENOS PINOT NOIR
    BV CARNEROS CHARDONNAY
    BV ENSEMBLE
    BV NAPA SERIES
    BV NAPA VALLEY SAUVIGNON BLANC
    BV NAPA VALLEY ZINFANDEL
    BV RESERVE
    BV RUTHERFORD/NAPA VALLEY CABER-
    NET
    BV SIGNET COLLECTION
    BV SYRAH
    BV TAPESTRY
    BV VIN GRIS DE PINOT NOIR
    BV VROGNIER

1255 Beaumont Products
1560 Big Shanty Dr NW
Kennesaw, GA 30144-7040   770-514-7400
      Fax: 770-514-7400 800-451-7096
           citrusii@citrusii@beaumontpr
                www.citrusmagic.com
    President: Hank Picken
Estimated Sales: $ 3 - 5 Million
Number Employees: 20-49

1256 Beaumont Rice Mills
1800 Pecos St
Beaumont, TX 77701-2500   409-832-2521
      Fax: 409-832-6927 info@bmtricemills.com
                www.bmtricemills.com
Manufacturer and exporter of brewers' rice and rice
bran
    President: Louis Broussard Jr
    VP: Ben Broussard
    Secretary: Sheryl Graham
    Assistant Secretary/Treasurer: Brenda Cook
Estimated Sales: $ 20 - 50 Million
Number Employees: 50-99
Type of Packaging: Consumer

1257 Beaver Enterprises
P.O.Box 712
Rockland, ME 04841-0712   207-596-2900
                              Fax: 207-596-2922

Owner: Wayne Stinson
Estimated Sales: $800,000
Number Employees: 5-9

1258 Beaver Meadow Creamery
415 Maple Ave
Du Bois, PA 15801   814-371-3711
Fax: 814-371-3713   800-262-3711
bmbutter@comcast.net
Processor and exporter of portion control butter, margarine and blends
President: J Kirk
Vice President: R Kirk
Estimated Sales: $20 - 50 Million
Sq. footage: 30000
Type of Packaging: Food Service, Private Label, Bulk
Brands:
BEAVER MEADOW

1259 Beaver Street Brewery
11 S Beaver St # 1
Flagstaff, AZ 86001-5500   928-779-0079
Fax: 928-779-0029
info@beaverstreetbrewery.com
www.beaverstreetbrewery.com
Processor of seasonal beers and porter
President/Owner: Evan Hanseth
VP: Winnie Hanseth
Estimated Sales: $2.5-5 Million
Number Employees: 100-249
Type of Packaging: Consumer, Food Service
Brands:
BRAMBLE BERRY BREW
HEFE WEIZEN
INDIA PALE ALE
MARZEN LAGER
PILSENER
R&r OATMEAL STOUT
RAIL HEAD RED ALE
VIENNA LAGER

1260 Beaver Street Fisheries
P.O.Box 41430
Jacksonville, FL 32203-1430   904-354-8533
Fax: 904-354-2607   800-874-6426
www.beaverfish.com
Processor, exporter and importer of frozen fish and seafood including stuffed shrimp, crabs and crab meat
President: Jeff Edwards
VP: Harry Frisch
Sales Manager: Carlos Sanchez
Estimated Sales: $$50-100 Million
Number Employees: 100-249
Parent Co: Beaver Street Fisheries
Type of Packaging: Consumer, Food Service, Private Label, Bulk

1261 Beaverton Foods
P.O.Box 687
Beaverton, OR 97075-0687   503-646-8138
Fax: 503-644-9204   800-223-8076
dombg@beavertonfoods.com
www.beavertonfoods.com
Processor and exporter of horseradish, mustard, garlic and sauces.
President: Gene Biggi
CEO: Bill Small
Foodservice Manager: Domonic Biggi
CEO: Bill Small
Marketing/Advertising Manager: Barbara Lutheran
Retail Grocery Sales Manager: Tom Murphy
Private Label Manager: Jan Westfall
Business/Customer Service Manager: Roger Klingsporn
Mail Order Manager: Mark Vander Yacht
Estimated Sales: $10-20 Million
Number Employees: 50-99
Sq. footage: 65000
Type of Packaging: Consumer, Food Service, Private Label, Bulk
Brands:
BEAVER
INGLEHOFFER
NAPA VALLEY
OLD SPICE

1262 Beck Farms
RR #8 12-7
Lethbridg, AB T1J 4P4
Canada   403-227-1020
Fax: 403-227-5414   Beck@tellesplanet.net
www.beckfarms.com
Processor and packer of carrots and parsnips
President: Peter Edgar
CEO: Peter Edgar
VP: Rod Bradsha
Sales Manager: Shelley Bradsha
Number Employees: 10-19
Brands:
Beck Farms
Beck Gourmet

1263 Beck Flavors
411 Gano Ave
St Louis, MO 63147-3210   314-436-7624
Fax: 314-436-1049   800-851-8100
usa.info@danisco.com   www.danisco.com
Manufacturer and exporter of vanilla and coffee extracts and flavors; also, sweet flavors
HR Administrator: Kim Hopkins
Operations Manager: Andy Zook
Estimated Sales: $ 20 - 50 Million
Number Employees: 50-99
Sq. footage: 120000
Type of Packaging: Bulk
Other Locations:
Ardsley NY
Bakersfield CA
Lakeland FL
New Century KS
Brands:
Beck Cafe
Beck Flavors

1264 Beck's Ice Cream
830 Roosevelt Ave
York, PA 17404-2830   717-848-8400
Fax: 717-846-5121
Ice cream
Owner: Jerry Beck
CEO: Lynne Beck
CFO: Kerry Beck
Estimated Sales: $250,000
Number Employees: 5-9
Brands:
Becks Ice Cream

1265 Beck's Waffles of Oklahoma
101 S Kickapoo Ave
Shawnee, OK 74801-7686   405-878-0615
Fax: 405-878-8546   800-646-6254
wafflman@swbell.net   www.beckswaffles.com
Processor of frozen Belgian waffles; wholesaler/distributor of waffle mix and irons
Sales: Doyle Beck
Estimated Sales: $1-3 Million
Number Employees: 20-49
Sq. footage: 20000
Type of Packaging: Consumer, Food Service

1266 Becker Food Company
4160 N Port Washington Road
Milwaukee, WI 53212-1030   414-964-5353
Fax: 414-964-4523
Manufacturer, importer and wholesaler/distributor of meats, frozen foods, poultry and seafood; serving the food service market
President: Stephen Becker
Estimated Sales: $100+ Million
Number Employees: 80
Sq. footage: 60000
Type of Packaging: Food Service

1267 Beckman & Gast Company
P.O.Box 307
St Henry, OH 45883-0307   419-678-4195
Fax: 419-678-3005   infobg@beckmangast.com
www.beckmangast.com
Processor of canned goods including tomato juice, tomatoes and cut green beans.
President: William Gast
Agriculture Manager: Bo Gast
Secretary/Treasurer: Trish Albers
Vice President: Nicholas Gast
Production: Gary Broering
Estimated Sales: $5-9.9 Million
Number Employees: 10-19
Type of Packaging: Consumer, Private Label
Brands:
BECKMAN'S

1268 Beckmann's Old World Bakery
2341 Mission St
Santa Cruz, CA 95060-5200   831-423-2566
Fax: 831-457-2269
Bread and baked goods
Manager: Beth Taiva
VP: Sharon May
Marketing Manager: Doug Eckley
Estimated Sales: $100-500 Million
Number Employees: 100-249

1269 Beckmen Vineyards
P.O.Box 542
Los Olivos, CA 93441-0542   805-688-8664
Fax: 805-688-9983   info@beckmenvineyards.com
www.beckmenvineyards.com
Wines
President: Tom Beckmen
Operations Manager: Steve Beckmen
Estimated Sales: $500-1 Million appx.
Number Employees: 1-4

1270 Bede Inc
PO Box 8263
Haledon, NJ 07538-0263   973-956-2900
Fax: 973-956-0600   866-239-6565
bedeinc@aol.com   www.bedenj.com
Processor and exporter of instant hot cereals including peanut porridge, banana, plantain, etc.; also, peanut-based health beverage mixes
President: Jasseth Cummings
CFO: Gloria Johnson
Buyer: Sam Cummings
Quality Control: King H
Estimated Sales: $2.5-5 Million
Number Employees: 1-4
Brands:
Cream of Peanut
Crema De Many
Malted Peanut
Quick Peanut Porridge
Vigorteen

1271 Bedell North Fork, LLC
36225 Main Rd
Cutchogue, NY 11935-1346   631-734-7537
Fax: 631-734-5788   wine@bedellcellars.com
www.bedellcellars.com
Wines
Manager: Trent Prezler
CEO: Michael Lynne
Senior VP Sales/Marketing: Jim Silver
COO: Trent Preszler
Plant Manager: Dave Thompson
Estimated Sales: $1-2.5 Million
Number Employees: 5-9
Other Locations:
Corey Creek Vineyards(Tasting Room)
Southold NY
Brands:
BEDELL CELLARS
COREY CREEK

1272 Bedford Cheese Store
P.O.Box 888
Shelbyville, TN 37162-0888   931-684-5422
Fax: 931-684-9584   800-264-1115
bedford@Bedfordcheese.com
www.bedfordcheese.com
Manufacturer of cheeses, sauces, dressings, meats, jams and jellies, gift trays and baskets, cakes and accessories.
Owner/President: Joe Madeo
Secretary: Martha Madeo
Estimated Sales: $1-2.5 Million
Number Employees: 10-19
Sq. footage: 7200

1273 Bedrock Farm Certified Organic Medicinal Herbs
106 Woodland Trl
Wakefield, RI 02879-1926   401-789-9943
ageary@bedrockfarmherbs.com
www.bedrockfarmherbs.com
Organic medicinal herbs
President: Angie Geary

1274 Bee International
2311 Boswell Rd # 5
Chula Vista, CA 91914-3512   619-710-1800
Fax: 619-710-1822   800-421-6465
www.beeinc.com

Manufacturer and importer of Easter, Valentine, Halloween, Christmans and novelty candy items
President/Owner: Louis Block
VP Marketing: Dan Blanchard
VP Sales: Dan Blanchard
Estimated Sales: $50-100 Million
Number Employees: 20-49
Sq. footage: 55000
Type of Packaging: Consumer
Brands:
CHICLE CHIPS
MICRO BMX BIKE
MICRO SCOOTER

1275 Bee Wayne Bakery
221 S 22nd Street
Saint Joseph, MO 64501-3135 816-232-8483
Fax: 816-238-0587
Bakery products
President: James Bunge
Estimated Sales: $500,000 appx.
Number Employees: 1-4

1276 Bee-Raw Honey
PO Box 1343
New York, NY 10013 212-941-1932
Fax: 646-607-2060 infobee@beeraw.com
www.beeraw.com
honey
President/Owner: Zeke Freeman
CEO: Sam Yocum

1277 Beech-Nut Nutrition Corporation
100 S 4th Street
Saint Louis, MO 63102-1800 314-655-2100
Fax: 314-436-7679 800-233-2468
Beech-Nut@Beech-Nut.com
www.beech-nut.com
Baby food formulated to supplement baby's diet of breast milk or formula. With no refined sugar, no added salt and no harsh spices. Juices and waters
Estimated Sales: $ 10 - 20 Million
Number Employees: 20-49
Brands:
CEREALS
STAGE 1
STAGE 2
TABLE TIME

1278 Beef Packers, Inc.
P.O.Box 12503
Fresno, CA 93778-2503 559-268-5586
Fax: 559-268-1352 www.beefpackers.com
Processor of beef; slaughtering services available
VP: Roger Hall
General Manager: Dennis Roth
Estimated Sales: $50-100 Million
Number Employees: 1,000-4,999
Sq. footage: 201550
Parent Co: Cargill Meat Solutions
Brands:
ANGUS PRIDE
CIRCLE T BEEF™
EXCEL
HONEYSUCKLE WHITE
MEADOWLAND FARMS™GROUND BEEF
PRAIRIE GROVE FARMS
PREFERRED ANGUS®BEEF
RANCHERS REGISTRY ANGUS® BEEF
RUMBA™
SHADY BROOK FARMS
STERLING SILVER
TENDER CHOICE
TENDER RIDGE™ANGUS BEEF
VALLEY™TRADITION BEEF

1279 (HQ)Beef Products
891 Two Rivers Dr
North Sioux City, SD 57049-5391 605-217-8000
Fax: 605-217-8001 sales@beefproducts.com
www.beefproducts.com
Manufacturer of partially de-fatted chopped beef and chopped pork; also, fat-reduced beef and pork
President/CEO: Eldon Roth
CFO/VP: Regina Roth
Estimated Sales: I
Number Employees: 100-249
Type of Packaging: Consumer, Food Service
Other Locations:
BPI Plant
South Sioux City NE
BPI Plant
Amarillo TX
BPI Plant
Garden City KS

BPI Plant
Waterloo IA
BPI Plant
Finney County KS

1280 Beehive Botanicals, Inc.
16297 W Nursery Rd
Hayward, WI 54843-7138 715-634-4274
Fax: 715-634-3523 800-233-4483
e-mail:beehivebotanicals.com
www.beehivebotanicals.com
Processor and exporter of health supplements derived from honey, propolis, pollen and royal jelly; also, sugar-free propolis chewing gum
President/CEO: Linda Graham
Estimated Sales: $5-10 Million
Number Employees: 20-49
Brands:
Beehive Botanicals
Honey Silk

1281 Beer Nuts
P.O.Box 1549
Bloomington, IL 61702-1549 309-827-8580
Fax: 309-827-0914 800-233-7688
info@beernuts.com www.beernuts.com
Processor of numerous nut products including: original peanuts; glazed old fashioned peanuts; almonds; cashews; macadamia nuts; honey mustard crunch nuts; sesame crunch nuts; bar mix; pecans, barbeque crunch nuts; chocolate coverednuts; spicy & hot peanuts; mixes; kettle cooked peanuts; and cajun crunch nuts.
Manager: James A Shirk
Marketing Manager: Cindy Shirk
Public Relations: Tom Foster
Media Relations: Georgia Dawson
Estimated Sales: $20-50 Million
Number Employees: 50-99
Type of Packaging: Food Service
Brands:
Beer Nuts

1282 Beetroot Delights
72 Spruceside Crescent
Foothill, ON L0S 1E1
Canada 888-842-3387
Fax: 905-892-1080 info@beetrootdelights.com
www.beetrootdelights.com
Manufacturer and exporter of beetroot condiments including cherry beet pepper and ginger beet jelly, spiced beet ketchup and beet relish
President: Grace Lallemand
Number Employees: 3
Sq. footage: 800
Type of Packaging: Consumer, Food Service
Brands:
BEETROOT DELIGHTS

1283 Behm Blueberry Farms
14904 Canary Drive
Grand Haven, MI 49417-8663 616-846-1650
Fresh blueberries
President: Howard Behm
VP: Sharon Behm
Estimated Sales: $ 3 - 5 Million
Number Employees: 10-19
Brands:
Blueberry King

1284 (HQ)Bel/Kaukauna USA
P.O.Box 1974
Kaukauna, WI 54130-7074 920-788-3524
Fax: 920-788-9725 800-558-3500
customerservicekk@belkauusa.com
www.kaukaunacheese.com
Manufacturer of nacho sauce, salsa and cheeses including cold pack, natural, mini goudas and processed spreads; importer of natural cheeses
President: Robert Gilbert
VP Finance: Alan Patz
VP: Al Patz
Director Marketing: Becky Ryan
VP Sales: David Peterson
Director Operations: Bob Eger
Estimated Sales: $258.6 Million
Number Employees: 250-499
Sq. footage: 120000
Parent Co: Fromageries Bel SA
Type of Packaging: Consumer, Food Service, Bulk
Brands:
CONNOISSEUR
KAUKAUNA
LAUGHING COW

MERKETS
MINI BABYBEL
OWLS NEST
PRICE'S
WISPRIDE

1285 BelGioioso Cheese
5810 County Road Nn
Denmark, WI 54208-8730 920-863-2123
Fax: 920-863-8791 877-863-2123
info@belgioioso.com www.belgioioso.com
Manufacturer of Italian cheeses including provolone, parmesan, romano, asiago, fontina, kasseri, mascarpone, gorgonzola, fresh mozzarella, pepato, peperoncino, parveggiano
President: Errico Auricchio
Marketing Director: Jay Wistenberg
Estimated Sales: $50-99.9 Million
Number Employees: 100-249
Number of Brands: 1
Number of Products: 15
Type of Packaging: Consumer, Food Service, Bulk
Brands:
BELGIOIOSO

1286 Belcolade
8030 National Hwy
Pennsauken, NJ 08110-1414 856-661-9123
Fax: 856-665-0005 kzimmermann@puratos.com
belcolade@aol.com
Manufacturer of couverture chocolate
Estimated Sales: $5-10 Million
Number Employees: 5-9
Parent Co: Belcolade NV/SA
Brands:
BELCOLADE
BELCOLADE
CARAT

1287 Belgravia Imports
275 Highpoint Ave
Portsmouth, RI 02871-1338 401-683-3323
Fax: 401-683-2717 800-848-1127
belgravia@belgraviaimports.com
www.belgraviaimports.com
Organic and natural foods
President: Donald Dick
Estimated Sales: $1-2.5 Million
Number Employees: 5-9

1288 Believe
3026 Mockingbird Lane
171
Dallas, TX 75205-2323 360-221-2919
Fax: 360-221-3604 800-428-7437
Vegan foods
President: Bruce Dearborn
Brands:
Eco Burger
Nogurt

1289 Bell & Evans
P.O.Box 39
Fredericksburg, PA 17026-0039 717-865-6626
Fax: 717-865-7046 info@bellandevans.com
www.bellandevans.com
Processor and exporter of fresh chicken, chicken nuggets, sausages, burgers, and diced IQF chicken breast
President/Owner: Scott Sechler
CEO: Bruno Schmalhofer
CEO: Mike Good
Estimated Sales: $50-100 Million
Number Employees: 1,000-4,999
Sq. footage: 100000
Brands:
Bell & Evans the Excellent Chicken
Farmers Pride Natural

1290 Bell Buckle Country Store
26 Railroad Sq E
Bell Buckle, TN 37020-2047 931-294-5906
Fax: 931-294-2120 800-707-0483
info@bellbuckle.com www.bellbuckle.com
Full line of jams, jellies, salad dressings, salsas, dessert topping and drink mixes
President: Larry Lowman
Marketing Director: Scott Bell
Estimated Sales: $ 1 - 3 Million
Number Employees: 10-19
Brands:
Captain Rodney's
Rose & Ivy

1291 Bell Buoy Crab Company
PO Box 680
Seaside, OR 97138-0680   503-738-6354
Fax: 503-738-8325   800-529-2722
bellbuoy@pacifier.com
www.bellbuoyofseaside.com
Processor of seafood including halibut, herring,
salmon, shrimp, smelt, squid, sturgeon, tuna, crabs
and clams; also, seafood cocktails.

Estimated Sales: $2.5-5 Million
Number Employees: 20-49
Type of Packaging: Consumer, Food Service, Private Label, Bulk

1292 Bell Dairy Products
201 University Ave
Lubbock, TX 79415-3426   806-293-1367
Fax: 806-765-5192
Processor of milk and buttermilk
VP: Bill Murphy
Plant Manager: Damon Mc Dermott
Purchasing Manager: Jim McGann
Estimated Sales: $50-99.9 Million
Number Employees: 100-249
Parent Co: Dean Foods Company
Type of Packaging: Consumer, Food Service, Private Label

1293 (HQ)Bell Flavors & Fragrances
500 Academy Dr
Northbrook, IL 60062-2497   847-291-8300
Fax: 847-291-1217   800-323-4387
infousa@bellff.com   www.bellff.com
Manufacturer and exporter of natural and artificial
flavoring extracts for food and beverages; also, spice
compounds
President/CEO: James Heinz
Controller: Julie Fox
VP/Technical Director: Mike Bloom
VP Marketing: Pete Healy
VP Plant Operations: Mike Bianco
Estimated Sales: $150 Million
Number Employees: 50-99
Sq. footage: 100000
Type of Packaging: Consumer, Food Service
Brands:
YUCCAFOAM

1294 Bell Foods
6761 Sierra Court
Suite F
Dublin, CA 94568-2692   925-803-2499
Fax: 925-803-2499   800-929-0777
www.bellfoods.com

1295 Bell Mountain Vineyards
P.O.Box 756
Fredericksburg, TX 78624-0756   830-685-3297
Fax: 830-685-3657
contactus@bellmountainwine.com
www.bellmountainwine.com
Wines
Owner: Robert P Oberhelman
VP: Ames Morrison
Estimated Sales: $2.5-5 Million
Number Employees: 5-9

1296 Bell-Carter Foods
3742 Mt Diablo Blvd
Lafayette, CA 94549-3601   925-284-5933
Fax: 925-284-1289   800-252-3557
www.bellcarter.com
Processor of California black ripe olives
President: H Jud Carter
Estimated Sales: $100+ Million
Number Employees: 250-499

1297 Bell-Carter Foods
3742 Mt Diablo Blvd
Lafayette, CA 94549-3601   925-284-5933
Fax: 925-284-1289   800-252-3557
contactus@bellcarter.com
Manufacturer and marketer of black ripe, spanish,
sicilian, kalamota, and other specialty olive products
President: Jud Carter
CEO: Tim Carter
COO: Ken Wienholz
Vice President: Mike McLaughlin
Estimated Sales: $ 20 - 50 Million
Number Employees: 20-49
Type of Packaging: Consumer, Food Service, Private Label, Bulk

Brands:
LINDSAY OLIVES

1298 Bella Chi-Cha Products
216-B Fern Street
Santa Cruz, CA 95060   831-423-1851
Fax: 831-423-0212   ccrusso@pacbell.net
www.bellachicha.com
Pesto and layered tortas
President/Owner: Chi-Cha Russo

1299 Bella Coola Fisheries
9829 River Road
Delta, BC V4G 1B4
Canada   604-583-3474
Fax: 604-583-4940   info@belcofish.com
www.belcofish.com
Processor and exporter of fresh and frozen herring
roe and salmon
President: Tim Turyk
Number Employees: 10-19
Type of Packaging: Consumer, Food Service, Private Label, Bulk

1300 Bella Cucina Artful Food
1050 N Highland Ave NE
Atlanta, GA 30306-3551   404-347-6476
Fax: 404-815-1826   800-671-3136
virginiahighlands@bellacucina.com
www.bellacucinaartfulfood.com
Manufacturer of quality Mediterranean inspired
food, such as olive oils and pestos
Manager: Reginald Weekes
Estimated Sales: $2.5-5 Million
Number Employees: 20-49
Type of Packaging: Private Label

1301 Bella Luna
228 E Main Street
Sun Prairie, WI 53590-2225   414-264-7676
Fax: 414-264-8940   800-884-8884
bellunainc@aol.com
Tuna
Sales Manager: Leah Krasno
Purchasing Manager: Jason Krasno
Estimated Sales: $2.5-5 Million
Number Employees: 10-19

1302 Bella Napoli Italian Bakery
721 River St
Troy, NY 12180-1233   518-274-8277
Fax: 518-274-2625   888-800-0103
www.bellanapolibakery.com
Manufacturer of Italian specialties
President: Dominic Mainella
Estimated Sales: $2.5-5 Million
Number Employees: 50-99
Other Locations:
Bella Napoli Italian Bakery
Latham NY

1303 Bella Ravioli
369 Main St
Medford, MA 02155-6149   781-396-0875
Fax: 781-396-0876
Processor of pasta
Owner: Mario De Pasquale
Estimated Sales: Less than $100,000
Number Employees: 1-4
Brands:
Bella Ravioli

1304 Bella Vista Farm
1002 SW Ard St
Lawton, OK 73505-9660   580-536-1300
Fax: 580-536-4886   866-237-8526
craig@peppercreekfarms.com
www.peppercreekfarms.com
Organic jams, honey, peanut butter, popcorn, all
nautral pasta sauces, organic pasta and organic olive
oil.
Owner: Craig Weissman
Estimated Sales: Less than $500,000
Number Employees: 5-9
Brands:
Bella Vista

1305 Bella Viva Orchards
3019 S Quincy Rd
Denair, CA 95316-9532   209-883-4146
Fax: 209-883-0215   800-552-8218
CustomerCare@BellaViva.com
www.bellaviva.com

Kosher dried fruit and chocolate fruits packaged for
gifts
Owner: Victor Martino
Estimated Sales: $1-2.5 Million
Number Employees: 20-49

1306 Bellacicco DistributionCompany
78 Livingston Street
Brooklyn, NY 11201-5043   718-206-1705
Fax: 718-206-7120   800-561-1705
Manufacturer of fresh baked breads and other bakery products
Estimated Sales: Less than $500,000
Number Employees: 1-4
Type of Packaging: Consumer, Food Service

1307 Bellatti Soybeans-Bellatti Soynuts
194 140th Avenue
Mount Pulaski, IL 62548   217-792-5503
soybeaniv@aol.com
Processor and exporter of soybeans including soy
nut snack foods
President: Mardy Bellatti
VP: Lou Bellatti
Number Employees: 5-9
Sq. footage: 15000
Type of Packaging: Food Service, Private Label
Brands:
Bellati Soy-A-Nuts
Bellatti Soybeans

1308 Belle Plaine Cheese Factory
N3473 Wisconsin Ave
Shawano, WI 54166-6609   715-526-2789
866-245-5924
Retailer of cheese including colby, cheddar,
monterey jack, rainbow and pepper jack
President: Donald Brandl
Estimated Sales: $50,000
Number Employees: 1-4
Type of Packaging: Consumer

1309 Belle River Enterprises
RR 3
Belle River, PE C0A 1B0
Canada   902-962-2248
Fax: 902-962-4276
Processor and exporter of rock crab combo and
minced crab, cocktail claws and salad meat
Number Employees: 50-99
Sq. footage: 8000
Brands:
Belle River

1310 BelleHarvest Sales
11900 Fisk Rd
Belding, MI 48809-9413   616-794-0320
Fax: 616-794-3961   800-452-7753
bellehar@iserv.net   www.belleharvest.com
Manufacturer, wholesaler/distributor, exporter and
packer of fresh fruits and vegetables
President: Mike Rothwell
Sales/Marketing: Tom Pletcher
Number Employees: 10-19
Parent Co: Belding Fruit Storage

1311 Belleco, Inc
P.O.Box 880
Saco, ME 04072-0880   207-854-8006
Fax: 207-283-8080   sales@bellecocooking.com
www.bellecocooking.com
Manufacturer of customized toasters, conveyor
Pizza Ovens and Heat Lamps
President: Russell Bellrose
CFO: Kevin Roche
Quality Control Manager: Gil Cole
Sales: Mike Clavet
Materials Manager: Ron Hevey
Type of Packaging: Food Service

1312 Belleisle Foods
880 Route 870
Belleisle Creek, NB E5P 1G4
Canada   506-485-2564
Fax: 506-485-2566
tellmemore@belleislefoods.com
www.belleislefoods.com
Manufacturer of frozen Chinese food and meat pies
and entrees
EVP: Peter Pope
Quality Assurance: Jeanette Sprague
Marketing/Sales: Shelly Bronnum
Number Employees: 100
Sq. footage: 33000

Type of Packaging: Consumer, Food Service, Private Label, Bulk
Brands:
BELLEISLE

1313 Bellerose Vineyard
435 W Dry Creek Rd
Healdsburg, CA 95448-9122   707-433-1637
     Fax: 707-433-7024 www.everettridge.com
Wines
President: Charles Richard
Founder/Owner: Charles Richard
Co-Owner: Charles Richard
Estimated Sales: $500,000 appx.
Number Employees: 5-9
Brands:
Bellerose

1314 (HQ)Belletieri Company
312 N 12th St
Allentown, PA 18102-2737   610-433-8300
    Fax: 610-433-4544   800-708-7280
Italian specialty foods
President: Louie Belletieri
Marketing Director: Lisa Kraftician
Estimated Sales: Under $500,000
Number Employees: 5-9

1315 Belleville Brothers Packing
2545 Insley Rd
North Baltimore, OH 45872-9776   419-257-3529
     Fax: 419-257-3529
Processor of meat products
President: James Belleville
Estimated Sales: $500,000
Number Employees: 1-4
Type of Packaging: Consumer, Bulk

1316 (HQ)Bellisio Foods, Inc.
PO Box 16630
Lakeville, MN 55816   952-469-2000
    Fax: 952-985-5822   800-368-7337
    michelinas@bellisiofoods.com
     www.michelinas.com
Processor of frozen entrees, sauces and soups
CEO: Joel Conner
CFO: Danette Bucsko
Director Research/Development: Kevin Towles
Senior VP Sales/Marketing: Charlie Pountney
Senior VP Operations: Jeff Wilson
Estimated Sales: $25-49.9 Million
Number Employees: 100
Sq. footage: 60000
Type of Packaging: Consumer, Food Service
Brands:
AUTHENTICO®
BUDGET GOURMET®
MICHELINA'S GRANDE
MICHELINA'S LEAN GOURMET®
MICHELINA'S PIZZA SNACK ROLLS
MICHELINA'S SIGNATURE®
ZAP'EMS®

1317 Bellville Meat Market
36 S Front St
Bellville, TX 77418-2406   979-865-5782
    Fax: 979-865-0550   800-571-6328
    sara@bellvillemeatmarket.com
     www.bellvillemeatmarket.com
Processor of regular and flavored beef and pork smoked sausage links including garlic, jalapeno, cayenne pepper, etc.; also, fresh pork links, dry, all beef summer and pan sausages and venison products available
Owner/Manager: Daniel Poffenberger Jr.
Plant Manager: Jerrod Poffenberger
Estimated Sales: $2.5-5 Million
Number Employees: 20-49
Sq. footage: 1500
Type of Packaging: Consumer, Food Service, Private Label, Bulk
Brands:
Poffenberger's Bellville

1318 Bellwether Farms
PO Box 299
Valley Ford, CA 94972-0299   707-963-2443
    Fax: 707-763-2443   888-527-8606
    info@bellwethercheese.com
     www.bellwethercheese.com
Fresh and aged cheese
Owner: Cynthia Callahan
Founder: Cindy Callahan
Vice President: Liam Callahan

Estimated Sales: Under $500,000
Number Employees: 5-9
Type of Packaging: Private Label
Brands:
Bellwether

1319 Belmar Spring Water Company
410 Grove St
Glen Rock, NJ 07452-1932   201-444-1010
     Fax: 973-423-4503
    service@belmarspringwater.com
     www.belmarspringwater.com
Processor and bottler of spring water
President: Wesley Outwater
Estimated Sales: $1-2.5 Million
Number Employees: 10-19
Type of Packaging: Consumer, Private Label

1320 Belmont Brewing Company
25 39th Pl
Long Beach, CA 90803-2806   562-433-3891
    Fax: 562-434-0604 www.belmontbrewing.com
Beer and micro brews
Owner: David Hansen
VP: Tom Avila
Estimated Sales: $2.5-5 Million
Number Employees: 50-99
Brands:
BITBURGER
BLACK & TAN
FRANZISKANER HEFE-WEISSE
GROWLER
LONG BEACH CRUDE
MARATHON
PENNY FOGGER
SHANDY
STRAWBERRY BLONDE
TOP SAIL AMBER
WOODCHUCK PEAR CIDER

1321 Belmont Chemicals
790 Bloomfield Ave # B3
Clifton, NJ 07012-1182   973-777-2225
    Fax: 973-777-6384   800-722-5070
     www.belmontchemicals.com
Processor and exporter of vitamins, nutritional and protein supplements, herbs and amino acids
Owner: Paul Egyes
Sales Manager: Paul Egyes
Public Relations: Mary Apuzzo
Estimated Sales: $10-20 Million
Number Employees: 5-9
Number of Products: 50
Type of Packaging: Bulk

1322 Belmont Peanuts of Southampton Inc
23195 Buckhorn Quarter Rd
Capron, VA 23829   800-648-4613
    info@belmontpeanuts.com
     www.belmontpeanuts.com
Peanut and peanut products
President/Owner: Patsy Marks
VP: Robert Marks

1323 Belton Foods
P.O.Box 13605
Dayton, OH 45413-0605   937-890-7768
    Fax: 937-890-7780   800-443-2266
    dsipos@beltonfoods.com   www.belton.com
Beverages, concentrates, pancake and table syrups, vinegars, drink mixes, enhancing syrups and slush base.
President: David Sipos
Vice President: Cynthia Gillespie
Marketing Director: Don Fox
Sales Director: Don Fox
Production Manager: Joe Reece
Purchasing Manager: Ted Dorow
Estimated Sales: $20-50 Million
Number Employees: 20-49
Number of Brands: 20
Number of Products: 120
Sq. footage: 24
Type of Packaging: Consumer, Food Service, Private Label, Bulk

1324 Belvedere Vineyards & Winery
250 Center St
Healdsburg, CA 95448-4402   707-431-4442
    Fax: 707-433-2429   800-433-8296
     www.belvederewinery.com

Wines
CFO: Tom Christenson
Winemaker: Alison Rosenelum
Plant Manager: Proy McEndry
Estimated Sales: $10-20 Million
Number Employees: 20-49
Sq. footage: 24
Type of Packaging: Private Label
Brands:
Belvedere
Grove Street
Hambrecht Vineyards

1325 Belvedere Winery
250 Center St
Healdsburg, CA 95448-4402   707-431-4442
     800-433-8296
     www.belvederewinery.com
Assortment of wines such as: Chardonnay, Russian River Wine and Renot Noir
Winemaker: Troy McEnery
Estimated Sales: $ 10 - 20 Million
Number Employees: 20-49

1326 (HQ)Ben & Jerry's Homemade
30 Community Dr # 1
South Burlington, VT 05403-6834   802-846-1500
    Fax: 802-846-1555 www.benjerry.com
Processor of ice cream, frozen yogurt, sorbet and smoothies
President/CEO: Perry Odak
CEO: Walt Freese
Director Quality Control: Mary Kamm
Public Relations Manager: Sean Greenwood
Estimated Sales: $50-99.9 Million
Number Employees: 500-999
Parent Co: Unilever USA
Type of Packaging: Consumer
Other Locations:
Ben & Jerry's
Waterbury VT
Brands:
Ben & Jerry's
Ben & Jerry's Frozen Smoothies
Ben & Jerry's Ice Cream

1327 Ben B. Schwartz & Sons
7201 W Fort St # 27
Detroit, MI 48209-2995   313-841-8300
     Fax: 313-841-1253
Grower of fruits and vegetables including apples, peaches, pears, cucumbers, lettuce and potatoes
Owner: Chris Billmeyer
Manager: Gary Schwartz
Estimated Sales: $10-20 Million
Number Employees: 20-49
Type of Packaging: Consumer

1328 Ben E. Keith DFW
P.O.Box 901001
Fort Worth, TX 76101-2001   817-654-3663
    Fax: 817-759-6886 www.benekeith.com
Wholesaler/distributor of frozen food, produce, groceries, dairy products, meats, etc.; serving the food service market
President: Mike Roach
CEO: Robert Hallam
CFO: Mel Cockrell
Director Marketing: Bill Sewell
Senior VP Sales: Ron Boyd
Estimated Sales: $100-500 Million
Number Employees: 20-49
Sq. footage: 591000
Parent Co: Ben E. Keith Company
Type of Packaging: Food Service, Private Label, Bulk
Brands:
ADMIRAL OF THE FLEET™
BEKO®
CEYLON TEA GARDENS®
CORTONA®
ELLINGTON ROASTING COMPANY®
FRESH FROM KEITH'S®
GOLDEN HARVEST®
KEITH'S CHOICE
KEITH'S ESSENTIALS
KEITH'S EXCLUSIVE
KEITH'S HOMESTYLE
KEITH'S PREMIUM
MARKRON COOPERATIVE®
SWEET D'LITE®

1329 Ben Heggy's Candy Company
743 Cleveland Ave NW
Canton, OH 44702-1807   330-455-7703
Fax: 330-455-9865 info@heggys.com
www.heggys.com
Manufacturer of Old Fashioned Candies and Hand-crafted Chocolates
President/Owner: Richard Wollenberg
Estimated Sales:$10-20 Million
Number Employees: 20-49
Type of Packaging: Private Label

1330 Ben Hill Griffin, Inc.
P.O.Box 127
Frostproof, FL 33843-0127   863-635-2251
Fax: 863-635-7333
Manufacturer of fresh citrus fruits including grape-fruit and oranges
President: Ben Hill Griffin
CFO: Stewart Hurst
CEO: Ben Hill Griffin Iii
Sales: Steve Maxwell
Operations: Larry Gray
Purchasing Manager: Dick Peavy
*Estimated Sales:*I
Number Employees: 250-499
Type of Packaging: Consumer, Bulk

1331 Ben-Bud Growers Inc.
Ste 203
1 N Federal Hwy
Boca Raton, FL 33432-3930   954-574-4040
Fax: 954-574-4041 www.ben-bud.com
Processor and importer of vegetables
President: Ben Litowich
Estimated Sales:$20-50 Million
Number Employees: 10-19
Type of Packaging: Consumer, Bulk

1332 Benbow's Coffee Roasters
16 Mount Desert St
Bar Harbor, ME 04609-1717   207-288-5271
Fax: 207-288-8227 Coffeeroaster@Benbows.com
www.benbows.com
Coffee roasters and jams
President: Ron Greenberg
CEO: Jaren Greenberg
Marketing Director: Ron Greenberg
Roast Maker: Dan Vashon
*Estimated Sales:*Less than $500,000
Number Employees: 1-4
Type of Packaging: Private Label
Brands:
Benbow's

1333 Bened Food Corporation
200 Food Center Dr
Bronx, NY 10474-7030   718-842-8644
Fax: 718-842-8582 www.bazzinionline.com
Nuts and dried fruits
President: Rocco Damato
Estimated Sales:$25-49.9 Million
Number Employees: 100-249

1334 Beneo Palatinit
2740 Rt 10 West
Suite 205
Morris Plains, NJ 07950-1258   973-867-2140
Fax: 973-867-2141 800-476-6258
info.usa@beneo.com www.beneo-palatinit.com
Supplier of Isomalt a bulk sugar replacer
President: Peter Strater
VP: Cees Boon
Estimated Sales:$170,000
Number Employees: 1-4
Brands:
Isomalt

1335 Benmarl Wine Company
156 Highland Ave
Marlboro, NY 12542-6304   845-236-4265
Fax: 845-236-7271 www.benmarl.com
Processor of wines including white, blended red, rose and Chardonnay
Owner: Victor Spaccerelli
Estimated Sales:$2.5-5 Million
Number Employees: 5-9
Type of Packaging: Consumer, Food Service
Brands:
Marlboro Village

1336 Bennett's Apples & Cider
944 Garners Road E
Ancaster, ON L9G 3K9
Canada   905-648-6878
Fax: 905-648-3647
Processor of sweet and mulled apple and apple cran-berry cider, apples, pumpkins and sweet corn; con-tract packaging available
CEO/President: Todd Bennett
VP Cider Mill: Richard Bennett
Number Employees: 10-19
Sq. footage: 10000
Type of Packaging: Consumer, Food Service, Pri-vate Label, Bulk
Brands:
Bennett's

1337 Bens Seafood Company
P.O.Box 276
Crescent, GA 31304-0276   912-832-5121
Fax: 912-832-2722
Fresh, frozen, smoked, live roe
Owner: Ben H Cox Jr

1338 (HQ)Benson Creamery
250 W Cerro Gordo St
Decatur, IL 62522-2102   217-429-2351
Fax: 217-429-2353
Processor of ice cream mixes, hard ice cream and frozen yogurt
President: Steve Miller
Plant Manager: Vince Shiflett
Estimated Sales:$5-10 Million
Number Employees: 20-49
Sq. footage: 15000
Type of Packaging: Food Service, Private Label, Bulk
Other Locations:
Benson Creamery
Decatur IL

1339 Benson's Bakery
P.O.Box 429
Bogart, GA 30622-0429   770-725-5711
Fax: 770-725-5888 800-888-6059
larrybenson@home.com
www.bensonsbakery.com
Processor of frozen and sourdough bread and pound and fruit cakes.
President: Larry Benson
Controller: Bob Mills
VP Sales/Marketing: Browning Adair
Plant Manager: Rich Preller
Estimated Sales:$10-20 Million
Number Employees: 50-99
Sq. footage: 100000
Parent Co: Benson's
Type of Packaging: Consumer, Food Service, Pri-vate Label, Bulk
Other Locations:
Benson's Old Home Kitchens
Athens GA
Brands:
BENSON'S
BENSON'S OLD HOME KITCHENS
HOLIDAY ISLAND
PERKINS WILLIAMS
SPECIALTY BREADS
SUN MAID
SUN-MAID FRUIT
VILLAGE FAIR
WES HEADLEY

1340 Benson's Bakery
P.O.Box 429
Bogart, GA 30622-0429   770-725-5711
Fax: 770-725-5888 800-888-6059
sales@bensonsbakery.com
www.bensonsbakery.com
Manufacturer of cakes and fruit cake
President: Larry Benson
Estimated Sales:$10-20 Million
Number Employees: 50-99
Type of Packaging: Private Label

1341 Benson's Gourmet Seasonings
P.O.Box 638
Azusa, CA 91702-0638   626-969-4443
Fax: 626-969-2912 800-325-5619
bensons4u@aol.com
www.bensonsseasonings.com
Manufacturer of kosher, salt-free and sugar-free sea-soning blends including herb/pepper, natural salty flavor, Southwestern, Jamaican, lemon and gar-lic/herb, big game, game bird and chili
President: Debbie Benson
*Estimated Sales:*Less than $500,000
Number Employees: 1-4
Sq. footage: 1000
Type of Packaging: Consumer, Food Service, Bulk

1342 Benton's Seafood Center
711 Central Ave S
Tifton, GA 31794-5212   229-382-4976
Fax: 229-382-0779
Seafood
President: Timothy Benton
Estimated Sales:$ 1 - 3 Million
Number Employees: 1-4

1343 Benzel's Pretzel Bakery
5200 6th Ave
Altoona, PA 16602-1435   814-942-5062
Fax: 814-942-4133 800-344-4438
pretzels@benzels.com www.benzels.com
Processor of pretzels
President: Ann Benzel
Vice President: William Benzel
Sales Director: Shaun Benzel
Production Manager: Erkin McCaulley
Plant Manager: Don Gority
Purchasing Manager: Angela Decker
Estimated Sales:$ 10 - 20 Million
Number Employees: 50-99
Number of Products: 36
Sq. footage: 180000
Type of Packaging: Consumer, Food Service, Pri-vate Label, Bulk
Brands:
BENZEL'S BRAND
PENNYSTICKS BRAND

1344 Benziger Family Winery
1883 London Ranch Rd
Glen Ellen, CA 95442-9728   707-935-3000
Fax: 707-935-3016 888-490-2739
greatwine@benziger.com www.benziger.com
Wines
President: Tim Wallace
National Sales Manager: Chris Benziger
General Manager: Mike Benziger
Estimated Sales:$20-50 Million
Number Employees: 50-99

1345 Bequet Confections
8235 Huffine Lane
Bozeman, MT 59718   406-586-2191
Fax: 406-586-7003 877-423-7838
sales@bequetconfections.com
www.bequetconfections.com
caramels and flavored caramels
President/Owner: Robin Bequet

1346 Berardi's Fresh Roast
12029 Abbey Rd
Cleveland, OH 44133-2637   440-582-4303
Fax: 440-582-4359 800-876-9109
www.berardis.com
Specialty coffees, estates, organic, signature blends, espresso and espresso pods. Green, black, organic and herbal teas
Manager: Sean Leneghan
Estimated Sales:$2.5-5 Million
Number Employees: 20-49
Type of Packaging: Private Label
Brands:
Berardi's
Berardi's Bodum
Berardi's Bunn
Berardi's Effie Mari
Berardi's Estate Col
Berardi's Estate-Dir
Berardi's Harvest Te
Berardi's Jet Tea Fr
Berardi's Joe To Go
Berardi's Melitta
Berardi's Minimints
Berardi's Monin
Berardi's Monin
Berardi's Nissan
Berardi's Oregon Cha
Berardi's Senza
Berardi's Technibrew
Berardi's Toddy
Berardi's Vita-Mix

1347 Berberian Nut Company
1503 S. Fresno Avenue
Stocton, CA 95206-1179   209-465-9181
                               Fax: 209-465-6008
Processor and exporter of walnuts, dry beans and rice
    Principal: Pete Turner
    General Manager: Terry Turner
    Plant Manager: Ren Fairbanks
Estimated Sales: $20-50 Million
Number Employees: 50-99
Parent Co: Farm Management Company
Type of Packaging: Consumer, Food Service, Private Label, Bulk

1348 Bergen Marzipan & Chocolate
205 S Washington Ave
Bergenfield, NJ 07621-2918   201-385-8343
                                    Fax: 201-385-0042
Confections, marzipan and chocolate
    Owner: Eddie Sarpon
Estimated Sales: $5-10 Million
Number Employees: 5-9

1349 Berger Foods
2520 Summeroak Drive
Tucker, GA 30084-3455   770-934-8983
        Fax: 770-934-8984 dan@bergerfoods.com
Manufacturer of dairy products
    President: R Daniel Berger
    CEO: Tom Berger
Estimated Sales: Less than $500,000
Number Employees: 1-4

1350 Bergey's Dairy Farm
2221 Mount Pleasant Road
Chesapeake, VA 23322-1252   757-482-4712
        Fax: 757-482-5439 leberg2221@cs.com
Milk, ice cream and butter
    President: Leonard Bergey
    Vice President: Elsa Bergey
Estimated Sales: $5-10 Million
Number Employees: 20-49

1351 Berghausen Corporation
4524 Este Ave
Cincinnati, OH 45232-1763   513-541-5631
        Fax: 513-541-1169 800-648-5887
    info@berghausen.com www.berghausen.com
Processor and finisher of quillaja and yucca extracts (powder and liquid forms) and food colors
    President: Fritz Berghausen
    Quality Control Manager: Tom Davlin
Estimated Sales: Below $5 Million
Number Employees: 10-19

1352 Bering Sea Fisheries
4413 83rd Avenue SE
Snohomish, WA 98290-5294   425-334-1498
Processor and exporter of frozen salmon
    President: H Bodey
Number Employees: 20-49
Type of Packaging: Private Label

1353 Bering Sea Raindeer Products
PO Box 42
Mekoryuk, AK 99630-0042   907-827-8940
                                 Fax: 907-827-8514

1354 Berke-Blake Fancy Foods, Inc.
150 National Pl # 140
Longwood, FL 32750-6431   407-831-7288
        Fax: 407-831-7065 888-386-2253
    info@anniepiesbakery.com
    www.anniepiesbakery.com
Manufacturer of cakes including cheesecakes, and pies
    CEO: Anne Resnick
    CEO: Ann Resnick
    Executive VP Sales/Marketing: Marnie Blake Zahn
    General Manager: Mark Hanft
    Production Manager: Daniele Sansone
Estimated Sales: $ 5 - 10 Million
Number Employees: 5-9
Number of Brands: 1
Number of Products: 100
Sq. footage: 9000
Type of Packaging: Food Service
Brands:
    Annie Pie's

1355 Berkeley Farms
25500 Clawiter Rd
Hayward, CA 94545-2739   510-265-8600
        Fax: 510-265-8748 www.berkeleyfarms.com
Manufacturer of dairy products
    Manager: Nick Kelble
    VP Sales/Marketing: Mike Lasky
Number Employees: 500-999
Parent Co: Dean Foods Company

1356 Berks Packing Company, Inc.
319 Bingaman St
Reading, PA 19602   610-376-7291
        Fax: 610-378-1210 800-882-3757
    marketingdept@berksfoods.com
    www.berksfoods.com
Processor of beef frankfurters, smoked sausage and kielbasa, roast beef, turkey breast, regular and reduced-sodium ham, deli meats, etc
    President: Mike Boylan
    Purchasing Director: David Boylan
Estimated Sales: $50-100 Million
Number Employees: 100-249

1357 Berkshire Brewing Company, Inc.
P.O.Box 251
South Deerfield, MA 01373-0251   413-665-7837
        Fax: 413-665-7837 877-222-7468
    frontdesk@berkshirebrewingcompany.com
    www.berkshirebrewingcompany.com
Processor of ale and seasonal beer
    Owner: Gary Bogoff
    VP: Gary Bogoff
Estimated Sales: $5-10 Million
Number Employees: 20-49
Type of Packaging: Consumer, Food Service
Brands:
    BERKSHIRE ALE
    CABIN FEVER ALE
    COFFEEHOUSE PORTER
    DRAYMAN'S PORTER
    GOLD SPIKE ALE
    HEFEWEIZEN
    HOLIDALE BARLEY WINE
    IMPERIAL STOUT
    LOST SAILOR INDIA PALE ALE
    MAILBOCK LAGER
    OKTOBERFEST LAGER
    RASPBERRY BARLEY WINE
    RIVER ALE
    SHABADOO BLACK AND TAN ALE
    STEEL RAIL EXTRA PALE ALE

1358 Berkshire Cold Storage
4550 S Packers Avenue
Chicago, IL 60609-3318   773-254-2424
        Fax: 773-254-2919 tedg@berkfoods.com
                            www.berkfoods.com
Warehouse providing cooler and freezer storage; also, labeling for refrigerated and frozen foods, import and export capabilities available
    President: Ted Zrzywacz
Estimated Sales: $10-20 Million
Number Employees: 50-99
Sq. footage: 490000
Parent Co: Berkshire Foods, Inc.
Type of Packaging: Consumer, Food Service

1359 Berkshire Dairy & Food Products
1258 Penn Ave
Wyomissing, PA 19610-2146   610-378-9999
        Fax: 610-378-4975 888-654-8008
    info@berkshiredairy.com
    www.berkshiredairy.com
Manufacturer, importer and exporter of analog extenders, dehydrated dairy products, powders, cheese, creamers, lactose, milk and whey, whole milk powder, Anhydreos milkfat butter, nonfat dry milk, permeate
    President: Dale Mills
    Sales Manager: Deb Haretty
    Operations Manager: Steve Cinegi
    Controller: Mark Moyer
Estimated Sales: $200 Million
Number Employees: 10-19
Sq. footage: 6000
Type of Packaging: Private Label, Bulk
Brands:
    Berk-Cap

1360 Berkshire Ice Cream
PO Box 510
West Stockbridge, MA 01266-0510   413-232-4111
        Fax: 413-232-0071 info@bershireicecream.com
                           www.berkshireicecream.com
Ice cream
    President: Matt White
    Manager: Beth White
Estimated Sales: $300,000-500,000
Number Employees: 5-9
Brands:
    Berkshire Ice Cream

1361 Berkshire Mountain Bakery
P.O.Box 785
Housatonic, MA 01236-0785   413-274-3412
        Fax: 413-274-6124 866-274-6124
    info@berkshiremountainbakery.com
    www.berkshiremountainbakery.com
Manufacturer of baked goods such as; sourdough bread, ciabatta bread, bread w/chocolate, oat pecan cookies, pizza crusts and pizza's
    President: Richard Bourdon
Estimated Sales: Less than $500,000
Number Employees: 10-19

1362 Berlin Natural Bakery
P.O.Box 311
Berlin, OH 44610-0311   330-893-2734
        Fax: 330-893-2157 800-686-5334
    bnb@tusco.net www.berlinnaturalbakery.com
Manufacturer of bakery products made with spelt
    Manager: Cindy Widder
    General Manager: Cindy Wittmen
Estimated Sales: $10-20 Million
Number Employees: 20-49
Type of Packaging: Private Label

1363 Bernadette Baking Company
85 Commercial St
Medford, MA 02155-4918   781-393-8700
        Fax: 781-393-0414 info@bernadettebaking.com
                           www.bernadettebaking.com
Crunchy biscotti dipped in brews, coffeees, teas, or wines
    President: Bernadette De Vergilio
    Vice President: Marie Cooke
    Plant Manager: Mario Ruiz
Estimated Sales: $5-10 Million
Number Employees: 5-9
Type of Packaging: Private Label
Brands:
    Bernadette's Biscotti
    Bernadette's Biscotti Soave
    Bernadette's Cookies

1364 Bernard & Sons
4011 Jewett Ave
Bakersfield, CA 93301-1113   661-327-4431
        Fax: 661-327-7461 www.bernardandsons.com
Meat
    President: Dennis Bernard
    General Manager: Hal Ulmer
Estimated Sales: $11,100,000
Number Employees: 20-49

1365 Bernard Food Industries
P.O.Box 1497
Evanston, IL 60204-1497   847-869-5222
        Fax: 800-962-1546 800-323-3663
    bernardfoods@bernardfoods.com
    www.bernardfoods.com
Manufacturer and exporter of mixes including dessert, soup, drink, baking, etc.; also, soup bases and gravy, textured vegetable protein, gelatin, syrup dessert toppings, dietary foods, etc.
    Owner: Steve Bernard
    CEO: Steven Bernard
    Vice President: Jules Bernard
    Purchasing Director: Steven Bernardi
Estimated Sales: $20-50 Million
Number Employees: 50-99
Sq. footage: 60000
Type of Packaging: Consumer, Food Service, Private Label, Bulk
Brands:
    BERNARD
    BETA-CARE
    CALORIE CONTROL
    HOLA
    KWIK-DISH
    LITE-95
    LONGHORN GRILL
    SANS SUCRE

TEX-PRO
THIXX

1366 Bernard Marcantel Company
PO Box 1149
Kinder, LA 70648-1149   318-738-5122
Fax: 401-783-2759
Owner: Bernard Marcantel

1367 Bernardi Italian Foods Company
595 W 11th St
Bloomsburg, PA 17815-3616   570-389-5500
Fax: 570-784-0293   www.windsorfoods.com
Processor of frozen and prepared Italian dinners and
cheese foods
  Manager: Howard Teufel
  Q/A Manager: Julie Simcox
  Plant Manager: Howard Toufel
  Purchasing: Sharon Lawrence
Estimated Sales: $20-50 Million
Number Employees: 100-249
Sq. footage: 70000
Parent Co: Windsor Frozen Foods
Type of Packaging: Consumer, Food Service, Private Label, Bulk

1368 Bernardo Winery
13330 Paseo Del Verano Norte
San Diego, CA 92128-1899   858-487-1866
Fax: 858-673-5376   jim@bernardowinery.com
www.bernardowinery.com
Manufacturer of wine
  Owner/President: Ross Rizzo
  CEO/VP: Rossi Rizzo
  Event Manager: Kathy Lieber
Estimated Sales: $500,000-$1 Million
Number Employees: 1-4
Type of Packaging: Private Label
Brands:
  Bernardo

1369 Bernardus Winery & Vineyards
P.O.Box 1800
Carmel Valley, CA 93924-1800   831-659-1900
Fax: 831-659-1676   888-648-9463
www.bernardus.com
Wines
  Owner: Ben Pon
  Operations Manager: Dean DeKorth
  Plant Manager: Matthew Shea
Estimated Sales: $5-10 Million
Number Employees: 20-49
Type of Packaging: Private Label
Brands:
  Bernardus

1370 Berner Cheese Corporation
10010 N Rock City Road
Rock City, IL 61070-9515   815-865-5136
Fax: 815-563-4017   rickz@bernerfoods.com
Processor of cheese
  President: Steve Kneubehl
  Office Manager: Nancy Germain
  Purchsiding Director: Melody Fuchs
Estimated Sales: $2.5-5 Million
Number Employees: 20-49
Parent Co: Berner Cheese Corporation
Type of Packaging: Consumer

1371 (HQ)Berner Cheese Corporation
2034 Cheese Factory Road
Dakota, IL 61018   815-563-4653
Fax: 815-623-1622   800-819-8199
sales@bernercheese.com   www.bernercheese.com
Processor of shelf stable, refrigerated and pasteurized cheese sauces
  President: Steve Kneubuehl
  Ctonroller: John Thoren
  Vice President: Edward Kneubuehl
  Research & Development: Laura Flores
  Quality Control: Deanna Ritschard
  Marketing Manager: Donna Noenning
  Plant Manager: Brian Markel
  Purchasing Director: Melody Fuchs
Estimated Sales: $20-50 Million
Number Employees: 50-99
Type of Packaging: Food Service, Bulk
Other Locations:
  Berner Cheese Corp.
  Rock City IL

1372 Berner Foods, Inc.
11447 2nd St # 6
Roscoe, IL 61073-9522   815-623-1722
Fax: 815-623-1622   800-819-8199
berner.sales@bernerfoods.com
www.bernerfoods.com
Processor of shelf stable cheese sauces and spreads,
shelf stable dips, and milk based retort beverages.
  Executive VP: Steve Fay
  Quality Control: Tammy Jacobs
  Marketing Manager: Dani Amman
Estimated Sales: $ 10 - 20 Million
Number Employees: 10-19
Parent Co: Illini Protein
Type of Packaging: Food Service, Private Label
Other Locations:
  Rock City IL
  Dakota IL
Brands:
  DAKOTA
  STEADFAST

1373 Bernheim Distilling Company
1416 S 3rd Street
Louisville, KY 40208-2117   502-638-1387
Fax: 502-585-9110   800-303-0053
Reservations@BernheimMansion.com
www.bernheimmansion.com
Spirits
  Owner: Bernard Bernheim
Estimated Sales: $300,000-500,000
Number Employees: 5-9

1374 Bernie's Foods
263 Classon Ave
Brooklyn, NY 11205-4321   718-417-6677
Fax: 718-417-0932   berniesfoods@aol.com
www.ratners.com
Ice-cream, sorbets and frozen foods
  President: Abraham Ostreicher
Number Employees: 20-49
Number of Brands: 3
Number of Products: 50
Sq. footage: 10000
Type of Packaging: Consumer, Food Service, Private Label
Brands:
  Frankel's Homestyle
  Tovli

1375 Berry Citrus Products
P.O.Box 459
Labelle, FL 33975-0459   863-675-2769
Fax: 863-675-2768   brenda@berryusa.com
www.berryusa.com
Manufacturer and exporter of citrus concentrates
  President: W E Kemper
  VP Sales/Marketing: Steve King
Estimated Sales: $ 20 - 50 Million
Number Employees: 100-249
Type of Packaging: Consumer, Food Service, Bulk

1376 Berry Processing
522 E Elm St
Watseka, IL 60970-1474   815-432-3264
Processor of beef and pork
  President: Catherine Berry
Estimated Sales: $500,000-$1 Million
Number Employees: 1-4
Type of Packaging: Consumer, Food Service, Private Label, Bulk

1377 Bertucci's
155 Otis St # 2
Northborough, MA 01532-2456   508-351-2500
Fax: 508-393-1231   www.bertuccis.com
Pizza restaurant chain, and manufacturer and grocer
  President: Rick Barbick
  CEO: Stephen Clark
  Purchasing Manager: Artie Morris
Estimated Sales: $100-500 Million
Number Employees: 5,000-9,999
Parent Co: NE Restaurant Company
Type of Packaging: Consumer

1378 Bessinger Pickle Company
537 N Court St
Au Gres, MI 48703-9204   989-876-8008
Fax: 989-876-8028
Manufacturer of dill pickles
  President: Craig Carruthers
Estimated Sales: $1 Million
Number Employees: 50-99
Sq. footage: 26000

Type of Packaging: Consumer

1379 Bessonet Bee Company
PO Box 303
Donaldsonville, LA 70346-0303   225-473-9428
Fax: 225-473-9409
Processor and exporter of honey
  President: Calvin Bessonet
  Secretary/Treasurer: Lynn Bessonet
Estimated Sales: $1-2.5 Million
Number Employees: 5-9
Type of Packaging: Consumer, Food Service, Private Label, Bulk
Brands:
  GULF BREEZE

1380 (HQ)Best Brands Corporate Office
1765 Yankee Doodle Rd
St Paul, MN 55121-1691   651-454-5850
Fax: 651-454-0062   800-328-2068
www.bestbrandscorp.com
Manufacturer of baking products. Continental Mill,
Inc. has completed the acquisition of the Pillsbury
foodservice small package dry mix business
  President/CEO: Scott Humphrey
  CFO: Jodi Anderson
  Data Processing: Mike Hayden
  SVP Sales: Mike Schultz
Estimated Sales: $156 Million
Number Employees: 100-249

1381 Best Brands Corporation
10741 Miller Rd
Dallas, TX 75238-1303   214-343-4816
Fax: 214-343-9462   800-969-2253
www.bestbrandscorp.com
Manufacturer of pies, cake layers and fillings, flavoring extracts, mixes, oils, etc.
  President: Brad Wadsten
  VP Sales/Marketing: Jeff Getzkin
  Plant Manager: Randy Stephens
Estimated Sales: $156 Million
Number Employees: 100-249
Sq. footage: 200000
Parent Co: Best Brands
Other Locations:
  Best Brands
  Eagan MN
  Best Brands
  Tampa FL
  Horizon Equipment
  Eagan MN
Brands:
  AMPCO

1382 Best Brands Corporation
6307 N 53rd St # 1
Tampa, FL 33610-4098   813-621-7802
Fax: 813-626-7897   800-282-0565
info@bestbrandscorp.com
www.bestbrandscorp.com
Manufacturer of baking mixes including bread, roll,
doughnut, pie, danish and cake, dough, icing and
filling
  Manager: John Smith
Estimated Sales: $20-50 Million
Number Employees: 50-99
Sq. footage: 65000
Parent Co: Best Brands
Type of Packaging: Food Service, Private Label, Bulk
Other Locations:
  Best Brands Colton
  Colton CA
  Best Brands Dallas
  Dallas TX
  Best Brands Eagan
  Eagan MN
Brands:
  8-GRAIN BREAD
  98% FAT FREE SWEET DOUGH
  98%FAT FREE BROWNIE MIX
  AMERICAN 100
  B.B. ANGEL CAKE MIX
  B.B. HONEY GLAZE
  B.B. ROLLING ICING
  BEST 501
  CLASSIC CHOCOLATE CAKE MIX
  CLASSIC WHITE CAKE MIX
  CUSTOM PEANUT BUTTER CHOCOLATE CHIP
  CUSTOM PEANUT BUTTER COOKIES
  DAINTEE SWEET DOUGH MIX
  DANISH COFFEE CAKE STRIP

GOURMET BISCUIT MIX
INSTANT VANILLA CREME
MILWAUKEE RYE BREAD MIX

1383 Best Chocolate In Town
880 Massachusetts Ave
Indianapolis, IN 46204-1633   317-636-2800
    Fax: 317-636-2822   888-294-2378
    info@bestchocolateintown.com
    www.bestchocolateintown.com
Manufacturer of hand-made chocolates
    Founder/President: Elizabeth Garber
Estimated Sales:$100,000
Number Employees: 5-9

1384 Best Ever Bake Shop
52 North Street
Mount Vernon, NY 10550-1150   914-665-7005
       Fax: 914-665-7005
Processor of sweet potato and pecan pie
    President/Owner: Connie Williams
Type of Packaging: Consumer

1385 Best Foods Baking Group
4613 Wedgewood Blvd
Frederick, MD 21703-7120   301-631-8185
       800-635-1700
    Controller: Clarence Jenkins
    Operations Manager: Mark Baugher
    Plant Manager: Gary Willis
Estimated Sales:$20-50 Million
Number Employees: 1-4
Parent Co: Unilever USA

1386 (HQ)Best Harvest Bakeries
530 S 65th St
Kansas City, KS 66111-2324   913-287-6300
    Fax: 913-287-5408   800-811-5715
       www.bestharvest.com
Processor of buns and rolls
    President: Ed Honesty Jr.
    CEO: Robert Beavers Jr.
    General Manager: Robert Young
    Plant Manager: Brad Wolf
Estimated Sales:$5-10 Million
Number Employees: 20-49
Type of Packaging: Consumer, Food Service

1387 Best Kosher Foods
1000 W Pershing Rd
Chicago, IL 60609-1426   773-650-6330
    Fax: 773-650-9046   888-800-0072
    slfconsumeraffairs@saralee.com
       www.bestkosherfoods.com
Kosher meats
    Manager: Damon Williams
    Sr Manager Facilities: John Empen
    Engineering: Roger Savastano
    Plant Manager: Robert Worth
Estimated Sales:$100+ Million
Number Employees: 250-499
Parent Co: Sara Lee Meat Group
Brands:
    Best's Kosher
    Oscherwitz
    Shofar
    Sinai Kosher

1388 Best Maid Cookie Company
1147 Benson St
River Falls, WI 54022-1594   715-426-2090
    Fax: 715-426-1950   888-444-0322
    customerservice@bestmaid.com
       www.bestmaidcookie.com
Processor of pre-formed frozen cookie dough and
baked cookies; also specialty products available.
    Co-President: Deb Dartsch
    Co-President: Ron Thielen
Number Employees: 50-99
Sq. footage: 20000
Type of Packaging: Food Service, Private Label

1389 Best Provision Company,Inc.
144 Avon Ave
Newark, NJ 07108-1995   973-242-5000
    Fax: 973-648-0041   800-631-4466
    bestprovco@aol.com   www.bestprovision.com
Processor and exporter of beef including corned,
roast, frankfurters and pastrami
    President: Leonard Karp
    General Manager: Larry Weinstein
Estimated Sales:$35 Million
Number Employees: 100-249
Sq. footage: 65000

Type of Packaging: Consumer, Food Service

1390 BestSweet
288 Mazeppa Rd
Mooresville, NC 28115-7928   704-664-4300
    Fax: 704-664-7493   888-211-5530
       www.bestsweet.com
Manufacturer of confectinery products, nutritional
supplements and cough drops
    CEO: Richard Zulman
    VP Marketing: Steve Berkowitz
Estimated Sales:$ 50 - 100 Million
Number Employees: 100-249
Type of Packaging: Private Label
Brands:
    BASKIN-ROBBINS SMOOTH & CREAMY
    HARD
    CANDY
    FIRE ANTZ
    GUMMY GUARD
    GUMMY WATCH
    SANTA PANTS

1391 Bestfoods Baking
1805 Shelburne Road
South Burlington, VT 05403-7719   802-862-2222
       Fax: 802-864-0270
    President: Peter Bouyea
    Sales Manager: Brian Carpentier
    Account Manager: Jason Driggers
Estimated Sales:$100-500 Million
Number Employees: 100-249
Parent Co: Unilever USA

1392 Bestfoods Foodservice
150 Pierce Street
Somerset, NJ 08873-4185   732-627-8722
       Fax: 732-627-8705
Manufacturer of processed food products. Soups,
soups bases, sauces, gravies, entrees and desserts in
a variety of formats such as frozen, dry, mixes,
canned and IMF paste
    Quality Assurance: William Kinell
Type of Packaging: Food Service

1393 Bestfoods Specialty Products
6 Sylvan Ave
Englewood Cliffs, NJ 07632-2431   401-644-4900
       800-338-8831
       www.unileverus.com
Pasta/noodles, ice cream, spaghetti sauce, butter,
mayonaise, peanut butter, salad dressings
    President: Michael B Polk
    VP Ethnic Market: Robert Allin
    VP Sales: Robert Jackson
*Estimated Sales:*K
Number Employees: 10,000+
Parent Co: Unilever
Type of Packaging: Consumer, Food Service
Brands:
    BEN & JERRY'S
    BERTOLLI
    BREYERS
    GOOD HUMOR
    HELLMAN'S
    I CAN'T BELIEVE IT'S NOT BUTTER
    KLONDIKE
    KNORR
    KNORR (LIPTON) SIDES
    LIPTON
    POPSICLE
    PROMISE
    RAGU
    SHEDD'S SPREAD COUNTRY CROCK
    SKIPPY
    SLIM-FAST
    WISH-BONE

1394 Beta Pure Foods
335 Spreckels Dr # D
Aptos, CA 95003-3952   831-685-6565
    Fax: 831-685-6569   nate.morr@sunopta.com
       www.betapure.com
Organic frozen fruits and vegetables, concentrates
and purees, sweeteners.
    President/CEO: Nate Morr
Number Employees: 5-9
Parent Co: SunOpta
Type of Packaging: Food Service, Private Label,
    Bulk

1395 BetaStatin Nutritional Rsearch
1187 Washington Street
Toms River, NJ 08753-6833   203-869-7778
    Fax: 203-869-7774   800-660-9570
       www.betastatin.com
    Managing Director: Dr Stephen L Newman

1396 Beth's Fine Desserts
591 Mercantile Drive
Cotati, CA 94931-3040   415-464-1891
    Fax: 415-925-9941   info@bethsfinedesserts.com
       www.beths.com
Manufacturer of bite-sized cookies and savory
cheese wafers, gourmet gift items, gingerbreads
Brands:
    Beth's
    Beth's Baking Basics
    Heavenly Little Cookies

1397 (HQ)Bethel Eckert Enterprises
P.O.Box 298
Collinsville, IL 62234-0298   618-345-1138
    Fax: 618-345-2032 www.bethel-eckert.com
Dry, chilled and frozen grocery: military only.
    President: Larry Eckert
    VP: Jim Eckert
    Marketing Director: Larry Lemma
Estimated Sales:$ 50 - 100 Million
Number Employees: 50-99
Other Locations:
    Bethel Eckert - Dry Warehouse
    Collinsville IL
    Bethel Eckert - Frozen/Dried/Chill
    Troy IL

1398 Bethel Heights Vineyard,Inc.
6060 Bethel Heights Rd NW
Salem, OR 97304-9733   503-581-2262
    Fax: 503-581-0943   info@bethelheights.com
       www.bethelheights.com
Wines
    President: Pat Dudley
    Marketing Director: Pat Dudley
    Plant Manager: Ted Castell
Estimated Sales:$5-10 Million
Number Employees: 20-49
Type of Packaging: Private Label

1399 Betsy's Cheese Straws
3761 Grandview Road
Millbrook, AL 36054   334-285-1354
    Fax: 800-625-9700   877-902-3141
       elizabeth@moonpie.com
       www.betsyscheesestraws.com
Cheese straws
    President/Owner: Betsy Parker
Number Employees: 6

1400 Bette's Diner Products
1807 4th St
Berkeley, CA 94710-1910   510-644-3230
Fax: 510-644-3209   bettesdiner@worldpantry.com
       www.bettesdiner.com
Manufacturer and exporter of pancake mixes includ-
ing buttermilk, oatmeal and buckwheat; also, scone
mixes including raisin, cranberry and lemon currant
    President: Manfred Kroening
    VP: Bette Kroening
Number Employees: 5-9
Type of Packaging: Consumer, Food Service
Brands:
    Bette's Oceanview Diner

1401 Better Bagel Bakery
4854 S Tamiami Trl
Sarasota, FL 34231-4352   941-924-0393
       Fax: 941-924-0358
Processor of baked goods such as; breads, rolls, ba-
gels, etc
    Owner: Jun Park
*Estimated Sales:*Less than $100,000
Number Employees: 1-4

1402 Better Baked Foods
56 Smedley St
North East, PA 16428-1632   814-725-8778
    Fax: 814-725-5021 www.betterbaked.com
Processor of frozen pasta and regular and French
bread pizza
    Owner: Bob Miller
    CEO: Joe Pacinelli
    Sales: Bob Miller
    Purchasing Director: John Shifler
Estimated Sales:$20-50 Million
Number Employees: 250-499

Type of Packaging: Private Label
Brands:
Better Baked Foods
Cardinal
Chestnut Hill
Empacadora Inter-Mex
King of the West
Land O'Sun
World Wide

1403 Better Beverages
10624 Midway Ave
Cerritos, CA 90703-1581   562-924-8321
        Fax: 562-924-6204 www.betbev.com
Processor of soft drinks; wholesaler/distributor of
soft drinks and juices; serving the food service
market
Owner: Ronald Harris
Estimated Sales: $ 20 - 50 Million
Number Employees: 20-49
Type of Packaging: Consumer, Food Service
Brands:
Rc Cola

1404 Better Living Products
208 Harvard Drive
Princeton, TX 75407   972-736-6691
        Fax: 972-734-1016 zetawize@yahoo.com
                www.betterlivingusa.com
Processor, importer of kava kava powder, aloe vera
juice and herbs
COO: Ed Carter
Estimated Sales: Less than $500,000
Number Employees: 1-4
Parent Co: Zeta Wize LLC Company
Brands:
KAVA KAVA
NONI NONU

1405 Better Meat North
P.O.Box 1100
Bay City, MI 48706-0100   989-684-6271
        Fax: 989-684-6390
Processor of potato chips, popcorn and cheese curls
and puffs; wholesaler/distributor of snack foods in-
cluding pork rinds, puffs and tortillas; private label-
ing and co-packing available
Manager: Mike Esseltine
Estimated Sales: $ 20 - 50 Million
Number Employees: 20-49
Parent Co: Cross & Peters
Type of Packaging: Consumer, Private Label
Brands:
Made Rite

1406 BetterBody Foods & Nutrition LLC
615 E Simpson Ave
Salt Lake City, UT 84106
        Fax: 801-456-2601 866-404-6582
        info@xagave.com www.xagave.com
President/Owner: Stephen Richards

1407 (HQ)Betty Jane Homemade Candies
3049 Asbury Rd
Dubuque, IA 52001-8459   563-582-4668
        Fax: 563-582-2150 800-642-1254
                www.bettyjanecandies.com
Manufacturer of candy
President/CEO: John Heinz Jr
Estimated Sales: $5-10 Million
Number Employees: 20-49
Type of Packaging: Consumer
Brands:
GREMLINS

1408 Betty Lou's Golden Smackers
P.O.Box 537
McMinnville, OR 97128-0537   503-434-5205
        Fax: 503-472-8643 800-242-5205
        bettylous@.onlinemac.com
                www.bettylousinc.com
Processor and exporter of oil and, low-fat oven
baked apple butter, low-fat and wheat-free fruit bars
and fat-free cookies, snack foods and candies, pro-
tein bars
Owner: Betty Carrier
VP Sales: John Sizemore
Estimated Sales: $2.5-5 Million
Number Employees: 20-49
Sq. footage: 9000
Type of Packaging: Consumer, Private Label

Brands:
Betty Lou's

1409 Bevco
9354 - 194th Street
Surrey, BC V4N 4E9
Canada   604-888-1455
        Fax: 604-888-2887 800-663-0090
                info@bevco.net www.bevco.net
Processor and co-packer of fruit juices, citrus drinks
and bottled water
President/CEO: Brian Lochansky
Sales/Marketing Director: Alan Hanson
Plant Manager: Julie Gurrittean
Purchasing Director: Andy Leait
Estimated Sales: $5-10 Million
Number Employees: 10-19
Type of Packaging: Consumer, Private Label
Brands:
Juicetyme Delites
O-Jay
Watertyme
Wild Springs

1410 (HQ)Beverage America
545 E 32nd St
Holland, MI 49423-5495   616-396-1281
        Fax: 616-396-8121
Bottled water, fruit beverages, Snapple
Plant Manufacturing: Dale Stein
Estimated Sales: $ 5 - 10 Million
Number Employees: 5-9

1411 Beverage Capital Corporation
2209 Sulphur Spring Rd
Halethorpe, MD 21227-2933   410-242-7003
        Fax: 410-247-2977 info@beveragecapital.com
                www.beveragecapital.com
Processor and exporter of bottled and canned soft
and juice drinks and juice; also, seltzer water; con-
tract packaging available
VP: Rick Smith
VP Sales: Rick Smith
Estimated Sales: $50-100 Million
Number Employees: 100-249
Sq. footage: 400000
Type of Packaging: Consumer, Private Label
Other Locations:
Whitehead Court Manufacturing
Baltimore MD
30th Street Manufacturing
Baltimore MD
Brands:
BEVNET
CADBURY SCHWEPPES
CANADA DRY
ENERGY BRAND
MISTIC
SNAPPLE

1412 Beverage House
400 High Point Rd SE
Cartersville, GA 30120   770-387-0451
        Fax: 770-387-1809 888-367-8327
        info@beveragehouse.com
                www.beveragehouse.com
Coffee, tea and beverage concentrates
Manager: Jimmy Garren
Marketing Manager: Robbin McCool
Estimated Sales: $10-20 Million
Number Employees: 10-19
Type of Packaging: Private Label
Brands:
NEW SOUTHERN TRADITION TEAS
REEDY BREW TEAS

1413 Beverage Specialties
196 Newton St
Fredonia, NY 14063-1354   716-673-1000
        Fax: 716-679-3444 800-828-8915
                www.carriagehousecos.com
Non-alcoholic cocktail mixes and Bloody Mary mix
under the Major Peters & Jero labels.
President: David Skarie
Quality Control: Joe Woloseyn
Marketing: Dan Bensur
Director Sales: Kevin Dress
Public Relations: Mary Jane Knight
Operations: Mark Chamberlain
Estimated Sales: I
Number Employees: 1,000-4,999
Number of Brands: 2
Parent Co: Ralcorp
Type of Packaging: Consumer

Brands:
JERO
MAJOR PETERS

1414 Beverage Technologies
5 Connerty Court
East Brunswick, NJ 08816-1633   888-204-4299
        Fax: 732-254-5736
Processor of coffee concentrates
Type of Packaging: Food Service
Brands:
La Spezzia

1415 Beverly International Nutrition
1768 Industrial Rd
Cold Spring, KY 41076-8610   859-781-3474
        Fax: 859-781-7590 800-888-3364
        support@beverlyintl.com
                www.bodybuildingworld.com
Manufacturer and exporter of multiple vitamin and
mineral packs; also, protein powders
Owner: Roger Riedinger
Owner: Sandy Riedinger
Estimated Sales: Less than $500,000
Number Employees: 10-19
Type of Packaging: Consumer, Food Service, Pri-
vate Label
Brands:
BEVERLY INTERNATIONAL

1416 Bi-O-Kleen Industry
PO Box 2679
Clackamas, OR 97015-2679   360-260-1587
        Fax: 503-557-7818 crluvearth@msn.com

1417 Biagio's Banquets
4242 N Central Ave
Chicago, IL 60634-1810   773-736-9009
        Fax: 773-587-3011 800-392-2837
        rperrye@aol.com   www.suparossa.com
Processor and exporter of pasta, breaded appetizers
and pizza including deep dish, thin crust, pan and
self-rising
President: Samuel Cirrincione
General Manager: Tom Cirrincione
Estimated Sales: $10-20 Million
Number Employees: 20-49
Sq. footage: 30000
Brands:
Suparossa

1418 Bianchi Winery
3333 W Coast Hwy # 400
Newport Beach, CA 92663-4042   949-646-9100
        Fax: 949-646-1600 sales@bianchiwine.com
                www.bianchiwine.com
Manufacturer and exporter of red and white wines
Owner: Glenn Bianchi
CFO: Mike Gardnier
Vice President: Albert Paul
Estimated Sales: $5 Million
Number Employees: 10-19
Number of Brands: 3
Number of Products: 20
Type of Packaging: Consumer, Food Service, Bulk
Brands:
Bianchi Vineyards
Chateau Cellars
Domaine Noel
Vista Verde

1419 Bias Vineyards & Winery
P.O.Box 93
Berger, MO 63014-0093   573-834-5475
        Fax: 573-834-2046 www.biaswinery.com
Wines
President: Carol Grass
VP: Kirk Grass
Purchasing Director: Carol Grass
Estimated Sales: $1-2.5 Million
Number Employees: 1-4
Type of Packaging: Private Label

1420 Biazzo Dairy Products
1145 Edgewater Ave
Ridgefield, NJ 07657-2102   201-941-6800
        Fax: 201-941-4151 info@biazzo.com
                www.biazzo.com
Processor and exporter of fresh, chunk and shredded
mozzarella, ricotta and string cheese.
President: John Iapichino Jr
Vice President: John Iapichino, Jr.
Sales Director: Tim Holden
Plant Manager: Joe Iapichino

Estimated Sales: $ 20 - 50 Million
Number Employees: 20-49
Sq. footage: 58000
Type of Packaging: Consumer, Food Service, Private Label, Bulk
Brands:
BIAZZO BRAND
PRIVATE LABEL

1421 Bick's Pickles
701 Broad Street E
Dunnville, ON N1A 1H2
Canada   905-774-7447
Fax: 905-774-5145
Manufacturer of horseradish, sauerkraut and pickles
VP Operations: Greg Mercer
Number Employees: 150
Parent Co: Robin Hood Multifoods
Type of Packaging: Consumer, Food Service
Brands:
Bick's
Gattuso
Habitant
McGaren's
Rose
Woodman's
Zest

1422 Bickel's Potato Chip Company
51 N Main St
Manheim, PA 17545-1503   717-665-2002
Fax: 717-665-5449 www.bickelssnacks.com
Warehouse location for Bickel's potato chips.
President: John Wareheine
Controller: Gary Knisely
Director Sales: Ed Dobkel
Plant Manager: Jay Epstein
Purchasing Director: Nellie Redding
Estimated Sales: $10-24.9 Million
Number Employees: 5-9
Type of Packaging: Consumer
Brands:
Bickel's

1423 (HQ)Bickel's of York SnackFoods
P.O.Box 2427
York, PA 17405-2427   717-843-0738
Fax: 717-843-5192   800-233-1933
customerservice@bickelssnacks.com
www.bickelssnacks.com
Processor of potato chips, pretzels, corn chips, popcorn, tortilla chips, party mix, pork skins, pellet snacks and cheese puffs.
Manager: Jeff Warhime
Controller: Gary Knisely
Sales: Michael Carter
Operations: Wade Fitzkee
Purchasing: Allen Young
Estimated Sales: $20-50 Million
Number Employees: 1,000-4,999
Parent Co: Hanover Foods
Type of Packaging: Private Label, Bulk
Brands:
BICKEL'S
BON-TON
CABANA
GOLDEN GOURMET
WEGE

1424 Bickels Snacks
P.O.Box 2427
York, PA 17405-2427   717-843-0738
Fax: 717-843-5192
customerservice@bickelssnacks.com
www.bickelssnacks.com
Snack food products
Manager: Jeff Warhime
Marketing/Advertising Manager: Jerry Neidigh
Sales Manager: Ed Doekel
Plant Manager: Gary Glatselter
Estimated Sales: $ 20-50 Million
Number Employees: 1,000-4,999
Type of Packaging: Private Label
Brands:
Bickle Snacks

1425 Bickford Daniel LobsterCompany
Lanes Is
Vinalhaven, ME 04863   207-863-4688
Fax: 207-863-4525
Lobster
Estimated Sales: $ 1 - 3 Million
Number Employees: 5-9

1426 Bickford Flavors
19007 Saint Clair Ave
Cleveland, OH 44117-1001   216-531-6006
Fax: 216-531-2006   800-283-8322
orders@bickfordflavors.com
www.bickfordflavors.com
Processor of extracts including vanilla and assorted flavoring
President: Scott Sofer
Operations: Heather Noel
Estimated Sales: $2.5-5 Million
Number Employees: 5-9
Number of Brands: 1
Number of Products: 150
Sq. footage: 15000
Type of Packaging: Private Label
Brands:
Bickford

1427 Bidwell Candies
1516 Lake Land Blvd # A
Mattoon, IL 61938-5751   217-234-3858
Fax: 217-234-3856   barbara@bidwellcandies.com
www.bidwellcandies.com
Manufactures chocolates and candies
Owner: Greg Kuhl
Plant Manager: Judy Brown
Estimated Sales: Less than $500,000
Number Employees: 5-9

1428 Bidwell Vineyard
18910 Middle Rd # 48
Cutchogue, NY 11935-1069   631-734-5200
Fax: 631-734-6763
Wines
Owner: Rose Pipia
Purchasing Director: James Bidwell
Estimated Sales: $1-2.5 Million appx.
Number Employees: 1-4
Brands:
CARBERNET SAUVIGNON
CHARDONNAY
COUNTRY GARDENS BLUSH BANQUET
MERLOT
SAUVIGNON BLANC
WHITE RIESLING

1429 Bien Padre Foods
P.O.Box 3748
Eureka, CA 95502-3748   707-442-4585
Fax: 707-442-4584   sales@bienpadre.com
www.bienpadre.com
Manufacturer and exporter of tortilla chips, corn and flour tortillas and salsas
President: Benito Lim
Estimated Sales: $1-2.5 Million
Number Employees: 20-49
Sq. footage: 14000
Type of Packaging: Consumer, Food Service, Private Label, Bulk

1430 Bieri's Jackson Cheese
3271 County Road P
Jackson, WI 53037-9793   262-677-3227
Fax: 262-677-3480   annette@bierischeese.com
www.bierischeese.com
Retailers of the finest Wisconsin cheeses
Owner: Annette Du Bois
Co-Owner/CEO: Wayne Dubois
Estimated Sales: $300,000-500,000
Number Employees: 5-9
Type of Packaging: Bulk

1431 Bierig Brothers
3539 Reilly Ct
Vineland, NJ 08360-1500   856-691-9765
Fax: 856-692-7869   sales@bierigbros.com
www.bierigbros.com
Processor of veal
President: Herbert Bierig
Purchasing Director: Herbert Bierig
Estimated Sales: $10-20 Million
Number Employees: 20-49

1432 Biery Cheese Company
6544 Paris Ave
Louisville, OH 44641-9544   330-875-3381
Fax: 330-875-5896   800-243-3731
www.bierycheese.com
Processor of cheese
President: Dennis Biery
Estimated Sales: $20-50 Million
Number Employees: 50-99
Type of Packaging: Consumer, Food Service, Private Label, Bulk
Brands:
Biery

1433 Bifulco Farms
590 Almond Road
Pittsgrove, NJ 08318-4070   856-692-0707
Fax: 856-696-5445 www.bifulco.com
Manufacturer of parsley, peppers, tomatoes and zucchini
Secretary: Mrs. Bifulco
Estimated Sales: $2.5-5 Million
Number Employees: 5-9
Type of Packaging: Consumer, Bulk
Brands:
Tall-Boy

1434 Big Al's Seafood
P.O.Box 293
Bozman, MD 21612-0293   410-745-3151
Fax: 410-745-9046
Manufacturer of wholesaler/distributor of crabs, clams, fish and oysters
Owner: Alan Poore
Estimated Sales: Less than $500,000
Number Employees: 5-9
Sq. footage: 6000
Type of Packaging: Consumer

1435 Big Apple Produce & Seafood Market
Us Route 13 N
Pocomoke City, MD 21851   410-957-1151
Fax: 410-957-1152
Manufacturer and packer of beef, lamb, veal and pork including sausage, cured and smoked ham and bacon; custom slaughtering available
President: Calvin Jones
Estimated Sales: $3 Million
Number Employees: 4
Sq. footage: 6000
Type of Packaging: Consumer, Food Service
Brands:
CORBIN
FARMER JONES
POCOMOKE

1436 Big B Distributors
P.O.Box 996
Evansville, IN 47706-0996   812-425-5235
Fax: 812-428-8432
Manufacturer of sauces, pepperoncinis, chili, pork barbecue, sloppy joes, vinegar, salsa and pickled products
President: Bob Bonenberger
CEO: Rich Bonenberger
Estimated Sales: $5-9.9 Million
Number Employees: 10-19
Type of Packaging: Consumer, Food Service, Private Label, Bulk
Brands:
Big B
Frontier Gold

1437 Big Bucks Brewery & Steakhouse
P.O.Box 214990
Auburn Hills, MI 48321-4990   989-732-5781
Fax: 989-732-3990   information@bigbuck.com
www.bigbuck.com
Processor of beer, ale, lager and stout
Manager: Tracy Dalman
Estimated Sales: $2.5-5 Million
Number Employees: 1-4
Type of Packaging: Consumer, Food Service

1438 Big Chief Meat Snacks
4235 17th Street SE
Calgary, AB T2G 3W7
Canada   403-264-2641
Fax: 403-262-9053
snacks@bigchiefbeefjerky.com
www.bigchiefbeefjerky.com
Manufacturer of snack meats including pepperoni and teriyaki sticks, beef jerky and kippered beef
Founder: William Klein
Number Employees: 17
Type of Packaging: Consumer
Brands:
Big Chief
Old Dutch

1439 Big City Reds
4430 S 110th Street
Omaha, NE 68137-1217   847-714-1640
Fax: 847-714-1647   800-850-8003
info@bigcityreds.com www.bigcityreds.com
Manufacturer of all beef hotdogs, frankfurters and sausage including Polish and cocktail
President: Michael Sternberg
VP Marketing: Rebecca Sternberg
National Sales Manager: Robin Warren
Estimated Sales:$5-10 Million
Number Employees: 5-9
Type of Packaging: Consumer, Food Service, Private Label
Brands:
Big City Reds

1440 Big Fatty's Flaming Foods
639 County Road 240
Valley View, TX 76272-5912   940-726-3741
Fax: 940-726-6257   888-248-6332
whatscookin@bigfattys.com
Spicy foods; biscotti, spice rubs and cornbread.
President/Owner: Gail Patterson
VP: Ricky Patterson
Estimated Sales:$300,000-500,000
Number Employees: 1-4

1441 Big Island Seafood, LLC
1201 University Drive NE
Atlanta, GA 30306-2504   404-366-8667
Fax: 404-366-9129
Tuna, swordfish, snapper, grouper, sea bass, mahi-mahi, tilapia, seafood

1442 Big J Milling & Elevator Company
733 W Forest St
Brigham City, UT 84302-2052   435-723-3459
Fax: 435-723-3450
Manufacturer of grain and flour
Owner: John Reese
VP: Ray Scott Reese
Estimated Sales:$10-15 Million
Number Employees: 10-19
Type of Packaging: Consumer, Food Service, Private Label

1443 Big Red Bottling
P.O.Box 20068
Waco, TX 76702-0068   254-772-7791
Fax: 254-772-2441 www.bigredltd.com
Manufacturer of carbonated soft drinks
CEO: Don Sharp
CEO: Gary Smith
Estimated Sales:$20-50 Million
Number Employees: 20-49

1444 Big River Seafood
PO Box 77980
Baton Rouge, LA 70879-7980   225-751-1116
Fax: 225-751-1108
Seafood
President: Lisa Porsche

1445 Big Rock Brewery
5555 76th Avenue SE
Calgary, AB T2C 4L8
Canada   403-720-3239
Fax: 403-236-7523 800-242-3107
ale@bigrockbeer.com www.bigrockbeer.com
Processor of beer, ale, stout and lager
President: E McNally
Marketing Director: Jessica Barrie
CFO: Tim Duffin
Number Employees: 50-99
Type of Packaging: Consumer, Food Service
Brands:
Traditional

1446 Big Shoulders Baking
4014 N Rockwell St
Chicago, IL 60618-3721   773-463-6328
Fax: 773-463-7101 800-456-9328
kat@littlemissmuffin.com
www.bigshouldersbaking.com
Four flavors of cookies
Owner: Staci Minic Mintz
Estimated Sales:$ 20 - 50 Million
Number Employees: 20-49

1447 (HQ)Big Sky Brands
253 College Street
Toronto, ON M5T 1R5
Canada   416-599-5415
Fax: 416-599-0392 luke@bigskybrands.com
www.bigskybrands.com
Candy and mints.
President/Owner: Ron Cheng
VP: Steve Yacht
Type of Packaging: Private Label
Other Locations:
Big Sky Brands
Chicago IL
Big Sky Brands
Buffalo NY
Big Sky Brands
Los Angeles CA
Brands:
CO2 HARD CANDY
DIABLO IGNITED SOURS
DRIVE ACTIVATED
GREEN-T ENERGY MINTS
JONES SODA CARBONATED CANDY
JONES SODA CARBONATED SOURS
JONES SODA ENERGY BOOSTERS
JONES SOURS
LOVE MINTS
MAKE OUT MINTS
PLAYBOY MINTS
WARP ENERGY MINTS
WARP MICRO HYPER CHARGED MINTS

1448 Big Sky Brewing Company
P.O.Box 17170
Missoula, MT 59808-7170   406-549-2777
Fax: 406-549-1919 800-559-2774
info@bigskybrew.com www.bigskybrew.com
Processor of ale and stout
President: Neal Leathers
VP: Bjorn Nabozney
Operations: Matt Long
VP Production: Kris Nabozney
Estimated Sales:$10-20 Million
Number Employees: 20-49
Sq. footage: 24000
Type of Packaging: Consumer, Food Service, Bulk
Brands:
BIG SKY IPA
MOOSE DROOL BROWN ALE
POWDER HOUND WINTER ALE
SCAPE GOAT PALE ALE
SUMMER HONEY SEASONAL ALE
TROUT SLAYER ALE

1449 Big Sky Manafacturing
P.O.Box 188
Roundup, MT 59072-0188   406-323-3580
Fax: 406-323-3599 877-293-3580
Info@BakingSystemsInc.com
www.totalbakingsolutions.com
President: Dave Roberts
VP Manufacturing: Mike Ninichuck
Operations Manager: John Eike
Estimated Sales:$ 3 - 5 Million
Number Employees: 10-19

1450 Big Steer Enterprises
P.O.Box 5413
Beaumont, TX 77726-5413   409-866-3198
Fax: 409-866-0734 800-421-4951
juwhi4@aol.com www.bigsteer.biz
Manufacturer microwave fudge and gourmet snack mixes
President: Grant Nichols
Estimated Sales:$1-2.5 Million
Number Employees: 1-4
Type of Packaging: Private Label

1451 Big Train
19732 Descartes
Foothill Ranch, CA 92610-2621 949-340-8800
Fax: 949-707-1000 800-244-8724
info@bigtrain.com www.bigtrain.com
Processor of ice blended coffees and flavored syrups.
Manager: Steve Schartg
CEO: Mike Dunn
CFO: Kevin Smith
VP, Supply Chain: Steve Scharetg
International Sales: Rachel Pena
Customer Service Supervisor: Shannon Haskill
Estimated Sales:$10-12 Million
Number Employees: 20-49
Sq. footage: 18000

Type of Packaging: Bulk

1452 Bigelow Tea
1 Corporate Dr # 136
Shelton, CT 06484-6208   203-929-2254
Fax: 203-926-0916 800-235-7072
sales@imsfood.com
www.bigelowtea.com/foodservice
Processor of tea bags and tea including loose, hot and iced
Owner: Arnold J D'Angelo
Estimated Sales:$ 5 - 10 Million
Number Employees: 20-49
Brands:
Bigelow

1453 Bijols
P.O.Box 189
Miami, FL 33242   305-634-9030
Fax: 305-634-7454 www.bijol.com
Contract packager and exporter of spices and herbs
President: Idi Borges
Estimated Sales:$2.5-5 Million
Number Employees: 10-19
Type of Packaging: Consumer

1454 Bilgore's Groves
PO Box 1958
Clearwater, FL 33757-1958   727-442-2171
Fax: 727-446-3998
Fruits
Manager: Evelyn Tumber
Estimated Sales:$500-1 Million appx.
Number Employees: 1-4

1455 Bill Grubb Sales
504 Beachview Drive
Saint Simons Island, GA 31522-4740 912-638-5777
Fax: 912-638-0666
President: William Grubb, Jr.

1456 Bill Holt Packing Plant
683 E 600 N
Salina, UT 84654   435-529-7203
Beef, beef products
Number Employees: 20-49

1457 Bill Lowden Seafood
PO Box 327
Warren, ME 04864-0327   207-273-2162
Fax: 207-273-1162
Seafood
Principal: Bill Lowden

1458 Bill Mack's Homemade Ice Cream
3890 Carlisle Rd
Dover, PA 17315-4418   717-292-1931
Manufacturer of ice cream including chocolate, vanilla, oreo cookie, peanut butter, raspberry, banana, caramel, strawberry, etc.
Owner: Todd Mc Daniel
Estimated Sales:$500,000-$1 Million
Number Employees: 20-49
Type of Packaging: Consumer
Brands:
Bill Mack's

1459 Bill's Seafood
9016 Belair Rd
Baltimore, MD 21236-2120   410-256-9520
Fax: 410-256-3491
Seafood
Owner: Bill Paulshock
Estimated Sales:$ 5 - 10 Million
Number Employees: 20-49

1460 Billie-Ann Plastics Packaging Corp
360 Troutman Stret
Brooklyn, NY 11237   718-497-5555
Fax: 718-497-6095 888-245-5432
info@billieannplastics.com
www.billieannplastics.com
manufacturer of cylinders and plastic boxes

1461 (HQ)Billingsgate Fish Company
630 7th Avenue SE
Calgary, AB T2G 0J7
Canada   403-571-7700
Fax: 403-571-7717 www.billingsgate.com

Processor and packager of fish, meat and deli products; wholesaler/distributor of meats and seafood; serving the food service market
  President: Bryan Fallwell
  Sales Representative: Brenda Shreindorfer
  Operations Manager: Mark Puffer
Number Employees: 50-99
Sq. footage: 35000
Type of Packaging: Consumer, Food Service
Other Locations:
  Billingsgate Fish Company
    Edmonton, Alberta
  Billingsgate Fish Company
    St. Albert, Alberta
Brands:
  Billingsgate
  King of Fish
  Plough Boy

1462 Billy's Seafood
P.O.Box 309
Bon Secour, AL 36511-0309   251-949-6288
      Fax: 251-949-6505 www.billys-seafood.com
Seafood
  Owner: Billy Parks
Estimated Sales: $2,000,000
Number Employees: 5-9

1463 Biltmore Estate Wine Company
1 Approach Rd
Asheville, NC 28803-8900   828-225-1333
      Fax: 828-225-6383   800-411-3812
    snowak@biltmore.com   www.bitmore.com
Wines
  President/CEO: William Cecil Jr.
  Marketing Director: Jerry Douglas
  Operations: Bernard Delille
Estimated Sales: $10-24.9 Million
Number Employees: 100-249

1464 Biltmore Trading LLC
4818 E Peak View Rd
Cave Creek, AZ 85331-6394   480-502-7500
                  Fax: 480-502-7503
Food broker
Estimated Sales: $ 3 - 5 Million
Number Employees: 1-4

1465 Bimbo Bakeries
480 S Vail Ave
Montebello, CA 90640-4947   323-720-6000
      Fax: 323-720-6015   877-224-7374
    contactBBU@bimbobakeriesusa.com
    www.bimbobakeriesusa.com
Processor of bread, buns and rolls.
  President: Reynaldo Reyna
Estimated Sales: $100-500 Million
Number Employees: 5-9
Parent Co: Bimbo Bakeries USA
Brands:
  BIMBO
  BOBOLI
  BOHEMIAN HEARTH
  ENTENMANN'S
  FRANCISCO INTERNATIONAL
  MARINELA
  MRS. BAIRD'S
  OLD COUNTRY
  OROWEAT
  THOMAS
  TIA ROSA
  WEBER'S

1466 Bimbo Bakeries
480 S Vail Ave
Montebello, CA 90640-4947   323-720-6000
                  Fax: 323-720-6015
Bread and bakery products
  Accounts Manager: Petra Castllanos
  Sales Director: Jeff Collins
Estimated Sales: $2.5-5 Million
Number Employees: 5-9
Brands:
  BIMBO
  MARINELA
  MRS. BAIRD'S
  TIA ROSA

1467 (HQ)Bimbo Bakeries
PO Box 976
Horsham, PA 19044-2861
        Fax: 610-320-9286   800-984-0989
      contactBBU@bimbobakeriesusa.com
        www.bimbobakeries.com

Breads, rolls, buns, tortillas, chips, snack cakes, cookies, donuts, cakes and pastries.
  President: Reynaldo Reyna
Estimated Sales: $1.2 Billion
Number Employees: 20-49
Brands:
  ARNOLD
  BIMBO
  BOBOLI
  BROWNBERRY
  ENTENMANN'S
  FRANCISCO
  FREIHOFER'S
  MARINELA
  MRS BAIRD'S
  OROWEAT
  STROEHMANN
  THOMAS'
  TIA ROSA

1468 Binding Brauerei USA
194 Main St
Norwalk, CT 06851-3502   203-229-0111
    Fax: 203-229-0105   bbusa@optonline.net
                  www.clausthaler.com
Beer and ale.
  President: Hans Schliebs
  CEO: Dilip Mehta
  VP Sales: Dave Deuser
  COO: Dilip Mehta
Estimated Sales: $5-10 Million
Number Employees: 10-19
Parent Co: Radeberger Gruppe GmbH
Brands:
  CLAUSTHALER
  DAB
  KRUSOVICE
  RADEBERGER
  TUCHER

1469 Binkert's Meat Products
8805 Philadelphia Rd
Baltimore, MD 21237-4310   410-687-5959
                  Fax: 410-687-5023
Sausage and other prepared meats
  Owner: Sonya Weber
  President: Sonya Weber
Estimated Sales: $300,000-$310,000
Number Employees: 1-4
Brands:
  Binkert's

1470 Binns Vineyards & Winery
1501 S Don Roser Dr
Las Cruces, NM 88011-4538   575-522-2211
                  Fax: 575-522-1112
Wines
  Owner: Eddie Binns
  Vice President: Glenn Binns
Estimated Sales: $1-4.9 Million
Number Employees: 5-9
Type of Packaging: Private Label

1471 Bio San Laboratories/MegaFood
P.O.Box 325
Derry, NH 03038-0325   603-432-5022
      Fax: 603-434-4736   800-848-5022
    info@biosan.net   www.biosanlabs.com
Processor of food nutrients; exporter of food supplements
  President: Carl Jackson
  V.P. Mfg.: Richard Lafond
Estimated Sales: $20-50 Million
Number Employees: 50-99
Type of Packaging: Consumer
Brands:
  Daily Foods
  Essentials
  Megafood
  Nutritional Therapeutix

1472 Bio-Foods
P.O.Box 622
Pine Brook, NJ 7058-622   973-808-5856
      Fax: 973-396-2999   bobkoetzner@aol.com
                  www.biofoodsltd.com
Manufacturer and exporter of nutrients
  President: Bharat Patel
  Vice President: Robert Koetzner
Number Employees: 6
Sq. footage: 9000
Type of Packaging: Bulk
Brands:
  BIO-FOODS

1473 Bio-Hydration Research Lab
2091 Rutherford Rd
Carlsbad, CA 92008-7320   760-268-0808
      Fax: 760-268-0808   800-531-5088
                  www.pentawater.com
Manufacturer of Bio-Hydration; a molecular restructured water that hydrates faster and provides enhanced performance and healthy living
  CEO: Bill Holloway
  CEO: Dennis O'Bryan
  Public Relations Manager: Jeffrey Pizzino
Estimated Sales: $ 5 - 10 Million
Number Employees: 50-99
Number of Brands: 1
Number of Products: 2
Sq. footage: 110000
Type of Packaging: Consumer
Brands:
  PENTA

1474 Bio-K + International
495 Boulevard Armand - Frappier
Laval, QC H7V 4B3
Canada   450-978-2465
      Fax: 450-978-9729   info@biokplus.com
                  www.biokplus.com
  President: Claude Chevalier
  Marketing Director: Michael Sirdemt
  CFO: Michael Rheault
Brands:
  Bio K

1475 Bio-Nutritional Products
119 Rockland Ave
Northvale, NJ 07647-2144   201-784-8200
                  Fax: 201-784-8201
  President: Stephen Difolco
Brands:
  Eugalan
  Lacto

1476 Bio-Tech Pharmacal
P.O.Box 1927
Fayetteville, AR 72702-1927   479-443-9148
      Fax: 479-443-5643   800-345-1199
    service@bio-tech-pharm.com
                  www.bio-tech-pharm.com
Manufacturer of hypo-allergenic nutraceuticals, vitamins, minerals, herbals, anti-oxidants, amino acids, etc
  Owner: Dale Benedict
  CFO: Martha Bendike
Estimated Sales: $ 10 - 20 Million
Number Employees: 10-19
Type of Packaging: Consumer, Private Label, Bulk
Brands:
  Bio-Tech Pharmacal

1477 BioSynergy
P.O.Box 16833
Boise, ID 83715-6833   208-342-6660
      Fax: 208-342-0880   800-554-7145
    email@biosynergy.com   www.biosynergy.com
Processor of health related products
  President: Ted Kremer
  Marketing Director: Hidemi Kremer
Estimated Sales: $200,000
Number Employees: 1-4
Brands:
  Nojo

1478 (HQ)BioTech Corporation
107 Oakwood Dr # E
Glastonbury, CT 06033-2481   860-633-8111
      Fax: 860-682-6863   800-880-7188
    info@biotechcorp.com   www.biotechcorp.com
Nutraceuticals and nutritional supplements.
  President: Gregory Kelly
Estimated Sales: $ 5 - 10 Million
Number Employees: 10-19

1479 Bioforce USA
6 Grandinetti Drive
Ghent, NY 12075   518-828-9111
      Fax: 888-798-7555   800-641-7555
    Info@BioforceUSA.com   www.bioforceusa.com
Natural products, vitamins, etc.
  President: Paul Ross
  Sales Manager: Rich Manziello
  Operations Manager: Roberts Sheets
Estimated Sales: $300,000-500,000
Number Employees: 1-4

Brands:
A. Vogel

1480 Biomist Inc
573 N Wolf Rd
Wheeling, IL 60090-3027   847-850-5530
Fax: 847-803-0875   prmartin@biomistinc.com
www.biomistinc.com/index.html
Manufacturer of Biomist Power Disinfecting System Spray.
Owner: Robert Cook
Vice President: Robert Cook II
Vice President Customer Service: Eileen Bowery
Director of Sales and Operations: Peter Martin

1481 Bionutritional ResearchGroup
20331 Irvine Ave
Santa Ana, CA 92707-5623   714-427-6990
Fax: 714-427-6998   nadine@bnrg.com
www.bnrg.com
Nutritional products, protein powder and bars, supplements.
President/CEO: Kevin Lawrence
VP Sales: Ken Braunstein
VP Operations: Tom Williams
Estimated Sales:$15 Million
Number Employees: 5-9
Brands:
ALPHA GLUTAMINE
CELL CHARGE®
POWER CRUNCH®
PROTO WHEY®

1482 Biotec AZ Laboratories
20809 N 19th Avenue
Suite 1
Phoenix, AZ 85027-3519   800-218-6979
Fax: 623-576-2285 www.biotechazlabs.com
Supplements and vitamins.
President: Tyler Rosales

1483 Biothera
3388 Mike Collins Dr
Eagan, MN 55121-2410   651-675-0300
Fax: 651-657-0400   info@biotheraopharma.com
www.biopolymer.com
Markets food-grade immune-enhancing ingredients for the nutritional supplement, functional food, cosmetic and the animal feed nutrition markets.
Founder: Dan Conners
President/CEO: Richard G Mueller
CFO: Julie R Streed
CEO: Richard Mueller
VP Sales and Marketing: Allen F Porter
Estimated Sales:$ 3 - 5 Million
Number Employees: 10-19
Type of Packaging: Bulk

1484 Birch Street Seafoods
PO Box 675
Digby, NS B0V 1A0
Canada   902-245-6551
Fax: 902-245-6554
Processor and exporter of fresh and frozen salted groundfish
Plant Manager: Alan Frankland
Number Employees: 20-49
Type of Packaging: Consumer, Food Service, Private Label, Bulk

1485 Birchwood Foods
P.O.Box 639
Kenosha, WI 53141-0639   262-859-2881
Fax: 262-859-2078 800-541-1685
bwinfo@bwfoods.com   www.bwfoods.com
Manufactuer and exporter of cryogenically frozen and vacuum-packed fresh ground beef in bulk and patties; importer of boneless beef
President/CEO: Dennis Vignieri
CFO: Jerry King
VP Sales/National Accounts: David Van Kampen
Corporate HR/Safety Director: Phyllis Murray
EVP Operations & Procurement: John Ruffolo
Estimated Sales:$300 Million
Number Employees: 250-499
Parent Co: Kenosha Beef International
Type of Packaging: Consumer, Food Service, Private Label, Bulk
Other Locations:
Frankfort Manufacturing Facility
Frankfort IN
Columbus Manufacturing Facility
Columbus OH
Atlanta Manufacturing Facility
Atlanta GA

1486 Bird Creek Brewery
Hc 52
Box 8503
Indian, AK 99540-9601   907-344-2473
Fax: 907-522-2739
Beer
President: Ike Kelly
Treasurer: Mary Kelly
Plant Manager: Allen Ellis
Estimated Sales:$5-9.9 Million
Number Employees: 1-4
Brands:
Anchorage
Denali Style Ale
Old 55

1487 Bird-In-Hand Farms, Inc.
1708 Columbia Ave
Lancaster, PA 17603-4550   717-291-5855
Fax: 717-291-1990   ted.bloom@bihfarms.com
www.bihfarms.com
Poultry
President: Fred Bloom
VP Sales: Ted Bloom
Estimated Sales:$5-10 Million
Number Employees: 5-9
Type of Packaging: Private Label
Other Locations:
Bird-In-Hand Farms
Chapin SC
Bird-In-Hand Farms
Jackson MI
Bird-In-Hand Farms
Huntington IN
Bird-In-Hand Farms
Nacogdoches TX
Bird-In-Hand Farms
Monett MO
Bird-In-Hand Farms
Topsail Beach NC
Bird-In-Hand Farms
Russellville AR
Bird-In-Hand Farms
Southern Pines NC
Brands:
BIRD-IN-HAND
TRULY DUTCH

1488 Birdie Pak Products
3925 W 31st St
Chicago, IL 60623-4934   773-247-5293
Fax: 773-247-4280   Kevin@birdiepak.com
www.birdiepak.com
Processor and distributor of frozen beef, poultry and fish
President: Thomas Krueger
VP: Kevin Krueger
Estimated Sales:$2.5-5 Million
Number Employees: 10-19
Type of Packaging: Consumer, Food Service, Private Label
Brands:
Birdie Pak

1489 (HQ)Birds Eye Foods
90 Linden Oaks
Rochester, NY 14625   585-383-1850
Fax: 585-385-2857 800-999-5044
www.birdseyefoods.com
Frozen vegetables and prepared meals
President/COO: Christopher Puma
Chairman/CEO: Neil Harrison
EVP/CFO: Linda Nelson
Estimated Sales:$930 Million
Number Employees: 1,000-4,999
Parent Co: Pinnacle Foods Group LLC
Type of Packaging: Consumer, Food Service, Bulk
Other Locations:
Fennville MI
Waseca MN
Fulton NY
Berlin PA
Algona WA
Tacoma WA
Darien WI
Green Bay WI
Brands:
BERNSTEIN'S
BIRDS EYE
BIRDS EYE C&W
BIRDS EYE FRESHLIKE
BIRDS EYE STEAMFRESH
BROOKS
COMSTOCK WILDERNESS
FRESHLIKE

GREENWOOD
HUSMAN'S
LARSEN FRESHLIKE FOODS
MARINER'S COVE CLAM CHOWDER
MCKENZIE'S
MCKENZIE'S
NALLEY
NALLEY'S CHILI & STEWS
NALLEY'S DRESSINGS
NALLEY'S PICKLES
NATURALLY GOOD FRUITS & VEGETABLES
ORCHARD FARM CANNED VEGETABLES
ORCHARD FRESH FROZEN FRUITS
OREGON'S FINEST
PIXIE CANNED CORN & CHUTNEYS
POPEYE POPCORN
POPS RITE POPCORN
PUFF-N-CORN
QUALITY BRAND
QUE PASA CHEESE SAUCE & SALSA
RIVIERA
RIVIERA CANNED ITALIAN SOUPS
SAVORAL SALT & OILS
SILVER FLOSS SAUERKRAUT
SNYDER OF BERLIN
SNYDER OF BERLIN SNACK PRODUCTS
SOUTH LAND FROZEN FOODS
SOUTHERN FARMS PRODUCE
SPOON BRAND
STIR CRAZY
THANK YOU FRUIT FILLINGS
TIM'S CASCADE CHIPS
TIM'S CASCADE SNACKS
TROPIC ISLE FROZEN COCONUT
VICTOR SAUERKRAUT
VIOLA
WEST BAY PIE FILLINGS
WILDERNESS

1490 Birds Eye Foods
1313 Stadium St
Berlin, PA 15530-1401   814-267-4641
Fax: 814-267-5648   rhayman@birdseyefoods.com
www.birdseyefoods.com/snyder
Manufacturer of pretzels, potato chips and chips, cheese curls and popcorn
Chairman/President/CEO: Neil Harrison
VP: John Blough
VP Human Resources/Purchasing: John Blough
Production Manager: John Lahm
Plant Engineer: Dennis Brant
Estimated Sales:$50 Milion
Number Employees: 250-499
Parent Co: Agrilink Foods
Type of Packaging: Consumer
Brands:
BERNSTEIN'S
BIRD'S EYE
BIRD'S EYE VOILA
BROOKS
C&W
COMSTOCK
FRESHLIKE
GREENWOOD BEETS
HUSMAN'S
MARINER'S COVE
MCKENZIE'S
NALLEY PRODUCTS
RIVIERA
SYNDER OF BERLIN
TIM'S CASCADE SNACKS
WILDERNESS

1491 Birdsall Ice Cream Company
518 N Federal Ave
Mason City, IA 50401-3216   641-423-5365
Manufacturer of ice cream
Owner: Vaughn Escher
Owner: Dave Escher
Estimated Sales:$1 Million
Number Employees: 10-19
Type of Packaging: Consumer, Food Service

1492 Birdseye Dairy
2325 Memorial Dr
Green Bay, WI 54303-6399   920-494-5388
Fax: 920-494-4388
Processor of apple and orange juice; wholesaler/distributor of dairy products including milk, ice cream, butter and sour cream; serving the food service market
President: Steven Williamss

Estimated Sales: $10-20 Million
Number Employees: 10-19
Type of Packaging: Consumer, Food Service, Private Label, Bulk
Brands:
Birdseye
Morning Glory

1493 (HQ)Birdsong Corporation
P.O.Box 1400
Suffolk, VA 23439-1400   757-539-3456
                               Fax: 757-539-7360
Manufacturer and exporter of raw peanuts
President: Jeff Johnson
CEO: George Birdsong
CFO: Stephen Huber
CEO: George Y Birdsong
Estimated Sales: $395.4 Million
Number Employees: 500-999
Parent Co: Birdsong Peanuts
Type of Packaging: Food Service
Other Locations:
Birdsong Corp.
Gorman TX

1494 Birdsong Peanut Company
P.O.Box 698
Gorman, TX 76454-0698   254-734-3153
                               Fax: 254-734-2029
pduke@birdsong-peanuts.com
Manufacturer of raw peanuts and peanut products
including seeds, meal and oil, shellers and crushers
President: Thomas H Birdsong Iii
VP/General Manager: Max Grice
VP Sales/Officer Manager: D Presley Duke Jr
Estimated Sales: $100-500 Million
Number Employees: 100-249
Parent Co: Birdsong Peanuts
Type of Packaging: Bulk
Other Locations:
Birdsong Peanuts
Blakely GA
Birdsong Peanuts
Suffolk VA

1495 Birkett Mills
P.O.Box 440
Penn Yan, NY 14527-0440   315-536-3311
Fax: 315-536-6740   service@theberkettmills.com
www.thebirkettmills.com
Processor of flour
President: Jeff Gifford
COO: Jeff Giffond
VP Marketing: Cliff Orr
Estimated Sales: $1-2.5 Million
Number Employees: 20-49
Type of Packaging: Consumer, Private Label, Bulk
Brands:
Bessie
Pocono
Puritan
Wolffs

1496 Birkholm's Jr Danish Bakery
1555 Mission Drive
Solvang, CA 93463-2607   805-688-3872
          Fax: 805-693-1027 www.birkholms.com
Breads, rolls, pastries, cakes
Owner: Danish Birkholm Jr
Estimated Sales: Less than $500,000
Number Employees: 5-9
Brands:
Birkholm's Jr. Danish

1497 Birmhall Foods Company
P.O.Box 34232
Memphis, TN 38184-0232   901-377-9016
Fax: 901-377-0476   ps139@brimsnacks.com
www.brimsnacks.com
President: Terry Brimhall
VP: Becki Brimhall
General Manager: Michael Patrick
Estimated Sales: $ 20 - 50 Million
Number Employees: 50-99
Brands:
Brim's

1498 Birnn Chocolates
314 Cleveland Ave
Highland Park, NJ 08904-1845   732-545-4400
Fax: 732-545-4494   info@birnnchocolates.com
www.birnnchocolates.com
Chocolate confections
President: John Cunnell

Estimated Sales: $500,000-$1 Million
Number Employees: 10-19
Type of Packaging: Private Label

1499 Birnn Chocolates of Vermont
102 Kimball Ave # 4
South Burlington, VT 05403-6800   802-860-1047
                               Fax: 802-860-1256 800-338-3141
www.birnn.com
Manufacturer of premium wholesale truffles
President/Owner: Jeff Birnn
VP: Bill Birnn
Estimated Sales: $5-10 Million
Number Employees: 20-49
Type of Packaging: Private Label

1500 (HQ)Biscomerica Corporation
P.O.Box 1070
Rialto, CA 92377-1070   909-877-5997
          Fax: 909-877-3593 info@biscomerica.com
www.biscomerica.com
Cookies and candy
President: Nadi Soltan
CEO: Nadi Soltan
Estimated Sales: $30 Million
Number Employees: 250-499
Sq. footage: 225000
Brands:
CHECKERS COOKIES
GRANNY'S OVEN
KNOTT'S BERRY FARMS

1501 Biscottea
23216 SE 135th Ct
Issaquah, WA 98027   425-313-1993
          Fax: 425-427-0709 info@biscottea.net
www.biscottea.net
Organic, all natural flavored shortbread
President/Owner: Laurance Milner
Number Employees: 2

1502 Biscotti Goddess
3910 Amberleigh Blvd
Richmond, VA 23236   804-745-9490
jan@biscotti-goddess.com
www.biscotti-goddess.com
Biscotti

1503 Bishop Baking Company
1335 S Ocoee St
Cleveland, TN 37311-2610   423-472-1561
          Fax: 423-472-6355 info@bishoptaboli.com
www.flowersfoods.com
Processor and exporter of snack cakes
President: Kent Feagans
Controller: Craig Parrish
Estimated Sales: $50-100 Million
Number Employees: 250-499
Parent Co: President Baking Company
Type of Packaging: Consumer, Private Label

1504 Bishop Brothers
P.O.Box 814
Bristow, OK 74010-0814   918-367-2270
          Fax: 918-367-2270 800-859-8304
info@bishoptaboli.com   www.bishoptaboli.com
Wholesaler/distributor of bulgur wheat including
tabbouleh; custom packaging services available
Owner: Eddie Bishop
Estimated Sales: $2.5-5 Million
Number Employees: 5-9
Type of Packaging: Consumer, Food Service, Bulk

1505 Bishop Farms Winery
500 S Meriden Rd
Cheshire, CT 06410-2968   203-272-8243
                               Fax: 203-272-7344
Wines
President: John Romanik
Marketing Director: Mary Romanik
Estimated Sales: $500,000-$1 Million
Number Employees: 1-4

1506 Bismarck Enterprises
680 N Lake Shore Dr # 2030
Chicago, IL 60611-3496   312-943-3310
                               Fax: 312-943-7898
Catering services, concessions
President: Peter Wirtz
Estimated Sales: $7,600,000
Number Employees: 10-19

1507 Bison Brewing Company
PO Box 4821
Berkeley, CA 94704-4821   510-697-1537
          Fax: 510-217-4332 info@bisonbrew.com
www.bisonbrew.com
Organic Beer
Owner: Dan DelGarande
Sales Representative: Rich Schwanbeck
Estimated Sales: $5-10 Million
Number Employees: 10-19
Brands:
BARLEY WINE ALE
BELGIAN ALE
CHOCOLATE STOUT
FARMHOUSE SAISON
GINGERBREAD ALE
HONEY BASIL ALE
INDIA PALE ALE
RED ALE
WINTER WARMER

1508 Bissett Produce Company
P.O.Box 279
Spring Hope, NC 27882-0279   252-478-4158
          Fax: 252-478-7798 800-849-5073
Bissettproducecompanyinc@msn.com
Grower, packer and exporter of sweet potatoes, pickling cucumbers and banana and specialty peppers
and seedless watermelons
Manager: Don Sparks II
Vice President: Lee Bissett II
Sales Director: Don Sparks
Estimated Sales: $2.5-5 Million
Number Employees: 20-49
Sq. footage: 60000
Type of Packaging: Consumer, Food Service, Private Label, Bulk
Brands:
Bissett's
Rue's Choice

1509 Bissinger's HandcraftedChocolatier
3983 Gratiot Street
St Louis, MO 63110
          Fax: 314-534-2419 800-325-8881
sales@bissingers.com   www.bissingers.com
boxed chocolates, sugar free chocolate and classic
gourmet candies

1510 Bittersweet Herb Farm
635 Mohawk Trl
Shelburne Falls, MA 01370-9775   413-625-6523
          Fax: 413-625-0166 800-456-1599
info@bittersweetherbfarm.com
www.bittersweetherbfarm.com
Wasabi ginger sauce, lemon garlic sauce, strawberry
jam and all natural seasonings. Also flavored oils
and balsamic vinegars
President: David Wallace
Estimated Sales: $1-2.5 Million
Number Employees: 10-19

1511 Bittersweet Pastries
385 Chestnut St
Norwood, NJ 07648-2001   201-768-7005
          Fax: 201-768-5980 800-537-7791
salesinfo@bittersweetpastries.com
www.bittersweetpastries.com
Processor of desserts including tarts, layer cakes,
and flourless chocolate truffle cakes. Also sold
frozen
President: Phyllis Trier
VP: Louis Florencia
Estimated Sales: $1-5 Million
Number Employees: 20-49
Sq. footage: 4500
Parent Co: Fairfield Gourmet Foods Corporation
Type of Packaging: Food Service

1512 Bizerba USA
1088 E 900th Road
Lawrence, KS 66047-9587   913-491-1093
                               Fax: 913-491-0033
Sales Director: Dean Dunlap

1513 Bjorneby Potato Company
P.O.Box 317
Minto, ND 58261-0317   701-248-3482
          Fax: 701-248-3508 lonewolf@uslink.net
www.lonewolffarms.com

Supplier of potatoes
President: Keith Bjorneby
VP: Dean Bjorneby
Sales Manager: Chris Bjorneby
Production Manager: Chris Bjorneby
Estimated Sales: $ 10 - 20 Million
Number Employees: 16
Type of Packaging: Consumer, Bulk

1514 Black Bear
PO Box 296
St Johnsbury, VT 05819-0296   802-748-5888
Fruit spreads

1515 Black Diamond Cheese
405 The West Mall
10th Floor
Toronto, ON M9C 5J1
Canada   613-969-0593
    Fax: 613-969-2199 800-263-2858
            www.blackdiamond.ca
Natural cheese, cheese slices and cheese spread
President: Mike Rosici
Director Operations: Bob Mitro
Number Employees: 300
Sq. footage: 100000
Parent Co: Parmalat Finanziaria SpA.
Type of Packaging: Food Service, Private Label
Brands:
BLACK DIAMOND

1516 Black Duck Cove Lobster
PO Box 42
Beals, ME 04611-0042   207-497-2232
                    Fax: 215-925-1779
Lobster
President: Marianne Beal

1517 Black Garlic Inc
2499 American Ave
Hayward, CA 94546
                               888-811-9065
    info@blackgarlic.com www.blackgralic.com
Garlic

1518 Black Hound New York
111 N 10th St
Brooklyn, NY 11211-1942   718-782-0154
    Fax: 718-782-1608 800-344-4417
    customerservice@blackhoundny.com
            www.blackhoundny.com
Hard, soft and chocolate candies, cakes and delectibles
President: Amiram Dror
Estimated Sales: $500,000-$1 Million
Number Employees: 10-19

1519 Black Jewell Popcorn
Rr 1
St Francisville, IL 62460   618-948-2303
    Fax: 618-948-2505 carole@blackjewell.com
                www.blackjewell.com
Popcorn
President: Carole Klein
Estimated Sales: $ 5 - 10 Million
Number Employees: 10-19
Brands:
Black Jewell
Crimson Jewell

1520 Black Jewell®Popcorn
Rr 1
St Francisville, IL 62460   618-948-2303
        Fax: 618-948-2505 800-948-2302
bjsales@blackjewell.com www.blackjewell.com
Black and red popcorn
President: Carole Klein
Estimated Sales: $2.5-5 Million
Number Employees: 10-19
Type of Packaging: Private Label
Brands:
BLACK JEWELL®
CRIMSON JEWELL®

1521 Black Mesa Winery
P.O.Box 308
Velarde, NM 87582-0308   505-852-2820
    Fax: 505-852-2820 800-852-6372
            www.blackmesawinery.com
Processor of wine
Co-Owner: Jerry Burd
Co-Owner: Lynda Burd
Estimated Sales: $500,000-$1 Million
Number Employees: 1-4

Type of Packaging: Private Label
Brands:
Black Mesa
Coyote Wine

1522 Black Mountain Brewing Company
6245 E Cave Creek Rd
Cave Creek, AZ 85331-8655   480-488-3553
    Fax: 480-488-0482 chili1!ix.netcom.com
                www.chilibeer.com
Beer
Owner: Glory Agenter
VP: Dick Chilleen
Operations Manager: Juan Olguin
Estimated Sales: $10-20 Million
Number Employees: 5-9
Type of Packaging: Private Label
Brands:
BLACK MOUNTAIN GOLD
CAVE CREEK CHILI BEER
FROG LIGHT
JUANDERFUL WHEAT
OCOTILLO AMBER
SOUTH OF THE BORDER PORTER

1523 Black Prince Distillery, Inc.
P.O.Box 1999
Clifton, NJ 07015-1999   973-365-2050
    Fax: 973-365-0746 rickn@blackprincedist.com
            www.blackprincedistillery.com
Processor of liquor, liqueurs and cordials
President: Robert Guttag
Estimated Sales: $25 Million
Number Employees: 50-99
Brands:
BLACK PRINCE
DEVILS SPRING
DORADO
LLORD'S
TJ TOAD

1524 Black Ranch Organic Grains
5917 Eastside Road
Etna, CA 96027-9753   530-467-3387
Processor of seven grain cereals including wheat and barley
Owner: Dave Black
Co-Owner: Dawn Black
Estimated Sales: Under $500,000
Number Employees: 1-4
Type of Packaging: Consumer, Food Service
Brands:
Black Ranch Gourmet Grains

1525 Black Sheep Vintners
P.O.Box 1851
Murphys, CA 95247-1851   209-728-2157
    Fax: 209-728-2157 info@blacksheepwinery.com
                www.blacksheepwinery.com
Wines
Owner: Steve Millier
CEO: David Olson
Marketing Director: Janis Olson
Estimated Sales: Less than $500,000
Number Employees: 1-4
Type of Packaging: Private Label

1526 Black Shield
5356 Pan American E Freeway NE
Albuquerque, NM 87109-2306   505-880-1112
                Fax: 505-884-5643 800-653-9357
Specialty gourmet popcorn
President: Marc Moore
Estimated Sales: Less than $500,000
Number Employees: 1-4

1527 Black's Barbecue
215 N Main St
Lockhart, TX 78644-2121   512-398-2712
    Fax: 512-398-6000 blacksbbq@sbcglobal.net
                www.blacksbbq.com
Manufacturer of barbequed sausage; wholesaler/distributor of meats including brisket, ribs, chicken, pork and loin.
Manager: Steve Cloud
CEO: Terry Black
Estimated Sales: $300,000-500,000
Number Employees: 20-49
Type of Packaging: Bulk

1528 Blackbear Coffee Company
318 N Main St
Hendersonville, NC 28792-0407   828-692-6333
                    Fax: 828-692-6333
        www.mountainshops.com/bear.html
Coffee
Manager: Bo Rodriquez
Estimated Sales: Less than $500,000
Number Employees: 5-9

1529 Blackberry Patch
92 Genesis Pkwy
Thomasville, GA 31792-3517   229-558-9996
    Fax: 229-558-9998 800-853-5598
        mail@blackberrypatch.com
        www.blackberrypatch.com
Manufacturer of natural fruit syrups, jams, jellies, chocolate sauces and pancake mixes
Owner: Harry Jones
Estimated Sales: $5-9.9 Million
Number Employees: 10-19
Number of Brands: 2
Number of Products: 48
Type of Packaging: Consumer, Private Label

1530 Blackey's Bakery
639 22nd Avenue NE
Minneapolis, MN 55418-3554   612-789-5326
                    Fax: 612-789-2924
Processor of bakery products
Owner: Rob Reding
Estimated Sales: $1-2.5 Million
Number Employees: 10-19

1531 Blackwell Wine Company
Star Route
Box 337
Lost Hills, CA 93249   661-397-2622
                    Fax: 661-397-2627
Wines
Chairman/President: Peter Lewis
CFO: Leon Elwclo
Estimated Sales: $500,000 appx.
Number Employees: 20-49

1532 Blair's Death Sauces & Snacks
188 Bay Ave
Highlands, NJ 07732-1624   732-872-0755
    Fax: 732-872-2035 www.extremefood.com
Sauces and snack foods
Owner: Blair Lazar
Estimated Sales: $ 10 - 20 Million
Number Employees: 10-19

1533 Blake's Creamery
46 Milford St
Manchester, NH 03102-4799   603-623-7242
    Fax: 603-623-7244 info@blakesicecream.com
            www.blakesicecream.com
Manufacturer of ice cream and frozen yogurt
Owner: Ann Mirageas
Owner: Rick Marquis
Estimated Sales: $25-49.9 Million
Number Employees: 100-249
Type of Packaging: Consumer, Food Service, Private Label, Bulk

1534 Blakely Freezer Locker
PO Box 7055
Thomasville, GA 31758-7055   229-723-3622
                    Fax: 229-723-9156
    sales@blakelyfreezerlocker.com
    www.blakelyfreezerlocker.com
Manufacturer of frozen beef, pork and chicken
Owner: Douglas Huey Johnson
Owner: Deeann Benton Johnson
Estimated Sales: $2.5-5 Million
Number Employees: 5-9
Type of Packaging: Consumer
Other Locations:
Blakely GA

1535 Blalock Seafood
24822 Canal Rd
Orange Beach, AL 36561-3894   251-974-5811
        Fax: 251-974-5812 www.blalockseafood.com
Seafood
President: Peter Blalock
Estimated Sales: $4,000,000
Number Employees: 10-19
Type of Packaging: Consumer

1536 Blanc Industries
88 King Street
Dover, NJ 07801   973-537-0090
          Fax: 973-537-0906   888-332-5262
     email@blancind.com   www.blancind.com
Manufacture, design and print point of sale promotional signage, displays and fixtures for the food and retail industry.
     President: Didier Blanc

1537 Bland Farms
PO Box 2119
Reidsville, GA 30453-2119   912-654-4973
          Fax: 912-654-4280   800-752-0206
Frozen foods

1538 Blansh International
6560 Rolling Oaks Drive
San Jose, CA 95120-4562   408-997-8284
                    Fax: 408-279-8444
Ethnic foods
     President: Atoor Eliasnia
Estimated Sales: $250,000
Number Employees: 1-4

1539 Blanton's
246 Jarco Dr
Sweetwater, TN 37874   423-337-3487
                    Fax: 423-337-3487
Manufacturer of hard stick candy, molded and regular chocolate; also, seasonal products available
     Owner: Harld Blanton
     Vice President: Betty Blanton
Estimated Sales: $500,000
Number Employees: 5-9
Type of Packaging: Consumer
Brands:
     Blanton's

1540 Blaser & Wolthers Specialty
905 Brickell Bay Drive
Suite 228
Miami, FL 33131-2923   305-374-7111
          Fax: 305-374-4020   www.bankruptcdata.com
Coffee
     Vice President: Christian Wolthers
     Office Manager: Marco Figueiredo
Estimated Sales: $1-2.5 Million
Number Employees: 1-4

1541 Blaser's USA, Inc.
P.O.Box 36
Comstock, WI 54826-0036   715-822-2437
          Fax: 715-822-8479   mail@blasersusa.com
                    www.blasersusa.com
Cheese
     President: Anthony Curella
     National VP Sales/Marketing: Jim Grande
     Operations Manager: Thomas Messicci
Estimated Sales: $500,000-$1 Million
Number Employees: 1-4
Type of Packaging: Private Label
Brands:
     BLASER'S

1542 Blau Oyster Company
11317 Blue Heron Rd
Bow, WA 98232-9326   360-766-6171
          Fax: 360-766-6115   contact@blauoyster.com
                    www.blauoyster.com
Processor and exporter of oysters.
     President: Paul Blau
     Marketing Manager: Pete Nordlund
     Director of Operations: Paul Blau
Estimated Sales: $2.5-5 Million
Number Employees: 10-19
Type of Packaging: Consumer, Food Service, Private Label, Bulk

1543 Blaze Products Corporation
1101 Isaac Shelby Dr
Shelbyville, KY 40065-9128   502-633-0650
          Fax: 502-633-0685   aaper@sky1.net
                    www.blazeproducts.com
Manufacture chafing dish fuel
     COO: Cindy Foster

1544 Blazzin Pickle Company
6105 N 32nd Street
McAllen, TX 78504-5006   956-630-0733
Processor of pickles including chips and spears
     President: Craig Johnson
     VP: Kathy Johnson

Number Employees: 1-4
Sq. footage: 2000
Type of Packaging: Consumer, Food Service
Brands:
     Blazzin

1545 Blend Pak
P.O.Box 458
Bloomfield, KY 40008-0458   502-252-8000
          Fax: 502-252-8001 www.blendpak.com
Processor and contract packaging of dry ingredients including breadings, batters, seasonings, marinades, forzen desserts, baking mixes and low carb pancake batters, muffins and seasoned cooking mixes.
     President: Dan Sutherland
     VP: Sue Sutherland
     R&D: Linda Mikels
     Quality Controll: Rob Elkin
     Public Relations: Vickie Byrnes
     Plant Manager: Matt Elder
Estimated Sales: $5-10 Million
Number Employees: 20-49
Type of Packaging: Food Service, Private Label, Bulk
Brands:
     Blend Pak
     Bloomfield Farms
     Pier Fresh

1546 Blendco
8 J M Tatum Industrial Dr
Hattiesburg, MS 39401-8341   601-544-9800
          Fax: 601-544-5634   800-328-3687
     csr@blendcoinc.com   www.blendcoinc.com
Dry food manufacturer, do customize blending and packaging as well as private labeling and contract packaging
     President: Charles N Mc Caffrey Jr
     Public Relations: Ken Hrdlica
     Purchasing Director: Charles Prescott
Estimated Sales: $10-20 Million
Number Employees: 20-49
Type of Packaging: Consumer, Food Service, Private Label, Bulk
Brands:
     EZY TIME
     HOME SENSATIONS

1547 Blendex Company
11208 Electron Dr
Jeffersontown, KY 40299-3875   502-267-1003
          Fax: 502-267-1024   800-626-6325
     sales@blendex.com   www.blendex.com
Breadings, seasonings, flavors and marinades
     President: Jacquelyn Bailey
     CEO: Ronald Pottinger
     CEO: Ronald W Pottinger
     VP Research/Development: Jordan Stivers
     Chief Marketing Officer: Olin Cook
     VP Operations: Wayne McDowell
Estimated Sales: $10-20 Million
Number Employees: 50-99

1548 Blenheim Bottling Company
N Highway 301 & I-95
Hamer, SC 29547   843-774-0322
          Fax: 843-774-4018   800-270-9344
                    blenheimga@aol.com
Jamaican ginger ale
     President: Alan Schafer
     CEO: Mackie Hayes
     Sales Director: Sheila McDowell
Estimated Sales: $2.5-5 Million
Number Employees: 5-9
Brands:
     Blenheim

1549 Blessed Herbs
109 Barre Plains Rd
Oakham, MA 01068-9675   508-882-3839
          Fax: 508-882-3755   800-489-4372
     info@blessedherbs.com   www.blessedherbs.com
Manufacturer, importer and exporter of organic and wildcrafted dried herbs, extracts, formulas and tablets; also, echinacea angustifolia root; exporter and importer of dried herbs
     Co-Founder: Michael Volchok
     Co-Founder: Martha Volchok
     Marketing Director: Shalom Volchok
Estimated Sales: $500,000-$1 Million
Number Employees: 5-9
Sq. footage: 6000
Type of Packaging: Consumer, Bulk

1550 Bletsoe's Cheese
8281 3rd Ln
Marathon, WI 54448-9522   715-443-2526
                    Fax: 715-443-6407
Cheese
     President: David Bletsoe
     Marketing Director: Bonnie Bletsoe
Estimated Sales: $5-10 Million
Number Employees: 10-19
Brands:
     Bletsoe's Cheese

1551 Bliss Brothers Dairy, Inc.
P.O.Box 2288
Attleboro, MA 02703-0039   508-222-2884
          Fax: 508-226-6320   800-622-8789
                    www.blissdairy.com
Manufacturers of ice cream, frozen yogurt, sherbert, sorbet, and ice cream mixes
     President: David Bliss
Estimated Sales: $1-2.5 Million
Number Employees: 50-99

1552 Blissfield Canning Company
PO Box 127
Blissfield, MI 49228-0127   517-486-3815
                    Fax: 517-486-4032
Canning
     President: George Waigle
     VP: Jerry Roessler
Estimated Sales: $2.5-5 Million
Number Employees: 20-49

1553 Bloch & Guggenheimer
P.O.Box 850
Hurlock, MD 21643-0850   410-943-4933
          Fax: 410-943-4729   800-541-2809
                    www.bgfoods.com
Roasted peppers, pickles, relishes, pickled cauliflower, pickled onions, pickled peppers, spices
     CFO: Robert C Cantwell
     CEO: David L Wenner
     VP Operations: Jim DePrima
Estimated Sales: $50-100 Million
Number Employees: 100-249
Brands:
     Ac'cent
     B&G
     Joan of Arc
     Ortega
     Polaner
     Red Devil
     Regina
     Vermont Maid

1554 (HQ)Blommer Chocolate Company
600 W Kinzie St
Chicago, IL 60654-5585   312-226-7700
          Fax: 312-226-4141   800-621-1606
                    www.blommer.com
Processor and exporter of chocolate ingredients for the bakery, dairy and confectionery industries including milk and dark chocolate, confectioner and pastel coatings, cookie drops, chocolate liquor, cocoa butter, cocoa powder, icecream ingredients, etc
     CFO: Linda Melampy
     VP: Rich Blommer
Estimated Sales: $500 Million +
Number Employees: 358
Sq. footage: 500000
Type of Packaging: Bulk

1555 Blommer Chocolate Company
1101 Blommer Dr
East Greenville, PA 18041-2140   215-679-4472
          Fax: 215-679-4196   800-825-8181
     klhicks@uc.blommer.com   www.blommer.com
Manufacturer of chocolate
     President: Peter Blommer
Estimated Sales: Less than $500,000
Number Employees: 100-249
Type of Packaging: Bulk
Other Locations:
     Chicago IL
     Union City CA

1556 Bloomer Candy Company
2200 Linden Ave.
Po Box 905
Zanesville, OH 43702-0905   740-452-7501
      Fax: 740-452-7865   800-452-7501
            feedback@bloomercandy.com
                  www.bloomercandy.com
Manufacturer and wholesaler/distributor of choco-
late candy
      President: Bill Barry
      VP Sales: Bob Barry
Estimated Sales:$20-50 Million
Number Employees: 100-249
Type of Packaging: Food Service, Private Label,
Bulk
Brands:
      STAR
      STARLINE SWEETS

1557 Bloomfield Bakers
10711 Bloomfield St
Los Alamitos, CA 90720-2503   562-594-4411
      Fax: 562-742-0408   800-594-4111
            info@bloomfieldbakers.com
                  www.bloomfieldbakers.com
Broker of dairy/deli products; serving food proces-
sors; manufacturers of cookies
      President: Sam Calderon
      Owner/CEO: William Ross
      National Sales Manager: John Gutteridge
      Office Manager: Susanne Decando
Estimated Sales:$5-10 Million
Number Employees: 850
Sq. footage: 80000
Type of Packaging: Private Label

1558 Bloomington Brewing Company
1795 E 10th St
Bloomington, IN 47408-3975   812-323-2112
                  Fax: 812-333-3200
Processor of ale and stout
      Manager: Michael Fox
      CFO: Lennie Busch
      Marketing Director: Sera Shikh
Number Employees: 1-4
Parent Co: One World Enterprises
Type of Packaging: Consumer, Food Service, Bulk
Brands:
      Bloomington Brewing
      Quarrymen Pale

1559 Bloomsberry & Co
92 Jackson St
Salem, MA 01970   978-745-9100
      Fax: 978-745-9150   800-745-5154
            sales@bloomsberry.com   www.bloomsberry.com
chocolates
      President/Owner: Paul Pruett
      VP: Kerry Francis
Number Employees: 5

1560 Blossom Farm Products
545 State Rt 17 # 2003
Ridgewood, NJ 07450-2035   201-493-2626
      Fax: 201-493-2666   800-729-1818
            kblossom@rcn.com
Processor, importer and exporter of dairy products
including milk powders, dry blends, whey,
caseinates, lactose, butter fats, etc.
      Manager: Kathy Oviedo
      VP: Paul Podell
      Operations Manager: Kathy Oviedo
Number Employees: 5-9
Type of Packaging: Consumer, Food Service, Bulk

1561 (HQ)Blount Seafood Corporation
630 Currant Rd
Fall River, MA 02720-4713   774-888-1300
      Fax: 774-888-1399   info@blountseafood.com
                  www.blountseafood.com
Processor of frozen seafood products including
chopped clams, lobster bisque, clam chowder, meat
and hearty soups.
      President: F Nelson Blount
      Marketin: David Vittorio
      VP Sales/Marketing: Bob Sewald
      Operations: Jonathan Areno
      Purchasing: Ed Sheehan
Estimated Sales:$20-50 Million
Number Employees: 100-249
Type of Packaging: Consumer, Food Service, Pri-
vate Label, Bulk
Brands:
      BLOUNT

GOURMET STUFFED CLAMS
POINT JUDITH
SAMS CLAMS
WHITE CAP

1562 Blue Bell Creameries
P.O.Box 1807
Brenham, TX 77834-1807   979-836-7977
      Fax: 979-830-7398   www.bluebell.com
Manufacturer of ice milk mix, ices, ice cream and
frozen yogurt
      President/CEO: Paul Kruse
      CEO: Paul W Kruse
Number Employees: 1,000-4,999
Type of Packaging: Consumer, Food Service
Other Locations:
      Sylacauga AL
      Broken Arrow OK
      Brenham TX
Brands:
      Blue Bell

1563 (HQ)Blue California Company
30111 Tomas
Rancho Santa Margarita, CA 92688-2929 949-635-1991
            Fax: 949-635-1988
            info@bluecal-ingredients.com
                  www.bluecal-ingredients.com
Manufacturer of botanical extracts and specialty in-
gredients
      President: Steven Chen
      Quality Control Manager: Carl Lai
      VP Sales/Marketing: Cecilia McCollum
Estimated Sales:$ 10 - 20 Million
Number Employees: 5-9
Other Locations:
      Rockaway NJ

1564 Blue Chip Group
432 W 3440 S
Salt Lake City, UT 84115-4228   801-263-6667
      Fax: 801-269-9666   800-878-0099
            customerservice@bluechipgroup.net
                  www.bluechipgroup.net
Processor of milk drinks including tofu, rice and soy.
Also health food additives, wheat gluten, dough
enhancers, dry food mixes, baking mixes and leci-
thin granules and powders. Custom blending and
packaging also available
      President: Philip Augason
      CEO: Jacqueline Augason
      R&D: Jeff Lund
      Quality Control: Jeff Olsen
      Sales: Jeffery Augason
      Prouction: Jeff Hatch
      Purchasing: Mark Augason
Estimated Sales:$5 Million
Number Employees: 20-49
Number of Brands: 16
Number of Products: 160
Sq. footage: 17500
Type of Packaging: Consumer, Food Service, Pri-
vate Label, Bulk
Brands:
      BLUE CHIP BAKER
      BLUE CHIP GROUP
      MORNING MOO'S
      SWISS WHEY D'LITE

1565 Blue Crab Bay Company
29368 Atlantic Dr
Melfa, VA 23410-3354   757-787-3602
      Fax: 757-787-3430   800-221-2722
            baybeyond@esva.net   www.bluecrabbay.com
Processor and exporter of Bloody Mary mixes, sea-
food soups, seasonings, snacks, preserves, crab
meat; sea salt, and sweet potato chips
      President: Pamela Barefoot
      Treasurer: Dawn Colona
Estimated Sales:$1-3 Million
Number Employees: 10-19
Sq. footage: 12400
Parent Co: Bay Beyond
Type of Packaging: Consumer
Brands:
      Barnacles Snack Mix
      Blue Crab Bay
      Crab House Nuts
      Salmonberry
      Sting Ray Bloody Mary Mixer
      Watts Island Trading

1566 Blue Crab Bay Company
29368 Atlantic Dr
Melfa, VA 23410-3354   757-787-3602
      Fax: 757-787-3430   800-221-2722
            sales@bluecrabbay.com   www.bluecrabbay.com
Specialty foods
      President: Pamela Barefoot
      Public Relations: Susan Tyler
Estimated Sales:$5-9.9 Million
Number Employees: 10-19
Sq. footage: 24000
Type of Packaging: Private Label
Brands:
      BARNACLES®
      CRAB HOUSE CRUNCH™
      CRAB HOUSE NUTS®
      SEA SALT NUTS™
      SHUCKERS™
      SKIPJACKS™
      STING RAY®

1567 Blue Diamond Growers
1802 C Street
Sacramento, CA 95814   916-442-0771
      Fax: 916-446-8461   feedback@bdgrowers.com
                  www.bluediamond.com
Processor, grower and exporter of almonds,
macadamians, pistachios and hazelnuts. Two thousand almond products in many cuts, styles, sizes and
shapes for use in confectionery, bakery, dairy and
processed foods. In house R/D for customproducts
      President/CEO: Douglas Youngdahl
      CFO: Robert Donovan
Estimated Sales:$709 Million
Number Employees: 1100
Type of Packaging: Consumer, Food Service, Private Label, Bulk
Brands:
      ALMOND BREEZE
      ALMOND TOPPERS
      BLUE DIAMOND
      BLUE DIAMOND ALMONDS
      BLUE DIAMOND HAZELNUT
      BLUE DIAMOND MACADAMIAS
      BREEZE
      NUT THINS
      SMOKEHOUSE

1568 Blue Dog Bakery
1210 E Shelby St # D
Seattle, WA 98102-3854   206-323-6958
      Fax: 206-666-3835   888-749-7229
            BlueDog@bluedogbakery.com
                  www.bluedogbakery.com
Company produces a variety of premium, natural,
low fat dog biscuits and treats.
      President/Owner: Margot Kenly
Estimated Sales:$ 1 - 3 Million
Number Employees: 1-4
Type of Packaging: Private Label
Brands:
      Mariner Biscuits
      Original Sesame Low Fat Crackers
      Parmesan Low Fat Crackers
      Sweet Onion Low Fat Crackers
      Sweet Pepper Low Fat Crackers

1569 Blue Gold Mussels
42 Spring Street
Suite 40
Newport, RI 02840-2979   508-993-2635
                  Fax: 508-994-9508
Processor of fresh and frozen mussel products and
calamari salad
      Director Marketing: Joe Jeffrey
Type of Packaging: Consumer, Food Service, Pri-
vate Label
Brands:
      Blue Gold

1570 Blue Grass Dairy Foods
1117 Cleveland Ave
Glasgow, KY 42141-1011   270-651-2146
      Fax: 270-651-8844   www.bluegrassdairy.com
Dairy and nondairy foods
      CEO: Billy Joe Williams
      Plant Manager: Mike Caron
Estimated Sales:$10-24.9 Million
Number Employees: 50-99

1571 Blue Grass Quality Meat
P.O.Box 17658
Covington, KY 41017-0658   859-331-7100
                         Fax: 859-331-4273
                    www.bluegrassqualitymeats.com
Manufacturer of smoked meats and sausage
    President: Paul Rice
Estimated Sales: $10-24.9 Million
Number Employees: 50-99
Type of Packaging: Consumer, Food Service, Private Label, Bulk

1572 Blue Hills Spring WaterCompany
134 Penn St
Quincy, MA 02169-7599   617-472-4200
         Fax: 617-770-2720 www.monadnock.com
Bottled water
    President: Mike Verachi
    COO: Mark Okum
Estimated Sales: $2.5-5 Million
Number Employees: 50-99
Brands:
    Monadnock Mountain Spring Water

1573 Blue Jay Orchards
125 Plumtrees Rd
Bethel, CT 06801-3102   203-748-0119
    Fax: 203-748-4814 www.bluejayorchardsct.com
Processor of apple butter, sauce and chutney; also, pear butter
    President: Paul Patterson
    VP: Mary Patterson
Estimated Sales: $5-10 Million
Number Employees: 5-9
Sq. footage: 10000
Type of Packaging: Consumer, Private Label
Brands:
    Blue Jay Orchards

1574 Blue Lakes Trout Farm
133 Warm Creek Rd
Jerome, ID 83338   208-734-7151
                 Fax: 208-733-0325
Rainbow trout

Estimated Sales: $2.5-5 Million
Number Employees: 20-49
Type of Packaging: Consumer, Food Service
Brands:
    GREENE'S

1575 Blue Marble Brands
96 Executive Avenue
Edison, NJ 08817   732-650-9905
    Fax: 732-650-9969 www.bluemarblebrands.com
organic, natural, specialty, ethnic and functional foods.

1576 Blue Moon Foods
568 N Main Street
White River Junction, VT 05001-7026 802-295-1165
                         Fax: 802-295-2553
Ice cream and frozen desserts.
    President: John Donaldson
Estimated Sales: $440,000
Number Employees: 7
Brands:
    Blue Moon Tea

1577 Blue Mountain Flavors
4000 Commerce Dr
Kinston, NC 28504-7906   252-522-1544
    Fax: 252-522-2599 800-522-1544
         bluemtnflavors@earthlink.net
         www.bluemountainflavors.com
Manufacturer of savory flavors for the food industry, also contract manufacturing and packaging
    President: William Baugher PhD
    Corporate Secretay/Treasurer: Teresa Baugher
    Quality Control: Margaret Jones
    Customer Service: Maureen Suggs
    Plant Manager: Laura Lassiter
Estimated Sales: $3 Million
Number Employees: 13
Number of Products: 150
Sq. footage: 30000
Parent Co: Blue Mountain Enterprises
Type of Packaging: Private Label, Bulk

1578 Blue Mountain Vineyards
7627 Grape Vine Dr
New Tripoli, PA 18066-3726   610-298-3068
Fax: 610-298-8616 info@bluemountainwine.com
                 www.bluemountainwine.com

Wines
    President/Owner: Joseph Greff
    VP: Vickie Greff
Estimated Sales: $2.5-5 Million
Number Employees: 10-19

1579 (HQ)Blue Pacific Flavors & Fragrances
1354 Marion Ct
City of Industry, CA 91745-2418   626-934-0099
    Fax: 626-934-0089 800-248-7499
    bpflavors@aol.com www.bluepacificflavors.com
Basic manufacturer of natural flavors, extracts, essences and functional ingredients to the beverage, dairy, confectionery, baking and pharmaceutical industries
    President: Donald Wilkes
Estimated Sales: $ 10 - 20 Million
Number Employees: 20-49
Sq. footage: 40000
Type of Packaging: Food Service, Private Label, Bulk
Other Locations:
    Blue Pacific Asia
    Malaysia
    Blue Pacific China
    Beijing, China
    Blue Pacific Korea
    Seoul, Korea
Brands:
    Cafe Extract
    Instacafe
    Naturessence
    Sun-Ripened
    Synature

1580 Blue Planet Foods, Inc.
P.O.Box 2178
Collegedale, TN 37315-2178   423-396-3145
    Fax: 423-396-3479 877-396-3145
         sales@blueplanetfoods.net
         www.blueplanetfoods.net
Manufacturer of grain based products, granola, nutrition and granola bar components, bread bases and nutritional fillers; exporter of granola products
    President/CFO: Deris Bagli
    Sales Director/Manager: Deris Bagli
    Industrial/Co-Packaging Sales Assistant: Sherry Poole
    Plant Manager: Frank Park
Estimated Sales: $100 Million
Number Employees: 250-499
Number of Products: 5
Sq. footage: 250000
Parent Co: McKee Foods Corporation
Type of Packaging: Consumer, Food Service, Private Label, Bulk

1581 Blue Ribbon Dairy
827 Exeter Ave
Exeter, PA 18643-1728   570-655-5579
                         Fax: 570-655-5637
Ice cream
    President: Ken Sorick
Estimated Sales: $5-10 Million
Number Employees: 10-19

1582 Blue Ribbon Meat Company
P.O.Box 633
Sparks, NV 89432-0633   775-358-8116
    Fax: 775-358-0992 www.blueribbonmeat.com
Processor and wholesaler/distributor of meat; serving the food service market.
    Owner: Scott Taylor
    Owner: Aaron Taylor
Estimated Sales: $20-50 Million
Number Employees: 20-49

1583 Blue Ribbon Meats
3316 W 67th Pl
Cleveland, OH 44102-5243   216-631-8850
                         Fax: 216-631-8934
Meats
    President: Albert Radis
Estimated Sales: $28.6 Million
Number Employees: 100-249

1584 Blue Ribbon Meats
200 S Biscayne Blvd
Miami, FL 33131-2310   305-960-2244
    Fax: 305-888-3917 800-522-6115
         www.brmeatsinc.com

Processor and exporter of portion controlled ground beef products, steaks and chops
    VP: Ira Bregman
Estimated Sales: $20-50 Million
Number Employees: 100-249
Type of Packaging: Consumer, Food Service, Private Label, Bulk
Brands:
    BLUE RIBBON
    QUALITY CUTS

1585 Blue Ridge Farms
5115 S Millard Avenue
Chicago, IL 60632-3736   708-748-4405
    Fax: 773-581-9833 brfarms@aol.com
         www.blueridgefarms.com
Processor of gelatin and mousse.
    Vice President: Maggie Scherette
    Research & Development: Deepak Dhotre
    General Manager II Division: John Slafkosky
    Production Manager: E Martinez
Estimated Sales: $5-10 Million
Number Employees: 20-49
Parent Co: Blue Ridge Farms
Type of Packaging: Consumer
Brands:
    Ez Cuisine
    Grilled Line
    Home Meal Replacements
    Jashua's Kosher Items
    Mendel's Haymish Brand
    Ultra Plus Salads

1586 Blue Ridge Farms
3301 Atlantic Ave
Brooklyn, NY 11208-1946   718-827-9000
    Fax: 718-647-0052 www.blueridgefarms.com
Processor of specialty foods including salads, pickles, desserts and frozen foods.
    CEO: Andrew Themis
    CEO: Seymour Siegel
    Sales Manager: David Charif
Estimated Sales: $ 5 - 10 Million
Number Employees: 10-19
Sq. footage: 20000
Type of Packaging: Consumer, Food Service, Private Label, Bulk
Brands:
    Blue Ridge Farms
    CHLOE FARMS
    EZ CUISINE
    JOSHUA'S KOSHER KITCHEN
    TEXAS SUPERIOR MEATS
    THE COOKIE STORE

1587 Blue Ridge Farms
3301 Atlantic Ave
Brooklyn, NY 11208-1946   718-827-9000
    Fax: 718-647-0052 www.blueridgefarms.com
Condiments and relishes
    President: Dr Robert Wallace
    CEO: Seymour Siegel
    CEO: Seymour Siegel
Estimated Sales: $ 50-100 Million
Number Employees: 250-499
Brands:
    Chloe

1588 Blue Ridge Poultry
145 Oneta Street
Athens, GA 30601-1838   706-546-6767
Processor of fresh and frozen poultry including turkey; wholesaler/distributor of poultry and eggs
    President: Robert Harris
Estimated Sales: $ 1 - 3 Million
Number Employees: 5-9
Sq. footage: 4500
Type of Packaging: Consumer

1589 Blue Ridge Tea & Herb Company
26 Woodhull St
Brooklyn, NY 11231-2643   718-625-3100
    Fax: 718-935-1874 pr@blueridgetea.com
         www.blueridgetea.com
Custom herbal and teabag formulations for private label. Also sales agent for teabags with ten vitamins; flavored
    President: Roger Rigolli
    Vice President: Paulette Rigolli
Estimated Sales: $4.5 Million est.
Type of Packaging: Private Label
Brands:
    Blue Ridge Teas

1590 Blue Runner Foods
P.O.Box 207
Gonzales, LA 70707-0207   225-647-3016
                    Fax: 225-647-4017
customerservice@bluerunnerfoods.com
www.bluerunnerfoods.com
Processor and canner of Cajun and Creole creamed
beans, peas and heat and serve entrees
   Manager: Sarah Muller
Estimated Sales: $5-10 Million
Number Employees: 20-49
Type of Packaging: Consumer, Food Service
Brands:
   Blue Runner

1591 Blue Sky Natural Beverage Company
510 Don Gaspar Avenue
Santa Fe, NM 87505-2626   505-995-9761
   Fax: 505-982-4004 heather@bleuskysoda.com
www.blueskysoda.com
Manufacturer and exporter of natural and energy so-
das; also sparkling and artesian drinking water
   President/CEO: Robert Black
   Executive VP/CFO: Mike Rising
   VP Sales: Frank McGuinn
Estimated Sales: $10+ Million
Number Employees: 7
Brands:
   Blue Sky
   Blue Sky Artesian Water
   Blue Sky Natural Soda
   True Seltzer

1592 Blue Smoke Salsa
119 E Main St
Ansted, WV 25812   304-658-3800
   Fax: 304-658-5400 888-725-7298
orders@bluesmokesalsa.com
www.bluesmokedsalsa.com
Jams and jellys, barbecue sauces, sparkling cider,
honey, gourmet mustards, specialty butters, pickles,
marinades and sauces, salsa, hot and spicy foods,
seasonings, and dry mixes
   President/Owner: Robin Hildebrand
Number Employees: 7

1593 Blue Wave Seafoods
PO Box 20
Port Mouton, NS B0T 1T0
Canada   902-683-2044
                    Fax: 902-683-2366
Processor of fresh and frozen groundfish and shell-
fish
   President: Sylvain D'Eon
   CEO: Sylvain D'Eon
   Marketing: Sylvain D'Eon
Type of Packaging: Consumer, Food Service, Pri-
vate Label, Bulk

1594 Blue Willow Tea Company
4059 Emery Street
Emeryville, CA 94608-3601   510-420-5777
                    800-328-0353
info@bluewillowtea.com
www.bluewillowtea.com
Manufacturer of teas
   President/CEO: Lynn Mallard
Estimated Sales: Under $500,000
Number Employees: 5-9
Brands:
   BLUE WILLOW
   WU WEI

1595 BlueWater Seafoods
1640 Brandon Crescent
Lachine, QC H8T 2N1
Canada   514-637-1171
   Fax: 514-637-5250 888-560-2539
www.bluewaterfish.com
Manufacturer of frozen seafood including fish cakes,
sticks and fillets, fish and chips, cod, sole, pollack,
shrimp, haddock and breaded scallops
   Sales/Marketing Director: Guy Emard
Number Employees: 225
Parent Co: Gortons USA
Type of Packaging: Consumer, Food Service

1596 Blueberry Hill Foods
7 Zane Grey St
El Paso, TX 79906-5213   915-779-8807
   Fax: 915-779-8181 800-451-8664
sales@blueberryhillfoods.com
www.blueberryhillfoods.com
Manufacturer of confectioneries, jaw breakers,
jellyies and more
   SVP Sales/Marketing: Scott Frey
   National Sales Manager: Jim Kelm
Estimated Sales: $ 10 - 20 Million
Number Employees: 10-19
Brands:
   ARBOR
   BLUEBERRY HILL
   BRADFORD FINE CANDIES
   SIMPLY SMART

1597 (HQ)Blueberry Store
P.O.Box 322
Grand Junction, MI 49056-0322   269-637-6322
   Fax: 269-434-6997 877-654-2400
jvannatter@blueberries.com
www.theblueberrystore.com
Manufacturer of all natural blueberry preserve, blue-
berry salsa, blueberry BBQ sauce, blueberry juice,
chocolate covered blueberries, blueberry syrup,
blueberry mustard, blueberry vinegar and chutney
   CEO: Jennifer Montgomery
   CFO: Jeff Van Natter
Estimated Sales: $300,000-500,000
Number Employees: 1-4
Number of Products: 20
Parent Co: Michigan Blueberry Growers Associa-
tion

1598 Bluebird
P.O.Box 378
Peshastin, WA 98847-0378   509-548-1700
                    Fax: 509-548-0288
Manufacturer and exporter of apples and pears
   President: Ron Gonvales
Estimated Sales: $35 Million
Number Employees: 500-999
Brands:
   Blue Bird
   Skookum

1599 Bluebird Restaurant
19 N Main St
Logan, UT 84321-4542   435-752-3155
Candy and confectionery
   Owner: Ansheng Xu
Estimated Sales: $1-2.5 Million
Number Employees: 20-49

1600 Bluegrass Brewing Company
3929 Shelbyville Rd
St Matthews, KY 40207-3120   502-899-7070
   Fax: 502-899-7051 pathagan@bbcbrew.com
www.bbcbrew.com
Brewer of ale, stout and lager
   Owner: Pat Hagan
Estimated Sales: $10-20 Million
Number Employees: 50-99
Type of Packaging: Consumer, Food Service, Bulk
Brands:
   ALTBIER
   AMERICAN PALE ALE
   BLUEBIRD RESTAURANT
   DARK STAR PORTER
   NUT BROWN ALE

1601 Bluepoint Bakery
1721 E 58th Ave
Denver, CO 80216-1505   303-298-1100
   Fax: 303-298-9797 sales@bluepointbakery.com
www.bluepointbakery.com
Bakery products
   President: Fred Bramhall
Estimated Sales: $20-50 Million
Number Employees: 50-99

1602 Blumenhof Vineyards-Winery
P.O.Box 30
Dutzow, MO 63342-0030   636-433-2245
   Fax: 636-433-5224 800-419-2245
info@blumenhof.com www.blumenhof.com
Wines
   President: Mark Blumenberg
Estimated Sales: $1-2.5 Million
Number Employees: 10-19

1603 Blundell Seafoods
11351 River Road
Richmond, BC V6X 2Z6
Canada   604-270-3300
   Fax: 604-270-6513 www.blundellseafoods.com
Processor and exporter of fresh and frozen salmon
and wall fish
   Manager: Bill Leung
Number Employees: 50-99
Type of Packaging: Consumer, Food Service, Pri-
vate Label, Bulk

1604 Bo-Ling's Products
9000 Bond Street
Overland Park, KS 66214-1723   913-888-8223
Vegetarian, Chinese curry
Estimated Sales: Less than $500,000
Number Employees: 1-4

1605 Boar's Head Provision Company
24 Rock St
Brooklyn, NY 11206-3812   718-417-3600
   Fax: 718-417-0504 www.boarshead.com
Processor of premium deli meats and cheeses.
Number Employees: 100-249
Type of Packaging: Consumer, Food Service

1606 Boar's Head Provisions Company
17 Parkway Pl
Edison, NJ 08837-3717   732-225-3111
   Fax: 732-225-3748 800-794-7180
www.boarshead.com
Processor of premium deli meats and cheeses.
Estimated Sales: $ 1 - 3 Million
Number Employees: 5-9

1607 Boar's Head Provisions Company
P.O.Box 929
Forrest City, AR 72336-0929   870-630-1638
   Fax: 870-630-0274 www.boarshead.com
Gourmet meat and poultry products.
   Manager: Ken Bosnert
Estimated Sales: $100+ Million
Number Employees: 500-999

1608 Boar's Head Provisions Company
1950 Industrial Rd
Petersburg, VA 23805-1100   804-733-7100
   Fax: 804-863-1409 www.boarshead.com
Processor of premium deli meats and cheeses.
   Plant Manager: Rachelle Harris
Estimated Sales: $100+ Million
Number Employees: 250-499

1609 Boar's Head Provisions Company
2905 Wurtsboro Lane
Holland, MI 49424-8528   616-738-7549
   Fax: 616-394-4866 www.boarshead.com
Premium deli meats, cheeses and condiments.
Number Employees: 450
Sq. footage: 180000

1610 Boar's Head Provisions Company
P.O.Box 277
Jarratt, VA 23867-0277   434-535-0129
   Fax: 434-535-8255 www.boarshead.com
Premium deli meats and cheeses, sausage.
   Plant Manager: Jeff Szymanski

1611 (HQ)Boar's Head Provisions Company
7025 Professional Pkwy E
Sarasota, FL 34240-8412   941-907-4192
   Fax: 941-907-3981 888-884-2627
www.boarshead.com
Processor of premium deli meats and cheeses.
   Owner: Robert Fox
   CEO: Robert Martin
   CFO: Alex Baruch
   Director Marketing: RuthAnn LaMore
Estimated Sales: $300,000-500,000
Number Employees: 1-4
Type of Packaging: Consumer
Brands:
   BOAR'S HEAD

1612 Boardman Foods
P.O.Box 786
Boardman, OR 97818-0786   541-481-3000
                    Fax: 801-881-8999
debbieradie@boardmanfoodsinc.com
www.boardmanfoodsinc.com

Processor of onions including IQF and peeled
President: Brian Maag
Operations: Debbie Radie
Quality Control: Deanna Goodeve
VP Sales: Thomas Flaherty
Operations Manager: Debbie Radie
Estimated Sales: $20-50 Million
Number Employees: 100-249
Type of Packaging: Bulk

1613 Bob Evans Farms
200 N Wolcott Street
Hillsdale, MI 49242-1762   517-437-3349
www.bobevans.com
Manufacturer of fresh sausage, refrigerated mashed
potatoes and side dishes and frozen breakfast
Manager: Dave Brummett
Manager: Tery Camp
Number Employees: 100
Type of Packaging: Consumer, Bulk
Other Locations:
Food Production Facilities
Hillsdale MI
Galva IL
Bidwell OH
Springfield OH
Xenia OH
Richardson TX
Sulphur Springs TX
Distribution Center
Springfield OH
Brands:
BOB EVANS®
BOB EVANS® RESTAURANT
MIMIS CAFE
OWENS®

1614 (HQ)Bob Evans Farms
3776 South High Street
Columbus, OH 43207   614-491-2225
Fax: 614-492-4949   800-272-7675
www.bobevans.com
Manufacturer of fresh sausage, refrigerated mashed
potatoes and side dishes and frozen breakfast
President: Harvey Brownlee
Chairman, CEO: Stephen Davis
CFO: Tod Spornhauer
Estimated Sales: $1.75 Billion
Number Employees: 44,086
Type of Packaging: Consumer, Bulk
Brands:
BOB EVANS
BOB EVANS RESTAURANTS
MIMIS CAFE
OWENS

1615 Bob Evans Farms
1001 Sw 2nd Street
Galva, IL 61434-1605   309-932-2194
www.bobevans.com
Manufacturer of fresh sausage, refrigerated mashed
potatoes and side dishes and frozen breakfast
Plant Manager: David Swanson
Secretary/Vice President: Larry Beckwith
Number Employees: 62
Type of Packaging: Consumer, Bulk

1616 Bob Evans Farms
363 Green Valley Drive
Bidwell, OH 45614-9240   740-446-2612
www.bobevans.com
Manufacturer of fresh sausage, refrigerated mashed
potatoes and side dishes and frozen breakfast
Manager: Dave Morgan
Secretary/Manager: Jim Bush
Number Employees: 90
Type of Packaging: Consumer, Bulk

1617 Bob Evans Farms
2110 W Jefferson Street
Springfield, OH 45506-1122   937-324-3356
www.bobevans.com
Manufacturer of fresh sausage, refrigerated mashed
potatoes and side dishes and frozen breakfast
Manager: Roger Burnett
Number Employees: 50
Type of Packaging: Consumer, Bulk

1618 Bob Evans Farms
640 Birch Road
Xenia, OH 45385-7600   937-372-8067
www.bobevans.com
Manufacturer of fresh sausage, refrigerated mashed
potatoes and side dishes and frozen breakfast
Manager: Thomas Sefton

Number Employees: 7
Type of Packaging: Consumer, Bulk

1619 Bob Evans Farms
1403 E Lookout Drive
Richardson, TX 75082-3074
www.bobevans.com
Manufacturer of fresh sausage, refrigerated mashed
potatoes and side dishes and frozen breakfast
Project Manager: Ismael Martinez
Number Employees: 50
Type of Packaging: Consumer, Bulk

1620 Bob Gordon & Associates
4500 S Western Avenue
Chicago, IL 60609-3025   773-247-0588
Fax: 773-247-3418
Processor and importer of green and black olives,
maraschino cherries, pickled onions, pickled mush-
rooms and Greek pepperoncini
President: Roberta Gordon
Vice President: Aaron Spefeldt
VP of Sales: Marcel Seefeldt
Controller: James Gosling
Estimated Sales: $5-10 Million
Number Employees: 10-19
Type of Packaging: Food Service, Private Label,
Bulk
Brands:
Marquis
Splinter

1621 Bob's Candies
PO Box 3170
Albany, GA 31706-3170   229-430-8300
Fax: 229-430-8331   800-841-3602
info@bobscandies.coms   www.bobscandies.com
Peppermint candy and candy.
President: Gregory McCormack
VP: Julie Roth
VP Sales: Ed Hudson
Purchasing Director: Mary Helen Dykes
Estimated Sales: $20-50 Million
Number Employees: 500-999
Type of Packaging: Private Label
Brands:
BOBS CANDY CANES
BOBS SUGAR FREE
OLD TIMEY
SWEET STRIPES

1622 Bob's Custom Cuts
PO Box 6189
Bonnyville, AB T9N 2G8
Canada   780-826-2627
Fax: 780-826-2138
Processor of fresh and frozen beef, pork, lamb, elk,
jerky, deer, buffalo, wild boar, ostrich and game sau-
sage
President: Paulette Dargis
Plant Manager: Ken Wychopen
Number Employees: 10-19
Sq. footage: 9500
Parent Co: Dargis Land & Cattle
Type of Packaging: Consumer, Food Service, Pri-
vate Label, Bulk

**1623 (HQ)Bob's Red Mill Natural
Foods**
13521 SE Pheasant Ct
Milwaukie, OR 97222-1248   503-654-3215
Fax: 503-653-1339   800-349-2173
www.bobsredmill.com
Processor of milled whole grain flours, cereals and
corn meal; also, mixes, bean flour and fat replacers
President: Bob Moore
CEO: Dennis Gilliam
CFO: John Wagner
VP Sales/Marketing: Dennis Gilliam
Estimated Sales: $25-49.9 Million
Number Employees: 100-249
Sq. footage: 320000
Type of Packaging: Consumer, Food Service, Bulk
Brands:
Bob's Red Mill

1624 Bob's Texas Style Potato Chip
3500 S La Cometa
Goodyear, AZ 85338-3606   623-932-6200
www.poorebrothers.com

6 flavors of potato chips and snacks
CEO: Eric Kufel
COO: Terry McDaniel
CFO: Thomas Freeze
Sr VP Marketing: Steven Sklar
Estimated Sales: $100 Million
Parent Co: Poore Brothers

1625 Boboli International Inc
3439 Brookside Rd # 104
Stockton, CA 95219-1754   209-473-3507
Fax: 209-473-0492 bobint@mail.com
www.boboli-intl.com
Frozen and unfrozen bakery products, pizza crusts
President/CEO: George Visgilio
VP: Tom Wise
VP: Art Bray
Genral Manager: Rick Todd
Estimated Sales: $5-10 Million
Number Employees: 10-19
Type of Packaging: Food Service
Brands:
AMBRETTA
DUTCH CHOCK FACTORY
PATISSA
TULIP STREET BAKERY
VAN DIERMAN

1626 Boca Bons, Inc.
4240 NW 120th Ave
Coral Springs, FL 33065-7603   954-346-0494
Fax: 954-346-0497 800-314-2835
bocabons@aol.com   www.bocabons.com
Manufacturer and exporter of a certified kosher
chocolate that is a combination of a truffle, fudge,
and a brownie.
President: Susan Kanter
Estimated Sales: $1-3 Million
Number Employees: 20-49
Sq. footage: 5000
Type of Packaging: Consumer, Food Service, Pri-
vate Label, Bulk
Brands:
Boca Bons

1627 Boca Foods Company
901 Mayer Avenue
Madison, WI 53704-4256   608-285-6950
Fax: 608-285-6741 www.bocaburger.com
Manufacturer of meatless burgers and more
President: Kevin Scott
Estimated Sales: $20-50 Million
Number Employees: 100-249
Parent Co: Kraft Foods
Brands:
BOCA®

1628 Boca Grande Foods
3245 N Berkeley Lake Rd NW
Duluth, GA 30096-3054   770-622-1500
Fax: 770-814-0046   800-788-8026
customerservice@bocagrandefoods.com
Portion control packaging
President: Herb Sodel
Marketing: Mark Katz
Office Manager: Melinda England
Estimated Sales: $5-10 Million
Number Employees: 100-249
Type of Packaging: Bulk
Brands:
GRANDE GOURMET
POCO PAC

1629 Bocconcino Food Products
140 W Commercial Ave
Moonachie, NJ 07074-1703   201-933-7474
Fax: 201-933-1530
Processor of frozen pizza and pizza bagels including
regular and bite-size; exporter of pizza bagels
Owner: Frank Lagalia
VP: Eric Silbeerman
Office Manager: Fay Campisi
Production Manager: Dan D'Amico
Estimated Sales: $5-10 Million
Number Employees: 20-49
Sq. footage: 19000
Type of Packaging: Consumer, Food Service, Pri-
vate Label
Brands:
Bocconcino

1630 Bodacious Food Company
339 Gennett Dr
Jasper, GA 30143-1140   706-253-1153
          Fax: 706-253-1156   800-391-1979
          cathy@bodaciousfoods.com
          www.bodaciousfoods.com
Processor of cheese straws and shortbread, ginger-
bread, key lime, chocolate and sugar-free brownie
bites
    President: Cathy Cunningham
    Purchasing Manager: Dave Hays
Estimated Sales: $1.4 Million
Number Employees: 20-49
Sq. footage: 8000
Type of Packaging: Consumer
Brands:
    Geraldine's Bodacious

1631 Bodek Kosher Produce
1294 E 8th St
Brooklyn, NY 11230-5106   718-377-4163
          Fax: 718-377-0782   mail@bodek.com
          www.bodek.com
Grade A, California grown produce, strictly super-
vised from seedling to harvest to production under
the Central Rabbinical Congress, OU, and Rabbi
Gissinger.
    Owner: Jack Whyman
Estimated Sales: $1-$2.5 Million
Number Employees: 5-9

1632 Bodin Foods
704 Avenue D
New Iberia, LA 70560-0527   337-367-1344
          Fax: 337-364-4968   daniel@cajun-recipes.com
          www.cajun-recipes.com
Manufacturer of frozen Cajun foods, browning/sea-
soning sauce, pork boudin, shrimp boudin, crawfish
boudin, dressing mix, crawfish pies, meat pies,
shrimp and crabmeat pies, and crawfish and crab-
meat pies
    Owner: Dennis Higginebotham
    CEO: Madine Pacetti
Estimated Sales: $500,000
Number Employees: 5-9
Number of Brands: 2
Number of Products: 11
Sq. footage: 8545
Type of Packaging: Consumer, Food Service, Pri-
vate Label
Brands:
    Bodin's
    Brown Kwik
    Cajun Bites

1633 Body Ammo Research Center
3423 Investment Blvd # 3
Hayward, CA 94545-3821   510-259-1690
          Fax: 510-782-7815   800-346-2303
          customerservice@bodyammoproducts.com
          www.bodyammoproducts.com
Processor and exporter of energy food powder,
weight loss systems and health and nutritional supplements, including anabolic, joint rehab formulas,
etc
    Owner: Kai Wang
    Sales Manager/Consumer/Retail: Hence Singleton

    Sales Manager/Distribution: Robert Tyson
    Scientist: Cleve Phillips
Estimated Sales: $10-20 Million
Number Employees: 10-19
Sq. footage: 30000
Brands:
    ACTI VIN
    BODY AMMO

1634 Body Breakthrough
561 Acorn St # I
Deer Park, NY 11729-3600   631-243-2443
          Fax: 631-243-2464   800-874-6299
          trimaxx@earthlink.com
          www.bodybreakthrough.com
Processor and exporter of teas including herbal, di-
etary and antioxidant; also, weight loss aids
    President: Cori Lichter
    Executive Director: Glenn Lichter
Estimated Sales: $2.5-5 Million
Number Employees: 5-9
Sq. footage: 5000
Type of Packaging: Consumer, Private Label
Brands:
    ANTI OXIDANT EDGE

TRIM MAXX
YOHIMBE

1635 Bodyonics Limited
200 Adams Blvd
Farmingdale, NY 11735-6615   516-822-1230
          Fax: 516-822-1252 www.greatearth.com
Sports nutrition, vitamins, herbs and supplements.
    President: Mel Rich
    Sales/Marketing: Andy Fishman
Number Employees: 50-99

1636 Boeckman JJ Wholesale Meats
1218 N Keowee St
Dayton, OH 45404-1546   937-222-4679
Manufacturer of ham and bologna
    President: James Weller
Estimated Sales: $1-2.5 Million
Number Employees: 1-4
Type of Packaging: Consumer, Food Service, Pri-
vate Label, Bulk

1637 Boeger Winery
1709 Carson Rd
Placerville, CA 95667-5195   530-622-8094
          Fax: 530-622-8112   800-655-2634
sue@boegerwinery.com   www.boegerwinery.com
Wines
    President: Greg Boeger
    Vice President: Susan Boeger
    Sales Director: Carl Keinert
Estimated Sales: $2.5-5 Million
Number Employees: 20-49
Type of Packaging: Private Label

1638 Boehringer Ingelheim
39w879 Hoeweed Lane
Saint Charles, IL 60175-6979   630-377-5150
          Fax: 630-377-5150   tomgush@avenew.com
Organic mineral salts

1639 (HQ)Boekhout Farms
2592 Ridge Rd
Ontario, NY 14519-9503   315-524-4041
          Fax: 315-524-4041
Grower of peaches, plums, rhubarb and apples. Dis-
tributer of frozen fruits; raspberries, strawberries,
blackberries, blueberries, cherries, aplles, peaches
and rhubarb.
    President: William Schwarz
Estimated Sales: $10 Million
Number Employees: 1-4
Number of Brands: 1
Number of Products: 30
Sq. footage: 15900
Type of Packaging: Consumer, Private Label, Bulk
Brands:
    BOEKHOUT FARM

1640 Boesl Packing Company
2322 Belair Rd
Baltimore, MD 21213-1283   410-675-1071
          Fax: 410-327-4131
Manufacturer and packer of meat products including
smoked frankfurters, knockwurst, bologna, salami
and bacon; pig tails, neck bones and chitterlings;
sausage: hot, smoked and Polish
    Owner: Jeffery Burton
Estimated Sales: $5.6 Million
Number Employees: 20-49
Type of Packaging: Consumer

1641 Boetje Foods
2736 12th St
Rock Island, IL 61201-5330   309-788-4352
          Fax: 309-788-4365   877-726-3853
boetje1889@aol.com   www.boetjefoods.com
Processor of gourmet mustard
    President: Robert Kropp
    Treasurer: Dorothy Kropp
    General Manager: Will Kropp
    Production Manager: Stuart Soliz
Estimated Sales: $2.5-5 Million
Number Employees: 1-4
Sq. footage: 6000
Type of Packaging: Consumer, Food Service, Pri-
vate Label, Bulk
Brands:
    DUTCH BOY

1642 Bogdon Candy Company
2316 Troost Ave
Kansas City, MO 64108-2835   913-262-6425
          Fax: 913-262-6885   800-821-6641
info@bogdoncandy.com   www.bogdoncandy.com
Manufacturer of candy
    Founders/Owners: Bogdon Family
Estimated Sales: $ 3 - 5 Million
Number Employees: 40
Brands:
    BOGDON
    DOUBLE DIPS
    RECEPTION STICKS

1643 Bogdon Candy Company
2316 Troost Ave
Kansas City, MO 64108-2835   913-262-6425
          Fax: 913-262-6885   800-821-6641
info@bogdoncandy.com   www.bogdoncandy.com
Manufacturer of mint, lemon, orange and cinnamon
flavored candy sticks dipped in dark chocolate and
individually wrapped
    President: Mr. Bogdon
    Sales Manager: Bob Zender
Estimated Sales: $5-10 Million
Number Employees: 20-49
Type of Packaging: Consumer, Food Service, Private Label, Bulk

1644 Boggiatto Produce
P.O.Box 2266
Salinas, CA 93902-2266   831-424-4864
          Fax: 831-424-1974   produce@boggiatto.com
          www.boggiattoproduce.com
Processor of artichokes, broccoli, Brussels sprouts,
cabbage, celery, cilantro, squash, lettuce, romaine
lettuce hearts, kale, onions, leeks, peas, parsley,
beets, green beans, rapini, spinach, etc
    Owner: Michael Boggiatto
    Sales Manager: Kraig Kuska
    Sales: Don Day
Estimated Sales: $2.5-5 Million
Number Employees: 10-19
Type of Packaging: Consumer, Food Service
Brands:
    Boggiatto
    Garden Hearts

**1645 Boghosian Raisin Packing
Company**
P.O.Box 338
Fowler, CA 93625-0338   559-834-5348
          Fax: 559-834-1419 www.boghosianraisin.com
Processor of raisins
    Owner: Philip Boghosian
    Owner: Peter Boghosian
    Owner: Paul Boghosian
    Plant Manager: Richard Lokey
Estimated Sales: $10-20 Million
Number Employees: 50-99
Type of Packaging: Consumer, Bulk

1646 Bogland
300 Oak Street
Pembroke, MA 02359-1984   781-829-9549
          Fax: 781-829-9567   janbaird@costalclassics.com
Cranberry chutney, cranberry mustard, cranberry
grill sauce, cranberry cabernet vinaigrette, cranberry
orange marmalade, cranberry blueberry preserves,
Szechuan peanut sauce, margarita madness mustard,
port mustard, seafood mustard
    President: Jan Baird
Estimated Sales: $2.5-5 Million
Number Employees: 1-4
Brands:
    Bogland
    Bogland By the Sea
    Boglandish

1647 Bogle Vineyards
37783 County Road 144
Clarksburg, CA 95612-5009   916-744-1139
          Fax: 916-744-1187   info@boglewinery.com
          www.boglewinery.com
Wine
    President: Patty Bogle
    VP: Warren Bogle
    Marketing Manager: Christopher Catterton
    Public Relation Manager: Kristen Alling
    Winemaker: Christopher Smith
Estimated Sales: $2.5-5 Million
Number Employees: 10-19
Type of Packaging: Private Label

1648 Bohea Associates
400 Union Avenue
Brooklyn, NY 11211-3429   718-387-6034
                           Fax: 718-387-2040
   President: Diana Fong
Estimated Sales:$2,300,000
Number Employees: 8

1649 Bohemian Biscuit Company
258 Littlefield Avenue
South San Francisco, CA 94080-6922323-935-6667
          Fax: 650-952-2439 800-443-6737
                           jhsosnick@sosnick.com
Wholesaler/distributor and importer of candy includ-
ing sugar-free, gourmet chocolate, lollipops and
gummies
   President: Jeffrey Sosnick
   Sales Director: Wayne Sosnick
Estimated Sales:$30 Million
Number Employees: 50-99
Sq. footage: 35000
Parent Co: J. Sosnick & Son
Type of Packaging: Consumer, Food Service, Pri-
   vate Label, Bulk
Brands:
   Droste
   Ferrero
   Ghirardelli
   Haribo
   La Vosigienne
   Lindt
   Royal Flush
   Walkers

1650 Bohemian Brewery
94 E 7200 S
Midvale, UT 84047-1532   801-566-5474
                           Fax: 801-566-5321
              jpetras@bohemianbrewery.com
                 www.bohemianbrewery.com
Manufacturer of ale and lager
   Owner: Joe Petras
Estimated Sales:$ 20 - 50 Million
Number Employees: 20-49
Type of Packaging: Consumer, Food Service
Brands:
   Bohemian

**1651 Bohrer & Moore Packing
Company**
816 County Road 25a
Wapakoneta, OH 45895-7751   419-738-7719
                           Fax: 419-738-6883
Casein and milk protein
   Owner: Robert Kelly
Estimated Sales:$2.5-5 Million
Number Employees: 5-9

1652 Boisset America
2320 Marinship Way
Suite 140
Sausalito, CA 94965-2830   415-339-9393
          Fax: 415-979-0305 800-878-1123
              info@ boissetamerica.com
                 www.boissetamerica.com
Wines
   President: Jean Charles Boisset
   CFO: Kelley Nowrouzk
   VP: Alain Leonnet
   Marketing: Lisa Heisinger
   Sales: Raymond Nantel
   Operations: Alain Leonnet
Estimated Sales:$10-20 Million
Number Employees: 5-9
Brands:
   BOUCHARD AINE FILS
   Boisset Classic
   Boisset Mediterranee
   Charles De Fere
   Christophe Cellars
   Evoluna Estate
   Fog Mountain
   J MOREAU FILS
   Jean-Claude Boisset
   Joliesse Vineyards
   LES DOMAINES BERNARD
   Lyeth Estate
   Oceana Coastal
   Ropiteall
   Summerlake
   Vienot
   William Wheeler Winery

1653 Boissons Miami Pomor
704 Boulevard Guimond
Longueuil, QC J4G 1T5
Canada   450-677-3744
          Fax: 450-677-7826 877-977-3744
              administration@boissonsmiami.com
                 www.boissonsmiami.com
Processor of juices, concentrates and crystals
   Administration: Lise Huneault
   Administration: Yves Brisebois
   Administration: Andre Brisebois
Number Employees: 12
Sq. footage: 6750

1654 Boja's Foods
P.O.Box 602
Bayou La Batre, AL 36509-0602   251-824-4186
                           Fax: 251-824-7339
Crab meat stuffing
   Manager: Greg Malone
Estimated Sales:$5-9.9 Million
Number Employees: 20-49
Brands:
   Boja's
   Boja's Chef's Delight
   Paulines

1655 Bold Coast Smokehouse
224 County Rd
Lubec, ME 04652-3611   207-733-8912
          Fax: 207-733-8986 888-733-0807
   vinny@boldcoastsmokehouse.com www.rier.com
Processor of hot and cold smoked Atlantic salmon,
smoked salmon, smoked salmon pate and lox,
smoked trout pate, finnan haddie, smoked mackeral,
smoked salmon kabobs, graulax, smoked lobster
products, smoked mussels and smokescallops.
   President/Owner: Vinny Gartmayer
Estimated Sales:$ 1 - 3 Million
Number Employees: 5-9
Type of Packaging: Consumer, Private Label

1656 Bolner's Fiesta Products
426 Menchaca St
San Antonio, TX 78207-1295   210-734-6404
          Fax: 210-734-7866 info@fiestaspices.com
                 www.fiestaspices.net
Processor and importer of dehydrated vegetables,
liquid extracts and spices, herbs and seasonings, in-
cluding: bay leaves, cinnamon, cloves, cumin, sage,
nutmeg, oregano, paprika, onion salt, anise, caraway,
garlic, celery and mustardseeds, black pepper.
   President: Clifton Bolner
   CEO: Rosalie Bolner
   CFO: George Paz
   Marketing Director: Chris Bolner
   Sales Director: Michael Bolner
   Operations Manager: Tim Bolner
   Plant Manager: James Morris
Estimated Sales:$10-24.9 Million
Number Employees: 100-249
Type of Packaging: Consumer, Food Service, Pri-
   vate Label, Bulk
Brands:
   FIESTA
   LYNWOOD FARMS
   PAPA JOE'S
   RIVER ROAD
   SPICE CHOICE
   SPICE RANCH
   SPICE STAR

1657 Bolthouse Farms
7200 E Brundage Ln
Bakersfield, CA 93307-3099   661-366-7205
          Fax: 661-366-7289 800-467-4683
          raust@bolthouse.com www.bolthouse.com
   President/CEO: Andre Hdant
   VP: Tim McCorkle
   Marketing Director: Bryan Reese
   Sales Director: Tim McCorkle
Estimated Sales:$ 5 - 10 Million
Number Employees: 20-49
Brands:
   Earth Unt Farm
   Green Gaint

1658 Bombay Breeze SpecialtyFoods
Box 67019
Mississauga, ON L5L 5V4
Canada   416-410-2320
          Fax: 416-410-2320 bombaybreeze@usa.com
                 www.bombaybreeze.com

Exotic tropical fruit juices, jams, chutney, sauce, or-
ganic soups, and Indian curries.
   President: Raju Tripathi
Brands:
   SAHARA

1659 Bon Appetit Gourmet Foods
7863 W Mossy Cup St # 1
Boise, ID 83709-2987   208-345-0475
                           Fax: 208-384-5461
Distributor of frozen food.
   Owner: John Lee
Estimated Sales:$ 1 - 3 Million
Number Employees: 10-19

1660 Bon Secour Fisheries
P.O.Box 60
Bon Secour, AL 36511-0060   251-949-7411
          Fax: 251-949-6478 800-633-6854
              bonsec@bonsecourfisheries.com
                 www.bonsecourfisheries.com
Manufacturer, exporter and wholesaler of fresh and
frozen flounder, whiting, snapper, shrimp, oysters,
scallops, crawfish, snow, soft shell and king crab,
lobster, cod, catfish, tuna, grouper, pollock, shark,
mahi, talapia, etc.; alsoalligator meat.
   CEO: John Ray Nelson
   CFO/Secretary/Treasurer: B Frank Bailey
   Sales: Kenny Crawford
   Purchasing Director: Carl Haynes
Estimated Sales:$20-50 Million
Number Employees: 100-249
Sq. footage: 60000
Type of Packaging: Consumer, Food Service, Bulk
Brands:
   BON SECOUR
   NELSON'S

1661 Bon Ton Products
275 E Hintz Rd
Wheeling, IL 60090-6002   847-520-3102
                           Fax: 847-520-8396
Meat buyer, boxed beef and pork cuts.
   Manager: James Cristy
   Marketing Director: Dave Centino
Estimated Sales:$17 Million
Number Employees: 5-9

1662 Bonert's Slice of Pie
2727 S Susan St
Santa Ana, CA 92704-5817   714-540-3535
          Fax: 714-540-9615 susanm@bonertspies.com
                 www.bonertspies.com
Manufacturer of fruit, creme, meringue, no sugar
added, and. no top-ready to finish pies.
   CEO: Michael Bonert
   Sales Rep: Susan Mahoney
Estimated Sales:$ 5 - 10 Million
Number Employees: 5-9

1663 Bongard's Creameries
110 3rd Ave NE
Perham, MN 56573-1831   218-346-4680
                           Fax: 218-346-4684
Processor of dairy products including cheese and
whey
Number Employees: 100-249
Parent Co: Land O'Lakes
Type of Packaging: Consumer, Private Label

1664 Bongards Creameries
13200 County Road 51
Norwood, MN 55368-9743   952-466-5521
          Fax: 952-466-5556 800-877-6417
              customerservice@bongards.com
                 www.bongardcheese.com
Manufacturer of butter, cheese and whey powder
   President: Curtis Wolter
   CEO: Roger Engelman
   Sales Manager: Stu Kringen
Estimated Sales:$172 Million
Number Employees: 250-499
Type of Packaging: Private Label

1665 (HQ)Bongrain Cheese
400 S Custer Ave
New Holland, PA 17557-9220   717-355-8500
          Fax: 717-355-8561 www.bongrain.com
Cheese and cream cheese
   President: Frank Otis
   President: James Williams
   Marketing Director: Jon Gutknecht
   Purchasing Manager: Nancy Henry

Estimated Sales:$ 20 - 50 Million
Number Employees: 50-99
Brands:
  Aloutte
  Chaumes
  Creme De Brie
  Cremeux
  Gerard
  La Cheesierie
  Mamie
  New Hoolland
  Quaker
  Real Fresh
  Short Cuts
  St. Albray
  Tartare
  Ultra Delight
  Zausner

1666 Bongrain North America
International Boulevard
Suite 400
Mahwah, NJ 07495   201-512-8825
          Fax: 201-512-8718 bna1@aol.com
Processor of cheese and cheese products
  President/CFO: Tom Swartele
Number Employees: 1-4
Parent Co: Bongrain USA
Type of Packaging: Consumer, Food Service
Brands:
  Allouette
  Charrie
  Delico
  Fleur De Lait
  Isle de Francis
  Montracheti
  Real Fresh

1667 Bonjour
80 Berry Drive
Pacheco, CA 94553-5601   925-676-1444
          Fax: 925-676-3082 800-266-5687
Gourmet foods
  President: Frank Brady
  VP: Pamela Almassy
Estimated Sales:$2.5-5 Million
Number Employees: 20-49

1668 Bonnie Baking Company
P.O.Box 426
La Porte, IN 46352-0426
          219-362-4561
          Fax: 219-325-0030
Bread, rolls
  Manager: John West
Estimated Sales:$ 20 - 50 Million
Number Employees: 100-249

1669 Bonnie Doon Ice Cream Corporation
2941 Moose Trl
Elkhart, IN 46514-8230
          574-264-3390
          Fax: 574-264-6208
Manufacturer of ice cream
  President: Samuel Dugan II
  Vice President: Jim Otis
Estimated Sales:$ 10 - 20 Million
Number Employees: 20-49
Type of Packaging: Food Service, Bulk

1670 Bonnie's Ice Cream
21 Leaman Road
Paradise, PA 17562-9660   717-687-9301
  President: Lou Termini
Estimated Sales:$1-2.5 Million
Number Employees: 10-19

1671 Bonny Doon Vineyard
328 Ingalls St
Santa Cruz, CA 95060-5849   831-425-3625
          Fax: 831-425-3856
          grahmcru@bonnydoonvineyard.com
          www.bonnydoonvineyard.com
Wines
  General Manager: David Amadia
  Marketing Manager: Ted Pearson
  Controller-Operations: Jim Fullmer
  President/CEO: Randall Graham
Estimated Sales:$10 Million
Number Employees: 20-49
Type of Packaging: Private Label

1672 Bonterra Vineyard
12625 E Side Road
Hopland, CA 95449   707-744-7575
          Fax: 707-744-1844
Wines
Brands:
  Bonterra

1673 Boones Abattoir
100 Old Bloomfield Pike
Bardstown, KY 40004-2000   502-348-3668
          Fax: 502-348-4046 www.boonesbutchershop.com
Packer of processed beef and pork products
  President: Luel Boone
Estimated Sales:$6 Million
Number Employees: 20-49

1674 Booneway Farms
167 Glades Road
Berea, KY 40403-1369   859-986-2636
          Fax: 859-986-3583
Processor of mustards, hamburger marinades, jellies,
preserves, seasonings and spices
  President: Williams Arant, Jr.
Estimated Sales:$2.5-5 Million
Number Employees: 20-49
Type of Packaging: Private Label

1675 Boordy Vineyards
12820 Long Green Pike
Hydes, MD 21082-9541   410-592-5015
          Fax: 410-592-5385 wineinfo@boordy.com
          www.boordy.com
Wines
  President/Owner: Robert Deford
  Marketing Director: Susan Daniels
  Public Relations: Rory Calhoun
  Production Manager: Tom Burns
Estimated Sales:$2.5-5 Million
Number Employees: 10-19
Type of Packaging: Private Label
Brands:
  Boordy Vineyards

1676 Boothbay Region Lobsterman
97 Atlantic Ave
Boothbay Harbor, ME 04538-2220 207-633-4900
          Fax: 207-633-4077
Lobster
Estimated Sales:$ 3 - 5 Million
Number Employees: 10-19

1677 Boquet's Oyster House
6645 Highway 56
Chauvin, LA 70344-2630   504-594-5574
          Fax: 253-761-0504
Fresh, frozen, shucked oysters
  President: Lawrenece "Bouquet, Jr."

1678 Borden
P.O.Box 3047
Tulsa, OK 74101-3047   918-587-2471
          Fax: 918-582-4605 800-733-2230
Manufacturer of dairy products
  Sales Director: Joan Farmer
  General Manager: George Streetman
  Plant Manager: Dave Schirmer
Number Employees: 50-99
Parent Co: Suiza Dairy Group
Type of Packaging: Consumer, Bulk

1679 Borden Foods
2001 Polaris Parkway
Columbus, OH 43240-2000   614-233-3759
          Fax: 614-233-3701 www.prince.com
Manufacturer of dry pasta, jarred pasta sauce, dry
soups and boullion
  VP Quality/Purchasing: Lloyd Moberg
Parent Co: Suiza Dairy Group
Brands:
  PRINCE

1680 Borden's Bread
1771 Winnipeg Street
Regina, SK S4P 1G1
Canada   306-525-3341
          Fax: 306-522-5303
Manufacturer of baked goods including bread, rolls,
cakes, cookies, pies and pastries
  Co-Owner: Leif Ellefson
  Co-Owner: Ruth Ellefson
Type of Packaging: Consumer, Food Service

1681 Border Foods Inc
4065 J St SE
Deming, NM 88030-7164   575-546-8863
          Fax: 575-546-8676 888-737-7752
          customerservice@borderfoodsinc.com
          www.borderfoodsinc.com
Manufacturer of canned Mexican food including
green chile peppers, sauces and salsa.
  President: John Bowman
  Chief Financial Officer: Leslie Berriman
  Senior VP: Bob Gats
  SVP/Marketing & Sales: Bob Gats
  Customer Service: Dela King
Estimated Sales:$100-500 Million
Number Employees: 250-499
Sq. footage: 7000
Parent Co: Border Foods
Type of Packaging: Food Service, Private Label,
  Bulk
Other Locations:
  Basic American Foods
  Vacaville CA
Brands:
  CLASSIC CASSEROLE
  GOLDEN GRILL
  NATURE'S OWN
  POTATOE PEARLS
  QUICK START
  REDI SHRED
  REGIONAL RECIPE
  SANTIAGO

1682 (HQ)Border Foods Inc
1750 Valley View Ln
Suite 350
Farmers Branch, TX 75234-9028 972-406-3300
          Fax: 972-406-3390 888-737-7752
          customerservice@borderfoodsinc.com
          www.borderfoodsinc.com
Manufacturer of green chile pepper, jalapeno pepper,
and enchilada products.
  President: John Bowman
  Senior VP: Bob Gats
  SVP/Marketing & Sales: Bob Gats
  Director Sales Retail: Roy Eliasen
  Director Sales Foodservice East: Mose Munro
  Director Sales Foodservice West: Susan Westphal

  Director Sales Industrial: David Darling
  Manager Sales Industrial: Reuben Marin
Number Employees: 500-999
Sq. footage: 234000
Type of Packaging: Food Service
Other Locations:
  Border Foods Plant
  Deming NM
  Border Foods Plant
  Las Cruces NM
Brands:
  DOS AMIGOS
  RIO LUNA

1683 Border's Market
135 Trux St
Plymouth, OH 44865-1061   419-687-2634
Processor of beef, pork, veal and lamb
  Owner: Mike Bauer
  Owner: Sandy Bauer
  President: Mary Ganzhorn
Estimated Sales:$1-2.5 Million
Number Employees: 5-9
Type of Packaging: Consumer

1684 Bordoni Vineyards
RR 4
Box 885k
Vallejo, CA 94591-9802   707-642-1504
Wines
  President: Jim Bordoni
Estimated Sales:$5-10 Million
Number Employees: 1-4

1685 Borgattis Ravioli
632 E 187th St
Bronx, NY 10458   718-367-3799
          Fax: 718-367-2229 www.borgattis.com
Pasta
  Owner: Mario Borgatti
Estimated Sales:$1-2.5 Million
Number Employees: 1-4

1686 Borgnine Beverage Company
4355 Sepulveda Boulevard
Apt 215
Sherman Oaks, CA 91403-3961   818-501-5312
        Fax: 818-788-6096   borg9cs@aol.com
        www.borgininescoffesoda.com
Manufacturer of Coffee, soda
Number Employees: 1-4

1687 Borinquen Biscuit Corporation
PO Box 1607
Yauco, PR 00698-1607   787-856-3030
        Fax: 787-856-5339 www.prtc.net
Manufacturers of quality soda crackers, cookies and
biscuits.
        President: Antonio Rodriguez Zamora
        VP: Herberto Yordan Torres
        Purchasing Manager: Antonio Rodriguez Morales

Number Employees: 140
Sq. footage: 58000
Type of Packaging: Consumer, Private Label
Brands:
        Cien En Boca
        Florecitas
        Rica
        Royal Borinquen Export
        Vanilla Imperial

1688 Borinquen Macaroni Corporation
PO Box 3045
Yauco, PR 00698-3045   787-856-1450
        Fax: 787-856-5630   pexcelsior@coqui.net
                www.pastasexcelsior.com
Manufacturer of pasta: spaghetti, macaroni, lasagna,
elbow, ditali, shells and ziti
        President: Heberto Yordan-Torres
        GM: David Cabassa
Estimated Sales: $2.5-5 Million
Number Employees: 50-99
Type of Packaging: Private Label
Brands:
        Excelsior
        Pastas Exelsior

1689 Bornstein Seafoods
45 NE Harbor
Warrenton, OR 97146   503-861-1233
        Fax: 503-861-3229 www.bornstein.com
Processor of canned fish and fresh and frozen
dungeness crab
        President: Jay Bornstein
        Sales: Colin Bornstein
Number Employees: 5-9
Parent Co: Bornstein Seafoods
Type of Packaging: Consumer, Food Service
Brands:
        Pacific Best
        Stormy

1690 Bornstein Seafoods
1001 Hilton Ave
Bellingham, WA 98225-2908   360-734-7990
        Fax: 360-734-5732   doug@bornstein.com
                www.bornstein.com
Live, fresh and frozen seafood
        President: Jay Bornstein
        CEO: JAY Bornstein
        Marketing: Meyer Bornstein
Estimated Sales: $20-50 Million
Number Employees: 100-249
Brands:
        Bornstein

1691 Bornt Family Farms
2307 E Us Highway 98
Holtville, CA 92250-9543   760-356-1066
        Fax: 760-356-1066
Organic vegetables
        Owner: Alan Bornt
        CFO: Mary Bornt
        VP Marketing/Sales: John Prock
Estimated Sales: $20-50 Million
Number Employees: 50-99
Brands:
        Bornt Family Farms
        Ocean Organics

1692 Borra Vineyards
1301 E Armstrong Rd
Lodi, CA 95242-9423   209-368-2446
        Fax: 209-369-5116   info@borravineyards.com
                www.borrawinery.com

Manufacturer of wine
        Owner: Steve Borra Sr
        CEO: Beverly Borra
        VP Marketing: Gina Granlees
Estimated Sales: $ 1 - 3 Million
Number Employees: 1-4
Type of Packaging: Private Label
Brands:
        BORRA

1693 Borthwicks Flavors
330 Motor Pkwy # 102
Hauppauge, NY 11788-5117   631-273-6200
        Fax: 631-273-6346   800-255-6837
Flavors
Estimated Sales: $50-100 Million
Number Employees: 1-4

1694 Bos Smoked Fish Inc
1175 Patullo Avenue
Woodstock, ON N4S 7W3
Canada   519-537-5000
        Fax: 519-537-5522   bossmokedfish@bellnet.ca
Procesor and exporter of smoked herring, trout,
salmon, whitefish, mackerel fillets, mackerel, (various spices) marinated products
        VP: Klaas Bos
Type of Packaging: Consumer, Food Service, Private Label, Bulk

1695 Bosco Products
441 Main Road
Towaco, NJ 07082-1201   973-334-7534
        Fax: 973-334-2617   800-438-2672
boscomail@earthlink.net   www.boscoworld.com
Chocolate and flavored syrup and drink products
        President: Steven Sanders
Number Employees: 50-99
Brands:
        Bosco

1696 Bosell Foods
17212 Miles Ave
Cleveland, OH 44128-3427   216-991-7600
        Fax: 216-991-7739   questions@bosellfoods.com
                www.bosellfoods.com
Processor of fresh and frozen prepared salads and
meats
        Manager: Nick Ryan
        VP: Jack Lain
Estimated Sales: $10-20 Million
Number Employees: 20-49
Type of Packaging: Consumer, Food Service, Pri-
vate Label
Brands:
        Bosell
        Brookside
        Homestead

1697 Boskovich Farms
P.O.Box 1352
Oxnard, CA 93032-1352   805-487-2299
        Fax: 805-487-5189
marketing@boskovichfarms.com
                www.boskovichfarms.com
Processor and exporter of fresh and frozen vegeta-
bles and strawberries.
        President: Joe Boskovich
        CEO: George Boskovich Jr
        Marketing Manager: Lindy Martinez
Estimated Sales: $50-100 Million
Number Employees: 100-249
Type of Packaging: Consumer, Food Service

1698 Boskydel Vineyard
7501 E Otto Rd
Lake Leelanau, MI 49653-9419   231-256-7272
        userg@jimrink.com
        www.boskydel.com
Wines
        Owner: Bernard Rink
        President: Jim Rink
        Vineyard Manager: Andrew Rink
Estimated Sales: Less than $500,000
Number Employees: 1-4
Type of Packaging: Private Label
Brands:
        Boskydel

1699 Boston America Corporation
325 New Boston St
Woburn, MA 01801-6273   617-923-1111
        Fax: 617-923-8839
customerservice@bostonamerica.com
        www.bostonamerica.com
Manufacturer of tinned candies and cookies
Estimated Sales: $ 1 - 3 Million
Number Employees: 20-49
Brands:
        BUBBLEGUM
        GRINCH
        MY LITTLE PONY
        POWERPUFF GIRLS
        SCOOBY DOO
        SPIDER-MAN
        STRAWBERRY SHORTCAKE

1700 (HQ)Boston Beer Company
50 Franklin St # 408
Boston, MA 02110-1306   617-422-0009
        Fax: 617-368-5500   800-372-1131
                www.bostonbeer.com
Manufacturer and exporter of beer
        Owner: Alex Bok
        CFO: Richard Lindsay
        VP Brand Development: Robert Hall
        COO: Jeffrey White
Estimated Sales: $190 Million
Number Employees: 50-99
Type of Packaging: Consumer, Food Service
Brands:
        HARDCORE
        SAMUEL ADAMS
        TWISTED TEA
        UTOPIAS

1701 Boston Chowda Company
101 Phoenix Ave
Lowell, MA 01852-4930   978-970-1144
        Fax: 978-970-0450   800-992-0054
                www.bostonchowda.com
Processor and exporter of frozen soups and chow-
ders
        President: Richard Lamattina
        CFO: Stephen Post
        Marketing Director: Lindsay Lamattina
Estimated Sales: $20-50 Million
Number Employees: 10-19
Sq. footage: 13000
Brands:
        Bay State Chowda

1702 Boston Direct Lobster
1501 Whitney Avenue
Gretna, LA 70056-5103   504-834-6404
        Fax: 504-834-6402
        President: Earl Duke III

**1703 Boston Fruit Slice &
Confectionery Corporation**
250 Canal St
Lawrence, MA 01840-1642   978-686-2699
        Fax: 978-686-5898   rick@bostonfruitslice.com
                www.bostonfruitslice.com
Manufacturer of jellied fruit slices
        Manager: Richard Hiera
Estimated Sales: $5 Million
Number Employees: 20-49
Brands:
        BOSTON FRUIT SLICES
        POLLY ORCHARD

1704 Boston Sea Farms
1 Fitchburg Street
Somerville, MA 02143-2136   617-547-3474
        seafarms@ziplink.net
Processor, wholesaler/distributor, importer and ex-
porter of seafood including fish and shellfish
        President/CEO: Adam Weinberg
Estimated Sales: $300,000-500,000
Number Employees: 5-9
Sq. footage: 18000

1705 Boston Spice & Tea Company
12207 Obannons Mill Rd
Boston, VA 22713-4161   540-547-3907
        Fax: 540-547-3656   800-966-4372
                bst@erols.com

Processor of herbal tea, vinegar, seasonings, mustard, sherry-pepper hot sauce, wassil, mulling and corned beef spices and dry bean soup mixes
President: Joann Neal
Marketing Director: Greaner Neal
Manager Sales: Greaner Neal
Estimated Sales: $ .5 - 1 million
Number Employees: 5-9
Type of Packaging: Consumer
Brands:
Boston spices
Logyan's Garden
Logyn's Garden Soups
O'Bannon's
Stews and Sauces

1706 Boston Stoker
P.O.Box 548
Vandalia, OH 45377-0548   937-890-6401
          Fax: 937-890-6403   800-745-5282
Coffee
President: Donald Dean
CFO: Sally Dean
Sales Manager: Ed Dunn
Plant Manager: John McWilliams
Estimated Sales: $500,000-$1 Million
Number Employees: 10,000+
Type of Packaging: Private Label

1707 Boston Tea Company
560 Hudson St # 1-5
Hackensack, NJ 07601-6638   201-440-3004
          Fax: 201-440-5380   800-800-2633
owner@bostontea.com   www.bostontea.com
Manufacturer of teas
President: Andy Jacobs
Vice President: Mary Jacobs
Estimated Sales: Under $500,000
Number Employees: 1-4
Brands:
Beddy By
Lemon Dew
Magic Mountain
Ming Cha
Natco
Pick O' the Bushel
Razzle Dazzle
Spice Bouquet

1708 Boston's Best Coffee Roasters
43 Norfolk Ave
South Easton, MA 02375-1190   508-238-8393
          Fax: 508-230-0298   800-323-4889
sales@bostonsbestcoffee.com
www.bostonsbestcoffee.com
Manufacturer, importer and exporter of coffee mixers and filters; processor, importer and exporter of coffee including freeze-dried, spray-dried, agglomerated, decaffeinated, whole bean, ground gourmet, spray dried, agglomen, flavoredand instant
President: Michael Dovner
CEO: Stephen Fortune
Production Manager: Rocky Raposa
Estimated Sales: $10 - 15 Million
Number Employees: 50-99
Sq. footage: 45000
Type of Packaging: Consumer, Food Service, Private Label, Bulk
Brands:
BOSTON'S BEST

1709 (HQ)Botanical Laboratories
1441 W Smith Rd
Ferndale, WA 98248-8933   360-384-5656
          Fax: 360-384-1140   800-232-4005
info@botlab.com   www.botlab.com
Processor, exporter and contract packager of herbal and homeopathic food supplements in liquid, tablet and topical forms
President/CEO: Jim Coyne
CEO: Brian Halverson
CEO: Jim Thornton
Director R&D: Mary Beth Watkins
Quality Control: John McKnight
Marketing Director: Jeff Kuklenski
Estimated Sales: $100-500 Million
Number Employees: 50-99
Type of Packaging: Consumer, Private Label
Brands:
Bioallers
CompliMed
Natrabio
Nico-Rx

Symtec
Zand Hebs For Kids

1710 Botanical Products
34725 Bogart Drive
Springville, CA 93265-9602   559-539-3432
          Fax: 559-539-2058
desertprideyuca@onemain.com
Processor and exporter of tablets, capsules, extracts and powders made from yucca and melatonin
President: Gordon Bean
VP: Joyce Bean
Estimated Sales: $1-2.5 Million
Number Employees: 1-4
Sq. footage: 2000
Type of Packaging: Consumer
Brands:
Desert Pride
Desert Wonder

1711 Botanicals International Extracts
1321 Poplar St
Denver, CO 80220-3024   303-322-3859
          Fax: 303-772-9054 www.hauser.com
Herbal extracts
CEO: Ken Cleveland
Research & Development: Dr. David Bailey
Quality Control: Rod Lenoble
Sales Director: Peter Hafermann
Estimated Sales: 100-500 Million
Number Employees: 1-4
Parent Co: Hauser
Type of Packaging: Bulk

1712 Botsford Fisheries
2112 Route 950
Petit-Cap, NB E4N 2J8
Canada   506-577-4327
     Fax: 506-577-2846 botsford@nbnet.nb.ca
Processor and exporter of fresh and smoked herring
President: William LeBlanc
Export Sales Manager: Janice Ryan
Plant Manager: Clement LeBlanc
Estimated Sales: $2.5 Million
Number Employees: 50-99
Sq. footage: 40000
Type of Packaging: Consumer, Food Service, Private Label, Bulk

1713 Bottineau Cooperative Creamery
517 Thompson St
Bottineau, ND 58318-1205   701-228-2216
          Fax: 701-228-3426
Manufacturer of dairy products including butter, milk and ice cream
President: Daniel Managelo
Plant Manager: Jeff Byer
Estimated Sales: $ 10 - 20 Million
Number Employees: 5-9
Type of Packaging: Consumer, Food Service, Bulk
Brands:
Pride

1714 Bottle Green Drinks
2375 Tedlo Street
Unit 1
Mississauga, ON L5A 3W7
Canada   905-273-6137
     Fax: 905-273-3186 info@bottle-green.com
          www.bottle-green.com
Manufacturer of flavours, organic fruit sodas, cordials beverages
Number Employees: 1-4
Sq. footage: 3000
Type of Packaging: Consumer, Food Service, Private Label

1715 Bottle Green Drinks Company
2375 Tedlost
Unit 1
Mississauga, ON L5A 3W7
Canada   905-273-6137
     Fax: 905-273-3186 info@bottle-green.com
          www.bottle-green.com
Processor of nonalcoholic and carbonated beverages including limeflower, elderflower, cranberry and lemongrass
President: Andrew James
CFO: Corrie James
Number Employees: 5-9
Number of Brands: 2
Number of Products: 9
Type of Packaging: Consumer, Food Service, Private Label

Brands:
Bottle Green

1716 Bottomline Foods
10021 Pines Blvd
Pembroke Pines, FL 33024-6191   954-843-0562
          Fax: 954-843-0568   info@blf.com
          www.blf.com
Distributor and packer, exporter for frozen foods, meats, cheese, groceries, seafood, spices, etc.
President: Howard Blitz
CEO: Larry Blitz
CFO: Bob Blitz
Purchasing Manager: Mark Roberts
Number Employees: 5-9
Sq. footage: 2000
Type of Packaging: Food Service, Private Label, Bulk

1717 Bouchaine Vineyards
1075 Buchli Station Rd
Napa, CA 94559-9716   707-252-9065
          Fax: 707-252-0401   800-654-9463
          www.bouchaine.com
Wines
Manager: Mike Richmond
Marketing Director: Carole Loomis
Sales Director: Jan Novotny
Controller: Steven Stoner
Winemaker: David Stevens
Estimated Sales: $2.5-5 Million
Number Employees: 10-19

1718 Bouchard Family Farm
3 Strip Rd
Fort Kent, ME 04743-1550   207-834-3237
          Fax: 207-834-7422   800-239-3237
bouchard@ployes.com   www.ployes.com
Processor and exporter of buckwheat pancake mixes and flour
President: Joseph Bouchard
Sales/Marketing Executive: Elaine Mininger
Estimated Sales: $500,000-$1 Million
Number Employees: 5-9
Sq. footage: 110000
Type of Packaging: Consumer, Food Service
Brands:
Bouchard Family Farm

1719 Boudreaux's Foods
5401 Toler St
New Orleans, LA 70123-5222   504-733-8440
     Fax: 504-866-1965 bfoods@bellsouth.net
          www.boudreauxsfoods.com
Processor of refrigerated entrees, salad dressings, breads, whole wheat pasta, soups, etc
President: Vince Hayward
Estimated Sales: $ 1 - 3 Million
Number Employees: 1-4
Sq. footage: 2000
Type of Packaging: Consumer
Brands:
Author's Choice
Boudreaux's

1720 Boulder Bar
2635 Ariane Drive
San Diego, CA 92117-3422   858-274-1049
          Fax: 858-274-1207
Marketing & Advertising: Lorie Zapf

1721 Boulder Brownie Company
132 Heritage Hill Road
Apt C
New Canaan, CT 06840-4631   203-323-1945
          Fax: 203-323-2010   800-309-9995
Richardheller@boulderbrownie.com
          www.boulderbrownie.com
All-natural, gourmet brownies, blondies, bar cookies and sheet cakes available in six individually packaged flavors
Estimated Sales: $5-10 Million
Number Employees: 10-19
Brands:
Boulder Brownies

1722 Boulder Creek Brewing Company
13040 Highway 9
Boulder Creek, CA 95006-9154   831-338-7882
          Fax: 831-338-7583   brewco@hwy9.com
          www.bouldercreekbrewery.net
Beer, ale, lager
Owner: Nancy Long

*Estimated Sales:*Less than $500,000
Number Employees: 10-19
Brands:
Boulder Creek
Redwood Ale

1723 Boulder Sausage
513 S Pierce Ave
Louisville, CO 80027-3019   303-665-6302
Fax: 303-665-3109 www.bouldersausage.com
Meat
VP: Tom Griffiths
Operations Manager: Tom Griffiths
Estimated Sales:$5-10 Million
Number Employees: 20-49
Number of Products: 14
Type of Packaging: Consumer, Food Service, Private Label, Bulk
Brands:
Boulder Sausage Products
Private Label Products
Rocky Mountain Products

1724 Boulder Street Coffee Roaster
332 N Tejon St
Colorado Springs, CO 80903-1224 719-577-4291
Fax: 719-577-4291
www.coloradospringsfictionwritersgroup.org
Coffee
Owner: Iwao Green
Estimated Sales:$5-10 Million
Number Employees: 10-19

1725 Boulevard Brewing Company
2501 Southwest Blvd
Kansas City, MO 64108-2345   816-474-7095
Fax: 816-474-1722 fineales@blvdbeer.com
www.blvdbeer.com
Processor of ale, lager, stout and seasonal beer
Manager: Steven Pauwels
CFO: Jeff Krum
Marketing Director: Bob Sullivan
Production Manager: Larry Dunaway
Plant Manager: Steven Pauwels, Head Brewer
Estimated Sales:$7 Million
Number Employees: 20-49
Type of Packaging: Consumer, Food Service

1726 Bouma Meats
PO Box 925
Provost, AB T0B 3S0
Canada   780-753-2092
Fax: 780-753-4939
Processor of beef and pork including fresh, frozen, portion controlled, sausage and deli cuts; also, bacon and ham
President: Ben Richter
Co-Owner: Tim Rachinski
Number Employees: 10-19
Type of Packaging: Consumer, Food Service, Private Label, Bulk
Brands:
Bouma

1727 Bountiful Pantry
PO Box 179
Nantucket, MA 02554-0179   508-228-6964
Fax: 508-325-0203 888-832-6466
judy@bountifulpantry.com
www.bountifulpantry.com
Manufacturer of soup mixes, side dishes, waffle mixes, bread, roll, scone and biscuit mixes, cookie and dessert mixes and teas and coffees

1728 Bourbon Ball
P.O.Box 4215
Louisville, KY 40204-0215   502-634-3300
Fax: 502-895-4403 800-280-0888
www.thebourbonball.com
Processor of chocolate liquor-filled candy
President: Jim Patton
Estimated Sales:$250,000
Number Employees: 5-9
Type of Packaging: Private Label
Brands:
Bourbon Ball

1729 Boutique Seafood
1326 White St SW
Atlanta, GA 30310-1648   404-752-8852
Fax: 404-752-6634
Seafood, red snapper, sea bass, lobster meat, crabmeat, grouper
President: Pano Karatassos

Estimated Sales:$1.3 Million
Number Employees: 5-9

1730 Bouvry Exports Calgary
312-222 58 Avenue SW
Calgary, AB T2H 2S3
Canada   403-253-0717
Fax: 403-259-3568
103241.2622@compuserve.com
www.egsood-alliance.ab.ca
Processor of horse meat, bison and beef
President: Claude Bouvry
CEO: John McNaughton
General Manager: Darin Sjonger
Sales: Alain Bouvry
Type of Packaging: Consumer, Bulk

1731 Bove's of Vermont
68 Pearl St
Burlington, VT 05401-4332   802-864-6651
Fax: 802-651-9371 888-545-2321
sauceboy10Boves.com www.boves.com
Marinara sauce, roasted garlic sauce, chianti mushroom sauce, romano pomodoro sauce.
Owner: Richard Bove
Estimated Sales:$500,000-$1 Million
Number Employees: 20-49
Brands:
Bove's of Vermont

1732 Bow Valley Brewing Company
109 Boulder Crescent
Canmore, AB T1W 1L4
Canada   403-678-2739
Fax: 403-678-8813 bvbc@telusplanet.net
www.beerexpedition.com
Processor of lager
President: Hugh Hancock
Number Employees: 5-9
Type of Packaging: Consumer, Food Service
Brands:
Bow Valley

1733 Bowman & Landes Turkeys
6490 Ross Rd
New Carlisle, OH 45344-8801   937-845-9466
Fax: 937-845-9998 www.bowmanlandes.com
Processor of poultry
CEO/President: Dan Landes
Estimated Sales:$10-20 Million
Number Employees: 100-249
Type of Packaging: Consumer, Bulk

1734 Bowman Apple Products Company
P.O.Box 817
Mt Jackson, VA 22842-0817   540-477-3111
Fax: 540-477-2353 877-426-9626
bap@bowmanappleproducts.com
www.bowmanappleproducts.com
Processor of apple sauce, juice and butter, diced apples and juice cocktail drinks
President: Gordon D Bowman Ii
President: Gordon Bowman
CFO: Benjamin Amoss II
Point of Sale Manager: Sam Wenger
Production Manager: George Hollida
Plant Manager: Gene Bodkin
Purchasing Manager: Timothy Proctor
Estimated Sales:$20-50 Million
Number Employees: 100-249
Type of Packaging: Consumer, Private Label
Brands:
Bowman
Bowman's
New Yorker
Old Virginia

1735 Bowness Bakery
4280-23rd Street NE
Calgary, AB T2E 6X7
Canada   403-250-9760
Fax: 403-291-9129
Processor of specialty breads, pretzels and pizza shells
President: Shams Habib
CEO: Shams Habib
Marketing Manager: Shams Habib
General Manager: Sm\Hams Habib
Number Employees: 20-49
Type of Packaging: Consumer, Food Service, Bulk
Brands:
Bowness Baker

Frisches Brot
Pretzeland

1736 Bowser Meat Processing
513 S Palmberg St
Meriden, KS 66512-9313   785-484-2454
Processor of meat including sausage
Manager: Kirsti Petesch
Manager: Kirsti Petesch
Estimated Sales:$1-2.5 Million
Number Employees: 5-9
Type of Packaging: Consumer

1737 Boyajian, Inc
144 Will Dr
Canton, MA 02021-3704   781-828-9966
Fax: 781-828-9922 800-965-0665
customerservice@boyajianinc.com
www.boyajianinc.com
Processor and importer of flavored vinegars, infused oils including olive, garlic, lemon, lime, orange, peanut, pepper, sesame and pure Asian and natural flavorings including strawberry, raspberry, cherry, spearmint, clove, peppermintcinnamon and wintergreen, etc
Owner: John Boyajian
Marketing: Amy Ferrara
Estimated Sales:$5-10 Million
Number Employees: 20-49
Sq. footage: 20000
Type of Packaging: Consumer, Food Service, Private Label, Bulk
Brands:
Boyajian

1738 (HQ)Boyd Coffee Company
19730 NE Sandy Blvd.
Portland, OR 97230   503-666-4545
Fax: 503-669-2223 800-545-4077
info@boyds.com www.boyds.com
Manufacturer of coffees teas, cocoa, hot and frozen beverages, soups, sauces, gravies and flour products.
Co-President/Co-CEO: David Boyd
Co-President/Co-CEO: Dick Boyd
SVP: Doug McKay
Estimated Sales:$59 Million
Number Employees: 500-999
Type of Packaging: Food Service
Other Locations:
Boyd Coffee Company
Coeur D Alene ID
Brands:
BOYD'S COFFEE
COFFEE HOUSE ROASTERS
ISLAND MIST ICED TEA
ITALIA D'ORO COFFEE
TECHNI-BREW
TODAY
VIAGGIO COFFEE

1739 Boyd Sausage Company
626 Highway 1 S
Washington, IA 52353-9786   319-653-5715
Manufacturer of beef jerky, bologna and deer meat products including sausage
Owner: George Statler
GM: Brandon Statler
*Estimated Sales:*Under $400,000
Number Employees: 5-9
Sq. footage: 3500
Type of Packaging: Consumer, Bulk

1740 Boyer Candy Company
821 17th St
Altoona, PA 16601-2074   814-944-9401
Fax: 814-944-4923 www.boyercandies.com
Processor of chocolate confectionery products including shell molded chocolates, cup candy and seasonal novelties
CEO: Robert Faith
Estimated Sales:$20-50 Million
Number Employees: 100-249
Sq. footage: 150000
Type of Packaging: Consumer, Private Label, Bulk
Brands:
Bartons
Boxer
Boyer
Casanova
Hill of Westchester
Kron
Schrafft's
Winters

1741 Boyer Coffee Company
7295 N Washington St
Denver, CO 80229-6707   303-289-3345
Fax: 303-289-2133 800-452-5282
boyers@usa.net   www.boyerscoffee.com
Coffee
President: W Boyer
Marketing Director: Bonnie Rine
Plant Manager: L Smith
Purchasing Manager: L Smith
Estimated Sales: $2.5-5 Million
Number Employees: 20-49
Type of Packaging: Private Label

1742 Boylan Bottling Company
74 Lee Avenue
Haledon, NJ 07508-1202   973-790-7093
Fax: 973-790-9097 800-289-7978
boylan@cybernex.net
Bottled soft drinks
President/CEO: Ronald Fiorina
Executive VP: Mark Fiorina
COO: David Fiorina, Jr.
Estimated Sales: $1-2.5 Million
Number Employees: 20-49

1743 Boyle Meat Company
1638 Saint Louis Ave
Kansas City, MO 64101-1130   816-221-6283
Fax: 816-221-3888 800-821-3626
christysteaks@boylesteaks.com
www.boylescornedbeef.com
Manufacturer and exporter of meat products
President: Tom Stratton
VP: Christy Chester
Estimated Sales: $20 - 50 Million
Number Employees: 20-49
Sq. footage: 45000
Type of Packaging: Consumer, Food Service
Brands:
BOYLE'S FAMOUS

1744 Boyle Meat Company
1638 Saint Louis Ave
Kansas City, MO 64101-1130   816-221-6283
Fax: 816-221-3888 800-821-3626
christysteaks@worldnet.att.net
www.boylescornedbeef.com
Steaks, corn beef, pastrami and pot roast
President: Don Wendl
VP: Christy Chester
Estimated Sales: $20-50 Million
Number Employees: 20-49
Sq. footage: 10000
Type of Packaging: Food Service, Private Label, Bulk

1745 Boyton Shellfish
RR 2
Box 85a
Ellsworth, ME 04605   207-667-8580
Fax: 619-474-6103
Owner: Dean Smith

1746 (HQ)Brach's Confections
19111 Dallas Parkway
Dallas, TX 75287-3199   972-930-3600
Fax: 972-930-3612 800-999-0204
www.brachs.com
Manufacturer of candy
President/CEO: Charles Haak
CFO: James Hagedorn
Estimated Sales: $20 - 50 Million
Number Employees: 20-49
Parent Co: Barry-Callebaut
Type of Packaging: Consumer
Brands:
Brach's
DOUBLE DIPPERS
FRUTIO'S
SPECIAL TREASURES
STAR BRITES
STARS

1747 Brad's Organic
7 Hoover Ave
Haverstraw, NY 10927   845-429-9080
Fax: 845-429-9089 sales@bradsorganic.com
www.bradorganic.com
organic, all-natural salsa, tortilla chips, honey, jams and peanut butter

1748 Brad's Taste of New York
P.O.Box 20475
Floral Park, NY 11002-0475   516-354-9004
Fax: 516-354-9004 bradstasteofny@aol.com
www.bradstasteofny.com
Manufacturer of gourmet mustard, pretzel dip, honey wheat pretzel, sourdough honey mustard nuggets, and kettle potato chips
Owner: Bradley Knese
Estimated Sales: $1 - 3 Million
Number Employees: 5-9

1749 Bradley Creek Seafood
2700 Gregory St # 200
Savannah, GA 31404-1432   912-484-3510
Fax: 912-897-7815 tastycrab@mindspring.com
www.bradleycreek.com
Manufacturer of crab au gratin pastries; deviled crab; and crab cakes.
President/CEO: Michael Simmons
Type of Packaging: Food Service

1750 Bradshaw's Food Products
1425 Somerset Avenue
Dighton, MA 02715-1215   508-669-6088
Processor of pickled beef tripe
Partner: D Bradshaw
Partner: R Bradshaw
Estimated Sales: $1-2.5 Million
Number Employees: 1-4

1751 Brady Farms
14786 Winans St
West Olive, MI 49460-9613   616-842-3916
Fax: 616-842-8357 bradyfarms@nefonecom.net
Processor of blueberries including fresh, frozen and puree
President: Robert Brady
Sales: Ronald Benson
Sales Director: Ron Benson
Plant Manager: Juana Chavez
Estimated Sales: $9 Million
Number Employees: 50-99
Type of Packaging: Consumer, Food Service, Private Label, Bulk

1752 Bradye P. Todd & Son
2 Sunset Ln
Cambridge, MD 21613-1308   410-228-8633
www.toddseafood.com
Manufacturer of seafood including crabs, seafood delicatessen and restaurant
Owner: Roy Todd
Estimated Sales: $3 Million
Number Employees: 20-49
Sq. footage: 4000
Parent Co: T.A. Ocean Odyssey
Type of Packaging: Consumer

1753 Bragg-Live Food Products
P.O.Box 7
Santa Barbara, CA 93102-0007   805-968-1020
Fax: 805-968-1001 800-446-1990
info@bragg.com   www.bragg.com
Health foods
President: Patricia Bragg
Estimated Sales: $3-4 Million
Number Employees: 20-49
Brands:
Bragg Raw Organic Cider Vinegar

1754 Braham Food Locker Service
P.O.Box 554
Braham, MN 55006-0554   320-396-2636
Processor of meat products including beef, goat and pork; also, smoked and cured sausage
President: Nicholas Grote
CEO: Diane Grote
Estimated Sales: $250,000
Number Employees: 5-9
Type of Packaging: Consumer

1755 Brakebush Brothers
N4993 6th Dr
Westfield, WI 53964-8200   608-296-2121
Fax: 608-296-3192 800-933-2121
brakebushrep@brakebush.com
www.brakebush.com
Manufacturer of frozen chicken
President: William Brakebush Jr
EVP: Carl Brakebush
QA Manager: Donna Halbach
Marketing Manager: Steve Ross
Director Sales/Marketing: Scott Sanders
Production Manager: Dave Robinson
Purchasing Manager: Chris Brakebrush
Estimated Sales: $100-500 Million
Number Employees: 500-999
Number of Brands: 1
Type of Packaging: Consumer, Food Service

1756 Brand Aromatics International
4 Countryview Road
Holmdel, NJ 07733-1806   732-706-3411
Fax: 732-706-3411 brandaroma@sprynet.com
Flavors and seasonings

1757 Brand Castle
23945 Mercantile Rd
Suite G
Beachwood, OH 444122   216-292-7700
Fax: 216-292-7701 www.brandcastle.com
cookie making kits and decorations
VP Sales/Marketing: Jim Shlonsky
Operations Manager: Jeff Berger
Number Employees: 5

1758 Brandborg Cellars
PO Box 506
Elkton, OR 97436-0506   510-215-9553
Fax: 415-282-6179 terryb@nbn.com
Wine
President: Terry Brandborg
Number Employees: 20-49

1759 Brander Vineyard
P.O.Box 92
Los Olivos, CA 93441-0092   805-688-2455
Fax: 805-688-8010 800-970-9979
info@Brander.com   www.brander.com
Manufacturer of red and white wines
Owner/Winemaker: C Frederic Brander
Office Manager: Kathy Forner
Operations Assistant: Drew Horton
Estimated Sales: $900,000
Number Employees: 5-9
Type of Packaging: Consumer, Food Service
Brands:
Brander

1760 Brandmeyer Popcorn Company
3785 NE 70th Ave
Ankeny, IA 50021-9734   515-262-3243
Fax: 866-400-8884 800-568-8276
www.lottapop.com
Processor and exporter of popcorn including gift boxes and specialty items
President: Arlie Brandmeyer
Estimated Sales: Less than $100,000
Number Employees: 1-4
Brands:
Iowa State
Lotta-Pop

1761 Brandt Farms
6040 Avenue 430
Reedley, CA 93654-9008   559-638-6961
Fax: 559-638-6964 sales@treeripe.com
www.treeripe.com
Processor, exporter and importer of fresh fruits including kiwifruit, apricots, nectarines, plums, peaches and table grapes
President: Wayne Brandt
CEO: Eleanor Brandt
CFO: Jack Brandt
Domestic Sales: Michael Reimer
Public Relations: Dave Maddox
Estimated Sales: $50 - 100 Million
Number Employees: 100-249
Sq. footage: 30000
Brands:
BRANDT
CRYSTAL FOODS
CRYSTAL R-BEST

1762 Brandt Mills
P.O.Box L
Mifflinville, PA 18631-0491   570-752-4271
Fax: 570-752-8712
Manufacturer of flour including pastry and whole wheat
Owner: Richard Brandt Jr

Estimated Sales: $ 10 - 20 Million
Number Employees: 10-19

1763 Brans Nut Company
581 W Bonner Rd
Wauconda, IL 60084-1186   847-526-0700
Fax: 847-526-4093   800-238-0400
t_weber@juno.com
Processor, importer and packager of snack and natural foods, roasted nuts, preservs, apple cider, fruit products candy and chocolate
  President: Richard Breeden III
  VP Sales: Thomas Weber Jr
  Secretary: Francic Collins
  Plant Manager: Jan Ikhtiari
  Purchasing: Thomas Weber
Estimated Sales: $1-2.5 Million
Number Employees: 5-9
Number of Brands: 3
Sq. footage: 25000
Type of Packaging: Consumer, Food Service, Private Label, Bulk
Brands:
  Brans
  ORCHARD GROVE
  WUACONDA ORCHARDS

1764 Braren Pauli Winery
7051 N State St
Redwood Valley, CA 95470-9629   707-485-0322
Fax: 707-485-6784   800-423-6519
info@brarenpauli.com   www.brarenpauli.com
Wines
  President: Charlie Barra
  Co-Owner/CEO: Bill Pauli
  Marketing Director: Larry Braren
  Sales Director: Larry Braren
  Winemaker: Larry Braren
Estimated Sales: $ .5 - 1 million
Number Employees: 20-49
Brands:
  Braren Pauli

1765 Brass Ladle Products
P.O.Box 39
Glen Mills, PA 19342   610-558-4403
Fax: 610-565-8665   800-955-2353
frontdesk@brassladle.com   www.brassladle.com
Manufacturer of all-natural gourmet cake mixes including carrot, mocha mud(chocolate) and lemon poppy seed.
  Owner: Skip Achuff
Estimated Sales: $1,000,000
Number Employees: 1-4
Number of Brands: 1
Number of Products: 3
Sq. footage: 3000
Type of Packaging: Consumer, Food Service, Private Label, Bulk
Brands:
  Brass Ladle
  Mocha Mud
  Mocha Mud Cake Mix

1766 Brasserie Brasel Brewery
8477 Rue Cordner
Lasalle, QC H8N 2X2
Canada   514-365-5050
Fax: 514-365-2954   800-463-2728
Processor and exporter of lager beers
  President: Marcel Jagermann
  Managing Director: Stan Jagermann
Number Employees: 10-19
Sq. footage: 12000
Type of Packaging: Consumer, Food Service, Private Label
Brands:
  Brasal Bock
  Brasal Legere
  Brasal Special Amber
  Hopps Aux Pommes
  Hopps Brau

1767 Brassica Protection Products
2400 Boston St
Baltimore, MD 21224-4723   410-732-1200
Fax: 410-732-1980   877-747-1277
mail@brassica.com   www.brassica.com
Food ingredients, supplements, nutraceuticals, functional foods (cander preventive products)
  CEO: Anthony Talalay
  CEO: Antony Talalay
  VP Business Development: Earl Hauserman

Estimated Sales: $2,000,000
Number Employees: 5-9
Brands:
  Brassica
  Brassica Teas with SGS
  BroccoSprouts

1768 Braswell Food Company
226 N Zetterower Ave
Statesboro, GA 30458   912-764-6191
Fax: 912-489-1572
customerservice@braswells.com
www.braswells.com
Preserves, special teas, seafood collection, braswell's organics, braswell's select, flavoring mixes, dressings, salsas and dips, sauces, hot sauces, seasonings and rubs, marinades, jams, jellies, hors d'oeuvre jellies, fruit buttersfruit spreads, marmalades, mustards, pickles, relishes, syrups, honeys, toppings, chutneys, chow chows
  President/Owner: Andy Oliver
  Production: Frank Farr
Estimated Sales: $12.4 Million
Number Employees: 95

1769 Braswell's Winery
7556 Bankhead Highway
Dora, AL 35062-2041   205-648-8335
Fax: 205-648-8335
Wines
  President: Wayne Braswell
  Owner: Ruth Braswell
Estimated Sales: $1-4.9 Million
Number Employees: 1-4

1770 Brateka Enterprises
15680 SW 23rd Avenue
Ocala, FL 34473-4278   352-307-5459
Fax: 352-307-5459   877-549-3227
brateka@aol.com   www.lizabbasauce.com
Processor of gourmet sauces in gift baskets
  CEO: Hyacinth Thomas
Number Employees: 10-19
Brands:
  Lize Jamaican Style Gourmet BBQ

1771 (HQ)Braum's Inc
PO Box 25429
Oklahoma City, OK 73125-0429   405-478-1656
Fax: 405-475-2460 www.braums.com
Frozen desserts, dairy and milk
  CEO: Drew Braum
  CFO: Mark Godwin
  Marketing Director: Terry Holden
  Purchasing Manager: Kenny McDonald
Type of Packaging: Food Service

1772 Braun Seafood Company
P.O.Box 971
Cutchogue, NY 11935-0971   631-734-5550
Fax: 631-734-7462   info@braunseafood.com
www.braunseafood.com
Processor of oysters and frozen scallops
  President: Kenneth Homan
  VP: Wayne Phillips
  VP: James Andrews
  General Manager: Richard Olsen-Harbich
  Purchasing Manager: Michael Checklick
Estimated Sales: $5-9.9 Million
Number Employees: 20-49
Brands:
  Peconic Bay
  Robins Island

1773 Bravard Vineyards & Winery
15000 Overton Rd
Hopkinsville, KY 42240-9451   270-269-2583
jbravard@apex.net
www.commercecenter.org/visitors/bravard/
Processor of wines including dry, semi-dry, semi-sweet and sweet in white, blush, rose and red
  Owner: Jim Bravard
Estimated Sales: $500,000-$1 Million
Number Employees: 1-4
Sq. footage: 250
Type of Packaging: Private Label
Brands:
  Bravard
  Countryside Red
  Foch
  Fruit Hill White
  Lady Genevieve
  Pennyroyal

1774 Bravo Farms
PO Box 1205
Visalia, CA 93279-1205   559-627-3525
Fax: 559-625-0490   info@whitecheddar.com
www.bravofarm.com
Cheese
  Owner: William Boersma
  Cheesemaker: Patt Boersma
Estimated Sales: $5-10 Million
Number Employees: 5-9

1775 Brazos Legends/Texas Tamale Co
9087 Knight Rd
Houston, TX 77054-4305   713-795-5500
Fax: 713-795-5534   800-882-6253
sbailey@texastamale.com   www.texastamale.com
Gourmet food products
  Manager: Shirley Bailey
  Sales Director: Shirley Bailey
  Operations Manager: Shirley Bailey
  Plant Manager: Ana Flores
Estimated Sales: $3-5 Million
Number Employees: 20-49
Number of Brands: 5
Number of Products: 125
Sq. footage: 25000
Type of Packaging: Consumer, Food Service, Private Label, Bulk
Brands:
  Brazos Legends
  Red Eye

1776 Bread & Chocolate
P.O.Box 692
Wells River, VT 05081-0692   802-429-2920
Fax: 802-429-2990   800-524-6715
breadcho@togther.net
www.breadandchocolatevt.com
Manufacturer of gourmet lemonade, cocoa, pancake mixes, jams, mustards and iced tea mixes
  President: Jonathan Rutstein
  Vice President: Fran Rutstein
Estimated Sales: $500,000-900,000
Number Employees: 1-4
Brands:
  BEAR RIVER
  BREAD & CHOCOLATE
  MOOSE MOUNTAIN
  SNOWMAN
  STORYTIME

1777 Bread Alone Bakery
3958 Route 28
Shokan, NY 12481   845-657-3328
Fax: 845-657-6228   800-769-3328
info@breadalone.com   www.breadalone.com
Processor of whole grain and organic bread
  Owner/President: Daniel Leader
  Co Owner: Sharon Burns-Leader
Estimated Sales: $20-50 Million
Number Employees: 20-49
Brands:
  Bread Alone

1778 Bread Box
445 7th Avenue S
Virden, NB R0M 2C0
Canada   204-748-1513
Processor of bread and buns
  President: Debby Andrews
  Co-Owner: Irene Plaisier
  Co-Owner: Dianna Careme
Number Employees: 1-4
Sq. footage: 1000
Type of Packaging: Consumer

1779 Bread Dip Company
PO Box 42782
Philadelphia, PA 19101-2782   215-563-9455
Fax: 215-563-9144   laura@breaddipcompany.com
www.breaddipcompany.com
Manufacturer of gourmet spreads
  Owner: Laura Sterbenz

1780 Bread Dip Company
378 Terrace Drive
Friday Harbor, WA 98250-8931   360-378-6070
breaddip@interisland.net
2152639455
Flavored bread dips: sun-dried tomato, olive and herb, artichoke and caper, peppers and spice and feta and pink peppercorn
  President: Laura Sterbenz

Estimated Sales: Under $500,000
Number Employees: 1-4

1781 Breadsmith
9871 Montgomery Rd
Cincinnati, OH 45242-6424   513-791-8817
        Fax: 513-791-8851 www.breadsmith.com
Baked goods
    Owner: Bob Harris
Estimated Sales: Less than $500,000
Number Employees: 20-49
Type of Packaging: Consumer

1782 Breadworks Bakery & Deli
923 Preston Ave # A
Charlottesville, VA 22903-4446   434-296-4663
    Fax: 434-971-6740 info@breadworks.org
                www.breadworks.org
Processor of breads including American and French
sourdough, twelve grain, Jewish rye, challah, semo-
lina, Irish soda and baguettes; also, cookies, muffins,
scones, danish, pies, cakes and deli products
    Manager: Jim Baber
    Chairman: Marc Bridenhagen
    Vice President: John Satoski
    Manager: Jim Baber
    Production/Sales: Priscilla Fox
Estimated Sales: $ 1 - 3 Million
Number Employees: 10-19
Parent Co: Worksource Enterprises
Type of Packaging: Consumer, Food Service

1783 Breakfast at Brennan's
417 Royal St
New Orleans, LA 70130-2191   504-525-9711
        Fax: 504-525-2302 800-888-9932
                brennansno@aol.com
                www.brennansneworleans.com
Coffees, muffins, jellies, Bananas Foster sauce mix,
Royal Delite cookies, Coffee-on-the-Rocks concen-
trate, beignet mix, frozen drink mixes
    Owner: Owen Brennan
    Owner: Ted Brennan
    Co-Owner: Jimmy Brennan
Estimated Sales: $ 5 - 10 Million
Number Employees: 100-249
Brands:
    Breakfast At Brennan's

1784 Breaktime Snacks
7723 Somerset Blvd
Paramount, CA 90723-4104   562-633-6200
    Fax: 562-633-8789 800-677-1868
        popcornconnection@earthlink.net
            www.popcornconnection.com
Gourmet popcorn
    President/CEO: Roger Glade
Estimated Sales: $1-2.5 Million
Number Employees: 5-9
Brands:
    Corn Appetit

1785 Breakwater Fisheries
14 O'Briens Hill
St. John's, NL A1B 4G4
Canada   709-754-1999
    Fax: 709-754-9712 rrbarnes@nf-sympatico.ca
Processor and exporter of frozen snow crab, capelin,
turbot, cod, mackerel, herring, squid and shrimp; im-
porter of frozen squid
    President: Randy R Barnes
    CEO: Lemuel C White
Number Employees: 250-499
Sq. footage: 75000
Brands:
    Breakwater

1786 Breakwater Seafoods
306 S F St
Aberdeen, WA 98520-4144   360-532-5693
                Fax: 360-533-6488
Seafoods
    Owner: Don Henry
Estimated Sales: $2 Million
Number Employees: 5-9

1787 Breaux Vineyards
13876 Harpers Ferry Rd
Purcellville, VA 20132   540-668-6299
    Fax: 540-668-6283 800-492-9961
        info@breauxvineyards.com
        www.breauxvineyards.com

Manufacturer of wines
    Owner: Paul Breaux
    Co-Owner: Alexis Breaux
    Sales Director: Jennifer Breaux Blosser
    Operations Manager: Chris Blosser
    Wine Maker: Dave Collins
Estimated Sales: $ .5 - 1 million
Number Employees: 20-49
Sq. footage: 20000
Type of Packaging: Consumer, Private Label, Bulk

1788 Brechet & Richter Company
6005 Golden Valley Rd
Minneapolis, MN 55422-4439   763-545-0201
                Fax: 763-545-0201
Baking ingredient doughnut and cake mixtures
    President: Tom Moore
Estimated Sales: $10-20 Million
Number Employees: 20-49
Type of Packaging: Private Label

1789 Breckenridge Brewery
471 Kalamath St
Denver, CO 80204-5019   303-623-2739
    Fax: 303-573-4877 www.breckenridge.com
Processor of ale and stout
    Owner: Ed Cerkovnik
    General Manager: Graham Squire
Estimated Sales: $1-2.5 Million
Number Employees: 20-49
Parent Co: Breckenridge Brewery
Type of Packaging: Consumer, Food Service, Bulk
Brands:
    AUTUMN ALE
    AVALANCHE ALE
    CHRISTMAS ALE
    HEFE PROPER
    OATMEAL STOUT
    PANDORA'S BOCK
    SUMMERBRIGHT ALE
    TRADEMARK PALE ALE

1790 Brede
19000 Glendale St
Detroit, MI 48223-3424   313-273-1079
    Fax: 313-273-4110 info@bredefoods.com
                www.bredefoods.com
Processor and exporter of horseradish and horserad-
ish sauce.
    President/CEO: Michael Brede
    Vice Presiddent: Craig Brede
Estimated Sales: $1-2.5 Million
Number Employees: 5-9
Sq. footage: 12000
Type of Packaging: Consumer, Food Service, Pri-
vate Label, Bulk
Brands:
    BREDE OLD FASHIONED
    FARMERS
    HI PRAIZE
    OLD FASHIONED
    POZNANSKI

1791 Breitenbach Wine Cellars
5934 Old Route 39 NW
Dover, OH 44622-7787   330-343-3603
    Fax: 330-343-8290 amishwine@tusco.net
                www.breitenbachwine.com
Wines
    President/CEO: Cynthia Bixler
    Director Manufacturing: Dalton Bixler
Estimated Sales: $2.5-5 Million
Number Employees: 10-19
Brands:
    Breitenbach
    Charming Nancy
    Dardenella
    Dusty Miller
    Festival
    First Crush
    Frost Fire
    Roadhouse Red
    Rosebarb
    Silver Seyual

1792 Bremner Biscuit Company
4600 Joliet St
Denver, CO 80239-2922   303-371-8180
    Fax: 303-371-8185 800-722-1871
        bremner@worldpantry.com
        www.bremnerbiscuitco.com
Processor and exporter of gourmet, snack and oyster
crackers
    Manager: Neil Bremner

Estimated Sales: $5-10 Million
Number Employees: 20-49
Sq. footage: 42000
Parent Co: Dare Foods
Type of Packaging: Consumer, Food Service, Pri-
vate Label, Bulk
Brands:
    BREMNER
    BREMNER WAFERS
    BREWSKI SNACK

1793 Bremner Company
400 Industrial Blvd
Poteau, OK 74953-3706   918-647-8630
                Fax: 918-647-8518
        www.bremnercookies-crackers.com
Processor and exporter of cookies and crackers
    Quality Director: Garry Caufield
    Operations Director: Steve Hickman
    Plant Manager: Jeff Hollis
    Purchasing Manager: Becky Broussard
Estimated Sales: $100+ Million
Number Employees: 250-499
Sq. footage: 250000
Parent Co: Ralcorp Holdings
Type of Packaging: Consumer, Food Service, Pri-
vate Label

1794 Brennan Snacks Manufacturing
1220 W 7th Street
Bogalusa, LA 70427-3406   800-290-7486
                Fax: 985-732-5397
Processor of snacks and cotton candy
    Co-Owner: Bernie "Brennan, Jr."
    Co-Owner: Christi Brennan
Number Employees: 20-49
Type of Packaging: Food Service, Private Label
Brands:
    Oboy's

1795 Brenner's Bakery of Arlington
2000 14th St N
Arlington, VA 22201-2500   703-534-0211
                Fax: 703-534-0200
Manufacturer of breads, rolls, cakes, pastries, pies
and doughnuts
    President: Bill Runner
    VP/Co-Owner: William Christian
Estimated Sales: $500,000-$1 Million
Number Employees: 250-499
Sq. footage: 7500

1796 Brenntag
81 W Huller Lane
Reading, PA 19605   610-926-4151
    Fax: 610-926-4160 888-926-4151
        northeast.salesadmin@brenntag.com
            www.brenntagnortheast.com
Distributor of food ingredients and specialty chemi-
cals
    Chairman/President: Markus Klaehn
    President: Anthony Medaglia
    VP: Dennis Eisenhofer
Estimated Sales: K
Number Employees: 500

1797 Brenntag Pacific
10747 Patterson Pl
Santa Fe Springs, CA 90670-4043   562-903-9626
    Fax: 562-906-5287 brenntag@brenntag.com
Beverages, confectionery, canned foods, processed
cheese, bakery, meat, seafood, dairy
    President: Steven M Pozzi
    VP, National Accounts: Robert L Moser Jr
Estimated Sales: $ 50-100 Million
Number Employees: 50-99
Brands:
    Brenntag Pacific

1798 Brent & Sam's Cookies
30 Collins Industrial Pl
N Little Rock, AR 72113-6555   501-562-4300
    Fax: 501-568-9777 800-825-1613
        perfectcookies@brentandsams.com
                www.brentandsams.com
Gourmet cookies.
    President: Brent Bumpers
    VP Sales: John Merck
Estimated Sales: $10-20 Million
Number Employees: 20-49
Type of Packaging: Private Label
Brands:
    BUTTER PECAN WITH CINN. OATS, RAIS.
    CARIBBEAN CRUNCH

CHOCOLATE CHIP WITH PECANS
EXTRA CHOCOLATE CHIP NO NUTS
KEY LIME WHITE CHOCOLATE
LEMON WHITE CHOCOLATE
RASPBERRY CHOCOLATE CHIP
WHITE CHOCOLATE MACADAMIA NUT

1799 Breslow Deli Products
1209 N Hancock Street
Philadelphia, PA 19122-4505   215-739-4200
            Fax: 215-423-4199
Processor of beef including smoked and dried
    President: Jon Breslow
Estimated Sales: $5-10 Million
Number Employees: 5-9
Type of Packaging: Consumer, Food Service

1800 Brewfresh Coffee Company
2375 S West Temple
South Salt Lake, UT 84115-2633   801-486-3334
            Fax: 801-486-9714   888-486-3334
    info@BrewFresh.com   www.brewfresh.com
Manufacturer of the largest coffee roaster in Utah.
We also produce; hot cocoa mixes, powder coffee
creamers and powdered shake mixes
    President: Larry Brog
    Sales/Marketing Manager/EVP: Anton Broq
Estimated Sales: $500,000-$1 Million
Number Employees: 10-19

1801 Brewski's Brewing Company
142 Arena Street
El Segundo, CA 90245-3901   310-202-9400
            Fax: 310-322-6700 www.ibeerman.com
Beer
    President: Sandy Saemann
    Vice President: Stephen Hogan
    Production Manager: Jane Gaillard
Estimated Sales: Under $500,000
Number Employees: 20-49
Brands:
    Bar Room Ale
    Bar Room Blonde
    Bar Room Honey Red
    Brewski's
    Holiday Salute

1802 (HQ)Brewster Dairy
P.O.Box 98
Brewster, OH 44613-0098   330-767-3492
            Fax: 330-767-3386   800-874-0874
            hr@brewstercheese.com
            www.brewstercheese.com
Processor and exporter of cheese including natural,
Swiss, cheddar, colby, jack and muenster; also, whey
    President: Brad Nelson
    VP Finance: Thomas Kiegler
    R&D: Gene Hong, Ph.D.
    Marketing: Jim Straughn
    Operations Manager: Brad Nelson
    Director Manufacturing: Lloyd Bryant
    Plant Manager: Tom Beck
    Purchasing: Paul Snyder
Estimated Sales: $50-100 Million
Number Employees: 100-249
Type of Packaging: Consumer, Food Service, Pri-
    vate Label, Bulk
Other Locations:
    Brewster Dairy
    Stockton IL

1803 Brewster Foods TestLab
7121 Canby Avenue
PO Box 306
Reseda, CA 91335-0306   818-881-4268
            Fax: 818-881-6370 rob@testlabinc.com
            www.testlabinc.com/
Processor and exporter of enzymes, flavors and in-
gredients.
    President: Gregory Brewster
    Customer Service: Rob Brewster
    Customer Service: Mike Latauska
Estimated Sales: $1100000
Number Employees: 15
Sq. footage: 4000
Brands:
    Brewster
    Testlab
    Vitalfa

1804 Briar's USA
P.O.Box 7902
North Brunswick, NJ 08902   732-821-7600
            Fax: 732-821-2898   887-327-4277
    info@briars.com   www.highgradebeverage.com
Manufacturer of soft drinks
    President: Guy Dattatlia
    CEO: Joseph Demarco

1805 Briceland Vineyards
5959 Briceland-Shelter Cove Rd
Redway, CA 95560   707-923-2429
Wines and champagnes
    President: Margaret Carey
Estimated Sales: $1-2.5 Million
Number Employees: 1-4

1806 Brick Brewery
181 King Street S
Waterloo, ON N2J 1P7
Canada   519-576-9100
            Fax: 519-576-0470   800-505-8971
    info@brickbeer.com   www.brickbeer.com
Manufacturer and exporter of light and dark lager
beers; also, ale
    Founder/Executive Chairman: Jim Brickman
    President/CEO: Doug Berchtold
    CFO: Graydon Moore
    VP Marketing: Norm Pickering
    VP Operations: Mike Baumken
Number Employees: 50-99
Sq. footage: 45000
Type of Packaging: Consumer
Brands:
    ALGONQUIN HONEYBROWN
    ANDECHS
    ANNIVERSARY BOCK
    BRICK PREMIUM
    CONNERS BEST BITTER
    FIX
    FORMOSA DRAFT
    HENNINGER KAISER PILS
    LAKER FAMILY OF BEERS
    PACIFIC REAL DRAFT
    RED BARON
    RED CAP
    WATERLOO DARK

1807 Bricker Labs
PO Box 338
Jackson, WI 53037-0338   262-334-7047
            Fax: 262-334-7651   800-274-2537
            www.brickerlabs.com
Processor of nutritional supplements
    Sales/Marketing Manager: Tami Dechairo
Estimated Sales: $1-2.5 Million
Number Employees: 20-49
Type of Packaging: Consumer, Food Service, Pri-
    vate Label, Bulk

1808 Bridenbaughs Orchards
316 Orchard Ln
Martinsburg, PA 16662-8145   814-793-2364
Grower and packer of apples, peaches, cherries,
strawberries and raspberries; exporter of apples
    Co-Owner: Glenn Bridenbaugh
    Co-Owner: David Bridenbaugh
Estimated Sales: Less than $500,000
Number Employees: 1-4
Sq. footage: 4000
Type of Packaging: Consumer, Bulk

1809 Bridenbaughs Orchards
P.O.Box 720
West Sacramento, CA 95691-0720   916-739-6540
            Fax: 916-739-0162
Fruits
    Owner: David Levin
Estimated Sales: $500,000-$1 Million
Number Employees: 5-9

1810 Bridge Brand Chocolate
286 12th Street
San Francisco, CA 94103   415-677-9194
            Fax: 415-362-2080   888-732-4626
            www.sfchocolate.com
gourmet chocolates

1811 Bridgetown Coffee
2330 NW 31st Ave
Portland, OR 97210-2034   503-224-3330
            Fax: 503-224-9529   800-726-0320
            www.bridgetowncoffee.com

Processor and exporter of coffee; wholesaler/distrib-
utor and exporter of tea; serving the food service
market
    President/Owner: Don Jensen
    CEO: Timothy Timmins
    Operations Manager: David Brathwait
Estimated Sales: $5-$10 Million
Number Employees: 20-49
Number of Brands: 6
Number of Products: 21
Sq. footage: 40000
Type of Packaging: Consumer, Food Service, Pri-
    vate Label, Bulk
Brands:
    BRIDGETOWN

1812 Bridgeview Winery
P.O.Box 609
Cave Junction, OR 97523-0609   541-592-4688
            Fax: 541-592-2127   877-273-4843
            www.bridgeviewwine.com.
            www.bridgeviewwine.com
Wine
    President: Robert Kerivan
Estimated Sales: $ 10 - 20 Million
Number Employees: 20-49

1813 (HQ)Bridgford Foods
P.O.Box 3773
Anaheim, CA 92803-3773   714-526-5533
            Fax: 714-526-4360   800-527-2105
    info@bridgford.com   www.bridgford.com
Manufacturer of frozen dough, pre-baked biscuits,
shelf-stable dry and semi-dry sausage products and
an assortment of frozen micro-ready sandwiches
    Chairman: Allan Bridgford
    President: Robert Schulze
    CFO: Raymond Lancy
Estimated Sales: $20-50 Million
Number Employees: 500-999
Type of Packaging: Consumer
Other Locations:
    Bridgford Foods Plant
    Dallas TX
    Bridgford Foods Plant
    Chicago IL
    Bridgford Foods Plant
    Statesville NC

1814 Bridgford Foods Corporation
P.O.Box 3773
Anaheim, CA 92803-3773   714-526-5533
            Fax: 714-526-4360   800-527-2105
    info@bridgford.com   www.bridgford.com
Manufacturer and distributor of frozen products, re-
frigerated and snack food products such as; biscuits,
bread dough, dry sausage, various sandwiches and
sliced luncheon meats
    Chairman: Allan Bridgford
    President: William Bridgford
    CFO: Raymond Lancy
Estimated Sales: I
Number Employees: 500-999
Type of Packaging: Consumer, Food Service
Other Locations:
    Bridgford Plant
    Dallas TX
    Bridgford Plant
    Chicago IL
    Bridgford Plant
    Statesville NC
Brands:
    BRIDGFORD JERKY

**1815 Bridgford Foods Corporation
Superior Foods Division**
P.O.Box 3773
Anaheim, CA 92803-3773   714-526-5533
            Fax: 714-526-4360   800-527-2105
    info@bridgford.com   www.bridgford.com
Processor of baked goods including frozen dinner
rolls and biscuits
    President: William Bridgford
    Chairman: Alan Bridgford
    Senior VP Sales/Marketing: Daniel Yost
    Director Public Relations: Lorene Salcido
Estimated Sales: $5-10 Million
Number Employees: 500-999
Type of Packaging: Food Service
Brands:
    BERTOLINI
    BERTOLINO
    BRIDGFORD
    BRIDGFORD BRANDS

FROZEN RITE
FROZEN-RITE

1816 Bridgford Foods Corporation
P.O.Box 3773
Anaheim, CA 92803-3773   714-526-5533
Fax: 714-526-4360   800-527-2105
www.bridgford.com
Processor and exporter of frozen dough, processed
meat, dry sausage and microwaveable sandwiches;
importer of boneless beef
Chairman, CEO: Allen Bridgford
President, CFO: Robert Schulze
VP, Treasurer: Raymond Lancy
Secretary: William Bridgford
*Estimated Sales:*1
Number Employees: 500-999
Sq. footage: 400000
Type of Packaging: Consumer, Food Service
Brands:
BERTOLINO
BRIDGFORD
FROZEN-RITE

1817 Bridor
1370 Rue Graham Bell
Boucherville, QC J4B 6H5
Canada   450-641-1265
Fax: 450-641-2428
Processor and exporter of frozen bread dough,
breads, croissants and danish; also, par-baked bread
President: Gerald Peooetier
Number Employees: 100-249
Parent Co: Bridor Products
Type of Packaging: Consumer, Food Service

1818 Brier Run Farm
Hc 32
Box 73
Birch River, WV 26610-9729   304-649-2975
Manufacturer of certified organic fresh chevre
cheese
Co-Owner: Greg Sava
Co-Owner: Verena Sava
Estimated Sales:$200,000
Number Employees: 5
Sq. footage: 2000
Type of Packaging: Consumer, Food Service
Brands:
Brier Run
Brier Run Chevre

1819 (HQ)Briess Industries
PO Box 229
Chilton, WI 53014-0229   920-849-7711
Fax: 920-849-4277   info@briess.com
www.briess.com
Manufacturer of all-natural food ingredients includ-
ing malts, natural sweeteners (grain and
starch-based), natural colorants, tapioca
maltodextrins, reduced cook-time grains,
pregelatinized flakes, and toasted grains. Many are
wholegrain. Non-GMO, Kosher Certified, USDA
Certified Organics.
President: Gordon Lane
CEO: Monica Briess
CFO: Craig Kennedy
Research & Development: Bob Hansen
Purchasing: Leana Prupson
Number Employees: 125
Type of Packaging: Bulk
Other Locations:
Briess Ingredients Company
Chilton WI
Waterloo WI
Brands:
BRIESS
CBW
INSTA GRAINS
MALTOFERM
MALTOROSE

1820 Briggs Ice Cream
5110 Buchanan St
Hyattsville, MD 20781-2488   301-277-8787
Fax: 301-927-4527   info@briggsicecream.com
www.briggsicecream.com
Ice cream
Owner, President: David Rosin
Sales Manager: Steve Williams
General Manager: Robert Strahorn
Purchasing: Steve Williams
Estimated Sales:$10-20 Million
Number Employees: 10-19

Brands:
ELAN FROZEN YOGURT

1821 Brighams
46 Mill Street
Arlington, MA 02476-4700   781-648-9000
Fax: 781-646-0507   800-274-4426
brighams-mail@brighams.com
www.brighams.com
Processor of ice cream, frozen yogurt, whipped
cream and fudge topping
President: Chuck Green
Operations: Claudia Kost
Estimated Sales:$2.5-5 Million
Number Employees: 50
Sq. footage: 110000
Type of Packaging: Consumer, Private Label, Bulk
Brands:
BRIGHAM'S
ELAN

1822 Bright Harvest Sweet Potato Company
P.O.Box 528
Clarksville, AR 72830-0528   479-754-6313
Fax: 479-754-7794   800-793-7440
swinter@brightharvest.com
www.brightharvest.com
Sweet potato patties, mashed sweet potatoes, sweet
potato sticks, center cut sweet potatoes, sweet potato
casserole
President: Rex King
President: Rex King
Quality Control: Jeff Hannon
VP Marketing/Sales: Sam Winterberg
Regional Sales Representative: John Coniglio
VP Operations: John Eyberg
Customer Service: Patricia Melton
Estimated Sales:$20-50 Million
Number Employees: 50-99
Sq. footage: 22000
Type of Packaging: Consumer, Food Service

1823 Brightwood Baking Company
24950 Mount Pleasant Road
Cicero, IN 46034-9470   317-356-2449
Processor of frozen baked goods including dough-
nuts and sweet rolls
Sales Manager: Gul Dansuinie
Bakery Manager: Jerry Miller
Estimated Sales:$10-20 Million
Number Employees: 20-49
Type of Packaging: Food Service, Private Label,
Bulk

1824 Brimstone Hill Vineyard
61 Brimstone Hill Rd
Pine Bush, NY 12566-5400   845-744-2231
Fax: 845-744-4782   bhvwine@frontiernet.net
brimstonehillwine.com
Manufacturer of still and sparkling wines
Owner: Richard Eldridge
Owner: Valerie Eldridge
Estimated Sales:$500,000-750,000
Number Employees: 1-4
Type of Packaging: Food Service
Brands:
Brimstone Hill

1825 Brinkley Dryer and Storage
25 W White Oak St
Brinkley, AR 72021   870-734-1616
Fax: 870-734-2113 www.achfood.com
Rice specialties
Manager: Donnie Parsley
VP, CFO, Treasurer: E Ray Wayne, Jr
Executive VP, Assistant Secretary: W David
Hanks
Marketing Director: Nelson Wurth
Operations Manager: Rick Wade
Production Manager: Patrick Roy
Plant Manager: Perry Willingham
Estimated Sales:$50 Million
Number Employees: 100-249
Sq. footage: 50
Parent Co: Riviana Foods
Type of Packaging: Private Label
Brands:
FIESTA BRAND
ISLAND GIRL BRAND

1826 Briny Sea Delicacies
715 78th Avenue SW
Tumwater, WA 98501-5700   360-956-1797
Fax: 360-956-1986
Processor of seafood including fresh, vac-
uum-packed smoked salmon
President: Jay Garrison
*Estimated Sales:*Less than $500,000
Number Employees: 1-4
Type of Packaging: Consumer, Food Service

1827 Brisk Coffee Company
507 N 22nd St
Tampa, FL 33605-6084   813-248-6264
Fax: 813-248-2947   800-899-5282
rperez@briskcoffee.com   www.briskcoffee.com
Processor and exporter of roasted coffee; also, leas-
ing of coffee equipment available
President/CEO: Richard Perez
Division President Sales: Phil Cooke
Sales Manager National/Government Accts:
Vicky Moore
National Sales Manager: Bill Watson
Division President Production: Randy Gonzalez
Estimated Sales:$10-20 Million
Number Employees: 20-49
Sq. footage: 20000
Type of Packaging: Food Service
Brands:
BRISK
GOLD PLUS
INNKEEPERS CHOICE

1828 Bristle Ridge Vineyard
P.O.Box 95
Knob Noster, MO 65336-0095   660-422-5646
800-994-9463
edward@brvwine.com   www.brvwine.com
Wines
President: Edward Smith
Co-Owner: Vickie Smith
General Manager: Todd Smith
Estimated Sales:$5-9.9 Million
Number Employees: 5-9
Brands:
Bristle Ridge

1829 Bristol Brewing Company
1647 S Tejon St
Colorado Springs, CO 80905-2215   719-633-2555
Fax: 719-633-2145   info@bristolbrewing.com
www.bristolbrewing.com
Processor of ale and stout
Manager: Josh Osperhoudp
Marketing: Megan Cram
Sales/Distribution: Bob Catalano
Operations: Josh Osterhoudt
Production: Jason Yester
Estimated Sales:$5-10 Million
Number Employees: 20-49
Type of Packaging: Consumer, Food Service, Bulk
Brands:
BEEHIVE
EDGE CITY IPA
EDGE CITY PILSNER
LAUGHING LAB
MASS TRANSIT
OLD NO.23
RED ROCKET
SCOTTISH
WINTER WARLOCK

1830 (HQ)Bristol Myers-Squibb Company
345 Park Ave
New York, NY 10154   212-546-4000
Fax: 212-546-4020 www.bms.com
Manufacturer of pharmaceuticals and related health
care products
Chairman: James Cornelius
President/CEO: Lamberto Andreotti
CFO: Charles Bancroft
Estimated Sales:$19 Billion
Number Employees: 28,000
Brands:
ENFACARE LIPIL
ENFALYTE
ENFAMIL GENTLE EASE LIPIL
ENFAMIL LIPIL LOW IRON
ENFAMIL WITH IRON
EXPECTA LIPIL
FER-IN SOL
KINDERCAL
LOCTOFREE LIPIL

NEXT STEP LIPIL
NEXT STEP PROSOBEE LIPIL
NUTRAMIGEN LIPIL
POLY-VI-SOL
PROGESTIMIL
PROSOBEE LIPIL
TRI-VI-SOL LIQUID

1831 Bristol Pork Company
533 Maple Street
Bristol, PA 19007-3510   215-788-3356
Processor of pork
President: Ed Mittleman
Estimated Sales:$5-10 Million
Number Employees: 10-19
Type of Packaging: Bulk

1832 Britannia Natural Products
PO Box 4554
New Windsor, NY 12553-0554   845-534-1335
          Fax: 845-534-1312   bnpusa@aol.com
Beverage ingredients, fruit, essential oils, natural
chemicals, flavors, concentrates
Estimated Sales:$500,000-$1 Million
Number Employees: 1-4

1833 British American Tea & Coffee
1320 Old Oxford Road
Durham, NC 27704-2470   919-471-1357
                Fax: 919-471-1357
Tea and coffee.
President: Christopher Hulbert
CFO: Elizabeth Albert
*Estimated Sales:*Under $500,000
Number Employees: 20-49
Sq. footage: 2
Type of Packaging: Private Label

1834 Brittle Bark Company
215 W Main Street
PO Box 1064
Mechanicsburg, PA 17055-1064   717-697-6950
    Fax: 717-731-9081   diane@brittlebark.com
                www.brittlebark.com
Brittle candy made with assorted nuts, dried fruits
and premium chocolate.
President/Owner: Diane Krulac

1835 Brittle Kettle
700 York Street
Lebanon, TN 37087-2960   615-449-6257
    Fax: 615-449-6263   bkettle@bellsouth.net
                www.brittlekettle.com
Processor of peanut brittle
President: Deanna Wilson
VP: Howard Wilson
Estimated Sales:$1-2.5 Million
Number Employees: 5-9
Type of Packaging: Consumer

1836 Brix Chocolates
PO Box 9111
Youngstown, OH 44513   330-657-5864
    Fax: 330-726-0749   866-613-2749
        sales@brixchocolate.com
            www.brixchocolate.com
Chocolate

1837 Broad Run Vineyards
10601 Broad Run Rd
Louisville, KY 40299-5417   502-231-0372
            finewine@iclou.com
        www.broadrunvineyards.com
Dry table and dessert wines
Owner/Grower/Vintner: Gerald Kushner
Manager of Sales/Marketing: Marilyn Kushner
Assistant Vintner: Lloyd Hyatt
Estimated Sales:$1-2.5 Million
Number Employees: 1-4
Sq. footage: 2000
Type of Packaging: Food Service
Brands:
  BROAD RUN VINEYARDS

1838 Broad Street Coffee Roasers
302 E Pettigrew Street
Suite 104
Durham, NC 27701-3796   919-688-5668
    Fax: 919-683-6377   800-733-9916
        www.broadstreetcoffee.com

Coffee
Founder, President: Larry Hayes
VP Administration: Terry Mancour
VP Operations, Roastmaster: Mark Leatherwood
Production: Jasmine Page
Estimated Sales:$2.5-5 Million
Number Employees: 1-4
Type of Packaging: Private Label

1839 Broadaway Ham Company
500 N Culberhouse St
Jonesboro, AR 72401-1690   870-932-6688
            ham-man@sbcglobal.net
Manufacturer of meat products including deli barbe-
cued ham and snack sticks
Owner: Bruce Broadway
Plant Manager: John Collins
Estimated Sales:$1-3 Million
Number Employees: 1-4
Sq. footage: 5000
Type of Packaging: Consumer
Brands:
  CROWLEY RIDGE

1840 Broadbent's B&B Foods
257 Mary Blue Rd
Kuttawa, KY 42055-6299   270-388-0609
    Fax: 270-388-0613   800-841-2202
        manager@broadbenthams.com
            www.broadbenthams.com
Manufacturer of cured ham, bacon and sausage
Owner: Ronny Drennan
*Estimated Sales:*Less Than $1 Million
Number Employees: 10-19

1841 Broadleaf Venison USA
5600 S Alameda St
Vernon, CA 90058-3428   323-826-9890
    Fax: 323-826-9830   800-336-3844
        mm@broadleafgame.com
            www.broadleafgame.com
Processor, importer and exporter of chilled and
frozen venison, wagyu beef ground venison sausage,
ostrich, buffalo and wild boar; wholesaler/distributor
of frozen foods and meats; serving the food service
market
President: Mark Mitchell
CEO: Pat McGowan
CFO: Ara Temuryan
Vice President: Annie Mitchell
Sales Director: Nathan Cooney
Operations Manager: Pierre La Breton
Plant Manager: Jose Madera
Purchasing Manager: Jamie Ferguson
Estimated Sales:$20-30 Million
Number Employees: 20-49
Sq. footage: 56000
Type of Packaging: Consumer, Food Service
Brands:
  BROADLEAF
  BROADLEAF CERVENA

1842 Broadley Vineyards
25158 Orchard Tract Rd
Monroe, OR 97456-9455   541-847-5934
    Fax: 541-847-6018   broadley@peak.org
        www.broadleyvineyards.com
Wines
President: Craig Broadley
Estimated Sales:$1-2.5 Million
Number Employees: 1-4

1843 Broadmoor Labs
4564 Telephone Rd
Ventura, CA 93003-5661   805-650-0996
    Fax: 805-650-0997   800-822-3712
    lfp@jetlink.net   www.happyhealth.net
Processor, exporter and importer of health products
including nutritional supplements
Owner: Larry Permen
VP: Larry Permen
Estimated Sales:$ 3 - 5 Million
Number Employees: 1-4
Brands:
  Bread, Rice & Pasta Lovers Diet
  Dermagest
  Natragest
  Sound Sleep

1844 Brock Seed Company
PO Box 549
El Centro, CA 92244-0549   760-353-1632
    Fax: 760-353-1693   brockasparagus@prodigy.net
        www.brockaspargus.com

Manufacturer and exporter of asparagus and aspara-
gus seed
Manager: Don Brock
Type of Packaging: Consumer, Food Service, Pri-
vate Label
Brands:
  Brock

1845 Brockles Foods Company
322 E Buckingham Road
Garland, TX 75040-4712   972-272-5593
Mayonnaise and sauces
President: Grover Howard
Estimated Sales:$5-9.9 Million
Number Employees: 5-9
Brands:
  Brockles

1846 Brockmann Chocolates
Unit 16-4751 Shell Road
Richmond, BC V6X 3H4
Canada   604-273-2230
    Fax: 604-279-8809   888-494-2270
        info@brockmannchocolate.com
            www.brockmannchocolate.com
Manufacturer of chocolates
Founder: Willy Brockmann
President: Norbert Brockmann
CEO: Marianne Brockmann
Type of Packaging: Private Label
Brands:
  TRUFFINI

**1847 Brockton Beef & Provisions
Corporation**
994 Crescent Street
Brockton, MA 02302-3409   508-583-4703
Manufacturer of hamburgers and sausage; Retail
Sales
President: Alan D'Ambrosio
Estimated Sales:$100,000-$150,000
Number Employees: 1-4

1848 Brokay Products
9999 Gantry Road
Philadelphia, PA 19115-1001   215-676-4800
                Fax: 215-677-1973
Candy and confectionery, bulk supplier

1849 Broken Bow Pack
518 E South E St
Broken Bow, NE 68822-2716   308-872-2833
Processor of meat products
Owner: Gary Voss
Estimated Sales:$2.5-5 Million
Number Employees: 1-4
Type of Packaging: Consumer

1850 Brolite Products
1900 S Park Ave
Streamwood, IL 60107-2944   630-830-0340
    Fax: 630-830-0356   888-276-5483
        info@bakewithbrolite.com
            www.bakewithbrolite.com
Processor of flavors, stabilizers, yeast foods, dough
accelerators and conditioners, egg yolk and whole
egg substitutes and fudge, English muffin and bread
bases; exporter of white and rye sour dough flavors
President: Virgil Delghingaro
Executive VP: David Del Ghingaro
R&D: Daniel Garcia
Marketing/Sales VP: Tom MacDonald
Estimated Sales:$2.5-5 Million
Number Employees: 50-99
Sq. footage: 36000
Type of Packaging: Bulk
Brands:
  ALL SOFT
  B5000
  BRO EGCELLENT
  BRO WHITE SOUR
  BROLITE IA
  BROSOFT
  EGG-O-LITE
  FEVER SOURS
  VITA PLUS

1851 Brom Food Group
5595 Cote De Liesse
St. Laurent, QC H4M 1V2
Canada   514-744-5152
                Fax: 514-744-8195

Processor, importer and exporter of frozen foods and frozen and fresh pierogies including cheese, potato/onion, beef and chicken
  Director Mareksting: Tom Luczak
  Director Operations: Bruce Luczak, M.B.A.
Sq. footage: 18000
Type of Packaging: Consumer, Food Service, Private Label, Bulk
Brands:
  Granny's
  Ogi's

1852 Brome Lake Ducks Ltd
40 Centre Road
PO Box 3430
Knowlton, QC J0E 1VO
Canada   450-242-3825
        Fax: 450-243-0497 888-956-1977
                     info@bromelakeducks.com
                     www.bromelakeducks.com
Duck products
  President: Claude Trottier
  CFO: Genevieve Grenier CMA
  R&D Director: Jennifer Caron
  Quality Control: Jennifer Caron
  Marketing Coordinator: Pier-Luc Fiest
  VP Sales/Marketing: Bruno Giuliani
  Human Resources Director: Michele Cote
  COO: Claude Trottier
  Plant Manager: Guy Ducharme

1853 Bronco Wine Company
P.O.Box 789
Ceres, CA 95307-0789   209-538-3131
        Fax: 209-538-4634 800-692-5780
winekid3@home.com   www.broncowine.com
Manufacturer of wine
  Owner: Fred Franzia
  Co-President: Joseph Franzia
  CEO: Fred Franzia
Estimated Sales: $250 Million
Number Employees: 250-499
Type of Packaging: Private Label
Brands:
  CHARLES SHAW
  ESTRELLA
  FORESTVILLE
  FOXHOLLOW
  GRAND CRU
  HACIENDA
  MONTPELLIER
  NAPA RIDGE
  RUTHERFORD VINTNERS
  SILVER RIDGE

1854 Brook Locker Plant
P.O.Box 451
Brook, IN 47922-0451   219-275-2611
Processor of meat products and fresh and frozen foods including beef, pork, chicken and veal; also, slaughtering available
  Owner: Jeff Laffoon
  Vice President: Chris Schoonveld
Estimated Sales: $1-2.5 Million
Number Employees: 5-9
Type of Packaging: Consumer, Bulk

1855 Brook Meadow ProvisionsCorporation
716 Security Rd
Hagerstown, MD 21740-4143   301-739-3107
Manufacturer of pork, beef and sausage
  Owner: Donald Hoffman
Estimated Sales: $5-10 Million
Number Employees: 1-4
Type of Packaging: Consumer

1856 Brookema Company
1120 Commerce Drive
West Chicago, IL 60185-2680   630-562-2290
                          Fax: 630-562-2291
Processor and contract packager of dry mixes including cake, soup, cocoa, coffee and coffee creamer
  President: Dan Clery
Estimated Sales: $2.5-5 Million
Number Employees: 20-49
Type of Packaging: Bulk

1857 Brookfield Farms
219 N Green Street
Chicago, IL 60607-1701   773-468-1739
                          Fax: 312-829-4788

Processor and exporter of fresh and frozen pork and beef
  President: Frank Swan
Estimated Sales: $ 20 - 50 Million
Number Employees: 100-249
Type of Packaging: Consumer, Food Service

1858 Brooklyn Bagel Company
PO Box 120027
Staten Island, NY 10312-0027   718-349-3055
           Fax: 718-349-1107 800-349-3055
Processor of frozen bagels
  Sales Manager: Stanley Silverman
  Sales Manager: Arnie Lichtenstein
  General Manager: Donald Santman
Estimated Sales: $1-2.5 Million
Number Employees: 20-49
Sq. footage: 20000
Type of Packaging: Consumer, Food Service, Bulk

1859 Brooklyn Baking Company
8 John St
Waterbury, CT 06708-3515   203-574-9198
Manufacturer of baked goods including sourdough, white and rye bread and cookies
  Manager: Art Lessier
Estimated Sales: Less than $500,000
Number Employees: 5-9
Type of Packaging: Consumer, Bulk
Brands:
  Brooklyn Baking Pumpernickel Bread
  Brooklyn Baking Rye Bread

1860 Brooklyn Bottling Company
P.O.Box 808
Milton, NY 12547-0808   845-795-2171
        Fax: 845-795-2589 emiller@nsbottle.com
                     www.brooklynbottling.com
Processor and bottler of juice drinks, apple juice and cider, iced tea and carbonated beverages including Latin American soda
  President: Eric Miller
  Quality Control: Luis Gonzalez
  Sales Director: Tom Marigliano
Estimated Sales: $10-20 Million
Number Employees: 100-249
Number of Brands: 25
Number of Products: 200
Type of Packaging: Private Label, Bulk
Brands:
  APPLE DANDY
  COUNTRY CLUB
  D&G
  NATURE'S OWN
  POSTOBON
  TROPICAL FANTASY

1861 Brooklyn Brewery
79 N 11th St
Brooklyn, NY 11211-1913   718-486-7422
        Fax: 718-486-7440 www.fansforfairplay.com
Processor of ale, stout and lager
  President: Steve Hindy
  President: Steve Hindy
  Controller: Debra Bascome
  VP New York Sales: Mike Vitale
  VP Out of State Sales: Robin Ottaway
  Brewmaster: Garrett Oliver
  General Manager: Eric Ottaway
Estimated Sales: $20-50 Million
Number Employees: 20-49
Type of Packaging: Consumer, Food Service, Bulk
Brands:
  BROOKLYN
  CHIMAY
  DUVEL
  PAULANER
  SAMUEL SMITH
  SIERRA NEVADA

1862 Brookmere Vineyards
107 Brookmere Farm Ln
Belleville, PA 17004-9303   717-935-5380
Fax: 717-935-5349 brookemere@nittanylink.com
                     www.brookmerewine.com
Wines
  Owner: Cheryl Glick
Estimated Sales: $2.5-5 Million
Number Employees: 5-9
Type of Packaging: Bulk

1863 Brooks County Sausage
610 S Highland Rd
Quitman, GA 31643-2922   229-263-7920
        Fax: 229-263-8458 800-342-4111
Processor of meat products including pork
  Manager: Pam Jones
  Plant Manager: Steve Twedell
Estimated Sales: $20-50 Million
Number Employees: 1-4
Parent Co: Sunnyland Foods
Type of Packaging: Consumer, Food Service, Private Label

1864 (HQ)Brooks Food Group Corporate Office
940 Orange St
Bedford, VA 24523-3303   540-586-8284
        Fax: 540-587-3137 800-873-4934
customerservice@brooksfoodgroup.com
                     www.brooksfoodgroup.com
Manufacturer of frozen foods including onion rings, french toast, breaded vegetables and cheese sticks; also, protein products including nuggets, patties, sticks, strips; exporter of onion rings
  Chairman/CEO: Robin Brooks
Estimated Sales: $20-50 Million
Number Employees: 250-499
Sq. footage: 90000
Other Locations:
  Brooks Food Group Plant
  Monroe NC
Brands:
  GOLDEN WEST FOODS

1865 Brooks Food Group, Inc
2701 Simpson St
Monroe, NC 28112-4120   704-289-8300
        Fax: 704-283-7623 800-873-4934
                     sales@brooksfoodgroup.com
                     www.brooksfoodgroup.com
Battered and breaded beef steak patties, chicken patties, mozzarella cheese sticks, breaded okra
  President: Harold Marshall
  VP Finance: Alan Kolody
  Executive VP: Jolene Belk
  Quality Control: John Schultz
  Plant Manager: Harold Marshall
  Purchasing Manager: Libby Lawrence
Estimated Sales: $100-500 Million
Number Employees: 100-249
Type of Packaging: Private Label, Bulk

1866 Brooks Meat
106 N Main St
Walton, KY 41094-1113   859-485-7104
                          Fax: 606-485-1541
Meat
  President: Steve Brooks
Estimated Sales: $ .5 - 1 million
Number Employees: 1-4

1867 Brooks Peanut Company
P.O.Box 305
Samson, AL 36477-0305   334-898-7194
                          Fax: 334-898-7196
Processor of peanuts
  Owner: Fleming G Brooks
  Vice President: Barrett Brooks
Estimated Sales: $1-2.5 Million
Number Employees: 5-9
Type of Packaging: Bulk

1868 Brooks Tropicals
P.O.Box 900160
Homestead, FL 33090-0160   305-247-3544
        Fax: 305-242-7393 800-327-4833
                     maryo@brookstropicals.com
                     www.brookstropicals.com
Grower, packer and shipper of papayas, avocados, starfruit, limes, passion fruit, mangos, guavas, uglyfruit and other tropical produce.
  President: Neil Brooks
  CEO: Craig Wheeling
  CEO: Craig Wheeling
  Director Marketing: Mary Ostlund
  VP Sales Management: Bill Brindle
  VP Human Resources: Susan Kruse
Estimated Sales: $ 10 - 20 Million
Number Employees: 100-249
Type of Packaging: Bulk

1869 Brooks Tropicals
P.O.Box 900160
Homestead, FL 33090-0160   305-247-3544
Fax: 305-242-7393   800-327-4833
info@brookstropicals.com
www.brookstropicals.com
Tropical foods and vegetables
President: Neal Brooks
VP Sales Management: Bill Brindle
R & D: Frank Sesto
CEO: Craig Wheeling
Quality Control: Billy Pritchett
Marketing Manager: Mary Ostlund
Estimated Sales: $ 30-50 Million
Number Employees: 100-249
Type of Packaging: Bulk

1870 Brookside Foods
3899 Mt. Lehman Road
Abbotsford, BC V4X 2N1
Canada   604-852-5940
Fax: 604-607-7012   877-793-3866
info@brooksidefoods.com
www.brooksidefoods.com
Processor of base concentrates, fruit fillings, custom ice cream inclusions, confectionery coatings, and paned and deposited chocolate confections, etc. Importer of cocoa butter, cocoal powder, chocolate liquer, etc. Exporter of realfruit chips, chocolate, paned and deposited chocolate confections, etc. Custom dry blending and private labeling.
President: Denis McGuire
Director Sales: Alan Whitteker
Parent Co: Brookside Foods
Type of Packaging: Consumer, Private Label, Bulk

1871 Brookview Farms
V354 County Road 24
Archbold, OH 43502-9502   419-445-6366
Fax: 419-445-0503
Processor of fresh and frozen meat including beef, pork, lamb and venison
President: Jack Lugbill
Estimated Sales: $5-10 Million
Number Employees: 10-19
Sq. footage: 7000
Type of Packaging: Consumer, Food Service, Bulk

1872 Brost International Trading Company
180 N Stetson Ave # 3400
Chicago, IL 60601-6740   312-861-7100
Fax: 312-225-4444
Processor and exporter of nuts, cheese flavored balls, nacho cheese, potato and corn chips, potato sticks and canned whole kernel corn and diced carrots
President: David Brost
VP: Elayne Brost
Estimated Sales: $ 3 - 5 Million
Number Employees: 20-49
Sq. footage: 10000
Type of Packaging: Consumer, Private Label
Brands:
Regal
Regal Farms

1873 Brother Bru Bru's Produce
PO Box 2964
Venice, CA 90294-2964   310-396-9033
Fax: 301-455-7221   brobrubru@aol.com
Natural salt-free sauces
President: Bruce Langhorne
Vice President: Janet Bachelor
Sales Director: Cynthia Riddle
Estimated Sales: $ 5 - 10 Million
Number Employees: 5-9
Type of Packaging: Private Label

1874 Brother's Bakery
47 Old Turnpike Road
Southington, CT 06489-3675   860-628-5455
Fax: 860-621-0729
Breads and rolls
Estimated Sales: $5-10 Million
Number Employees: 10-19

1875 Brotherhood Winery
P.O.Box 190
Washingtonville, NY 10992-0190   845-496-3661
Fax: 845-496-8720   wine@frontiernet.net
www.wines.com/brotherhood
Wines
President: Cesar Baeza
Vice President: James Cimino
Treasurer: Michael Venieri
Estimated Sales: $25-49.9 Million
Number Employees: 20-49
Type of Packaging: Private Label
Brands:
BROTHERHOOD

1876 Brothers International Desserts
1682 Kettering
Irvine, CA 92614-5614   949-655-0080
Fax: 949-655-0081 www.brothersdesserts.com
Processor sorbet, fruit bars and ice cream including vanilla, chocolate and strawberry; importer of chocolate and fruits; exporter of fruit bars
President: Gary Winkler
Number Employees: 50-99
Sq. footage: 30000
Type of Packaging: Food Service, Private Label
Brands:
Big Kahuna
Brothers
Kid Kobruno
Le Gourmet Sorbet
The Classic Sundae
Tropical Treat

1877 Brothers International Food Corp
23-38 Ganson Ave
Batavia, NY 14020   585-343-3007
Fax: 585-343-4218   888-842-7477
info@brothersallnatural.com
www.brothersallnatural.com
All-natural, freeze dried fruit and potato Crisps
CEO: Travis Betters
CFO: Matthew Betters
Estimated Sales: $4.1 Million
Number Employees: 22

1878 Brothers Juniper Bakery
463 Sebastopol Avenue
Santa Rosa, CA 95401-8502   707-542-6546
Fax: 707-542-6682
Bread and bakery products
President/CFO/VP Marketing: Lorene Colvin
Merchandise Support Manager: Dave Martin
Quality Control: Ron Colvin
Estimated Sales: $2.5-5 Million
Number Employees: 20-49

1879 Broughton Cannery
7909 Broughton Pike
Paulding, OH 45879-9639   419-399-3182
Fax: 419-399-3189
Processor of canned meat
Partner: Rex Bowersock
Estimated Sales: $5-10 Million
Number Employees: 10-19
Sq. footage: 14700
Type of Packaging: Consumer, Food Service, Private Label

1880 Broughton Foods
P.O.Box 656
Marietta, OH 45750-0656   740-373-4121
Fax: 740-373-2861   800-283-2479
www.deanfoods.com
Manufacturer and distributor of dairy products including milk, ice cream, cottage cheese, half and half, whipping cream, creamers, yogurt and dips, also; nondairy aerosol whipped topping
GM: David Broughton
Controller: Mike McIlyar
Marketing Director: Tim Duty
Production Manager: Tracy Augenstein
Plant Manager: Mike DePue
Estimated Sales: $75 Million
Number Employees: 250-499
Parent Co: Dean Foods Company
Type of Packaging: Food Service
Brands:
BROUGHTON
DAIRYLANE

1881 Brown & Haley
P.O.Box 1596
Tacoma, WA 98401-1596   253-620-3000
Fax: 253-272-6742   info@brown-haley.com
www.brown-haley.com
Manufacturer and exporter of confectionery items including Almond Roca.
President: Pierson Clair
CEO: Pierson E Clair Iii
VP Sales: Mark Greenhall
Number Employees: 100-249
Type of Packaging: Consumer, Private Label, Bulk
Brands:
MOUNTAIN BAR
ROCA
ZINGOS MINTS

1882 Brown & Jenkins TradingCompany
P.O.Box 236
Cambridge, VT 05444-0236   802-862-2395
Fax: 802-864-7336   800-456-5282
coffee@brownjenkins.com
www.brownjenkins.com
Coffee
Owner: Sandy Riggens
Marketing Director: Sarah Squirrell
Estimated Sales: $1-2.5 Million
Number Employees: 1-4
Brands:
Brown & Jenkins Fresh Roasted

1883 Brown County Wine Company
4520 State Road 46 E
Nashville, IN 47448-8673   812-988-6144
Fax: 812-988-8285   888-298-2984
bcwinfo@browncountywinery.com
www.browncountywinery.com
Wines
President: David Schrodt
Marketing Manager: Cynthia Schrodt
Estimated Sales: $1-2.5 Million
Number Employees: 1-4
Sq. footage: 5000
Type of Packaging: Bulk

1884 Brown Cow Farm
3810 Delta Fair Blvd
Antioch, CA 94509-4008   925-757-9209
Fax: 925-757-9160   888-429-5459
www.browncowfarm.com
Processor of yogurt
Manager: Steve Jerkins
Office Manager: Jennifer Wyneken
Estimated Sales: $10-20 Million
Number Employees: 20-49
Type of Packaging: Consumer
Brands:
Brown Cow Farm

1885 Brown Dairy
P.O.Box 98
Coalville, UT 84017-0098   435-336-5952
Fax: 435-355-6079
Dairy products
Owner: Glen Brown

1886 Brown Family Farm
56 Sugar House Road
Alstead, NH 03602-4307   802-387-8718
Fax: 802-387-4759   866-254-8718
maple@sover.net
www.brownfamilyfarmmaple.com
Maple products
Estimated Sales: $1-2.5 Million
Number Employees: 10-19

1887 Brown Family Farm
74 Cotton Mill Hl # A106
Brattleboro, VT 05301-7837   802-254-4554
Fax: 802-254-5022   866-254-8718
info@brownfamilyfarmmaple.com
www.brownfamilyfarmmaple.com
Maple products, gourmet foods, confections
Executive Director: Arnold Coombs
CFO: Nancy Adams
Estimated Sales: $ 3 - 5 Million
Number Employees: 10-19
Brands:
BROWN FAIRY FARM

1888 Brown Family Farm
74 Cotton Mill Hl # A106
Brattleboro, VT 05301-7837   802-254-4554
Fax: 802-254-5022   888-556-2753
www.brownfamilyfarmmaple.com

Processor of maple syrup, flavored syrups, pancake mixes, salad dressings, roasting sauces and ketchups
Executive Director: Arnold Coombs
Sales/Marketing Manager: Kevin Butler
Estimated Sales:$ 5-10 Million
Number Employees: 10-19

1889 Brown Foods
P.O.Box 953
Dallas, GA 30132-0017   770-445-4554
                              Fax: 770-445-5349
Poultry, pork, seafood, produce, beef
Owner: Graham Kirkman

1890 Brown Packing Company
P.O.Box 130
Gaffney, SC 29342-0130   864-489-5723
                              Fax: 864-487-3210
Processor and exporter of meat products including beef carcasses and primal cuts
President: Walter Brown
Sales/Transportation Manager: Johnny Price
Purchasing Agent: Sloan Bradford
Estimated Sales:$50-100 Million
Number Employees: 250-499
Type of Packaging: Consumer, Bulk

1891 Brown Packing Company
1 Dutch Valley Dr
South Holland, IL 60473-1967   708-849-7990
Fax: 708-849-8094   800-832-8325
Processor and exporter of veal
CEO/President: John Oedzes
VP: Brian Oedzes
Controller: Harold Gatlin
Estimated Sales:$20-50 Million
Number Employees: 50-99
Sq. footage: 1000000
Type of Packaging: Consumer, Food Service, Private Label

1892 Brown Produce Company
P.O.Box 265
Farina, IL 62838-0265   618-245-3301
                              Fax: 618-245-3552
Processor and exporter of eggs and egg products including frozen, liquid, whites, whole and yolk
President: Larry Seger
Vice President: Larry Pemberton
Plant Supervisor: Larry Jahraus
Estimated Sales:$10-20 Million
Number Employees: 50-99
Sq. footage: 10000000
Type of Packaging: Consumer, Bulk

1893 Brown Thompson & Sons
139 State Route 339 N
Fancy Farm, KY 42039   270-623-6321
                              Fax: 270-623-6928
Beef, beef products
Owner: Penny Lamb
Estimated Sales:$ .5 - 1 million
Number Employees: 1-4

1894 Brown's Bakery
505 Downs Street
Defiance, OH 43512-2927   419-784-3330
                              Fax: 419-784-5346
Processor of baked goods including breads and rolls
President: David Graham
CEO: Richard Graham
Sales Manager: Glenn Vinz
Treasurer: Bill Franzdorf
Plant Manager: Ernest Lopshire
Estimated Sales:$10-20 Million
Number Employees: 100-249
Sq. footage: 49720
Type of Packaging: Consumer, Food Service, Private Label, Bulk
Brands:
Bunny
Country Kitchen

1895 (HQ)Brown's Dairy
P.O.Box 52559
New Orleans, LA 70152-2559   504-529-2221
Fax: 504-529-9267   info@brownsdairy.com
                     www.brownsdairy.com
Milk
President: Kennon Davis
Sales Director: Lauren Barre
Plant Manager: John Brousard

Estimated Sales:$300,000-500,000
Number Employees: 1-4
Parent Co: Suiza Dairy Group
Type of Packaging: Consumer
Brands:
Brown's Dairy
Bulgarian Style
Hershey's Milkshake
Luzianne Ready-to-Drink
Nesquik

1896 Brown's Ice Cream
3501 Marshall St NE # 150
Minneapolis, MN 55418-0073   612-378-1075
                              Fax: 612-331-9273
Manufacturer of ice cream
Owner: Robert Nelson
Estimated Sales:$3 Million
Number Employees: 1-4
Parent Co: Upper Lakes Foods
Type of Packaging: Consumer, Food Service, Bulk

1897 (HQ)Brown-Forman Beverages Worldwide
850 Dixie Highway
Louisville, KY 40210   502-585-1100
Fax: 502-774-7876   brown-forman@b-f.com
                     www.brown-forman.com
Manufacturer, importer and exporter of wine, tequila, champagne, whiskey, gin, vodka, and liqueurs.
Chairman & CEO: Paul Varga
Executive VP/CFO: Don Berg
SVP/Chief Brands Officer: Kris Sirchio
SVP/Global Human Resources: Lisa Steiner
Executive VP/COO: James Bareuther
SVP/Chief Production Officer: Jill Jones
Estimated Sales:$3.2 Billion
Number Employees: 4120
Number of Brands: 25
Type of Packaging: Consumer
Other Locations:
Toronto, Ontario, Canada
Louisville KY
Versailles KY
Braintree MA
Dallas TX
Lebanon TN
Lynchburg TN
Nashville TN
Atlanta GA
Hopland CA
Newport Beach CA
San Rafael CA
Windsor CA
Brands:
BEL ARBOR® WINES
BONTERRA® VINEYARDS
CAHMBORD® LIQUEUR
CANADIAN MIST®
DON EDUARDO® TEQUILAS
EARLY TIMES® KENTUCKY WHISKY
EL JIMADOR® TEQUILAS
FETZER® WINES
FINLANDIA® VODKAS
FIVE RIVERS® WINES
GENTLEMAN JACK® RARE TN WHISKY
HERRADURA® TEQUILAS
JACK DANIEL'S® COUNTRY COCKTAIL
JACK DANIEL'S® SINGLE BARREL
JACK DANIEL'S® TN WHISKY
JEKEL® VINEYARDS
KORBEL® CALIFORNIA CHAMPAGNES
LITTLE BLACK DRESS® WINES
OLD FORESTER® KY STRAIGHT B-W
PEPE LOPEZ® TEQUILAS
SANCTUARY® WINES
SONOMA-CUTRER® WINES
SOUTHERN COMFORT®
TUACA® LIQUEUR
WOODFORD RESERVE® KY STRAIGHT

1898 Brownie Baker
4870 W Jacquelyn Ave
Fresno, CA 93722-5027   559-277-7070
Fax: 559-277-7077   800-598-6501
RWRoss1222@aol.com   www.browniebaker.com
Manufacturer of baking products such as; muffins, cakes, brownies, cookies, danish, mexican pastries, poundcake slices and cheesecakes
President: Dennis Perkins
Director Business Development: Adam Maples
VP Sales: Bob Ross
Estimated Sales:$ 20 - 50 Million
Number Employees: 50-99
Sq. footage: 45000

Brands:
PRO TREATS
THE BROWNIE BAKER

1899 Brownie Products Company
423 Industry Ave
Gardner, IL 60424-6321   815-237-2163
                    Fax: 815-237-2644 www.kelloggs.com
Processor of frozen pizza crusts
President: Ronald Westman
CEO: Don Wilson
Quality Assurance Manager: Marion Baranski
Controller: Jeff Grober
Estimated Sales:$20-50 Million
Number Employees: 50-99
Type of Packaging: Consumer, Food Service, Private Label

1900 Browniepops LLC
12008 Wenonga
Leawood, KS 66209   816-797-0715
Fax: 913-491-0788   email@browniepops.com
                     www.browniepops.com
Brownies with a crisp chocolate exterior on a stick lik lollipops. Available in 11 unique flavors.
President/Owner: Marsha Pener Johnston

1901 Browns Dairy
55 Monroe St
Valparaiso, IN 46383-5535   219-464-4141
                              Fax: 219-462-9785
Manufacturer of ice cream, frozen yogurt and sherbet
President: Mike Brown
VP: Mark Brown
Estimated Sales:$500,000
Number Employees: 10-19
Sq. footage: 2000
Parent Co: Valpo Velvet Ice Cream Company
Type of Packaging: Consumer, Food Service
Brands:
Valpo Velvet

1902 Browns' Ice Cream Company
P.O.Box 269
Bowling Green, KY 42102-0269   270-843-9882
Distributor of ice cream
Owner: Jerry Conder
Estimated Sales:$500,000
Number Employees: 5-9
Type of Packaging: Consumer, Food Service, Bulk

1903 Brownsdale Meat Service
105 Main Street W
Brownsdale, MN 55918   507-567-2211
                              Fax: 507-567-2212
Manufacturer of fresh and frozen poultry, beef, pork and seafood
President: Eugene Gerhardt
Number Employees: 9
Type of Packaging: Consumer, Food Service, Private Label

1904 Bruce Baking Company
229 Union Avenue
New Rochelle, NY 10801-6048   914-636-0808
                              Fax: 914-636-0808
Baked goods, macrobiotic food
Owner: Bruce Merbaum
*Estimated Sales:*Under $500,000
Number Employees: 5-9
Brands:
Bruce Baking
Tahini Crunch

1905 Bruce Church
950 E Blanco Road
Salinas, CA 93901-4419   831-758-4421
Fax: 831-422-6714   800-538-2861
Grower of lettuce
CEO: Steve Taylor
Estimated Sales:$100-500 Million
Number Employees: 100-249
Parent Co: Fresh International
Type of Packaging: Consumer, Food Service, Bulk
Brands:
Friendly
Red Coach

1906 Bruce Foods Corporation
P.O.Box 1030
New Iberia, LA 70562-1030   337-365-8101
Fax: 337-364-3742   800-299-9082
info@brucefoodsla.com   www.brucefoods.com

Manufacturer of true Cajun and Tex Mex food products such as; hot sauce, peppers, chili mix, chili powder, burrito seasoning mix, cajun seafood seasonings, canned yams and injectable flavoring
Owner: Si Brown
CEO: Joseph S Brown Jr
Estimated Sales:$10-20 Million
Number Employees: 100-249
Sq. footage: 250000
Type of Packaging: Consumer, Food Service, Bulk
Other Locations:
Bruce Foods Plant
El Paso TX
Bruce Foods Plant
Wilson NC
Bruce Foods Plant
Lozes LA
Bruce Foods Plant
Kerkrade, Netherlands
Brands:
BRUCE'S SWEET POTATO PANCAKE MIX
BRUCE'S YAMS
CAJUN INJECTOR
CAJUN KING
CASA FIESTA
LOUISIANA GOLD
MEXENE
THE ORIGINAL LOUISIANA

1907 Bruce Foods Corporation
P.O.Box 1030
New Iberia, LA 70562-1030   337-365-8101
Fax: 337-364-3742 info@brucefoodsla.com
www.brucefoods.com
Manufacturer of Cajun and Tex Mex products
CEO: Joseph S Brown Jr
Estimated Sales:$50-100 Million
Number Employees: 100-249
Number of Brands: 9
Number of Products: 350
Parent Co: Bruce Foods Corporation
Other Locations:
Bruce Foods Corporation
Lozes LA
Bruce Foods Corporation
Wilson NC
Bruce Foods Corporation
El Paso TX
Brands:
BRUCE'S
BRUCE'S YAMS
CAJUN INJECTOR
CAJUN KING
CASA FIESTA
LOUISIANA GOLD
LOUISIANA WING SAUCE
MEXENE CHILI
ORIGINAL

1908 Bruce Packing Company
P.O.Box 540
Silverton, OR 97381-0540   503-874-3000
Fax: 503-769-5081 800-899-3629
info@brucepac.com www.brucepac.com
Cooked and seasoned meats
President: Larry Bruce
VP: Rob Bruce
Marketing Manager: Jay Hansen
COO: Peter Larson
Production Manager: Cameron Cooper
Purchasing Manager: Duane Tipton
Estimated Sales:$5-10 Million
Number Employees: 100-249
Brands:
Brucepac
Early West
World Kitchen's

1909 Brucia Plant Extracts
3855 Dividend Dr
Shingle Springs, CA 95682-8485   530-676-2774
Fax: 530-676-0574 brucia@naturex.com
www.naturex.com
A leading manufacturer of high quality natural antioxidants, colors, herbs & spices oleoresins and essential oils, and botanical extracts for the food, flavor and nutraceutical industries
President: Jacques Dikansky
VP: Stephane Ducroux
Marketing: Thomas Capogis
Sales: David Yuengniaux
Plant Manager: Chris Young
Purchasing Manager: Romain Bayzelon
Estimated Sales:$45 Million
Number Employees: 20-49
Number of Brands: 10
Number of Products: 400
Sq. footage: 85000
Parent Co: Naturex
Type of Packaging: Bulk
Brands:
Theraplant

1910 Brum's Dairy
216 Hincks St.
Pembroke, ON K8A 4N8
Canada   613-735-4686
Fax: 613-735-2068 bdairy@webhart.net
http://www.webhart.net
Process and distribute fresh dairy products as well as fresh juice
President/CEO: S Brum
CFO/VP Finance: S Brum
VP Sales: T Brum
Quality Control: D Fleury
Sales Manager: Peter Rumohr
VP Production: B Brum
Estimated Sales:$10 Million +
Number Employees: 20-49
Sq. footage: 20000
Type of Packaging: Consumer, Private Label
Brands:
Nature's Pride

1911 Brunkow Cheese Company
17975 County Road F
Darlington, WI 53530-9310   608-776-3716
Fax: 608-776-3716
Processor of natural, cold pack and raw milk cheeses including cheddar, colby, monterey jack, mild, sharp, garlic, bacon, onion, dill, wine, jalapeno, Italian herb, smoked, etc
Owner: Karl Geissbuhler
CEO: Karl Geissbuhler
Estimated Sales:$2.5-5 Million
Number Employees: 5-9
Sq. footage: 3200
Type of Packaging: Bulk
Brands:
Brunkow Cheese

1912 Bruno Specialty Foods
208 Cherry Ave
West Sayville, NY 11796-1223   631-589-1700
Fax: 631-589-6357 info@brunofoods.com
www.brunofoods.com
Processor of frozen kosher and nonkosher Italian food products including tomato sauces, tortellini, regular and vegetable lasagnas, eggplant parmagiana, ravioli, manicotti and stuffed shells
President: Louis D'Agrosa
Estimated Sales:$5-10 Million
Number Employees: 20-49
Number of Brands: 2
Number of Products: 150
Sq. footage: 10000
Type of Packaging: Consumer, Food Service, Private Label, Bulk
Brands:
Bruno
Tova's Best

1913 Bruno's Cajun Foods & Snacks
210 Provosty Drive
Slidell, LA 70461-1413   985-726-0544
Fax: 985-726-0532 cause4paws@charter.net

Manufacturer and Distributor of Cajun Food Snacks, Porkskins and Cracklins' Caramel Popcorn, Cotton Candy, Roasted Peanuts, and candy
President: Brandon Halligan
CEO: Melody Halligan
VP: Everett Halligan
Marketing: Erin Halligan
Sales: Michael Halligan
Public Relations: Tracy Stricklin
Plant Manager: Katie Halligan
Purchasing Director: Everett Halligan
Estimated Sales:$70 Million
Number Employees: 6
Number of Products: 8
Sq. footage: 2000
Type of Packaging: Consumer, Private Label
Brands:
BRUNO'S

1914 Brush Locker
14250 County Road 15
Fort Morgan, CO 80701-8610   970-842-2660
Fax: 970-842-4831
Processor and packer of meat
Owner: Laura Teague
Owner: Gary Teague
Manager: Neil Allen
Plant Manager: Iram Khan
Estimated Sales:$5-10 Million
Number Employees: 10-19

1915 Bruss Company
3548 N Kostner Ave
Chicago, IL 60641-3898   773-282-2900
Fax: 773-282-6966 800-621-3882
customer.bruss@tyson.com
www.giftsteaksonline.com
Manufacturer of portion controlled steaks, pork, lamb and veal
President/CEO: Jeff DeLapp
CFO: Mike Porcaro
VP: Gary Heymann
Director Marketing: Al Iverhouse
National Account Sales: Frank Cardone
Estimated Sales:$85.6 Million
Number Employees: 10-19
Sq. footage: 52000
Parent Co: Tyson Foods
Type of Packaging: Consumer, Food Service
Brands:
GOLDEN TROPHY STEAKS

1916 Brutocao Cellars
P.O.Box 780
Hopland, CA 95449-0780   707-744-1066
Fax: 707-744-1046 800-433-3689
brutocoa@netdex.com www.brutocaocellars.com
Wines, gourmet foods
President: Len Brutocao
Estimated Sales:$1-2.5 Million
Number Employees: 20-49

1917 Bryan Foods
PO Box 1177
West Point, MS 39773-1177   662-494-3741
Fax: 662-495-4501
Processor of fresh and frozen sausage
CEO/President: John Bryan III
VP/CFO: Cal Jenness
R&D: Frank Mello
Operations: John Zobl
Food Safety Manager: Gay Baird
Number Employees: 1,000-4,999
Parent Co: Sara Lee Packaged Meats
Type of Packaging: Consumer, Food Service
Brands:
Bryan
Picnic
Prairie Belt
Redbird
Savoy
Smoky Hollow
Sweet Sue

1918 Bryant Preserving Company
P.O.Box 367
Alma, AR 72921-0367   479-632-2401
Fax: 479-632-2505 800-634-2413
sales@bryantpreserving.com www.oldsouth.com

Processor of pickled fruits and vegetables including sweet watermelon rinds and cucumber relish, baby carrots, green tomatoes and mild and hot okra.
President: Morgan Bryant
General Manager: Steve Bryant
Sales Manager: Leguetta Yates
Secretary/Treasurer: Morgan Bryant
COO: Steve Bryant
Plant Manager: Morgan Bryant
Estimated Sales:$1-2.5 Million
Number Employees: 5-9
Sq. footage: 25000
Type of Packaging: Consumer, Food Service, Private Label, Bulk
Brands:
OLD SOUTH

1919 Bryant Vineyard
1454 Griffitt Bend Road
Talladega, AL 35160-7255   256-268-2638
Wines
President: Susan Bryant
Co-Owner: Dan Bryant
Vice President: Kelly Bryant
Number Employees: 20-49
Brands:
Bryant Autumn Blush
Bryant Country White
Bryant Dixie Blush
Bryant Festive Red
Bryant Vineyard

1920 Bryant's Meats
P.O.Box 321
Taylorsville, MS 39168-0321   601-785-6507
                          Fax: 601-785-6507
Processor of meat products including smoked sausage, pork and chicken
Owner: Robert Hunt
Co-Owner: Robert Hunt
Estimated Sales:$5-10 Million
Number Employees: 20-49
Type of Packaging: Consumer
Brands:
River Road
Sunrise

1921 Bubbies Homemade Ice Cream
99-1267 Waiua Pl # B
Aiea, HI 96701-5642   808-487-7218
                          Fax: 808-484-5800
bubbiesicecream@hawn.rr.com
www.bubbiesicecream.com
Mocha ice cream
President: Keith Robbins
CFO: Sandra Robbins
VP: Gertrude Robbins
Quality Control: Jayci Robbins
Marketing: Cara Nagao
Public Relations: Jo Lacar
Estimated Sales:$2.5-5 Million
Number Employees: 5-9
Sq. footage: 18000
Type of Packaging: Bulk
Brands:
Bubbies Homemade Ice Cream
Mountain Apple
Tutus

1922 Bubbles Baking Company
15215 Keswick St
Van Nuys, CA 91405-1050   818-786-1700
              Fax: 818-786-3617 800-777-4970
Bubbles@aol.com
Gourmet baked goods
Manager: Torben Jensen
Manager: Torben Jenson
Plant Manager: Armando Berumen
Estimated Sales:$10-20 Million
Number Employees: 50-99
Brands:
Bubbles
Granny Gourmet Goodi

1923 Bubbles of San Francisco
2940 Chauncy Cir
Stockton, CA 95209-1617   209-951-6071
       Fax: 209-957-9413 info@bubbies.com
www.bubbies.com
Kosher pickle products
Co-Owner/CEO: John Gray
Co-Owner/COO: Kathy Gray
Estimated Sales:$500,000-$1 Million
Number Employees: 1-4

Type of Packaging: Private Label, Bulk

1924 Buccia Vineyard
518 Gore Rd
Conneaut, OH 44030-2914   440-593-5976
bucciwin@suite224.net
www.bucciavineyard.com
Wine
Owner/President: Alfred Bucci
Owner: Joanna Bucci
*Estimated Sales:*Under $1 Million
Number Employees: 1-4
Type of Packaging: Bulk

1925 Buchanan Hollow Nut Company
6510 Minturn Rd
Le Grand, CA 95333-9710   209-389-4594
          Fax: 209-389-4321 800-532-1500
sharleen@bhnc.com   www.bhnc.com
Manufacturer and grower of organic pistachio, almonds, variety of nuts, dried fruit and candies
Owner: Sharleen Robson
Owner: Bob Robson
Estimated Sales:$500,000-$1 Million
Number Employees: 5-9
Sq. footage: 4000
Type of Packaging: Bulk

1926 Buck's Spumoni Company
229 Pepes Farm Rd
Milford, CT 06460-3671   203-874-2007
                          Fax: 203-877-5777
Manufacturer of ice cream specialties including nut roll, spumoni and tortoni
President: Charles A Buck Jr
Estimated Sales:$ 10 - 20 Million
Number Employees: 20-49
Type of Packaging: Food Service, Bulk

1927 Buckeye Pretzel Company
1253 Deerfield Drive
Williamsport, PA 17701-9307   570-547-6295
          Fax: 570-547-6719 800-257-6029
Pretzels
President: John Best
Executive VP: Susan Best
Number Employees: 30
Brands:
BUCKEYE

1928 Buckhead Beef Company
2194 Marietta Blvd NW
Atlanta, GA 30318-2136   404-355-4400
          Fax: 404-355-4541 800-888-5578
info@buckheadbeef.com
www.buckheadbeef.com
Manufacturer and wholesaler/distributor of fresh and frozen specialty cut meat products including beef, veal, lamb and pork for food service operators
Founder/CEO: Howard Halpern
President: John Foster
CFO: Clay Jordan
Number Employees: 250-499
Type of Packaging: Food Service

1929 Buckhead Gourmet
4060 Peachtree Rd NE # D-272
Atlanta, GA 30319-3020   404-256-1399
          Fax: 404-256-1335 800-605-5754
customerservice@buckheadgourmet.com
www.buckheadgourmet.com
Manufacturer of prepared sauces including fat-free gourmet, barbecue, bordeaux, hunter, peppercorn, maderia, marinades, spice ribs, salad dressings, jams, relishes and salsas
President: Stephan Gosch
CEO: Rupert Crawford
Estimated Sales:$1,000,000
Number Employees: 1-4
Number of Brands: 1
Number of Products: 35
Type of Packaging: Consumer, Food Service, Private Label, Bulk
Brands:
Buckhead Gourmet

1930 Buckingham Valley Vineyards
P.O.Box 371
Buckingham, PA 18912-0371   215-794-7188
          Fax: 215-794-3606 ask@pawine.com
www.pawine.com

Wine
President: Kathy Forest
Vice President: Gerald Forest
Winemaker: Jon Forest
Plant Manager: Kevin Forest
Estimated Sales:$5-9 Million
Number Employees: 5-9
Brands:
Buckingham

1931 (HQ)Buckmaster Coffee
4893 NW 235th Ave
Hillsboro, OR 97124-5801   503-693-0796
          Fax: 503-681-0944 800-962-9148
Processor of roasted whole bean gourmet coffee
VP: Joe Schlichte
Sales Manager: Paul Hoffmann
VP of Sales: Joe Schlichte
Estimated Sales:$2.5-5 Million
Number Employees: 5-9
Type of Packaging: Consumer

1932 Bucks County Coffee Company
2250 W Cabot Boulevard
Langhorne, PA 19047   215-741-1855
          Fax: 215-741-1799 800-844-8790
help@buckscountycoffee.com
www.buckscountycoffee.com
Coffee
President: Rodger Owen
CFO: Debby Prentice
VP/Retail Operations: Kathy Owen
Sales Director: Roseann O'Connel
Purchasing Manager: Chris Vacearella
Estimated Sales:$19,600,000
Number Employees: 5-9
Type of Packaging: Private Label
Brands:
Bucks County Coffee

1933 Buddy's
626 E Lewis St
Pocatello, ID 83201-5863   208-233-1172
President: Steve Piper
Estimated Sales:$1-2.5 Million
Number Employees: 20-49

1934 Buds Kitchen
826 Gardner Center Road
New Castle, PA 16101-6020   724-654-9216
          Fax: 724-654-9216 bud301@libcom.com
Hot sauce

1935 (HQ)Buedel Food Products
3850 W North Ave
Chicago, IL 60647-4641   773-235-3637
                          Fax: 773-235-0534
Processor of refrigerated horseradish and frozen smoked fish
Owner: Pat Bedolla
Vice President: Kristin Buedel
Sales Director: Fred Buedel
Estimated Sales:$ 3 - 5 Million
Number Employees: 10-19
Type of Packaging: Consumer, Private Label
Brands:
Prince Gourmet Foods

1936 Buehler Vineyards
820 Greenfield Rd
St Helena, CA 94574-9529   707-963-2155
          Fax: 707-963-3747 buehlers@pacbell.net
www.buehlervineyards.com
Wine
President: John Buehler
Manager Sales/Marketing: Misha Chelini
Winemaker: David Tronin
Office Manager: Lori Sax
Estimated Sales:$2.5-5 Million
Number Employees: 5-9
Type of Packaging: Private Label

1937 Buena Vista Carneros Winery
P.O.Box 182
Sonoma, CA 95476-0182   707-252-7117
          Fax: 707-252-0392 800-678-8504
estate@buenavistawinery.com
www.buenavistawinery.com
Manufacturer, importer and exporter of wine and also, importer of champagne
President/CEO: Harry Parsley
CFO/VP: Peter Kasper
Human Resources: Dorothy Kines

Estimated Sales: $5-10 Million
Number Employees: 5-9
Sq. footage: 80000
Type of Packaging: Consumer, Private Label
Brands:
    CARNEROS

1938 Bueno Food Products
P.O.Box 293
Albuquerque, NM 87103-0293   505-243-2722
    Fax: 505-242-1680   800-888-7336
info@buenofoods.com   www.buenofoods.com
Manufacturer of frozen Mexican food including
green chile and corn and flour tortillas, chile pep-
pers, spices and dry chile powders
    President: Jacqueline Baca
    VP: Gene Baca
    R&D: Catherine Baca
    Public Relations: Ana Baca
Estimated Sales: $10-100 Million
Number Employees: 20-49
Parent Co: El Encanto
Type of Packaging: Consumer, Food Service, Pri-
vate Label
Brands:
    Bueno
    Chimayo

1939 Buffalo Bill Brewing Company
1082 B St
Hayward, CA 94541-4108   510-886-9823
    Fax: 510-886-8157

Processor of ale, stout and lager
    President: Jeff Harries
    Co-Owner: Jeff Harries
Estimated Sales: $20-50 Million
Number Employees: 50-99
Type of Packaging: Consumer, Food Service, Bulk
Brands:
    Alimony Ale
    Billy Bock
    Buffalo Brew
    Pumpkin Ale
    Tasmanian Devil
    White Buffalo

1940 Buffalo Bill's Snack Foods
P.O.Box 16346
Denver, CO 80216-0346   303-298-0705
    Fax: 303-298-0216   info@tortilla-chips.com
    www.tortilla-chips.com
Tortilla chips in a variety of stone-ground and natu-
ral flavors, salsa and hot sauce
    President: William A Ralston
Estimated Sales: $ 20 - 50 Million
Number Employees: 50-99
Brands:
    Buffalo Bill's
    Wild West

1941 Buffalo Bob's Everything Sauce
389 Edwin Dr
Virginia Beach, VA 23462-4548   757-490-9186
    Fax: 757-490-9494
Manufacturer of meat sauces
    President: Bob Buchanan
Estimated Sales: $300,000-$500,000
Number Employees: 1-4
Sq. footage: 4300
Parent Co: Festive Foods

1942 Buffalo Trace Distillery
P.O.Box 619
Frankfort, KY 40602-0619   502-223-7641
    Fax: 502-875-5553   800-654-8471
    thunder@buffalotrace.com
    www.buffalotrace.com
Bourbon and rum; importer of wine
    President: Mark Brown
    VP of Operations: Joseph Darmand
Estimated Sales: $100-500 Million
Number Employees: 100-249
Parent Co: Sazerac Company
Type of Packaging: Bulk

1943 Buffalo Wild Wings
600 Highway 169 S
Suite 1919
Minneapolis, MN 55426-1205   763-546-1891
    Fax: 952-593-9787   info@buffalowildwings.com
    www.buffalowildwings.com
    Owner: Jim Disbrow
    Co-Owner: Scott Lowery

Estimated Sales: $300,000-500,000
Number Employees: 10-19

1944 Bull Run Roasting Company
16790 W Us Highway 63
Hayward, WI 54843-7214   715-634-3646
    Fax: 715-634-8336   info@bullrunroasters.com
    www.bullrunroasters.com
Produce three outstanding families of coffee blends
for coffeehouses and restaurants plus two premium
teas. Offer the following roasting degrees: Full
City, Vienna, French and Italian
    Owner: Granville Harlow
    Owner: Greg Hoyt
Estimated Sales: $10-24.9 Million
Number Employees: 5-9

1945 Bullock's Country Meats
2020 Sykesville Rd
Westminster, MD 21157-7312   410-848-6786
    Fax: 410-848-8685
Manufacturer of beef, pork, chicken and turkey;
also, frozen seafood; slaughtering services available
    Owner: Clyde Hirt
Estimated Sales: $3 Million
Number Employees: 10-19

1946 Bully Hill Vineyards
P.O.Box 458
Hammondsport, NY 14840-0458   607-868-3610
    Fax: 607-868-3205   generalinfo@bullyhill.com
    www.bullyhillvineyards.com
Wines, champagne and grape juice
    President: Lillian Taylor
    VP Quality Control: Gregg Learned
    Sales: Adam LaPierre
    Operations: Gregg Learned
Estimated Sales: $5-9.9 Million
Number Employees: 5-9
Type of Packaging: Consumer
Brands:
    AURORA BLANC
    BANTY RED
    BARNYARD RED
    BULLDOG BACO NOIR
    CHAMBOURCIN
    CHARDONNAY ELISE
    EQUINOX
    EQUINOX
    ESTATE RED
    FELICITY
    FISH MARKET WHITE
    FOCH
    FUSION
    GARNET
    GOAT WHITE
    GROWER'S RED
    GROWERS BLUSH
    GROWERS WHITE
    HARBOR LIGHTS
    IVES
    LE GOAT BLUSH
    LIGHTHOUSE WHITE
    LOVE MY GOAT RED
    MEAT MARKET RED
    MISS LOVE WHITE
    MOTHER SHIP OVER PARIS CHAMPAGNE
    NIAGARA
    OH, BE JOYFUL
    PINOT NOIR
    RAVAT BLANC
    RIELSING
    SEASONS
    SEYVAL BLANC
    SEYVAL BLANC BRUT CHAMPAGNE
    SPACE SHUTTLE RED
    SPACE SHUTTLE WHITE
    SPECIAL RESERVE RED
    SPECIAL RESERVE WHITE
    SPRING BLUSH
    SPRING WHITE
    STATE CAPITAL RED
    SWEET WALTER RED
    SWEET WALTER WHITE
    VERDELET BLANC
    WALTER S. RED

1947 Bumble Bee Seafoods
PO Box 85362
San Diego, CA 92186-5362   858-715-4000
    Fax: 858-560-6045   www.bumblebee.com

Manufacturer, importer and exporter of canned tuna,
chicken, salmon, shrimp, crab, sardines & mackerel,
oysters, clams; also ready to eat meals
    President/CEO: Christopher Lischewski
    EVP/CFO: Kent McNeil
    EVP/COO: J Douglas Hines
Estimated Sales: $700 Million
Number Employees: 500
Sq. footage: 40000
Parent Co: Centre Partners
Type of Packaging: Consumer, Food Service, Pri-
vate Label, Bulk
Other Locations:
    Bumble Bee Canning Facility
    Mayaguez, PR
    Bumble Bee Canning Facility
    Sante Fe Springs CA
Brands:
    BUMBLE BEE
    CLOVER LEAF
    CORAL
    KING OSCAR
    LIBBY'S
    ORLEANS

1948 Bungalow Brand Foods
1310 Panchita Place
Santa Barbara, CA 93103-2223   805-899-4747
    Fax: 805-899-4747   800-899-5267
    bungalo@silcom.com
Spreadable fruits, tropical fruit butters, jellies, chut-
ney and scone mixes
    President: Diane Bock
    CFO: John Bock
    Vice President: Bryan Bock
Estimated Sales: $75,000
Number Employees: 1-4
Type of Packaging: Private Label

1949 Bunge Beverage & Dairy Ingredients
11720 Borman Drive
St Louis, MO 63146-1000   314-292-2000
    bna.ebusiness@bunge.com
    www.bungefoods.com
Supplier of grains, oilseeds and corn meals, flours,
industrial starch products
    President: Kain James
    Senior VP: Tim Gallagher
    Plant Manager: Edd Baranski
Number Employees: 50-99

1950 Bunge Canada
2190 S Service Road
Oakville, ON L6L 5N1
Canada   905-825-7930
    Fax: 905-469-2018   800-361-3043
    onpack@canamerafoods.com
    www.canamerafoods.com
Oil seeds, protein meals and edible oil products
    President/CEO: Carl Hausmann
    R&D: Dave Forster
    Quality Control: Rolf Mantei
    National Manager (Packaged Products): Larry
    Sigmundson
    Sales Manager: Liz Micallef
    Public Relations: Jim Francis
    VP Operations: Herb Schafer
    Plant Manager: Calvin Eyben
Number Employees: 500-999
Parent Co: Central Soya
Brands:
    Canaplus

1951 Bunge Corporation
1833 Haining Road
Vicksburg, MS 39183-9036   601-638-3824
    Fax: 601-634-0822   rneyer@bunge.com
    www.bungenorthamerica.com
Processor and exporter of soybean oil and meal
    Facility Manager: W Prestage
Estimated Sales: $ 50 - 100 Million
Number Employees: 2000
Type of Packaging: Consumer, Bulk

1952 Bunge Foods
15601 Mosher Ave
Tustin, CA 92780-6426   714-258-1223
    Fax: 714-258-1520
Bread and rolls.
    Manager: Joe Barsotti
    Quality Control Manager: Peter Fadul
    Plant Manager: Joe Barsotti

Estimated Sales: $ 20 - 50 Million
Number Employees: 100-249

1953 Bunge Ingredients
1001 John St
Seattle, WA 98109-5320   206-623-7740
          Fax: 206-224-9135 www.dawnfoods.com
Industrial ingredients; bulk supplier
     Manager: Brendan Caile
Estimated Sales: $100-500 Million
Number Employees: 20-49

1954 (HQ)Bunge North America
P.O.Box 28500
St Louis, MO 63146-1000   314-569-1339
     Fax: 314-292-2521 www.bungenorthamerica.com
Manufacturer and exporter of a wide range of
shortenings, oils, margarines, mixes, frozen products, toppings and fillings for the foodservice, food
processor and bakery industries
     President/CEO: Carl Hausmann
     Sr. VP/CFO: Michael Scharf
     Sr. VP/GM, Grain Division: Tim Gallagher
     Sr. VP/GM, Oilseed Processing Division: Larry
     Clarke
     Sr. VP/GM, Bunge Milling: Fred Luckey
     Sr. VP/GM, Bunge Oils: Richard Goodman
Estimated Sales: $100-500 Million
Number Employees: 1,000-4,999
Parent Co: Bunge Unlimited
Type of Packaging: Consumer, Food Service, Private Label, Bulk
Other Locations:
     Bradley IL
     Chattanooga TN
     Effingham IL
     Fort Worth TX
     Mexico MO
     Modesto CA
     Pawtucket RI
     Seattle WA
     St. Louis MO
     Tustin CA
     Decatur AL
     Danville IL
     Crete NE
Brands:
     VILLA SIERRA

1955 Bungy Oils
38 Colfax St
Pawtucket, RI 02860-3422   401-724-3800
          Fax: 401-724-4313 www.centralsoya.com
Edible vegetable oil and shortening
     CEO: Soren Schroder
     Plant Manager: David Parrillo
Estimated Sales: $50-100 Million
Number Employees: 20-49
Number of Products: 1
Parent Co: Central Soya
Type of Packaging: Private Label, Bulk

1956 Bunker Hill Cheese Company
6005 County Road 77
Millersburg, OH 44654-9045   330-893-2131
          Fax: 330-893-2079 800-253-6636
          info@heinis.com www.heinis.com
Processor of yogurt cultured and natural cheeses
     President: Peter Dauwalder
     Treasurer: Nancy Dauwalder
     Marketing Director: LeeAnne Dauwalder-Martin
     VP Sales: Lisa Troyer
     VP Operations: Robert Troyer
Estimated Sales: $7-10 Million
Number Employees: 50-99
Type of Packaging: Consumer, Bulk
Brands:
     AMISH VALLEY FARMS
     HEINI'S BRAND CHEESE

1957 Bunker Hill Foods
1621 15th St
Augusta, GA 30901-3929   706-733-7765
          Fax: 706-733-5079 info@castleberrys.com
          www.castleberrys.com
Processor of canned beef, gravy, chili, hot dog
sauce, beef stew, hash, barbecue products, soups and
chowder.
     General Manager: John Vaeth
     Sales: Roy Bryant
     Director Operations: Jack Bowersox
     Plant Manager: J Keith Griffis
Estimated Sales: $ 1 - 3 Million
Number Employees: 100-249

Sq. footage: 120000
Parent Co: Castleberry/Snow's Brands
Type of Packaging: Consumer, Food Service, Private Label
Brands:
     JAMES RIVER
     PARAMOUNT
     PRUDENCE

1958 Bunny Bread
19399 Helenberg Road
Suite 205
Covington, LA 70433-5392   504-241-1206
          Fax: 504-241-0953 www.bunnybread.net
Processor of bread.
     President: Daniel Brinson
     VP: Darryl Trainer
     Plant Manager: Daryl Mitchell
Estimated Sales: $17 Million
Number Employees: 240
Type of Packaging: Consumer

1959 Bunny Bread Company
833 Broadway St
Cape Girardeau, MO 63701-5515   573-332-7349
Processor of sweet rolls, fruit bread, doughnuts and
danish; wholesaler/distributor of bread
     President: Jack Lewis
Estimated Sales: $5-10 Million
Number Employees: 5-9
Parent Co: Flowers Foods
Type of Packaging: Consumer, Food Service, Private Label

1960 Buns & Roses Organic Wholegrain Bakery
6519-111th Street NW
Edmonton, AB T5K 3M6
Canada   780-438-0098
          Fax: 780-437-8805
Processor of breads and specialty baked products including organic whole grain and gluten-free
     President: Dhammika Jayawickrama
     Marketing Manager: Dhammika Jayawickrama
     Owner: Dhammika Jayawickrama
Number Employees: 1-4
Sq. footage: 2400
Type of Packaging: Consumer, Food Service
Brands:
     Buns & Roses

1961 Buns & Things Bakery
25 Brackley Point Road
Charlottetown, PE C1A 6Y1
Canada   902-892-2600
          Fax: 902-892-2620
          rob.deblois@pei-sympatico.ca
Processor of baked goods including danish, cinnamon rolls, bread, cookies, bagels, pies, rolls, etc
     President: Robert DeBlois
     CEO: Robert DeBlois
     Secretary: Elaine DeBlois
     Marketing Director: Robert DeBlois
Number Employees: 10-19
Sq. footage: 2600

1962 Buns Master Bakery
307 Nash Road
North Hamilton, ON L8H 7P4
Canada   905-560-5011
          info@bunmaster.com
     www.bunmaster.com / www.countrystyle.ca
Manufacturer of baked goods such as; breads and
bakery products
     Owner/Operations: Eric Munnik
Number Employees: 18
Sq. footage: 6000
Type of Packaging: Consumer, Food Service, Bulk

1963 Buns Master Bakery
405 Stafford Drive N
Lethbridge, AB T1H 2A7
Canada   403-320-2966
Processor of baked goods including bread and rolls
     President: Hugh McKee
Number Employees: 10-19
Parent Co: Buns Master Bakery Systems
Type of Packaging: Consumer, Food Service
Brands:
     Buns Master

1964 Buon Italia
75 9th Ave # 17
New York, NY 10011-7029   212-633-9090
          Fax: 212-633-9717 info@buonitalia.com
                    www.buonitalia.com
Processor and importer of gourmet Italian foods including pasta, rice, mushrooms, truffles, flour, jams,
oils, cheeses, vinegar, fruit mustard, cookies, biscuits and sweets
     Owner: Mimmo Majiulo
Estimated Sales: $ 3 - 5 Million
Number Employees: 10-19
Sq. footage: 10000
Parent Co: Misono Food
Type of Packaging: Consumer, Food Service, Private Label, Bulk

1965 Buona Vita
1 S Industrial Blvd
Bridgeton, NJ 08302-3401   856-453-7972
          Fax: 856-453-7978 info@buonavitainc.com
                    www.buonavitainc.com
Processor of Italian specialties including meatballs,
meatloaf, beef bracioli, eggplant, pasta and pizza
toppings
     President: Paul Infranco
     VP: John Taormina
     Production Manager: Blake Christy
Estimated Sales: $20-50 Million
Number Employees: 20-49
Sq. footage: 25000
Type of Packaging: Consumer, Food Service, Private Label, Bulk
Brands:
     Buona Vita
     Mama Mia

1966 Burch Farms
P.O.Box 399
Faison, NC 28341-0399   910-267-5781
          Fax: 910-267-1133 800-466-9668
     butch@intrastar.net   www.burchfarms.com
Processor of sweet potatoes
     President: Jimmy Burch
     CEO: Jimmy Burch
     Owner: Teresa Burch
     Marketing Director: Jimmy Burch Jr
Estimated Sales: $ 10 - 20 Million
Number Employees: 100-249
Brands:
     Candy Yams
     Georgiana
     Sugar & Spice

1967 Burger Dairy
3535 Rolling Hills Dr
Cleveland, OH 44124-5802   216-896-9100
                    Fax: 219-831-3494
Fluid and condensed milk
     President: Alan Berger
     Sales Manager: Gary Protsman
     Controller: Mark Niezgodski
     Production Manager: Terry Wuthrich
     Plant Manager: Marty Crook
Estimated Sales: $25-49.9 Million
Number Employees: 1-4
Parent Co: Suiza Dairy Group

1968 Burgers Smokehouse
32819 Highway 87
California, MO 65018-3227   573-796-3134
          Fax: 573-796-3137 800-624-5426
          service@smokehouse.com
                    www.smokehouse.com
Smoked meats, country cured ham, spare ribs, St.
Louis ribs, baby back ribs, pork chops, canadian bacon, spiral sliced ham, smoked bacon, summer sausage, smoked turkey, smoked chicken, smoked quail,
smoked pheasant, and smoked duck
     President: Steven Burger
     CEO: Morris Burger
     CFO: Ted Rohrbach
     Vice President: Philip Burger
     Marketing Director: Chris Mouse
     Operations Manager: Keith Fletcher
     Production Manager: Jeffery Kilgore
     Plant Manager: Kenneth Phillips
Estimated Sales: $20-50 Million
Number Employees: 250-499
Sq. footage: 200000
Type of Packaging: Consumer, Food Service, Private Label, Bulk

1969 Burke Brands
503 NE 189th St
Miami, FL 33179-3909   305-249-5628
          Fax: 305-651-6018   877-436-6722
info@cafedonpablo.com   www.cafedonpablo.com
Manufacturer of fine specialty coffee and gourmet
food products.
    President: Darron Burke
    Vice President: Eliana Burke
    Sales: Wilma Perez
    Production: Gladys Menjura
Estimated Sales: $1.3 Million
Number Employees: 5-9
Number of Brands: 4
Number of Products: 27
Sq. footage: 10000
Type of Packaging: Consumer, Food Service, Private Label, Bulk
Other Locations:
    Burke Brands
    N Miami Beach FL
Brands:
    Cafe Don Pablo

1970 Burke Candy & Ingredient Corporation
3840 N Fratney St
Milwaukee, WI 53212-1341   414-241-4369
          Fax: 414-964-7644   888-287-5350
info@burkecandy.com   www.burkecandy.com
Manufacturer of chocolate candies and confectionery. Products are certified kosher
    Owner/Chef: Julia Burke
    Owner/Chef: Tim Burke
Estimated Sales: Less than $500,000
Number Employees: 1-4

BURKE
Always make it your best®

1971 Burke Corporation

P.O.Box 209
Nevada, IA 50201-0209   515-382-3575
          Fax: 515-382-2834   800-654-1152
sales_info@burkecorp.com   www.burkecorp.com

Always make it your best® with Burke fully cooked meats. We specialize in Italian sausage, beef, and pork toppings, meatballs, taco meats, shredded meats, pepperoni, bacon, Canadian-style bacon, chicken and beef strips.Additionally, we offer a variety of specialty products: Hand-Pinched Style® brand toppings, chorizo, gyro topping, andouille sausage, and breakfast patties and links.

    Marketing Director: Liz Hertz
    VP Sales/Marketing: Doug Cooprider
Number Employees: 350
Type of Packaging: Food Service, Private Label, Bulk
Brands:
    Burke
    MagniFoods®
    NaturaSelect™
    Premoro®
    Tezzata®

1972 Burleigh Brothers Seafoods
PO Box 11
Ellerslie, PE C0B 1J0
Canada   902-831-2349
Processor of fresh shellfish, mollusk, trout and smelt
    CEO: Roger Burleigh
    President: Proy Burleigh
    Marketing Director: Tom Bradstaw
Number Employees: 100-249

Type of Packaging: Consumer, Food Service, Private Label, Bulk

1973 Burleson's
P.O.Box 578
Waxahachie, TX 75168-0578   972-937-4810
          Fax: 972-937-8711   jimcburlesons-honey.com
                    www.burlesons-honey.com
Honey
    President: Thomas E Burleson Jr
    CEO: T Burleson
    CFO: Walter Shugart
    Marketing Director: Jim Phillips
    Public Relations: Nina Swen-Kohler
    Office Manager: Walter Shugert
    Production Manager: Tim Burleson
    Plant Manager: Steve Chambers
    Purchasing Manager: LaWanna Ford
Estimated Sales: $10-20 Million
Number Employees: 20-49
Sq. footage: 45
Type of Packaging: Private Label
Brands:
    Burleson Pure Honey

1974 Burlington Bio-Medical Corporation
71 Carolyn Blvd
Farmingdale, NY 11735-1527   631-694-4700
          Fax: 631-694-9177   bscchemny@aol.com
                    www.amerolcorp.com
Processor and exporter of bittering agents and colors
    President: Melvin Blum
    VP Operations: Bill Rudy
Estimated Sales: $7.5 Million
Number Employees: 20-49
Sq. footage: 7
Type of Packaging: Bulk
Brands:
    Bitter Guard

1975 Burn Brae Farms
301 Ellor Street
Strathroy, ON N7G 2L5
Canada   519-245-1630
          Fax: 519-245-1690   General@burnbraefarms.com
                    www.burnbraefarms.com
Packager of eggs
    President: Joe Hutson
    Marketing Director: Margaret Hutson
    COO: Bob Anderson
    General Manager: Earl Powers
Number Employees: 50-99
Parent Co: Burnbrae Farm
Type of Packaging: Consumer, Food Service
Brands:
    Free Run
    Nature's Best
    Omega Pro
    Organic Shell Eggs

1976 Burnett & Son Meat Company
1420 S Myrtle Ave
Monrovia, CA 91016-4153   626-357-2165
          Fax: 626-357-7115   info@burnettandson.com
                    www.burnettandson.com
Processor of meat including taco, London broil, shredded beef and pork, corned and roast beef, pot roast, steak, pork loin, etc; also, entrees including beef stew, chile, meat loaf, corned beef and cabbage, spaghetti and meatballsetc
    Principal: Don Burnett
    Principal: David Kruse
Estimated Sales: $20-50 Million
Number Employees: 50-99
Type of Packaging: Consumer, Food Service

1977 Burnette Dairy Cooperative
11631 State Road 70
Grantsburg, WI 54840-7135   715-689-2468
          Fax: 715-689-2135   cheese@win.bright.net
                    www.burnettdairy.com
Processor of cheese including mozzarella, provolone, colby, cheddar and monterey jack
    President: Dale Olson
    Director: Gary Peterson
Estimated Sales: $20-50 Million
Number Employees: 100-249
Type of Packaging: Consumer, Food Service, Private Label, Bulk
Brands:
    Fancy Brand

1978 Burnette Foods
701 Us Highway 31
Elk Rapids, MI 49629-9525   231-264-8116
          Fax: 231-264-9597   info@burnettefoods.com
                    www.burnettefoods.com
Pasta products, pie fillings, apple sauce, apple juice, vegetables and maraschinos.
    Owner/Manager: William Sherman
    Owner/Manager: Fred Sherman
Estimated Sales: $ 40 Million
Number Employees: 50-99
Type of Packaging: Consumer, Food Service, Private Label, Bulk
Brands:
    Burnetti's
    Mother's Maid
    Romeo

1979 Burnette Foods
87171 County Road 687
Hartford, MI 49057-8602   616-621-3181
          Fax: 616-621-4504   info@burnettefoods.com
                    www.burnettefoods.com
Processor of canned and glass packed apple sauce, potatoes, pie fillings and juices including tomato and apple
    Operaitons Manager: Jack Wyatt
Estimated Sales: $10-20 Million
Number Employees: 50-99
Type of Packaging: Consumer, Food Service, Private Label, Bulk
Brands:
    Mother's Maid

1980 (HQ)Burnette Foods
701 Us Highway 31
Elk Rapids, MI 49629-9525   231-264-8116
          Fax: 231-264-9597   info@burnettefoods.com
                    www.burnettefoods.com
Manufacturer and exporter of canned fruits and vegetables including cherries, apples, plumbs, kidney beans, asparagus, green beans and potatoes
    Owner/Manager: William Sherman
    Owner/Manager: Fred Sherman
Estimated Sales: $40-$50 Million
Number Employees: 50-99
Type of Packaging: Consumer, Food Service
Other Locations:
    Burnette Foods Plant
    East Jordan MI
    Burnette Foods Plant
    Hartford MI
Brands:
    BURNETTI'S
    MOTHERS MAID
    ROMEO

1981 Burnley Vineyards and Daniel Cellars
4500 Winery Ln
Barboursville, VA 22923-1833   540-832-2828
          Fax: 540-832-2280   info@burnleywines.com
                    www.burnleywines.com
Wines
    Owner/President: C Reeder
    Owner: Lee Reeder
    Sales Manager: Pat Reeder
    Customer Service Manager: Dawn Reeder
Estimated Sales: $5-9.9 Million
Number Employees: 1-4

1982 Burris Mill & Feed
1012 Pearl St
Franklinton, LA 70438-1804   985-839-3400
          Fax: 985-839-3404   800-928-2782
burris@burrismill.com   www.cargill.com
Processor and exporter shrimp, alligator, redfish, etc
    Manager: Pedro Curry
    Manufacturing/Production: Robert Burris
Estimated Sales: $10-20 Million
Number Employees: 20-49
Type of Packaging: Private Label, Bulk

1983 (HQ)Bush Boake Allen
521 W 57th Street
New York, NY 10019-2929   212-765-5500
          Fax: 212-708-7132   iff.information@iff.com
                    www.iff.com

Manufacturer and exporter of essential oils, flavors, fragrances, aroma chemicals, vanilla extract, enzyme modified dairy ingredients, spices and seasonings
  Chairman/CEO: Richard Goldstein
  COO: Jim Dunsdon
  Sr. VP/CFO: Douglas Wetmore
  EVP Global Operations: D Wayne Howard
Number Employees: 1900

1984 Bush Brothers & Company
1016 E Weisgarber Rd
Knoxville, TN 37909-2678   865-588-7685
    Fax: 865-584-9429 www.bushbeans.com
Dry edible beans and other value-added food products
    President: James Ethier
Estimated Sales:$ 50 - 100 Million
Number Employees: 100-249

1985 Bush Brothers & Company
W7841 Smith Street
Shiocton, WI 54170-8640   920-986-3816
                                   Fax: 920-986-3476
Processor of sauerkraut
    General Manager: King Pharr
Estimated Sales:$5-10 Million
Number Employees: 20-49
Parent Co: Bush Brothers & Company
Type of Packaging: Consumer, Food Service
Brands:
    Bush's Best

1986 Bush Brothers & Company
3304 Chestnut Hill Rd
Dandridge, TN 37725-7224   865-509-2361
    Fax: 865-509-2339 www.bushbeans.com
Processor and exporter of dry packed beans, greens and hominy
    President: Ronnie Scott
Estimated Sales:$2.5-5 Million
Number Employees: 250-499

1987 Bush Brothers & Company
600 S Bush Brothers Dr
Augusta, WI 54722-7205   715-286-2211
    Fax: 715-286-1179 www.bushbeans.com
Manufacturer of canned vegetables, baked beans and pork and beans
    Chairman/CEO: Jim Ethier
    Plant Manager: Joe Bried
Estimated Sales:$ 50 - 100 Million
Number Employees: 100-249
Sq. footage: 200000
Type of Packaging: Consumer, Food Service, Private Label
Other Locations:
    Chestnut Hill TN
Brands:
    Bush's Best
    Showboat

1988 Bush Brothers Provision Company
1931 N Dixie Hwy
West Palm Beach, FL 33407-6084   561-832-6666
    Fax: 561-832-1460 800-327-1345
              Harry@bushbrothers.org
              http://www.bushbrothers.org
Processor and exporter of fresh and frozen portion cut beef, veal, lamb, pork and poultry; wholesaler/distributor of dairy products; serving the food service market.
    President: Harry Bush
    VP: Billy Bush
Estimated Sales:$10-20 Million
Number Employees: 10-19
Sq. footage: 10000
Type of Packaging: Consumer, Food Service, Private Label, Bulk

1989 Busken Bakery
2675 Madison Rd
Cincinnati, OH 45208-1389   513-871-2114
    Fax: 513-871-2662 www.busken.com
Cookies, cakes, doughnuts, breads, rolls, pies and muffins.
    President: Dan Busken
    CEO: Page Busken
    Vice President: Steve Snowden
    Catering Operations: Larry Bossert
    Production Manager: Tom Rinear
Estimated Sales:$5-10 Million
Number Employees: 100-249

1990 Busseto Foods
1351 N Crystal Ave
Fresno, CA 93728-1142   559-485-9882
    Fax: 559-485-9926 800-628-2633
                         www.busseto.com
Processor of specialty meats, salami, peperoni, prosciutto, chubs, pancetta and genoa
    President/CEO: G Michael Grazier
    CFO: C Laizure
Estimated Sales:$10-20 Million
Number Employees: 20-49
Parent Co: IBIS
Type of Packaging: Consumer, Food Service, Private Label, Bulk
Brands:
    Busseto
    Busseto Special Reserve

1991 Bustelo Coffee RoastingCompany
P.O.Box 520845
Miami, FL 33152-0845   305-592-7302
    Fax: 305-592-9471 www.javacabana.com
Processor, importer and exporter of coffee; importer and wholesaler/distributor of coffee equipment and supplies including filters
    President: Jose Souto
    General Manager of Sales: Angeo Soupo
Estimated Sales:$2.5-5 Million
Number Employees: 20-49
Sq. footage: 25000
Parent Co: Tetley USA
Type of Packaging: Consumer, Food Service, Private Label
Brands:
    Cafe Bustelo

1992 Butcher Shop
PO Box 698
Beaverlodge, AB T0H 0C0
Canada   780-354-8600
                                Fax: 780-354-8418
Processor of beef and pork sausages
    Manager: Bob Geib
    President: Bob Geib
    Marketing Director: Bob Geib
Number Employees: 1-4
Sq. footage: 2000
Type of Packaging: Consumer, Bulk

1993 Butler Winery
1022 N College Ave
Bloomington, IN 47404-3589   812-339-7233
              vineyard@butlerwinery.com
              www.butlerwinery.com
Manufacturer of wine and wine making supplies
    President/CEO: James Butler
Estimated Sales:$500,000-$1 Million
Number Employees: 1-4
Brands:
    Butler

1994 Butter Baked Goods
4321 Dunbar Street
Vancouver, BC V6S 2G2   604-221-4333
    Fax: 604-685-8563 info@butterbakedgoods.com
              www.butterbakedgoods.com
Scones, muffins, cinnamon buns, cookies, bars, cupcakes, cakes, pies, tarts and mini tarts, loaves, and marshmallow

1995 Butter Krust Baking Company
249 N 11th St
Sunbury, PA 17801-2450   570-286-5845
    Fax: 570-286-6975 800-282-8093
              www.butterkrust.com
Manufacturer of bread, rolls and donuts
    President: James G Apple
Estimated Sales:$300,000-500,000
Number Employees: 5-9
Type of Packaging: Consumer, Private Label, Bulk
Other Locations:
    Northumberland PA
Brands:
    BUTTER-KRUST COUNTRY
    HOLSUM
    MILANO

1996 (HQ)Butter Krust Baking Company
249 N 11th St
Sunbury, PA 17801-2450   570-286-5845
    Fax: 570-286-6975 www.butterkrust.com

    President: James Apple
    Vice President: John Apple
    Sales Manager: Thomas Gresh
    Controller: John Mertz
    Plant Manager: Barry Hulsizer
    General Manager: Brenda Swisher
Estimated Sales:$20-50 Million
Number Employees: 5-9

1997 (HQ)Butterball Farms
1435 Buchanan Ave SW
Grand Rapids, MI 49507-1699   616-243-0105
    Fax: 616-243-9169 ron.s@butterballfarms.com
              www.butterballfarms.com
Processor of butter and margarine; embossed designs available. Butter pats and butter balls certified kosher and dairy; Halal certification
    President/CEO: Mark Peters
    CFO: David Riemersma
    Vice President: Tina Collins
    Research & Development: Kasey Komdeur
    Marketing/Sales: Kelly Andrus
    Customer Service Manager: Ron Schalow
    Operations Manager: Carol Schipper
Estimated Sales:$100+ Million
Number Employees: 250-499
Type of Packaging: Food Service, Private Label
Brands:
    BUTTERBALL
    FIGURE-MAID
    PACK OF THE ROSES
    POP-OUT
    SWEETCORN

1998 Butterball Turkey Company
411 N Main St
Carthage, MO 64836-1327   417-358-5914
    Fax: 417-358-6553 800-641-4228
              www.butterball.com
Frozen and refrigerated turkeys
    President: Timothy Harris
    COO: Randy Counts
    Plant Manager: Jerry Lankford
*Estimated Sales:*Under $500,000
Number Employees: 20-49
Parent Co: ConAgra Refigerated Prepared Foods
Brands:
    Butterball
    Cook's
    Crunch'n Munch
    David
    Decker
    Gilroy
    Golden Cuisine
    Hunt's
    Libbys
    Louis Kemp
    Luck's
    Pen Rose
    Peter Pan

1999 Butterbuds Food Ingredients
2330 Chicory Rd
Racine, WI 53403-4113   262-598-9900
    Fax: 262-598-9999 800-426-1119
    bbfi@bbuds.com www.bbuds.com
Processor and exporter of cholesterol-free butter flavored oils and sprays; also, natural dairy concentrates including butter, cheese and cream
    President: Allen Buhler
    VP: John Buhler
    Applications Scientist: Adam Small
    International Marketing Manager: Thomas Buhler

Estimated Sales:$5-10 Million
Number Employees: 20-49
Sq. footage: 5000
Parent Co: Cumberland Packing Corporation
Type of Packaging: Consumer, Food Service, Private Label, Bulk
Brands:
    ALFREDOBUDS
    BUTTER FLO
    BUTTERBUDS
    BUTTERMIST
    CHEESEBUDS

2000 Butterfield Foods Company
225 Hubbard Ave
Butterfield, MN 56120-9452   507-956-5103
                                Fax: 507-956-5751
    mdowns@downsfoodgroup.com
              www.tonydownsfoods.com

Processor of poultry including fresh and frozen chicken; also, slaughtering services available.
President: Mike Downs
Finance Director: Patty Anderson
Vice President: Greg Cook
Vice President: Mitch Forstie
Sales & Marketing: Leo Zachman
Estimated Sales: $5-10 Million
Number Employees: 100-249
Parent Co: Tony Downs Foods
Type of Packaging: Consumer, Food Service

2001 Butterfields Brewing Company
777 E Olive Ave
Fresno, CA 93728-3350   559-264-5521
    Fax: 559-264-6033 www.sequoiabrewing.com
Processor of seasonal beer, ale, stout, lager and pilsner
President: Scott Kendall
Operations Manager: Holly Bragg
Director Manufacturing: Kevin Cox
Estimated Sales: $1-2.5 Million
Number Employees: 50-99
Type of Packaging: Consumer, Food Service
Brands:
    Bridalveil Ale
    San Joaquin Golden Ale
    Tower Dark Ale

2002 Butterfields/Sweet Concepts
2155 S Old Franklin Rd
Nashville, NC 27856-8952   252-459-7771
    Fax: 252-459-7606 800-945-5957
    bpugh@butterfieldscandy.com
    www.butterfieldscandy.com
Processor of hard candy.
President: Tracey West
Estimated Sales: Under $500,000
Number Employees: 10-19

2003 Butterfly Creek Winery
4063 Triangle Rd
Mariposa, CA 95338-9031   209-966-2097
    Fax: 209-742-5019 wine@yosemite.net
    www.yosemite.com
Wines
President: John Gerken
General Manager: Bob Gerken
Estimated Sales: $500-$1 Million
Number Employees: 1-4
Type of Packaging: Private Label

2004 Butternut Bread
1325 Edna St SE
Grand Rapids, MI 49507-3748   616-245-8292
    Fax: 616-245-8371
Processor of bread including whole wheat, rye, white, etc
Product Manager: Dwayne Scheacher
Plant Manager: Dave Erno
Purchasing Agent: Keith Morrow
Estimated Sales: $50-100 Million
Number Employees: 20-49
Parent Co: Interstate Brands Corporation
Type of Packaging: Consumer, Food Service, Private Label

2005 Butternut Mountain Farm
37 Industrial Park Dr
Morrisville, VT 05661-8533   802-888-3491
    Fax: 802-888-5909 800-828-2376
    stuart@vermontmaplesugarcompany.com
Manufacturer of pure maple syrup, handmade maple candy, maple sugar, maple butter, maple spreads, cake mixes, honey, and honey spreads
Owner: David R Marvin
Sales Manager: Stuart Macfarland
Purchasing Manager: Stuart Macfarland
Estimated Sales: $1-2.5 Million
Number Employees: 20-49
Parent Co: The Vermont Maple Syrup Company

2006 Buttonwood Farm Winery
1500 Alamo Pintado Rd
Solvang, CA 93463-9756   805-688-6160
    Fax: 805-688-6168 800-715-1404
    imbibers@buttonwoodwinery.com
    www.buttonwoodwinery.com
Wines
President: Bret Davenport
CFO: Elizabeth Williams
VP: Seyburn Zorthian
Estimated Sales: $500,000-$1 Million
Number Employees: 20-49

2007 Buxton Foods
401 Broadway
Buxton, ND 58218-4003   701-847-2110
    800-726-8057
Manufacturer of gourmet frozen pinto beans and chili fully cooked and packaged in oven/microwaveable trays and boil-in-bags
President: Paul Siewert
CEO: Eileen Siewert
Estimated Sales: $ 10 - 20 Million
Number Employees: 1-4
Sq. footage: 4500
Type of Packaging: Consumer, Food Service
Brands:
    Paul's Pintos

2008 BuyWell Coffee
4850 North Park Drive
Colorado Springs, CO 80918   719-598-7870
    Fax: 877-294-6246 main@buywellcoffee.com
    www.buywellcoffee.com
organic coffee

2009 Buzz Food Service
4818 Kanawha Blvd E
Charleston, WV 25306-6328   304-925-4781
    Fax: 304-925-1502 buzzfood@charter.net
    www.buzzfoodsvc.com
Manufacturer of frozen beef, chicken, ribs, pork, turkey, veal and lamb
President: Dick Gould
GM: John Haddy
Estimated Sales: $50-100 Million
Number Employees: 50-99
Sq. footage: 25000
Type of Packaging: Consumer, Food Service

2010 Buzzards Bay Trading Company
PO Box 600
Fairhaven, MA 02719-0600   508-996-0242
    Fax: 508-996-2421
Fresh and frozen seafood

2011 Buzzn Bee Farms
4700 N Flagler Dr
West Palm Beach, FL 33407-2907   561-881-1551
    Fax: 561-881-7023 www.buzznbee.com
Honey
Owner/Beekeeper: David Rukin
Estimated Sales: $2.5-5 Million
Number Employees: 1-4
Brands:
    Buzzn Bee Farms
    Sweet Squeeze

2012 Byblos Bakery
2479 23rd Street NE
Calgary, AB T2E 8J8
Canada   403-250-3711
    Fax: 403-291-4095 info@byblosbakery.com
    www.byblosbakery.com
Processor of Middle Eastern baked goods including pita bread, bagels, baklava and tortilla wraps
President: Sal Daklala
VP: George Daklala
Number Employees: 50-99
Number of Brands: 1
Type of Packaging: Consumer, Food Service, Private Label, Bulk
Brands:
    Byblos

2013 Byesville Aseptics
P.O.Box 280
Byesville, OH 43723-0280   740-685-2548
    Fax: 740-685-6550
Cocktail mixes, citrus juices, noncitrus fruit juices, vegetable juices
General Manager: Thomas Szymaniak
Plant Manager: Tom Szymaniak
Purchasing Agent: George Bussington
Estimated Sales: $50-100 Million
Number Employees: 100-249
Type of Packaging: Bulk

2014 Byington Winery & Vineyards
21850 Bear Creek Rd
Los Gatos, CA 95033-9438   408-354-1111
    Fax: 408-354-2782 tastingroom@byington.com
    www.byington.com
Wines
Manager: Frank Ashton
VP: Sheryl Byington Brissenden
General Manager: Rod Bravo
Estimated Sales: $1-2.5 Million
Number Employees: 5-9
Sq. footage: 15
Type of Packaging: Private Label
Brands:
    Byington

2015 Byrd Cookie Company
P.O.Box 13086
Savannah, GA 31416-0086   912-355-1716
    Fax: 912-355-4431 800-291-2973
    custserv@byrdcookiecompany.com
    www.byrdcookiecompany.com
Cookies
President: Jeff Repella
Vice President: Geoff Repella
Research & Development: Shawn Curl
Marketing Director: Amy Waddell
Sales Director: Geoff Repella
Public Relations: Amy Waddell
Operations/Plant Manager: Shawn Curl
Production Manager: Shawn Curl
Purchasing Manager: Shawn Curl
Estimated Sales: $5-10 Million
Number Employees: 50-99
Number of Brands: 3
Number of Products: 75
Sq. footage: 65000
Type of Packaging: Consumer, Private Label
Brands:
    BYRD BASICS
    BYRD COOKIE COMPANY
    SECKINGER-LEE BISCUITS

2016 Byrd Mill Company
14471 Washington Hwy
Ashland, VA 23005   804-798-3627
    Fax: 804-798-9357 888-897-3336
    sales@byrdmill.com www.byrdmill.com
Manufacturer of specialty mixes including bread, pound cake, cookie, fruit cobbler, biscuit, pancake, waffle, muffin, spoon bread, shortbread, corn bread, hushpuppy, stoneground grits, etc
President: Todd Attkisson
Estimated Sales: $300,000-$500,000
Number Employees: 1-4
Sq. footage: 1650
Type of Packaging: Consumer, Food Service, Private Label, Bulk

2017 Byrd's Pecans
Rr 3 Box 196
Butler, MO 64730-9418   660-679-5583
    Fax: 660-679-3783 866-679-5583
    goodbye1@ckt.net byrdspecans.com
Pecans
Owner: Loyle Byrd
Owner: Mary Byrd
Estimated Sales: Less than $500,000
Number Employees: 1-4
Type of Packaging: Private Label
Brands:
    Byrd Missouri Grown
    Byrd's Hoot Owl Pecan Ranch Pecans

2018 Byrd's Seafood
101 Potomac St
Crisfield, MD 21817-1448   410-968-0990
    Fax: 410-968-1424 www.byrdsseafood.com
Crabmeat
Manager: Patti Marshall
Estimated Sales: $ 3 - 5 Million
Number Employees: 5-9

2019 Byrne & Carlson
121 State St
Portsmouth, NH 03801-3825   603-559-9778
    Fax: 603-559-9778 888-559-9778
    info@byrneand carlson.com
    www.byrneandcarlson.com
Manufacturer of chocolates and confections
Owner: Chris Carlson
Owner: Christopher Carlson
Estimated Sales: Less than $500,000
Number Employees: 1-4

2020 Byrne Dairy
240 Oneida St
Syracuse, NY 13202-3373   315-475-2111
        Fax: 315-471-0930   800-899-1535
        mary.fietkiewicz@byrnedairy.com
        www.byrnedairy.com
Processor of dairy products including fresh milk,
cream and juice, UP milk and creams and ice cream.
    President: William Byrne
    Production: Nick Marsella
Estimated Sales: $100 Million
Number Employees: 100-249
Type of Packaging: Consumer, Food Service, Private Label, Bulk
Brands:
    Byrne Dairy

2021 Byrnes & Kiefer Company
131 Kline Ave
Callery, PA 16024   724-538-5200
        Fax: 724-538-9292   877-444-2240
        www.bkcompany.com
Baked goods
    President: Jay Thier
    CEO: Ed G Byrnes Jr
    Operations Manager: Donald Yoest
    Purchasing: Tom Byrnes
Estimated Sales: $5-9.9 Million
Number Employees: 20-49
Type of Packaging: Private Label

2022 Byrnes Packing
P.O.Box 8
Hastings, FL 32145-0008   904-692-1643
        Fax: 904-692-2002
Grower and packer of whole potatoes
    Owner: Danny Byrnes
Estimated Sales: $2.5-5 Million
Number Employees: 10-19
Type of Packaging: Consumer

2023 Byron Vineyard & Winery
5475 Chardonnay Ln
Santa Maria, CA 93454-9600   805-934-4770
        info@byronwines.com
        www.byronwines.com
Manufacturer of wines
    Manager: Jonathan Nagy
    Winemaker/General Manager: Ken Brown
    VP Winemaker: Byron Brown
Estimated Sales: $5-10 Million
Number Employees: 10-19
Type of Packaging: Private Label

2024 C C Conway Seafoods
2567 Conway Oyterhouse Road
Wicomico, VA 23184   804-642-2853
Fish and seafood
    President: C Conway III
Estimated Sales: $500,000-$1 Million
Number Employees: 1-4
Type of Packaging: Food Service, Bulk

2025 C&C Packing Company
P.O.Box 157
Stamps, AR 71860-0157   870-533-2251
        Fax: 870-533-4309   www.candcpacking.com
Processor of meat
    Owner: Randy Camp
Estimated Sales: $1-2.5 Million
Number Employees: 5-9
Type of Packaging: Consumer

2026 C&E Canners
P.O.Box 229
Hammonton, NJ 08037-0229   609-561-1078
        Fax: 609-567-2776
Processor, exporter and canner of sauces and
ketchup
    President: Robert Cappuccio
    COO: David Cappuccio
    Vice President: Joseph Cappuccio II
    Director Manufacturing: Stephen Cappuccio
    Purchasing: Robert Cappuccio
Estimated Sales: $5-10 Million
Number Employees: 20-49
Sq. footage: 80000
Type of Packaging: Consumer
Brands:
    C & E SUGAR
    CAPPUCCIO
    NA PO'OKELA O HONAUNAU

2027 (HQ)C&F Foods
15620 Valley Blvd
City of Industry, CA 91744-3926   626-723-1000
        Fax: 626-723-1212   www.cnf-foods.com
Processor and exporter of dried beans, lentils, popcorn, peas and rice
    President: Manuel Fernandez
    CFO: Jose Fernandez
Estimated Sales: $32.6 Million
Number Employees: 100-249
Type of Packaging: Consumer, Food Service, Private Label
Other Locations:
    C&F Foods
    Hansen ID
    C&F Foods
    Sikeston MO
    C&F Foods
    Manvel ND
    C&F Food
    Raleigh NC
Brands:
    EL ORGULLO DE MI TIERRA
    KANGA BEANS
    PREMIER FIELDS

2028 C&G Salsa
P.O.Box 6085
Fishers, IN 46038-6085   317-569-9099
        Fax: 317-569-8666   sales@cgsalsa.com
        www.cgsalsa.com
Produces a variety of salsa (mild/medium/hot) and
chili sauce (mild/zesty) products.
    Co-Owner: Charlie Ferguson
    Co-Owner: Glenda Ferguson
Type of Packaging: Food Service

2029 (HQ)C&H Sugar Company
830 Loring Ave
Crockett, CA 94525
        Fax: 510-787-1791   800-729-4840
        steve.tan@chsugar.com   www.chsugar.com
Manufacturer of refined pure cane sugar including
granulated, brown, powedered, liquid, cubes, raw
and organic sugars, exporter of pure cane sugar
    President/CEO: David Koncelik
    CFO: Robert Guilbert
    VP: William Duff
    VP Sales: William Duff
Estimated Sales: $500 Million-$1 Billion
Number Employees: 500-999
Type of Packaging: Consumer, Food Service, Private Label, Bulk
Brands:
    C&H BAKER'S SUGAR
    C&H DARK BROWN SUGAR
    C&H GOLDEN BROWN SUGAR
    C&H GRANULATED SUGAR
    C&H POWDERED SUGAR
    C&H SUPERFINE SUGAR
    C&H WASHED RAW SUGAR

2030 (HQ)C&H Sugar Company
830 Loring Ave
Crockett, CA 94525-1104   510-787-2121
        Fax: 510-787-1791   edgn.orr@cgsugar.com
        www.chsugar.com
Manufacturer of cane sugar and molasses
    President/CEO: David Koncelik
    CFO: Robert Guilbualt
    VP: William Duff
Estimated Sales: $169 Million
Number Employees: 500-999
Type of Packaging: Consumer, Food Service, Private Label, Bulk
Brands:
    C&H

2031 C&H Sugar/Sweetener Products
4570 Campus Dr
Newport Beach, CA 92660-8809   714-475-2665
        Fax: 949-475-2677   mkh4665@home.com
        www.chsugar.com
Sugar products
    President: David G Koncelik
    CEO: David G Koncelik
    CFO: Robert Guilbualt
Brands:
    C&H Sugar

2032 C&J Tender Meat
324 E Intl Airport Rd
Anchorage, AK 99518-1215   907-562-2838
        Fax: 907-561-5846

Owner: Steve Jones
Vice President: Arlita Jones
Estimated Sales: $1,300,000
Number Employees: 5-9

2033 C&J Trading
1140 Revere Ave
San Francisco, CA 94124-3423   415-822-8910
        Fax: 415-822-7526
Oriental food
    Owner: C Wo
Estimated Sales: $1-2.5 Million
Number Employees: 5-9
Type of Packaging: Private Label

2034 C&S Wholesale Meat Company
973 Confederate Ave SE
Atlanta, GA 30312-3799   404-627-3547
        Fax: 404-627-3549
Processor of portion cut meat including pork and
beef
    President: Jay Bernath
    CEO: Stanley Berneth
    Chairman of the Board: Stanley Bernath
    Marketing Administrator: Ronnie Berneth
Estimated Sales: $10-20 Million
Number Employees: 20-49
Type of Packaging: Food Service, Bulk
Brands:
    C&S

2035 C&T Refinery
7110 Forest Ave
Richmond, VA 23226-3786   804-287-1340
        Fax: 804-285-9168   800-284-6457
        jonathan_gilbert@ctrefinery.com
        www.cargill.com
Processor and exporter of vegetable oil
    President: C Sauer IV
    VP: Robert Holden
Parent Co: C.F. Sauer Company
Type of Packaging: Consumer, Food Service, Private Label, Bulk
Brands:
    C&T

2036 C-B Beverage Corporation
P.O.Box 49
Hopkins, MN 55343-0049   952-935-9905
        Fax: 952-938-2731   www.cocknbull.com
Beverages; ginger beer, sarsaparilla, sparkling juice,
root beer, etc.
    President: Daniel Meyers
Estimated Sales: Less than $300,000
Number Employees: 1-4

2037 C. Gould Seafoods
PO Box 14566
Scottsdale, AZ 85267-4566   480-314-9250
        Fax: 480-314-9240
Seafood
    President: Carla Gould
    Secretary/Treasurer: Helen Sambrano
    Vice President: Robert Llewellyn

2038 C. Howard Company
1007 Station Rd
Bellport, NY 11713-1552   631-286-7940
        Fax: 631-286-7947
        inquire@chowardcompany.com
        www.chowardcompany.com
Processor of confectionery products including hard
candy, mints and chewing gum
    President: Kenneth Pratz
    VP of Sales: Arthur Pratz
Estimated Sales: $1-2.5 Million
Number Employees: 5-9
Type of Packaging: Consumer, Private Label
Brands:
    Chowards

2039 C. Roy Meat Products
7756 Brockway Rd
Brockway, MI 48097   810-387-3957
        Fax: 810-387-3957
Processor of meat products including bologna
    Owner: Richard Roy
    Manager: Nancy Roy
Estimated Sales: $ 10 - 20 Million
Number Employees: 20-49
Type of Packaging: Consumer

2040 C.B.S. Lobster Company
48 Union Wharf
Portland, ME 04101-4607   207-772-9056
    Fax: 207-772-0169 www.mainelobsterdirect.com
Lobster
    Owner: Lee Kressbach
Estimated Sales: $ 5 - 10 Million
Number Employees: 20-49

2041 C.C. Graber Company
P.O.Box 511
Ontario, CA 91762-8511   909-983-1761
    Fax: 909-984-2180 800-996-5483
info@graberolives.com   www.graberolives.com
Vegetables, gourmet foods, olives
    President: Clifford Graber
    Co-Owner: Robert Graber
Estimated Sales: $20-50 Million
Number Employees: 100-249
Brands:
    Graber Olives

2042 C.E. Fish Company
P.O.Box 128
Jonesboro, ME 04648-0128   207-434-2631
    Fax: 207-434-6940
Processor and exporter of seafood including shucked
soft shelled and steamer clams
    President: Barbara Fish
Estimated Sales: $300,000
Number Employees: 5-9
Sq. footage: 3500
Type of Packaging: Consumer
Brands:
    UNI

2043 C.E. Zuercher & Company
1032 W Fulton Market
Chicago, IL 60607-1256   312-666-6992
    Fax: 847-324-0396 www.zuercher.biz
Processor and importer of cheese
    President: Joe Zuercher Jr
    CFO: John Lull
Estimated Sales: $5-10 Million
Number Employees: 5-9
Type of Packaging: Consumer, Food Service, Private Label, Bulk
Brands:
    E-Z
    Little Swiss

2044 C.F. Burger Creamery
8101 Greenfield Rd
Detroit, MI 48228-2296   313-584-4040
    Fax: 313-584-9870 800-229-2322
        www.cfburger.com
Processor of aerosol whip cream, ready-to-drink
milkshakes, coconut beverages and natural Swiss
goat's milk
    Co-Chairman: Thomas "Angott, Sr"
    CEO: Larry Angott
    COO: Larry Angott
    VP: James Brackett
    Quality Control: Arvind Patel
    Sales Manager: chris Angott
    COO: Larry Angott
Estimated Sales: $20-50 Million
Number Employees: 50-99
Type of Packaging: Consumer, Food Service, Private Label, Bulk
Brands:
    C.F. Burger
    Goody Shake
    Natures Fountain

2045 C.F. Gollott & Son Seafood
P.O.Box 1191
Biloxi, MS 39533-1191   228-392-2747
    Fax: 228-392-8848 866-846-3474
        www.century21.com
Importer of frozen shrimp
    President: Armond Gollott
    Secretary/Treasurer: Arny Gollot, Jr.
    VP Sales/Marketing: Arnie Gollott Jr.
Estimated Sales: $20-50 Million
Number Employees: 50-99
Sq. footage: 7800
Type of Packaging: Consumer, Food Service, Private Label
Brands:
    Gollott
    Gollott's Brand
    Merimaid Supreme
    Mermaid Supreme

2046 C.F. Sauer Company
728 N Main St
Mauldin, SC 29662-1918   864-288-3211
    Fax: 864-288-4933 800-688-5676
        consumer-information@cfsauer.com
            www.cfsauer.com
Processor of salad dressings and mayonnaise
    President: Conrad F Sauer IV
    VP: Bradford B Sauer
    Vice President: Jerry Zajaczek
    VP Sales: Mark A Sauer
    Operations Manager: George Jameson
    Plant Manager: Joe Burst
Estimated Sales: $20-50 Million
Number Employees: 100-249
Parent Co: C.F. Sauer Company
Type of Packaging: Consumer, Food Service, Private Label
Brands:
    Duke's Mayonnaise & Retail Salad Pr
    Gold Medal Spices, Flavorings & Mix
    Sauer's Flavorings & Extracts
    Sauer's Spices & Mixes

2047 (HQ)C.F. Sauer Company
2000 W Broad St
Richmond, VA 23220-2000   804-359-5786
    Fax: 804-358-4396 800-688-5676
        www.cfsauer.com
Processor of condiments, relishes, oils, shortenings,
salad dressings, mayonnaise, sauces, spices and seasonings
    President: Conrad F Sauer Iv
    CFO: Richard Coppolo
    Vice President: Richard Winger
    Quality Control: Chuck Adams
    Purchasing Agent: Anne Reager
Estimated Sales: $250 Million
Number Employees: 1,000-4,999
Type of Packaging: Consumer, Food Service, Private Label
Other Locations:
    C.F. Sauer Company
    San Luis Obispo CA
Brands:
    C.F. SAUER COMPANY

2048 C.H. Guenther & Son
129 E Guenther
San Antonio, TX 78204-1402   210-227-1401
    Fax: 210-227-1409 800-531-7912
        respinoza@chguenther.com
            www.chguenther.com
Flour meal and prepared mixes, frozen bakery products
    President/CEO: C.H. Guenther
    CEO: C.H. Guenther
    CFO: Walter Moede
    CEO: Dale W Tremblay
    Research & Development: Ron Spies
    Quality Control: Ron Spies
    Corporate Accounts VP: Mike Toti
    Food Service President: Steve Stroud
    Sr. VP Supply Chair: Dennis Daniels
    Plant Manager: Paul Chupp
    Purchasing Manager: Jim Sharp
Estimated Sales: $100+ Million
Number Employees: 250-499
Type of Packaging: Consumer, Food Service, Private Label, Bulk
Brands:
    Pioneer
    White Lily
    White Wings

2049 C.J. Distributing
PO Box 2344
Cpu Surf City, NC 28445-9821   910-329-1681
    Fax: 910-329-1286 800-990-2366
        peanutsrus@aol.com
Processor of peanuts and snack food items
    CEO: E Howell
Number Employees: 1-4
Sq. footage: 5000
Type of Packaging: Consumer, Private Label, Bulk

2050 C.J. Vitner Company
4202 W 45th St
Chicago, IL 60632-4390   773-523-7900
    Fax: 773-523-9143 www.vitners.com
Processor of pretzels, popcorn and tortilla, corn and
potato chips
    President: William Vitner

Estimated Sales: $20-50 Million
Number Employees: 100-249
Sq. footage: 250
Parent Co: C.J. Vitner Company
Type of Packaging: Consumer, Food Service, Private Label, Bulk

2051 C.L. Deveau & Son
PO Box 1
Salmon River, NS B0W 2Y0
Canada   902-649-2812
    Fax: 902-649-2838
Processor and exporter of salted hake, cusk, pollack
and cod; also, frozen herring roe
    President: Irvan Paul Deveau
Number Employees: 10-19
Type of Packaging: Consumer, Food Service, Private Label, Bulk

2052 C.N.L. Trading
1117 Westminster Avenue
Alhambra, CA 91803-1234   626-282-1938
    Fax: 626-282-1908
    Proprietor: John Chan

2053 C.S. Steen's Syrup Mill
119 N Main St
Abbeville, LA 70510-4603   337-893-1654
    Fax: 337-893-2478 800-725-1654
        steens@steensyrup.com   www.steensyrup.com
Processor of molasses and syrup
    Owner: Charlie Steen
    Marketing Director: Cole Thompson
    General Manager: Charley Steen
Estimated Sales: $ 5 - 10 Million
Number Employees: 20-49
Type of Packaging: Bulk
Brands:
    Steen's Cane Cured Pheasant

2054 C.W. Brown & Company
161 Kings Highway
Mount Royal, NJ 08061-1011   856-423-3700
    Fax: 856-423-8894
Processor of sausage and lard
    President: Robert Botto
Estimated Sales: $10-20 Million
Number Employees: 20-49
Type of Packaging: Consumer, Bulk
Brands:
    BOTTO'S ITALIAN

2055 CA Fortune
514 S Main St
Westby, WI 54667-1386   608-634-2468
    Fax: 608-634-2400
Producers of dairy products, specialty foods, pizza
toppings, pizza crusts and bread.
    Administrator: Rhonda Powers
    Purchasing: Ralph Johnson
Estimated Sales: $1-2.5 Million
Number Employees: 1-4
Type of Packaging: Private Label
Brands:
    BURLLE MEATS
    NEW HOLSTEIN CHEESE
    ROTELLA BREAD

2056 CAL Sun Produce Company
511 Mountain View Ave
Oxnard, CA 93030-7203   805-985-2262
    Fax: 805-486-5022 www.calsunproduce.com
Processor of strawberries
    Owner: S Taylor
    CFO: T Burt
    Purchasing Agent: Rick Meck
Estimated Sales: $10-20 Million
Number Employees: 500-999
Sq. footage: 48000
Type of Packaging: Bulk

2057 CB Seafoods
PO Box 299
Inverness, NS B0E 1N0
Canada   902-895-8181
    Fax: 902-895-8180
Processor and exporter of fresh and frozen lobster,
mackerel and sea urchins
    President/CEO: Bernard MacLennan
Number Employees: 50-99
Type of Packaging: Consumer, Food Service, Private Label, Bulk

2058 CBC Foods Inc
305 Main
PO Box 396
Little River, KS 67457-0396   620-897-6665
          Fax: 620-897-5599   800-276-4770
          carolyn@cookiehouse.com
Manufacture frozen cookie dough
     President: Carolyn Wright
Estimated Sales:$1 Million
Number Employees: 6
Sq. footage: 5000
Type of Packaging: Consumer, Food Service, Private Label, Bulk

2059 CBP Resources
5533 York Hwy
Gastonia, NC 28052-8729   704-868-4573
          Fax: 704-861-9252
Processor of hydrogenated fats
     President: Jj Smith
     Plant Manager: Rick Stradtman
Estimated Sales:$ 20 - 50 Million
Number Employees: 100-249
Parent Co: Carolina By-Products Company

2060 CBS Food Products Corporation
770 Chauncey St
Brooklyn, NY 11207-1120   718-452-2500
          Fax: 718-452-2516
Vegetable oil
     President: Chaim Stein
     Purchasing Agent: Bob Green
Estimated Sales:$10-20 Million
Number Employees: 10-19
Type of Packaging: Consumer, Food Service, Private Label
Brands:
     CBS

2061 CC Pollen Company
3627 E Indian School Rd # 209
Phoenix, AZ 85018-5134   602-957-0096
          Fax: 602-381-3130   800-875-0096
          royden@earthlink.net   www.ccpollen.com
Bee pollen and beehive products
     President: Bruce Brown
     CEO: C Brown
     CFO: I Pettit
     Marketing Director: M Hudnall
     Purchasing: Bruce Brown
Estimated Sales:$10-20 Million
Number Employees: 20-49
Type of Packaging: Consumer, Food Service, Private Label, Bulk
Brands:
     24-HOUR ROYAL JELLY
     ALLER BEE-GONE
     BEE PROPOLIS
     BUZZ BARS
     DYNAMIC TRIO
     HIGH DESERT
     POLLENERGY

2062 CCPI/Valley Foods
525 E Lindmore St
Lindsay, CA 93247-2559   559-562-5169
          Fax: 559-562-5691
Orange juice concentrate
     Owner: Tommy Elliott
     CEO: John Barkley
     Purchasing Agent: Tommy Elliott
Estimated Sales:$9 Million
Number Employees: 20-49
Sq. footage: 40000

2063 CE International Trading Corporation
13450 SW 134th Ave
Miami, FL 33186-4530   305-254-3448
          Fax: 305-254-3182   800-827-1169
          info@ceinternationaltrading.com
          http://ceinternational.marcorojas.com/index.htm
Manufacturer of vibratory and separation systems.
Food and beverage usage includes batch operations
to screen and scalp powders, granules, or liquids in
different locations.
     Sales Representative: Edwin Rojas

2064 CGI Desserts
1 King Arthurs Ct
Sugar Land, TX 77478-3145   281-240-1200
          Fax: 281-240-1242

Dessert manufacturer: layer cakes, sheet cakes,
cheesecake, ice cream cake, mousse cakes, pies, single serve desserts, bars, brownies and minipuffs.
     President: Sam Stolbun
     Vice President: Mike Newlin
     VP/Director Marketing: Cindy Newlin
Estimated Sales:$ 5 - 10 Million
Number Employees: 100-249
Type of Packaging: Consumer, Food Service, Private Label, Bulk

2065 CHR Foods
P.O.Box 608
Watsonville, CA 95077-0608   831-728-0157
          Fax: 831-728-0459
Processor of frozen mixed vegetables and strawberries including whole and puree
     President/CEO: Ray Rodriguez
     CFO: Julis Skelton
Estimated Sales:$ 5 - 10 Million
Number Employees: 5-9
Type of Packaging: Food Service
Brands:
     CHR
     New Harvest Foods

2066 CHR Hansen
440 Business Park Cir
Stoughton, WI 53589-3397   608-877-8970
          Fax: 608-877-8984 www.chr-hansen.com
Tablet excipients and coating for pharmaceuticals
and dietary supplements.
Parent Co: Chr Hansen

2067 CHR Hansen
P.O.Box 483
Gretna, LA 70054-0483   504-367-7727
          Fax: 504-367-8832 www.chr-hansen.com
Specialty sweeteners, molasses and fondants. Certified organic facility.
     Manager: Cory Breaux
Estimated Sales:$ 10 - 20 Million
Number Employees: 10-19
Parent Co: Chr Hansen

2068 CHR Hansen
2400 E 130th St
Chicago, IL 60633-1725   773-646-2203
          Fax: 773-646-6346 www.ch-humanhealth.com
Sweeteners, rice syrups, malt syrups and molasses.
Certified organic facility.
     Vice President: Knud Vindfeldt
     Sales Director: Robert Ciero
     Plant Manager: Chuck Stader
Estimated Sales:$ 5 - 10 Million
Number Employees: 20-49
Parent Co: Chr Hansen

2069 CHR Hansen
3558 NW 97th Boulevard
Gainesville, FL 32606-7323   352-332-9455
          Fax: 352-332-9939 www.chr-hansen.com
Processor of meat and poultry starter cultures, spice
extracts, seasoning blends and natural antioxidants.
     FID Industry Group Leader: Kim Bright
     Senior Applications Advisor: Jim Bacus
Estimated Sales:$500,000-$1 Million
Number Employees: 5-9
Parent Co: Chr. Hansen Group
Type of Packaging: Bulk

2070 CHR Hansen
110 Liberty Court
Elyria, OH 44035-2237   440-324-6060
          Fax: 440-324-2747 www.chr-hansen.com
Liquid and dry seasonings and spice blends.
     Sales Manager: Don Bachourus
*Estimated Sales:*Under $500,000
Number Employees: 1-4

2071 CHR Hansen
P.O.Box 14428
Milwaukee, WI 53214-0428   414-607-5700
          Fax: 414-607-5959   800-343-4680
          www.ch-humanhealth.com
Health nutritionals and savory, sweet, dairy and
compound blend flavors.
     Human Resources: Chris Beaudry
Estimated Sales:$50-100 Million
Number Employees: 1,000-4,999

2072 (HQ)CHR Hansen Inc
P.O.Box 14428
Milwaukee, WI 53214-0428   414-607-5700
          Fax: 414-607-5959   800-558-0802
          info@dk.chr-hansen.com
          www.ch-humanhealth.com
Manufacturer of dairy cultures, dairy flavors, natural
and artificial colors, enzymes, probiotics for human
health, and silage inoculants and direct-fed microbial products for animal health.
     President/CEO: David Carpenter
     Human Resources: Chris Beaudry
     Product Development Manager: Priscilla Reeves
     Web Editor: Trine Koch-Nielsen
     SVP Sales/Marketing: Don Cox
     Communications Director: Lars Wodschow
     Public Relations Consultant: Kristine Ahrensbach

     Communications/Journalist: Helle Rexen
Estimated Sales:$65.5 Million
Number Employees: 1,000-4,999
Type of Packaging: Food Service, Bulk

2073 (HQ)CHS
5500 Cenex Drive
Inver Grove Heights, MN 55077   651-355-6000
          800-232-3639
          lani.jordan@chsinc.com   www.chsinc.com
Miller and exporter of semolina, durum and bakery
flours; producer of refined vegetable oils, textured
soy protein, confectionary sunflower seeds, small
grains and processed nut ingredients.
     President & CEO: John Johnson
     Executive VP & CFO: John Schmitz
     Executive VP & COO Ag Business: Mark Palmquist
     Executive VP & COO Processing: Jay Debertin
Estimated Sales:$32+ Billion
Number Employees: 8113
Type of Packaging: Consumer, Food Service, Private Label, Bulk

2074 CHS Oilseed Processing & Refining
2020 S Riverfront Drive
Mankato, MN 56001-1613   507-625-7911
          Fax: 507-345-2254   800-525-6237
          daveschosthet@chsinc.com   www.chsinc.com
Soybean crushing and refined soybean meal, soybean flour, refined oils
     President: Jim Graham
     VP Manufacturing: James Amlie
Estimated Sales:$500 Million to $1 Billion
Number Employees: 100
Brands:
     Teneric

2075 CHS Sunflower
P.O.Box 169
Grandin, ND 58038-0169   701-484-5313
          Fax: 701-484-5657   sunflower@chsinc.com
          www.chssunflower.com
Processor of confection sunflower. We buy directly
from contracted growers and sell directly to buyers.
     President/CEO: James Krogh
     Research & Development: Joel Schaefer
     Sales Director: Bruce Fjelde
     Plant Superintendent: Arvid Terry
     Controller: Chuck Schmidt
Estimated Sales:$100+ Million
Number Employees: 100-249
Parent Co: CHS, Inc.
Type of Packaging: Consumer, Food Service, Private Label, Bulk

2076 CHS, Inc.
3500 Cenex Drive
Inner Grove Heights, MN 55077-1099   651-355-6000
          800-232-3639
          www.chsinc.com
Flavored condiments, sauces and dressings,
barbacue sauce and imitation bacon bits
     President/CEO: John Johnson
*Estimated Sales:*Below $ 5 Million
Number Employees: 50-99
Brands:
     Curley's Famous
     I Magic
     Imagic Baken
     Imagic Imitation Sau
     Imagic Meat Mix
     Imagic Sloppy Joe Mi
     Imitation Bacon Chip
     Imitation Chicken Flavor

Imitation Ham Flavor
Imitation Pepperoni
Imitation Pepperoni
Imitation Pepperoni
Imitation Pepperoni
RK
TSP
Ultra-Soy

2077 CJ America
1 Executive Dr
Fort Lee, NJ 07024-3309   201-461-7407
        Fax: 201-461-9926
Processor, importer and distributer of MSG and nucleotides; importer and exporter of food additives including citric acid
    President: Joonmo Suh
    Vice President: Stephen Chang
    National Sales Manager: Gene Moon
    Product Manager: Chris Lee
    Purchasing Agent: Jane Cho
Estimated Sales: $ .5 - 1 million
Number Employees: 1-4
Parent Co: Cheiljedang

2078 CJ Dannemiller Company
5300 S Hametown Rd
Norton, OH 44203-6199   330-825-7808
        Fax: 330-825-3793   800-624-8671
            www.cjdannemiller.com
Processor of roasted nuts and popcorn
    President: JA Dannemiller
    Secretary: TW Dannemiller
    Purchasing Manager: JA Dannemiller
Estimated Sales: $5-10 Million
Number Employees: 20-49
Sq. footage: 22000
Type of Packaging: Bulk

2079 CJ Vitner Company
4202 W 45th St
Chicago, IL 60632-4390   773-523-7900
        Fax: 773-523-9143 www.vitners.com
Producer of potato chips, corn chips, tortilla chips, popcorn and corn curls
    President/CEO: William Vitner
    CFO: Ron Jastrzebski
    VP Sales & Marketing: Phil Bremser
Estimated Sales: $ 20 - 50 Million
Number Employees: 100-249
Brands:
    VITNER'S

2080 CJ's Seafood
125 Dixie Drive
Des Allemands, LA 70030-3320   985-758-1237
Processor of fresh and frozen catfish
    President: Curtis Matherne
Number Employees: 1-4
Sq. footage: 280
Type of Packaging: Consumer, Food Service

2081 CK Mondavi Vineyards
P.O.Box 191
St Helena, CA 94574-0191   707-967-2200
        Fax: 707-967-2291   info@ckmondavi.com
            www.charleskrug.com
Manufacturer of wines
    President: Peter Mondavi Sr
    CFO: Tom Fossey
    Sales Director: Larry Challacombe
Estimated Sales: $5-9.9 Million
Number Employees: 100-249
Type of Packaging: Private Label
Brands:
    CK Mondavi Cabernet
    CK Mondavi Chardonnay
    CK Mondavi MERLOT
    CK Mondavi WHITE ZIN
    CK MondaviSAUVIGNON
    CK MondaviZINFANDEL

2082 CMT Packaging & Designs,Inc.
312 Amboy Ave
Metuchen, NJ 08840-1833   732-321-4029
    Fax: 732-549-3615   info@cmtpackaging.com
            www.cmtpackaging.com
A custom packaging company for the food and perfume industry.
    President: Preshal Iyar
Estimated Sales: $5,000
Sq. footage: 5000

2083 CNS Confectionery Products
33 Hook Rd
Bayonne, NJ 07002-5006   201-823-1400
        Fax: 201-823-2452   888-823-4330
    sales@cnscoinc.com   www.cnscoinc.com
Importer, processor and national distributor of sweetened, toasted and desiccated coconut as well as other sweet, dry baking ingredients. Certified kosher.
    Chief, Production/Purchasing: Eva Deutsch
    CFO: Irene Fishman
    VP Sales: Miriam Gross
Estimated Sales: $1-2.5 Million
Number Employees: 10-19
Type of Packaging: Private Label
Brands:
    CNS

2084 COBE Chem Labs
8616 Slauson Ave
Pico Rivera, CA 90660-4435   562-942-2426
        Fax: 562-942-9985   sales@cobechem.com
            www.cobechem.com
    President: Sergio Quinones
    CEO: Sergio Quinones
    Marketing Manager: Sergio Quinones
Estimated Sales: $ 20 - 50 Million
Number Employees: 50-99
Brands:
    Cobe

2085 CP Kelco
123 N Wacker Dr # 2000
Chicago, IL 60606-1753   312-554-7800
        Fax: 312-554-7810   800-535-2687
    solutions@cpkelco.com   www.cpkelco.com
Manufactures and sells a broad spectrum of texturizing and stabilizing ingredients. Food ingredients include pectin, carrageenan, xanthan gum and gellan gum, locust bean gum and microparticulated whey protein concentrate.
    President/Chief Executive Officer: Don Rubright
    Vice President/Chief Financial Officer: Torben Wetche
    CEO: Thomas B Lamb
    Vice President Research & Development: Akvia Gross Ph.D
    Vice President Business Management: Didier Viala
    Vice President Commercial Operations: Rick Calk
    Vice President & General Counsel: Edward Castorina
    Vice President Operations: Russ Jordan
    Vice President Supply Chain & Services: Gerald Coughlin
Estimated Sales: $480 Million
Number Employees: 50-99
Number of Brands: 10
Number of Products: 24
Parent Co: J.M. Huber Company
Other Locations:
    CP Kelco Production Plant
    Okmulgee OK
    CP Kelco Production Plant
    San Diego CA
Brands:
    GENU
    GENU GEL
    GENU PLUS
    GENULACTA
    GENUTINE
    GENUVISCO
    KELCOGEL
    KELGUM
    KELTROL
    SIMPLESSE

2086 CP Vegetable Oil
10 Carson Court
Unit 2
Brampton, ON L6T 4P8
Canada   905-792-2309
    Fax: 905-792-9461   ngonsalves@cpvegoil.com
            www.cpvegoil.com
Processor of vegetable oils
    Manager: Nigel Gonsalves
Number Employees: 5-9
Type of Packaging: Food Service, Bulk
Brands:
    C.P.

2087 CR Manufacturing
P.O.Box 590
Waverly, NE 68462-0590   402-786-2000
        Fax: 402-786-2096   877-789-5844
            info@crmfg.com   www.crmfg.com
US manufacturer of plastic supplies and smallwares to the food service, food prep, bakery, restaurant, scoop and scoop accessories, specialty items, pourers and pourer accessories, bar supply and bar accessories markets. Part finishingincluding hot stamping, pad printing, silk screening, sonic welding, sub assemblies and packaging.
    VP Operations: Daryl Chapelle
    Marketing/Sales: Sheila Camprecht
    Plant Manager: Bob Cooper
Estimated Sales: $20 Million
Number Employees: 100-249
Number of Brands: 27
Number of Products: 29
Sq. footage: 120000
Parent Co: PMC Group Companies
Type of Packaging: Food Service, Private Label, Bulk
Brands:
    3-Cup Measurer
    Betterway Pourers
    CR Scoops
    CR food baskets
    Cake Comb
    Crystal shooter tubes
    Drip catchers
    Econo pourer
    Exacto-Pour tester
    Ezy-Way pourer
    Jigg-All
    Jumbo Straws
    Kover All dust cap
    Lid-Off Pail Opener
    Magic-Mesh
    Marga-Ezy
    Pizza slicer
    Polar pitcher
    Posi-Pour 2000 pourer
    Posi-Pour pourer
    Pour Mor
    Pro-Flo pourer
    Roxi rimming supplies
    Roxi sugar and salt spices/flavors
    Shakers prepackaged accessories
    Shotskies gelatin mixes
    Steakmarkers
    Super Slicer
    Whisky gate pourer

2088 CSP Foods
6632 Rue Abrams
Mont-Royal, QC H4S 1Y1
Canada   514-731-7621
        Fax: 514-731-8466
Processor of cake icing, piping jelly, doughnut filling, glazes, jam, marmalades, etc.; importer of chocolates, raisins and nuts; wholesaler/distributor of yeast, mousse, flour, etc.; serving the food service market
Number Employees: 100-249
Sq. footage: 100000
Type of Packaging: Consumer, Food Service, Private Label, Bulk

2089 CSV Sales
44450 Pinetree Dr
Plymouth, MI 48170-3869   734-453-4544
        Fax: 734-453-1118   sales@csvsales.com
            www.csvsales.com
Supplier of closeouts, surplus, salvage and liquidator items including baked goods, poultry, meats and off-grade, frozen and value added foods
    President: Bud Zecman
    Sales Representative: Michael Neely
    Operations Manager: Justin Sarrach
    Purchasing/Sales Support: Roger Cary
Estimated Sales: $5-10 Million
Number Employees: 5-9
Brands:
    Awrey's
    Bakery Chef
    House of Raeford
    Pierre
    Pilgrim's Pride
    Tyson

2090 CTC International
11 York Ave
West Caldwell, NJ 07006-6486   973-228-2300
          Fax: 973-228-7076   info@ctcint.com
                              www.ctcint.com
    President: E L Herbert
Estimated Sales: $ 10 - 20 Million
Number Employees: 20-49

2091 CTC Manufacturing
B12, 416 Meridian Road SE
Calgary, AB T2A 1X2
Canada   403-235-3408
          Fax: 403-272-9558 800-668-7677
                              candytree@sprint.ca
Processor and exporter of gourmet lollypops
    President: G Paul Allen
    Sales Manager: David Skultety
    Plant Manager: Malcolm Steel
Number Employees: 10-19
Sq. footage: 3450
Parent Co: Candy Tree Company
Type of Packaging: Consumer, Food Service, Private Label
Brands:
    The Candy Tree

2092 CTL Foods
507 Pine St
Colfax, WI 54730-9186   715-962-3121
          Fax: 715-962-4030 800-962-5227
          foods@ctlcolfax.com   www.ctlcolfax.com
Processor of malted milk powder, dry-form syrup
bases and flavored slush drinks and bases; manufac-
turer of dry powder dispensers; also, custom blend-
ing and packaging services available
    President: Michael Bean
Estimated Sales: $1.5 Million
Number Employees: 5-9
Sq. footage: 10000
Type of Packaging: Food Service, Private Label
Brands:
    Glacier Ice
    Soda Fountain

2093 CVC Specialties
4510 S Boyle Ave
Vernon, CA 90058-2418   323-581-0178
          Fax: 323-589-6667 800-421-6175
          ronald@cvc4health.com   www.cvc4health.com
Processor of vitamins, supplements and energy prod-
ucts
    President: Ron Beckfield
    VP Sales: Greg Faull
    VP Operations: Bill Swan
Estimated Sales: $2.5-5 Million
Number Employees: 20-49
Sq. footage: 100000
Type of Packaging: Consumer, Private Label, Bulk
Brands:
    Pep'n Energy
    Unit Pac

2094 CVP Systems
2518 Wisconsin Ave
Downers Grove, IL 60515-4230   630-852-1190
          Fax: 630-852-1386 800-422-4720
          sales@cvpsystems.com   www.cvpsystems.com
    Owner: Wes Bork
    CFO: Wes Bork
    COO: Chris Van Wandelen
Estimated Sales: $ 10 - 20 Million
Number Employees: 20-49
Brands:
    C.V.P. Systems

2095 CW Resources
200 Myrtle St
New Britain, CT 06053-4160   860-229-7700
          Fax: 860-229-6847 rbuccilli@cwresources.org
                              www.cwresources.org
Processor of gourmet products including flavored
vinegars and oils, salsas, sauces, jellies, baking
mixes, dips/dip mixes, baked goods, rubs and salad
dressings
    President: Ronald Buccilli
    Sr. VP: Bob Williams
    VP Sales/Production: Alix Capsalors
    Production: Bill Blonski
Estimated Sales: $10-20 Million
Number Employees: 100-249
Sq. footage: 100000
Type of Packaging: Consumer, Food Service, Private Label, Bulk

Brands:
    B&B
    Sumptuous ions

2096 CaJohns Fiery Foods
2040 Oakland Park Ave
Columbus, OH 43224-3848   614-418-0808
          Fax: 614-418-0800 888-703-3473
          cajohns@cajohns.com   www.cajohns.com
Salsas, hot sauce, barbecue sauce, rubs, spice
blends, mixes and mustards.
    President/Owner: John Hard
Estimated Sales: $125,000
Number Employees: 1-4
Brands:
    CaJohns
    Nate Dog's

2097 Cable Car Beverage Corporation
555 17th Street
Denver, CO 80202-3950   303-298-9038
          Fax: 303-298-1150
Beverages
    Chairman/President: Samuel Simpson
Number Employees: 20-49
Brands:
    Stewart's Cherries N' Cream
    Stewart's Classic Ke
    Stewart's Cream Soda
    Stewart's Diet Cream
    Stewart's Diet Orang
    Stewart's Diet Root
    Stewart's Ginger Bee
    Stewart's Grape Soda
    Stewart's Lemon Meri
    Stewart's Orange N'
    Stewart's Root Beer

2098 Cabo Rojo Enterprises
Hc 1
Box 2693
Boqueron, PR 00622-9661   787-254-0015
          Fax: 787-254-2048
Processor and importer of salt
    President: Santos Padilla
Number Employees: 20
Type of Packaging: Consumer

2099 Cabot Creamery
1 Home Farm Way
Montpelier, VT 05602-8243   802-229-9361
          Fax: 802-371-1200 888-792-2268
          info@cabotcheese.com   www.cabotcheese.com
Processor of cheddar cheese, specialty and flavored
cheeses, Monterey Jack and light chesses, plus a va-
riety of other dairy products.
    President/CEO: Rich Stammer
    Master Cheddar Maker: Marcel Gravel
Estimated Sales: $ 10 - 20 Million
Number Employees: 50-99
Sq. footage: 150000
Parent Co: Agri-Mark
Type of Packaging: Consumer, Food Service, Private Label, Bulk
Brands:
    CABOT

2100 Cache Cellars
RR 2 Box 2780
Davis, CA 95616-9604   530-756-6068
          Fax: 530-756-6463
Wines
    President: Charles Lowe
Estimated Sales: $1-2.5 Million
Number Employees: 5-9
Type of Packaging: Private Label

2101 Cache Creek Foods
P.O.Box 180
Woodland, CA 95776-0180   530-662-1764
          Fax: 530-662-2529 matt@cachecreekfoods.com
                              www.cachecreekfoods.com
Custom flavoring and wholesale manufacturing of
almond, cashew, pistachio, nut products and nut
butters
    Manager: Matthew Moorehart
    CEO: Matthew Morehart
Estimated Sales: $3-5 Million
Number Employees: 10-19
Number of Products: 75
Sq. footage: 30000
Type of Packaging: Consumer, Food Service, Private Label, Bulk

Brands:
    PRIVATE LABEL

2102 (HQ)Cacique
14940 Proctor Ave
City of Industry, CA 91746-3219   626-961-3399
          Fax: 626-369-5780 www.caciqueusa.com
Processor and exporter of mozzarella and fresco
cheese
    President: Gilbert L De Cardenas
    Vice President: Will Parker
    Marketing Director: Alberto Fernandez
Estimated Sales: $50-100 Million
Number Employees: 250-499
Sq. footage: 200000
Other Locations:
    Cacique
    Cedar City UT
Brands:
    Black & Gold
    Cacique
    Nochebuena
    Ranchero
    Yonique

2103 Cactu Life Inc
PO Box 349
Corona Del Mar, CA 92625-0349   949-640-8991
          Fax: 949-640-8992 800-500-1713
          info@cactulife.com   www.cactulife.com
Health food supplements
    President: Jeff Liebfreid
Estimated Sales: $500,000
Number Employees: 1-4
Brands:
    Cactu Life

2104 Cactus-Creek
PO Box 671169
Dallas, TX 75367-1169   972-869-4600
          Fax: 972-869-8050 800-471-7723
          info@truco.com   www.cactus-creek.com
Manufactures a variety of salsas, mixes, tortilla
chips and candies.
Estimated Sales: $2.5-5 Million
Number Employees: 20-49
Parent Co: Truco Enterprises
Brands:
    CACTUS CREEK BRAND

2105 Cadbury Adams
5000 Yonge Street
Toronto, ON M2N 7E9
Canada   416-590-5000
          Fax: 416-590-5600
          consumer.relations@brandspeoplelove.com
                              www.chocolate.ca/
Manufacturer of a variety of confectionery products.
    Executive Chairman: John Sunderland
    Chief Executive Officer: Todd Stitzer
    Chief Financial Officer: Ken Hanna
    Chief Legal Officer: Michael Clark
    Chief Science & Technology Officer: David MacNair
    President Americas Beverages: Gil Cassagne
    President Europe/Middle East/Africa: Matt Shattock
    Group Strategy Director: Mark Reckitt
    Chief Legal Officer: Hank Udow
    Chief Human Resources Officer: Bob Stack
    Group Secretary: Hester Blanks
    President Americas Confectionery: Jim Chambers

    President Global Supply Chain: Steve Drive
Number Employees: 1,000-4,999
Parent Co: Cadbury Schweppes
Type of Packaging: Consumer, Food Service, Bulk

2106 Cadbury Beverages CanadaInc
30 Eglinton Avenue W
Mississauga, ON L5R 3E7
Canada   905-712-4121
          Fax: 905-712-8635
          consumer.relations@brandspeoplelove.com
                              www.cadburyschweppes.com

Beverage brands include 7 UP, Canada Dry, Clamato, Dr. Pepper, Hawaiian Punch, Mott's, Schweppes and Snapple.
    Executive Chairman: John Sunderland
    Chief Executive Officer: Todd Stitzer
    Chief Financial Officer: Ken Hanna
    Chief Legal Officer: Michael Clark
    Chief Science & Technology Officer: David MacNair
    President Americas Beverages: Gil Cassagne
    President Europe/Middle East/Africa: Matt Shattock
    Group Strategy Director: Mark Reckitt
    Chief Legal Officer: Hank Udow
    Chief Human Resources Officer: Bob Stack
    Group Secretary: Hester Blanks
    President Americas Confectionery: Jim Chambers

    President Global Supply Chain: Steve Drive
Number Employees: 1,000-4,999
Parent Co: Cadbury Schweppes
Type of Packaging: Consumer, Food Service, Bulk
Brands:
    CADBURY CHOCOLATE
    CADBURY DAIRY MILK
    CADBURY DARK
    CADBURY FAVOURITES
    CADBURY THINS
    CARAMILK

2107 Cadbury Schweppes
P.O.Box 869077
Plano, TX 75086-9077   972-673-7000
    Fax: 972-673-7980   800-696-5891
consumer.relations@brandspeoplelove.com
www.drpeppersnapplegroup.com
Beverage concentrates and confections.
    Executive Chairman: John Sunderland
    Chief Executive Officer: Todd Stitzer
    Chief Financial Officer: Ken Hanna
    CEO: Larry Young
    Chief Science & Technology Officer: David MacNair
    President Americas Beverages: Gil Cassagne
    President Europe/Middle East/Africa: Matt Shattock
    Chief Legal Officer: Hank Udow
    Chief Human Resources Officer: Bob Stack
    Group Secretary: Hester Blanks
    President Americas Confectionery: Jim Chambers

    President Global Supply Chain: Steve Drive
Estimated Sales: $50-100 Million
Number Employees: 10,000+
Parent Co: Cadbury Schweppes
Type of Packaging: Consumer, Food Service, Bulk
Brands:
    7 UP
    BASSETT'S
    BUBBAS
    BUTTERKIST
    CADBURY
    CADBURY CREME EGG
    CADBURY DAIRY MILK
    CADBURY ECLAIRS
    CADBURY ROSES
    CANADA DRY
    CLAMATO
    DENTYNE
    DENTYNE ICE
    DIET DR PEPPER
    DR PEPPER
    HALLS
    HAWAIIAN PUNCH
    HOLLYWOOD
    MAYNARDS
    MOTT'S
    ORANGINA
    PIBB ZERO
    SCHWEPPES
    SNAPPLE
    SOUR PATCH KIDS
    STIMOROL
    TREBOR
    TRIDENT

2108 Cadbury Trebor Allan
277 Gladstone Avenue
Toronto, ON M6J 3L9
Canada   416-530-4055
    Fax: 416-530-0048   800-565-6541
Chocolate
    President: Arthur Soler
Number Employees: 2700

2109 (HQ)Cadbury Trebor Allan
850 Industrial Boulevard
Granby, QC J2J 1B8
Canada   450-372-1080
    Fax: 450-378-4256   800-387-3267
consumer.relations@brandspeoplelove.com
www.ctai.ca OR www.cadburyschweppes.com
Manufacturer of candy including hard, filled hard, toffee, mints, licorice, gums, taffy kisses, penny goods, cough drops, jellies and lollypops, chocolates
    General Manager: Jerome Milcent
    Brand Manager: Michelle Bell
    VP Finance: Malcom Baxton Forman
    Cadbury Trebor Bassett Marketing: Louise Munton
    Cadbury Trebor Allan Supply Chain Mgr: Martin Spencer
Number Employees: 3030
Parent Co: Cadbury Schweppes PLC
Type of Packaging: Consumer, Food Service, Private Label, Bulk
Brands:
    Trebor

2110 Caddo Packing Company
P.O.Box 327
Marshall, TX 75671-0327   903-935-2211
Processors and butchers of beef and pork.
    President: Pat Parrish
Estimated Sales: $2.5-5 Million
Number Employees: 5-9
Type of Packaging: Consumer

2111 Cadick Poultry Company
PO Box 686
Grandview, IN 47615-0686   812-649-4491
                    Fax: 812-649-5327
Processor of poultry.
    President/Purchasing: John Cadick
Estimated Sales: $50-100 Million
Number Employees: 50-99
Type of Packaging: Consumer

2112 Cadillac Coffee Company
1801 Michael St
Madison Heights, MI 48071-4100   248-545-2266
    Fax: 248-584-4184   800-438-6900
info@cadillaccoffee.com
www.cadillaccoffee.com
Processor of tea and coffee
    Owner: Guy Gehlert
    VP Sales: Lisa Adkins
    Controller: Pat Hardy
    V.P., Contract Packaging: Gary Clark
    V.P.: Tom Pavloff
Estimated Sales: $20-50 Million
Number Employees: 20-49
Type of Packaging: Consumer, Food Service, Private Label, Bulk
Brands:
    Cadillac Coffee

2113 Cady Bag
P.O.Box 68
Pearson, GA 31642-0068   912-422-3298
                    Fax: 912-422-3155
    President: William Cady
    Vice President: John Moore
Estimated Sales: $ 20 - 50 Million
Number Employees: 100-249

2114 Cady Cheese Factory
126 State Road 128
Wilson, WI 54027-2604   715-772-4218
    Fax: 715-772-4224   info@cadycheese.com
www.cadycheese.com
Cheese
    President: Dale Marcott
    Treasurer: Wendy Marcott
    Marketing Manager: Dale Marcott
    Office Manager: Gay Wang
    Production Manager: Sandy Lee
    Purchasing: Dale Marcott
Estimated Sales: $50-99.9 Million
Number Employees: 50-99
Brands:
    GOLD'N JACK
    HOT PEPPER
    VEG'Y JACK

2115 Caesar's Pasta Products
1001 Lower Landing Rd # 311
Blackwood, NJ 08012-3124   856-227-2585
    Fax: 856-227-1910 www.caesarspasta.com
Processor of frozen pre-cooked and raw pasta specialties including ravioli, stuffed shells, manicotti with crepes, gnocchi, cavatelli, spaghetti, fettuccine, linguine, angel hair, agnolotti, ravioletti, tortelloni, cheese lasagnaetc
    President: Michael Lodato
    Secretary: Raymond Lodato
    VP: Ronald Lodato
    Purchasing Manager: Ronald Lodato Sr
Estimated Sales: $1-2.5 Million
Number Employees: 20-49
Sq. footage: 30000
Parent Co: Sicilian Chef's
Type of Packaging: Consumer, Food Service, Private Label, Bulk
Brands:
    CAESAR'S
    SICILIAN CHEFS

2116 Cafe Appassionato Coffee Company
4001 21st Ave W
Seattle, WA 98199-1201   206-281-8040
    Fax: 206-282-5218   888-522-2333
                    www.caffeappassionato.com
Coffee
    President/CEO: Phil Sancken
    CFO: Tim Schondelmayer
    Vice President: Tucker McHugh
    VP of Marketing: Tucker McHugh
    Roastmaster: Richard Oakes
    Production Manager: David Crumb
    Plant Manager: Jeffrey Craig
    Purchasing Manager: Phil Sancken
Estimated Sales: $5-10 Million
Number Employees: 50-99
Type of Packaging: Private Label
Brands:
    CAFE APPASSIONATO

2117 Cafe Cartago
3931 Holly St # A
Denver, CO 80207-1200   303-297-1212
    Fax: 303-316-3325   800-443-8666
                    www.cafecartago.com
Coffee
    Owner: Steve Larsen
    Partner: Chuck Ask
    Purchasing Manager: Steve Larsen
Estimated Sales: $2.5-5 Million
Number Employees: 5-9
Type of Packaging: Private Label, Bulk

2118 Cafe Chilku
433 Bay Rd
Colchester, VT 05446-7916   802-878-4645
Producer of BBQ sauces and dipping sauce
    Owner: Chilku Yi

2119 Cafe Del Mundo
229 E 51st Ave
Anchorage, AK 99503-7207   907-562-2326
    Fax: 907-562-3278 www.cafedelmundo.com
Coffee, espresso equipment
    Owner: Perry Merkel
    Purchasing: Perry Merkel
Estimated Sales: $20-50 Million
Number Employees: 10-19
Type of Packaging: Private Label, Bulk
Brands:
    CAFE DEL MUNDO

2120 Cafe Descafeinado de Chiapas
3625 NW 82nd Avenue
Suite 404
Doral, FL 33166-7602   305-499-9775
    Fax: 305-499-9776 www.deschiusa.com
Coffee importers
    President: Daniel Robles
    Director: Arandio Muguira
    Director: Luis Demetrio
Estimated Sales: $500,000-$1 Million
Number Employees: 1-4
Type of Packaging: Private Label

2121 Cafe Du Monde
1039 Decatur St
New Orleans, LA 70116-3309   504-587-0835
    Fax: 504-587-0847   office@cafedumonde.com
                    www.cafedumonde.com

Processor and exporter of beignet doughnut mix, coffee and roasted chicory for coffee flavoring
Manager: Burt Benrud
CFO: J Roman III
Manager: Robert Maher
Estimated Sales: $500,000 appx.
Number Employees: 5-9
Sq. footage: 15000
Other Locations:
Cafe Du Monde-French Market
New Orleans LA
Cafe Du Monde-Riverwalk Marketplace
New Orleans LA
Care Du Monde-New Orleans Centre
New Orleans LA
Cafe Du Monde-Oakwood Mall
Gretna LA
Cafe Du Monde-Lakeside Mall
Metairie LA
Cafe Du Monde-Esplanade Mall
Kenner LA
Cafe Du Monde-Veterans Boulevard
Metairie LA
Brands:
Cafe Du Monde

2122 Cafe Fanny
1619 5th St
Berkeley, CA 94710-1714   510-526-7664
Fax: 510-526-7486   800-441-5413
www.cafefanny.com
Organic granola.
Owner: James Maser
Manager: Leslie Wilson
Estimated Sales: $1-2.5 Million
Number Employees: 20-49

2123 Cafe La Semeuse
55 Nassau Ave
Brooklyn, NY 11222-3143   718-387-9696
Fax: 718-782-2471   800-242-6333
contactus@cafelasemeuse.com
www.cafelasemeuse.com
Coffee
Manager: Andi Billow
Estimated Sales: Under $500,000
Number Employees: 1-4
Brands:
Cafe La Semeuse
Classique
Espresso

2124 Cafe Moak
509 E Division Street
Rockford, MI 49341-1342   616-866-7625
Fax: 616-866-6422   800-757-8776
russos@russospizza.com   www.russospizza.com
Processor of bread sticks, subs, pizzas and coffee;
importer of coffee
Owner: Sal Russo
Administrative Assistant: Becky Fate
Brands:
Russo's

2125 Cafe Moto
2619 National Ave
San Diego, CA 92113-3617   619-239-6686
Fax: 619-239-9344   800-818-3363
www.cafemoto.com
Imported tea and roasted coffee
President: Torrey Lee
CFO: Kimberly Lee
Production Manager: Michael Figgins
Estimated Sales: Under $500,000
Number Employees: 20-49
Type of Packaging: Private Label

2126 Cafe Salvador
P.O.Box 29002
San Francisco, CA 94129-0002   415-751-7630
Fax: 415-387-7201
President: M Newman
Estimated Sales: $2.5-5 Million
Number Employees: 5-9

2127 Cafe Sark's Gourmet Coffee
22800 Savi Ranch Parkway
Yorba Linda, CA 92887-4623   626-579-6000
Gourmet coffee
President: Jeff Shamburger
Estimated Sales: Under $500,000
Number Employees: 5-9

2128 Cafe Society Coffee Company
2910 N Hall Street
Dallas, TX 75204-2310   214-922-8888
Fax: 214-922-0280   800-717-6000
info@cafesocietycoffee.net
Flavored and organic coffee and tea
President: Lauri Sanderfer
Sales Representative: Byron Laszlo
General Manager: Jessie Nickerson
Estimated Sales: $1-$1.4 Million
Number Employees: 11
Type of Packaging: Private Label

2129 Cafe Sol de Oro International
2366 Yonge Street
Toronto, ON M4P 2E6
Canada   416-322-8182
www.soldeoro.com
Roaster and importer of single origin unblended Arabica coffees from the Venezuelan Andes. Bulk, food service and retail in regular, organic and flavored
President: Mark Morgan

2130 Cafe Tequila
967 N Point Street
San Francisco, CA 94109-1111   415-264-0106
Fax: 415-674-1740   jfielder@cafetequila.com
www.cafetequila.com
Manufacturer of tequila sauces
President/CEO: John Fielder
Sales/Marketing Executive: Julie Fielder
Number Employees: 1-4
Type of Packaging: Consumer, Food Service
Brands:
Cafe Tequila

2131 Cafe Terra Cotta
6064 N Pinnacle Ridge Dr
Tucson, AZ 85718-3501   520-577-8100
Fax: 520-577-9015   800-492-4454
feedback@terracotta.com
www.cafeterracotta.com
Contemporary Southwest cuisine
President: Don Luria
Vice President: Donna Nordin
Marketing Director: Michael Luria
Purchasing: Michael Luria
Estimated Sales: $2.5-5 Million
Number Employees: 100-249
Type of Packaging: Private Label
Brands:
CREATIVE CONDIMENTS

2132 Cafe Yaucono/Jimenez & Fernandez
1103 Avenue Fernandez Juncos
Po Box 13097
Santurce, PR 00907-4713   787-721-3337
Fax: 787-722-5590   info@yaucono.com
www.yaucono.com
Processor of coffee
President: Jose Jimenez
VP: Julio Torres
Comp/Treasurer: Julio Torres
Marketing Manager: Joaquin Class
Number Employees: 20
Sq. footage: 25000
Type of Packaging: Consumer
Brands:
Yaucono

2133 Caffe D'Amore
1107 S Mountain Ave
Monrovia, CA 91016-4258   626-932-0050
Fax: 626-932-0152   800-999-0171
www.caffedamore.com
Processor of instant cappuccino
President: Chris Julius
Director Marketing: Cheri Hays
President: Chris Julius
Estimated Sales: $1 - 3 Million
Number Employees: 20-49
Type of Packaging: Consumer, Food Service

2134 Caffe D'Amore Gourmet Beverages
1107 S Mountain Ave
Monrovia, CA 91016-4258   626-932-0050
Fax: 626-932-0152   800-999-0171
support@caffeedamore.com
www.caffeedamore.com

Manufacturer: Frap Freeze specialty coffee beverages, Green Tea Smoothies, Botanica Fruitea, Bellagio Coffee, Espresso, Sipping Chocolate and European-style cocoas
President: Paul Comi
CEO: Chris Julius
Estimated Sales: $ 30 - 50 Million
Number Employees: 50-99

2135 Caffe D'Oro
14020 Central Avenue
Suite 580
Chino, CA 91710-5524   909-591-9493
Fax: 909-522-8844   800-200-5005
info@caffedoro.com   www.caffedoro.com
Processor of specialty coffee and cappuccino
President: Pamela Abbadessa
V P Marketing: Frank Abbadessa
Number Employees: 5-9
Parent Co: Brad Barry Company
Type of Packaging: Private Label
Brands:
Caffe D'Oro Cappuccino & Cocoa

2136 Caffe D'Vita
14020 Central Avenue
Suite 580
Chino, CA 91710-5524   909-591-9493
Fax: 909-627-3747   800-200-5005
info@caffedvita.com   www.caffedvita.com
Processor of instant cappuccino
President: Al Greene
CFO: Bob Greene
Vice President: Frank Abbadessa
Marketing Director: Frank Greene
Operations Manager: Frank Abbadessa
Estimated Sales: Under $500,000
Number Employees: 20-49
Parent Co: Brad Barry Company
Type of Packaging: Private Label
Brands:
Chai Delite
Chill-A-Ccino
Enhanted Chai
Horchata D'Vita

2137 Caffe Darte
719 S Myrtle St
Seattle, WA 98108-3426   206-762-4381
Fax: 206-763-4665   800-999-5334
sales@caffedarte.com   www.caffedarte.com
Coffee beans
Manager: Joe Mancuso
Vice President: Mauro Cipolla
Marketing Director: Joey Mancuso
Coffee Roaster: Sergio Barella
Plant Manager: Manuel Gonzalez
Purchasing Agent: Terri Trudeau
Estimated Sales: $5-10 Million
Number Employees: 5-9
Type of Packaging: Private Label
Brands:
CAFFE DARTE

2138 Caffe Luca
885 Industry Dr
Tukwila, WA 98188-3411   206-575-2720
Fax: 206-575-0537   800-728-9116
www.caffeluca.com
Processor, exporter and importer of espresso and blended coffee; also, custom roasting available
Owner: Carol Dema
Estimated Sales: $2.5-5 Million
Number Employees: 1-4
Sq. footage: 2000
Type of Packaging: Consumer, Food Service
Brands:
ANTONIO
CASA LUCA
GIOVANNI
GREGORIO
LEONARDO
MISTO
MISTO DARK

2139 Caffe Trieste Superb Coffees
1465 25th St
San Francisco, CA 94107-3403   415-550-1107
Fax: 415-550-1239   info@caffetrieste.com
www.caffetrieste.com
Coffee
President: F Giotta
Estimated Sales: $10-20 Million
Number Employees: 10-19

Type of Packaging: Private Label
Brands:
CAFFE TRIESTE COFFEE BEANS

2140 Cafferata
158 Prospect Avenue
San Anselmo, CA 94960-2521   510-620-1010
     Fax: 510-620-1019   800-626-8115
     info@cafferata.com   www.cafferata.com
Processor of pasta, prepared foods, pesto sauce and
fillings; contract packaging available
   President: Rick Hirsch
   Research & Development: Maurice Sainte-Yves
   Operations Manager: Paul Marner
   Plant Manager: Paul Marner
Estimated Sales: $10-20 Million
Number Employees: 20-49
Sq. footage: 26000
Parent Co: Viking Foods Company
Type of Packaging: Consumer, Food Service, Private Label, Bulk
Brands:
10 CARB RAVIOLI
MAGICAL MUSHROOM
NUTTY GORGONZOLA
OKI DOKI ARTICHOKE
OLOTA OLIVE
PESTO MANIFESTO
SOY GOOD 4U
SQUASH BY GOSH
SUNNY AND CHEESE

2141 Cagle's
P.O.Box 376
Collinsville, AL 35961-0376   256-524-2147
     Fax: 256-524-2910 www.cagles.net
Processor and exporter of poultry
   Manager: Ronnie Adrian Sr
   Chairman/CFO: Mark M Ham IV
   VP: George Douglas Cagle
   VP: James David Cagle
Estimated Sales: $100-500 Million
Number Employees: 500-999
Sq. footage: 131000
Parent Co: Cagle's
Type of Packaging: Bulk

2142 (HQ)Cagle's Inc
P.O.Box 4664
Atlanta, GA 30302-4664   678-904-2980
     Fax: 678-355-9326   800-476-2820
     marketing@cagles.net   www.cagles.net
Processor of poultry products
   President/CEO: C Douglas Cagle
   Chairman/CFO: Mark M Ham IV
   VP: George Douglas Cagle
   VP: James David Cagle
Estimated Sales: $100-500 Million
Number Employees: 1,000-4,999
Type of Packaging: Consumer, Food Service, Private Label, Bulk

2143 (HQ)Cagnon Foods Company
206 Crescent St
Brooklyn, NY 11208-1606   718-647-2244
Processor of soup and gravy bases; also, dehydrated
soups and vegetables
   Partner: Jeffrey Posner
Estimated Sales: $300,000-500,000
Number Employees: 1-4
Sq. footage: 5000
Type of Packaging: Consumer, Food Service, Bulk

2144 Cahoon Farms
P.O.Box 190
Wolcott, NY 14590-0190   315-594-8081
     Fax: 315-594-1678 www.dryhousefruits.com
Processor of frozen apples and cherries
   Owner: Duane Cahoon Jr
   Operations/Sales Manager: Chuck Frederick
Estimated Sales: $10-20 Million
Number Employees: 100-249
Type of Packaging: Consumer

2145 Caiazza Candy Company
202 W Washington Street
New Castle, PA 16101-3945   724-652-9492
                      800-651-1171
     sales@caiazzausa.com   www.caiazzausa.com
Manufacturer of chocolate, raspberry, mint and peanut butter
   Partner: Matt Caiazza
   Marketing Director: Felicia Fincesel

Estimated Sales: $10-20 Million
Number Employees: 20-49
Type of Packaging: Private Label
Brands:
Caiazza
Millennium Meltaways
Pretzel Smooth

2146 Cain Vineyard & Winery
3800 Langtry Rd
St Helena, CA 94574-9772   707-963-1616
     Fax: 707-963-7952   winery@cainfive.com
            www.cainfive.com
Wines
   Manager: Christopher Howell
   Owner: Nancy Meadlock
   Marketing Coordinator: Shari Coloumbe
   General Manager/Winemaker: Christopher
   Howell
   Production Manager: Francois Bugue
   Purchasing Agent: Francois Bugue
Estimated Sales: $5-10 Million
Number Employees: 20-49

2147 Cain's Coffee Company
540 N Cedarbrook Ave # A
Springfield, MO 65802-6324   417-865-7414
     Fax: 417-869-1201   800-641-4025
            www.saralee.com
Processor of roasted coffee
   Owner: Steve Flowers
   Regional Manager: Stephen Flwoer
   Purchasing Manager Assoc.: Steve McCreary
Estimated Sales: $500,000-$1 Million
Number Employees: 5-9
Type of Packaging: Consumer, Food Service
Brands:
Cains
Superior

2148 Cains Foods
P.O.Box 347
Ayer, MA 01432-0347   978-772-0300
     Fax: 978-772-9254 www.cainsfoods.com
Manufacturer of dressings, condiments, sauces and
crackers
   President: Denis Keaveny
   CFO: Ronald Adams
   VP Operations: Rick Duggan
Estimated Sales: $10-20 Million
Number Employees: 50-99
Type of Packaging: Food Service, Bulk
Brands:
CAINS
CAROLINE'S
OLDE CAPE COD
WESTMINSTER

2149 (HQ)Cains Foods/Olde Cape Cod
P.O.Box 347
Ayer, MA 01432-0347   978-772-0300
     Fax: 978-772-9254   800-225-0601
     info@cainsfoods.com   www.cainsfoods.com
Processor and exporter of mayonnaise, dressings,
sauces, soups, and crackers
   President/CEO: Denis Keaveny
   CFO: Ronald Adams
   VP Operations: Rick Dugan
Estimated Sales: $40 Million
Number Employees: 50-99
Number of Brands: 4
Sq. footage: 70000
Type of Packaging: Consumer, Food Service, Private Label, Bulk
Brands:
Cains
Cole Farms
Olde Cape Cod
Westminster

2150 Caito Fisheries
P.O.Box 1370
Fort Bragg, CA 95437-1370   707-964-6368
     Fax: 707-964-6439 www.caitofisheries.com
Processor of fresh and frozen ground fish, troll king
salmon, Dungeness crab, swordfish and albacore
   President: Joe Caito
   Purchasing: Jim Caito
Estimated Sales: $20-50 Million
Number Employees: 100-249
Type of Packaging: Consumer, Food Service, Private Label, Bulk
Brands:
CAITO

2151 Cajun Bayou Distributors & Management
PO Box 4106
Baton Rouge, LA 70821-4106   225-356-0387
                    Fax: 225-356-0284
   Vice President: Stephen Bowman

2152 Cajun Boy's Louisiana Products
6413 Airline Highway
Baton Rouge, LA 70805-3212   225-929-7269
     Fax: 225-357-6888   800-880-9575
            hicks3421@aol.com
Processor and exporter of seasoned beans, blended
seasonings and mixes
   Owner/President: Gerald Hicks
Number Employees: 1-4
Type of Packaging: Consumer
Brands:
Cajun Boy's Louisiana

2153 Cajun Chef Products
P.O.Box 248
St Martinville, LA 70582-0248   337-394-7112
     Fax: 337-394-7115 www.cajunchef.org
Processor of peppers including pickled, sport,
tobasco, cherry, jalapeno, yellow chile, banana and
serrano; also, prepared mustard, pure and imitation
pepper and flavoring extracts, pickled okra and tomatoes and sauces including hotworcestershire, etc.
   Founder: George Bulliard
Estimated Sales: $10-20 Million
Number Employees: 100-249
Type of Packaging: Consumer, Food Service, Private Label, Bulk
Brands:
BIG CHIEF
CAJUN CHEF
EVANGELINE
TIFFE'S

2154 Cajun Crawfish Distributors
360 Highway 1185
Cottonport, LA 71327-4290   504-341-9911
     Fax: 504-341-7627   800-525-6813
Processor of popcorn crawfish tail and seafood
gumbo; wholesaler/distributor of seafood
   Owner/President: Elton Bernard
Estimated Sales: $30 Million
Number Employees: 4

2155 Cajun Creole Products
5610 Daspit Rd
New Iberia, LA 70563-8961   337-229-8464
     Fax: 337-229-4814   800-946-8688
     info@cajuncreole.com   www.cajuncreole.com
Processor of coffee, in-shell and spicy hot peanuts,
Cajun seasonings for meat, poultry and fish. Exporter of in-shell and spiced hot nuts. Broker of
spices, peanuts and coffee
   President: Joel Wallins
   VP: Sandra Wallins
Estimated Sales: $5-10 Million
Number Employees: 5-9
Type of Packaging: Consumer, Food Service, Bulk
Brands:
CAJUN CREOLE
CAJUN CREOLE COFFEE
CAJUN CREOLE HOT NUTS
CAJUN CREOLE JALAPEANUTS
JALAPEANUTS

2156 Cajun Fry Company
P.O.Box 609
Pierre Part, LA 70339-0609   985-252-6438
     Fax: 985-252-8010   888-272-2586
     cajunfrycompany@aol.com   www.cajunfry.com
Cajun rice mixes, jambalaya, spices
   President: Clarence Cavalier Jr Jr
   Vice President: Marilyn Cavalier
Estimated Sales: $1-2.5 Million
Number Employees: 5-9
Brands:
Cajun Creole Coffee & Chicory
Jalapeanuts
Smokeless Blackened Seasoning

2157 Cajun Injector
Highway 67 Street
Clinton, LA 70722   225-683-4490
     Fax: 225-683-4401   800-221-8060
            www.cjuninjecter.com

Marinades, honey praline ham kit
President: Reece William
CEO: Reece William
Vice President: Don Pallie
Estimated Sales: $5-10 Million
Number Employees: 20-49
Brands:
Cajun Injector
Flavors of the World

2158 Cajun Seafood Enterprises
9650 Highway 52 E
Murrayville, GA 30564-6901   706-864-9688
Fax: 706-864-9688
www.cajunseafoodenterprises.com
Seafood

2159 Cakebread Cellars
P.O.Box 216
Rutherford, CA 94573-0216   707-963-5221
Fax: 707-967-4012   800-588-0298
cellars@cakebread.com   www.cakebread.com
Wines
President: John Cakebread
Director Sales: Dennis Cakebread
Purchasing Agent: Cathy Baldwin
Estimated Sales: $20-50 Million
Number Employees: 50-99
Brands:
CAKEBREAD

2160 Cal India Foods International
13591 Yorba Ave
Chino, CA 91710-5071   909-613-1660
Fax: 909-613-1663   infospecialityenzymes.com
www.systemicenzymetherapy.com
Processor and exporter of fruit juices, purees and
concentrates including apple and pineapple; also,
enzymes including papain, bromelin, proteases,
amylases and cellulases; importer of juice concen-
trates including apple, grapepineapple and mango
puree
President: Vic Rathi
Quality Control: Vilas Amin
Purchasing Agent: Priscilla Ferreri
Estimated Sales: $5-7 Million
Number Employees: 20-49
Sq. footage: 12000
Parent Co: Specialty Enzymes and Biochemicals
Company
Type of Packaging: Bulk
Brands:
CAL INDIA

2161 Cal Java International
19519 Business Center Dr
Northridge, CA 91324-3402   818-718-2707
Fax: 818-718-2715   800-207-2750
caljava@hotmail.com   www.cakevisions.com
Cake decorating supplies
Owner: Daniel Budiman
Estimated Sales: $ 5 - 10 Million
Number Employees: 5-9

2162 Cal Trading Company
32 Adrian Ct
Burlingame, CA 94010-2101   650-697-4615
Fax: 650-692-1049
Green coffee
Manager: Rick Johnson
Purchasing Agent: Steven McLaughlin
Estimated Sales: $10-100 Million
Number Employees: 5-9
Type of Packaging: Private Label
Brands:
100% KONA COFFEE

2163 Cal-Grown Nut Company
P.O.Box 69
Hughson, CA 95326-0069   209-883-4081
Fax: 209-883-0305
frankassali@californiagrown.com
www.californiagrown.com
Processor and exporter of almonds
President: Frank Assali
Vice President: Marie Assali
Office Manager: Linda Thomas
Estimated Sales: $ .5 - 1 million
Number Employees: 5-9

2164 Cal-Harvest Marketing
8700 Fargo Ave
Hanford, CA 93230-9771   559-582-4000
Fax: 559-582-0683   www.calharvest.com

Fresh fruits and vegetables
Owner: John Sagundes
Purchasing: John Fagundes
Estimated Sales: $5-10 Million
Number Employees: 5-9
Type of Packaging: Consumer, Private Label, Bulk
Brands:
CAL-KING
FRESH HARVEST
GOLDEN HARVEST

2165 Cal-Maine Foods
P.O.Box 2960
Jackson, MS 39207-2960   601-948-6813
Fax: 601-969-0905   IR@cmfoods.com
www.calmainefoods.com
Manufacturer and exporter of shell eggs
President/COO/Director: Adolphus Baker
Chairman/CEO: Fred Adams Jr
VP/CFO/Treasurer/Secretary/Director: Timothy
Dawson
CEO: Fred R Adams Jr
Estimated Sales: $375 Million
Number Employees: 1,000-4,999
Type of Packaging: Food Service, Private Label,
Bulk

2166 Cal-Maine Foods
P.O.Box 2960
Jackson, MS 39207-2960   601-948-6813
Fax: 601-969-0905   ir@cmfoods.com
www.calmainefoods.com
Processor of eggs
President/COO/Director: Adolphus Baker
Chairman/CEO: Fred Adams, Jr.
VP/CFO/Treasurer/Director: Timothy Dawson
CEO: Fred R Adams Jr
Estimated Sales: $ .5 - 1 million
Number Employees: 1,000-4,999
Type of Packaging: Consumer, Food Service, Pri-
vate Label, Bulk

2167 Cal-Maine Foods
P.O.Box 758
Pine Grove, LA 70453-0758   225-222-4148
Fax: 225-222-4154   www.calmainefoods.com
Processor of eggs
Manager: Michael Ermon
Purchasing Agent: Robert Lewis
Estimated Sales: $50-100 Million
Number Employees: 50-99
Parent Co: Cal-Maine Foods
Type of Packaging: Consumer, Food Service, Pri-
vate Label, Bulk

2168 Cal-Sun Produce Company
511 Mountain View Ave
Oxnard, CA 93030-7203   805-985-2262
Fax: 805-486-5022
Strawberries
President: Steve Taylor
General Manager: Jim Nahas
Purchasing: Rick Meck
Estimated Sales: $10-20 Million
Number Employees: 500-999
Brands:
CAL-SUN

2169 Cal-Tex Citrus Juice
402 Yale Street
Houston, TX 77007   713-869-3471
Fax: 713-869-3277   800-231-0133
gary.van.liew@cal-texjuice.com
www.cal-texjuice.com
Package fruit juices and fruit drinks from concen-
trate.
President: Gary Van Lieu
Quality Control: Alvaro Falquez
Sales: Vicki White
Operations: Danny Teague
Purchasing: Kory Mason
Estimated Sales: $40 Million
Number Employees: 50-99
Number of Brands: 3
Number of Products: 63
Type of Packaging: Consumer, Food Service, Pri-
vate Label
Brands:
CAL-TEX
CITRUS PRIDE
VITA-FRESH
VITA-MOST

2170 CalSungold
P.O.Box 1540
Indio, CA 92202-1540   760-399-5646
Fax: 760-399-1968   info@calsungold.com
www.calsungold.com
Dates and fruitbaskets.
Plant Manager: Jim Carter
Estimated Sales: $50-100 Million
Number Employees: 20-49

2171 Calabro Cheese Corporation
P.O.Box 120186
East Haven, CT 06512-0186   203-469-1311
Fax: 203-469-6929   www.calabrocheese.com
Processor of ricotta, mozzarella and grated cheese
CEO: Joseph Calabro
Purchasing Agent: Frank Angeloni
Estimated Sales: $50-100 Million
Number Employees: 100-249
Sq. footage: 54000
Type of Packaging: Consumer, Food Service, Pri-
vate Label, Bulk
Brands:
CALABRO

2172 Calafia Cellars
629 Fulton Ln
St Helena, CA 94574-1014   707-963-0114
Fax: 707-963-0114
Wines
President: Randle Johnson
VP Marketing: Mary Lee Johnson
Operations Manager: Randle Johnson
Estimated Sales: Less than $500,000
Number Employees: 1-4
Brands:
Calafia Wines

2173 (HQ)Calavo Foods
P.O.Box 751
Santa Paula, CA 93061-0751   805-525-5511
Fax: 805-525-1151   800-422-5280
www.calavo.com
Avacado pulp and puree, fresh avacado, papaya
President: Chuck Redman
Operations: Gary Gunther
Sales Manager: Corky Taylor
Purchasing Agent: Mario Guizar
Estimated Sales: $100-500 Million
Number Employees: 500-999
Type of Packaging: Consumer, Food Service, Bulk
Other Locations:
Temecula Packinghouse
Temecula CA
Santa Paula Packinghouse
Santa Paula CA
Calavo Processing Plant
Santa Paula CA
Brands:
CALAVO

2174 Calbee America
2064 Gravenstein HWY
Unit A
N. Sebastopol, CA 95473   310-370-2500
Fax: 310-328-8344   tkatsunoi@aol.com
http://www.calbeeamerica.com
Processor and exporter of potato chips
Sales Manager: Hiroshi Kosuge
Purchasing Manager: Taka Katsunoi
Estimated Sales: $2.5-5 Million
Number Employees: 1-4

2175 Calcium Springs Water Company
1800 Prospector Ave # 101
Park City, UT 84060-7319   435-615-7700
Fax: 435-615-7600   cool@calciumsprings.com
www.calciumsprings.com
Water
Owner: Lavelle Klobes

2176 Calco of Calgary
Bay C 1007 55th Avenue NE
Calgary, AB T2E 6W1
Canada   403-295-3578
Fax: 403-516-0286   calco1@telus.net
Processor and packer of bean sprouts, pre-cut vege-
tables, frozen Chinese dumplings, spring and egg
rolls and steamed noodles
President: Wing Tam
General Manager: May Yu
Production: Grace Tam
Number Employees: 10-19
Parent Co: Fung Nin Fine Foods
Type of Packaging: Consumer, Food Service

Brands:
Calgo
Mr. Egg Roll
Noodle Delights

2177 Caleb Haley & Company
14 Fulton Fish Market
New York, NY 10038-1903   212-732-7474
                              Fax: 212-349-2991
Seafood, seafood products
President: Neil Smith
Vice President: Michael Driansky
Production Manager: Joseph Serrantonio
Estimated Sales:$20-50 Million
Number Employees: 20-49
Brands:
Angel
Callaway
Ocean Harvest

2178 Calera Wine Company
11300 Cienega Road
Hollister, CA 95023-9619   831-637-9170
    Fax: 831-637-9070 info@calerawine.com
                        www.calerawine.com
Wines
President: Josh Jensen
COO: Diana Vita
Number Employees: 20-49
Brands:
CALERA
Central Coast
Doe Mill
Mills
Mt. Harlan
Reed
Selleck
VIOGNIER

2179 Calgary Italian Bakery
5310 5th Street SE
Calgary, AB T2H 1L2
Canada   403-255-3515
    Fax: 403-255-7016 800-661-6868
Processor of baked goods including bread, buns,
pastries and English muffins
President: Luigi Bontorin
CEO: Luigi Bontorin
Marketing Manager: Ralph Knipsthilb
Office Manager: Louis Bontorin
Plant Manager: Dave Bontorin
Number Employees: 50-99
Sq. footage: 30000
Type of Packaging: Consumer, Food Service
Brands:
Calgary Italian
Country Boy
Golden Rich

2180 Calhoun Bend Mill
7603 Highway 71 S
Alexandria, LA 71302-9272   318-619-8710
    Fax: 318-339-9099 800-519-6455
    info@calhounbendmill.com &
        info@orchardmills.com
    www.calhounbendmill.com &
        www.orchardmills.com
Products include mixes for Peach Cobbler mix, Ap-
ple Cinnamon Crisp mix, Cherry Oatmeal Crunch
mix, Awesome Onion Coating mix, Fish Fry & Sea-
food coating, Stoneground Cornmeal, Cornbread &
Muffin mix, Mexican Cornbread mix, Honey
ButterCornbread mix, Pecan Pie mix and Sopapilla
mix. Food services sizes in Fruit Cobblers, Corn-
meal and Fish Fry & Seafood coating.
President/CEO: Patrick Calhoun
R&D: Patrick Calhoun
Quality Control: Martie Hoover
Marketing: Patrick Calhoun
Sales Manager: Emma Lou Cash
Operations Manager: Martie Hoover
Estimated Sales:$2 Million
Number Employees: 20-49
Number of Brands: 2
Number of Products: 25
Sq. footage: 17000
Type of Packaging: Consumer, Food Service, Pri-
vate Label, Bulk
Brands:
CALHOUN BEND MILL
ORCHARD MILLS

2181 Calico Cottage
210 New Hwy
Amityville, NY 11701-1116   631-841-2100
    Fax: 631-841-2401 800-645-5345
    info@calicocottage.com www.calicocottage.com
Equipment, ingredients and merchandising concepts
for a profitable, small-space, fudge marketing
program
President: Mark Wurzel
VP: Larry Wurzel
Estimated Sales:$5-10 Million
Sq. footage: 45000
Brands:
CALICO COTTAGE FUDGE MIX
MISTER FUDGE

2182 Calidad Foods
PO Box 535008
Grand Prairie, TX 75053-5008   972-933-4100
                              Fax: 972-933-4120
Tortillas and other mexican food products.
CEO/President: Bing Graffunder
CFO: Sam Hillin
V.P Sales/Marketing: Gary Fraizer

2183 California & WashingtonCompany
2 Bryant Street
Suite 220
San Francisco, CA 94105-1641   415-344-5200
                              Fax: 415-344-5215
Vegetables
CFO: Jim Kunkel
Sales Director: Lynn Brown
Purchasing Manager: Jim Kunkel
Estimated Sales:$5-10 Million
Number Employees: 5-9
Type of Packaging: Private Label
Brands:
C & W
C & W BROCCOLETTES
C & W EARLY HARVEST
C & W VALENCIA
C & W VEGETABLE STAND COMBINATION

2184 California Almond Packers
21275 Simpson Rd
Corning, CA 96021-9509   530-824-3836
    Fax: 530-824-3899 capex@dm-tech.net
                        www.almondboard.com
Processor of almonds
Manager: Mathieu Esteve
*Estimated Sales:*Less than $500,000
Number Employees: 50-99
Brands:
California Almond

2185 California Blending Corpany
2603 Seaman Ave
El Monte, CA 91733-1929   626-448-1918
            califblending@earthlink.net
            www.californiablending.com
Processor of pizza spices, dough mixes, dressing
mixes, steak salts, and garlic blends. Also provided;
custom blending
President: Bill Morehart
VP: William Morehart, Jr.
*Estimated Sales:*Less than $500,000
Number Employees: 1-4
Sq. footage: 7300
Type of Packaging: Private Label, Bulk

2186 California Brands Flavors
411 Pendleton Way
Oakland, CA 94621-2115   510-562-2371
    Fax: 510-562-1279 800-348-0111
    webinfo@mane.com www.mane.com
Processor of customized natural and artificial fla-
vors, flavor extracts, beverages bases and frozen
dessert variegates
Manager: Gina Pinales
President: Michel Mane
VP: John Ashby
VP Sales: William Painter
Estimated Sales:$20-50 Million
Number Employees: 20-49
Parent Co: Mane
Type of Packaging: Food Service, Bulk

2187 California Cereal Products
1267 14th St
Oakland, CA 94607-2246   510-452-4500
    Fax: 510-452-4545 californiacereal@msn.com

Processor and exporter of rice, cereal and flour
Owner: Sterling Savely
Chairman: Robert Sterling Savely
Estimated Sales:$ 50 - 100 Million
Number Employees: 50-99
Sq. footage: 150000
Type of Packaging: Consumer, Private Label, Bulk

2188 California Citrus Producer
525 E Lindmore St
Lindsay, CA 93247-2559   559-562-5169
    Fax: 559-562-5691 kimberly@ccti.diz
                        www.ccti.diz
Processor of citrus fruits including oranges
President: Tomy Elliott
Marketing Director: Tomy Elliott
Estimated Sales:$ 5 - 10 Million
Number Employees: 20-49
Brands:
Citrus Juices

2189 California Citrus Pulp Company
PO Box 667
Lindsay, CA 93247-0667   626-332-1101
                              Fax: 559-562-1014
Orange peel, citrus ingredients
President: Jim Boyles
CEO: Jim Boyles
Marketing Director: Jim Boyles
General Manager: Paul Gottschall

2190 California Creative Foods
649 Benet Rd
Oceanside, CA 92058-1208   760-757-2622
    Fax: 760-721-2600 info@chachies.com
                        www.sbsalsa.com
Processor of refrigerated salsa, shelf stable foods
and sauces. Co-packer of specialty foods.
President: Doug Pearson
VP Purchasing: Patrick Hickey
Estimated Sales:$10-15 Million
Number Employees: 1-4
Sq. footage: 19000
Type of Packaging: Consumer, Food Service
Brands:
CHACHIES
CON GUSTO
SAN DIEGO SALSA
SANTA BARBARA SALSA
TIO TIO

2191 California Custom Fruits & Flavors
15800 Tapia St
Irwindale, CA 91706-2178   626-736-4130
    Fax: 626-736-4145 877-558-0056
    info@ccff.com www.ccff.com
California Custom Fruits and Flavors, in Irwindale,
CA is an industry leader in the manufacture of fruit
products and flavors. With an in-house flavor de-
partment and fully staffed lab, California Custom
can respond to any flavorrequest. Employing the lat-
est trends and technology, CCFF can bring your
ideas to fruition
Owner: Rose Ann Hall
Marketing Manager: Christine Long
Director Operations: Jack Miller
Production Manager: Eric Nielsen
Purchasing Director: Phyllis Ferguson
Estimated Sales:$20-35 Million
Number Employees: 50-99
Sq. footage: 33000
Type of Packaging: Bulk
Brands:
B2B
CCFF
PRIVATE LABEL

2192 California Dairies
755 F St
Fresno, CA 93706-3416   559-233-5154
    Fax: 559-268-5101 www.californiadairies.com
Co-op/processor of dairy products including butter,
buttermilk, skim milk and powdered milk
Plant Manager: Bob Ray
VP Operations: Dave Bush
Estimated Sales:$50-100 Million
Number Employees: 100-249
Type of Packaging: Consumer, Food Service, Bulk
Brands:
Challenge
Dairy America
Danish Creamery

2193 California Dairies
P.O.Box 6210
Artesia, CA 90702-6210 562-865-1291
Fax: 562-860-8633
cdistore@CaliforniaDairies.com
www.californiadairies.com
Processor of powdered milk
CEO: Gary Korsmeier
President: Gary Korsmeier
Quality Control: Ronald Thompson
Marketing Director: William Koot
Operations Manager: Keith Gomes
Operations Manager: Steve Cooper
Number Employees: 500-999
Type of Packaging: Consumer, Bulk

2194 (HQ)California Day Fresh
533 W Foothill Blvd
Glendora, CA 91741-2476 626-852-2560
Fax: 626-852-2560 800-800-0986
consumeraffairs@nakedjuice.com
www.nakedjuice.com
Processor of fresh and frozen fruit and vegetable
juices
General Manager: Dave Sperry
VP Purchasing: Richard Ziff
Controller: Wendy Morgan
Quality Control: Dominic Marlia
Sales Director: Paul Johnson
PR/Promotions Manager: Heidi Meinholz
Director Operations: Tom Guenther
Purchasing Manager: Ron Marks
Estimated Sales: $50-100 Million
Number Employees: 250-499
Sq. footage: 61000
Type of Packaging: Consumer, Food Service, Private Label, Bulk
Brands:
Ferraro's Earth Juice
Mojave Magic
Naked Juice

2195 California Farms & Canners
601 Montgomery Street
Suite 1115
San Francisco, CA 94111-2614 415-433-3522
Fax: 415-391-9240
Processor, importer and exporter of canned, fresh
and frozen foods including fruits and vegetables;
processor of soft drinks
President: B Lawrence
Estimated Sales: $5-10 Million
Number Employees: 5-9
Sq. footage: 3000
Parent Co: B.M. Lawrence & Company
Type of Packaging: Consumer, Food Service, Private Label, Bulk
Brands:
California Farms
U.S. Cola

2196 California Fresh Salsa
P.O.Box 948
Woodland, CA 95776-0948 530-662-0512
Fax: 530-662-9418
Manufacturer of condiments, beans and sprouts
President: Steve Mendez
Estimated Sales: $2.5-5 Million
Number Employees: 10-19

2197 California Fruit
2730 S De Wolf Ave
Sanger, CA 93657-9770 559-266-7117
Fax: 559-266-0988 www.californiafruitbasket.com
Processor of dried apricots, peaches, pears and nectarines
President: Mark Melkonian
Estimated Sales: $2.5-5 Million
Number Employees: 10-19
Type of Packaging: Bulk

2198 California Fruit & Nut
295 South Avenue
Gustine, CA 95322 209-854-6887
Fax: 209-854-1819 888-747-8224
fruitnnut@fruitnnut.com www.fruitnnut.com
Processor of flavored nuts including pistachios, peanuts and cashews; also, dried fruit and fruit rolls including apricot
President: Zaher Shahbaz
Estimated Sales: Less than $500,000
Number Employees: 5-9
Sq. footage: 5400

Type of Packaging: Consumer, Food Service
Brands:
Cal-Fruit

**2199 California Fruit Packing
Company**
1321 Harter Road
Yuba City, CA 95993-2604 530-822-9020
Fax: 530-822-0199
Fruit packing
President: Chris Rufer
Controller: Randy Lew
Sales: Ray Summers
Estimated Sales: Less than $500,000
Number Employees: 1-4
Brands:
California Fruit

2200 California Fruit Processors
2851 Bozzano Rd
Stockton, CA 95215-9152 209-931-1760
Fax: 209-931-0784 vfo@lightspeed.net
Brined cherries
President: Alan Corradi
Manager: Allan Corradi

**2201 California Fruit and Tomato
Kitchens**
2906 Santa Fe Street
Riverbank, CA 95367-2223 209-869-9300
Fax: 209-869-9060 bethclare@calfruittom.com
www.calfruittom.com
Manufacturer of canned goods including tomato
products and peaches
President: Barbara Langum
Plant Manager: Ed Harmon
Estimated Sales: $ 10 - 20 Million
Number Employees: 20-49
Type of Packaging: Food Service, Private Label
Brands:
Dinapoli
Flotta
Paradise

2202 California Garden Products
14 Rancho Cir
Lake Forest, CA 92630-8325 949-215-0000
www.hungrysultan.com
Canned beans
President: Fouad El-Abd
Public Relations: Laura El-Adb
Estimated Sales: $5-9.9 Million
Number Employees: 1-4

2203 California Garlic Co
2707 Boston Avenue
San Diego, CA 92113 951-506-8883
Fax: 951-699-9155 info@garlicking.net
www.garlicking.net
Garlic, ginger, shallots, green onion, herbs and other
President: John Rosingana
Vice President: Peter Tarantino
Quality Control/Production: Larry George
Marketing: Jeff Crace
Sales Director: John Rosingana
Estimated Sales: $5 Million
Number Employees: 35
Number of Brands: 4
Number of Products: 60
Sq. footage: 24000
Type of Packaging: Consumer, Food Service, Private Label, Bulk

**2204 California Independent Almond
Growers**
PO Box 1
Ballico, CA 95303-0001 209-667-4855
Fax: 209-667-4854 ciag@almond-growers.com
www.almond-growers.com
Growers, packers, processors and shippers worldwide. California grown whole natural almonds direct
from the source. State-of-the-art equipment
President: Karen Barstow
Marketing Director/Director Trade Promo: Jana
Nairn
General Manager: Jim Barstow
Estimated Sales: $2.5-5 Million
Number Employees: 50-99
Sq. footage: 30000
Type of Packaging: Consumer, Food Service, Private Label, Bulk
Brands:
California Independent Brand

2205 California Natural Products
P.O.Box 1219
Lathrop, CA 95330-1219 209-858-2525
Fax: 209-858-2556
joehall@californianatural.com
www.californianatural.com
Processor of rice starch, oligodextrin, syrup/syrup
solids, protein, etc.; also, soy milk and low acid
aseptic beverages and soups; co-packer of low acid
and aseptic beverages, soups, and teas; exporter of
rice syrup, protein andoligodextrin
President: Pat Mitchell
VP, Head R&D: Cheryl Mitchell
Technical Sales Manager: John Ashby
VP Operations: Marc Weinstein
Estimated Sales: $5-10 Million
Number Employees: 100-249
Type of Packaging: Private Label
Brands:
DACOPA

2206 California Nuggets
23073 S Frederick Rd
Ripon, CA 95366-9616 209-599-7131
Fax: 209-599-6320 info@californianuggets.com
www.californianuggets.com
President: Steve Gikas
Marketing Director: Diana Gikas
CFO: Nancy Knocks
Estimated Sales: $ 5 - 10 Million
Number Employees: 20-49
Brands:
California Nuggets

2207 California Oils Corporation
1145 Harbour Way S
Richmond, CA 94804-3618 510-233-7660
Fax: 510-233-1329 800-225-6457
sales1@caloils.com www.caloils.com
Processor of vegetable oils and meal; exporter of
corn and safflower oils
President: Sihira Ito
VP Sales & Trading: Joevic Fabregas
Number Employees: 20-49
Parent Co: Mitsubishi

2208 California Olive Growers
8427 N Millbrook Avenue
Suite 101
Fresno, CA 93720-2197 559-674-8741
Fax: 559-673-3960 888-965-4837
info@californiaolivegrowers.com
www.californiaolivegrowers.com
Packer of canned California ripe olives, olive oil, tomatoes and pizza sauce
President: Lewis Johnson
CEO: Tom Lindemann
CEO: Fred Avalli
Quality Control: Larry Newby
Production Manager: Bob Marshall
Plant Manager: Tom Annotti
Estimated Sales: $10 Million
Number Employees: 100-249
Number of Brands: 2
Number of Products: 10
Sq. footage: 300000
Type of Packaging: Consumer, Food Service, Private Label, Bulk
Brands:
MADERA
OBERTI

2209 California Olive Oil Corporation
120 Canal St # B
Salem, MA 01970-4651 978-744-7840
Fax: 508-744-3492 800-386-6457
customerservice@gem-ecoo.com
www.olive-oil.com
Processor and exporter of oils including garlic, sesame, peanut, olive, canola, mineral, soybean, citrus,
infused, organic, cold pressed and unrefined; also,
balsamic vinegar and cooking wines; importer of kosher certified soy sauce
Owner: Claudia Siniawski
Vice President: Robert Mandia
CFO: Dave Lofgren
VP Sales/Marketing: Mark Moffitt
Estimated Sales: $10-20 Million
Number Employees: 10-19
Sq. footage: 38000
Parent Co: East Coast Olive Corporation
Type of Packaging: Consumer, Food Service, Private Label, Bulk

Brands:
California Classics
Montebello
Oishii
Virginia

2210 California Orchards
9000 Crow Canyon Road
Suite S-384
Danville, CA 94506-1189   925-648-1500
                                Fax: 925-648-4471
Dried fruits, nuts and chocolate
    President: Ali Hashemian
Estimated Sales: $5-10 Million
Number Employees: 50-99
Type of Packaging: Private Label

2211 California Pie Company
7066 Las Positas Rd # G
Livermore, CA 94551-5134   925-373-7700
    Fax: 925-373-8303 www.horizonsnackfoods.com
Pies
    Owner: Bob Sharp
    Controller: Brett Howell
Estimated Sales: $2.5-5 Million
Number Employees: 10-19

2212 California Pretzel Company
P.O.Box 3143
Visalia, CA 93278-3143   559-651-0600
                                Fax: 559-651-0604
Processor and exporter of pretzels including regular
and peanut butter filled
    VP: Ed Desrosiers
    Director Operations/Manufacturing: Ed
    Desrosiars
Estimated Sales: $100+ Million
Number Employees: 100-249
Brands:
    Peanut Butter Nuggets

2213 California Prune Packing Company
2200 Encinal Road
Live Oak, CA 95953-9763   530-671-4200
                                Fax: 530-695-3654
Processor and packer of dried fruits including
prunes
Estimated Sales: $20-50 Million
Number Employees: 50-99
Type of Packaging: Private Label

2214 California Shellfish Company
1600 W Redondo Beach Boulevard
Gardena, CA 90247-3226   310-538-4197
                        hallmark@harborside.com
Processor and exporter of frozen cod
    President: Kenene Yanagita
Number Employees: 5-9

2215 California Shellfish Company
P.O.Box 2028
San Francisco, CA 94126-2028   415-923-7400
                                Fax: 415-923-1677
Processor of crab, smoked salmon, halibut and snap-
per
    President: Eugene Bugatto
    Manager: Richard Amundsen
Estimated Sales: $5-10 Million
Number Employees: 5-9
Type of Packaging: Consumer, Food Service, Pri-
    vate Label, Bulk

2216 California Smart Foods
2565 3rd St # 341
San Francisco, CA 94107-3159   415-826-0449
                                Fax: 415-826-0435
Breads, rolls, baked goods
    Owner: Rudy Melnitzer
Estimated Sales: $20-50 Million
Number Employees: 20-49

2217 California Snack Foods
2131 Tyler Ave
South El Monte, CA 91733-2754   626-444-4508
    Fax: 626-579-3038 info@calsnacks.com
                        www.cal-snacks.com
Snack food
    Owner: Ken Wong
    Marketing Manager: Mary Ohms
    Production Manager: John Ohms
Estimated Sales: $5-10 Million
Number Employees: 20-49

2218 California Specialty Farms
2420 Modoc St
Los Angeles, CA 90021-2916   323-587-2200
    Fax: 323-587-0050 800-437-2702
                        specfarms@aol.com
                www.californiaspecialtyfarms.com
Processor of gourmet specialty produce; importer
and exporter of baby squash, French beans and fresh
herbs
    Founder: Horacio Bellofiore
    VP Sales: Bruce Hoffman
Estimated Sales: $10-20 Million
Number Employees: 100-249
Parent Co: Worldwide Specialties
Brands:
    California Specialty Farms

2219 California Style Gourmet Products
6161 El Cajon Boulevard
Suite 200
San Diego, CA 92115-3922   619-265-1988
    Fax: 619-265-0893 800-243-5226
                        castylegor@aol.com
Processor, importer, exporter and co-packer of bar-
becue/raspberry and dessert sauces, mustards, salad
dressings, salsas, jams, preserves and fudge
    President: John Payne
    Research & Development: Marielaina Payne
    Marketing: John Payne
Estimated Sales: $750,000
Number Employees: 1-4
Sq. footage: 5000
Type of Packaging: Consumer, Food Service, Pri-
    vate Label
Brands:
    A Taste of the West
    California Style Gourmet

2220 California Treats
2131 Tyler Ave
South El Monte, CA 91733-2754   626-444-4508
    Fax: 626-579-3038 800-966-5501
    info@caltreats.com www.cal-snacks.com
Gourmet foods
    Owner: Ken Wong
Estimated Sales: $2.5-5 Million
Number Employees: 20-49
Type of Packaging: Private Label
Brands:
    Betty Clark's Confections
    Harmon's Gourmet

2221 California Watercress
P.O.Box 874
Fillmore, CA 93016-0874   805-524-4808
                                Fax: 805-524-5295
Processor of herbal supplements and herbs including
cilantro and chives; also, vegetables including
mixed, watercress and leeks
    President: Alfred Beserra
    Office Manager: Susan Barbera
Estimated Sales: $10 - 20 Million
Number Employees: 50-99
Type of Packaging: Consumer, Food Service, Bulk
Brands:
    Al's Best

2222 California Wholesale Nut Company
1925 Manzanita Ave
Chico, CA 95926-1763   530-895-0512
                                Fax: 530-345-1263
Processor of nuts
    Owner: Naomi Mc Dermott
Estimated Sales: $100,000
Number Employees: 1-4

2223 California Wild Rice Growers
41577 Osprey Rd
Fall River Mills, CA 96028-9750   530-336-5222
    Fax: 530-336-5265 800-626-4366
    info@frwr.com www.frwr.com
Wild Rice
    Manager: Walt Oiler
    Manager: Hiram Oilar
    PLant Manager: Tony Knight
Estimated Sales: $3 - 5 Million
Number Employees: 5-9
Brands:
    Fall River

2224 California-Antilles Trading Consortium
3735 Adams Ave
San Diego, CA 92116-2220   619-283-4834
    Fax: 619-283-4834 800-330-6450
                        caliantilles@worldnet.att.net
                www.calantilles.com
Hot sauces, salsas, barbecue sauces
    President: Richard E Gardner
    Operations: Tevor Dyer
    Production: Robert Davis
Estimated Sales: $2.5-5 Million
Number Employees: 1-4
Number of Brands: 2
Number of Products: 25
Type of Packaging: Consumer, Private Label

2225 Califrance
PO Box 491327
Los Angeles, CA 90049-9327   310-440-0729
    Fax: 310-440-0879 califrance@formula9.com
                www.formula9.com
Ketchups
Brands:
    Formula 9

2226 Calihan Pork Processing
1 South St
Peoria, IL 61602-1851   309-674-9175
    Fax: 309-674-3003 calihanpork@aol.com
                www.calihanpork.com
Processor of pork products including pre-rigor,
boneless hams, Canadian bacon, back ribs and
offals.
    President, Co-Owner: Tom Landon
    Co-Owner: Lou Landon
    General Manager: Jim Forbes
    Plant Supervisor: Bill Murphy
Estimated Sales: $20-50 Million
Number Employees: 20-49
Type of Packaging: Bulk

2227 Calio Groves
675 Cedar Street
Berkeley, CA 94710-1731   707-402-4700
    Fax: 707-402-4747 800-865-4836
    letters@caliogroves.com www.caliogroves.com
Processor of olive oil and extra virgin olive oil; im-
porter of olive oil
    President: Brendan Frasier
    VP Production & Farming: Bob Singletary
Estimated Sales: $20-50 Million
Number Employees: 20-49
Parent Co: NVK Realty
Type of Packaging: Consumer, Food Service, Pri-
    vate Label, Bulk
Brands:
    Calio Groves
    EVO
    Olio Santo
    Stutz Olive Oil
    VG Buck California Foods

2228 Calise & Sons Bakery
2 Quality Dr
Lincoln, RI 02865-4266   401-334-3444
    Fax: 401-334-0938 800-225-4737
    Info@calisebakery.com www.calisebakery.com
Processor of fresh Italian bread, rolls and pizza
shells.
    Founder: Francesco Calise
    Treasurer: Joseph Calise
    CEO: Peter Petrocelli
    Sales/Marketing Manager: Michael Calise
    Production Manager: James Fontaine
    Purchasing Manager: Anthony Capuzli
Estimated Sales: $15 Million
Number Employees: 100-249
Number of Products: 150
Sq. footage: 70000
Type of Packaging: Consumer, Food Service, Pri-
    vate Label
Brands:
    CALISE
    SUN RAY

2229 Calistoga Food Company
171 E 74th Street
New York, NY 10021-3221   212-879-4940
                                Fax: 212-879-5005
    President: Martin Kreinik
Estimated Sales: $2.5-5,000,000
Number Employees: 5-9

Brands:
Calistoga Food

2230 Calkins & Burke
800 - 1500 West Georgia St.
Vancouver, BC V6G 2Z6
Canada   604-669-3741
Fax: 604-699-9732 http://www.calbur.com
Processor and exporter of fresh and frozen halibut,
salmon and crab
Director: David Calkins
VP: Micheal Kolinn
Head of Marketing: Ken Jonn
Type of Packaging: Consumer, Food Service, Private Label
Brands:
Astra
Norden
Royal Canadian

2231 Callahan Ridge Winery
340 Busenbark Lane
Roseburg, OR 97470-9692   541-673-7901
Fax: 541-673-5580 800-695-4946
winenet@rosenet.net www.callahanridge.com
Wines
President: Mary Sykes
Tasting Room/Public Relations: Traci Kimball
VP Operations: Jerry Dawkins
Estimated Sales: $1-5 Million
Number Employees: 5-9
Type of Packaging: Private Label
Brands:
Callahan Ridge Wines

2232 Callard & Bowser-Suchard
Ei-3 250 N Street
White Plains, NY 10573   914-345-3311
Fax: 914-345-3303 877-226-3900
President: Jerry Finard
National Sales Manager: John Kernan
Senior Product Manager: Mark Sugden
Estimated Sales: $5-10 Million appx.
Number Employees: 10-19

2233 Callaway Packing Company
P.O.Box 572
Delta, CO 81416-0572   970-874-9743
Fax: 970-874-7842 800-332-6932
calpack@montrose.net
Meat packer of beef, pork and lamb
President: David Dillie
Contact: Erlene Grover
Estimated Sales: $20-50 Million
Number Employees: 10-19
Type of Packaging: Consumer

2234 Callaway Vineyards & Winery
P.O.Box 9014
Temecula, CA 92589-9014   951-676-4001
Fax: 951-676-5209 800-472-2377
www.callawaywinery.com
Processor of red and white wine
President: Mike Jellison
Director: Lori Lyn Narlock
VP/Winemaker: Dwayne Helmuth
Associate Public Relations Manager: Kelly Keagy

Vineyard Manager: Craig Weaver
Cellar Foreman: Joe Vera
Plant Manager: Jose Ceja
Estimated Sales: $20-50 Million
Number Employees: 50-99
Parent Co: Hiram Walker-Allied Domeq.
Type of Packaging: Consumer, Food Service

2235 Callie's Charleston Biscuits LLC
498-A Meeting Street
Charleston, SC 29403   843-577-1198
carrie@calliesbiscuits.com
www.calliesbiscuits.com
Biscuits
President/Owner: Callie White

2236 Callis Seafood
353 Callis Rd
Lancaster, VA 22503-4112   804-462-7634
Fax: 804-435-6808 callissfd@rivernet.net
www.callissfd.net
Processor of oysters, crabs and frozen shrimp
President: Diane Callis-Haydon
CEO/VP: Diane Haydon
Estimated Sales: $200,000
Number Employees: 1-4

2237 Calmar Bakery
PO Box 585
Calmar, AB T20 2J2
Canada   780-985-3583
Fax: 780-985-3583
Processor of baked goods including fruit cakes and
Danish almond rings and wedding cakes
President: Doug Campbell
CEO: Doug Campbell
Marketing Director: Doug Campbell
Manager: Tork Kristiansen
Number Employees: 5-9
Type of Packaging: Consumer, Food Service
Brands:
Calmar Bakery

2238 Calpro Ingredients
1138 W Rincon Street
Corona, CA 92880-9601   909-493-4890
Fax: 909-493-4845 cnorthup@dfamilk.com
www.goldencheese.com
Processor and exporter of whey protein concentrates
President: Garry Johns
Operations: Carole Northup
Number Employees: 5-9
Sq. footage: 3000
Parent Co: Golden Cheese Company of California
Type of Packaging: Bulk
Brands:
Calpro

2239 Caltex Foods
9045-A Eton Ave
Canoga Park, CA 91304   818-700-8657
Fax: 818-700-0285 800-522-5839
www.caltexrecords.com
Processor of dehydrated vegetables, canned soups,
meat stews and vegetarian canned foods; also, Middle Eastern gourmet products
President/Secretary: Mehrdad Pakravan
Estimated Sales: $1,200,000
Number Employees: 5-9
Sq. footage: 6000
Parent Co: Caltex Trading
Brands:
Aasan
Aviva
Beit Hashita
Jaffer

2240 Calumet Diversified Meat Company
10000 80th Ave
Pleasant Prairie, WI 53158-2803   262-947-7200
Fax: 262-947-7209 service@porkchops.com
www.porkchops.com
Processor of pork including cutlets, loin, barbecued
ribs, tenderloins, chops, etc
President: Larry Becker
National Accounts Manager: Joy Huskey
Estimated Sales: $36.5 Million
Number Employees: 100-249

2241 Calvert's
909 Texas Ave
El Paso, TX 79901-1524   915-544-3434
Fax: 915-544-7552 www.elpasochile.com
Lemonade mix
Owner: William Parker
Estimated Sales: $ 10 - 20 Million
Number Employees: 20-49

2242 Camara Raisin Packing Company
8427 N Millbrook Avenue
Suite 101
Fresno, CA 93720-2197   559-661-3780
Fax: 559-661-8123
Dried raisins
Owner: Ronald Camara
Estimated Sales: $20-50 Million
Number Employees: 20-49
Type of Packaging: Bulk

2243 Camas Prairie Winery
110 S Main St
Moscow, ID 83843-2806   208-882-0214
Fax: 208-882-0214 800-616-0214
scottcamas@turbonet.com
www.camasprairiewinery.com
Processor of wine
Co-Owner/President: Stuart Scott
Co-Owner/CFO: Susan Scott

Estimated Sales: $150,000
Number Employees: 1-4
Number of Products: 22
Type of Packaging: Private Label
Brands:
Camas

2244 Cambria Winery & Vineyard
5475 Chardonnay Ln
Santa Maria, CA 93454-9600   805-937-8091
Fax: 805-934-3589 888-339-9463
www.cambriawines.com
Wines
President: Barbara Banke
Marketing: Holly Evans
Customer Relations: Karen Readey
Public Relations: Elaine Mellis
General Manager: Keith W Moak
Vineyard Manager: Pat Huguenard
Winemaker: Denise Shurtleff
Estimated Sales: $5-10 Million
Number Employees: 50-99
Brands:
CAMBRIA

2245 Cambridge Brands
810 Main St
Cambridge, MA 02139-3588   617-491-2500
Fax: 617-547-2381
Manufacturer of candy: bagged, bars, caramels,
chocolate, chocolate covered cherries, fudge, holiday, gums and jellies, hard, jelly beans, licorice,
lollypops, mints, nougats and coated nuts; also,
chocolate and cocoa products forbakers, confectioners, etc.
VP: John "Newlin,"
President: Ellen Gordon
VP Finance: G Howard Ember Jr
Plant Manager: Gerald Chesser
Number Employees: 100-249
Parent Co: Tootsie Roll Industries
Type of Packaging: Consumer, Food Service
Brands:
Charleston Chew
Chuckles
Junior Mints,
Pearson
Pom Poms
Sugar Babies
Sugar Daddy
Sugar Mama

2246 Cambridge Food
2801 Salinas Hwy # F
Monterey, CA 93940-6401   831-373-2300
Fax: 831-373-7167 800-433-2584
info@cambridgedietusa.com
www.cambridgedietusa.com
Meal replacement formulas, cereals, soups, nutrition
bars
Manager: Janet Bishop
Research & Development: Dr Robert Nesheim
Estimated Sales: $300,000-500,000
Number Employees: 1-4
Brands:
Cambridge Food

2247 Cambridge Packing Company
41 Food Mart Rd # 43
Boston, MA 02118-2801   617-464-6000
Fax: 617-269-0266 800-722-6726
info@campcosteaks.com
www.cambridgepacking.com
Processor of portion controlled steaks; wholesaler/distributor of fine meats and fresh and frozen
seafood; serving the food service market
President, Co-Owner: Bruce Rodman
Executive VP, Co-Owner: Alan Roberts
Estimated Sales: $50-100 Million
Number Employees: 50-99
Sq. footage: 30000

2248 Cambridge Slaughtering
110 N East Rd
Cambridge, IL 61238-1185   309-937-2455
Processor of beef, pork and lamb
Owner: Sharon Helg
Estimated Sales: $2.5-5 Million
Number Employees: 1-4

2249 Camellia Beans
P.O.Box 23751
New Orleans, LA 70183-0751 504-733-8480
Fax: 504-733-8155 info@camelliabeans.com
www.lhhco.com
Manufacturer and exporter of dried beans, peas and lentils
Partner: Ken Hayward
Partner: Connely Hayward
Estimated Sales: $ 10 - 20 Million
Number Employees: 20-49
Type of Packaging: Consumer, Food Service, Bulk
Brands:
Camellia

2250 Camellia General Provision
1333 Genesee St
Buffalo, NY 14211-2227 716-893-5352
Fax: 716-895-7713 contact@camelliafoods.com
www.camelliafoods.com
Processor of meat including smoked, sausage and ham
Owner/President: Edmund Cichocki
Estimated Sales: $5-10 Million
Number Employees: 20-49

2251 Cameo Confections
543 Juneway Drive
Bay Village, OH 44140-2606 440-871-5732
Fax: 440-892-8656
Confections
President: Gail Barker

2252 Cameo Metal Products Inc
127 12th St
Brooklyn, NY 11215-3891 718-788-1106
Fax: 718-788-3761 cameosales@cameometal.com
OR beverage@cameometal.com
www.cameometal.com
Cameo Metal Products Manufactures metal closures for the food and beverage industry.
President: Vito Di Maio
Director of Operations: Anthony Di Maio
Sq. footage: 100000

2253 Cameron Birch Syrup & Confections
951 Hermon Road
Suite 6
Wasilla, AK 99654-7379 907-373-6275
Fax: 907-373-6274 800-962-4724
admin@birchsyrup.com www.birchsyrup.com
Processor and exporter of birch syrup, marinades, salad dressing and candy
President: Marlene Cameron
Number Employees: 1-4
Sq. footage: 2500
Type of Packaging: Consumer, Food Service, Private Label, Bulk
Brands:
Birch Bark
Birch Logs
Black Tie
Cameron
Cameron's
Sesame Birch Sticks

2254 Cameron Seafood Processors
PO Box 1228
Cameron, LA 70631-1228 318-775-5510
Fax: 318-755-5529 www.cameronseafood.com
Seafood
President: Bruce Bang

2255 Camino Real Foods
2638 E Vernon Ave
Vernon, CA 90058-1825 323-585-6599
Fax: 323-585-5420 800-421-6201
customerservice@crfoods.com
www.crfoods.com
Processor of frozen burritos and stuffed microwaveable sandwiches
President: Howard Wang
Marketing: Clark Metcalf
CFO: Stephen Wilson
CEO: Robert Cross
VP Sales: Terry McMartin
Parent Co: Nissan Foods
Type of Packaging: Consumer, Food Service
Brands:
Taxco
Tina's Las Campanas

2256 Camp Holly Springs
4100 Diamond Springs Dr
Richmond, VA 23231-7538 804-795-2096
Fax: 804-795-1280 www.camphollysprings.com
Bottled spring water, bulk spring water
Owner: Dusty Dowdy
General Manager: Roland "Dowey, Jr."
CFO: Jeannie Pierce
Estimated Sales: $500,000-$1 Million
Number Employees: 5-9

2257 Campagana Winery
10950 West Road
Redwood Valley, CA 95470-9741 707-485-1221
Fax: 707-485-1225
george@campagnawinery.com
Winery
Chairman: Joseph Campagna
CEO: Tony Coturri
CFO/COO: George Pruden
Marketing Director: Paul White
Sales Director: Paul White
Production Manager: Nic Coturri
Estimated Sales: $3 Million
Number Employees: 8
Type of Packaging: Private Label
Brands:
GABRIELLI
GABRIELLI WINERY

2258 Campagna
P.O.Box 2403
Lebanon, OR 97355-0995 541-258-6806
Fax: 541-258-7806 800-959-4372
mgpcampagna@msn.com
www.campagnagourmet.com
Processor of cooking sauces, fruit, savory, and mustard flavors; hot pepper and garlic jellies
President: Marlene Peterson
CFO: Joseph Peterson
Estimated Sales: $1-2.5 Million
Number Employees: 5-9
Type of Packaging: Private Label

2259 Campagna-Turano Bakery
6501 Roosevelt Rd
Berwyn, IL 60402-1100 708-788-9220
Fax: 708-788-3075 info@turano-baking.com
www.turanobaking.com
Baked goods, bread
President: Renato Turano
VP Sales: Bill Carlson
Quality Control Manager: Les Messina
Executive VP Sales/Marketing: Giarcarto Turano
Operations Manager: Umberto Turano
Executive VP Production/Operations: Tony Turano
Estimated Sales: $10-20 Million
Number Employees: 250-499
Type of Packaging: Private Label

2260 Campari
55 E 59th St # 9
New York, NY 10022-1112 212-891-3600
Fax: 212-891-3661 www.mps.it
Alcoholic beverages
Manager: Gennaro Miccoli
Estimated Sales: $2.5-5 Million
Number Employees: 10-19
Parent Co: Campari
Brands:
Campari

2261 Campbell Company of Canada
60 Birmingham Street
Toronto, ON M8V 2B8
Canada 416-251-1131
Fax: 416-253-8611 800-575-7687
www.campbellsoup.ca
Manufacturer of canned foods including condensed soups, broth, chili and ready to serve soups.
President: P Donne
VP/CFO: E Ellis
VP/Marketing: M Childs
President Food Service: K Matier
Number Employees: 800
Type of Packaging: Consumer, Food Service, Private Label
Brands:
BISTO
BROTHS
CAMPBELLS READY TO ENJOY SOUPS
CAMPBELLS SOUP AT HAND
CHUNKY READY TO GO BOWLS
CHUNKY READY TO SERVE SOUPS/CHILI
GARDENNAY
GODIVA
HABITANT
HEALTHY REQUEST READY TO SERVE SOUP
PACE
PEPPERIDGE FARM
RED & WHITE CONDENSED SOUPS
V8
V8 SPLASH
V8 VGO

2262 Campbell Sales Company
68 Fulbright Lane
Schaumburg, IL 60194-5168 847-297-0900
Processor of canned soup
Manager: Pete Barber
Parent Co: Campbell Soup Company
Type of Packaging: Consumer, Food Service

2263 (HQ)Campbell Soup Company
1 Campbell Place
Camden, NJ 08103-1701 856-342-4800
Fax: 856-342-3878 800-257-8443
www.campbellsoup.com
Manufacturer of prepared convenience foods, baked goods, instant breakfast foods, soups, chili, chowders, stew, spaghetti, vegetable juice, gravies, relishes, sauces, beans, candy, etc.; importer of cooked beef; exporter of prepareddentrees and soups.
President & CEO: Douglas Conant
SVP/CFO: B Craig Owens
SVP/Chief Information Officer: Joseph Spagnoletti
SVP Global R&D/Quality: George Dowdie
SVP/Human Resources & Communications: Nancy Reardon
Estimated Sales: $7.5 Billion
Number Employees: 18,700
Type of Packaging: Consumer, Food Service, Bulk
Other Locations:
Campbell Soup Co.
Redmond WA
Beverage Plant
Napoleon OH
Pepperidge Farms HQ
Norwalk CT
Brands:
ARNOTT'S
CAMPBELL'S ® SUPPER BAKES
CAMPBELL'S AWAY FROM HOME
CAMPBELL'S SEEDS
CAMPBELL'S® SOUPS
CAMPBELL'S® TOMATO JUICE
PACE® SAUCES
PEPPERIDGE FARM®
PREGO®
SWANSON®
V8®

2264 Campbell Soup Company
1 Campbell Pl
Camden, NJ 08103-1799 856-342-4800
Fax: 856-342-3878 800-257-8443
ken_nye@campbellsoup.com
www.campbellsoup.com
Processor of canned soup
President: Douglas Conant
SVP/CFO/Chief Administrative Officer: B Craig Owens
VP Manufacturing: Robert Furbee
SVP Public Affairs: Jerry Buckley
Plant Manager: Dave Parcher
Purchasing Agent: Dan Ginter
Estimated Sales: K
Number Employees: 10,000+
Parent Co: Campbell Soup Company
Type of Packaging: Consumer, Food Service
Brands:
Campbell Away From Home
Campbell's Seeds
Campbell's Soup at Hand
Campbell's Supper Bakes
Campbell's Tomato Juice
Pace Sauces
Prego Pasta Sauces
Swanson Broth
V8 beverages

2265 Campbell Soup Company of Canada
1400 Mitchell Avenue
Listowel, ON N4W 3B3
Canada   519-291-3410
Fax: 519-291-2551 800-575-7687
Processor and co-packer of frozen dinners, entrees, pastries, soups and sauces; also, powder gravy mixes and bottled sauces; exporter of frozen entrees, soup and meat balls
President: Philip Donne
VP, CFO: G J Arnold
Director R&D: S Graham
VP Marketing: R Weyersberg
Director Corporate Communications: J Nelson
Purchasing Director: Paul Martin
Number Employees: 500-999
Parent Co: Campbell Soup Company
Type of Packaging: Consumer, Private Label
Other Locations:
Campbell Heat Process Plant
Listowel ON
Campbell Frozen Foodservice Plant
Etobicoke ON
Brands:
CAMPBELLS

2266 Campbell Wrapper Corporation
1415 Fortune Ave
De Pere, WI 54115-8104   920-983-7100
Fax: 920-983-7300
calawaym@campbellwrapper.com
www.campbellwrapper.com
Manufactures Horizontal Fin Seal Wrappers for food and nonfood applications. Shrink and Polyethylene Wrappers for magazines, cards, and coupons. Dual Lane Wrappers for a variety of products. Side Seal Wrappers for the printing andmailing industries. On-Edge Wrappers for cookies and crackers. In-line Feed Systems for confectionery and bakery. Bar Distribution Systems for health bars, confectionery, bakery, etc.
President: John Dykema
VP Finance & Administration: Todd Goodwin
R&D Manager/Electrical Engineering Mgr: Jeff Ginzl
Mechanical Engineering Manager: Gary LeTourneau
Vice President Sales & Marketing: Don Stelzer
Product Manager: Steve Joosten
Service Manager: Marv Calaway
Materials Manager/Wrapper Assembly Mgr: Jeff Jende
Estimated Sales: $ 10 - 20 Million
Number Employees: 50-99
Type of Packaging: Consumer

2267 Campbell's Quality Cuts
2551 Michigan St
Sidney, OH 45365-9083   937-492-2194
Fax: 937-492-4044
Processor of lamb, beef and pork
Owner: Dennis Campbell
Estimated Sales: $300,000-$500,000
Number Employees: 1-4
Type of Packaging: Consumer, Bulk

2268 Camrose Packers
5320 47th Street
Camrose, AB T4V 3B6
Canada   780-672-4887
Processor of fresh beef and pork and wild game including deer, elk and moose
Owner: Andrew Anderson
Manager: Debilyn Witvoet Parent
Type of Packaging: Consumer
Brands:
Camrose

2269 Can Am Seafood
PO Box 940
Lubec, ME 04652   207-733-2267
Fax: 207-733-0927
Seafood
President: William Jackson

2270 Can-Oat Milling
Box 520
Portage la Prairie, MB R1N 3W1
Canada   204-857-9700
Fax: 204-857-9500 800-663-6287
www.can-oat.com

Processor and exporter of oats including rolled, bran, instant, steel cut, whole groats and flour; importer of whole oat groats
President: Karl Gerrand
Number Employees: 100-249
Parent Co: Saskatchewan Wheat Pool
Type of Packaging: Bulk

2271 CanAmera Foods
406-1780 Wellington Avenue
Winnipeg, NB R3H 1B3
Canada   204-324-6481
Fax: 204-774-3314
Processor of shortenings, margarines, oils, lard, whipped toppings, stabilizers and emulsifiers including lecithin
Sales Rep.: Greg Christensen

2272 Canada Bread
1704 Seymour Street
North Bay, ON P1B 8G4
Canada   705-474-3970
Fax: 705-474-6847 800-461-6122
www.canadabread.ca
Manufacturer and distributor of fresh bakery products, frozen partially baked and fresh pasta and sauces
GM: Greg Chadbourn
Number Employees: 7,000
Parent Co: Maple Leaf
Type of Packaging: Consumer, Food Service
Brands:
BEN'S
DEMPSTERS
OLAFSON'S
OLIVIERI
POM

2273 Canada Bread
10 Four Seasons Place
Etobicoke, ON M9B 6H7
Canada   416-622-2040
Fax: 416-622-9525 www.canadabread.ca
Processor and exporter of pre-baked pizzas, shells and sauces
President/CEO: Richard Lan
Chairman: Michael McCain
CFO: Michael Vels
Senior VP Finance: Steve Weinberger
Number Employees: 100-249
Sq. footage: 46000
Parent Co: Corporate Foods/Canada Bread Company
Type of Packaging: Consumer, Food Service, Private Label, Bulk
Brands:
Denpster
Dough Delight
Olivieri

2274 Canada Bread Atlantic
67 O'Leary Avenue
PO Box 8245
St. John's, NL A1B 3N4
Canada   709-722-5410
Fax: 709-722-7802
Manufacturer of bread and rolls
Account Representative: Steve Hillyard
Regional Sales Manager: Keith Vokey
Operations Manager: Weldon Peddle
Type of Packaging: Consumer, Food Service

2275 Canada Bread Company
12151 160th Street NW
Edmonton, AB T5V 1M4
Canada   780-451-4663
Fax: 780-447-6566
Processor of bread and rolls
Sales Manager: Andy Chamberlain
Brands:
Country
Homestead

2276 Canada Bread Company
6350 203 Street
Langley, BC V2Y 1L9
Canada   604-532-8200
Fax: 604-532-8207 800-465-5515
investorrelations@mapleleaf.ca
www.canadabread.ca

Processor of baked goods including bread, rolls and English muffins
President: Michael McCain
Chairman: John L Bragg
COO: Richard A Lan
VP Sales: D Bagnall
Communications Manager: Catherine Harling
Parent Co: Corporate Foods/Canada Bread Company
Type of Packaging: Consumer, Food Service, Private Label, Bulk
Brands:
Ben
Dempsters
Olafsons
Olivieri
POM
Tenderflake

2277 Canada Dry Bottling Company
11202 15th Ave
Flushing, NY 11356-1428   718-661-4265
Fax: 718-353-5235
consumer_relations@dpsu.com
www.dpsu.com
Manufacturer/bottler of sodas, seltzer and mineral water including diet
President: Dennis Berberich
Estimated Sales: $100-500 Million
Number Employees: 250-499
Parent Co: Cadbury Schweppes
Type of Packaging: Consumer, Food Service, Private Label
Brands:
A&W
CANADA DRY
COUNTRY TIME
DIET RITE
DR. PEPPER
HAWAIIAN PUNCH
HIRES ROOT BEER
RC COLA
SCHWEPPES
SEVEN UP
SLUSH PUPPIE
SQUIRT
SUNDROP
SUNKIST
VERNORS
WELCH'S

2278 Canada West Foods
4312 51st Street
Innisfail, AB T4G 1A3
Canada   403-227-3386
Fax: 403-227-1661
Processor of case-ready lamb, veal and bison; also, custom processing available (very little)
President: Gary Haley
CEO: Gary Haley
Vice President: Don Finstad
Plant Manager: Miles Kliner
Number Employees: 100-249
Parent Co: Canada West Foods
Type of Packaging: Consumer

2279 Canadian Fish Exporters
PO Box 411
Watertown, MA 02471-0411   617-924-8300
Fax: 617-926-8214 800-225-4215
cfe@cfeboston.com www.cfeboston.com
Processor, importer and exporter of saltfish including bacalao, pollock, hake, cusk, haddock, herring, mackerel and cod; importer of Italian cheeses and canned tomatoes
President: Robert Metafora
CEO: Robert Metafora
CFO/Treasurer: Janelle Calamari
VP: James Scannell
Estimated Sales: $ 10 - 20 Million
Number Employees: 10-19
Type of Packaging: Consumer, Private Label, Bulk
Brands:
BACALA RICO
BUENA VENTURA
CRISTOBAL

2280 (HQ)Canadian Harvest
1001 Cleveland St S
Cambridge, MN 55008-1150   763-689-5800
Fax: 763-689-5949 888-689-5800
miker@skypoint.com www.sunopta.com

Processor of stabilized fiber ingredients including bleached oat fibers, red and white wheat brans, corn brans, oat blends, wheat germs and customized grain blends
   Marketing Manager: Mike Rudquist
   General Manager: John White
   Plant Manager: Paul Empanger
Estimated Sales:$10-20 Million
Number Employees: 20-49
Other Locations:
   Canadian Harvest
   St. Thomas ON
Brands:
   Snowite

2281 Canadian Mist Distillers
202 MacDonald Road
Collingwood, ON L9Y 4J2
Canada   705-445-4690
                       Fax: 705-445-7948
Processor and exporter of whiskey
   Manager Admin./Commodities: Steve Sly
   Manager Production: Don Jaques
   Plant Manager: Harold Ferguson
Number Employees: 20-49
Sq. footage: 500000
Parent Co: Brown-Forman Corporation
Type of Packaging: Consumer, Food Service
Brands:
   Canadian Mist

2282 Canadian Salt Company Limited
Suite 700
Pointe Claire, QC H9R 5M9
Canada   514-630-0900
   Fax: 514-694-2451 tferrara@windsorsalt.com
                       www.windsorsalt.com
Manufacaturer and exporter of salt including table, food processing, water conditioning and ice melting
   President/CEO: Guy Leblanc
   VP Finance: Francois Allard
   Marketing Manager: Michel Prevost
   VP Sales/Marketing: Luc Savoic
   Human Resources Manager: Nicole Gagnon
Estimated Sales:$300+ Million
Number Employees: 700
Parent Co: Morton International
Type of Packaging: Consumer, Food Service, Bulk
Other Locations:
   Canadian Salt Company
   Pugwash, Nova Scoti
   Canadian Salt Company
   Mines Seleine, Quebec
   Canadian Salt Company-Warehouse
   Goderich, Ontario
   Canadian Salt Company-Warehouse
   Clarkson, Ontario
   Canadian Salt Company-Warehouse
   Anjou, Quebec
   Canadian Salt Company
   Ojibway, Ontario
   Canadian Salt Company
   Windsor, Ontario
   Canadian Salt Company
   Regina, Saskatchewan
   Canadian Salt Company
   Lindbergh, Alberta
Brands:
   WINDSOR

2283 Canadian Silver Herring
PO Box 792
Cap-Pele, NB E4N 3B3
Canada   506-577-6426
                       Fax: 506-577-2846
Processor and exporter of smoked herring
   Owner: Janice Ryan
Number Employees: 20-49
Type of Packaging: Bulk

2284 Canal Fulton Provision
2014 Locust St S
Canal Fulton, OH 44614-9477   330-854-3502
          Fax: 330-854-3502 800-321-3502
                       www.canalfultonpro.com
Processor of portion cut poultry and meats including beef, lamb and pork
   President: George Mizarek
Estimated Sales:$20-50 Million
Number Employees: 20-49
Type of Packaging: Consumer, Food Service, Private Label, Bulk
Brands:
   Corn King
   Flavor Pack
   Weaver

2285 Canandaigua Wine Concentrate
P.O.Box 99
Madera, CA 93639-0099   559-673-7071
   Fax: 559-661-3424 greg.magill@cwine.com
                       www.cwine.com
Wine industry ingredients
   President: Anil Shirkhande
   Vice President: Mike Martin
   Plant Manager: Chris Bonner
Estimated Sales:$100-500 Million
Number Employees: 500-999

2286 Canasoy Enterprises
57 Lakewood Drive
Vancouver, BC V5L 4W4
Canada   604-255-1304
       Fax: 604-255-5659 800-663-1222
   info@canasoy.com www.canasoy.com
Processor, importer and exporter of health foods, including grains and pasta
   President: Hau Cheong Chau
   Marketing/Sales: Gregory Chan
Number Employees: 10-19
Number of Products: 3000
Sq. footage: 25000
Type of Packaging: Consumer, Food Service, Private Label

2287 Candelari's Specialty Sausage
6002 Washington Ave
Houston, TX 77007-5015   832-200-1474
       Fax: 281-568-8098 800-953-5343
   emaillist@candelaris.com www.candelaris.com
Sausage
   President: Michael May
   CFO: Michael Freeman
Estimated Sales:$500,000-$1 Million
Number Employees: 5-9
Type of Packaging: Private Label
Brands:
   Candelari's

2288 Candone Fine Natural Foods
3343 Peachtree Road NE
Suite 1115
Atlanta, GA 30326-1430   404-469-2348
                       Fax: 404-364-3499
   President: Elvaina Candoni De Zan

2289 Candy Bouquet of Elko
3362 Dux Avenue
Elko, NV 89801-4432   775-777-9866
       Fax: 775-777-3200 888-855-3391
                       hopkins@sierra.net
Manufacturer of candy bouquets
   Co-Owner: Judy Hopkins
   Co-Owner: Diane Noble
   Manager: Angie Demars
Number Employees: 1-4

2290 Candy Cottage Company
465 Pike Rd
Huntingdon Vly, PA 19006-1620   215-953-8288
   Fax: 215-357-3035 info@candycottageco.com
                       www.candycottageco.com
Manufacturer of chocolate covered ultimate pretzels
   Co-Owner: Al Palagruto
   Co-Owner: Joan Palagruto
   Human Resources: Joan Simon
Estimated Sales:$5-10 Million
Number Employees: 50-99
Type of Packaging: Consumer, Food Service, Private Label, Bulk
Brands:
   Ultimate Petite Pretzels
   Ultimate Pretzel
   Ultimate Pretzel Rods
   Ultimate Pretzel Sculptures

2291 Candy Factory
25067 Viking St
Hayward, CA 94545-2703   510-293-6887
       Fax: 510-293-6890 800-736-6887
                       www.knudsens.com
Processor of gourmet chocolates including bon bons, creams, regular and caramel nut clusters, truffles, etc.; also, private labeling available
   President: Gary Love
   Chairman: David Knudsen
   Treasurer/Secretary: Kathy Knudsen
   Vice President: Tod Knudsen
   Marketing Director: Tod Knudsen
   Purchasing Manager: Tod Knudsen

Number Employees: 20-49
Sq. footage: 36000
Type of Packaging: Consumer, Private Label
Brands:
   Enjoymints
   Tropical Wonders

2292 (HQ)Candy Flowers
9350 Mercantile Drive
Mentor, OH 44060-4525   888-476-6467
   Fax: 508-842-3065 www.candyflowersinc.com
Processor of chocolate and candy flowers, chocolate covered pretzels, coffee spoons and cookies and theme wrapped chocolate bars; exporter of candy flowers; importer of chocolates
   President: Joanne Henry
   Marketing: Anthony Henry
Number Employees: 20-49
Sq. footage: 21000
Type of Packaging: Food Service
Brands:
   CANDY FLOWER BOUQUETS
   SPOONFUL OF FLAVORS
   SWEET BLOSSOMS

2293 Candyrific
3738 Lexington Rd
Louisville, KY 40207-3010   502-893-3626
   Fax: 502-893-3951 sales@candyrific.com
                       www.candyrific.com
Candy
Brands:
   COOL POPS
   CRAYOLA
   ETCH-A-SKETCH
   MARVEL
   PEEPS
   SLINKY BRAND CANDY

2294 Canelake's
414 Chestnut St
Virginia, MN 55792-2526   218-741-1557
       Fax: 218-741-1557 888-928-8889
   candy@canelakes.com www.canelakes.com
Processor and exporter of candies and chocolates; importer of nuts
   President: James Cina
Estimated Sales:$1-2.5 Million
Number Employees: 10-19
Sq. footage: 2000
Type of Packaging: Consumer

2295 Cangel
60 Paton Road
Toronto, ON M6H 1R8
Canada   416-532-5111
       Fax: 416-532-6231 800-267-4795
                       b.imai@cangel.com
Manufacturer and exporter of food, hydrolyzed and technical gelatins
   Sales/Marketing Rep.: Brian Imai
Number Employees: 50-99
Sq. footage: 80000
Type of Packaging: Bulk

2296 Cannery Row
PO Box 120
Cordova, AK 99574-0120   907-424-5920
                       Fax: 907-424-5923
Seafood

2297 Cannoli Factory
75 Wyandanch Ave
Wyandanch, NY 11798-4441   631-643-2700
   Fax: 631-643-2777 cannolifactory@aol.com
                       www.cannolifactory.net
Processor and exporter of Italian and New York style cheesecake, tiramisu, lobster tail pastries and cannoli products including chocolate covered shells, cream and tarts
   Owner: Michael Zucaro
Estimated Sales:$ 50 - 100 Million
Number Employees: 50-99
Type of Packaging: Food Service

2298 Cannon Potato Company
P.O.Box 880
Center, CO 81125-0880   719-754-3445
   Fax: 719-754-2227 sales@canonpotato.com
                       www.canonpotato.com
Potato packer and shipper
   President: Jim Tonso
   Sales Manager: David Tonso

Estimated Sales:$10-20 Million
Number Employees: 20-49
Type of Packaging: Private Label

2299 Cannon's Sweets Hots
2724 Tennessee Street NE
Albuquerque, NM 87110-3732   505-294-7018
     Fax: 505-292-4581   877-630-7026
sweethot@sweethots.com   www.sweethots.com
Hot sauces and chili
   Co-Owner/President: John Cannon
   Co-Owner/CEO: Diane Cannon
*Estimated Sales:*Under $500,000
Number Employees: 1-4

2300 Canoe Lagoon Oyster Company
118 Bayview Ave
Coffman Cove, AK 99918   907-329-2253
     Fax: 425-643-7266
Oyster
   Owner: Sharon Gray
   Owner: Don Nicholson
Estimated Sales:$500,000
Number Employees: 1-4
Type of Packaging: Consumer, Food Service, Bulk

2301 Cantare Foods
7678 Miramar Rd
San Diego, CA 92126-4202   858-578-8490
   Fax: 858-578-8065 www.cantarefoods.com
Manufacturer of fresh mozzarella, ricotta, mascarpone, burratta, and baked brie en croute
   President: Bob Fisher
   Marketing Director: Diane Bailey
Estimated Sales:$5-10 Million
Number Employees: 50-99

2302 (HQ)Cantisano Foods
815 Whitney Road W
Fairport, NY 14450-1030   585-377-9151
     Fax: 716-377-8150
Pizza sauce, tomato sauce, meatless spaghetti sauce, kosher spaghetti sauce, barbecue sauce
   Chairman: John Lidestri
   President/CEO: John LiDestri
   Production Manager: Santi LiDestri
Estimated Sales:$50-100 Million
Number Employees: 100-249
Brands:
   Cantisano
   Francesco Rinaldi

2303 Canton Noodle
481 W 26th St
Chicago, IL 60616-2235   312-842-4900
     Fax: 312-225-2262
Chinese foods and noodles
   President: Mitta Moy
Estimated Sales:$2.5-5 Million
Number Employees: 10-19

2304 Canton Noodle Corporation
101 Mott St
New York, NY 10013-4697   212-226-3276
     Fax: 212-226-8037
Processor of Chinese canned noodles
Estimated Sales:$1-2.5 Million
Number Employees: 5-9
Type of Packaging: Consumer

2305 Cantrell's Seafood
Sabino Road
Bath, ME 04530   207-442-7261
     Fax: 207-770-1600
Seafood
   President: S C Cantrell

2306 Cantwell's Old Mill Winery
403 S Broadway
Geneva, OH 44041-1844   440-466-5560
   Fax: 440-466-2099   winedoc@ncweb.com
     www.oldmillwinery.com
Gourmet foods, wines
   Owner: Dave Froelich
   Winemaker: Bill Turgeon
   Marketing Director: Shirley Barnett
Estimated Sales:$1-2.5 Million appx.
Number Employees: 1-4

2307 Canus Fisheries
PO Box 149
Clark's Harbour, NS B0W 1P0
Canada   902-745-2888
     Fax: 902-745-2526   canus@auracom.com

Processor and exporter of fresh lobster and salted and fresh fish
   President: Margot Swim
Number Employees: 50-99
Type of Packaging: Consumer, Food Service, Private Label, Bulk

2308 Canyon Specialty Foods
PO Box 35154
Dallas, TX 75235-0154   214-352-1771
   Fax: 214-352-3118   877-815-3663
     aconally@canyonfoods.com
     www.canyonfoods.com
Gourmet shelf and frozen food, salsa and sauces
   Owner, President: Anne Connally
   Production Manager: Tara McConnell
Estimated Sales:$10-20 Million
Number Employees: 10-19
Type of Packaging: Private Label

2309 Cap Candy
50 Technology Court
Napa, CA 94558-7519   707-251-9321
     Fax: 707-251-9482
Candy
   VP of Marketing: Deirdre Gonzalez
   General Manager: Tom Pritchard
Number Employees: 250-499
Parent Co: Hasbro

2310 Cap Rock Winery
408 E Woodrow Rd
Lubbock, TX 79423-7809   806-863-2704
   Fax: 806-863-2712   800-546-9463
     www.caprockwinery.com
Wines
   President: Don Roark
   VP Sales/Marketing: John Bratcher
   Plant Manager: Kim McPherson
Estimated Sales:$5-10 Million
Number Employees: 10-19
Type of Packaging: Private Label

2311 Capalbo's Gift Baskets
339 Passaic Ave
Nutley, NJ 07110-2779   973-235-0879
   Fax: 973-450-1199   800-252-6262
     www.capalbosgiftbaskets.com
Gift baskets for the specialty food industry
   Manager: Ruth Mac
   President: Francis Capalbo
   Marketing Director: Maria Rodriguez
Estimated Sales:$ 10 - 20 Million
Number Employees: 50-99
Brands:
   Capalbo's

2312 Caparone Winery
2280 San Marcos Rd
Paso Robles, CA 93446-5322   805-467-3827
     info@caparone.com
     www.caparone.com
Wines
   President: M Caparone
*Estimated Sales:*Under $500,000
Number Employees: 20-49

2313 Capay Canyon Ranch
P.O.Box 508
Esparto, CA 95627-0508   530-662-2372
     Fax: 530-662-2306
Processor and exporter of almonds, walnuts and grapes, and inshell chandler walnuts.
   President/Owner: Stan Barth
   Quality Control: Todd Barth
   Sales Director: Leslie Barth
   Operations Manager: Javier Quiroz
   Production: Todd Barth
   Plant Manager: Todd Barth
Estimated Sales:$14 Million
Number of Brands: 2
Number of Products: 8
Sq. footage: 10000
Type of Packaging: Bulk
Brands:
   Capay Canyon Ranch
   STAN BARTH FARMS

2314 Capco Enterprises
34 Deforest Ave # 3
East Hanover, NJ 07936-2832   973-884-0044
   Fax: 973-884-8711   800-252-1011
     www.capcoenterprisesinc.com

Almonds, licorice, baked beans, sugar-coated pistachios and chick peas
   Owner: Carole Lapone
Estimated Sales:$2.5-5 Million
Number Employees: 5-9

2315 Cape Ann Seafood
417 Main St
Gloucester, MA 01930-3006   978-282-3286
     Fax: 978-282-1870
Seafood
   Owner: Larry Misuraca
Estimated Sales:$300,000-500,000
Number Employees: 1-4

2316 Cape Ann Tuna
88 Commercial Street
Gloucester, MA 01930-5025   978-283-8188
     Fax: 978-281-6584
Tuna
   Owner: William Raymond
Estimated Sales:$ .5 - 1 million
Number Employees: 1-4

2317 Cape Cod Chowders
141 Falmouth Rd
Hyannis, MA 02601-2755   508-771-0040
     Fax: 508-771-0883
     www.cataniahospitalitygroup.com
Chowder
   President: Vincent J Catania
   Vice President: Richard Catenia
   Sales Director: Dan Sheehan
   Purchasing Manager: Paul Rumel
*Estimated Sales:*F
Number Employees: 500-999
Type of Packaging: Private Label
Brands:
   Cape Cod Clam Chowder
   Cape Cod Lobster Cho

2318 Cape Cod Coffee Roasters
348 Main St
Mashpee, MA 02649-2045   508-477-2400
     Fax: 508-477-2989 www.cccoffee.com
Coffee
   Owner: Demos Young
Estimated Sales:$5-9.9 Million
Number Employees: 5-9

2319 Cape Cod Potato Chip Company
100 Breeds Hill Rd
Hyannis, MA 02601-1886   508-775-3917
     Fax: 508-775-2808
   customer.service@capecodchips.com
     www.capecodchips.com
Processor and exporter of popcorn including white cheddar cheese, natural and butter; also, kettle-cooked potato chips
   President: Vincent Fantegrossi
   VP Sales/Marketing: Bill Germano
Estimated Sales:$20-50 Million
Number Employees: 100-249
Sq. footage: 30000
Parent Co: Lance
Type of Packaging: Consumer
Brands:
   Cape Cod

2320 Cape Cod Provisions
31 Jonathan Bourne Drive
Unit 1
Pocasset, MA 02559   508-564-5840
Fax: 508-564-5844   mail@capecodprovisions.com
     www.capecodprovisions.com
Chocolate covered cranberries, chocolate covered fruit, fruit truffles

2321 Cape Cod Specialty FoodsIncorporated
PO Box 519
Sagamore, MA 02561-0519   508-888-7099
   Fax: 508-888-6616   bogbeans@rcn.com
     www.bogbeans.com
Wholesaler/distributor of gourmet condiments including lemon pepper mustard, cranberry chutney, relish and sauces, schnappy peach preserves, chocolate covered cranberries, bog beans, etc.; also mail order available
   President: Mike Duryea
Estimated Sales:$2.5-5 Million
Number Employees: 1-4
Sq. footage: 2000
Type of Packaging: Consumer, Food Service

2322 Capital Brewery
7734 Terrace Ave
Middleton, WI 53562-3163   608-836-7100
Fax: 608-831-9155   capital@capital-brewery.com
www.capital-brewery.com
Brewer of lager and ale
    President, CEO: Carl Nolen
    Brewmaster: Kirby Nelson
Estimated Sales: $5-10 Million
Number Employees: 20-49
Type of Packaging: Consumer, Food Service, Bulk
Brands:
    Gartenbrau

2323 Capital City Processors
P.O.Box 94148
Oklahoma City, OK 73143-4148   405-232-5511
                                  800-473-2731
Processor of cooking oils
    Manager: Randy Mc Kiddie
Estimated Sales: $20-50 Million
Number Employees: 10-19
Type of Packaging: Bulk

2324 Capital Packers
12907-57th Street NW
Edmonton, AB T5A 0A6
Canada   780-476-1391
        Fax: 780-478-0083 800-272-8868
info@capitalpackers.ca www.capitalpackers.ca
Processor of cooked and smoked meats including
beef, pork and veal
    President: Brent Komarnicki
    Sales Manager: Peter Andreassen
    Plant Manager: Cor Van Miltenburg
Number Employees: 50-99
Number of Brands: 3
Number of Products: 850
Type of Packaging: Food Service, Private Label,
    Bulk
Brands:
    Bavarian Brand Sausage
    Cajun Brand Sausage
    Ham Sausage
    Polish Sausage

2325 Capital Seaboard
8005 Rappahanock Ave
Jessup, MD 20794-9438   443-755-1733
                                 Fax: 443-755-0282
Seafood
    Owner: Troy Geller

2326 Capitol Foods
PO Box 751541
Memphis, TN 38175-1541   662-781-9021
                                 Fax: 662-781-0697
Processor of canned vegetables, diced peaches,
mixed fruits and edible oils; exporter of canned veg-
etables; wholesaler/distributor of bakery, dairy and
grocery products, soups and bases, produce, syrups,
oils, pasta, meats; serving thefood service markets
    President: Kenneth Porter
    CFO: Phillip Duncan
Number Employees: 10-19
Sq. footage: 10000
Type of Packaging: Consumer, Food Service
Brands:
    Capitol Foods
    Orchard Naturals

**2327 (HQ)Capitol Wholesale
MeatsCCompany**
8751 W 50th St
Mc Cook, IL 60525-3132   708-485-4800
        Fax: 708-485-9600 800-331-6328
info@fontanini.com www.fontanini.com
Breakfast sausage, meat balls, meat loaf, pot roast,
pizza toppings, beef, etc.
    President: Gene Fontanini
    Vice President: Joanne Fontanini
    Director Quality Control: Anthony Pavel
    General Manager: Charles Brown
    Director Operations: Mike Catania
Estimated Sales: $100-500 Million
Number Employees: 100-249
Sq. footage: 240000
Type of Packaging: Consumer, Food Service
Brands:
    Diamanti
    Fontanini

2328 Capolla Foods
25 Lepage Court
North York, ON M3J 3M3
Canada   416-633-0389
    Fax: 416-633-7718 www.triple.coppolafood.com
Processor of packaged luncheon meats including
beef and pork
    President: Rick De Vincenzo
    CEO: Rick De Vincenzo
    Marketing Director: Francefca Ivas
    Sales/Marketing: Dion McGuire
    Purchasing Agent: John Capolla
Number Employees: 50-99
Parent Co: J.M. Schneider
Type of Packaging: Consumer
Brands:
    Capolla Foods

2329 Capone Foods
14 Bow St
Somerville, MA 02143-2915   617-629-2296
    Fax: 617-776-0318 albert@caponefoods.com
                       www.caponefoods.com
Pasta and sauces
    Owner: Albert Capone
Estimated Sales: $5-10 Million
Number Employees: 5-9

2330 Caporale Winery
910 Enterprise Way
Napa, CA 94558-6209   707-253-9230
                                 Fax: 707-253-9232
Wines
    President: Mark Caporale
Estimated Sales: $500-1 Million appx.
Number Employees: 20-49

2331 Cappello Foods
11 W Baltimore Street
Apt 817
Hagerstown, MD 21740-4302   301-745-6641
    Owner: Anthony Cappello

2332 Cappiello Dairy Products
534 Broadway
Schenectady, NY 12305   518-374-5064
        Fax: 518-374-4015 info@Cappiello.com
                            www.cappiello.com
Processor of cheeses including ricotta, mozzarella,
scamorza and Italian hand-crafted
    Owner: Peter Cappiello
    VP Marketing: Julianne Cappiello-Miranda
    VP Sales: Julianne Cappiello-Miranda
    Director Of Operations: Peter Cappiello
Estimated Sales: $20-50 Million
Number Employees: 50-99
Type of Packaging: Consumer, Private Label, Bulk
Brands:
    Cappiello

2333 Cappola Foods
92 Cartwright Avenue
Toronto, ON M6A 1V2
Canada   416-256-1084
                                 Fax: 416-787-1535
Processor and exporter of Italian flavored ices
    Owner: Dom Cappola
Type of Packaging: Consumer, Food Service

2334 Cappuccine
1285 N Valdivia Way
Palm Springs, CA 92262-5428   760-864-7355
        Fax: 760-864-7360 800-511-3127
    sales@cappuccine.net www.cappuccine.net
Gourmet instant powder beverage mixes in chai, va-
nilla, chocolate, fruit, toffes and coconut flavors
    Founder/President/CEO: Michael Rubin
    General Manager/COO: John Strohm
    Executive VP: Charles Jennings
    Director Sales: Harry van Kamp
    Operations Manager: Kayvon McMains
Estimated Sales: $5 Million
Number Employees: 5-9
Number of Brands: 1
Number of Products: 18
Sq. footage: 3600
Type of Packaging: Consumer, Food Service, Pri-
    vate Label, Bulk
Brands:
    Cappuccine
    Cappuccino Exotic Island Smoothies

2335 Capri Bagel & Pizza Corporation
215 Moore St
Brooklyn, NY 11206-3745   718-497-4431
                                 Fax: 718-497-7567
Manufacturer and exporter of pizza, pizza bagels
and mini pizzas
    President: Adrian Cooper
    Plant Manager: Ikey Tuachi
Estimated Sales: $500,000-$1 Million
Number Employees: 20-49
Sq. footage: 31000
Type of Packaging: Consumer, Food Service, Pri-
    vate Label
Brands:
    Big Time
    Boardwalk

2336 Capriccio
10021 1/2 Canoga Avenue
Chatsworth, CA 91311-0981   818-718-7620
    Fax: 818-718-0204 capriccio@worldnet.att.net
Manufacturer and exporter of food ingredients
    CEO: Jack Barsoumian
Estimated Sales: $500,000-$1 Million
Number Employees: 1-4
Type of Packaging: Food Service

2337 Capricorn Coffees
353 10th St
San Francisco, CA 94103-3855   415-861-1771
        Fax: 415-621-9875 800-541-0758
                            www.capricorncoffees.com
Coffee
    Manager: Megan Patterson
Estimated Sales: $1-2.5 Million
Number Employees: 10-19
Type of Packaging: Private Label

2338 Caprine Estates
3669 Centerville Road
Bellbrook, OH 45305-0307   937-848-7406
    Fax: 937-848-7437 info@caprineestates.com
Processor of goat milk cheese, fudge and bottled
milk
    President: Dennis Dean
    VP: Patti Dean
    Sales/Marketing VP: Ron Best
Estimated Sales: $250,000
Number Employees: 5
Sq. footage: 15000
Type of Packaging: Consumer, Food Service, Pri-
    vate Label, Bulk

2339 Caps Italian Foods
195 N Dixie Highway
Saint Anne, IL 60964-5562   815-427-6522
                                 Fax: 815-427-6522
Frozen foods
    Chairman: Jay Capriotti
    Vice President: Mark Capriotti
Estimated Sales: $500,000-$1 Million
Number Employees: 20-49
Brands:
    All Star
    Cap's
    Capriotti's
    Good Times
    Mr. B'S
    Mr. C'S
    Packer's Supreme
    Prestige
    Seline

2340 Capsule Works
10 Cartwright Loop
Bayport, NY 11705-1115   631-472-2817
        Fax: 631-472-2817 800-920-6090
    sales@capsuleworks.com
                            www.capsuleworks.com
Vitamins
    President: Kazuo Kawabata
    CFO: Jean-Marc Huët
Estimated Sales: $ 10 - 20 Million
Number Employees: 20-49
Brands:
    Capsule Works

2341 Captain Alex Seafood
8874 N Milwaukee Ave
Niles, IL 60714-1752   847-803-8833
                                 Fax: 847-803-9854
Seafood
    Owner: Alex Malidis

Estimated Sales:$680,000
Number Employees: 5-9

2342 Captain Bob's Jet Fuel
2216 Ladue Ln
Fort Wayne, IN 46804-2794   260-436-3895
                              877-486-6468
customerservice@captainbobs.com
www.captainbobs.com
Processor of hot sauces including habanero-garlic,
smoked serrano jalapeno and chile de arbol; also,
hot barbecue sauces
   President: Robert Kitto
Estimated Sales:$1-2.5 Million
Number Employees: 1-4
Brands:
   Captain Bob's Jet Fuel

2343 Captain Collier Seafood
P.O.Box 540
Coden, AL 36523-0540   251-824-4925
                         Fax: 251-824-2374
Seafood
   Owner: Phil Brannon
Estimated Sales:$ 3 - 5 Million
Number Employees: 5-9

2344 Captain Cook Coffee Company
P.O.Box 818
Captain Cook, HI 96704-0818   808-322-2087
   Fax: 808-322-2087 www.captaincoffee.com
Coffee
   President/CEO: Steven McLaughlin
Estimated Sales:$5-10 Million
Number Employees: 10-19

2345 Captain Joe & Sons
95 E Main St
Gloucester, MA 01930-3860   978-283-1454
   Fax: 978-283-1466 www.wholesalelobster.com
Seafood
   Co-Owner: Joe Ciaramitaro
   Co-Owner: Frank Ciaramitaro
Estimated Sales:$300,000-500,000
Number Employees: 1-4

2346 Captain Ken's Foods
344 Robert St S
St Paul, MN 55107-2200   651-298-0071
   Fax: 651-298-0849 jtraxler@captainkens.com
www.captainkens.com
Processor of frozen foods including chili, oven
baked beans and au gratin potatoes, taco meat,
meatloaf, macaroni and beef
   President, CEO: John Traxler
   Chairman, Owner: Mike Traxler
   Controller: Linda Traxler
   VP Business Development: Tom Traxler
   VP Sales: Don Keis
   Operations Manager: Kevin Kosel
   Plant Manager: Richard Gavin
Estimated Sales:$5-9.9 Million
Number Employees: 20-49
Sq. footage: 62000
Type of Packaging: Consumer, Food Service
Brands:
   Captain Ken's

2347 Captain Ottis Seafood
711 Shepard Street
Morehead City, NC 28557-4206   252-247-3569
                                 Fax: 252-726-7097
Frozen flounder, scallops, shrimp
   President: Doug Brady
Estimated Sales:$5-10 Million
Number Employees: 10-19

2348 Captain's Choice
29629 11th Pl S
Federal Way, WA 98003-3727   253-941-1184
   Fax: 253-946-2852 captainschoice@juno.com
www.captains-choice.com
Honey brine smoked salmon products and gift packages
   President: Donald Buchanan
   Public Relations: Rosalie Buchanan
*Estimated Sales:*Under $300,000
Number Employees: 1-4
Type of Packaging: Consumer, Food Service, Private Label
Brands:
   Captain's Choice Honey Brine
   Smoked Salmon
   Smoked Spices

2349 Captiva
45 Us Highway 206 # 104
Augusta, NJ 07822-2044   973-579-7883
                           Fax: 973-579-2509
Processor and exporter of bottled water including
stilled, carbonated and flavored; also, sports/health
drinks
   Owner: Don Destefano
   VP: Mary Ann Bell
Estimated Sales:$ 3 - 5 Million
Number Employees: 1-4
Sq. footage: 3000
Type of Packaging: Consumer, Food Service, Private Label, Bulk
Brands:
   Nature's Mist
   Pro-Life

2350 Captn's Pack Products
7135 Minstrel Way
Suite 203
Columbia, MD 21045-5294   410-720-6668
                            Fax: 410-381-6868
Seafood
   President: Benjamin Sha
Estimated Sales:$ 5 - 10 Million
Number Employees: 5-9

2351 Cara Mia Foods
10838 Cara Mia Parkway
PO Box 1307
Castroville, CA 95012-3211   831-633-2423
                               Fax: 831-633-9025
Frozen artichokes and artichoke hearts
   Purchasing Manager: Robert Epperson
Estimated Sales:$20-50 Million
Number Employees: 250-499

2352 Cara Mia Products
4652 E Date Ave
Fresno, CA 93725-2123   559-498-2900
                          Fax: 559-498-2910
consumerrelations@caramiaproducts.com
www.caramiaproducts.com
Processor of artichokes, brussels sprouts and mushrooms; contract packager of vegetables
   President: Jerry Maynard
   VP Marketing: Jim Scattini
   Purchasing Manager: Robert Epperson
Estimated Sales:$10-24.9 Million
Number Employees: 20-49
Type of Packaging: Consumer, Food Service, Private Label, Bulk
Brands:
   Cara Mia

2353 Caracollillo Coffee Mills
4419 N Hesperides St
Tampa, FL 33614-7618   813-876-0302
   Fax: 813-875-6407 800-682-0023
info@ccmcoffee.com   www.ccmcoffee.com
Coffee
   President: Michael Faedo
   VP/Owner: Julian Faedo
Estimated Sales:$ 3 - 5 Million
Number Employees: 5-9
Type of Packaging: Consumer, Food Service, Private Label
Brands:
   CAFE QUISQUEVA
   Cafe Caracolillo Decafe
   Cafe Caracolillo Expresso
   Cafe Caracolillo Gourmet
   Cafe Regil
   Cafe Rico Rico
   Cafe Riquisimo

2354 Carando Gourmet Frozen Foods
500 Worthington St
Springfield, MA 01105-1709   413-730-4205
                               Fax: 413-789-1653
Processor of frozen food and entrees including roast
beef, corned beef, pastrami, sauces, Italian stuffed
pastas, gourmet meatballs, cabbage and sweet
peppers
   Owner: Peter Carando Jr
   Director Sales: Brian Kelly
Parent Co: Carando Gourmet
Type of Packaging: Consumer, Food Service, Private Label, Bulk
Brands:
   Carando Gourmet

2355 Caraquet Ice Company
20 Rue Du Quai
Caraquet, NB E1W 1B6
Canada   506-727-7211
            Fax: 506-727-6769
Processor of fresh and frozen seafood
   President: Richard Albert
Type of Packaging: Bulk
Brands:
   Caraquet

2356 Caravan Company
237 Chandler St
Worcester, MA 01609-2935   508-752-3777
                             Fax: 508-753-4717
Manufacturer of coffee
   President: George Drapos
Estimated Sales:$10 Million
Number Employees: 10-19

2357 (HQ)Caravan Products Company
P.O.Box 1004
Totowa, NJ 07511-1004   973-256-8886
   Fax: 973-256-8395 800-526-5261
info@caravanproducts.com
www.caravanproducts.com
Manufacturer, wholesaler and exporter of bakery ingredients
   President: John Stone
   VP: Joseph Solimini
   Quality Control: Mark Carlson
Estimated Sales:$20-50 Million
Number Employees: 100-249
Other Locations:
   Caravan Products Co.
   Totowa NJ
Brands:
   DABUBE SEVEN
   HEART OF RYE
   SURFAX

2358 Caravan Trading Company
33300 Western Ave
Union City, CA 94587-2211   510-487-2600
                              Fax: 510-487-4100
Baked goods
   President: Joseph Maroun Sr
   VP Operations: William Maroun
Estimated Sales:$20-50 Million
Number Employees: 250-499

2359 Carberry's Home Made Ice Cream
42 Rose St
Merritt Island, FL 32953-4730   321-452-8900
   Fax: 321-459-5090 jc@carberrysbakery.com
Processor of ice cream including pies and cheesecake
   President: Stephen Carberry
   CEO: Kay Jackson
*Estimated Sales:*Less than $100,000
Number Employees: 1-4
Type of Packaging: Consumer, Food Service

2360 Carbolite Foods
1325 Newton Avenue
Evansville, IN 47715-2207
   Fax: 812-485-0002 888-524-3314
consumer@carbolitefoods.com
Manufacturer of low-carb items such as ice cream,
soy shakes, zero-carb bake mix and low carb bread
mix as well as low-carb candy bars, snack bars, candies and protein shakes.
   President: Gerry Morrison
   CEO: Jeff Greder
   CFO: Mike Lish
   VP: Roeland Polet
   R&D/Quality Control: Gordon Brown
   Marketing: William Dugan
   Operations Manager: Scott Gagnon
Number Employees: 24
Number of Products: 75
Type of Packaging: Food Service
Brands:
   Jolle Desserts

2361 Carbon's Golden Malted
4101 William Richardson Dr
South Bend, IN 46628-9485   574-247-2270
   Fax: 574-247-2280 800-686-6258
retail@goldenmalted.com
www.goldenmalted.com

Manufacturer and market flour mix for pancakes and waffles
President: Rick Mc Keel
CFO: Robert Spencer
National Account Sales Manager: Thomas Anderson
VP Sales/Marketing: Robert Coquillard
Number Employees: 1-4

2362 Carbon's Golden Malted
4101 William Richardson Dr
South Bend, IN 46628-9485   574-247-2270
   Fax: 574-247-2280   800-253-0590
   newcarbon@qtm.net   www.goldenmalted.com
Waffle and pancake flour
President: Rick Mc Keel
Estimated Sales:$ 10 - 20 Million
Number Employees: 20-49

2363 Carbon's Golden Malted Pancake & Waffle Flour Mix
PO Box 71
Buchanan, MI 49107-0071   574-247-2270
   Fax: 574-247-2280   800-253-0590
   newcarbon@goldenmalted.com
   www.goldenmalted.com
Manufacturer of gourmet malted pancake and waffle flour mixes.
President/CEO: Rick McKeel
CFO: Robert Spencer
VP Sales/Marketing: Robert Coquillard
National Account Sales Manager: Thomas Anderson
Number Employees: 1-4

2364 Carbonator Rental Service
6500 Eastwick Ave
Philadelphia, PA 19142-3399   215-726-8000
   Fax: 215-726-6367   800-220-3556
   info@carbonatorrental.com
   www.carbonatorrental.com
Processor of soda water syrups and bar mixes; wholesaler/distributor of beverage dispensing equipment
Chairman: Herbert Pincus
President: Andrew Pincus
Corporate Secretary: Susan Pincus
Estimated Sales:$5-10 Million
Number Employees: 20-49
Sq. footage: 40000

2365 Cardi Foods
1003 Sethcreek Drive
Fuquay Varina, NC 27526-5156   973-983-8818
   Fax: 973-627-6273   schwcscs@cs.com
Yeast extracts, kosher flavors
Vice President: Charles Schweizer
Estimated Sales:$500,000
Number Employees: 10-19
Number of Brands: 5
Number of Products: 10
Type of Packaging: Consumer, Food Service
Brands:
CARDI C

2366 Cardinal Meat Specialists
2396 Stanfield Road
Mississauga, ON L4Y 1S1
Canada   905-672-1411
   Fax: 905-672-0450   800-363-1439
Processor of hamburger patties and steaks
President: Mark Cator
COO: Bret Cator
Purchasing Manager: Scott Zies
Number Employees: 50-99
Type of Packaging: Food Service
Brands:
Cardinal Kettle
Roadhouse

2367 Cardinale Winery
P.O.Box 328
Oakville, CA 94562-0328   707-944-2807
   Fax: 707-944-5628   info@cardinale.com
   www.cardinale.com
Wines
Manager: Chantal Leruitte
Winemaker: Christopher Carpenter
Vineyard Manager: Pete Richmond
Estimated Sales:$20-50 Million
Number Employees: 50-99

2368 Care Ingredients
3141 W North Ave
Melrose Park, IL 60160-1108   708-450-3260
   Fax: 708-450-1034 www.kerryingredients.com
Processor of dry breading and baking mixes
Manager: Jim Braglia
Plant Manager: Jim Cisler
Estimated Sales:$20-50 Million
Number Employees: 100-249
Type of Packaging: Consumer, Food Service, Private Label, Bulk

2369 Cargill
15407 McGinty Rd W
Wayzata, MN 55391-2399   952-742-7575
   Fax: 952-742-7393   800-227-4455
   www.cargill.com
An international provider of food, agricultural and risk management products and services.
President: Dan Dye
Senior VP/CFO: David MacLennan
Corporate VP, Corporate Affairs: Bonnie Raquet
Number Employees: 10,000+
Parent Co: Cargill, Inc
Type of Packaging: Consumer, Food Service, Private Label, Bulk
Brands:
ANGUS PRIDE
BREAKFAST TAC-GO
CARMEL APPLE CINAMMON FRENCH TOAST
CERTIFIED ANGUS BEEF
CIRCLE T BEEF
COUNTRY CLASSIC
CULINARY EDGE
EGGS ASAP
ESL
EXCEL
EXCEL SUPREME
HONEYSUCKLE WHITE
JOBE'S
MEADOWLAND FARMS
OUR OWN KITCHEN
PECK/EXCEL
PRAIRIE GROVE FARMS
PREFERRED ANGUS BEEF
RANCHER'S REGISTRY ANGUS BEEF
RUMBA
SHADY BROOK FARMS
SKILLET FRITTATAS
SKILLET OMELETS
STERLING SILVER
STONESIDE PORK
SUN BREAK SCRAMBLED EGG MIX
SUNNY FRESH
SUNNY FRESH FREE
TENDER CHOICE
TENDER RIDGE ANGUS BEEF
THE BREAKFAST CLUB
TNT
VALLEY TRADITION BEEF
WIS-PAK FOODS

2370 Cargill Corn Milling
400 E Diehl Rd # 330
Naperville, IL 60563-3533   630-505-7788
   Fax: 630-505-7840   800-344-1633
   bill_gruber@cargill.com   www.cargill.com
Processor of liquid and dry dextrose corn syrups, high fructose and high maltose corn syrups, sodium and potassium citrates, sodium and potassium benzoates, citric acid, starches and CO2; exporter of citric products
VP: Pete Richter
Marketing Manager: Diane Pederson
Estimated Sales:$ 20 - 50 Million
Number Employees: 20-49
Parent Co: Cargill Foods
Type of Packaging: Bulk

2371 Cargill Dry Corn Ingredients
P.O.Box 550
Paris, IL 61944-0550   217-247-2143
   Fax: 217-463-1644   800-637-6481
Processor and exporter of milled corn products including crude oil, pre-gelatinized flour, meal, grits, masa, bran, etc
Manager: Rick Sims
Vice President: Mary Thompson
Research/Development Scientist: Dr. Ansui Xu
Quality Assurance Manager: Keith Smith
Number Employees: 250-499
Parent Co: Cargill Foods

2372 Cargill Dry Corn Ingredients
P.O.Box 550
Paris, IL 61944-0550   217-247-2143
   Fax: 217-463-1644   800-637-6481
   stephanie_gosnell@cargill.com   www.cargill.com
Corn grits, corn meal, corn flour
Manager: Rick Sims
R&D Scientist: Ansui Xu
Quality Assurance Manager: Keith Smith
Production Scheduler: Jeffrey Chandler
Estimated Sales:$50-100 Million
Number Employees: 100-249

2373 Cargill Flour Milling
12700 Whitewater Drive
Minneapolis, MN 55440   952-742-7575
   Fax: 612-742-7934   800-227-4455
   www.cargill.com
Processor and exporter of wheat flour
Chairman/CEO: Gregory Page
SVP/CFO: David MacLennan
Corporate VP R&D: Christopher Mallett
Corporate VP Human Resources: Peter Vrijsen
Corporate VP Operations: Thomas Hayes
*Estimated Sales:*K
Number Employees: 10,000+
Parent Co: Cargill Foods
Type of Packaging: Consumer, Food Service, Private Label, Bulk

2374 (HQ)Cargill Foods
P.O.Box 9300
Minneapolis, MN 55440-9300   952-742-7575
   Fax: 780-962-0862   800-227-4455
   info@cargill.com   www.cargill.com
Manufacturer grain, cotton and sugar. Cargill Foods has acquired Degussa AG's food ingredients business. Also; in talks is to buy Intercontinental Specialty Fats SDN, a Malaysian based palm oil refinery
Chairman/CEO: Warren Staley
Vice Chairman: Robert Lumpkins
President/COO: Gregory Page
CEO: Gregory R Page
Estimated Sales:$70 Million
Number Employees: 10,000+
Type of Packaging: Food Service

2375 Cargill Foods
505 S Old Missouri Road
Springdale, AR 72764-4715   479-750-6816
   www.honeysucklewhite.com
Turkey products
President: John O'Carroll
Controller: Mike Peirson
Director Sales/Marketing: Lin Lauve
Operations Manager: Andy Southerly
Estimated Sales:$ 10 - 20 Million
Number Employees: 10-19
Type of Packaging: Private Label
Brands:
HONEYSUCKLE WHITE
MEDALLION
PLANTATION
RIVERSIDE

2376 Cargill Juice Products
100 E 6th Street
Frostproof, FL 33843-2300   863-635-2211
   Fax: 863-635-8180   800-227-4455
   jon_hysell@cargill.com   www.carillfoods.com
Juice and juice ingredients, essential oils and orange essence
President: Martin Dudley
VP: Tom Abrahamson
Sales Director: Pat Rain
Estimated Sales:$100-500 Million
Number Employees: 100-249
Type of Packaging: Private Label

2377 Cargill Meat Solutions
480 Coop Dr
Timberville, VA 22853-9527   540-896-7041
   Fax: 540-896-6625 www.cargill.com

Processor and exporter of cooked turkey and chicken products including salami, bologna and ham; also, breasts
  Plant Manager: Wesley Carter
  Operations Manager: Milt McPike
  Purchasing Agent: George Miller
Estimated Sales: $300,000-500,000
Number Employees: 1-4
Sq. footage: 112708
Parent Co: Rocco
Type of Packaging: Consumer, Food Service, Private Label
Other Locations:
  Rocco Quality Foods
  Edinburg VA

2378 Cargill Meats
P.O.Box 2006
Milwaukee, WI 53201-2006   414-645-6500
          Fax: 414-645-6762 800-558-4242
          www.cargill.com
Manufacturer, importer and exporter of boxed and processed beef
  President: Bill Rupp
  Controller: Richard Cundy
  VP R&D: Thomas Rourke PhD
  VP Public Affairs: Robert Segel
Estimated Sales: $100-500 Million
Number Employees: 1,000-4,999
Parent Co: Excel Corporation
Type of Packaging: Consumer, Food Service
Brands:
  BERNHARDT PECK
  COUNTRY CLASSICS
  DELI RITE
  EMMBER CLASSIC
  EMMBER COUNTRY CLASSIC
  EMMBER COUNTRY MAGIC
  EMMBER DELI RITE
  EMMBER FAT FREE LEAN 'N TENDER
  EMMBER HEARTY CLASSIC
  EMMBER LEAN 'N TENDER
  EMMBER OUR OWN KITCHEN
  EMMBER REDI-ROAST
  EMMBER THICK 'N TENDER
  EMMBER TONIGHT'S CHOICE
  HEARTY CLASSICS
  OUR OWN KITCHEN
  PECK MEAT PACKING
  THICK N' TENDER
  TONIGHT'S CHOICE

2379 Cargill Refined Oils
PO Box 5625
Minneapolis, MN 55440-5625   952-742-6782
          Fax: 208-522-0794 800-323-6232
          willie_loh@cargill.com
          www.clearvalleyoils.com
Salad and cooking oils, frying and baking shortenings, soybean, winterized soybean, corn, cottonseed, canola, creamy liquid soybean and canola oil, pan and grill oil, peanut oil, all-purpose, animal and vegetable blends, and flavoredroll-in
  Sales: Stephanie Quah

2380 Cargill Specialty Oils
P.O.Box 9300
Minneapolis, MN 55440-9300   952-742-7575
          Fax: 952-742-5503 800-851-8331
          vickie_lacroix@cargill.com www.cargill.com
Manufacturer of specialty cooking and ingredient oils
  CEO: Gregory R Page
  Marketing Director: Connie Tobin
Estimated Sales: K
Number Employees: 10,000+
Parent Co: Cargill Foods
Type of Packaging: Food Service, Bulk
Brands:
  Clear Valley Oils
  Elitra Premium Vegtable Oils
  Odessey Oils
  Popwise Oils

2381 Cargill Sweeteners
P.O.Box 5621
Minneapolis, MN 55440-5621   952-984-8280
          Fax: 952-984-3256 800-227-4455
          cargillfoods@cargill.com www.cargillsalt.com

Dry sweeteners, food starches, high fructose corn syrup
  President: Mike Venker
  President/COO: Gregory Page
  Senior VP/Director Corporate Affairs: Robin Johnson
  C.V.P. Public Affairs: Bonnie Raquet
Estimated Sales: less than $ 500,000
Number Employees: 10,000+
Number of Products: 19

2382 Cargill Texturizing Solutions
308 6th Avenue SE
Cedar Rapids, IA 52401   877-650-7080
  Fax: 319-399-6170 For Cultures & Enzymes:
    800-342-5724; For Hydrocolloids & Blends:
          800-241-9485
          www.cargilltexturizing.com
Developer and marketer of specialty ingredient systems, including native and modified food starches, soy flour, pectin, maltodextrins, dextrins, lecithin, cultures, enzymes, stabilizer blends, hydrocolloids, liquid vitamins for foodand pharmaceutical applications. Applications include bakery, beverage, confectionery, dairy, meats, convenience foods, and snacks/cereals/bars.
  President: Ralph Apple
  R&D: Joe Holtwick
  Marketing: Jim Kubczak
  Sales: Andy Dederich
  Operations: Bernard Cerles
  Plant Manager: Mike Rizor
Number Employees: 100-249
Parent Co: Cargill Inc
Type of Packaging: Food Service, Bulk
Brands:
  ActiStar
  Amylogel
  Aubygum
  Battercrisp
  Biogarde
  Cargill Dry MD
  Cargill Dry Set
  Cargill Gel
  Cargill Set
  Cargill Tex
  Clean Set
  Cream Gel
  Cream Tex
  Daritech
  Deli Tex
  EZ Fill
  Em Cap
  Em Tex
  Emulfluid
  Emulpur
  Flanogen
  HiForm
  Polar Tex
  Prolia
  Prosante
  Pulp Tex
  Salioca
  Satiagel
  Satialgine
  Satiaxane
  Stabi Tex
  Topcithin
  Unipectine
  ViscoGum

2383 Cargill Vegetable Oils
5858 Park Ave
Minneapolis, MN 55417-3120   612-378-0551
          Fax: 612-742-5503 www.crcmeetings.com
Processor of vegetable and soybean oils; also, soybean meal
  Owner: Lisa Cargill
  National Accounts Sales: Bill Bohmer
Estimated Sales: $300,000-500,000
Number Employees: 1-4
Parent Co: Cargill Foods
Type of Packaging: Bulk

2384 Cargill Worldwide Acidulants
400 E Diehl Rd # 330
Naperville, IL 60563-3533   630-505-7788
          Fax: 630-505-7840 800-344-1633
          tim_bauer@cargill.com www.cargill.com
Food acidulants
  VP: Pete Richter
  Director Sales/Marketing: Tim Bauer

Estimated Sales: $100-500 Million
Number Employees: 20-49
Parent Co: Cargill Foods
Type of Packaging: Bulk

2385 Caribbean Coffee Company
116 E Yanonali St
Santa Barbara, CA 93101-1823   805-962-3201
          Fax: 805-962-5074 info@caribbeancoffee.com
          www.caribbeancoffee.com
Specialty coffee and tea
  President: John Goerke
  Marketing Manager: Putnam Fairbanks
Estimated Sales: $20-50 Million
Number Employees: 10-19
Type of Packaging: Private Label

2386 Caribbean Cookie Company
515 Central Drive
Suite 103
Virginia Beach, VA 23454-5274   757-631-6767
          Fax: 757-631-1725 800-326-5200
          jumbia@norfold.infi.net
          www.caribbeancookie.com
Gourmet cookies
  President: Charles Phelps
  Marketing Director: Leo Palomo
Estimated Sales: $1-2.5 Million
Number Employees: 10-19

2387 Caribbean Distributors
43 Penwood Road
Brentwood, MD 20722   301-403-2929
          Fax: 301-403-2931
  President: Miguel Cangas, Jr.

2388 Caribbean Food Delights
117 Route 303 - A
Tappan, NY 10983   845-398-3000
          Fax: 845-398-2316
          info@caribbeanfooddelights.com
          www.jerkqzine.com
Manufacturer and exporter of Jamaican baked goods including breads, fruit cakes and buns; also, beef, chicken and vegetable patties, jerk chicken, sausage, curried goat, rice, peas, etc
  President, CEO: Vincent HoSang
  CEO: Vincent Hosang
Estimated Sales: $10-20 Million
Number Employees: 20-49
Sq. footage: 60000
Parent Co: Royal Caribbean Bakery
Type of Packaging: Consumer, Food Service, Private Label, Bulk

2389 Caribbean Food Products
1936 2nd Avenue N
Jacksonville Beach, FL 32250-2734   904-246-0149
          Fax: 904-246-7273 trinidad@bellsouth.net
Hot sauces
  President: Mary Jane Barnes
  CFO: Robert Barnes
  VP Marketing: Carl Nelson
Estimated Sales: $2.5-5 Million
Number Employees: 10-19
Brands:
  Isle of Palms Salad Dressings
  Tobago Keys Gourmet
  Trinidad Gourmet Sauces

2390 Caribbean Products
3624 Falls Rd
Baltimore, MD 21211-1847   410-235-7700
          Fax: 410-235-1513 www.loyoladonsalumni.com
Manufacturer and also processor and packager of beef and pork products.
  President: Brian Hartman
Estimated Sales: $ 13 Million
Number Employees: 20-49
Type of Packaging: Consumer, Food Service

2391 Caribou Coffee Company
3900 Lake Breeze Ave
Brooklyn Center, MN 55429-3921   763-592-2200
          Fax: 763-592-2300 888-227-4268
          www.cariboucoffee.com
Coffee
  Co Chairman/Founder: Rosalyn Mallet
  CEO: Michael Coles
  CFO: George Mileusnic
  CEO: Michael Tattersfield
  VP R&D: Eddie Boyle
  VP Marketing: Chris Toal
  Sales Director: Henry Stein

Estimated Sales:$10-100 Million
Number Employees: 5,000-9,999

2392 (HQ)Carl Buddig & Company
950 West 175th Street
Homewood, IL 60430   708-798-0900
Fax: 708-798-3178 800-621-0868
buddigconsumers@buddig.com
www.buddig.com
Processor and exporter of luncheon meats including
chipped beef, ham, turkey, chicken, pastrami and
turkey ham; also, specialty sausage and meat snacks
President: John Buddig
CEO: Robert Buddig
Executive VP: Tom Budding
Quality Control: Joe Buchanan
Estimated Sales:$200-250 Million
Number Employees: 800
Number of Brands: 6
Type of Packaging: Consumer, Food Service, Private Label, Bulk
Brands:
BUDDIG ORIGINAL
BUDDIG PREMIUM LEAN SLICES
BUDDIG VALUE PACK

2393 Carl Colteryahn Dairy
1601 Brownsville Rd
Pittsburgh, PA 15210-3903   412-881-1408
Fax: 412-881-0460
Milk, cream and juices
Owner: Carl Colteryahn
VP, General Manager: Carl Colteryahn III
Operations Manager: Shaun Michael
Plant Manager: Shawn Niziol
Estimated Sales:$5-10 Million
Number Employees: 20-49

2394 Carl Rittberger Sr.
1900 Lutz Ln
Zanesville, OH 43701-9260   740-452-2767
Fax: 740-452-6001 info@rittbergermeats.com
www.rittbergermeats.com
Processor of beef and pork
President: Andy Rittberger
VP: George Rittberger
Estimated Sales:$10-20 Million
Number Employees: 20-49
Type of Packaging: Consumer, Bulk

2395 Carl Streit & Son Company
P.O.Box 157
Neptune, NJ 07754-0157   732-775-0803
Fax: 732-775-2274
Processor and wholesaler/distributor of poultry, Italian sausage and special cuts of beef, lamb, veal and
pork
Owner: Jim Robinson Jr Jr
VP: Judith Robinson
Estimated Sales:$10-20 Million
Number Employees: 5-9
Sq. footage: 4000
Brands:
Allen
Hatfield

2396 Carl Venezia Meats
1007 Germantown Pike
Plymouth Meeting, PA 19462-2449 610-239-6750
Fax: 610-239-6751 www.carlveneziameats.com
Processor and packer of meat
President: Carl Venezia
Sales Manager: Don Venezia
Estimated Sales:$500,000
Number Employees: 1-4

2397 Carla's Pasta
50 Talbot Ln
South Windsor, CT 06074-5401   860-436-4042
Fax: 860-436-4073 800-957-2782
info@carlaspasta.com www.carlaspasta.com
Processor of frozen pastas including ravioli and lasagna as well as sauces
President: Carla Squatrito
Director Sales: Sandro Squatrito
Manager, Productions: Sergio Squatrito
Estimated Sales:$21.20 Million
Number Employees: 50-99
Sq. footage: 13000
Type of Packaging: Food Service, Private Label, Bulk

2398 Carlisle Cereal Company
PO Box 2775
Bismarck, ND 58502-2775   701-222-3531
Fax: 701-222-3531 800-809-6018
chuck@hometownstars.com
www.hometownstars.com
Cereal
President: Charles Fleming
Estimated Sales:$1 Million
Number Employees: 5-9
Type of Packaging: Private Label
Brands:
Hometown Stars

2399 Carlson Vineyards
461 35 Rd
Palisade, CO 81526-9518   970-464-5554
Fax: 970-464-5442 888-464-5554
www.carlsonvineyards.com
Wines
President: Parker Carlson
Estimated Sales:$1-2.5 Million
Number Employees: 5-9

2400 Carlson Vitamins
15 W College Dr
Arlington Hts, IL 60004-1985   847-255-1600
Fax: 847-255-1605 888-234-5656
carlson@carlsonlabs.com www.carlsonlabs.com
Full line of nutritional food supplements and fish
oils
President: John Carlson
CEO: Susan Carlson
CFO: Trish Lange
Vice President: Robert Meyer
Quality Control: Melissa Wilson
Marketing Coordinator: Carilyn Anderson
Sales Director: Vicki Accardi
Public Relations: Kirsten Meyer
Operations Manager: Robert Meyer
Production Manager: Michael Anderson
Purchasing Manager: Lindy Eck
Estimated Sales:$ 50 - 100 Million
Number Employees: 100-249
Number of Brands: 2
Number of Products: 275
Sq. footage: 40000

2401 Carlton Farms
10600 NW Westside Rd
Carlton, OR 97111   503-852-7166
Fax: 503-852-6263 800-932-0946
www.carltonfarms.com
Processor of meats
President, CEO: John Duyn
Director Food Safety & Food Quality: Jacob Burns
Sales Manager: Forrest Peterson
Plant Manager: Bill Orton
Estimated Sales:$50-100 Million
Number Employees: 50-99

2402 Carmadhy's Foods
282 Marsland Drive
Waterloo, ON N2J 3Z1
Canada   519-746-0551
Fax: 519-746-0280 carol@carmadhys.ca
www.carmadhys.ca
Processor of flavored popcorn including caramel,
butter, cheese, white cheddar, pizza, barbecue,
ranch, salt and vinegar, sour cream and onion, dill
pickle, jalapeno, custom packaging and popcorn
seasoning
President: Carol Lang
Number Employees: 5-9
Sq. footage: 4500
Type of Packaging: Consumer, Private Label, Bulk
Brands:
Country Style
Olde Fashioned

2403 Carmel Meat/Specialty Foods
3345 Paul Davis Dr
Marina, CA 93933-2242   831-883-3555
Fax: 831-883-3599 800-298-5823
www.sierrameat.com
Processor of lamb, beef, poultry, veal, game and seafood
Manager: Jim Pryor
VP Marketing: Janetta Lucas
VP Sales: Bob Furter
Estimated Sales:$50-100 Million
Number Employees: 50-99
Type of Packaging: Food Service

2404 Carmela Vineyards
P.O.Box 795
Glenns Ferry, ID 83623   208-366-2539
Fax: 208-366-2458 info@carmelavineyards.com
www.carmelawinery.com
Wines
Manager: Neil Glancey
Winemaker: Neil Glancy
Estimated Sales:$1-2.5 Million
Number Employees: 20-49

2405 Carmela's Gourmet
415 English Ave
Monterey, CA 93940-3810   831-373-6291
Fax: 831-375-5313
carmelasgourmet@comcast.net
www.carmelasgourmet.com
Salad dressings
Owner: Carmela Cantisani
Co-Owner: Carmela Cantisani
*Estimated Sales:*Under $500,000
Number Employees: 1-4
Type of Packaging: Private Label
Brands:
Carmela's

2406 Carmelita Provisions Company
2901 W Floral Dr
Monterey Park, CA 91754-3626   323-262-6751
Fax: 323-262-3503 www.carmelitachorizo.com
Processor of pigs' feet including crackling and pickled; also, chorizo
Owner: Mario Lopez
Estimated Sales:$ .5 - 1 million
Number Employees: 20-49
Type of Packaging: Consumer, Food Service

2407 (HQ)Carmi Flavor & Fragrance Company
P.O.Box 911400
Los Angeles, CA 90091-1237   323-888-9240
Fax: 323-888-9339 800-421-9647
sales@carmiflavors.com www.carmiflavors.com
Manufacturer of high quality natural and artificial
flavors in liquid or powder form; supplier of packaging products.
President: Eliot Carmi
CEO: Frank Carmi
Account Manager: Jennifer Montgomery
Public Relations: Jasmine Lee
Plant Manager: Roger Speakman
Purchasing Director: Judy Montgomery
Estimated Sales:$5-10 Million
Number Employees: 20-49
Number of Brands: 1
Number of Products: 500
Sq. footage: 30000
Type of Packaging: Private Label, Bulk
Other Locations:
Carmi Flavor & Fragrance
Port Coquitlam, Canada
Carmi Flavor & Fragrance
Waverly LA
Brands:
CARMI FLAVORS
FLAVOR DEPOT

2408 Carmine's Bakery
2100 Country Club Road
Sanford, FL 32771-4051   407-324-1200
Fax: 407-324-1209 marlafrede@aol.com
Baked goods

2409 Carneros Creek Winery
P.O.Box 6828
Napa, CA 94581-1828   707-253-9464
Fax: 707-253-9465 wineinfo@carneroscreek.com
www.mahoneyvineyards.com
Wines
President: Francis Mahoney
Winemaker: Ken Foster
Vice President: Scot Rich
Sales Director: Hadden Guridie
Plant Manager: Greg Opitz
Estimated Sales:$5-10 Million
Number Employees: 10-19
Type of Packaging: Bulk
Brands:
CARNEROS
CARNEROS CREEK
COTE DE CARNEROS
FLEUR DE CARNEROS

2410 Carnival Brands
535 S Clark St
New Orleans, LA 70119-7007   504-734-8851
    Fax: 504-734-5886 800-925-2774
gumboking@aol.com   www.carnivalbrands.com
Processor of French bisques, alligator sauce
piquante, dry seasoning, boneless stuffed chicken,
sauce mix and seafood entrees including gumbo,
crab and shrimp cakes, shrimp Creole and crawfish
etouffee
    Owner: Jean Pigeon
    Marketing: E Alexander Stafford
    Public Relations: Simone Rathle
Estimated Sales: $1-2.5 Million
Number Employees: 1-4
Sq. footage: 7000
Type of Packaging: Consumer, Food Service
Brands:
    Baby Cakes
    Carnival Cajun Classics
    Chef Creole
    Zipp

2411 Caro Foods
2324 Bayou Blue Rd
Houma, LA 70364-4301   985-872-1483
    Fax: 985-876-0825 www.carofoods.com
Fresh meat and produce, canned and dry goods.
    President: Ricky Thibodaux
    Human Resources: Mike Latour
Number Employees: 100-249
Parent Co: Performance Food Group Company
Brands:
    HERITAGE OVENS

2412 Carob Tree
1008 N Santa Anita Ave
Arcadia, CA 91006-2330   626-445-0215
    Fax: 626-445-0215 thecarobtree@earthlink.net
Natural groceries and vitamins
    Owner: Hyun Chung
Estimated Sales: $160,000
Number Employees: 1-4
Type of Packaging: Consumer, Bulk

2413 Carol Hall's Hot PepperJelly
330 N Main St
Fort Bragg, CA 95437-3406   707-961-1899
    Fax: 707-961-0879 866-737-7379
hall@mcn.org   www.hotpepperjelly.com
Jams and condiments
    President: Carol Hall
    CFO: Albert Hall
    Marketing Director: John Temples
    Production Manager: Bill Hall
Estimated Sales: $1-2.5 Million
Number Employees: 5-9
Type of Packaging: Private Label

2414 Carol Lee Products
PO Box 3314
Lawrence, KS 66046-0314   785-842-5489
Processor of blended mixes for bakery products in-
cluding yeast raised and cake doughnuts, danish,
breads and cookies
    President: O Lee Scott
    VP: Agnes Scott
Number Employees: 4
Sq. footage: 9330
Type of Packaging: Consumer
Brands:
    Carol Lee

2415 Carol's Country Cuisine
2546 Warm Springs Road
Glen Ellen, CA 95442-8712   707-996-1124
    Fax: 707-996-1124 carolco@vom.com
        www.carolscountrycuisine.com
Marinades, dressings, sauces
    Partner: Carol Frankenfield
    Sales Director: Susan Wise
    Production Manager: Carol Frankenfield
Estimated Sales: $5-10 Million
Number Employees: 5-9
Type of Packaging: Private Label

2416 Carole's Cheesecake Company
1272 Castlefield Avenue
Toronto, ON M6B 1G3
Canada   416-256-0000
Fax: 416-256-0001 info@carolescheesecake.com
        www.carolescheesecake.com

Processor of cheesecakes including praline, lemon,
blueberry, raspberry and strawberry; also, pies,
low-fat salad dressings, pasta sauces and toppings
for cakes and ice cream; exporter of cakes and salad
dressings; vegetarian soups
    President: Carole Ogus
    CFO: Alexander Ogus
    Executive VP: Michael Ogus
    General Manager: Edison Carbajal
    Production: Maria Arias
Estimated Sales: $1-5 Million
Number Employees: 30
Number of Brands: 2
Number of Products: 160
Sq. footage: 15000
Type of Packaging: Consumer, Food Service, Pri-
vate Label, Bulk
Brands:
    CAROLE'S
    CAROLE'S TOPS
    POSITIVELY BLUEBERRY
    POSITIVELY PRALINES
    POSITIVELY STRAWBERRY

**2417 Carolina Atlantic Seafood
Enterprises**
PO Box 158
Beaufort, NC 28516-0158   252-504-2663
    Fax: 252-726-7097 case@mail.clis.com
Processor of frozen seafood
    President: Doug Brady
    CEO: Walter C Brady
Estimated Sales: $5-10 Million
Number Employees: 10-19
Type of Packaging: Private Label
Brands:
    Carolina Atlantic Seafood

**2418 (HQ)Carolina Beverage
Corporation**
1413 Jake Alexander Blvd S
Salisbury, NC 28146-8359   704-637-5881
    Fax: 704-633-7491 custserv@cheerwine.com
        www.cheerwine.com
Processor of syrups and beverage concentrates; ex-
porter of soft drinks and concentrates; whole-
saler/distributor of soft drinks and water
    President: Cliff Ritchie
    VP Marketing: Tom Barlinda
    Director Sales: Jim Lelona
    VP Operations: David Swaim
Estimated Sales: $ 10 - 20 Million
Number Employees: 20-49
Sq. footage: 25000
Parent Co: Cheerwine & Diet Cheerwine
Type of Packaging: Consumer
Other Locations:
    Carolina Beverage Corp.
    Hickory NC
    Carolina Beverage Corp.
    Greenville SC
Brands:
    CHEERWINE
    CHEERWINE SOFT DRINK
    DIET CHEERWINE
    SAVAGE ENERGY

2419 Carolina Blueberry Association
11375 Us Highway 701 N
Garland, NC 28441   910-588-4220
        Fax: 910-588-4093
    dennis@carolinablueberry.com
        www.carolinablueberry.com
Manufacturer of fresh and frozen blueberries
    General Manager: Dennis Harrell
    Process Manager: Steve Kuepker
Estimated Sales: $50-100 Million
Number Employees: 5-9
Type of Packaging: Consumer, Food Service, Bulk
Brands:
    BONNIE BLUE

2420 Carolina Brewery
460 W Franklin St
Chapel Hill, NC 27516-2313   919-942-1800
    Fax: 919-942-1809 www.carolinabrewery.com
Processor of ale, stout and lager
    Owner: Robert Poitras
    Co-Owner: Chris Rice
Estimated Sales: $2.5-5 Million
Number Employees: 50-99
Sq. footage: 8000
Type of Packaging: Consumer, Food Service, Bulk

Brands:
    Copperline Amber
    Franklin Street
    Old North State

2421 Carolina By-Products Company
P.O. Box 3588
Winchester, VA 22604-2586   540-877-2590
    Fax: 540-877-3215 www.valleyproteins.com
Processor and exporter of rendering meats including
poultry and bone meal; also, by-products
    President: David Evans
Estimated Sales: $ 50 - 100 Million
Number Employees: 20-49
Parent Co: Valley Proteins, Inc.
Type of Packaging: Food Service, Bulk

2422 Carolina Classic Catfish
P.O.Box 10
Ayden, NC 28513-0010   252-746-2818
    Fax: 252-746-3947 www.cccatfish.com
Processor of fresh and frozen catfish
    President: Robert Mayo
    Sales Manager: Doug Doering
    Sales Manager: Jeff Betcher
    General Manager: Mike McCready
    Controller: Mark Lomis
Estimated Sales: $20-50 Million
Number Employees: 100-249
Type of Packaging: Consumer, Food Service
Brands:
    Carolina Classics

2423 Carolina Cracker
P.O.Box 374
Garner, NC 27529-0374   919-779-6899
    Fax: 919-779-6899 www.carolinacracker.com
Manufacturer of nut crackers for soft shell nuts,
shelled pecans in bulk
    President: Dot Woodruff
    CEO: Harold Woodruff
Estimated Sales: $1-2.5 Million
Number Employees: 10-19
Number of Brands: 3
Sq. footage: 1
Type of Packaging: Bulk
Brands:
    The Carolina Cracker

2424 Carolina Culinary
1964 Old Dunbar Road
West Columbia, SC 29172-3922   803-739-8920
        Fax: 843-739-8920
Processor of value-added poultry and cooked
bone-in, breaded and roasted chicken
    President: Sheldon Phillips
    Manager: Ellen Burgin
    Manager: Bob Harris
Estimated Sales: $50 Million
Number Employees: 300

2425 Carolina Cupboard
505 Eno St
Hillsborough, NC 27278-2357   919-245-1654
    Fax: 800-646-1118 800-400-3441
customerservice@carolinacupboard.com
        www.southernseason.com
Cheesestraws, BBQ sauces, lemon drops, cookies,
jams and jellies
    Owner: Michael Barefoot
    Marketing Director: Deborah Miller
Brands:
    Carolina Cupboard

2426 Carolina Fine Snack Foods
209 Citation Ct
Greensboro, NC 27409-9026   336-605-0773
        Fax: 336-605-0721
Nutrional snacks
    President: Phil Kosak
Estimated Sales: $2.5-5 Million
Number Employees: 5-9

2427 Carolina Foods
1807 S Tryon St
Charlotte, NC 28203-4471   704-333-9812
        Fax: 704-940-0040 800-234-0441

Processor of baked goods including sweet rolls, fresh and frozen fried pies, yeast raised doughnuts and cakes, fruit turnovers and pie dough.
President: Paul Scarborough
Marketing Director: Paul Deer
Plant Manager/Operations: Bob Schumacher
General Manager: Kent Byrom
Purchasing Manager: Joanna Houchins
Estimated Sales: $20-50 Million
Number Employees: 250-499
Sq. footage: 110000
Type of Packaging: Consumer, Food Service, Private Label
Brands:
DUCHESS
O'BOY
SUNBEAM

2428 Carolina Ingredients
1595 Cedar Line Drive
Rock Hill, SC 29730   803-323-6550
Fax: 803-323-6535   cs@carolinaingredients.com
www.carolinaingredients.com
ingredients
President: Doug Meyer-Cuno
Sales/Marketing Direcotr: Allen Heavey
Production Manager: Richard Dawes
Purchasing Director: Glenn Shishido

2429 Carolina Packers
P.O.Box 1109
Smithfield, NC 27577-1109   919-934-6183
Fax: 919-989-6794   800-682-7675
info@carolinapackers.com
www.carolinapackers.com
Processor of hot dogs, bologna and smoked sausage and ham.
President: John Johnes Jr
Controller: Linwood Thornton II
VP: Hilton Byrd
Plant Manager: Johnny Hayes
Estimated Sales: $20-50 Million
Number Employees: 50-99
Type of Packaging: Consumer
Brands:
BRIGHTLEAF

2430 Carolina Pride Products
24488 Highway 561
Enfield, NC 27823   252-445-3154
Fax: 252-445-1033
Processor of sweet potatoes
President: Jake Taylor
Estimated Sales: $1-2.5 Million
Number Employees: 1-4
Brands:
Carolina Pride

2431 Carolina Products
1990 Hood Rd
Greer, SC 29650-1011   864-879-3084
Fax: 864-877-5736   cliffstar@cliffstar.com
www.cliffstar.com
Processor of bottled apple juice
President, CEO: Sean McGirr
Quality Control: Karen O'Keefe
Sales: Monica Consonery
VP Human Resources: Kevin Sanvidge
Plant Manager: Chris Neilson
Purchasing: Chris Roberts
Estimated Sales: $10-20 Million
Number Employees: 20-49
Sq. footage: 29000
Parent Co: Cliffstar
Type of Packaging: Consumer, Private Label
Brands:
CAROLINA GOLD

2432 Carolina Seafoods
P.O.Box 396
Mc Clellanville, SC 29458-0396   843-887-3713
Fax: 843-887-3318
Manufacturer and importer of seafood including shrimp, oysters and clams
President: Rutledge Leland
Estimated Sales: $5-10 Million
Number Employees: 10-19
Sq. footage: 10000
Type of Packaging: Consumer

2433 Carolina Treet
2957 N Kerr Ave
Wilmington, NC 28405-8678   910-762-1950
Fax: 910-762-1438   800-616-6344
info@carolinatreet.com   www.carolinatreet.com
Processor and importer of barbecue sauce, condiments, syrups, brewed tea, bar mixes and beverage concentrates
President: Joe King
Vice President: Lenwood King
General Manager: Allen Finberg
Estimated Sales: $2.5-5 Million
Number Employees: 10-19
Number of Brands: 5
Number of Products: 20
Sq. footage: 20000
Type of Packaging: Consumer, Food Service, Private Label, Bulk
Brands:
AUNT BERTIE'S
CAROLINA TREET

2434 Carolina Turkeys
P.O.Box 589
Mt Olive, NC 28365-0589   919-658-6743
Fax: 919-658-5865   800-523-4559
jcoleman@carolinaturkeys.com
www.carolinaturkeys.com
Manufacturer and exporter of fresh and frozen turkey
President/CEO: C Daniel Blackshear
CFO: Ed Kascuta
CEO: Keith Shoemaker
Estimated Sales: $330 Million
Number Employees: 1,000-4,999
Type of Packaging: Consumer, Food Service
Brands:
CAROLINA TURKEYS

2435 Carolyn Candies
PO Box 120861
Clermont, FL 34712-0861   352-394-8555
Fax: 877-394-3452

2436 Carolyn's Caribbean Heat
283 Boot Road
Malvern, PA 19355-3315   610-647-0336
Processor of hot sauces and condiments; also, importer of sauces, condiments and ingredients for production
Owner: Carolyn Thomas
Sales Manager: Robert Thomas
Number Employees: 1-4
Sq. footage: 500
Brands:
Carolyn's Caribbean Heat

2437 Carolyn's Gourmet
PO Box 1221
Concord, MA 01742-1221   800-656-2940
Fax: 978-371-0639   800-656-2940
info@40parklake.com   www.40parklake.com
Pecans, walnuts, peanuts, English toffee, chocolate bars
President: Hans van Putten
Executive VP: Tracey van Putten
Sales: Jennifer Bennett
Estimated Sales: $5-10 Million
Number Employees: 5-9
Parent Co: 40ParkLake, LLC
Type of Packaging: Consumer, Private Label, Bulk
Brands:
TULIP

2438 Carothers Research Laboratories
2438 Corunna Rd
Flint, MI 48503-3359   810-235-2055
Edible fats and oils
Manager: Marie Killein
Estimated Sales: $5-9.9 Million
Number Employees: 1-4

2439 Carousel Cakes
11 Seeger Dr
Nanuet, NY 10954-2323   845-627-2323
Fax: 845-627-0258   800-659-2253
www.carouselcakes.com
Processor of fresh and frozen cakes, mousse, cheesecakes and pies, kosher pdairy and non-dairy products
Owner: David Finkelstein
Estimated Sales: $500,000-$1 Million
Number Employees: 10-19
Type of Packaging: Consumer, Food Service

Brands:
Carousel Cakes

2440 Carousel Candies
5130 W 26th Street
Cicero, IL 60804-2993   708-656-1552
Fax: 708-656-0010   888-656-1552
info@carouselcandy.com
www.carouselcandy.com
Processor of candy including caramel, caramel apples, caramel sauce, chocolates, chocolate covered strawberries, gift boxes, gift baskets, assortments, bulk, and special occasion gift bags for holidays and special events.
President/CEO: Mary Jane Silvestri
Vice President: Andy Silvestri
Estimated Sales: $2.5-5 Million
Number Employees: 10-19
Type of Packaging: Food Service, Bulk
Brands:
CAROUSEL

2441 Carr Cheese Factory/GileCheese Company
116 N Main St
Cuba City, WI 53807-1538   608-744-8455
Fax: 608-744-3457
Cheese and cheese products
Owner: John Gile
Owner: Diane Gile
Estimated Sales: $2.5-5 Million
Number Employees: 1-4

2442 Carr Valley Cheese Company
S3797 County Road G
La Valle, WI 53941-9738   608-986-2781
Fax: 608-986-2906   800-462-7258
www.carrvalleychesse.com
Monterey jack, cheddar and colby cheese
President: Sid Cook
Estimated Sales: $10-20 Million
Number Employees: 10-19

2443 Carrabassett Coffee Roasters
P.O.Box 197
Kingfield, ME 04947-0197   207-265-2326
Fax: 207-265-3527   888-292-2326
info@carrabassettcoffee.com
www.carrabassettcoffee.com
Roaster and wholesaler of coffee
President: Tom Hildreth
CEO: Steve Skaling
Estimated Sales: $450,000
Number Employees: 5-9
Number of Brands: 35
Number of Products: 1
Sq. footage: 1800
Type of Packaging: Bulk
Brands:
35

2444 Carriage Charles
196 Newton St
Fredonia, NY 14063-1354   716-673-1000
Fax: 716-679-3444   800-828-8915
www.carriagehousecos.com
Sauces and dressings
Chairman: William Stiritz
President, Co-CEO: David Skarie
CEO: David P Skarie
Purchasing Manager: Mark Miller
Estimated Sales: $50-100 Million
Number Employees: 1,000-4,999
Parent Co: Ralcorp
Brands:
BEAZUR
FARM KING
RED WING

2445 Carriage House Companies
196 Newton St
Fredonia, NY 14063-1354   716-673-1000
Fax: 716-679-3444   800-828-8915
klanacm@carriagehousecos.com
www.carriagehousecos.com

Manufacturer and exporter of preserves and jellies, peanut butter, pasta sauce, salad dressing, table syrup, flavored syrup, barbecue sauce, mexican sauce, steak sauce/marinade, and cocktail sauce.
President/CEO: David Skarie
CFO: Dan Zoellner
CEO: David P Skarie
Quality Control: Joe Woloszyn
EVP Sales/Marketing: Mary Jane Knight
VP Marketing: Mike Klanac
Corporate VP/Director Human Resources: Jack Owczarczak
Estimated Sales: $389.2 Million
Number Employees: 1,000-4,999
Parent Co: Ralcorp
Type of Packaging: Consumer, Food Service, Private Label, Bulk
Other Locations:
Carriage House Companies - Plant Dunkirk NY
Carriage House Companies - Plant Streator IL
Carriage House Companies - Plant Buckner KY

2446 Carriage House Foods
1131 Dayton Ave
Ames, IA 50010-6408   515-232-2273
Fax: 515-232-3003 www.carriagehousefoods.com
Processor of frozen meat products
Primary Contact Person: Ryan Mallo
Estimated Sales: $ 10 - 20 Million
Number Employees: 20-49
Type of Packaging: Consumer, Food Service, Private Label
Brands:
Carriage House

2447 Carrie's Chocolates
9216-63 Avenue
Edmonton, AB T6E 0G3
Canada   780-435-7900
                             877-778-2462
carrie@compusmart.ab.ca
www.candybarwrapper.ca
Processor and exporter of handmade novelty and gift chocolates, promotional bars, and wedding candy
Owner: Carrie MacKenzie
Number Employees: 2
Sq. footage: 450
Type of Packaging: Consumer, Food Service, Private Label, Bulk

2448 Carriere Foods Inc
8615 Boul St Laurent
#200
Montreal, QC H2P 2M9
Canada   514-384-4281
                             Fax: 514-384-7992
marketing@carrierefoods.com
www.carrierefoods.com
Manufacturer and exporter of frozen and canned vegetables and fruits including peas, waxed beans, chick peas, green beans, asparagus and corn, dried beans, blueberries, cranberries, rasberries, rhubarb, strawberries, soups and sauces;importer of asparagus, carrots and spinach
President: Marcel Ostiguy
Number Employees: 990perm 180
Type of Packaging: Consumer, Private Label
Brands:
ARCTICA GARDENS
Avon
Carriere
Festino
Graves
Paula
SUNNY FARM
Stokely

2449 Carrington Foods
P.O.Box 509
Saraland, AL 36571-0509   251-675-9700
Fax: 251-679-8721 www.carringtonfoods.com
Processor of frozen seafood including stuffed flounder, crab and shrimp
President: David Carrington Sr
Secretary: Sally Carrington
Estimated Sales: $10-20 Million
Number Employees: 100-249
Type of Packaging: Consumer, Food Service
Brands:
MISS SALLY'S

2450 Carrousel Cellars
2825 Day Road
Gilroy, CA 95020-8827   408-847-2060
                             Fax: 831-424-1077
Wines
Winemaker: John DeSantis
Number Employees: 20-49

2451 Carson & Company
P.O.Box 30
Bon Secour, AL 36511-0030   251-949-7474
                             Fax: 251-949-5042
President: Carson Kimbrough
Estimated Sales: $ 10 - 20 Million
Number Employees: 100-249
Brands:
Carson & Co.

2452 Carson City Pickle Company
7451 S Garlock Rd
Carson City, MI 48811-8532   989-584-3148
                             Fax: 517-879-2146
Processor of produce including cucumbers, pickles and pickled and brined vegetables
Manager: Mike Zwerk
Manager: Rudy Montoya
Estimated Sales: $1-2.5 Million
Number Employees: 1-4
Parent Co: Funk Enterprises
Type of Packaging: Consumer, Food Service, Bulk

2453 Carta Blanca
3912 Frutas Ave
El Paso, TX 79905-1316   915-544-6367
                             Fax: 915-544-0109
Beer
Manager: Carmen Bitar
General Manager: Miriam De La Vega
Estimated Sales: $ 1 - 3 Million
Number Employees: 1-4

2454 Cary Randall's Sauces &Dressings
PO Box 363
Highlands, NJ 07732-0363   732-872-6353
Fax: 732-872-2035 www.deathsauce.com
Fat-free all natural salad dressing, hot sauce
Contact: Cary Lazon
Estimated Sales: Under $500,000
Number Employees: 1-4

2455 Cary's of Oregon
413 Union Ave
Grants Pass, OR 97527   541-474-0030
Fax: 541-474-5924   888-822-9300
purchases@carysoforegon.com
www.carysoforegon.com
English toffee in 7 different flavors.
Number Employees: 14

2456 Casa De Oro Foods
4433 S 94th St
Omaha, NE 68127-1203   402-339-7740
Fax: 402-339-0140 www.cdof.com
Producer of corn and flour tortillas, tortilla chips, taco shells, pre-cut chips, gordidas, flatbreads, tostadas, mexican dinner kits and low carbohydrate products.
President: Ted Longacre
CEO: Ray Murphy
VP: Charles Kraut
VP Product Development/Quality Assurance: Charles Kraut PhD
Director/Quality Assurance: Greg Power
VP Sales: Chuck Sinon
VP Operations: John Heussner
Plant Manager: Rod Hardenbergh
Estimated Sales: $100+ Million
Number Employees: 250-499
Brands:
CHI-CHI'S
Casa de Oro
Mesa

2457 Casa Di Bertacchi
1910 Gallagher Dr
Vineland, NJ 08360-1545   856-696-5600
Fax: 856-696-3341   800-818-9261
consumerrelations@rich-seapak.com
www.richs.com
Processor and exporter of frozen Italian meat balls, filled pasta and sausage
Chairman/Founder: Robert E Rich
President: Robert E Rich Jr
Executive VP Innovation: Mindy Rich
COO: Bill Gisel
Plant Manager: James Shradick
Purchasing Director: Steve Owens
Estimated Sales: $ 20 - 50 Million
Number Employees: 100-249
Sq. footage: 100000
Parent Co: Rich Products Corporation
Type of Packaging: Consumer, Food Service

2458 Casa DiLisio Products
486 Lexington Ave
Mt Kisco, NY 10549-2758   914-666-5021
Fax: 914-666-7209   800-247-4199
casadi@aol.com   www.casadilisio.com
Processor, importer and exporter of frozen Italian sauces including walnut and sun dried tomato pesto, clam, marinara, puttanesca, basil pesto, cilantro pesto provencal,alfredo and roasted red peppers pest
Owner: Lou Dilisio
VP: Lucy DiLisio
Sales: Linda DiLisio
Estimated Sales: $ 20 - 50 Million
Number Employees: 50-99
Number of Brands: 1
Number of Products: 25
Sq. footage: 4000
Type of Packaging: Consumer, Food Service, Private Label, Bulk
Brands:
Casa Dilisio

2459 Casa Larga Vineyards
P.O.Box 400
Fairport, NY 14450-0400   585-223-4210
Fax: 585-223-8899   info@casalarga.com
www.casalarga.com
Wines
President, VP: John Colaruotolo
Vineyard Manager: Andrew Colaruotolo
CFO: Ann Colaruotolo
Estimated Sales: $10-$24.9 Million
Number Employees: 20-49
Sq. footage: 20
Type of Packaging: Private Label

2460 Casa Nuestra
3451 Silverado Trl N
St Helena, CA 94574-9662   707-963-5783
Fax: 707-963-3174   866-844-9463
info@casanuestra.com   www.casanuestra.com
Wine
Owner: Gene Kirkham
Marketing Manager/Apprentice Winemaker: Stephanie Zacharia
Chief Winemaker: Allen Price
Vineyard Manager/Cellar Master: Rigoberto Nava

Estimated Sales: $500,000
Number Employees: 5-9
Brands:
Casa Nuestra

2461 Casa Sanchez Restaurant
2778 24th St
San Francisco, CA 94110-4263   415-282-2402
                                Fax: 415-550-4463
Mexican food
President: James Sanchez
Estimated Sales: $5-10 Million
Number Employees: 1-4
Type of Packaging: Private Label, Bulk

2462 Casa Valdez
502 E Chicago St
Caldwell, ID 83605-3337   208-459-6461
Fax: 208-459-4154 www.casavaldez.com
Corn and flour tortillas
Owner: Jose Valdez
Sales/Marketting: Joe Romero
Estimated Sales: $10-20 Million
Number Employees: 20-49

2463 (HQ)Casa Visco Finer Food Company
819 Kings Rd
Schenectady, NY 12303-2627   518-377-8814
Fax: 518-377-8269   888-607-2823
info@casavisco.com   www.casavisco.com

Processor of kosher products including spaghetti and barbecue sauces, salsa and mustard; exporter of spaghetti sauce
President: Joseph Viscusi
VP: Michael Viscusi
Marketing Director: Adine Gallo
Production Manager: Michael Viscusi, Jr.
Estimated Sales: $1-2.5 Million
Number Employees: 5-9
Sq. footage: 25000
Parent Co: Casa Visco Finer Food
Type of Packaging: Consumer, Food Service, Private Label, Bulk
Brands:
CASA VISCO
MY COUNTRY SWEET
SCHABERS

2464 Casa di Carfagna
1405 E Dublin Granville Rd
Columbus, OH 43229-3357   614-846-6340
Fax: 614-846-0937 www.carfagnas.com
Manufacturer of Italian sausages, frozen Italian meals and sauces
President: Sam Carfagna
Estimated Sales: $ 5 - 10 Million
Number Employees: 50-99
Brands:
Carfagna

2465 Casados Farms
P.O.Box 852
San Juan Pueblo, NM 87566-0852   505-852-2433
Manufacturer of dried and dehydrated fruits
President: Peter Casados
Estimated Sales: $200,000
Number Employees: 10-19
Type of Packaging: Consumer

2466 Casani Candy Company
5301 Tacony St # 208
Philadelphia, PA 19137-2309   215-535-0110
Fax: 215-535-8110
Confectionery ingredients
Manager: John Lees
VP: Joseph Lees
Estimated Sales: $2.5-5 Million
Number Employees: 10-19

2467 Cascade Cheese Company
P.O.Box 188
Cascade, WI 53011-0188   920-528-8221
Fax: 920-528-7473
Provolone, mozzarella
President: Keith Babler
Treasurer: Elizabeth Babler
Estimated Sales: $10-20 Million
Number Employees: 20-49

2468 Cascade Clear Water
1600 Port Drive
Burlington, WA 98233-3106   360-757-4441
Fax: 360-757-3534 www.clearly.ca
Clear water
President, CEO: Douglas Mason
Managing Director International Div: Robert Allen
Estimated Sales: $2.5-5 Million
Number Employees: 20-49
Parent Co: Cleary Canadian Beverage Company

2469 Cascade Coffee
1525 75th St SW # 100
Everett, WA 98203-7007   425-347-3995
Fax: 425-347-5076 www.cascadecoffeeinc.com
Coffee
President: Tim Kristine
Estimated Sales: $20-50 Million
Number Employees: 50-99
Brands:
ORGANIC ALTURA
ORGANIC MEXICAN ALTURA
ORGANIC SIERRA MADRE BLEND

2470 Cascade Continental Foods
1500 E Kentucky Avenue
Woodland, CA 95776-6107   415-668-6194
casfoods@aol.com
Contract packager of oils, nuts, beans and mixes including dry baking and soup
President: Gary Spakosky
Operations Manager: Peter Olson

Estimated Sales: $5-9.9 Million
Number Employees: 25
Sq. footage: 25000
Type of Packaging: Consumer, Food Service, Private Label

2471 Cascade Cookie Company
P.O.Box 618
St Louis, MO 63188-0618   314-877-7000
Fax: 314-877-7797
investorrelations@ralcorp.com
www.ralstonfoods.com
Manufacture of store brand products
President: Kevin Hunt
Estimated Sales: $1-3 Million
Number Employees: 1,000-4,999
Parent Co: Ralcorp Holdings
Brands:
Bremner
CARRIAGE HOUSE
Cascade Cookie
NUTCRACKER BRANDS

2472 Cascade Fresh
P.O.Box 33576
Seattle, WA 98133-0576   206-363-0991
Fax: 206-363-8191 800-511-0057
yogurt@cascadefresh.com
www.cascadefresh.com
Fat free, low fat and whole milk yogurts, as well as Greek and Mediterranean style yogurts, sour cream and acai, peach, raspberry and strawberry smoothies.
President: Satshakti Khalsa
Estimated Sales: $2,600,000
Number Employees: 10-19
Brands:
Cascade Fresh

2473 Cascade Mountain Winery& Restaurant
835 Cascade Rd
Amenia, NY 12501   845-373-9021
Fax: 845-373-7869 cascademt@mohawk.net
www.cascademt.com
Processor and exporter of dry and semi-dry and nonsweet table wines
Owner: William Wathmore
CEO: Margaret Wetmore
Estimated Sales: $ 3 - 5 Million
Number Employees: 5-9
Number of Products: 8
Sq. footage: 6000
Type of Packaging: Consumer

2474 Cascade Specialties
P.O.Box 583
Boardman, OR 97818-0583   541-481-2522
Fax: 541-481-2640 www.cascadespec.com
Dehydrated onions
Owner: Fraser Hawley
VP: Mike Kilfoy
Quality Assurance: Jeff Hermanson
Sales: Dan Biondi
Estimated Sales: $5-10 Million
Number Employees: 20-49
Brands:
CASCADE SPECIALTIES

2475 Cascadian Farm & MUIR Glen; Division of General Mills
719 Metcalf St
Sedro Woolley, WA 98284-1456   360-855-0100
Fax: 360-855-0444 www.smallplanetfoods.com
Processor, importer, manufacturer and marketer of frozen organic foods including fruits, vegetables and juice concentrates; also pickles and fruit spreads.
President: Maria Morgan
CEO: Steve Sanger
Estimated Sales: $10-20 Million
Number Employees: 50-99
Sq. footage: 14465
Parent Co: Small Planet Foods
Type of Packaging: Consumer, Food Service, Bulk
Other Locations:
Cascadian Farm
Napa CA
Brands:
CASCADIAN FARM
FANTASTIC FOODS
MUIR GLEN
SMALL PLANET FOODS

2476 Casco Bay Brewing
386 Fore St # 302
Portland, ME 04101-7406   207-797-2020
Fax: 207-797-4495 cascobaybrewing@msn.com
www.cascobaybrewing.com
Beer
Owner/President: Bryan Smith
Brewmaster: Bryan Smith
Production: Jim Walters
Estimated Sales: $1 Million
Number Employees: 10-19
Type of Packaging: Private Label
Brands:
Carrabassett
Casco Bay

2477 Case Farms of North Carolina
P.O.Box 308
Morganton, NC 28680-0308   828-438-6900
Fax: 828-437-8566 dturner@casefarms.com
http://www.casefarms.com
Processor of chicken
President: Thomas Shelton
International Sales Manager: David Turner
Plant Manager: Tom Shelton Jr
Estimated Sales: $250 Million
Number Employees: 500-999

2478 Case Farms of Ohio
P.O.Box 185
Winesburg, OH 44690-0185   330-359-7141
Fax: 330-359-6482 www.casefarms.com
Processor of fresh ice and tray packed poultry
President: John Turner
Vice President: Wayne Jones
General Manager: Wayne Jones
Plant Manager: Paul Nelson
Estimated Sales: $33 Million
Number Employees: 250-499
Sq. footage: 32500
Parent Co: Case Foods
Type of Packaging: Private Label
Brands:
CASE FARMS AMISH COUNTRY

2479 Case Side Holdings Company
PO Box 738
Kensington, PE C0B 1M0
Canada   902-836-4214
Fax: 902-836-3297 www.marysbakeshoppe.com
Processor of bread, muffins, biscuits, scones, doughnuts, cookies, pastries, cakes and pies
President: Don Caseley
VP: Trudy Caseley
Secretary: Roy Hogan
Managing Director: Trudy Caseley
Number Employees: 10-19
Type of Packaging: Private Label

2480 Casey Fisheries
PO Box 86
Digby, NS B0V 1A0
Canada   902-245-5801
Fax: 902-245-5552
Processor and exporter of fresh and frozen scallops and salmon
Plant Manager: Duncan Casey
Type of Packaging: Consumer, Food Service, Private Label, Bulk

2481 Casey's Food Products
PO Box 448
Blakely, GA 39823-0448   229-723-3411
Fax: 229-723-5130
danny.kilgore@peanutcorp.com
www.peanutcorp.com
Processor of peanuts and peanut products including oil roasted, granulated, dry roasted, honey roasted, peanut butter, retail and private label nuts.
Owner/President: Stewart Parnell
QA Manager: Jeff McFay
Sales Director: David Voth
Operations Manager: Danny Kilgore
Maintenance Manager: Steve Hutto
Director Purchasing: Manual Brubaker
Estimated Sales: $500,000-$1 Million
Number Employees: 10-19
Type of Packaging: Consumer, Food Service, Private Label

2482 Casey's Seafood
807 Jefferson Ave
Newport News, VA 23607-6117   757-928-1979
Fax: 757-928-0257   caseyseafood@prodigy.net
www.caseysseafood.com
Processor of canned and frozen blue crab meat; also,
heat and serve gourmet crab cakes and deviled crabs
and crawfish cakes
Owner: Jim Casey
Marketing Director: Mike Casey
Estimated Sales:$3 Million
Number Employees: 50-99
Sq. footage: 10000
Type of Packaging: Consumer, Food Service
Brands:
CASEY'S
CHESAPEAKE BAY'S FINEST

2483 Casino Bakery
P.O.Box 5828
Tampa, FL 33675-5828   813-242-0311
Fax: 813-242-4691
Processor of Cuban bread
Owner: Mark N Muhsen
Estimated Sales:$1-2.5 Million
Number Employees: 10-19
Type of Packaging: Consumer, Food Service

2484 Casper Foodservice Company
1041 W Carroll Ave
Chicago, IL 60607-1201   312-226-2265
Fax: 312-226-2686
President: Thomas Casper
Estimated Sales:$ 1 - 3 Million
Number Employees: 10-19

2485 Casper's Ice Cream
11805 N 200 E
Richmond, UT 84333-1408   435-258-2477
Fax: 435-258-5633   800-772-4182
FatBoy@FatBoyIceCream.com
www.fatboyicecream.com
Manufacturer of ice cream novelties including sand-
wiches and nut sundaes on a stick
President: Keith Merrill
Vice President: Paul Merrill
Estimated Sales:$20-50 Million
Number Employees: 50-99
Sq. footage: 46000
Type of Packaging: Consumer
Brands:
FAT BOY

2486 Cass Clay
PO Box 2947
Fargo, ND 58108-2947   701-232-1566
Fax: 701-232-9234   chadf@cassclay.com
www.cassclay.com
Processor of parmesan cheese
President: Jim Hageman
Quality Control: Chad Flores
VP Sales: Greg Hansen
VP Production: Al Nielson
VP/Procurement: Tom Kludt
Estimated Sales:$20-50 Million
Number Employees: 340
Type of Packaging: Consumer

2487 Cass Clay Creamery
200 20th St N
PO Box 3126
Fargo, ND 58108-3126   701-293-6455
Fax: 701-241-9154   salesinfo@cassclay.com
www.cassclay.com
ice cream, dips, sour cream, cream and butter, juice,
cottage cheese and yogurt
Quality Assurance Manager: Steve Lieser
Sales Director: Paul Morlock
Plant Manager: Troy Anderson
Estimated Sales:$50-100 Million
Number Employees: 125
Type of Packaging: Consumer, Food Service, Pri-
vate Label, Bulk
Brands:
CASS-CLAY

2488 Casson & Sons
3407 Delaware Avenue
Des Moines, IA 50313-4709   515-266-3197
Processor of beef, pork and chicken
Owner: Russ Casson
Estimated Sales:$5-10 Million
Number Employees: 5-9
Type of Packaging: Consumer, Food Service

2489 Castella Imports
60 Davids Dr
Hauppauge, NY 11788-2041   631-231-5500
Fax: 631-777-1022   866-227-8355
info@castellaimports.com
www.castellaimports.com
Castella Imports, Inc. is one of the country's largest
importer, manufacturer and distributor of specialty
foods; bringing gourmet flavor to your table from
around the world. From cheeses and spices to olives
and olive oils, CastellaImports offers only the best in
quality, service and price. Through hard work and
dedication, Castella is continually adding to and improving to this extensive line of quality products.
Owner: Bill Valsamos
Estimated Sales:$100+ Million
Number Employees: 100-249
Sq. footage: 66000

2490 (HQ)Castellini Company
P.O.Box 721610
Newport, KY 41072-1610   859-442-4600
Fax: 859-442-4266   800-442-3520
info@castellinicompany.com
www.castellinicompany.com
Processor of produce; also, transportation company
offering a 48 state authority of transporting
Owner: William Schuler
President: Bill Schuler
Number Employees: 20-49
Type of Packaging: Consumer, Food Service, Bulk

2491 Castello Di Borghese
17150 County Road 48
Cutchogue, NY 11935-1041   631-734-5111
Fax: 631-734-5485   800-734-5158
info@castellodiborghese.com
www.castellodiborghese.com
Vineyard and winery
Owner: Marco Borghese
Owner: Ann Marie Borghese
Estimated Sales:$500-1 Million appx.
Number Employees: 10-19
Type of Packaging: Private Label
Brands:
Hargrave Vineyards

2492 Castle Beverages
105 Myrtle Ave
Ansonia, CT 06401-2099   203-734-0883
Carbonated beverages
President: David Pantalone
General Manager: David Pantalone
Estimated Sales:$2.5-5 Million
Number Employees: 5-9
Brands:
Castle Beverages
Castle Carbonated Beverages

2493 (HQ)Castle Cheese
2850 Perry Hwy
Slippery Rock, PA 16057-6308   724-368-3022
Fax: 724-368-9456   800-252-4373
castlecheese@adelphia.net
www.castlecheeseinc.com
Processor and exporter of cheese foods including
substitutes, imitation and natural blends
President: George Myrter
VP: Michelle Sabol
Marketing: Joe Sabol
Plant Manager: Mike Conway
Purchasing Manager: Michelle Sabol
Estimated Sales:$20-50 Million
Number Employees: 50-99
Sq. footage: 55000
Type of Packaging: Consumer, Food Service, Pri-
vate Label, Bulk
Other Locations:
Castle Cheese
Vernon BC
Brands:
CASTLE CHEESE
VERNON BC

2494 Castle Hill Lobster
333 Linebrook Rd # R
Ipswich, MA 01938-1146   978-356-3947
Fax: 978-356-9883
Whole seafoods; lobsters
Owner: Robert Marcaurelle
Estimated Sales:$2 Million
Number Employees: 1-4
Type of Packaging: Food Service

2495 Castle Rock Meats
P.O.Box 16323
Denver, CO 80216-0323   303-292-0855
Fax: 303-292-0680
Meats
President: Michael Andrade
Plant Manager: Allen Rigby
Estimated Sales:$20-50 Million
Number Employees: 20-49

2496 Castleberry's Meats
748 Donald Lee Hollowell Pkwy
Atlanta, GA 30318-6775   404-873-1804
Fax: 404-873-4736
Manufacturer of beef, pork, veal and lamb
Owner: Russell Paulsen
Estimated Sales:$1-2.5 Million
Number Employees: 5-9
Sq. footage: 20000
Type of Packaging: Consumer, Food Service, Pri-
vate Label

2497 (HQ)Castleberry/Snow Brands
1621 15th St # 25
Augusta, GA 30901-3929   706-733-5827
Fax: 706-736-5061   800-241-3520
info@castleberrys.com   www.castleberrys.com
Manufacturer and exporter of canned meat products,
sloppy joe sauce, chili, gravy, stew, hash, chicken
and noodles, barbecue products, pork and canned
chicken.
President/CEO: Robert Kirby
Vice President: Mike Davis
VP Marketing and Strategic Planning: David
Melbourne Jr
Estimated Sales:$330 Million
Number Employees: 250-499
Sq. footage: 215000
Type of Packaging: Consumer, Food Service, Pri-
vate Label
Brands:
CASTLEBERRY
SNOW'S

2498 Casual Gourmet Foods
4500 140th Avenue N
Suite 113
Clearwater, FL 33762-3827   727-298-8307
Fax: 727-298-0616   info@cgfoods.com
www.cgfoods.com
Fully-cooked, all-natural chicken sausages and
chicken burgers. Turkey sausage
Marketing/Sales: David Canarelli
Public Relations: Ben Rizzo
Operations/Production/Plant Manager: Robert
Hapanowicz
Number Employees: 5-9

2499 Catahoula Crawfish
1006 Pete Guidry Rd
St Martinville, LA 70582-6304   337-394-4223
Fax: 337-394-4236
Crawfish
Owner: Terry Guidry
Estimated Sales:$ 3 - 5 Million
Number Employees: 10-19

2500 Catamount Brewing Company
Windsor Industrial Park
Windsor, VT 05089   802-674-6700
Fax: 802-674-6736 www.harpoonbrewery.com
Processor and bottler of ale and lager
Founder, CEO: Rich Doyle
VP Sales: Lee Tussing
Quality Control: Ben Turner
Marketing Director: Barbara Mason
Sales Director: Lee Tussing
Media Contact: Liz Melby
Plant Manager: Ron Schmidt
Estimated Sales:$3-4 Million
Number Employees: 20-49
Sq. footage: 10000
Parent Co: Harpoon Brewery
Brands:
CATAMOUNT AMBER ALE
CATAMOUNT AMERICAN WHEAT
CATAMOUNT ANNIVERSARY ALE
CATAMOUNT CHRISTMAS ALE
CATAMOUNT GOLD
CATAMOUNT OATMEAL STOUT
CATAMOUNT OCTOBERFEST
CATAMOUNT PALE ALE
CATAMOUNT PORTER

2501 Catamount Specialties ofVermont
1880 Mountain Rd
Stowe, VT 05672-4638   802-253-4525
          Fax: 802-253-6933   800-820-8096
          greenmt@warwick.net
          www.catamountspecialties.com
Produces mustards, salsas, BBQ sauces, pepper jellies, pasta sauces and seasonings
    Co-Owner: Don Mugford
    Co-Owner: George Gooss
Estimated Sales:$ .5 - 1 million
Number Employees: 1-4

2502 Catania Bakery
1404 N Capitol St NW
Washington, DC 20002-3342   202-332-5135
          info@cataniabakery.com
          www.cataniabakery.com
Italian bread and biscotti
    President: Micolt Tramonte
    General Manager: Carolyn Craig
Estimated Sales:$5-10 Million
Number Employees: 5-9

2503 Catania-Spagna Corporation
P.O.Box J
Ayer, MA 01432-0227   978-772-7900
          Fax: 978-772-7970   800-343-5522
          oils@cataniausa.com   www.cataniausa.com
Processor, packer, importer and exporter of oils including canola, coconut, cooking, corn, cottonseed, vegetable, olive, peanut and soybean
    President: Anthony Basile
    VP: Robert Basile
    Quality Control: Paul Sampson
    Marketing: David Masciolli
    Sales: Joseph Basile
    Production: Sam Bellino
    Plant Manager: Steve Sampson
    Director Purchasing: Brad Eisold
Estimated Sales:$40-60 Million
Number Employees: 50-99
Sq. footage: 55000
Type of Packaging: Consumer, Food Service, Private Label, Bulk
Brands:
    Atlantic Organic
    Atlantic Rose
    La Spagnola
    Marconi
    Sicilia

2504 Catawissa Bottling Company
450 Fisher Ave
Catawissa, PA 17820-1022   570-356-2301
          Fax: 570-356-2304   800-892-4419
          epg@sunlink.net   www.catawissabottlingco.com
Soft drinks
    Partner: Joseph Gregorowicz
    Controller: Michael Gregorowicz
    Plant Manager: Stephen Gregorowicz
    Purchasing: Paula Clark
Estimated Sales:$10-20 Million
Number Employees: 20-49

2505 Catelli Brothers
50 Ferry Ave
Camden, NJ 08103-3006   856-869-9293
          Fax: 856-869-9488   www.catellibrothers.com
Processor of veal and lamb
    President: Anthony Catelli
Estimated Sales:$100+ Million
Number Employees: 250-499
Brands:
    American Lamb
    Ami
    Namp

2506 Cateraid
1167 Fendt Dr
Howell, MI 48843-6501   517-546-8217
          Fax: 517-546-8674   800-508-8217
          cateraidinc@provide.net   www.cateraid.com
Processor of frozen European style tortes, cakes, cheesecakes, miniature pastries and hors d'oeuvres
    Owner: Rob Katz
    Co-Founder/VP Marketing: Robert Katz
    Plant Manager: Lise Holman
    Purchasing Manager: Suanne Brow
Estimated Sales:$2.5-5 Million
Number Employees: 20-49
Number of Brands: 2

Number of Products: 85
Sq. footage: 17000
Type of Packaging: Food Service, Private Label
Brands:
    CATERAID
    CATERED GOURMET

2507 Cates & Sons
354 N Faison Ave
Faison, NC 28341-7608   910-267-4711
          Fax: 910-267-4862   www.armorcotings.com
Processor of pickles including sweet, sour, dill, etc
    Plant Manager: Bill Scott
Estimated Sales:$100+ Million
Number Employees: 100-249
Parent Co: Dean Pickle & Specialty Products Company
Type of Packaging: Consumer, Food Service

2508 Cates Addis Company
P.O.Box 146
Parkton, NC 28371-0146   910-858-3439
          Fax: 910-858-3074   800-423-1883
Manufacturer and exporter of fresh and brined cucumbers for pickles
    President: John Cates
    VP/Treasurer: John Cates
Estimated Sales:$2.5-5 Million
Number Employees: 5-9
Type of Packaging: Bulk

2509 Catfish Wholesale
P.O.Box 759
Abbeville, LA 70511-0759   337-643-6700
          Fax: 337-643-1396   800-334-7292
          jimrich@catfishewholesale.com
          www.catfishwholesale.com
Processor and distributor of catfish, garfish, crawfish, shrimp, crabs, flounder and trout
    President: James Rich
    Sales Manager: Sheb Calahan
    Palnt Manager: Sheb Calahan
Estimated Sales:$ 5-10 Million
Number Employees: 50-99
Number of Brands: 1
Sq. footage: 8000
Type of Packaging: Consumer, Food Service, Private Label, Bulk

2510 Cathay Foods Corporation
960 Massachusetts Ave # 2
Boston, MA 02118-2690   617-427-1507
          Fax: 617-427-4083
Processor of frozen spring, cocktail and full sized egg rolls including shrimp, lobster, vegetable, pizza, spinach and cheese; also, egg roll wrappers and crab rangoons
    President: Victor Wong
    Sales: Nancy Tashjian
Estimated Sales:$5-10 Million
Number Employees: 20-49
Sq. footage: 18000
Type of Packaging: Consumer, Food Service, Private Label, Bulk
Brands:
    CATHAY FOODS

2511 Catoctin Vineyards
805 Greenbridge Road
Brookeville, MD 20833-1924   301-774-2310
          Fax: 301-774-2310   wineman1@starpower.net
Wines
    President: Bob Lyon
Estimated Sales:Less than $500,000
Number Employees: 1

2512 Catoris Candy
981 5th Ave
New Kensington, PA 15068-6307   724-335-4371
          Fax: 724-335-1759
Processor of confectionery items
    Owner: John Gentile
Estimated Sales:$5-10 Million
Number Employees: 10-19
Type of Packaging: Consumer

2513 Catskill Mountain Specialties
1411 Route 212
Saugerties, NY 12477-3040   845-246-0900
          Fax: 845-246-5313   800-311-3473
          mtmanfire@aol.com
          www.newworldhomecooking.com

Processor of condiments including roasted habanero, chipotle, barbecue, Jamaican jerk, etc.; importer of hot peppers, spices, etc.; also, co-packer of acidified foods
    Owner: Liz Corrado
    VP: Edward Palluth
Number Employees: 1-4
Sq. footage: 2000
Type of Packaging: Consumer, Food Service, Private Label, Bulk
Brands:
    Mountainman
    New World Home Cooking Co.

2514 Cattaneo Brothers
797 Caudill St
San Luis Obispo, CA 93401-5729   805-543-8166
          Fax: 805-543-4698   800-243-8537
          catteneo@cattaneobros.com
          www.cattaneobros.com
Processor of jerky, pepperoni sticks and sausage
    Owner: Mike Kanney
    Marketing Director: Katelyn Kaney
    Operations Manager: Jim Douglass
Estimated Sales:$2.5-5 Million
Number Employees: 20-49
Number of Brands: 1
Number of Products: 50
Sq. footage: 8500
Type of Packaging: Consumer, Food Service, Private Label
Brands:
    CATTANEO BROTHERS

2515 Cattle Boyz Foods
1735 33rd Avenue SW
Calgary, AB T2T 148
Canada   403-262-9366
          Fax: 403-262-5829   888-662-9366
          sales@cattleboyzsauce.com
          www.cattleboyzsauce.com
Manufacturer and exporter of unique latchtop bottle containing versatile gourmet sauces for barbecuing, marinades, glaze for all meats and seafoods. Available in 17 and 35 oz. sizes
    Managing Partner/Owner: Karen Hope
    Managing Partner: Joe Ternes
    Quality Control: Roxanne Quest
    Sales: Karen Hope
Number Employees: 1-4
Number of Brands: 1
Number of Products: 4
Type of Packaging: Consumer, Food Service, Private Label, Bulk
Brands:
    Cattle Boyz

2516 Cattleman's Meat Company
1825 Scott St
Detroit, MI 48207-2031   313-833-2700
          Fax: 313-833-7164   www.cattlemansmeat.com
Processor of fresh and frozen beef; exporter of frozen beef
    Chairman, Treasurer: Markus Rothbart
    CEO/President: David Rothbart
    Comptroller: Jerry Fowler
    CEO: David S Rohtbart
Estimated Sales:$20-50 Million
Number Employees: 100-249
Sq. footage: 65000
Type of Packaging: Bulk
Brands:
    CATTLEMEN'S

2517 Caudill Seed Company
1402 W Main St
Louisville, KY 40203-1328   502-583-4402
          Fax: 502-583-4405   800-626-5357
          hf@caudillseed.com   www.caudillseed.com
Manufactures organic and kosher foods, dried fruits, nuts, snacks, popcorn and basic foods
    President: Dan Caudill
    Vice President: Michael Cline
    Sales Director: Jack Donahoe
Estimated Sales:$20 Million
Number Employees: 20-49
Number of Brands: 5
Number of Products: 400
Sq. footage: 275000
Type of Packaging: Private Label, Bulk
Brands:
    WHOLE ALTERNATIVES

2518 Caughman's Meat Plant
P.O.Box 457
Lexington, SC 29071-0457   803-356-0076
                                  Fax: 803-356-4413
Manufacturer of sausage, liver pudding, barbecue
hash and beef chili
    President: Marguerite Caughman
    VP: Ronald Caughman
Estimated Sales: $20-50 Million
Number Employees: 20-49
Type of Packaging: Consumer
Brands:
    LEXINGTON

2519 (HQ)Cave Creek Coffee Company
P.O.Box 4650
Cave Creek, AZ 85327-4650   480-488-0603
    Fax: 480-595-1565   info@cavecreekcoffee.com
                        www.cavecreekcoffee.com
Processor of coffee
    Owner: Todd Newman
    Co-Owner: David Anderson
    Roastmaster: David Anderson
Estimated Sales: $5-10 Million
Number Employees: 20-49

2520 Cavender Castle Winery
142 Mitchell Street SW
Suite 300
Atlanta, GA 30303-3432   706-864-4759
Wines
    Vineyard Manager: Gerry Carty
Number Employees: 20-49

2521 Cavendish Farms
100 Midland Drive
Dieppe, NB E1A 6X4
Canada   506-858-7777
    Fax: 506-859-5152   888-883-7437
    webadmin@cavendishfarms.com
            www.cavendishfarms.com
Processor and exporter of frozen potato products
    President: Robert Irving
    VP Finance: Michael Fox
Parent Co: Irving Group
Type of Packaging: Consumer, Food Service
Brands:
    CAVENDISH FARMS
    DOUBLE R
    FAIR ISLE
    SCOTCH MAID

2522 Cavendish Farms
25 Mall Rd
Burlington, MA 01803-4156   781-273-2777
    Fax: 781-221-2154   888-88 -7437
    webadmin@cavendishfarms.com
            www.cavendishfarms.com
Processor of potato products
    President: Robert Irving
Estimated Sales: $10-20 Million
Number Employees: 5-9
Parent Co: The Irving Group
Brands:
    Always Crips
    Cavendish Farms
    County Fair
    Double R
    Scotch Maid

2523 Cavendish Farms
1200 boul Chomedy
Bureau 825
Laval, QC H7V 3Z3
Canada   450-973-1952
    Fax: 450-973-1955 www.cavendishfarms.com
Processor of frozen French fries
    General Manager: Michael Johnston Johnston
    VP Operations: Ron Clow
    VP: Claude Valler
    Sr. Account Manager: Greg Foster
Number Employees: 10-19
Parent Co: Cavendish Farms
Type of Packaging: Consumer, Food Service, Private Label
Brands:
    Always Crisp
    Cavendish Farms

2524 Cavendish Farms
5855 3rd St SE
Jamestown, ND 58401-6800   701-252-5222
    Fax: 701-252-6863   888-284-5687
            www.cavendishfarms.com

Processor of frozen potatoes including French fries
(various cut sizes) and formed potato products
(rounds, patties, tots, etc.), roastable products, whole
baked potatoes, european potato line; hashbrowns,
parfried, churros(nonpotato), dessert and snack
    President: Jeff Rinehart
    CFO: Ad Nieuwenhuis
    VP: Ron Clow
    Marketing: Kandy Jenkins
    VP Sales: Dan Koontz
    VP Operations: G Scott Piper
    Purchasing Agent: Dean Snow
Estimated Sales: $50-100 Million
Number Employees: 250-499
Brands:
    DAKOTA GOLD
    DAKOTA SKINS
    NORTHERN GROWN
    PRAIRIE SELECT

2525 Cavens Meats
P.O.Box 400
Conover, OH 45317-0400   937-368-3841
                                Fax: 937-368-3849
Processor and wholesaler/distributor of meat products; serving the food service market
    President: Victor Caven
    VP: Dean Caven
Estimated Sales: $10-20 Million
Number Employees: 10-19
Sq. footage: 15000
Type of Packaging: Consumer, Food Service

2526 Caver Shellfish
PO Box 187
Beals, ME 04611-0187   207-497-2629
                              Fax: 207-497-2770
Shellfish
    President: Albert Carver

2527 Caviness Packing Company
P.O.Box 790
Hereford, TX 79045-0790   806-357-2443
    Fax: 806-357-2277 www.cavinessbeefpackers.com
Manufacturer of meat products; slaughtering services available
    President: Terry Caviness
    VP: Trevor Caviness
Estimated Sales: $150-200 Million
Number Employees: 100-249

2528 Cawy Bottling Company
2440 NW 21st Ter
Miami, FL 33142-7182   305-634-2291
    Fax: 305-634-2291   877-917-2299
    cawy@cawy.net   www.cawy.net
Manufacturer of soft drinks
    President: Vincent Cossio
    CEO/VP/Public Relations: Vincent Cossio Jr
    Quality Control: Ramon Mesa
    Marketing Director: Vincent Cossio
    Sales Director: Harris Padron
    Public Relations: Vincent Cossio Jr
    Operations Manager: Mayra Alfonsin
    Production Manager: Carlos Garcia
    Plant Manager: Carlos Garcia
    Purchasing Manager: Harris Padron
Estimated Sales: $10-20 Million
Number Employees: 20-49
Sq. footage: 60000
Type of Packaging: Consumer, Food Service
Brands:
    CAWY CC
    CAWY LEMON-LIME
    CAWY WATERMELON
    CHAMP'S COLA
    COCO SOLO
    JUPINA
    MALTA CAWY
    MALTA RICA
    MATERVA
    QUINABEER
    RICA MALT TONIC
    TRIMALTA

2529 Caymus Vineyards
P.O.Box 268
Rutherford, CA 94573-0268   707-967-3010
    Fax: 707-963-5958 www.caymus.com
Wines
    President: Chuck Wagner
    VP: Karen Perry
    Public Relations: Phyllis Turner

Estimated Sales: $300,000-500,000
Number Employees: 1-4
Number of Brands: 1
Number of Products: 2
Brands:
    CAYMUS

2530 Cayuga Grain
P.O.Box 336
Cayuga, IN 47928-0336   765-492-3324
Processor of grain
    Manager: Nancy Martin
Estimated Sales: $500,000-$1 Million
Number Employees: 5-9
Type of Packaging: Food Service, Bulk

2531 Cayuga Ridge Estate Winery
6800 State Route 89
Ovid, NY 14521-9599   607-869-5158
    Fax: 607-869-3412   800-598-9463
    crew@fltg.net   www.cayugaridgewinery.com
Wines
    Owner: Tom Challen
    Owner: Susie Challen
Estimated Sales: $1-2.5 Million
Number Employees: 1-4

2532 Ce De Candy
1091 Lousons Rd
Union, NJ 07083-5097   908-624-9107
    Fax: 908-964-0911   800-631-7968
    cede@smarties.com   www.smarties.com
Processor and exporter of lollypops and novelty
candy items including lipsticks, fruit, money and
watches; also, sweet and sour wafers; importer of
candy necklaces
    Owner: Jonathan Dee
    VP Sales/Marketing: Eric Ostrow
    VP Operations: Karen Connell
Estimated Sales: $20-50 Million
Number Employees: 100-249
Type of Packaging: Consumer
Brands:
    SMARTIES

2533 Ce De Candy Southern Inc
1091 Lousons Rd
Union, NJ 07083-5097   908-624-9107
                              800-341-2254
Processor and importer of candies including filled,
lollypops, hard, mints, holiday novelties, taffy, toffee, rolls, bagged and packaged for fund raising and
vending; exporter of lollypops and hard candies
    Owner: Jonathan Dee
    VP Sales: Kenneth Bissett
Estimated Sales: $ 20 - 50 Million
Number Employees: 100-249
Sq. footage: 55000
Type of Packaging: Consumer, Private Label, Bulk
Brands:
    Matlow
    Swizzels

2534 Cebro Frozen Foods
2100 Orestimba Rd
Newman, CA 95360-9788   209-862-0150
    Fax: 209-862-0717 cffrich@inreach.com
            www.cebrofrozenfoods.com
Frozen foods
    President: Richard Brown
Estimated Sales: $2.5-5 Million
Number Employees: 10-19

2535 Cecchetti Sebastiani Cellar
PO Box 1607
Sonoma, CA 95476-1607   707-996-8463
                              Fax: 707-996-0424
Processor of wine
    Owner/President: Roy Cecchetti
    CEO: Don Sebastiani
    SVP Sales: Jim O'Connor
    SVP/Winemaker: Bob Broman
Estimated Sales: Less than $500,000
Number Employees: 1-4
Type of Packaging: Private Label
Brands:
    Brandy
    Cecchetti Sebastiani Napa Valley
    Pepperwood Grove
    Quatro
    Wines

2536 Cedar Creek Winery
N70w6340 Bridge Rd
Cedarburg, WI 53012-2099   262-377-8020
Fax: 262-375-9428   800-827-8020
info@cedarcreekwinery.com
www.cedarcreekwinery.com
Manufacturer of bottler of wine
Manager: Steve Danner
Estimated Sales:$5-9.9 Million
Number Employees: 10-19
Sq. footage: 12000
Type of Packaging: Consumer, Food Service, Private Label
Brands:
CEDAR CREEK

2537 Cedar Crest Specialties
P.O.Box 260
Cedarburg, WI 53012-0260   262-377-7252
Fax: 262-377-5554   800-877-8341
info@cedarcresticecream.com
www.cedarcresticecream.com
Processor of premium ice cream and no-fat ice cream, frozen yogurt, sherbet and Tom and Jerry mix
President: Ken Kohlwey
CEO: Bill Kohlwey
VP: Robert Kohlwey
Marketing Manager: Charlene Leach
Sales: Robert Kohlwey
Purchasing: Nadine Schmitt
Estimated Sales:$16 Million
Number Employees: 50-99
Number of Brands: 2
Number of Products: 400
Sq. footage: 45000
Parent Co: Cedar Crest Specialties
Type of Packaging: Consumer, Food Service, Private Label, Bulk
Brands:
CEDAR CREST
GUSTAFSON'S

2538 Cedar Grove Cheese
E5904 Mill Rd
Plain, WI 53577-9674   608-546-5284
Fax: 608-546-2805   800-200-6020
cheese@cedargrovecheese.com
www.cedargrovecheese.com
Organic cheese and specialty artisan crafted cheese
President: Robert Wills
Vice President: Beth Nachreiner
Marketing Director: Robert Wills
General Manager: Peter DeWaard
Estimated Sales:$2.5-5 Million
Number Employees: 20-49
Number of Brands: 3
Number of Products: 50
Type of Packaging: Consumer, Food Service, Private Label, Bulk
Brands:
CEDAR GROVE
FAMILY FARMER
SQUEAKS

2539 Cedar Hill Seasonings
P.O.Box 4055
Edmond, OK 73083-4055   405-340-1119
Fax: 405-340-7673
info@cedarhillseasonings.com
www.cedarhillseasonings.com
Manufacturer of seasonings, bottled products and packaged mixes, Cedar Hill Seasonings produces a variety of food items including taco mixes; dip mix with seasonings; cheese ball mixes; marinara and sauce mixes, in addition to offeringgift packages and combo samplers.
Co-Owner: Felicia Schaefer
Co-Owner: Helen Schaefer
Type of Packaging: Food Service

2540 Cedar Key Aquaculture Farms
PO Box 1430
Riverview, FL 33568-1430   352-543-9131
Fax: 352-543-9132   888-252-6735
custserv@cedarkeyclams.com
www.cedarkeyclams.com
Processor of fresh and frozen clams including hors d'oeuvres
President: Dan Solano
Operations Manager: Mike Smith
Type of Packaging: Food Service
Brands:
Cedar Key

2541 Cedar Lake Foods
P.O.Box 65
Cedar Lake, MI 48812-0065   989-427-5143
Fax: 989-427-5392   800-246-5039
cedarlakemgm@nethawk.com
www.cedarlakefoods.com
Processor and exporter of canned and frozen vegetable protein entrees including meat analogs; also, dry soy milk and vegetarian foods
President: Alejo Pizzaro
Contact: Cheri Graves
Production Manager: John Sias
Plant Manager: John Sias
Purchasing Manager: Ann Britten
Estimated Sales:$5-9.9 Million
Number Employees: 10-19
Type of Packaging: Consumer, Food Service, Private Label, Bulk
Brands:
CEDAR LAKE
MGM

2542 Cedar Mountain Winery
7000 Tesla Rd
Livermore, CA 94550-9151   925-373-6636
Fax: 925-373-6694   cedarmtn@neal.verio.com
www.cedarmountainwinery.com
Wines
President/CEO: Linda Eve Ault
Winemaker: Earl Ault
Marketing Manager: Sigrid Laing
VP Operations/Production Manager: R Michael Hasbrouck
Estimated Sales:$5-9.9 Million
Number Employees: 50-99
Type of Packaging: Private Label
Brands:
Cedar Grove
Cedar Mountain

2543 Cedar Valley Cheese
W3115 Jay Rd
Belgium, WI 53004-9769   920-994-9500
Fax: 920-994-2317   email
contact@cedarvalleycheese.com
www.cedarvalleycheese.com
Cheese
President: Jeff Hiller
Estimated Sales:$20-50 Million
Number Employees: 20-49

2544 Cedar Valley Fish Market
218 Division St
Waterloo, IA 50703-4902   319-236-2965
Fax: 253-761-0504
Seafood
Owner: Marilyn Ruvino
Estimated Sales:$370,000
Number Employees: 5-9

2545 Cedaredge Meats
PO Box 128
Cedaredge, CO 81413-0128   970-856-3517
Fax: 970-856-3517
Manufacturer of frozen sausage; custom cut meat available
General Manager: Randy Sunderland
Estimated Sales:$1-2.5 Million
Number Employees: 12-15
Type of Packaging: Consumer, Food Service, Private Label
Brands:
COLORADO CLASSIC

2546 Cedarlane Foods
1864 22nd Street
Carson, CA 90058   213-745-4255
Fax: 213-745-4253   800-826-3322
feedback@cedarlanefoods.com
www.cedarlanefoods.com
Processor of natural refrigerated and frozen foods including enchiladas, burritos, pot pies, tortillas, specialty breads, pizza and lasagna; varieties include vegetarian, low-fat and cholesterol and lactose-free
President: Robert Atallah
Vice President: Terry Mayo
Number Employees: 50-99
Sq. footage: 16000
Type of Packaging: Consumer, Food Service, Private Label
Brands:
CEDARLANE
SOYPREME

2547 Cedarlane Natural Foods
1135 E Artesia Blvd
Carson, CA 90746-1602   310-886-7720
Fax: 310-886-7733 www.cedarlanefoods.com
Natural foods
Owner: Robert Atallah
Estimated Sales:$ 50 - 100 Million
Number Employees: 250-499

2548 Cedarvale Food Products
11 Wiltshire Avenue
Toronto, ON M6N 2V7
Canada   416-656-6330
Fax: 416-656-6803   lounsbury@lounsbury.ca
Processor of mustard and sauces including horseradish, cocktail, mint and tartar; importer of tomato paste
VP: David Higgins
Manager Export Sales/Marketing: Tim Higgins
General Manager: Gil Marks
Number Employees: 10-19
Sq. footage: 15000
Parent Co: Lounsbury Foods
Type of Packaging: Consumer, Food Service, Private Label, Bulk
Brands:
CEDARVALE
LOUNSBURY
WILTSHIRE

2549 Ceilidh Fisherman's Cooperative
PO Box 99
Inverness, NS B0E 1N0
Canada   902-787-2666
Fax: 902-787-2388
Processor and exporter of salted cod, live lobster and crab
Manager: Bonnie MacDonald
Number Employees: 10-19
Type of Packaging: Consumer, Food Service, Private Label, Bulk

2550 Celebration Foods
1 Celebration Way
New Britain, CT 6053-1480   800-322-4848
Fax: 860-257-8859   800-322-4848
cranaldi@carvelcorp.com
www.celebrationfoods.com
Ice cream, frozen desserts
President: Steve Fellingham
CFO: George Brooks-Gonyer
Director: Jayne Minigell
Marketing Coordinator: Maggie Collin
Sales Director: Tom Fuchs
Public Relations: Melody Macary
Operations Manager: Greg Demadis
Purchasing Manager: Richard Carlo
Estimated Sales:$10-$100 Million
Number Employees: 50-99
Brands:
CARVEL
FLYING SAUCERS

2551 Celebrity Cheesecake
655 Nova Drive
Suite 304
Davie, FL 33317   954-625-6920
Fax: 954-625-6923   877-986-2253
Cheesecakes, pies, cakes
Owner: Anita Phillips
President: Susie Bernstein
Estimated Sales:$500,000-$1 Million
Number Employees: 10-19
Sq. footage: 6000
Brands:
Celebrity Cheesecakes

2552 Celentano Brothers
120 Bloomfield Ave
Verona, NJ 07044   973-239-2557
Fax: 973-239-7649
Processor of frozen Italian entrees including eggplant, shells and ravioli
President: Domenick Celentano
Vice President: Bob Carlucci
Sales Manager: Thomas Finn
Estimated Sales:$20-50 Million
Number Employees: 100-249
Parent Co: Rosina Holdings
Type of Packaging: Consumer
Brands:
CELENTANO
VEGETARIAN SELECT

2553 Celestial Seasonings Teas
4600 Sleepytime Dr
Boulder, CO 80301-3292   303-530-5300
Fax: 303-581-1332 www.celestialseasonings.com
Processor and exporter of black and herbal teas including powdered and bags; also, bottled iced teas
President: Steve Hughes
CEO/Chairman: Mo Siegel
VP: Michael A Bloom
Estimated Sales: $300,000-500,000
Number Employees: 10-19
Parent Co: Hain Food Group
Type of Packaging: Consumer, Food Service
Brands:
Celestial Seasonings

2554 Cell Tech International
P.O.Box 609
Klamath Falls, OR 97601-0329   541-882-5406
Fax: 541-885-5458 strausj@celltech.com
www.celltech.com
Processor and exporter of blue green algae products
President/CEO: Marta Carpenter
COO: Justin Straus
CEO: Bob Underwood
VP Marketing/Strategy: Victor Bond
Number Employees: 20-49
Sq. footage: 250000
Brands:
ALPHA GOLD
ELZ SUPER ENZYMES
OMEGA GOLD
OMEGA SURO
PLANET FOOD
SPECTRABIOTIC
SUPER BLUE GREEN ENZYMES
SUPER Q10

2555 Cella's Confections
7401 S Cicero Ave
Chicago, IL 60629-5885   773-838-3400
Fax: 773-838-3435 www.tootsie.com
Processor of confectionery products including boxed chocolates, chocolate covered cherries and holiday novelties
CEO: Melvin J Gordon
Plant Manager: Charles Musso
Estimated Sales: 1
Number Employees: 1,000-4,999
Parent Co: Tootsie Roll Industries
Type of Packaging: Consumer, Food Service, Bulk

2556 Cellone Bakery
P.O.Box 16288
Pittsburgh, PA 15242-0288   412-922-5335
Fax: 412-922-6940 800-334-8438
cellone@cellonebakery.net
www.cellonebakery.com
Bread and rolls
President: Jay Cellone
Owner: Randy Cellone
Public Relations: Tony Feeney
Operations Manager: Gary Cellone
Production Manager: Dean Cellone
Estimated Sales: $5-10 Million
Number Employees: 5-9
Type of Packaging: Private Label

2557 Cellu-Con
P.O.Box 185
Strathmore, CA 93267-0185   559-568-0190
Fax: 559-568-0271 cellucon@ocsnet.net
www.cellucon.com
Processor of natural yucca extract
Owner: John Yale
VP R&D: John Yale
Administrative Assistant: Kelly Smith
Estimated Sales: $1-3 Million
Number Employees: 10-19
Sq. footage: 10000

2558 Celplast Metallized Products Limited
67 Commander Boulevard
Unit 4
Toronto, ON M1S-3M7   416-293-4330
Fax: 416-293-9198 800-866-0059
jim@celplast.com http://cmp.celplast.com
Producer and manufacturer of metallized films for the food industry.
President/Founder: Chuck Larsen
Vice President: Bill Hellings
Technical Representative: Dante Ferrari
Sales Representative: Jim Lush
Sales Representative: Naomi Otta

2559 Cemac Foods Corporation
19 W 44th Street
Suite 1402
New York, NY 10036-6101   212-869-5633
Fax: 212-869-6177 800-724-0179
info@cemacfoods.com www.cemacfoods.com
Processor and exporter of cheese blends and analogs including soy cheese; importer of health foods including dairy products, pastas and snack chips. Manufacturer of full fat and low-fat cheesecake. Private labels
President: Tom May
CFO: Mildred Nash
VP: Mel Persily
Quality Control/Operations: Josef Zahal
Marketing: David Abuschinow
Contact: Kate Stoughton
Type of Packaging: Consumer, Food Service, Private Label, Bulk
Brands:
NU TOFU
ORGRAN PASTAS
SOY CHEESE
UNBELIEVABLE CHEESECAKE

2560 Cemac Foods Corporation
1821 E Sedgley Avenue
Philadelphia, PA 19124-5655   215-288-7440
Fax: 215-533-8993 800-724-0179
Processor of cheesecake and cut and shredded cheese; also, soy protein cheese substitutes: importer of soy chips and organic pasta
Director R&D/Plant Manager: Yoseph Zahal
National Sales Manager: Zachary Scott
VP Plant Operations: Morris Lowenthal
Number Employees: 20-49
Sq. footage: 28000
Brands:
Nutofu
Organ Pastas
Soy Cheese
Soy-A-King Soy Chips
Unbelievable Brand

2561 Centennial Farms
199 Jackson St
Augusta, MO 63332-1721   636-228-4338
centfarmaug@aol.com
www.centennialfarms.biz
Apple butters
Owner: Robert Knoernschild
Estimated Sales: $125,000
Number Employees: 5-9
Number of Brands: 1
Number of Products: 8
Type of Packaging: Consumer, Private Label

2562 (HQ)Centennial Food Corporation
4043 Brandon Street SE
Calgary, AB T2G 4A7
Canada   403-287-2525
Fax: 403-287-0789
http://www.centennialfood.com
Processor and exporter of fresh and frozen meat products including spiced and formed ground beef, beef patties, battered and breaded steaks and cutlets, vacuum sealed and aged beef cuts, bacon wrapped scallops and marinated short ribs;importer of beef and seafood
Chairman: Ron Kovitz
CEO/President: J Kalef
VP/General Manager: Nashir Vasanji
Number Employees: 250-499
Type of Packaging: Consumer, Food Service, Private Label, Bulk
Other Locations:
Centennial Food Corp.
Calgary AB
Brands:
Canadian Gourmet
Centennial
Mastercut

2563 Centennial Mills
601 1st St
Cheney, WA 99004-1653   509-235-6216
Fax: 509-235-2144
Processor of flour
Manager: Luke Burger
Estimated Sales: Under $500,000
Number Employees: 10-19
Parent Co: Archer Daniels Midland Company
Type of Packaging: Consumer, Food Service, Bulk

2564 Center Locker Service Company
P.O.Box 290
Center, MO 63436-0290   573-267-3343
Fax: 573-267-3392
Processor of beef, pork, sausage and meat and meat products
Owner: Dennis Mc Millen
Co-Owner: Debby McMillen
Estimated Sales: $500,000-$1 Million
Number Employees: 1-4
Type of Packaging: Food Service, Bulk

2565 Centflor Manufacturing Company
545 W 45th St
New York, NY 10036-3490   212-246-8307
Fax: 212-262-9717
Processor and exporter of essential oils and aromatic chemicals
President: Robert Beller
General Manager: Gloria Rose
Estimated Sales: $10-20 Million
Number Employees: 5-9

2566 Central Bakery
711 Pleasant St
Fall River, MA 02723-1001   508-675-7620
Fax: 508-677-4523
Processor of bread & other bakery products
Owner: Tibeiro Lopes
Estimated Sales: $2.3 Million
Number Employees: 10-19

2567 Central Bean Company
P.O.Box 215
Quincy, WA 98848-0215   509-787-1544
Fax: 509-787-4040 info@centralbean.com
www.centralbean.com
Processor of dry beans including pinto, black, navy, small red, great northern, light red kidney, pink, dry bean flour and seven bean soup mix.
President: Tom Grebb
Estimated Sales: $20-50 Million
Number Employees: 10-19
Sq. footage: 62000
Type of Packaging: Consumer, Food Service, Private Label, Bulk

2568 Central Beef
P.O.Box 399
Center Hill, FL 33514-0399   352-793-3671
Fax: 352-793-2227
Processor of beef
Owner: Thomas Bryan
Estimated Sales: $ 20 - 50 Million
Number Employees: 50-99
Type of Packaging: Consumer, Food Service

2569 Central California Raisin Packers
5316 S Del Rey Ave
Del Rey, CA 93616   559-888-2195
Fax: 559-888-2298
Dried apricots, mixed fruit, peaches, prunes, raisins
President: Dan Milinovich
Estimated Sales: $10-20 Million
Number Employees: 10-19
Brands:
DEL CARA

2570 Central Coast Coffee Roasting
1172 Los Olivos Ave
Los Osos, CA 93402-3231   805-528-7317
Fax: 805-528-1150 800-382-6837
www.slowroasted.com
Coffee
Owner: Norman Galloway
Owner: Chirs Galloway
Owner: Joe Galloway
Estimated Sales: Less than $500,000
Number Employees: 10-19
Type of Packaging: Food Service

2571 (HQ)Central Coast Seafoods
5495 Traffic Way
Atascadero, CA 93422-4246   805-462-3474
          Fax: 805-466-6613   800-273-4741
     info@ccseafood.com   www.ccseafood.com
Wholesaler/distributor and exporter of fresh seafood; serving the food service market in California
     President: Giovanni Comin
     Secretary: Molly Comin
     Vice President: Michael Anthony Degarimore
Estimated Sales: $10-20 Million
Number Employees: 10-19
Sq. footage: 15000
Other Locations:
     Central Coast Seafoods
     Morro Bay CA

2572 Central Coca-Cola Bottling Company
1706 Roseneath Road
Richmond, VA 23230-4436   804-359-3759
          Fax: 804-358-5822   800-359-3759
               www.centralcoke.com
Processor and bottler of flavored and regular iced teas, soft drinks, bottled and soda waters, fruit juices and drinks including sport, fruit and chocolate
     Chairman Board/President: Betty Sams Christian
     Director Administration: Scott Nally
     VP Production/Distribution: W Lee Christian
Estimated Sales: $10-20 Million
Number Employees: 20-49
Type of Packaging: Consumer

2573 Central Dairies
PO Box 8588
Station A
St Johns, NL A1B 3P2
Canada   709-364-7531
     Fax: 709-364-8714   800-563-6455
     centdair@nfld.com   www.centraldairies.com
Processor of dairy products and juice
     VP: Deve Collins
     CEO: Kennetch Peacock
     VP/General Manager: David Collins
     Manager Sales/Marketing: Ron Croke
     Plant Manager: Clarence Chaytor
Parent Co: Farmers Co-op Dairy
Type of Packaging: Consumer
Brands:
     Farmers Ice Cream
     Flavoured Milk

2574 Central Dairy Company
610 Madison St
Jefferson City, MO 65101-3199   573-635-6148
          Fax: 573-634-3028
Milk and ice cream
     President: Gale Hackman
     CEO: Chris Hackman
     VP: Steve Raithel
Estimated Sales: $20-50 Million
Number Employees: 50-99

2575 Central Grocers Cooperative
P.O.Box 1269
Franklin Park, IL 60131-8269   847-451-0660
     Fax: 847-288-8710   sales@central-grocers.com
               www.central-grocers.com
Wholesaler/distributor of equipment and fixtures, frozen foods, general line items, produce, meat products, etc
     President/CEO: Joseph Caccamo
     CEO: Jim Denges
Estimated Sales: $500,000-$1 Million
Number Employees: 250-499

2576 Central Meat & Provision Company
1603 National Ave
San Diego, CA 92113-1095   619-239-1391
          Fax: 619-239-1634
Processor of beef, pork and veal
     Owner: Robert Kuhlken
     VP Operations: Bert Risley
Estimated Sales: $10-20 Million
Number Employees: 20-49

2577 Central Michigan Foods
622 N Ball Street
Owosso, MI 48867-2310   517-723-3846
          pommypat@shianet.org
Processor and exporter of breakfast cereal and fruit juice concentrates
     President: Tom Creager

Type of Packaging: Consumer, Bulk
Brands:
     Scot Pride

2578 Central Milling Company
122 E Center St
Logan, UT 84321-4607   435-752-6625
     Fax: 435-753-7960 www.centralmilling.com/
Processor of pancake flour, Golden West All Purpose Flour, Red Rose All Purpose Flour, whole wheat flour, and Germade.
     President: H Roscoe Weston
     Quality Control: Jeff Daniels
     Mill Manager: Manuel Solis
     Mill Manager: Nathan Shumway
     Mill Manager: Melvin Alberta
     Secretary: James Weston
     Mill Manager/Electrician: Kurtis Williams
     Plant Manager: Fred Weston
Estimated Sales: $10-20 Million
Number Employees: 10-19
Type of Packaging: Consumer, Food Service
Brands:
     GOLDEN WEST
     RED ROSE

2579 Central Snacks
1700 N Pearl St
Carthage, MS 39051-8635   601-267-3112
     Fax: 601-267-5249   porkskin@aol.com
Pork skins
     President: N Carson
Estimated Sales: $2.5-5 Million
Number Employees: 10-19

2580 Central Soya
38 Colfax St
Pawtucket, RI 02860-3422   401-724-3800
          Fax: 401-724-4313   800-556-6777
               www.centralsoya.com
Processor of shortenings and edible oils including corn, canola, peanut, cottonseed, coconut, vegetable and soybean; exporter and importer of popcorn and frying oils and shortenings
     President: Sidney Dressler
     VP Sales/Marketing: Larry Dressler
     Plant Manager: David Parrillo
Estimated Sales: $50-100 Million
Number Employees: 20-49
Type of Packaging: Bulk
Brands:
     COLFAX
     GOLDLINE
     POPSIT

2581 Central Valley Dairymen
PO Box 576767
Modesto, CA 95357-6767   209-551-2667
          Fax: 209-551-2672
Cooperative of dairy product processors
     Chairman Board: Joe Machado
     Controller: Dee Wooldridge
Number Employees: 1-4

2582 Centreside Dairy
61 Lorne Street N
Renfrew, ON K7V 1L1
Canada   613-432-2914
          Fax: 613-432-5157
Processor of ice cream; wholesaler/distributor of dairy products
     President: Mark Tracey
     General Manager: Melany Tracey
Number Employees: 50-99
Type of Packaging: Consumer, Food Service, Private Label
Brands:
     ECONOMY
     PREMIUM
     TRACEY'S

2583 Century Foods International
400 Century Ct
Sparta, WI 54656-2468   608-269-1900
          Fax: 608-269-1910   800-269-1901
     info@centuryfoods.com   www.centuryfoods.com

Century Foods International is a manufacturer of nutritional powders and ready-to-drink beverages under private label and contract manufacturing agreements for food, sports, health and nutritional supplement industries. Other services provided include agglomeration, blending and instantizing, research and development, analytical testing, and packaging from bulk to consumer size.
     President: Tom Miskowski
     VP R&D: Julie Wagner
     VP Sales/Marketing: Kevin Meyer
     VP Operations: Wade Nolte
Number Employees: 250-499
Sq. footage: 420000
Parent Co: Hormel Foods Corporation
Type of Packaging: Private Label, Bulk
Brands:
     CENPREM
     LACEY DELITE
     PIZAZZ
     READY CHEESE

2584 (HQ)Cereal Food Processors
2001 Shawnee Mission Pkwy #110
Mission, KS 66205-2097   913-890-6300
     Fax: 913-890-6382   info@cerealfood.com
               www.cerealfood.com
Manufacturer and exporter of flour
     President: J Breck Barton
     President: J Breck Barton
     VP Sales: Don Shields
     VP Operations: John Erker
Estimated Sales: $20-50 Million
Number Employees: 20-49
Type of Packaging: Consumer
Other Locations:
     Cereal Food Processors Plant
     Los Angeles CA
     Cereal Food Processors Plant
     Kansas City MO
     Cereal Food Processors Plant
     McPherson KS
     Cereal Food Processors Plant
     Billings MT
     Cereal Food Processors Plant
     Great Falls MT
     Cereal Food Processors Plant
     Cleveland OH
     Cereal Food Processors Plant
     Portland OR
     Cereal Food Processors Plant
     Ogden UT
     Cereal Food Processors Plant
     Salt Lake City UT
     Cereal Food Processors Plant
     Montreal QC

2585 Cereal Food Processors
404 E 4500 S # B34
Salt Lake City, UT 84107-2700   801-265-3855
     Fax: 801-355-1152   info@cerealfood.com
               www.allstate.com
Processor of wheat flour
     Owner: Jaymie B Carroll
     Plant Superintendant: Max Horrocks
Estimated Sales: $10-24.9 Million
Number Employees: 10-19
Parent Co: Cereal Food Processors

2586 Cereal Food Processors
2001 Shawnee Mission Pkwy #110
Mission, KS 66205-2097   913-890-6300
     Fax: 913-890-6382   info@cerealfood.com
               www.cerealfood.com
Processor of flour
     President: J Breck Barton
     Chairman: Fred Merrill
     Vice Chairman: David Mattson
     Executive VP/Administration and Finance:
     Steven Heeney
     Senior VP Sales: Timothy Miller
     VP Operations: John Erker
Estimated Sales: $20-50 Million
Number Employees: 20-49
Parent Co: Cereal Food Processors
Type of Packaging: Consumer, Food Service, Private Label, Bulk

2587 Cereal Food Processors
1635 Merwin Ave
Cleveland, OH 44113-2476   216-621-3206
          Fax: 216-621-0404
Processor of flour
     Owner: Fred Merrill
Estimated Sales: $20-50 Million
Number Employees: 20-49

Type of Packaging: Private Label, Bulk

2588 Cereal Food Processors
2001 Shawnee Mission Pkwy #110
Mission, KS 66205-2097   913-890-6300
Fax: 913-890-6382   info@cerealfood.com
www.cerealfood.com
Cereals
President: J Breck Barton
Sales: Mark Dobbins
Estimated Sales: $20-50 Million
Number Employees: 20-49

2589 Cereal Ingredients
10835 NW Ambassador Dr
Kansas City, MO 64153-1241   816-891-1055
Fax: 816-891-7606   cereal@cerealingredients.com
www.cerealingredients.com
Proprietary, specialized ingredients developed from
wheat fiber concentrates
Chairman, CEO: Bob Hatch
Executive VP Sales/Marketing: James Thomasson

Estimated Sales: $1-2.5 Million
Number Employees: 50-99

2590 Cereal Ingredients
10835 NW Ambassador Dr
Kansas City, MO 64153-1241   816-891-1055
Fax: 816-891-7606   www.cerealingredients.com
Cereal ingredients
Owner: Robert Hatch
Executive VP: James Thomasson
Sales Manager: Vance Allred
Estimated Sales: $1-2.5 Million
Number Employees: 50-99

2591 Ceres Fruit Juices
7270 Woodbine Avenue
Suite 201
Markham, ON L3R 4B9
Canada   905-474-4450
Fax: 905-474-2536   800-905-1116
www.ceresjuices.com
All natural, 100% pure fruit juice

2592 Cerestar USA
1030 State Docks Rd
Decatur, AL 35601-7538   256-355-8815
Fax: 256-351-8012   www.cargill.com
Manufacturer of high-fructose corn syrup; also, corn
starch
President: Mitch Gardner
VP Operations: Gary Thompson
Estimated Sales: $100-500 Million
Number Employees: 100-249
Parent Co: Eridania Beghin-Say
Brands:
TRU-SWEET

2593 Cerestar USA
1100 S Indianapolis Boulevard
Hammond, IN 46320-1094   800-348-9896
Fax: 219-473-6601   jrohrer@us.ebsworld.com
www.cerestar.com
Manufacturer and exporter of specialty corn starch,
corn syrup solids, maltodextrin, dextrin and
cyclodextrin
President/CEO: Carl Hausmann
VP Sales/Marketing: Kevin Weber
General Manager: Thad Jones
Estimated Sales: $160 Million
Number Employees: 600
Parent Co: Eridania Beghin-Say
Type of Packaging: Food Service, Bulk
Brands:
AMAIZO
CAVITRON
FRO-DEX
LO-DEX

2594 Cericola Farms
RR 1
Bradford, ON L3Z 2A4
Canada   905-939-2962
Fax: 905-939-8423   877-939-4449
Processor of chicken and turkey also, fresh and
frozen eggs and egg products
President: Amedeo Cericola
VP: Anthony Cericola
Co-Owner: Anthony Cericola
Co-Owner/VP: Mary Cericola
Marketing Director: Amedeo Cericola
Number Employees: 100-249

Type of Packaging: Consumer, Food Service, Private Label, Bulk
Brands:
SureFresh Foods

2595 Certi-Fresh Foods
7410 Scout Ave
Bell Gardens, CA 90201-4932   562-806-1100
Fax: 562-806-2047   info@certi-fresh.com
www.certi-fresh.com
seafood processing and distribution
President/CEO/Owner: Nino Palma
President: Larry Cirin
CFO: Scott Obel
Quality Control: Michael Jamehdor
VP Marketing and Merchandising: Dave Versak
Sales: Pete Palma
Plant Manager: Tom Dukescherer
Purchasing: Revi Ayla
Estimated Sales: $75 Million
Number Employees: 130
Type of Packaging: Consumer, Food Service
Brands:
CERTI-FRESH

2596 Certified Grocers Midwest
1 Certified Dr
Hodgkins, IL 60525-4894   708-352-1232
Fax: 708-354-7502   www.certisaver.com
President: James Bradley
CEO: Jim Denges
Number Employees: 100-249

2597 Certified Processing Corporation
184 Us Highway 22
Hillside, NJ 07205-1895   973-923-5200
Processor of caffeine
President: Paul Iacono
Estimated Sales: $ 1 - 3 Million
Number Employees: 1-4
Sq. footage: 35000

2598 Certified Savory
5315 Dansher Road
Countryside, IL 60525-3101   800-328-7656
Fax: 847-244-5612   800-328-7656
dgoral@certifiedsavory.com
www.certifiedsavory.com
Processor of anchovy pastes, anchovy powders, fish
sauces
President: John Novak Jr.
CFO: Luigi Buffone
VP: Ralph Pirritano
Quality Control: Galina Mann
Sales: Dan Goral
Production: Tracy Swanson
Plant Manager: Galvin Reynolds
Purchasing: Andrew Kaminski
Estimated Sales: $ 20 - 50 Million
Number Employees: 50-99
Number of Brands: 2
Sq. footage: 25000
Parent Co: Sokol and Company
Type of Packaging: Food Service, Bulk

2599 Cervantes Foods Products
5801 Gibson Blvd SE
Albuquerque, NM 87108-4833   505-262-2253
Fax: 505-262-2253   877-982-4453
nmchile@earthlink.net
www.nmchileproducts.com
Chiles: red and green; fresh, dried, canned, frozen
Owner: Roberta Finley
Estimated Sales: $ 1 - 3 Million
Number Employees: 20-49

2600 Chaddsford Winery
632 Baltimore Pike
Chadds Ford, PA 19317-9305   610-388-6221
Fax: 610-388-0360   cfwine@chaddsford.com
www.chaddsford.com
Wines
Owner: Eric Miller
Winemaker: Eric Miller
Special Events Planner: Betsie Williamson
Marketing Director: Lee Miller
Sales Director: William Harris
Public Relations: Larry D'Antonio
Operations Manager: James Osborn
Estimated Sales: $1-2.5 Million
Number Employees: 5-9
Type of Packaging: Private Label
Brands:
CHADDSFORD

2601 Chadler
400 Eagle Ct
Swedesboro, NJ 08085-1758   856-467-0099
Fax: 856-467-8024   www.barry-callebaut.com
Processor and exporter of cocoa products, including
powder, butter and liqueur
President: Bill Mahaffy
Estimated Sales: $50-100 Million
Number Employees: 50-99
Parent Co: Chadley

2602 Chalet Cheese Cooperative
N4858 County Rd N
Monroe, WI 53566-9355   608-325-4343
Fax: 608-325-4409
Cheese
Manager: Myron Olson
Marketing Director: Myron Olson
Plant Manager: Myron Olson
Estimated Sales: $10-20 Million
Number Employees: 20-49
Type of Packaging: Private Label

2603 Chalet Debonne Vineyards
7743 Doty Rd
Madison, OH 44057-9512   440-466-3485
Fax: 440-466-6753   info@debonne.com
www.debonne.com
Wines and vineyard
Owner: Anthony Debevc
Treasurer: Rose Debevc
Vice President: Tony Debevc
Estimated Sales: $2.5-5 Million
Number Employees: 10-19

2604 Chalet Desserts
33063 Western Avenue
Union City, CA 94587-2156   510-783-8300
Fax: 510-783-1268
Processor and exporter of frozen desserts including
cheesecake, layer cake, mousse cake, brownies and
sheet cake; also, custom frozen desserts
President: Gordon Everett
Plant Manager: Chris Mahar
Estimated Sales: $20-50 Million
Number Employees: 50-99
Sq. footage: 34000
Parent Co: Harte Foods
Type of Packaging: Consumer, Food Service, Private Label, Bulk
Brands:
CALIFORNIA
CHALET
CHALET DESSERTS
LINDY'S

2605 Chalk Hill Estate Vineyards & Winery
10300 Chalk Hill Rd
Healdsburg, CA 95448-9558   707-838-4306
Fax: 707-838-9687   estatevine@aol.com
www.chalkhill.com
Wines
President: Frederick Furth
CEO: Peggy Furth
CFO: Melina Hobby
VP Winemaker: Steven Laveque
Marketing Director: Nancy Bailey
VP Sales: Craige Bennett
VP Vineyard Operations: Mark Lingenfelder
Estimated Sales: $10-20 Million
Number Employees: 20-49
Type of Packaging: Private Label
Brands:
CHALK HILL ESTATE BOTTLED
CHALK HILL ESTATE SELECTION

2606 Challenge Dairy Products
P.O.Box 2369
Dublin, CA 94568-0706   925-828-6160
Fax: 925-551-7591   800-733-2479
www.challengedairy.com
Processor and exporter of butter and dehydrated
milk; wholesaler/distributor of butter and frozen
foods; serving the food service market
President, CEO: John Whetten
CFO: Alan Maag
CEO: Irv Holmes
VP of Retail: Bud Tuohy
Estimated Sales: $100+ Million
Number Employees: 50-99
Type of Packaging: Consumer, Food Service, Private Label, Bulk

Brands:
CHALLENGE
CHALLENGE DANISH

2607 Chalmette Packing Company
17145 Million Dollar Road
Covington, LA 70435-7968   504-271-6241
                                Fax: 504-271-5559
Processor of meat products including luncheon, beef
and pork
Owner: Keith Pageaglia
Estimated Sales: $10-20 Million
Number Employees: 10-19
Type of Packaging: Consumer, Food Service, Bulk

2608 (HQ)Chalone Wine Group
621 Airpark Rd
Napa, CA 94558-6272   707-254-4200
Fax: 707-254-4201 pr@chalonewinegroup.com
                   www.chalonewinegroup.com
Wines
President/CEO: Kendall-Jackson Winery
CEO: Kendall-Jackson Winery
CEO: Thomas B Selfridge
Sales Director: Sara Brewer
Public Relations: Ken Morris
Estimated Sales: $6 Million
Number Employees: 100-249

2609 Champignon North America
600 E Palisade Ave # 25
Englewood Cliffs, NJ 07632-1826   201-871-7211
                                    Fax: 201-871-7214
customerservice@champignon-usa.com
                www.champignon-usa.com
Gourmet cheeses.
President: Birgit Bernhard
VP: Olaf Glaser
Estimated Sales: $8 Million
Number Employees: 5-9
Number of Brands: 2
Brands:
BRIE W/GARLIC DE LUXE
CAMBOZOLA
CHAMPIGNON
HOFMEISTER
MIRABO
MONTAGNOLO
ROUGETTE
ROYAL BAVARIAN

2610 Champion Beverages
44 Talmadge Hill Road
Darien, CT 06820-2125   203-655-9026
                             Fax: 203-655-0676
Beer, dairy drinks
President/CEO: Joseph Tighe
Estimated Sales: $1-2.5 Million
Number Employees: 1-4
Brands:
ERIN'S ROCK AMBER AND STOUT
SMOOTHIE SPARKLING CHOC.EGG CREAM
STALLION X MALT LIQUOR

2611 Champion Nutrition
1301 Sawgrass Corporate Pkwy
Sunrise, FL 33323-2813   925-689-1790
Fax: 925-689-0821 800-225-4831
info@champion-nutrition.com
www.champion-nutrition.com
Processor and exporter of sports nutrition supple-
ments
CEO/Preisent: Michael Zumpano
Industry Contact: Christy Olson
Estimated Sales: $10-20 Million
Number Employees: 50-99
Brands:
HEAVYWEIGHT GAINER 900
MET-MAX
METABOLOL
MUSCLE NITRO
OXI PRO METABOLOL
REVENGE

2612 Champlain Valley Apiaries Company
P.O.Box 127
Middlebury, VT 05753-0127   802-388-7724
Fax: 802-388-1653 800-841-7334
cva@together.net
www.champlainvalleyhoney.com

Processor of liquid and natural crystallized honey
Owner: Charles Mraz
Office Manager: Sue Synder
Bee Keeper: James Gabriel
Estimated Sales: $2.5-5 Million
Number Employees: 1-4
Type of Packaging: Consumer

2613 Champlain Valley Milling Corporation
P.O.Box 454
Westport, NY 12993-0454   518-962-4711
Fax: 518-962-8799 cvm@westelcom.com
                   http://www.westelcom.com
Processor of organic and kosher whole grain flour
including spring wheat, stone ground, soy, rye,
white, whole pastry, pancake, etc
President: Samuel Sherman
Vice President: Paul Barton
Operations Manager: Donald White
Estimated Sales: $5-9.9 Million
Number Employees: 5-9
Type of Packaging: Private Label
Brands:
CHAMP

2614 Champoeg Wine Cellars
10375 Champoeg Rd NE
Aurora, OR 97002-8657   503-678-2144
                             Fax: 503-678-1024
champoeg@champoegwine.com
www.champoegwine.com
Wines
Owner: Lounna Eggert
Estimated Sales: $1-2.5 Million
Number Employees: 1-4

2615 Chandler Foods
2727 Immanuel Rd
Greensboro, NC 27407-2515   336-299-1934
Fax: 336-854-4649 800-537-6219
cfoods@triad.rr.com www.carolinabarbecue.com
Manufacturer of barbecue products including pork,
chicken and beef; also, chili products including
frozen, hot dog and con carne
CEO: John Chandler
EVP: Jeff Chandler
Estimated Sales: $5-9.9 Million
Number Employees: 20-49
Sq. footage: 39900
Type of Packaging: Food Service
Brands:
CHANDLR FOODS

2616 Chang Food Company
13941 Nautilus Dr
Garden Grove, CA 92843-4026   714-265-9990
                                   Fax: 714-265-9996
Processor of process frozen egg rolls, spring rolls,
soba noodle, egg noodle bowls (stir fried tofu, vege-
table, etc)
President: Van Ntuyen
Manager: Nhuan Nguyen
Estimated Sales: $2.5-$3 Million
Number Employees: 20-49
Sq. footage: 9800
Type of Packaging: Consumer, Food Service, Pri-
vate Label, Bulk
Brands:
Chang Food

2617 Channel Fish ProcessingCompany
18 Food Mart Rd
Boston, MA 02118-2802   617-464-3366
Fax: 617-464-3377 info@channelfish.com
                   www.channelfish.com
Fresh and frozen seafood
President: John Zaffiro
CFO: Kevin Pickett
Inventory Control: Paul D'Agostino
COO: Roy Zaffiro
Production Supervisor: James Gallagher
Plant Manager: John Roberts
Estimated Sales: $10-20 Million
Number Employees: 50-99

2618 Channing Rudd Cellars
PO Box 426
Middletown, CA 95461-0426   707-987-2209
Wines
President: J Rudd
Number Employees: 20-49

2619 Chappaqua Crunch
65 Tedesco St
Marblehead, MA 01945-1039   781-631-8118
                                 Fax: 781-631-8113
Granola, snack foods
President: Debbie Waugh
Estimated Sales: Under $500,000
Number Employees: 1-4

2620 Chappellet Winery
1581 Sage Canyon Rd
St Helena, CA 94574-9628   707-963-7136
Fax: 707-963-7445 800-494-6379
info@chappellet.com www.chappellet.com
Wines
Founder/President: Donn Chappellet
Founder: Molly Chappallet
Marketing/Sales: Cyril Chappellet
Director National Sales: Steve Tamburelli
Winery/Vineyard Operations: Jon-Mark
Chappellet
Winemaker: Phillip Corallo-Titus
Vineyard Manager: David Pirio
Purchasing Manager: Carissa Chappellet
Estimated Sales: $5-10 Million
Number Employees: 20-49
Type of Packaging: Private Label
Brands:
CHAPPALLET

2621 Chappellet Winery
1581 Sage Canyon Rd
St Helena, CA 94574-9628   707-963-7136
Fax: 707-963-7445 800-494-6379
winery@chappellet.com www.chappellet.com
Wines
Founder: Donn Chappellet
Co-Founder: Molly Chappellet
Director National Sales: Steve Tamburelli
Estimated Sales: $ 10 - 20 Million
Number Employees: 20-49

2622 Char Crust
3017 N Lincoln Ave
Chicago, IL 60657-4242   773-528-0600
Fax: 773-472-1101 800-311-9884
charcrust@charcrust.com www.charcrust.com
Dry-rub seasonings for all meat and fish
President: Bernard Silver
Estimated Sales: $500,000-$1 Million
Number Employees: 5-9
Brands:
CHAR CRUST

2623 Char-Wil Canning Company
6818 Hunting Creek Road
Hurlock, MD 21643-3318   410-943-3580
                              Fax: 410-943-3580
Processor and canner of whole and peeled tomatoes
Owner/Partner: Charles Adams
Number Employees: 6
Type of Packaging: Consumer, Food Service, Pri-
vate Label, Bulk
Brands:
Char-Wil

2624 Charcuterie LaTour Eiffel
485 Rue Lavoie
Vanier, QC G1M 2J8
Canada   418-687-2840
              Fax: 418-688-9558
Processor and exporter of fresh and frozen pork
Marketing Director: Francois Couture
Parent Co: McCain Foods USA
Type of Packaging: Bulk
Brands:
Bilopage
Tour Eiffel

2625 Charles B. Mitchell Vineyards
8221 Stoney Creek Rd
Somerset, CA 95684-9231   530-620-3467
Fax: 530-620-1005 800-704-9463
cbmvwine@inforum.net
www.charlesbmitchell.com
Wine
Owner: Michael Conti
Estimated Sales: $2.5-5 Million
Number Employees: 5-9
Type of Packaging: Private Label

2626 Charles Boggini
733 Bread and Milk St
Coventry, CT 06238-1014   860-742-2652
Fax: 860-742-7903   glen@bogginicola.com
www.chasbcola.com
Manufacturer and exporter of flavoring extracts
President: Glen Boggini
VP: David Boggini
Estimated Sales: $5-10 Million
Number Employees: 5-9
Type of Packaging: Consumer

2627 Charles Clay Ltd
110 Post Road
Darien, CT 06820   203-662-0125
Fax: 203-662-1229
admin@englishribbonsbows.com
www.englishribbonsbows.com
English ribbons and bows

2628 Charles Dennery Pillsbury
1520 Kuebel St
New Orleans, LA 70123-6972   504-733-2331
Fax: 504-733-8669
Manufacturer and exporter of bakery and ice cream
supplies
Estimated Sales: $5-10 Million
Number Employees: 1-4
Parent Co: DCA Food Industries
Type of Packaging: Food Service, Bulk

2629 Charles H. Baldwin & Sons
P.O.Box 372
West Stockbridge, MA 01266-0372   413-232-7785
Fax: 413-232-0114 www.baldwinextracts.com
Manufacturer of flavoring extracts and flavors, ma-
ple table syrup and supplier of baking supplies.
Owner: Earl Moffatt
Estimated Sales: $500,000-$1 Million
Number Employees: 1-4
Brands:
Baldwin

2630 Charles H. Parks & Company
P.O.Box 100
Fishing Creek, MD 21634-0100   410-397-3400
Fax: 410-397-3400
Manufacturer of fresh, canned and pasteurized crab-
meat; also, fresh crabs
President: Virgil Ruark Jr Jr
Estimated Sales: $3-5 Million
Number Employees: 10-19
Sq. footage: 3000
Type of Packaging: Consumer
Brands:
CAPTAIN CHARLIE

2631 Charles Heitzman Bakery
804 Eastern Pkwy
Louisville, KY 40217-2262   502-635-2651
Fax: 502-634-1197
Baked goods
President: Tony Osting
Estimated Sales: $500,000-$1 Million
Number Employees: 5-9

2632 Charles J. Ross
401 Egle Road
Reading, PA 19601   610-685-5161
Fax: 717-843-0592
Estimated Sales: $300,000-500,000
Number Employees: 1-4

2633 Charles Jacquin Et Cie
2633 Trenton Ave
Philadelphia, PA 19125-1837   215-425-9300
Fax: 215-425-9438   800-523-3811
feedback@ou.org   www.chambordonline.com
Wines and liquors
President: Norton Cooper
CFO: Mark Small
CFO: Mark Small
V.P., National Sales Manager: Kevin O'Brien
VP: John Cooper
Sales Director: Mark Small
Operations Manager: Dr. Paul Stefan
Plant Manager: William Heinz
Estimated Sales: $50-100 Million
Number Employees: 100-249
Type of Packaging: Private Label
Brands:
BIRELL
Bocador
Botticelli

Canadian Whiskey
Devonshire Royal
Royale Montaine
Savory & James
Witenheim

2634 Charles Krug Winery
P.O.Box 191
St Helena, CA 94574-0191   707-967-2200
Fax: 707-967-2291   charleskmg@pmondavi.com;
information@pmondavi.com
www.charleskrug.com
Processor of wines
Proprietor: Peter Mondavi, Jr.
CEO/President: Peter Mondavi, Sr.
Proprietor: Marc Mondavi
CEO: Peter Mondavi Sr
Estimated Sales: $20 Million
Number Employees: 100-249
Brands:
Charles Krug
Ck Mondavi

2635 Charles M. Cook
PO Box 12
Bailey Island, ME 04003-0012   207-833-6641
Fax: 207-833-5851
President: Norman Parent
Estimated Sales: $ 3 - 5 Million
Number Employees: 50-99

2636 Charles Poultry Company
2943 Charlestown Rd
Lancaster, PA 17603-9758   717-872-7621
Fax: 717-872-9570
Processor of free range and all natural chicken and
turkey including whole cut up, cutlets, legs, wings,
whole breasts, drums, thighs, etc
President: Ken Charles
VP: Richard Charles
Estimated Sales: $20-50 Million
Number Employees: 20-49
Sq. footage: 9000
Parent Co: Charles Poultry Live Broker
Type of Packaging: Consumer, Food Service, Pri-
vate Label, Bulk

2637 Charles Rockel & Son
4303 Smith Rd
Cincinnati, OH 45212-4236   513-631-3009
Fax: 513-631-3083
Food brokers of dairy/deli products, frozen foods,
general merchandise, groceries, industrial ingredi-
ents, etc
President: Charles Rockel
CFO: Don Rockel
Estimated Sales: $2.5-5 Million
Number Employees: 3

2638 Charles Smart Donair Submarine
8952 82nd Avenue NW
Edmonton, AB T6C 0Z3
Canada   780-468-2099
Fax: 780-462-4647
Processor of raw, cooked, fresh and frozen spiced
beef
President: Chawki El Homeira
Number Employees: 5-9
Type of Packaging: Food Service
Brands:
Son Bake Kita
Son's Bun

2639 Charles Spinetta Winery
12557 Steiner Road
Plymouth, CA 95669-9510   209-245-3384
Fax: 209-245-3386
www.charlesspinettawinery.com
Table wine including wines for bulk market
Owner: Charles Spinetta
Estimated Sales: $1-2.5 Million
Number Employees: 1-4
Brands:
Charles Spinetta Barbera
Charles Spinetta Primitivo
Charles Spinetta Zinfanel

2640 Charles' Chips
Livermore Road
Calhoun, KY 42327   270-273-3282
Manager: Michael Scibona

2641 Charleston Tea Plantation
6617 Maybank Hwy
Wadmalaw Island, SC 29487-7006   843-559-0383
Fax: 843-559-3049   800-443-5987
chastea@awod.com
Tea
Co-President: Bill Hall
Estimated Sales: $2,900,000
Number Employees: 20-49
Brands:
American Classic Tea

2642 Charlie Beigg's Sauce Company
4 Heritage Lane
Windham, ME 04062-4984   888-502-8595
sales@charliebeiggs.com
www.charliebeiggs.com
Manufacturer of BBQ sauce and salsa.
Head of Sales/Marketing: Paula Standley
Parent Co: Equitythink Holdings, LLC

2643 Charlie Palmer Group
372 5th Ave
New York, NY 10018-8106   212-967-6942
Fax: 212-750-8613   888-287-3653
info@charliepalmer.com
www.charliepalmer.com
Pan sauces, dessert sauces
Owner: Charlie Lee
Estimated Sales: $2.5-5 Million
Number Employees: 50-99
Brands:
Charlie Palmer

2644 Charlie Trotter Foods
816 W Armitage Ave
Chicago, IL 60614-4308   773-248-6228
Fax: 773-248-6088   info@charlietrotters.com
www.charlietrotters.com
Sauces, smoked salmon and natural products
Owner, Chef: Charlie Trotter
Estimated Sales: $ 1 - 3 Million
Number Employees: 50-99

2645 Charlie's Country Sausage
4005 Burdick Expy E
Minot, ND 58701-5462   701-838-6302
Manufacturer of meat products including salami,
honey ham and sausage
Owner: Charles Weiskopf
Estimated Sales: $1-2.5 Million
Number Employees: 6

2646 Charlie's Pride Meats
P.O.Box 58204
Los Angeles, CA 90058-0204   323-585-3358
Fax: 323-587-7317   877-866-0982
info@cpmhotline.com   www.cpmhotline.com
Processor and exporter of roast beef, corned beef
and pastrami
President: Charles Dickman
VP: James Dickman
Regional Sales Manager: Phil Tanico
Plant Manager: James Miller
Estimated Sales: $ 50 - 100 Million
Number Employees: 50-99
Number of Products: 50
Type of Packaging: Consumer, Food Service, Pri-
vate Label, Bulk

2647 Charlie's Specialties
2500 Freedland Rd
Hermitage, PA 16148-9022   724-346-2350
Fax: 724-346-1110   charlies@htol.net
Fancy cookies
President: John Thier
Sales: Joe Webb
Plant Manager: Frank Keck
Purchasing Manager: Frank Keck
Estimated Sales: $5-10 Million
Number Employees: 100-249
Number of Products: 45
Sq. footage: 24000

2648 Charlotte's Confections
1395 El Camino Real
Millbrae, CA 94030-1410   650-589-1126
Fax: 650-589-1923   800-798-2427
lisa@charlottesconfections.com
www.charlottesconfections.com

Boxed chocolates, taffy, caramel, brittle, fudge, marshmallow, and holiday specialties.
President: Jeffrey Sosnick
Vice President: Sean Callaway
Marketing Director: Susan Muniak
Production Coordinator: Jim Macintire
Purchasing Manager: Jim Macintire
Estimated Sales: $5 Million
Number Employees: 50-99
Sq. footage: 24000
Type of Packaging: Consumer, Food Service, Private Label, Bulk

2649 Charlton Deep Sea Charters
P.O.Box 637
Warrenton, OR 97146-0637   503-338-0569
      Fax: 503-861-3229 www.charltoncharters.com
Seafood, including halibut, salmon, sturgeon, tuna, bottomfish
President: Mark Charlton
Purchasing Manager: Mark Charlton
Estimated Sales: $2.5-5 Million
Number Employees: 1-4

2650 Chartrand Imports
P.O.Box 1319
Rockland, ME 04841-1319   207-594-7300
      Fax: 207-594-8098   800-473-7307
            www.chartrandimports.com
Import broker of organic wine
President: Paul Chartrand
Estimated Sales: $ 1 - 3 Million
Number Employees: 1-4
Number of Brands: 50
Number of Products: 150
Type of Packaging: Consumer, Private Label

2651 Chase Brothers Dairy
P.O.Box 1272
Oxnard, CA 93032-1272   805-487-4981
      Fax: 805-487-2529   800-438-6455
Processor of milk and related products including fluid, half and half, chocolate, low-fat, nonfat, buttermilk, eggnog and shakes; also, juices, concentrates and drinks including orange, etc
Manager: Ken Mercer
General Manager: Ken Mercer
Operations Manager: Jonathan Chase
Purchasing: Ken Mercer
Estimated Sales: $50-100 Million
Number Employees: 20-49
Sq. footage: 7000
Parent Co: Hailwood
Type of Packaging: Consumer, Food Service
Brands:
CHASE BROTHERS
GOLD COAST

2652 Chase Candy Company
P.O.Box 698
St Joseph, MO 64502-0698   816-279-1625
      Fax: 816-279-1997   800-786-1625
info@cherrymash.com   www.cherrymash.com
Processor of candy including bagged, bar, brittle, chocolate, coconut, fund raising, multi-pack, vending, Christmas, Easter, Halloween and Valentine
President: Barry Yantis
Purchasing Manager: Barry Yantis
Estimated Sales: $ 10 - 20 Million
Number Employees: 20-49
Sq. footage: 20000
Type of Packaging: Consumer, Bulk
Brands:
CHERRY MASH
POE BRANDS

2653 Chase Farms
Rr 1 Box 158
Walkerville, MI 49459   231-873-3337
      Fax: 231-873-5699   info@chasefarms.org
            www.chasefarmsinc.com
Frozen fruits, fruit juices and vegetables.
President/General Manager: Michael Chase
VP/Agriculture Manager: Brett Chase
Quality Control: Michelle Shaddock
Sales: Lorraine Chase
Plant Manager: Vince Vinskowski
Estimated Sales: $2.5-5 Million
Number Employees: 250-499
Type of Packaging: Consumer, Food Service, Private Label, Bulk
Brands:
Chase Farms

Eagle Valley
Hillcrest

2654 Chases Lobster Pound
PO Box 1
Port Howe, NS B0K 1K0
Canada   902-243-2408
      Fax: 902-243-3334
Processor and exporter of fresh and frozen lobster
Owner/Manager: Earl Chase
Number Employees: 10-19
Type of Packaging: Consumer, Food Service, Private Label, Bulk

2655 Chateau Anne Marie
6580 NE Mineral Springs Rd
Carlton, OR 97111-9529   503-864-2991
      Fax: 503-864-2203 www.anneamie.com
Wines
Owner: Robert Pamplin Jr
Purchasing: Scott Huffman
Estimated Sales: $5-10 Million
Number Employees: 20-49

2656 Chateau Boswell
3468 Silverado Trl N
St Helena, CA 94574-9662   707-963-5472
      josh@chateauboswellwinery.com
            www.chateauboswellwinery.com
Manufacturer of wines
President: Dr Thronton Boswell
COO: Susan Boswell
Operations Manager: Joshua Peeples
Estimated Sales: Less than $500,000
Number Employees: 1-4
Type of Packaging: Consumer
Brands:
Chateau Boswell
Chateau Boswell Estate
Jacquelynn Cuv'e
Jacquelynn Syrah

2657 Chateau Chevre Winery
2030 Hoffman Ln
Napa, CA 94558-9301   707-944-2184
      Fax: 707-944-2408
Wines
Owner: Jerry Hazen
Estimated Sales: Less than $100,000
Number Employees: 1-4
Type of Packaging: Private Label

2658 Chateau Diana Winery
6195 Dry Creek Rd
Healdsburg, CA 95448-8100   707-433-6992
      Fax: 707-433-0401   info@chateaud.com
            www.chateaudiana.com
Wines
President: Corey Manning
VP Marketing: Dawn Manning
VP Marketing: Dawn Manning
Estimated Sales: $5-10 Million
Number Employees: 20-49
Brands:
Chateau Diana

2659 Chateau Food Products
6137 W Cermak Rd
Cicero, IL 60804-2024   708-863-4207
      Fax: 708-863-5806 www.chateaufoods.com
Processor of frozen potato and bread dumplings
President: Donald Shotola
VP: Anita Shotola
Production: Jon Shotola
Estimated Sales: $1 Million
Number Employees: 5-9
Sq. footage: 10000
Type of Packaging: Consumer, Food Service
Brands:
Chateau
Mihel

2660 Chateau Grand Traverse
12239 Center Rd
Traverse City, MI 49686-8558   231-223-7355
      Fax: 231-223-4105 www.cgtwines.com

Wines
Owner: Ed Okeefe
Founder/CEO: Edward O'Keefe, Sr
VP/Trade Relations: Sean O'Keefe
Operations Manager/Controller: Terrie McClelland
Productions/shipping/Warehouse: Mark Groenevelt
Purchasing Manager: Mark Groenevelt
Estimated Sales: $2.5-5 Million
Number Employees: 10-19

2661 Chateau Julien Winery
8940 Carmel Valley Rd
Carmel, CA 93923-9577   831-624-2600
      Fax: 831-624-6138 www.chateaujulien.com
Wines
Owner: Robert Brower
VP National Sales: Tom Kencheloe
Winemaker: Bill Anderson
Estimated Sales: $1-2.5 Million
Number Employees: 10-19
Brands:
CHATEAU JULIEN
EMERALD BAY COASTAK
GARLAND RANCH

2662 Chateau LaFayette Reneau
P.O.Box 238
Hector, NY 14841-0238   607-546-2062
      Fax: 607-546-2069   800-469-9463
support@clrwine.com   www.clrwine.com
Wine
Owner: Dick Reno
CEO: Dick Reno
Vice President: Betty Reno
Purchasing Manager: Dick Reno
Estimated Sales: $5-10 Million
Number Employees: 20-49
Type of Packaging: Private Label

2663 Chateau Montelena Winery
1429 Tubbs Ln
Calistoga, CA 94515-9726   707-942-5105
      Fax: 707-942-4221 www.montelena.com
Wines
President: James Barrett
Marketing Director: Greg Ralston
Public Relations: Tom Inlay
Operations Manager: Bo Barrett
Estimated Sales: $10-20 Million
Number Employees: 20-49
Brands:
Chateau Montelena
Silverado Cellars

2664 Chateau Morisette Winery
P.O.Box 766
Meadows of Dan, VA 24120-0766   540-593-2865
      Fax: 540-593-2868   info@thedogs.com
            www.chateaumorrisette.com
President: David Morrisette
Purchasing Manager: Nora Cooper
Estimated Sales: $10-20 Million
Number Employees: 20-49

2665 Chateau Potelle Winery
4 Blackberry Dr
Napa, CA 94558-7016   707-255-9440
      Fax: 707-255-9444   info@chateaupotelle.com
            www.chateaupotelle.com
Wines
President: Jean Noel Fourmeaux
Purchasing Manager: Ulysses Montre
Estimated Sales: $2.5-5 Million
Number Employees: 5-9
Brands:
CHATEAU POTELLE

2666 Chateau Ra-Ha
P.O.Box 428
Jerseyville, IL 62052-0428   618-639-4841
      Fax: 618-639-0510   866-639-4832
chateauraha@gtec.com   www.gtec.com
Wines
Owner: Paul Arnold
Estimated Sales: $500,000-$1 Million
Number Employees: 1-4

2667 Chateau Sassenage
PO Box 1606
Truth or Consequences, NM 87901-4605   505-894-7244
      Fax: 505-894-9156

Wines
President: Jean-Marie Guillaume
Estimated Sales:$500,000-$1 Million
Number Employees: 1-4

2668 Chateau Souverain
PO Box 528
Geyserville, CA 95441-0528   707-433-3141
Fax: 707-433-5174 www.chateausouverain.com
Processor of cabernet sauvignon, merlot, sauvignon blanc, chardonnay and zinfandel
President: Dan Leese
Purchasing Manager: John Peavey
Estimated Sales:$20-50 Million
Number Employees: 50-99
Type of Packaging: Private Label
Brands:
CHATEAU SOUVERAIN

2669 Chateau St. Jean Vineyards
P.O.Box 293
Kenwood, CA 95452-0293   707-833-4134
Fax: 707-833-4200 www.chateaustjean.com
Processor of table wine
Manager: Margo Van Stafvaren
Winemaker/Operation Director: Margo Anstaavern
Public Relations Manager: Nicole Breier
Wine Maker: Steven Reeder
Estimated Sales:$10-24.9 Million
Number Employees: 50-99
Parent Co: Beringer Wine Estates
Type of Packaging: Consumer

2670 Chateau Thomas Winery
6291 Cambridge Way
Plainfield, IN 46168-7905   317-837-9463
Fax: 317-837-8464 888-761-9463
info@chateauthomas.com
www.chateauthomas.com
Premium vinifera wines made from West Coast grapes
President: Charles Thomas
Purchasing Manager: Tommy England
Estimated Sales:$5-9.9 Million
Number Employees: 20-49
Type of Packaging: Private Label
Brands:
CHATEAU THOMAS

2671 Chateau des Charmes Wines
PO Box 280
St. Davids, ON L0S 1P0
Canada   905-262-4219
Fax: 905-262-5548 800-263-2541
www.chateaudescharmes.com
Processor of wines and champagnes, ice wine
President: Paul Bosc
Secretary: Rodger Gordon
Director Marketing: Paul-Andre Bosc
Sales Director: Dianne McDonald
Number Employees: 100-249

2672 Chatham Foods
620 S Chatham Avenue
448
Siler City, NC 27344-3910   919-742-2141
Fax: 919-742-2141
Processor of sausage
President: Jerry Wood III
Number Employees: 20-49
Type of Packaging: Consumer

2673 Chatila's Bakery
254 N Broadway
Salem, NH 03079-2132   603-898-5459
Fax: 603-893-1586
customercare@chatilasbakery.com
www.chatilasbakery.com
All sugar-free items. Chatila's muffins, cookies, pastries, cheesecakes, donuts, bagels, pies, breads, chocolates and ice cream. All items sweetend with Splenda and/or Melltitol, low carb, low cal, low fat, low cholestrol, notrans-fat.
President: Mohamad Chatila
Sales: Jennifer Marks
Estimated Sales:$650,000-700,000
Number Employees: 10-19
Number of Brands: 1
Number of Products: 100+
Sq. footage: 12000
Type of Packaging: Consumer, Food Service, Private Label, Bulk

2674 Chatom Vineyards
P.O.Box 2730
Murphys, CA 95247-2730   209-736-6500
Fax: 209-736-6507 800-435-8852
info@chatomvineyards
www.chatomvineyards.com
Wines
President: Gay Callan
Production Manager: Scott Klann
Purchasing Manager: Mari Wells
Estimated Sales:$1-2.5 Million
Number Employees: 10-19
Number of Products: 7
Sq. footage: 4200
Brands:
SANGIOVESE
SYRAH

2675 Chattanooga Bakery
P.O.Box 111
Chattanooga, TN 37401-0111   423-267-3351
Fax: 423-266-2169 800-251-3404
linda@moonpie.com www.moonpie.com
Manufacturer of marshmallow snack cakes and sandwiches
President/CEO: Sam Campbell IV
CEO: Sam H Campbell Iv
VP Marketing: Tory Johnston
VP Sales: John Campbell
Estimated Sales:$20-50 Million
Number Employees: 100-249
Type of Packaging: Consumer
Brands:
MOON PIE

2676 Chattem Chemicals
3708 Saint Elmo Ave
Chattanooga, TN 37409-1235   423-822-5000
Fax: 423-825-0507
customerservice@chattemchemicals.com
www.chattemchemicals.com
Manufacturer of glycine and creatine monohydrate
Marketing Manager: Art Pavilidis
Business Manager: Milton Boyer
Executive VP: Jim Friederichsen
VP Sales/Marketing: Jim Kedrowski
Managing Director: Rodney Sergent
Estimated Sales:$5-10 Million
Number Employees: 5-9
Parent Co: Elcat
Type of Packaging: Bulk

2677 Chatz Roasting Company
PO Box 2765
Ceres, CA 95307-7765   510-265-1600
Fax: 510-265-1734 800-792-6333
chatzcoffee@linkline.com www.chatz.com
Gourmet coffee, tea, cocoa
President: Linda Blaney
CEO: Robert Heinz
DirecterMarketing: Robert Heinz
Estimated Sales:$10-20 Million
Number Employees: 20-49
Brands:
Chatz

2678 Chauvin Coffee Corporation
4160 Meramec St
St Louis, MO 63116-2518   314-772-0700
Fax: 314-772-0722 800-455-5282
info@chauvincoffee.com
www.chauvincoffee.com
Coffee
President: Dave Charleville
Sales Manager: Sonya Miller
Estimated Sales:$ 1 - 3 Million
Number Employees: 10-19
Type of Packaging: Private Label

2679 Chazy Orchards
P.O.Box 147
Chazy, NY 12921-0147   518-846-7171
Fax: 518-846-8171 chazyapples@westel.com
www.chazy.com
Grower of apples
Owner: Donald F Green Iii III
Estimated Sales:$ 5 - 10 Million
Number Employees: 20-49

2680 Cheddar Box Cheese House
264 Alpine Dr
Shawano, WI 54166-2039   715-526-5411
Fax: 715-524-9930 info@cheddarbox.com
www.cheddarbox.com
Processor of cheese spreads
President: James O'Betts
Estimated Sales:$400,000
Number Employees: 1-4
Brands:
CHEDDAR BOX CHEESE

2681 (HQ)Cheese Factory
19724 Huber Road
Borden, IN 47106-8309   812-923-8861
Cheese
President: Pat Huffman
General Manager: LaDonna Mitchell
Estimated Sales:$5-9.9 Million
Number Employees: 1-4

2682 Cheese Smokers
360 Johnson Ave
Brooklyn, NY 11206-2802   718-456-0531
Fax: 718-381-0534
Processor of naturally smoked cheeses including Swiss, kosher, cheddar, mozzarella and provolone; also, bars and deli loaves; contract smoking available
President: Irving Binik
VP: Bary Binik
VP Sales: Barry Binik
Estimated Sales:$1-2.5 Million
Number Employees: 10-19
Sq. footage: 12000
Type of Packaging: Consumer, Food Service, Private Label, Bulk
Brands:
Hic-O-Ree
La-natural

2683 Cheese Straws & More
5717 Desiard Street
Monroe, LA 71203-4793   318-343-4666
Fax: 318-343-6333 800-997-1921
schwab@cheesestraws.com
www.cheesestraws.com
Processor of straws including Cajun cheese and southern tea; also, pecan pralines, candied pecans and pecan brittle
President: Brenda Schwab
Number Employees: 1-4

2684 CheeseLand
P.O.Box 22230
Seattle, WA 98122-0230   206-709-1220
Fax: 206-709-1818
Cheese
President: Jan Kos
Estimated Sales:$1-2.5 Million
Number Employees: 1-4

2685 Cheesecake Aly
530 Broad St
Glen Rock, NJ 07452-1308   201-444-8590
Fax: 201-444-8454 800-555-8862
chzcakealy@aol.com www.cheesecakealy.com
Processor of cheesecakes and desserts
President: Aly Boyd
Estimated Sales:$1-3 Million
Number Employees: 10-19
Sq. footage: 4000
Type of Packaging: Consumer, Food Service, Bulk
Brands:
Cheesecake Aly

2686 Cheesecake Etc. Desserts
400 Swallow Dr
Miami Springs, FL 33166-4432   305-887-0258
Fax: 305-888-5463 cheesecakeemail@aol.com
Cheesecakes, key lime pies, diner style layer cakes, individual dessert cups; including all varieties of layer cakes, cheesecake, and key lime pie
President: Dr. William Wolar
Vice President: Suzanne Conlon
Production: Dionis Reyes
Estimated Sales:$5-9.9 Million
Number Employees: 5-9
Number of Brands: 3
Number of Products: 25
Sq. footage: 10000
Type of Packaging: Food Service
Brands:
Florida Key Lime Pie

2687 Cheesecake Factory
26901 Malibu Hills Rd
Calabasas Hills, CA 91301-5354   818-871-3000
    Fax: 818-871-3100 www.cheesecakefactory.net
Cheesecakes
    President/CEO: David Overton
Estimated Sales: $37,800,000
Number Employees: 10,000+
Brands:
    Cheesecake Factory

2688 Cheesecake Momma
200 W Henry St
Ukiah, CA 95482-4355   707-462-2253
    Fax: 707-468-9056 momma@pacific.net
        www.cheesecakemomma.com
Processor and wholesaler of cheesecake including
all natural and 100% organic
    President: Robin Collier
    Vice President: Alana Rouse
    Purchasing Manager: Robin Collier
Estimated Sales: $2.5-5 Million
Number Employees: 20-49

2689 Cheeze Kurls
3711 Dykstra Drive NW
Grand Rapids, MI 49544-9745   616-784-6095
    Fax: 616-784-7445 www.cksnacks.com
Processor of snack foods including popcorn and
cheese curls
    President: Ed DeDinas
    VP: Bob Franzak
Number Employees: 20-49
Sq. footage: 30000
Type of Packaging: Consumer, Food Service, Private Label, Bulk
Brands:
    CK

2690 Cheezwhse.Com
111 Business Park Dr
Armonk, NY 10504   914-273-1400
    Fax: 914-273-2052 800-243-3994
    sales@cheezwhse.com   www.cheezwhse.com
Dairy products
    President/Owner: Joseph Gellert
Estimated Sales: $6.2 Million
Number Employees: 30

2691 Chef America
9601 Canoga Ave
Chatsworth, CA 91311-4115
        www.chefamerica.com
    818-718-8111
Processor of prepared frozen foods including stuffed
sandwiches and croissants, pizza snacks and waffles
    CEO: Paul Merage
    CFO: Glenn Lee
    VP: Larry Johnson
    Research & Development: Phil Mason
    V P Finance: Glenn Lee
    Manufacturing Development Manager: John Spinner
    Purchasing Director: George Turner
    Purchasing Manager: Russ Shroyer
    Plant Manager: Mike Crawford
Number Employees: 500-999
Type of Packaging: Consumer, Food Service

2692 Chef America East
150 Oak Grove Drive
Mount Sterling, KY 40353-9087   859-498-4300
        www.chefamerica.com
Processor of prepared frozen foods including stuffed
sandwiches and croissants, pizza snacks and waffles
    CEO: Paul Merage
    CFO: Glenn Lee
    VP: Larry Johnson
    Research & Development: Phil Mason
    V P Finance: Glenn Lee
    Manufacturing Development Manager: John Spinner
    Purchasing Director: George Turner
    Purchasing Manager: Russ Shroyer
    Plant Manager: Mike Crawford
    Purchasing Manager: George Turner
Number Employees: 100-249
Type of Packaging: Consumer, Food Service

2693 Chef Francisco of Pennsylvania
250 Hansen Access Road
King of Prussia, PA 19406-2448   610-265-7400
    Fax: 610-265-8314

Processor of frozen soups
Estimated Sales: $50-100 Million
Number Employees: 250-499
Parent Co: Heinz USA
Type of Packaging: Food Service, Private Label

2694 Chef Hans Gourmet Foods
310 Walnut St
Monroe, LA 71201-6712   318-322-2334
    Fax: 318-322-2340 800-890-4267
    ckorrodi@bayou.com
    www.chefhansgourmetfoods.com
Processor and exporter of soup bases, batter, spices,
seafood, breading, seasonings, wild rice pilaf, rice,
desserts, bran, jambalaya, gumbo, etouffee, etc.
    President: Hans Korrodi
Estimated Sales: $1-2.5 Million
Number Employees: 5-9
Sq. footage: 22000
Brands:
    Chef Hans

2695 Chef Merito
PO Box 260948
Encino, CA 91426-0948   800-637-4861
        info@chefmerito.com
        www.chefmerito.com
Processor, importer and exporter of dried spices,
seasonings, seasoned rice, batters, breading mixes,
soups and sauces
    President/CEO: Plinio Garcia, Jr
Estimated Sales: $10-20 Million
Number Employees: 20-49
Sq. footage: 30000
Type of Packaging: Consumer, Food Service, Bulk
Brands:
    CHEF MERITO
    PIKOS PIKOSOS
    PPEPPERS
    SABROSITO

2696 Chef Paul Prudhomme's Magic Seasonings Blends
P.O.Box 23342
Harahan, LA 70123   504-731-3590
    Fax: 504-731-3576 800-457-2857
    info@chefpaul.com   www.chefpaul.com
Seasonings and spices
    President: Shawn Mc Bride
    President/CEO: Shawn McBride
    CFO: Paula LaCour
    Marketing VP: John McBride
    Production Manager: David Hickey
    Purchasing Agent: Carol Mauthe
Estimated Sales: $10-20 Million
Number Employees: 50-99
Sq. footage: 30000
Type of Packaging: Private Label
Brands:
    CHEF PAUL PRUDHOMME'S

2697 Chef Shells Catering & Roadside Cafe
2639 24th St
Port Huron, MI 48060-6418   810-966-8371
    Fax: 810-966-8372 info@jabars.com
        www.chefshells.com
Processor of wine vinaigrettes, sauces, seasonings
and dip mixes; gourmet catering available
    Owner: Michelle Wrubel
Estimated Sales: $1-2.5 Million
Number Employees: 5-9
Number of Products: 45
Sq. footage: 1800
Type of Packaging: Consumer, Food Service, Private Label, Bulk

2698 Chef Solutions
1000 Universal Drive N
North Haven, CT 06473-3151   856-848-5314
    Fax: 856-853-9247 www.chefsolutions.com
Processor of frozen dough
    CFO: Carl Warschausky
    CIO: MICHAEL Casula
    Manager: Joe Mascelli
Estimated Sales: $100-500 Million
Number Employees: 100-249
Parent Co: Van den Bergh Foods
Brands:
    Chef Solutions

2699 Chef Solutions
100 N Youngman Rd
Baxter Springs, KS 66713-3226   620-856-2203
    Fax: 620-856-5697 www.chefsolutions.com
Manufacturers of fresh, refrigerated foods such as
deli-style salads, compnent kit salads, mashed potatoes and side dishes, fresh cut fruit, dips and salad
dressing.
    VP Human Resources: Bryan Glancy
    Plant Engineer: Mike Wilcox
    Purchasing Agent: Debbie Shafer
Estimated Sales: $500+ Million
Number Employees: 100-249
Parent Co: Questor
Type of Packaging: Consumer, Food Service

2700 Chef Zachary's Gourmet Blended Spices
216 Bagley Street
Detroit, MI 48221-0053   313-226-0000
    Fax: 313-226-0000 zach4spice@aol.com
        www.chefzachary.com
Natural, gourmet spice blends
    Owner/President: Chef Zachary Smith
Estimated Sales: $300,000-500,000
Number Employees: 1-4
Type of Packaging: Consumer
Brands:
    Blackening Spice
    Chelsea Spice
    Mediterranean
    Shana Spice

2701 Chef's Requested Foods
P.O.Box 82096
Oklahoma City, OK 73148-0096   405-239-2610
    Fax: 405-239-2616 800-256-0259
    customerservice@chefsrequested.com
        www.chefsrequested.com
Processor of fresh and frozen meats
    President: John Williams
Estimated Sales: $50-100 Million
Number Employees: 100-249
Type of Packaging: Food Service

2702 Chef-A-Roni
2832 S County Trl
East Greenwich, RI 02818-1742   401-884-8798
Processor of spaghetti sauce
    President: Henry Caniglia
    Marketing Manager: Henry Caniglia
Estimated Sales: $500,000-$1 Million
Number Employees: 5-9
Type of Packaging: Consumer, Food Service
Brands:
    Chef-A-Roni

2703 Chefmaster
10871 Forbes Ave
Garden Grove, CA 92843-6507   714-554-4410
    Fax: 714-546-2721 800-333-7443
    Chefmaster@BKCOMPANY.COM
        www.bkcompany.com
Manufacturer of ingredients for the bakery, confectionery and food industries. Items such as; gels,
liqua-gels, airbrush and candy colors, as well as
other decorating items such as piping gel, pastry
bags and meringue powders
    Manager: Ed Larrarte
Estimated Sales: $10-20 Million
Number Employees: 20-49
Sq. footage: 60000
Type of Packaging: Food Service, Private Label
Brands:
    CHEFMASTER

2704 Chelan Fresh
317 Johnson St
Chelan, WA 98816   509-682-5133
    Fax: 509-923-2329 www.chelanfresh.com
Grower of apples and pears
    CEO: Steve Terry
    Marketing Manager: Terry Braithwaite
    Office Manager: Susan Campbell
    Sales Manager: Doug McClellan
    Sales: Troy Burnett
    General Manager: Gerald Mineard
Estimated Sales: $ 10 - 20 Million
Number Employees: 100-249
Type of Packaging: Consumer
Brands:
    Chelan Fresh
    Frutrition

2705 Chella's Dutch Delicacies
6024 Jean Road
Suite C150
Lake Oswego, OR 97035-5330   503-534-9888
Fax: 503-635-1399   800-458-3331
Shortbread pastry and bread
Purchasing Agent: Jake Raymond
Estimated Sales: $10-20 Million
Number Employees: 10-19

2706 Chelsea Market Baskets
75 9th Ave # 1
New York, NY 10011-7047   212-727-1111
Fax: 212-727-1778   888-727-7887
info@chelseamarketbaskets.com
www.chelseamarketbaskets.com
Custom made gift baskets for various occasions
President: David Porat
Estimated Sales: $500,000-$1 Million
Number Employees: 10-19
Brands:
Chelsea Market Baskets
Cottage Delight
Shortbread Housf

2707 (HQ)Chelsea Milling Company
P.O.Box 460
Chelsea, MI 48118-0460   734-475-1361
Fax: 734-475-4630 www.jiffymix.com
Processor of mixes including cake, frosting, muffin,
brownie, pizza crust, biscuit, etc.
President: Howard Holmes
Vice President: Jack Kennedy
Plant Manager: Mike Williamson
Purchasing Manager: Ed Hofpstadter
Estimated Sales: $50-100 Million
Number Employees: 250-499
Type of Packaging: Consumer
Other Locations:
Chelsea Milling Co.
Marshall MI
Brands:
JIFFY MIX

2708 Chelten House Products
P.O.Box 434
Bridgeport, NJ 08014-0434   856-467-1600
Fax: 856-467-4769 info@cheltenhouse.com
www.cheltenhouse.com
Manufacturer of organic and all-natural dressings,
sauces, marinades, salsa and ketchup. QAI certified
and OU approved.
CEO: Steven Dabrow
Estimated Sales: $40 Million
Number Employees: 20-49
Sq. footage: 140000
Type of Packaging: Consumer, Food Service, Private Label
Brands:
CHELTEN HOUSE
MARINADE BAY
SIMPLY NATURAL

2709 Chempacific Corporation
6200 Freeport Ctr
Baltimore, MD 21224-6524   410-633-5771
Fax: 410-633-5808 sales@ChemPacific.com
www.chempacific.com
President: Dr Dean Wei
COO: Tony Liang
CEO: Rebecca Chiu
VP Sales/Marketing: Jim Havlin
Director Sales: Tony Liang
Estimated Sales: $ 3 - 5 Million
Number Employees: 20-49

2710 Cher-Make Sausage Co(Smokey Valley Meat Products Co)
P.O.Box 1267
Manitowoc, WI 54221-1267   920-683-5980
Fax: 920-682-2588 www.cher-make.com
Processor of smoked meats including sausage, jerky,
poultry, ham, bacon, venison, beef, turkey and bison
President: Arthur Chermak Jr
Estimated Sales: Less than $200,000
Number Employees: 10-19

2711 (HQ)Cher-Make Sausage Company
P.O.Box 1267
Manitowoc, WI 54221-1267   920-683-5980
Fax: 920-682-2588   800-242-7679
www.cher-make.com

Processor and exporter of kippered beef, sausage
and meat snacks; importer of frozen meat.
President: Tom Chermak
Director Finance: Larry Franke
Director Sales/Marketing: Rod Nedvedr
Plant Manager: Chuck Hoefner
Purchasing Manager: Jim Coulson
Estimated Sales: $10-20 Million
Number Employees: 100-249
Sq. footage: 80000
Type of Packaging: Consumer, Private Label
Brands:
CHER-MAKE SAUSAGE
HOME GAME
SMOKEY MESQUITE
SMOKY VALLEY

2712 Cheraw Packing
578 Highway 1 S
Cheraw, SC 29520-3812   843-537-7426
Fax: 843-537-6699
Processor of beef and pork
President: John Weeks
Purchasing: John Weeks
Estimated Sales: $5-10 Million
Number Employees: 10-19
Type of Packaging: Consumer, Food Service, Private Label, Bulk

2713 Cherbogue Fisheries
PO Box 326
Yarmouth, NS B5A 4B3
Canada   902-742-9157
Fax: 902-742-7708
Processor and exporter of fresh and frozen seafood
VP: Alfred LeBlanc
Number Employees: 20-49
Type of Packaging: Bulk

2714 Cherchies
1 N Bacton Hill Rd # 107
Malvern, PA 19355-1032   610-640-9440
Fax: 610-644-7937   800-644-1980
staff@cherchies.com   www.cherchies.com
Processor of gourmet foods including mustard, peppers, pepper jellies, sauces, soups, chowders, preserves and seasonings; also, chili and freeze-dried
soup and chowder mixes
President: Anthony Spallone
VP: Patti Spallone
Marketing: Joe Shrum
Operations: Lori Hughes
Purchasing: Gayle Snyder
Estimated Sales: $1-2.5 Million
Number Employees: 10-19
Number of Brands: 1
Number of Products: 60
Sq. footage: 1400
Type of Packaging: Consumer, Food Service, Private Label
Brands:
CHERCHIES

2715 Cheri's Desert Harvest
1840 E Winsett St
Tucson, AZ 85719-6548   520-623-4141
Fax: 520-623-7741   800-743-1141
help@cherisdesertharvest.com
www.cherisdesertharvest.com
Jellies, marmalade, bread, candies, syrup
Owner: Cheri Romanoski
Vice President: Jon Romanaski
Production Manager: Nancy Howes
Purchasing Manager: Cheryl Romanaski
Estimated Sales: $1-2.5 Million
Number Employees: 5-9
Brands:
CHERI'S DESERT HARVEST

2716 Cherith Valley Gardens
P.O.Box 12040
Fort Worth, TX 76110-8040   817-922-8822
Fax: 817-922-8884   800-610-9813
terriw@cherithvalley.com
www.cherithvalley.com
Processor, importer and exporter of gourmet pickles,
pickled vegetables, salsas, jellies, fruit toppings,
peppers, relishes and hors d'oeuvres
President: Alan Werner
Public Relations: Terri Werner
Operations Manager: Christa Werner
Estimated Sales: $ 5 - 10 Million
Number Employees: 10-19
Sq. footage: 6000

Type of Packaging: Consumer, Food Service
Brands:
Cherith Valley Gardens

2717 Chermont Winery
RR 1
Box 59
Esmont, VA 22937-9801   804-286-2211
Wines
Owner: George Wiltshire
Estimated Sales: Under $500,000
Number Employees: 1-4

2718 Cherokee Trout Farms
P.O.Box 525
Cherokee, NC 28719-0525   828-497-9227
Fax: 828-497-4330   800-732-0075
Processor of fresh and frozen trout including rainbow, hickory and smoked; also, trout cakes and dip
Owner: Dale Owen
Processing Mgr.: James Pheasant
Farm Manager: Ron Blankenship
Estimated Sales: $ .5 - 1 million
Number Employees: 1-4
Sq. footage: 8000
Type of Packaging: Consumer, Bulk
Brands:
Native American Foods

2719 Cherry Central Cooperative Inc
P.O.Box 988
Traverse City, MI 49685-0988   231-946-1860
Fax: 231-941-4167 info@cherrycentral.com
www.cherrycentral.com
Manufacturer and exporter of canned, frozen and
dried blueberries, cherries, apples and plums.
President/General Manager: Richard Bogard
Chairman: Claude Rowley
Controller: Laura Reed
VP Sales: James Giannestras
Estimated Sales: $100-500 Million
Number Employees: 50-99
Sq. footage: 15500
Type of Packaging: Consumer, Food Service, Private Label, Bulk
Brands:
CHERRY CENTRAL
FRUIT PATCH
GRAND TRAVERSE
INDIAN SUMMER
MONTMORENCY
NORTH BAY
REDDI MAID
TRAVERSE BAY
WILDERNESS

2720 Cherry Growers
6331 Us Highway 31
Grawn, MI 49637-9620   231-276-9241
Fax: 231-276-7075   800-530-9030
orders@cherrygrowers.net
www.cherrygrowers.net
processor and exporter of canned and frozen cherries, apples and juices.
President: Thomas Rochford
Quality Control: Barb Schilling
Sales Director: Tim Daly
Plant Manager: Ron Gallop
Estimated Sales: $1-2.5 Million
Number Employees: 1-4
Parent Co: Cherry Growers
Type of Packaging: Private Label
Brands:
VERMONT JACK'S
VERMONT VILLAGE

2721 Cherry Growers
6331 Us Highway 31
Grawn, MI 49637-9620   231-276-9241
Fax: 231-276-7075 orders@cherrygrowers.net
www.cherrygrowers.net
Processor and exporter of canned and frozen cherries, apples and juices.
President: Thomas Rochford
Quality Control: Barb Schilling
Sales: Tim Daly
Plant Manager: Ron Gallop
Estimated Sales: $20-50 Million
Number Employees: 500-999
Number of Brands: 2
Type of Packaging: Consumer, Food Service, Private Label, Bulk

Brands:
VERMONT JACK'S
VERMONT VILLAGE

2722 Cherry Hill Orchards Pelham
RR 3, Highway #20
Fenwick, ON L0S 1C0
Canada   905-892-3782
                        Fax: 905-892-7808
Processor and packer of fresh and frozen red tart cherries for pies and desserts.
President: Lawrence Haun
Secretary: Mary Lou Haun
Plant Manager: Stephen Haun
Number Employees: 24
Sq. footage: 25000
Type of Packaging: Consumer, Food Service
Brands:
Tree Ripe

2723 Cherry Hut
2345 N Us Highway 31 N
Traverse City, MI 49686-3755   231-938-8888
            Fax: 231-938-3333 888-882-4431
                        www.cherrytreeinn.com
Products made from cherries, including sauces, jams, jellies, conserves, preserves
Manager: Jonathan Pack
Owner: Brenda Case
Production VP: Leonard Case
Estimated Sales: Less than $500,000
Number Employees: 1-4

2724 Cherry Lane Frozen Fruits
4230 Victoria Avenue
Vineland Station, ON L0R 2E0
Canada   905-562-4337
        Fax: 905-562-5577 www.cherrylane.net
Processor of cherries and peaches
President: John Smith
Number Employees: 100
Type of Packaging: Consumer, Food Service

2725 Cherry Point Products
RR 1
Box 9
Milbridge, ME 04658-9703   207-546-7056
                        Fax: 207-546-7079
Owner: Drusilla Ray

2726 Cherrybrook Kitchen Inc
20 Mall Rd
Suite 410
Burlington, MA 01803   781-272-0400
Fax: 781-272-4460 www.cherrybrookkitchen.com
Peanut free, dairy free, egg free and nut free cake, cookie and brownie mixes, cookies, frostings, breakfast mixes, and wheat free and gluten free mixes
President/Owner: Chip Rosenberg
CEO: Chip Rosenberg
VP Marketing: Laura Kuykendall
VP Sales: Sallie Bowling
Finance/HR Manager: Sue Giannetti
Number Employees: 7

2727 Cherrydale Farms
1035 Mill Rd
Allentown, PA 18106-3101   610-366-1606
        Fax: 610-391-9284 800-333-4525
info@cherrydale.com www.cherrydalefarms.com
Manufacturer of chocolate and confections featuring nuts, caramel, creams, crunch products and more; packaged in a variety of tin shapes, sizes and designs for fundraising programs.
President: Richard Toltzis
Co-President: Richard Toltzis
Vice President: Jack Bucchioni
Senior Sales Representative: Larry Brown
Vice President Manufacturing: John Cooke
Estimated Sales: 10-100 Million
Number Employees: 500-999
Type of Packaging: Consumer, Private Label, Bulk

2728 Cherryfield Foods
P.O.Box 128
Cherryfield, ME 04622-0128   207-255-8364
                        Fax: 207-255-8341
        sales@oxfordfrozenfoods.com
            www.oxfordfrozenfoods.com
Blueberries
COO: Jeff Vose
Estimated Sales: $ 50 - 100 Million
Number Employees: 100-249
Parent Co: Oxford Frozen Foods

2729 Cheryl & Company
646 McCorkle Blvd
Westerville, OH 43082-8708   614-891-8822
        Fax: 614-891-8799 www.cherylandco.com
Cookies, brownies, cakes and pies
President: Cheryl Krueger-Horn
CFO: Dennis Hicks
CEO: Cheryl Krueger
Marketing Director: Lisa Henry
Production Planner: Scott Miller
Purchasing Director: Rob Salter
Estimated Sales: $50-100 Million
Number Employees: 250-499
Type of Packaging: Private Label
Brands:
CHERYL & CO.

2730 Chesapeake Bay Gourmet
8805 Kelso Dr
Essex, MD 21221-3112   410-780-0444
        Fax: 410-780-0511 800-432-2722
info@cbgourmet.com www.cbcrabcake.com
A specialty line of handmade, hand picked Jumbo Lump crab cakes and other gourmet seafood products.
President: Ron Kauffman
CEO: Margie Kauffman
CEO: Steve Cohen
Estimated Sales: $ 20 - 50 Million
Number Employees: 100-249
Sq. footage: 35000

2731 Chesapeake Feed Company
PO Box 23
Beltsville, MD 20704-0023   301-419-2433
Feed
President: Lingard Klein
Estimated Sales: $1-2.5 Million appx.
Number Employees: 1-4

2732 Chesapeake Spice Company
9341k Philadelphia Road
Baltimore, MD 21237   410-391-2100
        Fax: 410-391-2596 csc@chesapeakespice.com
                        www.chesapeakespice.com
Processor and importers of spices and seasoning blends
Estimated Sales: $5-10 Million
Number Employees: 20-49
Sq. footage: 50000
Type of Packaging: Bulk

2733 Chester Carr Company
PO Box 575
Saint Martinville, LA 70582-0575   318-332-4120
                        Fax: 318-981-3126

2734 Chester Dairy Company
P.O.Box 605
Chester, IL 62233-0605   618-826-2394
        Fax: 618-826-2395 www.conagra.com
Dairy
Plant Manager: Doyle Lueders
Estimated Sales: $10-24.9 Million
Number Employees: 20-49
Parent Co: ConAgra

2735 Chester Fried
2750 Gunter Park Drive W
Montgomery, AL 36109-1016   334-272-3528
        Fax: 334-272-3561 800-288-1555
jenniferp@gilesent.com www.chesterfried.com
Manufacturer and exporter of fried chicken products including breading mixes, seasonings, packaging supplies, deep fryers, fry kettles, marinades, warmers, breading tables, etc
President/CEO: Ted Giles
COO: David Byrd
Purchasing: Bryan Gonseth
Estimated Sales: $10-100 Million
Number Employees: 100-249
Sq. footage: 100000
Brands:
CHESTER FRIED CHICKEN
CHESTERFRIED

2736 Chester Inc.
P.O.Box 2237
Valparaiso, IN 46384-2237   219-465-7555
        Fax: 219-462-2652 800-778-1131
clark@chesterinc.com www.buy.chesters.com

Processor and exporter of popcorn
Chairman/CEO: Peter Peuquet
President: Larry Holt
EVP: Leonard Clark
Estimated Sales: $5-10 Million
Number Employees: 50-99
Type of Packaging: Consumer, Private Label
Other Locations:
Francesville IN
Gary IN
Troy MI
Brands:
Chester Farms
Chester Farms Popping Corn
Golden

2737 Chester River Clam Co, Inc
305 Roe Ingleside Rd
Centreville, MD 21617-2012   410-758-3810
                        Fax: 410-758-4089
Clams
President: Melvin Hickman
Estimated Sales: $2,100,000
Number Employees: 5-9

2738 Chester W. Howeth & Brother
P.O.Box 446
Crisfield, MD 21817-0446   410-968-1398
                        Fax: 410-968-0670
Processor of fresh and frozen seafood
Manager: Arthur Tawes
Estimated Sales: $5-10 Million
Number Employees: 20-49
Sq. footage: 4200
Type of Packaging: Food Service
Brands:
Chas. W. Howeth & Bro.

2739 Chestertown Foods
27030 Morgnec Rd
Chestertown, MD 21620-3112   410-778-3131
        Fax: 410-778-6386 cfoods@crosslink.net
                        www.chestertownfoods.com
Poultry
Manager: Jack Laird
CEO: Louis Rothman
Vice President: William Schroeder
Manager Industrial Sales: Michael Carrow
Plant Manager: Jack Laird
Estimated Sales: $5-10 Million
Number Employees: 250-499
Type of Packaging: Private Label
Brands:
Chestertown

2740 Chestnut Mountain Winery
1123 Highway 124
Hoschton, GA 30548-3421   770-867-6914
                        Fax: 770-867-6914
Wines
President: James Laikam
General Manager: Jim O'Dell
Estimated Sales: $1-2.5 Million
Number Employees: 1-4

2741 Chevalier Chocolates
39 Eastgate Lane
Enfield, CT 06082-6213   860-741-3330
                gifts@chevalierchoc.com
                        www.chevalier.ws
Belgian chocolates, pralines, truffles, mints, also chocolate, cordial, and brandy covered cherries
President: Linda Chevalier
Brands:
Chevalier Chocolates

2742 Chewys Rugulach
7795 Arjons Dr
San Diego, CA 92126-4366   858-271-1234
        Fax: 858-271-1346 800-241-3456
chewy123@aol.com www.chewys.com
Processor of filled rugulach including baked, unbaked and frozen
President: Ahmad Paksima
Vice President: Emily Paksima
Marketing Director: Shahriar Paksima
Purchasing Manager: Shahriar Paksima
Estimated Sales: $2.5-5 Million
Number Employees: 20-49
Sq. footage: 6240
Parent Co: Ahuramazda
Type of Packaging: Consumer, Food Service, Private Label, Bulk

Brands:
CHEWY'S

2743 Chex Finer Foods
39 Franklin R McKay Rd # Z
Attleboro, MA 02703-4625   508-226-0660
  Fax: 508-226-7060 800-322-2434
  www.chexfoods.com
Processor and importer of gourmet foods including
biscuits, confectionery items, specialties, etc
  President: David Isenberg
  Controller: Donald Robillard
  Purchasing: Dan Powers
Estimated Sales:$10-20 Million
Number Employees: 5-9
Type of Packaging: Consumer

2744 Chi & Hing Food Service
4545 N 43rd Ave
Phoenix, AZ 85031-1509   623-939-8889
  Fax: 623-340-8887
  President: Chi Tsang
Estimated Sales:$28,010,403

2745 Chi Company/Tabor Hill Winery
185 Mount Tabor Rd
Buchanan, MI 49107-8326   269-422-1165
  Fax: 269-422-2787 800-283-3363
  www.taborhill.com
Wines and champagnes
  President: David Upton
  Purchasing Manager: Patsy Wyman
Estimated Sales:$10-20 Million
Number Employees: 50-99

2746 Chia I Foods Company
2131 Tyler Avenue
South El Monte, CA 91733-2754 626-401-3038
  Fax: 626-579-3038
Spices and dehydrated fruits
  President: Ann Huang
  Vice President: Steve Huang
  Purchasing Manager: Mary Nelson
Estimated Sales:$10-24.9 Million
Number Employees: 10-19

2747 Chianti Cheese Company
P.O.Box 157
Wapakoneta, OH 45895-157   609-894-0900
  Fax: 609-894-4206 800-220-3503
info@chianticheese.com www.chianticheese.com
Manufacturer of hard grated cheese, parmesan and
romano cheese, in all sizes. Also available fresh
mozzarella, ricotta, pecorino romano, provolone,
pizza cheese, impastata, parmigiano, grana panado,
grated or shredded, domestic orimported cheese
  Sales: Jack Salemi
Estimated Sales:$20 Million
Number Employees: 90
Number of Brands: 10
Number of Products: 200
Sq. footage: 80000
Parent Co: Kantner Group
Type of Packaging: Consumer, Food Service, Private Label, Bulk
Other Locations:
  Chianti Cheese Company
  Phila PA
Brands:
  CHIANTI
  PAISANO MIO
  PARMILLANO

2748 Chiappetti Wholesale Meat
3900 S Western Ave
Chicago, IL 60609-2226   773-927-9476
  Fax: 773-847-3837 www.lambandveal.com
Processor and packer of veal and lamb
  President: Dennis Chiappetti
  VP: Bryan Chiappetti
  Purchasing Manager: Dennis Chiappetti
Estimated Sales:$50-100 Million
Number Employees: 100-249
Type of Packaging: Food Service, Private Label

2749 Chicago 58 Food Products
56 Lippincott Street
Toronto, ON M5T 2R5
Canada
  416-603-4244
  Fax: 416-603-4242

Processor of meat products including beef, pastrami,
smoked salami, frankfurters; also, herring, condi-
ments and cheese; importer of beef cuts
  President: Sid Starkman
  Secretary: Harold Bernholtz
  VP: Max Reiken
Number Employees: 20-49
Sq. footage: 15000
Type of Packaging: Consumer, Food Service, Pri-
vate Label, Bulk
Brands:
  Chicago 58
  Deli-Dogs
  Lanky Franky

2750 Chicago Baking Company
40 E Garfield Boulevard
Chicago, IL 60615-4603   773-536-7700
  Fax: 773-536-7692
Bread and rolls
  Controller: Richard Wilson
  VP/General Manager: Larry Anaszewicz
  Production Manager: Kevin Koenig
Estimated Sales:$50-100 Million
Number Employees: 250-499

2751 Chicago Coffee Roastery
11880 Smith Ct
Huntley, IL 60142-7390   847-669-1156
  Fax: 847-669-1114 800-762-5402
  sales@chicagocoffee.com
  www.chicagocoffee.com
Coffee, instant cocoa, instant cappuccio, tea
  Owner: Sandra Knight
  Vice President: Brian Gosell
  Purchasing Manager: Brian Gosell
Estimated Sales:$2 Million
Number Employees: 5-9
Sq. footage: 8000
Type of Packaging: Consumer, Food Service, Pri-
vate Label, Bulk

2752 Chicago Food Market
2245 S Wentworth Ave
Chicago, IL 60616-2011   312-842-4361
  Fax: 312-842-6448
  President: Matthew Chan
Estimated Sales:$2,500,000
Number Employees: 10-19

2753 Chicago Meat Authority
1120 W 47th Pl
Chicago, IL 60609-4302   773-254-0020
  Fax: 773-254-5841 www.chicagomeat.com
Processor, exporter and packer of portion control
meats including hamburgers
  President: Jordan Dorfman
  Purchasing Manager: Jennifer Bandish
Estimated Sales:$50-100 Million
Number Employees: 100-249
Sq. footage: 15000
Type of Packaging: Consumer, Food Service, Pri-
vate Label, Bulk

2754 Chicago Oriental Wholesale
2160 S Archer Ave
Chicago, IL 60616-1514   312-842-9993
  Fax: 312-808-1787
  Manager: Phil Chen
Estimated Sales:$ 20 - 50 Million
Number Employees: 20-49

2755 Chicago Pizza & Brewery
16162 Beach Boulevard
Suite 100
Huntington Beach, CA 92647-3828 714-848-3747
  Fax: 714-374-0015 dianne@bjsbrewhouse.com
Processor of beer, ale and lager; also, pizza
  President/CEO: Jerry Deitchle
*Estimated Sales:*9,302,000
Number Employees: 10-19
Parent Co: BJ's Restaurants Inc
Brands:
  BJ Beer

2756 Chicago Steaks
824 W Exchange Ave
Chicago, IL 60609-2507   773-847-5400
  Fax: 773-847-3364 800-776-4174
  blackangus@chicagosteaks.com
  www.chicagosteaks.com
Manufacturer of meat products, value added products, and gift steaks
  President/CEO: Tom Campbell

Estimated Sales:$9 Million
Number Employees: 20-49
Number of Brands: 5
Sq. footage: 1640
Type of Packaging: Food Service, Private Label
Brands:
  CHICAGO STEAK

2757 Chicago Sweeteners
1700 E Higgins Rd # 610
Des Plaines, IL 60018-5615   847-299-1999
  Fax: 847-299-6217 rfriedman@chisweet.com
  www.chisweet.com
Manufacturer of sugar
  President: Abel Friedman
  Quality Assurance: Kate Capek
  Ingredient Sales: Brian Abendroth
Estimated Sales:$50-100 Million
Number Employees: 50-99
Parent Co: Dot Foods, Inc

2758 Chicama Vineyards
PO Box 430
West Tisbury, MA 02575-0430   508-693-0309
  Fax: 508-693-5628 888-244-2262
  info@chicamavineyards.com
  www.chicamavineyards.com
Wines, vinegar and dressings
  President: Catherine Mathiesen
  Co-Owner: George Mathiesen
  Purchasing Manager: Catherine Mathiesen
Estimated Sales:$5-9.9 Million
Number Employees: 1-4
Brands:
  CHICAMA

2759 Chick-Fil-A
PO Box 500367
Atlanta, GA 31150-0367   404-765-8000
  Fax: 404-765-8140 800-232-2677
  www.chick-fil-a.com
Manufacturer of chicken
  Founder/Chairman: S Truett Cathy
  President/COO: Dan Cathy
  SVP: Donald Cathy
  SVP/General Counsel: Bureon Ledbetter Jr.
  SVP Finance/CFO: James McCabe
  Sr. Manager Public Relations: Jerry Johnston
  SVP Operations: Tim Tassopoulos
Number Employees: 250-499
Brands:
  Chick-Fil-A

2760 Chickasaw Foods
335 Cumberland Street
Memphis, TN 38112-3350   901-323-5467
Potato chips
  President: Jon M Buhler
Estimated Sales:$5-10,000,000 appx.
Number Employees: 20-49

2761 Chickasaw Trading Company
PO Box 1418
Denver City, TX 79323-1418   806-592-3515
  Fax: 806-592-3460 800-848-3515
  joe@texaslean.com
Processor and exporter of lean beef jerky and
smoked turkey breast strips
  Co-Owner: Linda Kay
  Co-Owner: Joe Kay
Number Employees: 1-4
Sq. footage: 5000
Type of Packaging: Private Label
Brands:
  Texas Lean

2762 Chicken of the Sea
P.O.Box 85568
San Diego, CA 92186-5568   858-558-9662
  Fax: 858-597-4566 www.chickenofthesea.com
  President: Danny Muffell
  CEO: Shue Wing Chan
Estimated Sales:$ 100-500 Million
Number Employees: 1,000-4,999

2763 Chicken of the Sea International
P.O.Box 85568
San Diego, CA 92186-5568   858-558-9662
  Fax: 858-597-4566 800-678-8862
  www.chickenofthesea.com

Canner and importer of tuna, salmon, shrimp, crab, oysters, clams, mackerel and sardines
President/CEO: Dennis Mussell
CEO: Shue Wing Chan
Senior VP Marketing: Don George
Senior VP Sales: Tony Montoya
Estimated Sales: $60 Million
Number Employees: 1,000-4,999
Parent Co: Tri-Union Seafoods
Type of Packaging: Consumer, Food Service, Private Label
Brands:
CHICKEN OF THE SEA
CHICKEN OF THE SEA SINGLES
CHICKEN OF THE SEA TUNA SALAD KIT
GENOVA TONNO
JACK MACKEREL

2764 Chico Nut Company
2020 Esplanade
Chico, CA 95926-2222   530-891-1493
Fax: 530-893-5381 almonds@chiconut.com
www.chiconut.com
Processor, exporter and packer of almonds
Owner: Peter D Peterson
Estimated Sales: $ 3 - 5 Million
Number Employees: 20-49
Type of Packaging: Bulk

2765 Chicopee Provision Company
19 Sitarz Ave
Chicopee, MA 01013-1342   413-594-4765
Fax: 413-594-2584 800-924-6328
info@bluesealkielbasa.com
www.bluesealkielbasa.com
Manufacturer of kielbasa and table ready meats, including polish kielbasa, baked loaf, hot dogs, cold cuts, and sausage
President: Fred Mamuszka
Office Manager: Carolyn Donnelly
Operations/Marketing: Thomas Bardon
Estimated Sales: $4.5 Million
Number Employees: 20-49
Number of Brands: 220
Number of Products: 610
Sq. footage: 24000
Type of Packaging: Consumer, Food Service, Private Label, Bulk
Brands:
BLUE SEAL

2766 Chief Tonasket Growers
PO Box 14490
Portland, OR 97293-0490   509-486-2914
Fax: 509-486-1815
Cooperative selling and exporting apples, cherries and pears
Mktg.: Rich Hutchins
Marketing: Katy Tibbs
General Manager: Robert Green
Number Employees: 50-99
Brands:
Alpine Fresh
Chief Tonasket
Husky

2767 Chief Wenatchee
1705 N Miller St
Wenatchee, WA 98801-1585   509-662-5197
Fax: 509-662-9415
Grower and exporter of apples, cherries and pears
President: Brian Birsall
Operations Manager: Skip Coonfield
Number Employees: 250-499
Type of Packaging: Bulk
Brands:
Chief Chelan
Chief Supreme
Chief Wenatchee
Wenatchee Gold

2768 Chieftain Wild Rice Company
P.O.Box 550
Spooner, WI 54801-0550   715-635-6401
Fax: 715-635-6415 800-262-6368
info@chieftainwildrice.com
www.chieftainwildrice.com

Processor of wild rice and blends; also, specialty beans and grains. Rice River Farms is a retail line sold to specialty stores, Chieftian Wild Rice is a food service line for restaurants
President: Donald Richards
CEO: Jim Deutsch
Marketing Director: Keith Kappel
General Manager: Joan Gerland
Plant Manager: Jim Deutsch
Estimated Sales: $2-5 Million
Number Employees: 20-49
Number of Brands: 2
Sq. footage: 16000
Type of Packaging: Consumer, Food Service
Brands:
AUTUMN HARVEST
BANQUET BLEND
CALICO BLEND
CHIEFTAIN WILD RICE
COUNTRY HARVEST
FESTIVAL BLEND
HOUSE BLEND
LOWER CARB BLEND
MIDWEST MEDLEY
PASTA RICE BLEND
QUINOA CONFETTI
RICE RIVER FARMS
SAVORY BLEND
SPECIAL BASMATI

2769 ChildLife-Nutrition forKids
4051 Glencoe Ave # 11
Marina Del Rey, CA 90292-5646   310-305-4640
Fax: 310-305-4680 800-993-0332
mailroom@childlife.net   www.childlife.net
Liquid supplements & vitamins for infants to children up to twelve years old
Founder: Dr. Murray C Clarke
VP: Helen Mauchi
Estimated Sales: $300,000-500,000
Number Employees: 1-4
Number of Products: 9

2770 Chile Today - Hot Tamale
2000 McKinnon Ave.,Bldg. 428,#5
San Francisco, CA 94124-1621   800-758-0372
Fax: 415-401-9107 800-758-0372
chiletoday@aol.com   www.chiletoday.com
Processor of trail mixes, gourmet hot sauce, salsa, seasoned pretzels, dried chiles and chile powders
President: Rob Polishook
VP: David Lipson
Purchasing Manager: David Lipson
Estimated Sales: $1-2.5 Million
Number Employees: 1-4
Sq. footage: 7000
Type of Packaging: Consumer, Food Service
Brands:
CHILE
FIRE NUGGET
SMOKED HABANERO PRETZELS

2771 Chili Dude
397 Dal Rich Vlg
348
Richardson, TX 75080-5715   972-907-0998
info@thechilidude.com
www.thechilidude.com
Chili
Director: Corrine Lovato
Brands:
Chili Dude

2772 Chill & Moore
3221 May Street
Fort Worth, TX 76110-4124   505-769-2649
Fax: 505-762-0571 800-676-3055
steph2@airmail.net
Processor of frozen ices
Sales Manager (Food Service): Bob Moore
Sales Manager (Retail): Jay Jackson
Type of Packaging: Consumer, Food Service

2773 Chimere
1800 Sequoia Drive
Santa Maria, CA 93454-7645   805-922-9097
Fax: 805-922-9143
Wines
President: Gary Mosby
Estimated Sales: $1-2.5 Million
Number Employees: 5-9

2774 China Bowl Trading Company
830 Post Road E
Westport, CT 06880-5222   203-222-0381
Fax: 203-226-6445
Processor, importer and exporter of Oriental foods including pasta, noodles, sauces, spices, vinegar, wine, oils, curry powder, chili pepper, etc
President: Henry Ellett
Estimated Sales: Under $300,000
Number Employees: 1-4
Sq. footage: 2500
Type of Packaging: Consumer, Food Service
Brands:
Bascom's
China Bowl
Dinny Robb
Sinatra
Tasti-Diet
Wye River

2775 China D Food Service
2535 S Kessler Street
Wichita, KS 67217-1044   316-945-2323
Fax: 316-945-5557
Food service and management
Purchasing: Lisa Diez
Estimated Sales: $300,000-500,000
Number Employees: 1-4
Type of Packaging: Food Service

2776 China Doll Company
100 Jacintoport Boulevard
Saraland, AL 36571-3304   251-457-7641
Fax: 251-457-4569
gbagget@achfoodcompany.com
Processor and exporter of rice, dried beans and peas, lentils, popcorn and raw shelled peanuts
CEO: Dan Antonelli
CFO: Daryl Vrbas
VP: Steve Robinson
Marketing/Sales: Gerald Baggett
Manager: Gerald Baggett
Production: Deprest Turner
Plant Manager: Gordan McElhenney
Purchasing: Gerald Bagget
Estimated Sales: $1-2.5 Million
Number Employees: 20-49
Number of Brands: 4
Number of Products: 38
Sq. footage: 40000
Parent Co: ACH Food Companies
Type of Packaging: Consumer, Food Service, Private Label, Bulk
Brands:
China Boy
China Doll
Jocko
Paddy
Silver King
Southern Charm

2777 China Food Merchant Corporation
2731 E Regal Park Drive
Fullerton, CA 92831   714-630-6896
Fax: 714-773-1082 877-465-2582
info@foodsonsale.com   www.foodsonsale.com
Processor of canned pineapples, mandarin oranges, kiwis, sliced mushrooms, rice, dried noodles and rice sticks, pasta, teas and dehydrated garlic products
Vice President: Susan Fu
Manager: Mike Young
Type of Packaging: Food Service
Brands:
Wintersweet

2778 China Mist Tea Company
7435 E Tierra Buena Ln
Scottsdale, AZ 85260-1608   480-998-8807
Fax: 480-443-8384 800-242-8807
info@chinamist.com   www.chinamist.com
China mist and leaves pure teas
President: Rommie Flammer
Chairman: Dan Schweiker
CFO: Rommie Dresher
VP: Marci Hendrickson
Plant Manager: Tom Renner
Estimated Sales: $10-20 Million
Number Employees: 20-49
Sq. footage: 17500
Brands:
CHINA MIST

FRENZY MIST
GREEN STAR

2779 China Pharmaceutical Enterprises
8323 Ohara Court
Baton Rouge, LA 70806-6513   225-924-1423
Fax: 225-924-4154   800-345-1658
Processor and importer of ascorbic acid, caffeine anhydrous and vitamin B-12
Office Manager: Susan Giska
Type of Packaging: Bulk

2780 (HQ)Chincoteague Seafood Company
7056 Forest Grove Rd
Parsonsburg, MD 21849-2096   443-260-4800
Fax: 443-260-4900   gourmetsoups@hotmail.com
www.chincoteagueseafood.com
Processor and distributor of gourmet specialty seafood items: canned and frozen products including fried clams, stuffed clams, New England/Manhattan clam chowders, corn chowder, lobster/clam/shrimp/lobster and cheddar bisques, cream ofcrab/vegetable crab/crab and cheddar soups, white/red clam sauces, chopped clams, clam juice
President: Leonard Rubin
CEO: Bernard Rubin
CFO: Toby Rubin
Estimated Sales: $1-2.5 Million
Number Employees: 5-9
Number of Brands: 4
Number of Products: 25
Sq. footage: 6000
Type of Packaging: Consumer, Food Service, Private Label, Bulk
Brands:
CAPE COD
CAPT'N DON'S
CAPT'N EDS
CHINOTEAGUE

2781 Chinese Spaghetti Factory
83 Newmarket Sq
Boston, MA 02118-2619   617-445-7714
Fax: 617-427-5918   www.chinesespaghetti.com
Processor of Peking ravioli, chicken and pork dumplings, scallops with bacon and shrimp spring rolls
President: Lai Fou Sou
General Manager: Henry Moy
Operations Manager: Ken Moy
Estimated Sales: $ 20 - 50 Million
Number Employees: 20-49
Sq. footage: 16000
Type of Packaging: Consumer, Food Service, Private Label, Bulk

2782 Chino Meat Provision Corporation
13564 Central Ave
Chino, CA 91710-5105   909-627-1997
Fax: 909-628-5147
Processor and packer of meat products
Owner: Orestes Blanco
Estimated Sales: $2.5-5 Million
Number Employees: 10-19
Sq. footage: 6000
Brands:
El Paso

2783 Chino Valley Ranchers
5611 Peck Road
Arcadia, CA 91006-5851   800-354-4503
Fax: 626-652-0893
david@chinovalleyranchers.com
www.chinovalleyranchers.com
Processor of fresh organic, cage free, free range and fertile white and brown eggs
Marketing Director: David Will
Plant Manager: Mario Gonzalez
Type of Packaging: Consumer, Food Service, Private Label
Brands:
Chino Valley
Humane Harvest
Mothers Free Range
Nutrifresh
Veg-A-Fed

2784 Chip Steak & Provision Company
232 Dewey St
Mankato, MN 56001-2330   507-388-6277
Fax: 507-388-6279

Wholesales meat & meat products; wholesales packaged frozen foods
President: Michael Miller
Secretary: Mike Miller
Estimated Sales: $5-9.9 Million
Number Employees: 5-9
Sq. footage: 4000
Type of Packaging: Consumer, Food Service, Bulk

2785 Chipotle Chile Company
510 Highland Avenue
174
Milford, MI 48381-1516   248-496-8308
www.dancingcow.com
Peppers
Brands:
Dancing Cow Steak Sauce

2786 Chipper Snax
1750 S 500 W # 700
Salt Lake City, UT 84115-1890   801-977-0742
Fax: 801-977-0743   info@chipperjerky.com
www.chipperjerky.com
Beef jerky
Manager: Jeffrey Labrum
Executive Vice President: Jeffrey Labrum
National Sales Manager: Steve Pich
Estimated Sales: $ 10 - 20 Million
Number Employees: 20-49
Brands:
CHIPPER BEEF JERKY

2787 Chiquita Brands
250 E 5th St
Cincinnati, OH 45202-5190   513-784-8000
Fax: 513-784-8030   www.chiquita.com
Manufacturer of bananas, melons, grapes and other fruits along with some vegetables
Chairman/President/CEO: Fernando Aguirre
SVP/CFO: Michael Sims
VP/CIO: Manjit Singh
Estimated Sales: $3 Billion
Number Employees: 21,000
Type of Packaging: Consumer, Food Service, Private Label, Bulk
Brands:
CHIQUITA
FRESH EXPRESS

2788 (HQ)Chiquita Brands International
250 East 5th Street
Cincinnati, OH 45202   513-784-8000
Fax: 513-564-2920   800-438-0015
www.chiquita.com
Grower, processor, importer and exporter of bananas; processor of fruits, fresh and canned vegetables, wet and dry salads, and fruit juices for consumer, manufacturing, and food service industries
President & CEO: Fernando Aquirre
President, North America: Brian Kocher
SVP & CFO: Michael Sims
Pres. Global Innovation/Emerg Mkts & CMO: Tanios Viviani
SVP Product Supply Organization: Waheed Zaman
Estimated Sales: $3.6 Billion
Number Employees: 23000
Type of Packaging: Consumer, Food Service, Private Label, Bulk
Brands:
CHIQUITA
FRESH EXPRESS

2789 Chiquita Brands International
250 E 5th St
Cincinnati, OH 45202-5190   513-784-8000
Fax: 513-564-2920   877-833-5551
mmitchell@chiquita.com   www.chiquita.com
Processor of canned corn, potatoes, carrots and rutabagas
President/CEO: Fernando Aguirre
VP Business Process Development: Anne L Gehring
Plant Manager: David Podoski
Estimated Sales: $5-10 Million
Number Employees: 10,000+
Parent Co: Chiquita Processed Foods
Type of Packaging: Private Label
Brands:
Chiquita Blue Label
Chiquita Jingle
Miss Chiquita

2790 Chiquita Processed Foods
1008 S Mill Street
Milton Freewater, OR 97862-1112   541-938-4461
www.chiquita.com
Processor and exporter of canned vegetables including asparagus, peas, peas and onions, peas and carrots, beans, corn and carrots
President: Robert Kistinger
Production Manager: Larry Jorgenson
Estimated Sales: $100-500 Million
Number Employees: 250-499
Parent Co: American Fine Foods
Type of Packaging: Consumer, Food Service, Private Label
Brands:
Bits O Honey
Cimmeron
Garden Grown
Inland Valley
Tom Thumb
Walla Walla

2791 Chiquita Processed Foods
Rr 1
Markesan, WI 53946   920-398-2386
Fax: 920-398-3924
Processor, packager and exporter of canned corn
Plant Manager: Richard Koehler
Purchasing Agent: Craig Giese
Estimated Sales: $ 1 - 3 Million
Number Employees: 5-9
Type of Packaging: Consumer, Private Label

2792 Chisesi Brothers Meat Packing Company
P.O.Box 19083
New Orleans, LA 70179-0083   504-822-3550
Fax: 504-822-3916
Manufacturer of hams, frankforters, and sausage
President: Phillip Chisesi
Estimated Sales: $15-20 Million
Number Employees: 100-249
Type of Packaging: Consumer, Food Service

2793 Chisholm Bakery
128 8th Street NW
Chisholm, MN 55719-1656   218-254-4006
Baked goods
Owner: Todd Renke
Estimated Sales: $500,000-$1 Million
Number Employees: 5-9

2794 (HQ)Chloe Foods Corporation
3301 Atlantic Ave
Brooklyn, NY 11208-1946   718-827-3600
Fax: 718-647-0052   www.blueridgefarms.com
Manufacturer of nonkosher, kosher and parve salads, knishes, cream cheeses, frozen hot entrees, desserts, pickles, and other ready-to-eat foods.
President: Andrew Themis
CEO: Andrew Themis
CFO: Annette Apergis
VP Sales North American: Ronnie Loeb
Estimated Sales: $80 Million
Number Employees: 250-499
Brands:
BLUE RIDGE FARMS
CHLOE FARMS
EZ CUISINE
JOSHUA'S KOSHER KITCHEN
TEXAS SUPERIOR MEATS
THE COOKIE STORE

2795 Chmuras Bakery
12 Pulaski Street
Indian Orchard, MA 01151-2215   413-543-2521
Fax: 413-543-2507
Rye bread and bakery products
President: Joe Albes
CEO: Joe Albes
Estimated Sales: $1-2.5 Million
Number Employees: 20-49

2796 Chock Full O'Nuts
65 West 36th St Suite 600   212-532-0300
Fax: 212-532-0401   888-246-2598
cad@saralee.com   www.chockfullonuts.com
Manufacturer of regular, decaffeinated, ground roast, instant and specialty coffees
President: Peter Wirth
VP: Richard Walker

Estimated Sales:$100-500 Million
Number Employees: 1,275
Parent Co: Sara Lee
Type of Packaging: Consumer, Food Service, Private Label
Other Locations:
  Chock Full O'Nuts Corp.
  Brooklyn NY
Brands:
  CHOCK FULL O'NUTS
  NEW YORK CLASSICS

2797 Chocoholics Divine Desserts
P.O.Box 730
Clements, CA 95227-0730   209-759-3320
  Fax: 209-759-3350   800-760-2462
  info@gourmetchocolate.com
  www.gourmetchocolate.com
Processor of chocolate dessert toppings, carmel sauces, double fudge cookies, truffles and chocolate novelties
  President: Ernie Schenone
  VP Sales & Operations: Mary Schenone
Estimated Sales:$5-10 Million
Number Employees: 10-19
Type of Packaging: Private Label

2798 Chocolat
2039 Bellevue Sq
Bellevue, WA 98004-5028   425-452-1141
  Fax: 425-452-1142   800-808-2462
  www.globalgourmet.com
Beverages
  President: Will Deeg
  Director Marketing: Rob Scott
Brands:
  Neuhaus
  Teuscher

2799 Chocolat Belge Heyez
45 Rue Saigneuriale Ouest
St. Bruno, QC J3V 4E4
Canada   450-653-5616
  Fax: 450-653-1445
Processor and importer of chocolates
  President: Hubert Heyez
  VP: Janine Heyez
Number Employees: 10-19
Sq. footage: 4000
Type of Packaging: Consumer, Private Label

2800 Chocolat Jean Talon
4620 Boulevard Thimens
St. Laurent, QC H4R 2B2
Canada   514-333-8540
  Fax: 514-333-8542   888-333-8540
  info@jtalon.ca
Processor of molded hollow chocolates for Easter
  President: Robert Poirier
  VP/Marketing: Richard Poirier
  Sales Manager: Johanne Lavallee
  Plant Manager: Lyne Lacharite
  Purchasing Manager: Marc Plante
Estimated Sales:$6 Million
Number Employees: 93
Number of Products: 100
Sq. footage: 55000
Type of Packaging: Food Service
Brands:
  Chocolat Jean Talon

2801 Chocolate By Design
700 Union Pkwy # 4
Ronkonkoma, NY 11779-7427   631-737-0082
  Fax: 631-737-0188   ChocoBD@aol.com
  www.chocolatebydesigninc.com
Processor of gourmet chocolate novelties and coins; also, custom molding available
  President: Ellen Motlin
  CEO: Richard Motlin
Estimated Sales:$500,000
Number Employees: 5-9
Number of Products: 350
Sq. footage: 5000
Type of Packaging: Consumer, Private Label

2802 Chocolate Chix
501 N College Street
Waxahachie, TX 75165-3361   214-744-2442
  Fax: 214-744-2449   csurana@chocolatechix.com
  www.chocolatechix.com
Processor of meringue cookies
  President: Cheryl Surana

*Estimated Sales:*Less than $500,000
Number Employees: 1-4
Brands:
  Just Meringues
  Mushroom Meringue Cookies

2803 Chocolate Creations
2501 Colorado Blvd # F
Los Angeles, CA 90041-1055   323-340-1576
  Fax: 323-340-4021   800-229-4140
  sales@chocolateart.com   www.chocolateart.com
Full line of specialty and seasonal chocolate gifts
  Owner: Jean Girard
  Purchasing Manager: J Dirard
Estimated Sales:$5-10 Million
Number Employees: 5-9

2804 Chocolate Fantasies
340 Shore Drive
Burr Ridge, IL 60527   630-572-0045
  Fax: 630-572-0039
  contactus@espressosecrets.net
  www.espressosecrets.net
all natural darck chocolate confections married to rich espresso coffee.
  CEO: Leonard Defranco

2805 Chocolate House
4121 S 35th St
Milwaukee, WI 53221-1807   414-281-7803
  Fax: 414-423-2484   800-236-2022
  candy@chocolatehouse.com
  www.chocolatehouse.com
Manufacturer and exporter of chocolate
  Manager: Irene Hyducki
Estimated Sales:$10-20 Million
Number Employees: 50-99
Type of Packaging: Consumer
Brands:
  ABSOLUTELY ALMOND
  CHOCOLATE MINT MELTAWAYS
  FUDGIE BEARS
  POSITIVELY PECAN

2806 Chocolate Moon
2000 Riverside Dr # 42f
Asheville, NC 28804-2062   828-253-6060
  Fax: 828-253-1020   800-723-1236
  info@chocolatemoon.com
  www.bluemoonwater.com
Chocolate covered dried cherries, blueberries and apricots, toffee, cocoa and cappuccino chocolate almonds and pistachios
  Owner: Chris Mathis
  Operations Manager: Jennifer Donnell
  Purchasing Manager: Jennifer Donnell
Estimated Sales:$1-2.5 Million
Number Employees: 10-19
Brands:
  DAVINCI GOURMET
  GHIARDELLI
  GUITTARD
  LINDT
  MARICH
  OREGON CHAI

2807 Chocolate Potpourri
1814 Johns Drive
Glenview, IL 60025   847-729-8878
  Fax: 847-729-8879   info@chocolatetruffles.com
  www.chocolatetruffles.com
chocolates
  President/Owner: Richard Gordon
  VP: Marsha Gordon
  Sales Staff Director: Michael Gordon
Number Employees: 11

2808 Chocolate Potpourri
1814 Johns Dr
Glenview, IL 60025-1657   847-729-8878
  Fax: 847-729-8879   888-680-1600
  micheal@chcilatetruffles.com
  www.chocolatetruffles.com
Processor of Pretzel rod dipped in caramel, rolled in fresh pecans and drizzled with rich, thick streams of chocolate, freshly popped corn dusted with white chocolate
  President: Richard Gordan
Estimated Sales:$ 5 - 10 Million
Number Employees: 10-19
Brands:
  Dipped Oreos
  Pop Au Chocolat
  Pretzel Twists

2809 Chocolate Shoppe Ice Cream Company
2221 Daniels St
Madison, WI 53718-6745   608-221-8640
  Fax: 608-221-8650
  www.chocolateshoppeicecream.com
Frozen desserts
  Owner: C B Deadman
  Vice President: Dave Deadman
  Purchasing Manager: Dave Deadman
Estimated Sales:$2.5-5 Million
Number Employees: 20-49

2810 Chocolate Street of Hartville
460 E Maple St
Hartville, OH 44632-8806   330-877-1898
  Fax: 330-877-1100   888-853-5904
Processor of custom chocolate products including 3-D corporate logos, bars and personalized gold foil wrapped coins; also, private label available; exporter of chocolate processing equipment including cooling tunnels, vibration tablesmeasuring pumps, etc
  General Manager: Robert Barton
Estimated Sales:$ 10 - 20 Million
Number Employees: 20-49
Sq. footage: 13000
Type of Packaging: Consumer, Food Service, Private Label, Bulk
Brands:
  Chocolate Street of Hartville

2811 Chocolate Studio
142 W Germantown Pike # A
Norristown, PA 19401   610-272-3872
  Fax: 610-272-3872
  sales@ChocolateStudioOnline.com
  www.chocolatestudioonline.com
Chocolates
  Owner: John Giaimo
Estimated Sales:$2.5-5 Million
Number Employees: 5-9
Type of Packaging: Consumer, Bulk

2812 Chocolaterie Bernard Callebaut
1313 1st SE
Calgary, AB T2G 5L1
Canada   403-265-5777
  Fax: 403-265-5738   800-661-8367
  bernardcallebaut.com
Processor and exporter of quality chocolates and chocolate products, including spreads, sauces and ice cream bars
  President/CEO: Bernard Callebaut
Number Employees: 20-49
Type of Packaging: Consumer, Private Label
Brands:
  Chocolaterie Bernard Callebaut

2813 Chocolaterie Stam
2814 Ingersoll Ave
Des Moines, IA 50312-4013   515-282-9575
  Fax: 515-282-9763   877-782-6246
  chocolate@stamchocolate.com
  www.stamchocolate.com
Quality Dutch chocolates
  President: Ton Stam
Estimated Sales:$500,000-$1 Million
Number Employees: 10-19
Brands:
  Stam

2814 Chocolates El Rey
P.O.Box 853
Fredericksburg, TX 78624-0853   830-997-2200
  Fax: 830-997-2417   www.chocolateselrey.com
Premium chocolates. Retail/wholesale, block, discos and chips
  President: Randall Turner
Estimated Sales:$2.5-5 Million
Number Employees: 1-4
Brands:
  CARENERO
  EL REY
  RIO CARIBE

2815 Chocolates Turin
Granite Parkway
Suite 200
Plano, TX 75024   972-731-6771
  Fax: 972-731-6774
  customerservice@turin.com.mx
  www.turin.com.mx

Chocolates
National Sales Manager: Jim Hutchins

2816 Chocolates a la Carte
28455 Livingston Ave
Valencia, CA 91355-4173   661-257-3700
Fax: 661-257-4999   800-818-2462
cus@candymaker.com
www.chocolatesalacarte.com
Processor, importer and exporter of chocolate designs for desserts, amenities and gifts including pianos, swans, sea shells, etc
President: Rena L Pocrass
Estimated Sales: $10-20 Million
Number Employees: 50-99
Sq. footage: 110000
Type of Packaging: Food Service
Brands:
CHOCOLATES A LA CARTE

2817 Chocolates by Mark
1039 Del Norte Street
Houston, TX 77018-1422   713-683-3866
Fax: 603-925-8000   mark@chocolatesbymark.com
www.chocolatesbymark.com
Processor of custom chocolate wedding/party favors, gifts
President: Mark Caffey
Number Employees: 1-4
Sq. footage: 2200
Type of Packaging: Private Label, Bulk

2818 Chocolates by Mr. Robert
505 NE 20th St
Boca Raton, FL 33431-8141   561-392-3007
Fine chocolates and truffles, chocolate-covered fruit
Owner: Heinz Robert Goldschneider
Estimated Sales: Less than $500,000
Number Employees: 1-4

2819 Chocolati Handmade Chocolates
7708 Aurora Ave N
Seattle, WA 98103-4752   206-784-5212
Fax: 206-525-4574   information@chocolati.com
www.chocolati.com
Processor of candy including mint truffles
President: Christian Wong
VP: John Berg
Estimated Sales: $100000
Number Employees: 5-9
Sq. footage: 5100
Type of Packaging: Consumer, Private Label, Bulk

2820 Chocolatier
27 Water St
Exeter, NH 03833-2440   603-772-5253
Fax: 603-772-0793   888-246-5528
the.chocolatier@verizon.net
www.the-chocolatier.com
Molded corporate chocolate candy
Owner: Jayne Welcome
Estimated Sales: $220,000
Number Employees: 5-9

2821 Chocolatique
11030 Santa Monica Blvd
#301
Los Angeles, CA 90025   310-479-3849
Fax: 310-479-8448 www.choclatique.com
chocolates, bars, marshmallows, nuts and novelties, sauces, ganaches and beverages, and baking ingredients
Co-Founder: Ed Engoron
Co-Founder: Joan Vieweger

2822 Chocolove Premium Chocolate
P.O.Box 18357
Boulder, CO 80308-1357   303-786-7888
Fax: 303-440-8850   888-246-2656
chocolove@worldnet.att.net
www.chocolove.com
Belgian chocolate bars
President: Timothy Moley
CEO: Timothy Moley
Estimated Sales: $2.5-5 Million
Number Employees: 5-9
Brands:
CHOCOLOVE

2823 Choctaw Maid Farms
PO Box 577
Carthage, MS 39051-0577   601-298-5300
Fax: 601-298-5497

Processor, importer and exporter of fresh and frozen chicken parts
Owner: Tammy Etheridge
Purchasing Agent: Ruthie Harper
Number Employees: 250-499
Type of Packaging: Bulk

2824 Choice One Foods
4020 Compton Ave
Los Angeles, CA 90011-2228   323-231-7777
Fax: 323-231-2007
Poultry and meats
CEO: Gary Rodkin
Estimated Sales: $101 Million
Number Employees: 100-249
Parent Co: ConAgra

2825 Choice Organic Teas
2414 SW Andover St
Seattle, WA 98106-1153   206-525-0051
Fax: 206-523-9750   choice@granum-inc.com
www.choiceorganicteas.com
Processor and exporter of organic teas including black, green and herbal
Owner: Blake Rankin
Estimated Sales: $1-$2.5 Million
Number Employees: 20-49
Type of Packaging: Consumer, Food Service, Private Label, Bulk
Brands:
Choice
Choice Organic Teas
Granum
Kaiseki Select
Mitoku Macrobiotic
Sound Sea Vegetables

2826 Choice of Vermont
305 Tequesta Drive
Destin, FL 32541-5715   802-888-6261
Fax: 802-888-6244   800-444-6261
gourmetfood@vtusa.net
Processor of mustard, hummus, black bean salsa, bruschetta toppings, maple pumpkin butter, pesto sauce and horseradish jam
President: Jim Peterson
Sales Director: Kevin Butler
Operations Manager: Robert Nelson
Estimated Sales: $1 Million
Number Employees: 5-9
Number of Brands: 1
Number of Products: 28
Sq. footage: 10000
Type of Packaging: Consumer, Food Service, Private Label
Brands:
Choice of Vermont

2827 Chong Mei Trading
1130 Oakleigh Drive
Atlanta, GA 30344-1821   404-768-3838
Fax: 404-768-0008
Pork, beef, seafood, chicken, dry goods, dairy, produce, Oriental grocery items
President: Kai Chen Wong
Estimated Sales: $1 - 3 Million
Number Employees: 10-19

2828 Chooljian Brothers Packing Company
3192 S Indianola Ave
Sanger, CA 93657-9716   559-875-5501
Fax: 559-875-6618   raisinnic@aol.com
www.californiaraisins.com
Processor and exporter of raisins
President: Leo Chooljian
Sales Manager: Nicholas Boghosian
Estimated Sales: $500,000
Number Employees: 50-99
Parent Co: Chooljian Brothers Packing Company
Type of Packaging: Consumer, Food Service, Private Label, Bulk
Brands:
Chooljian
Prize

2829 Chooljian Brothers Packing Company
3192 S. Indianola Avenue
P.O. Box 395
Sanger, CA 93657   559-875-5501
Fax: 559-875-1582

Raisin packer
President: Dan Milinovich
Estimated Sales: $ 10 - 20 Million
Number Employees: 10-19

2830 Chouinard Vineyards
33853 Palomares Rd
Castro Valley, CA 94552-9616   510-582-9900
Fax: 510-733-6274 www.chouinard.com
Wines
President: George Chouinard
Estimated Sales: $1-2.5 Million
Number Employees: 1-4
Brands:
ALICANTE BOUSCHET
CALIFORNIA CHAMPAGNE
CENTRAL COAST CHARDONNAY
CHOUINARD RED
CHOUINARD ROSE
GRANNY SMITH APPLE
LODI ZINFANDEL
MONTEREY CABERNET SAUVIGNON
MONTEREY CHARDONNAY
MONTEREY PETITE SYRAH
PASO ROBLES CABERNET SAUVIGNON
PASO ROBLES ORANGE MUSCAT

2831 Chowan Milling Company
PO Box 308
Ellicott City, MD 21041-0308   252-398-4238
Processor of corn meal
Plant Manager: Dean Wagenback
Number Employees: 5-9
Parent Co: Rogers Wilkins
Brands:
Beattie Brothers
Cross
Old Time

2832 Choyce Produce
3140 Ualena St # 206
Honolulu, HI 96819-1965   808-839-1502
President: Edmund Choy
Estimated Sales: $ 5 - 10 Million
Number Employees: 5-9

2833 Chr Hansen
110 Liberty Court
Elyria, OH 44035-2237   440-324-6060
Fax: 440-324-2747   800-558-0802
Manufacturer and exporter of seasonings, mixes, bacon bits, flour, oils, salt, binders, etc
President: John Cole
Estimated Sales: $3-5 Million
Number Employees: 1-4
Type of Packaging: Food Service, Private Label, Bulk

2834 Chris A. Papas & Son Company
921 Baker St
Covington, KY 41011-2007   859-431-0499
Fax: 859-431-0499
Candy and confectionery
President: Carl Papas
Vice President: Chris Papas
Estimated Sales: $1-2.5 Million
Number Employees: 1-4
Number of Products: 15
Sq. footage: 12000
Type of Packaging: Consumer, Private Label, Bulk
Brands:
Chocolate Marshmallow
It's a Boy
It's a Girl
Sugar Sticks

2835 Chris Candies
1557 Spring Garden Ave
Pittsburgh, PA 15212-3632   412-322-9400
Fax: 412-322-9402 www.chriscandies.com
Processor of chocolate bars and novelties; also, custom molds, labels and imprints available. Organic and kosher certified
President: Tim Rogers
CEO: Karl Lex
CFO: Jim Spadel
Quality Control: Kelly Scott
Purchasing Manager: Jim Spadel
Estimated Sales: $5-9.9 Million
Number Employees: 50-99
Sq. footage: 32000
Type of Packaging: Consumer, Food Service, Private Label

2836 Chris Hansen Seafood
134 Chris Ln
Port Sulphur, LA 70083-2814 504-564-2888
Fax: 580-564-2888
Seafood
Owner: Chris Hansen

2837 Chris Parker Company
55 Hearthstone Drive
Stockbridge, GA 30281-2801 770-474-6091
Fax: 770-474-7091

2838 Chris' Farm Stand
Worcester Rd
Hubbardston, MA 01452 978-928-4732
Processor of organic produce and jams and jellies
President: Thomas Holopainen
Estimated Sales: Less than $500,000
Number Employees: 5-9
Type of Packaging: Consumer

2839 Christensen Ridge
489 Gabriel Ln
Madison, VA 22727 540-923-4800
info@christensenridge.com
www.christensenridge.com
Wine
President/Owner: J D Hartman
Estimated Sales: $ 3 - 5 Million
Number Employees: 5-9

2840 Christie Cookie Company
1205 3rd Ave N
Nashville, TN 37208-2703 615-242-3817
Fax: 615-242-5572 www.christiecookies.com
Gourmet cookies and frozen ready to bake dough
President: Fleming Wilt
Plant Manager: Steve Meyers
Purchasing Manager: Robert Shefton
Estimated Sales: $10-20 Million
Number Employees: 20-49

2841 Christie Food Products
220 Canton Street - Stoughton
Randolph, MA 02072 781-341-3341
Fax: 781-341-3340 800-727-2523
hlemovitz@christiefoods.com
www.christiefoods.com
Processor and contract packager of drink mixes,
condiments, salad dressings, specialty foods, sauces
and seasonings.
Dried/Dehydrated Fruits Vegetables
VP: Raymond Smith
General Manager: Raymond Smith
Estimated Sales: $1-2.5 Million
Number Employees: 20-49
Sq. footage: 30000
Parent Co: Vision Specialty Foods
Type of Packaging: Consumer, Food Service, Private Label, Bulk
Brands:
Christie's Instant-Chef

2842 Christie-Brown
200 Deforest Avenue
East Hanover, NJ 07936-2833 973-503-4000
Fax: 973-503-3660
President: Chip Clothier
CEO: Chip Clothier
Estimated Sales: Under $500,000
Number Employees: 5-9

2843 Christine & Rob's
41103 Stayton Scio Rd SE
Stayton, OR 97383-9400 503-769-2993
Fax: 503-769-1291 bartell@wvi.com
www.christineandrobs.com
Manufacturer of old-fashioned oatmeal and preserves
Owner: Christine Bartell
Owner: Rob Bartell
Estimated Sales: $200,000
Number Employees: 1-4

2844 Christine Woods Winery
3155 Highway 128
Philo, CA 95466 707-895-2115
Fax: 707-895-2748 sales@christinewoods.com
www.christinewoods.com

Wines
Owner: Vernon Rose
Owner: Jo Rose
Partner: Edward Rose
Partner: Lisa Rose
Estimated Sales: $500,000-$1 Million
Number Employees: 1-4
Type of Packaging: Private Label

2845 Christmas Point Wild Rice Company
14803 Edgewood Dr
Baxter, MN 56425-8455 218-828-0603
Fax: 218-828-0543 www.christmaspoint.com
Wild rice products
Manager: Scott Goehring
Public Relations: Scott Goehring
Estimated Sales: $500,000-$1 Million
Number Employees: 20-49

2846 Christopher Creek Winery
6195 Dry Creek Rd
Healdsburg, CA 95448-8100 707-433-6992
Fax: 707-433-0401 fwasserm21@netcom.com
Wines
Owner: Diana Manning
CFO: Fred Wasserman
Estimated Sales: $ 10 - 20 Million
Number Employees: 20-49
Sq. footage: 3
Type of Packaging: Private Label

2847 Christopher Joseph Brewing Company
125 E 5th Street
Tempe, AZ 85281-3701 480-966-4438
Fax: 480-966-5300
Beer
President: Joseph Mocca
Estimated Sales: Under $500,000
Number Employees: 10-19
Brands:
Bandersnatch Milk Stout
Big Horn Premium
Cardinal Pale Ale

2848 Christopher Norman Chocolates
60 New St
New York, NY 10004-2303 212-402-1243
Fax: 212-402-1249
sales@ChristopherNormanChocolates.com
www.christophernormanchocolates.com
Manufacturers of hand made chocolates
Founder/Owner: John Down
Estimated Sales: $300,000-500,000
Number Employees: 1-4
Brands:
Christopher Norman Chocolates

2849 Christopher Ranch
305 Bloomfield Ave
Gilroy, CA 95020-9565 408-847-1100
Fax: 408-847-0139 chrsrnch@garlic.com
www.christopher-ranch.com
Processor, importer and exporter of garlic, ginger,
bell peppers, corn, cherries and shallots
Owner: Don Christopher
VP Marketing: Patsy Ross
Estimated Sales: $50-100 Million
Number Employees: 500-999
Type of Packaging: Consumer, Food Service, Bulk

2850 Christopher Ranch
305 Bloomfield Ave
Gilroy, CA 95020-9565 408-847-1100
Fax: 408-847-0139
garlicia@christopherranch.com
www.christopher-ranch.com
Vegetables
CEO: Bill Christopher
VP of Marketing: Patsy Ross
Sales Director: Jeff Stokes
Operations Manager: Don Christopher
Purchasing: Bridget Dunning
Estimated Sales: $100+ Million
Number Employees: 500-999
Brands:
CHRISTOPHER RANCH

2851 Chuao Chocolatier
2345 Camino Vida Roble
Carlsbad, CA 92011 760-476-1668
Fax: 760-476-1355 888-635-1444
info@chuaochocolatier.com
www.chuaochocolatier.com
Chocolates
CEO: Richard Antonorsi

2852 Chuck's Seafoods
P.O.Box 5502
Charleston, OR 97420-0616 541-888-5525
Fax: 541-888-2121 www.chucksseafoods.com
Processor and canner of seafood including salmon,
tuna, clams, crabs and shrimp
President: Jack Hampel
Secretary: Diana Hampel
Estimated Sales: $5-10 Million
Number Employees: 5-9
Type of Packaging: Consumer
Brands:
Vandon Sea-Pack

2853 Chudleigh's
8501 Chudleigh Way
Milton, ON L9T 0L9
Canada 905-878-8781
Fax: 905-878-6979 800-387-4028
farm@chudleighs.com www.chudleighs.com
Processor of fresh fruit pies and baked fruits
President: Dean Chudleigh
CFO: Robert Bolono
Brands:
Chudleigh's

2854 Chugwater Chili Corporation
P.O.Box 92
Chugwater, WY 82210-0092 307-422-3345
Fax: 307-422-3357 800-972-4454
chugchili@direcway.com
www.chugwaterchili.com
Processor of chili products including dip and dressing mixes, chili nuts red pepper jelly and ingredients
including spices, seasoning blends and peppers, and
also steak rub which is new.
Owner: Marcelyn Brown
CEO: Del Ficanz
VP: Karl Wilkerson
Marketing Director: Raece Wilkerson
Sales Director: Raece Wilkerson
Public Relations: Marcelyn Brown
Estimated Sales: $2.5-5 Million
Number Employees: 10-19
Number of Brands: 1
Number of Products: 5
Sq. footage: 2560
Type of Packaging: Consumer, Food Service
Brands:
Chugwater Chili

2855 Chukar Cherries
P.O.Box 510
Prosser, WA 99350-0510 509-786-2055
Fax: 509-786-2591 800-624-9544
sales@chukar.com www.chukar.com
Cherries, dried fruit, trail mixes, chocolates, preserves, sauces, baking mixes, tea and fresh cherries
President: Pam Auld
Head of Production: Kathlene Yound
Estimated Sales: $20-50 Million
Number Employees: 20-49

2856 Chula Vista Cheese Company
P.O.Box 69
Browntown, WI 53522-0069 608-439-5211
Fax: 608-439-5295
Cheese
President/CEO: Jim Meives
Manager: James Meives
Estimated Sales: $10-20 Million
Number Employees: 20-49

2857 Chung's Gourmet Foods
3907 Dennis St
Houston, TX 77004-2520 713-741-2118
Fax: 713-741-2330 800-824-8647
www.chungsfoods.com
Processor of juice, drinks, beverages and cranberry
sauce products
President: David Huddle
CEO: Tarrus Richardson
CEO: Vreij A Kolandjian
Sr. VP: Michael Cooper

Estimated Sales:$ 10 - 20 Million
Number Employees: 100-249
Type of Packaging: Consumer, Food Service, Private Label
Brands:
Chung's

2858 Chungs Gourmet Foods
3907 Dennis St
Houston, TX 77004-2520   713-741-2118
Fax: 713-741-2330 www.chungsfoods.com
Processor and importer of Oriental frozen entrees and appetizers including egg rolls
President: Gene Chung
CEO: Vreij A Kolandjian
Production Manager: Bob Lee
Purchasing Manager: Lynn Tri
Estimated Sales:$10-20 Million
Number Employees: 100-249

2859 Chupa Chups USA
1200 Abernathy Rd NE
Atlanta, GA 30328-5662   770-730-6200
Fax: 678-443-3157   800-843-1858
Candy
President: Xavier Bernat
VP/General Manager: Allan Slimming
Director of Trade Marketing: Mike Grindstaff
VP Sales: Jeff Goodman
Brand Manager: Kimberly Liss
Estimated Sales:$50 Million
Brands:
CHUPA CHUPS
CRAZY DIPS
POP ROCKS
SMINT
WHISTLE POPS

2860 (HQ)Church & Dwight Company
469 N Harrison St
Princeton, NJ 08540-3510   609-683-5900
Fax: 609-497-7269   800-221-0453
www.churchdwight.com
Manufacturer and exporter of leavening agents including sodium, ammonium and potassium bicarbonates; including Arm & Hammer Baking Soda.
Chairman/President/CEO: James Craigie
EVP Finance & CFO: Matthew Farrell
EVP & CMO: Bruce Fleming
VP Human Resources: Dennis Moore
EVP Global Operations: Mark Conish
Estimated Sales:$2.5 Billion
Number Employees: 3700
Type of Packaging: Consumer, Food Service, Bulk
Other Locations:
Lakewood NJ
London OH
Green River WY
Old Fort OH
Madera CA
Oskaloosa IA
Princeton NJ
Colonial Heights VA
North Brunswick NJ
Harrisonville MO
Brands:
ARM & HAMMER®

2861 Churchill's Confectionery
3232 SW 2nd Avenue
113-115
Fort Lauderdale, FL 33315-3330   954-764-8195
Fax: 954-764-2985
Processor of confectionery gifts.
Estimated Sales:$1-2.5 Million
Number Employees: 1-4

2862 Churny Company
705 W Fulton Street
Waupaca, WI 54981-1403   715-258-4040
Fax: 715-258-4046 www.philipmorrisusa.com
Processor of cheese
Sr. VP: Pascal Fernandez
Controller: Mark Hausman
Asset Manager: Dave Edel
Operations/Plant Manager: Michael Spence
Estimated Sales:$10-20 Million
Number Employees: 100-249
Sq. footage: 42000
Parent Co: Kraft Foods
Type of Packaging: Consumer, Food Service, Private Label
Brands:
Hoffmans

2863 (HQ)Ciao Bella Gelato Company
231 40th St
Irvington, NJ 07111-1154   973-373-1200
Fax: 973-373-1224   800-435-2863
info@ciaobellagelato.com
www.ciaobellagelato.com
Processor of gelato and sorbet
Owner: Charles Apt
CEO: F W Pearce
Estimated Sales:$5-10 Million
Number Employees: 5-9
Sq. footage: 10000
Type of Packaging: Consumer, Food Service, Private Label, Bulk
Other Locations:
Ciao Bella Gelato Co.
San Francisco CA
Ciao Bella Gelato Co.
Los Angeles CA
Brands:
Ciao Bella
Gelato
Gotham Dairy
Sarabeth's

2864 Ciao Bella Gellato Company
2215 S La Brea Ave
Los Angeles, CA 90016-2221   323-965-8690
Fax: 323-965-8692 info@ciaobellagelato.com
www.ciaobellagelato.com
Processor of gelato and sorbet
Manager: Enrique Lerma
Estimated Sales:$ 3 - 5 Million
Number Employees: 1-4
Parent Co: Ciao Bella Gelato
Other Locations:
Ciao Bella Gelato Company
Los Angeles CA

2865 Ciao Bella Gellato Company
2211 Quesada Ave
San Francisco, CA 94124-1921   415-824-3000
Fax: 415-824-3003 www.ciaobellagelato.com
Processor of gelato and sorbet
Manager: Bruno Martin
Parent Co: Ciao Bella Gelato Company
Other Locations:
Ciao Bella Gelato Company
San Francisco CA

2866 Cibao Meat Product
630 Saint Anns Ave
Bronx, NY 10455-1404   718-993-5072
Fax: 718-993-5638 www.cibaomeat.com
Processor and exporter of Spanish sausage and salami.
CEO: Heinz Vielus
Estimated Sales:$5-10 Million
Number Employees: 20-49
Type of Packaging: Food Service, Bulk
Brands:
CAMPESINO JAMONETA
DON PEDRO JAMONADA
INDUVECA
LONGANIZA CIBAO
PAVOLAMI
SALAMI CAMPESINO
SALAMI DEL PUEBLO
SALAMI SOSUA
SALAPENO SALAMI
VER-MEX
VILLA MELLA

2867 Cibolo Junction Food & Spice
3013 Aztec Road NE
Albuquerque, NM 87107-4301   505-888-1987
Fax: 505-888-1972 info@chimayotogo.com
www.chimayotogo.com
Soup, stew and bread mixes, salsas, pretzels, herbs, spices and seasonings
President: Brian McKinsey
Vice President: Susan McKinsey
Estimated Sales:$1-4.9 Million
Number Employees: 5-9
Type of Packaging: Private Label

2868 Cienega Valley Winery/DeRose
9970 Cienega Rd
Hollister, CA 95023-9617   831-636-9143
Fax: 831-636-1435 info@derosewine.com
www.derosewine.com

Producers of red, white and port wines.
Owner: Pat De Rose
Winemaker: Al DeRose
Assistant Winemaker: Ralph Hurd IV
Estimated Sales:$5-10 Million
Number Employees: 1-4
Type of Packaging: Private Label
Brands:
DE ROSE VINEYARDS

2869 Cifelli & Sons
38 Obert St
South River, NJ 08882-1235   732-238-0090
Fax: 732-238-7768
Processor of Italian sausage
President: Anthony Cifelli
VP: James Cifelli
Estimated Sales:$10-20 Million
Number Employees: 10-19
Sq. footage: 3500
Type of Packaging: Private Label

2870 Cimarron Cellars
P.O.Box 8
Caney, OK 74533-0008   580-889-5997
Fax: 580-889-6312 cimcel@atoka.net
Wine
Owner/Winemaker: Dwayne Pool
Owner: Suze Pool
President: Linda Pool
Estimated Sales:$1-2.5 Million
Number Employees: 1-4
Brands:
Cimarron Cellars

2871 Cimpl Meats
P.O.Box 80
Yankton, SD 57078-0080   605-665-1665
Fax: 605-665-8908
Manufacturer and packer of sausage and beef
VP: Dave Frankforter
Estimated Sales:$50-100 Million
Number Employees: 100-249

2872 Cincinnati Preserves Company
3015 E Kemper Rd
Cincinnati, OH 45241-1514   513-771-2000
Fax: 513-771-8381   800-222-9966
Processor of fruit preserves
Owner: Andrew Liscow
CEO: Andy Liscow
VP: Dan Cohen
Estimated Sales:$5 Million
Number Employees: 10-19
Sq. footage: 750000
Parent Co: Cincinatti Preserving Company
Type of Packaging: Consumer
Brands:
Clearbrook Frams
Spreadable Fruit

2873 Cinderella Cheese Cake Company
208 N Fairview St
Riverside, NJ 08075-3113   856-461-6302
Fax: 856-461-5813
Processor/Manufacturer of frozen cheesecake
President/CEO: Joseph Makin
Estimated Sales:$10-20 Million
Number Employees: 10-19
Type of Packaging: Consumer, Food Service
Brands:
Cinderella

2874 Cinnabar Specialty Foods
1134 Haining St # C
Prescott, AZ 86305-1693   928-778-3687
Fax: 928-778-4289   866-293-6433
info@cinnabarfoods.com
www.cinnabarfoods.com
Processor and exporter of sauces including ethnic and barbecue; also, fruit chutneys, dry spice blends, Caribbean salsa, kashmiri marinade, rice mixes, soup enhancers, etc
President: Neera Tandon
Vice President: Ted Schleicher
Estimated Sales:$1-4.9 Million
Number Employees: 1-4
Sq. footage: 1000
Type of Packaging: Consumer, Food Service, Private Label, Bulk
Brands:
Cinnabar Specialty Foods
Neera's

2875 Cinnabar Vineyards & Winery
P.O.Box 245
Saratoga, CA 95071-0245   408-741-5858
     Fax: 408-741-5860 www.cinnabarwine.com
Wines
     President: Suzanne Frontz
     General Manager: Suzan Franz
Estimated Sales:$2.5-5 Million
Number Employees: 5-9

2876 Cinnamon Bakery
121 Hancock Street
Braintree, MA 02184-7040   781-843-2867
     Fax: 781-849-0015   800-886-2867
cinbak@aol.com   www.cinnamonbakery.com
Processor of cinnamon, raspberry and chocolate
sticks, pecan sticky buns and cinnamon rolls
     President: Tom Pattavina
     Treasurer: Frances Pattavina
Estimated Sales:$2.5-5 Million
Number Employees: 5-9
Brands:
     Boston Bakers Exchange
     Cinnamon Bakery

2877 Cipriani's Spaghetti & Sauce Company
1025 W End Ave
Chicago Heights, IL 60411-2742   708-755-6212
     Fax: 708-755-6272 www.cipspasta.com
Processor and exporter of pasta including angel hair,
vermicelli, linguine, fettuccine, lasagna, spinach,
etc.; also, pasta sauces
     President: Annett Johnson
     Executive VP: Arthur Petrarca
     Purchasing Manager: Annette Johnson
Estimated Sales:$5-10 Million
Number Employees: 10-19
Sq. footage: 10893
Type of Packaging: Consumer, Food Service, Private Label, Bulk
Brands:
     Cipriani's Classic Italian
     Cipriani's Premium

2878 Circle B Meat Company
PO Box 578
Groom, TX 79039-0578   806-248-7332
          Fax: 806-248-7911
Manufacturer of Meat
     President/Owner: Bill Bohr
Estimated Sales:$1-2.5 Million
Number Employees: 5-9
Type of Packaging: Consumer

2879 Circle Packaging Machinery Inc
2020 American Blvd
De Pere, WI 54115-9139   920-983-3420
          Fax: 920-983-3421
dstelzer@circlepackaging.com
     www.circlepackaging.com
Manufacturer of vertical and horizontal
form/fill/seal machines. F/F/S machines can be used
to package a wide verity of liquids, tablet, capsules
and other food and beverage products.
     President: John Dykema
     VP Marketing & Sales: Don Stelzer
     Product Manager: Craig Stelzer
     Production Manager: Steve Joosten
     Parts & Service Manager: Ralph Ruggiero
*Estimated Sales:*Less than $ 500,000
Number Employees: 20-49
Type of Packaging: Consumer

2880 Circle R Ranch Gourmet Foods
5901 Cross Timbers Rd
Flower Mound, TX 75022-3142   817-430-1561
     Fax: 817-430-8108   800-247-3077
          www.circlerranch.org
Processor of sauces including black bean salsa,
jalapeno jelly, green chili salsa, cheese and spice
blend, corn relish and mesquite barbecue; also,
snacks including jalapeno popcorn, habanero popcorn and snack mix
     Manager: Wendy Foster
     CEO: Alan Powdermaker
*Estimated Sales:*Less than $500,000
Number Employees: 10-19
Parent Co: Sunset Trails
Type of Packaging: Consumer, Private Label
Brands:
     Circle R Gourmet Foods

2881 Circle V Meat Company
609 Arrowhead Trail Rd
Spanish Fork, UT 84660-9237   801-798-3081
     Fax: 801-798-8671 www.circlevmeat.com
Manufacturer of beef and pork including roasts, ham
and bacon
     Owner: Cliff Voorhees
Estimated Sales:$3 Million
Number Employees: 10-19

2882 Circle Valley Produce
P.O.Box 51260
Idaho Falls, ID 83405-1260   208-524-2628
          Fax: 208-524-2630
Processor and exporter of potatoes
     President: Kent Cornelison
Estimated Sales:$ 50 - 100 Million
Number Employees: 100-249
Type of Packaging: Consumer, Bulk
Brands:
     Throughbred
     Valley Gold

2883 Circus Man Ice Cream Corporation
1000 Fulton St
Farmingdale, NY 11735-4245   516-249-4400
          Fax: 516-249-4435
Processor of ice cream
     Owner: Blaise Graziano
Estimated Sales:$1.8 Million
Number Employees: 10-19
Brands:
     CIRCUS MAN

2884 Ciro Foods
PO Box 44096
Pittsburgh, PA 15205-0296   412-771-9018
     Fax: 412-771-9018   cirofoods@usa.net
Processor of roasted red pepper spread, Italian salsa,
sauces including pizza, barbecue and cooking and
hot honey mustard; wholesaler/distributor of hot
pepper sauce; serving the food service market; importer of vinegar; exporter ofhot honey mustard
     President: Robert Pasquarelli
     VP: Josephine Proto
     Marketing Executive: Armand Pasquarelli
Number Employees: 20
Type of Packaging: Consumer, Food Service, Private Label

2885 Cisco Brewers
P.O.Box 2928
Nantucket, MA 02584-2928   508-325-5929
     Fax: 508-325-5209   brewers@nantucket.net
          www.ciscobrewers.com
Processor and exporter of ale and lager
     Owner: Randy Hudson
Estimated Sales:$600,000
Number Employees: 1-4
Sq. footage: 3200
Type of Packaging: Consumer
Brands:
     Baggywrinkle
     Bailey's
     Captain Swain's Extra
     Celebration Libation
     Dubbel Felix Caspian
     Moor
     Nobadeer Ginger
     Summer of Lager
     Whale's Tale

2886 Citadelle Maple Syrup Producers Cooperative
2100 St. Laurent, C.P. 310
Plessisville, CN G6L 2Y8   819-362-2830
          citadelle@citadelle-camp.coop
          www.citadelle-camp.coop
Maple syrup.

2887 (HQ)Citadelle Maple Syrup Produce Cooperative
Cp 310
Plessisville, QC G6L 2Y8
Canada   819-362-3241
          Fax: 819-362-2830
          citadelle@citadelle-camp.coop
          www.citadelle-camp.coop

Processor and exporter of fruit spreads, honey, pure
maple syrup and maple sugar
     CEO: Luc Lussier
     Marketing: Sylvie Chapron
Number Employees: 150
Sq. footage: 90000
Type of Packaging: Consumer, Food Service, Private Label, Bulk
Other Locations:
Brands:
     Camp
     Canada Gold
     Citadelle
     O'Canada

2888 Citica
300 S Harbor Blvd # 808
Anaheim, CA 92805-3720   714-778-8891
          Fax: 714-778-0324
     Owner: John Sun
Estimated Sales:$ 3 - 5 Million
Number Employees: 5-9

2889 Citrico
155 Revere Dr # 1
Northbrook, IL 60062-1558   847-835-4368
     Fax: 847-945-7405   888-625-8516
rtv2@citrico.com   www.creativeimpactgroup.com
An independent manufacturer of citrus products for
the food, beverage, pharmaceutical and nutraceutical
industries. Citrico operates companies in the
Cayman Islands, United States, Mexico, Argentina,
Ireland, Germany and South Africa.Our two largest
prod
     Owner: Joanne Brooks
     VP Technical Sales: Robert Vieregg
     Sales: Timothy Grano
Estimated Sales:$4.8 Million
Number Employees: 10-19
Number of Brands: 20
Parent Co: Citrico International
Brands:
     Citrico

2890 Citrop
5707 W Sligh Avenue
Tampa, FL 33634-4435   813-249-5955
          Fax: 813-249-5956
Suppliers of natural flavoring
     President/CEO: Jorge Figueredo
Estimated Sales:$1-2.5 Million
Number Employees: 5-9

2891 Citrus Citrosuco North America
5937 State Road 60 E
Lake Wales, FL 33898-9279   863-696-7400
     Fax: 863-696-1303   800-356-4592
Processor of orange juice and concentrates; importer
of frozen orange and apple concentrates and not
from concentrate orange juice; exporter of frozen orange juice concentrates and not from concentrate
orange juice
     President: Nick Emanuel
     Secretary: Dennis Helms
     Sales Manager: Michael DuBrul
Estimated Sales:$ 50 - 100 Million
Number Employees: 100-249
Type of Packaging: Bulk

2892 Citrus International
210 Salvador Sq
Winter Park, FL 32789-5619   407-629-8037
          Fax: 407-629-8195
Citrus juice
     President: Brian Albertson
*Estimated Sales:*Under $500,000
Number Employees: 1-4

2893 Citrus Service
120 S Dillard St
Winter Garden, FL 34787-3560   407-656-4999
     Fax: 407-656-4999   beroper@iag.net
Manufacturer and exporter of frozen organic citrus
juices and frozen juice concentrates
     President: Bert Roper
     CEO: Charles Roper
Estimated Sales:$4 Million
Number Employees: 20-49
Sq. footage: 14000
Type of Packaging: Bulk
Brands:
     GROVE SWEET

2894 Citterio USA Corporation
2008 State Route 940
Freeland, PA 18224-3256   570-636-3171
Fax: 570-636-1267   800-435-8888
sales@citteriousa.com   www.citteriousa.com
Processor and importer of Italian Speciality deli
meat products
President/COO: Osvaldo Vanucci
Chairman/CEO: Enrico Citterio
CEO: Nick Dei Tos
VP Sales: Joseph Petruce
VP Manufacturing: Michael Zieminski
Estimated Sales: $5-10 Million
Number Employees: 100-249
Parent Co: Giuseppe Citterio Spa
Type of Packaging: Consumer, Food Service, Private Label, Bulk

2895 City Baker
906 1st Avenue NE
Calgary, AB T2E 0C5
Canada   403-263-8578
Fax: 403-237-0453
Processor of baked goods including breads, pastries,
cakes and frozen proofed dough products
President: George Weston
VP Operations: ED HOLIK
Sales Manager: Rick San Salvador
Number Employees: 50-99
Type of Packaging: Consumer, Food Service
Brands:
City Bakery

2896 City Bakery
P.O.Box 331
Hallettsville, TX 77964-331   361-798-2843
800-272-9416
billcho@webtv.net
Bakery
Owner: Bill Chovanetz
Estimated Sales: $100,000
Number Employees: 2
Sq. footage: 2000
Brands:
SAF

2897 City Bakery
3 W 18th St # 1
New York, NY 10011-4610   212-366-1414
Fax: 212-645-0810   877-328-3687
waxpoetic@thecitybakery.com
www.thecitynakery.com
Pretzel croissants and baked goods
Owner: Maury R Rubin
Estimated Sales: $ .5 - 1 million
Number Employees: 10-19
Brands:
Maury's Cookie Dough
The City Bakery

2898 City Bean
26042 Tennyson Lane
Stevenson Ranch, CA 91381-1018   310-208-0108
Fax: 310-208-4554   888-248-9232
info@citybean.com   www.citybean.com
Coffee, tea
President: James Marcotte
Estimated Sales: $500,000-$1 Million
Number Employees: 5-9

2899 City Brewery Latrobe
119 Jefferson St
Latrobe, PA 15650   724-537-5545
Fax: 724-537-4035 www.rollingrock.com
Manufacturer and exporter of beer
Brewer: Joe Gruss
Estimated Sales: $3 Billion
Number Employees: 1000
Parent Co: Stichting Anheuser-Busch Inbev
Type of Packaging: Consumer

2900 City Brewing Company
925 3rd St S
La Crosse, WI 54601-4411   608-785-4200
Fax: 608-785-4333   contact@citybrewery.com
www.citybrewery.com
Processor of beer and malt beverages
Manager: Julie Ann Wilkins
Sales/Marketing Executive: Randy Hull
Brewmaster: Randy Hughes
Purchasing Director: Jeff Glynn
Estimated Sales: $10-20 Million
Number Employees: 10-19
Type of Packaging: Consumer

Brands:
CITY LAGER
CITY LIGHT
CITY SLICKER
KUL
LACROSS LAGER
LACROSS LIGHT

2901 City Cafe Bakery
215 Glynn St S
Fayetteville, GA 30214-2039   770-461-6800
Fax: 770-461-2161 www.citycafeandbakery.com
Bakery products
Owner: Jorg Schatte
Estimated Sales: $ 3 - 5 Million
Number Employees: 20-49

2902 City Farm/Rocky Peanut Company
1545 Clay Street
Detroit, MI 48211-1911   313-871-5100
Fax: 313-871-5106   800-437-6825
info@rockypeanut.com
rocky-peanut.com/city-farm.com
Holiday snack items
President: Joe Russo
Purchsing Director: Joe Russo
Estimated Sales: $2.5-5 Million
Number Employees: 5-9

2903 City Foods
P.O.Box 09190
Chicago, IL 60609-0190   773-523-1566
Fax: 773-523-1414   kennymeat@aol.com
www.beasbest.com
Processor, importer and exporter of frozen beef
products including corned beef brisket, short ribs,
corned, sliced, roast beef, pastrami,and beef bacon
President: Eugene Kohn
VP: Kenneth Kohn
Estimated Sales: $20-50 Million
Number Employees: 50-99
Sq. footage: 43000
Type of Packaging: Consumer, Food Service, Private Label, Bulk
Brands:
Bea's Best Corned beef
Chef's Pride
SILVER LABEL

2904 City Market
1508 Gloucester St
Brunswick, GA 31520-7143   912-265-4430
Fax: 912-261-2191
Fish and seafood
Manager: Frank Owens
Estimated Sales: $3,500,000
Number Employees: 5-9

2905 City Seafood Company ofMonroe
1508 Siddon Street
Monroe, LA 71201-5026   318-323-3281
Fax: 318-388-4539
President: Carey Messina

2906 Clabber Girl Corporation
P.O.Box 150
Terre Haute, IN 47808-0150   812-232-9446
Fax: 812-478-7181   info@clabbergirl.com
www.clabbergirlb2b.com
Processor and exporter of single and double-acting
baking powder, cornstarch, baking soda, baking
mixes
CEO: Gary Morris
R&D: Mark Bormann
Quality Control: Keith Lee
Marketing: Lori Danielson
Sales: Eric Gloe
Plant Manager: Archie Kappel
Purchasing Manager: Bruce West
Number Employees: 100-249
Number of Products: 50
Parent Co: Hulman & Company
Type of Packaging: Consumer, Food Service, Private Label, Bulk
Brands:
Clabber Girl
Rumford

2907 Claeys Candy
P.O.Box 1535
South Bend, IN 46634-1535   574-287-1818
Fax: 574-287-4184   800-348-2239
claeysinc@aol.com   www.claeyscandy.com

Candy, old fashioned hard candies, cream fudge,
gourmet peanut brittle, chocolate charlie gift boxes,
bulk, private label
President: Gregg Claeys
Plant Manager: Brian Machalleck
Estimated Sales: $10-20 Million
Number Employees: 20-49
Type of Packaging: Consumer, Private Label, Bulk
Brands:
CHOCOLATE CHARLIE
CLAEYS GOURMET CREAM FUDGE
CLAEYS GOURMET PEANUT BRITTLE
CLAEYS OLD FASHION HARDS CANDIES

2908 Claiborne & Churchill Vintners
2649 Carpenter Canyon Rd
San Luis Obispo, CA 93401-8934   805-544-4066
Fax: 805-544-7012   info@clabornechurchill.com
www.claibornechurchill.com
Wines
Owner/President: Claiborne Thompson
Owner/CEO: Fredericka Churchill
Estimated Sales: $500,000-$1 Million
Number Employees: 1-4
Brands:
Claiborne & Churchill

2909 Claire's Grand River Winery
5750 Madison Rd
Madison, OH 44057-9001   440-298-9838
Fax: 440-298-1861
Wines
Manager: Cindy Lindberg
Vice-President: William Worthy
Estimated Sales: $2.5-5 Million
Number Employees: 5-9

2910 Clara Foods
100 First Avenue SE
Clara City, MN 56222-0457   320-847-3680
Fax: 320-847-3939   888-844-8518
snacks@hcnet.net
Processor of snack foods, pretzels, cereal, baking ingredients and extruded products
President: Massoud Kazemzadeh
Research & Development: Massoud Kazemzadeh
VP Sales/Marketing: Tom Condon
Purchasing Manager: Joe Jeanotte
Estimated Sales: $1.5 Million
Number Employees: 40

2911 Clarendon Flavor Engineering
P.O.Box 21069
Louisville, KY 40221-0069   502-634-9215
Fax: 502-634-1438   info@clarendonflavors.com
www.clarendonflavors.com
Manufactures natural and artificial flavors to food
and beverage industry. Specializes in natural soft
drinks, juice added and flavored sparkling waters
President: Richard Rigney
Estimated Sales: $5-10 Million
Number Employees: 5-9
Sq. footage: 20000
Type of Packaging: Bulk

2912 Clark Bar America
135 American Legion Hwy
Revere, MA 02151-2405   781-485-4500
Fax: 781-485-4509   www.necco.com
Manufacturer and exporter of confectionery products including candy bars, caramels, coconuts, taffy
and seasonal items
President/CEO: Domenic Antonellis
CFO: Andrew Vosnak
CEO: Richard S Krause
VP Operations: William Leva, Jr
Estimated Sales: $100+ Million
Number Employees: 1,000-4,999
Sq. footage: 820000
Parent Co: UIS
Type of Packaging: Consumer, Private Label, Bulk
Brands:
Clark Bar

2913 Clark Foodservice
950 Arthur Ave
Elk Grove Vlg, IL 60007-5217   847-956-1730
Fax: 847-956-0199 www.clarknational.com

Wholesaler/distributor of groceries, meats, produce, dairy/frozen foods and seafood; serving the food service market
President: Tom Ruszkowski
CEO: Ronald Hindman
CEO: Donald D Hindman
Marketing Director: Bob Hoffer
Sales Director: Jeff Ireland
Purchasing Manager: Bob Hoffer
Estimated Sales: $100+ Million
Number Employees: 100-249
Number of Products: 8000
Sq. footage: 165000
Parent Co: Clark Foodservice
Type of Packaging: Food Service

2914 (HQ)Clark Foodservice
950 Arthur Ave
Elk Grove Vlg, IL 60007-5217   847-956-1730
        Fax: 847-956-0199   800-504-3663
                clark@clarkproducts.com
                www.clarknational.com
Wholesaler/distributor of general line products and general merchandise including food, paper products and chemicals; serving the food service market
CEO: Don Hindman
CEO: Donald D Hindman
Purchasing Agent: John Combest
Estimated Sales: $50-100 Million
Number Employees: 50-99
Other Locations:
    Clark Foodservice
    West Palm Beach FL

2915 Clark Spring Water Company
319 Clark St
Pueblo, CO 81003-3591   719-543-1594
        Fax: 719-543-6334   info.clark@aol.com
Processor and bottler of water
President: William Clark
CEO: William Clark
Marketing Director: William Clark
Estimated Sales: $2.5-5 Million
Number Employees: 5-9
Type of Packaging: Consumer
Brands:
    Alpine

2916 (HQ)Clarks Joe Fund RaisingCandies & Novelties
621 E 1st Ave
Tarentum, PA 15084-2005   724-226-0866
                888-459-9520
        ourcard@nuwavemedia.com
Processor of chocolate candy including mints, nougats, boxed and fund raising; also, importer of raw chocolate
Owner: Bob Clark
Estimated Sales: $ 3 - 5 Million
Number Employees: 5-9
Type of Packaging: Consumer
Brands:
    Joe Clark's Candies, Inc.

2917 Clarkson Scottish Bakery
1715 Lakeshore Road W
Mississauga, ON L5J 1J4
Canada   905-823-1500
Processor of Scottish baked goods including pies, pastries and breads; importer of Scottish and English meats, candies and chocolates
Proprietor: Catherine Whitelaw
Number Employees: 1-4
Sq. footage: 450

2918 Clarmil Manufacturing Corporation
30865 San Clemente St
Hayward, CA 94544-7136   510-476-0700
        Fax: 510-476-0707   888-252-7645
info@clarmilmfg.com   www.goldilocks-usa.com
Manufacturers a full line of breads, rolls, buns, filled buns and pies, pastries, sweet goods, cookies, crackers and snack items. Cakes-pound cake, sponge, devil, chiffon, snack cakes and other specialty cake items. Processes soupssauces, side dishes, stews, processed meat products, meat and vegetable fillings, hors d'ouvers, specialty snacks and appetizers.
President: Marion Ortiz Luis
Estimated Sales: Less than $500,000
Number Employees: 5-9
Number of Products: 200+
Sq. footage: 57000

Type of Packaging: Consumer, Food Service, Private Label, Bulk

2919 Clasen Quality Coatings
2910 Laura Ln
Middleton, WI 53562-1747   608-831-6750
        Fax: 608-831-7489   877-459-4500
        info@clasen.us   www.clasen.us
Manufacturer of confectioners' coatings and chocolate products
President: Jay Jensen
CFO: Dan Dietzel
Director, Research & Innovation: Kelly Austin
Director Of Sales: Rose Defiel
Plant Manager: Scott Broesch
Estimated Sales: $10-20 Million
Number Employees: 20-49
Sq. footage: 65000
Type of Packaging: Consumer, Bulk
Brands:
    CLASEN

2920 Classic Commissary
126 E Arterial Highway
Binghamton, NY 13901-1656   800-929-3486
        Fax: 607-722-1415   classicommissary@aol.com
Processor of fresh salads and fruits; also, frozen dinners, sandwiches and bagels; for the vending and convenience food industry
Owner: Tara Gianfrate
Manager: Cataldo Gianfrate
Number Employees: 50-99
Number of Products: 125
Sq. footage: 22000
Type of Packaging: Food Service, Private Label, Bulk
Brands:
    Classic Commissary

2921 Classic Confectionery
PO Box 573
Fort Worth, TX 76101-0573   847-674-4490
        Fax: 847-674-4435   800-674-4435
                TomDetective@Yahoo.com
        www.candydetective.com/clascon.html
Candy and confectionery
President: Cory Rogin
Co-Founder: Thomas Allen
President: Gail Robinson
General Manager: Trevor Toppen
Estimated Sales: $10-24.9 Million
Number Employees: 50-99

2922 Classic Confections
25 Enterprise Blvd SW
Atlanta, GA 30336-2131   404-691-1211
        Fax: 404-691-5001   800-359-7351
                sales@dessertinnovations.com
                www.dessertinnovations.com
Processor of cream chocolate truffles and chocolate dessert shells
President: Anthony Ereddia
CFO: Rolf Fchiggli
General Manager: Tim Guidry
Operations Manager: Rolf Schittli
Production Manager: Ralph Ferdinand
Estimated Sales: $10-20 Million
Number Employees: 20-49
Brands:
    Classic Confections
    Custom Up Cakes
    Singel serving Sundae

2923 Classic Delight
P.O.Box 367
St Marys, OH 45885-0367   419-394-7955
        Fax: 419-394-3199   800-274-9828
        classicdelight@classicdelight.com
                www.classicdelight.com
Processor and co-packer of USDA and FDA frozen and refrigerated sandwiches, meat and entrees
President: D Harkleroad
Vice President: J Harkleroad
Quality Control: Thresia Buscher
Sales Director: D Harkleroad
Plant Manager: Joe Tebbe
Purchasing Manager: Tracy Miley
Estimated Sales: $8 Million
Number Employees: 50-99
Number of Brands: 25
Number of Products: 60
Sq. footage: 18500
Type of Packaging: Consumer, Food Service, Private Label, Bulk

Brands:
    CLASSIC DELIGHT
    EXPRESS DELIGHTS
    SENSIBLE DELIGHTS

2924 Classic Flavors & Fragrances
125 E 23rd St # 400
New York, NY 10010-4582   212-777-0004
        Fax: 212-353-0404   cffi125@aol.com
Manufacturer, importer and exporter of flavors, essential oils, aromatics, etc
Owner: George Ivolin
CEO: George Ivolin
Estimated Sales: $2.5-5 Million
Number Employees: 5-9
Sq. footage: 1800
Type of Packaging: Bulk

2925 Classic Foods
1592 Union Street
49
San Francisco, CA 94123-4531   800-574-8122
        Fax: 866-235-9993   custserv@kettleclassics.com
                www.kettleclassics.com
Family owned manufacturer of top quality branded snack foods distributed throughout the United States and Canada.
President: Florencio Cuetara
VP of Sales - Food Service: Shane Gray
Director of Sales - Vending: Lynn Marie Robles
Public Relations: Army Nix
Estimated Sales: $5-10 Million
Number Employees: 100-249
Brands:
    Baked Classics
    Kettle Classics
    Kids Klassics
    Stoned Classics

2926 (HQ)Classic Tea
649 Innsbruck Court
Libertyville, IL 60048-1845   630-680-9934
Processor, importer and exporter of ceylon (black) tea, liquid tea syrup and iced tea concentrates
Managing Dir.: Thomas Rielly
Dir.: F Court Bailey
Number Employees: 20-49
Sq. footage: 20000
Type of Packaging: Consumer, Food Service, Private Label, Bulk
Other Locations:
    Classic Tea Ltd.
    Chicago IL
Brands:
    Ceylon Classic
    Classic Ceylon
    Pearl

2927 Classy Delites
P.O.Box 340189
Austin, TX 78734-0004   512-266-7157
        Fax: 512-266-7198   800-440-2648
        classydelites@calssydelites.com
                www.classydelites.com
Processor of all-natural, artichoke marvelous melody, basalmic bean sauce, reduced carbs tweed tortilla chips, jamaican sauce, spinach - avacado sauce and portabella sauce.
Owner: Debbie Westbrook
CEO: Drew Westbrook
Estimated Sales: $1-2.5 Million
Number Employees: 1-4
Type of Packaging: Consumer
Brands:
    Classy Delites

2928 Claudia B Chocolates
663 W Rhapsody Dr
San Antonio, TX 78216-2608   210-366-0319
        Fax: 210-375-4602
        customerservice@claudiab.com
                www.claudiab.com
Chocolates
President: Don Bankler
Estimated Sales: $ 1 - 3 Million
Number Employees: 1-4
Sq. footage: 4000
Type of Packaging: Consumer, Private Label, Bulk

2929 Claudia Springs Winery
849 Bird Avenue
San Jose, CA 95125-1613   408-895-3926
Wines
President: Claudia Klindt

2930 Claudio Corallo Chocolate
1715 NW Market St
Seattle, WA 98109   206-859-3534
                    Fax: 206-204-0629
chocolate@claudiocorallo.com
www.claudiocorallochocolate.com
chocolates

2931 Claudio Pastry Company
7308 W North Avenue
Elmwood Park, IL 60707-4234   708-453-0598
                    Fax: 708-453-9043
Cakes and pastries
    President/Owner: John Golella
    CEO: John Golella
Estimated Sales: Less than $500,000
Number Employees: 5-9

2932 Claussen Pickle Company
1300 Claussen Dr
Woodstock, IL 60098-2155   815-338-7000
        Fax: 815-338-9244   800-435-2817
                    www.kraft.com
Processor and exporter of kosher sauerkraut, toma-
toes and pickles including garlic-free, whole, spears,
halves, slices, mini, chips and sweet and sour
    President: Richard Lerner
    Maintenance Manager: Jim Darby
    Production Manager: Paul Homola
    Plant Manager: Gerry Lales
Estimated Sales: $100-500 Million
Number Employees: 250-499
Sq. footage: 200000
Parent Co: Kraft Foods
Type of Packaging: Consumer, Food Service

2933 Claxton Bakery
203 West Main Street
P.O. Box 367
Claxton, GA 30417-0367   912-739-3441
    Fax: 912-739-3097   800-841-4211
service@claxtonfruitcake.com
www.claxtonfruitcake.com
Manufacturer and exporter of fruit cake and pecans
    President: Mid Parker
    VP: Betty Parker
    VP: Dale Parker
    VP: Paul Parker
Estimated Sales: $20-50 Million
Number Employees: 100-249
Type of Packaging: Consumer
Brands:
    Claxton

2934 Claxton Cold Storage
P.O.Box 673
6424 Highway 301
Claxton, GA 30417-2093   912-739-9800
Fax: 912-739-3271   info@claxtoncoldstorage.com
                    www.claxtoncoldstorage.com
Warehouse providing freezer storage and labeling
for frozen foods
    Mgr.: Norman Fries, Jr.
    Asst. G.M.: John Ryan
    Operations Manager: Jeff Willoughby
    Plant Manager: Pam Powell
Estimated Sales: $5-10 Million
Number Employees: 50 to 99

2935 Clay Center Locker Plant
212 6th St
Clay Center, KS 67432-3312   785-632-5550
                    Fax: 785-632-5550
Processor of beef, pork, lamb, buffalo and ostrich
    Owner: Brad Dieckmann
Estimated Sales: $ 3 - 5 Million
Number Employees: 5-9
Type of Packaging: Consumer, Food Service

2936 Clayton's Coffee & Tea
1016 H St
Modesto, CA 95354-2317   209-522-7811
    Fax: 209-576-1123   sales@claytoncoffee.com
                    www.claytonrestaurant.com
Coffee and tea
    Owner: Mitch Maiseti
Estimated Sales: $1-2.5 Million
Number Employees: 1-4
Type of Packaging: Bulk
Brands:
    Clayton Coffee & Tea

2937 Claytons Crab Company
5775 Us Highway 1
Rockledge, FL 32955-5729   321-639-0161
                    Fax: 321-636-4631
Processor of crab meat; wholesaler/distributor of
fresh, frozen and canned seafood and meat; serving
the food service market
    Owner: Clayton M Korecky Jr
Estimated Sales: $1-3 Million
Number Employees: 20-49

2938 Clean Foods
760 E Santa Maria St
Santa Paula, CA 93060-3634   805-933-3027
        Fax: 805-933-9367   800-526-8328
    contact@cafealtura.com   www.cafealtura.com
Processor, importer and exporter of organic coffee
    President: Chris Shepard
    Sales Manager: Elizabeth Blatz
Estimated Sales: $2.5-5 Million
Number Employees: 5-9
Sq. footage: 1000
Parent Co: Clean Foods
Brands:
    Cafe Altura

2939 Clear Creek Distillery
2389 NW Wilson St
Portland, OR 97210-2319   503-248-9470
                    Fax: 503-248-0490
steve@clearcreekdistillery.com
www.clearcreekdistillery.com
Wine and liquor
    President: Stephen R Mc Carthy
    Vice President: Rachel Showaiter
    Plant Manager: Rachel Showaiter
Estimated Sales: $5-10 Million
Number Employees: 5-9
Type of Packaging: Private Label
Brands:
    BARTLETT
    BLUE PLUMB BRANDY
    CLEAR CREEK GRAPPAS
    FLAMBOISE
    KIRSCHWASSER (CHERRY BRANDY)
    MCCARTHY'S OREGON SINGLE MALT
    PEAR BRANDY
    PURE FRUITE

2940 Clear Lake Bakery
8400 Maryland Avenue
Saint Louis, MO 63105-3647   641-357-5264
                    Fax: 641-357-7911
Bakery products
    President: Jim McQuaid
    Sales/Marketing Manager: Matthew Miller
    General Manager: Terry Olinger
Estimated Sales: $5-9.9 Million
Number Employees: 20-49

2941 Clear Mountain Coffee Company
9155 Brookville Rd
Silver Spring, MD 20910-1810   301-587-2233
Fax: 301-587-7158 www.clearmountaincoffee.com
Fourteen varieties of organic and wood roasted cof-
fees, syrups, Choice Tea, Ghiradelli Chocolate
    President: Robert Dasilva
Estimated Sales: $1-2.5 Million
Number Employees: 10-19
Number of Brands: 10
Brands:
    10

2942 Clear Springs Foods
P.O.Box 712
Buhl, ID 83316-0712   208-543-4316
        Fax: 208-543-5608   800-635-8211
    csf@clearsprings.com   www.tommytrout.com
Processor of fresh and frozen rainbow trout; breaded
trout portions, shapes and melts
    President: Larry Cope
    VP Sales: Don Riffle
Estimated Sales: $20-50 Million
Number Employees: 10-19
Sq. footage: 43000
Parent Co: Clear Springs Foods
Type of Packaging: Consumer, Food Service, Pri-
    vate Label
Brands:
    CLEAR SPRINGS KITCHEN®
    CLEAR SPRINGS®
    CLEARùCUTS®
    SPLASH®

2943 Clear Springs Foods
14 Oakley Court
Cherry Hill, NJ 08003-2225   856-424-9412
        Fax: 856-751-0147   800-635-8211
    csf@clearsprings.com   www.clearsprings.com
Processor of fresh and frozen rainbow trout, appetiz-
ers, roulades, and breaded portions
    President: Larry Cope
    CFO: Keith Quigly
    Research & Development: Randy McMillan
    Quality Control: Julie Sradleman
    Marketing Director: Chris Howard
    Sales Director: Don Riffle
    Operations Manager: Tim Harrifan
Estimated Sales: $ .5 - 1 million
Number Employees: 1-4
Parent Co: Clear Springs Foods
Type of Packaging: Food Service, Private Label

2944 Clear-Vu Industries
200 Homer Avenue
Suite 3
Ashland, MA 01721-1716   508-881-9100
    Fax: 508-881-9111   info@clear-vuindustries.com
                    www.clear-vuindustries.com
Bulk Candy System
    President: Robert McCann
Estimated Sales: $1-2.5 Million
Number Employees: 10-19

**2945 Clearly Canadian Beverage
Corporation**
2267 W 10th Avenue
Vancouver, BC V6K 2J1
Canada   604-742-5300
        Fax: 607-742-5301   800-663-0227
    info@clearly.ca   www.clearly.ca
Processor and exporter of water including sparkling
fruit, carbonated mineral and artesian
    President: Brent Lokash
    CEO: Andrew Strang
Estimated Sales: $10 Million
Number Employees: 50
Type of Packaging: Consumer, Food Service
Brands:
    CLEARLY CANADIAN
    CLEARLY CANADIAN O+2
    ORBITZ
    QUENCHER
    TRE' LIMONE

2946 Clearwater Coffee Company
711 Rose Rd
Lake Zurich, IL 60047-1542   847-540-7711
                    Fax: 847-540-7719
Coffee
    President: Jim Ludwig

2947 Clearwater Fine Foods
757 Bedford Highway
Bedford, NS B4A 3Z7
Canada   902-443-0550
                    Fax: 902-443-8365
Processor and exporter of frozen shrimp, lobster,
scallops, crabs and clams
    President: John Risley
Number Employees: 100-249
Type of Packaging: Consumer, Food Service

2948 Clem Becker
PO Box 133
Two Rivers, WI 54241-0133   920-793-1391
    Fax: 920-793-1393   clembeckerinc@lakefield.net
Processor of smoked pork products
    President: Peter Becker
Estimated Sales: $ 5 - 10 Million
Number Employees: 25
Type of Packaging: Consumer, Food Service, Pri-
    vate Label

2949 Clem's Refrigerated Foods
181 Virginia Ave
Lexington, KY 40508-3238   859-233-0821
        Fax: 859-233-0868   800-544-5571
Processor of beef and pork products
    Owner: William Clem
    Sales Manager: Bill Mahan
Estimated Sales: $20,000,000
Number Employees: 20-49
Type of Packaging: Consumer, Food Service, Bulk
Brands:
    Clem's Custom Cut Cattle

2950 Clem's Seafood & Specialties
4505 Mattingly Ct
Buckner, KY 40010-8830   502-222-7571
                            Fax: 502-222-7598
    Owner: Michael Mc Alister
Estimated Sales: $ 3 - 5 Million
Number Employees: 1-4

2951 Clement Pappas & Company
10 N Parsonage Road
Seabrook, NJ 08302   856-455-1000
    Fax: 856-455-8746   800-257-7019
    customerservice@clementpappas.com
            www.clementpappas.com
Manufacturer and exporter of juices including apple,
blueberry, grape, papaya and cranberry sauce
    President: Peter Pappas
    Vice President: Michael Strickland
Estimated Sales: $100+ Million
Number Employees: 106
Sq. footage: 170000
Type of Packaging: Consumer, Private Label, Bulk
Other Locations:
    Clement Pappas Food Plant
    Springdale AR
    Clement Pappas Food Plant
    Seabrook NJ
    Clement Pappas Food Plant
    Mountain Home NC
    Clement Pappas Food Plant
    Ontario CA
Brands:
    CLEMENT PAPPAS

2952 (HQ)Clements Foods Company
P.O.Box 14538
Oklahoma City, OK 73113-0538   405-842-3308
    Fax: 405-843-6894   800-654-8355
            www.clementsfoods.com
Processor of apple butter, preserves, jellies, salad
dressings, pie fillings, mayonnaise, mustard, sauces,
syrups, vinegar, peanut butter and imitation vanilla;
exporter of salad dressings and mustards
    President/CEO: Edward Clements
    CEO: Robert Clements
    Vice President: Gunnar Anderson
    Quality Control: Tom Johnson
    Operations Manager: Richard Meadors
    Plant Manager: Louis LeFlore
Estimated Sales: $ 50 - 100 Million
Number Employees: 100-249
Sq. footage: 150000
Type of Packaging: Consumer, Food Service, Private Label
Other Locations:
    Clements Foods Company
    Lewisville TX
Brands:
    American
    Delicious
    Dorcheste
    Garden Club
    Little Pig
    PAR
    Savory
    Win You

2953 Clements Pastry Shop
3355 52nd Ave # B
Hyattsville, MD 20781-1033   301-277-6300
    Fax: 301-277-2897   800-444-7428
            www.clementspastry.com
Custom manufacturing of specialty dessert and
pastry items
    CEO: Teresa Walls
    VP of Sales: John Barrazotto
Estimated Sales: $100+ Million
Number Employees: 100-249
Number of Brands: 1
Number of Products: 200
Type of Packaging: Food Service, Private Label
Brands:
    CLEMENTS PASTRY SHOP

2954 Clermont
PO Box 604
Hillsboro, OR 97123-0604   503-648-8544
                            Fax: 503-861-8054
Produces frozen fruits, fruit juice concentrate and
fruit purees
Estimated Sales: $10-25 Million
Number Employees: 100-249

2955 Cleugh's Frozen Foods
6571 Altura Blvd
Buena Park, CA 90620-1019   714-521-1002
                            Fax: 714-670-1731
Manufacturer and importer of frozen produce in-
cluding strawberries, red, yellow and green bell pep-
pers, rhubarb, small whole potatoes, brussels sprouts
and exporter of strawberries and peppers
    President: Serge Verela
Estimated Sales: $50 Million
Number Employees: 20-49
Sq. footage: 45000
Parent Co: Sunopta, Inc.
Type of Packaging: Consumer, Food Service, Pri-
    vate Label, Bulk
Brands:
    Cleugh's

2956 Cleveland Syrup Corporation
P.O.Box 91959
Cleveland, OH 44101-3959   216-883-1845
                            Fax: 216-883-6204
Processor of syrup and powdered sugar
    Manager: Jim Chaney
    VP: James Chaney
    President: Virginia Chaney
Estimated Sales: $1-2.5 Million
Number Employees: 1-4
Type of Packaging: Food Service, Bulk

2957 Clic International Inc
2185 Avenue Francis Hugues
Laval, QC H7S 1N5
Canada   450-669-2663
    Fax: 450-667-6799   clic@clicfoods.com
            www.clicfoods.com
rice, beans and lentils, cereals, spices, dried fruits,
oil and shortenings, gravy, cans and juices, milk
products, pickles, Asiatic, Indian and African, coffee, nuts and desserts
    President/Owner: M Assaad Abelnour
Estimated Sales: $24.5
Number Employees: 123

2958 Cliff Bar
1610 5th St
Berkeley, CA 94710-1715   510-558-7855
    Fax: 510-558-7872   800-884-5254
Healthy energy bars
    Owner: Gary Erickson
    Marketing/Sales: Terrye Parker
Estimated Sales: $ .5 - 1 million
Number Employees: 1-4
Type of Packaging: Private Label
Brands:
    Cliff Bars
    Luna Bars

2959 (HQ)Cliffstar Corporation
1 Cliffstar Ave
Dunkirk, NY 14048-2899   716-366-6100
    Fax: 716-366-6161   800-777-2389
    sales@cliffstar.com   www.cliffstar.com
Manufacturer, importer and exporter of juice and
drinks
    President: Paul Harder
    CEO: Dale Payne
    VP: Kevin Sanvidge
    EVP New Business Development: Jack Hutton
    EVP Procurement and Logistics: Janet Tharp
    EVP Sales and Marketing: Monica Consonery
Estimated Sales: $272 Million
Number Employees: 1,300
Type of Packaging: Consumer, Food Service, Pri-
    vate Label, Bulk
Other Locations:
    Cliffstar Manufacturing Plant
    East Freetown MA
    Cliffstar Manufacturing Plant
    Fontana CA
    Cliffstar Manufacturing Plant
    Fredonia NY
    Cliffstar Manufacturing Plant
    Greer SC
    Cliffstar Manufacturing Plant
    Joplin MO
    Cliffstar Manufacturing Plant
    N East PA
    Cliffstar Manufacturing Plant
    Walla Walla WA
    Cliffstar Manufacturing Plant
    Warrens WI
Brands:
    Cliffstar
    Golden Crown

2960 Cline Cellars
24737 Arnold Dr
Sonoma, CA 95476-9216   707-940-4000
    Fax: 707-940-4034   800-543-2070
    epcline@sonic.net   www.clinecellars.com
Wines
    Owner: Frederic Cline
    CFO: Nancy Cline
    Operations Manager: Chuck Elliott
    Sales/Marketing Manager: Tina Martin
    Special Events Director: Pepe Burns
    Production Manager: Matt Cline
Estimated Sales: $10-20 Million
Number Employees: 100-249
Type of Packaging: Private Label
Brands:
    Cline Cellars

2961 Clinton Milk Company
353 Morris Avenue
Newark, NJ 07103-2695   973-642-3000
                            Fax: 973-642-3457
Milk and juices
    President: Kelly Marx
    VP: Dan Marx
    Plant Manager: Lawrence Dineen
Estimated Sales: $50-100 Million
Number Employees: 50-99

2962 Clinton Vineyards
450 Schultzville Rd
Clinton Corners, NY 12514-2402   845-266-5372
    Fax: 845-266-3395   info@clintonvineyards.com
            www.clintonvineyards.com
Processor of white, dessert and sparkling wines
    President: Ben Feder
    VP: Phyllis Feder
    Marketing Director: Phyllis Rich Feder
    Production Manager: Mike Kelsey
    Plant Manager: Bill Wentzel
Estimated Sales: $ 1 - 3 Million
Number Employees: 1-4
Type of Packaging: Consumer
Brands:
    Clinton Victory
    DUET
    Embrace
    NUIT
    PEACH GAL
    Romance
    Seyval Blanc
    Seyval Naturel

2963 Clipper City Brewing
4615 Hollins Ferry Rd # B
Baltimore, MD 21227-4624   410-247-7822
            Fax: 410-247-7829 www.ccbeer.com
Brewer of beer and ale
    President: Hugh Sisson
    General Manager: Mike Jaeger
Estimated Sales: $ 10 - 20 Million
Number Employees: 10-19
Type of Packaging: Consumer, Food Service

**2964 (HQ)Clofine Dairy & Food
Products**
P.O.Box 335
1407 New Rd
Linwood, NJ 08221-0335   609-653-1000
    Fax: 609-653-0127   800-441-1001
    fsmith@clofinedairy.com   www.clofinedairy.com
Manufacturer and distributor of a full line of fluid
and dried dairy products, proteins, cheeses, milk re-
placement blends, tofu and soymilk powders, vital
wheat gluten, etc.
    Owner: Larry Clofine
    VP Finance: Butch Harmon
    Marketing - Fluid Products: Dawn Sink
    VP Sales: Rich Eluk
Estimated Sales: $20-50 Million
Number Employees: 10-19
Number of Brands: 2
Number of Products: 100
Type of Packaging: Food Service, Private Label,
    Bulk
Brands:
    Fine-Mix Dairy
    Food Blends
    Soy Products
    Soyfine
    Soymilk

2965 Clos Du Bois
P.O.Box 940
Geyserville, CA 95441-0940 707-857-1651
Fax: 707-857-1667 800-222-3189
thewinespot.com www.closdubois.com
Wines
President: Bill Newlands
VP: Jan Casebeer
Product Manager: Charles Stewart
Estimated Sales:$50-100 Million
Number Employees: 100-249

2966 Clos Du Muriel
27230 Madison Ave # A
Temecula, CA 92590-5639 951-296-5400
Fax: 909-676-9606
Wines
Manager: Mike Stasi

2967 Clos Pegase Winery
1060 Dunaweal Ln
Calistoga, CA 94515-9642 707-942-4981
Fax: 707-942-4993 800-866-8583
cp@clospegase.com www.clospegase.com
Wines
President: Jon Shrem
Controller/Business Manager: Abbe Bailon
VP: Theodore Sanford
Sales Director: Shannon Beglin
Winemaker: Steven Rogstad
Purchsing Manager: Theodore Sanford
Estimated Sales:$5-10 Million
Number Employees: 10-19

2968 Clos du Lac Cellars
P.O.Box 1164
Ione, CA 95640-1164 209-274-2238
Fax: 209-274-4147 www.closdulac.com
Wines
President/CEO: Timothy Evans
CFO: Robert Neumann
Vice President: Peter Evans
Winemaker: Francois Cardesse
Cellar Manager: Kelly Evans
Estimated Sales:$2.5-5 Million
Number Employees: 5-9

2969 Clos du Val Wine Company
P.O.Box 4350
Napa, CA 94558-0567 707-259-2200
Fax: 707-252-6125 800-993-9463
cdv@closduval.com www.closduval.com
Producer and exporter of wines
CFO: Bill Cambron
VP: Robert Saiz
VP/Marketing: Debra Eagle
VP/Sales: Robert Salz
PR Manager: Michaela Baltasar
Estimated Sales:$ 50 - 100 Million
Number Employees: 100-249
Brands:
Clos Du Val

2970 Cloud Nine
14855 Wicks Boulevard
San Leandro, CA 94577-6605 201-358-8588
Fax: 201-216-0383 cloud9choc@aol.com
www.cloudninecandy.com
Processor and exporter of hard candy, organic breath
mints, caramel popcorn and natural, gourmet, dairy,
nondairy, low-fat and organic chocolate bars
President: Josh Taylor
CFO: Lana Nguyen
Marketing Director: Robert Wagg
Sales Director: Sharon Desser
Director Operations: Andrew Spector
Number Employees: 10-19
Sq. footage: 2000
Type of Packaging: Consumer, Private Label
Brands:
Cloud Nine
Cloud Nine All-Natural Chocolate
Environments
Sorrento Valley Organics
Tropical Source
Tropical Source Dairy-Free Gourmet
Tropical Source Organic

2971 Cloud's Meat Processing
2051 S Paradise Ln
Carthage, MO 64836-8452 417-358-5855
Fax: 417-358-7639

Processor of smoked meat; slaughtering services
available
President: Mike Cloud
Marketing Director: Mike Cloud
Estimated Sales:$ 5 - 10 Million
Number Employees: 20-49

2972 Cloudstone Vineyards
27345 Deer Springs Way
Los Altos Hills, CA 94022-4352 650-948-8621
Wines
President: Peter Wolken
CEO: Judith Wolken
Number Employees: 1-4

2973 Clougherty Packing Company
P.O.Box 58870
Los Angeles, CA 90058-0870 323-583-4621
Fax: 323-584-1699 farmerjohn@farmerjohn.com
www.farmerjohn.com
Manufacturer of pork and pork products including a
full line of lean, fresh cut pork, sausages, weiners,
franks, Polish sausage, bacon in varied thicknesses,
boneless smoked fully cooked ham, liver spreads,
pre-packaged ready to eatlunch meats and more.
President: Greg N Longstreet
VP Finance: James Stephenson
VP Technical Services: Bob Delmore
VP Marketing: Steve Kolodin
Director Public Relations: Ronald Smith
Estimated Sales:$420 Million
Number Employees: 1,000-4,999
Parent Co: Hormel Foods
Type of Packaging: Consumer, Bulk
Brands:
FARMER JOHN
FARMER JOHN MEATS

2974 Clover Blossom Honey
P.O.Box 75
La Fontaine, IN 46940-0075 765-981-4443
Fax: 765-981-4086
Manufacturer of honey
President/Co-Owner: David Shenefield
VP/Co-Owner: Don Shenefield
Estimated Sales:$5-10 Million
Number Employees: 5-9
Type of Packaging: Consumer, Food Service, Pri-
vate Label, Bulk

2975 Clover Farms Dairy Company
P.O.Box 14627
Reading, PA 19612-4627 610-921-9111
Fax: 610-921-9913 800-323-0123
contact@cloverfarms.com www.cloverfarms.com
Milk
President/CEO: Richard Hartman
VP: Richard Rothenberger
Treasurer: John Rothenberger
VP of Sales: Thomas Mullery
Manager Plant Operations: Dennis Dietrich
Plant Manager: Royce Haag
Purchasing Manager: Craig Saul
Estimated Sales:$50-100 Million
Number Employees: 100-249

2976 Clover Hill Vineyards &Winery
9850 Newtown Rd
Breinigsville, PA 18031-1808 610-395-2468
Fax: 610-366-1246 800-256-8374
www.cloverhillwinery.com
Wines
Owner: John Skrip Jr
Owner: Pat Skrip
Estimated Sales:$2.5-5 Million
Number Employees: 10-19

2977 Clover Leaf Cheese
1201 45th Avenue NE
Calgary, AB T2E 2P2
Canada 403-250-3780
Fax: 403-291-9782 888-835-0126
chris@cheese-please.com
Packer and wholesaler/distributor of cheese
President: John Downey
Sales Manager: Chris Cameron
General Manager: John Downey
Plant Manager: Brad Lake
Number Employees: 20-49

2978 Clover Stornetta Farms
P.O.Box 750369
Petaluma, CA 94975-0369 707-778-8448
Fax: 707-778-0509 800-237-3315
www.clover-stornetta.com
Dairy products
President: Marcus Benedetti
CEO: Gary Imm
CEO: Kevin Imm
Sales Director: Mike Keefer
Estimated Sales:$50-100 Million
Number Employees: 100-249

2979 Clover Valley Food
RR 2
Box 134
Pierce, NE 68767-9668 402-329-4025
Fax: 402-329-4993
Canner of beef
President: Lawrence Polt
Estimated Sales:$500,000-$1 Million
Number Employees: 1-4
Type of Packaging: Consumer, Food Service

2980 (HQ)Cloverdale Foods Company
P.O.Box 667
Mandan, ND 58554-0667 701-663-9511
Fax: 701-663-0690 800-669-9511
www.cloverdalefoods.com
Manufacturer and wholesaler/distributor of meat
products including hickory smoked franks, bacon,
ham and sausages, along with other quality pork
products.
President/CEO: TJ Russell
VP Sales/Marketing: Scott Russell
Estimated Sales:$50-100 Million
Number Employees: 250-499
Sq. footage: 114000
Type of Packaging: Consumer, Food Service, Pri-
vate Label, Bulk
Other Locations:
Cloverdale Foods Plant
Minot ND
Brands:
Cloverdale
Teardrop

2981 Cloverdale Packing
PO Box 3346
Parkersburg, WV 26103-3346 304-485-5409
Fax: 304-428-3091
Meats
President: Jack Kincaid
Owner: David Winans
Estimated Sales:$5-9.9 Million
Number Employees: 10-19

2982 Cloverhill Bakery-Vend Corporation
2035 N Narragansett Ave
Chicago, IL 60639-3842 773-745-9800
Fax: 773-745-1647 bakery@cloverhill.com
www.cloverhill.com
Processor and exporter of sweet goods, doughnuts,
cakes and muffins.
President: William Gee
Executive VP: Edward Gee
Quality Control: Dan Gee
VP Sales: Robert Gee
Production Manager: Richard Salkowski
Estimated Sales:$20-50 Million
Number Employees: 100-249
Sq. footage: 140000
Type of Packaging: Consumer, Food Service
Brands:
CLOVER HILL

2983 Cloverland Dairy
PO Box 329
Saint Clairsville, OH 43950-0329 740-699-0509
Processor of portion controlled butter and buttermilk
President: Robert Hyest
Estimated Sales:$ .5 - 1 million
Number Employees: 300
Type of Packaging: Consumer, Private Label, Bulk

2984 Cloverland Green SpringDairy
2701 Loch Raven Rd
Baltimore, MD 21218-4731 410-235-4477
Fax: 410-889-3690 www.cloverlanddairy.com

Manufacturer of fluid milk, sour cream, cream cheese, nondairy coffee creamers, cottage cheese and juice
President/CEO: Ralph Kemp
Purchaing Director: John Evens
Estimated Sales:$20-50 Million
Number Employees: 250-499
Type of Packaging: Consumer

2985 Cloverland Green SpringDairy
2701 Loch Raven Rd
Baltimore, MD 21218-4731   410-235-4477
Fax: 410-889-3690   800-876-6455
www.cloverlanddairy.com
Manufacturer of fluid milk and dairy
President: Ralph Kemp
VP: John Kemp
Estimated Sales:$100-499.9 Million
Number Employees: 250-499
Brands:
CLOVERLAND

2986 Cloverland Sweets/Priester's Pecan Company
P.O.Box 381
Fort Deposit, AL 36032-0381   334-227-4301
Fax: 334-227-4294   800-523-3505
www.priesterpecans.com
Pecan candies, pies, baked goods, and chocolates.
Pecan shellers
President: Ned T Ellis Jr
Owner: Ellen Burkett
Vice President: Ellen Burkett
Public Relations: Faye Hood
Plant Manager: Jim Wheeler
Estimated Sales:$ 20 - 50 Million
Number Employees: 50-99
Type of Packaging: Food Service, Private Label, Bulk
Brands:
Cloverland Sweets
Priester's Pecans

2987 Cloverleaf Dairy
W10903 County Road N
Stanley, WI 54768   715-669-3145
Fax: 715-720-9332
Colby, cheddar, monterey jack cheeses
President: Daeo Paul
VP: Erlene Paul
Estimated Sales:$10-20 Million
Number Employees: 10-19
Type of Packaging: Private Label
Brands:
Cloverleaf

2988 Clovervale Farms
1833 Cooper Foster Park Rd
Amherst, OH 44001-1206   440-960-0146
800-433-0146
sales@clovervale.com   www.clovervale.com
Provides nutritious, pure, and safe food products.
Product line includes; individual preportioned servings of entrees, vegetables, sandwiches, fruits, cobblers, butter and jelly bars, frozen yogurts, sherbets, italian ices, frozenjuice pops and milk
Manager: Ted Geishart
CEO: Don Russel
Executive VP: Jim Miller
Marketing/Sales Manager: Ray Kautzman
Procurement: Neal Feist
Plant Engineer: Larry Huether
Purchasing Manager: Pam Stotler
Estimated Sales:$20-50 Million
Number Employees: 100-249
Brands:
CHEF'S PASTRY
CLOVERDALE

2989 Clown-Gysin Brands
3184 Doolittle Dr
Northbrook, IL 60062-2409   847-564-5950
Fax: 847-564-9076   800-323-5778
info@clown-gysin.com   www.clown-gysin.com
Producer and importer of marshmallows, snack foods, breadsticks, toasted onion bits, sesame dots, confectionery, and caramel apple dip items; importer of toasted onion bits and breadsticks
President: Herb Horn
Estimated Sales:$7-10 Million
Number Employees: 5-9
Number of Brands: 2
Sq. footage: 2000
Parent Co: Food Network

Type of Packaging: Food Service

2990 Club Chef
3776 Lake Park Dr
Covington, KY 41017-9826   859-578-3100
Fax: 859-578-3374 http://www.clubchef.com
Processor of wet and dry chopped salad items including lettuce, onions and cabbage
Owner: Bob Castelline
VP Retail Sales: Jeff Klare
Estimated Sales:$1-2.5 Million
Number Employees: 250-499
Sq. footage: 90000
Parent Company: Castellini Company
Type of Packaging: Consumer, Food Service, Private Label, Bulk
Brands:
Club Chef
Farm Fresh
Readypac

2991 Clutter Farms
7283 Millersburg Road
Gambier, OH 43022-9775   740-427-3515
Processor of popcorn including microwaveable
President: Gordon Clutter
V.P.: Larry Clutter
V.P.: Larry Clutter
Sq. footage: 7000
Type of Packaging: Consumer
Brands:
Clutters Indian Fields

2992 Clyde's Italian & German Sausage
3655 Inca St
Denver, CO 80211-3030   303-433-8744
Manufacturer of Italian and German sausage
President: Clyde Archer
Estimated Sales:$10 Milion
Number Employees: 1-4
Type of Packaging: Consumer

2993 Clydes Delicious Donuts
1120 W Fullerton Ave
Addison, IL 60101-4304   630-628-6555
Fax: 630-628-6838 www.clydesdonuts.com
Baked goods, bagels, danish, coffee cakes, sweet rolls, frozen and fresh yeast and cake donuts. Also apple, blueberry, maple, and cherry fritters
President: Kent Bickford
COB: William Bickford
Vice President: Kim Bickford
Research & Development: Mike Faherty
Quality Control: Rob LaScola
Marketing Director: Sue Nieues
Sales Director: Dave Bennett
Operations Manager: Larry Frank
Purchasing Manager: Dave Kells
Estimated Sales:$16-20 Million
Number Employees: 100-249
Number of Products: 125
Sq. footage: 160000
Type of Packaging: Consumer, Food Service, Private Label, Bulk

2994 Co-Hen Egg Farms
PO Box 758
Kennebunk, ME 04043-0758   207-985-9772
Fax: 207-224-7288
Processor and exporter of shelled eggs
Sales Manager: Fred Hersey
Type of Packaging: Consumer, Bulk

2995 Coach Dairy Goat Farm
105 Mill Hill Rd
Pine Plains, NY 12567-6103   518-398-5325
Fax: 518-398-5329   800-999-4628
coachfarm@taconic.net   www.coachfarm.com
Processor of goat's milk products including soft cheese and yogurt
President: Miles Cahn
General Manager: Phil Peeples
Plant Manager: Rosie Parsons
Estimated Sales:$10-20 Million
Number Employees: 20-49
Type of Packaging: Private Label
Brands:
Coach Farm
Yo-Goat

2996 Coach's Oats
22735 La Palma Ave
Yorba Linda, CA 92887-4772   714-692-6885
Fax: 714-692-6887 www.coachsoats.com
Oats
Owner: Lynn Rogers
Estimated Sales:$ 1 - 3 Million
Number Employees: 5-9

2997 Coast Packing Company
3275 E Vernon Ave
Vernon, CA 90058-1820   323-277-7700
Fax: 323-277-7712 www.coastpacking.com
Manufacturer of quality shortening products for the restaurant, baking and food industries. Also the leading supplier of animal fats and vegetable oil shortenings.
President: Ronald R Gustafson
Sales: Dieter Rehnberg
Estimated Sales:$50-100 Million
Number Employees: 50-99
Type of Packaging: Consumer, Food Service

2998 Coast Seafoods Company
14711 NE 29th Pl # 111
Bellevue, WA 98007-8612   425-702-8800
Fax: 425-702-0400   800-423-2303
info@coastseafoods.com
www.coastseafoods.com
Processor and exporter of fresh oysters and clams
President: John Petrie
CFO: Kay Christopher
Manager: Jim Donaldson
Estimated Sales:$2.5-5 Million
Number Employees: 1-4
Parent Co: Coast Seafoods Company
Type of Packaging: Consumer, Food Service

2999 Coast to Coast Seafood
9803 19th Avenue NE
Seattle, WA 98115-2311   425-889-2862
Fax: 425-822-3960
Seafood, seafood products
Estimated Sales:$50-100 Million
Number Employees: 20-49

3000 Coastal Classics
P.O.Box 1751
Duxbury, MA 2331-1751   508-746-6058
Fax: 508-746-6063 info@ciastalclassics.com
www.coastalclassics.com
Processor of cranberry chutney, cranberry mustard, cranberry preserves, cranberry hot sauce, cranberry orange marmalade, cranberry blueberry grilling sauce, peanut sauce
President: Jan Baird
Brands:
Bogland
Bogland By the Sea
Coastal Gourmet

3001 .Coastal Promotions
8828 Marlamoor Lane
West Palm Beach, FL 33412   561-202-5915
Fax: 561-626-8961 info@tasteoffl.com
www.tasteoffl.com
Manufacturer of beverage mixers
President: Doug McWhorter
Operations Manager: Kevin Blankenship
Number of Brands: 3
Number of Products: 21
Type of Packaging: Consumer, Food Service
Brands:
Taste of Florida
Wild Olive

3002 Coastal Seafood Partners
4647 N Lincoln Ave
Chicago, IL 60625-2024   773-989-7788
Fax: 773-989-7799
Seafood
President: Chris Costello
Estimated Sales:$ 1 - 3 Million
Number Employees: 20-49

3003 Coastal Seafood Processors
134 Brookhollow Esplanade
Harahan, LA 70123-5102   504-734-9444
Fax: 504-736-9447
Seafood
President: Brian Quartano

3004 Coastal Seafoods
P.O.Box 455
Ridgefield, CT 06877-0455   203-431-0453
                                   Fax: 203-438-7099
Seafood
    President: Robert Iseley
    CFO/Secretary: Linda Iseley
    Operations: Manuel Reyes
    Plant Manager: Manuel Reyes
Estimated Sales: $2.5-5 Million
Number Employees: 20-49
Sq. footage: 2500
Type of Packaging: Food Service, Private Label

3005 Coastlog Industries
45380 W 10 Mile Rd
Novi, MI 48375-3000   248-344-9556
    Fax: 248-344-9559 andy@coastlog.com
                                   www.coastlog.com
Aseptic shelf stable juice and milk products
    President: R K Sridharan
    VP Sales: Andy Larkin
Type of Packaging: Food Service
Brands:
    Coastlog

3006 Coastside Lobster Company
P.O.Box 151
Stonington, ME 04681-0151   207-367-2297
                                   Fax: 207-367-5929
Lobster
    President: Peter Collin
    Purchsing Director: Karen Rains
Number Employees: 5-9

3007 Coating Place
P.O.Box 930310
Verona, WI 53593-0310   608-845-9521
    Fax: 608-845-9526 info@encap.com
                                   www.encap.com
Contract manufacturer specializing in wurster fluid
bed coating services for encapsulation of solid par-
ticulate materials such as powders, grenules, crystals
and capsules
    President: Tim Breuning
    R&D: Charles Frey
    Quality Control: Scott Young
    Purchasing Director: Kurt Schmidt
Estimated Sales: $10-20 Million
Number Employees: 20-49
Sq. footage: 110000
Type of Packaging: Bulk

3008 Cobb Hill Chesse
5 Linden Rd
Hartland, VT 05048-8104   802-436-1612
    gailholmes@cobbhill.org
    www.vermontcheese.com
Cheese
    President: Gail Holmes

3009 Cobi Foods
51 Prince Street
Hantsport, NS B0P 1P0
Canada   902-684-1430
    Fax: 902-684-1437 800-565-8229
    cobifood@istar.ca
Processor and exporter of frozen quiche and meat
pies, beverages, fruit, juice concentrates and vegetables including: green, wax and lima beans, mixes,
brussels sprouts, turnips squash, chick peas, peppers,
beans, onions, pepperscarrots, corn, broccoli and
cauliflower
    President: George Bishop
    COO: Nick Betts
    VP Finances: David Perry
Number Employees: 100-249
Type of Packaging: Consumer, Food Service, Private Label, Bulk
Brands:
    Cobi
    Hilo
    Honeydew
    Kirkwod Kitchen

3010 Cobraz Brazilian Coffee
450 Park Ave
New York, NY 10022-2644   212-759-7700
                                   Fax: 212-725-1170
Coffee
    Managing Director: Francisco Barreto
Estimated Sales: $500,000-$1 Million
Number Employees: 5-9

3011 Cobscook Bay Seafood
PO Box 252
Perry, ME 04667-0252   207-853-2890
                              Fax: 208-459-3712
Seafood
    President: Joyce Pottle

3012 Coburg Dairy
P.O.Box 63448
North Charleston, SC 29419-3448   843-554-4870
Fax: 843-745-5502 marv.ervin@coburgmilk.com
                                   www.coburgdairy.com
Processor of dairy products including butter, butter-
milk, low-fat and regular cottage cheese and sour
cream; also, milk including homogenized, chocolate,
low-fat and skim
    Manager: Gary Rackley
    General Manager: Marv Ervin
    Vice President: Craig McCutcheon
    Operations Manager: Marv Ervin
Estimated Sales: $ 20 - 50 Million
Number Employees: 100-249
Type of Packaging: Consumer, Food Service, Bulk
Brands:
    Coburg

3013 (HQ)Coby's Cookies
48 Ashwarren Road
North York, ON M3J 1Z5
Canada   416-633-1567
                Fax: 416-633-9812
Processor and exporter of frozen cookie dough, muf-
fin and brownie batter; also, retail pack rice crispy
squares and brownies
    President: Joseph Bergman
    Executive VP: Jay Punwasee
Number Employees: 20-49
Sq. footage: 15000
Type of Packaging: Consumer, Food Service, Pri-
vate Label
Other Locations:
    Coby's Cookies
    Downsview ON
Brands:
    Coby's Cookies, Inc.
    Just Great Bakers, Inc.

3014 Coca-Cola Bottling Company
949 Mapunapuna St
Honolulu, HI 96819-4418   808-839-6711
    Fax: 808-834-7718 schow@na.cokecce.com
                                   www.cokecce.com
Processor of fruit juices, bottled water, soft drinks
and fountain syrup.
    President: Dan Whitford Jr
    SVP/Corporate Chief Information Officer: Jean
    Michel Ares
    SVP/Corporate External Affairs Director: Ingrid
    Saunders Jones
    General Manager: Stanley Chow
Estimated Sales: $50-100 Million
Number Employees: 100-249
Parent Co: Coca-Cola Bottling Company
Type of Packaging: Consumer

3015 Coca-Cola Bottling Company
91-233 Kalaeloa Blvd
Kapolei, HI 96707-1817   808-682-5778
    Fax: 808-682-4123 800-682-5778
                                   www.cokecce.com
Processor of syrups for soft drinks.
    President/COO North America Operations: J
    Alexander Douglas Jr
    SVP/Corporate Chief Information Officer: Jean
    Michel Ares
    SVP/Corporate External Affairs Director: Ingrid
    Saunders Jones
    General Manager: Jim Hood
Estimated Sales: $5-10 Million
Number Employees: 10,000+
Parent Co: Coca-Cola Bottling Company
Type of Packaging: Consumer, Food Service, Bulk

3016 Coca-Cola Bottling Company
15 Westcreek Boulevard
Brampton, ON L6T 5T4
Canada   905-874-7500
    Fax: 800-992-9672 800-926-5301
                                   www.cokecce.com

Processor of soft drinks.
    President/COO North America Operations: J
    Alexander Douglas Jr
    Canada Business Unit Operations: Vincent
    Timpano
    SVP/Corporate Chief Information Officer: Jean
    Michel Ares
    SVP/Corporate External Affairs Director: Ingrid
    Saunders Jones
    Manager: Daphine Walker
Number Employees: 275
Parent Co: Coca-Cola Bottling Company
Type of Packaging: Consumer, Food Service

3017 Coca-Cola Bottling Company
4100 Coca-Cola Plaza
Charlotte, NC 28211   704-557-4400
    Fax: 704-551-4646 800-777-2653
                                   www.cokebottling.com
Processor of soft drinks
    Chairman/CEO: J Frank Harrison III
    President/COO: William Elmore
    SVP/CFO: Steven Westphal
    CEO: J Frank Harrison Iii
    SVP/Chief Marketing Officer: Melvin Landis III
    SVP/Sales: C Ray Mayhall Jr
    SVP/Chief Information Officer: Jolanta Zwirek
    SVP/Human Resources: Kevin Henry
Estimated Sales: $1.4 Billion
Number Employees: 6000
Parent Co: Coca-Cola Bottling Company
Type of Packaging: Consumer, Food Service
Brands:
    Coca-Cola

3018 Coca-Cola Bottling Company
9000 Marshall Dr
Lenexa, KS 66215-3842   913-492-8100
    Fax: 913-599-9364 ccemail@na.cokecce.com
                                   www.cokecce.com
Processor of regular and diet soft drinks.
    Manager: Kevin Shea Jr
    SVP/Corporate Chief Information Officer: Jean
    Michel Ares
    SVP/Corporate External Affairs Director: Ingrid
    Saunders Jones
    Plant Manager: Karen Marshall
Estimated Sales: $100+ Million
Number Employees: 100-249
Parent Co: Coca-Cola Enterprises
Type of Packaging: Consumer, Food Service
Brands:
    Coca-Cola

3019 Coca-Cola Bottling Company
11001 Gateway Blvd W
El Paso, TX 79935-5003   915-593-2653
    Fax: 915-594-6977 800-288-3228
    ccemail@na.cokecce.com www.cokecce.com
Processor of soft drinks.
    Chairman/Interim CEO: Lowry F Kline
    Branch Manager: John Chavarria
    Telecommunications: Fred Calderon
    Branch Manager: Lui Rivera
    Operations Manager: Dave Kurzweg
Estimated Sales: $100-500 Million
Number Employees: 250-499
Parent Co: Coca-Cola Enterprises
Type of Packaging: Food Service
Brands:
    Coca-Cola

3020 Coca-Cola Bottling Company
1400 Rainer Rd
West Memphis, AR 72301-3965   870-732-1460
    Fax: 870-732-3018 www.cokecce.com
Canner of soft drinks
    Manager: Larry Colbert Jr
    SVP/Corporate Chief Information Officer: Jean
    Michel Ares
Estimated Sales: $20-50 Million
Number Employees: 50-99
Parent Co: Coca-Cola Bottling Company
Type of Packaging: Consumer
Brands:
    Coke

3021 (HQ)Coca-Cola Enterprises
2500 Windy Ridge Pkwy
Atlanta, GA 30339   770-989-3000
    Fax: 770-989-3788 800-233-7210
                                   www.cokecce.com/

Manufacturer, marketer and distributor of a full range of beverage categories, including sodas, energy drinks, still and sparkling waters, juices, sports drinks, milk-based products, fruit drinks, coffee-based beverages and teas.
Chairman & CEO: John Brock
EVP/CFO: William Douglas III
SVP Human Resources: Pamela Kimmet
Estimated Sales: $21+ Billion
Number Employees: 72000
Type of Packaging: Consumer, Food Service, Bulk
Brands:
5-ALIVE
ANDINA
APPOLLINARIS
AQUANA
AQUARIUS
BACARDI MIXERS
BARQ'S
BEAT
BISTRONE
BODY STYLE WATER
BONAQUA
BRIGHT & EARLY
BURN
BUZZ
CAMPBELL'S V8
CANADA DRY
CANNING'S
CARIBOU COFFEE
CHAUDFONTAINE
CHERRY COKE
COCA-COLA
CRUSH
DASANI
DELAWARE PUNCH
DIET COKE
DR PEPPER
EARTH & SKY
ENVIGA
EVIAN
FANTA
FAR COAST
FRESCA
FRUITOPIA
FULL THROTTLE
FUZE
GALCEAU FRUIT WATER
GODIVA BELGIAN BLENDS
GOLD PEAK
HI-C
KINLEY
LIFT
MELLO YELLO
MINUTE MAID JUICES
MONSTER
MR PIBB
NESTEA
NORTHERN NECK
NOS
ODWALLA
POWERade
RED FLASH
REHAB
SEAGRAM'S
SIMPLY JUICES
SMARTWATER
SPRITE
SUPER CAFFEINATED CANNED COFFEE
SUPER CAFFEINATED COFFEE
THE WELLNESS FROM COCA-COLA
VITAMINWATER

3022 Coca-Cola North America
2455 Watkins Rd
Columbus, OH 43207-3488   614-491-6305
Fax: 614-491-0342 www.coca-cola.com
Processor of beverage syrups.
Manager: Willie Peet Jr
SVP/Chief Corporate Information Officer: Navel Idell
CFO: Gary Fayard
Vice President: Lisa Lowe
SVP/Corporate External Affairs Director: Ingrid Saunders Jones
General Manager: Terry McGann
Purchasing Agent: Sherry Smailes
Estimated Sales: $100-500 Million
Number Employees: 100-249
Parent Co: Coca-Cola Enterprises
Type of Packaging: Consumer, Bulk
Brands:
Coca-Cola
Sugar Free Full Throttle

3023 Cocina de Mino
P.O.Box 851280
Yukon, OK 73085-1280   405-632-0600
Fax: 405-632-1394 www.cocinademino.com
Ethnic foods
Owner: Tim Wagner
Marketing Manager: Emeleo Perez
Estimated Sales: $ 1 - 3 Million
Number Employees: 20-49
Brands:
Cocina de Mino

3024 Coco Lopez
3401 SW 160th Ave # 350
Miramar, FL 33027-6306   954-450-3100
Fax: 954-450-3111 800-341-2242
customerservice@cocolopez.com
www.cocolopez.com
Canned fruits and vegetables, preserves, jams and jellie. Also manufacturer of cream of coconut, coconut milk, and coconut juice.
President: Leonardo Vargas
VP: Gisela Sanchez
Estimated Sales: $1,888,884
Number Employees: 10-19
Brands:
Coco Lopez

3025 Coco Rico
3907 St. Laurent Boulevard
Montreal, QC H2W 1X9
Canada   514-849-5554
Processor, importer and exporter of coconut extract
President: Carlos M Fuertes
Plant Manager: Roberto Villafana

3026 Cocolalla Winery
463254 Highway 95 N
Cocolalla, ID 83813   208-263-3774
Fax: 208-263-7605 cocolalla@idahowine.com
Wines
President/Owner: Mike Wagoner
VP: Vivian Merkeley
Estimated Sales: $1-4.9 Million
Number Employees: 1-4
Brands:
Cocolalla

3027 (HQ)Cocoline Chocolate Company
689 Myrtle Ave
Brooklyn, NY 11205-3984   718-522-4500
Fax: 718-522-4500 cocolichoc@aol.com
Processor and exporter of chocolate products including bars, boxed, bagged, jimmies, chips and coatings; also, cocoa powder, carob candy, etc.; importer of cocoa beans

Estimated Sales: $2.5-5 Million
Number Employees: 10-19
Sq. footage: 100000
Type of Packaging: Consumer, Food Service, Private Label, Bulk
Brands:
America's Best
Coveretts
Greeting Bars
Topping King

3028 Cocomira Confections
21 Goodrich Road
Unit 1
Toronto, ON M8Z 6A3
Canada   416-253-4867
Fax: 416-946-1749 866-413-9049
info@cocomira.com www.cocomira.com
Chocolates, hazelnut crunch, dark chocolate crunch, espresso crunch and maple crunch.
President/Owner: Anna Janes

3029 Codino's Italian Foods
704 Corporation Park
Scotia, NY 12302-1091   518-372-3308
Fax: 518-372-2787 800-246-8908
teresa@codinos.com www.codinos.com
Processor of frozen pasta including lasagna, manicotti, stuffed shells and rigatoni, ravioli, gnocchi and cavatelli
Owner: Leno Codino
Marketing Director: Scott DeVantier
Estimated Sales: $5-10 Million
Number Employees: 20-49

Type of Packaging: Consumer, Food Service, Private Label, Bulk
Brands:
Codino's

3030 Cody Consulting Services
509 Whitney
Cedar Hill, TX 75104   972-291-7268
debbiecody@sbcgloabl.net
www.codyconsultingservices.com
Customized quality and food safety program development. Food safety audits, audit preparation.
President: Deborah Cody
Number of Products: 4

3031 (HQ)Coffee & Tea
2000 NE Court
Bloomington, MN 55425-5506   952-853-1148
Fax: 952-853-0590
Coffee and tea
President: Lee Cone
Vice President: Jim Cone
Estimated Sales: Less than $500,000
Number Employees: 5-9
Type of Packaging: Private Label

3032 (HQ)Coffee Associates
178 Old River Road
Edgewater, NJ 07020   201-945-1060
Fax: 201-945-4887
Coffee
President/CEO: Constantine Callas
General Manager: William Callas
Estimated Sales: $20-50 Million
Number Employees: 50-99

3033 Coffee Barrel
2446 Jolly Rd
Okemos, MI 48864-3514   517-349-3888
Fax: 517-349-3036 www.thecoffeebarrel.com
Coffee
President: William DeGrow
Manager: Mary Vegrow
CEO: Tim Brenner
Estimated Sales: $2.5-5 Million
Number Employees: 5-9
Type of Packaging: Private Label
Brands:
Bis Train
David Rio
Ghiradelli Syrup
Guidparg Chocolates
Stirling Syrup

3034 Coffee Bean
1630 W Evans Ave
Englewood, CO 80110-1098   303-922-1238
Fax: 303-937-6336
Coffee
Owner: Carlo Rondn
Estimated Sales: Under $500,000
Number Employees: 1-4
Brands:
Country Spice Tea
Panache Cocoa and Blender Mix
Panache Gourmet Coffee
Xanadu Exotic Tea

3035 Coffee Bean & Tea Leaf
1945 S La Cienega Blvd
Los Angeles, CA 90034-1601   310-237-2326
800-832-5323
info@coffeebean.com www.coffeebean.com
Coffee, tea and blended drinks
Manager: Amber Rivero
CEO: Sunny Sassoon
VP of Finance: Kenneth A DiLillo
VP of Real Estate and Construction: Paul Goldman
Production Manager and Tea Buyer: David DeCandida
General Counsel/Sr. Director: Terry Phillip Mansky
Sr. Director, Marketing/Strategic All.: Tami Clark

Sr. Director of Store Operationa: Jay McDonald
Sr. Director/Green Coffee Mft/Distrib.: John 'Jay' Anthony Isais
Estimated Sales: $300,000-500,000
Number Employees: 10-19

3036 Coffee Bean International
9120 NE Alderwood Rd
Portland, OR 97220-1366   503-227-4490
     Fax: 503-225-9604   800-877-0474
     products@coffeebeanintl.com
     www.coffeebeanintl.com
Processor of roasted coffee, teas, cocoa, syrups and
confectionery products; manufacturer of coffee
equipment; importer of coffee beans and teas
     President: Patrick Critecer
     CFO: Kevin Burton
     Vice President: Karen Hunt
     Marketing Director: Kusa Wakjer
Estimated Sales: $10-20 Million
Number Employees: 50-99
Sq. footage: 125000
Type of Packaging: Consumer, Food Service, Private Label, Bulk
Brands:
     BLUE PARROT AUSSIE-STYLE TEA
     CAFE TIERRA
     COUNTRY SPICE TEA
     PANACHE

3037 Coffee Bean of Leesburg
110 S King St # A
Leesburg, VA 20175-3009   703-777-9556
     Fax: 703-777-4515   800-232-6872
     dion@mindspring.com   www.beanusa.com
Coffee
     Manager: Juanita Frye
Estimated Sales: $250,000
Number Employees: 5-9

3038 Coffee Beanery
3429 Pierson Pl
Flushing, MI 48433-2498   810-733-1020
     Fax: 810-733-1536   800-728-2326
     kevins@beanerysupport.com
     www.coffeebeanery.com
Coffee
     President: Joann Shaw
     VP Development: Kevin Shaw
     Marketing Director: Dee Kasmier
     Purchasing Manager: Audrey Brown
Estimated Sales: $20.4 Million
Number Employees: 100-249
Type of Packaging: Private Label
Brands:
     Coffee Beanery Franchise

3039 Coffee Brothers
1204 Via Roma
Colton, CA 92324-3909   909-370-1100
     Fax: 909-370-1101   888-443-5282
     ilcaffe@aol.com   www.coffeebrothers.com
Processor of coffee and espresso; importer and
wholesaler/distributor of espresso machines
     Owner: Cal Amodemo
     General Manager: Max Amodeo
Estimated Sales: $2.5-5 Million
Number Employees: 1-4
Sq. footage: 11000
Type of Packaging: Private Label, Bulk
Brands:
     Coffee Brothers
     Il Caffe
     Sigma

3040 Coffee Butler Service
3660 Wheeler Avenue
Alexandria, VA 22304-6403   703-823-0028
     Fax: 703-823-6943
Coffee
     President: H Steve "Swink, Ph.D."
     COO: Mike Kelsey

3041 Coffee Concepts
10836 Grissom Lane
Suite 110
Dallas, TX 75229-3544   214-363-9331
     Fax: 972-241-1619   espresso@ont.com
     www.coffeeconcepts.com
Roaster of arabica coffees, flavor syrups, granita machines and mixes, espresso bar supplies, consulting,
employee training, private labeling and unique customized signature blends
Estimated Sales: $ 1 - 5 Million
Number Employees: 20-49

3042 Coffee Creations
PO Box 10038
Lahaina, HI 96761-0038   808-575-9735
     Fax: 808-575-9759
     coffeecreations@worldnet.att.net
Coffee
     President: Jeff Ferguson
     Secretary/Treasurer: Diane Boyd
Estimated Sales: $1-2.5 Million
Number Employees: 1-4

3043 Coffee Creations
PO Box 10765
Portland, OR 97296-0765   503-224-9798
     Fax: 503-224-9796   800-245-5856
Manufacturer of coffee products including carbonated coffee sodas and Latte mixes
Estimated Sales: $5-10 Million
Number Employees: 5-9

3044 Coffee Culture-A House
1311 O Street
Lincoln, NE 68508-1512   402-438-8456
     Fax: 402-474-3535
Coffee
     General Manager: Terrance Alan Reis
     Operations Manager: Gregory Looney
Estimated Sales: Less than $500,000
Number Employees: 1-4

3045 Coffee Enterprises
32 Lakeside Ave
Burlington, VT 05401-5242   802-865-4480
     Fax: 802-865-3364   800-375-3398
     info@coffee-ent.com   www.coffee-ent.com
Processor of coffee extracts and chilled coffee-based
beverage concentrates; laboratory specializing in the
testing and analyzing services for coffee; consultant
specializing in the marketing and promotion of
coffee
     Owner/President: Dan Cox
     Director Coffee Operations: Paul Songer
Estimated Sales: $ 1 - 3 Million
Number Employees: 10-19
Sq. footage: 3500
Type of Packaging: Bulk

3046 Coffee Exchange
207 Wickenden St
Providence, RI 02903-4348   401-273-1198
     Fax: 401-273-4440   800-263-3339
     coffeex@ids.net   www.coffeexchange.com
Processor and importer of regular and decaffeinated
whole bean organic coffee; gift baskets available
     President: Charles Fishbein
     CEO: Susan Wood
Estimated Sales: $1-2.5 Million
Number Employees: 20-49
Brands:
     Coffee Exchange
     Mel's
     Roasting Coffee Daily

3047 Coffee Express Company
47722 Clipper St
Plymouth, MI 48170-2437   734-459-4900
     Fax: 734-459-5511   800-466-9000
     info@coffeeexpressco.com
     www.coffeexpressco.com
Wholesaler roaster of specialty coffees; distributors
of associated products.
     President: Tom Isaia
     Production: Scott Novak
Number Employees: 10-19
Number of Brands: 8
Number of Products: 20
Sq. footage: 8000
Type of Packaging: Consumer, Food Service, Private Label, Bulk
Brands:
     Coffee Express
     Mountain Country

3048 Coffee Grounds
1579 Hamline Ave N
St Paul, MN 55108-2107   651-644-9959
     Fax: 651-776-1143   coffee_grounds@comcast.net
     www.photofred.net
Coffee flavorings
     Owner: David Lawrence
Estimated Sales: $420,000
Number Employees: 5-9

3049 Coffee Holding Company
4401 1st Ave # 1507
Brooklyn, NY 11232-4201   718-832-0800
     Fax: 718-832-0892   800-458-2233
     sales@coffeeholding.com
     www.coffeeholding.com
Roaster, vemdor and packer of regular and green
coffee; also, packer of instant coffees
     President: Andrew Gordon
     CFO: David Gordon
     Quality Control: S Gordon
     Marketing, Specialty Coffee: Karen Gordon
     Food Service Sales: Dominic Caruso
     Plant Manager: D Rodriguez
Estimated Sales: $25 Million
Number Employees: 50-99
Number of Brands: 6
Sq. footage: 22000
Type of Packaging: Consumer, Food Service, Private Label, Bulk
Brands:
     5th Avenue
     Cafe Caribe
     Cafe Supremo
     Don Manuel 100% Colombian
     S&W
     Via Roma

3050 Coffee Masters
P.O.Box 460
Spring Grove, IL 60081-0460   815-675-0088
     Fax: 815-675-3166   800-334-6485
     cmaster@coffeemasters.com
     www.coffeemasters.com
Gourmet coffee, tea and cocoa
     Owner: Mike Ebert
     President: Mike Ebert
     Marketing Director: Betsy Summers
     Sales Director: Alan Denek
     Operations Manager: Tony Nowak
Number Employees: 50-99
Sq. footage: 46500
Type of Packaging: Consumer, Food Service, Private Label, Bulk
Brands:
     ASHBY'S ICED TEAS
     ASHBY'S TEAS OF LONDON
     BELLA CREMA
     BREW-A-CUP: PERFECT POTFULS
     COCOA AMORE
     COFFEE MASTERS

3051 Coffee Masters
511 Lake Zurich Rd
Barrington, IL 60010   847-382-9786
     Fax: 847-382-9786
Coffee and tea
Estimated Sales: $5-10 Million
Number Employees: 5-9

3052 Coffee Mill Roastery
108 Branchwood Drive
Elon, NC 27244-9384   919-929-1727
     Fax: 919-929-5899   800-729-1727
     coffeemill@bellsouth.net
Coffee and tea
     Owner: Jan Lawrence
Estimated Sales: $1-2.5 Million
Number Employees: 10-19
Type of Packaging: Private Label

3053 Coffee Mill Roasting Company
598 Falconbridge Road
Sudbury, ON P3A 5K6
Canada   705-525-2700
     Fax: 705-525-2790
Processor and packer of coffee
     President: Geoff Hong
Number Employees: 1-4
Type of Packaging: Food Service
Brands:
     The Coffee Mill

3054 Coffee Millers & Roasting
926 SE 9th Ln # B
Cape Coral, FL 33990-3121   239-573-6800
     Fax: 239-573-3693   ed@coffeemillers.com
     www.coffeemillers.com
Domestic and European coffees and blends. Over
150 varieties
     President: Marcell Miller
Estimated Sales: $1-2.5 Million
Number Employees: 1-4

3055 Coffee People
3590 SW Cedar Hills Boulevard
Beaverton, OR 97006-8951   503-619-0051
     Fax: 503-672-9013   800-354-5282
customerservice@coffeepeople.com
www.coffeepeople.com
Specialty coffees and teas
    Customer Service: Patti Graves
Estimated Sales: $ .5 - 1 million
Parent Co: Diedrich Coffee

3056 Coffee Process Technology
6005 N Shepherd Dr # G1
Houston, TX 77091-4253   713-695-7530
     Fax: 713-695-7530   www.emperorcoffee.com
Coffee
    Owner: Carlos De Aldecoa
    CFO: Larissa De Aldeco
    Vice President: Maria Carmen De Aldecoa
Estimated Sales: $1-2.5 Million
Number Employees: 10-19
Type of Packaging: Private Label
Brands:
    Uvvw Decaff

3057 Coffee Reserve
2030 W Quail Ave
Phoenix, AZ 85027-2610   623-434-0939
     Fax: 623-434-0946   www.coffeereserve.com
Coffee roasting
    President/CEO: Richard Grayson Jr
    Production Manager: Jeff Jackson
Estimated Sales: $ 5 - 10 Million
Number Employees: 10-19
Type of Packaging: Bulk

3058 Coffee Roasters
29 Edison Ave
Oakland, NJ 07436-1307   201-337-8221
     Fax: 201-337-0622   www.coffeeroastersinc.com
Coffees
    President: Lance Wetzel
Estimated Sales: $1,300,000
Number Employees: 10-19

3059 Coffee Roasters of New Orleans
712 Orleans Avenue
New Orleans, LA 70116-3111   504-827-0878
     Fax: 800-743-5711   800-737-5464
nolajava@iomenca.net   www.orleanscoffee.com
Coffee
    President: Bill Fiamers
    Director Sales/Marketing: Kathleen Siemers
    General Manager: William Siemers
    Production Supervisor: Robert Arceneaux
Estimated Sales: $5-9.9 Million
Number Employees: 5-9

3060 Coffee Up
2201 S Halsted Street
Chicago, IL 60608-4585   847-288-9330
     Fax: 847-288-9334
Coffee
    President: Chris Chacko
Estimated Sales: Under $500,000
Number Employees: 1-4

3061 Coffee Works
3418 Folsom Blvd
Sacramento, CA 95816-5312   916-452-1086
     Fax: 916-452-9134   800-275-3335
js@coffeeworks.com   www.coffeeworks.com
Coffee
    President: John Shahabian
    Sales: Greg Ward
Estimated Sales: $1-2.5 Million
Number Employees: 20-49
Brands:
    Balthazar's Blend
    Dark Star
    Jump Start
    Sweetfire

3062 Cognis
5051 Estecreek Rd
Cincinnati, OH 45232-1446   513-482-2100
     Fax: 513-482-5503   www.cognis.com

Suppliers of bulk nutritional raw materials for the
food industry
    Manager: Paul Allen
    CEO: Antonio Trius
    CFO: Klaus Edelmann
    Vice President: Paul Allen
    Managing Director: Paul Allen
Estimated Sales: $1-2.5 Million
Number Employees: 500-999

3063 Cohen's Bakery
1132 Broadway St
Buffalo, NY 14212-1502   716-892-8149
     Fax: 716-892-8150
Manufacturer of fresh bread, rolls and pastries; also,
frozen raw bread, pizza and roll dough
    President: John J Blando
Estimated Sales: $20-50 Million
Number Employees: 20-49
Sq. footage: 25000
Brands:
    Al Cohen's

3064 Cohen's Original Tasty Coddie
6639 Chippewa Dr
Baltimore, MD 21209-1542   410-539-0111
    President: Esther Cohen
Estimated Sales: Under $500,000
Number Employees: 1-4

3065 Colavita
2537 Brunswick Ave
Linden, NJ 07036-2433   908-862-5454
     Fax: 908-862-4382   usa@colavita.com
www.colavita.com
Processor, importer and wholesaler/distributor of ol-
ive and blended oils, pasta and grains.
    President/CEO: John Profaci
    CFO: John Profaci Jr
    VP Sales/Marketing: John Manginelli
Estimated Sales: $50-100 Million
Number Employees: 50-99
Brands:
    COLAVITA 25-STAR GRAN RISERVA VIN.
    COLAVITA BALSAMIC VINEGAR
    COLAVITA CLASSIC HOT SAUCE
    COLAVITA EXTRA VIRGIN OLIVE OIL
    COLAVITA FAT FREE CLASSIC HOT SAUCE
    COLAVITA FAT FREE GARDEN STYLE SAU.
    COLAVITA FAT FREE MARINARA SAUCE
    COLAVITA FAT FREE MUSHROOM SAUCE
    COLAVITA GARDEN STYLE SAUCE
    COLAVITA HEALTHY SAUCE
    COLAVITA MARINARA SAUCE
    COLAVITA MARINATED VEGETABLES
    COLAVITA MUSHROOM SAUCE
    COLAVITA PASTA
    COLAVITA PASTA PLUS
    COLAVITA PUTTANESCA SAUCE
    COLAVITA RED CLAM SAUCE
    COLAVITA WHITE CLAM SAUCE

3066 Colchester Bakery
96 Lebanon Ave
Colchester, CT 06415-1289   860-537-2415
     Fax: 860-537-4742   info@colchesterbakery.com
www.colchesterbakery.com
Manufacturer of baked breads
    Owner: Ursula Paredes
Estimated Sales: $1-2.5 Million
Number Employees: 20-49
Type of Packaging: Consumer

3067 Colchester Foods
P.O.Box 187
Bozrah, CT 06334-0187   860-886-2445
     Fax: 860-886-1138   800-243-0469
Processor and exporter of brown and white eggs
    VP: Kevin O'Brien
Number Employees: 50-99
Parent Co: Kofkoff Egg Farm
Type of Packaging: Consumer, Food Service, Pri-
    vate Label
Brands:
    New England Farms Eggs

3068 Cold Fusion Foods
8787 Shoreham Drive
Apt 308
West Hollywood, CA 90069-2227   310-287-3244
     Fax: 310-287-3242   react@colfusionfoods.com
www.coldfusionfoods.com
Processor of protein enriched frozen juice bars
    President: Collin Madden

3069 Cold Hollow Cider Mill
P.O.Box 420
Waterbury Center, VT 05677-0420   802-244-8771
     Fax: 802-244-7212   800-327-7537
info@coldhollow.com   www.coldhollow.com
Processor of apple products including cider, cider
jelly, butters, syrup, sauce, preserves and juices; ex-
porter of cider jelly; wholesaler/distributor of health
and specialty foods, general merchandise, private la-
bel items andproduce
    President: Paul Brown
    Vice President: Gayle Brown
Estimated Sales: $ 5 - 10 Million
Number Employees: 20-49
Sq. footage: 10000
Type of Packaging: Consumer, Food Service, Bulk
Brands:
    Cold Hollow Cider Mill

3070 Cold Spring Bakery
308 Main St
Cold Spring, MN 56320-2597   320-685-8681
     Fax: 320-685-3634   www.coldspringbakery.com
Bakery goods
    President: Dale Schurman
    Treasurer: Lynn Schurman
Estimated Sales: $10-20 Million
Number Employees: 50-99

3071 Cold Spring Brewing Company
P.O.Box 476
Cold Spring, MN 56320-0476   320-685-8686
Fax: 320-685-8318   info@coldspringbrewery.com
www.coldspringbrewery.com
Processor and exporter of beer and soda - 8oz &
16oz energy drinks
    President: Maurice Bryan
    President: Maurice Bryan
    Sr VP Marketing: Dave Pergl
    Sr VP Sales: Dave Pergl
    Head Brewmaster: Mike Kneip
Estimated Sales: $50-99.9 Million
Number Employees: 250-499
Type of Packaging: Private Label
Brands:
    Doppelbock
    Dunkel
    Gluek Golden Light
    Gluek Golden Pilsner
    Gluek Honey Bock
    Hefe Weiss
    Marzen
    Stite

3072 Cold Springs Farm
PO Box 100
Thamesford, ON N0M 2M0
Canada   519-285-3940
     Fax: 519-285-3181   800-265-1978
brenda@coldsp.com   www.coldspringfarm.com
Processor and exporter of fresh and frozen, whole
and de-boned turkey, fresh cooked roasts, marinated
turkey kabobs
    President: George Leroux
    VP: Brian Cram
    VP/Domestic Sales & Marketing: Peter Tessaro
    GM/Manufacturing Production Operations: John
    Alderman
Number Employees: 500-999
Sq. footage: 250000
Type of Packaging: Consumer, Food Service, Pri-
    vate Label, Bulk
Brands:
    Cold Springs Farms
    Golden Acres

3073 Colder Products Company
1001 Westgate Dr
St Paul, MN 55114-1092   651-645-0091
     Fax: 651-645-6938   800-444-2474
brad.ferstan@colder.com   www.colder.com
    President: Gary Rychley
Number Employees: 100-249

3074 Coldwater Fish Farms
PO Box 1
Lisco, NE 69148-0001   308-772-3474
     Fax: 308-772-3845   800-658-4450
cwsalmon@btigate.com
www.wheatbelt.com/cwfish_farm.htm

Fish
President: Walter Queen
Sales Director: Molly Vogler
Production Manager: Lloyd Harding
Estimated Sales:$5-10 Million
Number Employees: 20-49
Type of Packaging: Private Label

3075 Coldwater Seafood Corporation
190 Enterprise Dr
Newport News, VA 23603-1368   410-228-7500
Fax: 410-228-9222
Manufacturer of frozen seafood
President/CEO: Magnus Gustafsson
Plant Manager: Jay Book
Estimated Sales:$31.4 Million
Number Employees: 250-499
Parent Co: Icelandic Freezing Plants Corporation
Type of Packaging: Consumer, Food Service
Brands:
Icelandic

3076 Coldwater Seafood Corporation
501 Merritt 7
Norwalk, CT 06851-1181   203-846-8897
Fax: 203-866-4871
Manufacturer and importer of frozen fish and seafood including cod, haddock, pollack, perch, lobster tails, shrimp and salmon; also, catfish fillets, sticks and portion cuts
President/CEO: Magnus Gustafsson
Estimated Sales:$174 Million
Number Employees: 500
Parent Co: Coldwater Seafood
Type of Packaging: Consumer, Food Service, Private Label, Bulk
Brands:
ICELANDIC SEAFOOD
SEASTAR

3077 Cole's Quality Foods
1188 Lakeshore Dr
Muskegon, MI 49441-1613   231-722-1651
Fax: 231-722-6860 info@coles.com
www.coles.com
Processor of fresh and frozen garlic bread.
President: Scott Devon
VP: Jeffrey R Lewandoski
Quality Control: Robert Lewandoski
Plant Manager: Bob Lewandoski
Estimated Sales:$20-50 Million
Number Employees: 100-249
Type of Packaging: Consumer, Food Service
Brands:
Home Style

3078 Cole's Quality Foods
25 Ottawa Ave SW # 400
Grand Rapids, MI 49503-4052   616-975-0081
Fax: 616-975-0267 www.coles.com
Processor of frozen garlic bread and garlic spreads
President: John Sommabilla
CEO: John Sommavilla
Estimated Sales:$10-20 Million
Number Employees: 10-19
Type of Packaging: Consumer, Food Service
Brands:
Cole's

3079 Colegate Processing & Convenience Market
144 Groves Avenue
Marietta, OH 45750-2547   740-373-5699
Processor of beef and pork
President: Linda Beaver
Co-Owner: John Antill
Co-Owner: Sandy Antill
Estimated Sales:$2.5-5 Million
Number Employees: 10-19
Type of Packaging: Private Label

3080 Coleman Dairy
6901 Interstate 30
Little Rock, AR 72209-3162   501-748-1700
Fax: 501-568-9581 www.colemandairy.com
Processor of milk
President: Wc Coleman
Estimated Sales:$20-50 Million
Number Employees: 100-249
Parent Co: Turner Holdings
Type of Packaging: Consumer, Food Service

3081 (HQ)Coleman Purely Natural Brands
1767 Denver West Marriott Road
Suite 200
Golden, CO 80401   303-273-9444
Fax: 303-297-0426 877-810-8291
info@colemannatural.com
www.colemannatural.com
Processor and exporter of natural and organic beef and lamb.
President: Mel Coleman Sr
Chairman: Mel Coleman Jr
VP: Chuck Fletcher
Media: Ken Trantowski
Media: Robyn Nick
Plant Manager: Phil Wieke
Purchasing Manager: Ann DuPilka
Estimated Sales:$ .5 - 1 million
Number Employees: 100-249
Sq. footage: 25000
Type of Packaging: Food Service
Brands:
Coleman Natural Angus
Coleman Natural Beef

3082 Colgin Companies
2230 Valdina St
Dallas, TX 75207-6106   214-951-8687
Fax: 214-951-8668 888-226-5446
www.colgin.com
Processor of barbecue sauces including mesquite, apple and hickory liquid smoke
President: Elizabeth Thornhill
CEO: Kerry Thornhill
Estimated Sales:$2.5-5 Million
Number Employees: 5-9
Type of Packaging: Consumer, Bulk
Brands:
Chigarid
Colgin

3083 Colibri Pepper CompanyLLC
21 Burrough Cemetery Rd
Elmer, LA 71424   316-730-6528
chilecabro@gmail.com
www.colibrihotsauce.com
Pepper sauce
President: Eric Miller
Estimated Sales:$25,000
Number Employees: 2
Number of Brands: 1
Number of Products: 1
Sq. footage: 700
Type of Packaging: Consumer

3084 Colin Ingram
P.O.Box 146
Comptche, CA 95427-0146   707-937-1824
Fax: 707-937-5834
Manufacturer, importer and exporter of essential oils
President: John Weir
Estimated Sales:$2.5-5 Million
Number Employees: 1-4
Type of Packaging: Consumer, Food Service, Private Label, Bulk

3085 Collbran Locker Plant
P.O.Box 122
Collbran, CO 81624-0122   970-487-3329
Processor of meat products including beef, deer and elk
Owner: Frank Jones
*Estimated Sales:*Less than $500,000
Number Employees: 1-4

3086 College Coffee Roasters
115 N Donerville Rd # I
Mountville, PA 17554-1512   717-285-9561
Fax: 717-872-8554
www.collegecoffeeroasters.com
Coffee
President/Owner: Susan Lithgoe
VP: George Kerekgyarto
*Estimated Sales:*Less than $500,000
Number Employees: 1-4

3087 College Hill Poultry
P.O.Box 10
Fredericksburg, PA 17026-0010   717-865-2136
Fax: 717-865-0302 800-533-3361
info@raisedright.com www.raisedright.com

Manufacturer of fresh organic chicken. The Hain Celestial Group acquired the poultry processing facility assets of College Hill Poultry
VP Sales: Mike Yourison
Plant Manager: Lee Lebbon
Estimated Sales:$25-49.9 Million
Number Employees: 5-9
Parent Co: Hain Celestial Group, Inc.
Type of Packaging: Food Service
Brands:
RAISED RIGHT

3088 Collier's Fisheries
102 Bayou Road
Des Allemands, LA 70030-4433   985-758-7481
Fax: 985-454-8669
Seafood
President: Glay Collier

3089 Collin Street Bakery
P.O.Box 79
Corsicana, TX 75151-0079   903-872-8111
Fax: 903-872-6879 800-504-1896
cbsinfo@collinstreet.com
www.collinstreetbakery.com
Processor and exporter of fruit cakes.
President: Bob McNutt
CFO: Scott Holloman
VP Marketing: John Crawford
Operations: Jerry Grimmett
Plant Manager: John Watson
Purchasing: Marcia Lougo
Estimated Sales:$20-50 Million
Number Employees: 50-99
Sq. footage: 125000
Brands:
APPLE CINNAMON PECAN CAKE
APRICOT PECAN CAKE
BRITTLE DUET
CHEESECAKE SLICER
CINCHONA COFFEE
DEEP DISH PECAN PIKE
DELUXE FRUITCAKE
DOUBLE DEEP FUDGE PECAN PIE
GOLDEN RUM CAKE
KEY LIME CHEESECAKE
LEMON POPPY SEED CAKE
NEW YORK STYLE CHEESECAKE
ORANGE PARADISE CAKE
PECAN COFFEE CAKE
PECAN DUET
PECAN HALVES & PIECES
PINEAPPLE PECAN CAKE
PRALINE PECAN CHEESECAKE
TRIO OF CHEESECAKE
TRIPLE CHOCOLATE CAKE

3090 Collins Caviar Company
113 York St
Michigan City, IN 46360-3653   219-809-8100
Fax: 219-809-8105 cavco@collinscaviar.com
www.collinscaviar.com
American freshwater caviar, caviar creme spreads and custom compound butters
President/Owner: Carolyn Collins
CEO: Carolyn Collins
VP: Rachel Collins
Estimated Sales:$500,000-$1 Million
Number Employees: 1-4
Type of Packaging: Private Label

3091 Coloma Frozen Foods
4145 Coloma Rd
Coloma, MI 49038-8967   269-849-0500
Fax: 269-849-0415 800-642-2723
cffi@colomafrozen.com www.colomafrozen.com
Processor, importer and exporter of frozen fruits and vegetables including asparagus, apples, blackberries, blueberries, raspberries, strawberries, cherries, plums and rhubarb; also, apple juice, cider and fruit concentrates
President: Brad Wendzel
Sales Manager: Brad Wendzel
Plant Manager: Larry Endfield
Purchasing Manager: George Cuthbert
Estimated Sales:$20-50 Million
Number Employees: 100-249
Type of Packaging: Food Service, Bulk
Brands:
Coloma

3092 Coloma Meat Products
N979 County Road Ch
Coloma, WI 54930-9111   715-228-4080
          Fax: 715-228-4082 www.colomameats.com
Processor of sausage
     President: Tim Boss
     Sales Manager: Gary Hake
     Plant Manager: Mark Henke
Estimated Sales: $ 5 - 10 Million
Number Employees: 10-19
Type of Packaging: Consumer, Food Service
Brands:
     Royal

3093 Colombian Coffee Federation
140 E 57th St # 2
New York, NY 10022-2765   212-421-8300
     Fax: 212-758-3816 lfsamper@juanvaldez.com
               www.cafedecolombia.com
Green coffee trading
     President: Juan Orduz
     Marketing Director: Mary Petitt
     Operations Manager: Miguel Salazar
Estimated Sales: $1-2.5 Million
Number Employees: 10-19

3094 Colombo Bakery
1329 Fee Dr
Sacramento, CA 95815-3911   916-648-1011
                    Fax: 916-649-2534
Processor of bread, buns and rolls
     Plant Manager: Paul Gonzalez
Estimated Sales: $300,000-500,000
Number Employees: 5-9
Parent Co: Metz Group
Type of Packaging: Consumer, Food Service, Private Label, Bulk

3095 Colonial Beef Company
2060 E Tioga St
Philadelphia, PA 19134-2635   215-289-7042
          Fax: 215-288-4445 www.buonobeef.com
Processor of frozen portion-controlled beef and pork
     Manager: Debbie Wilson
     General Manager: Carl Scheifele
Estimated Sales: $ 5 - 10 Million
Number Employees: 20-49
Brands:
     Colonial Beef

3096 Colonial Coffee Roasters
3250 NW 60th St
Miami, FL 33142-2125   305-638-0885
     Fax: 305-634-2538 info@colonial-coffee.com
               www.colonial-coffee.com
Coffee roaster
     President: L Rafael Acevedo
     Vice President: Melvin Weinkle
     Operations Manager: Al Reyes
Estimated Sales: $5-9.9 Million
Number Employees: 10-19
Number of Brands: 3
Sq. footage: 30000
Type of Packaging: Food Service, Private Label, Bulk
Brands:
     Cafe Europa
     Cafe Latino
     Colonial International

3097 Colonna Brothers
P.O.Box 808
North Bergen, NJ 07047-0808   201-864-1115
                    Fax: 201-864-0144
     customerservice@colonnabrothers.com
               www.colonnabrothers.com
Manufacturer of bread crumbs, grated cheese, sauces, olive oil & vinegar, soups, stuffing mix, roasted peppers, marinated mushrooms, pepperoncini, chopped garlic, artichoke hearts and bread sticks
     President: Peter Colonna
     Secretary/Treasurer: Diane Maniscalco
     VP: Mark Colonna
Estimated Sales: $5.6 Million
Number Employees: 100-249
Type of Packaging: Consumer, Food Service
Brands:
     COLONNA

3098 Colony Foods
439 Haverhill St
Lawrence, MA 01841-4324   978-682-9677
                    Fax: 978-687-8448 www.colonyfoods.net

President: Dereck Barbagallo
Estimated Sales: $ 10 - 20 Million
Number Employees: 20-49

3099 (HQ)Colorado Baking Company
245 Rosevelt Road
Building 9-63
West Chicago, IL 80907-5177   630-231-6804
                    Fax: 630-231-1472
Bakery products
     Chairman/CEO: Steve Beaman
Estimated Sales: $2.6 Million
Number Employees: 4
Type of Packaging: Private Label, Bulk

3100 Colorado Bean Company/Greeley Trading
14574 County Road 64
Greeley, CO 80631-9317   970-356-1032
          Fax: 970-351-6003   888-595-2326
     wayne@coloradobeancompany.com
          www.coloradobeancompany.com
Processor of dried and refried beans
     Owner: Andrew Orris
Estimated Sales: 10,500,000
Number Employees: 100-249
Type of Packaging: Consumer, Food Service, Bulk

3101 (HQ)Colorado Boxed Beef Company
302 Progress Rd
Auburndale, FL 33823   863-967-0636
     Fax: 863-965-2222   j.rattigan@cbbcorp.com
               www.coloradoboxedbeef.com
Processor, exporter and wholesaler/distributor of fresh and frozen beef, veal, pork, lamb and poultry; also, portion control available; importer of lamb; transportation service and warehouse providing storage for meat products
     President and CEO: John Rattigan
     Senior VP: Bryan Saterbo
     COO: John Rattigan Jr.
Number Employees: 500-999
Type of Packaging: Consumer, Food Service, Private Label, Bulk
Other Locations:
     Colorado Boxed Beef Co.
     North Miami Beach FL
Brands:
     CASTRICUM BROTHERS
     CEDAR CREEK
     COLORADO GOLD
     COLORADO SUPREME
     DUTCH VALLEY VEAL
     EXCEL
     GREAT FISH COMPANY
     GWALTNEY
     IBP
     NATIONAL BEEF
     PACKERLAND PACKING
     PROVIMI VEAL
     SMITHFIELD PORK

3102 Colorado Cellars Winery
3553 E Rd
Palisade, CO 81526-9588   970-464-7921
          Fax: 970-464-0574 www.coloradocellars.com
Wines
     President: Richard Turley
     Treasurer: Padte Turley
Estimated Sales: $1-2.5 Million
Number Employees: 1-4

3103 Colorado Cereal
4129 Shoreline Dr
Fort Collins, CO 80526-4818   970-282-9733
          Fax: 970-223-4302   rmpop@webaccess.net
               www.coloradocereal.com
Processor and distributor of breakfast cereals in boxes and bags
     President: Bernie Blach
     Secretary: Cindy Blach
Estimated Sales: Less than $150,000
Number Employees: 1-4
Sq. footage: 20000
Type of Packaging: Consumer, Food Service, Private Label, Bulk
Brands:
     Colorado's Kernels
     Las Palomas Grandes
     Pop'n Snak

3104 Colorado Mountain Jams & Jellies
3573 G Rd
Palisade, CO 81526   970-464-0745
                    www.plumdaisy.com
fruit jams and wine jellies

3105 Colorado Popcorn Company
320 Oak St
Sterling, CO 80751-3306   970-522-7612
     Fax: 970-522-8630   800-238-2676
          popcorn@coloradopopcorn.com
               www.coloradopopcorn.com
Processor of gourmet popcorn
     Owner: Kathleen Littler
Estimated Sales: $100,000
Number Employees: 1-4
Number of Products: 13
Type of Packaging: Consumer, Food Service

3106 Colorado Salsa Company
1228 W Littleton Blvd
Littleton, CO 80120-5800   303-932-2617
                    Fax: 303-297-7752
     info_salsacolorado@yahoo.com
               www.salsacolorado.com
Processor of salsa
     Owner: David Karas
     CEO: Patricia Parkos
Estimated Sales: $1-2.5 Million
Number Employees: 1-4
Sq. footage: 1500
Type of Packaging: Consumer
Brands:
     Denver

3107 Colorado Spice
6350 Gunpark Dr
Boulder, CO 80301-3588   303-581-9586
     Fax: 303-581-9288   800-677-7423
               tzieglerne@prodigy.net
Processor of custom packed spice and herb blends; also, tea and tea blends
     President: Tim Ziegler
     CEO: Rod Smith
Estimated Sales: $900,000 appx.
Number Employees: 20-49
Sq. footage: 10200
Type of Packaging: Food Service, Private Label, Bulk
Brands:
     Cinnamon Ridge
     Shadow Mountain Foods, Inc.
     The Colorado Spice Co.
     The Spice Box
     The Spice Co.

3108 Colorado Sweet Gold
1722 S Golden Road
Lakewood, CO 80401   303-384-1101
     Fax: 303-384-1118 www.coloradosweetgold.com
Manufacturers of sweeteners and food ingredients
     President: Charlie Gilbert
     Executive: Tom Herrmann
Estimated Sales: $500,000-$1 Million
Number Employees: 1-4
Number of Products: 6
Type of Packaging: Private Label

3109 Colors Gourmet Pizza
6106 Avenida Encinas
Suite F
Carlsbad, CA 92011-1007   760-431-2203
     Fax: 760-431-0914   martial@colorspizza.com
               www.colorspizza.com
Manufacturer of gourmet pizza, handmade crusts, focaccia and panini bread
     President: Martial Bricnet
     Director of Sales/Distribution: James Tuckwell
Estimated Sales: $ 1 - 3 Million
Number Employees: 20
Sq. footage: 7500
Brands:
     Colors Gourmet Pizza

3110 Colts Chocolates
609 Overton St
Nashville, TN 37203-4149   615-251-0100
                    Fax: 615-251-0120
     information@coltschocolates.com
               www.coltschocolates.com
Chocolate candy and pies
     President: MacKenzie Colt

Estimated Sales:$1-2.5 Million
Number Employees: 20-49
Brands:
  Animal Crackers
  Brownies & Roses
  Butter Grahams
  Chocolate Covered Marshmallows
  Colts Bolts
  Gooey Butter Bar, NEW!
  Happy Trails T-Shirts
  Marie McGhee's
  Roy Rogers Happy Trails
  Truffle Babies

3111 Coltsfoot/Golden Eagle Herb
P.O.Box 5205
Grants Pass, OR 97527-0205   541-476-8267
              Fax: 541-476-0205 800-736-8749
              gldneagle@grantspass.com
              www.goldeneaglechew.com
Herbs
  Owner: Robert Anderson
  Owner: Joni Anderson
Estimated Sales:$ 3 - 5 Million
Number Employees: 5-9

3112 Columbia Brewery
PO Box 1950
Creston, BC V0B 1G0
Canada   250-428-9344
                          Fax: 250-428-3433
Processor and exporter of brewed beer and ale
  Manager: Murray Oswald
  Brewmaster: Scott Stokes
Number Employees: 104
Parent Co: Labatt Breweries
Type of Packaging: Consumer
Brands:
  Kokanee
  Kootenay True

3113 Columbia Coffee & Tea Company
4-505 Clayton Road
Weston, ON M9M 2G7
Canada   416-745-4235
          Fax: 416-745-4560 k00m@yahoo.com
Processor and importer of coffee; importer and
wholesaler/distributor of gourmet syrups; whole-
saler/distributor of tea, hot chocolate, drink crystals
and hot beverage equipment, groceries, meats, etc.;
serving the food servicemarket
  President/CEO: Maria McLean
Number Employees: 10-19
Sq. footage: 12000
Type of Packaging: Food Service, Private Label
Brands:
  Columbia

3114 Columbia County Fruit Processors
204 E Washington Street
Hanson, MA 02341-1137   508-763-5257
  Fax: 508-763-3830 www.northeastcranberry.com
Cranberries and cranberry products
  Plant Manager: Michael Kelly

3115 Columbia Empire Farms
31461 NE Bell Rd
Sherwood, OR 97140-8504   503-538-2156
                          Fax: 503-537-9693
              moreinfo@columbiaempirefarms.com
              www.nutworld.com
Manufacturer of hazelnuts, hazelnut candies, straw-
berries, red and black raspberries, Marion blackber-
ries, honey, preserves and Oregon wines
  President: Floyd Aylor
Estimated Sales:$5-10 Million
Number Employees: 20-49
Number of Brands: 5
Number of Products: 15
Sq. footage: 50000
Type of Packaging: Consumer, Food Service, Pri-
  vate Label, Bulk
Brands:
  AMERICA NORTHWEST
  COLUMBIA EMPIRE FARMS
  DOODLEBERRY
  FILBERT ACRES
  NORTHWEST GOURMAT
  NUTWORLD

3116 (HQ)Columbia Empire Farms
31461 NE Bell Rd
Sherwood, OR 97140-8504   503-554-9060
                          Fax: 503-538-4393
              jpendergrass@columbiaempirefarms.com
              www.yournw.com
Processor of Salted and roasted hazelnuts
  Partner: Linda Strand
Estimated Sales:$5-10 Million
Number Employees: 5-9
Type of Packaging: Private Label
Brands:
  America's Northwest
  Chateau Beniot
  Columbia Empire Farms
  Doodleberry
  Northwest Gourmet
  Nutworld

3117 Columbia Foods
P.O.Box 249
Snohomish, WA 98291-0249   360-568-0838
                          Fax: 360-568-4202
Processor and exporter of frozen vegetables
  President: Jay Cedergreen
  VP Sales: Ky Carlton
Estimated Sales:$1-2.5 Million
Number Employees: 5-9
Type of Packaging: Consumer, Food Service, Pri-
  vate Label, Bulk

3118 Columbia Foods
P.O.Box 605
Quincy, WA 98848-0605   509-787-1585
                          Fax: 509-787-1735
Processor and exporter of frozen vegetables includ-
ing peas, corn and carrots
  President: Jay Cedergreen
  Plant Manager: John Cedergreen
Estimated Sales:$20-50 Million
Number Employees: 100-249
Type of Packaging: Consumer, Food Service, Pri-
  vate Label

3119 Columbia Packing Company
2807 E 11th St
Dallas, TX 75203-2099   214-946-8171
          Fax: 214-946-2424 800-460-8171
              info@columbiapacking.com
              www.columbiapacking.com
Meat packers, cattle and hog slaughterers and dis-
tributors of boxed beef, boxed pork and sausage
items
  Pesident: Joseph Ondrusek
Estimated Sales:$20-50 Million
Number Employees: 50-99

3120 Columbia Snacks
P.O.Box 90424
Columbia, SC 29290-1424   803-776-0133
                          Fax: 803-776-0145
Snack products
  Owner: Steve Mims
Estimated Sales:$1-2.5 Million
Number Employees: 10-19

3121 Columbia Winery
P.O.Box 1248
Woodinville, WA 98072-1248   425-488-2776
                          Fax: 425-488-3460
              contact@columbiawinery.com
              www.columbiawinery.com
Processor and exporter of wine
  CEO: Jon Moramarco
  VP: Glenn Coogan
  Quality Control: Bruce Watson
  Marketing: Mike Jaeger
  Sales: Jim Icocoloski
  Public Relations: Lisa Farrell
Estimated Sales:$20-50 Million
Number Employees: 50-99
Parent Co: Canandaigua Wine Company
Type of Packaging: Consumer

3122 Columbus Bakery
4093 Cleveland Ave
Columbus, OH 43224-1699   614-645-2275
                          Fax: 614-462-2043

Processor of bread, buns, danish pastry, crackers and
cookies.
  QA/QC Manager: Ronald Kamer
  QA/QC Manager: Danielle Swineheart
  Sales Manager: Greg Mallory
  Product Manager: Tim Hatem
  General Manager: John Masa
Estimated Sales:$ .5 - 1 million
Number Employees: 1-4
Type of Packaging: Consumer, Private Label

3123 Columbus Brewing Company
525 Short St
Columbus, OH 43215-5614   614-464-2739
  Fax: 614-221-3316 www.columbusbrewingco.com
Beer
  Manager: Doug Griggs
  Vice President: Ben Pridgeon
Estimated Sales:$500,000-$1 Million
Number Employees: 20-49
Brands:
  1859 Porter
  Apricot Ale
  Columbus Pale Ale
  Nut Brown Ale

3124 Columbus Foods Company
30 E Oakton St
Des Plaines, IL 60018-1945   773-265-6500
          Fax: 773-265-6985 800-322-6457
              info@columbusfoods.com
              www.columbusfoods.com
Processor of almond, canola, coconut, cottonseed,
peanut, safflower, soybean, sunflower, cooking, pop-
corn, vegetable, flavored and olive oils; also, pan re-
leases, lard and animal fats; for retail, food service,
industrial, privatelabel and export, soy methyl esters,
canola methyl esters, methyl soyate.
  President: Paulette Gagliardo
  CFO: Rick Gerbatsch
  Quality Control: Rick Cumminsford
  Sales: Bob Bartilotta
  Public Relations: Kathy Miller
  Manufacturing Director: Joe Feely
Estimated Sales:$75-100 Million
Number Employees: 50-99
Sq. footage: 150000
Type of Packaging: Consumer, Food Service, Pri-
  vate Label, Bulk
Brands:
  BUTCHER BOY
  CODE 123
  EAGLE BRAND
  ENVIRO SAVER
  GOLDEN BUTCHER BOY
  LA SPAGNOLA
  MIKE
  NATURE'S SECRET
  PENOLA
  SORRENTO
  SUN
  SUNRISE 2000

3125 Columbus Gourmet
302 Brown Ave
Columbus, GA 31903-1253   706-687-0161
          Fax: 706-682-1528 800-356-1858
              www.columbusgourmet.com
Supplier of gourmet spirit cakes, pecans and cook-
ies.
  President/CEO: Brian Stone
  General Manager: Stacey Chambers
  Accounting: Karl McLure
  Sales Manager: Brad Arnholt
  COO: Jonothan Field
Sq. footage: 60000
Type of Packaging: Food Service, Private Label
Other Locations:
  Atlanta GA
  Cartersville GA
  Jacksonville FL
  Evansville IN
  Columbus GA
Brands:
  DODGE CITY STEAKS
  KENDRICK PECAN
  LA PICCOLINA

3126 Columbus Vegetable Oils
30 E. Oakton Avenue
Des Plaines, IL 60018   773-265-6500
          Fax: 773-265-6985 800-322-6457
              www.columbusvegoils.com

Manufacturer and supplier of vegetable oils, liquid & solid shortenings, bakery, specialty & organic oils, and balsamic vinegar.

3127 Colusa Canning Company
6229 Myers Rd
Williams, CA 95987-5803   530-473-2871
Fax: 530-473-2138 www.skfoods.com
Manufacturer of tomatoes, organic and non-organic
Manager: Rich Freitas
GM: Rich Freitas
Estimated Sales: $100-500 Million
Number Employees: 50-99
Parent Co: SK Foods
Brands:
COLUSA

3128 Comanche Tortilla Factory
107 S Nelson St
Fort Stockton, TX 79735-6707   432-336-3245
Processor of Mexican products including peppers, tortillas and tamales
President: Joe Ben Gallegos
Estimated Sales: $2.5-5 Million
Number Employees: 1-4
Type of Packaging: Consumer

3129 Comanzo & Company Specialty Bakers
10 Industrial Dr
Smithfield, RI 02917-1500   401-231-2361
Fax: 401-232-9826   888-352-5455
licette@comanzobiscotti.com
www.comanzosbiscotti.com
Biscotti, European style shortbread
President: Liz Walker
Estimated Sales: Less than $500,000
Number Employees: 1-4

3130 Comax Flavors
130 Baylis Rd
Melville, NY 11747-3808   631-249-0609
Fax: 631-249-9255   800-992-0629
info@comaxflavors.com
Flavors
President: Peter Calabretta
CFO: Virginia Wyan
Vice President: Paul Calabretta
Research & Development: Agneta Weisz
Quality Control: Frank Vollaro
Marketing Director: Catherine Armstrong
Sales Director: Norman Katz
PR/Communications Manager: Laura Ferrante
Production Manager: Jorge Quintanilla
Plant Manager: Marion Cunningham
Purchasing Manager: Michael Keppel
Estimated Sales: $25-50 Million
Number Employees: 50-99

3131 Comeau's Sea Foods
PO Box 39
Saulnierville, NS B0W 2Z0
Canada   902-769-2101
Fax: 902-769-3594 www.comeauseafoods.com
Processor and exporter of fresh, frozen and processed sea foods, herring, smoked salmon
President: Marcel Comeau
Vice President: Kim d'Entremont
VP Marketing: Sandy Clark
Number Employees: 100-249
Type of Packaging: Consumer, Food Service, Private Label, Bulk

3132 Comeaux's
2807 Kaliste Saloom Rd
Lafayette, LA 70508-7141   337-988-0516
Fax: 337-989-0091   800-323-2492
Sonja@comeaux.com   www.comeaux.com
Processor of vacuum packed seafood including crawfish boudin, oysters, seafood boudin, shrimp, pork and tasso
Owner: Ray Comeaux
Co-Owner: Sonja Comeaux
Estimated Sales: $300,000-500,000
Number Employees: 5-9
Type of Packaging: Consumer, Food Service
Brands:
Comeaux's Andouille Sausage
Comeaux's Crawfish Tails
Comeaux's Tasso

3133 Comet Rice
P.O.Box 2587
Houston, TX 77252-2587   281-272-8800
Fax: 281-272-9707 www.amrice.com
Processor and exporter of rice, pasta and olives
President: Lee Adams
Estimated Sales: $ 20 - 50 Million
Number Employees: 50-99
Type of Packaging: Consumer, Food Service
Brands:
AA BRAND
ADOLPHUS
BLUE RIBBON
BLUE RIBBON GOLDEN
COLUSA RICE
COMET RICE
DRAGON RICE
GREEN PEACOCK
PEAR BLOSSOM
WONDER RICE

3134 Comfort Food's
25 Commerce Way # 5
North Andover, MA 01845-1002   978-557-0009
Fax: 978-557-0131 www.harmonybaycoffee.com
Coffee
President/CEO: Michael Sullivan
VP of Marketing: Stephan Liff
Operations Manager: John Sullivan
Estimated Sales: $5-10 Million
Number Employees: 10-19
Type of Packaging: Private Label
Brands:
Benley's Irish Creme
Harmony Bay

3135 Comfort Foods
PO Box 1777
Tijeras, NM 87059-1777   505-281-7083
Fax: 505-281-4626   800-460-5803
www.comfortfoods.com
Soups and dip mixes
President/CEO: Mark Harden
VP: Matthew Cox
Handles Marketing/Sales: Matthew Coxler
Estimated Sales: $1.5 Million
Number Employees: 15
Number of Brands: 2
Number of Products: 80
Sq. footage: 35000
Type of Packaging: Private Label
Brands:
COUNTRY GARDENS CUISINE
DESERT GARDENS CHILE AND SPICE

3136 Commerce Foods
120 W 45th Street
New York, NY 10036-4041   212-398-0991
Fax: 212-944-7617
President: Stephen Roth
Estimated Sales: $500,000-$1 Million
Number Employees: 5-9

3137 Commercial Creamery Company
159 S Cedar St
Spokane, WA 99201-7047   509-747-4131
Fax: 509-838-2271   800-541-0850
megan@cheesepowder.com
www.cheesepowder.com
Processor of dried cheese and yogurt powders; processor and exporter of snack seasoning and spray dried dairy flavors
President: Michael Gilmartin
CFO: David Foedisch
VP: Peter Gilmartin
R&D: Staurt Terhune
Senior Project Leader: Kelly Curry
Estimated Sales: $10-20 Million
Number Employees: 5-9

3138 Commissariat Imports
PO Box 64271
Los Angeles, CA 90064-0271   310-475-5628
Fax: 310-475-8246 info@bombaybrand.com
www.bombaybrand.com
Processor, importer and exporter of indian chutneys, pickles, curry powder and pastes including curry, biryani, ginger, garlic and tandoori; certified kosher available
President/CEO: Parvez Commissariat
VP: Aban Commissariat
Estimated Sales: Over $500,000
Number Employees: 2
Type of Packaging: Food Service, Private Label

Brands:
Bombay

3139 Commodities Marketing, Inc.
2 Stephenville Pkwy
Edison, NJ 08820-3024
USA   732-516-0700
Fax: 732-516-0600 weldonrice@usa.net
www.weldonfoods.com
Importer and Wholesaler distributors of private label, specialty and ethnic food products to retail markets, national distributors and food service companies. Jasmine rice, Basmati rice, Coconut drinks, Coconut milk, Fruits, BeansGuar gum, Fruit juices and Cashews, Almonds, Saffron (Spain) White Rice/Parboiled Rice. We pack any size in rice.
President: Harbinder Sahni
CEO: Gagandeep Sahni
CFO: Soena Sahni
VP: Avneet Sodhi
R&D: Manoj Hedge
Marketing: Harbinder Singh Sahni & Melvin Medina
Sales: Avneet Sodhi
Public Relations: Mr. Dough & Harshida Shaw
Operations: Harshida Shah
Production: Mr Nobpsaul
Plant Manager: Mr Chandej
Estimated Sales: $10+ Million
Number Employees: 10-19
Number of Brands: 3
Number of Products: 6
Sq. footage: 1500
Type of Packaging: Consumer, Food Service, Private Label, Bulk
Brands:
MEHER
PRIVATE LABEL
WELDON

3140 Common Folk Farm
PO Box 141
Naples, ME 04055-0141   207-787-2764
Fax: 207-787-3894 www.commonfolk.com
Processor and exporter of herbal teas, seasonings and culinary mixes
Owner: Betz Golon
Owner: Dale Golon
Type of Packaging: Consumer, Private Label, Bulk
Brands:
Common Folk Farm, Inc.

3141 Commonwealth Brands
P.O.Box 51587
Bowling Green, KY 42102-5887   270-781-9100
Fax: 270-843-8607
www.commonwealthbrands.com
President: Bill Milton
CEO: John C Poling Ii
Estimated Sales: $2.5-5 Million
Number Employees: 20-49

3142 Commonwealth Brewing Company
138 Portland Street
Boston, MA 02114-1706   617-523-8383
Fax: 617-523-1037 www.commfish.com
Beer
Owner: Joe Quappeski
Estimated Sales: $1-2.5 Million
Number Employees: 50-99

3143 Commonwealth Fish & Beer Company
138 Portland Street
Boston, MA 02114-1706   617-523-8383
Fax: 617-523-1037
Brewer of beer
President: Austin O'Connor
Chef: Gwen Jordan
General Manager: Bill Goodwin
Chef: Gwen Jordan
Estimated Sales: $1-2.5 Million
Number Employees: 50-99
Sq. footage: 8000

3144 Community Bakeries
4501 W Fullerton Ave
Chicago, IL 60639-1933   773-384-1900
Fax: 773-384-3661 www.ralcorpfrozen.com
Muffins
Executive Director: Laura Rivera

Estimated Sales:$5-9.9 Million
Number Employees: 1-4
Brands:
Community Bakeries

3145 Community Coffee Specialty
P.O.Box 2311
Baton Rouge, LA 70821-2311   225-291-3900
        Fax: 225-368-4582   800-525-5583
        www.communitycoffee.com
Processor of coffee and tea; importer of green coffee; wholesaler/distributor of coffee creamer; serving the food service market
    President: Randall Russ
    CFO: Stephen Smith
    CEO: Matthew Saurage
    Director Green Coffee: George Guthrie
    Sales Director: Kevin Stevenson
    Purchasing Manager: Judy Landry
Number Employees: 1,000-4,999
Type of Packaging: Consumer, Food Service, Private Label, Bulk

3146 Community Market & Deli
P.O.Box 454
Lindstrom, MN 55045-0454   651-257-1128
        Fax: 651-257-3069
Manufacturer of beef, pork, lamb, goat, veal, venison, elk, ostrich, buffalo, smoked poultry, bacon, ham and sausage; private labeling available
    Owner: Martin Ziegler
Estimated Sales:$300,000
Number Employees: 10-19
Type of Packaging: Consumer, Private Label

3147 Community Mill & Bean
267 State Route 89
Savannah, NY 13146-9711   315-365-2664
        Fax: 315-365-2690   800-755-0554
        cmbs@mail.teds.net   www.crusoeisland.com
Organic flour milling
    President: Richard Corichi
    CEO: Richard Corichi
Estimated Sales:$1-2.5 Million
Number Employees: 1-4

3148 Community Orchard
2237 160th St
Fort Dodge, IA 50501-8547   515-573-8212
    Fax: 515-576-0489 www.communityorchards.com
Processor of apple cider, pie and dumplings
    President: Greg Baedke
Estimated Sales:$2.5-5 Million
Number Employees: 20-49

3149 Compact Industries
3945 Ohio Ave
St Charles, IL 60174-5467   630-513-9600
        Fax: 630-513-9655   800-513-4262
        www.compactind.com
Private label and contract packager: dry product packaging, in-house blending, formulating. AIB Superior Rating, flexible pouches, form/fill/seal, composite cans, plastic jars, fibre drums, super-sacks. kosher, R/D - lab. Manufacturerof cappuccino, hot cocoa, soluable coffee, creamers, dry mixes, cheese sauces, nutraceuticals, breakfast drinks, dietary drinks, powdered granita and smoothie mixes
    President/CEO: Michael Brown
    VP: Gary Johnson
    Purchasing Director: William Izzo
Estimated Sales:$50-100 Million
Number Employees: 50-99
Sq. footage: 150000
Type of Packaging: Consumer, Food Service, Private Label, Bulk
Brands:
Casa Verde
Cool Off
Geneva Freeze
John Foster Green

3150 Company of a Philadelphia Gentleman
2824 N 2nd St
Philadelphia, PA 19133-3515   215-427-2827
        Fax: 215-739-0871   sim4033@aol.com
Teas
    Owner: Morton Simkins
Estimated Sales:$500,000-$1 Million
Number Employees: 5-9

3151 Compass Foods/Eight O'Clock Coffee
P.O.Box 418
Montvale, NJ 07645-0418   201-573-9700
        Fax: 201-571-8719   800-299-2739
        scutarof@aptea.com   www.aptea.com
Supermarket coffee
    President: Christine Halp
    Group CEO: Michael J Bailey
    CEO: Eric Claus
    Marketing Director: Don Sommerville
    Plant Manager: Pete Notard
Estimated Sales:$100-500 Million
Number Employees: 10,000+
Brands:
BURGER KING
Caffè Ritazza
EIGHT O'CLOCK
Harry Ramsden's
Royale
Sbarro
Upper Crust

3152 Compass Minerals
9900 W 109th St # 600
Overland Park, KS 66210-1436   913-344-9200
        Fax: 913-338-7932   877-462-7258
        gentrade@compassminerals.com
        www.compassminerals.com
Food grade salt products
    Chairman/President/CEO: Angelo Brisimitzakis
    VP/CFO: Rodney Underdown
    VP/CIO: Jerry Smith
    Research & Development: Jerry Poe
    Quality Control: Jerry Poe
    Marketing Director: David Gruner
    Sales Director: Greg Jennings
    Public Relations: Peggy Landon
    Operations Manager: Larry Schultz
    Production Manager: Larry Schultz
    Purchasing Manager: Mike Runyon
Estimated Sales:$963 Million
Number Employees: 1,792
Type of Packaging: Consumer, Food Service, Private Label, Bulk

3153 Compton Dairy
25 Walker Street
Shelbyville, IN 46176-1332   317-398-8621
        Fax: 317-392-9777
Milk, dairy products-noncheese
    President: Dan Compton
Estimated Sales:$2.5-5 Million
Number Employees: 10-19

3154 Comstock's Marketing
PO Box 424
Barton, VT 05822-0424   802-754-2426
        Fax: 802-754-2428
Beef, beef products
    President: Dean Comstock
Estimated Sales:$2.5-5 Million
Number Employees: 1-4

3155 Con Agra Food Coperative
4530 Mobile Highway
Montgomery, AL 36108-5110   334-288-8660
        Fax: 334-286-6770   webmaster@conagra.com
        www.conagra.com
Beef processing
    CEO: Ronald Roskens
    Plant Manager: Richard Schulcz
    Quality Control: Patrick Trygstad
Estimated Sales:$ 100-499.9 Million
Number Employees: 300
Brands:
Act II
Butterball
David
Decker
Fernando's
FireCrackers
Gilroy

3156 Con Agra Foods
P.O.Box 116
Holly Ridge, NC 28445-0116   910-329-9061
        Fax: 910-329-1999
        denise.queen@lambweston.com
        www.lambweston.com

Processor of frozen turnovers including apple, cherry, peach, lemon, blueberry, chocolate, sweet potato, pumpkin, pineapple and meat/vegetable; also, custom formulations available
    VP Sales: Ed Buchanan
    VP Manufacturing: Allen Padgett
    Plant Manager: Charlie Jennings
Estimated Sales:$ 20 - 50 Million
Number Employees: 100-249
Sq. footage: 22000
Parent Co: ConAgra Foods
Type of Packaging: Food Service, Private Label
Brands:
Pixie Pie
Pocket Taco

3157 Con Agra Foods
P.O.Box 3768
Omaha, NE 68103-0768   402-475-6700
        Fax: 402-475-4772 www.cooksham.com
Processor of smoked ham
    COO: Gene Dimkowski
    Sales: Rick Ruge
    Sales/Marketing Executive: Rick Ruge
    VP Operations: Joe Gallagher
*Estimated Sales:*I
Number Employees: 1,000-4,999
Parent Co: ConAgra Refrigerated Prepared Foods
Type of Packaging: Consumer, Food Service

3158 Con Agra Store Brands
7700 France Ave S # 200
Edina, MN 55435-5867   952-835-6900
        Fax: 952-469-5550 www.conagra.com
Processor and exporter of natural and ready to eat cereals, granola bars, fruit flavored snacks and preformed graham cracker pie crusts
    Manager: David Dart
Estimated Sales:$ 20 - 50 Million
Number Employees: 50-99
Type of Packaging: Consumer

3159 Con Agro Food
3311 S State Road 19
Peru, IN 46970-7476   765-473-3086
        Fax: 765-473-5147
Canned meat spreads, bacon bits, bacon chips, bacon ipzza topping, meat analogs
    CEO: Bruce Rhode
    Plant Manager: Mike Firtz
Estimated Sales:$100+ Million
Number Employees: 250-499

3160 Con Pac
1041 Constance Street
New Orleans, LA 70130-3828   504-586-8783
        Fax: 504-596-4274
    President: Lee Barsic
    Vice President: Steve Gibson

3161 Con Piacere Italian Specialty
3110 Mission Beach Road
Tulalip, WA 98271-9735   360-653-7563
        Fax: 360-659-0729   800-204-3594
Italian foods
    President: Karen Mitchelli

3162 Con Yeager Spice Company
144 Magill Rd
Zelienople, PA 16063-3424   724-452-4120
        Fax: 724-452-6171   800-222-2460
        sales@yeagerspice.com   www.yeagerspice.com
Processor of seasonings and meat cures and binders; wholesaler/distributor of meat casings and spices
    President: William Kreuer
    Research & Development: Rodney Schaffer
    Sales Rep.: Rod Schaffer
    Production Manager: William Wolford
Estimated Sales:$1-2.5 Million
Number Employees: 10-19
Sq. footage: 18000
Type of Packaging: Consumer, Food Service, Private Label, Bulk
Brands:
Con Yeager Spices

3163 ConAgra Beef Company
RR 1
Box 957
Garden City, KS 67846-9801   620-275-9661
        Fax: 620-275-5273

Processor and exporter of meat products including beef
Plant Manager: Dennis Sydow
Purchasing Manager: Gayla Allsbury
Number Employees: 2000
Type of Packaging: Consumer

3164 ConAgra Beef Company
410 N 200 W
Hyrum, UT 84319-1024   435-245-6456
Fax: 435-245-6634 www.eamiller.com
Processor, packer and exporter of beef
President: Ted Miller
Sales Manager: Bruce Miller
Estimated Sales:$ 50 - 100 Million
Number Employees: 250-499
Type of Packaging: Consumer, Private Label, Bulk

3165 ConAgra Beef Company
1770 Promontory Cir
Greeley, CO 80634-9039   970-506-8000
Fax: 970-506-8307 www.jbsswift.com
Processor and exporter of beef
President: Wesley Bagista
VP (East): John DeMoney
Director Merchandising: John Lichtfuss
Estimated Sales:$100+ Million
Number Employees: 10,000+
Parent Co: ConAgra Foods
Type of Packaging: Consumer, Food Service

3166 ConAgra Beef Company
38002 County Road N
Yuma, CO 80759-7929   970-395-8226
Fax: 970-395-8903 http://www.conagrafoods.com
Processor and exporter of beef, pork and lamb
President: John Simons
VP Human Resources: Kathryn Danko-Lord
Estimated Sales:$50-100 Million
Number Employees: 100-249
Parent Co: ConAgra Foods
Type of Packaging: Consumer, Food Service, Private Label, Bulk
Other Locations:
ConAgra Beef Co.
Grand Island NE

3167 ConAgra Broiler Company
433 S Hamilton St
Dalton, GA 30720-8218   706-278-3212
Fax: 706-275-7123 www.pilgrimspride.com
Processor and exporter of fresh and frozen chicken
Division Controller: Laddie Toney
Complex Manager: Mike McCoure
Plant Manager: Bobby Phillips
Estimated Sales:$100+ Million
Number Employees: 500-999
Parent Co: ConAgra Poultry
Type of Packaging: Food Service, Private Label

3168 ConAgra Dairy Foods
8501 Page Ave
Overland, MO 63114-6001   314-429-3636
Fax: 314-253-6070
www.conagrafoods.com/index.jsp
Processor of egg substitutes
President/CEO: Gary Rodkin
EVP/Chief Financial Officer: Andre Hawaux
EVP/Research & Development & Quality: Al Bolles Ph.D
EVP/Chief Marketing Officer: Joan Chow
Plant Manager: Brian Fox
Estimated Sales:$ 20 - 50 Million
Number Employees: 100-249
Parent Co: ConAgra Foods
Type of Packaging: Consumer, Food Service

3169 ConAgra Dairy Foods
4300 W 62nd St
Indianapolis, IN 46268-2520   317-329-3700
Fax: 317-329-3715
Processor of dairy products
Plant Manager: Tamer Abuaita
Number Employees: 50-99
Parent Co: ConAgra Dairy Foods
Type of Packaging: Consumer, Food Service
Brands:
Blue Bonnet
Chiffon
Egg Beaters
Fleischmann's
Move Over Butter
Parkay
Touch of Butter

3170 ConAgra Dairy Foods
4300 W 62nd St
Indianapolis, IN 46268-2520   317-329-3700
Fax: 317-329-3715
Processor of margarine
Plant Manager: Tamer Abuaita
Estimated Sales:$100+ Million
Number Employees: 250-499
Parent Co: ConAgra Dairy Foods
Type of Packaging: Consumer, Food Service

3171 ConAgra Flour Milling
2020 E Steel Rd
Colton, CA 92324-4008   909-825-7630
Fax: 909-825-7157   800-736-2212
www.conagrafoods.com
Processor of flour including potato, wheat, rye and rice, yellow corn meal and oat. Daily capacity 1.15 million pounds of flour.
President Flour Milling: Darek Nowakowski
Estimated Sales:$5-10 Million
Number Employees: 10-19
Type of Packaging: Food Service, Bulk
Brands:
American Beauty
Kyrol
Magnifico Special
Occident

3172 ConAgra Flour Milling
4545 E 64th Ave
Commerce City, CO 80022-3107   303-289-6141
Fax: 303-287-4942 www.conagra.com
Manufacturer and exporter of milled flour
President: Darek Nowakowski
VP Sales: Don Brown
Plant Manager: John Mason
Estimated Sales:$50-100 Million
Number Employees: 100-249
Parent Co: ConAgra Foods
Type of Packaging: Consumer, Food Service, Private Label, Bulk

3173 ConAgra Flour Milling
P.O.Box 280
Macon, GA 31202-0280   478-743-5424
Fax: 478-745-4116 www.conagra.com
Processor of soft wheat flour
Milling Superintendent: Scott Freebern
Plant Manager: Charles Dawson
Estimated Sales:$10-20 Million
Number Employees: 10-19
Parent Co: ConAgra Foods
Type of Packaging: Bulk

3174 ConAgra Flour Milling
1 Conagra Dr
Omaha, NE 68102-5003   402-595-4000
Fax: 402-595-4447   800-214-0349
www.conagrafoods.com
Processor of flour including wheat
President/Chairman/CEO: Bruce Rhode
Senior VP/Controller: John F Gehring
CEO: Gary M Rodkin
VP/Strategic Development: Patrick J Koley
Estimated Sales:$10-20 Million
Number Employees: 10,000+
Type of Packaging: Bulk

3175 ConAgra Flour Milling
P.O.Box 369
Chester, IL 62233-0369   618-826-2371
Fax: 618-826-4154 www.conagrafoods.com
Processor of wheat flour
Manager: Alan Bindel
VP Sales/Marketing: Bruce Rohde
Executive VP/CFO: Frank S Sklarsky
Plant Manager: Eric Schmidt
Estimated Sales:$20-50 Million
Number Employees: 20-49
Parent Co: ConAgra Trading & Processing Companies
Type of Packaging: Bulk
Brands:
Andy Capp's
Armour
Banquet
Big Mama
Blue Bonnet
Butterball
Cook's
David
Decker

Eckrich
Fernando's
Firecracker
Gilroy
Golden Cuisine
Louis Kemp
Parkay
Peter Pan
Singleto
Slim Jim
Swiss Miss
Wesson
Wolfgang Puck

3176 ConAgra Flour Milling
125 S Broad St
Fremont, NE 68025-5658   402-721-4200
Fax: 402-721-1016 www.conagra.com
Processor of wheat flour
Manager: D Zongker
EVP/Legal & External Affairs: Rob Sharpe Jr
EVP/Chief Financial Officer: Andre Hawaux
EVP Research/Quality/Innovation: Al Bolles PhD
EVP/Chief Marketing Officer: Joan Chow
EVP/Human Resources: Pete Perez
Plant Superintendent: Todd Peterson
Plant Manager: Travis Kapusta
Estimated Sales:$10-20 Million
Number Employees: 20-49
Parent Co: ConAgra Trading & Processing Companies
Type of Packaging: Bulk

3177 ConAgra Flour Milling
P.O.Box 193
Martins Creek, PA 18063-0193   610-253-9341
Fax: 610-250-2003 www.conagra.com
Processor of milled wheat flour
Manager: Scott Dillingham
EVP Research/Quality/Innovation: Al Bolles PhD
EVP/Chief Marketing Officer: Joan Chow
General Manager: John Mason
Estimated Sales:$20-50 Million
Number Employees: 50-99
Parent Co: ConAgra Trading & Processing Companies
Type of Packaging: Consumer, Bulk

3178 ConAgra Flour Milling
321 Taylor Ave
Red Lion, PA 17356-2211   717-244-4559
Fax: 717-244-8072 www.conagra.com
Processor of wheat flour
Chief Executive Officer: Gary Rodkin
EVP Chief Financial Officer: Andre Hawaux
EVP Research/Quality/Innovation: Al Bolles PhD
Chief Marketing Officer: Joan Chow
Office Manager: Timothy Royer
Plant Manager: Matthew Fanshier
Purchasing Agent: Gus Gentzler
Estimated Sales:$5-10 Million
Number Employees: 5-9
Parent Co: ConAgra Trading & Processing Companies
Type of Packaging: Food Service, Bulk

3179 ConAgra Flour Milling
2800 Black Bridge Rd
York, PA 17406-9704   717-846-7773
Fax: 717-845-9534 www.conagra.com
Processor of wheat flour
Chief Executive Officer: Gary Rodkin
EVP/Chief Financial Officer: Andre Hawaux
EVP Research/Quality/Innovation: Al Bolles PhD
Chief Marketing Officer: Joan Chow
Plant Manager: Curt Aarons
Estimated Sales:$10-20 Million
Number Employees: 10-19
Sq. footage: 10000
Parent Co: ConAgra Trading & Processing Companies
Type of Packaging: Bulk

3180 ConAgra Flour Milling
408 E Magnolia St
Sherman, TX 75090-7049   903-893-8111
Fax: 903-892-7711
Processor and exporter of wheat flour
Plant Manager: Randy Garvert
Estimated Sales:$20-50 Million
Number Employees: 50-99
Parent Co: ConAgra Foods
Type of Packaging: Consumer, Food Service, Private Label, Bulk

3181 ConAgra Flour Milling
145 W Broadway
Alton, IL 62002-6222   618-463-4411
                        Fax: 618-463-4419
Processor and exporter of flour
    Plant Manager: Mark Zimitisch
Estimated Sales:$50-100 Million
Number Employees: 100-249
Parent Co: ConAgra Foods
Type of Packaging: Food Service, Bulk

3182 (HQ)ConAgra Food Ingredients
1 Conagra Dr
Omaha, NE 68102-5003   402-595-4000
    Fax: 402-595-4447 800-872-9236
            www.conagrafoods.com
Manufacturer of savory flavors, seasonings, food
bases, advanced flavoring systems
    President/COO: Gregory Heckman
    CEO: Gary M Rodkin
    VP Sales/Marketing: Thomas Burrows
Estimated Sales:$75-100 Million
Number Employees: 10,000+
Number of Brands: 60
Number of Products: 3000
Sq. footage: 104000
Parent Co: ConAgra Foods
Type of Packaging: Bulk
Brands:
    SPICETEC

3183 ConAgra Food Store Brands
7700 France Ave S # 200
Edina, MN 55435-5867   952-469-4981
                        Fax: 952-469-5550
Fruit snack, chewy granola bars, crisp rice bars, fruit
and grain bars, graham cracker pie crust, ready - to -
eat cereal, marshmallows; canned meats, beans,
chili, pasta, beef stew
    Plant Manager: Robert Marando

3184 ConAgra FoodsGrain Processing
420 Pearl Street
Milan, MO 63556-1240   660-265-1243
                        www.conagra.com
Wholesale and processer of grain and field beans
Number Employees: 9
Parent Co: ConAgra Foods
Type of Packaging: Consumer, Food Service

**3185 ConAgra FoodsLamb Weston®
Headquarters**
8701 W Gage Blvd
Kennewick, WA 99336-1034   509-736-0456
                        Fax: 509-787-9220
            herb.sprinkel@conagrafoods.com
    www.lamb-weston.com / www.conagra.com
Manufacturer of frozen potato products including
French fries
    CFO: Craig Treen
    Regional Sales Manager: Herb Sprinkel
    Manager: Don Odegard
Estimated Sales:$100+ Million
Number Employees: 600
Parent Co: ConAgra Foods
Type of Packaging: Consumer, Food Service, Pri-
    vate Label, Bulk
Brands:
    GENERATION 7 FRIES
    LAMBS SUMPREME
    LW PRIVATE
    STEALTH FRIES
    SUPREME STARZ
    SWEET THINGS
    TIMESAVOR
    aMAIZEing

**3186 ConAgra FoodsLamb Weston
Plant**
2013 Saint St
Richland, WA 99354-5302   509-375-4181
                        Fax: 509-375-5808
            herb.sprinkel@conagrafoods.com
                www.lambweston.com /
                www.conagrafoods.com
Manufacturer of frozen seasoned and regular French
fries
    Regional Sales Manager: Herb Sprinkel
    Plant Manager: Rick Gardner
Estimated Sales:$100+ Million
Parent Co: ConAgra Foods

Type of Packaging: Consumer, Food Service, Private Label, Bulk
Brands:
    LAMB WESTON

3187 ConAgra Foods
PO Box 2819
Tampa, FL 33601-2819   813-241-1500
                        Fax: 813-247-2019
            www.conagrafoods.com/index.jsp
Processor of frozen oysters, scallops, shrimp, crab
and fish
    President/CEO: Gary Rodkin
    EVP/Chief Financial Officer: Andre Hawaux
    EVP/Research & Development & Quality: Al
    Bolles Ph.D
    EVP/Chief Marketing Officer: Joan Chow
    Plant Manager: Steve Marlette
Estimated Sales:$300,000-500,000
Parent Co: ConAgra Foods Inc
Type of Packaging: Consumer, Food Service, Pri-
    vate Label
Brands:
    Florida Sea
    Gulf Harvest
    Peninsular

3188 ConAgra Foods
1910 Fair Rd
Sidney, OH 45365-8906   937-498-4511
        Fax: 937-497-8786 800-736-2212
            valeries.barlage@congrafoods.com
                www.conagrafoods.com
Italian, frozen entrees and pizza
    President: Bill Mackin
    Director Corporate Relations: Scott Deitz
    COO: Mike Gilardi
    VP of Sales/Marketing: Ed Korkki
    VP Sales: Mike Keenan
    Sales Director: Rick Slad
    Plant Manager: Walter Minch
    Purchasing Manager: David Gilardi
Estimated Sales:$10-20 Million
Number Employees: 250-499
Brands:
    Gilardi's
    Mama Rosa
    Old Italian
    Spanky's

3189 (HQ)ConAgra Foods Inc
1 Conagra Dr
Omaha, NE 68102-5003   402-240-4000
                        Fax: 402-240-4707
        consumeraffairs@conagrafoods.com
                www.conagrafoods.com
Processor, importer and exporter of stir fry dinners,
entrees, fish, seafood, sausage, hot dogs, cold cuts,
chicken, grains, spices, prepared foods, canned
goods, etc.
    President/CEO: Gary Rodkin
    EVP/CFO: John Gehring
    EVP Chief Administrative Officer: Owen Johnson

    EVP Research/Development/Quality: Al Bolles
    Ph.D
    EVP Chief Marketing Officer: Joan Chow
    Senior VP Communications: Timothy McMahon
    President Sales Division: Doug Knudsen
    EVP Legal and External Affairs: Rob Sharpe Jr
    President/COO Consumer Foods Division: Dean
    Hollis
    President/COO Commerical Products: Greg
    Heckman
Estimated Sales:$12 Billion
Number Employees: 25,600
Type of Packaging: Consumer, Food Service
Other Locations:
    ConAgra
    Los Angeles CA
Brands:
    ACT II
    ANDY CAPP'S
    ANGELA MIA
    ARMOUR
    AWARD
    BANQUET
    BIG MAMA SAUSAGE
    BLUE BONNET
    BROWN 'N SERVE
    BUTTERBALL
    CHEF BOYARDEE
    CHUN KING
    COOK'S

    COUNTRY LINE
    CRUNCH 'N MUNCH
    CULTURELLE
    DAVID
    DECKER
    DENNISON'S
    ECKRICH
    EGG BEATERS
    FERNADO'S
    FIRE CRACKER
    FLEISCHMANN'S
    GEBHARDT
    GILARDI FOODS
    GILROY BRAND
    GOLDEN CUISINE
    GOLDEN'S
    HEALTHY CHOICE
    HEBREW NATIONAL
    HOMESTYLE BAKES
    HUNT'S
    HUNT'S SNACK PACK
    ISLAND VALLEY
    JHS - J. HUNGERFORD SMITH
    JIFFY POP
    KID CUISINE
    KNOTT'S BERRY FARM
    LA CHOY
    LAMB WESTON
    LIBBY'S
    LIGHTLIFE
    LONGMONT
    LOUIS KEMP
    LUCK'S
    LUNCH MARKERS
    MAMA ROSA'S
    MANWICH
    MARGHERITA
    MARIE CALLENDER'S
    MERIDEN
    MOVE OVER BUTTER
    ORVILLE REDENBACHER'S
    PAM
    PARKEY
    PATIO
    PEMMICAN
    PENROSE
    PETER PAN
    RANCH STYLE
    READY CRISP
    REDDI-WIP
    RO*TEL
    ROSARITA
    SINGLETON
    SLIM JIM
    ROSARITA
    SINGLETON
    SLIM JIM
    SQUEEZE 'N GO
    SWISS MISS
    WOLFGANG PUCK'S

3190 ConAgra Foods Trenton Plant
1401 Harris Ave
Trenton, MO 64683-1963   660-359-3913
            Fax: 660-359-4260 www.conagra.com
Manufacturer and exporter of canned meats
    President/CEO: Gary Rodkin
    EVP/Chief Financial Offiicer: Andre Hawaux
    Human Resources: Teresa Morse
    EVP/Research & Development & Quality: Al
    Bolles Ph.D
    EVP/Chief Marketing Officer: Joan Chow
    Plant Manager: James Waits
Estimated Sales:$100+ Million
Number Employees: 500-999
Parent Co: Conagra Grocery Products
Type of Packaging: Consumer, Food Service, Pri-
    vate Label

3191 ConAgra Foods/Eckrich
1 Conagra Dr
Omaha, NE 68102   402-595-4000
        Fax: 402-240-4707 800-327-4424
                www.conagrafoods.com
Processor and exporter of sausage, sliced bacon,
boneless ham and processed beef
    President/CEO: Gary Rodkin
    Chairman: Steven Goldstone
    EVP/CFO: John Gehring
    EVP/Chief Marketing Officer: Joan Chow
    Plant Manager: Buz Sameuelson
    EVP/Product Supply: Jim Hardy Jr
Estimated Sales:$12 Billion
Number Employees: 25600

Sq. footage: 167260
Parent Co: ConAgra Foods Inc
Type of Packaging: Consumer, Food Service

3192 ConAgra Foods/International Home Foods
4825 Pettit Avenue
Niagara Falls, ON L2E 7B8
Canada 905-356-2661
Fax: 905-356-2633 www.congrafoods.com
Manufacturer and exporter of popcorn, stews and canned macaroni dinners including ravioli and spaghetti
Chairman/CEO: C Dean Metropoulas
EVP, Operational/Support Information: Kevin Adams
Number Employees: 250
Parent Co: ConAgra Foods
Type of Packaging: Consumer
Brands:
BUMBLE BEE
CHEF BOYARDEE
GULDEN'S
PAM

3193 ConAgra Frozen Foods Company
204 Vine St
Macon, MO 63552-1657 660-385-3184
Fax: 660-385-3566
www.conagrafoods.com/index.jsp
Processor and exporter of frozen chicken
President/CEO: Gary Rodkin
EVP/Chief Financial Officer: Andre Hawaux
Human Resources: Bonnie Seehase
EVP/Research & Development & Quality: Al Ph.D
EVP/Chief Marketing Officer: Joan Chow
Office Manager: Dave Ripley
Plant Manager: Kevin Arlin
Purchasing Agent: Dean Van Sickle
Estimated Sales: $50-100 Million
Number Employees: 250-499
Parent Co: ConAgra Frozen Foods
Type of Packaging: Consumer, Food Service, Private Label, Bulk

3194 ConAgra Frozen Foods Company
200 N Banquet Dr
Marshall, MO 65340-1718 660-886-3301
Fax: 660-886-3301
brian.lovell@conagrafoods.com
www.conagrafoods.com
Manufacturer of frozen and prepared meals; as well as snacks, mustard, whip cream and cooking oils.
CEO: Gary Rodkin
EVP/CFO: John Gehring
EVP/General Counsel: Colleen Batchler
EVP Research & Quality: Al Bolles PhD
EVP/Chief Marketing Officer: Joan Chow
Manager: Brian Cooke
Purchasing Agent: Ed Duvall
Estimated Sales: $3 Billion
Number Employees: 60
Parent Co: ConAgra Foods
Type of Packaging: Consumer
Brands:
ACT II
BANQUET
CHEF BOYARDEE
CRUNCH 'N MUNCH
DAVID SEEDS
EGG BEEATERS
GULDEN'S
HEALTHY CHOICE
HEBREW NATIONAL
HUNT'S
KID CUISINE
LA CHOY
MANWICH
MARIE CALLENDER'S
ORVILLE REDENBACHER'S
PAM
PARKAY
PETER PAN
REDDI-WIP
RO*TEL
SLIM JIM
SNACK PACK
SWISS MISS
VAN CAMP'S
WESSON

3195 ConAgra Frozen Foods Company
P.O.Box 240
Clinton, AR 72031-0240 501-745-2416
Fax: 501-745-8344 www.pilgrimspride.com
Processor of chicken
Plant Manager: Roger Hooper
Estimated Sales: $20-50 Million
Number Employees: 100-249
Parent Co: ConAgra Frozen Foods
Type of Packaging: Bulk

3196 ConAgra Frozen Foods Company
1 Conagra Dr
Omaha, NE 68102-5003 402-595-4000
Fax: 402-595-4447 www.conagrafoods.com
Processor of prepared frozen foods including seafood, pasta, chicken, meat and Mexican
CEO: Gary Rodkin
EVP/CFO: John Gehring
EVP/General Counsel: Colleen Batchler
EVP Research/Quality & Development: Al Bolles PhD
EVP/Chief Marketing Officer: Joan Chow
Estimated Sales: $2 Billion
Number Employees: 10,000+
Type of Packaging: Consumer, Food Service, Private Label, Bulk

3197 ConAgra Grocery Products
1645 W Valencia Drive
Fullerton, CA 92833-3860 714-680-1000
Fax: 714-680-2269 800-736-2212
info@conagrafoods.com www.conagrafoods.com
CEO: Greg Heckman
CFO: Bruce Rohde
CFO: Andr, Hawaux
Vice President: Rob Sharpe
COO: Dennis F O'Brien
Sales Director: Doug Knudsen
Estimated Sales: $ 3 - 5 Million
Number Employees: 1-4
Brands:
Andy Capps's
Angela Mia
Armour
Banquet
Cook's Ham
Fernando's

3198 ConAgra Grocery Products
901 Stryker St
Archbold, OH 43502-1053 419-445-8015
Fax: 419-446-9278 www.conagra.com
Processor and exporter of canned and frozen Chinese food including chop suey, chow mein, egg rolls, sauces and vegetables
President/CEO: Gary Rodkin
EVP/Research Development & Quality: Al Bolles Ph.D
EVP/Chief Marketing Officer: Joan Chow
Plant Manager: Ron Corkins
Estimated Sales: $100+ Million
Number Employees: 250-499
Parent Co: ConAgra Grocery Products
Type of Packaging: Consumer, Food Service
Brands:
La Choy

3199 ConAgra Grocery Products
3353 Michelson Drive
Irvine, CA 92612-7622 714-680-1000
www.conagra.com
Processor and exporter of beans, ketchup, dessert preparations and mixes, egg rolls, gravies, tomato juice, mustard, noodles, nuts, oils, tomato paste, canned and frozen fruits, jalapeno peppers, popcorn, sauces, cocoa mixes, etc
President: Ronald Roskens
Vice President: Rob Sharpe
Sales Director: Doug Knudsen
Director Corporate Communications: Kay Carpenter
Number Employees: 1,000-4,999
Parent Co: ConAgra Foods
Type of Packaging: Consumer, Food Service, Private Label, Bulk

3200 ConAgra Grocery Products
29180 Glenwood Rd
Perrysburg, OH 43551-3021 419-661-4400
Fax: 419-666-6362 www.conagrafoods.com

Processor and canner of tomatoes and shelf stable puddings
President: Greg Heckman
CEO: Gary Rodkin
EVP/Research Development & Quality: Al Bolles Ph.D
Sales/Marketing Executive: Denny Miller
Plant Manager: Barry Fiszhetto
Estimated Sales: $100+ Million
Number Employees: 250-499
Parent Co: ConAgra Foods
Type of Packaging: Consumer, Food Service, Private Label, Bulk
Brands:
Armour Brown 'N Serve
Banquet
Kid Cuisine

3201 ConAgra Grocery Products
1 Conagra Dr
Omaha, NE 68102-5003 402-595-4000
Fax: 402-595-4447 www.conagrafoods.com
Canned sliced apples, baked beans w/meat, pork and beans, dry beans, greens, dried peas, chicken and noodles, pizza sauce, packaged stovetop popcorn
CEO: Bruce Rhode
CFO: James O'Donnell
CEO: Gary M Rodkin
Estimated Sales: $27.1 Million
Number Employees: 10,000+
Number of Brands: 1
Number of Products: 50
Other Locations:
Conagra Grocery Products
Irvine CA
Brands:
Chef Boy-Ar-Dee
Jiffy Pop
Luck's Country Style

3202 ConAgra Mexican Foods
1805 N Santa Fe Ave
Compton, CA 90221-1009 310-223-1499
Fax: 310-223-1698 http://www.conagrafoods.com
Processor of frozen Mexican entrees and appetizers
Manager: Roger Mucino
Senior VP Sales/Marketing: Brett Schrock
General Manager: Abe Haymahmoud
Estimated Sales: $25-49.9 Million
Number Employees: 250-499
Parent Co: ConAgra Foods
Type of Packaging: Consumer, Food Service, Bulk

3203 ConAgra Mills
11 ConAgra Drive
Omaha, NE 68102 651-437-3161
Fax: 651-437-0133 800-851-9618
leroy.bertsch@conagramills.com
www.conagramills.com
Processor milled flours and whole grains sold to food manufacturing and foodservice industries; offers risk managment and product development services.
Manager: Gary Bidney
Plant Manager: Randy Garvert
Estimated Sales: $50-100 Million
Parent Co: ConAgra Foods
Type of Packaging: Consumer, Food Service, Private Label, Bulk
Brands:
ConAgra Mills
Sustagrain®
Ultragrain®

3204 ConAgra Mills
13825 Wyandotte Street
Kansas City, MO 64145 816-942-3700
Fax: 816-501-3892
www.conagrafoodingredients.com/about/index.jsp
Processor and exporter of bakery flour
President/CEO: Gary Rodkin
EVP/Chief Financial Officer: Andre Hawaux
EVP/Research & Development & Quality: Al Bolles Ph.D
EVP/Chief Marketing Officer: Joan Chow
Office Manager/Warehouse Supervisor: Fred Hankerson
Estimated Sales: $20-50 Million
Number Employees: 50-99
Parent Co: ConAgra Foods
Type of Packaging: Food Service, Private Label, Bulk

3205 ConAgra Mills
110 S Nebraska Ave
Tampa, FL 33602-5530   813-223-4741
        Fax: 813-221-5284   800-582-1483

www.conagrafoodingredients.com/products/conagr
        amills.jsp
Processor of multi-purpose flours including
ultragrain, whole grains, bakery flours, cake and
pastry flours, and durum flours.
    Manager: Alan Mersnick
    EVP/Chief Financial Officer: Andre Hawaux
    EVP/Chief Administrative Officer: Owen Johnson

    EVP/Research & Development & Quality: Al
    Bolles Ph.D
    EVP/Chief Marketing Officer: Joan Chow
    EVP/Legal And External Affairs: Rob Sharpe Jr
    President/COO Consumer Foods Division: Dean
    Hollis
    EVP/Product Supply: Jim Hardy Jr
    Plant Manager: Joseph Doyle
Estimated Sales: $ 20 - 50 Million
Number Employees: 20-49
Sq. footage: 100000
Parent Co: ConAgra Food Ingredients/ConAgra
Foods Inc
Type of Packaging: Private Label, Bulk

3206 ConAgra Mills
1 ConAgra Drive
Omaha, NE 68103-0500
        Fax: 402-595-4111   877-717-1694
        www.conagramills.com
Processor and exporter of grain and flour including
wheat, oat, barley and corn
    CEO: Bruce Rhode
Estimated Sales: $1 Billion+
Number Employees: 250-499
Parent Co: ConAgra Foods
Brands:
    ARMOUR
    CONAGRA FOODS
    GILROY
    SPICETEC

3207 ConAgra PV Grain
PO Box 2085
Superior, WI 54880-0456   715-398-3541
        Fax: 715-398-6480 www.conagra.com
Processor of oats
    President/CEO: Gary Rodkin
    EVP/Chief Financial Officer: Andre Hauwaux
    EVP/Chief Administrative Officer: Owen Johnson

    EVP/Research Development & Quality: Al Bolles
    Ph.D
Estimated Sales: $2.5-5 Million
Number Employees: 5-9
Sq. footage: 23000
Parent Co: ConAgra Foods
Type of Packaging: Bulk

3208 ConAgra Poultry Company
P.O.Box 1091
Chattanooga, TN 37401-1091   423-756-2471
        Fax: 770-232-4255
Processor of fresh chicken
    Manager: Leonard Polacek
    Sales/Marketing Executive: Rodney Walter
    General Manager: Terry Paschall
    Purchasing Agent: Steve Harwood
Estimated Sales: $100-500 Million
Number Employees: 1,000-4,999
Parent Co: ConAgra Poultry
Type of Packaging: Food Service

3209 (HQ)ConAgra Poultry Company
2475 Meadowbrook Parkway
Duluth, GA 30096-2366   770-232-4200
        Fax: 770-232-4255   800-609-6050
Processor of frozen chicken products including
frankfurters
    President: Blake Lovette
    VP: David Strawn
    Marketing Director: Steve Berman
Estimated Sales: $200,000
Number Employees: 2
Parent Co: CanAgra Foods
Type of Packaging: Consumer, Food Service
Other Locations:
    ConAgra Poultry
    Omaha NE

3210 ConAgra Refrigerated Foods International
5645 N 90th St
Omaha, NE 68134-1807   402-595-4000
        Fax: 970-506-8309   800-624-4724
        www.conagra.com
Manufacturer and exporter of beef, pork, chicken
and turkey products, processed meats, cheeses and
refrigerated dessert toppings.
    President/COO: Gary Rodkin
    EVP/Chief Financial Officer: Andre Hawaux
    EVP/Research & Development & Quality: Al
    Bolles Ph.D
    EVP/Chief Marketing Officer: Joan Chow
Estimated Sales: $70 Million
Number Employees: 50-99
Parent Co: ConAgra Foods
Type of Packaging: Consumer, Food Service, Bulk

3211 (HQ)ConAgra Refrigerated Prepared Foods
2001 Butterfield Road
Suite 1900
Downers Grove, IL 60515-1096   630-857-1000
        Fax: 630-512-1133 www.conagra.com
Manufacturer and exporter of meat products includ-
ing ham, poultry, beef, pork, veal
    President/CEO: Gary Rodkin
    EVP/Chief Financial Officer: Andre Hawaux
    EVP/Chief Administrative Officer: Owen Johnson

    EVP/Research Development & Quality: Al Bolles
    Ph.D
    Quality Control: Keith Drickey
    Sales Director: Mike Barker
    Public Relations: Julie DeYoung
    Operations Manager: Terry O'Dea
Number Employees: 1
Parent Co: ConAgra Foods
Type of Packaging: Consumer, Food Service, Pri-
vate Label, Bulk
Brands:
    Armour Swift-Eckrich
    Butterball Turkey
    Cook Family Foods
    El Extremo
    Lightlife
    National Foods
    The Max

3212 ConAgra Shrimp Companies
PO Box 2819
Tampa, FL 33601-2819   813-241-1501
        Fax: 813-248-6030
Processor of frozen seafood including shrimp,
clams, crabs, lobsters, oysters, scallops, fish patties
and cakes and stir fry seafood dinners
    President: Jesse Gonzalez
Parent Co: ConAgra Frozen Foods
Type of Packaging: Consumer, Food Service, Pri-
vate Label, Bulk

3213 ConAgra Snack Foods
1744 Junction Ave
San Jose, CA 95112-1018   408-436-0329
        Fax: 408-436-0156 www.conagrafoods.com
Processor and exporter of beef jerky and meat sticks
    Manager: Eddie Bell
Estimated Sales: $50-100 Million
Number Employees: 100-249
Type of Packaging: Consumer, Private Label

3214 ConAgra Snack Foods Group/Act II Popcorn
7700 France Ave S # 200
Edina, MN 55435-5867   952-835-6900
        Fax: 952-469-5550   800-328-6286
        www.actii.com OR www.conagrafoods.com
Processor and exporter of microweaveable popcorn
    Manager: David Dart
    EVP/Chief Financial Officer: Andre Hawaux
    EVP/Research Development & Quality: Al Bolles
    Ph.D
    EVP/Chief Marketing Officer: Joan Chow
Number Employees: 500-999
Parent Co: ConAgra Grocery Products
Type of Packaging: Consumer, Food Service, Pri-
vate Label, Bulk
Brands:
    ACT II POPCORN

3215 ConAgra Trading and Processing
11 Conagra Dr
Omaha, NE 68102-5011   402-595-5775
        www.conagrafoods.com
Processor of dry beans; also, cleaning services avail-
able
    Operations Manager: Greg Konsor
    Director: Bill Liebermann
Estimated Sales: K
Number Employees: 10,000+
Sq. footage: 1010000
Parent Co: ConAgra Foods

3216 ConFish
P.O.Box 271
Isola, MS 38754-0271   662-962-3101
        Fax: 662-962-0114   800-228-3474
Processor and exporter of farm raised catfish
    Owner/President: Dick Stevens
    VP Sales/Marketing: Jack Perkins
    VP Operations: Frank Davis
Estimated Sales: $10-20 Million
Number Employees: 500-999
Sq. footage: 240000
Type of Packaging: Consumer, Food Service, Pri-
vate Label, Bulk
Brands:
    Country Select

3217 Concannon Vineyard
4590 Tesla Rd
Livermore, CA 94550-9002   925-456-2500
        Fax: 925-456-2501   800-258-9866
        info@concannonvineyard.com
        www.concannonvineyard.com
Processor and exporter of bottled wines; grower of
grapes
    Manager: Adam Richardson
    CEO: Jim Concannon
    Sales Director: Jeremy Levenberg
    Wine Maker/General Manager: Tom Lane
Estimated Sales: $ 10 - 20 Million
Number Employees: 20-49
Parent Co: Wine Group
Type of Packaging: Consumer, Private Label
Brands:
    Concannon Vineyard

3218 Concept 2 Bakers
7350 Commerce Lane NE
Minneapolis, MN 55432-3113   800-266-2782
        Fax: 763-574-2210 heidi.wolter@c2b
        www.c2b.com
Frozen baked goods.
Parent Co: McGlynn Bakeries
Brands:
    EARL OF SANDWICH
    PANNE' PROVINCIO

3219 Conco Food Service
918 Edwards Ave
Harahan, LA 70123-3125   504-733-5200
        Fax: 504-734-5270   800-488-3988
        www.concofoods.com
Wholesaler/distributor of frozen foods, groceries,
dairy products, general line items, general merchan-
dise, produce, meats, seafood and equipment and
fixtures; serving the food service market
    President: Winn Chadwick
    VP Procurement: Dick Bachtell
    VP Sales: Robert Breaux
Estimated Sales: $100-500 Million
Number Employees: 100-249
Sq. footage: 200000
Parent Co: Consolidated Companies

3220 Concord Brewery
199 Cabot Street
Lowell, MA 01854-3611   978-937-1200
        Fax: 978-937-1423 www.concordbrew.com
Processor of ale
    President: Brett Pacheco
Estimated Sales: $1-2.5 Million
Number Employees: 1-4
Number of Brands: 4
Sq. footage: 5000
Type of Packaging: Consumer
Brands:
    Concord Grape Ale
    Concord Junction Porter
    Concord North Woods Ale
    Concord Pale Ale

3221 Concord Confections
345 Courtland Avenue
Concord, ON L4K 5A6
Canada   905-660-8989
         Fax: 905-660-8979 800-267-0037
                     info@dubblebubble.com
                www.concordconfectionsinc.com
Processor and exporter of gum including bubble,
chewing, filled and balls; also, dextrose and novelty
candy
    VP Sales: Virgil Lloyd
    Plant Manager: Howard Smuschkowitz
Number Employees: 250-499
Sq. footage: 300000
Brands:
    DUBBLE BUBBLE
    RAZZLES
    TEAR JERKERS
    TONGUE SPLASHERS
    TWINKLES

3222 Concord Farms
2811 Faber St
Union City, CA 94587-1203   510-429-8855
         Fax: 510-429-8844 www.concordfarms.com
Grower of fresh shiitake and oyster mushrooms
    Owner: Grace Tung
    Owner: David Tung
Number Employees: 10-19
Type of Packaging: Consumer, Private Label, Bulk
Brands:
    Oringer
    Reddy Glaze

3223 Concord Foods
10 Minuteman Way
Brockton, MA 02301-7508   508-580-1700
    Fax: 508-584-9425 roringer@concordfoods.com
                         www.concordfoods.com
Variegated fruit purees, stabilized fruit, caramel for
frozen desserts, bakery and confectionery including
sugar free, flavors systems — dry mixes for seafood,
chicken
    President: Peter Nevell
    Sales Manager: Rich Renna
    Research & Development: Diane Douglas
    Quality Control: Scott Lufz
    Sales Director: Rod Oringer
    VP of Manufacturing: Jesse Salfia
Estimated Sales:$10-20 Million
Number Employees: 249
Sq. footage: 190000
Type of Packaging: Bulk
Brands:
    Concord Foods
    Concord Mills
    Oringer
    Red E Made
    Tempo

3224 Condaxis Coffee Company
1805 W Beaver St
Jacksonville, FL 32209-7596   904-356-5330
                         Fax: 904-358-2027
Coffee
    President: Peter Condaxis
Estimated Sales:$500,000-$1 Million
Number Employees: 5-9

3225 Conecuh Sausage Company
P.O.Box 327
Evergreen, AL 36401-0327   251-578-3380
         Fax: 251-578-5408 800-726-0507
                sales@conecuhsausage.com
                www.conecuhsausage.com
Processor of meat products including sausage
    Owner: John Crum Sessions
    Manager: Ronny Elliot
Estimated Sales:$10-20 Million
Number Employees: 50-99
Type of Packaging: Consumer
Brands:
    Cajun Smoked Sausage
    Hickory Smoked Sausage
    Original Smoked Sausage
    Spicy and Hot Hickory Sausage

3226 Confection Solutions
12428 Gladstone Ave
Sylmar, CA 91342-5320   818-365-6619
         Fax: 818-365-8519 800-284-2422
                info@confectionsolutions.com
                www.confectionsolutions.com

Manufacturer and exporter of truffle, fruit juice
sweetened and chocolate chip cookies, cashew clus-
ters, peanut brittle and crunch, chocolate spoons,
chocolate covered graham crackers, etc
    President: Scott Goodspeed
Estimated Sales:$5-9.9 Million
Number Employees: 10-19
Sq. footage: 10000
Type of Packaging: Consumer, Food Service, Pri-
vate Label, Bulk
Brands:
    Beverly Hills Confection Line
    Coffee Companions
    Gourmet Delight
    More Than a Box

3227 Confectionately Yours
160 Lexington Drive
Suite D
Buffalo Grove, IL 60089-6929   847-537-5761
         Fax: 847-537-7178 800-875-6978
                info@confectionately-yours.com
                www.confectionately-yours.com
Processor of pretzel rods, English toffee and other
homemade style candies
    CEO: Thomas Fish
Estimated Sales:$600,000
Number Employees: 1-4
Number of Products: 35
Sq. footage: 4000
Type of Packaging: Consumer, Food Service, Pri-
vate Label, Bulk
Brands:
    Big Yummy
    Blasting Powder
    Bola Pop's
    Fizz Wiz
    Fun Stuff
    Joy Stiks
    Lumpy Logs
    Lumpy Lous
    Monster
    Monster Chews
    Nasty Tricks
    Ninja Sticks
    Oogly Eyes
    Rock 'n Roll Chews
    Stickers
    Sweet Stirrings
    Tuesday Toffee

3228 Confectionery Treasures
PO Box 418
Cumberland, MD 21501-0418   301-478-2245
                         Fax: 301-478-2245
Syrups and maple products
    Sales Manager: Alan Grub

3229 Confish
P.O.Box 271
Isola, MS 38754-0271   662-962-3101
                         Fax: 662-962-0114
Sea food
    President: Dick Stevens
    VP Sales/Marketing: Jack Perkins
    Operations Manager: Frank Davis
Estimated Sales:$10-20 Million
Number Employees: 500-999
Brands:
    Country Skillet

3230 Congdon Orchards
P.O.Box 2725
Yakima, WA 98907-2725   509-965-2886
                         Fax: 509-966-4447
Processor of apples and pears
    President: Dick Woodin
    CFO: Paul Pert
    Marketing Director: Tim Maddin
    Sales Manager: Dick Woodin
Estimated Sales:$100-500 Million
Number Employees: 250-499
Type of Packaging: Consumer, Food Service

3231 Conifer Specialties Inc
15500 Woodinville-Redmond Rd
Suite C-400
Woodinville, WA 98072   425-486-3334
         Fax: 425-398-0301 800-588-9160
         ldolstad@conifer-inc.com www.conifer-inc.com
Soups, breads, desserts and Fisher scones
    CEO: Mike Maher
Estimated Sales:$2.7 Million
Number Employees: 75

3232 Conlin Food Sales
PO Box 489
Placentia, CA 92871-0489   714-572-1088
         Fax: 800-429-1137 800-429-1136
                conbrokbill3@prodigy.net
Cheese, bacon, sour cream, various meats
    President: Walter Conlin
*Estimated Sales:*Under $500,000
Number Employees: 5-9

3233 Conn Creek Winery
8711 Silverado Trl S
St Helena, CA 94574-9577   707-963-5133
         Fax: 707-963-7840 800-793-7960
                         www.conn-creek.net
Wines
    President: Allen Shoup
    COO: David Lawrence
Estimated Sales:$5-10 Million
Number Employees: 10-19

**3234 (HQ)Conn's Potato Chip
Company**
1805 Kemper Ct
Zanesville, OH 43701-4634   740-452-4615
         Fax: 740-452-9272 866-486-4615
         conns@connschips.com www.connschips.com
Potato chips
    Co-Owner: Monte Hunter
    Co-Owner: Thomas George Sr
Estimated Sales:$5-10 Million
Number Employees: 20-49
Brands:
    CONN'S BBQ PORK RINDS
    CONN'S BEAN DIP
    CONN'S CARAMEL POPCORN
    CONN'S CHEESE CORN POPCORN
    CONN'S CHEESE CURLS
    CONN'S CHEESE DIP
    CONN'S CORN CHIPS
    CONN'S CORN POPS POPCORN
    CONN'S GREEN ONION
    CONN'S HONEY BBQ JERKY
    CONN'S HONEY MUSTARD DIP
    CONN'S JALAPENO DIP
    CONN'S NACHO TORTILLA CHIPS
    CONN'S OAT BRAN PRETZELS
    CONN'S ORIGINAL
    CONN'S ORIGINAL BEEF JERKY
    CONN'S PARTY MIX
    CONN'S PICANTE DIP
    CONN'S PORK RINDS
    CONN'S PRETZEL RODS
    CONN'S PRETZEL STICKS
    CONN'S PRETZEL THINS
    CONN'S PRETZEL TWISTS
    CONN'S RESTAURANT TORTILLA CHIPS
    CONN'S ROUND TORTILLA CHIPS
    CONN'S SALSA SUPREME DIP
    CONN'S SALT & VINEGAR
    CONN'S SOUR CREAM
    CONN'S WAVY

3235 Conneaut Cellars Winery
P.O.Box 5075
Conneaut Lake, PA 16316-5075   814-382-3999
         Fax: 814-382-6151 877-229-9463
                         www.ccw-wine.com
Wines
    President: Joel Wolf
    Sales/Office Manager: Jackie Elliot
Estimated Sales:$2.5-5 Million
Number Employees: 5-9

3236 Connection Source
5515 Taylor Road
Alpharetta, GA 30022-2600   770-667-1051
                         Fax: 770-667-1283
Manufacturer of vitamins, minerals, herbs, soft gelatin capsules and amino acids; manufacturer of
printed folding cartons; private label packaging
available
    President: Andrew Compain
Type of Packaging: Private Label, Bulk
Brands:
    Q GEL

3237 Connors Aquaculture
P.O.Box 263
Eastport, ME 04631-0263   207-853-6081
                         Fax: 207-853-6056
    Owner: Glen Cooke
    Plant Manager: David Morang

3238 Conpac
131 Industrial Drive
Warminster, PA 18974-1434   215-322-2755
Contract packaging
    President: Sam Gerbino
Estimated Sales: Less than $500,000
Number Employees: 1-4

3239 Conquest International LLC
1108 SW 8th St
Plainville, KS 67663-3106   785-434-2483
    Fax: 785-434-2736 conquest@ruraltel.net
        www.envirolyteconquestusa.com
Water treatment and purification systems, and bottled water plants
    President: Ned Colburn
Estimated Sales: Under $300,000
Number Employees: 1-4
Sq. footage: 10000
Brands:
    Natural Pure

3240 Conrad Rice Mill
307 Ann St
New Iberia, LA 70560-4719   337-364-7242
    Fax: 337-365-5806   800-551-3245
        sales@conradricemill.com
        www.conradricemill.com
Manufacturer of packed rice including yellow, herb, curry, ranch and wild; also, rice mixes including paella, long grain and wild
    President: Michael Davis
Estimated Sales: $20-50 Million
Number Employees: 20-49
Type of Packaging: Consumer, Food Service
Brands:
    CONRAD-DAVIS
    HOL GRAIN
    KONRIKO
    R.M.QUIGGS

3241 Conrotto A. Winery
1690 Hecker Pass Road
Gilroy, CA 95020-8800   408-847-2233
Wine
    President: James Burr
Estimated Sales: $1-2.5 Million
Number Employees: 1-4

3242 Conroy Foods
906 Old Freeport Rd
Pittsburgh, PA 15238-4163   412-781-1446
    Fax: 412-781-1409 beanos@conroyfoods.com
        www.conroyfoods.com
Deli and seafood condiments
    President: Jon Conroy
    CEO: Jon Conroy
Estimated Sales: $2.5-5 Million
Number Employees: 10-19
Brands:
    Beanos's

3243 Conserverie Larose
281 Beauce
Calixa-Lavallee, QC J0L 1A0
Canada   450-583-6438
    Fax: 450-583-6059
Exporter and canner of corn-on-the-cob
    President: Onil Larose
Number Employees: 20-49
Type of Packaging: Consumer
Brands:
    Larose/Lavalee

3244 (HQ)Consolidated Biscuit Company
312 Rader Rd
Mc Comb, OH 45858-9751   419-293-2911
    Fax: 419-293-3366   800-537-9544
        dan.bash@cbcbakery.com
Manufacturer and exporter of cookies, crackers, biscuits, nuts and snack foods; exporter of cookies; contract packaging available
    President/Owner: Jim Appold
    Vice President: Walter Kinsey
Estimated Sales: $100-500 Million
Number Employees: 1,000-4,999
Type of Packaging: Consumer, Food Service, Private Label, Bulk
Other Locations:
    Consolidated Biscuit Facility
    Michigan City IN
    Consolidated Biscuit Facility
    London KY
    Consolidated Biscuit Facility
    Willmar MN
    Consolidated Biscuit Facility
    Louisville KY
Brands:
    Fireside
    Gurley
    Gurley Golden Recipe
    Royal Crest

3245 Consolidated Biscuit Company
502 W Us Highway 20
Michigan City, IN 46360-6836   219-873-1880
    Fax: 219-873-1882 info@cbiscuits.com
        www.cbiscuits.com
Nut brittle
    President: Jeff Schuster
    VP: William Varney
    Vice President: Martin Seidler
    CEO: Michael Rienhard
Estimated Sales: $10-20 Million
Number Employees: 250-499
Brands:
    Tal-Furnar
    Venezini

3246 Consolidated Brands
821 17th Street
Altoona, PA 16601-2074   814-941-2200
    Fax: 814-943-2354
Chocolate candy
    President: Roger Raybuck
    Manager Sales/Marketing: Lorretta Brown
Estimated Sales: $50-100 Million
Number Employees: 100-249

3247 Consolidated Distilled Products
2600 W 35th Street
Chicago, IL 60632-1602   773-927-4161
    Fax: 773-927-8105
Distributor of liquor
    President/CEO: John Wittert
    CFO: Steve O'Malley
Number Employees: 100-249
Brands:
    Amaretto Corso
    Bambuca
    Barbarossa
    Benevento
    Canadian Reserve
    Chila
    Classic
    Conte
    Desert Island
    Dimitri
    E.S.T.
    Georgia
    Grand Suzette
    Grommes & Ullrich
    Gusano Grande
    Hannah & Hogg
    Kampai
    Karlof
    Lautrec
    McGuires Original
    Merlin
    Mme Lautrec
    Monastery
    Royal Islander
    Schranck's
    Sunset
    Vogue

3248 (HQ)Consolidated Factors
2959 Monterey Salinas Highway
Monterey, CA 93940-6400   831-375-5121
    Fax: 831-375-0754 max@confacto.com
Fresh and frozen fish, seafood, fruits and vegetables
    President/CEO: Warren Nobusada
    Executive VP/COO: Alan Nobusada
    VP of Sales: Max Boland
Estimated Sales: $50 Million+
Number Employees: 10-19
Brands:
    Crescent
    Red Rose Farms
    Sea Diamond
    Sea Jade
    Sea Pearl

3249 Consolidated Mills
7190 Brittmoore Rd # 150
Houston, TX 77041-3233   713-896-4196
    Fax: 713-896-4199 cto@hypercon.com
        www.consolidatedmills.com
Processor of frozen drink bases, slush flavors, flavoring extracts, sundae toppings, sno-cone syrups and custom spice blends
    Owner: Chuck Rodner
    Vice President: Mark Estep
Estimated Sales: $1-3 Million
Number Employees: 10-19
Sq. footage: 15000
Parent Co: Consolidated Mills
Type of Packaging: Consumer, Food Service
Brands:
    C&D
    COOL & DELICIOUS
    SOUTHERN FLAVORS

3250 Consolidated Sea Products
250 N Water St
Mobile, AL 36602-4000   251-433-3240
    Fax: 251-433-6721
Manufacturer of seafood
    Owner: Paul William
Estimated Sales: $ .5 - 1 million
Number Employees: 1-4

3251 Consolidated Seafood Enterprises
4718 E Cactus Road
188
Phoenix, AZ 85032-7706   480-348-9548
    Fax: 480-348-9587
    President: Karen Lamarche Blyth
    Vice President: David Phelps

3252 Consolidated Simon Distributor
1835 Burnet Ave
Union, NJ 07083-4282   973-674-2124
    Fax: 973-687-9132 www.candycentral.com
Candy and confections
    President: Ken Simon
Estimated Sales: $10-20 Million
Number Employees: 50-99

3253 Consolidated Tea Company
300 Merrick Rd # 202
Lynbrook, NY 11563-2503   516-887-1144
    Fax: 516-887-1643
Tea
    President: Elliot Labiner
Estimated Sales: $5-10 Million
Number Employees: 5-9

3254 Constantia Multifilm Corporation
1040 N McLean Blvd
Elgin, IL 60123-1709   847-695-7600
    Fax: 847-695-7645   800-837-9727
    info@multifilm.com   www.multifilm.com
Constantia Multifilm is an integrated manufacturer of flexible packaging solutions for the food, beverage, and confectionery industries.
    President/CEO: Olle Mannertorp
    Vice President Finance: Robert Tate
    Graphics Manager: Terry Piatkowski
    New Business Development Manager: Marcus Magnusson
    Vice President Sales and Marketing: Chris Rogers

    Customer Service: Nancy Jung
    Production Manager: Mike Huey
    Plant Manager: Dave Rohrschneider
    Purchasing & Planning Manager: Chris Bailey
Estimated Sales: Below $5 Million
Number Employees: 10-19
Type of Packaging: Consumer

3255 Consumer Guild Foods
5035 Enterprise Blvd
Toledo, OH 43612-3839   419-726-3406
    Fax: 419-726-8771
Processor of salad dressings and oils, mayonnaise, condiments and relishes
    President: W Ascham
    Quality Control: R Fuller
    VP Production: R Petrick
Estimated Sales: $10-20 Million
Number Employees: 20-49
Type of Packaging: Consumer, Food Service, Private Label, Bulk
Brands:
    Amhurst Kitchens

Annie's Supreme
Cg Supreme

3256 Consumer Packing Company
Plum & Liberty Streets
Lancaster, PA 17604   717-397-6141
Fax: 717-397-0322
wanda.hart@handoverfoods.com
General grocery
Estimated Sales: $ 1 - 3 Million
Number Employees: 5-9
Type of Packaging: Private Label

3257 Consumers Flavoring Extract Company
921 McDonald Ave
Brooklyn, NY 11218-5600   718-435-0201
Processor and exporter of flavoring extracts and essential oils including vanilla
President: L Fontana
Estimated Sales: $10-20 Million
Number Employees: 10-19

3258 Consumers Packing Company
1301 Carson Dr
Melrose Park, IL 60160-2970   708-344-0047
Fax: 708-345-9052   800-356-9876
www.consumerspacking.com
Meat products
President: William Schutz
Estimated Sales: $ 10 - 20 Million
Number Employees: 20-49

3259 Consumers Vinegar & Spice Company
4723 S Washtenaw Ave
Chicago, IL 60632-2097   773-376-4100
Fax: 773-376-6224
Processor of vinegar, spices and dehydrated garlic and onion
President: Stanley Zarno
Estimated Sales: $5-10 Million
Number Employees: 10-19
Sq. footage: 40000
Type of Packaging: Consumer, Food Service, Private Label, Bulk
Brands:
Burma
Consumers

3260 Consun Food Industries
123 Gateway Blvd N
Elyria, OH 44035-4923   440-233-7501
Fax: 440-322-8196   denniswalter@alltel.com
Packaged milk, fruit juices and ice cream
President: Dennis Walter
Quality Control: Dennis Diedrick
Marketing Director: Jerry Lattimer
Sales Director: Steve Cannon
Operations Manager: Ron Lattimer
Plant Manager: Paul Meiss
Estimated Sales: $10-24.9 Million
Number Employees: 500-999
Number of Brands: 1
Type of Packaging: Consumer, Food Service, Private Label, Bulk

3261 Contact International
8001 Lincoln Ave
Skokie, IL 60077-3695   847-324-4411
Fax: 847-229-1386   info@contactamt.com
Processor of liquid and powder flavor extracts, natural spring water, liquid tea, juices and carbonated soft drinks, RTD Beverages, CSD
President: Sumner Katz
VP: Phillip Ross
VP: Robert Goodman
Estimated Sales: $5-10 Million
Number Employees: 10-19
Type of Packaging: Private Label
Brands:
Artica

3262 Conte Luna Foods
760 S 11th St
Philadelphia, PA 19147-2614   215-923-3141
Fax: 215-925-4298   Sales@ConteLuna.com
www.conteluna.com
Processor and exporter of pasta and noodles for soups, frozen foods and shelf-stable foods, etc
President: Luke Marano
Estimated Sales: $ 5 - 10 Million
Number Employees: 5-9
Type of Packaging: Bulk

3263 Conte Luna Foods
40 Jacksonville Rd
Warminster, PA 18974-4804   215-441-5220
Fax: 215-441-8934   Sales@ConteLuna.com
www.conteluna.com
President: Max E Powell
VP: John Briggs
Plant Manager: Dan Graboyes
Purchasing Agent: Joe Rees
Estimated Sales: $10-20 Million
Number Employees: 20-49

3264 Conte's Pasta Company
310 E Wheat Rd
Vineland, NJ 08360   856-697-3400
Fax: 856-697-1757   800-211-6607
customer_service@contespasta.com
www.contespasta.com
Wheat and gluten free pasta, pizza, pierogi and more
President/Owner: Adelina Portillo

3265 Contessa Food Products
222 W 6th St # 800
San Pedro, CA 90731-3356   310-832-8000
Fax: 310-832-8333   contessa@contessa.com
www.contessa.com
Manufacturer and importer of frozen shrimp, scallops, calamari, shrimp and chicken convenience meals and pineapple chunks
President/CEO: John Blazevich
Estimated Sales: $100-500 Million
Number Employees: 100-249
Brands:
Contessa
Islander
Shanghai

3266 Conti Packing Company
P.O.Box 23025
Rochester, NY 14692-3025   585-424-2500
Fax: 585-424-2504
Manufacturer and importer of fresh and frozen meats including lamb, pork, beef, veal and sausage
President: Douglas Conti
Treasurer: Thomas Conti
Estimated Sales: $5-10 Million
Number Employees: 10-19

3267 Contigroup Companies
4110 Continental Dr
Oakwood, GA 30566-2800   770-538-2120
Fax: 770-538-2121   Information@Conti.com
www.waynefarmsllc.com
Poultry
President: Elton Maddox
Chairman/CEO: Paul Fribourg
VP/CFO: Kathy McManus
CEO: Paul Fribourg
Director Of Sales: Stan Haymaen
Number Employees: 10,000+
Type of Packaging: Bulk
Brands:
DUTCH QUALITY HOUSE
Wayne Farms

3268 Continental Coffee Products Company
235 N Norwood St
Houston, TX 77011-2311   713-928-6281
Fax: 713-924-9870   800-323-6178
www.saralee.com
Coffee, tea
President: Peter JW Roorda
Sales Manager: Scott Kolber
Plant Manager: Dan Hickman
Number Employees: 5-9

3269 Continental Culture Specialists
1358 E Colorado Street
Glendale, CA 91205-1474   818-240-7400
Fax: 818-243-3601   vasacont@aol.com
www.continentalyogurt.com
Processor of yogurt, kefir and lebni cheese and liquid acidophilus culture
President: Martha Frazier
Quality Control: M Josie Uy
Marketing Director: Martha Frazier
National Sales Manager: Gary Correll
Production Manager: Erroll McGowen
Estimated Sales: $50-100 Million
Number Employees: 50-99
Sq. footage: 22000
Type of Packaging: Consumer

Brands:
Continental
Continental Yogurt
Lebini-Kefer Cheese

3270 Continental Custom Ingredients
1170 Invicta Drive
Oakville, ON L6H 6G1
Canada   905-815-8158
Fax: 905-815-9194   rhames@cci-can.net
www.cci-can.net
Specializes in the design and application of stabilization, emulsification, and functional ingredient systems to impart the desired body and texture characteristics and self life stability to processed foods, beverage and dairyproducts.
Number Employees: 20-49
Type of Packaging: Private Label, Bulk
Brands:
AQUAMIN
DURAFRESH
FARGO

3271 Continental Deli Foods
1300 S Lake St
Cherokee, IA 51012-2177   712-225-5161
Fax: 712-225-6513 www.tyson.com
Processor of meats including smoked, cured, pork, ham, beef, hot dogs and cold cuts
President: Jerry Menke
General Manager: Jerry Menke
Asst. Plant Manager: Mark Fassler
Estimated Sales: $100-500 Million
Number Employees: 500-999
Sq. footage: 175000
Parent Co: FoodBrands America
Type of Packaging: Consumer, Food Service, Private Label
Brands:
American Favorite
Black Forest
Fresh Cut
Wilson Continental D

3272 Continental Food Products
P.O.Box 540928
Flushing, NY 11354-0928   718-358-7894
Fax: 718-463-6580 www.betzios.com
Processor of frozen pizzas
President: Elias Betzios
Controller: Richard Betzios
VP: Paul Betzios
Estimated Sales: $20-50 Million
Number Employees: 50-99
Brands:
Betzios

3273 (HQ)Continental Grain/ContiGroup Companies
277 Park Ave
New York, NY 10172   212-207-5930
Fax: 212-207-2910   information@conti.com
www.contigroup.com
Processor and exporter of poultry, meat, grain, flour and feed.
Chairman/CEO: Paul Fribourg
EVP/CFO: Michael Zimmerman
EVP Human Resources: Teresa McCaslin
Estimated Sales: K
Number Employees: 14,200
Type of Packaging: Bulk
Brands:
WAYNE FARMS

3274 Continental Group
21062 Brookhurst St # 203
Huntington Beach, CA 92646-7404   858-391-5670
Fax: 858-965-0260   norm_tcg@sbcglobal.net
Manufacturer of sardines, tuna, olive oils, balsamic vinegar, and pasta
Owner: Dean Beerbower

3275 Continental Mills
P.O.Box 88176
Seattle, WA 98138-2176   253-872-8400
Fax: 253-872-7954 www.continentalmills.com

Manufacturer and exporter of baking products including dry flour mixes. Continental Mills has acquired the Pillsbury foodservice small package dry mix business from Best Brands Corporation
President: John Heily
CFO: Michael Castle
Vice President: Bob Wallach
Research & Development: Dan Donahue
Quality Control: Christy Johnson
Marketing Director: Steve Donley
Sales Director: Steve Giuditta
Public Relations: Clyde Walker
Operations Manager: Mark Harris
Production Manager: Mike Meredith
Estimated Sales: $43.2 Million
Number Employees: 500-999
Sq. footage: 300000
Type of Packaging: Consumer, Food Service, Private Label, Bulk
Brands:
   ALPINE
   CLASSIC HEARTH
   EAGLE MILLS
   GHIRARDELLI
   KRUSTEAZ
   KRUSTEAZ CARBSIMPLE
   SNOQUALMIE FALLS LODGE

3276 Continental Sausage
911 E 75th Ave
Denver, CO 80229-6401   303-288-9787
   Fax: 303-288-9789 www.continentalsausage.com
Meats, sausage
   President: Eric Gutknecht
   Vice President: Ursula Gutknecht
   Purchasing Manager: Eric Gutknecht
Estimated Sales: $2.5-5 Million
Number Employees: 5-9

3277 Continental Seasoning
1700 Palisade Ave
Teaneck, NJ 07666-3798   201-837-6111
      Fax: 201-837-9248 800-631-1564
         info@continentalseasoning.com
         www.continentalseasoning.com
Processor, importer and exporter of sauces, spices, seasonings and food additives
   President: Pete Federer
   CFO: Jeffrey Bovit
   Vice President: Edward Levine
   Quality Control: Marty Haas
   VP Production: Ann Davis
   Plant Manager: Steve Wagner
Estimated Sales: $5-10 Million
Number Employees: 50-99
Sq. footage: 20000
Type of Packaging: Food Service, Private Label, Bulk

3278 Continental Vitamin Company
5410 S Boyle Ave
Vernon, CA 90058   323-581-0176
      Fax: 323-589-6667 800-421-6175
   ronald@cvc4health.com   www.cvc4health.com
Vitamins
   President: Ron Deckenfield
   CEO: Hal Frank
Estimated Sales: $5 - 10 Million
Number Employees: 50-99
Brands:
   Cvc Specialties
   Superior Source

3279 Continental Yogurt
1358 E Colorado Street
Glendale, CA 91205-1474   818-240-7400
                        Fax: 818-243-3601
Processor of yogurt
   Sales Manager: Gary Correll
   Purchasing Agent: Juan Garcia
Estimated Sales: $1 - 3 Million
Number Employees: 10-19
Type of Packaging: Food Service

3280 Contract Comestibles
2004 Beulah Ave
East Troy, WI 53120-1202   262-642-9400
   Fax: 262-642-9404 www.contractcomestibles.com
   Owner: Matt Nitz
   Purchasing: Matthew Nitz
Estimated Sales: $1-2.5 Million
Number Employees: 10-19

3281 Controlled Food Systems
PO Box 360
Oakmont, PA 15139-0360   412-828-2844
                        Fax: 412-828-2495
Manufacturer and exporter of stabilizers and emulsifiers
   President: John Morris
   CEO: Lois Harkness
Number Employees: 10-19
Sq. footage: 10000
Type of Packaging: Private Label

3282 Convenience Food Suppliers
607 Ellis Road
Suite 52a
Durham, NC 27703-6008   919-596-9338
   Fax: 919-596-9339 800-922-1586
         cfspop@mindspring.com
Processor of popcorn; wholesaler/distributor of popcorn machinery and concession supplies; serving the food service market
   Owner: Harold Pittman
Estimated Sales: Less than $500,000
Number Employees: 1-4
Sq. footage: 8500

3283 Conway Import Company
11051 Addison Ave
Franklin Park, IL 60131-1496   847-455-5600
      Fax: 847-455-5630 800-323-8801
         conwaydressings@minspring.com
            www.conwaydressings.com
Processor of oils, mayonaise, salad dressings, maple syrup, sauces and marinades.
   President: Scott Heineman
   VP: Gregg Haineman
   VP Marketing: Robert Burns
   VP Sales: Robert Burns
Estimated Sales: $50-100 Million
Number Employees: 50-99
Number of Products: 600
Type of Packaging: Food Service, Private Label, Bulk

3284 Cook Inlet Processing
909 W 9th Ave
Anchorage, AK 99501-3322   907-243-1166
                        Fax: 907-243-4231
   VP Operations: Tim Blott
Estimated Sales: $ 1 - 3 Million
Number Employees: 1-4

3285 (HQ)Cook Inlet Processing
P.O.Box 8163
Nikiski, AK 99635-8163   907-776-8174
      Fax: 907-776-5302 www.oceanbeauty.com
Processor and exporter of frozen seafood including crab, salmon, halibut, clams, etc
   President: Mike Schupe
   COO: Mel Morris
   Accounts Payable: Norma Johnson
   Controller, Plant Manager: Pat Hardina
   Production Manager: Tuck Bonney
   Plant Manager: Wayne Kvasinkoff
Estimated Sales: $20-50 Million
Number Employees: 100-249
Parent Co: Polar Equipment
Type of Packaging: Consumer, Food Service, Bulk
Brands:
   Cook Inlet Processing

3286 Cook Natural Products
2109 Frederick St
Oakland, CA 94606-5317   510-534-2665
      Fax: 510-534-2509 800-537-7589
         brendan@cooknaturally.com
            www.cooknaturally.com
Organic flour, grains, seeds, beans
   Owner: Brendan Mc Entee
   CEO: Brendan McEntee
   Vice President: Jeffrey Barnes
Estimated Sales: $1-2.5 Million
Number Employees: 10-19

3287 Cook Natural Products
2109 Frederick St
Oakland, CA 94606-5317   510-534-2665
      Fax: 510-534-2509 800-537-7589
         brendan@cooknaturally.com
            www.cooknaturally.com
Organic grains
   President/CEO: Brendan Mc Entee
Estimated Sales: $1-2.5 Million
Number Employees: 10-19

3288 Cook's Gourmet Foods
5821 Wilderness Ave
Riverside, CA 92504-1004   951-352-5700
   Fax: 951-352-5710 www.triplehfoods.com
Co-packers of gourmet foods
   President: Tom Harris Jr
Estimated Sales: $500,000-$1 Million
Number Employees: 50-99

3289 Cook-In-The-Kitchen
P.O.Box 961
White River Junction, VT 5001-961 802-333-4141
      Fax: 802-333-4624 info@citk.com
            www.cookinthekitchen.com
All natural pancake, bakery and soup mixes.
   President: Mary Spata
   VP/General Manager: Murray Burk
Estimated Sales: $1-2.5 Million
Number Employees: 3
Number of Products: 20
Type of Packaging: Consumer, Private Label

3290 Cooke Aguaculture
874 Main Street
Blacks Harbour, NB E5H-1E6
Canada   506-456-6600
   Fax: 506-456-6652 nhalse@cookeaqua.com
            www.cookeaqua.com/
Distributor of fresh and smoked salmon.
   CEO: Glenn Cooke
   CFO: Peter Buck
   VP Marketing: Jean Lamontagne
   VP Sales: Alan Craig
   VP Public Relations/Communications: Neil Halse

   Purchasing Director: Don Bourque
Number Employees: 20-49
Number of Brands: 3
Number of Products: 60
Sq. footage: 2500
Brands:
   APPLEDORE
   HORTON'S

3291 Cooke Tavern Ltd
4158 Penns Valley Rd
Spring Mills, PA 16875   814-422-7657
      Fax: 814-422-8752 866-422-7687
         info@cooketavernsoups.com
            www.cooketavernsoups.com
Soups
   President/Owner: Greg Williams
Number Employees: 5

3292 Cookie Cupboard Baking Corporation
12 Commerce Rd
Fairfield, NJ 07004-1602   973-575-4365
      Fax: 973-882-6998 800-217-2938
            www.davidscookies.com
Baked goods
   Owner: Ari Margulies
Estimated Sales: $10-20 Million
Number Employees: 20-49
Brands:
   DAVID'S COOKIES

3293 Cookie Kingdom
1201 E Walnut St
Oglesby, IL 61348-1344   815-883-3331
                        Fax: 815-883-3332
Processor of baked goods
   President: Cliff Sheppard
Estimated Sales: $8.5 Million
Number Employees: 100-249

3294 Cookie Specialties
482 N Milwaukee Ave
Wheeling, IL 60090-3067   847-537-3888
      Fax: 847-537-6709 matt@mattscookies.com
            www.mattscookies.com
Processor of cookies
   President: Grant Pierce
   VP: Matthew Pierce
Estimated Sales: $10-20 Million
Number Employees: 10-19
Type of Packaging: Consumer, Food Service, Private Label
Brands:
   MATT'S COOKIES

3295 Cookie Tree Bakeries
P.O.Box 57888
Salt Lake City, UT 84157-0888   801-268-2253
                Fax: 801-265-2727   800-998-0111
                        www.cookietree.com
Processor and exporter of frozen gourmet cookies
and cookie dough; also, fat-free available
    President: Greg Schenk
    Purchasing: Wayne Davis
Estimated Sales:$20-50 Million
Number Employees: 1-4
Type of Packaging: Consumer, Food Service, Private Label, Bulk
Brands:
    COOKIETREE BAKERIES

3296 Cookies & More
P.O.Box 2381
Lewiston, ME 4241-2381   207-923-4227
                pat@mainebaked.com
                www.mainebaked.com
Producer of gingerbread houses. Also dog biscuits,
cookies and pies
    Owner/President: Pat Guvala
Number Employees: 20-49
Sq. footage: 27000

3297 Cookies Food Products
P.O.Box 339
Wall Lake, IA 51466-0339   712-664-2662
                Fax: 712-664-2676   800-331-4995
                        www.cookiesbbq.com
Processor of barbecue and taco sauces
    President: Speed Herrig
    Purchasing Manager: Jeff Herrig
Estimated Sales:$10-20 Million
Number Employees: 10-19
Sq. footage: 61000
Type of Packaging: Consumer, Food Service
Brands:
    COOKIES

3298 Cookietree Bakeries
P.O.Box 57888
Salt Lake City, UT 84157-0888   801-268-2253
                Fax: 801-265-2727   800-998-0111
                cheryl@cookietree.com   www.cookietree.com
    Owner: Greg Schenk
    VP Sales: Mike Dougherty
Estimated Sales:$ 20 - 50 Million
Number Employees: 50-99

3299 Cookshack
2304 N Ash St
Ponca City, OK 74601-1100   580-765-3669
                Fax: 580-765-2223   800-423-0698
                sales@cookshack.com   www.cookshack.com
US Manufacturers of the World Famous Smart
Smokers, Smokette, Fast Eddy's OVens Barbeque
Sauces & Spices, Smoking Wood Accessories for
Better Barbeque, Cookshack Smoked Foods Cookbooks & more
    CEO: Stuart Powell
    CEO: Stuart Powell
    Marketing Coordinator: Cayley Armstrong
    Sales Manager: John Shiflet
    Production Manager: Jim Linnebur
Estimated Sales:$ 10 - 20 Million
Number Employees: 50-99
Number of Brands: 2
Number of Products: 1
Type of Packaging: Consumer, Food Service, Private Label, Bulk
Brands:
    Cookshack

3300 Cool
801 E Campbell Rd # 348
Richardson, TX 75081-1866   972-437-9352
                Fax: 972-644-7231
    Manager: Dan C Cole
Estimated Sales:$500-1 Million appx.
Number Employees: 1-4
Brands:
    Cool Natural Sodas
    Cool Quencher Sports

3301 Cool Beans Coffee Company
5063 NW 171st Place
Portland, OR 97229-7332   503-520-0836
                Fax: 503-520-9485
            info@coolbeanscoffeecompany.com
            www.coolbeanscoffeecompany.com

Coffee beans
    President/CEO: Aurelio Lewis
    President: Bruce Luong
    Marketing Director: Pete Sanida
    Director Manufacturing: Denise Shurtleff
Brands:
    Costa Rican Tarrazu
    French Roast
    Guatamalan Antigua
    Jamaican Blue Mountain
    Mexican Altura
    Pete's Bust Ass Blend
    Venezuela Maracaibo

3302 (HQ)Cool Brands International
4175 Veteran's Memorial Highway
3rd Floor
Ronkonkoma, NY 11779   631-737-9700
            Fax: 631-737-9792 www.coolbrandsinc.com
Ice cream and ice cream novelties
    President/CEO: David Kewer
    General Manager: Antonio Brooks
Number Employees: 20-49
Parent Co: CoolBrands International

3303 Cool Cargo
5324 Georgia Highway 85
Forest Park, GA 30297-2475   770-994-0338
    Manager: Tonya Cobb

3304 Cool Mountain Beverages
1065 E Prairie Ave
Des Plaines, IL 60016-3341   847-759-9330
            Fax: 847-759-9332 www.coolmountain.com
Produces gourmet flavored sodas.
    President: Bill Daker
Estimated Sales:$ 3 - 5 Million
Number Employees: 1-4
Brands:
    COOL MOUNTAIN GOURMET SODA

3305 Coombs Vermont Gourmet
74 Cotton Mill Hl # A106
Brattleboro, VT 05301-7837   802-257-8100
                                    888-266-6271
    info@maplesource.com   www.maplesource.com
Processor, importer and exporter of pure maple
syrup and sugar; also, organic and kosher varieties
available
    President: Arnold Coombs
Estimated Sales:$ .5 - 1 million
Number Employees: 1-4
Number of Brands: 3
Type of Packaging: Consumer, Food Service, Private Label, Bulk
Brands:
    COOMBS FAMILY FARMS

3306 Cooper Farms
6793 Us Route 127
Van Wert, OH 45891-9601   419-238-4056
            Fax: 419-238-1587 www.cooperfarms.com
Processor of fresh turkey products
    Manager: Greg Cooper
    Product Development Manager: Dale Siebeneck
    Regional Sales Manager: Scott Habben
    Human Resources Manager: Paula Flemming
    Production Superintendent: Mike Parker
    Plant Operations Manager: Greg Cooper
    Purchasing Manager: Duaine Hampton
Estimated Sales:$10-20 Million
Number Employees: 100-249

3307 Cooper Mountain Vineyards
20100 SW Leonardo Ln
Beaverton, OR 97007-7871   503-649-0027
                Fax: 503-649-0702
            sales@coopermountainwine.com
                www.coopermountainwine.com
Wines
    Owner: Robert Gross
    Sales Director: Susan Baltus
    Winemaker: Rich Cushman
Estimated Sales:$1-2.5 Million
Number Employees: 5-9
Type of Packaging: Private Label

3308 Cooper Vineyards
13372 Shannon Hill Rd
Louisa, VA 23093-3929   540-894-5253
            Fax: 804-285-8773 www.coopervineyards.com
Wine
    Owner: Jaque Hogge

Estimated Sales:$ 1 - 3 Million
Number Employees: 1-4

3309 Cooperative Cosecheros de Cidra
PO Box 985
Adjuntas, PR 00601-0985   787-829-2845
                Fax: 787-829-0250
Processor of citron slices in heavy syrup; exporter of
citron peel in brine
    General Manager: Joe Maldonado

3310 Cooperative Elevator
P.O.Box 619
Pigeon, MI 48755-0619   989-453-4500
    Fax: 989-453-3942 co-opinquiry@coopelev.com
                        www.coopelev.com
Processor of dried beans
    President/CEO: Pat Anderson
    Chairman: Kurt Ewald
    Finance VP: Mike Wehner
    VP: Barry Albrecht
Estimated Sales:$500,000-$1 Million
Number Employees: 1-4

3311 Cooperative Elevator Company
P.O.Box 619
Pigeon, MI 48755-0619   989-453-4500
    Fax: 989-453-3942 co-opinquiry@coopelev.com
                        www.coopelev.com
Processor and exporter of beans, wheat, barley, oats
and corn
    President/CEO: Pat Anderson
    Purchasing Manager: Michelle Sting
Estimated Sales:$ 50 - 100 Million
Number Employees: 100-249
Type of Packaging: Bulk

3312 Cooperstown Cookie Company
418 Public Landing Rd
PO Box 64
Cooperstown, NY 13326   607-435-5789
            Fax: 607-547-2673   888-269-7315
            goodies@cooperstowncookie.com
            www.cooperstowncookie.com
all natural baseball cookies
    President/Owner: Pati Grady

3313 (HQ)Coors Brewing Company
17735 W 32nd Avenue
Golden, CO 80401-1217   303-279-6565
            Fax: 303-277-2805   800-642-6116
                        www.coors.com
Manufacturer and exporter of malt beverages, ale
and beer including regular, light, seasonal and
nonalcoholic. Principle subsidiary is Coors Brewing
Company, the nation's third-largest brewer.
    President/CEO: Peter Swinburn
    CFO: Bill Waters
    VP/CIO: John Crowther
    Chief Marketing Officer: Andrew England
Estimated Sales:$900 Million
Number Employees: 2000
Parent Co: Molson Coors Brewing Company
Type of Packaging: Consumer
Other Locations:
    Shenandoah Facility
    Elkton VA
    Sandlot Brewery
    Denver CO
    Coors Brewing Company
    Canada
    Coors Brewing Company
    Puerto Rico
    Coors Brewing Company
    Carribean
    Coors Brewing Company
    United Kingdom
    Coors Brewing Company
    China
    Coors Brewing Company
    Japan
Brands:
    BLUE MOON™
    COORS LIGHT®
    COORS NON-ALCOHOLIC®
    COORS® BANQUET
    EXTRA GOLD™LAGER
    KEYSTONE®
    KILLIAN'S® IRISH RED™
    WINTERFEST
    ZIMA®

3314 Copia Trading Company
500 1st St
Napa, CA 94559-2629   707-265-5800
    Fax: 707-257-8601   info@copia.org
                        www.copia.org
    President: Arthur Jacobus
    COO: Kurt Nystrom
    Chief Marketing Officer: Larry Tsai
Estimated Sales: $500,000-$1 Million
Number Employees: 20-49

3315 Copper Hills Fruit Sales
4337 N Golden State Boulevard
Suite 102
Fresno, CA 93722-3801   559-277-1970
    Fax: 559-277-6971
Packers of peaches, plums, nectarines, apricots, pomegranates, and persimmons

3316 Copper Tank Brewing Company
504 Trinity Street
Austin, TX 78701-3714   512-854-9380
    Fax: 512-478-1832
Processor of seasonal beer, ale, stout, lager and porter
    President: Aaron Scharff
    Purchasing: Patrick Bradshaw
Estimated Sales: $2.5-5 Million
Number Employees: 50-99
Type of Packaging: Food Service

3317 Cora Italian Specialties
9630 Joliet Rd
Countryside, IL 60525-4138   708-482-4660
    Fax: 708-482-4663   800-696-2672
info@corainc.com   www.corainc.com
Importer and exporter of espresso machinery, pasta cookers and panini grills. Midwest distributor of Monin syrups, Oregon chai, Guitiard and Ghirardelli chocolates, Mocafe, Jet tea etc
    President: John Cora
    Sales: Paul Rekstad
Estimated Sales: $5-10 Million
Number Employees: 1-4
Sq. footage: 15000
Type of Packaging: Food Service
Brands:
    DANESI
    DOLCE
    GHIRARDELLI
    GUITTARD
    JET TEA
    MOCAFE
    MONIN
    MUSETTI
    NIKOLA'S BISCOTTI
    NUMI TEA
    OREGON CHAI
    SOY DREAM
    WHITE WAVE

3318 Cora-Texas Manufacturing Company
P.O.Box 280
White Castle, LA 70788-0280   225-545-3679
    Fax: 225-545-8360 www.coratexas.com
Processor of raw sugar and blackstrap molasses
    President: Paul Buckley Kessler
    Assistant Manager: Charles Schudmak
Estimated Sales: $20-50 Million
Number Employees: 100-249
Type of Packaging: Bulk

3319 Corbin Foods-Edibowls
P.O.Box 28139
Santa Ana, CA 92799-8139   714-966-6695
    Fax: 949-640-0279   800-695-5655
                        www.edibowls.com
Processor and exporter of edible bowls for salads, desserts and tarts; club packs available
    Manager: R J Hill
Estimated Sales: $5-10 Million
Number Employees: 5-9
Sq. footage: 100000
Type of Packaging: Consumer, Food Service, Bulk
Brands:
    EDIBOWL

3320 Corby Distilleries
193 Yonge Street
Toronto, ON M5B 1M8
Canada   416-369-1859
    Fax: 416-369-9281   800-367-9079
    corbyweb@adsw.com   www.corby.ca
Processor and importer of whiskey, Scotch whiskey, Irish whiskey, bourbon, rum, gin, vodka, tequila, cognac and brandy.
    VP Sales: Jim Keon
    VP SP/Customer Service: Chris Chan
Number Employees: 100-249
Parent Co: Allied Lyons
Type of Packaging: Consumer, Food Service
Brands:
    BALLANTINE'S FINEST
    BARCLAY'S
    BEEFEATER DRY
    BELVEDERE
    CANADIAN CLUB
    CHOPIN
    COURVOISIER
    D'EAUBONNE VSOP NAPOLEON
    DE KUYPER GENEVA
    GLENDRONACH
    HORNITOS SAUZA
    LAMB'S NAVY
    LAMB'S PALM BREEZE
    LAMB'S WHITE
    LAPHROAIG
    LEMON HART
    MAKER'S MARK
    MALIBU COCONUT RUM
    POLAR ICE TASSEL
    REVELSTOKE
    ROYAL RESERVE
    SAUZA COMMEMORATIVO
    SAUZA EXTRA GOLD
    SAUZA SILVER
    SAUZA TRIADA
    SCAPA SINGLE MALT
    SILK TASSEL
    SPECIAL OLD
    STOLICHNAYA
    STOLICHNAYA RAZBERI
    STOLICHNAYA RED
    STOLICHNAYA VANIL
    TEACHER'S HIGHLAND CREAM
    TRES GENERACIONES
    TULLAMORE DEW
    WISER'S DELUXE
    WISER'S SPECIAL BLEND
    WISER'S VERY OLD

3321 Cordon Bleu International
8383 Rue J Rene Ouimet
Anjou, QC H1J 2P8
Canada   514-352-3000
    Fax: 514-352-3226
Processor and exporter of pickled food products, sauces, gravies, chicken broth, meat pates, beef and chicken entrees and red kidney beans in tomato sauce.
    Director Advertising/Promotions: Michelle Guibord
    Director Sales: Jacques LeGare
    Purchasing: Kristen Gerard
Number Employees: 100-249
Parent Co: J-R Ouimet
Type of Packaging: Consumer, Private Label

3322 Corea Lobster Cooperative
199 Crowley Island Rd
Corea, ME 04624   207-963-7936
    Fax: 207-963-5952
Lobster
    Manager: Dwight Rodgers
Estimated Sales: $ 1 - 3 Million
Number Employees: 5-9

3323 (HQ)Corfu Foods
755 Thomas Dr
Bensenville, IL 60106-1624   630-595-2510
    Fax: 630-595-3884
Processor and exporter of pita bread, honey mustard sauce and beef and chicken gyro products including cones, patties, deli kits, sauce and loaves; importer of cheese, olives and stuffed grape leaves.
    President: Vasilios Memmos
    VP: Sophie Maroulis
    Purchasing Agent: Ron Fallot
Estimated Sales: $ 10 - 20 Million
Number Employees: 50-99
Sq. footage: 70000
Other Locations:
    Corfu Foods
    Long Island City NY
Brands:
    CORFU
    GYROS USA
    OMEGA
    TASTY

3324 Corfu Tasty Gyros
755 Thomas Dr
Bensenville, IL 60106-1624   630-595-2510
    Fax: 630-595-3884
Gyros
    President: Vasilios Memmos
Estimated Sales: $ 10 - 20 Million
Number Employees: 50-99

3325 Corim International Coffee
1116 Industrial Pkwy
Brick, NJ 08724   732-840-0544
    Fax: 732-840-1608   800-942-4201
Coffee
    President: Rame Teren
Estimated Sales: $1-2.5 Million
Number Employees: 20-49

3326 Corky's Bar-B-Q
5259 Poplar Ave
Memphis, TN 38119-3513   901-685-9744
    Fax: 901-685-1102   800-926-7597
pbqinfo@corkysbbq.com   www.corkysbbq.com
Processor of frozen barbecue ribs, pork shoulders and beef brisket
    President: Barry Pelts
    CEO: Andrew Woodman
    Marketing Director: Barry Pelts
Estimated Sales: $5-10 Million
Number Employees: 100-249
Type of Packaging: Consumer, Food Service

3327 Cormier Rice Milling Company
P.O.Box 152
De Witt, AR 72042-0152   870-946-3561
    Fax: 870-946-3029 www.cormierrice.com
Processor and exporter of long and medium grain, milled, brown and organic brown rice
    Owner: Carol Ellis
    VP: Jimmy Byens
    VP: J Ferguson
Estimated Sales: $10-20 Million
Number Employees: 20-49
Type of Packaging: Consumer, Food Service, Private Label, Bulk
Brands:
    Lone Pine
    Regal
    Snow Goose

3328 Corn Poppers
PO Box 620156
San Diego, CA 92162-0156   858-231-2617
    Fax: 858-231-2985 info@cornpoppers.com
                        www.cornpoppers.com
Processor of flavored, organic and plain popcorn.
    President: Richard Kratze
    CFO: Betty Melton
    General Manager: Jose Alves
Number Employees: 20-49
Parent Co: Corn Poppers
Brands:
    POPCORN DIPPERS

3329 (HQ)Corn Products International
5 Westbrook Corporate Center
Westchester, IL 60154   708-551-2600
    Fax: 708-551-2700 info@cornproducts.com
                        www.cornproducts.com

Processor, importer and exporter of corn oils, starches, gluten and sweeteners including high fructose syrups, dextrose and meltodextrin.
  Chairman, President & CEO: Ilene Gordon
  VP & CFO: Cheryl Beebe
  VP & President, North America Division: Jack Fortnum
Estimated Sales: $3.94 Billion
Number Employees: 7800
Type of Packaging: Bulk
Other Locations:
  Corn Products International
  Etobicoke ON
Brands:
  ABC CARRIER
  BREWER'S CRYSTALS
  BUFFALO
  CERELOSE
  ENZOSE
  FIBERBOND
  GLOBE
  GLOBE PLUS
  INVERTOSE HFCS
  PROFERM
  ROYAL
  ROYAL-T
  STABLEBOND
  SUREBOND
  ULTRABOND
  UNIDEX

3330 Cornell Beverages
105 Harrison Pl
Brooklyn, NY 11237-1403   718-381-3000
                   Fax: 718-381-3001
Carbonated soft drinks
  President/CEO: Allan Hoffman
  CFO: Allan Hoffman
  Vice President: Alan Hoffman
  Marketing Manager: Allan Hoffman
Estimated Sales: $10-20 Million
Number Employees: 20-49
Brands:
  Cornell Beverages

3331 Cornerstone Floorings &Linings
750 Patrick Pl
Brownsburg, IN 46112-2211   317-852-6433
           Fax: 317-852-6433 800-659-7699
           info@cornerstoneflooring.com
  www.cornerstoneflooring.com/industries/industrie
                   s.shtml
Manufacturer and installer of high performance polymer flooring, lining and coating materials for a variety of industries including that of food and beverage.
  Sales Manager: Tracy Figley
Estimated Sales: $ 1 - 5 Million
Number Employees: 20-49

3332 Corona College Heights Orange & Lemon Associates
8000 Lincoln Ave
Riverside, CA 92504-4343   951-688-1811
           Fax: 951-689-5115 www.cchcitrus.com
Processor and exporter of oranges, lemons and grapefruit.
  President: John Demshki
  Purchasing: Dale Stogner
Estimated Sales: $100-500 Million
Number Employees: 100-249
Type of Packaging: Consumer, Bulk

3333 Corrin Produce Sales
665 E Dinuba Avenue
Reedley, CA 93654-3533   559-638-3970
     Fax: 559-638-3957 Sharonb@corrin.com
                   www.corrin.com
Grower and exporter of fresh fruit including peaches, plums, nectarines and table grapes; also, raisins
  President: Bob Greiner
  VP Operations: Jim Krause
  Administration: Lisa Macedo
Number Employees: 20-49
Type of Packaging: Bulk

3334 Corsair Pepper Sauce
1110 42nd Avenue
Gulfport, MS 39501-2663   228-452-9238
                   Fax: 228-452-9148
Pickled fruits and vegetables, vegetable sauces and seasonings and salad dressings.
  President: Martha Murphy

Estimated Sales: $120,000
Number Employees: 2

3335 Corsetti's Pasta Products
1001 N Evergreen Ave
Woodbury, NJ 08096-3557   856-853-0999
           Fax: 856-853-7438 800-989-1188
Manufacturer of various pasta products such as lasagna and spaghetti.
  Owner: Dan Pellegrino
  Plant Manager: Michael Corsetti
  Purchasing: Michael Corsetti
Estimated Sales: $2.5-5 Million
Number Employees: 5-9
Type of Packaging: Bulk

3336 Corte Provisions
574 Ferry Street
Newark, NJ 07105-4402   201-653-7246
     Fax: 201-653-2271 leao51@aol.com
                   www.cortesausage.com
Processor of Spanish, Portuguese and Brazilian sausages and serrano-style hams.
Estimated Sales: $2 Million
Number Employees: 10-19
Number of Brands: 6
Number of Products: 20
Sq. footage: 15000
Parent Co: Seabrite Corporation
Type of Packaging: Consumer, Private Label, Bulk
Brands:
  CORTE'S
  EL BATURRO
  EL RICO

3337 Corus Brands
14030 NE 145th St
Woodinville, WA 98072-6994   425-806-2600
           Fax: 425-488-3460 info@corusbrands.com
                   www.corusbrands.com
Producers of various red, white and blush wines.
Estimated Sales: $5-10 Million
Number Employees: 5-9
Brands:
  ALDER RIDGE
  BATTLE CREEK
  SAWTOOTH
  ZEFINA

3338 Cosa de Rio Foods
3701 W Magnolia Ave
Louisville, KY 40211-1635   502-772-2500
           Fax: 502-772-7300 www.cdof.com
Manufactures tortilla products and flatbreads.
  President: Ted Longacre
  Director Operations: Richard Sawyer
Estimated Sales: $25-49.9 Million
Number Employees: 100-249
Type of Packaging: Private Label
Brands:
  CHI-CHI'S

3339 Cosco International
1826 N Lorel Ave
Chicago, IL 60639-4376   773-889-1400
           Fax: 773-889-0854 800-621-4549
                   www.sethnessgreenleaf.com
Manufacturer of flavors.
  President: Patrick Carney
  CFO: Joe Hughes
  Purchasing Agent: Ken Ciukowski
Estimated Sales: $1-$2.5 Million
Number Employees: 20-49
Brands:
  APPLE SIDRA
  COSCO FLAVORS

3340 Cosentino Winery
P.O.Box 2818
Yountville, CA 94599-2818   707-944-1220
           Fax: 707-944-1254 800-764-1220
           finewines@cosentinowinery.com
                   www.cosentinowinery.com
Manufactures fine red and white wines.
  President: Mitch Cosentino
  Marketing Director: Shawn Lutwalla
  Public Relations: Julie Weinstock
Estimated Sales: $5-10 Million
Number Employees: 10-19
Type of Packaging: Private Label

3341 Cosgrove Distributors
120 S Greenwood St
Spring Valley, IL 61362-2014   815-664-4121
                   Fax: 815-663-1433
Wholesaler/distributor of general line products; serving the food service market.
  President: Nora Cosgrove
  Purchasing Manager: Nora Cosgrove
Estimated Sales: $2.5-5 Million
Number Employees: 10-19

3342 Cosmo's Food Products
200 Callegari Dr
West Haven, CT 06516-6234   203-933-9323
           Fax: 203-937-7283 800-933-6766
           claudano@cosmosfoods.com
                   www.cosmosfoods.com
Processor, packer and importer of olives, artichokes, capers, peppers, marinated mushrooms and roasted peppers; also, sun-dried tomatoes, hot cherry peppers, pepperoncini and garlic.
  President: Cosmo Laudano
  VP: Lisa Laudano
  Sales Manager: Mario Laudano
  Production: Peter Merola
  Purchasing: Cosmo Laudano
Estimated Sales: $5-10 Million
Number Employees: 20-49
Number of Products: 39
Sq. footage: 22500
Type of Packaging: Consumer, Food Service, Private Label, Bulk
Brands:
  COSMO'S

3343 Cosmopolitan Foods
138 Essex Avenue
Glen Ridge, NJ 07028-2409   973-680-4560
  President: Nick Ten Velde
  Purchasing Manager: Nick Ten Velde
Number Employees: 5-9

3344 Cossack Caviar
5200 172nd St NE
Arlington, WA 98223-4703   360-435-6600
Processor, importer and exporter of salmon roe for caviar
  President: Gary Shaw
  Secretary: Barbara Estenson
Estimated Sales: $2.5-5 Million
Number Employees: 20-49
Sq. footage: 54000
Type of Packaging: Consumer, Bulk

3345 Costa Deano's Gourmet Foods
PO Box 6367
Canton, OH 44706-0367   330-453-1555
           Fax: 330-453-9766 800-337-2823
Processor and exporter of gourmet pasta sauces in glass jars
  President: Dean Bacopoulos
  VP: Bill Bacopoulos
Number Employees: 5-9
Sq. footage: 15000
Parent Co: Costa Deano's Enterprises
Type of Packaging: Consumer, Food Service, Private Label, Bulk
Brands:
  Costa Deano's

3346 Costa Macaroni Manufacturing
PO Box 32308
Los Angeles, CA 90032-0308
           Fax: 323-225-1667 800-433-7785
           info@costapasta.com www.costapasta.com
Manufacturer of homemade various shapes and sizes of pastas
  VP, Southwest Region: Stephen Zoccoli
  General Sales Manager: Buzz Weisman
Estimated Sales: $5-10 Million
Number Employees: 20-49
Type of Packaging: Food Service, Bulk
Brands:
  COSTA

3347 Costa's Pasta
2045 Attic Pkwy NW
Kennesaw, GA 30152-7610   770-514-8814
           Fax: 770-514-9766 www.costaspasta.com
Fresh pasta
  President: Mary Costa
  CFO: Joe Costa
  Vice President: Stephen Zoccoli
  Sales Director: Stephen Saferite

Estimated Sales: $2.5-5 Million
Number Employees: 5-9
Brands:
   Costa's Pasta

3348 Costadeanos Gourmet Foods
PO Box 6367
Canton, OH 44706-0367   330-453-1555
                              Fax: 330-493-9766
Gourmet foods
   President: Dean Bacopoulos
Estimated Sales: $5-10 Million
Number Employees: 20-49
Sq. footage: 10
Type of Packaging: Private Label
Brands:
   Costadeanos Gourmet

3349 Cotswold Cottage Foods
9820 W 60th Ave
Arvada, CO 80004-4948   303-423-2987
         Fax: 303-423-2987 800-208-1977
                        cotscotfds@aol.com
                 www.marthasuescookies.com
Scone mixes, gingerbread mixes, stuffing mixes,
lemon curd, jams, and tea
   President: Tricia Mackell
Estimated Sales: $300,000-500,000
Number Employees: 5-9
Type of Packaging: Consumer

3350 Cott Beverage
4211 W Boy Scout Boulevard
Suite 290
Tampa, FL 33607-5769   813-313-1800
         Fax: 610-376-1230 888-260-3776
         publicaffairs@cott.com www.cott.com
Carbonated and noncarbonated soft drinks
   President: John Sheppard
   CFO: Charles Linck
   Quality Control: Carie Finch
   Operations Manager: David Winner
   Plant Manager: Joseph Peters
   Purchasing Manager: Paul Kiler
Estimated Sales: $ 110 Million
Number Employees: 300
Number of Brands: 6
Number of Products: 1200
Sq. footage: 500000
Brands:
   Cott

3351 Cott Beverage West
4810 76th Avenue SE
Calgary, AB T2C 2V2
Canada   403-279-6677
                              Fax: 403-279-2260
Processor and exporter of nonalcoholic beverages
   Sales Manager (Western Canada): Lou Pituello
   General Manager: Mark Wiens
Number Employees: 100-249
Parent Co: GH Beverage
Type of Packaging: Consumer, Food Service
Brands:
   Cott
   RC
   Sun Mountain

3352 (HQ)Cott Beverages
4211 W Boy Scout Boulevard
Suite 290
Tampa, FL 33607-5769   813-313-1800
         Fax: 813-313-1811 www.cott.com

Manufacturer of soft drinks and other beverages
   President/CEO: David Bluestein
   Sales: Mike Duffy
   Operation Director: Dave Blood
   Director of Concentrates: Toby Polhamus
   Manufacturing Support Manager: Stanley
   Matthew
Estimated Sales: $20-50 Million
Number Employees: 20-49
Brands:
   American Fare
   Bi-Lo
   Classic Selection
   Delchaup's Select
   Desert Drinx
   Diet Dr. Schnee
   Diet Vess
   Dr. Schnee
   Exclaim
   First In Value
   Food Folks
   Great Buy
   Great Taste
   It's A
   Lady Lee
   Marquee Premium
   Master Choice
   Maxi Cola
   Nature's Classics
   Our Best
   President's Choice
   Private Selection
   Quality Value
   Randalls
   Rite Taste
   Safeway Select
   Sam's American Choice
   Schnuck's
   Smith's
   Vess
   Vess Distilled Water
   Vess Purified Water
   Whistle Orange
   World Classic
   Yes!

**3353 Cott Concentrates/RoyalCrown
Cola International**
P.O.Box 1440
Columbus, GA 31902-1440   706-494-7500
         Fax: 706-571-9189 800-652-5642
                        www.cott.com
Processor of soft drinks
   VP Manufacturing: Mike Wise
   Plant Manager: Toby Polhamus
Estimated Sales: $ 50 - 100 Million
Number Employees: 100-249
Parent Co: Cott Beverages
Type of Packaging: Consumer, Food Service

3354 Cottage Bakery
1831 S Stockton St
Lodi, CA 95240-6302   209-333-8044
         Fax: 209-333-7428 info@cottagebakery.com
                 www.cottagebakery.com
Bakery products
   President: Terry Knutson
Estimated Sales: $20-50 Million
Number Employees: 500-999

3355 Cottage Street Pasta
167 S Main Street
Barre, VT 05641-4813   802-476-4024
                        pastajules@aol.com
Manufactures a variety of fresh pasta and ravioli.
   Purchasing Agent: Karen Gordon
Estimated Sales: $300,000-500,000
Number Employees: 1-4

3356 Cotton Baking Company
4151 Viking Dr
Bossier City, LA 71111-7408   318-747-3168
         Fax: 318-747-0118 800-777-1832
                 www.interstatebakeriescorp.com
Processor of baked products including bread
   Manager: David Amos
   Sales Manager: Slade Cooper
Estimated Sales: $20-50 Million
Number Employees: 20-49
Type of Packaging: Consumer
Brands:
   Holsum Bread
   Wonder Bread

3357 Cottonwood Canyon Vineyards
3940 Dominion Rd
Santa Maria, CA 93454-9678   805-937-8463
   Fax: 805-937-8418 info@cottonwoodcanyon.com
                 www.cottonwoodcanyon.com
Wines
   Proprietor: Norman Beko
   Winemaker: Norman Beko
Estimated Sales: $1-2.5 Million
Number Employees: 5-9
Brands:
   Cottonwood Canyon

3358 Cottonwood Canyon Winery
3940 Dominion Rd
Santa Maria, CA 93454-9678   805-937-8463
   Fax: 805-937-8418 info@cottonwoodcanyon.com
                 www.cottonwoodcanyon.com
Wine
   Owner/Winemaker: Norman Beko
   VP: Stephen Beko
Estimated Sales: $1-2.5 Million
Number Employees: 5-9
Number of Products: 24
Brands:
   Cottonwood Canyon

3359 Couch's Country Style Sausages
4750 Osborn Rd
Cleveland, OH 44128-3184   216-587-2333
                              Fax: 216-663-3311
Processor of sausage including pork, beef and turkey
   President: Ludie Couch
   Manager: Stanley Redd
Estimated Sales: $500,000-$1 Million
Number Employees: 5-9
Sq. footage: 3500
Type of Packaging: Consumer, Bulk

3360 Couch's Original Sauce
5323 E Nettleton Ave
Jonesboro, AR 72401-6650   870-932-0710
         Fax: 870-910-0619 800-264-7535
                 www.couchsbbq.com
Processor of barbecue sauce
   Chairman: Beth Couch
   General Manager: Sharon Spurlock
Estimated Sales: $ .5 - 1 million
Number Employees: 20-49
Sq. footage: 6200
Brands:
   Couch's Original

**3361 Cougar Mountain Baking
Company**
4224 24th Ave W
Seattle, WA 98199-1216   206-467-5044
                              Fax: 206-467-0993
                 comments@cougar-mountain.com
                        www.cmbc.com
Producers of bakery products.
   Owner: David Saulnier
   Marketing/Sales: David Saulnier
   Customer Service: Dana Pantley
Estimated Sales: $300,000-500,000
Number Employees: 5-9
Brands:
   COUGAR MOUNTAIN

3362 Country - Fed - Meats Company
633 Roberts Drive
Riverdale, GA 30274-2913   770-991-5888
         Fax: 770-991-0469 800-637-7559
Meat
   CEO: Harry Peaden, Jr.

3363 Country Bob's
P.O.Box 706
Centralia, IL 62801-9111   618-533-2375
         Fax: 618-533-7828 800-373-2140
                 www.countrybobs.com
Producers of sauces and seasonings.
   President: Terry Edson
Estimated Sales: $2.5-5 Million
Number Employees: 10-19

3364 Country Butcher Shop
524 E Water St
Palmyra, MO 63461-1758   573-769-2257
         Fax: 573-769-4652 edent@socket.net
                 www.tendersticks.com

Processor and distributor of lamb, beef and pork.
President: Edward Dent
Purchasing Agent: Edward Dent
Estimated Sales: $10-20 Million
Number Employees: 5-9
Type of Packaging: Private Label

3365 Country Choice Naturals
9531 W 78th St # 230
Eden Prairie, MN 55344-8000   952-829-8824
Fax: 952-833-2090
www.countrychoiceorganic.com
Manufacturer of organic hot cereals, cookies and
cocoas.
President: Chuck Endersen
Number of Brands: 1
Number of Products: 35
Type of Packaging: Consumer
Brands:
COUNTRY CHOICE

3366 Country Club Bakery
1211 Country Club Rd
Fairmont, WV 26554-2318   304-363-5690
Fax: 304-363-6099   pallotajcp2@aol.com
Processor of bread, sandwich rolls, hoagie buns and
pepperoni rolls
Owner: Chris Pallotta
Owner: Chris Pallotta
Estimated Sales: $5-10 Million
Number Employees: 5-9
Type of Packaging: Consumer, Food Service

3367 Country Clubs Famous Desserts
83 Bustleton Pike
Langhorne, PA 19053-6465   215-322-0700
Fax: 215-322-1534   800-843-2253
Desserts
Owner: Brian Rothaus
VP Sales: Bruce Davidsen
Estimated Sales: $20-50 Million
Number Employees: 50-99

3368 Country Cupboard
P.O.Box 673
Virginia City, NV 89440-0673   775-847-7300
Fax: 775-847-7722   beanman01@aol.com
www.countrycupboard.com
Processor of dehydrated soups, pastas, rices, sauces,
relish, jams, beans, sugar-free chocolates, cornbread,
honey and salsa, among other products.
Owner: Beverly Cowan
Estimated Sales: $5-10 Million
Number Employees: 5-9

3369 Country Delight Farms
P.O.Box 25210
Nashville, TN 37202-5210   615-320-1440
Fax: 615-329-3017
Dairy products
Marketing Director: Jim Greaving
Public Relations: Royce McClintock
Operations Manager: Charles Hilton
Plant Manager: Rodney Hillis
Estimated Sales: $25-49.9 Million
Number Employees: 100-249
Brands:
Country Delight

3370 Country Delite
P.O.Box 25210
Nashville, TN 37202-5210   615-320-1440
Fax: 615-329-3017
Milk
Director: Suzie Lusk
Plant Manager: Rodney Hillis
Estimated Sales: $ 50 - 100 Million
Number Employees: 100-249
Parent Co: Suiza Dairy Group
Type of Packaging: Bulk
Brands:
Country Delite

3371 Country Estate Pecans
PO Box 7
Sahuarita, AZ 85629-0007   520-791-2062
Fax: 520-629-0119   800-473-2267
sales@pecans.com   www.pecans.com
Pecans, snacks
President: Liz Alexander
General Manager: DeWayne McCasland
Estimated Sales: $ 20 - 50 Million
Number Employees: 250-499
Parent Co: Fermers Investment

Type of Packaging: Private Label

3372 Country Foods
P.O.Box 571
Polson, MT 59860-0571   406-883-4384
Fax: 406-883-3275 www.countrypasta.com
Manufacturers of pasta.
President: Fred Kellogg
Vice President: Linda Knutson
Marketing Director: Dan Johnson
Operations Manager: Gary Ivory
Estimated Sales: $2.5-5 Million
Number Employees: 20-49
Type of Packaging: Private Label
Brands:
COUNTRY PASTA

3373 Country Fresh
31700 Enterprise Dr
Livonia, MI 48150   734-261-7980
Fax: 734-261-2633   800-968-7980
Manufacturer of milk.
Manager: Jerry Shannon
Purchasing Agent: Bruce Evans
Estimated Sales: $100+ Million
Number Employees: 100-249
Parent Co: Suiza Dairy Group

3374 Country Fresh
2555 Buchanan Ave SW
Grand Rapids, MI 49548-1091   616-243-0173
Fax: 616-954-2813   800-748-0480
www.deanfoods.com
Processor of dairy products including ice cream, yo-
gurt, sour cream, cottage cheese and milk
CEO: Gregg Engles
EVP/CFO: Jack Callahan Jr
VP: Pete Reynolds
Estimated Sales: $ 10 - 20 Million
Number Employees: 250-499
Parent Co: Suiza Dairy Group
Type of Packaging: Consumer, Food Service, Pri-
vate Label
Brands:
Country Fresh

3375 (HQ)Country Fresh Farms
432 W 3440 S
Salt Lake City, UT 84115-4228   801-266-1783
Fax: 801-269-9666   800-878-0099
www.countryfreshfarms.com
Producers of whey drinks, dairy products and dry
mixes.
Owner: Jackuie Augason
Estimated Sales: $10 Million
Number Employees: 5-9
Sq. footage: 10600
Type of Packaging: Consumer, Food Service, Pri-
vate Label, Bulk
Brands:
COUNTRY FRESH FARMS
SWISS WHEY D'LITE

**3376 Country Fresh Food &
Confections**
P.O.Box 604
Oliver Springs, TN 37840-0604   865-435-2655
Fax: 865-435-1930   800-545-8782
info@countryfreshfood.com
www.countryfreshfood.com
Manufacturer of Country Fresh Fudge, regular &
sugar-free, Pamela Ann Classic Confections, Jim
Bean Fudge, Kahula Fudge, Papa Joe's Downhome
Gourmet.
President: Edward Stockton
Estimated Sales: $1-2.5 Million
Number Employees: 20-49
Number of Brands: 6
Number of Products: 150
Sq. footage: 8000
Type of Packaging: Consumer, Food Service, Pri-
vate Label, Bulk
Brands:
Country Fresh
Country Fresh Fudge
Papa Joe's Downhome

3377 Country Fresh Golden Valley
31770 Enterprise Dr
Livonia, MI 48150-1960   734-261-7980
Fax: 734-261-1049
Manufacturer of fluid and frozen milk
President: Jerry Shannon
Plant Manager: Ken Andrews

Estimated Sales: $50-100 Million
Number Employees: 100-249
Type of Packaging: Consumer, Food Service, Pri-
vate Label, Bulk
Brands:
Burger
Country Fresh
Frost Bite
McDonald's

3378 Country Fresh Mushrooms
P.O.Box 489
Avondale, PA 19311-0489   610-268-3033
Fax: 610-268-0479
www.countryfreshmushrooms.com
Processor of mushrooms including exotic, fresh,
processed, whole and sliced.
President: Mickey Brosius
Purchasing Manager: Ed Sourney
Estimated Sales: $20-50 Million
Number Employees: 100-249
Sq. footage: 30750
Type of Packaging: Consumer, Food Service, Pri-
vate Label, Bulk
Brands:
COUNTRY FRESH

3379 Country Harbor Sea Farms
RR 1
Country Harbor, NS B0H 1J0
Canada   902-387-2364
Fax: 902-387-2526
Processor and exporter of mussels
President: Bruce Hancock
Number Employees: 5-9
Type of Packaging: Bulk

3380 Country Hearth Bread
855 Scott St
Murfreesboro, TN 37129-2735   615-893-6041
Fax: 615-893-1463
Bread
Manager: Rick Hardesty
Manager: Ray Ping
Estimated Sales: $20-50 Million
Number Employees: 100-249

3381 Country Home Bakers
21100 S Western Avenue
Torrance, CA 90501-1700   310-533-6010
Fax: 310-328-2608   800-672-6277
www.countryhomebakers.com
Processor of bread, cookies and fruit pies
President: Judith Borck
G.M.: Jesse Rodriguez
Vice President: Doris Zelinsky
Research & Development: Bob Tetrault
Quality Control: George Rupp
Marketing Director: Katy Callahan
VP Operations: Kevin McDonough
Purchasing Manager: Dick Warren
Estimated Sales: $10-20 Million
Number Employees: 100-249
Parent Co: Country Home Bakers
Type of Packaging: Consumer, Food Service, Pri-
vate Label, Bulk
Brands:
Jessie Lord
Readi Bake
Sanders

3382 Country Home Bakers
720 Metropolitan Pkwy SW
Atlanta, GA 30310-2000   404-758-5581
Fax: 404-527-6690   800-241-6445
Processor of frozen dough including danish, dough-
nut, roll and cookie and frozen bread dough includ-
ing jalapeno/cheese, salsa,
spinach/mushroom/cheese, vegetable, focaccia, etc.;
also, frozen baked and unbaked pies, frozen
cakestoppings, ice cream and candy
President: Judith L Borck
Manager: Kevin McDonough
Senior VP: V Wolczek
COO: Doris Zelinsky
Regional Sales Manager: Jim Rasmussen
General Manager: Roy Lowery
Plant Manager: Mike Harvison
Estimated Sales: $20-50 Million
Number Employees: 100-249
Sq. footage: 80000
Parent Co: Borck's Country Home Bakery
Type of Packaging: Consumer, Food Service, Pri-
vate Label, Bulk

Other Locations:
    Country Home Bakers
    Highland Park MI
Brands:
    Chop Block Breads
    Country Home Bakers
    Jessie Lord, Inc.
    Sanders
    Warme Bakker

3383 Country Home Creations
P.O.Box 126
Goodrich, MI 48438-0126   810-244-7348
        Fax: 810-244-5348   800-457-3477
    chcdips@countryhomecreations.com
    www.countryhomecreations.com
Processor and exporter of mixes including cheese-
cake, cookie, dip and soup.
    Owner: Shirley Kautman Jones
Estimated Sales:$-5 Million
Number Employees: 20-49
Sq. footage: 10000
Type of Packaging: Consumer, Private Label
Brands:
    CAMP MIXES
    CLASSIC COUNTRY
    COUNTRY HOME CREATIONS
    GINGER KIDS
    MY MOM'S MIXES
    PERFECT PARTY MIXES

3384 Country Life
180 Motor Pkwy
Hauppauge, NY 11788-5175   631-232-5400
        Fax: 631-231-2331   800-645-5768
    info@country-life.com www.country-life.com
    CEO: Halbert Drexler
Estimated Sales:$ 10 - 20 Million
Number Employees: 100-249
Brands:
    BIOCHEM
    COUNTRY LIFE
    IRON-TEK
    LONG LIFE BEVERAGES
    NATURAL PERSONAL CARE

3385 Country Maid
1919 S Kinnickinnic Ave
Milwaukee, WI 53204-4000   414-383-3970
        Fax: 414-383-9809   800-628-4354
        www.countrymaid.com
Processor of refrigerated salads, entrees and desserts
    President: Wayne Becker
    CEO: Jane Rodebaugh
    CFO: John Plotkin
Estimated Sales:$6-10 Million
Number Employees: 50-99
Sq. footage: 40000
Type of Packaging: Consumer, Food Service, Pri-
vate Label
Brands:
    Country Maid

3386 Country Pies
PO Box 255
Coombs, BC V0R 1M0
Canada
                    250-248-6415
        Fax: 250-248-4590
Processor of frozen meat pies including pork,
cornish, steak/kidney, steak/onion, steak/mushroom
and chicken/vegetable; also, sausage rolls
    President: Brian Forseth
    CEO: Brian Forseth
    Marketing Director: Brian Forseth
Type of Packaging: Bulk
Brands:
    Country Pies

3387 Country Pure Foods
681 W Waterloo Rd
Akron, OH 44314-1547   330-753-2293
    Fax: 330-745-7838 www.countrypurefoods.com
Manufacturer of juices
    President: Raymond Lee
    CEO: Tom Kolb
    Quality Control: Susan Woods
    Marketing Director: Joe Koch
    Sales Director: Jon Hanley
    Sr VP Operations: Paul Sukalich
*Estimated Sales:*I
Number Employees: 250-499
Type of Packaging: Consumer, Food Service, Pri-
vate Label

Other Locations:
    Ellington CT
    Deland FL
Brands:
    ARDMORE FARMS

3388 Country Pure Foods
58 West Rd
Ellington, CT 06029-4200   860-872-8346
    Fax: 860-875-6539 www.countrypurefoods.com
Manufacturer and exporter of fruit drinks, bottled
spring water and juices including apple, orange,
grape and pineapple
    President/CEO: Ray Lee
    VP: Jon Hanley
Estimated Sales:$50-100 Million
Number Employees: 100-249
Sq. footage: 80000
Parent Co: Country Pure Foods
Type of Packaging: Consumer, Food Service, Pri-
vate Label
Brands:
    GLACIER VALLEY
    NATURAL COUNTRY
    SUNFLO
    SUNNY LEA

3389 (HQ)Country Pure Foods
681 W Waterloo Rd
Akron, OH 44314-1547   330-753-2293
        Fax: 330-745-7838   877-995-8423
        www.countrypurefoods.com
Processor of fruit juices, drinks and nectars for food
service and retail
    President: Ray Lee
    CEO: Ricardo Alvarez
    CFO: Tom Kolb
    Vice President: Rick Conrad
    Quality Control: Jeff Ross
    Marketing Director: Joe Koch
    Sales Director: Rick Conrad
    Public Relations: Janet Dye
    Operations Manager: Paul Sukalich
    Plant Manager: Tim Hunter
    Purchasing Manager: Dan Goric
*Estimated Sales:*I
Number Employees: 250-499
Number of Brands: 3
Number of Products: 500
Sq. footage: 111000
Type of Packaging: Consumer, Food Service, Pri-
vate Label
Other Locations:
    Country Pure Foods
    Deland FL
    Country Pure Foods
    Ellington CT
Brands:
    Ardmore Farms Grove
    Glacier Valley
    Natural Country

3390 Country Smoked Meats
PO Box 171
Bowling Green, OH 43402-0171   419-353-0783
        Fax: 419-352-7330   800-321-4766
Processor and exporter of chunked, sliced and deli
style Canadian bacon, smoked sausage, pork loins,
hocks, turkey parts and ham, pepperoni, bratwurst,
kielbasa, chorizos, egg and muffin sandwiches, fresh
link sausage and freshboneless pork loins and ten
    National Sales Manager: Bruce Schroeder
Estimated Sales:$2.5-5 Million
Number Employees: 20-49
Sq. footage: 21000
Type of Packaging: Consumer, Food Service, Private Label, Bulk

3391 Country Village Meats
401 N Pennsylvania St
Sublette, IL 61367-9400   815-849-5532
Processor of beef, pork, lamb, veal, sausage, hot
dogs, etc.; slaughtering services available
    Owner: Edward Morrissey
    Co-Owner: Edward Morrissey
Estimated Sales:$1-2.5 Million
Number Employees: 1-4
Type of Packaging: Consumer, Bulk

3392 Counts Sausage Company
P.O.Box 390
Prosperity, SC 29127-0390   803-364-2392
        Fax: 803-364-1570

Processor and wholesaler/distributor of pork and
beef products; serving the food service market
    President: Jimmy Counts
Estimated Sales:$20-50 Million
Number Employees: 20-49
Type of Packaging: Consumer, Food Service, Bulk

3393 County Gourmet Foods, LLC
751 Chestnut Road
Sewickley, PA 15143-1143   412-741-8902
        Fax: 412-741-9176 www.wolfganpucksoup.com
Gourmet foods
    Quality Control: Thomas MacMurray, Ph.D.

3394 Coupla Guys Foods
401 N Racine Ave
Chicago, IL 60642-5839   312-829-2332
        Fax: 312-829-8866 ute@couplaguys.com
        www.couplaguys.com
Manufacturer of pasta sauces including: sesame;
arrabiata; puttanesca; tapenade; buoy base; marinara; and creme de la crimini sauce.
    General Manager: Joe Rowley
    Sales Manager: Ute Rowley
    Sales Representative: Rob Ryan
Type of Packaging: Food Service

3395 Coutts Specialty Foods
1190 Liberty Square Road
Boxborough, MA 01719-1115   978-263-2952
        Fax: 978-263-2953   800-919-2952
        csf@couttsspecialtyfoods.com
        www.couttsspecialtyfoods.com
Mother's Prize - sweet red pepper, hot sweet red
pepper, corn, picclilli relishes, apple butter, and
applesauce (with and with no sugar). No preserva-
tives or fillers are added to any of our products.
Mother's Pure Preserves - jamsjellies, and marma-
lades
    President: Alison Coutts Chateawneuf
Estimated Sales:$ 3 - 5 Million
Number Employees: 2
Number of Brands: 2
Number of Products: 38
Type of Packaging: Consumer, Food Service
Brands:
    MOTHER'S PRIZE
    MOTHER'S PURE PRESERVES

3396 Couture Farms
P.O.Box 569
Kettleman City, CA 93230-0569   559-945-2226
        Fax: 559-945-2936 cfhuron@aol.com
Processor and importer of asparagus, pistachios and
mixed melons
    Co-Partner: Steve Couture
    Co-Partner: Christina Couture
Estimated Sales:$50-100 Million
Number Employees: 20-49
Sq. footage: 30000
Type of Packaging: Consumer, Food Service, Pri-
vate Label, Bulk

3397 Couture's Maple Shop
560 Vt Rte 100
Westfield, VT 05874-9791   802-744-2733
        Fax: 802-744-6275   800-845-2733
        jcouture@together.net
        www.maplesyrupvermont.com
Maple syrup and candy
    Co-Owner: Jacques Couture
    Co-Owner: Pauline Couture
Estimated Sales:$ 1 - 3 Million
Number Employees: 1-4

3398 Covemaker Packing Company
5109 27th Avenue
Moline, IL 61265-5609   309-764-1480
Processor of beef, pork and poultry
    President: Sylvia Ferguson
Estimated Sales:$1-2.5 Million
Number Employees: 1-4
Type of Packaging: Consumer, Food Service

**3399 Covered Bridge Potato Chip
Company**
35 Alwright Ct
Waterville, NB E7P 0A5   506-375-2447
        Fax: 506-375-2448
        info@coveredbridgechips.com
        www.coveredbridgechips.com

Old fashioned kettle style potato chips
Marketing Manager/Customer Relations: Krysten Scott
Production: Mike McCartney
Estimated Sales: $2 Million
Number Employees: 14

3400 Cow Girl Creamery
P.O.Box 594
Point Reyes Sta, CA 94956-0594   415-663-8153
Fax: 415-663-5418 www.cowgirlcreamery.com
Manufacturers of cheese.
President: Sue Conley
Estimated Sales: $500,000-$1 Million
Number Employees: 20-49
Type of Packaging: Private Label
Brands:
COWGIRL CREAMERY

3401 Cow Palace Too
1631 N Liberty Rd
Granger, WA 98932-9713   509-829-5777
Fax: 509-829-5495 cowpal@dolsenco.com
Processor of milk
Manager: Jeff Boivin
Estimated Sales: $20-50 Million
Number Employees: 50-99
Type of Packaging: Consumer, Food Service
Brands:
Dairy Gold

3402 Cowart Seafood Corporation
755 Lake Landing Dr
Lottsburg, VA 22511-2503   804-529-6101
Fax: 804-529-7374
Manufacturer of seafood including fresh, frozen, and breaded oysters, frozen softshell crabs, and canned herring roe
President: Samuel Cowart
VP: Lake Cowart Jr
Estimated Sales: $10-20 Million
Number Employees: 50-99
Sq. footage: 10000
Type of Packaging: Food Service, Private Label
Brands:
CHESAPEAKE PRIDE
MANNINGS
SEA MIST

3403 Cowboy Caviar
169 Fairlawn Drive
Berkeley, CA 94708-2107   510-594-8051
Fax: 510-594-8058 877-509-1796
cowboycaviar@earthlink.net
Processor of spreads and chunky marinara sauces
President: Gary Forbes
Estimated Sales: $1-2.5 Million
Number Employees: 1-4
Type of Packaging: Private Label

3404 Cowboy Foods
770 Canyon View Road
Bozeman, MT 59715-1610   406-587-5489
Fax: 406-522-9337 800-759-5489
hucklebuddy@hotmail.com
Processor of natural barley without hulls; also, barbecue and bean sauces, bean soups, pancake, bread and baking mixes, flours, cereals and whole grains
Co-Owner: Jean Clem
Co-Owner: Bud Clem
Estimated Sales: $ 1 - 3 Million
Number Employees: 1-4
Number of Products: 30
Sq. footage: 2800
Type of Packaging: Consumer, Food Service, Bulk
Brands:
Cowboy Foods

3405 Cowgirl Chocolates
P.O.Box 8961
Moscow, ID 83843-1461   208-882-4098
Fax: 208-882-0265 888-882-4098
cowgirl@moscow.com
www.cowgirlchocolates.com
Manufacturers of chocolate candies.
Manager: Marilyn Coates
Estimated Sales: $ .5 - 1 million
Number Employees: 5-9
Brands:
COWGIRL CHOCOLATES

3406 Cowie Wine Cellars
101 N Carbon City Rd
Paris, AR 72855-4630   479-963-3990
Fax: 479-963-3990
bettekay@cowiewinecellars.com
www.cowiewinecellars.com
Wines
President: Robert Cowie
Sales Room Manager: Katie Cowie
Estimated Sales: Less than $50,000
Number Employees: 1-4
Brands:
COWIE

3407 Cozy Harbor Seafood
P.O.Box 389
Portland, ME 04112-0389   207-879-2665
Fax: 207-879-2666 800-225-2586
jnorton@cozyharbor.com   www.cozyharbor.com
Buys, processes and distributes premium quality seafood products
President/CEO: John Norton
Operations VP: Joseph Donovan Norton
Estimated Sales: $ .5 - 1 million
Number Employees: 100-249
Type of Packaging: Consumer, Food Service, Bulk

3408 Crab King Seafood Specialties
PO Box 99350
Seattle, WA 98139-0350   206-283-2722
Fax: 206-283-0253
Processor, importer and exporter of frozen fish and seafood
President: Norm Ursin
Estimated Sales: $ 1 - 3 Million
Number Employees: 1-4
Type of Packaging: Consumer, Food Service, Bulk
Brands:
Alaska Captain
Ursin

3409 Crab Quarters
2909 Eastern Blvd
Baltimore, MD 21220-2870   410-686-2222
Fax: 410-686-0343
President: James Myrick
Estimated Sales: $ 1 - 3 Million
Number Employees: 20-49

3410 Craby's Fish Market
303 S Black Horse Pike
Blackwood, NJ 08012-2893   856-227-9743
Seafood
Manager: Stephen Palo
Estimated Sales: Less than $500,000
Number Employees: 1-4

3411 Crain Ranch
10660 Bryne Ave
Los Molinos, CA 96055-9560   530-527-1077
Fax: 530-529-4143 crainranch@snowcrest.net
www.crainranch.com
Processor, grower and exporter of walnuts in the shell. Also packs for domestic markets
Partner: C Crain
Partner: W Crain
Estimated Sales: $300,000-500,000
Number Employees: 20-49
Sq. footage: 80000
Type of Packaging: Consumer, Private Label, Bulk
Brands:
Crain Ranch

3412 Cranberry Isles Fisherman's Cooperative
P.O.Box 258
Islesford, ME 04646-0258   207-244-5438
Fax: 207-244-9479
Manager: Mark Neighman
Estimated Sales: $ .5 - 1 million
Number Employees: 1-4

3413 Cranberry Products
703 W Pine Street
Eagle River, WI 54521-9336   715-479-4466
Fax: 715-479-6371
Manufacturer of cranberry products
President: Mark Goldsworthy
Estimated Sales: $890,000
Number Employees: 10

3414 Cranberry Sweets Company
1005 Newmark Ave
Coos Bay, OR 97420-3102   541-888-9824
Fax: 541-888-2824 cranberrysweets@att.net
www.cranberrysweetsandmore.com
Manufacturers of cranberries, jellies and candies.
Owner: Clayton Shaw
Estimated Sales: $1-2.5 Million
Number Employees: 20-49
Brands:
CRANBERRY SWEETS
OREGON BERRIES
SWEET BASICS

3415 Crane & Crane
P.O.Box 277
Brewster, WA 98812-0277   509-689-3447
Fax: 509-689-2214 www.cranefamilyorchards.com
Grower and exporter of apples and pears
President: Bob Brammer
CFO/President: Bob Brammer
Secretary: Sam McKee
Estimated Sales: $100+ Million
Number Employees: 250-499
Type of Packaging: Consumer, Food Service, Private Label, Bulk
Brands:
Crane's Aqua Line
Crane's Blue Line
Crane's Gray Line
Crane's Maroon Line
Crane's Red Line

3416 Crane's Pie Pantry Restaurant
6054 124th Ave
Fennville, MI 49408-9440   269-561-2297
Fax: 269-561-5545 pies@cranespiepantry.com
www.cranespiepantry.com
Pies
Owner: Beckey Crane-Hagger
Owner: Lue Crane
Co-Owner: Lue Crane
Winemaker: Rob Crane
Estimated Sales: $500,000-$1 Million
Number Employees: 20-49

3417 Crater Meat Packing Company
2811 Biddle Rd
Medford, OR 97504-4114   541-772-6966
Processor of meat products
Owner: James Cearley
Estimated Sales: Less than $100,000
Number Employees: 1-4
Type of Packaging: Consumer
Brands:
Crater's Meats

3418 Crave Natural Foods
104 Main St
Northampton, MA 01060-3160   413-587-7999
comments@craveorganic.com
www.craveorganic.com
Processor of nondairy whipped cream, dressings, ice cream and cheese sauce
Owner: Sally A Conway
Number Employees: 1-4
Sq. footage: 400
Type of Packaging: Consumer

3419 Craven Crab Company
PO Box 3321
New Bern, NC 28564-3321   252-637-3562
Fax: 252-637-3562
Crab
President: Gaston Fulcher
Brands:
Craven Crab

3420 Crawford Sausage Company
2310 S Pulaski Rd
Chicago, IL 60623-3098   773-277-3095
Fax: 773-277-7749 866-653-2479
csjudy@crawfordsausage.com
www.crawfordsausage.com
Bratwursts, frankfurters, polish sausage, other linked sausage, slicing lunchmeats, fresh sausages, smoked meats and gift boxes.
President: John Zicha
Estimated Sales: $5-10 Million
Number Employees: 20-49
Type of Packaging: Consumer, Food Service, Bulk
Brands:
Daisy Brand Meat Products

3421 Crazy Jerry's
P.O.Box 891
Roswell, GA 30077-0891   770-993-0651
    Fax: 770-993-8201   info@crazyjerrysinc.com
      www.crazyjerrysinc.com
Processor of sauces, can mixed nuts, garlic mushrooms, maters in spicy vermouth, stuffed olives, can beef stew, soup mix and gumbo mix
    President: Jerry Gualtieri
Estimated Sales: $1 Million
Number Employees: 1-4
Type of Packaging: Private Label
Brands:
    Crazy Jerry's

3422 Crazy Mary's
321 138th Street S
Tacoma, WA 98444-4749   253-536-8690
      bozenverry@aol.com
      www.flavor2die4.com

3423 CreAgri
25565 Whitesell St
Hayward, CA 94545-3614   510-732-6478
    Fax: 510-732-6493   info@supremooil.com
      www.creagri.com
Extra virgin olive oil
    Founder/Chairman: Roberto Crea
Estimated Sales: $1 Million
Number Employees: 5-9
Type of Packaging: Consumer, Food Service, Bulk
Brands:
    Integrale
    Supremo

3424 CreaFill Fibers Corporation
10200 Worton Rd
Chestertown, MD 21620-3545   410-810-0779
    Fax: 410-810-0793   800-832-4662
      www.creafill.com
Processor and exporter of powdered cellulose and pure vegetable fibers
    President: Paolo Fezzi
    Sales Associate: Sara Emgland
Estimated Sales: $10-20 Million
Number Employees: 20-49
Type of Packaging: Bulk
Brands:
    QC FIBERS
    SC FIBERS

3425 Cream O'Weaver Dairy
4282 W 1730 S
Salt Lake City, UT 84104-4805   801-973-9922
    Fax: 801-977-5073   www.creamoweber.com
Processor of buttermilk and milk including whole, 1% and 2%; wholesaler/distributor of cottage cheese, yogurt, ice cream and butter
    Marketing: Dave Gardner
    Plant Manager: Walt Kohl
Estimated Sales: $50-99.9 Million
Number Employees: 100-249
Parent Co: Dean Foods Company
Type of Packaging: Consumer, Food Service

3426 Cream of the West
P.O.Box 2909
Harlowton, MT 59036-2909   406-632-4804
      800-477-2383
cotw@mtintouch.net   www.creamofthewest.com
Company products line includes cereals, pancake mixes, jams and jellies, honey, coffee and gift baskets.
    Manager: Freida Robertson
Estimated Sales: $1-2.5 Million
Number Employees: 1-4
Sq. footage: 6000
Type of Packaging: Consumer, Food Service, Bulk
Brands:
    CREAM OF THE WEST

3427 Creamland Dairies
P.O.Box 25067
Albuquerque, NM 87125-0067   505-247-0721
      Fax: 505-246-9696
      connie_holdren@deanfoods.com
      www.creamland.com
Manufacturer of dairy products including ice cream, milk, cultured, cottage cheese, sour cream and dips.
    CEO: Howard Miller
    Public Relations: Connie Holdren
Number Employees: 20-49
Parent Co: Dean Foods Company

Type of Packaging: Consumer
Brands:
    CREAMLAND
    DEAN'S

3428 Creative Bakers
242 S 1st Street
Brooklyn, NY 11211-4503   718-384-5312
    Fax: 718-387-5337   800-247-7864
      info@brooklyncheesecake.com
      www.brooklyncheesecake.com
Processor and exporter of cheesecake
    President: Ron Schutte
Estimated Sales: $5-10 Million
Number Employees: 1-4
Sq. footage: 18000
Type of Packaging: Consumer, Food Service
Brands:
    Cheezecake

3429 Creative Confections
945 Bermuda Dunes Pl
Northbrook, IL 60062-3125   847-291-4128
      alicia@creativeconfections.net
      www.creativeconfections.com
Processor of gourmet candy including chocolate and English toffee
    President: Alicia Russell
Estimated Sales: $ 1 - 3 Million
Number Employees: 5-9
Type of Packaging: Consumer
Brands:
    Creative Confections

3430 Creative Flavors
P.O.Box 23307
Chagrin Falls, OH 44023-0307   440-543-9881
    Fax: 440-543-8707   800-848-9043
      info@creativeflavorsinc.com
      www.creativeflavorsinc.com
Flavors and ingredients for the dairy industry including cherries, flavors and core powders for novelty bars and sour cream dip bases
    President: Michael Ramsey
    Public Relations: Cindy Ramsey
Estimated Sales: $2.5-5 Million
Number Employees: 5-9

3431 Creative Flavors & Specialties LLP
991 E Linden Avenue
Linden, NJ 07036-2416   908-862-4678
    Fax: 908-862-7458   creativeflavors@aol.com
Manufacturer of flavors for coffee, candy, fruit drinks, bagels, ice cream, ice tea, coffee syrups, snack seasonings, spices and much more. We also customize any flavors, spray drieds and blending
    President: Esther Baita
    CEO: Mike DiPierro
    VP: Danielle Lau
    Quality Control: Esther Baita
    Production: Fredy Lau
    Plant Manager: Fredy Lau
Estimated Sales: $100,000
Number Employees: 5
Number of Products: 5000
Sq. footage: 5000
Type of Packaging: Bulk

3432 Creative Foods
P.O.Box 368
Osceola, AR 72370-0368   870-563-2601
    Fax: 870-563-3824   800-643-0006
      manderson@creativefoodsllc.com
      www.creativefoodsllc.com
Margarine, cheese, salsa
    President: Mart Massey
    CFO: Jason Collard
    Executive VP: Mike Anderson
    Executive VP: Mike Anderson
    VP Sales: Mike Anderson
Estimated Sales: $100+ Million
Number Employees: 100-249
Brands:
    Creative Foods

3433 Creative Foodworks
1011 S Acme Rd
San Antonio, TX 78237-3218   210-212-4761
      Fax: 210-212-4919

Manufacturer of private label condiments
    President: Dorothea Garcia
    CEO: Roqke Garcia, Jr.
    Quality Control: Michael Billings
    Operations Manager: Emilio Herrera
    Plant Manager: Norman Diggec
    Purchasing Manager: Chris Boynton
Estimated Sales: $5-10 Million
Number Employees: 10-19
Type of Packaging: Consumer, Food Service, Private Label, Bulk

3434 Creative Seasonings
34 Audubon Road
Wakefield, MA 01880-1203   617-246-1461
    Fax: 617-246-5381   www.conagrafoods.com
Seasonings
    President/CEO: Greg Heckman
    CEO: Gary Rodkin

3435 Creative Spices
33436 Western Avenue
Union City, CA 94587-3202   510-471-4956
      Fax: 510-471-9174
Bread and bakery products
    President: Carmella Hagman
    Treasurer: Virginia Holmes
    VP: Donna Hagman
Estimated Sales: $10-24.9 Million
Number Employees: 20-49
Brands:
    Creative Spices

3436 Creekside Mushrooms
1 Moonlight Dr
Worthington, PA 16262-9730   724-297-5491
      Fax: 724-297-5101
      mailbox@creeksidemushrooms.com
      www.creeksidemushrooms.com
Manufacturer of fresh mushrooms
    Chief Executive: Roger Claypoole
    VP: Dan Lucovich
Estimated Sales: $99 Million
Number Employees: 500-999
Sq. footage: 375000
Type of Packaging: Consumer, Food Service, Private Label, Bulk
Brands:
    MOONLIGHT MUSHROOMS

3437 Creemore Springs Brewery
PO Box 369
Creemore, ON L0M 1G0
Canada   705-466-2240
    Fax: 705-466-3306   800-267-2240
      thefolks@creemoresprings.com
      www.creemoresprings.com
Processor of lager beer
    President/CEO: Peter Amirault
    VP: Kurtis Zeng
    VP Marketing: Karen Gautin
Number Employees: 20-49
Type of Packaging: Consumer, Food Service
Brands:
    Creemore Springs Premium Lager
    Creemore Springs Urbock

3438 Creighton Brothers
P.O.Box 220
Atwood, IN 46502-0220   574-267-3101
    Fax: 574-267-6446   brianhayward@cb-cl.com
      www.cb-cl.com
Processor of fresh, frozen and hard cooked eggs
    President: Ron Pruex
    Quality Assurance: Tad Borchers
    Sales Manager: Brian Hayward
    Public Relations: Mindy Creighton
    Plant Manager: Bill Kelly
Estimated Sales: $20,800,000
Number Employees: 10-19
Type of Packaging: Consumer, Food Service, Private Label, Bulk
Brands:
    Good News Eggs
    Grandpa's Choice

3439 Creme Curls Bakery
P.O.Box 276
Hudsonville, MI 49426-0276   616-669-6230
    Fax: 616-669-2468   800-466-1219
      www.cremecurls.com

Processor of puff pastries, eclairs, seafoam candy, cream puffs, turnovers, strudels, bread cones, creme horns and puffs and frozen pie dough
President: Gary Bierling
CFO: Lees Geboer
CFO: Lee W Deboer
Quality Control: Paul Bierling
Sales Manager: Jerry Veldkamp
Plant Manager: Gary Bierling
Estimated Sales: $20-50 Million
Number Employees: 100-249
Sq. footage: 57000
Type of Packaging: Consumer, Food Service, Private Label, Bulk
Brands:
Creme Curls

3440 Creme D'Lite
7411 Hines Place
Dallas, TX 75235-4022   214-637-1010
Processor of a frozen nondairy cream beverage
President: Don Allen
Estimated Sales: $300,000-500,000
Number Employees: 10-19
Sq. footage: 2500
Type of Packaging: Consumer, Food Service, Private Label, Bulk
Brands:
Creme D'Lite
Tropic D'Lite

3441 (HQ)Creme Glacee Gelati
8390 Le Creusot
St Leonard, QC H1P 2A6
Canada   514-322-0111
Fax: 514-322-0250   888-322-0116
domenic@italgelati.com   www.italgelati.com
Processor and exporter of kosher frozen desserts including gelato, sherbet, spumoni, ice cream cakes, cassata, granita and tartufo.
Estimated Sales: $1-3 Million
Number Employees: 20-49
Sq. footage: 13000
Type of Packaging: Consumer, Food Service, Private Label
Other Locations:
Creme Glacee Ital Gelati
Plattsburg NY
Brands:
ITAL GELATI
ITALIAN GELATO NOVELTIES
LA BELLA ITALIANA
TARTUFO

3442 Cremer North America
3202 Francis Hughes
Laval, QC H7L 5A7
Canada   450-629-2229
Fax: 450-629-4666   sales.na@cremer.com
www.cremer.com
President: Fred Cremer
Marketing: Dennis Hebert
CEO: Fred Cremer
Brands:
Cremer Cunter

3443 Cremes Unlimited
600 Holiday Plaza Dr # 520
Matteson, IL 60443-2238   708-748-1336
Fax: 708-748-4985   800-227-3637
Non-dairy whipped toppings and icings
Manager: John Evans
Estimated Sales: $10-20 Million
Number Employees: 5-9
Brands:
Cremes

3444 Creole Delicacies Pralines
533 Saint Ann St
New Orleans, LA 70116-3318   504-523-6425
Fax: 504-523-4787   info@cookincajun.com
Manufacturer of pralines
President: Harry Verlander
Estimated Sales: $2.5-5 Million
Number Employees: 5-9
Type of Packaging: Consumer
Brands:
Cookin' Cajun
Creole Delicacies

3445 Creole Fermentation Industries
7331 Ben Frederick Rd
Abbeville, LA 70510-2374   337-898-9377
Fax: 337-898-9376
Processor of vinegar including white distilled; manufacturer of vinegar production equipment
President: Albert Steen
General Manager: Bill Tribados III
Plant Manager: Bill Tribaldos
Estimated Sales: $5-10 Million
Number Employees: 5-9
Type of Packaging: Bulk

3446 Crepinicafe.Com
101 Castleton Street
Pleasantville, NY 10570   914-533-6645
Fax: 914-206-4848   paula@crepinicafe.com
www.crepinicafe.com
organic crepes
President/Owner: Paula Rimer

3447 Crescent City Crab Corporation
PO Box 2668
New Orleans, LA 70176-2668   504-646-6645
Fax: 504-649-5064
Crabs
President: Gary Bauer

3448 Crescent City Seafoods
55 Holomua St
Hilo, HI 96720-5142   808-961-0877
Fax: 808-935-1603   www.hilofish.com
Seafood
President: Charles Umamoto
Estimated Sales: $ 20 - 50 Million
Number Employees: 20-49

3449 Crescent Duck Farm
P.O.Box 500
Aquebogue, NY 11931-0500   631-722-8700
Fax: 631-722-5324
Processor and exporter of frozen whole ducklings and parts
President: Douglas Corwin
Plant Manager: Arnold Tilton
Estimated Sales: $ 7 Million
Number Employees: 50-99
Type of Packaging: Consumer, Food Service
Brands:
Crescent
Peconic Bay
White Pekin

3450 Crescent Ridge Dairy
355 Bay Rd
Sharon, MA 02067-1399   781-784-2740
Fax: 781-784-8446   800-660-2740
info@crescentridge.com   www.crescentridge.com
Fluid milk
President: Mark Parrish
VP: Jim Carroll
Estimated Sales: $2.5-5 Million
Number Employees: 50-99
Type of Packaging: Private Label
Brands:
Crescent Ridge Dairy

3451 Crescini Wines
PO Box 216
Soquel, CA 95073-0216   831-462-1466
Wines
President: Richard Crescini
Co-Owner: Paula Crescini
Estimated Sales: $1-2.5 Million
Number Employees: 5-9
Sq. footage: 3
Type of Packaging: Private Label

3452 Cresinco
PO Box 23725
Overland Park, KS 66283-3725   913-897-4220
Fax: 913-897-5820
General grocery
Director: Diane Devine

3453 Crest Foods Company
P.O.Box 371
Ashton, IL 61006-0371   815-453-7411
Fax: 815-453-2646   800-435-6972
www.crestfoods.com
Processor of food ingredients including emulsifying agents, proteins, caseinates, whey, stabilizers and flavors for dips, bases and seasonings; contract packaging available
President: Jeff Meiners
CEO: Shirley Reif
VP Quality Assurance: Marty Barclay
VP Corporate Sales: Steven Meiners
VP Manufacturing: Mike Meiners
Estimated Sales: $20-50 Million
Number Employees: 250-499
Type of Packaging: Consumer, Food Service, Private Label

3454 Crest International Corporation
P.O.Box 83309
San Diego, CA 92138-3309   619-296-4300
Fax: 619-296-3624   800-548-1232
service@crestinternational.net
www.crestinternational.com
Fresh or frozen fish and seafoods, fresh and frozen packaged seafood
Owner: Stephen Willis
Corporate Secretary: Lourdes Garber
Estimated Sales: $5-10 Million
Number Employees: 10-19
Type of Packaging: Food Service, Bulk

3455 Crestar Crusts
1104 State Route 22 NW
Washington Ct Hs, OH 43160   740-335-4813
Fax: 740-335-3908   www.richelieufoods.com
Frozen pizza crusts
Controller: Martin Roberts
VP/General Manager: Richard Hayward
Sales: Don Farrow
Plant Manager: Jason Yoakum
Estimated Sales: $20-50 Million
Number Employees: 50-99

3456 Crestmont Enterprises
1420 Crestmont Ave
Camden, NJ 08103-3104   856-966-0700
Fax: 856-966-6137
Processor of flavors and extracts
President: Amy Baskin
VP: Joseph Shediack, Jr.
VP: Annette Rapaport
Estimated Sales: $ 5 - 10 Million
Number Employees: 10-19

3457 Crestwood Bakery
7400 95th Street
Pleasant Prairie, WI 53158-2714   414-453-4790
Fax: 414-453-2439
Processor of baked goods including bread, cakes, pies and rolls
General Manager: Duane Bunting
Number Employees: 250-499
Parent Co: Flemming
Type of Packaging: Consumer, Food Service, Bulk

3458 Creuzebergers Meats
3001 6th Avenue
Duncansville, PA 16635   814-695-3061
Meat processing
Owner: Sieglinde Creuzberger
Estimated Sales: Less than $500,000
Number Employees: 1-4

3459 Crevettes Du Nord
Cp 6380
Gaspe, QC G4X 2R8
Canada   418-368-1414
Fax: 418-368-1812   gesco@globetrotter.qc.ca
Processor and exporter of fresh and frozen shrimp
President: Gaetan Denis
Manager: Amedee La Pierre
Number Employees: 50-99
Type of Packaging: Bulk

3460 Cribari Vineyards

4180 W Alamos Ave
Fresno, CA 93722-3943   559-277-9000
Fax: 559-277-2420   800-277-9095
bulk@cribari.net   www.cviwines.com

Processor and exporter of high quality California bulk wine. Cribari Vineyards, Inc. has been involved in the California wine industry for more than four generations. Our commitment to quality and service is unsurpassed. We arecompetitive in our pricing and can furnish many varieties of California wine blended to our customers' specifications. Some of our most popular products are Cabernet Sauvignon, Merlot, Chardonnay, Sauterne, Sherry, Chablis, Marsala, and Chianti.

Presidnt/CEO/CFO: John Cribari
Sales: Ben Cribari
Operations: Kris Anson
Manufacturing Supervisor: Kristine Staebler
Estimated Sales: $25 Million
Number Employees: 9
Number of Brands: 7
Type of Packaging: Bulk
Brands:
CVI BULK WINES

3461 Crickle Company
90 Genesis Parkway
Thomasville, GA 31792   229-225-1902
Fax: 229-225-2116   800-237-8689
www.crickle.com
brittle and popcorn
President/Owner: Harry Jones
VP: Jerry Hunter
Number Employees: 12

3462 Cricklewood Soyfoods
250 Sally Ann Furnace Road
Mertztown, PA 19539-9036   610-682-4109
Fax: 717-484-4789   cricklewood@aol.com
Processor of kosher vegetarian soy-based foods including burgers and low-fat three bean, organic soy and three grain tempeh, organic and GMO free foods
President: Karl Krummenoehl
VP: Renate Krummenoehl
Estimated Sales: $150,000
Number Employees: 5-9
Number of Products: 5
Sq. footage: 600
Type of Packaging: Consumer, Food Service, Bulk
Brands:
Cricklewood Soyfoods
Cricklewood Soyfoods

3463 Criders Poultry
P.O.Box 398
Stillmore, GA 30464-0398   912-562-4435
Fax: 912-562-9286   800-342-3851
cpcorp@cridercorp.com   www.cridercorp.com
Processor and exporter of fresh, frozen, canned and further processed chicken
Owner/CEO: William Crider Jr
CFO: Max Harrell
CEO: William A Crider
Research & Development: Phil Hudspeth
Quality Control: Stan Wallen
Operations: Lee Thompkins
Plant Manager: Kenneth Houghton
Purchasing: Ritchie Young

Estimated Sales: $ 20 - 50 Million
Number Employees: 500-999
Type of Packaging: Food Service, Private Label, Bulk
Brands:
CRIDER

3464 Crillon Importers
80 E State Rt 4 # 108
Paramus, NJ 07652-2657   201-368-8878
Fax: 201-368-4450
support@crillonimporters.com
www.crillonimporters.com
Wines and liquors
Owner: Michel Roux
CEO: Michael Roux
Estimated Sales: $ 10 - 20 Million
Number Employees: 10-19
Brands:
ABSENTE
AGAVERO
AQUAVITS
DOUCE PROVENCE
ELISIR MP ROUX
HB PASTIS
MAGELLIN GIN
RHUM BARBANCOURT
RINQUINQUIN
TALAPA MEZCAL
UNICUM ZWACK

3465 Crispy Bagel Company
230 N Franklintown Rd
Baltimore, MD 21223-1039   410-566-4102
Fax: 410-945-8783   800-522-7655
Processor of fresh and frozen bagels
President: John Paterakis
Office Manager: Ken Peluso
General Manager: Barry Ansel
Director Plant Operations: Travis Talbert
Estimated Sales: $10-20 Million
Number Employees: 50-99
Brands:
Crispy Bagel

3466 Crispy Green
144 Fairfield Road
Fairfield, NJ 07004   973-679-4515
Fax: 973-755-0358   866-582-5577
info@crispygreen.com   www.crispygreen.com
Freeze-dried fruits
President: Angela Liu

3467 Cristom Vineyards
6905 Spring Valley Rd NW
Salem, OR 97304-9779   503-375-3068
Fax: 503-391-7057 www.cristomwines.com
Wines
Co-Owner: Paul Gerrie
Co-Owner: Eileen Gerrie
Estimated Sales: $2.5-5 Million
Number Employees: 10-19
Type of Packaging: Private Label

3468 Critchfield Meats
2285 Danforth Dr
Lexington, KY 40511-1087   859-255-6021
Fax: 859-281-1129   800-866-3287
orders@critchfieldmeats.com
www.critchfieldmeats.com
Meats
Owner: Larry Mc Millan
Secretary/Treasurer: Mike Critchfield
Estimated Sales: $ 50 - 100 Million
Number Employees: 20-49
Brands:
Critchfield Meats

3469 Critelli Olive Oil
747 Skyway Court
Napa, CA 94558-7510   707-265-8641
Fax: 707-265-6827   800-865-4836
info@critelli.com   www.critelli.com
Organic extra virgin olive oils and oils crushed with lemons or fresh garlic
Director Food Service: Mike Brossier Mike Brossier
President: Serafino Bianchi
Brands:
Critelli

3470 Criterion Chocolates
125 Lewis St
Eatontown, NJ 07724-3454   732-542-7847
Fax: 732-542-0045   800-804-6060
criterion@criterionchocolates.com
www.criterionchocolates.com
Chocolates
President: George Karagias
VP: James Samaras
Marketing Director: Ron Boyadjian
Estimated Sales: $5-10 Million
Number Employees: 20-49
Brands:
Criterion

3471 Crocetti Oakdale Packing
378 Pleasant St
East Bridgewater, MA 02333-1349   508-587-0035
Fax: 508-587-8758
Packer of hamburger meat and sausage
President: Carl Crocetti
Marketing Director: Carl Crocetti
CFO: Carl Crocetti
Estimated Sales: $5-10 Million
Number Employees: 20-49
Type of Packaging: Consumer, Food Service, Bulk

3472 Crockett-Stewart Honey Company
1040 W Alameda Dr
Tempe, AZ 85282-3332   480-731-3936
Fax: 480-731-3938   bnipper@crocketthoney.com
www.crocketthoney.com
Processor and exporter of honey
President: Harold Nipper
Secretary: Linda Nipper
VP: Brian Nipper
Estimated Sales: $5-10 Million
Number Employees: 10-19
Sq. footage: 12000
Type of Packaging: Consumer, Food Service, Bulk
Brands:
Crockett's
Mrs. Crockett's

3473 Croda, Inc.
300A Columbus Circle
Edison, NJ 08837-3907   732-417-0800
Fax: 732-417-0804   www.croda.com
Super refined marine and plant oils, proteins, and peptides for nutraceuticals, functional foods and dietary supplements.
President: Kevin Gallagher
Marketing Head: Kavin Gallaghar
Estimated Sales: $20-50 Million
Number Employees: 20-49
Parent Co: Croda International P/C

3474 Croft's Crackers
504 14th Avenue
Monroe, WI 53566-1140   608-325-1223
Fax: 608-325-1289   crofts@mail.tds.net
Crackers, granola, cookies
President: John King
Public Relations: John or Kathy King
Estimated Sales: $500,000-$1 Million
Number Employees: 1-4

3475 Crofton & Sons
P.O.Box 698
Brandon, FL 33509-0698   813-685-7745
Fax: 813-689-4535   800-878-7675
Processor of beef and pork smoked sausage, Italian sausage and smoked turkey links; also, full line of smoked meats
President/CEO: Kevin Crofton
General Manager: Kevin Crofton
Production Manager: Joseph Yates
Estimated Sales: $10-20 Million
Number Employees: 50-99
Sq. footage: 40000
Type of Packaging: Consumer, Food Service, Private Label, Bulk
Brands:
Bean Brothers
Smokehouse Favorite
Uncle John's Pride

3476 (HQ)Crompton Corporation
1 American Ln
Greenwich, CT 06831-2560   203-552-2000
Fax: 203-552-2010   800-295-2392
www.cromptoncorp.com

Processor of chemical ingredients and food additives
CEO and President: Robert Wood
CEO: Robert Wood
CFO: Stephen Forsyth
Vice President: Stephen Forsyth
Global Market Manager: Bob Ruckle
Sales Director: Rick Beitel
Number Employees: 20-49
Other Locations:

3477 Cronin Vineyards
11 Old La Honda Road
Woodside, CA 94062-2604   650-851-1452
                                Fax: 650-851-5696
www.travelenvoy.com/wine/SantaCruz/Cronin-Vin
                                          eyard
Wines
Prorietor: Duane Cronin
VP: Mora Cronin
Estimated Sales: $300,000
Number Employees: 1-4
Type of Packaging: Consumer
Brands:
Cizonin Vineyards
Portola Hills

3478 Crooked River Brewing Company
1101 Center St
Cleveland, OH 44113-2405   216-771-2337
                                Fax: 216-771-7990
Processor of beer, ale, stout, lager and porter
Owner: Stephen Danckers
CO-Owner: Stuart Sheridan Stuart Sheridan
General Manager: Stuart Sheridan
Estimated Sales: $5-9.9 Million
Number Employees: 10-19
Type of Packaging: Consumer, Food Service, Bulk
Brands:
Cool Mule
Crooked River Brewing
Lighthouse Gold

3479 Crookes & Hanson
PO Box 46033
Bedford, OH 44146-0033   216-426-1111
          Fax: 216-426-1120   800-999-0263
Processor and exporter of English shortbread
President: Miles Small
Sales Manager: Jay Tener
Type of Packaging: Consumer, Food Service, Private Label, Bulk
Brands:
Crookes & Hanson

3480 Crookston Bean
P.O.Box 53
Crookston, MN 56716-0053   218-281-2567
                                Fax: 218-281-2567
Processor and exporter of dried edible beans
Owner: Bob Seaver
Manager: Dave Seaver
Estimated Sales: $10-20 Million
Number Employees: 1-4
Type of Packaging: Private Label, Bulk

3481 Cropp Cooperative-Organic Valley
PO Box 159
La Farge, WI 54639-0159   888-444-6455
     Fax: 608-625-2600   organic@organicvalley.com
                         www.organicvalley.com
Organic dairy, eggs, meat, produce
Estimated Sales: $30 Million
Number Employees: 100-249
Type of Packaging: Private Label

3482 Crosby Molasses Company
PO Box 2240
St. John, NB E2L 3V1
Canada   506-634-7515
     Fax: 506-634-1724   crosbys@nb.aibn.com
                         www.crosbys.com
Processor of molasses, drink crystals, table syrup, pancake mix and iced tea; importer and exporter of molasses
General Manager: Lorne Goodman
Type of Packaging: Consumer, Food Service, Private Label, Bulk
Brands:
Crosby

3483 Cross & Peters Company
10148 Gratiot Ave
Detroit, MI 48213-3211   313-925-4774
                                Fax: 313-925-6028
Processor and exporter of cheese twists, potato chips and popcorn
Manager: Mike Schena
Estimated Sales: $20-50 Million
Number Employees: 100-249
Type of Packaging: Consumer, Food Service
Brands:
Better Made

3484 Cross Creek Foods
PO Box 1328
Fayetteville, NC 28302-1328   910-323-9477
                                Fax: 910-609-1704
President: J Stancil
CEO: J Stancil
Vice President: Charles Manis
Marketing Director: J Stancil
Brands:
Cross Creek

3485 Crossroad Farms Dairy
400 S Shortridge Rd
Indianapolis, IN 46219-7403   317-229-7600
          Fax: 317-357-6719 www.kroger.com
Dairy products
General Manager: George coark
Marketing Manager: Ralph Strope
CEO: George Clark
Production Manager: Mike Hanisch
Estimated Sales: $100-499.9 Million
Number Employees: 250-499
Brands:
Crossroad

3486 Crowley Beverage Corporation
526 Boston Post Road
Wayland, MA 01778-1835   508-358-7177
          Fax: 978-358-0057   800-997-3337
Soft drinks
President/CEO: Hill Crowley
Chairman: Edward Crowley
Marketing Director: Jill Crowley
Estimated Sales: $3 Million
Number Employees: 10-19
Brands:
Razcal

3487 Crowley Cheese
14 Crowley Ln
Mt Holly, VT 05758-9656   802-259-2340
          Fax: 802-259-2347 www.crowleycheese.com
Processor of cheese including colby, sage, pepper, smoked, dill, garlic and caraway
Manager: Cindy Dawley
General Manager: P Smith
Estimated Sales: $ 5 - 10 Million
Number Employees: 5-9
Type of Packaging: Consumer, Food Service, Private Label, Bulk
Brands:
Crowley

3488 (HQ)Crowley Foods
95 Court Street
Binghamton, NY 13901   607-779-3289
          Fax: 607-779-3440   800-637-0019
          linda.farley@crowleyfoods.com
                         www.crowleyfoods.com
Manufactures and distributes a full line of dairy products, refrigerated beverages, frozen desserts, and specialty products.
President/CEO: John Kaneb
VP/CFO: Gail Glover
Consumer Affairs: Linda Farley
Chief Operating Officer: Joseph Cervantes
Estimated Sales: $2 Billion
Number Employees: 1,660
Number of Brands: 6
Parent Co: HP Hood LLC
Type of Packaging: Consumer, Food Service, Private Label, Bulk
Other Locations:
Crowley Foods
Albany NY
Binghamton NY
Hatfield PA
Philadelphia PA
Arkport NY
Bristol VA
LaFargeville NY

Sodus NY
Walcott NY
Brands:
AXELROD
CROWLEY
HELUVA GOOD
MAGGIO CHEESE
PENN MAID DAIRY
ROSENBERGER'S DAIRY

3489 Crowley Foods
PO Box 549
Binghamton, NY 13902-0549   607-779-3289
          Fax: 315-434-9809   800-247-6269
          linda.farley@crowleyfoods.com
                         www.crowlyfoods.com
Processor of dairy products
Founder: J K Crowley
COO: Joe Cervantes
Division Manager: George Rogers
Estimated Sales: $20-50 Million
Number Employees: 20-49
Type of Packaging: Consumer, Food Service, Private Label, Bulk
Brands:
Crowley
Heluva Good
Maggio
Penn Maid
Rosenbergers

3490 Crowley Foods
20700 State Route 411
La Fargeville, NY 13656-3228   315-658-2221
          Fax: 315-658-2825   800-247-6269
          Linda.Farley@crowleyfoods.com
                         www.crowleyfoods.com
Processor of dairy products including cottage cheese, sour cream, yogurt and cream cheese
Manager: Tony Wahl
Manager: Milton Cutway
Estimated Sales: $100-500 Million
Number Employees: 100-249
Parent Co: Crowley Foods
Type of Packaging: Food Service, Bulk
Brands:
Axelrod
Heluva Good
Maggio Cheese
Penn Maid Dairy
Rosenberger's Dairy

3491 Crowley Foods
25 Hurlbut St
Arkport, NY 14807-9706   607-295-7451
          Fax: 607-295-7046   800-637-0019
          Linda.Farley@crowleyfoods.com
                         www.crowleyfoods.com
Processor of fresh and frozen yogurt, cottage cheese, dips, sour cream and mixes including ice cream and frozen yogurt
Manager: Robert Simmons
COO: Joe Cervantes
CFO: Gary R Kaneb
Division Manager: Rick Mitchell
Plant Manager: Rick Kovaritz
Estimated Sales: $50-100 Million
Number Employees: 100-249
Parent Co: Crowley Foods
Type of Packaging: Consumer, Private Label
Brands:
Axelrod
Heluva Good
Maggio
Penn Maid
Rosenburger's

3492 Crowley Foods
PO Box 549
Binghamton, NY 13902-0549   607-779-3289
          Fax: 518-482-4992   800-637-0019
          Linda.Farley@crowleyfoods.com
                         www.crowleyfoods.com
Processor of fresh milk
COO: Joe Cervantes
President: Joe Cervantes
VP Sales: Mark Cleveland
Sales Manager: Mark Clevland
Division Manager: Ron Gaidusk
Estimated Sales: $50-100 Million
Number Employees: 100-249
Type of Packaging: Consumer, Food Service, Private Label, Bulk

Brands:
Axelrod
Crowley
Heluva Good
Maggio Cheese
Penn Maid Dairy
Rosenberger's Dairy

3493 Crown Candy Corporation
P.O.Box 6273
Macon, GA 31208-6273   478-781-4911
Fax: 478-781-5649   800-241-3529
info@crowncandy.com   www.crowncandy.com
Processor and exporter of confectionery products including brittles, chocolate, coconut, peanut and pecan candies and fudge.
CEO: James Weatherford
Estimated Sales: $10-24.9 Million
Number Employees: 100-249
Type of Packaging: Consumer, Private Label, Bulk
Brands:
DELIGHTS
ROYAL RECIPE

3494 Crown City Brewery
P.O.Box 50366
Pasadena, CA 91115-0366   626-577-5548
Fax: 626-577-5590
Brewers of beer.
Manager: Mike Hansen
Estimated Sales: $1-2.5 Million
Number Employees: 20-49
Type of Packaging: Private Label
Brands:
ARROYO AMBER ALE
BLACK BEAR STOUT
BLACK CLOUD STOUT
DOO DAH PALE ALE
FATHERCHRISTMAS WASSAIL
GOLD LABEL
MASTER'S TOUCH
MOUNT WILSON
MOUNT WILSON WHEAT BEER
OOM PAH PAH OKTOBERFEST
YORKSHIRE PORTER

3495 Crown Pacific Fine Foods
8809 S 190th St
Kent, WA 98031-1270   425-251-8750
Fax: 425-251-8802   contact@cpff.net
www.cpff.net
Specialty foods
President: Tony Ataee
Estimated Sales: $20-50 Million
Number Employees: 20-49

3496 (HQ)Crown Packing Company
P.O.Box 247
Salinas, CA 93902-0247   831-424-2067
Fax: 831-424-7812
Grower and packer of lettuce, celery and cauliflower; exporter of lettuce and celery
President: Chris Bunn
Sales Manager: Rob Steitz
Sales: Tonya Tempalski
Estimated Sales: $ 3 - 5 Million
Number Employees: 5-9
Type of Packaging: Consumer, Food Service, Private Label, Bulk
Brands:
Bunny

3497 Crown Point
P.O.Box 309
St John, IN 46373-0309   219-365-3200
Fax: 219-365-1944   www.crownpt.com
Processor and exporter of canned and frozen products including tomato paste, vegetables, nuts, juice concentrates, flexible packaging and spices.
President: Kevin Gates
VP Sales Export: Scott Copes
Estimated Sales: $10,000,000
Number Employees: 5-9
Parent Co: Unaka Corporation
Type of Packaging: Consumer, Food Service, Private Label, Bulk
Brands:
Crown Point

3498 Crown Prince
P.O.Box 3568
City of Industry, CA 91744-0568   626-912-3700
Fax: 626-854-0350   800-255-5063
webmaster@crownprince.com
www.crownprince.com
Processors and packers of specialty canned seafood.
President: Robert Hoffman
Marketing Manager: Denise Hines
Sales Director: Gary Gruettner
Estimated Sales: $ 20 - 50 Million
Number Employees: 50-99
Number of Products: 3
Type of Packaging: Consumer, Private Label
Brands:
CROWN PRINCE NATURAL
CROWN PRINCE SEAFOOD
OCEAN PRINCE SEAFOOD

3499 Crown Prince Naturals
PO Box 447
Petaluma, CA 94953-0447   707-766-8575
Fax: 707-766-8582   cpnatural@earthlink.net
www.crownprince.com
Family owned, canned seafood importer in business since 1948. Anchovies, tuna, salmon, sardines, crab, mackerel, oysters and clams.
CEO: Dustan Hoffman
CFO: Chris Bruno
Quality Control: Colette Tauzin
Marketing Director: Denise Hines
Sales Director: Gary Gruettner
Operations Manager: Jeanie Stobaugh
Number Employees: 40
Number of Brands: 4
Number of Products: 125
Type of Packaging: Consumer, Private Label
Brands:
Crown Prince

3500 Crown Processing Company
PO Box 1
Bellflower, CA 90707-0001   562-865-0293
Processor, importer and exporter of citrus rinds including graded, sliced, cooked and canned
President: John Bowen
Estimated Sales: $5-10 Million
Number Employees: 20-49
Sq. footage: 27000
Type of Packaging: Food Service
Brands:
Crown

3501 Crown Regal Wine Cellars
586 Montgomery St
Brooklyn, NY 11225-3130   718-604-1430
Fax: 718-384-1336   ywine@hotmail.com
Wine and grape juice
Owner: Joseph Baycount
Estimated Sales: $2.5-5 Million
Number Employees: 5-9

3502 Crown Valley Food Service
P.O.Box 2101
Beaumont, CA 92223-1001   951-769-8786
Fax: 951-769-8788
President: Sheldon Zaritsky
CEO: Mike Cavanaugh
Estimated Sales: $ 1 - 3 Million
Number Employees: 10-19

3503 Crum Creek Mills
700 Old Marple Road
Springfield, PA 19064-1236   413-581-3501
Fax: 413-581-3501   888-607-3500
rich@crumcreek.com   www.crumcreek.com
Soy-based pastas, breadsticks and soy powders
President: Dr Ara Yeramyan

3504 (HQ)Crunchy Foods
1070 40th St
Oakland, CA 94608-3617   510-923-0446
Fax: 510-923-0344   800-211-5903
info@crunchyfoods.com
www.crunchyfoods.com
Biscotti
Owner: Karen Jackson
CEO: Karen Jackson
Estimated Sales: $5-9.9 Million
Number Employees: 5-9
Type of Packaging: Consumer, Food Service, Private Label, Bulk
Brands:
BISCOTTI DI SUZY™

3505 Cruse Vineyards
1683 Woods Road
Chester, SC 29706-9403   803-377-3944
Wines
Owner: Kenneth Cruse
Owner: susan Cruse
Estimated Sales: $1-4.9 Million
Number Employees: 1-4
Brands:
Cruse Vineyards
Red Vines

3506 Crustacean Foods
5369 W Pico Blvd
Los Angeles, CA 90019-4037   323-460-4387
Fax: 323-460-2628   866-263-2625
info@anfamily.com   www.anfamily.com
Manufacturer of gourmet sauces.
Owner: Elizabeth An
Estimated Sales: $300,000-500,000
Number Employees: 5-9

3507 Crustaces de la Malbaie
PO Box 6380
Gaspe, QC G4X 2R8
Canada   418-368-1414
Fax: 418-368-1812   gesco@globetrotter.qc.ca
Processor of live lobster
President: Gaetan Denis
Number Employees: 50-99
Type of Packaging: Bulk

3508 Crystal & Vigor Beverages
174 Sanford Ave
Kearny, NJ 07032-5920   201-991-2342
Fax: 201-991-1882
Alcoholic and non-alcoholic beverages
Owner: Martinho Oliveira
Estimated Sales: $2.5-5 Million
Number Employees: 10-19
Type of Packaging: Private Label

3509 (HQ)Crystal Cream & Butter Company
8340 Belvedere Ave
Sacramento, CA 95826-5902   916-447-6455
Fax: 916-381-0187   www.crystal-milk.com
President: Don Hanson
CEO: Donald Hansen
Quality Control: Gina Dezzani
Marketing: Kevin Nagle
Sales & Distribution: David Walker
Public Relations: Kim Patterson
Estimated Sales: $160 Million
Number Employees: 500-999
Type of Packaging: Consumer, Food Service, Private Label, Bulk
Other Locations:
Crystal Cream & Butter Co.
Sacramento CA
Brands:
Crystal

3510 Crystal Farms
P.O.Box 7101
Chestnut Mtn, GA 30502-0101   770-967-6152
Fax: 770-967-7248   scotthordon@bellfouth.net
www.crystalfarmsga.com
Processor of eggs
President: Jim Brock
CEO: Ban lancaster
Marketing Manager: Ban lancaster
Sales Manager: Jackie Jones
Estimated Sales: $50-100 Million
Number Employees: 20-49

3511 Crystal Foods
P.O.Box 4009
Brick, NJ 08723-1209   732-477-0073
Fax: 732-477-0073
Processor and exporter of dehydrated flavors and beverage bases
President: Peter Kewitt
VP: Wendy Kewitt
Estimated Sales: $5-10 Million
Number Employees: 5-9
Sq. footage: 10000
Type of Packaging: Food Service, Private Label, Bulk
Brands:
Sun Country

3512 Crystal Geyser Roxanne LLC
6300 Pensacola Blvd
Pensacola, FL 32505-1999   850-476-8844
          Fax: 850-476-4341 www.saturn.com
Processor, bottler and exporter of beer, ale, lager,
stout and seasonal; also, natural and sparkling bot-
tled spring water
     Manager: Stan Williams
     VP/General Manager: Ken Janowitz
     Executive VP: Mark Wiggins
     Controller: Jack Mayer
     Plant Manager: Jim Sullivan
     Purchasing Manager: Frank Benham
Estimated Sales: $5-10 Million
Number Employees: 50-99
Sq. footage: 45000
Type of Packaging: Consumer, Food Service
Brands:
     CASTLE SPRINGS

3513 Crystal Geyser Water Company
P.O.Box 304
Calistoga, CA 94515-0304   707-942-0500
          Fax: 707-942-0647 800-726-6121
               sfrecept@crystalgeyser.com
                    www.crystalgeyser.com
Bottler of natural beverages including spring water,
sparkling mineral water, java tea and juices
     President: Peter Gordon
     Chairman: Peter Gordon
     Plant Manager: Carmen Maib
Estimated Sales: $5-10 Million
Number Employees: 50-99
Brands:
     Juice Squeeze
     Tejava

3514 Crystal Geyser Water Company
55 Francisco St # 410
San Francisco, CA 94133-2115   415-616-9590
          Fax: 415-616-9595
          customerservice@crystalgeyserasw.com
               www.crystalgeyserwater.com
Bottler of natural beverages including spring water,
sparkling mineral water, java tea and juices.
     Manager: Karen Kimen
Estimated Sales: $5-10 Million
Number Employees: 10-19

3515 (HQ)Crystal Lake
P.O.Box 248
Decatur, AR 72722-0248   479-752-5100
                    800-382-4425
               www.petersonfarms.com
Processor and exporter of chicken
     Manager: Daryl Hopkins
     Sr Director, Commodity Sales: Bruce Bayley
     VP Human Resources: Janet Wilkerson
     Sr VP, Development: Dennis Martin
Estimated Sales: $500,000-$1 Million
Number Employees: 5-9
Type of Packaging: Food Service, Private Label,
     Bulk
Other Locations:
     Crystal Lake
     North Kansas City MO
Brands:
     Crystal Lake

3516 Crystal Lake
6500 W Crystal Lake Rd
Warsaw, IN 46580-8986   574-858-2514
          Fax: 574-858-9886
Liquid, frozen and fresh egg products
     VP/Sales Manager: Douglas Hoffer
     Production Manager: Glen Yoder
     Plant Manager: Bruce Andrews
Estimated Sales: $10-20 Million
Number Employees: 100-249

**3517 Crystal Rock Spring Water
Company**
343 Boston Post Rd
Waterford, CT 06385   860-443-5000
          Fax: 860-443-6995
Processor of spring water; also, office coffee service
available
     Director: Cheryl Gustafson
Estimated Sales: $500,000-$1 Million
Number Employees: 1-4
Type of Packaging: Consumer

3518 Crystal Seed Potato Company
652 6th St
Crystal, ND 58222-4021   701-657-2143
          Fax: 701-657-2366
Processor of seed potatoes
     President: Bruce Otto
     Partner: Robert Otto
Estimated Sales: $600,000
Number Employees: 1-4
Type of Packaging: Consumer
Brands:
     Dr. Red Norland
     Goldrush
     Norchip
     Red Lasoda
     Shephody
     Snowden

3519 Crystal Springs
1200 Britannia Road East
Mississauga, ON L4W 4T5
Canada   905-795-6500
          Fax: 905-670-3628 800-822-5889
               www.crystalsprings.ca
Bottled water
     Marketing Manager: Jeff Smith
     Retail Manager: Steve Bondmini
     General Manager: Paul Elliot
     Production Manager: Eric Chastain
Estimated Sales: $5-10 Million
Number Employees: 100-249
Type of Packaging: Private Label
Brands:
     Crystal Springs
     Value Glacier

3520 Crystal Springs Water Company
5331 NW 35th Ter
Fort Lauderdale, FL 33309-6372   954-484-0100
          Fax: 954-733-7913 800-432-1321
               customerservice@water.com
                    www.crystalspringswater.com
Bottler of drinking, distilled and spring water
     Owner: David Cappadona
Estimated Sales: $20-50 Million
Number Employees: 100-249
Parent Co: Suntory Water Group
Brands:
     Belmont Springs
     Crystal Springs
     Crystal Springs
     Hinckley Springs
     Kentwood Springs
     Sierra Springs
     Sparkletts

3521 Crystal Star Herbal Nutrition
1542 N Sanborn Rd
Salinas, CA 93905-4760   831-422-7500
          Fax: 800-260-4349 info@crystalstar.com
                    www.crystalstar.com
Processor, importer and exporter of herbal extracts,
capsules, teas, powdered drink mixes and sports nu-
trition products
     Manager: Julie Lu
     Founder: Linda Page PhD
     VP Sales: Scott Seabaugh
     VP Operations: Glenn Korando
Estimated Sales: Less than $500,000
Number Employees: 1-4
Sq. footage: 10000
Parent Co: Jones Products International
Type of Packaging: Consumer, Bulk

3522 Crystal Water Company
3866 Shader Rd
Orlando, FL 32808-3145   407-291-7631
          Fax: 407-578-7790 800-444-7873
               sales@crystalspringswater.com
                    www.crystalspringswater.com
Processor of bottled water
     Owner/Operator: David Cappadona
     Plant Manager: Larry Caldwell
Number Employees: 1-4
Parent Co: Suntory Water Group
Type of Packaging: Consumer, Food Service, Pri-
     vate Label, Bulk
Brands:
     Crystal Springs

3523 Cuba Lockers
600 S 4th Street
Cuba, IL 61427-5313   309-785-2211
          Fax: 309-785-8601

Processor of beef and pork; slaughtering services
available.
Estimated Sales: $2.5-5 Million
Number Employees: 5-9
Type of Packaging: Consumer, Food Service, Bulk

3524 Cucina Antica Foods Corporation
254 Route 117 By Pass Rd
Bedford Hills, NY 10507-2142   914-244-9700
          Fax: 914-244-1794 877-728-2462
info@cucina-antica.com www.cucina-antica.com
     Owner: Niel Fusco
Estimated Sales: $5-10 Million
Number Employees: 5-9

3525 Cudlin's Market
8 Cox Rd
Newfield, NY 14867-9420   607-564-3443
Processor of meat products; also, slaughtering ser-
vices available
     Owner: Vince Distefano
Estimated Sales: Less than $500,000
Number Employees: 1-4
Type of Packaging: Consumer

3526 Cugino's Gourmet Foods
1000 Meyer Dr
Crystal Lake, IL 60014-8166   815-455-7242
          Fax: 847-458-8785 888-592-8446
          godell@cuginos.com www.cuginos.com
Garlic bread spread, gourmet soups, pasta sauce,
BBQ sauce and marinades
     Owner: Dan Hochstatter
Estimated Sales: $ 10 - 20 Million
Number Employees: 10-19

3527 Cuisinary Fine Foods
PO Box 8300-539
Dallas, TX 75205   214-521-8814
          Fax: 214-559-2131 888-283-5303
               cuisinary@aol.com
Gourmet chocolate cookies, chocolate and pretzel
snacks, assorted gourmet coffees, white choco-
late/liquer, toppings, bourbon-pecan
     President: Sandra Goodloe
Type of Packaging: Consumer, Food Service, Pri-
     vate Label
Brands:
     Creme and Chocolate
     Dolce Praline
     Twigs & Bark

3528 Cuisine Perel
1001 Canal Blvd # A
Richmond, CA 94804-3524   510-232-0343
          Fax: 510-232-0321 800-887-3735
          info@cuisineperel.com www.cuisineperel.com
Processor of chocolate, salad dressings, flavored
grapeseed oil, mayonnaise, pasta and barbecue
sauces, dry pastas and mustard; private label
available
     Owner: Mark Birchall
Estimated Sales: $2.5-5 Million
Number Employees: 5-9
Sq. footage: 6000
Type of Packaging: Private Label

3529 Cuisine Solutions
2800 Eisenhower Ave
Alexandria, VA 22314-5204   703-270-2900
          Fax: 703-750-1158 888-285-4679
               www.cuisinesolutions.com
Manufacturers of prepared foods.
     CEO: Stanislas Vilgrain
Estimated Sales: $10-24.9 Million
Number Employees: 250-499
Sq. footage: 44000
Brands:
     CUISINE SOLUTIONS
     FIVE LEAF

3530 Cuizina Food Company
18744 142nd Ave NE
Woodinville, WA 98072-8523   425-486-7000
          Fax: 425-486-1148 www.cuizina.com
Processor of sauces including alfredo, marinara,
primavera and spaghetti; also, minestrone soup and
croppino soup and pastas including frozen, filled,
extruded and vegetable blends.
     President: Ric Ferrera
Estimated Sales: $5-10 Million
Number Employees: 20-49
Sq. footage: 10000

Type of Packaging: Consumer, Food Service, Private Label, Bulk
Brands:
CUIZINA ITALIA

3531 Culinaire
1111 W Exposition Ave
Denver, CO 80223-2335   303-592-9100
     Fax: 303-592-7619   877-502-9100
admin@culinaire.com   www.culinairefoods.com
Hand made gourmet hors d oeuvres and entrees.
Custom production available
   President: Leo Reiff
Number Employees: 50-99
Number of Brands: 2
Number of Products: 110+
Sq. footage: 10000
Type of Packaging: Consumer, Food Service, Private Label
Brands:
BISTRO FAIRE
CULINAIRE

3532 Culinar Canada
380 Rue Notre Dame N
Ste. Marie De Beauce, QC G6A 3B3
Canada   418-387-5421
     Fax: 418-387-4746
Processor of cakes
   President: Yvan Grégoire
   CEO: Yvan Grégoire
   VP: Real Menard
Number Employees: 500-999
Parent Co: Culinar Canada
Brands:
Frenzi

3533 Culinary Farms, Inc.
1244 E Beamer St
Woodland, CA 95776   916-375-3000
     Fax: 916-375-3010   888-383-2767
info@culinaryfarms.com
www.culinaryfarms.com
Processors of dried tomatoes, tomato paste and mexican chile peppers.
   President: Kirk Bewley
Estimated Sales: $5-10 Million
Number Employees: 10-19
Sq. footage: 6000
Type of Packaging: Bulk

3534 Culinary Foods
4201 S Ashland Ave
Chicago, IL 60609-2305   773-650-1814
     Fax: 773-650-4501   800-621-4049
Processor and exporter of prepared and frozen foods including chicken, turkey, veal, cornish hens, hors d'oeuvres, omelets, crepes, quiche and sauces
   Owner/President: Wayne Butler
   Sales/Marketing Executive: Rick Trainor
   Purchasing Agent: Rick Trainor
Number Employees: 1,000-4,999
Parent Co: Tyson Foods
Brands:
Lady Aster

3535 Culinary Imports
100 Schillhammer Road
Jericho, VT 05465-3046   802-899-4505
     Fax: 802-899-4678   800-958-7678
Vinegar and mustards
   Owner: Bill Wheater
Estimated Sales: $2.5-5 Million
Number Employees: 1-4
Type of Packaging: Private Label
Brands:
Guldener Dutch Sugar Beet Vinegar
Guldener Fine Ground Mustard
Guldener Spiced Sugar Beet Vinegar
Guldener Sweet Coarse Mustard
Guldener Whole Grain Mustard

3536 Culinary Masters Corporation
6755 Shiloh Road E
Suite 109
Alpharetta, GA 30005-2227   770-667-1688
     Fax: 770-667-1682   800-261-5261
holzer@culinarymasters.com
www.culinarymasters.com

Wholesaler/distributor and importer of specialty foods, baked goods, equipment and tools; serving the food service market; exporter of spices, blends and specialty equipment
   Master Chef/President: Helmut Holzer
   Controller: Beth Ann Jackson
   Vice President: Sara Jane Holzer
   Sales: Michelle Brayley
Estimated Sales: $ 3 - 5 Million
Number Employees: 5-9
Sq. footage: 4000
Type of Packaging: Food Service, Private Label
Brands:
Affiorato
DreiMeister
Ravifruit
Stubi
Symphony Pastries
Vincotto

3537 Culinary Revolution
1320 Inspiration Drive
La Jolla, CA 92037-6810   323-939-1099
     Fax: 323-939-4844   chefakasha@aol.com
www.chefakasha.com

3538 Culinary Standards Corporation
P.O.Box 4547
Louisville, KY 40204-0547   502-587-8877
     Fax: 502-587-0150   800-778-3434
www.culinarystandards.com
Manufacturer of frozen prepared foods including soups, entrees, barbecue and cooked meats, side dishes, vegetables, chilies, sauces & gravies, dips & spreads as well as Mexican foods.
   President: Joe Stefanutti
Estimated Sales: $20-30 Million
Number Employees: 100-249
Sq. footage: 65000
Type of Packaging: Consumer, Food Service
Brands:
ALL AMERICAN SOUP COLLECTION
HALL'S
KENTUK

3539 (HQ)Culligan Water Technologies
1 Culligan Parkway
Northbrook, IL 60062-6287   847-205-6000
     Fax: 847-205-6030   feedback@culligan.com
www.culligan.com
Water
   President: Douglas Pertz
   CFO/VP Finance: M E Salvati
   Chairman: Ralph Hubley
   Secretary: E A Christensen
Estimated Sales: $50-100 Million
Number Employees: 1,000-4,999
Brands:
Culligan

3540 Culture Systems
3224 N Home St
Mishawaka, IN 46545-4436   574-258-0602
     Fax: 574-258-1136 www.culturesystems.net
Processor, exporter and wholesaler/distributor of dairy ingredients; also, researcher for the food industry
   President: Hyung Kim
Estimated Sales: $1-2.5 Million
Number Employees: 10-19
Sq. footage: 4000

3541 Cultured Specialties
P.O.Box 3248
Fullerton, CA 92834-3508   714-772-8861
     Fax: 714-956-1478 www.deanfoods.com
Processor and exporter of milk, yogurt and cottage cheese
   Manager: Rick Struble
   Sales/Marketing Executive: Jim Duffy
   Plant Manager: Ed Stewart
   Purchasing Agent: Lorraine Coulter
Estimated Sales: $50-100 Million
Number Employees: 100-249
Parent Co: Morningstar-Avoset
Type of Packaging: Consumer, Food Service

3542 Cultured Specialties
P.O.Box 3248
Fullerton, CA 92834-3508   714-772-8861
     Fax: 714-956-1478 www.deanfoods.com
   Manager: Rick Struble
   Operations Manager: Michael Buchanan

Estimated Sales: $ 50 - 100 Million
Number Employees: 100-249

3543 Culver Duck
P.O.Box 910
Middlebury, IN 46540-0910   574-825-9537
     Fax: 574-825-2613   800-825-9225
info@culverduck.com   www.culverduck.com
Processor and exporter of duck, chicken and sausage products.
   President: Herbert R Culver
Estimated Sales: $20-50 Million
Number Employees: 100-249
Sq. footage: 30000
Type of Packaging: Food Service
Brands:
CULVER DUCK

3544 Culver's Fish Farm
1316 W Kansas Ave
Mc Pherson, KS 67460-6053   620-241-5200
     Fax: 620-241-5202   800-241-5205
www.culverfishfarm.com
Fish
   Owner: Brent Culver
Estimated Sales: $300,000-500,000
Number Employees: 5-9

3545 Cumberland Dairy
P.O.Box 308
Rosenhayn, NJ 08352-0308   856-451-1300
     Fax: 856-451-1332
ccatalana@cumberlanddairy.com
www.cumberlanddairy.com
Processor and exporter of ice cream mixes, juices, soy products and milk including whole, skim, 1% and 2%; processor of ice cream
   President: Carmine C Catalana Iv IV
   Sales Director: David Catalana
   Director Operations: Frank Catalana
Estimated Sales: $20-50 Million
Number Employees: 100-249
Type of Packaging: Consumer, Food Service, Private Label, Bulk
Brands:
Cumberland Dairy

3546 Cumberland Gap Provision Company
P.O.Box 1797
Middlesboro, KY 40965-3797   606-248-4286
     Fax: 606-248-6517   800-331-7154
bmarsee@eastky.net   www.cumbgap.com
Processor of fresh smoked sausage and ham
   President/CEO: Ray Mc Gregor
   Vice President: Ron Bakies
   Quality Control: Kim Treiter
   Sales Director: Tim Kreiter
   Purchasing Manager: Gary Evans
Estimated Sales: $20-50 Million
Number Employees: 250-499
Parent Co: Hilander Ice
Type of Packaging: Consumer, Food Service, Private Label
Brands:
Cumberland Gap
Hickory Hills
Old Kentucky

3547 Cumberland Packing Corporation
2 Cumberland St
Brooklyn, NY 11205-1000   718-858-4200
     Fax: 718-858-6386 info@cpack.com
www.cpack.com
Processor and exporter of artificial sweeteners and butter flavor spreads
   Chairman: Benjamin Eisenstadt
   President: Marvin Eisenstadt
   VP: Jeff Eisenstadt
Estimated Sales: $100-500 Million
Number Employees: 250-499
Type of Packaging: Consumer
Brands:
SWEET 'N LOW

3548 Cumberland Pasta
PO Box 238
Cumberland, MD 21501-0238   301-777-1270
     Fax: 301-777-1330   800-572-7821
www.nevy.org
Macaroni and egg noodles
   President: Robert Bratti
   Plant Manager: Richard Crawford

Estimated Sales:$10-24.9 Million
Number Employees: 50-99
Brands:
American Eagle
Marco Polo

3549 Cumberland Seafood Corporation
40 Macondray St
Cumberland, RI 02864-8131   401-728-6088
Frozen fish
Owner: John Clairo
Estimated Sales:$5-9.9 Million
Number Employees: 1-4

3550 Cummings Lobster Company
5 Alewive Park Road
Kennebunk, ME 04043-6134   207-985-1677
Fax: 207-985-1686
Lobster
President: William Cummings
Estimated Sales:$1,400,000
Number Employees: 5

3551 Cummings Studio Chocolates
679 E 900 S
Salt Lake City, UT 84105-1101   801-328-4858
Fax: 801-328-4801 800-537-3957
candy@CummingsStudioChocolates.com
www.cummingsstudiochocolates.com
Processors of candy including chocolates
President: Marion Cummings
CEO: Marion Cumming
VP: Marion Cummings
Marketing Manager: Jolend Proter
Estimated Sales:$2.5-5 Million
Number Employees: 50-99
Sq. footage: 7000

3552 Cuneo Cellars
9360 SE Eola Hills Road
Amity, OR 97101-2416   503-835-2782
Wines
Partner: Gino Cuneo
*Estimated Sales:*Less than $500,000
Number Employees: 1-4

3553 Cupid Candies
7637 S Western Ave
Chicago, IL 60620-5871   773-925-8191
Fax: 773-925-7736 www.cupidcandies.com
Processor of candy
CEO: John Stefanos
Estimated Sales:$10-20 Million
Number Employees: 50-99
Type of Packaging: Consumer, Private Label

3554 Cupoladua Oven
PO Box 266
Wexford, PA 15090   412-592-5378
info@cupoladuaoven.com
www.cupoladuaoven.com
all natural baked goods, sweet treats and savory
snacks.

3555 (HQ)Cupper's Coffee Company
331 5th Street S
Lethbridge, AB T1J 2B4
Canada
403-380-4555
Fax: 403-328-8004
Importer and exporter of coffee
President: Al Anctil
Number Employees: 20-49

3556 Curly's Custom Meats
P.O.Box 123
Jackson Center, OH 45334-0123   937-596-6518
Fax: 937-596-6518
Meats
President: Larry Edwards
Estimated Sales:$2.5-5 Million
Number Employees: 1-4

3557 Curly's Dairy
475 North Second Ave
Stayton, OR 97383   503-399-1984
Fax: 503-363-3050 800-785-1335
curleys@wvi.com http://www.wvi.com

Processor of dairy products including ice cream and
milk
President: Jim Wilcox
CEO: Barry Wilcox
CFO: Ted Hartshone
VP Marketing: Kirk Hofstetter
Operations Manager: J T Wilcox
Production Manager: Steve Campbell
Plant Manager: Roland Lethe
Estimated Sales:$10-20 Million
Number Employees: 50-99
Type of Packaging: Consumer, Food Service
Brands:
Curley's Butter
Curley's Cottage Che
Curley's Cream Chees
Curley's Milk
Curley's Sour Cream
Flavor Pack
Quality Chek'd

3558 Curly's Foods
5201 Eden Ave # 265
Edina, MN 55436-2365   612-920-3400
Fax: 612-920-9889 www.curlys.com
Processor of beef including roast, corned, barbecued
and cooked and frozen ribs.
President: John Pauley
Senior VP: Ken Feinberg
Estimated Sales:$100-150 Million
Number Employees: 500-999
Type of Packaging: Consumer, Food Service, Private Label, Bulk
Brands:
CURLY'S

3559 Curran's Cheese Plant
W8850 Davis Rd
Browntown, WI 53522-9741   608-966-3361
Fax: 608-966-3309
Cheese products
Owner: James Curran
Estimated Sales:$10-24.9 Million
Number Employees: 10-19
Brands:
Curran Cheese

3560 Curry King Corporation
P.O.Box 413
Waldwick, NJ 07463-0413   201-652-6228
Fax: 201-447-3291 800-287-7987
curryusa@aol.com www.curryking.com
Processor and importer of curry, balti and tandoori
sauce; also, mango chutney; exporter of curry sauce
Owner: Lall Kwatra
Estimated Sales:$5-10 Million
Number Employees: 1-4
Sq. footage: 2500
Type of Packaging: Food Service, Private Label,
Bulk
Brands:
Curry King

3561 Curtice Burns Foods
Center St
Fennville, MI 49408   269-927-2111
Fax: 616-561-2758
Processor of canned fruits and vegetables
Manager: Luke Plamondon
Estimated Sales:$ 1 - 3 Million
Number Employees: 5-9
Parent Co: Curtice Burns
Type of Packaging: Consumer, Food Service, Private Label

3562 Curtis Packing Company
P.O.Box 1470
Greensboro, NC 27402-1470   336-275-7684
Fax: 336-275-1901
www.curtispackingcompany.com
Processor of pork and beef
President: Douglas B Curtis
CEO: Douglas Branch
Co-Owner: Earl Branch
Founder: John A Curtis
Estimated Sales:$10-20 Million
Number Employees: 50-99
Type of Packaging: Consumer, Food Service, Bulk
Brands:
Curtis
Ga Best

3563 Curtis Packing Company
P.O.Box 1470
Greensboro, NC 27402-1470   336-275-7684
Fax: 336-275-1901
www.curtispackingcompany.com
Packer of meat products including frankfurters, bo-
logna, bacon, ham, beef and fresh pork
President: Douglas Curtis
Secretary: Paul Hale Jr
Controller: Paul Hale
Consultant: Neil Webb
Sales: John Curtis
Plant Manager: Doug Grantham
Estimated Sales:$50-100 Million
Number Employees: 50-99
Type of Packaging: Consumer
Brands:
Beef Master
Curtis
IBP
Mbpxl
Monfort
Porter House

3564 Cusack Wholesale Meat Company
P.O.Box 25111
Oklahoma City, OK 73125-0111   405-232-2114
Fax: 405-232-2127 800-241-6328
cusack@cusackmeats.com
www.cusackmeats.com
Processor of beef, pork, lamb, veal and poultry
Owner: Donnie Cusack
General Manager: Al Cusack
Estimated Sales:$20-50 Million
Number Employees: 20-49
Type of Packaging: Food Service

3565 Cusano's Baking Company
213 NW 4th Ave
Hallandale Beach, FL 33009-4014   954-458-1010
Fax: 954-458-1052 sales@cusanosbakery.com
www.cusanosbakery.com
Italian bread and bakery products
Owner: Mike Greco
General Manager: Mike Grego
Estimated Sales:$5-10 Million
Number Employees: 20-49
Brands:
Cusano's

3566 Cushner Seafood
4141 Amos Ave
Baltimore, MD 21215-3309   410-358-5564
Fax: 410-358-5558
Fish & Seafood
Owner: Jack Deckelbaum
Estimated Sales:$1,600,000
Number Employees: 1-4

3567 Custom Brands Unlimited
PO Box 500
Solebury, PA 18963-0500   215-297-9842
Fax: 215-297-0161 customerbran@aol.com
Private-label gourmet mixes, candy, tea, snack items
and fruit

3568 Custom Confections & More
PO Box 62
Algonquin, IL 60102-0062   888-457-4676
Fax: 208-342-5996
stacey@customconfectionsandmore.com
www.customconfectionsandmore.com
Hard candy, lollipops
President: Lowell Fugal
Estimated Sales:$5-10 Million
Number Employees: 20-49

3569 Custom Cuts
2842 S 5th Ct
Milwaukee, WI 53207-1472   414-483-0491
Fax: 888-888-3717 www.ccuts.com
Processor of pre-washed and cut lettuce, cabbage,
onions, potatoes, melons, pineapples and watermel-
ons
Owner: Brad Beckman
Director Sales: Andy Siegel
General Manager: Monty Vikse
Estimated Sales:$100-500 Million
Number Employees: 250-499
Type of Packaging: Food Service, Private Label

3570 Custom Food Processors International
450 Bailey Ave
New Hampton, IA 50659-1061   641-394-4802
Fax: 641-394-4735 www.bayvalleyfoods.com
Contract packager and exporter of spray dried products including nondairy creamer, powdered milk, mixes, etc
President: John Nicolaisen
Plant Manager: Bob Sanford
Estimated Sales: $ 5 - 10 Million
Number Employees: 50-99
Type of Packaging: Bulk

3571 Custom Food Products
5145 W 123rd Street
Alsip, IL 60803-3105   708-388-8883
Fax: 630-928-4899 www.customculinary.com
Processor and exporter of tenderizers, seasonings and bases including soup, gravy and sauce
Director Culinary Services: Mike Minor, CEC, AAC, HGT
CEC: Mike Sperenza
Estimated Sales: $20-50 Million
Number Employees: 10-19
Sq. footage: 90000
Type of Packaging: Food Service, Bulk
Brands:
Custom Gold Label
Custom Master's Touch
Custom Whisk & Serve
Gold Label
Master's Touch
Saucery

3572 Custom Food Service
719 E Jackson St
Phoenix, AZ 85034-2284   602-254-1876
Fax: 602-256-6216 www.customfoodservice.com
President: Carl Schnitzer
VP: Nadine Schnitzer
Vice President: David Schnitzer
Estimated Sales: $ 20 - 50 Million
Number Employees: 20-49

3573 Custom Food Solutions
2505 Data Drive
Louisville, KY 40299   502-671-6966
Fax: 502-671-6906 800-767-2993
www.customfoodsolutions.com
A USDA, FDA and AIB inspected food manufacturing facility specializing in custom batchh, fresh ingredient production of soups, sauces, fillings and Sous Vide cooked proteins in flexible sized pouches.
Sales: Karen Reid
Number Employees: 30
Number of Products: 50
Sq. footage: 65000
Type of Packaging: Food Service

3574 Custom House Coffee Roasters
PO Box 694281
Miami, FL 33269-1281   305-651-0110
Fax: 305-651-4535 888-563-5282
roastabean@earthlink.net
Specialty coffees; including flavored coffees
President: Corey Colaciello
CEO: Joe Colaciello
Sales Director: Barbara Colaciello
Estimated Sales: $750,000-$1 Million
Number Employees: 5-9
Number of Brands: 115
Sq. footage: 3000
Type of Packaging: Food Service, Private Label, Bulk

3575 Custom House Seafoods
P.O.Box 7112
Portland, ME 04112-7112   207-773-2778
Fax: 207-761-9458
Fish and seafood.
President: Craig Johnson
Estimated Sales: $820,000
Number Employees: 1-4

3576 Custom Industries
9807 S 40 Dr
St Louis, MO 63124-1103   314-787-2828
Fax: 314-787-2828   sales@cusombits.com
www.custombits.com
Confectionery bits for baking and cereal industries, chocolate dairy powders, ice cream inclusion and fruit drinks for dairies
CEO: Dale Musick

Estimated Sales: $ 20 - 50 Million
Number Employees: 100-249
Type of Packaging: Bulk

3577 Custom Ingredients
1614 N Ih 35
New Braunfels, TX 78130-2502   830-608-0915
Fax: 830-625-7914 800-457-8935
info@customingredients.com
www.customingredients.com
Ingredients, snacks, dips, bakery, sauces, tortilla
President: James Curry PhD
Marketing: D Ames
Operations: Grey Baker
Production: R Nahn
Estimated Sales: $2.5-5 Million
Number Employees: 20-49
Type of Packaging: Bulk

3578 Custom-Pak Meats
PO Box 5377
Knoxville, TN 37928-0377   865-687-0871
Fax: 865-688-3276 800-457-4437
Packer of meat
President: C Hobbs
Executive VP: Christopher Satterfield
Number Employees: 42
Sq. footage: 24800
Type of Packaging: Food Service
Brands:
Nugget
Pocahontas

3579 Cut Above Foods
6100 Avenida Encinas
Suite A
Carlsbad, CA 92011-1052   760-931-6777
Fax: 760-931-5749
Processor and importer of raw and roasted garlic, shallots, ginger and IQF fire-roasted vegetables including onions, tomatoes, peppers, eggplant, squash, etc
Owner/President: Michael Crouse
COO: John Rosingana
National Sales: Keith Shelby
Estimated Sales: $20-50 Million
Number Employees: 20-49
Sq. footage: 12200
Type of Packaging: Consumer, Food Service, Private Label, Bulk
Brands:
A Cut Above

3580 Cutie Pie Corporation
443 W 400 N
Salt Lake City, UT 84103-1227   801-533-9550
Fax: 801-355-8021 800-453-4575
www.horizonsnackfoods.com
Processor and exporter of frozen fruit snack pies
Manager: Frank Kieffer
VP Sales/Marketing: Bob Nelson
Food Service Division: Scott Pollack
Retail Division: Randy Healey
Estimated Sales: $50-100 Million
Number Employees: 50-99
Type of Packaging: Consumer, Food Service
Brands:
Cutie Pies

3581 Cutler Egg Products
P.O.Box 578
Abbeville, AL 36310-0578   334-585-2268
Fax: 334-585-2473 cutleregg@ala.net
www.cutleregg.com
Processor and exporter of dried, frozen, liquid and extended shelf life egg products
Manager: Jeff Cutler
VP: Harold Cutler
VP Manufacturing: Joel Cutler
Estimated Sales: $100-500 Million
Number Employees: 100-249
Parent Co: Cutler Dairy Products
Type of Packaging: Food Service, Bulk

3582 Cutone Specialty Foods
145 Market Street
Chelsea, MA 02150   617-889-1122
Fax: 617-884-3944
customerservice@cutonespecialtyfoods.com
www.cutonespecialtyfoods.com
marinated and blanched mushrooms
President/Owner: Mario Cutone III

3583 Cutrale Citrus Juices
602 McKean St
Auburndale, FL 33823-4070   863-965-5000
Fax: 863-965-5149 information@cutrale.com
www.cutrale.com
Manufacturer of grapefruit and orange juices
President: Hugh Thompson III
Estimated Sales: $150 Million
Number Employees: 250-499
Parent Co: Sucocitrico Cutrale Ltd
Type of Packaging: Consumer, Food Service, Private Label, Bulk

3584 Cutrale Citrus Juices
11 Cloud St
Leesburg, FL 34748-5306   352-728-7800
Fax: 352-728-7840 information@cutrale.com
www.cutrale.com
Processor of pasteurized orange juice and concentrate
Operations Manager: Jim Fitzgerald
Plant Manager: Jose Zamperlini
Estimated Sales: $100-500 Million
Number Employees: 100-249
Type of Packaging: Consumer

3585 Cuvaison Vineyard
4550 Silverado Trl
Calistoga, CA 94515-9604   707-942-6266
Fax: 707-942-5732 www.cuvaison.com
Processor of red and white wines.
President: Jay Schuppert
Estimated Sales: $10-20 Million
Number Employees: 20-49
Type of Packaging: Consumer, Food Service

3586 Cyanotech Corporation
73-4460 Queen Kaahumanu Hwy
Kailua Kona, HI 96740-2632   808-326-1353
Fax: 808-329-4533 800-395-1353
info@cyanotech.com www.cyanotech.com
Cyanotech Corporation, the world's leader in microalgae technology, produces high-value natural products from microalgae, and is the world's largest commercial producer of natural astaxanthin from microalgae. Products include HawaiiamSpirulina Pacifica, a nutrient-rich dietary supplement; BioAstin, a natural astaxanthin, a powerful antioxidant with expanding applications as a human nutraceutical
Executive VP: Gerald R Cysewski
VP Sales/Marketing: Robert Capelli
Sales Manager: Jeane Vinson
Estimated Sales: F
Number Employees: 50-99
Number of Brands: 3
Number of Products: 2
Sq. footage: 653400
Parent Co: Cyanotech Corporation
Type of Packaging: Consumer, Private Label, Bulk
Brands:
BioAstin Natural Astaxanthin
Spirulina Hawaiian Spirulina

3587 Cybros
P.O.Box 851
Waukesha, WI 53187-0851   262-547-1821
Fax: 262-547-8946 800-876-2253
sales@cybrosinc.com www.cybrosinc.com
Manufacturer of fine breads, rolls, cookies and other products
Owner: Debbie Brooks
General Manager: Paul Geboy
Estimated Sales: $2.5-5 Million
Number Employees: 10-19
Sq. footage: 8000

3588 Cyclone Enterprises
146 Knobcrest Dr
Houston, TX 77060-1213   281-872-0087
Fax: 281-872-7645 www.cyclone-ent.com
Processor and importer of Mexican food including hot sauce and peppers. Distributors of dry, canned, processed and frozen grocery items including juices, drinks, dairy products, meats, cheeses, deli products, specialty foods, herbsspices, candy and snac
President: Mark Mendenhall
CEO: Mark Mindenhall
VP Sales: Ronny Thomas
Customer Support: Dora Mendoza
General Information: Martha Gibbs
Purchasing: Ted Spafford
Estimated Sales: $2.5-5 Million
Number Employees: 100-249

Type of Packaging: Consumer, Food Service, Private Label

3589 Cygnet Cellars
PO Box 1956
Hollister, CA 95024-1956   831-637-7559
Wine
    Partner: Jim Johnson
Estimated Sales: $500,000 appx.
Number Employees: 1-4
Brands:
    Cygnet

3590 Cypress Grove Chevre
1330 Q St
Arcata, CA 95521-5740   707-825-1100
    Fax: 707-825-1101 cypgrove@aol.com
    www.cypressgrovechevre.com
Maker of goat's milk cheeses including Humboldt
Fog, Bermuda Triangle, chevre, Fromage Blanc,
cheddar, hub and ash coated chevre.
    President: Mary Keehn
Estimated Sales: $1-5 Million
Number Employees: 20-49
Number of Brands: 2
Number of Products: 18
Sq. footage: 6000
Type of Packaging: Consumer, Food Service, Private Label, Bulk
Brands:
    CYPRESS GROVE CHEVRE
    CYPRESS GROVE CREAM

3591 (HQ)Cyril's Bakery Company
2890 W State Road 84
Unit 103
Fort Lauderdale, FL 33312   954-797-1272
    Fax: 413-473-9708 800-929-7457
    cyril@cyrils.com www.cyrils.com
Frozen bakery products including breads and pastries.
    VP: Adam Weizer
    Marketing: Kelly Wechsler
    Public Relations: Shannon Campbell
    Operations: Steve Tarrick
Estimated Sales: $15 Million
Number Employees: 18
Number of Brands: 1
Number of Products: 75
Type of Packaging: Consumer, Food Service

3592 Cytodyne Technologies
1920 Swarthmore Avenue
Suite 2
Lakewood, NJ 08701-4589   732-942-0393
    Fax: 732-886-2066 www.cytodyne.com

3593 Czech-Am Brands
235 W 75th St
New York, NY 10023-1700   212-799-7134
    Fax: 212-724-1054
    Owner: Dave Borasho
Estimated Sales: Less than $500,000
Number Employees: 1-4

3594 Czepiel Millers Dairy
PO Box 277
Ludlow, MA 01056-0277   413-589-0828
    Fax: 413-589-0828
Dairy
    President: Stanly Czepiel

3595 Czimer's Game & Sea Foods
13136 W 159th St
Homer Glen, IL 60491-8768   708-301-0500
Meat and fish
    Owner: Richard Czimer Jr
Estimated Sales: $300,000
Number Employees: 1-4

3596 D & D Foods
3715 4th Ave
Columbus, GA 31904-7441   706-322-4507
    Fax: 706-327-4121 ddfoods@aol.com
    www.ddfoods.com
Manufacturer of barbecue sauces, marinades and
salad dressings; also, contract packaging available
    President: Marlene Dodelin
    CFO: Fred Dodelin
Estimated Sales: $3-5 Million
Number Employees: 5-9
Type of Packaging: Consumer, Food Service, Private Label, Bulk

Brands:
    FOY'S B.B.Q. SAUCE

3597 D Seafood
2723 S Poplar Avenue
Chicago, IL 60608-5915   312-808-1086
    Fax: 312-808-0869
Seafood
    Owner: De Trinh

3598 D Steengrafe & Company
1726 Main St
Pleasant Valley, NY 12569-5611   845-635-4067
    Fax: 845-635-4239
Manufacturer and importer of beeswax, botanicals,
kola nuts and nut powder, quassia chips, dried ginger and spices
    VP: Margot Nordenholt
    VP: Carl Schmidt
Estimated Sales: $5 Million
Number Employees: 1-4
Type of Packaging: Bulk

3599 D Waybret & Sons Fisheries
3 Clam Point
Shelburne, NS B0T 1W0
Canada   902-745-3477
    Fax: 902-745-2112
Manufacturer and exporter of fresh and salted haddock, cod, halibut and hake; also, fresh lobster
    President/Co-Owner: Dewey Waybret
    Manager/Co-Owner: Cecil Waybret
Number Employees: 50
Type of Packaging: Bulk

3600 D&A Foodservice
PO Box 2762
Dartmouth, NS B2W 4R4
Canada   902-468-4715
    Fax: 902-468-4715
Manufacturer of sandwiches, chicken wings,
chicken wing sauces and prepared dinners
    President/Owner: Pat McCluskey
    VP: Gary Keigan
Number Employees: 9
Type of Packaging: Food Service
Brands:
    DAVE'S
    KOKOMO'S

3601 D&M Seafood
135 N King St # 2b
Honolulu, HI 96817-5084   808-531-0687
    Fax: 808-531-4947 www.shrimphawaii.com
Seafood
    Owner: Hansen Chong

3602 D' Luke Seafood
7332 Grand Caillou Road
Dulac, LA 70353-2700   504-563-2328
    Fax: 504-563-4218
Shrimp
    President: David Luke

3603 D'Arrigo Brothers Company of California
P.O.Box 850
Salinas, CA 93902-0850   831-424-3955
    Fax: 831-424-3136 800-995-5939
    promero@darrigo.com www.andyboy.com
Manufacturer of vegetables: broccoli, fennel, hearts
of romaine, broccoli rabe, cauliflower and cactus
pear.
    Chairman: Andrew D'Arrigo
    President: John D'Arrigo
    Director Sales: Dave Martinez
    EVP Operations: Margaret D'Arrigo-Martin
Estimated Sales: $79.9 Million
Number Employees: 1,000-4,999
Type of Packaging: Consumer, Bulk
Brands:
    ANDY BOY
    GREEN HEAD

3604 D'Artagnan
280 Wilson Ave
Newark, NJ 07105-3844   973-344-0565
    Fax: 973-465-1870 800-327-8246
    orders@dartagnan.com www.dartagnan.com

Manufacturer of pates, game sausages, smoked
items, ducks, meats, game birds, mushrooms and
specialty products
    President: Ariane Daguin
    Marketing: Donna Brunnguell
    Purchasing: Kris Kelleher
Estimated Sales: $30 Million
Number Employees: 100-249
Type of Packaging: Consumer, Food Service, Bulk

3605 D'Oni Enterprises
5152 Sepulveda Boulevard
207
Sherman Oaks, CA 91403-1154   818-888-3664
    Fax: 818-348-5632 888-997-7423
    janisd@d-oni.com www.d-oni.com
Sauces
    President: Janis Dallessandro
    Vice President: David Dallesandro
    Shipping/Receiving: Linda Trudeau

3606 D'Orazio Foods
960 Creek Rd
Bellmawr, NJ 08031-1672   856-931-1900
    Fax: 856-931-1907 888-328-7287
    web@dorazio.com www.dorazio.com
Manufacturer and exporter of all natural frozen Italian food including ravioli, stuffed shells, manicotti
and lasagna
    President: Anthony D'Orazio
    SVP Sales/Business Development: Michael
    Novosel
Estimated Sales: $20-50 Million
Number Employees: 100-249
Brands:
    DORAZIO

3607 D-Liteful Baking Company
9012 NW 105 Way
Medley, FL 33178   305-883-6449
    Fax: 305-883-8797 www.d-litefulbaking.com
Product line includes that of Heavenly Desserts featuring a variety of sugar free products such as
cheesecakes and meringues available in vanilla,
chocolate, cappuccino, strawberry and lemon flavors. Their Heavenly Harvest lineincludes sugar
free baked products such as sesame and wheat
crackers.
    Founder: Jorge Guevara Sr
Type of Packaging: Food Service

3608 (HQ)D. Merlino & Sons
1001 3rd Street
Suite 8
Oakland, CA 94607-2507   510-568-2151
    Fax: 510-568-2220
Manufacturer of pasta products including semolina,
organic and specialty
    Chairman: Richard Merlino
    President: Rico Merlino
Estimated Sales: $10 Million
Number Employees: 15
Type of Packaging: Consumer, Food Service, Private Label, Bulk
Brands:
    ALITA

3609 D.D. Williamson & Company
P.O.Box 6001
Louisville, KY 40206-1   209-529-1820
    Fax: 209-529-0810 866-412-6567
    info@ddwmson.com www.caramel.com
Manufacturer and exporter of caramel coloring
    President: Alexander Nixon
    CEO: Ted Nixon
    Plant Manager: Henry Ackerman
Estimated Sales: $5-10 Million
Number Employees: 5-9
Sq. footage: 10000
Parent Co: D.D. Williamson & Company
Type of Packaging: Consumer, Bulk
Other Locations:
    DDW Support Center
    Louisville KY
    D.D. Williamson Ireland
    Cork, Ireland
    D.D. Williamson Ingredients
    Shanghai, China
    D.D. Williamson do Brazil
    Manaus, Brazil
    D.D. Williamson & Company
    Louisville KY
    Colormaker
    Anaheim CA
    D.D. Williamson

Matsapha, Swaziland
D.D. Williamson UK
Manchester UK
Brands:
WILLIAMSON'S

3610 DB Kenney Fisheries
PO Box 1210
Westport, NS B0V 1H0
Canada   902-839-2023
                              Fax: 902-839-2070
dbkenney@dbkenneyfisheries.com
www.dbkenneyfisheries.com
Manufacturer and exporter of scallops, lobster, cod
and haddock
President: Daniel Kenney Jr
Number Employees: 50-99
Type of Packaging: Bulk

3611 DCI Cheese Company
3018 Helsan Drive
Richfield, WI 53076   262-677-3407
Fax: 262-677-8325 thickey@dcicheeseco.com
www.dcicheeseco.com
imported cheeses, dips, spreads, hummus and other
exotic and flavorful offerings
President/Owner: Timothy Omer
VP: Dominique Delugeau
Estimated Sales: $12.8 Million
Number Employees: 200

3612 DCL
628 Laumaka St
Honolulu, HI 96819-2312   808-845-3834
                              Fax: 808-845-4901
Manufacturer of various fresh Hawaiian seafoods
President: Dennis Goto
Estimated Sales: $ 5 - 10 Million
Number Employees: 10-19

3613 DD Williamson & Company
100 S Spring St
Louisville, KY 40206-1945   502-895-2438
Fax: 502-895-7381 800-227-2635
info@ddwmson.com   www.caramel.com
Manufacturer and exporter of caramel color
President: T H Nixon
Estimated Sales: $ 20 - 50 Million
Number Employees: 50-99
Parent Co: Williamson Group
Type of Packaging: Bulk

3614 DDC
931 Calle Negocio
San Clemente, CA 92673-6224   949-498-0030
ddcprod@ddcproducts.com
www.hgh4life.com
Vitamins, supplements

3615 DE Wolfgang Candy Company
50 E 4th Ave
York, PA 17404-2507   717-843-5536
Fax: 717-845-2881 800-248-4273
info@wolfgangcandy.com
www.wolfgangcandy.com
Manufacturer of confectionery products including
chocolate and peanut brittle
Partner: Benjamin McGlaughlin
Managing Partner/Marketing: Mike Schmid
Managing Partner/Sales: Steve Schmid
Managing Partner: Brad McGlaughin
Managing Partner/Operations: Robert Wolfgang
III
Managing Partner/Finance/Adminsitration:
Benjamin McGlaughin
Estimated Sales: $20-50 Million
Number Employees: 100-249
Type of Packaging: Consumer

3616 DF Stauffer Biscuit Company
360 S Belmont St
York, PA 17403-2616   717-843-9016
Fax: 717-843-0592 800-673-2473
www.stauffers.net
Manufacturer of animal crakers, cookies and other
snacks.
President: Marc Garrett
CFO: Carlous Sutton Jr
VP: Scott Stauffer
Quality Control: Janet Dunlap
Sales: Rodney Stauffer
Operations: Gary Shortt
Purchasing: Diane Toomey

Estimated Sales: $50-100 Million
Number Employees: 500-999
Parent Co: Meiji Seika
Type of Packaging: Consumer, Food Service, Private Label, Bulk
Other Locations:
DF Stauffer Biscuit Company
Blandon PA
DF Stauffer Biscuit Company
Cuba NY
DF Stauffer Biscuit Company
Santa Ana CA
Brands:
STAUFFERS
YORK FARMS

3617 DG Yuengling & Son
P.O.Box 539
Pottsville, PA 17901-0539   570-622-4141
Fax: 570-622-4011 www.yuengling.com
Manufacturer of beer including ale, porter, lager and
light
Owner: Richard L Yuengling Jr Jr
Estimated Sales: $50-100 Million
Number Employees: 100-249
Brands:
YUENGLING

3618 DGZ Chocolates
6909 Ashcroft Dr # 315
Houston, TX 77081-5819   713-777-3444
Fax: 713-777-9444 877-949-9444
www.dgzchocolates.com
Chocolates, caramel apples, popcorn covered in
chocolate and caramel
Owner: Debbie Zissman
Purchasing: Deborah Zissman
Estimated Sales: $5-10 Million
Number Employees: 1-4
Brands:
APPLERAZZI
POPARAZZI
TOFFARASSI
TURTLERAZZI

3619 DL Geary Brewing
38 Evergreen Dr
Portland, ME 04103-1066   207-878-2337
Fax: 207-878-2388 www.gearybrewing.com
Manufacturer of beers.
President: David Geary
Marketing: Kelly Lucas
Purchasing: Kelly Lucas
Estimated Sales: $10-20 Million
Number Employees: 20-49
Brands:
DL GEARY BREWING

3620 DMH Ingredients
1228 American Way
Libertyville, IL 60048-3936   847-362-9977
Fax: 847-362-9988 www.dmhingredients.com
Confectionery, gums and stabilizers, cheese and
dairy powders, fruit and vegetable products, powdered cellulose, savory flavors, flavor enhancers,
sweet flavors, coffee, tea and botanicals, vitamins,
amino acids and food chemicalsgrain products, meat
aspartama
President: David Damlich
Purchasing: David Damlich
Estimated Sales: $5-10 Million
Number Employees: 5-9

3621 DMH Ingredients
1228 American Way
Libertyville, IL 60048-3936   847-362-9977
Fax: 847-362-9988
customerservice@dmhingredients.com
www.dmhingredients.com
Specialty ingredient brokerage/distribution firm
which supplies the industrial food and pharmaceutical industries - innovative trendsetter of food
ingredient technology
Owner: David Damlich
Estimated Sales: $ 5 - 10 Million
Number Employees: 5-9

3622 DMV International Nutritional
1712 Deltown Plaza
Delhi, NY 13753-3100   607-746-0100
Fax: 607-746-2710 www.dmv-international.com
Manufacturer of food additives including hydrolized
proteins, bioactive peptides and protein fractions
Purchasing Agent: Peggy Urban

Estimated Sales: $50-100 Million
Number Employees: 100-249
Parent Co: DMV International
Brands:
AERION
ESPRION
GLUTAMINE
LACTOPEROXIDASE
LACTOVAL
PEPTIDE FM
PHARMATOSE
PRIMELLOSE
PRIMOJEL
RESPITOSE
TEXTRION

3623 DNE World Fruit Sales
1900 Old Dixie Hwy
Fort Pierce, FL 34946-1423   772-465-1110
Fax: 772-465-1181 800-327-6676
www.dneworld.com
Grower, packer, marketer, and importer of citrus
fruit including navel oranges, clementines, lemons
and limes; exporter of grapefruit, oranges, tangerines and juice
President: Gregory Nelson
VP: David Mixon
Manager Fresh Juices: Robert Poyner
Estimated Sales: $20-50 Million
Number Employees: 100-249
Parent Co: Bernard Egan & Company
Type of Packaging: Consumer, Food Service, Private Label, Bulk
Brands:
INDIAN RIVER PRIDE
OCEAN SPRAY
PRIDE

3624 DNO
4561 E 5th Ave # 8-12
Columbus, OH 43219-1896   614-231-3601
Fax: 614-231-5032 800-686-2366
dno@core.com   www.dnoinc.com
Manufacturer of pre-cut prepackaged fresh fruit and
vegetables
Owner: Tony Dinovo
Sales Representative: Jim Davis
Sales Representative: Jim Fryer
Purchasing Manager: Tony DiNovo
Estimated Sales: $10-20 Million
Number Employees: 20-49
Sq. footage: 10000
Type of Packaging: Consumer, Food Service, Private Label, Bulk
Brands:
FRESH HEALTH
OLD FASHIONED CARAMEL APPLE

3625 DPI Dairy Fresh Products Company
601 S Rockefeller Avenue
Ontario, CA 91761-7871   909-605-7300
Fax: 909-975-7259
Dairy products
President: James De Keyser
Purchasing: Cheryl Hopson
Estimated Sales: $5-10 Million
Number Employees: 5-9
Brands:
DPI DAIRY

3626 DPI Midwest
600 E Brook Dr
Arlington Hts, IL 60005-4622   847-364-9704
Fax: 847-364-9702 www.distribution-plus.com
Distributor of specialty perishable foods from
around the world, all natural and all organic, 6,000
items carried
President: Andrew Kramer
CFO: John Byrne
Director Sales/Marketing: Tom Bowker
Operations: Jim Thigpen
Purchasing: Robert Fisher
Estimated Sales: $100+ Million
Number Employees: 50-99
Sq. footage: 66000
Type of Packaging: Food Service, Private Label
Other Locations:
DPI Corporate
Wilmette IL
DPI Rock Mountain
Henderson CO
DPI Northwest
Tualatin OR

DPI West
Ontario CA
DPI Southwest
Albuquerque NM
DPI Arizona
Mesa AZ
DPI Mid Atlantic
Upper Marlboro MD

3627 (HQ)DS Waters of America
5660 New Northside Dr NW # 500
Atlanta, GA 30328   770-933-1400
          Fax: 770-956-9495   800-728-5508
customerservice@water.com   www.water.com
Manufacturer and distributor of bottled water
    President/CEO: Stewart Allen
    CFO: Dillon Schickli
    COO: Tom Harrington
Estimated Sales:$800 Million
Number Employees: 4500
Parent Co: Suntory Water Group
Type of Packaging: Consumer, Food Service, Private Label, Bulk
Brands:
    ALHAMBRA®
    BELMONT SPRINGS®
    CRYSTAL SPRINGS®
    HINCKLEY SPRINGS®
    KENTWOOD SPRINGS®
    NURSERY® WATER
    ROAST2COAST®
    SIERRA SPRINGS®
    SPARKLETTS®

3628 DS Waters of America
5660 New Northside Drive
Suite 500
Atlanta, GA 30328   770-933-1400
          Fax: 770-956-9495   800-728-5508
customerservice@water.com   www.water.com
Bottled water
    President/CEO: Stewart Allen
    CFO: Dillon Schickli
    COO: Tom Harrington
*Estimated Sales:*J
Number Employees: 4700
Parent Co: Hinkley & Schmitt
Brands:
    Anjou

3629 DSM Food SpecialtiesPeptoPro
26689 Peachwood Drive
Murrieta, CA 92563   951-461-1619
    Fax: 951-461-1638   reto.rieder@dsm.com OR
          info.Peptopro@dsm.com
          www.peptopro.com
DSM Food Specialties is a producer of value-added ingredient solutions for the international food, feed and beverage industries.
    President: A Wessels
    Finance & Control: G Nieboer
    Legal Affairs: R De Graaf
    Research & Development: B Poldermans
    QESH & M: J Van Lemmen
    Strategy & Marketing Services: A Stikkers
    National Account Manager: Reto Rieder
    Human Resources: A Twigt
    Demand & Supply Chain Management: T Brett

3630 DSM Food Specialties
2675 Eisenhower Avenue
Eagleville, PA 19403-2316   610-650-8480
    Fax: 610-650-8599   800-662-4478
          www.dsm-foodspecialties.com
Manufacturer of yeast extracts and flavor enhancers
    President: Richard Calk Jr
Estimated Sales:$ 5 - 10 Million
Number Employees: 7
Parent Co: DSM

3631 DSM Food Specialties
N89w14475 Patrita Drive
Menomonee Falls, WI 53051-2360   262-255-7955
          Fax: 262-255-7732   800-423-7906
Yeast extracts, flavor systems, inactive dry yeast, fermentation nutrients, beverage enzymes, wine yeasts, coagulants, starter cultures, starter media, preservation systems and antibiotic residue tests
    Marketing: Jim Whitt

3632 DSM Specialties
2675 Eisenhower Avenue
Norristown, PA 19403-2316   610-650-8480
    Fax: 610-650-8599   800-662-4478
          www.gist-brocades.com

Food ingredients
Estimated Sales:$ 5 - 10 Million
Number Employees: 20-49

3633 Da Vinci Gourmet
7224 1st Ave S
Seattle, WA 98108-4103   206-768-7401
          Fax: 206-768-1855   800-640-6779
          info@davincigourmet.com
          www.davincigourmet.com
Manufacturers flavored syrups, gourmet sauces, and confections
    Manager: Gary Sletten
Estimated Sales:$14 Million
Number Employees: 50-99
Number of Products: 120+
Sq. footage: 65000
Type of Packaging: Consumer, Food Service, Private Label, Bulk

3634 Dabruzzi's Italian Foods
417 2nd St
Hudson, WI 54016-1509   715-386-3653
          Fax: 715-549-5202
Manufacturer of ravioli, garlic butter bread and red and white sauces
    Owner: Sharon Ellstrom
    Manager: Nancy Cramer
Estimated Sales:$1-2.5 Million
Number Employees: 5-9

3635 Daerim America
195 W Spring Valley Ave # 5
Maywood, NJ 07607-1730   201-587-8989
          Fax: 201-587-8959   800-635-0781
          soh@daesangamerica.com
Manufacturer, importer and exporter of frozen seafood and fish products including yellowfin sole, Alaska pollack, cod, hoki, salmon and oysters
    President: Hwan Yoon
    Chief Representative: Dae Park
    VP: H Kim
    Sales Director: David Lee
    Sales Manager: Thomas Park
Estimated Sales:$5-10 Million
Number Employees: 10-19
Sq. footage: 20000
Parent Co: Daerim Fishery Company
Type of Packaging: Food Service
Brands:
    AQUAROYALE
    DAERIM

3636 Dagoba Organic Chocolate
1105 Benson Way
Ashland, OR 97520-9540   541-482-2001
    Fax: 541-482-5661   800-482-5661
          oracle@dagobachocolate.com
          www.dagobachocolate.com
Organic chocolates
    Founder: Frederick Schilling
    Plant Manager: Doug Massey
Estimated Sales:$ 10 - 20 Million
Number Employees: 20-49

3637 (HQ)Dahlgren & Company
1220 Sunflower St
Crookston, MN 56716-2480   218-281-2985
          Fax: 218-281-6218   800-346-6050
          cconsidine@sunflowerseed.com
          www.sunflowerseed.com
Manufacturer and exporter of in-shell and kernel sunflower seeds, soynuts including roasted, salted and flavored. Custom roasting and packaging also available
    President: Charlie Considine
    Quality Systems Manager: Ronald Klinge
    Central Region Sales Manager: Lois Helland
    Senior Executive International Sales: Thomas Miller
    Human Resources Director: Mary Ellen Swenson
    Senior Executive International Sales: Thomas Miller
Estimated Sales:$20.2 Million
Number Employees: 100-249
Type of Packaging: Consumer, Food Service, Bulk
Other Locations:
    Dahlgren & Company
    Grace City ND
    Dahlgren & Company
    Fargo ND

3638 Dahm's Foods
5234 Brown Street
Skokie, IL 60077-3616   847-673-0653

Salad dressings, jellies and jams
    President: Bruce Dahm
Estimated Sales:$1-4.9 Million
Number Employees: 3
Brands:
    DAHM'S

3639 Daily Foods
3535 S 500 W
Salt Lake City, UT 84115-4205   801-269-1998
          Fax: 801-269-1409   www.dailymeats.com
Bacon
    President: Russell Wilcox
    Production Manager: Russ Wilcox
Estimated Sales:$100-500 Million
Number Employees: 250-499
Brands:
    DAILY FOODS

3640 Daily Juice Products
1 Daily Way
Verona, PA 15147-1199   412-828-9020
          Fax: 412-828-8876   800-245-2929
          www.ambev.com
Manufacturer of cocktail mixes including pina colada, strawberry colada, whiskey sour, strawberry daiquiri and juice concentrates; also, pancake syrup
    President: Tony Battaglia
    VP Finance/Administration: Peter Chiappa
    Research & Development: Jack Cornelius
    VP Sales/Marketing: Paul Beranek
    VP Operations: Don Bonaroti
    Director Engineering: Kevin Tappa
    Plant Manager: John Reynolds
    Purchasing Manager: Ron Trant
Estimated Sales:$50-99.9 Million
Number Employees: 500-999
Parent Co: American Beverage Corporation
Type of Packaging: Consumer, Food Service, Private Label, Bulk
Brands:
    BIG JUICY

3641 Daily Soup
134 E 43rd St # 1
New York, NY 10017-4019   212-949-7687
          Fax: 212-687-7839   888-393-7687
soup@dailysoup.com   www.dailysoup.com
Fresh soups
    Owner: Young Yoon
    Executive Chef: Leslie Kaul
*Estimated Sales:*Less than $500,000
Number Employees: 10-19
Brands:
    DAILY MADE

3642 Dainty Confections
PO Box 523
Valley Stream, NY 11582-0523   516-825-0943
          Fax: 516-568-9214
Candy
    President: Catherine Diehl

3643 Dairiconcepts
3253 E. Chestnut Expressway
Springfield, MO 65802   417-829-3400
          Fax: 417-829-3401   877-596-4374
          dcinfo@dairiconcepts.com
          www.dairiconcepts.com
Dairy powders and replacement systems, cheese powders and cheese concentrates, block and grated Italian cheeses.

3644 Dairy Chem Inc
9120 Technology Lane
Fishers, IN 46038   317-849-8400
    Fax: 317-849-8213   cservice@dairychem.com
          www.dairychem.com
Manufacturer and exporter of starter distilled flavors including buttermilk, sour cream, butter and cream for dairy and bakery products
    President: Daniel Church
Estimated Sales:$ 3 - 5 Million
Number Employees: 5-9
Type of Packaging: Private Label, Bulk

3645 Dairy Concepts
W7014 County Road Mm
Greenwood, WI 54437-8409   715-267-5400
          Fax: 715-267-5409   888-680-5400

Fresh/dry, grated and shredded parmesan cheese, romano cheese, asiago cheese. Retail, food service/ingredients
Quality Control: Loni Duell
Plant Manager: Scott Anderson
Estimated Sales:$20-50 Million
Number Employees: 20-49
Type of Packaging: Consumer, Food Service, Private Label, Bulk

3646 Dairy Farmers Of America
10220 N. Ambassador Drive
Kansas City, MO 64153   816-801-6455
webmail@dfamilk.com
www.dfamilk.com
Manufacturer of dairy products, cheese and butter.

3647 (HQ)Dairy Farmers of America
1950 Washington St
Franklinton, LA 70438-2135   985-839-4481
Fax: 985-839-4028   800-735-2038
www.dfamilk.com
Manufacturer of butter, condensed milk solids and nonfat dry milk
Manager: Rodney Ervin
Quality Control: Lavern Jenkins
Manager: Rodney Ervin
Estimated Sales:$5-10 Million
Number Employees: 50-99
Sq. footage: 24000
Parent Co: Dairy Farmers of America
Type of Packaging: Consumer, Food Service

3648 Dairy Farmers of AmericaGoshen Plant
1110 S 9th St
Goshen, IN 46526-4316   574-533-3141
Fax: 574-533-2708   800-758-0269
www.dfamilk.com
Manufacturer of nonfat dry milk
Chairman: Tom Camerlo
Safety Foreman: Andy Gall
Plant Manager: Robert Gehlke
Estimated Sales:$ 20 - 50 Million
Number Employees: 20-49
Parent Co: Dairy Farmers of America
Type of Packaging: Consumer

3649 Dairy Farmers of America
6350 N 2150 W
Smithfield, UT 84335-9700   435-563-3281
Fax: 435-563-3388   800-453-2820
www.dfamilk.com
Manufacturer of cheese and whey powder
Manager: Don Hansen
VP Environmental Affairs: Dennis Treacy
COO: Greg Yando
Chief Grader: Judy Capparelli
Plant Manager: Rex Gleason
Estimated Sales:$5-10 Million
Number Employees: 100-249
Parent Co: Dairy Farmers of America
Type of Packaging: Consumer, Food Service, Private Label, Bulk

3650 Dairy Farmers of America
8600 NW 107th Ter
Kansas City, MO 64153-1239   816-801-6200
Fax: 816-891-7294 www.dfamilk.com
Manufacturer of powdered and condensed milk and cream
Manager: Bob Shaffer
Plant Manager: Damon Kustes
Estimated Sales:$2.5-5 Million
Number Employees: 10-19
Sq. footage: 20000
Parent Co: Dairy Farmers of America
Type of Packaging: Bulk

3651 Dairy Farmers of America
1140 S 3200 W
Salt Lake City, UT 84104-4561   801-977-3000
Fax: 801-977-3090 www.dfamilk.com
Cooperative of dairy processors
Manager: Don Jensen
COO: Greg Yando
Estimated Sales:$ 10 - 20 Million
Number Employees: 20-49
Type of Packaging: Consumer

3652 Dairy Farmers of America
PO Box 1837
Springfield, MO 65801-1837   417-865-9641
Fax: 816-801-6491   800-243-2479
www.dfamilk.com
Manufacturer and exporter of shelf stable canned nutritional beverages; also, instant nonfat dry milk powder
President/CEO: Gary Hanman
COO: Sam McCroskey
Manager Formula Manufacturing: John Weidner
Estimated Sales:$100+ Million
Number Employees: 200
Sq. footage: 240000
Parent Co: Dairy Farmers of America
Type of Packaging: Consumer, Food Service, Private Label, Bulk

3653 (HQ)Dairy Farmers of America
10220 NW Ambassador Dr
Kansas City, MO 64153-1367   816-801-6455
Fax: 816-801-6456   888-332-6455
webmail@dfamilk.com   www.dfamilk.com
Milk and milk products
President/CEO: Gary Hanman
COO: Jim Hahn
CFO: Jerry Bos
CEO: Rick Smith
VP Quality Assurance/Regulatory Affairs: James Carroll
Media/Public Relations: Agnes Schaffer
Estimated Sales:$5-10 Million
Number Employees: 1,000-4,999
Type of Packaging: Private Label, Bulk
Brands:
DAIRY FARMERS

3654 Dairy Farmers of America
PO Box 1837
Springfield, MO 65801-1837   417-865-9641
Fax: 417-829-2501   800-435-7269
www.dfamilk.com
Formulated dairy foods
President: Gary Hanman
Estimated Sales:$ 100-500 Million
Number Employees: 160

3655 Dairy Farmers of America
10220 NW Ambassador Dr
Kansas City, MO 64153-1367   816-801-6200
Fax: 816-801-6201 www.dfamilk.com
Manufacturer of cheese and dried whey
President/CEO: Richard Smith
Senior VP Finance: David Meyer
VP Quality Assurance & Regulatory Affair: James Carroll
Marketing: John Wilson
Senior VP Human Resources: Annette Regan
Estimated Sales:$11.7 Million
Number Employees: 250
Parent Co: Dairy Farmers of America
Type of Packaging: Private Label, Bulk

3656 Dairy Farmers of America
P.O.Box 939
Sulphur Springs, TX 75483-0939   903-885-6518
Fax: 903-885-9590 www.dfamilk.com
Manufacturer of milk including condensed, skim, butter, whole, 1% and 2%; also, cream
Manager: Mark Gunderson
SVP/COO: David Jones
Q/C Manager: Amanda Ballard
Plant Superintendant: Harvey Shumaker
Estimated Sales:$2.5-5 Million
Number Employees: 50-99
Parent Co: Dairy Farmers of America
Type of Packaging: Bulk

3657 Dairy Farms of America
925 State Route 18
New Wilmington, PA 16142-5023   724-946-8729
Fax: 724-946-2261   800-837-5214
www.dfamilk.com
Manufacturers of dairy products
President: Shawn Koddoura
Plant Manager: Tim Sallman
Estimated Sales:$ 50 - 100 Million
Number Employees: 250-499
Brands:
SAVOLDI CHEESE

3658 Dairy Fresh
2221 Patterson Ave
Winston Salem, NC 27105-6036   336-723-0311
Fax: 336-723-0353   800-446-5577
Milk, dairy products
President: Barney Meredith
Sales: Sam Garrett
Operations Manager: Robert Paxton
Plant Manager: Robert Paxton
*Estimated Sales:*I
Number Employees: 250-499
Parent Co: Suiza Dairy Group
Brands:
DAIRY FRESH

3659 Dairy Fresh Corporation
P.O.Box 159
Greensboro, AL 36744-0159   334-624-3041
Fax: 334-624-4889   800-239-5114
www.dairyfreshcorp.com
Manufacturer of dairy products including ice cream, milk, sour cream and dip
President: Betty Morrison Gist
Estimated Sales:$50-100 Million
Number Employees: 20-49
Type of Packaging: Consumer, Food Service, Bulk
Brands:
DAIRY FRESH
NESTLE

3660 (HQ)Dairy Fresh Foods
21405 Trolley Industrial Dr
Taylor, MI 48180-1811   313-295-6300
Fax: 313-295-6950 jfarber@dairyfreshfoods.com
www.dairyfreshfoods.com
Manufacturer of beverages, cheeses, deli foods and frozen foods; importer of cheese and meats including corned beef and ham; exporter of cheese
President: Alan Must
Chairman: Mike Must
Truck Operator: Joel Must
Estimated Sales:$50-100 Million
Number Employees: 100-249
Sq. footage: 90000
Type of Packaging: Consumer, Food Service, Bulk
Brands:
BRITTNIA
DAIRY FRESH
DELI-FRESH
GOURMET
MARLA
OCEEN FRESH
PURE MAID

3661 Dairy Group
366 N Broadway # 410
Jericho, NY 11753-2000   516-433-0080
Fax: 516-433-7657 ndorman@dairygroup.com
www.thedairygroup.com
Cheese
Owner: Ned Dorman
Estimated Sales:$1-3 Million
Number Employees: 1-4
Brands:
DAIRY GROUP

3662 Dairy House
150 Larkin Williams Industrial Court
Fenton, MO 63026   636-343-5444
Fax: 314-772-4280 www.dairyhouse.com
Manufacturer and suppliers of cocoa, chocolate dairy powders and beverage flavors.
President: Carl Fitzwater
Vice President: John Hutchinson
*Estimated Sales:*4.6 Million
Number Employees: 30

3663 Dairy Ingredients
10465 Enterprise Dr
Davisburg, MI 48350-1313   248-922-0900
Fax: 248-370-0113 www.dairyingredientsinc.com
Dairy blends
President: Finn Nielsen
Estimated Sales:$2.5-5 Million
Number Employees: 10-19

3664 Dairy King Milk Farms/Foodservice
PO Box 3605
Glendale, CA 91221-0605   818-243-6455
Fax: 818-243-2455 themilkguy@aol.com
www.dairyking.net

Manufacturer of dairy products, frozen vegetables and dry goods; wholesaler/distributor of frozen foods, general merchandise, general line products, produce, meats and seafood; serving the food service market
VP: Joseph Goldstein
Number Employees: 50-99
Sq. footage: 10000
Type of Packaging: Consumer

3665 Dairy Land
2255 Gray Hwy
Macon, GA 31211-1058   478-742-6461
                Fax: 478-745-3673 www.dairylandinc.com
Processor of citrus drinks and dairy products including ice cream
President: George Bush
VP: Sam Standard
Area Sales Manager: Harold Cross
Estimated Sales: $ 20 - 50 Million
Number Employees: 20-49
Parent Co: Atlanta Dairies
Type of Packaging: Consumer
Brands:
NEW ATLANTA
PARMALAT

3666 Dairy Maid Dairy
259 E 7th St
Frederick, MD 21701-5227   301-663-5114
                Fax: 301-695-0431 www.dairymaiddairy.com
Manufacturer of milk, sour cream, yogurt, buttermilk, juices and drinks
President/Co-Owner: Jody Vona
Co-Owner: James Vona
Controller: Clyde Faucheux
VP: Joseph Vona
Distribution Manager: Bill Fulmer
Production Supervisor: Robert Cullum
Plant Manager: Tony Vona
Office Manager: Cheryl Cowan
Estimated Sales: $20-50 Million
Number Employees: 100-249

3667 Dairy Maid Ravioli Manufacturing Corporation
216 Avenue U
Brooklyn, NY 11223-3825   718-449-2620
                Fax: 718-449-3206 dairymaid1@aol.com
                www.dairymaidravioli.com
Manufacturer and distributor of pasta products including ravioli and tortellini
President/Co-Owner: Louis Ballarino
Co-Owner: Salvatore Ballarino
Vice President: Anthony Ballarino
Estimated Sales: $1-2.5 Million appx.
Number Employees: 5-9
Sq. footage: 11000
Type of Packaging: Consumer, Private Label, Bulk
Brands:
DAIRY MAID

3668 Dairy Management
10255 W Higgins Rd # 900
Rosemont, IL 60018-5638   847-803-2000
                Fax: 847-803-2077 800-248-8829
                Amys@rosedmi.com
                www.nationaldairycouncil.org
Manufacturer of bleaching compounds, chocolate, cultures, dairy powders, nonfat dry milk, milk, protiens, vegetable, sweetners
SVP Nutrition/Product Innovation: Greg Miller, PhD, FACN
CEO: Thomas P Gallagher
VP Nutrition Research: Doug DiRenzom, PhD, FACN
Brand Development Director: Jose Cubillos
Number Employees: 50-99
Parent Co: National Dairy Council

3669 Dairy Queen of Georgia
730 Dekalb Industrial Way
Decatur, GA 30033-5704   404-292-3553
                Fax: 404-292-5535
Manufacturer of soft serve ice cream
Manager: Joe Denmark
VP: David Lyle
Plant Manager: Robert Crements
Estimated Sales: $500,000-$1 Million
Number Employees: 10-19
Parent Co: International Dairy Queen
Type of Packaging: Consumer

3670 Dairy State Foods
6035 N Baker Rd
Milwaukee, WI 53209-3701   414-228-1240
                Fax: 414-228-9747 800-435-4499
                larry@dairystatefoods.com
                www.dairystatefoods.com
Manufacturer and exporter of juvenile cookies and animal, oyster crackers, also contract packaging available
President: Lawrence Rabin
Estimated Sales: $1-2.5 Million
Number Employees: 20-49
Sq. footage: 40000
Type of Packaging: Consumer, Food Service, Private Label
Brands:
ALPHABET COOKIES
CIRCUS WAGON SPRINKLED ANIMAL CRACK
TOY BUS ANIMAL CRACKERS
WILD JUNGLE ANIMAL CRACKERS

3671 (HQ)Dairy-Mix
3020 46th Ave N
St Petersburg, FL 33714-3863   727-525-6101
                Fax: 727-522-0769 ecoryn@dairymix.com
Manufacturer and exporter of ice cream, ice milk and milk shake mixes, frozen dessert
President: Edward Coryn
Secretary: Ann Coryn
VP: John Coryn
Estimated Sales: $8 Million
Number Employees: 10-19
Type of Packaging: Food Service, Bulk

3672 DairyAmerica
4974 E Clinton Way # C221
Fresno, CA 93727-1531   559-251-0992
                Fax: 559-251-1078 800-722-3110
                webmaster@dairyamerica.com
                www.dairyamerica.com
Manufacturer and exporter of milk including low heat, medium heat, high heat, whole and dry buttermilk
President/SVP: Keith Gomes
Controller: Jean McAbee
CEO: Rich Lewis
Director Marketing: Doug White
COO: Richard Lewis
Estimated Sales: $1-2.5 Million
Number Employees: 20-49
Type of Packaging: Bulk
Brands:
DAIRYAMERICA

3673 Dairyfood USA Inc
2819 Highway F South
Blue Mounds, WI 53517   608-437-5598
                Fax: 608-437-8850 800-236-3300
                customerservice@dairyfoodusa.com
                www.dairyfoodusa.com
cheeses, as well as candies, coffees, sausages and crackers
President/Owner: Daniel Culligan
Human Resources Manager: Teddy White
Purchasing: Vicki Mosure
Estimated Sales: $14.2 Million
Number Employees: 100

3674 Dairyland Ice Cream Company
487 Chancellor Ave
Irvington, NJ 07111-4002   973-923-7625
                Fax: 973-923-2557
Ice cream and frozen desserts
President: Arthur Anastasia
Estimated Sales: $5-10 Million
Number Employees: 5-9
Type of Packaging: Private Label
Brands:
DAIRYLAND

3675 Dairyman's/Land O' Lakes
380 S M St
Tulare, CA 93274   559-687-8287
                Fax: 559-685-6947 www.landolakesinc.com
Manurfactuer of whole and powdered milk, cheese, butter and yogurt
President/CEO: Jack Gherty
CEO: Bill Schrieber
Sr VP Marketing/Product Development: Lee Blakeley
Purchasing Agent: Brian Gilbert

Estimated Sales: $ .5 - 1 million
Number Employees: 5-9
Parent Co: Land O'Lakes
Type of Packaging: Private Label
Brands:
BETTY CROCKER POP SECRET
DAIRY EASE
LAND O'LAKES ALL NATURAL EGGS
LAND O'LAKES BUTTER
LAND O'LAKES CAPPUCCINO CLASSICS
LAND O'LAKES COCOA CLASSICS
LAND O'LAKES DAIRY CASE CHEESE
LAND O'LAKES DELI CHEESE
LAND O'LAKES FLAVORED BUTTER
LAND O'LAKES INTERNATIONAL PASTA
LAND O'LAKES LAKE TO LAKE CHEESE
LAND O'LAKES MACRONI AND CHEESE
LAND O'LAKES MARGARINE, BLENDS/SP.
LAND O'LAKES SOUR CREAM
LAND O'LAKES ULTRA CREAMY BUTTER

3676 (HQ)Dairymen's
3068 W 106th Street
Cleveland, OH 44111-1899   216-671-2300
                Fax: 216-671-1560
Dairy
President: Russell Dzurec
Estimated Sales: $50-100 Million
Number Employees: 250-499
Parent Co: Suiza Dairy Group

3677 Dairytown Products Ltd
49 Milk Board Road
Sussex, NB E4E 5L2
Canada   506-432-1950
                Fax: 506-432-1940 800-561-5598
                admin@dairytown.com www.dairytown.com
Manufacturer of butter and skim milk, whole milk and buttermilk powders
CEO: Derek Roberts
Quality Assurance: Wendy Palmer
VP Sales/Marketing: George MacPhee
Operations Manager: Lynn McLaughlin
Type of Packaging: Private Label

3678 Daisy Brand
12750 Merit Dr # 600
Dallas, TX 75251-1261   972-726-0800
                Fax: 972-726-0115 877-292-9830
                narr_br@daisybrand.com www.daisybrand.com
Manufacturer and exporter of sour cream
President: David Sokolsky
Information Systems Manager: Kevin Brown
Estimated Sales: $20-50 Million
Number Employees: 20-49
Type of Packaging: Consumer, Food Service, Private Label, Bulk
Brands:
DAISY LIGHT BRAND SOUR CREAM
DAISY NO FAT BRAND SOUR CREAM
DAISY REGULAR BRAND SOUR CREAM

3679 (HQ)Dakota Brands International
2121 13th St NE
Jamestown, ND 58401-3568   701-252-5073
                Fax: 701-251-1047 800-844-5073
                dearle@dakotabrands.com
                www.dakotabrands.com
Manufacturer of bagels, rolls and frozen roll dough
President: Rex King
CEO: Donald Kerr
Financial Manager: Sharon Schultz
R&D/QA Manager: Colleen Miller
Plant Superintendent: Reuben Moser
Estimated Sales: $11.20 Million
Number Employees: 20-49
Number of Products: 60
Sq. footage: 10500
Type of Packaging: Consumer, Food Service, Private Label, Bulk
Brands:
BAGELS
BAKEABLE
DAKOTA

3680 Dakota Country Cheese
2909 Twin City Dr
Mandan, ND 58554-3870   701-663-0246
                Fax: 701-663-9412 dakcoche@btigate.net
Manufacturer of cheese
President: Virgil Johnson
Estimated Sales: $10-24.9 Million
Number Employees: 20-49
Sq. footage: 17000

Type of Packaging: Consumer
Other Locations:
Dakota Country Cheese - Plant
Mandan ND
Brands:
DAKOTA COUNTRY

3681 Dakota Gourmet
896 22nd Ave N
Wahpeton, ND 58075-3026   701-642-3068
Fax: 701-642-9403 800-727-6663
info@dakotagourmet.com
www.dakotagourmet.com
Manufacturer of roasted sunflower nuts, soynuts, and toasted corn
Manager: Lucy Spiekermeier
General Manager: Lucy Spiekermeier
Estimated Sales: $2.5-5 Million
Number Employees: 20-49
Sq. footage: 40000
Parent Co: Sonne
Type of Packaging: Consumer, Food Service, Private Label, Bulk
Brands:
GIANTS

3682 Dakota Growers Pasta Company
1 Pasta Ave
Carrington, ND 58421-2500   701-652-2855
Fax: 701-652-3552
webmaster@dakotagrowers.com
www.dakotagrowers.com
Manufacturer of traditional and unique pastas including organic.
President/Chief Executive Officer: Timothy Dodd

Chief Financial Officer: Edward Irion
Estimated Sales: l
Number Employees: 250-499
Type of Packaging: Consumer, Food Service, Private Label, Bulk
Brands:
DAKOTA GROWERS PASTA
PASTA SANITA
ZIA BRIOSA

3683 Dakota Organic Products
500 19th Street Southwest
P.O. Box 815
Watertown, SD 57201-0815   605-884-1100
Fax: 605-884-1133 800-243-7264
hescoinc@hesco-inc.com www.hesco-inc.com
Processor and exporter of wheat, millet, durum, flour, sorghum meal, oat flour, flakes, triticale and rye flakes; organic forms available
President: Colleen Hestad
CEO: Bruce Hestad
VP: Rick Hanson
Quality Control: Michael Britt
Sales: Brad Hennrich
Plant Manager: Layne Glines
Purchasing: Travis Sitter
Estimated Sales: $ 50 - 100 Million
Number Employees: 20-49
Sq. footage: 15000
Parent Co: Hesco, Inc.
Type of Packaging: Bulk
Brands:
Enhanced Oat Fiber
Flaxgrain
Flaxmeal

3684 Dakota Prairie Organic Flour Company
500 North Street West
Harvey, ND 58341   701-324-4330
Fax: 701-324-4334 www.dakota-prairie.com
Organic white & wheat flours, gluten free flour, bread, brownie, cake & cookie mixes.

3685 Dakota Premium Foods
100 Bridgepoint Curv
South St Paul, MN 55075-5506   651-552-8230
Fax: 651-552-2107
Manufacturer and exporter of beef
Manager: Pat Devitt
CEO: Thomas Rosen
COO: Greg Benedict
Plant Manager: Steve Cortinas
Estimated Sales: 169 Million
Number Employees: 5-9
Parent Co: Rosen Diversified
Type of Packaging: Consumer, Food Service, Private Label, Bulk

3686 (HQ)Dale T. Smith & Sons Meat Packing Corporation
P.O.Box 479
Draper, UT 84020-0479   801-571-3611
Fax: 801-571-3685 www.smithmeats.com
Manufacturer of beef, pork and lamb, packing service
President: Dale Smith
Co-Owner: Darrell Smith
Production Manager: Roger McNicol
Estimated Sales: $22.60 Million
Number Employees: 50-99
Type of Packaging: Consumer, Food Service

3687 Dale and Thomas Popcorn
One Cedar Lane
Englewood, NJ 07631   201-645-4600
Fax: 201-645-4848 800-767-4444
info@daleanfthomaspopcorn.com
www.daleandthomaspopcorn.com
flavored popcorn
Estimated Sales: $40.8 Million
Number Employees: 250

3688 Daley Brothers
215 Water Street, Suite 301
St John's, NL A1C 6C9
Canada   709-364-8844
Fax: 709-364-7216 sales@daleybrothers.com
www.daleybrothers.com
Manufacturer and exporter of fresh and frozen seafood
President: Terry Daley
CEO: Steve Hoskins
Sales Manager: Rosemary Buckingham
Number Employees: 20-49
Type of Packaging: Bulk

3689 Dalla Valle Vineyards
P.O.Box 329
Oakville, CA 94562-0329   707-944-2676
Fax: 707-944-8411 www.dallavalleyineyards.com
Wines
President: Naoko Dalla Valle
Estimated Sales: $2.5-5 Million
Number Employees: 5-9
Type of Packaging: Private Label
Brands:
DALLA

3690 Dallas City Packing
3049 Morrell Ave
Dallas, TX 75203-4000   214-948-3901
Fax: 214-942-2039
Manufacturer and exporter of boxed and carcass beef; also, cooked sausage products
President: Alan Rubin
Estimated Sales: $75 Million
Number Employees: 100-249
Type of Packaging: Food Service, Private Label

3691 Dallas Dressed Beef
1348 Conant St
Dallas, TX 75207-6006   214-638-0142
Fax: 214-631-0765
Manufacturer of frozen meat patties including beef and pork
President: David Hampton
Estimated Sales: $20-50 Million
Number Employees: 10-19
Type of Packaging: Consumer, Food Service

3692 Dallis Brothers
10030 Atlantic Ave
Jamaica, NY 11416-1795   718-845-3010
Fax: 718-843-0178 800-424-4252
info@dallisbros.com www.dallisbros.com
Coffee and tea
President: Marcello Crescent
Sales: Jim Monahan
Operations Manager: Charles Bosworth
Estimated Sales: $20-50 Million
Number Employees: 20-49
Type of Packaging: Private Label
Brands:
DALLIS BROS. COFFEE

3693 Dalton's Best Maid Products
P.O.Box 1809
Fort Worth, TX 76101-1809   817-335-5494
Fax: 817-534-7117 www.bestmaidproducts.com

Manufacturer of a variety of pickles, sauces, dressings and condiments
Chairman: Gary Dalton
President: Brian Dalton
Marketing Director: Roger Fort
Estimated Sales: $50.4 Million
Number Employees: 100-249
Type of Packaging: Consumer
Brands:
BEST MAID
DEL-DIXI

3694 Dalton's Best Maid Products
P.O.Box 1809
Fort Worth, TX 76101-1809   817-335-5494
Fax: 817-534-7117 800-447-3581
www.bestmaidproducts.com
Pickles, dressings
President: Brian Dalton
Sales Director: Noah Bass
Estimated Sales: $50-100 Million
Number Employees: 100-249
Brands:
DALTON'S

3695 Damon Industries
822 Packer Way
Sparks, NV 89431-6445   775-331-3200
Fax: 775-331-3980 info@fruitful.com
www.fruitful.com
Manufacturer of shelf stable juice and beverage concentrates
President: Douglas Damon
Quality Control: Richard Johnson
Sales Manager: Larry Grant
Productions: Gary Messerli
Estimated Sales: $5-10 Million
Number Employees: 20-49
Brands:
FRUITFUL JUICE PRODUCTS
JUICE DIRECT

3696 Damron Corporation
4433 W Ohio St
Chicago, IL 60624-1054   773-265-2724
Fax: 773-826-6004 800-333-1860
info@damrontea.com www.damroncorp.com
Tea
President/CEO: Ronald Damper
Estimated Sales: $20-50 Million
Number Employees: 20-49
Type of Packaging: Bulk
Brands:
DAMRON
HARVEST DELIGHTA

3697 Dan Carter
PO Box 282
Richfield, WI 53076-0282   920-387-5740
Fax: 920-387-2194 800-782-0741
www.dcicheeseco.com
Manufacturer of cheese
President: Timothy Omer
Estimated Sales: $500,000-$1 Million
Number Employees: 20-49
Brands:
DAN CARTER

3698 Dan Tudor & Sons
11081 Zachary Ave
Delano, CA 93215-9596   661-792-3176
Fax: 661-792-6488
Packer and exporter of table grapes
Owner: John Buksa
Sales Manager: Anthony Buksa
Estimated Sales: $2.5-5 Million
Number Employees: 5-9
Type of Packaging: Consumer, Food Service, Bulk

3699 Dan's Feed Bin
806 Hammond Ave
Superior, WI 54880-6631   715-394-6639
Fax: 715-394-5333
Manufacturer of flour
Owner: Dan Wicklund
Estimated Sales: $1-2.5 Million
Number Employees: 10-19

3700 Dan's Prize
P.O.Box 2997
Gainesville, GA 30503-2997   770-503-1881
Fax: 770-503-7710 800-233-5845

Roast beef, full line deli meat
President/CEO: Joe Smith
Senior VP: James W Cavanaugh
VP Sales: Patrick Hutzel
Operations: Bob Uhlenkamp
Number Employees: 10-19
Parent Co: Hormel
Brands:
DAN'S PRIZE

3701 Dan-D Foods Ltd
11760 Machrina Way
Richmond, BC V7A-4VA
Canada 604-274-3263
Fax: 604-274-3268 info@dan-dpak.com
www.dan-dpak.com
Fine food importer, manufacturer and distributor of cashews, dried fruits, rice crackers, snack foods, spices etc. from around the world.
Chairman/President/CEO/Founder: Dan On
Number Employees: 500
Type of Packaging: Food Service, Bulk

3702 Dan-Dee Pretzel & Chip Company
4553 Johnston Pkwy
Cleveland, OH 44128-2954 216-341-1764
Fax: 216-341-9386 www.troyerfarms.com
Snack products
Manager: Gene Stiffler
Estimated Sales: $ 20 - 50 Million
Number Employees: 50-99
Brands:
DAN DEE

3703 Dancing Deer Baking Company
65 Sprague St # 1
Hyde Park, MA 02136-2062 617-442-7300
Fax: 617-442-8118 888-699-3337
info@dancingdeer.com www.dancingdeer.com
Manufacturer of all natural cakes and cookies
President/CEO: Patricia Karter
CFO: James Tyson
Marketing: Duane Lefevre
Sales: Dave Lamlein
Production: Lissa McBurney
Estimated Sales: $20-50 Million
Number Employees: 20-49
Number of Brands: 1
Number of Products: 25
Sq. footage: 14000
Type of Packaging: Consumer, Food Service, Private Label, Bulk

3704 Dancing Paws
17575 Pacific Coast Highway
Pacific Palisades, CA 90272-4148 310-230-9898
Fax: 310-230-6777 888-644-7297
werndog@dancingpaws.com
www.dancingpaws.com
Manufacturer of all natural dog and cat supplements that are human quality made
President: Werner Forster
COO: Buzz Truitt
Number Employees: 9
Brands:
COAT SHINE PREMIUM
DANCING PAWS
EDIBLE COAT CONDITIONER
HI-POTENCY JOINT RECOVERY
HOWLIN' GOURMET
HUMAN QUALITY MADE FOR PETS
JOINT MAINTENANCE
NATURAL FLEA EZE
SHAKE'N'ZYME

3705 Dandy US
11n357 Hickory Court
Hampshire, IL 60140-8650 847-683-2868
Fax: 847-683-7803 www.dandygroup.com
Sales Development Manager: Daniel Lynn

3706 Dangold
13843 78th Road
Flushing, NY 11367-3241 718-591-5286
Fax: 718-591-5193
Confectioneries and cookies
President/Public Relations: Daniel Gross
Number Employees: 1-4
Type of Packaging: Private Label
Brands:
DANGOLD

3707 Daniel Weaver Company
P.O.Box 508
Lebanon, PA 17042-0508 717-274-6100
Fax: 717-274-6103 800-932-8377
dweaverco@onemain.com www.godshalls.com
Beef, beef products
Manager: Jerry Landuyt
CFO: Toni Spangler
VP: Hugh Millen
Marketing: Hugh Miller
Estimated Sales: $10-20 Million
Number Employees: 20-49
Type of Packaging: Private Label
Brands:
BAUM'S SWEET BOLOGNA
WEAVER'S BEEF JERKY
WEAVER'S BEEF STICKS
WEAVER'S FAMOUS LEBANON BOLOGNA
WEAVER'S WOOD SMOKED BACON
WEAVER'S WOOD SMOKED HAMS

3708 Daniel Webster Hearth NKettle
141 Falmouth Rd
Hyannis, MA 02601-2755 508-771-0040
Fax: 508-771-0883 888-774-5511
www.cataniahospitalitygroup.com
Fresh and frozen soups and chowders
President: Vincent J Catania
VP: Richard Catonia
Estimated Sales: $500,000-$1 Million
Number Employees: 500-999
Type of Packaging: Private Label
Brands:
CAPE COD CLAM CHOWDER
CAPE COD LOBSTER BISQUE
CAPE COD LOBSTER CHOWDER
LOBSTER CHOWDER
MINESTRONE

3709 Daniel's Bagel & Baguette Corporation
414 36th Avenue SE
Calgary, AB T2G 1W4
Canada 403-243-3207
danbagel@telusplanet.net
Manufacturer of baked goods including specialty breads, bagels and pretzels
President: D Oppenheim
Number Employees: 6
Type of Packaging: Consumer, Food Service

3710 Daniele Imports
1150 University Ave # 8
Rochester, NY 14607-1694 585-244-3140
Fax: 585-461-2234 800-298-9410
info@eurocafeimports.com
www.eurocafeimports.com
Biscotti, chocolate, espresso, flavoring. Distributors of cafe and restaurant products
Owner: Barb Campbell
Public Relations: Danny Daniele
Estimated Sales: $1-2.5 Million
Number Employees: 5-9

3711 Daniels Seafood Company
Mill Landing Road
Wanchese, NC 27981 252-473-5779
Seafood
President: Mickey Daniels
Estimated Sales: $2.5-5 Million
Number Employees: 10-19
Brands:
DANIELS

3712 Danisco USA
3919 Kidron Road
Lakeland, FL 33811-1293 863-646-0165
Fax: 863-646-0991 usa.info@danisco.com
www.danisco.com
Manufacturer of natural fruit flavors
President: Kevin McCole
Director Business Development: Gil Escobar
Innovation Director: Robert Kryger
Director Operations: Paul Jones
Estimated Sales: $25-49.9 Million
Number Employees: 1-4

3713 Danisco-Cultor
430 Saw Mill River Rd
Ardsley, NY 10502-2605 914-674-6300
Fax: 914-674-6538 www.danisco.com

Ingredients for beverage products, including flavor enhancers, and functional botanicals, xylitol, industrial enzymes, sugar
President: Robert Mayer
CEO: Tom Knutzen
VP: Philippe Lavielle
Estimated Sales: $ 5 - 10 Million
Number Employees: 20-49

3714 Danish Baking Company
15215 Keswick St
Van Nuys, CA 91405-1050 818-786-1700
Fax: 818-786-3617 800-777-4970
Manufacturer and exporter of fresh and frozen baked goods including brownies, muffins, pastries, fruit tortes, bread and cakes: individual portions available
Manager: Torben Jensen
CFO/General Manager: Torben Jensen
Estimated Sales: $ 10 - 20 Million
Number Employees: 50-99
Sq. footage: 20000
Type of Packaging: Consumer, Food Service, Private Label, Bulk
Other Locations:
Brands:
BUBBLES BAKING CO.
GRANNY'S GOURMET GOODIES

3715 Danish Creamery Association
755 F St
Fresno, CA 93706-3416 559-233-5154
Fax: 559-268-5101 www.californiadairies.com
Creamery
Executive VP: Jim Gomes
Plant Manager: Bob Ray
Estimated Sales: $50-100 Million
Number Employees: 100-249
Sq. footage: 135
Brands:
DANISH CREAMERY

3716 Danish Maid Butter Company
8512 S Commercial Ave
Chicago, IL 60617-2533 773-731-8787
Fax: 773-731-9812
danishmaidbutter@hotmail.com
www.danishmaid.com
Manufacturer of dairy products including anhydrous milkfat, butter oil and regular and whipped butter; also, packaging services available
President: Susan Wagner
Plant Manager: Matthew Wagner
Estimated Sales: $5-9.9 Million
Number Employees: 10
Sq. footage: 18000
Type of Packaging: Consumer, Food Service, Private Label, Bulk

3717 (HQ)Dankworth Packing Company
P.O.Box 584
Ballinger, TX 76821-0584 325-365-3552
Fax: 325-365-2367
Manufacturer of pork products including ham, bacon and sausage; also, barbecue meats and gift boxes available, packing services available
President: Michael Dankworth
Estimated Sales: $17 Million
Number Employees: 50-99
Type of Packaging: Consumer

3718 Danner Salads
P.O.Box 10585
Peoria, IL 61612-0585 309-691-0289
Fax: 309-691-5267 jenellesummas@yahoo.com
Manufacturer of prepared salads including potato
President: Jenelle Summers
VP Treasurer: Doreen Cunningham
Production Manager: Paula Riddle
Plant Manager: Chuck Summers
Estimated Sales: $ 3 Million
Number Employees: 20-49
Number of Products: 50
Type of Packaging: Food Service, Private Label, Bulk

3719 Dannon Company
1300 W Peter Smith St
Fort Worth, TX 76104-2116 817-332-1264
Fax: 817-877-0854 800-211-6565
www.dannon.com

Manufacturer of yogurt
President/CEO: Juan Carlos Dalto
CFO: Tony Cicio
SVP Marketing: Andreas Ostermayr
Plant Manager: Mike Weidman
Estimated Sales: $100-500 Million
Number Employees: 250-499
Parent Co: Danone Group
Type of Packaging: Consumer, Food Service
Other Locations:
Dannon Plant
Minster OH
Dannon Plant
West Jordan UT
Brands:
DANNON

3720 Dannon Company
P.O.Box 122
Minster, OH 45865-0122   419-628-3861
          Fax: 419-628-4008 www.dannon.com
Manufacturer of yogurt
Manager: Didier Menu
CFO: Tony Cicio
VP R&D North America: Hans Leijtens
VP Quality Management: Todd Brown
SVP Marketing: Andreas Ostermayr
SVP Sales: Nick Krzyzaniak
VP Regulatory Affairs: Philippe Caradec
VP Manufacturing: Alain Foulgoc
VP Purchasing: Francois Blanckaert
Estimated Sales: $100-499.9 Million
Number Employees: 250-499
Parent Co: Groupe Danone
Other Locations:
Dannon Company
Minster OH
Dannon Company
Fort Worth TX
Dannon Company
West Jordan UT
Brands:
DANNON
DANONE

3721 (HQ)Dannon Company
100 Hillside Ave # 3
White Plains, NY 10603-2863   914-872-8400
          Fax: 914-366-2805   877-326-6668
                    www.dannon.com
Manufacturer of yogurt products
President/CEO: Juan Carlos Dalto
CFO: Tony Cicio
CEO: Gustavo Valle
VP Quality Management: Todd Brown
Sales: Jim Murphy
Sr Director Public Relations: Michael Neuwirth
VP Purchasing: Francois Blankaert
Number Employees: 500-999
Parent Co: Dannon Groupe
Other Locations:
Dannon Company Plant
West Jordan UT
Dannon Company Plant
Fort Worth TX
Dannon Company Plant
Minster OH
Brands:
DANNON

3722 Danny's Poultry
2129 S Erie Hwy
Hamilton, OH 45011   513-737-7780
                    Fax: 513-868-7372
Poultry
Estimated Sales: $1-2.5 Million
Number Employees: 10-19
Brands:
DANNY'S

3723 (HQ)Danone Waters of North America
3280 E Foothill Boulevard
Suite 400
Pasadena, CA 91107-3190   626-585-1000
          Fax: 626-585-8703 www.evian.com,
                    www.dannon.com
Manufacturer of bottled water
President: Thomas Kunz
CEO: William Holl
CFO: Dan Redfern
VP Marketing: Conrad Smits
Sales: Pascal Rigaud

Estimated Sales: $10-20 Million
Number Employees: 50-99
Parent Co: Danone Group
Type of Packaging: Consumer
Brands:
ALHAMBRA
DANNON
EVIAN
SPARKLETTS

3724 Danvers Bakery
114 Water Street
Danvers, MA 01923-3751   978-774-9186
Breads, rolls, pastries, cakes
Estimated Sales: Less than $500,000
Number Employees: 5-9
Brands:
DANVERS

3725 Daphne Baking Company
One Landmark Lane
PO Box 417
Kent, CT 06757   860-927-1818
          Fax: 646-349-4164   info@daphnebaking.com
                    www.daphnebaking.com
Frozen tarts, shells and cakes
Number Employees: 5

3726 Daprano & Company
203 E Harris Avenue
South San Francisco, CA 94080-6807650-588-5417
          Fax: 650-588-4996   800-722-6333
          angelo@daprano.com   www.daprano.com
Manufacturer of designer chocolates, bonbons, novelties, Italian cookies, biscotti, madeleines, shortbread
President: Angelo Daprano
Brands:
AMARETTI VIRGINIA
BONBON BARNIER
CAFFAREL
CANTATTI
FLAMIGNI
GATSBY'S/PIERRE KOENIG
JILA & JOLS
REINHARDT

3727 Darbo
145 Grand St
Carlstadt, NJ 07072-2106   201-939-5656
          Fax: 201-939-5613   800-727-8791
                    www.parisgourmet.com
President: Xavier Noel
Parent Co: Paris Gourmet

3728 Darby Plains Dairy
9870 Us Highway 42 S
Plain City, OH 43064-9561   614-873-4574
                    Fax: 614-873-8304
Milk, dairy products
Owner: Derrick Yoder
Estimated Sales: $500,000-$1 Million
Number Employees: 10-19
Brands:
DARBY PLAINS

3729 Dare Foods
4600 Joliet Street
Denver, CO 80239-2922   800-722-1871
          Fax: 303-371-8185   cmollohan@darefoods.com
                    www.darefoods.com
Manufacturer of cookies and crackers
President: Carl Doerr
Plant Manager: Jeff Wilson

3730 (HQ)Dare Foods
2481 Kingsway Drive
PO Box 1058
Kitchener, ON N2G 4G4
Canada   519-893-3233
          Fax: 519-893-8369   800-865-8225
                    www.darefoods.com
Manufacturer and exporter of sweet biscuits, cookies and crackers; also, chocolate, regular and gummy candies
President: Lee Andrews
CFO: Lois Norris
Research & Development: Aubrey Williams
Marketing Director: Heather McTavish
Sales Director: Johnathan Taylor
Operations Manager: Tim Yoworski
Number Employees: 1000
Type of Packaging: Consumer, Food Service, Private Label, Bulk

Other Locations:
Dare Foods Ltd.
Milton ON
Brands:
BREMNER
BRETON
CABARET
DARE
GRISSOL
REALFRUIT GUMMI'S
SUNMAID
VIVANT

3731 Dare Foods
143 Tycos Drive
Toronto, ON M6B 1W6
Canada   416-787-1495
          Fax: 416-787-5406   800-665-5817
                    nvoutt@darefoods.com
Manufacturer and exporter of cookies, candies and crackers; also, ground cookie ingredients
National Sales Manager: Neil S Voutt
Type of Packaging: Bulk

3732 Dare Foods
51 Atlantic Avenue
Suite 9
Marblehead, MA 01945-3045   781-639-1808
          Fax: 781-639-2286   mthompson@darefoods.com
                    www.darefoodsinc.com
Cookies and crackers
President: Graham Dare
VP/General Manager: Michael Thompson
Estimated Sales: $500,000-$1 Million
Number Employees: 1-4
Type of Packaging: Private Label
Brands:
BREALETINE COOKIES
BRENNER WAFERS
BRETON
COBRANT
DARE COOKIES
VINTA CRACKERS
VIVANT CRACKERS

3733 Dare Foods Incorporated
248 Kingway Drive
PO Box 1058
Kitchener, ON N2G 4G4   519-893-5500
          Fax: 519-893-2644   800-265-8222
          akueneman@darefoods.com   www.darefoods.com
cookies, crackers, fine breads and candy

3734 Daregal Gourmet
100 Overlook Center
2nd Floor Suite 2014
Princeton, NJ 08540   609-375-2312
          Fax: 609-651-8356   info@daregalgourmet.com
                    www.daregalgourmet.com
forzen chopped herbs

3735 Darifair Foods
4131 Sunbeam Rd
Jacksonville, FL 32257-6027   904-268-8999
          Fax: 904-268-8666   info@darifair.com
                    www.darifair.com
Manufacturers of cultured dairy ice cream and dessert
President: Andrew Block
CFO: William Block
VP Business Development: Jeffrey Block
VP Marketing: Michele Block
VP Operations: Ed Stevens
Estimated Sales: $2.5-5 Million
Number Employees: 10-19
Type of Packaging: Private Label
Brands:
DAIRFAIR

3736 Darigold
1130 Rainier Ave S
Seattle, WA 98144   206-284-7220
          Fax: 206-722-2569   800-333-6455
                    www.darigold.com
Milk, butter, sour cream, yogurt, cottage cheese, half & half/creamers/whipping cream and buttermilk
President/CEO: John Underwood
SVP Finance/CFO: John Wells
Sales Manager: Scott Campbell
SVP Operations: Jim Wegner
Plant Manager: Todd Aarons
Purchasing Agent: Ralph Goeckner
Estimated Sales: $2 Billion
Number Employees: 1,240

Type of Packaging: Consumer, Food Service, Private Label, Bulk
Brands:
Fred Meyer
Haggen
Safeway
Sysco Products
Western Family

3737 Darigold
P.O.Box 79007
Seattle, WA 98119-7907   360-354-2151
Fax: 360-354-1010 www.darigold.com
Manufacturer of butter, milk, yogurt, sour cream, cottage cheese and frozen desserts
CEO: John Mueller
Plant Manager: Wayne Eskew
Estimated Sales: $50-100 Million
Number Employees: 50-99
Parent Co: Darigold Farms
Brands:
DAIRYMEN'S

3738 Darigold Inc
1130 Rainier Ave S
Seattle, WA 98114   206-286-6832
Fax: 206-722-2569 800-333-6455
www.darigold.com
Milk, butter, sour cream, yogurt, cottage cheese, half & half/creamers, whipping cream, buttermilk
President/CEO: John Underwood
SVP Finance/CFO: John Wells
VP: Steve Harper
Quality Control: Stephanie Olmsted
Marketing: Randy Eronimous
Public Relations: David Coburn
SVP Operations: Jim Wegner
Purchasing: George Johnson
Estimated Sales: $ 1-5 Billion
Number Employees: 1240
Type of Packaging: Consumer, Food Service, Private Label, Bulk
Other Locations:
Darigold Boise ID
Darigold Caldwell ID
Darigold Chehalis WA
Darigold Issaquah WA
Darigold Jerome ID
Darigold Los Angeles ID
Darigold Lynden WA
Darigold Medford OR
Darigold Portland OR
Darigold Seattle WA
Darigold Sunnyside WA
Brands:
Darigold

3739 Darisweet Farms
21707 66th Avenue W
Mountlake Terrace, WA 98043-2103 425-771-5007
Fax: 425-774-8767 info@darisweet.com
www.darisweet.com
Manufacturer of portion control whipped and garlic butter and margarine blend; wholesaler/distributor of cheese; serving the food service market
President: Litsa Stamlous
General Manager: Paula Stamlous
Estimated Sales: $5-10 Million
Number Employees: 5-9
Sq. footage: 8000
Type of Packaging: Consumer, Food Service, Private Label, Bulk

3740 Dark Mountain Winery and Brewery
13605 E Benson Highway
Vail, AZ 85641-9027   520-762-5777
Fax: 520-762-5898
Wine and beer
President: H Clarke Romans
Estimated Sales: $1-2.5 Million
Number Employees: 1-4
Brands:
DARK MOUNTAIN

3741 Dark Tickle Company
PO Box 191
Griquet, NL A0K 2X0
Canada   709-623-2354
Fax: 709-623-2354 darktickle@nf.sympatico.ca
www.darktickle.com
Manufacturer and exporter of wild berry jams, toppings, beverage concentrate, relish and vinegars
President: Stephen Knudsen
Number Employees: 6
Sq. footage: 2500
Type of Packaging: Consumer
Brands:
DARK TICKLE

3742 Darling International
4734 S 27th St
Omaha, NE 68107-2732   402-733-3010
Fax: 402-733-8460 www.darlingii.com
Manufacturer of edible oils; also, partially defatted chopped beef and beef tissue
General Manager: Mike Musgrave
Estimated Sales: $2.5-5 Million
Number Employees: 10-19
Parent Co: Darling Delaware

3743 (HQ)Darling International
3275 W 65th St
Cleveland, OH 44102-5509   216-651-9300
Fax: 216-651-5675 www.darlingii.com
Manufacturer of rendered grease
General Manager: Mike Musgrave
Plant Manager: Lori Horvath
Estimated Sales: $5-10 Million
Number Employees: 20-49

3744 Darmex Division of Fuchs
2140 S 88th Street
Kansas City, KS 66111-1756   913-441-7143
Fax: 913-441-2333 www.darmex.com

3745 Daume Winery
300 S Lewis Rd
Camarillo, CA 93012-6619   805-484-0597
Fax: 805-484-0597 800-559-9922
Wines
President: John Daume
Estimated Sales: Less than $500,000
Number Employees: 1-4
Sq. footage: 2
Type of Packaging: Private Label
Brands:
DAUME

3746 Dave Kingston Produce
477 Shoup Ave # 207
Idaho Falls, ID 83402-3658   208-522-2365
Fax: 208-552-7488 800-888-7783
www.kingstonmarketing.com
Manufacturer, packager, shipper and exporter of produce including potatoes and onions
Owner: Dave Kingston
Contact: Jody Boline
Estimated Sales: $20-50 Million
Number Employees: 100-249
Brands:
AWESOME
RUSSETTS

3747 Dave's Bakery
1235 Main St
Honesdale, PA 18431-2062   570-253-1660
Manufacturer of baked goods including bread, cakes, cookies, rolls and pies
President: Edwin Day
Estimated Sales: $500,000-$1 Million
Number Employees: 10-19
Type of Packaging: Consumer

3748 Dave's Gourmet
2000 McKinnon Ave # 428-5
San Francisco, CA 94124-1621   415-401-9100
Fax: 415-401-9107 800-758-0372
info@davesgourmet.com
www.davesgourmet.com
Manufacturer and exporter of hot sauce, mayonnaise, salsa, salad dressing, nuts, cheese and snacks; wholesaler/distributor of three-beer mustard; serving the food service market
Owner: Dave Hrischcop
Estimated Sales: $10-20 Million
Number Employees: 5-9
Sq. footage: 20000

Type of Packaging: Consumer, Food Service, Private Label, Bulk
Brands:
BONSAL & LLOYD
GARLIC MASTERPIECE
INSANITY
JUMP UP & KISS ME
SOLES

3749 Dave's Hawaiian Ice Cream
96-1361 Waihona St
Pearl City, HI 96782-1971   808-453-0500
Fax: 808-456-8078
www.daveshawaiianicecream.com
Manufacturer of ice cream including Hawaiian flavors available in pints; also, frozen yogurt, sherbet, ice cream pies and cakes
President, CEO: David Leong
Estimated Sales: $2.5-5 Million
Number Employees: 10-19
Sq. footage: 5000
Type of Packaging: Private Label, Bulk

3750 David Berg & Company
2501 N Damen Ave
Chicago, IL 60647-2101   773-489-4711
Fax: 773-278-4759 info@davidberg.com
www.davidberg.com
Manufacturer of beef products including frankfurters, Polish sausage, bratwurst, knockwurst, pastrami, salami, beef sticks, corned beef and roast beef.
President: Jim Einsenberg
VP Sales: Craig Campbell
Estimated Sales: $100-500 Million
Number Employees: 250-499
Type of Packaging: Consumer, Food Service
Brands:
DAVID BERG

3751 David Bradley Chocolatier
P.O.Box 458
Windsor, NJ 08561-0458   609-443-4747
Fax: 609-443-8762 877-289-7933
mhicks4794@aol.com www.dbchocolate.com
Confectionery
President/CEO: Bob Hicks
Vice President: Marcy Hicks
Estimated Sales: $ 1 - 3 Million
Number Employees: 50-99
Type of Packaging: Private Label
Brands:
Gourmet Snack Bags
Sophisticated Chocol
Zany Pretzels

3752 David Bruce Winery
21439 Bear Creek Rd
Los Gatos, CA 95033-9429   408-354-4214
Fax: 408-395-5478 800-397-9972
dbw@davidbrucewinery.com
www.davidbrucewinery.com
Wines
Owner: David Bruce
Director Sales/Marketing: Joe Kimbro
Director Vineyard Operations: Greg Stokes
Production Manager, Winemaker: Eric Glomski
Cellar Master, Winemaker: Mike Sones
Estimated Sales: $2.5-5 Million
Number Employees: 20-49
Type of Packaging: Private Label
Brands:
DAVID BRUCE

3753 David Elliott Poultry Farms
300 Breck St
Scranton, PA 18505-1602   570-344-6348
Fax: 570-344-6349
Manufacturer and exporter of poultry
President: David Fink
VP: Moshe Fink
Estimated Sales: $ 10 - 20 Million
Number Employees: 50-99
Type of Packaging: Consumer

3754 David Gollott Seafood
PO Box 553
Biloxi, MS 39533-0553   228-374-2555
Fax: 228-374-2561
Refrigerated oysters, frozen shrimp
President: David Gollott, Sr.
Sales Manager: David Gollot, Jr.
Estimated Sales: $10-20 Million
Number Employees: 50-99

Brands:
DAVID'S BEST
GOLLOT

3755 David Michael & Company
10801 Decatur Rd
Philadelphia, PA 19154-3298   215-632-3100
     Fax: 215-637-3920   800-363-5286
dmflavor@dmflavors.com   www.dmflavors.com
Manufacturer and exporter of flavors including beef
extract replacement, savory, nut, fruit, vanilla extract
and raisin juice concentrate; also, stabilizers
President: William B Rosskam Iii
President/COO: Skip Rosskam
Estimated Sales:$100+ Million
Number Employees: 100-249
Number of Brands: 45
Number of Products: 26k
Sq. footage: 86000
Type of Packaging: Consumer, Private Label, Bulk
Brands:
BEEFMATE
COCOAMATE
DM CHOICE
DM OLE
FAIRWAY
GORILLA VANILLA
HONEYMATE
MICHAELOK
MICHTEX
PREMIER
RAISINMATE
SUPER SUPREME
SUPERVAN
SUPREME

3756 David Mosner Meat Products
E8 Hunts Point Co Op Mkt # E8
Bronx, NY 10474-7559   718-328-5600
     Fax: 718-842-6693   info@davidmosner.com
                www.davidmosner.com
Manufacturer and packer of veal and lamb
President: Michael Mosner
CEO: Philip Mosner
Sales/Production Manager: Benjamin Mosner
Directs Lamb Program: Larry Breth
Estimated Sales:$ 20 - 50 Million
Number Employees: 20-49
Type of Packaging: Consumer, Food Service, Private Label
Brands:
MVP

3757 David Rio Coffee & Tea
P.O.Box 885462
San Francisco, CA 94188-5462   415-543-2733
     Fax: 415-543-2749   800-454-9605
     chai@davidrio.com   www.davidrio.com
Chai and loose leaf teas
President: Scott Lowe
VP: Rio Miura
Sales: Laure Macanes
Estimated Sales:$2 Million
Number Employees: 10-19
Number of Brands: 2
Number of Products: 20
Sq. footage: 3150
Parent Co: David Rio San Francisco
Type of Packaging: Consumer, Food Service, Private Label, Bulk
Brands:
DAVID RIO CHAI

3758 David's Cookies
12 Commerce Rd
Fairfield, NJ 07004-1602   973-808-8248
     Fax: 973-882-6998 oliver@davidscookies.com
                www.davidscookies.com
Manufacturers fresh and frozen cookie dough,
scones, crumbcake rugulach, butter cookies, brownies and mini-muffins
President: Ari Margulies
Estimated Sales:$10-20 Million
Number Employees: 20-49
Sq. footage: 20000
Parent Co: Fairfield Gourmet Foods
Brands:
COOKIE CUPBOARD
DAVID'S COOKIES

3759 David's Fish Market
257 Davis St
Fall River, MA 02720-5129   508-676-1221
                Fax: 508-659-1223

Seafood
Owner: Maria Sardinha
Estimated Sales:$ 1 - 3 Million
Number Employees: 1-4

3760 Davidson Meat Processing Plant
6490 Corwin Ave
Waynesville, OH 45068-9722   513-897-2971
Manufacturer of frozen meats including beef, pork
and lamb
President: Adam Davidson
Estimated Sales:$1-2.5 Million
Number Employees: 1-4

3761 Davidson Meat Products
424 S 2nd Street
New Bedford, MA 02740-5749   508-999-6293
                Fax: 508-991-4533
Manufacturer of frozen and fresh meat products including sausage, hamburger patties, frankfurters,
kielbasa, salami, etc
Estimated Sales:$ 5 - 10 Million
Number Employees: 10-19
Type of Packaging: Consumer, Food Service
Brands:
DAVIDSON'S
MAC GREGOR

3762 Davidson of Dundee
P.O.Box 800
Dundee, FL 33838-0800   863-439-2284
     Fax: 863-439-5049 800-654-0647
          sales@davidsonofdundee.com
          www.davidsonofdundee.com
Manufacturer of fresh citrus fruit including; oranges,
ruby red grapefruits, all natural citrus candies, coconut patties, citrus marmalades, citrus jellies, butters
and orange blossom honey. Gift baskets available
President: Glen Davidson
CEO: Tom Davidson
Estimated Sales:$6 Million
Number Employees: 100-249
Number of Brands: 1
Number of Products: 112
Sq. footage: 150000
Type of Packaging: Consumer, Private Label

3763 Davidson's Organic Tea
PO Box 11214
Reno, NV 89510   775-356-1690
     Fax: 775-356-3713   800-882-5888
info@davidsonstea.com   www.davidsonstea.com
Organic teas

3764 Davidsons
PO Box 11214
Reno, NV 89510-1214   775-356-1690
     Fax: 775-356-3713   800-882-5888
tea@davidson.reno.nv.us   www.davidsontea.com
Manufacturer, exporter and importer of teas, spices,
and accessories for the specialty trade and retail use
Estimated Sales:$5-10 Million
Number Employees: 5-9
Sq. footage: 25000
Brands:
DAVIDSON'S INC

3765 Davis Bakery & Delicatessen
4572 Renaissance Pkwy
Cleveland, OH 44128-5702   216-464-5599
     Fax: 216-932-8282 www.davisbakery.net
Manufacturer of specialty baked goods including
cakes, doughnuts and low-sodium
President: Joel Davis
VP Treasurer: Sheldon Davis
Supervisor Sales: Janice Davis
VP Deli Operations: Sam Perkul
Estimated Sales:$1-2.5 Million
Number Employees: 10-19
Brands:
KIDDIE KAKES
SODEX

3766 Davis Bread & Desserts
720 Olive Dr
Davis, CA 95616-4740   530-757-2700
          www.davisbreadanddesserts.com
Breads, rolls and desserts
Estimated Sales:$10-20 Million
Number Employees: 10-19
Brands:
DAVIS BREAD

3767 Davis Bynum Winery
239 Theresa Ct
Healdsburg, CA 95448-3445   707-431-0339
     Fax: 707-433-4309   800-826-1073
info@davisbynum.com   www.davisbynum.com
Wines
President: Davis Bynum
CFO: Susie Bynum
Purchasing: Hampton Bynum
Estimated Sales:$2.5-5 Million
Number Employees: 10-19
Number of Brands: 2
Type of Packaging: Private Label
Brands:
DAVIS BYNUM
RIVER BEND

3768 Davis Cookie Company
P.O.Box 430
Rimersburg, PA 16248-0430   814-473-8181
     Fax: 814-473-3042 sales@daviscookie.com
                www.daviscookie.com
Cookies
President: Dana Davis
VP: Dan Davis
Estimated Sales:$20-50 Million
Number Employees: 50-99
Brands:
DAVIS COOKIE

3769 Davis Custom Meat Processing
206 W 1st
Overbrook, KS 66524-9565   785-665-7713
Manufacturer of meat products and custom butchering
Owner: Aaron Higbie
Estimated Sales:$1-3 Million
Number Employees: 5-9
Type of Packaging: Consumer

3770 Davis Food Company
P.O.Box 16118
Plantation, FL 33318-6118   954-791-5868
                Fax: 440-461-2261
ddwoskin@stadiummustard.com
          www.stadiummustard.com
Mustard
President: Peggy D Davis
Estimated Sales:$1-2.5 Million
Number Employees: 1-4
Brands:
STADIUM MUSTARD

3771 Davis Strait Fisheries
71 McQuade Lake Crescent
Halifax, NS B3S 1C4
Canada   902-450-5115
     Fax: 902-450-5006 admin@davisstrait.com
Manufacturer of northern shrimp, scallops,
snowcraf, cod, haddock, pollock
Marketing Director: John Andrews
Manager: Grant Stonehouse
Estimated Sales:$48 Million
Number Employees: 75
Type of Packaging: Bulk
Brands:
DAVIS STRAIT FISHERIES LTD

3772 Davis Street Fish Market
P.O.Box 5173
Evanston, IL 60204-5173   847-869-3474
                Fax: 847-869-6435
          www.davisstreetfishmarket.com
Seafood
Manager: Matt Sherry
Estimated Sales:$ 3 - 5 Million
Number Employees: 50-99

3773 Davisco Foods International
11000 W 78th St # 210
Eden Prairie, MN 55344-8012   952-914-0400
     Fax: 952-914-0887   800-757-7611
          polly@daviscofoods.com
          www.daviscofoods.com
Manufacturer in whey proteins
Manager: Dana Bellanger
CFO: Jim Ward
VP Finance/Business Administration: John
Velgersdyk
Director Quality Assurance: Matt Davis
VP Sales/Marketing/Business Development:
Pauline Olson
General Manager: Martin Davis

Estimated Sales:$10-20 Million
Number Employees: 20-49

3774 Davisco International
11000 W 78th St
Suite 210
Eden Prairie, MN 55344-8012   952-914-0400
        Fax: 952-914-0887   800-757-7611
info@daviscofoods.com   www.daviscofoods.com
Manufacturer and exporter of spray dried dairy
products including whey protein concentrate and
isolate, lactose, sweet dairy whey and whey powder;
custom processing and agglomeration available
    Manager: Dana Bellanger
    CFO: Jim Ward
    VP Finance/Business Administration: John
    Velgersdyk
    Director Quality Assurance: Matt Davis
    VP Sales/Marketing: Pauline Olson
    General Manager: Martin Davis
Estimated Sales:$ 20 - 50 Million
Number Employees: 20-49
Brands:
    BI-PRO
    VERSA PRO

3775 Dawes Hill Honey Company
P.O.Box 429
Nunda, NY 14517-0429   585-468-2535
        Fax: 585-468-5995   888-800-8075
            info@onceagainnutbutter.com
            www.onceagainnutbutter.com
Manufacturer, exporter and importer of honey, royal
jelly and fruit honey cream spread
    Owner: Sandi Alexander
    Comptroller: Sandra Alexander
    Purchasing Agent: Lloyd Kirwan
Estimated Sales:$10-20 Million
Number Employees: 10-19
Sq. footage: 20000
Parent Co: Once Again Nut Butter
Type of Packaging: Consumer, Private Label, Bulk
Brands:
    BEE SUPREME

3776 Dawn Food Products
P.O.Box 14032
Louisville, KY 40214-0032   502-361-8471
        Fax: 502-368-9437   800-626-2542
            louisville@dawnfoods.com
            www.dawnfoods.com
Manufacturer of baking mixes, fillings, icings and
frozen baked goods
    Manager: David Lightheiser
    CEO: Ron Jones
    Executive VP: Miles Jones
    Marketing: Frank Sliwinski
    Product Manager: Sarah Jones
Estimated Sales:$20-50 Million
Number Employees: 100-249
Type of Packaging: Consumer, Food Service
Brands:
    AMERICAN TRADITION
    BAKERS' ADVANTAGE
    C.K.'S GOURMET PRETZEL STRIPS
    CHOC-O-LOTA FUDGE BASE
    CHOCOLATE QUIK
    CRATER CONE
    CRATER CONE MIX
    DAWN
    DAWN/BAKER BOY
    DAWN/BESCO
    DELUX PANCAKE/WAFFLE MIX
    DERBY SCONE MIX
    DIP QUIK
    DUTCHESS
    EMPRESS
    ENERGY BAR BASE CARROTS
    ENGLISH MUFFIN MIX LORD BENCHLEY'S
    EXTRA MOIST DEVILS'S FOOD CAKE MIX
    FUL-O-FRUIT
    GRISANTIS DEEP CRUST PIZZA
    HARVEST DELIGHT
    HERITAGE
    HOMESTYLE BISCUIT
    HONEYBUN
    ICE'N BASE, CHOCOLATE
    KING KORN
    KOUNTRY KWIK
    LIBERTY
    LITTLE CEASAR'S SUGAR BLEND
    LORD BENCHLEY
    MAJESTIC
    MASTER BLEND

O.J.
ORIGINATOR
PIZZA MIX, PAN STYLE
PRINCESS
REGENCY
SELECT
SELECT WHITE BUT-R CREME BASE
SOFT ROLL MIX
SPREAD N GLOSS
YOLAY

3777 Dawn Food Products
3333 Sargent Rd
Jackson, MI 49201-8847   517-789-5285
        Fax: 517-789-4465   800-248-1144
            www.dawnfoods.com
Manufacturer of cake doughnuts, danish pastry,
sweet rolls and cakes
    President/CEO: Ronald Jones
    CFO: Jerry Baglieon
    CEO: Carrie Jones-Barber
    National Account Manager: Sam Barber
    VP Operations: Rick Dahlin
    Product Manager: Sarah Jones
Estimated Sales:$5-10 Million
Number Employees: 1,000-4,999
Sq. footage: 40000
Type of Packaging: Consumer, Food Service, Pri-
vate Label, Bulk
Brands:
    BROTHERS DONUTS
    COUNTY FARMS

3778 Dawn Food Products
3701 Concord Rd
York, PA 17402-9101   717-840-0044
        Fax: 717-840-9070   800-405-6282
            www.dawnfoods.com
Manufacturer and exporter of cakes
    Manager: John Duda
    CEO: Ron Jones
    Executive VP: Miles Jones
    Product Manager: Sarah Jones
Estimated Sales:$50-100 Million
Number Employees: 5-9
Parent Co: Dawn Food Products
Type of Packaging: Consumer, Food Service, Pri-
vate Label
Brands:
    KNAUB'S

3779 Dawn Food Products
3333 Sargent Rd
Jackson, MI 49201-8847   517-789-4400
        Fax: 517-789-4465   800-248-1144
            web-admin@dawnfoods.com
            www.dawnfoods.com
Doughnut, cake, brownie and other dry mixes, icings
and fillings, frozen products
    CEO: Carrie Jones-Barber
    National Account Manager: Sam Barber
    Product Manager: Sarah Jones
    General Manager, Phoenix: Aaron Jones
Estimated Sales:$1.4 Billion
Number Employees: 3,500

3780 Dawn's Foods
1530 La Dawn Dr
Portage, WI 53901-8823   608-742-2494
        Fax: 608-742-1806 www.dawnsfoodsinc.com
Jellies
    President: Greg Drewsen
Estimated Sales:$20-50 Million
Number Employees: 20-49
Brands:
    DAWN'S FOODS

3781 Day Spring Enterprises
45 Benbro Dr
Cheektowaga, NY 14225-4805   716-685-4340
        Fax: 716-685-0810   800-879-7677
info@rainbowpops.com   www.rainbowpops.com
Manufacturer and exporter of hard candy and
lollypops; also, seasonal items available
    President: Roselyn Baran
    Sales Manager: Jeff Baran
    Plant Manager: George Sparks
Estimated Sales:$5-9.9 Million
Number Employees: 20-49
Sq. footage: 16000
Type of Packaging: Consumer, Food Service, Pri-
vate Label, Bulk
Brands:
    RAINBOW POPS

3782 Day's Bakery
1235 Main St
Honesdale, PA 18431-2062   570-253-1660
            Fax: 570-253-1462
Baked goods
    President: Edwin Day
Estimated Sales:$500,000-$1 Million
Number Employees: 10-19
Number of Brands: 1
Number of Products: 25
Sq. footage: 2400
Brands:
    DAY'S

3783 Day's Crabmeat & Lobster
1269 Route 1
Yarmouth, ME 04096-6964   207-846-5871
            Fax: 207-846-3423
Manufacturer and wholesaler/distributor of crabmeat
and lobster
    President/Owner: Sandy Thebeau
Number Employees: 1-4

3784 Day-Lee Foods
10350 Heritage Park Dr # 11
Santa Fe Springs, CA 90670-3787   562-903-3020
        Fax: 562-906-5080   info@day-lee.com
            www.day-lee.com
Manufacturer of meats and poultry
    President/CEO: Sumio Somura
    CEO: Takahito Okoso
    General Manager: Yasushi Yokozeki
    Director Manufacturing: Toshiyuki Iho
Estimated Sales:$50-100 Million
Number Employees: 5-9
Parent Co: Nippon Meat Packers
Brands:
    DAY-LEE FOODS

3785 Daybreak Coffee Roasters
2377 Main St # 4
Glastonbury, CT 06033-2021   860-657-4466
        Fax: 860-633-6614   800-882-5282
            freshcoffee@daybreakcoffee.com
            www.daybreakcoffee.com
Coffee
    President: Thomas Clarke
    Sales: Cathy Reynolds
Estimated Sales:$500,000-$1 Million
Number Employees: 10-19
Brands:
    DAYBREAK

3786 Daybreak Foods
609 6th St NE
Long Prairie, MN 56347-1003   320-732-2966
            Fax: 320-732-3690
Egg products
    President/CEO: William Rehm
    Plant Manager: Steven Masia
Estimated Sales:$10-20 Million
Number Employees: 20-49
Type of Packaging: Bulk
Brands:
    DAYBREAK FOODS

3787 (HQ)Daybrook Fisheries
Highway 11 S
Empire, LA 70050   985-657-9711
            Fax: 985-657-9916
Manufacturer of fish meal and fish oil
    President: Gregory Holt
    VP: Borden Wallace
Estimated Sales:$30 Million
Number Employees: 2
Type of Packaging: Bulk

3788 Dayhoff
802 N Belcher Road
Clearwater, FL 33765-2103   727-443-5544
        Fax: 727-467-0272   800-354-3372
            www.dayhoffinc.com
Candy
    President/CEO: Uday Lele
Estimated Sales:$15 Million
Number Employees: 16
Brands:
    CONNOISSEYR CHOCOLATES
    CREAM SWIRLS
    JUICEE GUMMEE
    JUICEE JELLIE
    JUST FRUITEE
    JUST JUICEE

3789 Dayhoff
1947 Clarke Avenue
Pocomoke City, MD 21851   410-957-4301
     Fax: 410-957-4171
Candy
   President: Dave Lele
   CFO: Aditi Lele
   Sales: Marianne Pihl
   Plant Manager: Kathy Karmine
Estimated Sales: $4 Million
Number Employees: 10-19
Sq. footage: 120
Type of Packaging: Private Label
Brands:
   DAYHOFF

3790 Daymar Select Fine Coffees
460 Cypress Ln # B
El Cajon, CA 92020-1647   619-444-1155
   Fax: 619-444-1985   800-466-7590
     daymarcoffee@pacbell.net
Manufacturer of chocolates, syrups, teas and coffees
including flavored, organic, roast, ground, whole
beans and instant
   President: Roy Gallegos
   Secretary: Diana Gallegos
Estimated Sales: $5-10 Million
Number Employees: 10-19
Type of Packaging: Consumer, Food Service, Private Label, Bulk
Brands:
   CAFE EL MARINO

3791 Dayton Nut Specialties
919 N Main St
Dayton, OH 45405-4694   937-223-3225
   Fax: 937-223-9456   800-548-1304
     info@daytonnut.com
     www.riverdalefinefoods.com
Confectionery and nuts
   President: Stanley Maschino
   VP: Kyle Maschino
   Productions: Kurt Maschino
Estimated Sales: $10-20 Million
Number Employees: 20-49
Type of Packaging: Private Label
Brands:
   CANDY FARM
   FRIESINGER'S FINE CHOCOLATES
   RIVERDALE

3792 Dazbog Coffee Company
1090 Yuma St
Denver, CO 80204-3838   303-892-9999
   Fax: 303-893-9999 www.coffeeandtea.net
Manufacturer of coffee
   President: Tony Yuffa
   VP: Leo Yuffa
Estimated Sales: $5-10 Million
Number Employees: 10-19
Brands:
   DAZBOG

3793 De Bas Chocolate
5877 E Brown Avenue
Fresno, CA 93727-1364   559-294-7638
   Fax: 559-348-2289   888-461-1276
Candy and confectionery
   President: Guy DeBas
Estimated Sales: $10-20 Million
Number Employees: 20-49
Brands:
   DEBAS

3794 De Bas Chocolatier
5877 E Brown Avenue
Fresno, CA 93727-1364   559-294-7638
   Fax: 559-348-2289 www.debas.com
Manufacturer of truffles, wine-filled biscotti and
chocolate bars with fruits and nut meat
   President: Guy De Bas
Estimated Sales: $10-20 Million
Number Employees: 20-49
Type of Packaging: Consumer
Brands:
   DE BAS VINEYARD
   INCOGNITO

3795 De Beukelaer Corporation
P.O.Box 1697
Madison, MS 39130-1697   601-856-7454
   Fax: 601-856-1462   timsullivan@pirouline.com
     www.pirouline.com

Manufacturer of cookies
   Owner: Peter De Beukelaer
   VP Sales: Joe Snyder
   Plant Manager: Joe Couch
Estimated Sales: $50-100 Million
Number Employees: 100-249
Brands:
   DE BEUKELAER

3796 De Bilio Food Distributors
605 E Commercial Street
Anaheim, CA 92801-2591   714-773-9323
     Fax: 714-738-0245
   President: Joseph DeBilio
   VP: Joseph DeBilio
Estimated Sales: $ 10 - 20 Million
Number Employees: 10-19

3797 De Bruyn Produce Company
P.O.Box 76
Zeeland, MI 49464-0076   616-772-2102
   Fax: 616-772-4242   800-733-9177
     debruyn@michcomm.com
     www.debruynproduce.com
Manufacturer and exporter of onions and carrots
   President: Robert De Bruyn
   Manager: Jill Philip
Estimated Sales: $50-100 Million
Number Employees: 5-9
Type of Packaging: Consumer, Food Service
Brands:
   CITATION
   DEBCO
   GOLD RIM
   GULF

3798 De Ciantis Ice Cream Company
45 Quaker Ln
West Warwick, RI 02893-2119   401-821-2440
     Fax: 401-821-2440
Ice cream and frozen desserts
   Owner: Stephen De Ciantis
Estimated Sales: $500,000-$1 Million
Number Employees: 10-19
Brands:
   DE CIANTIS

3799 De Cio Pasta Primo
37801 Basin Road
Cave Creek, AZ 85331   480-488-4114
   Fax: 480-488-8126   800-397-0770
Macaroni and spaghetti
   Owner: Rebecca DeFalco
   VP: Gary Ciminello
Estimated Sales: $500,000-$1 Million
Number Employees: 1-4
Brands:
   DECIO PASTA

3800 De Coty Coffee Company
1920 Austin St
San Angelo, TX 76903-8704   325-655-5607
   Fax: 325-655-6837   800-588-8001
     www.decotycoffee.com
Coffee, teas, spices, breading mix
   President/CEO: Michael Agan
   Purchasing/Point of Sales Manager: Bryan Baker
   Public Relations: Charles Ducote
   Director Operations: Ronnie Wallace
   Productions: Eric Fischer
   Plant Manager: Ronnie Wallace
   Purchasing: Mark Sedden
Estimated Sales: $20-50 Million
Number Employees: 20-49
Sq. footage: 34
Type of Packaging: Private Label
Brands:
   DE COTY

3801 De Lima Company
P.O.Box 4813
Syracuse, NY 13221-4813   315-457-3725
   Fax: 315-457-3730   800-962-8864
   info@delimacoffee.com   www.delimacoffee.com
Coffee roasters
   President: Peter Miller
   CEO: Paul Lima
   CEO: W J Drescher Jr
   Marketing Manager: Wells Neale
   Regional Sales Manager: Charles Miller
   Plant Manager: Bill Neuman
   Purchasing: Paul Michaud
Estimated Sales: $50-100 Million
Number Employees: 50-99

Type of Packaging: Private Label
Brands:
   DE LIMA

3802 De Loach Vineyards
1791 Olivet Road
Santa Rosa, CA 95401-3898   707-526-9111
   Fax: 707-526-4151 www.deloachvineyards.com
Wines
   President: Cecil DeLoach
   VP: Christine DeLoach
   Marketing: Walt Averill
Estimated Sales: $20-50 Million
Number Employees: 50-99
Brands:
   DE LOACH

3803 De Lorimier Winery
PO Box 487
Geyserville, CA 95441-0487   707-857-2000
   Fax: 707-857-3262   800-546-7718
     discover@delorimierwinery.com
     www.delorimierwinery.com
Wines
   President: Alfred De Lorimier
   Marketing: John Woodward
Estimated Sales: $2.5-5 Million
Number Employees: 8
Number of Brands: 1
Number of Products: 10
Type of Packaging: Private Label
Brands:
   DE LORIMEIR

3804 De Soto Confectionery &Nut Company
PO Box 70
De Soto, GA 31743-0070   229-874-1200
   Fax: 229-874-7277   800-237-8689
   nsc@sowega.net   www.cricklecompany.com
Manufacturer of nuts and candy
   Owner: Nancy Carlan
Estimated Sales: $5-10 Million
Number Employees: 20-49
Sq. footage: 8000
Type of Packaging: Consumer
Brands:
   CRICKLE BRITTLE
   TJ'S SUGAR

3805 De-Iorio's Frozen Dough
624 Elizabeth Street
Utica, NY 13501-2413   315-732-7612
   Fax: 315-732-7621   800-649-7612
   deiorios@prodigy.net   www.deiorios.com
Frozen dough
   President: Benjamin DeIorio
   Marketing: James Viti
   Sales: Bob Horth
   Operations: Larry Evans
   Purchasing: Tim Manion
Estimated Sales: $5-10 Million
Number Employees: 20-49
Number of Brands: 1
Number of Products: 87
Type of Packaging: Consumer, Food Service, Private Label
Other Locations:
   De-Iorio's Frozen Dough
   Utica NY
Brands:
   DE-IORIO'S
   MAMA DEIORIO

3806 DeBenedetto Farms
P.O.Box 9760
Fresno, CA 93794-9760   559-276-3447
     Fax: 559-276-0797
Fresh figs
   Owner: Maurice Debenedetto

3807 DeBragga & Spitler
826 Washington St # D
New York, NY 10014-1406   212-924-1311
   Fax: 212-206-8437 debragga@aol.com
     www.debraggaandspitler.com
Manufacturer of beef, veal, lamb and pork; wholesaler/distributor of further processed beef, veal,
lamb and pork; serving the food service market
   President: Marc Sarrazin
Estimated Sales: $20-50 Million
Number Employees: 50-99
Type of Packaging: Food Service, Bulk

Brands:
NATURAL CERTIFIED ANGUS BEEF

3808 DeChoix Specialty Foods
5825 52nd Avenue
Woodside, NY 11377-7402 718-507-8080
Fax: 718-335-9150 800-332-4649
dechoix@dechoix.com
Specialty foods including chocolate, vegetables, imported cheeses, specialty meats, pate, caviar, smoked fish, oils and vinegars from Europe, Asian products and pastry and baking products.
President: Henry Kaplan
Parent Co: Amazon Coffee & Tea Company
Type of Packaging: Food Service, Bulk
Other Locations:
DeChoix Specialty Foods
San Francisco CA

3809 DeConna Ice Cream
P.O.Box 39
Orange Lake, FL 32681-0039 352-591-1530
Fax: 352-591-4418 800-824-8254
www.deconna.com
Manufacturers and distributors of ice cream
Owner: Vince Deconna
Sales: Jim Carpenter
Estimated Sales:$20-50 Million
Number Employees: 50-99
Type of Packaging: Bulk
Brands:
DECONNA

3810 DeFluri's Fine Chocolates
130 N Queen Street
Martinsburg, VA 25401 304-264-3698
Fax: 304-264-3698 sales@defluris.com
www.defluris.com
truffles, nuts, crunches and chews, creams
President/Owner: Brenda Casabona

3811 DeFrancesco & Sons
PO Box 605
Firebaugh, CA 93622-0605 209-364-7000
Fax: 209-364-7001 mrde@mrde.com
www.mrde.com
Manufacturer and exporter of dehydrated onion, garlic and vegetable products
CEO/President: Mario DeFrancesco, Jr.
CFO: Tom Abert
Sales: Mario DeFrancesco III
Estimated Sales:$100+ Million
Number Employees: 500-999
Sq. footage: 500000
Type of Packaging: Private Label, Bulk

3812 (HQ)DeMedici Imports
P.O.Box 482
Elizabeth, NJ 7207-482 845-651-4400
Fax: 845-651-5759 info@demedici.com
www.demedici.com
Gourmet specialty foods
President: Paul Farber
Operations: Marilyn O'Daniels
Estimated Sales:$5-10 Million
Number Employees: 5-9
Type of Packaging: Private Label
Brands:
COLONNA

3813 DeSouza International
P.O.Box 395
Beaumont, CA 92223-0395 951-849-5172
Fax: 951-849-1348 800-373-5171
info@desouzas.com www.desouzas.com
Manufacturer of solar-dried sea salt; also, chlorophyll liquid, tablets and capsules
President/CEO: Rosalie DeSouza
VP Operations: K Hill
Estimated Sales:$1-2.5 Million
Number Employees: 1-4
Sq. footage: 8000
Type of Packaging: Private Label

3814 Dean & Deluca
560 Broadway # 404
New York, NY 10012-3945 212-226-6800
Fax: 212-334-6183 800-999-0306
www.deandeluca.com
Gourmet foods
President: John Richards
CEO: Mark Daley
Purchasing: Jeff Morgan
Estimated Sales:$10-20 Million
Number Employees: 250-499

Brands:
DEAN & DELUCA

3815 Dean Dairy Products
1858 Oneida Ln
Sharpsville, PA 16150-9638 724-962-7801
Fax: 724-962-8566 800-942-8096
www.deanfoods.com
Manufacturer of milk and fruit juices
CEO: Joseph Neubauer
Number Employees: 250-499
Parent Co: Dean Foods Company
Type of Packaging: Consumer, Food Service, Private Label
Brands:
DEAN

3816 Dean Distributing Inc
1215 Ontario Road
Green Bay, WI 54311 920-469-6500
Fax: 920-469-6505
customerservice@deandist.com
www.abwslr.com/deandistributing/home
Manufacturer of beers and malt beverages.
President: Jim Dean
Chairman/CEO: Robert Dean
Marketing Director: Jim Gibbons
VP Sales: Ken Eggen
Team Leader: Denis Gillis
Team Leader: Pat Petasek
Team Leader: Wayne Wasurick
Team Leader: Mark Williquette
Estimated Sales:$700 Million
Number Employees: 100
Parent Co: Dean Foods Company
Type of Packaging: Consumer, Food Service, Private Label, Bulk
Other Locations:
Deans Specialty Foods
LaJunta CO
Deans Specialty Foods
New Hampton IA
Deans Specialty Foods
Chicago IL
Deans Specialty Foods
Dixon IL
Deans Specialty Foods
Pecatonica IL
Deans Specialty Foods
Plymouth IN
Deans Specialty Foods
Benton Harbor MI
Deans Specialty Foods
Waylan MI
Deans Specialty Foods
Faison NC
Deans Specialty Foods
Portland OR
Brands:
BACARDI SILVER
BUDWEISER
BUSCH
MICHELOB
O'DOUL'S

3817 (HQ)Dean Distributors
1350 Bayshore Highway
Suite 400
Burlingame, CA 94010-1813 650-340-1754
Fax: 800-928-2090 800-792-0816
corporate@deandistributors.com
www.deandistributors.com
Manufacturer of specialty foods including soup and gravy bases, dry dressing, pudding, gelatin, mousse and beverage mixes, seasonings, nutritional supplements, syrups, flavors, extracts and sauces; exporter of gravy bases.
Owner: Mark Schulz
Founder/President: Ralph Schulz
Director Sales/Marketing: Mark Schulz
Purchasing Manager: John Garinger
Estimated Sales:$15 Million
Number Employees: 55
Sq. footage: 70000
Type of Packaging: Food Service, Private Label, Bulk
Brands:
BFF
CAMBRIDGE
DEAN
FLAVORGLOW
NATURAL HIGH
NUTRICARE

3818 Dean Distributors
1350 Bayshore Highway
Suite 400
Burlingame, CA 94010-1813 650-340-1754
Fax: 800-928-2090 800-227-3112
corporate@deandistributors.com
www.deandistributors.com
Manufacturer of specialty food products including sauces, kosher and Mexican soups and gravy bases, tenderizers and aid, consomme, smoke and cheese flavors, syrups, extracts and nutritional supplements
President: Ralph Schulz
Director Sales/Marketing: Mark Schulz
Estimated Sales:$15 Million
Number Employees: 5-9
Sq. footage: 70000
Parent Co: Dean Distributors
Type of Packaging: Food Service
Brands:
BERNARD FINE FOODS
DEAN
FLAVOR-GLOW

3819 Dean Foods
2515 McKinney Ave # 1200
Dallas, TX 75201-1945 214-303-3400
Fax: 214-303-3499 www.deanfoods.com
Frozen foods
President: Mike Keown
CEO: Gregg L Engles
Director Operations: Thomas Roth
*Estimated Sales:*Under $500,000
Number Employees: 10,000+
Brands:
Alta Dena
Barber's
Brown's Diary
Creamland
Dean Foods
Gandy's
Melody Farms
Oak Farm Diary
Silk SoyMilk
Stroh
T G Lee Diary

3820 Dean Foods Company
2515 McKinney Ave # 1200
Dallas, TX 75201-1945 214-303-3400
Fax: 214-303-3499 warren@deanfoods.com
www.deanfoods.com
Manufacturer of ice cream
Chairman/CEO: Mike Keown
EVP/CAO/General Counsel & Corp Secretary: Joseph Scalzo
EVP/CFO: Jack Callahan
CEO: Gregg L Engles
SVP/Corporate Development: Ronald Klein
SVP/Chief Information Officer: Arthur Fino
SVP/Human Resources: Robert Dunn
Plant Manager: Mike Warren
Estimated Sales:$50-100 Million
Number Employees: 10,000+
Parent Co: Dean Foods Company
Type of Packaging: Consumer, Food Service

3821 Dean Foods Company
2515 McKinney Ave # 1200
Dallas, TX 75201-1945 214-303-3400
Fax: 214-303-3499 www.deanfoods.com
Manufacturer of fresh and sour cream, aerosol dessert toppings and flavored milk.
CEO: Gregg L Engles
SVP/Corporate Development: Ronald Klein
SVP/Government & Industry Relations: Bill Tinklepaugh
Sales Director: Tom Yates
SVP/Chief Information Officer: Arthur Fino
SVP/Human Resources: Robert Dunn
Estimated Sales:$100+ Million
Number Employees: 10,000+
Parent Co: Dean Foods Company
Type of Packaging: Consumer, Food Service, Private Label

3822 Dean Foods Company
1126 Kilburn Ave
Rockford, IL 61101-5996 815-962-0647
Fax: 815-962-0684 www.deanfoods.com

Manufacturer of cottage cheese, cream, dips, sour cream.
Chairman/CEO: Gregg Engles
EVP/CAO/General Counsel & Corp Secretary: Michelle Goolsby
EVP/Chief Financial Officer: Jack Callahan
SVP/Government & Industry Relations: Bill Tinklepaugh
SVP/Corporate Development: Ronald Klein
SVP/Chief Information Officer: Arthur Fino
SVP/Human Resources: Robert Dunn
Plant Manager: David Holcomb
Estimated Sales: $50-100 Million
Number Employees: 100-249
Parent Co: Dean Foods Company
Type of Packaging: Consumer, Food Service

3823 Dean Foods Company
P.O.Box 508
Rochester, IN 46975-0508   574-223-2141
       Fax: 574-223-2544 800-336-7215
                        www.deanfoods.com
Manufacturer of milk, cottage cheese, buttermilk and juice/drinks.
Chairman/CEO: Gregg Engles
EVP/CAO/General Counsel & Corp Secretary: Michelle Goolsby
EVP/Chief Financial Officer: Jack Callahan
SVP/Government & Industry Relations: Bill Tinklepaugh
SVP/Corporate Development: Ronald Klein
SVP/Chief Information Officer: Arthur Fino
SVP/Human Resources: Robert Dunn
Plant Manager: Shawn Condon
Estimated Sales: $50-100 Million
Number Employees: 100-249
Parent Co: Dean Foods Company
Type of Packaging: Consumer, Food Service

3824 Dean Foods Company
11713 Mill St
Huntley, IL 60142-7398   847-669-5123
       Fax: 847-669-5236 www.deanfoods.com
Manufacturer of milk and juice/drinks.
Manager: Greg Warren
EVP/CAO/General Counsel & Corp Secretary: Michelle Goolsby
EVP/Chief Financial Officer: Jack Callahan
SVP/Government & Industry Relations: Bill Tinklepaugh
SVP/Corporate Development: Ronald Klein
SVP/Chief Information Officer: Arthur Fino
SVP/Human Resources: Robert Dunn
Plant Manager: Greg Warren
Estimated Sales: $50-100 Million
Number Employees: 100-249
Parent Co: Dean Foods Company
Type of Packaging: Consumer, Food Service

3825 Dean Foods Company
10255 W Higgins Road
Suite 500
Rosemont, IL 60018-5612   847-699-8310
       Fax: 847-375-8459 800-323-1571
       michelle_hooper@deanfoods.com
                        www.amboyfoods.com
Manufacturer of milk, ice cream, nondairy creamers, pickles, cheese sauces, pudding, dips and dressings
VP Dairy Division: Vic Deguilio
VP Sales/Marketing: Doug Parr
Number Employees: 100-249
Parent Co: Dean Foods Company
Type of Packaging: Consumer, Food Service, Private Label

3826 Dean Foods Company
215 W 3rd St
Pecatonica, IL 61063-7002   815-239-1632
       Fax: 815-239-1632 www.deanfoods.com
Manufacturer of powdered milk
Estimated Sales: $50-100 Million
Number Employees: 100-249
Parent Co: Dean Foods Company
Type of Packaging: Consumer, Food Service, Private Label

3827 (HQ)Dean Foods Company
2515 McKinney Ave # 1200
Dallas, TX 75201-1945   214-303-3400
       Fax: 214-303-3499 800-431-9214
                        www.deanfoods.com

Manufacturer and distributor of milk, dairy products, soy products, water, juices and drinks, ice cream and novelties, yogurt, cottage cheese, sour cream and dips.
Chairman/CEO: Gregg Engles
EVP Chief Administrative Officer: Michelle Goolsby
EVP Chief Financial Officer: Jack Callahan
SVP/Dpty General Counsel/Ast Secretary: Steven Kemps
SVP Corporate Development: Ronald Klein
SVP Chief Accounting Officer: Ronald McCrummen
SVP Government & Industry Relations: Bill Tinklepaugh
SVP Chief Information Officer: Arthur Fino
SVP Human Resources: Robert Dunn
Estimated Sales: $280 Million
Number Employees: 10,000+
Type of Packaging: Food Service
Brands:
ADOHR FARMS
ALTA DENA
BARBE'S
BERKELEY FARMS
BORDEN
BROUGHTON
BROWN'S DAIRY
CELTA
COUNTRY DELITE
COUNTRY FRESH
CREAMLAND
DAIRY
DAIRY FRESH
DEAN'S
FOREMOST
GANDY'S
GARELICK
LAND O' LAKES
MAYFIELD DAIRY FARMS
MCARTHUR DAIRY
MEADOW BROOK
MODEL DAIRY
OAK FARMS
PET
PRICE'S
PURITY
REITER DAIRY
ROBINSON DAIRY
SCHENKEL'S
SCHEPPS
SUIZA
SWISS
T.G. LEE DAIRY
TUSCAN
ULTRA
VERIFINE
WENGERT'S DAIRY

3828 Dean Foods Company/Country Fresh
2555 Buchanan Ave SW
Grand Rapids, MI 49548-1091   616-243-0173
       Fax: 616-954-2813 www.deanfoods.com
Manufacturer of sherbert, frozen desserts, ice cream, juice/drinks, sorbet, milk, cream, half & half, buttermilk.
Chairman/CEO: Gregg Engles
EVP/CAO/General Counsel & Corp Secretary: Michelle Goolsby
EVP/Chief Financial Officer: Jack Callahan
VP: Pete Reynolds
SVP/Corporate Development: Ronald Klein
SVP/Chief Information Officer: Arthur Fino
SVP/Human Resources: Robert Dunn
Estimated Sales: $5-10 Million
Number Employees: 5-9
Parent Co: Dean Foods Company
Type of Packaging: Consumer, Food Service, Private Label

3829 Dean Foods/Land O'Lakes
P.O.Box 430
Bismarck, ND 58502-0430   701-222-3131
       Fax: 701-355-1041 www.deanfoods.com

Manufacturer of cream, milk, buttermilk, fresh whipped cream, eggnog, half & half.
Manager: Jim Wolf
EVP/CAO/General Counsel & Corp Secretary: Michelle Goolsby
EVP/Chief Financial Officer: Jack Callahan
SVP/Government & Industry Relations: Bill Tinklepaugh
SVP/Corporate Development: Robert Klein
SVP/Chief Information Officer: Arthur Fino
SVP/Human Resources: Robert Dunn
Estimated Sales: $100-500 Million
Number Employees: 100-249
Parent Co: Dean Foods Company
Type of Packaging: Private Label

3830 Dean Foods/Verifine Dairy Products
P.O.Box 879
Sheboygan, WI 53082-0879   920-457-7733
       Fax: 920-457-5372 800-236-6455
                        www.deanfoods.com
Processor of milk, juice drinks, eggnog.
Manager: Steve Weinreich
EVP/CAO/General Counsel & Corp Secretary: Michelle Goolsby
EVP/Chief Financial Officer: Jack Callahan
SVP/Corporate Development: Ronald Klein
SVP/Government & Industry Relations: Bill Tinklepaugh
SVP/Chief Information Officer: Arthur Fino
SVP/Human Resources: Robert Dunn
Estimated Sales: $ 1 - 3 Million
Number Employees: 50-99
Parent Co: Dean Foods Company
Type of Packaging: Consumer, Food Service, Private Label

3831 Dean Milk Company
4420 Bishop Ln
Louisville, KY 40218-4506   502-451-9111
       Fax: 502-459-7858 800-451-3326
                        www.deanfoods.com
Manufacturer of milk; wholesaler/distributor of cream, cottage cheese, butter and orange juice; serving the food service market.
Chairman/CEO: Gregg Engles
EVP/CAO/General Counsel & Corp Secretary: Michelle Goolsby
EVP/Chief Financial Officer: Jack Callahan
VP: Steve Gurley
SVP/Corporate Development: Ronald Klein
SVP/Chief Information Officer: Arthur Fino
SVP/Human Resources: Robert Dunn
Estimated Sales: $100+ Million
Number Employees: 100-249
Parent Co: Dean Foods Company
Type of Packaging: Consumer, Food Service, Private Label

3832 Dean Sausage Company
P.O.Box 750
Attalla, AL 35954-0750   256-538-6082
       Fax: 256-538-2584 800-228-0704
       deansausage@deansausage.com
                        www.deansausage.com
Manufacturer of sausage.
President/Treasurer: Marsue Lancaster
Vice President: Garry Shirley
Marketing Director: Hugh Miller
Estimated Sales: $10-20 Million
Number Employees: 100-249
Sq. footage: 25000
Type of Packaging: Consumer, Food Service, Private Label
Brands:
DEAN'S COUNTRY
KENTUCKY FARM

3833 Dearborn Sausage Company
2450 Wyoming St
Dearborn, MI 48120-1518   313-842-2375
       Fax: 313-842-2640 info@dearbornbrand.com
                        www.dearbornsausage.com
Sausage
President: Donald Kosch
Marketing Manager: Leo Tomoson
VP Sales/Marketing: Todd Meier
Estimated Sales: $10-20 Million
Number Employees: 20-49
Brands:
DEARBORN SAUSAGE

3834 Deaver Vineyards
12455 Steiner Rd
Plymouth, CA 95669-9504   209-245-4099
                              Fax: 209-245-5250
deaverwinery@deavervineyard.com
www.deavervineyard.com
Wines
    President/Marketing Manager: Ken Deaver
    Purchasing: Ken Deaver
Estimated Sales:$2.5-5 Million
Number Employees: 10-19
Number of Brands: 19
Number of Products: 1
Type of Packaging: Private Label
Brands:
    19
    DEAVER VINEYARDS WINE

3835 Deb-El Foods
2 Papetti Plz
Elizabeth, NJ 07206-1421   908-351-0330
                              Fax: 908-351-0334   800-421-3447
mgrossman@debelfoods.com
www.debelfoods.com
Manufacturer of egg products
    Owner/President/CEO: Elliot Gibber
Estimated Sales:$50-100 Million
Number Employees: 50-99
Brands:
    JUST WHITES
    SCRAMBLETTES

3836 Debbie D's Jerky & Sausage
2210 N Main St
Tillamook, OR 97141-7724   503-842-2622
debbiedssausage@oregoncoast.com
www.debbiedssausage.com
Manufacturer of smoked beef jerky and sausage
    President: Debbie Downie
Estimated Sales:$1-2.5 Million
Number Employees: 1-4
Type of Packaging: Consumer, Bulk
Brands:
    DEBBIE D'S

3837 Decadent Desserts
103 1019-17 Avenue SW
Calgary, AB T2T 0A7
Canada   403-245-5535
www.decadentdesserts.ca
Manufacturer of cakes including cheese and wedding; also, pies and cookies
    President: Pamela Fortier
Number Employees: 6
Type of Packaging: Consumer, Food Service

3838 Decas Cranberry Products
219 Main Street
Wareham, MA 02571-2134   508-295-0147
                            Fax: 508-291-1417   800-649-9811
paradise@decascranberry.com
www.decascranberry.com
All-natural cranberry and fruit products
    President/CEO: John Decas
    VP Sales: Nick Decas
Estimated Sales:$ 5 - 10 Million
Number Employees: 100

3839 Decatur Dairy
W1668 County Road F
Brodhead, WI 53520-9505   608-897-8661
                            Fax: 608-897-4587 www.decaturdairy.com
Brick, muenster, farmer cheese, pavarti
    President: Steven Stettler
Estimated Sales:$500,000-$1 Million
Number Employees: 10-19
Brands:
    DECATUR DAIRY

3840 Decker & Son Company
1500 Arch St
Colorado Springs, CO 80904-4199   719-634-8311
Manufacturer of sausages: pork, Italian, mild, medium and hot; also, sausage patties: mild, medium and hot
    Manager: Carrol Ellis
    VP: Mary Decker
    Plant Manager: Robert Lilley
Estimated Sales:$500,000-$1 Million
Number Employees: 5-9
Sq. footage: 4000
Type of Packaging: Food Service
Brands:
    PIG-IN-THE-SACK

3841 Decker Farms
12475 SW River Road
Hillsboro, OR 97123-9314   503-628-1532
            Fax: 503-628-3696   marvin@deckerfarm.com
www.deckerfarm.com
Manufacturer of frozen fruits including red and black raspberries and strawberries; also, frozen filberts and hazelnuts
    President: Marvin Decker
Type of Packaging: Bulk
Brands:
    DECKER FARMS FINEST

3842 Decko Products
2105 Superior St
Sandusky, OH 44870-1891   419-626-5757
            Fax: 419-626-3135   800-537-6143
shumphrey@decko.com   www.decko.com
Manufacturer and exporter of edible cake and candy decorations and packaged rings, gels
    President: F William Niggemyer
    Marketing Director: Sara Humphrey
Estimated Sales:$10 Million
Number Employees: 100-249
Sq. footage: 35000
Type of Packaging: Private Label
Brands:
    ROYAL ICING DECORATION

3843 Decoty Coffee Company
1920 Austin St
San Angelo, TX 76903-8704   325-655-5607
            Fax: 325-655-6837   800-588-8001
www.decotycoffee.com
Manufacturer and importer of cappuccino, flavored and regular coffees, teas, etc
    CEO/President: Michael Agan
    Sales/Marketing: Bryan Baker
    Operations: Ronnie Wallace
Estimated Sales:$20-50 Million
Number Employees: 20-49
Sq. footage: 50000
Type of Packaging: Food Service, Private Label, Bulk

3844 Dee Lite Bakery
1930 Dillingham Blvd
Honolulu, HI 96819-4021   808-847-5396
            Fax: 808-842-7056 www.stghi.com
Breads, rolls, bakery products
    Owner: Shigeru Shilohara
Estimated Sales:$5-10 Million
Number Employees: 50-99
Brands:
    DEE LITE

3845 (HQ)Dee's All Natural Baking Company
PO Box 1262
Bettendorf, IA 52722   319-359-8500
            Fax: 319-359-8901   800-358-8099
Manufacturer of frozen bakery products except bread
    President: Diane Benge
    VP Sales/Marketing: Lonny Benge
Brands:
    DEE'S ALL

3846 (HQ)Dee's Cheesecake Factory/Dee's Foodservice
3300 Menaul Blvd NE
Albuquerque, NM 87107-1819   505-884-1777
            Fax: 505-884-2242
smager@deesfoodservice.com
www.deescheesecakefactory.com
Manufacturer of frozen desserts including cheesecake, strudel, brownies, carrot cake, etc.; licensed distributor of Certified Angus Beef; full line unipro food service distributor
    President/CEO: Steven Mager
    Purchasing: Mike Abramovich
Estimated Sales:$30 Million
Number Employees: 20-49
Number of Products: 4500
Sq. footage: 37000
Type of Packaging: Consumer, Food Service, Private Label
Other Locations:
    Dee's Cheesecake Factory/Dee'
    Albuquerque NM
Brands:
    DEE'S CHEESECAKE FACTORY
    DEE'S FAMOUS DESSERTS

3847 Deen Meat Company
813 E Northside Dr
Fort Worth, TX 76102-1017   817-335-2257
            Fax: 817-338-9256   800-333-3953
webmaster@deenmeat.com   www.deenmeat.com
Meat
    President: Danny Deen
    VP Sales: Craig Deen
    Production: Joe Cholopisa
    Purchasing Manager: David Burns
Estimated Sales:$50-100 Million
Number Employees: 20-49
Brands:
    DEEN
    DOUBLE L

3848 Deep Creek Custom Packing
P.O.Box 39229
Ninilchik, AK 99639-0229   907-567-3395
            Fax: 907-567-1041   800-764-0078
dccp@ptialaska.net
www.deepcreekcustompacking.com
Manufacturer and exporter of fresh, frozen, smoked, canned and vacuum packed halibut, cod and salmon
    Owner/President/Sales Contact: Jeff Berger
    Plant Manager: Chris Baobo
Estimated Sales:$10-20 Million
Number Employees: 50-99
Sq. footage: 20000

3849 Deep Foods
1090 Springfield Rd # 1
Union, NJ 07083-8147   908-810-7500
            Fax: 908-810-8482 www.deepfoods.com
Manufacturer of frozen Indian, Thai and Chinese vegetable and nonvegetable entrees, ice cream, bread and snacks; importer of basmati rice, spices, canned goods and miscellaneous groceries
    President: Arvind Amin
    Director Marketing: Archit Amin
    Sales Director: Chet Trivedi
Estimated Sales:$5-10 Million
Number Employees: 100-249
Sq. footage: 80000
Type of Packaging: Consumer, Food Service, Bulk
Other Locations:
    Deep Foods
    Mississagua, CANADA ON
Brands:
    BANSI
    CURRY CLASSICS
    DEEP FOODS
    GREEN GURU
    MIRCH MASALA
    REENAS

3850 Deep River Snacks
PO Box 373
Old Lyme, CT 06371   860-434-7347
            Fax: 860-434-7512   sales@deepriversnacks.com
www.deepriversnacks.com
chips and popcorn
    President/Owner: Jim Goldberg
Estimated Sales:$2 Million
Number Employees: 6

3851 Deep Rock Fontenelle Water Company
4110 S 138th St
Omaha, NE 68137-1113   402-330-9000
            Fax: 402-330-9769   800-433-1303
www.deeprockwater.com
Manufacturer of bottled distilled and mineral water
    Manager: Tom Somers
    General Manager: Tom Somers
Estimated Sales:$1-2.5 Million
Number Employees: 10-19
Sq. footage: 30000
Parent Co: Deep Rock Water Company
Type of Packaging: Consumer, Food Service, Private Label, Bulk
Brands:
    DEEP ROCK FONTENELLE

3852 (HQ)Deep Rock Water Company
2640 California St
Denver, CO 80205-2931   303-292-2020
            Fax: 303-296-8812   800-695-2020
questions@deeprockwater.com
www.deeprockwater.com

Manufacturer of bottled spring, artesian and distilled water
President/CEO: Colleen Porterfield
CEO: Tom Schwein
Estimated Sales: $10-20 Million
Number Employees: 100-249
Type of Packaging: Consumer, Food Service
Brands:
DEEP ROCK

3853 Deep Rock Water Company
225 Thomas Ave N
Minneapolis, MN 55405-1098   612-374-2253
Fax: 612-374-2397   800-800-8986
info@deeprockwater.com
www.deeprockwater.com
Processor and bottler of water
Manager: John Monahan
General Manager: Craig Puhr
Estimated Sales: $10-20 Million
Number Employees: 100-249
Type of Packaging: Consumer, Food Service
Brands:
Glenwood-Inglewood

3854 (HQ)Deep Sea Foods
13050 N Wintzell Ave
Bayou La Batre, AL 36509-2110   251-824-7000
Fax: 251-824-2349
Manufacturer of frozen shrimp; warehouse providing freezer and cold storage of seafood and poultry
Number Employees: 5-9

3855 (HQ)Deep South Products
255 Jacksonville Hwy
Fitzgerald, GA 31750-8927   229-423-1121
Fax: 229-424-9039
Manufacturer of carbonated beverages, ketchup, sauces, cooking oils, peanut butter, mayonnaise, jams, jellies, marmalades and preserves; importer of olives, olive oil and Greek peppers; exporter of carbonated beverages
President: Tim Lahrs
Controller: Tommy Treadway
Plant Beverage Support: Lee Siler
Plant Food Support: Jerome Thomas
Plant Manager: Dale Williams
Estimated Sales: $74 Million
Number Employees: 250-499
Sq. footage: 425000
Parent Co: Winn Dixie
Type of Packaging: Private Label
Brands:
ASTOR
CHEK
DEEP SOUTH
TROPICAL

3856 (HQ)Deepsouth Packing Company
3536 Lowerline Street
New Orleans, LA 70125-1004   504-488-4413
Fax: 504-488-4432
Seafood, seafood products
President: Eric Skrmetta
VP: Dennis Skrmetta
Number Employees: 20-49
Type of Packaging: Private Label
Brands:
DEEPSOUTH PACKING

3857 Deer Creek Honey Farms
551 E High St
London, OH 43140-9521   740-852-0899
Fax: 740-852-4530
Manufacturer of kosher certified honey and molasses
President: Chris Dunham
Estimated Sales: $5-10 Million
Number Employees: 5-9
Type of Packaging: Consumer, Food Service, Private Label, Bulk
Brands:
DEER CREEK

3858 Deer Meadow Vineyard
199 Vintage Lane
Winchester, VA 22602-3247   540-877-1919
Fax: 540-877-1919   800-653-6632
info@dmeadow.com   www.dmeadow.com
Wines
Estimated Sales: Under $500,000
Number Employees: 1-4
Type of Packaging: Private Label

Brands:
DEER MEADOW

3859 Deer Mountain Berry Farms
P.O.Box 257
Granite Falls, WA 98252-0257   360-691-7586
Manufacturer of preserves including strawberry, blackberry and raspberry
Owner: Barb Neal
Estimated Sales: $1-2.5 Million
Number Employees: 1-4
Type of Packaging: Consumer

3860 Deer Park Winery
14936 Malberg Road
Elk Creek, MO 65464-9610   707-963-5411
Wines
President: David Clark
Estimated Sales: $500,000-$1 Million
Number Employees: 1-4
Brands:
DEER PARK

3861 Deer River Wild Rice
P.O.Box 296
Deer River, MN 56636-0296   218-246-2713
Fax: 218-246-8722
Manufacturer of wild rice
President: Judy Myers
Manager: Tim Blanchard
Estimated Sales: $50-100 Million
Number Employees: 50-99
Type of Packaging: Consumer, Food Service, Bulk

3862 Deerfield Bakery
201 N Buffalo Grove Rd
Buffalo Grove, IL 60089-1748   847-520-0068
Fax: 847-520-0135 sheila@deerfieldbakery.com
www.deerfieldsbakery.com
Cakes and full service bakery
Owner: Kurt Schmitt
Estimated Sales: Less than $500,000
Number Employees: 100-249
Type of Packaging: Private Label
Brands:
DEERFIELD

3863 Dehlinger Winery
4101 Vine Hill Rd
Sebastopol, CA 95472-2300   707-823-2378
Fax: 707-823-0918 www.dehlingerwinery.com
Wines
President: Tom Dehlinger
Estimated Sales: $2.5-5 Million
Number Employees: 10-19
Brands:
DEHLINGER

3864 Dehydrates Inc
1251 Peninsula Blvd
Hewlett, NY 11557-1223   516-295-3700
Fax: 516-295-3777   800-983-4443
dehydrates123@hotmail.com
www.dehydratesinc.com
Manufacturer, and importer of dehydrated vegetables including beets, broccoli, cabbage, carrots, celery, mushrooms, corn, bell and jalapeno peppers, green beans, parsley, etc.; also, processor of citrus peels, parsley, spinach, tomatoes well as custom blends. Freeze dried products and certified organic products are also available. Kosher certified
President: Steven Reich
Marketing: Gail Whiteford
Public Relations: Lori Zahler
Estimated Sales: $5-10 Million
Number Employees: 1-4
Sq. footage: 20000
Type of Packaging: Food Service, Private Label, Bulk
Brands:
DEHYDRATES

3865 Del Campo Baking Company
PO Box 2510
Wilmington, DE 19805-0510   302-656-6676
Fax: 302-652-4678 www.delcampo.com
Manufacturer of fresh and frozen hearth baked bread and rolls.
President/CEO: John Del Campo
Purchasing: Tom Pacchioli
Estimated Sales: $20-50 Million
Number Employees: 100-249
Sq. footage: 42000

3866 Del Grosso Foods
P.O.Box 337
Tipton, PA 16684-0337   814-684-5880
Fax: 814-684-3943   800-521-5880
dgfoods@delgrossofoods.com
www.delgrossofoods.com
Manufacturer and importer of traditional spaghetti sauce, pizza sauce, salsa, sloppy joe sauce, country garden spaghetti sauce and meatballs.
President: James Del Grosso
R&D: Sean Etters
Quality Control: Fredrick Del Grosso
Sales Manager: Robert DelGrosso
Public Relations: Sean Albright
Manager: Joseph Del Grosso
Estimated Sales: $10-20 Million
Number Employees: 50-99
Sq. footage: 105000
Type of Packaging: Consumer, Food Service
Brands:
DEL GROSSO

3867 Del Mar Food Products Corporation
P.O.Box 891
Watsonville, CA 95077-0891   831-722-3516
Fax: 831-722-7690
Apples, applesauce, apricots, strawberries, peaches, peppers
President: P Mecozzi
Estimated Sales: $50-100 Million
Number Employees: 250-499
Brands:
DEL MAR

3868 (HQ)Del Monte Foods
1 Market @ The Landmark
San Francisco, CA 94105   415-247-3000
Fax: 415-247-3565   800-543-3090
www.delmonte.com
Manufacturer and exporter of fruit, vegetable and tomato products, as well as broths.
Chairman/President/CEO: Richard Wolford
Executive VP, Administration & CFO: David Meyers
SVP/CAO/Controller: Richard French
SVP & CMO: William Pearce
EVP Sales: Tim Cole
SvP/Chief Human Resources Officer: Richard Muto
COO: Nils Lommerin
Estimated Sales: $3.6 Billion
Number Employees: 5400
Type of Packaging: Consumer, Food Service, Private Label
Other Locations:
Del Monte Foods
Cambria WI
Brands:
COLLEGE INN
CONTADINA
DEL MONTE
S&W

3869 Del Monte Foods
P.O.Box 140
Mendota, IL 61342-0140   815-539-9361
Fax: 815-538-1446 www.delmonte.com
Manufacturer of canned lima beans, peas, mixed vegetables and corn including whole kernel, creamed, etc.
Chairman/President/CEO: Richard Wolford
SVP/General Counsel & Secretary: James Potter
EVP/Chief Financial Officer: David Meyers
SVP/Marketing & Innovation: Barry Shepard
EVP/Sales: Tim Cole
EVP/Operations: Nils Lommerin
SVP/Human Resources: RoJean DeChantal
Plant Manager: Scott Jamieson
SVP/Supply Chain Operations: David Allen
Estimated Sales: $100-500 Million
Number Employees: 50-99
Parent Co: Del Monte Foods
Type of Packaging: Consumer, Food Service, Private Label
Brands:
DEL MONTE

3870 Del Monte Foods
P.O.Box 237
Cambria, WI 53923-0237   920-348-5121
Fax: 920-348-5094 www.delmonte.com

Manufacturer of canned and frozen fruits and vegetables, tuna fish, soups and baby food.
Manager: Dean Meeusen
SVP/General Counsel & Secretary: Richard Wolford
EVP/Chief Financial Officer: David Meyers
Vice President: Timothy Cole
SVP/Marketing & Innovation: Barry Shepard
EVP/Sales: Timothy Cole
EVP/Operations: Nils Lommerin
SVP/Human Resources: RoJean DeChantal
Estimated Sales:$100-500 Million
Number Employees: 250-499
Parent Co: Del Monte Foods
Type of Packaging: Consumer, Food Service, Private Label
Brands:
COLLEGE INN
CONTADINA
DEL MONTE
S&W
STARKIST

3871 Del Monte Fresh ProduceCompany
241 Sevilla Ave
Suite 200
Coral Gables, FL 33134-6600   305-520-8400
Fax: 305-567-0320   800-950-3683
office@freshdelmonte.com
www.freshdelmonte.com
Manufacturer, marketers and distributor of high quality fresh and fresh-cut fruit and vegetables, as well as a producer and distributor of prepared fruit and vegetables.
President/CEO: Hani Naffy
EVP/Chief Financial Officer: John Inserra
VP: Bryce Edmonson
VP/Research-Development Agricultural Svc: Thomas Young Ph.D
SVP/North American Sales & Product Mgmt: Emanuel Lazopoulos
VP/Human Resources: Marissa Tenazas
SVP/North American Operations: Paul Rice
Purchasing: Pablo Zamora
Estimated Sales:$1.7 Billion
Number Employees: 1050
Parent Co: Del Monte Foods
Type of Packaging: Consumer, Food Service, Bulk
Brands:
DE LORA
DEL MONTE
GOLDEN RIPE
JUST JUICE
MISSION
ROSY
UTC

3872 Del Monte Fresh ProduceCompany
14 Stuart Dr
Kankakee, IL 60901-8946   815-936-7400
Fax: 815-936-7409   office@freshdelmonte.com
www.freshdelmonte.com
Processor of fresh vegetables including lettuce, carrots, potatoes and onions; also, fruit.
Manager: John Mc Conaghy
President/Chief Operating Officer: Hani El-Naffy
EVP/Chief Financial Officer: John Inserra
SVP/General Counsel & Secretary: Bruce Jordan
VP/Research-Development Agricultural Svs: Thomas Young Ph.D
SVP/North American Sales & Product Mgmt: Emanuel Lazopoulos
VP/Human Resources: Marissa Tenazas
SVP/North American Operations: Paul Rice
Estimated Sales:$ 50 - 100 Million
Number Employees: 100-249
Parent Co: Del Monte Fresh Produce Company
Type of Packaging: Consumer, Food Service

3873 Del Rey Packing Company
5287 S Del Rey Ave
Del Rey, CA 93616   559-888-2031
Fax: 559-888-2715
gchooljian@delreypacking.com
www.delreypacking.com
Manufacturer and exporter of raisins
President: Carl Chooljian
Treasurer/Secretary: Gerald Chooljian
Vice President: Kenneth Chooljian
Estimated Sales:$20-50 Million
Number Employees: 50-99

Type of Packaging: Consumer, Food Service, Private Label, Bulk
Brands:
DELUXE
REGENT

3874 Del Rey Tortilleria
5201 W Grand Ave
Chicago, IL 60639-3007   773-637-8900
Fax: 773-637-5195   800-446-1459
Manufacturer of Mexican products including tortillas, tostadas, burrito shells, tortilla chips, nacho cheese, salsa cheese and chorizo
President: Jeannette Toledo
Estimated Sales:$20-50 Million
Number Employees: 50-99
Type of Packaging: Consumer, Food Service, Private Label, Bulk

3875 Del Rio Nut Company
P.O.Box 396
Livingston, CA 95334-0396   209-394-7945
Fax: 209-394-7955   delrio@evansinet.com
www.delrionut.com
Manufacturer and exporter of all varieties of natural almonds
President: David Arakelian
Estimated Sales:$ 3 - 5 Million
Number Employees: 20-49
Sq. footage: 18000
Type of Packaging: Consumer, Food Service, Private Label, Bulk
Brands:
DEL RIO

3876 Del Sol Food Company
PO Box 2243
Brenham, TX 77834-2243   979-836-5978
Fax: 979-836-6953
info@briannassaladdressing.com
www.briannassaladdressing.com
Salad dressings
President: Jerry Brown
Director Sales/Marketing: Betty O'Connor
Estimated Sales:$5-9.9 Million
Number Employees: 35
Number of Brands: 1
Number of Products: 10
Sq. footage: 20000
Type of Packaging: Consumer, Food Service
Brands:
BRIANNAS

3877 Del's Lemonade & Refreshments
1260 Oaklawn Ave
Cranston, RI 02920-2628   401-463-6190
Fax: 401-463-7931 www.dels.com
Lemonade
Owner: Bruce De Lucia
VP: Joe Padula
Estimated Sales:$3 Million
Number Employees: 20-49
Brands:
DEL'S
DEL'S ITALIAN ICES
DEL'S LEMONADE

3878 Del's Pastry
344 Bering Avenue
Etobicoke, ON M8Z 3A7
Canada   416-231-4383
Fax: 416-231-3254
Manufacturer of muffins, turnovers, pies, tea biscuits, cakes and danish
President: Benno Mattes

3879 Del's Seaway Shrimp & Oyster Company
PO Box 648
Biloxi, MS 39533-0648   228-432-2604
Fax: 228-432-8919
Manufacturer of frozen shrimp
President: George Higginbotham
Executive VP: Paul Delcambre
Estimated Sales:$10-20 Million
Number Employees: 50-99
Type of Packaging: Consumer, Food Service
Brands:
SEAWAY

3880 Del-Rey Tortilleria
5201 W Grand Ave
Chicago, IL 60639-3007   773-637-8900
Fax: 773-637-5195

Flour tortilla shells
President: Jeannette Toledo
Estimated Sales:$20-50 Million
Number Employees: 50-99
Brands:
DEL-RAY TORTILLERIA

3881 Delallo Italian Foods
6390 State Route 30
Jeannette, PA 15644-3188   724-523-5000
Fax: 724-523-0981 http://www.delallo.com
Olives
Manager: Eric Baker
Estimated Sales:$2.5-5 Million
Number Employees: 20-49
Brands:
DELALLO

3882 Delancey Dessert Company
573 Grand St
New York, NY 10002-4381   212-254-0977
Fax: 212-253-8902   800-254-5254
delancey@babka.com   www.babka.com
Candy and confectionery
Owner: Zvia Levi
Estimated Sales:$1-2.5 Million
Number Employees: 1-4
Brands:
DELANCEY DESSERT

3883 (HQ)Delano Growers Grape Products
32351 Bassett Ave
Delano, CA 93215-9699   661-725-3255
Fax: 661-725-0279
Manufacturer and exporter of white grape juice concentrate
President: Ray Cox
Sales: Luis Caratan
Production: Herold Nelson
Estimated Sales:$26.30 Million
Number Employees: 50-99
Type of Packaging: Bulk

3884 Delectable Gourmet LLC
1110 Route 109 # 1
Lindenhurst, NY 11757-1025   631-957-1350
Fax: 631-957-1013   800-696-1350
info@icebakers.com
www.intercountybakers.com
Pesto, cranberry sauce, and gourmet cranberry juice
President: Ted Heim Sr
Estimated Sales:$ 20 - 50 Million
Number Employees: 50-99

3885 Delftree Farm
234 Union St
North Adams, MA 01247-3522   413-664-4907
Fax: 413-664-4908   800-243-3742
Gourmet foods and vegetables
Manager: Lori Garvey
VP: Steve Rich
Estimated Sales:$2.5-5 Million
Number Employees: 20-49
Brands:
DELFTREE

3886 Deli Express/EA Sween Company
16101 W 78th St
Eden Prairie, MN 55344-5798   952-937-9440
Fax: 952-937-0186   800-328-8184
tsween@deliexpress.com   www.deliexpress.com
Prepackaged individual sandwiches
President/CEO: Tom Sween
CFO: Dick Pearson
VP: Bill Bastian
R&D: Grant Nellis
VP Product Safety: Lavonne Kucera
Marketing: Cheryl Peterson
Production: Curt Karger
Plant Manager: Curt Karger
Purchasing: Janet Robling
Estimated Sales:$100-150 Thousand
Number Employees: 250-499
Parent Co: E.A. Sween Company
Type of Packaging: Consumer
Brands:
DELI EXPRESS
SENSIBLE CARBS

3887 Delicae Gourmet
1310 E Lake Dr
Tarpon Springs, FL 34688-8110   727-942-2502
Fax: 727-942-1837   800-942-2502
sales@delicaegourmet.com
www.delicaegourmet.com
Bread topppers, slow cooker meals, spice rubs,
mustards, relishes, chutneys, jams, jellies, spices, in-
fused oils and vinegars.
Owner: Barbara Macaluso
CEO: Barbara Macaluso
CFO: Linda Parish
VP: Leonard Macaluso
R&D: Eugene Mann
Quality Control: James Parish
Marketing: Janice Strayer
Sales: Janice Strayer
Public Relations: Barbara Macaluso
Operations: James Parish
Production: Scott Shepard
Purchasing Director: Scott Shepard
Estimated Sales:$1,500,000
Number Employees: 10-19
Number of Brands: 1
Number of Products: 120
Sq. footage: 10000
Type of Packaging: Consumer, Food Service, Pri-
vate Label, Bulk

3888 (HQ)Delicato Vineyards
455 Devlin Rd # 201
Napa, CA 94558-7562   707-265-1700
Fax: 707-265-7837   877-824-3600
info@delicato.com   www.delicato.com
Manufacturer and exporter of wine
President/CEO: Chris Indelicato
SVP Operations: Jay Indelicato
CFO: Don Allen
VP Marketing: Steve Morgan
VP National Sales: Charles Spelman
VP Human Resources: Lillian Bynum
Estimated Sales:$100-500 Million
Number Employees: 250-499
Sq. footage: 250000
Type of Packaging: Consumer, Food Service, Pri-
vate Label, Bulk
Brands:
DELICATO

3889 Delicato Vineyards
455 Devlin Rd # 201
Napa, CA 94558-7562   707-265-1700
Fax: 707-265-7837
wine@delicato.com/info@delicato.com
www.delicato.com
Wine
President/CEO: Eric Morham
CFO: Chris Indelicato
CEO: Chris Indelicato
VP of Marketing: Kathy McAfee
Estimated Sales:$100+ Million
Number Employees: 250-499
Brands:
DELICATO FAMILY

3890 Delicious Brands
2070 Maple Street
Des Plaines, IL 60018-3019   847-699-3200
Fax: 847-699-3201   800-247-2848
www.deliciousbrands.com
Cookies and crackers
President/CEO: Tom Guinan
CFO: Jeff Weiner
Marketing: Doreen Lindsey
Production Manager: Judy Grossman
Number Employees: 100-249
Brands:
DELICIOUS
FROOKIE
MAMA'S
SALERNO

3891 Delicious Desserts
785 5th Ave
Brooklyn, NY 11232-1750   718-680-1156
Fax: 718-369-6665 www.deldes.com
Manufacturer of Italian desserts including spumoni,
tartufo, tortoni, tiramisu, cannolis and cakes; im-
porter of fruit sorbet and Italian cakes
President: Joe Fusceo
Estimated Sales:$1-2.5 Million
Number Employees: 1-4
Sq. footage: 2000
Type of Packaging: Private Label

3892 Delicious Food ProductsCompany
5520 N Northwest Highway
Chicago, IL 60630-1116   773-763-5553
Fax: 773-763-0141
Manufacturer and exporter of honey, molasses and
syrups
Manager: Sam Tang
Estimated Sales:$1-2.5 Million
Number Employees: 1-4
Type of Packaging: Consumer, Food Service, Pri-
vate Label, Bulk

3893 (HQ)Delicious Frookie Company
2070 Maple Street
Des Plaines, IL 60018-3019   847-699-5900
Fax: 847-699-5940
Cookies, crackers
President: Chuck Enderson
Marketing: Judy Grossman
Estimated Sales:$500,000 appx.
Number Employees: 20-49

3894 Delicious Popcorn Company
P.O.Box 188
Waupaca, WI 54981-0188   715-258-7683
Fax: 715-258-1514 www.wisnack.com
Manufacturer of potato chips and popcorn; whole-
saler/distributor of pretzels, tostados, tortillas, baked
and fried corn curls, party snack mix, corn chips,
raw popcorn and popping oil and gourmet popcorn
products
President/Co-Owner: James Hollnbacher
CEO/Co-Owner: Jeff Hollnbacher
Marketing/Sales: Jeff Hollnbacher
Production Manager: James Hollnbacher
Purchasing Manager: James Hollnbacher
Estimated Sales:$2-5 Million
Number Employees: 10-19
Type of Packaging: Consumer, Food Service, Pri-
vate Label, Bulk
Brands:
DE-LISH-US
WISNACK

3895 Delicious Valley FrozenFoods
1200 E Ridge Rd # 9
McAllen, TX 78503-1528   956-631-7177
Fax: 956-630-1757
Frozen foods
Manager: Sylvia Villarreal
Estimated Sales:$ .5 - 1 million
Number Employees: 1-4

3896 Dell'Amore Enterprises
948 Hercules Dr # 1
Colchester, VT 05446-5926   802-655-6264
Fax: 802-655-6262   800-962-6673
info@dellamore.com   www.dellamore.com
All natural pasta sauces
President: Frank Dell'amore
VP: David Dell'Amore
Estimated Sales:$2.5-5 Million
Number Employees: 5-9
Type of Packaging: Private Label

3897 Dellaco Classic Confections
8002 352nd Ave
Burlington, WI 53105-8938   262-537-2656
Fax: 262-843-1634   dellaco@busynet.net
www.pamperedpetscatalog.com
Confections and nuts
Chairman: Cynthia Delligatti
President: Laura Delligatti
Sales/Marketing: Margaret Delligatti
Estimated Sales:$2.5-5 Million
Number Employees: 10-19

3898 (HQ)Delmonico's Winery
182 15th Street
Brooklyn, NY 11215-4806   718-768-7020
Fax: 718-768-8825
Manufacturer and exporter of sherry flavors
President/Winemaker: Gerald Della Monica
Estimated Sales:$3 Million
Number Employees: 1-4
Type of Packaging: Bulk

3899 Delphos Poultry Products
205 S Pierce Street
Delphos, OH 45833-1924   419-692-5816
Fax: 419-692-1606   simtom@1m3.com
Manufacturer of chicken products including mari-
nated breasts, breaded, breast fillets, hot wings,
wingettes and gizzards
President: Thomas Schimmoller
Estimated Sales:$1-2.5 Million
Number Employees: 10-19
Sq. footage: 7000
Type of Packaging: Consumer, Food Service, Pri-
vate Label, Bulk
Brands:
VOLCANO WINGS

3900 Delsa Foods Processors
PO Box 489
Delisle, SK S0L 0P0
Canada   306-493-2400
Fax: 306-493-2211   delsa@delsa.sk.ca
Manufacturer of deli salads including potato, cole
slaw, macaroni and specialty; concentrated soups in-
cluding oreo, potato, broccoli cheese, vegetable bar-
ley, tomato, minestrone
President: Sydney Hill
Operations Manager: Don Melanson
Number Employees: 20
Sq. footage: 15000
Type of Packaging: Food Service, Private Label,
Bulk
Brands:
DELSA

3901 Delta BBQ Sauce Company
6231 Pacific Ave # A2
Stockton, CA 95207-3700   209-472-9284
Fax: 209-472-9284 www.spfloraldesigns.com
Manufacturer of marinades and barbecue sauces
Owner: Katie Wendland
Estimated Sales:$300,000-$500,000
Number Employees: 1-4
Sq. footage: 1800
Type of Packaging: Consumer, Food Service
Brands:
DELTA
RIVERBOAT

3902 Delta Catfish Products
PO Box 99
Eudora, AR 71640-0099   870-355-4192
Fax: 714-778-0998
Catfish
President/CEO: Thomas Marshall

3903 Delta Distributors
610 Fisher Rd
Longview, TX 75604-5201   903-759-7151
Fax: 903-759-7845   800-945-1858
www.deltadist.com
Beverages, confectionery, canned foods, processed
cheese, bakery, meat, seafood, dairy
President: Tom Corcoran
Product Manager: Mike Leahy
Number Employees: 50-99

3904 Delta Food Products
10557 114th Street NW
Edmonton, AB T5H 3J6
Canada   780-424-3636
Fax: 780-424-1536   deltafoods@shaw.ca
Manufacturer of frozen Chinese dim sum, fresh noo-
dles, egg and spring rolls, microwaveable Oriental
dinners and green onion cakes
President/Sales: Frankie Yeung
Manager: Mei-ling Chan
Number Employees: 22
Sq. footage: 15000
Type of Packaging: Consumer, Food Service, Pri-
vate Label
Brands:
DELTA FOODS
WOK MENU

3905 Delta Pacific Seafoods
6001 60th Avenue
Delta, BC V4K 4E2
Canada   604-946-5160
Fax: 604-946-5157   800-328-2547
customerservice@icicleseafoods.com
www.icicleseafoods.com
Processor of fresh and frozen salmon, hake, sar-
dines, halibut
Contact: Don Pollard
Number Employees: 50-99
Type of Packaging: Consumer, Food Service

3906 Delta Packing Company of Lodi
6021 E Kettleman Ln
Lodi, CA 95240-6400   209-334-0689
Fax: 209-334-0811 mail@deltapacking.com
                        www.deltapacking.com
Packer/shipper of produce including cherries, on-
ions, juice grapes, pears, asparagus and bell peppers
    Manager: Paul Poutre
    CEO: Jeff Rostomily
    Sales Manager: Paul Poutre
Estimated Sales: $20-50 Million
Number Employees: 100-249
Type of Packaging: Consumer, Food Service, Pri-
    vate Label
Brands:
    DELTA FRESH

3907 Delta Pride Catfish
P.O.Box 850
Indianola, MS 38751-0850   662-887-5401
    Fax: 662-887-5950 800-421-1045
    walterh@deltapride.com   www.deltapride.com
Manufacturer of farm-raised catfish and whole-
saler/distributor of fresh and frozen farm raised cat-
fish and hush puppies
    President/CEO: Steve Osso
    CEO: David Allen
    Quality Control Director: Kathy Boyette
    Eastern Division Manager: Greg Griffith
    VP Sales: Daryl Cargile
    Production/Transportation Manager: Pam Walker
Estimated Sales: $30 Million
Number Employees: 500-999
Parent Co: Delta Pride Catfish

3908 Delta Valley Farms
1365 N Highway 6
Delta, UT 84624-7471   435-864-2725
                        Fax: 435-864-4823
Natural and processed cheese
    President: Elwin Johnson
Estimated Sales: $5-10 Million
Number Employees: 5-9

3909 Deluxe Ice Cream Company
P.O.Box 12459
Salem, OR 97309-0459   503-581-4923
        Fax: 503-370-8516 800-304-7172
                www.deluxeicecream.com
Manufacturer of ice cream novelties
    President: Bill McMillan
    Controller: Norma Morlock
    Plant Manager: Harry Price
Estimated Sales: $50-100 Million
Number Employees: 100-249
Type of Packaging: Consumer, Food Service, Pri-
    vate Label, Bulk

3910 Demaria Seafood
12544 Warwick Blvd
Newport News, VA 23606-2644   757-930-3474
                        Fax: 757-930-4847
Catfish, cod, flounder, haddock, halibut, mackerel,
perch, salmon, shad, tuna, monkfish fillets, blue
crabmeat, clams, shrimp
    Owner: John De Maria
Estimated Sales: $500,000-$1 Million
Number Employees: 5-9
Brands:
    DEMARIA SEAFOOD

3911 Demeter Agro
PO Box 189
Lethbridge, AB T1J 3Y5
Canada   403-329-4111
    Fax: 403-329-4418 800-661-1450
    demeter@agricoreunited.com
                www.agricoreunited.com
Manufacturer and exporter of spices, herbs, spice
seeds, bird seed complete, mustard seed, peas seed
    President/Sales Manager: Walter Dyck
    Export Sales/Marketing: M L Dyck
    Unit Manager: Blair Roth
Estimated Sales: $20 - 50 Million
Number Employees: 35
Sq. footage: 60000
Parent Co: Agricore United
Other Locations:
    Demeter Agro
    Warner AB
Brands:
    DEMETER AGRO
    WARNER AB

3912 Demitri's Bloody Mary Seasonings
1705 S 93rd St # F1
Seattle, WA 98108-5150   206-764-6006
    Fax: 206-764-3163 800-627-9649
                www.demitris.com
Manufacturer of concentrated Bloody Mary Season-
ings
    President: Demitri Pallis
Estimated Sales: Under $300,000
Number Employees: 1-4
Sq. footage: 1200
Parent Co: Gourmet Mixes
Type of Packaging: Consumer, Food Service, Bulk
Brands:
    DEMITRI'S BLOODY MARY SEASONINGS

3913 Dempseys Restaurant
50 E Washington St
Petaluma, CA 94952-3115   707-765-9694
        Fax: 707-762-1259 www.dempseys.com
Beer
    President/CEO: Bernadette Burrell
    CFO: Peter Burrell
Estimated Sales: $1-2.5 Million
Number Employees: 20-49
Sq. footage: 6000
Brands:
    GOLDEN EAGLE ALE
    RED ROOSTER ALE
    SONOMA BREWING
    UGLY DOG STOUT

3914 (HQ)Denatale Vineyards
11020 Eastside Road
Healdsburg, CA 95448-9487   707-431-8460
    Fax: 707-431-8736 www.denatalevineyards.net
Wines
    President: Ron DeNatale
Estimated Sales: $500,000-$1 Million
Number Employees: 1-4

3915 Deneen Company
34 Uss Thresher Ln
Belen, NM 87002-8233   505-988-1515
                        Fax: 505-988-1300
Manufacturers and distributors for variety of food
products ranging from salsa to orange juice
    President: Greg Deneen
Estimated Sales: $5-10 Million
Number Employees: 20
Type of Packaging: Private Label

3916 Deneen Foods
33859 United Avenue
Pueblo, CO 81001   719-948-2050
    Fax: 719-948-2051 800-264-5535
    info@santafeseasons.com
        www.santafeseasons.com
Sauces
    President: Greg Deneen
    VP: Edith Deneen
Estimated Sales: $1-2.5 Million
Number Employees: 39009
Number of Brands: 3+
Number of Products: 5+
Sq. footage: 17000
Type of Packaging: Consumer, Food Service, Pri-
    vate Label, Bulk
Brands:
    Coyote Cocina
    Santa Fe Seasons

3917 Dengler's Bakery
16 E Summit Street
Souderton, PA 18964-1337   215-723-2706
                denglersbakery@erols.com
Manufacturer of baked goods including pies
    President: Brent Halteman
Estimated Sales: $500,000-$1 Million
Number Employees: 10-19
Type of Packaging: Consumer

3918 Dennco
14350 S Saginaw Ave
Chicago, IL 60633-2008   708-862-0070
                        Fax: 708-862-0097
Bakery products and bakery ingredients
    President: Dennis Slomski
Estimated Sales: $10-20 Million
Number Employees: 10-19

3919 Dennison Meat Locker
P.O.Box 128
Dennison, MN 55018-0128   507-645-8734
Manufacturer of frankfurters and sausage
    Owner: Dori Gregory
Estimated Sales: $ 1 - 3 Million
Number Employees: 1-4
Type of Packaging: Consumer

3920 Denzer's Food Products
PO Box 5632
Baltimore, MD 21210-0632   410-889-1500
        Fax: 410-235-7032 jake@denzer.com
Conch chowder, crab soup, lima bean soup, peanut
soup. Southeastern and US regional foods
    President: Jacob Slagle
Estimated Sales: $1-3 Million
Number Employees: 1-4
Type of Packaging: Consumer

3921 Depaul Industries
4950 NE M L King Blvd
Portland, OR 97211-3354   503-281-1289
        Fax: 503-284-0548 800-518-6637
        lfletcher@depaulindustries.com
                www.depaulindustries.com
DePaul Industries provides food and consumer
goods packaging services.
    CEO: Bennett Johnson
    Business Development Manager: Lori Fletcher
    Foods & Consumer Goods Packaging Manager:
    Chris Cusack
Type of Packaging: Consumer

3922 Depoe Bay Fish Company
PO Box 1650
Newport, OR 97365-0121   541-265-8833
        Fax: 541-265-2145 dbfc@newportnet.com
Manufacturer fresh seafood including groundfish,
shrimp, crab, salmon, whiting, herring, tuna and
swordfish
    President: Gerald Bates
    VP: Mike Freels
Estimated Sales: $100-500 Million
Number Employees: 200
Sq. footage: 32000
Type of Packaging: Consumer, Food Service
Brands:
    DEPOE BAY
    PACIFIC TRAWLER

3923 Deppeler Cheese Factory
P.O.Box 788
Monroe, WI 53566-0788   608-325-6311
                        Fax: 608-325-6935
Cheese and cheese products
    Manager: Silvan Blum
    Plant Manager: Silvan Blum
Estimated Sales: Less than $500,000
Number Employees: 5-9
Type of Packaging: Private Label

3924 (HQ)Derby Cone Company
PO Box 99157
Louisville, KY 40269-0157   502-491-1220
        Fax: 270-499-9580 buttermann@aol.com
Manufacturer and exporter of ice cream cones
    President: Garry Butterman, Jr
    Executive VP: Garry Butterman III
    Sales Manager: Garry Butterman Iv
    Operations: Dan McCarthy
Estimated Sales: $20-50 Million
Number Employees: 50-99
Type of Packaging: Consumer, Food Service, Bulk
Brands:
    BUTTERMAN'S WAFFLE CRISP
    CRISPY CONES
    DIPPER MATE
    EV-R-CRISP
    EVERCRISP

3925 Derco Foods
2670 W Shaw Ln
Fresno, CA 93711-2772   559-435-2664
    Fax: 559-435-8520 leond@dercofoods.com
                www.dercofoods.com
Manufacturer of dried fruits, nuts and specialty
foods; importer of dried fruits, nuts, pineapple,
mushrooms and canned fruit; exporter of dried and
canned fruit, nuts, mushrooms, beans and popcorn
    Owner: Leon Dermenjian
Estimated Sales: $20-50 Million
Number Employees: 10-19
Sq. footage: 6000

Brands:
DERCO

3926 Derlea Foods
953 Dillingham Road
Pickering, ON L1W 1Z7
Canada   905-839-7212
          Fax: 905-839-7217 888-430-7777
     derlea@fympatico.ca www.derlea.com
Manufacturer of fresh garlic
     President: Salvatore Geraci
Number Employees: 20-49
Type of Packaging: Consumer, Food Service, Private Label, Bulk

3927 Derst Baking Company
P.O.Box 22849
Savannah, GA 31403-2849   912-233-2235
          Fax: 912-234-3611 www.derst.com
Manufacturer of bread products including bread, rolls, and cakes.
     President: Paul Frankum Jr
     CEO: Edward Derst Jr
     Executive VP/Assistant CEO: Morgan Derst
     Secretary/Treasurer: Catherine Derst
Estimated Sales:$100-500 Million
Number Employees: 250-499

3928 Deschutes Brewery
901 SW Simpson Ave
Bend, OR 97702-3118   541-385-8606
     Fax: 541-383-4505 www.deschutesbrewery.com
Manufacturer of seasonal beer, ale, stout, lager and porter
     President: Gary Fish
     VP Sales/Marketing: John Bryant
Estimated Sales:$20-50 Million
Number Employees: 100-249
Type of Packaging: Consumer, Food Service
Brands:
     BLACK BUTTE
     CASCADE ALE
     MIRROR POND PALE ALE
     OBSIDIAN STOUT

3929 Deseret Dairy Products
784 W 700 S
Salt Lake City, UT 84104-1415   801-240-7350
                    Fax: 801-240-7352
Fluid milk
     Manager: Bill Beane
     Production Supervisor: Curtis Frame
Estimated Sales:$10-24.9 Million
Number Employees: 20-49

3930 Desert King International
3802 Main Street
Suite 10
Chula Vista, CA 91911-6248   800-982-2235
     Fax: 619-427-9041 rkramer@desertking.com
Manufacturer and exporter of quillaja and yucca extracts for root beer and oil flavors
     President: Paul Hiley
     VP: Joel Powers
     Regional Sales Manager: Raymond Kramer
Estimated Sales:$3-5 Million
Number Employees: 65
Sq. footage: 15000
Type of Packaging: Private Label, Bulk
Brands:
     FOAMATION

3931 Desert Valley Date
86740 Industrial Way
Coachella, CA 92236-2718   760-398-0999
     Fax: 760-398-1514 sales@desertvalleydate.com
                    www.desertvalleydate.com
Dates
     President: George Kirkjan
Estimated Sales:$10-20 Million
Number Employees: 50-99

3932 Designed Nutritional Products
P.O.Box 1242
Orem, UT 84059-1242   801-224-4518
                    Fax: 801-434-8270
          info@designednutritional.com
          www.designednutritional.com

Manufacturer of dietary supplements including organic germanium, saw palmetto extracts, ascorbigen, melatonin and indole-3-carbinol; exporter of melatonin, gramine, bisindolylmethane and glycogen
     President: David Parish
     Marketing: Omar Filippelli
     Purchasing Director: Craig Hansen
Estimated Sales:$10-20 Million
Number Employees: 5-9
Sq. footage: 5000
Type of Packaging: Bulk

3933 Desserts by David Glass
1280 Blue Hills Ave
Bloomfield, CT 06002-5317   860-769-5570
     Fax: 860-242-4408 david@davidglass.com
                    www.davidglass.com
Manufacturer and exporter of desserts including chocolate truffle cake, cheesecake and chocolate mousse balls
     President: David Glass
Estimated Sales:$10-20 Million
Number Employees: 20-49
Sq. footage: 10000
Type of Packaging: Consumer, Food Service
Brands:
     DESSERTS BY DAVID GLASS

3934 Desserts of Distinction
5365 SE International Way
Milwaukie, OR 97222-4605   503-654-8370
     Fax: 503-654-1322 desserts2@aol.com
                    www.dessertsofdistinction.com
Manufacturer of baked goods including frozen cheesecake
     Owner: Sue Sanders
Estimated Sales:$10-20 Million
Number Employees: 20-49
Type of Packaging: Food Service

3935 Destileria Serralles
PO Box 198
Mercedita, PR 00715-0198   787-723-0107
     Fax: 787-840-1155 aleman@donq.com
                    www.donq.com
Manufacturer of rum, vodka, gin, cordials and wine; importer of scotch; exporter of rum; wholesaler/distributor of general merchandise
     President/CEO: Felix Serralles, Jr.
     VP Sales: Jose Higuera
Estimated Sales:$118 Million
Number Employees: 376
Sq. footage: 300000
Type of Packaging: Consumer, Private Label, Bulk

3936 Detroit Chili Company
21400 Telegraph Rd
Southfield, MI 48033-4245   248-440-5933
          Fax: 248-440-5945 www.dtigroup.biz
Manufacturer of frozen chili
     Owner: Tim Keros
     Purchasing Agent: Terry Keros
Estimated Sales:$500,000-$1 Million
Number Employees: 10-19
Sq. footage: 5000
Type of Packaging: Consumer, Food Service

3937 Detroit City Dairy
15004 3rd Street
Highland Park, MI 48203-3718   313-868-5511
                    Fax: 313-868-0134
Dairy foods
     President/Marketing: Alan Must
Estimated Sales:$50-100 Million
Number Employees: 100-249
Type of Packaging: Private Label

3938 Deutsch Kase Haus
11275 W 250 N
Middlebury, IN 46540-7708   574-825-9511
                    Fax: 574-825-1102
Cheese
     CEO/Plant Manager: Richard Bylsma
     CEO: Dick Bylsma
Estimated Sales:$20-50 Million
Number Employees: 50-99

3939 Devansoy
P.O.Box 885
Carroll, IA 51401-0885   712-792-9600
          Fax: 712-792-2712 800-747-8605
     info@devansoy.com www.devansoy.com

Manufacturer and exporter of powdered and liquid soy milk and soy flours;. Organic and parve available
     President: Elmer Schettler
     VP/Sales & Mktg: Montgomery Kilburn
     VP/Operations: Deb Wycoff
Estimated Sales:$ 1 - 3 Million
Number Employees: 1-4
Number of Products: 8
Type of Packaging: Food Service, Private Label, Bulk
Brands:
     ENZACT
     SOY ROAST

3940 Devault Foods
P.O.Box 587
Devault, PA 19432-0587   610-644-2536
          Fax: 610-644-2631 800-426-2874
          devault@devaultfoods.com
          www.devaultfoods.com
Manufacturer of fresh and frozen portion controlled ground beef, hamburgers, pre-cooked meat balls and Philadelphia-style sandwich steaks
     President: Tom Fillippo
     CFO: Carl Sorzano
     Marketing Manager: Mark Pepe
     VP Sales/Marketing: Gerry Mello
Estimated Sales:$ 50 - 100 Million
Number Employees: 100-249
Sq. footage: 114000
Parent Co: Devault Packing Company
Type of Packaging: Food Service, Private Label, Bulk
Brands:
     MINUTE MENU
     MRS DIFILLIPPO'S
     STEAKWICH
     STEAKWICH LITE

3941 Devine Foods
8 S Plum St
Media, PA 19063-3309   610-566-2400
                              888-338-4631
     denise@devinefoods.com www.devinefoods.com
Beverages, frozen confections
     President: Denise Devine
     Operations: Jerome Renners
Estimated Sales:$ 5 - 10 Million
Number Employees: 5-9
Brands:
     DEVINE NECTAR
     FIBRYMID
     FRUICE
     SIMPLY DEVINE

3942 Devine Meat Company
1201 N Windy Knoll Drive
Devine, TX 78016-1507   830-663-4621
Manufacturer of beef and pork
     President: Dennis Haass
Estimated Sales:$1-2.5 Million
Number Employees: 1-4

3943 Devlin Trading Company
PO Box 701
Wayzata, MN 55391-0701   952-475-0259
Manufacturer and importer of spices including mustard powder and horseradish
Estimated Sales:$500,000-$1 Million
Number Employees: 1-4
Type of Packaging: Bulk

3944 Devlin Wine Cellars
PO Box 728
Soquel, CA 95073-0728   831-476-7288
     Fax: 831-479-9043 www.webwinery.com/devlin
Wines
     President: Cheryl Devlin
Estimated Sales:Less than $500,000
Number Employees: 1-4
Type of Packaging: Private Label

3945 Devro, Inc.
P.O. Box 11925
Columbus, SC
                    enquiries@devro-casings.com
                    www.devro.plc.uk
Manufacturer of casings for sausages, hams, salami, as well as other meat products.
Estimated Sales:28.8 Million
Number Employees: 373

3946 Dewey's Bakery
1930 3121 Indiana Avenue
Winston-Salem, NC 27105 336-722-8633
Fax: 336-748-0501 800-274-2994
mike@deweys.com www.deweys.com
Bakery products
Owner/President: Guy Wilkerson
Estimated Sales: $5-10 Million
Number Employees: 100-249

3947 (HQ)Dewied International
5010 E Interstate Highway 1
San Antonio, TX 78219 210-661-6161
Fax: 210-662-6112 800-992-5600
hq@dewiedint.com www.dewied.com
Manufacturer, importer and exporter of natural and synthetic sausage casings specializing in hog, sheep and beef casings
President: Howard deWied
CEO: Howard W Dewied
VP Sales: George Burt
Estimated Sales: $10-20 Million
Number Employees: 50-99
Brands:
DEWIED

3948 Dhidow Enterprises
PO Box 285
Oxford, PA 19363-0285 610-932-7868
Fax: 509-753-0570 dhidow@brandywine.net
Manufacturer of nonvinegar based hot sauces
President: Dhidow Stephens
CEO: Paulette Colman
Estimated Sales: $300,000
Number Employees: 2
Type of Packaging: Consumer, Food Service, Bulk
Brands:
DHIDOW ENTERPRISE 150X
DHIDOW ENTERPRISE 20X
DHIDOW ENTERPRISE 50X
DHIDOW ENTERPRISE ZERO

3949 Di Camillo Bakery
811 Linwood Ave
Niagara Falls, NY 14305-2584 716-282-2341
Fax: 716-282-2596 800-634-4363
dicamillo@dicamillobakery.com
www.dicamillobakery.com
Cakes, biscuits, biscotti, cookies, crispbreads and flatbreads
President/CEO/CFO/Sales: David Di Camillo
VP Marketing: Michael Di Camillo
Estimated Sales: $20-50 Million
Number Employees: 50-99

3950 Di Grazia Vineyards
131 Tower Rd
Brookfield, CT 06804-3654 203-775-1616
Fax: 203-775-3195 800-230-8853
wine@prodigy.net www.digrazia.com
Wine
Owner: Paul Di Grazia
VP: Paul DiGrazia
Sales: Matthew Guglielmo
Estimated Sales: $500,000-$1 Million
Number Employees: 1-4
Brands:
CONVETUAL FRANCISCAN FRIARS
DI GRAZIA VINEYARDS

3951 Di Paolo Baking Company
598 Plymouth Ave N
Rochester, NY 14608-1691 585-232-3510
Fax: 585-423-5975 sales@dipaolobread.com
www.dipaolobread.com
Breads, rolls and pastries
Owner: Genario Della Porta
CEO: Dominick P Massa
Estimated Sales: $10-20 Million
Number Employees: 50-99

3952 DiCarlo's Bakery
1701 N Gaffey Street
San Pedro, CA 90731-1274 310-831-2524
Muffins and buns
Estimated Sales: $25-49.9 Million
Number Employees: 5-9

3953 DiGregorio Food Products
2232 Marconi Ave
St Louis, MO 63110-3114 314-776-1062
Fax: 314-776-3954 www.digregoriofoods.com

Manufacturer of sausage, meat balls and spaghetti sauce
President: Dora Di Gregorio
CEO: John DiGregorio
Estimated Sales: $ .5 - 1 million
Number Employees: 20-49
Sq. footage: 50000
Type of Packaging: Food Service, Private Label

3954 (HQ)DiMare International
82025 Avenue 44
Indio, CA 92201-2244 760-564-3762
Fax: 760-347-0858 www.dimareinc.com
Manufacturer, importer and exporter of lemons, oranges, grapefruit, dates, asparagus, grapes, green onions and mixed vegetables
Owner: Thomas Dimare
VP Government Relations: Dominic DiMare
General Sales Manager: Jim DiMare
General Manager: Thomas DiMare
Estimated Sales: $20-50 Million
Number Employees: 100-249
Sq. footage: 45000
Type of Packaging: Consumer, Food Service, Private Label, Bulk
Brands:
BERMUDA DUNES
DI-MARE GOLD LABEL
RANCHO PALM SPRINGS
SEA VIEW

3955 DiPasquale's
3700 Gough St
Baltimore, MD 21224-2539 410-276-6787
Fax: 410-276-0161 mustogusto@aol.com
www.depasquales.com
Distributor of fine Italian foods and specialties.
Owner: Joseph Di Pasquale
Estimated Sales: $20-50 Million
Number Employees: 20-49
Type of Packaging: Consumer, Food Service

3956 (HQ)Diageo United Distillers
801 Main Avenue
Norwalk, CT 06851-1127 203-602-5000
Fax: 203-359-7402
global.general.information@diageo.com
www.diageo.com
Alcoholic beverages
President/CEO/COO: Paul Clinton
CFO: Greg Au
EVP Consumer Strategy/Marketing: Mark Waller
Estimated Sales: $18,759,000
Number Employees: 20-49
Parent Co: Diageo
Brands:
BAILEY'S
BARTON & GUESTIER
BEAULIEU VINEYARD
BUSHMILLS
CAPTAIN MORGAN
CROWN ROYAL
CUERVO
GUINNESS
HARP
J&B
JOHNNIE WALKERS
KILKENNY
SMIRNOFF
SMITHWICK'S
STERLING VINEYARD
TANQUERAY

3957 (HQ)Diamond Bakery Company
756 Moowaa Street
Honolulu, HI 96817-4405 808-845-8200
Fax: 808-847-7482 info@diamondbakery.com
www.diamondbakery.com
Manufacturer and exporter of crackers and cookies
President: Brent Kunimoto
Estimated Sales: $ 20 - 50 Million
Number Employees: 48
Number of Products: 50+
Sq. footage: 50500
Type of Packaging: Consumer, Food Service, Private Label, Bulk
Brands:
DIAMOND BAKERY

3958 Diamond Blueberry
548 Pleasant Mills Rd
Hammonton, NJ 08037-8931 609-561-3661
Fax: 609-567-4423

Manufacturer and packer of fresh and frozen blueberries
President: John Bertino
Sales: Tim Wetherbee
Estimated Sales: $500,000-$1 Million
Number Employees: 1-4
Brands:
DIAMOND

3959 Diamond Creek Vineyards
1500 Diamond Mountain Rd
Calistoga, CA 94515-9669 707-942-6926
Fax: 707-942-6936
www.diamondcreekvineyards.com
Wines
President: Al Brounstein
Estimated Sales: $2.5-5 Million
Number Employees: 5-9
Type of Packaging: Private Label

3960 Diamond Crystal
P.O.Box 9177
Savannah, GA 31412-9177 912-651-5112
Fax: 912-650-3500 800-227-4455
www.diamondcrystal.com
Manufacturer of saccharin, aspartame and sugar including granulated, light and dark brown
President: Karl Kaiser
Estimated Sales: $60 Million
Number Employees: 250-499
Sq. footage: 300000
Parent Co: Homel Foods
Type of Packaging: Consumer, Food Service
Brands:
DIAMOND CRYSTAL

3961 Diamond Crystal Brands
P.O.Box 9177
Savannah, GA 31412-9177 912-651-5112
Fax: 912-650-3500 www.diamondcrystal.com
Manufacturer and exporter of low-sodium mixes including soup, milk shake, ice cream, sauce, sugar-free dessert and fruit drink; also, instant breakfast beverages, cookies, nutritional chocolate bars and portion packed condimentsincluding jelly, mustard, etc
President: Karl Kaiser
VP Finances: Dave Lewis
Estimated Sales: $100-500 Million
Number Employees: 250-499
Sq. footage: 305500
Parent Co: Imperial Holly Corporation
Type of Packaging: Food Service, Private Label
Other Locations:
Diamond Crystal Specialty Foo
Aurora ON
Brands:
DIAMOND CRYSTAL
DIAMOND SHAKERS
DIET KIT
MIGHTYSHAKES
PACKET
SINGLE SERV

3962 Diamond Crystal Specialty Foods
1600 2nd St NE
Bondurant, IA 50035-1144 515-967-3737
Fax: 515-967-3578
Manufacturer and exporter of flavoring extracts, sweeteners, food colors, stabilizers, ice cream mixes and powdered milk
President: Walter Lehnies
Plant Manager: Brent Canny
Estimated Sales: $17.70 Million
Number Employees: 20-49
Parent Co: Diamond Crystal
Type of Packaging: Food Service, Bulk
Other Locations:
Diamond Crystal Specialty Foods
Perryburg OH

3963 Diamond Foods
11899 Exit 5 Pkwy
Fishers, IN 46037-7938 317-845-5534
Fax: 317-577-3588 www.goldenstream.com
Manufacturer, importer and wholesaler/distributor of dried fruit, seeds, fruit and nuts
President/CEO: Michael Mendes
Estimated Sales: $20-50 Million
Number Employees: 20-49
Type of Packaging: Consumer, Bulk

3964 (HQ)Diamond Foods Inc
1050 Diamond St
Stockton, CA 95205-7020   209-467-6000
Fax: 209-467-6709 aburke@diamondfoods.com
www.diamondnuts.com
Manufacturer of walnuts, almonds, pecans, hazelnuts, pine nuts, Brazil nuts and raw Spanish peanuts.
President/CEO/Director: Michael Mendes
EVP/COO: Gary Ford
EVP/CFO: Seth Halio
VP General Counsel: Stephen Kim
VP Marketing: Andrew Burke
VP Investor Relations/Treasurer: Robert Philips
VP Corporate Affairs/Human Resources: Sam Keiper
Estimated Sales: $350 Million
Number Employees: 500-999
Type of Packaging: Food Service
Other Locations:
Diamond Foods Processing Plant
Stockton CA
Diamond Foods Processing Plant
Linden CA
Diamond Foods Processing Plant
Modesto CA
Diamond Foods Processing Plant
Lemont IL
Diamond Foods Processing Plant
Robertsdale AL
Brands:
DIAMOND

3965 Diamond Fruit Growers
P.O.Box 185
Odell, OR 97044-0185   541-354-5300
Fax: 541-354-2123 MartinC@diamondfruit.com
www.diamondfruit.com
Cooperative grower, packer, shipper and exporter of apples, pears and cherries
President/GM: Ron Girardelli
VP Finance: David Garcia
VP Sales: Neil Galone
Operations Manager: Robert Wymore
Information Services Manager: Martin Cohen
Estimated Sales: $ 20 - 50 Million
Number Employees: 500-999
Type of Packaging: Bulk

3966 Diamond Nut Company
16500 103rd Street
Lemont, IL 60439-9600   630-739-3000
Fax: 630-739-1446 www.diamondofcalifornia.com
Manufacturer, importer and exporter of almonds, pecans, Brazils, filberts, walnuts and mixed nuts; also, tropical fruits, and onions
Chairman: John Gilbert
President/CEO: Michael Mendes
General Manager: Larry Rehmann
Estimated Sales: $45 Million
Number Employees: 125
Parent Co: Diamond Walnut Growers
Type of Packaging: Consumer, Private Label, Bulk

3967 Diamond Oaks Vineyard
PO Box 433
Cloverdale, CA 95425-0433   707-894-3191
Wines
President: Dinesh Maniar

3968 Diamond Seafood
204 N Edgewood Avenue
Wood Dale, IL 60191-1610   630-787-1100
Fax: 630-787-1309
Seafood
President: Thomas Hannagan
Estimated Sales: $ 5 - 10 Million
Number Employees: 10-19

3969 Diamond Water
P.O.Box 1610
Hot Springs, AR 71902-1610   501-623-1251
Fax: 501-623-2648
Manufacturer of bottled spring water
Plant Manager: Brian Hinds
Estimated Sales: $5-10 Million
Number Employees: 10-19
Parent Co: Mountain Valley Water
Type of Packaging: Consumer

3970 Diamond of California
PO Box 1727
Stockton, CA 95201-1727   925-251-3816
Fax: 925-251-3820 www.diamondnuts.com
Nuts
President: Michael Mendes
CEO: Michael Mendes
CFO: Seth Halio
VP: Mario Alioto
Sales: Frank Morgan
Public Relations Manager: Vicki Zeigler

3971 Diana Fruit Company
651 Mathew St
Santa Clara, CA 95050-2928   408-727-9631
Fax: 408-727-9890 tklevay@dianafruit.com
www.dianafruit.com
Producer and supplier of high quality Maraschino Cherries.
President: Gene Acronico
VP Sales/Marketing: Thomas Klevay
Estimated Sales: $ 20 - 50 Million
Number Employees: 50-99
Parent Co: Gene Acronico Canners & Packing
Type of Packaging: Bulk

3972 Diana Naturals
707 Executive Drive
Valley Cottage, NY 10989   845-268-5200
Fax: 845-268-4626
contact@diana-naturals-inc.com
www.diana-naturals.com
Ingredients
Manager: Karina Giusto
Parent Co: Diana Naturals

3973 Diana's Specialty Foods
2305 Aurora Dr
Pingree Grove, IL 60140-6442   847-683-1200
Fax: 847-683-1207 dsf@elnet.com
Maunfacturer of Vinegar, fancy gifts, Italian riviera and provencial bread dippers, grapeseed oils, miniature bread dipping oils, salsa, jams, jelly, mustard, herb mayonnaise, and olive oil
Manager: Mark Pagnoni
Estimated Sales: $12,000
Number Employees: 10-19
Sq. footage: 3000
Type of Packaging: Private Label

3974 Dianne's Gourmet Desserts
410 W Industrial St
Le Center, MN 56057-1200   507-357-4161
Fax: 507-357-2247 800-289-7437
stevenlen@diannesdesserts.com
www.diannesdesserts.com
Desserts
Plant Manager: Bruce Heckman
Estimated Sales: $100+ Million
Number Employees: 250-499

3975 Dick & Casey's Gourmet Seafoods
P.O.Box 2392
Harbor, OR 97415-0313   541-469-9494
Fax: 541-469-0757 800-662-9494
inquire@gourmetseafood.com
www.gourmetseafood.com
Manufacturer of canned and frozen seafood including shrimp, lobster, crab meat, etc
Owner: Julie Tomlinson
Estimated Sales: $500,000-$1 Million
Number Employees: 1-4
Type of Packaging: Consumer, Food Service
Brands:
DICK & CASEY'S

3976 (HQ)Dick Garber Company
7900 SW 245h Street
Suite 202
Davie, FL 33324   954-236-0456
Fax: 954-236-0468 dgarber@garbersales.com
Cheese, meat, bakery specialties
President/CEO: Dick Garber
CFO: Rosalie Garber
Sales: Mark Finocchio
Estimated Sales: $5-10 Million
Number Employees: 5-9
Type of Packaging: Private Label

3977 Dick's Packing Company
1207 Rogers St
Columbia, MO 65201-4796   573-449-2995
Fax: 573-449-3163
Manufacturer of beef, pork and venison
Estimated Sales: $20-50 Million
Number Employees: 20-49
Type of Packaging: Food Service

3978 Dick's Packing Plant
7745 State Route 37 E
New Lexington, OH 43764-9512   740-342-4150
Manufacturer of fresh meats
Owner: Dick Knipe
Co-Owner: Blanche Knipe
Estimated Sales: $5-10 Million
Number Employees: 5-9
Type of Packaging: Consumer, Food Service, Bulk

3979 Dickinson Frozen Foods
600 NW 21st St
Fruitland, ID 83619-5052   208-452-5200
Fax: 208-452-5365
www.dickinsonfrozenfoods.com
Manufacturer of frozen onions and bell peppers
President: Paul Fox
Finance: Chuck White
VP Marketing: Charles Murphy
Sales/Marketing: Aaron Mann
VP Operations: Craig Culver
VP Production: Bob Pedracini
Plant Manager: Roger Ingebritsen
Estimated Sales: $100-500 Million
Number Employees: 100-249
Type of Packaging: Consumer, Food Service, Private Label
Brands:
DICKINSON FROZEN FOODS

3980 Dickson Company
930 S Westwood Ave
Addison, IL 60101-4997   630-543-3747
Fax: 630-543-0498 800-323-2448
dicksoncsr@dicksonweb.com
www.dicksonweb.com
Data loggers, chart recorders and indicators.
President: Michael Unger
Marketing: Kathy Donovan
Estimated Sales: $ 5 - 10 Million
Number Employees: 50-99

3981 Dickson's Pure Honey
4331 Hatchery Road
San Angelo, TX 76903-1513   915-655-9233
Pure honey
President: Andrew Dickson
Estimated Sales: $1-2.5 Million appx.
Number Employees: 1
Brands:
DICKSON'S PURE HONEY

3982 Dicola Seafood
10754 S Western Ave
Chicago, IL 60643-3199   773-238-7071
Fax: 773-238-8337
Seafood
Owner: Robert Di Cola
Estimated Sales: $ 5 - 10 Million
Number Employees: 20-49

3983 Diedrich Coffee
28 Executive Park # 200
Irvine, CA 92614-4741   949-260-1600
Fax: 949-260-1610 800-354-5282
java@diedrich.com www.diedrich.com
Manufacturer of coffee
President/CEO: Roger Laverty
Executive VP/CFO: Martin Lynch
CEO: J Russell Philips
VP Operations: Greg Macisaac
Director Purchasing: Steve Leach
Estimated Sales: $75 Million
Number Employees: 100-249
Brands:
COFFEE PEOPLE
DIEDRICH COFFEE
GLORIA JEANS

3984 Dieffenbach Potato Chips
51 Host Rd
Womelsdorf, PA 19567-9421   610-589-2385
Fax: 610-589-2866 www.dieffenbachs.com
Potato chips
Owner: Elan Dieffenbach
Estimated Sales: $ 5 - 10 Million
Number Employees: 10-19

3985 Diehl Food Ingredients
24 N Clinton St
Defiance, OH 43512-1807   419-782-5010
Fax: 419-783-4319 800-251-3033
diehl@bright.net www.diehlinc.com

Manufacturer and exporter of lactose free beverages, powdered fat, coffee creamers and whip topping bases.
President: Charles Nicolais
CFO: Darren Lane
CEO: Peter Diehl
Research & Development: Joan Hasselman
Quality Control: Kelly Roach
Marketing Director: Dennis Reid
Sales Director: Jim Holdrieth
Number Employees: 100-249
Parent Co: Diehl
Type of Packaging: Consumer, Food Service, Bulk
Brands:
CHOCOMITE
VITAMITE

3986 Dietrich's Milk Products
100 McKinley Ave
Reading, PA 19605-2117   610-929-5736
                                800-526-6455
www.dietrichsmilk.com
Manufacturer and exporter of cream and powdered and condensed milk; contract drying services available for nondairy powders
President/CEO: Thomas Dietrich
Estimated Sales: $50-75 Million
Number Employees: 50-99
Sq. footage: 60000
Parent Co: Dairy Farmers of America
Type of Packaging: Bulk
Brands:
CHOCOLATE CRUMB POWDER

3987 Dietz & Watson
5701 Tacony St
Philadelphia, PA 19135-4394   215-831-9000
Fax: 215-831-8719 800-333-1974
www.dietzandwatson.com
Manufacturer of meat products including sausage, deli ham, turkey breast, frankfurters, etc
President: Butch Dietz
Finance: Cindi Eni Yingling
Marketing/QA/Product Development: Louis Eni
VP Sales/Marketing: Rich Wright
Design/Operation: Chri Eni
Estimated Sales: $50-100 Million
Number Employees: 500-999
Sq. footage: 240000
Type of Packaging: Consumer, Bulk
Brands:
DIETZ & WATSON

3988 Difiore Pasta Company
556 Franklin Ave
Hartford, CT 06114-3024   860-296-1077
Fax: 860-296-5635
Pasta
Owner: Louise Di Fiore
Estimated Sales: $1-2.5 Million
Number Employees: 5-9
Brands:
DIFIORE PASTA

3989 (HQ)Diggs Packing Company
1207 Rogers St
Columbia, MO 65201-4796   573-449-2995
Fax: 573-449-3163
Manufacturer of beef, ham, sausage, meat packing services, distributes fresh meat, provides slaughtering
Owner: Dale Diggs
Public Relations: Dan Reynolds
Estimated Sales: $14.10 Million
Number Employees: 20-49
Type of Packaging: Consumer

3990 Dilettante Chocolates
19016 72nd Ave S
Kent, WA 98032-1005   206-328-1530
Fax: 206-709-0309 888-600-2462
patricksnider@dilettante.com
www.seattlegourmetfoods.com
Candy and confectionery
President: David Taylor
CEO: Brian Davenport
Director Sales/Marketing: Tom Davis
Sales Manager: Chris Ratliff
Production Manager: Brian Hubbard
Estimated Sales: $1-2.5 Million
Number Employees: 5-9

3991 Dillanos Coffee Roasters
1607 45th St E
Sumner, WA 98390-2202   253-826-1682
Fax: 253-826-1827 800-234-5282
www.dillanos.com
Manufacturer and importer of coffee
Owner: Chris Heyer
VP: Keith Hayward
Estimated Sales: $10-20 Million
Number Employees: 20-49
Type of Packaging: Food Service

3992 Dillard's Bar-B-Q Sauce
3921 Fayetteville St
Durham, NC 27713-1135   919-544-1587
Fax: 919-361-3410
Manufacturer of barbecue sauce
Co-Partner: Geneva Dillard
Co-Partner/General Manager: Wilma Dillard
Estimated Sales: Less than $500,000
Number Employees: 10-19
Type of Packaging: Consumer
Brands:
DILLARD'S

3993 Dillman Farm
4955 W State Road 45
Bloomington, IN 47403-9362   812-825-6878
Fax: 812-825-4650 800-359-1362
dillman@dillmanfarm.com
www.dillmanfarm.com
Manufacturer of fruit butters, preserves, jellies, salsa, mustard, bbq, no preservatives, cane sugar or grape juice to sweeten products
President/Production: Cary Dillman
Estimated Sales: $5-10 Million
Number Employees: 9
Sq. footage: 15000
Brands:
DILLMAN FARM
DILLMAN'S ALL NATURAL

3994 Dillon Candy Company
19927 Highway 84 E
Boston, GA 31626-2666   229-498-2051
Fax: 229-498-2201 800-382-8338
margarer@dilloncandy.com
www.dilloncandy.com
Manufacturer of candy including peanut and pecan log rolls, sand brittles, divinity, coated pecans, pralines and pecan puffs
Owner/President: Oscar Cook
Sales: Michele Tull
Estimated Sales: $10-20 Million
Number Employees: 20-49
Type of Packaging: Consumer

3995 Dillon Companies
P.O.Box 1608
Hutchinson, KS 67504-1608   620-665-5511
Fax: 620-669-3167 www.dillons.com
Supermarket chain
President: John Bays
Plant Manager: Albert Garcia
Parent Co: Kroger

3996 Dillon Dairy Company
5512 Leetsdale Dr
Denver, CO 80246-1432   303-388-1645
Fax: 303-388-0514
Milk, dairy products
Manager: William Weyhrich
Estimated Sales: $10-20 Million
Number Employees: 20-49

3997 Dimare
827 W Center Ave
Visalia, CA 93291-6013   559-627-0821
Fax: 559-627-2605 www.dimarefresh.com
Processor of citrus fruits including oranges, lemons, grapefruit, tangerines and limes
Manager: Stewart Lockwood
General Manager: Allan Dodge
Estimated Sales: $ 1 - 3 Million
Number Employees: 1-4
Parent Co: Fresh America Corporation

3998 Dimitria Delights
81 Creeper Hill Rd
North Grafton, MA 01536-1421   508-839-3035
Fax: 508-839-1685 800-763-1113
sales@dimitriadelights.com
www.dimitriadelights.com

Manufacturer of frozen baked and nonbaked desserts including spinach pies, puff pastries, fruit strudels, regular and filled danish and croissant dough
President/Production Manager: John Colorio
Vice President: Mary Colorio
Estimated Sales: $10-20 Million
Number Employees: 50-99
Sq. footage: 35000
Type of Packaging: Consumer, Food Service, Private Label
Brands:
MARY'S
PITA
STRUDELKINS

3999 Dimock Dairy Products
P.O.Box 26
Dimock, SD 57331-0026   605-928-3833
Fax: 605-928-1410 dimockdairy@santel.net
www.dimockdairy.com
Manufacturer of cheese
Manager: Roger Swemby
Manager: Mike Royston
Estimated Sales: $5-10 Million
Number Employees: 5-9
Sq. footage: 4500
Type of Packaging: Consumer

4000 Dimond Tager Company Products
2801 E Hillsborough Ave
Tampa, FL 33610-4410   813-238-3111
Fax: 813-238-3114
Manufacturer and wholesaler/distributor of produce
Owner/President: Ray Charlton
Estimated Sales: $ 1 - 3 Million
Number Employees: 5-9
Sq. footage: 4000
Type of Packaging: Consumer, Food Service, Bulk

4001 Dimpflmeier Bakery
26 Advance Road
Toronto, ON M8Z 2T4
Canada   416-239-3031
Fax: 416-239-5370
carolm@dimpflmeierbakery.com
Manufacturer and exporter of German-style breads including rye, pumpernickel, sourdough and monastery; also, rolls and buns
President: Alfonse Dimpflmier
Number Employees: 170
Type of Packaging: Consumer, Food Service
Brands:
HOLZOFEN
KLOSTERBROT
MUENCHNER/STADTBROT

4002 Dina's Organic Chocolate
39 Smith Ave
Mt Kisco, NY 10549   914-242-0124
Fax: 914-242-5289 888-625-2008
dina@dinakhader.com www.dinakhader.com
organic chocolate bars in four different flavors
President/Owner: Dina Khader

4003 Dinkel's Bakery
3329 N Lincoln Ave
Chicago, IL 60657-1107   773-281-7300
Fax: 773-281-6169 800-822-8817
norm@dinkels.com www.dinkels.com
Manufacturer of baked goods including chocolate chip butter cookies, cakes, pecan fudge brownies and snacks; contract baking available
President: Norman Dinkel
Estimated Sales: $5-10 Million
Number Employees: 20-49
Sq. footage: 17000
Type of Packaging: Consumer, Food Service, Private Label, Bulk
Brands:
DINKEL'S
DINKEL'S FAMOUS STOLLEN
DINKEL'S SIP'N
DINKEL'S SOUTHERN DOUBLE

4004 Dinner Bell Meat Product
P.O.Box 11404
Lynchburg, VA 24506-1404   434-847-7766
Fax: 434-847-6305
Manufacturer of sausage
President: Butch Anderson
Estimated Sales: $10-20 Million
Number Employees: 10-19
Type of Packaging: Consumer

4005 Dino's Sausage & Meat Company
722 Catherine St
Utica, NY 13501-1304   315-732-2661
    Fax: 315-732-3094
Manufacturer of sausage and beef products; wholesaler/distributor of bacon, ham, pork, lamb, etc
    President: Carmen Bossone
Estimated Sales: $10-20 Million
Number Employees: 10-19
Type of Packaging: Consumer
Brands:
    DINO'S

4006 Dino-Meat Company
PO Box 95
White House, TN 37188-0095   615-643-1022
    Fax: 615-643-1022   877-557-6493
dinomeatco@bellsouth.net   www.dinomeat.com
Manufacturer of emu meat including steaks, ground, breakfast sausage, summer sausage, hot dogs, hot links, meat balls, snack sticks and jerky. Also emu oil and emu oil products
    President: Neil Williams
Type of Packaging: Consumer, Food Service
Brands:
    BACK COUNTRY EMU PRODUCTS
    DINE-MEAT EMU PRODUCTS

4007 Dip Seafood
1870 Dauphin Island Pkwy
Mobile, AL 36605-3000   251-479-0123
    Fax: 251-479-9869
Seafood
    Owner: Trina Nguyen
Estimated Sales: $300,000-500,000
Number Employees: 1-4

4008 Dipasa
6600 Fm 802
Brownsville, TX 78526-6953   956-831-5893
    Fax: 956-831-5893   info@dipasausa@com
    www.dipasausa.com
Manufacturer, importer and exporter of tahini and sesame seeds, raisins, oil, flour and candy; wholesaler/distributor of onion and cheese breadsticks, baked snacks, halvah and confectionery items, natural colors, oleoresins
Estimated Sales: $8 Million
Number Employees: 10-19
Number of Brands: 2
Number of Products: 10
Sq. footage: 20000
Parent Co: Dipasa De C.V.
Type of Packaging: Consumer, Food Service, Private Label, Bulk
Brands:
    BILADI
    BILADI TOHINA
    DE CHAMPAQUE BAKERY SNACKS
    DIPASA BILADI
    DIPASA DE CHAMPAGNE
    DIPASA USA
    SESAMIN

4009 Dippin' Dots
5101 Charter Oak Dr
Paducah, KY 42001-5209   270-443-8994
    Fax: 270-443-8997   slaes@dippindots.com
    www.dippindots.com
Ice cream, yogurt, flavored ices and sherbets
    President: Tom Leonard
    CFO: Connie Ulrich
    Director Sales: Tammy Wilson
    Public Relations: Terry Reeves
    Director Operations: Steve Schiff
Estimated Sales: G
Number Employees: 100-249
Brands:
    DIPPIN' DOTS

4010 Dippy Foods
10554 Progress Way
Suite K
Cypress, CA 90630-4724   714-816-0150
    Fax: 714-816-0153   800-819-8551
erin@dippyfoods.com   www.dippyfoods.com
Single-serving meals to schools and other institutional food servers
    President: Jon Stevenson
    VP: Erin Stevenson
Brands:
    EARTH'S BEST

    HAIN KIDZ
    HEALTH VALLEY

4011 Discovery Foods
2395 American Ave
Hayward, CA 94545-1807   510-293-1838
    Fax: 510-293-1830 www.lingling.com
Manufacturer of ethnic and frozen foods
    President: Clarence Mou
    Public Relations: Charlene Crosby
Estimated Sales: $ 20 - 50 Million
Number Employees: 100-249

4012 Dismat Corporation
336 N Westwood Ave
Toledo, OH 43607-3343   419-531-8963
    Fax: 419-531-8965 www.mckaysseasoning.com
Manufacturer and exporter of powdered soup mixes and seasonings
    President: John Donofrio
    Operations VP: Sandra Lee Jones
Estimated Sales: $1-$2 Million
Number Employees: 5-9
Number of Brands: 1
Number of Products: 3
Sq. footage: 12000
Type of Packaging: Consumer, Bulk
Brands:
    MCKAY'S

4013 Distant Lands Coffee Roaster
11754 State Highway 64 W
Tyler, TX 75704-6934   903-592-8014
    Fax: 903-593-2699   800-346-5459
    sales@dlcoffee.com   www.dlcoffee.com
Roasters of organic, flavored and fair-trade coffees.
    President: Bill McAlpin
Estimated Sales: $20-50 Million
Number Employees: 50-99
Type of Packaging: Private Label, Bulk
Brands:
    COUNTRY COFFEE

4014 Distant Lands Coffee Roaster
11754 State Highway 64 W
Tyler, TX 75704-6934   903-592-8014
    Fax: 903-593-2699   800-346-5459
    sales@dlcoffee.com   www.dlcoffee.com
Coffee, tea
    President/ CEO: William McAlpin
    Marketing: Kristin Jones
Estimated Sales: $2.5-5 Million
Number Employees: 50-99
Type of Packaging: Private Label

4015 Distillata Company
1608 East 24th St
Cleveland, OH 44114   216-771-2900
    Fax: 216-771-1672   800-999-2906
    ClevelandCustomerService@Distillata.com
    www.distillata.com
Manufacturer and bottler of spring and distilled water
    President: Keith Schroeder
Estimated Sales: $10-20 Million
Number Employees: 100-249
Type of Packaging: Consumer, Food Service, Private Label, Bulk
Brands:
    DISTILLATA

4016 Distillerie Stock USA
Apt 11b
400 E 77th St
New York, NY 10075-2325   718-651-9800
    Fax: 718-651-7806   800-323-1884
    jill@stockusaltd.com
Manufacturer and importer of vermouth, brandy, liqueur, Asti, French and Italian wines, Grand gala triple orange, Keglevich vodka and liqueur, Glengoyne single highland malt whisky
    President: David Morel
    Executive VP: Todd Bernier
Estimated Sales: $20-50 Million
Number Employees: 50-99
Parent Co: Eckes, AG
Brands:
    STOCK VERMOUTH

4017 Distinctive Brands
1095 Cottonwood Cir
Golden, CO 80401-1796   303-273-9049
    Fax: 303-444-9049

All natural beef jerky and meat snack products
    CEO: Rob Calianno

4018 Distribution Plus Incorporated (DPI)
P.O.Box 5940
Mesa, AZ 85211-5940   480-969-9333
    Fax: 480-461-3645 www.epicurean-foods.com
Distributor of imported and domestic specialty foods along with multi-unit and school foodservice
    President: Chip Forster
Estimated Sales: $ 50 - 100 Million
Number Employees: 50-99

4019 Diversified Avocado Products
25950 Acero Street
Suite 360
Mission Viejo, CA 92691-7900   949-837-6464
    Fax: 949-837-6464   800-879-2555
    bswartwout@dapguacamole.com
    www.dapguacamole.com
Manufacturer of frozen guacamole and fresh avocados
    Director Sales/Marketing: Ray Flores
Number Employees: 5-9
Sq. footage: 100000
Type of Packaging: Consumer, Food Service

4020 (HQ)Diversified Foods
3115 6th St
Metairie, LA 70002-1712   504-831-6651
    Fax: 504-831-8288   dfi@diversifiedfoods.com
    www.diversifiedfoods.com
Manufacturer of ready-to-eat cereal, Cream of Coconut, Powder Drink Mixes, Powder Gelatins, Fruit Juice Concentrates, UHT Milk and Flavored Milk, Shelf Stable Milk, Aseptic UHT, Milk Products, Textured Vegetable Protein and many otherFood Service Products.
    Co-President: Tab Damiens
    Co-President: Michelle Damiens
Estimated Sales: $ 10 - 20 Million
Number Employees: 10-19
Type of Packaging: Food Service, Private Label, Bulk

4021 Diversified Foods & Seasoning
1012 S Harimaw Ct
Metairie, LA 70001   504-846-5090
    Fax: 504-834-0395
Manufacturer of frozen beans, gravy, sauce and soups; also, dry mixes, meat glazes and seasonings
    Operations Manager: Conrad Howe
Estimated Sales: $20-50 Million
Number Employees: 100-249
Parent Co: A.L. Copeland
Type of Packaging: Food Service, Private Label
Brands:
    CHIEF'S CREATIONS

4022 Divine Chocolate
418 7th Street SE
Washington, DC 20003   202-332-8913
Fax: 202-332-8916   info@divinechocolateusa.com
    www.divinechocolateusa.com
chocolate bars
    CEO: Erin Gorman
Estimated Sales: $1 Million
Number Employees: 3

4023 Divine Delights
1250 Holm Rd
Petaluma, CA 94954-1106   707-559-7099
    Fax: 707-559-7098   800-443-2836
    divinedelights@sbcglobal.com
    www.divinedelights.com
Premium petit fours and petite confections
    President: Angelique Fry
Estimated Sales: $5-10 Million
Number Employees: 20-49
Type of Packaging: Private Label, Bulk
Brands:
    CHECKERBITES
    DIVINE DELIGHTS
    MICE-A-FOURS
    TRUFFLECOTS

4024 Divine Ice Cream Company
4256 N Arlington Heights Road
Arlington Heights, IL 60004-1300   847-398-0095
Ice Cream
    President: Billy Griffin
Estimated Sales: Under $500,000
Number Employees: 1

Brands:
FRESH FROZEN

4025 Division Baking Corporation
250 Dyckman St
New York, NY 10034-5354   212-567-4500
Fax: 212-942-7682   800-934-9238
Manufacturer of cheese cake
Owner: Robert Gruenebaum
Estimated Sales: $5-10 Million
Number Employees: 20-49

4026 Divvies
700 Oakridge Common
South Salem, NY 10590   914-533-0333
madetoshare@divvies.com
www.divvies.com
dairy free, egg free, peanut free, tree nut free food snacks

4027 Dixie Brewing Company
6221 S Claiborne Avenue
New Orleans, LA 70125-4142   504-822-8711
Fax: 504-827-0410
Brewery of fine beers
President: Kendra Bruno
CEO: Joseph Bruno
Brewmaster: Peter Cadoo
Director of Brewing: Kevin Stuart
Estimated Sales: $25-49.9 Million
Number Employees: 75
Type of Packaging: Consumer, Private Label
Brands:
AMBER LIGHT
DIXIE
DIXIE BLACKENED VOODOO LAGER
DIXIE CRIMSON VOODOO ALE
DIXIE JAZZ
DIXIE WHITE MOOSE

4028 Dixie Dairy Company
1200 W 15th Avenue
Gary, IN 46407-1014   219-885-6101
Fax: 219-882-7533
Manufacturer of milk, cream, eggs, cottage cheese
and butter
President: Thomas Eskilson
Estimated Sales: $20-50 Million
Number Employees: 80
Type of Packaging: Consumer

4029 Dixie Dew Products
PO Box 18310
Erlanger, KY 41018-0310   859-283-1050
Fax: 859-282-3781   800-867-8548
info@dixiedewproducts.com
www.dixiedewproducts.com
Manufacturer of fruit glazes, dips, puddings, toppings, day blends and specialty sauces; contract processing and packaging available
Purchasing: Krista Reese
Estimated Sales: $5-10 Million
Number Employees: 10-19
Sq. footage: 40000
Type of Packaging: Consumer, Food Service, Private Label, Bulk
Brands:
CLASSIC TRADITIONS
HARRY'S CHOICE
HERITAGE FANCY FOODS

4030 Dixie Egg Company
5139 Edgewood Ct
Jacksonville, FL 32254-3601   904-783-0950
Fax: 904-786-6227   800-394-3447
kjkeggs@aol.com   www.dixieegg.com
Manufacturer and exporter of fresh shell eggs
President: Jacques Klempf
CEO: Edward Klempf
Controller: Paul Stevenson
Operations/General Manager: John Reece
Feed/Production Manager: Dennis Hughes
Number Employees: 250-499
Parent Co: Foodonics International
Type of Packaging: Consumer, Bulk

4031 Dixie Rice
600 Pasquiere St
Gueydan, LA 70542   337-536-9276
Fax: 337-536-5099
Rice
Manager: Keith Hensgens
Number Employees: 1-4

Brands:
DIXIE

4032 Dixie Trail Farms
PO Box 4082
Wilmington, NC 28406-1082   800-665-3968
Fax: 800-765-7482   info@dixietrail.com
www.dixietrail.com
Grilling sauces and marinades

4033 Dixie USA
P.O.Box 1969
Tomball, TX 77377-1969   281-290-6010
Fax: 281-516-3070   800-233-3668
info@dixieusa.com   www.dixiediner.com
Manufacturer of meat analogs, tofu, soy products and low carb products; exporter of soy
Owner: Bob Beeley
Executive VP: Jim Oswalt
Estimated Sales: $5-10 Million
Number Employees: 20-49
Sq. footage: 30000
Type of Packaging: Consumer, Food Service, Private Label, Bulk
Brands:
BEEF NOT
CHICKEN NOT
DUTLETTES

4034 Dixon Associates
PO Box 1250
Mechanicsburg, PA 17055-1250   717-691-0800
Fax: 717-691-4153
Specialty dairy beverages
President: John Kober
Estimated Sales: $25-49.9 Million
Number Employees: 1-4

4035 Dixon Canning Company
P.O.Box 340
Dixon, CA 95620-0340   707-678-4406
Fax: 707-441-3718
Manufacturer of canned tomato products including diced and paste
Plant Manager: Pete Imhoff
Estimated Sales: $50-100 Million
Number Employees: 250-499
Parent Co: Campbell Soup Company
Type of Packaging: Bulk

4036 Dixon's Fisheries
1807 N Main St
East Peoria, IL 61611-2193   309-694-6823
Fax: 309-694-0539
Seafood
President: Robert Dixon
Estimated Sales: $ 20 - 50 Million
Number Employees: 50-99

4037 Dobake
810 81st Ave
Oakland, CA 94621-2510   510-834-3134
Fax: 510-834-4408   800-834-3134
dobeinc@aol.com   www.dobake.com
Gourmet and premium baked sweet goods.
Manager: David Shenson
VP Marketing/Sales: Jack Dellert
Number Employees: 100-249
Brands:
DOBAKE

4038 Doc Miller's Fish & Seafood Company
PO Box 426
Syracuse, IN 46567-0426   574-457-8469
Fax: 547-457-5887
Seafood
President: Gary Miller
Estimated Sales: $ 5 - 10 Million
Number Employees: 20-49

4039 Dockside Market
PO Box 1002
Key Largo, FL 33037   305-283-6678
Fax: 305-397-2389   800-813-2253
donna@docksidemarket.com
www.docksidemarket.com
cakes, cookies, salsa, sauces, hot sauces, coffee & tea

4040 Doctor's Best
1120 Calle Cordillera # 101
San Clemente, CA 92673-6299   949-498-0036
Fax: 949-498-3952   800-333-6977
www.drbvitamins.com
Manufacturer of food supplements
President: Ken Halvorsrude
VP Operations: Ranate Halvorsrude
Estimated Sales: $1-2.5 Million
Number Employees: 10-19
Sq. footage: 5000

4041 (HQ)Doerle Food Services
PO Box 9230
New Iberia, LA 70562-9230   337-367-8551
Fax: 337-367-9717   www.doerlefoodservice.com
Manufacturer and distributor of fresh and frozen meats and poultry, a wide variety of beverages and chemical supplies, also includes seafood, gourmet foods, fresh produce, dry groceries, dairy products, disposables, small ware andtable top items, specialty healthcare products and janitorial supplies
President/CEO: Carolyn Doerle-Ray
Estimated Sales: $ 20 - 50 Million
Number Employees: 100-249
Other Locations:
Doerle Food Service
Shreveport LA

4042 Dogfish Head Craft Brewery
22 Nassau Commons
Lewes, DE 19958-1607   302-644-4660
Fax: 302-644-4140   888-834-3474
dogfish@dogfish.com   www.dogfish.com
Manufacturer of beer
President: Sam Caglione
Estimated Sales: $10-20 Million
Number Employees: 10-19
Brands:
CHICORY STOUT
IMMORT ALE
INDIAN BROWN ALE
RAISON D'ETRE
SHELTER PALE ALE

4043 Dogwood Brewing Company
1222 Logan Cir NW
Atlanta, GA 30318-2857   404-367-0500
Fax: 404-367-0505   www.dogbrewing.com
Manufacturer of ale and stout
President: Crawford Moran
Estimated Sales: $1-2.5 Million
Number Employees: 1-4
Type of Packaging: Consumer, Food Service
Brands:
DOGWOOD

4044 Dohar Meats
1979 W 25th St
Cleveland, OH 44113-3455   216-241-4197
Manufacturer of pork including sausage and deli meats
Owner: Angela Dohar
Manager: Mike Szucs
Estimated Sales: Less than $500,000
Number Employees: 1-4
Type of Packaging: Consumer, Bulk

4045 Dol Cice Italian FrozenTreats
1317 Revere Road
Yardley, PA 19067-4347   215-493-9000
Fax: 215-493-6348   www.dolcice.com
Manufacturer and wholesaler/distributor of Italian water ices
President: Laurence Dobelle
Type of Packaging: Food Service, Private Label

4046 Dolav
P.O.Box 478
Totowa, NJ 07511-0478   973-785-1700
Fax: 973-785-9899   800-842-5033
info@spc-volta.com   www.spc-volta.com
Flavor and fragrance materials
Chairman: Boaz Raam
President/CEO: Alon Natanson
CEO: Alon Natanson
Estimated Sales: $ 20 - 50 Million
Number Employees: 50-99

4047 Dolce Nonna
162-43 12th Avenue
Whitestone, NY 11357   718-767-3501
Fax: 718-767-3501   info@dolcenonnas.com
www.dolcenonnas.com

Marinated string beans, agri-dolce peppers and marinated eggplant
President/Owner: Gisella Civale

4048 Dold Foods
2929 Ohio St
Wichita, KS 67219-4320   316-838-9101
          Fax: 316-838-9053 www.hormel.com
Manufacturer of fresh and frozen ham and bacon
Manager: Terry W Hadden
Plant Manager: Mark Coffey
Number Employees: 250-499
Sq. footage: 100000
Parent Co: Hormel Foods Corporation
Type of Packaging: Consumer

4049 (HQ)Dole & Bailey
16 Conn St
Woburn, MA 01801-5699   781-935-1234
          Fax: 781-935-9085 iluvcab@ix.netcom.com
          www.doleandbailey.com
Meats, seafood, gourmet groceries
President: Nancy Matheson-Burns
CEO: Aileen Darragh
Marketing: Jennifer Hertig
Estimated Sales: $45 Million
Number Employees: 100-249
Brands:
CHEF'S SIGNATURE

4050 Dole Food Company
1 Dole Dr
Westlake Village, CA 91362   818-879-6600
          Fax: 818-879-6615 www.dole.com
Manufacturer and importer of apples
President/CEO: David DeLorenzo
Chairman: David Murdock
EVP/CFO: Joseph Tesoriero
Marketing VP: Kevin Fiore
Regional Manager: Scott Deyoe
Estimated Sales: $7.6 Billion
Number Employees: 75,800
Parent Co: Castle & Cooke
Type of Packaging: Consumer, Bulk

4051 (HQ)Dole Food Company
1 Dole Drive
Westlake Village, CA 91362   818-879-6600
          Fax: 818-879-6615 www.dole.com
Manufacturer of more than 200 products, such as;
fresh fruit, fresh vegetables and packaged foods
Chairman: David Murdock
President/COO/Director: David DeLorenzo
EVP/CFO: Joseph Tesoriero
Estimated Sales: $7.6 Billion
Number Employees: 75,800
Parent Co: Coastal Berry Company
Type of Packaging: Consumer, Food Service, Private Label, Bulk
Brands:
CAMEO
CINNARAISINS
COSMIC
DOLE
DOLE CAESAR SALAD
DOLE CANNED FRUIT
DOLE CLASSIC COLESLAW
DOLE DRIED FRUIT AND NUTS
DOLE FRESH CUT VEGETABLES
DOLE HERB RANCH
DOLE PINEAPPLE
DOLE RAISINS
DOLE SHREDDED RED CABBAGE
DOLEWHIP
FRUITBOWLS
FUN SHAPES
GREENER SELECTION
LUNCH FOR ONE
SEA CREATURES

4052 Dole Fresh Vegetable Company
32655 Camphora Gloria Rd
Soledad, CA 93960-9600   831-678-5030
          Fax: 831-678-5391 800-333-5454
          www.dole.com
Manufacturer and grower of fresh broccoli, lettuce
and salad mixes
Manager: Tony Stanton
Estimated Sales: $100+ Million
Number Employees: 1,000-4,999
Parent Co: Tropicana
Type of Packaging: Consumer, Food Service

4053 Dole Fresh Vegetables
2959 Salinas Hwy
Monterey, CA 93940-6400   831-422-8871
          Fax: 831-422-3627 www.dole.com
Fresh Vegetables
President/CEO: Lawrence Kern
VP: Rick Bravo
Plant Manager: Lenny Pelifian
Estimated Sales: $100-500 Million
Number Employees: 1,000-4,999
Parent Co: Dole Food Company
Type of Packaging: Food Service
Brands:
DOLE

4054 Dole Nut Company
P.O.Box 845
Orland, CA 95963-0845   530-865-5511
          Fax: 530-865-7864 tmdduchenut.com
          www.duchenut.com
Food and almond processing
Manager: John Wilson
Sales: Steve Spellman
Estimated Sales: $500,000-$1 Million
Number Employees: 20-49
Type of Packaging: Private Label
Brands:
T.M. DUCHE NUT

4055 Dole Pond Maple Products
PO Box 841
Jackman, ME 04945-0841   418-653-5322
          Fax: 418-653-5322
          www.dolepondmapleproducts.com
Manufacturer of maple syrup
President: Jean-Claude Pare

4056 Dolefam Corporation
2821 N Vista Rd
Arlington Hts, IL 60004-2108   847-577-2122
          Fax: 708-577-4244
Manufacturer of sauces, dips and dressings
Owner: Arlen Gould
Executive VP: Arlen Gould
Brands:
DOLEFAM

4057 Dolisos America
1710 Whitney Mesa Dr
Henderson, NV 89014-2055   702-871-7153
          Fax: 702-871-9670 800-365-4767
dolisos@earthlink.net   www.santeactiveusa.com
Homeopathic medicines.
President/CEO: Luc Clouatre

4058 Dollar Food Manufacturing
1410 Odlum Drive
Vancouver, BC V5L 4X7
Canada   604-253-1422
          Fax: 604-253-2226
Manufacturer of salted and/or dried salmon, sausage
cured, golden pork hock
Director: Kelly Chow
Number Employees: 35
Type of Packaging: Consumer, Food Service

4059 Dolly Madison Bakery
3080 N National Rd
Columbus, IN 47201-3236   812-376-7432
          Fax: 812-378-4482
Manufacturer of cakes, pies, muffins, biscuits, rolls
and bread
Manager: Pam Smith
General Manager: Don Dorr
Purchasing Agent: Keith Ritzline
Estimated Sales: $100+ Million
Number Employees: 1,000-4,999
Parent Co: Interstate Brands Corporation
Type of Packaging: Consumer, Food Service, Private Label, Bulk

4060 Dolores Canning Company
1020 N Eastern Ave
Los Angeles, CA 90063-3214   323-263-9155
          Fax: 323-269-4876 chilibrick@earthlink.net
          www.dolorescanning.com
Manufacturer of pickled pork products, chili bricks
and specialty Mexican items
President: Steve Munoz
Marketing: David Munoz
Sales: Bert Munoz
Estimated Sales: $10-20 Million
Number Employees: 20-49

Type of Packaging: Consumer, Food Service, Private Label
Brands:
DOLORES

4061 Dolphin Natural Chocolates
1975 Woodview Avenue
Cambria, CA 93428-5168   805-927-7103
          Fax: 805-927-1251 800-236-5744
          hank@dolphinnatural.com
          www.dolphinnatural.com
Manufacturer and exporter of sugar and dairy-free
chocolates; also, chocolate dipped apricots, papaya
and pineapple
Owner: Henry McKowen
Estimated Sales: $2.5-5 Million
Number Employees: 5-9
Sq. footage: 1000
Type of Packaging: Consumer
Brands:
DOLPHIN NATURAL

4062 Dom's Sausage Company
10 Riverside Park
Malden, MA 02148-6781   781-324-1310
          Fax: 781-322-6776 www.domsausage.com
Meats
President: Buddy Botticelli
Plant Manager: Vinnie Bono
Estimated Sales: $20-50 Million
Number Employees: 20-49
Type of Packaging: Bulk
Brands:
DOM'S

4063 Domaine Chandon
1 California Dr
Yountville, CA 94599-1426   707-944-2892
          Fax: 707-944-1123 800-242-6366
          info@chandon.com   www.chandon.com
Sparkling and aperitif wines
President/CEO: John Wright
CFO: Dan Marotto
CEO: Malcolm Dunbar
Marketing: Allison Evanow
Public Relations: Sue Furdek
Engineer: Michael Morris
Estimated Sales: $20-50 Million
Number Employees: 250-499
Parent Co: LVMH Moet-Hennessy Louis Vitton
Type of Packaging: Consumer
Brands:
BLANC DE NOIRS
BRUT CLASSIC
CHARDONNAY
MT. VEEDER BLANC DE BLANCS
PINOT MEUNIER
PINOT NOIR
RESERVE BRUT
RESERVE BRUT ROSE
RICHE
VINTAGE

4064 Domaine Montreaux
4242 Big Ranch Road
Napa, CA 94558-1301   707-252-9380
          Fax: 707-253-1019 800-743-6668
          102543,3256@compuserve.com
Wines
President: Stephen Corley
Estimated Sales: $1-2.5 Million
Number Employees: 20
Sq. footage: 10
Type of Packaging: Private Label
Brands:
DOMAINE MONTREAUX BRUT

4065 Domaine St. George Winery
1141 Grant Ave
Healdsburg, CA 95448-9570   707-433-5508
          Fax: 707-433-5736 dswines@domstgeo.com
          www.domainesaintgeorge.com
Wines
Presdient: Somchai Likitprakong
Estimated Sales: $5-10 Million
Number Employees: 20-49
Type of Packaging: Private Label
Brands:
DOMAINE ST

4066 Dominex
P.O.Box 5069
St Augustine, FL 32085-5069   904-692-1348
Fax: 904-692-2348   800-282-1030
dominexjl@aol.com   www.dominexeggplant.com
Manufacturer of eggplant cutlets and appetizers; including peeled, breaded, battered, deep fried and IQF. All natural fully cooked breaded in italian crumbs, eggplant appetizers and cutlets
President: Jim Lacerenza
CFO: J Peters
Marketing Director: Chris Crosby
Sales: Deirdre Teagarden
VP of Operations: Bob Harvey
Estimated Sales:$5-10 Million
Number Employees: 50-99
Number of Brands: 10
Number of Products: 145
Type of Packaging: Food Service, Private Label, Bulk
Brands:
DOMINEX

4067 Dominion Wine Cellars
PO Box 1057
Culpeper, VA 22701-1057   540-825-8772
Fax: 540-829-0377
Wine
President: Wade D Sampson

4068 Domino Foods
1 Federal Street
Yonkers, NY 10705-1079   914-963-2400
Fax: 914-963-5113 www.dominosugar.com
Fully integrated refiner of cane sugar. Product line includes liquid sugar, granulated sugar, brown and powdered sugar in addition to a full line of specialty ingredients that are sucrose based
President/CEO: Brian O'Malley
CFO: Gregory Smith
Vice President: Armando Tabernilla
Director Marketing/Sales: Kevin McElvanry
Senior Director: Gary Black
VP Production: Joseph Goodwin
Estimated Sales:$10-50 Million
Number Employees: 25-100
Parent Co: Con Agra Foods
Type of Packaging: Consumer, Food Service, Private Label, Bulk
Brands:
DOMINO SUGAR

4069 Domino Specialty Ingredients
1100 E Key Hwy
Baltimore, MD 21230-5123   410-752-6150
Fax: 410-783-8612   800-446-9763
www.dominospecialtyingredients.com
Brownulated brown sugars, icings sugars, molasses sugars, honey sugars, invert sugars, fondant sugars.
President: Richard Baker
Estimated Sales:$100+ Million
Number Employees: 250-499

4070 Domino Sugar Corporation
1100 E Key Hwy
Baltimore, MD 21230-5123   410-752-6150
Fax: 410-783-8612 www.dominosugar.com
Manufacturer of sugar including crystallized and granulated; also, honey, molasses and brown sugar
President: Richard Baker
Sales Manager: David Poust
Estimated Sales:$100+ Million
Number Employees: 250-499
Type of Packaging: Consumer, Private Label
Brands:
DOMINO
QUIK-FLO

4071 Don Alfonso Foods
7218 McNeil Drive
Austin, TX 78729-7980   512-335-2370
Fax: 512-335-0636   800-456-6100
Mexican food ingredients (prepared moles) dried chiles, spices and sauces
President: Jose Marmolejo
Brands:
DON ALFONSO

4072 Don Francisco Coffee Traders
PO Box 58271
Los Angeles, CA 90058-0271   800-697-5282
Fax: 804-385-5333 www.don-francisco.com

Gourmet coffee products
Brands:
DON FRANCISCO

4073 Don Hilario Estate Coffee
3003 W Harbor View Avenue
Tampa, FL 33611-1644   813-254-1900
Fax: 813-254-6030   800-799-1903
info@donhilario.com   www.donhilario.com
Coffee
CEO/Marketing Director: Russell Versaggi
Estimated Sales:$2.5-5 Million
Number Employees: 1-4
Type of Packaging: Private Label
Brands:
DON HILARIO ESTATE COFFEE

4074 Don Jose Foods
4140 Oceanside Boulevard
159-315
Oceanside, CA 92056-6005   760-631-0243
Fax: 760-945-0651 www.donjosefoods.com
Fruit and juice beverages, chocolate drinks and assorted non-dairy items
President: Chuck Kuhlman
Vice President: Robby Kuhlman
Sales Manager: Enrique Ibarra
Parent Co: Paradise Valley Foods
Type of Packaging: Private Label
Brands:
CEREAL MATCH
CHOCO D' LITE
DON JOSE HORCHATA

4075 Don Miguel Mexican Foods
1501 W Orangewood Ave
Orange, CA 92868-2006   714-634-8441
Fax: 714-978-3743 www.donmiguel.com
Manufacturer of frozen Italian and Mexican foods including burritos, enchiladas, entrees and dinners
President: Steve Charton
CFO: Saralyn Brown
VP: Mike Morales
Estimated Sales:$50-99.9 Million
Number Employees: 100-249
Number of Brands: 4
Number of Products: 100
Type of Packaging: Consumer, Food Service, Bulk
Brands:
DON MIGUEL
EL CHARRITO
LEAN OLE
LUCCA
PINATA
XLNT

4076 Don Sebastiani & Sons
PO Box 1248
Sonoma, CA 95476   707-933-1704
Fax: 707-939-7115   hbast@donandsons.com
www.donandsons.com
wine
President/Owner: Don Sebastiani
VP: Don Staaveren
VP Marketing: Robert Carroll
Sales Manager: Rusty Boddeker
President/COO: Mike Holden
Estimated Sales:$9.4 Million
Number Employees: 10

4077 Don Tango Foods
PO Box 3153
Sterling, VA 20167-3153   703-406-8303
Fax: 703-406-8955   877-406-4064
btoruno@bellatlantic.net
www.dontangofoods.com
Chimichurri: Argentine grilling and marinade
*Estimated Sales:*Less than $500,000
Number Employees: 1-4

4078 Don's Dock Seafood
1220 E Northwest Hwy
Des Plaines, IL 60016-3352   847-827-1817
Fax: 847-827-1846 www.donsdockseafood.com
Manufacturer of fresh seafood
Co-Owner: Andy Johnson
Co-Owner: George Johnson
Co-Owner: Don Johnson
Estimated Sales:$ 3 - 5 Million
Number Employees: 10-19

4079 Don's Food Products
4461 Township Line Road
Schwenksville, PA 19473   888-321-3667
www.donssalads.com
salads, cream cheeses, commodity salads, soups and desserts
President/Owner: Victor Skloff

4080 Dona Yiya Foods
PO Box 1623
San Sebastian, PR 00685-9502   787-896-4007
Fax: 787-280-1430   donyiyafoods@PRtC.net
www.donayiya.com
Manufacturer, exporter and importer of spices and seasonings including garlic in oil or water, soffritto, condiments and tropical candies
President: Javier Denis
VP: Luis Denis
Plant Manager: Luis Denis
Estimated Sales:$2.5 Million
Number Employees: 10
Number of Brands: 2
Number of Products: 23
Sq. footage: 10000
Type of Packaging: Consumer, Food Service, Private Label, Bulk

4081 Donald E. Hunter Meat Company
4612 Turkey Rd
Hillsboro, OH 45133-7044   937-466-2311
Manufacturer of beef
Owner: Donald Hunter
Estimated Sales:$1-2.5 Million
Number Employees: 1-4
Type of Packaging: Consumer

4082 Donald McCoun
541 Mundys Lane
Versailles, KY 40383-9468   859-873-4650
Manufacturer of sorghum syrups
*Estimated Sales:*Under $300,000
Number Employees: 1
Sq. footage: 80000
Type of Packaging: Consumer, Food Service, Private Label
Brands:
SWEET SORGHUM

4083 Donaldson's Finer Chocolates
600 S State Road 39
Lebanon, IN 46052-9401   765-482-3334
Fax: 765-482-7994
www.donaldsonschocolates.com
Manufacturer of chocolates and candy
President: George Donaldson
Estimated Sales:$5-10 Million
Number Employees: 5-9
Type of Packaging: Consumer

4084 Donatoni Winery
10604 S La Cienega Boulevard
Inglewood, CA 90304-1115   310-645-5445
Fax: 310-645-5445
Wines
President/CEO: Mark Donatoni
Manager Sales: Tina Donatoni
*Estimated Sales:*Less than $500,000
Number Employees: 1-4
Brands:
DONATONI

4085 Donells' Candies
201 E 2nd St # 2
Casper, WY 82601-2576   307-234-6283
Fax: 307-235-9119   877-461-2009
sales@donnellschocolates.com
www.donnellschocolates.com
Manufacturer of confectionery products including hand-dipped chocolates and fudge
Partner: Donald Stepp
President: Mike Stepp
Estimated Sales:$1-2.5 Million
Number Employees: 5-9
Type of Packaging: Consumer

4086 Dong Kee Company
2252 S Wentworth Ave
Chicago, IL 60616-2042   312-225-6340
Fax: 312-567-9119
Manufacturer of canned Chinese products including egg rolls, water chestnuts, bamboo shoots, mushrooms and fortune and almond cookies
Owner: Herman Wong

Estimated Sales:$500,000-$1 Million
Number Employees: 5-9
Type of Packaging: Consumer, Food Service

4087 Donsuemor Madeleines
2080 N Loop Rd
Alameda, CA 94502   510-865-6406
          Fax: 510-865-6947   888-420-4441
                    remember@donsuemor.com
                    www.donsuemor.com
gourmet french madeleine cookies

4088 Donut Tree & Deli
943 E 15th Avenue
Anchorage, AK 99501-5407   907-274-6969
                    Fax: 907-274-6969
Donuts
Brands:
    DONUT TREE

4089 Door Country Potato Chips
3840 N Fratney St
Milwaukee, WI 53212-1341   414-964-1428
          Fax: 414-964-1484   swsherbi@aol.com
Potato chips and pasta and contract packaging
    Owner: Jamie Swisher
Number Employees: 1-4
Brands:
    DOOR COUNTY POTATO CHIPS
    STRENDGE PASTA

4090 Door County Fish Market
2831 Dundee Rd
Northbrook, IL 60062-2501   847-559-9229
                    Fax: 847-559-9273
Seafood
    Manager: Eric Rayan
Estimated Sales:$ .5 - 1 million
Number Employees: 1-4

4091 Door-Peninsula Winery
5806 State Highway 42
Sturgeon Bay, WI 54235-9767   920-743-7431
          Fax: 920-743-5999   800-551-5049
          DPW@DCwis.com   www.dcwine.com
Wines
    Owner: Bob Polman
    VP: Robert Pollman
    Marketing: Bob Pollman
Estimated Sales:$2.5-5 Million
Number Employees: 10-19
Sq. footage: 8
Type of Packaging: Private Label
Brands:
    DOOR-PENINSULA

4092 (HQ)Dorchester Crab Company
2076 Wingate Bishops Head Rd
Wingate, MD 21675-2015   410-397-8103
                    Fax: 410-376-3179
Manufacturer of fresh and frozen seafood, shellfish
including crabs and crab meat
    Owner: Zach Seaman
Estimated Sales:$1.70 Million
Number Employees: 10-19
Type of Packaging: Consumer, Bulk

4093 (HQ)Dorina/So-Good
P.O.Box 403
Union, IL 60180-0403   815-923-2144
                    Fax: 815-923-2151
Manufacturer and exporter of shelf stable barbecue
beef and pork; also, mustard, sauces, salsa, salad
dressings, chip dips, olive salad and cheesespreads
    President: Tim Young
    CEO: Darwin Young
Estimated Sales:$.5-1 Million
Number Employees: 20-49
Sq. footage: 8000
Type of Packaging: Consumer, Food Service, Private Label, Bulk
Brands:
    BAR-B-Q FIESTA
    BAR-B-Q TREAT
    CONEY ISLAND
    DUFFY
    FARM COUNTRY
    OLD WEST BAR-B-Q DELIGHT
    SO-GOOD BAR-B-Q DELIGHT
    SO-GOOD PORK BAR-B-Q
    SUPER
    YOUNG'S BREADING

4094 Dorothy Dawson Foods Products
251 W Euclid Ave
Jackson, MI 49203-4101   517-788-9830
          Fax: 517-788-7852 www.dawsonfoods.com
Manufacturer of all-natural, ready-to-use frozen
soups, sauces, batters, breadings and mixes includ-
ing soup, marinade and steak au jus; also, pizza
products including sauces, mixes and seasoning
blends
    President: Phillip Dawson Sr
    VP: David Elias
Estimated Sales:$ 10 - 20 Million
Number Employees: 20-49
Type of Packaging: Food Service, Private Label,
Bulk
Brands:
    EMILY'S GOURMET
    FRESHDRY
    KETTLE GOURMET
    SIMON'S
    STARTERS
    ZIP

4095 Dorothy Timberlake Candies
2351 Eaton Rd
Madison, NH 03849-6201   603-447-2221
    Fax: 603-447-2221   faith@timberlakecandies.com
                    www.timberlakecandies.com
Hard candy and lollipops
    President: William Timberlake
Estimated Sales:$1-2.5 Million
Number Employees: 1-4
Brands:
    DOROTHY

4096 Dorset Fisheries
179 Water Street
St. John's, NL A1C 1B1
Canada   709-739-7147
    Fax: 709-739-0586   dorsetfish@roadrunner.nf.net
Manufacturer and exporter of fresh lobster and cod
    President: Derick Philpott
Number Employees: 100-249
Type of Packaging: Bulk

4097 Dorval Trading Company
P.O.Box 620
Nanuet, NY 10954-0620   845-624-3031
          Fax: 845-624-8137   800-367-8252
info@dorvaltrading.com   www.dorvaltrading.com
Importer of candy including, licorice, lollipops,
mints, sourballs, hard and filled, caramels, choco-
lates, gift items, gift boxes and gum.
    President: Roberta Cappel
    Sales/Marketing Manager: Lance Reiter
Estimated Sales:$ 10 - 20 Million
Number Employees: 10,000+
Sq. footage: 2000
Type of Packaging: Consumer, Private Label, Bulk

4098 Doscher's Candies
24 W Court St
Cincinnati, OH 45202-1062   513-381-8656
                    Fax: 513-381-8656
Manufacturer of candy including bars, canes and
taffy products
    President: Greg Clark Sr
    VP: Harry J Doscher
Estimated Sales:$1-2.5 Million
Number Employees: 5-9
Sq. footage: 8400
Type of Packaging: Consumer
Brands:
    FERNCH CHEW

4099 Double B Distributors
1031 W New Circle Rd
Lexington, KY 40511-1843   859-255-8822
                    Fax: 859-233-1241
Manufacturer of meat snack foods
    Owner: Bob Heim
Estimated Sales:$ 5 - 10 Million
Number Employees: 10-19

4100 Double B Foods
PO Box A
Schulenburg, TX 78956-0060   979-725-9444
          Fax: 979-725-9501   800-472-6661
                    www.doubleb.com
Manufacturer of chicken, eggs, frankfurters and
Mexican foods
    President: Bill Bucek
    VP: Andy Bosl

Estimated Sales:$25-49.9 Million
Number Employees: 20-49

4101 Double Play Foods
500 E 77th Street
Apt 3525
New York, NY 10162-0011   212-535-4224
          Fax: 212-570-4488 www.overloadcup.com
Peanut butter cups

4102 Double Rainbow Gourmet Ice Creams
275 S Van Ness Ave
San Francisco, CA 94103-3733   415-861-5858
          Fax: 415-861-5872   800-489-3580
                    www.doublerainbow.com
Manufacturers of ice cream and nondairy desserts
    President: Steve Fink
Number Employees: 10-19

4103 Double Wrap Cup & Container
317 Ronnie Dr
Buffalo Grove, IL 60089-1149   312-337-0072
    Fax: 312-337-0104 www.comfortgripwrap.com
Manufacturer of high quality,low cost insulated
wrap for paper coffee cups.
    CEO: Ted Alpert
    VP: Ted Alpert
    Marketing Director: Ted Alpert
    Sales Director: Ted Alpert
    Public Relations: Ted Alpert
    Operations Manager: Ted Alpert
Estimated Sales:$ 3 - 5 Million
Number Employees: 10-19
Type of Packaging: Food Service

4104 Double-Cola Company
537 Market St # 100
Chattanooga, TN 37402-1229   423-267-5691
          Fax: 423-267-0793   info@double-cola.com
                    www.double-cola.com
Soft drinks
    President: Alnoor Dhanini
    VP Sales/Marketing: Gilford Thomas
    Production: Roy Chisenall
Estimated Sales:$5-10 Million
Number Employees: 5-9
Brands:
    CHASER
    DIET CHASER
    DIET DOUBLE-COLA
    DIET SKI
    DOUBLE DRY GINGERALE
    DOUBLE-COLA
    DOUBLE-DRY MIXERS
    JUMBO FLAVORS
    SKI

4105 Doug Hardy Company
Mountainville Rd
Deer Isle, ME 04627   207-348-6604
                    Fax: 207-348-6100
Manufacturer of seafood
    Owner: Doug Hardy
Estimated Sales:$ 3 - 5 Million
Number Employees: 5-9

4106 Dough Delight
144 Viceroy Road
Concord, ON L4K 2L8
Canada   905-738-1242
          Fax: 905-738-5056   800-465-5515
Manufacturer of Italian flat and pita breads, kosher
bagels, coffee cakes, frozen muffin batters,
par-baked breads and frozen danish and puff pastry
doughs; exporter of bagels, par-baked, flat and pita
breads and frozen Danish and puffpastry doughs
    Director Marketing: Michael Taras
    VP Sales: Michael Pflanzer
    VP Operations: Walter Miller
Estimated Sales:$100 Million
Number Employees: 700
Sq. footage: 200000
Parent Co: Corporate Foods/Canada Bread
Company
Type of Packaging: Consumer, Food Service, Private Label, Bulk
Brands:
    DEMPSTER'S
    HARVEST HEARST
    JERUSALEM PITA
    OLIVIERI
    PITA DELIGHT

PLATINA
THE BAKERS BAKERY

4107 Dough Works Company
710 Oak Ln
Horicon, WI 53032-1708   920-485-4550
Fax: 920-485-4035   800-383-8808
info@doughworks.biz www.doughworks.biz
Manufacturer of frozen bakery products, organic cookies and bread/specialty distributor of food products and supply goods 80% of WI/Chicago
President: Robert Scott
VP: Kim Gassner
Sales: Robert Scott
Estimated Sales: $500,000-$1 Million
Number Employees: 11
Sq. footage: 32000

4108 Dough-To-Go
3535 De La Cruz Blvd
Santa Clara, CA 95054-2112   408-727-4094
Fax: 408-727-4095 betsyl@doughtogo.com
www.dough-to-go.com
Manufacturer of frozen raw dough and cookies, scones and brownies
President: Elizabeth Sanders
Sales/Marketing: Barbara Christensen
Purchasing: Tom Natusch
Estimated Sales: $20-50 Million
Number Employees: 20-49
Sq. footage: 10000
Type of Packaging: Food Service
Brands:
DOUGH-TO-GO
JANE DOUGH

4109 Douglas Cross Enterprises
2030 5th Ave
Seattle, WA 98121-2505   206-448-1193
Fax: 206-448-1979 richmond@tomdouglas.com
www.tomdouglas.com
BBQ Sauces
President: Tom Douglas
Estimated Sales: $5-10 Million
Number Employees: 10-19

4110 Doumak
2201 Touhy Ave
Elk Grove Vlg, IL 60007-5327   847-437-2100
Fax: 847-437-1809   800-323-0318
www.doumak.com
Manufacturer of marshmallows
President: Barry Blum
VP Manufacturing: Barry Blum
Estimated Sales: $2.5-5 Million
Number Employees: 10-19
Sq. footage: 40000
Type of Packaging: Consumer, Food Service, Private Label
Brands:
FIRESIDE
WONDERFOOD

4111 Dove Mushrooms
P.O.Box 340
Avondale, PA 19311-0340   610-268-3535
Fax: 610-268-3099   800-441-9928
www.modernmush.com
Manufacturer of fresh, canned and dried mushrooms
President: Chuck Ciarrocchi
VP Marketing: Paul Frederic
Estimated Sales: $20-50 Million
Number Employees: 20-49
Sq. footage: 25000
Parent Co: Modern Mushroom Farms
Type of Packaging: Consumer, Food Service, Private Label, Bulk
Brands:
MODERN
SHER ROCKEE

4112 Dover Industries Limited
4350 Harvester Road
Burlington, ON L7L 5S4
32   905-333-1515
Fax: 905-333-1584 info@dovergrp.com
www.dovergrp.com
Manufacturer of wheat; warehouse providing dry storage for bagged goods
President: Howard Rowley
SVP/Chief Financial Officer: Brian Short
Sales Manager: Dan Vida
VP/Director Operations: Bill Campbell
Parent Co: Dover Industries Limited

Type of Packaging: Consumer, Food Service, Bulk
Other Locations:
Acton ON
Halifax NS

4113 Dover Industries Limited
4350 Harvester Road
Burlington, ON L7L 5S4
Canada   905-333-1515
Fax: 905-333-1584   800-387-7316
info@dovergrp.com www.dovergrp.com
Manufacturer and exporter of flour and flour based products, such as ice cream cones, hot and cold paper cups
Chairman: Kenneth Campbell
President/CEO: Howard Rowley
Estimated Sales: $148 Million
Number Employees: 525
Type of Packaging: Consumer, Food Service, Private Label, Bulk

4114 Dover Metals
4768 Highway M-63
Coloma, MI 49038   269-849-1411
Fax: 269-849-2903 sales@dovermetals.com
www.dovermetals.com
accessories and supplies for the food service and hospitality industry
President/Owner: Deborah Bedwell
VP: Nick Anders
Estimated Sales: $2.8 Million
Number Employees: 8

4115 Dow Distribution
524 Ohohia St
Honolulu, HI 96819-1934   808-836-3511
Fax: 808-833-3634
President: Craig Mitchell
Estimated Sales: $ 10 - 20 Million
Number Employees: 10-19

4116 Dowd & Rogers
1641 49th Street
Sacramento, CA 95819-4404   916-451-6480
Fax: 916-736-2349 info@dowdandrogers.com
www.dowdandrogers.com
Premium wheat free and gluten free products
President: Derek Dowd
Number of Brands: 2
Number of Products: 8
Type of Packaging: Consumer, Food Service, Private Label, Bulk
Brands:
DOWD AND ROGERS

4117 Down East Specialty Products/Cape Bald Packers
171 Virginia St
Portland, ME 04103-3943   207-878-9170
Fax: 207-878-9104   800-369-6327
cnally@capebaldpackers.com
www.capebaldpackers.com
Manufacturer of lobster, mussels, rock crab and red crab
Manager: Kathy Nally
Manager: Patrice Landry
Estimated Sales: $ 1 - 3 Million
Number Employees: 1-4
Parent Co: Cape Bald Packers
Type of Packaging: Private Label
Brands:
DOWNEAST

4118 Downeast Candies
P.O.Box 25
Boothbay Harbor, ME 04538-0025   207-633-5178
decinc@dwi.net
Manufacturer of fudges and taffy
President: David Carmolli
VP: Elaine Miller
Production Manager: Rick Carmolli
Estimated Sales: $1-2.5 Million
Number Employees: 1-4
Type of Packaging: Consumer, Private Label, Bulk
Brands:
DOWNEAST CANDIES

4119 Downeast Coffee
259 East Avenue
Pawtucket, RI 02860-3801   207-878-8300
Fax: 207-878-3820   800-922-6287
jpeterman@downeastcoffee.com

Coffee
President/CEO: William Kapos
CFO: Frank DeLuca
VP: James Peterman
Marketing: Mark Bishop
Plant Manager: Ron Yanko
Estimated Sales: $1-2.5 Million
Number Employees: 10-19
Type of Packaging: Private Label
Brands:
DOWNEAST

4120 Downeast Pasta
47 India Street
Portland, ME 04101-4209   207-775-3839
Fax: 207-775-3843   800-587-2782
info@downeastpasta.com
www.downeastpasta.com
Manufacturer of novelty shaped pasta; also, gourmet long noodles
President: Hilary Tounge
VP Marketing: Jeffrey Tounge
Estimated Sales: $2.5-5 Million
Number Employees: 5-9
Sq. footage: 28000
Type of Packaging: Consumer, Private Label

4121 Doyon & Doyon
68 Tycos Drive
Toronto, ON M6B 1V9
Canada   416-789-4391
Fax: 416-789-9112   888-851-3110
info@billybee.com www.mieldoyon.com
Manufacturer of beeswax and honey; exporter of honey; importer of pollen
President: Paul Doyon
CEO: David Sugarman
Number Employees: 15
Sq. footage: 15000
Type of Packaging: Consumer, Food Service, Bulk
Brands:
DOYON
PURE HONEY

4122 Dr Kracker
10490 Miller Rd
Dallas, TX 75238   214-503-1971
Fax: 214-503-1939 alan.konecny@drkracker.com
www.drkracker.com
organic flatbreads, snacker krackers, snack chips and snack flats.
President: Carsten Kruse
Sales/Marketing Director: George Eckrich
Estimated Sales: $1.1 Million
Number Employees: 21

4123 Dr McDougall's Right Foods
105 Associate Road
South San Francisco, CA 94080   650-583-4993
Fax: 650-583-6376 rits@sfspice.com
www.rightfoods.com
instant meal cups
President/Owner: John McDougall MD

4124 Dr Pepper/Seven Up
5950 Sherry Ln
Dallas, TX 75225-6533   214-530-5000
Fax: 214-530-5036   800-527-7096
www.dpsubg.com
Carbonated soft drinks and fountain syrup concentrate
Owner: Jim Turner
Chief Legal Officer: Hank Udow
Chief Financial Officer: Ken Hannas
Group Strategy Director: Mark Reckitt
Chief Science and Technology Officer: David Macnair
Marketing Director: Randy Gier
Chief Human Resources Officer: Bob Stock
Estimated Sales: $ .5 - 1 million
Number Employees: 500-999
Parent Co: Cadbury Schweppes PLC
Type of Packaging: Consumer, Food Service, Bulk
Brands:
7 UP
A&W
CANADA DRY
COUNTRY TIME
DEJA BLUE
DIET RITE
DR. PEPPER
HAWAIIAN PUNCH
HIRES ROOT BEER
RASING COW

RC COLA
RED FUSION
SCHEPPES
SLUSH PUPPIES
SQUIRT
SUNDROP
SUNKIST
VERNORS
WELCH'S
dnL

4125 Dr Pete's

2224 Gamble Rd
Savannah, GA 31405-2833   912-233-3035
          Fax: 912-233-0001   888-599-0047
          info@dr-petes.com www.dr-petes.com
Manufacturer of sauces, marinades and dressings
     CEO: Joel Coffee
Estimated Sales: $600,000
Number Employees: 5-9
Type of Packaging: Consumer, Food Service
Brands:
     Dr. Pete's

4126 Dr. Christopher's Original Foods

1195 Spring Creek Place
Springville, UT 84663-3040   801-373-8978
          Fax: 801-489-7207   800-453-1406
          www.drchristopher.com
Manufacturer and exporter of supplements and
herbal formulas
     Sales/Marketing: Troy Fukumitsu
Estimated Sales: $20-50 Million
Number Employees: 20-49
Type of Packaging: Consumer, Private Label, Bulk

4127 Dr. Cookie

2112 6th Ave
Seattle, WA 98121-2513   206-389-9321
          orderdesk@drcookie.com
          www.drcookie.com
Cookies, breads, rolls
     Manager: Steve Krendall
Estimated Sales: $1-5 Million appx.
Number Employees: 1-4
Brands:
     DR COOKIE

4128 Dr. Frank's Vinifera Wine Cellar

9749 Middle Rd
Hammondsport, NY 14840-9612   607-868-4884
          Fax: 607-868-4888   800-320-0735
     info@drfrankwines.com   www.drfrankwines.com
Manufacturer and exporter of table wine and cham-
pagne
     Chairman: Willie Frank
     President: Fred Frank
Estimated Sales: $ 5 - 10 Million
Number Employees: 10-19
Type of Packaging: Consumer
Brands:
     CHATEAU FRANK CHAMPAGNE CELLARS
     DR. KONSTANTIN FRANK

4129 Dr. Konstantin Frank Vinifera Wine Cellars

9749 Middle Rd
Hammondsport, NY 14840-9612   607-868-4884
          Fax: 607-868-4888   800-320-0735
     frankwines@aol.com   www.drfrankwines.com
Wines and champagne. Founded by Dr. Konstantin
Frank, pioneer grower of European wine grape vari-
eties in Eastern United States.
     President: Fredrick Frank
     VP: Eric Volz
Estimated Sales: $5-9.9 Million
Number Employees: 10-19
Type of Packaging: Private Label
Brands:
     DR KONSTANTIN FRANK
     SALMON RUN

4130 Dr. Pepper/Seven-Up

3131 Phillips Ave
Racine, WI 53403-3547   262-634-3369
          Fax: 262-634-8870   800-696-5891
          www.dpsu.com
Manufacturer of bottled beverages including soft
drinks
     Manager: Tom Andersen
     Sales Manager: Brad Allbee
Estimated Sales: $12 Million
Number Employees: 1-4
Parent Co: Cadbury Schweppes & Carlyle Group

Brands:
     7 UP
     A&W
     CANADA DRY
     COUNTRY TIME
     DEJA BLUE
     DIET RITE
     DR PEPPER
     HAWAIIAN PUNCH
     HIRES ROOT BEER
     RAGING COW'S
     RC COLA
     RED FUSION
     SCHWEPPES
     SLUSH PUPPIE
     SQUIRT
     SUNDROP
     SUNKIST
     VERNORS
     WELCHOS
     dnL

4131 Dr. Pete's

2224 Gamble Rd
PO Box 24089
Savannah, GA 31403   912-233-3035
     Fax: 912-233-0001   info@dr-petes.com
          www.dr-petes.com
sauces, marinades, dressings, baking mixes
     CEO: Joel Coffee
     VP: Jan Coffee
Number Employees: 5

4132 Dr. Praeger's Sensible Foods

9 Boumar Pl
Elmwood Park, NJ 07407-2615   201-703-1300
     Fax: 201-703-9333   nurit@drpraegers.com
          www.drpraegers.com
Manufacturer of kosher natural frozen products such
as veggie burgers, fish sticks and potato pancakes
     President: Dr Peter Praeger
     Director Sales/Marketing: Larry Praeger
Estimated Sales: $ 20 - 50 Million
Number Employees: 50-99
Type of Packaging: Food Service
Brands:
     DR PRAEGER'S
     UNGAR'S

4133 Dr. Smoothie Brands

1730 Raymer Avenue
Fullerton, CA 92833   714-449-9787
          Fax: 714-449-9474   888-466-9941
     info@drsmoothie.com or
          www.cafeessentials.com
Dr. Smoothie Brands is a full line beverage company
manufacturing shelf-stable , liquid natural fruit
smoothies and powdered cocoa, mocha, latte, and
chai blends. Manufactures nutritional blends ranging
from raw, whole food nutritionbars to a full range of
botanicals, including medically endorsed products
like The Complete Meal, and Amino line.
Number of Brands: 6
Number of Products: 93
Type of Packaging: Consumer, Food Service

4134 Dr. Tima Natural Products

131 Groverton Pl
Los Angeles, CA 90077-3732   310-472-2181
          Fax: 310-652-9884
Natural health products and soda
     Owner: Potito Depaolis
     VP: Mary Caronna
Estimated Sales: $2.5-5 Million
Number Employees: 5-9
Brands:
     DR TIMA

4135 Drader Manufacturing Industries

5750-50 Street NW
Edmonton, AB T6B 2Z8
Canada   780-440-2231
          Fax: 780-440-2244   800-661-4122
          bakery@drader.com   www.drader.com
Manufacturer of custom carriers, bread baskets, bak-
ery trays, hand trucks, dollies and bakery shelving
     President/General Manager: Gordon McTavish
     Account Manager: Chris Gaucher
     Sales Manager: Jeff McTavish
     Manager: Glenn Eckert
Number Employees: 60
Sq. footage: 35000

4136 Dragnet Fisheries

4141 B St
Anchorage, AK 99503-5940   907-276-4551
          Fax: 907-274-3617
Manufacturer of fresh and frozen herring, black cod,
halibut and salmon
     President: Jay Cherrier
Estimated Sales: Less than $500,000
Number Employees: 1-4
Type of Packaging: Consumer, Food Service
Brands:
     DRAGNET

4137 Dragoco

300 North St
Teterboro, NJ 07608-1204   201-288-3200
          Fax: 201-288-0843 www.symrise.com
Manufacturer and exporter of natural and artificial
concentrated food flavors
     President: Klaus Stanzl
Estimated Sales: $50-100 Million
Number Employees: 1,000-4,999
Sq. footage: 250000
Parent Co: Dragoco
Brands:
     EXTRAPONES
     MICROSEAL
     NEOROM

4138 Drake's Ducks Woodstream Specialty Foods

PO Box 1120
Keene, NH 03431-1120   603-357-5858
          Fax: 603-352-8986 cdrake@top.monad.net
Manufacturer of all-natural pesto sauces including
original, basil, sundried tomato, Sicilian olive,
cilantro pumpkinseed, sweet red pepper, fat-free
chili tomato, white and rosemary roasted garlic
     President: C Drake
     Director R&D: Marie Drake
Estimated Sales: $3-5 Million
Number Employees: 15
Sq. footage: 10000
Type of Packaging: Consumer, Food Service
Brands:
     Drake's Ducks

4139 Drakes Brewing

1933 Davis Street
Suite 177
San Leandro, CA 94577-1256   510-562-0866
     Fax: 510-382-1479   drinkdrakes@jbrfoods.com
          www.drinkdrakes.com
Beer
     Principal: Adolfo Carrera
     CFO: Peter Rogers
     Director Manufacturing: Roger Lind
Estimated Sales: $ 1-2.5 Million
Number Employees: 100
Brands:
     AUTUMN FEST
     BLOOD RED
     CHOCOLATE MILK STOUT
     DRAKES AMBER ALE
     DRAKES BLOND ALE
     DRAKES HEFE-WEIZEN
     DRAKES IPA
     EXPEDITION
     HARVEST ALE BRITISH ESB
     IMPERIAL IPA BLACK PILSNER
     IMPERIAL IPA PILSNER
     IMPERIAL STOUT
     JOLLY ROGERS
     SIR FRANCIS STOUT
     ZATEC PILSNER

4140 Drakes Fresh Pasta Company

P.O.Box 5072
High Point, NC 27262-5072   336-861-5454
          Fax: 336-861-4823 www.drakesfreshpasta.com
Pasta products
     President: Richard Drake
     Sales: Ginger Edward
Estimated Sales: $20-50 Million
Number Employees: 50-99
Brands:
     DRAKES FRESH

4141 Drangle Foods

300 S Riverside Dr
Gilman, WI 54433-9300   715-447-8241
          Fax: 715-447-8242

Flavored processed cheese
Owner: Tom Hant
CEO: Tom Hand
Estimated Sales: $20-50 Million
Number Employees: 50-99
Sq. footage: 20
Type of Packaging: Private Label
Brands:
  DRANGLE

4142 Draper Valley Farms
P.O.Box 838
Mt Vernon, WA 98273-0838   360-424-7947
                    Fax: 360-424-1666
Manufacturer and exporter of poultry including
fresh and frozen chicken and turkey
President/Co-Owner: Jim Koplowitz
CEO/Co-Owner: Richard Koplowitz
VP: John Jefferson
VP: Jim Calhoun
Comptroller: Mel Call
Sales Manager: Larry Morris
Human Relations Manager: Colleen Helergson
Trucking Supervisor: Mark Anderson
Plant Manager: Jerry Lindquist
Estimated Sales: $74 Million
Number Employees: 250-499
Sq. footage: 59000
Type of Packaging: Consumer, Food Service

4143 (HQ)Dream Confectioners
540 Cedar Ln
Teaneck, NJ 07666-1742   201-836-9000
                    Fax: 201-836-9015
Manufacturer and exporter of pretzels
President: Joseph Podolski
Estimated Sales: $2.5-5 Million
Number Employees: 1-4
Type of Packaging: Consumer, Private Label, Bulk
Brands:
  GREAT

4144 Dream Time
343 Soquel Ave # 271
Santa Cruz, CA 95062-2355   831-464-6702
          Fax: 831-464-6703   info@dreamtimeinc.com
                    www.dreamtimeinc.com
Manufacturer of natural ingredient health products
Owner: Judy Day
Estimated Sales: $ 1 - 3 Million
Number Employees: 10-19

4145 Dreamous Corporation
2720 Monterey St # 401
Torrance, CA 90503-7231   310-787-7002
          Fax: 310-787-7276   800-251-7543
          info@dreamous.com   www.dreamous.com
Manufacturer and distributor of all natural health
supplements, homeopathic formula, and beauty
products
Owner: Susan Negus
VP Product Development: Dr Howard Davis
Estimated Sales: $ 20 - 50 Million
Number Employees: 20-49
Type of Packaging: Private Label

4146 Dresden Stollen Company
7 Heathcote Drive
Albertson, NY 11507   516-746-5802
                    Fax: 516-746-5918
gourmet foods
President/Owner: Joan Greenfield
Number Employees: 1

4147 Dressed in Style/Chase
PO Box 15515
Atlanta, GA 30333-0515   404-377-3757
          Fax: 404-872-3211   888-368-2698
          chasefood@mindspring.com
                    www.chasefood.com
Salad dressings, sauces and marinades
President: Sue Shuster
Estimated Sales: $300,000
Number Employees: 4
Brands:
  DRESSED

4148 (HQ)Dressel Collins Fish Company
5131 S Director St
Seattle, WA 98118-5105   206-725-0121
                    Fax: 206-725-1354
Manufacturer of canned and smoked salmon
President: Mike Bonney

Estimated Sales: $10 Million
Number Employees: 1-4
Type of Packaging: Consumer, Food Service

4149 Drew's
PO Box 8181
Brattleboro, VT 05304-8181   800-228-2980
          Fax: 413-367-9357   800-228-2980
          chefdrew@chefdrew.com   www.chefdrew.com
Hot sauces
President: Andrew Starkweather
CFO: Catherine Wescott
Marketing/Public Relations: Michelle Swedick
Plant Manager: Joe Brent
Estimated Sales: $ 1.5 Million
Number Employees: 11
Type of Packaging: Private Label

4150 Drew's All Natural
926 Vt Route 103 S
Chester, VT 05143-8461   802-875-1184
          Fax: 413-367-9357   800-228-2980
          chefdrew@chefdrew.com   www.chefdrew.com
All natural salad dressings and salsa, Certified Or-
ganic
President/CEO: Andrew Starkweather
Assistant Controller: Rob Feakes
Plant Manager: Joe Brent
Estimated Sales: $1.5 Million
Number Employees: 10-19
Type of Packaging: Consumer, Private Label
Brands:
  DREW'S ALL NATURAL

4151 Dreyer Sonoma
161 Fox Hollow Rd
Woodside, CA 94062-3607   650-851-9448
          Fax: 650-851-3268   jdreyer@dreyerwine.com
                    www.dreyerwine.com
Wines
Co-Owner: Walter Dreyer
Co-Owner: Bettina Dreyer
General Manager: Jonathan Dreyer
Estimated Sales: $2.5-5 Million
Number Employees: 5-9
Brands:
  Dreyer Wine

4152 (HQ)Dreyer's Grand Ice Cream
5929 College Ave
Oakland, CA 94618-1391   510-652-8187
          Fax: 570-301-4538   877-437-3937
          dsbailey@dreyers.com   www.dreyers.com
Manufacturer of ice cream, packaged and novelties
President/CEO: Mike Mitchell
EVP/CFO: Steve Barbour
Research & Development: Donald Birnbaum
Director Consumer Communications: Dori Sera
Bailey
Public Relations Premium Brands: Kim Goeller
Johnson
Public Relations Super Premium Brands: Diane
McIntyre
Estimated Sales: $1 Billion
Number Employees: 7500
Number of Brands: 5
Type of Packaging: Consumer, Food Service
Other Locations:
  Dreyer's Grand Ice Cream
  Fort Wayne IN
Brands:
  DIBS
  DREAMERY
  DREAMERY BANANA SPLIT
  DREAMERY BLACK RASPBERRY AVA-
  LANCHE
  DREAMERY CARAMEL TOFFEE BAR
  HEAVEN
  DREAMERY CASHEW PRALINE PARFAIT
  DREAMERY CHERRY CHIP BA DA BING
  DREAMERY CHOCOLATE ALMOND BAR
  DREAMERY CHOCOLATE PEANUT BUTTER
  CH
  DREAMERY CONEY ISLAND WAFFLE
  CONE
  DREAMERY COOL MINT
  DREAMERY DEEP DISH APPLE PIE
  DREAMERY DULCE DE LECHE
  DREAMERY GRANDMA'S COOKIE DOUGH
  DREAMERY HARVEST PEACH
  DREAMERY NEW YORK CHEESECAKE
  DREAMERY NOTHING BUT CHCOLATE
  DREAMERY NUTS ABOUT MALT
  DREAMERY RASPBERRY BROWNIE ALA

  MODE
  DREAMERY STRAWBERRY FIELDS
  DREAMERY TIRAMISU
  DREAMERY TRUFFLE EXPLOSION
  DREAMERY VANILLA
  EDY'S
  GODIVA
  M&M/MARS
  STARBUCKS
  WHOLE FRUIT

4153 (HQ)Dreyers Grand Ice Cream
5929 College Ave
Oakland, CA 94618-1391   510-652-8187
          Fax: 510-601-4405   www.dreyers.com
Manufacturer and exporter of frozen desserts includ-
ing ice cream yogurt, sherbet, sorbet and novelties;
also, manufacturer and exporter of frozen yogurt dis-
pensing equipment
Chairman: T Gary Rogers
President/CEO: William Cronk
EVP/CFO: Doug Holdt
CEO: Mike Mitchell
EVP/COO: Timothy Kahn
Purchasing Manager: Linda Shuck
Estimated Sales: $15 Million
Number Employees: 5,000-9,999
Sq. footage: 100000
Parent Co: Dreyer's Grand Ice Cream
Type of Packaging: Consumer, Food Service
Brands:
  DREYERS
  EDY'S
  PORTOFINO
  STARBUCKS

4154 Dreymiller & Kray
P.O.Box 238
Hampshire, IL 60140-0238   847-683-2271
          Fax: 847-683-2272 www.dreymillerandkray.com
Packer/processor of sausage, ham and bacon
President: Ed Reiser
Estimated Sales: $500,000-$1 Million
Number Employees: 10-19
Type of Packaging: Consumer

4155 Drier's Meats
14 S Elm St
Three Oaks, MI 49128-1122   269-756-3101
          Fax: 616-756-9285   info@driers.com
                    www.driers.com
Smoked meats
Owner: Carolyn Drier
Estimated Sales: Less than $500,000
Number Employees: 1-4
Brands:
  DRIER MEATS

4156 Driftwood Dairy
P.O.Box 5508
El Monte, CA 91734-1508   626-444-9591
          Fax: 626-448-7649 www.driftwooddairy.com
Manufacturer of dairy products
President: James Dolan
CEO: Mike Dolan
VP: Jeep Dolan
COO: Tom Dolan
Estimated Sales: $100-500 Million
Number Employees: 250-499
Type of Packaging: Consumer, Food Service, Bulk

4157 Driscoll Strawberry Associates
P.O.Box 50045
Watsonville, CA 95077-5045   831-763-3050
          Fax: 831-724-4530 www.driscolls.com
Grower and exporter of fresh organic strawberries,
raspberries, blackberries and blueberries
Manager: Rick Reyes
Marketing Manager: Mark Munger
Sales Manager: Randy Benko
Estimated Sales: $20-50 Million
Number Employees: 10-19
Brands:
  ASSOCIATES
  DRISCOLL'S
  DSA
  ISLANDER

4158 Drohan Company
PO Box 770708
Woodside, NY 11377-0708   718-898-9672
                    Fax: 718-335-7815
Manufacturer of fresh and frozen poultry
President: John Howell

Estimated Sales:$10-20 Million
Number Employees: 10-19

4159 Droubi's Imports
7333 Hillcroft Street
Houston, TX 77081-6203 713-988-7138
Fax: 713-988-9506
Manufacturer, importer and wholesaler/distributor of tea and coffee
President: A Droubi
VP: Sharon Droubi
Estimated Sales:$1-2.5 Million
Number Employees: 20-49
Sq. footage: 12000
Parent Co: Droubi's Bakery & Delicatessen
Brands:
GOLD STAR

4160 Drum Rock Specialty Company
P.O.Box 7001
Warwick, RI 02887-7001 401-737-5165
Fax: 401-737-5060 www.drumrockproducts.com
Manufacturer and exporter of fritter breading and batter mixes for vegetables, seafood and poultry; also, custom dry blending and mixing and private labeling services available
President: Stephen Hinger
Sales Manager: Paul Skorupa
Estimated Sales:$1-2.5 Million
Number Employees: 5-9
Type of Packaging: Food Service, Private Label, Bulk
Brands:
FIS-CHIC WONDER BATTER

4161 Drusilla Seafood Packing & Processing Company
3482 Drusilla Ln # D
Baton Rouge, LA 70809-1800 225-923-0896
Fax: 225-928-4936 800-364-8844
www.drusillaplace.com
Manufacturer and packer of seafood, spices, salad dressings and breading mixes
President: James Zito
Marketing Manager: Nancy Zito
Estimated Sales:$300,000-$500,000
Number Employees: 100-249
Sq. footage: 2500
Parent Co: Seafood Restaurant
Brands:
DRUSILLA

4162 Dry Creek Vineyard
3495 Dry Creek Rd
Healdsburg, CA 95448-9712 707-433-4171
Fax: 707-433-5329 800-864-9463
dcv@drycreekvineyard.com www.dcgstore.com
Wines
Owner: Gina Gallo
VP: Don Wallace
VP Marketing: Kim Stare-Wallace
Estimated Sales:$10-20 Million
Number Employees: 10-19
Type of Packaging: Consumer, Food Service
Brands:
LATE HARVEST ZINFANDEL-LIMITED ED.
MERITAGE
REGATTA
SOLEIL-LATE HARVEST SAUVIGNON BLANC

4163 Dryden & Palmer Company
16 Business Park Dr
Branford, CT 06405-2964 203-481-3725
Fax: 203-488-8085 info@rockcandy.com
www.rockcandy.com
Rock candy
President: Stephen Besse
Estimated Sales:$10-20 Million
Number Employees: 20-49

4164 Dryden Provision Company
1016 E Washington St
Louisville, KY 40206-1821 502-583-1777
Fax: 502-583-3006 www.drydenprovidin.com
Manufactuer of beef, meat products
President: William Dryden
Estimated Sales:$20-50 Million
Number Employees: 10-19
Brands:
DRYDEN

4165 Dubois Seafood
P.O.Box 10218
Houma, LA 70363-0218 985-876-2514
Fax: 985-851-6147
Seafood
President: Kerry Dubois
Estimated Sales:$ 1 - 3 Million
Number Employees: 5-9

4166 Duck Pond Cellars
23145 N Highway 99w
Dundee, OR 97115 503-538-3199
Fax: 503-538-3190 800-437-3213
duckpond@duckpondcellars.com
www.duckpondcellars.com
Wines
President: Doug Fries
CFO: Jo Ann Fries
Sales: Scott Jenkins
VP Operations: Lisa Jenkins
Estimated Sales:$1-2.5 Million
Number Employees: 10-19
Type of Packaging: Private Label
Brands:
DUCK POND CELLARS

4167 Duckhorn Vineyards
1000 Lodi Ln
St Helena, CA 94574-9713 707-963-7108
Fax: 707-963-7595 888-354-8885
welcome@duckhorn.com
www.duckhornvineyards.com
Wines
President: Daniel Duckhorn
VP Marketing/Sales: Margaret Duckhorn
Estimated Sales:$10-20 Million
Number Employees: 50-99
Brands:
DECOY
DUCKHORN VINEYARDS
GOLDENEYE
KING EIDER
PARADUXX

4168 Ducktrap River Fish Farm
57 Little River Dr
Belfast, ME 04915-6036 207-338-6280
Fax: 207-338-6288 800-434-8727
smoked@ducktrap.com www.ducktrap.com
Manufacturer, importer and exporter of pate and smoked seafood including trout fillets, Atlantic salmon, peppered and herb mackerel, mussels, scallops and shrimp
Manager: Don Cynewski
CFO: John Thibodeau
Purchasing: Bill McLellan
Estimated Sales:$50-100 Million
Number Employees: 100-249
Sq. footage: 25000
Type of Packaging: Consumer, Food Service, Bulk
Brands:
DUCKTRAP
KENDALL BROOK
SPRUCE POINT
WINTER HARBOR

4169 Duda Redifoods
P.O.Box 620257
Oviedo, FL 32762-0257 407-365-2189
Fax: 407-365-2001 www.duda.com
Manufacturer of canned and frozen celery
Manager: Joseph Duda
Estimated Sales:$10-20 Million
Number Employees: 20-49
Parent Co: A. Duda & Sons
Type of Packaging: Consumer, Bulk

4170 Dufflet Pastries
41 Dovercourt Drive
Toronto, ON M8W 1V8
Canada 416-536-1330
Fax: 416-538-2366 dufflet@dufflet.com
www.dufflet.com
Manufacturer of cakes, tortes, pies, flan, tarts, brownies, cookies, etc
President: Dufflet Rosenberg
Marketing: Karin Jensen
production: Thomas Zetlian
Plant Manager: Laws Gatsos
Number Employees: 65
Number of Products: 100
Sq. footage: 10000
Type of Packaging: Consumer, Food Service

4171 Dufour Pastry Kitchens
25 9th Avenue
New York, NY 10014-1209 212-929-2800
Fax: 212-645-8460
info@dufourpastrykitchens.com
www.dufourpastrykitchens.com
Manufacturer of frozen puff pastry products including hors d'oeuvres, doughs, snacks, lunch products, tart shells, etc
President: Judi Arnold
Vice President: Carla Krasner
Estimated Sales:$20-50 Million
Number Employees: 50
Sq. footage: 9600
Type of Packaging: Consumer, Food Service, Bulk
Brands:
DUFOUR PASTRY KITCHENS

4172 Dugdale Beef Company
4224 W 71st St
Indianapolis, IN 46268-2259 317-291-9660
Fax: 317-298-7608
Manufacturer of meat products, and meat packer
President: Jean Deering
Estimated Sales:$ 20 - 50 Million
Number Employees: 20-49
Type of Packaging: Consumer

4173 Duguay Fish Packers
1062 Bas-Cap-Pele Road
Cap-Pele, NB E4N 1K9
Canada 506-577-2287
Fax: 506-577-1995
Manufacturer of smoked herring fillets hand-cured, alewives pickled
Owner: Omer Duguay
Contact: Bobby Duguay
Number Employees: 10-19
Type of Packaging: Food Service

4174 (HQ)Duis Meat Processing
1991 E 6th St
Concordia, KS 66901-2621 785-243-7850
800-281-4295
duis@dustdevil.com
Manufacturer of fresh and frozen meat including sausages, buffalo and smoked meats
President: Toby Duis
Estimated Sales:$1-3 Million
Number Employees: 5-9
Sq. footage: 3200
Type of Packaging: Consumer, Food Service, Private Label, Bulk
Other Locations:
Duis Meat Processing
Salina KS

4175 Dulce de Leche DelcampoProducts
15908 NW 48th Ave
Hialeah, FL 33014-6410 305-620-1444
Fax: 305-624-2728 877-472-9408
info@delcampoproducts.com
www.delcampoproducts.com
Manufacturer of dulce de leche, cholesterol-free white cheese, guava spread and filling
President: Carlos Ruiz DeLuque
Estimated Sales:$ 3 - 5 Million
Number Employees: 10-19
Type of Packaging: Consumer, Food Service, Private Label, Bulk
Brands:
DEL CAMPO

4176 Duma Meats
857 Randolph Rd
Mogadore, OH 44260-9343 330-628-3438
Fax: 330-628-3438
www.dumameatsfarmmarket.com
Manufacturer of fresh and frozen beef, lamb and pork; slaughtering services available
President: David Duma Jr
Estimated Sales:$1-2.5 Million
Number Employees: 20-49
Type of Packaging: Consumer, Food Service, Bulk

4177 Dummbee Gourmet Foods
PO Box 70159
Albany, GA 31708-0159 229-435-4800
Fax: 229-420-4108 800-569-1657
Gourmet foods
President: Tammy Barber
Owner: Steve Barber
*Estimated Sales:*Under $500,000
Number Employees: 1

Brands:
DUMMBEE GOURMET

4178 Dunbar Foods
P.O.Box 519
Dunn, NC 28335-0519   910-892-3175
                    Fax: 910-892-6311
Manufacturer of canned sweet potatoes and peppers
President: Stanley K Dunbar
Estimated Sales:$50-100 Million
Number Employees: 250-499
Parent Co: Moody Dunbar
Type of Packaging: Consumer, Food Service, Private Label

4179 Duncan Peak Vineyards
P.O.Box 358
Hopland, CA 95449-0358   707-744-1129
      Fax: 925-283-3632   wine@duncanpeak.com
                    www.duncanpeak.com
Wines
President: Hubert Lenczowski
*Estimated Sales:*Less than $500,000
Number Employees: 1-4
Type of Packaging: Private Label
Brands:
DUNCAN

4180 Dundee Brandied Fruit Company
PO Box 445
Dundee, OR 97115-0445   503-537-2500
      Fax: 503-538-8599   sadler@dundeefruit.com
Manufacturer of brandied fruit
Owner: Richard Sadler
*Estimated Sales:*Under $500,000
Number Employees: 5
Brands:
DUNDEE BRANDIED

4181 Dundee Candy Shop
2112 Bardstown Rd
Louisville, KY 40205-1916   502-452-9266
      Fax: 502-459-7981   VOLINDAHJ@aol.com
                    www.dundeecandy.com
Candy
Owner: Maria Moore
Estimated Sales:$1-2.5 Million
Number Employees: 5-9
Brands:
DUNDEE CANDY SHOP

4182 Dundee Citrus Growers
P.O.Box 1739
Dundee, FL 33838-1739   863-439-1574
      Fax: 863-439-1535   800-447-1574
            info@dun-d.com   www.dun-d.com
Manufacturer of all varieties of Florida citrus fruits
including oranges, grapefruit, tangerines and red
grapefruit
President: Steven Callahan
CFO: Jon Marone
VP Operations: Greg Dunnahoe
Estimated Sales:$58.9 Million
Number Employees: 500-999
Sq. footage: 125000
Type of Packaging: Consumer, Food Service
Brands:
DUN-D

4183 Dundee International
3 Center Plz # 440
Boston, MA 02108-2086   617-742-4000
      Fax: 617-742-5000   www.oldrepublic.com
Manufacturer of fish and seafood
VP: Stephen Wilson

4184 Dundee Wine Company
P.O.Box 220
Dundee, OR 97115-0220   503-538-3922
      Fax: 503-538-2055   888-427-4953
wine@argylewinery.com   www.argylewinery.com
Wines
Administrator: Rob Daykin
Sales: Craig Eastman
Estimated Sales:$1-2.5 Million
Number Employees: 5-9
Type of Packaging: Private Label
Brands:
DUNDEE

4185 Dunford Bakers
509 W Spring St
Fayetteville, AR 72701-5056   479-521-3000
      Fax: 479-521-3006   donuts@coastlink.com
                    www.flyingburritoco.com
Donuts, danish, muffins, cookies, cakes, pan breads,
specialty breads, and bagels
Owner: Mike Rohrbach
VP/CEO: Gary Gottfredson
CFO: Stephen Ames
Production: Bevin Crowther
Plant Manager: Ronald Stevens
Estimated Sales:$10-20 Million
Number Employees: 100-249
Brands:
DUTCH DELIGHT
HARVEST HAVEN

4186 Dunford Bakers Company
8556 S 2940 W
West Jordan, UT 84088-9660   801-304-0400
      Fax: 801-304-0511   donuts@coastlink.com
                    www.dunfordbakers.com
Manufacturer of doughnuts
Manager: Coelen Williamson
Estimated Sales:$ 5 - 10 Million
Number Employees: 100-249
Type of Packaging: Consumer, Private Label, Bulk

4187 Dunham Hill Bakery
61 Central Street
Woodstock, VT 05091-1121   802-457-3121
                    802-218-3121
Baked goods, frozen desserts and pastry
President/CEO: Barbara Kennedy
CFO: Ronald Behrns
*Estimated Sales:*Under $500,000
Number Employees: 10-19

4188 Dunham's Lobster Pot
60 Mt Blue Pond Rd
Avon, ME 04966-3301   207-639-2815
      Fax: 207-639-2815   durhamsfish@tds.net
Manufacturer of fresh seafood including fish, clams,
haddock, scallops, crab meat, mussels, oysters,
shrimp, lobster and rib-eye steaks
Owner: Tom Philbrick
Estimated Sales:$300,000-500,000
Number Employees: 1-4
Type of Packaging: Food Service, Bulk

4189 Dunham's Meats
5999 E State Route 29
Urbana, OH 43078-9752   937-834-2411
                    Fax: 937-834-2411
Manufacturer of meat products; also, slaughtering
services available
Owner/VP: Barry Dunham
Estimated Sales:$1-2.5 Million
Number Employees: 5-9
Type of Packaging: Consumer, Bulk

4190 Dunkin Brands Inc.
130 Royall Street
Canton, MA 02021   781-737-3000
      Fax: 781-737-4000   800-458-7731
                    www.dunkinbrands.com
coffee and ice cream
Chairman: Jon Luther
CEO: Nigel Travis
CFO: Kate Lavelle
SVP/General Counsel: Richard Emmett
Chief Marketing Officer: John Costello
SVP Human Resources: Christine Deputy
*Estimated Sales:*K
Number Employees: 1,126
Type of Packaging: Food Service
Brands:
BASKIN ROBBINS
DUNKIN DONUTS

4191 Dunn Vineyards
805 White Cottage Rd N
Angwin, CA 94508-9616   707-965-3642
      Fax: 707-965-3805   www.dunnvineyards.com
Wines
Owner: Randall Dunn
Estimated Sales:$1-2.5 Million
Number Employees: 1-4
Brands:
DUNN

4192 Duo Delights
P.O.Box 8919
Madison, WI 53708-8919   608-837-8535
      Fax: 608-825-6463   800-303-4416
      info@duodelights.com   www.mille-lacs.com
Confections
President: Jay Singer
Estimated Sales:$ 5 - 10 Million
Number Employees: 20-49

4193 Duplin Wine Cellars
P.O.Box 756
Rose Hill, NC 28458-0756   910-289-3888
      Fax: 910-289-3094   800-774-9634
info@duplinwinery.com   www.duplinwinery.com
Wines
Owner: David Fussell Jr
Marketing/Sales: Bill Hatcher
Estimated Sales:$5-10 Million
Number Employees: 20-49
Type of Packaging: Private Label
Brands:
DUPLIN

4194 Dupont Cheese
P.O.Box 96
Marion, WI 54950-0096   715-754-5424
      Fax: 715-754-1313   800-895-2873
                    dupontcheese@yahoo.com
                    www.dupontcheeseinc.com
Manufacturer of cheese including colby, mini-horus
and longhorn
President: Fred Laack
Estimated Sales:$10-20 Million
Number Employees: 20-49
Type of Packaging: Consumer

4195 Durango Brewing
3000 Main Ave
Durango, CO 81301-5951   970-247-3396
                    www.durangobrewing.com
Beer
Owner: Mark Harvey
Estimated Sales:$1-2.5 Million
Number Employees: 5-9
Brands:
DURANGO

4196 Durey-Libby Edible Nuts
100 Industrial Rd
Carlstadt, NJ 07072-1614   201-939-2775
      Fax: 201-939-0386   800-332-6887
      info@dureylibby.com   www.dureylibby.com
Custom roasting
President: Wnedy Dicker
CEO: Billy Dicker
Plant Manger: William Dicker
Estimated Sales:$1-2.5 Million
Number Employees: 20-49
Sq. footage: 30000
Type of Packaging: Bulk

4197 Durham/Ellis Pecan Country Store
308 S Houston St
Comanche, TX 76442-3237   325-356-5291
      Fax: 325-356-3161   www.durhams.com
Manufacturer of pecans and other nuts
President: Oldie Dollins
Estimated Sales:$4 Million
Number Employees: 50-99

4198 Durkee-Mower
P.O.Box 470
Lynn, MA 01903-0570   781-593-8007
                    Fax: 781-593-6410
customerservice@marshmallowfluff.com
            www.marshmallowfluff.com
Manufacturer and exporter of marshmallow creme
President: Donald D Durkee
CEO: Donald Durkee
Treasurer: Jonathan Durkee
VP Sales: Dan Quirk
Factory Manager: Paul Walker
Estimated Sales:$ 5 - 10 Million
Number Employees: 20-49
Sq. footage: 35000
Type of Packaging: Consumer, Food Service
Brands:
MARSHMALLOW FLUFF

4199 Durney Vineyards
67 E Carmel Valley Rd
Carmel Valley, CA 93924-9652   831-659-6220
      Fax: 831-659-6226   800-625-8466
info@hellerestate.com   www.durneywines.com
Manufacturer and exporter of wine
   General Manager: Rene Schober
Estimated Sales: $1-2.5 Million
Number Employees: 10-19
Type of Packaging: Consumer

4200 Durrett Cheese Sales
188 Volunteer Ct
Manchester, TN 37355-6492   931-723-3422
      Fax: 931-723-3435   800-209-6792
greg@durrettcheese.com
www.durrettcheese.com
Manufacturer of cheeses specializing in slicing,
chunking and cubing; serving delis, meat depart-
ments and food service operations
   President: Bill Hemperly
Estimated Sales: Less than $500,000
Number Employees: 20-49
Type of Packaging: Consumer, Food Service

4201 Dutch Ann Foods Company
14 Moran Rd
Natchez, MS 39120   601-445-5566
      Fax: 601-445-8738   sales@dutchann.com
Manufacturer of frozen pie crusts
   President: William Jones Jr
Estimated Sales: $ 1 - 3 Million
Number Employees: 5-9
Type of Packaging: Consumer, Food Service, Pri-
   vate Label
Brands:
   BEST WAY
   DUTCH ANN

4202 Dutch Farms Inc
700 E 107th St
Chicago, IL 60628-3806   773-660-0900
      Fax: 773-660-1044   800-637-3447
lbultema@dutchfarms.com
www.dutchfarms.com
Manufacturer/processor of eggs, cheeses, dairy
products, deli, bakery and meat items.
   Chairman: Archie Boomsma
   President: Brian Boomsma
   Executive Officer: Bruce Boomsma
   Administration/Customer Service: Linda Bultema
   Customer Service Representative: Cindi
   Richardson
Number Employees: 100-249
Type of Packaging: Food Service

4203 Dutch Girl Donuts
19000 Woodward Ave
Detroit, MI 48203-1903   313-368-3020
Manufacturer of doughnuts
   Owner: Jon Timmer
   CEO: Gene Timmer
Estimated Sales: $300,000 appx.
Number Employees: 10-19

4204 (HQ)Dutch Gold Honey, Inc.
2220 Dutch Gold Dr
Lancaster, PA 17601-1997   717-393-1716
      Fax: 717-393-8687   800-338-0587
info@dutchgoldhoney.com   www.dutchgold.org
Manufacturer, exporter, importer and packer of
honey and honey products.
   President/CEO: Nancy Gamber Olcott
   CEO: Nancy J Gamber
   VP Sales/Marketing: Jill Clark
   VP Operations: Joe Semmelman
Estimated Sales: $20-50 Million
Number Employees: 20-49
Sq. footage: 100000
Type of Packaging: Consumer, Food Service, Pri-
   vate Label, Bulk
Other Locations:
   Dutch Gold Honey
   Littleton NH
Brands:
   BLOSSOM HILL
   DUTCH GOLD
   HONEY IN THE ROUGH

4205 Dutch Henry Winery
4300 Silverado Trl
Calistoga, CA 94515-9603   707-942-5771
      Fax: 707-942-5512   888-224-5879
info@Dutchhenry   www.dutchhenry.com

Wines
   Owner: Scott Chafen
   VP: Scott Chafen
Estimated Sales: $2.5-5 Million
Number Employees: 5-9
Type of Packaging: Private Label
Brands:
   DUTCH HENRY

4206 Dutch Kitchen Bakery
12 John Fitch Hwy
Fitchburg, MA 01420-5902   978-345-1393
      Fax: 978-345-6651
Breads, rolls, cakes and pastries
   President: Joseph Raimo
Estimated Sales: $1-2.5 Million
Number Employees: 20-49
Brands:
   DUTCH KITCHEN

4207 Dutch Packing Company
4115 NW 28th St
Miami, FL 33142-5691   305-871-3640
      Fax: 305-871-3668   dutchplayer@msn.com
Manufacturer of sausage
   President: Guillermo Rodriguez
   VP Sales: William Rodriguez
   VP Production: Victor Rodriguez
Estimated Sales: Less than $500,000
Number Employees: 20-49
Type of Packaging: Consumer, Food Service
Brands:
   GARCIA

4208 Dutch Valley Veal
1 Dutch Valley Dr
South Holland, IL 60473-1967   708-849-7990
      Fax: 708-849-8094   800-832-8325
sales@dutchvalleyveal.com
www.dutchvalleyveal.com
Manufacturer and packer of meat including beef and
pork
   President: John Oedzes
   VP/National Sales Manager: Brian Oedzes
   VP/Operations Director, Livestock: Bryan Scott
Estimated Sales: $ 20 - 50 Million
Number Employees: 50-99
Type of Packaging: Consumer
Brands:
   Holly

4209 Dutchess Bakery
715 Bigley Ave
Charleston, WV 25302-3356   304-346-3210
Manufacturer of cookies
   Owner: Edward S Rada Iii Jr
Estimated Sales: $500,000-$1 Million
Number Employees: 5-9
Type of Packaging: Consumer

4210 Dutchie Sales Corporation
570 Carlisle St
Hanover, PA 17331-2163   717-632-9343
      Fax: 717-632-4190   wege@supernet.com
www.wege.com
Pretzels
   Manager: Carol Arentz
   VP: Tony Laughman
Estimated Sales: $500-1 Million appx.
Number Employees: 50-99
Type of Packaging: Private Label
Brands:
   DUTCHIE

4211 Dutchland Frozen Foods
205 N Main Street
Lester, IA 51242   712-478-4349
      Fax: 712-478-4554   888-497-7243
info@dutchlandfrozenfoods.com
www.dutchlandfrozenfoods.com
butter pastry puffs

4212 Dutterer's Home Food Service
2700 Lord Baltimore Drive
Baltimore, MD 21244-2648   410-298-3663
      Fax: 410-298-1625
Manufacturer of meats including frankfurters, pas-
trami, roast and corned beef and poultry products
   President: Mark Mules
Estimated Sales: $ 10 - 20 Million
Number Employees: 10-19
Type of Packaging: Consumer, Private Label

4213 Duval Bakery Products
1733 Evergreen Ave
Jacksonville, FL 32206-4730   904-354-7878
      Fax: 904-354-7828
Manufacturer of stuffing and bread crumbs
   Owner: Robert Gorsuch
Estimated Sales: $500,000-$1 Million
Number Employees: 5-9
Sq. footage: 6000
Type of Packaging: Food Service, Private Label,
   Bulk

**4214 Duxbury Mussel & Seafood
Corporation**
8 Joseph St # B
Kingston, MA 02364-1122   781-585-5517
      Fax: 781-585-2976
Seafood
   President: Robert Marconi

4215 Dwayne Keith Brooks Company
6628 Fiesta Lane
Orangevale, CA 95662-3554   916-988-1030
      Fax: 916-988-4442   dkbrooksco@home.com
Manufacturer of school and institutional frozen
foods including mini buns, dinner rolls, bread sticks,
jumbo burger buns; manufacturer of oven baskets,
transport dollies and speed line baskets; serving
food service operators andwholesalers/distributors
   President: Dwayne Brooks
Estimated Sales: $10-20 Million
Number Employees: 6
Sq. footage: 1800
Parent Co: SA Products Company
Type of Packaging: Food Service, Bulk

4216 DynaPro International
860 W Riverdale Road
Ogden, UT 84405-3758   801-621-8224
      Fax: 801-621-8258   800-877-1413
sales@dynaprointernational.com
www.dynaprointernational.com
Manufacturer and exporter of vitamins and herbal
supplements
   President: Rowene Visser
   Accounting Director: Tammy Hair
   Marketing Director: Gary Hoffman
Estimated Sales: $ 1 - 3 Million
Number Employees: 9
Sq. footage: 3900

4217 Dynagel
10 Wentworth Ave
Calumet City, IL 60409-2744   708-891-8400
      Fax: 708-891-8432   888-396-2435
dynagel@aol.com   www.dynagel.com
Manufacturer and exporter of gelatin including hy-
drolyzed
   Manager: Nicholas Liu
   CEO: Chuck Markham
   CFO: Rib Mayberry
   Plant Manager: Conrad Heisner
Estimated Sales: $20-50 Million
Number Employees: 50-99
Sq. footage: 70000
Type of Packaging: Bulk
Brands:
   SOL-U-PRO

4218 Dynamic Coatings Inc
3628 W Holland Ave
Fresno, CA 93722-7808   559-225-4605
      Fax: 559-225-4606   dycoatings@aol.com
www.dynamiccoatingsinc.net
Product and service line is concrete restoration and
protective coating products for floors and walls applications of which include that of food processing
plants, kitchens, wineries, dairies, bakeries and
breweries.
   Owner: Jose A Gonzales
   IT/Webmaster: Dennis Stemper
   Sales Representative: Jose Gonzalez

4219 Dynamic Confections
119 East 200 North
Alpine, UT 84004   801-756-6916
      Fax: 801-756-7791   800-377-4368
info@dynamicconfections.com
www.dynamicconfections.com
candy

4220 Dynamic Foods
1001 E 33rd St
Lubbock, TX 79404-1816   806-762-0780
Fax: 806-723-5680   jsullivan@dynamicfoods.com
www.furrs.net
Manufacturer of baked goods, cakes, muffins, cornbread, pies, cobblers, frozen dinner rolls, casseroles, side dishes, soups, sauces, glazes, mexican foods, breaded fish, bread sticks
President: Mike Blasdell
Controller: Todd Hill
Research & Development: Beth Tay
Quality Control: George Railsback
Sales Director: Justine Sullivan
Production Manager: Richard Hill
Purchasing Manager: Connie Carpenter
Estimated Sales: $50-100 Million
Number Employees: 100-249
Number of Products: 100+
Sq. footage: 225000
Type of Packaging: Food Service, Private Label
Brands:
DYNAMIC FOODS
PRIVATE LABEL

4221 Dynamic Health Labs
110 Bridge St # 2
Brooklyn, NY 11201-1575   718-858-0100
Fax: 718-392-9301   800-396-2214
information@dynamic-health.com
www.dynamichealth.com
Manufacturer of liquid diet supplements, certified kosher
President: Bruce Burwick
Estimated Sales: $ 3 - 5 Million
Number Employees: 20-49

4222 (HQ)Dynic USA Corporation
4750 NE Dawson Creek Dr
Hillsboro, OR 97124-5799   503-693-1070
Fax: 503-648-1185   800-326-1249
cesar@dynic.com   www.dynic.com
Manufactures complementary product lines to serve the needs of the labeling and printing industry
President: Shigeru Tamura
Sales Director: Cesar Santa
Estimated Sales: $ 5 - 10 Million
Number Employees: 50-99
Parent Co: Dynic Corporation
Other Locations:
Dynic UK Ltd
Cardiff, South Wales UK
Dynic Corporation
Minatoku, Tokyo, Japan HK
Brands:
CABIN AIR FILTERS
CETUS TEXTILE FABRICS
OLED DESICCANT
SIRIUS TTR

4223 E U Blending Company
1221 West Gila Bend Highway
Casa Grande, AZ 85222   520-374-2603
www.erifoods.com
Manufacture of dry blending, extrusion, milling, grinding and pouch packaging machines.
President: David Reisenbigler
Sq. footage: 200000
Parent Co: Erie Foods, Inc.

4224 E&G Food
5600 1st Ave # 4nb
Brooklyn, NY 11220-2550   718-680-1300
Fax: 718-680-2392   888-525-8855
Chicken, turkey
President: Meir Grunbaum
Plant Manager: Ignacio Quirch
Estimated Sales: $1-2.5 Million
Number Employees: 5-9

4225 E&H Packing Company
2453 Riopelle St
Detroit, MI 48207-4524   313-567-8286
Fax: 313-567-8287
Manufacturer of beef
Owner/President: Robert Buzar
Treasurer: Bob Buzar
Estimated Sales: $1-2.5 Million
Number Employees: 5-9
Type of Packaging: Consumer, Food Service

4226 (HQ)E&J Gallo Winery
600 Yosemite Boulevard
Modesto, CA 95354-2760   209-341-3111
Fax: 209-341-8857 www.gallo.com
Manufacturer of wines, brandy and sparkling wine
Chairman: James E Coleman
Co-Chairman, President, and CEO: Josepy Gallo
Co-Chairman: Robert Gallo
VP Operations: Steven Kidd
Estimated Sales: $2 Billion
Number Employees: 5,000
Type of Packaging: Consumer, Food Service
Other Locations:
E&J Gallo Winery
Mississauga ON
Brands:
ANAPAMU®
ANDRE®
BALLATORE®
BAREFOOT BUBBLY®
BAREFOOT® CELLARS
BARTLES & JAYMES®
BELLA SERA®
BLACK SWAN®
BOONE'S FARM®
BRIDLEWOOD® ESTATE WINERY
CARLO ROSSI®
CASK & CREAM®
CLARENDON HILLS
DANCING BULL®
DAVINCI
DON MUGUEL GASCON
E. & J.® VS BRANDY
E. & J.®VSOP BRANDY
ECCO DOMANI®
ESTATE
FREI BROTHERS®
FRUTEZIA®
GHOST PINES®
HORNSBY'S®
INDIGO HILLS®
LAS ROCAS®
LIBERTY CREEK®
LIVINGSTON CELLARS®
LOUIS M. MARTINI®
MACMURRAY RANCH®
MARCELINA®
MARTIN CODAX®
MASO CANALI®
MATTIE'S PERCH®
MCWILLIAM'S®
MIRASSOU®
NEW AMSTERDAM® GIN
PETER VELLA®
POLKA DOT®
RANCHO ZABACO®
RED BICYCLETTE®
RED ROCK WINERY®
REDWOOD CREEK®
RESERVE®
SEBEKA®
SINGLE VINEYARD
SONOMA
STARBOROUGH™
TISDALE VINEYARDS®
TURNING LEAF®
TURNING LEAF® SONOMA RESERVE
TWIN VALLEY®
WHITEHAVEN®
WILD VINES®
WILLIAM HILL ESTATE™
WYCLIFF® SPARKLING

4227 E&J Gallo Winery
5610 E Olive Ave
Fresno, CA 93727-2707   559-458-2480
Fax: 559-453-2411 www.ejgallo.com
Manufacturer of white, red and pink wines
Plant Manager: Gary Schmidt
Purchasing: Sharon Kirby
Estimated Sales: $50-100 Million
Number Employees: 1-4
Type of Packaging: Consumer, Food Service

4228 E&J Gallo Winery
18000 River Rd
Livingston, CA 95334-9514   209-394-6219
Fax: 209-394-4425 www.ejgallo.com
Manufacturer of wine
Manager: Thomas Green
Estimated Sales: $100-500 Million
Number Employees: 100-249
Type of Packaging: Consumer, Food Service

4229 E&J Gallo Winery
10-5155 Spectrum Way
Mississauga, ON L4W 5A1
Canada   905-602-4575
Fax: 905-602-9709
Manufacturer of brandy and wine
Director Sales: Tim Maletich
Number Employees: 65
Type of Packaging: Consumer, Food Service

4230 E-Fish-Ent Fish Company
1941 Goodridge Road
Sooke, BC V0S 1N0
Canada   250-642-4007
Fax: 250-642-4057 www.e-fish-ent.ca
Manufacturer and exporter of smoked salmon in retort pouch; meat products in pouch, stews, chili, curry.
President: Bryan Mooney
VP: Linda Mooney
Number Employees: 5-9
Sq. footage: 8000
Type of Packaging: Private Label

4231 E. Gagnon & Fils
405 Route 132 CP 37
St Therese-De-Gaspe, QC G03 3B0
Canada   418-385-3011
Fax: 418-385-3021
Manufacturer and exporter of frozen snow crabs, crab
President: Roger Gagnon
Number Employees: 250-499
Type of Packaging: Food Service

4232 E. Harris
117 Hamilton Avenue
Farrell, PA 16121-2145   724-346-4664

4233 E. Waldo Ward & Son Corporation
273 E Highland Ave
Sierra Madre, CA 91024-2014   626-355-1218
Fax: 626-355-5292   800-355-9273
jelly@waldoward.com   www.waldoward.com
Manufacturer and importer of gourmet foods including olives, preserves, jellies, marmalades, brandied fruits and sauces including meat, relish and seafood cocktail; exporter of marmalades. Services, private labeling and anufacturing tolarge and small companies. Also offers consulting services
President: Richard Ward
VP: Jeffrey Ward
Estimated Sales: $5 Million
Number Employees: 10-19
Number of Brands: 2
Number of Products: 150
Sq. footage: 10000
Type of Packaging: Consumer, Private Label
Brands:
E. WALDO WARD
SIERRA MADRE BRAND

4234 E.B. Evans Company
2324 Hampton Avenue
Saint Louis, MO 63139-2909   215-425-0558
Fax: 215-425-0560
Syrups, toppings, beverage bases
President: Guy Mc Clellan
COO: John McClellan
Estimated Sales: $5-9.9 Million
Number Employees: 5-9

4235 E.C. Phillips & Son
PO Box 8235
Ketchikan, AK 99901-3235   907-225-3121
Fax: 907-225-7249
Manufacturer of smoked Alaska salmon
President: Larry Elliott
Estimated Sales: $ 10 - 20 Million
Number Employees: 100-249
Type of Packaging: Consumer

4236 E.D. Smith & Sons
944 Highway 8
Winona, ON L8E 5S3
Canada   905-643-1211
Fax: 905-643-3328   inquiry@edsmith.com
www.edsmith.com

Manufacturer and exporter of jams, ketchup, pie fillings, barbecue and pasta sauces, fruit toppings, salsas and syrups
President/CEO: Michael Burrows
VP Finance: David Smith
VP Operations: Dorothy Pethick
Estimated Sales:$120 Million
Number Employees: 250-490
Sq. footage: 400000
Parent Co: Imperial Capital Corporation
Type of Packaging: Consumer, Food Service, Private Label, Bulk
Brands:
E.D. SMITH
HABITANT
LEA & PERRINS

4237 E.E. Mucke & Sons
2326 Main St
Hartford, CT 06120-2061   860-246-5609
Fax: 860-541-6403   800-726-5598
Manufacturer of meat products including sausage, kielbasa, frankfurters, salami and liverwurst
President: Ernest Mucke Iii
VP: Ernest Mucke III
Estimated Sales:$5-10 Million
Number Employees: 20-49
Type of Packaging: Consumer, Food Service, Private Label
Brands:
Circle M

4238 E.F. Lane & Son
744 Kevin Ct
Oakland, CA 94621-4040   510-569-8980
Fax: 510-569-0240
Manufacturer and exporter of honey and peanut products
Manager: Phyllis Tut
Estimated Sales:$500,000-$1 Million
Number Employees: 1-4
Type of Packaging: Consumer, Food Service, Private Label, Bulk

4239 E.J. Cox Company/Sachs Nut Company
P.O.Box 550
Clarkton, NC 28433-0550   910-647-4711
Fax: 910-647-0301   800-732-6933
ejcox@weblnk.net   www.sachspeanuts.com
Manufacturer of in-shell peanuts
President: Nathan Cox
Sales Secretary: Ruth Cox-Church
Estimated Sales:$100+ Million
Number Employees: 50-99
Sq. footage: 10000
Type of Packaging: Consumer, Food Service, Bulk
Brands:
SACHS

4240 E.J. Green & Company
PO Box 99
Winterton, NL A0B 3MO
Canada
709-583-2670
Fax: 709-583-2804   ejgreen@nf.sympatico.ca
Manufacturer of sea urchins
President: Derek Green
Type of Packaging: Food Service

4241 E.W. Bowker Company
22 New Lisbon Road
Pemberton, NJ 08068-1820   609-894-9508
Fax: 609-894-2165   ewbowker@yahoo.com
Manufacturer of fresh cranberries and blueberries
President: Ernest Bowker
Vice President: Betty Minkus
*Estimated Sales:*500,000-$1 Million
Number Employees: 5-9
Type of Packaging: Consumer, Food Service, Bulk

4242 (HQ)E.W. Knauss & Son
625 E Broad St
Quakertown, PA 18951-1713   215-536-4220
Fax: 215-536-1129   800-648-4220
sales@knaussfoods.com   www.alderfermeats.com
Manufacturer of sliced dried beef products including beefsticks, beef jerky, hot sausage and pickled meat products.
President: Sherry Russell
Chairman: E William Knauss
VP Sales: Richard Harlan
Estimated Sales:$20-50 Million
Number Employees: 50-99
Sq. footage: 100000

Type of Packaging: Consumer, Food Service, Private Label, Bulk
Brands:
BEARDSLEY
BULL
CARSON
HANNAH
KNAUSS

4243 EB Botanicals
50 Church St
Montclair, NJ 07042-2772   973-655-9585
Fax: 973-696-7666   service@eccobella.com
www.eccobella.com
Botanicals
President: Sally Malagna

4244 EFCO Products
130 Smith St
Poughkeepsie, NY 12601-2109   845-452-4715
Fax: 845-452-5607   800-284-3326
info@efcoproducts.com   www.efcoproducts.com
Leading supplier of mixes, fruit and creme style fillings, jellies, jams and concentrated icing fruits to the baking industry.
President: Jack Effron
Executive VP: Ira Effron
Estimated Sales:$2.5-5 Million
Number Employees: 50-99

4245 EMD Chemicals
480 S Democrat Rd
Gibbstown, NJ 08027-1239   856-224-0742
Fax: 914-592-9469   800-364-4535
www.emdchemicals.com
Manufacturer of food additives and preservatives including ascorbic acid, niacin, niacinamide, d-Bioton, etc.; also, vitamins, minerals, salts and nutraceuticals
President: Douglas Brown
Estimated Sales:$100+ Million
Number Employees: 100-249
Parent Co: K&A Merck
Type of Packaging: Bulk

4246 EOS Estate Winery
P.O.Box 1287
Paso Robles, CA 93447-1287   805-239-2562
Fax: 805-239-2317   800-349-9463
info@eosvintage.com   www.eosvintage.com
Wines
President: Kerry Vix
CFO: Pati Withers
Marketing: Christopher Vix
Sales: Luis Cota
Public Relations: Denise McLean
Operations: Steve Felten
Production: Leslie Melendez
Plant Manager: Gary Cargill
Purchase Manager: Pat Withers
Estimated Sales:$1-2.5 Million
Number Employees: 5-9
Number of Brands: 4
Type of Packaging: Private Label
Brands:
ARUERO
CUPAGRANOLS
EOS
NOVELLA

4247 EPI Breads
1757 Tullie Cir NE
Atlanta, GA 30329-2305   404-325-1016
Fax: 404-325-0735   800-325-1014
bdoan@epibreads.com   www.epibreads.com
Manufacturers of bread
Owner: Nick Mulliez
Estimated Sales:$100+ Million
Number Employees: 100-249
Brands:
EPI

4248 EPI De France Bakery
1757 Tullie Cir NE
Atlanta, GA 30329-2305   404-325-1016
Fax: 404-325-0735   800-325-1014
info@epibreads.com   www.epibreads.com
Manufacturer and exporter of fresh and frozen bread; importer of machinery
President: Nic Mulliez
Estimated Sales:$20-50 Million
Number Employees: 100-249
Sq. footage: 42500
Type of Packaging: Consumer, Food Service, Private Label, Bulk

Brands:
Epi De France
Graines De Vie

4249 ERBL
P.O.Box 131135
Carlsbad, CA 92013-1135   760-599-6088
Fax: 760-599-6089   800-275-3725
info@cormega.com   www.coromega.com
Omega-3 dietary supplements.
Manager: Suzanne Goodrich
Estimated Sales:$ 5 - 10 Million
Number Employees: 10-19

4250 Eagle Agricultural Products
PO Box 1451
Huntsville, AR 72740-1451   501-738-2203
Fax: 501-738-2203
Manufacturer of organic unbleached white, whole wheat, corn and rice flour, corn meal, white and brown basmati and long grain rice
Owner/CEO: Kathy Turner
Owner: Gary Turner
Estimated Sales:$1-4.9 Million
Number Employees: 1
Sq. footage: 10000
Type of Packaging: Private Label, Bulk
Brands:
Eagle Agricultural Products

4251 (HQ)Eagle Coffee Company
1019 Hillen St
Baltimore, MD 21202-4197   410-752-1229
Fax: 410-528-0369   800-545-4015
info@eaglecoffee.com   www.eaglecoffee.com
Manufacturer, importer and wholesaler/distributor of restaurant and gourmet coffees, coffee machines and grinders and coffee beans; serving the food service market
Owner: Nick Constantine
Vice President: Arthur Constantinides
Estimated Sales:$1-2.5 Million
Number Employees: 10-19
Sq. footage: 40000
Type of Packaging: Food Service, Private Label
Other Locations:
Eagle Coffee Co.
Baltimore MD

4252 Eagle Crest Vineyards
7107 Vineyard Rd
Conesus, NY 14435-9521   585-346-2321
Fax: 585-346-2322
Wines
President: Michael Secretan
VP: Sarah Brown
Estimated Sales:$2.5-5 Million
Number Employees: 5-9

4253 Eagle Eye Produce
P.O.Box 460
Iona, ID 83427-0460   208-522-2343
Fax: 208-522-2345 www.eagleeyeproduce.com
President: Newman Giles
*Estimated Sales:*Under $500,000
Number Employees: 1-4

4254 Eagle Family Foods
735 Taylor Rd # 200
Columbus, OH 43230-6274   614-501-4200
Fax: 614-501-4299   888-656-3245
corporate@effinc.com
www.eaglefamilyfoods.com
Sweetened condensed milk, citrus juices, lemonade concentrate, nondairy creamers
President/CEO: John Nugent
CEO: Craig A Steinke
Number Employees: 5-9
Brands:
BORDEN
CREMORA
EAGLE BRAND
KAVA
NONE SUCH
REALEMON
REALIME

4255 Eagle Rock Food Company
1225 12th St NW
Albuquerque, NM 87104-2113   505-323-1183
eaglerock@abq.com
Meat
Owner: Mike Perea

Estimated Sales: $ 1 - 3 Million
Number Employees: 1-4

4256 Eagle Seafood Producers
56 N 3rd Street
Brooklyn, NY 11211-3925   718-963-0939
     Fax: 718-963-1306 info@eagleseafood.com
          www.eagleseafood.com
Manufacturer of fresh and frozen seafood
     President: Mark Rudes
     VP: Donald Draghi
Estimated Sales: $10-20 Million
Number Employees: 20-49
Type of Packaging: Food Service

4257 Earl's Candy Company
430 Raines Avenue
Macon, GA 31206-1557   229-781-6858
Sugar stick candy
     President: Earl Mc Afee
     General Manager: Sammy Mc Afee
Estimated Sales: $1-2.5 Million
Number Employees: 5-9

4258 Earle Brothers Fisheries
PO Box 250
Carbonear, NL A1Y 1B6
Canada   709-596-5166
               Fax: 709-596-3801
Manufacturer of fresh and frozen fish including
salted, pickled and meal
     President: Fred Earle, Sr.
     Manager: Frederick Earle, Jr.
Number Employees: 50

4259 Earth & Vine Provisions
PO Box 1637
Loomis, CA 95650   916-434-8399
     Fax: 916-434-8398 888-723-8463
tressac@earthnvine.com www.earthnvine.com
jams, sauces, beverage elixirs and dressings
     President/Owner: Tressa Cooper
     CFO: Ron Cooper
Number Employees: 10

4260 Earth & Vine Provisions
160 Flocchini Cir
Lincoln, CA 95648-1700   916-434-8399
     Fax: 916-434-8398 888-723-8463
customerservice@earthnvine.com
               www.earthnvine.com
Manufacturer of jams, cooking sauces, vinaigrettes,
chutneys, relishes and dessert sauces
     President: Tressa Cooper
Estimated Sales: $ 3 - 5 Million
Number Employees: 10-19

4261 Earth Ade Beverages
1373 E Morehead Street
Charlotte, NC 28204-2947   704-343-9990
Beverages
     President: Richard Mullin
     Marketing Director: Catherine Page
Number Employees: 5-9

4262 Earth Fire Products
507 N East Ave
Viroqua, WI 54665-1412   608-735-4711
Manufacturer of organic food, miso
     President: Robert Ribbens
Estimated Sales: $5-10 Million
Number Employees: 5-9

4263 Earth Friendly Products
44 Green Bay Rd
Winnetka, IL 60093-4006   847-446-4441
     Fax: 847-446-4437 800-335-3267
jv@ecos.com www.ecos.com

President: John Vlahakis
CEO: Val Osakada
Estimated Sales: $ .5 - 1 million
Number Employees: 5-9

4264 Earth Island Natural Foods
P.O.Box 9400
Canoga Park, CA 91309-0400   818-725-2820
     Fax: 818-725-2812 www.followyourheart.com
Manufacturer of prepared deli salads, vegetarian
specialties, nondairy cheese alternative, meat ana-
logues, egg-free mayonnaise and dressings
     President/Co-Owner: Robert Goldberg
     Co-Owner: Paul Lewin
Estimated Sales: $1-3 Million
Number Employees: 20-49
Sq. footage: 6000
Type of Packaging: Consumer, Food Service, Pri-
     vate Label, Bulk
Brands:
     FOLLOW YOUR HEART
     VEGENAISE

4265 Earth Mother Foods Company
1788 Charles Avenue
Arcata, CA 95521-6816   707-825-6723
     Fax: 707-825-6723 vegatus@northeast.com
               www.earthmotherfoods.com

4266 Earth Products
2320 Cousteau Ct # 100
Vista, CA 92081-8363   760-494-2000
     Fax: 760-494-2005 randersn@connectnet.com
Manufacturer of nutritional products, chia seed
     President: Bob Andersen
     CEO: Jeff Larsen
Estimated Sales: D
Number Employees: 50-99

4267 Earth Science
475 N Sheridan St
Corona, CA 91720   909-371-7565
               Fax: 909-371-0509
Manufacturer of creams, lotions, AHA/BHA, Vita-
min C products, shampoos, conditioners, styling
aids, body care, liquid vitamins
     President: Kristine Schoenauer
     VP: Michael Rutledge
     Contract Sales Manager: Diane Smart
Number Employees: 100-249
Sq. footage: 80000
Type of Packaging: Consumer, Bulk

4268 Earth Song Whole Foods
4880 San Juan Avenue
Suite 216
Fair Oaks, CA 95628-4719   916-332-1355
     Fax: 916-332-1355 877-327-8476
julie@earthsongwholefoods.com
               www.earthsongwholefoods.com
Vegan natural food products
     Owner: Julie Rogers
Estimated Sales: $300,000-500,000
Number Employees: 1-4
Brands:
     EARTH SONG WHOLE FOOD BARS
     GRANDPA'S SECRET OMEGA-3 MUESLI

4269 Earthen Vessels Herb Company
PO Box 1375
Hockessin, DE 19707-5375   302-234-7667
               Fax: 302-234-7667
Manufacturer of Seasonings, spices
     President: Timothy Rodden
Estimated Sales: $500,000-$1 Million
Number Employees: 1-4

4270 Earthgrains Company
8400 Maryland Avenue
St. Louis, MO 63105-3668   314-259-7000
     www.earthgrains.com / www.saralee.com
Manufacturer of fresh packaged bread, baked goods
and refrigerated dough products
     Chairman/CEO: Barry Beracha
     COO/EVP: John Iselin, Jr
     VP/CFO: Mark Krieger
     VP/Secretary: Joseph Noelker
Estimated Sales: $300,000-500,000
Number Employees: 200
Parent Co: Sara Lee Corporation
Type of Packaging: Consumer
Brands:
     Old Home
     Sara Lee

4271 Earthrise Nutritionals
424 Payran Street
Petaluma, CA 94952-5905   559-855-3804
     Fax: 707-778-9028 707-778-9078
info@earthrise.com www.earthrise.com
Manufacturer of Spirulina based green food nutri-
tional products
     VP: Walter Rick
Number Employees: 65
Type of Packaging: Private Label

4272 Easley Winery
205 N College Ave
Indianapolis, IN 46202-3799   317-636-4516
     Fax: 317-974-0128 indygrape@cs.com
               www.easleywinery.com
Manufacturer of table wine
     President/Co-Owner: Mark Easley
     Co-Owner: Meredith Easley
Estimated Sales: $5-9.9 Million
Number Employees: 10-19
Type of Packaging: Consumer, Food Service, Pri-
     vate Label, Bulk
Brands:
     Cape Sandy Vineyards
     Easley's

4273 East & West Gourmet
PO Box 61769
Honolulu, HI 96839-1769   808-262-2453
     Fax: 808-261-2726 800-378-6978
Gourmet foods
     President: Alan Tang
     Public Relations: Alicia Tang
Estimated Sales: $5-10 Million
Number Employees: 5-9
Brands:
     Sassy Tropics Hawaii

4274 East Balt Bakery
4701 E 50th Avenue
Denver, CO 80216-3106   303-377-5533
               Fax: 303-388-0258
Manufacturer of buns and rolls

4275 East Balt Bakery
1108 Collins Dr
Kissimmee, FL 34741-4697   407-933-2222
               Fax: 407-933-5367
Manufacturer and exporter of buns
     Manager: Tim Weitfeldt
     Plant Manager: Tim Weitfeldt
Estimated Sales: $50-100 Million
Number Employees: 50-99
Sq. footage: 45000
Type of Packaging: Food Service

4276 (HQ)East Balt Commissary
1801 W 31st Pl
Chicago, IL 60608-6199   773-376-4444
     Fax: 773-376-8137 www.eastbalt.com
Bread
     President: John Petenes
     CFO: John Kent
     Plant Manager: George Guiness
Estimated Sales: $20-50 Million
Number Employees: 100-249
Type of Packaging: Private Label

**4277 East Beauregard Meat Processing
Center**
5362 Highway 113
Deridder, LA 70634-8119   337-328-7171
               Fax: 337-328-8132
Manufacturer of beef, pork, mutton, venison and
goat meat; also, custom slaughtering available
Estimated Sales: $ 1 - 3 Million
Number Employees: 1-4
Type of Packaging: Private Label

4278 East Coast Fresh Cuts Company
8704 Bollman Place
Savage, MD 20763-9747   410-799-9900
               Fax: 410-799-8000
mgeorge@eastcoastfreshcuts.com
               www.eastcoastfreshcuts.com
Manufacturer of fresh cut vegetables including on-
ions, peppers, carrots, celery, etc
     President: John Phillip Muth
     Sales: Tom Brown
Estimated Sales: $100+ Million
Number Employees: 250-499

Sq. footage: 30000
Parent Co: Coastal Sun Belt
Type of Packaging: Food Service, Private Label, Bulk

4279 East Coast Olive Oil
75 Wurz Avenue
Utica, NY 13502-2524   315-797-3151
          Fax: 315-797-6981 gem-ecoo.com
Olive oil
    President: Stephen Mandia
    VP: Robert Mandia
    Sales Manager: Tim Morrison
    Operations: Roger Bateman
    Plant Manager: Fran Mandia
Estimated Sales: $5-10 Million
Number Employees: 20-49

4280 East Coast Seafood of Phoenix
2311 E Jones Ave
Phoenix, AZ 85040-1455   602-268-3313
          Fax: 602-268-3988
Manufacturer of Seafood
    Manager: Anwer Haider
Estimated Sales: $ 20 - 50 Million
Number Employees: 50-99

4281 East Dayton Meat & Poultry
1546 Keystone Ave
Dayton, OH 45403-3396   937-253-6185
          Fax: 937-253-1040
Manufacturer of beef, pork and poultry
    President: Kim Lakey
Estimated Sales: $ 20 - 50 Million
Number Employees: 10-19

4282 East India Coffee & TeaCompany
1933 Davis St # 308
San Leandro, CA 94577-1259   510-638-1300
    Fax: 510-638-0760 800-829-1300
          www.rogersfamilyco.com
Manufacturer of Coffee and teas
    President: Jon Rogers
    Sales Director: Mike Carlin
    Operations Manager: Pete Rogers
    Purchasing Manager: Tom Garber
Estimated Sales: $20-50 Million
Number Employees: 50-99
Type of Packaging: Private Label

4283 East Indies Coffee & Tea Company
7 Keystone Dr
Lebanon, PA 17042-9791   717-228-2000
    Fax: 717-228-2540 800-220-2326
    mstea@pa.online.com www.eastindies.com
Gourmet and flavored coffees and teas
    President: Walter Progner
    VP: Mim Enck
Estimated Sales: Less than $500,000
Number Employees: 5-9

4284 East Kentucky Foods
P.O.Box 33
Winchester, KY 40392-0033   859-744-2218
          Fax: 859-744-8511
Healthy snacks
    President: Greg Ginter
Estimated Sales: $ 10 - 20 Million
Number Employees: 5-9

4285 East Point Seafood Company
P.O.Box 127
South Bend, WA 98586-0127   360-875-5507
    Fax: 360-875-5417 888-317-8459
    info@eastpointseafood.com
          www.eastpointseafood.com
Seafood
    Owner: Joel Van Ornun
Estimated Sales: $ 1 - 3 Million
Number Employees: 5-9
Type of Packaging: Private Label

4286 East Poultry Company
P.O.Box 6499
Austin, TX 78762-6499   512-476-5367
    Fax: 512-476-5360 epoultry@att.net
          www.eastpoultry.com
Poultry and eggs
    President: Kenneth J Aune
Estimated Sales: $4.5 Million
Number Employees: 10-19
Sq. footage: 13500
Type of Packaging: Food Service, Bulk

4287 East Shore Specialty Foods
P.O.Box 379
Hartland, WI 53029-0379   262-367-8988
    Fax: 262-367-9081 800-236-1069
    customerservice@eastshorefoods.com
          www.eastshorefoods.com
Manufacturer of gourmet mustards, pretzels, chocolate sauces
    President: Jeri Mesching
    CEO: Kristin Graves
Estimated Sales: $10-20 Million
Number Employees: 10-19
Type of Packaging: Private Label

4288 East Side Winery/Oak Ridge Vineyards
P.O.Box 440
Lodi, CA 95241-0440   209-369-4768
          Fax: 209-369-0202
    eswinery@oakridgevineyards.com
          www.oakridgewinery.com
Manufacturer of bottled wines
    Owner: Rudy Maggio
Estimated Sales: $10-20 Million
Number Employees: 20-49
Type of Packaging: Consumer, Food Service, Private Label, Bulk

4289 East Wind Nut Butters
Hc 3 Box 3370
Tecumseh, MO 65760-9503   417-679-4682
          Fax: 417-679-4684 www.eastwind.org
Manufacturer of peanut and organic peanut butters; also, cashew and almond butters and tahini
    Manager: Lena Berglund
    Sales Director: Sam Lucas
Estimated Sales: $1-3 Million
Number Employees: 10-19
Sq. footage: 7000
Parent Co: East Wind Community
Type of Packaging: Consumer, Food Service, Private Label
Brands:
    East Wind
    East Wind Almond
    East Wind Cashew
    East Wind Organic Peanut Butter
    East Wind Peanut
    East Wind Tahini

4290 Eastern Brewing Corporation
329 Washington Street N
Hammonton, NJ 08037-1537   609-561-2700
          Fax: 609-561-9441
Beer
Estimated Sales: Less than $500,000
Number Employees: 1-4

4291 (HQ)Eastern Fish Company
300 Frank W Burr Blvd # 30
Teaneck, NJ 07666-6719   201-801-0800
    Fax: 201-801-0802 800-526-9066
    dkapar@easternfish.com www.easternfish.com
Manufacturer and importer of farm raised shrimp and other seafood, bay and sea scallops, lobster, king crab legs and claws, snow crab clusters, yellow fin tuna
    President: Eric Bloom
    CEO: William Bloom
    VP: Lee Bloom
Estimated Sales: $200 Million
Number Employees: 10-19
Type of Packaging: Private Label
Other Locations:
    Norwestern Sales Office
    Kingston WA
    Western Sales Office
    Anaheim CA
    Northeastern Sales Office
    Gloucester MA
    Southeastern Sales Office
    South Springs FL
Brands:
    SAIL

4292 Eastern Food Industries
2832 S County Trl
East Greenwich, RI 02818-1742   401-884-8798
Manufacturer of Pasta sauces
    President: Henry Caniglia
    VP/Treasurer: Stephen Caniglia
    Purchasing Manager: Henry Caniglia

Estimated Sales: $5-10 Million
Number Employees: 5-9

4293 Eastern Foods NaturallyFresh
1000 Naturally Fresh Blvd
College Park, GA 30349-2909   404-765-9000
          Fax: 404-765-9016 www.naturallyfresh.com
Salad dressings, dips and sauces
    President: Robert Brooks
    CEO: Jerry Greene
    Plant Manager: Jerry Greene
    Purchasing Agent: Cindi Mullis
Estimated Sales: $50-100 Million
Number Employees: 1-4

4294 Eastern Marketing Service
P.O.Box 6530
Lakeland, FL 33807-6530   863-701-8214
          Fax: 863-607-9610
Manufacturer of fruit including watermelon
    Manager: Karen Mason
Estimated Sales: Less than $500,000
Number Employees: 1-4
Type of Packaging: Bulk

4295 Eastern Quebec Sea Foods
1600 Matane-Sur-Mer
Matane, QC G4W 3M6
Canada   418-562-1273
    Fax: 418-562-5407 fmeq@matane-shrimp.ca
Manufacturer and exporter of frozen seafood including shrimp
    Sales Coordinator: Francine Gaudreau
    General Manager: Genevieve Emond
    Contact: George Frafer
Number Employees: 50-99
Type of Packaging: Consumer, Food Service, Private Label, Bulk
Brands:
    Matane

4296 Eastern Sea Products
11 Addison Avenue
Scoudouc, NB E4P 3N3
Canada   506-532-6111
    Fax: 506-532-9111 800-565-6364
    maurice@easternsea.ca www.easternsea.ca
Manufacturer and exporter of salted and smoked seafood: herring, mackerel, salmon
    President: Maurice Allain
    Operations: Donald Richard
Estimated Sales: $1-3 Million
Number Employees: 10-19
Number of Brands: 2
Number of Products: 10
Sq. footage: 12000
Type of Packaging: Consumer, Private Label
Brands:
    Cape Royal
    Seapro

4297 Eastern Seafood Company
1020 W Hubbard St
Chicago, IL 60642-6526   312-243-2090
          Fax: 312-243-9467
Seafood
    President: Mario Falco
Estimated Sales: $ 3 - 5 Million
Number Employees: 5-9

4298 Eastern Shore Seafood Products
P.O.Box 38
Mappsville, VA 23407-0038   757-824-5651
    Fax: 757-987-6543 800-466-8550
          www.easternshoreseafood.com
Manufacturer and exporter of clams and clam products including juice, prepared, canned, frozen, whole, chopped, minced, etc
    President: Rick Myers
    Sales: Denise Chance
    Sales: Scott James
Estimated Sales: $25-49.9 Million
Number Employees: 250-499
Parent Co: Eastern Shore Seafood Products
Type of Packaging: Consumer, Bulk

4299 Eastern Shore Tea
9 W Aylesbury Rd # T
Lutherville, MD 21093-4121   410-561-5079
    Fax: 410-561-4816 800-823-1408
    bct@baltcoffee.com www.easternshoretea.com

Manufacturer of tea including whole leaf and bagged
President: Stanley Constantine
CEO: Janice Burns
Estimated Sales: $5-9.9 Million
Number Employees: 5-9
Type of Packaging: Consumer
Brands:
Baltimore Tea

4300 Eastern Tea Corporation
1 Engelhard Drive
Monroe Township, NJ 08831-3722   609-860-1100
Fax: 609-860-1105   800-221-0865
Manufacturer, importer and exporter of packaged and loose tea; also, tea bags and tapioca
President: Paul Barbakoff
Vice President: Ira Barbakoff
VP of Manufacturing: Glenn Barbakoff
Estimated Sales: $5-10 Million
Number Employees: 50-99
Sq. footage: 90000
Type of Packaging: Consumer, Food Service, Private Label

4301 Eastman Chemical Company
PO Box 431
Kingsport, TN 37662   423-229-2000
Fax: 423-229-2145   800-327-8626
jstokes@eastman.com   www.eastman.com
Chemical, fibers and plastics that are used in the packaging and health and wellness industries as well as many other industries.
President/CEO: James Rogers
SVP/CFO: Curt Espeland
Estimated Sales: $5 Billion
Number Employees: 10,000
Brands:
Nutriene
Tenox

4302 Eastrise Trading Corporation
16281 Gale Ave
City of Industry, CA 91745-1719   626-330-0933
Fax: 626-330-0205 teas@eastrise.com
www.eastriseteas.com
Manufacturer of Teas; certified organic
Owner: Stephen Chau
Estimated Sales: $1-2.5 Million
Number Employees: 5-9
Brands:
RARE TEAS

4303 Eastside Deli Supply
2601 W Main St
Lansing, MI 48917-4344   517-485-4630
Fax: 517-485-7904   800-349-6694
www.eastsidedeli.com
Manufacturer of fresh prepared deli sandwiches and beef jerky
Owner: Tom Jakovac
VP: Thomas Jakovac
Estimated Sales: $10 - 20 Million
Number Employees: 20-49
Sq. footage: 2500
Type of Packaging: Food Service
Brands:
Eastside Deli
Fresh From the Deli
Tillamook Country Smoker

4304 Eastside Seafood
1248 Jeffersonville Rd
Macon, GA 31217-4335   478-743-1888
Fax: 478-272-5800
Manufacturer of Seafood
Owner: Riccardo Del Mastro
Estimated Sales: $300,000-500,000
Number Employees: 1-4

4305 Eat This
PO Box 2474
Breckenridge, CO 80424-2474   970-389-1853
Gourmet sauces, marinades, salsas
President: Roy Leinfuss
Estimated Sales: $300,000-500,000
Number Employees: 1-4
Brands:
Eat This Oriental Marinade
Eat This Strawberry Habenero Sauce

4306 Eat Your Heart Out
332 Bleecker St
New York, NY 10014-6492   212-989-8303
Fax: 212-691-8661
snackgirl@eatyourheartout.com
www.neighborhoodoffice.com
Freze-dried fruit and vegetables snack foods
Owner: Helen Lally
Estimated Sales: $ .5 - 1 million
Number Employees: 1-4
Number of Products: 5

4307 Eatem Foods Company
1829 Gallagher Dr
Vineland, NJ 08360-1548   856-692-1663
Fax: 856-692-0847   800-683-2836
jrandazzi@eatemfoods.com
www.eatemfoods.com
Manufacturer and exporter of all natural food bases including certified organic, GMO-free, kosher and vegetarian; also, flavor and seasoning concentrates, cheese, pepper, gravy and sauce bases and shelf stable broth bases
Owner: Robert Buono
CFO: Bob Buono
Research & Development: Thomas Shaw
Marketing/Sales: Jim Gervato
VP Sales: Jim Gervato
Public Relations: Bob Buono
Plant Manager: Carol Patton
Purchasing: Jerry Santos
Estimated Sales: $50-100 Million
Number Employees: 50-99
Sq. footage: 56000
Type of Packaging: Consumer, Food Service, Bulk
Brands:
Eatem

4308 Eau Galle Cheese Factory Shop
N6765 State Highway 25
Durand, WI 54736-4209   715-283-4211
Fax: 715-283-0711   800-283-1085
info@eaugallecheese.com
www.eaugallecheese.com
Cheese
President: John Buhlman
Estimated Sales: $10-20 Million
Number Employees: 20-49

4309 Eberhard Creamery
PO Box 845
Redmond, OR 97756-0186   541-548-5181
Fax: 541-548-7009
Manufacturer of dairy products and frozen foods
Owner: Jack Eberhard
President: Bob Eberhard
Production Manager: Richard Eberhard
Plant Manager: Jack Eberhard
Estimated Sales: $10-24.9 Million
Number Employees: 40
Type of Packaging: Consumer, Food Service

4310 Eberle Winery
P.O.Box 2459
Paso Robles, CA 93447-2459   805-238-9607
Fax: 805-237-0344 sales@eberlewinery.com
www.eberlewinery.com
Wine
Owner: Gary Eberle
Estimated Sales: $5-10 Million
Number Employees: 20-49

4311 Eberly Poultry
1095 Mount Airy Rd
Stevens, PA 17578-9804   717-336-6440
Fax: 717-336-6905 www.eberlypoultry.com
Poultry
President: Robert Eberly
Estimated Sales: $10 - 20 Million
Number Employees: 50-99

4312 Ebro Foods
1330 W 43rd St
Chicago, IL 60609-3308   773-696-0150
Canned vegetables and sausage
Owner: Silvio Vega
Sales: Marta Jimenez
Production: Steve Abreu
Plant Manager: Silvio Vega
Estimated Sales: $10-24.9 Million
Number Employees: 50-99

4313 Echo Farms Puddings
573 Chesterfield Rd
Hinsdale, NH 03451-2210   603-336-7706
Fax: 603-336-5964   866-488-3246
www.echofarmpuddings.com
Desserts, pudding
Owner: Robert Hodge
Estimated Sales: $ 10 - 20 Million
Number Employees: 10-19
Brands:
ECHO FARM PUDDING

4314 Echo Lake Farm Produce Company
P.O.Box 279
Burlington, WI 53105-0279   262-763-9551
Fax: 262-763-4593 c.bull@echoforeggs.com
www.echoforeggs.com
Frozen and liquid egg processing, pancakes, French toast, waffle, crepe and blintz manufacturing
Manager: Jerry Warntjes
VP: Jerry Warntjes
Sales Manager: Scott Hall
Operations: David Warntjes
Estimated Sales: $20-50 Million
Number Employees: 100-249
Type of Packaging: Consumer, Food Service, Private Label, Bulk

4315 Echo Spring Dairy
706 Oscar St
Eugene, OR 97402-5322   541-342-1291
Fax: 541-342-8379
Manufacturer of dairy products
Manager: Mike Miller
Estimated Sales: $10-20 Million
Number Employees: 20-49
Parent Co: Darigold
Type of Packaging: Consumer, Food Service

4316 Eckert Cold Storage
905 Clough Rd
Escalon, CA 95320-8647   209-838-4040
Fax: 209-838-4049 eckert@thevision.net
Manufacturer of IQF red, green and yellow bell and jalapeno peppers, cabbage leaves, diced cabbage, bok choy, kabocha and mangos
President: G P Thompson
VP: Craig West
VP Quality Control: Mark Thompson
Estimated Sales: $100+ Million
Number Employees: 250-499
Sq. footage: 100000
Type of Packaging: Bulk

4317 (HQ)Eckhart Corporation
7110 Redwood Blvd # A
Novato, CA 94945-4141   415-898-9528
Fax: 415-898-1917   800-200-4201
info@eckhartcorp.com   www.eckhartcorp.com
Manufacturer and exporter of vitamins, food supplements and diet aids including antioxidants, royal jelly, fish oil, fiber, herbs, amino acids, beta carotene, etc.; importer of vitamins
President: Deepak Chopra
Marketing/Sales: Ryan Friman
Purchasing: Kathleen McClendon
Estimated Sales: $20-50 Million
Number Employees: 10-19
Sq. footage: 160000
Type of Packaging: Consumer, Food Service, Private Label, Bulk
Brands:
Nature's Edge
Stay Well

4318 Eckhart Seed Company
P.O.Box 7176
Spreckels, CA 93962-7176   831-758-0925
Fax: 831-758-0388 baney12@aol.com
Manufacturer of dried beans
President: Andrew Smith
Secretary: Peter Eckhart
VP: Richard Eckhart
Estimated Sales: Less than $500,000
Number Employees: 10-19
Type of Packaging: Bulk

4319 Eckroat Seed Company
1106 N Martin Luther King Ave
Oklahoma City, OK 73117-4226   405-427-2484
Fax: 405-427-7174 www.eckroatseed.com

Manufacturer, importer and exporter of mung beans
President: Robert Eckroat
VP: Don Eckroat
Estimated Sales: $5-10 Million
Number Employees: 10-19
Sq. footage: 100000
Type of Packaging: Consumer, Food Service, Private Label, Bulk
Brands:
Green Dragon

4320 Eclectic Institute
36350 Industrial Way
Sandy, OR 97055-7377   503-668-4120
Fax: 503-668-3227
customerservice@eclecticherb.com
www.eclecticherb.com
Organic alcohol extracts, alcohol free glycerins and
nutritional supplements.
Owner: Edward Alstat
Estimated Sales: $ 5 - 10 Million
Number Employees: 50-99

4321 Eclipse Sports Supplements
PO Box 79
Scranton, PA 18504-0079   800-320-0062
Fax: 570-504-1503   eclipseCEC@exite.com
www.eclipse2000.com
Sports supplements
Brands:
ECLIPSE2000

4322 Eco Foods
2905 W Main Street
St Charles, IL 60175-1020   630-443-1646
Fax: 630-377-2996   866-326-1646
www.ecobar.com
Manufacturer of energy snacks
Brands:
ECOBAR

4323 Eco-Cuisine
P.O.Box 19006
Boulder, CO 80308-2006   303-444-6634
Fax: 303-444-6647   ron@eco-cuisine.com
www.ecocycle.org
Manufacturer of vegetarian, organic and kosher
mixes for bakery items and meat analogs, vegetarian
broth powders, instant soy puddings, pancakes
Executive Director: Eric Lombardi
VP: Nancy Loving
Estimated Sales: $ 20 - 50 Million
Number Employees: 50-99
Number of Brands: 13
Number of Products: 25
Type of Packaging: Consumer, Food Service, Private Label, Bulk
Brands:
Eco-Cuisine

4324 EcoNatural Solutions
997 Dixon Rd
Boulder, CO 80302-8798   303-527-1554
Fax: 303-527-3885   877-684-5159
customerservice@econaturals.com
www.stclaires.com
Manufacturer and exporter of organic sweets
CEO: Debra St Claire
Estimated Sales: $2.5-5 Million
Number Employees: 5-9
Type of Packaging: Consumer
Brands:
St. Claire

4325 Ecom Agroindustrial Corporation Ltd
17 State Street
23rd Floor
New York, NY 10004   212-248-7475
Fax: 212-248-1816   www.ecomtrading.com
Cocoa powder, cocoa butter, cocoa liquor, cocoa
beans
Vice President: Pablo Esteve
Research & Development: Nar Lin
Estimated Sales: $2 Billion
Number Employees: 1000
Type of Packaging: Consumer
Brands:
AMSA
ECOM COCOA

4326 Ecom Manufacturing Corporation
80 Telson Road
Markham, ON L3R 1E5
Canada   905-477-2441
Fax: 905-477-2511   dsoknacki@ecomcanada.com
www.ecomcanada.com
Manufacturer of natural colors and flavors including
garlic, onion, rosemary, allspice, turmeric, jalapeno,
cilantro and nutmeg
President: David Soknacki
Sales/Marketing: Kan Husband
Plant Manager: Hoody Minski
Number Employees: 20-49
Type of Packaging: Bulk

4327 Ed & Don's Candies
4462 Malaai St
Honolulu, HI 96818-3134   808-423-8200
Fax: 808-423-0550
eddons.generalmanager@verizon.net
www.edanddons.com
Manufacturer of Chocolate candies
President: Earl Kurisu
Sales Manager: Gladys Ornellas
Estimated Sales: $5-9.9 Million
Number Employees: 20-49
Type of Packaging: Private Label
Brands:
Ed & Don's Chocolate Macadamias
Ed & Don's Macadamia Brittles
Ed & Don's Macadamia Chews

4328 Ed Kasilof's Seafoods
P.O.Box 18
Kasilof, AK 99610-0018   907-262-7295
Fax: 907-262-1617   800-982-2377
eks@alaska.net   www.kasilofseafoods.com
Seafood
President: James Trujillo
Estimated Sales: $ 5 - 10 Million
Number Employees: 10-19

4329 Ed Miniat
1055 175th St # 201
Homewood, IL 60430-4616   708-957-3800
Fax: 708-957-7413   www.miniat.com
Processor of cooked beef and pork products; also,
shortenings and oils
Owner/President: Dave Miniat
COO: Don Ervin
Sales/Marketing Executive: Chuck Nalon
Estimated Sales: $ 5 - 10 Million
Number Employees: 20-49
Type of Packaging: Bulk

4330 (HQ)Ed Miniat
1055 175th St # 201
Homewood, IL 60430-4616   708-957-3800
Fax: 708-957-7413   www.miniat.com
Frozen prepared meats
President: Ed Miniat
Executive VP: Michael Miniat
Sales Manager: Chuck Nalon
Production: David Jackson
Plant Manager: Neil Brodrick
Purchasing: Richard Krups
Estimated Sales: $ 5 - 10 Million
Number Employees: 20-49

4331 Ed Oliveira Winery
156 Center Street
Arcata, CA 95521-6056   707-822-3023
Manufacturer of Wines
President: Douglas Oliveira
Estimated Sales: Under $500,000
Number Employees: 1-4

4332 Ed's Honey Company
497 10th Ave SE
Dickinson, ND 58601-7421   701-225-9223
Manufacturer of honey
Owner: Ed Fetch
Estimated Sales: $2.5-5 Million
Number Employees: 1-4
Type of Packaging: Consumer

4333 Eda's Sugarfree Candies
4900 N 20th St
Philadelphia, PA 19144-2402   215-324-3412
Fax: 215-324-3413   edasugarfree@msn.com
www.edasugarfree.com
Processor and exporter of sugar-free hard candies
President: Brian Berry
Vice President: Dan Harasewyah

Number of Brands: 1
Number of Products: 28
Sq. footage: 20000
Parent Co: Lehman Sugarfree Confectionery
Type of Packaging: Consumer, Food Service, Private Label, Bulk
Brands:
EDA SUGARFREE HARD CANDIES

4334 Eddy's Bakery
380 N Five Mile Rd
Boise, ID 83713-8959   208-377-8100
Fax: 208-322-7823
Manfuacturer of baked goods including bread and
cakes
Sales Manager: Gary Davis
Estimated Sales: $ 3 - 5 Million
Number Employees: 1-4
Type of Packaging: Consumer

4335 Edelman Meats
P.O.Box 433
Antigo, WI 54409-0433   715-623-7686
Fax: 715-623-7688
Manufacturer of beef, pork, chicken, fish, etc
President: Joseph Edelman
Estimated Sales: $20-50 Million
Number Employees: 10-19
Type of Packaging: Food Service

4336 (HQ)Edelmann Provision Company
517 Commercial Drive
Fairfield, OH 45014-7594   513-881-5801
Fax: 513-881-5803   www.freshsausage.com
Manufacturer of fresh sausage
President: James Frondorf
Estimated Sales: $14.10 Million
Number Employees: 50

4337 Edelweiss Patisserie
56 Roland St # 200
Charlestown, MA 02129-1233   617-628-0225
Fax: 617-628-0882   rcebi@edelweisspastry.com
www.hbook.com
Manufacturer of baked goods including cakes, pastries, muffins, croissants, pullman and tea loaves, rustic breads, cookies, etc
Manager: Roger Sutton
Estimated Sales: $20-50 Million
Number Employees: 50-99
Type of Packaging: Food Service

4338 (HQ)Eden Foods Inc
701 Tecumseh Rd
Clinton, MI 49236-9599   517-456-7424
Fax: 517-456-6075   800-248-0320
info@edenfoods.com   www.edenfoods.com
Manufacturer, importer and exporter of natural and
organic foods including pasta, soymilk, green tea,
beans, tomatoes, spaghetti sauce, etc
President/CEO: Michael Potter
CFO: Jay Hughes
Vice President: Jim Fox
Quality Control: Jon Solomon
Marketing VP: Sue Becker
Sales: Demian Potter
VP Operations: William Swaney
Estimated Sales: $20-50 Million
Number Employees: 100-249
Type of Packaging: Food Service
Brands:
EDEN
EDEN ORGANIC
EDENBALANCE
EDENBLEND
EDENSOY
EDENSOY EXTRA

4339 Eden Organic Pasta Company
9104 Culver St
Detroit, MI 48213-2237   313-921-2053
Fax: 313-921-0282   800-248-0320
info@edenfoods.com   www.edenfoods.com
Manufacturer of organic and vegetable pastas
Manager: Steven Swaney
Vice President: Jim Fox
Chief Financial Officer: Jay Hughes
General Manager: Steve Swaney
Operations Manager: William Swaney
Estimated Sales: $2.5-5 Million
Number Employees: 10-19
Parent Co: Eden Foods
Type of Packaging: Food Service

Other Locations:
Eden Foods Plant
Detroit MI
Eden Foods Plant
Union City CA
Brands:
EDEN'S

4340 Eden Processing
100 East Street
Poplar Grove, IL 61065-9787   815-765-2000
Fax: 815-765-2777 www.edencherry.com
Manufacturer of bakers' and confectioners' supplies
including maraschino cherries, sweetened coconut,
mince meat pie fillings, orange, lemon, melon,
grapefruit and citron peels, etc
President, CEO: Louis Tenore, Jr.
Marketing Director: Pam McDowell
Estimated Sales: $3.10 Million
Number Employees: 14
Sq. footage: 55000
Type of Packaging: Bulk
Brands:
True Blue

4341 Eden Vineyards Winery
19709 Little Ln
Alva, FL 33920-3706   239-728-9463
info@edenwinery.com
www.edenwinery.com
Wines
President: Earl Kiser
Estimated Sales: $1-2.5 Million
Number Employees: 1-4

4342 Edgar A. Weber Company
562 Chaddick Dr
Wheeling, IL 60090-6056   847-215-1980
Fax: 847-215-2073 800-558-9078
info@weberflavors.com www.weberflavors.com
Manufacturer and exporter of flavoring extracts for
wine, liquor, baked goods and ice cream
Owner: Andrew Plennert
Customer Service: Linda DeLeo
Sales Administration: Judith Turyna
Estimated Sales: $20-50 Million
Number Employees: 50-99
Brands:
Hy Van
Simply Natural
Simply Natural-Like

4343 Edge Labs
PO Box 33067
Trenton, NJ 08629-3067   732-617-1100
Fax: 732-536-9179 866-334-3522
info@edgelabsproducts.com www.edgelabs.com
Powdered drink dietary suuplements.
Marketing Manager: Cindy Filippone

4344 Edgewood Estate Winery
607 Airpark Road
Napa, CA 94558-6272   800-755-2374
Fax: 707-254-4920 sales@edgewoodestate.com
www.edgewoodestate.com
Wines
CEO: Jeff O'Neill
CFO: John Kelleher
Sales: Steve Lindsay
Purchasing: David Weckerle
Estimated Sales: $1-2.5 Million
Number Employees: 7
Number of Brands: 1
Number of Products: 14
Sq. footage: 70000
Parent Co: Golden State Vintners
Type of Packaging: Consumer, Private Label
Brands:
EDGEWOOD ESTATE

4345 (HQ)Edlong Dairy Flavors
225 Scott St
Elk Grove Vlg, IL 60007-1212   847-439-9230
Fax: 847-439-0053 888-698-2783
info@edlong.com www.edlongflavors.com

Concentrated Dairy flavors. Flavors are available in
liquid, powder, emulsion, paste and spray-dried
forms and a variety of solubilities. Specialties in-
clude cheese, butter, dairy, dairy brown and func-
tional dairy flavors.
President: Laurie Smith
CEO: Eugene Rondenet
CFO: Harold Stover
Finance VP: Paul Simkus
R&D VP: Eric Johnson
Marketing/Sales VP: Paula Gallagher
Public Relations: David Booth
Purchasing: Cindy Johnson
Estimated Sales: $50-100 Million
Number Employees: 50-99
Sq. footage: 90000
Type of Packaging: Food Service, Private Label,
Bulk
Other Locations:
Edlong Dairy Flavors
Suffolk
Edlong Dairy Flavors
United Kingdom
Edlong Dairy Flavors
Mexico City
Brands:
CAPSULONG
CHEOLONG
ED-VANCE
VISION

4346 Edmac Foods
PO Box 467
Woodruff, WI 54568-0467   715-356-5394
Fax: 715-358-2989
Meat packing
Chairman/President: Edward McFadden
General Manager/Sales: Ed McFadden
Production Manager: Mike McFadden
Brands:
Edmac

4347 Edmonds Chile Company
3236 Oregon Ave
St Louis, MO 63118-3004   314-772-1499
Fax: 314-664-7735
Manufacturer of sliced pork and gravy, sliced beef
and gravy, beef au jus, vegetable soup, beef stew,
meat sauce, beef chili, chili con carne, beef patties
and tamales
President: Mark Adelman
Estimated Sales: $2.5-5 Million
Number Employees: 10-19
Type of Packaging: Consumer

**4348 Edmonton Meat Packing
Company**
8310 Yellowhead Trail NW
Edmonton, AB T5B 1GS
Canada   780-474-2471
Fax: 780-479-6167 800-361-6328
Manufacturer and exporter of fresh and frozen beef,
pork, lamb, veal, smoked meats, sausage and sea-
food
Plant Manager: Bruce Larson
Number Employees: 100-249
Type of Packaging: Consumer, Food Service, Bulk

4349 Edmonton Potato Growers
12220 170th Street NW
Edmonton, AB T5V 1L7
Canada   780-447-1860
Fax: 780-447-1899 admin@epg.ab.ca
www.epg.ab.ca
Manufacturer and exmporter of potatoes including
table, seed and processed, onions
President: Wayne Groot
Sales: Darcy Olson
General Manager: Bob Jensen
Number Employees: 35
Type of Packaging: Consumer, Food Service, Bulk
Brands:
CANADA GOOSE

4350 Edmunds St. John
1331 Walnut St
Berkeley, CA 94709-1408   510-981-1510
Fax: 510-981-1610 www.edmundstjohn.com
Wine
President: Steve Edmunds
Estimated Sales: $1-2.5 Million
Number Employees: 1-4

4351 Edna Valley Vineyard
2585 Biddle Ranch Rd
San Luis Obispo, CA 93401-8319   805-544-5855
Fax: 805-544-0112 info@ednavalley.com
www.ednavalley.com
Manufacturer of table wines including chardonnay
and pinot noir
Manager: Harry Hansen
Estimated Sales: $5-10 Million
Number Employees: 20-49
Parent Co: Chalone Company
Type of Packaging: Consumer, Food Service, Pri-
vate Label
Brands:
Edna Valley
Videyards

4352 Edner Corporation
1200 Zephyr Ave
Hayward, CA 94544-7937   510-441-8504
Fax: 510-441-9395
Manufacturer of breads (specialty), cakes, cookies,
croissants (filled and unfilled), muffins, pastries, &
scones (filled and unfilled)
President: Ed Kirschner
VP Technical Sales: Mark Aquilar
Estimated Sales: $10-20 Million
Number Employees: 10-19
Parent Co: Edner Corporation
Type of Packaging: Consumer, Food Service, Pri-
vate Label, Bulk
Brands:
Edna Foods
Extreme
Huckleberry
Jonathan International Foods
La Patisserie
Warfarers

4353 (HQ)Edom Laboratories
100 E Jefryn Blvd # M
Deer Park, NY 11729-5729   631-586-2266
Fax: 631-586-2385 800-723-3366
www.edomlaboratories.com
Manufacturer, exporter and wholesaler/distributor of
vitamins and dietary supplements
President: Arthur Pollack
Estimated Sales: $20-50 Million
Number Employees: 1-4
Type of Packaging: Consumer, Private Label, Bulk

**4354 Edward & Sons Trading
Company**
P.O.Box 1326
Carpinteria, CA 93014-1326   805-684-8500
Fax: 805-684-8220 info@edwardsons.com
www.edwardandsons.com
Manufacturer, importer and exporter of natural, or-
ganic and specialty foods: condiments, confection-
ery products, crackers, vegetarian soup mixes, snack
foods, canned organic vegetables, vegetarian bouil-
lon cubes, cake decorationsorganic coconut milk
President: Joel Dee
Vice President: Alison Cox
Operations Manager: Dean Seicher
Estimated Sales: $ 5 - 10 Million
Number Employees: 10-19
Type of Packaging: Consumer, Food Service, Pri-
vate Label
Brands:
EDWARD&SONS
HERITAGE SOUPS
LET'S DO
LET'S DO ORGANIC
NATIVE FOREST
ORGANIC COUNTRY
PREMIER JAPAN
RAINFOREST ORGANIC
TROY'S
WIZARDS

4355 Edwards Baking Company
1 Lemon Ln NE
Atlanta, GA 30307-2860   404-377-0511
Fax: 404-378-2074 800-241-0559
www.edwardsbaking.com
Frozen dessert pies
Manager: Brian Schneider
Executive VP: J Riesch
Sales/Marketing Manager: Jerry Hanna
Operations Director: Joe Leonardo
Plant Manager: Joe Leonardo
Estimated Sales: $20-50 Million
Number Employees: 250-499

4356 Edwards Mill
P.O.Box 17
Point Lookout, MO 65726-0017   417-334-6411
        Fax: 417-335-2618   800-222-0525
        admiss4@cofo.edu   www.cofo.edu
Manufacturer of whole grains that are blended into mixes; pancake, waffle, biscuit, muffin, fruitcakes, jams, jelly, preserves, apple butter
    President: Jerry Davis

4357 Edy's Grand Ice Cream
601 Wall St
Glendale Heights, IL 60139-1906   630-924-7755
        Fax: 630-924-8336   888-377-3397
                        www.edys.com
Manufacturer and wholesaler/distributor of ice cream and frozen yogurt; serving the food service market
    Finance Executive: Marshall Osterloh
    Business Development Manager: Nick De Pinto
    Sales/Marketing Executive: Patty SanFilippo
    Regional Manager: Mike Olsen
Estimated Sales: $100-500 Million
Number Employees: 100-249
Parent Co: Dreyer's Grand Ice Cream
Type of Packaging: Consumer, Food Service

4358 Edy's Grand Ice Cream
301 Round Hill Drive
Rockaway, NJ 07866-1224   973-627-5935
        Fax: 973-627-7005   800-362-7899
Manufacturer of ice cream cones and sandwiches, ice pops, fruit bars and frozen yogurt; serving retail grocery markets
    Division Marketing Manager: Ellen Sparano
    Division Manager (Northeast): Stan Fabian
Estimated Sales: $100-500 Million
Number Employees: 250-499
Parent Co: Dreyer's Grand Ice Cream
Type of Packaging: Consumer
Brands:
    EDY'S

4359 Edy's Grand Ice Cream
3255 Meridian Pkwy
Weston, FL 33331-3503   954-384-7133
        Fax: 954-384-0815
Manufacturer of dairy products including ice cream and frozen yogurt; serving supermarket chains and restaurants
    Manager: Gary Bruner
    District Manager: Mark Servaes
Estimated Sales: $50-100 Million
Number Employees: 50-99
Sq. footage: 20000
Parent Co: Dreyer's Grand Ice Cream
Type of Packaging: Consumer, Food Service

4360 Edy's Grand Ice Cream
3426 N Wells St
Fort Wayne, IN 46808-4043   260-483-3102
        Fax: 260-482-4152   www.edys.com
Manufacturer of ice cream, sherbet and frozen yogurt
    Manager: Wayne Clive
    Plant Manager: John Williams
    Purchasing Agent: Dan Tague
Estimated Sales: $50-100 Million
Number Employees: 250-499
Parent Co: Dreyer's Grand Ice Cream
Type of Packaging: Consumer, Food Service

4361 Efco Products
130 Smith St
Poughkeepsie, NY 12601-2109   845-452-4715
        Fax: 845-452-5607   800-284-3326
                service@efcoproducts.com
                www.efcoproducts.com
Bakery mixes and ingredients, fruit and creme-style fillings, jellies, jams, and concentrated icing fruits
    Chairman: Jack Effron
    President: Ira Effron
Estimated Sales: $2.5-5 Million
Number Employees: 50-99

4362 Effie's Homemade
One Westinghouse Plaza
Hyde Park, MA 02136   617-364-9300
        Fax: 617-364-9333   info@effieshomemade.com
                www.effieshomemade.com
all natural oatcakes and crispy corncakes
    President/Owner: Joan MacIsaac

4363 Egg Company
756 Sizer Road
Gurnee, IL 60031-3173   847-367-8553
        Fax: 847-367-8554   onlyegg@aol.com
Egg and chicken products dried
Estimated Sales: $20 Million
Number Employees: 1-4

4364 Egg Cream America
633 Skokie Boulevard
Suite 205
Northbrook, IL 60062-2858   847-559-2703
        Fax: 847-559-2709   getcreamed@aol.com
                www.getcreamed.com
Dairy based carbonated beverages
Estimated Sales: $1-5 Million
Number Employees: 5-9

4365 Egg Low Farms
35 W State St
Sherburne, NY 13460-9424   607-674-4653
        Fax: 607-674-9216   www.egglowfarms.com
Fresh eggs including diced and scrambled. Also salad ready diced eggs and tray ready scrambled eggs; all fresh
    President: Helen Dunckel
    CEO: David Dunckel
Estimated Sales: $1-2.5 Million
Number Employees: 5-9
Sq. footage: 40000
Type of Packaging: Food Service, Private Label
Brands:
    Egg Low Farms
    The Unbeatable Eatable Egg

4366 Egg Roll Fantasy
PO Box 7895
Auburn, CA 95604-7895   530-887-9197
        Fax: 530-887-9199
Manufacturer of gourmet egg rolls
    President: Louie Buendia
    VP: Robert DiMiceli
Estimated Sales: $500,000-$1 Million
Number Employees: 10
Number of Brands: 3
Number of Products: 20
Sq. footage: 4000
Type of Packaging: Consumer, Food Service, Private Label, Bulk

4367 Eggland's Best Foods
860 First Ave # 842
King of Prussia, PA 19406-4033   610-265-6500
        Fax: 610-265-8380   888-922-3447
        ataylor@eggland.com   www.eggland.com
Manufacturer of Dairy, organic eggs
    President/CEO: Charles Lanktree
    Director Quality Assurance: Bart Slaugh PhD
    Marketing Manager: Francis Kane
Estimated Sales: $10-20 Million
Number Employees: 10-19
Type of Packaging: Private Label
Brands:
    Cage Free Organic
    Eggland's Best
    Eggs & More
    Eggs To Go

4368 Eggology
6728 Eton Ave
Canoga Park, CA 91303-2813   818-610-2222
        Fax: 818-610-2223   information@eggology.com
                www.eggology.com
Manufacturer of pure liquid egg whites
    President: Brad Halpern
Estimated Sales: $5 - 10 Million
Number Employees: 20-49

4369 Egon Binkert Meat Products
8805 Philadelphia Rd
Baltimore, MD 21237-4310   410-687-5959
        Fax: 410-687-5023
Manufacturer and distributor of German style lunch meats and sausages
    Owner: Sonya Weber
Estimated Sales: $300,000-500,000
Number Employees: 1-4
Sq. footage: 2800

4370 Egypt Star Bakery
2225 Macarthur Rd
Whitehall, PA 18052-4521   610-434-3762
        Fax: 610-443-1915

Breads, rolls
    President: Esther Erdossy
Estimated Sales: $500,000-$1 Million
Number Employees: 10-19

4371 Ehmann Olive Company
1800 Idora St
Oroville, CA 95966-6767   530-533-3303
        Fax: 530-534-8137
Manufacturer of green and black olives
    Manager: Jose Gonzales
Estimated Sales: $ 10 - 20 Million
Number Employees: 20-49
Parent Co: George DeLallo
Type of Packaging: Consumer, Food Service, Private Label
Brands:
    Delallo
    Ehmann

4372 Ehresman Packing Company
P.O.Box 403
Garden City, KS 67846-0403   620-276-3791
        Fax: 620-276-1916
Manufacturer of meat products; also, custom butchering available
    Co-Owner: Mike Plankenhorn
    Co-Owner: Velda Plankenhorn
Estimated Sales: $5-10 Million
Number Employees: 10-19
Type of Packaging: Consumer, Private Label

4373 Ehrle Brothers Winery
P.O.Box 10
Homestead, IA 52236-0010   319-622-3241
        Fax: 319-622-6085
Manufacturer of wines including grape and rhubarb
    President: Don Krauss
    Sales Manager: Ray Krauss
Estimated Sales: $3-5 Million
Number Employees: 5-9
Type of Packaging: Consumer

4374 Eickman's Processing
P.O.Box 118
Seward, IL 61077-0118   815-247-8451
        Fax: 815-247-8463
Manufacturer of beef, pork, lamb and wild game
    President: Mike Eickman
Estimated Sales: $2.5-5 Million
Number Employees: 20-49
Type of Packaging: Consumer, Food Service

4375 Eidon Mineral Supplements
12330 Stowe Dr
Poway, CA 92064-6802   858-668-0900
        Fax: 858-668-3593   800-700-1169
        questions@eidon.com   www.eidon.com
Manufacturer of mineral supplements
    Manager: Deborah Stewart
    VP: Fred Elsner
    Sales Director: Barbara G.
    Production Manager: Cory Wagner
    Plant Manager: Cory Wagner
Estimated Sales: $1 Million
Number Employees: 5-9
Number of Brands: 1
Number of Products: 30
Sq. footage: 11500
Type of Packaging: Consumer, Private Label, Bulk

4376 Eilenberger Bakery
P.O.Box 710
Palestine, TX 75802-0710   903-729-2253
        Fax: 903-723-2915   800-831-2544
                sales@eilenbergerbakery.com
                www.eilenberger.com
Manufacturer of gourmet cakes and brownies
    President: Tresas Smith
Estimated Sales: $ 3 - 5 Million
Number Employees: 20-49

4377 Eiserman Meats
900b S Main Street Ss 3
Slave Lake, AB T0G 2A3
Canada   780-849-5507
        Fax: 780-849-6097   info@eisermanmeats.com
                www.eisermanmeats.com
Manufacturer of fresh beef, pork, sausage and wild game; also, beef jerky; slaughtering services available
    President/Co-Owner: Russell Eiserman
    Co-Owner: Annellen Eiserman
Type of Packaging: Consumer

4378 El Aguila Food Products
42 W Market St
Salinas, CA 93901-2653   831-422-3629
Fax: 831-422-3328   800-398-2929
www.elaguila.com
Manufacturer of corn and flour tortillas and other mexican food products
President: Russel Chisum
Estimated Sales: $50-100 Million
Number Employees: 50-99
Type of Packaging: Consumer, Food Service, Private Label, Bulk
Brands:
EL AGUILIA

4379 El Brands
267 Van Heusen Drive
Ozark, AL 36360-1054   334-445-2828
Fax: 334-352-7263
Manufacturer of peanuts
CEO: Ed Lindley
VP Sales/Marketing: Steve Ratliff

4380 El Charro Mexican Food Industries
1711 S Virginia Ave
Roswell, NM 88203-1829   575-622-8590
Fax: 575-622-8590   ectortilla@yahoo.com
Manufacturer and exporter of chili sauce and tortilla chips
Owner: Michael Trujillo
Owner: Mireya Trujillo
Estimated Sales: $5-10 Million
Number Employees: 10-19
Type of Packaging: Consumer, Food Service, Private Label, Bulk
Brands:
EL CHARRO
LA PABLANITA

4381 El Charro Mexican Foods
1711 S Virginia Ave
Roswell, NM 88203-1829   575-622-8590
Fax: 575-622-8590
Tortillas
President: Michael Trujillo
Estimated Sales: $500-1 Million appx.
Number Employees: 10-19
Type of Packaging: Private Label
Brands:
Don Jose's
Elcharro
Lapoblanita

4382 El Dorado Coffee
5675 49th St
Flushing, NY 11378-2012   718-418-4100
Fax: 718-418-4500   800-635-2566
info@eldoradocoffee.com
www.eldoradocoffee.com
Manufacturer and roaster of coffee
President: Segunda Martin
Vice President: John Canal
VP: Andres Martin
Estimated Sales: $20-50 Million
Number Employees: 20-49
Type of Packaging: Consumer, Food Service, Private Label
Brands:
EL DORADO COFFEE ROASTERS

4383 El Galindo
3709 Promontory Point Drive
Austin, TX 78744-1112   512-478-5756
Fax: 512-478-5839
Manufacturer of corn and flour tortillas, tortilla chips, tostadas, taco shells and chalupa shells
President/Owner: Ernestine Galindo
Estimated Sales: $50-100 Million
Number Employees: 50-99
Type of Packaging: Consumer, Food Service
Brands:
EL GALINDO

4384 El Grano De Oro
1710 Francisco Blvd
Pacifica, CA 94044-2515   650-355-8417
Fax: 650-355-7705
Mexican Restaurant
Owner: Mauricio Garcia
Estimated Sales: $1-2.5 Million
Number Employees: 10-19

4385 El Matador Foods
7201 Bayway Dr
Baytown, TX 77520-1303   281-838-1375
Fax: 281-838-1375
Manufacturer of Tortilla chips
Owner: Erick Ybarra
Director: John Eric Ybrra
Estimated Sales: $10-24.9 Million
Number Employees: 5-9
Brands:
El Matador Tortilla Chip

4386 El Molino Winery
P.O.Box 306
St Helena, CA 94574-0306   707-963-3632
Fax: 707-963-1647   info@elmolinowinery.com
www.elmolinowinery.com
Manufacturer of Wine
Sales/Marketing: Mimi Buttenheim
General Manager: Lily Oliver
Winemaker: Jon Berlin
Labelling/Foiling Wines: Altagracia Rincon
Estimated Sales: Less than $500,000
Number Employees: 1-4

4387 El Paso Chile Company
909 Texas Ave
El Paso, TX 79901-1524   915-544-3434
Fax: 915-544-7552   888-472-5727
info@alpasochile.com   www.elpasochile.com
Manufacturer of Salsas, condiments, barbecue sauce, trail mixes, nuts, drink mixes, spices and fixings
Owner: William Parker
VP: Norma Kerr
Estimated Sales: $10-20 Million
Number Employees: 20-49
Type of Packaging: Private Label

4388 El Paso Meat Company
1523 Myrtle Ave
El Paso, TX 79901-1796   915-838-8600
Fax: 915-533-3997
Manufacturer of fresh and frozen beef and pork; slaughtering services available
Owner: Francis Ramos
General Manager: Javier Garcia
Estimated Sales: $3-5 Million
Number Employees: 5-9
Type of Packaging: Consumer, Food Service

4389 El Paso Winery
742 Broadway
Ulster Park, NY 12487-5407   845-331-8642
www.elpasowinery.com
Manufacturer of red, white and rose wines
Owner: Maryl Marino-Vogel
Co-Owner: Maryl Vogel
Operations Manager: Felipe Beltra
Estimated Sales: Less than $500,000
Number Employees: 1-4
Type of Packaging: Consumer, Food Service

4390 El Perico Charro
204 N 7th St
Garden City, KS 67846-5519   620-275-6454
Manufacturer and retailers of Mexican foods, tortillas
President/CEO: Natividad Hernandez
Estimated Sales: $500,000-$1 Million
Number Employees: 1-4
Number of Products: 2
Type of Packaging: Consumer, Food Service

4391 El Peto Products
65 Saltsman Drive
Cambridge, ON N3H 4R7
Canada   519-650-4614
Fax: 519-650-5692   800-387-4064
info@elpeto.com   www.elpeto.com
Manufacturer and exporter of wheat, gluten and milk-free products including baking mixes, breads, muffins, cakes, buns, pies, cookies, frozen doughs and batters, pastas, soups and specialty flours
President: Elisabeth Riesen
VP: Peter Riesen
Number Employees: 19
Number of Brands: 3
Sq. footage: 4500
Type of Packaging: Consumer, Food Service, Bulk
Brands:
El Peto

4392 El Ranchito
19422 SE Stark St
Portland, OR 97233-5755   503-665-4919
Fax: 503-669-2503
Manufacturer of Mexican spices
Owner: Francisco Sanchez
VP Sales/Marketing: Paul Bradley
Estimated Sales: $ .5 - 1 million
Number Employees: 10-19
Type of Packaging: Consumer, Food Service

4393 El Rancho Tortilla
623 New Laredo Hwy
San Antonio, TX 78211-1929   210-922-8411
Fax: 210-922-9159
Manufacturer of corn and flour tortillas, tostadas, taco shells and picante sauce
Owner: Ruben Martinez
Estimated Sales: $2.5-5 Million
Number Employees: 10-19
Type of Packaging: Consumer

4394 El Segundo Bakery
219 W Grand Avenue
El Segundo, CA 90245-3740   310-322-3422
Fax: 310-322-8760
Manufacturer of cakes, danish, bread, rolls, cookies, decorated cakes and wedding cakes
President: Arthur Miltenberger
VP: Lisa Miltenberger
Sales: Peter Miltenberger
Production: Arthur Miltenberger
Estimated Sales: $900,000
Number Employees: 10
Sq. footage: 45800
Type of Packaging: Consumer, Food Service

4395 El Toro Food Products
504 El Rio Street
Watsonville, CA 95076-3540   831-728-9266
Fax: 831-688-8766   oeltoro@pacbell.net
Manufacture of canned salsas varieties including sauces and vegetables
President: Richard Thomas
Estimated Sales: $5-10 Million
Number Employees: 5-9
Number of Brands: 6
Number of Products: 10
Sq. footage: 6000
Type of Packaging: Food Service, Private Label, Bulk

4396 El-Milagro
3050 W 26th St
Chicago, IL 60623-4130   773-847-9407
Fax: 773-650-4692   www.elmilagro.com
Manufacturer and exporter of Mexican foods including corn flour tortillas and tortilla chips
President: Raphael Lopez
Director Marketing: Jesus Lopez
Estimated Sales: $20-50 Million
Number Employees: 50-99
Type of Packaging: Consumer, Food Service

4397 El-Rey Foods
6190 Bermuda Dr
Ferguson, MO 63135-3298   314-521-3113
Manufacturer and exporter of frozen foods including chili, tamales, roast and barbecued beef, taco meat and pork; also, barbecue sauce
Owner: Joseph Frisella
Estimated Sales: $10-20 Million
Number Employees: 5-9
Sq. footage: 2000
Type of Packaging: Consumer, Food Service
Brands:
Chef's Helper
Menu a La Carte

4398 Elan Chemical Company
268 Doremus Ave
Newark, NJ 07105-4875   973-344-8014
Fax: 973-344-1948   sales@elan-chemical.com
www.elan-chemical.com
Manufacturer and exporter of organic kosher certified vanilla extract, flavoring and synthetic and natural aromatic chemicals
President: Jocelyn Manship
VP Sales: Mike Shragher
Estimated Sales: $20-50 Million
Number Employees: 50-99
Type of Packaging: Bulk

4399 Elan Nutrition
4490 44th St SE
Grand Rapids, MI 49512-4011   616-940-6000
    Fax: 616-940-9971 www.elannutrition.com
Manufacturer of Nutritional products
    President/CEO: David Finnigan
    Accounts Manager: Pam Lauroff
    CEO: Tom Olive
    Sales: Lee Covert
Estimated Sales: $75-125 Million
Number Employees: 100-249
Sq. footage: 230000
Type of Packaging: Private Label

4400 Elba Custom Meats
405 Alabama Highway 203
Elba, AL 36323-4217   334-897-2007
Manufacturer of meat products
    Owner: Billy F Hudson
    General Manager: F Hudson
Estimated Sales: $1 - 3 Million
Number Employees: 1-4
Type of Packaging: Consumer

4401 (HQ)Eldorado Artesian Springs
P.O.Box 445
Eldorado Springs, CO 80025-0445   303-499-1316
    Fax: 303-499-1339 info@eldoradosprings.com
        www.eldoradosprings.com
Bottled water
    President/CEO: Douglas Larson
    VP Marketing: Jeremy Martin
    VP Operations: Kevin Sipple
Estimated Sales: $5.3 Million
Number Employees: 50-99
Type of Packaging: Private Label
Brands:
    Eldorado Natural Spring Water
    Eldorado Spring Water

4402 Eldorado Coffee Distributors
2520 Decatur Street
New Orleans, LA 70117-8696   504-949-8416
        Fax: 504-945-3695
Coffee
    Manager: Willy Ordonez
Estimated Sales: $500,000 appx.
Number Employees: 1-4

4403 Eldorado Seafood
55 Old Bedford Road
Lincoln, MA 01773-1125   781-259-4290
    Fax: 781-721-4376 800-416-5656
        www.eldoradoseafood.com
Manufacturer of shrimp including breaded, cooked,
peeled and deveined
    President: Christinne Randazzo
    VP: Laura Randazzo
Estimated Sales: $2.5-5 Million
Number Employees: 1-4
Type of Packaging: Consumer, Food Service, Private Label
Brands:
    Eldorado
    Max-Sea

4404 Elegant Desserts
275 Warren St
Lyndhurst, NJ 07071-2017   201-933-0770
    Fax: 201-933-7309 info@elegantdesserts.com
        www.elegantdesserts.com
Manufacturer and wholesaler/distributor of pastries
including tarts and miniature grand viennas; serving
the food service market
    President: John Mazur
Estimated Sales: $20-50 Million
Number Employees: 20-49
Type of Packaging: Food Service, Private Label

4405 Elegant Edibles
3311 Mercer St
Houston, TX 77027-6019   713-522-2884
    Fax: 713-522-1777 800-227-3226
        info@elegantedibles.com
        www.elegantedibles.com
All natural, gourmet confections, snacks, and recipe
ready ingredients
    Owner: Diane Dagostino
    R&D: Francis Jacquinet
    Operations: Lori Lake
    Production: Amanda Stults
    Plant Manager: Ana Olmedo

Estimated Sales: Less than $500,000
Number Employees: 5-9
Number of Brands: 8
Type of Packaging: Consumer, Food Service, Private Label, Bulk
Brands:
    Mrs. Powell's Gourmet

4406 Elegant Gourmet
11836 NE 112th St
Kirkland, WA 98033-4511   425-814-2500
    Fax: 425-823-2345 christa@elegantgourmet.com
        www.elegantgourmet.com
Manufacturer of chocolate almond toffee, chcolate
shapes, caramels, holiday candies, cookies, and hot
cocoa
    Owner: Louisa Davis
Estimated Sales: $5-10 Million
Number Employees: 50-99
Type of Packaging: Private Label, Bulk
Brands:
    Elegant Sweets
    Hannah's Delishts
    Kingsley's Caramels

4407 Elena's
2650 Paldan Dr
Auburn Hills, MI 48326-1824   248-373-1100
    Fax: 248-373-1120 800-723-5362
        info@elenas.com   www.elenas.com
Manufacturer and exporter of pasta, pasta sauce and
pasta salad
    President: Elena Houlihan
    VP Operations: John Houlihan
Estimated Sales: $2.5-5 Million
Number Employees: 20-49
Parent Co: Houlihan's Culinary Traditions
Type of Packaging: Food Service, Private Label, Bulk
Brands:
    Bella Mercato
    Bruschetta

4408 Elena's Food Specialties
405 Allerton Ave
S San Francisco, CA 94080-4818   650-871-8700
        Fax: 650-871-0502 800-376-5368
    peter@elenasfoods.com   www.elenasfoods.com
Manufacturer of frozen Mexican foods including enchiladas and burritos
    President: Peter Sartorio
    VP Product Development: Nathan Steck
    R&D Manager: Mark Cooley
    Eastern Regional Sales Manager: Alice Pager
    Western Regional Sales Manager: Susan Turtletaub
    Plant Manager: Manuel Lara
    Office Manager: Crystal Snearing
Estimated Sales: $5-10 Million
Number Employees: 50-99
Type of Packaging: Consumer, Food Service

4409 Eleni's Cookies
75 9th Ave
New York, NY 10011-7006   212-255-6804
    Fax: 212-255-8923 info@elenis.com
        www.elenis.com
Cookies
    Owner: Eleni Giamopulos
Estimated Sales: $300,000-500,000
Number Employees: 5-9

4410 Elgin Dairy Foods
3707 W Harrison St
Chicago, IL 60624-3622   773-722-7100
    Fax: 773-722-3230 800-786-9900
        www.elgindairy.com
Manufacturer of ice cream, frozen yogurt, dairy and
nondairy whipped toppings, sour cream and dairy
mixes
    President: Edward Gignac
    Marketing/Sales: James Gignac
    Operations: John Hartline
    Purchasing: Vanessa Jackson
Estimated Sales: $20-50 Million
Number Employees: 50-99
Sq. footage: 29000
Brands:
    Flav'r Top
    Freeze-Thaw

4411 Eli's Bread
403 E 91st St
New York, NY 10128-6800   212-831-4800
    Fax: 212-423-9078 info@elizabar.com
        www.elizabar.com
Hearth-baked European-style breads, rolls, bagels
and crisps based on traditional European recipes
    Owner: Eli Zabar
    Administrative Executive: Uzziah Phillips
    Director Sales: Judah Zweiter
Estimated Sales: $ 5 - 10 Million
Number Employees: 100-249
Sq. footage: 15000

4412 Eli's Cheesecake Company
6701 W Forest Preserve Ave
Chicago, IL 60634-1405   773-736-3417
    Fax: 773-736-1169 800-999-8300
        sales@elicheesecake.com
        www.elicheesecake.com
Manufacturer of frozen cakes including cheese and
carrot
    President: Marc Schulman
    CEO: Jolene Worthington
    CFO: Bob Monn
    VP Sales: Pete Filippelli
    R&D: Diana Moles
    Marketing: Debbie Littmann
    Public Relations: Maureen Schulman
    Operations: Jolene Worthington
    Purchasing: Jeff Anderson
Estimated Sales: $20-50 Million
Number Employees: 100-249
Sq. footage: 60000
Brands:
    Eli's

4413 Elite Bakery
709 Atlantic Avenue
Rochester, NY 14609-7422   585-482-5857
        Fax: 585-482-1740 877-791-7376
Manufacturer of baked goods
    Sales: Kathy Ewart
    Operations: Tom Quinn
Type of Packaging: Consumer, Food Service, Private Label, Bulk
Brands:
    ELITE BAKERY

4414 Elite Industries
6800 Jericho Tpke
Suite 216w
Syosset, NY 11791-4488   516-682-0479
    Fax: 516-921-0228 888-488-3458
        laurel@eliteconfections.com
Manufacturer of confections
Type of Packaging: Private Label

4415 Elite Spice
7151 Montevideo Rd
Jessup, MD 20794-9308   410-796-1900
    Fax: 410-379-6933 800-232-3531
    jbrandt@elitespice.com www.elitespice.com
Manufacturer and importer of spices and seasonings;
also, custom blending available
    President: Isaac Samuel
    Executive VP: Anton Samuel
    Research & Development: Leslie Krause
    Quality Control: Dave Anthony
    Marketing: Judy Brandt
    VP Sales: Paul Kurpe
    Operations: George Mayer
    Plant Manager: Kathy Lyons
    Purchasing Manager: Margie Singer
Estimated Sales: $20-50 Million
Number Employees: 100-249
Sq. footage: 60000
Type of Packaging: Private Label

4416 Elk Cove Vineyards
27751 NW Olson Rd
Gaston, OR 97119-8042   503-985-7760
    Fax: 503-985-3525 info@elkcove.com
        www.elkcove.com
Wines
    President: Patricia Campbell
    Sales Manager: Shirley Brooks
Estimated Sales: $5-9.9 Million
Number Employees: 10-19

4417 Elk Run Vineyards
15113 Liberty Rd
Mt Airy, MD 21771-9502   410-775-2513
        Fax: 410-875-2009   800-414-2513
        elk_run@msn.com   www.elkrun.com
Wines
    President/Winemaker: Fred Wilson
    Treasurer: Neil Bassford
    Marketing Director: Carol Wilson
Estimated Sales: $1-2.5 Million
Number Employees: 1-4
Type of Packaging: Private Label
Brands:
    ELK RUN

4418 Elkhart Locker Plant
P.O.Box 608
Elkhart, KS 67950-0608   620-697-4424
Manufacturer of beef
    Owner: Randy Lewis
    Manager: Randy Lewis
Estimated Sales: $500,000
Number Employees: 1-4

4419 Ellie's Country Delights
PO Box 1059
Wainscott, NY 11975   631-478-5200
        Fax: 631-267-3854
        sales@elliescountrydelights.com
        www.elliescountrydelights.com
Ratatouille
    President/Owner: Ellenka Baumrind

4420 Elliott Bay Baking Co.
8300 Military Road S
Seattle, WA 98108-3951   206-762-7690
    Fax: 206-762-7679   paula@elliottbaybaking.com
Manufacturer of Biscotti bites, java mocha cookies,
European tea biscuits
    President: Paula Lukoff
Estimated Sales: $ 2.5-5 Million
Number Employees: 20-49
Brands:
    Ii Biscotto Della Nonna
    My Bubby's

4421 Elliott Seafood Company
53 Stevens Lane
Cushing, ME 04563-3730   207-354-2533
        Fax: 207-354-2533
Manufacturer of Seafood
    President: Stan Elliott

4422 Ellis Coffee Company
2835 Bridge St
Philadelphia, PA 19137-1895   215-537-9500
        Fax: 215-534-5311   800-822-3984
        www.elliscoffee.com
Coffee
    President: Eugene Kestenbaum
    Executive VP: Frank Parker
    VP Sales/Marketing: James O'Ferrell
Estimated Sales: Less than $500,000
Number Employees: 5-9

4423 (HQ)Ellis Foods
5051 Edison Avenue
Chino, CA 91710-5716   909-613-0030
        Fax: 909-613-0321
Food products
    Owner: Gino Marinelli
    CFO: Mike Schuster
    President: Phil Harper
    Marketing Manager: Bob Albaugh
    Marketing Director: Bill Corcoran
    Purchasing Manager: Gary Cleveland
Estimated Sales: Less than $500,000
Number Employees: 1-4
Parent Co: Ellis Foods
Type of Packaging: Private Label
Brands:
    Nouget Fluffs
    Simply Sugar Free
    Taffy Whips

4424 (HQ)Ellis Popcorn Company
101 Poplar St
Murray, KY 42071-2533   270-753-5451
        Fax: 270-753-7002   800-654-3358
        mailto:epc@ellispopcorn.com
        www.ellispopcorn.com

Manufacturer and exporter of yellow popcorn
    President: Ann Kelly Ellis
    Sales Manager: Dave Roberts
    Fundraising Coordinator: John Youngerman
    Field Supervisor: Gerald Ray
    Director Customer Service: Frances Wyatt
    Customer Service: Michael Sunderland
Estimated Sales: $500,000-$1 Million
Number Employees: 10-19
Type of Packaging: Consumer, Food Service, Private Label, Bulk
Brands:
    BLUE RIBBON
    CALLOWAY COUNTY'S BEST

4425 Ellison Bakery
P.O.Box 9087
Fort Wayne, IN 46899-9087   260-747-6136
        Fax: 260-747-1954   800-711-8091
        todd@ebakery.com   www.ellisonbakery.com
Manufacturer of cookies, ice-cream sandwich wafers, crunch and inclusion products
    Chairman: William Ellis
    President: Robert Ellis
    Executive VP: Richard Smith
    Account Executive: David Barton
    Plant Manager: David Barton
Estimated Sales: $20-50 Million
Number Employees: 50-99
Type of Packaging: Consumer, Food Service, Bulk
Brands:
    ARCHWAY

4426 Ellison Milling Company
PO Box 400
Lethbridge, AB T1J 3Z2
Canada   403-328-6622
    Fax: 403-327-3772   sales@ellisonmilling.com
        www.ellisonmilling.com
Manufacturer and exporter of Durum Semolina,
Hard and Soft Wheat Flours
    President: Michael Greer
    Quality Control: Paolo Santangelo
    Marketing Director: Bob Grebinsky
    Sales Director: Bob Grebinsky
    General Manager: M Greer
    Operations Manager: B McConnell
    Production Manager: K Novakowski
    Plant Manager: B McConnell
    Purchasing Manager: B McConnell
Number Employees: 65
Parent Co: Parrish & Heimbecker
Type of Packaging: Food Service, Private Label, Bulk
Brands:
    ALEBRTA
    BAKER'S GOLD
    DREAM
    ELLISON'S
    ROYAL PASTRY
    U-BAKE

4427 Elliston Vineyards
463 Kilkare Rd
Sunol, CA 94586-9415   925-862-2377
        Fax: 925-862-0316   elliston@elliston.com
        www.elliston.com
Wines
    President: Donna Flavetta
    VP: Mark Piche
Estimated Sales: $1-2.5 Million
Number Employees: 20-49
Type of Packaging: Private Label

4428 Ellsworth Cooperative Creamery
P.O.Box 610
Ellsworth, WI 54011-0610   715-273-4311
        Fax: 715-273-5318   info@eaugallecheese.com
Dairy cooperative that is a distributor or butter,
cheese, whey powder, cheese curds and other dairy
items.
    Manager: Ken Mc Mahon
    CEO/General Manager: Ken McMahon
Estimated Sales: $101,000,000
Number Employees: 50-99
Type of Packaging: Consumer, Private Label, Bulk
Brands:
    Ellsworth Cheese Curds

4429 Ellsworth Foods
1510 Eastman Dr
Tifton, GA 31793-8228   229-386-8448
        Fax: 229-387-9749

Grocery products
    Owner: Ken Ellsworth Jr
Estimated Sales: $ 10 - 20 Million
Number Employees: 20-49

4430 Ellsworth Ice Cream Company
120 Division Street
Saratoga Springs, NY 12866-3003   518-584-1684
        Fax: 518-584-1657   elsworth@nycap.rr.com
        www.ellsworthicecrm.com
Manufacturer of novelty ice cream bars, cups, sandwiches, pints, pop juice bars, citrus juice bars, dry
coat bars and sherbet
    President: Tabor Ellsworth
Estimated Sales: $10-20 Million
Number Employees: 160
Type of Packaging: Consumer
Other Locations:
    Ellsworth Ice Cream
    Springfield VT
Brands:
    ELLSWORTH

4431 Ellsworth Locker
P.O.Box 85
Ellsworth, MN 56129-0085   507-967-2544
Manufacturer of sausage, beef, pork and venison
    Co-Owner/Treasurer: Brian Chapa
    Co-Owner: Kathy Chapa
Estimated Sales: $1-2.5 Million
Number Employees: 5-9
Type of Packaging: Consumer

4432 Elm City Cheese Company
2240 State St
Hamden, CT 06517-3798   203-865-5768
        Fax: 203-865-8303
Manufacturer of grated parmesan cheese
    President: Richard Weinstein
Estimated Sales: $5-10 Million
Number Employees: 10-19
Type of Packaging: Consumer

4433 Elmer Candy Corporation
P.O.Box 788
Ponchatoula, LA 70454-0788   985-386-6166
        Fax: 985-386-6245   800-843-9537
        www.elmercandy.com
Manufacturer and exporter of candy including chocolate, hard, lollypops, mints, taffy, holiday, etc.; also,
nut sundae toppings
    President/CEO: Allan Nelson
    VP: Robert Nelson
    VP Sales/Marketing: Roch Lemieux
    Customer Development Manager: Mike Martin
Estimated Sales: $50-100 Million
Number Employees: 250-499
Type of Packaging: Consumer
Brands:
    FIDDLERS
    GOLD BRICK
    HEAVENLY HASH
    JUST NUTS
    SMALL TALK CONVERSATION HEARTS
    SWEET OCCASION

4434 Elmer's Fine Foods
P.O.Box 3117
New Orleans, LA 70177-3117   504-949-2716
        Fax: 504-948-2537   a.elmer@worldnet.att.net
        www.elmerscheewees.com
Manufacturer of snack foods including potato chips,
popcorn and cheese curls
    President: Allen Elmer
    VP/CEO: Rob Nelson
Estimated Sales: $3-5 Million
Number Employees: 10-19
Type of Packaging: Consumer

4435 Elmwood Dairy
Hc 61
Box 13
Newport, VT 05855   802-334-8125
Dairy
    President: James Palin
Estimated Sales: $500-1 Million appx.
Number Employees: 5-9

4436 Elmwood Lockers
P.O.Box 603
Elmwood, IL 61529-0603   309-742-8929
        Fax: 309-742-7071
Manufacturer of sausage jerky, beef sticks and bratwurst
    Owner: John Powers

Estimated Sales:$500,000-$1 Million
Number Employees: 1-4
Type of Packaging: Consumer, Bulk
Brands:
J & J

4437 Elmwood Pastry
1136 New Britain Ave
West Hartford, CT 06110-2413   860-233-2029
                            Fax: 203-865-8303
Manufacturer of hard rolls, bread, doughnuts, cakes and cookies
  President: Richard S Winalski Jr
Estimated Sales:$500,000-$1 Million
Number Employees: 10-19
Type of Packaging: Consumer

4438 (HQ)Elore Enterprises
7224 NW 25th Street
Miami, FL 33122-1701   305-477-1650
    Fax: 305-477-2291   elore@bellsouth.net
              www.chorizoquijote.com
Manufacturer of Spanish sausage
  President: Joe Alanso
  VP: Juan Alanso
Estimated Sales:$1-2.5 Million
Number Employees: 5-9
Type of Packaging: Consumer, Food Service

4439 Elwell Farms
P.O.Box 1099
South Gate, CA 90280-1099   714-546-9280
                        Fax: 714-546-6496
Manufacturer of poultry
Estimated Sales:$10-20 Million
Number Employees: 50-99
Type of Packaging: Consumer, Food Service

4440 Elwha Fish
801 Marine Dr
Port Angeles, WA 98363-2103   360-457-3344
      Fax: 360-457-1205   www.elwhafish.com
Manufacturer of smoked and vacuum-packed salmon including no salt salmon and albacore tuna.
  Manager: Ed Bedford
Estimated Sales:$5-9.9 Million
Number Employees: 5-9
Type of Packaging: Consumer, Private Label, Bulk
Brands:
  ELWHA
  HEGG & HEGG
  NORTHWEST

4441 Elwood International
89 Hudson St
Copiague, NY 11726-1505   631-842-6600
  Fax: 631-842-6603   info@elwoodintl.com
                www.elwoodintl.com
Manufacturer and exporter of regular and dietetic portion controlled condiments including dressings, jellies, mayonnaise, mustard, ketchup, peanut butter, table syrups, private label and contract packaging
  President: Stuart Roll
  Vice President: Richard Roll
Estimated Sales:$2.90 Million
Number Employees: 10-19
Number of Brands: 3
Number of Products: 40
Sq. footage: 23000
Type of Packaging: Consumer, Food Service, Private Label, Bulk
Brands:
  Elwood
  RENAISSANCE
  Winston

4442 Embasa Foods
4340 Eucalyptus Ave
Chino, CA 91710-9705   909-631-2000
    Fax: 909-631-2100   888-236-2272
                    www.embasa.com
Manufacturer and distributor of full line ,high quality Mexican food products: chiles, salsa and nopalitos.
  President: Ted Gardner
Estimated Sales:$5-10 Million
Number Employees: 20-49
Parent Co: Authentic Specialty Foods
Brands:
  EMBASA
  LA GLORIA
  PUEBLITO

4443 Embassy Flavours Ltd.
5 International Drive Unit #1
Brampton, ON L6T 5V9
Canada   905-789-3200
    Fax: 905-789-3201   800-334-3371
             sales@embassyflavours.com
             www.embassyflavours.com
Manufacturer and exporter of extracts, flavors, colors, essential oils, bases and mixes including cake, pastry and bread
  President: Martino Brambilla
  R&D: Anne Klingerman
  National Sales/Marketing Manager: Mike Taras
Number Employees: 20-49
Sq. footage: 14400
Type of Packaging: Consumer, Food Service, Private Label, Bulk
Brands:
  Batter-Moist
  Elite
  Embassy
  Prairie Sun

4444 Embassy Wine Company
10615 Foster Avenue
Brooklyn, NY 11236-2211   718-272-0600
  Fax: 718-272-7845   abe@embassywines.com
             www.embassywines.com
Manufacturer, exporter and importer of kosher wines
  President: William Max Bauer
  VP: Eli Fink
Estimated Sales:$10-20 Million
Number Employees: 10-19

4445 Embassy of Spain TradesCommission
405 Lexington Ave
New York, NY 10174-0002   212-907-6481
      Fax: 212-867-6055   newyork@mcx.es
             www.spainbusines.com
Manufacturer of Spanish foods
  President: M Sanse
  VP: Jeffrey Shaw
*Estimated Sales:*Under $500,000
Number Employees: 20-49

4446 Emerald Valley Kitchen
90472 Woodruff St
Eugene, OR 97402-9612   541-688-3297
                    Fax: 541-688-0136
        www.emeraldvalleykitchen.com
Fresh organic sauces
  Owner: Mel Bankoff
  Plant Manager: Ken Eldrich
Estimated Sales:$5-10 Million
Number Employees: 10-19
Type of Packaging: Private Label

EMERLING INTERNATIONAL FOODS, INC.

4447 Emerling International Foods
2381 Fillmore Ave
Suite 1
Buffalo, NY 14214-2197   716-833-7381
    Fax: 716-833-7386   pemerling@emerfood.com
          www.emerlinginternational.com

> We supply food manufacturers and food service customers worldwide (since 1988) with bulk ingredients including: Fruits & Vegetables; Juice Concentrates; Herbs & Spices; Oils & Vinegars; Flavors & Colors; Honey & Molasses. We alsoproduce PURE MAPLE SYRUP.

  President: J P Emerling
  Sales: Amanda Karaszewski
  Public Relations: Jenn Burke
Estimated Sales:$10-20 Million
Number Employees: 20-49
Sq. footage: 250000

4448 Emery Smith Fisheries Limited
PO Box 14
Shag Harbour, NS B0W 3B0
Canada   902-723-2115
    Fax: 902-723-2372   emfish@klif.com
          www.hazem@bar.auracom.com
Manufacturer and exporter of salt fish
  President: Emery Smith
Number Employees: 20-49
Type of Packaging: Bulk

4449 Emil Lerch
PO Box 102
Hatfield, PA 19440-0102   215-855-2233
                    Fax: 215-855-0550
Mushrooms
  President/COO: Emil Lerch
  Marketing Director: Thomas Golden
Estimated Sales:$5-9.9 Million
Number Employees: 20-49
Type of Packaging: Private Label

4450 Emil's Original
1345 Germantown Ave
Philadelphia, PA 19122-4407   215-763-3311
                    Fax: 215-763-9755
       emilshomestyle@compuserve.com
Deli meats
  President: Ron Ramstead
  Plant Manager: Lernik Achikyan
Estimated Sales:$ 20 - 50 Million
Number Employees: 20-49

4451 Emilio Guglielmo Winery
1480 E Main Ave
Morgan Hill, CA 95037-3299   408-779-2145
  Fax: 408-779-3166   info@guglielmowinery.com
             www.guglielmowinery.com
Manufacturer and exporter of wines and vintner
  Owner: George E Guglielmo
  VP: Gene Guglielmo
  VP Sales: Gary Guglielmo
Estimated Sales:$10-20 Million
Number Employees: 20-49
Type of Packaging: Consumer, Private Label, Bulk
Brands:
  EMILE'S
  GUFLIELMO RESERVE
  GUGLIELMO
  GUGLIELMO VINEYARD SELECTION

4452 Emkay Trading Corporation
P.O.Box 504
Elmsford, NY 10523-0504   914-592-9000
    Fax: 914-347-3616   emkay@iname.com
             www.emkaytrading.org
Manufacturer and distributor of cheese including cream, bakers, neuchatel, lite, tvorog (Russian style soft cheese) and quark, also, bulk cream, custom fluid diary blends, bulk skim, sour cream, bulk cultured buttermilk and condensedskim milk. All above items may be EEUU certified, and are OU kosher
  Owner: Howard Kravitz
  CEO: Howard Kravitz
Estimated Sales:$8 Million
Number Employees: 1-4
Sq. footage: 200000
Type of Packaging: Consumer, Food Service, Private Label, Bulk
Brands:
  Emkay

4453 Emkay Trading Corporation
P.O.Box 504
Elmsford, NY 10523-0504   914-592-9000
    Fax: 914-347-3616   www.emkaytrading.org
Gourmet cheese
  Owner: Howard Kravitz
*Estimated Sales:*Less than $500,000
Number Employees: 1-4

4454 Emmy's Candy from Belgium
9816 Emerald Point Drive
Unit 3
Charlotte, NC 28278-6536   704-588-5445
    Fax: 704-588-2729   emmy@emmyscandy.com
             www.emmyscandy.com
Candies

4455 Empire Beef Company
Ste 500
36 W Main St
Rochester, NY 14614-1703　585-235-7350
　　　Fax: 585-235-3674　800-462-6804
　　　www.empirebeef.com
Manufacturer and exporter of fresh beef; wholesaler/distributor of fresh and frozen poultry, pork, lamb and veal
　　President/CEO: Steven Levine
　　Portion Department Supervisor: Steve Gerasimchik
　　General Manager: Chis Ciretta
Estimated Sales:$100-500 Million
Number Employees: 100-249
Type of Packaging: Bulk

4456 Empire Cheese
4520 Haskell Rd
Cuba, NY 14727-9598　585-968-1552
　　Fax: 585-968-2660 www.greatlakescheese.com
Manufacturer of whey and cheese including cheddar and mozzarella, provolone
　　Sales/Marketing Executive: John Sleggs
　　Production Manager: Steve Scott
　　Manager: John Sleggs
　　Manufacturing Manager: Joseph Miner
　　Plant Manager: Tom Eastham
Estimated Sales:$5-10 Million appx.
Number Employees: 100-249
Parent Co: Great Lakes Cheese Company
Type of Packaging: Private Label
Other Locations:
　　Great Lakes Cheese of New York
　　Adams NY
　　Great Lakes Cheese of Utah
　　Fillmore UT
　　Great Lakes Cheese Company - HQ
　　Hiram OH
　　Great Lakes Cheese of La Crosse
　　La Crosse WI
　　Great Lakes Cheese of Wisconsin
　　Plymouth WI

4457 Empire Foods
P.O.Box 1118
Bellmore, NY 11710-0310　516-679-1414
　　　　　　　　　Fax: 516-679-1419
Manufacturer of cheese
　　President: Leonard Epstein
Estimated Sales: Less than $500,000
Number Employees: 1-4

4458 Empire Kosher Foods
Rr 5 Box 228
Mifflintown, PA 17059-9409　717-436-5921
　　Fax: 717-436-7070　800-367-4734
empire@acsworld.net　www.empirekosher.com
Manufacturer of kosher poultry
　　President/CEO: Rob Van Naarden
　　CFO: Richard Berger
　　CEO: Rob Van Naarden
　　Rabbinic Administrator: Rabbi Israel Weiss
　　Director QA/Food Technology: Dr Stan Wallen
　　VP Sales/Marketing: Barry Rosenbaum
　　Director Human Resources: Jeff Brown
　　VP Operations: Cloyd Bowsman
　　Director Live Operations: Keith Flanders
　　Plant Manager: Mike Goguts
　　Director Pricing/Inventory Control: Deb Fitzpatrick
Estimated Sales:$50-100 Million
Number Employees: 1,000-4,999
Type of Packaging: Private Label
Brands:
　EMPIRE KOSHER POULTRY PRODUCTS

4459 Empire Spice Mills
908 William Avenue
Winnipeg, NB R3E 0Z8
Canada　204-786-1594
　　　　　Fax: 204-783-2847
Manufacturer and importer of flavoring extracts and whole ground and blended spices, herbs and seeds, seasonings
　　President: Don Ramage
Estimated Sales:$20-50 Million
Number Employees: 8
Sq. footage: 16000
Type of Packaging: Consumer, Food Service, Private Label, Bulk
Brands:
　EMPIRE'S BEST

4460 Empire SweetsOswego Growers and Shippers
8011 State Route 104
Oswego, NY 13126-5624　315-343-2157
　　Fax: 315-343-5371 www.empire-sweets.com/
Grows and distributes Empire Sweets Onions.
　　President: John Zappala
　　Vice President: Sam Zappala Jr
　　Vice President: Jim Zappala
Type of Packaging: Food Service

4461 Empire Tea Services
1965 St James Pl
Columbus, IN 47201-2805　812-375-1937
　　Fax: 812-376-7382　800-790-0246
　　sales@empiretea.com　www.empiretea.com
Importer of tea in tins, black tea, green tea, herb tea bulk tea, tea bags in wood boxes and various forms of packing
　　President: Lalith Guy Paranavitana
Estimated Sales:$200,000
Number Employees: 1-4
Number of Brands: 3
Number of Products: 27
Sq. footage: 2000
Type of Packaging: Consumer, Food Service, Private Label, Bulk
Brands:
　GUY'S TEA
　TEA TEMPTATIONS

4462 Empresa La Famosa
PO Box 51968
Toa Baja, PR 00950-1968　787-251-0060
　　Fax: 787-251-2270 www.empresalafamosa.com
Juice
　　VP Operations: Sandy Martin

4463 (HQ)Empresas La Famosa/CocoLopez
PO Box 51968
Toa Baja, PR 00950-1968　787-251-0060
　　Fax: 787-251-2270　mvillegas@coqui.net
　　　　www.empresaslafamosa.com
Manufacturer of fruit juices, coconut, cream & milk, beans and tomato willow
　　President: Jose Coripio
　　Plant Manager: Rosalia Prieto
Estimated Sales:$10-100 Million
Number Employees: 100-249
Brands:
　COCO LOPEZ, USA

4464 Empress Chocolate Company
5518 Avenue N
Brooklyn, NY 11234-4006　718-951-2251
　　Fax: 718-951-2254　800-793-3809
　　　sales@empresschocolate.com
　　　www.empresschocolate.com
Manufacturer and exporter of custom and stock molded chocolate novelties, cream filled chocolates, truffles and gift boxes
　　President: Ernie Grunhut
　　VP: Jack Grunhut
Estimated Sales:$5-10 Million
Number Employees: 20-49
Sq. footage: 20000
Parent Co: Ernex Corporation
Type of Packaging: Consumer, Private Label
Brands:
　EMPRESS CHOCOLATES

4465 Empress Foods
1525 Erin Street
Winnipeg, NB R3E 2T2
Canada　204-775-0344
　　　　　Fax: 204-775-4705
Manufacturer of bread and rolls
　　Plant Manager: Paul Jhooty
Number Employees: 100-249
Parent Co: Lucerne Foods
Type of Packaging: Consumer, Food Service
Brands:
　NATURE'S BLEND
　STONE HEDGE

4466 En Garde Health Products
7702 Balboa Blvd # 9
Van Nuys, CA 91406-2244　818-901-8505
　　Fax: 818-786-4699 www.engardehealth.com
Health products
　　CEO: Roberta Gabor

Estimated Sales:$ 1 - 3 Million
Number Employees: 1-4

4467 Endangered Species Chocolate
5846 W 73rd St
Indianapolis, IN 46278-1742　317-387-4372
　　Fax: 317-844-4951　800-293-0160
info@chocolatebar.com　www.chocolatebar.com
Processor of Gourmet Belgian chocolate, chocolate squares
　　CFO: Sylvia Parks
　　CEO: Wayne Zink
Estimated Sales:$5-10 Million
Number Employees: 50-99
Brands:
　BUG BITES
　ENDANGERED SPECIES CHOCOLATE BARS

4468 Endico Potatoes
160 N MacQuesten Pkwy
Mt Vernon, NY 10550-1099　914-664-1151
　　　　　　　　　Fax: 914-664-9267
Manufacturer and exporter of frozen French fried potatoes
　　Manager: Robert Hanna
　　General Manager: Bob Hanna
Estimated Sales:$20-50 Million
Number Employees: 20-49
Parent Co: Snow Fresh Foods
Type of Packaging: Consumer, Food Service

4469 (HQ)Ener-G Foods
P.O.Box 84487
Seattle, WA 98124-5787　206-767-3928
　　Fax: 206-764-3398　800-331-5222
　　samiii@ener-g.com　www.ener-g.com
Manufacturer and exporter of wheat and gluten-free bread, hamburger buns, cereals, cookies, pasta, mixes, etc.; also, dairy-free drinks and allergy-free foods; importer of gluten-free pasta and starches. Medical and diet foods, lowprotein foods for PKU a
　　President: Sam Wylde Iii
　　CEO: Sam Wylde III
　　Marketing/Sales: Jerry Colburn
　　Production Manager: Roger Traynor
　　Purchasing Manager: Sabina Melovie
Estimated Sales:$3 Milion
Number Employees: 20-49
Number of Brands: 2
Number of Products: 200
Sq. footage: 20000
Type of Packaging: Consumer, Food Service, Private Label
Brands:
　ENER-G
　OLD WORLD

4470 (HQ)Energen Products
14631 Best Ave
Norwalk, CA 90650-5258　562-926-5522
　　Fax: 562-921-0039　800-423-8837
　　　　　www.theadlgroup.com
Manufacturer and exporter of vitamins, wheat germ oil and brewers' yeast
　　President: Joseph Bensler
Estimated Sales:$3 Million
Number Employees: 10-19
Number of Brands: 13
Number of Products: 250
Sq. footage: 75000
Type of Packaging: Food Service, Private Label
Brands:
　AMERICAN DIETARY
　REAL LIFE
　THE PIERSON COMPANY
　VEGETRATES

4471 Energenetics International
PO Box 845
Keokuk, IA 52632-0845　217-453-2340
　　Fax: 217-453-6759　egi@adams.net
　　　　www.energeticsusa.com
Manufacturer of corn-based protein
　　President: Sammy Pierce
Number Employees: 5-9

4472 Energique
P.O.Box 121
Woodbine, IA 51579-0121　712-647-2499
　　Fax: 712-647-2588　800-869-8078
　　jesse@energiqueherbal.com
　　　www.energiqueherbal.com
Manufacturer of liquefied herbal extracts
　　President: Jesse Rettig

Estimated Sales: $ 3 - 5 Million
Number Employees: 10-19
Type of Packaging: Private Label, Bulk
Brands:
  ENERGIQUE®

4473 Energy Brands/Haute Source
1720 Whitestone Expy
Flushing, NY 11357-3000   718-746-0087
        Fax: 718-747-5900   800-746-0087
ebi@energybrands.com   www.energybrands.com
Manufacturer of distilled water
    President/CEO: J Darius Bikoff
    CEO: Darius Bitkoff
Estimated Sales: Less than $500,000
Number Employees: 1-4
Type of Packaging: Consumer, Food Service
Brands:
  FRUIT WATER
  GLACEAU VITAMINWATER
  GO-GO DRINKS
  SMART WATER
  SOY WATER
  VITAMIN WATER

4474 Energy Club
12950 Pierce St
Pacoima, CA 91331-2526   818-834-8222
        Fax: 818-834-8218   800-688-6887
eclub@energyclub.com   www.eclub.com
Hispanic snacks, candy, nuts, stoys, trail mix extra
large packages, salty snacks, beef jerky, accessories
and supplies
    President: Arnold Zane
    VP: Miron Aviv
    National Sales Manager: Vincent Guiliano
Estimated Sales: $5-10 Million
Number Employees: 100-249
Number of Products: 300
Sq. footage: 50000
Type of Packaging: Consumer, Private Label

4475 Energy Drinks
125 Hempstead Gardens Drive
Apt E2b
West Hempstead, NY 11552-2609   516-481-0872
        Fax: 516-481-4834
Energy drinks, vitamin drinks and sports supple-
ments

4476 Enfield Farms
1064 Birch Bay Lynden Rd
Lynden, WA 98264-9490   360-354-3019
    Fax: 360-354-0503 berries@enfieldfarms.com
        www.enfieldfarms.com
Manufacturer and packer of frozen red raspberries
and blueberries
    President: Marv Enfield
Estimated Sales: $50-100 Million
Number Employees: 250-499
Sq. footage: 17200
Type of Packaging: Food Service, Private Label,
  Bulk
Brands:
  ENFIELD FARMS

4477 Engel's Bakeries
4709 14 Street
Bay 6
Calgary, AB T2E 6S4
Canada   403-250-9560
    Fax: 403-250-5381 engelbak@telus.net
Manufacturer of baked and frozen ready-to-bake
products including breads, pastries, sausage rolls,
cakes, etc
    President: Mithoo Gillani
    R&D: Brian Hinton
    Marketing/Sales: Ron Clappison
    Sales Manager: Aaron Goss
    Production Manager: Greg Zub
    Purchasing: Danoz McKinnon
Number Employees: 50-99
Sq. footage: 16000
Type of Packaging: Food Service

4478 English Bay Batter
4491 Dunleary Dr
Dublin, OH 43017-8442   614-760-9921
        Fax: 614-760-9983
Manufacturer of frozen batter and baked goods
Estimated Sales: $ 5 - 10 Million
Number Employees: 5-9
Parent Co: English Bay Batter

Type of Packaging: Consumer, Food Service, Pri-
  vate Label, Bulk
Brands:
  ENGLISH BATTER

4479 Enjoy Foods International
10601 Beech Ave
Fontana, CA 92337-7204   909-823-2228
    Fax: 909-355-1573 info@EnjoyBeefJerky.com
        www.enjoybeefjerky.com
Manufacturer and exporter of beef and turkey jerky
and meat snacks; exporter of steak kabobs
    Owner: Waleed Saab
    VP Sales/Marketing: Sue McCarty
    Sales Manager (Western Region): Mike Shinkwin

    Sales Manager (Midwest/Eastern): Jerry Houseer
Estimated Sales: $ 10 - 20 Million
Number Employees: 20-49
Type of Packaging: Consumer

4480 Ennio International
1005 N. Commons Drive
Aurora, IL 60504-4100   630-355-1655
    Fax: 630-851-7744   info@enniousa.com
        www.enniousa.com
Manufacturer and supplier of high quality netting
and casings for the meat and poultry industries.
    Director Of Sales: Ralph Schuster

4481 Enon Valley Cheese Compay
1671 State Route 351
Enon Valley, PA 16120-3435   724-336-5207
        Fax: 724-336-1200
Manufacturer of Swiss cheese
    Owner: Thomas Bussers
Estimated Sales: $5-9.9 Million
Number Employees: 1-4
Type of Packaging: Bulk

4482 Enrico's/Ventre Packing
6050 Court Street Rd
Syracuse, NY 13206-1711   315-463-2384
        Fax: 315-463-5897   888-472-8237
enrico@enricos-ventre.com   www.ventre.com
Sauces and salsas.
    President: Marty Ventre
    Manager Quality Control: Kurt Alpha
    Eastern Regional Sales Manager: Rick Alesia
Estimated Sales: $ 10 - 20 Million
Number Employees: 10-19

4483 Ensemble Beverages
600 S Court Street
Suite 460
Montgomery, AL 36104-4106   334-324-7719
        www.ensemblebeverage.com
Manufacturer, importer and exporter of beverages
including carbonated, sports drinks, nutritional
shakes, iced tea and powders
    President: James Harris
    CFO: Cornelius Blanding, Jr
Number Employees: 10-19

4484 Enslin & Son Packing Company
89 Scenic Dr
Hattiesburg, MS 39401-8102   601-582-9300
        Fax: 601-544-2010   800-898-4687
Manufacturer, packer and wholesaler/distributor of
sausage
    President: August F Enslin Iii Jr
Estimated Sales: $10-20 Million
Number Employees: 20-49
Sq. footage: 8000
Type of Packaging: Consumer, Private Label, Bulk
Brands:
  BOWIE RIVER
  COUNTRY MORNING
  GLENDALE
  HICKORY

4485 (HQ)Enstrom Candies
P.O.Box 1088
Grand Junction, CO 81502-1088   970-683-1000
        Fax: 970-683-1011   800-367-8766
candy@enstrom.com   www.enstrom.com
Manufactures and sells confectionery products in-
cluding almond toffee, chocolates, brittles and
fudges
    President: Douglas Simons
    Secretary/Treasurer: Jamee Enstorm Simons
    Plant Manager: Clint Miller
Estimated Sales: $7 Million
Number Employees: 100-249

Number of Brands: 1
Sq. footage: 19360
Parent Co: Enstrom Candies
Type of Packaging: Consumer
Other Locations:
  Enstrom Candies
  Denver CO
Brands:
  DENVER CO
  ENSTROM CANDIES

4486 Entenmann's-Oroweat/BestFoods
264 S Spruce Ave
S San Francisco, CA 94080-4589   650-875-3100
        Fax: 650-875-3140
Manufacturer of whole grain bread, pizza dough and
frozen bagels.
    Director Sales: Jack Neugebaurer
    General Manager: Noel Corpus
    General Manager: Thad Mikols
Estimated Sales: $50-100 Million
Number Employees: 250-499
Sq. footage: 100000
Parent Co: Unilever USA
Type of Packaging: Consumer, Food Service

4487 Enterprise Foods
5315 Tulane Drive SW
Atlanta, GA 30336-2343   404-351-2251
        Fax: 404-351-3969
Wholesale bakery ingredients and emulsifiers,
dough conditioners, bromate replacers
    President: Gerald Anderson
Estimated Sales: $1 Million
Number Employees: 10-19
Number of Brands: 1
Number of Products: 10
Sq. footage: 75000
Type of Packaging: Bulk
Brands:
  ENTERPRISE
  SIP
  ZEELANCO

4488 Enterprises Pates et Croutes
1540 Rue De Coulomb
Boucherville, QC J4B 8A3
Canada   450-655-7790
        Fax: 450-655-8037
Manufacturer and exporter of frozen pie dough and
shells; processor of baked muffins
    President: Luc Benoit
Number Employees: 20-49
Type of Packaging: Consumer, Food Service

4489 Entner-Stuart Premium Syrups
1852 Fescue St SE
Albany, OR 97322-7075   541-812-8000
    Fax: 541-812-8010   800-377-9787
        info@enterstuartsyrups.com
        www.allannbroscoffee.com
Tea and coffee syrups
    President/CEO: Allan Stuart
Estimated Sales: $ 5 - 10 Million
Number Employees: 10-19

4490 EnviroPAK Corporation
4203 Shoreline Dr
Earth City, MO 63045-1209   314-739-1202
        Fax: 314-739-2422 sales@enviropak.com
        www.enviropak.com
Manufacturer of pulp packaging for numerous in-
dustries including that of food and beverage.
    President: John Wichlenski
    Accounting Manager: Stacey Bealke
    Design: Mike Lembeck
    Vice President Sales & Marketing: Bill Noble
    Sales & Marketing Administrator: Kim Bryant
    Vice President Manufacturing: Rodney Heenan
Sq. footage: 20000

4491 Enway/Northwood
16940 SE 130th Avenue
Clackamas, OR 97015-8945   503-657-9334
        Fax: 503-657-9346 www.enway.com
Potatoes
    President: Neal Pearson
    Sales Manager: William Miller
    Plant Manager: Steven Gersch
Estimated Sales: $5-9.9 Million
Number Employees: 50-99
Brands:
  ENWAY POTATOES

4492 Enz Vineyards
1781 Limekiln Rd
Hollister, CA 95023-9172 831-637-3956
Fax: 831-637-9382
Manufacturer of Wine
President: Robert Enz
Estimated Sales: $500,000-$1 Million
Number Employees: 1-4

4493 Enzymatic Therapy
825 Challenger Dr
Green Bay, WI 54311-8328 920-406-3612
Fax: 920-469-4400 800-783-2286
etmail@enzy.com www.enzy.com
Nutritional supplements
President/CEO: Randy Rose
CEO: Randy Rose
CFO: Mike Devereux
VP Scientific Affairs: Bob Doster
Quality Control: Bob Doster
SVP: Matt Schueller
Sales Director: Mike Devereux
Public Relations: Toni Weiss
Operations SVP: Cathy Stone
Production SVP: Cathy Stone
Plant Manager: Tom Krojewski
Purchasing Manager: Greg Kolarik
Estimated Sales: $ 50 - 100 Million
Number Employees: 250-499
Number of Products: 350
Type of Packaging: Consumer, Private Label

4494 Enzyme Development Corporation
360 W 31st St
New York, NY 10001-2833 212-736-1580
Fax: 212-279-0056
info@enzymedevelopment.com
www.enzymedevelopment.com
Manufacturer, importer and exporter of industrial
and specialty enzymes
President: Phillip Nelson
Marketing/Sales: C Peter Moodie
Estimated Sales: $ 20 - 50 Million
Number Employees: 20-49
Type of Packaging: Bulk
Brands:
ASPERZYME
ENZECO
LIQUIPANOL
PANOL

4495 Enzyme Formulations
6421 Enterprise Ln
Madison, WI 53719-1116 608-273-8100
Fax: 608-273-8111 800-614-4400
info@loomisenzymes.com
www.naturalenzymes.com
Supplements
President: Howard Loomis

4496 Eola Hills Wine Cellars
501 S Pacific Hwy W
Rickreall, OR 97371-9728 503-623-2405
Fax: 503-623-0350 800-291-6730
www.eolahillswinery.com
Wines
President: Tom Huggins
Marketing: Julie Brink
Estimated Sales: $5-10 Million
Number Employees: 20-49

4497 Eola Specialty Foods
3213 Waconda Rd NE
Gervais, OR 97026-9709 503-390-1425
Fax: 503-390-9526
codybell@eolaspecialtyfoods.com
www.eolacherry.com
A food processor, manufacturer specialized in
co-packing
President: Craig Bell
CFO: Paul Leipzig
Marketing Director: Cody Bell
VP Sales: Doug Zibell
Plant Manager: Monica Guzman
Estimated Sales: $65,000
Number Employees: 20-49
Parent Co: Bell Farms
Type of Packaging: Consumer, Food Service, Private Label, Bulk
Brands:
EOLA

4498 EpicCure Princess of Yum
PO Box 1202
San Luis Obispo, CA 93406-1202 805-466-3655
Fax: 805-466-3642 info@princessofyum.com
www.princessofyum.com
Manufactuer of Naturally flavored sugars

4499 (HQ)Epicurean Butter
6701 Stapleton Drive North
Denver, CO 80216 720-261-8175
Fax: 303-254-5381 epicureanbutter@msn.com
ww.epicureanbutter.com
compound butters, both sweet and savory.
President/Owner: John Hubschman
VP: Janey Hubschman
Estimated Sales: $6.4 Million
Number Employees: 12

4500 (HQ)Epicurean International
P.O.Box 13242
Berkeley, CA 94712-4242 510-477-8894
Fax: 510-675-9045 800-967-7424
info@thaikitchen.com www.thaikitchen.com
Manufacturer, importer and exporter of Thai ingredients including coconut milk, sauces, pastes, rice
mixes, noodles, soups and teas; custom formulations
available
President: Seth Jacobson
Estimated Sales: $ 5 - 10 Million
Number Employees: 10-19
Number of Products: 45
Type of Packaging: Consumer
Brands:
Thai Kitchen

4501 Epicurean Specialty
PO Box 2209
Sebastopol, CA 95473-2209 707-829-3881
Fax: 707-829-3826 800-500-0065
epispec@aol.com www.epicureanspecialty.com
Manufacturer of gourmet mushrooms, saffron, vanilla, herbs and spices
President: Craig Kodros
Estimated Sales: $5-10 Million
Number Employees: 5-9

4502 Equal Exchange
50 United Dr
West Bridgewater, MA 02379-1026 774-776-7400
Fax: 781-830-0282 info@equalexchange.com
www.equalexchange.com
Cooperative providing traded organic coffees
President: Rink Dickinson
Marketing: Bruce McKinnon
Sales: Mark Sweet
Director Operations: Mark Souza
Purchasing: Rob Everts
Estimated Sales: $20-50 Million
Number Employees: 50-99
Sq. footage: 10000
Type of Packaging: Bulk

4503 Equinox Enterprises
22040 Twp Road 520
Suite 101
Sherwood Park, AB T8E 1E7 780-922-5170
Fax: 780-922-4909 888-378-7364
Cereals, wheat, barley etc
Owner: Velma McKinney
Estimated Sales: $30 Million
Number Employees: 10-19
Type of Packaging: Private Label

4504 Equity Group
P.O.Box 1436
Reidsville, NC 27323-1436 336-342-6601
Fax: 336-349-2940
Manufacturer of chicken products including prepared, frozen, patties and nuggets
Manager: Tom Harris
Plant Manager: Kaylan Adams
Estimated Sales: $50-100 Million
Number Employees: 250-499
Parent Co: Keystone Food Corporation
Type of Packaging: Food Service

4505 Erath Vineyards Winery
9409 NE Worden Hill Rd
Dundee, OR 97115-9146 503-538-3318
Fax: 503-538-1074 800-539-5463
info@erath.com www.erath.com
Wines
Owner/President: Dick Erath
VP: Dana Ramos
Marketing/Sales Manager: Steve Vuylsteke
Estimated Sales: $5-10 Million
Number Employees: 20-49
Number of Brands: 1
Number of Products: 1
Type of Packaging: Private Label, Bulk

4506 (HQ)Erba Food Products
2550 E New York Ave
Brooklyn, NY 11207-2323 718-272-7700
Fax: 718-272-7711 sales@haddar.com
Manufacturer, importer and exporter of kosher foods
including vegetables, juices, coffee, spices, seasonings, baked goods, fruits, condiments, fish, nuts,
oils, etc
Manager: Heeren Patel
VP of Marketing: Abraham Perkowski
Sales: Jen O'Connor
Number Employees: 10-19
Type of Packaging: Consumer, Food Service
Brands:
EMBASSY WINES
HADDAR

4507 Erbrich-Sewell ProductsCompany
PO Box 55107
Indianapolis, IN 46205-0107 317-925-6433
Fax: 317-921-5023
Manufacturer of mustard and vinegar; manufacturer
of household cleaners
President: John J Heidt Jr
General Manager: Brian King
Estimated Sales: $10-20 Million
Number Employees: 50
Sq. footage: 90000
Type of Packaging: Consumer, Food Service, Private Label
Brands:
GOURMET CHOICE
TIME SAVER
WORK SAVER

4508 Erevia Products
8951 Buchanan Road
Brighton, MI 48116-6230 810-225-0460
Fax: 810-225-0460
Snacks, pasta sauces
Brands:
Erevia
Four Sisters

4509 (HQ)Erie Foods International
401 Seventh Ave
PO Box 648
Erie, IL 61250-0648 309-659-2233
Fax: 309-659-2822 800-447-1887
glindsy@eriefoods.com www.eriefoods.com
Manufacturer and exporter of co-dried and concentrated milk proteins; also sodium, calcium, combination and acid-stable caseinates and dairy blends;
importer of milk proteins
President/CEO: David Reisenbigler
CFO: Mark Delaney
Executive VP: Jim Klein
Research & Development: Craig Air
Quality Control: Jo Air
Marketing Director: Ryan Tranel
Operations Manager: Jim Jacoby
Production Manager: Jim Jacoby
Plant Manager: Jim Naftzgak
Purchasing Manager: Shawn Larson
Estimated Sales: $1-2.5 Million
Sq. footage: 30000
Parent Co: Erie Foods International Inc
Type of Packaging: Bulk
Other Locations:
Erie Foods International
Beenleigh QLD
Brands:
ECCO
ERIE
PRO-GIM

4510 Erivan Dairy
105 Allison Rd
Oreland, PA 19075-1808 215-887-2009
Fax: 215-885-3679
Manufacturer of yogurt
President: Harry Fereshetian
Plant Manager: Paul Fereshetian

Estimated Sales:$1-2.5 Million
Number Employees: 20-49
Type of Packaging: Consumer

4511 Errol Cajun Foods
126 Daniel Street
Pierre Part, LA 70339-4204   985-252-6003
                                          Fax: 985-252-9176
Manufacturer of stuffed and frozen jalapeno peppers
and value added seafood products including crab
and shrimp; also, seafood gumbo and shrimp
etouffee and patties
    Owner: Errol Perera
Estimated Sales:$2.5-5 Million
Number Employees: 5-9
Type of Packaging: Consumer, Food Service

4512 Ervan Guttman Company
8208 Blue Ash Rd
Cincinnati, OH 45236-1997   513-791-0767
        Fax: 513-891-0559   800-203-9213
                                  hguttman@fuse.net
                              theervanguttmancompany.com
Manufacturer and exporter of candy making equip-
ment and supplies including release papers and fla-
vorings
    Owner: Harold Guttman
Estimated Sales:$500,000-1 Million
Number Employees: 1-4
Sq. footage: 1000
Type of Packaging: Bulk

4513 Escalon Premier Brand
1905 McHenry Ave
Escalon, CA 95320-9601   209-838-7341
        Fax: 209-838-6206 www.escalon.net
Manufacturer of canned tomatoes and tomato prod-
ucts including sauces
    Controller: Steve Kelly
    Human Resource Executive: Susan McCready
    Product Manager: Dan Milazzo
    Plant Manager: John Raggio
    Purchasing Agent: Tom Muller
Number Employees: 100-249
Parent Co: Heinz USA
Type of Packaging: Consumer, Food Service
Brands:
    6-in-1
    BELL 'ORTO
    BELLA ROSA
    CHRISTINA'S ORGANIC
    HENIZ
    MAMA LINDA

4514 Eschete's Seafood
229 New Orleans Blvd
Houma, LA 70364-3345   985-872-4120
                                          Fax: 504-851-6147
Seafood
    Owner: John Eschete
Estimated Sales:$300,000-500,000
Number Employees: 1-4

4515 (HQ)Esco Foods
1035 Howard St
San Francisco, CA 94103-2823   415-864-2147
                                          Fax: 415-822-2969
Manufacturer of syrups, toppings, salad dressings,
marinades, bbq sauce, flavors
    President: Marc Bosschart
Estimated Sales:$2.5-5 Million
Number Employees: 20-49

4516 Eskimo Candy
P.O.Box 1106
Kihei, HI 96753-1106   808-879-5686
        Fax: 808-874-0504   eskimo@maui.net
                              www.eskimocandy.com
Seafood and other fine foods.
    President: Jeffrey Hansen
Estimated Sales:$ 10 - 20 Million
Number Employees: 20-49

4517 (HQ)Eskimo Pie Corporation
4175 Veterans Memorial Highway
3rd Floor
Ronkonkoma, NY 11779-7639   631-737-9700
        Fax: 631-737-9792 info@eskimopie.com
                              www.eskimopie.com

Manufacturer and exporter of dairy specialties including ice cream novelties, fruit flavors for ice
cream, sherbets, frozen yogurt, sorbet, cottage
cheese, egg nog concentrate and chocolate coating
    Owner: David Clark
    President: David Kewer
    Executive VP: L Bradford Armstrong
    VP Sales: Steve Kangisser
    Sales Director: WC Breed
    Director Marketing: Louise Fecteau
    General Manager Sales: Neal Glaeser
    Investor Relations Director: James Cheatham
    Purchasing Manager: Thomas Foss
Number Employees: 50-99
Parent Co: CoolBrands International
Type of Packaging: Consumer, Bulk
Brands:
    Atkins Endulge
    Better Kids
    Breyers
    Carb Solutions
    Care Bears
    Crayola
    Dogsters
    Dreamery
    Eskimo Pie
    Eskimo Pie Chipwich
    Fruit-A-Freeze
    Godiva
    Justice League
    No Pudge
    Snapple
    Trix
    Tropicana
    Welch's
    Whole Fruit
    Yoplait

4518 (HQ)Esper Products DeLuxe
2793 N Orange Blossom Trl
Kissimmee, FL 34744-1375   407-847-3726
                                        800-268-0892
                              colleen1014@webtv.com
Jellies and preserves
    President: Andrew McFarland
Estimated Sales:$2.5-5 Million
Number Employees: 5-9
Brands:
    ESPER DELUXE

4519 Espresso Vivace
901 E Denny Way
Suite 100
Seattle, WA 98122-8400   206-860-5869
        Fax: 206-860-1567   vivace@speakeasy.net
                              www.espressovivace.com
Coffee
    President: David Schomer
Estimated Sales:$1-2.5 Million
Number Employees: 20-49

4520 Essaic Canada International
PO Box 365
Lake Worth, FL 33460-0365   561-585-7111
    Fax: 561-585-7145 maloney@essiac-canada.com
                              www.essiac-canada.com
Manufacturer and exporter of herbal dietary supple-
ments
    President: Kevin Maloney
Number of Brands: 2
Number of Products: 2
Parent Co: Essiac Canada International
Type of Packaging: Consumer, Food Service
Brands:
    ESSIAC (EXTRACT)
    ESSIAC (POWDER)

4521 Essen Nutrition
1414 Sherman Rd
Romeoville, IL 60446-4046   630-739-6700
        Fax: 630-739-6464 essen@essen-nutrition.com
                              www.essen-nutrition.com
Dietetic and health foods
    President: Madhavan Anirudhan
    Director Sales: Joe Martin
Estimated Sales:$5-10 Million
Number Employees: 20-49
Type of Packaging: Private Label

4522 Essentia Water
5050 N 40th Street
Suite 340
Phoenix, AZ 85018-2194   602-912-9500
        Fax: 602-912-9595   877-293-2239
                              www.essentiawater.com
Purifying drinking water
    President: James Tonkin
    Marketing/Sales: Wayne Addison
Estimated Sales:$300,000-500,000
Number Employees: 1-4

4523 Essential Flavors & Fragrances, Inc
1521 Commerce St
Corona, CA 92880-1730   951-737-3889
        Fax: 951-737-4237   888-333-9935
                              www.essentialflavors.com
Manufacturer of drink based concentrates, flavor-
ings, herbal extracts and body building formulas
    President: Michael Gulan
Estimated Sales:$5-10 Million
Number Employees: 5-9
Type of Packaging: Bulk

4524 Essential Nutrients
PO Box 5183
Cerritos, CA 90703-5183   562-407-5457
        Fax: 562-407-5458   800-767-8585
                              www.superkmh.com
Deal in nutrients
    President: Randy Haringa
    Vice President: Vicki Heringa
Estimated Sales:$58,000
Number Employees: 1-4
Type of Packaging: Private Label
Brands:
    Super Kmh

4525 Essential Products Company
Apt 5b
1250 Ocean Pkwy
Brooklyn, NY 11230-5178   212-344-4288
Manufacturer and exporter of flavoring extracts
    President: Barry Striem
*Estimated Sales:*Less than $500,000
Number Employees: 1-4
Type of Packaging: Consumer, Food Service
Brands:
    MELLOW BLENDER

4526 Essential Products of America
6710 Benjamin Road
Suite 700
Tampa, FL 33634-4314   813-886-9698
        Fax: 813-886-9661   800-822-9698
                    info@aromatherapyproducts.info
                    www.aromatherapyproducts.info
Manufacturer, importer and exporter of essential oils
    President: Michael Alexander
    Sales Manager: Michael Alexander
Estimated Sales:$2.5-5 Million
Number Employees: 5
Sq. footage: 1200
Type of Packaging: Consumer, Private Label, Bulk
Brands:
    WHOLE SPECTRUM

4527 Esteem Products
1800 136th Pl NE # 5
Bellevue, WA 98005-2343   425-562-1281
        Fax: 425-562-1284   800-255-7631
                    amy@esteemproducts.com
                    www.esteemproducts.com
Manufacturer, wholesaler/distributor and exporter of
nutritional supplements and specialty vitamins. All
combination formulas for consumer simplicity
    CEO/President: John Sheaffer
    VP: Linda Sheaffer
    Marketing: Amy Braisford
Estimated Sales:$500,000-$1 Million
Number Employees: 5-9
Sq. footage: 5000
Brands:
    ARTHO LIFE
    CARDIO LIFE
    ESTEEM PLUS
    GOLDEN LIFE
    IMMUNE LIFE
    SUPER LIFE
    TOTAL MAN
    TOTAL WOMAN
    TRIM & FIRM AM/PM

4528 Esterlina Vineyard & Winery
P.O.Box 2
Philo, CA 95466-0002   707-895-2920
Fax: 707-895-2972 info@esterlinavineyards.com
www.esterlinavineyards.com
Wines
President: Craig Sterling
CEO: Eric Sterling
Marketing Manager: Steve Sterling
Estimated Sales: Under $500,000
Number Employees: 5-9
Brands:
Esterlina

4529 Esther Price Candies & Gifts
1709 Wayne Ave
Dayton, OH 45410-1711   937-253-2121
Fax: 937-253-6034 800-782-0326
mvnp8la@prodigy.com www.estherprice.com
Chocolates
President: James Day
Estimated Sales: $20-50 Million
Number Employees: 50-99
Type of Packaging: Consumer, Private Label

4530 Ethical Specialty Products
2843 Hopyard Road
Suite 170
Pleasanton, CA 94588-5241   925-462-3824
Fax: 925-462-1168
www.healthyheritagehoney.com
President: Alper Aziz

4531 Ethnic Edibles
2186 5th Avenue
Apt 17a
New York, NY 10037-2720   718-320-0147
Fax: 718-320-0147 ethnicedibles@aol.com
www.ethnicedibles.com
Cookies and cookie cutters with African and Puerto
Rico themes
President: Heather McCartney
Brands:
COQUI COOKIES
ETHNIC EDIBLES

4532 Ethnic Gourmet Foods
700 Old Fern Hill Rd
West Chester, PA 19380-4274   610-692-7575
Fax: 610-719-6399
Manufacturer of frozen gourmet foods
Manager: Richard Alexander
Estimated Sales: $20 Million
Number Employees: 50-99
Parent Co: Heinz Frozen Foods Company

4533 Etna Brewing Company
P.O.Box 757
Etna, CA 96027-0757   530-467-5277
Fax: 530-567-3083 www.etnabrew.com
Manufacturer of Beer
Owner: Dave Krell
Brewer: Luke Hurlimann
Estimated Sales: $500,000-$1 Million
Number Employees: 10-19
Brands:
DARK LAGER
ETNA ALE
ETNA BOCK
ETNA DOPPELBOCK
ETNA OKTOBERFEST
ETNA WEIZEN
EXPORT LAGER

4534 (HQ)Ettlinger Corporation
175 Olde Half Day Rd # 247
Lincolnshire, IL 60069-3063   847-564-5020
Fax: 847-564-0802
Manufacturer of cereal grains, barley & wheat, re-
duced lactose whey
President: Edward Ettlinger
Estimated Sales: $1-2.5 Million
Number Employees: 5-9
Type of Packaging: Food Service, Bulk

4535 Euphoria Chocolate Company
4080 Stewart Rd
Eugene, OR 97402-5408   541-344-4914
Fax: 541-344-5223 www.euphoriachocolate.com
Chocolate truffles, trail mix
President/CEO: Bob Bury
Estimated Sales: Less than $500,000
Number Employees: 1-4

4536 Eureka Lockers
P.O.Box 194
Eureka, IL 61530-0194   309-467-2731
Fax: 309-467-2731
Manufacturer of beef, pork and lamb
President: Scott Bittner
Estimated Sales: $500,000-$1 Million
Number Employees: 1-4
Type of Packaging: Consumer

4537 Eureka Springs Winery
194 Spring St
Eureka Springs, AR 72632-3150   479-253-8754
Fax: 479-253-7807
Wines
Manager: Jean Elderwind
General Manager: Robert Cowie
Estimated Sales: Under $500,000
Number Employees: 1-4

4538 Eureka Water Company
729 S W Third Street
Oklahoma City, OK 73109   405-235-8474
Fax: 405-235-6344 800-310-8474
info@ozarkah2o.com www.ozarkah2o.com
Manufacturer of bottled water
President/CEO: Steve Raupe
Plant Manager: Robert DeShazo
Estimated Sales: $5-10 Million
Number Employees: 50-99
Type of Packaging: Consumer, Private Label, Bulk
Brands:
MOUNTAIN VALLEY
OZARKA
SHAMROCK

4539 Euro Chocolate Fountain
2647 Ariane Dr
San Diego, CA 92117-3422   858-270-9863
Fax: 858-270-6801 800-423-9303
info@eurochocolate.com
www.eurochocolatefountain.com
Bakery products, chocolate confections and spe-
cialty baking
Owner: Urs Huwyler
VP: Don Rein
Estimated Sales: Below $ 5 Million
Number Employees: 1-4
Brands:
Euro Chocolate

4540 Euro Source Gourmet
220 Little Falls Road
Unit 2
Cedar Grove, NJ 07009-1255   973-857-6000
Fax: 973-857-8862 tjvambass@aol.com
www.eurosourcegourmet.net
Gourmet foods
Owner: Thomas Calvaruso
Sales: Janka Delatte

4541 EuroAm
1302 S 293rd Place
Federal Way, WA 98003-3756   253-839-5240
Fax: 253-839-4171 888-839-2702
euroaminc1@aol.com www.scorpa.com
Coffee
President: Vito Rizzo
VP: Anita Goransson
Estimated Sales: Under 100,000
Number Employees: 1-4
Number of Brands: 10
Number of Products: 20
Sq. footage: 1800
Parent Co: Euro Am Imports

4542 Eurobubblies
725 Arizona Ave # 100
Santa Monica, CA 90401-1734   310-319-1100
Fax: 310-319-1105 800-273-0750
info@eurobubblies.com www.eurobubblies.com
Beverage and food products from Europe
Manager: Robert Birgit
Sales Director: Laurent Masliah
Estimated Sales: $10 Million
Number Employees: 5-9
Type of Packaging: Consumer, Food Service, Pri-
vate Label, Bulk
Brands:
BASILIC PISTOU
BEL NORMANDE - SPRITZERS
CLOS NORMAND
DUPONT D'ISIGNY - CANDIES
EAT NATURAL
EFFERVE
EUROBUBBLIES
EUROSUPREME
HARRGATE
HOBGOBLIN - BEER
JOKER - FRUIT JUICE
LORINA - LEMONADE
PAMPRYL
PRIMEL
SEASONING SALT
SIRACUSE
SPOONTY
ST PETER'S
TERRAFOOD
WYCHWOOD

4543 Eurocaribe Packing Company
PO Box 29046
Rio Piedras, PR 00929-0046   787-752-8181
Fax: 787-752-8983 europak@coqui.net
Manufacturer of smoked meats
President: Jose Casanova
CFO: John Erickson
Purchasing: Hiram Morales
Estimated Sales: $10-20 Million
Number Employees: 100-249
Type of Packaging: Private Label, Bulk
Other Locations:
Zona Industrial
Carolina PR

4544 Eurodrinks
2555 W Bluff Avenue
Unit 105
Fresno, CA 93711-0379   559-449-9463
Fax: 559-432-5524 bonyhadi@earthlink.net
Wine industry additive agents
President: Daniel Bonyhadi
Estimated Sales: $20 Million
Number Employees: 1-4

4545 Europa Foods
400 Lyster Avenue
Saddle Brook, NJ 07663-5910   201-368-8929
Fax: 201-368-2065
Manufacturer of baked products, sauces, mustard
President: Larry LaPane
Estimated Sales: $5-10 Million
Number Employees: 10-19
Type of Packaging: Private Label
Brands:
Barral
China's Secret
DEA
Duke of Modena
Gawler Park
Haudecoeur
Louis Regis
Pyett
Saslins
Toastalettes
Valade
Viniberra
Viniberra

4546 Europa Sports Products
11401 Granite St
Charlotte, NC 28273-6400   704-525-0792
Fax: 704-405-2025 800-447-4795
info@eurosports.com www.europasports.com
Sports foods
Owner: Eric Hillman
Estimated Sales: $ 50 - 100 Million
Number Employees: 50-99

4547 European Bakers
5055 S Royal Atlanta Dr
Tucker, GA 30084-3097   770-723-6180
Fax: 770-939-6632
Manufacturer of baked goods including breads and
buns
President: James Allen
Estimated Sales: $10-20 Million
Number Employees: 100-249
Sq. footage: 130000
Parent Co: Flowers Baking Company
Type of Packaging: Consumer

4548 European Coffee
1401 Berlin Rd
Cherry Hill, NJ 08034-1402   856-428-7202
Fax: 856-428-7262 www.melitta.com

Manufacturer of Coffee
President/CEO: H Radtke
VP: John Masters
Plant Manager: Vincent Tagliaferro
Estimated Sales: $5-10 Million
Number Employees: 20-49
Brands:
FRAC-PACKS

4549 European Egg Noodle Manufacturing
14815 Yellowhead Trail
Edmonton, AB T5L 3C4
Canada   780-453-6767
      Fax: 780-453-6769 pastatime@sprint.ca
Manufacturer of frozen pastas, sauces, sausages and pizzas
President/Sales: Fausto Chinellato
Operations: Dorothy Chinellato
Number Employees: 10-19
Type of Packaging: Consumer
Brands:
BELLA FESTA
PASTA TIME

4550 European Roasterie
250 W Bradshaw St
Le Center, MN 56057-1121   507-357-2272
      Fax: 507-357-4478 888-469-2233
      sales@euroroast.comom www.euroroast.com
Coffee
President/CEO: Timothy Tulloch
Sales: Cindy Dorzinski
Operations: Thomas Dotray
Estimated Sales: $20-50 Million
Number Employees: 20-49
Type of Packaging: Private Label

4551 European Style Bakery
112 N Hamilton Drive
Unit 107
Beverly Hills, CA 90211-2279   818-368-6876
Manufacturer of blueberry filling, cakes and bakery items
President: Vladimir Landa
Estimated Sales: Less than $500,000
Number Employees: 5-9

4552 Eva Gates Homemade Preserves
P.O.Box 696
Bigfork, MT 59911-0696   406-837-4356
      Fax: 406-837-4376 800-682-4283
      evagates@digisys.net www.evagates.com
Fruit preserves and fruit syrups
President: Gretchen Gates
Estimated Sales: $2.5-5 Million
Number Employees: 10-19
Type of Packaging: Private Label

4553 Evan Hall Sugar Cooperative
33389 Highway 1 N
Donaldsonville, LA 70346   225-473-8241
      Fax: 225-473-7425
Manufacturer of raw sugar and molasses
President: James Thibaut
VP: Charles Thibaut
Estimated Sales: $10-20 Million
Number Employees: 50-99
Type of Packaging: Bulk

4554 Evan's Food Products
4118 S Halsted St
Chicago, IL 60609-2612   773-254-7400
      Fax: 773-254-7791 www.evansfood.com
Manufacturer of low carb snacks
President: Alex Silva
Number Employees: 100-249

4555 Evans Bakery
P.O.Box 284
Cozad, NE 69130-0284   308-784-2409
      Fax: 308-784-3630 800-222-5641
      e_bakery@cozadtel.net www.evansbakery.com
Manufacturer of frozen breads, rolls, cakes, cookies, buns and bagels
Manager: Jerry Armagost
Estimated Sales: $10-20 Million
Number Employees: 50-99

4556 Evans Creole Candy Company
848 Decatur St
New Orleans, LA 70116-3375   504-522-7111
      Fax: 504-522-7113 800-637-6675
      www.evanscreolecandy.com

Praline, chocolate candy and syrup
President: Hope Cuccia
Estimated Sales: $1-2.5 Million
Number Employees: 5-9
Type of Packaging: Bulk

4557 Evans Food Products Company
4118 S Halsted St
Chicago, IL 60609-2612   773-254-7400
      Fax: 773-254-7791 866-254-7400
      sales@evansfood.com www.evansfood.com
Manufacturer and exporter of rendered pork rinds
President/CEO: Alex Silva
Sales Manager: William Connor
Consumer Contact: Mike Pannito
Operations Manager: Humberto Iniguez
Estimated Sales: $20-50 Million
Number Employees: 100-249
Sq. footage: 104000
Type of Packaging: Consumer

4558 Evans Properties
12833 Us Highway 301
Dade City, FL 33525-5812   352-567-5662
      Fax: 352-567-3683
Frozen citrus juices
President: James Evans
Estimated Sales: $5-10 Million
Number Employees: 1-4

4559 Evco Wholesale Foods
P.O.Box D
Emporia, KS 66801-7343   620-343-7000
      Fax: 620-343-6375 www.evcofoods.com
Coffee, wholesale foods
President: Charles Evans
Estimated Sales: $20-50 Million
Number Employees: 50-99

4560 Evensen Vineyards
PO Box 127
Oakville, CA 94562-0127   707-944-2396
Wines
President: Richard Evensen

4561 Ever Fresh Fruit Company
35855 SE Kelso Rd
Boring, OR 97009-7064   503-668-8026
      Fax: 503-668-5823 800-239-8026
      keithm@everfreshfruit.com
      www.everfreshfruit.com
Manufacturer and importer of frozen strawberries, red raspberries, blackberries, boysenberries, rhubarb, apples, loganberries, blueberries and cranberries; also, fresh sliced apples
Owner: Kurt Mc Knight
VP: LeAnn Miller
Estimated Sales: $10-20 Million
Number Employees: 50-99
Type of Packaging: Consumer, Food Service, Private Label
Brands:
NATURE'S QUEST

4562 Everfresh Beverages
6600 E 9 Mile Rd
Warren, MI 48091-2673   586-755-9500
      Fax: 586-755-9587
      everfreshmail@nationalbeverages.com
      www.everfreshjuice.com
Manufacturer and exporter of soft drinks and fruit juices including orange and grape
President/CEO: Stan Sheridan
Telecommunications: Ray Laurinaitis
Operations: Dave Piontkowski
Plant Manager: Matt Filipovitch
Purchasing Director: Walter Koziara
Number Employees: 50-99
Sq. footage: 125000
Parent Co: National Beverages Corporation
Type of Packaging: Consumer, Private Label
Brands:
EVERFRESH
LACROIX

4563 Everfresh Food Corporation
501 Huron Blvd SE
Minneapolis, MN 55414-3199   612-331-6393
      Fax: 612-331-1172 george_edgar@yahoo.com
Manufacturer of chow mein noodles and vanilla including pure and imitation; importer of bamboo shoots and water chesnuts including whole and sliced
VP: Rita Sorsveen

Estimated Sales: $5-10 Million
Number Employees: 10-19
Type of Packaging: Consumer, Food Service, Private Label, Bulk
Brands:
CHINA BOY

4564 Everglades Foods
PO Box 595
Labelle, FL 33975-0595   863-675-2221
      Fax: 863-675-2289 800-689-2221
      everglades92@aol.com
      www.evergladeseasoning.com
Manufacturer of seasonings
President: Seth Howard
Estimated Sales: $1-2.5 Million
Number Employees: 5-9
Type of Packaging: Consumer, Food Service
Brands:
EVERGLADES
EVERGLADES HEAT
EVERGLADES ORIGINAL

4565 Evergood Sausage Company
1389 Underwood Ave
San Francisco, CA 94124-3308   415-822-4660
      Fax: 415-822-1066 800-253-6733
      salesinfo@evergoodfoods.com
      www.evergoodfoods.com
Manufacturer of deli meats including corned beef, pastrami, and roast beef, skinless frankfurters, old world frankfurters and sausages.
President: Harlan Miller
Quality Control Manager: Christopher Ham
VP Sales/Marketing: Don Miller
Plant Manager: Richard Bower
Estimated Sales: $20-50 Million
Number Employees: 50-99
Type of Packaging: Consumer

4566 Evergreen Juices
PO Box 1
Ontario, CA 91762-8001   905-886-8090
      877-915-8423
      info@evergreenjuices.com
      www.evergreenjuices.com
Juice
President: Don Mills

4567 Evergreen Sweeteners, Inc

19495 Biscayne Blvd # 800
Aventura, FL 33180-2321   305-931-1321
      Fax: 305-692-7942
      info@evergreensweeteners.com
      www.evergreensweeteners.com

Evergreen Sweeteners is a full service sweetener distributor serving the entire state of Florida. From bulk liquid sweeteners to bagged sweeteners, Evergreen provides its customers with industry-leading service and unsurpassed quality.

President/CEO: Arthur Green
VP: Mark Gilden
Estimated Sales: $40 Million
Number Employees: 50-99
Number of Products: 40
Sq. footage: 150000
Type of Packaging: Food Service, Bulk
Other Locations:
Evergreen Sweeteners
Atlanta GA
Evergreen Sweeteners
Sanford FL
Evergreen Sweeteners
Miami FL

4568 Everix Bakery
55 W Pioneer Road
Fond Du Lac, WI 54935-6151   920-921-2250
                              Fax: 920-921-1235
Manufacturer of Bakery products
   President: E Everix
   Production: John Marion
Estimated Sales: $2.5-5 Million
Number Employees: 50-99

4569 Everson Spice Company
P.O.Box 6097
Long Beach, CA 90806-0097   562-595-4785
         Fax: 562-988-0219   800-421-3753
kenh@eversonspice.com   www.eversonspice.com
Manufacturer of seasonings, dry rubs, stuffing mixes
and marinades
   Chairman: Tom Everson
   President: Ken Hopkins
   CEO: Kim Everson
Estimated Sales: $2.5-5 Million
Number Employees: 20-49
Type of Packaging: Food Service

4570 Everything Yogurt
1100 Pennsylvania Ave NW
Washington, DC 20004-2501   202-842-2990
Yogurt, salad products
   Owner: January Kwak
Estimated Sales: Under $500,000
Number Employees: 20-49

**4571 Evesham Wood Vineyard
&Winery**
3795 Wallace Road NW
Salem, OR 97304-9703   503-371-8478
      Fax: 541-763-6015   eversham@open.org
                        www.evershamwood.com
Wines
   President: Russell Raney
   CFO: Mary Raney
Estimated Sales: Under $500,000
Number Employees: 1-4
Type of Packaging: Private Label

4572 Eweberry Farms
30377 Brownsville Rd
Brownsville, OR 97327-9525   541-466-3470
         eweberry@proaxis.com
                        www.eweberry.com
Manufacturer of gourmet jams and syrups
   Owner: John Morrison

4573 Excalibur Seasoning Company
1800 Riverway Dr
Pekin, IL 61554-9307   309-347-1221
      Fax: 309-347-9086   800-444-2169
            jay@excaliburseasoning.com
            www.excaliburseasoning.com
Seasoning
   President: Jay Hall
Estimated Sales: $ 5 - 10 Million
Number Employees: 50-99

4574 Excel Corporation
2901 N Mead Street
Wichita, KS 67219-4242   316-832-7500
      Fax: 316-291-2590 www.excelmeats.com
Processor and packer of meat
   President: William Buckner
   CFO: Derek Kennedy
   VP Sales/Marketing: Matthew Wineinger
Number Employees: 30,000

4575 Exceldor Cooperative
460 Rue Principale
St. Anselme, QC G0R 2N0
Canada   418-885-4451
      Fax: 418-885-4271   aforcicer@exceldor.com
                        www.exceldor.com
Manufacturer and exporter of fresh and frozen
chicken
   President: Jean-Guy Guillet
Number Employees: 500
Parent Co: Group Dorchester
Type of Packaging: Consumer, Private Label, Bulk
Brands:
   EXCELDOR EXPRESS

4576 Excellent Coffee Company
259 East Ave
Pawtucket, RI 02860-3800   401-724-6393
      Fax: 401-724-0560   800-345-2007
excelcoffee@aol.com   www.excellentcoffee.com

Coffee
   President/CEO: William Kapos
   CFO: Frank DeLuca
   Marketing: Mark Bishop
   Production Manager: Ron Yanku
   Plant Manager: Ron Yanku
   Purchasing: Judy Hahn
Estimated Sales: $50-100 Million
Number Employees: 20-49
Type of Packaging: Private Label
Brands:
   EXCELLENT COFFEE'S DOWNEAST
   EXCELLENT COFFEE'S MICRO ROAST
   EXCELLENT COFFEE'S OCEAN

4577 (HQ)Excelline Foods
20232 Sunburst St
Chatsworth, CA 91311-6218   818-701-7710
      Fax: 818-701-5904   info@excellinefoods.com
                        www.excellinefoods.com
Manufacturer of frozen Mexican foods
   Owner: Silvia Donhue
Estimated Sales: $25-49.9 Million
Number Employees: 50-99
Number of Brands: 1
Number of Products: 25
Type of Packaging: Consumer, Food Service, Pri-
vate Label, Bulk
Brands:
   EXCELLINE

**4578 Excelpro Manufacturing
Corporation**
3760 E 26th Street
Los Angeles, CA 90023-4506   323-268-1918
      Fax: 323-268-1993   pernsterjr@excelpro.com
Manufacturer of cheese and baking proteins includ-
ing hydrolyzed proteins, sodium, calcium and potas-
sium caseinates and blends
   Chairman: John Ernster
   President: Peter Ernster
Estimated Sales: $20-50 Million
Number Employees: 34
Sq. footage: 45000
Parent Co: Excelpro
Other Locations:
   Excelpro Manufacturing Corp.
   Wellsville UT

4579 Excelsior Dairy
458 Kekuanaoa Street
Hilo, HI 96720-4319   808-961-3608
Manufacturer of Milk, nectar, juice drinks

4580 Excelso Coffee Company
6700 Dawson Blvd # 3a
Norcross, GA 30093-1006   770-449-8140
      Fax: 770-448-6698   800-241-2138
                        dan@excelso.com
Manufacturer of Coffee
   President: Geoffrey Paul
   Sales Manager: Daniel Lane
Estimated Sales: $10-20 Million
Number Employees: 100-249

4581 Exclusive Smoked Fish
43 Mulock Avenue
Toronto, ON M6N 3C3
Canada   416-766-6007
                              Fax: 416-766-7313
Manufacturer and exporter of fresh and frozen
smoked scallops and salmon
Number Employees: 5-9
Type of Packaging: Consumer, Food Service, Pri-
vate Label, Bulk

**4582 Exeter Produce & Storage
Company**
215 Thames Road W
Exeter, ON N0M 1S3
Canada   519-235-0141
      Fax: 519-235-3515 www.exterproduce.com
Manufacturer, importer and exporter of rutabagas,
snap beans, bell peppers, cauliflower, cabbage, car-
rots, onions and potatoes
   President: Leonard Veri
   Director: James Veri
   Director: Michael Veri
Estimated Sales: $5-10 Million
Number Employees: 250-499
Sq. footage: 55000
Type of Packaging: Bulk

Brands:
   Huron Pride
   Veri Fine

4583 Exquisita Tortillas
P.O.Box 1078
Edinburg, TX 78540-1078   956-383-6712
                              Fax: 956-383-1012
            folvera@exquisitatortillas.com
Manufacturer of corn and flour tortillas
   Owner: Humberto Rodriguez
Estimated Sales: $100-500 Million
Number Employees: 100-249
Brands:
   EXQUISITA

4584 Extracts Plus
2460 Coral St
Vista, CA 92081-8430   760-597-0200
      Fax: 760-597-0734 www.pluspharm.com
Manufacturer of herbs, gelatin and vegetarian capsules

4585 Extreme Creations
P.O.Box 4785
El Dorado Hills, CA 95762-0024   916-941-0444
      Fax: 916-941-1777   usa@extremepops.com
                        www.extremepops.com
Manufacturer of jellied lollipops
   Manager: Kamal Naim
Estimated Sales: $ .5 - 1 million
Number Employees: 1-4

4586 Exxter Trading
940 Del Ganado Road
San Rafael, CA 94903-2312   415-492-1820
   President: H Osadchuk

4587 Eyrie Vineyards
P.O.Box 697
Dundee, OR 97115-0697   503-472-6315
      Fax: 503-472-5124 www.eyrievineyards.com
Wines
   President: David Lett
Estimated Sales: $5-10 Million
Number Employees: 20-49

4588 Ezzo Sausage Company
PO Box 7784
Columbus, OH 43207-0784   614-445-8841
      Fax: 614-445-8843   800-558-8841
                              www.ezzo.com
Sausage, pepperoni
   President: Bill Ezzo
Number Employees: 10-19

4589 F Gavina & Sons Inc
2700 Fruitland Ave
Vernon, CA 90058   323-582-0671
      Fax: 323-581-1127   800-428-4627
            sales@gavina.com   www.gavina.com
whole bean coffee, ground coffee, espresso, teas,
specialty drink mixes
   President/Owner: Pedro Gavi□a
   CEO: Jos, Gavi□a
   VP: Leonor Gavi□a-Valls
   Sales: Yolanda Sanchez
Estimated Sales: $88.1 Million
Number Employees: 295

4590 F R LePage Bakeries
P.O.Box 1900
Auburn, ME 04211-1900   207-783-9161
                              Fax: 207-784-4634
Manufacturer of bread, buns, rolls and bagels
   Chairman: Albert LePage
   President/CEO: Andrew Barowsky
   CEO: Andrew P Barowsky
Estimated Sales: $300,000-500,000
Number Employees: 1-4

4591 F&A Cheese Corporation
P.O.Box 19127
Irvine, CA 92623-9127   949-221-8255
      Fax: 949-221-8256   800-634-4109
                        www.facheese.com
Manufacturer of mozzarella and provolone cheese
   Owner: Frank Terranova
   VP Sales: Michael Fray
Estimated Sales: $10-20 Million
Number Employees: 10-19
Type of Packaging: Food Service, Private Label,
Bulk

Brands:
F&A
GOLDEN RIBBON
GOLDEN STATE
GOLDEN STATE PREMIUM

4592 F&A Dairy Products
P.O.Box 278
Dresser, WI 54009-0278 715-755-3485
Fax: 715-755-3480 mike@fadairy.com
www.fadairy.com
Manufacturer of cheese including mozzarella,
provolone, romano and parmesan; importer of pecor-
ino romano
President/Owner: Jeffrey Terranova
Controller: Clyde Loch
CFO: Jay Benusa
QC: Ralph Ramos
Sales: Chris Slavek
Sales: Renzo Sciortino
Human Resources: Carl Gutierrez
VP Wisconsin Operations: Mike Breault
VP New Mexico Operations: Bob Snyder
Estimated Sales:$10-24.9 Million
Number Employees: 50-99
Type of Packaging: Food Service
Other Locations:
F&A Dairy Products
Las Cruces NM
Brands:
F&A

4593 F&A Dairy of California
P.O.Box 578
Newman, CA 95360-0578 209-862-1732
Fax: 209-862-1043 800-554-6455
Manufacturer of cheddar, monterey jack, mozzarella,
provolone, custom blends, shredded and diced
cheeses
VP: Joe Gaglio
QC Manager: Glenn Lewis
General Manager: Joseph Smith
Plant Supervisor: Joseph Gaglio
Estimated Sales:$50-100 Million
Number Employees: 100-249
Type of Packaging: Bulk

4594 F&F Foods
3501 W 48th Pl
Chicago, IL 60632-3028 773-927-1521
Fax: 773-927-3906 800-621-0225
webmaster@fffoods.com www.fffoods.com
Manufacturer and exporter of vanilla, chocolate and
strawberry cookie wafers, chewable vitamins and
bagged hard candies, cough drops and mints; also,
seasonal and vending varieties available
President: Dave Barnett
Estimated Sales:$20-50 Million
Number Employees: 100-249
Sq. footage: 125000
Type of Packaging: Consumer, Private Label, Bulk
Brands:
Daily C
F&F Dietary Supplements
Fast Dry Zinc
Foxes Candy Mint Rolls
Polar Blast Breath Mints
Sen-Sen
Smith Brothers Cough Drops
SmokersGuard

4595 F&M Brewery
71 King Street N
Waterloo, ON N2J 2X2
Canada 519-824-1194
Fax: 519-822-8201 877-316-2337
beer@fmbrewery.com www.fmbrewery.com
Manufacturer and exporter of beer, lager and cask
condition ale
President: Mordechai Rozanski
Brewmaster: Charles MacLean
Brewery Manager: Brian Reilly
Number Employees: 4
Type of Packaging: Consumer, Food Service
Brands:
ERAMOSA HONEY WHEAT
F AND M SPECIAL DRAFT
MACLEANS CASK CONDITIONED
MACLEANS PALE
OAC GOLD
ROYAL CITY
SAINT ANDRE VIENNA
STONE HAMMER PILSNER

4596 F&M Food Products
1001 N Damen Ave
Chicago, IL 60622-4388 773-862-2432
Canned food products
Manager: Eddie Redman
Estimated Sales:$1-4.9 Million
Number Employees: 1-4

4597 F&S Produce Company
P.O.Box 17
Rosenhayn, NJ 08352-0017 856-453-0316
Fax: 856-453-0494 800-886-3316
mstetser@f-and-s-produce.com
www.freshcutproduce.com
Manufacturer of fresh, whole and pre-cut produce
including peppers, onions, lettuce, carrots, spinach,
cabbage, tomatoes and cucumbers; brine products
including vegetables, cherry and bell peppers, on-
ions and jalapenos; also, salad and vegetable trays
President: Sam Pipitone
CEO: Sam Pipitone Jr
*Estimated Sales:*10-20 Million
Number Employees: 100-249
Type of Packaging: Consumer, Food Service, Private Label, Bulk

4598 F&Y Enterprises
716 Merritt Court
Naperville, IL 60540-8106 630-637-8519
Fax: 630-637-8628
Manufacturer and exporter of hickory smoked meat
snacks including sausage sticks and beef jerky
President: Frank Vitek
VP: Bonnie Vitek
Estimated Sales:$5-10 Million
Number Employees: 5-9
Parent Co: F&Y Enterprises
Type of Packaging: Consumer, Food Service, Pri-
vate Label
Brands:
TEXAS BRAND

4599 F. Gavina & Sons
2700 Fruitland Ave
Vernon, CA 90058-2893 323-582-0671
Fax: 323-581-1127 sales@gavina.com
www.gavina.com
Manufacturer of coffee beans.
President: Pedro Gavina
CFO: Jose Gavina
Vice President: Leonor Gavina-Valls
Estimated Sales:$63 Million
Number Employees: 100-249
Sq. footage: 220000
Type of Packaging: Consumer, Food Service, Pri-
vate Label, Bulk
Brands:
CAFE GAVINA ESPRESSO
CAFE LA LLAVE ESPRESSO
DON FRANCISCO GOURMET COFFEE

4600 F. Soderlund Company
9240 Bonita Beach Rd # 1101
Bonita Springs, FL 34135-4250 239-498-0600
Fax: 239-498-0606 soderlund@aol.com
Manufacturer of dairy products
Manager: Michael Cunningham
Estimated Sales:$2.5-5 Million
Number Employees: 1-4
Type of Packaging: Private Label

4601 F.M. Brown Sons
797 Commerce St
Sinking Spring, PA 19608-1308 610-678-3353
Fax: 610-678-6640 800-345-3344
marybethruh@fmbrown.com www.fwbrown.com
Small animal food
Manager: Marianne Egolf
Vice President: Marianne Etolf
Manager: Harvey Brown
Estimated Sales:$20-50 Million
Number Employees: 10-19

4602 F.X. Matt Brewing Company
811 Edward St
Utica, NY 13502-4092 315-624-2400
Fax: 315-624-2452 800-690-3181
info@saranac.com www.saranac.com
Manufacturer, brewer and exporter of beer, ale,
stout, lager and malt; also, soft drinks and juices
President: Nicholas Matt
Vice President: Fred Matt II
Public Relations: Marie McNamara
Operations Manager: Frank Vlossak
Plant Manager: Dave Campbell
Estimated Sales:$50-100 Million
Number Employees: 100-249
Sq. footage: 350000
Type of Packaging: Consumer, Food Service, Pri-
vate Label, Bulk
Brands:
ADIRONDACK AMBER
AMERICAN PLSENER
BLACK AND TAN
BLACK FOREST
ENGLISH PALE ALE
LIGHT
MOUNTAIN BERRY
SARANAC DIET ROOT BEER
SARANAC GINGER BEER
SARANAC ORANGE CREAM
SARANAC ROOT BEER
TRADITIONAL LAGER

4603 FB Washburn Candy Corporation
PO Box 3277
Brockton, MA 02304-3277 508-588-0820
Fax: 508-588-2205 info@fbwashburgncandy.com
www.fbwashburncandy.com
Manufacturer and exporter of candy including hard,
ribbon, rock, lollypops and Christmas novelties;
available bagged, boxed and packaged for racks
President/Co-Owner: James Gilson
Treasurer/Co-Owner: Douglas Gilson
Sales: Robert Gilson
Estimated Sales:$5-10 Million
Number Employees: 50
Sq. footage: 150000
Type of Packaging: Consumer, Food Service, Pri-
vate Label, Bulk
Brands:
BAY STATE
SEVIGNY
TRINITY
WALEECO
WASHBURN

4604 FBC Industries
500 Remington Rd # 300
Schaumburg, IL 60173-4558 847-839-0880
Fax: 847-839-0884 888-322-4637
info@fbcindustries.com www.fbcindustries.com
Manufacturer of industrial ingredients including
dipotassium phosphate, calcium chloride, sodium
and potassuim citrates, lactates and benzoates used
as buffering agents, emulsifers, firming agents, pre-
servatives, antioxidantsflavorings, etc
President: Robert Bloom
VP: John Tramontana
Estimated Sales:$ 1 - 3 Million
Number Employees: 10-19
Type of Packaging: Bulk

4605 FCC Coffee Packers
8801 NW 15th Street
Doral, FL 33172-3027 305-591-1128
Fax: 305-591-1367 sales@fcccoffee.com
Coffee, instant coffee
President: Mike Ferrara
CFO: Alex Ramirez
VP: Ignacio Perez-Echeverria
Plant Manager: Jim Saenz
Estimated Sales:$2.5-5 Million
Number Employees: 20-49
Brands:
ROMA

4606 FDP
398 Tesconi Ct
Santa Rosa, CA 95401-4653 707-547-1776
Fax: 707-545-5270 sales@fdpusa.com
www.fdpusa.com
Manufacturer of dehydrated fruits and vegetables
President: Mark Martindill
Quality Control: Scott Klinger
Sales: Nancy Costa
Estimated Sales:$20-50 Million
Number Employees: 20-49
Parent Co: FDP GmbH
Brands:
SOUBRY INSTANT PASTA
TAURA URC

4607 FNI Group LLC
188 Lake Street
Sherborn, MA 01770-1606   508-655-8816
Fax: 508-655-8816 fnigrouplc@attbi.com
www.essensmart.com
Manufacturer of all natural cookies that are choles-
terol and lactose free
President/Founder: Josephine Ho
Estimated Sales: $ 5 - 10 Million
Number Employees: 5-9
Brands:
ESSEN SMART GLUTEN FREE
ESSEN SMART SINGLE COOKIE 2
ESSEN SMART SINGLE COOKIE 3
ESSEN SMART SOY COOKIES

4608 FSI/MFP
135 Front Ave
West Haven, CT 06516-2811   203-934-5233
Fax: 203-933-8506
Frozen hors d'oeuvres-shrimp, egg rolls, pizza rolls,
seafood rolls, stuffed clams
Manager: Willie Taylor
VP Sales: Marvin Gutkin
Estimated Sales: $100+ Million
Number Employees: 100-249
Brands:
CRYSTAL BAY
MATLAW'S

4609 FW Bryce
8 Pond Rd
Gloucester, MA 01930-1833   978-283-7080
Fax: 978-283-7647 fwbryce@fwbryce.com
www.fwbryce.com
Manufacturer of frozen seafood
Chairman: Carl Moores
President: Keith Moores
Financial Controller: Robert Caldwell
General Counsel: Ian Moores
Quality Assurance Manager: Justin Moores
Inventory Control Manager: Mary Murch
Director Sales: Glenn Hale
VP Sales: Joe Flammia
Logistics Manager: Frank Souza
Warehousing/Logistics: Ralph Pierce
Number Employees: 10-19
Sq. footage: 26000

4610 FW Thurston
P.O.Box 178
Bernard, ME 04612-0178   207-244-3320
Fax: 207-244-3320
Manufacturer of fresh lobster
Owner: Michael Radcliffe
Estimated Sales: $ 3 - 5 Million
Number Employees: 20-49

4611 FW Witt & Company
1106 S Bridge St
Yorkville, IL 60560-1765   630-553-6366
Fax: 630-553-6599 www.newlywedsfoods.com
Manufacturer of spices, seasonings and soy products
President: Dennis Baxter
Estimated Sales: $ 20 - 50 Million
Number Employees: 50-99
Type of Packaging: Consumer

4612 Fabbri Sausage Manufacturing
166 N Aberdeen St
Chicago, IL 60607-1606   312-829-6363
Fax: 312-829-0396 info@fabbrisausage.com
www.fabbrisausage.com
Manufacturer of Italian meats and other pizza sup-
plies including italian sausage, meatballs, italian
roast beef, italian style gravy, italian chili.
President: Ray Fabbri
Estimated Sales: $2.5-5 Million
Number Employees: 20-49
Sq. footage: 25000
Type of Packaging: Consumer, Food Service, Pri-
vate Label, Bulk

4613 Fabe's Natural Gourmet
18115 Saticoy Street
Reseda, CA 91335-3120   818-562-1804
Fax: 818-562-1849
Manufacturer of Gourmet
President/Owner: Lorraine Fabes
Estimated Sales: $10-20 Million
Number Employees: 20-49

4614 Faber Foods and Aeronautics
1153 Evergreen Parkway
Suite M105
Evergreen, CO 80439-9501   800-237-3255
Fax: 303-670-0971 mariafaber@earthlink.net
Manufacturer of low-fat muesli cereal including
strawberry/banana, cranberry/apricot, papaya/peach,
blueberry/peach, raspberry/apple, etc.; also, custom
blend cereals; exporter of extruded crisp rice, edible
seeds, canned oats driedfruit raisins and nuts
President: Maria Faber
Estimated Sales: $300,000-500,000
Number Employees: 10-19
Sq. footage: 10000
Type of Packaging: Consumer, Food Service, Pri-
vate Label, Bulk
Brands:
LOW FAT BODY MUESLIX

4615 Fabio Imports
PO Box 1009
Bonsall, CA 92003-1009   760-726-7040
Fax: 760-726-5731
Estimated Sales: $5-10 Million
Number Employees: 5-9

4616 Fabrique Delices
1610 Delta Ct # 1
Hayward, CA 94544-7043   510-441-9500
Fax: 510-441-9700 sespinas@ix.netcom.com
www.fabriquedelices.com
Manufacturer of Foie gras, terrine, block and
mousse, smoked meats, mousses
CEO: Marc Poinsignon
VP Sales: Sebastian Espinasse
Estimated Sales: $2.5-5 Million
Number Employees: 20-49

4617 Fabulous Chocolate Confections
PO Box 1548
Valdosta, GA 31603-1548   912-244-7000
Fax: 912-247-9000   800-755-5785
Chocolate, soft and hard candy
Public Relations: Kelley Warren
Estimated Sales: $5-9.9 Million
Number Employees: 5-9
Brands:
Chocolate Confetti
Merry Madeline's Cho

4618 Facciola Meat
P.O.Box 14160
Fremont, CA 94539-1360   510-438-8600
Fax: 510-498-1909
Meat
VP: Dennis Welsh
Plant Manager: Richard Ficker
Estimated Sales: $50-100 Million
Number Employees: 10-19

4619 Fage USA
2526 50th St
Flushing, NY 11377-7823   718-204-5323
Fax: 718-204-1842 info@fageusa.com
www.fageusa.com
Greek yogurt and feta cheese
Manager: Antonios Maridakis
Estimated Sales: $ 5 - 10 Million
Number Employees: 5-9

4620 Faidley Seafood
203 N Paca St
Baltimore, MD 21201   410-727-4898
Fax: 410-837-6495 www.faidleyscrabcakes.com
Seafood
President: Nancy Devine
Estimated Sales: $ 3 - 5 Million
Number Employees: 10-19

4621 Fair Oaks Farms
7600 95th St
Pleasant Prairie, WI 53158-2713   262-947-0320
Fax: 262-947-0340 www.fairoaksfarms.com
Manufacturer of cooked and uncooked pork, turkey
and chicken sausage
President/CEO: Michael Thompson
Operations Manager: Michael Duerson
Estimated Sales: $50-100 Million
Number Employees: 100-249

4622 Fair Scones
P.O.Box 177
Medina, WA 98039-0177   425-486-3334
Fax: 425-398-0301   800-588-9160
rebecca.olson@fairscones.com
www.conifer-inc.com
Manufacturer of bean soup and chili mixes, bread,
breakfast, dessert and beverage mixes
President: Michael Maher
Estimated Sales: $ 10 - 20 Million
Number Employees: 20-49

4623 Fairbury Food Products
601 2nd St
Fairbury, NE 68352   402-729-3379
Fax: 402-729-2437
Processor of bacon bits
President: Arden Schacht
Number Employees: 20-49
Parent Co: Fairbury Food
Type of Packaging: Food Service, Private Label

4624 Fairchester Snacks Corporation
100 Lafayette Ave
White Plains, NY 10603-1612   914-761-9430
Salty biscuits
Owner: John Barisano
Estimated Sales: $300,000-500,000
Number Employees: 1-4

4625 Fairfield Farm Kitchens
P.O.Box 333
Tamworth, NH 3886-333   508-584-9300
Fax: 508-580-9910
www.fairfieldfarmkitchens.com
Manufacturer and custom packer of frozen soups,
entrees, side dishes, sauces, gravies, layer, sheet and
pound cakes, etc
President/CEO: Frank Carpenito
Estimated Sales: $20-50 Million
Number Employees: 100-249
Sq. footage: 170000
Brands:
BASIC AMERICAN FROZEN FOODS
FAIRFIELD FARM

4626 Fairhaven Cooperative Flour Mill
1115 Railroad Ave
Bellingham, WA 98225-5007   360-734-9947
Fax: 360-734-9947
Manufacturer and exporter of flour including whole
grain, wheat, rye, corn, buckwheat, rice, etc
President: Bill Distler
Manager: Bill Distler
Estimated Sales: $1-2.5 Million
Number Employees: 1-4
Type of Packaging: Consumer, Bulk

4627 Fairmont Foods of Minnesota
905 E 4th St
Fairmont, MN 56031-4014   507-238-9001
Fax: 507-238-9560 morris@fairmontfoods.com
www.fairmontfoods.com
Manufacturer of frozen entrees including beef,
chicken, chili, pork, lasagna, burritos and soups
President: Larry McGuire
Estimated Sales: $50-100 Million
Number Employees: 250-499

4628 Fairmont Products
15 S Kishacoquillas St
Belleville, PA 17004-8617   717-935-2121
Fax: 717-935-5473
Manufacturer of cultured dairy products including
cottage cheese, sour cream, ice cream mix and cream
Manager: John Lacombe
VP Sales: Peter Menard
Plant Manager: John Lacombe
Estimated Sales: $20-50 Million
Number Employees: 50-99
Parent Co: Dean Foods Company
Type of Packaging: Private Label

4629 Fairmont Snacks Group
6133 Rockside Rd # 404
Cleveland, OH 44131-2244   216-573-2777
Fax: 216-642-0748
Peanuts and snack items
Estimated Sales: $10-20 Million
Number Employees: 20-49

4630 Fairview Swiss Cheese
1734 Perry Hwy
Fredonia, PA 16124-2720   724-475-4154
                          Fax: 724-475-4777
Manufacturer of cheeses
   President: Richard Koller
Estimated Sales: $5-10 Million
Number Employees: 10-19
Type of Packaging: Consumer, Food Service, Private Label, Bulk

4631 Fairwinds Gourmet Coffee
25 Nolls Farm Rd
Auburn, NH 3032-3334   603-626-0135
      Fax: 603-668-0888   800-645-4515
               khybsch@jbfroods.com
               www.fairwindscoffee.com
Manufacturer of gourmet Coffee and tea
   President: Kathy Hybsch
Estimated Sales: $2.5-5 Million
Number Employees: 1-4
Parent Co: JBR Gourmet Foods
Type of Packaging: Bulk
Brands:
   EAST INDIA COFFEE AND TEA
   FAIRWINDS COFFEE
   ORGANIC COFFEE CO

4632 Fairytale Brownies
4610 E Cotton Center Blvd #100
Phoenix, AZ 85040-8898   602-489-5100
      Fax: 602-489-5133   800-324-7982
      julieg@brownies.com   www.brownies.com
Brownies, cookies
   Owner/President: Eileen Spitalny
   Marketing: Julie Gaffney

4633 Faith Dairy
3509 72nd Street E
Tacoma, WA 98443-1299   253-531-3398
                          Fax: 253-536-2782
Manufacturer of ice cream
   President/CEO: Sid Mensonides
   COO: John Mensonides
Estimated Sales: $5-10 Million
Number Employees: 10-19
Type of Packaging: Consumer

4634 Falcon Rice Mill Inc
P.O.Box 771
Crowley, LA 70527-0771   337-783-3825
      Fax: 337-783-1568   800-738-7423
      charles@falconrice.com   www.falconrice.com
Manufacturer and exporter of white and popcorn rice
   President: Mona Trahan
   CFO/Office Manager: Linda Thibodeaux
   VP: Randy Falcon
   General Manager: Tom Dew
   Plant Manager: Russell Cormier
Estimated Sales: $20-50 Million
Number Employees: 20-49
Type of Packaging: Consumer, Food Service, Private Label, Bulk

4635 Falcone's Cookieland
1648 61st St
Brooklyn, NY 11204   718-236-4200
                       Fax: 718-259-6133
Manufacturer of regular and dietetic cookies; also, crackers, biscuits, breadsticks and flatbread
   President: Carmine Falcone
   Vice President: Angelo Falcone
Estimated Sales: $5-9.9 Million
Number Employees: 20-49
Type of Packaging: Consumer, Food Service, Private Label, Bulk
Brands:
   FALCONE'S
   FALCONE'S BAKED GOODS
   FALCONE'S COOKIES
   FALCONE'S FLATBREAD

4636 Fall Creek Vineyards
1402 San Antonio St # 200
Austin, TX 78701-1623   512-476-4477
               Fax: 512-476-6116 www.fcv.com
Wine
   President: Ed Auler
   VP: Chad Auler
   Operations Manager: Roy Nobles
Estimated Sales: $ 3 - 5 Million
Number Employees: 5-9
Type of Packaging: Bulk

4637 Fall River Wild Rice
41577 Osprey Rd
Fall River Mills, CA 96028-9750   530-336-5222
      Fax: 530-336-5265   800-626-4366
      wildrice@frwr.com   www.frwr.com
Manufacturer of wild rice
   Manager: Walt Oiler
Estimated Sales: $20-50 Million
Number Employees: 5-9
Brands:
   FALL RIVER

4638 (HQ)Falla Imports
P.O.Box 1532
Greenville, ME 4441-1532   609-476-4106
                          Fax: 609-476-0412
Importers of coffee
   President: Roderick Falla
Number Employees: 1-4

4639 Fama Sales
450 W 44th St
New York, NY 10036-5205   212-757-9433
      Fax: 212-765-4193   famasales@aol.com
                      www.famasales.com
Food products
   President: Ugo Quazzo
Estimated Sales: $1-2.5 Million
Number Employees: 10-19

4640 Famarco
1381 Air Rail Ave
Virginia Beach, VA 23455-3301   757-460-3573
      Fax: 757-460-2621   info@famarco.com
                      www.famarco.com
Raw material importer and processor for spice, botanicals and craob
   President: Bruce Martin
   VP: Ken Hartfelder
   Quality Control: Darrick Bargher
   Marketing: Mark Herrick
   Plant Manager: James O'Neil
Estimated Sales: $10 Million
Number Employees: 20-49
Sq. footage: 40000
Parent Co: B&K International
Type of Packaging: Private Label, Bulk
Brands:
   Martin's Virginia Roast
   Virginia Roast

4641 Famco Automatic SausageLinkers
P. O. Box 8647
Pittsburgh, PA 15221   412-241-6410
      Fax: 412-242-8877   info@famcousa.com
                      www.famcousa.com
Manufacturer of linking machines for sausage and frankfurter production
   President: Charles Allen
   Vice President: R. Robert Allen
   Sales: Dick Carson

4642 Family Brand International
P.O.Box 429
Lenoir City, TN 37771-0429   865-986-8005
      Fax: 865-986-7171 www.fbico.com
Manufacturer of fresh and frozen pork products
   President: John Wampler
   CEO: Harry Wampler
   VP: Tim Wampler
   Marketing: Clay Jones
   Plant Manager: Bob Epley
Estimated Sales: $20-50 Million
Number Employees: 100-249
Type of Packaging: Consumer, Food Service
Brands:
   Cades Cove
   Dinner Delight
   Elm Hill
   Frosty Morn
   Houser
   Jubilee
   Sycamore

4643 Family Sweets Candy Company
1099 Pratt Boulevard
Elk Grove Village, IL 60007-5120   336-788-5068
      Fax: 336-784-6708   800-334-1607
                      www.familysweets.com
Candy
   President: LeRoy Mansson

4644 Family Tradition Foods
PO Box 869
Wheatley, ON N0P 2P0
Canada   519-825-4673
      Fax: 519-825-3134 www.familytradition.com
Manufacturer and importer of frozen fruits and vegetables; exporter of canned corn and IQF vegetables
   President/CEO: John Omstead
Number Employees: 100-249
Sq. footage: 321000
Type of Packaging: Consumer, Food Service
Other Locations:
   Family Tradition Foods
   Tecumseh, Ontario
Brands:
   FAMILY TRADITIONS
   JOHN O'S

4645 Family Tree Farms
41646 Road 62
Reedley, CA 93654-9124   559-591-6280
      Fax: 559-595-7795 www.familytreefarms.com
Manufacturer, packer, shipper, exporter, and distributor of fresh fruit
   President: David Jackson
   CFO: Dan Clenney
   Quality Control: Mary Ortiz
Estimated Sales: $ 20 - 50 Million
Number Employees: 250-499
Brands:
   EAT SMART
   GREAT WHITES

4646 Famous Chili
1421 N 7th St
Fort Smith, AR 72901-1320   479-782-0096
      Fax: 501-782-6825 www.famouschili.com
Manufacturer of chili and salsa
   President: David Korkames
Estimated Sales: $5-10 Million
Number Employees: 5-9
Sq. footage: 5000
Type of Packaging: Consumer, Food Service, Private Label
Brands:
   FAMOUS
   FOUR STAR
   HEAT & SERVE
   STAR

4647 Famous Pacific Dessert Company
2414 SW Andover Street
Building C
Seattle, WA 98106-1153   206-935-1999
      Fax: 206-935-2535   800-666-1950
                      mherna9334@aol.com
               www.greatfood.com/pacificdessert
Gourmet tortes, cheesecakes, brownies, dessert bars and shortbreads
   President: Anthony Rayner
   CFO: Michelle Hernandez
   Plant Manager: Tina McLaughlin
Estimated Sales: $20-50 Million
Number Employees: 20-49
Sq. footage: 15
Type of Packaging: Private Label
Brands:
   CHOCOLATE DECADENCE
   CHOCOLATE THUNDER/WHITE LIGHTNING
   ELEPHANT BAR
   ESPRESSO DECADENCE
   FAMOUS PACIFIC DESSERT COMPANY
   GORILLA BAR
   JUNGLE BARS
   LINZER TORTE MONKEY BAR
   RHINO BAR
   RUBY SLIPPERS
   ZEBRA BAR

4648 Famous Specialties Company
55 Saratoga Blvd # B
Island Park, NY 11558-1114   516-889-9099
      Fax: 516-889-9099   877-273-6999
               craig@famousspecialties.com
               www.famousspecialties.com
Manufacturer of raw prepared strudel dough
   President: Craig Tropp
Estimated Sales: $2.5-5 Million
Number Employees: 1-4
Sq. footage: 2500
Brands:
   BARNEY'S TOWN & COUNTRY
   BEEF INTERNATIONAL
   BLUE RIDGE FARMS

BRANDT
CAESAR'S
CREATIVE BAKERS
FANCY FOODS
FANCY'S FINEST
FANTASIA
GILDA
HEATH & HEATHER
HIGH MEADOWS
LEAVES
REDI PREP STRUDEL
SILVER LAKE
STAHL MEYER
SWEET STREET

4649 Fancy Farms Popcorn
P.O.Box 209
Bernie, MO 63822-0209   573-276-3315
          Fax: 573-276-2287   800-833-8154
          sales@fancyfarmpopcorn.com
          www.fancyfarmpopcorn.com
Manufacturer of portion-packed popcorn
  President: Chris Tanner
  Sales: J Smith
Estimated Sales:$500,000-$1 Million
Number Employees: 5-9
Parent Co: St. Francis River Farming
Type of Packaging: Food Service, Bulk
Brands:
  FANCY FARM

4650 Fancy Lebanese Bakery
PO Box 9192, Station A
Halifax, NS B3K 5M8
Canada   902-429-0400
          Fax: 902-429-0403
Manufacturer of pita bread and submarine sandwich
buns
  President: Mary Laba
  Manager: Maura Fougere
Estimated Sales:$.5-1 Million
Number Employees: 20-49
Type of Packaging: Consumer, Food Service, Private Label
Brands:
  FANCY LEBANESE BAKERY
  FLB

4651 Fancy's Candy's
5601 Twin Creeks Trl
Rougemont, NC 27572-8657   919-644-2573
          Fax: 919-732-2070   888-403-2629
          akeller@fancyscandys.com
          www.fancyscandys.com
Toffee, milk chocolate, dark chocolate, hazelnuts,
white chocolate, and pecans
  Director: Anne Keller
Estimated Sales:$ 1 - 3 Million
Number Employees: 1-4

4652 (HQ)Fanestil Packing Company
P.O.Box 629
Emporia, KS 66801-0629   620-342-6354
          Fax: 620-342-8190 www.fanestils.com
Manufacturer of sausage, ham and bacon
  President: Dan Smoots
Estimated Sales:$20-50 Million
Number Employees: 50-99
Type of Packaging: Consumer, Food Service
Brands:
  FANESTIL

4653 Fannie May Candies
22 Danada Sq W
Wheaton, IL 60187-1000   630-653-3088
Manufacturer of candy including chocolate, hard
and gummies
  President: Larry Small
*Estimated Sales:*Less than $500,000
Number Employees: 5-9
Parent Co: Fannie Mae Candies
Type of Packaging: Consumer
Brands:
  CELEBRATED COLLECTION
  FANNIE MAY CANDIES

4654 Fannie May/Fanny Farmer
8550 W Bryn Mawr Ave # 550
Chicago, IL 60631-3225   773-693-9100
                                800-333-3629
          questions@archibaldcandy.com
          www.fanniemay.com

Chocolates
  President: Ted Shepherd
  CEO: David Taiclet
Number Employees: 5-9
Parent Co: Archibald Candy Corporation

4655 Fanny Mason Farmstead Cheese
13 Boggy Meadow Ln
Walpole, NH 03608-4200   603-756-3300
          Fax: 603-756-9645   info@fannymasoncheese.com
          www.fannymasoncheese.com
Cheese
  Owner: Marcus Lovell-Smith
  CEO: Scott Lyndecker
  CFO: Sharlene Braldey
  Plant Manager: Mark Whitney
Estimated Sales:$ .5 - 1 million
Number Employees: 5-9
Number of Products: 3
Type of Packaging: Private Label

4656 Fantasia
PO Box 1267
Sedalia, MO 65302-1267   660-827-1172
                           Fax: 660-827-3653
Frozen cakes
  President: Robert Wright
  VP Sales: Thad Bagnato
  Plant Manager: Trent Wanamaker
  Purchasing Agent: Mike Mallory
Estimated Sales:$10-20 Million
Number Employees: 147

4657 Fantastic Foods
580 Gateway Dr
Napa, CA 94558-7517   707-254-3700
          Fax: 707-259-0219   800-288-1089
          jforaker@consorzio.com
          www.fantasticfoods.com
Manufacturer of vegetarian convenience foods in-
cluding soups and rice; importer of rice
  Founder: Jim Rosen
  President/CEO: John Foraker
  CEO: John Foraker
  VP Marketing: Sarah Bird
  VP Sales: Karen Borie
  VP Operations: J Randy Hopkins
Estimated Sales:$20-50 Million
Number Employees: 1-4
Sq. footage: 76000
Type of Packaging: Consumer
Brands:
  FANTASTIC
  JUMPING BLACK BEANS
  NATURE'S BURGER MIX
  TABOULI SALAD MIX
  TOFU BURGER MIX
  TOFU SCRAMBLER MIX

4658 Fantasy Chocolates
2885 S Congress Ave # A
Delray Beach, FL 33445-7336   561-276-9007
          Fax: 561-265-0027   800-804-4962
          fantasychocolate@aol.com
Manufacturer and exporter of chocolate novelties
and gourmet pretzels including chocolate, keylime,
chocolate pizza, caramel and chocolate apple
  President: Becky Gardner
  Products: Bill Gardner
Estimated Sales:$2.5-5 Million
Number Employees: 5-9
Type of Packaging: Consumer, Private Label, Bulk
Brands:
  CHOCOLATE OREOS
  CHOCOLATE PIZZA
  FORBIDDEN FRUIT
  KEYLIME GRAHAM CRACKERS
  LOGO CHOCOLATES
  NOVELTY CHOCOLATES
  PARTY PRETZELS
  PEANUT BUTTER DREAM

4659 Fantasy Cookie Company
12322 Gladstone Ave
Sylmar, CA 91342-5318   818-361-6901
          Fax: 818-365-0040   800-354-4488
          www.fantasycookie.com
Manufacturer of cookies including low fat, fruit
juice sweetened and holiday; also, gingerbread
houses
  President/CEO: Joseph Semder
  VP Sales: Richard Semder
Estimated Sales:$ 3 - 5 Million
Number Employees: 5-9

Type of Packaging: Private Label, Bulk

4660 Fantazzmo Fun Stuff
425 N Martingale Road
Suite 1680
Schaumburg, IL 60173-2214   847-413-1700
          Fax: 847-413-1885   mikecavalier@fantazzmo.com
          www.fantazzmo.com
Manufacturer of Novelty candy
  VP Marketing: Deirdre Gonzalez
Brands:
  CANDY WHISTLER
  SLIDE POPS
  SPORT TOTOE 'EMS
  TOTE 'EMS
  WONKA
  WONKA PIXY STIX MIXERS
  XTREME NERDS

4661 Fantini Baking Company
375 Washington St
Haverhill, MA 01832-5398   978-373-1273
          Fax: 978-373-6250   800-343-2110
Breads
  President: Robert Fantini
  VP: Joe Fantini
Estimated Sales:$1-2.5 Million
Number Employees: 100-249

4662 Fantis Foods
60 Triangle Blvd
Carlstadt, NJ 07072-2701   201-933-6200
          Fax: 201-933-8797 www.fantisfoods.com
Manufacturer of cheese and frozen Greek and Mid-
dle Eastern pastries; importer of wine, Greek and
Italian cheeses, olive oil and olives
  President: George Makris
Estimated Sales:$10-20 Million
Number Employees: 20-49
Sq. footage: 50000
Type of Packaging: Consumer

4663 Far Eastern Coconut Company
200 Corporate Plaza
Central Islip, NY 11749-1552   631-851-8800
          Fax: 631-851-7950   flakes350@aol.com
          www.fareasterncoconut.com
Manufacturer and importer of desiccated and sweet-
ened coconut
  President: Mitchell Bauman
  VP: Anthony Armen
Estimated Sales:$ 3 - 5 Million
Number Employees: 10
Sq. footage: 4000
Type of Packaging: Food Service, Bulk
Brands:
  PALM FLAKE

4664 Far Niente Winery
P.O.Box 327
Oakville, CA 94562-0327   707-944-2861
          Fax: 707-944-2312 www.farniente.com
Wines
  President/CEO/Marketing: Larry Maguire
  CFO: Laura Harwood
  Public Relations: Mary Grace
Estimated Sales:$10-20 Million
Number Employees: 50-99

4665 Far West Rice Inc
P.O.Box 370
Durham, CA 95938-0370   530-891-1339
          Fax: 530-891-0723   greg@greatrice.com
          www.farwestrice.com
Mill, paakage and market rice for food service and
retail demands.
  President: C W Johnson
  CEO: Greg Johnson
  Research & Development: Steve Ross
  Marketing Director: Greg Johnson
  Operations Manager: Steve Ross
Estimated Sales:$10 Million
Number Employees: 20-49
Number of Brands: 10
Number of Products: 100
Type of Packaging: Consumer, Food Service, Private Label, Bulk
Brands:
  CALROSE RICE
  FUKUSUKE RICE
  KOMACHI PREMIUM RICE
  VALLEY SUN ORGANIC BROWN RICE

4666 Farallon Fisheries
207 S Maple Ave
S San Francisco, CA 94080-6305   650-583-3474
Fax: 650-583-0137
Manufacturer of seafood
    Manager: Juan De Alva
    Contact: Aiden Coburn
Estimated Sales:$500,000-$1 Million
Number Employees: 10-19
Brands:
    Farallon Foods

4667 Farb's
241 Pismo St
San Luis Obispo, CA 93401-4203   805-543-1412
    Owner: Barbara Farber
Estimated Sales:$5-10 Million
Number Employees: 10-19

4668 Farbest Foods
P.O.Box 480
Huntingburg, IN 47542-0480   812-683-4200
    Fax: 812-683-4226 www.farbestfoods.com
Manufacturer of turkey and turkey products
    President: Charles La Rue
    Plant Manager: Charlie LaRue
    Purchasing Manager: S Jean Mikula
Estimated Sales:$82 Million
Number Employees: 500-999
Type of Packaging: Consumer, Food Service, Private Label, Bulk
Brands:
    COUNTRY FESTIVAL
    FARBEST FOODS
    HERITAGE PRIDE

4669 (HQ)Farbest-Tallman Foods Corporation
160 Summit Ave # 2
Montvale, NJ 07645-1721   201-573-4900
    Fax: 201-573-0404 dwhobrey@farbest.com
    www.farbest.com
Manufacturer of dairy and soy proteins, carbohydrate sytems, vitamins, and nutraceuticals
    President: Daniel Meloro
Estimated Sales:$20-50 Million
Number Employees: 20-49
Type of Packaging: Bulk
Other Locations:
    Farbest Brands
    Louisville KY
    Farbest Brands
    Huntington Beach CA
    Farbest Brands - Manufacturing
    Plain City OH
Brands:
    FARBEST

4670 Farella-Park Vineyards
2222 N 3rd Ave
Napa, CA 94558-3840   707-254-9489
    www.farella.com
Wines
    Owner: Frank Farella
Estimated Sales:$ 1 - 3 Million
Number Employees: 1-4

4671 Farfelu Vineyards
13058 Crest Hill Road
Flint Hill, VA 22627-1814   540-364-2930
    Fax: 540-364-3930 c-info@farfeluwine.com
    www.farfeluwine.com
Wines
    Owner: C Raney
Estimated Sales:$500,000-$1 Million
Number Employees: 1-4

4672 Fargo Packing & SausageCompany
307 Main Ave E
West Fargo, ND 58078-1834   701-282-3211
    Fax: 701-282-0325 www.qualitymeats.com
Manufacturer and packer of meat and meat products including ham, bacon and sausage
    Manager: Roger Mammenga
Estimated Sales:$20-50 Million
Number Employees: 20-49
Parent Co: Quality Boneless Beef Company
Type of Packaging: Consumer, Food Service

4673 Faribault Dairy Company
222 3rd Street NE
Faribault, MN 55021   507-334-5260
    Fax: 507-332-9011 www.faribaultdairy.com

cheese
    President/Owner: Sarah Arhameault
    CEO: Jeff Jirik
    VP: Michael Gilbertson
Estimated Sales:$3.5 Million
Number Employees: 21

4674 (HQ)Faribault Foods
222 S 9th St # 3380
Minneapolis, MN 55402-3820   612-333-6461
    Fax: 612-342-2908 MKTG@faribaultfoods.com
Manufacturer of canned beans, chicken, chili, pasta, soups, stews and vegetables including peas, corn and green beans.
    President: Reid V Mac Donald
    EVP/CFO: Gary Kindseth
    EVP Research/Engineering: Jim Nelson
    EVP Sales/Marketing: Frank Lynch
    VP Strategic Sourcing: Jim Montealegre
    Director Human Resources: Amy Dellis
    VP Manufacturing: Scott King
    VP Purchasing/Contract Management: Andy Murray
Estimated Sales:$164 Million
Number Employees: 5-9
Type of Packaging: Consumer, Private Label
Other Locations:
    Faribault Foods Distribution
    Faribault MN
    Faribault Foods Plant
    Cokato MN
Brands:
    BUTTER KERNEL
    CHILLI MAN
    FINEST
    KUNERS
    MRS GRIMES
    PASTA SELECT
    PRIDE
    SEASIDE
    SUN VISTA

4675 (HQ)Faribault Foods
222 S 9th St # 3380
Minneapolis, MN 55402-3820   612-333-6461
    Fax: 612-342-2908 www.faribaultfoods.com
Manufacturer and exporter of canned food products including dried beans, peas, corn and pasta
    President: Reid V Mac Donald
    CEO: Reid MacDonald
    Exec VP/Treasurer: Gary Kindseth
    Exec VP Marketing: Mike Peroutka
    Exec VP Sales: Mike Peroutka
    VP Operations: Mike Cureton
    Production Superintendent: Brenda Probst
    Plant Manager: Dave Cross
    VP Purchasing/Contract Management: Andy Murray
Estimated Sales:$50-100 Million
Number Employees: 5-9
Type of Packaging: Consumer, Private Label
Other Locations:
    Faribault Foods
    Faribault MN
    Faribault Foods - Mondovi Plant
    Mondovi WI
    Faribault Foods - Grimes Dist.
    Grimes IA
    Faribault Foods - Kuner's Dist.
    Brighton CO
    Faribault Foods - Cokato Plant
    Cokato MN
Brands:
    BUTTER KERNEL®
    CHILLIMAN® CHILI
    KUMER'S SOUTHWESTERN®
    KUNER'S®
    MRS. GRIMES®
    PASTA SELECT®
    PRIDE®
    S&W BEANS®

4676 Faribault Foods
P.O.Box 339
Cokato, MN 55321-0339   320-286-2166
    Fax: 320-286-5142 www.faribaultfoods.com

Manufacturer and exporter of canned corn and pasta products
    CEO: Reid McDonald
    EVP Corporate Research/Engineering: Jim Nelson
    Senior QA Manager: Jean Berger
    Product Development Manager: Judene Smahal
    Food Technologist Manager: Phyllis Nichols
    HR Supervisor/Office Manager: Kathy Nowak
    Maintenance Superintendent: Ray Youngkrantz
    Production Manager: Tina Noyes
    Plant Manager: Allen Anderson
    Purchasing Coordinator: Terry Hauth
Estimated Sales:$ 50 - 100 Million
Number Employees: 100-249
Parent Co: Faribault Foods
Type of Packaging: Consumer

4677 Faridault Food
13512 Business Center Dr NW
Elk River, MN 55330-4612   763-241-7343
    Fax: 763-241-7412 service@spftpacinc.com
    www.fairbaultfoods.com
Flexible packaging
    president: John Ambrose
    Marketing Manager: chris Ambrose
    Plant Manager: John Anderson
Brands:
    Faridault

4678 Farley Candy Company
2945 W 31st St
Chicago, IL 60623-5104   773-254-0900
    Fax: 773-254-0795 www.kelloggs.com
Chocolate candy
    President: Williams Sampson
    Sales: Keith Barton
    Plant Manager: Larry Carroll
Estimated Sales:$50-99.9 Million
Number Employees: 100-249

4679 (HQ)Farley's & Sathers CandyCompany
P.O.Box 28
1 Sathers Plaza
Round Lake, MN 56167-0028   507-945-8181
    Fax: 507-945-8343
    comments@farleysandsathers.com
    www.farleysandsathers.com
Manufactures and distributes confections and snacks
    President/COO: Dennis J Nemeth
    CFO: Tammy Koller
    VP Operations: Kurt Schultz
Estimated Sales:$ 400 Million
Number Employees: 1800
Type of Packaging: Private Label
Other Locations:
    Farley's & Sathers - Distribution
    Chattanooga TN
    Farley's & Sathers - Manufacturing
    Des Plaines IL
    Farley's & Sathers - Manufacturing
    Reynosa MX
Brands:
    BOBS®
    BRACH'S®
    CHUCKLES®
    FARLEY & SATHERS
    FARLEY'S®
    FRUIT STRIPES®
    HEIDE®
    NOW AND LATER®
    RAINBLO®
    SATHERS®
    SUPER BUBBLE®
    TROLLI®

4680 Farley's & Sathers Candy Company
1 Sather Plaza
PO Box 28
Round Lake, MN 56167   507-945-8181
    Fax: 507-945-8343   800-533-0330
    comments@farleysandsathers.com
    www.farleysandsathers.com

Processor and exporter of candy including butter-scotch, caramels, chocolate, jelly beans, hard, lico-rice, lollypops, mints, marshmallows, nougats, etc.
President: Dennis Nemeth
CEO: Liam Killeen
CFO: Tammy Koller
R&D: John Flanyak
Marketing: Matthew Fenton
Sales: Mike Sprinkle
Public Relations: Theresa Neuburger
Operations: Kevin McElvain
Estimated Sales: $600 Million
Parent Co: Farley's & Sathers Candy Company
Type of Packaging: Food Service, Private Label, Bulk
Brands:
ANDES CANDIES
AUTUMN LEAVES
BEAR PAKS
BEST OF BROCK
BLUE RASPBERRY
BRACH
BRACH'S CANDY
BRACH'S TDS
BUNNY PRINTS
BUNNY TAILS
BUTTERLETS
CANDY DISH
CHAMPS COLLEGE
CHATTANOOGA CHOO CHOO
CHRISTMAS CRITTERS
CHUBBY SANTA
COOL BLUE
CORDIALLY YOURS
DOUBLE DIPPERS
EASTER BUTTERCREME CRITTERS
EASTER HUNT CANDIES
EASTER JORDAN
EASTER PARADE
FRIGHT BITES
FRITOS
FRUIT BASKET
FRUIT SNACKERS
GUM DINGER
GUMMY SQUIRMS
HECTOR RABBIT
HIDE A PAKS
HIDE-A-WAY EGGS
KENTUCKY MINTS
LOVE
MEMORY
MINI-MONSTERS CANDY
MINT COOLERS
MINT PEARLS
MINTS JOTS
MY OWN BUNNY
NIK NAKS
NINJA TROLLS
NUBBINS
OLD FASHIONED
OLDE WORLD GOURMET GUMMIES
PERKY'S
POWER PLUS
PUCKER HUSTLE
PUTTERS
SANTA SNACKS
SASSY HEARTS
SCARY POPS
SCARY TARTS
SCHULER
SIZZLE HEART
SOUR BEASTIES GUM
SOUR SPOTS JELLY BIRD EGGS
SPARKLES
SPEARMINTLETS
SPECIAL TREASURES
SPERRY
SPRING BOUQUET
SQUIRMS
STARS
TARGETS
TREE TRIMMERS
VILLA CHERRIES
TARGETS
TREE TRIMMERS
VILLA CHERRIES
YUMMY GUMMY MUMMIES

4681 Farm 2 Market
PO Box 124
Roscoe, NY 12776-0124   607-498-5448
Fax: 607-498-5275   800-663-4326
info@farm-2market.com
www.farm-2-market.com

Manufacturer of seafood including farm raised shrimp, freshwater prawns, scallops, crawfish and oysters; importer of Australian crawfish and fresh-water prawns
President: Marshall Shnider
Estimated Sales: $3-5 Million
Number Employees: 10-19
Type of Packaging: Consumer, Food Service
Brands:
SWEET-WATER

4682 (HQ)Farm Boy Food Service
P.O.Box 996
Evansville, IN 47706-0996   812-428-8436
Fax: 812-428-8432   800-852-3976
www.farmboyfoodservice.com
Manufacturer of beef and pork; wholesaler/distribu-tor of frozen, refrigerated and dry food products, meat, equipment and fixtures, etc.; serving the food service market
President/Co-Owner: Bob Bonenberger
VP/Co-Owner: Rich Bonenberger
Estimated Sales: $38 Million
Number Employees: 50-99
Type of Packaging: Consumer, Food Service, Pri-vate Label

4683 Farm Fresh Bakery
1433 SE 1st Street
Lawton, OK 73501-5733   580-355-3485
Fax: 580-581-4181
Bread
Estimated Sales: $10-20 Million
Number Employees: 100-249
Parent Co: New Mexico Farm Fresh Dairy Produc-ers

4684 Farm Fresh Catfish Company
1616 Rice Mill Road
Hollandale, MS 38748   662-827-2204
Fax: 662-827-2005   800-647-8264
www.farmfreshcatfish.com
Manufacturer and exporter of fresh and frozen farmed raised catfish
President/CEO: Willard Fehr
Purchasing Director: Jimmy Sanders
Estimated Sales: $50-99.9 Million
Number Employees: 250-499
Type of Packaging: Consumer, Food Service, Pri-vate Label, Bulk
Brands:
FARM FRESH

4685 Farm Fresh Frozen
123 Industrial Boulevard
Americus, GA 31719-8116   912-928-5600
Fax: 912-928-8828
Frozen vegetables
President: Calvin Canedy
Estimated Sales: $5-9.9 Million
Number Employees: 20-49

4686 Farm Pak Products
7840 Old Bailey Hwy
Spring Hope, NC 27882-8393   252-459-3101
Fax: 252-459-9020 www.farmpak.com
Manufacturer and exporter of produce including sweet potatoes
Owner/President: Carson Barnes
Sales: Eddie Lee
Packhouse Manager: Frank Salinas
Estimated Sales: $20-50 Million
Number Employees: 50-99
Type of Packaging: Consumer, Bulk

4687 Farm Stores
18001 Old Cutler Rd # 370
Palmetto Bay, FL 33157-6434   305-471-5141
Fax: 305-513-4176   800-726-3276
www.farmstores.com
Ice cream and dairy products
President/CEO: Carlos Bared
VP Marketing: Manuel Portuondo
Estimated Sales: $50-99.9 Million
Number Employees: 1,000-4,999

4688 Farm T Market Company
P.O.Box 727
Somerville, TN 38068-0727   901-465-2844
Fax: 901-465-6812
Produce
President: Frank Boswell
Estimated Sales: $ 1 - 3 Million
Number Employees: 10-19

4689 Farm to You
PO Box S
Carmel, CA 93921-0589   408-626-8357
Fax: 408-625-6067
farm-to-you@thejamesranch.com
www.farm-to-you.com
Fresh farm grown food and products from direct market farms. A comprehensive farmer directory to enable the farmer to consumer connection to grow and to prosper. Farm direct, products can be found by state and by category
President: Dale Pressow
Estimated Sales: $500,000-$1 Million
Number Employees: 1-4

4690 FarmGro Organic Foods
101-2445 13th Avenue
Regina, SK S4P 0W1
Canada   306-522-0092
Fax: 306-721-3130 info@farmgro-organic.com
Manufacturer of organic food
President: Bruce Johnson
CFO: Dennis Puff
Purchase Manager: Tim Beard

4691 Farmacopia
23600 Big Basin Way
Saratoga, CA 95070-9755   831-335-8401
Fax: 831-335-5601   888-827-3623
roberta@sosbee.com   www.farmacopia.com
Condiments, dressings and sauces
Owner: Bette Mermis
Vice President: John Mermis
Estimated Sales: $5-9.9 Million
Number Employees: 5
Brands:
Saveur

4692 Farmdale Creamery
1049 W Base Line St
San Bernardino, CA 92411-2310   909-889-3002
Fax: 909-888-2541 www.farmdale.net
Creamery
Owner: Nick Sibilio
VP: Mark Hannay
Estimated Sales: $20-50 Million
Number Employees: 50-99

4693 (HQ)Farmer Brothers Company
P.O.Box 2959
Torrance, CA 90509-2959   310-787-5200
Fax: 310-787-5246   800-735-2878
info@farmerbroscousa.com
www.farmerbroscousa.com
Manufacturer of coffees, teas, beverage mixes and spices
Chairman/President/CEO: Guenter Berger
CFO/Treasurer: John Simmons
CEO: Roger M Laverty Iii
Estimated Sales: $193,600,000
Number Employees: 1,000-4,999
Type of Packaging: Food Service

4694 Farmers Co-operative Grain Company
P.O.Box 246
Kinde, MI 48445-0246   989-874-4200
Fax: 989-874-5793 kindecoop@centurytel.net
www.kindecoop.com
Manufacturer of dried beans
President: Jeff Kreh
CEO: Dan Gottschalk
Estimated Sales: $10-20 Million
Number Employees: 20-49
Type of Packaging: Consumer

4695 Farmers Cooperative Creamery
700 NE Highway 99w
McMinnville, OR 97128-2795   503-227-5133
Fax: 503-472-3821 www.farmerscoop.org
Manufacturer and exporter of butter and powdered milk
President: Dan Bansen
CEO/Secretary: Mike Anderson
CEO: Michael Anderson
Estimated Sales: $50-100 Million
Number Employees: 20-49
Type of Packaging: Consumer, Food Service, Bulk

4696 (HQ)Farmers Cooperative Dairy
PO Box 8118
Halifax, NS B3K 5Y6
Canada   902-835-3373
                                    Fax: 902-835-1583
customerservice@farmersdairy.ca
www.farmersdairy.ca
Manufacturer of dairy products including milk, yo-
gurt, ice cream, cheese, sour cream, etc
    CEO/President: Kenneth Peacock
    Export Manager: Alfred Jennings
Estimated Sales: $100+ Million
Number Employees: 500-999
Type of Packaging: Consumer, Food Service, Pri-
    vate Label
Other Locations:

4697 Farmers Dairies
7321 North Loop Dr
El Paso, TX 79915-2598   915-772-2736
                                    Fax: 915-772-0907
Dairy products
    Plant Manager: Ovidio Matamores
Estimated Sales: $20-50 Million
Number Employees: 100-249

4698 Farmers Grain Company
PO Box 58
Morganfield, KY 42437-0058   270-822-4241
        Fax: 270-822-4425   800-339-4241
Manufacturer and exporter of soybeans and grains
including wheat and specialty white and yellow corn
Estimated Sales: $1-2.5 Million
Number Employees: 10-19
Parent Co: Geico Corporation
Type of Packaging: Bulk

4699 Farmers Hen House
1956 520th St SW
Kalona, IA 52247-9173   319-683-2206
                                    Fax: 319-683-2256
Manufacturer of eggs; commercial, organic and cage
free
    President: Mark Miller
Estimated Sales: $10-20 Million
Number Employees: 10-19
Brands:
    FARMERS HEN HOUSE

**4700 (HQ)Farmers Investment
Company**
P.O.Box 7
Sahuarita, AZ 85629-0007   520-791-2852
                                    Fax: 520-791-2853
    President/CEO: Richard Walden
    Plant Manager: Albert Celaya
Estimated Sales: $20-50 Million
Number Employees: 20-49

4701 Farmers Meat Market
Box 961
Viking, AB T0B 4N0
Canada   780-336-3193
                                    Fax: 780-336-0180
Processor of bologna, cured meats and wild game in-
cluding deer, elk and moose, famous original viking
wieners
    President: Eugene Miskew
    Sales: Shirley Miskewn
    Purchasing Manager: Chris Ferguson
Estimated Sales: $150,000
Number Employees: 2
Type of Packaging: Private Label

4702 Farmers Produce
103 Melby Ave
Ashby, MN 56309-4707   218-747-2749
Manufacturer of chicken
    Owner: Paul Ellingson
Estimated Sales: $ 3 - 5 Million
Number Employees: 10-19
Type of Packaging: Consumer

4703 Farmers Rice Milling Company
P.O.Box 3704
Lake Charles, LA 70602-3704   337-433-5205
        Fax: 337-433-1735   sales@FRMCO.com
www.frmco.com
Manufacturer and exporter of rice and rice bran
    President: Jamie Warshaw
    CFO: Gregory Mack
    Vice President: Charles Miia
    VP Sales: Charles Miia
    Production Manager: Richard Deville

Estimated Sales: $50-100 Million
Number Employees: 50-99
Parent Co: Powell Group
Type of Packaging: Consumer, Food Service
Brands:
    Cajun Pride Rice

4704 Farmers Seafood Company
P.O.Box 1225
Shreveport, LA 71163-1225   318-221-9957
        Fax: 318-424-2029   800-874-0203
farmersseafood@aol.com
www.farmersseafood.com
Wholesaler/distributor of groceries, dairy products
and seafood; serving the food service market
    President: Alexander Mijalis
Estimated Sales: $5-10 Million
Number Employees: 50-99

4705 Farmers' Rice Cooperative
P.O.Box 15223
Sacramento, CA 95851-0223   916-923-5100
        Fax: 916-920-4295   800-326-2799
www.farmersrice.com
Domestic, international, institutional, bulk and pack-
aged rice milling and marketing
    President/CEO: Robert Sandrock
    CFO/VP: James Dodson
Estimated Sales: $100-500 Million
Number Employees: 20-49

4706 Farmington Food
7419 Franklin St
Forest Park, IL 60130-1016   708-771-3600
        Fax: 708-771-2643   800-609-3276
info@farmingtonfoods.com
www.farmingtonfoods.com
Manufacturer and wholesaler/distributor and packer
of meat
    President: Frank Dijohn
Estimated Sales: $50-100 Million
Number Employees: 100-249

4707 Farmland Dairies
520 Main Ave
Wallington, NJ 07057-1892   973-777-2500
        Fax: 973-777-7648   888-727-6252
questions@farmlanddairies.com
www.roorbachflowers.com
Formerly, Parmalat USA we are a manufacturer of
milk, ice cream, yogurt, juice and ice tea
    President/CEO: Martin Margherio
    VP Finance: Anthony Mayzun
Estimated Sales: $200+ Million
Number Employees: 1,000-4,999
Sq. footage: 80000
Type of Packaging: Consumer
Other Locations:
    Farmland Dairies Facility
    Wallington NJ
    Farmland Dairies Facility
    Newark NJ
    Farmland Dairies Facility
    Grand Rapids MI
Brands:
    ALTANTA DAIRY
    CLINTON'S
    FARMLAND
    SUNNYDALE FARMS
    WELSH FARMS

4708 Farmland Dairies
5252 Clay Ave SW
Grand Rapids, MI 49548-5658   616-538-3822
        Fax: 616-538-3844   www.farmlanddairies.com
Contract packager of aseptic packaged juice and
dairy and soy products; exporter of aseptic packaged
milk
    Principal: Mike Rozixki
    VP: Mark Sherman
    VP Operations North America: Barry Dyer
Estimated Sales: $1 Billion
Number Employees: 50-99
Sq. footage: 105000
Parent Co: Parmalat USA

4709 Farmland Dairies
520 Main Ave
Wallington, NJ 07057-1892   973-777-2500
                                    Fax: 973-777-7648
questions@farmlanddairies.com
www.roorbachflowers.com

Manufacturer of milk, ice cream, cream, yogurt,
juice and ice tea
    President/CEO: Martin Margherio
    VP Finance: Anthony Mayzun
Estimated Sales: $289 Million
Number Employees: 1,000-4,999
Brands:
    ATLANTA DAIRIES
    CLINTON'S
    FARMLAND
    SUNNYDALE FARMS
    WELSH FARMS

4710 Farmland Foods
401 N Grant Road
Carroll, IA 51401-2907   712-792-1660
        Fax: 712-792-1372   www.farmlandfoods.com
Manufacturer and canner of ham
    Plant Superintendent: Kevin Boger
    Plant Manager: Jeff Bowden
Estimated Sales: $50-100 Million
Number Employees: 120
Parent Co: Farmland Industries
Type of Packaging: Consumer, Food Service, Pri-
    vate Label, Bulk
Brands:
    FARMLAND

4711 Farmland Foods
800 Industrial Dr
Denison, IA 51442-2714   712-263-5002
        Fax: 712-263-7330   800-831-1812
rxcarlson@farmland.com
www.farmlandfoods.com
Manufacturer, exporter and packager of pork; also,
slaughtering services available
    Manager: Todd Gerken
    Mannufacturing/Operations Director: Jim
    Schaben
    Plant Manager: Jerry Behrens
    Purchasing Manager: Larry Schwarte
Estimated Sales: $500 Million-$1 Billion
Number Employees: 900
Sq. footage: 382000
Parent Co: Farmland Industries
Type of Packaging: Consumer, Food Service

4712 (HQ)Farmland Foods
PO Box 20121
Kansas City, MO 64195-0121   816-243-2700
        Fax: 816-243-3343   888-327-6526
info@farmlandfoods.com
www.farmlandfoods.com
Manufacturer and exporter of fresh and frozen ba-
con, ham, hot dogs, deli & lunch meat and sausage.
    President: James Sbarro
    CFO: Shelly Phalen
    VP Human Resources: Mark Garrett
Estimated Sales: $1 Billion
Number Employees: 6,123
Type of Packaging: Consumer, Food Service, Pri-
    vate Label, Bulk
Other Locations:
    Farmland Foods Plant
    Monmouth IL
    Farmland Foods Plant
    Denison IA
    Farmland Foods Plant
    Wichita KS
    Farmland Foods Plant
    Springfield MA
    Farmland Foods Plant
    Crete NE
    Farmland Foods Plant
    New Riegel OH
    Farmland Foods Plant
    Carroll IA
    Farmland Foods Plant
    Salt Lake City UT
Brands:
    CARANDO
    FARMLAND
    OHSE
    ROEGELEIN

4713 Farmland Foods
P.O.Box 98
Carroll, IA 51401-0098   712-792-1660
        Fax: 712-792-1372   www.farmlandfoods.com
Manufacturer of meats
    VP: Tom Farner
    Plant Manager: Jeff Bowden
Estimated Sales: $25-49.9 Million
Number Employees: 100-249

4714 Faroh Candies
14840 Indian Creek Drive
Cleveland, OH 44130-6663 440-842-4070
Fax: 440-842-4013
Manufacturer of confectionery products including boxed chocolates, chocolate cherries and popcorn specialties.
Owner: George Faroh
Purchasing: Donna Parrot
Estimated Sales: $5-10 Million
Number Employees: 20-49
Type of Packaging: Consumer

4715 Farr Candy Company
345 D St
Idaho Falls, ID 83402-3532 208-522-8215
Fax: 208-523-3307 www.farrcandy.com
Manufacturer of confectionery products including cherry cordials, peanut clusters and malo nuts; also, ice cream
President/Owner: Kevin Call
Estimated Sales: $ 3 - 5 Million
Number Employees: 10-19

4716 Farrell Baking Company
26 Stefanak Dr
West Middlesex, PA 16159-3138 724-342-7906
Bread and bakery products
President: Rick Vatavuk
Owner: Richard Vatavuk
Estimated Sales: $1-2.5 Million
Number Employees: 10-19
Brands:
Farrell Baking

4717 Fast Fixin Foods
1481 Us Highway 431
Boaz, AL 35957-1552 256-593-7221
Fax: 256-593-7208
Manufacturer of fast foods
Owner: Ricky Ragsdale
Estimated Sales: $ 10 - 20 Million
Number Employees: 10-19

4718 Fast Food Merchandisers
PO Box 800
Rocky Mount, NC 27802-0800 252-450-4000
Fax: 252-985-6605
Producers of prepared foods.
Estimated Sales: Under $500,000
Number Employees: 10-19

4719 Fastachi
598 Mount Auburn Street
Watertown, MA 02472-4124 617-924-8787
800-466-3022
info@fastachi.com www.fastachi.com
Produces candy, chocolate, dried fruits and nuts.
Estimated Sales: $300,000-500,000
Number Employees: 1-4

4720 Fastachi
598 Mount Auburn Street
Watertown, MA 02472-4124 617-924-8787
Fax: 617-924-8844 800-466-3022
souren@fastachi.com www.fastachi.com
Processor of almonds, cashews, pistachios, hazelnuts, peanuts and sunflower seeds; also, gift baskets available
President/CEO: Souren Etyenezian
Estimated Sales: Less than $500,000
Number Employees: 1-4
Brands:
Fastachi

4721 (HQ)Fasweet Company
P.O.Box 5000
Jonesboro, AR 72403-5000 870-932-1562
Fax: 870-932-1114
Manufacturer of sugar substitutes
President: Jake Morse
Estimated Sales: $5-10 Million
Number Employees: 5-9
Sq. footage: 10000
Parent Co: Morse Company
Type of Packaging: Consumer, Food Service
Brands:
Fasweet

4722 Fat Witch Bakery
75 Ninth Avenue
New York, NY 10011 212-807-1335
Fax: 212-807-7993 888-419-4824
patwitch@fatwitch.com www.fatwitch.com
brownies

4723 FatBoy Cookie Company
18-01 River Road
Fair Lawn, NJ 07410 201-796-1000
Fax: 201-475-3501 888-328-2690
fatboycookies@aol.com
www.outrageouscookiedough.com
cookie dough
President/Owner: Joel Ansh

4724 Father Sam's Bakery
105 Monsignor Valente Dr
Buffalo, NY 14206-1815 716-853-1071
Fax: 716-853-1062 800-521-6719
info@fathersams.com OR
dziolkowski@fathersams.com
www.fathersams.com
Manufactures regular and large pocket bread, mini pocket bread, and wraps.
Founder: Albert Sam
President: William Sam
Marketing: Dennis Ziolkowski
VP Sales: Glenn Povitz
Estimated Sales: $ 20 - 50 Million
Number Employees: 50-99
Type of Packaging: Food Service

4725 Father Sam's Syrian Bread
105 Monsignor Valente Dr
Buffalo, NY 14206-1815 716-853-1071
Fax: 716-853-1062 800-521-6719
dziclkowski@fathersams.com
www.fathersams.com
Manufacturer of Syrian-style pocket bread, tortilla shells and thin-style pita bread
President: William Sam
Marketing: Dennis Ziolkowski
VP Sales: Glenn Povitz
Estimated Sales: $20-50 Million
Number Employees: 50-99
Sq. footage: 40000
Type of Packaging: Consumer, Food Service, Private Label
Brands:
FATHER SAM'S POCKET BREADS
FATHER SAM'S TORTILLAS
FATHER SAM'S WRAPS

4726 Father's Country Hams
P.O.Box 99
Bremen, KY 42325-0099 270-525-3554
Fax: 270-525-3333 www.fatherscountryhams.com
Ham, bacon, and smoked sausage
President: Charles Gatton Jr
Estimated Sales: $ .5 - 1 million
Number Employees: 5-9

4727 Fauchon
575 Madison Ave
New York, NY 10022-2511 212-605-0495
Fax: 212-605-0421 877-605-0130
Chocolate, tea, coffee, cookies, mustard, oil
Estimated Sales: Less than $500,000
Number Employees: 1-4

4728 Favorite Brands International
2121 Waukegan Road
Suite 300
Bannockburn, IL 60015-1831 847-374-0900
Fax: 847-374-0952
Marshmallow cream
President: Steve Kaplan
CEO: Richard Harshman
VP Sales: Paul Hervey
Brands:
Kidd's
Sweet Shop

4729 Favorite Brands International
75 Tri State International
Suite 400
Lincolnshire, IL 60069-4428 847-405-5814
Fax: 847-374-0148 betchick_j@favbrands.com
www.favbrands.com
Industrial confectionery and candy products to food processors

4730 Favorite Foods
6934 Greenwood Street
Burnaby, BC V5A 1X8
Canada 604-420-5100
Fax: 604-420-9116
Manufacturer and exporter of sauces including light and dark soy, oyster, teriyaki, marinade, barbecue, black bean, stir fry, Szechuan spicy hot and plum
Manager: Henry Lam
Number Employees: 10-19
Sq. footage: 35000
Type of Packaging: Consumer, Food Service, Private Label, Bulk
Brands:
Golden Dragon

4731 Favreau's Cheese
42 1/2 George Street
Green Island, NY 12183-1104 518-273-1146
Fax: 518-273-1146
Cheese
President: Danny Favreau

4732 Fayes Bakery Products
216 E Business Us Highway 60
Dexter, MO 63841-1222 573-624-4920
Manufacturer of bakery products
Owner: Dale Parks
Estimated Sales: $ .5 - 1 million
Number Employees: 1-4

4733 Faygo Beverages
3579 Gratiot Ave
Detroit, MI 48207-1892 313-925-1600
Fax: 313-571-7611 800-347-6591
www.faygo.com
Manufacturer of carbonated soft drinks
President: Stan Sheridan
CEO: Nick A Caporella
Number Employees: 500-999
Parent Co: National Beverage Company
Type of Packaging: Consumer, Private Label

4734 Fayter Farms Produce
69400 Jolon Rd
Bradley, CA 93426-9676 831-385-8515
Fax: 831-385-0833 fayterfarms@earthlink.net
Fresh herbicide pesticide-free Kiss of Burgundy globe artichokes.
President: Thomas Fayter
Estimated Sales: $300,000-500,000
Number Employees: 1-4
Type of Packaging: Private Label, Bulk
Other Locations:
Fayter Farms Produce
Bradley CA
Brands:
Globe Artichoke
Kiss of Burgundy

4735 Fearn Natural Foods
6425 W Executive Dr
Mequon, WI 53092-4482 262-242-2400
Fax: 262-242-2751 800-877-8935
modernfearn@aol.com www.modernfearn.com
Manufacturer and exporter of natural food products including baking, pancake and dehydrated soup mixes, soybean and rice flour, breakfast cereals, wheat germ and powdered milk
President: Gaylord Palermo
Estimated Sales: $ 10 - 20 Million
Number Employees: 20-49
Sq. footage: 70000
Parent Co: Modern Products
Type of Packaging: Consumer, Food Service, Private Label, Bulk
Brands:
FEARN®
GAYELORD HAUSER®

4736 Fearnow Brothers
994 Ocean Dr
Cape May, NJ 08204-5400 609-884-0440
Fax: 609-898-2409 fearnow@lov-stew.com
www.lov-stew.com
Canned foods
Controller: Larry Rossello
Estimated Sales: $5-9.9 Million
Number Employees: 100-249
Brands:
MRS. FEARNOW'S

4737 Feaster Foods
11808 W Center Rd
Omaha, NE 68144-4434   402-691-8800
    Fax: 402-691-7920   800-228-6098
        www.mariolive.com
Real bacon bits, sunflower kernels, imitation bacon bits
    CEO: Dick Westin
    Purchasing Manager: Scott Bailey
Estimated Sales: F
Number Employees: 20-49

4738 Feature Foods
15 Meteor Drive
Etobicoke, ON M9W 1A3
Canada
                    416-675-7350
    Fax: 416-675-7428   info@featurefoods.com
        www.featurefoods.com
Manufacturer and exporter of pickled eggs and herring; also, herb horseradish
    President: Reva Krongold
Number Employees: 20-49
Type of Packaging: Consumer

4739 Federal Pretzel Baking Company
638 Federal Street
Philadelphia, PA 19147-4845   215-467-0505
        Fax: 215-467-3153
Manufacturer of soft pretzels
    Owner: Florence Sciambi
Estimated Sales: $1-2.5 Million
Number Employees: 20-49
Type of Packaging: Consumer

4740 Federal Pretzel Baking Company
638 Federal Street
Philadelphia, PA 19147-4845   215-467-0505
        Fax: 215-467-3153
Manufacturer of pretzels, cookies
    President: Florence Sciambi
    Plant Manager: Rich Bezila
Estimated Sales: $1-2.5 Million
Number Employees: 20-49
Brands:
    Federal Pretzel

4741 Federation of Southern Cooperatives
2769 Church St
East Point, GA 30344-3258   404-765-0991
    Fax: 404-765-9178   fsc@mindspring.com
        www.federation.coop
Manufacturer and exporter of fresh vegetables
    Executive Director: Ralph Paige
    Executive Director: Ralph Paige
Estimated Sales: $500,000-$1 Million
Number Employees: 20-49
Type of Packaging: Consumer, Bulk

4742 Fee Brothers
453 Portland Ave
Rochester, NY 14605-1597   585-544-9530
    Fax: 585-544-9530   800-961-3337
    info@feebrothers.com   www.feebrothers.com
Manufacturer and exporter of cocktail mixes including whiskey sour, daiquiri, margarita, pina colada, etc.; also, slush bases, bitters, nonalcoholic cordials, tea and juice concentrates, grenadine, coffee flavoring syrups, maraschinocherries, olives, cocktail
    President: John Fee
    CEO: Ellen Fee
    Treasurer: Joe Fee
Estimated Sales: $1 Million
Number Employees: 5-9
Number of Brands: 1
Number of Products: 90
Sq. footage: 32000
Type of Packaging: Food Service, Private Label, Bulk
Brands:
    Fee Brothers

4743 Fehr Foods
5425 N 1st St
Abilene, TX 79603-6424   325-691-5425
    Fax: 325-691-5471   jdoll@fehrfoods.com
        www.fehrfoods.com
Manufacturer of Lil' Dutch Main Sandwich Center wirecut cookies
    President/CEO: Steven Fehr
    Controller: Bruce Foreman
    VP Marketing: Doug Veazey
    VP Sales: Doug Veazey

Estimated Sales: $19.60 Million
Number Employees: 100-249

4744 Felbro Food Products
5700 W Adams Blvd
Los Angeles, CA 90016-2402   323-936-5266
    Fax: 323-936-5946   800-335-2761
    bart@felbro.com   www.felbrofoods.com
Manufacturer, importer and exporter of fountain syrups, sauces, soup, gravy and beverage bases, ice cream toppings, flavors, colors and extracts; also, custom formulations and private labeling available
    President: Barton Feldmar
    Operations Manager: John Pesce
Estimated Sales: $20-50 Million
Number Employees: 20-49
Sq. footage: 40000
Type of Packaging: Consumer, Food Service, Private Label, Bulk
Brands:
    Coffee Express
    Food Tone

4745 Felix Custom Smoking
17461 147th St SE # 2a
Monroe, WA 98272-1070   425-485-2439
        Fax: 425-485-2439
Manufacturer of smoked and vacuum-packed salmon, cod and halibut
    Owner: Diane Zollinger
Estimated Sales: Less than $500,000
Number Employees: 5-9
Type of Packaging: Private Label

4746 Felix Roma & Sons
P.O.Box 5547
Endicott, NY 13763-5547   607-748-3336
    Fax: 607-748-3607   800-640-3336
        www.felixroma.com
Manufacturer of bread, bagels and rolls
    President: Eugene Roma Jr
    VP/Master Baker: Barry Roma
    VP/Sales Manager: Anthony Roma Jr
    Office Manager: Mary Consentio
    Bakery General Manager: James Wasley
    VP/Frozen Foods Manager: Michael Roma
    Production Manager: Brian Bertoni
    Plant Manager: Eugene Roma Jr
Estimated Sales: $20-50 Million
Number Employees: 50-99
Type of Packaging: Consumer, Food Service, Private Label, Bulk
Brands:
    FELIX ROMA

4747 Fellom Ranch Vineyards
17075 Montebello Road
Cupertino, CA 95014-5439   408-741-0307
    Fax: 408-741-0307 www.fellom.com
Wines
    Owner/Winemaker: Roy Fellom
    Consulting Winemaker: Dan Barwick
    Wine Sales/Marketing: Karen Fellom
    Vineyard Manager: Javier Garcia
Estimated Sales: $1-2.5 Million
Number Employees: 5-9
Type of Packaging: Private Label

4748 Fendall Ice Cream Company
470 S 700 E
Salt Lake City, UT 84102-2860   801-355-3583
    Fax: 801-521-0133   gunter@fendalls.com
        www.fendalls.com
Manufacturer and wholesaler/distributor of ice cream, sherbet, water ices, sorbets and frozen yogurt
    Owner: Carol Radinger
Estimated Sales: $1-2.5 Million
Number Employees: 5-9
Type of Packaging: Consumer
Brands:
    Cream of Weber
    Fendall's

4749 Fenestra Winery
83 Vallecitos Rd
Livermore, CA 94550-9603   925-447-5246
    Fax: 925-447-4655   800-789-9463
        www.fenestrawinery.com
Wines
    Owner: Lanny Replogle
Estimated Sales: $500,000-$1 Million
Number Employees: 1-4
Type of Packaging: Private Label

Brands:
FENESTRA WINERY

4750 (HQ)Fenn Valley Vineyards
6130 122nd Ave
Fennville, MI 49408-9457   269-561-2396
    Fax: 269-561-2973   800-432-6265
    winery@fennvalley.com   www.fennvalley.com
Wines
    President: Douglas Welsch
Estimated Sales: $500,000-$1 Million
Number Employees: 10-19

4751 Fennimore Cheese
860 Lincoln Ave
Fennimore, WI 53809-1538   608-822-3599
    Fax: 608-822-6007   888-499-3778
    igo@fennimorecheese.com   www.fennimore.com
Manufacturer of cheese
    Manager: Linda Parrish
Estimated Sales: $2.5-5 Million
Number Employees: 5-9
Type of Packaging: Consumer, Private Label, Bulk
Brands:
    Bahl Baby

4752 Fentimans North America
141 Camino Amigo Ct
Danville, CA 94526   925-837-9995
        Fax: 925-837-9996
    gwarwick@drinkfentimans.com
        www.fentimans.com
botanically brewed beverages-natural sodas
    President/Owner: Greg Warwick

4753 Fenton & Lee Chocolatiers
35 E 8th Avenue
Eugene, OR 97401-2906   541-343-7629
    Fax: 541-343-6385   800-336-8661
        www.fentonandlee.com
Chocolates and confections
    President: Janele Smith
Estimated Sales: $2.5-5 Million
Number Employees: 5-9

4754 Ferko Meat Company
P.O.Box 170966
Milwaukee, WI 53217-8086   414-967-5500
        Fax: 414-967-5515
Manufacturer of beef, chicken, veal, lamb and pork
    President: Craig Nevins
    Purchasing Manager: Craig Nevins
Estimated Sales: $20-50 Million
Number Employees: 20-49
Sq. footage: 28000
Type of Packaging: Food Service

4755 Ferme Ostreicole Dugas
675 Saint Pierre W Boulevard
Caraquet, NB E1W 1A2
Canada   506-727-3226
        Fax: 506-727-4950
Manufacturer of fresh oysters
    Purchasing: Gaetan Dugas
Number Employees: 5-9
Type of Packaging: Consumer, Food Service

4756 Fernandez Chili Company
8267 County Road 10 S
Alamosa, CO 81101-9176   719-589-6043
        Fax: 719-587-0485
Manufacturer and importer of chili and taco sauces, spices and prepared chili mixes; also, Mexican corn products
    President: Donald Fernandez
Estimated Sales: $5-10 Million
Number Employees: 5-9
Sq. footage: 15000
Type of Packaging: Consumer, Food Service, Bulk

4757 Fernando C Pujals & Bros
PO Box 364245
San Juan, PR 00936-4245   787-792-3080
        Fax: 787-792-8797
Manufacture of candy
    President: Fernando Pujals
Number Employees: 50

4758 Ferolito Vultaggio & Sons
5 Dakota Dr
New Hyde Park, NY 11042-1109   516-812-0300
    Fax: 516-326-4988   800-832-3775

Manufacturer of beverages, general grocery
President: John Ferolito
CEO: Rick Adonailo
CEO/CFO: Richard Adonailo
CFO: Rick Adonailo
VP Corporate Communications: Francie Patton
Estimated Sales:$10-100 Million
Number Employees: 500-999
Type of Packaging: Private Label
Brands:
 Arizona Iced Tea
 Ferolito Vultaggio

4759 Ferrante Winery & Ristorante
5585 State Route 307
Geneva, OH 44041   440-466-6046
 Fax: 440-466-7370 info@ferrantewinery.com
 www.ferrantewinery.com
Manufacturer of wines
President: Peter Ferrante
VP: Nicholas Ferrante
General Manager: Mary Jo Ferrante
Estimated Sales:$10-20 Million
Number Employees: 20-49
Brands:
 Ferrante

4760 Ferrara Bakery & Cafe
195 Grand St
New York, NY 10013-3717   212-226-6150
 Fax: 212-226-0667 information@ferraracafe.com
 www.ferraracafe.com
Manufacturer and importer of confectionery products including candies, novelties, Italian and seasonal products; also, syrups, coffee and baked goods
Owner: Ernest Lepore
Owner: Peter Lepore
Estimated Sales:$5-10 Million
Number Employees: 100-249
Type of Packaging: Consumer, Private Label

4761 Ferrara Pan Candy Company
7301 Harrison St
Forest Park, IL 60130-2083   708-366-0500
 Fax: 708-366-5921 800-323-1168
 www.ferrarapan.com
Manufacturer of candy including gummy, glazed nuts, sour balls, Valentine, jelly beans, licorice, hard candies, etc
President/COO: Salvatore Ferrara II
CEO/Chairman: Nello Ferrara
CFO/Secretary: James Buffardi
CEO: Salvatore Ferrara Ii II
VP International Sales: Louis Buffardi
Estimated Sales:$50-100 Million
Number Employees: 250-499
Type of Packaging: Consumer
Brands:
 Atomic Fireball
 Jaw Busters
 Lemonheads
 Original Boston Baked Beans
 Red Hots
 The Original Black Forest

4762 Ferrara Winery
1120 W 15th Ave
Escondido, CA 92025-5548   760-745-7632
Manufacturer of wines
Owner: Gasper D Ferrara
CEO: Vera "Ferrara,"
Estimated Sales:$1-2.5 Million
Number Employees: 5-9
Brands:
 Ferrara

4763 Ferrari-Carano Vineyards& Winery
8761 Dry Creek Rd
Healdsburg, CA 95448-9133   707-433-6700
 Fax: 707-431-1742 800-831-0381
 info@ferrari-carano.com
 www.ferrari-carano.com
Manufacturer of wines
President: Don Carano
Director, Vineyard Operations: Steve Domenichelli
Controller: David James
Marketing Director: Steve Meisner
Public Relations Director: Nancy Gilbert
Winemaker: George Bursick
Estimated Sales:$20-50 Million
Number Employees: 100-249
Type of Packaging: Private Label

4764 Ferrero USA
600 Cottontail Ln
Somerset, NJ 08873-1233   732-764-9300
 Fax: 732-764-2700 800-337-7376
 www.ferrerousa.com
Manufacturer of confectionery items including breath mints, chocolates, chocolate and hazelnut wafers and spread; also, chocolate espresso coffee
COO: Michael Gilmore
CEO: Michael Gilmore
VP Sales: Lawrance Fineburg
Estimated Sales:$10-20 Million
Number Employees: 100-249
Parent Co: Ferrero, SPA
Type of Packaging: Consumer
Brands:
 MON CHERI
 RAFFAELLO
 ROCHER
 SILVERS
 TIC TAC

4765 Ferrigno Vineyard & Winery
17301 State Route B
St James, MO 65559-8583   573-265-7742
Manufacturer of wine
Owner: Richard Ferrigno
Estimated Sales:$500,000-$1 Million
Number Employees: 5-9

4766 Ferrigno Vineyards & Winry
17301 State Route B
St James, MO 65559-8583   573-265-7742
 ferrigno@fidnet.com
 www.ferrignovineyards.com
Wines
President: Dick Ferrigno
Estimated Sales:$140,000
Number Employees: 1-4
Type of Packaging: Private Label
Brands:
 Ferrigno

4767 Ferris Organic Farm
3565 Onondaga Rd
Eaton Rapids, MI 48827-9608   517-628-2506
 Fax: 517-628-8257 800-628-8736
 ferrisorganicfarm@excite.com
 www.ferrisorganicfarm.com
Manufacturer, grower and exporter of organic beans including black, soy, black turtle and pinto; also, grains including wheat and barley; wholesaler/distributor of organic natural foods
Co-Owner: Richard Ferris
Estimated Sales:$1-2.5 Million
Number Employees: 1-4
Sq. footage: 7000
Type of Packaging: Bulk

4768 (HQ)Ferris Stahl-Meyer Packing Corporation
P.O.Box 5600
Bronx, NY 10460   718-328-0059
 Fax: 718-328-0729
Manufacturer of frankfurter and meat products
Manager: Melissa Torres
Purchasing: Guillermo Gonzalez
Estimated Sales:$63.70 Million
Number Employees: 10-19
Number of Brands: 5
Number of Products: 50
Type of Packaging: Consumer, Food Service, Private Label, Bulk
Brands:
 FERRIS
 STAHLMEYER
 SWEET MEADOW FARMS

4769 Ferroclad Fishery
Highway 17 N
Batchawana Bay, ON P0S 1A0
Canada   705-882-2295
 Fax: 705-882-2297
Manufacturer, importer and exporter of herring, trout, whitefish and caviar
Owner: Gary Symons
Number Employees: 20-49
Parent Co: Presteve Foods Limited
Type of Packaging: Consumer, Food Service

4770 Fess Parker Winery
P.O.Box 908
Los Olivos, CA 93441-0908   805-688-1545
 Fax: 805-686-1130 800-446-2455
 www.fessparker.com
Wines
Manager: Rosemary Williams
Estimated Sales:$5-10 Million
Number Employees: 20-49
Sq. footage: 9
Type of Packaging: Private Label
Brands:
 AMERICAN TRADITION RESERVE
 PINOT NOIR SANTA BARBARA COUNTY
 SANTA BARBARA COUNTY
 SYRAH SANTA BARBARA COUNTY
 VIOGNIER SANTA BARBARA COUNTY

4771 Festida Food
P.O.Box 326
Cedar Springs, MI 49319-0326   616-696-0400
 Fax: 616-696-0496 www.festidafoods.com
Corn, tortilla chips and flour tortillas
President: Raul Vega
VP: Gloria Vega
Purchasing: Robert Robbins
Estimated Sales:$500,000-$1 Million
Number Employees: 20-49
Type of Packaging: Private Label

4772 Festive Finer Foods
12220 Merrick Boulevard
Jamaica, NY 11434-1916   718-341-2100
 Fax: 718-978-0764
Beverages and Drink Mixes, Cereals and Grains, Fruits & Vegetables, Tomato products

4773 Festive Foods
389 Edwin Dr
Virginia Beach, VA 23462-4548   757-490-9186
 Fax: 757-490-9494
Manufacturer and exporter of sauces including spicy and extra spicy
President: Robert Buchanan
Purchasing: Robert Buchanan
Estimated Sales:$ .5 - 1 million
Number Employees: 1-4
Type of Packaging: Consumer
Brands:
 BUFFALO BOB'S EVERYTHING SAUCE

4774 Fibred-Maryland
P.O.Box 3349
Cumberland, MD 21504-3349   301-724-6050
 Fax: 301-722-7131 800-598-8894
 dennis@fibred.com www.fibred.com
Manufacturer of soy fiber
Owner: Karen Ort
SVP/Director Sales: Rick Thayer
Estimated Sales:$10-20 Million
Number Employees: 20-49
Type of Packaging: Bulk
Brands:
 F1-1 Soy Fibre

4775 Ficklin Vineyards
30246 Avenue 7 1/2
Madera, CA 93637-9198   559-674-4598
 www.ficklin.com
Wines
President: Peter Ficklin
Estimated Sales:$500,000-$1 Million
Number Employees: 1-4

4776 Fidalgo Bay Coffee
856 N Hill Blvd
Burlington, WA 98233-4640   360-757-8818
 Fax: 360-757-8810 800-310-5540
 www.fidalgobaycoffee.com
Coffee
Owner: Gary Swoyer
CEO: David Evans
Purchasing: Gary Sawyer
Estimated Sales:$1-2.5 Million
Number Employees: 20-49

4777 Fiddlers Green Farm
P.O.Box 254
Belfast, ME 04915-0254   207-338-3872
 Fax: 207-338-3872 800-729-7935
 fiddlers@fiddlersgreenfarm.com
 www.fiddlersgreenfarm.com

Manufacturer of organic and stone ground grains, flour and corn meal
Owner: Laine Alexander
Owner: Judy Ottmann
Vice President: Laine Alexander
Estimated Sales: Under $500,000
Number Employees: 1-4
Sq. footage: 300
Type of Packaging: Consumer, Food Service
Brands:
Belleweather
Bertha's
Bread & Biscuits
Fiddle Cakes
Fiddlers Green Farms
Islander's Choice
Oatbran & Brown Rice
Penobscot Porridge
Spice
Toasted Buckwheat

4778 Fidelity Flavors & Fragrances
17 Ridgeview Ter
Goshen, NY 10924-5310   845-294-5356
                                Fax: 845-294-5356
Manufacturer of natural and artificial flavors including outdoor fragrances
President: Jefferson Schiller
VP of Sales: George Schiller
Number Employees: 5-9
Sq. footage: 3800
Type of Packaging: Bulk

4779 Field Stone Winery & Vineyard
10075 Highway 128
Healdsburg, CA 95448-9025   707-433-7266
     Fax: 707-433-2231   800-544-7273
                       fieldstone1@earthlink.com
                       www.fieldstonewinery.com
Manufacturer of Wines
President: John Staten
CFO: Ben Staten
Vice President: Katrina Staten
Tasting Room Manager: Helen Weber
Public Relations: Roger Hull
Winemaker: Tom Milligan
Estimated Sales: $2.5-5 Million
Number Employees: 10-19

4780 Field's
P.O.Box 7
Pauls Valley, OK 73075-0007   405-238-7381
     Fax: 405-238-5075 www.fieldspies.com
Manufacturer of frozen pies including pecan, German chocolate and lemon chess
President: Chris Field
Purchasing Manager: Chris Field
Estimated Sales: $20-50 Million
Number Employees: 20-49
Sq. footage: 12500
Type of Packaging: Consumer, Food Service, Private Label, Bulk
Brands:
FIELD'S

4781 Fieldale Farms
1540 Monroe Dr
Gainesville, GA 30507-7317   770-536-3899
     Fax: 770-297-9261   800-241-5400
     danwhite@fieldale.com   www.fieldalefarms.com
Manufacturer of fresh chicken including whole and parts
Manager: Claude Sullens
CEO: Joe Hatfield Jr
VP/Director Sales/Marketing: Gus Arrendale
Estimated Sales: $100+ Million
Number Employees: 500-999
Parent Co: Fieldale Farms
Type of Packaging: Consumer, Food Service, Private Label, Bulk

4782 (HQ)Fieldale Farms Corporation
P.O.Box 558
Baldwin, GA 30511-0558   706-778-5100
     Fax: 706-776-3191   800-241-5400
     donclick@fieldale.com   www.fieldale.com
Manufacturer of fresh and frozen chicken
Chairman/CEO: Joe Hatfield
President: Tom Arrendale
VP of Marketing/Sales: Gus Arrendale
Sales Director: Sammy Franklin
Sales Manager: Jeff Paschall
Sales Manager: Jim McGahee
Sales Manager: Don Click

Estimated Sales: $ 50 - 100 Million
Number Employees: 50-99
Type of Packaging: Consumer, Food Service, Private Label, Bulk

4783 (HQ)Fieldale Farms Corporation
P.O.Box 558
Baldwin, GA 30511-0558   706-778-5100
     Fax: 706-776-3191   www.fieldale.com
Manufacturer of fresh and frozen poultry
Chairman: Joe Hatfield
CEO: Joe Hatfield
VP: Steven Collier
VP/CFO: Thomas Hensley
Director Sales/Marketing: Thomas Arrendale III
Estimated Sales: $470 Million
Number Employees: 1-4
Type of Packaging: Consumer, Food Service, Private Label, Bulk

4784 (HQ)Fieldbrook Farms
P.O.Box 1318
Dunkirk, NY 14048-6318   716-366-5400
     Fax: 716-366-3588   800-333-0805
                       www.fieldbrookfarms.com
Manufacturer and exporter of ice cream, sorbet, sherbet, fudge, juice and fruit bars, regular and fat-free frozen yogurt and frozen novelties, and whipped topping
President: Kenneth Johnson
Manager Operations: Kevin Grismore
Estimated Sales: $50-100 Million
Number Employees: 500-999
Sq. footage: 280000
Type of Packaging: Consumer, Food Service, Private Label, Bulk
Other Locations:
Fieldbrook Farms
Columbus GA
Brands:
DEERING
HOWARD JOHNSON
MY FAVORITE

4785 Fieldbrook Valley Winery
4241 Fieldbrook Rd
McKinleyville, CA 95519-8130   707-839-4140
                       www.fieldbrookwinery.com
Manufacturer of Wines
President: Dr Robert Hodgson
COO: Judith Hodgson
Estimated Sales: $1-2.5 Million
Number Employees: 1-4

4786 Fields of Fair Whiskey
RR 1
Box 19
Paxico, KS 66526-9708   785-636-5460
                                Fax: 785-636-5365
Manufacturer of Alcoholic beverages
President: Mont Dennis
Estimated Sales: $5-10 Million
Number Employees: 10-19

4787 Fiera Foods
220 Norelco Drive
North York, ON M9L 1S4
Canada   416-744-1010
     Fax: 416-744-7777 www.fierafoods.com
Manufacturer of frozen French pastries including croissants, danish and turnovers; also, muffin mixes
President/Co-Founder/COO: Alex Garber
VP/Co-Founder: Boris Serebryany
VP Sales/Marketing: Robert Shapiro
Estimated Sales: $20-50 Million
Number Employees: 250-499
Sq. footage: 200000
Type of Packaging: Food Service

4788 Fiesta Candy Company
25 Old Dover Rd # I
Rochester, NH 03867-3490   603-926-6053
                 Fax: 603-926-6628   800-285-9735
Manufacturer of Candy
President: Jose Mayoral
Estimated Sales: $ 5 - 10 Million
Number Employees: 5-9

4789 Fiesta Canning Company
8071 N Central Highway
Mc Neal, AZ 85617-9513   520-364-7541
                                Fax: 520-642-3271

Manufacturer of canned chili pepper paste
President: Gary Johnson
CFO: Bob Myers
VP: Stephen Johnson
Marketing: Ernie Jayme
Sales: Sharisse Johnson
Plant Manager: Bob Godfrey
Sq. footage: 10000
Brands:
Cochise Farms
Fiesta Del Sole
Macayo Mexican Foods

4790 Fiesta Farms
350 Commercial Ave
Nyssa, OR 97913-3712   541-372-2248
     Fax: 541-372-2474   fiesta@fmtc.com
Manufacturer and exporter of onions including red, yellow and white
President: Garry Bybee
Secretary: Tamara Bybee
VP: Marc Bybee
Estimated Sales: $ 10 - 20 Million
Number Employees: 20-49
Type of Packaging: Consumer, Food Service, Private Label, Bulk
Brands:
Bloombuilder
Bybee's
FF
Ru-Bee
Zoombees

4791 Fiesta Gourmet of Tejas
42 Oak Villa Road
Canyon Lake, TX 78133-3102   210-212-5233
     Fax: 210-212-5240   800-585-8250
                       www.fiestagourmetoftejas.com
Manufacturer and exporter of Texas-made wines, chiles, salsas, sauces, jellies, oils, coffees and teas; custom-made gift baskets available
Owner: Maricela Smith
Estimated Sales: Less than $500,000
Number Employees: 1-4
Sq. footage: 2000
Parent Co: Fiesta Gourmet del Sol
Type of Packaging: Consumer, Food Service, Private Label
Brands:
FIESTA DEL SOL
POBLANOS
SERRANOS
TEJAS SIZZLE

4792 Fiesta Mexican Foods
979 G St
Brawley, CA 92227-2615   760-344-3577
                                Fax: 760-344-3580
Tortillas
President: Carmelita Halton
Estimated Sales: $20-50 Million
Number Employees: 20-49

4793 Fife Vineyards
3620 Rd 8
Redwood Valley, CA 95470   707-485-0323
     Fax: 707-485-0832   info@fifevineyards.com
                       www.fifevineyards.com
Wines
President: Dennis Fife
Estimated Sales: $2.5-5 Million
Number Employees: 5-9

4794 Fife Vineyards
3620 Rd 8
Redwood Valley, CA 95470   707-485-0323
     Fax: 707-485-0832   info@fifevineyards.com
                       www.fifevineyards.com
Wine
President: Dennis Fife
Owner: Karen MacNeil
Co-Owner: Dennis Fife
Estimated Sales: $ 3 - 5 Million
Number Employees: 5-9
Type of Packaging: Bulk

4795 Fig Garden Packing
P.O.Box 13157
Fresno, CA 93794-3157   559-271-9000
     Fax: 559-271-1332   mike@figgardenpacking.com
                       www.figgardenpacking.com

Manufacturer, exporter and packer of dried and
diced figs and fig paste including regular and
crushed seed
President/CEO: Mike Jura Jr
Estimated Sales:$10-20 Million
Number Employees: 50-99

4796 Figamajigs
133 White Oak Circle
Petaluma, CA 94952   707-992-0023
        Fax: 707-581-1753 mel@figamajigs.com
                www.figamajigs.com
all natural, gluten free, low fat, kosher fig bars and
fig pieces covered in chocolate

4797 Figaro Company
3601 Executive Blvd
Mesquite, TX 75149-2711   972-288-3587
        Fax: 972-288-1887 dave@figaroco.com
                www.figaroco.com
Manufacturer and exporter of hickory liquid smoke,
mesquite liquid smoke, fajita marinade, brisket
cooking sauce
    Owner: J K Mc Kenney
    CEO: Dave McCormack
    Sales: Dave McCormack
    Public Relations: Linda Willett
    Operations: Anita Watson
    Production: C Platero
Number Employees: 10-19
Number of Products: 6
Sq. footage: 21000
Type of Packaging: Consumer, Food Service, Private Label
Brands:
    FIGARO

4798 Figuerola Laboratories
PO Box 1569
Santa Ynez, CA 93460-1569   805-688-6626
        Fax: 805-688-8099 800-219-1147
        customerservice@figuerola-labs.com
                www.figuerola-laboratories.com
Manufacturer of dietary supplements
    President: Rossana Figuerola
    Executive Marketing Director: Antonio Figuerola
Brands:
    Figuerola

4799 Fiji Ginger Company
2801 Ocean Park Boulevard
Suite 232
Santa Monica, CA 90405-2905   310-452-0878
        Fax: 310-452-7977 info@fijiginger.com
                www.fijiginger.com
Manufacturer of Ginger products

4800 Fiji Water Company
361 Southside Drive
Basalt, CO 81621-9170   970-920-1780
                877-426-3454
        info@fijiwater.com www.fijiwater.com
Natural artesian water known for its signature soft,
smooth taste and well-balanced mineral content including a high level of silica, a youth-preserving
antioxidant
    Owner: David Gilmour
    CEO: Doug Carlson
Brands:
    FIJI

4801 Fiji Water LLC
11444 W Olympic Blvd # 210
Los Angeles, CA 90064-1559   310-312-2850
        Fax: 310-312-2828 888-426-3454
        info@fijiwater.com www.fijiwater.com
Manufacturer of bottled water
    President: John Edward Cochran
    CEO: Doug Carlson
Parent Co: Roll International Corporation
Brands:
    FIJI

4802 Filippo Berio Brand
255 S State Rt 17 # 203
Hackensack, NJ 07601-1085   201-525-2900
        Fax: 201-525-0805 www.filippoberio.com
Manufacturer of Olive oil
    President: Thomas Mueller
Estimated Sales:$20-50 Million
Number Employees: 10-19
Brands:
    Casale Degli Ulivi
    Centanni

FILIPPO BERIO EXTRA
FILIPPO BERIO EXTRA
FILIPPO BERIO EXTRA
FILIPPO BERIO EXTRA
FILIPPO BERIO GREEN/
    Farmhouse
Fattoria Dell'ulivo
Filippo Berio
Filippo Berio Olive
Francesconi
Sagri
Tiger Brand

4803 Fillmore Piru Citrus Association
P.O.Box 350
Piru, CA 93040-0350   805-521-1781
        Fax: 805-521-0990 800-524-8787
                www.fillmorepirucitrus.com
Manuafacturer, packer and exporter of oranges
    President: Thomas Hardison
    Corporate Secretary/Treasurer: Lois Yates
    VP: Brian Edmonds
Estimated Sales:$ 20 - 50 Million
Number Employees: 20-49
Type of Packaging: Consumer, Food Service
Brands:
    AIRSHIP
    BELLE OF PIRU
    CUPID
    CYCLE
    DESIRABLE
    GLIDER
    HOME OF RAMONA
    MANSION
    ORIOLE
    WEAVER

4804 Fillo Factory
P.O.Box 155
Dumont, NJ 07628-0155   201-439-1036
        Fax: 201-385-0012 800-653-4556
        ronrex@bellatlantic.net www.fillofactory.com
Manufacturer of gourmet appetizers, baklava, stru-
del, pastries and fillo dough; importer of dough
    President: Ron Rexroth
    VP Sales: Tony Falletta
Estimated Sales:$1-3 Million
Number Employees: 10-19
Sq. footage: 12000
Type of Packaging: Consumer, Food Service, Private Label, Bulk
Brands:
    Fillo Factory

4805 Filsinger Vineyards & Winery
39050 De Portola Rd
Temecula, CA 92592-8833   951-302-6363
        Fax: 909-302-6650 www.filsingerwinery.com
Wines
    President: William Filsinger
Estimated Sales:$500-1 Million appx.
Number Employees: 5-9

4806 Filtration Solutions Inc
4361 Charlotte Hwy # 301
Lake Wylie, SC 29710-7063   803-831-8379
        Fax: 803-831-8476 803-831-8476
        sales@filtrationsolutions.com
                www.filtrationsolutions.com
Filtration products and systems.
    President: Billie Wells
    Office Manager: Tamara Hartman
    Engineernig Consultant: Larry Seitz
    Sales Representative: April Sadler
    Sales Representative: Pete Dawes
    Customer Service Representative: Robbie Putnam

4807 Finchville Farms
P.O.Box 56
Finchville, KY 40022-0056   502-834-7952
                800-678-1521
                www.finchvillefarms.com
Manuafacturer of country ham
    President: William Robertson
Estimated Sales:$ 5 - 10 Million
Number Employees: 10-19
Type of Packaging: Consumer

4808 Fine Choice Foods
23111 Fraserwood Way
Richmond, BC V6V 1B3
Canada   604-522-3110
        Fax: 604-522-3114 info@finechoicefoods.com
                www.finechoicefoods.com
Manufacturer of dim sum, frozen Chinese entrees
and egg rolls
    President: Charles Lui
    Operations Manager: Christina Lui
Estimated Sales:$1-3 Million
Number Employees: 10-19
Sq. footage: 10000
Type of Packaging: Consumer, Food Service, Private Label, Bulk

4809 Fine Dried Foods International
2553 Mission St # A
Santa Cruz, CA 95060-5745   831-426-1413
        Fax: 831-426-0870 awesomefruit@yahoo.com
Natural and organic tropical dried fruits
    President: Rusty Brown
Estimated Sales:$2.5-5 Million
Number Employees: 1-4
Type of Packaging: Private Label
Brands:
    True Fruit

4810 Fine Foods International
9907 Baptist Church Rd
St Louis, MO 63123-4903   314-842-4473
        Fax: 314-843-8846 ffinylp@aol.com
Tea and coffee industry bags (brick packs), coffee
and cappuccino mixes
    Manager: Carole Garnett
    VP: Keith Sheller
    Operations: Carole Garnett
*Estimated Sales:*Less than $500,000
Number Employees: 1-4
Type of Packaging: Bulk

4811 Fine Foods Northwest
12736 35th Ave NE
Seattle, WA 98125-4508   206-361-7960
        Fax: 206-361-7985 800-862-3965
        info@mochamax.com www.mochamax.com
Manufacturer of Chocolate covered dried strawber-
ries, chocolate peanut butter pretzels, chocolate cov-
ered espresso beans, nuts, fruits, coffee and
chocolate covered nuts
Estimated Sales:$1-2.5 Million
Number Employees: 1-4
Brands:
    MOCHA MAGIC
    MOCHA MARBLES

4812 Fine Line Seafood
4 Terry Dr # 14
Newtown, PA 18940-1838   215-860-1144
                Fax: 215-598-7235
Manufacturer of Seafood
    President: Herbert Young
Estimated Sales:$5-10 Million
Number Employees: 1-4

4813 (HQ)Fineberg Packing Company
P.O.Box 80432
Memphis, TN 38108-0432   901-458-2622
                Fax: 901-458-7449
        richard@finebergpacking.com
                www.finebergpacking.com
Manufacturer of meat products: boloney, hot dogs,
bacon, smoked hams, packing services available
    President: Richard Freudenberg
Estimated Sales:$13.8 Million
Number Employees: 50-99

4814 Finer Foods
3100 W 36th St
Chicago, IL 60632-2304   773-579-3870
                Fax: 773-890-1115
Manufacturer of frozen foods
    President: James Fitzgerald
Estimated Sales:$ 10 - 20 Million
Number Employees: 50-99

4815 Finestkind Fish Market
855 Us Route 1
York, ME 03909-5835   207-363-5000
        Fax: 207-363-2664 800-288-8154
        info@finestkindlobster.com
                www.finestkindlobster.com

Manufacturer and Wholesaler full service seafood company.
Owner: Tom Robinson
Estimated Sales: $ 3 - 5 Million
Number Employees: 10-19

4816 Finger Lakes Coffee Roasters
6081 State Route 96
Farmington, NY 14425-1062   585-742-6218
Fax: 585-742-6211   800-420-6154
mail@fingerlakescoffee.com
www.fingerlakescoffee.com
Manufacturer of fresh roasted coffee
Manager: Kierna McGhan
VP: Robert Cowdery
Estimated Sales: Less than $500,000
Number Employees: 10-19
Sq. footage: 1100
Brands:
CANANDAIGUA BLEND
LAKE BLEND
SENECA BLEND

4817 Finkemeier Bakery
3103 Strong Avenue
Kansas City, KS 66106-2113   913-831-3103
Manufacturer of Bakery products
President: Bill Crum
Estimated Sales: $500,000 appx.
Number Employees: 5-9

4818 (HQ)Finlandia Cheese
2001 Us Highway 46 # 303
Parsippany, NJ 07054-1315   973-316-6699
Fax: 973-316-6609   www.finlandiacheese.com
www.finlandiacheese.com
Cheese, dairy
President: Christopher Franco
VP Marketing: Jyrki Heimino
Sales Manager: Carol Nicolay
Estimated Sales: $5-10 Million
Number Employees: 10-19
Brands:
FINLANDIA LAPPI
FINLANDIA NATURALS
FINLANDIA SWISS
HEAVENLY LIGHT
MUENSTER
SANDWICH NATURALS

4819 Finlay Tea Solutions
10 Early St
Morristown, NJ 07960-3813   973-538-1701
Fax: 973-538-8366   tea@finlayusa.com
www.finlayusa.com
Tea extracts.
Owner: Herb Finlay
CFO: Jim Klucharits
Quality Control: Joe Stout
Marketing Director: E Fernando
Sales Director: L Malkin
Manager Tea Extract Sales: Gary Vorsheim
Estimated Sales: $ 10-20 Million
Number Employees: 1-4
Type of Packaging: Bulk

4820 Fiore Winery
3026 Whiteford Rd
Pylesville, MD 21132-1212   410-452-0132
Fax: 410-879-4926   fiore@verison.net
www.fiorewinery.com
Wines
President: Michael Fiore
VP: Erich Fiore
Estimated Sales: $1-2.5 Million
Number Employees: 5-9

4821 Fiori-Bruna Pasta Products
5395 NW 165th St
Hialeah, FL 33014-6232   305-621-0074
Fax: 305-621-4997   fiori.bruna@worldnet.att.net
www.fioribrunapasta.com
Manufacturer and exporter of frozen cheese tortellini, ravioli, cavatelli and potato gnocchi; also, dry egg fettuccine and linguine
President: Jose Yimin
VP Sales/Co-Founder: Cesare Bruna
Estimated Sales: $2.5-5 Million
Number Employees: 10-19
Sq. footage: 10000
Type of Packaging: Consumer, Food Service, Private Label, Bulk
Brands:
Fiori-Bruna

4822 Fiorucci Foods
1800 Ruffin Mill Rd
Colonial Heights, VA 23834-5910   804-520-7775
Fax: 804-520-7180 800-524-7775
www.fioruccifoods.com
Manufacturer and exporter of Italian speciality meats including prosciutto ham, salami, pepperoni, genoa, mortadella and other dry cured meats; also, importer of Parma prosciutto
President: Claudio Colmignoli
VP/Marketing: Jack Kelly
Sales: Beth Nolan
Operations: Bill McCall
Plant Manager: Mark Bragalone
Estimated Sales: $10-20 Million
Number Employees: 50-99
Sq. footage: 100000
Parent Co: Cesare Fiorucci
Type of Packaging: Consumer, Food Service, Private Label, Bulk
Brands:
Colosseum
Fiorucci

4823 Fire Island Fisheries
9 Degnon Boulevard
Bay Shore, NY 11706-8910   631-666-0942
Seafood
President: Jeff Kirchner
Estimated Sales: Under $500,000
Number Employees: 1-4

4824 Firefly Fandango
3217 33rd Avenue S
Seattle, WA 98144-6901   206-760-3700
Fax: 206-721-0909
fireflyfandango@earthlink.com
Chocolate and cookies
Estimated Sales: $300,000-500,000
Number Employees: 5-9

4825 Firelands Wine Company
917 Bardshar Rd
Sandusky, OH 44870-1507   419-625-5474
Fax: 419-625-4887 800-548-9463
info@firelandswinery.com
www.firelandswinery.com
Wines
Manager: Claudio Salvador
Plant Manager: Claudio Salvador
Estimated Sales: $5-10 Million
Number Employees: 10-19

4826 Fireside Kitchen
3430 Prescott Street
Halifax, NS B3K 4Y4
Canada   902-454-7387
Fax: 902-453-0275   info@prescottgroup.ca
www.prescottgroup.ca
Manufacturer of natural jams, marmalades, cranberry sauce, cookies, muffins and fruit cakes; also, available in gift packs
Sales Coordinator: Cindy Kingwell
Production Supervisor: Karen Walters
Brands:
FIRESIDE KITCHEN

4827 Firestone Packing Company
P.O.Box 61928
Vancouver, WA 98666-1928   360-695-9484
Fax: 360-695-0040 sales@firestonepacking.com
Wine
President: Stanley Firestone
Estimated Sales: $2.5-5 Million
Number Employees: 100-249

4828 Firestone Vineyard
P.O.Box 244
Los Olivos, CA 93441-0244   805-688-3940
Fax: 805-686-1256 info@firestonewine.com
www.firestonevineyard.com
Wines
President: Adam Firestone
Controller: Heather McCollum
National Sales Director: Steve Mann
Estimated Sales: $10-20 Million
Number Employees: 20-49
Brands:
CABERNET SAUVIGNON
CHARDONNAY
GEWURZTRAMINER
MERLOT
RIESLING
SAUVIGNON BLANC
SYRAH
ZINFANDEL

4829 Fireworks Popcorn Company
PO Box 461
Belgium, WI 53004-0461   262-285-4800
Fax: 262-285-4820 877-668-4800
kathy@popcornlovers.com
www.popcornlovers.com
Manufacturer of gourmet popcorn in fourteen varieties, and carmel corn in six different types
President: Rick Hercules
Sales: Don Sothman
Operations: Kaye Croatt
Purchasing Director: Rick Hercules
Estimated Sales: $1 Million
Number Employees: 10-19
Number of Brands: 4
Number of Products: 60
Sq. footage: 20000
Type of Packaging: Consumer, Food Service, Private Label, Bulk
Brands:
Settler's Popcorn

4830 Firmenich
250 Plainsboro Rd
Plainsboro, NJ 08536   609-452-1000
Fax: 609-452-6077 800-452-1090
www.firmenich.com
Manufacturer of flavors and fragrances
CEO: Patrick Firmenich
CEO: Patrick Firmenich
Purchasing Director: Linda Campbell
Estimated Sales: $Over 500 Million
Number Employees: 5,680
Other Locations:
Firmenich Chemical Plant
Newark NJ
Fermenich Citrus Center
Safety Harbor FL

4831 (HQ)First Colony Coffee & Tea Company
P.O.Box 11005
Norfolk, VA 23517-0005   757-622-2224
Fax: 757-623-2391 800-446-8555
sales@firstcolonycoffeeinc.com
www.firstcolonycoffee.com
Processor, importer and exporter of teas and coffees including varietal, blends and flavored
President/CEO: Charles Cortellini
Controller: Barbara Devaney
CEO: Miguel A Abisambra
Inventory Control Analyst: Don Burnside
Estimated Sales: $12.3 Million
Number Employees: 50-99
Sq. footage: 75000
Type of Packaging: Consumer, Food Service, Private Label, Bulk
Brands:
BENCHELEY
CAROLAN'S
FIRST COLONY
FRANGELICO
GHIRARDELLI
JACK DANIEL'S
SOUTHERN COMFORT

4832 First Colony Winery
1650 Harris Creek Rd
Charlottesville, VA 22902-7820   434-979-7105
Fax: 434-293-2054 877-979-7105
info@firstcolonywinery.com
www.firstcolonywinery.com
Wine
Owner: Randolph Mc Elroy
Estimated Sales: $ 3 - 5 Million
Number Employees: 5-9

4833 First District Association
101 S Swift Ave
Litchfield, MN 55355-2800   320-693-3236
Fax: 320-693-6243   1stdist@hutchtel.net
www.firstdistrict.com

Manufacturer of dairy products including lactose blends and mixes, specialty cheeses, cream, wheys, whey protein concentrates and milk powders; exporter of lactose, whey protein concentrates and dairy calcium
President: Clint Fall
Quality Control/Lab Manager: Kevin Hagen
Plant Manager: Doug Anderson
Human Resources/Purchasing Manager: Dean Grabow
Estimated Sales: $267 Million
Number Employees: 100-249
Sq. footage: 180000
Brands:
Fieldgate

4834 First Foods Company
P.O.Box 560029
Dallas, TX 75356-0029   214-637-0214
                              Fax: 214-905-0605
Manufacturer of gelatins for desserts, salads, etc
President: Burke Hogan
Estimated Sales: $ 5 - 10 Million
Number Employees: 20-49
Type of Packaging: Consumer, Food Service, Private Label, Bulk

4835 First Oriental Market
2774 E Ponce De Leon Ave
Decatur, GA 30030-2715   404-377-6950
                              Fax: 404-377-7505
Tilapia, flounder, catfish, mackerel, oriental food items
Owner: Diane Bounngaseng
Estimated Sales: $ 5 - 10 Million
Number Employees: 5-9

4836 First Original Texas Chili Company
P.O.Box 4281
Fort Worth, TX 76164-0281   817-626-0983
Fax: 817-626-9105   sales@texaschilicompany.cm
                              www.texaschili.com
Manufacturer of frozen chili con carne, chili sauce and beef taco filling
President: Danny Owens
Estimated Sales: $5-10 Million
Number Employees: 5-9
Type of Packaging: Consumer, Food Service, Private Label
Brands:
Our Famous Texas Chili
Sloppy Joe
Tex-O-Gold
Texas One Step

4837 First Roasters of Central Florida
863 N Highway 17/92
Longwood, FL 32750-3167   407-699-6364
                              Fax: 407-699-6301
Manufacturer of Coffee
Manager: Leomild Lamascus
Estimated Sales: $2.5-5 Million
Number Employees: 1-4
Brands:
First Roasters of Central Florida

4838 (HQ)First Spice Mixing Company
3333 Greenpoint Ave
Long Island City, NY 11101-2084   718-361-2556
            Fax: 718-361-2515   800-221-1105
info@firstspice.com   www.firstspice.com
Manufacturer, importer and exporter of seasonings, binders and curing compounds; also, textured vegetable protein, hydrolyzed dairy products, nonfat dry milk, curing ingredients, phosphate compounds, MSG-flavor boosters and spices
President: Peter Epstein
Vice President: Vickie Miller
Research & Development: Marcy Epstein
Estimated Sales: $ 5 - 10 Million
Number Employees: 10-19
Other Locations:
First Spice Mixing Company
San Francisco CA
Brands:
Albunate
Flavolin
Flavor 86
Savorlok
Texite
Tietolin
Vegolin Hvp

Vita-Curaid
Vitaphos

4839 First Spice Mixing Company
3333 Greenpoint Ave
Long Island City, NY 11101-2084   718-361-2556
            Fax: 718-361-2515   800-221-1105
info@firstspice.com
Manufacturer and exporter of food ingredients including seasonings, spices, soy products, antioxidants, flavor enhancers, etc.; wholesaler/distributor of gelatin, garlic and marinades; also, custom packaging and product development services available.
President: Peter Epstein
VP: Vicki Miller
VP: Elizabeth Miller
Plant Manager: Glenn Davis
Estimated Sales: $5+ Million
Sq. footage: 50000
Parent Co: First Spice Mixing Company
Type of Packaging: Consumer, Food Service, Private Label, Bulk
Other Locations:
San Francisco CA
Toronto, Canada
Brands:
ALBUNATE
FLAVOLIN
FLAVOR 86
SAVORLOK
TEXITE
TIETOLIN
VEGOLIN HVP
VITA-CURAID
VITAPHOS

4840 First You Make A Roux
238 Meeting House Lane
Brattleboro, VT 05301-8987   802-257-9336
                    FYMAR@aldelphia.net
Spice mixes for cajun entrees

4841 Firth Maple Products
22418 Firth Rd
Spartansburg, PA 16434-3222   814-654-2435
            Fax: 814-654-7265   firth2@earthlink.net
Maple syrup
President: Troy Firth
Estimated Sales: $5-10 Million
Number Employees: 1-4

4842 (HQ)Fis USA
30003 Bainbridge Road
Solon, OH 44139-2205   440-248-1820
            Fax: 440-349-3334   800-233-3133
            information@us.fisflavors.com
                    www.fisflavors.com
Manufacturer of dry ingredients including compound flavors
President/Owner: Frank Giotto
Estimated Sales: Less than $500,000
Number Employees: 10-19
Parent Co: Nestle SA
Type of Packaging: Food Service

4843 Fischer & Wieser Specialty Foods
411 S Lincoln St
Fredericksburg, TX 78624-4502   830-997-7194
            Fax: 830-997-0455   800-880-8526
            case@jelly.com   www.jelly.com
Manufacturer of jams, jellies, preserves, marmalades, mustard, sauces, salsa, syrup, honey and snacks
President/CEO: Case Fischer
Purchasing: Jenny Wieser
Estimated Sales: $1-3 Million
Number Employees: 100-249
Type of Packaging: Consumer, Food Service, Private Label
Brands:
FISCHER & WIESER
MOM'S
OLD CHISHOLM TRAIL

4844 Fischer Honey Company
2001 N Poplar St
N Little Rock, AR 72114-2999   501-758-1123
                              Fax: 501-758-8601
Manufacturer of honey including table, creamed and bakers
President: Joe Callaway
Estimated Sales: $5-10 Million
Number Employees: 5-9
Sq. footage: 25000

Type of Packaging: Consumer, Food Service, Private Label, Bulk

4845 Fischer Meats
85 Front St N
Issaquah, WA 98027-3237   425-392-3131
                              Fax: 425-392-0168
Manufacturer of meat
Owner: Chris Chiechi
Estimated Sales: Less than $500,000
Number Employees: 1-4
Type of Packaging: Consumer, Food Service

4846 Fish Breeders of Idaho
10215 W. Emerald Street,Suite #160
Boise, ID 83704   208-947-3678
            Fax: 208-837-6254   888-414-8818
            fpi@cyberhighway.net
            http://www.cyberhighway.net
Manufacturer and exporter of fresh and frozen farm-raised trout, catfish, tilapia, sturgeon and alligator
Owner/President: Leo Ray
Estimated Sales: $5-10 Million
Number Employees: 20-49
Parent Co: Fish Processors
Type of Packaging: Consumer, Food Service
Brands:
Pride of Idaho

4847 Fish Brothers
P.O.Box 416
Blue Lake, CA 95525-0416   707-668-9700
            Fax: 707-668-9701   800-244-0583
            fishbro@fishbrothers.com
                    www.fishbrothers.com
Manufacturer of smoked fish including, salmon, nova lox and albacore
Owner: Scott Bradshaw
Estimated Sales: $500,000-1 Million
Number Employees: 1-4
Sq. footage: 2500
Type of Packaging: Consumer, Food Service, Private Label, Bulk
Brands:
Fish Brothers

4848 Fish Express
3343 Kuhio Hwy # 10
Lihue, HI 96766   808-245-9918
                              Fax: 808-246-9188
Seafood
President: David Wada
Estimated Sales: $ 3 - 5 Million
Number Employees: 10-19

4849 Fish Hopper
700 Cannery Row # O
Monterey, CA 93940-1036   831-372-8543
            Fax: 831-372-2026 www.fishhopper.com
Manufacturer of canned clam chowder
Owner: Sabu Shake
CEO: Sabu Shake Jr
Estimated Sales: $2.5-5 Million
Number Employees: 50-99
Type of Packaging: Private Label

4850 Fish King Processors
710 Squalicum Way
Bellingham, WA 98225   360-733-9090
                              Fax: 360-733-9152
Processor of smoked salmon
CEO: Terrill Beck
Estimated Sales: $ 10 - 20 Million
Number Employees: 20-49
Parent Co: Unisea Foods
Type of Packaging: Consumer, Food Service
Brands:
Pride of Alaska
Salmon Bay

4851 Fish Market
1032 W Market Street
Louisville, KY 40202-2630   502-589-6636
                              Fax: 502-589-5869
Seafood
President: Steven Smith

4852 Fish Market
6226 Prospect Avenue
Kansas City, MO 64130   816-444-3474
Fish
Estimated Sales: $500,000-$1 Million
Number Employees: 1-4

4853 Fish Processors
P.O.Box 479
Hagerman, ID 83332-0479   208-837-6114
    Fax: 208-837-6254   fpi@cyberhighway.net
Manufacturer of frozen fish and seaford, Rainbow
trout, channel catfish
    President: Leo Ray
    Marketing/Plant Manager: Sandra Paatton
Estimated Sales:$5-10 Million
Number Employees: 20-49
Brands:
    Pride of Idaho

4854 FishKing
13842 Shell Belt Road
Bayou La Batre, AL 36509-2348   334-824-2118
    Fax: 334-824-7181
Processor of seafood including breaded and IQF
scallops, shrimp and calamari
    President: Tom Furuckawa
Number Employees: 125
Type of Packaging: Consumer, Food Service

4855 Fisher Honey Company
1 Belle Ave # 21
Lewistown, PA 17044-2433   717-242-4373
    Fax: 717-242-3978
    fisherhoney@fisherhoney.com
    www.fisherhoney.com
Manufacturer and exporter of honey, beeswax,
beekeepers supplies, containers, glass, metal and
plastic
    President: W Dyson Fisher
    Plant Supervisor: Scott Fisher
Estimated Sales:$1-2 Million
Number Employees: 1-4
Sq. footage: 20000
Type of Packaging: Consumer, Food Service, Pri-
    vate Label, Bulk
Brands:
    Fisher Honey
    Stewarts Honey

4856 Fisher Rex Sandwiches
1519 Brookside Dr
Raleigh, NC 27604-2099   919-832-6494
    Fax: 919-832-4865   fisherrex@aol.com
Manufacturer of sandwiches, pastries and snack
foods
    Owner: W T Fisher Jr
    VP: Tom Fisher
Estimated Sales:$7.9 Million
Number Employees: 50-99
Type of Packaging: Consumer

4857 Fisher Ridge Wine Company
529 Sheridan Cir
Charleston, WV 25314-1054   304-342-8702
Wines
    Owner: Wilson Ward
Estimated Sales:$1-2.5 Million
Number Employees: 1-4

4858 Fisher Vineyards
6200 Saint Helena Rd
Santa Rosa, CA 95404-9692   707-539-7511
    Fax: 707-539-3601   info@fishervineyards.com
    www.fishervineyards.com
Wines
    President: Fred Fisher
    Sales/Marketing/Public Relations: Whitney Fisher

Estimated Sales:$5-10 Million
Number Employees: 10-19
Type of Packaging: Private Label

4859 Fisher's Bakery
8143 Main St
Ellicott City, MD 21043-4618   410-461-9275
    Fax: 410-750-8556 www.fishersbakery.com
Breads, muffins, and cakes
    Owner: Chris Sikora
Estimated Sales:$1-2.5 Million
Number Employees: 5-9
Sq. footage: 2000

4860 Fisher's Popcorn
200 S Boardwalk
Ocean City, MD 21842-4075   410-289-1399
    Fax: 410-289-1720   888-395-0335
    fishers@dmv.com   www.fisherspopcorn.com
Caramel-coated popcorn
    Owner: Donald Fisher

Number Employees: 50-99

4861 Fisherman's Market International
607 Bedford Highway
Halifax, NS B3M 2L6
Canada   902-445-3474
    Fax: 902-445-2555   mjs@fmii.com
    www.fmii.com
Manufacturer of live lobster and fresh or frozen sea-
food
    President: Fred Greene
    Director International Marketing: Gino Nadalini
    Sales: J R Ewing
    General Manager: Monte Snow
    Plant Administrator: Bill Murphy
Estimated Sales:$20+ Million
Number Employees: 100-249
Sq. footage: 20000
Type of Packaging: Consumer, Food Service, Pri-
    vate Label, Bulk

**4862 Fisherman's Reef
ShrimpCompany**
P.O.Box 26006
Beaumont, TX 77720-6006   409-842-9528
    Fax: 409-842-6905
Manufacturer of frozen domestic shrimp
    President: Vikki Jones
    Sales: Trudy Verdine
Number Employees: 100-249
Parent Co: Farmer Boys Catfish International
Type of Packaging: Food Service, Private Label
Brands:
    Fisherman's Reef

4863 Fishermens Net
849 Forest Ave
Portland, ME 04103-4162   207-772-3565
    Fax: 207-828-1726
Seafood
    Owner: Benjamin Lindner
Estimated Sales:$6 Million
Number Employees: 5-9

**4864 (HQ)Fishery Products
International**
18 Electronics Ave
Danvers, MA 01923-1011   978-777-2660
    Fax: 978-777-6849   800-374-4700
    www.fpil.com
Manufacturer and importer of fresh and frozen sea-
food including shrimp, crab, cod, flounder, perch,
pollack, tilapia and salmon
    President: Kevin Murphy
    CEO: Derrick Rowe
    Executive: Bill Dimento
    Research & Development: Bob Saville
    Quality Control: William DiMento
    Marketing Director: Dave Jermain
Estimated Sales:$100-500 Million
Number Employees: 1-4
Sq. footage: 105000
Parent Co: Fishery Products International
Type of Packaging: Consumer, Food Service
Other Locations:
    Fishery Products
    Seattle WA
Brands:
    BLATIN REDFISH
    CARIBOU
    FPI
    LUXURY
    MIRABEL
    SEA CUISINE
    SEA NUGGETS
    SEA STRIPS
    SEAFOOD ELITE
    SHOREGRILL
    SIMPLE SERV
    TREASURE ISLE

4865 Fishery Products International
2001 Western Ave # 300
Seattle, WA 98121-2164   206-782-9979
    Fax: 206-782-0209   800-374-4700
    webmaster@fisheryproducts.com
    www.fisheryproducts.com
Manufacturer of fresh and frozen seafood
    Manager: Grimes Williams
Estimated Sales:$5-10 Million appx.
Number Employees: 10-19
Number of Brands: 8
Parent Co: Fisher Products International

Brands:
    Acadian Supreme
    FPI
    Luxury
    Margaritaville
    Mirabel
    Sea Cuisine
    Tiki Island
    Upper Crust

4866 Fishhawk Fisheries
P.O.Box 715
Astoria, OR 97103-0715   503-325-5252
    Fax: 503-325-8786
Manufacturer of crab, shrimp, canned fish, salmon,
sturgeon, shad, smelt, halibut and black cod
    President: Steve Fick
Estimated Sales:$5-10 Million
Number Employees: 10-19
Sq. footage: 6000
Type of Packaging: Bulk
Brands:
    Fishhawk

4867 Fishking
PO Box 1068
Bayou La Batre, AL 36509-1068   251-824-2118
    Fax: 334-824-7181
Manufacturer of Seafood
    President/CEO: Eugene Laurendeau
Estimated Sales:$20-50 Million
Number Employees: 100-249

4868 (HQ)Fishking Processors
PO Box 21385
Los Angeles, CA 90021-0385   213-746-1307
    Fax: 213-746-4008   877-677-3329
Manufacturer of frozen fish and seafood including
cod, halibut, sole, pollack, New Zealand whiting,
hoki, perch, shrimp, scallops and oysters; also,
frozen seafood hors d'oeuvres
    President/CEO: Dennis Delaye
    Senior Director Finance: Ed Shelly
    VP Foodservice Sales/Marketing: Tim Farno
Estimated Sales:$50-100 Million
Number Employees: 250-499
Parent Co: Nippon Suisan USA
Type of Packaging: Consumer, Food Service
Other Locations:
    Fish King Processors
    Bayou La Batre AL
Brands:
    PRIDE OF ALASKA

4869 Fishland Market
117 Ahui Street
C
Honolulu, HI 96813-5545   808-523-6902
    Fax: 808-523-6905
Manufacturer of Aku, ahi, a'u, bottomfish, reef fish,
Kona crab, white crab, Hawaiian crab
    President: Paul Nishimoto

4870 Fishmarket Seafoods
1406 W Chestnut St
Louisville, KY 40203-1706   502-587-7474
    Fax: 502-587-7503 fseafoods@aol.com
Manufacturer of frozen seafood
    President: Steven Smith
Estimated Sales:$5-10 Million
Number Employees: 5-9
Sq. footage: 7000
Type of Packaging: Consumer, Food Service, Pri-
    vate Label
Brands:
    Fishmarket Seafoods

4871 Fitzkee's Candies
2352 S Queen St
York, PA 17402-4997   717-741-1031
    Fax: 717-741-5176
Manufacturer of assorted chocolates
    President: Robert Fitzkee
Estimated Sales:$2.5-5 Million
Number Employees: 10-19
Type of Packaging: Consumer

4872 Fitzpatrick Winery & Lodge
7740 Fairplay Rd
Somerset, CA 95684-9208   530-620-3248
    Fax: 530-620-6838   800-245-9166
    brian@fitzpatrickwinery.com
    www.fitzpatrickwinery.com

Wines
President: Brian Fitzpatrick
VP: Diana Fitzpatrick
Estimated Sales: $500,000-$1 Million
Number Employees: 1-4
Brands:
Fitzpatrick

4873 Five Ponds Farm
1933 E Mill Road
Lineville, AL 36266-3767 256-396-5217
Fax: 256-386-5899
President: Edward Donlon

4874 Five Star Food Base Company
865 Pierce Butler Rte
St Paul, MN 55104-3073 651-488-2300
Fax: 651-488-2094
cjoyce@fivestarfood.com www.fivestarfood.com
Soup bases and blended seasonings
President: Sid Larson
Estimated Sales: $5-10 Million
Number Employees: 10-19

4875 Fizz-O Water Company
809 N Lewis Ave
Tulsa, OK 74110-5365 918-834-3691
Fax: 918-832-0899 www.fizzowater.com
Bottler and wholesaler/distributor of spring, drinking and distilled water
President: Harry R Doerner
Owner: Hency Doerner
CFO: Rick Doerner
Plant Manager: Rick Malkey
Estimated Sales: $1-3 Million
Number Employees: 20-49
Number of Brands: 4
Sq. footage: 10000
Type of Packaging: Consumer
Brands:
DOUBLEPURE DISTILLED
MOUNTAIN VALLEY
OZARKA
SPRING HOUSE

4876 Fizzle Flat Farm
18773 E 1600th Avenue
Yale, IL 62481-2215 618-793-2060
Fax: 618-793-2060
Manufacturer and exporter of organic popcorn and food grade certified organic grains including white, yellow and blue corn, wheat, soybeans, buckwheat, rye, barley, oats and spelt
Owner: Marvin Manges
Estimated Sales: $1-3 Million
Number Employees: 1-4
Sq. footage: 10000
Type of Packaging: Private Label, Bulk
Brands:
Fizzle Flat Farm

4877 Fizzy Lizzy
265 Lafayette St
New York, NY 10012-4035 212-966-2155
Fax: 212-966-6621 800-203-9336
liz@fizzylizzy.com www.fizzylizzy.com
All-natural spritzer
President: Lizzy Marlin
Brands:
FIZZY LIZZY

4878 Fizzy Lizzy
265 Lafayette St
Suite D20
New York, NY 10012 212-966-3232
Fax: 212-966-6621 800-203-9336
love@fizzylizzy.com
whole fruit juice and sparkling water.
VP: Amy Drown
Estimated Sales: $1.1 Million
Number Employees: 5

4879 Fjord Pacific Marine Industries
2400 Simpson Road
Richmond, BC V6X 2P9
Canada 604-270-3393
Fax: 604-270-3826 jbomhof@fjordpacific.com
Manufacturer and exporter of pickled herring, smoked salmon and salmon and halibut portions and steaks
President: Grant Keays
Sales Manager: John Bomhof
General Manager: Don Pollard

Number Employees: 20-49
Sq. footage: 10000
Type of Packaging: Consumer, Food Service, Private Label
Brands:
Dutch Boy
Fjord

4880 Flagstaff Brewing Company
16 E Route 66
Flagstaff, AZ 86001-5792 928-773-1442
Fax: 928-773-7772 www.flagbrew.com
Beer
Owner: Jeff Thorsett
Estimated Sales: $10-20 Million
Number Employees: 20-49
Brands:
AGASSIZ AMBER
BITTERROOT EXTRA SPECIAL BITTER
BLACKBIRD PORTER
BUBBAGANOUJ IPA
GREAT GOLDEN ALE
SASQUATCH STOUT
THREE-PIN PALE ALE

4881 Flaherty
9047 Terminal Ave
Skokie, IL 60077-1570 847-966-1005
Fax: 847-966-1072
Manufacturer of mustard
Owner: Catherine Flaharty
Estimated Sales: $10-24.9 Million
Number Employees: 10-19

4882 Flair Flexible Packaging
2605 S Lakeland Dr
Appleton, WI 54915-4193 920-722-1779
Fax: 920-722-1789 csusa@flairpackaging.com
www.flairpackaging.com/
Flair Flexible Packaging is a fully integrated packaging solutions company providing complete in-house services within the United States and Canada since 1992. Product line includes printing and manufacturing of rolls and bags:multilayer lamination; dry lamination; extrusion lamination and tandem extrusion lamination.
Owner: Cheryl Miller Balster
Vice President Sales & Marketing: Charles Miller

Type of Packaging: Consumer

4883 Flamin' Red's Woodfired
Robinson Hill Rd
Pawlet, VT 05761 802-325-3641
Fax: 802-325-3641 woodfire@vermontel.net
Pizza crusts made with organic flour
Owner: Carson Lake
Estimated Sales: $300,000-500,000
Number Employees: 1-4

4884 (HQ)Flamm Pickle & Packing Company
P.O.Box 500
Eau Claire, MI 49111-0500 269-461-6916
Fax: 269-461-6166
Manufacturer of pickle relish
President/General Manager: Gina Flamm
Estimated Sales: $4.20 Million
Number Employees: 10-19
Sq. footage: 30000
Type of Packaging: Food Service, Bulk
Brands:
Flamm's

4885 Flamous Brands
2500 East Colorado Blvd
Suite 205
Pasadena, CA 91107 626-799-7909
Fax: 626-548-5891 www.flamousbrands.com
vegetarian chips and dips

4886 (HQ)Flanders Provision Company
P.O.Box 720
Waycross, GA 31502-0720 912-283-5191
Fax: 912-283-6228 info@flandersprovisions.com
Manufacturer, distributor and packager of beef patties
President/CEO: Huey Dubberly
CEO: Chris Huff
Sales: Hollis Yarn
Estimated Sales: $36.80 Million
Number Employees: 100-249

4887 Flanigan Farms
9522 Jefferson Blvd
Culver City, CA 90232-2918 310-836-8437
Fax: 310-838-0743 800-525-0228
nuts@flaniganfarms.com
www.flaniganfarms.com
Manufacturer and exporter of nut mixes and dried organic persimmons
President: Patsy Flanigan
Operations: C Flanigan
Estimated Sales: $3 Million
Number Employees: 10-19
Number of Products: 42
Sq. footage: 12000
Type of Packaging: Consumer, Food Service, Private Label
Brands:
Nuts 'n' Fruit
Nuts 'n' Things

4888 Flannery Seafood Company
3445 California St
San Francisco, CA 94118-1836 415-346-1303
Fax: 415-346-1304 cohan@earthlink.net
Manufacturer of fresh swordfish, tuna and exotic seafoods
President/CEO: Walker Flannery
Plant Manager: Alex Guerrero
Estimated Sales: $10-20 Million
Number Employees: 10-19
Type of Packaging: Private Label

4889 Flapjacks
4808 Ogram Road
Santa Barbara, CA 93105-9732 805-964-4743
Fax: 805-967-8877
English flapjacks

4890 Flat Enterprises
5424 W Roosevelt Road
Chicago, IL 60644-1489 312-666-1830
Fax: 312-666-3671
President: Brian Flynn

4891 Flathau's Fine Foods
211 Greenwood Place
Hattiesburg, MS 39402 601-582-9629
Fax: 601-544-2333 888-263-1299
info@flathausfinefoods.com
www.flathausfinefoods.com
flavore shortbread cookies covered with powdered sugar

4892 Flaum Appetizing
288 Scholes St
Brooklyn, NY 11206-1728 718-821-1970
Fax: 718-821-9051 www.flaum.com
Manufacturer of sour pickles, sauerkraut, pickled herring, cole slaw, lox spreads and potato, whitefish, tuna and eggplant salads
President: Morris Grunhut
Production Manager: Salomon Benatar
Estimated Sales: Less than $500,000
Number Employees: 10-19
Sq. footage: 25000
Parent Co: M&M Food Products
Type of Packaging: Consumer, Food Service, Private Label, Bulk

4893 Flavex Protein Ingredients
25 Commerce Dr
Cranford, NJ 07016-3605 908-709-4045
Fax: 908-709-9221 800-851-1052
info@arnhemgroup.com www.arnhemgroup.com
Owner: Michael J Bonner
CEO: Michael Bonner
Estimated Sales: $ 3 - 5 Million
Number Employees: 1-4

4894 (HQ)Flavor & Fragrance Specialties
3 Industrial Ave
Mahwah, NJ 07430-3595 201-825-2025
Fax: 201-825-4785 800-998-4337
ffsample@aol.com www.ffs.com
Manufacturer of flavor concentrates and fragrance extracts
President: Michael Bloom
VP Sales: William Palmer
Estimated Sales: $2.5-5 Million
Number Employees: 20-49
Sq. footage: 40000
Type of Packaging: Bulk

Brands:
   Ammonia Guard
   E.O.C.
   High Impact

4895 (HQ)Flavor & Fragrance Specialties
300 Corporate Dr
Mahwah, NJ 07430-3605   201-825-2025
         Fax: 201-828-9449   800-998-4337
             info@ffs.com   www.ffs.com
Manufacturer and exporter of flavors and flavoring agents; also, fragrances
   President: Robert Maleeny
   VP: Steve Vanata
   R&D: Michael Bloom
   Marketing: Michelle Bloom
   VP Sales: William Palmer
Estimated Sales:$10-20 Million
Number Employees: 20-49
Sq. footage: 50000
Type of Packaging: Bulk
Other Locations:
   Flavor & Fragrance Specialties
   Baltimore MD
Brands:
   AMMONIA GUARD
   EFS ENHANCED FLAVOR SYSTEMS
   ENHANCER 21
   EOC ENVIRONMENTAL ODOR CONTROL
   HIGH IMPACT

4896 Flavor Consortium
2017 Camfield Avenue
Los Angeles, CA 90040-1501   323-724-1010
                  Fax: 323-724-3183
Manufactures flavors extracts, syrups and related products
Estimated Sales:$5-10 Million
Number Employees: 10-19

4897 Flavor Dynamics
640 Montrose Ave
South Plainfield, NJ 07080-2602   908-822-8855
         Fax: 908-822-8547   888-271-8424
   customercare@flavordynamics.com
       www.flavordynamics.com
Manufacturer and exporter of flavors for confectionery products, baked goods, desserts, meats, cheeses, vegetables, coffee and tea, cocoa and chai, and soft drinks, energy drinks and juices.
   Owner: Dolf DeRovira
   VP: Marilyn DeRovira
   VP Quality Control: Dolf DeRovira Jr
   VP Sales: Colleen Roberts
   Customer Service: Helen Mossa
   Plant Manager: Ken Warren
Estimated Sales: $ 20 - 50 Million
Number Employees: 26
Sq. footage: 23000
Type of Packaging: Food Service, Private Label, Bulk
Other Locations:
   Flavor Dynamics
   Glenview IL
   Flavor Dynamics
   Corona Del Mar CA
   Flavor Dynamics
   Cape Charles VA

4898 Flavor House
PO Box 98
Adelanto, CA 92301-0098   760-246-9131
                  Fax: 909-599-3517
Manufacturer and exporter of flavor concentrates including meat, poultry and seafood; also, hydrolyzed vegetable proteins and liquid and dry soy sauce
   President/Manager: Richard Staley
Estimated Sales: $ 20 - 50 Million
Number Employees: 20-49
Sq. footage: 42000
Type of Packaging: Bulk

4899 Flavor Innovations
220 Saint Nicholas Ave
South Plainfield, NJ 07080-1810   908-754-2020
         Fax: 908-753-2557   800-536-2030
             flavorpros@msn.com
Manufacturer of flavor bases for food and beverages; also, private label packaging and mixing available
   President: Charlene Brach
   VP Operations: Richard Brach
   Purchasing Agent: Mary McGuire

Estimated Sales:$20-50 Million
Number Employees: 20-49
Sq. footage: 75000
Type of Packaging: Private Label

4900 Flavor Right Foods Group
2200 Cardigan Ave
Columbus, OH 43215-1092   614-488-2536
         Fax: 614-488-0307   888-464-3734
   info@flavorright.com   www.instantwhip.com
Dessert and pastry toppings and icings, frozen dessert mixes.
   President: Doug Smith
Estimated Sales:$ 5 - 10 Million
Number Employees: 10-19
Brands:
   FESTEJOS
   WHIP N ICE
   WHIP N TOP

4901 (HQ)Flavor Sciences
7 Gleason Avenue
Stamford, CT 06902-5101   203-363-0300
         Fax: 203-348-3116   800-535-2867
       information@flavorscience.com
           www.flavorsciences.com
Manufacturer of natural and artificial flavors and essential oils; exporter of natural and artificial flavors and extracts
   President: Roger Kiley
   Executive VP: Joyce Kiley
   Sales Manager: Scott Derrick
Estimated Sales:$ 3 - 5 Million
Number Employees: 5-9

4902 Flavor Specialties
790 E Harrison St
Corona, CA 92879-1348   951-734-6620
   Fax: 951-734-4214   flavspec@earthlink.net
           www.flavorspecialties.com
Liquid and dry ingredients and flavors including natural beverage flavors-mango, guava, tropical, kiwi strawberry; botanical bases for carbonated and noncarbonated beverages; herbal tea and green tea beverage base blends
   President: Bob Dayton
Estimated Sales:$20-50 Million
Number Employees: 20-49

4903 Flavor Systems International
9950 Commerce Park Drive
Cincinnati, OH 45246-1332   513-870-4900
         Fax: 513-870-4909   800-498-2783
       info@flavorsystems.com
           www.flavorsystems.com
Manufacturer and exporter of custom flavorings and specialty food systems
   President: William Wasz
   CEO: John Disebastian
   CFO: William Baker
   VP: Robert Bahashy
   R&D: Angie Lantman
   Quality Control: Alan Baker
   Sales: Earl Fisher
   Public Relations: Linda Weeks
   Plant Manager: Rick Messinger
   Purchasing: Roger Sage
Estimated Sales:$5 Million
Number Employees: 20-49
Sq. footage: 25000
Type of Packaging: Bulk

4904 Flavor Waves
1012 Poplar Drive
Novato, CA 94945-1116   415-899-0084
                  Fax: 415-898-9096
Flavorings, liquid coffee extracts and concentrates, liquid tea concentrates

4905 Flavorbank
4710 Eisenhower Boulevard
Suite E8
Tampa, FL 33634-6336   813-885-1797
                  Fax: 813-887-5652
Tea and coffee industry coffee and cappuccino mixes, creamers, flavors, herbs and spices

4906 Flavorbank Company
6372 E Broadway Blvd
Tucson, AZ 85710-3538   520-747-5431
         Fax: 520-790-9469   800-835-7603
   spices@flavorbank.com   www.flavorbank.com

Manufacturer of Spices and seasonings
   Owner: Jennifer English
   Public Relations: Jan Jorden
   Operations: Jackie Brooks
   Production: James Husser
   Plant Manager: Ramona Flores
Estimated Sales:$1-2.5 Million
Number Employees: 1-4
Type of Packaging: Private Label
Brands:
   DANIEL ORR
   FLAVORBANK

4907 Flavorchem
1525 Brook Dr
Downers Grove, IL 60515-1024   630-932-8100
         Fax: 630-932-4626   800-323-1301
   info@flavorchem.com   www.flavorchem.com
Manufacturer and exporter of flavorings and food colorings; processor of pure vanilla extract; importer of fine chemicals and essential oils
   President: Ken Malinowski
   VP Sales/Marketing: Phil Sprovieri
Estimated Sales:$20-50 Million
Number Employees: 100-249
Sq. footage: 150000
Type of Packaging: Consumer, Food Service, Private Label, Bulk
Brands:
   Spicery Shoppe Natural

4908 Flavorganics
268 Doremus Ave
Newark, NJ 07105-4875   973-344-8014
   Fax: 973-344-1948   jason@flavorganics.com
           www.elan-chemical.com
Manufacturer and exporter of organic extracts including vanilla, almond, peppermint, lemon and orange
   President: Jocelyn Manship
Estimated Sales:$ 20 - 50 Million
Number Employees: 50-99
Parent Co: Elan
Type of Packaging: Private Label, Bulk
Brands:
   Flavorganics
   Kogee

4909 (HQ)Flavormatic Industries
230 All Angels Hill Rd
Wappingers Falls, NY 12590-3327 845-297-9100
   Fax: 845-297-2881   sales@flavormatic.com
           www.flavormatic.com
Manufacturer, importer and exporter of flavors, fragrances and essential oils
   President: Judith Back
   Executive VP: Ronald Black
Estimated Sales:$2.5 Million
Number Employees: 20-49
Sq. footage: 21000
Type of Packaging: Bulk
Other Locations:

4910 Flavors
250 W Side Mall # 217
Edwardsville, PA 18704-3106   570-287-8642
                  Fax: 717-284-2892
Flavors
   President: Bruce Gutterman
Estimated Sales:$1-2.5 Million
Number Employees: 1-4

4911 Flavors from Florida
203 Bartow Air Base
Bartow, FL 33830-9599   863-533-0408
   Fax: 863-533-9478 www.flavorsfromflorida.com
Manufactures Ice cream, sherbert, drink base flavoring, flavoring extracts and syrups
   President: Robert K Prendes
   General Manager/Contact: Mike Benewiat
Estimated Sales:$25-50 Million
Number Employees: 20-49

4912 Flavors of Hawaii
945 Waimanu St
Honolulu, HI 96814-3319   808-597-1727
                  Fax: 808-597-1728
Coconut syrup, guava syrup, cocopine syrup
   President: Alexander Lee
   VP: Henry Mau
Estimated Sales:$5-10 Million
Number Employees: 5-9
Brands:
   Hawaii

4913 Flavors of North America
1900 Averill Rd
Geneva, IL 60134-1601   630-462-1414
          Fax: 630-578-8601   800-308-3662
info@fona.com   www.fonaflavors.com
Flavors, creation and manufacture of confection flavors, beverage flavors, cereal flavors, snack flavors, bakery flavors, dessert flavors, dairy flavors and flavors for use in functional food, prepared food and animal foodindustries.creates and manufactures a full line of quality flavors for the food, beverage, pharmaceutical and nutraceutical industries
          President: Robert Allen
          CEO: Joseph J Slawek
          R&D: Sue Johnson
          Quality Control: Carol Lund
          Marketing: Tracy Bergfeld
          Sales: TJ Widuch
          Purchasing: Terry Emmel
Estimated Sales: $50-100 Million
Number Employees: 100-249

4914 Flavors of the Heartland
P.O.Box 136
Rocheport, MO 65279-0136   573-698-2063
                                   800-269-3210
Manufacturer of Gourmet foods
          Manager: Roger Pilkinton
Estimated Sales: Less than $500,000
Number Employees: 1-4
Brands:
          Flavors of the Heartland

4915 Flavouressence Products
1-6750 Davand Drive
Mississauga, ON L5T 2L8
Canada   905-795-0318
          Fax: 905-795-0317   866-209-7778
                    info@flavouressence.com
                    www.flavouressence.com
Manufacturer of beverage syrups, juices, bar mixes and slush; exporter of juices, bar mixes and beverage syrups
          President/CEO: Mark Weber
          CFO: Brain Ferry
          Marketing: Bob Graham
          Sales: Jolene Davies
          Plant Manager: David Milner
Estimated Sales: $5 Million
Number Employees: 5-9
Sq. footage: 10500
Type of Packaging: Food Service, Private Label, Bulk

4916 Flavours Inc
24855 Corbit Pl
Yorba Linda, CA 92887-5543   714-463-1440
          Fax: 951-520-1151   gmichaud@flavoursinc.com
                    www.flavoursinc.com/
Products and services includes that of: development of dietary supplements, nutraceutical enhanced products, and low/high acid shelf stable beverages; flavor development and manufacturing; spun matrix micro-encapsulation technology;aseptic dosing of vitamins, flavors, nutraceutical/herbal extracts; and PET/HDPE filling for clinical trials and market testing.
          Director of Aseptic Packaging: Geramy Michaud

4917 Flavtek
1916 S Tubeway Avenue
Los Angeles, CA 90040-1612   323-588-5880
          Fax: 323-588-0178   800-562-5880
                    flavtek@flavtek.com
Manufacturer of flavors, oils, extracts and emulsions to the dairy, beverage, wine, bakery and confectionery industries.
          President: Cary Chow
          VP: Dan Yang
Estimated Sales: $10-20 Million
Number Employees: 10-19
Parent Co: Geneva Ingredients
Type of Packaging: Private Label, Bulk
Brands:
          Flavtek, Inc.

4918 Flavurence Corporation
1916 S Tubeway Ave
Commerce, CA 90040-1612   323-727-1957
          Fax: 323-728-8380   800-717-1957
                    www.flavurence.com
Manufacturer and exporter of flavors
          Manager: Chris Long

Estimated Sales: $25 Million
Number Employees: 5-9
Sq. footage: 60000
Type of Packaging: Private Label, Bulk

4919 Fleet Fisheries
20 Blackmer St
New Bedford, MA 02744-2614   508-996-3742
                                     Fax: 508-996-3785
Manufacturer and wholesale of scallops
          Owner: Lars Jerud
Estimated Sales: $ 5 - 10 Million
Number Employees: 10-19

4920 Fleischer's Bagels
1688 Wayneport Rd
Macedon, NY 14502-8765   315-986-9999
          Fax: 315-986-7200   marc@fleischersbagels.com
                    www.fleischersbagels.com
Manufacturer and exporter of fresh, frozen and refrigerated bagels
          President: Marc Fleischer
          VP: Jody Fleischer
          National Sales Manager: Aaron Fleischer
          Production: Eric Kestenblatt
Estimated Sales: $10-20 Million
Number Employees: 100-249
Sq. footage: 45000
Type of Packaging: Consumer, Food Service, Private Label, Bulk
Brands:
          Fleischer's

4921 Fleischmann's Vinegar
12604 Hiddencreek Way # A
Cerritos, CA 90703-2137
Canada   562-483-4600
          Fax: 562-483-4644   800-443-1067
                    http://www.fleischmannsvinegar.com
Manufacturer of vinegar
          President: Daniel Muth
          CEO: Ken Simril
Number Employees: 1-4
Parent Co: Burns Philp Foods
Type of Packaging: Consumer, Food Service, Private Label, Bulk
Brands:
          Allens
          Fleischann's
          Spice Islands

4922 Fleischmann's Yeast
1350 Timberlake Manor Pkwy
Chesterfield, MO 63017-6042   636-349-8800
          Fax: 636-349-8825   800-247-7473
consumerinfo@bpna.com   www.breadworld.com
Manufacturer and exporter of active and inactive yeasts, vinegars, leaveners and mold inhibitors; also, technical consulting for bakeries available
          President: Andrew Armstrong
          VP: Brian Thronquist
          Marketing Manager: Keith Dierberg
          Sales Manager: Rick Mercuri
          Operations Manager: Terry Strang
          VP Industrial Production: Rex Mercuri
          Plant Manager: Bob Williams
Estimated Sales: $50-100 Million
Number Employees: 1,000-4,999
Parent Co: Burns Philp Foods
Type of Packaging: Food Service, Bulk

4923 Fleischmanns Vinegar
12604 Hiddencreek Way # A
Cerritos, CA 90703-2137   562-483-4600
          Fax: 562-483-4644   800-443-1067
                    vinegar@fvinegar.com
                    www.FleischmannsVinegar.com
Leading manufacturer and marketer of industrial vinegar in North America. We offer a full line of standard and specialty vinegars and cooking wines
          CEO: Daniel Muth
          CFO: Larry McKeown
          CEO: Ken Simril
          R&D/Quality Control: Sylvain Norton
          Public Relations: Daniel Muth
Type of Packaging: Bulk
Brands:
          FLEISCHMANNS VINEGAR
          FLEISCHCMANNS COOKING WINE

4924 Fletcher's Fine Foods
7550 40th Avenue, Bag 5641
Red Deer, AB T4P 2H8
Canada   403-343-8700
                                   Fax: 403-343-7545
Manufacturer and exporter of pork and by-products
          President/CEO: Fred Knoedler
Number Employees: 500-999
Parent Co: Fletcher's Fine Foods
Type of Packaging: Food Service, Bulk
Brands:
          Fletcher's
          Goodlife

4925 Fleur De Lait Foods
400 S Custer Ave
New Holland, PA 17557-9220   717-355-8500
                                     Fax: 717-355-8561
          President: Jesse Hogan
Estimated Sales: $ 20 - 50 Million
Number Employees: 250-499

4926 Fleurchem
33 Sprague Ave
Middletown, NY 10940-5128   845-341-2170
          Fax: 845-341-2121   info@fleurchem.com
                    www.fleurchem.com
Manufacturer, importer and exporter of natural and synthetic flavoring agents and fragrances including acidulants, anethole, citronellal, eucalyptol, furfural, geraniol, heptanal, methyl actetate, etc
          CEO: George Gluck
          CFO: Sara Gluck
          CEO: George Gluck
          Quality Control: Brian Merdler
          VP Marketing: Jack Snicolo
          Operations Manager: Louis Mercun
          Production Manager: Larry Costa
          Purchasing Manager: Angie Roman
Estimated Sales: $10-20 Million
Number Employees: 10-19
Sq. footage: 200000
Type of Packaging: Private Label, Bulk

4927 Fliinko
PO Box 80102
South Dartmouth, MA 02748-0102   508-996-9609
                                   Fax: 508-990-1281
          President: Ingrid Flynn
          Marketing: Thomas Flynn
Estimated Sales: $1-22.5 Million
Number Employees: 1-4
Type of Packaging: Private Label
Brands:
          Nectarade

4928 Flint Hills Foods
PO Box 340
Wamego, KS 66547-0340   785-765-3396
                                Fax: 785-765-2294
Manufacturer of cooked and portion controlled steaks
          President: Bernie Hansen
Estimated Sales: $50 Million
Number Employees: 50-99
Sq. footage: 50000
Type of Packaging: Consumer, Food Service
Brands:
          FLINT HILLS

4929 Flippin-Seaman
5529 Crabtree Falls Hwy
Tyro, VA 22976-3103   434-277-5828
          Fax: 434-277-9057   info@flippin-seaman.com
                    www.flippin-seaman.com
Growers, packer and shippers of fine fruit.
          Owner: Bill Flippin
          Owner: Richard Seaman
Estimated Sales: $10-20 Million
Number Employees: 20-49
Brands:
          Seaman Orchard
          Silver Creek

4930 Flora
P.O.Box 73
Lynden, WA 98264-0073   360-354-2110
          Fax: 360-354-5355   800-446-2110
                    www.florahealth.com

Manufacturer of cold pressed and unrefined oils including flax, canola, sunflower, safflower, sesame, pumpkin, almond and walnut; also, herbal teas and alcohol-free Swedish bitters
President: Thomas Greither
Marketing Manager: Gabriel Lightfriend
Estimated Sales: $10-20 Million
Number Employees: 50-99
Type of Packaging: Consumer
Brands:
Flor-Essence
Flora

4931 (HQ)Flora Manufacturing & Distributing
7400 Fraser Park Drive
Burnaby, BC V5J 5B9
Canada   604-436-6000
         Fax: 604-436-6060 888-436-6697
bonnie@florahealth.com   www.florahealth.com
Manufacturer of natural health products, herbal remedies
President/CEO: Thomas Greither
Quality Control: Summer Sit
Marketing: Guru Simran Khalsa
Sales: Amber Davies
Public Relations Coordinator: Jasmin Tamdoo
Number Employees: 50-99
Sq. footage: 40000
Brands:
FLORA

4932 Flora Springs Wine Company
677 Saint Helena Hwy S
St Helena, CA 94574-2209   707-967-8032
         Fax: 707-967-8036 info@florasprings.com
                    www.florasprings.com
Wines
Manager: Margaret Meraz-Ha
Estimated Sales: $5-10 Million
Number Employees: 5-9

4933 Florasynth
PO Box No
New York, NY 10150   212-371-7700
Manager: Bill Calbo

4934 Florence Macaroni Manufacturing
1312 W 2nd Street
Los Angeles, CA 90026-5808   323-232-7269
                            Fax: 323-232-7143
Manufacturer of macaroni products
President: Roy Pier-Dominici
Merchandising Manger: Joseph Esposito
Plant Manager: Matt Koch
Estimated Sales: $1-2.5 Million
Number Employees: 1-4
Sq. footage: 20000
Type of Packaging: Consumer, Food Service

4935 Florence Macaroni Manufacturing
4334 W Chicago Ave
Chicago, IL 60651-3422   773-252-6113
         Fax: 773-252-7085 800-647-2782
                    florencemacaroni@aol.com
Manufacturer of macaroni products including regular/orangic semolina and whole wheat
Manager: Tom Behnke
Plant Manager: Thomas Benhke
Estimated Sales: $5-10 Million
Number Employees: 20-49
Type of Packaging: Consumer, Food Service, Private Label, Bulk

4936 Florence Pasta & Cheese
115 W College Drive
Marshall, MN 56258-1747   800-533-5290
         Fax: 507-537-8159 info@foodpros.com
                    www.foodpros.com
Manufacturer of frozen pasta and dehydrated cheese
President: Alfred Schwan
Parent Co: Schwann's Sales
Type of Packaging: Consumer, Food Service, Bulk

4937 Florentyna's Fresh Pasta Factory
1864 E 22nd St
Vernon, CA 90058-1034   213-742-9374
         Fax: 310-677-2782 800-747-2782
jascha@freshpasta.com   www.freshpasta.com

Manufacturer of fresh and fresh frozen pasta products for the food service industry
Manager: Jascha Smuloviez
Estimated Sales: $1-4.9 Million
Number Employees: 20-49
Number of Products: 60
Type of Packaging: Food Service, Private Label, Bulk

4938 Florida Bottling
P.O.Box 420708
Miami, FL 33242-0708   305-324-5900
  Fax: 305-325-9573 info@floridabottling.com
                    www.floridabottling.com
Manufacturer and exporter of glass-packed fruit juices including apricot nectar, black cherry, carrot orange, cranberry blend, grape, mango, orange pineapple, passion fruit, pina colada, pineapple, raspberry, red papaya, strawberrythree berry
Manager: Julian Galeote
Sales Manager: Ana Inguanzo
Operations: Holly Newberry
Estimated Sales: $10-20 Million
Number Employees: 20-49
Type of Packaging: Consumer, Food Service, Bulk
Brands:
Coconut Grove
Lakewood
Rainberry
Summer Song

4939 Florida Brewery
202 Gandy Rd
Auburndale, FL 33823-2726   863-965-1825
                            Fax: 863-967-6965
info@thefloridabreweryinc.com
                    www.floridabreweryinc.com
Beer
President: Ramon Campos
CFO: James Biggs
Operations: Erich Schalk
Purchasing: R Campos
Estimated Sales: $20-50 Million
Number Employees: 20-49
Sq. footage: 62
Type of Packaging: Private Label

4940 Florida Carib Fishery
1301 NW 89th Ct
Doral, FL 33172-3034   305-696-2896
                            Fax: 305-547-2772
Manufacturer of frozen prepared, whole fresh and fillet seafood including conch meats, kingfish steaks, mullet roe, cooked whole lobsters and lobster tails
VP: Carlos Sanchez
Plant Manager: Jesse Alonso
Estimated Sales: $1-2.5 Million
Number Employees: 1-4
Parent Co: Beaver Street Fisheries
Type of Packaging: Consumer, Food Service, Private Label

4941 Florida Citrus
3546 N 40th Street
Tampa, FL 33605-1694   813-626-5580
         Fax: 813-664-1576 john@citrusbarn.com
Manufacturer of fruit cocktails, juice and syrup. Product categories are vegetables, canned fruits and fresh fruits
President: John Roberts
VP: Scott Stallard
Estimated Sales: $5-10 Million
Number Employees: 10-19
Type of Packaging: Consumer

4942 Florida Crystals
P.O.Box 4671
West Palm Beach, FL 33402-4671 561-655-4153
         Fax: 561-366-5158 877-835-2828
heather_forbes@floridacrystals.com
                    www.floridacrystals.com
Sugar cane and rice, including premium white rice, sem-chi rice, organic foods
President: Jose Fanjul
CEO: Alfonso Fanjul
CFO: Luis Fernandez
Estimated Sales: $ 5 - 10 Million
Number Employees: 20-49
Brands:
FLORIDA CRYSTALS
SEMI-CHI

4943 Florida Deli Pickle
200 NW 20th Avenue
Fort Lauderdale, FL 33311-8724   954-463-0222
                            Fax: 954-463-5992
Manufacturer of pickles, relishes and pickled products; wholesaler/distributor of meats, cheese, poultry, salads and frozen foods
President: George Bell
Type of Packaging: Consumer, Food Service, Private Label, Bulk

4944 Florida Distillers Company
530 N Dakota Ave
Lake Alfred, FL 33850-2130   863-956-3477
         Fax: 863-956-3979 oyu@todhunter.com
                    www.todhunter.com
Alcoholic and nonalcoholic beverages
President/CEO: Terry Karr
CFO: Troy Edwards
Executive VP: Ron Call
Sales Director: Dennis Mitchell
Production: Lee Stewart
Plant Manager: Bob Miller
Purchasing: Frank Dieling
Estimated Sales: $100-499.9 Million
Number Employees: 250-499
Type of Packaging: Private Label
Brands:
Albertsons
Bacardi
Cruzan
Jacquins
Porfidio
Ron Matusalem
Seagrams

4945 (HQ)Florida Food Products
2231 W County Road 44
Eustis, FL 32726-2628   352-357-4141
         Fax: 352-483-3192 800-874-2331
contact@floridafood.com   www.floridafood.com
Vegetable juice concentrates, aloe vera gel, fruit juice powders, vegetable juice powders
President: Jerry Brown
Vice President: Tom Brown
Research & Development: Scott Ruppe
Plant Manager: Keith Burt
Purchasing Manager: James Arnett
Estimated Sales: $15-20 Million
Number Employees: 50
Sq. footage: 100000
Other Locations:
Florida Food Products
Sabila
Brands:
FLORIDA FOOD PRODUCTS
VEG CON BEET
VEG CON CARROT
VEG CON CELERY

4946 Florida Fruit Juices
7001 W 62nd St
Chicago, IL 60638-3924   773-586-6200
                            Fax: 773-586-6651
Manufacturer of fruit juices including apple, grape, orange, grapefruit, pineapple, etc
President: Donald Franko Sr
CEO: Don Franko
VP: Don Franko, Jr.
Estimated Sales: $ 5 - 10 Million
Number Employees: 20-49
Type of Packaging: Consumer, Food Service, Private Label

4947 Florida Juice Products
PO Box 3628
Lakeland, FL 33802-3628   863-802-4040
                            Fax: 863-686-3649
Manufacturer of Orange and grapefruit juice
President: Ronald Grigsby
Estimated Sales: $50-99.9 Million
Number Employees: 5-9

4948 Florida Key West
5470 Division Dr
Fort Myers, FL 33905-5010   239-694-8787
         Fax: 239-694-0402 juice@florida-juice.com
                    www.florida-juice.com
Lemon and key lime juices
President: Earl Tanner
VP: Sandra Tanner
Estimated Sales: $1-2.5 Million
Number Employees: 5-9

Type of Packaging: Consumer, Food Service, Private Label, Bulk
Brands:
Florida Key West

4949 Florida Natural Flavors
P.O.Box 181125
Casselberry, FL 32718-1125   407-834-5979
Fax: 407-834-6333 800-872-5979
info@floridanaturalflavors.com
www.floridanaturalflavors.com
Manufacturer, exporter and importer of juice and beverage concentrates including carbonated, noncarbonated and frozen products
President: David Erdman
VP: Garry Erdman
Estimated Sales:$10-20 Million
Number Employees: 20-49
Parent Co: Florida Natural Flavors
Type of Packaging: Private Label
Brands:
DIET RITE
Davy's Mix
Juicemaster
MISTIC ICED TEA
NEHI FLAVORS
Polynesian Pleasure
R-Own Cola
STEWART'S
Tropical Pleasure

4950 Florida Shortening Corporation
7360 NW 35th Avenue
Miami, FL 33147-5808   305-691-2992
Fax: 305-691-2997 flshortening@aol.com
Manufacturer, importer and exporter of shortenings, margarines, oils, puff paste, pan releases and spices including garlic; packaging services available
President: Calvin Theobald
Sales Director: Gerald Delmonico
Estimated Sales:$2.5-5 Million
Number Employees: 1-4
Number of Brands: 20
Number of Products: 9
Sq. footage: 20000
Type of Packaging: Food Service, Private Label, Bulk

4951 Florida Veal Processors
6712 State Road 674
Wimauma, FL 33598   813-634-5545
Fax: 813-633-1405
Manufacturer of fresh and frozen veal
Co-Owner: Richard Nusman
Co-Owner: Max Nusman
Accountant: David Gauthier
Estimated Sales:$5.70 Million
Number Employees: 20
Type of Packaging: Consumer, Food Service

4952 Florida's Natural Brand
P.O.Box 1111
Lake Wales, FL 33859-1111   863-676-1411
Fax: 863-676-1640 888-657-6600
www.floridasnatural.com
Manufacturer, canner and exporter of frozen fruit juices, concentrates and blends including grapefruit, orange, lemonade, lime, apple and grape; also, frozen sections
Owner/President: Frank Hunt
CEO: Steve Caruso
CEO: Stephen M Caruso
VP Sales/Marketing: Walt Lincer
Estimated Sales:$100+ Million
Number Employees: 500-999
Parent Co: Citrus World
Type of Packaging: Consumer, Food Service, Private Label
Brands:
ADAMS
BIG TEX
BLUEBIRD
DONALD DUCK
FLORIDA'S NATURAL
LAKE WALES

4953 Florida's Natural Growers
P.O.Box 1111
Lake Wales, FL 33859-1111   863-676-1411
Fax: 863-676-1640 info@nextdigital.com
www.floridasnatural.com
Manufacturer of juices
CEO: Stephen M Caruso
VP Sales/Marketing: Walter Lincer

Estimated Sales:$422 Million
Number Employees: 500-999
Brands:
FLORIDA'S NATURAL

4954 Florida's Natural Growers
38851 State Road 19
Umatilla, FL 32784-8843   352-669-2101
Fax: 352-669-3120 800-366-4440
www.floridasnatural.com
Manufacturer of Florida juice and fresh fruit packs
President: Ralph Hayes
SVP: Martin Stevens
Plant Manager: Mark Hopkins
Estimated Sales:$100-500 Million
Number Employees: 100-249
Type of Packaging: Private Label

4955 Floron Food Services
2545 96th Street
Edmonton, AB T6N 1E3
Canada   780-438-9300
Fax: 780-438-9200 info@floron.com
www.floron.com
Manufacturer of mozzarella and cheddar cheese, manufacturer of private label pasta sauce, full line distribution
President: Greg Lamorie
VP: Stephen Robbins
Estimated Sales:$20 Million
Number Employees: 40
Sq. footage: 20000
Type of Packaging: Consumer, Food Service

4956 Flower Bakeries
501 E 4th St
London, KY 40741-4108   606-864-5161
Fax: 606-864-3462 800-568-3476
Flowers@CustomerService.com
www.flowersfoods.com
Processor of fresh and frozen pies
President: Kerry Phelps
CFO: Jimmy M Woodward
Controller: Anne Stivers
Chairman: Amos McMullian
Purchasing Agent: Glenn Benge
Estimated Sales:$100+ Million
Number Employees: 500-999
Parent Co: Mrs. Smiths Bakeries
Type of Packaging: Consumer
Brands:
Flower Bakeries
Mrs. Freshley's

4957 Flower Essence Services
P.O.Box 1769
Nevada City, CA 95959-1769   530-265-0258
Fax: 530-265-6467 800-548-0075
info@fesflowers.com www.fesflowers.com
Manufactuer of flower essences
Owner: Richard Katz
Estimated Sales:$ 1 - 3 Million
Number Employees: 10-19

4958 (HQ)Flower Foods, Inc.
1919 Flowers Cir
Thomasville, GA 31757-1137   229-226-9110
Fax: 229-225-3806 www.flowersfoods.com
Fresh and frozen bakery foods including breads, buns, and rolls to snack cakes and pastries.
President: Allen Shiver
Chairman/CEO: George Deese
EVP/CFO: R Steve Kinsey
EVP: Stephen Avera
EVP/COO: Gene Lord
Estimated Sales:$2.6 Billion
Number Employees: 8,800
Brands:
BLUE BIRD
BUNNY
COBBLESTONE MILL
EUROPEAN BAKERIES
MI CASA
MRS FRESHLEY'S
NATURE'S OWN
SUNBEAM

4959 (HQ)Flowers Bakeries
1919 Flowers Cir
Thomasville, GA 31757-1137   229-226-9110
Fax: 229-225-3823 800-226-2429
www.flowersbakeries.com

Producer and marketer of packaged bakery foods
President: Allen Shiver
Chairman/CEO: George Deese
EVP/CFO: R Steve Kinsey
EVP/General Counsel/Secretary: Stephen Avera
VP Marketing: Charlie Moon
EVP Corporate Relations: Marta Jones Turner
EVP/COO: Gene Lord
Estimated Sales:$2.6 Billion
Number Employees: 5,000-9,999
Parent Co: Flowers Foods
Type of Packaging: Consumer
Brands:
AUNT HATTIE'S
BLUE BIRD
BUNNY 'S OWN
BUTTERKRUST
CAPTAIN JOHN DERST'S
COBBLESTONE MILL
EUROPEAN BAKERS
EVANGELINE MAID
HOLSUM
MARY JANE
MARY JANE & FRIENDS
MI CASA
MRS. FRESHLEY'S
NATURE'S OWN
SUNBEAM
WHITEWHEAT

4960 Flowers Bakeries
1925 Flowers Cir
Thomasville, GA 31757-1137   229-226-9110
Fax: 229-225-3823 800-568-3476
www.flowersbakeries.com
Manufacturer and exporter of breads, rolls and buns
President: John Deleu Sr
Executive VP: Gene Lord
Sales Assistant: Renee Fortino
Number Employees: 5,000-9,999
Parent Co: Flowers Baking Company
Type of Packaging: Consumer

4961 Flowers Bakeries
1925 Flowers Cir
Thomasville, GA 31757-1137   229-226-9110
Fax: 229-225-3823 800-568-3476
www.flowersbakeries.com
Manufacturer of baked goods including breads, rolls and buns
President: Calvin Rhodes
Executive VP: Gene Lord
VP Sales: Steve Bordeaux
Estimated Sales:$100+ Million
Number Employees: 5,000-9,999
Parent Co: Flowers Baking Company
Type of Packaging: Consumer

4962 Flowers Bakeries
1925 Flowers Cir
Thomasville, GA 31757-1137   229-226-9110
Fax: 229-225-3823 800-568-3476
www.flowersbakeries.com
Manufacturer of baked goods including breads, buns and rolls
President: Debbie Broussard
Executive VP: Gene Lord
Estimated Sales:$ 50 - 100 Million
Number Employees: 5,000-9,999
Parent Co: Flowers Baking Company
Type of Packaging: Consumer

4963 Flowers Bakeries
1925 Flowers Cir
Thomasville, GA 31757-1137   229-226-9110
Fax: 229-225-3823 800-568-3476
www.flowersbakeries.com
Manufacturer of breads, buns and rolls
President: William Bueck
Executive VP: Gene Lord
Estimated Sales:$ 20 - 50 Million
Number Employees: 5,000-9,999
Parent Co: Flowers Baking Company
Type of Packaging: Consumer

4964 Flowers Bakeries
1925 Flowers Cir
Thomasville, GA 31757-1137   229-226-9110
Fax: 229-225-3823 800-568-3476
www.flowersbakeries.com
Manufacturer of baked goods including buns, rolls and breads
President: Bradley Alexander
Executive VP: Gene Lord

Estimated Sales:$ 3 - 5 Million
Number Employees: 5,000-9,999
Parent Co: Flowers Baking Company
Type of Packaging: Consumer

4965 Flowers Bakeries
P.O.Box 308
Bluefield, WV 24701-0308   304-327-3561
        Fax: 304-325-5410 800-327-1630
Manufacturer of baked goods including bread, buns
and rolls
    President: Robbie Watkins
    VP Sales: Richard Mayse
Estimated Sales:$ 50 - 100 Million
Number Employees: 100-249
Sq. footage: 70000
Parent Co: Flowers Baking Company
Type of Packaging: Consumer

4966 Flowers Bakeries
1925 Flowers Cir
Thomasville, GA 31757-1137   229-226-9110
        Fax: 229-225-3823 800-568-3476
                www.flowersbakeries.com
Manufacturer of baked goods including breads, buns
and rolls
    President: John Coate
    Executive VP: Gene Lord
    VP Sales: Mike McCall
Estimated Sales:$100+ Million
Number Employees: 5,000-9,999
Parent Co: Flowers Baking Company
Type of Packaging: Consumer

4967 Flowers Bakeries
1925 Flowers Cir
Thomasville, GA 31757-1137   229-226-9110
        Fax: 229-225-3823 800-568-3476
                www.flowersbakeries.com
Manufacturer of baked goods including breads, buns
and rolls
    President: Jackie Forrest
    Executive VP: Gene Lord
Estimated Sales:$300,000-500,000
Number Employees: 5,000-9,999
Parent Co: Flowers Baking Company
Type of Packaging: Consumer

4968 Flowers Bakery of Montgomery
140 Folmar Pkwy
Montgomery, AL 36105-5501   334-281-7030
        Fax: 334-284-6119 april_bagi@flocorp.com
Manufacturer of breads, buns, rolls, frozen dough,
biscuits
    President: Larry Brewer
Estimated Sales:$ 10 - 20 Million
Number Employees: 100-249
Parent Co: Flowers Baking Company
Type of Packaging: Consumer, Food Service, Pri-
    vate Label

4969 Flowers Bakery of Winston-Salem
PO Box Ab
Winston Salem, NC 27108-0467   336-785-8700
        Fax: 336-785-8723 800-334-5260
        info@royalcake.com www.royalcake.com
Manufacturer of snack cakes and cookies. The com-
pany was previously known as Royal Cake Com-
pany until Flower Foods Specialty Group acquired
the company
    President: James Whitney
    COO: Florence Burnette
    Corporate Controller: G Kyle Norman
    VP Sales/Marketing: Charles Forrest
Estimated Sales:$25.7 Million
Number Employees: 200
Number of Brands: 35
Number of Products: 18
Parent Co: Flowers Foods
Type of Packaging: Consumer, Food Service, Pri-
    vate Label, Bulk
Brands:
    BAKERS BEST
    ROYAL

4970 Flowers Baking
6000 NE Loop 410
San Antonio, TX 78218-5424   210-661-2361
    Fax: 210-661-4037 ryan_barrios@flocorp.com
                www.butterkrust.com

Manufacturer and exporter of cakes, cookies, sweet
rolls, doughnuts, biscuits and tortillas.
    President: Ryan Barrios
    Quality Control Director: Jeff Loose
    Human Resources Director: David Harpek
    Production Manager: Bob Cummins
    Plant Manager: Richard Richter
    Purchasing Agent: Neal Sintek
Estimated Sales:$500 Million to $1 Billion
Number Employees: 290
Sq. footage: 100000
Parent Co: Richter Bakeries
Type of Packaging: Consumer, Food Service, Pri-
    vate Label
Brands:
    Butterkrust
    Colonial
    Cozy Kitchen
    Sunbeam

4971 Flowers Baking Company
P.O.Box 1774
Morristown, TN 37816-1774   423-586-2471
        Fax: 423-586-3728 www.flowersfoods.com
Manufacturer of baked goods including buns and
rolls.
    President: Craig White
Estimated Sales:$ 20 - 50 Million
Number Employees: 100-249
Parent Co: Flowers Baking Company
Type of Packaging: Consumer, Food Service, Pri-
    vate Label, Bulk

4972 Flowers Baking Company
801 W Main St
Jamestown, NC 27282-9562   336-841-8840
        Fax: 336-841-6433 www.flowersfoods.com
Manufacturer of baked goods including breads, rolls
and buns
    President: Roger Tooley
Estimated Sales:$ 50 - 100 Million
Number Employees: 250-499
Parent Co: Flowers Baking Company
Type of Packaging: Consumer

4973 Flowers Baking Company
P.O.Box 12579
Jacksonville, FL 32209-0579   904-353-8293
                Fax: 904-634-4829
Manufacturer of baked goods including breads, rolls
and buns
    President: Rick Mc Combs
Estimated Sales:$100+ Million
Number Employees: 100-249
Parent Co: Flowers Baking Company
Type of Packaging: Consumer

4974 Flowers Baking Company
P.O.Box 7413
Pine Bluff, AR 71611-7413   870-534-0221
        Fax: 870-534-4768 www.flowersfood.com
Manufacturer of rolls and buns
    President: James Welch
    CEO: Larry Ruth
Estimated Sales:$3-5 Million
Number Employees: 50-99
Parent Co: Flowers Industries
Type of Packaging: Consumer, Food Service, Pri-
    vate Label

4975 (HQ)Flowers Foods Bakeries
1919 Flowers Cir
Thomasville, GA 31757-1137   229-226-9110
        Fax: 229-225-3806 www.flowersfoods.com
Breads, bins, rolls, snack cakes and pastries
    President: Allen Shiver
    Chairman/CEO: George Deese
    EVP/CFO: R Steve Kinsey
    EVP: Stephen Avera
    EVP/COO: Gene Lord
Estimated Sales:$2.6 Billion
Number Employees: 5,000-9,999
Type of Packaging: Consumer, Food Service, Pri-
    vate Label, Bulk
Other Locations:
    Atlanta GA
    El Paso TX
    Fort Smith AK
    Goldsboro NC
    Houston TX
    Lafayette LA
    New Orleans LA
    Pine Bluff AR
    San Antonio TX

Brands:
    AUNT HATTIE'S
    BLUE BIRD
    BUNNY
    BUTTERKRUST
    CAPTAIN JOHN DERST'S
    COBBLESTONE MILL
    EUROPEAN BAKERS
    EVANGELINE MAID
    HOLSUM
    MARY JANE
    MARY JANE & FRIENDS
    MI CASA
    MRS. FRESHLEY'S
    NATURE'S OWN
    SUNBEAM
    WHITEWHEAT

4976 Flowers Snack of Tennessee
P.O.Box 495
Crossville, TN 38557-0495   931-484-6101
        Fax: 931-484-3657 www.flowersfoods.com
Manufacturer of pecan spins, sweet rolls and
cake/doughnut sticks
    President: Frank Shipley
Estimated Sales:$100-500 Million
Number Employees: 250-499
Sq. footage: 270000
Parent Co: Flowers Baking Company
Type of Packaging: Consumer

4977 Flying Dog Brewery
2401 Blake St # 2
Denver, CO 80205-2251   303-292-5027
        Fax: 303-296-0164 www.flyingdogales.com
Manufacturer of seasonal beer, ale, stout and porter
    President/CEO: Eric Warner
    CFO: Kelly McElroy
    Sales: Rich Graham
Estimated Sales:$20-50 Million
Number Employees: 20-49
Parent Co: Wynkoop
Type of Packaging: Consumer, Food Service
Brands:
    Flying Dog
    Railyard

4978 Flying Seafood Incorporated
73-4776 Kanalani St # 8
Kailua Kona, HI 96740-2625   808-326-7708
        Fax: 808-329-3669 www.hilofish.com
Manufacturer of fresh, frozen seafood
    Owner: Kerry Umamoto
Estimated Sales:$ 5 - 10 Million
Number Employees: 10-19

4979 Flynn Vineyards Winery
2200 N Pacific Hwy W
Rickreall, OR 97371-9774   503-623-8683
        Fax: 503-623-0908 888-427-4953
                www.flynnvineyards.com
Wines
    President: Howard Rossbach
Estimated Sales:$5-10 Million
Number Employees: 5-9
Type of Packaging: Private Label

4980 (HQ)Fmali Herb
831 Almar Avenue
Santa Cruz, CA 95060-5899   831-423-7913
        Fax: 831-429-5173 sales@fmali.com
Manufacturer and contract packager of ginseng, hi-
biscus flowers, orange and lemon peels, herbal,
green and black teas and chamomile; importer of
ginseng, royal jelly and panax extractum; exporter of
herbal teas and orange and lemonpeels
    President/Co-Founder: Ben Zaricor
    Executive VP/Co-Founder: Louise Veninga
Estimated Sales:$14.0 Million
Number Employees: 50-99
Sq. footage: 42000
Type of Packaging: Consumer, Food Service, Pri-
    vate Label, Bulk
Brands:
    FAMLI
    GOOD EARTH
    WILDCRAFT

4981 Foell Packing Company
PO Box 4595
Naperville, IL 60567-4595   919-776-0592
        Fax: 919-774-1627 info@foellpacking.com
                www.foellpacking.com

Manufacturer and exporter of canned meats including tripe, Vienna sausage and pork brains; also, contract packaging available
President: D Johnson
Vice President: T O'Shea
Estimated Sales: $5-10 Million
Number Employees: 20-49
Sq. footage: 36000
Type of Packaging: Consumer, Private Label
Brands:
Beverly
Rose

4982 Fogo Island CooperativeSociety
PO Box 70
Seldom, NL A0G 320
Canada   709-627-3452
                Fax: 709-627-3495
Manufacturer and exporter of live and frozen crabs
President: Cecil Godwin
General Manager: Keith Watts
Number Employees: 500-999
Type of Packaging: Consumer, Food Service, Bulk

4983 Fold-Pak East, Inc.
33 Powell Dr
Hazleton, PA 18201-7360   570-454-0433
          Fax: 570-454-0456   800-486-0490
                east@gsdpackaging.com
                www.gsdpackaging.com
Wire handled square paper food containers, round cup style closeable food and soup containers, square closeable paper food containers (microwaveable, carry out and storage capable)
Manager: Charlie Mattson
Marketing Director: Wes Gentles
Sales Director: Jim Keitges
Corporate Credit Manager: William Moon
Plant Manager: Lee King
Number Employees: 5,000-9,999
Number of Brands: 16
Number of Products: 66
Sq. footage: 104000
Parent Co: Rock-Tenn Company
Type of Packaging: Consumer, Food Service, Private Label

4984 Foley Estates Vineyards& Winery
1711 Alamo Pintado Rd
Solvang, CA 93463-9712   805-688-8554
          Fax: 805-688-9327   info@foleywines.com
                www.foleywines.com
Wines
President: Robert Lidquist II
Marketing Manager: Lisa Schaeffer
Sales: Mike Keonig
Production Manager: Norm Yost
Estimated Sales: $2.5-5 Million
Number Employees: 10-19
Type of Packaging: Private Label

4985 Foley's Candies
12671 No 5 Road
Richmond, BC V7A 4E9
Canada   604-274-2131
          Fax: 604-275-1682   888-236-5397
                info@foleyscandies.com
                www.foleyscandies.com
Manufacturer of chocolate and confectionery products including wafers, blocks, chips, almond barks, squares, mints, yogurt covered almonds, raisins, peanuts and coffee beans
Sales Manager: Scott Oswald
Number Employees: 20-49
Type of Packaging: Private Label, Bulk

4986 Folgers Coffee Company
1 Strawberry Lane
Orrville, OH 44667-0280   513-983-1100
          Fax: 513-983-4905   877-693-6543
                www.folgers.com
Manufacturer of roasted, ground, regular and decaffeinated coffee. Also, Folgers is the licensed manufacturer and distributor of Dunkin' Donuts retail coffee brand.
Executive Chairman/Co-CEO: Richard Smucker
Chairman/Co-CEO: Tim Smucker
Estimated Sales: $1 Billion
Number Employees: 1038
Parent Co: J.M Smucker Company
Type of Packaging: Consumer
Brands:
FOLGERS

4987 Folie a Deux Winery
P.O.Box 248
St Helena, CA 94574-0248   707-963-1160
          Fax: 707-963-9223   800-473-4454
          tasting@folieadeux.com   www.folieadeux.com
Wines
Manager: Paul Scholfield
CEO: Richard Peterson
CFO: George Schofield
Marketing: Cardace Guridi
Public Relations: David Foster
Operations: Carla Clift
Production: Alejandro Pantoja
Purchasing: Marc Norwood
Number Employees: 10-19
Number of Brands: 3
Type of Packaging: Consumer
Brands:
Fantaisie
Folie a Deux
La Grande Folie
La Petite Folie

4988 Folklore Foods
9 N B St
Toppenish, WA 98948-1312   509-865-4772
                Fax: 509-865-7363
Manufacturer and exporter of espresso syrups and granita concentrate
President/CEO: Daniel Hanson
Estimated Sales: $5-10 Million
Number Employees: 5-9
Sq. footage: 8200
Type of Packaging: Consumer, Food Service, Private Label
Brands:
Folklore
Folklore Cream Soda
Folklore Gourmet Syrups
Folklore Sasaparilla
Folklore Sparkling Beverages

4989 Follmer Development/Americana
850 Tourmaline Dr
Newbury Park, CA 91320-1290   805-498-4531
Fax: 805-376-2404 www.follmerdevelopment.com
Vegetable oil cooking sprays
President: Christopher Follmer
VP: Garrett Follmer
Marketing: David McKenzie
Estimated Sales: $20-50 Million
Number Employees: 20-49
Type of Packaging: Consumer, Food Service, Private Label

4990 Foltz Coffee Tea & Spice Company
7733 Edinburgh Street
New Orleans, LA 70125-1505   504-486-1545
                Fax: 504-486-1545
Coffee and tea
President: George Foltz
Estimated Sales: $2.5-5 Million
Number Employees: 10-19

4991 Fontana's Casa De La Pasta
115 Grant Avenue
Vandergrift, PA 15690-1229   724-567-2782
                Fax: 724-567-1429
Dried pasta and ravioli
President: William Fontana
Estimated Sales: $5-9.9 Million
Number Employees: 1-4
Sq. footage: 4
Type of Packaging: Private Label

4992 Fontanini Italian Meats& Sausages
911 W 37th Place
Chicago, IL 60609-1412   773-890-0600
          Fax: 773-890-1680   800-331-6328
          info@fontanini.com   www.fontanini.com

Manufacturer of meatballs, breakfast items, pizza toppings, beef
President: Gene Fontanini
Account Executive: Rita Rufo
VP: Joanne Fontanini
Controller Midwest: Eric Divelbiss
Director QC: Anthony Pavel
General Manager: Charles Brown
Regional Manager: Jim Doherty
West Coast Regional Manager: Gene Borgomainero
Director Operations: Mike Catania
Estimated Sales: $100-500 Million
Number Employees: 250
Sq. footage: 240000
Parent Co: Capital Wholesale Meats Company
Type of Packaging: Consumer, Food Service
Brands:
MAMA RANNE

4993 Fontazzi/Metrovox Snacks
6116 Walker Avenue
Maywood, CA 90270-3447   323-771-3221
          Fax: 323-771-2429   800-428-0522
          metrovox@aol.com   www.giftbasketsupplies.com
Popcorn, pretzels, snack mixes, gift packs, gift boxes, sourdough truffles
President: Paul Voxrand
Estimated Sales: $300,000-500,000
Number Employees: 1-4

4994 (HQ)Fontina Foods
485 NW Enterprise Drive
Port Saint Lucie, FL 34986-2202   561-878-1400
          Fax: 561-878-8196   800-966-7107
Manufacturer and exporter of refrigerated herbs and spices in blended canola oil, herb blends and pesto sauces, custom product development services for chain restaurants; also, importer of olive oil
President: J Michael Buscaino
Manager of Purchasing: Folker Raynolds
Estimated Sales: $10-20 Million
Number Employees: 20-49
Sq. footage: 27000
Parent Co: Cargill
Type of Packaging: Food Service, Private Label, Bulk
Brands:
FONTINA FOODS

4995 Food & Paper Supply
7247 S South Chicago Ave
Chicago, IL 60619-1295   773-752-0700
                Fax: 773-752-0747
President: Bruce Goldberg
Estimated Sales: $ 10 - 20 Million
Number Employees: 50-99

4996 Food & Vine
68 Coombs St # I-2
Napa, CA 94559-3966   707-251-3900
          Fax: 707-251-3939   info@grapeseedoil.com
                www.grapeseedoil.com
Manufacturer of grapeseed oil
President: Valentin Humer
VP/Public Relations: Nanette Humer
Estimated Sales: $5-10 Million
Number Employees: 1-4
Sq. footage: 1000
Type of Packaging: Consumer, Food Service, Private Label, Bulk
Brands:
Salute Sante
Salute Sante! Grape Oil

4997 Food & Vine
68 Coombs St # I-2
Napa, CA 94559-3966   707-251-3900
                www.grapeseedoil.com
Grapeseed oil
President: Valentin Humer

4998 Food City Pickle Company
2501 N Damen Ave
Chicago, IL 60647-2101   269-781-9135
                Fax: 616-781-3422
Manufacturer of sweet relish, dill relish, whole dill pickles, dill slices, sweet pickles, pepperoncini and peppers including hot and mild banana
President: Ron DeRuiter
Estimated Sales: $2.5-5 Million
Number Employees: 5-9
Sq. footage: 22000

Type of Packaging: Consumer, Food Service, Private Label, Bulk
Brands:
  King's Choice

4999 Food City USA
4752 W 60th Ave # A
Arvada, CO 80003-6900   303-321-4447
         Fax: 303-428-4143
     information@grandmaspasta.com
Manufacturer of fresh and frozen pre-cooked pasta including wide egg noodles, linguini, fettuccine and angel hair
  Owner: Moni Piz-Wilson
Estimated Sales: $ 3 - 5 Million
Number Employees: 5-9
Parent Co: Grandma's Pasta Products
Type of Packaging: Consumer, Food Service
Brands:
  Grandma's

5000 Food Concentrate Corporation
921 NW 72nd Street
Oklahoma City, OK 73116-7107   405-840-5633
         Fax: 405-843-6832
Manufacturer of barbecue sauce concentrate and muffin and seasoning mixes
  President: Walter Seideman
Estimated Sales: $2.5-5 Million
Number Employees: 1-4
Sq. footage: 4000
Type of Packaging: Consumer, Food Service, Private Label
Brands:
  Food Concentrate Corp.
  Oat-N-Bran
  Uncle Walter's

5001 Food Factory
875 Waimanu St # 535
Honolulu, HI 96813-5266   808-593-2633
         Fax: 808-591-2943
  President: David Phillips
Estimated Sales: $300,000-500,000
Number Employees: 5-9

5002 Food Ingredients
2425 Alft Ln
Elgin, IL 60124-7864   847-683-0001
     Fax: 847-683-0007   800-500-7676
         leonardra@aol.com
Manufacturer of Dairy and flavor products, colloids, cereal and legumes, fats and oils, sweeteners, process enrichment aids, surficatants, peanut butter and fruit flakes
  President: Robert Leonard
Estimated Sales: $5-10 Million
Number Employees: 1-4
Sq. footage: 7000

5003 Food Ingredients Solutions
300 Corporate Dr
Blauvelt, NY 10913-1144   845-353-8501
     Fax: 212-541-9087   jgreaves@foodcolor.com
         www.foodcolor.com
Manufacturer and distributor of Ingredients for barbeque sauces, spices, seasonings, colors, flavors, gums
  President/CEO/CFO: Jeff Greaves
Estimated Sales: $6 Million
Number Employees: 1-4
Number of Brands: 2
Number of Products: 80
Type of Packaging: Food Service, Private Label, Bulk
Other Locations:
  Food Ingredients Solutions
  Signal Hill CA
Brands:
  Grill-In-A-Bottle
  Safrante

5004 Food Masters
300 W Broad St
Griffin, GA 30223-2904   770-227-0330
     Fax: 770-228-4281   888-715-4394
  sales@foodmasters.com   www.foodmasters.com
Mesquite BBQ sauce, Caesar, cucumber dressing and dip, sea sauce, honey mustard, dill delight, vinaigrette, poppy seed
  President: Pradeep Kumarhia
Estimated Sales: $1-2.5 Million
Number Employees: 5-9

5005 Food Merchants
5431 W 103rd Avenue
Westminster, CO 80020-4132   303-466-5574
     Fax: 303-469-9630   jc@foodmerchants.com
         www.foodmerchants.com
Manufacturer of organic polenta, polenta pasta, and Kamut pasta
  President: Don McKinley
Estimated Sales: $1 Million
Number Employees: 1-4
Type of Packaging: Private Label
Brands:
  Cleopatra Kamit Pasta Products
  Gabriele Pasta Produ
  San Gennaro Original

5006 Food Mill
3033 Macarthur Blvd
Oakland, CA 94602-3299   510-482-3848
     Fax: 510-482-0344   www.foodmillonline.com
Manufacturer of nut butter, cookies and breads
  President/Co-Owner: Kirk Watkins
  Treasurer/Co-Owner: Arthur Watkins
Estimated Sales: $1-2.5 Million
Number Employees: 20-49
Sq. footage: 12000
Type of Packaging: Consumer, Bulk
Brands:
  Food Mill

5007 Food Processor of New Mexico
PO Box 3672
Albuquerque, NM 87190-3672   505-881-4921
     Fax: 505-797-2505   877-634-3772
         fpnm@comcast.net
     www.foodprocessorsofnm.com
Manufacturer of bar-b-que sauces, green chile, red chile, habanero
  Co-Owner: Phillip Clark
  Co-Owner: Wanda Clark

5008 Food Products Corporation
3121 E Washington St
Phoenix, AZ 85034-1519   602-273-7139
         Fax: 602-275-9429
Manufacturer of Mexican foods including flour and corn tortillas, tortilla chips and masa
  CEO: David Brennan
  Plant Manager: Joaquin Amaro
Estimated Sales: $5-10 Million
Number Employees: 50-99
Sq. footage: 40000
Parent Co: Sparta Foods
Type of Packaging: Consumer, Food Service, Private Label, Bulk
Brands:
  ARIZONA

5009 (HQ)Food Reserves
P.O.Box 88
Concordia, MO 64020-0088   660-463-2158
     Fax: 660-463-2159   800-944-1511
         info@goodforyouamerica.com
         www.goodforyouamerica.com
Manufacturer and exporter of emergency and survival food tablets and canned freeze-dried foods; importer of bulk ingredients and freeze-dried foods
  Manager: Deborah Collins
  Manager: Landy Coldwell
Estimated Sales: $ 3 - 5 Million
Number Employees: 5-9
Sq. footage: 10000
Type of Packaging: Consumer, Private Label, Bulk
Other Locations:
  Food Reserves - Laboratory
  Kansas City MO
  Food Reserves
  Syracuse NY
Brands:
  FOOD RESERVES
  STOREHOUSE FOODS

5010 (HQ)Food Reserves/Good ForYou America
P.O.Box 88
Concordia, MO 64020-0088   660-463-2158
     Fax: 660-463-2159   800-944-1511
         info@FoodReserves.com
         www.goodforyouamerica.com
Processor, importer and exporter of natural snack foods
  Manager: Deborah Collins
  General Manager: Jennifer Winklebauer

Estimated Sales: $ 3 - 5 Million
Number Employees: 5-9
Sq. footage: 10000
Type of Packaging: Consumer, Private Label, Bulk
Brands:
  Good For You America
  The Original Food Tab

5011 Food Sciences Corporation
821 E Gate Dr
Mt Laurel, NJ 08054-1239   856-778-8080
     Fax: 856-778-4192   800-320-7928
         www.foodsciences.com
Manufacturer of Nutritional shakes, puddings; protein snack bars, chips; soups, pastas, hot beverages, other nutritional food supplements
  Owner: Robert Schwartz
Estimated Sales: $ 10 - 20 Million
Number Employees: 50-99

5012 Food Should Taste Good
PO Box 776
Needham Heights, MA 02494   781-455-8500
         Fax: 781-455-8550
     james@foodshouldtastegood.com
         www.foodshouldtastegood.com
flavored tortilla chips
  CEO: Peter Lascoe
  CFO: Bob Craig
Estimated Sales: $5 Million
Number Employees: 8

5013 Food Source
2200 Redbud Blvd
McKinney, TX 75069-8217   972-548-9001
     Fax: 972-542-0884   www.foodsourcelp.com
Manufacturer of frozen custom-made lasagna, manicotti, cannelloni and ravioli; also, soups and sauces
  President: Richard Riccardi
  Executive VP: Anita Riccardi
  VP: Carmine Riccardi
Estimated Sales: $20-50 Million
Number Employees: 50-99

5014 Food Source Company
1335 Fewster Drive
Mississauga, ON L4W 1A2
Canada   905-625-8404
         Fax: 905-238-9160
Manufacturer, exporter and importer of salad dressings, sauces and fat-free mayonnaise
Estimated Sales: $5-10 Million
Number Employees: 20-49
Sq. footage: 20000
Type of Packaging: Consumer, Food Service, Private Label

5015 Food Specialties
1727 Expo Ln
Indianapolis, IN 46214-2334   317-271-0862
         Fax: 317-634-8482
Manufacturer of salad dressing, mayonnaise, prepared mustard and barbecue sauce
  President: John Bradshaw
Estimated Sales: $.5-1 Million
Number Employees: 5-9
Sq. footage: 20000
Type of Packaging: Food Service, Private Label, Bulk
Brands:
  Ambassador
  Tasty Rich

5016 Food Specialties Company
12 Sunnybrook Dr
Cincinnati, OH 45237-2191   513-761-1242
         Fax: 513-821-3733
Manufacturer of mayonnaise, tartar sauce, salad dressings, salsa and sandwich spreads
  Owner: Susan Rollman
  VP/GM: Stuart Schulman
  Plant Manager: Ron Simmons
Estimated Sales: $5-10 Million
Number Employees: 10-19
Sq. footage: 35000
Type of Packaging: Consumer, Food Service, Private Label, Bulk
Brands:
  Caddy
  Lady Rose

5017 Food Systems of Louisiana
1540 Lobdell Avenue
Baton Rouge, LA 70806-8244 225-343-3401
Fax: 225-343-6764
President: Mickey Montalbano

5018 Food for Life Baking Company
P.O.Box 1434
Corona, CA 92878-1434 951-279-5090
Fax: 951-279-1784 www.foodforlife.com
Baked goods including sprouted grain breads
President: Jim Torres
CEO: Larry Cappetto
VP: Charlie Torres
Estimated Sales:$10-20 Million
Number Employees: 50-99

5019 Food of Our Own Design
1988 Springfield Ave
Maplewood, NJ 07040-3437 973-762-0985
Fax: 973-762-7895
www.foodofourowndesign.com,
www.maplewoodonline.com
Manufacturer of cakes, pastries, brownies and
crunch bars
Owner: Timothy Quickel
VP Sales/Operations: Tisha Jackson
Estimated Sales:$10-20 Million
Number Employees: 10-19
Sq. footage: 4000

5020 FoodMatch Inc
575 Eight Avenue
New York, NY 10018 212-244-5050
Fax: 212-334-5042 800-350-3411
info@foodmatch.com www.foodmatch.com
olives, fig spreads and dolmas
President/Owner: Philip Meldrum
Estimated Sales:$2.5 Million
Number Employees: 23

5021 FoodScience of Vermont
20 New England Dr
Essex Junction, VT 05452-2896 802-878-5508
Fax: 802-878-0549 800-874-9444
info@foodscienceofvermont.com
www.foodsciencecorp.com
Manufacturer and exporter of vitamin supplements,
joint and immune support supplements and specialty
nutritional formulas
President: Dom Orlandi
CEO: Dale Metz
CFO: Tricia Wunsch
QC: Mary Helrich
Sales/Marketing: Mark Ducharme
Operations: Sarah Oliveira
Estimated Sales:$300,000-500,000
Number Employees: 1-4
Parent Co: FoodScience Corporation
Brands:
AANGAMIK DMG
CHITOLEAN
DISCOVERY
HERB ALCHEMY

5022 Foodbrands America
840 Research Pkwy
Oklahoma City, OK 73104-3616 405-290-4000
Fax: 405-879-5325 www.labcorp.com
Manufacturer of kosher and breaded and battered
appetizers, gourmet hors d'oeuvres, pastries, soups,
sauces, lasagna, burritos, pizza toppings and crusts,
snacks, side dishes and meat products including
boneless ham, bologna, salamifrankfurters, sausage,
etc
President: Richard Bond
CEO: Richard Bond
CFO: Wade Miquelon
VP: William Lovette
Plant Manager: Bert Kock
Purchasing Agent: Randy Allison
Number Employees: 50-99
Parent Co: IBP
Type of Packaging: Consumer, Food Service, Pri-
vate Label, Bulk
Other Locations:
Foodbrands America
Buffalo NY

5023 Foodmark
180 Linden Street
Wellesley, MA 02482 781-237-7088
Fax: 781-237-7455 ggavris@foodmark.com
www.foodmark.com

Broker of dairy/deli products, frozen foods, grocer-
ies, meat products and private label items. Also
product development and marketing services for ice
cream novelties and pizza available
Partner: George Gavris
Partner: Rob Simmons
Partner: Lee Gavris
Estimated Sales:$10-20 Million
Number Employees: 10-19

5024 Fool Proof Gourmet Products
PO Box 2442
Grapevine, TX 76099-2442 817-329-1839
Fax: 817-329-1819
chefmark@foolproof-foods.com
www.foolproof-foods.com
Manufacturer and exporter of gourmet seasonings,
spices, sauces, etc
President: Mark Pierce
VP: Jeff Covington
Estimated Sales:$1-3 Million
Number Employees: 5-9
Sq. footage: 10000
Parent Co: Coulton Associates
Type of Packaging: Consumer, Food Service
Brands:
Fool Proof Gourmet

5025 (HQ)Foothills Creamery
4207-16th Street SE
Calgary, AB T2G 3S2
Canada 403-263-7725
Fax: 403-237-5051 800-661-4909
www.foothillscreamery.com
President: Don Bayrack
Vice President: Barry Northfield
Sales Manager: Randy Wagner
Estimated Sales:$250,000 - $1,000,000
Number Employees: 200
Number of Brands: 3
Number of Products: 24
Type of Packaging: Consumer, Food Service, Pri-
vate Label, Bulk
Brands:
Jersey Supreme
Lone Pine Country
Rocky Mountain

5026 Foothills Creamery
4207 16th Street SE
Calgary, AB T2G 352
Canada 403-263-7725
Fax: 403-237-5051
foothills.cream@cadvision.com
www.foothillscreamery.com
Manufacturer of ice cream, butter and ice cream
cones
President: Don Bayrack
Type of Packaging: Consumer
Brands:
Foothills
Unique Cones

5027 Foppiano Vineyard
12707 Old Redwood Hwy
Healdsburg, CA 95448-9241 707-433-7272
Fax: 707-433-0565 louis@foppiano.com
www.foppiano.com
Manufacturer and exporter of wines
President: Louis Foppiano
Winemaker: Bill Regan
Estimated Sales:$ 10 - 20 Million
Number Employees: 20-49
Type of Packaging: Consumer
Brands:
FOPPIANO
FOX MOUNTAIN
RIVERSIDE

5028 Forakers Joy Orchard
3696 Hamlin Road
Malaga, WA 98828-9759 509-663-6097
FRUITS

5029 Foran Spice Company
P.O.Box 109
Oak Creek, WI 53154-0109 414-764-1220
Fax: 414-764-8803 800-558-6030
foran@foranspice.com www.foranspice.com

Manufacturer of re-cleaned and sterilized spices,
custom engineered seasonings, and value-added
food products
President: Patty Goto
Research & Development: Greg Gamble
Public Relations: Joy Kuhns
Operations Manager: Joe Basilo
Engineer: Alan Goto
Purchasing Director: Joanne Allbaugh
Estimated Sales:$50-100 Million
Number Employees: 100-249
Sq. footage: 71000
Type of Packaging: Food Service, Private Label,
Bulk

5030 Forbes Candies
2692 Dean Drive
Virginia Beach, VA 23452-7405 757-486-5515
Fax: 757-486-0646 800-626-5898
www.forbescandies.com
Manufacturer of confectionery products including
salt water taffy, fudge, assorted brittle, and peanuts.
President: William Lawton
Sales Manager: Lynn Watson
Estimated Sales:$5-10 Million
Number Employees: 20-49
Type of Packaging: Consumer

5031 Forbes Chocolate
15620 Industrial Parkway
Cleveland, OH 44135-3316 216-433-1090
Fax: 216-433-1093 800-433-1090
sales@forbeschocolate.com
Chocolate
President: Keith Geringer
Estimated Sales:$ 5 - 10 Million
Number Employees: 10-19

5032 Forbes Chocolates
15620 Industrial Parkway
Cleveland, OH 44135-3316 216-433-1090
Fax: 216-433-1093 800-433-1090
rstunek@forbeschocolate.com
www.forbeschocolate.com
Manufacturer and exporter of chocolate-flavored
powders for milk and ice cream
President: Darwin Geringer
VP: Keith Geringer
Director Marketing: Rick Stunek
Estimated Sales:$5-10 Million
Number Employees: 10-19
Sq. footage: 17000
Type of Packaging: Bulk

5033 Ford Gum & Machine Company
18 Newton Ave
Akron, NY 14001-1099 716-542-4561
Fax: 847-542-4610 800-225-5535
www.fordgum.com
Manufacturer and exporter of value added gums and
sour balls; also, vending machines
President: George Stege
VP Marketing: Stephen Gold
VP Sales: Steven Gold
Production Manager: Jim Monteleone
Estimated Sales:$20-50 Million
Number Employees: 100-249
Parent Co: Ford Gum
Type of Packaging: Consumer, Food Service, Pri-
vate Label, Bulk
Brands:
CAROUSEL
CHUNK A CHEW
YOWSER!!

5034 Ford's Fancy Fruit
1109 Agriculture St
Raleigh, NC 27603-2373 919-833-9621
Fax: 919-821-5781 800-446-0947
sales@bonesuckin.com www.bonesuckin.com
Manufacturer of Sauces, mustards, salsa and nuts
President: Sandi Ford
VP: Patrick Ford
Estimated Sales:$5-10 Million
Number Employees: 50-99
Type of Packaging: Private Label
Brands:
Big Chunks Salsa
Blessing's Mustard
Bone Suckin' Sauce
Ford's Foods
Hiccuppin' Hot Sauce
J. Berrie Brown Wine Nuts
We're Talking Serious Salsa

5035 Fords Gourmet Foods
1109 Agriculture Street
Raleigh, NC 27603   919-833-7447
Fax: 919-821-5781   800-446-0947
patford@bonesuckin.com   www.bonesuckin.com
sauces, marinades, mustards, and nuts

5036 Foreign Candy Company
1 Foreign Candy Dr
Hull, IA 51239-7499   712-439-1496
Fax: 712-439-1434   800-831-8541
jc.reichter@foreigncandy.com
www.foreigncandy.com
Distributors of confectionery
CEO: Peter DeYager
CEO: Peter Deyager
VP Marketing: Art Zito
VP Sales: Jim Finelli
Estimated Sales: $5-10 Million
Number Employees: 50-99
Type of Packaging: Private Label
Brands:
MEGA WARHEADS
RIPS TOLL

5037 Foremost Dairies-Hawaii
2277 Kamehameha Highway
Honolulu, HI 96819   808-841-5831
Fax: 808-841-4834
Processor of dairy products including milk, and
cream
President: Takeshi Arao
VP: Jon Nishimura
Marketing Director: Kimberly Gerhardt
Sales Director: Ed Kini
Plant Manager: Terry Inouye
Purchasing Manager: Roy Sekigawa
Estimated Sales: $20-50 Million
Number Employees: 100-249
Sq. footage: 180000

5038 Foremost Farms
830 Allamakee St
Waukon, IA 52172-1048   563-568-3474
www.foremostfarms.com
Manufacturer and exporter of powdered buttermilk
and whey solids
President: Dave Fuhrmann
VP Finance: Duaine Kamenick
VP Fluid Products Division: Joe Weis
Plant Manager: Jon Ebner
Estimated Sales: $5-10 Million
Number Employees: 20-49
Parent Co: Foremost Farms USA
Type of Packaging: Food Service, Private Label,
Bulk
Brands:
Golden Guernsey Dairy Products
Morning Glory Products

5039 Foremost Farms
3101 Fish Hatchery Rd
Fitchburg, WI 53713-3126   608-271-3000
Fax: 608-271-1072   www.foremostfarms.com
Manufacturer and co-packer of chilled juices and
juice beverages; importer of fruit juice concentrates
Manager: Robert Voss
Quality Assurance Manager: Jerry LaBelle
General Manager: Bob Voss
Plant Manager: Robert Voss
Purchasing Manager: Donald Storhoff
Estimated Sales: $20-50 Million
Number Employees: 100-249
Sq. footage: 60000
Parent Co: Foremost Farms USA
Type of Packaging: Consumer, Food Service, Private Label

5040 Foremost Farms
2101 Delafield St
Waukesha, WI 53188-2299   262-547-1700
Fax: 262-312-5026   800-289-7787
katie.salverson@foremostfarms.com
www.foremostfarms.com
Dairy cooperative manufacturer of bottled milk and
cultured buttermilk
President/Purchasing: Donald Storhoff
Human Resources: Jeff Hayes
Sales/Marketing: Bob Rusch
Plant Manager: Eric Van Der Huevel
Estimated Sales: $100-500 Million
Number Employees: 100-249
Parent Co: Foremost Farms USA

5041 (HQ)Foremost Farms
E 10889 Penny Lane
Baraboo, WI 53913-8115   608-355-8700
Fax: 608-356-5458   800-365-9196
linda.strachan@foremostfarms.com
www.foremostfarms.com
Manufacturer of cheese, butter and a host of
value-added whey ingredients. Also supply bulk
fluid milk to handlers.
President: David Fuhrmann
VP Finance/CFO: Michael Doyle
VP Marketing: Douglas Wilke
VP HR/Safety/Communications: Michael
McDonald
VP Manufacturing: Michael Pronschinske
Plant Manager: Terry Sutton
Estimated Sales: $1.6 Billion
Number Employees: 1,370
Type of Packaging: Bulk
Other Locations:
Foremost Farms USA Coop.
Plover WI
Brands:
Foremost Farms
Natural Choice

5042 Foremost Farms
P.O.Box 399
Preston, MN 55965-0399   507-765-3831
Fax: 507-765-4430   www.foremostfarms.com
Manufacturer of dried dairy products
Plant Manager: Bruce Snitker
Estimated Sales: $20-50 Million
Number Employees: 20-49
Parent Co: Foremost Farms USA
Type of Packaging: Bulk

5043 Foremost Farms
W12215 County Road Ff
Alma Center, WI 54611-8409   715-964-7411
Fax: 715-964-1122   www.foremostfarms.com
Manufacturer of mozzarella cheese
Manager: Gordon Kleba
Estimated Sales: $20-50 Million
Number Employees: 50-99
Parent Co: Foremost Farms USA
Type of Packaging: Bulk

5044 Foremost Farms
PO Box 1317
Appleton, WI 54912-1317   920-738-1555
Fax: 920-738-1549   www.foremostfarms.com
Manufacturer of dried whey
Sales: Patrick Mathiowetz
Plant Manager: Ed Fallon
Estimated Sales: $20-50 Million
Number Employees: 50-99
Parent Co: Foremost Farms USA
Type of Packaging: Bulk

5045 Foremost Farms
684 S Church St
Richland Center, WI 53581-2737   608-647-2186
Fax: 608-647-2955   www.foremostfarms.com
Manufacture of mozzarella cheese
Plant Manager: Dan Williams
Estimated Sales: $50-100 Million
Number Employees: 100-249
Parent Co: Foremost Farms USA
Type of Packaging: Bulk

5046 Foremost Farms
100 Main St N
Clayton, WI 54004-9121   715-948-2166
Fax: 715-355-6726   www.foremostfarms.com
Manufacturer of mozzarella cheese
Manager: Andrew Vanheuklom
Estimated Sales: $20-50 Million
Number Employees: 50-99
Parent Co: Foremost Farms USA
Type of Packaging: Bulk

5047 Foremost Farms
487 State Road 128
Wilson, WI 54027-2449   715-772-4211
Fax: 715-772-3210   www.foremostfarms.com
Manufacturer of mozzarella sticks, whey protein
concentrate
Plant Manager: Kelton Greenway
Estimated Sales: $20-50 Million
Number Employees: 20-49
Parent Co: Foremost Farms USA

Type of Packaging: Consumer, Food Service, Private Label

5048 Foremost Farms
2541 Foremost Rd
Plover, WI 54467-3401   715-341-0101
Fax: 715-341-5332   www.foremostfarms.com
Manufacturer of whey edible lactose, reduced minerals whey protein concentrate
QC/Waste Plant Supervisor: David Voelker
Plant Manager: Scott Oberfelt
Estimated Sales: $20-50 Million
Number Employees: 50-99
Parent Co: Foremost Farms USA
Type of Packaging: Bulk

5049 Foremost Farms USA
932 N Madison St
Lancaster, WI 53813-1139   608-723-7681
Fax: 608-723-6811   www.foremostfarms.com
Manufacturer of cheddar cheese
Plant Manager: Tom Matthews
Estimated Sales: $20-50 Million
Number Employees: 50-99
Parent Co: Foremost Farms USA
Type of Packaging: Bulk

5050 Foremost Farms USA
427 E Wisconsin St
Sparta, WI 54656-2456   608-269-3126
Fax: 608-269-5094   www.foremostfarms.com
Manufacturer of whole milk powder, nonfat dry
milk, buttermilk
Production Associate: Mike Gastrau
Plant Manager: Alan Schroeder
Estimated Sales: $20-50 Million
Number Employees: 20-49
Parent Co: Foremost Farms USA
Type of Packaging: Bulk

5051 Foremost Farms USA
684 S Church St
Richland Center, WI 53581-2737   608-647-2186
Fax: 608-647-2955   www.foremostfarms.com
Cheese and dairy products
President: Alan Buchholz
Plant Manager: Dan Williams
Estimated Sales: $25-49.9 Million
Number Employees: 100-249

5052 Forest Packing Company
P.O.Box D
Forest, MS 39074-0558   601-469-3321
Fax: 601-469-4251
Poultry
President: William Haralson
Estimated Sales: $25-49.9 Million
Number Employees: 100-249

5053 Forge Mountain Foods
1215 Greenville Hwy
Hendersonville, NC 28792-6207   828-692-9470
Fax: 828-692-6135   800-823-6743
pbrim@forgemountain.com
www.forgemountain.com
Specialty foods company with over 250 varieties of
old timey food products; jams and jellies, pickles
and relishes and more
President: Brian Pawling
VP Sales/Marketing: Paul Brim
Estimated Sales: $500,000-$1 Million
Number Employees: 5-9
Number of Products: 250+
Brands:
FORGE MOUNTAIN

5054 Foris Vineyards
654 Kendall Rd
Cave Junction, OR 97523-9721   541-592-3752
Fax: 541-592-4424   foris@foriswine.com
www.foriswine.com
Wines
President: Ted Gerber
Estimated Sales: $2.5-5 Million
Number Employees: 10-19
Number of Brands: 10
Type of Packaging: Private Label

5055 Forkless Gourmet Inc
10 S Riverside Plz
Chicago, IL 60606-3728   312-474-5746
Fax: 312-474-6127   www.forklessgourmet.com/

Manufacturers forkless bun meals available in several varieties including: chicken sesame teriyaki; thai style chicken; beef & broccoli; pork & vegetables with Five Fortune BBQ Sauce; kung pao shrimp (spicy); vegetarian feast withtofu & edamame; chipotle chicken (spicy); margarita chicken; beef asada; pork & vegetable with Ancho Honey BBQ Sauce, and black bean adobo.
  Bun Meal Pioneer: Gregory Stahl
  Bun Meal Pioneer: Christopher Scott
  Bun Meal Pioneer: Katie Torres
  Bun Meal Pioneer: Steven Spiegel
  Bun Meal Pioneer: Susan Schneider
Type of Packaging: Food Service

5056 Forman Vineyards
P.O.Box 343
St Helena, CA 94574-0343   707-963-3900
    Fax: 707-963-5384 www.formanvineyard.com
Wines
  President: Rick Forman
Estimated Sales: Under $500,000
Number Employees: 5-9

5057 Formax/Provisur Technologies
9150 W 191st Street
Mokena, IL 60448   708-479-3500
    Fax: 708-479-3598 info@provisur.com
        www.provisur.com
Food processing equipment: forming machines, multi-loaf slicers and automatic transport equipment
Number Employees: 250-499

5058 Formost Friedman Company
152 Frankel Boulevard
Merrick, NY 11566-4033   516-378-4919
        Fax: 516-379-8301
General grocery
  President: William MacMelville
Estimated Sales: $1-2.5 Million
Number Employees: 1-4

5059 Fort Boise Produce Company
PO Box 1545
Nyssa, OR 97913-0045   541-372-3837
        Fax: 541-372-3326
Packed onions
  President: Thomas Stephens
Estimated Sales: $1-2.5 Million
Number Employees: 50-99

5060 Fort Garry Brewing Company
130 Lowson Crescent
Winnipeg, NB R3P 2H6
Canada   204-487-3678
    Fax: 204-487-0839 info@fortgarry.com
        www.fortgarry.com
Manufacturer of beer
  President/CEO: Doug Saville
  CFO: Denis Chabbert
  Marketing: Wayne Vanlandeghem
  Sales: Orest Horechko
Number Employees: 23
Number of Brands: 13
Number of Products: 1
Sq. footage: 25000
Type of Packaging: Private Label, Bulk

5061 Forte Stromboli Company
3129 S 13th Street
Philadelphia, PA 19148-5234   215-463-6336
        Fax: 215-463-8616
Manufacturer of frozen stromboli
  President: Ronald Conti
Estimated Sales: $ 5 - 10 Million
Number Employees: 5-9
Type of Packaging: Consumer, Food Service

5062 Fortella Fortune Cookies
214 W 26th St
Chicago, IL 60616-2204   312-567-9000
        Fax: 312-567-9119
Manufacturer of fortune, almond and specialty cookies
  Owner: Herman Wong
  Company Manager: Brenda Wong
Estimated Sales: $1-2.5 Million
Number Employees: 10-19
Type of Packaging: Consumer, Food Service

5063 Fortenberry Ice Company
3128 Fortenberry Rd
Kodak, TN 37764-2020   865-933-2568
        Fax: 865-933-2568

Manufacturer of ice
  Owner: Jeff Fortenberry
Estimated Sales: $1-2.5 Million
Number Employees: 5-9
Type of Packaging: Consumer
Other Locations:
  Fortenberry Ice Company
  Kodak TN

5064 Fortino Winery
4525 Hecker Pass Rd
Gilroy, CA 95020-8807   408-842-3305
    Fax: 408-842-8636 888-617-6606
        gino@fortinowinery.com
        www.fortinowinery.com
Wines
  Owner: Gino Fortino
Estimated Sales: $5-10 Million
Number Employees: 5-9

5065 (HQ)Fortitech
2105 Technology Dr
Schenectady, NY 12308-1151   518-372-5155
    Fax: 518-372-5599 800-950-5156
    info@fortitech.com www.fortitech.com
Manufacturer and exporter of vitamin and mineral pre mixes
  President: Walt Borisenok
  CFO: Brian Wilcox
  Research & Development: Ram Chaudhari Ph.D
  Marketing (Global): Rich Schleif
  VP Sales: Sam Sylvestky
  Production Manager: Ed Webster
  Purchasing Manager: Tom Morba
Estimated Sales: $100 Million
Number Employees: 250-499
Sq. footage: 100000
Type of Packaging: Food Service
Other Locations:
  Fortitech
  Europe
  Fortitech
  South America
  Fortitech
  Mexico

5066 Fortitude Brands LLC
6925 Almansa Street
Coral Gables, FL 33146-3809   305-439-9763
    Fax: 305-662-4977 fstanzl@aol.com
        www.fortitudebrands.com
Manufacturer and importer of exotic and natural tropical food products
  CEO: Franco Stanzione
  CFO: Juan Serna
  Marketing: Robert Hunt
  Sales: Bob Ottmar
  Public Relations: Renee Morales
Estimated Sales: $400,000
Number Employees: 21
Number of Brands: 5
Number of Products: 14
Type of Packaging: Consumer
Brands:
  CASABE RAINFOREST CRACKERS
  ISABO HEARTS OF PALM
  SAMAI

5067 Fortress Systems LLC
2132 S 156th Cir
Omaha, NE 68130-2503   402-333-3532
    Fax: 402-333-3536 888-331-6601
        www.8-ballnutrition.com
Manufacturer of dietary supplements
  CEO: Mike Carnazzo
  VP R&D: Joseph Carnazzo BS, RPh
  Consultant: Dr Martha Garcia, PharmD
  Consultant: Dr Brian Sakurada, PharmD
Number Employees: 1-4
Parent Co: FSI Nutrition

5068 Fortuna Cellars
2124 Fortuna Court
Davis, CA 95616-0603   530-756-6686
Wines
  President: Gerald Bowes

5069 Fortunate Cookie
PO Box 1386
Stowe, VT 05672-1386   802-888-5706
    Fax: 802-888-5563 866-266-5337
        portico@stowevt.net
        www.thefortunatecookie.com

Specialty cookies/gift baskets made from scratch and to order signature offering: fortune cookies in 4 sizes and 19 flavors
  President: Portia Arthur
  CEO: Portia Arthur
Type of Packaging: Consumer

5070 Fortune Brands
300 Tower Pkwy
Lincolnshire, IL 60069-3665   847-541-9500
    Fax: 847-541-5750 www.accobrands.com
Manufacturer of liquor
  Chairman/CEO: Norman Wesley
  CEO: Robert J Keller
Estimated Sales: $160 Million
Number Employees: 5,000-9,999
Parent Co: Jim Beam Brands Worldwide
Type of Packaging: Consumer, Food Service, Private Label
Other Locations:
  Fortune Brands
  Fairhaven MA
Brands:
  ABSOLUT VODKA
  AFTER SHOCK
  ALBERTA SPRINGS
  BAKER'S
  BANFF ICE
  BOOKER'S
  CALVERT
  CANYON ROAD
  CHINACO TEQUILA
  COURVOISIER
  DALMORE
  DALMORE SCOTCH
  DE PON FELIPE
  DEKUYPER
  DISTILLERS MASTERPIECE
  EL TESCERO
  GEYSER PEAK
  GILBEY'S
  JIM BEAM
  KAMCHATKA
  KESSLER
  KNOB CREEK
  LEROUX
  LORD CALVERT
  OLD CROW
  OLD GRAND DAD
  OLD OVERHOLT
  RONRICO
  SOURZ
  TAGLE RIDGE
  VOX
  WILD HORSE
  WINDSOR
  WOLFSCHMIDT

5071 Fortune Cookie Factory
261 12th St
Oakland, CA 94607-4440   510-832-5552
        Fax: 510-832-2565
Fortune cookies
  President: Andrew Wong
Estimated Sales: $2.5-5 Million
Number Employees: 5-9

5072 Fortune Seas
42 Rogers Street
Gloucester, MA 01930-5000   978-281-6666
    Fax: 978-281-8519 fseas@aol.com
Seafood
  President/CEO: Donald Short
  VP Sales: Charles Bencal
Brands:
  FORTUNE'S CATCH
  OCEAN DELI

5073 Fortunes International Teas
11 Tunnel Way
Mc Kees Rocks, PA 15136-2525   412-771-8327
    Fax: 412-771-2122 800-551-8327
    teaman3000@cs.com www.fortunescoffee.com
Black, green and herbal teas
  Owner: Richard Cefola Sr
  VP Marketing: Michael Brunk
Estimated Sales: $500,000-$1 Million
Number Employees: 1-4
Type of Packaging: Private Label
Brands:
  Commonwealth
  Fortunes
  London Herb & Spice
  Ridgways

5074 Forty Second Street Bagel Cafe
1726 W 9th St
Upland, CA 91786-5603   909-949-7334
                              Fax: 909-949-0721
Manufacturer of Bagels and rolls
    Owner: Robert Hall
Estimated Sales: $ 3 - 5 Million
Number Employees: 5-9

5075 Fosselman's Ice Cream Company
1824 W Main St
Alhambra, CA 91801-1897   626-282-6533
    Fax: 626-282-0246   info@fosselmans.com
                              www.fosselmans.com
Ice cream, sherbet
    President: F Fosselman
    VP: Christian Fossleman
Estimated Sales: $2.5-5 Million
Number Employees: 10-19
Type of Packaging: Consumer, Bulk

5076 Fossil Farms
294 W Oakland Ave
Oakland, NJ 07436   201-651-1190
    Fax: 201-651-1191   sales@fossilfarms.com
                              www.fossilfarms.com
farm raised game and all natural meats
    CEO/Co-Owner: Lance Appelbaum
    Sales Manager: Sturgess Spanos
    COO/Co-Owner: Todd Appelbaum
    Warehouse Manager: Jose Rivera
Estimated Sales: $1.1 Million
Number Employees: 7

5077 Foster Family Farm
90 Foster
South Windsor, CT 06074   860-648-9366
                              www.fosterfarms.com
Manufacturer and exporter of pickled asparagus and
beans
    President: Chris Foster
    Co-Owner: Teresa Robertson
Estimated Sales: $10-20 Million
Number Employees: 50-99

5078 Foster Farms
P.O.Box 70
Demopolis, AL 36732-0070   334-289-5082
    Fax: 334-289-1774 www.fosterfarms.com
Packing
Estimated Sales: $ 3 - 5 Million
Number Employees: 5-9

5079 (HQ)Foster Farms
1000 Davis Street
Livingston, CA 95334   209-537-1121
    Fax: 209-394-6342   800-255-7227
    comments@fosterfarms.com
    www.fosterfarms.com
Manufacturer and exporter of chicken and turkey
products including frankfurters and corn dogs
    CEO: Ron Foster
    SVP/CFO: John Landis
    Plant Manager: Mark Silvas
Estimated Sales: $2 Billion
Number Employees: 10,000
Sq. footage: 25000
Type of Packaging: Consumer, Food Service, Private Label, Bulk
Other Locations:
    Foster Farms
    Porterville CA
Brands:
    FIRCREST FARMS
    FOSTER FARMS
    FOSTER FARMS DAIRY PRODUCTS
    FOSTER FARMS DELI MEAT
    FOSTER FARMS POULTRY
    VALCHRIS FARMS

5080 Foster Farms
P.O.Box 70
Demopolis, AL 36732-0070   334-289-5082
    Fax: 334-289-1774   800-255-7227
                              www.fosterfarms.com
Manufacturer of meat products including sausage;
wholesaler/distributor of corn dogs
    President/CEO: Ron Foster
Estimated Sales: $500,000-$1 Million
Number Employees: 5-9
Type of Packaging: Consumer

5081 Foster Farms
P.O.Box 8
Creswell, OR 97426-0008   541-895-2161
    Fax: 541-895-2166 www.fosterfarms.com
Manufacturer of fresh and frozen chicken and turkey
    President: Mike Avalos
Estimated Sales: $25-49.9 Million
Number Employees: 100-249
Parent Co: Foster Farms
Type of Packaging: Consumer, Food Service
Brands:
    FOSTER FARM

5082 Foster Farms
855 NW 8th Street
Corvallis, OR 97330-6210   541-754-6211
    Fax: 541-757-0276 www.fosterfarms.com
Manufacturer and exporter of chicken products including frankfurters
Estimated Sales: $50-100 Million
Number Employees: 50-99
Parent Co: Foster Farms
Type of Packaging: Consumer, Food Service, Private Label, Bulk

5083 Foster Farms Dairy
415 Kansas Ave
Modesto, CA 95351-1515   209-576-3470
    Fax: 209-576-2397
    mzanos@fosterdairyfarms.com
    www.fosterfarms.com
Manufacturer and exporter of cottage cheese, yogurt,
sour and heavy cream, milk, butter, ice cream, milk
powder and juice
    President/CEO: Ron Foster
    Plant Manager: Larry Diggory
Estimated Sales: $10-20 Million
Number Employees: 250-499
Parent Co: Foster Farms
Type of Packaging: Consumer, Food Service, Bulk

5084 Foster Farms Dairy
3380 W Ashlan Ave
Fresno, CA 93722-4448   559-244-2200
    Fax: 559-244-2003   800-241-0008
    www.fosterfarmsdairy.com
Manufacturer of milk
    Owner/President: Ron Foster
    Sales Manager: Dennis Roberts
    Plant Manager: Dennis Bettencourt
Estimated Sales: $50-100 Million
Number Employees: 1-4
Type of Packaging: Consumer, Food Service, Private Label, Bulk
Brands:
    KNUDSEN

5085 (HQ)Foulds
520 E Church St
Libertyville, IL 60048-2300   847-362-3062
    Fax: 847-362-6658 www.fouldspasta.com
Macaroni, spaghetti and egg noodles
    Owner: Chris Bradley
    VP: Joseph Bradley
    Marketing: Gary Heinke
    Sales: Lowell Wilkins
    Plant Manager: Thomas Smith
    Purchasing: James Bauspies
Estimated Sales: $20-50 Million
Number Employees: 20-49
Brands:
    KABOODLES
    NO YOLKS EGG NOODLES
    WACKY MAC

5086 Fountain Products
220 Persimmon Dr
St Charles, IL 60174-5604   630-443-1113
                              Fax: 630-443-1344
Manufacturer of equipment
    President: Paul Lamb
    Inside Sales: Sue Bellecomo
    Sales Representative: PJ Lamb
Estimated Sales: $ 1 - 3 Million
Number Employees: 1-4
Brands:
    Dynamic
    Leer
    SSP

5087 Fountain Shakes/MS Foods
PO Box 26263
Minneapolis, MN 55426-0263   952-988-6940
    Fax: 952-988-6941   877-988-6940
    astone2454@aol.com   www.fountainshake.com
Fountain shake in six flavors: chocolate malt, cappuccino, strawberry, vanilla, banana and chocolate
    President: Alan B Stone
    Marketing: Lou Ann Stone
    Public Relations: Melanie Stone
Parent Co: MS Foods
Type of Packaging: Consumer, Food Service
Brands:
    FOUNTAIN SHAKE

5088 (HQ)Fountain Valley Foods
1420 Aviation Way
Colorado Springs, CO 80916-2712   719-573-6012
    Fax: 303-695-0284
    mark@fountainvalleyfoods.com
    www.fountainvalleyfoods.com
Manufacturer of salsa and packaged dips including,
bean; Jalapenos, serranos and specialty sauces.
Wholesaler/distributor of cheese sauces; importer of
jalapeno peppers; exporter of cheese sauces and
jalapeno peppers
    President: James Loyacono
Estimated Sales: $10-20 Million
Number Employees: 1-4
Sq. footage: 10000
Type of Packaging: Consumer, Food Service, Private Label, Bulk
Other Locations:
    Den-Mar Products
    Trinidad CO
Brands:
    Galante
    Long Tree Farms
    Nacho Grande
    Queso Del Sol

5089 Fountainhead Water Company
3280 Green Pointe Parkway
Suite 300
Norcross, GA 30092-6656   864-944-1993
    Fax: 864-944-0001 www.fountainheadwater.com
Bottled water
    President: Kevin McClanahan
    VP: Mark Rehl
    Production: Gene Wells
Estimated Sales: $10-15 Million
Number Employees: 50-99
Number of Brands: 1
Brands:
    FOUNTAINHEAD BOTTLED WATER

5090 Four C Foods Corporation
580 Fountain Ave
Brooklyn, NY 11208-6002   718-272-4242
    Fax: 718-272-2899 www.4c.com
Bread crumbs, grated cheese, iced tea mix, soup
mixes, coating mixes
    President: John Celauro
    CEO: Sally McCracken
    VP: Nathan Celuaro
    Operations: Wayne Celuaro
    Purchasing: Paul Korba
Estimated Sales: $20-50 Million
Number Employees: 100-249
Brands:
    4C INSTANT ICED TEA MIX

**5091 Four Chimneys Farm Winery
Trust**
211 Hall Rd
Himrod, NY 14842-9783   607-243-7502
    Fax: 607-243-8156
    info@fourchimneysorganicwine.com
    www.fourchimneysorganicwines.com
Manufacturer of organically grown grape juice,
wine, cooking wine and vinegar
    Owner: Scott Smith
    Sales Manager: W Daniel
Estimated Sales: Less than $500,000
Number Employees: 5-9
Type of Packaging: Consumer, Bulk

5092 Four Percent Company
16145 Hamilton Ave
Highland Park, MI 48203-2615   313-345-5880
    Fax: 313-345-8686   singerextract@msn.com
                              www.singerextract.com
Flavors
    President: Harold Samhat

Estimated Sales:$500,000-$1 Million
Number Employees: 1-4
Type of Packaging: Food Service, Private Label
Brands:
SEELY

5093 Four Sisters Winery
10 Doe Hollow Ln
Belvidere, NJ 07823-2661 908-475-3671
Fax: 908-475-3555 matty@goes.com
www.matarazzo.com
Wines
President: Robert Matarazzo
Production: Valerie Tishuk
Estimated Sales:$1-2.5 Million
Number Employees: 5-9
Type of Packaging: Private Label

5094 Four Star Meat Company of Louisiana
P.O. Box 429
Amite, LA 70422-0429 985-748-8134
Fax: 985-748-8137 800-444-5228
Manufacturer of ham and cooked roast beef; importer of beef
President: Anthony Graphia
Secretary: Mickey Graphia Jr
VP: Russel Autin
Plant Manager: Mickey Graphia Jr
Estimated Sales:$20-50 Million
Number Employees: 100-249
Sq. footage: 36000
Type of Packaging: Consumer, Food Service, Private Label
Brands:
BIG CAJUN
CHEF MASTER
FOUR STAR

5095 Fowler Cooperative Association
215 W Santa Fe Ave
Fowler, CO 81039-1166 719-263-4266
Cooperative of pinto bean growers
Executive Director: Julie Pharr
Estimated Sales:$1-3 Million
Number Employees: 5-9
Sq. footage: 30000
Parent Co: La Junta Company
Type of Packaging: Consumer, Food Service, Private Label, Bulk

5096 Fowler Packing Company
8570 S Cedar Ave
Fresno, CA 93725-8905 559-834-5911
Fax: 559-834-5272 www.fowlerpacking.com
Manufacturer of peaches, nectarines, plums, apricots, grapes and pomegranates
Owner: Dennis Parnagian
Estimated Sales:$ 20 - 50 Million
Number Employees: 50-99

5097 Fox Deluxe Foods
370 N Morgan St
Chicago, IL 60607-1321 312-421-3737
Fax: 312-421-8067
Owner: Sam Samano
Estimated Sales:$ 50 - 100 Million
Number Employees: 50-99

5098 Fox Hollow Farm
10 Old Lyme Rd
Hanover, NH 03755-4806 603-643-6002
Fax: 603-643-2540
Manufacturer sweet and spicy mustard sauce used as a glaze, marinade and a mustard on meat, fish, chicken and sandwiches
President: Phyllis Fox
Estimated Sales:$500,000-$1 Million
Number Employees: 1-4
Type of Packaging: Consumer
Brands:
FOX HOLLOW FARM MUSTARD
FOX-MORE THAN A MUSTARD

5099 Fox IV Technologies
6011 Enterprise Dr
Export, PA 15632-8969 724-387-3500
Fax: 724-387-3516 foxiv@foxiv.com
www.foxiv.com
President/CEO: Rick Fox
Estimated Sales:$ 10 - 20 Million
Number Employees: 20-49

5100 Fox Meadow Farm
1439 Clover Mill Road
Chester Springs, PA 19425-1108 610-827-9731
President: Harry Mandell, Jr.
Estimated Sales:$500,000 appx.
Number Employees: 1-4

5101 Fox Meadow Farm of Vermont
135 N Main St # 5
Rutland, VT 05701-3238 802-775-5460
Fax: 802-773-2242 888-754-4204
hoermann@mt-mainsfield.com
www.vtgrocers.org
Dry seasoning and herb blends, dry mixes
President: James Harrison
Estimated Sales:$300,000-500,000
Number Employees: 1-4

5102 Fox Run Vineyards
670 State Route 14
Penn Yan, NY 14527-9622 315-536-4616
Fax: 315-536-1383 800-636-9786
info@foxrunvineyards.com
www.foxrunvineyards.com
Wines
President: Scott Osborn
Estimated Sales:$5-10 Million
Number Employees: 10-19
Sq. footage: 6

5103 Fox Vineyards Winery
225 Highway 11 S
Social Circle, GA 30025-5003 770-787-5402
Fax: 770-787-5402
Wines
President: John Fuchs
Estimated Sales:$1-2.5 Million
Number Employees: 1-4

5104 Fox's Fine Foods
303 Broadway St
Laguna Beach, CA 92651-1816 949-497-8910
Fax: 949-497-1763 888-522-3697
foxsfine@aol.com www.foxfinefoods.com
Pestos, relishes, condiments, soups
President: Kim Fox
*Estimated Sales:*Under $500,000
Number Employees: 5-9
Type of Packaging: Private Label

5105 Foxen Vineyard
7200 Foxen Canyon Rd
Santa Maria, CA 93454-9581 805-937-4251
Fax: 805-937-0415 www.foxenvineyard.com
Wines
President: Richard Dore
Estimated Sales:$1-2.5 Million
Number Employees: 5-9

5106 Foxtail Foods
6880 Fairfield Business Ctr
Fairfield, OH 45014-5476 513-881-7900
Fax: 513-881-7910 800-323-6944
www.foxtailfoods.com
Manufacturer of pancake flour, syrups, cookies, cakes, muffins and pies
President: Jim Barrasco
National Accounts Manager - Retail: Rich Ferris
VP: Watt Daniel
VP Sales: Watt Daniel
Northeast Regional Manager: Nick Malta
Southcentral Regional Manager: Stuart Ginsberg
Northwest Regional Manager: Cameron Austin
Midcentral Regional Manager: Geoff Grosz
Southwest Regional Manager: Mark Miller
Southeast Regional Manager: Rusty Sigmon
Estimated Sales:$10-20 Million
Number Employees: 50-99
Sq. footage: 25000
Parent Co: Perkins
Type of Packaging: Consumer, Food Service, Private Label, Bulk
Other Locations:
Foxtail Foods - Corporate
Memphis
Foxtail Foods - Corporate
Tennese
Foxtail Foods - R&D
Cincinnati
Brands:
FOXTAIL

5107 Frair & Grimes
PO Box 3647
Kent, WA 98089-0210 206-935-0134
Fax: 206-935-7937 sales@frairandgrimes.com
www.frairandgrimes.com
Manufacturer of teas including darjeeling, black, green, oolong, fruit blends, flavored, etc
Owner: Timothy Frair
Number Employees: 1-4

5108 Fralinger's
1325 Boardwalk # 1
Atlantic City, NJ 08401-7287 609-345-2177
Fax: 609-344-0758 800-938-2339
sales@fralingers.com www.seashoretaffy.com
Taffy and candy
Manager: Barbara Brennan
VP: Arthur Gager
VP Marketing/Sales: Lisa Glaser
Operations: Susan Saraceni
Estimated Sales:$500,000-$1 Million
Number Employees: 5-9
Type of Packaging: Private Label

5109 Fran's Chocolates
1300 E Pike Street
Seattle, WA 98122 206-322-0233
Fax: 203-322-0452 800-422-3726
andriab@franschocolates.com
www.franschocolates.com
chocolates
President/Owner: Fran Bigelow
Estimated Sales:$5 Million
Number Employees: 30

5110 Fran's Gifts to Go
4733 Dwight Evans Road
Charlotte, NC 28217-0906 704-561-0070
Fax: 704-561-0078 800-476-6887
info@franspecans.com www.franspecans.com
Roasted and chocolate pecans, coated almonds, peanuts, pretzels, coffee beans, pastel chocolate fruits, gift baskets and baked products
Owner: Mike Mc Nabb
Type of Packaging: Private Label

5111 Fran's Healthy Helpings
840 Hinckley Road
Suite 128
Burlingame, CA 94010-1505 650-652-5772
Fax: 650-652-5773
Health foods
President: Fran Lent
VP Operations: Ada Chang
Estimated Sales:$1-2.5 Million
Number Employees: 5-9
Brands:
FRAN'S HEALTHY HELPINGS

5112 (HQ)France Croissant
227 W 40th St
New York, NY 10018-1513 212-888-1210
Fax: 212-719-5940
Manufacturer of frozen muffin doughs and baked goods including croissants, danishes, puff pastries and breads
Owner: Fanny Paderganana
Number Employees: 10-19
Type of Packaging: Private Label, Bulk

5113 France Delices
5065 Ontario E
Montreal, QC H1V 1V2
Canada 514-259-2291
Fax: 514-259-1788
Manufacturer and exporter of cakes including fresh, frozen and gourmet
VP: Laurent Durot
Estimated Sales:$5-10 Million
Number Employees: 100-249
Sq. footage: 50000
Type of Packaging: Consumer, Food Service

5114 Franciscan Oakville Estates
P.O.Box 407
Rutherford, CA 94573-0407 707-963-7111
Fax: 707-963-7867 800-529-9463
www.franciscan.com
Manufacturer of Wines, liquors, mixers
President: Jean-Michael Valette
Director Public Relations: Lisa Supple
Senior Winemaker: Larry Levin
Production: Bill Skowronski
Plant Manager: Lee Isola

Estimated Sales: $10-20 Million
Number Employees: 100-249
Parent Co: Constellation Brands

5115 Franciscan Vineyards
P.O.Box 407
Rutherford, CA 94573-0407   707-963-7111
      Fax: 707-963-7867   800-529-9463
      winemaker@franciscan.com
      www.franciscan.com
Manufacturer and exporter of fine wines
    President/CEO: Agustin Francisco Huneems
    CFO: Bill Skwronski
    Marketing: Kathryn De Maignet
    Sales: Jon Sweeney
    Public Relations: Gaven McGill
    Production: Jim De Bonis
    Plant Manager: Lee Isola
Estimated Sales: $ 50 - 100 Million
Number Employees: 100-249
Number of Brands: 7
Parent Co: Canandaigua Wine Company
Type of Packaging: Consumer
Brands:
    ESTANCIA
    FRANCISCAN OAKVILLE ESTATE
    MT VEEDER
    QUINTESSA
    SIMI RAVENSWOOD
    VERAMONTE

5116 Franco's Cocktail Mixes
121 SW 5th Ct
Pompano Beach, FL 33060-7909   954-782-7491
      Fax: 954-786-9253 800-782-4508
      Francocktl@aol.com
      www.francoscocktailmixes.com
Manufacturer and exporter of liquid and dry cocktail
mixes; also, colored margarita salt and colored rim-
ming sugars
    President: Brenda Franco
    Quality Controll: Guy Haret
    Public Relations: Laura Schnell
Estimated Sales: $10-24.9 Million
Number Employees: 10-19
Number of Brands: 12
Number of Products: 100+
Sq. footage: 25000
Type of Packaging: Food Service, Private Label
Brands:
    CROWN'S PRIDE
    FLORIDA STRAITS RUM RUNNER
    FLORIDA'S GOLD COCKTAIL
    FLORIDA's PRIDE
    FRANCO'S MARGARITA SALT SOMBRERO
    JOSE CUERVO MARGARITA SALT SOM-
    BRERO
    PAT O'BRIEN'S
    SAUZA MARGARITA SALT WITH JUICER
    TOUT FINI COCKTAIL MIXES

5117 Frank & Dean's CocktailMixes
1395 Coronet Avenue
Pasadena, CA 91107-1639   626-351-4272
      Fax: 909-596-4640
Bloody Mary, margarita, pina colada, mai tai, straw-
berry margarita, lime juice and grenadine
    President: Frank Abbadessa
    CFO: John Kennick
    VP: Dean Carbone
Number Employees: 1-4
Type of Packaging: Private Label
Brands:
    FRANK & DEAN'S COCKTAIL MIXES

5118 Frank Capurro & Son
P.O.Box 450
Moss Landing, CA 95039-0450   831-728-3904
      Fax: 831-728-0241   info@capurromkt.com
      www.capurromkt.com
Manufacturer, packer and exporter of produce in-
cluding parsley, radishes, endive, escarole, spinach,
collards, kale, brussels sprouts, Italian squash, beets,
bell peppers, etc
    Partner: Kris Capurro
    Partner: John Manfre
    Controller: Lavelle Brown
    Director Marketing: Rick Osterhues
    Sales Manager: Steve Timsak
    General Manager: Frank Capurro
    Production Manager: Gary Bertone
    Facilities Manager: Robert Bertone
Estimated Sales: $20-50 Million
Number Employees: 100-249

Type of Packaging: Consumer, Food Service, Bulk
Brands:
    TOPLESS

5119 Frank Family Vineyard
1091 Larkmead Ln
Calistoga, CA 94515-9675   707-942-0859
      Fax: 707-942-2581
      www.frankfamilyvineyards.com
Wines
    Owner: Richard Frank
    Director Marketing/Sales: Emily Kaufman
Estimated Sales: $ 10 - 20 Million
Number Employees: 20-49
Type of Packaging: Private Label

5120 Frank Korinek & Company
4828 W 25th St
Cicero, IL 60804-3432   773-242-1917
      Fax: 773-242-1917
Pastry fillings, fruit pie filling, donut mixes
    President: George Korinek
Estimated Sales: $1-2.5 Million
Number Employees: 5-9
Brands:
    BOHEMIAN MAID
    KORINEK

**5121 Frank Mattes & Sons Reliable
Seafood**
2327 Edwards Lane
Bel Air, MD 21015-5001   410-879-5444
      Fax: 410-734-6061
Seafood

5122 Frank Pagano Company
1527 S State Street
Lockport, IL 60441-3550   815-838-0303
      Fax: 815-723-9861
Manufacturer of quality meats
    President/CEO: Mary Pagano

5123 Frank Wardynski & Sons
336 Peckham St
Buffalo, NY 14206-1717   716-854-6083
      Fax: 716-854-4887   info@wardynski.com
      www.wardynski.com
Smoked polish sausage, italian sausage, natural cas-
ing wieners, tender casing weiners, skinless weiners,
knockwurst, bologna, cooked salami, liver sausage,
kiska, blood tongue, sweet or sour head cheese.
    Chairman/President: Raymond Wardynski
Estimated Sales: $ 5 - 10 Million
Number Employees: 20-49
Sq. footage: 35000

5124 Frank's Foods
1141 W Kawailani St
Hilo, HI 96720-3299   808-959-9121
      Fax: 808-959-1330   franksfd@interpac.net
Manufacturer and packer of meat products
    President: Michael Frenz
Estimated Sales: $5-10 Million
Number Employees: 5-9
Type of Packaging: Consumer

5125 Frank-Lin Distillers
650 Lenfest Rd
San Jose, CA 95133-1614   408-259-8900
      Fax: 408-258-9527   production@frank-lin.com
      www.frank-lin.com
Alcoholic beverages
    President: Frank Lin
    Sales/Marketing: Michael Maestri
Estimated Sales: $ 3 - 5 Million
Number Employees: 1-4
Type of Packaging: Bulk

**5126 Frankford Candy & Chocolate
Company**
9300 Ashton Rd
Philadelphia, PA 19114-3464   215-735-5200
      Fax: 215-735-0721   800-523-9090
      www.frankfordcandy.com
Processor of solid, hollow chocolate molded
novelties and nonchocolate candies for Christmas,
Easter, Halloween and Valentine's Day
    CEO: Stu Selarnik
    CEO: Stuart Selarnick
    VP Marketing: Kurt Dungan
Estimated Sales: $20-50 Million
Number Employees: 250-499
Sq. footage: 65000
Type of Packaging: Bulk

Brands:
    BARBIE
    BEATRIX POTTER
    BRACH
    FRANKFORD
    HOT WHEELS
    NICKELODEON
    PETER PAN
    PETER RABBIT
    POWER PUFF GIRLS
    ROCKET POWER
    RUGRATS
    SCOOBY DOO
    SIMPSONS
    SPONGE BOB SQUARE PANTS
    THE GRINCH WHO STOLE CHRISTMAS

5127 Frankfort Cheese
F1705 County Rd N
Edgar, WI 54426-9648   715-352-2345
      Fax: 715-352-2346
Cheese
    President: Dennis Telschow
Estimated Sales: Less than $500,000
Number Employees: 5-9

5128 Franklin Baking Company
P.O.Box 228
Goldsboro, NC 27533-0228   919-735-0344
      Fax: 919-705-2029   800-248-7494
Manufacturer of baked goods including breads,
bisuits and rolls
    President: Tom Buffkin
    Data Systems Manager: Kevin Bailey
Estimated Sales: $50-100 Million
Number Employees: 500-999
Sq. footage: 340000
Type of Packaging: Consumer
Brands:
    BLUEBIRD
    BUNNY
    COBBLESTONE MILL
    MARY JANE
    NATURE'S OWN
    ROMAN MEAL
    SUNBEAM

5129 Franklin Baking Company
2004 N Queen Street
Kinston, NC 28501-1621   252-527-1155
      Fax: 252-527-9871   800-248-7494
Bakery items
    President: Eugene Franklin
    Production: Randy Brock
Estimated Sales: $10-24.9 Million
Number Employees: 100-249

5130 (HQ)Franklin Farms
P.O.Box 18
North Franklin, CT 06254-0018   860-642-3019
      Fax: 860-642-3024 www.franklinfarms.com
Manufacturer of organic mushrooms
    CEO: Wilheim Meya
Estimated Sales: $100+ Million
Number Employees: 500-999

5131 Franklin Farms
P.O.Box 18
North Franklin, CT 06254-0018   860-642-3019
      Fax: 860-642-3024 www.franklinfarms.com
Manufacturer, importer and exporter of mushrooms
including white button, portobello, shiitake, crimini
oyster and maitake; also, vegetarian burgers; im-
porter of mushrooms
    President: Wilhelm Meya
Estimated Sales: $100-500 Million
Number Employees: 500-999
Type of Packaging: Consumer, Food Service, Pri-
vate Label, Bulk
Brands:
    FRANKLIN FARMS
    FRANKLIN FOODS

5132 Franklin Foods
P.O.Box 486
Enosburg Falls, VT 05450-0486   802-933-4338
      Fax: 802-933-2300   800-933-6114
      info@franklinfoods.com   www.franklinfoods.com
Manufacturer of baker's cheese, regular and flavored
cream cheese, salsa and cream cheese dips
    President/CEO: Jon Gutknecht
    Sales Director: Steve Barrows
    Plant Manager: John Ovitt

Estimated Sales:$25-49.9 Million
Number Employees: 100-249
Sq. footage: 43000
Type of Packaging: Consumer, Food Service, Private Label, Bulk
Brands:
ALL SEASON'S KITCHENS
BRUEGGERS
HAHN'S
LOMBARDI'S ITALIAN CLASSICS
VERMONT GOURMET

5133 Franklin Hill Vineyards
7833 Franklin Hill Rd
Bangor, PA 18013-4039   610-588-8708
Fax: 610-588-8158   888-887-2839
franklinhill@enter.net
www.franklinhillvineyards.com
Wines
Owner: Elaine Pivinski
Estimated Sales:$2.5-5 Million
Number Employees: 5-9
Type of Packaging: Private Label

5134 (HQ)Franklin Mushroom Farms
P.O.Box 18
North Franklin, CT 06254-0018   860-642-3019
Fax: 860-642-3024 www.franklinfarms.com
Mushrooms
President: Wilhelm Meya
Estimated Sales:$100-500 Million
Number Employees: 500-999

5135 Franklin Reister & Sons
1718 Gooding Street
Conklin, MI 49403-9793   616-887-9689
Fax: 616-887-8415
Manufacturer and packer of apples
President: Bob Reister
Estimated Sales:$500,000-$1 Million
Number Employees: 1-4
Parent Co: Reisters Grower Services
Type of Packaging: Consumer, Bulk

5136 Franklin Supply Company
337 W 4th Street
Rushville, IN 46173-1613   765-932-3928
Manufacturer of feed and sunflower seeds
Owner: Jeff Tebbe
Owner: Scott Tebbe
Estimated Sales:$3-5 Million
Number Employees: 5-9

5137 Frankly Natural Bakers
7740 Formula Pl
San Diego, CA 92121-2419   858-536-5910
Fax: 858-536-5911 800-727-7229
mail@franklynatural.com
www.franklynatural.com
Manufacturer of brownies, cookies, energy bars, etc
Owner: Jerry Sarnow
Estimated Sales:$3-5 Million
Number Employees: 10-19
Number of Brands: 3
Number of Products: 26
Sq. footage: 10000
Type of Packaging: Consumer, Private Label, Bulk
Brands:
98% FAT-FREE
AMAZINGLY TASTY
BEACH
COAST
FRANKLY NATURAL3
FRANKLY ORGANIC
RICE CRUNCHIES
VEGAN DECADENCE

5138 Franz Bakery
P.O.Box 14769
Portland, OR 97293-0769   503-232-2191
Fax: 503-234-7036
Bakery products
President/CEO: Bob Albers
Marketing: Jill Spitznass
Number Employees: 250-499

5139 Franzia Winery
P.O.Box 897
Ripon, CA 95366-0897   209-599-4111
Fax: 209-599-5892
Manufacturer of wines
Plant Manager: Lou Dambrosio
Estimated Sales:$10-20 Million
Number Employees: 250-499

Type of Packaging: Consumer, Food Service, Private Label

5140 Fratelli Perata
1595 Arbor Road
Paso Robles, CA 93446-9669   805-238-2809
Fax: 805-238-2809 www.fratelliperata.com
Wines
Owner: Gene Perata
*Estimated Sales:*Under $500,000
Number Employees: 1-4

5141 Fratello Coffee
4021 9th Street SE
Calgary, AB T2G 3C7
Canada   403-265-2112
Fax: 403-263-3255 800-465-7227
info@fratellocoffee.com www.fratellocoffee.com
Processor of gourmet coffee
President: Henry Kutarna
VP: Jason Prefontaine
Marketing Director: David Selley
Type of Packaging: Consumer, Food Service
Brands:
Fratello

5142 Frazier Nut Farms
10830 Yosemite Blvd
Waterford, CA 95386-9637   209-522-1406
Fax: 209-874-9638 fraznut@aol.com
Manufacturer and exporter of nuts including shelled and in-shell English walnuts and shelled almonds
President: Jim Frazier
VP: Steve Slacks
Estimated Sales:$2.5-5 Million
Number Employees: 100-249
Type of Packaging: Bulk
Brands:
FRAZIER'S FINEST

5143 Fred Busch Foods
Apt 3
904 Michigan Ave
Evanston, IL 60202-5421   773-545-2650
Fax: 773-545-2441 www.fredbuschfoods.com
Manufacturer of sausage
Estimated Sales:$5-10 Million
Number Employees: 20-49

5144 Fred Meyer Bakery
16253 SE 122nd Ave
Clackamas, OR 97015-9136   503-650-2000
Fax: 503-650-2128 www.fredmeyer.com
Bread and bakery products
Manager: Warren Ali
Estimated Sales:$10-24.9 Million
Number Employees: 100-249

5145 Fred Usinger
1030 N Old World 3rd St
Milwaukee, WI 53203-1300   414-276-9105
Fax: 414-291-5277 800-558-9998
allenw@usinger.com www.usinger.com
Sausages
President: Frederick Usinger IV
VP Marketing/Sales: John Gabe
Estimated Sales:$20-50 Million
Number Employees: 1-4
Brands:
SAUSAGE A LA CARTE

5146 (HQ)Freda Quality Meats
1007 W Oregon Ave
Philadelphia, PA 19148-4420   215-755-1899
Fax: 215-336-1353 800-443-7332
jimfreda@aol.com www.fredatech.com/home
Manufacturer and wholesaler/distributor of deli items including proscuitto, salami, pepperoni, sopprasata, panchetta, cappicola, frozen pork chops, butter, pickles, vinegar, relish, peppers, meat balls, steaks, mozzarella stickbuffalo wings, etc
President: James Giuffrida
Account Manager: Charles Sedlack
Plant Manager: Matthew Oorsaro
Estimated Sales:$300,000-500,000
Number Employees: 1-4
Parent Co: Freda

5147 Frederick Brewing Company
4607 Wedgewood Blvd
Frederick, MD 21703-7120   301-694-7899
Fax: 301-694-2971 888-258-7434
www.frederickbrewing.com

Manufacturer and exporter of beer, ale, stout, lager and porter
CEO: David Snyder
CEO: Eric Warner
VP Marketing: Julie Stolzer
VP Sales: Kirk Larimore
VP Operations: John Niziolek
*Estimated Sales:*1-2.5 Million
Number Employees: 20-49
Sq. footage: 57000
Type of Packaging: Private Label
Brands:
BLUE RIDGE
BRIMSTONE
HEMPEN
WILD GOOSE

5148 Frederick Wildman & Sons
307 E 53rd St
New York, NY 10022-4985   212-355-0700
Fax: 212-355-4719 800-733-9463
info@frederickwildman.com
www.frederickwildman.com
Manufacturer and importer of wines
President: Richard Cacciato
CFO: Rocco Lombardo
Senior VP: Vincenzo Marino
Marketing Director: Roger Bohmrich
Sales Director: Peter Ascher
Public Relations: Odila Gaier-Noel
VP/Director Operations: Joseph Losardo
Estimated Sales:$20-50 Million
Number Employees: 50-99
Brands:
KANONKOP
POL ROGER

5149 Fredericksburg Herb Farm
P.O.Box 927
Fredericksburg, TX 78624-0927   830-997-8615
Fax: 830-997-5069 800-259-4372
info@fredericksburgherbfarm.com
www.fredericksburgherbfarm.com
Gourmet herbs and vinegars
Owner: Bill Varney
Estimated Sales:$1-2.5 Million
Number Employees: 20-49

5150 Fredericksburg Lockers/OPA's Smoke
P.O.Box 487
Fredericksburg, TX 78624-0487   830-997-3358
Fax: 830-997-9916 800-543-6750
comments@opassmokedmeats.net
www.opassmokedmeats.net
Manufacturer of smoked and fresh sausage, ham, jerky and poultry products.
President: Helen Wahl
Controller: Ken Wahl
COO: Michael Schandua
Estimated Sales:$ 20 - 50 Million
Number Employees: 50-99
Type of Packaging: Consumer, Food Service
Brands:
OPA'S

5151 Freed, Teller & Freed
P.O.Box 553
Burlingame, CA 94011-0553   650-589-8500
Fax: 650-589-0711 800-370-7371
info@freedscoffeetea.com
www.freedscoffeetea.com
Manufacturer of tea, coffee, preserves, candy, oil, herbs and spices
President: Augi Tethiera
Operations: Karen Techeira
Estimated Sales:$2.5-5 Million
Number Employees: 5-9
Number of Brands: 10
Number of Products: 275
Type of Packaging: Consumer, Private Label, Bulk
Brands:
DEPENDABLE
FREED'S
FREED, TELLER & FREDD

5152 Freeda Vitamins
4725 34th St
Long Island City, NY 11101-2410   718-433-4337
Fax: 718-433-4373 800-777-3737
info@freedavitamins.com
www.freedavitamins.com

Manufacturer and exporter of kosher yeast-free vitamins and supplements including garlic
President/CEO: P Zimmerman
VP: S Zimmerman
R&D: Eliyahu Zimmerman
Production Manager: R Zimmerman
Estimated Sales: $2.5 Million
Number Employees: 10-19
Number of Brands: 1
Number of Products: 200
Sq. footage: 9150
Type of Packaging: Consumer
Brands:
  FREEDA

5153 Freedman's Bakery
803 Main St
Belmar, NJ 07719-2783   732-681-2334
                Fax: 732-681-1269
Bakery items
President: Herb Freedman
VP: Mark Freedman
Estimated Sales: $500,000-$1 Million
Number Employees: 100-249

5154 Freedom Gourmet Sauce
278 Cathy Jo Drive
Nashville, TN 37211-3840   615-333-9063
        freedomsauce@webtv.net
        www.freedomsauce.com
Gormet sauces

5155 Freeland Bean & Grain
1000 E Washington Rd
PO Box 515
Freeland, MI 48623-8439   989-695-9131
    Fax: 989-695-5241 800-447-9131
        freeland.i@att.net
    www.freelandbeanandgrain.com
Manufacturer and exporter of dried beans and grains
Owner/President: John Hupfer
VP: Elenor Hupfer
Estimated Sales: $3.8 Million
Number Employees: 5-9
Type of Packaging: Bulk

5156 Freeman Industries
P.O.Box 415
Tuckahoe, NY 10707-0415   914-961-2100
    Fax: 914-961-5793 800-666-6454
   freeman@lanline.com www.freemanllc.com
Manufacturer of dairy vitamin concentrates and zein. Importer and exporter of dried fruits and vegetables, pectin, herbal extracts and natural colors. Processor of citrus bioflavonoids and rice bran and rice bran derivates
President/CEO: Joel G Freeman
VP: Paul Freeman
Estimated Sales: $1-3 Million
Number Employees: 10-19
Sq. footage: 5000
Type of Packaging: Bulk
Brands:
  A/D/F
  D' SOL

5157 Freemark Abbey Winery
3022 St. Helena Highway North,P.O. Box
Helena, CA 94574   800-963-9698
    Fax: 707-963-0554 800-963-9698
        www.freemarkabbey.com
Manufacturer and exporter of wines including cabernet sauvignon, chardonnay and johannisberg riesling
Estimated Sales: $5-9.9 Million
Number Employees: 20-49
Type of Packaging: Food Service
Brands:
  FREEMARK ABBEY

5158 Freestone Pickle Company
P.O.Box 160
Bangor, MI 49013-0160   269-427-7702
    Fax: 269-427-5542 877-874-2553
  freestonepickles@freestonepickles.com
        www.freestonepickles.com
Manufacturer of pickles, relish and pickled peppers and cauliflower; also, individually packed pickles available
President/CEO: Michael Hescott
Estimated Sales: $10-20 Million
Number Employees: 20-49
Type of Packaging: Consumer, Food Service, Private Label, Bulk

Brands:
  FREESTONE
  HOLIDAY ROYAL
  PARTETIME

5159 Freeze-Dry Products
398 Tesconi Ct
Santa Rosa, CA 95401-4653   707-547-1776
    Fax: 707-545-5270 sales@fdpusa.com
        www.fdpusa.com
Industrial ingredients, dehydrated and freeze dried vegetables, freeze dried fruit, dairy and meat products
President: Alan Anger
VP: Mark Martindill
Estimated Sales: $20-50 Million
Number Employees: 20-49

5160 Freezer Queen Foods
975 Fuhrmann Blvd
Buffalo, NY 14203-3135   716-826-2500
    Fax: 716-824-4258 800-828-8383
        info@freezerqueen.com
        www.freezerqueenfoods.com
Manufacturer and contract packager of prepared frozen entrees; salisbury steak, chicken nuggets, veal, pot roast, stew, meat balls, sliced turkey, sliced beef, meat loaf, chicken and turkey croquettes, lasagna, rigatoni, vegetable andpasta dishes
Manager: Matt Kwasek
Director Finance: Michael Bradley
Research & Development Manager: Karen Centofani
Marketing Director: Jerry Brozowski
Transportation Services: Bob Lewandowski
Plant Manager: William Rouse
Purchasing Manager: Sharon Piehlei
Estimated Sales: $100-500 Million
Number Employees: 250-499
Sq. footage: 58000
Parent Co: Home Market Foods
Type of Packaging: Consumer, Food Service, Private Label, Bulk
Brands:
  FREEZER QUEEN

5161 Freezer Queen Foods
975 Fuhrmann Blvd
Buffalo, NY 14203-3135   716-826-2500
    Fax: 716-824-4258 800-828-8383
        info@freezerqueen.com
        www.freezerqueenfoods.com
Manufacturer of pulled and diced poultry, all white meat, natural proportion (white and dark), pulled dark/white and all dark; canned poultry; chunk white chicken, white and dark chicken and premium chunk white turkey
President: Matthew W Kwasek
Research & Development Manager: Karen Centofanti
Traffic Manager, Freight Services: Bob Lewandowski
Plant Manager: William Rouse
Purchasing Manager: Sharon Piehler
Estimated Sales: $20-50 Million
Number Employees: 250-499
Sq. footage: 58000
Type of Packaging: Consumer, Food Service, Private Label, Bulk
Brands:
  Valley Fresh

5162 (HQ)Freixenet
P.O.Box 1949
Sonoma, CA 95476-1949   707-996-4981
    Fax: 707-996-0720 info@freixenetusa.com
        www.freixenetusa.com
Manufacturer and importer of Spanish champagnes and wines; also, processor of California wines
President: Juan Furne
Executive VP: Eva Bertran
VP Marketing: David Brown
VP Sales: Peter Zilocchi
Estimated Sales: $75 Million
Number Employees: 50-99
Type of Packaging: Consumer
Brands:
  CASTELLBLANCH
  FREIXENET SPANISH WINES
  FREIXENET WINES
  GLORIA FERRER
  HENRI ABELE
  RENE BARBIER
  SEGURA VIUDAS

5163 Fremont Beef Company
P.O.Box 908
Fremont, NE 68026-0908   402-727-7200
             Fax: 402-727-0907
Meats
President: Les Leech
Estimated Sales: $25-49.9 Million
Number Employees: 100-249

5164 Fremont Company
802 N Front St
Fremont, OH 43420-1917   419-334-8995
    Fax: 419-334-8120 sales@sauerkraut.com
        www.fremontcompany.com
Manufacturer of tomatoes, sauerkraut, salsa and barbecue sauces
President: Don Slessman
CEO: Richard Smith
Quality Control: Diane Pfanner
Marketing Manager: Christopher Smith
Purchasing Manager: William Armstrong
Estimated Sales: $20-50 Million
Number Employees: 50-99
Type of Packaging: Consumer, Food Service, Private Label
Brands:
  FRANKS
  HIAWATHA
  MILFORD
  SNOW FLOSS
  WATOUGA

5165 Fremont Special Brands
802 N Front Street
Fremont, OH 43420   419-334-8995
    Fax: 419-334-8120 sales@sauerkraut.com
        www.fremontcompany.com
tomato based sauces, sauerkraut, ketchup and bbq

5166 French Baking
429 Soundview Avenue
Stratford, CT 06615-5664   203-378-7381
             Fax: 203-378-7253
Bakery products
Estimated Sales: $1-2.5 Million
Number Employees: 10-19

5167 French Creek Seafood
1097 Lee Road
Parksville, BC V9P 2E1
Canada   250-248-7100
    Fax: 250-248-7197 seafood@nanaimo.ark.com
Manufacturer and exporter of fresh and frozen seafood
President: Gordon McLean
Production Manager: Brad McLean
Number Employees: 20-49
Type of Packaging: Bulk

5168 French Gourmet
500 Kuwili St
Honolulu, HI 96817-5355   808-524-4000
    Fax: 808-528-0329 linda@frenchgourmet.com
        www.frenchgourmet.com
Manufacturer of frozen dough, croissants, danish, puff pastry, breads, and muffin, cookie batters
President: Patrick Novak
VP: Linda Coffman
Estimated Sales: $10-20 Million
Number Employees: 20-49
Number of Brands: 1
Number of Products: 57
Sq. footage: 50000
Type of Packaging: Food Service, Private Label, Bulk

5169 French Meadow Bakery
2610 Lyndale Ave S
Minneapolis, MN 55408-1321   612-870-7855
    Fax: 612-870-0907 877-669-3278
        bread@frenchmeadow.com
        www.frenchmeadow.com
Manufacturer of certified organic yeast-free and functioned bread
Owner: Steve Shapiro
VP: Steven Shapiro
Plant Manager: Michael Simon
Purchasing: Debra Gordon
Estimated Sales: $5-9.9 Million
Number Employees: 20-49
Number of Brands: 4
Number of Products: 32
Sq. footage: 24000

Type of Packaging: Consumer, Food Service, Private Label, Bulk
Other Locations:
French Meadow Bakery
Auburn WA
Brands:
HEALTHSEED
HEALTHY HEMP
MENS BREAD
WOMENS BREAD

5170 French Patisserie
1090 Palmetto Ave
Pacifica, CA 94044-2216   650-738-4990
Fax: 650-738-4995   800-300-2253
fpatis@frenchpatisserie.com
www.frenchpatisserie.com
Frozen cakes, tarts, and dessert sauces
President: Marta Spasic
Estimated Sales:$5-10 Million
Number Employees: 20-49

5171 French Quarter Seafood
2933 Paris Road
Chalmette, LA 70043-3346   504-277-1679
Fax: 504-277-1679
Seafood
Owner: Philippe Despointes

5172 French and Brawn
1 Elm St
Camden, ME 04843-1902   207-236-3361
Fax: 207-236-4880   mail@frenchandbrawn.com
www.frenchandbrawn.com
Manufacturer of choice meats, lobsters, soups and sandwiches
President: Todd Anderson
Estimated Sales:$ 5 - 10 Million
Number Employees: 20-49

5173 French's Coffee
1400 Central Rd
Walnut Creek, CA 94596-3794   925-978-6105
Coffee
Owner: Chet Parker
*Estimated Sales:*Under $500,000
Number Employees: 1-4

5174 French's Flavor Ingredients
4343 E Mustard Way
Springfield, MO 65803-7139   800-437-3624
Fax: 417-837-1801
elyse.stufft@reckittbenckiser.com
www.frenchsflavoringredients.com
Manufacturer of mustard and sauces including barbecue and hot sauce
Technical Sales: Rhonda McRae
Estimated Sales:$100+ Million
Number Employees: 250-499
Parent Co: Reckitt & Benckiser
Type of Packaging: Consumer, Food Service, Private Label, Bulk
Brands:
CATTLEMEN'S
FRANK'S
FRENCH'S
REDHOT

5175 French's Ingredients
4343 E Mustard Way
Springfield, MO 65803-7139   417-837-1813
Fax: 417-837-1801
elyse.stufft@reckittbenokiser.com
www.frenchsingredients.com
Manufacturer and exporter of mustard, mustard flours and sauces including barbecue, worcestershire and hot
Parent Co: Reckitt & Colman PLC
Type of Packaging: Bulk

5176 Fresca Mexican Foods
11193 W Emerald St
Boise, ID 83713-8932   208-376-6922
Fax: 208-375-2330   frescamexfoods@quest.net

Flour and corn tortillas and flavored wraps
President: Andy Savin
VP: Richard Kay
R&D: Richard Kay
Quality Control: Jim Anderson
Marketing: Chuck Shaw
Sales: Keith Snyder
Public Relations: Rick Kay
Operations: Jim Anderson
Production: Jim Anderson
Plant Manager: Jim Anderson
Purchasing: Jim Anderson
Estimated Sales:$15-31 Million
Number Employees: 100-249
Number of Brands: 1
Number of Products: 60
Type of Packaging: Food Service, Private Label

5177 Fresh Express
9501 Nevada Ave
Franklin Park, IL 60131-3331   847-288-2200
Fax: 847-288-2205   800-242-5472
www.freshexpress.com
Manfuacturer of ready made salads, carrots and coleslaw and salad kits.
Manager: Stuart Wilcox
CEO: Steve Taylor
VP Operations: Brian Hill
Estimated Sales:$72 Million
Number Employees: 500-999
Parent Co: Performance Food Group
Brands:
Fresh Express

5178 Fresh Express
P.O.Box 80599
Salinas, CA 93912-0599   831-775-2300
Fax: 831-751-7482 www.freshexpress.com
Manufacturer of fruits and vegetables. Chiquita Brands International has acquired the assets of Fresh Express
Chairman: Steve Taylor
President/CEO: Mark Drever
Plant Manager: Phil Bradway
Estimated Sales:$100+ Million
Number Employees: 1,000-4,999
Parent Co: Chiquita Brands International
Brands:
FRESH EXPRESS FARMS SALADS

5179 Fresh Farm
7255 Sheridan Boulevard
Arvada, CO 80003-3301   303-429-1536
Fax: 303-429-1252
Estimated Sales:$2.5-5 Million
Number Employees: 10-19

5180 Fresh Fish
2700 Avenue D
Birmingham, AL 35218-2139   205-252-0344
Fax: 205-252-3432
Seafood
President: George Drakos
VP: George Sarris

5181 Fresh Frozen Foods
P.O.Box 215
Jefferson, GA 30549-0215   706-367-9851
Fax: 706-367-4646   800-277-9851
fffga@alltel.net
Manufacturer of frozen vegetables, branded products, packer and distributor
President: Billy Griffin
VP: Billy Griffin, Jr
Estimated Sales:$50-100 Million
Number Employees: 50-99

5182 Fresh Hemp Foods
15.2166 Notre Dame Avenue
Winnipeg, NB R3H 0K1
Canada   800-665-4367
Fax: 204-956-5984 www.freshhempfoods.com
Hemp food products
President/CEO: Mike Fata
Type of Packaging: Bulk

5183 Fresh Island Fish Company
312 Alamaha St # G
Kahului, HI 96732-2430   808-871-1111
Fax: 808-871-6818 www.freshislandfish.com
Seafood
President: Mike Lee
Estimated Sales:$ 10 - 20 Million
Number Employees: 20-49

5184 Fresh Juice Company
280 Wilson Avenue
Newark, NJ 07105-3844   973-465-7100
Fax: 973-465-7170
Manufacturer and exporter of fresh and fresh-frozen juices including citrus and blended
Estimated Sales:$ 20 - 50 Million
Number Employees: 20-49
Parent Co: Saratoga Beverage
Type of Packaging: Consumer, Food Service
Brands:
Florida Pik't
Fresh Pik't
Just Pik't

5185 Fresh Mark
1600 Harmont Avenue NE
Canton, OH 44705   330-430-5686
Fax: 330-430-7660   800-860-6777
www.freshmark.com
Bacon, ham, weiners, deli and luncheon meats, dry sausage and other specialty meat items.
President/COO: Harry Valentino
Chairman/CEO: Neil Genshaft
Administrative VP/CFO: David Cochenour
Plant Manager: Rick Hawley
Estimated Sales:$500 Million-$1 Billion
Number Employees: 500-999
Parent Co: Superiors Brand Meats
Type of Packaging: Consumer, Food Service, Private Label

5186 Fresh Market Pasta Company
43 Exchange Street
Portland, ME 04101-5009   207-773-7146
Fax: 207-871-7156
Manufacturer of Pasta, noodles of all kinds, including ginger and squid's ink
President: Alex Gingrich
Estimated Sales:$500,000-$1 Million
Number Employees: 10-19

5187 Fresh Pack Seafood
PO Box 1008
Waldoboro, ME 04572-1008   207-832-7720
Fax: 207-832-7795
Manufacturer of fresh seafood
President: Frank Minio
VP/General Manager: Roger Greene

5188 Fresh Roast Systems
1341 N McDowell Blvd
Petaluma, CA 94954-7137   707-763-1050
Fax: 707-763-1946 www.frestroastsystems.com
Coffee roaster
President: Roger Allington
Estimated Sales:$5-10 Million
Number Employees: 5-9
Type of Packaging: Private Label

5189 Fresh Roasted Almond Company
22511 Telegraph Road
Westland, MI 48185   734-466-9577
sales@freshroastedalmond.com
www.freshroastedalmondco.com
Manufacturer of dry roasted, sweetened and flavored kosher nut confections including almonds, pecans, cashews, peanuts and walnuts flavored in cinnamon, honey, maple, vanilla, cherry and spices
President: Dan Levy
Estimated Sales:$1-3 Million
Number Employees: 10-19
Sq. footage: 4500
Type of Packaging: Consumer, Private Label, Bulk
Brands:
KARS
RITTER

5190 Fresh Samantha
84 Industrial Park Road
Saco, ME 04072-1840   207-284-0011
Fax: 207-284-8331   800-658-4635
www.freshsamantha.com
Manufacturer of fresh juice
CEO: Doug Levin
*Estimated Sales:*Less than $500,000
Number Employees: 1-4
Type of Packaging: Consumer
Brands:
FRESH SAMANTHA

5191 Fresh Seafood Distributors
P.O.Box 1641
Daphne, AL 36526-1641   251-626-1106
                                Fax: 251-626-1109
    President: Steve Miller
Estimated Sales:$ 3 - 5 Million
Number Employees: 5-9

5192 Fresh Squeezed Juice Company
PO Box 780312
Sebastian, FL 32978-0312   561-589-0390
Juice and jellies
    President: Robert Kordick

5193 Fresh Start Bakeries
649 S 7th Ave
City of Industry, CA 91746-3174   626-961-2525
    Fax: 626-330-9890 www.freshstartbakeries.com
Manufacturer of buns and English muffins
    President: Craig Olsen
    Plant Manager: Bob Mitchell
Estimated Sales:$5-10 Million appx.
Number Employees: 100-249
Parent Co: Fresh Start Bakeries
Type of Packaging: Consumer, Food Service

5194 Fresh Start Bakeries
920 Shaw Rd
Stockton, CA 95215-4014   209-943-9200
    Fax: 209-462-3618 www.freshstartbakeries.com
Manufacturer of hamburger buns
    Manager: Scott Parker
Estimated Sales:$ 10 - 20 Million
Number Employees: 50-99
Sq. footage: 40000
Parent Co: Fresh Start Bakeries
Type of Packaging: Food Service
Other Locations:
    Fresh Start Bakeries
    Brea CA
    Fresh Start Bakeries
    City of Industry CA
    Fresh Start Bakeries
    Waipahu HI
    Best Harvest Bakeries
    Kansas City KA
    Tennessee Bun Company
    Dickson TN
    Nashville Bun Company
    Nashville TN
    Galasso's Bakery
    Mira Loma CA

5195 (HQ)Fresh Start Bakeries
P.O.Box 9939
Brea, CA 92822-1939   714-256-8900
    Fax: 714-256-8916 www.freshstartbakeries.com
Manufacutrer of baked goods including hamburger
buns and English muffins
    President: Craig Olson
    Senior VP/CMO: Mike Ward
    VP Engineer: Clyde Kawamoto
Estimated Sales:$50-100 Million
Number Employees: 20-49
Sq. footage: 60000
Parent Co: Fresh Start Bakeries
Type of Packaging: Food Service

5196 Freshco
7929 SW Jack James Drive
Stuart, FL 34997-7243   772-595-0070
                                Fax: 561-595-9522
Manufacturer of bottled orange and grapefruit juice
    President: J Patrick Shirard
    CEO: Clifford Burg
Estimated Sales:$13.80 Million
Number Employees: 82
Type of Packaging: Consumer, Food Service, Pri-
    vate Label
Brands:
    INDIAN RIVER SELECT

5197 Freshmark Foods Corporation
22613 76th Avenue S
Kent, WA 98032-1922   253-872-9426
                                Fax: 253-395-6525
Food brokers

5198 Freshwater Farms of Ohio
2624 N Us Highway 68
Urbana, OH 43078-9537   937-652-3701
    Fax: 937-652-3481 800-634-7434
                                www.fwfarms.com
    Owner: Dave Smith

Estimated Sales:$1-2.5 Million
Number Employees: 10-19

5199 Freshwater Fish Marketing
8542 126th Avenue NW
Edmonton, AB T5B 1G9
Canada   780-495-5103
    Fax: 780-495-5384 800-345-3113
                edmonton@freshwaterfish.com
                www.freshwaterfish.com
Manufacturer of freshwater fish, whitefish and
northern pike
    President: Tom Dunn
    Sales Manager: Doug Clayton
Type of Packaging: Consumer, Food Service

5200 Freund Baking Company
611 Sonora Ave
Glendale, CA 91201-2338   818-502-1400
    Fax: 818-502-1338 www.freundbaking.com
Bread and bakery products
    President: James Freund
Estimated Sales:$100+ Million
Number Employees: 100-249

5201 Frey Vineyards
14000 Tomki Rd
Redwood Valley, CA 95470-6135   707-485-5177
    Fax: 707-485-7875 800-760-3739
    info@freywine.com   www.freywine.com
Wines
    President: Paul Frey
    VP: Jonathan Frey
    VP Marketing/Sales: Katrina Frey
Estimated Sales:$5-10 Million
Number Employees: 10-19
Type of Packaging: Private Label

5202 Frick Winery
23072 Walling Road
Sacramento, CA 95829   415-776-7331
    Fax: 415-776-7331 frick@frickwinery.com
                www.frickwinery.com
    OWner: Bill Frick

5203 Fricks Meat Products
360 M E Frick Drive
Washington, MO 63090-1050   636-239-3313
    Fax: 636-239-2200 800-241-2209
                frickmeats@frickmeats.com
                www.frickmeats.com
Manufacturer of cured and smoked meats including
sausage and ham
    Sales Director: David King
Estimated Sales:$10-20 Million
Number Employees: 50-99

5204 Fried Provisions Company
P.O.Box F
Evans City, PA 16033-0310   724-538-3160
                                Fax: 724-538-3262
Manufacturer of cheese, luncheon meats, chopped
ham, poultry and sausage
    President: James Deily
    Sales Manager: Tim Deily
Estimated Sales:$1.40 Million
Number Employees: 1-4
Parent Co: Fort Pitt Brand Meats
Type of Packaging: Consumer, Food Service, Pri-
    vate Label, Bulk
Brands:
    Fort Pitt
    Harmony

5205 Frieda's
4465 Corporate Center Dr
Los Alamitos, CA 90720-2561   714-826-6100
    Fax: 714-816-0277 800-421-9477
    mail@friedas.com   www.friedas.com
Exotic fruits and vegetables
    President/CEO: Karen Caplan
    VP: Jackie Caplan Wiggins
    Marketing: Tristan Millar
Estimated Sales:$50-100 Million
Number Employees: 100-249

5206 Friendly Ice Cream Corporation
1855 Boston Rd
Wilbraham, MA 01095-1098   413-731-4000
    Fax: 413-773-1447 800-966-9970
                www.friendlys.com

Manufacturer of ice cream including low-fat and
sugar-free; also, frozen yogurt
    President/CEO: Ned Lidvall
    CFO: Steve Sanchioni
    SVP Marketing: Lawrence Rusinko
    SVP Company Operations: John Bowie
Estimated Sales:$575 Million
Number Employees: 12,787
Type of Packaging: Consumer, Food Service, Pri-
    vate Label, Bulk
Brands:
    FRIENDLY ICE CREAM

5207 (HQ)Friendship Dairies
1 Jericho Plz # 107
Jericho, NY 11753-1668   516-719-4000
                                Fax: 516-719-3866
    myfriends@friendshipdairies.com
                www.friendshipdairies.com
Manufacturer of all natural cultured dairy products
such as; cottage cheese, sour cream, buttermilk and
yogurt and cheese
    President: Joe Murgolo
    VP: Douglas Gerbosi
    Marketing Manager: Marc Silverstein
    VP Sales: Bob Grasso
Estimated Sales:$6.7 Million
Number Employees: 20-49
Type of Packaging: Consumer, Food Service, Pri-
    vate Label, Bulk
Brands:
    FRIENDSHIP
    METCO
    SOUR TREAT

5208 Friendship Dairies
6701 County Road 20
Friendship, NY 14739-8660   585-973-3031
    Fax: 585-973-2401 www.friendshipdairies.com
Manufacturer of dairy products including cottage
cheese and whey and whey powders including acid
and neutralized; also, calcium lactate powder and so-
dium lactate
    President: David Buteyan
    Plant Manager: Greg Knapp
Estimated Sales:$50-100 Million
Number Employees: 100-249
Parent Co: Friendship Dairies
Type of Packaging: Consumer, Food Service

5209 Friendship International
PO Box 1005
Camden, ME 04843-1005   207-594-1111
    Fax: 207-203-4622 waaddman@hotmail.com
Manufacturer and exporter of live sea urchins
    President: Jim Wadsworth

5210 Frio Foods
8600 Wurzbach Road
Suite 500
San Antonio, TX 78240-4331   210-278-4525
                                Fax: 210-278-1094
Processes frozen foods
    President: Ron Trine
Brands:
    FRIO

5211 Frionor U.S.A.
P.O.Box 2087
New Bedford, MA 02741-2087   508-997-0031
    Fax: 508-991-6432 800-343-8046
                www.americanprideseafoods.com
Cod, haddock, pollock, salmon, whiting, great silver
smelt, fishsticks
    President: John Cummings
    Director Sales: Bob Bruno
Estimated Sales:$50-100 Million
Number Employees: 100-249
Sq. footage: 210000
Brands:
    ARCTIC CAPE
    BAYSIDE
    BISTRO
    BUNCH O'CRUNCH
    FRIONER
    NORTH CAPE
    OCEAN CUTS

5212 Frisco Baking Company
621 W Avenue 26
Los Angeles, CA 90065-1095   323-225-6111
                                Fax: 323-225-3554
Baked goods
    President: James Pricco

Estimated Sales: $100-500 Million
Number Employees: 100-249

5213 Frisinger Cellars
2277 Dry Creek Road
Napa, CA 94558-9723   707-255-3749
   Fax: 707-963-7867 www.francisanico.com
Wines
   President: Raymond Reyes
Estimated Sales: $5-9.9 Million
Number Employees: 10-19
Parent Co: Consolation Brand

5214 (HQ)Frito-Lay
PO Box 660634
Dallas, TX 75266-0634   972-334-7000
   Fax: 972-334-2019 800-352-4477
   beth.struckell@fritolay.com   www.fritolay.com
Manufacturer and exporter of potato, tortilla and
corn chips, pretzels, popcorn, peanuts and cookies.
   President/CEO: Al Carey
   CFO: Nancy Loewe
   VP/General Counsel: Marc Kesselman
   Group VP R&D: Mike Zbuchalski
   SVP/CMO: Anindita Mukherjee
   SVP/Sales: Randy Melville
   SVP Human Resources: Michele Thatcher
   SVP/Operations: Leslie Starr Keating
Estimated Sales: $12 Billion
Number Employees: 40,000
Parent Co: PepsiCo Inc
Type of Packaging: Consumer, Food Service
Brands:
   100 CALORIE MINI BITES
   BAKED!
   BAKEN-ETS®
   CHEETOS®
   CRACKER JACK®)
   CRACKERS
   DORITOS®
   EL ISLENO®
   FRITO-LAY® DIPS
   FRITO-LAY® NUTS AND SEEDS
   FRITOS®
   FRITOS® DIPS
   FUNYUNS®
   GAMESA®
   GRANDMA'S®
   LAY'S®
   LAY'S® DIPS
   MATADOR
   MAUI STYLE®
   MISS VICKIE'S®
   MUNCHIES®
   MUNCHOS®
   NATURAL
   NUT HARVEST®
   QUAKER®
   ROLD GOLD®
   RUFFLES®
   SABRITONES®
   SMARTFOOD® POPCORN
   SMARTFOOD® POPCORN CLUSTERS
   SPITZ®
   STACY'S®
   SUNCHIPS®
   TOSTITOS®
   TOSTITOS® DIPS AND SALSAS
   TRUENORTH®

5215 Frito-Lay
4236 SW Kirklawn Avenue
Topeka, KS 66609-1266   785-266-2439
   Fax: 785-266-9785 www.fritolay.com
Manufacturer of potato, tortilla and corn chips; serv-
ing the food service market
   President/CEO: Al Carey
   Chief Financial Officer: Dave Rader
   VP/General Counsel: Kelly Tullier
   SVP/Research & Development: Rocco Papalia
   Chief Marketing Officer: Jaya Kumar
   SVP/Sales: Randy Melville
   VP/Public Affairs: Charles Nicolas
   SVP/Operations: Rich Beck
   SVP/Human Resources: Michele Thatcher
Estimated Sales: $5-10 Million
Number Employees: 5-9
Parent Co: PepsiCo Inc
Type of Packaging: Food Service

5216 Frito-Lay
2800 Silver Star Rd
Orlando, FL 32808-3941   407-295-1810
   Fax: 407-290-8041 www.fritolay.com

Manufacturer of potato, tortilla and corn chips
   President/CEO: Al Carey
   Chief Financial Officer: Dave Rader
   VP/General Counsel: Kelly Tullier
   SVP/Research & Development: Rocco Papalia
   Chief Marketing Officer: Jaya Kumar
   SVP/Sales: Randy Melville
   VP/Public Affairs: Charles Nicolas
   SVP/Operations: Rich Beck
   Manufacturing Manager: Mark Billington
   Plant Manager: Chris Henry
Estimated Sales: $500 Million-$1 Billion
Number Employees: 364
Parent Co: PepsiCo Inc
Type of Packaging: Consumer

5217 Frito-Lay
948 Avenue H E
Arlington, TX 76011-7786   817-385-5834
   Fax: 817-640-3026 www.fritolay.com
Manufacturer of jalapeno bean dip and snacks
   President/CEO: Al Carey
   Chief Financial Officer: Dave Rader
   VP/General Counsel: Kelly Tullier
   SVP/Research & Development: Rocco Papalia
   Chief Marketing Officer: Jaya Kumar
   SVP/Sales: Randy Melville
   VP/Public Affairs: Charles Nicolas
   SVP/Operations: Rich Beck
   SVP/Human Resources: Michele Thatcher
   Plant Manager: Daniel Knox
Estimated Sales: $50-100 Million
Number Employees: 50-99
Parent Co: PepsiCo Inc
Type of Packaging: Consumer, Food Service, Bulk

5218 Frito-Lay
701 N Wildwood Dr
Irving, TX 75061-8831   972-579-2111
   Fax: 972-579-2137 www.fritolay.com
Manufacturer of snack foods including potato, torti-
lla and corn chips
   President: David Strickland
   Chief Financial Officer: Dave Rader
   VP/General Counsel: Kelly Tullier
   SVP/Research & Development: Rocco Papalia
   Chief Marketing Officer: Jaya Kumar
   SVP/Sales: Randy Melville
   VP/Public Affairs: Charles Nicolas
   SVP/Operations: Rich Beck
   SVP/Human Resources: Michele Thatcher
   Plant Manager: Willie Leggett
Estimated Sales: $500 Million-$1 Billion
Number Employees: 800
Parent Co: PepsiCo Inc
Type of Packaging: Consumer, Food Service, Pri-
vate Label, Bulk

5219 Frito-Lay
2121 Plantside Dr
Jeffersontown, KY 40299-1923   502-491-9616
   Fax: 502-491-9936 www.fritolay.com
Manufacturer of potato and tortilla chips; also, corn
products
   Manager: Ken Thomas
   Chief Financial Officer: Dave Rader
   VP/General Counsel: Kelly Tullier
   SVP/Research & Development: Rocco Papalia
   Chief Marketing Officer: Jaya Kumar
   SVP/Sales: Randy Melville
   VP/Public Affairs: Charles Nicolas
   SVP/Operations: Rich Beck
   SVP/Human Resources: Michele Thatcher
Estimated Sales: $75-120 Million
Number Employees: 250-499
Parent Co: PepsiCo Inc
Type of Packaging: Consumer

5220 Frito-Lay
26706 Road L34
Underwood, IA 51576-3884   712-322-5561
   Fax: 712-322-6127 www.fritolay.com
Manfuacturer of corn chips
   President/CEO: Al Carey
   Chief Financial Officer: Dave Rader
   VP/General Counsel: Kelly Tullier
   SVP/Research & Development: Rocco Papalia
   Chief Marketing Officer: Jaya Kumar
   SVP/Sales: Randy Melville
   VP/Public Affairs: Charles Nicolas
   SVP/Operations: Rich Beck
   SVP/Human Resources: Michele Thatcher
Number Employees: 50-99
Parent Co: PepsiCo North America

Type of Packaging: Consumer

5221 Frito-Lay
1626 Old Mansfield Rd
Wooster, OH 44691-9056   330-262-0387
   Fax: 330-262-0105 www.fritolay.com
Manufacturer of snack foods including potato, torti-
lla and corn chips
   Manager: Mike Kulbacki
   Chief Financial Officer: Dave Rader
   VP/General Counsel: Kelly Tullier
   SVP/Research & Development: Rocco Papalia
   Chief Marketing Officer: Jaya Kumar
   SVP/Sales: Randy Melville
   VP/Public Affairs: Charles Nicolas
   SVP/Operations: Rich Beck
   SVP/Human Resources: Michele Thatcher
Estimated Sales: $100-500 Million
Number Employees: 250-499
Parent Co: PepsiCo Inc
Type of Packaging: Consumer

5222 Frito-Lay
2810 Kennedy Dr
Beloit, WI 53511-3998   608-365-7112
   Fax: 608-365-2905 www.fritolay.com
Manufacturer of snack foods including potato and
corn chips
   President/CEO: Al Carey
   Chief Financial Officer: Dave Rader
   Manager: John Arnold
   SVP/Research & Development: Rocco Papalia
   Chief Marketing Officer: Jaya Kumar
   SVP/Sales: Randy Melville
   VP/Public Affairs: Charles Nicolas
   SVP/Operations: Rich Beck
   SVP/Human Resources: Michele Thatcher
Estimated Sales: $500 Million-$1 Billion
Number Employees: 20
Parent Co: PepsiCo Inc
Type of Packaging: Consumer, Food Service, Pri-
vate Label, Bulk

5223 Frito-Lay
2911 Nevada Blvd
Charlotte, NC 28273-6434   704-588-2840
   Fax: 704-588-3250 www.fritolay.com
Manufacturer of potato and corn chips and
multi-grain snacks
   President/CEO: Al Carey
   Chief Financial Officer: Dave Rader
   VP/General Counsel: Kelly Tullier
   SVP/Research & Development: Rocco Papalia
   Chief Marketing Officer: Jaya Kumar
   SVP/Sales: Randy Melville
   VP/Public Affairs: Charles Nicolas
   Manufacturing/Operations Director: Xavier
Perpad
   Manager: Tieun Brayboy
Estimated Sales: $500 Million-$1 Billion
Number Employees: 500
Sq. footage: 350000
Parent Co: PepsiCo Inc
Type of Packaging: Consumer

5224 Frito-Lay
1450 W Maricopa Hwy
Casa Grande, AZ 85293-5599   520-836-2363
   Fax: 520-426-6216 www.fritolay.com
Manufacturer of potato, tortilla and corn chips
   President/CEO: Al Carey
   Chief Financial Officer: Dave Rader
   VP/General Counsel: Kelly Tullier
   SVP/Research & Development: Rocco Papalia
   Chief Marketing Officer: Jaya Kumar
   SVP/Sales: Randy Melville
   VP/Public Affairs: Charles Nicolas
   SVP/Operations: Rich Beck
   SVP/Human Resources: Michele Thatcher
   Plant Manager: Wendy Vitiritto
Estimated Sales: $100-500 Million
Number Employees: 250-499
Parent Co: PepsiCo Inc
Type of Packaging: Consumer, Food Service

5225 Frito-Lay
4855 Greatland
San Antonio, TX 78218-5380   210-662-2100
   Fax: 210-661-2023 www.fritolay.com

Manufacturer of snack foods including corn chips
  Manager: Wendy Agee
  Chief Financial Officer: Dave Rader
  VP/General Counsel: Kelly Tullier
  SVP/Research & Development: Rocco Papalia
  Chief Marketing Officer: Jaya Kumar
  SVP/Sales: Randy Melville
  VP/Public Affairs: Charles Nicolas
  SVP/Operations: Rich Beck
  SVP/Human Resources: Michele Thatcher
Estimated Sales:$20-50 Million
Number Employees: 20-49
Parent Co: PepsiCo Inc
Type of Packaging: Consumer, Food Service

5226 Frito-Lay
18100 Oakwood Blvd # 207
Dearborn, MI 48124-4085   313-271-3000
          Fax: 313-271-6457 www.fritolay.com
Manufacturer of potato, tortilla and corn chips; importer and exporter of potato chips
  Owner: K Thavarajah
  Chief Financial Officer: Dave Rader
  VP/General Counsel: Kelly Tullier
  SVP/Research & Development: Rocco Papalia
  Chief Marketing Officer: Jaya Kumar
  SVP/Sales: Randy Melville
  VP/Public Affairs: Charles Nicolas
  SVP/Operations: Rich Beck
  SVP/Human Resources: Michele Thatcher
Estimated Sales:$500 Million-$1 Billion
Number Employees: 500-999
Parent Co: PepsiCo Inc
Type of Packaging: Consumer

5227 Frito-Lay
3310 Highway 36 N
Rosenberg, TX 77471-9716   281-232-2363
          Fax: 281-232-1516 www.fritolay.com
Manufacturer and exporter of snack foods including potato, tortilla and corn chips
  President: Kevin Brightwell
  Chief Financial Officer: Dave Rader
  VP/General Counsel: Kelly Tullier
  SVP/Research & Development: Rocco Papalia
  Chief Marketing Officer: Jaya Kumar
  SVP/Sales: Randy Melville
  VP/Public Affairs: Charles Nicolas
  Manufacturing/Operations Director: Latane Brackett
  Manager: Lance O'Pry
Estimated Sales:$500 Million-$1 Billion
Number Employees: 300
Sq. footage: 400000
Parent Co: PepsiCo Inc
Type of Packaging: Consumer, Food Service

5228 Frito-Lay
323 S County Road 300 W
Frankfort, IN 46041-8780   765-659-1831
          Fax: 765-654-6610 www.fritolay.com
Manufacturer of potato, tortilla and corn chips
  President: Frank Armetta
  Chief Financial Officer: Dave Rader
  VP/General Counsel: Kelly Tullier
  SVP/Research & Development: Rocco Papalia
  Chief Marketing Officer: Jaya Kumar
  SVP/Sales: Randy Melville
  VP/Public Affairs: Charles Nicolas
  Manufacturing/Operations Director: Dave Hendricks
*Estimated Sales:*Over $1 Billion
Number Employees: 500
Parent Co: PepsiCo Inc
Type of Packaging: Consumer, Food Service

5229 Frito-Lay
P.O.Box 3096
Williamsport, PA 17701-0096   570-326-4136
          Fax: 570-323-8016 www.fritolay.com
Manufacturer and exporter of snack foods including tortilla and corn chips
  Manager: John Susko
  Chief Financial Officer: Dave Rader
  VP/General Counsel: Kelly Tullier
  SVP/Research & Development: Rocco Papalia
  Chief Marketing Officer: Jaya Kumar
  SVP/Sales: Randy Melville
  VP/Public Affairs: Charles Nicolas
  SVP/Operations: Rich Beck
  SVP/Human Resources: Michele Thatcher
Estimated Sales:$20-50 Million
Number Employees: 20-49
Parent Co: PepsiCo Inc

Type of Packaging: Consumer

5230 Frito-Lay
9846 4th Street
Rancho Cucamonga, CA 91730-5720 909-948-3600
          Fax: 909-948-3614 www.fritolay.com
Manufacturer of corn chips
  President/CEO: Al Carey
  Chief Financial Officer: Dave Rader
  VP/General Counsel: Kelly Tullier
  SVP/Research & Development: Rocco Papalia
  Chief Marketing Officer: Jaya Kumar
  SVP/Sales: Randy Melville
  VP/Public Affairs: Charles Nicolas
  SVP/Operations: Rich Beck
  SVP/Human Resources: Michele Thatcher
  Manager: George Smith
Estimated Sales:$500 Million-$1 Billion
Number Employees: 26
Parent Co: PepsiCo Inc
Type of Packaging: Consumer

5231 Frito-Lay
28801 Highway 58
Bakersfield, CA 93314-9000   661-328-6000
          Fax: 661-328-6077 www.fritolay.com
Manufacturer and exporter of potato, tortilla and corn chips; also, pretzels
  President/CEO: Al Carey
  Chief Financial Officer: Dave Rader
  VP/General Counsel: Kelly Tullier
  SVP/Research & Development: Rocco Papalia
  Chief Marketing Officer: Jaya Kumar
  SVP/Sales: Randy Melville
  VP/Public Affairs: Charles Nicolas
  Operations/Manufacturing Director: Steve Bouholtz
  Manager: Jerry Matthews
Estimated Sales:$1+ Billion
Number Employees: 800
Parent Co: PepsiCo Inc
Type of Packaging: Consumer

5232 Fritsch Cheese
Highway G
Cobb, WI 53526   608-623-2205

5233 Friuli Sorbet
225 Lafayette Street
Room 400
New York, NY 10012-4015   212-966-3073
          Fax: 212-966-9354
Manufacturer of frozen fruit sorbet including nonfat, nondairy and kosher
  President: Susan Friuli
Estimated Sales:$1-3 Million
Number Employees: 1-4
Sq. footage: 400
Type of Packaging: Consumer, Food Service
Brands:
  FRUILI

5234 Froedtert Malt
500 W 3rd St
Winona, MN 55987-2800   507-454-1535
          Fax: 507-454-1041 minimaul@hbci.com
Manufacturer and exporter of barley malt
  President: Gabriel Pujol
  Logistics Coordinator: Bonny Maul
  Plant Manager: Steve Kukla
Estimated Sales:$20-50 Million
Number Employees: 20-49
Parent Co: International Malting Company
Type of Packaging: Bulk

5235 Froedtert Malt Company
3830 W Grant St
Milwaukee, WI 53215-2355   414-671-1166
          Fax: 414-671-1166 info@froedtert.com
Malt
  President: Dale West
Estimated Sales:$100+ Million
Number Employees: 100-249

5236 Froedtert Malt Corporation
7455 181st Ave SE
Wahpeton, ND 58075-9707   701-642-9269
          Fax: 701-642-2003 800-493-4886
Manufacturer of malt
  Manager: David Peterson
  General Manager: Dave Peterson
Estimated Sales:$1-3 Million
Number Employees: 5-9
Type of Packaging: Bulk

5237 Froedtert Malt Corporation
PO Box 712
Milwaukee, WI 53201   414-649-0205
          Fax: 414-649-0285 800-493-4886
Manufacturer and exporter of barley malt and grain
  Manager: Dave Peterson
Estimated Sales:$20-50 Million
Number Employees: 20-49
Parent Co: International Malting Company
Type of Packaging: Bulk

5238 Frog City Cheese
PO Box 94
106 Messer Hill Road
Plymouth Notch, VT 05056   802-672-3650
          Fax: 802-672-1629 frogcity@vermontel.net
Manufacturer of granular curd (whole milk) cheese
  Co-Owner: Jackie McCuin
  Co-Owner: Tom Gilbert
Estimated Sales:$3-5 Million
Number Employees: 10-19
Type of Packaging: Consumer

5239 Frog Ranch Foods
5 S High St
Glouster, OH 45732-1001   740-767-3705
          Fax: 740-767-4658 800-742-2488
          info@frogranch.com www.frogranch.com
Traditional style salsas, pickles, peppers, tortilla chips
  President: Craig Cornett
Estimated Sales:$2.5-5 Million
Number Employees: 1-4
Type of Packaging: Private Label

5240 Frog's Leap Winery
P.O.Box 189
Rutherford, CA 94573-0189   707-963-4704
          Fax: 707-963-0242 800-959-4704
          greenmailbox@frogsleap.com
          www.frogsleap.com
Wines
  President: John Williams
Estimated Sales:$5-10 Million
Number Employees: 20-49
Brands:
  CABERNET SAUVIGNON
  CHARDONNAY
  MERLOT
  SAUVIGNON BLANC
  ZINFANDEL

5241 Frolic Candy Company
20 Central Avenue
Farmingdale, NY 11735-6906   516-756-2255
  President: L Hirshheimer
Estimated Sales:$2.5-5 Million
Number Employees: 5-9

5242 From Oregon
2787 Olympic Street
Suite 4
Springfield, OR 97477-7809   541-747-4222
          Fax: 541-747-5456
Jams, marmalades and berries
  President: Bonnie Koenig
Estimated Sales:$1-4.9 Million
Number Employees: 1-4

5243 Froma-Dar
378 rue Principale
St. Boniface, QC G0X 2L0
Canada   819-535-3946
          Fax: 819-535-7010
Manufacturer of dairy products including cheddar, curd and partly skim cheeses
  President: Michel Veillette
Number Employees: 50-99
Sq. footage: 20000
Type of Packaging: Consumer, Food Service, Private Label, Bulk
Brands:
  DES COTEAUX
  FROMA-DAR
  JUNEAU

5244 Frontenac Point Vineyard
9501 State Route 89
Trumansburg, NY 14886-9211   607-387-9619
          contactus@frontenacpoint.com
          www.frontenacpoint.com

Wines
*Estimated Sales:*Under $500,000
Number Employees: 1-4

5245 Frontera Foods
449 N Clark St # 205
Chicago, IL 60654-4500   312-595-1624
Fax: 312-595-1625 800-509-4441
brownson@fronterafoods.com
www.fronterakitchens.com
Processor of tortilla chips, sauces, spices, salsas, nut
mixes, and drink mixes
President: Manuel Valdes
Founder/Owner: Rick Bayless
Estimated Sales:$5-9.9 Million
Number Employees: 5-9
Type of Packaging: Food Service
Brands:
FRONTERA FOODS
SALPICA

5246 Frontier Beef Company
PO Box 927
Huntingdon Valley, PA 19006-0927 215-663-2120
Beef
President: Bill Hardimon

5247 Frontier Commodities
8255 Country Club Road W
Byron, MN 55920-4201   507-775-2174
Fax: 507-775-7049 soybn@aol.com
www.puregrain.net/frontier/frontier.htm
Manufacturer of a wide of variety of grains
Partner: Randy Brown

5248 (HQ)Frontier Cooperative Herbs
2990 Wilderness Place
Boulder, CO 80301-2388   303-449-8137
Fax: 800-717-4372 800-669-3275
customercare@frontiercoop.com
www.frontiercoop.com
Herbs and spices packaging
President: Rick Stewart
Marketing: Clint Landis
Sales: Tony Bedard
Production: Lana Miller
Plant Manager: Tony Bedard
*Estimated Sales:*Less than $500,000
Number Employees: 1-4

5249 Frontier Game Company
3801 N Grove St
Fort Worth, TX 76106-3720   817-624-1136
Fax: 817-624-4594 888-432-1581
www.frontiermeats.com
Meat products
President: Eric Nauwelares
Accounts Department: Tulio Bustillo
Operations Manager: Ann Heusele
Estimated Sales:$20-50 Million
Number Employees: 50-99
Brands:
Frontier

5250 Frontier Ingredients
3021 78th St
PO Box 299
Norway, IA 52318   319-227-7996
Fax: 319-227-2041 800-669-3275
info@frontiercoop.com www.frontiercoop.com
organic spices

5251 Frontier Natural Co-op
PO Box 299
Norway, IA 52318-0299   303-449-8137
Fax: 303-449-8139 bob.fan@frontiercoop.com
www.frontier.coop.com
Certified organic coffee
VP: Adam Strauss
Sales: Bob Fan
Purchasing: Rob Stephen
Type of Packaging: Private Label
Brands:
FRONTIER ORGANIC COFFEE
JOE BEAN ORGANIC COFFEE

5252 Frontier Soups
895 S Northpoint Blvd
Waukegan, IL 60085-8277   847-688-1200
Fax: 847-688-1206 800-300-7867
info@frontiersoups.com www.frontiersoups.com
Manufacturer of dried soup and pasta salad mixes
President: Trisha Anderson
Production: Eva Dantoja

Estimated Sales:$2.5-5 Million
Number Employees: 10-19
Sq. footage: 8000
Type of Packaging: Consumer
Brands:
FRONTIER
HEARTY ORIGINALS
HOMEMADE IN MINUTES
I'LL BRING THE SALADD
ILLINOIS PRAIRIE
MINNESOTA HEARTLAND
NEW LINE HOMEMADE
WISCONSIN LAKESHORE

5253 Frookie
2070 Maple Street
Des Plaines, IL 60018-3019   847-699-3200
Fax: 847-699-3201
Cookies.
President: Phil Roos

5254 Frostbite
4117 Fitch Rd
Toledo, OH 43613-4007   419-473-9621
Fax: 419-473-3183 800-968-7711
bob_strayer@deanfoods.com
www.deanfoods.com
Manufacturer and exporter of frozen dessert novel-
ties including yogurt, ice cream and water ices; also,
baked goods for ice cream novelties
Plant Manager: Randy Bevier
Estimated Sales:$20-50 Million
Number Employees: 250-499
Sq. footage: 100000
Parent Co: Suiza Dairy Group
Type of Packaging: Consumer, Food Service, Pri-
vate Label
Brands:
CHILLY THINGS
FROSTBITE
YOPLAIT

5255 Frostproof Sunkist Groves
P.O.Box 1098
Fort Meade, FL 33841-1098   863-635-4873
Fax: 863-635-3447 www.frostproofgroves.com
Owner: John Stephens
Estimated Sales:$ 1 - 3 Million
Number Employees: 1-4

5256 Frozen Specialties
P.O.Box 410
Archbold, OH 43502-0410   419-445-9015
Fax: 419-445-9465
Manufacturer of frozen pizza bites, sandwiches, egg
rolls and stuffed clams
Chairman/President/CEO: Eugene Welka
CFO: Ken Dippman
VP Operations: Ron Zaleski
Plant Manager: Brian Replogle
Purchasing Manager: Jeff Miller
Estimated Sales:$102 Million
Number Employees: 100-249
Type of Packaging: Consumer, Private Label
Brands:
FOX DELUXE
G&W
MR P'S
NATLANS
PIZZA BITES

5257 Frozfruit Corporation
14805 S San Pedro Street
Gardena, CA 90248-2030   310-217-1034
Fax: 310-715-6943
Manufacturer and exporter of frozen ice cream nov-
elties and fruit bars
President: Tom Guinan
Director Marketing: Michael Armer
Estimated Sales:$500,000-$1 Million
Number Employees: 5-9
Sq. footage: 75000
Type of Packaging: Consumer, Food Service, Pri-
vate Label, Bulk
Brands:
FROZFRUIT
FROZFRUIT ALL NATURAL FRUIT BARS
SUMMER NATURALS

5258 (HQ)Frozsun Foods
166 E Lajolla Pl
Anaheim, CA 92806   714-630-2170
Fax: 714-630-0920 dyvanovi@frozsun.com
www.frozsun.com

Manufacturer, exporter and importer of frozen
strawberries and purees
President: Doug Circle
CFO: Tim Graven
Estimated Sales:$10-20 Million
Number Employees: 250-499
Sq. footage: 500000
Type of Packaging: Consumer, Food Service, Pri-
vate Label, Bulk
Other Locations:
Frozsun Foods
Oxnard CA
Brands:
FROZSUN

5259 Fruit A Freeze
12919 Leyva St
Norwalk, CA 90650-6855   562-407-2881
Fax: 562-407-2889 www.fruitafreeze.com
Frozen fruit products
President/CEO: David Stein
Estimated Sales:$5-10 Million
Number Employees: 20-49

5260 (HQ)Fruit Acres
P.O.Box 23
La Crescent, MN 55947-0023   507-895-4750
Fax: 507-895-8353 rpyates@acegroup.cc
Manufacturer of Apples
Manager: Ralph Yates
Secretary: Ralph Yates
Estimated Sales:$.5-1 Million
Number Employees: 1-4
Sq. footage: 4000
Brands:
King

5261 Fruit Acres Farm Marketand U-Pick
2559 Friday Rd
Coloma, MI 49038-9712   269-468-5076
peaches@parrett.net
www.fruitacresfarms.com
230 acre fruit farm growing sweet cherries, apples,
sweet corn and peaches. Also sells gourmet jams,
jellies, honey, sauces, pickles and country gifts.
Co-Owner: Annette Bjorge
Co-Owner: Randy Bjorge
Estimated Sales:$ 5 - 10 Million
Number Employees: 10-19

5262 Fruit Belt Foods
P.O.Box 81
Lawrence, MI 49064-0081   269-674-3939
Fax: 269-674-8354 office@fruitbeltfoods.com
www.fruitbeltfoods.com
Manufacturer, wholesaler/distributor of fruits and
vegetables such as; asparagus, red tart cherries and
strawberries
President: David Frank
Vice President: Warren Frank
Marketing/Sales: Jim Armstrong
Estimated Sales:$5-9.9 Million
Number Employees: 20-49
Type of Packaging: Food Service, Private Label,
Bulk
Brands:
Fruit Belt
Solar

5263 Fruit Fillings
2531 E Edgar Ave
Fresno, CA 93706-5410   559-237-4715
Fax: 559-237-0728 www.fruitfillings.com
Pie and pastry filling, fruit glazes, pectin based jams,
fresh California fruit
President: Stephen Norcross
Estimated Sales:$2.5-5 Million
Number Employees: 20-49

5264 Fruit Growers MarketingAssociation
112 N Bridge St
Newcomerstown, OH 43832-1004   740-498-8366
Fax: 740-498-8367 800-466-5171
fruitgrow@tusco.net   www.web.tusco.net
Cooperative group supplying apples and apple cider
Manager: Bill Dodd
Sales: Lorrie Jurin
General Manager: David Gress
Assistant Manager: Peggy Caudill
Estimated Sales:$ 3 - 5 Million
Number Employees: 1-4
Sq. footage: 1200

Type of Packaging: Consumer, Private Label, Bulk
Brands:
  AUTUMN PRIDE
  GROWERS PRIDE
  ORCHARD GEM

5265 Fruitcrown Products Corporation
250 Adams Blvd
Farmingdale, NY 11735-6615   631-694-5800
        Fax: 631-694-6467   800-441-3210
    info@fruitcrown.com   www.fruitcrown.com
Aseptic fruit flavors and bases for beverage, dairy
and baking industries
    President: Robert Jagenburg
Number Employees: 50-99
Type of Packaging: Bulk
Brands:
  ASP
  EXQUIZITA
  FRUITCROWN
  HUNTINGCASTLE

5266 Fruithill
6501 NE Highway 240
Yamhill, OR 97148-8507   503-662-3926
    Fax: 503-662-4270 fruithilee@worldnet.att.net
    www.fruithill.yamhillbusiness.com
Manufacturer of frozen cherries, plums and fruit pu-
rees
    President: Lee W Schrepel
    EVP/Sales: Lee Schrepel
Estimated Sales: $10-20 Million
Number Employees: 50-99
Type of Packaging: Food Service, Private Label

5267 (HQ)FrutStix Company
1525 State St # 203
Santa Barbara, CA 93101-6512   805-965-1656
        Fax: 805-963-8288   info@frutstix.com
        www.frutstix.com
Manufacturer of fresh frozen fruit bars, fudge bars
    Owner: William Mc Kinley
    Operations Assistant: Lynne Burton
Estimated Sales: $ 5 - 10 Million
Number Employees: 5-9
Type of Packaging: Food Service, Private Label
Other Locations:
    FrutStix - Manufacturing Plant
    San Diego CA

5268 Frutarom Meer Corporation
9500 Railroad Ave
North Bergen, NJ 07047-1422   201-861-9500
        Fax: 201-861-8711 800-526-7147
    fmeernj@aol.com   www.frutarom.com
Manufacturer, exporter and importer of botanicals,
extracts, gums, stabilizers, oleoresins, natural colors,
enzymes and hydrocolloids
    President: William Graham
    VP R&D: Tom Gluckson
    Executive VP Marketing/Development: Clayton
    Bridges
Estimated Sales: $20-50 Million
Number Employees: 100-249
Sq. footage: 100000
Parent Co: Frutarom
Type of Packaging: Bulk
Brands:
  MERECOL
  MERETEC
  MEREZAN
  STAMERE

5269 Fry Foods
P.O.Box 837
Tiffin, OH 44883-0837   419-448-0831
        Fax: 419-448-8363 800-626-2294
    sales@fryfoods.com   www.fryfoods.com
Manufacturer and importer of frozen and breaded
appetizers such as; onion rings, cheese sticks, mush-
rooms, jalapeno, zucchini sticks and cauliflower
    President: Norman Fry
    VP: David Fry
Estimated Sales: $20-50 Million
Number Employees: 50-99
Sq. footage: 45000
Type of Packaging: Food Service
Brands:
  FRY FOODS

5270 Fry Krisp Food Products
P.O.Box 127
Jackson, MI 49204-0127   517-784-8531
        Fax: 517-784-6585 frykrisp@tds.net
        www.frykrisp.com
manufacturer of batter mixes for poultry and sea-
food, funnel cake, corn dogs and onion ring for fairs,
and breakfst items such as pancakes, cornbread, bis-
cuit mix and distributor of yellow corn grits.
    President: Richard Neuenfeldt
    VP: Richard Nuenfeldt
Estimated Sales: $2.5-5 Million
Number Employees: 10
Number of Brands: 2
Number of Products: 15
Sq. footage: 8000
Type of Packaging: Consumer, Food Service, Pri-
vate Label, Bulk
Brands:
  FRY KRISP
  FRY KRISP BATTER MIXES
  OVEN KRISP COATING MIXES

5271 Fudge Farms
PO Box 90
South Bend, IN 46624-0090   616-695-2722
        Fax: 616-695-2733 800-874-0261
    goldenfarmcandies@goldenfarmcandies.com
        www.goldenfarmcandies.com
Manufacturer of confectionery products including
hard and soft, sugar-free, salt-free, caramels, nou-
gats, taffy, fruit chews, coffee, boxed chocolates,
candy bars, and sugar-free lollipops
    President: Kenneth Harrington
    CEO: Michele Fadely
Estimated Sales: $2-2.5 Million
Number Employees: 10-19
Sq. footage: 21500
Brands:
  GOLDEN FARM CANDIES

5272 Fudge Fatale
President
Los Angeles, CA 90034-2617   310-287-0600
    Fax: 310-287-0603 888-923-8343
    sales@fudgefatale.com   www.fudgefatale.com
Manufacturer of fudge
    President: Alexander Black
    Sales: Rich Pariseau
Estimated Sales: $ 3 - 5 Million
Number Employees: 5-9

5273 Fuji Foods
6206 Corporate Park Dr
Browns Summit, NC 27214-8302   336-375-3111
    Fax: 336-375-3663 info@fujifoodsusa.com
        www.fujifoodsusa.com
Manufacturer of chicken, pork and beef broths in-
cluding concentrated pastes and powders; also, sa-
vory flavors, soup bases; and spray dried flavor
powders; spray drying services available
    President: Yasushi Muranaka
    CFO: Timm Phillips
    Vice President: Mike Russell
    Research & Development: Dr Ben Cheng
    Quality Control: Pat Pittman
    Plant Manager: Jarrett Pearman
Estimated Sales: $20-50 Million
Number Employees: 20-49
Parent Co: Fuji Foods Corporation
Type of Packaging: Food Service, Bulk

5274 Fuji Foods
4340 Glencoe St
Denver, CO 80216-4508   303-377-3738
    Fax: 303-377-9397 sales@fujifoodsus.com
        www.fujifoodsus.com
Manufacturer and exporter of frozen, boxed, sliced
and marinated beef and pork; importer of beef slic-
ers
    President/CEO: Maria Keating
    Human Resources: Eva Walz
Estimated Sales: $10-20 Million
Number Employees: 50-99
Number of Products: 50
Type of Packaging: Food Service
Brands:
  Fuji Food

5275 Fuji Vegetable Oil
1 Barker Ave # 290
White Plains, NY 10601-1535   914-761-7900
        Fax: 914-761-7919 fvonyk@aol.com

Vegetable and other oil
    Manager: Andre Cormeau
    Quality Control: Thomas McBrayer
Estimated Sales: $2.5-5 Million
Number Employees: 5-9

5276 Fujiya
454 Waiakamilo Rd
Honolulu, HI 96817-4941   808-845-2921
        www.fujiyahawaii.com
Manufacturer of Japanese cookies including moliti,
tea cakes and nut
    VP: Junko Iwata
Estimated Sales: $2.5-5 Million
Number Employees: 10-19
Type of Packaging: Consumer, Food Service

5277 Ful-Flav-R Foods
P.O.Box 82
Alamo, CA 94507-82   510-339-9618
        Fax: 510-339-3789
    customerservice@ffrfoods.com
        www.fulflavr.com
Manufacturer of Premium Ground Garlic, Minced
Garlic (in oil & water), Ground and Minced Ginger,
Ground Roasted Garlic, Ground Onion, diced Sweet
Bell Peppers, Ground and Diced Jalepeno's, Fire
Roasted Anaheim chili's, GroundChili-Garlic
Blends and other unique custom formulated blends.
All of our products are pasteurized and pH
controlled.
    President: Joseph Farrell
    Chief Operations Officer: Glen Farrell
    Director Sales/Marketing: Steve Linzmeyer
    Plant Manager: John Small
Estimated Sales: $1-2.5 Million
Number Employees: 5-9
Type of Packaging: Food Service, Bulk
Brands:
  Ful-Flav-R

5278 Fulcher's Point Pride Seafood
P.O.Box 250
Oriental, NC 28571-0250   252-249-0123
    Fax: 252-249-2337 fulchers@always-online.com
        www.bluecrabusa.net
Manufacturer of seafood
    President: Chris Fulcher
    Purchasing: Ralph Bard
Estimated Sales: $20-50 Million
Number Employees: 50-99
Type of Packaging: Consumer, Food Service, Bulk

5279 Fulgenzi Foods
2100 S Illini Rd
Leland Grove, IL 62704-4366   217-787-7495
        Fax: 217-787-7495
    President: Danielle Fulgenzi
Estimated Sales: Under $500,000
Number Employees: 1-4

5280 Full Sail Brewing Company
506 Columbia St
Hood River, OR 97031-2000   541-386-2281
    Fax: 541-386-7316 fullsail@fullsailbrewing.com
        www.fullsailbrewing.com
Brewing
    CEO: Jerome Chicvara
    CEO: Irene Firmat
    Marketing/Sales: Sandra Evans
Estimated Sales: $20-50 Million
Number Employees: 50-99
Brands:
  FULL SAIL ALES AND LAGERS

5281 (HQ)Full Service Beverage Company
2900 S Hydraulic St
Wichita, KS 67216-2403   316-524-3201
        Fax: 316-529-1608 800-540-0001
Manufacturer and importer of soft drinks and bottled
water
    Manager: Jerry Mc Broom
Estimated Sales: $20-50 Million
Number Employees: 100-249
Type of Packaging: Consumer, Food Service
Other Locations:
    Full Service Beverage Co.
    Denver CO
Brands:
  7-UP
  CRYSTAL LITE
  DIET-RITE

EVIAN
SNAPPLE

5282 Fulton Provision Company
16123 NE Airport Way
Portland, OR 97230-4953   503-254-3000
        Fax: 503-408-5640   800-333-6328
Manufacturer of meats
    CEO: Carl F Walther
    Sales Contact: Tom Semke
Estimated Sales: $20-50 Million
Number Employees: 50-99
Parent Co: Sysco

5283 Fumoir Grizzly
159 Amsterdam
St-Augustin, Quebec, QC G3A 2V5
Canada   418-878-8941
        Fax: 418-878-8942   info@grizzly.qc.ca
                www.grizzly.qc.ca
Manufacturer and exporter of smoked salmon, trout,
halibut
    Partner/CEO: Pierre Fontaine
    VP/Partner/Sales: Bernard Ruby
    Quality Control Inspector/R&D: Michele Tessier
    Sales Representative - Quebec: Normand Richard
    Production Supervisor: Johanne Laroche
Number Employees: 20-49
Type of Packaging: Consumer, Food Service, Private Label, Bulk

5284 Fun City Popcorn
3211 Sunrise Ave
Las Vegas, NV 89101-4835   702-367-2676
        Fax: 702-876-1099   800-423-1710
Manufacturer of caramel, cheese and butter popcorn;
manufacturer of popcorn processing machinery
    President/CEO: Richard Falk
    CFO: Maryann Talavera
Estimated Sales: $1-3 Million
Number Employees: 5-9
Sq. footage: 20000
Type of Packaging: Consumer, Food Service, Private Label, Bulk

5285 Fun Factory
6223 W Forest Home Avenue
Milwaukee, WI 53220-1916   414-543-5887
        Fax: 414-543-7850   877-894-6767
Gum, candy
    President: Mike Dunlap
Brands:
    FACE TWISTERS SOUR BUBBLE GUM

5286 Fun Foods
99 Murray Hill Pkwy # D
East Rutherford, NJ 07073-2143   201-896-4949
        Fax: 201-896-4911   800-507-2782
                funfoodspasta@yahoo.com
Manufacturer and exporter of bi- and tri-colored holiday shaped gourmet pasta including Christmas
trees, hearts, bunnies, stars and stripes, Jack
O'Lanterns, star of David, angels, etc
    President: Sharon Nicklas
Estimated Sales: $5-10 Million
Number Employees: 5-9
Sq. footage: 4000
Type of Packaging: Consumer, Food Service, Private Label, Bulk
Brands:
    ALL-AMERICAN SPORTS PASTA
    BUNNY PASTA
    FUNFOODS HOLIDAY PASTA
    FUNFOODS PREMIUM
    HARVEST PASTA
    HOLIDAY PASTA
    I LOVE PASTA
    LUCKY PASTA
    PASTA DELLA FESTA
    PATRIOTIC PASTA
    STAR OF DAVID PASTA

5287 Fun Foods
99 Murray Hill Pkwy # D
East Rutherford, NJ 07073-2143   201-896-4949
        Fax: 201-896-4911   800-507-2782
                funfoodspasta@yahoo.com
Custom-shaped pastas
    President: Sharon Nicklas
Estimated Sales: $5-10 Million
Number Employees: 5-9
Type of Packaging: Private Label
Brands:
    PASTA DELLA FESTA

5288 Functional Foods
15765 Sturgeon Street
Roseville, MI 48066-1816   586-445-0550
        Fax: 586-445-1118   877-372-0550
                www.smartchocolate.com
Chocolate
    President/CEO: Thomas Morley, Jr
Brands:
    SMARTCHOCOLATES

5289 Functional Foods
470 Route 9
Englishtown, NJ 07726-8239   732-972-2232
        Fax: 732-536-9179   800-442-9524
                yshah5462@aol.com
                www.functionalfoodscorp.com
Manufacturer of microcrystalline and hydroxypropyl
cellulose, cellulose and psyllium fiber, gum arabic
and guar, cellulose and vegetable gums
    Marketing Manager: Alpa Nanavati
    Manufacturing Manager: Yogi Shah
Estimated Sales: $2.5-5 Million
Number Employees: 20-49

5290 Functional Products LLC
1179 Atlantic Blvd
Atlantic Beach, FL 32233-2516   904-249-8074
        Fax: 904-249-8467   800-628-5908
                sales@functional-products.com
                www.functional-products.com
Vitamins and food supplements.
    Owner: Dirk Mueggenburg
    CEO: Dirk Mueggenburg
    Sales: Laura Lambs
Estimated Sales: $ 1 - 3 Million
Number Employees: 1-4

5291 Fungi Perfecti
P.O.Box 7634
Olympia, WA 98507-7634   360-426-9292
        Fax: 360-426-9377   800-780-9126
                www.fungi.com
Gourmet and medicinal mushrooms.
    Owner: Paul Stamets
Estimated Sales: $ 3 - 5 Million
Number Employees: 20-49

5292 FungusAmongUs Inc
PO Box352
Snohomish, WA 98291   360-568-3403
    Fax: 360-563-2663   orders@fungusamongus.com
                www.fungusamongus.com
gourmet organic mushrooms

5293 Funkandy Corporation
1180 Olympic Drive
Suite 206
Corona, CA 92881-3393   909-371-6282
        Fax: 909-371-6291   866-386-2263
Candy
Brands:
    ALIEN EX-TREME
    TONGUE ROLLER LOLLIPOP
    TUBE-A-GOO

5294 FunkyChunky
7452 W 78th Street
Edina, MN 55439   952-938-6663
        Fax: 952-938-2294   888-473-8659
                info@funkychunkyinc.com
                www.funkychunkyinc.com
chocolate covered pretzels, chocolate popcorn, caramel corn and bars

5295 FunniBonz
3 Lake View Court
West Windsor, NJ 08850
        Fax: 609-845-1806   877-300-2669
                info@funnibonz.com   www.funnibonz.com
bbq sauces, rubs and marinades
    President/Owner: Jim Barbour
    CEO: Ryan Marrone

5296 (HQ)Furmano Foods
P.O.Box 500
Northumberland, PA 17857-0500   570-473-3516
        Fax: 570-473-7367   877-877-6032
                www.furmanos.com
Manufacturer of canned pizza sauce and tomatoes
including pureed, crushed, stewed and whole peeled
    President/CEO: Dave Geise
    VP Sales/Marketing: Robert Vanderhook

Estimated Sales: $ 20 - 50 Million
Number Employees: 500-999
Type of Packaging: Consumer, Food Service
Brands:
    FURMANO'S

5297 Furst-McNess Company/Terrapin Ridge
120 E Clark St # 130
Freeport, IL 61032-3300   815-235-6151
        Fax: 815-232-9724   800-999-4052
                www.furstmcness.com
Manufacturer of spices, extracts, puddings and mustard; exporter of vanilla tablets
    President: Martha Furst
    CEO: Frank Furst
    CFO: Terry Gogel
    Marketing Director: Susan Furst
    Public Relations: Kelly Monigold
Estimated Sales: $100-500 Million
Number Employees: 50-99
Type of Packaging: Private Label

5298 Furukawa Potato Chip Factory
P.O.Box 1129
Captain Cook, HI 96704-1129   808-323-3785
                Fax: 808- 32-3 37
Potato chips and snack foods
    Owner: Jerome Furukawa
Estimated Sales: $ 1 - 3 Million
Number Employees: 1-4

5299 Fusion Gourmet
16927 S Main St # B
Gardena, CA 90248-3139   310-532-8938
        Fax: 310-532-8991   abc-usa@world.att.net
                www.fusiongourmet.com
Specializes in authentically prepared, fines quality
and all-natural cooking sauces, marinades, and dips
from Southeast Asia
    President: Annie Chu
Estimated Sales: $ 3 - 5 Million
Number Employees: 1-4
Brands:
    ABC
    BALI'S BEST
    FATAL ATTRACTION
    PEARL EMPRESS
    SWEET SEDUCTION

5300 Future Bakery & Cafe
106 N Queen Street
Etobicoke, ON M8Z 2E2
Canada   416-231-1491
        Fax: 416-231-1879   www.futurebakery.com
Manufacturer of specialty and artisan breads, European pastries and cheesecakes
    President: Borys Wrzesnewskyj
Number Employees: 50-99
Sq. footage: 22000
Type of Packaging: Consumer
Brands:
    FUTURE BAKERY

5301 FutureCeuticals
300 West 6th Street
Momence, IL 60954
        Fax: 815-472-3850   888-472-3545
                Sales@futureceuticals.com
www.jopling.co.uk/ingredients/frame_future.html
Primary processor of nutraceuticals, functional foods
and cosmetic ingredients. Processing capabilities include: fermentation, refining, IQF freezing, freeze
drying, drum drying, air drying, spray drying, vacuum evaporationextraction, synthesis, milling,
grinding and blending.
    President: Jeff Van Drunen
    Director New Business Development Europe:
    Zheko Kounev Ph.D
    Vice President Business Development: John
    Hunter
    Vice President Research & Development:
    Zbigniew Pietrzkowski Ph.D
    Director Quality Control: Boris Nemzer Ph.D
    FutureCeuticals Technical Sales: Kit Kats
Sq. footage: 6000000

5302 Futurebiotics
70 Commerce Dr
Hauppauge, NY 11788-3936   631-273-6300
        Fax: 631-273-1165   800-645-1721
info@futurebiotics.com   www.futurebiotics.com

Manufacturer and distributor of natural health food supplements and vitamins
Owner: Saisul Kibria
Marketing Director: Ed Keenan
Public Relations: Ed Keenan
Director Operations: Wendy L Kauffman
Estimated Sales: $10-20 Million
Number Employees: 5-9
Type of Packaging: Consumer, Private Label, Bulk
Brands:
VITAL K

5303 Fuzz East Coast
140 Sylvan Avenue
3rd Floor
Englewood Cliffs, NJ 07632   866-438-3893
Fax: 201-461-1091   info@fuzebev.com
www.drinkfuze.com/
Manufacturers a variety of Fuze Health Infusions drinks including green tea and fruit juice flavored beverages.
Co-Founder: Lance Collins
Co-Founder: Joe Rosamilia
Co-Founder: Bruce Lewin
Co-Founder: Paula Grant
Type of Packaging: Food Service

5304 Fuzzy's Wholesale Bar-B-Q
408 W End Blvd
Madison, NC 27025-1646   336-548-2283
Fax: 336-548-2272
Frozen pork barbecue, brunswick stew, gourmet chicken pot pies, home replacement meals.
President: Fred Nelson
Estimated Sales: Less than $500,000
Number Employees: 1-4

5305 G & F Manufacturing Company
5555 W 109th St
Oak Lawn, IL 60453-5070   708-424-4170
Fax: 708-424-4922   866-865-1591
www.gandf.com
Designing and manufacturing high quality chemical resistant, durable and rugged Stainless steel products such as steel tanks, filling machines, piston filters, cappers, and labeling.
President: Ron Bais
Purchasing Manager: Ron Bais
Number Employees: 10-19
Sq. footage: 15000
Type of Packaging: Food Service

5306 G & R Food Sales
5736 W Loma Lane
Glendale, AZ 85302-5938   602-939-7337
Fax: 602-939-7337
Partner: Juanita Linder
Partner: Fridolin Linder

5307 G A Food Service
12200 32nd Ct N
St Petersburg, FL 33716-1847   727-573-2211
Fax: 727-572-8209   frankc@gafoods.net
www.sunmeadow.net
Manufacturer of pre-plated frozen meals including frozen fruit cups, shelf stable emergency day meal packs, dry milk packs and school lunch sandwiches designed for elderly nutrition and health care markets
President: James Lobianco
VP: Kenneth Lo Bianco
Estimated Sales: G
Number Employees: 100-249
Sq. footage: 50000
Parent Co: G.A. Food Service of Pinellas County
Type of Packaging: Consumer, Food Service, Private Label
Brands:
SUN MEADOW

5308 G B Ratto & Company International
821 Washington St
Oakland, CA 94607-4089   510-832-6503
Fax: 510-836-2250   800-325-3483
Full line of imported Italian foods and ingredients. Olives, oils and spices - a 'specialty food emporium'.
Owner: Elena Voiron
General Manager: Susan Nelson
Estimated Sales: $2.5-5 Million
Number Employees: 5-9

5309 G Cefalu & Brothers
P.O.Box 946
Jessup, MD 20794-0946   410-799-3414
Fax: 410-799-8694   jessup29@aol.com
Processor/repacker of tomatoes and all types of produce.
Owner: John Cefalu
Estimated Sales: $10-20 Million
Number Employees: 20-49
Type of Packaging: Consumer, Food Service, Bulk

5310 G Di Lullo & Sons
P.O.Box 126
Westville, NJ 08093-0126   856-456-3700
Fax: 856-456-7161
Manufacturer and exporter of canned foods including chili con carne, beef cubes, meatballs in sauce, meatballs, in gravy and also, sauces including spaghetti, Creole, parmigiana, etc.; importer of canned and frozen meat
President: Ugo Di Lullo
Estimated Sales: $1-3 Million
Number Employees: 5-9
Number of Products: 25
Sq. footage: 15000
Type of Packaging: Food Service

5311 (HQ)G E Barbour
165 Stewart Avenue
Sussex, NB E4E 3H1
Canada   506-432-2300
Fax: 506-432-2323 www.barbours.ca
Processor of food colors and mustards; importer of teas, coffees, spices, cheeses, food colors, extracts, syrups and mustards
President: Grant Brenan
VP: Sylvia MacVey
Marketing: Don Macleod
Number Employees: 100-249
Type of Packaging: Consumer, Food Service, Private Label
Other Locations:
G.E. Barbour
St. John NB
Brands:
BARBOURS
KING COLE

5312 G E Hawthorn Meat Company
164 Guy Hawthorn Ln
Hot Springs, AR 71901-9149   501-623-8111
Manufacturer of fresh pork and beef; also, slaughtering services available
President: Richard Hawthorn
Estimated Sales: $1-3 Million
Number Employees: 1-4
Sq. footage: 250000
Type of Packaging: Consumer

5313 G H Bent Company
7 Pleasant St
Milton, MA 02186-4514   617-698-5945
Fax: 617-696-7730   info@bentscookiefactory.com
www.bentscookiefactory.com
Processor of cookies, brownies and crackers.
Owner: Eugene Pierotti
CEO: Eugene Pierotti
VP: James Pierotti
Sales: Eugene Pierotti, Sr
Estimated Sales: $500,000-$1 Million
Number Employees: 10-19
Sq. footage: 20000
Type of Packaging: Food Service
Brands:
BENT'S

5314 G H Ford Tea Company
PO Box 947
Wappingers Falls, NY 12590-0947   845-298-8900
Fax: 845-296-0375   info@ghfordtea.com
www.ghfordtea.com
Processor, importer and exporter of whole leaf teas in tea ball packaging. Offers 30 to 50 blends and flavors utilizing original blending formulas and all natural flavoring.
President: Keith Capolino
Estimated Sales: $2.5-5 Million
Number Employees: 5-9
Type of Packaging: Consumer, Food Service, Private Label, Bulk
Brands:
G.H. Ford

5315 G H Leidenheimer BakingCompany
1501 Simon Bolivar Ave
New Orleans, LA 70113-2399   504-525-1575
Fax: 504-525-1596   800-259-9099
info@leidenheimer.com   www.leidenheimer.com
Have a full line of breads that meet every foodservice needs. Established since 1896
President: Robert J Whann Iv III
Estimated Sales: $10-20 Million
Number Employees: 50-99

5316 G J Shortall
107 Clyde Avenue
Mount Pearl, NL A1N 4R9
Canada   709-747-0655
Fax: 709-747-2223
Processor, exporter and wholesaler/distributor of dried and frozen squid, capelin, herring and mackerel
President: Steve Shortall
Number Employees: 10-19
Type of Packaging: Bulk

5317 G L Mezzetta
105 Mezzetta Ct
American Canyon, CA 94503-9604   707-648-1050
Fax: 707-648-1060   consumerinfo@mezzetta.com
www.mezzetta.com
Leading manufacturer of imported and domestic peppers, roasted peppers, fancy stuffed olives, green and specialty olives, imported olive oil and capers, pickled vegetables, cocktail and appetizer specialties, assorted gourmetspecialties.
President: Jeff Mezzetta
Senior VP: Thomas Rickard Jr
Midwest Sales Manager: Tony Guidio
Sales Manager: Paul Kastl
Food Technologist: Shea Rosen
Estimated Sales: $20-50 Million
Number Employees: 100-249
Type of Packaging: Consumer, Food Service, Private Label
Brands:
KONA COAST
MEZZETTA
TULELAKE

5318 G M Allen & Son
P.O.Box 454
Blue Hill, ME 04614-0454   207-469-7060
Fax: 207-469-7060
www.gmallenwildblueberries.com
Processing of frozen wild blueberries.
President/CEO: Wayne Allen
VP Operations: Kermit Allen
Estimated Sales: $50-100 Million
Number Employees: 50-99

5319 G S Dunn & Company
80 Park Street N
Hamilton, ON L8R 2M9
Canada   905-522-0833
Fax: 905-522-4423   contact us@gsdunn.com
www.gsdunn.com
Global supplier of dry mustard products and currently exports to over 45 countries on six continents. Complete line of mustard flours, ground mustards, brans and deactived mustard makes us the premier supplier of these products to theworld.
President: Ron Kramer
Number Employees: 20-49
Sq. footage: 35000
Type of Packaging: Food Service, Private Label, Bulk

5320 G S Robins & Company
126 Chouteau Ave
St Louis, MO 63102-2490   314-621-5155
Fax: 314-621-1216   800-777-5155
info@gsrobins.com   www.gsrobins.com
Supplier for hundreds of specialty chemical products and services that meet your chemical needs.
President: G Stephen Robins
Sales: Doug Kutz
Estimated Sales: $50-100 Million
Number Employees: 20-49

5321 G Scaccianoce & Company
1165 Burnett Pl
Bronx, NY 10474-5716   718-991-4462
Fax: 718-991-0154

Processor and exporter of confectionery items including Jordan almonds, French mints and licorice
President: Donald Beck
Estimated Sales:$2.5-5 Million
Number Employees: 5-9
Type of Packaging: Consumer, Food Service, Private Label, Bulk

5322 G&G Foods
322 Bellevue Ave
Santa Rosa, CA 95407-7711   707-542-6300
        Fax: 707-542-6370 www.gandgfoods.com
Strive to produce restaurant quality, convenient, entertaining and snacking products which include specialty and fat-free cheese spreads, gourmet cheese, hummus and dips
President: Rich Goldberg
Operations: David Blair
Estimated Sales:$100-500 Million
Number Employees: 100-249
Type of Packaging: Consumer
Brands:
    GOLDY'S
    LA TORTA
    MEZA

5323 G&G Marketing
315 Dunes Boulevard
Apt 1003
Naples, FL 34110-6432   239-593-4564
    Fax: 239-593-0937 gary@athenamelons.com
            www.athenamelons.com
Growers, exporters, and distributors of melons, and other fresh fruits and vegetables

5324 G&G Sheep Farm
11406 Boston Road
Boston, KY 40107-8602   502-833-4863
Processor of lamb
*Estimated Sales:*Under $300,000
Number Employees: 1-4
Type of Packaging: Consumer

5325 G&J Land and Marine Food Distributors
506 Front St
Morgan City, LA 70380-3708   985-385-2620
        Fax: 985-385-3614   800-256-9187
                www.gjfood.com
Full service food distributor dedicated to providing an extensive grocery and janitorial product line to the offshore oil and gas, commercial shipping and restaurant industry.
President: Mike Lind
VP/Sales: Mike Lind
Operations: Adam Mayon
Purchasing: Jarrod Leonard
Estimated Sales:$ 10 - 20 Million
Number Employees: 100-249

5326 G&J Pepsi-Cola Bottlers
P.O.Box 360540
Columbus, OH 43236-0540   614-253-8771
        Fax: 614-253-3306 www.pbg.com
Processor of regular, diet and caffeine-free soft drinks
President: Thomas R Gross
Senior VP: Thomas Gross, Jr
Sales/Marketing: Gregory Ramsey
Estimated Sales:$50-100 Million
Number Employees: 250-499
Parent Co: PepsiCo Bottling Group
Type of Packaging: Consumer, Food Service

5327 G&W Packing Company
824 W Exchange Ave
Chicago, IL 60609-2507   773-847-5400
        Fax: 773-847-3364 tschicagosteak@aol.com
                www.chicagosteaks.com
Meat packaging
Owner: Tom Campbell
Estimated Sales:$ 10 - 20 Million
Number Employees: 20-49

5328 G.E.F. Gourmet Foods Inc
35584 County Road 8
Mountain Lake, MN 56159-2106   507-427-2631
        Fax: 507-427-6762   800-692-6762
            Comments@GLADCORN.com OR
greatsnack@frontiernet.net   www.gladcorn.com/
Manufactures Glad Corn A-maizing Corn Snacks.
Founder/Co-Owner: Stan Friesen
Founder/Co-Owner: Gladys Friesen
Type of Packaging: Food Service

5329 G.L. Mezzetta Inc
105 Mezzetta Court
American Canyon, CA 94503   707-648-1050
        Fax: 707-648-1060 info@mezzetta.com
                www.mezzetta.com
glass-packed peppers and olives
President/Owner: Ronald Mezzetta
Estimated Sales:$12.3 Million
Number Employees: 80

5330 GAF Seelig
5905 52nd Ave
Flushing, NY 11377-7480   718-899-5000
        Fax: 718-803-1198 sales@gafseelig.com
                www.gafseelig.com
Distributor of fine baked foods to restaurants, hotels, hospitals and cooperative businesses.
President: Rodney Seelig
Estimated Sales:$5-10 Million
Number Employees: 100-249
Type of Packaging: Private Label

5331 GCI Nutrients (USA)
1163 Chess Dr # H
Foster City, CA 94404-1119   650-697-4700
        Fax: 650-697-6300 walter@gcinutrients.com
                www.gcinutrients.com
Processor, importer and exporter of vitamins and supplements including beta carotene, essential fatty acids, herbal products, botanical extracts, food supplements, bulk ingredients, premium raw materials for nutritional and beverageindustries with over 33 years of experience
President: Richard Merriam
CFO: Jennifer Evich
R&D: William Forgach
Marketing Director: Walter Rick
Production: Mike Cronin
Plant Manager: Mike Crowin
Purchasing Manager: Derek Cronin
Estimated Sales:$10 Million
Number Employees: 10-19
Number of Brands: 10
Number of Products: 300
Sq. footage: 10000
Brands:
    ABG
    CM - 22
    ELEUTHEROGEN
    GAMMA - E
    GE - OXY 132
    LIPO - SERINE
    OLIVIR
    OXI - GAMMA
    OXI - GRAPE

5332 GEM Berry Products
804 Airport Way
Sandpoint, ID 83864-8200   208-263-7503
        Fax: 208-263-3247   800-426-0498
                gamberry92@hotmail.com
Processor and exporter of spreads, jams and syrups including raspberry and huckleberry; berry filled chocolates, berry barbecue sauce and many other berry products.
President: Jack O' Brien
CFO: Betty Menser
Marketing: Harry Menser
Production: Elizabeth O Brien
Estimated Sales:$50,000-100,000
Number Employees: 1-4
Sq. footage: 2500
Type of Packaging: Food Service, Bulk
Brands:
    GEM BERRY
    LITEHOUSE
    TASTE THE BEAUTY OF NORTH IDAHO
    TASTE THE BEAUTY OF THE ROCKIES

5333 GEM Cultures
30301 Sherwood Rd
Fort Bragg, CA 95437-6100   707-964-2922
                www.gemcultures.com
Manufacturer and exporter of shelf stable starters for cultured vegetarian foods including tempeh, miso, shoyu, natto, sourdough, nonyogurt and dairy cultures; importer of koji and natto starters
Owner: Betty Stechmeyer
Public Relations: Gordon McBride
Estimated Sales:$35,000
Number Employees: 1-4
Sq. footage: 1000
Type of Packaging: Private Label

Brands:
    GEM

5334 GFA Brands
115 W Century Rd # 260
Paramus, NJ 07652-1431   201-568-9300
        Fax: 201-568-6374 pdray@gfabrands.com
                www.smartbalance.com
Manufacturer of cheese, margarine, mayonnaise, cereals, salad dressings, pickles and oils
President: Robert Harris
CEO: Steve Hughes
Estimated Sales:$1-3 Million
Number Employees: 10-19
Type of Packaging: Consumer
Brands:
    GFA
    H-O
    MRS FANINGS
    SPIN BLEND

5335 GFF
145 Willow Avenue
City of Industry, CA 91746-2047   323-232-6255
Fax: 323-726-0934 wjperry@girardsdressing.com
                www.girardsdressing.com
Salad dressings, marinades, sauces and mayonnaise
President/Co-CEO: William Perry
Chairman/Co-CEO: Jack Tucey
CFO: Tim Schoenbaum
Research & Development: Jeff Stalley
Marketing: Dottie Dinkheller
Sales Manager: Steve Shapiro
Corporate Chef/Trade Show Market Coordin: Malcolm Hackett
Plant Manager: Dennis Tyler
Estimated Sales:$22.5 Million
Number Employees: 50-99
Number of Brands: 3
Number of Products: 175
Sq. footage: 20000
Type of Packaging: Food Service, Private Label, Bulk
Brands:
    CHEFS IDEAL
    GIRARDS
    STATE FARM

5336 (HQ)GFI Premium Foods
2815 Blaisdell Ave
Minneapolis, MN 55408-2312   612-872-6262
        Fax: 612-870-4955   800-669-8996
            customerservice@gfiamerica.com
                www.gfipremiumfoods.com
Processors beef, poultry, and pork for its food service and institutional customers
President: Robert Goldberger
VP Sales: Joe Goldberger
Estimated Sales:$100+ Million
Number Employees: 250-499
Type of Packaging: Consumer, Food Service, Private Label, Bulk
Other Locations:
    GFI Premium Foods
    Rapid City SD
Brands:
    SMART MEAT STEAKS & HAMBURGERS
    THE NATURAL

5337 GINCO International
Ste C
725 Cochran St
Simi Valley, CA 93065-1974   805-520-2592
                        800-284-2598
            sales@gincointernational.com
                www.ginsengcompany.com
The choice of nine different types of ginseng. We hand select and pure-grind our products.
President: Gary Raskin
Vice President: Linda Raskin
Director Marketing: Rick Seibert
Estimated Sales:$ 1 - 3 Million
Number Employees: 10-19

5338 GKI Foods
7926 Lochlin Dr
Brighton, MI 48116-8329   248-486-0055
        Fax: 248-486-9135 chuck@gkifoods.com
                www.gkifoods.com

Manufacturer of milk chocolate, sugar free chocolate, yogurt and cards products, panned and enrobed, bulk or packaged. Also produces custom granola (all natural, highly nutritional, low in fat and fat free), trail mixes, etc. Customformulation. Aid certified, GMP and HACCP accreditation.
President: Chuck Wilts
Number Employees: 20-49
Type of Packaging: Consumer, Private Label, Bulk

5339 GLCC Company
39149 W Red Arrow Hwy
Paw Paw, MI 49079-9389   269-657-3167
Fax: 269-657-4552   glcc@triton.net
www.glccflavors.com
Processor of flavors, juice concentrates and blends; custom repackaging available
President: Johnathan Davis
Estimated Sales: $ 10 - 20 Million
Number Employees: 20-49
Sq. footage: 100000
Type of Packaging: Bulk

5340 GLG Life Tech Corporation
Suite 519 World Trade Center
999 Canada Place
Vancouver, BC V6C 3E1
Canada   604-641-1368
Fax: 604-844-2830   info@glglifetech.com
www.glglifetech.com
Supplier of Stevia, which is a natural, zero calorie sweetening additive used in the food and beverage industries.
President/Vice Chairman: Brian Palmieri
Chairman & CEO: Dr. Luke Zhang
Vice President, Marketing: James Kempland
Vice President, Sales: Jack Tokarczyk

5341 GMB Specialty Foods
P.O.Box 962
San Juan Cpstrno, CA 92693-0962   949-240-3053
Fax: 949-240-3086   800-809-8098
info@gmbfoods.com
Quaility foods for the gourmet industry.
President: Greg Bloom
Marketing Director: Helen Bloom
Estimated Sales: $1 Million
Number Employees: 5-9
Type of Packaging: Private Label
Brands:
BASITAN'S
EDELWEISS DRESSINGS
NORMAN BISHOP
SALLIE'S
SCOTTSDALE MUSTARD CO

5342 GMF Corporation
54 Commercial Street
Gloucester, MA 01930-5025   978-283-0479
Fax: 978-283-8738

5343 GMI Products
2525 Davie Road
Suite 330
Plantation, FL 33317-7403   305-474-9608
Fax: 954-474-0989   800-999-9373
Gelatin and flavors

5344 (HQ)GMI Products/Originates
1301 Sawgrass Corporate Pkwy
Sunrise, FL 33323-2813   954-233-3300
Fax: 954-233-3301   800-999-9373
info@gmi-originates.com
www.natures-products.com
Manufacturer and supplier of raw materials specializing in gelatin, flavors, active pharmaceuticals, botanicals and pharmaceutical additives. Providing import/export services, warehousing and freight forwarding to and from the UnitedStates and worldwide
President: Jose Minski
Number Employees: 100-249
Type of Packaging: Private Label, Bulk
Brands:
CURT GEORGI FLAVORS & FRAGRANCES
GMI GELATIN
HEALTH ASSURE

5345 GMP Laboratories
2931 E La Jolla St
Anaheim, CA 92806-1306   714-630-2467
Fax: 714-237-1374   info@gmplabs.com
www.gmplabs.com

Leading contract manufacturer of high quality vitamins and nutritional supplements. Our laboratories can assist you in formulating, manufacturing, packaging your products while always maintaining absolute confidentiality.
President/CEO: Mo Ishaq
Estimated Sales: $ 20 - 50 Million
Number Employees: 50-99

5346 GNS Food
2109 E Division St
Arlington, TX 76011-7817   817-795-4671
Fax: 817-795-4673   sales@gnsfoods.com
www.gnsfoods.com
Processor of raw and roasted nuts, packaged pecan candy and dried fruits including raisins, mango, pineapple, apple, banana chips, apricots and mixed; wholesaler/distributor of specialty foods; serving the food service market
President: Kim Peacock
Estimated Sales: $5-10 Million
Number Employees: 20-49
Sq. footage: 12596
Type of Packaging: Consumer, Food Service, Private Label, Bulk
Brands:
GROVE ON THE GO
GROVE, JR
PECAN STREET SWEETS
THE GROVE

5347 GNS Spices
PO Box 90
Walnut, CA 91788-0090   909-594-9505
Fax: 909-594-5455   800-870-6657
Processor and exporter of red savina and orange habanero peppers including pods, flakes and ground
President: Frank Garcia Jr
VP: Mary Garcia
Operations Manager: Frank Garcia Sr
Estimated Sales: $300,000-500,000
Number Employees: 1-4
Type of Packaging: Bulk

5348 GNT USA
203 Redwood Shores Pkwy
Redwood City, CA 94065-1198   650-596-0900
Fax: 650-596-0911   info@gntusa.com
www.gntusa.com
Manufacturer of colouring foodstuffs, natural colours and phytochemicals.
Managing Director: Paul Collins
Managing Director: Stefan Hake
Managing Director: Wolfgang Quehl
Managing Director: Peter Van De Riet
Senior Food Scientist: Rachael Rothman

5349 GPI USA LLC.
931 Hill Street
Athens, GA 30606   706-850-7826
Fax: 706-850-7827   www.gumproducts.com
www.gumproducts.com
Specialize in carageenan used for stabilization and as an additive for both dairy products and in the red meat and poultry industries.

5350 GPR Company
400 Old Reading Pike # C
Stowe, PA 19464-3781   610-326-4777
Fax: 610-327-1171   gprco123@aol.com
Manufacturer and exporter of chocolate chips, cocoa powder, chocolate liqueur, powdered beverage base mixes and milked based and water based, hot and cold and cocoa drinks, powdered iced tea, powdered orange beverage drink, Belgianpancake and waffle mixes; and sweetened coconut and green tea and black cion, and flavored tea; importer of chocolate, coconut, coffee, dry milk solids, chips, snack mixes, crackers, oatmeal, grits, liqueurs and covertures; Packaged in cans, jars andbags
President: Greg Roberts
VP: Albert Roberts
Quality Control: Ken Frazee
VP Sales/Marketing: Wayne Karghey
Purchasing Director: Albert Roberts
Estimated Sales: $10-20 Million
Number Employees: 20-49
Sq. footage: 95000
Type of Packaging: Private Label, Bulk
Brands:
Penny Roberts

5351 GS-AFI
238 Saint Nicholas Avenue
South Plainfield, NJ 07080-1810   908-753-9100
Fax: 908-753-9635   800-345-4342
dhiller@gsafi.com   www.gsafi.com
Specialty premixes, spices and seasonings
President: David Hiller
Contact: Dagmar Hiller
Number Employees: 250-499

5352 GSB & Associates
3115 Cobb International Blvd
Kennesaw, GA 30152-4354   770-424-1886
Fax: 770-422-1732   877-472-2776
sales@gsbflavorcreators.com
www.gsbflavorcreators.com
To provide the flavor industry with new innovative flavor creations that never been tasted before. Our products include natural, natural and artifical, artificial, water or oil soluble, liquid and spray dried flavors. Flavors areKosher Certified. We also offer a line of Certified Organic Flavors.
President: Eugene Buday
Estimated Sales: $5-10 Million
Number Employees: 10-19
Type of Packaging: Bulk

5353 GTC Nutrition Company
523 Park Point Dr # 300
Golden, CO 80401-9364   303-216-2489
Fax: 303-216-2477   800-522-4682
generalinfo@gtcnutrition.com
www.gtcnutrition.com
A leading provider of high-quality, science based nutritional ingredients for today's healthy lifestyles. Proudly takes a multi-disciplinary approach to it's business by offering customer support that reaches beyond standard needs.Areas of expertise include scientific and technical counsel, marketing and brand development, applications innovation, logistics and regulatory support and customer service.
CEO: Patrick Smith
Marketing: Trina O'Brien
Estimated Sales: $5-10 Million
Number Employees: 20-49

5354 GWB Foods Corporation
PO Box 228
Brooklyn, NY 11204-0228   718-686-9600
Fax: 718-686-6161 www.gwbfoods.com
Processor, exporter, importer and wholesaler/distributor of specialty and frozen foods including cookies, candies, crackers, rice cakes, vegetables in jars, bottled water, pickles and pimiento peppers
President: Joshua Weinstein
Export Manager: S Williams
Sales Manager: Jack Yhumns
Estimated Sales: $2.5-5 Million
Number Employees: 10-19
Sq. footage: 40000
Parent Co: President Baking Company
Type of Packaging: Consumer, Food Service, Private Label, Bulk
Brands:
Presidor

5355 GYMA IQF Herbs, Garlic & Mushrooms & Vegetables
PO Box 113
Stroudsburg, PA 18360-0113   570-422-6311
Fax: 570-422-6301   888-496-2872
gjgyma@pnpa.net
Processor, importer and exporter of IQF herbs, garlic, mushrooms, leeks, asparagus, string beans, etc
VP Industrial Sales: Pierre Hellivan
Sales Manager Technical: Ghislaine Joly
Estimated Sales: $5-10 Million
Number Employees: 10-19
Parent Co: GYMA Group
Type of Packaging: Bulk
Brands:
Gyma

5356 Gabilas Knishes
120 S 8th Street
Brooklyn, NY 11211-6099   718-387-0750
Fax: 718-384-8621
Processor and exporter of frozen knishes
President: Gloria Gabay
Partner: Sophie Levy
Controller: Linda Ghignone
Estimated Sales: $1-2.5 Million
Number Employees: 20-49
Type of Packaging: Consumer

Brands:
KING OF POTATO PIES

5357 Gabriele Macaroni Company
P.O.Box 90564
City of Industry, CA 91715-0564   626-964-2324
Fax: 626-912-1058   sales@gabrielepasta.com
www.gabrielepasta.com
Manufactures macaroni, egg noodles, whole wheat
pasta, flavored and organic pasta.
President/CEO: Victor Fusano
Estimated Sales: $5-10 Million
Number Employees: 10-19
Sq. footage: 20000
Type of Packaging: Consumer, Private Label, Bulk
Brands:
GABRIELE
HEALTH BEST
HEALTH VALLEY
PURE & SIMPLE
TRADER JOE'S

5358 Gad Cheese Company
2401 County Road C
Medford, WI 54451-9009   715-748-4273
Fax: 715-748-4299
Processor of cheddar cheese, cheese curds, monterey
jack, specialty cheese and more than 30 varieties.
Retail outlet and an observation window.
President: Bruce Albrecht
VP: Diane Albrecht
Estimated Sales: $500,000-$1 Million
Number Employees: 10-19
Type of Packaging: Consumer, Food Service, Private Label, Bulk

5359 Gadot Biochemical Industries
1440 Hicks Road
Suite B
Rolling Meadows, IL 60008-1234   847-259-1809
Fax: 847-259-6984   888-424-1424
gadot@jstewartandcompany.com
www.gadotbio.com
Gadot is a producer of citric acid, sodium citrate, potassium citrates, fumaric acid, calcium citrate, magnesium citrate, zinc citrate, tri calcium phosphate,
and mono potassium phosphate
President: Jim Stewart
Estimated Sales: $5-10 Million
Number Employees: 5-9
Parent Co: Haifa Bay
Type of Packaging: Bulk

5360 Gadoua Bakery
150 Industrial Boulevard
Napierville, QC J0J 1L0
Canada   450-245-3326
Fax: 450-245-7609
Processor and exporter of bread and buns
President/CEO: Benoit Gregoire
Estimated Sales: $40-60 Million
Number Employees: 550
Sq. footage: 150000
Type of Packaging: Food Service
Brands:
GADOUA

5361 Gadsden Coffee/Caffe
P.O.Box 460
Arivaca, AZ 85601-0460   520-398-3251
Fax: 520-398-2001   888-514-5282
roaster@gadsdencoffee.com
www.gadsdencoffee.com
Specialty coffees
President: Tom Shook
Estimated Sales: $2.5-5 Million
Number Employees: 10-19

5362 Gai's Northwest Bakeries
P.O.Box 24327
Seattle, WA 98124-0327   206-322-0931
Fax: 206-726-7533
Bread rolls, buns
Manager: Barry Ware
Estimated Sales: Under $500,000
Number Employees: 1,000-4,999

5363 Gaia Herbs
101 Gaia Herbs Rd
Brevard, NC 28712-8930   828-884-4242
Fax: 828-883-5960   800-831-7780
www.gaiaherbs.com

Organic processor of herbal extracts. Plant specific
methods for extraction are used to assure that we obtain the highest yields from the plant with disturbing
the plant's natural chemical profile. We are one of
the few herbal extractcompanies in the world that
controls production from seed selection and plant
horticulture, through every phase of extraction, concentration and testing, to the product that you can
rely upon to deliver theraputic results.
President: Richard Scalzo
CFO: Jon Green
VP: Eston Brandberg
Estimated Sales: $10-20 Million
Number Employees: 100-249
Sq. footage: 16000
Brands:
ECHINACEA
ECHINACEA/GOLDENSEAL SUPREME
GINSENG EXTRACT

5364 Gainey Vineyard
3950 E Highway 246
Santa Ynez, CA 93460   805-688-0558
Fax: 805-688-5864   www.gaineyvineyard.com
To create wines of uncompromising quality with optimum flavor and aromatic components that reflect
the unique characteristics of the vineyards from
which they come. Our varieties consist of Bordeaux
varieties, Pinot Nois, Chardonnayand Syrah.
President: Daniel Gainey
Estimated Sales: $5-10 Million
Number Employees: 10-19

5365 Gaiser's European StyleProvisions
2019 Morris Ave
Union, NJ 07083-6013   908-206-9822
Fax: 908-686-7131
Processor, exporter and wholesaler/distributor of
sausage, liverwurst and smoked ham
Owner: Efem Rablov
Estimated Sales: $500,000-$1 Million
Number Employees: 10-19
Brands:
GAISER'S

5366 Galante Vineyards
18181 Cachagua Rd
Carmel Valley, CA 93924   831-659-2649
Fax: 831-624-3200   800-425-2683
wine@galantevineyards.com
www.galantevineyards.com
Recognized as one of the premier Cabernet Sauvignon producers in Monterey county in all of California.
President: Jack Galante
Purchasing: Jack Galante
Estimated Sales: Less than $500,000
Number Employees: 1-4
Type of Packaging: Private Label
Brands:
BLACKJACK PASTURE CABERNET
GALANTE WINES
RANCHO GALANTE CABERNET
RED ROSE HILL CABERNET

5367 Galassos Baking Company
10820 San Sevaine Way
Mira Loma, CA 91752-1116   951-360-1211
Fax: 951-360-0427   webmaster@galassos.com
www.galassos.com
A complete line of Hearth Baked breads, buns, soft
rolls, and variety breads. Also specialize in
Par-baked breads and rolls.
President: John Galasso
VP: John Roundtree
Plant Manager: Armando Ramirez
Estimated Sales: $100+ Million
Number Employees: 100-249
Sq. footage: 110000
Type of Packaging: Consumer, Food Service, Private Label, Bulk
Brands:
GALASSO

5368 Galaxy Dairy Products, Incorporated
700 Lake St # E
Ramsey, NJ 07446-1246   201-818-2030
Fax: 201-818-1969   galxdairy@aol.com
Import and export dairy products.
President: Thomas Phiebig
VP: Carole Phiebig
Estimated Sales: $30 Million+
Number Employees: 5-9

Type of Packaging: Private Label

5369 Galaxy Desserts
1100 Marina Way S # D
Richmond, CA 94804-3727   510-439-3160
Fax: 415-439-3170   800-225-3523
indulgence@galaxydesserts.com
www.galaxydesserts.com
Worldwide leader in individual gourmet desserts
producing the finest individual mousse cakes, tarts
and cheesecakes.
President/CEO: Paul Levitan
Sales/Marketing: Dan Brooking
Estimated Sales: $20-50 Million
Number Employees: 100-249
Sq. footage: 20000
Type of Packaging: Consumer, Food Service
Brands:
GALAXY DESSERTS

5370 Galaxy Nutritional Foods
6280 Hazeltine National Dr
Orlando, FL 32822-5114   407-855-5500
Fax: 407-855-7485   800-441-9419
www.galaxyfoods.com
Leading producer of healthy diary products such as
soy based dairy, low-fat, and cholestral-free. Category leader in both supermarkets and health food
stores.
President: Angelo Morini
CEO: Michael Broll
CFO: Salvatore Furnari
CEO: Michael E Broll
Operations: Thomas Perno
Estimated Sales: $50-100 Million
Number Employees: 20-49
Brands:
FORMGG
GALAXY NUTRITIONAL FOODS
LITE BAKERY
NATURE'S ALTERNATIVE
SOYCO
SOYMAGE
VEGGIE
VEGGIE CAFE
VEGGIE LITE BAKERY
WHOLESOME VALLEY

5371 Galco Food Products
318 Orenda Road
Brampton, ON L6T 1G1
Canada   905-793-5757
Fax: 905-793-2513   888-793-5291
shawnkowalyshyn@olymel.com
Processor and exporter of fresh and frozen chicken
including whole and parts
Number Employees: 250-499
Parent Co: Galco Foods
Type of Packaging: Consumer, Food Service, Private Label, Bulk

5372 Galegher Farms
PO Box 242
Thompson, ND 58278-0242   701-847-2151
Fax: 701-599-2376
Grower of round white processing potatoes
President: John Galegher, Jr.
Estimated Sales: $2.5-5 Million
Number Employees: 5-9
Type of Packaging: Bulk

5373 Galena Canning Company
PO Box 265
Chicago, IL 60690-0265   773-645-9388
Fax: 773-477-5627   info@galenacanning.com
www.galenacanning.com
Specialties in salsas, pasta sauce, BBQ sauces, chili,
relishes, pickles, hot sauces, mustard, jams and jellies, fruit butter, syrups, toppings, flavored oils and
vinegar.
Owner: Ivo Puidak
Estimated Sales: $ 1 - 3 Million
Number Employees: 10-19

5374 Galena Cellars Winery
P.O.Box 207
Galena, IL 61036-0207   815-777-3330
Fax: 815-777-3335   800-397-9463
wine@galenacellars.com   www.galenacellars.com

Producers, bottles and cellars a variety of wines using grapes, juice and fruit from across the US. Classic dry wines such as Chardonay, Cabernot Sauvignon, White Zinfandel, semi-dry and semi-sweet wines, selection of fruit wines anddessert ports.

Owner/President: Scott Lawlor
VP: Karen Lawlor
Estimated Sales:$1.8 Million
Number Employees: 20-49
Number of Products: 32
Type of Packaging: Consumer, Bulk
Brands:
GALENA CELLARS

5375 Galilean Seafoods
P.O.Box 1140
Bristol, RI 02809-0903   401-253-3030
Fax: 401-253-9207   galileansf@aol.com
www.galileanseafoods.com
Largest and most respected hand shucked clam supplier in the country. Frozen and refrigerated clams, hard shell clams, scallops, conch, and mussels and a full line of hand shucked breaded clam items.
President: Mark Montopoli
Estimated Sales:$10-20 Million
Number Employees: 50-99
Brands:
GALILEAN
KING CONCH
PURE BRAND PRODUCTS

5376 Galileo Foods
2411 Baumann Ave
San Lorenzo, CA 94580-1801   510-276-1300
Fax: 510-278-2177 www.saralee.com
Manufacturer, importer and exporter of processed meats such as; salami, pepperoni, dried/cured sausages, Italian specialty meats, roast beef, pastrami and corned beef
Manager: Alfred Yu
Estimated Sales:$100-500 Million
Number Employees: 250-499
Type of Packaging: Consumer, Food Service, Bulk
Brands:
GALILEO

5377 Gallands Institutional Foodservice
P.O.Box 3007
Bakersfield, CA 93385-3007   661-631-5505
Fax: 661-631-5513
Distributors of a full service food line, exceptions produce and meat.
President: Joan Galland
CFO: Leonard Galland
Estimated Sales:$ 3 - 5 Million
Number Employees: 10-19

5378 Galleano Winery
4231 Wineville Ave
Mira Loma, CA 91752-1412   951-685-5376
Fax: 951-360-9180 info@galleanowinery.com
www.galleanowinery.com
Processor of wines and wine grapes
President: Donald Galleano
Estimated Sales:$5-10 Million
Number Employees: 100-249
Type of Packaging: Consumer, Private Label, Bulk
Brands:
GALLEANO
GREEN VALLEY

5379 (HQ)Galliker Dairy
P.O.Box 159
Johnstown, PA 15907-0159   814-266-8702
Fax: 814-266-4619 800-477-6455
info@gallikers.com www.gallikers.com
Processor and distributor of milk, ice cream, orange juice and iced tea.
Chairman: Louis Gilliker III
President: Charles Price
CEO: Mark Duray
Estimated Sales:$86,100,000
Number Employees: 250-499
Brands:
GALLIKER'S
POTOMAC FARMS
QUALITY CHEKD
SLIM 'N' TRIM

5380 Galloway Company
601 S Commercial St
Neenah, WI 54956-3392   920-722-7741
Fax: 920-722-1927 800-722-8903
info@gallowaycompany.com
www.gallowaycompany.com
Processor of sweetened condensed milk and candy and frozen dessert mixes. Also custom industrial ingredients and beverage bases
President: Doug Dietrich
CEO: Timothy Galloway
VP Sales/Marketing: Ted Galloway
Sales Manager: Pat Galloway
Estimated Sales:$20-50 Million
Number Employees: 20-49
Type of Packaging: Food Service, Private Label, Bulk
Brands:
GOLDEN CREST

5381 Galluccio Estate Vineyards
PO Box 1269
Cutchogue, NY 11935-0885   631-734-7089
Fax: 631-734-7114 info@gallucciowineries.com
www.gristinawines.com
Wines such as Chardonney, Mirlot and Cabernet Sauvignon
Owner: Vince Galluccio
Estimated Sales:$2.5-5 Million
Number Employees: 10-19

5382 Gallup Sales Company
530 E Highway 66
Gallup, NM 87301-6098   505-863-5241
Fax: 505-863-4219
Distributors of beer and wine.
President: Reed Ferrari
Estimated Sales:$1-2.5 Million
Number Employees: 10-19

5383 Gama Products
11725 NW 100th Rd # 3
Medley, FL 33178-1013   305-883-1200
Fax: 305-883-0741 info@gamaproducts.com
www.gamaproducts.com
Processor, importer and exporter of oils including corn, soy, canola, vegetable, rice bran and cottonseed.
President: Alberto Abrante
Estimated Sales:$20-50 Million
Number Employees: 20-49
Parent Co: ARA Group
Type of Packaging: Private Label
Brands:
BEKAL
REAL

5384 Gamay Flavors
2770 S 171st St
New Berlin, WI 53151-3510   262-785-5104
Fax: 262-789-5149 888-345-4560
dawnm@gamayflavors.com
www.gamayflavors.com
Supplier to the food industry with products such as heat stable cheese flavorings, complete flavor systems and thermostable fillings. Gamay flavors include enzyme modified cheeses, natural cheese flavors, lipolyzed butter oils andcreams, natural butter and cream flavors, starter distillate replacers, liquid flavors, sweet flavors, savory flavors, and food colors. Flavors and colors are manufactured in New Berlin, Wisconsin and shipped throughout the world.
President: Dr. Aly Gamay
Operations: Randy Cook
Estimated Sales:$1-5 Million
Number Employees: 5-9
Parent Co: Gamay Flavors

5385 (HQ)Gambino's
2308 Piedmont St
Kenner, LA 70062-7960   504-712-0809
Fax: 504-466-1507 www.gambinos.com
Distribution of confections, specialty cakes, italian cookies and pastries, internet specialties, Mardi Gras packages, Doberge cakes and King Cake packaging. Every cake is baked fresh daily and we now ship overnight.
Owner: Sam Scelfo
Estimated Sales:$300,000-500,000
Number Employees: 1-4

5386 (HQ)Gambrinus Company
14800 San Pedro Ave
San Antonio, TX 78232-3785   210-490-9128
Fax: 210-490-9984 www.gambrinusco.com
Best known as importer of the Grupo Modelo brand portfilio for the eastern US. Also imports Moosehead Lag from Canada. Includes more than 300 corporate, sales, distribution, brewing and support personnel and markets five brandportfolios throughout the US and Caribbean. Modelo brands include Corona Extra and the fast growing Corona Light, Modelo Especial, Negra Modelo and Pacifico Clara.
President/CEO: Carlos Alvarez
CFO: James Bolz
*Estimated Sales:*Under $500,000
Number Employees: 50-99
Brands:
KOSMOS LAGER
LORUNITA EXTRA
MODELO ESPECIAL
NEGRA MODELO
PACIFICO CLARA
SHINER BOCK
SHINER PREMIUM

5387 Ganong Acosta Head Office West
827 Belgrave Way
Suite 101
New Westminster, BC V3M 5R8
Canada   604-520-6002
Fax: 604-520-6898 888-270-8222
feedback@ganong.com www.ganong.com
Acosta branch office of Ganong Bros. Ltd., a chocolate/confectionery company that processes and exports a varity of products including bagged candy, boxed chocolate and fruit snacks, varieties of which include milk caramel, chocolatetruffles, peanut butter cups, double dipped cherries and the original chicken bones candies.
President: David Ganong
Chief Financial Officer: Doug Gaudett
VP/Chief Information Officer: Marc Lefebvre
VP/Business Development: Danay Branscombe
VP/Marketing & Sales: Greg Fash
VP/Sales United States Region: Terry Arthurs
Chief Operating Officer: David Pigott
Logistics Manager: Harold Ryan
Industrial/Custom Products/Private Label: Bryana Ganong
Number Employees: 250-499
Type of Packaging: Consumer, Private Label, Bulk

5388 Ganong Atlantic Sales Division
633 Main Street
Suite 650
Moncton, NB E1C 9X9
Canada   506-389-7898
Fax: 506-854-5826 888-270-8222
feedback@ganong.com www.ganong.com
Sales division office of Ganong Bros. Ltd., a chocolate/confectionery company that processes and exports a varity of products including bagged candy, boxed chocolate and fruit snacks, varieties of which include milk caramel, chocolatetruffles, peanut butter cups, double dipped cherries and the original chicken bones candies.
President: David Ganong
Chief Financial Officer: Doug Gaudett
VP/Chief Information Officer: Marc Lefebvre
VP/Business Development: Danay Branscombe
VP/Marketing & Sales: Greg Fash
VP/Sales United States Region: Terry Arthurs
Chief Operating Officer: David Pigott
Logistics Manager: Harold Ryan
Industrial/Custom Products/Private Label: Bryana Ganong
Number Employees: 250-499
Type of Packaging: Consumer, Private Label, Bulk

5389 (HQ)Ganong Bros LimitedCorporate Office
One Chocolate Drive
St. Stephen, NB E3L 2X5
Canada   506-465-5600
Fax: 506-465-5610 888-426-6647
feedback@ganong.com www.ganong.com

Processor and exporter of confectionery products including bagged candy, boxed chocolate and fruit snacks. Many old fashion varieties such as rich milk caramel, sinful chaocolate truffles, peanut butter cups, delicious double dippedcherries and the one and only chicken bones.
> President: David Ganong
> Chief Financial Officer: Doug Gaudett
> VP/Business Development: Dana Branscombe
> Quality Control: Craig Ivey
> VP/Marketing & Sales: Greg Fash
> Chief Operating Officer: David Pigott
> Plant Manager: Rob Snow
> Purchasing Director: Larry Kirk
> *Number Employees:* 250
> *Type of Packaging:* Consumer, Private Label, Bulk
> *Brands:*
> BETWEEN FRIENDS PROMOTIONAL CANDY
> DELECTO CHOCOLATES
> FUN FRUITS FRUIT SNACKS-SUNKIST
> GANONG CHICKEN BONES
> GANONG CHOCOLATES
> GANONG FRUITFULL
> GANONG SUGAR CONFECTIONS
> PAL-O-MINE CHOCOLATE BARS
> SUNKIST FLAVOUR BURSTS
> SUNKIST FRUIT FIRST FRUIT SNACKS
> TIFFANY BAGGED CANDY
> WILDFRUIT FRUIT SNACKS

5390 Ganong Ontario and National Sales Division
10 Kingsbridge Garden Circle
Suite 704
Mississauga, ON L5R 3K6
Canada   905-502-3473
          Fax: 905-502-3475 888-270-8222
feedback@ganong.com   www.ganong.com
Ontario and National Sales Division branch office of Ganong Bros. Ltd., a chocolate/confectionery company that processes and exports a variety of products including bagged candy, boxed chocolate and fruit snacks, varieties of whichinclude milk caramel, chocolate truffles, peanut butter cups, double dipped cherries and the original chicken bones candies.
> President: David Ganong
> Chief Financial Officer: Doug Gaudett
> VP/Chief Information Officer: Marc Lefebvre
> VP/Business Development: Danay Branscombe
> VP/Marketing & Sales: Greg Fash
> VP/Sales United States Region: Terry Arthurs
> Chief Operating Officer: David Pigott
> Logistics Manager: Harold Ryan
> Industrial/Custom Products/Private Label: Bryana Ganong
> *Number Employees:* 250-499
> *Type of Packaging:* Consumer, Private Label, Bulk

5391 Ganong USA Division
8170 Corporate Park Dr # 137
Cincinnati, OH 45242-3306
Canada   513-489-8439
          Fax: 513-489-2728 888-270-8222
feedback@ganong.com   www.ganong.com
United States regional division branch office of Ganong Bros. Ltd., a chocolate/confectionery company that processes and exports a variety of products including bagged candy, boxed chocolate and fruit snacks, varieties of which includemilk caramel, chocolate truffles, peanut butter cups, double dipped cherries and the original chicken bones candies.
> President: David Ganong
> Chief Financial Officer: Doug Gaudett
> VP: Terry Arthurs
> VP/Business Development: Danay Branscombe
> VP/Marketing & Sales: Greg Fash
> VP/Sales United States Region: Terry Arthurs
> Chief Operating Officer: David Pigott
> Logistics Manager: Harold Ryan
> Industrial/Custom Products/Private Label: Bryana Ganong
> *Number Employees:* 250-499
> *Type of Packaging:* Consumer, Private Label, Bulk

5392 Ganong Western Canada Division
1400-1500 West Georgia Street
Vancouver, BC V6G 2Z6
Canada   604-688-6772
          Fax: 604-688-7723 888-270-8222
feedback@ganong.com   www.ganong.com

Vancouver/Western Canada Division branch office of Ganong Bros. Ltd., a chocolate/confectionery company that processes and exports a varity of products including bagged candy, boxed chocolate and fruit snacks, varieties of whichinclude milk caramel, chocolate truffles, peanut butter cups, double dipped cherries and the original chicken bones candies.
> President: David Ganong
> Chief Financial Officer: Doug Gaudett
> VP/Chief Information Officer: Marc Lefebvre
> VP/Business Development: Danay Branscombe
> VP/Marketing & Sales: Greg Fash
> VP/Sales United States Region: Terry Arthurs
> Chief Operating Officer: David Pigott
> Logistics Manager: Harold Ryan
> Industrial/Custom Products/Private Label: Bryana Ganong
> *Number Employees:* 250-499
> *Type of Packaging:* Consumer, Private Label, Bulk

5393 Garber Farms
3405 Descannes Hwy
Iota, LA 70543-3118   337-824-6328
          Fax: 337-824-2676 800-824-2284
                          www.garbergifts.com
Processor and exporter of long grain white rice and yams
> General Partner: Walter Garber
> Sales/Marketing Partner: Wayne Garber
> Production Manager: Earl Garber
> *Estimated Sales:* $1-2.5 Million
> *Number Employees:* 10-19
> *Sq. footage:* 100000
> *Type of Packaging:* Consumer, Food Service, Private Label, Bulk
> *Brands:*
> CREOLE CLASSIC
> CREOLE DELIGHTS
> CREOLE ROSE
> LOUISIANA MINI

5394 Garber Ice Cream Company
P.O.Box 3265
Winchester, VA 22604-2465   540-662-5422
          Fax: 540-722-5088 800-662-5422
Manufacturing of ice cream and frozen desserts and yogurt.
> President: David Garber
> *Estimated Sales:* $5-10 Million
> *Number Employees:* 50-99
> *Type of Packaging:* Consumer, Private Label

5395 Garcias Mexican Foods
2920 Old Norcross Road
Duluth, GA 30096-4952   770-638-0881
                          Fax: 770-638-1485
Mexican cuisine at its best.
> *Estimated Sales:* $5-10 Million
> *Number Employees:* 10-19

5396 (HQ)Garcoa
24007 Ventura Blvd # 135
Calabasas, CA 91302-2568   818-225-0375
          Fax: 818-225-9251 800-831-4247
                          www.garcoa.com
Processor and exporter of vitamins and supplements. Manufacturer skin care, hair care, powder, oral care. Private label/contract
> President: Gregory Rubin
> VP/Sales: Terry Williams
> *Estimated Sales:* $ 10 - 20 Million
> *Number Employees:* 10-19
> *Sq. footage:* 750000
> *Type of Packaging:* Consumer, Private Label
> *Brands:*
> CLEAN N' NATURAL
> NATURE'S BEAUTY
> NATURE'S GLORY
> VITAMIN CLASSICS

5397 Garden & Orchard Foods
1301 39th Street N
Fargo, ND 58102-2865   701-282-2300
          Fax: 701-281-9074 800-370-3682
Grocery stock items such as: bakery, baked goods, cakes and pastries, confectionery, candy novelties, dietetic, health, natural and organic foods, dry grocery: bases, soup and gravy, cookies, crackers and biscuits.
> President: Richard Blajsczak
> *Brands:*
> CHARLOTTE CHARLES
> GARDEN & ORCHARD
> M A O'HALLORAN

5398 Garden & Valley Isle Seafood
225 N Nimitz Hwy # 3
Honolulu, HI 96817-5349   808-524-4847
          Fax: 808-528-5590 800-689-2733
info@gvisfd.com   www.gvisfd.com
Processor of ahi, sashimi, swordfish and snapper; importer and exporter of fresh seafood; wholesaler/distributor of smoked fish and general merchandise
> President: Robert Fram
> VP: Dave Marabella
> Operations: Cliff Yamauchi
> Purchasing: James Lee
> *Estimated Sales:* $20-50 Million
> *Number Employees:* 20-49
> *Sq. footage:* 9000
> *Type of Packaging:* Bulk

5399 (HQ)Garden Complements
920 Cable Rd
Kansas City, MO 64116-4244   816-421-1090
          Fax: 816-421-4220 800-966-1091
gardcomp@sprintmail.com   www.sauceman.com
Processor of sauces including barbecue, Mexican, Italian and Asian marinades, salsas, salad dressing, gourmet products
> President: Don Blackman
> Marketing Director: Jim Pirotte
> *Estimated Sales:* $1-2.5 Million
> *Number Employees:* 5-9
> *Sq. footage:* 15000
> *Type of Packaging:* Consumer, Food Service, Private Label, Bulk
> *Brands:*
> AMIGO
> AUSSIE
> AUSSIE SAUCE
> BEST CHOICE
> CAMPFIRE
> GAETANO'S
> HERITAGE
> OLD SOUTHERN
> PRIMO

5400 Garden Fresh Salsa
1505 Bonner St
Ferndale, MI 48220-1973   248-336-8486
          Fax: 248-336-8487 866-725-7239
info@gardenfreshsalsa.com
                          www.gardenfreshsalsa.com
Family owned fresh made salsa company.
> Owner/President: Jack Aronson
> *Estimated Sales:* $ 5 - 10 Million
> *Number Employees:* 10-19

5401 Garden Herbs
26021 Business Center Drive
Redlands, CA 92374-4553   909-796-2569
          Fax: 909-796-2376 800-388-9397
Processor of pesto sauces and frozen common and exotic herbs including basil, dill, chervil, oregano, cilantro, rosemary, thyme, apple mint and lemon and Thai basil; also, contract packaging available
> President: Robert Christman
> VP: Gay Christman
> *Estimated Sales:* $2.5-5 Million
> *Number Employees:* 1-4
> *Sq. footage:* 5300
> *Type of Packaging:* Consumer, Food Service, Private Label, Bulk

5402 Garden Row Foods
10929 Franklin Ave # N
Franklin Park, IL 60131-1430   847-455-2200
          Fax: 847-455-9100 800-555-9798
                          hotfood@xnet.com
Manufacturer and distribuor of hot sauces and other products, including Endorphin Rush, Pyromania, Brutal Bajan and 350 more products.
> Owner: Gary Poppins
> *Estimated Sales:* $2.5-5 Million
> *Number Employees:* 10-19
> *Type of Packaging:* Consumer, Food Service, Bulk
> *Brands:*
> BRUTAL BAJAN
> ENDORPHIN
> MONGO
> PYROMANIA

5403 Garden Row Foods
411 Stone Drive
St Charles, IL 60174-3301   800-555-9798
Fax: 847-455-9110   800-505-9999
gardenrowfoods@eathot.com
Manufacturer and distributor of hot sauces and other
products, including Engorphin Rush, Pyromania,
Brutal Bajan, and 350 more products.
President: George Kosten
Number of Products: 15
Sq. footage: 2500
Parent Co: Garden Row Foods
Brands:
CARIBBEAN MARKETPLACE
GREAT GRUB RUBS
TROPICAL CHILE CO

5404 (HQ)Garden Spot Distributors
191 Commerce Dr
New Holland, PA 17557-9114   717-354-4936
Fax: 717-354-4934   800-829-5100
info@gardenspotsfinest.com
www.gardenspotdist.com
Processor and wholesaler/distributor of organic
foods for allergy and chemically-sensitive people in-
cluding bread, granolas, cooking cereals and flour.
Features organic produce, dairy, poultry and beef.
President: John Clough
Marketing Director: Peter Horvath
Sales Director: Jean O'Donnell
Purchasing Manager: Mark Drury
Estimated Sales:$8 Million
Number Employees: 20-49
Number of Brands: 100+
Sq. footage: 20000
Type of Packaging: Consumer, Private Label, Bulk
Other Locations:
Garden Spot Distributors
Sulphur Springs AR

5405 Garden State Farms
3333 S Front St
Philadelphia, PA 19148-5605   215-463-8000
Fax: 215-467-1144 www.procaccibrothers.com
Lettuces, peaches, tomato
Owner: Joe Procacci
CEO: Joseph Procacci
Estimated Sales:$100-500 Million
Number Employees: 5-9

5406 Garden Valley Foods
850 Garden Valley Cir
Sutherlin, OR 97479-9860   541-459-9565
Fax: 541-459-1865 gvc@rosenet.net
Dehydrated vegetables: peas, lentils and legumes
Owner: Mark M Sterner
Estimated Sales:$2.5-5 Million
Number Employees: 10-19

5407 Garden of the Gods Seasonings
2028 W Cucharras St
Colorado Springs, CO 80904   719-473-5181
Fax: 719-577-4896   877-229-1548
godsseasonings@aol.com
www.godsseasonings.com
A multi-faceted gourmet company. A unique blend
of seasonings and spices, plus a variety of fresh and
frozen specialty foods.
President: Sandy Vanderstoup
*Estimated Sales:*Less than $500,000
Number Employees: 5-9

5408 Gardenburger
P.O.Box 160427
Clearfield, UT 84016-0427   801-773-8855
Fax: 801-773-1955 www.whfoodsco.com
Frozen veggie patties
President: Scott Wallace
Marketing: Mary Dillon
Plant Manager: David Samuelson
Estimated Sales:$25-49.9 Million
Number Employees: 5-9
Type of Packaging: Private Label, Bulk
Brands:
ALMOND CHEESE
GARDENBURGER
GARDENDOG
GARDENMEXI
GARDENSAUSAGE
GARDENSTEAK
GARDENVEGAN
GARDENVEGGIE
WHITE ALMOND BEVERAGE

5409 Gardner Pie Company
191 Logan Pkwy
Akron, OH 44319-1188   330-245-2030
Fax: 330-245-2036 www.gardnerpie.com
Manufacturer of frozen pies
Owner: Robert Goff
CEO: Tom Gardner
Estimated Sales:$3-5 Million
Number Employees: 50-99
Sq. footage: 18000
Type of Packaging: Consumer, Food Service, Pri-
vate Label

5410 Gardner's Gourmet
45450 Industrial Pl # 3
Fremont, CA 94538-6474   510-490-6106
Fax: 510-490-4563   800-676-8558
info@greatdrink.com   www.greatdrink.com
Processor and exporter of frosted caffe ghiaccio,
granitas, iced cappuccino and smoothie mixes, our
original fruit ices, concentrates, frozen cocktails,
fruit purees and flavoring syrups.
Owner: Beverly Fritz
Estimated Sales:$ 3 - 5 Million
Number Employees: 1-4
Brands:
GHIACCIO
X-TREME FREEZE

5411 Gardners Candies
30 W 10th St
Tyrone, PA 16686-1506   814-684-0857
Fax: 814-684-2304   800-242-2639
info@gardnerscandies.com
www.gardnerscandies.com
Processor of confectionery products including choc-
olate candy and the original peanut butter meltaway
and peanut butter.
Manager: Kristin Barrett
Estimated Sales:$25-49.9 Million
Number Employees: 50-99
Type of Packaging: Consumer

5412 Gardunos Mexican Food
180 E 6th St
Pomona, CA 91766-3301   909-469-6611
Mexican foods
Owner: Martha Santiago
Estimated Sales:$10-100 Million
Number Employees: 1-4

5413 Garelick Farms
626 Lynnway
Lynn, MA 01905-3030   781-599-1300
Fax: 781-599-7810 800-487-8700
www.deanfoods.com
Processor of milk, ice cream and juice
President: Arthur Pappathanasi
VP: Phillip Drexler
Estimated Sales:$100+ Million
Number Employees: 500-999
Parent Co: Suiza Dairy Group
Type of Packaging: Consumer, Food Service, Pri-
vate Label, Bulk

5414 (HQ)Garelick Farms
1199 W Central St
Franklin, MA 02038-3109   508-528-9000
Fax: 508-520-0307   800-343-4982
http://www.garelickfarms.com
Processor of milk, juice, spring water, cider and egg-
nog
President: Marty Devine
Sales/Marketing: Chris Keyes
Purchasing: Steve Stewart
Number Employees: 1,000-4,999
Parent Co: Suiza Dairy Group
Type of Packaging: Consumer, Food Service
Other Locations:
Garelick Farms 508 473-0550
Mendon MA
Garelick Farms 800 343-4982
Franklin MA
Garelick Farms 800 648-0135
Burlington NJ
Brands:
ALL NATURAL
GARELICK

5415 Garelick Farms
504 3rd Ave Ext
Rensselaer, NY 12144-5613   518-283-0820
Fax: 518-283-9524 www.deanfoods.com

Produces milk, chocolate milk and orange juice
VP: Chris Inzerello
Sales: Rich Gold
Plant Manager: Charles Smith
Estimated Sales:$300,000-500,000
Number Employees: 1-4
Parent Co: Suiza Dairy Group

5416 Garlic Company
18602 Zerker Rd
Bakersfield, CA 93314-9747   661-393-4212
Fax: 661-393-9340 www.thegarliccompany.com
Peeled and process garlic and jalapenos to the
foodservice
Marketing: Tiffany Lane
Sales: Bob Lords
Plant Manager: John Merkle
Estimated Sales:$ 50 - 100 Million
Number Employees: 100-249

5417 Garlic Festival Foods
P.O.Box 1145
Gilroy, CA 95021-1145   408-842-7088
Fax: 408-842-7087 888-427-5423
info@garlicfestival.com   www.garlicfestival.com
Processor of garlic seasoning, sauce, mustard and
dressing
President: Caryl Simpson
VP: Tom Reed
Estimated Sales:$500,000-$1 Million
Number Employees: 5-9
Sq. footage: 10300
Parent Co: Randan Corporation
Type of Packaging: Consumer, Bulk
Brands:
GARLI GARNI
GARLIC FESTIVAL
GOURMET GOLD

5418 Garlic Survival Company
32422 Alipaz St # G
San Juan Cpstrno, CA 92675-4187   415-822-7112
Fax: 415-822-6224   800-342-7542
garlicsurv@aol.com
Garlic sauces, spices and gift packs
President: Scott Seay
*Estimated Sales:*Less than $500,000
Number Employees: 1-4
Brands:
GARLIC SURVIVAL

5419 Garlic Valley Farms Inc
624 Ruberta Ave
Glendale, CA 91201-2335   818-247-9600
Fax: 818-247-9828   800-424-7990
anderson@garlicvalleyfarms.com
www.garlicvalleyfarms.com
Processor, importer and exporter of liquid garlic
products including juices and purees
President: William Anderson
CFO: Sonja Anderson
R&D: Bill Brock
Estimated Sales:$1.2 Million
Number Employees: 5-9
Number of Products: 2
Sq. footage: 15000
Type of Packaging: Consumer
Brands:
GARLIC JUICES

5420 Garon Industries
PO Box 339
Mosinee, WI 54455-0339   715-693-1593
Fax: 715-693-1594 info@garonfoods.com
wwwgaronfoods.com
Manufactures peppers including jalapenos,
habaneros and bell, vegetables, herbs and fruits.
President: Gary Griesbach
Estimated Sales:$ 5 - 10 Million
Number Employees: 12
Number of Brands: 1
Type of Packaging: Bulk
Brands:
EL GUSTO

5421 Garrard's Sausage Company
3263 Rose of Sharon Rd # A
Durham, NC 27712-3129   919-383-4657
Fax: 919-383-6673
Processor of meat products
President: Issac Garrard
Estimated Sales:$5-10 Million
Number Employees: 5-9

Type of Packaging: Consumer, Food Service, Private Label, Bulk

5422 Garratt & Gunn
3565 Airway Dr
Santa Rosa, CA 95403-1605   707-578-8192
                              Fax: 707-578-5221
Health foods
    Owner: Duncan Garrett
Estimated Sales: Under $500,000
Number Employees: 1-4

5423 Garrett Popcorn Shops
676 N Saint Clair Street
Chicago, IL 60611-2927   312-944-8155
    Fax: 312-280-9611   888-476-7267
              www.garrettpopcorn.com
Several varieties of popcorn caramel crisp, cheese corn, cashew caramel crisp, macadamia caramel crisp
    President: Karen Galaba
Estimated Sales: $300,000-500,000
Number Employees: 1-4
Type of Packaging: Bulk

5424 Garry Packing
P.O.Box 249
Del Rey, CA 93616-0249   559-888-2126
    Fax: 559-888-2848   800-248-2126
info@garrypacking.com www.garrypacking.com
Dried fruit and nuts, gift packing (trays, baskets, crates), gift components
    President: James Garry
    VP: Jessie Garry
    Sales Manager: Tamara Garry
Estimated Sales: $20-50 Million
Number Employees: 250-499
Sq. footage: 125000
Type of Packaging: Consumer
Brands:
    GARRY'S
    GARRY'S DRIED FRUIT & NUTS

5425 Garuda International
P.O.Box 44380
Lemon Cove, CA 93244-0380   559-594-4380
    Fax: 559-594-4689 garudainfo@garudaint.com
              www.garudaint.com
We have specialized in the development, manufacturing and the marketing of ingredients derived from natural sources for more than 23 years. Our products provide a variety of nutraceutical benefits to foods, beverages, dietarysupplements and cosmeceuticals. A well known and globally recognized for the pioneering and development of natural milk calcium in the United States. Garuda manufactures the COWCIUM® Natural Milk Calcium and the equally recognizedLesstanol®.
    President/CEO: J Roger Matkin
    Marketing/Sales: Bassam Faress
Estimated Sales: $500,000-$1 Million
Number Employees: 5-9
Sq. footage: 15000
Type of Packaging: Private Label, Bulk
Brands:
    COWCIUM
    LESSTANOL
    MILCAL
    MILCAL-FG
    MILCAL-TG
    MOO-CALCIUM
    OCTACOSANOL GF
    VEGe-COAT

5426 Gary Farrell Wines
PO Box 342
Santa Rosa, CA 95402-0342   707-433-6616
    Fax: 707-433-9060 http://garyfarrellwines.com
Producer of a 1982 Russian River Valley Pinot Noir. Also produces premium Chardonnay, Merlot, Cabernet Sauvignon and Zinfandel.
    President: Gary Farrell

5427 Gary's Frozen Foods
109th S University Avenue
Lubbock, TX 79452-2348   806-745-1933
                          Fax: 806-745-3141
Manufacturer of barbecue beef, frozen smoked beef brisket, corn dogs and super dogs
    Owner: Gary Tidwell
Estimated Sales: Under $500,000
Number Employees: 1
Type of Packaging: Consumer, Food Service

5428 Gaskill Seafood
124 Spencer Street
Bayboro, NC 28515   252-745-4211
                     Fax: 252-745-3170
Fish and shrimp
    President: Clifton Gaskill
Estimated Sales: $500,000-$1 Million
Number Employees: 1-4

5429 Gaslamp Popcorn Company
330 Heron Lane
Riverside, CA 92507-1500   877-237-8276
    Fax: 619-671-5858   877-237-8276
customer.service@gaslamppopcorn.com
              http://www.gaslamppopcorn.com
Popcorn and kettle corn
    Senior VP: Hap Eliott
Estimated Sales: $ 1 - 3 Million
Number Employees: 10-19

5430 Gaspar's Sausage Company
384 Faunce Corner Rd
North Dartmouth, MA 02747-1257   508-998-2012
    Fax: 508-998-2015   800-542-2038
CustomerCare@GaspersSausage.com
              www.linguica.com
Processor and exporter of sausage including Portuguese linguica and chourico
    President: Fernando Gaspar
    Sales Manager: Robert Gaspar
    Plant Manager: Charles Gaspar
Estimated Sales: $5-9.9 Million
Number Employees: 20-49
Sq. footage: 35000
Type of Packaging: Consumer, Food Service, Private Label

5431 Gaston Dupre
1000 Italian Way
Suite 200
Excelsior Springs, MO 64024-8016   817-629-6275
    Fax: 816-502-6722   mrsleepers@aipc.com
              www.mrsleeperspasta.com
Wheat products - pasta
    President: Terri Webb McMillin
    Co-owner: Michelle Muscat
Estimated Sales: $10-20 Million
Number Employees: 20-49
Brands:
    Eddie's
    Michelle's

5432 Gateway Food Products Company
1728 N Main St
Dupo, IL 62239-1045   618-286-4844
    Fax: 618-286-3444   877-220-1963
traines@gatewayfoodproducts.com
              www.gatewayfoodproducts.com
Processor of syrups, vegetable oils and shortenings; exporter of corn syrup; wholesaler/distributor of general line items; also shortening flakes, popcorn oils and butter toppings
    President: John Crosley
    Quality Control: Jeremy Gray
    Marketing Director: Teresa Raines
    Sales Director: Teresa Raines
    Operations Manager: Jeremy Gray
    Production Manager: Jim Raines
    Plant Manager: Jim Raines
    Purchasing Manager: John Crosley
Estimated Sales: $10-20 Million
Number Employees: 10-19
Number of Products: 9
Sq. footage: 25000
Type of Packaging: Food Service, Private Label, Bulk
Brands:
    DU CROSE
    DU GLAZE
    DU SWEET
    GATEWAY - DU BAKE

5433 Gator Hammock
P.O.Box 360
Felda, FL 33930-0360   863-675-0687
    Fax: 863-675-4938   800-664-2867
hotgator@iline.com www.gatorsauce.com
Manufacturer of hot and spicy sauces, dressings, mustard, cabbage, pickles, and jam. Contains no MSG - only natural ingredients.
    President: Buddy Taylor
    VP: David Romano, PE
    Purchasing: Judy Stewart

Estimated Sales: Less than $500,000
Number Employees: 1-4
Type of Packaging: Private Label

5434 Gaucho Foods
PO Box 307
Westmont, IL 60559-0307   630-889-4241
    Fax: 630-241-3917   mscinc@aol.com
              www.gauchofoods.com
Processor of beef including frozen, barbecue, Southern-brand in barbecue sauce and regular gravy and Italian style and gravy; also, spaghetti sauce with meat
    President: Jack Lachmann
Estimated Sales: $5-9.9 Million
Number Employees: 15
Sq. footage: 6000
Type of Packaging: Consumer, Food Service, Private Label, Bulk
Brands:
    GAUCHO

5435 Gaudet & Ouellette
PO Box 335
Cap-Pele, NB E4N 3B3
Canada   506-577-4016
           Fax: 506-577-4006
Processor and exporter of smoked herring
    President: Normand Ouellette
Number Employees: 20-49
Type of Packaging: Bulk

5436 Gay & Robinson
PO Box 156
Kaumakani, HI 96747-0156   808-335-3133
    Fax: 808-335-6424 gnr@gayandrobinson.com
Sugar and condiments
    President: E Alan Kennett
    VP: Bruce Robinson
Estimated Sales: $20-50 Million
Number Employees: 250-499

5437 Gay's Wild Maine Blueberries
PO Box 129
Cherryfield, ME 04622-0129   978-649-3256
                              Fax: 978-649-3811
Blueberry
    President: Paul Gay

5438 Gayle's Sweet 'N Sassy Foods
269 S Beverly Dr # 472
Beverly Hills, CA 90212-3851   310-246-1792
    Fax: 310-246-1794   sassybbq@aol.com
              www.gaylesbbq.com
Processor of barbecue sauce
    Owner: Gayle Gannes
Estimated Sales: Under $500,000
Number Employees: 5-9

5439 Gazin's
PO Box 19221
New Orleans, LA 70179-0221   504- 48-2 03
    Fax: 504- 48-8 62   800-262-6410
gazins@aol.com www.gazins.com
Gumbo roux
    Owner: Kary Le Fleur
Brands:
    Kary's Gumbo Roux

5440 Gecko Gary's
PO Box 15185
Scottsdale, AZ 85267-5185   602-765-3756
    Fax: 602-765-3450 gary@geckogarys.com
              www.gecogarys.com
    Co-Owner: Gary Soultanian
    Co-Owner: Cindy Soultanian

5441 Geeef America
19550 S Dominguez Hills Drive
Compton, CA 90220-6418   310-944-9485
                          Fax: 310-944-9476
Gum, candy
    President: Stanley Park
Brands:
    BUBBLE POP
    CHOCO POP
    IMAGE LOLLIPOP CANDY
    MAGIC POP

5442 Geetha's Gourmet of India
1589 Imperial Road
Las Cruces, NM 88011-4805   505-522-5740
    Fax: 505-522-0930   800-274-0475

Processor and exporter of natural Indian pastas, sauces, marinades, chutneys, salsas, curries, lentil soup and tempura mixes, basmati rice pilaf, spiced tea, garam masala and honey sticks
President: Geetha Pai
Estimated Sales: Under $500,000
Number Employees: 5-9
Sq. footage: 4000
Type of Packaging: Consumer, Food Service
Brands:
FIESTA OLE
GEETHA'S GOURMET OF INDIA

5443 Gehl Guernsey Farms
P.O.Box 1004
Germantown, WI 53022-8204 262-251-8570
Fax: 262-251-8744 800-434-5713
www.gehls.com
Processor of canned puddings, cheese sauces, condensed milk, nutritional drinks and iced cappuccino
President: John Gehl
National Sales Manager: Tracy Propst
VP Operations: John Shaugnessy
Estimated Sales: $20-50 Million
Number Employees: 100-249
Sq. footage: 60000
Type of Packaging: Food Service
Brands:
GEHL MAINSTREAM CAFE
GEHL'S GOURMET

5444 Gel Spice Company, Inc
48 Hook Rd
Bayonne, NJ 07002-5007 201-339-0700
Fax: 201-339-0024 800-922-0230
jacob@gelspice.com www.gelspice.com
A full line of bulk, food service and retail spices, seeds and bakery ingredients.
President: Andre Engle
Vice President: Jacob Engel
Marketing Director: Sherman Engel
Purchasing Manager: Gershon Engel
Number Employees: 100-249
Sq. footage: 250000
Type of Packaging: Consumer, Food Service, Private Label, Bulk

5445 Gelati Celesti
612 Meyer Ln # 2
Redondo Beach, CA 90278-5274 310-372-2593
Fax: 310-798-0043 800-550-7550
www.gelaticelesti.com
Processor of gelati, sorbets and gelato truffles
President: Steve Edmonds
Estimated Sales: $2.5-5 Million
Number Employees: 10-19
Type of Packaging: Consumer, Food Service, Private Label, Bulk
Brands:
GELATI CELESTI

5446 Gelato Fresco
60 Tycos Drive N York
Toronto, ON M6B 1V9
Canada 416-785-5415
Fax: 416-781-3133
Processor of natural ice cream, sorbet and tartufo
President: Hart Melvin
Number Employees: 10-19
Sq. footage: 10000
Type of Packaging: Consumer, Food Service
Brands:
GELATO FRESCO

5447 Gelato Giuliana LLC
168 N Plains Industrial Rd
Wallingford, CT 06492 203-269-2200
Fax: 203-294-9495 gelatogiuliana@sbcglobal.net
www.gelatogiuliana.com
gelatos and flavored gelatos
President/Owner: Giuliana Maravalle

5448 Gelita USA
P.O.Box 927
Sioux City, IA 51102-0927 712-943-5516
Fax: 712-943-3372 888-456-5435
service.na@gelita.com www.gelatin-gmia.com
Research, manufacture and marketing of high-quality gelatines
President: Charles Markham
CFO: Robert Mayberry
VP: George Riedenfield
R & D: John Dolphin
Quality Control: Deck Schaeser

Estimated Sales: $ 50-100 Million
Number Employees: 250-499
Sq. footage: 150000
Brands:
Gelita

5449 (HQ)Gelita/Kind & Knox Gelatine
PO Box 927
Sioux City, IA 51102-0927 712-943-1636
Fax: 712-943-1644 888-456-5435
service.na@gelita.com www.gelita.com
Processor of gelatine.
President/CEO: Charles Markham
CFO: Rob Mayberry
VP Communications: Michael Teppner
Research & Development: Dr J Michael Dunn
National Sales/Marketing Manager: John Harty
Sales Director: George Riejenfeld
Number Employees: 250
Brands:
GELITA

5450 Gelsinger Food Products
2209 Honolulu Ave
Montrose, CA 91020-1616 818-248-7811
Fax: 818-957-2545
Frozen and refrigerated beef, game meats, lamb, pork, veal, smoked meats, poultry, cured meats, cooked meats
President: Ron Gelsinger
Sales/Marketing Manager: Kirk Gelsinger
Estimated Sales: $2.5-5 Million
Number Employees: 20-49

5451 (HQ)Gem Berry Products
804 Airport Way
Sandpoint, ID 83864-8200 208-263-7503
Fax: 208-263-3247 800-426-0498
gemberry92@hotmail.com
Jams, jellies, syrups, gift packs
President: Jack O' Brien
Sales Director: Harry Menser
Production Manager: Elizabeth O'Brien
Estimated Sales: $500,000-$1 Million
Number Employees: 1-4
Type of Packaging: Private Label

5452 Gem Meat Packing Company
515 E 45th St
Boise, ID 83714-4896 208-375-9424
Fax: 208-375-1568
Processor and packer of beef, pork and sausages including kitchen cured and smoked; slaughtering services available
Owner: Brent Compton
Estimated Sales: $ 7 Million
Number Employees: 20-49

5453 Gemini Food Industries
559 Main St
Fiskdale, MA 01518 508-347-2800
Fax: 508-347-1945
Processor and importer of frozen foods including marinated, breaded and battered chicken, par-baked and full-baked goods, cooked and sliced beef, boil-bag sauces and soups and glazed, breaded and battered seafood; importer of baby backribs, riblets, etc
President: Warren Kenniston
Chairman/CEO: Robert Gibson
Number Employees: 20-49
Sq. footage: 7500
Type of Packaging: Consumer, Food Service, Private Label, Bulk

5454 Genarom International
6 Santa Fe Way
Cranbury, NJ 08512-3288 609-409-6200
Fax: 609-409-6500
Processor and exporter of marinades, sauces and flavors including beef, chicken, turkey, pork, ham, cheese, seafood and creams
President: Bob Gallatine
Co-Founder/Chairman: Werner Hiller
Number Employees: 20-49
Sq. footage: 30000
Type of Packaging: Food Service, Bulk
Brands:
DOHLAR
GENAROM

5455 Gene & Boots Candies
2939 Pittsburgh Rd
Perryopolis, PA 15473-1005 724-736-2701
800-864-4222
www.geneandboots.com
Processor of candy including chocolate-covered caramels, jellies and fudge
President: Bob Ferguson
Estimated Sales: $5-9.9 Million
Number Employees: 10-19
Type of Packaging: Consumer

5456 Gene Belk Fruit Packers
10380 Alder Ave
Bloomington, CA 92316-2302 909-877-1819
Fax: 909-877-2460
Fruit and vegetable by-products
Manager: Curtis Belk
Estimated Sales: $ 20 - 50 Million
Number Employees: 20-49

5457 Gene's Citrus Ranch
P.O.Box 996
Palmetto, FL 34220-0996 941-723-0504
Fax: 941-723-3620 888-723-2006
www.citrusranch.com
Grower of oranges and grapefruit; processor of fresh orange and grapefruit juice
President: Gene Mixon
Estimated Sales: $10-20 Million
Number Employees: 10-19
Type of Packaging: Consumer, Food Service

5458 Genencor International
2600 Kennedy Dr
Beloit, WI 53511-3992 608-365-1112
Fax: 608-365-4526 www.genencor.com
Manufacturer and exporter of carbohydrate enzymes for wet milling, baking, brewing, etc
Chairman/CEO: Robert Mayer
President: Thomas Pekich
SVP Technology: Michael Arbige PhD
SVP Global Supply: Carol Beth Cobb
Estimated Sales: $ 10 - 20 Million
Number Employees: 10-19
Parent Co: Danisco Company
Type of Packaging: Bulk
Brands:
G-ZYME

5459 General Henry Biscuit Company
300 Bakery Blvd
Du Quoin, IL 62832-4414 618-542-6222
Fax: 618-542-5099
Biscuits, breads, rolls
Plant Manager: Steven Scaff
Estimated Sales: $ 50 - 100 Million
Number Employees: 100-249

5460 General Mills
704 W Washington St
West Chicago, IL 60185-2797 630-231-1140
Fax: 630-231-6968 800-248-7310
www.generalmills.com
Branch division manufacturers cereals, foods preparations and pasta products.
Chairman/Chief Executive Officer: Stephen Sanger
President/Chief Operating Officer: Kendall Powell
Vice Chairman/Chief Financial Officer: James Lawrence
SVP/General Counsel & Governance: Siri Marshall
SVP/Strategic Technology Development: Rory Delaney
SVP/External Relations: Christina Shea
SVP/Human Resources & Corporate Services: Michael Peel
Parent Co: General Mills Inc
Type of Packaging: Food Service

5461 (HQ)General Mills
PO Box 9452
Minneapolis, MN 55440
Fax: 763-764-8330 800-248-7310
www.generalmills.com

Manufacturer and exporter of ready-to-eat breakfast cereals, dry packaged dessert, main meal and side dish mixes, fruit and grain snacks, microwave popcorn, flour, baking mixes, refrigerated and soft-frozen yogurt, food serviceproducts and bakery flours.
    Chairman/CEO: Kendall Power
    EVP/CFO: Donal Mulligan
    SVP/Chief Marketing Officer: Mark Addicks
    SVP International Sales/Marketing: Peter Capell
    SVP/Global Human Resources: Michael Davis
    EVP/COO International: Christopher O'Leary
Estimated Sales: $14.7 Billion
Number Employees: 30,000
Type of Packaging: Consumer, Food Service
Other Locations:
    General Mills
    Covington GA
    General Mills
    Chelsea MA
    General Mills
    Swedesboro NJ
    General Mills
    Chanhassen MN
Brands:
    BETTY CROCKER
    BIG G CEREALS
    BIG T BURGERS
    BISQUICK
    BUGLES
    CASCADIAN FARM
    CHEERIOS
    CHEX
    CINNAMON TOAST CRUNCH
    DIABLITOS UNDERWOOD
    FIBER ONE
    FRESCARINI
    FRUIT SNACKS
    GARDETTO'S
    GOLD MEDAL
    GREEN GIANT
    HAAGEN-DAZS
    HAMBURGER HELPER
    JUS-ROL
    KIX
    KNACK & BACK
    LA SALTENA
    LARABAR
    LATINA
    LUCKY CHARMS
    MACARONI GRILL
    MONSTERS
    MUIR GLEN
    NATURE VALLEY
    OLD EL PASO
    PILLSBURY
    PILLSBURY ATTA
    PROGRESSO
    TOTAL
    TOTINO'S/JENO'S
    TRIX
    V.PEARL
    WANCHAI FERRY
    WHEATIES
    YOPLAIT

5462 General Mills
P.O.Box 129
Federalsburg, MD 21632-0129   410-479-4800
    Fax: 410-479-3980 www.solocup.com
Manufacturer of specialty crumbs and croutons
    Chairman/CEO: Stephen Sanger
    President/COO: Kendall Powell
    Vice Chairman/CFO: James Lawrence
    EVP/CTO Worldwide Ops & Technology: Randy Darcy
    EVP/Worldwide Health/New Business Dvlpmt: Y Marc Belton
    EVP/Worldwide Sales/Channel Development: Jeffrey Rotsch
    EVP/COO International: Christopher O'Leary
    EVP/COO US Retail: Ian Friendly
Estimated Sales: $50-100 Million
Number Employees: 500-999
Parent Co: General Mills
Type of Packaging: Food Service, Bulk

5463 General Mills
100 Justin Dr
Chelsea, MA 02150-4032   617-884-9800
    Fax: 617-889-0281 800-370-7834
    www.generalmills.com

Processor of frozen and par-baked goods including French bread
    Manager: Tony Rodrigues
    Maintenance Supervisor: Noe Rodriguez
Number Employees: 100-249
Sq. footage: 100000
Parent Co: Pillsbury Company
Type of Packaging: Food Service, Private Label

5464 General Spice
238 Saint Nicholas Avenue
South Plainfield, NJ 07080-1810   908-753-9100
    Fax: 908-753-9635 800-345-7742
    khillerl@crfc.com
Food development, fire roasted, sauteed and roasted vegetable bases, Kosher meat flavors and bases, glazes and marinades
    President: Werner Hiller
    Co-Owner: Dagmar Hiller Laramie
Number Employees: 10-19
Type of Packaging: Bulk

5465 General Taste Bakery
5830 Triangle Dr
Commerce, CA 90040-3637   323-888-2170
Estimated Sales: Less than $500,000
Number Employees: 1-4

5466 Generation Farms
1109 NE McKinney St
Rice, TX 75155-9734   903-326-4263
    Fax: 903-326-6511 generationfarms@pflash.com
    www.generationfarms.com
Grower of fresh culinary herbs and edible flowers
    President: Ethan Milkes
Estimated Sales: $ 5 - 10 Million
Number Employees: 50-99
Type of Packaging: Food Service, Private Label, Bulk

5467 Generation Foods Too
20969 Ventura Blvd
Woodland Hills, CA 91364-2305   818-887-5858
    Fax: 626-331-0040
Candy
    Owner: David Ginsberg
    VP: Steffani Corri-Dolivo
    Director Of Sales: Scott Corri
Estimated Sales: $ 10 - 20 Million
Number Employees: 20-49
Brands:
    MOUTH FOAMING GUMBALLS
    SHAVING CREAM CANDY FUN FOAM
    SOUR LIQUID CANDY
    SOUR POWDER CANDY

5468 Generation Tea
6 Sydell Ln
Spring Valley, NY 10977-6018   845-352-1216
    Fax: 845-352-2973 866-742-5668
    contact@generationtea.com
    www.generationtea.com
Manufacturer of premium whole leaf chinese tea - contains no additives or preservatives
    President/Co-Owner: Michael Sanft
    Co-Owner: Marci Sanft
Estimated Sales: $300,000-500,000
Number Employees: 1-4

5469 (HQ)Genesee Farms
10 Irving Parkway
Oakfield, NY 14125-1109   716-343-5878
    President: Alvin Scrogen
    Marketing Director: Rollin Scrogen
Estimated Sales: $10-20 Million
Number Employees: 100-249
Sq. footage: 18
Type of Packaging: Private Label

5470 Genesis Research Corporation
918 Sherwood Drive
Lake Bluff, IL 60044-2204   847-810-3416
    Fax: 847-234-5545 888-225-2201
    www.genesisresearchonline.com
    CEO: Mark Nottoli
    Marketing Director: Bill Froese
    Purchasing Manager: Ernie Hughes
Type of Packaging: Private Label, Bulk

5471 Geneva Foods
119 Commerce Way # B
Sanford, FL 32771-3085   407-323-5518
    Fax: 407-323-4394 800-240-2326
    Lysanders@genevafoods.com
    www.lysanders.com
Dried beans, soups, marinades, dip mixes and seasoning blends
    President: Tom Vandermar
    Senior Partner: Pete Corteville
Estimated Sales: $10-20 Million
Number Employees: 10-19

5472 (HQ)Geneva Ingredients
413 Moravian Valley Rd
Waunakee, WI 53597-9593   608-849-9440
    Fax: 608-850-3762 800-828-5924
    jwick@terracom.net www.mastertaste.com
Processor and exporter of flavors including butter, fish, meat, pork, poultry, seafood and vegetable; also, natural antioxidants, beef extract replacements, broths, hydrolyzed vegetable protein replacers, meat bases, sauces and bonestocks
    President: Warren Meyer
    VP Technical Service: Jay Wickeham
    Plant Manager: Dan Hoeft
Estimated Sales: $20-50 Million
Number Employees: 20-49
Type of Packaging: Bulk
Other Locations:
    Geneva Ingredients
    Union NJ

5473 Geni
1250 Conner St # 201
Noblesville, IN 46060-2900   317-219-0355
    Fax: 317-776-3750 888-656-4364
    info@geniherbs.com www.geniherbs.com
Boswellia Serrata Extract
    Owner/President/CEo: Ajay Patel
    Research & Development: Dr Lal Hingorani
    Marketing Director: Sonya Bucklew
    Sales Director: Nipen Lavingia
Estimated Sales: $ .5 - 1 million
Number Employees: 10-19
Number of Brands: 2
Number of Products: 30
Brands:
    WOKVEL

5474 Genisoy Food Company
100 W 5th Street
Suite 700
Tulsa, OK 74103   866-606-3829
    888-437-4769
    info@genisoy.com www.genisoy.com
Mission is to provide convenient, delicious and affordable soy products that make it easy to incorporate the benefits of soy in the average person's everyday diet. Products include bars, shakes, powders, soy nuts, trail mixes, soycrisps, potato soy crisps and low carb bars.
    Founder/President: Paul Wenner
Type of Packaging: Food Service

5475 Genisoy Products Company
100 W. 5th Street,Suite 700
Suite C
Tulsa, OK 74103   800-228-4656
    Fax: 707-399-2518 800-228-4656
    www.mloproducts.com
Mission is to provide convenient, delicious and affordable soy products that make it easy to incorporate the benefits of soy in the average person's everday diet. Products include bars, shakes, powders, soy nuts, trail mixes, soycrisps, potato soy crisps and low carb bars.
    President/CEO: Doug Williamson
    CFO: Al Larson
    Director Of Marketing: Sharon Jacobson
    VP Sales/Marketing: Duke Field
Estimated Sales: $ .5 - 1 million
Number Employees: 350
Brands:
    GENISOY SOY PRODUCTS
    MLO SPORTS NUTRITION

5476 Gentile Brothers Company
10310 Julian Dr
Cincinnati, OH 45215-1131   513-771-5579
    Fax: 513-771-5569 800-877-7954
    www.gentilebros.com

Serving and processor of quality produce to the retail chains and foodservice distributors around the world
President/COO: Ed Sabin
CEO: Glen Bryant
West Virginia Sales Director: Ernie Coe
Director Marketing: Tom Rettig
VP Sales/Logistics: Dave Schirman
Sales/Product Manager: Chris Deier
Specialist/Banana/Pineapple: Jim Flehmer
Type of Packaging: Consumer

5477 Gentilini's Italian Products
55415 Lazy River Dr
Sunriver, OR 97707-2539 541-593-5053
Fax: 541-593-5609 pasta@teleport.com
www.gentilinis.com
Processor of fresh pastas including egg and gluten-free, fettucine, angel hair, linguine, seafood and herb and vegetable stuffed, cheese free pesto, fresh tomato sauce; also, sauces including pesto, marinara and alfredo; gift basketsavailable
Owner: Wesley Vinc Acker
Co-Owner: Becky Gentilini
Estimated Sales: $5-10 Million
Number Employees: 1-4
Sq. footage: 5000

5478 Gentle Ben's Brewing Company
P.O.Box 3458
Tucson, AZ 85722-3458 520-624-4177
Fax: 520-884-9776 www.gentlebens.com
Manufacturing of beer and ale
President: Dennis Arnold
Estimated Sales: $1-2.5 Million
Number Employees: 50-99
Type of Packaging: Private Label
Brands:
Copperhead Pale Ale
Gentle Ben Winter Brau
Nolan Porter
Red Cat Amber
Taylor Jane's Raspberry Ale
Tucson Blonde

5479 Gentry's Poultry Company
P.O.Box 38
Ward, SC 29166-0038 864-445-2161
Fax: 864-445-2331 800-926-2161
Processor of poultry
Manager: Wesley M Gentry Iii Jr
VP: Wesley Gentry III
Estimated Sales: $ 5 - 10 Million
Number Employees: 5-9
Type of Packaging: Consumer, Food Service

5480 Geon Technologies
35 Melanie Ln
Whippany, NJ 07981-1638 973-929-3700
Fax: 973-889-4340 800-303-3041
mediadept@goengroup.com www.trimspa.com
President: Alex Goen
Public Relations Specialist: Chrissy Kulig
Estimated Sales: $ 20 - 50 Million
Number Employees: 100-249
Brands:
TrimSpa
Winsuel

5481 George A Dickel & Company
P.O.Box 490
Tullahoma, TN 37388-0490 931-857-9313
Fax: 931-857-9313 www.dickel.com
Processor of whiskey
Master Distiller: John Lunn
Plant Manager: Jennings Backus
Estimated Sales: $10-20 Million
Number Employees: 20-49
Parent Co: Guiness PLC
Type of Packaging: Consumer

5482 George A Jeffreys & Company
504 Roanoke St
Salem, VA 24153-3552 540-389-8220
Fax: 540-387-7418 www.novozymes.com
Manufacturer and exporter of enzymes
Manager: Doug Acksel
Estimated Sales: $5-10 Million
Number Employees: 10-19
Sq. footage: 50000

5483 George Braun Oyster Company
P.O.Box 971
Cutchogue, NY 11935-0971 631-734-7770
Fax: 631-734-7462
Processor and distributor of oysters
Estimated Sales: $2.5-5 Million
Number Employees: 20-49

5484 George Chiala Farms
15500 Hill Rd
Morgan Hill, CA 95037-9516 408-778-0562
Fax: 408-779-4034 georgejr@gcfarm-inc.com
www.gcfarmsinc.com
Processor of tomatillos, garlic and peppers including jalapeno, chile, bell, habanero, kosher, organic, etc
President: George Chiala
CFO: Alan Chiala
Marketing/Sales: George Chiala, Jr
Sales Director: Don Hall
Plant Manager: Pat Connelly
Estimated Sales: $20-50 Million
Number Employees: 100-249
Number of Products: 300
Sq. footage: 40000
Type of Packaging: Food Service, Bulk

5485 George E De Lallo Company
101 Lincoln Hwy E
Jeannette, PA 15644 724-523-6577
Fax: 724-523-0198 800-307-0198
delallo@delallo.com www.delallo.com
Importer and packer of Italian foods including pasta, sauces, grocery products, olives, oils, etc
President: Francis De Lallo
Purchasing Agent: J Panichella
Estimated Sales: $500,000-$1 Million
Number Employees: 5-9
Type of Packaging: Consumer

5486 George F Brocke & Sons
P.O.Box 159
Kendrick, ID 83537-0159 208-289-4231
Fax: 208-289-4242
Garbanzo beans, rapeseed
President: George Brocke
General Manager: Dean Brocke
Estimated Sales: $10-20 Million
Number Employees: 20-49

5487 George H Hathaway Coffee Company
6210 S Archer Rd
Summit Argo, IL 60501-1721 708-458-7668
Fax: 708-458-7668
Coffee
President: B Gordon

5488 George H Leidenheimer Baking
1501 Simon Bolivar Ave
New Orleans, LA 70113-2399 504-525-1575
Fax: 504-525-1596 800-259-9099
www.leidenheimer.com
Bread, rolls
President: Robert J Whann Iv III
Estimated Sales: $10-20 Million
Number Employees: 50-99

5489 George L. Wells Meat Company
P.O.Box 37011
Philadelphia, PA 19122-0711 215-627-3903
Fax: 215-922-7648 800-523-1730
www.wellsmeats.com
Processor of beef, pork, veal, seafood, frozen vegetables, frozen desserts, butter, eggs and processed chicken
President/Owner: James Conboy
VP Sales/Marketing: Shawn Padgett
Estimated Sales: $100-500 Million
Number Employees: 50-99

5490 George Noroian
5700 Balboa Drive
Oakland, CA 94611-2315 510-591-7044
info@fruitfulvalley.com
Processor of canned peaches including white nectar, Elberta and organic; also, frozen peach puree and canned and frozen orange slices
Proprietor: George Noroian
Estimated Sales: $50-100 Million
Number Employees: 100-249
Sq. footage: 100000

5491 George Richter Farm
4512 70th Ave E
Fife, WA 98424-3710 253-922-5649
Fax: 253-926-0621
Grower, processor and exporter of fresh and frozen raspberries, blackberries, tayberries and nectarberries; also, currants and rhubarb
President: George Richter
Estimated Sales: $100+ Million
Number Employees: 10-19
Number of Brands: 1
Sq. footage: 6000
Type of Packaging: Consumer, Food Service
Brands:
RICHTERS

5492 George Robberecht Seafood
440 McGuires Wharf Rd
Montross, VA 22520-3603 804-472-3556
Fax: 804-472-4800
Processor and exporter of live blue crab, soft-shell crab, oyster meats, eel, croaker, spot, and striped bass.
President/CEO: Maurice Bosse
Estimated Sales: $2.5-5 Million
Number Employees: 1-4

5493 George W Saulpaugh & Sons
1790 Route 9
Germantown, NY 12526-5512 518-537-6500
Fax: 518-537-5555
Processor and exporter of apples, pears, grapes and prunes
President: Alan Saulpaugh
VP: David Jones
Estimated Sales: $10-20 Million
Number Employees: 20-49
Type of Packaging: Consumer, Food Service, Bulk
Brands:
CLERMONT

5494 George Weston Bakeries
1724 5th Ave
Bay Shore, NY 11706-3444 631-242-2222
800-356-3314
www.gwbakeries.com
Processor of pizza, garlic bread, cookies, pies, English muffins and low-fat cakes
Owner/Presiednt: Gary Prince
VP Finance: Bill Petersen
Estimated Sales: $100-500 Million
Number Employees: 1-4
Parent Co: Unilever USA
Type of Packaging: Consumer
Brands:
ANZIO AND SONS
ARNOLD
AUGUST BROTHERS
BOBOLI
BOUYEA FASSETTS
BROWNBERRY
COTTAGE HOUSE, ENTENMANN'S
FREIHOFER'S
HEALTHY HOME
LEVY'S
STROEHMANN
THOMAS'

5495 (HQ)George Weston Bakeries
3325 NW 62nd Street
Hollywood, FL 33023 305-836-4900
Fax: 305-835-1349 800-356-3314
www.gwbakeries.com
Manufacturer and exporter of baked goods
Sales Manager: Mike Martinez
Estimated Sales: $3-$5 Million
Type of Packaging: Consumer
Brands:
Boboli
Freihofer's

5496 George Weston Bakeries
1 Petra Ln
Albany, NY 12205-4961 518-456-4792
Fax: 518-482-0419 800-531-4002
www.gwbakeries.com
Manufacturer of baked goods including brownies, pastries, cookies, danish and cakes; also, fat-free cakes, chocolate chip loaf and raspberry cheese buns
Manager: George Weston
Sales/Marketing Executive: Tim Howe
GM: Pete Rollins
Number Employees: 1,000-4,999
Parent Co: Weston Foods

5497 George Weston Bakeries
300 W North Avenue
Northlake, IL 60164-2404   708-562-6311
          Fax: 708-409-4232 www.gwbakeries.com
Manufacturer of bread, cakes, pies, danish, cookies
and muffins
GM/VP: John Speaker
Number Employees: 200
Type of Packaging: Consumer

5498 George Weston Bakeries
1724 5th Ave
Bay Shore, NY 11706-3444   631-242-2222
                                  800-356-3314
                             www.gwbakeries.com
Manufacturer of baked goods
VP Finance: Bill Petersen
Sales Director: Joan Dogery
Operations Manager: Charles Loschman
Estimated Sales: $ 5 - 10 Million
Number Employees: 5-9
Type of Packaging: Consumer

5499 George Weston Bakeries
2300 Old Dixie Hwy
Riviera Beach, FL 33404-5456   561-848-9705
                                 Fax: 561-844-6182
Manufacturer of Baked goods such as cakes, breads,
etc.
Estimated Sales: $100-500 Million
Number Employees: 100-249
Type of Packaging: Consumer

5500 George's
P.O.Box G
Springdale, AR 72765   479-927-7500
          Fax: 479-927-7525 877-855-3447
                    jlossing@george'sinc.com
Frozen chickens whole raw, chicken parts, chicken
prepared
President: Monty Henderson
CEO: Gary George
Executive VP: Otto Jech
Field Operations Manager: Fred Edwards
Plant Manager: Pat Mareth
Estimated Sales: $50-100 Million
Number Employees: 50-99
Type of Packaging: Private Label
Brands:
GEORGE'S
TASTE O'SPRIING

5501 George's Chicken
19992 Senedo Rd
Edinburg, VA 22824-3172   540-984-4121
                            Fax: 540-984-8360
Poultry business
President: Robert Kenney
President: Bob Feather
Marketing Director: Don Stroud
Estimated Sales: $100+ Million
Number Employees: 1,000-4,999
Type of Packaging: Private Label
Brands:
George's Chicken

5502 Georges Chicken
19992 Senedo Rd
Edinburg, VA 22824-3172   540-984-4121
                            Fax: 540-984-8360
Manufacturer and exporter of fresh and frozen tur-
key and chicken including whole, without giblets,
livers, legs, leg quarters, pieces and hot dogs
President: Robert Kenney
Contact: Gary Richman
Estimated Sales: $100+ Million
Number Employees: 1,000-4,999
Sq. footage: 130000
Parent Co: Rocco
Type of Packaging: Consumer, Food Service, Bulk

5503 (HQ)Georgetown Farm
P.O.Box 106
Free Union, VA 22940-0106   434-973-6761
          Fax: 434-973-7715 888-328-5326
info@georgetownfarm.com   www.eatlean.com
Processor of piedmontese beef and bison meat in-
cluding sausage and jerky products
Production: Craig Gibson
Plant Manager: Matt Albert
Estimated Sales: $3-5 Million
Number Employees: 5-9

Brands:
GEORGETOWN FARM BISON
GEORGETOWN FARM PIEDMONTESE

5504 Georgetown Fisherman's Co-Op
79 Moores Tpke
Georgetown, ME 04548-3925   207-371-2950
                             Fax: 207-371-2907
Seafood
Manager: Mohamed Khan
Estimated Sales: $ .5 - 1 million
Number Employees: 1-4

5505 Georgia Fruit Cake Company
5 S Duval St
Claxton, GA 30417-2027   912-739-2683
                          Fax: 912-739-3419
          www.georgiafruitcakecompany.com
Processor and exporter of canned fruit cakes
President: Ira S Womble Jr
CEO: Ira Womble Jr
Estimated Sales: $5-10 Million
Number Employees: 5-9
Number of Brands: 2
Number of Products: 2
Sq. footage: 10000
Type of Packaging: Consumer
Brands:
GEORGIA
GEORGIA FRUIT CAKE

5506 Georgia Nut Company
7500 Linder Ave
Skokie, IL 60077-3270   847-324-3600
          Fax: 847-674-1173 800-621-1264
Processor of nut meats and candies including malted
milk balls, chocolate raisins, double dip peanuts and
coated pretzels
CEO: Rick Drehobl
CEO: Richard A Drehobl
VP Sales & Marketing: Rick Lytle
Sales Manager: Steve Coryea
Estimated Sales: $20-50 Million
Number Employees: 100-249
Type of Packaging: Private Label
Brands:
DRIZZLS!
GEORGIA'S
MALT TEENIES
SPECKLS!
TEENIES

5507 Georgia Nut Ingredients
7500 Linder Ave
Skokie, IL 60077-3270   847-324-3600
          Fax: 847-674-1173 877-674-2993
sgi@solofoods.com   www.georgianuts.com
Processor of fruit and nut fillings, European pastry
fillings, marshmallow creme, toffees, malt balls,
brittles, etc
President: Tom Musso
Marketing Manager: Alet Schneider
R & D: Carol Anderson
CEO: Richard A Drehobl
CFO: Rick Trehobl
CFO: Arends Jack
Estimated Sales: $ 20-50 Million
Number Employees: 100-249
Sq. footage: 2000
Parent Co: Georgia Nut Company
Type of Packaging: Bulk
Brands:
Georgia's
Solo

5508 Georgia Seafood Wholesale
5634 New Peachtree Rd
Chamblee, GA 30341-2508   770-936-0483
                            Fax: 770-936-9332
Scallops, frozen seafood, shrimp
Owner: Jack Wong
Estimated Sales: $ 3 - 5 Million
Number Employees: 5-9

5509 Georgia Spice Company
3600 Atlanta Industrial Pky NW
Atlanta, GA 30331-1004   404-696-6200
          Fax: 404-696-4546 800-453-9997
                    gaspice@aol.com
Processor, importer and exporter of blended spices
and seasonings for snacks, poultry and meat; also,
custom blending and kosher available
Owner: Selma Shapiro

Estimated Sales: $5-10 Million
Number Employees: 20-49
Sq. footage: 25000
Type of Packaging: Food Service, Private Label,
Bulk

5510 Georgia Sun
50 Amlajack Blvd
Newnan, GA 30265-1016   770-251-2500
Processor and importer of beverage bases and juice
concentrates
President: Walter Loesche
Estimated Sales: Less than $500,000
Number Employees: 1-4
Sq. footage: 40000
Type of Packaging: Consumer, Food Service, Pri-
vate Label, Bulk
Brands:
Georgia Sun

5511 Georgia Vegetable Company
P.O.Box 2037
Tifton, GA 31793-2037   229-386-2374
                          Fax: 229-386-2500
          georgiavegetable@surfsouth.com
Processor of produce including snap beans, pole
beans, cabbage, corn, cucumbers, eggplant, peppers,
squash, etc
President: Billy Thomas
Co-Owner: Rebecca Kilby
Co-Owner: Shay Briggs
Estimated Sales: $5-10 Million
Number Employees: 10-19
Type of Packaging: Consumer, Bulk

5512 Georgia Winery
I-75 Exit 350 Battlefield Parkway
Ringgold, GA 30736   706-937-2177
                    info@georgiawines.com
                    www.georgiawines.com
Winery - red wines such as: concord, blackberry,
raspberry, roses and blushes and white wines.
Founder: Dr Maurice Rawlings Sr
Estimated Sales: $5-9.9 Million
Number Employees: 1-4

5513 Georis Winery
4 Pilot Rd
Carmel Valley, CA 93924-9515   831-659-1050
          Fax: 831-659-1054 info@georiswine.com
                    www.georiswine.com
Grows, producers and bottles only the finest Merlot
and Cabernet Sauvignon wines.
President: Walter Georis
Purchasing: Sylvia Georis
Estimated Sales: $500,000-$1 Million
Number Employees: 5-9
Type of Packaging: Private Label
Brands:
ESTATE CABERNET SAUVIGNON
ESTATE MERLOT

5514 Gerard's French Bakery
4226 County Road 22
Longmont, CO 80504-9403   303-772-4710
          Fax: 303-581-0212 gerard@aol.com
Processor of focaccia, sourdough, baked and
par-baked breads, croissants and hamburger buns
President: Gerry Watson
VP Operations: Gary Hoerner
Estimated Sales: $20-50 Million
Number Employees: 100-249
Parent Co: Mountain View Harvest Cooperative
Type of Packaging: Food Service, Private Label
Brands:
GERARD'S FRENCH BAKERY
MOUNTAINVIEW HARVEST BAKERY

5515 Gerawan Farming
P.O.Box 67
Sanger, CA 93657-0067   559-787-8780
          Fax: 559-787-8798 primasales@gerawan.com
                    www.gerawan.com
Grower and exporter of grapes and tree fruit
President: Dan Gerawan
Sales Manager: Karen Osborn
Estimated Sales: $100-500 Million
Number Employees: 50-99
Type of Packaging: Bulk
Brands:
PRIMA

5516 (HQ)Gerber Products Company
200 Kimball Dr
Parsippany, NJ 07054-2173   973-503-8000
Fax: 973-503-8450   800-443-7237
www.novartis.com
More than 350 Gerber and NUK branded products.
Processor and importer of banana flakes, essence
and nonhomogenized frozen banana purees and con-
centrates. Aseptic, organic, kosher and homogenized
available. ISD-9002 certified, HACCPmonitored
President/CEO: Frank Palantoni
CFO: Kurt Furger
CEO: Larry Allgaire
VP R&D/Quality Control: Jan Relford
Marketing Director: David Yates
Public Relations: Terry Boylan
Number Employees: 100-249
Parent Co: Novartis Consumer Health
Type of Packaging: Food Service, Bulk
Brands:
  GERBER 1ST FOODS
  GERBER 2ND FOODS
  GERBER 3RD FODOS
  GERBER GRADUATES

5517 Gerber Products Company
26 Lote
Carolina, PR 00984   787-769-7745
Baby foods
Parent Co: Gerber Products Company

5518 Gerbers Poultry
P.O.Box 206
Kidron, OH 44636-0206   330-857-2731
Fax: 330-857-1841   800-362-7381
mgerber@gerbers.com   www.gerbers.com
Processor of poultry
President: D Michael Gerber
Controller: John Metzger CPA
VP Sales/Distribution: Timothy Gerber
Estimated Sales: $20-50 Million
Number Employees: 250-499

5519 Gerhard's Napa Valley Sausage
910 Enterprise Way
Napa, CA 94558-6209   707-252-4116
Fax: 707-252-0879   gnvs@jps.net
www.gerhardsausage.com
Processor of gourmet sausage
Owner: Gerhard Twele
Estimated Sales: $10-20 Million
Number Employees: 50-99
Sq. footage: 27000
Type of Packaging: Consumer

5520 Gerhart Coffee Company
224 Wohlsen Way
Lancaster, PA 17603-4043   717-397-8788
Fax: 717-397-3677   800-536-4310
sales@gerhartcoffee.com
www.gerhartcoffee.com
Processor of coffee that is available in decaf, fla-
vored and blended. Food service available to: hotels,
coffee houses, fund raisers, schools and colleges, ba-
gel shops, grocery stores, gift shops, etc.
Owner/President: Charles Braungard
Representative: Donald Platt
Representative: Darrel Burns
Representative: Peter Bard
Estimated Sales: $1-2.5 Million
Number Employees: 1-4
Sq. footage: 4200

5521 Gerhart Coffee Company
224 Wohlsen Way
Lancaster, PA 17603-4043   717-397-8788
Fax: 717-397-3677   800-536-4310
www.gerhartcoffee.com
Coffee
President: Charles Braungard
Sales Director: Charles Braungard
Estimated Sales: $1-2.5 Million
Number Employees: 1-4
Type of Packaging: Private Label

5522 Gerkens CacaoWilbur Chocolate Company
20 N Broad Street
Lititz, PA 17543-1005   717-626-3450
Fax: 717-626-3488   800-233-0139
gerkenscocao@cargill.com
www.gerkenscocoa.com
Manufacturer of chocolate
President: William Shaughnessy

Parent Co: Cargill Incorporated

5523 Germack Pistachio Company
2140 Wilkins St
Detroit, MI 48207-2123   313-393-2000
Fax: 313-393-0636   800-872-4006
questions@germack.com   www.germack.com
Processor and importer of dried fruit, chocolate and
nuts including cashews, filberts, peanuts and pista-
chios
Owner: Frank Germack
Estimated Sales: $1-2.5 Million
Number Employees: 20-49
Type of Packaging: Consumer, Food Service

5524 Germain-Robin
P.O.Box 175
Ukiah, CA 95482-0175   707-462-0314
Fax: 707-462-8885   800-782-8145
alambic@pacific.net
Distiller and exporter of brandy. Marketing of spe-
cialty spirits
President: Ansley J Coale Jr
Estimated Sales: $1-2.5 Million
Number Employees: 1-4
Sq. footage: 20000
Type of Packaging: Consumer, Private Label

5525 Germain-Robin/Alambic
P.O.Box 175
Ukiah, CA 95482-0175   707-462-0314
Fax: 707-462-8885
Distilled spirits
President: Ansley J Coale Jr
Co-Founder: Hubert Germain-Robin
Estimated Sales: $1-2.5 Million
Number Employees: 1-4
Type of Packaging: Private Label

5526 German Bakery at Village Corner
6655 James B Rivers Dr
Stone Mountain, GA 30083-2232   770-498-0329
Fax: 770-498-9863   866-476-6443
germanrestaurant@aol.com
www.germanrestaurant.com
Full line of bakery products, breads and rolls
Owner: Hilde Friese
Co-Owner: Clause Friese
Estimated Sales: $ 1 - 3 Million
Number Employees: 10-19
Brands:
  Bailey's Irish Cream

5527 German Village Products
P.O.Box 417
Wauseon, OH 43567-0417   419-335-1515
Fax: 419-337-0514
Processor and exporter of dried pasta
Estimated Sales: $10-20 Million
Number Employees: 20-49
Sq. footage: 80000
Parent Co: Campbell Soup Company
Type of Packaging: Bulk

5528 Germanton Winery
3530 Highway 8
Germanton, NC 27019   336-969-2075
Fax: 336-969-6559   800-322-2894
sales@germantongallery.com
www.germantongallery.com
Wine list consists of chardonnay, seyval blanc, white
zinfandel, vermillion, merlot, niagara, and sweet red
wines.
President: David Simpson
Treasurer: Judy Simpson
Estimated Sales: Less than $500,000
Number Employees: 1-4

5529 Gertrude & Bronner's Magic Alpsnack
P.O.Box 28
Escondido, CA 92033-0028   760-743-2211
Fax: 760-745-6675   allone@drbronner.com
www.drbronner.com
Manufacturer of energy snack bars that contain
hemp nut
President: David Bronner
VP: Ralph Bronner
Estimated Sales: $ 1 - 3 Million
Number Employees: 1-4
Type of Packaging: Consumer
Brands:
  Dr. Bronner's

5530 Gertrude Hawk Chocolates
9 Keystone Park
Dunmore, PA 18512   570-342-7556
Fax: 570-342-0266   800-706-6275
www.markavenuechocolates.com
milk chocolate, dark chocolate, nno-chocolate con-
fections, sugar-free chocolates and white chocolate
President: David Hawk
CFO/VP: Steven Arling
VP Sales/Marketing: Christopher Cuneo
Human Resources Director: David Garton
VP Operations/Producstion/Manufacturing: Steve
Liddic
Purchasing Manager: Sandra Koch

5531 Gertrude Hawk Chocolates
9 Keystone Industrial Park
Dunmore, PA 18512-1544   570-342-7556
Fax: 570-342-0261   800-822-2032
webmaster@gertrudehawk.com
www.gertrudehawkchocolates.com
Processor of chocolates including truffles, molds
and bulk chocolates, sugar-free chocolates
President: David Hawk
Chairman: Ethan Hawk
CEO: Bill Aubrey
Estimated Sales: $20-50 Million
Number Employees: 500-999

5532 Gertrude Hawk Ingredients
5117 Pine Top Pl
Orlando, FL 32819-3846   407-876-6785
Fax: 407-876-8671   800-822-2032
chrisbyrd@aol.com
Chocolate confections for bakery and frozen des-
serts
President: David Hawk
Chairman: Ethan Hawk

5533 Gesco ENR
Cp 830
Gaspe, QC G4X 6H4
Canada   418-368-1414
Fax: 418-368-1812   gesco@globetrotter.qc.ca
Processor and exporter of fresh and frozen shrimp
President: Gaetan Denis
Number Employees: 20-49
Type of Packaging: Consumer, Food Service, Pri-
vate Label, Bulk

5534 Getchell Brothers
1 Union St
Brewer, ME 04412-2040   207-989-7335
Fax: 207-989-7810   800-949-4423
Wines
President: Willard Farnham
Estimated Sales: $2.5-5 Million
Number Employees: 20-49

5535 Geyser Peak Winery
P.O.Box 25
Geyserville, CA 95441-0025   707-857-9463
Fax: 707-857-3545   800-945-4447
geyserpk@sonic.net   www.geyserpeakwinery.org
Processor and exporter of table wines
Manager: Lisa Flohr
VP/Winemaker: Daryl Groom
Public Relations: Tim McDonald
Production Manager: Paul White
Estimated Sales: $20-50 Million
Number Employees: 50-99
Parent Co: Jim Beam Brands Worldwide
Brands:
  CANYON ROAD
  GEYSER PEAK
  VENEZIA

5536 Ghirardelli Chocolate Company
150 John F Kennedy Parkway
Suite 100
Short Hills, NJ 07078-2701   908-898-0021
Fax: 510-297-2649   800-877-9338
Processor of confections and chocolate baking prod-
ucts including chips, bars and powders; also, hot
beverages
Sr. VP Sales: Andrew Nestler
VP Sales: Mark Greenhall
Number Employees: 150
Type of Packaging: Food Service

5537 Ghirardelli Chocolate Company
1111 139th Ave
San Leandro, CA 94578-2616   510-483-6970
Fax: 510-297-2649   800-877-9338
www.ghirardelli.com
Manufacturer of chocolate and cocoa
President/CEO: Fabrizio Parini
CFO: Jurgen Auerbach
VP Sales/Marketing: Marty Thompson
Estimated Sales:$100-500 Million
Number Employees: 250-499
Type of Packaging: Private Label
Brands:
GHIRARDELLI

5538 Ghirardelli Ranch
371 Jewett Rd
Petaluma, CA 94952-8117   707-795-7616
Grower of fresh produce including zucchini, leeks,
lettuce and beets
Co-Owner: Dorothy Ghirardelli
Co-Owner: Gildo Ghirardelli
Number Employees: 10-19
Type of Packaging: Consumer, Bulk
Brands:
GHIRARDELLI RANCH

5539 Ghyslain Chocolatier
350 W Deerfield Rd
Union City, IN 47390-1039   765-964-7905
Fax: 765-964-9138   866-449-7524
ghyslain@pop.skyenet.net   www.ghyslain.com
Artisan chocolates
President: Ghyslain Maurais
Estimated Sales:$2.5-5 Million
Number Employees: 10-19

5540 Gia Russa
65 Coitsville Hubbard Rd
Coitsville, OH 44505   330-743-6050
Fax: 330-743-0739   800-527-8772
customers@giarussa.com   www.giarussa.com
pasta and sauces

5541 Giacorelli Imports
20423 State Road 7
Boca Raton, FL 33498-6797   561-451-1415
Fax: 561-451-1618   giacorelli@aol.com
All-natural, sparkling fruit juice imported from Italy
President: Thomas Spirelli
Estimated Sales:$2 Million
Number Employees: 5-9
Brands:
GIACOBAZZI JUICE SPA
PEACH-STRAWBERRY-RASPBERRY-SPAR-
KLE
RED & WHITE GRAPE JUICE
TANGERINE SPARKLING BEVERAGE

5542 Giambri's Quality Sweets
26 Brand Ave
Clementon, NJ 08021   856-783-1099
Fax: 856-783-6377   dave@giambris.com
www.giambris.com
hard candies, creamy fudge and chocolates
President/Owner: David Giambri
VP: Josephine Giambri
Number Employees: 6

5543 Giant Food
10515 Greenbelt Rd
Lanham, MD 20706-2213   301-666-1181
Fax: 301-618-4967   888-469-4426
www.giantfood.com
Processor of baked products including bread, rolls,
cakes, pies, sweetgoods, doughnuts and cookies
Manager: Tarjani Shah
Executive VP/General Manager: Bill Holmes
VP Quality Control: David Richman
Public Relations: Barry Scher
Manufacturing Director: Walter Auman
Number Employees: 5,000-9,999
Type of Packaging: Consumer

5544 Giasi Winery
4194 State Route 14
Rock Stream, NY 14878-9612   607-535-7785
Wines
Estimated Sales:$300,000-500,000
Number Employees: 1-4

5545 Gibbon Packing
P.O.Box 730
Gibbon, NE 68840-0730   308-468-5771
Fax: 308-468-5262
Manufacturer of boneless beef and offal products
President: Wesley Hodge
Estimated Sales:$100-500 Million
Number Employees: 250-499
Parent Co: IBP
Type of Packaging: Consumer

5546 Gibbons Bee Farm
314 Quinnmoor Dr
Ballwin, MO 63011-2515   636-394-5395
Fax: 636-256-0303   877-736-8607
info@gibbonsbeefarm.com
www.gibbonsbeefarm.com
Processor of honey, salad dressing and honey mus-
tard
Owner: Sharon Gibbons
Sales Manager: John Gibbons
Estimated Sales:$ 1 - 3 Million
Number Employees: 1-4
Type of Packaging: Consumer
Brands:
GIBBONS

5547 Gibbsville Cheese Company
W2663 County Road Oo
Sheboygan Falls, WI 53085-2971   920-564-3242
Fax: 920-564-6129   sales@gibbsvillecheese.com
www.gibbsvillecheese.com
Manufacturer of fine cheddar, colby, montery jack,
and two-tone (montery and colby) cheeses
Owner: Phillip Van Tatenhove
Estimated Sales:$1-2.5 Million
Number Employees: 10-19
Sq. footage: 5000
Type of Packaging: Consumer

5548 Gibson Wine Company
1720 Academy Ave
Sanger, CA 93657-3799   559-875-2505
Fax: 559-875-4761
Processor and exporter of table wines
President: Leland Herman
Sales: Leland Herman
Production: Glenn Nilmeier
General Manager: Kim Spruance
Estimated Sales:$20-50 Million
Number Employees: 50-99
Sq. footage: 144000
Parent Co: Bronco Wine Company
Type of Packaging: Consumer, Private Label, Bulk
Brands:
GIBSON VINEYARDS

5549 Gibsonburg Canning Company
401 S Gibson St
Gibsonburg, OH 43431-1306   419-637-2221
Fax: 419-637-2003
Canned whole tomatoes, diced tomatoes, stewed to-
matoes, no salt added tomatoes, Italian style stewed
tomatoes
President: Jerry Schuett
Estimated Sales:$1-2.5 Million
Number Employees: 5-9
Brands:
J & J

5550 Gielow Pickles
5260 Main St
Lexington, MI 48450-9393   810-359-7680
Fax: 810-359-2408 www.gielowpickles.com
Manufacturer, importer and exporter of pickles,
sweet relish
President: Douglas Gielow
VP Sales: Craig Gielow
Sales Representative: Sue Burgess
Order/Receiving: Lisa Disser
Assistant Plant Manager: Dennis Coker
Purchasing: Doug Gielow
Estimated Sales:$10-20 Million
Number Employees: 20-49
Sq. footage: 30000
Type of Packaging: Food Service, Private Label
Brands:
COOL CRISP

5551 Gifford's Dairy
25 Hathaway St
Skowhegan, ME 04976   207-474-9821
Fax: 207-474-6120 giffords@kynd.com
www.giffordsicecream.com

Processor of ice cream and sugar-free and nonfat yo-
gurt
President: Roger Gifford
Treasurer: John Gifford
Estimated Sales:$ 10 - 20 Million
Number Employees: 20-49
Type of Packaging: Consumer, Food Service
Brands:
GIFFORD'S

5552 Gifford's Ice Cream & Candy Co
8810 Brookville Rd
Silver Spring, MA 20910   800-708-1938
info@giffords.com   www.giffords.com
ice cream and candy
President/CEO: Marcelo Ramagem
VP: Neal Lieberman
Number Employees: 5

5553 Gift Basket Supply World
815 Haines Street
Jacksonville, FL 32206-6050   904-353-6278
Fax: 904-633-8764   800-786-4438
www.gbswimports.com
Gourmet foods
Estimated Sales:$2.5-5 Million
Number Employees: 5-9

5554 Gift Factory/Beverly Hills
12432 Gladstone Ave
Sylmar, CA 91342-5320   818-365-6619
Fax: 818-365-8519   800-365-6619
Manufacturer of Truffle cookies and confections,
packaged snacks and confections, flavored chocolate
spoons for coffee service and gift sales, keepsake
greeting boxes filled with candies
President: Scott Goodspeed
Estimated Sales:$ 5 - 10 Million
Number Employees: 10-19
Type of Packaging: Consumer, Private Label, Bulk
Brands:
BEVERLY HILLS COLLECTION
COFFEE COMPANION
GOURMET DELIGHT
MORE THAN A BOX
MUNCHKINS
SNACK CAFE
SWEET WRAPS
TRUFFIE COOKIES

5555 Gil's Gourmet Gallery
577 Ortiz Ave
Sand City, CA 93955-3522   831-394-3305
Fax: 831-394-9144   800-438-7480
www.gilsgourmet.com
Condiments, salsa, pasta sauce, olives
President: Gil Tortolani
VP: Dylan Tortolani
Marketing Manager: Dave Elgin
Estimated Sales:$1-2.5 Million
Number Employees: 5-9
Type of Packaging: Private Label, Bulk

5556 Gilardi Foods
1910 Fair Rd
Sidney, OH 45365-8906   937-498-4511
Fax: 937-497-8786
Processor of frozen and refrigerated foods including
pizza, lasagna and submarine sandwiches
President: Bill Mackin
Plant Manager: Ken Baptist
Estimated Sales:$100+ Million
Number Employees: 250-499
Type of Packaging: Consumer, Food Service, Pri-
vate Label, Bulk
Brands:
GILARDI
MA MA ROSA
OLD ITALIAN
OUR DELI
SPANKY'S

5557 Gilda Industries
P.O.Box 133355
Hialeah, FL 33013-0355   305-887-8286
Fax: 305-888-4064 www.gildaindustries.com
Crackers
President/Owner: Juan Blazquez
Estimated Sales:$20-50 Million
Number Employees: 50-99
Type of Packaging: Private Label

5558 Gile Cheese Company
116 N Main St
Cuba City, WI 53807-1538   608-744-3456
Fax: 608-744-3457 www.gilecheese.com
Cheese, cheese products
　Co-Ower/President: John Gile
　Co-Owner: Diane Gile
　Marketing: Tim Gile
Estimated Sales:$2.5-5 Million
Number Employees: 1-4

5559 Gilette Foods
1001 Stuyvesant Ave
Union, NJ 07083-6024   908-688-0500
Fax: 908-688-0012
Supplier and importer of juices and concentrates
　Manager: Luis Rodriguez
Estimated Sales:$10-20 Million
Number Employees: 10-19

5560 Gill's Onions
1051 Pacific Ave
Oxnard, CA 93030-7254   805-240-1983
Fax: 805-271-1932 800-348-2255
www.gillsonions.com
Processor of onions
　President: Steve Gill
　Sales Manager: Susan Schmidt
Estimated Sales:$50-100 Million
Number Employees: 100-249
Sq. footage: 80000
Type of Packaging: Food Service, Bulk

5561 Gillam Brothers Peanut Sheller
P.O.Box 550
Windsor, NC 27983-0550   252-794-3435
Fax: 252-794-9167
Processor of peanuts
　Manager: Dawson Rascoe
　General Manager: David Cobb
Number Employees: 20-49
Parent Co: Gillam Brothers Peanut Sheller
Type of Packaging: Consumer, Bulk

5562 Gilleshammer Thiele Farms
P.O.Box 261
St Thomas, ND 58276-0261   701-257-6634
Agriculture farming, vegetables, meats
　President: Orville Gilleshammer
Estimated Sales:$1-2.5 Million
Number Employees: 5-9

5563 (HQ)Gilliam Candy Brands
PO Box 1060
Paducah, KY 42002-1060   270-443-6532
Fax: 270-442-1922 800-445-3008
jwyatt@gilliamcandybrands.com
www.gilliamcandybrands.com
Processor and exporter of candy, including hard,
mints taffy sticks and brittles, lollypopa, and
sugar-free candy.
　President: Brian Duwe
　CEO: Bill Lacy
　VP Sales: Jeff Wyatt
Estimated Sales:$10-20 Million
Number Employees: 50-99
Sq. footage: 30000
Type of Packaging: Consumer, Food Service, Private Label, Bulk
Other Locations:
　Gilliam Candy Brands
　Edwardsville KS
Brands:
　GILLIAM CANDY
　KITS & BB BATS
　SLO POKE
　SOPHIE MAE BRITTLE

5564 Gillies Coffee Company
150 19th St
Brooklyn, NY 11232-1005   718-499-7766
Fax: 718-499-7771 800-344-5526
info@gilliescoffee.com www.gilliescoffee.com
Processor, importer, exporter and wholesaler/distributor of roasted specialty coffees and blended specialty teas; exporter of roasted coffee
　President/CEO: Donald Schoenholt
　CFO/VP: Hy Chabbott
Estimated Sales:$10-20 Million
Number Employees: 10-19
Sq. footage: 14000
Type of Packaging: Food Service, Private Label, Bulk

Brands:
　BROOKLYN JAVA
　GILLIES
　LONG ISLAND ICED TEA

5565 Gilly's Hot Vanilla
P.O.Box 1991
Lenox, MA 01240-4991   413-637-1515
Fax: 413-637-1515
Processor of hot vanilla drink mixes
　Owner: Joanne Deutch
　Production Manager: Carl Deutch
Estimated Sales:$5-10 Million
Number Employees: 5-9
Type of Packaging: Consumer, Food Service, Bulk
Brands:
　GILLY'S HOT VANILLA

5566 Gilmore's Seafoods
131 Court St
Bath, ME 04530-2054   207-443-5231
Fax: 207-386-3271 800-849-9667
gilmore@gilmoreseafood.com
www.gilmoreseafood.com
Seafood
　Co-Owner: Kevin Gilmore
　Co-Owner: Ben Gilmore
Estimated Sales:$300,000-500,000
Number Employees: 1-4

5567 Gilroy
9301 Lacey Blvd
Hanford, CA 93230-4765   559-584-2711
Fax: 559-583-0370
　Executive Director: Mike Fry
　Marketing/Sales Coordinator: Juanita Smith
Estimated Sales:$100+ Million
Number Employees: 250-499

5568 (HQ)Gilroy Foods
1350 Pacheco Pass
Gilroy, CA 95020-9559   408-846-7817
Fax: 408-846-3523 800-921-7502
customerservice@gilroyfoods.com
www.gilroyfoods.com
Fresh, dehydrated, frozen or pureed garlic and onion, flavor systems and seasonings.
　Branch Manager: Randall Stuewe
　Director Specialty Sales: Cathy Katavich
　Purchasing Manager: Dan Hager
Estimated Sales:$1 Billion+
Number Employees: 100
Parent Co: ConAgra Foods
Type of Packaging: Food Service, Private Label, Bulk
Brands:
　AIRE FREEZ DRIED
　CERTIFIED ORGANIC
　DEHYDROFROZEN
　DIAL-A-HEAT
　ENDURACOLOR
　GARDENFROST
　GILROY FRESH
　PUFF DRIED
　QUICK COOK
　REDI-MADE/HI-FLAVOR

5569 Gilroy Foods
705 E Whitmore Ave
Modesto, CA 95358-9408   209-538-1071
Fax: 209-538-5423 www.gilroyfoods.com
Processor of freeze-dried and dehydrated vegetables
including asparagus, beets, cucumbers, green cabbage and carrots
　President: Dennis Wittchow
　COO: Mike Smyth
Parent Co: ConAgra Foods
Type of Packaging: Private Label, Bulk
Brands:
　CVC VEGETABLES
　DIAL-A-HEAT
　FRESH FLAVOR
　SNOW WHITE
　SUN SPICED

5570 Gilster Mary Lee/JasperFoods
311 W Mercer St
Jasper, MO 64755-9345   417-394-2567
Fax: 417-394-3003 800-777-2168
www.gilstermarylee.com

Processes raw popcorn and packages both poly and
microwave popcorn.
　President/CEO: Donald Welge
　CFO: Michael Welge
　VP Technical Sales: Tom Welge
　Plant Manager: Jim Cook
Estimated Sales:$300,000-500,000
Number Employees: 1-4
Sq. footage: 60000
Type of Packaging: Consumer, Food Service, Private Label, Bulk
Brands:
　Ozark
　Pop 'n Snak
　Wyman's Wild Blueberries
　Wyman's Wild Raspberries

5571 (HQ)Gilster-Mary Lee Corporation
P.O.Box 227
Chester, IL 62233-0227   618-826-2361
Fax: 618-826-2973 800-851-5371
webmaster@gilstermarylee.com
www.gilstermarylee.com
Manufacturer and exporter of baking mixes,
ready-to-eat and hot breakfast cereals, macaroni and
cheese, chocolate, pasta, instant potatoes,
microwaveable popcorn, dinner mixes, hot cocoa
mix, instant cocoa mix, sugar-sweetened
drinkmixes, specialty potatoes, and stuffing mixes
　President/CEO: Donald Welge
　CFO: Michael Welge
Estimated Sales:$100-500 Million
Number Employees: 1,000-4,999
Sq. footage: 165000
Type of Packaging: Consumer, Food Service, Private Label, Bulk
Brands:
　DUFF'S
　HOSPITALITY
　PY-O-MY

5572 Gilt Edge Flour Mills
P.O.Box 7
Richmond, UT 84333-0007   435-258-2425
Fax: 435-258-2428
customerservice@giltedgeflour.com
www.giltedgeflour.com
Processor of flour
　President: Keith Giusto
　VP: Evan Perry
Estimated Sales:$5-10 Million
Number Employees: 20-49
Type of Packaging: Consumer, Food Service, Private Label, Bulk
Brands:
　GILT EDGE

5573 Gimbal's Fine Candies
250 Hillside Blvd
S San Francisco, CA 94080-1644   650-588-4844
Fax: 650-588-0150 800-344-6225
info@gimbals.net www.gimbalscandy.com
Processor of licorice, confectionery products, fruit
slices and candy including sour balls, jelly beans and
seasonal
　President/CEO: Lance Gimbal
　VP Sales/Marketing: Estle Kominowski
　Purchasing: Ward Sims
Estimated Sales:$5-10 Million
Number Employees: 20-49
Number of Brands: 1
Number of Products: 100
Sq. footage: 30000
Type of Packaging: Consumer, Bulk
Brands:
　JELLY BEAN
　KLEERGUM
　LOWCOOM
　SOFT CHEWS
　TAFFY DELIGHT
　TAFFY LITE
　ULTIMATE

5574 Gimbal's Fine Candy
250 Hillside Blvd
S San Francisco, CA 94080-1644   650-588-4844
Fax: 650-588-0150 800-344-6225
www.gimbalscandy.com
Candy
　President: Lance Gimbal
Estimated Sales:$ 10 - 20 Million
Number Employees: 20-49

5575 Ginco International
725 Cochran St # C
Simi Valley, CA 93065-1974   805-520-7500
          Fax: 805-520-7509   800-423-5176
          ginseng@ginsengcompany.com
          www.ginsengcompany.com
Processor, importer and exporter of ginseng products
     President: Gary Raskin
Estimated Sales: $ 1 - 3 Million
Number Employees: 10-19
Sq. footage: 15000

5576 Gindi Gourmet
1845 Range Street
Boulder, CO 80301-2745   303-473-9177
          Fax: 303-473-9158
Gourmet foods

5577 Ginger People®
2700 Garden Road
Suite G
Monterey, CA 93940-5337   831-645-1090
          Fax: 831-645-1094   800-551-5284
          info@gingerpeople.com www.gingerpeople.com
Over 80 ginger products and receipes. Crystallized
ginger made in Australia to premium fresh Hawaiian
ginger. The spice has endless versatility and impres-
sive medical properties.
Estimated Sales: $ 1 - 3 Million
Number Employees: 10-19
Parent Co: Royal Pacific Foods

5578 Gingro Corp
5103 Main Street
Manchester Center, VT 05255   802-362-0836
          Fax: 802-362-0741 candeleros@gmail.com
          www.candeleros.net
ethnic cuisine and all-natural, gourmet sauces, salsas
and snacks

5579 Ginkgoton
1225 W 190th Street
Suite 225
Gardena, CA 90248-4322   310-538-8383
          Fax: 310-538-8651 shelle@ ginkgoton.com
     President: Seung Choi
Estimated Sales: $2.5-5 Million
Number Employees: 1-4

5580 Ginseng America
PO Box 246
Roxbury, NY 12474-0246   607-326-3123
Ginseng
     President: Steven Roth

5581 Ginseng Up Corporation
390 5th Ave # 8
New York, NY 10018-8104   212-696-1930
          Fax: 212-779-0493 mling10@aol.com
          www.ginsengup.com
Processor and exporter of natural soft drinks; con-
tract packaging and tunnel pasteurization available
     President: Sang Han
Estimated Sales: $ 3 - 5 Million
Number Employees: 1-4
Parent Co: One Up
Type of Packaging: Consumer
Brands:
     COLD/HOT PACK TUNNEL PASTERIZED
     FLAVOR
     GINSENG UP

5582 Giorgio Foods
P.O.Box 96
Temple, PA 19560-0096   610-926-2139
          Fax: 610-926-7012   800-220-2139
          lbortz@giorgiofoods.com
          www.giorgiofoods.com
Manufacturer and exporter of fresh and frozen
mushrooms and frozen breaded cheese sticks,
pierogies, breaded pierogies, portabella burgers, and
veggie burgers
     President: John Majewski
     CFO: Mike Butto
     Sr. Customer Service Coordinator: LuAnn Bortz
     VP Sales/Marketing: Brian Threlfall
     Regional Sales Manager: Lisa Hemker
Estimated Sales: $100-500 Million
Number Employees: 250-499
Type of Packaging: Consumer, Food Service, Pri-
vate Label, Bulk
Brands:
     BRANDYWINE

DUTCH COUNTRY
GIORGIO
PENNSYLVANIA

5583 Giovanni Food Company
114 W Oneida St
Oswego, NY 13126-2462   315-342-3451
          Fax: 315-342-9276 giovanni@dreamscape.com
          http://www.dreamscape.com
Spaghetti sauce
     President: L John DeMent
     Vice President: Louis DeMent
     Production Manager: Jim Doyen
     Plant Manager: Rick Latimer
Estimated Sales: $ 20 - 50 Million
Number Employees: 20-49
Type of Packaging: Private Label
Brands:
     DIMENTO
     LUIGI GIOVANNI
     MARIA ANGELINA

5584 Giovanni's Appetizing Food Products
P.O.Box 26
Richmond, MI 48062-0026   586-727-9355
          Fax: 586-727-3433 INFO@GIOAPP.COM
          www.gioapp.com
Processor, canner and exporter of gourmet foods in-
cluding antipasto, pickled mushrooms, chopped
chicken liver and pates: meat, fish and poultry; also,
fish pastes: anchovy, lobster, shrimp and smoked
salmon; importer of saltedanchovies.
     President: Philip Ricossa
     Secretary/Treasurer: Elvira Ricossa
Estimated Sales: $2.5-5 Million
Number Employees: 10-19
Sq. footage: 16000
Type of Packaging: Consumer, Food Service
Brands:
     CHAMPAGNE DELIGHT
     GIOVANNI'S

5585 Girard Spring Water
1100 Mineral Spring Ave
North Providence, RI 02904-4104   401-725-7298
          Fax: 401-725-7913   800-477-9287
Manufacturer of spring water and water coolers
     President: John Ponton
Estimated Sales: $500,000-$1 Million
Number Employees: 5-9
Sq. footage: 2500
Type of Packaging: Consumer, Private Label, Bulk

5586 Girard Winery/Rudd Estates
P.O.Box 105
Oakville, CA 94562-0105   707-944-8577
          Fax: 707-944-2823 www.ruddwines.com
Processor and exporter of wines
     Owner: Leslie Rudd
     Marketing/Sales Coordinator: Gaby Terrill
     Director Sales/Marketing: Ellen Hunt
     Winery Manager: Vickie Gomez
     Vineyard Manager: Terry Mathison
Estimated Sales: $5-10 Million
Number Employees: 20-49
Brands:
     GIRARD

5587 Girard's Food Service Dressings
145 Willow Avenue
City of Industry, CA 91746-2047   323-724-2519
          Fax: 323-726-0934   888-327-8442
          wjperry@girardsdressings.com
          www.girardsdressings.com
Processor and exporter of mayonnaise, salad dress-
ings, sauces and marinades
     Chairman/Co-CEO: Jack Tucey
     President/Co-CEO: William Perry
     Controller: Tim Schoenbaum
     Quality Control/R&D Manager: Jeff Stalley
     Marketing/Sales Coordinator: Dottie Dinkheller
     Sales Manager Deli/Airline Retail Sales: Steve
     Shapiro
     Plant Manager: Dennis Tyler
     Purchasing/Logistics Manager: Walt Richmond
Estimated Sales: $24 Million
Number Employees: 60
Number of Brands: 3
Number of Products: 175
Sq. footage: 25000
Parent Co: T Marzetti Company
Type of Packaging: Consumer, Food Service, Bulk

Brands:
     GIRARD'S

5588 Girardet Wine Cellars
895 Reston Rd
Roseburg, OR 97471-8611   541-679-7252
          Fax: 541-679-9502 genuine@girardetwine.com
          www.girardetwine.com
Collection of wines such as: Baco Noir, Pinot Noir,
Cabernet Sauvignon, Riesling and Grande Rouge.
     President: Philippe Girardet
     CEO: Bonnie Girardet
     Winemaker/General Manager: Marc Girardet
Estimated Sales: $5-10 Million
Number Employees: 10-19
Type of Packaging: Private Label

5589 Giulia Specialty Food
10 Dell Glen Ave # 4
Lodi, NJ 07644-1740   973-478-3111
          Fax: 973-478-1133
          giuliaspecialty@worldnet.att.net
Mineral water, balsamic vinegar, olive oil, coffee,
Easter eggs, rice
     VP: Carmelo Lamonto
Estimated Sales: $2.5-5 Million
Number Employees: 1-4
Brands:
     BASSO
     LASANTA MARIA
     MAKO
     PASTA MALTAGLIATI

5590 Giuliano's Specialty Foods
12132 Knott St
Garden Grove, CA 92841-2801   714-895-9661
          Fax: 714-373-6872
          http://www.giulianopeppers.com
Vegetables, pepperoncini
     President: Errol Giuliano
     Quality Control: Lance Giuliano
     Sales: Brian Giuliano
Estimated Sales: $1-2.5 Million
Number Employees: 10-19
Type of Packaging: Consumer, Food Service, Pri-
vate Label
Brands:
     ESG
     GIULIANO

5591 Giumarra Companies
3646 Avenue 416
Reedley, CA 93654-9111   559-897-5060
          Fax: 559-897-8363 eblaylock@giumarra.com
          www.giumarra.com
Grapes, stonefruit, berries, apples/pears, tomatoes,
vegetables, avocados, emlons and kiwi
Estimated Sales: $ 3 - 5 Million
Number Employees: 5-9
Brands:
     ARRA GIUMARRA VINEYARDS
     ARRAcado
     BAUZA EXPORT
     CARLSBAD
     DAVID DEL CURTO S.A.
     FRESH
     FRUIT KING
     GRAPE KING GIUMARRA VINEYARDS
     LTD PERFECT PICK
     LTD TREE RIPENED FRUIT
     LUVYA
     NATURE'S PARTNER
     SOUTH HILLS
     STA TERESA
     YUMMY FRUIT COMPANY

5592 Giumarra Companies
15651 Old Milky Way
Escondido, CA 92027-7104   760-480-8502
          Fax: 760-489-1870 www.giumarra.com
Processor, exporter and importer of avocados
     Manager: Tom Vaughn
     VP: John Corsaro
     Sales Manager: Bruce Dowhan
Estimated Sales: $10-20 Million
Number Employees: 50-99
Sq. footage: 22000
Parent Co: Giumarra Brothers Fruit Company
Type of Packaging: Bulk
Other Locations:
     Giumarra Brothers
     Los Angeles CA
Brands:
     ARRACADO

5593 Giumarra Vineyards
P.O.Box 1969
Bakersfield, CA 93303-1969   661-395-7000
      Fax: 661-395-7195 www.giumarra.com
Processor and exporter of grape concentrate and
juice; co-packer of water, juices, wines, beers, dis-
tilled spirits cocktails, ciders and teas
      President: John Giumarra
Estimated Sales: $100 Million
Number Employees: 1,000-4,999
Sq. footage: 600000

5594 Giusto's Specialty Foods
344 Littlefield Ave
S San Francisco, CA 94080-6103   650-873-6566
      Fax: 650-873-2826   leslie@giustos.com
                              www.giustos.com
General grocery
      President: Fred Giusto
      Secretary/Treasurer: Albert Giusto
Estimated Sales: $10-20 Million
Number Employees: 20-49

5595 Givaudan
1199 Edison Dr
Cincinnati, OH 45216-2265   513-948-8000
      Fax: 513-948-3214   800-892-1199
      corp.communications@givaudan.com
                              www.givaudan.com
Manufacturer, exporter and importer of flavors and
extracts
      President: Michael Carlos
      VP: Michael Blanco
Estimated Sales: $100-500 Million
Number Employees: 250-499
Parent Co: Hercules
Type of Packaging: Bulk
Brands:
      ALDEMAX
      ASEPTILOK
      FLAV-O-LOK
      PRIME
      REDD
      SUGARONE

5596 Givaudan
231 Rock Industrial Park Dr
Bridgeton, MO 63044-1212   314-702-2000
      Fax: 314-291-3289   800-422-5444
      dick@givaudan.com   www.givaudan.com
Flavor enhancers
      Chairman: Dr Jurg Witmer
      CEO: Gilles Andrier
      Senior Food Scientist: David Watson
      Purchasing Manager: Kurt Scaturro
Estimated Sales: $ 50-100 Million
Number Employees: 100-249

5597 Givaudan Access
110 E 69th St
Cincinnati, OH 45216-2008   513-948-8000
      Fax: 513-948-5637   866-448-2832
      info@givaudanaccess.com   www.givaudan.com
Flavors, extracts
      President: Mike Davis
      VP Commercial-Global Lead: Daniel Offermann
      VP Marketing: Lori Smith
      VP Sales: Jean-Marc Dardier
Estimated Sales: $100+ Million
Number Employees: 250-499
Brands:
      Givaudan

5598 Givaudan Flavors
231 Rock Industrial Park Dr
Bridgeton, MO 63044-1212   314-702-2000
      Fax: 314-291-3289   800-422-5444
                              www.givaudan.com
Manufacturer and exporter of flavors, fruit drinks,
ice cream/yogurt flavors, cocoa, flavored base pow-
ders for milk, yogurt, fruit, sherbet bases, egg nog
bases, nondairy drinks and vitamins to fortify milk;
importer of cocoa
      Chairman: Dr Jurg Witmer
      Vice-Chairman: Dr Andres Leuenberger
Estimated Sales: $20-50 Million
Number Employees: 100-249
Parent Co: Givaudan
Brands:
      CHOCOLATE DELIGHT
      DINOSAUR
      GOLDEN
      GOLDEN DELIGHT

      GRAND PRIX
      LEMONADE STAND
      MOO-MANIA
      SKIM SELECT
      VITA-RITE

5599 Givaudan-Roure
1775 Windsor Rd
Teaneck, NJ 07666-3018   201-833-2300
      Fax: 201-833-8165 www.globalvillage.com
Manufacturer of flavors, perfume oils and fragrances
      President: Colin O'Neill
      CEO: Gilles Andrier
      CFO: Matthias Wahren
      SVP Chief Perfumer: Rene Morgenthaler
      SVP Development/Innovation: Tom McGee
Estimated Sales: $35 Million
Number Employees: 100-249

5600 Glacial Ridge Foods
24350 Joy Road
Suite 9
Redford, MI 48239-1265   612-239-2215
      Fax: 313-535-4466
Country grown multi-grain chips, pop-lite popcorn
and multi-grain pretzels
      President: Mark Shirkey
      National Sales Manager: Roger Spagnola
Estimated Sales: $500,000 appx.
Number Employees: 1-4
Brands:
      COUNTRY GROWN FOODS

5601 Glacier Bay Seafood & Meat Company
1900 W 31st Street
B-21
Lawrence, KS 66046-5505   785-832-2650
      Fax: 785-832-1192
Seafood, meat
      Owner: Chris McCue

5602 Glacier Fish Company
1200 Westlake Ave N # 9
Seattle, WA 98109-3543   206-298-1200
      Fax: 206-298-4750   info@glacierfish.com
                              www.glacierfish.com
Processor of frozen surimi, halibut roe and Alaskan
cod, pollack and salmon; also, frozen king,
dungeness and snow crabs; exporter of cod, pollack
and surimi
      President: John Bundy
      Owner/CEO: Erik Breivik
      CEO: Erik Breivik
      Director Human Resources: Renee Vargas
      Operations Manager: Erik Breivik
      Purchasing Manager: Angela Estep
Estimated Sales: $20-50 Million
Number Employees: 100-249
Type of Packaging: Food Service, Bulk
Brands:
      GLACIER FREEZE

5603 Glacier Foods
1117 K St
Sanger, CA 93657-3200   559-875-3354
      Fax: 559-875-3179
Processor, importer, domestic and exporter of frozen
and fresh fruit and vegetables
      Owner: Jack Mulvaney
      Plant Manager: Alvin McAvoy
      Assistant Plant Manager: Sheila Young
Estimated Sales: $ 10 - 20 Million
Number Employees: 50-99
Sq. footage: 748260
Parent Co: JR Wood
Type of Packaging: Consumer, Food Service, Pri-
vate Label, Bulk

5604 Gladder's Gourmet Cookies
1403 Industrial Blvd
Lockhart, TX 78644-3701   512-398-1970
      Fax: 512-398-6323   888-398-4523
      gladders.com   www.gladders.com
Processor of frozen raw cookie dough,
ready-to-bake brownies and thaw and serve cookies
and brownies
      Owner: Dusty Baker
      Marketing Director: Susan Glader
      VP Sales/Marketing: Dave Foreman
      Director Operations: Kevin Cobb
      General Manager: Mark Brown

Estimated Sales: $1-2.5 Million
Number Employees: 20-49
Sq. footage: 40000
Type of Packaging: Food Service
Brands:
      GLADDER'S GOURMET COOKIE

5605 Gladstone Candies
7480 Brookpark Road
Cleveland, OH 44129   216-472-0206
      Fax: 216-274-9200   888-729-1960
                              www.groovycandies.com
Processor of candy including lollypops, black anise,
red-hot cinnamon and molded Christmas, Easter,
Halloween and Valentine holiday candies.
      President: Ed Kitchen
      Chairman: Bert Hiddie
Estimated Sales: $5-9.9 Million
Number Employees: 20-49
Number of Brands: 1
Number of Products: 25
Sq. footage: 10000
Type of Packaging: Consumer, Private Label, Bulk
Brands:
      GLADSTONE CANDIES

5606 Gladstone Food ProductsCompany
P.O.Box 28010
Kansas City, MO 64188-0010   816-436-1255
      Fax: 816-436-1255
Mexican foods
      President: Joe Catalano
Estimated Sales: $1-2.5 Million appx.
Number Employees: 1-4

5607 Glanbia Foods
1373 Fillmore St
Twin Falls, ID 83301-3392   208-733-7555
      Fax: 208-733-9222   custsrv@glanbiausa.com
                              www.glanbia.com
Processor of cheese including Monterey and pepper
jack and natural, mild and sharp cheddar
      President/CEO: Jeff Williams
      Quality Assurance Manager: Mary Pierson
      Director Cheese Sales/Marketing: Dave Snyder
      VP Operations: John Lanigan
      Production Manager: Troy Thomas
      Plant Manager: Dan Carlbom
Estimated Sales: $625 Million
Number Employees: 50-99
Sq. footage: 40000
Parent Co: Glanbia PLC
Type of Packaging: Bulk

5608 (HQ)Glanbia Foods
1373 Fillmore St
Twin Falls, ID 83301-3392   208-733-7555
      Fax: 208-733-9222   800-427-9477
      custserv@glanbiausa.com   www.glanbia.com
Manufacturer of cheese including natural, barrel,
cheddar, Swiss and Monterey jack; also, processor
and exporter of whey protein concentrate and lactose
      President/CEO: Jeff Williams
      Director Cheese Sales/Marketing: Dave Snyder
Estimated Sales: $625 Million
Number Employees: 20-49
Parent Co: Glanbia PLC
Type of Packaging: Consumer, Food Service, Pri-
vate Label, Bulk
Brands:
      PROVON

5609 Glanbia Foods
1373 Fillmore St
Twin Falls, ID 83301-3392   208-733-7555
      Fax: 208-733-9222   custsrv@glanbiausa.com
                              www.glanbia.com
Natural and processed cheese
      President: Jeff Williams
      Director Human Resources: Shawn Athay
      Sales Manager: Steve Singer
      VP of Production: William Hanson
      Cheese Technology Director: Dave Perry
      Sales Director: Dave Snyder
      Mktg Services Mgr: Tammy Hasse-mcguir
      Operations Manager: Bjorn Sorensen
      Plant Manager: Tim Opper
      Plant Manager: Hugh Royal
Estimated Sales: $25-49.9 Million
Number Employees: 20-49
Brands:
      Glanbia Foods

5610 Glanbia Nutritionals
523 6th St
Monroe, WI 53566   608-329-2800
Fax: 608-329-2828   800-336-2183
nutrition@glanbiausa.com
www.glanbianutritionals.com
Provide innovative, science-based nutritional solutions. A leader in production of natural whey protein isolates, whey protein concentrates, whey fractions, heat-stable whey proteins, protein blends, milk proteins, lactose and dairycalcium. They also offer flax seed products and vitamins and minerals.
    President: Jerry O'Dea
    CEO: Kevin Toland
    CFO: Alan Morris
    VP: Robert Beausire
    R&D: Eric Bastian
    Quality Control: Mary Pierson
    Marketing Manager: Eric Borchardt
    Operations: Carl Garcia
Number Employees: 50-99
Number of Brands: 12
Number of Products: 7
Parent Co: Glandia Ingredients, PLC
Type of Packaging: Consumer, Private Label, Bulk
Brands:
    AVONLAC™
    BARFLEX®
    BARGAIN™
    BARPRO™
    CFM®
    PROLIBRA®
    PROVON®
    SALIBRA®
    SOLMIKO MILK PRODUCTS
    THERMAX®
    TRI-FX®
    TRUCAL®

5611 Glasco Locker Plant
P.O.Box 175
Glasco, KS 67445-0175   785-568-2364
Processor of beef, pork and lamb; also, slaughtering and curing available
    Owner: Kelly L Cool
Estimated Sales: $1-2.5 Million
Number Employees: 5-9
Type of Packaging: Consumer

5612 Glatech Productions
325 2nd St
Lakewood, NJ 08701-3329   732-364-8700
Fax: 732-886-2131   glatech@gmail.com
www.koshergelatin.com
Producers of kolatin kosher gelatin and Elyon confectionery products
    VP: Moshe Eider
Type of Packaging: Consumer, Bulk

5613 Glazier Packing Company
3140 State Route 11
Malone, NY 12953-4708   518-483-4990
Fax: 518-483-8300
Processor of sausage and frankfurters; wholesaler/food service wholesaler distributor and importer of meat products; serving the food service market
    President/Owner: John Glazier
    Vice President: Shawn Glazier
    General Manager: Lynn Raymond
Estimated Sales: $10-11 Million
Number Employees: 20-49
Sq. footage: 30000
Type of Packaging: Consumer, Food Service
Brands:
    TAST-T
    TAST-T TENDER

5614 Glazier Packing Company
7170 Us Highway 11
Potsdam, NY 13676-3198   315-265-2500
Fax: 315-265-2502
Processor of sausage; wholesaler/distributor of fresh and frozen foods; serving the food service market
    Manager: Floyd Leminc
Estimated Sales: $5-10 Million
Number Employees: 10-19
Sq. footage: 25000
Type of Packaging: Consumer, Food Service, Bulk

5615 Glee Gum
305 Dudley Street
Providence, RI 02907   401-351-6415
Fax: 401-272-1204   info@gleegum.com
www.gleegum.com
cheing gum and candy making kits

5616 Glen Rose Meat Company
4561 Loma Vista Ave
Vernon, CA 90058-2601   323-589-3393
Fax: 323-589-3712
Grocery items
    CEO: Glen Rose
Estimated Sales: $10-20 Million
Number Employees: 20-49
Brands:
    Glen Rose Meat

5617 Glen Summit Springs Water Company
P.O.Box 127
Mountain Top, PA 18707-0127   570-287-3107
Fax: 570-474-9840   800-621-7596
www.glensummitspringswater.com
Processor of bottled spring water
    Manager: Kevin Duffy
Estimated Sales: $2.5-5 Million
Number Employees: 20-49

5618 Glen's Packing Company
P.O.Box 244
Hallettsville, TX 77964-0244   361-798-2601
Fax: 361-798-1201   800-368-2333
Manfuacturer of fresh meats, special cuts - quarters and halves, pork and beef sausage, slaughtering available
    President: Harold Dolezal
Estimated Sales: $5-10 Million
Number Employees: 10-19
Type of Packaging: Consumer

5619 Glencourt
1205 Hillview Ln
Napa, CA 94558-9789   707-944-4444
Fax: 925-944-4009   www.omnibrands.com
Processor and exporter of beverages, dairy products, baked goods, sauces, preserves, frozen concentrates, juices, peanut butter, mayonnaise, spices and natural cheeses
    Owner: Susie Hasenpusch
    VP Sales: David Maco
    Sales Manager: Dave Hackney
    Sales Manager: Dennis Drennon
    Export Sales Manager: Joanne Goh
    Sales Development Analyst: Christopher Hartig
    Export Sales Specialist: Joyce Stump
Number Employees: 1-4
Parent Co: Safeway Stores
Type of Packaging: Private Label

5620 Glendora Quiche Company
210 W Arrow Hwy
San Dimas, CA 91773-3360   909-394-1777
Fax: 909-394-1780
Processor of gourmet quiche including lorraine, broccoli, green chile, spinach and mushroom
    Owner: Todd Bilef
Estimated Sales: $ 1 - 3 Million
Number Employees: 1-4
Sq. footage: 3000
Parent Co: Kovar Companies
Type of Packaging: Consumer, Food Service, Private Label, Bulk
Brands:
    Glendora Quiche Co.

5621 Glenmark Food Processors
4545 S Racine Ave
Chicago, IL 60609-3371   773-927-4800
Fax: 773-847-2946   800-621-0117
Processor and exporter of frozen steak and veal, canned and frozen stews and beef patties
    Manager: Todd Ryan
    VP: Bob Martin
    Director Operations: John Dobias
Estimated Sales: $5-10 Million
Number Employees: 20-49
Parent Co: OSI Industries
Type of Packaging: Consumer, Food Service, Private Label, Bulk
Brands:
    Great Grilsby

5622 Glenmark Industries
4545 S Racine Ave
Chicago, IL 60609-3371   773-927-4800
Fax: 773-847-2946
Processor of ground beef patties, pork chopettes, ribettes and sausage, meatloaf, meatballs and breaded beef and poultry products
    Manager: Todd Ryan
    Controller: Robert Martin
    Research & Development: B Girdhar
    Quality Control: Sharon Birkett
    Marketing Manager: Connie Christoff
    Operations Manager: John Dobias
    Purchasing Manager: Dominic Pinto
Estimated Sales: $50-100 Million
Number Employees: 250-499
Brands:
    Blazer
    Glenmark
    Glenmark

5623 Glenn Sales Company
6425 Powers Ferry Rd NW
Atlanta, GA 30339-2908   770-952-9292
Fax: 770-988-9325
Seafood, Whiting, Sea Trout, Flounder, Croaker, Pollock
    President: Bruce Pearlman
Estimated Sales: $1,600,000
Number Employees: 5-9

5624 Glenn's Rabbit & Emu Farm
5731 Highway 31 W
Portland, TN 37148-8333   615-325-6903
Fax: 615-325-5097   877-325-6903
rabbirdman@aol.com
Processor of emu and rabbit meat including fresh and frozen
    President: Glenn Prochaska
Estimated Sales: $1-3 Milion
Number Employees: 8
Sq. footage: 3500
Type of Packaging: Consumer, Food Service, Private Label
Brands:
    Emu Meat

5625 Glennys
371 S Main St
Freeport, NY 11520-5114   516-377-1400
Fax: 516-377-9046   888-864-1243
www.glennys.com
Processor of natural snacks including soy veggie nuts and snack, soy crisps, animal cookies, vitamin C lollypops, hard candies, carob coated bee pollen, spirulina and ginseng, and moist'n chewy bars
    Manager: Rhonda Talbot
Estimated Sales: $5-10 Million
Number Employees: 20-49
Type of Packaging: Consumer, Food Service
Brands:
    Glenny's

5626 Glenoaks Food
11030 Randall St
Sun Valley, CA 91352-2621   818-768-9091
Fax: 818-767-0742   info@glenoaksfood.com
www.glenoaksfood.com
All natural meat snacks without preservatives or MSG. beef, turkey, buffalo, venison and ostrich jerky in 18 flavors
    Owner: John J Fallon Jr
Estimated Sales: $ 1 - 3 Million
Number Employees: 1-4
Sq. footage: 26000
Type of Packaging: Consumer, Private Label, Bulk
Brands:
    J.C. RIVERS GOURMET JERKY

5627 Glenora Wine Cellars
5435 State Route 14
Dundee, NY 14837-8804   607-243-5511
Fax: 607-243-5514   800-243-5513
info@glenora.com   www.glenora.com
Processor of sparkling and table wines - premium New York State wines including, Brut Sparkling, Chardonnay, Riesling, Merlot, Cabernet Sauvignon, Cayuga and Seyval
    Principal: Gene Pierce
    Principal: Ed Dalrymple
    Principal: Scott Welliver
    Director Marketing: Gail Fink
    Winemaker: Steve diFrancesco

Estimated Sales:$5-10 Million
Number Employees: 10-19
Sq. footage: 17500
Type of Packaging: Consumer, Food Service, Private Label
Brands:
  FINGER LAKES
  GLENORA
  PEACH ORCHARD FARMS
  TRESTLE CREEK

5628 Glier's Meats
533 Goetta Pl
Covington, KY 41011-2203   859-291-1800
        Fax: 859-291-1846 800-446-3882
                www.goetta.com
Processor of German breakfast sausage - contains pork, beef and steel-cut (pinhad oats) and seasonings.
  President: Daniel Glier
  Director Marketing: Mark Balasa
  Plant Manager: Tom Rabe
Estimated Sales:$2.2 Million
Number Employees: 10-19
Sq. footage: 12000
Type of Packaging: Food Service, Private Label
Brands:
  Glier's

5629 Global Bakeries
13336 Paxton St
Pacoima, CA 91331-2339   818-896-0525
        Fax: 818-896-3237 marksoeur@aol.com
                www.globalbakeriesinc.com
Manufacturer of baked goods including bagels, croissants, pita breads, rolls and pitochips.
  Owner: Albert Boyajian
Estimated Sales:$10-50 Million
Number Employees: 100-249
Number of Products: 5
Sq. footage: 40000
Type of Packaging: Consumer, Food Service, Private Label, Bulk

5630 Global Beverage Company
130 Linden Oaks # C
Rochester, NY 14625-2834   585-381-3560
        Fax: 585-381-4025 www.wetplanet.com
Carbonated soft drinks, ice teas, fruit juices, energy drinks and bottled water
  President: Cj Rapp
Number Employees: 20-49

5631 (HQ)Global Botanical
545 Welham Road
Barrie, ON L4N 8Z6
Canada   705-733-2117
  Fax: 705-733-2391 info@globalbotanical.com
                www.globalbotanical.com
Processor, wholesaler/distributor, importer and exporter of herbs, spices, oils, etc., also; custom formulation available
  President: Sandra Thuna
  Office Manager: Therese White
  General Manager: Joel Thuna
  Director Purchasing: Kathy Vessair-Skalitzky
Number Employees: 12
Sq. footage: 20000
Type of Packaging: Private Label, Bulk
Brands:
  Excalibur
  Global Botanical
  Kidz
  Naturalvalves
  Pure-Li Natural

5632 Global Citrus Resources
1835 Stonecrest Ct
Lakeland, FL 33813-2456   863-647-9020
        Fax: 863-683-0267
        sales@globalcitrusresources.com
        www.globalcitrusresources.com
Processor and exporter of frozen juice concentrates
  President: David Alpin
  CFO: Richard Reichler
  VP Sales/Marketing: Joe Hart
  Production Manager: David Tegreene
Estimated Sales:$20-50 Million
Number Employees: 5-9

5633 Global Egg Corporation
17 Newbridge Road
Etobicoke, ON M8Z 2L6
Canada   416-231-2409
        Fax: 416-231-8991 abk@globalegg.com
Processor of whole, cooked, liquid, frozen and pelletized eggs; also, salt and sugar egg yolks; exporter of frozen egg whites and whole eggs
  CEO: Aaron Kwinter
Number Employees: 20-49
Sq. footage: 25000
Type of Packaging: Food Service, Bulk
Brands:
  Egg King
  Global

5634 Global Express Gourmet
315 Edelweiss Drive
Bozeman, MT 59718-3928   406-587-5571
        Fax: 406-582-0614 www.eprovisions.com
Gourmet foods
  Marketing/Sales: Cameron Haag

5635 Global Food Industries
PO Box 489
Townville, SC 29689-0489   864-287-1212
        Fax: 864-287-1335 800-225-4152
                info@globalfoodindustries.com
                www.globalsoyfood.com
Processor of dairy, industrial ingredients, dehydrated foods, beverages, halal, and vegetarian foods
  President: Neal Pfeiffer
  Vice President: Paulette Harary
  Office Manager: Sandra Sanoh
Number Employees: 5-9
Number of Brands: 1
Number of Products: 30
Type of Packaging: Food Service, Bulk
Brands:
  Global Food

5636 Global Health Laboratories
548 Broadhollow Rd
Melville, NY 11747-3708   631-293-0030
        Fax: 631-293-0349
Processor and exporter of health products including nutritional drinks, energy bars, food and nutritional supplements, vitamins, herbs and weight loss products
  Administrator: Susan Mc Guckian
  Sales Director: James Gibbons
Type of Packaging: Consumer, Private Label
Brands:
  Herb Actives
  Nature's Plus
  Source of Life
  Spirutein
  Thermo Tropic

5637 (HQ)Global Marketing Associates
1901 N Roselle Road
Schaumburg, IL 60195-3176   847-490-6481
        Fax: 847-397-2354 james@gmaexports.com
                www.gmaexports.com
Processor of fruit juices, dry drink mixes and macaroni and cheese dinners; exporter of nonalcoholic beverages, confectionery products, ingredients, ketchup, mustard and salad dressings
  Managing Director: James Biesinger
Estimated Sales:$500,000-$1 Million
Number Employees: 1-4
Type of Packaging: Consumer, Private Label, Bulk
Brands:
  Suncoast

5638 Global Marketing Enterprises
1801 S Canal St # C
Chicago, IL 60616-1522   312-733-0000
                Fax: 312-733-8010
        www.globalmarketingchicago.com
  President: Eduardo Chua
Estimated Sales:$ 5 - 10 Million
Number Employees: 10-19

5639 Global Nutrition Research Corporation
3120 S Potter Dr
Tempe, AZ 85282-3141   602-454-2248
        Fax: 602-454-2249 shannon@gnrc.us

Provide a comprehensive database of herbal supplements, health products, and herbal companies available on the internet. We are not only an information provider, but also an herbal and alternative medicine community site.
  President: Ken Ardisson
  Sales Contact: Shannon Purcell
Estimated Sales:$ 20 - 50 Million
Number Employees: 20-49

5640 Global Preservatives
718 Ryan St
Lake Charles, LA 70601-4243   337-491-0816
        Fax: 337-433-5253 800-256-2253
                www.globalpreservatives.com
Manufactures Food Processing aids and preservatives for meats, produce and the bakery industry.
  President: William Woodward
  R&D: Damon Thibodeaux
  Operations Director: Tim Vaughan
  Plant Manager: Bryan Hymel
Estimated Sales:$2.5 -$5 Million
Number Employees: 1-4
Sq. footage: 20000

5641 Global Trading
Ste 200
6571 Altura Blvd
Buena Park, CA 90620-1020   864-288-7332
        Fax: 864-234-5815 www.globaltrading.net
Processor and exporter of frozen fruits and purees
  President: Arthur Price
  Accounting: Karen Gray
  Inventory Control: Joyce Lambert
  Information Technology: Kevin Martin
  Sales Manager: Terry Miller
  Office Manager: Karen Berry
  FDA/Customs Coordinator: Denise Roof
  Production Coordinator: Jeanice Messick
  Transportation: Pam Torres
  Purchasing: Beanie Lee
Estimated Sales:$2.5-5 Million
Number Employees: 5-9
Type of Packaging: Consumer, Bulk

5642 GlobeTrends
11 the Esplanade
Morris Plains, NJ 07950-1360   973-984-7444
        Fax: 973-984-7422 800-416-8327
        info@globetrends.com www.globetrends.com
Importer and distributor of Taylors of Harrogate teas from England, Harrisons and Crosfield teas. Also imports Granja San Francisco, Spain's #1 selling honey. We ship throughout the US
  President: Al Sharif
  Marketing/Public Relations: Cheryl Templeton
Estimated Sales:$500,000-$1 Million
Number Employees: 1-4
Type of Packaging: Private Label
Brands:
  British Honey Company
  Taylors of Harrogate

5643 Globus Coffee
426 Plandome Rd
Manhasset, NY 11030-1943   516-304-5780
                Fax: 516-364-4558
        globuscoffeeco@worldnet.att.net
Coffee traders
  Owner: Kurt Kappeli
  Member Manager: Kurt Kappeli
Estimated Sales:$5-10 Million
Number Employees: 5-9

5644 Gloria Ferrer Champagne
P.O.Box 1427
Sonoma, CA 95476-1427   707-996-7256
        Fax: 707-996-0720 info@gloriaferrer.com
                www.gloriaferrer.com
Most honored and accaimed sparkling wines
  President: Juan Furne
  EVP: Eva Bertran
  VP/Winemaker: Bob Iantosca
  VP/Vineyard Manager: Mike Crumly
  VP Marketing/Advertising: David Brown
Estimated Sales:$20-50 Million
Number Employees: 50-99
Brands:
  Freixenet Spanish Wines
  Freixenet Wines

5645 Gloria Jean's Gourmet Coffees
23141 Arroyo Vis # 100
Rcho Sta Marg, CA 92688-2613   949-589-5040
        Fax: 949-589-5041   800-354-5258
                www.seguecorp.com
Gourmet flavored coffees, varietals and blends, tea
and hot chocolate
    Manager: Lyle Peterson
    VP Marketing: Diane Hays-Hoag
    Cutsomter Service: Patti Graves
Estimated Sales:$100-500 Million
Number Employees: 50-99

5646 Gloria Winery & Vineyard
1648 E 8th St N
Springfield, MO 65802-2114   417-926-6263
Wines
    President: William Toben
Estimated Sales:$500,000-$1 Million
Number Employees: 1-4

5647 Gloria's Gourmet
36 Carver Street
New Britain, CT 06053-1302   860-225-9196
        Fax: 860-224-2602   gloria306870@aol.com
Dip and spread mixes, herbs and spices

5648 Glory Foods
901 Oak St
Columbus, OH 43205-1204   614-252-2042
        Fax: 614-252-2043 www.gloryfoods.com
Fresh and frozen vegetables, fresh - cut vegetables,
and gluten - free products
    President: Jaqui Neal
    Founder: Iris Cooper
    Founder/Plant Manager: Dan Charna
    Founder: Garth Henley
Estimated Sales:$5-10 Million
Number Employees: 20-49
Type of Packaging: Food Service, Bulk

5649 Glorybee Foods
P.O.Box 2744
Eugene, OR 97402-0277   541-689-0913
        Fax: 541-689-9692   800-456-7923
    info@glorybeefoods.com   www.glorybee.com
Started in the family garage of Dick and Pat
Turanski in 1975 with a dream of providing natural,
healthy ingredients for the people of their own town.
That spirit remains strong today, and Glorybee is
still a family-owned and operatedbusiness in Eugene
    President: Richard Turanski
    Quality Control: Gary Powell
    Marketing: Michele Lukowski
    Sales: Greg Wilson
    Operations: Alan Turanski
Estimated Sales:$2.5-5 Million
Number Employees: 50-99
Sq. footage: 30000
Type of Packaging: Food Service, Bulk

5650 Glorybee Natural Sweeteners
PO Box 2744
Eugene, OR 97402-0277   800-456-7923
        Fax: 541-607-8803   800-456-7923
    sales@glorybee.com   www.glorybee.com
Process retail natural sweeteners-both organic and
commercial. Manufactures all natural honeystix
    President: Richard Turanski
    Marketing Director: Rae Jean Wilson
    Plant Manager: Ron Okonski
Estimated Sales:$50-99.9 Million
Number Employees: 50-99
Sq. footage: 16
Type of Packaging: Private Label
Brands:
    Aunt Patty's Natural Sweetners
    Glorybee Foods Honeystix
    Glorybee Herbal Honey
    Glorybee Honey

5651 Glover's Ice Cream
705 W Clinton St
Frankfort, IN 46041-1824   765-654-6712
        Fax: 765-654-7977   800-686-5163
Manufacturer of ice cream, frozen yogurt and frozen
novelties
    President: Steve Glover
Estimated Sales:$3-5 Million
Number Employees: 5-9
Sq. footage: 6000
Type of Packaging: Consumer, Private Label

5652 Glucona America
114 E Conde Street
Janesville, WI 53546-3054   608-752-0449
        Fax: 608-752-7643   cfields@glucona.com
                www.glucona.com
Processor and importer of gluconates including fer-
rous, magnesium, potassium, sodium and zinc; also,
calcium supplements and glucono-delta lactone
(GDL); exporter of glucono-delta lactone
    Development Manager: Charles King
    Marketing Manager: Scott Wellington
    General Manager: Sean Trac
Estimated Sales:$20-50 Million
Number Employees: 20-49
Parent Co: Avebe
Type of Packaging: Food Service
Brands:
    Gluconal

5653 Glue Dots International
5515 S Westridge Dr
New Berlin, WI 53151-7900   262-814-8500
        Fax: 262-814-8505   888-688-7131
    info@gluedots.com   www.gluedots.com
Providing adhesive solutions to people, businesses
and industries worldwide. Packaging/product assembly, printing and bindery, direct mail/sales promotion, gift baskets, balloon decorating,
candlemaking, greeting cards, customproducts, kids
and school, scrapbooking and rubber stamping and
many more.
    Manager: John Downs
    Marketing/Communications Manager: Jennie
    Staghano
Estimated Sales:$ 10 - 20 Million
Number Employees: 10-19
Type of Packaging: Consumer, Bulk

5654 Glunz Family Winery & Cellars
888 E Belvidere Rd # 107
Grayslake, IL 60030-2569   847-548-9463
        Fax: 847-548-8038   winetogo@gfwc.com
                www.gfwc.com
Our wines consist of white, red, Chardonnay, White
Zinfandel, Merlot, Port, fruit wines (rasberry, black
currant) and hertiage wines such as: May Wine, San-
gria, and Glogg
    Owner: Matthew Glunz
    VP/Winemaker: Joe Glunz Jr
    Cellarmaster: Cipriano Luvieanos
Estimated Sales:$1-2.5 Million
Number Employees: 1-4

5655 (HQ)Glutino
2055 Boul Dagenais Quest
Laval, QC H7L 5V1
Canada
        Fax: 450-629-4781   800-363-3438
    info@glutino.com   www.glutino.com
Manufacturer and distributor specializing in gluten
free products. Our mission is provide a healthy lifestyle to all those with Celiac Disease and those who
follow a gluten-free/wheat-free diet.
    President: Steven Singer
    EVP: David Miller

5656 Go Lightly Candy
35 Hillside Avenue
Hillside, NJ 07205-1833   973-926-2300
        Fax: 973-926-4440   800-524-1304
    info@hillsidecandy.com   www.hillsidecandy.com
Manufacturer of Sugar free candy and 100% natural
candy
    President: Ted Cohen
    Marketing/Exports VP: Susan Rosenthal Jay
Estimated Sales:$ 5 - 10 Million
Number Employees: 40
Type of Packaging: Consumer, Food Service, Pri-
    vate Label, Bulk
Brands:
    GOLIGHTLY SUGAR FREE CANDY
    SHAKEN COUNTRY MEADOWS SWEETS

5657 Go-Rachel.com
8120 Penn Avenue S
Minneapolis, MN 55431-1358   952-884-2305
        Fax: 952-884-2307
Potato chips

5658 Godiva Chocolatier
355 Lexington Ave
New York, NY 10017-6603   212-681-2600
        Fax: 212-984-5901   800-946-3482
                www.godiva.com
Manufacturer of chocolates, coffee, biscuits and
biscotti
    President: Archie Van Beuren
    CEO: James A Goldman
    VP Marketing: Michael Simon
    National Sales: Scott Jones
Number Employees: 10,000+
Brands:
    GODIVA
    GODIVA CHOCOLATE

5659 Godiva Chocolatier
355 Lexington Ave
New York, NY 10017-6603   212-681-2600
        Fax: 212-984-5901   800-946-3482
    letters@godiva.com   www.godiva.com
Manufacturer of chocolate candy including boxed
and covered cherries, ice-cream, liqueur and coffee
    President, Worldwide: James Goldman
    SVP: Paul Amorello
    VP Marketing/Merchandising: Michael Simon
    Director PR/Promotions: Erica Lapidus
    Master Chocolatier: Thierry Muret
Number Employees: 10,000+
Parent Co: Campbell Soup
Type of Packaging: Consumer
Brands:
    Godiva
    Godiva Chocolate

5660 Godshall's Quality Meats
675 Mill Rd
Franconia, PA 18924   215-256-1108
        Fax: 215-256-4965   888-463-7425
                www.godshells.com
Processor and wholesaler/distributor of poultry,
beef, pork, lamb and veal; serving the food service
industry
    President: Mark Godshall
    Secretary: Kendall Godshall
    VP: Floyd Kratz
Estimated Sales:$300,000-500,000
Number Employees: 1-4
Sq. footage: 12000
Type of Packaging: Food Service

5661 Godwin Produce Company
P.O.Box 163
Dunn, NC 28335-0163   910-892-4171
        Fax: 910-892-2232   godwinproduce@aol.com
                www.sweettater.com
Manufacturer of produce including sweet potatoes,
watermelons and cantaloupes
    Owner: Anthony Godwin
    Owner: David Godwin
    Office Manager: Susan Moore
Estimated Sales:$5-10 Million
Number Employees: 5-9
Sq. footage: 85000
Type of Packaging: Consumer, Food Service, Pri-
    vate Label, Bulk
Brands:
    Dunn's Best
    Godwin
    Godwin Produce
    Godwin's Blue Ribbon
    Sweet Carolina

5662 Goebbert's Home Grown Vegetables
40 W Higgins Road
South Barrington, IL 60010-9319   847-428-6727
        Fax: 847-428-6850
Processor/grower of vegetables including tomatoes,
sweet corn, peppers, cabbage, eggplant, broccoli,
pumpkins and squash
    Owner: J.H. Goebbert
Estimated Sales:$1-2.5 Million
Number Employees: 10-19

5663 Goedens Fish Market
529 University Avenue
Madison, WI 53703-1909   608-256-1991
Seafood

5664 Goetze's Candy Company
3900 E Monument St
Baltimore, MD 21205-2980   410-342-2010
        Fax: 410-522-7681   800-638-1456
    office@goetzecandy.com   www.goetzecandy.com

Manufacturer and exporter of caramel creams, chocolate cow tales, strawberri cream candy
President: Randle Goetze
CEO: Spaulding Goetze
VP Administration: Mitchell Goetze
VP Sales: Marty Thompson
Estimated Sales:$20-50 Million
Number Employees: 50-99
Type of Packaging: Consumer, Food Service, Bulk
Brands:
GOETZE'S

5665 Goglanian Bakeries
3710 S Susan St
Santa Ana, CA 92704-6966   714-444-3500
          Fax: 714-444-3800 pattr@goglanian.com
Processor and exporter of pita bread, soft taco shells, flat breads and pizza crusts.
President: George Goglanian
VP: Sam Goglanian
Sales/Marketing Executive: Eric Porat
General Manager: Alex Goglanian
Estimated Sales:$5-10 Million
Number Employees: 250-499
Type of Packaging: Consumer, Food Service, Private Label

5666 Gold Coast Baking Company
1590 E Saint Gertrude Pl
Santa Ana, CA 92705-5310   714-545-2253
          Fax: 714-751-2253
mflaherty@goldcoastbakery.com
www.goldcoastbakery.com
Bread and bakery products
Manager: Rick Lamb
CFO: Mike Flaherty
Manager: Mike Martinez
Estimated Sales:$100-500 Million
Number Employees: 100-249

5667 Gold Coast Ingredients
2429 Yates Ave
Commerce, CA 90040-1917   323-724-8935
          Fax: 323-724-9354 800-352-8673
info@goldcoastinc.com www.goldcoastinc.com
A wholesale manufacturer of flavors and colors selling only to the wholesale segment of the food industry.
President: Jim Sgro
CEO: Chuck Brasher
Research & Development: C.M. Barnes
Quality Control: C.M. Barnes
Corporate Sales Manager: Michele Trent
Operations Manager: Jon Wellwood
Production Manager: Ted Rodriquez
Estimated Sales:$10-$20 Million
Number Employees: 20-49
Type of Packaging: Private Label, Bulk

5668 Gold Cup Farms
P.O.Box 116
Clayton, NY 13624-0116   315-686-2480
          Fax: 315-686-4701 800-752-1341
support@riverratcheese.com
www.riverratcheese.com
Distributor NYS Cheese, Adirondack Sausage
President: Richard Brown
CFO: Barb Leeson
VP: Cindy Major
Marketing/Sales: Dick Brown
Estimated Sales:$2,500,000
Number Employees: 10-19
Type of Packaging: Consumer, Food Service, Private Label, Bulk
Brands:
Adirondack Cheese
Gold Cup
Ny State River Rat Cheese

5669 Gold Dollar Products
6073 Mount Moriah Road Ext
Suite 12
Memphis, TN 38115-2666   901-326-6027
          Fax: 901-948-0309 800-971-8964
golddoll@bellsouth.net
Vinegar, mustard, hot sauce, lemon juice, bottled water
Owner: Sondra Abraham
VP, Consultant: Herbert Abraham
VP Marketing: George Abraham
Estimated Sales:$2.5-5 Million
Number Employees: 1-4
Brands:
Gold Dollar

Gold Dollar Lemon
Gold Dollar/Monedade'oro

5670 Gold Medal Bakery
21 Penn St
Fall River, MA 02724-1276   508-674-5766
          Fax: 508-674-6090 800-642-7568
www.goldmedalbakery.com
Processor of bread and rolls.
President: Roland Le Comte
VP Sales: Carl Culotta
Estimated Sales:$50-100 Million
Number Employees: 250-499
Type of Packaging: Private Label
Brands:
Holsum

5671 Gold Medal Baking Company
901 N 3rd St
Philadelphia, PA 19123-2205   215-627-4787
          Fax: 215-925-0179 www.goldmedalbakery.com
Processor of bread, cakes, rolls, muffins, etc
Owner: Stan Silverman
Marketing Director: Stan Silverman
Estimated Sales:$1-2.5 Million
Number Employees: 20-49
Type of Packaging: Consumer, Food Service
Brands:
Gold Medal Baking

5672 Gold Pure Foods Products Company
1 Brooklyn Rd
Hempstead, NY 11550-6619   516-483-5600
          Fax: 516-483-5798 800-422-4681
www.goldshorseradish.com
Processor and exporter of kosher salad dressings, horseradish, sauces, mustard, salsa, borscht, schav and vinegar; importer of horseradish roots, dried peaches and dried apricots
President: Steven Gold
VP: Herbert Gold
VP Sales: Marc Gold
Estimated Sales:$5-10 Million
Number Employees: 50-99
Sq. footage: 100000
Type of Packaging: Consumer, Food Service, Private Label, Bulk
Brands:
Baker
Baker's
Dip N' Joy
Gold's
Nathan's
Old World
Uncle Dave's

5673 Gold Seal Fruit Bouquet
6301 W Bluemound Rd
Milwaukee, WI 53213-4146   414-259-9552
          Fax: 414-258-9377 800-558-5558
fruitranchgifts@hotmail.com
www.fruitranch.com
Processor of fruit gift baskets. Wholesaler of baskets and supplies
Owner: Tanya Gearheart
Estimated Sales:$1 Million
Number Employees: 5-9
Sq. footage: 10000
Type of Packaging: Consumer, Private Label, Bulk

5674 Gold Standard Baking
3700 S Kedzie Ave # A
Chicago, IL 60632-2768   773-523-2333
          Fax: 773-523-7381 800-648-7904
www.gsbaking.com
Processor of fully and partially baked bakery products including breads, pizza crusts, croissants, etc.
President: Yianny Caparos
VP: Joe Chiodo
VP Business Development: Charles Chiodo
Estimated Sales:$2.5-5 Million
Number Employees: 5-9
Sq. footage: 50000
Type of Packaging: Consumer, Food Service, Private Label, Bulk
Brands:
Croissant De Paris
Gold Standard

5675 Gold Star Chocolate
250 Lorraine Street
Brooklyn, NY 11231-3806   718-330-0187
          Fax: 718-330-0534
Dkatz@goldstarchocolate.com
www.goldstarchocolate.com
Chocolate
VP: Doron Katz
Brands:
CANTALOU
CAXTON
CEMOI
COPPELLA
ELGORRIAGA
FOULLON
FRANKONIA
MR
PELLETIER
PHOSCAO
PUPIER
SAINT SIFFREIN

5676 Gold Star Coffee Company
51 Bridge St # A
Salem, MA 01970-4198   978-744-2672
          Fax: 978-744-8238 888-505-5233
Coffee
President: David Desimone
Estimated Sales:$10-20 Million
Number Employees: 10-19
Type of Packaging: Private Label

5677 Gold Star Dairy
6901 Interstate 30
Little Rock, AR 72209-3100   501-565-6125
          Fax: 501-568-5245
Fluid milk
Estimated Sales:$20-50 Million
Number Employees: 5-9

5678 Gold Star Sausage Company
2800 Walnut St
Denver, CO 80205-2236   303-295-6400
          Fax: 303-294-0495 800-258-7229
rick@goldstarsausage.com
www.goldstarsausage.com
Processor of smoked ribs, hot dogs, and sausage products
President: Rick Rue
Co-Owner: Eric Mohlke
Plant Manager: Ed Telgenhoff
Estimated Sales:$22,600,000
Number Employees: 50-99
Sq. footage: 50000
Type of Packaging: Consumer, Food Service, Private Label, Bulk
Brands:
Gold Star
Old Timer

5679 Gold Star Seafood
2300 W 41st St
Chicago, IL 60609-2214   773-376-8080
          Fax: 773-376-9879
Seafood
President: Van Giragosian
Estimated Sales:$ 10 - 20 Million
Number Employees: 10-19

5680 Gold Star Smoked Fish
570 Smith St
Brooklyn, NY 11231-3820   718-522-1545
          Fax: 718-260-9194 intl@goldstarco.com
www.goldstarco.com
Smoked fish and specialty foods from 20 European countries
President: Robert Pinkow
Estimated Sales:$ 10 - 20 Million
Number Employees: 20-49
Brands:
Cuetara
Denmark: Officer
Germany: Wessergold
Gerolsteiner
Gold Star
Hargita
Heine's
Iceland: Armant
Latvia: Unda
Poland: Solidarnosc
Teaports
Ukraine: Chumak, Nektar

5681 Gold Sweet Company
8949 North Fork Drive
Fort Myers, FL 33903   239-997-7656
Packer of honey for health food distributors and the
bakery industry
   Owner/Manager: Richard Phillips
Estimated Sales: $500,000-$1 Million
Number Employees: 1-4
Sq. footage: 3000
Type of Packaging: Consumer, Food Service, Bulk

5682 Gold'n Plump Poultry
P.O.Box 1106
St Cloud, MN 56302-1106   320-251-3570
   Fax: 320-240-6250 800-328-2838
                  www.goldenplump.com
Processor and exporter of poultry including
pre-packaged, roasters, parts and whole
   President: D Wooten
   CEO: Mike Hegelson
   VP Finance: Steve Jurek
   CEO: Michael Helgeson
   VP Sales: Tim Wensman
   Operations Manager: Mike Yeager
   Director Engineering: G Bennett
   Plant Manager: Brian Klepke
Estimated Sales: $50-100 Million
Number Employees: 50-99
Parent Co: JFC International
Type of Packaging: Consumer, Food Service, Bulk
Brands:
   Gold'n Plump

5683 Goldcoast Salads
3565 Plover Ave
Naples, FL 34117   239-304-0710
   Fax: 239-304-2156 pradno@goldcoastsalads.com
                  www.goldcoastsalads.com
maine lobster, blue crab and smoked salmon spreads
   President/Owner: Peter Radno Jr
   Plant Manager: Ruben Valenzuela

5684 Golden Alaska Seafoods
2200 6th Ave # 707
Seattle, WA 98121-1855   206-441-1990
   Fax: 206-441-8112 www.goldenalaska.com
Frozen seafood
   President: Lou Fleming
   CFO: Randy Adamson
   Sales Manager: Markna Franklyn
Estimated Sales: $1-2.5 Million
Number Employees: 5-9

5685 Golden Apples Candy Company
PO Box 735
Southport, CT 06890-0735   203-336-9188
   Fax: 203-336-9538 800-776-0393
          sales@goldenapplesinc.com
                  www.goldenapplesinc.com
Processor and exporter of confectionery items in-
cluding hard, bagged, packaged for racks, sugar-free
and all natural lollypops; also, sugar-free, all natural,
homeopathic and cough pops; importer of hard
candy
   President: Arthur Baltimore
   Vice President: Margaret Baltimore
   Sales Director: David Baltimore
Estimated Sales: $500,000-$1 Million
Number Employees: 1-4
Type of Packaging: Consumer, Bulk
Brands:
   7 Calorie Candy
   Golden Apples 7 Calorie Candy
   Kid's Choice Cough Pops
   Mother Natures Health Pops
   People Drops
   Peoplepops

5686 Golden Bounty Food Processors
7410 Scout Ave
Bell Gardens, CA 90201-4932   562-806-1100
   Fax: 562-806-2047 www.certi-fresh.com
   President: Salvatore Galletti
   CEO: Paul Demoss
   CEO: Nino Palma
Estimated Sales: $ 3 - 5 Million
Number Employees: 1-4

5687 Golden Boys Pies of SanDiego
2667 Camino Del Rio S
San Diego, CA 92108-3707   619-293-7400
   Fax: 619-293-3009 800-746-0280

Pies, breads
Estimated Sales: $10-20 Million
Number Employees: 10-19
Type of Packaging: Private Label

5688 Golden Brands
PO Box 398
Louisville, KY 40201-0398   502-636-3712
   Fax: 502-636-3904 800-622-3055
   shirleym@gfgb.com   www.gfgb.com
Manufacturer and exporter of shortenings including
flaked, creamy liquid and votated; also, soybean and
cottonseed oils; as well as identity preserved oils for
GMO-free market. Sell to industrial baking industry
and food service
   President/CEO: Timothy Helson
   EVP/VP Sales/Marketing: Jan Helson
   Director Business Development: Shirley Marple
   Director Sales/Service: Jason Glaser
   VP Technical Sales: Bob Delaney
   VP Operations/Plant Manager: Sam Marrillia
Estimated Sales: $100 Million
Number Employees: 150
Sq. footage: 250000
Type of Packaging: Food Service, Bulk
Brands:
   Golden Brands
   Golden Foods

5689 Golden Brown Bakery
421 Phoenix St
South Haven, MI 49090-1309   269-637-3418
   Fax: 269-637-7822 www.goldenbrownbakery.com
Full service retail bakery and cafe with wholesale
capabilities
   Owner: David Braschi
Estimated Sales: $1-1.5 Million
Number Employees: 45
Type of Packaging: Consumer, Food Service, Pri-
vate Label, Bulk

5690 Golden Cheese Company of California
1138 W Rincon St
Corona, CA 92880-9601   951-493-4700
                  Fax: 951-493-4749
Manufacturer of natural, processed and imitation
cheese and flavoring syrup
   President: David Simon
Estimated Sales: $100+ Million
Number Employees: 250-499
Type of Packaging: Consumer, Food Service, Bulk

5691 Golden Cheese of California
1138 W Rincon St
Corona, CA 92880-9601   951-493-4700
                  Fax: 951-493-4749 800-842-0264
Manufacturer of milk, cottage cheese, butter, sweet
and sour cream, orange juice and yogurt
   President: Dave Simon
   Plant Controller: Richard Pluimer
   VP International Sales: Gabriel Sevilla
   Sales/Marketing: Doug Moore
   Customer Service Manager: Christine Merritt
   Plant Manager: Dermot O'Brien
Estimated Sales: $ 1 - 3 Million
Number Employees: 10-19
Sq. footage: 420000
Parent Co: Dairy Farmers of America
Type of Packaging: Consumer, Food Service
Brands:
   GOLDEN CHEESE

5692 Golden City Brewery
920 12th St
Golden, CO 80401-1181   303-279-8092
                  Fax: 303-279-8092
Beer
   President: Jennie Sturdavant
   Director Manufacturing: Charles Sturdevant
Estimated Sales: $5-9.9 Million
Number Employees: 1-4
Type of Packaging: Private Label

5693 Golden City Meats
400 Vine St
Golden City, MO 64748-8276   417-537-8560
Processor of meat products including beef, pork and
ostrich
   Owner: Robert Long
Estimated Sales: $2.5-5 Million
Number Employees: 1-4

5694 Golden Creek Vineyard
4480 Wallace Road
Santa Rosa, CA 95404-1433   707-538-2350
Wines
   President: Ladi Danielik
Estimated Sales: Less than $500,000
Number Employees: 1-4
Type of Packaging: Private Label

5695 Golden Drop
1306 N San Fernando Rd
Los Angeles, CA 90065-1237   323-225-9161
                  Fax: 323-225-9163
Beverages
   President: Arthur Papazyan
Estimated Sales: $5-10 Million
Number Employees: 1-4

5696 Golden Eagle Olive Products
P.O.Box 390
Porterville, CA 93258-0390   559-784-3468
                  Fax: 559-784-2186
Processor of virgin, extra virgin and pure olive oil
   Owner: Jerry Padula
   Assistant Manager: Traci Padula
Estimated Sales: $5-10 Million
Number Employees: 1-4
Sq. footage: 10000
Type of Packaging: Consumer
Brands:
   Golden Eagle

5697 Golden Eagle Syrup Manufacturing Company
P.O.Box 690
Fayette, AL 35555-0690   205-932-5294
   Fax: 205-932-5296 info@goldeneaglesyrup.com
                  www.goldeneaglesyrup.com
Manufacturer of syrups including table, waffle and
pancake
   Co-Owner/President: Trent Mobley
   Co-Owner/Plant Manager: Vic Herren
   Office Manager: Martha Kimbrell
Estimated Sales: $2.5-5 Million
Number Employees: 5-9
Type of Packaging: Consumer, Food Service, Bulk

5698 Golden Eye Seafood
17640 Clarke Rd
Tall Timbers, MD 20690-2055   301-994-2274
                  Fax: 301-994-9960
Processor and wholesaler/distributor of seafood in-
cluding live and cooked blue crabs, oysters and soft
shelled
   Owner: Robert Lumpkins
   Treasurer: Nancie Lumpkins
   House Manager: Lee Deagle
Estimated Sales: $ 5 - 10 Million
Number Employees: 5-9

5699 Golden Flake Snack Food
1 Golden Flake Dr
Birmingham, AL 35205-3312   205-323-6161
   Fax: 205-458-7335 www.goldenflake.com
Snacks
   President/CEO: Mark McCutcheon
Estimated Sales: I
Number Employees: 500-999
Brands:
   GOLDEN FLAKE

5700 (HQ)Golden Flake Snack Foods
1 Golden Flake Dr
Birmingham, AL 35205-3312   205-323-6161
   Fax: 205-458-7335 www.goldenflake.com
Snacks-salted
   President: Mark McCutcheon
   Quality Control: Joe Elliott
   Marketing Director: June Strauss
   Sales Director: Randy Bates
   Operations Manager: Dave Jones
   Production Manager: Neil Hunt
   Purchasing Manager: Jeff Clemmons
Estimated Sales: $110 Million
Number Employees: 500-999
Number of Brands: 4
Sq. footage: 350000
Type of Packaging: Consumer, Food Service, Bulk
Other Locations:
   Golden Flake Manufacturing Plant
   Ocala FL
   Golden Flake Manufacturing Plant
   Birmingham AL

5701 (HQ)Golden Flake Snack Foods
3031 W Silver Springs Blvd
Ocala, FL 34475-5647 352-351-2277
Fax: 352-351-3197 800-239-2447
www.goldenflake.com
Processor of potato and tortilla chips
President/CEO: Mark W McCutcheon
VP/CFO: Mark Mccutcheon
CFO: Patty Townsend
Vice President: Randy Bates
Sales Director: Randy Bates
Production Manager: Larry Wood
Plant Manager: John Wagner
Estimated Sales:$20-50 Million
Number Employees: 20-49
Type of Packaging: Consumer, Private Label
Brands:
Golden Flake

5702 Golden Fluff Popcorn Company
118 Monmouth Ave
Lakewood, NJ 08701-3347 732-367-5448
Fax: 732-367-1028 goldenfluff@aol.com
www.goldenfluff.com
Pre-popped popcorn, potato sticks, microwave pop-
corn, tortilla chips, toppings, nuts & dried fruits,
elyon marshmallow and dontil sugar free chewing
gum.
President: Ephraim Schwinder
Estimated Sales: Less than $500,000
Number Employees: 10-19
Type of Packaging: Consumer, Bulk
Brands:
Dontil
Elyon
Golden Fluff

5703 Golden Foods
5743 Smithway St # 305
Commerce, CA 90040-1549 323-721-1882
Fax: 323-721-4526 800-350-2462
gsfoods@gowebway.com
Processor of confectionery products, cake and pie
fillings, syrups, dessert toppings, frozen edible coat-
ings and low-fat fudge variegates
President: Jonathan Freed
CEO: Kit Phillips
CFO: Ezekiel Freed
VP: Rose Freed
Purchasing Manager: Kit Phillips
Estimated Sales:$1-2.5 Million
Number Employees: 5-9
Sq. footage: 8000
Type of Packaging: Bulk
Brands:
Gelite
Pectose-Standard

5704 Golden Gate Foods
1618 W Commerce St
Dallas, TX 75208-1407 214-747-2223
Fax: 214-760-7611
Processor of chow mein, egg rolls, egg and pork
sausage rolls, egg and cheese rolls, noodles,
wontons, stir fry rice, sesame oil, soy sauce, dim
sum and pot stickers
President: Buck Jung
CEO: Helen Jung
CFO: Lai Chun Jung
Estimated Sales:$2.5-5 Million
Number Employees: 20-49
Number of Products: 10
Sq. footage: 13000
Type of Packaging: Consumer, Food Service, Pri-
vate Label, Bulk
Brands:
Golden Gate

5705 Golden Glow Cookie Company
1844 Givan Ave
Bronx, NY 10469-3155 718-379-6223
Fax: 718-379-4417 ggcookies@aol.com
www.goldenglowcookie.com
Processor of cookies, cakes and Italian pastries
President: Rose Florio
VP Sales: Sal Florio
VP Production: Joan Florio
Estimated Sales:$2.5-5 Million
Number Employees: 10-19
Brands:
Mama Rose

5706 Golden Grain
4576 Willow Rd
Pleasanton, CA 94588-2715 925-734-8800
Fax: 925-416-7065 www.pepsico.com
Dry pasta
President: Mark Shapiro
VP: Jim Richard
Estimated Sales:$100-500 Million
Number Employees: 100-249
Brands:
Golden Grain
Mission
Pasta Roni

5707 Golden Grain Company
7700 W 71st St
Bridgeview, IL 60455-1095 708-458-7020
Fax: 708-458-7023
Processor of pasta and rice products
Comptroller: Jerry Gates
Plant Manager: Dave Corazzi
Estimated Sales:$100-500 Million
Number Employees: 250-499
Parent Co: Quaker Oats Company
Type of Packaging: Consumer, Food Service, Pri-
vate Label

5708 Golden Gulf Coast Packing Company
642 Bayview Ave
Biloxi, MS 39530-2307 228-374-6121
Fax: 228-374-0599
Processor and exporter of frozen and breaded shrimp
President/Owner: Richard Gollott
Estimated Sales:$ 10 - 20 Million
Number Employees: 50-99
Sq. footage: 8000

5709 Golden Harvest Pecans
348 Vereen Bell Road
Cairo, GA 39828-4910 229-762-3233
Fax: 229-762-3335 800-597-0968
gharvest@rose.net
Processor, co-packer and exporter of certified or-
ganic pecans, gift baskets and southern delicacies
President/CEO: J Van Ponder
Estimated Sales:$2.5-5 Million
Number Employees: 5
Type of Packaging: Consumer, Food Service, Pri-
vate Label, Bulk

5710 Golden Heritage Food
P.O.Box 97
Latty, OH 45855-0097 419-399-5786
Fax: 419-399-4924 888-233-6446
info@ghfllc.com www.ghfllc.com
Premium honey
president: dwight Stoller
CEO: Brent Barkman
Estimated Sales: Below $ 5 Million
Number Employees: 20-49
Brands:
Busy Bee

5711 Golden Heritage Foods
P.O.Box 97
Latty, OH 45855-0097 419-399-5786
Fax: 419-399-4924 888-233-6446
info@ghfllc.com www.ghfllc.com
Processor and packager of honey and flavored honey
spreads
President: Dwight Stoller
Estimated Sales:$20 - 50 Million
Number Employees: 20-49
Sq. footage: 23000
Type of Packaging: Consumer, Food Service, Pri-
vate Label, Bulk

5712 Golden Kernel Pecan Company
P.O.Box 613
Cameron, SC 29030-0613 803-823-2311
Fax: 803-823-2080 800-845-2448
info@goldenkernel.com www.goldenkernel.com
Processor and exporter of pecans
President: David K Summers Jr
VP/Treasurer: J Williams Summers
Marketing Director: Bill Summers
Operations Manager: Jerry Fogle
Estimated Sales:$50 Million
Number Employees: 20-49
Sq. footage: 17100
Type of Packaging: Consumer, Private Label, Bulk
Brands:
GOLDEN KERNEL

5713 Golden Locker Cooperative
P.O.Box 279
Golden, IL 62339-0279 217-696-4456
Processor of beef and pork
Manager: Rick Huntley
Estimated Sales:$2.5-5 Million
Number Employees: 5-9
Type of Packaging: Consumer, Bulk

5714 Golden Malted
4101 William Richardson Drive
South Bend, IN 46628 574-247-2270
Fax: 574-247-2280 800-686-6258
retail@goldenmalted.com
www.goldenmalted.com
pancake and waffle flour

5715 Golden Moon Tea
Ste 204
1043 Sterling Rd
Herndon, VA 20170-3842 425-820-2000
Fax: 425-821-9700 877-327-5473
service@goldenmoontea.com
www.goldenmoontea.com
Specialty tea and fine chocolates, tea accessories
President: Cynthia Knotts
Number of Products: 30
Type of Packaging: Consumer, Food Service, Pri-
vate Label, Bulk
Brands:
Golden Moon Tea

5716 Golden Peanut Company
P.O.Box 488
Ashburn, GA 31714-0488 229-567-3311
Fax: 229-567-2006 www.goldenpeanut.com
Processor and exporter of shelled peanuts
Plant Manager: Bill Leverette
Estimated Sales:$ 5 - 10 Million
Number Employees: 100-249
Parent Co: Gold Kist Poultry
Type of Packaging: Bulk

5717 Golden Peanut Company
100 N Point Center E
Suite 400
Aplharetta, GA 30022 770-752-8205
Fax: 770-752-8306 www.goldenpeanut.com
Sheller and processor of peanuts and peanut prod-
ucts. Raw shelled and inshell peanuts, peanut flours,
peanut extracts, roasted aromatic and refined various
peanut oils, and peanut seed.
President/CEO: James Dorsett
CFO: Fritz Holzgrefe
Plant Manager: Craig Smith
Regional Procurement Manager: Milton Smith
Estimated Sales:$500 Million-$1 Billion
Number Employees: 1000
Type of Packaging: Consumer

5718 Golden Peanut Company
P.O.Box 279
Aulander, NC 27805-0279 252-345-1661
Fax: 252-345-1991 www.goldenpeanut.com
Processor and exporter of peanuts
President: John Monahan
Plant Manager: Merle Yates
Estimated Sales:$5-10 Million
Number Employees: 100-249
Parent Co: Golden Peanut
Type of Packaging: Consumer

5719 Golden Peanut Company
100 N Point Ctr E
Suite 400
Alpharetta, GA 30022 770-752-8205
Fax: 770-752-8306 www.goldenpeanut.com
Sheller and processor of peanuts and peanuts prod-
ucts including raw shelled and inshell peanuts, pea-
nut flours, peanut extracts, roasted aromatic and
refined various peanut oils and peanut seed.
President/CEO: James Dorsett
CFO: Fritz Holzgrefe
VP International Sales: Alex Izmirlian
Estimated Sales:$500 Million+
Number Employees: 1000
Type of Packaging: Bulk

5720 Golden Peanuts Company
100 N Point Ctr E # 400
Alpharetta, GA 30022-8262 770-752-8160
Fax: 770-752-8308 www.goldenpeanut.com

Sheller and processor of peanuts and peanut products. Golden's primary product lines include raw shelled and inshell peanuts, peanut flour, various peanut oils, and peanut seed.
President/CEO: Jimmy Dorsett
CFO: Fritz Holzgrefe
VP Sales: Bill Grant
Estimated Sales: $500,000-$1 Million
Number Employees: 1,000-4,999
Type of Packaging: Private Label

5721 Golden Platter Foods
37 Tompkins Point Rd
Newark, NJ 07114-2814   973-242-0291
      Fax: 973-242-5892   scott@goldenplatter.com
            www.goldenplatter.com
Processor and exporter of poultry products including frozen nuggets, patties and parts and turkey sausages; also, Halal meats
President: Scott Bennett
Estimated Sales: $5-10 Million
Number Employees: 20-49
Type of Packaging: Consumer, Food Service

5722 Golden River Fruit Company
P.O.Box 2090
Vero Beach, FL 32961-2090   772-562-4502
                    Fax: 772-567-6008
Grower and shipper of grapefruit
Owner: George Lambeth
VP: David Milwood
Purchasing Manager: Fred Van Antwerp
Estimated Sales: $5-10 Million
Number Employees: 10-19
Sq. footage: 95000
Type of Packaging: Bulk
Brands:
Bland Farms
Golden Eagle
Golden One
Golden River
Golden Sun
National Gold
National One
Sundance

5723 Golden Rod Broilers
2352 County Road 719
Cullman, AL 35055-9655   256-734-0941
                    Fax: 256-739-4024
Manufacturer and exporter of poultry
President: Forrest Ingram
VP: Wynona Cooley
Estimated Sales: $50-100 Million
Number Employees: 500-999
Parent Co: Ingram Farms
Type of Packaging: Consumer, Food Service, Private Label, Bulk

5724 Golden Specialty Foods
14605 Best Ave
Norwalk, CA 90650-5258   562-802-2537
                    Fax: 562-926-4491
Processor of canned dips, salad dressings, sauces, Mexican seasonings, chicken and beef bases, etc.; exporter of salsa and chili con carne
President: Phil Pisciotta
VP: Helga Kim
Quality Control: Shegun Olexoshevekan
Marketing Director: Jeff Chan
Estimated Sales: $5-9.9 Million
Number Employees: 50-99
Sq. footage: 32000
Type of Packaging: Consumer, Food Service, Private Label, Bulk

5725 Golden State Citrus Packers
P.O.Box 697
Woodlake, CA 93286-0697   559-564-3351
      Fax: 559-564-3865   vcpg@vcpg.com
            www.vcpg.com
Golden State Citrus Packers is a licensed commercial shipper of citrus products for Sunkist Growers, Inc.
General Manager: Cliff St Martin
Assistant Manager: John Clower
Plant Manager: Raul Gamez
Parent Co: Visalia Citrus Packing Group
Type of Packaging: Food Service

5726 (HQ)Golden State Foods
18301 Von Karman Ave
Suite 1100
Irvine, CA 92612   949-252-2000
      Fax: 949-252-2080 www.goldenstatefoods.com
sauces, dressings, syrups, jams/jellies and toppings, cooked beef, taco meat, chili and burrito fillings, produce, rolls and buns, elongated buns, and mini roll.
Chairman/President/CEO: Mark Wetterau
Estimated Sales: $4 Billion
Number Employees: 3,000
Other Locations:
Golden State Foods
Sixth of October City

5727 (HQ)Golden State Foods
18301 Von Karman Ave
Suite 1100
Irvine, CA 92612   949-252-2000
                    Fax: 949-252-2080
gsfinfo@goldenstatefoods.com
      www.goldenstatefoods.com
Manufacturer and exporter of portion packed ketchup, sauces, jams, jellies, meat patties, honey, etc
Chairman/CEO: Mark Wetterau
CFO: Mike Waitukaitis
Corporate Senior EVP: Frank Listi
Corporate SVP Human Resources: Steve Becker
Estimated Sales: $4 Billion
Number Employees: 3,000
Type of Packaging: Food Service
Other Locations:
Golden State Foods
City of Industry CA
Golden State Foods
Conyers GA
Golden State Foods
Greensboro NC
Golden State Foods
Columbia SC
Golden State Foods
Phoenix AZ
Golden State Foods
Portland OR
Golden State Foods
Rochester NY
Golden State Foods
Suffolk VA
Golden State Foods
Oak Brook IL
Golden State Foods
Earth City MO
Golden State Foods
Waipahu HI

5728 Golden State Foods
640 S 6th Ave
City of Industry, CA 91746-3086   626-968-6431
                    Fax: 626-333-3804
gsfinfo@goldenstatefoods.com
      www.goldenstatefoods.com
Processor of portion packed ketchup, sauces, jams, jellies, honey, etc.; exclusively for McDonald's
President: John Pooly
Vice President: Larry McGill
Sales/Marketing Executive: Larry Jacobsen
Plant Manager: Jorgue Hasbun
Purchasing Agent: Bill Calhoun
Estimated Sales: $100-500 Million
Number Employees: 250-499
Parent Co: Golden State Foods
Type of Packaging: Food Service
Brands:
McDonalds

5729 Golden State Vintners
38558 Road 128
Cutler, CA 93615-9755   559-528-3033
      Fax: 559-528-2627 www.gsvwine.com
Processor and exporter of wine, grape juice and brandy.
President/CEO: Jeffrey O'Neill
CFO: John Kelleher
Plant Manager: Ted Miller
Estimated Sales: $5-10 Million
Number Employees: 20-49
Type of Packaging: Consumer, Food Service, Private Label, Bulk
Brands:
BOUNTY
EDGEWOOD
LE BLANC
MONTHAVEN
SUMMERFIELD

5730 Golden Temple
1616 Preuss Rd
Los Angeles, CA 90035-4212   310-275-9891
      Fax: 310-275-2923 www.goldentemple.com
Natural foods, organic teas, natural and organic cereals, body care products and herbal supplements.
International Sales Administrator: Sarib Khalsa
Estimated Sales: $ 1 - 3 Million
Number Employees: 20-49

5731 (HQ)Golden Temple
2545 Prairie Rd
Eugene, OR 97402-9700   541-461-2160
      Fax: 541-461-2191   800-964-4832
      cs2006@kiit.com   www.yogitea.com
Processor and exporter of natural products including low-fat granola cereals and muesli, herbal tea blends and confectionery products; importer of herbs and spices
President: Sopurkh Khalsa
CEO: Kartar Khalsa
Director R&D: Gura Hari Shigh Khalsa
Sales Manager: Grundhan Khalsa
Estimated Sales: $ .5 - 1 million
Number Employees: 100-249
Sq. footage: 100000
Parent Co: Yogi Tea
Type of Packaging: Consumer, Food Service, Private Label, Bulk
Other Locations:
Golden Temple
Seattle WA
Brands:
Ancient Healing Formulas
Golden Temple
Herb Technology
Rain Forest
Sweet Home Farm
Yogi Tea

5732 Golden Temple, Sunshine& Yogi Tea
1616 Preuss Rd
Los Angeles, CA 90035-4212   310-275-9891
      Fax: 310-275-2923 800-225-3623
            www.goldentemple.com
Natural foods and health products and Yogi Tea
President: Yogi Bhajan
National Sales Manager: Gurudhan Singh Khalsa
Estimated Sales: $ 1 - 3 Million
Number Employees: 20-49
Brands:
Yogi Tea

5733 Golden Town Apple Products
PO Box 303
Thornbury, ON N0H 2P0
Canada   519-599-6300
                    Fax: 519-599-2103
keithc@goldentownapples.com
      www.goldentownapples.com
Specializing in apple processing, especially apple peeling and apple-juice production. Leading producer in Ontario
President: Thomas Kritsch
Business Manager: Gerry Williams
Technical Director: Doug Johnson
Office Administrator: Darlene Gardner
Maintenance/Engineering Manager: Ron McQuarrie
Juice Production Coordinator: Jennifer Rear
Plant Manager: Bryan Lowe
GM/Purchasing/Sales: Keith Cummings
Number Employees: 20-49
Sq. footage: 40000
Parent Co: A. Lassonde, Inc
Type of Packaging: Consumer, Bulk

5734 Golden Valley Dairy Products
1025 E Bardsley Ave
Tulare, CA 93274-5752   559-687-1188
      Fax: 559-685-6551 webamster@gvdairy.com
            www.saputo.com
Processor of cheese
Manager: Mike Kothbauer
CEO: John Prince
Estimated Sales: $500,000-$1 Million
Number Employees: 5-9
Parent Co: DCCA
Type of Packaging: Consumer
Brands:
Ben & Jerry
Breyers

Haagen Dazs
Klondike

5735 Golden Valley Foods
31632 Marshall Road
PO Box 1800
Abbotsford, BC V2S 7G3
Canada   604-855-7431
        Fax: 604-855-7439   888-299-8855
        gvfoods@goldenvalley.com
        www.goldenvalley.com
Egg production through grading, wholesaling, and
distribution of eggs
    President: Ken Funk
    Manager/Controller: Marion Juhasz
    Quality Assurance/Plant Manager: Frank Curtis
    Manager/Food Service Division: John Funk
    Director Sales/Marketing: Bryan Piazza
    Manager Human Resources: Carol Wayner
    General Manager: Walt Puetz
    VP Operations: Ralph Paine
Estimated Sales:$90 Million
Number Employees: 150
Type of Packaging: Consumer, Food Service, Private Label
Brands:
    FRASER VALLEY
    GOLDEN VALLEY FOODS

5736 Golden Valley Seed
P.O.Box 1600
El Centro, CA 92244-1600   760-337-3100
    Fax: 760-337-3135 info@goldenvalleyseed.com
        www.goldenvalleyseed.com
Processor, importer and exporter of tomato and
squash seeds
    President: Nassif Burkhuch
    CFO/Secretary: Clark Sarchet
    Vice President: Irene Davila
    Mgmt Information Systems/Accts Payable: Kevin
    Sarchet
    Warehouse Manager: Jerry Richardson
    Warehouse Supervisor: Miguel Izarraras
Estimated Sales:$5-10 Million
Number Employees: 10-19
Type of Packaging: Bulk

5737 Golden Walnut SpecialtyFoods
3200 16th St
Zion, IL 60099-1416   847-731-3200
    Fax: 847-731-6433   800-843-3645
            sales@goldenwalnut.com
            www.goldenwalnut.com
Processor of specialty food products including cook-
ies, cakes, cheesecakes, shortbread and candy; ex-
porter of cookies
    President: Mark Sigel
    Operations: Preston Came
    Production: Abel Pelaez
Estimated Sales:$5-10 Million
Number Employees: 20-49
Parent Co: EMAC International
Type of Packaging: Consumer, Private Label, Bulk
Brands:
    Almond Ingot
    Amelia's Sugar Free Shoppe
    Buckley's
    Golden Walnut
    Ingot
    Monica's
    Razzlenuts
    Sideboard Sweets & Savories
    Thimble

5738 Golden West Fruit Company
2151 Saybrook Ave
Commerce, CA 90040-1717   323-726-9419
        Fax: 323-726-9504 www.goldenwestfruit.com
Processes fruits, toppings, syrups, fillings & bottled
fruit & beverages.
    President: Donald Campolo
Estimated Sales:$280,000
Number Employees: 1-4
Sq. footage: 20000
Type of Packaging: Private Label, Bulk

5739 Golden West Nuts
1555 Warren Rd
Ripon, CA 95366-9532   209-599-6193
    Fax: 209-599-6013 steve@goldenwestnuts.com
            www.goldenwestnuts.com

Golden West Nuts, Inc. is a grower, processor and
shipper of California almonds. We offer natural and
blanched forms of whole, sliced, slivered and diced
almonds. We are also one of the largest shippers of
inshell almonds. For almondapplication ideas and
recent nutritional research on the health benefits of
almonds, visit the all about almonds section of our
web site at www.goldenwestnuts.com. Contact Steve
Gikas at (209)-599-6193 or at
steve@goldenwestnuts.com forinformation
    President: Jon Hoff
    CEO: Steve Gikas
Estimated Sales:$ 20 - 50 Million
Number Employees: 100-249
Type of Packaging: Bulk

5740 Golden West Nuts
1555 Warren Rd
Ripon, CA 95366-9532   209-599-6193
    Fax: 209-599-6013 sales@goldenwestnuts.com
            www.goldenwestnuts.com
Manufacturer of California almonds; offered inshel,
natural whole, blanched, sliced, slivered, diced, cus-
tom specifications
    President/Co-Owner: Jon Hoff
    Controller: Mark Vanlerberghe
    CEO: Steve Gikas
    Logistics Manager: Bonnie Pater
    Plant Manager: Miguel Fernandez
Estimated Sales:$60 Million
Number Employees: 100-249
Sq. footage: 32000
Type of Packaging: Bulk
Brands:
    Golden West

5741 Golden West Specialty Foods
300 Industrial Way
Brisbane, CA 94005   415-657-0123
        Fax: 415-657-0110   800-584-4481
    info@gwsfoods.com   www.gwsfoods.com
Gourmet foods, sauces, cookies, shortbread, pesto
sauce, cocktail sauce, BBQ sauce, marinades, dressings and chocolate poker chips.
    President: Lawrence Ames
Estimated Sales:$2-4 Million
Type of Packaging: Consumer, Food Service, Private Label, Bulk

5742 Golden Whisk
330 Shaw Road
PO Box 2131
South San Francisco, CA 94080-6616650-952-7677
        Fax: 650-952-9004   800-660-5222
            laregina@goldenwhisk.com'
            www.goldenwhisk.com
Processor, exporter and wholesaler/distributor of ol-
ive oil, pasta, vinegar, specialty sauces and condi-
ments including Asian, south-western and Mexican;
serving the retail and food service markets
    President/CEO: Elinor Hill-Courtney
    Executive VP: A Courtney
    Marketing Director: Julie Hutchinson
    Purchasing Manager: Elinor Hill-Courtney
Estimated Sales:$500,000-$1 Million
Number Employees: 5-10
Sq. footage: 10000
Type of Packaging: Consumer, Food Service, Pri-
vate Label, Bulk
Brands:
    A.J's Frisco B-B-Q
    Albear's Apri-Dijon
    Alla Primavera
    Aloha Gold
    Arti-Garlico
    Basically Basil
    Canzone Del Mare
    Cucina Della Regina
    Earl Grey Vinaigre Det
    Expressly Oriental
    Formaglio
    Garlirosti
    Golden Whisk
    Honeyed Ginger
    Jazzy Garlic Jazz
    La Regina's Balsamic
    Lala's Bar & Grill
    Marinara Mia
    Porcini Toscanini
    Really Garlicky
    Red Raspberry Razzle
    Salsa Di Marco Polo
    Smokey Lap-Souchang Vinaigre Det
    Star of Siam

Vinegar Paradiso
Vinegar Siam
Vinegar Tropicana
Wokin'n Tossin'
Zesta Italiana
Zia Maria's Verde

5743 Goldenberg Candy Company
7701 State Rd
Philadelphia, PA 19136-3405   215-335-4500
        Fax: 215-335-4510   800-727-2439
            info@goldenbergcandy.com
            www.peanutchews.com
Manufacturer and exporter of candy including
coated bars, and miniatures with syrup and peanuts,
Halloween, fund raising, etc
    VP: Mindy Goldenberg
Estimated Sales:$20-50 Million
Number Employees: 100-249
Sq. footage: 100000
Type of Packaging: Consumer, Food Service, Bulk
Brands:
    Chew-Ets
    Peanut Chews

5744 Goldenrod Dairy Foods/U C Milk Company
234 N Scott St
Madisonville, KY 42431-2067   270-821-7221
        Fax: 270-821-7292   800-462-2354
            www.goldenroddairy.com
Milk and dairy products
    General Manager: Tony Mayes
    Sales Manager: Mark Miller
    Human Resource Manager: Steve Shoots
    Plant Manager: Aaron Johnson
Estimated Sales:$ 50 - 100 Million
Number Employees: 155
Parent Co: National Dairy
Type of Packaging: Bulk

5745 Goldilocks Bakeshop
344 Littlefield Ave
S San Francisco, CA 94080-6103   650-873-6566
            Fax: 650-873-2826 www.giustos.com
Flour and other grains
    Owner: Albert Giusto
Estimated Sales:$5-9.9 Million
Number Employees: 20-49

5746 Golding Farms Foods
6061 Gun Club Rd
Winston Salem, NC 27103-9727   336-766-6161
            Fax: 336-766-3131
        information@goldingfarmsfood.com
            www.goldingfarmsfoods.com
Processor and private label co-packer of condiments
and sauces including barbecue, steak, cocktail, salad
dressing, tartar and salsa; also, honey, molasses and
relishes including chow chow and onion
    President/Owner: Tony Golding
    EVP: Ron Foster Jr
    Technical Director: Daniel Sortwell
    Director Sales: Tom Clayton
    Operations Manager: Preston Myers
    Production Manager: Lawrence Logan
*Estimated Sales:*2.5-5 Million
Number Employees: 50-99
Number of Products: 150
Sq. footage: 40000
Type of Packaging: Consumer, Food Service, Pri-
vate Label, Bulk
Brands:
    Golding
    Golding Farms
    Golding Gourmand
    Mrs. Campbells
    Naturally Healthy
    Old Laredo

5747 Goldrush Sourdough
491 W San Carlos Street
San Jose, CA 95110-2632   408-288-4090
    Fax: 408-286-1503 christine@commissary.com
            www.mccornbread.com
Distribution of cornbread
    President: Henry Down
    Marketing Director: Barry Johnson
    Purchasing Manager: Preston Myers
Estimated Sales:$2.5-5 Million
Number Employees: 10-19

5748 Goldwater's Food of Arizona
Salsa Express
PO Box 9846
Fredericksburg, TX 78624
Fax: 830-990-9481 800-488-4932
goldwaters@goldwaters.com
www.goldwaters.com
Processor of fruit salsa and bean dips, barbecue
sauces and chili
President: Carolyn Ross
Estimated Sales: $1-2.5 Million
Number Employees: 1-4
Type of Packaging: Consumer
Brands:
Goldwater's
Goldwater's Taste of the Southwest

5749 Golf Mill Chocolate Factory
332 Golf Mill Ctr
Niles, IL 60714-1221 847-635-1107
Fax: 847-390-1737
Processor of chocolate candy
Owner: Ella Faybysh
CEO: Lela Faybysh
Estimated Sales: $ 1-2.5 Million
Number Employees: 5-9
Type of Packaging: Consumer

5750 Goll's Bakery
234 N Washington St
Havre De Grace, MD 21078-2909 410-939-4321
Fax: 410-939-2556 www.grollsbakery.com
Family owned german style bakery, breads, wedding
cakes, birthday cakes, cookies baked fresh every
day.
Owner: Robert K Goll Jr
Estimated Sales: Less than $500,000
Number Employees: 5-9

5751 Gollott Brothers Seafood Company
555 Bayview Ave
Biloxi, MS 39530-2418 228-432-7865
Fax: 228-435-3820
Processor and importer of fresh shrimp and oysters
President: Larry Gollott Jr
Estimated Sales: $20-50 Million
Number Employees: 50-99
Type of Packaging: Consumer

5752 Gomax Foods
PO Box 944
Dimmitt, TX 79027-0944 806-647-3504
Fax: 806-647-3517
Frozen carrots, onions, jalapeno peppers, beef raw,
cooked beef
President: Glenn Odom
Estimated Sales: $5-10 Million
Number Employees: 10-19
Type of Packaging: Private Label
Brands:
Gomax
Renegade

5753 Gonard Foods
4139 Edmonton Trail NE
Calgary, AB T2E 3Y5
Canada
403-277-0991
Fax: 403-277-0664
Processor of frozen entrees, meat patties, chicken
products, veal cutlets, fresh entrees, packaged sand-
wiches, red and deli meats
President/Owner: Munir Lakha
Number Employees: 7

5754 Gondwanaland
PO Box 266
Corrales, NM 87048-0266 505-899-5660
Fax: 505-890-5315 larry@gondwanaland1.com
www.gondwanaland1.com
Processor of gourmet coffee including organic,
arabican, Columbian, Costa Rican, Indonesian,
Mexican, Ethiopian and Tanzanian
Owner: Larry Ward

5755 (HQ)Gonnella Baking Company
2002 W Erie St
Chicago, IL 60612-1318 312-733-2020
Fax: 312-733-7670 rabiera@gonnella.com
www.gonnella.com
Freshly baked, aromatic crisp crusted breads, a true
hearth-baked product and our frozen dough prod-
ucts.
President: Nicholas Marcucci
Vice President: Tom Marcucci
VP Sales: Paul Gonnella
Human Resources: Kathleen Heinzman
Productions Division: Rudy Abiera
Estimated Sales: $10-24.9 Million
Number Employees: 250-499

5756 Gonnella Frozen Products
1117 Wiley Rd
Schaumburg, IL 60173-4337 847-884-8829
Fax: 847-884-9469 www.gonnella.com
Frozen dough products
President: Ken Gonnella
Treasurer: George Mancucci
Sales: Ronald Lucchesi
Human Resources/Safety Manager: James
Mazukelli
Plant Manager: Kent Beernink
Estimated Sales: $20-50 Million
Number Employees: 250-499
Type of Packaging: Consumer, Food Service, Pri-
vate Label, Bulk

5757 Good 'N Natural
2100 Smithtown Avenue
Ronkonkoma, NY 11779-7347
800-544-0095
questions@goodnnatural.com
www.goodnnatural.com
Processor of vitamins and supplements

5758 (HQ)Good Earth® Teas
831 Almar Avenue
Santa Cruz, CA 95060-5804 831-423-7913
Fax: 831-429-5173 sales@goodearthteas.com
www.goodearthteas.com
Processor of highest quality standards and great tast-
ing flavors of teas such as: green, chai, red, black,
herbal, black and medicinal to name a few.
President/Plant Manager: Ben Zaricor
CEO: Louise Zaricor
VP Marketing: Clive Rowlandson
VP Sales: Randall Duarte
Manufacturing/Operations Director: Arn Parker
Estimated Sales: $13.8 Billion
Number Employees: 70
Parent Co: Tetley US Holdings Limited
Type of Packaging: Private Label
Brands:
China Collection Teas
Energy Supplements
Functional Teas
Good Earth Teas
Herbal Teas

5759 Good Food
P.O.Box 160
Honey Brook, PA 19344-0160 610-273-3776
Fax: 610-273-2087 800-327-4406
goodfood@goldenbarrel.com
www.goldenbarrel.com
Molasses, syrups, shoofly pie and funnel cake
mixes; vegetable, cotton seed, coconut, peanut, corn,
olive, canola and blended cooking oils
President: Larry Martin
CEO: Ean Johnson
Estimated Sales: $20-50 Million
Number Employees: 100-249

5760 Good Fortunes & Edible Art
6754 Eton Ave
Canoga Park, CA 91303-2813 818-595-1555
Fax: 818-595-1550 800-644-9474
order@goodfortunes.com
www.corporatecandyworks.com
Gourmet dipped fortune cookies, classical-sized
dipped and decorated fortune cookies, sourdough
pretzels sticks dipped in chocolate, Bavarian pret-
zels dipped
Owner: Karen Staitman
Brands:
A Dose of Good Fortunes
Candy Art
Cookie Art
Fractured Fortunes
Good Fortunes
Pretzel Twisters
Pretzel Wands
Sugar Art

5761 Good Harbor Fillet Company
21 Great Republic Dr
Gloucester, MA 01930-2276 978-675-9100
Fax: 978-675-9190 www.goodharborfillet.com
Specializes in the manufacture and distribution of a
complete line of made-to-order, processed seafood
products, as well as a variety of innovative specialty
items.
President: William Stride
Chief Financial Officer: Mike Joyce
Northeast Regional Manager: Ned Hawkins
Southeast Regional Manager: Dave Galloway
Quality Control Manager: Alan Pothier
VP Sales/Marketing: Annette Chalmers
West Coast Sales Manager: Joel Bortz
Chief Operating Officer: Dave Nelson
Purchasing Manager: Alan Gilbert
Number Employees: 50-99
Type of Packaging: Consumer, Food Service

5762 Good Harbor Vineyards
34 S Manitou Trl
Lake Leelanau, MI 49653-9589 231-256-7165
Fax: 231-256-7378 winery@goodharbor.com
www.goodharbor.com
Wines: White Riesling, Chardonnay, Fishtown
White, Trillium®, Pinot Grigio, Manitou, and spe-
cialty wines.
Winemaker/Owner: Bruce Simpson
Associate: Richard Flores
Associate: Rocky Flores
Retail Sales/Owner: Debbie Simpson
Operations: William Schaub
Operations: Gary Schaub
Assistant Winemaker: David Hooper
Growing/Management Workforce: Ovidio Chapa
Estimated Sales: Under $500,000
Number Employees: 1-4
Type of Packaging: Private Label

5763 Good Health Natural Foods
81 Scudder Avenue
Northport, NY 11768-2966 631-261-2111
Fax: 631-261-2147
francois@goodhealthnaturalfoods.com
Olive oil, potato chips, popcorn, pretzels, candy, ap-
ple chips crackers and cookies
Estimated Sales: $ 3 - 5 Million
Number Employees: 5-9

5764 Good Health Natural Foods
81 Scudder Avenue
Northport, NY 11768-2966 631-261-2111
Fax: 631-261-2147 info@e-goodhealth.com
www.goodhealthnaturalfoods.com
Good health natural snacks and energy-well high
protein snacks with soy, south of France natural
body care. Organic olive oil potato chips, popcorn,
pretzels, natural candy, apple chips and crackers.
President: Francois Bogrand
Estimated Sales: $2.5-5 Million
Number Employees: 1-4

5765 (HQ)Good Humor Breyers Ice Cream Company
2271 Hutson Road
Green Bay, WI 54303-4712 920-499-5151
Fax: 920-497-6523 www.breyers.com
Processor and exporter of ice cream and novelties
President: Eric Walsh
VP Finance: Pete Allcox
VP: Harold Vastag
Marketing Director: Terry Olson
VP Sales: Joe Culligan
VP Human Resources: Mark Freeman
Estimated Sales: $1.1 Billion
Number Employees: 2000
Parent Co: Unilever USA
Type of Packaging: Consumer, Food Service, Pri-
vate Label, Bulk
Brands:
Breyers
Good Humor
Klondike
Popsicle

5766 (HQ)Good Humor Breyers Ice Cream Company
2271 Hutson Road
Green Bay, WI 54307-9007 920-499-5151
Fax: 920-497-6523 866-204-9750
info@icecreamusa.com www.breyers.com

Processor of ice cream and novelties
President/CEO: Eric Walsh
VP: Harold Vastag
Logistics Director: Krik Heissel
Marketing/Development VP: Dan Hammer
VP Sales: Joe Colligan
VP Human Resources: Mark Freeman
Estimated Sales: $1+ Billion
Number Employees: 2000
Type of Packaging: Consumer, Food Service
Brands:
  All Natural
  Breyer's Blends
  Breyer's Dairy Products
  Breyer's Rainbow Ice
  Breyer's Romantica
  Breyer's Sherbet
  Fudgsicle
  Good Humor Homemade
  Good Humor-Breyers
  Incredible Hulk
  Klondike
  Lipton Original All
  Minute Main Soft Frozen
  Nickelodeon Ice Cream
  Popsicle Frozen Pops
  Power Ranger Ice Cream
  Reese's Peanut Butter
  Rosetto Pasta
  Rugrats Ice Cream

5767 Good Humor Breyers Ice Cream Company
490 Old Connecticut Path
Framingham, MA 01701-4589   508-620-4300
        Fax: 508-620-0707 www.unilever.com
Processor of ice cream and frozen yogurt
  President: Eric Walsh
  Plant Manager: Kevin Culver
  Controller: Larry Jones
  Plant Manager: Steve Rosemary
Estimated Sales: $100+ Million
Number Employees: 250-499
Parent Co: Good Humor Breyers Ice Cream Company
Type of Packaging: Consumer, Food Service, Bulk
Brands:
  Breyers
  Good Humor

5768 Good Humor Breyers Ice Cream Company
1100 Frederick St
Hagerstown, MD 21740-6867   301-797-9603
        Fax: 301-797-9026 www.breyers.com
Processor of ice cream novelties
  Manager: Ken Wells
  Plant Manager: Dean Palmer
Estimated Sales: $100+ Million
Number Employees: 250-499
Parent Co: Good Humor Breyers Ice Cream Company
Type of Packaging: Consumer, Food Service, Private Label
Brands:
  Breyers
  Good Humor
  Klondike
  Popsicle

5769 Good Humor Breyers Ice Cream Company
1001 Olsen Dr
Henderson, NV 89011-3006   702-564-0020
        Fax: 702-564-5811 www.breyers.com
Processor of ice cream and novelties
  President: Dick Foster
  Personnel Manager: Terry Griguts
  Plant Manager: Greg Hewkin
Estimated Sales: $100+ Million
Number Employees: 100-249
Parent Co: Good Humor Breyers Ice Cream Company
Type of Packaging: Consumer, Food Service, Private Label
Brands:
  Breyers

5770 Good Old Dad Food Products
185 Industrial Court B
Sault Ste. Marie, ON P6B 5Z9
Canada   705-253-7426
        Fax: 705-949-0871 800-267-7426
                           godfoods@shaw.ca
Processor of frozen and snack pasta, etc
  Manager: Richard Palarchio
  Sales: Richard Palarchio
Number Employees: 10-19
Sq. footage: 11000
Type of Packaging: Consumer, Food Service
Brands:
  Rico's

5771 Good Old Days Foods
3300 S Polk St
Little Rock, AR 72204-7823   501-565-1257
  Fax: 501-562-7439 www.goodolddaysfoods.com
Processor of frozen fruit cobblers, corn bread dressing, bread pudding, sweet potato casserole, pecan cobbler. Old fashioned, farm kitchen foods.
  President: Carroll Elder
  CFO: Jim Fletcher
Estimated Sales: $10-20 Million
Number Employees: 20-49
Sq. footage: 100000
Type of Packaging: Consumer, Food Service, Private Label

5772 Good Star Foods
9310 Prototype Drive
Reno, NV 89521-5907   775-851-2442
  Fax: 775-851-7436 nans@qualitycrisp.com
                       www.qualitycrisp.com
Processor and contract packager of crisped grains, protein crisps, extruded cereals and fat-free extruded cereal snacks; also, contract product development available
  President: Hans Bohner
Estimated Sales: $ 1 - 3 Million
Number Employees: 5-9
Sq. footage: 11000
Type of Packaging: Bulk

5773 Good Wives
86 Sanderson Ave # 3
Lynn, MA 01902-1965   781-596-0070
  Fax: 781-596-1131 800-521-8160
              customerservice@goodwives.com
                       www.goodwives.com
Manufacturer of frozen hors d'oeuvres, pastries, tortilla wraps, and flatbreads
  President: Chris Collias
  CFO: Bruce Robertson
  Marketing: Sandra Gamble
  Plant Manager: John Reardon III
Estimated Sales: Under $500,000
Number Employees: 100-249
Sq. footage: 10000
Type of Packaging: Consumer, Food Service, Private Label

5774 Good-O-Beverages Company
1801 Boone Ave
Bronx, NY 10460-5101   718-328-6400
        Fax: 718-328-7002 www.good-o.com
Processor, bottler and exporter of flavored soft drinks including coconut and strawberry
  Owner: Richard Hahn
  Plant Manager: Irving Mendelson
Estimated Sales: $10-20 Million
Number Employees: 20-49
Type of Packaging: Consumer
Brands:
  Coco Rico
  Kola Champagne
  Red Pop
  West Indian Kola

5775 GoodMark Foods
536 Fairfield Avenue
Stamford, CT 06902-7525   919-790-9940
        Fax: 919-790-6537 www.slimjim.com
Snacks
  Trade Marketing: Jeff Seccombe
Brands:
  ANDY CAPP'S
  PEMMICAN
  PENROSE
  SLIM JIM

5776 Goodart Candy
P.O.Box 901
Lubbock, TX 79408-0901   806-747-2600
                           Fax: 806-747-8330
Manufacturer of peanut patties and peanut brittle
  President: Ron Harbuck
  VP: Ron Harbuck
Estimated Sales: $500,000-$1 Million
Number Employees: 10-19
Sq. footage: 12500
Type of Packaging: Private Label, Bulk
Brands:
  Goodart's

5777 Goodheart Brand Specialty Foods
11122 Nacogdoches Rd
San Antonio, TX 78217-2314   210-637-1963
  Fax: 210-637-1391 888-466-3992
  tkennedy@goodheart.com www.goodheart.com
Processor and exporter of quail, venison, bison, wild boar, pheasant and Argentinian all-natural beef; importer of Argentinian beef
  Owner: Amalia Palmaz
  Director Sales: Chef Tim Kennedy
  Plant Manager: Demetrio Molales
Estimated Sales: $5-10 Million
Number Employees: 50-99
Sq. footage: 15000
Parent Co: Bluebonnet Company
Type of Packaging: Consumer, Food Service
Brands:
  Goodheart

5778 Goodman Manufacturing Company
P.O.Box 294
Carthage, MO 64836-0294   417-358-3231
  Fax: 417-358-3231 www.goodmansvanilla.com
Processor of flavoring extracts including vanilla
  President: Mike Kimrey
Estimated Sales: $2.5-5 Million
Number Employees: 1-4

5779 Goodnature Products
3860 California Road
Orchard Park, NY 1412722621   716-855-3325
  Fax: 716-855-3328 800-875-3381
  sales@goodnature.com www.goodnature.com
Manufacturer and exporter of food and juice processing equipment including juice presses, pasteurizers, evaporators, infusers, grinders, feed systems and auxiliary equipment for a variety of fruit, vegetables and herbs. Turnkeyprocessing plant/waste reduction equipment.
  President: Dale Wettlaufer
  Marketing: Kim Ranick
  Sales: Peter Whitehead
  Operations: Diane Massett
  Production: Michael Walters
Estimated Sales: $5-10 Million
Number Employees: 25
Number of Brands: 1
Number of Products: 21
Brands:
  CMP PASTEURIZER
  JUICE-IT
  MAXIMIZER
  SQUEEZEBOX
  X-1

5780 Goodson Brothers CoffeeCompany
138 Sherlake Ln
Knoxville, TN 37922-2307   865-693-3572
  Fax: 865-691-8578 sales@goodsonbrothers.com
                       www.goodsonbrothers.com
Coffee and tea products
  President: Jeff Goodson
Estimated Sales: $10-20 Million
Number Employees: 20-49

5781 Goose Island Brewing
1800 N Clybourn Ave
Chicago, IL 60614-4939   312-915-0071
  Fax: 312-915-0788 info@gooseisland.com
                       www.gooseisland.com
Processor of beer, ale, stout, lager and porter. Many specialities such as Oatmeal Stout, Kelgubbin Red Ale, (Irish style red ale), and craft sodas
  Manager: Rob England
  Brewmaster: Greg Hall
  General Manager: Tim Lane

Estimated Sales: $2.5-5 Million
Number Employees: 50-99
Sq. footage: 37000
Type of Packaging: Consumer, Food Service
Brands:
　Hey Nut
　Honkers
　IPA
　Oatmeal

5782　Goosecross Cellars
1119 State Ln
Yountville, CA　94599-9407　　　707-944-1986
　　　Fax: 707-944-9551　800-276-9210
　　　webmaster@goosecross.com
　　　www.goosecross.com
Specialize in limited production Chardonnay,
Viognier, Chenin Blanc, Merlot, Syrah, Zinfandel,
Cabernet, Pinot Noir and a very special blend of
Sangiovese and Cabernet we call Amerital.
　President/CEO: David Topper
　Vice President/Winemaker: Geoff Gorsuch
　Hospitality/Public Relations: Colleen Topper
　Business Development/Distribution: Pamela
　Topper
Estimated Sales: $2.5-5 Million
Number Employees: 10-19
Type of Packaging: Private Label
Brands:
　Aeros
　Bernard Pradel Cabernet
　Goosecreek
　Goosecross
　Goosecross Cabernet
　Goosecross Chardonnay
　Goosecross Chardonnay Winemaker
　Goosecross Eros
　Goosecross Goosecreek
　Goosecross Mountain Cabernet
　Goosecross Sauvignon Blanc
　Goosecross Syrah
　Goosecross Zinfandel

5783　Gorant Candies
P.O.Box 9068
Youngstown, OH　44513-0068　　　330-726-8821
　　　Fax: 330-726-0325　800-572-4139
　　　kris.stephens@amgreetings.com
　　　www.gorantcandiesofwarren.com
Processor of chocolate-coated candies
Estimated Sales: $50-99.9 Million
Number Employees: 500-999
Sq. footage: 60000
Parent Co: American Greetings
Type of Packaging: Consumer, Private Label
Brands:
　GORANT & YUM YUM CHOCOLATES

**5784　Gordon Biersch Brewing
Company**
33 E San Fernando St
San Jose, CA　95113-2508　　　408-294-6785
　　　Fax: 408-294-4052　info@gbrestaurants.com
　　　www.gordonbiersch.com
Beer
　Manager: Sean McKennan
　Marketing Director: Mike curtis
　CFO: Larry Nally
　Vice President: Dean Biersch
　CEO: Allin Strikli
　Sales Director: Mark Blecher
　Operations Manager: Eddie Sipple
Estimated Sales: $2.5-5 Million
Number Employees: 100-249
Brands:
　Gordon Biersch Blonde Black
　Gordon Biersch Golde
　Gordon Biersch Marzen
　Gordon Biersch Pilsner
　Maibock Hefeweizen
　Winter Block

5785　(HQ)Gordon Food Service
P.O.Box 1787
Grand Rapids, MI　49501-1787　　　616-530-7094
　　　Fax: 616-717-7600　888-437-3663
　　　info@gfs.com　www.gfs.com
Distributor of food, beverages, and supply items to
the food service industry
　President/CEO: Daniel A Gordon
　CFO: Jeff Maddox
　Treasurer: John M Gordon Jr
　Director Marketing/Procurement: Rob
　Vanrenterghem

Estimated Sales: I
Number Employees: 5,000-9,999
Parent Co: Gordon Food Service

5786　Gorman Fisheries
PO Box 10
Conception Bay, NL　A1X 2E2
Canada　　　709-229-6536
　　　Fax: 709-229-6864
Processor and exporter of fresh and frozen mackerel,
herring, squid, tuna, lumpfish roe, capelin and live
and frozen lobster
　President: Patrick Gorman
Number Employees: 100-249
Type of Packaging: Consumer, Food Service, Pri-
vate Label, Bulk

5787　Gormly's Orchard
695 Nowland Farm Rd
South Burlington, VT　05403-8102　802-483-2400
　　　Fax: 802-483-2698　800-639-7604
　　　info@gormlys.com　www.gormlys.com
Processor of pancake and scone mixes, jellies, pre-
serves, mustards, barbecue sauce and spiced apple
cider concentrate
　President: Bill Gormly
Estimated Sales: $500,000 appx.
Number Employees: 5-9
Sq. footage: 9500
Type of Packaging: Consumer, Food Service, Pri-
vate Label

5788　Gorton's Seafood
128 Rogers St
Gloucester, MA　01930-5005　　978-283-3000
　　　Fax: 978-281-7949 www.gortons.com
Processor, importer and exporter of frozen seafood
including clams, fish cakes, flounder, breaded sticks
and fillets, restaurant-style entrees, whiting, shrimp,
sole, crabs, lobster, scallops, etc.; also, batter
　Manager: Karen Carter
　CEO: Steve Warhover
　Director Marketing: Mark Lamothe
　Plant Manager: John Gates
　Purchasing Manager: Lisa Webb
Number Employees: 500-999
Parent Co: Unilever USA
Type of Packaging: Consumer, Food Service
Other Locations:
　Gorton's Seafood
　Cleveland OH
Brands:
　Batters & Breaders
　Blue Water
　Gorton's
　Gorton's Frozen Entrees
　Matlaws
　Specialty

5789　Goshen Dairy Company
3110 Oldtown Valley Rd SW
New Philadelphia, OH　44663-7932　330-339-1959
　　　Fax: 330-339-2252
Milk, ice cream and butter
　President: Jerry Bichsel
　VP/General Manager: Chris Bichsel
Estimated Sales: $5-9.9 Million
Number Employees: 20-49
Type of Packaging: Private Label

5790　(HQ)Gossner Food
P.O.Box 3247
Logan, UT　84323-3247　　　435-752-9365
　　　Fax: 435-713-6200　800-944-0454
　　　cheese@gossner.com　www.gossner.com
Processor and exporter of cheese and aseptic-pack-
aged milk
　President/CEO: Dolores Wheeler
　Vice President: Greg Rowley
　Marketing Director: James Liddle
　UHT Plant Manager: Kelly Luthi
　Cheese Plant Manager: Dave Larsen
Estimated Sales: $20-50 Million
Number Employees: 250-499
Type of Packaging: Consumer, Food Service, Pri-
vate Label, Bulk
Brands:
　Fridge Free

5791　Gotliebs Guacamole
PO Box 1036
Sharon, CT　06069-1036　　　860-364-0842

Guacamole
　President: Richard Gotlieb
　VP Marketing: Leslie MacKenzie
　Production Manager: Laura Mars
Estimated Sales: $500,000-$1 Million
Number Employees: 5-9
Brands:
　Gotliebs

5792　Gould's Maple Sugarhouse
Mohawk Trl
Shelburne Falls, MA　01370　　　413-625-6170
　　　info@goulds-sugarhouse.com
　　　www.goulds-sugarhouse.com
Processor of pure maple syrup and also a selection
of pies
　Owner/President: Edgar Gould
　Owner/President: Helen Gould
Estimated Sales: $1-2.5 Million
Number Employees: 5-9

5793　Gouldsboro Enterprises
14 Factory Rd
Gouldsboro, ME　04607-4222　　207-963-4024
　　　Fax: 212-925-1913
Lobster
　Owner: Leonard Bishko
Estimated Sales: $300,000-500,000
Number Employees: 1-4

5794　Gourmantra Foods
95 Silver Rose Crescent
Markham, ON　L6C 1W6
Canada　　　416-225-6711
　　　Fax: 416-225-6711　info@gourmanta.com
　　　www.gourmantra.com
spices
　CEO: Rachna Prasad
　VP R&D: Rekha Prasad
　COO: Mona Prasad
Number Employees: 5

5795　Gourme' Mist
10880 Wiles Rd
Coral Springs, FL　33076　　　954-608-6858
　　　Fax: 954-252-2247　866-502-8472
　　　info@gourmemist.com　www.gourmemist.com
oil and vinegar misters

5796　Gourmedas Inc
2661 Boulevard du Versant Nord
Quebec, QC　G1V 1A3
Canada　　　418-210-3703
　　　Fax: 418-948-4083　info@gourmedas.com
　　　www.gourmedas.com
chocolate
　President/CEO: Christoph Klein
　Director of Operations: Giordano Perini

5797　Gourmet Baker
4190 Lougheed Highway
Suite 502
Burnaby, BC　V5C 6A8
Canada　　　604-298-2652
　　　Fax: 604-298-9656　800-663-1972
　　　bchomatt@multifoods.com
　　　www.gourmetbaker.com
Manufacturer and marketer of baked and unbaked
desserts and breakfast pastries to the in-store bakery
and foodservice channels
　VP/General Manager: John Gebbie
Number of Brands: 2
Parent Co: Robin Hood Multifoods
Type of Packaging: Consumer, Food Service, Pri-
vate Label
Brands:
　Fantasia
　Gourmet Baker

5798　Gourmet Central
47 Industrial Park
Romney, WV　26757-1101　　　304-822-6047
　　　Fax: 304-822-3148　800-984-3722
　　　gourmetcentral@usa.net　www.chefharv.com
Jams, jellies, sauces, dressings, toppings, salsa
　Owner/President: Harvey Christie
　Owner/President: Christy Christie
Estimated Sales: $5-9.9 Million
Number Employees: 20-49
Number of Products: 200+
Sq. footage: 20000
Type of Packaging: Consumer, Food Service, Pri-
vate Label, Bulk

5799 Gourmet Concepts International
2855 Rolling Pin Lane
Suwanee, GA 30024-7218   770-491-2100
Fax: 770-326-6157   800-241-4166
www.hartmutgourmet.com
Desserts

Estimated Sales: $50-100 Million
Number Employees: 100-249
Sq. footage: 66
Type of Packaging: Private Label

5800 Gourmet Confections
PO Box 2004
Northbrook, IL 60065-2004   847-498-1200
Fax: 847-498-3343 gourmet@mc.com
www.gourmetconfections.com
Processor of candy including regular and sugar-free
chocolate, caramels and taffy
Controller: Warren Long
General Manager: H Williams
Estimated Sales: $ 1 - 3 Million
Number Employees: 5-9
Type of Packaging: Food Service, Private Label,
Bulk
Brands:
Mrs Carrol's

5801 Gourmet Conveniences Ltd
457 Bantam Road
Litchfield, CT 06759   860-567-3529
Fax: 860-631-1012 866-793-3801
sales@sweetsunshine.com
www.sweetsunshine.com
sauces
President/Owner: Paul Sarris
Number Employees: 4

5802 Gourmet Croissant
320 36th St
Brooklyn, NY 11232-2504   718-499-4911
Fax: 718-499-6394
Processor of fresh and frozen baked goods including
croissants, danish, yogurt muffins and loaves
Co-Owner: Dino Alatsas
Co-Owner: Teddy Alatsas
Estimated Sales: Less than $500,000
Number Employees: 1-4
Sq. footage: 8000

5803 Gourmet Food Mall
2400 Veteren's Boulevard
Suite 484
Kenner, LA 70062   504-733-2400
Fax: 504-733-0939 800-903-7553
info@gourmetfoodmall.com
www.gourmetfoodmall.com
Search engine for gourmet and speciality foods in-
cluding pasta, olive oil and spices
Founder: Andrew Restivo
Estimated Sales: $ 1 - 3 Million
Number Employees: 10-19

5804 Gourmet Foods
3434 Mynatt Avenue
Knoxville, TN 37919-4524   865-970-2982
Fax: 615-970-7681
Processor of sauces including steak, burger, hot pep-
per, Cajun and seafood; also, seasonings for meat
and seafood
Manager: Taylor Dulaney
Estimated Sales: $1-2.5 Million
Number Employees: 5-9
Sq. footage: 10000
Parent Co: William B. Reily & Company
Type of Packaging: Consumer, Food Service, Pri-
vate Label
Brands:
Cajun Sunshine
Caribbean Clipper
Peppervine
Tiger
Tryme
Tryme Tiger
Wine & Pepper

5805 (HQ)Gourmet Foods
2910 E Harcourt St
Compton, CA 90221-5502   310-632-3300
Fax: 310-632-0303 sales@gourmetfoodsinc.com
www.gourmetfoodsinc.com
Processor of hors d'oeuvres and banquet items
President: Heinz Naef

Estimated Sales: $5-10 Million
Number Employees: 250-499

5806 Gourmet Foods Market
5107 Kingston Pike
Knoxville, TN 37919-5152   865-584-8739
Fax: 865-584-5661
www.shopgourmetsmarket.com
Gourmet
President: Eric Nelson
CEO: Eric Nelson
Estimated Sales: $1-2.5 Million
Number Employees: 20-49
Brands:
Gourmet Foods Market

5807 Gourmet Ice Cream
225 Ware Street
Palmer, MA 01069-1558   413-283-3740
Fax: 413-283-5188 gourmay@samnet.net
Processor of ice cream products including spumoni,
rolls, decorated cakes, pies and chocolates
President: Richard Patnaude
Estimated Sales: $470,000
Number Employees: 8
Sq. footage: 10000
Type of Packaging: Consumer, Food Service
Brands:
Gourmay

5808 Gourmet Organics
44 Greenwood Ln
Waynesville, NC 28786-7123   828-452-7700
Fax: 828-452-7832 serenahd@earthlink.net
www.serenas.com
Frozen bakery products
President: Serena Dossenko
Marketing Director: Barry Dossenko
Estimated Sales: $1-2.5 Million
Number Employees: 1-4
Type of Packaging: Private Label

5809 Gourmet Products
PO Box 387
Thomaston, CT 06787-0387   860-283-5147
Fax: 860-283-6912
Sauces, mustards, relishes, salsas
Owner: A Yurgelun
Marketing Director: W Yurgelun
VP Operations: David Yurgelun
Production Manager: T Del Gadio
Purchasing Manager: T Curnell
Number Employees: 10-19
Sq. footage: 12000
Type of Packaging: Consumer, Private Label, Bulk
Brands:
GOURMET PRODUCTS
NEW CLASSICS
NEW ENGLAND

5810 Gourmet Treats
1860 W 220th St # 445
Torrance, CA 90501-3679   310-212-6975
Fax: 310-212-0709 800-444-9549
inquiry@gourmettreats.com
www.gourmettreat.com
Processor of gourmet regular and fat-free cakes and
cookies
President: Shaffin Jinnah
Estimated Sales: Less than $500,000
Number Employees: 1-4
Sq. footage: 3000
Type of Packaging: Consumer, Private Label
Brands:
Gourmet Lite
Gourmet Treats

5811 Gourmet Village
539 Village Rd
Morin Heights, QC J0R 1H0   450-226-7377
Fax: 450-226-8329 800-668-2314
sales@gourmetduvillage.com
www.gourmetduvillage.com
gourmet dips, coffee, tea and cool drinks, desserts,
hot chocolate and festive drinks
President/Owner: Mike Tott
VP North American Sales: Drew Bunn
VP Product Development: Linda Tott

5812 Gourmet's Finest
P.O.Box 160
Avondale, PA 19311-0160   610-268-6910
Fax: 610-268-2298 info@gourmetsfinest.com
www.gourmetsfinest.com

Fresh and processed mushrooms, mushroom salads,
and marinades
Owner: Richard Pia
Type of Packaging: Food Service, Private Label

5813 Gourmet's Secret
5304 Roseville Rd # F
North Highlands, CA 95660-5049   916-334-6161
Fax: 916-334-6161 gourmetsec@aol.com
www.thegourmetsecret.com
Beer-based marinade and sauce packaged in German
beer bottles, herb and fruit-flavored vinegars and
flavor-infused grapeseed oil bottled in European
glass bottles
Partner: Rita Nelson
Estimated Sales: $100,000
Number Employees: 1-4
Brands:
Bachelor's Brew
Java Jelly

5814 Gourmets Fresh Pasta
950 N Fair Oaks Ave
Pasadena, CA 91103-3009   626-798-0841
Fax: 626-798-3591 mayagjian@aol.com
www.gourmetpasta.com
Processor of refrigerated, frozen and precooked
pasta - sold to restaurantsand markets throughout the
US
President/CEO: Michael Yagjian
Estimated Sales: $2.5-5 Million
Number Employees: 20-49
Sq. footage: 30000
Type of Packaging: Consumer, Food Service, Pri-
vate Label, Bulk
Brands:
California Cuisine
Gourmet Fresh

5815 Gouw Quality Onions
5801-54 Avenue
Taber, AB T1G 1X4
Canada   403-223-1440
Fax: 403-223-2036
onions@gouwqualityonions.com
www.gouwqualityonions.com
Grower, importer and packer of onions, radish and
red beets
Chairman: Casey Gouw, Sr.
Sales Manager/Controller: Casey Gouw Jr
Warehouse/Plant Operations: Ken Gouw
Farm Manager: Kyle Gouw
Type of Packaging: Consumer

5816 Govadinas Fitness Foods
2651 Ariane Drive
San Diego, CA 92117-3422   858-270-0691
Fax: 858-270-0696 800-900-0108
blissbar@earthlink.net www.govindabars.com
Manufacturer of health food bars and natural snacks
President: Larry Gatpandan
CEO: Larry Gatpandan
Accountant: Alberto Hael
VP: Zenaida Gatpandan
Marketing: Michael Pugliese
Sales: Lisa Gatpandan
Production: Jose Marquez
Purchasing: Nila Morrill
Estimated Sales: $3 Million
Number Employees: 20-49
Number of Products: 25
Sq. footage: 5000
Type of Packaging: Private Label
Brands:
BLISS BAR
HEMP BAR
PRALINE PACK
RAW POWER

5817 Govatos
800 N Market St
Wilmington, DE 19801-3011   302-652-5252
Fax: 302-652-3418 888-799-5252
GVTSCANDY@AOL.COM
www.govatoschocolates.com
High quality assortment of homemade chocolates
President: Richard Govatos Jr
Estimated Sales: $1-2.5 Million
Number Employees: 10-19
Type of Packaging: Consumer

5818 (HQ)Goya Foods
100 Seaview Dr
Secaucus, NJ 07094-1887   201-348-4900
Fax: 201-348-6609 info@goya.com
www.goya.com
Beans, rice, regional specialities, condiments, beverages, pantry, frozen foods and reduced sodium and organic.
President: Robert Unanue
VP Finance: Miguel Lugo
EVP: Peter Unanue
VP General Counsel: Carlo Ortiz
VP Logistics: Rebecca Rodriguez-Llerena
VP Sales/Marketing: Conrad Colon
Public Relations Director: Rafael Toro
Estimated Sales: $1.3 Billion
Number Employees: 3,000
Type of Packaging: Consumer, Food Service
Brands:
Goya Beans
Goya Beverages
Goya Caribbean Specialties
Goya Central American Specialties
Goya Condiments
Goya Foods
Goya Frozen
Goya Mexican
Goya Refrigerated
Goya Rices
Goya South American Specialties
Goya Tropical Fruit Blast Drink
Sazon

5819 Goya Foods of Florida
P.O.Box 226110
Miami, FL 33222-6110   305-592-3150
Fax: 305-592-4093 info@goya.com
www.goyafoods.com
Wholesaler/distributor of Hispanic and Latin foods including olive oil, olives, beans, rice, fish preserves, canned meats, frozen foods, etc.
President: Frankie Unanue
VP: R Chavez
CFO: Joe Unanue
Chairman: Joseph Unanue
Purchasing Director: Luis Olarte
Estimated Sales: $ 20 - 50 Million
Number Employees: 100-249
Parent Co: Goya Foods

5820 Goya de Puerto Rico
PO Box 601467
Bayamon, PR 00960-6067   787-740-4900
Fax: 787-740-5040
Manufacturer, distribution and office for Goya Foods
President: Frank Unanue
Parent Co: Goya Foods

5821 Goya of Great Lakes NewYYork
P.O.Box 152
Angola, NY 14006-0152   716-549-0076
Fax: 716-549-7259 www.goya.com
Packer and canner of dry besns including pink, pinto, black, small white and red, cannellini, kidney, butter, roman and Great Northern
President: Robert Drago
Marketing Director: Rubin Montalvo
CFO: John Saccammano
VP Sales/Purchasing: Greg Drago
Estimated Sales: $ 50 - 100 Million
Number Employees: 50-99
Number of Brands: 1
Number of Products: 18
Parent Co: Goya Foods
Type of Packaging: Consumer
Brands:
Goya

5822 Grabill Country Meats
P.O.Box 190
Grabill, IN 46741-0190   260-627-3691
Fax: 219-627-2106 866-333-6328
grabillmeats@aol.com www.grabillmeats.com
Processor of canned beef, pork, chicken, and turkey products containing no preservatives or additives and no water added
President: Patrick Fonner
Estimated Sales: $5-10 Million
Number Employees: 10-19
Type of Packaging: Consumer

5823 Grace Baking Company
3200 Regatta Blvd # G
Richmond, CA 94804-6401   510-231-7200
Fax: 510-231-7210 gracebaking@mapleleaf.ca
www.gracebaking.com
Manufacturer of baked goods including breads; desserts; morning pastries, and focaccia.
Founder/Co-Owner: Glenn Mitchell
Co-Owner: Cindy Mitchell
Public Relations and Marketing: Fred Doar
Plant Manager: Mike Cassie
Parent Co: Maple Leaf Foods Inc
Type of Packaging: Food Service

5824 Grace Foods International
39-36 32nd Street #1
Astoria, NY 11106   718-433-4789
Fax: 718-433-0384 www.gracefoods.com
beverages, canned meats and fish, chips, coconut products, jams and jellies, ready mixes, rice combos, sauces and condiments, spices and seasoning, teas and veggie meals.

5825 Grace Tea Company
808 W End Ave # 1109
New York, NY 10025-5313   212-678-2008
Fax: 212-255-2935 graceraretea@aol.com
www.gracetea.com
Exporter, importer, blender and packer of gourmet loose orthodox teas
President: Marguerita Sanders
VP: Richard Verdery
Operations Director: Richard Sanders
Estimated Sales: Under $500,000
Number Employees: 1-4
Number of Brands: 1
Number of Products: 20
Sq. footage: 2000
Brands:
CHINA YUNNAN SILVER TIP CHOICE
CONNOISSEUR MASTER BLEND
DARJCELING SUPERB 6000
DEMITASSE AFTER DINNER TEA
EARL GREY SUPERIOR MIXTURE
FLOWERY JASMINE-BEFORE THE RAIN
FORMOSA OOLONG CHAMPAGNE OF TEA
GUN POWDER PEARL PINHEAD GREEN TEA
LAPSANG SOUCHONG SMOKY #1 BLEND
MOUNTAIN-GROWN FANCY CEYLON
OWNER'S BLEND PREMIUM CONGOU
PURE ASSAM IRISH BREAKFAST
RUSSIAN CARAVAN ORIGINAL CHINA
WINEY KEEMUN ENGLISH BREAKFAST

5826 Graceland Fruit
1123 Main St
Frankfort, MI 49635-9341   231-352-7181
Fax: 231-352-4881 800-352-7181
gracelandinfo@gracelandfruit.com
www.gracelandfruit.com
Infused dried fruits, and vegetables,
Fridg-N-Fresh™vegetables, and
Soft-N-Frozen™fruit products
President/CEO: Donald W Nugent
CFO: Troy Terwilliger
CEO: Donald Negent
VP R&D: Nirmal Sinha
Procurement Manager: Ken Fitzhugh
Marketing/Public Relations: Suzi Mills
National Sales Manager: Derek Klein
VP Operations: Douglas Pumstead
Director Engineering: Bob Donnan
Manager/Grower/Processor Relations: Ben Evans
Estimated Sales: $40 Million
Number Employees: 100-249
Number of Brands: 1
Number of Products: 50
Type of Packaging: Food Service, Private Label, Bulk
Brands:
GRACELAND FRUIT

5827 Graceland Fruit Inc
1123 Main Street
Frankfort, MI 49635   231-352-7181
Fax: 231-352-4711 800-352-7181
cwalrad@wildveggiesus.com
www.wildveggieus.com

fruit and vegetable products
President: Donald Nugent
CFO: Troy Terwilliger
VP R&D: Nirmal Sinha
Sales/Marketing Manager: Suzi Mills
National Sales Manager: Derek Klein
COO: Steve Nugent
Estimated Sales: $63.8
Number Employees: 70

5828 Gracie's Gourmet Shop
P.O.Box 1552
Stowe, VT 05672-1552   802-253-8741
Fax: 802-253-6888 888-472-2437
gracies@stoweaccess.com www.gracies.com
Processor of salad dressings, marinades, sauces and spice and bread mixes
Owner: Paul Archdeacon
Manager: Paul Archdeacon
Estimated Sales: $1-2.5 Million
Number Employees: 1-4
Type of Packaging: Consumer

5829 Gracious Gourmet
PO Box 218
Bridgewater, CT 06752   860-350-1213
Fax: 860-350-1214
info@thegraciousgourmet.com
www.thegraciousgourmet.com
chutneys, glazes, pestos, spreads and tapenades

5830 Graf Creamery
P.O.Box 49
Zachow, WI 54182-0049   715-758-2137
Fax: 715-758-8020 Jimb@ezwebtech.com
Processor of butter and condensed and powdered buttermilk
President/CEO: James Bleick
Plant Manager: Dale Hodmiewicz
Purchasing Director: Jay Winter
Estimated Sales: $10-24.9 Million
Number Employees: 50-99
Sq. footage: 56000
Type of Packaging: Private Label, Bulk
Brands:
CLOVERDALE
GOLD MEDAL
GOLDEN GLOW

5831 Graffam Brothers Lobster Company
PO Box 340R
Rockport, ME 04856-0340   207-236-3396
Fax: 207-236-2569 800-535-5358
sales@lobsterstogo.com www.graffambros.com
Distributor of fresh Maine lobsters and clams, cooked lobster meat and frozen lobster tails.
President/Co-Owner: James Graffam

5832 Grafton Village Cheese Company
P.O.Box 87
Grafton, VT 05146-0087   802-843-2221
Fax: 802-843-2210 800-472-3866
cheese@sover.net
www.graftonvillagecheese.com
Processor of cheddar cheese
President: Stephan Morse
VP Marketing: Peter Mohn
Media Contact: Melissa Gullotti
Cheesemaker: Kevin Bush
Cheesemaker: Scott Fletcher
Plant Manager: Brian Joslyn
Estimated Sales: $1-2.5 Million
Number Employees: 20-49
Parent Co: Windham Foundation
Type of Packaging: Consumer, Food Service, Private Label, Bulk
Brands:
Classic Reserve
Classic Reserve Ext Sharp Cheddar
Grafton Gold
Grafton Gold-Ext Aged Cheddar

5833 Graham & Rollins
19 Rudd Ln
Hampton, VA 23669-4029   757-723-3831
Fax: 757-722-3762 800-272-2728
johnny@grahamandrollins.com
www.grahamandrollins.com
Processors of bluecrab (live and steamed), soft-shell crab and crabmeat, fresh, pasteurized and frozen cakes and bites
President: John Graham Sr
VP: Johnny Graham Jr

Estimated Sales:$1-2.5 Million
Number Employees: 100-249

5834 Graham Cheese Corporation
P.O.Box 391
Washington, IN 47501-0391   812-692-5237
    Fax: 812-692-5650   800-472-9178
    www.grahamcheese.com
Cheese blocks, longhorns, pieces and spreads; including colby, cheddar, pepper, calico cheeses and cheese gifts
    President: Robert Graham Iii III
    Plant Manager: Jerry Sims
Estimated Sales:$10-24.9 Million
Number Employees: 10-19
Type of Packaging: Consumer, Food Service, Private Label, Bulk

5835 Graham Fisheries
13890 Shell Belt Rd
Bayou La Batre, AL 36509-2304   251-824-2890
    Fax: 251-824-7370   shrimp1951@aol.com
Processor of seafood -shrimp
    Owner: Darrell Graham
Estimated Sales:$ .5 - 1 million
Number Employees: 1-4

5836 Grain Bin Bakers
P.O.Box 1296
Carmel, CA 93921-1296   831-624-3883
    Fax: 831-624-1459 www.allsaintscarmel.org
Religious Leader: Richard Matters
*Estimated Sales:*Under $500,000
Number Employees: 5-9

5837 (HQ)Grain Millers
9531 W 78th St # 400
Eden Prairie, MN 55344-8006   952-829-8821
    Fax: 952-829-8819   800-232-6287
    info@grainmillers.com   www.grainmillers.com
Manufacturer of specialty grain products and organic grain products such as oats, wheat, barley, rye and corn
    President: Steven Eilertson
    SVP: Rick Schwein
    Sales/Marketing Manager: Kris Nelson
Estimated Sales:$ 20 - 50 Million
Number Employees: 20-49
Type of Packaging: Food Service, Private Label, Bulk
Brands:
    GRAIN MILLERS

5838 Grain Millers Eugene
315 Madison St
Eugene, OR 97402-5034   541-687-8000
    Fax: 541-343-7820   800-443-8972
    info@grainmillers.com   www.grainmillers.com
Manufacturer of flour and other grain mill products
President, West Coast Operations: Christian Kongsore
    Logistics Manager: Lorna Yarbourgh
    QA Manager: Mark Kruk
    VP Product Development: Robert Serrano
    VP Sales/Marketing: Darren Schubert
    VP Operations: Keith Horton
    Mix Plant Manager: Dick Green
    Plant Manager: Tony Selby
    VP Purchasing: Perry Anderson
Estimated Sales:$20-50 Million
Number Employees: 50-99

5839 Grain Place Foods
1904 N Highway 14
Marquette, NE 68854-2516   402-854-3195
    Fax: 402-854-2566   davegpf@hamilton.net
    www.grainplacefoods.com
Processor of grains, cereals
    President: David Vetter
Estimated Sales:$1-2.5 Million
Number Employees: 10-19
Type of Packaging: Consumer, Private Label, Bulk
Brands:
    Grain Place

5840 Grain Process Enterprises Ltd.
115 Commander Boulevard
Scarborough, ON M1S 3M7
Canada   416-291-3226
    Fax: 416-291-2159   800-387-5292
    gbjr@grainprocess.com   www.grainprocess.com

Processor of stone ground hard and soft wheat flours, granola cereals, grain, bread and muffin mixes, cereal blends, etc.; exporter of granolas and flours
    President: George Birinyi Sr
Number Employees: 20-49
Sq. footage: 75000
Type of Packaging: Consumer, Private Label, Bulk
Brands:
    Brimley Stone
    Grain-Pro
    Happy Home
    Millbrook

5841 Grain Processing Corporation
P.O.Box 349
Muscatine, IA 52761-0072   563-264-4211
    Fax: 563-264-4289   800-448-4472
    sales@grainprocessing.com
    www.grainprocessing.com
Manufacturer and worldwide marketer of corn-based products.
    President: Doyle Tubandt
    CEO: Gage Kent
    VP: Brian Tompoles
    R&D: Frank Barresi
    Quality Control: Rani Thomas
    Marketing/Public Relations: Diane Rieke
    Sales: Chad Christensen
    Operations: Ron Zitzow
    Purchasing: Brian Hasser
Number Employees: 1-4
Brands:
    INCOSITY
    INSTANT PURE-COTE
    MALTRIN
    MALTRIN QD
    PURE-BIND
    PURE-COTE
    PURE-DENT
    PURE-GEL

5842 Grain-Free JK Gourmet
303 Joicey Blvd
Toronto, ON M5M 2V8
Canada   416-782-0045
    Fax: 416-785-0686   800-608-0465
    info@jkgourmet.com   www.jkgourmet.com
all-natural, preservative-free granola, biscotti, almond flour and muffin loaves.
    President/Owner: Jodi Bager
Number Employees: 3

5843 Grainaissance
1580 62nd St
Emeryville, CA 94608-2014   510-547-7256
    Fax: 510-547-0526   800-472-4697
    amazake@grainaissance.com
    www.grainaissance.com
Food processing, producing 2 brown rice products, Mochi-bake and serve rice popover, Amazake-healthy rice shake. Both refrigerated.
    President: Tony Plotkin
Estimated Sales:$1.4 Million
Number Employees: 11
Type of Packaging: Consumer
Brands:
    Amazake
    Grainaissance
    Mochi

5844 Grainbakers Bakery
401 E Joe Orr Road
Chicago Heights, IL 60411-1202   708-758-8900
    Fax: 708-758-9220   grainbakers@earthlink.net
Bakery
    President: Patrick Riha
    CEO: Tom Dunck
    Marketing Director: Patrick Riha
Estimated Sales:$10 Million appx.
Number Employees: 20-49
Type of Packaging: Private Label
Brands:
    Grainbakers Bagel Bread
    Grainbakers Bagels

5845 (HQ)Graminex
95 Midland Rd
Saginaw, MI 48638-5770   989-797-5502
    Fax: 989-799-0020   877-472-6469
    graminex@graminex.co   www.graminex.com

Exclusive, original grower, harvester, processor and manufacturer and distributor of flower pollen extract and fabales - Red Clover Extract - other extracts include lactose, gluten and talc free
    President: Cynthia May
Estimated Sales:$ 3 - 5 Million
Number Employees: 1-4

5846 Grand Avenue Chocolates
1021 Detroit Avenue
Concord, CA 94518
    Fax: 925-682-1900   877-934-1800
    info@grandavenuechocolates.com
    www.grandavenuechocolates.com
Manufactures chocolate covered grahams, french cream truffles, crisp chashew thin brittles, bite sized cookies and the original unbelievable apple covered with carmel, chocolate and nuts
    Owner: Rachel Dunn
Estimated Sales:$10-20 Million
Number Employees: 10-19
Type of Packaging: Private Label
Brands:
    Ebird's
    Grand Avenue

5847 Grand Rapids Brewing Company
3689 28th St SE
Grand Rapids, MI 49512-1605   616-285-5970
    Fax: 616-285-5923   grbc17@aol.com
    www.michiganmenu.com
Processor of beer, ale, stout and lager
    Manager: Terry Mundwiler
    Chef: Kim Chase
    Manager: Missy Kroll
    Manager: Dan Mast
    Brewer: John Svoboda
    General Manager: Terry Mundwiler
Estimated Sales:$2.5-5 Million
Number Employees: 100-249
Type of Packaging: Consumer

5848 (HQ)Grand River Poultry Farm
10 Woodslee Avenue
Paris, ON N3L 4A5
Canada   519-442-5453
    Fax: 519-442-2648   800-853-5454
    crichardson@grandriverpoultry.com
    www.grandriverpoultry.com
Processor of roasters for further processing; importer of deboned chicken breast; exporter of chicken patties, giblets and legs
    President: Guy Gillyatt
    Director Business Development: Jeff Lanteigne
    Quality Assurance: John Wendell
    Director Retail Sales: Mike Reed
    VP Sales/Marketing: Dean Cebulski
    Production: Rob Sutor
    Transportation: Dale McLaren
Number Employees: 100-249
Sq. footage: 24000
Type of Packaging: Bulk

5849 Grand Teton Brewing
430 Old Jackson Hwy
Victor, ID 83455-5500   208-787-9000
    Fax: 208-787-4114   888-899-1656
    beermail@GrandTetonBrewing.com
    www.grandtetonbrewing.com
Processor of pale, amber and wheat beer; also, ale, stout and porter, as well as soda.
    President/CEO: Charlie Otto
    VP: Ernie Otto
Estimated Sales:$ 5-10 Million
Number Employees: 10-19
Type of Packaging: Consumer, Food Service
Brands:
    Grand Teton Brewing
    Teton

5850 Grand View Winery
P.O.Box 91
East Calais, VT 05650-0091   802-456-7012
    info@grandviewwinery.com
    www.grandviewwinery.com
Wines: Rhubarb, Foch, Seyval, Riesling, Montmorency Cherry, Pear Wine, Blueberry Apple, Dandelion Wine, Raspberry Infusion, Blueberry Wine, Elderberry Wine, Mac Jack Hard Cider
    Winemaker/Owner: Phil Tonks
Estimated Sales:$ 3 - 5 Million
Number Employees: 5-9

5851 Grande Cheese Company
P.O.Box 67
Brownsville, WI 53006-0067   920-583-3122
Fax: 920-269-7124   800-678-3122
elio.camilotto@grande.com   www.grande.com
Manufactures Mozzarella and FIOR-di-LATTE
Fresh Mozzarella, and whey products
President: Wayne Matzke
VP Marketing/Sales: Elio Camilotto Jr
Estimated Sales:$20-50 Million
Number Employees: 5-9
Type of Packaging: Consumer, Food Service

5852 Grande Custom Ingredients Group
Dairy Rd
Brownsville, WI 53006   920-269-7200
Fax: 920-269-7124   800-772-3210
gcig@grande.com   www.grande.com
Processor and exporter of specialty whey products
and lactose
CEO: Wayne Matzke
CEO: Wayne Matzke
R&D: Michelle Ludtke
Marketing Director: Stephen Dott
Operations: Mike Nelson
Purchasing Director: Kevin Hampton
Estimated Sales:$25 Million
Number Employees: 5-9
Sq. footage: 10000
Parent Co: Grande Cheese Company
Type of Packaging: Bulk
Brands:
Grande Bravo Whey Protein
Grande Gusto Natural Flavor
Grande Ultra Nutritional Whey Prot.

5853 Grande River Vineyards
P.O.Box 129
Palisade, CO 81526-0129   970-464-5867
Fax: 970-464-5427   800-264-7696
info@www.granderiverwines.com
www.granderiverwines.com
Estate grown and bottled - consisting of Sauvgnon
Blanc, Meritage white, barrel select Chardonnay,
Merlot, Syrah and Desert Blend and many more se-
lections.
Founder/Owner/Winemaker: Stephen Smith
Vineyard Manager: Jim Mayrose
General Manager/Marketing: Naomi
Shepherd-Smith
Assistant Winemaker: David Roy
Tasting Room/Sales: Jeanne Finch
Tasting Room/Sales: Barb Mark
Estimated Sales:$5-10 Million
Number Employees: 10-19
Type of Packaging: Private Label
Brands:
Grande River Vineyards
Grande River Vineyards Everyday
Grande River Vineyards Meritage

5854 Grande Tortilla Factory
914 N Grande Ave
Tucson, AZ 85745-2404   520-622-8338
Processor of flour and corn tortillas; also, tamales
including green, corn and beef
President: Frank Pesqueira Jr
Estimated Sales:$200,000
Number Employees: 5-9
Type of Packaging: Consumer

5855 Grandma Beth's Cookies
1221 Toluca Avenue
Alliance, NE 69301-2447   308-762-8433
Fax: 308-762-6165   cookie@premaonline.com
Old fashioned homemade cookies
Owner: Beth Fetcher
Estimated Sales:$500,000-$1 Million
Number Employees: 1-4
Type of Packaging: Private Label

5856 Grandma Brown's BeansInc
P.O.Box 230
Mexico, NY 13114-0230   315-963-7221
Fax: 315-963-4072
grandmabrownsbeans@verizon.net
Manufacturer of baked beans, saucepan beans, bean
soup and split pea soup under the Grandma Brown's
brand.
President: Sandra Brown
Estimated Sales:$2.5-3 Million
Number of Products: 4
Sq. footage: 36000

Type of Packaging: Consumer, Food Service
Brands:
GRANDMA BROWN'S

5857 Grandma Hoerner's Foods
31862 Thompson Rd
Alma, KS 66401   785-765-2300
Fax: 785-765-2303   hoerner@kansas.net
www.grandmahoerners.com
organic reduced sugar preserves, pie fillings, fruit
butters, hamburger relish and red pepper jelly
President/Owner: Duane McCoy
VP: Regina McCoy
Estimated Sales:$7.9 Million
Number Employees: 40

5858 Grandma Pat's Products
PO Box 158
Albin, WY 82050-0158   307-631-0801
Fax: 307-673-5765   waypal@daltontel.net
Soup and chili-bean mixes, popcorn, and winter
wheat
Co-Owner: Pat Palm
Co-Owner: Chuck Palm

5859 Grandma's Recipe Ruglactch
409 W 15th Street
New York, NY 10011-7006   212-627-2775
Fax: 212-463-8670
Bread and bakery related products
President: Patricia Alessi
Estimated Sales:$920,000
Number Employees: 18
Type of Packaging: Private Label

5860 Grandpops Lollipops
2600 Burlington St # A
Kansas City, MO 64116-3019   816-421-5282
Fax: 816-421-5599   800-255-7873
Lollipops and candy
President: Josh Sitzer
*Estimated Sales:*Under $500,000
Number Employees: 5-9
Brands:
Grandpops Lollipops

5861 Granello Bakery
5045 W Mardon Ave
Las Vegas, NV 89139-5521   702-361-0311
Fax: 702-361-0415   orders@granellobakery.com
www.granellobakery.com
Specialty baked goods such as breads, pastry, cake,
tarts, cookies and bar cookies.
Owner: Laurie Steed
Estimated Sales:$ 20 - 50 Million
Number Employees: 100-249

5862 Granite Springs Winery
5050 Granite Springs Winery Rd
Somerset, CA 95684-9386   530-620-6395
Fax: 530-620-4884   800-638-6041
latcham@directcon.net   www.latcham.com
Wines consisting of: Zinfandels, Chardonnay, Sauvi-
gnon Blanc, Merlot, Syrahplus Port and many other
varieties.
President: Jon Latcham
Winemaker: Craig Boyd
Estimated Sales:$1-2.5 Million
Number Employees: 5-9

5863 Granite State Potato Chip Company
P.O.Box 45
Salem, NH 03079-0045   603-898-2171
Fax: 603-894-5158
Proccesor of snack foods including nuts, popcorn
and potato chips
President/CEO: William Croft
General Manager: Buddy Croft
Estimated Sales:$1-2.5 Million
Number Employees: 1-4
Type of Packaging: Consumer, Food Service
Brands:
Granite State Potato Chip

5864 Granny Annie Jams
Old School Street
South Londonderry, VT 05155   802-824-6625
Fax: 802-824-6625
Jams flavors include: strawberry rhubarb, strawberry
blueberry, raspberry, raspberry blueberry, orange
rhubarb and pear apple honey

5865 Granny Blossom Specialty Foods
Route 30
Wells, VT 05774   802-645-0507
Fax: 802-645-0860   gblossom@sover.net
www.grannyblossomsspecialtyfoods.com
Producers specialty foods such as: fruit salsas, tradi-
tional salas, relishes, Bloody Mary mix, apple cider
BBQ sauce, picked garlic, dilly beans and spices.
Manufactured in West Pawlet and shipped nation-
wide.
Owner: Bob Kopp
Owner: Doris Kopp

5866 Granny's Best Strawberry Products
PO Box 9
Victoria, ON L7C 3L6
Canada   519-426-0705
Fax: 519-428-0211
Processor of frozen strawberry puree
President: Gary Cooper
Type of Packaging: Private Label

5867 Granny's Kitchens
178 Industrial Park Drive
Frankfort, NY 13340-4798   315-735-5000
Fax: 315-735-3200
Frozen doughnuts
President: Alan Rosenblum
VP: Barry Thaler
Estimated Sales:$10-20 Million
Number Employees: 100-249

5868 Granowska's
175 Roncesvalles Avenue
Toronto, ON M6R 2L3
Canada   416-533-7755
Fax: 416-533-3261
Manufacturer of baked goods including specialty
mousse cakes, cheesecakes, poppy seed cakes, fruit
flans, butter cream cakes, whipped cream cakes,
cookies and doughnuts
Co-Owner: E Klodas
Number Employees: 10-19
Sq. footage: 3500
Brands:
Granowska's

5869 Grant & Janet Brians
743 Shore Rd
Hollister, CA 95023-9427   831-637-8497
bob@ihollister.com
www.heirloom-organic.com
Organic vegetables
President: Grant Brians
Estimated Sales:$ .5 - 1 million
Number Employees: 5-9

5870 Grant Park Packing
842 W Lake St
Chicago, IL 60607-1720   312-421-4096
Fax: 312-421-1484   vince@grantparkpacking.com
www.grantparkpacking.com
Processor of meat products - pork, beef, and poultry
Owner: Vincent Maffei
Estimated Sales:$10-20 Million
Number Employees: 20-49
Type of Packaging: Consumer

5871 Grant's Yakima Brewery
1803 Presson Place
Yakima, WA 98903-2200   509-575-1900
Fax: 509-457-6782   www.grantsale.com
Beer
President: Ted Basler
Number Employees: 10-19
Type of Packaging: Private Label
Brands:
Grant's

5872 Grantstone Supermarket
8 W Grant Rd
Tucson, AZ 85705-5529   520-628-7445
Fax: 520-628-1259
Specializes in Chinese, Japanese, Korean, Thai and
Vietnamese products wholesale and retail. Fresh
Chinese fruit and produce.
President: Janet Hom
Estimated Sales:$ 3 - 5 Million
Number Employees: 20-49

5873 Granville Gates & Sons
RR 1
Hubbards, NS B0J 1T0
Canada   902-228-2559
   Fax: 902-228-2368 ed.granville@nssympatico.ca
Processor and exporter of dried and salted seafood
   Office Manager: Norma Young
      Plant Manager: Ed Grant
*Estimated Sales:*5,000,000 - 9,999,999
Number Employees: 32
Type of Packaging: Bulk

5874 Grapevine Trading Company
738 Wilson St
Santa Rosa, CA 95401-6249   707-576-3950
   Fax: 707-576-3945 800-469-6478
           sanvan@grapevinetrading.com
           www.grapevinetrading.com
Manufacturer of mustards, fruit and balsamic vinegars, olive oils, tapenades, wild mushrooms, chile peppers, pine nuts, dried tomatoes, polenta mixes, vanilla extract.
   President: Sandra Van Voorhis
Estimated Sales:$10-20 Million
Number Employees: 10-19
Brands:
   California Harvest
   Gourmet Fare
   Grapevine Trading Co.
   Wine Gift Packaging

5875 Graseby Goring Kerr
642 Blackhawk Drive
Westmont, IL 60559-1116   416-438-9711
                            Fax: 416-438-2340

5876 Grassland Dairy Products
P.O.Box 160
Greenwood, WI 54437-0160   715-267-6182
      Fax: 715-267-6044 800-428-8837
   email@grassland.com www.grassland.com
Processor and exporter of anhydrous milk fat and butter including whipped, salted, unsalted and oil
   President/Owner: Dallas Wuethrich
   VP Procurement: Tayt Wuethrich
   Director Marketing: Trevor Wuethrich
   VP/Director Sales/Marketing: Jill Cornman
   Director Operations: Laverne Gregorich
Estimated Sales:$50-100 Million
Number Employees: 100-249
Sq. footage: 70000
Type of Packaging: Consumer, Food Service, Private Label, Bulk
Brands:
   Fall Creek
   Grassland

5877 Grasso Foods
2111 Kings Highway
Woolwich Township, NJ 08085-3216856-467-2222
                            Fax: 856-467-5474
Processor of frozen fruit and vegetables
   President: Joseph Grasso
   Plant Manager: Tony Verchio
Estimated Sales:$25-49.9 Million
Number Employees: 100-249
Type of Packaging: Consumer, Food Service, Private Label, Bulk

5878 Grating Pacific/Ross Technology Corporation
3651 Sausalito St
Los Alamitos, CA 90720-2436   562-598-4314
   Fax: 562-598-2740 800-321-4314
           sales@gratingpacific.com
           www.gratingpacific.com
   President: Ron Robertson
Estimated Sales:$ 20 - 30 Million
Number Employees: 50-99

5879 Graves Mountain Cannery
Route 670
Syria, VA 22743   540-923-4747
                            Fax: 540-923-4312
   cannery@gravesmountain.com
           www.gravesmountain.com
Processor of pepper and cucumber relish, fruit preserves, jellies, chutney, apple butter and apple sauce
   President: James Graves
   VP: James Graves
   Plant Manager: Gail Ford
Estimated Sales:$300,000- $500,000
Number Employees: 8
Number of Brands: 1

Sq. footage: 10000
Parent Co: Graves Mountain Lodge
Type of Packaging: Consumer, Private Label
Brands:
   Colonial Williamsburg
   Graves Mountain

5880 (HQ)Gravymaster, Inc
16 Business Park Dr
Branford, CT 06405-2964   203-481-2276
         Fax: 203-488-8085 info@gravy.com
                            www.gravy.com
Processor of sauces including seasoning and browning
   President: Stephen Besse
   Consultant: John Mills Jr.
Estimated Sales:$10-20 Million
Number Employees: 20-49
Parent Co: Founders Equity
Type of Packaging: Consumer, Food Service
Brands:
   Gravy Master
   Gravymaster

5881 (HQ)Gray & Company
P.O.Box 218
Forest Grove, OR 97116-0218   503-357-3141
      Fax: 503-359-0719 800-551-6009
   fruitsales@cherryman.com www.cherryman.com
Processor and exporter of maraschino cherries, glazed fruit and chocate cherry cordials
   President: James G Reynolds
   Chief Executive Officer: Jim Reynolds Sr.
   Vice President Sales/Marketing: Josh Reynolds
*Estimated Sales:*H
Number Employees: 500-999
Brands:
   QUEEN ANNE CORDIAL CHERRIES
   QUEEN ANNE JUBILEES

5882 Gray & Company
P.O.Box 218
Forest Grove, OR 97116-0218   503-357-3141
   Fax: 503-359-0719 sales@cherryman.com
Processor and exporter of maraschino cherries, glace fruit and chocolate cherry cordials
   Chairman: James Reynolds
   CFO: Jeffrey Grimm
   Marketing Director: Josh Reynolds
   Senior VP Sales: Bob Vugar
   Operations Manager: Judd Marlatt
   Director Manufacturing: J Marlatt
   Plant Manager: P Lieber
*Estimated Sales:*H
Number Employees: 500-999
Type of Packaging: Consumer, Food Service, Private Label, Bulk
Brands:
   Cherryman
   Pennant
   Queen Anne
   Towie
   White Swan

5883 Gray Brewing Company
2424 W Court St
Janesville, WI 53548-3307   608-754-5150
      Fax: 608-752-0821 www.graybrewing.com
Processor of beer, ale, stout and porter
   Co-Owner: Fred Gray
   Brewmaster: Greg Hammond
Estimated Sales:$5-10 Million
Number Employees: 5-9
Type of Packaging: Consumer, Food Service

5884 Grays Ice Cream
16 East Rd
Tiverton, RI 02878-3599   401-624-4500
   Fax: 401-624-4500 graysicecream@excite.com
           www.graysicecream.com
Homemade ice cream, frozen desserts
   President: Marilyn Dennis
Estimated Sales:$10-20 Million
Number Employees: 20-49

5885 Graysmarsh Farm
6187 Woodcock Rd
Sequim, WA 98382-8144   360-683-5563
      Fax: 360-683-6509 800-683-4367
   grysmrsh@olypen.com www.graysmarsh.com

Processor of barley, jams, jellies, marmalades and processed raspberries. U-pick rasberries, strawberries, loganberries, blueberries and have fields of lavender.
   General Manager: Arturo Flores
   Production: Susan Trapp
Estimated Sales:$ 20 - 50 Million
Number Employees: 20-49
Type of Packaging: Consumer, Food Service, Bulk

5886 Great American Appetizers
216 8th St N
Nampa, ID 83687-3029   208-465-5111
         Fax: 208-465-5059 800-282-4834
   marco@appetizer.com www.appetizer.com
Processor and exporter of frozen, battered and breaded appetizers including vegetables, onion rings and cheese sticks; and other specialty appetizers; New Betty Crocker frozen homestyle mashed potatoes, mashed sweet potatoes andgourmet twice baked potatoes.
   President: Ellen Meyer
   CFO: Marco Meyer
   Vice President: Frank Benso
   Research & Development: Juan Larios
   Quality Control: Juan Larios
   Marketing Director: Debbie Lindley
   Sales Director: John Wills
   Operations Manager: Steve Cordova
   Plant Manager: Luis Garcia
   Purchasing Manager: Tammy Mika
Estimated Sales:$25-50 Million
Number Employees: 100-249
Number of Products: 100
Parent Co: Westin Foods
Type of Packaging: Consumer, Food Service, Private Label, Bulk
Brands:
   Big Red
   Brew House
   Questias
   Wahoo! Appetizers

5887 Great American BarbecueCompany
1078 Highway 90
Weimar, TX 78962-4402   510-865-3133
           catering@greatbbq.com
           www.greatbbq.com
Frozen and refrigerated beef prepared, chicken prepared
   Owner: Dave Mann
   Owner: Dan Ferreira
   VP Sales: Troy Gall
Brands:
   Great American Barbecue

5888 (HQ)Great American Dessert
P.O.Box 780208
Flushing, NY 11378-0208   718-894-3494
   Fax: 718-894-6105 www.juniorscheesecake.com
Processor of gourmet desserts including cakes, pies, tortes, rugulach and brownies, also cookies, petit fours, dried fruit, babkas, hammentaschen and puff pasteries.
   Owner: Michael Goodwin
   Public Relations: Theresa Kramer
   Purchasing: Grace Pavlak
Estimated Sales:$1-5 Million
Number Employees: 20-49
Type of Packaging: Private Label
Brands:
   Granny Cheesecakes
   Rode Lee

5889 Great American Foods Commissary
7566 Us Highway 259 N
Ore City, TX 75683-5639   903-968-8630
   Fax: 903-968-4376 www.davidbeards.com
Process foods including, catfish, tomato relish, hot sauce and hushpuppies
   President: David Beard
   Purchasing: Terry Simpler
Estimated Sales:$20-50 Million
Number Employees: 20-49
Brands:
   David Beards
   David Beards Texas Style

5890 Great American Popcorn Works of Pennsylvania
336 W Broad St
Telford, PA 18969-1931   215-721-0414
          Fax: 215-721-6082 800-542-2676
          info@popcornworks.com
          www.popcornworks.com
Gift tins filled with gourmet popcorn, bags of all natural and flavored popcorns, jars of kernels, and toppings
   Manager: Alice Barnes
   Vice President: Jack Egner
   Sales Director: Rob Rosen
   Public Relations: Giselle Wetzel
Estimated Sales: Less than $500,000
Number Employees: 1-4
Number of Products: 65
Sq. footage: 6000
Type of Packaging: Consumer, Food Service, Private Label, Bulk

5891 Great American Seafood Company
808 E 00n Rd
Dewey, IL 61840-9502   217-352-0986
          Fax: 217-352-0987
          contact@greatamericanseafood.com
          www.greatamericanseafood.com
Great American Seafood is a premier provider of quality seafood to America.
Estimated Sales: $300,000-500,000
Number Employees: 5-9

5892 Great American Smokehouse & Seafood Company
15657 Highway 101 S
Brookings, OR 97415-9556   541-469-6903
          Fax: 541-469-9692 800-828-3474
          nancy@smokehouse-salmon.com
          www.smokesalmon.com
Seafood
   Owner: Lee D Myers Sr
   Co-Owner: Nancy Myers
   Co-Owner: Lee Myers Jr
Estimated Sales: $500,000-$1 Million
Number Employees: 10-19

5893 Great Atlantic Trading Company
563 Seaside Rd SW
Ocean Isle Beach, NC 28469-6102 910-575-7979
          Fax: 910-575-7978 888-268-8780
          info@caviarstar.com www.caviarstar.com
Fresh and frozen seafood, American and imported caviar
   President: Dana Leavitt
Estimated Sales: $3.2 Million
Number Employees: 1-4
Sq. footage: 5000

5894 Great Cakes
8956 Ellis Avenue
Los Angeles, CA 90034-3302   310-287-0228
          Fax: 310-202-8305
Cakes, breads, rolls
   President: Pamela Freedman
Estimated Sales: $5-10 Million appx.
Number Employees: 10-19

5895 Great Circles
P.O.Box 495
Bellows Falls, VT 05101-0495   802-463-2111
          Fax: 802-463-2110 877-877-2120
          gcircles@sover.net http://www.sover.net
Health foods
   President: Dwane Kurisu
   CEO: Rich Kendall
Estimated Sales: $2.5-5 Million
Number Employees: 1-4

5896 Great Divide Brewing Company
2201 Arapahoe St
Denver, CO 80205-2512   303-296-9460
          Fax: 303-296-9464 info@greatdivide.com
          www.greatdivide.com
Processor of beer and ale. Offer a wide spectrum of ales, HotShot ESB and Ridgeline Amber, Denver Pale Ale, Hercules Double IPA, Old Ruffian Barley Wine. We introduced Titan IPA, Hercules Double IPA and Yeti Imperial Stout and twonewones, Old Ruffian Barley Wine and Oak Aged Yeti Imperial Stout.
   President/Brewmaster: Brian Dunn
   Vice President: Tara Dunn
   Vice President Operations: Mason Thomas
Estimated Sales: $5-10 Million
Number Employees: 10-19
Brands:
   Arapahoe
   Bee Sting
   Denver
   Hibernation
   Saint Brigid's
   WIT
   Whitewater
   Wild Raspberry

5897 Great Eastern Sun
92 McIntosh Rd
Asheville, NC 28806-1406   828-665-7790
          Fax: 828-667-8051 800-334-5809
          weborders@great-eastern-sun.com
          www.great-eastern-sun.com
Manufacturer and importer Asian organic and natural foods including miso, green and black teas, dressings, sweeteners, noodles, sea vegetables, etc
   Owner: Berry Evans
   Finance: Brett Martin
   Sales Manager: Mary Griffin
   VP Operations/Purchaser: Jan Paige
   Assistant Production Manager: Wendy Young
   Warehouse/Shipping: Joe Putnam
Estimated Sales: $ 5 - 10 Million
Number Employees: 20-49
Brands:
   Emerald Cove Sea Vegetables
   Emperor's Kitchen
   Haiku Teas
   Miso Master Miso
   One World Teas
   Organic Planet Asian Pastas

5898 Great Expectations Confectionery Gourmet Foods
1911 W Warren Boulevard
Chicago, IL 60612-2412   773-525-4865
          Fax: 773-281-5506
Candy and confections
   President: John Prescott
Estimated Sales: Under $100,000
Number Employees: 2
Type of Packaging: Consumer, Private Label
Brands:
   Great Expectations

5899 Great Garlic Foods
709 5th Ave
Bradley Beach, NJ 07720-1004   732-775-3311
          Fax: 732-774-9386
Garlic spreads, pesto sauces, chopped garlic in oil, chopped garlic in water
   Owner: Joe De Santis
Estimated Sales: $ 1 - 3 Million
Number Employees: 5-9
Type of Packaging: Consumer, Food Service, Private Label, Bulk

5900 Great Glacier Salmon
PO Box 1137
Prince Rupert, BC V8J 4H6
Canada   250-627-4955
          Fax: 250-627-7945 bob@stikine.bc.ca
          www.wildsalmon.ca
Small specialty fisherman owned salmon processor
   Accounting: Mary Allen
   General Manager: Robert Gould
Estimated Sales: $250,000 To 1,000,000
Number Employees: 20-49
Number of Brands: 2
Sq. footage: 3200
Type of Packaging: Private Label, Bulk
Brands:
   GLACIER CAVIAR
   GLACIER SALMON

5901 Great Grains Milling Company
P.O.Box 427
Scobey, MT 59263-0427   406-783-5588
          organic@greatgrainsmilling.com
          www.greatgrainsmilling.com
Processor of stone ground and whole organic hard red spring wheat flour and bran, cracked wheat cereal, pancake and waffle mix.
   President: Alvin Rustebakke
Estimated Sales: $500,000-$1 Million
Number Employees: 1-4
Sq. footage: 800
Type of Packaging: Consumer, Food Service, Private Label

5902 Great Hill Dairy
160 Delano Rd
Marion, MA 02738-2029   508-748-2208
          Fax: 508-748-2282 888-748-2208
          info@greathillblue.com www.greathillblue.com
Manufacturer of gourmet quality raw milk non-homogenized aged Blue cheese in 6 lbs wheels and 1.5 lb wedges wrapped in foil
   President: Tim Stone
   President: Nancy Weaver
Estimated Sales: $500,000-$1 Million
Number Employees: 1-4
Brands:
   Great Hill Blue

5903 Great Lakes Brewing
30 Queen Elizabeth Boulevard
Etobicoke, ON M8Z 1L8
Canada   416-255-4510
          Fax: 416-255-4907 800-463-5435
          info@greatlakesbeer.com
          www.greatlakesbeer.com
Premium Canadian malt and choice German hops are used in brewing of Golden Horseshoe Premium lager which contains no additives or preservatives.
   Vice President: Peter Bulut Jr
Number Employees: 20-49
Type of Packaging: Consumer, Food Service

5904 Great Lakes Brewing Company
2516 Market Ave
Cleveland, OH 44113-3434   216-771-4404
          Fax: 216-771-4466 info@greatlakesbrewing.com
          www.greatlakesbrewing.com
Processor of beer, ale, stout, lager and porter
   Manager: Jeff West
   Co-Owner: Daniel Conway
Estimated Sales: $50-100 Million
Number Employees: 100-249
Type of Packaging: Consumer, Food Service
Brands:
   Burning River
   Edmond Fitzgerald

5905 (HQ)Great Lakes Cheese Company
17825 Great Lakes Parkway
PO Box 1806
Hiram, OH 44234-1806   440-834-2500
          Fax: 440-834-1002
          glcinfo@greatlakescheese.com
Manufacturer and supplier of high quality cheese products
   President/CEO: Gary Vanic
   CFO: Russell Mullins
   VP Sales/Marketing: Bill Andrews
Estimated Sales: $2.2 Billion
Number Employees: 1,700
Type of Packaging: Private Label

5906 Great Lakes Cheese of NY
23 Phelps St
Adams, NY 13605-1096   315-232-4511
          Fax: 315-232-4055
          glcinfo@greatlakescheese.com
          www.greatlakescheese.com
Processor of cheddar cheese
   Plant Manager: John Jennings
   Plant Superintendent: Bob Mann
Estimated Sales: $50-100 Million
Number Employees: 50-99
Parent Co: Great Lakes Cheese Company
Type of Packaging: Consumer, Private Label

5907 Great Lakes Foods
101 Brockley Drive
Hamilton, ON L8E 3C4
Canada 905-560-4223
Fax: 905-560-5540 glfoods@interlynx.net
Processor of canned mushrooms, fruit and vegetable
canning, pickling and drying
President: Tom Ireland
Vice President: Johanne Ubbels
Manager: Richard Ubbels
Number Employees: 10-19
Parent Co: Ubbelea Farms
Type of Packaging: Consumer, Food Service, Private Label
Brands:
Chateau
Riviera

5908 Great Lakes Kraut Company
P.O.Box 217
Bear Creek, WI 54922-0217 715-752-4105
Fax: 715-752-3432
Manufacturer and exporter of canned, bagged and
glass packed sauerkraut and pickled asparagus; also,
bulk cabbage
Owner: Ryan Downs
VP of Sales: Ryan Downs
Estimated Sales:$2.5-5 Million
Number Employees: 20-49
Type of Packaging: Consumer, Food Service, Private Label, Bulk
Brands:
Flanagan
Pixie Pak
Symco

5909 (HQ)Great Lakes Kraut Company
P.O.Box 450
Shortsville, NY 14548-0450 585-289-4414
Fax: 585-289-4280 www.greatlakeskraut.com
Sauerkraut, cabbage products
President: David Flanagan
Controller: Shane Sieracki
Facility Manager: Thomas Holtby
Plant Manager: Mark Mette
Estimated Sales:$10-20 Million
Number Employees: 100-249
Type of Packaging: Bulk

5910 Great Lakes Packing Company
6556 Quarterline Rd
Kewadin, MI 49648-8907 231-264-5561
Fax: 231-264-5594
Processor of frozen cherries
President: Jon Veliquette
Estimated Sales:$50-100 Million
Number Employees: 250-499
Type of Packaging: Consumer, Private Label
Brands:
Great Lakes

5911 Great Lakes Products
2540 Ridge Road
Highland Park, IL 60035-1606 847-406-3076
Fax: 847-406-3077
President: Joe Schuetz

5912 Great Lakes Tea & SpiceCompany
6610 Western Ave-M109
PO Box 661
Glen Arbor, MI 49636 231-645-8327
Fax: 231-326-2333 877-645-9363
contact@glteaandspice.com
www.glteaandspice.com
loose teas, flowering teas and spices
President/Owner: Chris Sack

5913 Great Northern Baking Company
443 Hoover St NE
Minneapolis, MN 55413-2926 612-331-1043
Fax: 612-331-1052
Daniel@GreatNorthernBaking.com
www.greatnorthernbaking.com
Muffins, cakes, cookie bars and pretzels
President: Fred Johnson
Estimated Sales:$ 5-9.9 Million
Number Employees: 50-99
Brands:
Mrs Feldman's Desserts

5914 Great Northern Brewing Company
2 Central Ave
Whitefish, MT 59937-2547 406-863-1000
Fax: 406-863-1001 joe@greatnorthernbrewing.com
www.greatnorthernbrewing.com
Processor of beer and lager
Owner: Dennis Konopatzke
Accounts Management/Retail Sales: Pam Barberis

Tasting Room/Customer Service: Jessica
Stanhope
Production Manager: Dan Rasmussen
Estimated Sales:$2.5-5 Million
Number Employees: 1-4
Parent Co: McKenzie River Partners
Type of Packaging: Consumer, Food Service
Brands:
Black
Premium
Whitefish
Wild Huckleberry

5915 Great Northern Maple Products
331 Rue Principale
Saint Honor, De Shenley, QC G0M 1V0
Canada 418-485-7777
Fax: 418-485-6185
gary@greatnorthernmaple.com
www.greatnorthernmaple.com
Supply organic made maple and fruit syrups to distributors, supermarkets, importers and manufacturers
Director General: Gary Coppola
International Marketing Manager: Luc Tardiff

5916 Great Northern Products
P.O.Box 7622
Warwick, RI 02887-7622 401-490-4590
Fax: 401-633-6051 info@northernproducts.com
www.northernproducts.com
Processor of Natural Scallops, Cold Water Shrimp,
Farmed Atlantic Salmon, Snow Crab Products
President: George Nolan
Vice President: Tom Lucia
Export Manager: David Sussman
Estimated Sales:$85 Million
Number Employees: 10-19
Number of Brands: 4
Number of Products: 40
Brands:
Commonwealth
Fruits De Mer
Langlois
Sabana
Sealicious
Simmonds

5917 Great Pacific Seafoods
4201 Old Intl Airport Rd
Anchorage, AK 99502-1205 907-248-7966
Fax: 907-248-8190
Processor of fresh and frozen salmon
Manager: Roger Stiles
Estimated Sales:$10-20 Million
Number Employees: 50-99
Type of Packaging: Consumer, Food Service
Brands:
Great Pacific

5918 Great Plains Seafood
6360 Carter Street
Shawnee, KS 66203-3600 913-262-6060
Fax: 913-393-0238
Quality seafood products.
President: Doug Hensley
Estimated Sales:$ 20 - 50 Million
Number Employees: 20-49

5919 (HQ)Great Recipes Company
P.O.Box 647
Beaverton, OR 97075-0647 503-590-1108
Fax: 800-585-2331 800-273-2331
contactus@great-recipes.com
www.great-recipes.com
Processor of bread, cookie, cake, brownie and muffin mixes; custom mixes available such as beer
bread
President: Mark Bonebrake
Estimated Sales:$1-2.5 Million
Number Employees: 1-4
Type of Packaging: Private Label
Brands:
FIRENZA
Great Recipes

5920 (HQ)Great River Milling
P.O.Box 185
Fountain City, WI 54629-0185 608-687-9580
Fax: 608-687-3014
rhaverson@greatrivermilling.com
www.greatrivermilling.com
Supplier of certified organic grains, flour and mixes
Owner: Rick Halverson
Customer Service: Nadine Bayer
Estimated Sales:$300,000-500,000
Number Employees: 1-4
Type of Packaging: Bulk

5921 Great San Saba River Pecan Company
P.O.Box 906
San Saba, TX 76877-0906 325-372-6078
Fax: 325-372-5852 800-621-9121
info@greatpecans.com www.greatpecans.com
Processor of pecan preserves, pies, cakes, breads,
candies, spreads, toppings and pecan praline popcorn
Co-Owner/President: Larry Newkirk
Co-Owner/Vice President: Martha Newkirk
Estimated Sales:$ 5 - 10 Million
Number Employees: 1-4
Type of Packaging: Consumer
Brands:
Great San Saba River Pecan

5922 Great Spice Company
295 Distribution St
San Marcos, CA 92078-4359 760-759-2290
Fax: 760-744-0401 800-730-3575
jslatic@greatspice.com www.greatspice.com
Processor and exporter of dehydrated and fresh
herbs such as: Dill, Basil, Italian Parsley, Greek
Oregano, Marjoram and many other culinary herbs.
President: Jay Fishman
Inventory Manager: Steve Addison
Quality Manager: Ja Attaphongse
VP Sales: Jim Slatic
Founder/VP Operations: Jerry Tenenberg
Operations Manager: Dan Sullivan
Shipping Manager: Michael Tenenberg
Global Purchasing Coordinator: Rommina
Chavarria
Estimated Sales:$ 3 - 5 Million
Number Employees: 20-49
Type of Packaging: Food Service, Private Label,
Bulk

5923 Great Spring Waters
5215 Central Avenue
Richmond, CA 94804-5805 510-526-1810
Fax: 510-526-1645 800-950-9393
Spring waters
Specialty Food Manager: Tom Wright
*Estimated Sales:*Under $500,000
Number Employees: 50-99

5924 Great Valley Mills
1774 County Line Rd # A
Barto, PA 19504-8720 610-754-7800
Fax: 610-754-6490 800-688-6455
gvm1710@pdt.net www.greatvalleymills.com
Stone ground flour, pancake, muffin, bread and specialty dry food mixes.
Owner: Steve Kantoor
Estimated Sales:$690,000
Number Employees: 5-9
Sq. footage: 15000
Type of Packaging: Consumer, Food Service, Private Label
Brands:
1710
Covered Bridge Mills
Flip It
Great Valley Mills
Great Valley Mixes

5925 Great West of Hawaii
P.O.Box 3228
Honolulu, HI 96801-3228 808-593-9981
Fax: 808-593-2805
Wholesaler/distributor of frozen food, general line
products, provisions/meats and seafood; serving the
food service market
President: Robert Henrie
Estimated Sales:$10-20 Million
Number Employees: 5-9

5926 Great Western Brewing Company
519 Second Avenue N
Saskatoon, SK S7K 2C6
Canada   306-653-4653
        Fax: 306-653-2166   800-764-4492
        info@greatwesternbrewing.com
        www.greatwesternbrewing.com
A malt beverage company with an overriding commitment to quality. Processor of beer, lager and stout.
        President/CEO: Ron Waldman
        Brewmaster: Garry Johnston
Number Employees: 20-49
Type of Packaging: Consumer, Food Service

5927 (HQ)Great Western Juice Company
16153 Libby Rd
Cleveland, OH 44137-1298   216-475-5770
        Fax: 216-475-5772   800-321-9180
        suegwjuice@sbcglobal.net
        www.greatwesternjuice.com
Manufacturer and exporter of fruit juices, beverages syrups and cocktail mixes
        President: Bill Overton
        VP: William Overton
Estimated Sales: $2.5-5 Million
Number Employees: 20-49
Sq. footage: 50000
Type of Packaging: Food Service, Private Label

5928 Great Western Malting Company
P.O.Box 1529
Vancouver, WA 98668-1529   360-693-3661
        Fax: 360-696-8354   877-770-7055
        mblackmore@conagramalt.com
Processor and exporter of processed malt including brewers', distillers' and wheat
        Finance Executive: Steve Rosvold
        Contact: Marla Blackmore
Estimated Sales: $50-100 Million
Number Employees: 50-99
Parent Co: ConAgra Foods
Type of Packaging: Bulk

5929 Great Western Products Company
P.O.Box 6
Bismarck, MO 63624-0006   573-734-2210
        Fax: 573-734-6454
Processor and exporter of popcorn, popping corn oil, cotton candy, sno-cone syrup, candy apple coatings, funnel cakes, waffle cones, corn dog mix, etc.; manufacturer of concession equipment including corn poppers
        Manager: Marvin Scott
Estimated Sales: $500,000-$1 Million
Number Employees: 5-9
Type of Packaging: Consumer, Food Service, Private Label, Bulk

5930 Great Western Products Company
545 N Bowen Avenue
Bremen, IN 46506-2005   217-546-4010
        Fax: 217-546-2352 www.gwproducts.com
Processor and exporter of popcorn, popping corn oil, cotton candy, sno-cone syrup, candy apple coatings, funnel cakes, waffle cones, corn dog mix, etc.; manufacturer of concession supplies and equipment
Estimated Sales: $1-2.5 Million
Number Employees: 5-9
Type of Packaging: Consumer, Food Service, Private Label, Bulk

5931 Great Western Products Company
2047 E 1350 North Road
Assumption, IL 62510-8530   217-226-3241
        Fax: 217-226-3569
Processor and exporter of popcorn, popping corn oil, cotton candy, sno-cone syrup, candy apple coatings, funnel cakes, waffle cones, corn dog mix, etc.; manufacturer of concession supplies and equipment
Estimated Sales: $10-20 Million
Number Employees: 20-49
Type of Packaging: Consumer, Food Service, Private Label, Bulk

5932 Great Western Tortilla
P.O.Box 16346
Denver, CO 80216-0346   303-298-0705
        Fax: 303-298-0216 info@tortilla-chips.com
        www.tortilla-chips.com
Tortilla chips, nuts, salsa, hot sauces and snack mix
        Director Sales/Marketing: John Amerman

Estimated Sales: $10-20 Million
Number Employees: 50-99

5933 Greater Galilee Gourmet
2110 Wilshire Boulevard
Suite 829
Santa Monica, CA 90403-5704   310-459-9120
        Fax: 310-459-1276   800-290-1391
Gourmet foods - Israili seasonings
        President: Ehud Yonay

5934 (HQ)Greater Omaha Packing Company
P.O.Box 7566
Omaha, NE 68107-0566   402-731-1700
        Fax: 402-731-8020 info@greateromaha.com
        www.greateromaha.com
Processor and exporter of boxed beef
        President/CEO: Henry Davis
        Executive Vice President: Angelo Fili
        Vice President Technical Resources: Kathleen Krantz
        Vice President Sales/Marketing: Roy Wiggs
        Cattle Procurement Manager: Joe Goergen
Estimated Sales: $100+ Million
Number Employees: 500-999
Sq. footage: 200000
Type of Packaging: Consumer, Food Service, Private Label, Bulk

5935 Greaves Jams & Marmalades
PO Box 26
Niagara-on-the-Lake, ON L0S 1J0
Canada   905-468-3608
        Fax: 905-468-0071   800-515-9939
        greaves@greavesjams.com
        www.greavesjams.com
Processor of all natural jams, jellies, marmalades and condiments; exporter of portion controlled jams, marmalades and honey - 100% pure, no preservatives, no additives, no pectin -
        Production Manager: Rudy Doerwald
Number Employees: 10-19
Number of Products: 1
Sq. footage: 10000
Type of Packaging: Consumer, Private Label
Brands:
        Greaves

5936 Grebe's Bakery & Delicatessen
5132 W Lincoln Ave
Milwaukee, WI 53219-1684   414-543-7000
        Fax: 414-543-8863   800-356-9377
Manufacturer of bread, rolls, doughnuts and cakes.
        Manager: Joan Janczak
Estimated Sales: $10-20 Million
Number Employees: 100-249
Sq. footage: 31000
Type of Packaging: Consumer, Bulk
Brands:
        GREBE'S

5937 Grecian Delight Foods
1201 Tonne Rd
Elk Grove Vlg, IL 60007-4925   847-364-1010
        Fax: 847-364-1077   800-621-4387
        www.greciandelight.com
Processor of ethnic frozen baked goods, meat products, pita bread, gyros, Greek entrees and desserts
        President/CEO: Peter Parthenis
        Research/Development Manager: John Matchuk
Estimated Sales: $50-100 Million
Number Employees: 250-499
Sq. footage: 200000
Type of Packaging: Consumer, Food Service, Private Label
Brands:
        Athenian
        Chicago Style
        Pita Folds

5938 Greek Gourmet Limited
38 Miller Avenue PMB 510
Mill Valley, CA 94941   415-480-8050
        Fax: 617-833-6056 info@greekgourmet.com
        www.greekgourmet.com
Importer of chocolate, rolled wafers, olives, olive oil, salad dressings, preserves, peppers, spreads, teas, spices, coffee
        President: George Nassopoulos
        Vice President: Diane Nassopoulos
        Sales Director: James Contis
        Production Manager: P Margaritidis

Estimated Sales: $2.5-5 Million
Number Employees: 5-9
Number of Brands: 4
Number of Products: 35
Sq. footage: 10000
Type of Packaging: Consumer, Food Service, Private Label, Bulk
Brands:
        7 Day Round
        Bolero
        Chelsea
        Greek Gourmet
        Santorina

5939 Greeley Elevator Company
700 6th St
Greeley, CO 80631-3902   970-352-2575
        Fax: 970-352-6390 greecal@aol.com
Processor of dried beans
        Owner: Matt Geib
        General Manager: Matthew Geib
Estimated Sales: $1-2.5 Million
Number Employees: 5-9
Type of Packaging: Consumer, Food Service, Bulk

5940 Green Bay Cheese Company
P.O.Box 11766
Green Bay, WI 54307-1766   920-434-3233
        Fax: 920-434-3262 jayw@greenbaycheese.com
        www.greenbaycheese.com
Cheese (cutting, shredding and packaging)
        President: Thomas Vorpahl
        Plant Manager: Dean Zaretzke
Estimated Sales: $20-50 Million
Number Employees: 100-249
Parent Co: DCI Cheese Company

5941 Green County Foods
PO Box 2813
Monroe, WI 53566-1364
        Fax: 608-328-8648   800-233-3564
        greencity@tds.net   www.greencountyfoods.com
petitfours, tortes-bite-sized desserts-contract bakery, fudge, gingerbread
        President: Gene Curran
        Sales: Wally Wagner
        Public Relations: Jim Mason
        Operations: Sharee Marzolf
Estimated Sales: $2.5-5 Million
Number Employees: 10-19
Parent Co: Swiss Colony
Type of Packaging: Consumer, Food Service, Private Label, Bulk
Brands:
        Richly Deserved
        Sweet Treasures

5942 Green Foods Corporation
320 Graves Avenue
Oxnard, CA 93030-5184   805-983-7470
        Fax: 805-983-8843   800-777-4430
        gfc@greenfoods.com   www.greenfoods.com
Processor, importer and exporter of health foods including barley and vegetable juice powders, green magma, wheat germ extracts, etc
        President: Takahiko Amano
        Technical Service Manager: Bob Terry PhD
        Office Manager: Deborah Pollack
Estimated Sales: $10-20 Million
Number Employees: 10-19
Sq. footage: 9800
Type of Packaging: Consumer
Brands:
        Green Essence

5943 Green Garden Food Products
5851 S 194th St
Kent, WA 98032-2125   253-395-4460
        Fax: 253-395-0408   800-304-1033
        info@ggfoods.com   www.ggfoods.com
Processor of salad dressings, sauces, marinades, dips, salsas, mayonnaise
        President: Mark Hockman
        Director Technical Services: Kyle Anderson
Estimated Sales: $25,000,000
Number Employees: 50-99
Type of Packaging: Consumer, Food Service

5944 Green Gold Group
13905 Stettin Dr
Marathon, WI 54448-9476   715-842-8546
        Fax: 715-842-4614   888-533-7288

Processor, wholesaler/distributor and exporter of ginseng, herbs, whole roots, prong, fiber, capsules, tablets and extracts
Owner: Sam Chen
CEO: Phouangmala Chen
Estimated Sales:$ 1 - 3 Million
Number Employees: 10-19
Sq. footage: 7200
Type of Packaging: Consumer, Bulk

5945 Green Grown Products
P.O.Box 3383
Santa Monica, CA 90408-3383   310-828-1686
Fax: 310-453-3039
Processor and importer of herbs, royal jelly, propolis, bee pollen, chia and sesame seeds, apricot kernels and turbinado sugar; exporter of herbs, propolis, bee pollen and royal jelly
President: Hal Neiman
CEO: Teri Bernardi
Estimated Sales:$2 Million
Number Employees: 1-4
Sq. footage: 8000
Parent Co: Earth Commodities
Type of Packaging: Private Label, Bulk

5946 Green House
PO Box 497
San Luis Rey, CA 92068-0497   760-439-6515
Fax: 760-439-4163
Fresh herbs
President: Megan Williams
Estimated Sales:$1-2.5 Million
Number Employees: 20-49

5947 Green House Fine Herbs
PO Box 231069
Encinitas, CA 92023-1069   760-942-5371
Processor of fresh and dehydrated herbs including mint, edible flowers, basil, chives and dill; also, industrial blends available
New Bus.: Mike Murphy
Number Employees: 250-499
Sq. footage: 40000
Type of Packaging: Consumer, Food Service, Private Label, Bulk
Brands:
Green House
Herb Farm

5948 Green Mountain Chocolates
835 W Central St # 1
Franklin, MA 02038-3189   508-520-7160
Fax: 508-520-7161
info@greenmountainchocolate.com
www.greenmountainchocolate.com
Chocolate candies (Petite Truffles, Chocolate Covered Potato Chips, Butter Crunch, Desssert Truffles, Turtles, Bark)
Manager: Karen Tyler
Estimated Sales:$2.5-5 Million
Number Employees: 1-4
Brands:
GREEN MOUNTAIN CHOCOLATE TRUFFLE

5949 Green Mountain Cidery
153 Pond Ln
Middlebury, VT 05753-1190   802-388-0700
Fax: 802-388-0600   gmbinfo@gmbeverage.com
www.woodchuck.com
Processor of hard cider (Woodchuck Draft Cider, Strongbow, Woodpecker, Cider Jack)
President: Joseph Cerniglia
VP: Dan Rowell
Director Marketing: Alan MacDonald
General Manager: Rob Hyman
Estimated Sales:$2.5-5 Millioin
Number Employees: 20-49
Sq. footage: 50
Type of Packaging: Private Label
Brands:
WOODCHUCK DRAFT CIDER

5950 Green Mountain Gringo
PO Box 4329
Winston Salem, NC 27115-4329   802-875-3117
Fax: 802-875-3140   gmgringo@sover.net
www.greenmountaingringo.com
Manufacturer of salsa, hot, medium, and mild

5951 Green Mountain Gringo
P.O.Box 4329
Winston Salem, NC 27115-4329   336-661-1550
Fax: 336-661-1901
info@greenmountaingringo.com
www.greenmountaingringo.com
Manufacturer of salsa,(hot, medium, mild) roasted garlic, roasted Chile peppers and tortilla strips - all homemade.
President: Ralph Garner
VP: Ann Garner Riddle
Estimated Sales:$3.5 Million
Number Employees: 10-19
Parent Co: TW Garner Food Company
Type of Packaging: Private Label

5952 Green Options
17 Paul Dr # 104
San Rafael, CA 94903-2043   415-883-6100
Fax: 415-526-1453   888-473-3667
info@vegiedeli.com   www.greenoptions.net
Health foods, Vegi-Deli®, Vegi-Deli®Slices, Vegi-Jerky™, Vegi-Deli® Quick Stick
Manager: Michael Madden
Sales Manager: Jill Koperweis
Estimated Sales:$ 1 - 3 Million
Number Employees: 5-9

5953 Green River Chocolates
P.O.Box 421
Hinesburg, VT 5461-421   802-246-2652
info@grchocolates.com
www.grchocolates.com
Vermont maple syrup. chocolates, (and sugar free), chocolate sauce, fresh butter corn syrup, crepes and pancake mixes, ice cream and pepper sauces
Estimated Sales:$ 1 - 3 Million
Number Employees: 5-9

5954 Green Spot Packaging
100 S Cambridge Ave
Claremont, CA 91711-4842   909-625-8771
Fax: 909-621-4634   800-456-3210
Processor, importer and exporter of juices, juice concentrates, drinks, flavors and fragrances; aseptic packaging services available
CEO: Mike Staudt
Plant Manager: Roy Cooley
Estimated Sales:$6.5 Million
Number Employees: 20-49
Sq. footage: 100000
Type of Packaging: Consumer, Food Service, Private Label, Bulk
Brands:
Action Ade
Apple Delight
Apple Royal
Awesome Orange
Black Cherry Royal
Citrus Royal
Galactic Grape
Good Buddies
Green Spot
Peach Royal
Superstar Strawberry
Tropical Royal

5955 Green Turtle Bay Vitamin Company
P.O.Box 642
Summit, NJ 07902-0642   908-277-2240
Fax: 908-273-9116   800-887-8535
mail@energywave.com   www.energywave.com
Processor and exporter of vitamin supplement formulas including herbal antioxidants, oils and herbs
President: Karen Horbatt
CEO: Gloria Mckenna
Quality Control: Monica Harris
Marketing: Michele Murphy
*Estimated Sales:*Under $10 Million
Number Employees: 20-49
Number of Brands: 8
Number of Products: 8
Type of Packaging: Consumer
Brands:
Diabetiks
Maple Melts
Powermate
Powersleep
Powervites
Primrose Oile
Signal 369
Sunnie

5956 Green Turtle Cannery & Seafood
PO Box 585
Islamorada, FL 33036-0585   305-664-9595
Fax: 305-664-9564
Manhattan clam chowder, New England clam chowder, turtle chowder, turtle consumme, conch chowder, New England fish chowder, key lime pie filling
President: Henry "Rosenthal, Jr."
Estimated Sales:$1-2.5 Million
Number Employees: 20-49
Brands:
Sid and Roxie's

5957 (HQ)Green Valley Apples of California
14322 Di Giorgio Rd
Arvin, CA 93203-9519   661-854-4436
Fax: 661-854-0810   grnvby@lightseed.com
www.greenvalleypackers.com
Apples: sliced, diced, concentrates
Owner: Bruce Goren
General Manager: Jim Carlisle
Estimated Sales:$ 20 - 50 Million
Number Employees: 50-99
Type of Packaging: Private Label

5958 Green Valley Foods
P.O.Box 456
Tranquility, NJ 07879-0456   908-852-8300
Fax: 908-852-0021   800-853-8399
Importer and wholesaler/distributor of cheese, meats, pates, cookies, crackers, breads, jams, jellies, preserves, soups, snack foods, pasta and confections; custom packer of domestic and imported cheeses
President: Philip Stites
Estimated Sales:$2,100,000
Number Employees: 5-9
Sq. footage: 60000

5959 Green Valley Packing
2992 Green Valley Rd
Claysville, PA 15323-1360   724-948-3321
Fax: 724-948-3340   800-522-9970
brian@albertsmeats.com   www.albertsmeats.com
Processor of meat products: luncheon meats, sausage, wieners and hams.
Owner: George P Weiss
Sales Manager: Brian Weiss
Estimated Sales:$20-50 Million
Number Employees: 50-99
Type of Packaging: Consumer

5960 Green Valley Pecan Company
P.O.Box 7
Sahuarita, AZ 85629-0007   520-791-2880
Fax: 520-629-0119   800-533-5269
bcaris@greenvalleypecan.com
www.greenvalleypecan.com
Processor, sheller, importer and exporter of shelled pecans, namely Western Schley and Wichita
President: Richard Walden
Chief Financial Officer: Heather Triana
Telecommunications: Connie Karsten
Director Sales/Marketing: Bruce Caris
Estimated Sales:$20-50 Million
Number Employees: 20-49
Parent Co: Farmers Investment Company
Type of Packaging: Consumer, Bulk
Brands:
GREEN VALLEY PECANS

5961 Greenberg Cheese Company
3163 Beaudry Ter
Glendale, CA 91208-1744   213-617-1180
Fax: 213-617-1188   800-301-4507
Cheese, cheese products
President/CEO: Michael Greenberg
CFO: Merilyn Greenberg
Vice President: Douglas Smith
Operations Manager: Michael Burns
Estimated Sales:$30 Million
Number Employees: 20-49
Number of Products: 300
Sq. footage: 100000
Parent Co: Dairy Commodities Corporation
Type of Packaging: Food Service, Bulk

5962 Greene Brothers Specialty Coffee Roaster
313 High Street
Hackettstown, NJ 07840-1908   908-979-0022
info@greenesbeans.com
http://www.greenesbeans.com/
Processor of regular, flavored and decaffeinated
whole bean coffees, espresso and loose tea
Co-President: David Greene
Co-Presidemt: Brian Greene
Estimated Sales: $ 1 - 3 Million
Number Employees: 10-19
Sq. footage: 1500

5963 Greenfield Mills
750 N 10505 E
Howe, IN 46746   260-367-2394
customerservice@newrinkelflour.com
http://www.newrinkelflour.com/
Processor of wheat and buckwheat flour; also, pan-
cake mixes, Certified Organic whole wheat and
white soft wheat flour
President: Howard Rinkel
Vice President: Joyce Rinkel
Secretary/Treasurer: Helen Rinkel
Estimated Sales: $300,000-500,000
Number Employees: 1-4
Sq. footage: 8000
Type of Packaging: Consumer, Food Service
Brands:
New Rinkel

5964 Greenfield Noodle & Specialty Company
600 Custer Street
Detroit, MI 48202-3128   313-873-2212
Fax: 313-873-0515
Processor of sheeted noodles; wholesaler/distributor
of specialty and kosher foods
Owner: Ken Michaels
Estimated Sales: $ 5 - 10 Million
Number Employees: 10-19
Sq. footage: 25000
Type of Packaging: Consumer, Food Service, Pri-
vate Label, Bulk
Brands:
Greenfield
Mrs. Asien

5965 Greenfield Wine Company
401 Saint Helena Highway S
Saint Helena, CA 94574-2200   707-963-2335
Fax: 707-963-8537
Wines
General Manager: Tony Cartlidge
Estimated Sales: $10-24.9 Million
Number Employees: 20-49

5966 Greenhills Irish Bakery
780 Adams Street
Dorchester, MA 02124   617-825-8187
Fax: 617-698-0335 cquinn3k@comcast.net
www.greenhillsbakery.com
Bakery products; Irish brown bread and soda bread,
scones, cakes, pastries
Co-Owner: Dermot Quinn
Co-Owner: Cindy Quinn
Estimated Sales: $10-20 Million
Number Employees: 10-19

5967 Greens Today®
91 Commercial St # 2
Plainview, NY 11803-2409   516-576-1665
Fax: 516-576-1662 800-473-3641
www.greenstoday.com
Processor and exporter of powdered nutritional sup-
plements
President: Ellen Piernick
Estimated Sales: $ 1 - 3 Million
Number Employees: 5-9
Parent Co: Nature's Answer, Inc.
Type of Packaging: Bulk
Brands:
Greens Today
The Organic Frog

5968 Greenwell Farms
345 Popcorn Rd
Morganfield, KY 42437-6638   270-389-3289
Fax: 270-389-3307 greenwellfarms@prodig.net
www.greenwellfarms.com

Processor of coffee, chocolate covered coffee beans,
chocolate covered macadamia nuts, hawaiian choco-
late bars, sugar, honey
Owner/President: Tom Greenwell
CEO: Jennifer Greenwell
Estimated Sales: $1-2.5 Million
Number Employees: 10-19
Type of Packaging: Consumer, Food Service, Pri-
vate Label, Bulk
Brands:
GREENWELL FARMS

5969 Greenwood Associates
600 Central Ave # 240
Highland Park, IL 60035-5605   847-242-7900
Fax: 847-579-5501
info@greenwoodassociates.com
www.greenwoodassociates.com
Processor, distributor and re-packer of fruit concen-
trates and purees including lemon, grape, apple,
berry, lime, grapefruit, peach, apricot, tropical,
cherry, tangerine and pineapple. All to custom specs
President: Ron Kaplan
Estimated Sales: $5-10 Million
Number Employees: 50-99
Sq. footage: 1000
Type of Packaging: Bulk

5970 Greenwood Ice Cream Company
4829 Peachtree Rd
Chamblee, GA 30341-3113   770-455-6166
Fax: 770-455-4152 www.greenwoodicecream.com
Ice cream, frozen desserts
President: Mitchell Williams
Owner: Mitchell Williams
General Manager: George Normandy
Estimated Sales: $10-20 Million
Number Employees: 20-49
Brands:
Greenwood

5971 Greenwood Packing Plant
P.O.Box 188
Greenwood, SC 29648-0188   864-229-5611
Fax: 864-330-1118 cpridesales@emeraldis.com
www.greenwoodpacking.com
Manufacturer of fresh pork and bacon, smoked
meats and processed luncheon meats including deli
loaves and bologna; exporter of skinned jowls, pork
kidneys, liver and stomachs, flat belly skins, etc
Owner: Bill Barnette Ii
Vice President: Lee Miles
Estimated Sales: $100 Million
Number Employees: 5-9
Sq. footage: 450000
Type of Packaging: Consumer, Food Service, Pri-
vate Label, Bulk
Brands:
CAROLINA PRIDE
COTTAGE BRAND
GREENWOOD
GREENWOOD FARMS

5972 Greenwood Ridge Vineyards
5501 Highway 128
Philo, CA 95466-9477   707-895-2002
Fax: 707-895-2001
everybody@greenwoodridge.com
www.greenwoodridge.com
Wines consisting of White Riesling, Cabernet, Sau-
vignon, Merlot and Pinot Noir
Owner: Allan Green
Estimated Sales: $1-2.5 Million
Number Employees: 5-9

5973 Greg's Lobster Company
PO Box 295
Harwich Port, MA 02646-0295   508-432-8080
Fax: 508-432-2203
Lobster
President: Leslie Sykes
Estimated Sales: $ 1 - 3 Million
Number Employees: 1-4

5974 Gregerson's Foods
P.O.Box 1460
Gadsden, AL 35902-1460   256-549-0644
Fax: 256-549-1435 clubgreg@aol.com
Supermarket chain
President: Greg Gregerson
CEO: Peter V Gregerson Jr
Estimated Sales: G
Number Employees: 100-249

5975 Gregg Candy & Nut Company
4715 Woodhill Drive
Munhall, PA 15120-3537   412-461-0301
Candy

5976 Gregory Packaging
P.O.Box 5188
Newark, NJ 07105-0188   973-465-1113
Fax: 973-465-7307
Processor of portion controlled frozen juices includ-
ing apple, grapefruit, cranberry and orange
President: Edward Gregory
Vice President: Daniel Gregory
Estimated Sales: $20-50 Million
Number Employees: 50-99
Type of Packaging: Consumer, Food Service, Pri-
vate Label, Bulk
Brands:
Draft Cider
Woodchuck

5977 Gregory's Foods
1301 Trapp Rd
Eagan, MN 55121-1247   651-454-0277
Fax: 651-454-2254 800-231-4734
ghelland@mn.mediaone.net
www.gregorysfoods.com
Processor of frozen baked goods, mixes and bases;
wholesaler/distributor of bakery ingredients and
supplies; serving the food service market
President: Greg Helland
Quality Control: Tom Hoebbel
Sales/Marketing: Randy Clemons
Estimated Sales: $5-10 Million
Number Employees: 20-49
Sq. footage: 22000
Type of Packaging: Food Service, Private Label,
Bulk

5978 Gregory-Robinson Speas
4647 Bronze Way
Dallas, TX 75236-2009   214-352-1761
Fax: 214-339-7245
Processor of vinegar including white distilled, cider
and wine
Plant Manager: Palmer Mamola
Estimated Sales: $$10-20 Million
Number Employees: 20-49
Parent Co: Speaco Foods
Type of Packaging: Consumer, Food Service, Pri-
vate Label, Bulk

5979 Greinoman's/Unified Industries
PO Box 562
Cumming, GA 30028-0562   770-889-8233
Fax: 770-889-1476
Liquid tea concentrates, fountain syrups, food fla-
vorings and food colors.
President: Lee Horning
Plant Manager: Dave Baxter
Estimated Sales: $5-10 Million
Number Employees: 12
Sq. footage: 16000
Type of Packaging: Food Service, Private Label

5980 Grennan Meats
P.O.Box 180
Rochelle, IL 61068-0180   815-562-5565
Fax: 815-562-7262
Meat products
President: John Grennan
Estimated Sales: $1 Million
Number Employees: 5-9

5981 Gress Poultry
992 N South Rd
Scranton, PA 18504-1412   570-561-0150
Fax: 570-314-1299
Processor and exporter of frozen chicken parts: legs,
wings, breasts, thighs and drumsticks
President: Edward Gress
VP/General Manager: Keith Gress
VP Marketing: Glenn Gress
Estimated Sales: $5-10 Million
Number Employees: 20-49
Type of Packaging: Food Service, Bulk

5982 Grey Eagle Distributors
2340 Millpark Dr
Maryland Heights, MO 63043-3569   314-429-9100
Fax: 314-429-9137 www.greyeagle.com

Anheuser-Busch and Budweiser products
President/Chief Operating Officer: Steven Nolan
Chief Executive Officer: David Stokes
Accountant: Catherine Bowen
CEO: David M Stokes
Manager Information Systems: Raymond Schrempf
Inventory Control Coordinator: Jeffrey Paluczak
Marketing Manager: Shawn Freeman
Director Sales/Marketing: James Bannes
Director Communications/Public Affairs: James Hubbard
Vice President Operations: Neil Komadoski
Delivery Office/Warehouse: Steve Clawson
Estimated Sales:$50-100 Million
Number Employees: 100-249
Brands:
Hy-5
Sports Drinks

5983 Grey Owl Foods
510 11th St S.E.
Grand Rapids, MN 55744　　　218-327-2281
Fax: 218-327-2283　800-527-0172
Processor and exporter of wild rice and gourmet rice blends; specializing in lake harvested Canadian jumbo wild rice
Director Sales/Marketing: Jim McCool
Estimated Sales:$10-20 Million
Number Employees: 10-19
Sq. footage: 6000
Parent Co: SIAP Marketing Company
Type of Packaging: Consumer, Food Service, Bulk

5984 Greyston Bakery
104 Alexander St
Yonkers, NY 10701-2535　　　914-375-1510
Fax: 914-375-1514　800-289-2253
info@greystonbakery.com
www.greystonbakery.com
Cakes, tarts, brownies and other baked goods
President/CEO: Julius Walls, Jr.
CEO: Julius Walls Jr
Estimated Sales:$20-50 Million
Number Employees: 100-249
Type of Packaging: Consumer, Food Service

5985 Griffin Food Company
111 S Cherokee St
Muskogee, OK 74403-5420　　　918-687-6311
Fax: 918-687-3579　800-580-6311
griffin@ok.azalea.net　www.griffinfoods.com
Contract packager and wholesaler/distributor of sauces, vegetables and condiments including jams and syrups; serving the food service, retail and private label markets
President: John Griffin
VP Sales/Marketing: Sam Ramos
Director Midwest Sales: D C Smith
Director Southeast Region Sales: Wayne Fuller
Estimated Sales:$10-20 Million
Number Employees: 50-99
Sq. footage: 216099
Type of Packaging: Consumer, Food Service, Private Label, Bulk
Brands:
CHEROKEE MAID
DELTA
GRIFFIN
LUCKY DUTCH
OLD SANTA FE
OLDE FARM
PRIZE TAKER

5986 (HQ)Griffin Industries
4221 Alexandria Pike
Cold Spring, KY 41076　　　859-781-2010
Fax: 859-572-2575　sales@griffinind.com
www.griffinind.com
Manufacturer of meat products including chicken and bone meal
Chairman: John Griffin
CEO: Robert Griffin
CFO: Anthony Griffin
Estimated Sales:$2.5 Billion
Number Employees: 1,800
Parent Co: Griffin Industries
Type of Packaging: Private Label, Bulk
Brands:
BAKERY FEEDS
BIO G-3000
NATURE SAFE
VERSAGEN

5987 Griffin Industries
11313 SE 52nd Ave
Starke, FL 32091-6801　　　904-964-8083
Fax: 904-964-8483　sales@griffinind.com
Processor of meat and poultry meal; also, tallow rendering
President: Dennis Griffin
Estimated Sales:$20-50 Million
Number Employees: 50-99

5988 Griffin Seafood
P.O.Box 640
Golden Meadow, LA 70357-0640　985-396-2453
Fax: 985-396-2459
Seafood
Owner: Archie Dantin
*Estimated Sales:*Under $500,000
Number Employees: 5-9

5989 Griffith Laboratories
757 Pharmacy Avenue
Scarborough, ON M1L 3J8
Canada　　　416-288-3050
Fax: 416-288-8910
contactsalesna@griffithlabs.com
www.griffithlabs.com
Processor of binders, bread crumbs and croutons, breading, meat flavors, batters, seasonings, spices and stuffing; also, agricultural and regular analytical, custom sterilization and packaging services available
President: David Morrison
Vice President Technical: Ken Darley
Number Employees: 325
Parent Co: Griffith Laboratories
Type of Packaging: Food Service, Bulk
Brands:
Imperial
Krusto
Robust

5990 (HQ)Griffith Laboratories Worldwide
1 Griffith Ctr
Alsip, IL 60803-4701　　　708-371-0900
Fax: 708-389-4055　800-346-4743
sandersen@griffithlabs.com
www.griffithlabs.com
Processor of food ingredient mixes including gravy, breading, salad dressings, batter, sauces, soups, spices, etc.; also, flavors
Chairman: Dean Griffith
Worldwide President/CEO: Herve de la Vauvre
Executive Vice President/CFO: Joe Maslick
CEO: Herve De La Vauvre
Chief Chemist: Dr Lloyd Hall
Senior Director Marketing: Christine Carr
Vice President National Sales: Mike Kregor
Associate Communications Manager: Susan Andersen
Estimated Sales:$ 150 - 200 Million
Number Employees: 1,000-4,999
Type of Packaging: Food Service, Private Label, Bulk

5991 Grimaud Farms
1320 S Aurora St # A
Stockton, CA 95206-1616　　　209-466-3200
Fax: 209-466-8910　800-466-9955
grimaud@grimaud.com　www.grimaud.com
Processor and exporter of muscovy ducks and guinea fowl
President: Rheal Cayer
Accounting Manager: Ciba Williams
Vice President Sales: Jim Galle
Customer Service: Cecile Halverson
Live Production: Diego Davalos
Estimated Sales:$50-100 Million
Number Employees: 100-249
Sq. footage: 25000
Parent Co: Groupe Grimaud
Type of Packaging: Consumer, Food Service, Private Label, Bulk
Brands:
Grimaud Farms
Grimaud Farms Muscovy Ducks
Sonoma Foie-Gras

5992 Grimm's Fine Food
7680 Alderbridge Way
Richmond, AB VX6 2A2
CA　　　780-415-4331
Fax: 780-477-5287
georgemccorry@grimmsfood.com
Processor and exporter of processed meats and sausages
President: Rick Grimm
Plant Manager: George McCorry
Number Employees: 50-99
Parent Co: Fletcher's Fine Foods
Type of Packaging: Consumer, Food Service, Private Label, Bulk
Brands:
Deli Flavor
Fletchers

5993 Grimm's Locker Service
P.O.Box 4524
Sherwood, OH 43556-0524　　　419-899-2655
Fax: 419-899-2655
Canned meat and poultry
Owner: Michael Oskey
*Estimated Sales:*Below $ 5 Million
Number Employees: 1-4

5994 (HQ)Grimmway Farms
P.O.Box 81498
Bakersfield, CA 93380-1498　　　661-845-2296
Fax: 661-845-9745　800-301-3101
pboman@grimmway.com　www.grimmway.com
Processor of carrots and organic produce
Manager: Fred Rappleye
Director Marketing: Patty Boman
Vice President Marketing: Phil Gruszka
Vice President Foodservice Sales: Lisa McNeece
Estimated Sales:$1-2.5 Million
Number Employees: 20-49
Type of Packaging: Consumer, Food Service
Other Locations:
Grimmway Farms
Bakersfield CA
Brands:
Grimmway

5995 Grimmway Frozen Foods
P.O.Box 81498
Bakersfield, CA 93380-1498　　　661-845-2296
Fax: 661-845-9745　www.grimmway.com
Frozen green beans, carrots, celery, red bell peppers, whole or sliced potatoes, vegetables for soup or stew
Manager: Fred Rappleye
Executive VP: Michael Davis
Number Employees: 1,000-4,999
Type of Packaging: Private Label
Brands:
Grimmway

5996 Grinde Sausage House
Box 5282
Drayton Valley, AB T7A 1R4
Canada　　　780-542-4625
Fax: 780-542-6313　866-621-1755
hjgrinde@telusplanet.net
Processor of beef, pork, wild game, sausage, pepperoni and salami
Co-Owner: Allan Grinde
Co-Owner: Margaret Grinde
CFO: Holly Grinde
Number Employees: 20-49

5997 Grindle Point Lobster Company
RR 1
Box 4690
Lincolnville, ME 04849　　　207-763-4142
Fax: 207-763-3861
Lobster
Owner: David Aho

5998 Grippo's Food Products
6750 Colerain Ave
Cincinnati, OH 45239-5542　　　513-923-1900
Fax: 513-923-3645　info@grippos.com
www.grippopotatochips.com
Manufacturer of snack foods including potato chips and pretzels.
President: Ralph Pagel
Purchasing: Ralph Pagel
Estimated Sales:$10-20 Million
Number Employees: 50-99
Sq. footage: 33000
Type of Packaging: Consumer

5999 Grist Mill Confections
7700 France Ave S # 200
Edina, MN 55435-5867   952-469-4981
    Fax: 612-469-5550 www.grist-maill.com
Processor of jelly candy and fruit snacks
    CEO: Glen S Bolander
    Quality Control: Tom Johnson
    Plant Manager: Anthony Rocco
Estimated Sales: $10-20 Million
Number Employees: 50-99
Parent Co: Grist Mill Company
Type of Packaging: Consumer, Private Label
Brands:
    Performed Pie Crust

6000 Groeb Farms
P.O.Box 269
Onsted, MI 49265-0269   517-467-7100
    Fax: 517-467-2840 www.groebfarms.com
Processor, importer and exporter of honey, honey
powder, mustard, peanut butter, molasses, molasses
powder and fresh salsa
    Owner: Ernest Groeb
Estimated Sales: $80 Million
Number Employees: 50-99
Type of Packaging: Consumer, Food Service, Private Label, Bulk
Brands:
    GOURMET JOSE
    GROEB FARMS

6001 Groezinger Provisions
1200 7th Ave
Neptune, NJ 07753-5190   732-775-3220
    Fax: 732-775-3223   800-927-9473
    www.alexianpate.com
Processor of pates, mousses and specialty meats
    President: Laurie Groezinger
Estimated Sales: $10-20 Million
Number Employees: 10-19

6002 Groff Meats
33 N Market St
Elizabethtown, PA 17022-2087   717-367-1246
    Fax: 717-367-1952
Processor of smoked ham and bacon, bologna and
beef mince meat
    President: Frank Groff
    VP: Virginia Groff
    VP: Virginia Groff
Estimated Sales: $10-20 Million
Number Employees: 20-49
Sq. footage: 9000
Type of Packaging: Consumer, Food Service, Private Label

6003 Grossinger's Home Bakery
244 W 54th St
New York, NY 10019-5515   212-362-8672
    Fax: 212-362-8627   800-479-6996
    hrgrsin@aol.com
Ice cream cakes
    Owner: Herb Grossingers
Estimated Sales: $140,000
Number Employees: 5-9
Brands:
    Bombe Glaze

6004 Grosso Foods
2111 Kings Highway
Woolwich Township, NJ 08085-3216 856-467-2222
    Fax: 856-467-5762
Frozen peppers (green bell, red bell, mixed red and
green, yellow bell)
    President: Joseph Grasso
Estimated Sales: $ 50 - 100 Million
Number Employees: 100-249

6005 Grote & Weigel
76 Granby St
Bloomfield, CT 06002-3512   860-242-8528
    Fax: 860-242-4162
    customerservice@groteandweigel.com
    www.groteandweigel.com
Processor of low sodium processed meats including
frankfurters, kielbasa, hams, ham steaks and specialty sausages
    Owner: Mike Grenier
    VP/Owner: Arthur Haskins
    Purchasing: Michael Greiner
Estimated Sales: $ 5 - 10 Million
Number Employees: 20-49
Sq. footage: 15000

Brands:
    CLEARFIELD
    GROTE & WEIGEL
    JERSEY BOARDWALK
    MARCELLO
    MEINEL
    RILEY'S BEEF SAUSAGE
    TEXAN WIENER

6006 Grote Bakery
9285 Princeton Glendale Rd
Hamilton, OH 45011-8952   513-874-7436
    Fax: 513-874-5299
Bread, rolls and cakes
    President: Joseph Grote
    Sales Manager: Robert Grote
    Plant Manager: Tony Grote
Estimated Sales: $5-10 Million
Number Employees: 5-9

6007 Groth Vineyards & Winery
P.O.Box 390
Oakville, CA 94562-0390   707-944-0290
    Fax: 707-944-8932   info@grothwines.com
    www.grothwines.com
Wines such as Cabernet Sauvignon, Chardonnay,
Sauvignon Blanc
    President: Dennis Groth
    Vice President: Judith Groth
    Marketing Director: Ken Uhl
    National Sales Manager: Ken Uhl
    Winemaker: Michael Weis
    Vineyard Manager: Ben Benson
Estimated Sales: $5-10 Million
Number Employees: 10-19
Type of Packaging: Private Label

6008 Grounds for Thought
133 W Wooster St
Bowling Green, OH 43402-2802   419-354-2326
    Fax: 419-354-7512 www.groundsforthought.com
Processor of fresh roasted gourmet coffees including
Arabica blends
    Owner: Kelly Wicks
Estimated Sales: Under $500,000
Number Employees: 1-4
Sq. footage: 3000
Type of Packaging: Consumer, Food Service, Private Label, Bulk
Brands:
    BLACK SWAMP
    BLUEGRASS
    GROUNDS FOR THOUGHT
    JOHN Z'S BIG CITY

6009 (HQ)Groupe Paul Masson
110-50, Rue De La Barre
Longueuil, QC J4K 5G2
Canada   514-878-3050
    Fax: 450-651-5453
Processor of beverages including wines, ciders,
coolers and aperitifs; importer of wines and coolers;
exporter of coolers
    President: Jean Denis Cote
    VP Marketing Development: Alain Lecours
Number Employees: 100-249
Type of Packaging: Consumer
Brands:
    Aperossimo
    Bau Maniere
    Castelet
    De Lescot
    Dubleuet
    El Condor
    Foret Noire
    L'Ombrelle
    Nobella
    Pica
    Robert De Serbie
    Valentino

6010 Grouse Hunt Farms
458 Fairview St
Tamaqua, PA 18252-4718   570-467-2850
    Fax: 570-467-2850
Processor of dressings, relishes, mustards, sauces,
seasonings, jellies, preserves, butters, fruits, horse-
radish, etc
    President: Paul Zukovich
Estimated Sales: $1 Million
Number Employees: 10-19
Number of Brands: 2
Number of Products: 108
Sq. footage: 20000

Type of Packaging: Private Label
Brands:
    Grouse Hunt Farms
    Pennsylvania Dutch Foods
    Wos-Wit

6011 Grove Fresh Distributors
7553 S South Chicago Avenue
Chicago, IL 60619-2604   773-288-2065
    Fax: 773-288-2065
    President: Cecil Troy

6012 Grow Company
55 Railroad Ave
Ridgefield, NJ 07657-2109   201-941-8777
    Fax: 201-342-9127   growco@aol.us
    www.growco.us
Processor and exporter of vitamins, minerals and flavors
    President: Andrew Szalay
    VP: Massoud Avanaghi
Estimated Sales: $1-2.5 Million
Number Employees: 10-19
Sq. footage: 45600
Brands:
    Re-Natured

6013 Grow-Pac
2220 SW Lafollett Rd
Cornelius, OR 97113-6033   503-357-9691
    Fax: 503-357-2155
Frozen blackberries, blueberries, strawberries,
marionberries
    President: Lloyd Duyck
Estimated Sales: $5-10 Million
Number Employees: 10-19
Brands:
    Grow-Pac

6014 Grower Shipper Potato Company
P.O.Box 432
Monte Vista, CO 81144-0432   719-852-3569
    Fax: 719-852-5917
Processor and exporter of potatoes
    Manager: Mark Lounsbury
    Manager: Ken Shepherd
Estimated Sales: $10-20 Million
Number Employees: 20-49
Sq. footage: 40000
Type of Packaging: Consumer, Food Service, Bulk
Brands:
    Big Ram
    Colorado Gold
    Diamond
    Jackpot

6015 (HQ)Growers Cooperative Grape Juice Company
112 N Portage St
Westfield, NY 14787-1054   716-326-3161
    Fax: 716-326-6566   growersb@cecomet.net
    www.concordgrapejuice.com
Processor and exporter of grape juice and juice concentrate
    President: Steve Baran
    Quality Assurance Manager: Jim Gillespie
    General Manager: David Momberger
    Plant Manager: Todd Donato
Estimated Sales: $5-10 Million
Number Employees: 20-49
Type of Packaging: Bulk

6016 Growth Products
1638 Taylor Avenue
Racine, WI 53403-2120   262-637-9287
    President: Allen Buhler

6017 Gruet Winery
8400 Pan American Fwy NE
Albuquerque, NM 87113-1832   505-821-0055
    Fax: 505-857-0066   888-897-9463
    nathalie@gruetwinery.com
    www.gruetwinery.com
Wines: Brut, Blanc, Rose, Demi-sec, Gruet Grande
Reserve, Gruet Chardonnay, Pinot Noir
    President/Winemaker: Laurent Gruet
    Vice President: Farid Himeur
Estimated Sales: $1-2.5 Million
Number Employees: 5-9
Type of Packaging: Private Label
Brands:
    Domaine St. Vincent
    Gruet Winery

6018 GuS Grown-up Soda
424 E 57th St
Suite 3C
New York, NY 10022   212-355-7454
    Fax: 212-208-4444   info@drinkgus.com
    www.drinkgus.com
sodas made with real juice and real flavor extracts
President/Owner: Steve Hersh

6019 Guapo Spices Company
6200 E Slauson Avenue
Los Angeles, CA 90040-3012   213-322-8900
    Fax: 213-627-0601
Seasonings, spices

Estimated Sales:$2.5-5 Million
Number Employees: 20-49
Type of Packaging: Private Label

6020 Guayaki Sustainable Rainforest Products
6782 Sebastopol Ave
Sebastopol, CA 95472-3861   707-823-3442
    Fax: 707-824-6607   888-482-9254
    info@guayaki.com   www.guayaki.com
Organic rainforest herbs
Co-Founder: Alex Pryer
Co-Founder: David Karr
Chief Executive Officer: Chris Mann
CEO: Chris Mann
Sales Manager: Eileen McHale
Vice President Operations: Richard Bruehl
Estimated Sales:$3 Million
Number Employees: 10-19
Number of Brands: 1
Number of Products: 13
Sq. footage: 15000
Type of Packaging: Consumer, Food Service, Bulk
Brands:
ORGANIC GUAYAKI YERBA MATE

6021 Guerra Nut Shelling Company
P.O.Box 1117
Hollister, CA 95024-1117   831-637-4471
    Fax: 831-637-1358   info@guerranut.com
    www.guerranut.com
Processor and exporter of walnuts including shelled
President: Anthony Guerra
Estimated Sales:$5-10 Million
Number Employees: 50-99
Sq. footage: 50000
Type of Packaging: Bulk
Brands:
Cal Best
Hillcrest

6022 Guers Dairy
P.O.Box 513
Pottsville, PA 17901-0513   570-277-6611
    Fax: 570-277-0135
Milk and milk products
President: Daniel Guers
Treasurer: William Yaag
VP: Edward Guers
Purchasing Manager: Dwight Manbeck
Estimated Sales:$10-20 Million
Number Employees: 50-99

6023 Guggisberg Cheese
5060 State Route 557
Millersburg, OH 44654-9266   330-893-2500
    Fax: 330-893-3240   800-262-2505
    info@guggisberg.com   www.babyswiss.com
Processor of cheese including swiss, lace, farmer, baby swiss and butter.
President: Richard Guggisberg
Estimated Sales:$20-50 Million
Number Employees: 20-49
Sq. footage: 60000
Type of Packaging: Consumer, Food Service, Bulk
Brands:
AMISH FARM
GUGGISBERG
ORIGINAL BABY

6024 Guida's Milk & Ice Cream
433 Park Street
New Britain, CT 06051
    Fax: 860-612-5394   800-832-8929
    www.supercow.com

Processor of dairy products which includes milk, ice cream, orange juice, drinks and water
President: Michael Guida
Sr VP/Secretary: James Guida
VP/Treasurer: Michael Young
Product Quality Manager: Hugh O'Hare
Director Plant Operations: Wesley Sliwinski
Estimated Sales:$149 Million
Number Employees: 300
Number of Brands: 75
Sq. footage: 75000
Type of Packaging: Consumer, Food Service, Private Label
Brands:
GUIDA'S

6025 Guido's International Foods
1669 La Cresta Dr
Pasadena, CA 91103-1260   626-296-1427
    Fax: 626-296-0306   877-994-8436
    guidoserious@earthlink.net
    www.guidoseriousbbq.com
Manufacturer all-purpose spicy-seasonings and roots, BBQ sauce and hot sauce
President: Guido Meindl
Estimated Sales:$150,000
Number Employees: 1-4
Number of Brands: 7
Type of Packaging: Consumer, Food Service, Private Label, Bulk
Brands:
GUIDO'S SERIOUS

6026 Guidry's Catfish
1093 Henderson Hwy
Breaux Bridge, LA 70517-7728   337-228-7546
    Fax: 337-228-7544
Processor of fresh catfish
Owner: Bobby Jules
Administrative Executive: Sandra Robertson
Operations: Sandra Guidry-Robertson
Estimated Sales:$ 10 - 20 Million
Number Employees: 100-249

6027 Guilliams Winery
3851 Spring Mountain Rd
St Helena, CA 94574-9678   707-963-9059
    Fax: 707-963-9059
Family owned business - wines consisting of:
Cabernet Sauvignon, Merlot and Cab Franc
President: John Guilliams
Estimated Sales: Less than $500,000
Number Employees: 1-4

6028 Guiltless Gourmet
One Harmon Plaza,10th Floor
Secaucus, NJ 07094   201-453-5200
    Fax: 201-333-8475   www.guiltlessgourmet.com
Processor and exporter of natural, low-fat baked snacks including tortilla and potato chips; also, non-fat dips and salsas
President: Michael Shaw
VP Finance: Bart Glaser
VP Sales/Marketing: Robert Greenberg
Number Employees: 20-49
Type of Packaging: Consumer, Food Service, Private Label, Bulk
Brands:
Guiltless Gourmet

6029 Guiltless Gourmet®
One Harmon Plaza
Tenth Floor
Secaucus, NJ 07094   512-389-0770
    Fax: 512-443-5052   www.guiltlessgourmet.com
dessert bowls, sandwich wraps, chips and dips, potato crisp, tortilla chips, salsa and bean dip, hummus
President/CEO: Michael Schall
VP Marketing, RAB Food Group: David Rossi
Estimated Sales:$ .5 - 1 million
Number Employees: 1-4
Parent Co: R.A.B. Food Group, LLC
Brands:
GUILTLESS GOURMET

6030 Guinness-Bass Import Company
6 Landmark Square
Stamford, CT 06901-2704   203-323-3311
    Fax: 203-359-7209   800-521-1591
    guinness@consumer-care.net   www.guiness.com
Processor and importer of beer and stout
President: Tim Kelly
Chief Information Officer: Lynda Gutman
Vice President Operations: Colin Funnell

Number Employees: 50-99
Parent Co: Guiness PLC
Type of Packaging: Consumer
Brands:
Asahi
Bass Ale
Furstenberg
Guinness Stout
Harp Lager
Kaliber

6031 Guittard Chocolate Company
10 Guittard Rd
Burlingame, CA 94010-2203   650-697-4427
    Fax: 650-692-2761   800-468-2462
    sales@guittard.com   www.guittard.com
Manufactures chocolate and pastel coatings, cocoa cookie drops, chocolate liqueurs and bulk and bitter white cocoa
President/CEO: Gary Guittard
Director Sales/Marketing: Mark Spini
Estimated Sales:$20-50 Million
Number Employees: 100-249
Brands:
Chocolate Products
Dick Servaes
Melt-N-Mold
Smooth-N-Melty

6032 Gulf Atlantic Freezers
PO Box 2493
Gretna, LA 70054-2493   504-392-3590
    Fax: 504-392-3443

6033 Gulf Central Seafood
PO Box 373
Biloxi, MS 39533-0373   228-436-6346
    Fax: 228-374-1207
Custom seafood, fresh, live and frozen shrimp
President: Rock Sekul
Estimated Sales:$2.5-5 Million
Number Employees: 20-49
Brands:
Gulf Central
Gulf Star
Treasure Bay

6034 Gulf City Marine Supply
PO Box 625
Bayou La Batre, AL 36509-0625   251-824-4154
    Fax: 251-824-7980
Processor of seafood including shrimp, oysters and stuffed flounder
President: Charles Graham
Estimated Sales:$500,000-$1 Million
Number Employees: 5-9
Parent Co: Gulf City Seafood

6035 (HQ)Gulf City Seafoods
411 Cedar Street
Pascagoula, MS 39567   228-762-3271
    Fax: 228-762-3962   800-666-3300
Packer and importer of fresh and frozen crabs, scallops, shrimp and oysters
President/CEO: Charles Graham
Controller: Ron Jones
Quality Control: Betty Roach
Director Manufacturing: David Graham
Plant Manager: Jim Cooney
Estimated Sales:$20-50 Million
Number Employees: 100-249
Type of Packaging: Consumer, Food Service, Private Label, Bulk
Brands:
Grand Bay
Gulf City

6036 Gulf Crown Seafood
P.O.Box 198
Delcambre, LA 70528-0198   337-685-4721
    Fax: 337-685-4241
Peeled shrimp, shell-on shrimp
President: John Floyd
VP: Jeffrey W Floyd
Telecommunications: Crystal Marceaux
Estimated Sales:$ 20 - 50 Million
Number Employees: 100-249
Brands:
Gulf Crown

6037 (HQ)Gulf Food Products Company
509 Commerce Pt
New Orleans, LA 70123-3203   504-733-1516
    Fax: 504-733-1517 roberthoy@worldnet.att.net
Wholesaler/distributor, importer and exporter of seafood; serving the food service market
    Owner: Albert Lin
Estimated Sales: Less than $500,000
Number Employees: 1-4
Sq. footage: 4000

6038 Gulf Island Shrimp & Seafood
3935 Ryan St
Lake Charles, LA 70605-2817   985-563-4586
    Fax: 985-563-4202
Processor of shrimp, frozen and fresh
Estimated Sales: $5-9.9 Million
Number Employees: 20-49

6039 (HQ)Gulf Island Shrimp & Seafood
3935 Ryan Street
Lake Charles, LA 70605   985-563-4586
    Fax: 985-563-4586 888-626-7264
        info@gulfislandsshrimp.com
        www.gulfislandsshrimp.com
Shrimp processing plant
    Contact: Steve Loga
Estimated Sales: $ 20 - 50 Million
Number Employees: 20-49

6040 Gulf Marine & Industrial Supplies
5501 Jefferson Hwy # 116
New Orleans, LA 70123-4237   504-525-6252
    Fax: 504-525-4761 800-886-6252
    service@gulfmarine.net   www.gulfmarine.net
Wholesaler/distributor of seafood, pork, beef, poultry, canned and frozen foods, fresh vegetables, beer, wine and general merchandise
    Owner: Steve Cotsoradis
    Marketing: Dimitris Karmoukos
Estimated Sales: $10-20 Million
Number Employees: 50-99
Sq. footage: 250000

6041 Gulf Marine Products Company
501 Louisiana St
Westwego, LA 70094-4141   504-436-2682
    Fax: 504-436-1585
        sales@gulfmarineproducts.com
        www.lapack.com/index.htm
Gulf Marine is a processor of domestic and imported shrimp, crawfish tail meat and whole-cooked crawfish. Additional products include tilapia, redfish, imitation crab meat, salmon, grouper, frog legs, squid, mussels, and clams.
    President: David Lai

6042 Gulf Packing Company
P.O. Box 357
San Benito, TX 78586-0029   956-399-2631
    Fax: 956-399-2675
Processor/packer, exporter and wholesaler/distributor of meat including heifer calf and packaged meats
    President: Charlie Booth
    VP: Carlos Selainais
    Manager: Ace Delacerta
    Mngr: Frank Esquivel
Estimated Sales: $10-20 Million
Number Employees: 50-99
Type of Packaging: Consumer
Brands:
    Quality Minded

6043 Gulf Pecan Company
6522 Highway 90
Theodore, AL 36582-1820   334-661-2931
Salted and roasted nuts and seeds
    President: Danny Fritz
Estimated Sales: $5-9.9 Million
Number Employees: 5-9

6044 Gulf Performance Group
PO Box 309
Mandeville, LA 70470-0309
    Fax: 985-892-0707 800-562-7514
        brandon@stimostam.com
        http://www.stimostam.com/
Processor and exporter Supplements, Nutritional: Energy Mixes
    Contact: Quin Boylan

Estimated Sales: $300,000-500,000
Number Employees: 1-4
Sq. footage: 10000
Type of Packaging: Consumer
Brands:
    Stim-O-Stam

6045 Gulf Pride Enterprises
P.O. Box 355
Biloxi, MS 39533-0355   228-432-2488
    Fax: 228-374-7411 888-689-0560
Processor, importer and exporter of fresh frozen shrimp: peeled, shell-on headless, peeled & deveined. White, Grey, Neutral
    President: Janet Seymour
    Vice President: Wally Gollott
Estimated Sales: $ 10 Million - $50 Million
Number Employees: 50-99
Type of Packaging: Consumer, Private Label
Brands:
    Captain Pierre
    Gulf Pride
    Magnolia Bay

6046 Gulf Shrimp, Inc.
P.O. Box 2490
Fort Myers Beach, FL 33932-2490   239-463-8788
    Fax: 239-463-3550
Shrimp
    Owner: Dennis Henderson
    Manager: Dan Schribner
Estimated Sales: $2.5-5 Million
Number Employees: 20-49

6047 Gulf States Canners
1006 Industrial Park Dr
Clinton, MS 39056-3298   601-924-0511
    Fax: 601-924-7746
Processor of canned soft drinks
    Manager: Randy Lee
    Manager: Randy Lee
Estimated Sales: $50-100 Million
Number Employees: 50-99
Type of Packaging: Consumer, Food Service

6048 Gulf Stream Crab Company
P.O. Box 427
Bayou La Batre, AL 36509-0427   251-824-4717
    Fax: 251-824-7416
Crabs
    President: Bryan Cumbie
Estimated Sales: $ .5 - 1 million
Number Employees: 1-4

6049 Gum Technology Corporation
509 W Wetmore Rd
Tucson, AZ 85705-1521   520-888-5500
    Fax: 520-888-5585 800-369-4867
    info@gumtech.com   www.gumtech.com
Processor, importer and exporter of vegetable gums and stabilizers
    President/CEO: Allen Freed
    R&D/Laboratory Director: Aida Prenzno
    VP/Sales: Joshua Brooks
Estimated Sales: $ 5 - 10 Million
Number Employees: 5-9
Sq. footage: 3000
Type of Packaging: Bulk
Brands:
    COYOTE
    COYOTE STAR

6050 Gumix International
2160 N Central Rd # 202
Fort Lee, NJ 07024-7547   201-947-6300
    Fax: 201-947-9265 800-248-6492
    info@gumix.com   www.gumtragacanth.com
Processor and exporter of natural water-soluble gums including karaya, gum ghatti, carageenan, tragacanth, arabic (acacia), guar, locust bean, agar agar and xanthan.
    President: Sean Katir
Estimated Sales: $2.5-5 Million
Number Employees: 1-4

6051 Gumpert's Canada
2500 Tedlo Street
Mississauga, ON L5A 4A9
Canada   905-279-2600
    Fax: 905-279-2797 800-387-9324
    info@gumpert.com   www.gumpert.com

Processor, importer and exporter of dessert preparations, mixes, toppings, canned sauces and desserts
    President: George Johnson
    R&D/QA Manager: Erica Tulloch
Number Employees: 20-49
Number of Products: 200
Sq. footage: 53000
Type of Packaging: Bulk
Brands:
    Gumpert's

6052 Gumtech International
246 E Watkins St
Phoenix, AZ 85004-2926   602-252-7425
        www.gum-tech.com
Processor of chewing gum
    CEO/President: Gary Kehoe
    R&D Engineer: Stephen Roman
Estimated Sales: $ 5 - 10 Million
Number Employees: 5-9

6053 Gundlach Bundschu Winery
2000 Denmark St
Sonoma, CA 95476-9615   707-938-5277
    Fax: 707-938-9460 info@gumbun.com
        www.gunbun.com
Wines consisting of: Chardonnay, Pinot Nois, Merlot, Zinfandel, Red Bearitage, Mountain Cuvee
    President: Jeff Bundschu
    Director Business: Mark Stornetta
    Director Marketing: Susan Sueiro
    Winemaker: Linda Trotta
    Winegrower: Jim Bundschu
Estimated Sales: $ 20 - 50 Million
Number Employees: 50-99
Number of Brands: 3

6054 Gunnoe Farms-Sausage & Salad Company
2115 Oakridge Dr
Charleston, WV 25311-1499   304-343-7686
    Fax: 304-343-4748 gunnoefarm@aol.com
Manufacturer of meat including sausage
    President: Glenn Gunnoe
    Vice President: Joy Gunnoe
Estimated Sales: $15 Million
Number Employees: 20-49
Type of Packaging: Consumer

6055 Gunsberg Corned Beef
3925 Tillman Street
Detroit, MI 48208-2445   313-894-6600
    Fax: 313-894-8307
Processor of roast beef, corned beef, and pastrami.
    President: Louis Gunsberg
Number Employees: 500-999
Sq. footage: 150000
Type of Packaging: Consumer, Food Service, Private Label, Bulk

6056 Guptill's Farms
PO Box 129
Machias, ME 04654-0129   207-255-8536
    Fax: 207-255-6176

6057 Gurley's Foods
P.O. Box 88
Willmar, MN 56201-0088   320-235-0600
    Fax: 320-235-0659 800-426-7845
        www.gurleysfoods.com
Bakery foods, snacks, candy, gum, general groceries
    President: Mike Mickelson
Estimated Sales: $ 20 - 50 Million
Number Employees: 50-99
Brands:
    GURLEY'S CANDY
    GURLEY'S GOLDEN RECIPE NUTS
    GURLEY'S NATURES HARVEST
    ROCKY MOUNTAIN

6058 Gustafsons Dairy
P.O. Box 338
Green Cove Spgs, FL 32043-0338   904-284-3750
    Fax: 904-284-5570 hmiller@gustafsonsdairy.com
        www.gustafsonsdairy.com
Manufacturer of dairy products
    President: Randy Peck Jr.
    Plant Manager: David Plumley
Estimated Sales: $21.7 Million
Number Employees: 250-499
Type of Packaging: Consumer

6059 Gutheinz Meats
520 Cedar Ave
Scranton, PA 18505-1191   570-344-1191
                                 Fax: 570-344-1193
Processor of prepared meat products
    President: Alan Leach
Estimated Sales: $2.5-5 Million
Number Employees: 5-9
Type of Packaging: Consumer

6060 Guttenplan's Frozen Dough
100 Highway 36
Middletown, NJ 07748
            Fax: 732-495-2415 888-422-4357
info@guttenplan.com   www.guttenplan.com
Frozen rolls, bread, dough and bagels, sweet goods
    Owner/President: Jack Guttenplan
Estimated Sales: $10-25 Million
Number Employees: 50-99
Number of Products: 7
Sq. footage: 70000
Type of Packaging: Private Label

6061 Guy's Food
405 S Leonard Street
Liberty, MO 64068-2520   816-781-6700
        Fax: 816-792-9546 800-821-2405
                                www.guysnacks.com
Snacks
    President: Ron Hirasawa
    CEO: John Morris
    CFO: Thomas Price
    VP of Sales: Reid Bennett
    Operations Manager: Thomas Anderson
    Plant Manager: George Flughum
Number Employees: 500-999
Type of Packaging: Private Label
Brands:
    Guy's

6062 Guylian USA
560 Sylvan Ave
Englewood Cliffs, NJ 07632-3137   201-871-4144
        Fax: 201-871-3632 800-803-4123
                                guylian@intac.com
Confectionery imports
    President/CEO: Leslie Coopersmith
Estimated Sales: $360,000
Number Employees: 1-4
Type of Packaging: Private Label
Brands:
    Guylian

6063 Gwaltney Food Service
108 Wake Robin Cir
Spartanburg, SC 29301-2624   864-587-7761
                                    Fax: 864-587-2966
Processor and exporter of fresh and frozen pork and
pork products
    National Account Manager: Fred Bailey
Parent Co: Smithfield Foods
Type of Packaging: Consumer, Food Service, Private Label, Bulk
Brands:
    Gwaltney

6064 Gwaltney of Smithfield
P.O.Box 489
Smithfield, VA 23431-0489   757-357-3131
        Fax: 757-357-1576 800-888-7521
                                www.gwaltneyfoods.com
Processor and exporter of fresh and processed meat
products including ham, bacon, frankfurters and
sausage
    CEO: Clarry Pope
    VP Marketing: Bob Darrell
    VP Sales: Ron Marsh
    VP Operations: Rob Bogaard
Number Employees: 1,000-4,999
Parent Co: Smithfield Foods
Type of Packaging: Consumer, Food Service, Private Label
Brands:
    Gwaltney

6065 Gwaltney of Smithfield
2175 Elmhurst Lane
Portsmouth, VA 23701-2626   757-465-0666
                                   Fax: 757-465-1745
Processor of frankfurters, lunch meats and sausage
    President: Timothy A Seely
    VP: Daniel G Stevens's
    Plant Manager: Jim Honnoll

Estimated Sales: $100-500 Million
Number Employees: 250-499
Parent Co: Smithfield Foods
Type of Packaging: Consumer, Private Label
Brands:
    Gwaltney of Smithfield

6066 Gwinn's Foods
6190 Bermuda Dr
St Louis, MO 63135-3264   314-521-8792
                                 Fax: 314-521-8792
Beef, beef products, hot tamales
    Owner: Joseph Frisella
Estimated Sales: $1-2.5 Million
Number Employees: 5-9

6067 Gyma
115 Seven Bridge Road
East Stroudsburg, PA 18301-9100   570-422-6311
An IQF, frozen food company

6068 H & A Canada, Inc.
1160 Tapscott Road
Toronto, ON M1X 1E9
Canada   416-412-9518
    Fax: 416-293-9066 sales@hacanada.com
Flavor enhancers, preservatives, sweeteners, food
gums/hdrocolloids, shrink bags and casings.

6069 H Cantin
1910 Av Du Sanctuaire
Beauport, QC G1E 3L2
Canada   418-663-3523
        Fax: 418-663-0717 800-463-5268
                                cantinh@microtec.ca
Processor of jams, pie fillings, pudding mixes, ma-
ple syrup, soup bases, bakery products and candies;
importer of frozen fruit; exporter of marshmallow
cones and caramels
    President/General Manager: Leonce Tremblay
Number Employees: 50-99
Sq. footage: 60000
Parent Co: Bon Bons Associates
Type of Packaging: Consumer, Food Service, Private Label, Bulk

6070 H Coturri & Sons Winery
P.O.Box 396
Glen Ellen, CA 95442-0396   707-525-9126
        Fax: 707-542-8039 866-268-8774
                                www.coturriwinery.com
Producers of red and white wines.
    Manager: Tony Coturri
    Marketing Director: Harry Coturo
    Operations Manager: Tony Coturri
Estimated Sales: $500,000-$1 Million
Number Employees: 1-4

6071 H E Williams Candy Company
1230 Perry St
Chesapeake, VA 23324-1334   757-545-9311
Candy
    Owner: Lillie Williams
Estimated Sales: $220,000
Number Employees: 5-9

6072 H H Dobbins
99 West Ave
Lyndonville, NY 14098-9744   585-765-2271
        Fax: 585-765-9710 877-362-2467
                                hhdobbins@wnyapples.com
                                www.wnyapples.com
Processor and exporter of produce including apples,
cabbage, pears and prunes; also, apple packers
    Owner/President: Howard Dobbins
Estimated Sales: $3 - 5 Million
Number Employees: 20-49
Type of Packaging: Consumer, Food Service, Bulk
Brands:
    Old Dobbin

6073 H R Nicholson Company
6320 Oakleaf Ave
Baltimore, MD 21215-2213   410-580-0975
        Fax: 410-764-9125 800-638-3514
        410-764-2323@yahoo.com
                                www.hrnicholson.com
Canned fruit juice concentrates and beverage bases
    President: Bob Nicholson
    Regional Manager Mid-Atlantic: Scott Thompson

Estimated Sales: $25-50 Million
Number Employees: 20-49

6074 H&B Packing Company
P.O.Box 2344
Waco, TX 76703-2344   254-752-2506
                             Fax: 254-752-1451
Processor of summer, hot and smoked link sausage
    President: Jake K Bauer
    Vice President: David Bauer
Estimated Sales: $20-50 Million
Number Employees: 50-99

6075 H&F Food Products Company
321 Ramsdell Avenue
Buffalo, NY 14216-1088   716-876-4345
Processor and importer of Spanish olives, Greek
pepperoncini, Israeli cocktail onions and mixed veg-
etables
    President: Thomas Amabile
Number Employees: 5-9
Sq. footage: 24000
Type of Packaging: Consumer, Food Service, Pri-
vate Label, Bulk
Brands:
    Hetty Fair

6076 H&H Bagels
2239 Broadway
New York, NY 10024-6201   212-595-8003
        Fax: 212-799-6765 800-692-2435
                                www.handhbagels.com
Processor, exporter and wholesaler/distributor of
fresh and frozen bagels; serving the food service
market
    President: Helmer Toro
Estimated Sales: $20-50 Million
Number Employees: 20-49
Sq. footage: 20000
Type of Packaging: Food Service
Brands:
    H&H BAGELS

6077 H&H Fisheries Limited
PO Box 172
Eastern Passage, NS B3G 1M5
Canada   902-465-6330
        Fax: 902-465-2572 rhartlen@hhseafood.com
                                www.fishbasket.com
Processor and exporter of fresh/frozen whole fish,
fresh fillets, salt fish, shellfish and lobster. Products
include: Lobster, Halibut, Cod, Haddock, Pollock,
Cusk, Catfish, Mackerel, Herring, Crab-Snow,
Shark, Swordfish, Tuna andAltantic Salmon
    Contact: R Hartlen
Number Employees: 20-49
Type of Packaging: Consumer, Food Service, Pri-
vate Label, Bulk

6078 H&H Foods
P.O.Box 358
Mercedes, TX 78570-0358   956-565-6363
        Fax: 956-565-0228 800-365-4632
                                www.hhfoods.com
Fully integrated meat company that produces raw as
well as fully cooked products.
    Owner: Libo Hinojosa
    CEO: Andrew Guerra
    CFO: Onder Ari
    Sales Director: Ruben Hinojosa Jr
    Operations Manager: Frederick Garcia
    Production Manager: Libo Hinojosa Jr
Estimated Sales: $50-100 Million
Number Employees: 250-499
Type of Packaging: Food Service, Private Label,
Bulk

6079 H&H Products Company
6600 Magnolia Homes Rd
Orlando, FL 32810-4285   407-299-5410
                                Fax: 407-298-6966
customerservice@hartleysbrand.com
                                www.hartleysbrand.com
Manufacturer of juices, drink bases, liquid teas and
syrups including fountain, fruit, pancake and waffle
    President: Morris Hartley
Estimated Sales: $6 Million
Number Employees: 20-49
Sq. footage: 40000
Type of Packaging: Food Service, Private Label
Brands:
    Bloody Mary Juice Burst
    Citrus Punch Sugar-Free
    Flavor Burst Liquid Citrus Tea
    Flavor Burst Liquid Sweet Tea
    Flavor Burst Liquid Unsweet Tea

Flavorburst
Hartley's
Juiceburst
Lemon/Lime Thristaway
Neutral Slush
Orange Thirstaway

6080 H&K Packers Company
420 Turenne Street
Winnipeg, NB R2J 3W8
Canada   204-233-2354
    Fax: 204-235-1258 hkpack@mb.sympatico.ca
Processor and exporter of pork and beef
    President: Albert Kelly
    Production Manager: Jake Penner
    Plant Manager: Andy Van Patter
Number Employees: 20-49
Sq. footage: 10000
Type of Packaging: Bulk
Brands:
    H&K Packers
    Kings Choice

6081 H&K Products-Pappy's Sassafras Teas
10246 Road P
Columbus Grove, OH 45830-9733   419-659-5110
    Fax: 419-659-5110 877-659-5110
        pappy@q1.net www.sassafrastea.com
Pappy's Sassafras Teas manufacture three teas, Sassafras, Green & Raspberry Teas along with two jellies, Sassafras & Raspberry
    President: Sandra Nordhaus
    CEO: Don Nordhaus
    Marketing/Sales: Jeff Nordhaus
    Production/VP: Jeff Nordhaus
Estimated Sales:$500,000
Number Employees: 5-9
Number of Brands: 1
Number of Products: 2
Sq. footage: 15000
Type of Packaging: Consumer, Food Service, Private Label, Bulk
Brands:
    Pappy's

6082 H&R Florasynth
300 North Street
Teterboro, NJ 07608-1204   888-473-5672
    Fax: 973-467-3514
    www.ajtsc.com/hr_Florasynth.htm
Flavors, fragrances and aroma chemicals
Number Employees: 250-499

6083 H&S Bakery
601 S Caroline St
Baltimore, MD 21231-2814   410-276-7254
    Fax: 410-522-5200 800-959-7655
                www.hsbakery.com
Artisan European hearth-baked bread varieties.
Sandwich and submarine rolls in a variety of flavors.
    President: John Paterakis
    Senior Vice President: William Paterakis
    Director Sales: Charlie Alves
Estimated Sales:$50-99.9 Million
Number Employees: 250-499

6084 H&S Edible Products Corporation
119 Fulton Lane
Mount Vernon, NY 10550-4697   914-664-4041
    Fax: 914-664-8304 800-253-3364
        info@hsbreadcrumbs.com
            www.hsbreadcrumbs.com
Dry bread crumbs, nuts
    President: Mari Rowan
    Vice President: Peter Rowan
    Marketing Director: P Rowan, Jr.
Estimated Sales:$2 Million
Number Employees: 20-49
Number of Products: 1
Sq. footage: 13000
Type of Packaging: Food Service, Private Label, Bulk
Brands:
    H&S Bread Crumbs

6085 H&W Foods
2029 Lauwiliwili St
Kapolei, HI 96707-1836   808-682-8300
    Fax: 808-841-8687 shawn@hwfoodservice.com
        www.hwfoodservice.com

Stock and distribute over 5,500 plus items of refrigerated, frozen and dry products - an in-house line of raw and cooked meat products
    Owner: Bill Loose
    Chief Executive Officer: Bill Loose
    Chief Financial Officer: Jeff Sakamoto
    IT Manager: Shelle Andrade
Estimated Sales:$ 5 - 10 Million
Number Employees: 5-9
Sq. footage: 90000

6086 H. Fox & Company
416 Thatford Ave
Brooklyn, NY 11212-5895   718-385-4600
    Fax: 718-345-4283 www.foxs-u-bet.com
Processor and exporter of chocolate and fruit flavored syrups; processor of imitation pancake and dietetic syrups, sundae toppings and juice mixes - been in existance for 100+ years
    President: David Fox
Estimated Sales:$10-20 Million
Number Employees: 20-49
Sq. footage: 36000
Type of Packaging: Food Service
Brands:
    FOX
    Fox's U-Bet
    No-Cal

6087 H. Gass Seafood
38945 Jacqueline Street
Hollywood, MD 20636   301-373-6882
                Fax: 301-884-8350
Processor of fresh oysters and crabs
    Owner: James Payne
    Manager: Benji Quade
Number Employees: 10-19
Sq. footage: 1000

6088 (HQ)H. Interdonati
P.O.Box 262
Cold Spring Hbr, NY 11724-0262   631-367-6611
    Fax: 631-367-6626 800-367-6617
            flavorplus@aol.com
Manufacturer, importer and exporter of ingredients including tartaric acid, chlorophyll, inositol, natural furanone, gamma deca lactone, bioflavonoids, menthol, fructose, sodium and calcium saccharin
    President: Robert Interdonati
    Sales Manager: Andrew Interdonati
Estimated Sales:$3 Million
Number Employees: 1-4
Sq. footage: 1000
Brands:
    Alnose

6089 H. Meyer Dairy Company
415 John St
Cincinnati, OH 45215-5400   513-948-8811
    Fax: 513-948-8837 800-347-6455
                www.meyerdairy.com
Fluid dairy products (milk and juice drinks) other dairy products such as eggs, cheese and yogurt.
    CEO: Mike Meyer
    Sales Manager: Mike Osborne
Number Employees: 250-499
Sq. footage: 60000
Parent Co: Dean Foods Company
Type of Packaging: Food Service

6090 H. Nagel & Son Company
2428 Central Pkwy
Cincinnati, OH 45214-1804   513-665-4550
                Fax: 513-665-4570
Processor and exporter of flour and flour based mixes including whole wheat, graham, cake and pastry
    President: W Nagel
    CEO: Mike Norris
    CFO: Brian Mitchell
    Operations Manager: Edward Nagel
Estimated Sales:$ 20 - 50 Million
Number Employees: 20-49
Type of Packaging: Food Service, Private Label, Bulk
Brands:
    Gilt Edge

6091 H. Naraghi Farms
20001 McHenry Ave
Escalon, CA 95320   209-577-5777
                Fax: 209-838-3299

Processor and exporter of grapes, peaches, apples, walnuts, pistachios and almonds
    Owner/President: H Naraghi
Number Employees: 20-49

6092 H. Reisman Corporation
377 Crane Street
PO Box 759
Orange, NJ 07051   973-882-1670
    Fax: 973-882-0323 lcullen@us.lycored.com
Processor, exporter and importer of vitamins including natural carotenoid products and standardized herbal extracts - supplier of saccharin, mannitol, quinine hydrochloride, vitamin food chemicals, cyclamates, luten, soy proteinsolvable products and many more
    Owner/President: Frank Molinaro
Estimated Sales:$5-10 Million
Number Employees: 20-49
Sq. footage: 100000
Parent Co: LycoRed Company
Type of Packaging: Bulk
Brands:
    Bionova
    Floraglow
    Lycomato
    Phyto Foods

6093 H. Shenson International Export
650 5th St
San Francisco, CA 94107-1536   415-318-7000
                Fax: 415-318-7001
Processor and exporter of meat products including beef, veal, lamb, pork and poultry; also, seafood
    President: Shelly Lazar
    Chairman: Merv Shenson
    VP: Michael Shenson
Estimated Sales:$300,000-500,000
Number Employees: 5-9
Sq. footage: 20000
Type of Packaging: Food Service
Brands:
    Shenson

6094 H.B. Dawe
PO Box 100
Cupids, NL A0A 2B0
Canada   709-528-4347
                Fax: 709-528-3463
Processor and exporter of fresh, frozen, salted and cooked groundfish and shellfish
    General Manager: Philip Hillyard
Number Employees: 100-249
Type of Packaging: Consumer, Food Service, Private Label, Bulk

6095 H.B. Taylor Co
4830 S Christiana Ave
Chicago, IL 60632-3092   773-254-4805
    Fax: 773-254-4563 www.hbtaylor.com
Manufacturer and exporter of flavorings, colors and food essentials; FDA approved; natural, artificial, vanilla, chocolate, fruit, citrus and nut; dairy products, butter, cheese and cheese flavors and cream; coffee creamers; powdersroasted sesame seed, dairy flavors, liquids, emulsions, spray dried; custom products
    General Manager: Saul Juskaitis
    R&D: Jon Sounders
    Quality Control: Eric Johnson
    Marketing Director: Woody Walmsley
    Sales Director: Peggy Drabek
    Customer Service Manager: Peggy Drabek
    Plant Manager: Ed Juskaitis
    Purchasing Manager: Mary Power
Estimated Sales:$ 5 - 10 Million
Number Employees: 10-19
Type of Packaging: Private Label, Bulk
Brands:
    Cocoa Replacers
    Dark Roast
    Golden Roast
    Hyskor
    Lipo Butter
    Liquimul Black
    Mahogany Black
    Sesa-Krunch
    Sesame Seed

6096 H.B. Trading
10 Taft Road
Totowa, NJ 07512-1006   973-812-1022
    Fax: 973-812-2191 nico@nideco.com
                www.nideco.com

Manufacturer and distributor of cookies and candies
Brands:
BRENT & SAM's
CAPE COD CRANBERRY C
COW-TOWN and RANCHER's

6097 H.C. Berger Brewery
1900 E Lincoln Avenue
Fort Collins, CO 80524-2750   970-493-9044
Fax: 970-493-4508   info@hcberger.com
www.hcberger.com
Brewer of beer, ale and lager
President: Peter Davidoff
Estimated Sales:$5-10 Million
Number Employees: 5-9
Type of Packaging: Consumer, Food Service

6098 H.C. Brill Company
1912 Montreal Rd
Tucker, GA 30084-5238   770-938-3823
Fax: 770-939-2934   800-241-8526
contactbrill@hcbrill.com   www.hcbrill.com
Processor and exporter of icings, fillings, frozen
cake/muffin batters, whipped toppings and cookie
dough
CEO: Bret Weaver
National Sales Manager: Keith Appling
Estimated Sales:$100-500 Million
Number Employees: 250-499
Parent Co: Carpro
Type of Packaging: Food Service

6099 (HQ)H.E. Butt Grocery Company
P.O.Box 839999
San Antonio, TX 78283-3999   210-938-8000
Fax: 210-938-8169   800-432-3113
customer.relations@heb.com   www.heb.com
Processor of ice cream, cottage cheese, milk, cook-
ies, chips and yogurt
President/Chief Operating Officer: James
Clingman
CEO/Chairman: Charles Butt
CEO: Charles C Butt
Director Public Affairs: Greg Flores
Plant Manager: John Elia
Purchasing Agent: Gary Sullivan
Estimated Sales:$20-50 Million
Number Employees: 10,000+
Type of Packaging: Consumer

6100 (HQ)H.J. Heinz Company
1 PPG Place
Suite 3100
Pittsburgh, PA 15222-5448   412-456-5700
Fax: 412-456-6128   800-872-2229
www.heinz.com
Manufacturer of beans, cheese pouches/condiments,
dry soup mixes, frozen appetizers, entrees, soups
and sauces, ketchup, pasta and pasta sauce, peanut
butter and jelly, pickles, relishes and vinegar. Also,
frozen foods and babyfood.
Chairman/President/CEO: William Johnson
EVP/CFO: Art Winkleback
EVP/General Counsel: Ted Bobby
Estimated Sales:$10 Billion
Number Employees: 32,500
Type of Packaging: Consumer, Food Service
Other Locations:
Heinz Factory
Atlanta GA
Heinz Factory
Cedar Rapids IA
Heinz Factory
Chatsworth CA
Heinz Factory
Dallas TX
Heinz Factory
Escalon CA
Heinz Factory
Fremont OH
Heinz Factory
Holland MI
Heinz Factory
Irvine CA
Heinz Factory
Jacksonville FL
Heinz Factory
King of Prussia PA
Heinz Factory
LeCentre MN
Heinz Factory
Mason OH
Heinz Factory
Muscatine IA
Brands:
BAGEL BITES

BOSTON MARKET
CHEF FRANCISCO
CLASSICO
DELIMEX
HEINZ
LEA & PERRINS
ORE-IDA
T.G.I. FRIDAYS
WEIGHT WATCHERS SMART ONES

6101 H.J. Heinz Company
P.O.Box 57
Pittsburgh, PA 15230-0057   412-237-5948
Fax: 412-237-5725 www.heinz.com
Manufacturer and exporter of ketchup, condiments,
sauces, frozen foods, beans and pasta. Heinz has
completed its acquisition of the HP Foods Group
which includes Lea & Perrins, HP sauces and a per-
petual license to market the Amoy Asiansauces
brands in Europe
Chairman/President/CEO: William Johnson
Senior Vice President/General Counsel: Theodore
Bobby
SVP Finance/Corporate Controller: Edward
McMenamin
Executive Vice President/CFO: Arthur
Winkleback
Executive Vice President: David Moran
SVP Business Development: Mitchell Ring
Global Marketing Officer: Andrew Towle
Number Employees: 1-4
Type of Packaging: Consumer, Food Service, Pri-
vate Label, Bulk
Brands:
HEINZ
ORE-IDA
WEIGHT WATCHERS

6102 (HQ)H.K. Canning
130 N Garden St
Ventura, CA 93001-2531   805-652-1392
hkcanning@earthlink.net
Processor, exporter and contract packager of canned
and dry beans, soup and mushrooms; also, kosher
approved
President: Henry Knaust
CFO: Richard Hanson
Vice-President: Carol Knaust
Estimated Sales:$4 Million
Number Employees: 40
Type of Packaging: Consumer, Food Service, Pri-
vate Label, Bulk
Brands:
Freshman
Henry's Kettle
Knaust Beans
Meridian Foods
Norteno
Sea Valley
Seaside

6103 H.P. Hood
233 Main St
Agawam, MA 01001-1851   413-786-7166
Fax: 413-786-5484 www.hphood.com
Processor of dairy products including milk, ice
cream, cottage cheese, sour cream, etc
Manager: Rick Kovavarik
VP Marketing: John Kaneb
CFO: Gary Kaneb
Vice President: Theresa Bresten
Sales Director: James Walsh
Operations Manager: Steve Pelkey
Estimated Sales:$100-500 Million
Number Employees: 250-499
Parent Co: H.P. Hood
Type of Packaging: Consumer
Brands:
Hood

6104 H.P. Hood
Six Kimball Lane
Lynnfield, ME 01940   617-887-3000
Fax: 207-773-2913   800-343-6592
hoodhomedelivery@hphood.com
www.hphood.com

Milk, calorie countdown, cottage cheese, cream,
eggnog, frozen novelties, ice cream, juice & drinks,
simply smart milk and sour cream
Chairman/President/CEO: John Kaneb
CFO: Gary Kaneb
EVP: Jeffrey Kaneb
SVP R&D/Engineering & Procurement: Mike
Suever
VP Marketing: Christopher Ross
EVP Sales: James Walsh
VP Public Relations: Lynne Bohan
SVP Operations: H Scott Blake
Estimated Sales:$2.2 Billion
Number Employees: 4500
Parent Co: H.P. Hood
Type of Packaging: Consumer
Brands:
AXELROD
BRIGHAM'S
CALORIE COUNTDOWN
CROWLEY
HELUVA GOOD
HOOD
KEMPS
LACTAID
MAGGIO
PENN MAID
ROSENBERGER'S
SIMPLY SMART

6105 H.P. Hood
219 Allen St
Barre, VT 05641-5433   802-476-6605
Fax: 802-476-7497   800-622-4468
www.hphood.com
Processor of milk
Manager: Jerry Booth
Vice President: H Scott Blake
VP Marketing: Barry Boehme
Regional Sales Manager: Joe Cafarelli
Distribution Manager: Doug Sikes
Plant Manager: Jerry Booth
Estimated Sales:$10-20 Million
Number Employees: 100-249
Parent Co: H.P. Hood
Type of Packaging: Consumer, Food Service, Pri-
vate Label
Brands:
Arizona Fresh Iced Tea
Coffee-mate
Hood Carb Countdown reduced carb da
Lactaid
Nesquik
Southern Comfort Eggnog
Stonyfield Farm Organic Milk

6106 H.P. Hood
P.O.Box 870
Vernon, NY 13476-0870   315-829-3004
Fax: 315-829-3108
Processor of milk, sour cream and cottage cheese
Chairman/President/CEO: John Kaneb
Operations: John Donley
Estimated Sales:$20-50 Million
Number Employees: 50-99
Parent Co: H.P. Hood
Type of Packaging: Consumer, Food Service, Pri-
vate Label

6107 (HQ)H.P. Hood
90 Everett Ave # 1
Chelsea, MA 02150-2389   617-884-0151
Fax: 617-887-8484   800-343-6592
www.hphood.com
Produces a variety of branded, private label, licensed
and franchise products including milk, culture foods,
citrus, extended shelf-life dairy, frozen desserts,
non-dairy and specialty drinks
Chairman/President/CEO: John Kaneb
Chief Financial Officer: Gary Kaneb
Vice President: Jeffery Kaneb
SVP R&D/Engineering/Procurement: Mike
Suever
Executive Vice President Sales: James Walsh
VP Public Relations/Government Affairs: Lynne
Bohan
Senior Vice President Operations: H Scott Blake
Estimated Sales:$100-500 Million
Number Employees: 50-99
Type of Packaging: Consumer, Food Service, Pri-
vate Label
Other Locations:
HP Hood
Agawab MA

HP Hood
Barre VT
HP Hood
Oneida NY
HP Hood
Portland ME
HP Hood
Suffield CT
HP Hood
Vernon NY
HP Hood
Winchester VA
Brands:
CARNATION
COFFEE-MATE
HENDRIE'S
HOOD
HORIZON
LACTAID
LAND O' LAKES
NESQUIK
ORGANIC COW
PEAK TREASURES
Shake-Ups
Simply Chocolate
Stix
Strassel's
Sunny Meadow
Ultimate Vanilla Bean

6108 H.R. Davis Candy
4713 Cleveland Avenue NW
Canton, OH 44709-1838   330-494-0155
Processor of confectionery products including caramels, butterscotch, coconut, chocolate and chocolate cherries, licorice, mints and seasonal items
Owner: Hugh Davis
Estimated Sales: $630,000
Number Employees: 15
Type of Packaging: Consumer
Brands:
Mrs. Davis' Homemade

6109 H.R. Nicholson Company
1332 Londontown Boulevard
102
Sykesville, MD 21784-6409   410-764-2323
Fax: 410-764-9125   800-638-3514
oakleaf@erols.com   www.hrnicholson.com
Processor, importer and exporter of fruit juice and tea concentrates, ready-to-serve juices and flavor bases
President: H Robert Nicholson
Secretary/Treasurer: Su Shaffer
VP Sales/Marketing: Bob Homewood
Number Employees: 35
Sq. footage: 38000
Type of Packaging: Consumer, Food Service
Brands:
Bombay Gold 100
Nicholson's Bestea
Nicholson's Bottlers
Nicholson's Chok-Nick

6110 H3O
PO Box 482
Beckley, WV 25802-0482   304-256-0436
Fax: 304-256-0520   888-436-9287
www.click-into.com/h30/contactus
Bottled water
President: Jamison Humphrey
Estimated Sales: Under $500,000
Number Employees: 1-4
Brands:
H3O

6111 HB Taylor Company
4830 S Christiana Ave
Chicago, IL 60632-3092   773-254-4805
Fax: 773-254-4563   sjukaitis@hbtaylor.com
www.hbtaylor.com
Manufacturing and exporter of flavorings, colors and food essentials, FDA approved, natural, artificial, vanilla, chocolate, fruit, citrus, and nut, dairy products, butter, cheese and cheese flavors and cream, coffee creamers, powdersroasted sesame seed, dairy flavors, liquids, emulsions, spray dried, custom products, custom blending/packaging
Owner: Saul Juskaitis
Sales Manager: Peggy Drabek
Plant Manager: Edward Juskaitis
Estimated Sales: $ 5 - 10 Million
Number Employees: 10-19
Type of Packaging: Bulk

6112 HBP Services
3114 Rockford Drive
Dallas, TX 75211-8922   214-337-3488
President: Gary Warthan
Estimated Sales: Under $500,000
Number Employees: 1-4

6113 HC Brill Company
1912 Montreal Rd
Tucker, GA 30084-5238   770-938-3823
Fax: 770-939-2934   800-241-8526
contactbrill@hcbrill.com   www.hcbrill.com
Ingredients and mixes; bulk supplier
President: Cefo Grteor
CEO: Bret Weaver
Estimated Sales: $5-10 Million
Number Employees: 50-99
Brands:
Brill's

6114 HEB Foods & Drugs
P.O.Box 839999
San Antonio, TX 78283-3999   210-938-8000
Fax: 210-938-8169   www.heb.com
General grocery
President: Fully Clingman
CEO: Charles Butt
CEO: Charles C Butt
Estimated Sales: K
Number Employees: 10,000+

6115 HFI Foods
17515 Northeast 6th Court
Redmond, WA 98074   425-883-1320
Fax: 425-861-8341
Processor of fresh and frozen surimi products, frozen entrees, frozen mousse desserts and pasta salads; exporter of frozen mousse desserts
President: Byron Kuroishi
CFO: Yoshinari Kuroishi
Vice President: Christina Gaimaytan
Quality Control: Jenel Lee
Marketing Director: Gwen McLellan
Sales Director: Nori Ishiwari
Public Relations: Cindy Fuller-Stephens
Production Manager: Kazue Yamada
Plant Manager: Kazuo Yamada
Purchasing Manager: Cindy Fuller-Stephens
Estimated Sales: $12 Million
Number Employees: 50-99
Sq. footage: 40000
Parent Co: JMS
Type of Packaging: Consumer
Brands:
Fitness First
Kibun
King Core
King Cove
Seastix

6116 HMC Marketing Group
13138 S Bethel Ave
Kingsburg, CA 93631-9216   559-897-1009
Fax: 559-897-1610   hmcinfo@hmcmarketing.com
www.hmcmarketing.com
Peaches, nectarines, persimmons, pomegranates, apricots, plums, grapes, satsumes, navels, valencias and vegetables
Owner: Harold Mc Clarty
Estimated Sales: $ 20 - 50 Million
Number Employees: 10-19

6117 HP Hood
6 Kimball Lane
Lynnfield, MA 01940   617-887-3000
Fax: 617-887-8484   800-343-6592
n_carroll@hphood.com   www.hphood.com
Milk, calorie countdown, cottage cheese, cream, eggnog, frozen novelties, ice cream, juice & drinks, simply smart milk, and sour cream
Chairman/President/CEO: John Kaneb
CFO: Gary Kaneb
EVP: Jeffrey Kaneb
SVP Research & Development Engineering: Mike Suever
VP Quality Systems/Regulatory Affairs: Margaret Poole
VP Marketing: Christopher Ross
EVP Sales: James Walsh
VP Public Relations/Government Affairs: Lynne Bohan
SVP Operations: H Scott Blake
Plant Manager: Bruce Diltz

Estimated Sales: $2.2 Billion
Number Employees: 4,500
Type of Packaging: Consumer, Food Service, Private Label
Brands:
Hood

6118 HP Schmid
231 Sansome St # 300
San Francisco, CA 94104-2322   415-765-5925
Fax: 415-765-5922   organic@hpschmid.com
www.hpschmid.com
Specializing in edible seeds: sesame, sunflower, poppy and caraway; dry peas, beans and lentils; dried fruits, nuts and organic products - dehydrated garlic and onions
President/International Sales: Hans Schmid
Sales North America: Analucia Melendez
Sales Organics: Marinda Thomas
Customer Service: Whitney Weaver
Estimated Sales: $20-50 Million
Number Employees: 5-9

6119 HVJ International
2609 N Spring Dr
Spring, TX 77373   281-288-8560
Fax: 281-288-9000   877-730-3663
info@hvj-international.com
Olives, pickled vegetables, sauces, salsas, condiments, pasta sauces, dressings, olive oil, hot sauces
President/CEO: Hank Van Joslin
Operations Manager: Jake Jalufka
Estimated Sales: $5-10 Million
Number Employees: 5-9
Number of Brands: 8
Number of Products: 240
Type of Packaging: Consumer, Food Service, Bulk
Brands:
0007
Cartagena
Fiorevante
HVJ
Joslin
Occasions
Peppers of the World
Rainforest
Spicy Jones

6120 HVR Company
1221 Broadway
Oakland, CA 94612-1837   510-271-7000
800-537-2823
Processor of Hidden Valley Ranch products
VP: George C Roeth
VP Marketing: George Roeth
Manager: John White
Estimated Sales: $100-500 Million
Number Employees: 100-249
Parent Co: Clorox Company

6121 Haas Baking Company
9769 Reavis Park Dr
St Louis, MO 63123-5315   314-631-6100
Fax: 314-631-3464   800-325-3171
joseph@haasbaking.com   www.haasbaking.com
Processor of frozen doughnuts, fat free pastry, danish, coffee cake
President: Joseph Haas
Estimated Sales: $ 20 - 50 Million
Number Employees: 100-249
Type of Packaging: Consumer, Food Service

6122 Haas Coffee Group
1110 Brickell Avenue
Suite 400
Miami, FL 33131   305-371-7473
Fax: 305-418-7384   info@haasgroup.com
www.haasgroup.com
Leading independent grower, processor, marketer and merchant of coffee - ground, instant and coffee extract. Also a leading independent processor and marketer of soft commodities and frozen foods which include meats (beef and pork)and poultry.
Contact: Michael Dibbs
Estimated Sales: $10-100 Million
Number Employees: 5-9

6123 Habby Habanero's Food Products
6475 Ferber Road
Jacksonville, FL 32277-1513   904-333-9758
mail@habbys.net
http://www.habbys.net/

Fire and brimstone barbecue sauces
Contact: Malcolm Quincy
Contact: Jerry Quincy

6124 Habersham Winery
P.O.Box 808
Helen, GA 30545-0808   706-878-9463
Fax: 706-878-8466 info@habershamwinery.com
www.habershamwinery.com
Collection of wines such as: Creekstone Wines,
Habersham Estate Wines and Southern Harvest
Wines
Manager: Steve Gibson
Winemaker: Andrew Beatty
Operations Manager: Russell Jones
General Manager: Steve Gibson
Vineyard Manager: Terri Haney
Estimated Sales: $2.5-5 Million
Number Employees: 10-19
Type of Packaging: Private Label
Brands:
Creekstone
Habersham Estates
Southern Harvest

6125 Haby's Alsatian Bakery
207 Us Highway 90 W
Castroville, TX 78009   830-931-2118
Fax: 830-931-2194
Processor of cookies, pies, cakes, apple fritters, stru-
dels, stollens, bread and coffeecakes.
President: Sammy Tschirhart
VP/Secretary/Treasurer: Yvonne Tschirhart
Estimated Sales: $500,000-$1 Million
Number Employees: 10-19
Sq. footage: 5400
Type of Packaging: Consumer

6126 Hach Company
5600 Lindbergh Drive
P.O. Box 389
Loveland, CO 80539   970-669-3050
800-227-4224
info@hach.com www.hach.com
manufacturer of oxygen sensors and water analysis
products for the beverage and water bottling industries. Also manufactures, designs, and distributes
test kits for testing the quality of water in food
industry applications.

6127 Hacienda De Paco
9564 Sidney Hayes Road
Orlando, FL 32824-8121   407-859-5417
Fax: 407-850-9317
Processor of Mexican foods including tortillas, ta-
males and burritos
President: Richard Dubler
Estimated Sales: $20-50 Million
Number Employees: 20-49
Type of Packaging: Food Service
Brands:
Hacienda

6128 Hadley Date Gardens
83555 Airport Blvd
Thermal, CA 92274-9341   760-399-5191
Fax: 760-399-1311 sdougherty@hadleys.com
www.hadleys.com
Processor and exporter of whole, pitted and diced
dates and date products
President: John Keck
CEO: Albert Keck
CFO: Melinda Dougherty
Marketing Director: Sean Dougherty, Sr.
Estimated Sales: $25 Million
Number Employees: 50-99
Sq. footage: 12000
Parent Co: Haldeys
Type of Packaging: Consumer, Food Service, Pri-
vate Label, Bulk
Brands:
Hadley Date Gardens

6129 Hafner
4609 Lewis Rd
Stone Mountain, GA 30083-1003   678-406-0101
Fax: 678-406-9222   888-725-4605
pieshells@hafner.com www.hafner.com
Pastry shells, cream puffs, puff pastries, cake kits,
savory shells and 17 Kosher desserts
President: Xavier M De Goursac
Estimated Sales: $5-10 Million
Number Employees: 5-9

6130 Hafner Vineyard
P.O.Box 1038
Healdsburg, CA 95448-1038   707-433-4606
Fax: 707-433-1240 info@hafnervineyard.com
www.hafnervineyard.com
Estate wines
Managing Partner: Parke Hafner
Managing Partner: Scott Hafner
Public Relations: Laurie Williams
Winemaker: Sarah Hafner
Estimated Sales: $ 5 - 10 Million
Number Employees: 10-19
Type of Packaging: Private Label
Brands:
Hafner

6131 Hagelin & Company
200 Meister Ave
Branchburg, NJ 08876-6033   908-707-4401
Fax: 908-707-4408   800-229-2112
flavors@hagelin.com www.hagelin.com
Processor and exporter of flavors, extracts, vanilla
and beverage bases including health drink contain-
ing antioxidants
President: Craig Hagelin
VP Operations: Barry Fielding
Estimated Sales: $20-50 Million
Number Employees: 20-49
Sq. footage: 26000
Brands:
Isotonic
Rebound

6132 Hagensborg Foods
1576 Rand Avenue
Vancouver, BC V6P 3G2
Canada   604-266-9092
Fax: 604-266-9919   877-554-7763
sales@hagensborg.com www.hagensborg.com
Exporter and importer of canned pate, chocolate and
confectionery items, olive oils, sherry vinegar; also,
exporter of smoked salmon fillets
President: Shelley Miller
Sales/Marketing Assistant: Rochelle Lockhart
Public/Media Relations: Chantelle Chouinard
Sales Manager: Karen Girardeau
Estimated Sales: $10-20 Million
Number Employees: 10-19
Sq. footage: 15000
Type of Packaging: Consumer, Food Service, Pri-
vate Label
Brands:
HAGENSBORG MELTAWAYS TRUFFLES
KISS ME FROG TRUFFLES
TRUFFLES TO GO

6133 Hagerty Foods
9847 Enterprise Street
Suite J
Orange, CA 92867   714-628-1230
Processor and contract packager of condiments, rel-
ishes, salad dressings, pasta sauces, salsas, BBQ
sauce and hot sauces
President: Francisco Esquivel
Estimated Sales: $220,000
Number Employees: 3
Sq. footage: 10000
Type of Packaging: Consumer, Food Service, Pri-
vate Label
Brands:
Hagerty Foods
La Napa
Winemaker's Choice

6134 Hahn & Company
601 Montgomery St # 840
San Francisco, CA 94111-2611   415-394-6512
Fax: 415-861-7400 www.hahncap.com
Owner: Elaine Hahn
Estimated Sales: $5-10 Million
Number Employees: 5-9

6135 Hahn Brothers
P.O.Box 395
Westminster, MD 21158-0395   410-848-4200
Fax: 410-848-1247   800-227-7675
wholesale@hahnsofwestminster.com
www.hahnsofwestminster.com
Processor of varieties of pork products and cooked
beef and corn beef
Owner: Ed Ladzinski
Vice President/Production Manager: Barbara
Brown

Sq. footage: 23000
Type of Packaging: Consumer, Food Service, Private Label

6136 Hahn Estates and Smith &Hook
P.O.Box C
Soledad, CA 93960-0167   831-678-4555
Fax: 831-678-0557
tastingroom@hahnestates.com
www.hahnestates.com
Estate Wines
Owner: William Leigon
President: William Leigon
Marketing/Public Relations: Sandy Martini-Coero

Winemaker: Adam LaZarre
Estimated Sales: $7.5 Million
Number Employees: 50-99
Sq. footage: 30
Type of Packaging: Private Label
Brands:
Smith & Hook Winery

6137 Hahn's Old Fashioned Cake Company
75 Allen Blvd
Farmingdale, NY 11735-5614   631-249-3456
Fax: 631-249-3492 www.crumbcake.net
Processor of coffee cake
Co-Owner: Andrew Hahn
Co-Owner: Regina Hahn
Chief Operating Officer: Andrew Hahn
Estimated Sales: $2.5-5 Million
Number Employees: 20-49
Type of Packaging: Consumer, Food Service

6138 Haight-Brown Vineyard
29 Chestnut Hill Rd
Litchfield, CT 06759-4101   860-567-4045
Fax: 860-567-1766   800-577-9463
haightvineyard@aol.com
www.haightvineyards.com
Wines: Chardonnay, Merlot, Riesling, Covertside
White, Barely Blush, Picnic Red, and an old New
England tradition Honey Nut Apple.
Manager: Sal Cimino
Co-Partner: Amy Brown
Cellar Master: Salvatore Cimino
Estimated Sales: $2.5-5 Million
Number Employees: 5-9
Brands:
Haight Vineyard Wines

6139 Haile Resources
2650 Freewood Dr
Dallas, TX 75220-2511   214-357-1471
Fax: 214-357-9381 800-357-1471
www.haileresources.com
Food and beverage ingredients
President: Howard Haile
Vice President: Debbie Haile
V.P. of Marketing: Cindy Soliday
Sales Manager: Pamela Klingele
Estimated Sales: $20 Million
Number Employees: 5-9
Type of Packaging: Private Label

6140 Hain Celestial Canada
1638 Derwent Way
Delta, BC V3M 6R9
Canada   604-525-1345
Fax: 604-525-2555 866-983-7834
yvc@yvesveggie.com www.yvesveggie.com
Processor of vegetarian foods including tofu hot
dogs, garden patties and veggie dogs
Chief Executive Officer: Philippe Woitrin
Managing Director: David Arrow
Director Marketing: Janice Harada
General Manager: Beena Goldenberg
Number Employees: 300
Number of Brands: 1
Number of Products: 30
Parent Co: Hain Celestial Group
Type of Packaging: Consumer, Food Service, Pri-
vate Label, Bulk
Brands:
CASBAH
EARTHS BEST
GARDEN OF EATEN
GOOD SLICE
HAIN
HEALTH VALLEY
PRIMA VEGGIE
TERRA

6141 (HQ)Hain Celestial Group
58 S Service Rd # 250
Melville, NY 11747-2338   631-730-2200
          Fax: 631-730-2550 800-434-4246
          www.hain-celestial.com
Manufacturer and exporter of natural and specialty soy beverages, snacks, canned goods, baked products and cereals. The company signed an agreement and plan of merger with Spectrum Organics Products in California
          Chairman/President/CEO: Irwin Simon
          EVP/CFO/Treasurer/Secretary: Ira Lamel
          EVP/President Grocery & Snacks: John Carroll
          Chief Marketing Officer Grocery & Snacks:
          Maureen Putman
          VP Operations Grocery & Snacks: James Meiers
Estimated Sales: C
Number Employees: 1,000-4,999
Brands:
          Agrain & Agrain
          Alba Foods
          Apple Corns
          Arrowhead Crunch
          Arrowhead Mills
          Bear Mush
          Bits'o Barley
          Boston Popcorn
          Breadshop
          Hains Celestial
          Natural Gourmet
          Nature O's
          Nature Puffs
          QBR
          Rice & Shine
          Seitan Quick Mix
          Simpler Life
          Terra Chips

6142 Haines City Citrus Growers Association
P.O.Box 337
Haines City, FL 33845-0337   863-422-4924
          Fax: 863-421-4754 800-422-4245
          www.hilltopcitrus.com
Grower of citrus fruits including oranges, grapefruits, tangerines, etc
          Finance Executive: Rod Hamric
          Director Field Operations: Charles Counter
          Packing House Manager: John Soles
Estimated Sales: $10-20 Million
Number Employees: 250-499
Parent Co: Citrus World

6143 Hains Celestial Group
58 S Service Rd # 250
Melville, NY 11747-2338   631-730-2200
          Fax: 631-730-2550 877-612-4246
          info@acirca.com www.hain-celestial.com
Processor of certified organic foods and beverages including soups, salsas, sauces and juices
          President/CEO: Irwin Simon
          General Manager: Maurene Putman
          CFO: William Urich
          VP, Sales: Terence Dalton
          Consultant: William Russell
Estimated Sales: C
Number Employees: 1,000-4,999
Brands:
          Fruitti Di Bosco
          Millina's Finest
          Moutain Sun
          Walnut Acres

6144 Hair Fitness
5318 E Second Street
345
Long Beach, CA 90803-5324   562-438-4247
          888-348-4247
          hairmail@healthandbodyfitness.com
          www.healthandbodyfitness.com
Designed not only for body fitness but hair fitness benefits - supplements plus hair conditioners -
          Founder/President: Jeannie Maxon
Estimated Sales: $300,000-500,000
Number Employees: 1-4

6145 Hair of the Dog BrewingCompany
4509 SE 23rd Ave
Portland, OR 97202-4771   503-232-6585
          Fax: 503-235-8743 www.hairofthedog.com
German style beer
          President/Founder: Alan Sprints
          Brewer: Pat Savage

Estimated Sales: $500,000-$1 Million
Number Employees: 1-4

6146 Halal Transactions
P.O.Box 4546
Omaha, NE 68104-0546   402-572-6120
          Fax: 402-572-4020 halal2eat@hotmail.com
Processing and certification of Halal meat-beef, lamb, goat and poultry. Brokerage of Halal meats.
          President: Ahmad Absy
          CEO: Dr. Ahmad Al-Absy
Estimated Sales: $ .5 - 1 Million
Number Employees: 10-19
Brands:
          All Halal

6147 Halben Food Manufacturing Company
8543 Page Ave
Overland, MO 63114-6096   314-426-4100
          Fax: 314-426-0391 800-888-4855
Processor of mixes including beverage, sauce, gravy, dressing and dessert; also, sauces, mayonnaise and dressings
          President: Bob Baker
          Sales Director: Joel Allen
Estimated Sales: $20-50 Million
Number Employees: 100-249
Sq. footage: 100000
Parent Co: Allen Foods
Type of Packaging: Food Service

6148 Haldin International
3 Reuten Dr
Closter, NJ 07624-2115   201-784-0044
          Fax: 201-784-2180 haldinus@haldin-natural.com
          www.haldin-natural.com
Began as importer of Indonesian vanilla beans and now has a wide range of products including essential oil to meet the flavor and fragrance industry. Items such as: betel peper liquid extract, citronella oil, and eurycoma longifaliapowder extract
          Manager: Khelly Boon
          Founder/Chief Executive Officer: Ali Haliman
Estimated Sales: $ 5 - 10 Million
Number Employees: 1-4
Sq. footage: 12000
Parent Co: Pt. Haldin Pacific Semesta
Type of Packaging: Bulk
Other Locations:
          Haldin International
          Cikarang, Bekasi

6149 Hale & Hearty Soups/Chelsea Markets
75 9th Ave
New York, NY 10011-7006   212-255-2400
          Fax: 212-929-9588 888-727-7887
          Info@ChelseaMarketBaskets.com
          www.haleandhearty.com
All fresh and homemade ingredients for our chowders, chicken vegetable with noodles soup and delicious roast beef sandwiches with shaved parmesan.
          President: Simon Jacobs
          Chief Executive Officer: Simon Jacobs
          Co-Owner: Jonathan Schnipper
Estimated Sales: $5-10 Million
Number Employees: 5-9

6150 Hale Indian River Groves
P.O.Box 700217
Wabasso, FL 32970-0217   772-581-9915
          Fax: 772-226-3503 800-562-4502
          customerservice@halegroves.com
          http://www.halegroves.com/
Processor of oranges, grapefruit, tangerines and fruit juice; manufacturer of fruit gift baskets
          President: Stephen Hale III
          VP: Fred Kuester
Estimated Sales: $20-50 Million
Number Employees: 50-99
Type of Packaging: Consumer, Bulk

6151 Hale's Ales
4301 Leary Way NW
Seattle, WA 98107-4538   206-706-1544
          Fax: 360-706-1572 pub@halesbrewery.com
          www.halesales.com

Beers such as: Hales cream, Wee Heavy Winter Ale, Irish style Nut Brown ale, O'Brien Harvest Ale, Pale American, Hales Dublin Style Stout and German Style Kolsch Ale
          President/Founder: Michael Hale
          Marketing Manager: Barbara Dollarhide
          Chief Operating Officer: David Metzger
          General Manager: Pat Foote
Estimated Sales: $20-50 Million
Number Employees: 50-99
Brands:
          Hale's Celebration Porter
          Hale's Pale American Ale
          Hale's Special Bitter
          Moss Bay Extra Ale
          Moss Bay Stout

6152 Half Moon Bay Trading Company
210 Mayport Rd
Atlantic Beach, FL 32233-3332   904-246-9493
          Fax: 904-246-9442 888-447-2823
          info@halfmoonbaytrading.com
          www.halfmoonbaytrading.com
Purveyors of fine imported condiments including hot pepper sauces, mixers, salsas and glaze toppings.
          President: Robin Shephard
          CFO: Jeff Hite
          VP: Tom Nuijens
          Marketing: Tom Nuijens
          Sales: Tom Nuijens
          Public Relations: Tina Kicklighter
          Operations Manager: Regina Story
Estimated Sales: Under $1 Million
Number Employees: 5-9
Number of Brands: 5
Number of Products: 21
Sq. footage: 10000
Type of Packaging: Consumer, Food Service, Private Label
Brands:
          BEESTING
          CARIBBEAN CONDIMENTS
          IGUANA
          SWEETSTING
          TAMARINDO BAY

6153 Half Moon Fruit & Produce Company
P.O.Box 428
Yolo, CA 95697-0428   530-662-1727
          Fax: 530-662-6072
Grower and packer of prunes, plums, melon
          President: B E Giovannetti
          Operations Manager: Richard Monford
Estimated Sales: $10-20 Million
Number Employees: 5-9
Brands:
          Buster
          Melo-Glow
          Morning Cheer
          Valley King

6154 Haliburton International Corporation
10891 Business Dr
Fontana, CA 92337-8235   909-428-8507
          Fax: 909-428-8521 877-980-4295
          info@haliburton.net www.haliburton.net
Processor and importer of fire roasted vegetables including peppers, tomatoes, tomatillos, onions, garlic, shallots, squash, zucchini; also, chili peppers and anchovy products
          Owner: Ian Schenkel
          Contact: Desiree Mettille-Schenkel
          Technical Contact: Joseph Antonio
Estimated Sales: $10-20 Million
Number Employees: 50-99
Type of Packaging: Food Service, Bulk

6155 Halifax Group
3264 McCall Dr
Doraville, GA 30340-3306   770-452-8828
          Fax: 770-457-4546 info@oakhillfarms.com
          www.oakhillfarms.com
Gourmet sauces, dressings, salsa, condiments and beverages
Estimated Sales: $ 5 - 10 Million
Number Employees: 10-19
Brands:
          Hill Farms
          Redneck Gourmet
          Scorned Woman

Southern Sensations
Wild Man

6156 Hall Brothers Meats
27040 Cook Rd
Cleveland, OH 44138-1111 440-235-3262
Fax: 440-235-6696 www.hallsqualitymeats.com
Processor of fresh and frozen beef, pork, poultry,
lamb and seafood
President: Richard Hall
Estimated Sales: $ 10 - 20 Million
Number Employees: 5-9
Type of Packaging: Consumer, Food Service, Bulk

6157 Hall Grain Company
101 W Railroad Ave
Akron, CO 80720-1419 970-345-2206
Fax: 970-345-6680
Processor of grains such as: millet, milo, safflower,
sunflower and wheat
Manager: Tim Mayes
Controller: Kevin Hall
VP: Pat Hall
Estimated Sales: $10-20 Million
Number Employees: 50-99

6158 Halladays Harvest Barn
6 Webb Ter
Bellows Falls, VT 05101-3157 802-463-3471
Fax: 802-463-2580 halladay@sover.net
www.halladays.com
Seasonings, dips, cheesecake mixes, dry soup mixes,
garlic oil, and vinegars - products are all natural -
contain no msg and many contain no salt -
Co-Owner: Rich Govotski
Co-Owner: Kathleen Govotski
Estimated Sales: $ 1 - 3 Million
Number Employees: 5-9

6159 Hallcrest Vineyards
379 Felton Empire Rd
Felton, CA 95018-9167 831-335-4441
Fax: 831-335-4450 info@hallcrestvineyards.com
www.hallcrestvineyards.com
Wines: Perez Estates Chardonnay, Andersen Cabernet/Merlot, Ciardella Pinot Noir, Belle Farms Pinot
Noir
Co-Owner/President: John Schumacher
Lab Director: Paul Bouswa
Sales Manager: Will Warto
Co-Owner/Public Relations: Lorraine
Schumacher
Cellar Master: Giovanni Jovel
Estimated Sales: $2.5-5 Million
Number Employees: 10-19
Type of Packaging: Private Label
Brands:
Hallcrest Vineyards
The Organic Wine Work
Vinatopia

6160 Hallman International
2935 Saint Xavier Street
Louisville, KY 40212-1936 502-778-0459
Fax: 502-778-0435
President: James Smith
CFO: Jay Broder
Sales Director: David Wallace
Plant Manager: Clarence Philpott
Estimated Sales: $10-20 Million
Number Employees: 20-49
Sq. footage: 20
Type of Packaging: Private Label

6161 Hallmark Fisheries
P.O.Box 5390
Charleston, OR 97420-0606 541-888-3253
Fax: 541-888-6814 info@hallmarkfisheries.com
www.hallmarkfisheries.com
Processor of fresh, frozen and canned seafood including crab meat, shrimp, tuna and boxed fillets
Inventory Specialist: Blair Samuelson
QC/HACCP Supervisor: Crystal Adams
Sales Manager: Judi Houston
General Manager: Jack Emmons
Production/Plant Manager: Scott Adams
Plant Manager: Scott Adams
Estimated Sales: $20-50 Million
Number Employees: 100-249
Parent Co: California Shellfish
Type of Packaging: Consumer, Food Service, Private Label, Bulk
Brands:
Hallmark

Peacock
Point St. George

6162 Halsted Packing House
445 N Halsted Street
Chicago, IL 60622-6518 312-421-5147
Fax: 312-421-4511
Processor of lamb, pork and goat meat
Co-Owner: William Davos
Co-Owner: Ann Davos
Estimated Sales: Less than $500,000
Number Employees: 1-4
Sq. footage: 6400
Type of Packaging: Consumer, Food Service

6163 Halton Flour Milling
45 Church Street West
Acton, ON L7J 1K1
Canada 519-853-2850
Fax: 519-853-0446 800-608-7694
doverhalton@dovergrp.com
Processor of wheat flour; wholesaler/distributor of
yeast, salt, sugar, mixes, fillings, etc
President/Co-Owner: Brian Dolotowicz
Co-Owner: Debbie Dolotowicz
Director Operations: Bruce McIntyre
Number Employees: 20-49
Parent Co: Dover Flour Mills
Type of Packaging: Food Service, Private Label,
Bulk

6164 Ham I Am
17618 Davenport Rd # 1
Dallas, TX 75252-5964 972-447-0440
Fax: 972-447-0460 800-742-6426
www.hamiam.com
Pork products, quail, duck, turkey, Texas BBQ, desserts, breakfast ideas, homemade tamales, hors
d'oeuvres, and party foods
President: Sharon Meehan
Estimated Sales: Under $500,000
Number Employees: 1-4
Type of Packaging: Private Label, Bulk

6165 Hama Hama Oyster®Company
35846 N Us Highway 101
Lilliwaup, WA 98555 360-877-5811
Fax: 360-877-6942 888-877-5844
Seafood: Oysters, Manila clams, native Little Neck
Clams and Geoducks
Owner: David Robins
Sales, Wholesale: Adam James
Estimated Sales: $500,000-$1 Million
Number Employees: 1-4
Type of Packaging: Private Label, Bulk

6166 Hamburg Industries
218 Pine St
Hamburg, PA 19526-1815 610-562-3031
Fax: 610-562-0209 800-321-6256
sales@hamburgindustries.com
www.hamburgindustries.com
Manufacturer and importer of brooms, brushes,
mops and handles
President/CEO/Marketing: Richard Stiller
CFO: Donna Ladd
VP: William Bast
Quality Control: Donald Banres
Sales: John Stevens
Operations: Donald Barnes
Plant Manager: Patty Frankenfield
Number Employees: 28
Sq. footage: 65000
Type of Packaging: Consumer, Private Label, Bulk

6167 Hamilos Brothers Inspected Meats
1117 Greenwood St
Madison, IL 62060-1278 618-451-7877
Fax: 618-876-3732
Processor of beef, pork, poultry and fresh and frozen
fish; wholesaler/distributor of canned goods, paper
products and pre-packaged meat
Owner: Mike Skinner
Owner: Jeff Skinner
Estimated Sales: $500,000-$1 Million
Number Employees: 5-9
Type of Packaging: Consumer

6168 Hamilton Provision Company
623 Walnut Street
Hamilton, OH 45012-0351 513-867-9500
Fax: 513-867-1522 800-328-9979

Processor of meats including beef patties, lamb,
pork and veal
President: Ben Douglas
Estimated Sales: $10-20 Million
Number Employees: 20-49
Type of Packaging: Food Service, Private Label,
Bulk

**6169 Hamilton Quality Convenience
Foods**
29411 Beverly Road
Romulus, MI 48174-4259 734-946-1800
Fax: 734-728-1909 hamiltonfoods@aol.com
www.hamiltonfoods.com
Processor of folded pizza, philly steaks, ham/cheese
sandwiches, pot pies and beef and chicken pastries
President: Richard Calleja
Estimated Sales: $20-50 Million
Number Employees: 20-49
Type of Packaging: Consumer, Food Service, Private Label

6170 Hamm's Custom Meats
213 N Tennessee St
McKinney, TX 75069-3922 972-542-3359
http://www.hammsmeats.com/
Honey Glazed Spiral-Cut Ham, Choice USDA
Steaks cut to order, Bacon, Chili, Cheese, Smoked
Brisket and Ribs, Honey Glazed Smoked Ribs.
Owner: Ken Uselton
Estimated Sales: $ .5 - 1 million
Number Employees: 1-4
Type of Packaging: Consumer, Food Service, Bulk

6171 Hammer Corporation
3765 Atlanta Industrial Dr NW
Atlanta, GA 30331-1031 404-696-4178
Fax: 404-696-4003 800-423-3138
www.tootarts.com
Processor and exporter of fat and calorie-free coffee,
tea, cappuccino, soft drink and water flavors
President: Armand Hammer
VP Sales: Al Silva
Estimated Sales: $20-50 Million
Number Employees: 50-99
Brands:
TPP TARTS KIDS KANDY

6172 Hammond Pretzel Bakery
716 S West End Ave
Lancaster, PA 17603-5050 717-392-7532
Fax: 717-392-8085 info@hammondpretzels.com
www.hammondpretzels.com
Processor of handmade pretzels and chocolate pretzels
President: Thomas Nicklaus
General Manager: Brian Nicklaus
Estimated Sales: $ 10 - 20 Million
Number Employees: 10-19
Type of Packaging: Consumer
Brands:
Hammond's

6173 Hammond's Candies
5735 Washington St
Denver, CO 80216-1321 303-333-5588
Fax: 303-333-5622 888-226-3999
www.hammondscandies.com
Chocolates and traditional hard candy and confections
Owner: Bob List
Manager: Eric Lane
Master Candymaker: Ralph Nafziger
Estimated Sales: $10-20 Million
Number Employees: 50-99

6174 Hammons Meat Sales
P.O.Box 40638
Bakersfield, CA 93384-0638 661-831-9541
Fax: 661-831-2656
Processor of fresh beef, lamb, pork and seafood -
some items are frozen
Owner/President: Craig Hammons
Estimated Sales: $ 50 - 100 Million
Number Employees: 20-49

6175 Hammons Products Company
P.O.Box 140
Stockton, MO 65785-0140 417-276-5121
Fax: 417-276-5187 888-429-6887
bwsalesdave@u-n-i.net www.black-walnuts.com
Processor and exporter of shelled black walnuts
President: Brian Hammons
VP Sales: David Steinmuller

Estimated Sales:$10-20 Million
Number Employees: 100-249
Sq. footage: 229000
Type of Packaging: Consumer, Food Service, Bulk
Brands:
   Hammons

6176   Hamner Provision Company
PO Box 831446
San Antonio, TX 78283-1446   210-736-3117
                                    Fax: 210-736-9118
Processor of fresh and frozen beef
   Owner/President: Edward Gomez
Estimated Sales:$10-20 Million
Number Employees: 20-49
Type of Packaging: Consumer, Food Service

6177   Hampton Associates & Sons
12728 Dogwood Hills Lane
Fairfax, VA 22033-3244   703-968-5847
                                   jamcola@hotmail.com
   CEO/Chairman: Hampton Brown III
*Estimated Sales:*Under $500,000
Number Employees: 1-4
Type of Packaging: Consumer, Food Service
Brands:
   Bahama Berry
   Bahama Black Cherry
   Bahama Blue Creme
   Bahama Grape
   Bahama Kiwi Strawberry
   Bahama Orange Mango
   Bahama Pink Lemonade
   Bahama Punch
   Bahama Strawberry
   Deep Purple
   Diet Clear Jazz
   Falcon Orange Soda
   Jazz Cola
   Rustler Root Beer

6178   Hampton Chutney Company
P.O.Box 273
Amagansett, NY 11930-0273   631-267-3131
Fax: 631-267-6169   hamptonchutney@verizon.net
                     www.hamptonchutney.com
Fresh chutneys including mango chutney, cilantro
chutney, tomato chutney, curry chutney, pumpkin
chutney and peanut chutney, continental, seafood
and southIndian foods
   Owner: Gary Mac Gurn
   Co-Owner: Isabel MacGurn
   Chef: Patty Gentry
*Estimated Sales:*Less than $500,000
Number Employees: 5-9

6179   Hampton Farms
PO Box 149
Severn, NC 27877-0149
          Fax: 757-654-0994   800-313-2748
          companystore@hamptonfarms.com
                     www.hamptonfarms.com
Premier roaster and marketer of in-shell peanuts and
peanut products
   VP Sales/Marketing: Thomas Nolan
   Operations: Dan Hutton
Estimated Sales:$25 Million
Number Employees: 100-249
Parent Co: Meherrin Chemical
Type of Packaging: Private Label, Bulk
Brands:
   Hamptom Farms

6180   Hampton House
9696 199a Street
Langley, BC V2Y 3H8
Canada   604-888-8662
          Fax: 604-888-0074   800-665-4355
Processor and exporter of poultry and meat products
including chicken strips, nuggets, burgers and fla-
vored boneless and skinless breasts; also, barbecued
baby back ribs, vegetarian patties and falafel
   President: Ken Thorpe
   Director Sales/Marketing: Hari Aroon
   General Manager: Don Davidson
Number Employees: 100-249
Sq. footage: 55000
Parent Co: J.D. Sweid
Type of Packaging: Consumer, Food Service, Pri-
vate Label, Bulk
Brands:
   Hampton House
   Sensations

6181   Hanan Products Company
196 Miller Pl
Hicksville, NY 11801-1826   516-938-1000
   Fax: 516-938-1925   info@hananproducts.com
                     www.hananproducts.com
Processor and exporter of kosher non-dairy creamer,
sour dressings, whipped toppings, icings, fillings,
and specialty desserts
   President: Frank Hanan
Estimated Sales:$2.5-5 Million
Number Employees: 20-49
Type of Packaging: Consumer, Food Service

**6182   Hancock Lobster
GourmetCompany**
104 Taylor Road
Cundys Harbor, ME 04079   207-725-1855
          Fax: 207-725-1856   800-552-0142
          service@hancockgourmetlobster.com
                     www.hancockgourmetlobster.com
frozen lobster, shrimp and crab dishes

6183   Hancock Peanut Company
PO Box 100
Courtland, VA 23837-0100   757-653-9351
                                   Fax: 757-653-2147
Processor and exporter of peanuts - cooked and raw
-
   President: J Matthew Pope
   VP Sales: Robert Pope
   Contact: Melissa Rose
Number Employees: 50-99
Type of Packaging: Consumer, Food Service

6184   Hancock's Old Fashioned
3484 Nc Highway 22 N
Franklinville, NC 27248-8254   336-824-2145
   Fax: 336-824-2312   mschields@asheboro.com
Processor of country ham and dry cure pork bellies
   President: Joseph Leuter
   Contact: Ray Jester
   Plant Manager: Lloyd Newman
Estimated Sales:$300,000-500,000
Number Employees: 65
Parent Co: Gwaltney of Smithfield

6185   Handley Cellars
3151 Highway 128
Philo, CA 95466   707-895-3876
          Fax: 707-895-2603   800-733-3151
                     info@handleycellars.com
                     www.handleycellars.com
Collection of wines such as: Zinfandel, Pinot Gris,
Ranch House Red, Water Tower White, Chardonnay,
Dry Creek Valley
   President/Winemaker: Milla Handley
   National Sales Manager: Andrea Lederle
   Retail Sales: Ellen Springwater
   Assistant Winemaker: Kristen Barnhisel
Estimated Sales:$5-10 Million
Number Employees: 10-19
Type of Packaging: Private Label

6186   (HQ)Handy Pax
500 N Main St # C
Randolph, MA 02368-6700   781-963-8300
Processor and wholesaler/distributor of snack foods
including crackers with peanut butter, cheese, pret-
zel sticks, brownies and cookies
   President: Jay Sussman
   Sales Manager: David Sussman
Number Employees: 10-19
Type of Packaging: Consumer, Private Label

6187   Hangzhou Sanhe Food Company
20536 Carrey Rd
Walnut, CA 91789-2459   909-869-6016
          Fax: 909-869-6015   aili28@hotmail.com
                     www.hzsanhe.com
Food additives
   Owner: Duan Zong
   Marketing Director: Alili Chen
Brands:
   Hangzhou Sanhe

6188   Hank's Beverage Company
4625 E Street Rd
Feastervl Trvs, PA 19053-6630   215-396-2809
          Fax: 215-396-8077   800-289-4722
                     info@hanksbeverages.com
                     www.hanksbeverages.net

Diversified line of classic old fashioned gourmet fla-
vors such as: Root Beer, Diet Root beer, Orange
Cream, Vanilla Cream and Black Cherry. Specialty
flavors as Birch Beer, Highland Berry;, Citrus and
Fruit Punch
   Manager: Jennifer Brady
Estimated Sales:$ 5 - 10 Million
Number Employees: 5-9

6189   Hanmi
5447 N Wolcott Ave
Chicago, IL 60640-1017   773-271-0730
          Fax: 773-271-1756 http://www.hanmi.com
Oriental and Korean foods
   Owner: Young Kim
   Contact: Sung Sohn
   CFO: Michael Winiarski
   Vice President: John Kim
Estimated Sales:$ 10 - 20 Million
Number Employees: 10-19

6190   Hanna's Honey
P.O.Box 17353
Salem, OR 97305-7353   503-393-2945
                                   Fax: 503-393-2945
Small business: We package and wholesale gourmet
Oregon honey. We also carry honey sticks-flavored
colored honey in straws
   President: Jean Hunter
   CEO: Claude Hunter
*Estimated Sales:*C
Number Employees: 1-4
Type of Packaging: Consumer
Brands:
   Hanna's

6191   (HQ)Hanover Foods Corporation
P.O.Box 334
Hanover, PA 17331-0334   717-632-6000
          Fax: 717-637-2890 www.hanoverfoods.com
Processor and importer of canned, frozen,
freeze-dried and fresh vegetables, beans, mush-
rooms, potato chips, pretzels, juices, sauces, salads,
entrees, soups, desserts, etc.; also, spaghetti and
meat balls in tomato sauce
   President/CEO: John Warehime
   Executive Vice President/CFO: Gary Knisely
   VP: Dave Still
   Research & Development: Tim Mechler
   Advertising/Marketing: Jerry Neidigh
   Retail Sales: Dan Schuchart
   Foodservice Sales: Kathy Shaffer
   Private Label Sales: Donna Bowser
   Senior Vice President Purchasing: Alan Young
Number Employees: 500-999
Type of Packaging: Consumer, Private Label, Bulk
Brands:
   Alcosa
   Aunt Kitty's
   Bickel's
   Casa Maid
   Clayton Farms
   Dawn Glo
   Dutch Farms
   Farmer Girl
   Gibbs
   Hanover
   Hanover Farms
   Lk Burman
   Maryland Chef
   Mitchell's
   Myers
   O & C
   Phillips
   Round the Clock
   Spring Glen
   Spring Glen Fresh Foods
   Sunnyside
   Sunwise
   Super Fine
   Superfine
   Vegetable Cocktail

6192   Hanover Foods Corporation
P.O.Box 334
Hanover, PA 17331-0334   717-632-6000
                                   Fax: 717-397-0322
Processor and exporter of freeze-dried vegetables,
poultry, meats, dairy products and ice
   VP: Dave Still
   Manager (Freeze-Dry/Support): Sue Haar
   Plant Manager: Arnold Bolman

Estimated Sales:$20-50 Million
Number Employees: 100-249
Parent Co: Hanover Foods Corporation
Type of Packaging: Consumer, Bulk

6193 Hanover Potato Products
P.O.Box 35
Hanover, PA 17331-0035   717-632-0700
                              Fax: 717-632-0756
Processor and wholesaler/distributor of fresh potato
products including fries, whole and diced; serving
the food service market
    President: Kendra Kauffman
Estimated Sales:$5-10 Million
Number Employees: 10-19
Type of Packaging: Food Service

6194 Hans Kissle Company
9 Creek Brook Dr
Haverhill, MA 01832-1548   978-372-2504
    Fax: 978-556-4612 info@hanskissle.com
                              www.hanskissle.com
Refrigerated salads - traditional, protein, contempo-
rary and heart healthy, quiches, stuffings and
desserts
    President/CEO: Steven Zenlea
    National Sales Manager: Kymberley Feldman
    Regional Sales Manager: Ken Boyle
    Vice President Operations: Mary Connolly
    Plant Technical Director: Robin Beane
Estimated Sales:$20-50 Million
Number Employees: 5-9
Sq. footage: 112000
Type of Packaging: Private Label

6195 Hansel 'N Gretel
7936 Cooper Ave
Flushing, NY 11385-7593   718-326-0041
    Fax: 718-326-2069 healthydeli@healthydeli.com
                              www.healthydeli.com
Processor of meats including cold cuts and sausage
and ham
    President: Milton Rattner
    CEO: Milton Rattner
    CFO: Steve Rosbash
    Vice President: Wayne Williamson
    COO: Ron Walsen
    Public Relations: Dawn Rattner
    Operations Manager: James Rowe
    Plant Engineer: John Krauss
    Plant Manager: John Dinisi
Estimated Sales:$20-50 Million
Number Employees: 100-249
Type of Packaging: Consumer, Bulk
Brands:
    Healthy Deli

6196 Hansen Beverage
550 Monica Cir # 201
Corona, CA 92880-5496   951-739-6200
    Fax: 951-739-6210 800-426-7367
                              www.hansens.com
Natural juices, sodas, teas, energy drinks
    Vice Chairman/President: Hilton Schlosberg
    Chairman/CEO: Rodney Sacks
    CEO: Rodney C Sacks
    Marketing: Tim Hansen
    SVP/National Sales Manager: Michael Schott
Estimated Sales:$10-20 Million
Number Employees: 250-499
Brands:
    Equator Products Teas
    Hansen Apple Juice
    Hansen Fruit Juice B
    Hansen Lemonades
    Hansen Smoothies
    Hansen Sodas
    Hansen Spring Water
    Hansen Tea
    Hansen's Healthy Ant
    Hansen's Healthy Imm
    Hansen's Healthy Int
    Hansen's Healthy Vit
    Hansen's Healthy Vit
    Lost Five-0
    Lost Perfect 10
    Monster Energy Khaos

6197 Hansen Caviar Company
881 State Route 28
Kingston, NY 12401-7216   845-331-5622
    Fax: 845-331-8075 800-735-0441
    hcaviar@aol.com www.hansencaviar.com

Caviar (Russian and American), foie gras, truffles,
smoked fish and other specialty food products
    President: Michael Hansen-Sturm
Estimated Sales:$500,000-$1 Million
Number Employees: 1-4
Type of Packaging: Private Label
Brands:
    Hansen
    Hansen-Norge
    St. Etienne

6198 Hansen Packing Meat Company
807 State Highway 16
Jerseyville, IL 62052-2813   618-498-3714
                              Fax: 618-498-5507
    info@hansenpackingmeats.com
    http://www.hansenpackingmeats.com/
Processor of meat
    President: Ron Hansen
    Customs Processor/Logistics Operations: Todd
    Pearse
    Customs Processor/Logistics Operations: Jim
    Woelfel
    Marketing/Sales Manager: Ryan Hansen
    Retail Manager/Daily Operations: Shon Kennedy
    Manager Administrative Operations: Terrie Perry
    Lead Meat Processor: Mike Pearse
    Livestock Consultant/Cattle Buyer: Ronnie
    Hansen
    Driver Wholesale Orders: Dan Monroe
Estimated Sales:$ 3 - 5 Million
Number Employees: 5-9
Type of Packaging: Bulk
Brands:
    Hansen

6199 Hansen's Juices
935 W 8th St
Azusa, CA 91702-2246   626-812-6022
    Fax: 626-334-6439 www.nakedjuice.com
Processor and exporter of fresh citrus and blended
juices including strawberry, lemon and apple
    CEO/President: Jeff Heavirland
    Telecommunications: Paul Lingenfelder
Estimated Sales:$10-20 Million
Number Employees: 100-249
Parent Co: Fresh Juice Company
Type of Packaging: Consumer, Food Service

6200 Hansen's Natural
1031 Rosecrans Ave # 104
Fullerton, CA 92833-1946   714-870-0310
    Fax: 909-739-6210 www.cdchealth.com
Number Employees: 250-499

6201 Hansmann's Mills
63 N Main Street
Bainbridge, NY 13733-1225   607-967-5080
Baking mixes, cakes, pastries and pies, pancakes and
waffles
    President: George Slilaty
    Owner: Robin Fellows
Estimated Sales:$5-10 Million
Number Employees: 5-9

6202 Hanson Thompson Honey Farms
P.O.Box 129
Redfield, SD 57469-0129   605-472-0474
Processor of honey
    President: Bruce Hanson
    Co-Owner: Adrian Thompson
*Estimated Sales:*Under $500,000
Number Employees: 1-4

6203 Hanzell Vineyards
18596 Lomita Avenue
Sonoma, CA 95476-4619   707-996-3860
    Fax: 707-996-3862 maildesk@hanzell.com
                              www.hanzell.com
Wines: Chardonnay, Pinot Noir and many others
    Proprietor: Alexander de Byre
    President: Jean Arnold Sessions
    Consulting Winemaker: Bob Sessions
    National Sales Manager: Armen Khatchaturian
    General Manager/Winemaker: Michael Terrien
Estimated Sales:$5-9.9 Million
Number Employees: 5-9

6204 Hapag-Lloyd America
245 Townpark Dr NW # 300
Kennesaw, GA 30144-5889   678-355-5025
    Fax: 678-801-8464 888-851-4083
    www.hapag-lloyd.com

International transportation, cold storage, box cars
    Senior VP: James I Newsome
    Director Sales: Stuart Sandlin
    Director Operations: John Palmer
Number Employees: 100-249

6205 Happy & Healthy Products
1600 S Dixie Hwy # 200
Boca Raton, FL 33432-7463   561-367-0739
    Fax: 561-368-5267 behappy@fruitfull.com
                              www.fruitfull.com
Committed to producing and supplying the highest
quality frozen fruit bars and other products such as
decadent dips, frozen dessert bars, fruit smoothies,
and healthy snacks that promote a happy and healthy
life-syle.
    President: Linda Kamm
    General Manager: Rosemary Harris
    Marketing Director: Tabitha Locke
    Customer Service Manager: Susan Scotts
    Public Relations: Mary Galinat
    Operations Manager: Len Murray
Estimated Sales:$4 Million
Number Employees: 20-49
Number of Brands: 5
Type of Packaging: Consumer, Food Service, Pri-
vate Label, Bulk
Brands:
    BE HAPPY 'N HEALTHY SNACKS
    FRUITFULL
    HAPPY INDULGENCE
    HAPPY INDULGENCE DELADENT DIPS

6206 Happy Acres Packing Company
PO Box 444
Petal, MS 39465-0444   601-584-8301
Sausage
    President: Helen Jernigan
Estimated Sales:$500-1 Million appx.
Number Employees: 1-4

6207 Happy Egg Dealers
3204 E 7th Ave
Tampa, FL 33605-4302   813-248-2362
                              Fax: 813-247-1754
Processor and exporter of eggs
    Owner: Frank Selph Sr
Estimated Sales:$ 10 - 20 Million
Number Employees: 10-19
Type of Packaging: Consumer, Bulk
Brands:
    Belle Mead

6208 Happy Herberts Food Company
444 Washington Boulevard
Apt 2524
Jersey City, NJ 07310-1916   201-386-0984
    Fax: 201-386-0984 800-764-2779
    info@happyherberts.com
                              www.happyherberts.com
Snacks
    Owner: Gary Plutchok
Estimated Sales:$500,000-$1 Million
Number Employees: 1-4
Brands:
    Happy Herberts

6209 Happy Hive
4476 Tulane Street
Dearborn Heights, MI 48125-2297   313-562-3707
                              Fax: 313-562-3707
Candy/confectionery
    Owner: Stanley Kozlowicz
*Estimated Sales:*Less than $100,000
Number Employees: 1-4
Type of Packaging: Consumer, Food Service, Bulk
Brands:
    Happy Hive

6210 Happy Refrigerated Services
900 Turk Hill Rd
Fairport, NY 14450-8747   585-388-0080
                              Fax: 585-388-0185
Ice
    President: David Blind
Estimated Sales:$2.5-5 Million
Number Employees: 20-49

6211 Happy's Potato Chip Company
3900 Chandler Dr NE
Minneapolis, MN 55421-4494   612-781-3121
                              Fax: 612-781-3125

Processor and exporter of snack foods including potato chips, popcorn, tostados and cheese puffs
Plant Manager: Finn Henrikssen
Estimated Sales:$10-20 Million
Number Employees: 50-99
Parent Co: Old Dutch Foods
Type of Packaging: Consumer, Food Service

6212 Harbar Corporation
320 Turnpike St
Canton, MA 02021-2703   781-828-0848
        Fax: 781-828-0849 800-881-7040
                www.harbar.com
Processor of fresh tortillas including white corn, blue corn, white flour, wholewheat and flavored flour
Owner: Ezequiel Montmayor
Estimated Sales:$3 Million
Number Employees: 50-99
Sq. footage: 40000
Type of Packaging: Consumer, Food Service, Private Label, Bulk
Brands:
Harbar's
It's a Wrap
La Sabrosa
Maria & Ricardo's Tortilla Factory
Real Chip
Wrappy

6213 Harbison Wholesale Meats
2115 County Road
Suite 401
Cullman, AL 35057   256-739-5105
        Fax: 256-739-8123
Meat
Proprietor: Gary Harbison

6214 Harbor Fish Market
9 Custom House Wharf
Portland, ME 04101-4708   207-775-0251
        Fax: 207-879-0611 info@harborfish.com
                www.harborfish.com
Processor of fresh fish; wholesaler/distributor of seafood, fresh swordfish, halibut, wild salmon, new shell lobsters, Maryland blue crabs, native steamers, oysters, mussels, lobster meat, crabmeat, and assorted smoked seafood.
Owner: Mike Alfiero
Estimated Sales:$5 Million
Number Employees: 20-49
Sq. footage: 6000

6215 Harbor Food Sales & Services
PO Box 21
Alameda, CA 94501-0321   360-405-0677
        Fax: 360-405-0752

6216 Harbor Lobster
Shag Harbor
Shelburne, NS B0T 1W0
Canada   902-723-2500
        Fax: 902-723-2568
Processor and exporter of live lobster and salted groundfish
President: Wayne Banks
Number Employees: 5-9
Type of Packaging: Bulk

6217 Harbor Seafood
969 Lakeville Rd
New Hyde Park, NY 11040-3000   516-302-8893
        Fax: 516-775-2407 800-585-0900
                www.harborseafood.com
Processor and importer of seafood
President: Peter Cardone
Finance Manager: Dill Jienke
Estimated Sales:$50-100 Million
Number Employees: 20-49

6218 Harbor Spice Company
P.O.Box 146
Forest Hill, MD 21050-0146   410-893-9500
        Fax: 410-893-9502 www.harborspice.com
Spices
Manager: Dan Sanchuck
Estimated Sales:$1-2.5 Million
Number Employees: 10-19

6219 Harbor Sweets Chocolates
85 Leavitt St
Salem, MA 01970-5599   978-745-7648
        Fax: 978-741-7811 800-243-2115
                infohs@harborsweets.com
                www.harborsweets.com
Processor of gift chocolates including wedding favors, perennial sweets, classics, dark horse collection, hunt collection, sweet treats, easter and spring gifts, custom chocolates and sugar-free
Owner: Phyllis Le Blanc
Estimated Sales:$50-100 Million
Number Employees: 100-249
Brands:
DARK HORSE CHOCOLATES
MARBLEHEAD MINTS
PERENNIAL SWEETS
SWEET SHELLS
SWEET SLOOPS
TOPIARY TOFFEE

6220 Harbor Winery
614 Harbor Blvd
West Sacramento, CA 95691   916-371-6776
Wines
Owner: Charles Myers
*Estimated Sales:*Less than $100,000
Number Employees: 1-4
Brands:
Harbor

6221 Hard-E Foods
3228 N Broadway
St Louis, MO 63147-3515   314-533-2211
        Fax: 314-533-2656 www.hardefoods.com
Processor of hard cooked and deviled egg products; also, fresh cut vegetables
President/CEO: Judy Rutz
Plant Manager: Larry Rutz
Estimated Sales:$2 Million
Number Employees: 20-49
Sq. footage: 50000
Type of Packaging: Consumer, Food Service, Private Label
Brands:
Hard-E Foods

6222 Hardin's Bakery
2121 14th St
Tuscaloosa, AL 35401-2926   205-344-6690
        Fax: 205-752-1780
Processor of baked goods including breads, buns and rolls.
Partner: Charles A Hardin
Estimated Sales:$ .5 - 1 million
Number Employees: 1-4
Parent Co: Flowers Baking Company
Type of Packaging: Consumer

6223 Hardscrabble Enterprises
PO Box 1124
Franklin, WV 26807-1124   304-358-2921
Processor and wholesaler/distributor of American dried shiitake mushrooms and maitake mushrooms
President: Paul Goland
*Estimated Sales:*Under $500,000
Number Employees: 1-4
Sq. footage: 3500
Type of Packaging: Consumer, Food Service, Bulk
Brands:
American Shiitake
Hen-Of-The-Woods

6224 Hardy Farms Peanuts
Rr 2 Box 2120
Hawkinsville, GA 31036-8945   478-783-3044
        Fax: 478-783-0606 888-368-6887
                info@hardyfarmspeanuts.com
                www.hardyfarmspeanuts.com
Processor of fresh green and boiled peanuts
President: Alex Hardy
Estimated Sales:$1 Million
Number Employees: 10-19
Number of Brands: 1
Number of Products: 3
Sq. footage: 100000
Type of Packaging: Consumer, Food Service, Bulk

6225 Harford Glen Water
P.O.Box 786
Seneca Falls, NY 13148-786   607-844-8351
        Fax: 607-844-8351 866-844-8351
                edsjet@yahoo.com www.deeprockaqua.com

Company is a supplier of natural spring water.
President/CEO: Edmund McHale
CFO/VP: Lura McHale
Number Employees: 6
Number of Brands: 2
Number of Products: 5
Sq. footage: 6000
Type of Packaging: Food Service, Private Label

6226 Hari Om Farms
8416 Shelbyville Hwy
Eagleville, TN 37060-9603   615-368-7778
        Fax: 615-368-7650 kkpaul@h2ofarms.ne
                www.h2ofarms.com
Processor of herbs and lettuce
Manager: Pedro Lopez
Estimated Sales:$1-2.5 Million
Number Employees: 1-4
Sq. footage: 60000
Type of Packaging: Consumer, Food Service, Bulk
Brands:
H2O
Hari Om Farms

6227 Haribo of America
1825 Woodlawn Dr # 204
Baltimore, MD 21207-4045   410-265-8890
        Fax: 410-265-8898 800-638-2327
                info@us.haribo.com www.haribo.com
Processor of Gummi and licorice candy products
President: Christian Jegen
Vice President Plant Operations: Ryan Schader
Estimated Sales:$5-10 Million
Number Employees: 10-19
Type of Packaging: Private Label
Brands:
HARIBO

6228 Haring's Pride Catfish
681 Pete Haring Rd
Wisner, LA 71378-4653   318-724-6133
        Fax: 318-724-6138 800-467-3474
                info@haringspridecatfish.com
                www.haringspridecatfish.com
Frozen and refrigerated catfish, catfish fillets, catfish nuggets, catfish strips, catfish tidbits, breaded catfish products
President/Owner: Carl Haring
Estimated Sales:$100-500 Million
Number Employees: 250-499

6229 (HQ)Harker's Distribution
P.O.Box 1308
Le Mars, IA 51031-1308   712-546-8171
        Fax: 712-536-3159 800-798-7700
                www.harkers.com
Wholesaler/distributor of frozen foods, meats, center-of-the-plate foods, poultry and seafood; serving the food service market
President: Ron Geiger
CEO: Jim Harker
Sr. VP Sales/Marketing: Stan Dickman
Purchasing Agent: Kevin Regan
Number Employees: 100-249
Other Locations:
Harker's Distribution
Denver CO

6230 Harlan Bakeries
7597 E Us Highway 36
Avon, IN 46123-7171   317-272-3600
        Fax: 317-272-1110 info@harlanbakeries.com
                www.harlanbakeries.com
Producer and supplier of premium quality Kosher bagels and bagel related products, cakes, cookies and pies.
President: Hugh Harlan
Executive VP: Doug Harlan
Estimated Sales:$100+ Million
Number Employees: 250-499
Sq. footage: 180000
Type of Packaging: Consumer, Food Service, Private Label, Bulk
Brands:
Colosso Bowl
Colosso Cones
Mickey's Parade

6231 Harlan Bakeries
7597 E Us Highway 36
Avon, IN 46123-7171   317-272-3600
        Fax: 317-272-1110 info@harlanbakeries.com
                www.harlanbakeries.com

Processor and importer of bagels including fresh, frozen, fully baked, partially baked and raw dough; also, breads, bialys, bagel sticks, muffins, cakes, cookies, pies.
President: Hugh P Harlan
Executive Vice President: Doug R Harlan
Director Research/Development: Keith Lockwood

EVP Sales/Marketing: Joseph Latouf
Vice President Operations: Michael L Hulsebos
Estimated Sales: $100-500 Million
Number Employees: 250-499
Sq. footage: 150000
Brands:
Bagel King
Bigger Better
Giant Gourmet
Harlan Bakeries
World's Best

6232 Harlan Bakeries, Inc.
7597 E Us Highway 36
Avon, IN 46123-7171   317-272-3600
Fax: 317-272-1110   info@harlanbakeries.com
www.harlanbakeries.com
Processor of baked goods including pita bread and bagels
President: Hugh Harlan
Executive VP/Co-Owner: Doug Harlan
Executive VP/Sales and Marketing: Joseph Latouf
Estimated Sales: $20-50 Million
Number Employees: 50-99

6233 Harlin Fruit Company
602 N 17th St
Monett, MO 65708-9178   417-235-7370
Fax: 417-235-7316
Fresh fruits and vegetables
Owner: Jerry Sutton
President: Dennis Hughes
Estimated Sales: $1-2.5 Million
Number Employees: 10-19
Type of Packaging: Consumer, Bulk
Brands:
Harlin Fruit

6234 Harlon's L.A. Fish, LLC
P.O.Box 486
Kenner, LA 70063-0486   504-467-3809
Fax: 504-466-1503
Seafood
Owner: Harlon Pearce
Estimated Sales: $ 10 - 20 Million
Number Employees: 20-49

6235 Harlow House Company
PO Box 12018
Atlanta, GA 30355   404-325-1270
Fax: 678-560-8355   sales@harlowhouse.com
Confectionery
President: David Swain
Estimated Sales: Less than $500,000
Number Employees: 4
Type of Packaging: Consumer, Bulk

6236 Harmon's Original Clam Cakes
P.O.Box 1113
Kennebunkport, ME 04046-1113   207-283-1091
Fax: 207-967-1008
steve@harmonsclamcakes.com
www.harmonsclamcakes.com
Clam Cakes

6237 Harmony Cellars
P.O.Box 2502
Harmony, CA 93435-2502   805-927-1625
Fax: 805-927-0256   800-432-9239
www.harmonycellars.net
Wines consisting of white, red, and blush
Co-Owner/Winemaker: Charles Mulligan
Co-Owner/Business Manager: Kim Mulligan
Estimated Sales: $500,000-$1 Million
Number Employees: 5-9
Brands:
Harmony Cellars

6238 Harmony Foods Corporation
11899 Exit Five Parkway
Fishers, IN 46038   317-567-2700
Fax: 317-577-3588   gummy@harmonyfoods.com
www.harmonyfoods.com

Processor and exporter of gummys, jelly beans, gels, yogurt, chocolate confections and sugar-free and natural candies; also, dried fruit, banana chips and snack and trail mixes
President: Jim Hanlon
Estimated Sales: $1-2.5 Million
Number Employees: 100-249
Sq. footage: 200000
Type of Packaging: Consumer, Food Service, Private Label, Bulk
Brands:
Bold Beans
Harmony Snacks
Planet Harmony

6239 Harmony Foods Corporation
11899 Exit Five Parkway
Fishers, IN 46038   317-567-2700
Fax: 317-577-3588   800-837-2855
info@harmonyfoods.com
www.harmonyfoods.com
Nourish healthy lifestyles by providing delicious and better snacks made with the highest quality wholesome ingredients. Such items are trail mixes, dried fruits, nuts and seeds, sweet snacks and sugar-free specialty sweets andorganic snacks
President: George Pappas
Estimated Sales: $10-20 Million
Number Employees: 100-249
Sq. footage: 125000

6240 Harner Farms
2191 W Whitehall Road
State College, PA 16801-2332   814-237-7919
Fax: 814-238-8349
Processor of produce including apples, cherries, plums and vegetables
Owner: Daniel Harner
Estimated Sales: $1-2.5 Million
Number Employees: 20
Type of Packaging: Consumer, Food Service

6241 Harney & Sons Tea Company
PO Box 665
Salisbury, CT 06068-0665   888-427-6398
Fax: 518-789-2100   ht@harney.com
www.harney.com
Processor, importer and exporter of teas including black, green, fruit, iced and herbal
President: John Harney
Sales: Michael Harney
Manager: Paul Harney
Purchasing: Elvira Cardenos
Estimated Sales: $2.5-5 Million
Number Employees: 5-9
Sq. footage: 12000
Type of Packaging: Consumer, Food Service, Private Label, Bulk
Brands:
Harney & Sons

6242 Harold Bozman Seafood
PO Box 195
Upper Fairmount, MD 21867-0195   410-651-0647
Prepared fresh or frozen fish & seafood
President: Harold Bozman
Estimated Sales: $1-2.5 Million
Number Employees: 5-9
Type of Packaging: Consumer

6243 Harold Food Company
15800 John J Delaney Drive
Suite 300
Charlotte, NC 28277-2981   704-588-8061
Fax: 704-588-4636
Processor of frozen fruit cobblers, salads, spreads, chili and barbecue products; wholesaler/distributor of dry, paper, frozen, fresh and refrigerated products; serving the food service market
President: Susan Yandle
Marketing Director: Tom Taylor
General Manager: Butch Summey
Director Purchasing: Phyllis Roach
Estimated Sales: $20-50 Million
Number Employees: 50-99
Sq. footage: 46500
Type of Packaging: Food Service, Private Label, Bulk
Brands:
Harold Food Co.

6244 Harold L. King & Company
1420 Stafford St
Redwood City, CA 94063-1076   650-368-2233
Fax: 650-368-3547   888-368-2233
kingcoffee@aol.com
Green coffee
President: Robert King
Secretary/Treasurer: John King
Vice President: Tim Kallok
Estimated Sales: $25 Million
Number Employees: 5-9
Type of Packaging: Consumer

6245 Harold M. Lincoln Company
2130 Madison Ave # 101
Toledo, OH 43604-5135   419-255-1200
Fax: 419-259-5631   800-345-4911
hmlincoln@aol.com
Broker of confectionery and dairy/deli products, frozen foods, general merchandise, groceries, etc. Marketing, sales planning and promotional tracking services available
President: David Lincoln
VP/Account Manager: J Lincoln
Chairman: H Lincoln
Estimated Sales: $20-50 Million
Number Employees: 5-9
Sq. footage: 7000

6246 Harper Seafood Company
1348 White Point Rd
Kinsale, VA 22488-2306   804-472-3310
Fax: 804-472-2682
Processor of refrigerated oysters
President: Robert Harper
Estimated Sales: $10-20 Million
Number Employees: 10-19
Type of Packaging: Consumer, Food Service
Brands:
Harper Seafood

6247 Harper's Country Hams
P.O.Box 122
Clinton, KY 42031-0122   270-653-2081
Fax: 270-653-2409   888-427-7377
info@hamtastic.com   www.hamtastic.com
Country ham
President: Gary Harper
Treasurer: Doris Harper
Vice President: Brian Harper
Plant Manager: John Mcauliffe
Purchasing Manager: Brant Dublin
Estimated Sales: $20-50 Million
Number Employees: 100-249

6248 Harper's Seafood
526 W Jackson St
Thomasville, GA 31792-5903   229-226-7525
Fax: 229-228-6446
Seafood
President: Wayne Harper
Estimated Sales: $ 3 - 5 Million
Number Employees: 10-19

6249 Harpersfield Vineyard
6387 State Route 307
Geneva, OH 44041   440-466-4739
info2@harpersfield.com
www.harpersfield.com
Wines
Manager: Adolf Ribic
Co-Owner: Wesley Gerlosky
Estimated Sales: $1-4.9 Million
Number Employees: 1-4
Type of Packaging: Private Label

6250 Harpo's
1001 Bishop St # 6
Honolulu, HI 96813-3429   808-537-3439
Fax: 808-735-6456   alohaharpos@hawaii.rr.com
www.harposdressings.com
Processor of gourmet salad dressings, marinades, and pizza
Manager: Ingrid Larsson
Number Employees: 1-4

6251 Harpoon Brewery
10 Tremont St # 4
Boston, MA 02108-2008   617-574-9551
Fax: 617-482-9361   800-427-7666
akeyser@harpoonbrewery.com
www.harpoonbrewery.com

Beer
    Owner: Patricia Michaels
    Co-Founder/President: Daniel Kenary
Estimated Sales:$10-100 Million
Number Employees: 50-99
Brands:
    Harpoon
    Pickwick
    U.F.O.

6252 Harrell Pecan Company
P.O.Box 508
Camilla, GA 31730-0508   229-336-7282
    Fax: 229-336-1177   800-526-8770
    info@harrellnut.com   www.harrellnut.com
Pecans
    President: Marty Harrell
Estimated Sales:$1-2.5 Million
Number Employees: 10-19
Number of Brands: 3
Brands:
    Camilla Pecan
    Harrell Nut
    Ole' Henry's Nuthouse

6253 Harrington's of Vermont
210 Main Rd
Richmond, VT 05477   802-434-7500
    Fax: 802-434-3166   info@harringtonham.com
                www.harringtonham.com
Smoked meats, cheese, maple syrup, seafood, sweets
& snacks, condiments and cakes and pastries
    Owner: Peter Klinkenberg
    Marketing: Carol Wiseley
Estimated Sales:$20-50 Million
Number Employees: 100-249

6254 Harris Baking Company
P.O.Box 129
Rogers, AR 72757-0129   479-636-3313
                Fax: 479-631-3895
Processor of baked products including bread and
buns.
    Manager: Josh Carosh
Estimated Sales:$100-500 Million
Number Employees: 100-249
Sq. footage: 70000
Type of Packaging: Consumer
Brands:
    Best Choice
    IGA
    Ozark
    Tender Crust

6255 Harris Farms
Rr 1 Box 400
Coalinga, CA 93210-9222   559-884-2859
        Fax: 559-884-2253   800-742-1955
    info@harrisfarms.com   www.harrisfarms.com
Processor of tomatoes, onions, melons, almonds,
bell peppers and garlic
    President: John Harris
    Senior VP: Donald Devine
Estimated Sales:$5-10 Million
Number Employees: 100-249
Type of Packaging: Consumer, Food Service, Pri-
    vate Label, Bulk
Brands:
    Harris Farms
    Harris Fresh
    Harris Ranch

6256 Harris Freeman & Company
3110 E Miraloma Ave
Anaheim, CA 92806-1906   714-765-1190
    Fax: 714-765-1199   800-275-2378
                charlene@harrisfreeman.com
                www.harrisfreeman.com
Distributor and importer of spices, teas and coffee
    Manager: Anil Shah
    Spices: Peter Shah
    Coffee: Aaron Zaris
Estimated Sales:$ 20 - 50 Million
Number Employees: 20-49

6257 Harris Moran Seed Company
P.O.Box 4938
Modesto, CA 95352-4938   209-579-7333
        Fax: 209-527-8684   www.harrismoran.com
Processor and exporter of vegetable seeds
    Finance Executive: Angie Rooney
Estimated Sales:$ 10 - 20 Million
Number Employees: 100-249
Parent Co: Groupe Limagrain

Brands:
    Niagra Seed

6258 Harris Ranch Beef Company
P.O.Box 220
Selma, CA 93662-0220   559-233-4116
    Fax: 559-896-3095   800-742-1955
                www.harrisranchbeef.com
Processor, packer and exporter of fresh beef prod-
ucts
    Corporate Chairman/Owner: John Harris
    CEO: Dave Wood
    CEO: Dave Wood
    Research & Development Manager: Bruce Hurley

    QA/Food Safety Director: Dr. Patrick Mies
    Vice President Marketing: Brad Caudill
    Director International Sales: Doug Fariss
Estimated Sales:$100-500 Million
Number Employees: 500-999
Sq. footage: 160000
Type of Packaging: Consumer, Food Service, Pri-
    vate Label, Bulk
Brands:
    Harris Ranch

6259 Harrisburg Dairies
P.O.Box 2001
Harrisburg, PA 17105-2001   717-233-8701
    Fax: 717-231-4584   800-692-7429
                sales@harrisburgdairies.com
                www.harrisburgdairies.com
Processor of frozen orange juice, spring water and
milk including regular and chocolate
    President: Fred Dewey
    CEO: Fred B Dewey Jr
    Operations Manager: Matthew Zehring
    Plant Manager: Ralph Watts
Estimated Sales:$50-100 Million
Number Employees: 100-249
Type of Packaging: Consumer
Brands:
    Harrisburg Dairies

6260 Harrison Napa Valley
1527 Sage Canyon Road
Saint Helena, CA 94574-9628   707-963-8271
    Fax: 707-963-4552   800-913-9463
                info@harrisonvineyards.com
                www.harrisonvineyards.com
Wines
    Owner/Winemaker: Lyndsey Harrison
    Consulting Winemaker: Marco DiGiulio
*Estimated Sales:*Less than $500,000
Number Employees: 1-4
Type of Packaging: Private Label
Brands:
    Harrison

6261 Harrison Poultry
P.O.Box 550
Bethlehem, GA 30620-0550   770-867-9105
                Fax: 770-867-0999
Manufacturer, hatcher, of fresh whole birds and
parts; exporter of frozen poultry parts
    Owner: Patsy Harrison
Estimated Sales:$50-100 Million
Number Employees: 500-999
Sq. footage: 150000
Type of Packaging: Consumer, Food Service, Pri-
    vate Label, Bulk
Brands:
    HARRISON GOLDEN GOODNESS
    PRIDE OF GEORGIA

6262 Harry & David
P.O.Box 712
Medford, OR 97501-0712   541-776-2121
    Fax: 541-864-2194   877-322-1200
                www.harryanddavid.com
Producer of fruit, frozen gourmet truffles, beef
steaks, ham, turkey, cakes, cheesecake, cookies and
cinnamon rolls
    President/CEO: Bill Williams
    EVP Sales/Marketing: Cathy Fultineer
    EVP Operations: Peter Kratz
Number Employees: 1,000-4,999
Parent Co: Bear Creek Corporation
Type of Packaging: Consumer, Food Service
Brands:
    Harry & David

6263 Harry H. Park Company
3539 W Lawrence Avenue
Chicago, IL 60625-5627   773-478-4424
                Fax: 773-478-2313
    Owner: Harry Park

6264 Harry London Candies
5353 Lauby Rd
North Canton, OH 44720-1572   330-494-0833
    Fax: 330-499-6902   800-321-0444
                customerservice@harrylondon.com
                www.harrylondon.com
Processor of chocolates, and truffles
    President: Terry Mitchell
    Chief Executive Officer: Rex Mason
    Chief Financial Officer: Matthew Anderson
    Vice President Business Development: Bob
    Happel
Estimated Sales:$50-100 Million
Number Employees: 100-249
Brands:
    HARRY LONDON CHOCOLATES
    HEARTLAND CHOCOLATES

6265 Harry's Cafe
3621 Route 103
Mount Holly, VT 05758   802-259-2996
                eat@harryscafe.com
                www.harryscafe.com
Manufacturer of sauces - also restaurant -
    Owner/Chef: Trip Pearce
Estimated Sales:$300,000-500,000
Number Employees: 5-9

6266 Hart Winery
P.O.Box 956
Temecula, CA 92593-0956   951-676-6300
    Fax: 951-676-6300   877-638-8788
                hartwinery@speedband.com
                www.thehartfamilywinery.com
Manufacturer of wines
    Owner/Winemaker: Joe Hart
    Owner/CEO: Nancy Hart
    Winemaker: Bill Hart
Estimated Sales:$1-2.5 Million
Number Employees: 1-4
Sq. footage: 3
Type of Packaging: Private Label
Brands:
    Hart Winery

6267 Harten Corporation
18 Commerce Road
Unit H
Fairfield, NJ 07004   973-808-9488
                Fax: 973-808-3966   866-642-7836
Supplier of herbal extracts, botanicals, powders, and
nutritional supplements for the health food industry.

6268 Hartford City Foam Packaging & Converting
P.O.Box D
Hartford City, IN 47348-0151   765-348-2500
    Fax: 765-348-1635   www.hartfordcityfoam.com
Processor of aseptic canned diced and whole toma-
toes and canned tomato paste; also, sauces including
pizza, marinara, salsa, picante and tomato; importer
of aseptic canned tomato paste
    President/CEO: John Jackson
    CEO: Russell Mitchel
Estimated Sales:$10-24.9 Million
Number Employees: 50-99
Sq. footage: 220000
Type of Packaging: Consumer, Food Service, Pri-
    vate Label, Bulk
Brands:
    Mama Rizzo

6269 Hartford Family Winery
8075 Martinelli Rd
Forestville, CA 95436-9255   707-887-1756
    Fax: 707-887-7158   800-588-0234
                hartford.winery@hartfordwines.com
                www.hartfordwines.com
Wines specializing in Pinot Noir, Chardonnay, and
Old-Vine Zinfandel
    Manager: Jeff Mangahas
    Co-Owner: Jennifer Hartford
    Events Manager: Melissa Cook
Estimated Sales:$ 5 - 10 Million
Number Employees: 10-19
Brands:
    HARTFORD
    HARTFORD COURT

6270 Hartford Provision Company
P.O.Box 1228
South Windsor, CT 06074-7228   860-583-3908
Fax: 860-583-6570 www.hpcss.com
President: Barry Pearson
CEO: Barry Pearson
Marketing Manager: Ken Annini
Estimated Sales:$50-100 Million
Number Employees: 50-99
Brands:
Heinz

6271 Harting's Bakery
P.O.Box 220
Bowmansville, PA 17507-0220   717-445-5644
Fax: 717-445-4818
www.hartingscountrymaidbky.com
Doughnuts and buns
President/CEO: Jocelyn Heft
COO: Thomas Lester
Plant Manager: William Burkhart
Estimated Sales:$1-2.5 Million
Number Employees: 20-49

6272 Hartley's Potato Chip Company
2157 Back Maitland Rd
Lewistown, PA 17044-7311   717-248-0526
Fax: 717-248-3512 http://www.hartleyschips.com
Processor and packager of potato chips, pretzels,
cheese curls
President: Dan Hartley
Operations: Kellie Johnson
Estimated Sales:$5-10 Million
Number Employees: 10-19
Sq. footage: 6400
Type of Packaging: Consumer, Food Service

6273 Hartog Rahal Foods
529 5th Ave
New York, NY 10017-4608   212-687-2000
Fax: 212-687-2659 info@hartogfoods.com
www.hartogfoods.net
Fruit juice concentrates, fruit purees, frozen fruits
and flavoring ingredients
President: Jack Hartog Jr
VP: Randy Loewis
Estimated Sales:$ 10 - 20 Million
Number Employees: 20-49
Parent Co: Hartog Rahal Foods

6274 Hartselle Frozen Foods
PO Box 544
Hartselle, AL 35640-0544   256-773-7261
Fax: 709-722-1116
President: Billy Wiley
Secretary/Treasurer: Sam Wiley
Vice President: Danny Wiley

6275 Hartsville Oil Mill
311 Washington St
Darlington, SC 29532-4755   843-393-2855
Fax: 843-395-2690
President/ Owner: Edgar Lawton
Estimated Sales:$20-50 Million
Number Employees: 50-99

6276 Hartville Kitchen
1015 Edison St NW # 1
Hartville, OH 44632-8510   330-877-9353
Fax: 330-877-2101 www.hartvillekitchen.com
Dressings, light dressings
President: Vernon Sommers
VP: Vernon Sommers Jr.
Estimated Sales:$5-10 Million
Number Employees: 250-499

6277 Hartville Locker
P.O.Box 7
Hartville, OH 44632-0007   330-877-9547
Beef processing
Owner: Young
Estimated Sales:$2.5-5 Million
Number Employees: 1-4

6278 Harvard Seafood Company
PO Box 208
Grand Bay, AL 36541-0208   251-865-0558
Fax: 251-865-2187
Seafood

6279 Harvest 2000
683 New York Drive
Pomona, CA 91768-3313   909-622-8039
Fax: 909-622-9789

Oriental dry mixes
President: Howard Goh
Public Relations: Grace Law
Estimated Sales:$1-2.5 Million
Number Employees: 5-9

6280 Harvest Bakery
84 Farmington Ave
Bristol, CT 06010-4293   860-589-8800
Fax: 860-583-4693
Processor of bread and pastries
President: Martin Hurwitz
Estimated Sales:$1-2.5 Million appx.
Number Employees: 20-49
Type of Packaging: Consumer
Brands:
Harvest Bakery

6281 (HQ)Harvest Day Bakery
6565 Knott Avenue
Buena Park, CA 90620-8100   714-739-6318
Fax: 714-739-6626

6282 Harvest Direct
P.O.Box 50906
Knoxville, TN 37950-0906   865-539-6305
Fax: 865-523-3372 800-838-2727
monty@harvestdirect.com
www.harvestdirect.com
Meat and milk alternatives
President: Roger Kilburn
Marketing Director: Monty Kilburn
Manager Wholesale Division: Mary Ellen Kilburn

Estimated Sales:$500,000-$1 Million
Number Employees: 5-9
Type of Packaging: Private Label
Brands:
Protflan
Solait
Veggie Ribs

6283 Harvest Food Products Company
1381 Franquette Avenue
Concord, CA 94520-7981   925-676-8208
dkkha@aol.com
Processor and importer of pot stickers, egg rolls,
wontons, barbecue pork buns and tempura shrimp
President: Danny Kha
Estimated Sales:$ 10 - 20 Million
Number Employees: 50-99
Sq. footage: 17000
Type of Packaging: Consumer, Food Service, Private Label, Bulk
Brands:
Harvest Foods

6284 Harvest Innovations
1210 North 14th Street
Indianola, IA 50125   515-962-5063
info@harvest-innovations.com
www.harvest-innovations.com
Manufacturer of natural ingredients such as legumes, soy & multigrain flours, cereal grains and
oilseeds for the food industry.
Director Of Research: Dr. Noel Rudie
Product Development & Quality Assurance:
Regena Butler
Director Food Technology: Dr. Wilmot Wijeratne

6285 Harvest States Milling
5500 Cenex Drive
Inver Grove Heights, MN 55077   651-355-6000
Fax: 651-306-6397 800-232-3639
bakeryflour@harveststates.com www.chsinc.com
refined vegetable oils, soy and wheat flours, textured
soy protein and confectionery sunflower seeds.
President/CEO: John Johnson
EVP/CFO: John Schmitz
COO: Thomas Larson
Estimated Sales:$25.7 Billion
Number Employees: 8,802
Type of Packaging: Food Service

6286 Harvest Time Foods
3857 Emma Cannon Rd
Ayden, NC 28513-7413   252-746-6675
Fax: 252-746-3160 impressions10@earthlink.net
www.annesdumplings.com
Processor of frozen dumplings
President: Bryan Grimes
VP: Wendy Grimes

Estimated Sales:$5-9.9 Million
Number Employees: 20-49
Sq. footage: 17000
Type of Packaging: Consumer, Food Service
Brands:
Anne's Chicken Base
Anne's Dumpling Squares
Anne's Dumpling Strips
Anne's Flat Dumplings
Anne's Old Fashioned
Anne's Pot Pie Squares
Mac's Dumplings

6287 Harvest Valley Bakery
348 N 30th Rd
La Salle, IL 61301-9710   815-224-9030
Fax: 815-224-9033
Cookies, brownies, and bar cookies. Offers diet and
kosher foods
President: Nancy Norton
Estimated Sales:$10-20 Million
Number Employees: 20-49
Sq. footage: 24000
Type of Packaging: Food Service, Private Label,
Bulk

6288 Harvest-Pac Products
RR 6
Chatham, ON N7M 5J6
Canada   519-436-0446
Fax: 519-436-0319 sales@harvestpac.com
www.harvestpac.com
Processor of canned pumpkin, dark red kidney
beans, chick peas and crushed and pureed tomatoes;
also, pizza sauce, tomato juice
President: Mark O'Neill
Type of Packaging: Food Service, Private Label
Brands:
Harvest-Pac
Mom's Choice

6289 Harvin Choice Meats
P.O.Box 939
Sumter, SC 29151-0939   803-775-9367
Fax: 803-775-9369 www.harvinmeats.com
Owner: S A Harvin Jr
Estimated Sales:$20-50 Million
Number Employees: 50-99

6290 Has Beans Coffee & Tea Company
1011 S Mount Shasta Boulevard
Mount Shasta, CA 96067-2722   530-926-3602
Fax: 530-926-6503 800-427-2326
coffeeorders@hasbeans.com www.hasbeans.com
Coffee roasting, wholesale coffee and tea
Owner: Anne Rivera
Estimated Sales:$10-20 Million
Number Employees: 10-19
Type of Packaging: Private Label

6291 Hastings Cooperative Creamery
P.O.Box 217
Hastings, MN 55033-0217   651-437-9414
Fax: 651-437-3547
Processor of milk
Manager: John Cook
General Manager: John Cook
Estimated Sales:$ 20 - 50 Million
Number Employees: 20-49
Type of Packaging: Consumer, Private Label

6292 Hastings Meat Supply
PO Box 1167
Hastings, NE 68902-1167   402-463-9857
Fax: 402-463-0446
Processor of meat
Owner: Jeff Andreasen
Estimated Sales:$ 1 - 3 Million
Number Employees: 1-4
Type of Packaging: Consumer, Food Service, Bulk

6293 (HQ)Hatfield Quality Meats
P.O.Box 902
Hatfield, PA 19440-0902   215-368-9174
Fax: 215-368-3018 800-523-5291
www.hqm.com
Processor and exporter of fresh and frozen pork
products including ham, sausage and frankfurters
Chairman: Philip Clemens
Sr VP: Kenneth Clemens
HR Director: David Kolesky
Estimated Sales:$100-500 Million
Number Employees: 1,000-4,999

Type of Packaging: Consumer, Food Service, Private Label
Other Locations:
  Hatfield Quality Meats
  Chester PA
Brands:
  Beaver Falls
  Butcher Wagon
  CVF
  Chef Pleaser
  Gold Ribbon
  Hatfield
  Medford
  Olde Philadelphia
  Prima Porta
  Tender Plus

6294 Haug North America
Units 14 & 15
Mississauga, ON L4W 2S7
Canada   905-206-9701
        Fax: 905-206-0859   800-714-8331
    haug@pathcom.com   www.haug-static.com
    President: Toby Wagener
Estimated Sales: Below $ 5 Million
Number Employees: 4

6295 Haug Quality Equipment
18443 Technology Dr
Morgan Hill, CA 95037-2822   408-465-8160
        Fax: 408-842-1265   sales@haugquality.com
                          www.haugquality.com
    President: Brian Haug
Estimated Sales: $ 1 - 3 Million
Number Employees: 5-9
Brands:
    Haug

6296 Haus Barhyte
P.O.Box 1499
Pendleton, OR 97801-0950   541-276-0259
        Fax: 503-691-8918   800-407-9241
                chris@mustardpeople.com
                www.mustardpeople.com
Processor, importer and exporter of gourmet and yellow mustards; private labeling and co-packing available
    Owner: Susan Barhyte
    Secretary/Treasurer: Irene Barhyte
    Director Sales Marketing: Chris Barhyte
Estimated Sales: $2.5-5 Million
Number Employees: 5-9
Brands:
    Aviator Ale Micro Brew Mustards
    Food and Wine
    Food and Wine Mustards
    Haus Barhyte Mustard
    Williamette Valley Mustard

6297 Hausbeck Pickle Company
1626 Hess Avenue
Saginaw, MI 48601-4903   989-754-4721
        Fax: 989-754-3855   866-754-4721
        tim@hausbeck.com   www.hausbeck.com
Processor and exporter of relish and pickles including dill, kosher, sweet, fresh pack kosher and hamburger sliced dill
    President: John Hausbeck
    Treasurer: Richard Hausbeck
    First Vice President: Gerald Hausbeck
    Second Vice President: Charles Hausbeck
    Sales Manager: John Schnepf
    General Manager: Tim Hausbeck
Estimated Sales: $5-10 Million
Number Employees: 10-19
Sq. footage: 30000
Type of Packaging: Consumer, Food Service

6298 Hauser Chocolate
59 Tom Harvey Rd
Westerly, RI 02891-3685   401-596-8866
        Fax: 401-596-0020   888-599-8231
            hauser@hauserchocolates.com
            www.hauserchocolates.com
Chocolate manufacturer
    Owner: Ruedi Hauser Sr Jr
    Vice President Research/Development: Ruedi Hauser Sr
Estimated Sales: $2.5-5 Million
Number Employees: 10-19

6299 Hauser Chocolates
137 Greenwood Ave
Bethel, CT 06801-2527   203-794-1861
        Fax: 203-792-1153   info@hauserchocolates.com
                www.hauserchocolates.com
Processor and exporter of assorted chocolates including Swiss style truffles
    President: Rudi Hauser Jr
Estimated Sales: $2.5-5 Million
Number Employees: 5-9
Type of Packaging: Consumer

6300 Havana's Limited
4420 Coquina Avenue
Titusville, FL 32780-6552   321-267-0513
        Fax: 321-267-5340   havanasltd@aol.com
                www.acebandito.com
Producing gourmet products of the highest quality with no additives - hot sauces, dry rubs and seasonings and BBQ sauces - use only whole fresh vegetables and high quality dry spices
    President/CEO: Mark Webber
    Vice President: Bruce Webber
Number of Brands: 1
Number of Products: 10
Sq. footage: 5000
Type of Packaging: Consumer, Food Service, Private Label, Bulk
Brands:
    ACE BANDITO

6301 Haven's Candies
87 County Rd
Westbrook, ME 04092-3807   207-772-1557
        Fax: 207-775-0086   800-639-6309
                havens@havenscandies.com
                www.havenscandies.com
Processor of chocolates, fudge, salt water taffy, cooked nuts and candy canes; custom chocolate molding available
    Owner: Andy Charles
    Marketing Director: Krista Viola
    Production Manager: Arthur Dillon
Estimated Sales: $1-2.5 Million
Number Employees: 20-49
Sq. footage: 8000
Type of Packaging: Consumer, Private Label, Bulk

6302 Havi Food Services Worldwide
227 South Blvd
Oak Park, IL 60302-4711   708-445-1700
                        Fax: 630-351-9479
Breads, rolls, baked goods
    President: Jeff Somers
    CEO: Jeff Somers
Number Employees: 50-99

6303 (HQ)Havoc Maker Products
121 Old Sachems Head Rd
Guilford, CT 06437-3120   203-453-4943
        Fax: 203-453-4943   800-681-3909
        havoc@snet.net   www.havocmaker.com
Processor of hot sauce, salsa, chili and hot sauce mixes, black bean dip, popcorn and bottled spices
    Owner: Ernest Neri
Number Employees: 1-4
Sq. footage: 500
Type of Packaging: Food Service, Private Label, Bulk
Other Locations:
    Havoc Maker Products
    Old Lyme CT
Brands:
    Havoc Maker

6304 Hawaii Baking Company
P.O.Box 2900
Honolulu, HI 96846-0001   808-694-8198
                Fax: 808-526-0964   www.boh.com
Processor of bread
    President: Ham Homan
    Chairman of the Board: James DeYoung
    Marketing Executive: Ray Sabanal
Parent Co: Holsum
Type of Packaging: Consumer
Brands:
    Holsum/Oroweat

6305 Hawaii Candy
2928 Ualena St
Honolulu, HI 96819-1937   808-836-8955
        Fax: 808-839-4040   info@hawaiicandy.com
                www.hawaiicandy.com
Processor and exporter of confectionery items, snacks, puff rice cakes, coconut balls and fortune cookies
    President: Keith Ohta
    Secretary: Richard Ohta
Estimated Sales: $5-10 Million
Number Employees: 20-49
Sq. footage: 11000
Type of Packaging: Consumer, Food Service, Private Label, Bulk
Brands:
    Hawaiian Island Crisp
    Hawaiian Island Crisp Cookies

6306 Hawaii Coffee Company
1555 Kalani St
Honolulu, HI 96817-4908   808-847-3600
        Fax: 808-847-3434   800-338-8353
    webinfo@hicoffee.com   www.lioncoffee.com
Processor of Kona coffee
    President: Jim Wayman
    Vice President Sales, Foodservice: Jim Lenhart
    VP Sales, Retail/Military/Int'l: Sharon Zambo-Fan
Estimated Sales: $28,000,000
Number Employees: 100-249
Parent Co: C. Brewer & Company

6307 Hawaii Coffee Company
1555 Kalani St
Honolulu, HI 96817-4908   808-847-3600
        Fax: 808-847-3434   800-338-8353
            lion@lioncoffee.com
A leader in premium delicious blends of Hawaiian coffees from Kona and the surrounding islands and delicious Hawaiian Island teas.
    President: Jim Wayman
    Marketing Coordinator: Tom Tsuhako
    Vice President/Sales: James Lenhart
    Vice President/Sales -Retail, Military: Sharon Zambo-Fan
    Wholesale US/International Customers: Kevin Chang
    Mailorder/Catalog Request/Online Orders: Eriko Fong
Estimated Sales: $9 Million
Number Employees: 100-249
Number of Brands: 4
Parent Co: Paradise Beverages
Brands:
    Hawaii Coffee Company
    Lion Coffee
    Royal Kona Coffee
    Tiger Tea

6308 Hawaii International Seafood
P.O.Box 30486
Honolulu, HI 96820-0486   808-839-5010
        Fax: 808-833-0712   www.cryofresh.com
Fish and seafood
    President: Bill Kowalski
Estimated Sales: $2,000,000
Number Employees: 5-9

6309 Hawaii Star Bakery
944 Akepo Ln # D
Honolulu, HI 96817-4588   808-841-3602
                        Fax: 808-842-7941
Processor of French, sourdough and rye bread, English muffins and rolls
    Owner: Liane Small
Estimated Sales: $10-20 Million
Number Employees: 20-49
Type of Packaging: Consumer, Food Service

6310 Hawaiian Bagel
753 Halekauwila Street
Honolulu, HI 96813-5318   808-596-0638
        Fax: 808-593-2434   hibagel@gte.net
Bagels and breads
    President: Steve Gelson
Estimated Sales: $5-9.9 Million
Number Employees: 20-49

6311 Hawaiian Candies & Nuts
707 Waiakamilo Rd
Honolulu, HI 96817-4312   808-841-3344
        Fax: 808-841-2551   hcn@iav.com
Chocolate-covered macadamia nuts
    President: Patrick Arakaki
    Controller: Kenneth Arakaki
    VP: Neal Arakaki
Estimated Sales: $5-10 Million
Number Employees: 20-49

6312 Hawaiian Fruit Specialties
P.O.Box 637
Kalaheo, HI 96741-0637   808-332-9333
                    Fax: 808-332-7650
customerservice@kukuibrand.com
                    www.kukuibrand.com
Tropical fruit mustard, sauces, mango chutney,
jams/preserves, guava jelly, tropical fruit marmalade,
fruit syrup
    Chief Executive Officer: George Morvis Jr
    CEO: Greg Shredder
    Consultant: Fay Tateishi
Estimated Sales: $2.5-5 Million
Number Employees: 5-9

6313 (HQ)Hawaiian Host
500 Alakawa St # 111
Honolulu, HI 96817-4576   808-848-0500
    Fax: 808-845-7466 888-529-4678
info@hawaiianhost.com   www.hawaiianhost.com
Created the chocolate covered Macadamia nut, premium chocolates, specialty chocolates, gift baskets,
tea, cofee and cookies
    President/CEO: Keith Sakamato
    CEO: Dennis Teranishi
    Vice President Sales: Tad Teraizumi
Estimated Sales: $20-50 Million
Number Employees: 100-249

6314 Hawaiian Housewares
P.O.Box 820
Aiea, HI 96701-0820   808-453-8000
                    Fax: 808-456-5043
    Owner: Diana Allen
Estimated Sales: $ 50 - 100 Million
Number Employees: 50-99

6315 Hawaiian Isles Kona Coffee Co
2839 Mokumoa St
Honolulu, HI 96819-4402   808-833-2244
    Fax: 808-833-6328 www.hawaiianisles.com
Coffee
    President: Sidney Boulware
Estimated Sales: $50-100 Million
Number Employees: 50-99

6316 Hawaiian King Candies
550 Paiea St # 501
Honolulu, HI 96819-1837   808-833-0041
    Fax: 808-839-7141 800-570-1902
                    dniiro@lava.net
Manufacturer of Foil-Bagged Macadamia Nuts,
Macadamia Nut Chocolates, Macadamia Nut
Cookies
    President: David Niiro
Estimated Sales: $10-24.9 Million
Number Employees: 50-99
Type of Packaging: Consumer, Food Service, Pri-
vate Label
Brands:
    AMERICA
    ENJOYING LAS VEGAS
    ENJOYING SAN FRANCISCO
    FAVORITES OF HAWAII
    HAWAIIAN DELIGHT
    HAWAIIAN JOYS
    HAWAIIAN KING
    HAWAIIAN MAJESTY
    NEW YORK CLUB
    PASSPORT
    SAN FRANCISCO BAY TRADERS
    THAT'S HOLLYWOOD
    USA

6317 Hawaiian Natural Water Company
98-746 Kuahao Pl # F
Pearl City, HI 96782-3125   808-483-0520
    Fax: 808-483-0536 hisprings@aol.com
                    www.hawaiianspring.com
Bottled spring water
    President/CEO: Marcus Bender
    CFO: Willard D Irwin
    CFO: David Leaha
    CEO: Tom Van Dixhorn
    Executive VP Marketing: Ray Riss
    Operations Manager: Tony Persson
Number Employees: 5-9
Type of Packaging: Private Label
Brands:
    Hawaiian Natural Water

6318 Hawaiian Salrose Teas
500 Alakawa St # 111
Honolulu, HI 96817-4576   808-848-0500
    Fax: 808-845-7466 www.hawaiianhost.com
Chocolate candies
    President: Dick Hollier
    CEO: Dennis Teranishi
    Public Relations: Harvey Hahn
Estimated Sales: $20-50 Million
Number Employees: 100-249

6319 Hawaiian Solar Dried Fruit
PO Box 1592
Pahoa, HI 96778-1592   808-965-8915
                    janus@ilhawaii.net
Processor of solar dried and organic tropical fruits
and spices including bananas, papayas, pineapples,
ginger, etc.; also, gift baskets available
    Sales: Janus Garramone
    Operations Engineer: Noah Becker

6320 Hawaiian Sun Products
259 Sand Island Access Rd
Honolulu, HI 96819-2227   808-845-3211
    Fax: 808-842-0532 mailorder@hawnsun.com
                    www.hawaiiansunproducts.com
Processes and cans tropical fruit juices; manufac-
tures macadamia nut candy
    President: Burt K Okura
Estimated Sales: $20-50 Million
Number Employees: 50-99
Brands:
    Hawaiian Sun
    Pokka

6321 Hawk Pacific Freight
PO Box 4080
Napa, CA 94558-0407   707-259-0266
                    Fax: 707-259-0120
    General Manager: Patrick Minehan
Estimated Sales: Under $500,000
Number Employees: 20-49

6322 (HQ)Hawkhaven Greenhouse International
4777 N Woodruff Avenue
Whitefish Bay, WI 53211   920-540-3536
    Fax: 920-787-4295 800-745-4295
    hgi@wirural.net   www.hawkhaven.com
Processor of certified organic fresh cut wheat grass
and fresh frozen organic wheat grass juice; exporter
of fresh-frozen certified organic wheat grass and
juice
    President: Timothy Paegelow
Estimated Sales: Under $300,000
Number Employees: 1-4
Sq. footage: 5000
Type of Packaging: Consumer
Brands:
    Grower's Pack
    Hawkhaven
    Verdegrass

6323 Hawkins Farms
PO Box 1
Pennfield, NB E5H 2M1
Canada   506-755-6241
                    Fax: 506-755-6241

6324 Hawthorne Valley Farm
327 County Route 21c
Ghent, NY 12075-1927   518-672-7500
    Fax: 518-672-4887 www.vspcamp.com
400 acre biodynamic® farm
    Executive Director: Nick Franceschelli
    Farm Tours: Rachel Schneider
Estimated Sales: $2.5-5 Million
Number Employees: 10-19
Type of Packaging: Private Label
Brands:
    Hawthorne Valley Farm

6325 Hayashibara International Inc
390 Interlocken Crescent
Suite 680
Broomfield, CO 80021   303-650-4590
                    Fax: 303-650-9860
ahashino@hayashibara-intl.com
                    www.hayashibara-intl.com
Trehlose, Pullulan and Maltose. Functional food in-
gredients made from starch.
    VP: Alan Richards
    Sales: Akihiro Hashino
Number Employees: 10

Type of Packaging: Bulk

6326 Haydel's Bakery
4037 Jefferson Hwy
Jefferson, LA 70121-1643   504-837-0190
    Fax: 504-837-5512 800-442-1342
                    www.haydelbakery.com
Mardi Gras cakes, other gourmet cakes and pastries
    Owner: David Haydel
Estimated Sales: $1-2.5 Million
Number Employees: 20-49

6327 Haydenergy Health
200 W 58th St # 2c
New York, NY 10019-1432   212-888-1008
    Fax: 212-246-9344 800-255-1660
                    www.naura.com
Processor of health food products including vitamins
and energy shakes
    President: Naura Hayden
    Vice President: Nancy Leonard
Estimated Sales: $2.5-5 Million
Number Employees: 1-4
Number of Brands: 1
Number of Products: 3
Sq. footage: 4000
Type of Packaging: Consumer
Brands:
    DYNAMITE ENERGY SHAKE
    DYNAMITE VITES

6328 Haypress Gourmet Pasta
7f Hoover Avenue
Haverstraw, NY 10927-1024   845-947-4580
                    Fax: 845-947-2147
Pasta
    General Manager: Nicholas DiNapoli
Estimated Sales: $5-10 Million
Number Employees: 5-9

6329 Haywood Enterprises
2700 Napa Valley Corporate # L
Napa, CA 94558-7558   707-261-5100
    Fax: 707-261-5111 info@perfectpuree.com
                    www.perfectpuree.com
Flavored purees for drinks, desserts and food
    President: Tracy Hayward
Estimated Sales: $ 1 - 3 Million
Number Employees: 10-19
Type of Packaging: Consumer, Bulk

6330 Hazel Creek Orchards
227 Smiling Apple Dr
Mt Airy, GA 30563-2714   706-754-4899
                    Fax: 706-754-1524
Processor of apples and apple juice; also, cider in-
cluding apple, cherry, peach, raspberry and blue-
berry
    Owner: Horace Yearwood
Estimated Sales: $1-2.5 Million
Number Employees: 1-4
Sq. footage: 8400
Type of Packaging: Consumer, Bulk
Brands:
    Hazel Creek

6331 Hazelnut Growers of Oregon
25 Lb.,$90.00
Premium, OR 24644   503-648-4176
    Fax: 503-648-9515 800-273-4676
    nutsales@hazelnut.com www.hazelnut.com
Processor, roaster and exporter of hazelnuts
    President: Len Spesert
    CFO: Ozzie Hyde
    Quality Control: Don Marshall
    VP Marketing: Troy Johnson
    Sales Director: Bob Hoffman
    VP Operations: Dick Vanderschuere
    Plant Manager: Ken Guinn
    Purchasing Manager: Mike Sook
Estimated Sales: $5-10 Million
Number Employees: 100-249
Type of Packaging: Consumer, Bulk
Brands:
    Oregan Orchard

6332 (HQ)Hazelwood Farm Bakeries
1 General Mills Boulevard
Minneapolis, MN 55426-1347   314-595-4150
                    Fax: 314-595-4728

Gourmet, cheese, chocolate, butter, junk cookie, oatmeal, raisin.
President: David Ockleshaw
CEO: Walt VanBenthuysen
VP Operations: Brent Baxter
Purchasing Manager: Paul Ray
Number Employees: 500

6333 Hazelwood Farms Bakery
155 Balta Dr
Rochester, NY 14623-3142   585-424-1240
     Fax: 585-424-1286 www.pillsbury.com
Processor of frozen pies
President: Peter Statt
Plant Manager: Rich Sychterz
Estimated Sales: $ 20 - 50 Million
Number Employees: 50-99
Parent Co: Pillsbury Company
Type of Packaging: Consumer, Food Service

6334 (HQ)Hazle Park Packing Company
260 Washington Ave
West Hazleton, PA 18202-1183   570-455-7571
     Fax: 570-455-6030   800-238-4331
     sales@hazlepark.com   www.hazlepark.com
Processor and packer of ham, sausage, bologna, frankfurters, pork and beef products.
President: Gary Kreisl
Estimated Sales: $20-50 Million
Number Employees: 20-49
Type of Packaging: Consumer, Food Service, Private Label, Bulk
Brands:
HAZLE

6335 Hazlitt's 1852 Vineyard
P.O. Box 53
Hector, NY 14841-0053   607-546-9463
     Fax: 607-546-5712   888-750-0494
     info@hazlitt1852.com   www.hazlitt1852.com
Producers of red and white wines.
VP: D Hazlitt
Estimated Sales: $5-10 Million
Number Employees: 10-19
Number of Brands: 2
Brands:
HAZLITT

6336 Hazy Grove Nuts
PO Box 2354
Lake Oswego, OR 97035-0601   503-670-8344
     Fax: 503-968-2111   800-574-6887
     lobbok7@gte.net   www.hazygrove.com
Processors of hazelnuts.
President: Karen Lobb
Number Employees: 1-4
Type of Packaging: Private Label

6337 Head Country Food Products
P.O. Box 2324
Ponca City, OK 74602-2324   580-762-1227
     Fax: 580-765-8867   888-762-1227
     chead@poncacity.net   www.headcountry.com
Manufacturer of BBQ sauces, seasonings and salsas
President: Danny Head
Office Manager/Accounting: Linda Groth
Marketing: Carey Head
Internet Sales: Kerenda Wood
General Manager: Paul Schatte
Estimated Sales: $5-10 Million
Number Employees: 10-19
Number of Brands: 1
Number of Products: 6
Type of Packaging: Consumer, Food Service, Private Label, Bulk
Brands:
HEAD COUNTRY

6338 Healing Light
22 Spring Street
Catskill, NY 12414-1416   518-537-8800
     Fax: 518-945-7703 www.thehealinglight.com

6339 Health & Nutrition Systems International
6615 Boyntn Bch Blvd # 117
Boynton Beach, FL 33437-3526   561-433-0733
     Fax: 888-478-8467 info@hnsglobal.com
     www.hnsglobal.com

Designed to help you with your individual diet goals, whether that is to lose weight or stop gaining. Our products include Original Carb Cutter, Carb Cutter Phase 2, Carb Cuttler A&B, Fat Cutter and Eat Less -
President: Christopher Tisi
Controller: Al Dugan
Marketing Director: Steven Sarafian
Marketing Assistant: Lindsay Garveyff
Product Development/Sales: Jamie Heithoff
Human Resources/Director Operations: Mona Lalia
Graphic Design: Derek Lopez
Graphic Design: Cathy Card
Shipping/Receiving: Tonya Davis
Number Employees: 10-19

6340 Health Asure
125 McPherson Street
Santa Cruz, CA 95060-5818   818-577-1100
     Fax: 818-577-1150 www.breathasure.com
Manufacturers of fresh breath capsules and mints.
Estimated Sales: $10-100 Million
Number Employees: 20-49
Brands:
MEGAMINTS
MINTASURE
ORABLAST CHEWY

6341 Health Concerns
8001 Capwell Dr
Oakland, CA 94621-2107   510-639-0280
     Fax: 510-639-9140   800-233-9355
     info@healthconcerns.com
     www.healthconcerns.com
Processor and exporter of Chinese herbs, medicinal mushrooms and energy tonics.
President: Andrew Gaeddert
Estimated Sales: $3-5 Million
Number Employees: 5-9
Sq. footage: 6000
Type of Packaging: Consumer
Brands:
HEALTH CONCERNS

6342 Health Enhancers
8139 Corunna Road
Flint, MI 48532-5505   810-635-9899
     Fax: 810-659-4949
President: Herbert Kinnee
Brands:
Health Enhancers

6343 Health Plus
13837 Magnolia Ave
Chino, CA 91710-7028   909-627-9393
     Fax: 909-591-7659   800-822-6225
     www.healthplusinc.com
Importer and exporter of psyllium and nutritional herbs, tablets and capsules.
President: Rita Mediratta
Estimated Sales: $1-2.5 Million
Number Employees: 20-49
Sq. footage: 17000
Type of Packaging: Bulk
Brands:
ADRENAL CLEANSE
ASTAZANTHIN
AZ-ONE
BLOOD CLEANSE
BRAIN VITA
COLON CLEANSE
ENER JET
FIREBALL FAT BURNER
HEART CLEANSE
JOINT CLEANSE
KIDNEY CLEANSE
LIVER CLEANSE
ORA-PLUS
PAT'S PSYLLIUM SLIM
PROSTATE CLEANSE
SHELLY'S HAIR CARE
SUPER FAT BURNER

6344 Health Products Corporation
1060 Nepperhan Ave
Yonkers, NY 10703-1432   914-423-2900
     Fax: 914-963-6001 zurion2@aol.com
     www.hpc7.com
Importer and exporter of psyllium and nutritional herbs, tablets and capsules; contract packager of blending and filling powders
President: J Lewin
Vice President: K Linnington

Estimated Sales: $ 50 - 100 Million
Number Employees: 50-99
Sq. footage: 45000
Parent Co: Health Products Corporation
Brands:
Aspi-Cor
Khg-7
Lactalins
Malpotane
Tick Stop

6345 Health Valley Company
16100 Foothill Boulevard
Irwindale, CA 91706   626-334-3241
     Fax: 626-334-0220   800-334-3204
Processor and exporter of natural foods including cookies, cereal bars, tarts, crackers, granola bars, cereals, chilis, soups, snacks, corn puffs and canned vegetarian entrees
President: Ben Brecher
CFO/Sr VP: Diane Beardsley
Number Employees: 250-499
Parent Co: Intrepid Food Holdings
Type of Packaging: Consumer, Food Service, Private Label, Bulk
Brands:
Health Valley

6346 Health from the Sun/ArkoPharma
19 Crosby Drive
Suite 300
Bedford, MA 01730-1401   781-276-0505
     Fax: 781-276-7335 www.healthfromthesun.com
Brands:
LEAN FOR LESS

6347 Health is Wealth Foods
217 Prosser Ave
Williamstown, NJ 08094-8600   856-728-1998
     Fax: 856-629-0378
     customerservice@healthiswealthfoods.com
     www.healthiswealthfoods.com
Processor of boxed, frozen and all natural egg rolls, spring rolls, appetizers, beef and chicken hot dogs, pot stickers and chicken including grilled cutlets, nuggets, patties and tenders. Also vegeterian and vegan items.
President: Val Vasilief
Vice President: Jerry Colt
Estimated Sales: $ 5 - 10 Million
Number Employees: 5-9
Sq. footage: 10000
Type of Packaging: Food Service, Private Label
Brands:
HEALTH IS WEALTH

6348 Health-Tech
PO Box 243759
Boynton Beach, FL 33424-3759
     Fax: 561-364-8158   800-600-2861
     sharon.lord@sweetbreath.com
     www.sweetbreath.com
Breath fresheners, energy strips, vitamin strips and cough and cold strips instant energy for your body and mind
Founder/President: Jeffrey Hirschman
National Account Manager: David Hirschman
Vice President Marketing: Roger Mascall
Brands:
ICE CHEWS
ICE CHIPS
ICE CHUNKS
SWEET BREATH XTREME INTENSE BREATH

6349 HealthBest
133 Mata Way # 107
San Marcos, CA 92069-2937   760-752-5230
     Fax: 760-752-1322 davegebhard@healthbest.com
     www.globalkaizen.com
Processor, importer and exporter of natural and organic beans, dried fruits, snack foods, grains, herbs, spices, seasonings, nuts, seeds, bee pollen, pasta, sugar-free candy, etc
President: Jamie Hickerson
Vice President: Jerry Johnston
Quality Control: Eric Pena
Sales Director: Bob Bonner
Operations Manager: Jamie Hickerson
Purchasing Manager: Mike Hantman
Estimated Sales: $3 Million
Number Employees: 20-49
Number of Brands: 2
Number of Products: 300

Sq. footage: 40000
Parent Co: Nature's Best
Type of Packaging: Consumer, Private Label, Bulk
Brands:
 Healthbest

6350 Healthco Canada Enterprises
PO Box 8249
Victoria, BC V8W 3R9
Canada   250-382-8384
        Fax: 250-868-2195 877-468-2875
 jb-rebar@shaw.ca www.healthcocanada.com
Manufactures organic nutrition bars.

6351 Healthmate Products
1510 Old Deerfield Rd # 103
Highland Park, IL 60035-3069   847-579-1051
        Fax: 847-579-1059 800-584-8642
 tburke@healthmateproducts.com
        www.healthmateproducts.com
    VP: Tim Burke
Estimated Sales: $1 Million
Number Employees: 1-4
Type of Packaging: Consumer, Food Service

6352 Healthwave
PO Box 4614
Santa Barbara, CA 93140-4614   805-899-4240
    Fax: 805-899-1113 info@aromapatches.com
        www.aromapatches.com
    President/CEO: Art Williams

6353 Healthy Grain Foods
4125 Yorkshire Ln
Northbrook, IL 60062-2915   847-272-5576
    Fax: 847-272-5576 www.healthygrainfoods.com
Research and development of frozen food products.
Cereal breakfast foods.
    President: Harold Zukerman
Estimated Sales: $1-2.5 Million
Number Employees: 5-9

6354 Healthy Oven
62 Grand Street
Croton on Hudson, NY 10520-2519 914-271-5458
    Fax: 914-271-9279 healthyovn@aol.com
        www.low-fat.com
    President: Sarah Phillips
Estimated Sales: Under $500,000
Number Employees: 1-4
Brands:
 Healthy Oven

6355 Healthy Times
13200 Kirkham Way
Suite 104
Poway, CA 92064-7126   858-513-1550
    Fax: 858-513-1533 htbaby@healthytimes.com
        www.healthytimes.com
    President: Rondi K Prescott
Estimated Sales: $5-10 Million appx.
Number Employees: 5-9

6356 Healthy'N Fit Nutritionals
435 Yorktown Rd
Croton on Hudson, NY 10520-3703 914-271-6040
    Fax: 914-271-6042 800-338-5200
 healthynfit@aol.com www.behealthynfit.com
Processor of vitamins, minerals and food supple-
ments; importer of herbs, nutraceuticals, ascorbic
acid and nutritional raw materials; exporter of food
and dietary supplements
    President: Robert J Sepe
    VP/CFO: Irene Sepe
    Public Relations: Denise O'Neill
Estimated Sales: $7 Million appx.
Number Employees: 10-19
Number of Products: 1000
Sq. footage: 40000
Type of Packaging: Consumer, Food Service, Pri-
vate Label, Bulk
Brands:
 DOCTOR'S NUTRICEUTICALS
 HEALTHY'N FIT NUTRITIONALS

6357 Heart Foods Company
2235 E 38th St
Minneapolis, MN 55407-3083   612-724-5266
    Fax: 612-724-5516 800-229-3663
        www.heartfoods.com
Processor of encapsulated herbal and high potency
cayenne formulas.
Estimated Sales: $1-2.5 Million
Number Employees: 1-4

Number of Brands: 1
Number of Products: 13
Sq. footage: 2500
Type of Packaging: Consumer

6358 Heart to Heart Foods
P.O.Box 6096
Logan, UT 84341-6096   435-753-9602
                    Fax: 435-753-9605
Ice cream products
    Owner: Craig Earl
Estimated Sales: $2.5-5 Million
Number Employees: 10-19

6359 Hearthstone Whole GrainBakery
4717 Meadow Lane
Bozeman, MT 59715-9631   406-586-1227
        Fax: 406-586-1227 800-757-7919
Bakery
    President: Gwen Phillips
    Manager: Mavis Mason

6360 Heartland Brewery
35 Union Sq W # 1
New York, NY 10003-3200   212-645-3400
    Fax: 212-645-8306 www.heartlandbrewery.com
Processor of ale, beer and lager
    President: John Bloostein
    CEO: John Bloostein
    Marketing Director: Bonnie Bernier
Estimated Sales: $2.5-5 Million
Number Employees: 50-99
Type of Packaging: Consumer, Food Service
Brands:
 Heartland

6361 Heartland Farms
1241 N Wells Street
Fort Wayne, IN 46808-2791   888-757-7423
        Fax: 888-757-7423 888-747-7423
 mail@spiceintel.com www.spiceintel.com
Bread mixes, mesquite and barbecue sauces, and
smoke powder

6362 Heartland Fields
4200 Corporate Dr # 106
West Des Moines, IA 50266-5903 515-225-1166
        Fax: 515-225-1177 www.heartlandfields.com
Manufacturers of prepared soy meals and snacks.
    Owner: John Schillinger
Estimated Sales: $ 5 - 10 Million
Number Employees: 5-9
Type of Packaging: Consumer

6363 Heartland Fields, LLC
4200 Corporate Dr # 106
West Des Moines, IA 50266-5903 515-225-1166
        Fax: 515-225-1177 866-769-7200
 heartland@heartlandfields.com
 www.heartlandfields.com
Manufacturer and exporter of soybeans
    President/Founder/CEO: John Schillinger PhD
    Marketing/Sales Director: Karen Labenz
Estimated Sales: $10-20 Million
Number Employees: 100-249
Parent Co: Monsanto
Type of Packaging: Consumer, Bulk
Brands:
 DEKALB

6364 Heartland Food Products
1901 W 47th Pl # 210
Shawnee Mission, KS 66205-1834 913-831-4446
                    Fax: 913-831-4004
 patkearney@heartlandfoodproducts.com
        www.heartlandfoodproducts.com
Processor and wholesaler/distributor of waffle and
pancake mixes for the institutional food market
    President: Bill Steeb
    Founder: Mary Steeb
Estimated Sales: Less than $500,000
Number Employees: 10-19
Type of Packaging: Bulk
Brands:
 Bascoms Paprika
 Bascoms Tapioca

6365 Heartland Gourmet Popcorn
131 Martin Lane
Elk Grove Village, IL 60007-1309 847-593-6471
        Fax: 262-743-1848 866-489-4676
 customerservice@heartlandpopcorn.com
        www.heartlandpopcorn.com

Packaged gourmet popcorn kernels, packaged or-
ganic popcorn kernels, all natural seasonings, canola
oil and sea salt, private label popcorn poppers and
caramelized popcorn bags
    President: Gary Petersen
    VP: Brent Petersen
Estimated Sales: $1-2 Million
Number Employees: 9
Number of Brands: 2
Number of Products: 19
Sq. footage: 10000
Parent Co: Leasetronix
Type of Packaging: Consumer, Food Service
Other Locations:
 Heartland Gourmet Popcorn
 Elkhorn WI
Brands:
 HEARTLAND FARMS
 HEARTLAND GOURMET

6366 Heartland Gourmet Popcorn
P.O. Box 483
Elkhorn, WI 53121-0483   262-743-1420
    Fax: 262-743-1848 866-489-4676
 customerservice@heartlandpopcorn.com
        http://www.heartlandpopcorn.com
Packaged gourmet popcorn kernels, packaged or-
ganic popcorn kernels, all natural seasonings, canola
oil and sea salt; private label popcorn poppers and
caramelized popcorn bags.
    Founder/President: Gary Petersen
    Vice President: Brent Petersen
Estimated Sales: $1-2 Million
Number Employees: 5-9
Number of Brands: 2
Number of Products: 19
Sq. footage: 10000
Parent Co: Leusetronix
Type of Packaging: Consumer, Private Label
Other Locations:
 Heartland Gourmet Popcorn
 Elkhorn WI

6367 Heartland Mill
124 N Highway 167
Marienthal, KS 67863-6368   620-379-4472
    Fax: 620-379-4459 info@heartlandmill.com
        www.heartlandmill.com
Grower, marketer, processor, importer and exporter
of organic grains, flour, oat products and sunflower
seeds. Organic and Kosher certified.
    President: Larry Decker
Estimated Sales: $10-20 Million
Number Employees: 20-49
Sq. footage: 100000
Type of Packaging: Food Service, Private Label,
Bulk
Brands:
 HEARTLAND MILL

6368 Heartland Vineyards
24945 Detroit Rd # G
Cleveland, OH 44145-2554   440-871-0701
        jwdover@aol.com
        www.heartlandvineyards.com
Wines
    Owner: Jerome M Welliver
Estimated Sales: $500-1 Million appx.
Number Employees: 1-4

6369 Heartland Wheat Growers
1030 E 15th Street
Russell, KS 67665-2255   785-483-5559
                    Fax: 785-483-5561
Processor and exporter of wheat starch and gluten
Number Employees: 50-99
Parent Co: Farmland Industries
Brands:
 Heartex
 Heartpro
 Heartstar

6370 Heartline Foods
830 Post Road E
Westport, CT 06880-5222   203-222-0381
                    Fax: 203-226-6445
Processor of paprika, beans, noodles, sauces, sea-
sonings, pasta, soups and tapiocas.
Estimated Sales: $ .5 - 1 million
Number Employees: 1-4
Brands:
 CHINA BOWL
 DINNY ROBB
 SINATRA
 WYE RIVER

6371 Heaven Hill Distilleries
P.O.Box 729
Bardstown, KY 40004-0729   502-348-3921
          Fax: 502-348-0162 www.heaven-hill.com
Manufacturer and distiller of spirits including bourbon, brandy, gin, whiskey, vodka, liqueurs and rum.
President: Max Shapira
Director Marketing: Kate Latts
Corporate Communications Manager: Josh Hafer
Master Distiller: Parker Beam
Master Distiller: Craig Beam
Estimated Sales: $100+ Million
Number Employees: 250-499
Type of Packaging: Consumer, Private Label, Bulk
Brands:
ANSAC COGNAC
ARANDAS
BURNETT'S CITRUS VODKA
BURNETT'S GIN
BURNETT'S ORANGE VODKA
BURNETT'S RASPBERRY VODKA
BURNETT'S VANILLA VODKA
BURNETT'S VODKA
CHRISTIAN BROTHERS
CLUNY
COPA DE ORO
CORONET VSQ BRANDY
DU BOUCHETT
DUBONNET
EL CONQUISTADOR
ELIJAH CRAIG
EVAN WILLIAMS
EVAN WILLIAMS EGG NOG
FIGHTING COCK
GLEN SALEN
HENRY MCKENNA
HPNOTIQ
ISLE OF JURA
KILBEGGAN
LAZZARONI
O'MARA'S IRISH COUNTRY CREAM
OLD FITZGERALD
RON LLAVE
TWO FINGERS
TYRCONNELL
WHALER'S

6372 Heaven Scent Natural Foods
2516 California Ave
Santa Monica, CA 90403-4610   310-829-9050
Fax: 310-829-6745 info@heavenscent-foods.com
          www.heavenscent.com
Processor of croutons, breadcrumbs, breadsticks and cookies including seasonal, butter, natural, wheat-free, fat-free and special dietary baked without refined sugar; also, gingerbread houses and cookies. We also do private label.
President: Tom Mosk
Estimated Sales: $2 Million approx.
Number Employees: 1-4
Sq. footage: 40000
Type of Packaging: Private Label
Brands:
HEAVEN SCENT WINDMILL COOKIES
Heaven Scent
Heaven Scent Butter Cookies
Heaven Scent Croutons
Heaven Scent Fat Free Cookies
Heaven Scent Natural Foods

6373 Heavenly Hemp Foods
PO Box 1794
Nederland, CO 80466-1794   303-938-0195
          Fax: 303-443-1869 888-328-4367
bhc@hempfoods.com   www.hempfoods.com
Health foods
President: David Almquist
Marketing Director: Tom White
Operations Manager: Kathleen Chippi
Brands:
Heavenly Hemp Blue Tortillas
Heavenly Hemp Garlic
Heavenly Hemp Spicy

6374 Heavenscent Edibles
402 E 90th Street
New York, NY 10128-5119   212-369-0310
          Fax: 212-369-0310
Brownies and holiday cookies

6375 Hebert Candies
575 Hartford Tpke
Shrewsbury, MA 01545-4002   508-845-8051
          Fax: 508-842-3065 866-432-3781
          www.hebertcandies.com
Processor of Kosher chocolate candies and confectionery products.
CEO: Tom O'Rourke
CFO: Jeff Goodman
CEO: Tom O'Rourke
Purchasing Manager: Bob Kerekon
Estimated Sales: $10+ Million
Number Employees: 100-249
Sq. footage: 50000
Type of Packaging: Consumer

6376 Heck Cellars
15401 Bear Mountain Winery Rd
Arvin, CA 93203-9743   661-854-6120
          Fax: 661-854-2876
Processor and exporter of table wine, wine coolers and brandy; also, juices and bottled water.
Owner: Gary Heck
Plant Manager: Tim Holt
Estimated Sales: $10-20 Million
Number Employees: 20-49
Sq. footage: 600000
Parent Co: F. Korbel & Brothers
Type of Packaging: Private Label, Bulk

6377 Hecker Pass Winery
4605 Hecker Pass Rd
Gilroy, CA 95020-8808   408-842-8755
Fax: 408-842-9799 carlo@heckerpasswinery.com
          www.heckerpasswinery.com
Wines
Owner/President: Mario Fortino
VP/Operations/Marketing: Carlo Fortino
Owner: Frances Fortino
Estimated Sales: $500,000-$1 Million
Number Employees: 1-4
Type of Packaging: Private Label
Brands:
Hecker Pass

6378 Hedgehaven Specialty Foods
PO Box 719
Ilwaco, WA 98624-0719   800-642-4711
Fax: 360-642-3014 inforequest@hedgehaven.com
          www.hedgehaven.com
Manufacturer of cookies, shortbread and bakery goods.
President: Linda Hedge
Estimated Sales: $5-9.9 Million
Number Employees: 5-9

6379 Hega Food Products
6 Santa Fe Way
Cranbury, NJ 08512-3288   609-409-6200
          Fax: 609-409-6500 800-345-7742
          www.conagrafoods.com
President: Greg Heckman
Estimated Sales: $10-20 Million
Number Employees: 20-49
Brands:
Butterball
Crunch N Munch

6380 Hegy's South Hills Vineyard & Winery
PO Box 727
Twin Falls, ID 83303-0727   208-599-0074
          Fax: 208-734-6369
Wines
Owner/Vineyard Manager: Frank Hegy
Estimated Sales: Under $500,000
Number Employees: 1-4
Brands:
South Hills

6381 Heidi's Cheese Products
1570 Baskin Road
Mundelein, IL 60060   847-362-5971
          Fax: 847-362-2670 heidicheese@aol.com
Processor of cheese including low-fat cheddar and muenster; also, farmer's, Swiss, etc
President: Jim Mahoney
Estimated Sales: $3 - 5 Million
Number Employees: 5
Type of Packaging: Consumer, Food Service, Bulk
Brands:
Garden Vegetable
Heidi Ann Brand Swiss cheese
Snappy Jack
lactose

6382 Heidi's Gourmet Desserts
1651 Montreal Cir
Tucker, GA 30084-6933   770-449-4900
          Fax: 770-326-6157 800-241-4166
Processor and exporter of frozen custom desserts including cheesecakes, multi-layer tortes, brownies a la mode and special occasion cakes; also, cheesecake batter.
President: Larry Obertfell
Operations Director: Brian Schendider
Estimated Sales: $10-20 Million
Number Employees: 100-249
Sq. footage: 67000
Type of Packaging: Consumer, Food Service, Private Label
Other Locations:
Heidi's Gourmet
Atlanta GA
Heidi's Gourmet
Sun Valley CA
Heidi's Gourmet
Salt Lake City UT

6383 (HQ)Heikes Produce Company
P.O.Box 4310
Medford, OR 97501-0164   541-772-5653
          Fax: 541-608-0747 www.sabroso.com
Processor, importer and exporter of frozen packed strawberries, cherries, blackberries, raspberries, boysenberries, blueberries and tropical fruits
President: Dwayne Heikes
President: Tony Miller
CEO: James Root
Estimated Sales: $100+ Million
Number Employees: 250-499
Type of Packaging: Food Service, Bulk
Brands:
Heikes Farms Finest

6384 Heineman's Winery
P.O.Box 300
Put In Bay, OH 43456-0300   419-285-2811
Fax: 419-285-3412 info@HeinemansWinery.com
          http://www.heinemanswinery.com/
Manufacturer of fruit juices and wine.
President/Winemaker: Ed Heineman
Vice President: Louis Heineman
Assistant Manager: Michael Bianichi
Estimated Sales: $500,000-$1 Million
Number Employees: 1-4
Parent Co: Heineman Beverage
Other Locations:
Heineman Distributing
Port Clinton OH
Brands:
CATAWBA GRAPE JUICE
HEINEMAN'S

6385 (HQ)Heinemann's
1300 E Locust St
Milwaukee, WI 53212-2693   414-265-1900
          Fax: 414-265-1915
          www.heinemannsrestaurants.com
Processor of baked goods and confectionery products
Executive Director: Brian Bielert
Manager: Jim Bergman
Estimated Sales: $300,000-500,000
Number Employees: 10-19
Type of Packaging: Consumer, Food Service

6386 Heinemann's Bakeries
3925 W 43rd Street
Chicago, IL 60632-3494   312-239-5592
          Fax: 773-523-7985 feedback@heinemanns.com
          www.heinmanns.com
Manufacturer of cakes, cookies, Danish, brownies, muffins and breads.
President: Vincent Graham
CFO: Andrew Geryol
Sales: John Termine
Purchasing: Paul Krug
Estimated Sales: $25 Million
Number Employees: 250
Number of Brands: 1
Number of Products: 150
Type of Packaging: Consumer, Food Service, Private Label, Bulk
Brands:
HEINEMANN'S

6387 Heiner's Bakery
P.O.Box 9247
Huntington, WV 25704-0247   304-523-8411
Fax: 304-525-9268 800-776-8411
http://www.heinersbakery.com
Processor of breads and buns.
President: E Heiner Jr
Production Manager: James Basler
Estimated Sales: $20-50 Million
Number Employees: 250-499

6388 Heinke Industrial Park
5365 Clark Rd
Paradise, CA 95969-6392   530-877-7864
Beef, beef products
Estimated Sales: $500,000-$1 Million
Number Employees: 1-4

6389 Heinkel's Packing Company
2005 N 22nd St
Decatur, IL 62526-4734   217-428-4401
Fax: 217-428-4403 800-594-2738
Processor of smoked meats including ham, bacon,
pork, turkey and smoked sausages; also, lunch meats
and fresh sausage available; wholesaler/distributor
of boxed beef and pork; serving the food service
market. Venison processing
President: Miles Wright
CFO: Neal Wright
Vice President: Dennis Heinkel
Estimated Sales: $5-9.9 Million
Number Employees: 10-19
Type of Packaging: Consumer, Food Service, Bulk
Brands:
Heinkel's

**6390 Heino's German-Style Wholesale
Bakery**
3951 Arnold Avenue
Naples, FL 34104-3358   941-643-3911
Baked goods
Estimated Sales: $5-10 Million
Number Employees: 5-9

6391 Heintz & Weber Company
150 Reading Ave
Buffalo, NY 14220-2156   716-852-7171
Fax: 716-852-7173 info@webersmustard.com
www.webersmustard.com
Processor of condiments including horseradish, hot
garlic and jalapeno mustard, dill pickle and hot
green tomato piccalilli relish, and hot texan sand-
wich sauce.
President: Steven Desmond
Executive VP: Suzanne Desmond
CEO: Steven Desmond
Estimated Sales: $5-10 Million
Number Employees: 5-9
Sq. footage: 24000
Type of Packaging: Consumer, Bulk
Brands:
Weber's Horseradish Mustard
Weber's Hot Garlic M
Weber's Hot Piocacic
Weber's Spicy Dill Pickles
Weber's Sweet Pickle

6392 Heinz
1200 N 5th St
Fremont, OH 43420-3900   419-332-7357
Fax: 419-332-3973 www.heinz.com
Processor of ketchup and barbecue and chili sauces
Manager: Jerry Kozicki
Vice President: Jeffrey P Berger
Sr. VP/President: David C Moran
Plant Manager: Jerry Kozicki
Purchasing Agent: Becky White
Estimated Sales: $100-500 Million
Number Employees: 500-999
Parent Co: H.J. Heinz Company
Type of Packaging: Consumer
Brands:
Heinz
Jack Daniel's
John West
Linda McCartney
Orlando
Plasmon
Poppers
Smart Ones
Watties
Wylers

6393 Heinz
1357 Isett Ave
Muscatine, IA 52761-4599   563-263-5711
Fax: 563-262-2304 www.hjheinz.com
Processor of canned soup, gravies and ketchup
Chairman/President/CEO: Lynn Swann
Vice President: Jeffrey P Berger
Sr. VP/President, Heinz Consumer Produ: David
C Moran
Plant Manager: Steve McNulty
Estimated Sales: $100-500 Million
Number Employees: 500-999
Parent Co: H.J. Heinz Company
Type of Packaging: Consumer
Brands:
Bagel Bites
Heinz
Jack Daniel's
John West
Linda McCartney
Mr Yoshida's
Orlando
Poppers
Smart Ones

6394 Heinz
P.O.Box 57
Stockton, CA 95201-3057   209-948-2782
Fax: 209-948-3165 800-253-3399
www.hjheinz.com
Processor of tomato paste
President: Reuben Peterson
CFO: Arthur B Winkleblack
Managing Director: Mary C Choksi
Plant Manager: Tom McMurtry
Purchasing Agent: Laura Smith
Estimated Sales: $100-500 Million
Number Employees: 100-249
Parent Co: H.J. Heinz Company
Type of Packaging: Consumer, Food Service
Brands:
Heinz Ketchup
Ore-Ida French Fries
Smart Ones

6395 Heinz
431 W 16th Street
Holland, MI 49423-3497   616-396-6557
Fax: 616-396-1797 800-528-5757
www.heinz.com
Processor of relish, pickles, peppers and vinegar
Chairman/President/CEO: Lynn Swann
Executive VP, Global Foodservice: Scott OHara
CFO: Arthur Winkleblack
Vice President: Jeffrey P Berger
Sr. VP/President, Heinz Consumer Produ: David
C Moran
Plant Manager: J Shoup
Purchasing Agent: Clarence Becker
Estimated Sales: $50-100 Million
Number Employees: 250-499
Parent Co: H.J. Heinz Company
Type of Packaging: Consumer
Brands:
Catelli
Farley,s
Heinz
John West
Linda McCartney
Orlando
Poppers
Smart Ones
Watties
Wylers

6396 Heinz Bakery Products
191 Bethpage Sweet Hollow Road
Old Bethpage, NY 11804-1314   631-249-3170
Baked goods
Estimated Sales: Under $500,000
Number Employees: 50-99

6397 Heinz Company
6 Neshaminy Interplex
Suite 117
Trevose, PA 19053-6942   215-639-2343
Fax: 215-639-9075
Processor of tomato products, condiments, soups,
pickles, canned entrees, etc
Regional Manager: Dan Peterson
Estimated Sales: $2.5-5 Million
Number Employees: 1-4
Parent Co: H.J. Heinz Company

Type of Packaging: Consumer, Food Service, Private Label

6398 Heinz Company of Canada
90 Shepherd Avenue
Suite 400
North York, ON M2M 4K6
Canada   416-226-5757
Fax: 416-226-7544 800-268-6641
Processor and exporter of beans, ketchup, mustard,
mayonnaise, relish, salad, salad dressing, olives,
pickles, sandwich spreads, sauces, tomato products,
tuna, vinegar, soups, stews, croutons, canned pasta
and frozen entrees
CEO/President: Mark Leckie
Number Employees: 100-249
Parent Co: H.J. Heinz Company
Type of Packaging: Consumer, Food Service, Pri-
vate Label
Other Locations:
H.J. Heinz Co. of Canada Ltd.
Wheatley ON

6399 Heinz North America
357 6th Avenue
Pittsburgh, PA 15222   412-237-5700
Fax: 412-237-3584 www.heinz.com
Processor and exporter of pudding, beans, canned
entrees, condiments, dietary drink mixes, gravy,
ketchup, mustards, peppers, pickles, pureed foods,
relishes, sauces, soups, tomato products and
vinegars
Chairman/President/CEO: William Johnson
EVP/CFO: Art Winkleblack
EVP/Pres/CEO, Heinz North America: Scott
O'Hara
VP/Chief Procurement Officer: Chris Stockwell
Estimated Sales: $10 Billion
Number Employees: 32,500
Parent Co: H.J. Heinz Company
Type of Packaging: Consumer, Food Service, Pri-
vate Label
Other Locations:
Heinz (USA)
Cedar Rapids IA
Brands:
BAGEL BITES
BELLA ROSSA
BOSTON MARKET
CATELLI
CHEF FRANCISCO
CLASSICO
DELI MEX
DIANNE'S
HEINZ
HEINZ NURTURE
JACK DANIEL'S SAUCES
KABOB
LEA & PERRINS
MR. YOSHIDA'S
NANCY'S
ORE-IDA
POPPERS
SMART ONES
T.G.I. FRIDAYS

6400 Heinz North America
5521 Division Dr
Fort Myers, FL 33905-5017   239-694-3663
Fax: 239-693-4498
heinzconsumeraffairs@hiheinz.com
www.bagelbites.com
Manufacturer and exporter of frozen mini bagel piz-
zas
Factory Manager: Tom Brahler
Estimated Sales: $50-100 Million
Number Employees: 250-499
Sq. footage: 75000
Parent Co: Heinz USA
Type of Packaging: Consumer, Food Service, Pri-
vate Label, Bulk
Brands:
BAGEL BITES
STUFFED BAGEL BITES

6401 Heise's Wausau Farms
2805 Valley View Rd
Wausau, WI 54403-8799   715-675-3584
Fax: 715-675-3256 800-764-1010
heisewausaufarms@yahoo.com
Processor and exporter of cultivated Wisconsin gin-
seng and bottled bee pollen capsules
President/Owner: Lyn Heise

Estimated Sales:$1-2 Million
Sq. footage: 4000
Brands:
    Heise's
    Jar-Lu

6402 Heisler Food Enterprises
5760 Broadway
A
Bronx, NY 10463-4143   718-543-0855
                      Fax: 718-543-2498
Kosher baked goods
    President: Judith Heisler
    Treasurer: Richard Heisler
Estimated Sales:$5-9.9 Million
Number Employees: 20-49

6403 Heitz Wine Cellar
500 Taplin Rd
St Helena, CA 94574-9537   707-963-3542
       Fax: 707-963-7454 www.heitzcellar.com
Processor and exporter of wine
    Owner: Kathleen Heitzmyers
    Winemaker: David Heitz
    COO: Kathleen Heitz-Myers
Estimated Sales:$5-10 Million
Number Employees: 10-19
Type of Packaging: Consumer
Brands:
    Heitz

6404 Heitzman Bakery
3800 Shepherdsville Rd
Louisville, KY 40218-3169   502-452-1891
     Fax: 502-452-6789 linda@heitzmanbakery.net
                    www.heitzmanbakery.net
Processor of donuts, cookies, brownies, desert
cakes, custom decorated ckaes and wedding cakes.
Also provides deli trays.
    President: Paul Osting
    Manager: Nancy Kasey
Estimated Sales:$500,000-$1 Million
Number Employees: 5-9
Type of Packaging: Consumer, Food Service
Brands:
    Springerlies

6405 Helen Grace Chocolates
2369 E Pacifica Pl
Compton, CA 90220-6216   310-638-8400
       Fax: 310-605-0704 800-367-4240
orders@helengrace.com   www.helengrace.com
Chocolate candy
    Partner: Robert Worth
    Partner: David Worth
    VP: Mike Harrigian
Estimated Sales:$5-10 Million
Number Employees: 20-49
Type of Packaging: Consumer
Brands:
    Helen Grace

6406 Helena View/Johnston Vineyard
3500 Highway 128
Calistoga, CA 94515-9715   707-942-4956
       Fax: 707-942-4956 info@helenaview.com
                    www.helenaview.com
Wines
    VP: Charles Johnston
    Manager Public Relations: Sarah Marie Johnston
    VP Administration: Charles Johnston
Brands:
    Helena View
    Moon Mountain

6407 Helens Pure Foods
301 Ryers Ave
Cheltenham, PA 19012-2113   215-379-6433
Vegetarian dips, salads and sandwiches
    President: Richard Goldberg
Estimated Sales:$5-9.9 Million
Number Employees: 5-9

6408 Hell on the Red
13716 E Fm 273
Telephone, TX 75488   903-664-2573
       Fax: 903-664-2301 hellonthered@gcsco.net
                    www.hellontheredinc.com
Pickled fruits and vegetables, vegetable sauces and
seasonings, & salad dressings. Manufacturer of
picante sauce hot mustard cheese dip and barbecue
sauce
    President: Thomas Baugh

Estimated Sales:$575,395
Number Employees: 5-9
Type of Packaging: Consumer, Private Label
Brands:
    Hell on the Red

6409 Heller Brothers PackingCorporation
P.O.Box 770249
Winter Garden, FL 34777-0249   407-656-4986
       Fax: 407-656-1751 www.hellerbros.com
Processor and exporter of citrus fruits including
grapefruit, tangelos, tangerines and oranges
    Controller: Jeff McKinney
    CEO: Harry H Falk
    Sales Manager: Rob Rath
    Manager: Harry Falk
Estimated Sales:$20-50 Million
Number Employees: 250-499
Type of Packaging: Consumer

6410 (HQ)Heller Seasonings
150 S Wacker Dr
Chicago, IL 60606-4103   312-346-1012
       Fax: 312-346-3140 800-323-2726
Seasonings
    VP Finance: Allen Marshall
Estimated Sales:$ 5 - 10 Million
Number Employees: 5-9

6411 Hells Canyon Winery
18835 Symms Rd
Caldwell, ID 83607-9513   208-454-3300
                     800-318-7873
              hellwine@yahoo.com
           www.hellscanyonwinery.org
Wines
    Owner: Steve Robertson
    Vineyard Manager: Stephen Robertson
*Estimated Sales:*Less than $500,000
Number Employees: 1-4
Brands:
    Hells Canyon

6412 Helms Candy Company
P.O.Box 607
Bristol, VA 24203-0607   276-669-2612
       Fax: 276-669-0150 www.helmscandy.com
Various candies and lollipops as well as
pharmaceuticals such as cough drops and medicated
lollipops
    President: George Helms III
    CEO: Helen Helms
    VP Candy Division: Buzz Helms
    VP Pharmaceutical Division: Mark Helms
    Accounting Department: Deborah Smith
Estimated Sales:$5-10 Million
Number Employees: 10-19
Sq. footage: 65000
Brands:
    Cool-E-Pops
    Happy Day Pops
    Helms
    Hot-C-Pops
    Hot-N-Coldpops
    Mint Lumps
    Mint Puffs
    Thank You Pops
    Virginia Beauty
    Zippy Pop

6413 Helmuth Country Bakery
6706 W Mills Ave
Hutchinson, KS 67501-8890   620-567-2301
       Fax: 620-567-2036 800-567-6360
              info@helmuthfoods.com
           www.helmuthfoods.com
Processor of cookies, candies, noodles and cotton
candy
    Owner: Jim Rein
    VP: Katie Helmuth
Estimated Sales:$1-4.9 Million
Number Employees: 5-9
Sq. footage: 3000
Type of Packaging: Consumer, Food Service
Brands:
    Cortland Manor
    Hatties
    Helmuth

6414 Helshiron Fisheries
6 Old Factory Round Turn Road
Grand Manan, NB E5G 2J4
Canada   506-662-3502
       Fax: 506-662-3786 lobfish@nbnet.nb.ca
Processor of salted cod, pollack and hake; also, fresh
sea urchins, lobster and scallops
    President: Ronald Benson
    Marketing Director: Morton Benson
    VP: Morton Benson
Number Employees: 10-19
Type of Packaging: Bulk
Brands:
    Helshiron

6415 Heluva Good Cheese
P.O.Box 410
Sodus, NY 14551-0410   315-483-6971
       Fax: 315-483-9927 hgcl@heluvagood.com
                    www.heluvagood.com
Processor of naturally aged cheese, dips, horserad-
ish, cocktail sauce, and mustard
    Owner/President: Martin Margherio
    COO: Bob Fratangelo
    Marketing Director: Neil Giudice
    Sales Director: John Snedeker
    Operations: Robert Fratangelo
    Plant Manager: Steve De Mass
    Purchasing Manager: Claudia Putman
Estimated Sales:$20-50 Million
Number Employees: 100-249
Sq. footage: 42000
Parent Co: Wessanen
Type of Packaging: Consumer, Food Service, Pri-
    vate Label, Bulk
Brands:
    Heluva Good Cheese

6416 Hemisphere Associated
7 High St # 400
Huntington, NY 11743-3417   631-673-3840
                      Fax: 631-673-3870
Processor, importer and exporter of apple, cherry,
grape, cranberry and strawberry fruit juice concen-
trates; also, mustard oil and mustard oil blends
    President: Dolores Mayoka
Estimated Sales:$870,000
Number Employees: 1-4
Sq. footage: 10000
Type of Packaging: Bulk

6417 HempNut
1286 Winter Solstice Avenue
Henderson, NV 89014-8869   707-576-7050
       Fax: 707-579-0940 infoweb@thehempnut.com
                    www.thehempnut.com
Tastes like sunflower seeds, looks like sesame seeds
and can be used in any recipe. High-quality protein,
most nutritious plant food available and very high in
vitamins
    Founder/President: Richard Rose

6418 Hena Coffee
660 Berriman St
Brooklyn, NY 11208-5304   718-272-8237
       Fax: 718-272-8391 www.henacoffee.com
Manufacturer of iced coffee, iced tea mix and liquid
concentrates.
    President: Scott Tauber
Estimated Sales:$ 5 - 10 Million
Number Employees: 5-9
Type of Packaging: Food Service, Private Label

6419 Henderson's Gardens
Box 214
Berwyn, AB T0M 0E0
Canada   780-338-2128
                      Fax: 780-338-2128
Processor and packer of corn, cucumbers, potatoes,
tomatoes, cabbage, peas, beans and peppers
    President: Robert Henderson
    Marketing Director: Robert Henderson
    Manager: Bob Henderson
    Manager: Bob Henderson
Number Employees: 5-9
Type of Packaging: Consumer, Food Service
Brands:
    Pride of Peace Vegetables

6420 Hendon & David
PO Box 836
Millbrook, NY 12545-0836   845-677-9696
       Fax: 845-677-9699 hendonco@aol.com

Macadamia nuts, cranberry grand marnier, exotic meat sauces, honeys, latin specialties, relishes, mustards
Owner: Helen Hendon
Brands:
Bushman's Best Mazavaroo
Clove Valley Farms
Hendon

6421 Hendricks Apiaries
4001 S Elati Street
Englewood, CO 80110-4555   303-789-3209
www.coloradosunshinehoney.com
Processor of specialty clover, alfalfa and knapweed honey
President: Paul Hendricks
Co-Owner: Linda Hendricks
Estimated Sales: Under $500,000
Number Employees: 1-4
Sq. footage: 3400
Type of Packaging: Consumer, Food Service, Private Label, Bulk
Brands:
Colorado Sunshine Honey

6422 Henggeler Packing Company
P.O.Box 313
Fruitland, ID 83619-0313   208-452-4212
Fax: 208-452-5416
Processor, exporter and packer of apples, plums and prunes
President: Gerald Henggeler
Estimated Sales: $20-50 Million
Number Employees: 50-99
Type of Packaging: Consumer, Bulk
Brands:
Fortress
Fruitland

6423 Henkel Corporation
5051 Estecreek Road
Cincinnati, OH 45232-1447   513-482-3000
Fax: 513-482-5513   800-543-7370
Processor and exporter of fatty acids and alcohol, glycerine, plasticizers, methyl esters and other chemicals
Sr Marketing Manager: Steve Kennedy
Marketing Manager: Jeff Mahaffey
Marketing Manager: Chris Scheider
Number Employees: 500-999
Parent Co: Henkel Corporation

6424 Henkel Corporation
5325 9th Ave
Countryside, IL 60525-3600   708-579-1123
Fax: 708-579-6150   800-328-6199
holgerbecker@henkel-americas.com
Processor, importer and exporter of food ingredients including natural antioxidants, bread and baking additives and whipped topping concentrates
Manager Food Ingredients: Holger Becker
Estimated Sales: $2.5-5 Million
Number Employees: 20-49
Sq. footage: 10000
Parent Co: Henkel Corporation
Brands:
Covi-Ox
Delios
Lamegin
Lamequick
Nutrilife
Spongolit

6425 Henning's Cheese
20201 Ucker Point Creek Rd
Kiel, WI 53042-4299   920-894-3032
Fax: 920-894-3022   kay@henningcheese.com
www.henningcheese.com
Processor of cheese including cheddar, colby, colby jack and mozzarella
President: Kay Henning
Estimated Sales: $10-20 Million
Number Employees: 10-19
Type of Packaging: Consumer, Food Service, Private Label, Bulk
Brands:
Henning's

6426 Henningsen Foods
14334 Industrial Road
Omaha, NE 68144-3398   402-330-2500
Fax: 402-330-0875   dianet@henningsenfoods.com
www.henningsenfoods.com

Processor of dried meats and eggs, and contract dehydration
Director Technical Services: David Slaughter
Research/Development: John Toney
Research/Development: Karen Moss
National Sales Manager: Mike McGuire
Sales/Marketing Associate: Sarah Hortz
Customer Service Coordinator: Diane Torpy
Estimated Sales: $5-10 Million
Number Employees: 500
Type of Packaging: Food Service, Private Label, Bulk

6427 Henningsen Foods
2700 Westchester Ave # 311
Purchase, NY 10577-2554   914-701-4020
Fax: 914-701-4050 www.henningsenfoods.com
Processor of cheese, eggs, poultry and dehydrated foods
Manager: Daves Splendour
Owner: Victor Henningsen Jr
CEO: Michael Cruger
Marketing Director: John Wankewicz
Manager: Earl Bals
Estimated Sales: $5-10 Million
Number Employees: 100-249
Parent Co: Henningsen Foods
Type of Packaging: Private Label, Bulk

6428 Henningsen Foods
2700 Westchester Ave # 311
Purchase, NY 10577-2554   914-701-4020
Fax: 914-701-4050   johnw@henningsenfoods.com
www.henningsenfoods.com
A manufacturer of frozen and dehydrated egg products for use in baking, mayonnaise, salad dressing, pasta and confectionary applications. Products include; egg whites, egg yolk, whole egg and egg blends. Henningsen also manufacturesdehydrated meat products for use in soups, side dishes, gravies and sauces. Meat products includes; chicken, turkey, beef, veal, pork and seafood. Custom manufacturing is also done for various protein and carbohydrate products
CEO: Michael Cruger
Vice President International Sales: Kit Henningsen
Sales Manager: Jamie Conetta
Vice President Operations: Mike Cruger
Estimated Sales: $50-100 Million
Number Employees: 100-249
Number of Products: 80
Type of Packaging: Bulk

6429 Henry & Henry
3765 Walden Ave
Lancaster, NY 14086-1405   716-685-4000
Fax: 716-685-0160   800-828-7130
elarson@henryandhenry.com
www.henryandhenry.com
Bakery ingredients, soda fountain toppings and syrups
President: Richard Gahlin
Estimated Sales: $50-100 Million
Number Employees: 100-249

6430 Henry Avocado Company
P.O.Box 300867
Escondido, CA 92030-0867   760-745-6632
Fax: 760-745-5043   phil@avacado.com
www.henryavocado.com
Processor and packaging of avacados
President: Charles Henry
Vice President: Phil Henry
Estimated Sales: $100+ Million
Number Employees: 250-499

6431 Henry Broch & Company/APK, Inc.
704 Florsheim Dr
Libertyville, IL 60048-5002   847-816-6225
Fax: 847-816-6238   sales@hbroch.com
www.hbroch.com

An industrial food brokerage representing natural food ingredients processors around the world. Henry Broch & Company markets more than 400 products - and more than 1,000 varieties of those products —including spray-dried, dehydratedand freeze dried vegetables, fruit concentrates and purees, spice oleoresins, spices and air-dried herbs, IQF herbs and onions, and mint and other herb extracts.
President: Jim Antonetti
Marketing Director: Jim Kuzma
VP: Jim Kuzman
Sales: JoAnne Stefanick
Director: Greg Antonetti
Estimated Sales: $1-2.5 Million
Number Employees: 5-9
Brands:
Henry Broch

6432 Henry Davis Company
3405 W 15th Ave
Gary, IN 46404-1964   219-949-8555
Fax: 219-949-9764
President: Henry Davis
Estimated Sales: $ 1 - 3 Million
Number Employees: 20-49

6433 Henry Estate Winery
687 Hubbard Creek Rd
Umpqua, OR 97486-9611   541-459-5120
Fax: 541-459-5146   800-782-2686
winery@henryestate.com   www.henryestate.com
Wines: Pinot Noir, Chardonnay, Gewurztraminer and White Riesling
President/Owner: Calvin Scott Henry III
Export Sales: Doyle Hinman
Public Relations Manager: Syndi Henry Beavers
Winemaker/Operations Manager: Calvin Scott Henry IV
Estimated Sales: $5-10 Million
Number Employees: 10-19
Brands:
HENRY ESTATE

6434 Henry H. Misner
1540 Harbour Street
Port Dover, ON N0A 1N0
Canada   519-583-1811
Fax: 519-583-1529
Processor of frozen shellfish and groundfish
President: Donald Misner
CFO: Nancy Misner
Marketing Director: Donald Misner
General Manager: Donald Misner
Number Employees: 20-49
Type of Packaging: Consumer, Food Service

6435 Henry Hill & Company
5 Financial Plz
Napa, CA 94558-3082   707-224-6565
Fax: 707-257-2990   bhill@billhill.com
Wines
Partner: William Hill
Estimated Sales: $1.5 Million
Number Employees: 20-49
Brands:
Broken Rock Cellars

6436 Henry J Meat Specialties
4460 W Armitage Ave
Chicago, IL 60639-3574   773-227-5400
Fax: 773-227-0414   800-242-1314
www.henryjmeats.com
Processor of sliced pastrami and corned, roast and Italian beef
President/CEO: Forrest Krisco
Vice President: James Dragatsis
Quality Control Supervisor: Nicole Stringer
QA/Plant Operations: Lorenzo Jackson
Director Marketing: Cindy Krisco
Customer Service: Alicia Vega
Estimated Sales: $ 5 - 10 Million
Number Employees: 10-19

6437 Henry J's Hashtime
4460 W Armitage Ave
Chicago, IL 60639-3574   773-227-5400
Fax: 773-227-0414   800-242-1313
www.henryjmeats.com
Prepared meats
President: Henry Juracic
Plant Manager: Forest Krisco
Estimated Sales: $5-10 Million
Number Employees: 10-19

6438 Henson & Courtner Ham House
Highway 67
Butler, TN 37640   423-369-1121
Ham and ham products

6439 Herb Bee's Products
210 Mallard Drive
Colchester, VT 05446-7013   802-864-7387
        sierrassong@aol.com
Jam, jelly, relish, quick breads, cheese spreads, and
vinegars

6440 Herb Connection
188 S Main St
Springville, UT 84663-1849   801-489-4254
        Fax: 801-489-8341
      www.drchristophersherbshop.com
Food supplements manufacturer, private label items,
herbs and health foods
    President: David Christopher
    Vice President: Ruth Christopher Bacalla
    Production Manager: James Webster
    Purchasing Manager: Josh Bruni
Estimated Sales: $ 1 - 3 Million
Number Employees: 5-9
Sq. footage: 7500
Type of Packaging: Private Label

6441 Herb Patch of Vermont
30 Island Street
Bellows Falls, VT 05101-1350   802-463-1400
    Fax: 802-463-1911   800-282-4372
        info@vermontnaturally.com
        www.vermontnaturally.com
Manufacturer of all natural cocoas, dessert bever-
ages, dips, teas and herb blends; exporter of cocoa
    Owner: John Molsis
Estimated Sales: Less than $500,000
Number Employees: 5
Sq. footage: 6500
Brands:
    Country Cow
    Country Cow Cocoa
    Cowpuccino Toppers

6442 Herb Pharm
P.O.Box 116
Williams, OR 97544-0116   541-846-6262
    Fax: 541-846-6112   800-348-4372
info@herb-pharm.com   www.herb-pharm.com
Health supplements and personal care products
    Founder/Co-Owner: Ed Smith
    Co-Owner: Sara Katz
Number Employees: 50-99

6443 Herb Society of America
9019 Kirtland Chardon Rd
Willoughby, OH 44094-5156   440-256-0514
    Fax: 440-256-0541   herbs@herbsociety.org
        www.herbsociety.org
Seasonings, spices
    Executive Director: Katrinka Morgan
    Administrative Assistant: Nancy Walczak
    Office Administrator: Michelle Milks
    Horticulturist: Robin Siktberg
    Librarian: Michele Meyers
Estimated Sales: $500,000-$1 Million
Number Employees: 5-9
Type of Packaging: Private Label
Brands:
    Herb Society of America

6444 Herb Tea Company
P.O.Box 1962
Oxnard, CA 93032-1962   805-486-6477
        Fax: 805-385-3216
Tea
    Religious Leader: Robert Cox
    Sales Coordinator: Robert Lessin
    Plant Manager: William Ashwell
Estimated Sales: $ 2.5-5 Million
Number Employees: 10-19
Type of Packaging: Consumer, Private Label

6445 Herb's Specialty Foods
112 Schoolhouse Road
Westampton, NJ 08060-3774   609-267-0276
    Fax: 609-261-1949   800-486-0276
        email@kaptainsketch.com
        www.kaptainsketch.com
Processor of frozen value-added poultry and seafood
    President: Nash Cohen

Estimated Sales: $10-20 Million
Number Employees: 20-49
Type of Packaging: Consumer, Food Service, Pri-
vate Label
Brands:
    Herb's Five Star
    Kaptain's Ketch
    Westhampton Farms

6446 HerbaSway Laboratories
P.O.Box 6098
Wallingford, CT 06492-0089   203-269-6991
    Fax: 203-269-9703   800-672-7322
herbs@herbasway.com   www.herbasway.com
Manufacturer of liquid dietary health supplements
    Owner: Franklin St John
    Founder/Owner: Lorraine St. John
Estimated Sales: $ 10 - 20 Million
Number Employees: 20-49

6447 Herbal Coffee International
120 28th Avenue S
Jacksonville Beach, FL 32250-6014   904-259-6350
        800-743-8774
    coffeephd@aol.com   www.herbalcoffee.com
Processor of herbal coffees
Number Employees: 5-9

6448 Herbal Magic
PO Box 70
Forest Knolls, CA 94933-0070   800-684-3722
    Fax: 415-488-1057   melren@aol.com
        www.herbalmagic.com
Herbs for colds, flu, immune system, feminine
needs, herbs for children, St. John's Wort, parasite
kit and femopause
    Founder/Master Herbalist: Renee Ponder
Estimated Sales: $300,000-500,000
Number Employees: 1-4

6449 Herbal Products & Development
PO Box 1084
Aptos, CA 95001-1084   831-688-4200
        info@centralcoastnutrition.com
        www.centralcoastnutrition.com
Processor and exporter of high energy food concen-
trates, digestive enzymes, antioxidants, probiotics,
tinctures, oils and liquid vitamins and minerals
    President: Paul Gaylon
Number Employees: 1-4
Sq. footage: 1200
Type of Packaging: Consumer, Private Label
Brands:
    Liquid Life Essential Day & Night
    Liver Restore
    Plant Power
    Power Plus
    Pro Plus
    Supreme 7

6450 Herbal Water
PO Box 800
Narberth, PA 19072   610-668-4000
    Fax: 610-642-4082   nerdosy@herbalwater.com
        www.herbalwater.com
organic naturally enhanced flavored water.
    President/Owner: Albert Cahana

6451 Herbalist & Alchemist
51 S Wandling Ave
Washington, NJ 07882-2192   908-689-9020
    Fax: 908-689-9071   herbalist@nac.net
        www.herbalist-alchemist.com
Herbal products: Osteo Herb Capsules, Throat
Spray, Herbal Formulas, Alcohol Free Formulas, Tea
Blends, Solid Extracts, Herbal Ointments, Astral Tea
Remedies, Single Extracts, Chinese Bulk Herbs,
Ceremonial Herbs, Herbal Oils, and 5LUNG
RE-LEAF™Formulas.
    President: David Winston
Estimated Sales: $ 1 - 3 Million
Number Employees: 10-19

6452 Herbco International
16661 W Snoqualmie River Rd NE
Duvall, WA 98019-9202   425-788-7903
    Fax: 425-844-9114   herbco@msn.com
        www.herbco.net
    Owner: Ted Andrews
Estimated Sales: $ 5 - 10 Million
Number Employees: 50-99

6453 Herbs Seafood
112 Schoolhouse Road
Westampton, NJ 08060-3774   609-267-0276
    Fax: 609-261-1949   800-486-0276
Prepared fish and poultry
    President: Nash Cohen
    Owner: Nash Cohen
    VP Sales: Gary Cannard
    Sales Manager: Richard Applebam
    Plant Manager: William Byrne
Estimated Sales: $10-20 Million
Number Employees: 20-49
Type of Packaging: Private Label
Brands:
    Herbs Seafood

6454 Herbs from China
PO Box 314
Chicago, IL 60690   312-240-0000
    Fax: 312-945-1111   866-823-4372
        service@herbsfromchina.com
        www.herbsfromchina.com
Chinese herbs
    Cheif Executive Officer: Thomas Lowrance
    CFO/Health Care Consultant: Cynthia Lowrance
    RN, BS, MBA
    Nutritionist/Sport Medicine Consultant: James
    Hicks PhD, MD
Estimated Sales: $ 20 - 50 Million
Number Employees: 20-49

6455 Herbs, Etc.
1345 Cerrillos Rd
Santa Fe, NM 87505-3508   505-982-1265
    Fax: 505-984-9197   888-433-1212
    retail@herbsetc.com   www.herbsetc.com
Manufacturer of bulk herbs, herbal remedies, sup-
plements and essential oils.
    Manager: B Siebel
Estimated Sales: $ .5 - 1 million
Number Employees: 5-9

6456 Herbs, Etc.
1345 Cerrillos Rd
Santa Fe, NM 87505-3508   505-982-1265
    Fax: 505-984-9197   888-694-3727
        www.herbsetc.com
Processor and exporter of liquid herbal extracts, and
fast acting softgel herbal medicines.
    Manager: B Siebel
Estimated Sales: $2.5-5 Million
Number Employees: 20-49
Sq. footage: 7000
Type of Packaging: Consumer
Brands:
    Allertonic
    Deep Chi Builder
    Deep Sleep
    Depiezac
    Echinacea Triple Source
    Herbs, Etc.
    Kidalin
    Lung Tonic
    Lymphatonic
    Singers Saving Grace

6457 Hercules Incorporated
1313 N Market Street Hercules Plaza
Wilmington, DE 19894-0001   302-594-5000
    Fax: 302-594-5204   800-345-8104
        www.herc.com
Manufacturer of pectin, carrageenan, fat replacers,
methylcellulose, hydroxypropyl cellulose,
hydroxypropyl methylcellulose, guar gum and cellu-
lose gum
    VP: Paul Raymond
    VP Human Resources: Edward V Carrington
    Director Sales/Marketing: Ross MacLaughlin
    Plant Manager: Thomas Strang
Estimated Sales: K
Number Employees: 4660
Parent Co: Hercules
Type of Packaging: Bulk
Brands:
    Aqualon
    FiberVisions
    Genu
    Slendid
    Supercol

6458 Heringer Meats
16 W 7th St
Covington, KY 41011-2302   859-291-2000
        Fax: 859-291-0052

Processor of fresh and frozen meat including pork, beef, veal and lamb
President: Ray Niemeyer Jr
Estimated Sales:$5-10 Million
Number Employees: 10-19
Type of Packaging: Consumer, Food Service
Brands:
 Kahns
 Plue Grass
 Sara Lee

6459 Heritage Cheese House
PO Box 376
Heuvelton, NY 13654-0376   315-344-2216
                          Fax: 315-344-2260
www.northcountrysidecybermall.com/heritage.htm
l
Producers of cheese, honey, bologna, cheese curd and maple syrup.
*Estimated Sales:*Less than $500,000
Number Employees: 1-4

6460 Heritage Dairy Stores
376 Jessup Rd
West Deptford, NJ 08086-2130   856-845-2855
          Fax: 856-845-8392 www.heritages.com
Milk, dairy products
 President: Harold R Heritage
Number Employees: 500-999

6461 Heritage Family Specialty Foods Inc
901 Santerre St
Grand Prairie, TX 75050-1939   972-660-6511
 Fax: 972-660-4567 info@hfsfoods.com
                        www.hfsfoods.com
Sauces, salsa, soups, salad dressings.
 President: Daniel Brackeen
 VP: Cheryl Brackeen
 CFO: Cheryl Brackeen
 Vice President: Johnny Lee Stanley
 Production Manager: Fred Bertschi
Estimated Sales:$20-50 Million
Number Employees: 20-49
Type of Packaging: Food Service, Private Label
Brands:
 Heritage Chipotle Roasted Salsa
 Heritage Fresh Salsa
 Heritage Garlic Mayo

6462 Heritage Fancy Foods Marketing
PO Box 18310
Erlanger, KY 41018-0310   859-282-3782
                          Fax: 859-282-3781
Gourmet foods
 President: Robert Carl
Brands:
 Heritage Fancy Foods

6463 Heritage Farms Dairy
1100 New Salem Rd
Murfreesboro, TN 37129-6914   615-895-2790
          Fax: 615-895-0570 www.kroger.com
Processor of fresh apple and orange juices; also, dairy products including cottage cheese, milk and yogurt
 Manager: Bill Crabtree
 General Manager: Bill McCarthy
 General Manager: Robert Allard
Number Employees: 100-249
Parent Co: Kroger Company
Type of Packaging: Consumer, Private Label, Bulk
Brands:
 Kroger

6464 (HQ)Heritage Foods
4002 Westminster Ave
Santa Ana, CA 92703-1310   714-775-5000
 Fax: 714-775-7677 www.heritage-foods.com
Processor of milk, cheese and cream
 Partner: Jon Newman
 CEO: Lou Stremick
 Sales Manager: Tom Gustafson
Estimated Sales:$100-500 Million
Number Employees: 100-249
Type of Packaging: Consumer, Food Service
Other Locations:
 Heritage Foods
 Riverside CA

6465 Heritage Foods
14515 124th Avenue
Edmonton, AB T5L 3B2
Canada   780-454-7383
 Fax: 780-454-2685 cheemo@cheemo.com
                        www.cheemo.com
Processor of frozen cabbage rolls and pierogies.
Type of Packaging: Consumer, Food Service, Private Label
Brands:
 CHEEMO

6466 Heritage Foods
PO Box 630
Holicong, PA 18928-0630   215-244-0900
                          Fax: 215-244-6122
Gefilte fish

6467 Heritage Northwest
625 W 7th St
Juneau, AK 99801-1803   907-586-1088
 Fax: 907-586-4446 info@heritagecoffee.com
                        www.heritagecoffee.com
Fair-trade, environmentally friendly coffees roasted to order.
Estimated Sales:$1-2.5 Million
Number Employees: 20-49
Brands:
 BLACK WOLF BLEND
 HERITAGE COFFEE

6468 Heritage Salmon
P.O.Box 263
Eastport, ME 04631-0263   207-853-6081
 Fax: 207-853-6056 www.heritagesalmon.com
Salmon
 President: Glen Cooke
 Marketing: Aian Craig
Number Employees: 100-249
Number of Products: 60
Brands:
 Heritage Salmon

6469 Heritage Salmon Company
100-12051 Horseshoe Way
Richmond, BC V7A 4V4
Canada   604-277-3093
                          Fax: 604-275-8614
Processor and exporter of fresh Atlantic salmon
 President: Ken Hirtle
 CFO: Rob Reisen
Type of Packaging: Bulk

6470 Heritage Shortbread
35 Hunter Rd
Suite F
Hilton Head Island, SC 29926   843-342-7268
 Fax: 888-744-6697 hshortbread@aol.com
                        www.heritageshortbread.com
shortbread cookies
 President/Owner: Thomas Cole

6471 Heritage Store
314 Laskin Rd
Virginia Beach, VA 23451-3020   757-428-0110
 Fax: 757-428-3632 heritage@caycecures.com
                        www.caycecures.com
Processor and exporter of essential oils, health foods, food supplements, vitamins, herbal teas, massage oils, castor oil, oral care products, herbal tonics and supplements
 Manager: Cindy Mills
 Marketing Director: David Riblet
Estimated Sales:$10-20 Million
Number Employees: 50-99
Sq. footage: 6000
Type of Packaging: Consumer, Private Label, Bulk

6472 Heritage Tymes/Pancake House
159 Dixon Road
3121
Spearsville, LA 71277-3547   806-765-8566
                          Fax: 806-765-8507
Processor and exporter of sweet potato pancake, muffin and waffle mixes
 Co-Owner/President: Scott Johnson
 Co-Owner/VP: Jane Johnson
 Co-Owner/VP: Jason Johnson
Number Employees: 20-49
Sq. footage: 4000
Type of Packaging: Consumer, Food Service, Private Label, Bulk
Brands:
 Jane's

6473 Heritage Wine Cellars
12162 E Main Rd
North East, PA 16428-3644   814-725-8015
 Fax: 814-725-8654 800-747-0083
bostwick@erie.net www.heritagewine.biz
Wine
 VP: Matthew Bostwick
 CEO: Robert Bostwick
 President: Josh Bostwick
 General Manager: Bob Bostwick
Estimated Sales:$2.5-5 Million
Number Employees: 5-9
Brands:
 Heritage

6474 Herkimer Foods
P.O.Box 310
Herkimer, NY 13350-0310   315-895-7832
 Fax: 315-895-4664 herkimer@cnymail.com
                        www.herkimerfoods.com
Manufacturer of cheese, spreads, dips, fudge, nuts, gelatine and jello snacks
 President/Director Marketing: Michael Basloe
Estimated Sales:$ 3 - 5 Million
Number Employees: 20-49
Type of Packaging: Consumer, Food Service, Private Label, Bulk
Brands:
 HERKIMER
 IDA MAE

6475 Herkimer Foods
P.O.Box 310
Herkimer, NY 13350-0310   315-895-7832
 Fax: 315-895-4664 www.herkimerfoods.com
Dairy foods
 President: Michael Basloe
 VP: Robert Basloe
Estimated Sales:$ 3 - 5 Million
Number Employees: 20-49

6476 Herlocher Foods
415 E Calder Way
State College, PA 16801-5663   814-237-0134
 Fax: 814-237-1893 800-437-5624
 info@herlocherfoods.com
                        www.herlocherfoods.com
Processor of dipping mustard and salsa, including licensed Penn State novelty dipping mustard.
 President: Neil Herlocher
Estimated Sales:$1-2.5 Million
Number Employees: 5-9
Brands:
 HERLOCHER'S DIPPING MUSTARD

6477 Herman Falter Packing Company
384 Greenlawn Ave
Columbus, OH 43223-2610   614-444-1141
 Fax: 614-445-3915 800-325-6328
 info@faltersmeats.com www.faltersmeats.com
Processor of meat
 President: James Falter
 General Sales Manager: Charles Honeycutt
Estimated Sales:$ 10 - 20 Million
Number Employees: 100-249

6478 Herman's Bakery Coffee Shop
130 Main St S
Cambridge, MN 55008-1621   763-689-1515
                          Fax: 763-689-9642
Bakery products
 President: Herman Oestreich
Estimated Sales:$1-2.5 Million
Number Employees: 20-49

6479 Hermann J. Wiemer Vineyard
P.O.Box 38
Dundee, NY 14837-0038   607-243-7971
 Fax: 607-243-7983 800-371-7971
 wines@wiemer.com www.wiemer.com
Wines
 Manager: Fred Merwarth
Estimated Sales:$5-10 Million
Number Employees: 10-19
Brands:
 Hermann J. Wiemer

6480 Hermann Laue Spice Company
119 Franklin Street
Uxbridge, ON L9P 1J5
Canada   905-852-5100
 Fax: 905-852-1113 hela@helacanada.com
                        www.helacanada.com

Processor, importer and exporter of custom blended spices, sodium erythorbate, carrageenan, potassium sorbate, ascorbic acid and sodium ascorbate for the meat and poultry industries; also, technical assistance available
President: Walter Knecht
Vice President: Paul Hoogenboom
Research & Development: Uwe Thode
Quality Assurance Supervisor: Crista Dagnall
Director Of Operations: Dr. Thomas Varga
Plant Manager: Tushar Patel
Purchasing Manager: Lisa Gay
Number Employees: 35
Sq. footage: 57000
Parent Co: Laue, Herman, GmbH
Type of Packaging: Food Service
Brands:
  HELA

6481 Hermann Pickle Farm
P.O.Box 347
Garrettsville, OH 44231-0347   330-527-2696
            Fax: 330-527-2327 800-245-2696
Processor of dill and kosher pickles, dill tomatoes and peppers
President/CEO: Larry Hermann
Treasurer: Ruth Hermann
Vice President: Don Hermann
Estimated Sales: $10-20 Million
Number Employees: 20-49
Type of Packaging: Consumer, Bulk
Brands:
  Hermann Pickle

6482 Hermann Wiemer Vineyards
P.O.Box 38
Dundee, NY 14837-0038   607-243-7971
            Fax: 607-243-7983 800-371-7971
wines@wiemer.com   www.wiemer.com
Vinter of vinifera wines; also, grafted grape vines.
Manager: Fred Merwarth
Estimated Sales: $ 5 - 10 Million
Number Employees: 10-19
Type of Packaging: Consumer
Brands:
  HERMANN J WIEMER

6483 Hermannhof Winery
104 Industrial Dr
Hermann, MO 65041-9650   573-486-5959
            Fax: 573-486-3415 800-393-0100
hermannhofinfo@hermannhof.com
www.hermannhof.com
Producers of red and white wines and champagne.
Manager: Paul Leroy
Estimated Sales: $10-20 Million
Number Employees: 20-49

6484 Hermany Farms
2338 Hermany Avenue
Room 1
Bronx, NY 10473-1130   718-823-2989
            Fax: 718-828-8110
Dairy products
President: Robert Marrow
Manager: Philip Carloson
Vice President: Sam Katz
Director Engineering: Mark Butler
Plant Manager: Phil Carlson
Estimated Sales: $2.5-5 Million
Number Employees: 50-99
Type of Packaging: Private Label
Brands:
  American DG
  Hermany

6485 Herold's Salad
17512 Miles Ave
Cleveland, OH 44128-3481   216-991-7500
            Fax: 216-991-9565 800-427-2523
www.heroldssalads.com
Processor of potato and pasta salads, side dish vegetables and desserts
President/Owner: Cathy Herold
Sales Manager: Ken Sanguedolce
Estimated Sales: $20-50 Million
Number Employees: 20-49
Type of Packaging: Consumer

6486 Heron Hill Winery
9301 County Route 76
Hammondsport, NY 14840-9685   607-868-4241
            Fax: 607-868-3435 800-441-4241
www.heronhill.com

Producers of red and white wines and champagne.
Owner: John Ingle
Estimated Sales: $5-10 Million
Number Employees: 20-49
Type of Packaging: Private Label

6487 Heronwood Farm
PO Box 1555
Kent, WA 98035-1555   877-203-5908
            Fax: 253-520-0282
Jams, jellies, fruit butters
President: Jeannie Hertel
Type of Packaging: Private Label
Brands:
  Heronwood Farm 100% Pure Honey
  Heronwood Farm Apple Butter
  Heronwood Farm Apricot Jam
  Heronwood Farm Apricot Jam
  Heronwood Farm Blackberry Jelly
  Heronwood Farm Blackberry Syrup
  Heronwood Farm Blueberry Jam
  Heronwood Farm Blueberry Syrup
  Heronwood Farm Cherry Jam
  Heronwood Farm Cranberry-Raspberry
  Heronwood Farm Jennifer Plum Jam
  Heronwood Farm Orange Marmalade
  Heronwood Farm Peach Butter
  Heronwood Farm Peach Jam
  Heronwood Farm Pear Butter
  Heronwood Farm Pear Jam
  Heronwood Farm Raspberry Jam
  Heronwood Farm Rhubarb Jelly
  Heronwood Farm Ruby Salmon Jelly
  Heronwood Farm Slug Butter
  Heronwood Farm Strawberry Jam
  Salmonberry

6488 Herr Foods
476 E 7th Street
Chillicothe, OH 45601-3455   740-773-8282
            Fax: 740-775-8286 800-523-8468
www.herrfoods.com
Processor and exporter of potato chips and pretzels
Branch Manager: Dale Garrison
Estimated Sales: $ 20 - 50 Million
Number Employees: 50-99
Type of Packaging: Consumer

6489 (HQ)Herr's Foods
P.O.Box 300
Nottingham, PA 19362-0300   610-932-3407
            Fax: 610-932-2137 800-344-3777
www.herrfoods.com
Processor of snack foods including potato chips, pretzels, popcorn, cheese curls, onion rings and corn, nacho and tortilla chips; also, kosher products available
Founder: James Herr
Chairman/CEO: J M Herr
President/Director: Ed Herr
Vice President Finance: Gerry Kluis
Vice President Sales/Marketing: Richard White
Vice President Manufacturing: Harold Blank
Estimated Sales: $100-500 Million
Number Employees: 1,000-4,999
Type of Packaging: Consumer
Brands:
  Herr's

6490 Herrell's Ice Cream
8 Old South St
Northampton, MA 01060-3847   413-586-9700
            Fax: 413-584-5320 www.herrells.com
Manufacturers of ice cream.
CEO: Stephen Herrell
Number Employees: 20-49

6491 Herring Brothers
P.O.Box 526
Dover Foxcroft, ME 04426-0526   207-876-2631
            treynjaime@netscape.net
www.herringbrothersmeats.com
Processor and wholesaler/distributor of meats
President: Andrea Gilbert
Estimated Sales: $5-10 Million
Number Employees: 5-9
Type of Packaging: Consumer

6492 Hershey
2350 Matheson Boulevard E
Mississauga, ON L4W 5E9
Canada   905-602-9200
      Fax: 905-602-8766 800-468-1714
cdnheadoffice@hersheys.com
www.hersheys.com
Processor of chocolate products including candy, chips, drinks and syrups; also, candy including mints, toffee, hard, licorice and chocolate covered almonds.
Chairman/President/CEO Corporate Office:
  Richard Lenny
VP/International Business Development: Bryan Crittenden
VP/International Commmerical Marketing:
  Richard Andrews
VP/Chief Information Officer: George Davis
Number Employees: 150
Parent Co: Hershey Company
Type of Packaging: Consumer

6493 Hershey Canada Inc
375 Pleasant Street
Dartmouth, NS B2Y 4N4
Canada   902-469-2470
      Fax: 902-469-7169 www.hersheycanada.com OR
www.hersheys.com
Manufactures, distributes and sells confectionery, snack, refreshment and grocery products in Canada.
Chairman/President/CEO Corporate Office:
  Richard Lenny
VP/Global Strategy Business Intelligence: Robert Goodpaster
VP/International Business Development: Bryan Crittenden
VP/International Commerical Marketing: Richard Andrews
VP/Chief Information Officer: George Davis
Number Employees: 650
Parent Co: Hershey Company
Type of Packaging: Consumer
Brands:
  CHIPITS
  EAT-MORE
  GLOSETTE
  HERSHEY'S
  JOLLY RANCHER
  OH HENRY!
  REESE
  TWIZZLER

6494 Hershey Chocolate & Confectionery Division
6130 Stoneridge Mall Rd # 140
Pleasanton, CA 94588-3770   925-460-0359
            Fax: 925-937-4139 www.hersheys.com
Processor of chocolate candy including bars
Chairman/President/CEO: Richard Lenny
VP/Finance & Planning: Humberto Alfonso
VP/International Business Development: Bryan Crittenden
VP/Quality & Regulatory Compliance: Donald Mastrorocco Jr
VP/International Marketing: Richard Andrews
VP/Global Strategy Business Intelligence: Robert Goodpaster
VP/Chief Information Officer: George Davis
EVP/Chief Operating Officer: David West
Estimated Sales: $10-20 Million
Number Employees: 50-99
Parent Co: Hershey Company
Type of Packaging: Consumer

6495 Hershey Company
1 Crystal A Drive
Hershey, PA 17033   717-534-4200
            Fax: 717-534-6760 800-468-1714
www.hersheys.com
Chocolate and chocolate candies
President/CEO: David West
SVP/CFO: Humberto Alfonso
SVP/General Council & Secretary: Burton Snyder

VP Global R&D: C Daniel Azzara
SVP/Global Chief Marketing Officer: Michele Buck
SVP/Chief People Officer: Charlene Binder
SVP Global Operations: Terence O'Day
Estimated Sales: $5.3 Billion
Number Employees: 13,000
Type of Packaging: Consumer, Food Service, Private Label, Bulk

Other Locations:
Hershey Foods Corp.
Lake Forest IL
Brands:
HERSHEY'S
ICE BREAKERS
JOLY RANCHER
KISSES
KIT KAT
REESE'S
SNACK
TWIZZLERS

6496 Hershey Company
14 E Chocolate Ave
Hershey, PA 17033-1329   717-534-4200
Fax: 717-534-6324 800-468-1714
PR@hersheys.com www.hersheys.com
Cocoa, baking chips, baking chocolate, syrups,
pourable peanut butter
President: David West
Marketing Director: Thomas K Hernquist
CFO: David J West
Parent Co: Hershey Foods Corporation
Brands:
Heath
Hershey's
Reese's

6497 (HQ)Hershey Corporation
P.O.Box 810
100 Crystal A Drive
Hershey, PA 17033-0810   717-534-4200
Fax: 717-534-6550 800-468-1714
Info@HersheyPA.com www.hersheys.com
Manufacturer of chocolate and sugar confectionery
products.
President/CEO: David West
SVP/Chief Financial Officer: Humberto Alfonso
SVP/General Counsel: Burton Snyder
VP/Global Research and Development: C Daniel
Azzara
SVP/Global Chief Marketing Officer: Michele
Buck
SVP/Global Operations: Terence O'Day
Estimated Sales: $5.3 Billion
Number Employees: 13,000
Type of Packaging: Consumer, Food Service, Private Label
Brands:
HERSHEY'S COOKIES & CREME
HERSHEY'S EXTRA CREAMY CHOCOLATE
HERSHEY'S MILK CHOCOLATE
HERSHEY'S MILK CHOCOLATE W/ALMONDS
HERSHEY'S SPECIAL DARK CHOCOLATE
HERSHEY'S SPECIAL DARK W/ALMONDS
ICE BREAKERS ALPINE SPLASH
ICE BREAKERS CINNAMON
ICE BREAKERS CITRUS FREEZE
ICE BREAKERS COOL MINT
ICE BREAKERS SPEARMINT
JOLLY RANCHER DOUBLE BLASTS
JOLLY RANCHER GUMMIES CANDY
JOLLY RANCHER JELLY BEANS
JOLLY RANCHER LOLLIPOPS
JOLLY RANCHER SOFT & CHEWY
JOLLY RANCHER SOUR BLASTS
JOLLY RANCHERS
KISSES
KISSES CHERRY CORDIAL
KISSES FILLED w/CARAMEL
KISSES HUGS
KISSES SPECIAL DARK
KISSES w/ALMOND
REESE'S BROWNIE
REESE'S CRISPY CRUNCHY
REESE'S EGG
REESE'S HEART
REESE'S PB & MILK CHOCOLATE BIG CUP
REESE'S PB & WHITE CHOCOLATE
REESE'S PB & WHITE CHOCOLATE BIG CU
REESE'S PEANUT BUTTER & MILK CHOC
REESE'S PUMPKIN
REESE'S SELECT CLUSTERS
REESE'S SNACK BARZ
REESE'S TREE
TWIZZLERS CHERRY
TWIZZLERS CHOCOLATE
TWIZZLERS LICORICE
TWIZZLERS STRAWBERRY

6498 Hershey Creamery Company
P.O.Box 1821
Harrisburg, PA 17105-1821 717-238-8134
Fax: 717-233-7195 888-240-1905
info@hersheyicecream.com
www.hersheyicecream.com
Processor of ice cream
Chairman/President/CEO: Richard Lenny
VP/Finance & Planning: Humberto Alfonso
CEO: George H Holder
VP/International Business Development: Bryan
Crittenden
VP/Quality & Regulatory Compliance: Donald
Mastrorocco Jr
VP/International Marketing: Richard Andrews
VP/Chief Information Officer: George Davis
EVP/Chief Operating Officer: David West
Estimated Sales: $50-100 Million
Number Employees: 100-249
Parent Co: Hershey Company
Type of Packaging: Consumer, Food Service, Bulk
Brands:
Hershey

6499 Hershey International
2700 S Commerce Parkway
Weston, FL 33331-3628 954-385-2600
Fax: 954-385-2625 exports@hersheys.com
www.thehersheycompany.com
Processor and exporter of chocolate and
nonchocolate confectionery products, cookies, biscuits and ice cream.
Chairman/President/CEO: Richard Lenny
VP/Finance & Planning: Humberto Alfonso
VP/Global Strategy Business Intelligence: Robert
Goodpaster
VP/International Business Development: Bryan
Crittenden
VP/Quality & Regulatory Compliance: Donald
Mastrorocco Jr
VP/Chief Information Officer: George Davis
EVP/Chief Operating Officer: David West
Number Employees: 1-4
Parent Co: Hershey Company
Type of Packaging: Consumer, Food Service, Bulk

6500 Hershey Pasta Group
2521 S Floyd Street
Louisville, KY 40209-1809 502-637-2563
Fax: 502-637-6328 800-468-1714
www.hersheys.com
Egg noodles, macaroni, spaghetti and crisp rice
Chairman/President/CEO: Richard H Lenny
CEO: Richard Lenny
VP/Finance & Planning: David West
Vice President: Marcella K Arline
VP/International Business Development: Bryan
Crittenden
VP/Quality & Regulatory Compliance: Donald
Mastrorocco Jr
VP/International Marketing: Richard Andrews
VP/Chief Information Officer: George Davis
EVP/Chief Operating Officer: David West
Estimated Sales: $25-50 Million
Number Employees: 100-249
Parent Co: Hershey Company
Brands:
Almond Joy
Hershey's
Jolly Rancher
Kit Kat

6501 Hess Collection Winery
P.O.Box 4140
Napa, CA 94558-0565 707-255-1144
Fax: 707-253-1682 877-707-4377
info@hesscollection.com
www.hesscollection.com
Wines
President: Clement Firko
Owner: Donald Hess
CEO: Max Leinhard
VP Director Winemaking: Dave Guffy
Winemaker: Julie Murrell
Estimated Sales: $10-100 Million
Number Employees: 50-99
Type of Packaging: Private Label
Brands:
ARTEZIN
HESS COLLECTION
HESS ESTATE
HESS SELECT

6502 Heterochemical Corporation
111 E Hawthorne Ave
Valley Stream, NY 11580-6319 516-561-8225
Fax: 516-561-8413
Processor and exporter of vitamin K products
President: Lynne Galler
VP: Raymond Berruti
Estimated Sales: $1,000,000
Number Employees: 1-4
Sq. footage: 20000

6503 Hetty Fair Foods Company
51 N Gates Avenue
Buffalo, NY 14218-1029 716-876-4345
Fax: 716-876-7455
Vegetables
President: Thomas Amabile
Estimated Sales: $1-2.5 Million
Number Employees: 6
Number of Brands: 1
Number of Products: 4
Type of Packaging: Consumer, Food Service, Private Label, Bulk

6504 Hey Brothers Ice Cream
8297 S Main Street
Dixon, IL 61021-9408 815-288-4242
Ice cream

6505 Heyerly Bakery
P.O.Box 391
Ossian, IN 46777-0391 260-622-4196
Processor of baked goods including cookies
Owner: Ron Heyerly
Estimated Sales: $500,000-$1 Million
Number Employees: 10-19
Type of Packaging: Consumer

6506 Hi Ball Energy
1862 Union Street
San Francisco, CA 94123 415-420-4801
Fax: 415-931-1096 info@hiballer.com
www.hiballer.com
naturally flavored sparkling energy water and sparkling energy waters.
President/Owner: Todd Berardi
Sales Director: Dan Craytor

6507 Hi Point Industries
4767 E 49th St
Vernon, CA 90058-2703 323-589-7211
Fax: 323-589-8270 800-959-7292
www.goldenovaleggs.com
Processor of egg products including whole fresh,
liquid and frozen; also, whites, frozen salted and
sugared yolks, substitute blends and powders; also,
salted and sweet butter
President: Fred Alejo
Estimated Sales: $20-50 Million
Number Employees: 20-49
Sq. footage: 45000
Type of Packaging: Food Service, Bulk
Brands:
Amatex
X-Mix

6508 Hi-Country Corona
PO Box 338
Selah, WA 98942-0338 909-272-2600
Fax: 909-272-8438 hicountrycorona@aol.com
Processor and exporter of fruit juices and concentrates including orange, grapefruit, lemon and lime;
also essential oils. Packer of juice and juice drinks in
Hot-Fill PET, 46 ounce cans, aluminum cans and
HDPE bottles
Industrial Sales: Norman Saldana
Sales Director: Cindy Henry
Plant Manager: Jolene Crosby
Estimated Sales: $10-20 Million
Number Employees: 50-99
Sq. footage: 161913
Type of Packaging: Consumer, Food Service, Private Label, Bulk
Brands:
Cal-Glory
Citra-Gold

6509 Hi-Country Foods Corporation
P.O.Box 338
Selah, WA 98942-0338 509-697-7292
Fax: 509-697-3498 hcfoods@hcfoods.com
www.yakamajuice1855.com

Processor of fruit juice concentrates, apple and fruit juices, bottled water, teas and new age beverages; exporter of apple and fruit juices
President/Owner: Otis Harlan
CFO: Richard Johnson
CEO: Pat Kelly
Quality Control: Judy Groves
VP/Operations/Marketing: Patrick Kelly
Estimated Sales: $10-20 Million
Number Employees: 50-99
Sq. footage: 75000
Type of Packaging: Food Service, Private Label, Bulk
Brands:
  Hi-Country
  Wenatchee Valley

6510 Hi-Point Beef Company
5265 W Cimarron Road
Ayr, NE 68925-2638   937-599-2115
         Fax: 937-599-4453
Processor and exporter of beef
Plant Manager: Gary Rose
Estimated Sales: $20-50 Million
Number Employees: 50-99
Parent Co: Lovett & Sons
Type of Packaging: Consumer, Food Service, Bulk

6511 Hi-Seas of Dulac
8345 Shrimpers Row
Dulac, LA 70353-2205   985-563-7155
         Fax: 985-563-2536
Shrimp
Owner: Eric Authamant
Estimated Sales: $ 5 - 10 Million
Number Employees: 10-19

6512 HiBix Corporation
5860 W Las Positas Blvd
Suite 21
Pleasanton, CA 94588   925-225-0800
   Fax: 925-225-0700   jdee@hibixcorp.com
         www.oobabeverage.com
all natural, refreshingly clean, sparkling beverage that infuses the pure extracts of the incredible hibiscus flower into every bottle.
President/CEO: John-David Enright
SMO: Janet DiGiovanna
VP Sales: James Curley

6513 (HQ)Hialeah Products Company
2207 Hayes Street
Hollywood, FL 33020-3437   954-923-3379
   Fax: 954-923-4010   800-923-3379
richnuts@aol.com   www.newurbanfarms.com
Packer of nuts, dried fruits, candy and snacks; wholesaler/distributor and exporter of dried fruits, pecans, Brazil nuts, almonds, walnuts, cashews, pistachios, peanuts, gourmet snack mixes and spicy snack mixes; all kosher; servingthe food service market
President: Richard Lesser
CEO: Kathy Lesser
Research & Development: Noah Lesser
Estimated Sales: $5-10 Million
Number Employees: 24
Number of Brands: 2
Number of Products: 200+
Sq. footage: 15000
Type of Packaging: Consumer, Food Service, Private Label, Bulk
Brands:
  OH NUTS

6514 Hibiscus Aloha Corporation
826 Queen St # 200
Honolulu, HI 96813-5286   808-591-8826
President: Elvira Lo
Estimated Sales: $ 1 - 3 Million
Number Employees: 5-9

6515 Hickey Foods
P.O.Box 2312
Sun Valley, ID 83353-2312   208-788-9033
         Fax: 208-788-8879
Manufacturer of vacuum-packed smoked trout
President: Thomas M Hickey
Estimated Sales: $ 1 - 3 Million
Number Employees: 5-9

6516 Hickory Baked Food
3221 Commerce Ct
Castle Rock, CO 80109-9458   303-688-2633
         Fax: 303-688-8431

Manufacturer of smoked and cured poultry and meats.
President: Robert Anderson
Purchasing Manager: Robert Anderson
Estimated Sales: $500,000-$1 Million
Number Employees: 1-4
Sq. footage: 6000
Parent Co: Hickory Baked Food
Type of Packaging: Consumer, Food Service, Private Label, Bulk
Brands:
  HICKORY BAKED
  HIGH VALLEY FARM

6517 Hickory Farms
P.O.Box 219
Maumee, OH 43537-2157   419-893-7611
   Fax: 419-893-0164 www.hickoryfarms.com
Manufacturer of beef, cheese, fruit, desserts, nuts, seafood and more
President/CEO: John Langdon
VP: James O'Neill
Estimated Sales: $16.3 Million
Number Employees: 500-999
Type of Packaging: Consumer, Food Service, Bulk

6518 Hickory Harvest Foods
900 Killian Rd
Akron, OH 44312-4705   330-644-6266
   Fax: 330-644-2501 www.hickoryharvest.com
Processor and importer of nuts and dried fruits; wholesaler/distributor of speciality candy
President: George Swiatkowski
Estimated Sales: $20-50 Million
Number Employees: 20-49
Sq. footage: 25000
Type of Packaging: Consumer, Food Service, Private Label, Bulk

6519 Hickory Specialties
2204 Highway 96
Burns, TN 37029-6289   615-446-7679
   Fax: 615-371-1780   800-251-2076
       info@hickoryspecialties.com
         www.hickoryspecialties.com
Manufacturer and exporter of natural liquid, oil and powder-based smoke flavors.
Owner: Edward Moore
CEO: Steven Davis
Estimated Sales: $ 3 - 5 Million
Number Employees: 20-49
Parent Co: Bob Evans Farms
Type of Packaging: Bulk
Brands:
  IMPERIAL SMOKE
  LIST-A-SMOKE
  ROYAL SMOKE
  ZESTI ADVANTAGE
  ZESTI CODE 425
  ZESTI MILD
  ZESTI SMOKE

6520 Hickory Valley Farm
Hc 1 Box 101s
Swiftwater, PA 18370-9725   570-839-6492
         Fax: 570-476-4197
Processor of meat products
Owner: Stavro Ladeas
Office Manager: Kathy Hulsizer
Estimated Sales: $5-10 Million
Number Employees: 5-9
Type of Packaging: Consumer

6521 Hidden Mountain Ranch Winery
2740 Hidden Mountain Rd
Paso Robles, CA 93446-8712   805-226-9907
         Fax: 805-238-4997
Wine
Owner: Richard Gumerman
Estimated Sales: $1-2.5 Million
Number Employees: 5-9

6522 Hidden Villa Ranch
310 N Harbor Blvd # 205
Fullerton, CA 92832-1954   714-680-3447
   Fax: 714-680-3380   800-326-3220
info@hiddenvilla.com   www.hiddenvilla.com
Manufacturer of Cheese and cheese products, liquid eggs
Founder/President: Timothy Luberski
Senior Vice President: Michael Sencer
Vice President, Pinehill Division: Robert Kelly
Estimated Sales: $50-100 Million
Number Employees: 100-249

Brands:
  Arizona Ranch Fresh
  California Ranch Fresh
  California Sunshine Dairy Pproducts
  Hidden Villa Ranch
  Horizon Orangic

6523 Hig-Country Corona
P.O.Box 698
Selah, WA 98942-0698   509-697-7950
   Fax: 909-272-8438   hccorona@hcfoodf.com
         www.hcfoods.com
Fruit and vegetable beverage bases
Owner: Leo Hogue
Estimated Sales: $10-20 Million
Number Employees: 1-4

6524 Higa Meat and Pork Market Limited
225 N Nimitz Hwy # 2
Honolulu, HI 96817-5349   808-531-3591
         Fax: 808-521-4951
Wholesale fresh meat; market meat
President: Marshall Higa
Estimated Sales: $ 50 - 100 Million
Number Employees: 20-49

6525 Higgins Seafood
2798 Jean Lafitte Blvd
Lafitte, LA 70067-5206   504-689-3577
Processor of frozen seafood including crabs and oysters
President: Denny Higgins
Estimated Sales: $300,000-500,000
Number Employees: 1-4
Type of Packaging: Consumer

6526 High Coffee Corporation
9601 Katy Freeway
Houston, TX 77024-1342   713-465-2230
   Fax: 713-465-5751   hi-co@msn.com
President: Antonio Pinero
Manager: Marcello Frau
Estimated Sales: Less than $500,000
Number Employees: 1-4

6527 High Country Elevators
P.O.Box 597
Dove Creek, CO 81324-0597   970-677-2251
   Fax: 970-677-2461   akmbr@yahoo.com
Processor of dried beans
Manager: Bruce Riddel
Estimated Sales: Less than $500,000
Number Employees: 1-4
Type of Packaging: Consumer, Food Service, Bulk

6528 High Country Gourmet
225 Mountain Way Drive
Orem, UT 84058-5121   801-426-4383
   Fax: 801-426-4385   hictrygrmt@aol.com
Procesor of dehydrated soup mixes
President: Rod Meldrum
Type of Packaging: Consumer, Food Service, Private Label, Bulk
Brands:
  HIGH COUNTRY GOURMET

6529 High Country Snack Food
P.O.Box 159
Lincoln, MT 59639-0159   406-362-4203
   Fax: 406-362-4275   800-433-3916
mt@hicountry.com   www.hicountry.com
Processor of high energy bars
President: James Johnson
CEO: James Johnson
Sales Manager: Randy Wagoner
Estimated Sales: $ 20 - 50 Million
Number Employees: 50-99
Parent Co: Hi Country Snack Foods
Type of Packaging: Consumer, Private Label
Brands:
  High Country
  Trekbarr

6530 High Country Snack Foods
P.O.Box 159
Lincoln, MT 59639-0159   406-362-4203
   Fax: 406-362-4275   800-433-3916
mt@highcountry.com   www.hicountry.com
Processor of beef jerky
President: James Johnson
Estimated Sales: $ 20 - 50 Million
Number Employees: 50-99
Type of Packaging: Consumer, Food Service

6531 High Falls Brewing
445 Saint Paul St
Rochester, NY 14605-1726   585-546-1030
          Fax: 585-546-8928 www.highfalls.com
Manufacturer of beer and ale
   President: Johnhen Henderson
   CEO: Tom Hubbard
   CEO: Norman Snyder
   Vice President/Marketing: David Boggs
   Sales: Donald Cotter
   Brew Master: David Schlosser
   Purchasing Manager: James Barber
Estimated Sales:$100-499.9 Million
Number Employees: 100-249
Type of Packaging: Consumer, Food Service
Brands:
   12 HORSE
   GENESEE BEER
   GENESEE LAGER
   GENESEE RED BEER
   GENNY CREAM ALE
   GENNY ICE
   GENNY LIGHT BEER
   GENNY NON-ALCOHOLIC
   GOLDEN ANNIVERSARY
   HONEY BROWN LAGER
   JW DUNDEE'S HONEY BROWN LAGER
   JW DUNDEE'S HONEY LIGHT
   MICHAEL SHEA'S BLACK & TAN
   MICHAEL SHEA'S IRISH AMBER
   SHEA'S BLACK & TAN
   TW DUNDEES CLASSIC LAGER

6532 High Falls Brewing Company
445 Saint Paul St
Rochester, NY 14605-1726   585-546-1030
          Fax: 585-546-8928 800-729-4366
          consumeraffairs@genbrew.com
          www.highfalls.com
Manufacturer of beer
   President/CEO: Tom Hubbard
   CEO: Norman Snyder
   Brewmaster: Dave Schlosser
Estimated Sales:$100-500 Million
Number Employees: 250-499
Type of Packaging: Consumer, Food Service
Brands:
   GENESEE
   GENNY LIGHT
   JW DUNDEE'S
   KOCH'S
   MICHAEL SHEA'S

6533 (HQ)High Liner Foods
100 Battery Point Road
PO Box 910
Lunenburg, NS B0J 2C0
Canada   902-634-9475
   Fax: 902-634-4785 info@highlinerfoods.com
          www.highlinerfoodservice.com
Manufacturer of fresh and frozen cod, haddock, sole,
perch, cured roe, pollack, halibut, grenadier and
salmon; also, kippers, cheese bites and pasta
   President/CEO: Henry Demone
   President/COO, USA: Mark Lamothe
   VP Corporate Services/CFO: Kelly Nelson
   VP Procurement: Paul Snow
   VP Business Development: Ronald Whynacht
   Director Human Resources: Joanne Brown CRHP
   VP/COO Canadian Operations: Mario Marino
   President/COO High Liner Foods USA: Richard
   Seban
Estimated Sales:$269 Million
Number Employees: 1400
Type of Packaging: Consumer, Food Service, Private Label, Bulk
Other Locations:
   High Liner Foods
   Secaucus NJ
Brands:
   40 FATHOMS
   FISHER BOY
   FLORESTA
   GINA ITALIAN VILLAGE
   HIGH LINER
   SEA FRESH

6534 High Liner Foods
P.O.Box 839
Portsmouth, NH 03802-0839   603-431-6865
          Fax: 603-430-9205 www.highlinerfoods.com

Frozen cod, flounder, perch, pollock, fish fillets, fish
portions, fish cakes, fishsticks
   President: Keith A Decker
   Vice President: Melissa Morasah
   VP Human Resources: Bob Korciusko
   VP Operations: Eric Conrad
Estimated Sales:$50-100 Million
Number Employees: 100-249
Brands:
   BOOTH
   FISHER BOY

6535 High Liner Foods USA
P.O.Box 839
Portsmouth, NH 03802-0839   603-431-6865
   Fax: 603-430-9205 info@highlinerfoods.com
          www.highlinerfoods.com
Seafood products
   President: Keith A Decker
   COO: Eric Conrad
   COO: Mario Marino
Estimated Sales:$ 10-100 Million
Number Employees: 100-249
Brands:
   Booth
   Fisher Boy
   Floresta®
   Gina Italian Village®
   High Liner®
   Italian Village Foods™
   Sea Fresh

6536 High Ridge Foods LLC
424 Ridgeway
White Plains, NY 10605-4208   914-761-2900
   Fax: 914-761-2901 alzerez@mindspring.com
Cultured dairy products, sugars, flowers, cheese, etc
   President: Nestor Alzerez
   Sales Manager: Nestor Alzerez, Jr
Estimated Sales:$2.5 Million
Number Employees: 1-4
Type of Packaging: Private Label, Bulk

6537 High Rise Coffee Roasters
2421 W Cucharras St
Colorado Springs, CO 80904-3048   719-633-1833
          Fax: 719-471-4815
Coffee
   President: Toby Anderson
Estimated Sales:$1-2.5 Million
Number Employees: 1-4

6538 High Sea Foods
188a Main Street N
Glovertown, NL A0G 2L0
Canada   709-533-2626
          Fax: 709-533-2627
Processor of frozen eel, catelin, herring, salmon,
smelt, sea urchin, lobster and whelk; also, fresh lobster
   President: Emerson Oram
   VP: Cory Oram
Number Employees: 20-49
Type of Packaging: Bulk

6539 High Tide Seafoods
P.O.Box 2141
Port Angeles, WA 98362-0407   360-452-8488
          Fax: 360-452-6710
Processor of fresh and frozen salmon
   Owner: Ernest Vail
Estimated Sales:$10-20 Million
Number Employees: 20-49
Type of Packaging: Consumer, Food Service
Brands:
   HIGH TIDE SEAFOODS

6540 High Valley Farm
3221 Commerce Court
Castle Rock, CO 80109-9458   303-634-2944
          Fax: 303-688-8431
Sausages and other processed meats
   President: Robert Anderson
   Plant Manager: Kenneth Trapp
Estimated Sales:$10-20 Million
Number Employees: 20-49

6541 High's Dairies
10630 Riggs Hill Rd
Jessup, MD 20794-9450   301-776-7727
          Fax: 301-776-2440
Dairy products
   President: Jack Sherman

6542 Highland Dairies
P.O.Box 2199
Wichita, KS 67201-2199   316-267-4221
   Fax: 316-267-1050 800-336-0765
          www.hilanddairy.com
Milk, dairy products
   Manager: Jerald Grey
   President: Gary Aggus
   Marketing Director: Ted Barlows
Number Employees: 100-249
Brands:
   Highland
   Old Chester

6543 Highland Fisheries
PO Box 459
Glace Bay, NS B1A 6C9
Canada   902-849-6016
          Fax: 902-849-7794
Processor and exporter of fresh and frozen finfish
   Plant Manager: Greg Mitchelitis
Number Employees: 100-249
Type of Packaging: Bulk

6544 Highland Laboratories
P.O.Box 199
Mt Angel, OR 97362-0199   503-845-9223
   Fax: 503-845-6364 888-717-4917
          answers@highlandvitamins.com
          www.highlandvitamins.com
Processor of vitamins, minerals and protein powders
   President: Candis Scott
   Owner: Kenneth Scott
   CFO: Virginia Myers
   Quality Control: John Mills
Estimated Sales:$20-50 Million
Number Employees: 20-49
Type of Packaging: Private Label

6545 Highland Manor Winery
2965 S York Hwy
Jamestown, TN 38556-5334   931-879-9519
Fax: 931-879-2907 www.highlandmanorwinery.net
Wine
   Co-Owner: Butch Campbell
   Co-Owner: Gertie Campbell
Estimated Sales:$2.5-5 Million
Number Employees: 5-9

6546 Highland Sugarworks
P.O.Box 58
Websterville, VT 05678-0058   802-479-1747
   Fax: 802-479-1737 800-452-4012
          sales@highlandsugarworks.com
          www.highlandsugarworks.com
Pure maple syrup and pancake mixes including apple cinnamon,buttermilk and blueberry; also, gift
packs available
   President: Jim Mac Isaac
   Sales/Marketing: Jim Close
   Operations: Deb Frimodig
Estimated Sales:$500,000-$1 Million
Number Employees: 10-19
Sq. footage: 15000
Type of Packaging: Consumer, Food Service, Private Label, Bulk
Brands:
   HIGHLAND SUGARWORKS

6547 Highlandville Packing
PO Box 186
Highlandville, MO 65669-0186   417-443-3365
   Fax: 417-443-3365 sales@hillbillymeats.com
          www.goatworld.com
Processor of meat products
   Owner: Neva Smith
Estimated Sales:$1-2.5 Million
Number Employees: 1-4

6548 Hightower's Packing
1713 Highway 518
Minden, LA 71055-8001   318-377-5459
          Fax: 318-377-5408
Processor of meat products
   President: Marvin Hightower
Estimated Sales:$2.5-5 Million
Number Employees: 10-19
Type of Packaging: Consumer, Bulk

6549 Highwood Distillers
PO Box 5693
High River, AB T1V 1M7
Canada   403-652-3202
    Fax: 403-652-4227 hwdistill@telusplanet.net
             www.highwooddistillers.com
Processor and exporter of whiskey, vodka, rums, liqueurs and tequila; also, pre-mixers
    President/Sales: Barry Wilde
    Chairman/CEO: W Miller
    VP: R Stothers
    Operations: Glen Hopkins
    Production: Larry Beutler
Number Employees: 20-49
Sq. footage: 30000
Type of Packaging: Consumer, Private Label
Brands:
    BUCCANEER
    CHINA WHITE
    COLITA
    HIGHWOOD
    MARUSHKA
    OLD MEXICO
    TRIPLE SEC
    WHITE LIGHTNING

6550 Hiland Dairy
P.O.Box 2199
Wichita, KS 67201-2199   316-267-4221
    Fax: 316-267-1050   800-336-0765
             www.hilanddairy.com
Milk
    Manager: Jerald Grey
    Sales Director: Larry Powers
    Plant Manager: Jeff Zielke
Estimated Sales:$100+ Million
Number Employees: 100-249
Type of Packaging: Bulk
Brands:
    Hiland

6551 Hiland Dairy Foods Company
P.O.Box 2270
Springfield, MO 65801-2270   417-862-9311
    Fax: 417-837-1106 www.hilanddairy.com
Manufacturer of dairy products including; ice cream, milk, butter, cheese, yogurt, dips, juice and to-go dairy drinks
    President/COO: Gary Aggus
*Estimated Sales:*1
Number Employees: 500-999
Parent Co: Prairie Farms Dairy/Dairy Farmers of America
Type of Packaging: Consumer, Food Service
Brands:
    HILAND DAIRY

6552 Hiland Dairy Foods Company
P.O.Box 2199
Wichita, KS 67201-2199   316-267-4221
    Fax: 316-267-1050 www.hilanddairy.com
Processor of milk and cottage cheese
    Manager: Jerald Grey
Estimated Sales:$20-50 Million
Number Employees: 100-249
Parent Co: Hiland Dairy
Type of Packaging: Consumer, Food Service

6553 Hiland Roberts Ice Cream Company
P.O.Box 19
Norfolk, NE 68702-0019   402-371-3660
    Fax: 402-371-0243 www.robertsdairy.com
Processor of ice cream and novelties
    Manager: Mitch Ayers
    Director Corporate Marketing: Al Streeter
    Division Manager: Bob Walker
Estimated Sales:$250 Million
Number Employees: 50-99
Parent Co: Roberts Dairy Company
Type of Packaging: Consumer, Food Service, Private Label

6554 Hill Nutritional Products
1950 Old Cuthbert Road
Suite M
Cherry Hill, NJ 08034-1439   856-857-0811
             hillherbal@aol.com
             www.hillherbal.com

6555 Hill Top Berry Farm & Winery
2800 Berry Hill Rd
Nellysford, VA 22958-2034   434-361-1266
    Fax: 434-361-1266 hilltop1@intelos.net
             www.hilltopberrywine.com
Wine
    Owner: Marlyn Allen
Estimated Sales:$ 3 - 5 Million
Number Employees: 5-9

6556 Hill of Beans Coffee Roasters
3438 W 43rd St
Los Angeles, CA 90008-4906   323-291-2160
    Fax: 213-665-7769   888-527-6278
Coffee Roasters
    Owner: Leo Hill
Estimated Sales:$5-10 Million appx.
Number Employees: 5-9

6557 Hillandale
370 Spicer Rd
Gettysburg, PA 17325-7613   717-334-1973
             Fax: 717-334-6623
Processor of eggs
    Owner: Donald Hershey
Estimated Sales:$10-20 Million
Number Employees: 100-249
Type of Packaging: Consumer, Food Service

6558 Hillard Bloom Packing Co
2601 Ogden Ave
Port Norris, NJ 08349-3141   856-785-0120
             Fax: 856-785-2341
             www.hillardbloomshellfish.com
Processor of fresh and frozen clams and oysters
    President: Hillard Bloom
    COO: Todd Reeves
    VP: Todd Reeves
Estimated Sales:$7600000
Number Employees: 10-19
Sq. footage: 2000
Parent Co: Tallmadge Brothers

6559 Hillbilly Smokehouse
1801 S 8th Street
Rogers, AR 72756-5998   479-636-1927
    Fax: 479-636-4590 hillbilly@ipa.net
             www.hillbillysmokehouse.com
Manufacturer of smoked ham, bacon, sausage, turkey, chicken, pork and beef
    President: Tom Baumgartner
    Vice President: Drew Baumgartner
Estimated Sales:$1 Million
Number Employees: 10
Number of Brands: 1
Number of Products: 20
Sq. footage: 5000
Type of Packaging: Consumer

6560 Hillcrest Orchard
101 Autumn Ter
Lake Placid, FL 33852-6275   865-397-5273
    Fax: 865-397-5273 ftpresto@tnni.net
Processor of apple butter and jellies including apple, peach, plum and grape; grape juice; grower of fresh apples and grapes
    Co-Owner: Frank Preston
    Co-Owner: Twylia Preston
*Estimated Sales:*Under $100,000
Number Employees: 1-4
Number of Brands: 1
Number of Products: 15
Sq. footage: 92000
Type of Packaging: Consumer, Food Service, Bulk
Brands:
    HILLCREST ORCHARD

6561 Hillcrest Vineyard
240 Vineyard Ln
Roseburg, OR 97471-9097   541-673-3709
             finewine@sorcum.com
Wines
    Manager: Della Terra
    Owner: Richard Sommer
Estimated Sales:$1-2.5 Million
Number Employees: 1-4

6562 Hiller Cranberries
131 Hiller Rd
Rochester, MA 02770-4031   508-763-5257
             Fax: 508-763-3204

Quince concentrate, currant concentrate, crabapple concentrate, fruit puree/pulp, noncitrus fruit juices
    Owner: Robert Hiller
    Owner: Robert Hiller III
Estimated Sales:$5-10 Million
Number Employees: 1-4

6563 Hillestad Pharmaceuticals
178 Us Highway 51 N
Woodruff, WI 54568-9501   715-358-2113
    Fax: 715-358-7812   800-535-7742
    info@hillestadlabs.com www.hillestadlabs.com
Manufacturer and exporter of nutritional products
    Marketing: Dan Hillestad
Estimated Sales:$10-20 Million
Number Employees: 10-19
Type of Packaging: Consumer, Private Label

6564 Hilliard Corporation
100 W 4th St
Elmira, NY 14901-2190   607-733-7121
    Fax: 607-737-1108 hilliard@hilliardcorp.com
             www.hilliardcorp.com
The Hilliard Corporation products offer a broad line of motion control products, oil filtration and reclaiming products, starters for industrial gas, diesel engines and gas turbines, and plate and frame filter presses used in the food and beverage industry.
    President: Paul Webb
    CEO: Nelson Mooers Van Den
    CEO: Nelson Mooers Van Den Blink
    Regional Sales Manager: Gerry Lachut
Estimated Sales:$ 50 - 75 Million
Number Employees: 500-999

6565 Hillman Shrimp & Oyster
10700 Hillman Dr
Dickinson, TX 77539-3058   281-339-1506
    Fax: 281-339-1509   800-582-4416
             info@hillmanoysters.com
             www.hillmanoysters.com
Processor of IQF shucked and cleaned oysters including topped, half shell, meats and pillow packed, scallops, clams, mussels, breaded seafood
    President: Steve Hillman
    CEO: Clifford Hillman
    VP Marketing: Chris Hillman
    Marketing Director: Tricia Roberts
    Sales: Dale Rymer
    Public Relations: Wendy Taylor
    COO: Steve Taylor
Estimated Sales:$15 Million
Number Employees: 250-499
Number of Brands: 1
Number of Products: 12
Sq. footage: 75000
Type of Packaging: Consumer, Food Service, Bulk
Brands:
    HILLMAN

6566 Hillsboro Coffee Company
4416 N Hubert Avenue
Tampa, FL 33614-7649   813-877-2126
             Fax: 813-879-0524
Custom coffee
    President: Neil McTague
    VP Sales: John Sakkis
Estimated Sales:$5-10 Million
Number Employees: 8

6567 Hillsboro Refrigerated Lockers
411 S Ash Street
Hillsboro, KS 67063-1403   316-947-3781
Processor of sausage and lard
Estimated Sales:$1-2.5 Million
Number Employees: 1-4
Type of Packaging: Consumer

6568 Hillside Candy
274 Hillside Ave
Hillside, NJ 07205-1803   973-926-2219
    Fax: 973-926-2214   800-524-1304
             sales@hillsidecandy.com
             www.townshipofhillside.org
Manufactures Sugar-free confections
    Manager: David Klurman
    CFO: Ray La Conte
    VP Marketing & Exports: Susan Rosenthal Jay
Estimated Sales:$2.5-5 Million
Number Employees: 10-19
Number of Brands: 3
Type of Packaging: Consumer, Private Label
Brands:
    BLUE BIRD TOFFE

GOLIGHTLY SUGAR FREE
SHAKER COUNTRY MEADOWSWEETS

6569 Hillside Dairy
W11299 Broek Rd
Stanley, WI 54768-8215
715-644-2275
Fax: 715-644-0720
Cheese
Owner: Randy La Grander
Estimated Sales: $1-2.5 Million
Number Employees: 20-49

6570 Hillside Lane Farm
160 Hillside Ln
Randolph, VT 05060-9178
802-728-0070
Fax: 802-728-0071 info@hillsidelane.com
www.hillsidelane.com
Organic maple pancake & baking mixes, infused
vinegars, body syrups
President: Cathy Bacon
Estimated Sales: $ 1 - 3 Million
Number Employees: 1-4
Number of Brands: 4
Number of Products: 17
Type of Packaging: Consumer, Food Service, Private Label, Bulk

6571 Hillson Nut Company
P.O.Box 602038
Cleveland, OH 44102-0038
216-961-4477
Fax: 216-961-4480 800-333-2818
nuts@hillsonnut.com www.hillsonnut.com
Roasted, raw salted nuts and peanut butter
President: Richard Hillson
Vice President: Troy Sawvel
Estimated Sales: $500,000-$1 Million
Number Employees: 10-19

6572 Hilltop Herb Farm & Restaurant
235 Chain O Lakes Resort
Cleveland, TX 77327-8698
832-397-4020
Fax: 281-592-6288 info@hilltopherbfarm.com
www.hilltopherbfarm.com
Processor of jams, jellies, pickles and relishes
Owner: James Smith
Executive Chef: Jim Condra
Number of Brands: 1
Number of Products: 100
Parent Co: Chain-O-Lakes Resort
Type of Packaging: Private Label
Brands:
HILL TOP FARM

6573 Hilltop Meat Company
US 29 North
Gantt, AL 36038
334-388-2393
Fax: 334-388-3131
Processor of meat products
President: William Green
Estimated Sales: $1-2.5 Million
Number Employees: 5-9
Type of Packaging: Consumer

6574 Hilltown Whole Food Company
445 Berkshire Trl
Cummington, MA 01026-9610
413-634-5677
Fax: 413-634-5409
Cereal, granola
President: Robert Berenson
Number Employees: 5-9
Type of Packaging: Private Label
Brands:
MY DAD'S CEREAL

6575 Hilmar Cheese Company
9001 Lander Ave
Hilmar, CA 95324-8320
209-667-6076
Fax: 209-634-1408 800-577-5772
info@hilmarcheese.com www.hilmarcheese.com
Manufacturer of Cheddar, Monterey Jack, Colby,
Colby Jack, flavored Jacks, Mozzarella and Hispanic
cheeses for use in food service, ingredients, retail
and the restaurant/fast food trade.
President/CEO: John Jeter
CFO: Donald Hicks
Vice President Sales/Marketing: Phil Robnett
Estimated Sales: $100-500 Million
Number Employees: 500-999
Type of Packaging: Consumer, Food Service, Private Label
Brands:
Gina Marie Cream Cheese

6576 Hilo Fish Company
55 Holomua St
Hilo, HI 96720-5142
808-961-0877
Fax: 808-935-1603 www.hilofish.com
President: Charles Umamoto
Estimated Sales: $ 20 - 50 Million
Number Employees: 20-49

6577 Himalaya
10440 Westoffice Dr
Houston, TX 77042-5309
713-863-1622
Fax: 713-863-1686 cdeans@himalayausa.com
www.himalaya-proselect.com
President/CEO: Nabeel Manal
CEO: Nabeel Manal
National Sales Manager: Connie Deans
Estimated Sales: $ 5 - 10 Million
Number Employees: 20-49

6578 Himalayan Heritage
N5821 Fairway Dr
Fredonia, WI 53021-9742
262-692-9500
Fax: 262-692-6387 888-414-9500
colin@himalayanheritge.com
www.blueskymassage.com
Processor, importer and exporter of herbal dietary
supplements
Co-Owner: Blair Lewis
Co_Owner: Karen Lewis
Estimated Sales: $ 1 - 3 Million
Number Employees: 10-19
Type of Packaging: Consumer, Food Service, Private Label, Bulk
Brands:
ATTNETION SPAN
ERJUV-POWDER
FIVE FORCES OF NATURE
IMMUNO FORCE
JOYFUL MIND

6579 Hinckley Springs Water Company
6055 S Harlem Ave
Chicago, IL 60638-3985
773-586-8600
Fax: 773-586-8613 www.water.com
Bottled water
President/CEO: George Schmitt
CFO: Chet Matykiewicz
VP: Mike Garrity
Director, Corporate Communications: Debbie
Lawrence
Estimated Sales: $500,000-$1 Million
Number Employees: 50-99
Sq. footage: 1500
Parent Co: DS Waters
Type of Packaging: Consumer, Food Service, Bulk
Brands:
ALHAMBRA®
BELMONT SPRINGS®
CRYSTAL SPRINGS®
HINCKLEY SPRINGS®
KENTWOOD SPRINGS®
NURSERY® WATER
SIERRA SPRINGS®
SPARKLETTS®

6580 Hingham Shellfish
25 Eldridge Court
Hingham, MA 02043-2203
781-749-1374
Fax: 405-631-8473
President/Treasure: Myrle Derbyshire
Estimated Sales: $ .5 - 1 million
Number Employees: 1-4

6581 Hinojosa Bros Wholesale
P.O.Box 901
Roma, TX 78584-0901
956-849-2386
Fax: 956-849-2386 800-554-4119
Candy and confectionary.
Owner: Antonio Hinojosa
Estimated Sales: $600,000
Number Employees: 1-4
Brands:
HINOJOSAS BROTHERS PORL
CRACKLINGS

6582 Hint
2124 Union Street
Suite D
San Francisco, CA 94123
415-513-4050
Fax: 415-276-1786 kara@drinkhint.com
www.drinkhint.com
naturally flavored water
CEO: Kara Goldin

6583 Hint Mint
2432 E 8th St
Los Angeles, CA 90021-1734
213-622-6468
Fax: 213-748-3189 info@hintmint.com
www.hintmint.com
Breathmints and peppermint
Owner: Cooper Bates
Estimated Sales: $ .5 - 1 million
Number Employees: 5-9
Brands:
HINT MINT

6584 Hinzerling Winery
1520 Sheridan Ave
Prosser, WA 99350-1140
509-786-2163
Fax: 509-786-2163 800-722-6702
info@hinzerling.com www.hinzerling.com
Wine, vinegar
President/Winemaker: Michael Wallace
Cellarmaster: Stan Kelly
Estimated Sales: $1-2.5 Million
Number Employees: 1-4
Type of Packaging: Private Label
Brands:
HINZERLING
WALLACE

6585 Hiram Walker & Sons
P.O.Box 2407
Fort Smith, AR 72902-2407
479-783-4191
Fax: 479-783-4195
www.canadianclubwhiskey.com
Manufacturer and importer of gin, tequila, vodka,
whiskey and liqueurs; exporter of liqueurs and
tequila
President: W S Walker Sr
Plant Manager: Brian Hastings
Estimated Sales: $10-20 Million
Number Employees: 20-49
Parent Co: Allied Domecq
Type of Packaging: Consumer
Brands:
BALLATINES
BEEFEATER
CANADIAN CLUB
CORVOISIER
IRISH MIST
KAHLUA
MAKER'S MARK
MALIBU
MIDORI
SAUZA
STOLICHNAYA

6586 (HQ)Hiram Walker & Sons
2072 Riverside Drive E
Windsor, ON N8Y 1A7
Canada
519-254-5171
Fax: 519-971-5717
Processor and exporter of blended whiskey, gin,
scotch, vodka, rum, liqueurs, etc
President: Ian Gourlay
Number Employees: 500-999
Parent Co: Allied Domecq
Type of Packaging: Consumer, Food Service
Brands:
BALLANTINE'S
BEEFEATER
CANADIAN CLUB
COURVOISIER
IRISH MIST
KAHLUA
MAKER'S MARK
MALIBU
MIDORI
SAUZA
STOLICHNAYA

6587 Hirsch Brothers & Company
1838 S Shore Drive
Holland, MI 49423-4343
616-335-5806
Fruits and vegetables.
President: L Hirsch
Estimated Sales: $500-1 Million appx.
Number Employees: 1-4

6588 (HQ)Hirzel Canning Company &Farms
411 Lemoyne Rd
Northwood, OH 43619-1699
419-693-0531
Fax: 419-693-4859 info@hirzel.com
www.hirzel.com

Manufacturer and exporter of canned tomatoes and tomato products, sauerkraut, sauces, salsa, tomato juice, tomato soup and more
President/CEO: Karl Hirzel Jr
Vice President: William Hirzel
Quality Control: Karl Hirzel
Retail Sales Manager: Steve Hirzel
Estimated Sales: $20-50 Million
Number Employees: 50-99
Number of Brands: 4
Number of Products: 30
Sq. footage: 500000
Type of Packaging: Consumer, Food Service, Private Label, Bulk
Brands:
Dei Fratelli
Silver Fleece
Starcross

6589 His Catch Value Added Products
PO Box 770
Homer, AK 99603-0770   800-215-7110
Fax: 907-235-1040   stuart@xyz.net
www.hiscatch.com
Processing plant, catch & process salmon and halibut as well as a variety of other fish and shellfish
President: Douglas Stuart
Vice President: Alexander Stuart IV

6590 Hiscock Enterprises
Keating Road
PO Box 40
Brigus, NL A0A 1K0
Canada   709-528-4577
Fax: 709-528-4575
Processor of frozen wild berries
President: Charles Hiscock
Managing Director: David Hiscock
Production Manager: Graham Hiscock
Number Employees: 5-9
Sq. footage: 15000

6591 Hitz Cheese Company
519 E Linwood Road
Linwood, MI 48634-9706   517-697-5932
Chesse
President: Dolores Hitz
Estimated Sales: $500,000 appx.
Number Employees: 1-4

6592 Hobarama Corporation
400 NW 26th St
Miami, FL 33127-4120   305-531-9708
Fax: 305-531-9709   880-439-2295
www.bawls.com
Manufacturer of beverages
President: Hobart Buppert
Senior VP: Christina Staalstrom
Estimated Sales: $2.5-5 Million
Number Employees: 10-19
Type of Packaging: Bulk

6593 Hobe Laboratories
6479 S Ash Ave
Tempe, AZ 85283-3657   480-413-1950
Fax: 480-413-2005   800-528-4482
hobelabs@aol.com   www.hobelabs.com
Processor and exporter of weight loss and herbal teas
President: Bill Robertson
Sales Director: Brenda Martin
Director Manufacturing: Peter Samuell
Estimated Sales: $10-20 Million
Number Employees: 10-19
Sq. footage: 12000
Type of Packaging: Consumer, Private Label
Brands:
SLIM
THERMO SLIM
ULTRA SLIM

6594 Hodgson Mill Inc
1100 Stevens Ave
Effingham, IL 62401-4265   217-347-0105
Fax: 217-347-0198   800-525-0177
paul.kirby@hodgsonmill.com
www.hodgsonmill.com
All natural and organic foods-flours, cereals, baking mixes, whole wheat pastas, gluten free pastas, gluten free mixes, baking ingredients-producers and manufacturers of whole grain foods. Co-packing for private label available
President: Robert Goldstein
Executive VP Sales/Marketing: Paul Kirby

Estimated Sales: $25-30 Million
Sq. footage: 120000
Brands:
DON'S CHUCK WAGON
HODGSON MILL
KENTUCKY KERNEL
PASTAMANIA
VIDALIA SWEET

6595 Hoechst Food Ingredients
PO Box 3053
Edison, NJ 08818-3053   800-344-5807
Manufacturer of artificial sweeteners
Parent Co: Hoechst Celanese Corporation
Brands:
SUNETT

6596 Hoekstra Meat Company
PO Box 2113
Kalamazoo, MI 49003-2113   616-321-0797
Fax: 616-345-9398
Processor of cooked, corned and case-ready ground beef and patties, portion cut steaks, cooked pork, pastrami and ready-to-eat entrees
President: M Hoekstra
VP: J Hoekstra
VP: T Hoekstra
Number Employees: 50-99
Sq. footage: 40000

6597 Hoff's Bakery
2 Sixth Street
Medford, MA 02155   781-396-8384
Fax: 781-396-7918   888-871-5100
www.hoffsbakery.com
cakes and tortes, cheesecakes, pies and tarts, 1/2 sheet tray, individual desserts, and trifle cups
President/Owner: Vincent Frattura
Estimated Sales: $1.5 Million
Number Employees: 20

6598 Hoff's United Foods
P.O.Box 145
Brownsville, WI 53006-0145   920-583-3734
Smoked sausage, bacon
Owner: Dorothy Hoff
Marketing: Tim Hoff
Estimated Sales: $1-2.5 Million
Number Employees: 10-19
Type of Packaging: Private Label, Bulk

6599 Hoffman Aseptic Packaging Company
PO Box 225
Hoffman, MN 56339-0225   320-986-2084
Fax: 320-986-2087   hapcoalx@rea-alp.com
Aseptic-packed sauces and puddings
President: Tom Ashley
Estimated Sales: $20-50 Million
Number Employees: 50-99

6600 Hoffman Sausage Company
2111 Kindel Avenue
Cincinnati, OH 45214-1841   513-621-4160
Fax: 513-621-7205   hoffmannsausage@aol.com
Processor of sausage and luncheon meats
Owner/President: Howard Tallen
Estimated Sales: $10-20 Million
Number Employees: 20-49
Type of Packaging: Consumer, Bulk

6601 Hofmann Sausage Company
6196 Eastern Ave
Syracuse, NY 13211-2209   315-437-7257
Fax: 315-437-2391   800-724-8410
sales@hofmannsausage.com
www.hofmannsausage.com
Processor of sausage including Polish, hot and bologna; also, hot dogs natural casings and skinless
President: Walter Flook
Estimated Sales: $10-20 Million
Number Employees: 20-49
Number of Brands: 15
Number of Products: 75
Type of Packaging: Consumer, Food Service, Bulk
Brands:
GERMAN
SANPPY'S

6602 Hog Haus Brewing Company
430 W Dickson St
Fayetteville, AR 72701-5107   479-521-2739
Fax: 479-442-0077   hops@ozarkbrew.com
www.hoghaus.com

ter
Processor of seasonal beer, ale, stout, lager and porter
President: Kari Larson
VP: Julie Sill
Managing Director: Kari Larson
Estimated Sales: Below $ 5 Million
Number Employees: 50-99
Type of Packaging: Consumer, Food Service
Brands:
HogHaus
Ploughman's Pils
WoodStock Wheat

6603 Hogtown Brewing Company
2351 Royal Windsor Drive
Unit 6
Mississauga, ON L5J 4S7
Canada   905-855-9065
Fax: 905-822-0990   hogman@infinity.net
www.hogtownbeer.com
Processor of beer; also, bottling services available
President: Maria Lopez
General Manager: Peter Lazaro
Number Employees: 5-9
Type of Packaging: Consumer, Food Service

6604 Hogtowne B-B-Q Sauce Company
1712 W University Ave
Gainesville, FL 32603-1839   352-375-6969
Fax: 352-373-6969 www.saltydogsaloon.com
Wholesaler/distributor of hot sauces, BBQ sauces, marinades and other specialty food products
Manager: Keith Singleton
Vice President: Pam Taylor-Kinard
Estimated Sales: $500,000-$1 Million
Number Employees: 20-49
Sq. footage: 2000
Parent Co: Original Alan's Cubana
Type of Packaging: Consumer, Food Service, Private Label, Bulk
Brands:
CAROLINA STYLE B-B-Q-SAUCE
HOGTOWNE
KINARD'S MARINADE
PRIME STEAK SAUCE

6605 Holey Moses Cheesecake
115 Gabreski Airport
Westhampton Beach, NY 11978-1200 631-288-8088
Fax: 631-288-0551   800-225-2253
www.holeymosescheesecake.com
Processor of cheesecake
President: Christopher Weber
Estimated Sales: Less than $500,000
Number Employees: 1-4

6606 Holistic Products Corporation
10 W Forest Avenue
Englewood, NJ 07631-4020   201-569-1188
Fax: 201-569-3224   800-221-0308
Processor, wholesaler/distributor and importer of health food products including propolis lozenges
President: Arnold Gans
VP Sales: Myra Gans
Number Employees: 10-19
Sq. footage: 8000
Parent Co: MNI Group

6607 Holland American International Specialties
10343 Artesia Blvd
Bellflower, CA 90706-6721   562-867-7589
Fax: 562-925-4507   sales@dutchmall.com
www.1dutchmall.com
European and domestic specialty gourmet foods.
Manager: Maria Cervantes
Estimated Sales: $ .5 - 1 million
Number Employees: 1-4

6608 Holland Sweeteners N A
1100 Circle 75 Parkway SE
Atlanta, GA 30339-3064   770-956-8443
Fax: 770-956-7102   800-757-9468
Processor of aspartame
President: Ken Dooley
CEO: Barbara Durrance
Estimated Sales: $5-10 Million
Number Employees: 5-9
Parent Co: Holland Sweeteners N.A.
Type of Packaging: Bulk

6609 Holland-American Wafer Company
PO Box 9877
Wyoming, MI 49509-0877   616-243-0191
Fax: 616-243-0342   800-253-8350
info@hawco.com   www.wafers.com
Processor of portable snack foods including sugar wafer cookies, confectionery wafer centers and granola.
President: Stuart Vanderheide
VP Sales/Marketing: Mark O'Toole
Plant Manager: Tom Huizinger
Estimated Sales: $100-500 Million
Number Employees: 250-499
Sq. footage: 200
Type of Packaging: Consumer, Food Service, Private Label, Bulk
Brands:
CLASSIC GRAINS
DUTCH TWINS

6610 Hollman Foods
1948 36 Rd
Minden, NE 68959-7116   308-468-5635
Fax: 308-468-6141   888-926-2879
info@hollmans.com   www.hollmans.com
Processor of barbecue sauce, seasonings, spices, smoked turkey, breading mixes, gourmet jellies and fruit butters; also, gift box items, dip mixes, and honey
Owner: Byron Holl
CEO: Judith Holl
Estimated Sales: $ 3 - 5 Million
Number Employees: 5-9
Number of Brands: 2
Number of Products: 30
Sq. footage: 3000
Type of Packaging: Consumer, Food Service, Private Label
Brands:
EDEN FARMS
HOLLMANS

6611 Hollow Road Farms
271 Hollow Road
Stuyvesant, NY 12173-1910   518-758-7214
Fax: 518-758-1899
Yogurt.
President: Joan Snyder
Estimated Sales: $500,000-$1 Million
Number Employees: 5-9

6612 Holly Hill Locker Company
8728 Old State Rd
Holly Hill, SC 29059   803-496-3611
Manufactuer of beef and pork
Owner: L Kenneth Folse Jr
Estimated Sales: Less than $500,000
Number Employees: 1-4
Type of Packaging: Consumer, Bulk

6613 Holmes Cheese Company
9444 State Route 39
Millersburg, OH 44654-9764   330-674-6451
Fax: 330-674-6673   rjramseyer@valkyrie.net
Manufacturer of cheese and whey
President: Robert Ramseyer
Estimated Sales: $10-20 Million
Number Employees: 20-49
Type of Packaging: Consumer, Food Service, Private Label, Bulk

6614 Holmes Foods
101 S Liberty Ave
Nixon, TX 78140-2401   830-582-1551
Fax: 830-582-1090
Poultry
President: Phillip A Morris
General Manager: Phillip Morris
Estimated Sales: $20-50 Million
Number Employees: 100-249

6615 (HQ)Holsum Bakery
P.O.Box 6690
Phoenix, AZ 85005-6690   602-252-2351
Fax: 602-252-6505   800-755-8167
www.holsumaz.com
Manufacturer of breads and rolls
Owner: L Edward Eisele Jr
Estimated Sales: $20-50 Million
Number Employees: 500-999
Other Locations:
Holsum Manufacturing Plant
Tempe AZ
Holsum Manufacturing Plant
Tolleson AZ
Brands:
Aunt Hattie's
Aunt Hattie's Quality Breads
Bar S
Holsum
LeFrancias
Roman Meal
Smart Kids

6616 Holsum Bakery
20.1 Carretera 2
Toa Baja, PR 00949   787-798-8282
Fax: 787-251-2060
Processor of baked goods
President: Ramon Calderon
VP Finance: Raul Buso
Number Employees: 1,000-4,999
Type of Packaging: Consumer, Food Service, Private Label, Bulk

6617 Holsum Bakery
P.O.Box 11468
Fort Wayne, IN 46858-1468   260-456-2130
Fax: 260-745-1404
Processor of bread including white, rye, whole wheat, low-fat, etc
President: Wayne Davidson
VP Sales: Frank Kerr
Number Employees: 100-249
Parent Co: Lewis Brothers Bakeries
Type of Packaging: Consumer, Food Service

6618 Holsum Bread
5120 8th Ave
Kenosha, WI 53140-3410   262-658-1396
Fax: 262-658-0029
Baked goods
President: Edward Eisele, Jr
Estimated Sales: $10-20 Million
Number Employees: 20-49

6619 Holt's Bakery
101 Sellers St
Douglas, GA 31533-4607   912-384-2202
Fax: 912-384-7467
Baked goods, pastries, cookies
Owner: Howard Holt
CEO/Manager: Cecil Holt, Jr
Purchasing Agent: Paul Spivey
Estimated Sales: $1-2.5 Million
Number Employees: 20-49

6620 Holten Meats
1682 Sauget Business Blvd
Sauget, IL 62206-1454   618-337-8400
Fax: 618-337-3292   800-851-4684
info@holtenmeat.com   www.holtenmeat.com
Processor of frozen beef, pork and veal patties
President: Mike Holten
Chairman/Chief Executive Officer: Jim Holten
COO: R Scott Hudspeth
Estimated Sales: $32 Million
Number Employees: 200
Sq. footage: 50000
Type of Packaging: Food Service
Brands:
EXTRA VALUE
HOLTEN

6621 Holton Food Products Company
500 W Burlington Ave
La Grange, IL 60525-2227   708-352-5599
Fax: 708-352-3788
Processor of ingredients for frozen pies, cakes and cookies including egg whites and stabilizers
President: Ross Holton
CEO: Paul Holton
Executive VP: John Holton
Estimated Sales: $2.5-5 Million
Number Employees: 10-19
Type of Packaging: Bulk

6622 Holton Meat Processing
701 Arizona Ave
Holton, KS 66436-1247   785-364-2331
Processor of beef
Owner: Ben Hartley
Estimated Sales: $ 1 - 3 Million
Number Employees: 1-4
Type of Packaging: Consumer

6623 Holy Mole
PO Box 203128
Austin, TX 78720-3128   512-310-8453
Fax: 512-671-4766   877-310-8453
info@holymole.comm
www.holymole.com/index2.ivnu
Manufacturer of salsa available in several flavors including hot red salsa, fire roasted habanero; gift packs available.
President: Pat Jones
Estimated Sales: $300,000-500,000
Number Employees: 1-4

6624 Homarus
476 Armour Circle NE
Atlanta, GA 30324-4002   404-877-1988
Fax: 404-877-1999   www.smoked.salmon.com
Processor and exporter of smoked salmon, nova, lox, sturgeon, trout, tuna loins, scallops, shrimp, mussels and whitefish; also, custom-cured salmon
Co-Owner/President: Peter Heineman
CEO: Chris Harvey
VP Sales: Thomas Marshall
Type of Packaging: Consumer, Food Service
Brands:
HOMARUS
RIVERBANK

6625 Hombres Foods
102 Cedar Ln
Cedar Creek, TX 78612-3204   512-303-4558
Fax: 515-303-4558   877-446-6273
Sales@HombresFoods.com
www.hombresfoods.com/start.html
Specializes in gourmet salsas, chili and cornbread fixins, dip mixes, soup, brownie mixes and BBQ seasonings.
President: Dennis Willms
Estimated Sales: $ .5 - 1 million
Number Employees: 1-4

6626 Home Baked Group
1084 S Rogers Cir
Boca Raton, FL 33487-2815   561-995-0767
Fax: 561-995-0294   www.homebaked.com
Fat-free and low-fat brownies, sugar-free baked goods
Estimated Sales: $1-4.9 Million
Number Employees: 5-9

6627 Home Bakery
304 S 2nd St # Main
Laramie, WY 82070-3648   307-742-2721
Fax: 307-745-3346
Manufacturer of baked goods and chocolate
President: Kim Campbell
Estimated Sales: $500,000-$1 Million
Number Employees: 10-19
Type of Packaging: Food Service

6628 Home Baking Company
900 16th St N
Birmingham, AL 35203-1017   205-252-1161
Fax: 205-323-7610
Manufacturer and exporter of hamburger buns
President: Carter Wood
Estimated Sales: $10-20 Million
Number Employees: 100-249
Sq. footage: 65000
Parent Co: Flowers Baking Company
Type of Packaging: Consumer

6629 Home Delivery Food Service
PO Box 215
Jefferson, GA 30549-0215   706-367-9551
Fax: 706-367-4646
Frozen foods, meats and chicken
President: William Griffin, Sr.

6630 Home Made Brand Foods Company
2 Opportunity Way
Newburyport, MA 01950-4043   978-462-3663
Fax: 978-462-7117   info@hmbf.com
www.hmbf.com
Processor of deli and meat salads, chilled entrees, quiche, pot pies, soups, stews, chowders, dips, spreads and desserts
President: Richard Walthers
CEO: John Palmieri
VP Operations: Dayne Wayhl
Estimated Sales: $20-50 Million
Number Employees: 100-249

6631 Home Maid Bakery
1005 Lower Main St
Wailuku, HI 96793-2008 808-244-7015
Fax: 808-242-8458 info@homemaidbakery.com
www.homemaidbakery.com
Bakery products
President: Jeremy Kozuki
Sales Director: Leighton Saito
Purchasing Manager: Steven Tarnoff
Estimated Sales: $4-5 Million
Number Employees: 50-99
Number of Brands: 1
Number of Products: 100+
Type of Packaging: Consumer, Private Label

6632 Home Market Foods
140 Morgan Dr # 100
Norwood, MA 02062-5076 781-948-1500
Fax: 781-702-6171 info@homemarketfoods.com
www.homemarketfoods.com
Cooked steak, cooked meatballs, sausage, Italian
sausage, cooked sausage
Administrator: Andy Stone
VP: Steve Smith
Director Sales: Dana Geremonte
Estimated Sales: $ 1 - 3 Million
Number Employees: 5-9
Brands:
CHEF'S CHOICE

6633 Home Roast Coffee
25126 State Road 54
Lutz, FL 33559-6256 813-949-0807
Fax: 813-948-6998
Coffee
Owner/President: Marvis Wood
Estimated Sales: $500,000-$1 Million
Number Employees: 1-4

6634 Home Run Inn Frozen Foods
1300 Internationale Pkwy
Woodridge, IL 60517-4928 630-783-9696
Fax: 630-783-0069 800-636-9696
gyarka@homerunn.com www.homerunn.com
Processor of frozen pizza including original thin
crust and deep dish varieties.
President/CEO: Joseph Perrino
Marketing Director: Gina Bolger
Operations: Dan Costello
Estimated Sales: $10-24.9 Million
Number Employees: 50-99
Type of Packaging: Consumer, Food Service, Private Label
Brands:
HOME RUN INN

6635 Home Style Bakery
924 N 7th St
Grand Junction, CO 81501-3108 970-243-1233
Processor of baked goods
President: Jan Wilke
Estimated Sales: $1-2.5 Million
Number Employees: 10-19
Sq. footage: 2000
Type of Packaging: Consumer, Food Service

6636 Homegrown Naturals
560 Gateway Dr
Napa, CA 94558-7517 707-254-3700
Fax: 707-259-0219 800-288-1089
erciborgstrom@fantasticfoods.com
www.homegrownnaturalfoods.com
Manufacturer of natural foods products
Chief Executive Officer: John Foraker
CEO: John Foraker
VP Research/Development: Bob Kaake
Brand Team: Kathryn Keslosky
Web Marketing Manager: Mark Berger
Human Resources Manager: Amy Barberi
Consumer Relations Associate: Corrie Aldous
Consumer Relations Manager: Sherrie Crespin
Number Employees: 20-49
Brands:
Annie's

6637 Homemade By Dorothy
5150 Montecito Pl
Boise, ID 83704-2355 208-375-3720
dorothys@micron.net
http://dorothys.cc/
Jellies, syrups, toppings, pancake and baking mixes,
soups, beverages, candy, gift crates and baskets, seasonal and holiday products.
President/Owner: Dorothy Baumhoff
Estimated Sales: $1-2.5 Million
Number Employees: 1-4

6638 Homer's Ice Cream
1237 Green Bay Rd
Wilmette, IL 60091-1699 847-251-0477
Fax: 847-251-0495 www.homersicecream.com
Processor of ice cream and sorbet
Owner: Dean Poulos
Marketing Director: Tean Poulous
VP: John Poulos
CEO: Stephen Poulous
Estimated Sales: $10-20 Million
Number Employees: 20-49
Sq. footage: 8000
Type of Packaging: Consumer, Food Service, Private Label, Bulk

6639 Homer's Wharf Seafood Company
43 Blackmer St
New Bedford, MA 02744-2613 508-997-0766
Fax: 508-999-9666
Processor of fish
Manager: Bruce Fontes
General Manager: Bruce Fontes
Estimated Sales: $10-20 Million
Number Employees: 50-99
Type of Packaging: Consumer

6640 Homes Packaging Company
PO Box 29
Millersburg, OH 44654-0029 330-674-2520
Fax: 330-674-5451 800-401-2529
Clay pot baked goods, baking mixes
Public Relations: Bruce Cameron
Estimated Sales: $1-2.5 Million
Number Employees: 1-4
Type of Packaging: Private Label

6641 (HQ)Homestead Baking Company
145 N Broadway
Rumford, RI 02916-2800 401-434-0551
Fax: 401-438-0542 800-556-7216
pvican@homesteadbaking.com
www.homesteadbaking.com
Processor of rolls, specialty breads and English muffins
President: Peter Vican
VP/Treasurer: William Vican
Sales Manager: Vinny Palmiotti
Estimated Sales: $10-20 Million
Number Employees: 100-249
Sq. footage: 40000
Type of Packaging: Food Service, Private Label, Bulk
Brands:
MATTHEWS ALL NATURAL
MRS KAVANAGH'S
NEW ENGLAND PREMIUM

6642 Homestead Dairies
41 Churchill Avenue
Massena, NY 13662-1630 315-769-2456
Fax: 315-769-8975
Dairy
President: Robert Squires
Estimated Sales: $10-100 Million
Number Employees: 1-4

6643 Homestead Fine Foods
315 S Maple Ave # 106
S San Francisco, CA 94080-6307 650-615-0750
Fax: 650-615-0764 www.homesteadpasta.com
Processor of fresh and frozen lasagna, ravioli,
gnocchi and tortellini; also, mushroom and meat
sauces
President: Terry Hall
Estimated Sales: $ .5 - 1 million
Number Employees: 10-19
Type of Packaging: Consumer, Food Service, Private Label
Brands:
HOMESTEAD

6644 Homestead Mills
P.O. Box 1115
Cook, MN 55723-1115 218-666-5233
Fax: 218-666-5236 800-652-5233
aho.uslink.net www.homesteadmills.com
Processor and exporter of grain and wild rice, hot
cereal and pancake mixes; also, corn and rye meal
and flour including whole wheat, cracked wheat,
rye, barley and buckwheat. Also backpacker meals
Owner/President: Keith Aho
Owner/Vice President: Carol Aho
Plant Manager: Anita Reinke
Estimated Sales: $1 Million
Number Employees: 5-9
Number of Brands: 2
Number of Products: 27
Sq. footage: 13000
Type of Packaging: Consumer, Food Service, Private Label, Bulk
Brands:
COUNTRY BLEND CEREAL
HOMESTEAD MILLS
NOPRTHERN LITES PANCAKES
POTATO PANCAKE MIX
SOUTH OF THE BORDER CHILI
SPECIALTY FLOUR
UNCLE WAYNES FISH BATTER

6645 Homestead Ravioli Company
315 S Maple Ave # 106
S San Francisco, CA 94080-6307 650-615-0750
Fax: 650-615-0764 www.homesteadpasta.com
Italian frozen specialties
President: Terry Hall
Estimated Sales: $5-9.9 Million
Number Employees: 10-19

6646 Homestyle Bread
3305 E Broadway Rd
Phoenix, AZ 85040-2829 602-268-0677
Fax: 602-276-1468
Bread and bakery products
President: James Boots
Vice President: Robert Schurman
Estimated Sales: $5-9.9 Million
Number Employees: 20-49

6647 Homestyle Foods Company
5163 Edwin St
Hamtramck, MI 48212-3388 313-874-3250
Fax: 313-874-1026 www.homestylefoods.com
Processor and exporter of fresh salads including
macaroni, potato and cole slaw.
President: Mike Kadian
Estimated Sales: $10-20 Million
Number Employees: 20-49
Type of Packaging: Private Label, Bulk

6648 Homewood Winery
23120 Burndale Rd
Sonoma, CA 95476-9722 707-996-6353
Fax: 707-996-6935 www.homewoodwinery.com
Wines
President/Vineyard Manager: David Homewood
Estimated Sales: Under $500,000
Number Employees: 1-4
Type of Packaging: Private Label

6649 Hommus Factory
143 Winter Street
Haverhill, MA 01830-5625 508-460-0212
Fax: 978-374-5252
Processor of specialty foods including hummus,
tabbouleh, baba ghanoush, stuffed grape leaves, baklava, falafel mix, tahini sauce and cracked wheat
salad; wholesaler/distributor of Italian cheeses and
health and specialty foods
Founder/President: Carol Coutrier
Sq. footage: 3000
Type of Packaging: Consumer, Food Service, Private Label, Bulk
Brands:
BAGEL HOMMUS
ORIGINAL AMERICAN HOMMUS

6650 Honest Tea
4827 Bethesda Ave
Bethesda, MD 20814-5240 301-652-3556
Fax: 301-652-3557 800-865-4736
mail@honesttea.com www.honesttea.com
Processor of organic bottled ice tea with wholeleaf
bags
President/CEO: Seth Goldman
Marketing/Sales Coordinator: Amy Ard
Estimated Sales: $ 5 - 10 Million
Number Employees: 10-19
Type of Packaging: Bulk

6651 Honey Acres
N1557 Highway 67
PO Box 346
Ashippun, WI 53003
Fax: 920-474-4018 800-558-7745
sales@honeyacres.com www.honeyacres.com
Processor and exporter of honey and honey products
including fruit bars and mustard
President/CEO: Eugene Brueggeman
National Sales Director: Kathy Sedan
Estimated Sales: $5-9.9 Million
Number Employees: 30
Number of Products: 50
Sq. footage: 36000
Type of Packaging: Consumer, Food Service, Private Label, Bulk
Brands:
1852
HI HONEY
HONEY ACRES

6652 Honey Baked Ham Company
11935 Mason Montgomery Rd #200
Cincinnati, OH 45249-3702 513-583-9700
Fax: 513-583-4190 www.honeybaked.com
Baked hams, turkey, frozen desserts and party trays
President/CEO: Craig Kurz
Estimated Sales: $5-10 Million
Number Employees: 20-49
Brands:
HONEY BAKED HAM

6653 Honey Bar/Creme de la Creme
335 Albany Avenue
Kingston, NY 12401 845-331-4643
Fax: 845-331-4576 rvezina@delacreme.com
www.delacreme.com/
Owner: Roger Vezina

6654 Honey Bear Fruit Basket
6321 Washington St # N
Denver, CO 80216-1100 303-297-3390
Fax: 303-297-3393 888-330-2327
info@honeybearbasket.com
www.honeybearbaskets.com
Fine wine jelly, sauce, scone mix, lemon curd
Owner: Carol Kincler
General Manager: Linda Wenz
Estimated Sales: $500,000-$1 Million
Number Employees: 1-4
Brands:
Penelope's

6655 Honey Bee Company
865 N Main St
Alpharetta, GA 30009-8371 770-753-8057
Fax: 770-612-0815 800-572-8838
joejmarcou@aol.com
www.honeybakedonline.com
Processor of flavored honey
Manager: Ray Grant
Estimated Sales: $2.5-5 Million
Number Employees: 1-4
Type of Packaging: Private Label, Bulk

6656 Honey Butter Products Company
103 S Heintzelman St
Manheim, PA 17545-1723 717-665-9323
Fax: 717-665-4422
Processor of bread spread: honey, butter and cinnamon blend
President/CEO: Kevin Sadd
Estimated Sales: $ 5 - 10 Million
Number Employees: 5-9
Type of Packaging: Consumer, Food Service
Brands:
DOWNEY'S

6657 Honey Cell
850 Union Avenue
PO Box 5187
Bridgeport, CT 06610-0187 203-925-1818
Fax: 203-367-5266 cellpak@aol.com
www.valleycontainer.com/honey
Manufacturer of packaging pallets, corrugated pallets, void fillers, corner protection, runners, dunnage, and separator pads.
Sales Manager: Bruce Padden
Sales Representative: Richard Jackson
Estimated Sales: $ 20-50 Million
Number Employees: 20-50
Sq. footage: 40000
Parent Co: Valley Containers
Type of Packaging: Consumer

6658 Honey Hut Ice Cream
4674 State Rd
Cleveland, OH 44109-5252 216-749-7077
Fax: 216-661-1883 HoneyHut@Adelphia.net
www.honeyhuticecream.com/
Ice cream, frozen desserts
President/Owner: Frank Page
Estimated Sales: Less than $500,000
Number Employees: 10-19

6659 Honey Ridge Farms
12310 NE 245th Avenue
Brush Prairie, WA 98606 360-256-0086
Fax: 360-883-2679 info@honeyridgefarms.com
www.honeyridgefarms.com
gourmet honey, honey cremes, balsamic honey vinegar, honey sauces
Owner: Leeanne Goetz

6660 Honey Rose Baking Company
PO Box 230394
Encinitas, CA 92023-0394 760-942-8996
Fax: 760-722-5203
Cookies, pies and tarts
President: Terry Cooper
Estimated Sales: $5-9.9 Million
Number Employees: 10-19
Type of Packaging: Private Label

6661 Honey Wafer Baking Company
13952 Kildare Ave
Crestwood, IL 60445-2357 708-388-9010
Fax: 708-388-9680 800-261-2984
honeywafer@yahoo.com
www.anisihoneywafer.com
Manufacturer of gourmet honey wafers, all naturally
made in the European style
Owner/President: Tony Lewandowski
Estimated Sales: $ 5 - 10 Million
Number Employees: 10-19
Type of Packaging: Consumer
Brands:
Anisi

6662 Honey World
P.O.Box 459
Parker, SD 57053-0459 605-297-4188
Fax: 605-297-4118 candles@iw.net
Processor of whipped honey, and flavored honey
President: Glen Wollman
Estimated Sales: $5-10 Million
Number Employees: 1-4
Type of Packaging: Private Label, Bulk

6663 HoneyRun Winery
2309 Park Ave
Chico, CA 95928-6706 530-345-6405
Fax: 530-894-6639 honeyrun@honeyrun.com
www.honeyrun.com
Wine in a variety of flavors including blackberry,
cherry, elderberry, and cranberry.
President: John Hasle
VP: Amy Hasle
Estimated Sales: $ .5 - 1 million
Number Employees: 1-4

6664 Honeybake Farms
P.O.Box 6124
Kansas City, KS 66106-0124 913-371-7777
Fax: 913-371-7799 nsloman@aol.com
www.chefspride.com
Processor of fresh and frozen sandwiches; also, salads, desserts and gourmet cinnamon rolls
President/CEO/Owner: Neil Sloman
Estimated Sales: $5-10 Million
Number Employees: 100-249
Sq. footage: 50000
Type of Packaging: Consumer, Private Label
Brands:
HONEYBAKE FARMS

6665 Honeydrop Foods
PO Box 6428
Bridgewater, NJ 08807-0428 908-203-1577
Fax: 908-203-9063
comments@honeydropfoods.com OR
funlayo@honeydropfoods.com
www.honeydropfoods.com
Authentic African Foods
Marketing/Sales/Product Information: Yvonne
Adedeji

Brands:
OBE SAUCE
OBE SAUCE MIX

6666 Honeypot Treats
642 Hillsboro Road
Camden, NY 13316-4411 315-245-2415
Fax: 315-245-3000 800-223-1024
Honey
President/CEO: Dan Russell

6667 Honeytree
247 S Main St
Adrian, MI 49221-2614 517-265-7872
Fax: 517-265-7046 888-682-1256
honeytree@tc3net.com www.tc3net.com
Honey, molasses
Owner: Joe Mattausch
Estimated Sales: $20-50 Million
Number Employees: 20-49

6668 Honeyville Grain
11600 Dayton Dr
Rancho Cucamonga, CA 91730-5525 909-980-9500
Fax: 909-980-6503 888-810-3212
info@honeyvillegrain.com
www.honeyvillegrain.com
Processor of bakery mixes, soy and corn products,
dry milk, whey powder, flour and rolled oats; wholesaler/distributor of ingredients including flour, corn
meal, edible oils, salt, etc.; exporter of beverages,
corn, flour, etc.
VP: John C Hadfield
Quality Assurance Manager: Jose Parra
VP Marketing/Sales: John Hadfield
Human Resources Manager: Jacob Walters
VP Operations: Richard Larsen
General Manager: Tyler Christensen
Assistant Mix Plant: Natalia Espinoza
Purchasing: Brian Davis
Estimated Sales: $3-5 Million
Number Employees: 1-4
Sq. footage: 25000
Type of Packaging: Food Service, Bulk

6669 Honeyville Grain
635 Billy Mitchell Rd # A
Salt Lake City, UT 84116-2980 801-972-2168
Fax: 801-972-8412 infoslc@honeyvillegrain.com
www.honeyvillegrain.com
Processor of bakery mixes, soy and corn products,
dry milk, whey powder, flour and rolled oats; wholesaler/distributor of ingredients including flour, corn
meal, edible oils, salt, etc.; exporter of beverages,
corn, flour, etc.
President: Bruce Merrell
VP Finance: Robert Anderson
Executive VP: Trevor Christensen
Director Marketing/Sales: Don Mann
Sales Manager: Craig Dunford
Assistant Operations Manager: Garth Rollins
Estimated Sales: $ 10 - 20 Million
Number Employees: 10-19
Sq. footage: 60000
Parent Co: Honeyville Grain
Type of Packaging: Consumer, Food Service, Private Label, Bulk

6670 Honeywood Winery
1350 Hines St SE
Salem, OR 97302-2521 503-362-4111
Fax: 503-362-4112 800-726-4101
info@honeywoodwinery.com
www.honeywoodwinery.com
Processor and exporter of specialty wines including
pinot gris, pinot noir, chardonnay, cranberry, peach,
fruit, etc.
President: Paul Gallick
VP: Marlene K Gallick
Estimated Sales: $1 Million+
Number Employees: 5-9
Number of Brands: 5
Number of Products: 45
Sq. footage: 22000
Type of Packaging: Private Label
Brands:
HONEYMAN & WOOD
HONEYWOOD GRANDE
HONEYWOOD NORTH AMERICAN GRAPE
HONEYWOOD PREMIUM

6671 Hong Kong Market Company
2425 S Wallace St
Chicago, IL 60616-1855   312-791-9111
                                Fax: 312-791-1324
Processor of bean sprouts, snow peas and other Chinese vegetables
    President: Gloria Lam
    VP: Thomas Lam
Estimated Sales: $1-2.5 Million
Number Employees: 10-19
Type of Packaging: Consumer, Food Service, Private Label, Bulk

6672 Hong Kong Noodle Company
2350 S Wentworth Ave
Chicago, IL 60616-2092   312-842-0480
    Fax: 312-842-7069 ron@hongkongnoodle.com
                        www.hongkongnoodle.com
Manufactures dry egg, plain or water noodles
    Manager: Glenn Jung
    Vice President/Co-Owner: Harry Chung
Estimated Sales: $2.5-5 Million
Number Employees: 20-49
Type of Packaging: Food Service

6673 Hong Kong Supermarket
4166 Buford Hwy NE
Atlanta, GA 30345-1081   404-325-3999
                                Fax: 404-325-3311
Oriental food items, ethnic foods, full line seafood
    Owner: Ly Tieu
Estimated Sales: $ 10 - 20 Million
Number Employees: 50-99

6674 Hong Tou Noodle Company
7059 N Figueroa St
Los Angeles, CA 90042-1276   323-256-3843
Noodles
    Owner: Peter Kwong
    General Manager: Peter Kong
Estimated Sales: $500,000-$1 Million
Number Employees: 1-4

6675 Hongar Farm Gourmet Foods
2121 Tucker Industrial Rd
Tucker, GA 30084-5017   770-938-9884
    Fax: 770-938-8964 888-296-7191
info@hongarfarms.com www.hongarfarms.com
Gourmet seasoned oils and vinegars, marinades, bread dippers, and specialty items.
    President: Joe Oxman
Estimated Sales: $1-2.5 Million
Number Employees: 5-9
Brands:
    HONGAR FARMS

6676 HongryHawg Products
16414 Chris Rd
Prairieville, LA 70769-5806   225-622-4011
    Fax: 225-622-0546 888-772-4294
                        answers@cajunsauce.com
www.hongryhawg.com OR www.cajunsauce.com
Hot sauce, barbecue sauce, jambalaya mix, cajun seasoning and gift boxes.
    Owner: Hiram Davis
Estimated Sales: $ 5 - 10 Million
Number Employees: 5-9

6677 Honickman Affiliates
8275 N Crescent Blvd
Pennsauken, NJ 08110-1435   856-665-6200
    Fax: 856-661-4684 800-573-7745
Processor, canner and bottler of soft drinks
    Chairman: Harold Honickman
    CEO: Jeffrey Honickman
    CFO: Walt Wilkinson
    Business Development Manager: Larry Linder
    Production Manager: Phil Forte
Estimated Sales: $ 10 - 20 Million
Number Employees: 20-49
Parent Co: PepsiCo North America
Type of Packaging: Consumer, Food Service
Brands:
    Cadbury Schweppes
    Coors
    Pepsi-Cola
    Snapple
    South Beach

6678 Honig Vineyard and Winery
P.O.Box 406
Rutherford, CA 94573-0406   707-963-5618
    Fax: 707-963-5639 800-929-2217
                        www.honigwine.com

Wines, including: Sauvignon Blanc, Rutherford Sauvignon Blanc, Cabernet Sauvignon, Bartolucci Vineyard Cabernet, Late Harvest Sauvignon Blanc.
    President: Michael Honig
    CFO: Tony Benedetti
    Marketing Director: Regina Weinstein
Estimated Sales: $5-9.9 Million
Number Employees: 5-9
Type of Packaging: Private Label

6679 Honolulu Fish & SeafoodCompany
3109 Koapaka St
Honolulu, HI 96819-1998   808-833-1123
    Fax: 808-836-1045 www.honolulufish.com
Offers more than 14 species of sashimi grade fish to restaurants around the world.
    President/CEO: Wayne Samiere

6680 Honso USA
4602 E Elwood St # 6
Phoenix, AZ 85040-1960   480-377-8787
    Fax: 480-377-6649 888-461-5808
    info@honso.com www.HonsoUSA.com
Manufacturer of Chinese herbal products.
    President: Dan Wen
Estimated Sales: $300,000-500,000
Number Employees: 1-4

6681 Hood River Coffee Company
1310 Tucker Rd
Hood River, OR 97031-8647   541-386-3908
    Fax: 541-386-3998 800-336-2954
    customerservice@hoodrivercoffeeco.com
                www.hoodrivercoffeeco.com
Coffee available in several varieties including: African, American, Indonesian, Organic, Dark Roast, Espresso, Decaffeinated; also organic teas, gifts and gear.
    Owner: Mark Hudon
Number Employees: 1-4

6682 Hood River Distillers
P.O.Box 240
Hood River, OR 97031-0062   541-386-1588
    Fax: 541-386-2520 HRDsales@HRDspirits.com
                        www.hrdspirits.com
Hood River Distillers creates, produces, imports and distributes 15 brands of spirits ranging from value to premium products: whisky, rum, gin, vodka, schnapps, Irish cream whiskey, scotch and liqueurs. Brands include: Pendleton, YaziBroker's, Cockspur, Ullr, Knicker's, Spudka, Monarch, and HRD.
    President/CEO: Ronald Dodge
    VP/General Manager: Lynda Webber
    Sales/Marketing Western USA: Erik Svenson
    Public Relations/Media: Olga Haley
Estimated Sales: $ 50 - 100 Million
Number Employees: 20-49
Number of Brands: 7
Number of Products: 46
Sq. footage: 53000
Brands:
    Baron Rothschild
    HRD
    Monarch

6683 Hood River Vineyards and Winery
4693 Westwood Drive
Hood River, OR 97031   541-386-3772
    Fax: 541-386-5880 hoodriverwines@gorge.net
            http://hoodrivervineyards.us/home/
Produces a variety of table and dessert wines including: Chardonnay, Pinot Noir, Zinfandel, Cabernet Sauvignon, Merlot, Riesling, Black Muscat, Zinfandel Port, Marionberry, and Black Cherry.
    President: Bernie Lerch
    VP: Anne Lerch
Estimated Sales: $1-2.5 Million
Number Employees: 1-4

6684 Hoodsport Winery
23501 N Us Highway 101
Hoodsport, WA 98548-9605   253-396-9463
    Fax: 253-877-9508 800-580-9894
    wine@hoodsport.com www.hoodsport.com
Produces a variety of wines; also offers gourmet coffee and chocolate wine truffles.
    President: Peggy Patterson
Estimated Sales: $5-10 Million
Number Employees: 10-19
Type of Packaging: Private Label

Brands:
    HOODSPORT

6685 Hoody Corporation
8344 Pateywoods Rd
Newark, MD 21841-2012   410-632-1766
    VP Sales/Marketing: Darryl Hamilton
    VP Operations: Sid Harvey
Estimated Sales: Under $500,000
Number Employees: 5-9

6686 Hook's Cheese Company
320 Commerce Street
Mineral Point, WI 53565-1240   608-987-3259
                                        Fax: 608-987-2658
Monterey jack, cheddar and colby cheese
    President: Tony Hook
Estimated Sales: $1-2.5 Million
Number Employees: 1-4

6687 Hoonah Cold Storage
P.O.Box 470
Hoonah, AK 99829-0470   907-945-3264
                                Fax: 907-945-3441

    Manager: Terrence Barry

6688 (HQ)Hoopeston Foods
101 W Burnsville Pkwy
Burnsville, MN 55337-2571   952-854-0903
                                    Fax: 952-854-6874
    choerning@hoopestonfoods.com
            http://hfinc3.qwestoffice.net/
Full line of canned dry beans, chili, stews, soups, sauces, tamales, meats in a variety of sizes.
    President: Eric Newman
    CEO: Tad Ballentyne
    SVP/CFO/CAO: Corey Hoerning
    CEO: Tad Ballantyne
    VP Sales/Marketing: Tony Trenkle
Estimated Sales: $ 5 - 10 Million
Number Employees: 5-9
Type of Packaging: Food Service, Private Label
Brands:
    NATURE'S GOLD
    TIO FRANCO

6689 Hoople Country Kitchens
714 N 5th St
Rockport, IN 47635-1103   812-649-2351
                                Fax: 812-649-2836
Processor of pork sausage, prepared salads, corn meal mush and horseradish
    President: David Caskey
    Sales Manager: Denise Caskey
Estimated Sales: $5-10 Million
Number Employees: 20-49
Type of Packaging: Consumer

6690 Hop Growers of America
P.O.Box 1207
Moxee, WA 98936-1207   509-248-7043
    Fax: 509-457-8561 info@usahops.org
                        www.usahops.org
Hop Growers of America represents and promotes the interests of U.S. growers both domestically and internationally. As the national organization, HGA provides support, coordination and communication to growers, brewers and the worldhop industry in areas of common interest, including; marketing statistics, promotion, education and research.
    Administrator: Ann George
    Public Relations: Michelle Palacios
Number Employees: 1-4

6691 Hop Kee
2425 S Wallace St
Chicago, IL 60616-1855   312-791-9111
                                Fax: 312-791-1324

    President: Gloria Lam

6692 Hop Kiln Winery
6050 Westside Rd
Healdsburg, CA 95448-8318   707-433-6491
    Fax: 707-433-8162 info@hopkilnwinery.com
                        www.hopkilnwinery.com
Producer of a variety of wines including: Rushin' River Red, Thousand Flowers, Zinfandel, Sauvignon Blanc, and Big Red. Also offers mustards, vinegars, pestos, oils, vinaigrettes, and dessert sauces.
    President: David Di Loreto
    Plant Manager: Erich Bradley
Estimated Sales: $5-9.9 Million
Number Employees: 10-19

Brands:
CHARDONNAY BARREL SELECT
LATE HARVEST ZINFANDEL
MARTY GRIFFIN BIG RED
PRIMIVITO ZINFANDEL
SONOMA COUNTY ZINFANDEL
THOUSAND FLOWERS
VALDIGUIE

6693 Hope Creamery
P.O.Box 42
Hope, MN 56046-0042   507-451-2029
Manufacturer of butter
President/Owner: Victor Mrotz
Operations: Gene Kruckeberg
Estimated Sales: $300,000-$500,000
Number Employees: 1-4
Sq. footage: 4000
Type of Packaging: Consumer, Bulk
Brands:
HOPE

6694 Hopkins Food Service
272 Oak Hill Road
Cairo, GA 39828-6119   229-872-3214
                             Fax: 229-872-3216
Estimated Sales: $ 1 - 3 Million
Number Employees: 5-9

6695 Hopkins Inn
22 Hopkins Rd
Warren, CT 06777-1016   860-868-7295
Fax: 860-868-7464 www.thehopkinsinn.com
Gourmet salad dressings
President: Beth Schober
Estimated Sales: $1-2.5 Million
Number Employees: 20-49
Brands:
HOPKINS INN CAESAR DRESSING
HOPKINS INN HOUSE DRESSING

6696 Hopkins Vineyard
25 Hopkins Rd
Warren, CT 06777-1015   860-868-7954
Fax: 860-868-1768 info@hopkinsvineyard.com
                   www.hopkinsvineyard.com
Wine
President: Hilary Hopkins
Estimated Sales: $1-2.5 Million
Number Employees: 5-9
Type of Packaging: Private Label
Brands:
HIGHLAND ESTATES
HOPKINS VINEYARD CABERNET FRANC
HOPKINS VINEYARD CHARDONNAY
HOPKINS VINEYARD HARD CIDER
HOPKINS VINEYARD HIGHLAND ESTATES
HOPKINS VINEYARD ROSE
HOPKINS VINEYARD SACHEM'S PICNIc
HOPKINS VINEYARD SPARKLING WINE
HOPKINS VINEYARD VIDAL BLANC
HOPKINS WESTWIND

6697 Hops Extract Corporation of America
305 N 2nd Ave
Yakima, WA 98902-2690   509-248-1530
Fax: 509-457-1639 sales@hopsteiner.com
                   www.hopsteiner.com
Processor of hops.
Manager: Dave Dunmham
Operations: Paul Signorotti
Estimated Sales: $20-50 Million
Number Employees: 20-49
Parent Co: S. S. Steiner, Inc.

6698 Hopson
PO Box 38
Ottumwa, IA 52501-0038   515-682-8164
                               Fax: 515-682-3123
President: Rodney Hopson

6699 Hopunion CBS
203 Division St
Yakima, WA 98902-4622   509-457-3200
Fax: 509-453-1551 800-952-4873
           hops@hopunion.com OR
ralph.olson@hopunion.com www.hopunion.com
Processor and exporter of hops and hops products
President/General Manager: Ralph Olson
Sales Director: Ralph Woodall
Plant Manager: Tracy McCorkle
Estimated Sales: $ 10 - 20 Million
Number Employees: 10-19

Type of Packaging: Bulk

6700 Horizon Organic Dairy
PO Box 17577
Boulder, CO 80308-7577   303-530-2711
           Fax: 303-652-1371 888-494-3020
                 info@horizonorganic.com
                 www.horizonorganic.com
Processor of organic dairy products including milk,
yogurt, sour cream, cottage cheese, cream cheese,
cheese, butter and dry milk
Public Relations: Jarod Ballentine
VP Operations: Jule Taylor
Estimated Sales: $29 Million
Number Employees: 50-99
Type of Packaging: Consumer

6701 Horizon Poultry
92 Cartwright Avenue
Toronto, ON M6A 1V2
Canada   519-364-3200
Fax: 519-364-4692 cphilipp@schneiderfoods.ca
                   www.schneiderfoods.ca/
Hatchery and processor of chickens; importer of
eggs
Quality Assurance: Cynthia Philippe MD
Number Employees: 165
Parent Co: J.M. Schneider
Type of Packaging: Consumer, Food Service, Private Label, Bulk

6702 Horizon Winery
PO Box 191
Santa Rosa, CA 95402-0191   707-544-2961
Wines
President: Paul Gardner

6703 Horlacher's Fine Meats
30 W 700 N
Logan, UT 84321-3214   435-752-1287
Processor of fresh and frozen ham, beef jerky and
roast beef
Owner: Betty Horlacher
Estimated Sales: $5-10 Million appx.
Number Employees: 1-4
Sq. footage: 8000
Type of Packaging: Consumer, Bulk

6704 Hormel Foods
P.O.Box 45
Rochelle, IL 61068-0045   815-562-4141
           Fax: 815-562-4149 800-523-4635
                 www.hormel.com
Processor of bacon, ham and sausage.
Manager: Cal Jacobs
Executive Vice President: Jeffrey Ettinger
SVP/Chief Financial Officer: Jody Feragen
VP/Finance & Treasurer: William Snyder
SVP/General Counsel: James Cavanaugh
Corporate Brand Information: Joan Hanson
Sales Director: Thomas Day
Corporate Media Information: Julie Craven
Number Employees: 1,000-4,999
Parent Co: Hormel Foods Corporation
Type of Packaging: Food Service, Private Label

6705 Hormel Foods Corporation
3000 Kennedy Dr
Beloit, WI 53511-3996   608-365-9501
           Fax: 608-365-8322 www.hormel.com
Processor and exporter of canned meat including
chicken, beef, turkey and pork.
Chairman/President/CEO: Jeffrey Ettinger
Executive Vice President: Ronald Fielding
SVP/Chief Financial Officer: Jody Feragen
SVP/General Counsel: James Cavanaugh
Media/Corporate Information: Julie Craven
Corporate/Brand Information: Joan Hanson
VP/Finance & Treasurer: Roland Gentzler
Plant Manager: Mike Lee
Estimated Sales: $100-500 Million
Number Employees: 100-249
Parent Co: Hormel Foods Corporation
Type of Packaging: Consumer

6706 Hormel Foods Corporation
P.O.Box 69
Fremont, NE 68026-0069   402-721-2300
           Fax: 402-721-0445 rrheisinger@hormel.com
                 www.hormel.com

Processor of canned and smoked meats, sausage,
ham, bacon and hot dogs; slaughtering services
available.
Manager: Mark Coffey
Executive Vice President: Ronald Fielding
SVP/Chief Financial Officer: Jody Feragen
VP/Finance & Treasurer: Roland Gentzler
Corporate Media Information: Julie Craven
Corporate Brand Informtation: Joan Hanson
General Manager: Bruce Schweitzer
Operations Manager: Randy R Heisinger
Estimated Sales: $100+ Million
Number Employees: 1,000-4,999
Parent Co: Hormel Foods Corporation
Type of Packaging: Consumer

6707 Hormel Foods Corporation
1118 Highway 18 E
Algona, IA 50511-1166   515-295-2477
           Fax: 515-295-2470 www.hormel.com
Processor of pepperoni
Manager: Pete Von Ruden
VP/Finance & Treasurer: Roland Gentzler
SVP/Chief Financial Officer: Johy Feragen
SVP/General Counsel: James Cavanaugh
Corporate Media Information: Julie Craven
Corporate Brand Information: Joan Hanson
Manager: Peter Von Ruden
Estimated Sales: $100-500 Million
Number Employees: 100-249
Parent Co: Hormel Foods Corporation
Type of Packaging: Consumer

6708 (HQ)Hormel Foods Corporation
1 Hormel Place
Austin, MN 55912-0800   507-437-5611
           Fax: 507-437-5129 800-523-4635
                 www.hormel.com
Processor of soups, entrees, desserts, broths, puddings, sauces and meats including ham, sausage, bacon, turkey, pre-packaged chicken and deli items.
Chairman/President/CEO: Jeffrey Ettinger
SVP/CFO: Jody Feragen
SVP/General Counsel: James Cavanaugh
Estimated Sales: $3.675 Billion
Number Employees: 10,000+
Type of Packaging: Consumer, Food Service, Private Label
Brands:
CHI-CHI'S
DILUSSO
DINTY MOORE
FARMER JOHN
HERBOX
HORMEL
JENNIE-O
LLOYD'S
NOT SO SLOPPY JOE
SAAG'S
SPAM
STAGG CHILI
VALLEY FRESH
WORLDFOOD

6709 Hormel Foods Corporation
3075 Southwestern Blvd # 210
Orchard Park, NY 14127-1236   716-675-7700
           Fax: 716-675-7700 www.hormel.com
Processor of fresh, frozen and canned meats, soups,
shelf-stable prepared entrees, pre-packaged chicken,
Oriental sauces, bouillon, olive oils, deli items and
Mexican, Indian and Mediterranean foods.
Manager: Scott Moore
Executive Vice President: Ronald Fielding
SVP/Chief Financial Officer: Jody Feragen
SVP/General Counsel: James Cavanaugh
VP/Finance & Treasurer: Roland Gentzler
Corporate Brand Information: Joan Hanson
Corporate Media Information: Julie Craven
Estimated Sales: $5-10 Million
Number Employees: 5-9
Parent Co: Hormel Foods Corporation
Type of Packaging: Consumer, Food Service

6710 Hormel Foods Corporation
10550 New York Ave # 201
Urbandale, IA 50322-3744   515-276-8872
           Fax: 515-276-2641 www.hormel.com

Processor of fresh and frozen ingredients, meats, soups, entrees, desserts, pre-packaged chicken, Oriental sauces, deli items and Mexican foods.
>   Manager: Joe Fleskoski
>   Executive Vice President: Ronald Fielding
>   SVP/Chief Financial Officer: Jody Feragen
>   VP/Finance & Treasurer: Roland Gentzler
>   SVP/General Counsel: James Cavanaugh
>   Corporate Brand Information: Joan Hanson
>   Corporate Media Information: Julie Craven
Estimated Sales: $10-20 Million
Number Employees: 10-19
Parent Co: Hormel Foods Corporation
Type of Packaging: Consumer, Food Service

6711 Hormel Foods Corporation
6760 Alexander Bell Dr # 240
Columbia, MD 21046-2263   410-290-1855
      Fax: 410-290-1855 www.hormel.com
Processor of fresh and frozen meat, pre-packaged chicken, Asian sauces and Mexican and deli items.
>   Manager: Justin Moses
>   Executive Vice President: Ronald Fielding
>   SVP/Chief Financial Officer: Jody Feragen
>   VP/Finance & Treasurer: Roland Gentzler
>   SVP/General Counsel: James Cavanaugh
>   Corporate Brand Information: Joan Hanson
>   Corporate Media Information: Julie Craven
Estimated Sales: $20-50 Million
Number Employees: 20-49
Parent Co: Hormel Foods Corporation
Type of Packaging: Consumer, Food Service

6712 Hormel Foods Corporation
16727 Park Row
Suite 220
Houston, TX 77084-5020   281-492-1770
Processor of fresh and frozen meats, soups, entrees, desserts, prepackaged chicken, Mexican foods, Oriental sauces and deli items
>   Regional Manager: Bill Keith
Estimated Sales: $10-20 Million
Number Employees: 10-19
Parent Co: Hormel Foods Corporation
Type of Packaging: Consumer, Food Service

6713 Hormel Foods Corporation
65 Germantown Ct # 226
Cordova, TN 38018-4257   901-753-4282
      Fax: 901-753-2762 www.hormel.com
Processor of fresh and frozen ingredients, meats, soups, entrees, prepackaged chicken, Mexican foods, Oriental sauces and deli items.
>   Manager: Mike Snyder
>   Executive Vice President: Ronald Fielding
>   SVP/Chief Financial Officer: Jody Feragen
>   VP/Finance & Treasurer: Roland Gentzler
>   SVP/General Counsel: James Cavanaugh
>   Corporate Brand Information: Joan Hanson
>   Corporate Media Information: Julie Craven
Estimated Sales: $10-20 Million
Number Employees: 10-19
Parent Co: Hormel Foods Corporation
Type of Packaging: Consumer, Food Service

6714 Hormel Foods Corporation
5000 Hopyard Road
Suite 440
Pleasanton, CA 94588-3352   925-225-9349
      Fax: 925-734-9888 www.hormel.com
Processor of meats, entrees, pre-packaged chicken, Oriental sauces and deli items.
>   Chairman/President/CEO: Jeffrey Ettinger
>   Executive Vice President: Ronald Fielding
>   SVP/Chief Financial Officer: Jody Feragen
>   VP/Finance & Treasurer: Roland Gentzler
>   SVP/General Counsel: James Cavanaugh
>   Corporate Brand Information: Joan Hanson
>   Corporate Media Information: Julie Craven
Estimated Sales: $20-50 Million
Number Employees: 20-49
Parent Co: Hormel Foods Corporation
Type of Packaging: Consumer, Food Service

6715 Hormel Foods Corporation
3501 NW 63rd Street
Oklahoma City, OK 73116-2237   405-843-5643
      Fax: 405-843-7614
Processor of fresh and frozen ingredients, meats, soups, entrees, desserts, pre-packaged chicken, Asian sauces and Mexican and deli items; also, olive oil
>   Sales Executive: Kalton Hill

Estimated Sales: $5-10 Million
Number Employees: 5-9
Parent Co: Hormel Foods Corporation
Type of Packaging: Consumer, Food Service

6716 Hormel Foods Corporation
8700 Monrovia St # 200
Shawnee Mission, KS 66215-3500   913-888-8744
      Fax: 913-492-6919 www.hormel.com
Processor of fresh and frozen meats, soups, entrees, desserts, pre-packaged chicken, Asian sauces and Mexican and deli items.
>   Manager: Alan Johnson
>   Executive Vice President: Ronald Fielding
>   SVP/Chief Financial Officer: Jody Feragen
>   VP/Finance & Treasurer: Roland Gentzler
>   SVP/General Counsel: James Cavanaugh
>   Corporate Brand Information: Joan Hanson
>   Corporate Media Information: Julie Craven
Estimated Sales: $20-50 Million
Number Employees: 20-49
Parent Co: Hormel Foods Corporation
Type of Packaging: Consumer, Food Service

6717 Hormel Foods Corporation
4416 74th Street
Suite 72
Lubbock, TX 79424-2315   806-796-3630
Processor of fresh and frozen ingredients, meats, soups, entrees, desserts, pre-packaged chicken, Asian sauces and Mexican and deli items
>   District Manager: Jim Coehnk
Estimated Sales: $1-2.5 Million
Number Employees: 1-4
Parent Co: Hormel Foods Corporation
Type of Packaging: Consumer, Food Service

6718 Hormel Foods Corporation
7300 SW 29th St
Oklahoma City, OK 73179-5201   405-745-3471
      Fax: 405-745-3675 www.hormel.com
Processor of ingredients, meats, soups, entrees, desserts and pre-packaged chicken.
>   Chairman/President/CEO: Jeffrey Ettinger
>   Executive Vice President: Ronald Fielding
>   SVP/Chief Financial Officer: Jody Feragen
>   VP: Greg Cook
>   SVP/General Counsel: James Cavanaugh
>   Corporate Brand Information: Joan Hanson
>   Corporate Media Information: Julie Craven
Estimated Sales: $100-500 Million
Number Employees: 100-249
Parent Co: Hormel Foods Corporation
Type of Packaging: Consumer, Food Service

6719 Hormel Foods Corporation
8848 Red Oak Blvd
Charlotte, NC 28217   704-527-4388
      Fax: 205-969-2482 www.hormel.com
Processor of fresh and frozen ingredients, meats, soups, entrees, desserts, pre-packaged chicken, deli items and sauces including Asian, Mediterranean, Greek and Indian.
>   Chairman/President/CEO: Jeffrey Ettinger
>   Executive Vice President: Ronald Fielding
>   SVP/Chief Financial Officer: Jody Feragen
>   VP/Finance & Treasurer: Roland Gentzler
>   SVP/General Counsel: James Cavanaugh
>   Corporate Brand Information: Joan Hanson
>   Corporate Media Information: Julie Craven
Estimated Sales: $5-10 Million
Number Employees: 5-9
Parent Co: Hormel Foods Corporation
Type of Packaging: Consumer, Food Service

6720 Hormel Foods Corporation
11840 Nicholas Street
Omaha, NE 68154-4475   402-493-8470
      Fax: 402-493-8536
Processor of fresh and frozen ingredients, meats, entrees, Mexican foods, Oriental sauces and deli items
>   Territory Manager: Craig Klein
Number Employees: 1-4
Parent Co: Hormel Foods Corporation
Type of Packaging: Consumer, Food Service

6721 Hormel Foods Corporation
4222 E Thomas Road
Suite 340
Phoenix, AZ 85018-7618   602-230-2400
      Fax: 602-230-2405 www.hormel.com

Processor of fresh and frozen ingredients, meats, soups, entrees, desserts, pre-packaged chicken, Mexican foods, Oriental sauces and deli items.
>   Chairman/President/CEO: Susan Marvin
>   SVP/General Counsel: James Cavanaugh
>   Corporate Brand Information: Joan Hanson
>   Corporate Media Information: Julie Craven
Estimated Sales: $5-10 Million
Number Employees: 5-9
Parent Co: Hormel Foods Corporation
Type of Packaging: Consumer, Food Service

6722 Hormel Foods Corporation
100 Corporate Dr # 202
Lebanon, NJ 08833-2200   908-236-7009
      Fax: 908-236-7767 www.hormel.com
Processor of fresh and frozen ingredients, meats, soups, entrees, desserts, pre-packaged chicken, deli items and sauces including Indian, Asian, Greek and Mediterranean; also, olives.
>   Chairman/President/CEO: Jeffrey Ettinger
>   Executive Vice President: Ronald Fielding
>   SVP/Chief Financial Officer: Jody Feragen
>   VP/Finance & Treasurer: Roland Gentzler
>   SVP/General Counsel: James Cavanaugh
>   Corporate Brand Information: Joan Hanson
>   Corporate Media Information: Julie Craven
Estimated Sales: $20-50 Million
Number Employees: 20-49
Parent Co: Hormel Foods Corporation
Type of Packaging: Consumer, Food Service

6723 Hormel Foods Corporation
4055 Executive Park Dr # 300
Cincinnati, OH 45241-4020   513-563-0211
      Fax: 513-563-5054 www.hormel.com
Processor of fresh and frozen ingredients, meats, soups, entrees, desserts, pre-packaged chicken, Asian sauces and Mexican and deli items.
>   Manager: Rick Barghini
>   Executive Vice President: Ronald Fielding
>   SVP/Chief Financial Officer: Jody Feragen
>   VP/Finance & Treasurer: Roland Gentzler
>   SVP/General Counsel: James Cavanaugh
>   Corporate Brand Information: Joan Hanson
>   Corporate Media Information: Julie Craven
Estimated Sales: $20-50 Million
Number Employees: 20-49
Parent Co: Hormel Foods Corporation
Type of Packaging: Consumer, Food Service

6724 Hormel Foods Corporation
4343 Commerce Court
Lisle, IL 60532-3615   630-577-6499
      Fax: 630-955-9829   800-533-2000
      www.hormel.com
Processor of fresh and frozen ingredients, meats, soups, entrees, desserts, pre-packaged chicken, Mexican foods, Oriental sauces and deli items.
>   Chairman/President/CEO: Jeffrey Ettinger
>   Executive Vice President: Ronald Fielding
>   SVP/Chief Financial Officer: Jody Feragen
>   VP/Finance & Treasurer: Roland Gentzler
>   SVP/General Counsel: James Cavanaugh
>   Corporate Brand Information: Joan Hanson
>   Corporate Media Information: Julie Craven
Estimated Sales: $50-100 Million
Number Employees: 20-49
Parent Co: Hormel Foods Corporation
Type of Packaging: Consumer, Food Service

6725 Hormel Foods Corporation
220 Morris Avenue
Suite 340
Salt Lake City, UT 84115-3292   801-487-8251
      Fax: 801-487-0279
Processor of fresh and frozen meats, entrees, desserts and pre-packaged chicken; also, ingredients, soups, Mexican foods, Oriental sauces and deli items
>   Manager/Meat Products: Jeff Schwartz
Estimated Sales: $5-10 Million
Number Employees: 5-9
Parent Co: Hormel Foods Corporation
Type of Packaging: Consumer, Food Service

6726 Hormel Foods Corporation
10201 W Lincoln Avenue
Suite 304
West Allis, WI 53227-2136   414-604-0570
      Fax: 414-321-8890

Processor of ingredients, meats, soups, entrees, desserts, pre-packaged chicken, Mexican foods, Asian sauces and deli items
    District Manager: Jody Russell
    Territory Manager: Jerry Hammes
Estimated Sales: $2.5-5 Million
Number Employees: 1-4
Parent Co: Hormel Foods Corporation
Type of Packaging: Consumer, Food Service

6727 Hormel Foods Corporation
8848 Red Oak Boulevard
Suite A
Charlotte, NC 28217-5595   704-527-4388
                      Fax: 704-527-6753
Processor of fresh and frozen ingredients, meats, soups, entrees, desserts, pre-packaged chicken, Mexican foods, Oriental sauces and deli items
    Area Manager: Roger Earnheart
Estimated Sales: $20-50 Million
Number Employees: 20-49
Parent Co: Hormel Foods Corporation
Type of Packaging: Consumer, Food Service

6728 Hormel Foods Corporation
4601 Hollow Tree Dr # 107
Arlington, TX 76018-1288   817-465-4735
        Fax: 817-468-4011 www.hormel.com
Processor and importer of fresh, frozen and canned ingredients, meats, soups, entrees, chicken, turkey, Asian sauces and Mexican and deli items.
    Chairman/President/CEO: Jeffrey Ettinger
    Executive Vice President: Ronald W Fielding
    SVP/Chief Financial Officer: Jody Feragen
    VP/Finance & Treasurer: Roland Gentzler
    SVP/General Counsel: James Cavanaugh
    Corporate Brand Information: Joan Hanson
    Corporate Media Information: Julie Craven
Estimated Sales: $20-50 Million
Number Employees: 20-49
Parent Co: Hormel Foods Corporation
Type of Packaging: Consumer, Food Service

6729 Hormel Foods Corporation
651 Holiday Dr
Pittsburgh, PA 15220-2740   412-921-7036
        Fax: 412-921-7018 www.hormel.com
Processor of ingredients, meats, soups, entrees, desserts, pre-packaged chicken, Asian sauces and deli items.
    Manager: Dick Gaffney
    Executive Vice President: Ronald Fielding
    SVP/Chief Financial Officer: Jody Feragen
    VP/Finance & Treasurer: Roland Gentzler
    SVP/General Counsel: James Cavanaugh
    Corporate Brand Information: Joan Hanson
    Corporate Media Information: Julie Craven
Estimated Sales: $10-20 Million
Number Employees: 10-19
Parent Co: Hormel Foods Corporation
Type of Packaging: Consumer, Food Service

6730 Hormel Foods Corporation
901 North Lake Destiny Rd #255
Maitland, FL 32751-4864   407-660-0808
        Fax: 407-660-1990 www.hormel.com
Processor of ham, bacon, beef, pork, frankfurters and sausage.
    Manager: Craig Drefcinski
    Executive Vice President: Ronald Fielding
    SVP/Chief Financial Officer: Jody Feragen
    VP/Finance & Treasurer: Roland Gentzler
    SVP/General Counsel: James Cavanaugh
    Corporate Brand Information: Joan Hanson
    Corporate Media Information: Julie Craven
Estimated Sales: $20-50 Million
Number Employees: 10-19
Parent Co: Hormel Foods Corporation
Type of Packaging: Consumer, Food Service

6731 Hormel Foods Corporation
500 Franklin Village Dr # 205
Franklin, MA 02038-4017   508-541-7112
        Fax: 508-541-7278 www.hormel.com

Processor of fresh and frozen ingredients, meats, entrees, pre-packaged chicken, deli items and sauces including Asian, Mediterranean, Greek and Indian; also, fresh and canned soups.
    Manager: Matthew King
    Executive Vice President: Ronald Fielding
    SVP/Chief Financial Officer: Jody Feragen
    VP/Finance & Treasurer: Roland Gentzler
    SVP/General Counsel: James Cavanaugh
    Corporate Brand Information: Joan Hanson
    Corporate Media Information: Julie Craven
Estimated Sales: $20-50 Million
Number Employees: 20-49
Parent Co: Hormel Foods Corporation
Type of Packaging: Consumer, Food Service

6732 Hormel Foods Corporation
P.O.Box 800
Austin, MN 55912-0800   507-437-5611
    Fax: 507-437-5129 carapelli@worldfood.com
                      www.hormel.com
Olive and grape seed oils, vinegars in addition to pre-packaged Carapelli Pasta and Sauce mixes.
    Chairman/President/CEO: Richard Sommese
    CEO: Jeffrey M Ettinger
    SVP/General Counsel: James Cavanaugh
    Corporate Brand Information: Joan Hanson
    Corporate Media Information: Julie Craven
Estimated Sales: $500,000-$1 Million
Number Employees: 10,000+
Parent Co: Hormel Foods Corporation

6733 Hormel Foods Pork Division
3367 Montreal Industrial Way
Tucker, GA 30084-5211   770-908-4000
        Fax: 770-908-4111 www.hormel.com
Manufacturer of pork products
    President: Tim Fritz
    Executive Vice President: Ronald Fielding
    SVP/Chief Financial Officer: Jody Feragen
    VP/Finance & Treasurer: Roland Gentzler
    SVP/General Counsel: James Cavanaugh
    Corporate Brand Information: Joan Hanson
    Corporate Media Information: Julie Craven
    Purchasing Director: Jeff Dahlgren
Estimated Sales: $3.25 Billion
Number Employees: 230
Parent Co: Hormel Foods Corporation
Type of Packaging: Consumer, Food Service
Brands:
    BUFALO
    CARPAPELLI
    CHI CHI'S
    CURE 81
    DI LUSSO
    DINTY MOORE
    DONA MARIA
    HERB-OX
    HERDEZ
    HORMEL
    HOUSE OF TSANG
    JENNIE-O TURKEY STORE
    LIGHT & LEAN
    LITTLE SIZZLERS
    LLOYDS
    MANNY'S
    MARRAKESH EXPRESS
    PATAK'S
    PELOPONNESE
    SPAM
    STAGG

6734 Hormel Health Labs
1 Hormel Place
Austin, MN 55912   507-437-5611
    Fax: 507-437-5129 800-866-7757
                      www.hormel.com
Products for people with disorders such as dysphagia and diabetes
    CEO: Jeffrey M Ettinger
    VP Engineering: Larry Pfeil
Estimated Sales: $6.5 Billion
Number Employees: 18,600
Brands:
    GLUTASORB
    L-EMENTAL
    PRO-PEPTIDE

6735 Hormel Health Labs
181 Kelly Road
Quakertown, PA 18951-4209   215-529-7405
    Fax: 215-529-7409 800-887-1553
                      limantour@aol.com
    www.hormelhealthlabs.com/home.asp

Processor of consistency modified foods for pureed, mechanical soft, Alzheimer and dysphagia diets.
    President: John Joel
    Vice President: Jose Limantour
    Sales Director: Ron Kline
    General Plant Manager: Jose Limantour
Estimated Sales: $3-5 Million
Number Employees: 10-19
Sq. footage: 14000
Parent Co: Hormel Foods Corporation

6736 Hornell Brewing Company
5 Dakota Dr
New Hyde Park, NY 11042-1109   516-812-0300
                      Fax: 516-326-4988
    President: John Ferolito
Estimated Sales: F
Number Employees: 500-999

6737 Horriea 2000 Food Industries
P.O.Box 975
Reynolds, GA 31076-0975
Canada   478-847-4186
    Fax: 478-847-4464 fathi.khattab@sympatyco.ca
                      www.taylororchards.com
    Owner: Jeff Wainwright
    VP Marketing: Hassan El Findi
    Production Manager: Mohamed El Findi
Estimated Sales: $11 Million
Number Employees: 10-19
Number of Products: 38
Type of Packaging: Private Label

6738 Hors D'Oeuvres Unlimited
4209 Dell Avenue
North Bergen, NJ 07047-2418   201-865-4545
    Fax: 201-865-1175 800-648-3787
    info@horsdoeuvresunlimited.com
Processor, importer and exporter of frozen hors d'oeuvres
    President: Allan Epstein
Estimated Sales: $5-10 Million
Number Employees: 20-49
Sq. footage: 5000
Type of Packaging: Consumer, Food Service, Private Label
Brands:
    HORS D'OEUVRES UNLIMITED

6739 Horst Alaskan Seafood
2315 Industrial Blvd
Juneau, AK 99801-8534   907-790-4300
    Fax: 907-790-5534 877-518-4300
    horsts@gci.net www.horstsalaskanseafood.com
Processor of fresh and frozen seafood (vacuum packed)
    President: Horst Schramm
Estimated Sales: Less than $500,000
Number Employees: 1-4
Type of Packaging: Consumer

6740 Horstmann Mix & Cream
3011 12th St
Long Island City, NY 11102-4097   718-932-4735
                      Fax: 718-932-4794
Dairy
    President: William Horstmann
Estimated Sales: $2.5-5 Million
Number Employees: 5-9

6741 Horton Cellars Winery
6399 Spotswood Trl
Gordonsville, VA 22942-7735   540-832-7440
    Fax: 540-832-7187 800-829-4633
    vawinee@aol.com www.hbwine.com
Wine
    President: Dennis Horton
Estimated Sales: $ 5 - 10 Million
Number Employees: 10-19

6742 Horton Fruit Company
4701 Jennings Ln
Louisville, KY 40218-2967   502-969-1371
    Fax: 502-964-1515 800-626-2245
                      www.hortonfruit.com
Re-packer of tomatoes and onions and a processor of spinach, kale, coleslaw, bananas, avocados, pineapples and caramel apples.
    Chairman/CEO: Albert Horton
    President/COO: Jackson Woodward
    Treasurer: Steve Edelen
    Vice President: Bill Benoit
    Sales/Procurement: Tom Smith
    Transportation Manager: Bobby Harlow

Estimated Sales:$50-100 Million
Number Employees: 250-499
Type of Packaging: Consumer, Food Service

6743 Hosemen & Roche Vitamins & Fine Chemicals
340 Kingsland Street
Building 787
Nutley, NJ 07110-1199   973-235-5000
          Fax: 973-235-7605   800-526-6367
     paul.paslaske@roche.com   www.roche.com
Processor of bulk vitamins, carotenoids and citric acids for food manufacturing
     President: Dr Franz B Humer
Estimated Sales: Less than $500,000
Number Employees: 1-4
Parent Co: Hoffman-La Roche
Type of Packaging: Bulk
Brands:
     Roche

6744 Hosford & Wood Fresh Seafood Providers
2545 E 7th Street
Tucson, AZ 85716-4701   520-795-1920
                    Fax: 520-795-1010
Seafood
     President: Anita Wood
     Secretary: Bruce Hosford

6745 Hosmer Mountain Bottling
217 Mountain St
Willimantic, CT 06226-3299   860-423-1555
          Fax: 860-423-2207   800-763-2445
          www.hosmersoda.com/index.php
Soft drinks
     President/CEO: Andrew Potvin
     VP Marketing Manager: Bill Potvin
Estimated Sales:$2.5-5 Million
Number Employees: 5-9
Type of Packaging: Private Label
Brands:
     HOSMER MOUNTAIN SOFT DRINKS

6746 Hoson Produce
PO Box 93910
Los Angeles, CA 90093-0910   323-550-8695
                    Fax: 323-550-8194
Processor of vegetables including lettuce, cabbage and carrots
Number Employees: 20-49
Type of Packaging: Consumer, Food Service, Bulk

6747 Hospitality Mints
P.O.Box 3140
Boone, NC 28607-3140   828-264-3045
          Fax: 828-264-6933   800-334-5181
     mints@boone.net   www.hospitalitymints.com
Processor of mints; also, sugar-free breath mints; kosher available
     President: Alan Peterson
     Sales: Kathi Guy
Estimated Sales:$ 3 - 5 Million
Number Employees: 50-99
Sq. footage: 65000
Type of Packaging: Food Service

6748 Hospitality Mints LLC
P.O.Box 3140
Boone, NC 28607-3140   828-264-3045
          Fax: 828-264-6933   800-334-5181
          mints@hospitalitymints.com
          www.hospitalitymints.com
Processor and exporter of dessert mint candies; custom printed packaging available
     President/CEO: Allen Peterson
     COO: Ira Wagner
     Vice President: Walter Kaudelka
Estimated Sales:$500,000-$1 Million
Number Employees: 100-249
Sq. footage: 63000
Type of Packaging: Consumer, Food Service, Private Label, Bulk
Brands:
     Hospitality

6749 Hostess Frito-Lay Company
1001 Bishop Street N
Cambridge, ON N3H 4V8
Canada
                    519-653-5721
                    Fax: 519-650-6194

Processor of snack foods including potato, corn and tortilla chips, cheese twists and popcorn
     Technical Manager: Alain Bedard
     Plant Manager: Dean Bordner
Number Employees: 250-499
Parent Co: Pepsico
Type of Packaging: Consumer

6750 Hot Licks Hot Sauces
2820 Via Orange Way
Spring Valley, CA 91978-1742   619-232-6444
          Fax: 619-660-7429   888-766-6468
     hotlicks@juno.com   www.2hotlicks.com
Hot sauces, salsas, mustards, condiments, snacks, mixes and seasonings, bbq sauces, marinades, and gifts.
Estimated Sales: Less than $500,000
Number Employees: 1-4
Brands:
     AMAZON PEPPER PRODUCTS
     CALIFORNIA JUST CHILE!
     DEATH VALLEY HABANERO
     HOT! HOT! HOT!
     OTTIMO
     PEPE'S SAUCE
     RING OF FIRE

6751 Hot Potato Distributor
1133 W Randolph St
Chicago, IL 60607-1620   312-243-0640
                    Fax: 312-243-0659
     President: Irwin Brottman
     VP: Wayne Newman
     VP Operations: Bill Ferkaluk
Estimated Sales:$ 20 - 50 Million
Number Employees: 20-49

6752 Hot Springs Packing Company
P.O.Box 2312
Hot Springs, AR 71914-2312   501-767-2363
          Fax: 501-767-9715   800-535-0449
     hspc@hotspringspacking.com
          www.arkansasmeat.com
Processor and exporter of polish sausage, andouille sausage, smoked sausage, hot links, pork and beef franks, knockwurst, deli meats and hams.
     President/CEO: John Stubblefield
Estimated Sales:$10-20 Million
Number Employees: 20-49
Type of Packaging: Consumer, Food Service

6753 Hot Wachula's
4960 Lakeland Commerce Pkwy #4
Lakeland, FL 33805-8592   863-665-0383
          Fax: 863-665-0358   877-883-8700
          www.hotwachulas.com
Gourmet dips and sauces, marinades
     President: Matt Barber
Estimated Sales:$1 Million
Number Employees: 5-9
Brands:
     HOT WACHULA'S GOURMET DIPS & SAUCES

6754 Houdini
4225 N Palm St
Fullerton, CA 92835-1045   714-525-0325
          Fax: 714-996-9605   rritts@houdini.com
                    www.houdiniinc.com
Manufacturer, importer and exporter of food and wine; manufacturer of gift baskets
     President: Timothy Dean
Estimated Sales:$ 500,000 - $ 1 Million
Number Employees: 50-99
Brands:
     CALIFORNIA PANTRY
     WINE COUNTRY

6755 Houlton Farms Dairy
P.O.Box 429
Houlton, ME 04730-0429   207-532-3170
                    Fax: 207-532-3613
Milk processing
     President: Leonard Lincoln
Estimated Sales:$5-10 Million
Number Employees: 10-19

6756 House Autry Mills
PO Box 460
Four Oaks, NC 27524-0460   910-594-0802
          Fax: 910-594-0739   800-849-0802
     info@house-autry.com   www.house-autry.com

Baking mixes including breaders, coating mixes, hushpuppy mixes, biscuit and cornbread mixes, corn meal.
     President: Roger Mortenson
Estimated Sales:$10-20 Million
Number Employees: 20-49
Type of Packaging: Private Label

6757 House Foods America Corporation
7351 Orangewood Ave
Garden Grove, CA 92841-1411   714-901-4350
          Fax: 714-901-4235 www.house-foods.com
Processor of tofu and tofu products; importer of curry, spices, ramen noodles and tea.
     President: Gerald Shirasaka
Estimated Sales:$100-$500 Million
Number Employees: 100-249
Sq. footage: 221600
Brands:
     HINOICHI
     HOUSE FOODS

6758 House of Coffee Beans
2348 Bissonnet St
Houston, TX 77005-1512   713-524-0057
          Fax: 713-795-5410   800-422-1799
     contact@houseofcoffeebeans.com
          www.houseofcoffeebeans.com
Processor of gourmet coffees including dark roasted and espresso, decaffeinated, flavored, and blended coffee.
     Owner: Roger Farber
Estimated Sales: Less than $500,000
Number Employees: 1-4
Sq. footage: 14000
Type of Packaging: Consumer, Food Service, Private Label, Bulk

6759 House of Flavors
110 N William St
Ludington, MI 49431-2092   231-845-7369
          Fax: 231-845-7371   800-930-7740
     flavors@houseofflavors.com
          www.houseofflavors.com
Processor and exporter of kosher ice cream and frozen novelties
     Owner: Robert Neil
Number Employees: 20-49
Type of Packaging: Consumer, Food Service

6760 House of Raeford Farms
P.O.Box 100
Raeford, NC 28376-0100   910-844-4100
          Fax: 910-844-3306   800-888-7539
     rhonda.murphy@houseofraeford.com
          www.houseofraeford.com
Manufacturer and exporter of poultry
     Chairman: E Marvin Johnson
     Vice Chairman/CEO: Bob Johnson
     President/COO: Don Taber
     CEO: Chris Chavis
     Commodity/Export Manager: Harold Brock
     Director Marketing: Rhonda Murphy
     VP Sales/Marketing: Brenda Branch
     Sales Manager: Tonya Smith
Estimated Sales:$100 Million
Number Employees: 1,000-4,999
Type of Packaging: Food Service
Other Locations:
     Further Processing Plant/Distrib.
     Raeford NC
     Chicken Processing Plant
     Arcadia LA
     Columbia Farms Chicken Processing
     Columbia SC
     Breaded Chicken & Turkey Products
     Hemingway SC
     Columbia Farms Chicken Plant
     Greenville SC
Brands:
     COLUMBIA FARMS

6761 (HQ)House of Raeford Farms
P.O.Box 100
Raeford, NC 28376-0100   910-875-5161
          Fax: 910-875-8300   800-888-7539
     raefrdtrky@aol.com   www.houseofraeford.com

Manufacturer and exporter of turkey and chicken products
President/COO: Don Tabor
Chairman: E Marvin Johnson
Vice Chairman/CEO: Bob Johnson
VP: Steve Dunn
Sales Manager: Tonya Smith
Marketing Director: Rhonda Murphy
VP Sales/Marketing: Brenda Branch
Commodity/Export Manager: Harold Brock
Complex Manager: Greg Steenblock
VP National Accounts: Steve Dunn
Plant Manager: Sherwood Locklear
Estimated Sales: $100-500 Million
Number Employees: 1,000-4,999
Type of Packaging: Consumer, Food Service, Private Label, Bulk
Brands:
HOUSE OF RAEFORD

6762 House of Spices
127-40 Willets Point Blvd
Flushing, NY 11368   718-507-4900
                    Fax: 718-507-4683
customerservice@hosindia.com
www.hosindia.com
daals, beans, nuts, spices, edible oils, flours, pickels, pastes, chutneys, frozen vegetables and frozen meals.
President/Owner: Gordhandas Soni
CFO: Chetan Soni
VP: Krishnakumar Soni
Estimated Sales: $28 Million
Number Employees: 65

6763 House of Spices India
12740 Willets Point Blvd
Flushing, NY 11368-1506   718-507-4600
                    Fax: 718-507-4798
customerservice@hosindia.com
www.hosindia.com
Processor of pickles, condiment pastes, chutney, snack foods, candy, ice cream and frozen foods; importer of Indian-Pakistani basmati rice, lentils, spices, oils and nuts; exporter of pickles, condiments and spices.
President: G Soni
CEO: Kumar Soni
Estimated Sales: $5-10 Million appx.
Number Employees: 50-99
Number of Brands: 25
Number of Products: 2000
Sq. footage: 300000
Type of Packaging: Consumer, Food Service, Private Label, Bulk
Brands:
A-1
GITZ
JANTA
LAXMI
MAAZA
MAGGIE
NESTLE
PARLE
ROOHAFZA
SHAMIANA
VICCO-ZANDVADILD

6764 House of Spices India
4030 Bluebonnet Dr
Stafford, TX 77477-3950   281-313-5224
                    Fax: 281-494-5963
customerservice@hosindia.com
www.houseofspices.com
Processor of pickles, condiment pastes, chutney, snack foods, candy, ice cream and frozen foods; importer of Indian-Pakistani basmati rice, lentils, spices, oils and nuts; exporter of pickles, condiments and spices.
Manager: Anu Goshavi
CEO: Kumar Soni
Parent Co: House of Spices
Type of Packaging: Consumer, Food Service, Private Label, Bulk

6765 House of Spices India
13821 Struikman Rd
Cerritos, CA 90703-1031   562-407-0711
                    Fax: 562-407-0712
customerservice@hosindia.com
www.hosindia.com/contact.html

Processor of pickles, condiment pastes, chutney, snack foods, candy, ice cream and frozen foods; importer of Indian-Pakistani basmati rice, lentils, spices, oils and nuts; exporter of pickles, condiments and spices.
President: G Soni
CEO: Kumar Soni
Parent Co: House of Spices
Type of Packaging: Consumer, Food Service, Private Label, Bulk

6766 House of Spices India
2411 United Ln
Elk Grove Vlg, IL 60007-6818   847-595-2929
                    Fax: 847-595-9595
customerservice@hosindia.com
www.hosindia.com/contact.html
Processor of pickles, condiment pastes, chutney, snack foods, candy, ice cream and frozen foods; importer of Indian-Pakistani basmati rice, lentils, spices, oils and nuts; exporter of pickles, condiments and spices.
Manager: Subhash Majmudar
CEO: Kumar Soni
Parent Co: House of Spices
Type of Packaging: Consumer, Food Service, Private Label, Bulk

6767 House of Spices India
7908 Fernham Ln
Forestville, MD 20747-4517   301-420-1088
                    Fax: 301-967-7001
customerservice@hosindia.com
www.hosindia.com
Processor of pickles, condiment pastes, chutney, snack foods, candy, ice cream and frozen foods; importer of Indian-Pakistani basmati rice, lentils, spices, oils and nuts; exporter of pickles, condiments and spices.
Manager: Gunvant Pabari
CEO: Kumar Soni
Parent Co: House of Spices
Type of Packaging: Consumer, Food Service, Private Label, Bulk

6768 House of Spices India
25377 Huntwood Ave
Hayward, CA 94544-2212   510-732-8014
                    Fax: 510-732-7829
customerservice@hosindia.com
www.hosindia.com/contact.html
Processor of pickles, condiment pastes, chutney, snack foods, candy, ice cream and frozen foods; importer of Indian-Pakistani basmati rice, lentils, spices, oils and nuts; exporter of pickles, condiments and spices.
Manager: Dushyant Jani
CEO: Kumar Soni
Parent Co: House of Spices
Type of Packaging: Consumer, Food Service, Private Label, Bulk

6769 House of Spices India
3445 Bartlett Boulevard
Orlando, FL 32811   407-841-4608
                    Fax: 407-841-4611
customerservice@hosindia.com
www.hosindia.com/contact.html
Processor of pickles, condiment pastes, chutney, snack foods, candy, ice cream and frozen foods; importer of Indian-Pakistani basmati rice, lentils, spices, oils and nuts; exporter of pickles, condiments and spices.
President: G Soni
CEO: Kumar Soni
Parent Co: House of Spices
Type of Packaging: Consumer, Food Service, Private Label, Bulk

6770 House of Spices India
6115 Northbelt Dr
Norcross, GA 30071-4649   770-263-0202
                    Fax: 770-797-9669
customerservice@hosindia.com
www.hosindia.com/contact.html
Processor of pickles, condiment pastes, chutney, snack foods, candy, ice cream and frozen foods; importer of Indian-Pakistani basmati rice, lentils, spices, oils and nuts; exporter of pickles, condiments and spices.
Manager: Piyusha Zope
CEO: Kumar Soni
Parent Co: House of Spices

Type of Packaging: Consumer, Food Service, Private Label, Bulk

6771 House of Spices India
243 Stafford St
Worcester, MA 01603-1168   508-757-6555
                    Fax: 508-757-6554
customerservice@hosindia.com
www.hosindia.com
Processor of pickles, condiment pastes, chutney, snack foods, candy, ice cream and frozen foods; importer of Indian-Pakistani basmati rice, lentils, spices, oils and nuts; exporter of pickles, condiments and spices.
Manager: Sejeal Vora
CEO: Kumar Soni
Parent Co: House of Spices
Type of Packaging: Consumer, Food Service, Private Label, Bulk

6772 House of Thaller
1600 Harris Rd
Knoxville, TN 37924-2215   865-689-5893
                    Fax: 865-689-7132 www.houseofthaller.com
Processor of refrigerated salads and sandwich spreads; also, custom foods
President: John Thaller
Estimated Sales: $5-10 Million
Number Employees: 20-49
Type of Packaging: Consumer, Food Service, Private Label, Bulk

6773 House of Tsang
2345 3rd St
San Francisco, CA 94107-3108   415-282-9952
                    Fax: 415-243-0157   lgmarconi@hormel.com
www.worldfood.com OR
www.hormelfoods.com/brands/worldFood/houseof
tsang.as
Processor of Asian sauces, marinades, oils, vegetables and sauce combinations.
Owner: David Haase
Estimated Sales: $1 Million
Parent Co: Hormel Foods International Corporation

6774 House of Webster
P.O.Box 1988
Rogers, AR 72757-1988   479-636-4640
                    Fax: 479-636-2974   800-369-4641
www.houseofwebster.com
Processor of apple butter, jelly, salsa, barbecue sauce and preserves, ice cream toppings, ham, bacon and sausage, candy and cheese, pancake mix and assorted gifts.
Manager: Craig Casterlon
Estimated Sales: $10-20 Million
Number Employees: 20-49
Sq. footage: 100000
Type of Packaging: Consumer, Private Label
Brands:
WEBSTER'S

6775 House-Autry Mills
7000 Us Highway 301 S
Four Oaks, NC 27524-7628   919-963-6200
                    Fax: 919-963-6458   800-849-0802
info@house-autry.com   www.house-autry.com
Processor of flour based dairy mixes and corn meal
President: Roger Mortenson
Chief Financial Officer: Tim Johns
Vice President: Ken Gilbert
Number Employees: 20-49
Sq. footage: 45000
Type of Packaging: Consumer, Food Service
Other Locations:
House-Autry Mills
Four Oaks NC
Brands:
GOLDEN EAGLE
HOUSE AUTRY
THOMPSON'S

6776 Houser Meats
Rr 2 Box 180b
Rushville, IL 62681-9656   217-322-4994
                    Fax: 217-322-4994 www.housermeats.com
Processor of beef, pork, lamb and venison
Partner: Douglas Houser
Partner: Terri Houser
Estimated Sales: $500,000-$1 Million
Number Employees: 5-9
Sq. footage: 2500
Type of Packaging: Bulk

6777 Houston Calco
2400 Dallas St
Houston, TX 77003-3604   713-236-8668
        Fax: 713-236-1920 kent@hypercon.com
Bean sprouts, egg rolls, wontons and tofu.
    Owner: Alice Chang
Estimated Sales: $5-10 Million
Number Employees: 20-49
Type of Packaging: Private Label
Brands:
    CALCO

6778 Houston Harvest
3501 Mount Prospect Rd
Franklin Park, IL 60131-1305   847-957-0980
        Fax: 847-957-8883 800-548-5896
            www.houstonharvestgifts.com
Manufacturer, importer and exporter of gourmet
popcorn and candy gifts packaged in ceramics,
wooden baskets and tins
    President/CEO: Brett Glass
    VP Sales: Ron Gerstung
Estimated Sales: $50-100 Million
Number Employees: 100-249
Sq. footage: 1000000

6779 Houston Tea & Beverage
1700 Wirt Rd
Houston, TX 77055-3506   713-956-6751
        Fax: 713-956-6751 800-585-4549
            wms@pdq.net
Processor and importer of blended and flavored teas
    President: Linda Williams
Estimated Sales: Less than $500,000
Number Employees: 1-4
Sq. footage: 8500
Type of Packaging: Private Label

6780 Howard Foods
P.O.Box 2072
Danvers, MA 01923-5072   978-774-6207
    Fax: 978-777-2384 howardfoods@verizon.net
            www.howardfoods.com
Howard's products include: sweet pepper relish, hot
pepper relish, green tomato piccalilli, ham glaze,
sugar free syrup, garlic and onion seasoning juices,
chopped and minced garlic in various sizes.
Estimated Sales: $1 - 3 Million
Number Employees: 5-9
Brands:
    HOWARD'S

6781 Howard Turner & Son
1659 Route 1 Highway 7
Marie Joseph, NS B0J 2G0
Canada   902-347-2616
        Fax: 902-347-2714
Processor and exporter of fresh and frozen lobster
and groundfish
    President: Randy Turner
Type of Packaging: Bulk

6782 Howards of Colorado
333 E 16th Avenue
Apt 313
Denver, CO 80203-1806   970-332-5662
        Fax: 970-332-5662
Processor and exporter of popcorn and all natural
salt/butter seasonings; also, gift packaging and fund
raising available
    President: Don Howard
Estimated Sales: $500,000-$1 Million
Number Employees: 1-4
Type of Packaging: Consumer, Food Service, Private Label, Bulk
Brands:
    COUNTRY GOLD
    PRIDE OF THE ROCKIES

6783 Howjax
PO Box 246063
Pembroke Pines, FL 33024-0117   954-441-2491
        Fax: 954-962-7258 info@howjax.com
            www.howjax.com
Gourmet condiments, and Caribean style chutney

6784 Howler Products
PO Box 601
Philo, CA 95466-0601   415-824-0686
        Fax: 415-824-0697 800-469-5377
        howlerprod@aol.com www.howler.com
Sorbets and gelato.
    President: Joe Hernandez

6785 Howson & Howson Limited
232 Westmoreland Street
Blyth, ON N0M 1H0
Canada   519-523-4241
        Fax: 519-523-4920
        howson@howsonandhowson.ca
            www.howsonandhowson.ca
Durum flour milling
    President: Jim Howson
    VP: Jeff Howson
    R&D/Plant Manager: Doug Howson
    Marketing: Dan Greyerbighl
    Operations/Purchasing: Jeff Howson
Estimated Sales: $30 Million
Number Employees: 35
Type of Packaging: Bulk

6786 Hoyt's Honey Farm
11711 Interstate 10 E
Baytown, TX 77523-0852   281-576-5383
        Fax: 281-576-2191 hoyts@imsday.com
            www.hoytshoney.com
Processor and importer of honey
    President: Gordon Brown
Estimated Sales: $5-10 Million
Number Employees: 5-9
Sq. footage: 7500
Type of Packaging: Consumer, Food Service, Private Label, Bulk
Brands:
    HOYT'S PURE HONEY
    HOYTS

6787 Hsin Tung Yang Foods Co.
405 S Airport Blvd
S San Francisco, CA 94080-6909   650-589-6789
        Fax: 650-589-3157 info@htyusa.com
            www.htyusa.com
Manufacturer and canner of Asian meat products in-
cluding beef jerky, pork jerky, sausage and ham
    President: Kailen Mai
    Director Manufacturing: Pin Chong
Estimated Sales: $10 - 20 Million
Number Employees: 50-99

6788 Hsu's Ginseng Enterprises
P.O.Box 509
Wausau, WI 54402-0509   715-675-2325
        Fax: 715-675-7832 800-826-1577
    info@hsuginseng.com www.hsuginseng.com
Processor and exporter of ginseng products, royal
jelly, bee pollen, astragalus, dong quai and
goldenseal
    President: Paul Hsu
    Vice President: Sharon Hsu
Estimated Sales: $5-10 Million
Number Employees: 50-99
Brands:
    ROOT TO HEALTH

6789 Hubbard Farms
PO Box 309
Pikeville, TN 37367-0309   501-262-1061
        Fax: 501-262-2322
Manufacturer and exporter of chickens including
broiler bred and day-old
    President: Don Johnson
Estimated Sales: $5-10 Million
Number Employees: 20-49
Parent Co: Hubbard Farms
Type of Packaging: Bulk

6790 Hubbard Meat Company
500 N Birdwell Ln
Big Spring, TX 79720-8204   432-267-7781
Processor of meats
    Owner: T Hubbard
Estimated Sales: $1-2.5 Million
Number Employees: 1-4

6791 Hubbard Peanut Company
P.O.Box 94
Sedley, VA 23878-0094   757-562-4081
        Fax: 757-562-2741 800-889-7688
    hubs@hubspeanuts.com www.hubspeanuts.com
Processor and exporter of cocktail peanuts
    President: Lynne Rabil
    Plant Manager: David Benton
Estimated Sales: $10-24.9 Million
Number Employees: 10-19
Sq. footage: 30000
Type of Packaging: Consumer, Food Service, Private Label

6792 Huber's Orchard Winery
19816 Huber Rd
Borden, IN 47106-8309   812-923-9813
        Fax: 812-923-3013 800-345-9463
    info@huberwinery.com www.huberwinery.com
Produces a variety of Wines in addition to offering
numerous fruits and vegtables at their farmer's market, including: strawberries, raspberries, blueberries,
black raspberries, and blackberries. Homegrown
summer vegetables includecorn, green beans, tomatoes, peppers, broccoli, and cauliflower.
    President: Ted Huber
    VP: Greg Huber
Estimated Sales: $5-10 Million
Number Employees: 20-49

6793 Huck's Seafood
508 Cynwood Dr # D
Easton, MD 21601-3892   410-770-9211
        Fax: 410-763-8811
Processor of crabs, oysters and clams; whole-
saler/distributor of fish including rock, perch, blue,
spot and flounder; serving the food service market
    Owner/President: James Ford, Jr
    Orders: Amber Ford
Estimated Sales: $.5 - 1 million
Number Employees: 1-4
Sq. footage: 2500
Type of Packaging: Consumer, Food Service, Bulk
Brands:
    HUCK'S

6794 Huckleberry Patch
P.O.Box 1
Hungry Horse, MT 59919-0001   406-387-5000
        Fax: 406-387-4444 800-527-7340
        info@huckleberrypatch.com
            www.huckleberrypatch.com
Wildberry jellies, syrups, jams, preserves
    Manager: Laurie Carpy
Estimated Sales: $5-10 Million
Number Employees: 10-19

6795 Hudson Valley Fruit Juice
33 White St
Highland, NY 12528-1621   845-691-8061
        Fax: 845-691-9056
Fruit and vegetable juices and vinegar
    President: Vincent Nemeth
Estimated Sales: $1-2.5 Million
Number Employees: 1-4

6796 Hudson Valley Homestead
102 Sheldon Ln
Craryville, NY 12521-5324   518-851-7336
        Fax: 518-851-7553
    sales@hudsonvalleyhomestead.com
        www.hudsonvalleyhomestead.com
Gourmet foods including vinegars, mustards, salad
dressings, sauces, spreads, oils, and jams.
    President: John King
Estimated Sales: Less than $500,000
Number Employees: 1-4
Type of Packaging: Private Label
Brands:
    BASHWHACBER'S MUSTARD
    BLOW HARD MUSTARD
    HUDSON VALLEY HOMESTEAD

6797 Hudsonville Creamery & Ice Cream
345 E 48th St # B
Holland, MI 49423-5381   616-928-0793
        Fax: 616-546-4020
    hello@hudsonvilleicecream.com
        www.hudsonvilleicecream.com
Processor of regular and low-fat ice cream, frozen
yogurt and sherbet
    Owner: Dennis Ellens
Estimated Sales: $5-10 Million
Number Employees: 20-49
Number of Brands: 2
Type of Packaging: Consumer, Bulk
Brands:
    HUDSONVILLE ICE CREAM

6798 Hue's Seafood
105 S 14th Street
Baton Rouge, LA 70802-4753   225-383-0809
        Fax: 225-383-0809
Seafood
    President: Tu Nguyen

6799 Hughes Company Inc
1200 W James St
Columbus, WI 53925-1028   920-623-2000
    Fax: 920-623-4098 Hughes@Powerweb.net
            www.hughescompany.biz
Manufacturer of machinery for the food processing
industry including air cleaners; bins; rotary blanchers and cookers; rotary coolers; bulk unloading feed-
ers; fillers; graders; inspection tables, etc.
    President: Todd Belz
    Sales Engineer: Dave Olson

**6800 Hughes Springs Frozen Food
Center**
P.O.Box 206
Hughes Springs, TX 75656-0206   903-639-2941
Meat packer
    Owner: Alvin Dannelley
Estimated Sales: $1-2.5 Million
Number Employees: 1-4
Type of Packaging: Consumer

6801 Hughson Meat Company
407 S Guadalupe Street
San Marcos, TX 78666-6837   512-392-3368
        Fax: 512-392-4190 877-462-6328
        http://www.hughson-meat.com/retail
Manufacturer of meat products; slaughtering also
available
    Owner: Marvin Rutkowski
Estimated Sales: $3-5 Million
Number Employees: 5-9
Type of Packaging: Consumer

6802 Hughson Nut Company
1825 Verduga Rd
Hughson, CA 95326-9675   209-883-0403
    Fax: 209-883-2973 info@hughsonnut.com
            www.hughsonnut.com
Almond nuts diced, sliced, slivered, milled,
blanched and dry toasted
    President: Martin Pohl
Estimated Sales: $2.5-5 Million
Number Employees: 10-19
Number of Brands: 1
Sq. footage: 75000
Type of Packaging: Consumer, Private Label, Bulk

6803 Huisken Meat Center
245 Industrial Blvd
Sauk Rapids, MN 56379   320-259-0305
    Fax: 320-240-0654 info@huiskenmeats.com
            www.huiskenmeats.com
Manufacturer and packer of meats and meat snacks
    President: James Hanson
Estimated Sales: $15.3 Million
Number Employees: 80
Parent Co: Branding Iron Holding Company
Type of Packaging: Consumer, Private Label
Brands:
    BESURE
    HUISKEN
    RG'S

6804 Hulman & Company
P.O.Box 150
Terre Haute, IN 47808-0150   812-232-9446
    Fax: 812-478-7181
    bakingpowder@brickyard.com
            www.clabbergirl.com
Processor and exporter of regular and double-acting
baking powder
    President: Anton Hulman George
    CEO: Tony George
Estimated Sales: $20-50 Million
Number Employees: 1,000-4,999
Parent Co: Clabber Girl Corporation

6805 Humble Cremery
1474 N Indiana St
Los Angeles, CA 90063-2518   323-269-9481
    Fax: 323-261-7555 800-697-9925
            www.humboldtcreamery.com
Processor of ice cream
    Plant Manager: Dale Killen
    Sales Manager: Don Baker
    Plant Manager: Kevin Creviston
Estimated Sales: $ 20 - 50 Million
Number Employees: 50-99
Parent Co: West Farm Foods
Type of Packaging: Consumer, Food Service, Pri-
    vate Label

Brands:
    Humble

6806 Humboldt Creamery Association
572 Highway One
Fortuna, CA 95540   707-725-6182
                Fax: 707-725-6186
    info@humboldtcreamery.comm
            www.humboldtcreamery.com
Processor and exporter of ice cream and milk includ-
ing specialty powders, whole, skim, 1% and 2%
    President/CEO: Rich Ghilarducci
Estimated Sales: $50-100 Million
Number Employees: 50-99
Type of Packaging: Consumer, Food Service, Bulk

6807 Humboldt Flour Mills
PO Box 400
Humboldt, SK S0K 2A0
Canada   306-682-2577
                Fax: 306-682-4486
Processor and exporter of flour, mustard seeds, len-
tils, peas, etc.; also, organic flour and bran
    President: Jim Hussin
Number Employees: 50-99
Parent Co: Humboldt Flour Mills
Type of Packaging: Consumer, Food Service, Bulk
Brands:
    SUPREME

6808 Humboldt Sausage Company
1515 15th St N
Humboldt, IA 50548-1017   515-332-4121
                Fax: 515-332-2629
Manufacturer of sausage and salami; exporter of
hard and Genoa salami and pepperoni
    Founder/General Manager: Roger Lawson
    Plant Manager: Gary Piearson
Estimated Sales: $25 Million
Number Employees: 50-99
Sq. footage: 45000
Parent Co: SMG
Type of Packaging: Consumer, Food Service, Pri-
    vate Label, Bulk
Brands:
    AQUILA D'ORA
    BEIRMEISTER
    BUON GIORNO
    GRATIFICA
    LIGURIA

6809 Humbolt Brewing Company
856 10th Street
Arcata, CA 95521-6232   707-826-1734
        Fax: 707-826-2045 www.humboldtbrews.com/
Processor of beer, ale and lager
    President: Mario Celotto
Number Employees: 50-99
Type of Packaging: Consumer, Food Service, Bulk
Brands:
    GOLD NECTAR
    RED NECTAR

6810 Humco
7400 Alumax Rd
Texarkana, TX 75501-0282   903-831-7808
        Fax: 903-334-6300 800-662-3435
            www.humco.com
Processor and exporter of OTC liquid and powder
herbal supplements
    CEO/Presidnet: Greg Pulido
    CEO: Greg Pulido
    CFO: Steve Woolf
    Vice President: Susan Hickey
    VP Quality/Regulatory Affairs: Steve Bryant
    VP Sales: Alan Fyke
Estimated Sales: $10-20 Million
Number Employees: 100-249

6811 Hume Specialties
PO Box 4329
Winston Salem, NC 27115-4329   802-875-3117
                Fax: 802-875-3140
Processor of salsa and tortilla chips and strips
    President: Christine Hume
    Executive VP/Production Manager: Dave Hume
    Sales Manager: Carl Lill
Estimated Sales: $2.5-5 Million
Number Employees: 10-19
Sq. footage: 7000
Type of Packaging: Consumer
Brands:
    GREEN MOUNTAIN GRINGO

6812 Humeniuk's Meat Cutting
PO Box 11
Ranfurly, AB T0B 3T0
Canada   780-658-2381
Processor of fresh and frozen beef and pork; also,
wild game including deer
    President: Nector Humeniuk
    Owner/Manager: Gerald Humeniuk
    Secretary: Oksana Humeniuk
Number Employees: 10-19
Sq. footage: 80000
Type of Packaging: Consumer, Food Service, Pri-
    vate Label, Bulk
Brands:
    GRANNY'S

6813 Hummel Brothers
180 Sargent Dr
New Haven, CT 06511-5958   203-787-4113
        Fax: 203-498-1755 800-828-8978
Manufacturer of cold cuts, frankfurters and sausage
    President: William C Hummel Sr
    Controller: Mary Ellen Hummel
Estimated Sales: $20-50 Million
Number Employees: 50-99
Sq. footage: 47000
Type of Packaging: Consumer, Private Label
Brands:
    HUMMEL MEATS

6814 Hummingbird Kitchens
PO Box 1286
Whitehouse, TX 75791-1286   903-839-6244
                800-921-9470
    wfaulkner@cox-internet.com
            www.hummingbirdkitchens.com
Processor of gourmet food mixes including bread,
soup, dip, salad dressing, tea, jambalaya, spice, sea-
soning and rice. Including American, Southwestern,
and Tex-mex style foods
    President: Janet Faulkner
    CEO: William Faulkner
Estimated Sales: $1-2.5 Million
Number Employees: 5-9
Number of Products: 51
Type of Packaging: Consumer, Private Label, Bulk

6815 Humphrey Blue Ribbon Meats
1821 S 15th St
Springfield, IL 62703-3298   217-544-7445
        Fax: 217-544-7518 800-747-6328
Processor of specialty sausage and hams
    President: T Humphrey
    Chairman: E Humphrey
Estimated Sales: $10-20 Million
Number Employees: 10-19
Sq. footage: 14600

6816 Humphrey Company
20810 Miles Pkwy
Cleveland, OH 44128-5508   216-662-6629
        Fax: 216-662-6619 800-486-3739
    humphreycompany@ameritech.net
            www.humphreycompany.com
Premium white popcorn
    Owner: Dudley Humphrey
    VP: Betsy Humphrey
Estimated Sales: $500,000-$1 Million
Number Employees: 10-19
Number of Brands: 1
Number of Products: 10
Sq. footage: 11000
Type of Packaging: Consumer, Private Label

6817 Humphreys Dairy
1675 Shady Grove Road
Hot Springs National Par, AR 71901-5943 262-1820
            http://www.pwhump.com
Milk
    President: Paul Humphreys
    VP: Charles Humphreys
    Sales Manager: Harris Humhpreys
    Plant Manager: Jim Humphrey
Estimated Sales: $1-2.5 Million
Number Employees: 10-19

6818 Humpty Dumpty Snack Foods
88 Pleasant Hill Road
Scarborough, ME 04074-8719   207-883-8422
        Fax: 207-885-0773 800-274-2447
            www.humptydumpty.com
Snacks
    President: Turk Thacher

Brands:
HUMPTY DUMPTY

6819 Humpty Dumpty Snack Foods
2100 Rue Norman
Lachine, QC H8S 1B1
Canada 514-367-3521
Fax: 514-639-5419 800-361-6440
reception@humptydumpty.com
www.humptydumpty.com
Processor of snack foods including kettle-style potato chips, popcorn, tortilla chips and extruded corn products
President: David Murphy
CFO: Lois Norris
Vice President: Lynda Murray
Marketing Director: Linda Murray
Director Sales: Gerard Pacull
Parent Co: Small Fry Snack Foods
Type of Packaging: Consumer, Food Service, Private Label
Brands:
Humpty Dumpty
Krunchers
Mexitos

6820 Hung's Noodle House
25-1410 40th Avenue NE
Calgary, AB T2E 6L1
Canada 403-250-1663
Fax: 403-291-0632
Processor of noodles including rice
President: Ricky Chung
Production: Cindy Chung
Parent Co: Hung Kee Holdings Company
Brands:
HUNG'S NOODLE HOUSE

6821 Hungerford J Smith Company
1500 N Central Ave
Humboldt, TN 38343-1798 731-784-3461
Fax: 731-784-2124 www.conagrafoodservice.com
Processor of ice cream toppings, syrups, coatings and shake base mixes.
Estimated Sales: $10-20 Million
Number Employees: 50-99
Parent Co: ConAgra Foods
Type of Packaging: Consumer, Private Label

6822 Hungry Sultan
14 Rancho Cir
Lake Forest, CA 92630-8325 949-215-0000
Fax: 949-215-0965 info@HungrySultan.com
www.hungrysultan.com
Mediterranean snack products
President: Fouad El-Abd
Public Relations: Darren El-Abd
Estimated Sales: Less than $500,000
Number Employees: 10-19

6823 Hunt Brothers Cooperative
P.O.Box 631
Lake Wales, FL 33859-0631 863-676-9471
Fax: 863-676-8362
Processor of citrus fruits including grapefruits, limes, oranges and tangerines
President: Frank Hunt Iii III
Estimated Sales: $20-50 Million
Number Employees: 250-499
Type of Packaging: Consumer, Food Service, Bulk
Brands:
SEALD SWEET
TREASURE PAK

6824 Hunt Country Foods
P.O.Box 876
Middleburg, VA 20118-0876 540-364-2622
Fax: 540-364-3112 info@send-best-of-luck.com
www.send-best-of-luck.com
Proceesor of specialty cookies, cakes, chocolates
Owner: Maggi Castelloe
Estimated Sales: Less than $500,000
Number Employees: 5-9
Brands:
BEST OF LUCK
BEST OF LUCK HORSESHOE CHOCOLATES
HORSESHOE CAKE
HORSESHOES AND NAILS

6825 Hunt Country Vineyards
4021 Italy Hill Rd
Branchport, NY 14418-9615 315-595-2812
Fax: 315-595-2835 800-946-3289
info@HuntWines.com www.huntwines.com

Processor and exporter of wines including red, white, table, late harvest, ice, wine, sherry, port
President: Joyce Hunt
CEO: Arthur Hunt
Marketing/Sales Manager: James Alsina
Operations Manager: David Mortensen
Estimated Sales: $500,000-$1 Million
Number Employees: 20-49
Sq. footage: 8000
Type of Packaging: Consumer, Private Label
Brands:
Fingerlakes Wine Cellars
Foxy Lady
Hunt Country Vineyards

6826 Hunt-Wesson Food Service Company
PO Box 25309
Rochester, NY 14625-0309 949-437-1000
800-633-1002
info@foodpros.com www.hunt-wesson.com
Frozen and prepared entrees, pasta, vegetables and sauces
President: Jeff Wayne
Number Employees: 500-999
Parent Co: ConAgra
Brands:
KNOTT'S BERRY FARM
LA CHOY
ROSARITA

6827 Hunt-Wesson Foods
PO Box 25309
Rochester, NY 14625-0309 209-847-0321
Fax: 209-848-7386 http://www.hwfoods.com
Processor of canned tomato sauce and juice
President: Kent Stacy
Parent Co: ConAgra Grocery Products
Type of Packaging: Consumer, Food Service, Private Label, Bulk

6828 Hunt-Wesson Foods
2239 Edgewood Avenue S
Minneapolis, MN 55426-2822 612-544-2761
Fax: 612-525-9274 www.hwfoods.com
Ice cream toppings and cones
President: Edward Snell
Estimated Sales: $25-49.9 Million
Number Employees: 100-249
Parent Co: ConAgra Foods

6829 Hunter Farms
1900 N Main St
High Point, NC 27262-2132 336-822-2300
Fax: 336-882-2341 800-446-8035
email@hunterfarms.net www.hunterfarms.com
Processor of dairy products including milk, ice cream, frozen yogurt and sour cream
VP: Dwight Moore
Sales Development: Karin Cavanaugh
Director Sales: Bob Cooke
General Manager: Dwight Moore
Estimated Sales: $10-24.9 Million
Number Employees: 50-99
Parent Co: Harris Teeter
Type of Packaging: Consumer

6830 Hunter Food Inc
3700 E Melville Way
Anaheim, CA 92806-2122 714-666-1888
Fax: 714-666-1222 www.hunterfood.com
Poultry processing plant specializing in various types of chicken breast, leg, thigh, and portion products.
Owner: Ricky Lee
CEO: Hsin Jung Le
Estimated Sales: $ 20 - 50 Million
Number Employees: 100-249

6831 Huppen Bakery
8721 Santa Monica Boulevard
Suite 201
Los Angeles, CA 90069-4507 323-656-7501
Fax: 323-656-1090
verticalsales@worldnet.att.net
Processor of swiss chocolates and wafer rolls
President: Urs Brauchli
Type of Packaging: Consumer, Bulk

6832 Hurd Orchards
17260 Ridge Rd
Holley, NY 14470-9353 585-638-8838
Fax: 585-638-5175 market@hurdorchards.com
www.hurdorchards.com

Processor of preserves, vinegars, brandied fruit, pickles, chili sauce, jams, marmalades, canned fruit and dried fruit
Owner: Susan Machamer
VP: Amy Machamer
Estimated Sales: $ .5 - 1 million
Number Employees: 1-4

6833 Hurd Orchards
17260 Ridge Rd
Holley, NY 14470-9353 585-638-8838
Fax: 585-638-5175 market@hurdorchards.com
www.hurdorchards.com
Preserves, vinegars, brandied fruit, pickles, chili sauce, jams, marmalades, conserves, canned and dried fruit
Owner: Susan Machamer
Owner: Amy Macharmer
Estimated Sales: $ .5 - 1 million
Number Employees: 1-4

6834 Hurst Vineyards
PO Box 220
Bosque, NM 87006-0220 505-864-1831
Fax: 505-864-1831
Wines

6835 (HQ)Husch Vineyards
4400 Highway 128
Philo, CA 95466-9476 707-895-3216
Fax: 707-895-2068 800-554-8724
www.huschvineyards.com
Produces a variety of wines including: Sauvignon Blanc, Pinot Noir, Cabernet Sauvignon, Chardonnay, Muscat Canelli, and Syrah.
President: Zach Robinson
VP: Amanda Robinson Holstine
Operations Manager: Al White
Production Manager: Brad Holstine
Estimated Sales: $2.5-5 Million
Number Employees: 5-9

6836 Huse's Country Meats
3697 State Highway 171
Malone, TX 76660-3053 254-533-2205
Fax: 254-533-2498 mcarpent@internetwork.net
Processor of smoked beef and pork sausage
Owner: Randy Huse
Estimated Sales: $5-10 Million
Number Employees: 10-19

6837 Huser Paul Company
3636 Illinois Rd
Fort Wayne, IN 46804-2062 260-432-0557
Fax: 260-432-0559
Manager: Steve Sczink
VP: Bernie Kaufman
Estimated Sales: $5-10 Million
Number Employees: 10-19

6838 Husman Snack Food Company
1621 Moore Street
Cincinnati, OH 45210 859-282-7490
Fax: 513-562-2646 www.birdseyefoods.com
Manufacturer of potato and tortilla chips
President/CEO: David Ray
Quality Assurance Manager: John Barlage
Plant Manager: Leroy Pennekamp
Number Employees: 100-249
Sq. footage: 70000
Parent Co: Birds Eye Foods
Type of Packaging: Consumer, Private Label, Bulk
Brands:
HUSMAN'S

6839 Hutchins-Logue
1348 Commerce Ln
Santa Cruz, CA 95060-3906 831-426-0600
Fax: 831-426-7758 800-959-7670
elaine@coolbeanmints.com www.codigacpa.com
Mints
Partner: Christopher Codiga
Brands:
COOL BEAN MINTS

6840 Huval Baking Company
P.O.Box 2339
Lafayette, LA 70502-2339 337-232-1611
Processor of baked goods including bread, buns and rolls
Comptroller: Kerry Schexnayder
VP: Ronald Harison

Estimated Sales: Less than $500,000
Number Employees: 5-9
Parent Co: Flowers Baking Company
Type of Packaging: Consumer

6841 Hybco USA
363 S Mission Rd
Los Angeles, CA 90033-3752   323-269-3111
      Fax: 323-269-3130 sales@hybco.com
                  www.hybco.com
Products include oils (soy, cottonseed, vegetable, corn, canola, peanut, and shortenings); long grain rice and long grain rice flour.
      President: David Kashani
Estimated Sales: $2.5-5 Million
Number Employees: 10-19

6842 Hyde & Hyde
13837 Bettencourt Street
Cerritos, CA 90703   562-926-9238
      Fax: 562-926-1915 sales@hydeandhyde.com
                  www.hydeandhyde.com
Condiments for the fresh-cut produce industry. Also offers custom packaging and co-packaging.
      President: Timothy Hyde
Number Employees: 100-249
Type of Packaging: Consumer

6843 Hyde Candy Company
1916 E Mercer Street
Seattle, WA 98112-4029   206-322-5743
Candy manufacturer
      President: Alfred Hyde

6844 Hyde Meat Packing
24362 Highway 190 E
Robert, LA 70455-0365   985-345-5756
                  Fax: 985-345-1259
Processor of beef
      Owner: Janice Hyde
Estimated Sales: $ 10 - 20 Million
Number Employees: 20-49
Type of Packaging: Consumer, Food Service, Bulk

6845 Hydroblend
1801 N Elder St
Nampa, ID 83687-3079   208-467-7441
      Fax: 208-467-2220
customerservice@hydroblendinc.com
      www.hydroblendinc.com
Crispy and crunchy coating for potatoes, appetizers, fish, chicken and vegetbles.
      President: Mike Guthrie
      CEO: Bill Cyr
      VP Sales/Marketing: Randy Hobert
      R&D: Henning Melvej
      Quality Control: Joshua Bevan
      Customer Service: Gay Tisdale
      Purchasing Director: Matt Haines
Estimated Sales: $ 10 - 20 Million
Number Employees: 100-249
Sq. footage: 110000
Type of Packaging: Bulk
Brands:
      HB Batters
      HB Breadings

6846 Hye Cuisine
4730 S Highland Ave
Del Rey, CA 93616-9716   559-834-3000
      Fax: 559-834-5882 hyecuisine@aol.com
Processor of specialty marinated vegetables and stuffed grape leaves; exporter of grape leaves
      President: Raffi Santikian
      Secretary: Hilda Santikian
Estimated Sales: $ 5 - 10 Million
Number Employees: 50-99
Sq. footage: 8000
Type of Packaging: Food Service, Private Label

6847 Hye Quality Bakery
2222 Santa Clara St
Fresno, CA 93721-2921   559-445-1511
      Fax: 559-445-1540 877-445-1778
info@hyequalitybakery.com
      www.hyequalitybakery.com
Processor of cracker breads, gourmet crackers and soft cracker bread.
      President: Sammy Ganimian
Estimated Sales: $10-20 Million
Number Employees: 10-19
Brands:
      HYE DELITES
      HYE ROLLER

6848 Hygeia Dairy Company
525 Beaumont Ave
McAllen, TX 78501-2737   956-686-0511
                  Fax: 956-630-6747
Manufacturer of dairy products including ice cream, ices, sherbets, chocolate milk, buttermilk, milk and cream; also, ice cream and ice milk mixes
      Manager: Jimmy Wallace
      General Manager: Jimmy Wallace
Estimated Sales: $3-5 Million
Number Employees: 50-99
Parent Co: Deans Foods
Type of Packaging: Consumer, Food Service

6849 Hygeia Dairy Company
5330 Ayers St
Corpus Christi, TX 78415-2104   361-854-4561
      Fax: 361-854-7267 www.deanfoods.com
Processor and exporter of regular and chocolate milk and orange juice
      Manager: Scott Mc Clarren
Estimated Sales: $20-50 Million
Number Employees: 20-49
Parent Co: Hygeia Dairy Company
Type of Packaging: Consumer, Food Service, Private Label, Bulk
Brands:
      HYGEIA
      SUPER GOOD

6850 Hygrade Ocean Products
P.O.Box 6918
New Bedford, MA 02742-6918   508-993-5700
            Fax: 508-991-5133 soaked@aol.com
Processor of fresh and frozen scallops including bay and sea and fillets including flounder, cod, yellow tail and haddock; importer of cod fish and scallops; exporter of scallops
      Owner: Carmine Romano
      CFO: Linda Wisnewski
Estimated Sales: $10-20 Million
Number Employees: 20-49
Sq. footage: 28000
Type of Packaging: Consumer, Food Service, Private Label, Bulk
Brands:
      DING GUA GUA
      HYDRADE
      OLD CAPE HARBOR
      TEDDY'S

6851 I & K Distributors
P.O.Box 369
Delphos, OH 45833-0369   419-692-6911
      Fax: 419-695-7585 800-869-6337
      custserv@ikdist.com www.ikdist.com
Manufacturer of frozen pizza
      President/CEO: Robert Fishbein
      Director Business Development: Tom Baker
      Director Human Resources: Jason Leffel
Estimated Sales: $347.5 Million
Number Employees: 250-499
Parent Co: Countryside Foods, LLC
Type of Packaging: Consumer
Brands:
      BERNEA FARMS
      MICHIGAN
      RENOS
      YODER

6852 I Rice & Company
11500 Roosevelt Blvd # D
Philadelphia, PA 19116-3080   215-533-3663
      Fax: 215-673-2616 800-232-6022
      sales@iriceco.com www.iriceco.com
Processor and exporter of syrups, flavorings, sundae toppings, fudge, bakery fillings and stabilizers
      President: Steve Kuhl
Estimated Sales: $20-50 Million
Number Employees: 20-49
Number of Brands: 3
Number of Products: 1000
Sq. footage: 85000
Type of Packaging: Food Service, Private Label, Bulk
Brands:
      RICE'S PRODUCTS

6853 I. Deveau Fisheries
PO Box 118
Meteghan, NS B0W 2J0
Canada   902-645-3036
                  Fax: 902-645-3109

Processor and exporter of fresh haddock and herring roe; also, live lobster
      President: Berton German
Number Employees: 5-9
Type of Packaging: Bulk

6854 I. Epstein & Sons
8 Joanna Court
East Brunswick, NJ 08816-2108   800-237-5320
                  Fax: 732-432-3928

6855 IBC Holsum
PO Box 100435
Atlanta, GA 30384-0435   305-888-3441
      Fax: 561-464-6931 800-465-7861
Processor of baked goods including bread, rolls, muffins and croissants
      President: Edward Eisele
      Marketing Manager: Scott Currie
Estimated Sales: $50-100 Million
Number Employees: 250-499
Parent Co: IBC
Type of Packaging: Consumer, Food Service

6856 IBP Foods
2000 Oak Industrial Drive NE
Grand Rapids, MI 49505-6012   616-774-0711
                  Fax: 616-774-2493
Processor of hot dogs, luncheon meats and fresh and smoked sausage
      VP: Larry Hopkins
      VP/General Manager: James Hatch
      Plant Manager: Jim Ledford
      Purchasing Agent: Mike Puh
Estimated Sales: $500 Million-$1 Billion
Number Employees: 500-999
Parent Co: Tyson Foods
Type of Packaging: Consumer, Private Label
Brands:
      Tyson

6857 IBP Foods
1090 Chicago Rd
Troy, MI 48083-4203   248-588-4710
      Fax: 248-585-8909 www.ibpcustompanels.com
Processor and exporter of meat products including boneless pork loins, slab and sliced bacon, fresh pork, sausage, poultry, beef, veal, smoked meats, frankfurters, luncheon meats, etc
      CEO/President: Clearance Johns
      Executive VP Sales/Marketing: Mike Vallaro
Estimated Sales: $ 3 - 5 Million
Number Employees: 20-49
Parent Co: Tyson Foods
Type of Packaging: Bulk

6858 IFive Brands
P.O.Box 9134
Seattle, WA 98109-0134   206-783-2498
      Fax: 206-789-1016 800-882-5615
adam@peppermints.com www.peppermints.com
Fat-free and sugar free mints
      Owner: Brett Canfield
Estimated Sales: $ 3 - 5 Million
Number Employees: 1-4
Brands:
      PENGUIN

6859 II Sisters
850 Airport St # 9
Moss Beach, CA 94038-9617   650-728-5613
      Fax: 650-728-5611 800-282-7058
                  summin_t@yahoo.com
Seasoned oils, herbal vinegars
      President/Owner: Sudi Taleghani
      CFO: Simmin Taleghani
Estimated Sales: $1-2.5 Million
Number Employees: 5-9
Brands:
      II Sisters
      Ii Sisters
      Sorrell Flavours

6860 IL HWA American Corporation
91 Terry St
Belleville, NJ 07109-3222   973-759-1996
      Fax: 973-450-0562 800-446-7364
                  support@ilhwaamerica.com
                  www.ilhwaamerica.com
Processor, importer, exporter and wholesaler/distributor of Korean ginseng
      President: Sang Kil Han
      Warehouse Manager: Edner Louis

Estimated Sales:$2.5-5 Million
Number Employees: 1-4
Brands:
Il Hwa

6861 IMAC
1702 N Sooner Rd
Oklahoma City, OK 73141-1222   405-424-8794
Fax: 405-424-4822   888-878-7827
Processor of dried foods including citrus, rice, grain, milk and cheese; also, anti-caking agents, flavor extenders, soy milk and cheese cultures
President: Jim Baird
Mananager: Ed Price
Manager: Alvin Thompson
Plant Manager: Bill Armstrong
Estimated Sales:$ 3 - 5 Million
Number Employees: 20-49
Sq. footage: 80000
Parent Co: ADFAC
Type of Packaging: Private Label, Bulk

6862 IMC-Agrico Company
7250 La 44
Convent, LA 70723-2418   225-562-3501
Fax: 225-562-2797 www.mosaicco.com
Manufacturer of phosphoric acid
General Manager: Robert Dennis
Estimated Sales:$ 50 - 100 Million
Number Employees: 250-499
Parent Co: Freeport Minerals Company

6863 IMEX Enterprises
110 Gerstley Rd
Hatboro, PA 19040-1911   215-672-2887
Fax: 215-672-9552 info@imexEnterprises.com
www.imexenterprises.com
Pepper, salt, nutmeg mills and coffee grinders, SS cookware, SS gadgets, SS serving ware, copper molds
President: Norbert Hein
Estimated Sales:$10-20 Million
Number Employees: 20-49
Brands:
Ultima
Zassenhaus

6864 IMO Foods
9-10 Ragged Lake Boulevard
Halifax, NS B3S 1C2
Canada   902-450-5060
Fax: 902-450-5061 fancyfoods@yahoo.com
www.websight.ns.ca/imo
Processor and exporter of canned fish including herring, mackerel, sardines, skinless/boneless salmon and herring roe; manufacturer of aluminum cans, lids, etc
President: Sidney Hughes
Executive VP/General Manager: Phillip Le Blanc
Director Marketing: David Jollimore
Number Employees: 100-249
Parent Co: IMO Foods
Type of Packaging: Consumer, Food Service, Private Label
Other Locations:
Brands:
Golden Treasure
Kersen
West Island

6865 IMS Food Service
1 Corporate Dr # 136
Shelton, CT 06484-6208   203-929-2254
Fax: 203-926-0916 800-235-7072
Processor of fine specialty teas including bags and loose
President: Arnie D'Angelo
VP: Tom O'Hara
Estimated Sales:$ 5 - 10 Million
Number Employees: 20-49
Parent Co: Bigelow Tea
Type of Packaging: Consumer, Food Service

6866 INCA Kola Golden Kola
17 James Street
Bloomfield, NJ 07003-3656   973-680-9700
Fax: 973-680-9833 rincakola@aol.com
www.incakola-usa.com
Processor and exporter of soft drinks
President: Roldofo Salas
VP Marketing: Randall Berman
Estimated Sales:$2.5-5 Million
Number Employees: 5-9

Type of Packaging: Consumer, Food Service, Private Label
Brands:
Golden Kola
Inca Kola

6867 IOE Atlanta
P.O.Box 267
Galena, MD 21635-0267   410-755-6300
Fax: 410-755-6367
Shellfish, sushi
Manager: Denise Ford
Chairman: Charles Cully Jr.
CFO: Denise For
Number Employees: 10-19

6868 ISE Farms
P.O.Box 267
Galena, MD 21635-0267   410-755-6300
Fax: 410-755-6367
Processor of fresh eggs
Manager: Denise Ford
President: Hikonobu Ise
CFO: Denise Ford
Estimated Sales:$100-500 Million
Number Employees: 10-19
Type of Packaging: Consumer, Food Service

6869 ISE Newberry
P.O.Box 758
Newberry, SC 29108-0758   803-276-5803
Fax: 803-276-4468 isenby@mindspring.com
www.iseamerica.com
Processor and exporter of eggs
VP: Gregg Clanton
Sales Manager: Kathy Price
Operations VP: Doug Wicker
Production Manager: Jerry Thomas
Plant Manager: Ned Kesler
Estimated Sales:$100-500 Million
Number Employees: 100-249
Parent Co: Ise America
Type of Packaging: Consumer, Food Service, Private Label, Bulk
Brands:
NEWBERRY
SOUTHERN BREAKFAST

6870 ISF Trading
P.O.Box 772
Portland, ME 04104-0772   207-879-1575
Fax: 207-761-5877 isfco@aol.com
www.seaurchinmaine.com
Manufacturer of Fresh Sea Urchin Roe, Live Sea Urchin, Dry Sea Urchin Shell, Live Lobster, Live Rock Crab, Live Whelk, Fresh Atlantic Salmon, Frozen Salmon Roe, Fresh Marine Shrimp, Fresh Pine Tree Mushroom.
Founder: Atchan Tamaki
Office Manager: Lan Gao
Estimated Sales:$ 50 - 100 Million
Number Employees: 10-19

6871 ISG-Avne Packaging Services
PO Box 2415
New York, NY 10021-0057   718-716-7600
Fax: 718-294-8416 800-722-2863
aven@avne.com www.avne.com
Contract packager of candy, cookies, premiums, coupons, etc
President: Daniel Solomon
VP Sales: Ralph Noveck
Estimated Sales:$20-50 Million
Number Employees: 250-499
Sq. footage: 100000

6872 ITW Dynatec
31 Volunteer Dr
Hendersonville, TN 37075-3156   615-824-3634
Fax: 615-264-5248 dynatec@itwdynatec.com
www.itwdynatec.com
President: Zent Myer
CFO: Doug Betew
CFO: Doug Detew
R & D: Marie McLain
Number Employees: 100-249

6873 IVC American Vitamin
500 Halls Mill Rd
Freehold, NJ 07728-8811   732-308-3000
Fax: 732-761-2878 800-666-8482
www.invernessmedical.com

Processor and exporter of vitamin supplements, herbal products and antioxidants
Manager: Barb McCleer
Number Employees: 250-499
Type of Packaging: Consumer

6874 Ians Natural Foods
176 Shirley Ave
Revere, MA 02151-3257   781-284-1999
Fax: 781-284-6888 info@iansnaturalfoods.com
www.iansnaturalfoods.com
Only all natural, antibiotic and hormone free line of beef, poultry and specialty french fry prepared foods in a retail packaged format. Allergen Free fish stick and chicken nuggets, funfoods, appetizers, breakfast, desserts, friesand entrees.
Manager: Terrence Dalton
VP Marketing: Jeff Canner

6875 (HQ)Iberia Sugar Cooperative
PO Box 11108
New Iberia, LA 70562-1108   337-367-9991
Fax: 337-365-0030 iberiasugar@aol.com
www.iberiasugar.com
Manufacturer of raw cane sugar and blackstrap molasses
President: Ronald Gonsoulin
Estimated Sales:$23 Million
Number Employees: 65
Sq. footage: 90000
Type of Packaging: Bulk

6876 Icco Cheese Company
1 Olympic Dr
Orangeburg, NY 10962-2514   845-398-9800
Fax: 845-398-1669 johna@iccocheese.com
www.iccocheese.com
Processor, importer and exporter of grated parmesan cheese in shaker canisters and glass jar containers; processor and exporter of bread crumbs
President: Joseph Angiolillo
Vice President: John Angiolillo
Estimated Sales:$10-15 Million
Number Employees: 50-99
Type of Packaging: Consumer, Food Service, Private Label, Bulk
Brands:
America's Choice
American Beauty
Berkley & Jensen
D'Agostino
Dominick's
Food Club
Giant
Icco Brand
Luigi Vitelli
Pastene
PathMark
Price Chopper
Reggano
Ronzoni
San Giorgio
Shop Rite
Splendido
Weis

6877 Ice Cream & Yogurt Club
1580 High Ridge Rd
Boynton Beach, FL 33426-8724   561-731-3331
Fax: 561-731-0311 info@icecreamclub.com
www.icecreamclub.com
Processor of ice cream, yogurt, ice cream cones, toppings and syrups; also, soft serve machines available
Co-President: Marie Lawson
CEO: Richard Draper
*Estimated Sales:*D
Number Employees: 20-49
Type of Packaging: Consumer, Food Service, Private Label, Bulk

6878 Ice Cream Specialties
P.O.Box 19766
St Louis, MO 63144-0166   314-962-3935
Fax: 314-962-1990 www.northstarfrozentreats.com
Processor of ice cream including novelties, bars, cups and pops
Marketing Intern: Chris McQueen
Plant Manager: Mary Luebbert
Estimated Sales:$50-100 Million
Number Employees: 100-249
Sq. footage: 250000
Parent Co: Prairie Farms Dairy
Type of Packaging: Consumer

6879 Ice Cream Specialties
P.O.Box 679
Lafayette, IN 47902-0679   765-474-2989
Fax: 765-474-6150 cotegolf@dwi.com
Processor of novelty ice cream including cones,
sandwiches and cups
President: Robert Theissen
CEO: Roger Capps
Sales: Tom Gueltzow
Production: John Fitz Simons
Plant Manager: Robert Thiessen
Estimated Sales: $20-50 Million
Number Employees: 100-249
Parent Co: Prairie Farms Dairy
Type of Packaging: Consumer

6880 Ice House
PO Box 430133
Big Pine Key, FL 33043-0133   305-872-1215
Owner: R Lucas

6881 Ice Land Corporation
5777 Baum Blvd
Pittsburgh, PA 15206-3745   412-441-9512
Fax: 412-441-9517 catchup@bellatlantic.net
Processor and exporter of plain and kosher frozen
pizza; also, Italian specialties including pasta
President: Daniel Paskoff
COO: Tonald Paskoff
Estimated Sales: $2.5-5 Million
Number Employees: 5-9
Type of Packaging: Consumer, Food Service, Pri-
vate Label, Bulk
Brands:
Cholov Yisrael
Tambellini

**6882 Icelandic Milk and
SkyrCorporation**
135 W 26th Street
2nd Floor
New York, NY 10001   212-966-6950
Fax: 646-536-8159 info@skyr.com
www.skyr.com
icelandic-style yogurt
CEO: Vicky Hilmarsson
Number Employees: 4

6883 Icelandic USA
190 Enterprise Dr
Newport News, VA 23603-1368   757-820-4000
Fax: 757-888-6250 http://www.icelandic.com/
Manufacturer, importer and exporter of frozen fish
including catfish, cod, haddock, pollock, whiting,
salmon, tilapia and flounder: precooked, breaded
and unbreaded, batter-fry and fish-in-batter portions,
IQF loins, tails and cakesnuggets, sticks and
portions
President/CEO: Evar Agnarsson
Executive Vice President: Daniel Murphy
VP Finance/Administration: Michael Thome
VP Supply Chain: Rick Barnhardt
VP Foodservice Distribution/Services: Robert
Mizek
VP Marketing: Tom Sherman
VP Human Resources: Christine Searles
VP Manufacturing: Steve Bloodgood
Estimated Sales: $25-49.9 Million
Number Employees: 250-499
Sq. footage: 170000
Parent Co: Icelandic Group HF
Type of Packaging: Consumer, Food Service, Pri-
vate Label
Other Locations:
Icelandic Processing Plant
Cambridge MD
Icelandic Processing Plant
Newport News VA
Brands:
ICELANDIC
SAMBAND

6884 (HQ)Icicle Seafoods
P.O.Box 79003
Seattle, WA 98119-7903   206-282-0988
Fax: 206-282-7222
customerservice@icicleseafoods.com
www.icicleseafoods.com

Manufacturer and exporter of fresh and frozen cod,
pollock, halibut, sablefish, herring, herring roe,
salmon, salmon roe, crabs, and surimi based prod-
ucts
President/CEO: Don Giles
Sr Executive Vice President, Asia: Larry Hill
National Sales Manager: Rick Speed
National Fresh Sales Manager: Mark Callaghan
Director Canned Sales: John Boynton
Estimated Sales: $100+ Million
Number Employees: 500-999
Type of Packaging: Consumer, Food Service, Pri-
vate Label, Bulk

6885 Icy Bird
1151 Jim Hennessee Road
Sparta, TN 38583-1115   931-738-3557
Processor of citrus juices and frozen juice bars in-
cluding grape, cherry/apple and orange
President: William Norvell
Number Employees: 1-4
Parent Co: M&B Products

6886 Idaho Beverages
2108 1st Ave N
Lewiston, ID 83501-1699   208-743-6535
Fax: 208-746-2273
Beverages
President: Gary Parsio
Estimated Sales: $5-10 Million
Number Employees: 10-19

6887 Idaho Candy Company
412 S 8th St
Boise, ID 83702-7105   208-342-5505
Fax: 208-384-5310 800-898-6986
info@idahospud.com www.idahospud.com
Processor of vending, boxed and bagged candy in-
cluding bars, butter toffee, mints, marshmallows,
hard, jelly beans, brittles, chocolate, Valentine,
glazed nuts, etc
Chairman: John Wagers
President: Dave Wagers
Estimated Sales: $10-20 Million
Number Employees: 20-49
Sq. footage: 28000
Type of Packaging: Consumer, Food Service, Bulk
Brands:
IDAHO SPUD
OLD FAITHFUL
OWYHEE

6888 Idaho Fresh-Pak/IdahoanFoods
P.O.Box 130
Lewisville, ID 83431-0130   208-754-4686
Fax: 208-754-8188 800-635-6100
ifp.talk@idahoan.com www.idahoan.com
Manufacturer of dehydrated potato products such as;
instant mashed potatoes, hash browns, scalloped, au
gratin as well as potato ingredients like flakes,
shreds and slices
President: Ryan Clement
CFO: Rodney Roberts
CEO: Gordon Lewis
VP Sales: Todd Clement
Plant Engineer: Todd Scott
Estimated Sales: $74.5 Million
Number Employees: 250-499
Type of Packaging: Food Service, Private Label
Brands:
IDAHOAN

6889 Idaho Milk Products
2249 S. Tiger Drive
Jerome, ID 83338   208-644-2882
Fax: 208-644-2899 www.idahomilkproducts.com
Supplier of milk cream derivatives, milk protein
concentrate and milk permeate used in the cheese,
yogurt and dairy food industries.

6890 Idaho Pacific Corporation
P.O.Box 478
Ririe, ID 83443-0478   208-538-6971
Fax: 208-538-5082 800-238-5503
ipc@idahopacific.com www.idahopacific.com

Manufacturer and exporter of dehydrated potato
flakes, granules, agglomerates, and flour.
CEO: Dick Nickel
CFO: Baden Burt
Executive VP/COO: Wally Browning
R&D: Jennifer Weekes
Quality Control: Jennifer Weekes
VP/Sales & Marketing: Jon Schodde
VP/Operations: Todd Sutton
Plant Manager: Steve McLean
Purchasing: Brian Hart
Estimated Sales: $40-50 Million
Number Employees: 100-249
Parent Co: AgraWest Foods
Type of Packaging: Food Service, Private Label,
Bulk
Brands:
Idaho-Pacific

6891 Idaho Supreme Potatoes
P.O.Box 246
Firth, ID 83236-0246   208-346-6841
Fax: 208-346-4104 info@idahosupreme.com
www.idahosupreme.com
Supplier of slices, diced, and shredded potatoes.
President/General Manager: Wade Chapman
CFO: Steve Prescott
VP: Art Polson
Estimated Sales: $ 37.60 Million
Number Employees: 250-499
Sq. footage: 100000
Type of Packaging: Consumer, Private Label
Brands:
Idaho Supreme

6892 Idaho Trout Company
P.O.Box 72
Buhl, ID 83316-0072   208-543-6444
Fax: 208-543-8476 866-878-7688
rainbowtrout@idahotrout.com
www.idahotrout.com
Processor and exporter of rainbow and golden trout
Manager: Harold Johnson
Vice President: Gregory Kaslo
Sales/Shipping: Janie Higgins
General Manager: Harold Johnson
Estimated Sales: $10-25 Million
Number Employees: 50-99
Type of Packaging: Food Service, Private Label,
Bulk
Brands:
Cold River
Idaho's Best
Rainbow Springs

6893 Idaho-Frank Associates
391 Taylor Blvd # 180
Pleasant Hill, CA 94523-2282   925-609-8458
Fax: 925-609-9318 info@idahofrank.com
www.idahofrank.com
Dehydrated potato granules, flakes, slices, dices,
frozen dices and flour
President: Mark Lyons
Estimated Sales: $5-10 Million
Number Employees: 1-4
Type of Packaging: Food Service, Private Label,
Bulk

6894 Idahoan
P.O.Box 130
Lewisville, ID 83431-0130   208-754-4686
Fax: 208-754-8188 800-635-6100
ifp.talk@idahoan.com www.idahoan.com
Processor of dehydrated mashed potatoes
President/CEO: Gale Clement
Controller: Rod Roberts
CEO: Gordon Lewis
Research & Development: Dena Shatila
Quality Control: Cal McCombes
Marketing Director: Drew Facer
Public Relations: Drew Forcer
COO: Norman Hart
Plant Manager: Gene Christiansen
Estimated Sales: $ 50 - 100 Million
Number Employees: 250-499
Type of Packaging: Consumer, Food Service
Brands:
Idahoan
Loaded Baked
Mashed Potatoes
Roasted Garlic

6895 (HQ)Idahoan Foods
529 N 3500 East
Lewisville, ID 83431-5035   208-754-4686
       Fax: 208-754-0094 800-635-6100
                              www.idahoan.com
Manufacturer of dehydrated potato products for retail and foodservice, as well as potato ingredients, and frozen fruits and vegetables. J.R. Simplot markets and distributes Idaho Fresh-Pack potato products under the Idahoan brand.
    Chairman: J R Simplot
    President: Bill Whitacre
    Sales Manager: Val Lambert
Estimated Sales:$98.7 Million
Number Employees: 361
Type of Packaging: Consumer, Food Service, Bulk
Other Locations:
    Simplot Potato Processing
    Aberdeen ID
    Simplot Potato Processing
    Caldwell ID
    Simplot Potato Processing
    Grand Forks ND
    Simplot Potato Processing
    Moses Lake WA
    Simplot Potato Processing
    Nampa ID
    Simplot Potato Processing
    Othello WA
    Simplot Vegetable Processing
    Pasco WA
    Simplot Vegetable Processing
    West Memphis AK
    Simplot Fertilizer Plant
    Brandon, Manitoba
    Simplot Fertilizer Plant
    Helm CA
    Simplot Fertilizer Plant
    Lathrop CA
    Simplot Fertilizer Plant
    Pocatello ID
    Simplot Fertilizer Plant
    Portland OR

6896 Ideal American
PO Box 70
Holland, IN 47541-0070   812-424-3351
                      Fax: 812-423-9809
Processor of milk including whole fat-free, low and reduced-fat and chocolate
    Plant Manager: Tim McAllister
Estimated Sales:$20-50 Million
Number Employees: 50-99
Parent Co: Prairie Farms Dairy
Type of Packaging: Consumer, Food Service

6897 Ideal Dairy
490 S Main St
Richfield, UT 84701-2873   435-896-5061
       Fax: 435-896-8360 www.idealdairy.com
Processor of dairy products including milk, cream and ice cream - also retail business
    Owner: Kristie Sorsen
    Co-Owner: Kristie Sorensen
Estimated Sales:$20-50 Million
Number Employees: 20-49
Sq. footage: 2500
Type of Packaging: Consumer, Food Service

6898 Ideal Distributing Company
23800 7th Place W
Bothell, WA 98021-8508   425-488-6121
                      Fax: 425-488-8159
Tea, coffee
    Principal: John Erdman
    Co-Ownr: Cathy Erdman

6899 Ideal Snacks
89 Mill St
Liberty, NY 12754-2038   845-292-7000
       Fax: 845-292-3100 www.idealsnacks.com
Snacks
    President: Zeke Alenick
    Director of Operations: LJ Goldstock
Estimated Sales:$ 3 - 5 Million
Number Employees: 100-249

6900 Iguana Tom's
44477 Parkmeadow Dr
Fremont, CA 94539-6581   704-847-5923
       Fax: 704-847-4857 888-827-2572
                  iguanatom@carolina.rr.com
                          www.iguanatoms.com
    Co-Owner: Ellen Siegler
    President: Tom Siegler

Brands:
    Iguana Tom's

6901 Il Gelato
2451 46th Street
Astoria, NY 11103-1007   718-937-3033
                      Fax: 718-786-5543
Processor of baked goods, gelato and individual desserts
    President: Dimitri Pauli
*Estimated Sales:*Less than $500,000
Number Employees: 10-19

6902 Il Giardino Bakery
2859 N Harlem Ave
Chicago, IL 60707-1638   773-889-2388
       Fax: 773-889-5990 www.ilgiardinobakery.com
Processor of cannoli shells, mini pasteries, butter cookies and cakes
    Owner: Maria Ventrella
*Estimated Sales:*Less than $500,000
Number Employees: 10-19
Type of Packaging: Consumer
Brands:
    Giardino

6903 Il Tiramisu
64 E Merrick Road
Suite G1
Valley Stream, NY 11580-5946   516-599-1010
                      Fax: 516-599-6540
Exporter and processor of Italian desserts including chocolate mousse, tiramisu, gelato, tartufo, tortoni and spumoni; importer of Italian cakes and pasta
    Owner/President: Aldo Antonoacci
Estimated Sales:$2.5-5 Million
Number Employees: 1-4

6904 Il Vicino Pizzeria
136 E 2nd St
Salida, CO 81201-2115   719-539-5219
                      Fax: 719-539-2918
Processor of beer, ale and stout
    Owner: Kathie Younghans
Estimated Sales:$1-2.5 Million
Number Employees: 20-49
Parent Co: Il Vicino Holding Company
Type of Packaging: Consumer, Food Service
Brands:
    Web Mountain

6905 Illes Seasonings & Flavors
2200 Luna Rd # 120
Carrollton, TX 75006-6559   214-689-1300
       Fax: 214-689-1381 800-683-4553
                  customerserv@illesseasonings.com
                          www.illesfood.com
Manufacturer and exporter of sauce bases, seasonings, flavors and worcestershire products
    Chairman/CEO: Rick Illes
    VP Administration: Linda Mullin
Estimated Sales:$20-50 Million
Number Employees: 1-4
Type of Packaging: Consumer, Food Service, Private Label

6906 Iltaco Food Products
1378 W Hubbard Street
Chicago, IL 60622-6453
              Fax: 312-421-0774 800-244-8935
                          www.iltaco.com
Processor of frozen pizza, pizza puffs, pasta with marinara sauce, burritos, tamales and taco puffs
    Owner/Vice President: Rebecca Shabaz
Estimated Sales:$10-20 Million
Number Employees: 50-99
Type of Packaging: Consumer, Food Service, Private Label
Brands:
    Iltaco

6907 Imaex Trading
5405 Buford Highway
Suite 350
Norcross, GA 30071-3982   770-825-0848
                      Fax: 770-825-0166
    President: Seng Angkawijana

6908 Image Development
PO Box 150028
San Rafael, CA 94915-0028   415-626-0485
                      Fax: 415-255-7597
*Estimated Sales:*Less than $500,000
Number Employees: 1-4

6909 Imagine Foods
58 S Service Rd
Melville, NY 11747-2344   631-730-2200
       Fax: 631-730-2550 800-333-6339
questions@imagine.com www.imaginefoods.com
Processor of kosher beverages, drink mixes, ice cream and frozen novelties
    President: Robert Nissenbaum
    CFO: Joe Marshall
    CEO: Irwin Simon
    Marketing Director: Ellen Weiser
    VP Sales: Ron Pieper
Estimated Sales:$5-9.9 Million
Number Employees: 100-249
Type of Packaging: Consumer, Food Service
Brands:
    IMAGINE NATURAL
    POWER DREAM
    RICE DREAM SUPREME
    SOY DREAM

6910 Imaginings 3
6401 W Gross Point Rd
Niles, IL 60714-4507   847-647-1370
       Fax: 847-647-0633 www.flixcandy.com
    President: Sidney Diamond
    VP Sales: Jeff Grossman
Estimated Sales:$ 5 - 10 Million
Number Employees: 20-49

6911 Immaculate Baking Company
PO Box 299
Flat Rock, NC 27831   828-696-1655
       Fax: 828-696-1663 info@immaculatebaking.com
                          www.immaculatebaking.com
cookies
    President/Owner: Scott Blackwell

6912 Immaculate Consumption
PO Box 299
Flat Rock, NC 28731-0299   828-696-1655
       Fax: 828-696-1663 888-826-6567
info@immaculateconsumption.com
              www.immamculatecomsumption.com
Processor of bakes goods, cookies, scones, biscotti, and mojos
    President/CEO: Scott Blackwell
    Vice President: Caroline Blackwell
    VP Sales: Don Porter
*Estimated Sales:*Under $1 Million
Number Employees: 10-19
Number of Brands: 1
Number of Products: 29
Sq. footage: 10000
Type of Packaging: Consumer, Food Service, Private Label
Brands:
    IMMACULATE CONSUMPTION

6913 Immediate Gratification
1840 41st Avenue
Suite 102-199
Capitola, CA 95010-2513   831-457-9602
                      Fax: 831-457-9602
    Owner: Andra Rudolph
*Estimated Sales:*Under $500,000
Number Employees: 1-4

6914 ImmuDyne
7453 Empire Dr # 300
Florence, KY 41042-2944   859-746-3909
       Fax: 859-746-8772 888-246-6839
sales@immudyne.com www.immudyne.com
Processor and exporter of beta glucan dietary natural supplements - helping our wold eat better, live healthier and look younger
    VP: Alfred Munoz
    Investor: Mark McLaughlin
Number Employees: 1-4
Type of Packaging: Consumer, Food Service, Bulk

6915 Impact Confections
888 Garden of the Gods Rd #200
Colorado Springs, CO 80907-9436 719-278-5400
       Fax: 719-268-6197 877-770-7677
info@impactconfections.com
                          www.impactconfections.com
Processor of confectionery products including gourmet, seasonal, custom made and novelty lollypops
    Founder/President: Brad Baker
    Director Marketing: Steve Moskowitz

Estimated Sales: $25-49.9 Million
Number Employees: 20-49
Number of Products: 40
Type of Packaging: Consumer
Brands:
    ALIEN POP
    ALIEN POPPIN' POPS
    CAROUSEL POP
    COLOR BLASTER
    GLOW POP
    HAPPY HEART LOLLIPOPS
    HOPPIN' POPS
    LILLIDAY POPS
    LOLLIPOP PAINT SHOP
    POP-A-BEAR
    SOCCER POPS

6916 Impact Nutrition
1155 S Havana Street
Suite 11-392
Aurora, CO 80012-4019   720-374-7111
    www.impactnutrition.com
Contract packager of vitamins, minerals, herbal and
nutritional supplements, sports nutrition products,
capsules, tablets and powders - true innovator in the
field of nutritional supplements and sports nutrition
    President: Patrick Frazier
    General Manager: Julene Frazier
Estimated Sales: $10-20 Million
Number Employees: 20-49
Sq. footage: 15000

6917 Imperia Foods
234 Saint Nicholas Avenue
S Plainfield, NJ 07080-1810   908-756-7333
    Fax: 908-756-6076 800-526-7333
General grocery
    President: Ira Weissman
Estimated Sales: $2.5-5 Million
Number Employees: 50-99
Sq. footage: 37
Type of Packaging: Private Label

6918 (HQ)Imperial Flavors Beverage Company
6300 W Douglas Ave
Milwaukee, WI 53218-1551   414-536-7788
    Fax: 414-536-7730 info@imperialflavors.com
    www.imperialflavors.com
Processor of bag-in-box juice and soda concentrates
including soda water; also, juice products for
soft-serve machines
    President: Jack Pettigrew
Estimated Sales: $10-20 Million
Number Employees: 10-19
Sq. footage: 12000
Type of Packaging: Consumer, Food Service, Private Label, Bulk
Brands:
    CAPTAIN JACK'S
    FRUIT N' JUICE
    JUICE PLUS
    JUICY ORANGE
    MILWAUKEE SELTZER COMPANY
    TROPICS

6919 Imperial Food Supply
4800 North St
Baton Rouge, LA 70806-3497   225-924-4222
    Fax: 225-924-3362
Owner/President: Michael Divincenti, Jr.

6920 Imperial Foods
5014 39th St
Long Island City, NY 11104-4508 718-784-3400
    Fax: 718-361-7993 www.imperialfoods.com
Processor and wholesaler/distributor of dairy prod-
ucts including Armenian string, Naboulsi, Akawi
and Syrian cheeses, yogurt and kefir spread
    General Manager: Charles Mkhitarian
Estimated Sales: $2.5-5 Million
Number Employees: 10-19
Sq. footage: 4000
Brands:
    GREENFIELD
    VICTOR'S

6921 Imperial Nougat Company
P.O.Box 2851
Santa Fe Springs, CA 90670-0851 562-693-8423
    Fax: 562-945-8852
Candy
    President: Al Maghsoudi

Estimated Sales: $2.5-5 Million
Number Employees: 5-9

6922 Imperial Salmon House
1632 Franklin Street
Vancouver, BC V5L 1P4
Canada   604-251-1114
    Fax: 604-251-3177 smokedsalmon@sprint.ca
Processor and exporter of smoked salmon
    President: Robert Blair
Number Employees: 5-9
Type of Packaging: Consumer, Food Service, Bulk

6923 Imperial Sensus
PO Box 9
Sugar Land, TX 77487-0009   281-490-9522
    Fax: 281-490-9615 pgalvin@imperialsensus.com
    www.isullc.com
Processor, importer and exporter of inulin, a natural
extract from chicory uses include as a texture modi-
fier, flavor masking and gut health benefits
    VP Sales/Marketing: Sally Brain
    VP of Technical Affairs: Bryan Tungland
Parent Co: Imperial Sugar Company
Type of Packaging: Food Service, Bulk
Brands:
    Frutafit
    Nutralin

6924 Imperial Sugar
433 Davies St
Ludlow, KY 41016-1462   859-261-1920
    Fax: 859-261-1869
Producer of sugar
    President/CEO: Robert Peiser
    VP Operations: Brian Harrison
    Plant Manager: Mike Kaminsky
Estimated Sales: $5-10 Million
Number Employees: 5-9
Parent Co: Imperial Holly Corporation
Type of Packaging: Consumer, Food Service, Private Label, Bulk

6925 Imperial Sugar Company
PO Box 9
Sugar Land, TX 77487-0009   281-491-9181
    Fax: 281-490-9530 800-727-8427
    Consumers@ImperialSugar.com
    www.imperialsugar.com
Sugar
    President/CEO: John Sheptor
    SVP/CFO: H P Mechler
    SVP/Secretary/General Counsel: Louis Bolognini
    VP Manufacturing/Engineering: Ralph Clements
Estimated Sales: J
Number Employees: 500-999
Brands:
    Dixie Crystals
    Imperial Sugar

6926 Imperial Sugar Company
8016 Highway 90A
Sugar Land, TX 77478   281-491-9181
    Fax: 281-490-9530 800-727-8427
    www.imperialsugar.com
Processor and marketer of refined sugar to grocery
customers, food manufacturers and food service dis-
tributors.
    President/CEO: John Sheptor
    Senior VP/CFO: H P Mechlar
    SVP/Secretary/General Counsel: Louis Bolognini
    VP Manufacturing/Engineering: Ralph Clements
Estimated Sales: $522 Million
Number Employees: 726
Sq. footage: 1000000
Type of Packaging: Consumer, Food Service, Private Label, Bulk
Other Locations:
    Cane Operations
    Gramercy LA
    Cane Operations
    Savannah GA
Brands:
    DIXIE CRYSTAL®
    HOLLY®
    IMPERIAL PURE SUGAR CANE®

6927 Imprint Plus
21320 Gordon Way
Unit 260
Richmond, BC V6W 1J8
Canada   604-278-7147
    Fax: 604-278-7149 800-563-2464
sales@imprintplus.com www.imprintplus.com

Imprint Plus is a designer, manufacturer and worldwide distributor of name badges, name badge systems, and accessories
    President: Ellen Flanders
    CEO: Marla Kott
    Marketing Director: Chuck Beebe
    Sales Director: Phil Coles
    Operations Manager: Kristin MacMillian
Number Employees: 65

6928 Impromtu Gourmet
141 Wooster Street
Apt 7d
New York, NY 10012-3199   212-475-4640
    Fax: 212-475-5794
ychi@impromptugourmet.com
www.impromptugourmet.com
Fresh gourmet foods
    Founder/CEO: Max Polaner

6929 Imsco Technology
40 Bayfield Drive
North Andover, MA 01845-6016 978-689-2080
    Fax: 978-689-2585
    Chairman/CEO: Timothy Keating
Estimated Sales: $500,000-$1 Million
Number Employees: 5-9

6930 Imus Ranch Foods
PO Box 282
Holtsville, NY 11742-0282
    Fax: 631-758-8360 888-284-4687
    service@imusranchfoods.com
    www.imusranchfoods.com
Processor of tortilla chips, salsa and coffee
    President: Fred Imus
Estimated Sales: $1-2.5 Million
Number Employees: 10-19
Type of Packaging: Consumer, Food Service
Brands:
    FRED IMUS SOUTHWEST
    FRED IMUS TURQUOISE
    IMUS BROTHERS COFFEE

6931 In Ranchito
PO Box 717
Zillah, WA 98953-0717   509-829-5880
    Fax: 509-829-6300
Processor of food, beverage and tobacco.
    Owner: Geoff Solomon
Estimated Sales: $5-10 Million
Number Employees: 20-49

6932 Inca Kola/Golden Kola
215 E 64th Street
New York, NY 10021-6662   212-688-1895
    Fax: 212-688-1895 973-688-0970
Processor of beverages.
    President: Rodolfo Salas
Estimated Sales: $5-10 Million appx.
Number Employees: 1-4

6933 Increda-Meal
PO Box 30
Cato, NY 13033-0030   315-626-2111
    Fax: 315-626-2777
Nutrition bars
Estimated Sales: $10-20 Million
Number Employees: 50-99

6934 Incredible Cheesecake Company
3161 Adams Ave
San Diego, CA 92116-1638   619-563-9722
    Fax: 619-563-1022 www.incrediblecheesecake.net
Processor of frozen cheesecakes
    Co-Owner/President: Michelle Satren
    Co-Owner/VP: Scott Satren
Estimated Sales: $1-2.5 Million
Number Employees: 10-19
Sq. footage: 3500

6935 (HQ)Indel Food Products
11415 Cedar Oak Dr
El Paso, TX 79936-6009   915-590-5914
    Fax: 915-590-5913 800-472-0159
    customerservice@indelfoods.com
    www.indelfoods.com
Red, green, mixed and roasted peppers and pimen-
tos, jalapenos, green chiles, cherry and banana pep-
pers. (Food service, private label, bulk)
    Owner: Gustavo Deandar
Estimated Sales: $2.5-5 Million
Number Employees: 1-4
Sq. footage: 20000

Type of Packaging: Food Service, Private Label, Bulk
Other Locations:
Indel Food Products
Delicias, Chihuahua
Brands:
DEL SOL

6936 Indel Food Products
11415 Cedar Oak Dr
El Paso, TX 79936-6009   915-590-5914
Fax: 915-590-5913 800-472-0159
indl@dzn.com www.indeofoods.com
Processor and exporter of canned hot, jalapeno nacho, whole jalapeno peppers:also, green and red salsa
President: Gustavo Deandar
Estimated Sales: $2.5-5 Million
Number Employees: 1-4
Parent Co: Agroindustrias Deandar
Type of Packaging: Consumer, Food Service, Private Label, Bulk
Brands:
DEL SOL

6937 Indena USA
811 1st Ave # 218
Seattle, WA 98104-1434   206-340-6140
Fax: 206-340-0863 greg@indenausa.com
www.indena.com
Processor of herbal extracts
President: Ezio Bombardelli
CEO: Dario Bonacorsi
VP: Greg Ris
VP Sales: Greg Ris
Estimated Sales: $1-2.5 Million
Number Employees: 1-4
Parent Co: Indena S.p.A.
Type of Packaging: Bulk

6938 Independent Bakers Association
1223 Potomac St NW
Washington, DC 20007-3212   202-333-8190
Fax: 202-337-3809
npyle@independentbaker.com
www.independentbaker.org
Baked goods
President: Robert Pyle
VP Sales: Nicholas Pyle

6939 Independent Dairy
126 N Telegraph Rd
Monroe, MI 48162-3299   734-241-6016
Fax: 734-241-1251
Ice cream
President: Michael Cheney
Estimated Sales: $5-9.9 Million
Number Employees: 50-99

6940 (HQ)Independent Food Processors Company
311 N 4th St # 204
Yakima, WA 98901-2467   509-457-6487
Fax: 509-457-7983 800-476-5398
glewis@indfoodpro.com
Canner and exporter of apples, apple sauce, cherries and pears
Manager: Jeff Goshorn
CEO: Jeff Goshorn
Sales Manager: Gary Lewis
Plant Manager: Mike Trader
Estimated Sales: $ 5 - 10 Million
Number Employees: 10-19
Type of Packaging: Consumer, Food Service, Private Label
Other Locations:
Independent Food Processors C
Sunnyside WA

6941 Independent Food Processors
P.O.Box 357
Sunnyside, WA 98944-0357   509-837-3806
Fax: 509-837-3573
Manufacturer and exporter of canned fruit including apples, pears and cherries
President: Peter Plath
Plant Manager: Mike Trader
Estimated Sales: $100-500 Million
Number Employees: 500-999
Parent Co: Independent Food Processing
Type of Packaging: Private Label

6942 Independent French Manufacturers
20 W 20th Street
Suite 303
New York, NY 10011   212-229-1633
Fax: 212-898-9024 franck@ifm-usa.com
www.ifm-usa.com
cookies (butter, chocolate and fruit), mushrooms, truffles, wildberries, mustards, mayonnaises, sauces and salad dressings

6943 Independent Master Casing Company
904111 Dice Road
Santa Fe Springs, CA 90670   562-946-1913
Fax: 562-946-1913 800-635-9518
President: Manil Whig
Vice President: Frank Drozdowski
Estimated Sales: $2.5-5 Million
Number Employees: 10-19

6944 Independent Meat Company
P.O.Box Ee
Twin Falls, ID 83303-0028   208-733-0980
Fax: 208-734-9702 info@salmoncreekfarms.com
www.independentmeat.com
Processor and packer of meat and sausage
President/CEO: Patrick Florence
Media Contact: Jeanne Bjorn
Estimated Sales: $20-50 Million
Number Employees: 250-499
Type of Packaging: Consumer

6945 Independent Packers Corporation
Suite C102
Seattle, WA 98119   206-285-6000
Fax: 206-285-9236
Custom processor and packer of fresh and frozen seafood including crab, cod, halibut, salmon and tuna
President/CEO: Bill Manning
Estimated Sales: $3-5 Million
Number Employees: 100-249
Sq. footage: 30000
Type of Packaging: Food Service, Private Label

6946 Indi-Bel
P.O.Box 878
Indianola, MS 38751-0878   662-887-1226
Fax: 662-887-5630
President: Lester Myers
Estimated Sales: $10-20 Million
Number Employees: 20-49

6947 India Tea Importers
8551 Loch Lomond Dr
Pico Rivera, CA 90660-2509   562-801-9600
Fax: 323-722-6368 tealand@aol.com
www.buybulktea.com
Tea
Owner: DeVan Shah
Estimated Sales: $2.5-5 Million
Number Employees: 1-4

6948 India Tree Gourmet Spices & Specialties
1421 Elliott Avenue W
Seattle, WA 98119   206-270-0293
Fax: 206-282-0587 800-369-4848
india@indiatree.com www.indiatree.com
purveyor of sugar, spices and other fine food products from around the world
President/Owner: Gretchen Gorren
Number Employees: 10

6949 (HQ)India's Rasoa
25 N Euclid Ave
St Louis, MO 63108-1445   314-727-1414
Fax: 314-727-8331 harinder@rasoi.com
www.rasoi.com
Indian specialties
President: Harinder Singh
Estimated Sales: Less than $500,000
Number Employees: 5-9

6950 Indian Bay Frozen Foods
PO Box 160
Centreville, NL A0G 4P0
Canada   709-678-2844
Fax: 709-678-2447 ackermans@ibffinc.com
www.ibffinc.com

Processor and exporter of blueberries, lingonberries, jams and pie fillings; also, fish including capelin
President: Calvin Ackerman
Controller: David Collins
Number Employees: 20-49
Sq. footage: 10000
Type of Packaging: Consumer, Private Label, Bulk
Brands:
ACKERMAN'S WILD

6951 Indian Foods Company
7575 Golden Valley Rd # 135
Minneapolis, MN 55427-4570   763-593-3000
Fax: 763-593-3003 kmehta@gotindia.com
www.sccnet.com
Processor of Indian naam pizzas
Owner: Erik Phorsell
Estimated Sales: $300,000-500,000
Number Employees: 1-4
Brands:
ASHOKA

6952 Indian Harvest
P.O.Box 910
Colusa, CA 95932-0910   530-458-8512
Fax: 530-458-8344 800-294-2433
Processor and exporter of rice, grain and bean products, soup and chili mixes, seasonings and pasta; importer of rice
Plant Manager: Don Kuiken
Estimated Sales: $5-10 Million
Number Employees: 20-49
Type of Packaging: Food Service, Private Label

6953 Indian Harvest Specialitifoods
P.O.Box 428
Bemidji, MN 56619-0428   218-751-8500
Fax: 218-751-8519 800-346-7032
www.indianharvest.com
Processor of heirloom beans and specialty rice blends and grains including red, wheat, wild, brown, white and basmati
Manager: Jenni Hillman
VP: John DeVos
Sales Manager: Joe Bofferding
Corporate Chef: Michael Holleman
Estimated Sales: $20-50 Million
Number Employees: 20-49
Type of Packaging: Consumer, Food Service, Private Label, Bulk
Brands:
GUEST CHEF
INDIAN HARVEST

6954 Indian Hollow Farms
15321 Us Hwy 14
Richland Center, WI 53581-5715   608-536-3499
800-236-3944
Processor of apples and apple cider
Owner: John Symons
Estimated Sales: $1-2.5 Million
Number Employees: 5-9
Sq. footage: 100000
Type of Packaging: Consumer, Food Service, Private Label, Bulk
Brands:
COUNTRY ROAD
IDDIAN HOLLOW

6955 Indian Ridge Shrimp Company
P.O.Box 177
Chauvin, LA 70344-0177   985-594-5869
Fax: 985-594-2168 594-5869(985)
www.triple-t-shrimp.com
Processor, importer and exporter of frozen shrimp
Owner: Andrew Blanchard
COO: Richard Fakier
Sales Manager: Daniel Babin
Estimated Sales: $2.5-5 Million
Number Employees: 50-99
Sq. footage: 25000
Type of Packaging: Consumer, Food Service
Brands:
PEARL

6956 Indian River Foods
3798 Selvitz Road
Fort Pierce, FL 34981-4723   561-462-2222
Fax: 561-462-2224

Processor and exporter of frozen orange and grape-fruit juices and concentrates; importer of orange, grape and apple concentrates
Sales Manager: Doug Burlan
Manager (Materials): Bruce Gowan
Plant Manager: Larry Gray
Number Employees: 100-249
Sq. footage: 150000
Parent Co: Becker Holding Corporation
Type of Packaging: Food Service, Private Label, Bulk

6957 Indian Rock Produce
P.O.Box 428
Perkasie, PA 18944-0428   215-536-9600
Fax: 215-529-9448   800-882-0512
Grower of organically grown vegetables and fruits including asparagus, beets, broccoli, cabbage, carrots, cauliflower, corn, eggplant, lettuce, onions, squash, tomatoes, etc
Co-Owner: Lu Ann Buehrer
Co-Owner: Albert Buehrer
Sales Contact: Bill Neely
Estimated Sales:$50-100 Million
Number Employees: 5-9
Type of Packaging: Consumer, Food Service, Bulk

6958 Indian Rock Vineyards
1154 Pennsylvania Gulch Rd
Murphys, CA 95247-9589   209-728-8514
www.indianrockvineyards.com
Wines
President: Boyd Thompson
Estimated Sales:$ 3 - 5 Million
Number Employees: 5-9

6959 Indian Springs Fresh Poultry
217 Hawkeye Ct
Columbus, OH 43235-1489   614-443-7473
Processor of poultry
President: Lindy O Brien
Office Manager: Dick Neblette
Estimated Sales:$500,000-$1 Million
Number Employees: 1-4

6960 Indian Springs Vineyards
P.O.Box 688
Browns Valley, CA 95918-0688   530-477-2237
Fax: 530-274-5954   800-375-9311
isv@gv.net   www.gv.net
Wines
President: David McCord
Production Manager: Julie Holmes
Estimated Sales:$10-20 Million
Number Employees: 20-49
Type of Packaging: Private Label

6961 Indian Valley Meats
Hc 52 Box 8809
Indian, AK 99540-9604   907-653-7511
Fax: 907-653-7694   ivm@alaska.net
www.indianvalleymeats.com
Processor of poultry, venison and fish including halibut and salmon; exporter of smoked fish and meats including sausage
President: Douglas Drum
Plant Manager: Renia Drum
Estimated Sales:$2.5-5 Million
Number Employees: 10-19
Sq. footage: 17000

6962 Indiana Beverage 7UP
1 N Bridge Street
Gary, IN 46404-1073   219-882-3100
Fax: 219-886-6811
Beverages
CEO: Jim Turner
Vice President: Tom Graham
Energy Manager: Jim Turner

6963 Indiana Botanic Gardens
3401 W 37th Ave
Hobart, IN 46342-1751   219-947-4040
Fax: 219-947-4148   www.botanicchoice.com
Processor of herbal products and vitamins
President: Tim Cleland
Estimated Sales:$10-100 Million
Number Employees: 100-249

6964 Indiana Grain Company
1700 Beason St
Baltimore, MD 21230-5347   410-685-6410
Fax: 410-685-0233   www.silopoint.com

Grain and flour
President: Patrick Turner
Number Employees: 20-49
Type of Packaging: Bulk

6965 Indiana Sugar
745 McClintock Dr
Burr Ridge, IL 60527-0880   630-986-9150
Fax: 630-986-1030
Processor of sugar
President: John Yonover
Executive VP: John Yonover
Estimated Sales:$5-10 Million
Number Employees: 10-19

6966 Indianola Pecan House
1013 Highway 82 E
Indianola, MA 38751   662-887-5420
Fax: 662-887-2906   800-541-6252
pecan@pecanhouse.com   www.pecanhouse.com
President/Owner: Wheeler Timbs III
Estimated Sales:$5.1 Million
Number Employees: 28

6967 Indianola Pecan House
P.O.Box 367
Indianola, MS 38751-0367   662-887-5420
Fax: 662-887-2906   800-541-6252
pecan@pecanhouse.com   www.pecanhouse.com
Processor of gourmet pecans, cookies and candies
President: Timmy Timbs
Vice-President: Wheeler Timbs
Estimated Sales:$2.5-5 Million
Number Employees: 5-9
Number of Brands: 1
Number of Products: 30

6968 Indigo Coffee Roasters
660 Riverside Dr # 1
Florence, MA 01062-2763   413-586-4537
Fax: 413-586-0019   800-447-5450
info@indigocoffee.com   www.indigocoffee.com
Artisan roaster of specialty coffees, organic coffee, fair trade coffee; custom roasting available
President: Lourdes Tallet
Number Employees: 5-9
Sq. footage: 1000
Type of Packaging: Consumer, Food Service, Private Label, Bulk
Brands:
INDIGO

6969 Indo Med
38 Millers Ln
New Hyde Park, NY 11040-4939   516-437-8390
Fax: 516-488-5117
Owner: Dan Wesler
Estimated Sales:$ 5 - 10 Million
Number Employees: 20-49

6970 Indochina Tea Company
8569 Wonderland Ave
Los Angeles, CA 90046-1463   323-650-8020
Fax: 323-650-8022
Indochina tea
President/CEO: Gabriella Karsch
*Estimated Sales:*Under $500,000
Number Employees: 1-4

6971 Industria Lechera de Puerto Rico
PO Box 360454
San Juan, PR 00936-0454   787-765-7545
Fax: 787-758-1126
Cheese and milk
President: Luis Fullana
Marketing Director: Jos, Passalacqua
Estimated Sales:$10-100 Million
Number Employees: 20-49
Type of Packaging: Private Label, Bulk

6972 Industrial ConstructionServices Inc
215 15th St S
St James, MN 56081-2438   507-375-4633
Fax: 507-375-7513   800-795-8315
cbrown@icsmn.com   www.icsmn.com

Design and construction of contamination controlled environments, services of which include biocontainment laboratories, clean rooms, antimicrobial atmospheres for pharmaceutical, biomedical, and nutraceutical development, and sanitaryenvironments for food and beverage processing and manufacturing.
President: Clint Brown
Sales Representative: Josh Brown

6973 Industrial Products
24 N Clinton St
Defiance, OH 43512-1807   419-782-5010
Fax: 419-783-4319   800-251-3033
diehl@bright.net   www.diehlinc.com
Evaporated milk, nondairy coffee creamer, whipped toppings, powdered shortening and dairy products
President: John Diehl
Estimated Sales:$50-100 Million
Number Employees: 100-249

6974 Ineeka Inc
2023 W Carroll Ave
Suite 263
Chicago, IL 60612   312-661-1550
Fax: 312-277-2555   sg@ineeka.co
www.ineeka.com
organic teas
Number Employees: 5

6975 Infraready Products Ltd.
850 C 56th Street E
Saskatoon, SK S7K 5Y8
Canada   306-242-4950
Fax: 306-242-4213   info@sk.sympatico.ca
www.infrareadyproducts.com
President: Glenn Bachmann

6976 Ingleby Farms
123 N Main Street
Dublin, PA 18917-2107   215-249-1118
Fax: 215-249-3722   877-728-7277
carin@peppersauces.com
www.peppersauces.com
Chilies, hot sauce and specialty foods
President: Carin Froehlich
Vice President: Dietrich Froehlich
Plant Manager: Hans Froehlich
Estimated Sales:$1-2.5 Million
Number Employees: 1-4
Type of Packaging: Private Label

6977 Ingleside Plantation Winery
5872 Leedstown Rd
Colonial Beach, VA 22443-5424   804-224-8687
Fax: 804-224-8573
Wine
Owner: Douglas Flemer
Director Sales: Doug Weaver
Estimated Sales:$20-50 Million
Number Employees: 10-19

6978 Ingomar Packing Company
P.O.Box 1448
Los Banos, CA 93635-1448   209-826-9494
Fax: 209-854-6292   staff@ingomarpacking.com
www.ingomarpacking.com
Processor of diced tomatoes and tomato paste
Managing Partner: Greg Pruett
Controller: Wayne Mosley
Quality Control: John Palombi
Marketing Director: William Cahill Jr
Director Operations: Timothy Durham
General Manager: Jim Murphy
Estimated Sales:$20-50 Million
Number Employees: 20-49
Type of Packaging: Bulk

6979 Ingredient Innovations
313 NW North Shore Dr
Kansas City, MO 64151-1455   816-587-1426
Fax: 816-587-4167
Roxanne@IngredientInnovations.com
www.ingredientinnovations.com
Processor of natural dairy, chemical and fruit flavors, cultures, probiotics and soy food ingredients
President: Roxanne Armstrong
Estimated Sales:$ 1 - 3 Million
Number Employees: 1-4

6980 Ingredients Corporationof America
676 Huron Ave
Memphis, TN 38107-1511   901-525-6660
        Fax: 901-525-4425   888-242-2669
kpeterson@memphi.net www.barzi.com
Manufacturer and packer of dried beans and spice
    President: Damon Arney
Estimated Sales: $1 Million
Number Employees: 1-4
Sq. footage: 5500
Brands:
    Barzi

6981 Ingredients Corporationof America
676 Huron Ave
Memphis, TN 38107-1511   901-525-6660
        Fax: 901-525-4425 ingred@mem.net
                www.barzi.com
Seasoning manufacturer; importer and processor of
spices, dehydrated vegetables, seeds, herbs, oils,
salt, soy products, oleos, etc
    Owner: Damon Arney
    Manager: Kathryn Peterson
Estimated Sales: $2.5-5 Million
Number Employees: 20-49
Sq. footage: 25000
Type of Packaging: Consumer, Food Service, Pri-
    vate Label, Bulk
Brands:
    Memphi
    Ole Yazoo

6982 Ingredients Unlimited
PO Box 3146
Bell Gardens, CA 90202-3146   562-806-7560
        Fax: 562-806-7562 info@ingunl.com
                www.ingunl.com
    President: Kathryn Hicks
Estimated Sales: $ 5 - 10 Million
Number Employees: 20-49
Type of Packaging: Private Label

6983 Ingredients, Inc.
1130 W Lake Cook Rd # 320
Buffalo Grove, IL 60089-1976   847-419-9595
    Fax: 847-419-9547   sales@ingredientsinc.com
                www.ingredientsinc.com
Supplies specialty ingredients to the food/beverage,
nutraceutical and pharmaceutical industries in North
America.
    President: James Stewart
Estimated Sales: $ 5-10 Million
Number Employees: 5-9
Parent Co: J. Stewart & Company
Type of Packaging: Bulk

6984 Ingretec
1500 Lehman St
Lebanon, PA 17046-3337   717-273-1360
    Fax: 717-273-1364 ingretec@poonline.com
Food ingredients, cheese flavors, cheese products,
spice blends, savory flavors, and dairy flavors
    President: Philippe Jallon
    Quality Control: Annabel Ries
    Operations Manager: Valerie Jalloy
Estimated Sales: $5 Million
Number Employees: 5-9
Number of Products: 50
Sq. footage: 30000
Type of Packaging: Food Service, Bulk

6985 Inko's White Iced Tea
205 Jackson St
Englewood, NJ 07631
                866-747-4656
                www.healthywhitetea.com
flavored white iced tea
    President/Owner: Andy Schamisso

6986 Inland Empire Foods
5425 Wilson St
Riverside, CA 92509-2434   951-682-8222
        Fax: 951-682-6275   888-452-3267
            janelle@inlandempirefoods.com
Precooked vegetables: beans, peas and lentils
    President: Mark Sterner
Estimated Sales: $20-50 Million
Number Employees: 20-49

6987 Inland Fresh Seafood Corporation
122 Menlo Drive
Atlanta, GA 30318   404-350-5850
                Fax: 404-350-5870
Seafood
    President/CEO: Joel Knox
    Purchasing Manager: Bill Demond
Number Employees: 100-249

6988 Inland Fruit Company
P.O.Box 158
Wapato, WA 98951-0158   509-877-2126
    Fax: 509-877-2012 gfjos@nwinfo.net
                www.inlandfruit.com
Apples, cherries, pears, apricots, nectarines,
peaches, plums, prunes as well as organic apples and
pears.
    President: Susan Putman
    IS Manager: Dale Panattoni
Estimated Sales: $20-50 Million
Number Employees: 100-249
Brands:
    Carriage Trade
    Extra Treat
    My Treat
    Royal Treat
    Tasty Treat

6989 Inland Northwest Dairies
P.O.Box 7310
Spokane, WA 99207-0310   509-489-8600
        Fax: 509-482-3402 www.dairygold.com
Processor of dairy products including buttermilk,
half and half, milk, eggnog and sour cream
    President: Jerrald Barsten
    Plant Manager: Bruce Senn
Estimated Sales: $20-50 Million
Number Employees: 50-99
Type of Packaging: Consumer, Food Service, Pri-
    vate Label
Brands:
    Albertson
    Broadview Dairy
    Janet Leigh

6990 Inland Products
PO Box 430
Carthage, MO 64836-0430   417-358-4046
                Fax: 417-358-7196
Animal and marine fats and oils
    Vice President: Jack Sweeny
Estimated Sales: $10-20 Million
Number Employees: 20-49

6991 Inland Seafood
P.O.Box 172
Milbridge, ME 04658-0172   207-546-7591
        Fax: 207-546-3334 www.inlandseafood.com
Seafood
    Manager: Billy Thinney
    VP: Bill Demmond
Estimated Sales: $ 1 - 3 Million
Number Employees: 10-19

6992 Inlet Salmon
PO Box 2146
Bothell, WA 98041-2146   425-487-0495
                Fax: 425-487-0527
Processor, importer and exporter of frozen halibut,
salmon and black cod
    President: Mark Powell
    Sales Manager: Jim Gonzalez
Estimated Sales: $500,000-$1 Million
Number Employees: 5-9
Parent Co: Inlet Fisheries
Type of Packaging: Food Service, Bulk
Other Locations:
    Inlet Salmon
    Kenai AK

6993 Inmark
PO Box 43309
Atlanta, GA 30336-0309   404-267-2020
                Fax: 404-267-2021
Packaging supplies, plastic food containers
    President: Brian Murphy
    Vice President: James Curlee
Estimated Sales: $ 20 - 50 Million
Number Employees: 50-99

6994 Inn Foods
310 Walker St
Watsonville, CA 95076-4585   831-724-2026
        Fax: 831-728-5708 www.innfoods.com
Processor of frozen fruits, vegetables and orange
juice
    President: Jack Randle
    CFO: Fred Haas
    Quality Control: Ralph Ramirez
    Sales Director: Arnie Hummel
    Production Manager: Matt Haas
Estimated Sales: $50-100 Million
Number Employees: 100-249
Type of Packaging: Consumer, Food Service
Brands:
    Freidel's Finest
    Gold Premium
    The Inn
    Valley Pokt

6995 Inn Maid Food
PO Box 1972
Lenox, MA 01240-4972   413-637-2732
        Fax: 413-499-3839 inmaidfood@aol.com
Processor of natural foods including multi-grain ce-
real, granola, sunflower seeds, trail mix, multi-grain
pancake and waffle mix and sugar-free fruit syrups
    President: Jane Peters
Estimated Sales: $1-2.5 Million appx.
Number Employees: 1-4
Sq. footage: 2000
Type of Packaging: Consumer, Food Service, Pri-
    vate Label, Bulk
Brands:
    Berrylicious
    Colonial Jacks
    New Granola

6996 Inniskillin Wines
RR 1
Niagara-On-The-Lake, ON L0S 1J0
Canada   905-468-2187
        Fax: 905-468-5355   888-466-4754
inniskil@inniskillin.com   www.inniskillin.com
Processor, exporter and importer of wines including
ice, red, white, dessert and limited editions
    President: Donald Ziraldo
    VP: Karl Kaiser
Number Employees: 20-49
Sq. footage: 16000
Type of Packaging: Consumer, Food Service
Brands:
    Inniskillin

6997 Innovative Fishery Products
25 Henry Street
Clarks Harbour, NS B0W 1P0
Canada   902-837-5163
                Fax: 902-837-5165
Processor and exporter of fresh, frozen and salted
clams, scallops, groundfish and lobster
    President: Mark Blinn
    VP: Doug Bertman
Number Employees: 20-49
Sq. footage: 16000
Type of Packaging: Bulk

6998 Innovative Food Corporation
6171 Atlantic Drive
Mississauga, ON L5T 1N7
Canada   905-670-8878
                Fax: 905-670-4642
Processor and exporter of salad dressings, mayon-
naise, peanut butter and margarine
    Purchasing Director: Lynn Jeffries
Type of Packaging: Consumer, Food Service, Pri-
    vate Label, Bulk

6999 Innovative Food Solutions LLC
4516 Kenny Road
Suite 320
Columbus, OH 43220-3711   614-326-1421
        Fax: 614-326-1443   800-884-3314
            jliebrec@columbus.rr.com
                www.innovativefoodsolutions.com
Innovative Food Solutions LLC is a food industry
R&D consulting firm ready to assist you to quickly
launch new food products and manufacturing processes, new food industry ingredients, perform technical troubleshooting and produceprototype samples
for trade shows and market research studies. Areas
of experience include organic, natural and
nutraceutical/functional food products, including
aseptic and retort liquids, and spray dried powders.
    President: Jeff Liebrecht
    R&D: Jeff Liebrecht

7000 Innovative Health Products
6950 Bryan Dairy Rd
Largo, FL 33777-1608   727-544-8866
          Fax: 727-544-4386 800-654-2347
victoriat@onlineihp.com www.onlineihp.com
Innovative Health Products, Inc. is a turn-key, contract manufacturer of cosmeceutical, nutraceutical and pharmaceutical products. IHP produces tablets, capsules, powders, liquids, creams, lotions and gels. Our services range fromformulation to fulfillment.
    President: Dr Sekharam Kotha
Estimated Sales:$ 5 - 10 Million
Number Employees: 5-9
Sq. footage: 100000

7001 Innovative Health Products
6950 Bryan Dairy Rd
Largo, FL 33777-1608   727-544-8866
          Fax: 727-544-4386 800-654-2347
victoriat@onlineihp.com www.onlineihp.com
Contract manufacturer of nutraceuticals, cosmeceuticals, and pharmacuticals. Produces tablets, capsules, powders, liquids, creams, lotions and gels.
    President: Kotha Sekharam
    CEO: Mihir Taneja
    Falcone: Carol Dore
    R&D: Colen Lanke
    Quality Control: Jose Vasquez
    VP Sales/Marketing: Victoria Travers
    Operations: Steve Kovalik
    Production/Plant Manager: Steve Kovalik
    Plant Manager: Liz Gifford
    Purchasing: Terry Crocket
Estimated Sales:$ 20 - 50 Million
Number Employees: 100
Sq. footage: 100000
Parent Co: Geopharma
Type of Packaging: Private Label, Bulk

7002 Innovative Ingredients
11620 Reisterstown Road
830
Reisterstown, MD 21136-3702   888-403-2907
          Fax: 435-655-8276
randy@innovativeingredients.com
www.innovativeingredients.com
Processor of dairy ingredients for prepared foods, dairy products, baked goods, beverages, dips, sports drinks and snacks. Custom formulations-color and flavor solutions
Brands:
    California Sunshine
    Doc's
    Yonkers

7003 Inny's Wholesale
1068 Puuwai St
Honolulu, HI 96819-4330   808-841-3172
          Fax: 808-841-1410
    President: Stanley Lum
Estimated Sales:$ 3 - 5 Million
Number Employees: 1-4

7004 (HQ)Inovatech USA
8400 St-Laurent Boulevard
Montreal, QC H2P 2M6
Canada   360-527-1919
          Fax: 360-527-1881 888-388-3447
info@inovatech.com www.inovatech.com
Produces whey protein isolates, concentrates and modified milk ingredients in our leading edge ulta-filtration facilities; produces high quality egg white proteins; and continually works to identified and refine new technology to meetthe needs of our customers
    President: Philip Vanderpol
    General Manager Bio-Products: Stephen Smith
    Research & Development: Jerry Middleton
    Quality Control: Dr. Peter Bertram
    Operations Manager: Mike Vanderpol
Estimated Sales:$ 5 - 10 Million
Number Employees: 10-19
Type of Packaging: Bulk
Brands:
    ALPHAPRO 34
    INPRO 80
    INPRO 90

7005 Inshore Fisheries
PO Box 118
Middle West Pubnico, NS B0W 2M0
Canada   902-762-2522
          Fax: 902-762-3464 inshore@atcon.com

Processor and exporter of fresh and frozen catfish, pollack, perch, haddock, cod, flounder and ground fish
    President: Claude d'Entremont
Number Employees: 50-99
Type of Packaging: Consumer, Food Service

7006 Instant Products of America
835 S Mapleton Street
Columbus, IN 47201-7359   812-372-9100
          Fax: 812-372-9132
Processor, importer and exporter of instant beverages, dry mixes, syrups, toppings and ready-to-drink beverages
    President: Joe Pavelich
    Quality Control: Linda Justus
    Sales Director: Timothy Scheidler
    General Manager: Shari Plimpton
    Plant Manager: Mike Brannan
Estimated Sales:$10-24.9 Million
Number Employees: 50-99
Sq. footage: 35000
Parent Co: Kruger Gmbh & Company
Type of Packaging: Consumer, Food Service, Private Label, Bulk
Brands:
    Impress
    Kruger

7007 Instantwhip: Arizona
2517 E Chambers Street
Phoenix, AZ 85040-3640   800-544-9447
          Fax: 614-488-0307 800-544-9447
          www.instantwhip.com
Processor and exporter of nondairy portion packaged creamers, half and half, ready-to-whip dessert toppings and sour dressing
    VP: Kyle Tillman
    VP Operations: Douglas Smith
Estimated Sales:$10-20 Million
Number Employees: 20-49
Sq. footage: 22000
Parent Co: Instantwhip Foods
Type of Packaging: Food Service, Private Label, Bulk

7008 Instantwhip: Chicago
1535 N Cicero Ave
Chicago, IL 60651-1690   773-235-5588
          Fax: 773-235-0578 800-933-2500
info@instantwhip.com www.instantwhip.com
Distributor of dairy and nondairy toppings, dairy products, egss, baked goods and desserts.
    President: Jim Ring
Estimated Sales:$10-20 Million
Number Employees: 10-19
Parent Co: Instant Whip
Type of Packaging: Private Label, Bulk
Brands:
    Instantwhip

7009 Instantwhip: Florida
3803 E Columbus Dr
Tampa, FL 33605-3220   813-621-3233
          Fax: 813-626-1516 www.instantwhipflorida.com
Processor and exporter of dairy products including dessert toppings; also, salad dressings
    President: William Tiller
Estimated Sales:$10-20 Million
Number Employees: 50-99
Parent Co: Tiller Foods
Type of Packaging: Consumer

7010 Instantwhip: Texas
1031 Hot Wells Blvd
San Antonio, TX 78223-2797   210-333-2771
          Fax: 210-333-0717 800-544-9447
lindalh@flash.net www.instantwhipfoods.com
Processor of dairy and nondairy coffee creamer, sour and whipped cream, salad dressing, etc.; processor and exporter of bakery toppings
    President: Lindal Hardwick
    Vice President: Lindal Hardwick
    Quality Control: Mylissa Rios
    Plant Manager: Dene Smith
Estimated Sales:$20-50 Million
Number Employees: 20-49
Sq. footage: 30000
Parent Co: Instantwhip Foods
Type of Packaging: Food Service, Private Label, Bulk

7011 Institut Rosell/Lallemand
8480 St Laurent Boulevard
Montreal, QC H2P 2M6
Canada   514-858-4627
          Fax: 514-383-4493 human@lallemand.com
          www.lallemand.com
Well researched, high quality yeast - cultures are fermented before being high density concentrated and granulated. Yeasts are then fluid bed-dried and bacteria are freeze-dried. Certified yeast for many of the wine countries aroundthe world.
    Sales Director: Aldo Fuoco

7012 Integrated Health
3535 Lomita Boulevard
Suite A
Torrance, CA 90505-5028   310-675-1164
          Fax: 310-675-4187 800-799-3232
Manufacturer and exporter of amino acids, vitamin/mineral formulations and specialty health supplement products
    National Sales Manager: Willy Coumans
    Operations Manager: Steve Gibson
Estimated Sales:$5-10 Million
Number Employees: 5-9
Sq. footage: 20000
Parent Co: Tyson Foods
Brands:
    Accuvite
    Amino Form
    Amino Health
    Aminolife
    Aminopro
    Aminotrate
    Freeform
    Geo Chrome
    Geo Mins
    Geo Zinc
    Mins Plus
    Pyridox
    San Tox
    Two-Day
    Viva-Lift
    Zap Tox

7013 (HQ)Integrated Therapeutics
3 Monroe Pkwy
Lake Oswego, OR 97035-1486   503-697-8697
          Fax: 503-582-0467 800-648-4755
          info@tyler-inz.com
Manufacturer, exporter and wholesaler/distributor of dietary supplements and medical nutritionals; also, specialty nutritional products for patients with end stage renal disease
    President: Steve Liberman
    General Manager: Reagen Miles
    Technical Director: Corey Resnick
Number Employees: 250-499
Sq. footage: 44000
Other Locations:
    Vitaline Formulas
    Oakdale CA
Brands:
    Biotin Forte
    Carni-Vite
    Phos-Ex
    Total Formula

7014 Inter-American Products
1015 Vine St
Cincinnati, OH 45202-1108   513-762-4900
          Fax: 513-762-4565 800-645-2233
          edi@inter-americanfoods.com
          www.interamericanproducts.com
Supplier of gelatins and puddings, nuts, powdered beverages, natural processed cheese, tea, extracts, peanut butter, coffee, soy sauce, steak and Worcestershire sauce, coconut, syrup, salad dressing, mayonnaise, preserves, jellies andbeverages.
    Senior Marketing Manager: Jeff Pahl
    Technical Director: Terry Shamblin
*Estimated Sales:*Under $500,000
Number Employees: 5-9
Parent Co: Kroger Company

7015 Inter-Continental Imports Company
149 Louis St
Newington, CT 06111-4517   860-665-1101
          Fax: 860-665-1085 800-424-4422
gitalia@grande-italia.com www.icaffe.com

Coffee roaster
President/CEO: Vincent Saccuzzo
Office Manager: Lucy Pluchino
Purchasing Manager: Vincent Saccuzzo
Estimated Sales: $5-10 Million
Number Employees: 5-9
Type of Packaging: Private Label
Brands:
   Grande Italia
   Miscela Bar
   Miscela Napoli

7016   Inter-Ocean Seafood Traders
1200 Industrial Rd # 12
San Carlos, CA 94070-4129   650-508-0691
                     Fax: 650-595-1261
Seafood
President: John Chen
Treasurer: Jeanne Chen
Vice President: Grace Chai
Estimated Sales: $25,000,000
Number Employees: 5-9

7017   Inter-State Cider & Vinegar Company
101 N Warwick Ave
Baltimore, MD 21223-1497   410-947-1529
    Fax: 410-947-7585 www.interstatevinegar.com
Worcestershire & steak sauce, sour beef mix; bottled
& herbal vinegar
President: Jeanne Lanciotti
VP: Richard Lanciotti, Jr.
Estimated Sales: $1-2.5 Million
Number Employees: 5-9
Sq. footage: 15000
Type of Packaging: Consumer, Food Service, Private Label, Bulk
Brands:
   Casa Vina
   Log Cabin

7018   InterHealth
5451 Industrial Way
Benicia, CA 94510-1010   707-751-2800
    Fax: 707-751-2801   800-783-4636
                info@interhealthusa.com
                www.interhealthusa.com
Processor, importer and exporter of specialty nutritional and botanical ingredients including niacin bound chromium, zinc monomethionine, grape seed and green tea extracts and garcinia cambogia
President: William Ceroy
CEO: Paul Dijkstra
Vice President: Debasis Bagchi
Marketing Cordinator: Cindy Reilly
VP Sales/Marketing: Michael Hogge
Operations Manager: Massood Moshrefi
Estimated Sales: $10 - 20 Million
Number Employees: 20-49
Type of Packaging: Private Label
Brands:
   ALLER-7
   CHROMEMATE
   L-OPTIZINC
   OPTIBERRY
   PROTYKIN
   SUPER CITRIMAX
   UC II
   ZMA

7019   Interbake Foods
29310 S Jackson Road
Canby, OR 97013-8512   503-651-3003
                     Fax: 503-651-3004
Processor and exporter of crackers and cookies
Sales Manager (Western Region): Shawn Roten
Sales Manager (Northwest Region): Benny Henderson
Parent Co: Interbake Foods
Type of Packaging: Consumer

7020   Interbake Foods
1122 Lincoln St
Green Bay, WI 54303-3630   920-497-7669
    Fax: 888-497-1893   804-576-3459
                     www.norse.com
Ice cream cones
Plant Manager: Steven Krotz
Estimated Sales: $5 - 10 Million
Number Employees: 5-9
Type of Packaging: Private Label

7021   Interbake Foods Corporate Office
2821 Emerywood Pkwy # 210
Richmond, VA 23294-3726   804-755-7107
    Fax: 804-755-7173   inquiries@interbake.com
                     www.interbake.com
Manufacturer of crackers and cookies
President/CEO: Ray Baxter
SVP/CFO: Donald Niemeyer
Number Employees: 1,000-4,999
Type of Packaging: Consumer, Food Service, Private Label, Bulk

7022   Intercorp Excelle Foods
1880 Ormont Drive
Toronto, ON M9L 2V4
Canada   416-744-2124
    Fax: 416-746-4369   888-476-2124
Processor of refrigerated and shelf stable sauces, marinades, dips and dressings
Co-Chairman/President: Renee Unger
Co-Chairman/CEO: Arnold Unger
CFO/COO/Secretary/Director: Fred Burke
Number Employees: 100
Sq. footage: 85000
Type of Packaging: Consumer, Food Service
Brands:
   EXCELLE
   RENEE'S GOURMET

7023   Interfrost
349 W Commercial St
East Rochester, NY 14445-2407   585-381-0320
    Fax: 585-381-1052 www.interfrost.com
Processor and importer of frozen fruits and vegetables
VP/General Manager: Thomas Crandall
Estimated Sales: $5-10 Million
Number Employees: 5-9
Parent Co: Cobi Foods

7024   Intergum North America
1365 Westgate Center Dr
Winston Salem, NC 27103-2980   336-760-5420
                     Fax: 336-760-5434

7025   Interhealth Nutraceuticals
5451 Industrial Way
Benicia, CA 94510-1010   707-751-2800
    Fax: 707-751-2801   800-783-4636
                info@interhealthusa.com
                www.interhealthusa.com
Nutraceuticals
President: William Ceroy
Executive VP: Gary Troxel
Purchasing: Joe Mies
Estimated Sales: $10 - 20 Million
Number Employees: 20-49

7026   (HQ)Interior Alaska Fish Processors
P.O.Box 81522
Fairbanks, AK 99708-1522   907-455-9469
    Fax: 907-456-3889   800-478-3885
                     www.alaskasbest.com
Salmon and salmon products
Owner: Kade Mendelowitz
Vice President: Marie Mitchell
Estimated Sales: $2.5-5 Million
Number Employees: 10-19
Type of Packaging: Private Label, Bulk

7027   Intermex Products
1375 Avenue S # 300
Grand Prairie, TX 75050-1293   972-660-2979
    Fax: 972-660-5941   j.lacy@intermexproducts.com
                     www.intermexproducts.com
Mexican dishes and sauces
President: David Hagli
CFO: Susen Hurt
CEO: Carlos Lorenzo
Plant Manager: Gonzalo Branch
Estimated Sales: $10-20 Million
Number Employees: 20-49

7028   Intermountain Canola Cargill
2300 N Yellowstone Hwy
Idaho Falls, ID 83401-1662   208-522-4113
    Fax: 208-522-0794   800-822-6652
Processor of specialty canola oils
President: Erwin Kelm
Finance Executive: Joann Wages
General Manager: Ernie Unger
Manager: R Covington
Estimated Sales: $10-20 Million
Number Employees: 10-19
Parent Co: Cargill Foods
Type of Packaging: Consumer, Food Service, Bulk

7029   International Bakers Services
1902 N Sheridan Street
South Bend, IN 46628-1592   574-287-7111
    Fax: 574-287-7161   800-345-7175
                ibsflavors@aol.com
                www.internationalbakers.com
Manufacturer of kosher certified flavors and flavor blends for the baking industry. Also manufacturers liquid and dry flavors, natural, and natural/artificial.
President/CEO: William Busse
Sales Contact: Christopher Lee
Estimated Sales: $10-20 Million
Number Employees: 20-49

7030   International Baking Company
5200 S Alameda St
Vernon, CA 90058-3457   323-583-9841
                     Fax: 323-588-3652
Processor of fresh bread, rolls and sweet goods
Owner/President: Simon Mani
VP: Dan Smith
Purchasing Director: Sam Abekian
Estimated Sales: $100+ Million
Number Employees: 250-499
Parent Co: Sara Lee Corporation
Type of Packaging: Consumer, Food Service, Private Label

7031   International Bar-B-Que
PO Box 5
Unionville, IN 47468-0005   812-988-6150
    Fax: 812-988-7039   ibbq12762@aol.com
Barbaque

7032   International Brownie
602 Middle Street
Weymouth, MA 02189-1130   781-340-1588
    Fax: 781-331-1900   800-230-1588
                info@internationalbrownie.com
                www.internationalbrownie.com
Processor of gourmet brownies including sugar-free; mail order available
President: Cindy Rice
Estimated Sales: Less than $500,000
Number Employees: 1-4
Sq. footage: 1500
Brands:
   INTERNATIONAL BROWNIE

7033   International Casein Corporation
111 Great Neck Rd
Great Neck, NY 11021-5402   516-466-4363
                     Fax: 516-466-4365
Processor and wholesaler/distributor of casein
Number Employees: 5-9

7034   (HQ)International Casing Group
4420 S Wolcott Avenue
Chicago, IL 60609-3159   773-376-9200
    Fax: 773-376-9292   800-825-5151
             sales@casings.com   www.casings.com
Processor, importer and exporter of natural beef, pork and lamb casings
Sales: Roberto Espinosa
Estimated Sales: $50 - 100 Million
Number Employees: 100-249
Sq. footage: 40000
Type of Packaging: Food Service
Other Locations:
   Tyrone GA
   Sante Fe Springs CA
   Montreal, Canada

7035   (HQ)International Casings Group
4420 S Wolcott Avenue
Chicago, IL 60609-3159   312-421-5234
    Fax: 773-376-9292   800-825-5151
    jgcreighton@casings.com   www.casings.com
Processor and exporter of natural sausage casings
President: Eric Svendsen
VP: Elliot Simon
Estimated Sales: $10-20 Million
Number Employees: 50-99
Type of Packaging: Food Service
Brands:
   NATURE'S BEST

7036 International Casings Group
12207 Los Nietos Rd # F
Santa Fe Springs, CA 90670-6137   562-946-2100
Fax: 562-946-1913   800-635-9518
www.casings.com
Processor, importer and exporter of natural sausage
casings including sheep, hog and beef
Manager: Peter Jimenez
Estimated Sales:$1-2.5 Million
Number Employees: 5-9
Sq. footage: 5200
Parent Co: International Casings Group
Brands:
REDI-2-STUF

7037 International Cheese Company
67 Mulock Avenue
Toronto, ON M6N 3C5
Canada   416-769-3547
Fax: 416-769-7153
Processor of Italian cheese
President: M Pelosi
Number Employees: 10-19
Sq. footage: 9999
Type of Packaging: Consumer, Food Service

7038 International Chemical
PO Box 188
Milltown, NJ 08850-0188   732-238-5160
Fax: 732-238-5970   800-914-2436
95263@msn.com   www.intl-chem.com
Processor, importer and exporter of acids including
ascorbic, citric, sorbic and tartaric; also, sodium ci-
trate, sodium ascorbate and vanillin
President: Jimmy Hsu
Number Employees: 20-49
Sq. footage: 50000
Type of Packaging: Private Label, Bulk
Brands:
ICI

7039 International Coconut Corporation
225 W Grand St
Elizabeth, NJ 07202-1205   908-289-1555
Fax: 908-289-1556
sales@internationalcoconut.com
www.internationalcoconut.com
Processor, wholesaler/distributor, importer and ex-
porter of coconut including sweetened, desiccated
and toasted
Owner: A Kaye
Vice President: Richard Kesselhaut
Estimated Sales:$2.5-5 Million
Number Employees: 5-9
Sq. footage: 11500
Type of Packaging: Consumer, Food Service, Pri-
vate Label, Bulk
Brands:
SNO-TOP

7040 International Coffee Corporation
300 Magazine St
New Orleans, LA 70130-2413   504-586-8700
Fax: 504-523-3301   intocof@worldnet.att.net
www.iccnola.com
Coffee traders and brokers
President: William Madary II
VP: Matthew Madary
Estimated Sales:$1-2.5 Million
Number Employees: 10-19

7041 International Cuisine
164 S Us Highway 17
East Palatka, FL 32131-4024   904-325-0002
Fax: 904-325-6600
Oriental frozen foods

7042 International Dehydrated Foods
P.O.Box 10347
Springfield, MO 65808-0347   417-881-7820
Fax: 417-881-7274   800-525-7435
customerservice@idf.com   www.idf.com
Processor and exporter of spray-dried meat and
poultry powders and fat and broth powders; also,
frozen and shelf stable chicken broth and liquid
chicken fat
President: Robert Bell
Technical Director: Marty Scabarozi
Public Relations: Ann Hollis
Purchasing Manager: Dennis Scholl
Estimated Sales:$20-50 Million
Number Employees: 5-9
Sq. footage: 85000

Type of Packaging: Bulk
Brands:
IDF

7043 International Dehydreated Foods
P.O.Box 10347
Springfield, MO 65808-0347   417-881-7820
Fax: 417-881-7274   800-641-6509
www.idf.com
Powdered chicken broth
Estimated Sales: $ 20 - 50 Million
Number Employees: 5-9
Type of Packaging: Food Service, Bulk

7044 International Delicacies
1485 Park Avenue
Emeryville, CA 94608-3559   510-428-9364
Fax: 510-428-2457 Intl_delicacies@msn.com
Olive oils, pasta, bastoncini, cookies, panettone,
pickles, balsamic vinegar, honey, infused oils, mus-
tard, dolma, dried figs, fruit preserves, artichokes
VP Sales/Marketing: Maxx Sherman
Brands:
AMIR
ANNA'S
AUDISIO & LORI
LOOZA
PAN DUCALE
RUBINO & VERO
VICENZI

7045 International Diverse Foods
189 Spence Ln
Nashville, TN 37210-2506   615-889-8345
Fax: 615-231-5983 www.diversefoods.com
General grocery
President: Philip Francis
CFO: Drew Nethery
Marketing: Connie Brown
Research Director: Rebecca Carothers
Estimated Sales:$10-100 Million
Number Employees: 250-499

7046 International Enterprises
PO Box 158
Herring Neck, NL A0G 2R0
Canada   709-628-7406
Fax: 709-628-7875
Processor and exporter of fresh cultivated mussels
President: Wayne Fudge
Number Employees: 5-9
Type of Packaging: Consumer, Food Service, Bulk

7047 International Equipment
163
Arecibo, PR 00612   787-879-3151
Fax: 787-879-1569   intequi@xsn.net
Processor of baked goods including bread, rolls and
pastries; wholesaler/distributor and importer of res-
taurant supplies including bakers' equipment and
supplies; serving the food service market
President: Juan Guzman
Number Employees: 20-49
Type of Packaging: Consumer, Food Service

7048 International Farmers Market
PO Box 81226
Chamblee, GA 30366-1226   770-455-1777
Fax: 770-451-7474
www.internationalfarmersmarket.com
Dairy, meats, seafood, general grocery items, poul-
try, blue crab, catfish, clams

7049 International Fiber Corporation
50 Bridge St
North Tonawanda, NY 14120-6895 716-693-4040
Fax: 716-693-3528   888-698-1936
info@ifcfiber.com   www.ifcfiber.com
Executive VP: Brian Finn
Executive VP: Jit Ang
CEO: Dan Muth
VP Industrial Sales: Steve Godin
Estimated Sales:$ 20 - 50 Million
Number Employees: 50-99
Brands:
Alpha-Cel
FloAm
Keycel
NutraFiber
QualFlo
SolkaFloc

7050 International Fiber Corporation
50 Bridge St
North Tonawanda, NY 14120-6895 716-693-4040
Fax: 716-693-3528   ifc@ifcfiber.com
www.ifcfiber.com
A leading manufacturer of dietry fiber.
President/CEO: Dan Muth
Executive VP: Mike Bailey
R&D: Jit Ang
Purchasing Manager: Steve Couladis
Number Employees: 50-99
Number of Brands: 10+
Type of Packaging: Bulk
Brands:
Justfiber

7051 (HQ)International Flavors &Fragrances
521 W 57th St
New York, NY 10019   212-765-5500
Fax: 212-708-7132 iff.information@iff.com
www.iff.com
Manufacturer of flavors and fragrances used in a
wide variety of consumer products, from fine fra-
grances to toiletries, to soaps, detergents, and other
household products, as well as food and beverage
products
Chairman/CEO: Doug Tough
EVP/CFO: Kevin Berryman
Marketing Director: Sharon Maes
VP Global Corporate Communications: Gail
Belmuth
EVP Global Operations: D Wayne Howard
Purchasing Director: Gladys Gabriel
Estimated Sales:$2.3 Billion
Number Employees: 5,400
Type of Packaging: Bulk

7052 International Flavors &Fragrances
P.O.Box 439
Dayton, NJ 08810-0439   732-329-4600
Fax: 732-274-6550   800-433-3528
iffusafragrances@iff.com   www.iff.com
Food flavorings, fragrances, ingredients
R & D: Clint Brooks
Chairman/CEO: Richard Goldstein
VP: Jim Dunsdon
Marketing Director: Sharon Maes
VP Global Corporate Communications: Gail
Belmuth
Purchasing Director: Glayds Gabriel
Estimated Sales: $ 100-500 Million
Number Employees: 250-499
Type of Packaging: Bulk

7053 International Food
N114w18937 Clinton Dr
Germantown, WI 53022-3009   262-251-9230
Fax: 414-255-8810   800-558-8696
pat.eckert@ifoodsolutions.com
www.ifoodsolutions.com
Seasonings
Estimated Sales:$20-50 Million
Number Employees: 100-249

7054 International Food Packers Corporation
7095 SW 47th Street
Miami, FL 33155-4653   305-669-1662
Fax: 305-669-1447
Processor, importer and exporter of canned corned
beef, frozen cooked beef and beef cuts; importer of
canned fish and rice
President: Richard Spradling
Estimated Sales:$2.5-5 Million
Number Employees: 5-9
Sq. footage: 6000

7055 International Food Products Corporation
PO Box 22106
Saint Louis, MO 63116-0106   314-776-2700
Fax: 314-776-4830   800-227-8427
Processor of salad dressings, sauces, syrups and con-
diments
President: Bill Holtgrieve
CEO: Fred Brown
Sales Manager: Ed Carle
Director Operations: Bob Bullock
COO: Clayton Brown
Warehouse Manager: Kirk Greer
VP Purchasing: John Hany

Estimated Sales: $10-100 Million
Number Employees: 50-99
Type of Packaging: Consumer, Food Service
Brands:
  IFP

7056 International Food Solutions
N114w18937 Clinton Dr
Germantown, WI 53022-3009   262-251-9230
       Fax: 630-983-8354 www.ifoodsolutions.com
Processor and exporter of flavors for sauces, season-
ings, bases and spices
    President: George Zabrycki
    Sales Manager: Carol Mayer
Estimated Sales: $20-50 Million
Number Employees: 100-249
Parent Co: Bestfoods

7057 International Food Technologies
PO Box 5555
Evansville, IN 47716-5555   812-853-9432
    Fax: 812-853-3157 ift@evansville.net
       www.internationalfoodtech.com
Processor and exporter of Powdered Dessert and
Beverage mixes including; ice cream mixes (hard
pack and soft serve), Low carbohydrate dessert
products, frozen yogurt, granita, cappuccino (hot
and cold), smoothie mixes, smoothieproteins, chai
and lemonade. Custom, private label, food service
    President: Joseph Greif
Number Employees: 10-19
Sq. footage: 10000
Type of Packaging: Food Service, Private Label,
  Bulk
Brands:
  CAPPUCCINO FREEZE
  JOE'S LOW-CARB
  POWER BOOSTS

7058 International Food Trade
Rural Route 6
Amherst, NS B4H 3Y4
Canada   902-667-3013
       Fax: 902-667-0350
Processor and exporter of IQF wild blueberries
    President: Chris Gaklis
Parent Co: International Food Trade
Brands:
  BLUE BOY
  CHRISTY CROPS

7059 International FoodcraftCorporation
1601 E Linden Ave
Linden, NJ 07036-1508   908-862-8810
    Fax: 908-862-8825 800-875-9393
sales@intlfoodcraft.com   www.intlfoodcraft.com
Manufacturer and exporter of anti-stick lubricants,
release agents and food color concentrates for the
food, confectionery, cosmetic and pharmaceutical
industries
    Owner: David Dukes
Estimated Sales: $5-10 Million
Number Employees: 10-19
Type of Packaging: Bulk
Brands:
  COLOREZE
  CONFECTO
  EEZ-OUT
  PANO

7060 International Foods & Confections
6590 Shiloh Rd E
Alpharetta, GA 30005-2260   770-887-0201
Gourmet delicacies
Estimated Sales: $ 10 - 20 Million
Number Employees: 10-19

7061 International Glace
351 Rancho Camino
Fallbrook, CA 92028-8488   760-731-3220
    Fax: 760-731-3221 800-884-5041
       alan@internationalglace.com
       www.internationalglace.com
Importer of ginger, brewers' yeast spread and glace
fruits including apricots, orange slices and peels,
pineapple, peaches, pears, figs and kiwifruit
    Manager: Marilyn Guest
    Vice President: Bill Davids
    Sales Director: Alan Sipole
Estimated Sales: $1-2.5 Million
Number Employees: 1-4
Type of Packaging: Consumer, Bulk

7062 International Glatt Kosher
5600 1st Avenue
Building A-1
Brooklyn, NY 11220-2558   718-491-2756
       Fax: 718-921-1542
Kosher foods
    President: Leib Chaimovitz
Estimated Sales: Less than $500,000
Number Employees: 1-4

7063 International Harvest
606 Franklin Ave
Mt Vernon, NY 10550-4518   914-939-1505
       Fax: 718-279-0623
Dry foods company
    President: Robert M Sterling

7064 International Home Foods
25 Marr Street
Milton, PA 17847-1520   973-359-9920
    Fax: 949-437-3382 www.intlhomefoods.com
Processor and exporter of canned beans, peas, ap-
ples, pasta, chicken, tomato paste and chili; also,
mustard, instant hot cereal, nonstick cooking spray
and glazed popcorn
    Chairman/CEO: C Dean Metropoulos
    SVP/CFO: Craig Steeneck
    President/COO: Lawrence Hathaway
    Sales/Marketing Executive: Mike Larney
Number Employees: 100
Parent Co: ConAgra Foods
Type of Packaging: Consumer
Brands:
  Bumble Bee
  Campfire
  Campfire Marshmallows
  Captain Jac
  Chef Boyardee
  Chef Boyardee Pastas
  Clover Leaf
  Crunch 'n Munch
  Crunch'n'munch Glazed Popcorn
  Dennison
  Dennison's
  Fireside
  Franklin Crunch 'n' Munch
  Golden Touch
  Gulden's
  Iron Kettle
  Jiffy Pop
  Libby's
  Louis Kemp
  Luck's
  Luck's Beans
  Maypo
  Orleans
  PAM
  Pam Cooking Spray
  Paramount
  Ranch Style
  Ranch Style Brand Beans
  Ro*Tel
  Royal Reef
  Seafest
  Swiftwater
  Tuxedo
  Western Gold
  Wheatena

7065 International Leisure Activities
107 Tremont City Rd
Springfield, OH 45502-9506   937-399-0783
    Fax: 937-399-0784 800-782-7448
       www.ilaproducts.com
Distributor of chocolate
    President: George Keriazes
Estimated Sales: $500,000-$1 Million
Number Employees: 5-9
Type of Packaging: Private Label

7066 International Malting Company
3830 W Grant St
Milwaukee, WI 53215-2355   414-671-1166
    Fax: 414-671-1385 info@imc-world.com
       www.imc-world.com
Processor and exporter of malt
    President: Steve Furcich
    COO: Dale West
Estimated Sales: $100+ Million
Number Employees: 100-249
Parent Co: Lesaffre International Corporation
Type of Packaging: Bulk

7067 International Meat Company
P.O.Box 35028
Elmwood Park, IL 60707-0028   773-622-1400
       Fax: 773-622-6829
Processor of meat products including fresh beef,
pork, poultry and veal
    President: Joseph Bomprezzi
Estimated Sales: $5-10 Million
Number Employees: 10-19
Type of Packaging: Food Service

7068 (HQ)International Multifoods Corporation
1 Strawberry Ln # 300
Orrville, OH 44667-1241   330-594-3300
    Fax: 330-684-3062 800-664-2942
Manufacturer, wholesaler/distributor, and exporter
of dessert and baking products, baking mixes and
frozen products to the food service industry in North
America. Manufacturer and marketer of consumer
foods in Canada
    President/COO: Dan Swander
    CEO: Gary Costley
    SVP Finance/CFO: John Byom
    Public Relations: Jill Schmidt
Estimated Sales: $2.5 Billion
Number Employees: 1,450
Type of Packaging: Consumer, Food Service, Pri-
  vate Label, Bulk
Other Locations:
  International Multifoods
  Windsor CT
Brands:
  FANTASIA

7069 International Noodle Company
32811 Groveland St
Madison Heights, MI 48071-1330   248-583-2479
       Fax: 248-583-3004
Chinese noodle, egg roll wrapper, pasta, perogi
wrapper
    President: Robert Ip
Estimated Sales: $1-2.5 Million
Number Employees: 5-9

7070 International Oceanic Enterprises of Alabama
P.O.Box 767
Bayou La Batre, AL 36509-0767   251-824-4193
    Fax: 251-824-7687 800-816-1832
Processor of IQF shrimp and crab
    President: Jens Sunde
    Vice President: Clinton Jones
Estimated Sales: $20-50 Million
Number Employees: 20-49
Type of Packaging: Private Label, Bulk
Brands:
  GOLDEN GULF
  LITTLE BAY
  MASTERMARINE

7071 (HQ)International Packers Corporation
31 Katherine Road
Watertown, MA 02472-4731   508-963-8214
       Fax: 617-924-2299
Processor and importer of low-fat pre-cooked Italian
sausage; portion control, IQF cooked and raw philly
style steaks; importer of boneless beef and trim-
mings; exporter of beef and fish
    CEO/President: Larry Greenburg
Number Employees: 20-49
Sq. footage: 59000
Type of Packaging: Consumer, Bulk
Brands:
  Perfect Foods

7072 International Seafood Distributors
P.O.Box 1130
Hayes, VA 23072-1130   804-642-1417
       Fax: 804-642-1009
       sales@internationalseafood.com
       www.internationalseafood.com
Processor of frozen squid; processor and exporter of
frozen scallops, dogfish, monkfish, conch meat,
croaker and crabs; importer of frozen scallops, pol-
lack, crawfish, frogs' legs and shrimp
    President: Thomas Fass
Estimated Sales: $50-100 Million
Number Employees: 20-49
Sq. footage: 30000

Type of Packaging: Food Service, Private Label, Bulk
Brands:
　Delicate Seas
　Ocean Classic

7073 International Seafoods of Chicago
1133 W Lake St
Chicago, IL 60607-1618　　　312-243-2330
　　　　　　　　　　　Fax: 312-243-1923
Seafood
　President: Inkie Hong
Estimated Sales: $1,800,000
Number Employees: 5-9

7074 International Seafoods of Alaska
P.O.Box 2997
Kodiak, AK 99615-2997　　　907-486-4768
　　　　　　　　　　　Fax: 907-486-4885
Prepared fresh or frozen fish and seafoods
　Administrator: Ted Kishimoto
Estimated Sales: $4,200,000
Number Employees: 5-9
Type of Packaging: Consumer, Food Service, Private Label
Brands:
　Internation Seafood of Alaska
　Kodiak Seafood

7075 International Service Group
4080 McGinnis Ferry Rd # 1403
Alpharetta, GA 30005-1774　　770-518-0988
　　　　　　　　　　　Fax: 770-518-0299
Processor and exporter of peanuts, popcorn
　President: John Kopec
Estimated Sales: $ 3 - 5 Million
Number Employees: 1-4
Type of Packaging: Consumer, Private Label, Bulk

7076 (HQ)International SpecialtySupply
820 E 20th St
Cookeville, TN 38501-1451　　931-526-1106
　Fax: 931-526-8338　sprouts@infoave.net
　　　　　　　　　　www.sproutnet.com
Manufacturer and exporter of commercial sprouting systems; grower and exporter of fresh alfalfa and bean sprouts. Also carry beansprouts, sunflower, cabbage, broccoli, onion, clover and pea sprouts
　Owner: Robert Rust
Estimated Sales: $ 5 - 10 Million
Number Employees: 20-49
Sq. footage: 105000
Type of Packaging: Consumer, Food Service, Private Label, Bulk
Brands:
　Rota Tech
　Sentrex
　Track I
　Wetlite

7077 International Trade Impa
30 Gordon Ave
Lawrenceville, NJ 08648-1033　　609-987-0550
　　　　　Fax: 609-987-0252　800-223-5484
　info@iTitropicals.com　www.ititropicals.com
Tropical juices
　Owner: Gerrit Van Manen
Estimated Sales: $2.5-5 Million
Number Employees: 5-9
Brands:
　iTitropicals

7078 International Trademarks
149 Leroy Avenue
Darien, CT 06820-3413　　　203-656-4046
　　　　　　　　　　　Fax: 203-655-1690
Import broker of soft drinks. Also marketing, importing and sales consultation
　President: Nicholas Ord
　VP: Stewart Warner

7079 International Trading Company
300 Portwall Street
Houston, TX 77029-1336　　　713-224-5901
　　　　　　　　　　　Fax: 713-678-1718
Importer of gourmet foods including Danish hams, cheeses, snails and pate
　Sales Manager: Lenny Yassie

7080 International Yogurt Company
5858 NE 87th Ave
Portland, OR 97220-1312　　　503-257-0210
　　　　　Fax: 503-256-3976　800-962-7326
　info@yocream.com　www.yocream.com
Frozen dessert, snacks and beverages
　Marketing Director: Suzanne Gardner
　Sales Director: Tyler Bargas
Estimated Sales: $ .5 - 1 million
Number Employees: 5-9
Type of Packaging: Consumer, Food Service, Private Label, Bulk
Brands:
　Sorbet By Yo Cream
　The Yogurt Stand
　Yo Cream
　Yo Cream Smoothies

7081 Internatural Foods
15 Prospect Street
Paramus, NJ 07652-2742
0　　　　　　　　　　　201-909-0808
　Fax: 973-338-1485　info@internaturalfoods.com
　　　　　　　　www.internaturalfoods.com
Organic and natural products; hot and cold cereal, pastas, crisp breads, soups, salad dressings and balsamic vinegar, chocolate and wafers
　President: Peter Leiendecker
　VP: Linda Palame
Estimated Sales: $1-2.5 Million
Number Employees: 1-4
Type of Packaging: Private Label
Brands:
　Bio-Familia
　Bisca
　Blanchard & Blanchard
　Cafix
　Clipper
　DaVinci
　DrSoy
　Eddie's
　Helwa
　Kavli
　McCann'S
　Monari Federzoni
　Mount Hagen
　Mrs Leeper's
　Pero
　Pritikin
　Ryvita
　Vivani

7082 Internova
1071 Ave Saint-Aime
BP 727
St Lambert-De-Levis, QC G0S 2W0
Canada　　　　　　　　　418-889-9929
　　　Fax: 418-889-9774　www.internova.com
　Marketing Director: Anne Gilbert

7083 Interstate Bakeries Corporation
747 W 5th Street
Cincinnati, OH 45203　　　　513-721-0212
　　　Fax: 513-721-6368　harnold@lakpr.com
　　　　　　www.interstatebakeriescorp.com
Processor of bread including white, rye and whole wheat
　Chairman: Leo Benatar
　President/CEO: Michael J Anderson
　Chief Marketing Officer: Richard C Seban
　General Sales Manager: Rob Plough
　Plant Manager: Daniel Hawkins
Estimated Sales: $100+ Million
Number Employees: 500-999
Parent Co: Interstate Brands Corporation
Type of Packaging: Consumer, Private Label
Brands:
　Bread du Jour
　Colombo
　Cotton's
　Eddy's Sweetheart
　Holsum Di Carlo
　J.J. Nissen
　Millbrook
　Mrs. Cubbison's
　Parisian

7084 Interstate Bakeries Corporation
200 Busch Dr E
Jacksonville, FL 32218　　　　904-696-1400
　　　　　　　　　　　Fax: 904-696-1410
　　　　　　www.interstatebakeriescorp.com

Processor of rolls and bread
　Chairman: Leo Benatar
　President/CEO: Michael J Anderson
　Controller: Dick Mason
　Sales: Gary Globis
　Chief Marketing Officer: Richard C Seban
　Sales Manager: Gary Globis
　Plant Manager: Keith Schueler
Estimated Sales: $10-20 Million
Number Employees: 250-499
Parent Co: Interstate Brands Corporation
Type of Packaging: Food Service, Private Label
Brands:
　Bread du Jour
　Colombo
　Cotton's
　Eddy's
　Marie Callender's
　Millbrook
　Parisian
　Sweetheart

7085 Interstate Bakeries Corporation
6007 S St Andrews Pl
Los Angeles, CA 90047-1310　　323-750-7204
　　　　　　　　　　　Fax: 323-778-1508
　　　　　　www.interstatebakeriescorp.com
Manufacturer of baked goods such as; twinkies, ding-dong's, ho-ho's, mini muffins and fruit pie
　Media Relations: Hannah Arnold
Estimated Sales: $100-500 Million
Number Employees: 5-9
Brands:
　HOSTESS

7086 Interstate Brands
1 Bakers Way
PO Box 8000
Biddeford, ME 04005　　　　207-286-1200
　　　　　　　　　　　Fax: 207-286-0883
Processor of baked goods including bread, rolls, cakes, pies, muffins, etc
　Manager: Lowell Hall
Estimated Sales: $500 Million to $1 Billion
Number Employees: 100
Type of Packaging: Consumer

7087 Interstate Brands
P.O.Box 5405
Alexandria, LA 71307-5405　　318-448-6600
　　　　　　　　　　　Fax: 318-448-6655
　　　　　　www.interstatebakeriescorp.com
Manufacturer of baked goods including breads and cakes
　President: Mike Kafoure
　EVP: Roy Shelter
　Plant Manager: Steve Cooper
Estimated Sales: $20-50 Million
Number Employees: 250-499
Parent Co: Interstate Brands Corporation
Type of Packaging: Consumer

7088 Interstate Brands
1 Bakers Way
Biddeford, ME 04005-4337　　207-286-1200
　　　　　　　　　　　Fax: 207-286-0883
　nightingale_zoeann@interstatebrands.com
　　　　　　www.interstatebakeriescorp.com
Processor of frozen dough
　Manager: Lowell Hall
Estimated Sales: $500 Million to $1 Billion
Number Employees: 100
Brands:
　Interstate Brands

7089 Interstate Brands Company/Drake Bakeries
75 Demarest Dr # 1
Wayne, NJ 07470-6701　　　973-696-5010
　　　　　　　　　　　Fax: 973-696-2485
　　　　　　www.interstatebakeriescorp.com

Processor of snack cakes and fruit pies.
Regional VP: Sam Coffman
Engineering Manager: Mike Morgan
VP Sales/Marketing: Vanessa Maskal
Production Manager: Fred Zalocha
Plant Manager: Stan Blondek
Purchasing Agent: Lisa Karlson
Estimated Sales: $ 50 - 100 Million
Number Employees: 50-99
Parent Co: Interstate Brands Corporation
Type of Packaging: Consumer

7090 Interstate Brands Corporation
2243 S Main St
Florence, SC 29501-9417   843-393-8895
Fax: 843-393-8343
Processor of bread, rolls and buns
Manager: Donald Gilbert
General Manager: Joseph Hutson
Purchasing Agent: Henry Paul
Estimated Sales: $20-50 Million
Number Employees: 250-499
Parent Co: Interstate Brands Corporation
Type of Packaging: Consumer, Food Service, Private Label, Bulk

7091 (HQ)Interstate Brands Corporation
P.O.Box 419627
Kansas City, MO 64141-6627   816-502-4000
Fax: 816-502-4126
www.interstatebakeriescorp.com
Processor of baked goods including bread, cakes, doughnuts, pies, buns and rolls.
President/CEO: Michael Kafoure
Corporate Secretary VP: Ray Sandy Sutton
CEO: Craig D Jung
Quality Control Manager: Steve Piland
Engineering Director: Brian Poulter
Sales: John McKinney
Manager Administration Services: Debbie Rosewell
Purchasing: Brian Stevenson
Number Employees: 100-249
Type of Packaging: Consumer, Food Service, Private Label
Brands:
Banama
Braun's
Buttercup
Butternut
Colombo Bread Bakery
Delmaid
Delmar
Devil Dogs
Diclaro
Dolly Madison
Dolly Madison Cakes
Drake's
Drake's Cakes
Eddy's
Holsum
Hostess
Merita
Millbrook
Mrs. Cubbison's
Nissen
Nu-Maid
Old Country
Parisian
Rainbo
Ring Dings
Roman Meal
San Francisco French Bread
Satin Gold
Sunmaid
Supreme
Sweetheart
Sweetheart Bread
Toscana
Weber's
Wonder
Wonder Bread
Yodels

7092 Interstate Brands Corporation
P.O.Box 928
Peoria, IL 61653-0928   309-674-9221
Fax: 309-672-1238
info@interstatebakeriescorp.com
www.interstatebakeriescorp.com

Processor of bread including whole wheat, rye, white, reduced-fat, etc
Manager: Robert Glenzinski
CEO: Antonio C Alvarez II
Chief Marketing Officer: Richard C Seban
Sales Manager: John Antonacci
Plant Manager: Bob Glenzinski
Estimated Sales: $100+ Million
Number Employees: 250-499
Parent Co: Interstate Brands Corporation
Type of Packaging: Consumer, Food Service, Private Label
Brands:
Bread du Jour
Colombo
Cotton's Holsum
Hostess
J.J. Nissen
Marie Callender's
Millbrook
Mrs. Cubbison's
Parisian
Sunbeam
Sweetheart
Twinkies
Wonder Bread

7093 Interstate Brands Corporation/Wonder Bread Bakery
6301 N Broadway
St Louis, MO 63147-2802   314-385-1600
Fax: 314-385-4059
www.interstatebakeriescorp.com
Processor of baked goods including breads, rolls, buns, breakfast items, tortillas, snack cakes, pies, doughnuts and muffins.
General Manager: Larry Worley
Plant Manager: Jim Hutton
Estimated Sales: $10-20 Million
Number Employees: 5-9
Parent Co: Interstate Brands Corporation
Type of Packaging: Consumer, Food Service

7094 Interstate Brands Corporation
P.O.Box 419627
Kansas City, MO 64141-6627   816-502-4000
Fax: 816-502-4126   800-777-8067
www.interstatebakeriescorp.com
Processor of buns
CEO: Richard C Seban
Executive VP Finance: Jacques Roizen
CEO: Craig D Jung
Board of Directors: Leo Benator
Production Supervisor: Brian Gordon
Production Manager: Jim Fostino
Purchasing Agent: Marc Eder
Estimated Sales: $10-20 Million
Number Employees: 100-249
Parent Co: Interstate Brands Corporation
Type of Packaging: Consumer, Food Service, Private Label, Bulk
Brands:
Bread Du Jour
Colombo
Cottons
Eddy's Sweetheart
Holsum Di Carlo
J.J. Nissen
Millbrook
Mrs. Cubbisons
Parisian

7095 Interstate Brands Corporation
1525 Industrial Rd
Emporia, KS 66801-6297   620-342-6811
Fax: 620-342-6033
www.interstatebakeriescorp.com
Manufacturer of cakes, doughnuts and sweet rolls.
Manager: Ben Burnett
CEO: Antonio Alvarez II
EVP/CFO: Ronald Hutchison
EVP/Chief Restructuring Officer: John Suckow
SVP Finance/Treasurer: J Randall Vance
Quality Control Manager: Brad Burchett
EVP/CMO: Richard Seban
VP/Corporate Controller: Laura Robb
Plant Manager: Ben Bernette
Purchasing Agent: Roy Turney
Estimated Sales: $100-500 Million
Number Employees: 500-999
Parent Co: Interstate Brands Corporation
Type of Packaging: Consumer, Private Label

Brands:
BEEFSTEAK
BREAD du JOUR
BUTTERNUT
COLOMBO
COTTON'S
DI CARLO
DOLLY MADISON
DRAKES
EDDY'S
HOLSUM
HOME PRIDE
HOSTESS
JJ NISSEN
MERITA
MILLBROOK
MRS CUBBISON'S
PARISIAN
SWEATHEART
WONDER

7096 Interstate Brands Corporation/Butternut Bread Bakeries
P.O.Box 478
Springfield, MO 65806   417-869-0711
Fax: 417-863-1454   info@twinkie.org
www.interstatebakeries.com
Processor of bread including white, wholewheat and rye
President: Mike Kaoure
Sales Manager: Mike Campbell
Plant Manager: Jim Hutton
Purchasing Agent: Melinda Wilsey
Estimated Sales: $100+ Million
Number Employees: 100-249
Parent Co: Interstate Brands Corporation
Type of Packaging: Consumer, Food Service, Private Label

7097 Interstate Brands Corporation/Merita Bread Bakery
2200 S Division Ave
Orlando, FL 32805-6231   407-843-5110
Fax: 407-841-3188
www.interstatebakeriescorp.com
Processor of baked goods including bread, buns, rolls and doughnuts
Manager: Leo Desroisers
Sales Director: Roberta Young
Production Manager: Gerald Hendrix
Estimated Sales: $100+ Million
Number Employees: 500-999
Parent Co: Interstate Brands Corporation
Type of Packaging: Consumer, Food Service
Brands:
Dolly Madison
Drakes
Merita

7098 Interstate Brands Corporation/Wonder/Hostess
9801 Blue Grass Rd
Philadelphia, PA 19114-1079   215-969-1200
Fax: 215-552-8677
http://www.interstatebakeriescorp.com
Processor of white bread and doughnuts.
Personnel Manager: Nancy Hudson
Plant Manager: Bill Hagan
Number Employees: 500-999
Parent Co: Interstate Brands Corporation
Type of Packaging: Consumer
Brands:
Hostess
Wonder

7099 Interstate Brands Corporation
P.O.Box 81250
Billings, MT 59108-1250   406-248-4800
Fax: 406-248-1499
www.interstatebakeriescorp.com
Processor of baked goods including bread and rolls
President: Mike Kafoure
COO: Jerry Valentine
Plant Manager: Mark Oconnell
Estimated Sales: $100+ Million
Number Employees: 250-499
Parent Co: Interstate Brands Corporation
Type of Packaging: Consumer, Food Service, Private Label

7100 Interstate Brands Corporation
3100 NW Park Drive
Knoxville, TN 37921-1000   865-947-6191
                            Fax: 865-523-5822
Processor of baked goods including bread and rolls;
wholesaler/distributor of cakes, doughnuts and general merchandise
    President: Mike Kafoure
    Plant Manager: John Collins
Estimated Sales:$300,000-500,000
Number Employees: 5-9
Parent Co: Interstate Brands Corporation
Type of Packaging: Consumer, Food Service, Private Label

7101 Interstate Brands Corporation/Dolly Madison Cakes
PO Box 2647
Columbus, GA 31902-2647   706-257-7000
                            Fax: 706-257-6782
        http://www.interstatebakeriescorp.com
Processor of baked goods including cakes, doughnuts and pies.
    Quality Control Manager: Priscilla Marshall
    Sales: Bill Hoskinson
    Operations Director: Douglas Gibson
    Production Manager: Bruce Cofone
    General Manager: Ron Wilson
Estimated Sales:$ 5 - 10 Million
Number Employees: 5-9
Parent Co: Interstate Brands Corporation
Brands:
    BLUE RIBBON CAKES
    COUNTESS CAKES
    DOLLY MADISON CAKES
    HOSTESS CAKES

7102 Interstate Brands Corporation/Butternut Bread Company
500 Main St
Boonville, MO 65233-1583   660-882-6107
                            Fax: 660-882-2265
        www.interstatebakeriescorp.com
Processor of hamburger and hot dog buns and rolls.
    President: Mike Kafoure
    General Manager: Gene Goodwin
    Production Manager: Mike Dilse
    Plant Manager: Cecil Monroe
Estimated Sales:$ 50 - 100 Million
Number Employees: 100-249
Parent Co: Interstate Brands Corporation
Type of Packaging: Consumer, Food Service, Private Label

7103 Interstate Brands Corporation
140 Dupree St
Charlotte, NC 28208-2926   704-398-2051
        www.interstatebakeriescorp.com
Processor of baked goods including bread and doughnuts
    Controller: George Lubejko
    Vice President: Bob McClellan
    Plant Manager: Ken Thomas
Estimated Sales:$ 5 - 10 Million
Number Employees: 5-9
Parent Co: Interstate Brands Corporation
Type of Packaging: Consumer, Private Label

7104 Interstate Brands Corporation
PO Box 10663
Birmingham, AL 35202-0663   205-841-6301
                            Fax: 205-322-1148
Processor of baked goods including hamburger and hot dog buns and white, autumn grain and stone-ground breads
    President: Mike Kafoure
    Production Manager: Robin Messer
    Plant Manager: Gary Goff
Estimated Sales:$ 5 - 10 Million
Number Employees: 5-9
Parent Co: Interstate Brands Corporation
Type of Packaging: Consumer, Private Label

7105 Interstate Brands Corporation
P.O.Box 591
Rocky Mount, NC 27802-0591   252-977-3400
                            Fax: 252-977-9029
        www.interstatebakeriescorp.com

Manufacturer of baked goods including bread and rolls.
    President/COO: Michael Kafoure
    CEO: Antonio Alvarez II
    EVP/CFO: Ronald Hutchison
    Plant Manager: Adam Ligon
Estimated Sales:$100-500 Million
Number Employees: 500-999
Type of Packaging: Consumer, Food Service, Private Label, Bulk
Brands:
    BEEFSTEAK
    DOLLY MADISON
    DRAKE'S
    EDDY'S
    HOLSUM
    HOME PRIDE
    HOSTESS
    JJ NISSEN
    MARIE'S CALLENER'S
    MILLBROOK
    PARISIAN
    WONDER

7106 Interstate Brands Corporation
2519 S Grand St
Monroe, LA 71202-3109   318-388-2244
                        Fax: 318-388-2613
        www.interstatebakeriescorp.com
Processor of white bread
    Manager: Mark Buchanan
    General Sales Manager: Ross Buchanan
    Production Manager: Jerry Ross
Estimated Sales:$100+ Million
Number Employees: 100-249
Parent Co: Interstate Brands Corporation
Type of Packaging: Consumer, Private Label

7107 Interstate Foods
P.O.Box 13068
Lansing, MI 48901-3068   517-372-5500
    Fax: 517-372-2870 www.paramountcoffee.com
Coffees
    President: Steve Morris
    CEO: James Elsesser
    VP: Robert Morgan
    Plant Manager: B Brown
Estimated Sales:$5-10 Million
Number Employees: 1-4

7108 Interstate Seed Company
PO Box 338
West Fargo, ND 58078-0338   701-282-3373
            Fax: 701-281-1888   800-437-4120
                        info@interstateseed.com
                        www.interstateseed.com
Processor of soybean seeds
    President: Bruce Hovland
    Marketing Coordinator: Gerri Leach
    Sales Director: Bill Webber
    Operations Manager: Vic Nordstrom
Estimated Sales:$2.5-5 Million
Number Employees: 20-49

7109 Intervest Trading Company
5435 Spring Garden Road
Halifax, NS B3J 1G1
Canada   902-425-2018
        Fax: 902-420-0763   info@intervest.ca
Processor and exporter of fresh and frozen groundfish and shellfish
    President: Jeff Whitman
Number Employees: 1,000-4,999
Type of Packaging: Bulk

7110 Inverness Dairy
1631 Woiderski Rd
Cheboygan, MI 49721-8969   231-627-4655
                            Fax: 231-627-4655
Milk and butter
    President: David Woiderski
Estimated Sales:$5-10 Million
Number Employees: 20-49

7111 Iowa Ham Canning
812 3rd St NW
Independence, IA 50644-1724   319-334-7134
                            Fax: 319-334-7259
Processor of ham and turkey
    President: Brooks Burkhart
    Quality Control: Brian Hayek
    Plant Manager: Paul Hunzinger
Estimated Sales:$ 50 - 100 Million
Number Employees: 100-249

Type of Packaging: Private Label

7112 Iowa Quality Meats
2075 NW 92nd Ct
Clive, IA 50325-5458   515-225-6868
        Fax: 515-224-4775   800-677-6868
Processor and exporter of portion-control and roast-ready pork products; also, custom processing available
    Manager: Craig Raecker
    National Account Sales: David Mercer
    Purchasing Agent: Matt George
    General Manager: Pat Watkins
Estimated Sales:$50-100 Million
Number Employees: 100-249
Sq. footage: 25000
Type of Packaging: Consumer, Food Service, Private Label
Brands:
    Iowa Quality Meats

7113 Iowa Turkey Products
PO Box 200
Marshall, MN 56258-0200   563-864-7676
                            Fax: 563-864-7636
        kburger@iowaturkeyproducts.com
Processor of fresh and frozen turkey
    President: Thomas Dietrick
    CEO: Keith Burger
    CFO: Ken Smith
    VP: Dennis Brechler
    Plant Manager: Todd Rhoades
Estimated Sales:$25-49.9 Million
Number Employees: 390
Type of Packaging: Consumer, Food Service, Private Label
Brands:
    Turkey Valley Farms

7114 Ipswich Bay Seafoods
19 Longmeadow Drive
Ipswich, MA 01938-1174   978-356-9292
                            Fax: 978-356-7979
Seafood
    President: Louis Malaquias

7115 Ipswich Maritime Product Company
P.O.Box 338
Ipswich, MA 01938-0338   978-356-9866
    Fax: 978-356-9894 www.ipswichmaritime.com
Seafood
    President: Peter Maistrellis
Estimated Sales:$ 10 - 20 Million
Number Employees: 10-19

7116 Ipswich Shellfish Company
P.O.Box 550
Ipswich, MA 01938-0550   978-356-6941
    Fax: 978-356-9235 www.ipswichfishmarket.com
Shellfish and shellfish products
    Manager: Zina Smith
Estimated Sales:$50-100 Million
Number Employees: 5-9

7117 Ira Higdon Grocery Company
PO Box 488
Cairo, GA 39828-0488   229-377-1272
                        Fax: 229-377-8756
Wholesaler/distributor of general line products
    President: I Higdon Jr
    VP: L Higdon
Estimated Sales:$50-100 Million
Number Employees: 50-99

7118 Ira Middleswarth & Son
250 Furnace Rd
Middleburg, PA 17842-9159   570-837-1431
        Fax: 570-837-1731   toddhestor@hotmail.com
Potato Chips
    President: Robert Middleswarth
Estimated Sales:$20-50 Million
Number Employees: 50-99
Type of Packaging: Private Label

7119 Irani & Company
PO Box 29297
Indianapolis, IN 46229-0297   317-894-4465
                            Fax: 317-894-4478
Teas

7120 Iron Horse Products
5109 W 48th St
Edina, MN 55436-1533 952-920-7722
Fax: 952-920-7722
Bottle and can soft drinks and carbonated waters
President: John Justice
Estimated Sales:$750,000
Number Employees: 1-4
Type of Packaging: Consumer, Food Service
Brands:
IRON HORSE

7121 Iron Horse Ranch & Vineyard
9786 Ross Station Rd
Sebastopol, CA 95472-2179 707-887-1212
Fax: 707-887-1337 info@ironhorsevineyards.com
www.ironhorsevineyards.com
Wines
Co-Founder: Barry Sterling
Vineyard Manager: Forrest Tancer
Co-Founder: Audrey Sterling
Marketing Director: Joy Anne Sterling
Estimated Sales:$10-20 Million
Number Employees: 20-49
Type of Packaging: Private Label

7122 Ironstone Vineyards
1894 6 Mile Rd
Murphys, CA 95247-9543 209-728-1251
Fax: 209-728-1275 kautz@goldrush.com
www.ironstonevineyards.com
Wines, brandies, grappa, port
President: Stephen Kautz
Controller: Lynn Gentry
Sales Director: Bob Reider
Public Relations: Jo Diaz
Operations Manager: John Kautz
Bottling Foreman: John McVarish
Estimated Sales:$50-100 Million
Number Employees: 100-249
Type of Packaging: Private Label
Brands:
Angels Creek
Creekside
Delta Bay

7123 Irresistible Cookie Jar
PO Box 3230
Hayden Lake, ID 83835-3230 208-664-1261
Fax: 208-667-1347
service@irresistiblecookiejar.com
www.irresistablecookiejar.com
Cookie and muffin mixes, cookie cutters and decorations
President: Wanda Hall
Estimated Sales:$300,000-500,000
Number Employees: 10
Brands:
Boyds' Kissa Bearhugs
Mimi's Muffins
Susan Winget

7124 Irving R. Boody & Company
11 Penn Plz
New York, NY 10001-2006 212-947-8300
Fax: 212-947-8301 info@boody.com
www.boody.com
Processor, exporter and importer of oils including
cod liver, fish, essential and edible
Owner: Irving R Boody
Estimated Sales:$50-100 Million
Number Employees: 1-4

7125 Isaar Cheese
N9310 Isaar Road
Seymour, WI 54165-9423 920-833-6190
Cheese products
Estimated Sales:$500,000 appx.
Number Employees: 5-9

7126 Isabel's Country Mustard
1213c Old Highway 63 N
Columbia, MO 65201-6319 573-441-9188
Fax: 573-442-4736 877-441-9188
Mustard and other condiments
President: Susan Stalcupgray
Estimated Sales:$1-2.5 Million
Number Employees: 1-4

7127 Isabella's Healthy Bakery
170 Muffin Ln
Cuyahoga Falls, OH 44223-3358 330-929-0000
Fax: 330-920-8329 800-476-6328
mramcharran@isabellashealthybakery.com
www.mainstreetmuffins.com
Supplier of healthy baked goods including muffins,
cookies & cakes. Specializing in sugar free, no sugar
added, fat free and whole grain categories. All products are certified kosher and packaged for retail.
CEO: Steve Marks
CEO: Harvey Nelson
President: Monica Curtis
Quality Control: Angela Stoughton
Marketing: Joe Schaefer
Sales/Marketing: Manorma Ramcharran
Plant Manager/Operations: Mike Braun
Production: Tommie Smith
Production: Bryan Smith
Purchasing Director: Jim Braun
Estimated Sales:$15 Million
Number Employees: 100-249
Number of Brands: 1
Number of Products: 39
Sq. footage: 65000
Parent Co: Feature Foods dba Main Street Gourmet
Type of Packaging: Consumer, Private Label, Bulk
Brands:
Isabella's

7128 Isadore A. Rapasadi & Son
P.O.Box 66
Canastota, NY 13032-0066 315-697-2216
Fax: 315-697-3300 www.rapasadi.com
Grower, packer and exporter of onions and potatoes
President: Samuel Rapasadi
CEO: Izzy Rapasadi
Sales Manager: Bob Rapasadi
Estimated Sales:$10-20 Million
Number Employees: 50-99
Sq. footage: 60000
Type of Packaging: Consumer
Brands:
Raps Blue Ribbon
Stars & Stripes

7129 Isernio Sausage Company
5600 7th Ave S
Seattle, WA 98108-2644 206-762-6207
Fax: 206-762-5259 888-495-8674
info@isernio.com www.isernio.com
Processor and exporter of pork, beef and lamb sausage
President: Frank Isernio
Estimated Sales:$2.5-5 Million
Number Employees: 20-49
Type of Packaging: Consumer, Food Service

7130 Island Aquaculture Company
PO Box 222
Bernard, ME 04612-0222 207-526-4144
Fax: 207-526-4433
Aquaculture

7131 Island Farms Dairies Cooperative Association
PO Box 38
Victoria, BC V8W 2R4
Canada 250-360-5200
Fax: 250-360-5220 info@islandfarms.com
www.islandfarms.com
Processor and wholesaler/distributor of a full range
of dairy products
President: George Aylard
CEO: David McMillan
CFO: Eric Erikson
Quality Control: Sam Arora
Marketing: Jona De Jesus
Sales: Art Paulo
Operations: Greg Martin
Plant Manager: Al Snedden
Purchasing Director: Steve Wainwright
Number Employees: 250-499
Number of Products: 500
Type of Packaging: Consumer, Food Service, Private Label, Bulk

7132 Island Lobster
PO Box 258
Matinicus, ME 04851-0258 207-366-3937
Fax: 207-366-3380
Lobster
Owner: Marc Ames

7133 Island Marine Products
PO Box 40
Clarks Harbour, NS B0W 1P0
Canada 902-745-2222
Fax: 902-745-3247
Processor and exporter of haddock, lobster and lobster meat and tuna
President: Cyril Swim
VP: Peter (E T) Swim
Number Employees: 20-49
Type of Packaging: Food Service, Bulk

7134 Island Oasis Frozen Cocktail Company
P.O.Box 769
Walpole, MA 02081-0769 508-660-1176
Fax: 508-660-1435 800-777-4752
vponline@mail.islandoasis.com
www.islandoasis.com
Processor and exporter of premium all-natural
nonalcoholic beverage mixes; manufacturer and exporter of ice shavers and blenders
President: J Michael Herbert
Research & Development: Bill Flynn
Marketing Director: Larry Painter
VP of Sales: Michael Walsh
Public Relations: Andrea Scavuzzo
VP of Production: Joseph Cunnane
Estimated Sales:$20-50 Million
Number Employees: 100-249
Number of Products: 16
Sq. footage: 25000
Brands:
SB-3X

7135 Island Princess
2846 Ualena St
Honolulu, HI 96819-1943 808-839-5222
Fax: 808-836-2019 866-872-8601
info@islandprincesshawaii.com
www.islandprincesshawaii.com
Manufacturer of specialty macadamia nut products,
luscious chocolates and unique gourmet coffees -
caramel popcorn, chocolate coffee beans and
macadamia nuts.
President: Michael Purdy
VP: Owen Purdy
Estimated Sales:$8 Million
Number Employees: 50-99
Number of Brands: 10
Number of Products: 100
Sq. footage: 12000
Type of Packaging: Consumer, Food Service, Private Label, Bulk
Brands:
HAWAIIAN PRINCESS SMOKE
ISLAND PRINCESS

7136 Island Scallops
5552 W Island Highway
Qualicum Beach, BC V9K 2C8
Canada 250-757-9811
Fax: 250-757-8370
islandscallops@bcsupernet.com
www.islandscallops.com
Processor of fresh and frozen scallops; also, marine
research hatchery
President/CEO: Robert Saunders
R&D: Barb Bunting
Processing Manager: Lorraine Hopps
Type of Packaging: Consumer, Food Service

7137 Island Seafood
32 Brook Dr
Eliot, ME 03903-1423 207-439-8508
Fax: 207-439-6609
Seafood
Owner: Randy Townsend
Estimated Sales:$ 3 - 5 Million
Number Employees: 20-49

7138 Island Seafoods
317 Shelikof St
Kodiak, AK 99615-6048 907-486-8575
Fax: 907-486-3007 800-355-8575
islandseafood@gci.net www.islandseafoods.com
Seafood such as king crab, halibut, salmon, scallops,
prawns, smoked salmon, rockfish and cod
Owner: Frank Tulcich
Estimated Sales:$ 5 - 10 Million
Number Employees: 20-49

7139 Island Spices
907 Bangs Avenue
Asbury Park, NJ 07712-6403   877-229-2900
Fax: 732-775-6840   sales@starlites.com
www.islandspice.com
Dry spices and sauces
Owner: Andre Schwab

7140 Island Spring
P.O.Box 747
Vashon, WA 98070-0747   206-463-9848
Fax: 206-463-5670   lakeskie@wolfenet.com
www.islandspring.com
Processor of organic soy and tofu products
President: W M Luke Lukoskie
R&D: Suni Kim Lukoskie
Estimated Sales:$2.5-5 Million
Number Employees: 10-19
Sq. footage: 4000
Type of Packaging: Consumer, Food Service, Private Label, Bulk
Brands:
Island Spring

7141 Island Sweetwater Beverage Company
825 Lafayette Road
Bryn Mawr, PA 19010-1816   610-525-7444
Fax: 610-525-7502 www.peacemountain.com
Processor, exporter and importer of soft drinks, bottled waters, energy drinks; exporter of beer
President: Michael Salaman
Sq. footage: 10000
Parent Co: A/S Beverage Marketing
Type of Packaging: Private Label
Brands:
4th of July Cola
Absolutenergy
Activin Energy
Beverly Hills
Citrimax
Citrimax - French Diet Cola
French Paradox
Island Sweetwater
Jazz
Kiwi Kola
Nicola
Rebound
Sangria Cola
Santa-Claus
Slender
Stampede

7142 Island Treasures MusselProcessing
PO Box 10
Little Bay, NL A0J 1J0
Canada   709-267-3146
Fax: 709-267-3149
Processor and exporter of fresh mussels
Co-Owner: Edward Sheppard
Co-Owner: Denyse Sheppard
Number Employees: 10-19
Type of Packaging: Consumer, Food Service, Bulk

7143 Island of the Moon Apiaries
17560 Company Road
85-B
Esparto, CA 95627   530-787-3993
Fax: 530-787-3993
Bee pollen, honey
President: Jerry Kaplan
Estimated Sales:$2.5-5 Million
Number Employees: 1-4

7144 Issimo Food Group
PO Box 1991
La Jolla, CA 92038-1991   619-260-1900
Fax: 619-260-8400   sales@issimo.com
www.issimo.com
White and dark chocolate specialty candies and desserts
President/Owner: Willing Howard
Sales Manager: Kathleen Hornbacher
Estimated Sales:$1-2.5 Million
Number Employees: 20-49
Brands:
Chef Howard's Williecake
Ecco!
Issimo Celebrations!
Issimo's Creme Br-L,
Lilycake

7145 It's It Ice Cream Company
865 Burlway Rd
Burlingame, CA 94010-1705   650-347-2122
Fax: 650-347-2703   800-345-1928
comments@itsiticecream.com
www.itsiticecream.com
Processor of ice cream novelties
President: Charles Shamieh
Manager: Charles Shamieh
Estimated Sales:$5-10 Million
Number Employees: 20-49
Brands:
It's It

7146 Ital Florida Foods
3805 W Gardenia Avenue
Weston, FL 33332-2464   305-769-0799
Fax: 305-681-2442
Pasta products
President: Vincenzo Dioguardi
Controller: Santiano Blanco
VP: Claudio Dioguardi
Marketing Director: Anthony Musto
Technical Services: Thailie Purica
Production Manager: Fiorenzo Bigolin
Plant Manager: Marco Dioguardi
Estimated Sales:$20-50 Million
Number Employees: 20-49
Type of Packaging: Private Label
Brands:
Dino & David

7147 Italia Foods
2365 Hammond Dr
Schaumburg, IL 60173-3815   847-397-4479
Fax: 847-397-6817   800-747-1109
info@italiafoods.com   www.italiafoods.com
Processor of frozen pasta and sauces
President: Philip Carabetta
VP: Peter Carabetta
Estimated Sales:$5-10 Million
Number Employees: 20-49
Brands:
Italia
Mama Lina

7148 Italian Bakery
205 1st St S
Virginia, MN 55792-2699   218-741-3464
Fax: 218-741-2531 www.potica.com
Processor of fresh pies
President: Joseph Prebonich
Estimated Sales:$1-2.5 Million
Number Employees: 20-49
Type of Packaging: Consumer

7149 Italian Baking Company
4028 Windsor Road
Youngstown, OH 44512-1019   330-782-1358
Fax: 330-788-9044
Processor of baked products including pizza
Owner/CEO: Greg Deniro
CEO: Heidi Deniro
Estimated Sales:$1-2.5 Million
Number Employees: 20-49

7150 Italian Baking Company
10644 97th Street NW
Edmonton, AB T5H 2L6
Canada   780-424-4830
Fax: 780-425-6577
Processor of Italian-style bread, cakes, pies, muffins and rolls
President/Owner: Antonio Frattin
Marketing Director: Frank Debenz
CFO: Tony Frattin
Number Employees: 10-19
Type of Packaging: Consumer, Food Service

7151 Italian Connection
55 W Shore Ave # B
Dumont, NJ 07628-2332   201-385-2226
Fax: 201-385-9026
Italian specialty foods
Owner: John Stracquadanio
Estimated Sales:$1-2.5 Million
Number Employees: 1-4

7152 Italian Foods
606 Ridgewood Avenue
Holly Hill, FL 32117-3618   904-255-5200

Italian foods

7153 Italian Foods Corporation
3640 Grand Ave
Suite 210
Oakland, CA 94610   510-444-9050
Fax: 510-444-9049   info@italianfoods.com
www.italianfoods.com
pasta, sauces, spreads & toppings, oil & vinegar, rice, risotto, gnocchi, snacks, grilled vegetables, pasta express
President/Owner: Elena Lapiana
Sales: Francesca Lapiana
Operations: Kirk Newcross

7154 Italian Foods Manufacturing
2317 Vestal Parkway E
Vestal, NY 13850-1900   607-754-1070
Fax: 607-786-0233   800-962-7700
Processor of frozen meatballs, sausage and Italian pasta products
President: Guido Iacovelli
President: Cameron Robert
Purchasing Manager: David Iacovelli
Sq. footage: 15000
Type of Packaging: Consumer, Food Service, Private Label, Bulk
Brands:
Chef Dreamblend

7155 Italian Gourmet Foods Canada
809 1st Avenue NE
Calgary, AB T2E 0C2
Canada   403-263-6996
Fax: 403-266-6061
Processor of fresh pasta
President: Peter Bellusci
Type of Packaging: Consumer, Food Service
Brands:
The Perfect Pasta

7156 Italian Peoples Bakery
31 Scotch Rd
Ewing, NJ 08628-2512   609-771-1369
Fax: 609-771-1369
Baked goods
Manager: Sandy Elmer
Secretary/Treasurer: Carmen Guagliardo
Estimated Sales:$ .5 - 1 million
Number Employees: 100-249
Parent Co: Italian Peoples Bakery

7157 Italian Rose Garlic Products
1380 W 15th St
West Palm Beach, FL 33404-5310   561-863-5556
Fax: 561-863-1462   800-338-8899
irg@italian-rose.com   www.italian-rose.com
Processor of garlic powder and sauces, gourmet garlic, roasted garlic products, toppings, dips, sauces and gifts
President: Ken Berger
VP: Aurthor Conlan
Marketing Director: Aurthor Conlan
Estimated Sales:$5-10 Million
Number Employees: 50-99
Type of Packaging: Consumer, Food Service, Private Label
Brands:
Italian Rose

7158 Italian Specialty Foods
5600 7th Avenue S
Seattle, WA 98108-2644   206-322-5790
Italian foods
President: Jerry Mascio
Estimated Sales:$50-100 Million
Number Employees: 50-99

7159 Italian Village Ravioli& Pasta Products
P.O.Box 839
Portsmouth, NH 03802-0839   603-431-6865
Fax: 603-430-9205
italianvillage@highlinerfoods.com
www.highlinerfoods.com
Processor of frozen ravioli, cavatelli and gnocchi
President: Keith A Decker
VP, Procurement: Paul W Snow
VP: Dave Johnson
VP Human Resources: Mario G Patenaude
Estimated Sales:$ 50 - 100 Million
Number Employees: 100-249
Parent Co: High Liner Foods

Type of Packaging: Consumer, Food Service, Private Label
Brands:
Gina Italian Village

7160 Itarca
400 Warren Ln
Inglewood, CA 90302-3116   310-419-6433
Fax: 310-677-2782 800-747-2782
www.florentyna.com
Processor of fresh and frozen Italian pasta including ravioli, tortellini, cavatelli, potato and cheese gnocchi, cannelloni and lasagna
Manager: Jascha Smuloviez
VP Sales: Ivan Andre Smulovitz
Estimated Sales: $5-10 Million
Number Employees: 20-49

7161 Itella Foods
1729 E 21st Street
Los Angeles, CA 90058-1006   213-765-0967
Fax: 213-745-3009
General grocery
Owner: Salveatore Gallatti
Vice President: Frank Brigulio
Estimated Sales: $20-50 Million
Number Employees: 100-249

7162 (HQ)Ito Cariani Sausage Company
3190 Corporate Pl
Hayward, CA 94545-3916   510-887-0882
Fax: 510-387-8323
Manufacturer and exporter of meat products including sausage, wine-flavored dry salami, roast and smoked beef, headcheese, pepperoni and bologna
President: Tony Nakashima
VP Finance: Allen Shiroma
Executive VP/General Manager: Ken Kamata
VP Sales: Al Lera
Estimated Sales: $10-20 Million
Number Employees: 50-99
Sq. footage: 85000
Type of Packaging: Consumer, Food Service, Private Label, Bulk
Other Locations:
Ito Cariani Sausage Co.
Nishinomiya
Brands:
Cariani Italian Dry Salami
Cariani Italian Specialty Loaves

7163 Itoen
125 Puuhale Rd
Honolulu, HI 96819-4992   808-847-4477
Fax: 808-841-4384 www.itoen-usa.com
Processor of fruit juice, sports drinks, iced tea and coffee, canned teas and frozen concentrates; also, Oriental noodles and soup bases
President: Shigeyuki Utsugi
Marketing Director: Alan Pollock
Estimated Sales: $20-50 Million
Number Employees: 50-99
Type of Packaging: Consumer, Food Service
Brands:
Aloha Maid
Itoen

7164 Ittella Foods
2050 Long Beach Avenue
Los Angeles, CA 90058-1022   213-746-6201
Fax: 213-745-3009
Pinto beans, tomato sauce, sauces, imitation crab salad, salsa, guacamole
President: Sam Galetti
VP Sales: Peter Roddy
Production Manager: Jose Reveles
Brands:
De La Casa
Del Rancho
El Pueblo

7165 Ittels Meats
P.O.Box 676
Howard Lake, MN 55349-0676   320-543-2285
Fax: 320-543-2285
Manufacturer of beef jerky and summer sausage
Owner: Don Schwartz
Estimated Sales: $1-3 Million
Number Employees: 1-4
Type of Packaging: Consumer, Food Service, Private Label, Bulk

7166 Ivanhoe Cheese Inc
11301 Highway 62 N
RR 5
Madoc, ON K0K 2K0
Canada   613-473-4269
Fax: 613-473-5016 ivanhoecheese@sympatico.ca
www.ivanhoecheese.com
Manufacturer, processor, importer and exporter of natural, process and cold pack cheeses including cheddar, swiss and parmesan; also, cheese sauces
President: Bruce Kingston
Executive VP: Paul McKinlay
Quality Control: Diane Musclow
Sales: Paul McKinlay
Plant Manager: Chris Spencer
Number Employees: 50-99
Type of Packaging: Consumer, Food Service, Private Label, Bulk
Brands:
Ivanhoe
Ivanhoe Classics
Ivanhoe Fresh

7167 Iversen Baking Company
PO Box 28
Bedminster, PA 18910-0028   215-636-5904
Fax: 215-575-5076
Cookies
President: David Collins
Estimated Sales: Under $500,000
Number Employees: 1-4

7168 Iveta Gourmet
2125 Delaware Ave # F
Santa Cruz, CA 95060-5758   831-423-5149
Fax: 831-423-5169 iveta@iveta.com
www.iveta.com
Natural scones, muffins and savory biscuit mixes. Imports jams, curds and clotted cream to serve with them.
Owner: John Bilanko
Co-Owner: Yvette Bilanko
Estimated Sales: $2.5-5 Million
Number Employees: 5-9
Brands:
Iveta Gourmet

7169 Ivy Cottage Scone Mixes
709 Adelaine Avenue
South Pasadena, CA 91030-2401   626-441-2761
Fax: 626-441-9657
Prepared mixes for scones
President: Elaine Osmond

7170 Ivy Foods
3851 E. Thunderhill Place
Phoenix, AZ 85044-6679   480-759-4849
Fax: 801-943-7311 877-223-5459
www.nutribase.com
Manufacturer of wheat based meat substitutes including chicken, sausage and burger analogs
President: Mira Blue Machlis
Operations Manager: Mark Machlis
Estimated Sales: $2.5-5 Million
Number Employees: 1-4
Sq. footage: 12000
Brands:
Meat of Wheat

7171 Ivydaro
PO Box 369
Putney, VT 05346-0369   802-387-5597
ivydaro@sover.net
Foiled wraped chocolate apples

7172 Iwamoto Natto Factory
143 Hana Hwy # C
Paia, HI 96779   808-579-9933
Fax: 808-579-9933
Natto and noodles
Owner: Robert Yamashita
Estimated Sales: $110,000
Number Employees: 1-4
Type of Packaging: Consumer, Food Service

7173 J & B Seafood
9301 Faith St
Coden, AL 36523-3057   251-824-4512
Fax: 251-824-1260
Seafood
President: Raymond Barbour
Estimated Sales: $7.7 Million
Number Employees: 50-99

7174 J Bernard Seafood & Processing
P.O.Box 623
Cottonport, LA 71327-0623   318-876-3885
Fax: 318-876-2925
Seafood
President: James Bernard
Estimated Sales: $3.2 Million
Number Employees: 10-19

7175 J Freirich Food Products
4601 5th St
Long Island City, NY 11101-5311   718-361-9111
800-221-1315
sales@freirich.com www.freirich.com
Cooked and cured meats including prime rib, corned beef, pastrami, smoked pork, pot roast and other specialty items.
President: Jerry Freirich
Estimated Sales: $25 Million
Number Employees: 10-19
Sq. footage: 35000
Type of Packaging: Consumer, Food Service
Brands:
Freirich Porkette
Regal Chef

7176 J G Townsend Jr & Company
P.O.Box 430
Georgetown, DE 19947-0430   302-856-2525
Fax: 302-855-0922
Processor of frozen vegetables including beans and peas
President: Paul Townsend
VP: John Townsend IV
Plant Manager: Soloman Henry
Estimated Sales: $ 2.5-5 Million
Number Employees: 20-49
Type of Packaging: Consumer, Food Service
Brands:
Country Fair
Townsend

7177 J G Van Holten & Son
P.O.Box 66
Waterloo, WI 53594-0066   920-478-2144
Fax: 920-478-2316 800-256-0619
info@vanholtenpickles.com
www.vanholtenpickles.com
Processor and exporter of pre-packaged pickles and relish
President: James D Byrnes
VP and General Manager: Steve Byrnes
VP of Sales: Stef Espiritu
Estimated Sales: $7000000
Number Employees: 50-99
Type of Packaging: Consumer, Private Label, Bulk
Brands:
BIG PAPA
GARLIC GUS
HOT MAMA
LIL' PEPE
VAN HOLTEN

7178 J J Gandy's Pies
3725 Alt 19 # A
Palm Harbor, FL 34683-1477   727-938-7437
Fax: 727-938-7437
Bakery items
President: Gay Schmidt
Estimated Sales: Less than $100,000
Number Employees: 1-4
Type of Packaging: Food Service

7179 J K Marley's LLC
5032 Willow Creek Road
Unit C
Machesney Park, IL 6115-8204   815-636-7712
Fax: 800-717-5043 www.bigpapasbarbecue.com
BBQ sauce
Number Employees: 5
Type of Packaging: Consumer

7180 J M Clayton Company
P.O.Box 321
Cambridge, MD 21613-0321   410-228-1661
Fax: 410-221-0216 800-652-6931
jmclayton@shorenet.net www.jmclayton.com
Processor of Chesapeake Bay blue crabs including whole and steamed; also, custom packaging in fresh pasteurized and frozen containers available
President: John C Brooks Jr
CEO: William Brooks

Estimated Sales: $3000000
Number Employees: 100-249
Sq. footage: 29000
Type of Packaging: Consumer, Food Service, Private Label, Bulk
Brands:
    EPICURE

7181 J Vineyards & Winery
P.O.Box 6009
Healdsburg, CA 95448-6009   707-431-3646
    Fax: 707-431-5410 800-885-9463
    winefolk@jwine.com www.jwine.com
Wines
    Marketing Director: Judy Jordan
    CEO: Bruce Lundquist
    CEO: Judy Jordan
    CFO: Bruce Lundquist
    Public Relations: Robin Oden
    Winemaker: Lisa Kashin
Estimated Sales: $ 5-9.9 Million
Number Employees: 50-99
Type of Packaging: Private Label
Brands:
    J Nicole Vineyard Pinot Noir
    J Russian River Vall
    J Sparkling Wine

7182 J W Allen Company
555 Allendale Dr
Wheeling, IL 60090-2638   847-459-5400
    Fax: 847-459-0314 marksr@ameritech.net
    www.richs.com
Baked goods
    President/CEO: William Allen Jr
    CFO: Ron Vantz
    VP Sales: Allan Foster
    Director Marketing: Jerry Widdick
    General Manager: J Joy
    General Manager-Cereal Mix Division: Don Colson
    Plant Manager: Rene Marcos
    Purchasing Manager: Dorothy Wood-Johnson
Estimated Sales: $ 50-100 Million
Number Employees: 100-249
Type of Packaging: Private Label

7183 J&B Meats Corporation
P.O.Box 69
Coal Valley, IL 61240-0069   309-799-7341
    Fax: 309-799-7633
Processor of fresh and frozen steaks, pork chops, beef patties, ground beef, pork and veal products; also, breaded beef, pork, chicken and veal
    President: Jeff Jobe
    CFO: Jobe Jeff
    Quality Control: Sandy Belfhaufe
    Plant Manager: James Sommer
Estimated Sales: $ 10 - 20 Million
Number Employees: 50-99
Type of Packaging: Consumer, Food Service

7184 J&B Sausage Company
P.O.Box 7
Waelder, TX 78959-0007   830-788-7511
    Fax: 830-788-7279 contact@jbfoods.com
    www.jbfoods.com
Processor and exporter of smoked sausage, bacon, ham and jerky; also, barbecued meat
    President: Danny Janecka
    CEO: Ron Bushaw
Estimated Sales: $42040000
Number Employees: 250-499
Type of Packaging: Consumer, Food Service, Private Label, Bulk
Brands:
    J Bar B Foods
    Singletree Farms
    Texas Smokehouse

7185 J&B Wholesale Distributing
P.O.Box 212
St Michael, MN 55376-0212   763-497-3913
    Fax: 763-497-9481 800-872-4642
    info@jbwhsle.com www.jbgroup.com
Wholesaler/distributor of frozen portion cut meat, fish, poultry and equipment and fixtures; serving the food service market; transportation firm providing LTL, TL, long, short and local haul trucking
    President: Robert Hageman
    President: Mike Hageman
Estimated Sales: $132300000
Number Employees: 250-499
Sq. footage: 180000

7186 J&G Cheese Company
847 Colony Way
Columbus, OH 43235-1755   614-436-1070
    Fax: 614-436-9683
Cheese
    Marketing Director: David Holmberg

7187 J&G Poultry
P.O.Box 2414
Gainesville, GA 30503-2414   770-536-5540
    Fax: 770-531-0829
Poultry
    Manager: Bob Gregory
Estimated Sales: $ 10 - 20 Million
Number Employees: 10-19

7188 J&J Produce Company
105 Frederick St
Hattiesburg, MS 39401-2457   601-582-1512
    Fax: 601-582-1515
Processor of produce
    President: Joseph R Forte
    Co-Owner: Joe Forte
Estimated Sales: $ 5 - 10 Million
Number Employees: 10-19

7189 J&J Snack Foods Corporation
6000 Central Hwy
Pennsauken, NJ 08109-4672   856-665-9533
    Fax: 856-663-8002 webmaster@jjsnack.com
    www.jjsnack.com
Manufacturer and exporter of various nutritional snack foods and beverages.
    Chairman/President/CEO: Gerald Shreiber
    CFO/VP/Secretary/Treasurer: Dennis Moore
    COO/Sr VP: Robert Radano
    SVP Marketing: Michael Karaban
Estimated Sales: $ 100 + Million
Number Employees: 1,000-4,999
Type of Packaging: Food Service, Private Label
Brands:
    BARQ'S
    CAMDEN CREEK
    CHILL
    ICEE
    LUIGI'S
    MAMA TISH'S
    MINUTE MAID
    MRS GOODCOOKIE
    PRETZEL FILLERS
    SHAPE UPS
    SUPERPRETZEL
    THE FUNNEL CAKE FACTORY
    TIO PEPE'S

7190 J&J Snack Foods Corporation
5353 S Downey Rd
Vernon, CA 90058-3756   323-581-0171
    Fax: 323-583-4732 800-486-7622
    www.jjsnack.com
Processor and exporter of health food cookies including fruit filled, fruit juice sweetened, wheat-free, dairy-free and fat-free as well as soft pretzels and cookie doughs for food service
    Manager: Mark Slakter
    R&D: Joyce Berham
    Vice President: Robert Radano
    Marketing Director: Michael Karabon
    Sales Director: Steve Taylor
Estimated Sales: $353187000
Number Employees: 250-499
Sq. footage: 150000
Parent Co: J&J Snack Foods Company
Type of Packaging: Consumer, Food Service, Private Label, Bulk
Brands:
    BAKERS BEST
    BAVARIAN
    CHURROS
    DUTCHIE
    FROSTAR
    FUNNEL CAKE
    ICEE
    LUIGI'S
    MAMA TISH'S
    MR. TWISTER
    MRS. GOODCOOKIE
    PRETZEL COOKIE
    PRETZEL FILLERS
    SHAPE-UPS
    SUPERJUICE
    SUPERPRETZEL
    TIO PEPE'S

7191 (HQ)J&J Snack Foods Corporation
6000 Central Hwy
Pennsauken, NJ 08109-4672   856-665-9533
    Fax: 856-663-8002 webmaster@jjsnack.com
    www.jjsnack.com
Manufacturer and exporter of various nutritional snack foods and beverages
    Chairman/President/CEO: Gerald Shreiber
    CFO/VP/Secretary/Treasurer: Dennis Moore
    COO/SVP: Robert Radano
    SVP Marketing: Michael Karaban
Estimated Sales: $50-100 Million
Number Employees: 1,000-4,999
Sq. footage: 170000
Type of Packaging: Food Service, Private Label
Brands:
    ARCTIC BLAST
    DUTCHIE
    FROSTAR
    ICEE
    LUIGI'S
    MR. IWISTER
    MRS. GOODCOOKIE
    PRETZEL FILLERS
    SHAPE-UPS
    SUPERJUICE
    SUPERPRETZEL
    TANGO WHIP
    TIO PEPE'S

7192 J&J Wall Baking Company
8800 Fruitridge Rd
Sacramento, CA 95826   916-381-1410
    Fax: 916-381-6008 www.jjwallbaking.com
Processor of frozen bread and rolls
    President: Janet Wall
Estimated Sales: $ 20 - 50 Million
Number Employees: 20-49
Type of Packaging: Consumer

7193 J&J Wholesale
2925 Industrial St
Junction City, KS 66441-8519   785-238-4721
    Fax: 785-762-6869
    President: Dan Coffey
    Plant Manager: Dirk Francis
Estimated Sales: $ 20 - 50 Million
Number Employees: 20-49

7194 J&K Ingredients
160 E 5th Street
Paterson, NJ 07524-1603   973-340-8700
    Fax: 973-340-4994 jkfoods1@aol.com
    www.jkingredients.com
Bakery flavorings, extracts and mold inhibitors
    President: Paul W Kinney
Estimated Sales: $ 10-25 Million
Number Employees: 20-30
Brands:
    Bred-Mate
    Sausville's

7195 J&L Grain Processing
12456 Addison Ave
Riceville, IA 50466-7096   641-985-4255
    Fax: 641-985-4256 800-244-9211
    jlgiain@omnitelcon.com
Processing of grain
    President/CEO: Joel Yorgey
Estimated Sales: Below $ 5 Million
Number Employees: 5-9

7196 J&L Seafood
P.O.Box 272
Bayou La Batre, AL 36509-0272   251-824-2371
    Fax: 251-824-2371
Seafood
    President: Joshua Alderman
Estimated Sales: $ 3 - 5 Million
Number Employees: 10-19

7197 J&M Food Products Company
P.O.Box 334
Deerfield, IL 60015-0334   847-948-1290
    Fax: 847-948-0468 sales@halalcertified.com
    www.halalcertified.com
Manufacturer of certified, halal and dhabiha halal meals, rations and food products
    President: Joseph D'Onofrio
    CEO: Mary Anne Jackson
Estimated Sales: $ .5 - 1 million
Number Employees: 1-4

Type of Packaging: Private Label
Brands:
 J&M

7198 J&M Foods
P.O.Box 250080
Little Rock, AR 72225-0080   501-663-1991
      Fax: 501-663-2822 800-264-2278
gparham@jm-foods.com www.jm-foods.com
Processor of flavored straws.
  President: Jamie Parham
  VP: Scott Thibault
  Director Sales/Marketing: Greg Parham
  Production Manager: Jeff Stockman
Estimated Sales: $ 10-20 Million
Number Employees: 20-49
Type of Packaging: Private Label

7199 J&M Industries
300 Ponchatoula Pkwy
Ponchatoula, LA 70454-8311   985-386-6000
      Fax: 985-386-9066 800-989-1002
              www.jm-ind.com
  President: Rene Gaudet
  Plant Manager: Al Bourgeois
Estimated Sales: $ 20 - 50 Million
Number Employees: 100-249

7200 J&M Meats
PO Box 370
Warburg, AB T0C 2T0
Canada   780-848-7598
      Fax: 780-848-7532 midge@telusplanet.net
Processor and exporter of fresh and frozen pork
  President: J McCullough
  Administrator Quality Control: Kevin
  McCullough
  Sales Manager: Nannette McCullough
Number Employees: 22
Sq. footage: 18000
Type of Packaging: Consumer, Food Service, Bulk

7201 J&R Fisheries
PO Box 3302
Seward, AK 99664-3302   907-224-5584
      Fax: 907-224-5572
Seafood
Estimated Sales: $300,000-500,000
Number Employees: 1-4

7202 J&R Foods
307 Morris Ave
Long Branch, NJ 07740   732-229-4020
      Fax: 732-229-0111
Processor of half shell mussels and marinara sauce
with mussels
  President: Rocco F Raimondi III
Estimated Sales: $1000000
Number Employees: 10-19
Type of Packaging: Consumer, Food Service

7203 J-N-D Company
11424 Tweedsmuir Run
Fort Wayne, IN 46814-8217   260-459-6206
      Fax: 219-485-9242
  President: James Davis
Estimated Sales: $ 5-10 Million
Number Employees: 6

7204 J. Crow Company
P.O.Box 172
New Ipswich, NH 03071-0172   603-878-1965
      Fax: 603-878-1965 800-878-1965
jcrow@jcrow.mv.com www.jcrow.com
Processor of herbs, spices, essential and fragrance
oils and teas
  Owner: Jeff Krouk
Estimated Sales: Less than $500,000
Number Employees: 1-4
Sq. footage: 50000
Type of Packaging: Consumer
Brands:
 J. Crow's

7205 J. Dickerson
291j Commerce Sq S
Irondale, AL 35210   205-956-0881
  President: Jerry Dickerson

7206 J. Filippi Winery
12467 Baseline Rd
Etiwanda, CA 91739-9522   909-899-5755
      Fax: 909-899-9196 jfilippiwinery@aol.com
              www.josephfilippiwinery.com

Wine
  President: Joseph Filippi
  CEO: Joseph Filippi
  Marketing Director: Gino Filippi
Estimated Sales: $ 10-20 Million
Number Employees: 20-49
Brands:
 J. Filippi

7207 J. Frasinetti & Sons
PO Box 292368
Sacramento, CA 95829-2368   916-383-2444
      Fax: 916-383-5825 www.frasinetti.com
Wine

7208 J. Fritz Winery
24691 Dutcher Creek Rd
Cloverdale, CA 95425-9742   707-894-3389
      Fax: 707-894-4781 info@fritzwinery.com
              www.fritzwinery.com
Wines
  President: Clayton Fritz
  Winemaker: Christina Pallmann
Estimated Sales: $ 2.5-5 Million
Number Employees: 10-19
Brands:
 Fritz

7209 J. Hoelting Produce
P.O.Box 2260
Decatur, IL 62524-2260   217-429-7774
      Fax: 217-429-8129
Produce
  President: Bob Tipsword
Estimated Sales: $ 20 - 50 Million
Number Employees: 20-49

7210 J. Matassini & Sons Fish Company
2111 N Boulevard
Tampa, FL 33602-1936   813-229-0829
      Fax: 813-229-0820
Processor of fresh and frozen seafood including cat-
fish, trout, lobsters, oysters, crabs, scallops, breaded
shrimp and crab cakes
  Founder: J Matassini
  Executive VP: Pat Matassini
  Executive VP: Louis Matassini
Estimated Sales: $ 1 - 3 Million
Number Employees: 5-9
Type of Packaging: Consumer, Food Service
Brands:
 Matassini Seafoods

7211 J. Moniz Company
91 Wordell St
Fall River, MA 02721-4307   508-674-8451
      Fax: 508-673-6464
Seafood
  President/Treasurer/Clerk: John Moniz
Estimated Sales: $1,000,000
Number Employees: 5-9

7212 J. Rettenmaier
16369 Us Highway 131 S
Schoolcraft, MI 49087-9150   269-679-2340
      Fax: 269-679-2364 877-243-4661
              info@jrsusa.com   www.jrusa.com
Fiber products: cellulose, wheat, oat, apple, orange,
tomato for bakery, cereal, snack food, pasta and diet
beverage markets
  Manager: Gerhard Goss
Estimated Sales: $ 10 - 20 Million
Number Employees: 50-99

7213 J. Stonestreet & Sons Vineyard
PO Box 46
Healdsburg, CA 95448-0046   707-473-3307
      Fax: 707-433-9469 800-723-6336
              www.stonestreetwines.com
Wines
  President: Jess Jackson
  Sales Manager: Mick Unti
Estimated Sales: $ 2.5-5 Million
Number Employees: 10
Brands:
 Alexander Valley
 Christopher's
 Legacy Red Wine

7214 J. Turner Seafoods
4 Smith St
Gloucester, MA 01930-2710   978-281-8535
      Fax: 978-281-1710

Seafood
Estimated Sales: $2,000,000
Number Employees: 5-9

7215 J. Weil & Company
5907 Clinton St
Boise, ID 83704-9304   208-377-0590
      Fax: 208-378-1682 800-755-3885
              www.jweil.com
Food service distributor
  President: Bill Tippetts
Estimated Sales: $ 5 - 10 Million
Number Employees: 20-49

7216 J.A.M.B. Low Carb Distributor
4100 N Powerline Road
Suite W3
Pompano Beach, FL 33073-3065   954-917-9881
      Fax: 954-917-2590 800-708-6738
mike@jambco.com www.jambco.com
Low carb and sugar free foods.
  CEO: Alan Beyda

7217 J.B. Peel Coffee Roasters
7582 N Broadway
Red Hook, NY 12571-1469   845-758-1792
      Fax: 845-758-1814 800-231-7372
jbpeel@citlink.net www.jbpeelcoffee.com
Gourmet coffee
  President: Gil Klein
  VP: Pat Klein
Estimated Sales: Less than $500,000
Number Employees: 10,000+
Number of Products: 200
Type of Packaging: Consumer, Private Label, Bulk

7218 J.B. Sons
564 Mile Square Rd
Yonkers, NY 10701-6333   914-963-5192
      Fax: 914-963-5192
Processor of ricotta cheese, hand-made mozzarella
cheese and pasta including ravioli, manicotti, stuffed
shells, cavatelli and gnocchi
  President: Joseph L Brunetto Jr
  Sales: Steven Brunetto
Estimated Sales: $ 5 - 10 Million
Number Employees: 5-9
Sq. footage: 3000
Type of Packaging: Consumer, Food Service, Pri-
vate Label, Bulk

7219 J.C. Watson Company
P.O.Box 300
Parma, ID 83660-0300   208-722-5141
      Fax: 208-722-6646 nancy@soobrand.com
              www.soobrand.com
Processor and exporter of produce including onions,
apples, potatoes and plums
  Manager: Kent Sutherland
  Sales Manager: Nancy Carter
  Transportation Manager: Melanie Steinhaus
Number Employees: 5-9
Type of Packaging: Consumer, Food Service
Brands:
 SOO

7220 J.D. Mullen Company
PO Box 130
Palestine, IL 62451-0130   618-586-2727
      Fax: 618-586-2718 mullins11@verizon.net
              www.mullensdressing.com
Processor of Imitation French, French, Creamy Ital-
ian and Special Salad Dressings, as well as BBQ
Sauce and Ham's Delight.
  President: Jeff Shaner
  CFO/Quality Control: Jeff Shaner
Estimated Sales: $300,000-500,000
Number Employees: 5-9
Sq. footage: 7500
Type of Packaging: Consumer, Food Service
Brands:
 Mullen's

7221 J.F.C. International
1925 N Norcross Tucker Rd
Norcross, GA 30071-3411   770-448-0070
      Fax: 770-263-9790 www.jfc.com
  Manager: Shoso Ota
Estimated Sales: $ 20 - 50 Million
Number Employees: 20-49

7222 J.G. British Imports
801 N Orange Ave
Sarasota, FL 34236-4116   941-926-1700
                    Fax: 941-926-1701 888-965-1700
                    info@ratherjolly.com
                    www.sarasotamilitaryacademy.com
Tea
    Administrator: Dan Kennedy
    Vice President: Fern Grace
Estimated Sales: $100,000
Number Employees: 50-99
Type of Packaging: Private Label
Brands:
    Rather Jolly Tea

7223 J.H. Verbridge & Son
6700 Lake Ave
Williamson, NY 14589-9569   315-589-2366
                    Fax: 315-589-7478
Processor of frozen cherries, pineapples and straw-berries
    President: Robert Verbridge
    Executive VP: Gerald Verbridge
    Plant Manager: Lloyd Verbridge
Estimated Sales: $1 Million
Number Employees: 20-49
Type of Packaging: Consumer, Food Service
Brands:
    Big V

7224 J.J. Andrade's Slaughterhouse
463675 Mamelehoa
Honokaa, HI 96727   808-775-0741
                    Fax: 808-429-1328
Processor of frozen meat including beef, pork and lamb
Estimated Sales: $ 5 - 10 Million
Number Employees: 10
Type of Packaging: Consumer, Food Service, Bulk

7225 J.L. DeGraffenried & Sons
2848 N Le Compte Rd
Springfield, MO 65803-5729   417-862-9411
                    Fax: 417-862-8615 www.jldpickle.com
Processor of canned pickles and relishes
    President: Teggy Henry
    Sales Manager: Dave McCalley
Estimated Sales: $ 20 - 50 Million
Number Employees: 50-99
Parent Co: DG Foods
Type of Packaging: Food Service, Private Label

7226 J.M. Schneider
254 Rue Principale
Saint Anselme, QC G0R 2N0
Canada   418-885-4474
            Fax: 418-885-9408 www.schneiders.ca
Processor of beef and pork
    Plant Manager: Narie Claude Lamontadne
    Plant Manager: Cal Petraszko
Number Employees: 100-249
Parent Co: J.M. Schneider
Type of Packaging: Consumer, Food Service
Brands:
    Schneider

7227 J.M. Smucker Company
1 Strawberry Lane
Orrville, OH 44667   330-682-3000
            Fax: 330-684-6410 info@smuckers.com
                    www.smuckers.com
Preserves, mustards, flavored mayonaise, honey des-sert sauces, fruit curds, fruit butters and all fruit spreads.
    Chairman/Co-CEO: Timothy Smucker
    Executive Chairman/Co-CEO: Richard Smucker
    SVP/CFO: Mark Belgya
    VP/General Counsel & Secretary: M Ann Harlan
    VP/Corporate Development: Barry Dunaway
    VP/Chief Information Officer: Andrew Platt
    VP/Human Resources: Robert Ellis
    VP/Logistics & Operations: Dennis Armstrong
Estimated Sales: $4.6 Billion
Number Employees: 4,850
Brands:
    ADAMS
    CRISCO
    CROSSE & BLACKWELL
    DICKINSON'S
    DUNKIN DONUTS
    DUTCH GIRL
    EAGLE BRAND
    FOLGERS
    HUNGRY JACK

JIF
KAVA
KNOTT'S BERRY FARM
LAURA SCUDDER'S
MAGNOLIA
MARTHA WHITE
MARY ELLEN
MILLSTONE
NATURAL BREW
NATURE'S PEAK
NONE SUCH
PET
PILLSBURY
R W KNUDSEN FAMILY
SANTA CRUZ ORGANIC
SMUCKER'S
WHITE LILY

7228 (HQ)J.M. Smucker Company
1 Strawberry Lane
Orrville, OH 44667-0280   330-682-3000
            Fax: 330-684-6410 www.smuckers.com
Fruit spreads, retail packaged coffee, peanut butter, shortening and oils, ice cream toppings, sweetened condensed milk, and health and natural foods beverages
    Chairman/Co-Chief Executive Officer: Timothy Smucker
    Executive Chairman/Co-CEO: Richard Smucker
    VP/Chief Financial Officer: Mark Belgya
    Human Resources: Angela Foldan
    SVP/Corporate & Organization Development: Barry Dunaway
    VP/Chief Information Officer: Andrew Platt
    VP/Marketing Communications: Christopher Resweber
    VP/U.S. Grocery Sales: James Brown
    VP/Logistics and Operations: Dennis Armstrong
Estimated Sales: $4.6 Billion
Number Employees: 4,850
Sq. footage: 130000
Type of Packaging: Consumer, Food Service
Brands:
    ADAMS
    CRISCO
    CROSSE & BLACKWELL
    DICKINSON'S
    DUNKIN DONUTS
    DUTCH GIRL
    EAGLE BRAND
    FOLGERS
    HUNGRY JACK
    JIF
    KAVA
    KNOTT'S BERRY FARM
    LAURA SCUDDER'S
    MAGNOLIA
    MARHTA WHITE
    MARY ELLEN
    MILLSTONE
    NATURAL BREW
    NATURE'S PEAK
    NONE SUCH
    PET
    PILLSBURY
    R.W. KNUDSEN FAMILY
    R.W. KNUDSEN FAMILY
    SANTA CRUZ ORGANIC
    SMUCKER'S
    WHITE LILY

7229 J.M. Smucker Company
1 Strawberry
Orrville, OH 44667-0280   330-682-3000
            Fax: 330-684-3951 888-550-9555
                    www.smuckers.com
Processor and exporter of jam, jelly and preserves, peanut butter, sanwich snacks, ice cream toppins and specialty items.
    Executive Chairman/President/Co-CEO: Richard K Smucker
    Chairman/Co-CEO: Timothy Smucker
    VP/CFO/Treasurer: Mark Belgya
    VP Quality Assurance: Albert Yeagley
    VP Marketing Services: Christopher Resweber
    National Foodservice Sales Manager: Greg Stiff
    VP Information Services/CIO: Andrew Platt
    VP Logistics/Operations Support: Dennis Armstrong
Estimated Sales: $3,757,000
Number Employees: 750
Type of Packaging: Consumer, Food Service
Brands:
    ADAMS

AFTER THE FALL
BICK'S (CANADA)
CRISCO
CROSSE & BLACKWELL
DICKINSON'S
DOUBLE FRUIT (CANADA)
DUTCH GIRL
GOLDEN TEMPLE (CANADA)
HUNGRY JACK
JIF
LAURA SCUDDER'S
MARTHA WHITE
MARY ELLEN
NATURAL BREW
PET
PILLSBURY
R.W. KNUDSEN FAMILY
RED RIVER (CANADA)
ROBIN HOOD (CANADA)
SANTA CRUZ ORGANIC
SHIRRIFF (CANADA)
SMUCKER'S

7230 J.M. Smucker Company
P.O.Box 608
Grandview, WA 98930-0608   509-882-1530
            Fax: 509-882-2212 www.smuckers.com
Processor of grape juice concentrate
    Manager: Randy Hecker
    Plant Manager: Randy Hecker
Estimated Sales: $ 5 - 10 Million
Number Employees: 20-49
Sq. footage: 12000
Parent Co: J.M. Smucker Company
Type of Packaging: Bulk

7231 J.M. Smucker Company
P.O.Box 280
Orrville, OH 44667-0280   330-682-3000
    Fax: 330-684-3951 pam.yates@jmsmucker.com
                    www.smuckers.com
Canner and exporter of jams, preserves and fruit syr-ups
    Chairman: Timothy P Smucker
    Plant Manager: Pat Campbell
    Purchasing Agent: Mark Lillie
Estimated Sales: $ 50-100 Million
Number Employees: 1,000-4,999
Parent Co: J.M. Smucker Company
Type of Packaging: Consumer, Food Service

7232 J.N. Bech
214 Dexter Street
Elk Rapids, MI 49629-9606   231-264-5080
            Fax: 231-264-5107 800-232-4583
                    sales@themustardwithauthority.com
                    www.themustardwithauthority.com
Processor of gourmet water-cooled stone ground mustards and barbecue glazes including addi-tive/preservative and fat-free
    President: John Bech
    Office Manager: Lynn Haveman
Estimated Sales: $600000
Number Employees: 7
Type of Packaging: Consumer, Food Service, Pri-vate Label
Brands:
    Bech

7233 J.P. Green Milling Company
P.O.Box 187
Mocksville, NC 27028-0187   336-751-2126
                    Fax: 336-751-1349
Processor of grits, feed, flour and corn meal
    President: Ralph Naylor
Estimated Sales: $ 5 - 10 Million
Number Employees: 10-19

7234 J.P. Shellfish
P.O.Box 666
Eliot, ME 03903-0666   207-439-6018
                    Fax: 207-439-7794
Seafood
    President: John Price
Estimated Sales: $ 10 - 20 Million
Number Employees: 20-49

7235 J.P. Sunrise Bakery
14728 119th Avenue NW
Edmonton, AB T5L 2P2
Canada   780-454-5797
    Fax: 780-452-7696 office@sunrise-bakery.com
                    www.sunrisebakery.com

Processor of baked goods including nanaimo bars
and tarts; exporter of cinnamon buns
President: Jary Huising
Sales: Hank Renzenrrink
Manager: Gary Huising
Number Employees: 80
Sq. footage: 30000
Type of Packaging: Consumer, Food Service

7236 J.R. Fish Company
PO Box 774
Wrangell, AK 99929-0774
907-874-2399
Fax: 907-874-2398
Seafood
President: Janell Privett
Secretary/Treasurer: William Privett

7237 J.R. Poultry
2924 Maus Road
Fults, IL 62244-1506
618-476-7342
Fax: 706-777-8690
Poultry

7238 J.R. Short Canadian Mills
54 Harding Boulevard
Toronto, ON M4G 2B5
Canada
416-421-3463
Fax: 416-421-2876 a.norris@jrshort.com
Processor and exporter of confectioners corn flakes,
corn meal, stablized wheat bran, wheat germ and
corn germ
Vice President: Alexa Norris
Parent Co: J.R. Short Milling Company

7239 (HQ)J.R. Short Milling Company
1580 Grinnell Rd
Kankakee, IL 60901-8246
815-937-2624
Fax: 815-937-3981 800-544-8734
info@shortmill.com www.shortmill.com
Manufacturer and exporter of corn grits, meal, flour,
brewer's flakes, heat stabilized fours and snack pel-
lets; also corn germ for flavor.
Sales: Judy Hunter
Estimated Sales: $25 Million
Number Employees: 100-249
Type of Packaging: Private Label, Bulk
Other Locations:
Short, J.R., Milling Co.
Kankakee IL
Brands:
CERATEX
SNO-FLUF
SUNLITE
WYTASE

7240 J.R. Short Milling Company
1580 Grinnell Rd
Kankakee, IL 60901-8246
815-937-2624
Fax: 815-937-3981 800-457-3547
judih@shortmill.com www.shortmail.com
Snack foodss, bakery dough improvers
General Manager: Dennis Bunck
Sales: Judy Hunter
Research & Development: Raleigh Wilkinson
Quality Control: Richard Cochran
Sales Director: Bruce Dunlap
Operations Manager: Dennis Bunck
Purchasing Manager: Don Pitzer
Estimated Sales: $ 50-100 Million
Number Employees: 100-249
Brands:
Sunlite

7241 (HQ)J.R. Simplot Company
999 Main Street
Suite 1300
Boise, ID 83702
208-336-2110
Fax: 208-389-7515 info@simplot.com
www.simplot.com
Processes potatoes, grains and vegetables to produce
fresh and frozen bulk, private label, and consumer
products.
President & CEO: Bill Whitacre
SVP Finance/CFO: Annette Elg
President, Food Group: Kevin Storms
VP Marketing, Food Group: Alan Kahn
VP Sales, Food Group: Steve Patterson
Director Corp Comm & PR: Rick Phillips
Purchasing: John Glerum
Estimated Sales: $4.5 Billion
Number Employees: 10,000
Type of Packaging: Consumer, Food Service, Pri-
vate Label
Other Locations:
J.R. Simplot Potato Processing

Aberdeen ID
J.R. Simplot Potato Processing
Caldwell ID
J.R. Simplot Potato Processing
Grand Forks ND
J.R. Simplot Potato Processing
Moses Lake WA
J.R. Simplot Potato Processing
Nampa ID
J.R. Simplot Potato Processing
Othello WA
J.R. Simplot Vegetable Processing
West Memphis AR
Brands:
CHEF'S CHOICE
CONQUEST®
CULINARY SELECT™
DEHYDROFROZEN
FIESTA
FREEZERFRIDGE®
GLORI FRI®
GRAND VALLEY®
HARVEST SUPREME™
IDAHOAN®
INFINITY®
JR BUFFALO®
KRUNCHIE WEDGES®
MARINER®
MEGACRUNCH®
NATURALCRISP®
OLD FASHIONED WAY®
PANCAKE PODS®
PAYETTE FARMS®
PLATE-PERFECT®
QUICKMASH®
RECIPE QUICK®
ROASTWORKS®
SAVORY
SEASONEDCRISP®
SELECT RECIPE®
SIMPLOT®
SIMPLOT® CULINARY FRESH™
SKINCREDIBLES®
SKINCREDIBLES® PLUS
SOUR CREAM & CHIVE
SPUDSTERS®
SUN CROP®
TASTEE SPUD™
TATER PALS®
TOP CAT®
TRADITIONAL
TRUE RECIPE®
ULTRA CLEAR®
UPSIDES®
WONDER FRY

7242 J.R. Simplot Company
PO Box 27
Boise, ID 83707
208-336-2110
Fax: 208-389-7515 jrs_info@simplot.com
www.simplot.com
Processor of frozen vegetables and French fried po-
tatoes; also fruits and vegetables
Owner: Dennis Facer
CEO: Bill Whitacre
Estimated Sales: $ 1-5 Billion
Number Employees: 9,970
Parent Co: J.R. Simplot Company
Brands:
Simplot

7243 J.R. Simplot Company
3630 Gateway Dr
Grand Forks, ND 58203-0826
701-746-6431
Fax: 701-780-7882 jrs_info@simplot.com
www.simplot.com
Avocado products, instant mashed potatoes, frozen
potatoes, fruits, roasted products, sweet potato prod-
ucts, and vegetables
VP: Fred Zerza
Director: Don J Simplot
Plant Manager: Dave Gotberg
Purchasing Agent: Rod Howell
Estimated Sales: $1-5 Billion
Number Employees: 250-499
Parent Co: J.R. Simplot Company
Type of Packaging: Consumer, Food Service, Bulk

7244 J.R. Simplot Company
PO Box 27
Boise, ID 83707
208-336-2110
Fax: 208-389-7515 jrs_info@simplot.com
www.simplot.com

Manufacturer of frozen potatoes, french, home fries,
mash potatoes, fruit and vegetables
Owner: Dennis Facer
CEO: Bill Whitacre
Estimated Sales: $4.5 Billion
Number Employees: 250-499
Type of Packaging: Consumer, Food Service, Pri-
vate Label, Bulk
Other Locations:
J.R. Simplot Food Plant
Aberdeen ID
J.R. Simplot Food Plant
Caldwell ID
J.R. Simplot Food Plant
Grand Forks ND
J.R. Simplot Food Plant
Moses Lake WA
J.R. Simplot Food Plant
Nampa ID
J.R. Simplot Food Plant
Othello WA
J.R. Simplot Food Plant
Pasco WA
J.R. Simplot Food Plant
West Memphis AR

7245 J.R. Simplot Food Group
5815 N Industrial Way
Pasco, WA 99301-9388
509-544-6700
Fax: 509-544-6799
Processor and exporter of frozen vegetables includ-
ing potatoes, sweet corn and carrots
President: Larry Ring
General Manager: Larry Ring
Purchasing Agent: Marvin Moore
Estimated Sales: $100+ Million
Number Employees: 500-999
Sq. footage: 160000
Parent Co: J.R. Simplot Company
Type of Packaging: Consumer, Food Service, Pri-
vate Label, Bulk

7246 J.R.'s Seafood
9908 Southwest Highway
Oak Lawn, IL 60453
708-422-4555
Fax: 914-624-0329
Seafood
President: Frank Cestro
Estimated Sales: $ 1 - 3 Million
Number Employees: 5-9

7247 J.S. McMillan Fisheries
PO Box 520
Prince Rupert, BC V8J 3R7
Canada
604- 25- 519
Fax: 604- 25- 460 sparkhill@jsm.bc.ca
www.bcseafoodonline.com
Processor of canned salmon and ground fish
President: Steve Parkhill
VP Sales: Guy Dean
Number Employees: 250-499
Parent Co: J.S. McMillan
Type of Packaging: Consumer, Food Service
Brands:
Hywave
J.S. McMillan
Pinnacle
Snow Cod

7248 J.S. McMillan Fisheries
2199 Commissioner Street
Vancouver, BC V5L 1A9
Canada
604-255-5191
Fax: 604-255-4600
Processor of canned salmon and frozen halibut
President: Tarry Mcmillan
Brands:
J.S. McMillan Fisheries

7249 J.T. Pappy's Sauce
1909 1/4 N Las Palmas Avenue
Los Angeles, CA 90068-3270
323-969-9605
Fax: 323-969-9659 saucecentral@aol.com
www.jtpappys.com
Manufacturer, sales and marketing of sauces and
marinades
Number Employees: 8
Number of Brands: 1
Number of Products: 12
Type of Packaging: Consumer, Food Service, Pri-
vate Label

7250 J.T. Ward Meats & Provisions
4561 Loma Vista Avenue
Vernon, CA 90058-2601
323-585-9935

Processor of meats
Estimated Sales:$ 2.5-5 Million
Number Employees: 1-4

7251 J.T.R.
Hc 32
Box 189
Sebasco Estates, ME 04565   207-389-1819
    Fax: 207-389-1819

7252 J.W. Haywood & Sons Dairy
1744 W Burnett Ave
Louisville, KY 40210-1740   502-774-2311
Processor of ice cream
    Owner: Charles Haywood
Estimated Sales:$300,000-500,000
Number Employees: 5-9
Type of Packaging: Consumer, Food Service

7253 J.W. Raye & Company
P.O.Box 2
Eastport, ME 04631-0002   207-853-4451
    Fax: 207-853-2937 800-853-1903
    mustards@rayesmustard.com
    www.rayesmustard.com
Processor of natural stone ground mustard and mustard sauces
    Owner: Karen Raye
    General Manager: Nancy Raye
Estimated Sales:$ 5 - 10 Million
Number Employees: 5-9
Type of Packaging: Consumer, Food Service, Bulk

7254 J.W. Raye & Company
PO Box 2
Mira Loma, CA 91752-0002   909-428-8630
    Fax: 909-428-6264
Mustard flavors
    General Manager: Nancy Raye
Estimated Sales:$5-10 Million
Number Employees: 5

7255 J.W. Treuth & Sons
328 Oella Ave
Baltimore, MD 21228-5499   410-465-4650
    Fax: 410-465-4867 info@jwtreuth.com
    www.jwtreuth.com
Processor of meat products
    President: Vernon L Treuth Jr Jr
Estimated Sales:$28.1 Million
Number Employees: 50-99
Type of Packaging: Consumer, Food Service

7256 JBR Coffee & Tea
1933 Davis St # 308
San Leandro, CA 94577-1259   510-638-1300
    Fax: 510-632-0839 800-829-1300
    sfbay_service@rogersfamilyco.com
    www.rogersfamilyco.com
Roasted coffee
    President: Jon B Rogers
    VP Sales: Jim Rogers
    Sales Director: Mike Carlin
    Operations Manager: Pete Rogers
    Purchasing Manager: Tom Garber
Estimated Sales:$ 10-24.9 Million
Number Employees: 50-99
Type of Packaging: Private Label
Brands:
    Fairwinds Coffee
    Jbr Coffee
    Organic Coffee Compa

7257 JBS Natural Products
5 Jacquelyn Lane
Suite A
Dallas, PA 18612-9107   800-565-6207
    Fax: 570-255-2501 jbs@naturalquit.com
    www.naturalquit.com
Supplier of natural smoking cessation program and other natural products for your health.
    Vice President: Bill Schechter

7258 JBS Packerland
PO Box 64395
Souderton, PA 18964-0395
    Fax: 215-723-5294 800-967-8325
Manufacturer and packer of boxed and ground beef. Also an exporter of fresh and frozen boxed beef and offals.
    President/CEO: Lee Delp
    VP Marketing: Bruce Blanton
    VP Sales: Bruce Blanton

Estimated Sales:$ .5 Billion
Number Employees: 1,600
Parent Co: Smithfield Foods
Type of Packaging: Consumer, Private Label, Bulk

7259 JBS Packing Company
P.O.Box 399
Port Arthur, TX 77641-0399   409-982-3216
    Fax: 409-982-3549 jimistring@aol.com
Processor of fresh and frozen shrimp
    President: Jack Hemmenway
    CFO: Terry Billenez
Estimated Sales:$ 20-50 Million
Number Employees: 100-249
Type of Packaging: Consumer, Food Service
Brands:
    Lucky Seas
    Sea Market

7260 JC World Foods
310 Johnson Avenue
Brooklyn, NY 11206-2801   347-386-1130
    Fax: 718-628-7400
Canned soups
Estimated Sales:$ 5-9.9 Million
Number Employees: 8

7261 JC'S Natural Bakery
1701 Naranca Avenue
El Cajon, CA 92019-1065   619-239-4043
Bakery products
    President: Joe Lewis
*Estimated Sales:*Below $ 5 Million
Number Employees: 3

7262 JC's Midnite Salsa
PO Box 89451
Tucson, AZ 85752-9451   520-574-3993
    Fax: 520-572-1151 800-817-2572
    jc@jcsmidnitesalsa.com
    www.jcsmidnitesalsa.com
Salsa
Estimated Sales:$300,000-500,000
Number Employees: 1-4

7263 JCW Tawes & Son
206 S 10th Street
Crisfield, MD 21817-1051   410-968-1288
Processor of seafood including fresh and pasteurized blue crabs and hard shell crabs
    Manager: Norman Tyler
Estimated Sales:$ 5 - 10 Million
Number Employees: 20-49
Type of Packaging: Consumer, Food Service, Private Label

7264 JE Bergeron & Sons
7 Rue St John Baptiste
Bromptonville, QC J0B 1H0
Canada   819-846-2761
    Fax: 819-846-6217 800-567-2798
    jebergeron@faltec.net www.nuvel.ca
Processor and exporter of shortening and margarine including soya, canola, vegetable, etc
    President: Philippe Bergeron
    Secretary: Berengere Bergeron
    VP: Danielle Bergeron
Number Employees: 20-49
Sq. footage: 30000
Parent Co: Margarine Thibault
Type of Packaging: Consumer, Food Service, Private Label, Bulk
Brands:
    BANQUET
    BERGERON
    CANOLEAN
    CHEF GASTON
    G BLANCHET
    REXPO
    SILVER
    TRADITION
    WONDER

7265 JEJ Food Company
7608 Fullerton Road
Springfield, VA 22153-2814   703-455-0155
    Fax: 703-451-8917

7266 JES Foods
4703 Broadway Ave
Cleveland, OH 44127-1007   216-883-8987
    Fax: 216-883-8984 info@jesfoods.com
    www.jesfoods.com

Processor of produce including carrots, onions, celery, peppers and melons
    President: Elaine R Freed
Estimated Sales:$ 5 - 10 Million
Number Employees: 10-19

7267 JF Braun & Sons Inc.
P.O.Box 1806
Westbury, NY 11590-0251   516-997-2200
    Fax: 516-997-2478 800-997-7177
    steve@jfbny.com www.jfbny.com
Imported dried fruits and nuts
    President: Stephen O'Mara
Number Employees: 20-49
Brands:
    J.F. Braun

7268 JF Clarke Corporation
173 Franklin Ave
Franklin Square, NY 11010-1441   516-328-8333
    Fax: 516-328-8346 800-229-7474
    jclarke@jfclarke.com www.jfclarke.com
Frozen shrimp and seafood
    President: James Clarke
Estimated Sales:$ 5-10 Million
Number Employees: 5-9
Type of Packaging: Food Service
Brands:
    Amazonas
    Avila
    Bee Gee
    Fresh Cargo
    Yutaka

7269 JFC International
7101 E Slauson Ave
Commerce, CA 90040-3622   323-513-1500
    Fax: 323-587-0597 800-633-1004
    info@jfc.com www.jfc.com
Processor of fortune cookies
    Manager: Koichi Inagaki
Estimated Sales:$2.5-5 Million
Number Employees: 10-19
Parent Co: JFC International
Type of Packaging: Consumer, Food Service

7270 JJ's Tamales & Barbacoa
1611 Culebra Rd
San Antonio, TX 78201-5914   210-737-1300
    Fax: 210-733-8133
Mexican foods
    Manager: Gilbert Aparipio
    Manager: M Rodriguez
*Estimated Sales:*Under $500,000
Number Employees: 1-4

7271 JK SucraLose Inc
131 Fieldcrest Ave
Edison, NJ 08831   732-512-0886
    Fax: 732-512-0188 jkusa@jksucralose.com
    www.jksucralose.com
sweetners, sucralose
    President/Owner: Hugh Zhang
    VP: Florey Ye
    Marketing: Elvis Arce
    Sales: Shawn Miller
    Public Relations: Lynn Cruzado
Estimated Sales:$25 Million
Number Employees: 219
Number of Brands: 1
Number of Products: 1
Sq. footage: 135000

7272 JLH European Trading
1179 Howard Street
San Francisco, CA 94103-3925   415-626-3672
    Fax: 415-626-3673
Confectionery, candy novelties, chocolate and non-chocolate candy.
    President: Jean-Luc Hoffer
*Estimated Sales:*Under $500,000
Number Employees: 1-4

7273 JM All Purpose Seasoning
PO Box 22162
Lincoln, NE 68542-2162   402-421-8326
    whollow@navix.net
    www.jmaps.com
Processor of seasonings herbs and spices for fish, chicken and beef
    Owner: James Meeks
Number Employees: 1-4

7274 JMH International
394 Williamstowne
Suite C
Delafield, WI 53018-2322   262-646-7460
                    Fax: 435-645-9109   888-741-4564
info@jmhpremium.com   www.jmhpremium.com
Processor of premium flavor base; soup, sauce, flavor bases
  President: Kirk Mellecker
  Sales Director: Michael Norman
Estimated Sales: $500,000-$1 Million
Number Employees: 1-4
Type of Packaging: Consumer, Food Service, Bulk
Brands:
  Jmh Premium

7275 JMP Bakery Company
P.O.Box 120307
Brooklyn, NY 11212-0307   718-272-5400
                    Fax: 718-272-5427
Processor of baked goods including Italian breads, egg twists, Kaiser breads, bagels, etc
  President: Chris Palagonia
  VP: Chris Palagonia
  VP Sales: Joe Palagonia
  Plant Manager: Richard Palagonia
Estimated Sales: $12 Million
Number Employees: 250-499
Sq. footage: 100000
Brands:
  Italian Bread Products
  Kaiser Rolls
  Palagonia
  Stuhmer's

7276 JMS Specialty Foods
126 Jefferson Street
Ripon, WI 54971-1383   920-748-2858
          Fax: 920-745-6150   800-535-5437
Processor of bottled fruit, peanut butter, barbacue and meat sauces, dessert toppings, maple syrup, jams, jellies, preserves and condiments
  Marketing Manager: Carrie Hogan
  General Manager: Ken Miller
  Plant Manager: Tim Carr
Number Employees: 100-249
Sq. footage: 120000
Parent Co: J.M. Smucker Company
Type of Packaging: Consumer, Food Service, Private Label

7277 JR Carlson Laboratories
15 W College Dr
Arlington Hts, IL 60004-1985   847-255-1600
          Fax: 847-255-1605   888-234-5656
carlson@carlsonlabs.com   www.carlsonlabs.com
Processor, importer and exporter of vitamins, minerals, food supplements, omega three fish oil capsules, liquid cod liver oil, amino acids and anti-oxidant formulas
  President/CEO: J Carlson
  CFO: Trish Lange
  VP: Susan Carlson
  R&D: Carilyn Anderson
  Quality Control: Dolores Rokos
  Marketing: Kirsten Carlson
  Sales: Vicki Accardi
  Public Relations: Toni Edwards
  VP Pharmaceuticals: S Carlson
  Production: Robert Meyer
  Plant Manager: Robert Meyer
  Purchasing Director: Lindy Eck
Estimated Sales: $ 50 - 100 Million
Number Employees: 100-249
Number of Brands: 40
Number of Products: 275
Sq. footage: 40000
Type of Packaging: Consumer, Private Label
Brands:
  Aces
  Carlson
  E-Gems
  Key-E
  Niacin-Time
  Super-1-Daily

7278 JR Laboratories
Smith Hill Rd
Honesdale, PA 18431   570-253-5826
          www.jrlaboratories.com/
Processor of Chinese herbal products and fluids
  President: Jainie Minogue
Estimated Sales: $300,000-500,000
Number Employees: 1-4

7279 JR Wood/Big Valley
P.O.Box 545
Atwater, CA 95301-0545   209-358-5643
          Fax: 209-358-6351   cswartz@jrwood.com
                    www.jrwood.com
Processor and exporter of frozen fruits including apricots, berries, peaches, importer of pineapples, mangos, blackberries, raspberries and melons
  CFO: Tim Nelson
  CEO: Grey Costley
  Quality Control: Lynette Jacob
  VP: Jerry Widick
  Sales Director: Rick Schmidt
  Operations Manager: Jerry Widick
  Production: Mitch Horntons
  Purchasing: Frank Abarla
Estimated Sales: $300,000-500,000
Number Employees: 1-4
Sq. footage: 1000000
Type of Packaging: Consumer, Food Service, Private Label, Bulk
Brands:
  Big Valley
  Flavorland

7280 (HQ)JRL
527 Bellevue Avenue
Hammonton, NJ 08037-1932   609-561-1572
          Fax: 609-561-8950   josephlucca@comcast.net
                    www.luccacoldstorage.com
Buy and sell blueberries and peaches fresh pack
  President: Joseph Lucca
Estimated Sales: Below $ 5 Million
Number Employees: 4

7281 JSL Foods
3550 Pasadena Ave
Los Angeles, CA 90031-1946   323-223-2484
          Fax: 323-223-9882   800-745-3236
tkishimoto@jslfoods.com   www.jslfoods.com
Processor of chilled and frozen pre-cooked noodles; also, nutritional/power bars and cookies
  President: Frank Kawana
  CFO: Jerry Chung
  Vice President: Terri Kishimoto
  R & D: Swee Seet
  Quality Control: Rhaun Turner
Estimated Sales: $ 100-500 Million
Number Employees: 100-249
Type of Packaging: Food Service, Private Label, Bulk
Brands:
  Amber Farms
  Fortune
  Stir fryNoodels

7282 JTM Food Group
200 Sales Ave
Harrison, OH 45030-1485   513-367-4900
          Fax: 513-367-1132   800-626-2308
                    comments@jtmfoodgroup.com
                    www.jtmfoodgroup.com
Processor of beef patties, buns, bread sticks, dinner rolls, French bread pizza, spaghetti and meatballs, chili, taco and barbecue sauce
  President: Anthony Maas
  Marketing Director: Amy Mcadams
  CFO: Bill Meier
  Sales Director: John Maas, Jr.
  VP Plant Operations: Joseph Maas
Estimated Sales: $ 50-100 Million
Number Employees: 250-499
Sq. footage: 120000
Type of Packaging: Consumer, Food Service
Brands:
  CHEF VITO PASTA MEALS
  Cincy Style
  J.T.M. Food Group
  Texas Jack's Tex-Mex
  VITO'S BAKERY

7283 JWS Delavau Company
10101 Roosevelt Blvd
Philadelphia, PA 19154-2105   215-671-1400
          Fax: 215-671-1401   info@delavau.com
                    www.delavau.com
Processor and exporter of nutritional products including garlic, gelatin, ginseng, calcium carbonate and oyster tablets
  President: Steve Bryan
  CEO: Richard Leff
  Operations Manager: Don Prosser
  Purchasing Manager: Linda Bridge
Estimated Sales: $34 Million
Number Employees: 250-499
Sq. footage: 20000
Type of Packaging: Consumer, Bulk
Brands:
  Herbal Capsules

7284 Ja-Ca Seafood Products
3 Center Plaza
Boston, MA 02108-2003   978-281-8848
                    Fax: 978-281-2247
Seafood
  President: Kenichi Kawauchi

7285 Jack & Jill Ice Cream Company
101 Commerce Dr
Moorestown, NJ 08057-4212   856-813-2300
          Fax: 856-813-2303   sv@jackjillicecream.com
                    www.jackjillicecream.com
Processor and exporter of ice cream and frozen yogurt; wholesaler/distributor of cakes and fancy desserts
  President: Jay Schwartz
  Marketing Director: Shawn Brady
  VP Sales: John Corral
  General Manager: Ken Schwartz
Number Employees: 500-999
Type of Packaging: Consumer, Food Service

7286 Jack Brown Produce
8035 Fruit Ridge Ave NW
Sparta, MI 49345-9758   616-887-9568
          Fax: 616-887-9765   800-348-0834
                    john@jackbrownproduce.com
                    www.jackbrownproduce.com
Processor and exporter of produce
  President: John Schaefer Ii
  Sales: Pat Chase
  Sales Manager: Norm Klein
Estimated Sales: $ 20 - 50 Million
Number Employees: 20-49
Type of Packaging: Consumer, Food Service, Private Label, Bulk
Brands:
  Apple Ridge
  Peach Ridge

7287 Jack Daniel's Distillery
280 Lynchburg Highway 55
Lynchburg, TN 37352-5271   931-759-4221
          Fax: 931-327-1551   www.jackdaniels.com
Processor and exporter of whiskey
  President: W L Lyons Brown
  Manager-Accounting: James Ramsey
  Manager (Lynchburg Promotions): Roger Brashears
  VP/Director Operations: William Roof
Estimated Sales: J
Number Employees: 300
Parent Co: Brown-Forman Corporation
Type of Packaging: Consumer
Brands:
  JACK DANIEL'S

7288 Jack Link Snack Foods
P.O.Box 397
Minong, WI 54859-0397   715-466-2234
          Fax: 715-466-5151   www.linksnacks.com
Beef products
  CEO: Jack Link
  President: Troy Link
  CFO: John Hermeier
Estimated Sales: $ 50-100 Million
Number Employees: 100-249
Brands:
  Jack Link's Beef Jerky

7289 Jack Miller's Food Products
P.O.Box 57
Ville Platte, LA 70586-0057   337-363-1541
          Fax: 337-363-4784   800-646-1541
                    jackmiller@jackmillers.com
                    www.jackmillers.com
Cajun barbecue and cocktail sauces
  President/CEO: Kermit Miller
Estimated Sales: Below $ 5 Million
Number Employees: 5-9
Sq. footage: 7000
Type of Packaging: Food Service, Bulk
Brands:
  Jack Miller

7290 Jack's Bean Company
PO Box 327
Holyoke, CO 80734-0327   970-854-3702
Fax: 970-854-3707   800-274-3702
Processor of dried beans including pinto, Great
Northern, light red kidney, navy and white
General Manager: Steve Brown
Manager: Steve Brown
Estimated Sales: $ 50 - 100 Million
Number Employees: 20
Sq. footage: 65000
Parent Co: ConAgra Foods
Type of Packaging: Consumer, Food Service, Private Label, Bulk

7291 Jack's Lobsters
Limited Oyster Pond
Musquodoboit Harbor, NS B0J 1P0
Canada   902-889-2771
Fax: 902-889-2720
Processor and exporter of fresh and frozen lobsters
President: Joseph Goyetche
Type of Packaging: Consumer, Food Service

7292 Jack's Wholesale Meat Company
719 S Pearl St
Trenton, TX 75490-3111   903-989-2293
Processor of beef and pork
President: Ricky Glasscock
Estimated Sales: $ 3 - 5 Million
Number Employees: 5-9
Type of Packaging: Consumer

7293 Jackson Brothers Food Locker
121 S Avenue H
Post, TX 79356-3330   806-495-3245
Fax: 806-495-3741
Processor of beef, pork and deer meat; slaughtering
services also available
Owner: Joe Rodriguez
Partner: Anna Wilson
Estimated Sales: $ 3 - 5 Million
Number Employees: 5-9
Type of Packaging: Consumer

7294 Jackson Frozen Food Center
13 W 6th Ave
Hutchinson, KS 67501-4650   620-662-4465
Manufacturer of meat products
Owner: Michael Jackson
Estimated Sales: $10-20 Million
Number Employees: 5-9
Type of Packaging: Consumer, Bulk

7295 Jackson Ice Cream Company
400 Yuma St
Denver, CO 80204-4820   303-534-2454
Fax: 303-534-7648
Processor of frozen dairy desserts, low calorie ice
cream and frozen yogurt
Plant Manager: M Day
Number Employees: 100-249
Parent Co: Dillon Corporation
Type of Packaging: Consumer, Food Service, Private Label
Other Locations:
Jackson Ice Cream Co.
Hutchinson KS

7296 Jackson Milk & Ice CreamCompany
2600 E 4th Avenue
Hutchinson, KS 67501-1902   620-663-1244
Processor of dairy products including milk, ice
cream and novelties; also, orange juice and bottled
water
Sales Manager: Mark Miller
General Manager: Joe Lockwood
Number Employees: 20-49
Parent Co: Kroger Company
Type of Packaging: Consumer, Food Service, Private Label, Bulk

7297 Jackson Valley Vineyards
4851 Buena Vista Road
Ione, CA 95640-9625   916-354-3200
Fax: 916-354-3208
Wines
Vineyard Manager: John Bree
Estimated Sales: $ 100-250 Million
Number Employees: 20

7298 Jacob & Sons Wholesale Meats
P.O.Box 217
Martins Ferry, OH 43935-0217   740-633-3091
Fax: 740-633-3106 www.jacobandsonsmeat.com
Manufacturer of fresh and frozen beef, pork and
poultry
Owner: Michael Jacob
Estimated Sales: $2.5 Million
Number Employees: 10-19
Type of Packaging: Consumer, Food Service, Bulk

7299 Jacob & Sons Wholesale Meats
P.O.Box 217
Martins Ferry, OH 43935-0217   740-633-3091
Fax: 740-633-3106 chops070@aol.com
www.jacobandsonsmeat.com
Wholesale meats
President: Michael Jacob
Estimated Sales: $ 20 - 50 Million
Number Employees: 10-19

7300 Jacobs Meats
8127 N State Route 66
Defiance, OH 43512-6724   419-782-7831
Fax: 419-782-8128 www.jacobsmeats.com
Manufacturer of beef, pork and poultry
President: Paul Stork
Estimated Sales: $1-3 Million
Number Employees: 10-19
Type of Packaging: Consumer, Food Service, Private Label, Bulk

7301 Jacobs, Malcolm, & Burtt
2001 Jerrold Ave
San Francisco, CA 94124-1604   415-285-0400
Fax: 415-285-2056
Processor of produce including asparagus and
melons
Owner: Leo Rolandeli
Estimated Sales: $54486391
Number Employees: 20-49
Type of Packaging: Consumer, Food Service, Bulk

7302 Jacobsmuhlen's Meats
1415 NW Susbauer Rd
Cornelius, OR 97113-6331   503-359-0479
Manufacturer of pork and beef
Owner: Harry Jacobsmuhlen
Estimated Sales: $15 Million
Number Employees: 5-9
Type of Packaging: Consumer

7303 Jacques' Bakery
27122b Paseo Espada
San Juan Capistrano, CA 92675-5706 949-496-5322
Fax: 949-496-2941
Bakery products

7304 Jaeger Bakery
918 W Somers Street
Milwaukee, WI 53205-2399   414-263-1700
Cookies
COO: William Metzler
Sales Manager: Randy Johnson
Estimated Sales: $ 100-500 Million
Number Employees: 250-499

7305 Jager Foods
18557 County 11
Long Prairie, MN 56347-4800   320-732-6925
Fax: 320-732-4047   800-358-7251
Dried soup mixes
President: Pete Jager
Owner: Pete Jager
Number Employees: 5-9
Brands:
Jager
Shitake Mushroom Soup Mixes (4)

7306 Jaguar Yerba Company
P.O.Box 1192
Ashland, OR 97520-0040   541-482-7745
Fax: 541-482-6780   800-839-0775
ecoteas@ecoteas.com   www.yerbamate.com
Yerba mate teas
Owner: Stefan Schachter
Co-Founder: Brendan Girardi
Partner: Joe Chermesino
Estimated Sales: $ 3 - 5 Million
Number Employees: 1-4

7307 Jagulana Herbal Products
P.O.Box 45
Badger, CA 93603-0045   559-337-2188
Fax: 559-337-2354 www.gynostemma.com
Dedicated to researching, developing and marketing
jiaogulan and jiaogulan-based herbal products of the
highest quality
President: Chris Gleen
Research: Michael Blumert
Technical Assistant: Chris Glenn
Estimated Sales: $ 1 - 3 Million
Number Employees: 1-4

7308 Jaindl's Turkey Farms
3150 Coffeetown Rd
Orefield, PA 18069-2511   610-395-3333
Fax: 610-395-8608   800-475-6654
jaindl2@aol.com   www.jaindl.com
Processor of turkey
Owner: David Jaindl
Sales/Marketing: Alice Brown
General Manager: David Jaindl
Estimated Sales: $ 20 - 50 Million
Number Employees: 100-249
Type of Packaging: Consumer, Food Service, Private Label, Bulk
Brands:
Grand Champion

7309 Jakeman's Maple Products
454414 Trillium Line
Beachville, ON N0J 1A0
Canada   519-539-1366
Fax: 519-421-2469   800-382-9795
bob@themaplestore.com
www.themaplestore.com
Processor and exporter of maple syrup, sugar, candy
and yogurt, coffee, tea and cookies
President: Bob Jakeman
CFO: Jane Henderson
Quality Control: Melissa Martin
Sales: Mary Jakeman
Production: Heather Crane
Number Employees: 15
Number of Brands: 1
Number of Products: 78
Sq. footage: 6620
Parent Co: Auvergne Farms
Type of Packaging: Consumer, Food Service, Private Label, Bulk

7310 Jakes Brothers Country Meats
6089 Clarksville Pike
Joelton, TN 37080-8997   615-876-2911
Cured meats
Owner: Johny Jakes
Estimated Sales: $ 1-2.5 Million
Number Employees: 1-4

7311 Jalapeno Foods Company
1215 W Imperial Highway
Suite 205
Brea, CA 92821-3735   714-521-9900
Fax: 714-521-9940   800-863-9198
ralbanol@aol.com/snavares@aol.com
http://www.aol.com/snavares
Condiments, ethnic foods
President: Arturo Pimiento
Sales Manager: Sabrina Navares
Estimated Sales: $ 5-10 Million
Number Employees: 20
Type of Packaging: Private Label
Brands:
Mi Mexico

7312 (HQ)Jalapeno Foods Company
1450 Lake Robbins Drive
Suite 350
The Woodlands, TX 77380-3252   281-363-4585
Fax: 281-364-8452   800-896-2318
www.jalapenofoods.com
Processor, importer, exporter and packager of red
and green Mexican salsas, chipotle and chile peppers, shelf-stable guacamole and jalapenos including
whole, nacho, sliced and diced
CEO: Carlos Gosselin
Vice President: Sue Doolittle
Estimated Sales: $ 5 - 10 Million
Number Employees: 5-9
Sq. footage: 60000
Type of Packaging: Consumer, Food Service, Private Label, Bulk

Brands:
Jake & Amos
Mi Mexico

7313 Jamae Natural Foods
PO Box 481096
Los Angeles, CA 90048-9696 323-937-3670
Fax: 323-937-0849 800-343-0052
crystal@jamae.com www.jamae.com
Cookies, soy nut crunch bars
President: Crystal You
Estimated Sales: $300,000
Number Employees: 5-9
Type of Packaging: Private Label
Brands:
Health Cookie
Soynut Crunch Bar
Soynuts

7314 Jamaica John
9140 Belden Ave
Franklin Park, IL 60131-3506 847-451-1730
Fax: 847-451-1590 sales@jamaicajohn.com
www.jamaicajohn.com
Manufacture, package and distribute liquid and
sauce food products
President: John Capozzoli
Quality Control: John Capozzoli Jr
Estimated Sales: $ 5-10 Million
Number Employees: 10-19

7315 Jamaican Gourmet CoffeeCompany
PO Box 8115
New Haven, CT 06530-0115 203-239-5633
Fax: 203-239-5192 sales@coffeeforless.com
www.jamaicancoffeeco.com
Coffee, tea
President: Lloyd Parchment
Estimated Sales: Below $ 5 Million
Number Employees: 20
Sq. footage: 13800

7316 James Candy Company
1519 Boardwalk
Atlantic City, NJ 08401-7012 609-344-1519
Fax: 609-344-0246 800-441-1404
sales@jamescandy.com www.jamescandy.com
Processor of confectionery products including salt-
water taffy, lollypops, fudge and macaroons
President: Frank Glaser
Marketing Director: Lisa Whitley
VP Operations: Susan Saraceni
Estimated Sales: $2 Million
Number Employees: 50-99
Type of Packaging: Consumer, Bulk
Brands:
James Chocolate Seal Taffy
James Cream Mints
James Salt Water Taffy
Mumsey

7317 James Cowan & Sons
20 Temple Street
Worcester, MA 01604-4118 508-754-5385
Processor and wholesaler/distributor of groceries,
dairy products, equipment and fixtures, fresh and
frozen fish, poultry and meat; serving the food ser-
vice market
Vice President: Anne Sibson
Comptroller: Debra Ross
Number Employees: 10-19
Sq. footage: 9600
Type of Packaging: Food Service

7318 James Finley & Company
23 Vreeland Rd # 106
Florham Park, NJ 07932-1510 973-539-8030
Fax: 973-539-4816 www.finlayusa.com
President: Patrick O'Keefe
Sales Director: Greg Vorshiem
Estimated Sales: $ 10 - 20 Million
Number Employees: 10-19

7319 James Frasinetti & Sons
PO Box 292368
Sacramento, CA 95829-2368 916-383-2444
Fax: 916-383-5825 www.frasinetti.com
Wines
Partner: Howard Frasinetti
Estimated Sales: $ 2.5-5 Million
Number Employees: 20-50

7320 James J. Derba Company
206 Commonwealth Avenue
Apt 9
Boston, MA 02116-2558 617-884-6700
Fax: 617-884-6764 800-732-3848
www.prime-steaks.com
Manufacturer of portion control premium steaks,
poultry and gourmet food
President: Paul Derba
Estimated Sales: $115 Million
Number Employees: 40
Sq. footage: 20000
Type of Packaging: Food Service

7321 James L. Mood Fisheries
PO Box 60
Wood's Harbour, NS B0W 2E0
Canada 902-723-2360
Fax: 902-723-2880 info@moodfisheries.com
www.moodfisheries.com
Processor and exporter of fresh seafood including
tuna, lobster, swordfish and groundfish
Owner & CEO: Cory Mood
Manager: Almond Mood
Estimated Sales: $ 5-10 Million
Number Employees: 20
Type of Packaging: Consumer, Food Service, Pri-
vate Label, Bulk

7322 James Skinner Company
4657 G St
Omaha, NE 68117-1410 402-734-1672
Fax: 402-734-0516 800-358-7428
www.skinnerbaking.com
Processor and exporter of frozen baked goods in-
cluding danish, pastries, muffins, cinnamon rolls and
coffee cakes
President: James Skinner
VP Marketing: Doug Dinnin
VP Sales: Doug Dinnin
VP Operations: Audie Keaton
Plant Manager: Tom Urzendowski
Estimated Sales: $7.6 Million
Number Employees: 100-249
Sq. footage: 75000
Type of Packaging: Consumer, Food Service, Pri-
vate Label, Bulk
Brands:
Skinner Bakery

7323 Jamesport Vineyards
P.O.Box 842
Jamesport, NY 11947-0842 631-722-5256
Fax: 631-722-5256
info@jamesport-vineyards.com
www.jamesport-vineyards.com
Wines
President: Ron Goerler Sr Sr
General Manager: Ronald Goerler Jr
Estimated Sales: $ 2.5-5 Million
Number Employees: 5-9
Type of Packaging: Private Label
Brands:
Cabernet Franc
Jamesport Vineyards
Marlot

7324 Jamieson Laboratories
Suite 1600
Toronto, QC M4V 1L5
Canada 519-974-8482
Fax: 519-974-4742 www.jamiesonvitamins.com
Manufacturer, importer and exporter of kefir, yogurt,
cod liver oil, vitamins, mineral supplements, water
purifying systems and filters
President: Vic Neufeld
Owner: Eric Margolis
Number Employees: 50-99
Sq. footage: 40000
Parent Co: Jamieson Pharmacal
Type of Packaging: Consumer
Brands:
Super Vita Vim

7325 Janca's Jojoba Oil & Seed Company
456 E Juanita Avenue
Suite 7
Mesa, AZ 85204-6538 480-497-9494
Fax: 480-497-1312 custsvc@jancas.com
www.jancas.com

Processor and exporter of vegetable oils and waxes,
rice bran oil and jojoba oil, butter, waxes and herbs;
also, essential oils and fragrances
President: Tom Janca
Vice President: Val Brown
VP Marketing: David Murphy
Sales Manager: Jennifer Hathaway
Sales Manager: Matt Drapcho
Production Manager: Mike Green
Purchasing Manager: Sam Flaherty
Estimated Sales: $ 1 - 3 Million
Number Employees: 1-4
Sq. footage: 2000
Type of Packaging: Private Label, Bulk
Brands:
Janca's

7326 Jane Specialty Foods
PO Box 19057
Green Bay, WI 54307-9057 920-497-7131
Fax: 920-497-4604 800-558-4700
Pickles and pickle relish
Plant Manager: Dave Schindler
Estimated Sales: Under $500,000
Number Employees: 250-499
Type of Packaging: Private Label

7327 Janes Family Foods
3340 Orlando Drive
Mississauga, ON L4V 1C7
Canada 905-673-7145
Fax: 905-677-0607 800-565-2637
info@janesfamilyfoods.com
www.janesfamilyfoods.com
Processor of frozen breaded and battered seafood,
poultry, vegetable and cheese products
National Sales Manager (Food Service): Cindy
Novak
National Sales Manager (Retail): Ken Clarkson
Estimated Sales: $17500000
Number Employees: 100
Sq. footage: 100000
Type of Packaging: Consumer, Food Service, Pri-
vate Label, Bulk
Brands:
Crisp & Delicious
Golden Gate
J&J Gourmet
Janes Family Favourites

7328 Janet's Own Home Sweet Home
1101 Dalton Lane
Austin, TX 78742-2807 512-385-4708
President: Janet Morgan
Estimated Sales: Under $500,000
Number Employees: 1-4

7329 Janowski's Hamburgers
15 S Long Beach Rd
Rockville Centre, NY 11570-5621 516-764-9591
Fax: 516-764-1908
www.janowskishamburgers.com
Butcher quality meats and Weber products
Owner: Bill Vogelsberg
Estimated Sales: $ 10-20 Million
Number Employees: 5-9

7330 Jarchem Industries
414 Wilson Ave
Newark, NJ 07105-4287 973-578-4560
Fax: 973-344-5743 info@jarchem.com
www.jarchem.com
Processor, importer and exporter of calcium chlo-
ride, acetic acid, sodium diacetate and sodium ben-
zoate
CEO: Arnold Stern
Mngr.: Howard Honing
Estimated Sales: $ .5 - 1 million
Number Employees: 1-4

7331 Jardine Foods
P.O.Box 1530
Buda, TX 78610-1530 512-312-0555
Fax: 512-295-3020 800-544-1880
customerservice@jardinefoods.com
www.jardinefoods.com
Ketchup, chilies, sauces, dips, salsa, BBQ sauce,
jelly
Manager: Scott Bolding
VP Sales/Mearketing: Garth Gardner
VP of Operations: Scott Jackson
Director: Craig Lieberman
Director: Brad Wallace

Estimated Sales: $ 5-10 Million
Number Employees: 100-249
Number of Brands: 20
Number of Products: 200
Type of Packaging: Consumer, Food Service, Private Label, Bulk
Brands:
    D.J. JARDINE

7332 Jardine Organic Ranch Co
910 Nacimiento Lake Dr
Paso Robles, CA 93446-8713   805-238-2365
    Fax: 805-239-4334   866-833-5050
order@jardineranch.com   www.jardineranch.com
Processor and exporter; gift baskets of nuts
    Owner: Bill Jardine
    Owner: Mary Jardine
    Manager: Duane Jardine
Estimated Sales: Less than $500,000
Number Employees: 1-4
Type of Packaging: Consumer, Food Service, Bulk

7333 Jarrow Industries
12246 Hawkins St
Santa Fe Springs, CA 90670-3365   562-906-1919
    Fax: 562-906-1979 info@jiimfg.com
    www.jiimfg.com
Manufacturing and packaging of the highest quality and clean vitamins and supplements for their customers.
    President/CEO: Silva Hari
Estimated Sales: $ 50 - 100 Million
Number Employees: 20-49

7334 Jasmine & Bread
RR 2
Box 256
S Royalton, VT 05068   802-763-7115
    Fax: 802-763-7115
Processor of condiments
    Owner: Sherrie Maurer
Estimated Sales: $500,000-$1 Million
Number Employees: 1-4
Type of Packaging: Private Label, Bulk

7335 Jasmine Vineyards
11239 Famoso Porterville Hwy
Delano, CA 93215-9460   661-792-2141
  Fax: 661-792-6365 jvine@jasminevineyards.com
    www.jasminevineyards.com
Processor, packer and exporter of grapes
    President: Martin Zaninovich
    Sales Manager: Jon Zaninovich
Estimated Sales: $13,556,816
Number Employees: 100-249
Type of Packaging: Consumer, Food Service, Bulk
Brands:
    HAVREN
    JASVINE
    MEV
    VINMAR

7336 Jason & Son Specialty Foods
2590 Mercantile Drive
Rancho Cordova, CA 95742-6244   916-635-9590
    Fax: 916-635-9711 800-810-9093
info@jasonson.com   www.jasonson.com
Processor of enrobed, panned and specialty packed confectionery items including trail mixes, nut clusters and raisins; also, sugar-free products available
    President: William Jason
    VP: Margaret Jason
    General Manager: Richard Antti
Estimated Sales: $1255895
Number Employees: 15
Type of Packaging: Consumer, Food Service, Private Label, Bulk
Brands:
    Jason & Son

7337 Jason Pharmaceuticals
11445 Cronhill Dr
Owings Mills, MD 21117-2283   410-581-8042
    Fax: 410-581-8070 800-638-7867
    www.medibix.com
Dietetic products
    President: John Hereford
    CEO: William Vitale
    Managing Director: William Vitale
Number Employees: 100-249
Brands:
    Jason Pharmaceuticals

7338 Jasper Products LLC
3877 E 27th St
Joplin, MO 64804-3306   417-206-2099
    Fax: 417-206-3434 877-769-7367
info@jasperproducts.com
www.jasperproducts.com
Soy products
    President: Ken Haubein
Estimated Sales: $ 50 - 100 Million
Number Employees: 250-499

7339 Jasper Wyman & Son
P.O.Box 100
Milbridge, ME 04658-0100   207-546-2311
    Fax: 207-546-2074 800-341-1758
jwyman@wymans.com   www.wymans.com
Processor of frozen, canned, dried and fresh wild blueberries, raspberries and cranberries; exporter of IQF wild blueberries
    President: Edward Flanagan
    Director International Sales: J Kim Higgins
Estimated Sales: $ 1 - 3 Million
Number Employees: 5-9

7340 Jasper Wyman & Son Canada
PO Box 205
Morell, PE C0A 1S0
Canada   902-961-3330
    Fax: 902-961-5610

7341 Java Cabana
P.O.Box 520845
Miami, FL 33152-0845   305-592-7302
    Fax: 305-592-9471 jc@javacabana.com
    www.javacabana.com
Produces a variety of coffee products - whole beans and ground in addition to instant; iced tea mixes; decaf; expresso; cappuccino; demitasse sets; expresso machines.
    Owner: Jose Souto
    Marketing Director: Beatriz Vescovacci
Estimated Sales: $2.5-5 Million
Number Employees: 20-49
Type of Packaging: Food Service, Private Label

7342 Java Jungle
208 W Main Street
Visalia, CA 93291-6212   559-732-5282
    Fax: 559-732-5282
Coffee
    President: Cruz Ann Borges
Estimated Sales: Less than $500,000
Number Employees: 5-9

7343 Java Sun Coffee Roasters
35 Atlantic Ave
Marblehead, MA 01945-3139   781-631-7788
Coffee
    Owner: Cheryl Burka
Estimated Sales: $500,000-$1 Million
Number Employees: 10-19

7344 Java-Gourmet/Keuka LakeCoffee Roaster
2792 Route 54A
Penn Yan, NY 14527   315-536-7843
    888-428-2739
susan@java-gourmet.com
www.java-gourmet.com
coffee, rubs, sauces and marinades, a brine mix, a dessert topper, a finishing salt, and a chocolate and espresso bean candy.
    President/Owner: Susan Atkisson

7345 Javalution Coffee Company
2485 E Sunrise Blvd # 201a
Fort Lauderdale, FL 33304-3100   954-568-1747
    Fax: 954-568-0854 877-528-2348
customerservice@javalution.com
www.javalution.com/index.php
Producer of Latin American gourmet arabica blend coffee products including diet plus; energy plus; gourmet diet plus, and single serve gourmet coffee.
    President: Scott Pumper
    CEO: Tony Sanzari
    Chief Science Officer: Jose Antonio
Type of Packaging: Food Service

7346 Jaxsons Ice Cream
128 S Federal Hwy
Dania, FL 33004-3695   954-923-4445
    Fax: 954-922-8293 jaxsons@bellsouth.net
    www.jaxsonsicecream.com

Ice cream, frozen desserts
    Owner: Monroe Udell
Estimated Sales: $ 1-2.5 Million
Number Employees: 20-49
Brands:
    Jaxsons

7347 Jay & Boots Meats
3701 Neal Drive
Knoxville, TN 37918-5314   865-922-3213
    Fax: 865-922-8095
Meat
    President: Jay Willard
    Vice President: Shannon Willard
    Operations Manager: Nancy Anderson
Brands:
    Jay & Boots Meats

7348 Jay Hoyt of California
1372 N McDowell Boulevard
Suite H
Petaluma, CA 94954-7102   707-762-1881
    Fax: 707-762-1950
Processor and exporter of frozen cheesecake
    Owner: Jay Hoyt
    Sales Director: Brook Havener
    Operations Manager: Jayne Cinquini
Number Employees: 5-9
Sq. footage: 5110
Type of Packaging: Consumer, Food Service, Private Label
Brands:
    Sonoma Valley

7349 Jay Poultry Corporation
1010 Haddonfield Berlin # 402
Voorhees, NJ 08043-3514   856-435-0900
    Fax: 856-435-3019 info@oakvalleyfarms.com
    www.oakvalleyfarms.com
Poultry
    President: Leo Rubin
    Co-Owner: Joseph Milgrim
Estimated Sales: $ 5-10 Million
Number Employees: 5-9
Brands:
    Oak Valley Farms

7350 Jay Shah Foods
1121 Meyerside Drive
Mississauga, ON L4T 1J6
Canada   905-696-0172
Processor of East Indian specialty snack foods and chutneys
    President: Jay Shah
    Sales/Marketing Manager: Jay Shah
    Purchasing Manager: Shushi Shah
Number Employees: 5-9
Sq. footage: 10000

7351 Jays Foods
B
5025 W 73rd St
Chicago, IL 60638-6611   773-731-8400
    Fax: 773-933-2100 www.jayfoods.com
Processor of snack foods including potato chips, popcorn, tortilla chips, etc
    CEO: Tim Healy
    Executive VP: Michael Vallero
    VP Sales/Marketing: Greg Spears
    VP Operations: Dan Madigan
    Plant Manager: Steve Green
Estimated Sales: $78 Million
Number Employees: 850
Type of Packaging: Consumer

7352 Jazz Fine Foods
5065 Ontario E Street
Montreal, QC H1V 3V2
Canada   514-255-0110
    Fax: 514-259-1788 laurent.durot@videotrona.ca

7353 Jazzie J. Enterprises
PO Box 2748
Grapevine, TX 76099-2748   817-481-3421
    Fax: 817-421-5383
    President: Janet Williams

7354 Jazzie Smoothie
14 Rue Royale
Metairie, LA 70002-1535   504-780-8429
    Fax: 504-455-7349 info@jazziesmoothie.com
    www.jazziesmoothie.com

Processor and exporter of fruit and coffee beverage mixes including all natural, nonfat, noncholesterol, caffeine free, reduced calorie and vitamin boosted; kosher available
President: Stan Middleton III
Number Employees: 5-9
Sq. footage: 1200
Parent Co: Commercial Holding Corporation
Type of Packaging: Consumer, Food Service, Private Label
Brands:
Berry Hill
Crescent City
Jazzy Java
Mango Mambo
Pete's Peach
Straw/Banana Twist

7355 (HQ)Jbs Packerland Inc
2580 University Ave
Green Bay, WI 54311-5824   920-468-4000
Fax: 920-468-7140 www.packerland.com
Meat packing and non-local trucking.
President & CEO: Richard V Vesta
CFO: Craig Liegel
Estimated Sales: $290 Million
Number Employees: 1000
Type of Packaging: Food Service, Bulk
Other Locations:
Packerland-Green Bay
Green Bay WI
Packerland-Plainwell
Plainwell MI
Moyer Packing Company
Souderton PA
Sun Land Beef Company
Tolleson AZ
Brands:
Grand River Ranch
Showcase Supreme

7356 Jeanerette Sugar Company
2304 Main St
Jeanerette, LA 70544-3321   337-276-4238
Fax: 337-276-9877 david@ijeanerettesugar.com
www.jeanerettesugar.com
Processor of raw sugar
President: Robert Roane
Estimated Sales: $27,000,000
Number Employees: 50-99
Type of Packaging: Bulk

7357 Jecky's Best
26450 Summit Cir
Santa Clarita, CA 91350-2991   661-259-1313
Fax: 661-259-5855 888-532-5972
info@jabfoods.com www.jabfoods.com
Frozen dough and unbaked goods
President: Jecky Bicer
VP: Areila Bicer
Estimated Sales: $ 5-10 Million
Number Employees: 20-49
Type of Packaging: Private Label
Brands:
Jecky's Best

7358 Jed's Maple Products
475 Carter Road
Westfield, VT 05874-9719   802-744-2095
Fax: 802-744-2095 866-478-7388
wheeler@jedsample.com www.jedsample.com
Maple syrup, candy, cream, lollipops salad dressings, and sauces
Co-Owner: Stephen Wheeler
Co-Owner: Amy Wheeler

7359 Jedwards International
39 Broad St
Quincy, MA 02169-4689   617-472-9300
Fax: 617-472-9359 info@jedwardsinc.com
www.codliveroil.com
Jedwards International, Inc. is a supplier of Specialty oils to the Food, Dietary Supplement, and Cosmetic industries in North America. Jedwards International, Inc. is a leading supplier of the omega-3 fatty acids: EPA and DHA, thepurest Cod Liver Oil and the finest GLA and omega-3 rich Seed oils.
President: Christos Iorio
Estimated Sales: $1,200,000
Number Employees: 5-9

7360 Jefferson Packing Company
765 Marlene Drive
Gretna, LA 70056-7639   504-366-4451
Fax: 504-366-9382

President: William Marciante

7361 Jefferson Vineyards
1353 Thomas Jefferson Pkwy
Charlottesville, VA 22902-7518   434-977-3042
Fax: 434-977-5459 800-272-3042
info@jeffersonvineyards.com
www.jeffersonvineyards.com
Wine
Manager: Chad Zakaib
Winemaker/Vineyard Manager: Frantz Ventre
Estimated Sales: $ 5 - 10 Million
Number Employees: 10-19

7362 Jel-Sert Company
P.O.Box 261
West Chicago, IL 60186-0261   630-231-7590
Fax: 630-231-3993 800-323-2592
www.jelsert.com
Manufacturer and exporter of powdered drink mixes, juices and novelty frozen ice pops.
Chairman: Charles Wegner IV
CEO: Gary Ricco
CFO: Tony D'Anna
Sales Manager: Vincent Morgan
Estimated Sales: $175 Million
Number Employees: 250-499
Sq. footage: 500000
Type of Packaging: Food Service
Brands:
FLA-VOR-AID
FLA-VOR-ICE
POP-ICE

7363 Jelks Coffee Roasters
P.O.Box 8667
Shreveport, LA 71148-8667   318-636-6391
Fax: 318-635-1384 info@jelkscoffee.com
www.jelks-coffee.com
Processor of regular, decaffeinated and flavored coffee including banana hazelnut, chocolate cheesecake, pumpkin spice, vanilla almond, orange creamsicle, victorian caramel, etc
President: Harvey Jelks
Estimated Sales: $ 2.5-5 Million
Number Employees: 5-9
Brands:
Toddy

7364 (HQ)Jelly Belly Candy Company
1 Jelly Belly Ln
Fairfield, CA 94533-6741   707-428-2800
Fax: 707-428-2863 800-522-3267
www.jellybelly.com
Processor and exporter of candy including bagged, cremes, jelly beans, candy corn, gums, jellies, Halloween, Valentine, Christmas, Easter, etc.
CEO: Herman Rowland
Director Of Marketing: John Harrington
Estimated Sales: $100+ Million
Number Employees: 250-499
Number of Brands: 2
Number of Products: 150
Type of Packaging: Consumer, Private Label
Brands:
GOELITZ
JELLY BELLY

7365 (HQ)Jelly Belly Candy Company
1 Jelly Belly Ln
Fairfield, CA 94533-6741   707-428-2800
Fax: 707-428-2863 800-522-3267
www.jellybelly.com
Processor and exporter of bagged, rack packaged and seasonal candy. Product line includes Jelly Belly Jelly Beans, Gummi Bears, Assorted Jordan Almonds, Cinnamon Bears, Peach Rings, Raspberries and Blackberries, Chocolate Dutch MintsCandy Corns and Licorice Pastels.
Chairman/Chief Executive Officer: Herman Rowland Sr
President/Chief Operations Officer: Robert Simpson
Founder of Company: Gustav Goelitz
Vice President Business Development: Ryan Schader
Vice President Plant Operations: Mike Bianco
Estimated Sales: $50-100 Million
Number Employees: 250-499
Type of Packaging: Consumer, Bulk
Brands:
Dutch
Goelitz Confections
Jelly Belly

Pet Rat
Pet Tarantula

7366 Jemm Wholesale Meat Company
4649 W Armitage Ave
Chicago, IL 60639-3405   773-523-8161
Fax: 773-523-8890
information@jemmburger.com
www.jemmburger.com
Processor of frozen portion controlled steaks and ground beef items including patties
President: Daniel Goldman
VP: Thomas Nacht
Plant Manager: Dominic Pinto
Estimated Sales: $14,100,000
Number Employees: 20-49
Type of Packaging: Consumer, Food Service
Brands:
Seasoned Delux

7367 Jenkins Foods
14245 Birwood St
Detroit, MI 48238-2207   313-834-0800
Fax: 313-834-0443 800-800-3286
sandy@unclerays.com www.unclerays.com
Snack foods
President: Raymond Jenkins
Marketing Director: Dennis BaPra
CFO: Sandra Subotich
CFO: Sandra Jenkins
General Manager: James Coomes
Estimated Sales: $ 20-30 Million
Number Employees: 100-249
Brands:
Unclerays

7368 Jennie-O Turkey Store
P.O.Box 778
Willmar, MN 56201-0778   320-235-2622
Fax: 320-231-7100 turkeyinfo@j-ots.com
www.jennie-oturkeystore.com
Processor and exporter of turkey products
President: Michael Tolbert
CEO: Jerry Jerome
CFO: Dwight York
VP Marketing: Bob Tegt
Sales Director: Jime Splinter
Public Relations: Dave Suheke
Operations Manager: Bob Wood
Purchasing Agent: Larry Hammond
Number Employees: 5,000-9,999
Parent Co: Hormel Foods Corporation
Type of Packaging: Consumer, Food Service

7369 Jenny Lee Bakery
620 Island Ave
Mc Kees Rocks, PA 15136-3293   412-331-8900
Fax: 412-331-8903
advertising@jennyleebakery.com
www.jennyleebakery.com
Manufacturer and wholesaler/distributor of breads, muffins and rolls; serving supermarkets and retail stores
Co-Owner: Bernard Baker
Co-Owner: Beverly Baker
VP: James Baker
Sales Manager: Scott Baker
Estimated Sales: $4 Million
Number Employees: 100-249
Sq. footage: 10000
Type of Packaging: Consumer

7370 Jenny's Country Kitchen
438 Main Street S
Dover, MN 55929-1509   507-932-3035
Fax: 507-932-4777 800-357-3497
info@jennyscountrykitchen.com
www.jennyscountrykitchen.com
Cocoa and coffee products
President: Jenny Wood
CEO: Dan Wood
VP: Dan Wood
Marketing Manager: Dan Wood
Estimated Sales: Below $ 5 Million
Number Employees: 10
Brands:
Jenny's Country Kitchen

7371 Jenport International Distributors
Suite 107
Coquitlam, BC V3K 6H1
Canada   604-464-9888
Fax: 604-464-8388

Processor, importer and exporter of frozen foods including fruit and seafood; also, polyethylene bags
President: Dato Tan
Estimated Sales: Below $5 Million
Number Employees: 10
Brands:
Deep Cove
Sea Pearl
Sun King
Tuff 'n' Tidy

7372 Jensen Luhr & Sons
P.O.Box 297
Hood River, OR 97031-0065   541-386-3811
Fax: 541-386-4917   info@luhrjensen.com
www.luhrjensen.com
Processor of sausage and brine mixes and seasonings and spices; also, sausage making kits, electric smokers and wood flavor fuels
President: Philip Jensen
Customer Service: Linda Gordon
Estimated Sales: $10-20 Million
Number Employees: 250-499
Sq. footage: 50000

7373 Jensen Meat Company
2525 Birch St
Vista, CA 92081-8433   760-727-6700
Fax: 760-727-8598   gebbley@jensenmeat.com
www.jensenmeat.com
Processor and exporter of ground beef
President: Robert Jensen
VP: Shirley Jenson
General Manager: Ken Duhram
Estimated Sales: $26.9 Million
Number Employees: 100-249
Type of Packaging: Consumer, Food Service, Private Label, Bulk

7374 Jensen Seafood Packing Company
P.O.Box 338
Dulac, LA 70353-0338   985-563-7022
Fax: 985-563-4858
Fish and seafood
President: Ken Trinh
Estimated Sales: $ 3 - 5 Million
Number Employees: 5-9

7375 Jensen's Old Fashioned Smokehouse
10520 Greenwood Ave N
Seattle, WA 98133-8721   206-364-5569
Fax: 206-364-0880
sales@jensenssmokehouse.com
www.jensenssmokehouse.com
Processor of smoked seafood
President: Michael Jensen
Estimated Sales: Below $ 5 Million
Number Employees: 5-9
Type of Packaging: Consumer, Food Service
Brands:
Wild Keta Salmon
Wild Keta Salmon
Wild Red King Salmon
Wild White King Salmon

7376 Jer's Handmade Chocolates
437 S Highway 101
Suite 205
Solana Beach, CA 92075   858-792-2287
Fax: 858-792-4196   800-540-7265
info@jers.com   www.jers.com
gourmet chocolate peanut butter bars, chocolate covered peanut brittle bites
President/Owner: Jerry Swain

7377 Jer-Mar Foods
PO Box 1114
Windsor, ON   N9A 6P8
Canada   519-256-3474
Fax: 519-258-4455
Processor and exporter of fresh and frozen fish including perch, pickerel and whitefish
President: Mark Goldhar
Type of Packaging: Consumer, Food Service, Private Label, Bulk

7378 Jerabek's New Bohemian Coffee House
63 Winifred St W
St Paul, MN 55107-1139   651-228-1245
Fax: 651-228-3011 www.jerabeks.com
Baked goods, coffees, collectables
Manager: Russell Sprangler

Estimated Sales: $500,000 appx.
Number Employees: 10-19

7379 Jerbeau Chocolate
1080 Avenida Acaso
Camarillo, CA 93012-8725   805-484-4686
Fax: 805-484-2477   800-755-3723
mary_decker@jerbeau.com   www.jerbeau.com
Chocolates
President: Katalin Coburn
Estimated Sales: $ 10-24.9 Million
Number Employees: 33

7380 (HQ)Jeremiah's Pick Coffee Company
1495 Evans Ave
San Francisco, CA 94124-1706   415-206-9900
Fax: 415-206-9542   800-537-3642
office@jeremiahspick.com
www.jeremiahspick.com
Roasted gourmet coffee
President: Jeremiah Pick
Operations Manager: Jay Meltesen
Estimated Sales: Below $ 5 Million
Number Employees: 20-49
Sq. footage: 14000
Type of Packaging: Consumer, Food Service, Private Label, Bulk
Brands:
Cafe Pick
Chocatal
Jeremiah's Pick

7381 Jerrell Packaging
802 Labarge Dr
Bessemer, AL 35022-8320   205-426-8930
Fax: 205-426-8989   john@jerrellpackaging.com
www.jerrellpackaging.com
Popcorn
President: John Lyon
Estimated Sales: Below $ 5 Million
Number Employees: 10-19

7382 Jerry's Nut House
2101 Humboldt St
Denver, CO 80205-5327   303-861-2262
Fax: 303-861-1214   888-214-0747
Products include raw, roasted and salted inshell; raw redskins, raw blanched, roasted snack peanuts, honey coated/roasted, granules, hot & spicy seasoned; chocolate covered, peanut bars/squares.
President: Claude Julia
Vice President: Wendy Julia
General Manager: Jim Ohrt
Estimated Sales: $2600000
Number Employees: 10-19
Sq. footage: 20000
Type of Packaging: Consumer, Food Service, Private Label, Bulk
Brands:
Jerry's
Jerry's Caramel Corn
Jerry's Cheese Corn
Jerry's Popcorn
Jerry's Snack Packs

7383 Jersey Fruit CooperativeAssociation
800 Ellis Mill Rd # B
Glassboro, NJ 08028-3204   856-863-9100
Fax: 856-863-9490   sales@jerseyfruit.com
www.jerseyfruit.com
Bluberries, peaches, nectarines, and cranberries.
President: Louis Deeugenio
Director of Sales: Francisco Allende
Estimated Sales: $ 10-20 Million
Number Employees: 20-49
Type of Packaging: Food Service

7384 Jersey Juice
186 Stanton Mountain Road
Lebanon, NJ 08833-3103   609-406-0500
Processor of fruit juice concentrates
Manager: Chuck Gandle
VP Sales: Chuck Gandle
VP Operations: David Montes
Number Employees: 20-49
Sq. footage: 24000
Type of Packaging: Food Service, Private Label, Bulk

7385 Jersey Pride
PO Box 10796
New Brunswick, NJ 08906   406-585-0014
Fax: 406-585-0035 http://www.jerseypride.org
President: George Dorsey
Estimated Sales: $500,000-$1 Million
Number Employees: 5-9

7386 Jerusalem House
2425 W 18th Ave
Eugene, OR 97402-3403   541-485-1012
Fax: 541-687-6853
Mideastern natural refrigerated foods: hummus, baba ghannouj, tabbouleh, tihini, baklava, spinich & artichoke dips and salads.
President: Simon Oueis
Estimated Sales: Less than $500,000
Number Employees: 1-4

7387 Jeryl's Jems
43 Eagle Lane
Tappan, NY 10983-1810   845-359-4715
Fax: 845-359-7386   info@jerylsjems.com
www.jerylsjems.com
Cake truffles, cookies, brownies
President: Jeryl Kipnis Kronish

7388 Jess Jones Farms
7179 Rio Dixon Road
Dixon, CA 95620-9645   707-678-3839
Fax: 707-678-3898
Processor, packer and exporter of popcorn
President: Jess Jones
CEO: Mary Ellen Jones
Estimated Sales: $700,000
Number Employees: 1-4
Sq. footage: 10000
Type of Packaging: Consumer, Bulk
Brands:
CALIFORNIA GOLDEN POP
CUSTOMER'S BAGS
JESS JONES FARMS

7389 (HQ)Jesse's Best
1201 Progress Road
Suffolk, VA 23434-2145   757-489-8383
Fax: 757-489-8382   dapeck@supremeonline.com
www.jessesbest.com
Processor of fresh and frozen meats including beef, pork and veal
President: Dave Peck
Manager: Tim Reeves
Number Employees: 10-19
Type of Packaging: Consumer, Food Service, Private Label
Other Locations:
Jesse's Best
Suffolk VA
Brands:
Jesse's Best

7390 Jesse's Fine Meats
100 Washburn Rd
Cherokee, IA 51012-7274   712-225-3637
Fax: 712-225-6113
www.advancefoodcompany.com
Manufacturer of meat specialty items including beef, pork and chicken
President/CEO: Larry Schlichting
Plant Manager: Paul Beermann
Estimated Sales: $8.5 Million
Number Employees: 50-99
Sq. footage: 13000
Type of Packaging: Consumer, Food Service, Private Label
Brands:
FARMLAND
FOOD MASTER
QUIK TO FIX
SYSCO

7391 Jessie's Ilwaco Fish Company
P.O.Box 800
Ilwaco, WA 98624-0800   360-642-3773
Fax: 360-642-3362   pierrem@ilwacofish.com
Processor, importer and exporter of fresh and frozen fish fillets, shrimp, salmon, perch, sturgeon, tuna, whiting, sardines, smelt, and Dungeness crab
Owner: Pierre Marchand
VP: Doug Ross
Marketing: George Alexander
Production: Phil Marchand

Estimated Sales:$20-40 Million
Number Employees: 100-249
Sq. footage: 25000
Type of Packaging: Consumer, Food Service, Private Label, Bulk
Brands:
Custom Lable
Seaside

7392 Jet's Le Frois Foods Corporation
56 High St
Brockport, NY 14420-2058   585-637-5003
                          Fax: 585-637-2855
Barbeque sauces and vinegars
Owner: Duncan Tsay
Estimated Sales:$ 5-10 Million
Number Employees: 5-9
Type of Packaging: Private Label

7393 Jewel Bakery
1955 W North Ave
Melrose Park, IL 60160-1131   708-531-6000
                          Fax: 708-343-9450
Breads
CEO: Stephen Bowater
Number Employees: 100-249

7394 Jewel Date Company
56474 Us Highway 111
Thermal, CA 92274   760-399-4474
          Fax: 760-399-4476 jeweldate@aol.com
                          www.jeweldate.com
Processor and exporter of natural and organic pecans, dates, raisins, nuts and dried fruits
President: Gregory Raumin
Estimated Sales:$1300000
Number Employees: 20-49
Parent Co: Covalda
Type of Packaging: Consumer

7395 Jianlibao America
420 5th Avenue
26th Floor
New York, NY 10018-2729   212-354-8898
          Fax: 212-354-8838 800-526-1688
sales@orientalfoodmaster.com   www.janlibo.com
Beverages, Oriental foodstuffs
President: Qishu Lin
Estimated Sales:$ 3 Million
Number Employees: 20

7396 Jillipepper
P.O.Box 7546
Albuquerque, NM 87194-7546   505-344-2804
          Fax: 505-344-6633 jilli@jillipepper.com
                          www.jillipepper.com
Salsas, sauces, dips
President: Jill Levin
VP: Lowell Levin
Production Manager: Martin Dobyns
Estimated Sales:$ 1 - 3 Million
Number Employees: 1-4
Type of Packaging: Private Label

7397 Jim Foley Company
1121 Chestnut Hill Cir SW
Marietta, GA 30064-4652   770-427-0999
                          Fax: 770-427-5102
Seafood
President: Jim Foley

7398 Jim's Cheese Pantry
410 Portland Rd
Waterloo, WI 53594-1200   920-478-3600
          Fax: 920-478-2320 800-345-3571
jpcheese@gdinet.com
                  www.jimscheesepantry.com
Processor of cheese sculptures and wholesaler/distributor of jams, jellies and crackers; serving the food service market
President: James Peschel
Estimated Sales:$6 Million
Number Employees: 50-99
Type of Packaging: Consumer, Food Service

7399 Jimbo's Jumbos
P.O.Box 465
Edenton, NC 27932-0465   252-482-2193
          Fax: 252-482-7857 800-334-4771
                          www.jimbosjumbos.com
Snacks and peanuts, custom formulation is available
Manager: Hal Burns
Number Employees: 100-249
Type of Packaging: Private Label

7400 Jimm's Pizza
1901 Durand Ave
Racine, WI 53403-3275   262-634-2164
                          Fax: 262-634-9929
Manufacturer of frozen pizzas
Manager: Brian Ehmcke
Estimated Sales:$10-20 Million
Number Employees: 10-19
Sq. footage: 6000
Type of Packaging: Consumer, Private Label
Brands:
JIMM'S
SPINUCHI'S

7401 Jimmy Dean Foods
PO Box 25111
Cincinnati, OH 45225-0111   513-281-9104
          Fax: 901-758-6709 800-925-3326
                          www.jimmydean.com
Processor of breakfast sandwiches and suasage.
President: Jerry Laner
VP Procurement: Jim Morey
Executive VP Retail Sales: Wes Jackson
Estimated Sales:$300,000-500,000
Number Employees: 1-4
Parent Co: Sara Lee Packaged Meats
Type of Packaging: Consumer, Food Service, Private Label, Bulk
Brands:
FRESH TASTE FAST!
JIMMY DEAN

7402 Jimmy's Chiles
9447 Maple Drive
Apt 3b
Rosemont, IL 60018-5017   708-429-2803
                          Fax: 847-685-4099
Chilie peppers and other vegetables
Owner: James Doyle

7403 Jimmy's Cookies
18-01 River Rd
Fair Lawn, NJ 07410   201-797-8900
                          Fax: 201-797-2090
Cookies
Owner: Jim Zorn
Estimated Sales:$ 5 - 10 Million
Number Employees: 20-49

7404 Jimtown Store
6706 Highway 128
Healdsburg, CA 95448-9634   707-433-1212
          Fax: 707-433-1252 jimtown@jimtown.com
                          www.jimtown.com
Vegetable spreads
President: Carrie Brown
Marketing Director: Haley Callahan
Catering: Susan Schmid
*Estimated Sales:*Less than $500,000
Number Employees: 10-19
Brands:
Chickpea Chipotle
Fig & Olive Tapenade
SPICY OLIVE

7405 Jitney Jungle Stores of America
3800 i 55 N
Suite B
Jackson, MS 39211-6324   601-965-8600
          Fax: 601-965-8171 800-647-2364
Processor and exporter of poultry products
National Sales/Marketing Manager: Peter Patota
Director Distribution Sales: Ira Fingerman
Director National Accounts: Bob Dreiling
Number Employees: 250-499

7406 Jo Mar Laboratories
583 Division St # B
Campbell, CA 95008-6915   408-374-5920
          Fax: 408-374-5922 800-538-4545
info@jomarlabs.com   www.jomarlabs.com
Wholesaler/distributor and exporter of health products including packaged amino acids and food supplements; also, contract packaging available
President: Joanne Brown
Estimated Sales:$ 1 - 3 Million
Number Employees: 10-19
Sq. footage: 3500
Parent Co: Jo Mar Labs
Type of Packaging: Consumer, Private Label

7407 Jo Mints
2101 E Coast Highway
Suite 250
Corona Del Mar, CA 92625-1928   310-401-1894
          Fax: 310-388-5647 877-566-4687
tom@jomints.com   www.jomints.com
Marketing: Tom Knutson
Sales: Tom Knutson
Public Relations: Ashley Talbott
Number Employees: 3
Number of Brands: 2
Number of Products: 3
Brands:
JO CITRUS
JOMINTS
M60 ENERGY MINTS

7408 Jo's Candies
2530 W 237th Street
Torrance, CA 90505   310-257-0260
          Fax: 310-257-0266 800-770-1946
sales@joscandies.com   www.jos-candies.com
chocolate graham crackers, s'mores, coco jo's, peppermint crunch, english toffee bars, chocolaty toffee corn, peanut butter meltaways, handmade meltaways, handmade turtles, buttery toffee corn, toffee nuggets, peanut brittle, englishtoffee, chocolate gift tower, marshmallow squares, lemon breeze

7409 Jo's Candies
2560 W 237th St
Torrance, CA 90505-5217   310-257-0260
          Fax: 310-257-0266 800-770-1946
sales@joscandies.com   www.joscandies.com
Manufacturer of gourmet chocolates, English toffee, chocolate graham crackers, caramels, chocolate covered peppermints, smores and toffee caramel corn.
President: Tom King
Controller: Grant Philders
Plant Manager: Dave Good
*Estimated Sales:*Below $ 5 Million
Number Employees: 5-9
Type of Packaging: Private Label, Bulk
Brands:
Chocolate Covered Graham Crackers
Dr. Peter's Peppermint Crunch
Jo's Candies
Jo's Original

7410 Jodar Vineyard & Winery
2393 Gravel Road
Placerville, CA 95667   530-621-0324
          Fax: 530-621-0324 jodarwinery@foothill.net
                          www.jodarwinery.com
Manufacturer of wines
President: Vaughn Jodar
Estimated Sales:$500,000-$1 Million
Number Employees: 1-4
Brands:
Jodar

7411 Jodie's Kitchen
736 Anclote Rd
Tarpon Springs, FL 34689-6719   727-939-3444
          Fax: 727-934-9967 800-728-3704
info@jodieskitchen.com   www.jodieskitchen.com
Processor of gourmet herb and spice blends, private label for dry mixes
President: Nobert Moore
VP: Vickey Auge
Estimated Sales:$300,000-500,000
Number Employees: 1-4
Sq. footage: 2400
Type of Packaging: Consumer, Private Label, Bulk
Brands:
Country Classic
Dip-Idy-Dill
Galloping Garlic
Garlic Galore
Magically Mexican
Obviously Onion

7412 Jodie's Kitchen
736 Anclote Rd
Tarpon Springs, FL 34689-6719   727-939-3444
          Fax: 727-939-3444 800-728-3704
admin@jodieskitchen.com
                          www.jodieskitchen.com
Food spice blends, dip mixes
President: Norbert Moore
Marketing Director: Norbert Moore
Estimated Sales:$ 5-9.9 Million
Number Employees: 5-9

Brands:
Dipidy Dill
Simply Spinach

7413 Jody Maroni's Sausage Kingdom
P.O.Box 2997
Venice, CA 90294-2997   310-822-5639
          Fax: 310-822-0065 www.jodymaroni.com
Processor of sausages
Owner: Jordan Monkarsh
VP Marketing: Richard Leivenberg
Number Employees: 50-99
Type of Packaging: Consumer, Food Service
Brands:
Jody Maroni

7414 Jody's Gourmet Popcorn
205 Laskin Rd
Virginia Beach, VA 23451   757-425-5639
          Fax: 757-425-0059 866-797-5639
          danny@jodyspopcorn.com
          www.jodyspopcorn.com
flavored popcorn and flavored fudge

7415 Joe Corbis' Wholesale Pizza
1430 Desoto Rd
Baltimore, MD 21230-1202   410-525-3810
          Fax: 410-525-0531 888-526-7247
          baltimore@joecorbi.com www.joecorbi.com
Pizza
President: Rocco Violi
CEO: Victor Corbi
Estimated Sales: $ 10-20 Million
Number Employees: 20-49
Brands:
Joe Corbi's

7416 Joe Fazio's Bakery
1717 Sublette Ave
St Louis, MO 63110-1926   314-645-6239
Fax: 314-645-2410 fazioinfo@faziosbakery.com
          www.faziosbakery.com
Bakery products
President: Charles Fazio
Estimated Sales: Below $ 5 Million
Number Employees: 100-249
Brands:
Fazio's

7417 Joe Fazio's Famous Italian
1008 Bullitt St
Charleston, WV 25301-1004   304-344-3071
          http://www.fazios.net
Italian foods, seafoods, steaks, sandwiches
President: Joe Fazio
Owner: Joe Fazio
Quality Control: Nell Fazio
Marketing Manager: Joe Fazio
Manager: Nell Fazio
Estimated Sales: Below $ 5 Million
Number Employees: 20-49
Brands:
Fazio's

7418 Joe Hutson Foods
8331 Sanlando Avenue
Jacksonville, FL 32211-5135   904-731-9065
          Fax: 904-731-9066 keithhutson@juno.com
Processor and exporter of spicy salsas and steak, hot
and cocktail sauces; also, gift baskets
President: Teresa Foster
CEO: Keith Hutson
Chairman Board: Joe Hutson
Number Employees: 1-4
Sq. footage: 1200
Parent Co: Joe Hutson Foods
Brands:
Put Me Hot

7419 Joe Patti Seafood Company
P.O.Box 12567
Pensacola, FL 32591-2567   850-432-3315
          Fax: 850-435-7843 800-500-9929
          www.joepattis.com
Seafood, seafood products
President: Frank Patti
Marketing Director: Maria Walker
Estimated Sales: $ 20-50 Million
Number Employees: 100-249

7420 Joe's Vegetables
PO Box 2494
Hollister, CA 95024-2494   831-636-3224
          Fax: 831-636-3226 joesveg@aol.com

Vegetables
President: Joe Herbert
VP: Catherine Herbert
Estimated Sales: Below $ 5 Million
Number Employees: 5
Type of Packaging: Private Label
Brands:
Organic Convenience

7421 Joel & Diane Laperyhouse Company
7241 Shoreline Drive
Chauvin, LA 70344-2425   504-594-9744
          Fax: 504-594-9744

7422 Joel Harvey Distributing
8800 Ditmas Ave
Brooklyn, NY 11236-1608   718-629-2690
          Fax: 718-629-2172 sales@joelharvey.com
          www.joelharvey.com
Chocolate, cookies, crackers, jellies and juices
President: Mark Statfeld
Estimated Sales: $ 1-2.5 Million
Number Employees: 10-19
Brands:
Ferrara
Guylian
Hero
Hershey
Kedem
Perugina
Venus

7423 Joelle's Choice Specialty Foods LLC
1829 Highway 1
Fairfield, IA 52566   641-472-2414
          Fax: 641-472-3774 800-880-2779
          sales@joelleschoice.com
          http://joelleschoice.com
Manufacturer of shelf stable soy puddings;
soymilks; rapid culture soy yogurts; gourmet gelatos
and sorbets; gourmet soy-brat hybrids; soy-sausage
brat hybrids, and soy-burger hybrids.
President: Larry Sutton
Type of Packaging: Food Service

7424 Joette's Sausage
PO Box 200
Kincaid, IL 62540-0200   217-789-6300
          Fax: 217-544-4444
Processor of pork sausage and patties
President: Joette Curtis
VP: Donald Curtis
Number Employees: 5-9
Sq. footage: 60000
Type of Packaging: Consumer, Food Service, Bulk

7425 Joey Oysters
P.O.Box 904
Amite, LA 70422-0904   985-748-7140
          Fax: 985-748-8300 800-748-1525
          oyster@i-55.com
Processor of oysters
President: Vito Caronna
VP: Frank Boudreaux
Estimated Sales: $ 20 - 50 Million
Number Employees: 100-249
Type of Packaging: Consumer, Food Service, Bulk
Brands:
Louisiana

7426 Joey's Fine Foods
135 Manchester Pl
Newark, NJ 07104-1722   973-482-1400
          Fax: 973-482-1597 sales@joeysfinefoods.com
          www.joeysfinefoods.com
Processor and wholesaler/distributor of mixes and
baked goods including danish, cakes, cookies, tarts
and muffins; wholesaler/distributor of bakery and
packaging equipment; exporter of muffins, bakery
mixes and bakery and packaging equipment
President: Aaron Aihini
VP Sales: Anthony Romano
Estimated Sales: $6 Million
Number Employees: 20-49
Sq. footage: 42000
Type of Packaging: Consumer, Food Service, Private Label, Bulk
Brands:
Cottage Bake
Joey's
New Englander

7427 Jogue Inc
P.O.Box 190
Northville, MI 48167-0190   248-349-1500
          Fax: 248-349-1505 800-521-3888
          info@jogue.com   www.jogue.com
Manufacturer of flavoring extracts, essential oils,
food colors, ice cream toppings, juices and syrups
President/Owner: Dattu Sastry
Technical Sales Manager: Gary Holtquist
Estimated Sales: $10-20 Million
Number Employees: 20-49
Type of Packaging: Food Service, Private Label, Bulk
Other Locations:
Jogue
Detroit MI
Western Syrup Company
Santa Fe Springs CA
High Mountain Manufacturing Company
Salt Lake City UT
Brands:
GOLD LABEL

7428 Johanna Foods
P.O.Box 272
Flemington, NJ 08822-0272   908-788-2409
          Fax: 908-788-2331 800-727-6700
          www.johannafoods.com
Manufacturer of yogurt and chilled, aseptic juices
and drinks
President/CEO: Robert Facchina
VP Marketing: Melinda Champion
VP Human Resources: Don Griffin
Estimated Sales: $97.5 Million
Number Employees: 500-999
Type of Packaging: Consumer, Food Service, Private Label, Bulk
Brands:
LA YOGURT
SABOR LATINO
SSIPS
TREERIPE

7429 Johlin Century Winery
3935 Corduroy Rd
Oregon, OH 43616-1811   419-693-6288
          Fax: 419-693-6429
Wines
President/Owner: Richard Johlin
Sales Director: Rich Johlin
Estimated Sales: $500,000-$1 Million
Number Employees: 1-4
Type of Packaging: Private Label

7430 John A. Vassilaros & Son
2905 120th St
Flushing, NY 11354-2505   718-886-4140
          Fax: 718-463-5037 sales@vassilaroscoffee.com
          www.vassilaroscoffee.com
Coffee and tea
President: John Vassilaros
Director: Ann Vassilaros
Estimated Sales: $ 10-20 Million
Number Employees: 20-49
Type of Packaging: Private Label

7431 John B Sanfilippo & Son
16435 Ih 35 N
Selma, TX 78154-1200   210-651-5300
          Fax: 210-651-6244 800-423-6546
          jasperjr@jbssinc.com www.jbssinc.com
Manufaturer of shelled nuts including walnuts, pecans, almonds, cashews and peanuts; packaged in
cellophane, jars, cans and bulk
Chairman/CEO: Mathias A Valentine
SVP/Secretary: Michael Valentine
Plant Manager: Ruben Roecker
Estimated Sales: $520 Million
Number Employees: 500-999
Type of Packaging: Consumer, Food Service, Private Label, Bulk
Other Locations:
John B. Filippo & Son
Bainbridge GA
John B. Filippo & Son
Garysburg NC
John B. Filippo & Son
Gustine CA
John B. Filippo & Son
Walnut CA
Brands:
EVON'S
FISHER
FLAVOR TREE

SUNSHINE COUNTRY
TEX PRIDE

7432 John B Sanfilippo & Son
29241 Cottonwood Rd
Gustine, CA 95322-9574   209-854-2455
          Fax: 209-854-3135   800-218-3077
ebulkfoods@jbssinc.com   www.jbssinc.com
Processor and exporter of almonds and walnuts
President: Sid Cortez
President: Mathias Valentine
Export Sales Manager: Kim Sziraki
Director West Coast Operations: Shirley Sietsema

Estimated Sales: $520 Million
Number Employees: 250-499
Parent Co: John B. Sanfilippo & Son
Type of Packaging: Bulk

7433 John B Sanfilippo & Son
1703 N Randall Road
Elgin, IL 60123-7820   847-289-1800
          Fax: 847-289-1843 www.fishernuts.com
Processor, marketer and distributor of nut based
snacking solutions
CEO: Jeffrey Sanfilippo
CFO: Michael Valentine
Sales: James Baker
SVP Human Resources: Tom Fordonski
Manager: Bill Schwann
Estimated Sales: $ 520 Million
Number Employees: 90
Parent Co: John B. Sanfilippo & Son
Type of Packaging: Consumer, Bulk
Brands:
Evon's
Fisher
Flavor Tree
Sunshine
Texas

7434 (HQ)John B Sanfilippo & Son
1703 N Randall Rd
Elgin, IL 60123-7820   847-289-1800
          Fax: 847-289-1843   ebulkfoods@jbssinc.com
          www.jbssinc.com
Nutmeats, snack foods
Chairman/ Chief Executive Officer: Jasper
Sanfilippo
EVP/Finance and Chief Financial Officer:
Michael Valentine
Research & Development: Russell Tietz
Controller: Herbert Marros
EVP/Sales and Marketing: Jeffrey Sanfilippo
EVP Operations: Jasper Brian Sanfilippo
Production Manager: Mark Bardon
Plant Manager: Jerry Needham
Purchasing Manager: Paul Rabe
Estimated Sales: $520 Million
Number Employees: 1,000-4,999
Number of Brands: 4
Type of Packaging: Consumer, Food Service, Pri-
vate Label, Bulk
Brands:
Evon's
Fisher
Flavor Tree
Sunshine
Texas Pride
VANDERMINT
WHALER'S RUM

7435 John B Sanfilippo & Son
8060 N Carolina Hwy 46
Garysburg, NC 27831   252-536-5111
          Fax: 252-536-5587
Runner and Virginia type peanuts
Manager: Barry Smith
Estimated Sales: $520 Million
Number Employees: 50-99
Parent Co: John B. Sanfilippo & Son

7436 John B Sanfilippo & Sons
16435 Ih 35 N
Selma, TX 78154-1200   210-651-5300
          Fax: 210-651-6244   800-423-6546
ebulkfoods@jbssinc.com   www.jbssinc.com
Pecans, almonds, walnuts, sunflowers, pistachios,
peanuts, pine nuts, macadamias, brazil nuts, ca-
shews, hazelnuts and mixed nuts
President: Michael Valentine
Plant Manager: Ruben Roecker
Estimated Sales: $ 20 - 50 Million
Number Employees: 500-999

Brands:
Evon's
Fisher
Flavor Tree
Sunshine Country

7437 John B. Wright Fish Company
427 Main Street
Gloucester, MA 01930-3006   978-283-4205
          Fax: 978-281-5944
Seafood
President: Brian Wright
Estimated Sales: $ 5 - 10 Million
Number Employees: 5-9

7438 John C. Meier Juice Company
6955 Plainfield Rd
Cincinnati, OH 45236-3733   513-891-2900
          Fax: 513-891-6370   800-346-2941
          info@meierswinecellars.com
          www.meierswinecellars.com
Juice, jams, jellies
President: John Lucia
CEO: Bob szabo
Chairman: Robert Gottesman
Marketing Director: Lyn Lubin
Estimated Sales: $ 5-10 Million
Number Employees: 20-49
Brands:
Breckenridge Farm Sparkling Juices
Meier's
Meier's Sparkling Ju

7439 John Conti Coffee Company
4023 Bardstown Rd
Louisville, KY 40218-2684   502-499-8600
          Fax: 502-499-2944   800-928-5282
          www.johnconti.com
Coffee
President: John Conti
VP Coffee Services: Tami Conti
Human Resources: Debbie Redmon
Operations Director: Mark Nethery
Estimated Sales: Under $500,000
Number Employees: 100-249

7440 John Copes Food Products
759 Long Road
Manheim, PA 17545-8613   717-367-5142
          Fax: 717-367-7317   800-745-8211
          larry@copefoods.com   www.copefoods.com
Processor of canned corn and frozen vegetables
President: Larry Jones
VP/Sales and Marketing: Steve Davis
CFO/Treasurer: Don Long
Controller: Stephen Gaukler
Estimated Sales: $ 30-50 Million
Number Employees: 130
Type of Packaging: Consumer, Private Label
Brands:
Copes
Dutch Delight

7441 John F. Davis Candy Company
PO Box 1142
Scranton, PA 18501-1142   570-342-7696
          Fax: 570-342-7697
Processor of confectionery products including choc-
olates and seasonal
Type of Packaging: Consumer

7442 John Garner Meats
P.O.Box 625
Van Buren, AR 72957-0625   479-474-6894
          Fax: 479-474-6897   800-543-5473
Processor of portion controlled pork, poultry and
beef including ground and frozen patties
CEO: John Garner
Owner: John Garner
Marketing Director: Ralph Farrar
Sales Director: Gary Scott
Public Relations: Steve Fow
Operations Manager: Rusty Underwood
Production Manager: Rusty Polk
Estimated Sales: $8 Million
Number Employees: 20-49
Sq. footage: 40000
Type of Packaging: Food Service, Private Label,
Bulk

7443 John Gust Foods & Products Corporation
1350 Paramount Pkwy
Batavia, IL 60510-1461   630-879-8700
          Fax: 630-879-8708   800-756-5886
          sales@northern-pines.com
          www.northern-pines.com
Processor of pancake, waffle and muffin mixes; also,
pancake and sugar-free syrups
President: John Koutselas
Estimated Sales: $1 Million
Number Employees: 5-9
Type of Packaging: Consumer, Food Service, Pri-
vate Label, Bulk
Brands:
Northern Pines Gourmet

7444 John Hene Specialty Meats
131 W 15th Street
Indianapolis, IN 46202-2311   317-972-9400
Meat
President: John Hene

7445 John Hofmeister & Son
2386 S Blue Island Ave
Chicago, IL 60608-4292   773-847-0700
          Fax: 773-847-6707   800-923-4267
          ehofmeis@hofhaus.com   www.hofhaus.com
Processor of smoked and boiled hams both boneless
and semi boneless and smoked turkeys.
President/Owner: Ed Hofmeister
VP: Robert Bukala
VP Sales: Mark Rataj
Production: Chris Chin
Plant Engineer: Justo Sanchez
Estimated Sales: $18 Million
Number Employees: 50-99
Sq. footage: 27000
Type of Packaging: Consumer, Food Service, Pri-
vate Label
Brands:
Hofmeister Haus

7446 (HQ)John I. Haas
5185 Macarthur Blvd NW # 300
Washington, DC 20016-3341   202-223-0005
          Fax: 202-777-4895   salesadmin@johnihaas.com
          www.johnihaas.com
Processor, importer and exporter of hops and hop
aroma extract and oils
President: Henry Von Eichel
Estimated Sales: $ 10-20 Million
Number Employees: 20-49
Type of Packaging: Food Service, Private Label,
Bulk
Other Locations:
Haas, John I.
Yuen Long, N.T.
Brands:
Aromahop
Beta Stab
Hepahop Gold
Isahop
Lacto Stab
Redihop
Tetrahop Gold

7447 John J. Nissen Baking Company
34 Abbott Street
Brewer, ME 04412-2202   207-989-7654
          Fax: 207-989-7654   contact@twinkies.com
          www.interstatebakeriescorp.com
Processor of baked goods including bread, pastries,
cakes and rolls
President: Michael D Kafoure
CEO: Antonio C Alvarez II
CFO: Ronald B Hutchison
Estimated Sales: $ 10 - 20 Million
Number Employees: 20-49
Brands:
Hostess
Wonder Bread

7448 (HQ)John J. Nissen Baking Company
PO Box 1158
Portland, ME 04104-1158   207-775-3460
          Fax: 978-791-5571
Processor of breads including white, whole wheat
and rye
President: Michael Kafoure
Estimated Sales: $ 5 - 10 Million
Number Employees: 5-9

7449 John Kelly Chocolates
1506 N Sierra Bonita Avenue
Los Angeles, CA 90046   323-851-3269
Fax: 323-851-1789   800-609-4243
service@johnkellychocolates.com
www.johnkellychocolates.com
chocolates

7450 John Koller & Sons
1734 Perry Hwy
Fredonia, PA 16124-2720   724-475-4154
Fax: 724-475-4777   rkoller54@aol.com
Manufacturer of cheese
President: Richard Koller
Estimated Sales: $ 10-20 Million
Number Employees: 10-19
Parent Co: Fairview Swiss Chesse
Brands:
Fairview Swiss Cheese

7451 (HQ)John Morrell & Company
805 E Kemper Road
Cincinnati, OH 45246   513-346-3540
Fax: 513-346-7556 www.johnmorrell.com
Smoked sausage, hams, off the bone lunchmeats. bacon, hot dogs, off the bone quarter hams, cocktail smokies, ham cuts and lunchmeat.
President/CEO: Joseph Sebring
EVP Sales/Marketing: John Pauley
VP Human Resources: Gary Junso
Estimated Sales: $1+ Billion
Number Employees: 6,565
Type of Packaging: Consumer, Food Service, Private Label
Other Locations:
JM Sioux Falls Plant
Sioux Falls SD
JM Sioux City Plant
Sioux City SD
JM Springdale Plant
Cincinnati OH
JM Great Bend Plant
Great Bend KS
Brands:
Dinner bell
E-Z-Cut
Farmers Hickory
Hunter
Iowa Quality
John Morrell
Kretschmar
Peytons
Rath Black Hawk
Rodeo
Shenson
Tobin's First Prize

7452 John Morrell & Company
1200 Bluff Road
Sioux City, IA 51106-5813   712-279-7360
Fax: 712-279-7351 www.johnmorrell.com
Smoked sausage, hams, off the bone lunchmeat, bacon, hot dogs, off the bone quarter hams, cocktail smokies, ham cuts, lunchmeat.
Manufacturing/Operations Director: Craig Schmidt
Manager: Carol Dermit
Estimated Sales: Over $ 1 Billion
Number Employees: 150
Parent Co: Smithfield Foods
Type of Packaging: Consumer, Food Service

7453 John Morrell & Company
11530 Century Blvd
Cincinnati, OH 45246-3305   513-346-5375
Fax: 605-330-3162 800-345-0743
www.johnmorrell.com
Processor and exporter of fresh and frozen pork and sausage products
President: Joe Sebring
General Manager: Steve Crim
Manager Human Resources: Buth Anderson
Purchasing Agent: Ben Flottman
Estimated Sales: Over $ 1 Billion
Number Employees: 1,000-4,999
Parent Co: Smithfield Companies
Type of Packaging: Consumer, Private Label, Bulk

7454 (HQ)John Morrell & Company
805 E Kemper Road
Cincinnati, OH 45240-5020   513-346-3540
Fax: 513-346-7556 www.johnmorrell.com

Smoked sausage, hams, off the bone lunchmeat, bacon, hot dogs, off the bone quarter hams, cocktail smokies, ham cuts, lunchmeat
Presdient/CEO: Joseph Sebring
EVP Sales/Marketing: John Pauley
VP Human Resources: Gary Junso
Estimated Sales: Over $1 Billion
Number Employees: 6,565
Parent Co: Smithfield Companies
Type of Packaging: Food Service, Private Label
Other Locations:
Sioux Falls SD
Sioux City IA
Des Moines IA
Great Bend KS
San Jose CA
Middlesboro KY
Brands:
ARMOUR AND ERICKSON
CURLY'S
DINNER BELL
E Z CUT
HUNTER
JOHN MORRELL
KRETSCHMAR
MOHAWK
PEYTON'S
RATH BLACK HAWK
RODEO
TOBIN'S FIRST PRIZE

7455 (HQ)John Morrell & Company
805 E Kemper Road
Cincinnati, OH 45246   513-346-3540
Fax: 513-346-7556 800-445-2013
jweiler@johnmorrell.com   www.johnmorrell.com
Smoked sausage, hams, off the bone lunchmeat, bacon, hot dogs, off the bone quarter hams, cocktail smokies, ham cuts, lunchmeat
President/CEO: Joseph Sebring
EVP Sales/Marketing: John Pauley
VP Human Resources: Gary Junso
Estimated Sales: $2 Billion
Number Employees: 6,565
Type of Packaging: Consumer, Food Service, Private Label
Brands:
CURLY'S
DINNER BELL
E Z CUT
HUNTER
JOHN MORRELL
KRETSCHMAR
MOHAWK
PEYTON'S
RATH BLACK HAWK
RODEO
TOBIN'S FIRST PRIZE

7456 John N Wright Jr
402 Railroad Ave
Federalsburg, MD 21632-1413   410-754-9044
Fax: 410-754-9045
Processor of canned tomatoes
President: Mary Harding
Estimated Sales: $100,000
Number Employees: 1-4

7457 John Paton
73 E State St
Doylestown, PA 18901-4359   215-348-7050
Fax: 215-348-8147
www.goldenblossomhoney.com
Honey
President/Chairperson: Jill Paton
Estimated Sales: $860,000
Number Employees: 5-9

7458 John R Morreale
216 N Peoria St
Chicago, IL 60607-1706   312-421-3664
Fax: 312-421-8928 morrealemeat@aol.com
Processor and wholesaler/distributor of beef and pork
Owner: John Lucachoni
VP: Mike Magrini
VP Operations: Steve Hurckes
Estimated Sales: $25,000,000
Number Employees: 50-99
Number of Products: 1
Sq. footage: 100000
Type of Packaging: Bulk

7459 John R. Daily
P.O.Box 16007
Missoula, MT 59808-6007   406-721-7007
Fax: 406-721-1540 wwilcox@dailybacon.com
www.seaboardfoods.com
Manufacturer of meat including bacon
President: Mark Wilson
VP: Mark Wilson
Estimated Sales: $30 Million
Number Employees: 50-99
Brands:
BIG SKY
HONEY CURED
PEPPERED

7460 John T. Handy Company
700 E Main St
Salisbury, MD 21804-5037   410-968-1772
Fax: 410-968-1592 800-426-3977
handyco@attglobal.net   www.handycrab.com
Processor and exporter of frozen seafood including soft shell crabs, crab and salmon cakes and stuffed crabs
President: Carol Haltaman
Sales Director: Nelda DiLauro
Director Operations: Benjamin White
Purchasing Manager: Arlene Wharton
Estimated Sales: $8000000
Number Employees: 100-249
Type of Packaging: Consumer, Food Service
Brands:
Handy

7461 John Volpi & Company
5258 Daggett Ave
St Louis, MO 63110-3026   314-772-8550
Fax: 314-772-0411 800-288-3439
www.volpifoods.com
Processor of Italian meat products including salami, dry cured coppa, mortadella, prosciutto ham, etc
President: Lorenza Pasetti
National Sales Manager: Christine Illuminato
General Manager: Lorenza Pasetti
Estimated Sales: $ 20 - 50 Million
Number Employees: 100-249
Type of Packaging: Consumer, Food Service, Private Label, Bulk
Brands:
Volpi Foods

7462 John Wm. Macy's Cheesesticks
80 Kipp Ave
Elmwood Park, NJ 07407-1036   201-791-8036
Fax: 201-797-5068 800-643-0573
ales@cheesesticks.com   www.cheesesticks.com
Processor of cheesesticks, cheescrisps and bread sticks
President: John William Macy
VP: Tim Macy
Estimated Sales: $5214599
Number Employees: 20-49
Sq. footage: 22000
Type of Packaging: Consumer, Food Service, Private Label, Bulk
Brands:
John Wm. Macy's Cheesecrips
John Wm. Macy's Cheesesticks
John Wm. Macy's Sweetsticks

7463 Johnny Harris Famous Barbecue Sauce
2801 Wicklow St
Savannah, GA 31404-4131   912-354-8828
Fax: 912-354-6567
Processor of barbecue sauce
President: Phillip Donaldson
VP: Norman Heidt
Estimated Sales: $ 5 - 10 Million
Number Employees: 5-9
Sq. footage: 3000
Type of Packaging: Consumer

7464 Johns Cove Fisheries
RR 3
Yarmouth, NS B5A 4B1
Canada   902-742-8691
Fax: 902-742-3574 sales@johnscove.com
www.johnscove.com
Processor and exporter of live lobster and herring roe and scallops
President: Don Cunningham
Number Employees: 60
Type of Packaging: Consumer, Food Service, Bulk

7465 Johnson Brothers Produce Company
P.O.Box 730
Whitakers, NC 27891-0730   252-437-2111
Fax: 252-437-2121 hbjfarms@coastalnet.com
Processor of sweet potatoes
President: Hursel Johnson
VP: Lou Johnson
Estimated Sales: $ 10 - 20 Million
Number Employees: 20-49
Type of Packaging: Bulk
Brands:
Norma Lou

7466 Johnson Canning Company
300 Warehouse Ave
Sunnyside, WA 98944-1310   509-837-4188
Fax: 509-839-3243 www.princesspickled.com
Processor of canned maraschino cherries and pickled vegetables
Manager: Pete Krause
CEO: George Jhonson
Marketing Director: George Jhonson
Manager: Gary Stonemetz
Manager: Pete Krause
Estimated Sales: $ 5 - 10 Million
Number Employees: 20-49
Parent Co: Johnson Canning Company
Type of Packaging: Consumer, Food Service, Private Label
Brands:
Princess
Sunnyside

7467 Johnson Concentrates
P.O.Box 955
Sunnyside, WA 98944-0955   509-837-4600
Fax: 509-837-5151
info@johnsonconcentrates.com
www.johnsonconcentrates.com
Processor, importer and exporter of fruit purees and concentrates
Owner: Gorge Johnson
CFO: Nyle Farmer
VP: David Watkins
Quality Control: Edward Thomas
Sales: Shannon Elkins
Plant Manager: Mike Kilian
Estimated Sales: $ 10 - 20 Million
Number Employees: 20-49
Sq. footage: 40000
Type of Packaging: Bulk
Brands:
Johnson Concentrates

7468 Johnson Estate Wines
P.O.Box 52
Westfield, NY 14787-0052   716-326-2191
Fax: 716-326-2131 800-374-6569
jwinery@cecomet.net   www.johnsonwinery.com
Processor of wine
President: Frederick Johnson
Marketing Contact: Bob Dahl
Operations Manager: Mark Lancaster
Estimated Sales: $ 3 - 5 Million
Number Employees: 5-9
Sq. footage: 15000
Type of Packaging: Consumer

7469 Johnson Fruit Company
P.O.Box 955
Sunnyside, WA 98944-0955   509-837-4600
Fax: 509-837-5151
info@johnsonconcentrates.com
www.johnsonconcentrates.com
Manufacturer and exporter of maraschino and dark sweet cherries, IQF asparagus and pickled vegetables including beans, peas, carrots, bell peppers, asparagus and dried tomatoes in oil
President: Gary Johnson
Estimated Sales: $ 10 - 20 Million
Number Employees: 20-49
Sq. footage: 20000
Type of Packaging: Consumer, Food Service, Private Label, Bulk

7470 Johnson Sea Products
P.O.Box 665
Coden, AL 36523-0665   251-824-2693
Fax: 251-824-7808
Seafood
Principal: Sean Johnson
Human Resources: Bridget Sprinkle

Estimated Sales: $100+ Million
Number Employees: 100-249

7471 Johnson's Alexander Valley Wines
8333 Highway 128
Healdsburg, CA 95448-9639   707-433-2319
Fax: 707-433-5302 800-888-5532
johnsons@funvacation.net
www.funvacation.net/johnsons.html
Wines
Owner/President: Ellen Johnson
CEO: Ellen Johnson
Marketing Director: Ellen Johnson
Estimated Sales: Below $ 5 Million
Number Employees: 1-4
Type of Packaging: Private Label
Brands:
Diamond Springs

7472 (HQ)Johnson's Food Products
1 Mt Vernon St
Dorchester, MA 02125-1604   617-265-3400
Fax: 617-265-1099
Processor of bakers' and confectioners' supplies including mixes, bases, flavorings and whipped toppings
President: Chris Anton
VP: Peter Anton
Estimated Sales: $ 5 - 10 Million
Number Employees: 10-19
Sq. footage: 20000
Type of Packaging: Consumer, Food Service, Bulk

7473 Johnson's Real Ice Cream
2728 E Main St
Columbus, OH 43209-2534   614-231-0014
Fax: 614-231-5450
jim@johnsonsrealicecream.com
www.johnsonsrealicecream.com
Processor of ice cream and sherbet
President: Jim Wilcoxon
Estimated Sales: $380000
Number Employees: 10-19
Sq. footage: 2400
Type of Packaging: Consumer, Food Service

7474 Johnson's Wholesale Meats
161 N Sixth St
Opelousas, LA 70570-2105   337-948-4444
Fax: 337-948-4495
Meat packer
Manager: David Comoeuax
Sales Manager: Billy Baque
Estimated Sales: $ 1 - 3 Million
Number Employees: 5-9
Type of Packaging: Consumer, Bulk

7475 Johnson, Nash, & Sons Farms
P.O.Box 699
Rose Hill, NC 28458-0699   910-293-7153
Fax: 910-293-4876 800-682-6843
Manufacturer of fresh poultry and eggs
Manager: Paul Gilbert
Vice Chairman/CEO: Robert Johnson
President/COO: Don Taber
Estimated Sales: $567.8 Million
Number Employees: 5-9
Type of Packaging: Consumer, Food Service, Bulk
Brands:
HOUSE OF RAEFORD

7476 Johnsonville Food Company
PO Box 786
Sheboygan, WI 53082-0786   920-459-6800
Fax: 920-459-7824
Processor of sausage
Type of Packaging: Consumer
Brands:
Hot'n Zesty Links
Johnsonville Bratwur
Johnsonville Country
Sage'n Pepper
Table Two Entree

7477 Johnston County Hams
P.O.Box 489
Smithfield, NC 27577-0489   919-934-8054
Fax: 919-934-1091 800-543-4267
www.countrycuredhams.com
Hams, bacon and turkey
Cure Master: Rufus Brown
Estimated Sales: Below $ 5 Million
Number Employees: 10-19

7478 Johnston Farms
P.O.Box 65
Edison, CA 93220-0065   661-366-3201
Fax: 661-366-6534 www.johnstonfarms.com
Packer, exporter and wholesaler/distributor of navel oranges, peppers and potatoes
President: Don Johnston
Co-Prtnr.: Gerald Johnston
Plant Manager: Steve Stacker
Number Employees: 250-499

7479 Johnston's Home Style Products
PO Box 1737
Charlottetown, PE C1A 7N4
Canada   902-629-1300
Fax: 902-368-1776
Processor of canned wild cranberry sauce, beef stew and chicken parts and stew
President: Harris Johnston
Type of Packaging: Food Service, Private Label

7480 Johnston's Winery
5140 Bliss Rd
Ballston Spa, NY 12020-2044   518-882-6310
Fax: 518-882-5551
Manufacturer of wine
President: Kurt Johnston
Estimated Sales: Less than $500,000
Number Employees: 1-4
Brands:
Johnston's Winery

7481 Jolina Foods
10516 Route 116
Hinesburg, VT 05461-8500   802-434-2185
Fax: 802-434-2784
Executive Director: Bob Barton
Estimated Sales: $ 1-2.5 Million appx.
Number Employees: 20

7482 Jon Donaire Pastry
12805 Busch Pl
Santa Fe Springs, CA 90670-3023   562-946-2536
Fax: 562-946-3781 877-366-2473
JDdesserts@rich.com   www.jondonaire.net
Cheese cake mousse
Dessert Specialist: Lisa Tanner
Estimated Sales: $ 30 Million
Number Employees: 100-249
Brands:
Jon Donaire

7483 Jonathan Lord Corporation
87 Carlough Rd
Bohemia, NY 11716-2921   631-563-4445
Fax: 631-563-8505 800-814-7517
jlcorp@optonline.net   www.jonathanlord.com
Bakery Products
Owner: Kathy Dancik
Sales Director: William Kentrup
Estimated Sales: Below $ 5 Million
Number Employees: 10-19
Type of Packaging: Consumer, Food Service, Private Label, Bulk

7484 Jonathan's Sprouts
P.O.Box 100
Rochester, MA 02770-0100   508-763-2577
Fax: 508-763-3316 bob@jonathansorganic.com
www.jonathansorganic.com
Manufacturer of alfalfa sprouts, mung bean sprouts, citrus fruits and vegetables. Certified packer and shipper of organic produce
Owner/President: Robert Sanderson
Owner/President: Barbara Sanderson
CEO: John Musser
Sales Director: Cathy Rounseville
Estimated Sales: $4 Million
Number Employees: 20-49
Sq. footage: 15000
Type of Packaging: Consumer
Brands:
Jonathan's Organics
Jonathan's Sprouts

7485 Jones Bakeries
1665 S Martin Luther King Jr D
Winston Salem, NC 27107-1310   336-720-9737
800-849-5663
Manufacturer of specialty breads and rolls; also, co-packing services available
Manager: Wayne Hall

Estimated Sales:$ 1 - 3 Million
Number Employees: 20-49
Sq. footage: 20000
Type of Packaging: Consumer, Food Service
Brands:
  OLDE SALEM

7486 Jones Brewing Company
P.O.Box 746
Smithton, PA 15479-0746   724-872-6626
    Fax: 724-872-6538 800-237-2337
info@stoneysbeer.com www.stoneysbeer.com
Processor and exporter of beers, lagers, nonalcoholic
beers and other malt beverages in kegs, cans and
bottles
  President: Sandra Podlucky
  Vice President: Sandra Podlucky
  Inventory Control: Joyce Winkler
  Production Manager: John Lonesky
Estimated Sales:$1.1 Million
Number Employees: 5-9
Type of Packaging: Consumer, Private Label
Brands:
  Equire
  Eureka
  Stoney's
  Stoney's Black & Tan
  Stoney's Harvest Gold
  Stoney's Light
  Stoney's Non-Alcoholic Brew

7487 (HQ)Jones Dairy Farm
P.O.Box 808
Fort Atkinson, WI 53538-0808   920-563-2431
    Fax: 920-563-6801 800-563-1004
jdfxprt@idcnet.com www.jonesdairy.com
Manufacturer, packer and exporter sausage, bacon
and ham products, maple syrup
  President/CEO: Philip Jones
  VP Finance: Loren Gray
  SVP Sales/Marketing: Richard Lowry
  Operations Manager: Roger Borchardt
  Natl. Food Service Accounts Manager: Richard
  Klippstein
Estimated Sales:$58 Million
Number Employees: 250-499
Type of Packaging: Consumer, Food Service, Bulk
Brands:
  JONES SAUSAGEST
  RALPH & PAULA ADAMS SCRAPPLE

7488 Jones Packing Company
22701 Oak Grove Rd
Harvard, IL 60033-8205   815-943-4488
Processor of beef, lamb, pork and goat
  Owner: Ray Jones
Estimated Sales:$4 Million
Number Employees: 10-19
Type of Packaging: Consumer, Food Service, Private Label

7489 Jones Potato Chip Company
265 Bowman St
Mansfield, OH 44903-1699   419-529-9424
    Fax: 419-529-6789 800-466-9424
chips@joneschips.com www.joneschips.com
Processor of potato chips
  President: Robert Jones
  Director Sales: Don Markov
  Office Manager: Jim Ford
  Production Manager: Roy Kehl
Estimated Sales:$6 Million
Number Employees: 20-49
Type of Packaging: Consumer, Food Service, Private Label
Brands:
  Jones
  Thomasson's
  Thomasson's Potato Chips

7490 Jones Produce
P.O.Box 487
Quincy, WA 98848-0487   509-787-3537
  Fax: 509-787-1275 merchant@jonesproduce.com
Vegetables, fuits
  Owner: Jack Jones
Estimated Sales:$ 20 - 50 Million
Number Employees: 20-49

7491 Jones Soda Company
234 9th Ave N
Seattle, WA 98109-5120   206-624-3357
    Fax: 206-624-6857 800-656-6050
www.jonessoda.com

Soda
  President/Founder: Peter van Stolk
  CEO: Peter van Stolk
  CFO/COO: Jennifer Cue
  CEO: Jonathan J Ricci
  Marketing Assistant: Diana Turner
  Sales Assistant: Anna Woolverton-Hiatt
  VP of Operations: Eric Chastain
  Production: Aaron Reed
  Purchasing Manager: Elijah Glenn
*Estimated Sales:*G
Number Employees: 50-99
Type of Packaging: Consumer
Brands:
  BERRY WHITE
  BETTY
  DAVE
  PURPLE CARROT

7492 Jones Soda Vancouver
13980 Bridgeport Road
Richmond, BC V6V 1V3
Canada   604-654-6050
    Fax: 604-253-4501 800-656-6050
www.jonessoda.com
Soda

7493 Jordahl Meats
25585 State Highway 13
Manchester, MN 56007-5020   507-826-3418
Processor of meat products including lamb, beef,
pork, veal, etc
  Owner: Brian Jordahl
Estimated Sales:$520,000
Number Employees: 1-4
Type of Packaging: Consumer, Food Service, Private Label, Bulk

7494 Josef Aaron Syrup Company
16541 Redmond Way
Suite 206
Redmond, WA 98052-4492   425-820-7221
    Fax: 425-702-9292
Tea and coffee flavors, syrups
  President: Judy Toller
Number Employees: 5-9

7495 Joseph Adams Corporation
P.O.Box 583
Valley City, OH 44280-0583   330-225-9135
    Fax: 330-225-9105
Processor and exporter of oleoresins, essential oils,
natural flavors and colors from spices and botanicals
  President: Patrick Adams
Estimated Sales:$3 Million
Number Employees: 10-19

7496 Joseph Bertman Foods
P.O.Box 6562
Cleveland, OH 44101-1562   216-431-4460
    Fax: 216-561-2232
Mustard, horseradish
  President: Pat Mazoh
Estimated Sales:$ 1 - 3 Million
Number Employees: 1-4
Brands:
  Bertman Raddish Sauce
  Joe Bertman's Ballpark Mustard
  Mustard
  Original

7497 Joseph D Teachey Produce
P.O.Box 965
Wallace, NC 28466-0965   910-285-4502
    Fax: 910-285-5491
Processor of sweet potatoes including Jewel,
Beauregard and Hernandez
  Owner: Joseph Teachey
Estimated Sales:$ 10-20 Million
Number Employees: 20-49
Brands:
  Mary Jo's Blueberries
  Mary Jo's Fancy

7498 Joseph Filippi Winery
12467 Baseline Rd
Etiwanda, CA 91739-9522   909-899-5755
    Fax: 909-899-9196 jfilippiwinery@aol.com
www.josephfilippiwinery.com
A variety of wines including: Cabarnet, Cinq
Vignobles, Alicante Bouschet,Ruby-Ruby Port, An-
gelica Elena, Syrah and Zinfandel.
  President: Joseph P Filippi
  VP Sales/Marketing: Gino Filippi

*Estimated Sales:*Below $ 5 Million
Number Employees: 20-49
Number of Brands: 2
Number of Products: 25
Type of Packaging: Private Label
Other Locations:
  Joseph Filippi Winery
  Guasti-Ontario, Canada
Brands:
  Guasti Altar Wines
  Joseph Filippi

7499 Joseph Foodservice
P.O.Box 1187
Valdosta, GA 31603-1187   229-242-0867
    Fax: 912-242-8877 800-333-2261
info@jfs.com www.ijconnect.com
Wholesaler/distributor of general line products;
serving the food service market
  Manager: Casey Kinker
  CEO: Luis Quintero
  VP Purchasing: Bobby Joseph
Estimated Sales:$30 Million
Number Employees: 20-49
Sq. footage: 150000
Parent Co: IJ Company

7500 Joseph Gallo Farms
10561 W Highway 140
PO Box 775
Atwater, CA 95301   209-394-7984
    Fax: 209-394-2392 jgfinfo@josephfarms.com
www.josephfarms.com
Processor of cheese
  Plant Manager: Mike Gallo
  CEO: Michael Gallo
*Estimated Sales:*Over $ 1 Billion
Number Employees: 250-499
Type of Packaging: Consumer, Food Service
Brands:
  Joseph Farms Cheese

7501 Joseph J. White
1 Pasadena Rd
Browns Mills, NJ 08015-7113   609-893-2332
    Fax: 609-893-2316
Processor of cranberries
  President: Joe Darlington
  Chairman Board: Thomas Darlington
Estimated Sales:$500,000-$1 Million
Number Employees: 10-19
Type of Packaging: Bulk

7502 Joseph Kirschner & Company
193 Riverside Dr
Augusta, ME 04330   207-623-3544
    Fax: 207-623-1557
Processor of meats
Estimated Sales:$100+ Million
Number Employees: 100-249

7503 Joseph McSweeney & Sons
P.O.Box 99
Windom, MN 56101-99   804-359-6024
    Fax: 804-359-4807
Processor of beef, lamb, pork, veal and poultry
  President: C B Baugher
  Vice President: Bruce Brooking
Estimated Sales:$ 50 - 100 Million
Number Employees: 100-249
Type of Packaging: Food Service, Bulk

7504 Joseph Phelps Vineyards
200 Taplin Rd
St Helena, CA 94574-9544   707-963-2745
    Fax: 707-963-4831 www.napavalleysearch.com
Processor and exporter of wines
  President: Tom Shelton
Estimated Sales:$100+ Million
Number Employees: 250-499
Type of Packaging: Consumer
Brands:
  Innisfree
  Myers Winery

7505 Joseph Sanders
P.O.Box 128
Custer, MI 49405-0128   231-757-4768
    Fax: 231-757-4786 800-968-5035
www.sandersmeats.com
Processor of beef and pork products; also, slaughter-
ing services available
  Owner: Dale Sanders
Estimated Sales:$ 5 - 10 Million
Number Employees: 10-19

Type of Packaging: Consumer

7506 Joseph Schmidt Confections
2000 Folsom St
San Francisco, CA 94110-1318   415-626-7900
        Fax: 415-626-7991   866-237-0152
                customercare@jsc.com
            www.josephschmidtconfections.com
Processor of Chocolate truffles and chocolate novelties
    President: Charles Huggins
    CFO: Jeff Smith
    CEO: Joseph Scmidt
    VP Marketing: Ellen Meuse
    Production Manager: Richard Chaeniot
Estimated Sales: $ 5-10 Million
Number Employees: 100-249
Brands:
    Chocolate Slicks

7507 Joseph and Sally Krusas
6539 Laurelwood Drive
Rockford, IL 61108-1568   815-395-1330
Polish foods
    President: Joseph Krusa

7508 Joseph's Gourmet Pasta & Sauces
133 Hale St
Haverhill, MA 01830-3969   978-521-1718
    Fax: 978-374-7917   800-863-8998
Processor of gourmet filled and cut pastas including
ravioli, triangoli, agnolotti, tortelloni, tortellini,
gnocchi and angel hair
    President: Joseph Faro
    Marketing: David Robinson
    Operations: Tom Bean
Estimated Sales: $ 50 - 100 Million
Number Employees: 100-249

7509 Joseph's Lite Cookies
3700 J St SE
Deming, NM 88030-7106   575-546-2839
        Fax: 575-546-6951
    customerservice@jospehslitecookies.com
            www.josephslitecookies.com
Sugar free cookies, fat free cookies, brownies, syrups and more.
    President: Joseph Semprevivo
Estimated Sales: $ 5-10 Million
Number Employees: 20-49
Sq. footage: 52000
Type of Packaging: Consumer

7510 Joseph's Pasta Company
PO Box 8211
Ward Hill, MA 01835-0711   978-521-1718
        Fax: 978-374-7917   888-327-2782
Manufacturers of fresh and frozen pasta, filled ravioli, pesto and sauces
Estimated Sales: $ 51 Million
Number Employees: 175

7511 Josh & John's Ice Cream
111 E Pikes Peak Ave
Colorado Springs, CO 80903-1803   719-632-0299
    Fax: 719-632-2833   800-530-2855
        joshjohn1@earthlink.com
            www.joshandjohns.com
Processor of ice cream products
    President/CEO/CFO: John Krakauer
Estimated Sales: $300,000-500,000
Number Employees: 100-249
Brands:
    Josh & John's Ice Cream

7512 Josh Early Candies
4640 W Tilghman Street
Allentown, PA 18104-3293   610-395-4321
            Fax: 610-398-8502
Candy and confections
    Marketing: Barry Bobil
    Public Relations: Lisa Medero
Estimated Sales: Below $ 5 Million
Number Employees: 10

7513 Josie's Best New Mexican Foods
PO Box 5525
Santa Fe, NM 87502-5525   505-473-3437
            Fax: 505-473-5808
Processor of tortillas, chili and posole
    Co-Owner: Nate Pino
    Co-Owner: Debbie Mixon
    Secretary: Betty Vinzant
Type of Packaging: Consumer

7514 Josuma Coffee Corporation
P.O.Box 1115
Menlo Park, CA 94026-1115   650-366-5453
        Fax: 650-366-5464   josuma@aol.com
                www.josuma.com
Coffee
    President: Joseph John
    Vice President: Urmila John
Estimated Sales: Under $300,000
Number Employees: 1-4
Type of Packaging: Private Label
Brands:
    Espresso Blend
    Green Coffee
    Malabar Gorld Premium
    Monsooned Malabar

7515 Jou Jou's Pita Bakery
166 W Valley Ave
Birmingham, AL 35209-3620   205-945-7482
        Fax: 205-945-6021 www.pita.net
Processor of plain and wheat pita bread
    Owner: Naji Constantine
Estimated Sales: Less than $500,000
Number Employees: 10-19
Sq. footage: 6000
Brands:
    Pito

7516 Joullian Vineyards
P.O.Box 1400
Carmel Valley, CA 93924-1400   831-659-2800
        Fax: 831-659-2802   877-659-2800
Wines
    Manager: Raymond E Watson Iii
    Owner: Jeannette Joullian Sias
    VP: Raymond Watson III
    CFO: Robert Fain
    General Manager/Winemaker: Ridge Watson
Estimated Sales: $ 2.5-5 Million
Number Employees: 5-9
Brands:
    Joullian Vineyards

7517 Joy Cone Company
3435 Lamor Rd
Hermitage, PA 16148-3097   724-962-5747
        Fax: 724-962-3470   800-242-2663
    joycone@joycone.com   www.joycone.com
Processor and exporter of ice cream cones
    President: Joseph George
    CFO: Scott Kaomanek
    Quality Control: Sharon George
    Director Food Service/Sales: Juergen Kloo
Estimated Sales: $ 100-500 Million
Number Employees: 250-499
Brands:
    Joy
    Scoopy

7518 Joy's Specialty Foods
300 N Willow Street
Mancos, CO 81328-9059   970-533-1500
        Fax: 970-533-2011   800-831-5697
    joy@joysfoods.com   www.joysfoods.com
Gourmet specialty foods that include salas and hot
sauces, marinades and grilling sauces, chile jams
and seasonings and dips
    President: Joy Kyzer
    Vice President: Dave Kyzer
Estimated Sales: $300,000-500,000
Number Employees: 5
Type of Packaging: Consumer, Bulk
Brands:
    Joy's

7519 Joyce Food Products
Boumar Place
Elmwood Park, NJ 07407   201-791-4300
            Fax: 201-791-0324
Dry baked goods
    President: Howard Freundlich
    Controller: Rhoda Sallay
    VP: Victor Ostreicher
    Operations Manager: Anthony Benzinger
    Purchasing Manager: Art Hersh
Estimated Sales: $ 20-50 Million
Number Employees: 200
Type of Packaging: Private Label

7520 Joyva Corporation
53 Varick Ave
Brooklyn, NY 11237-1589   718-497-0170
    Fax: 718-366-8504   richard@joyva.com
                www.joyva.com
Processor of confectionery products including
bagged, bars, boxes chocolate, fund raising, gums,
jellies, Halloween, hard, marshmallows, packaged
for racks, theatre packaging and vending; also, seasonal Passover and kosher products
    President: Milton Radutzky
    VP: Harry Radutzky
Estimated Sales: $ 20 - 50 Million
Number Employees: 50-99
Type of Packaging: Consumer

7521 Juanita's Foods
P.O.Box 847
Wilmington, CA 90748-0847   310-834-5339
            Fax: 310-834-5064
    customerservice@juanitasfoods.com
            www.juanitasfoods.com
Processor and exporter of Mexican foods including
soups, hot sauce, hominy and ready-to-serve mole
    President: George Delatorre
    CEO: Aaron De Latorre
    Sales Director: Bill Sneen
    Operations Manager: Mark De La Torre
    General Manager: Gina Harpur
    Plant Manager: Frank Andrade
    Purchasing Manager: Leo Medina
Estimated Sales: $41500000
Number Employees: 100-249
Type of Packaging: Consumer, Food Service, Private Label, Bulk
Brands:
    Juanita's
    Pico Pica
    Tia Anita

7522 Jubelt Variety Bakeries
216 W Main Street
Mount Olive, IL 62069-1639   217-999-7312
            Fax: 217-999-2613
Processor of cakes, breads, doughnuts and cookies
    President: Lance Jubelt
Estimated Sales: $1,200,000
Number Employees: 35
Number of Brands: 2
Sq. footage: 8000
Type of Packaging: Food Service, Bulk

7523 Jubilations
1536 Gardner Blvd # 8
Columbus, MS 39702-2891   662-328-9210
    Fax: 662-329-1558   cheesecakes@jubilations.com
                www.jubilations.com
Cheesecakes.
    President: Tamara Craddock
    Sales/Marketing: George Purnell
    Purchasing Manager: Ed Griffith
Estimated Sales: $984807
Number Employees: 5-9
Sq. footage: 6000
Type of Packaging: Consumer, Food Service, Private Label
Brands:
    Jubilations

7524 Jubilee Foods
PO Box 973
Bayou La Batre, AL 36509-0973   251-824-2110
    Fax: 251-824-7449   patrick@jubileefoods.com
                www.jubileeseafood.com
Processor of fresh and frozen shrimp
    President: Charles Walton Kraver
    Vice President: Frank Kawana
    Quality Control: Mike Williams
    Plant Manager: Charles Kraver
Estimated Sales: Below $ 5 Million
Number Employees: 15
Brands:
    Buyer Label
    Jubilee
    Southern Supreme

7525 Jubilee Gourmet Creations
PO Box 6305-0318
Manchester, NH 03108   603-625-0654
            Fax: 603-625-0654
Processor of brandied cherries, peaches and berries
    President: Joyce Davis
Type of Packaging: Consumer, Food Service, Bulk

7526 Jubilee-Sedgefield Salads
PO Box 29114
Greensboro, NC 27429-9114   336-288-6646
                                    Fax: 336-545-1880
Manufacturers of salami and sausages
    President: Jerry McMasters
Estimated Sales: $ 50-100 Million
Number Employees: 100

7527 Judicial Flavors
11400 Atwood Road
Auburn, CA 95603-9017   530-885-1298
    Fax: 530-888-0311 shyster@boothill.net
            www.judicialflavors.com
Products include hot sauces, barbecue sauces, coffe,
dressings, fruit sauces, marinades, mustards, nuts,
oils, salsa, spices & rubs
Estimated Sales: $ 1 - 3 Million
Number Employees: 5-9

7528 Judith Ann
1 Schuster Road
Falmouth, ME 04105-2531   207-871-0551
                                    Fax: 207-871-0167

7529 Judson-Atkinson Candies
P.O.Box 200669
San Antonio, TX 78220-0669   210-359-8380
    Fax: 210-359-8392 800-962-3984
    customerservice@judsonatkinsoncandies.com
            www.judsonatkinsoncandies.com
Processor of confectionery products including hard
candies, taffy, marshmallow candies, mints, jellies,
jelly beans, seasonal candy products and assorted
bagged goods; importer of gum, gummies and mints
    President/CEO/Chairman: Basil Atkinson Jr
    VP Finance: Rachel Espinosa
    VP Sales/Marketing: Doyle Huntsman
Estimated Sales: $100 Million
Number Employees: 100-249
Sq. footage: 123000
Type of Packaging: Consumer, Food Service, Pri-
    vate Label, Bulk
Brands:
    Chewy Pralines
    Sours-Soft Centers

7530 Judy's Cream Caramels
19995 SW Chapman Road
Sherwood, OR 97140-8606   503-819-5080
                                    Fax: 503-625-1602
Processor and exporter of cream caramels
    Owner: Debbie Judy
Number Employees: 5-9
Type of Packaging: Consumer

7531 Judyth's Mountain
PO Box 28201
Spokane, WA 99228-8201   509-484-5000
                                    Fax: 509-484-5500
    President: Jerry Johnson
Estimated Sales: $ 5-10 Million
Number Employees: 20

7532 Juice Bowl Products
2090 Us Highway 98 S
Lakeland, FL 33801-6557   863-665-5515
    Fax: 863-667-7116 www.juicebowl.com
Juices and juice drinks
    CEO: Paul Grady
    VP Operations: Terry Simmers
    VP: Carl Anderson
    Quality Control: Rey Dedmon
    Director Marketing/Sales: Kim Grady Brock
    Plant Manager: Carl Anderson
Estimated Sales: $12 Million
Number Employees: 100-249
Brands:
    JB

7533 Juice Guys
45 Dunster Street
Cambridge, MA 02138-5908   508-228-4464
    Fax: 781-868-5490 www.juiceguys.com
Processor of juice, juice products and cocktails, iced
tea and nutraceuticals
    President: Mark Hellendrung
    National Sales Manager: Ken Traenkle
Estimated Sales: $20-50 Million
Number Employees: 50-99

7534 Juice Mart
6758 Julie Lane
West Hills, CA 91307-2727   818-992-4442
    Fax: 818-992-4479 877-888-1011
    juice@juicemart.com www.juicemart.com
Juice concentrates and nutripaks. Design and set-up
of juice bars.
    President: Linda Renaud
Estimated Sales: $500,000-$1 Million
Number Employees: 1-4

7535 Juice Tyme
4401 S Oakley Ave
Chicago, IL 60609-3020   773-579-1291
    Fax: 773-579-1251 800-236-5823
    juicetyme@aol.com www.juicetyme.com
Juices
    President: Philip L Scott
    CFO: Thomas Martens
    Executive VP: Michael Schmidt
Estimated Sales: Below $ 5 Million
Number Employees: 20-49

7536 Juicy Whip
1668 Curtiss Ct
La Verne, CA 91750-5848   909-392-7500
    Fax: 626-814-8016 http://www.juicywhip.com
Processor of fruit juices; manufacturer of beverage
dispensers
    President: Gus Stratton
Estimated Sales: $5-10 Million
Number Employees: 5-9
Brands:
    Juicy Whip

7537 Julac
175 Chemin Marieville
Rougemont, QC J3L 3V9
Canada   514-861-2404
    Fax: 450-651-5453 alcours@paulmasson.com
Processor and exporter of blueberry aperitif
    President: Alain Lecours
Parent Co: Groupe Paul Masson
Type of Packaging: Consumer, Food Service

7538 Julius Sturgis Pretzel House
219 E Main St
Lititz, PA 17543-2011   717-626-4354
    Fax: 717-627-2682 info@sturgispretzel.com
            www.sturgispretzel.com
Pretzels
    Manager: Aerin Sturgis
    Co-Owner: Clyde Tshudy
    Co-Owner: Barbara Ann Tshudy
Estimated Sales: Under $ 1 Million
Number Employees: 10-19

7539 Jungbunzlauer
7 Wells Avenue
Newton, MA 02459-3261   617-969-0900
    Fax: 617-964-2921 800-828-0062
    info@jungbunzlauer-inc.com
            www.jungbunzlauer.com
Processor and wholesaler/distributor of acidulants,
gums, potassium, sodium, caffeine, etc
    President: George Mieling
    CEO: Jack Doyle
    Technical Service Manager: Tom West
Estimated Sales: $3300000
Number Employees: 16
Type of Packaging: Bulk

7540 Junior's Cheesecake
58-42 Maurice Avenue
PO Box 780-208
Maspeth, NY 11378   718-852-5257
    Fax: 718-260-9849 800-458-6467
    info@juniorscheesecake.com
            www.juniorscheesecake.com
traditional plain cheesecake, as well as flavored
cheesecake

7541 Juniper Valley Farms
15504 Liberty Ave
Jamaica, NY 11433-1000   718-291-3333
                                    Fax: 718-291-0560
    President: Ken Schlossberg
Estimated Sales: $ 5-10 Million
Number Employees: 20-49

7542 Juno Chef's
230-49 Street
Brooklyn, NY 11220   718-492-1300
                                    Fax: 718-492-1334

Processor of frozen breakfast foods, macaroni and
cheese and pasta with tomato sauce
    President: Julius Spessot
    General Manager: Onofrio Demattia
Estimated Sales: $10-20 Million
Number Employees: 50-99
Sq. footage: 20000
Type of Packaging: Food Service

7543 Junuis Food Products
800 E Northwest Hwy # 510
Palatine, IL 60074-6511   847-359-4300
                                    Fax: 847-359-4364
Processor and packer of frozen and fresh horseradish
    President: John Russell
Estimated Sales: Less than $500,000
Number Employees: 1-4
Type of Packaging: Consumer, Food Service

7544 Jurgielewicz Duck Farm
P.O.Box 68
Moriches, NY 11955-0068   631-878-2000
    Fax: 631-878-4281 800-543-8257
Processor of frozen ducklings including free range
long island duckling, kosher and parts
    Owner: Benjamin Jurgielewicz
    Partner: Tom Jurgielewicz
Estimated Sales: $ 10-20 Million
Number Employees: 50-99
Type of Packaging: Consumer, Food Service
Brands:
    South Shore
    South Side
    Twin Lake

7545 (HQ)Jus-Made
9761 Clifford Dr # 100
Dallas, TX 75220-5334   972-241-5544
    Fax: 972-241-3399 800-969-3746
    info@jus-made.com www.jus-made.com
Processor of bar mixes, fruit juices and drinks, fruit
granitas, coffee granitas and smoothies; also sells
beverage equipment
    President: Gene Barfield
    VP Sales: Jim Tanner
    Operations Manager: Mike Sayre
Estimated Sales: $ 1 - 3 Million
Number Employees: 50-99
Sq. footage: 3500
Type of Packaging: Consumer, Food Service, Pri-
    vate Label, Bulk
Other Locations:
    Jus-Made
    Houston TX
Brands:
    Floria Julep
    Orogold

7546 Just Born
1300 Stefko Blvd
Bethlehem, PA 18017-6672   610-867-7568
    Fax: 610-543-4981 800-445-5787
            www.justborn.com
Manufacturer of confectionery products including
boxed and bagged, chewy candy, holiday novelties,
jelly beans and marshmallow products
    Co-President: Ross Born
    CEO: David N Shaffer
    Director of Marketing: John Kerr
    Director of Sales: John Leipold
Estimated Sales: $ 20 - 50 Million
Number Employees: 250-499
Parent Co: Just Born
Type of Packaging: Consumer
Brands:
    Hot Tamales
    Marshmellow Peeps
    Mike and Ike
    Peanut Chews
    Teenee Beanee
    Zours

7547 Just Delicious Gourmet Foods
PO Box 2747
Seal Beach, CA 90740-1747   949-215-5341
    Fax: 714-870-0332 800-871-6085
    justdel@aol.com www.justdelicious.net
Processor of dry soup, bread and dip mixes; exporter
of dry soup mixes
    President: Diana Ferguson
Estimated Sales: $500,000 appx.
Number Employees: 5-9
Sq. footage: 10000
Type of Packaging: Consumer, Food Service, Bulk

Brands:
Just Delicious

7548 Just Desserts
1970 Carroll Avenue
San Francisco, CA 94124-2511   415-602-9245
   Fax: 415-468-4811   Mareya@justdesserts.com
Specialty cakes, pastries, cookies
   President: Elliot Hoffman
   Controller: Shyam Kataruka
   Marketing Manager: Mareya Ibrahim
   Director Retail: John Grubb
   Operations Manager: David Parker
Estimated Sales: $ .5 - 1 million
Number Employees: 100-249
Type of Packaging: Private Label

7549 Just Off Melrose
1196 Montalvo Way
Palm Springs, CA 92262-5441   714-533-4566
   Fax: 714-533-4567   800-743-4109
    inforequest@justoffmelrose.com
     www.justoffmelrose.com
Manufacturer of crisps, croutons, chips, biscotti and gourmet snacks.
   President: Brandon Tesmer
   Sales Rep: Ryan Niesen
Estimated Sales: Below $ 5 Million
Number Employees: 40
Brands:
   Just Chips
   Just Crisps
   Just Croutons

7550 Just Tomatoes Company
P.O.Box 807
Westley, CA 95387-0807   209-894-5371
   Fax: 209-894-3146   800-537-1985
   info@justtomatoes.com   www.justtomatoes.com
Processor of dried fruits and vegetables including tomatoes, red and green bell peppers, corn, peas, carrots, apples, persimmons, blueberries, mango, cherries, raspberries, etc.; also, mixed fruit and vegetable trail mix, crunchyraisins and dry roasted soy nuts. Food theme greeting cards, cookbooks
   Co-Owner: Karen Cox
   Co-Owner: Bill Cox
Estimated Sales: $ 50 - 100 Million
Number Employees: 50-99
Sq. footage: 7000
Type of Packaging: Consumer, Food Service, Private Label, Bulk
Brands:
   Hot Just Veggies
   Just Apples
   Just Bell Peppers
   Just Blackberries
   Just Blueberries
   Just Carrots
   Just Cherries
   Just Corn
   Just Crunch Onions
   Just Crunchy
   Just Fruit Munchies
   Just Fruit Snacks
   Just Green Onions
   Just Mango
   Just Peas
   Just Persimmon
   Just Persimmons
   Just Pineapple
   Just Raisins
   Just Raspberries
   Just Roasted Garlic
   Just Soy Nuts
   Just Strawberries
   Just Tomatoes
   Just Veggies
   Tomato Press

7551 Justin Lloyd Premium Tea Company
1111 E Watson Center Road
Carson, CA 90745-4217   310-834-4000
     Fax: 310-834-0300
Brands:
   Flavors & Fusions
   Herbals
   Traditional

7552 Justin Winery & Vineyard
11680 Chimney Rock Rd
Paso Robles, CA 93446-9792   805-238-6932
    Fax: 805-238-7382   800-726-0049
   info@justinwine.com   www.justinwine.com
Wines
   President: Justin Baldwin
   VP/Director Sales/Marketing: Rich Richardson
   VP/Director Finance/Human Resources: Cheryl Wieczorek
   Sales Manager: Paul Sowerby
Estimated Sales: $ 2.5-5 Million
Number Employees: 20-49
Type of Packaging: Private Label
Brands:
   Justin

7553 Justin's Nut Butter
409 Spruce Street
Boulder, CO 80302   303-449-9559
     Fax: 303-442-0881
   comments@justinsnutbutter.com
    www.justinsnutbutter.com
flavored nut butters
   President/Owner: Justin Gold
   Sales/Marketing: Lance Gentry
   Operations: Skip Latimer

7554 (HQ)Jyoti Cruisine India
PO Box 516
Berwyn, PA 19312-0516   610-522-2650
   Fax: 610-522-2652   jyoti@jyotifoods.com
     www.jyotifoods.com
Processor and exporter of Indian foods including vegetables, soups, bean products, frozen vegetarian meals and sauces
   President: Jyoti Gupta
   VP: Vijai Gupta
Type of Packaging: Consumer, Food Service, Private Label
Brands:
   INDIA HOUSE
   JYOTI

7555 Jyoti Cuisine India
816 Newtown Rd
Berwyn, PA 19312-2200   610-296-4620
   Fax: 610-889-0492   jyoti@jyotifoods.com
     www.jyotifoods.com
Sauces (masala, rogan josh, saffron cream), Indian foods, chhole, matar paneer, sambar karhi, saag, dal, basmati rice
   VP: Vijay Gupta
   President: Jyoti Gupta
Estimated Sales: $300,000-500,000
Number Employees: 10-19
Brands:
   Jyoti

7556 K Horton Specialty Foods
28 Monument Sq
Portland, ME 04101-6447   207-228-2056
   Fax: 207-228-2059   Kris@KHortonFoods.com
     www.khortonfoods.com
Specialty cheeses, olives, dried cured meats and meat pates, smoked seafood.
   President: Kris Horton

7557 K&B Company
P.O.Box 100
Schulenburg, TX 78956-0100   979-743-6555
   Fax: 979-743-4422 www.primeproductsinc.net
   President: Elgin Kristinik
Estimated Sales: $ 50-100 Million
Number Employees: 100-249

7558 K&F Select Fine Coffees
2801 SE 14th Ave
Portland, OR 97202-2203   503-234-7788
   Fax: 503-231-9827   800-558-7788
   sandyj@kfcoffee.com   kfcoffee.com
Wholesaler/distributor of coffee products from around the world, torami syrups and sauces, taza rica cocoas, powdered drink mixes, liquid fruit smoothie products, and allied coffee products
   President: Don Dominguez
   Director Sales/Marketing: Sandy Jumonville
   Sales: Steve O Brien
Estimated Sales: $3228000
Number Employees: 10-19
Type of Packaging: Consumer, Food Service, Private Label, Bulk

Brands:
   K&F
   TAZA RICA MEXICAN SPICED COCOA

7559 K&K Gourmet Meats
300 Washington St
Leetsdale, PA 15056-1004   724-266-8400
     Fax: 724-266-8402
Processor of frozen philly and chicken philly steaks; also, frozen chicken
   Owner: Art Kotz
Number Employees: 10-19
Type of Packaging: Consumer, Food Service

7560 K&K Laboratories
3305 Tyler St
Carlsbad, CA 92008-3056   760-434-6044
   Fax: 760-720-9888   knklabspacball.net
     kklabs.com
Formulator and technical services of vitamin tablets, hard-shell capsules and powders.
   President: Alex Kononchuk
Estimated Sales: $3500000
Number Employees: 20-49
Type of Packaging: Private Label, Bulk

7561 K&N Fisheries
Upper Port Latour
Shelburne, NS B0T 1W0
Canada   902-768-2478
     Fax: 902-768-2385
Processor and exporter of fresh and salted fish including cod, haddock and pollack
   Owner/Manager: Kirk Nickerson
   Plant Manager: Gregory Nickerson
Number Employees: 10-19
Type of Packaging: Bulk

7562 K&R Pretzel Bakery
1700 Flesher Ave
Dayton, OH 45420-3231   937-299-2231
Pretzels
   President: Ralph Glaze
Estimated Sales: $500,000-$1 Million
Number Employees: 1-4

7563 K&S Bakery Products
10637 172nd Street NW
Edmonton, AB T5S 1P1
Canada   780-481-8155
     ksbakery@telus.net
Processor of muffins, cakes, scones, dry mixes, doughs, batters and spreads
   President: Eric Kettner
   VP/Manager: Ruth Snider
   VP: Ruth Snider
   Manager: Earle Snider
Number Employees: 10-19
Type of Packaging: Consumer, Food Service
Brands:
   Cakes
   Jumbo Muffins
   K&S
   Scones

7564 K&S Riddle
5701 White Street
Buzzards Bay, MA 02542-1411   508-563-7333

7565 K.B. Hall Ranch
11999 Ojai Santa Paula Road
Ojai, CA 93023-8323   805-646-4512
   Manager: Thomas Hall

7566 K.B. Specialty Foods
P.O.Box 289
Greensburg, IN 47240-0289   812-663-8184
   Fax: 812-663-5680   ncortolillo@kroger.com
     www.kroger.com
Bakery items
   Manager: Nick Cortolillo
   Operation Manager: Rod Taylor
   Production Manager: Nick Cortolillo
   Purchasing Manager: R Stutes
Estimated Sales: $ 100-500 Million
Number Employees: 250-499

7567 K.L. Keller Imports
230 Madison St
Oakland, CA 94607-4520   510-839-7890
   Fax: 510-839-7895 www.klkellerimports.com
Distributors of fine foods
   Owner: Kitty Keller

7568 K.S.M. Seafood Corporation
PO Box 3057
Baton Rouge, LA 70821-3057   225-383-1517
Fax: 225-387-6641
Seafood
President: Bo Wallenhom
Estimated Sales: $ 10 - 20 Million
Number Employees: 50-99

7569 KB Electronics Inc
12095 NW 39th St
Coral Springs, FL 33065-2516   954-346-4900
Fax: 954-346-3377   info@kbelectronics.com
www.kbelectronics.com
KB Electronics manufactures a variety of AC
Drives, DC Drives, Fan Speed Controls, DC-DC
Low Voltage Battery Controls and RFI/EMI Filters
and Signals.
CFO: Fred Mush
CEO: Gilbert Knauer
Marketing Director: Gilbert Kanver
National Sales Manager: Richard Fritts
Plant Manager: Jason Morgan
Purchasing Manager: Omar Blackwood
Estimated Sales: $20-50 Million
Number Employees: 100-249
Number of Brands: 60
Sq. footage: 27000

7570 KBC Trading & Processing Company
PO Box 667
Stockton, CA 95201-3067   661-758-5178
Fax: 209-955-0664 www.conagrafoods.com
Processor of dried beans and rice.
Chief Executive Officer: Gary Rodkin
Executive Vice President/CFO: Andre' Hawaux
Executive Vice President: Al Bolles Ph.D
Executive VP/Chief Marketing Officer: Joan
Chow
Exec VP Operations: Mayo Schmidt
Estimated Sales: Less than $500,000
Number Employees: 10-19
Parent Co: ConAgra Foods
Type of Packaging: Bulk

7571 KDK Inc
1128 E 12400 S
Draper, UT 84020-9628   801-571-3506
Processor of milk including skim, whole, 1% and
2%
VP: L Fitzgerald
Number Employees: 20-49
Sq. footage: 28000
Type of Packaging: Consumer, Food Service, Private Label, Bulk
Brands:
Dairy Rich
Golden Dairy

7572 KHS-Bartelt
5501 N Washington Blvd
Sarasota, FL 34243-2249   941-359-4000
Fax: 941-359-4086 800-829-9980
mschroeder@barteltinc.com
www.barteltinc.com
Bakery, confectionery, biscuit/cracker, pharmaceutical products
President: Reno N Cruz
Marketing Manager: Samantha Bishop
Executive: Paul Rosile
Customer Service Manager: Michael Schroeder
Estimated Sales: $ 10-25 Million
Number Employees: 50-99
Brands:
Bartlett

7573 KMC Citrus Enterprises
P.O.Box 1819
Winter Haven, FL 33882-1819   352-821-3666
Fax: 352-821-1400
Processor of fresh and frozen orange puree and dried
citrus
President: Maristela Ferrari
VP: Keith Bowen
Estimated Sales: $ 1 - 3 Million
Number Employees: 10-19
Type of Packaging: Consumer, Bulk
Brands:
KMC Citrus

7574 KP USA Trading
500 S Anderson Street
Los Angeles, CA 90033-4222   323-881-9871
Fax: 323-268-3669
Processor, wholesaler/distributor and exporter of
soybean, corn, cottonseed, sesame and other vegetable oils; importer of oriental foods including jasmine, sweet rice, noodles, rice stick and candy
VP: Jerry Wong
Manager: Joe Beatly
Manager: Nancy Wong
Number Employees: 10-19
Sq. footage: 25000
Type of Packaging: Consumer, Food Service, Private Label, Bulk
Brands:
King Products
Mama

7575 KT's Kitchen
1065 E Walnut St # C
Carson, CA 90746-1384   310-764-0850
Fax: 310-764-0855 www.ktskitchens.com
Frozen pizza
President: Kathy Taggares
VP: Sheryl Schneider
Vice President: David Fortney
Quality Control: Mario Ayon
Sales Manager: Steve Redmond
Operations Manager: Joan Paris
Purchasing Manager: Curt Ramsey
Estimated Sales: $ 100-500 Million
Number Employees: 100-249
Type of Packaging: Private Label

7576 KTI-Keene Technology
14357 Commercial Pkwy
South Beloit, IL 61080-2621   815-624-8989
Fax: 815-624-4223   info@keenetech.com
www.keenetech.com
Manufacturer of automatic zero speed splicers, matrix iturret rewinders, web tension controls, infeeds,
unwind/rewind stands and related web handling
equipment.
President: John Keene
Sales Manager: Darrel Spors
Plant Manager: Bill Carpenter
Estimated Sales: $5-10 Million
Number Employees: 50-99
Sq. footage: 65000

7577 Kabco
2000 New Horizons Blvd
Amityville, NY 11701-1137   631-842-3600
Fax: 631-842-6002   skibria@aol.com
www.kabcopharm.com
Processor and exporter of vitamins and dietary supplements
Chairman: Abu Kabir
Director Purchasing: Rezaur Rahman Yousuf
Estimated Sales: $ 20 - 50 Million
Number Employees: 100-249
Sq. footage: 30000
Type of Packaging: Private Label

7578 Kabob's
5423 N Lake Dr
Morrow, GA 30260-3534   404-361-6283
Fax: 404-361-8008 800-732-9484
jherrera@kabobs.com   www.kabobs.com
Processor of hors d'oeuvres including mini-beef
Wellingtons, spanakopita and coconut chicken
Founder/Chairman: Perry Hunt
President/Executive Chef: Will Rece
CFO: Secott Barnett
Quality Control: Lisa Moris
R & D: Nilson Haynes
VP Sales/Marketing: Steve Law
Regional Sales Manager: Dan Grant
Purchasing: Ric Consuegra
Estimated Sales: $ 75-100 Million
Number Employees: 100-249
Type of Packaging: Food Service
Brands:
Kabob's

7579 Kachemak Bay Seafood
PO Box 4004
Homer, AK 99603-4004   907-235-2799
Fax: 907-235-2799
Various fishes and other seafoods
Estimated Sales: Less than $500,000
Number Employees: 1-4

7580 Kaffe Magnum Opus
636 E Landis Avenue
Vineland, NJ 08360-8007   856-794-8900
Fax: 856-327-9975 800-652-5282
support@Icafe.com   www.icafe.com
Regular, flavored and decaffeinated coffee
President: Robert Johnson
Estimated Sales: $500,000-$1 Million
Number Employees: 5-9
Brands:
Coffee Time
Kaffe Magnum Opus

7581 (HQ)Kagome
333 Johnson Rd
Los Banos, CA 93635-9768   209-826-8850
Fax: 209-826-8858 www.kagomeusa.com
Canned fruit, fruit beverages and sauces
President: Gregg Ishigure
CEO: Herosi Mori
Marketing Manager: Luis Be Olizeira
VP Sales/Marketing: Don Polk
General Manager: Steve Fukushima
Plant Manager: Louis De Oliveira
Estimated Sales: $ 50 - 100 Million
Number Employees: 100-249
Brands:
Kagome

7582 Kahiki Foods
3583 E Broad Street
Columbus, OH 43213-1141   614-237-5425
Fax: 614-237-3122
President: Michael Tsao
Plant Manager: Andy Chan
Estimated Sales: $ 2.5-5 Million
Number Employees: 100

7583 Kahns Bakery Company
4130 Rio Bravo St # B
El Paso, TX 79902-1024   915-544-6950
Fax: 915-534-0043
Bakery
Estimated Sales: Under $500,000
Number Employees: 1-4

7584 Kaiser Foods
500 York St
Cincinnati, OH 45214-2490   513-621-2053
Fax: 513-455-8284 888-291-0608
www.kaiserpickles.com
Processor of olives, peppers, pickles and sauerkraut
President: Ted G Kaiser
Chairman: David Kaiser
Estimated Sales: $ 10 - 20 Million
Number Employees: 20-49
Sq. footage: 250000
Type of Packaging: Consumer, Food Service, Private Label, Bulk

7585 Kajun Kettle Foods
698 Saint George Ave
New Orleans, LA 70121-1117   504-733-8800
Fax: 504-736-0517 mdavidson@kajunkettle.com
www.kajunkettle.com
Processor of sauces, gumbo and corn shrimp soup
President: Pierre Hilzim
VP: Monica Davidson
Estimated Sales: Below $ 5 Million
Number Employees: 20-49
Sq. footage: 86000
Type of Packaging: Consumer, Food Service, Private Label, Bulk
Brands:
Crawfish Monica

7586 (HQ)Kake Tribal Corporation
P.O.Box 263
Kake, AK 99830-0263   907-785-3465
Fax: 907-785-6407
Seafood and seafood products
President: Harold Martin
Estimated Sales: $2.4 Million
Number Employees: 10-19
Brands:
fuel

7587 Kaladi Brothers
6921 Brayton Dr # 105
Anchorage, AK 99507-5601   907-644-7400
Fax: 907-344-5935   sales@kaladi.com
www.kaladi.com

Coffee
President: Tim Gravel
Estimated Sales: $ 2.5-5 Million
Number Employees: 20-49

7588 Kalama Chemical
1725 Bank of California Center
Seattle, WA 98164   206-682-7890
          Fax: 206-682-1907   800-742-6147
Manufacturer and exporter of specialty chemicals including benzaldehyde, cinnamic aldehyde, benzyl benzoate, benzyl alcohol, benzylacetate, potassium benzoate, benzoic acid and sodium benzoate
President: James Hamberick
VP Marketing: Jim Harris
VP Engineering: Jarl Opgrande
Number Employees: 175

7589 Kalamar Seafoods
2490 W 78th Street
Hialeah, FL 33016-2762   305-822-5586
          Fax: 305-557-4418
          rvazquez@kalamarseafood.com
          www.kalamarseafood.com
Frozen seafoods
President: Roberto R Vazquez
Controller: Carl Johnson
Vice President: Barbara Vazquez
Estimated Sales: $ 10-20 Million
Number Employees: 20-50
Number of Products: 500
Type of Packaging: Private Label

7590 Kalamazoo Brewing Company
8938 Krum Ave
Galesburg, MI 49053-9558   269-382-2338
          Fax: 269-382-3820   fredb@bellsbeer.com
          www.bellsbeer.com
Processor of ale and stout
President: Larry Bell
VP: Angie Bell
Production Manager: J Mallett
Plant Manager: Michael Wachowski
Estimated Sales: $ 5-10 Million
Number Employees: 50-99
Type of Packaging: Consumer, Food Service
Brands:
Bell's Amber Ale
Bell's Best Brown Ale
Bell's Kalamazoo Stout
Bell's Oberon Ale
Bell's Pale Ale
Bell's Porter
Third Coast Beer
Two Hearted Ale

7591 Kalamazoo Creamery
706 Lake Street
Kalamazoo, MI 49001-2201   616-343-2558
          Fax: 616-343-1620
Dairy products
President: william Steers
CEO: William Steers
Brands:
Kalamazoo

7592 Kalashian Packing Company
1850 S Parallel Avenue
Fresno, CA 93702-4137   559-237-4287
          Fax: 559-237-4280
Figs, fig paste
President: Richard Kalashian
Controller: Deborah Fries
Vice President: Jerry Floratos
VP Sales/Marketing: Ron Garabedian

7593 Kalin Cellars
61 Galli Dr
Novato, CA 94949-5701   415-883-3543
          Fax: 415-883-3543   sales@kalincellars.com
          www.kalincellars.com
Wines
President: Terrance Leighton
Secretary: Frances Leighton
CFO: Frances Leighton
Estimated Sales: Under $500,000
Number Employees: 1-4
Brands:
Kalin Cellars

7594 Kalle USA, Inc.
5750-B Centerpoint Court
Gurnee, IL 60031   847-775-0781
          Fax: 847-775-0782   www.kalle.de

Manufacuturer of sausage casings. Also manufacture sponge cloths that can be used to wipe up large spills.
Sales Manager: John Lample
Brands:
PULLULAN
SUNMALT
TREHALOSE

7595 Kalman Floor Company
1202 Bergen Pkwy # 110
Evergreen, CO 80439-9559   303-674-2290
          Fax: 303-674-1238
          Karl.Johnson@kalmanfloor.com
          www.kalmanfloor.com
Manufacturer of seamless industrial concrete floors suitable for the food and beverage industries.
President: Carl Ytterberg
Sales Engineer: Karl Johnson

7596 Kalsec
P.O.Box 50511
Kalamazoo, MI 49005-0511   269-349-9711
          Fax: 269-382-3060   800-323-9320
          info@kalsec.com   www.kalsec.com
Processor and exporter of natural flavors, colors, extracts, spice oleoresins and essential oils
President: George Todd
Treasurer: Don Baird
Research & Development: Don Berdahl
Marketing Director: Bill Goodrich
VP Sales: Gary Hainrihar
Plant Manager: Harry Todd
Purchasing Manager: Walt Bower
Estimated Sales: $ 3 - 5 Million
Number Employees: 5-9
Parent Co: Kalamazoo Holdings
Type of Packaging: Food Service, Bulk
Brands:
Aquaresin Spices
Aquaresins
Durabrite
Durabrite Colors
Duralox
Duralox Blends
Herbalox
Herbalox Seasonings
Hexahydrolone
Hexalone
Hop Oil
Hoppy Drops
Hydraisolone
Hydrolone
Isolone
Kalsec
Kettle Aroma Extract
Strolone
Tetrahydrolone
Tetralone
Vegetone
Vegetone Colors

7597 Kalustyan Corporation
855 Rahway Ave
Union, NJ 07083-6633   908-688-6111
          Fax: 908-688-4415   info@kalustyan.com
          www.kalustyans.com
Manufacturer, importer and exporter of herbs, spices, rice, nuts, dried fruits, beans, seeds, oils, etc
President: John Bas
Estimated Sales: $3 Million
Number Employees: 20-49
Sq. footage: 100000
Type of Packaging: Food Service, Bulk

7598 Kalva Corporation
3940 Porett Dr
Gurnee, IL 60031-1280   847-336-1200
          Fax: 847-336-0712   800-525-8220
          info@kalvacorp.com   www.kalvacorp.com
Manufacturer of cone dips; chocolate, caramel and butterscotch toppings, hot fudge, syrups, variegates and ice cream bases; fruited shake bases and syrups; dry ice cream mix; caramel for candy manufacturers, bakeries and ice creammanufacturers
President: Robert Semred
VP: Allen Ballerini
VP Sales/Marketing: Allen Ballerini
Estimated Sales: $ 2.5-5 Million
Number Employees: 10-19
Sq. footage: 30000
Brands:
Kalva

7599 Kamish Food Products
3848 N Bell Ave
Chicago, IL 60618-3812   773-267-0400
          Fax: 773-267-0400
Processor and exporter of baking mixes, chocolate products, jams, jellies and dehydrated fruit nuggets
President: Ted Kamish
VP: R Kamish
Estimated Sales: $5000000
Number Employees: 20-49
Type of Packaging: Food Service, Private Label, Bulk

7600 Kammeh International Trade Co
1718 N Sayre Avenue
Chicago, IL 60707-4323   312-804-0800
          Fax: 773-804-0804
President: Reza Rezai
CEO: Morris Rezai
Marketing Director: Elham Jazab
Sales Director: Shon Barnette
Operations Manager: Alexander Rezai
Production Manager: Mike Simkhim
Plant Manager: Athena Uslander
Purchasing Manager: Charles Uslander
Estimated Sales: $ 6.8 Million
Number Employees: 32
Sq. footage: 12
Type of Packaging: Private Label
Brands:
Athena's Brownies
Athena's Cookies
Floryn
Isadora
Ixima
Pure Breath
Regal
Silverland
Tokyo

7601 Kan-Pac
1016 S Summit St
Arkansas City, KS 67005-3339   620-442-6820
          Fax: 620-442-6867
Juices, creamers, dairy, ice creams
VP: Steven Soza
President: Dennis Cohlmai
Estimated Sales: $ 10-20 Million
Number Employees: 50-99

7602 Kanai Tofu Factory
515 Ward Ave
Honolulu, HI 96814-4168   808-591-8205
          Fax: 808-591-8225
Prepared foods and soybean products
Owner: Richard Kanada
President: Mark Kaneda
Quality Control: Mark Kaneda
Sales Manager: Mark Kaneda
Estimated Sales: Below $ 5 Million
Number Employees: 20-49
Brands:
Kanai Tofu

7603 Kandia's Fine Teas
PO Box 797
Lewiston, ME 04243-0797   207-782-6300
          Fax: 207-225-2513   kandiasteas@cs.com
          www.kandiasteas.com
Herbal teas
Estimated Sales: $ 1-2.5 Million
Number Employees: 1-4

7604 Kang's Seafood
3000 S Shields Ave
Chicago, IL 60616-2630   312-225-2250
          Fax: 312-225-6495   800-269-8425
          srhea42781@aol.com   www.kangsseafood.com
Seafood
Owner: Steve Rhea
CEO: Seokjuh Rhea
CFO: Sunok Rhea
Estimated Sales: $5 Million
Number Employees: 5-9
Sq. footage: 15000
Type of Packaging: Food Service

7605 Kangaroo Brands
7620 N 81st St
Milwaukee, WI 53223-3836   414-355-9696
          Fax: 414-355-4295   800-798-0857
          sales@kangaroobrands.com
          www.kangaroobrands.com

Bread, pita bread, flat bread, pocket bread, wraps
President: John Kashou
Treasurer: Bill Podewils
VP: George Kashou
Marketing: Salem Kashou
Sales: Tony Schultz
Operations Manager: Kristina A Kashou
Plant Manager: John Kashou
Purchasing/Human Resources: Kristina Kashou
Estimated Sales: $ 5-10 Million
Number Employees: 50-99
Number of Brands: 1
Number of Products: 3
Type of Packaging: Private Label

7606 (HQ)Kantner Group
P.O.Box 157
Wapakoneta, OH 45895-0157   419-738-4060
      Fax: 419-738-4426 www.kantnergroup.com
Kantner Group includes Kantner Ingredients, Blue
Valley Foods and Chianti Cheese. Kantner Ingredi-
ents (formerly Euro Proteins) is a manufacturer and
distributor of dairy proteins and a custom/contract
dry blender. Blue Valley Foods isa manufacturer of
pi
President: Doug Kantner
General Manager: John Sadowsky
CFO: Mike Koon
Quality Control: Joe Chayka
Sales/Operations: Pam Jeffery
Sales: Jack Salemi
Purchasing: Paul Sharp
Purchasing: Mark Howell
Estimated Sales: $ 3 - 5 Million
Number Employees: 20-49
Type of Packaging: Food Service, Private Label,
Bulk
Other Locations:
Kantner Ingredients
Wapakoneta OH
Blue Valley Foods
Hebron NE
Chianti Cheese of New Jersey
Pemberton NJ
Brands:
Chianti Cheese

7607 Kapaa Bakery
PO Box 688
Kapaa, HI 96746-0688   808-822-4541
Baked goods
President: Paul Nishijo
Estimated Sales: $500,000 appx.
Number Employees: 5-9

7608 Kapaa Poi Factory
1181 Kainahola Rd
Kapaa, HI 96746-8926   808-822-5426
Processor of poi, tofu and kulolo
President: Kenneth Fujinaga
Estimated Sales: $500000
Number Employees: 1-4
Type of Packaging: Consumer

7609 Kaplan & Zubrin
P.O.Box 1006
Camden, NJ 08101-1006   856-964-1083
      Fax: 856-964-0510 800-334-0002
kz.pickles@verizon.net www.kzpickles.com
Institutional and private brand packers of pickled
products including pickles, condiments, relishes or
peppers.
President: Ronald Kaplan
Estimated Sales: $4773872
Number Employees: 20-49
Sq. footage: 72000
Type of Packaging: Food Service
Brands:
Garden State
K&Z
Shupak

7610 Kapono Sales
2688 Kilihau Bay H
Honolulu, HI 96823   808-839-2714
      Fax: 808-833-5444
President: Cal Odo

7611 Kara Chocolates
575 E University Pkwy # B43
Orem, UT 84097-7567   801-224-9515
Fax: 801-224-9588 800-284-5272
info@giftbasketsuppliers.com
www.giftbasketsuppliers.com

Chocolate candies
Manager: Susan Boren
Manager: Steve Peterson
Estimated Sales: $ 5-10 Million
Number Employees: 20-49
Brands:
Kara

7612 Karam Elsaha Baking Company
8195 Cazenovia Rd # 24
Manlius, NY 13104-8809   315-682-2780
      Fax: 315-682-2781
Processor of pita bread including white, wheat, on-
ion and cinnamon raisin; also, prepared pitas includ-
ing spinach turnovers, lentil, meat, pizza, apple,
cherry, blueberry and raspberry
Manager: Shawn Ryan
Marketing Director: Kay Dara
Number Employees: 10-19
Sq. footage: 5000
Type of Packaging: Consumer, Food Service, Pri-
vate Label
Brands:
Elsaha
Elsaha Cinnamon Raisin
Elsaha Wheat Pita

7613 Karen's Fabulous Biscotti
50 Main St
White Plains, NY 10606-1901   914-682-2165
      Fax: 914-328-4276 karen@biscotti-co.com
www.biscotti-co.com
Processor of bulk and wrapped shelf stable biscotti
and gourmet cookies
President: Gary Spirer
Marketing Director: Jerry O'Donnell
Sales Director: Debbie Rittberg
General Manager: Jerry O'Donnell
Number Employees: 10-19
Sq. footage: 9000
Type of Packaging: Consumer, Bulk
Brands:
Alex & Dani's Biscotti
Karen's Fabulous Biscotti

7614 Karen's Wine Country Cafe
P.O.Box 447
Sonoita, AZ 85637-0447   520-455-5282
      Fax: 520-455-0075 800-453-5650
President: Jennifer Wyrick
CEO: Jarde Wyrick
Estimated Sales: Less than $500,000
Number Employees: 5-9
Type of Packaging: Private Label

7615 Kargher Corporation
3131 Sandstone Dr
Hatfield, PA 19440-1939   215-822-1186
      Fax: 215-822-9666 800-355-1247
dlkcsk@aol.com
Chocolate chips, chocolate products, chocolate non-
pareils, confectionary coated pretzels
President: Douglas Kargher
CEO: Douglas Kargher
Estimated Sales: $ 5-10 Million
Number Employees: 20-49
Type of Packaging: Consumer, Food Service, Pri-
vate Label, Bulk
Brands:
Kargher Chocolate Chips
Kargher Milk Chocolate Chips
Kargher White Chocolate Chips

7616 Kari-Out Company
399 Knollwood Rd # 309
White Plains, NY 10603-1941   914-580-3200
      Fax: 914-580-3248 800-433-8799
info@kariout.com www.fresh-nap.com
Manufacturer and importer of sauces including hot,
mustard, soy and duck/sweet and sour; also, cooking
sherry, ketchup, vinegar and food colors
President: Howard Epstein
Sales Manager: David Chan
Estimated Sales: $ 50 - 100 Million
Number Employees: 100-249
Sq. footage: 40000
Parent Co: Perk-Up
Brands:
China Pack
Chinese-Lady
Kari-Out

7617 Karl Bissinger French Confections
32 Maryland Plz
St Louis, MO 63108-1526   314-367-9750
      Fax: 314-534-2419 800-325-8881
orders@bissingers.com www.bissingers.com
Processor and exporter of chocolate candy solids,
covered cream centers, covered cherries and nuts,
covered pretzels and half dipped oranges
Manager: Cindy Abrewczynski
Estimated Sales: $6000000
Number Employees: 5-9
Type of Packaging: Consumer, Bulk

7618 Karl Ehmer
6335 Fresh Pond Rd
Flushing, NY 11385-2623   718-456-8100
      Fax: 718-456-2270 800-487-5275
info@karlehmer.com www.karlehmer.com
Sausages and deli and smoked meats.
President: Mark Hanssler
Quality Control: Gary Durante
Production Manager/VP: Allen Hanssler
Marketing Director: Will Osanitsch
Purchasing Manager: Daniel Durante
Estimated Sales: $ 5-10 Million
Number Employees: 20-49
Brands:
KARL EHMER

7619 Karl Strauss Breweries
5985 Santa Fe St
San Diego, CA 92109-1623   858-273-2739
      Fax: 858-581-5691 www.karlstrauss.com
Brewer and importer of beer, amber lager and pale
ale
Owner: Karl Strauss
CFO: Matthew Rattner
Marketing Director: Brian Bolten
Sales: Paul Timm
Operations: Grant Gotteshon
Production: Paul Segura
Estimated Sales: $ .5 - 1 million
Number Employees: 10-19
Number of Brands: 25
Number of Products: 2
Sq. footage: 22000
Parent Co: Associated Micro Breweries
Brands:
DOWNTOWN AFTER DARK
ENDLESS SUMMER GOLD
Karl Strauss
RED TROLLEY ALE
STARGAZER
WINDANSEA WHEAT

7620 Karla's Smokehouse
P.O.Box 537
Rockaway Beach, OR 97136-0537   503-355-2362
Smoke fish
Owner: Karla Steinhauser
Estimated Sales: Less than $500,000
Number Employees: 1-4

7621 Karlin Foods Corporation
1845 Oak St # 19
Northfield, IL 60093-3022   847-441-8330
      Fax: 847-441-8640 karlin@karlinfoods.com
www.karlinfoods.com
Dry food products: dehydrated soup mixes
President: Mitchell Karlin
Estimated Sales: $ 10-20 Million
Number Employees: 10-19

7622 Karlsburger Foods
3236 Chelsea Rd W
Monticello, MN 55362-4667   763-295-2273
      Fax: 763-323-1745 800-383-6549
www.karlsburger.com
Processor of soup, sauce and gravy bases; also, sea-
sonings
President: Michael Maher
Estimated Sales: Below $ 5 Million
Number Employees: 10-19
Type of Packaging: Food Service
Brands:
Karlsburger

7623 Karly Wines
11076 Bell Rd
Plymouth, CA 95669-9516   209-245-3922
      Fax: 209-245-4874 karly@karlywines.com
www.karlywines.com

Manufacturer of wine
  Co-Owner: Karly Cobb
  Co-Owner: Lawrence Cobb
Estimated Sales: Under $500,000
Number Employees: 1-4
Brands:
  Karnival Pink Lemonade
  Plastic Fruit Drink

7624 Karn Meats
931 Taylor Ave
Columbus, OH 43219-2557   614-252-3712
          Fax: 614-252-8273   800-221-9585
kmi@karnmeats.com   www.karnmeats.com
Manufacturer of both cooked and raw meat products
that include; ground beef, beef patties, seasoned
hoagie steaks, breaded and floured cutlets, prime rib,
meatloaf, pork roast, pork chops, shredded chicken
and turkey legs
  President: Richard Karn
  R&D Director: Roger Clevinger
  Sales VP: Colby Karn
  Operations VP: Mike Furr
Estimated Sales: $25 Million
Number Employees: 50-99
Type of Packaging: Food Service, Private Label,
  Bulk

7625 Karoun Dairies
5117 Santa Monica Boulevard
Los Angeles, CA 90029-2413   323-666-6222
  Fax: 323-666-1501   contact@karouncheese.com
          www.karouncheese.com
Specialty cheeses in the Mediterranean style
  President: Anto Baghdassarian
Estimated Sales: $ 10-20 Million
Number Employees: 20-30
Brands:
  Karoun Dairies

7626 Karp's
Ste 530
1933 N Meacham Rd
Schaumburg, IL 60173-4342   847-593-5700
          Fax: 847-593-0749   800-593-5277
jeard@bakerbaker.com   www.bakerbaker.com
Processor and wholesaler/distributor of frozen
pre-baked biscotti and rugulach, icings, mixes, fruit
fillings and frozen cookie and muffin batters; also,
bakery equipment; serving the food service market
  CEO: Jack Karp
Estimated Sales: $100+ Million
Number Employees: 100-249

7627 Karp's
6 Mazel Way
Georgetown, MA 01833   800-373-5277
Processor and exporter of frozen muffin batters and
pre-baked breakfast desserts
  Sales Manager: Mark Ake
Number Employees: 10-19
Type of Packaging: Consumer, Food Service
Brands:
  Karp's
  Scoop-N-Bake

7628 Karpa Trading
PO Box 3877
Alhambra, CA 91803-0877   626-448-2223
          Fax: 626-448-2221
  President: Ashley Tsao
  General Manager: Joseph Chu

7629 Karsh's Bakery
5555 N 7th St # 116
Phoenix, AZ 85014-2574   602-264-4874
  Fax: 602-264-7986   gloria@karshsbakery.com
          www.karshsbakery.com
Bread and bakery products
  President: Wayne Kindig
  Marketing Director: Gloria Gardner
Estimated Sales: Below $ 5 Million
Number Employees: 20-49
Brands:
  AJ's Fine Foods
  Don & Charlies
  Miracle Mile
  Park Central Delis

7630 Kasel Engineering
5911 Wolf Creek Pike
Trotwood, OH 45426   937-854-8875
  Fax: 937-854-8875   don@kaselengineering.com
          www.kaselengineering.com

Bacon equipment, slicing machines and scales.
  Owner: Donald Kasel
Estimated Sales: A
Number Employees: 8

7631 Kashi Company
P.O.Box 8557
La Jolla, CA 92038-8557   858-274-8870
          Fax: 858-274-8894   info@kashi.com
          www.kashi.com
Processor and exporter of multi-grain products in-
cluding dry cereal, pilaf and specialty mixes
  President: Philip Tauber
  Co-founder: Gayle Tauber
  CFO: David Garner
  Product Manager: Karen Moyer
  Sales Director: Greg Fleishman
  Public Relations: Karen Meyer
  Purchasing Manager: Carolyn Reynolds
Estimated Sales: $6900000
Number Employees: 20-49
Type of Packaging: Food Service, Private Label
Brands:
  Golean Slimming Systems
  Kashi
  Kashi Medley
  Kashi Products

7632 Kashi Company
P.O.Box 8557
La Jolla, CA 92038-8557   858-274-8870
          Fax: 858-274-8894   info@kashi.com
          www.kashi.com
Ready to eat cereals
  General Manager: David Denholm
  Marketing Director: David Desoza
  CFO: David Garner
  CFO: David Carmor
Estimated Sales: $ 5-10 Million
Number Employees: 20-49
Brands:
  Kashi

7633 Kasilof Fish Company
3912 134th St NE
Marysville, WA 98271-7813   360-658-7552
          Fax: 360-653-3560   800-322-7552
  info@kasilof.com   www.kasilof.com
Processor of smoked salmon and smoked seafood
  President: Drew Ellison
  Production Manager: Michelle Ansley
  VP: Patti Moore
Estimated Sales: $ 5-10 Million
Number Employees: 10-19
Type of Packaging: Consumer, Food Service, Pri-
  vate Label, Bulk
Brands:
  Eagle RIVER Brand
  Kasilof Fish

7634 Kastner's Pastry Shop &Grocery
9467 Harding Ave
Surfside, FL 33154-2803   305-866-6993
Pastry
  Owner: Philip Cohen
Estimated Sales: Less than $500,000
Number Employees: 5-9

7635 Kate Latter Candy Company
2608 L and a Road
Metairie, LA 70001-5957   504-828-0041
          Fax: 504-828-0045   800-825-5359
          klcandy@bellsouth.net
          www.katelattercandy.com
New Orleans pralines, Southern candies, Cajun and
Creole food products
  President: Pam Randazza
  CEO: Pam Randazza
  Marketing Director: Pam Randazza
Estimated Sales: Below $ 5 Million
Number Employees: 12
Brands:
  Chef Hans
  Kate Latters Chocolates

7636 Kate's Vineyard
5211 Big Ranch Rd
Napa, CA 94558-1004   707-255-2644
          Fax: 707-966-2813   info@katesvineyard.com
          www.katesvineyard.com
Wine
  President: William Bryant
  VP: Sally Bryant
  Marketing VP: Kate Bryant

Estimated Sales: Below $ 5 Million
Number Employees: 1-4
Brands:
  Kate's
  Sedna

7637 Kathleen & Julie II
11 Harbor Road
Gloucester, MA 01930-3221   978-281-8815
          Fax: 978-281-8879
  President: Fred Bayley

7638 Kathryn Kennedy Winery
13180 Pierce Rd
Saratoga, CA 95070-4212   408-867-4170
          Fax: 408-867-9463
  cabernet@KathrynKennedyWinery.com
          www.kathrynkennedywinery.com
Manufacturer of wine
  President/Winegrower: Marty Mathis
Estimated Sales: Below $ 5 Million
Number Employees: 1-4
Brands:
  Kathryn Kennedy

7639 Kathy's Gourmet Specialties
PO Box 1058
Mendocino, CA 95460-1058   707-937-1383
  Fax: 707-937-1383   info@kathysgourmet.com
          www.kathysgourmet.com
Specialty sauces, mustards and condiments.
  Owner: Shelley Pittman
Number of Products: 8
Type of Packaging: Consumer, Food Service, Pri-
  vate Label, Bulk
Brands:
  KATHY'S GOURMET SPECIALTIES

7640 Katie's Korner
1105 Tibbetts Wick Rd
Girard, OH 44420-1137   330-539-4140
  Fax: 330-534-1412   kkinfo@zoominternet.net
          www.katiesicecream.com
Homemade ice cream and yogurt
  Owner/President: Katherine Martin
  Secretary/Treasurer: Keith Martin
Estimated Sales: Less than $500,000
Number Employees: 1-4

7641 Katrina's Tartufo
585 Bicycle Path
Port Jeffrsn Sta, NY 11776-3431   631-476-0863
          Fax: 631-331-1269   800-480-8836
Processor of ice cream
  Owner: Rob Dineon
Estimated Sales: Less than $500,000
Number Employees: 10-19
Sq. footage: 3000

7642 Katy's Smokehouse
P.O.Box 621
Trinidad, CA 95570-0621   707-677-0151
          Fax: 707-677-9328
  service@katyssmokehouse.com
          www.katyssmokehouse.com
Processor of smoked fish including salmon, stur-
geon, albacore, shark, swordfish and halibut
  President: Robert Lake
  CEO: Judy Lake
Estimated Sales: $500,000-$1 Million
Number Employees: 1-4
Type of Packaging: Consumer, Food Service
Brands:
  Katy's Smokehouse

7643 (HQ)Kauai Coffee Company
P.O.Box 530
Kalaheo, HI 96741-0530   808-335-5497
          Fax: 808-335-0036   800-545-8605
          greensales@kauaicoffee.com
          www.kauaicoffee.com
Coffee, green and roasted
  Manager: Donn Soares
  Manager: Donn Soares
  VP/General Manager: Frank Kiger
  Marketing Manager: Annette Burton
  Public Relations: Joan Morita
Estimated Sales: $ 10-100 Million
Number Employees: 5-9
Type of Packaging: Private Label
Brands:
  Kauai Coffee

7644 Kauai Kookie Kompany
P.O.Box 68
Eleele, HI 96705-0068   808-335-5003
Fax: 808-335-5186   800-361-1126
cookie@aloha.net   www.kauaikookie.com
Cookies and dressings
Marketing: Ruth R Hashisaka
Director Sales/Marketing: Ruth Hashisaka
Plant Manager: Ellen Albarado
Estimated Sales: $1 Million
Number Employees: 20-49
Number of Brands: 2
Brands:
Hawaiian Hula Dressing
Kauai Kookie

7645 (HQ)Kauai Organic Farms
PO Box 86
Kilauea, HI 96754   808-651-8843
Fax: 808-826-6809   phil@kauaiorganicfarms.com
www.kauaiorganicfarms.com
Growers of certified organic hawaiian yellow ginger.
Fresh ginger in season. Ginger puree. Ginger juice.
Owner/President: Phil Green
Quality Control: Phil Green
Marketing: Phil Green
Sales: Phil Green
Public Relations: Linda Green
Estimated Sales: $ .5 - 1 million
Number Employees: 5
Number of Products: 4
Sq. footage: 2000
Type of Packaging: Bulk

7646 Kauai Producers
3185 Oihana St
Lihue, HI 96766-1432   808-245-4044
Fax: 808-245-9061   kauai@hvcb.org
www.kauaivisitorsbureau.org
Wholesaler/distributor of produce and dairy, frozen,
dry and refrigerated products; serving the food ser-
vice market
President: Scott Nonaka
Marketing Manager: Merle Nonaka
Estimated Sales: $ 20-50 Million
Number Employees: 20-49

7647 Kauffman Turkey Farms
P.O.Box 205
Waterman, IL 60556-0205   815-264-3470
Fax: 815-264-7820   hoka@indianvalley.com
www.hokaturkeys.com
Processor of turkey
President: Robert Kauffman
General Manager: Tom Klopsentein
Estimated Sales: $1618790
Number Employees: 5-9
Type of Packaging: Consumer, Bulk
Brands:
Ho-Ka

7648 Kaufman Ingredients
P.O.Box 5609
Vernon Hills, IL 60061-5609   847-573-0844
Fax: 847-573-0945
Flour, wheat and grain
Owner: Michael Kaufman
Estimated Sales: $500,000-$1 Million
Number Employees: 1-4

7649 Kava King
123 N Orchard Street
Suite 4a
Ormond Beach, FL 32174-9514   386-677-5282
Fax: 386-671-9500   888-670-5282
info@kavaking.com   www.kavaking.com
Instant Kava drink mixes
VP: William Darby
Marketing Director: Jared White
Sales: Richard Bahmann
Estimated Sales: $300,000-500,000
Number Employees: 1-4
Type of Packaging: Consumer
Brands:
Kava King Beverage Mixes
Kava King Chocolates

7650 Kay Foods Company
1063 W Lincoln Avenue
Ionia, MI 48846-1457   616-527-0120

Processor of deli salads including potato, macaroni
and coleslaw; also, gourmet candies including pea-
nut brittles and clusters
President: Catherine Gallagher
VP Sales/Marketing: David Gallagher
VP Production: Paul Gallagher
Number Employees: 20-49
Sq. footage: 20000
Type of Packaging: Consumer, Food Service, Pri-
vate Label
Brands:
Kay Foods

7651 (HQ)Kayem Foods
75 Arlington St
Chelsea, MA 02150-2365   617-889-1600
Fax: 617-889-5931   800-426-6100
consumer.support@kayem.com
www.kayemfoods.com
Manufacturer and distributor of deli products and
also hot dogs, traditional italian sausages, deli
meats, and fresh gourmet chicken sausage
President: Ray Monkiewicz
CFO/ VP Finance: Ralph Smith
Marketing: Matt Monkiewicz
VP Operations: Ed Blanchette
Estimated Sales: $150000000
Number Employees: 250-499
Sq. footage: 200000
Type of Packaging: Consumer, Food Service, Pri-
vate Label, Bulk
Other Locations:
Genoa Sausage Company
Woburn MA
Brands:
Al Fresco Chicken Sausage
Genoa Sausage
Kayem Bratwurship
Kayem Old Tyme Hot Dogs
McKenzie of Vermont
Meisterchef
Schonland's Original Recipe
Triple M Spiral Hams

7652 Keebler Company
4375 Mead Road
Macon, GA 31206-1946   478-781-4620
Fax: 478-781-9430   www.keebler.com
Manufacturer of baked goods including biscuits,
cookies and crackers
Human Resource Manager: Monica Dunlap
Operations Manager: Mike Williams
Production Manager: Mike Jones
Plant Engineer: David Sitton
Estimated Sales: $622 Million
Number Employees: 400
Sq. footage: 325000
Parent Co: Kellogg Company
Type of Packaging: Consumer

7653 Keebler Company
PO Box Camb
Battle Creek, MI 49016-1986   419-332-1518
Fax: 419-332-1598   800-962-1413
media.hotline@kellogg.com   www.kelloggs.com
Processor of cheese and whey products
CEO: Carlos Gutierrez
Board Member: Claudio X Gonzalez
Managing Director: Benjamin S Carson
Plant Manager: John Chambers
Number Employees: 20-49
Sq. footage: 25000
Parent Co: Kellogg Company
Type of Packaging: Bulk
Brands:
Austin Crackers
Carr's Cookies
Carr's Crackers
Cheez-It Crackers
Famous Amos Cookies
Kellogg
Murray Sugar Free Cookies

7654 Keebler Company
51 Chubb Way
Branchburg, NJ 08876   973-254-2000
Fax: 732-254-8552
Processor and exporter of cookies, crackers and bis-
cuits
Manager: Rob Zaccaro
Plant Manager: Joe Henry
Number Employees: 500-999
Parent Co: Kellogg Company

Type of Packaging: Consumer, Food Service, Pri-
vate Label, Bulk
Brands:
Sunshine

7655 Keenan Farms
P.O.Box 99
Avenal, CA 93204-0099   559-945-1400
Fax: 559-945-1414   keenan@keenanpistachio.com
www.keenanpistachio.com
Pistachios
President: Robert Keenan
VP: Charles Keenan
Estimated Sales: Below $ 5 Million
Number Employees: 100-249
Brands:
Keenan Farms

7656 Keeter's Meat Company
P.O.Box 41
Tulia, TX 79088-0041   806-995-3413
800-456-5019
Manufacturer of meat products
Owner: Jerry Keeter
Owner: Kati Keeter
Estimated Sales: $3 Million
Number Employees: 1-4
Type of Packaging: Consumer

7657 Kehr's Kandy Kitchen
3533 W Lisbon Ave
Milwaukee, WI 53208-1954   414-344-4305
Fax: 414-933-2985   Paul@kehrs.com
http://www.kehrs.com
Candy
Owner: Paul Martinka
Estimated Sales: Less than $500,000
Number Employees: 5-9
Brands:
Kehr's Kandy

7658 Kelatron Corporation
1675 W 2750 S
Ogden, UT 84401-3200   801-394-4558
Fax: 801-394-4559   biomin@klatroncorp.com
www.kelatroncorp.com
Bioactive mineral nutrients
President: Robert Wilkins
Vice President of Technical Services: Brent
Hagen
Plant Manager: Venus Hall
Estimated Sales: $ 20 - 50 Million
Number Employees: 50-99

7659 Kelble Brothers
9111 Reiger Rd
Berlin Heights, OH 44814-9644   419-588-2015
Fax: 419-588-3116   800-247-2333
Processor of beef and lamb
Owner: Bill Fox
Estimated Sales: $ 5 - 10 Million
Number Employees: 10-19
Type of Packaging: Consumer, Food Service, Bulk

7660 Kelchner's Horseradish
P.O.Box 245
Dublin, PA 18917-0245   215-249-3439
Fax: 215-249-1931
Manufacturer of prepared horseradish, tartar sauce,
cocktail sauce, horseradish mustard and horseradish
with beets
President: John Slaymaker
Chairman of the Board: Walter Slaymaker
Production Manager: Richard Rankin
Estimated Sales: $4700000
Number Employees: 10-19
Sq. footage: 10000
Type of Packaging: Consumer, Food Service
Brands:
Kelchner's

7661 Kellbran Candies & Snacks
PO Box 266
Tallmadge, OH 44278-0266   330-794-1448
Fax: 330-794-1448
Snack foods
Owner: Jim Buck

7662 Keller's Bakery
1012 Jefferson St
Lafayette, LA 70501-7991   337-235-1568
Fax: 337-235-8817
Manufacturer of baked products
President: Kenneth Keller

Estimated Sales: $1-3 Million
Number Employees: 10-19

7663 (HQ)Keller's Creamery
855 Maple Ave
Harleysville, PA 19438-1037   215-256-8871
          Fax: 215-859-4001 800-535-5371
          www.kellerscreamery.com
Manufacturer of butter, butter oil, powdered milk,
cream cheese, cheese products, heavy cream
     President/CEO/Managing Partner: Frank Otis
     CFO/VP Administration: Mark Stinson
     VP: Larry Weaver
     Marketing Director: Joe Fallon
     VP Sales/Customer Satisfaction: Larry Weaver
Estimated Sales: $250 Million
Number Employees: 50-99
Sq. footage: 100000
Type of Packaging: Consumer, Food Service, Pri-
     vate Label, Bulk
Other Locations:
     Keller's Creamery - Production
     Winnsboro TX
Brands:
     BORDEN
     BREAKSTONES
     FALFURRIAS
     HOTEL BAR
     KELLER'S
     MID-AMERICA FARMS
     PLUGRA
     SCULPTURES

7664 Keller's Creamery
855 Maple Ave
Harleysville, PA 19438-1037   215-256-8871
          Fax: 215-859-4001 800-535-5371
          sales@kellerscreamery.com
          www.kellerscreamery.com
Processor of regular and unsalted butter
     President: Mark Korsneyer
     Marketing Director: Joe Sallon
     CFO: Mark Stinson
     VP: Larry Weaver
     Quality Control: Brent Nyce
     Sales/Marketing Executive: Larry Weaver
Estimated Sales: $ 300 Million
Number Employees: 50-99
Parent Co: Keller's Cremery LLC
Brands:
     Breakstone's
     Keller's
     Plugra

7665 Kelley Bean Company
P.O.Box 638
Torrington, WY 82240-0638   307-532-2131
          Fax: 307-532-4293 www.kelleybean.com
Processor of dried beans
     Manager: Jerry Notman
     Manager: Dan Smith
Estimated Sales: $ 5 - 10 Million
Number Employees: 10-19
Type of Packaging: Consumer, Food Service, Bulk
Brands:
     Buffalo

7666 Kelley Bean Company
P.O.Box 2488
Scottsbluff, NE 69363-2488   308-635-6438
          Fax: 308-635-7345 kkelley@kelleybean.com
          www.kelleybean.com
Manufacturer and exporter of dry beans and seeds
     President: Robert Kelley
Estimated Sales: $ 50 - 100 Million
Number Employees: 20-49
Type of Packaging: Consumer, Food Service, Bulk
Brands:
     BROWN'S BEST

7667 (HQ)Kelley Bean Company
P.O.Box 2488
Scottsbluff, NE 69363-2488   308-635-6438
          Fax: 308-635-7345 www.kelleybean.com
Processor and exporter of dried beans
Great Northern and pinto
     President: Robert Kelley
     CEO: Gary Kelley
     Sales Manager: Stephen Snyder
Estimated Sales: $500,000-$1 Million
Number Employees: 5-9
Sq. footage: 100000
Type of Packaging: Consumer, Food Service, Pri-
     vate Label, Bulk

7668 Kelley Foods of Alabama
P.O.Box 708
Elba, AL 36323-0708   334-897-5761
          Fax: 334-897-2712 eddiek@kelleyfoods.com
          www.kelleyfoods.com
Processor of sausage; wholesaler/distributor of
meats, dairy items, frozen foods, equipment and
fixturers, paper products, poultry, spices and catfish;
serving the food service market
     President: Eddie Kelley
     CEO: Eddie Kelley
     Vice President: J Kelley
     VP Marketing: C Kelley
     VP Operations: Dwight Kelley
Estimated Sales: $ 10 - 20 Million
Number Employees: 100-249
Type of Packaging: Food Service
Brands:
     Bryan
     Excel
     Hormel
     Kelley's

7669 Kelley Meats
8937 Beckwith Rd
Taberg, NY 13471-2805   315-337-4272
          Fax: 315-337-4272
Processor of beef, pork, veal, bacon, smoked ham
and sausage; also, custom slaughtering
     President: Dean Kelley
     CEO: Dean Kelley
Estimated Sales: $120,000
Number Employees: 1-4
Type of Packaging: Consumer

7670 Kelley's Katch Caviar
140 Jaggers Ln
Savannah, TN 38372-7515   731-925-7360
          Fax: 731-925-5631 888-681-8565
          americasfinest@kellyskatch.com
          www.kelleyskatch.com
Manufacturer of all-natural American paddlefish
caviar and sturgeon caviar.
     Owner: Vickie Kelley
Estimated Sales: Less than $500,000
Number Employees: 1-4

7671 Kelley's Katch Caviar
140 Jagger's Lane
Savannah, TN 38372   731-925-7360
          Fax: 731-925-5631 888-681-8565
          americasfinest@kellyskatch.com
          www.kelleyskatch.com
caviar

7672 Kelleys Island Wine Company
418 Woodford Rd
Kelleys Island, OH 43438   419-746-2678
          bretlynn@cros.net
          www.kelleysislandwine.com
Wines
     President: Kirt Zettler
     Owner: Toby Zettler
Estimated Sales: $ 5-9.9 Million
Number Employees: 5-9
Brands:
     Coyote White
     Inscription White
     Long Sweet Red
     Sunset Pink

7673 Kellogg Canada Inc
5350 Creekbank Road
Mississauga, ON L4W 5S1
Canada   905-290-5200
          Fax: 905-290-5388 888-876-3750
          diane.bellissimo@kellogg.com www.kelloggs.ca/
Processor of breakfast foods including cereals, natu-
ral grain waffles and toaster tarts.
     President: Gregory Peterson
     Public Relations/Media: Diane Bellissimo
Estimated Sales: 10 Billion
Number Employees: 850
Parent Co: Kellogg Company
Type of Packaging: Consumer

7674 Kellogg Company
2168 Frisco Ave
Memphis, TN 38114-4621   901-743-0250
          Fax: 901-745-9882
          paulina.ruiz-lang@kellogg.com
          www.kellogg.com
Processor and exporter of breakfast cereals.
     Quality Control Manager: Melissa Dunham
     Corporate Affairs Manager: Paulina Ruiz-Lang
     Personnel Assistant: Cindy Taylor
     General Manager: Tim Blair
     Plant Manager: Jim Ambrose
     Purchasing Agent: Robin Milligan
Estimated Sales: $500 Million to $1 Billion
Number Employees: 750
Parent Co: Kellogg Company
Type of Packaging: Consumer
Brands:
     ALL-BRAN®
     AUSTIN®
     BEAR NAKED®
     CHEEZ-IT®
     CHIPS DELUXE®
     CLUB®
     EGGO®
     FAMOUS AMOS®
     GARDENBURGER®
     KASHI®
     KEEBLER®
     KELLOGG'S®
     MINI-WHEATS®
     MORNINGSTAR FARM®
     MURRAY®
     NUTRI-GRAIN®
     POP-TARTS®
     RICE KRISPIES®
     SANDIES®
     SPECIAL K®
     STRETCH ISLAND(190

7675 Kellogg Company
P.O.Box 3866
Omaha, NE 68103-0866   402-331-7717
          Fax: 402-593-2688 rheylan@kellogg-fcu.org OR
          paulina.ruiz-lang@kellogg.com
          www.kellogg.com
Manufacturer of breakfast cereals.
     President/CEO: Roger B Hylen
     VP Lending: Linda Bohac
     Corporate Affairs Manager: Paulina Ruiz-Lang
     Plant Manager: Virgil Thomas
Estimated Sales: $ .5 - 1 million
Number Employees: 500-999
Parent Co: Kellogg Company
Type of Packaging: Consumer, Bulk

7676 (HQ)Kellogg Company
P.O.Box 3599
Battle Creek, MI 49016-3599   269-961-2000
          Fax: 269-961-2871 800-962-1413
          paul.fitzsimmons@kellogg.com
          www.kelloggs.com
Manufacturer of cereal and convenience foods, including cookies, crackers, toaster pastries, cereal
bars, frozen waffles, meat alternatives, pie crusts and
ice cream cones, fruit snacks.
     Chairman: James Jenness
     President/Chief Executive Officer: A D David
          MacKay
     EVP/Chief Financial Officer: John Bryant
     SVP/General Counsel & Development: Gary
          Pilnick
     EVP/Chief Marketing Officer: Alan Harris
     SVP/Chief Information Officer: Ruth Bruch
     EVP/COO: John Bryant
     SVP/Global Nutrition & Corporate Affairs:
          Celeste Clark Ph.D
Estimated Sales: $12.82 Billion
Number Employees: 30,900
Type of Packaging: Consumer
Other Locations:
     Plants & Bakeries
     1 - CA
     4 - GA
     2 - IL
     1 - KS
     3 - KY
     3 - MI
     1 - NE
     1- NJ
     2 - NC
     2 - OH
     2 - PA
     2 - TN
     1 - UT
Brands:
     ALL-BRAN
     APPLE JACKS
     BRAN BUDS
     COCOA RICE KRISPIES
     COMPLETE

COOUNTRY INN SPECIALTIES
CORN POPS
CRACKLIN' OAT BRAN
CRISPIX
EGGO
FROOT LOOPS
FROSTED FLAKES
FROSTED RICE KRISPIES
FRUIT HARVEST
GREYFIELD INN
HONEY CRUNCH CORN FLAKES
JUST RIGHT
KELLOGG'S
KELLOGG'S MINI-WHEATS BITE SIZE
KRAVE
MINI-WHEATS
MORNINGSTAR FARMS
MUESLIX
NATURAL TOUCH
NUTRI GRAIN
PRODUCT 19
RICE KRISPIES
RICE KRISPIES TREATS
SMART START
SMORZ
SPECIAL K

7677 Kellogg Company
322 S Egg Harbor Rd
Hammonton, NJ 08037-9439   609-567-2300
                                Fax: 609-567-4948
investor.relations@kellogg.com OR
paulina.ruiz-lang@kellogg.com
www.kellogg.com
Processor of frozen waffles.
　Chairman/CEO: James Jenness
　President/COO: A D David Mackay
　Executive VP: John A Bryant
　Corporate Affairs Manager: Paulina Ruiz-Lang
　Plant Manager: Patrick Taylor
Estimated Sales:$ 50 - 100 Million
Number Employees: 100-249
Parent Co: Kellogg Company
Type of Packaging: Consumer
Brands:
　Kellogg's

7678 Kellogg Company
475 Eggo Way
San Jose, CA 95116-1016   408-295-8656
                                Fax: 408-295-0794
paulina.ruiz-lang@kellog.com
www.kellogg.com
Processor and exporter of frozen waffles.
　President: David Mackay
　CEO: David Mackay
　President: John Bryant
　Vice President: Jeffrey Boromisa
　CFO: Jeffrey M Boromisa
　Plant Manager: Mark Haas
　Purchasing Agent: Patrick Yee
Estimated Sales:$22000000
Number Employees: 100-249
Parent Co: Kellogg Company
Type of Packaging: Consumer, Food Service

7679 Kellogg Company
2050 State Rd
Lancaster, PA 17601   717-898-0161
        Fax: 717-898-3487 www.kelloggs.com
Manufacturer of cereal and convenience foods in-
cluding: cookies, crackers, toaster pastries, cereal
bars, frozen waffles, meat alternatives, pie crusts and
ice cream cones.
　Administrator: Steve Harvey
　Director: Paul Ebersberger
　Corporate Affairs Manager: Paulina Ruiz-Lang
　Maintenance Manager: Tim Fritz
Estimated Sales:1+ Billion
Number Employees: 508
Type of Packaging: Consumer, Food Service
Brands:
　AUSTIN
　CARR'S
　CHEEZ IT
　EGGO
　FAMOUS AMOS
　KASHI
　KEEBLER
　KELLOGG'S
　MORNINGSTAR FARMS
　MURRAY
　NUTRI-GRAIN
　PLANTATION

POP-TARTS
READY CRUST
RICE KRISPIES

7680 Kellogg Company
1675 Fairview Rd
Zanesville, OH 43701-8890   740-453-7782
　Fax: 740-453-7789 www.morningstarfarms.com
Manufacturer and exporter of low-fat entrees includ-
ing meatless, pre-cooked, frozen and kosher; also,
breakfast sausages and veggie burgers
　Chairman/CEO: James Jenness
　SVP/CFO: Jeffrey Boromisa
　Human Resources: Carolyn Jarvis
Estimated Sales:$100+ Million
Number Employees: 250-499
Type of Packaging: Consumer, Food Service
Brands:
　AUSTIN
　CARR'S
　CHEEZ-IT
　EGGO
　FAMOUS AMOS
　KASHI
　KEEBLER
　KELLOGG'S
　MORNINGSTAR FARMS
　MURRAY
　NUTRI-GRAIN
　POP-TARTS
　RICE KRISPIES

7681 Kellogg Company Grand Rapids Bakery
310 28th St SE
Grand Rapids, MI 49548-1108   616-247-4841
paulina.ruiz-lang@kellogg.com
www.kelloggcompany.com
Manufacturer and exporter of baked goods including
cookies and crackers.
　Chairman/CEO: Carlos Gutierrez
　Manager: Bruce Malder
　Corporate Affairs Manager: Paulina Ruiz-Lang
Estimated Sales:$8 Billion
Number Employees: 500-999
Type of Packaging: Consumer
Brands:
　AUSTIN
　CHEEZ-IT
　EGGO
　KEEBLER
　MORINGSTAR FARMS
　MURRAY
　NUTRI-GRAIN
　POP TARTS
　RICE KRISPIES

7682 Kellogg Food Away From Home
545 Lamont Road
Elmhurst, IL 60126   630-956-9645
　Fax: 630-833-6880 susan.danner@kellogg.com
www.kelloggsfoodawayfromhome.com
Ready-To-Eat Cereal; Crackers; Grab 'N Go Snacks;
Cones, Pie Crusts, & Crushed Cookies; Cookies;
Waffles & Veggie Products.
　Operations Manager: Frank Costanza
Number Employees: 160
Parent Co: Kellogg Company
Type of Packaging: Food Service

7683 Kellogg Ingredients Company
1 Kellogg Square
Battle Creek, MI 49016   269-961-2000
        Fax: 269-961-2871 888-223-7723
paulina.ruiz-lang@kellogg.com
www.kelloggs.com
Cereals, breakfast foods and snack
　President/CEO: A D David Mackay
　EVP/COO: John Bryant
Estimated Sales:$12.6 Billion
Number Employees: 30,900
Parent Co: Kellogg Company

7684 Kellogg Snacks
801 Sunshine Rd
Kansas City, KS 66115-1121   913-342-2300
        Fax: 913-371-8190 800-229-4414
paulina.ruiz-lang@kellogg.com
www.kelloggcompany.com
Manufacturer of baked goods including crackers,
cookies and biscuits.
　President/CEO: Bradford Davidson
　Corporate Affairs Manager: Paulina Ruiz-Lang
　Plant Manager: Mike Hobson

Estimated Sales:$ 20 - 50 Million
Number Employees: 500-999
Type of Packaging: Consumer
Brands:
　CHEEZ-IT
　CHIP-A-ROOS
　GOLDEN FRUIT
　HI HO
　HYDROX
　KRISPY
　VIENNA FINGERS

7685 Kellogg US SnackDivision
1 Kellogg Square
Battlecreek, MI 49016-3599   269-961-2000
　Fax: 269-961-2871 www.keebler.com and
www.kelloggcompany.com
Manufacturer snack bars, novelties, sugar cones,
cookies, crackers and pie crusts.
　President: Todd Penegor
　SVP Marketing: Michael Allen
　Manager, Sales Keebler: Raymond Mangini
　SVP Operations: Mike McGrath
Estimated Sales:$2.2 Billion
Number Employees: 600
Parent Co: Kellogg Company
Type of Packaging: Consumer, Food Service, Bulk
Brands:
　AUSTIN®
　CARR'S®
　CHEEZ-IT®
　CHIPS DELUXE®
　CLUB®
　EL FUDGE®
　FAMOUS AMOS®
　FUDGE SHOPPE®
　GRIPZ®
　KASHI®
　KEEBLER®
　KELLOG'S®
　MUNCH'EMS
　MURRAY
　READY CRUST
　RICE KRISPIES TREATS®
　RIGHT BITES ®
　SANDIES®
　SANDWICH CRACKERS®
　SCOOBY-DOO®
　SOFT BATCH®
　STRETCH ISLAND®
　SUNSHINE KRISPY
　TOASTEDS®
　TOWNHOUSE®
　VIENNA FINGERS®
　WHEATABLES®
　ZESTA®

7686 Kellogg's
2945 W 31st St
Chicago, IL 60623-5104   773-254-0900
        Fax: 773-254-0795 800-323-4064
paulina.ruiz-lang@kellogg.com
www.kelloggs.com
Processor of jelly beans, jelly candies, fruit snacks
and candy corn.
　SVP Kellogg Company/President US Snacks:
　　Bradford Davidson
　Corporate Affairs Manager: Paulina Ruiz-Lang
　Plant Manager: Larry Carroll
Estimated Sales:$100+ Million
Number Employees: 100-249
Type of Packaging: Consumer, Private Label

7687 (HQ)Kelly Flour Company
1208 N Swift Rd
Addison, IL 60101-6104   630-678-5300
        Fax: 630-678-5311 info@foodblends.com
www.oxydry.com
Dry milk replacers and dry egg extenders
　Manager: Dan Hoberg
　Executive VP: Donald Kelly, Jr.
　Plant Manager: Samuel Vergara
Estimated Sales:$ 3-5 Million
Number Employees: 20-49
Sq. footage: 15
Type of Packaging: Food Service, Private Label
Brands:
　Chickadee Products
　Hi-Bak
　Kel-Yolk
　Thel-Egg

7688 Kelly Foods
513 Airways Boulevard
Jackson, TN 38301-5759   731-424-2255
info@kellyfoods.com
www.kellyfoods.com
Processor of canned meat products including hash,
chili, beef stew, corned beef, tamales, etc.; importer
of corned beef
President: Ann Koch
VP Operations: Mark Koch
Plant Manager: Bob James
Purchasing Manager: Mike Rushing
Estimated Sales: $5700000
Number Employees: 50
Sq. footage: 65000
Type of Packaging: Consumer
Brands:
Hypower
Kelly

7689 Kelly Gourmet Foods
2095 Jerrold Ave
San Francisco, CA 94124-1628   415-648-9200
Fax: 415-648-6164   edkelly@kellyfds.com
www.kellygourmetfoods.com
Processor and exporter of cooked, smoked and raw
chicken, sausage, roasters and chicken including
whole, parts, boneless, skinless, breast and legs
President: Rina Kelly
VP: Chris Kelly
Sales Director: Ed Kelly
Estimated Sales: Less than $500,000
Number Employees: 1-4
Type of Packaging: Consumer, Food Service, Bulk
Brands:
Fulton Organic Free Range Chicken
Fulton Valley Farms
Sierra Sausage Co.

7690 Kelly Kornbeef Company
3531 N Elston Ave
Chicago, IL 60618-5687   773-588-2882
Fax: 773-588-0810
Processor of beef hot dogs and deli foods including
corned beef and pastrami
President: Marvin Eisenberg
Estimated Sales: $510000
Number Employees: 20-49
Parent Co: Eisenberg Sausage Company
Brands:
Eisenberg
Kelly

7691 Kelly Packing Company
P.O.Box 27
Torrington, WY 82240-0027   307-532-2210
Fax: 307-532-8482
Manufacturer of meat products including beef, pork
and lamb; also, smoked turkey and honey ham avail-
able
President: David K Kelly
Estimated Sales: $4 Million
Number Employees: 5-9
Type of Packaging: Consumer
Brands:
KELLY

7692 Kelly Pickle Company
235 Cook Avenue
Oconto, WI 54153-1915   920-834-4433
Fax: 920-834-2598   dweslow@kellypickle.com
www.kellypickle.com
Processor and exporter of canned and glass-packed
pickles, peppers, relish, ketchup and mustard
V.P. Prod.: Michael Bittner
Number Employees: 50-99
Sq. footage: 115000
Type of Packaging: Food Service, Private Label,
Bulk
Brands:
Bond

7693 Kelly's Candies
9250 Highland Rd
Pittsburgh, PA 15237-4532   412-795-8922
Fax: 412-573-0044   800-523-3051
kellyscandies@comcast.net
www.kellycandies.com
Processor of homemade fudge and chocolate candies
Owner: Gina Broderick
Estimated Sales: $ .5 - 1 million
Number Employees: 5-9
Type of Packaging: Consumer, Private Label, Bulk

Brands:
Kelly's

**7694 Kelly-Eisenberg GourmetDeli
Products**
3531 N Elston Ave
Chicago, IL 60618-5687   773-588-2882
Fax: 773-588-0810   sales@kellyeisenberg.com
www.kellyeisenberg.com
Corned beef, hot dogs, roast beef, pastrami, Polish
sausage
President: Marvin Eisenberg
CEO: Marvin Eisenberg
VP: Cliff Eisenberg
VP: Howard Eisenberg
Marketing Director: Marvin Eisenberg
Operations Manager: Greg Timm
Estimated Sales: Below $ 5 Million
Number Employees: 20-49
Type of Packaging: Private Label
Brands:
Eisenberg Beef Hot Dogs
Eisenberg Corned Bee
Eisenberg Pastrami
Kelly Corned Beef

7695 Kelsen Bisca
40 Marcus Dr # 101
Melville, NY 11747-4200   631-694-8080
Fax: 631-694-8085   888-253-5736
pb@kelsen-us.com   www.kelsenbisca.com
Danish butter cookies
President: Lars Norgaard
Estimated Sales: $ 5 - 10 Million
Number Employees: 5-9
Number of Brands: 4
Brands:
Bisca
Karenvolf
Kjeldsens
Royal Dansk

7696 Kelson Creek Winery
19919 Shenandoah School Rd
Plymouth, CA 95669-9524   209-245-4700
Fax: 209-245-4707
sales@kelsoncreekwinery.com
www.kelsoncreekwinery.com
Manufacturer of wine; Formerly Sonora Winery and
Port Works
Manager: April Ysmael
CEO: Tim Tado
Estimated Sales: $500,000-$1 Million
Number Employees: 1-4
Type of Packaging: Private Label
Brands:
Kelson Creek

**7697 Kemach Food
ProductsCorporation**
9920 Farragut Rd
Brooklyn, NY 11236-2302   718-272-5655
Fax: 718-272-6226   888-453-6224
s.salzman@kemach.com   www.kemach.com
Company provides drink mixes, soup mixes, cook-
ies, crackers, flour, cereals, kosher, pasta, noodles,
breadsticks, flatbread, candy, chocolates, health
food, natural foods, chocolate syrup, juices, pasta
sauces, ices, cones, etc
President: Samuel Salzman
CFO: Aaron Daum
VP: Nik Salzman
Estimated Sales: $2.5-5 Million
Number Employees: 15
Sq. footage: 15000
Type of Packaging: Consumer, Food Service, Pri-
vate Label, Bulk
Brands:
A'Guania
Kemach
Matzo Meal
Mekach

7698 Kemin Health
600 E Court Ave # A
Des Moines, IA 50309-2098   515-248-4000
Fax: 515-248-4051   888-248-5040
info@kemin.com   www.kemin.com

Vitamin and supplement ingredients, natural preser-
vatives, FloraGLO lutein, natural antioxidant
preservatives
President: Rodney Ausich
VP: Charles Brice
Marketing Director: Andy Martin
Sales Manager: Linda Fullmer
Customer Service: Lori Barker
Number Employees: 10-19
Brands:
FloraGlo
Myco CURB
Naturox
Oro GLO
PALASURANCE
Paradigmox
Roseen
Satise
ZeniPRO

7699 Kemoo Farm Foods
1718 Wilikina Dr
Wahiawa, HI 96786-1498   808-622-8004
Fax: 808-545-4721
Processor and exporter of specialty items including
fruit thins and Hawaiian cakes
Owner: Robin Kirby
Estimated Sales: $ .5 - 1 million
Number Employees: 20-49
Type of Packaging: Consumer, Food Service
Brands:
Hawaiian Happy

7700 Kemp Foods
150 Roosevelt Avenue
Suite 100
York, PA 17401-3381   717-394-5601
Fax: 717-399-8584   800-233-2007
www.crowleyfoods.com
Manufacturer of milk, ice cream, frozen yogurt,
sherbert and novelties
President: Terri Webb
Operations: Rick Kovarik
Estimated Sales: $389 Million
Number Employees: 390
Parent Co: Crowley Foods
Type of Packaging: Consumer, Food Service, Pri-
vate Label, Bulk
Brands:
GREENS
KEMPS
PENN FARMS
PENSUPREME

7701 Kemper Bakery Systems
3 Enterprise Dr # 108
Shelton, CT 06484-4694   203-929-6530
Fax: 203-929-7089   pat@kemperusa.com
www.kemperusa.com
Manufacturer of bakery equipment
President: Patricia Kennedy
VP Marketing/Mixer Product Manager: Shawna
Goldfarb
Estimated Sales: $5 Million
Number Employees: 5-9

7702 Kemps
P.O.Box 287
Cedarburg, WI 53012-0287   262-377-5040
Fax: 262-377-9532   r.kraus@kemps.com
Processor of flavored fruit drinks and dairy products
including milk, cream and half and half
CEO: Jim Green
Operations Manager: Roy Roggentin
General Manager: Dave O'Connell
Estimated Sales: $ 50 - 100 Million
Number Employees: 50-99
Parent Co: Marigold Foods
Type of Packaging: Consumer, Food Service, Pri-
vate Label, Bulk

7703 Kemps
1270 Energy Ln
St Paul, MN 55108-5225   651-379-6500
800-322-9566
kempscrd@kemps.com   www.kemps.com
Products include frozen novelties, frozen yogurt, ice
cream, sherbert, milk and cultured products and
juices.
President: Jim Green
CEO: Jim Green
Distribution Manager: Roger Kraus
Estimated Sales: $ 1-2.5 Million
Number Employees: 5-9

7704 Ken's Foods
9 Stonehill Rd
Marlborough, MA 01752-1730   508-481-0711
        Fax: 508-485-6882   800-633-5800
    service@kensfoods.com   www.kensfoods.com
Manufacturer of salad dressings, mayonnaise and sauces
    Owner: Dorothy H Keene
    CEO: Andy Crowley
Estimated Sales: 100+ Million
Number Employees: 1-4
Other Locations:
    Ken's Plant Facility
    McDonough GA
    Ken's Plant Facility
    Las Vegas NV

7705 Kenai Custom Seafoods
PO Box 1649
Kenai, AK 99611-1649   907-283-9109
        Fax: 907-283-6475
Seafood
    Proprietor: James Hill

7706 Kenai Packers
PO Box 31179
Seattle, WA 98103-1179   206-433-6917
Salmon
    President: Hisashi Sugiyama
Estimated Sales: $ 10-100 Million
Number Employees: 20

7707 Kencraft
P.O.Box 1129
American Fork, UT 84003-6129   801-756-6916
        Fax: 801-756-7791   800-377-4368
        sales@kencraftcandy.com
        www.kencraftcandy.com
Manufacturer of Candy and other confectionery products
    President: David Taiclet
    CEO: David Taiclet
    VP Sales: Frank Trinnaman
Estimated Sales: $ 100-500 Million
Number Employees: 250-499
Number of Brands: 12
Parent Co: Alpine Confections
Brands:
    BUBBLEGUM BUDDIES
    CANDY CLIMBERS
    CHOCO PALS
    CHUMMY CHUMS
    CIRCUS STICKS
    KENCRAFT CLASSICS
    KOOKIE KAKES
    LIL' LOLLIES
    LOLLIPALS
    PUPPET PALS
    TWIST POPS
    TWISTIX

7708 Kendall Citrus Corporation
PO Box 157
Goulds, FL 33170   305-258-1628
        Fax: 305-258-2445
Citrus juice, oils, flavors, orange, grapefruit, lemon, lime
Estimated Sales: $ 10-25 Million
Number Employees: 30

7709 (HQ)Kendall-Jackson Wine
P.O.Box 1900
Windsor, CA 95492-1900   707-544-4000
        Fax: 707-569-0105   800-544-4413
        kjwines@kj.com   www.kj.com
Wines
    Chairman of the Board: Jesse Jackson Jr
    President: John Grant
    CFO: Alfred Rossow, Jr. Jr
    CEO: Lewis Platt
    Executive VP Finance/Administration: John Bridendall
    Sales Director: Bob Roux
    Public Relations: Jim Caudill
    Operations Manager: Chuck Shea
    Winemaster: Randy Ullom
Estimated Sales: $ 50-100 Million
Number Employees: 100-249
Type of Packaging: Private Label
Brands:
    Kendall-Jackson College
    Kendall-Jackson Grand Reserve
    Kendall-Jackson Great Estates
    Kendall-Jackson Vitner's Reserve
    Stuature

7710 Kendrick Gourmet Products
302 Brown Ave
Columbus, GA 31903-1253   706-687-0161
        Fax: 706-682-1528   800-356-1858
        info.kendrick@columbusgourmet.com
        www.columbusgourmet.com
Pecan candies/cakes/brownies
    President: Bryan Stone
    Vice President: Liz Kendrick
Estimated Sales: $ 5-9.9 Million
Number Employees: 10-19
Sq. footage: 60000
Parent Co: Columbus Gourmet

7711 Kenlake Foods
300 N Lp Miller St
Murray, KY 42071-2198   270-762-5100
        Fax: 270-759-1919   800-632-6900
        tcolson@kroger.com   www.kroger.com
Processor of hot chocolate mixes, breakfast drinks, instant teas and oatmeal; also, canned nuts
    Manager: Bob Beuhler
Number Employees: 10,000+
Parent Co: Kroger Company
Type of Packaging: Consumer, Private Label
Brands:
    Kenlake Foods

7712 (HQ)Kennebec Bean Company
PO Box 219
North Vassalboro, ME 04962-0219   207-873-3473
        Fax: 207-877-9280   info@kennebecbean.com
        www.kennebecbean.com
Manufacturer of dry and canned beans and lentils; also, contract packaging available
    President: Ronald Loubier
Estimated Sales: $12 Million
Number Employees: 22
Sq. footage: 35000
Other Locations:
    Kennebec Bean Co.
    China ME
Brands:
    A-1
    STATE OF MAINE

7713 Kennebec Fruit Company
2 Main St
Lisbon Falls, ME 04252-1505   207-353-8173
Moxie; yellow gentian based soft drink
    Owner: Frank Anicetti II
Estimated Sales: Less than $500,000
Number Employees: 1-4

7714 Kennedy Candy Company
1313 Energy Drive
Kilgore, TX 75662-5539   903-986-3227
        Fax: 903-986-3828   800-657-5258
Processor of chocolate flavored coffee beans, cinnamon sticks, pretzel rods, chocolate covered popcorn, fudge, margarita and Bloody Mary mixes, seasoned vinegar, pasta, etc
    Pres.: George Kennedy III
Number Employees: 100-249
Type of Packaging: Consumer, Private Label

7715 Kennedy Gourmet
9087 Knight Road
Houston, TX 77054-4305   866-986-3227
        Fax: 713-795-5534   800-882-6253
        info@kennedygourmet.com
        www.kennedygourmet.com
Manufacturer of gourmet candy and foods
    President: J Read Boles III
    Plant Manager: Sandy Lewis
    Purchasing Manager: Sue Williams
Estimated Sales: Below $ 5 Million
Number Employees: 50
Sq. footage: 40
Type of Packaging: Private Label
Brands:
    Brazos Legends
    Choc-Quitos
    Chocolate Covered Pretzels
    Chocolate Flavored Coffee Spoons
    Chocolate Fortune Cookies
    Graham Dunks
    Gram Dunks
    Nostalgic Creations
    Sir George Fudge
    Stirring Sticks
    Tea Sickles
    Which Ends

7716 Kennesaw Fruit & Juice
1300 SW 1st Ct
Pompano Beach, FL 33069-3204   954-782-9800
        Fax: 954-784-1222   800-949-0371
        www.kennesawfruitandjuice.com
Processor of citrus juices including orange, grapefruit, lemonade, etc.; also, cored and chunked pineapple, fresh orange and grapefruit slices and fruit salad available
    President: Len Roseberg
    V.P./Prtnr.: Ed Zukerman
Estimated Sales: $ 3 - 5 Million
Number Employees: 20-49
Sq. footage: 38000
Type of Packaging: Consumer, Food Service

7717 Kenny's Candy Company
P.O.Box 269
Perham, MN 56573-0269   218-346-2340
        Fax: 218-346-2343   800-782-5152
        www.klnenterprises.com
Licorice
    President: Kenneth Nelson
    CFO: Mike Holper
    VP: Shane Kangas
    National Sales Manager: Shane Kangas
Estimated Sales: $ 20-50 Million
Number Employees: 100-249
Sq. footage: 52000
Brands:
    JUICY TWISTS
    KENNY'S

7718 (HQ)Kenosha Beef International
P.O.Box 639
Kenosha, WI 53141-0639   262-859-2272
        Fax: 262-859-2078   800-541-1685
        bwinfo@bwfoods.com   www.bwfoods.com
Processor of meat products including frozen boxed beef patties
    Purchasing: Don Wirch
    CEO: Charles Vignieri
Number Employees: 500-999
Type of Packaging: Consumer, Food Service
Brands:
    K-Pack

7719 Kent Foods
P.O.Box 658
Gonzales, TX 78629-0658   830-672-7993
        Fax: 830-672-7223
Manufacturer of frozen and liquid egg products
    President: Daw Lu
Estimated Sales: $1-3 Million
Number Employees: 20-49
Sq. footage: 15000
Type of Packaging: Food Service, Bulk
Brands:
    KENT FOODS

7720 Kent Meats
703 Leonard St NW
Grand Rapids, MI 49504-4236   616-459-4595
        Fax: 616-459-5802   www.kentqualityfoods.com
Makes sausages
    President: Charles Soet Jr
Estimated Sales: $ 10-100 Million
Number Employees: 100-249

7721 Kent Quality Foods
703 Leonard St NW
Grand Rapids, MI 49504-4236   616-459-4595
        Fax: 616-459-5802   800-748-0141
        info@kentqualityfoods.com
        www.kentqualityfoods.com
Manufacturer and packer of meat products including skinless frankfurters and sausages
    President: Charles Soet Jr
Estimated Sales: $30 Million
Number Employees: 100-249
Type of Packaging: Consumer, Food Service, Private Label, Bulk

7722 Kent's Wharf
31 Steamboat Hl
Swans Island, ME 04685   207-526-4186
        Fax: 207-526-4291
Seafood
    Owner: David Niquette
Estimated Sales: $300,000-500,000
Number Employees: 1-4

7723 Kentucky Beer Cheese
P.O.Box 206
Nicholasville, KY 40340-0206 859-887-1645
Fax: 859-885-3555
kentuckybeercheese@alltel.net
www.kentuckybeercheese.com
Processor and wholesaler/distributor of cheese
spread and dip including hot, garlic and beer fla-
vored
Owner: Diane Evans
Estimated Sales:$500,000-$1 Million
Number Employees: 1-4
Sq. footage: 1000
Parent Co: Evans Gourmet Foods, LLC
Type of Packaging: Consumer, Food Service
Brands:
Kentucky Beer Cheese

7724 Kentucky Bourbon
P.O.Box 16
Westport, KY 40077-0016 502-222-6154
Fax: 502-222-1848 866-472-7797
tracy@bourbonQ.com www.bourbonQ.com
Gourmet sauces & spices
President: Shane Best
Estimated Sales:$300,000-500,000
Number Employees: 10-19
Brands:
BEAR CLAW
CULTURED RED NECK T-SHIRTS
FIGHTING COCK
KENTUCKY BOURBONQ
LADY IN RED
MOONSHINE MADNESS
PAPPY'S BEST PREMIMUM MARINADE
PAPPY'S XXX WHITE LIGHTININ
SAUCE FOR SISSIES
SHRIMP BUTLER
SMOKY MOUNTAIN TRAIL RUB

7725 Kenwood Vineyards
P.O.Box 447
Kenwood, CA 95452-0447 707-833-5891
Fax: 707-833-1146 info@kenwoodvineyards.com
www.kenwoodvineyards.com
Processor and exporter of Sonoma county table
wines
Manager: Alan Jensen
Sales/Marketing: Paul Young
Public Relations: Margie Healy
Winemaker: Mike Lee
Number Employees: 50-99
Sq. footage: 50000
Parent Co: Korbel Champagne
Type of Packaging: Consumer
Brands:
Kenwood Vineyards

7726 Kern Meat Distributing
Rr 2 Box 339
Brooksville, KY 41004 606-756-2255
Fax: 606-756-2114
Meat
President: Ed Kern
Estimated Sales:$ 10 - 20 Million
Number Employees: 20-49

7727 Kern Ridge Growers
P.O.Box 455
Arvin, CA 93203-0455 661-854-3141
Fax: 661-854-7229 scott@kernridge.com
www.kernridge.com
Processor, exporter and packer of carrots and bell
and chile peppers
Manager: Bob Girgosian
G.M.: Robert Giragosian
Estimated Sales:$25000000
Number Employees: 250-499
Type of Packaging: Consumer, Bulk
Brands:
Kern Ridge
Morn'n Fresh

7728 Kernel Season's
2401 E Devon Avenue
Elk Grove, IL 60007
Fax: 773-326-0869 866-328-7672
info@kernelseasons.com
www.kernelseasons.com
Manufacturer of popcorn seasonings, machines and
accessories.
Founder/Owner/President/CEO: Brian Taylor

7729 Kerr Brothers
956 Islington Avenue
Toronto, ON M8Z 4P6
Canada 416-252-7341
Fax: 416-252-6054
Manufacturer and exporter of confectionery prod-
ucts
Pres.: R Patterson

7730 Kerr Concentrates
2340 Hyacinth St NE
Salem, OR 97301-7566 503-378-0493
Fax: 503-378-1123 800-910-5377
info@kerrconcentrates.com
www.kerrconcentrates.com
Processor of frozen fruit and vegetable juice concen-
trates, purees and puree concentrates
CFO: David Gatti
Sales: Michael Roth
Research & Development: Mike January
Quality Control: Sam Grubb
Sales Director: Mike Roth
General Manager: Mike Alley
Plant Manager: Bart Hoopman
Purchasing: Jerry Mink
Estimated Sales:$ 5 - 10 Million
Number Employees: 50-99
Sq. footage: 48000
Parent Co: International Flavors & Fragrances
Type of Packaging: Bulk
Other Locations:
Kerr Concentrates Div.
Woodburn OR

7731 Kerr Jellies
PO Box 599
Dana, NC 28724-0599 828-685-8381
Fax: 828-685-8381 877-685-8381
Jellies
President: Kathy Thompson
Estimated Sales:$ 5-10 Million
Number Employees: 5-9

7732 Kerrobert Bakery
PO Box 454
Kerrobert, SK S0L 1R0
Canada 306-834-2461
Processor of bagel, bread, buns, pastries, doughnuts
and muffins
President: Eileen Mackay
VP: Eileen Mackay
Marketing Director: Eileen Mackay
Number Employees: 1-4
Sq. footage: 2000
Type of Packaging: Consumer, Food Service, Bulk
Brands:
Kerrobert Bakery

7733 (HQ)Kerry Ingredients
100 E Grand Ave
Beloit, WI 53511-6255 608-362-1651
Fax: 608-363-1490 www.kerryingredients.com
Manufacturer and exporter of confectionery prod-
ucts including brownie fudge bits, toffee crunches,
chocolate and fruit flakes, fruit syrups and chocolate
and carob coated nuts
Chairman: Denis Buckley
Chief Executive: Hugh Friel
Deputy Chief Executive: Denis Cregan
CEO: Jerry Behan
Chief Financial Officer: Brian Mehigan
Estimated Sales:$20-50 Million
Number Employees: 1,000-4,999
Type of Packaging: Bulk

7734 Kerry Ingredients
1515 Park St
Evansville, IN 47710-2259 812-464-9151
Fax: 812-464-9196 www.kerrygroup.com
Processor of bread crumbs and batter mixes
Manager: Joe Stellern
Materials Manager: Nina Jones
Estimated Sales:$ 50 - 100 Million
Number Employees: 100-249
Parent Co: Kerry Ingredients
Type of Packaging: Bulk

7735 Kerry Ingredients
Prince's Street
Tralee, Co. Kerry,
Ireland

Processor, importer and exporter of dehydrated food
ingredients including chicken broth, buttermilk,
cheese and sweet and sour cream
President: Phil Harn
Contllr.: Charlie Hadin
Number Employees: 113
Sq. footage: 120000
Type of Packaging: Bulk

7736 Kerry Ingredients
PO Box 968
Woodstock, ON N4S 8A4
Canada 519-537-3461
Fax: 519-537-8742 jboudreau@kerrygroup.com
www.kerryingredients.com
Ingredient innovations
President: Edin O'Connell
CFO: Claire Salmon
Type of Packaging: Bulk
Brands:
Kerry

7737 Kerry Ingredients & Flavours
3330 Millington Road
Beloit, WI 53511 608-362-1651
Fax: 608-363-1490 800-248-7310
sales@kerryingredients.com
www.kerryingredients.com
Processor of ingredients and flavorings
CEO: Stan McCarthy
CEO: Jerry Behan
Marketing Director: Jim Andrews
Sales Director: Verle Grove
Operations Manager: Michael Leahy
Purchasing Manager: Daryl Adei
*Estimated Sales:*J
Number Employees: 1,000-4,999
Parent Co: Kerry Group
Brands:
Baker's Aid
DCA
Golden Dipt
Modern Maid

7738 Kerry Sweets Ingredients
P.O.Box 427
Gridley, IL 61744-0427 309-747-3534
Fax: 309-747-2485 gregu@ringgerfoods.com
www.kerrygroup.com
Processor of cookie pieces and rice crisps for cere-
als, including soy crispies and flakes. Private label-
ing available
Manager: Marc Johnson
Eastern Sales Manager: Greg Umland
Research & Development: Jonathan Baner
Estimated Sales:$ 10-20 Million
Number Employees: 50-99
Sq. footage: 70000
Type of Packaging: Food Service, Private Label
Brands:
Kerry Sweets

7739 Kershenstine Beef Jerky
550 Industrial Park Rd
Eupora, MS 39744-2619 662-258-2049
Fax: 662-258-2002
Processor and exporter of beef jerky
President: Timothy Kershenstine
Estimated Sales:$710000
Number Employees: 5-9
Type of Packaging: Consumer

7740 Kess Industries Inc
130 37th St NE
Auburn, WA 98002-1707 253-735-5700
Fax: 253-735-2851 800-578-5564
ray@kessind.com www.kessind.com
Kess Industries produces an extensive array of stan-
dard and custom equipment for accumulating, chill-
ing, coating, depositing, distributing, drying,
dumping, metering, pasteurizing, transferring, wash-
ing and weighing products. Allequipment designs
are acc
President: K Jell Fogelgren
Sales and Estimating: Ray Cassingham
*Estimated Sales:*Below $5 Million
Number Employees: 10-19
Sq. footage: 12000

7741 Kessler's, Inc
P.O.Box 126
Lemoyne, PA 17043-0126 717-763-7162
Fax: 717-763-4982 800-382-1328
info@kesslerfoods.com www.kesslerfoods.com

Manufacturer of fresh and smoked sausage, franks, hams and deli meats
President/CEO: Bob Kessler Jr Jr
CFO: Lee Fake
Quality Control: Glen Sansom
Sales Director: Bob Kessler Jr
Operations/Production/Plant Manager: Richard Caramaga
Estimated Sales:$ 20 - 50 Million
Number Employees: 40
Number of Brands: 4
Number of Products: 600
Sq. footage: 39000
Type of Packaging: Consumer, Food Service, Private Label, Bulk
Brands:
KESSLER'S
NITTANY LION FRANKS
PRIMAL SCREAM
SUSQUEHANNA VALLEY

7742 (HQ)Keto Foods
3535 Highway 66
Suite 2
Neptune, NJ 07753-2624   732-922-0009
          Fax: 732-643-6677   email@keto.com
          www.keto.com
Processor of diet coffee, tea and creamer. Manufacturing and developmnet of largest line of low carbohydrate foods and snacks
President: Arnie Bey
Quality Control: Allan Nargolies
VP Corporation Counsel: Dan Majollo
Sales/Marketing Executive: Arnie Bey
Purchasing Agent: Megan Holman
Estimated Sales: $ 2.5-5 Million
Number Employees: 30
Sq. footage: 30000
Type of Packaging: Consumer, Food Service, Bulk
Brands:
Slim Diez

7743 Ketters Meat Market & Locker Plant
118 W Main Ave
Frazee, MN 56544   218-334-2351
Manufacturer of beef, pork, turtle and deer
President: Kenneth Ketter
Estimated Sales:$1-3 Million
Number Employees: 5-9
Type of Packaging: Consumer, Food Service

7744 Kettle Cooked Food
7401 Will Rogers Blvd
Fort Worth, TX 76140-6019   817-615-4500
          Fax: 817-551-1578 www.kprfoods.com
Producers and packages custom soups, sauces and side dishes
President: John Tyson
Plant Manager: Greg Irby
Estimated Sales:$ 50-100 Million
Number Employees: 100-249
Parent Co: Tyson Foods
Type of Packaging: Food Service, Private Label
Brands:
Tyson

7745 Kettle Cuisine
270 2nd St
Chelsea, MA 02150-1802   617-884-1219
          Fax: 617-884-1341 877-302-7687
sales@kettlecuisine.com www.kettlecuisine.com
Processor of fresh soups and chowders
President: Jerry Shafir
Estimated Sales:$ 20 - 50 Million
Number Employees: 100-249
Type of Packaging: Consumer, Food Service

7746 Kettle Foods
P.O.Box 664
Salem, OR 97308-0664   503-364-0399
          Fax: 503-371-1447 kettlejohn@aol.com
          www.kettlefoods.com

Processor of Kettle brand hand cooked potato chips; krinkle cut potato chips; pretzel chips; pita chips; tortilla chips; nut butters; and nuts, nut mixes and trail mixes.
President: Tim Fallon
Vice President Finance: Michael Bays
Kettle Foods Ambassador: Jim Green
Chief Flavor Architect: Carolyn Richards
Consumer Affairs: Janet Wilson
Vice President Sales: Greg Intlekofer
Public Relations: Jan Maxwell Muir
Vice President Operations: Jim McMullen
Vice President Human Resources: Bret Hughes
Estimated Sales: $ 50 - 100 Million
Number Employees: 500-999

7747 Kettle Foods
P.O.Box 664
Salem, OR 97308-0664   503-364-0399
          Fax: 503-371-1447 jgreen@kettlefoods.com
          www.kettlefoods.com
Processor of potato and tortilla chips, nuts, nut butters and popcorn
President: Tim Fallon
VP Sales: Jerry Siner
Estimated Sales:$72200000
Number Employees: 100-249

7748 Kettle Master
497 Farmers Market Rd
Hillsville, VA 24343-5106   276-728-7571
          sales@kettlemaster.com
          www.kettlemaster.com
Manufacturer of jellies, jams, salsa and sauces
Manager: Rex Horton
Marketing Sales Director: Ben Web
Operations Manager: Fred Jones
Number Employees: 5-9
Type of Packaging: Consumer, Private Label
Other Locations:
Chesapeake Bay Gourmet
Baltimore MD

7749 Kettle Valley Fruits
PO Box 1168
Summerland, BC V0H 1Z0
Canada   250-494-0335
          Fax: 250-494-0334 888-297-6944
          sales@kettlevalley.net www.kettlevalley.net
Processor, importer and exporter of fruit-based snacks and energy bars
President: John Boot
Number Employees: 50+
Sq. footage: 30000
Type of Packaging: Consumer, Food Service, Private Label, Bulk

7750 Kevton Gourmet Tea
385 Fm 416
Streetman, TX 75859-3024   903-389-2905
          Fax: 903-389-5607 888-538-8668
          kevtoen@kevtoenteatyme.com
          www.kevtoenteatyme.com
Honey, flavored mixes, sour cream, tea, cocoa
President: Tanya Miller
CEO: Tanya Miller
Marketing Director: Tanya Miller
Brands:
Bee My Honey
Good Stuff Cocoa
Not Just Jam
Tea Tyme Cookies
countrymixes
joy
tease

7751 Key Colony/Red Parrot Juices
P.O.Box 425
Lyons, IL 60534-0425   708-442-2007
          Fax: 708-447-0188 800-424-0868
Processor of bag-in-box juices
President: James Behrens
Estimated Sales: Below $ 5 Million
Number Employees: 5-9
Type of Packaging: Food Service
Brands:
Red Parrot

7752 Key Essentials
30322 Esperanza # 400
Rcho Sta Marg, CA 92688-2138   949-635-1000
          Fax: 949-636-1001 hhaget@keyessentials.com
          www.keyessentials.com

Beverage flavors, bakery flavors, candy flavors, beverage product development, coffee and tea flavors
Chairman: Thomas H Quinn
CEO: Hector Haget
Estimated Sales:$ 10-20 Million
Number Employees: 50-99

7753 Key III Candies
4211 Earth Dr
Fort Wayne, IN 46809-1513   260-747-7514
          Fax: 260-747-9898 800-752-2382
Processor of milk chocolate candies including cream peanut clusters, caramels and pretzels covered in chocolate or confectionery coatings
Manager: Gary Yarger
V.P./Co-Ownr.: Richard Dickmeyer
Estimated Sales:$ 3 - 5 Million
Number Employees: 10-19
Sq. footage: 10000
Type of Packaging: Consumer, Bulk
Brands:
Key Iii

7754 Key Ingredients
802 S 16th Street
Harrisburg, PA 17104-2601   717-233-0451
          Fax: 717-238-4017 800-227-4448
Cheese products, spaghetti sauce, dressings, prepared meals

7755 Key Largo Fisheries
P.O.Box 273
Key Largo, FL 33037   305-451-3782
          Fax: 305-451-3215 800-399-6970
          www.keylargofisheries.com
Processor of frozen fish including lobster
President: Tom Hill
Finance Manager: Rick Hill
Estimated Sales:$6838250
Number Employees: 20-49
Type of Packaging: Consumer, Food Service, Private Label

7756 Key Lime
5200 Highlands Parkway SE
Smyrna, GA 30082-5163   770-333-0840
          Fax: 770-436-4280
Processor and exporter of key lime pies, pie filling, sorbet and novelty desserts
President: Kenneth Burts
Plt. Mgr.: K Michael Miller
Quality Control: Slorence Clay
Estimated Sales:$ 5-10 Million
Number Employees: 20-50
Sq. footage: 12000
Type of Packaging: Food Service, Private Label
Brands:
Kenny's
Kenny's Island Style
Kenny's Key Lime Crunch

7757 Key West Key Lime Pie CoLLc
225 Key Deer Blvd
Big Pine Key, FL 33043-4905   305-872-7400
          Fax: 305-872-7600 877-882-7437
kwklpco@bwisk.net keywestkeylimepieco.com
Distribute/sell key lime products to food establishments
President: James Brush
Vice President: Alison Sloat
Estimated Sales:$400,000
Number Employees: 5-9
Number of Brands: 4
Number of Products: 100+
Sq. footage: 1200
Type of Packaging: Consumer, Food Service, Private Label
Brands:
KEY LIME PIE SLICES DIPPED IN CHOCO
KEY LIME PIES ASSORTED FLAVORS
PACKAGE BULK KEY LIME FILLING

7758 Keynes Brothers
1 W Front St
Logan, OH 43138-1825   740-385-6824
          Fax: 740-385-9076
Soft and whole wheat flour milling
President: William Keynes
Quality Control: Jeff Brown
Estimated Sales:$ 20-30 Million
Number Employees: 50-99

7759 Keyser Brothers
1146 Honest Point Rd
Lottsburg, VA 22511 804-529-6837
Fax: 804-529-5144 rkeyser@skyelink.com
Processor of fresh and frozen seafood including
crabs and pasteurized crab meat
President/CEO: R Calvin Keyser
Executive VP: Norman Keyser
Estimated Sales: $350,000
Number Employees: 20-25
Number of Brands: 1
Sq. footage: 17500
Type of Packaging: Private Label
Brands:
Potomac River
Potomac River Brand

7760 Keystone Coffee Company
2230 Will Wool Dr
San Jose, CA 95112-2605 408-998-2221
Fax: 408-998-5021 sales@keystonecoffee.com
www.keystonecoffee.com
Processor and exporter of gourmet coffee
President: Tim Wright
Estimated Sales: $3000000
Number Employees: 10-19
Brands:
Keystone

7761 Keystone Food Products
PO Box 326
Easton, PA 18044-0326 610-258-0888
Fax: 610-250-0721 800-523-9426
Key_Contact@Keystonefoods.com
www.keystonefoods.com
Processor of snack foods including pretzels, cheese
twists, popcorn, pork skins and corn and tortilla
chips
President: William Corriere Jr
Chairman: Herb Lottman
Estimated Sales: $18,000,000
Number Employees: 150
Type of Packaging: Consumer, Food Service, Private Label, Bulk
Brands:
BEST BUY
KEYSTONE
PRIZE

7762 Keystone Foods
P.O.Box 369
Camilla, GA 31730-0369 229-336-5211
Fax: 229-336-1818 www.keystonefoods.com
Processor of fresh and frozen chicken
Manager: Clay Banks
Estimated Sales: $750,000
Number Employees: 10-19
Parent Co: Keystone Food Corporation
Type of Packaging: Consumer, Bulk

7763 Keystone Foods Corporation
300 Barr Harbor Dr # 600
W Conshohocken, PA 19428-3809 610-667-6700
Fax: 610-667-1460
key.contact@keystonefoods.com
www.keystonefoods.com
Processor and exporter of beef hamburgers and
chicken
Chairman: Herbert Lotman
Pres.: Gerome Dean
CFO: John Coggins
CEO: Jerry Dean
President: Jerry Dean
Number Employees: 50-99
Type of Packaging: Bulk
Brands:
Keystone Foods

7764 Keystone Foods Corporation
6767 Old Madison Pike NW # 500
Huntsville, AL 35806-4522 256-964-1000
Fax: 256-533-4870 800-327-6701
key.contact@keystonefoods.com
www.keystonefoods.com
Manufactures and supplies beef, poultry, fish, pork
products and custom distribution services to the
food industry
Manager: Wendy Parker
VP: Jerry Wilson
Estimated Sales: $ 600 Million
Number Employees: 80
Type of Packaging: Food Service

7765 Keystone Pretzel Bakery
124 W Airport Rd
Lititz, PA 17543-9294 717-560-1882
Fax: 717-560-2241 888-572-4500
sales@keystonepretzels.com
www.keystonepretzels.com
Manufacturer of pretzels
President: George Phillips
Estimated Sales: $12 Million
Number Employees: 20-49
Type of Packaging: Consumer, Food Service, Bulk

7766 Khalsa International Trading
1616 Preuss Rd
Los Angeles, CA 90035-4212 310-275-9891
Fax: 310-275-2923
customerservice@yogitea.com
www.goldentemple.com
Medicinal teas, packaged cereal, bulk granolas
President: Sopurkh K Khalsa
Vice President: Sada Sat Kalsa
VP Marketing: Parampal Singh
Public Relations: Jagat Joti Khalsa
Operations Manager: Ajeet Khalsa
Estimated Sales: $ 20-50 Million
Number Employees: 20-49
Type of Packaging: Private Label
Brands:
Ancient Healing Formula
Golden Temple
Peace Cereal
Sunshine Spa
Wha Guru Chews
Yogi Tea

7767 Khatsa & Company
PO Box 50754
Bellevue, WA 98015-0754 425-649-5508
Fax: 425-649-0774 888-542-8728
info@khatsa.com www.khatsa.com
President: Dachs Kyaping
Vice President: Nanang Nornang
Public Relations: Dachen Kyaping
Estimated Sales: $500,000-$1 Million
Number Employees: 1-4
Brands:
Khatsa
Liberate Your Senses
Urban Nomad Food

7768 Kibun Foods
2101 4th Ave # 1240
Seattle, WA 98121-2323 206-467-6287
Fax: 206-467-6612 kibun@aloha.com
Beer
President: Tadahiko Mitsui
Estimated Sales: $7,500,000
Number Employees: 5-9

7769 Kid Care
4420 Via Real
Suite B
Carpinteria, CA 93013-1635 805-566-2473
Fax: 805-566-9211 kidbear1@aol.com
www.kidbear.com
Vegetarian company producing vegetarian gummy
supplements
VP Sales/Marketing: Alison Cox
Number of Brands: 1
Number of Products: 4
Type of Packaging: Consumer
Brands:
KID BEAR

7770 Kid's Kookie Company
1000 Calle Negocio
San Clemente, CA 92673-6205 949-661-7880
Fax: 949-498-5496 800-350-7577
info@kidscookies.com www.kidscookies.com
Processor of holiday, theme, decorated, specialty
shaped and pre-baked cookies
Owner: Dennis Sellers
VP: Gay Sellers
Estimated Sales: $ 5 - 10 Million
Number Employees: 5-9
Type of Packaging: Food Service
Brands:
Kids Cookie

7771 Kid's Pantry
215 NE Hillcrest Drive
Grants Pass, OR 97526-3593 541-476-8812
Fax: 541-476-8812 800-452-9551
President: Pat Enos

Estimated Sales: Under $500,000
Number Employees: 1-4

7772 Kids Cooking Club
PO Box 91192
San Diego, CA 92169-3192 858-539-1855
Fax: 858-539-2010 kidscook@kidscook.com
www.kidscook.com
Cooking projects for kids including pizza, pretzel
kits and other make, bake and decorate kits
Number Employees: 1-4

7773 Kidsmania
12332 Bell Ranch Dr
Santa Fe Springs, CA 90670-3356 562-946-8822
Fax: 562-946-8802 sales@candynovelties.com
www.candynovelties.com
Candy toys and novelties
Owner: Foreman Lam
Estimated Sales: $300,000-500,000
Number Employees: 1-4
Number of Products: 100

7774 Kiefer Company
1406 W Chestnut St
Louisville, KY 40203-1706 502-587-7474
Fax: 502-587-7503
Processor of meat
Owner: Steve Smith
Estimated Sales: $3000000
Number Employees: 20-49

7775 (HQ)Kikkoman International
P.O.Box 420784
San Francisco, CA 94142-0784 415-956-7750
Fax: 415-956-7760 dac@kikkoman.com
www.kikkoman-usa.com
Manufacturer of soy-based flavor enhancers and
sauces including soy and teriyaki
Chairman: Yuzaburo Mogi
Sales/Marketing Manager: Shigeru Nemoto
Estimated Sales: $110 Million
Number Employees: 100-249
Number of Brands: 1
Type of Packaging: Consumer, Food Service, Bulk
Other Locations:
Kikkoman Production Facility
Walworth WI
Kikkoman Production Facility
Folsom CA
Brands:
Kikkoman

7776 (HQ)Kikkoman International
P.O.Box 420784
San Francisco, CA 94142-0784 415-956-7750
Fax: 415-956-7760 www.kikkoman-usa.com
Processor and exporter of soy and teriyaki sauces
President: H Takamatsu
Executive VP: B Nelson
Estimated Sales: $ 3 - 5 Million
Number Employees: 100-249
Parent Co: Kikkoman Corporation
Type of Packaging: Consumer, Food Service
Other Locations:
Kikkoman Production Facility
Walworth WI
Kikkoman Production Facility
Folsom CA
Brands:
Kikkoman

7777 Kikkoman International
555 Republic Drive
Suite 200
Plano, TX 75074 972-516-4207
Fax: 972-516-4233 www.kikkoman-usa.com
Manufacturer of liquid and dehydrated soy sauces,
teriyaki sauce, specialty sauces, natural flavor
enhancers, and gravinol.
Exec. V.P.: H Takamatsu
V.P.: B Nelson
Estimated Sales: $ 5 - 10 Million
Number Employees: 5-9
Parent Co: Kikkoman Corporation
Type of Packaging: Consumer, Food Service

7778 Kikkoman International
2 Mid America Plz # 1022
Oakbrook Terrace, IL 60181-4720 630-954-1244
Fax: 630-954-1309 www.kikkoman-usa.com

Manufacturer of liquid and dehydrated soy sauces, teriyaki sauce, specialty sauces, natural flavor enhancers, and gravinol.
Manager: Tom Gufler
V.P.: B Nelson
Estimated Sales: $ 3 - 5 Million
Number Employees: 5-9
Parent Co: Kikkoman Corporation
Type of Packaging: Consumer, Food Service

7779 Kikkoman International
1979 Lakeside Pkwy # 930
Tucker, GA 30084-5870 770-496-0605
Fax: 770-496-0918 www.kikkoman.com
Processor and exporter of soy and teriyaki sauces
Manager: Earl Haraguchi
V.P.: B Nelson
Number Employees: 100-249
Parent Co: Kikkoman Corporation
Type of Packaging: Consumer, Food Service

7780 Kilauea Agronomics
PO Box 80
Kilauea, HI 96754-0080 808-828-1761
Fax: 808-828-1880
Estimated Sales: $ 20 - 50 Million
Number Employees: 50-99

7781 Kilgus Meats
3346 W Laskey Rd
Toledo, OH 43623-4030 419-472-9721
Processor of sausage including wieners, bratwurst and bologna; also, lunch meats
President: Erich Schiehlen
Estimated Sales: $5-9.9 Million
Number Employees: 5-9
Type of Packaging: Consumer, Food Service, Bulk

7782 Kilwons Foods
326 May Ave
Santa Cruz, CA 95060-4109 831-426-9670
Fax: 831-426-2720 kilwonsfoods@hotmail.com
www.kilwonsfoods.com
Manufactures sauce, gravy, dressing & dip mixes
Owner: Kilwon Poveromo
Estimated Sales: Under $500,000
Number Employees: 5-9
Brands:
Kilwons Foods

7783 Kimball Enterprise International
3129 S Hacienda Heights Boulevard
Suite 410
Hacienda Heights, CA 91745 213-276-8898
Fax: 213-947-1888 sales@garlicpeeler.com
www.garlicpeeler.com
Processor and exporter of roasted, peeled and chopped garlic, peeled and chopped shallots and garlic juice
President: Jimmy Tani
Estimated Sales: $ 2 Million
Number Employees: 20
Sq. footage: 15000
Type of Packaging: Consumer, Food Service, Private Label, Bulk
Brands:
Kimball

7784 Kimco World Trade Company
PO Box 39377
Los Angeles, CA 90039-0377 323-662-5836
Fax: 323-662-5956 kimco888@yahoo.com
www.kimcoworldtrade.com
Food, grains, beans, edamame and herbs
Supplier Chain Network: Peter Kim
Estimated Sales: $ 1 Million
Number Employees: 6
Number of Brands: 3
Number of Products: 12
Type of Packaging: Food Service
Brands:
Azuki
Green Soy
Kimco

7785 Kimes Cider Mill
P.O.Box 419
Bendersville, PA 17306-0419 717-677-7539
Fax: 717-677-7151 kimescid@cvn.net
www.kimescidermill.com
Processor of apple butter and cider
Partner: Rick Kime
Prtnr.: Randy Kimes

Estimated Sales: Below $ 5 Million
Number Employees: 10-19
Type of Packaging: Consumer
Brands:
Kimes

7786 Kimmie Candy Company
525 Reactor Way
Reno, NV 89502-4108 775-284-9200
Fax: 775-284-9206 888-532-1325
info@kimmiecandy.com www.kimmycandy.com
A manufacturer of quality panned candies. Located in Reno NV, we specialize in colorfull candy shells over chocolate or not centers. Branded products include sunbursts and choco rocks and corn bitz
President/CEO: Joseph Dutra
VP Sales/Marketing: Bernie Leas
Public Relations: Tina Norberg
Operations: John Dutra
Production: OoIn Jung
Estimated Sales: $ 1-5 Million
Number Employees: 20
Sq. footage: 20000
Type of Packaging: Consumer, Food Service, Private Label, Bulk
Brands:
Baby Dino Eggs
Choco Rocks
Kandy Kookies
Peanut Crunchers
Raisin Royales
Sunbursts

7787 Kimson Chemicals
24 Crescent Street
Waltham, MA 02453-4358 781-893-6878
Fax: 781-893-6881
Sodium citrate, ascorbic acid, sodium benzoate, citric acid, ammonium bicarbonate, potassium sorbate
Estimated Sales: Below $ 5 Million
Number Employees: 7

7788 King & Prince Seafood Corporation
P.O.Box 899
Brunswick, GA 31521-0899 912-265-5155
Fax: 912-264-4812 800-841-0205
sales@kpseafood.com www.kpseafood.com
Processor of shrimp including breaded, boil-in-bag, stuffed, battered, cooked, steamed, IQF scampi and steaks; also, lobster tails and stuffed fish; importer of frozen shrimp
President: Robert Brubaker
CEO: Russell Mentzer
Marketing Executive/ EVP: Russ Mentzer
Operations Director: Tom Sublett
Purchasing Manager: Howard Browning
Estimated Sales: $ 50 - 100 Million
Number Employees: 500-999
Sq. footage: 133747
Brands:
Flying Jib
Golden Shore
Gulf Stream
King & Prince

7789 King 888 Company
231 Third Street
Suite 210
Las Vegas, NV 89101 800-785-3674
Fax: 800-785-3674 info@king888.com
www.king888.com
Manufacturers an energy drink that is available in Silver Label (citrus blend flavor), Original Gold (ginger/lemon flavor) and Authentic Cola (natural cola flavor).
Sales Representative: Gary Larson
Type of Packaging: Food Service

7790 King Arthur Flour
135 Us Route 5 S
Norwich, VT 05055-9430 802-649-3881
Fax: 802-649-3323 bakers@kingarthurflour.com
www.kingarthurflour.com
Manufacturer of flour
President/CEO: Steve Voigt
Estimated Sales: $45 Million
Number Employees: 100-249
Number of Brands: 1
Sq. footage: 16600

7791 King B Meat Snacks
P.O.Box 397
Minong, WI 54859-0397 715-466-2234
Fax: 715-466-5151 800-346-6896
info@linksnacks.com www.kingbjerky.com
Manufacturer and exporter of jerky and meat snacks
CEO: Jack Link
VP Operations: Karl Paepke
Estimated Sales: $10-20 Million
Number Employees: 250-499
Type of Packaging: Consumer, Food Service, Private Label, Bulk
Brands:
B. King
Taylor Country Farms

7792 (HQ)King Brewing Company
1350 Gateway Blvd # A8
Fairfield, CA 94533-6905 707-428-4503
Fax: 707-864-2232
Wines
Owner: Tom King
Operations Manager: Robert Egelhoff
Estimated Sales: Under $500,000
Number Employees: 1-4
Sq. footage: 18
Type of Packaging: Private Label

7793 King Cole Ducks Limited
PO Box 185
Aurora, ON L4G 3H3
Canada 800-363-3845
Fax: 905-836-4440 800-363-3825
rgrant@kingcoleducks.com
www.kingcoleducks.com
Processor and exporter of fresh and frozen duck including parts, smoked, boneless breast, peppered, fully cooked, etc
President: James Murby
Export Sls.: Robert Grant
VP: Robert Murby
Number Employees: 100-249
Sq. footage: 1000
Type of Packaging: Consumer, Food Service, Private Label, Bulk
Brands:
King Cole

7794 King David's All NaturalFood
129 Marshall St # 1
Syracuse, NY 13210-1893 315-471-5000
Fax: 315-471-1310
Gourmet foods
President: Milad Hatem
VP: Madeo Hatem
Estimated Sales: Below $ 5 Million
Number Employees: 1-4

7795 King Estate Winery
80854 Territorial Hwy
Eugene, OR 97405-9715 541-942-9874
Fax: 541-942-9867 800-884-4441
info@kingestate.com www.kingestate.com
Wines
CEO: Ed King
Director Sales: Steve Thomson
CFO: Doyal Eubank
Estimated Sales: Less than $500,000
Number Employees: 20-49
Brands:
Oregon

7796 King Food Service
94-272 Pupuole St
Waipahu, HI 96797-2329 808-671-5464
Fax: 808-676-8888
Supplier of food products to hotels and restaurant. Cold storage leasing.
President: Dana H Y Chun
CEO: Bill Hughes
Assistant Controller: Lisa Tomihama
Estimated Sales: $ 24-34 Million
Number Employees: 50 to 99
Sq. footage: 38000

7797 King Food Service
7810 42nd St W
Rock Island, IL 61201-7319 309-787-4488
Fax: 309-787-4501
sales11@kingfoodservice.com
www.kingfoodservice.com

Providing superior service, quality & pricing since 1945. Specialists in seafood, poultry & meat, distributor, importer, broker and processor.
President/CEO: Mike Cutkomp
Marketing Director: Chef Albert Ames
Sales Director: Matt Cutkomp
Operations Manager/Purchasing: Rick White
Estimated Sales:$24 Million
Number Employees: 10-19
Number of Products: 1500

7798 King Juice
851 W Grange Ave
Milwaukee, WI 53221-4425 414-482-0303
Fax: 414-482-0719 inquiries@kingjuice.com
www.kingjuice.com
Juices
President: Tim Kezman
Estimated Sales:$500,000-$1 Million
Number Employees: 20-49
Brands:
Calypso
King Juice
Villa Quenchers

7799 King Kat
RR 2
Box 185
Carlisle, AR 72024-8607 870-854-8187
Fax: 209-464-8135

7800 King Kelly Marmalade Company
P.O.Box 1
Bellflower, CA 90707-0001 562-865-0291
Fax: 562-865-9318
Manufacturer of jams, jellies and orange marmalade
President: John Bowen
Estimated Sales:$ 5 - 10 Million
Number Employees: 20-49
Sq. footage: 25000
Type of Packaging: Consumer, Food Service, Private Label
Brands:
KING KELLY

7801 King Kold
837 N California Ave
Chicago, IL 60622 773-278-7711
Fax: 773-278-7783 info@kingkold.com
www.kingkold.com
Beef, potato pancakes, vegetable pancakes, maztoh balls
CEO: Michael K Hahn
Founder: Jacob Harmatz
Estimated Sales:$ 5-10 Million
Number Employees: 50-99
Brands:
Ratner's

7802 King Kold Meats
331 N Main St
Englewood, OH 45322-1333 937-836-2731
Fax: 937-836-5919 800-836-2797
kingkold@gte.net
Processor of portion packed frozen meat patties including beef, pork and veal. Also cooked entrees including barbecued beef and sloppy joes and chili
President: Douglas Smith
CFO: Sue Miller
VP Distribution: Michael DeFrances
Sales Manager: David Anticoli
Estimated Sales:$ 10 - 20 Million
Number Employees: 20-49
Number of Brands: 3
Number of Products: 125
Sq. footage: 10000
Type of Packaging: Consumer, Food Service, Private Label, Bulk
Brands:
EVELYN SPRAGUE
HEARTH & KETTLE
KINGKOLD

7803 King Meat
P.O.Box 58834
Los Angeles, CA 90058-0834 323-582-7401
Fax: 323-582-1813
Processor, exporter and importer of beef
President: Ray Rosenthel
Sls. Mgr.: Harry Slevove
Estimated Sales:$ 50 - 100 Million
Number Employees: 100-249
Type of Packaging: Food Service

7804 King Milling Company
P.O.Box 99
Lowell, MI 49331-0099 616-897-9264
Fax: 616-897-4350 jcantrell@kingflour.com
www.kingflour.com
Manufacturer of wheat and white flour
President: Brian Doyle
VP: Steve Doyle
SVP: James Doyle
Estimated Sales:$ 20 - 50 Million
Number Employees: 20-49
Type of Packaging: Food Service, Bulk
Brands:
Kimco
Pathfinder
Pure Gold
Sincerity
Super Kleaned Wheat

7805 King Neptune
21 Bay St
Winslow, ME 04901-7045 207-872-5015
Fax: 415-485-6921
Owner: Jeannine Hendsbee
Estimated Sales:$300,000-500,000
Number Employees: 1-4

7806 King Nut Company
31900 Solon Rd
Cleveland, OH 44139-3536 440-248-8484
Fax: 440-248-0153 800-860-5464
customer@kingnut.com www.kingnut.com
Manufacturer of snack mixes, chocolates, nuts and tropical fruit tins; exporter of salted nuts
President: Martin Kanan
VP Sales/Marketing: Matthew Kanan
Product Development: Debra Smith
Plant Operations: James Dedario
Estimated Sales:$35 Million
Number Employees: 100-249
Sq. footage: 50000
Parent Co: Kanan Enterprises/King Nut
Type of Packaging: Consumer, Food Service, Private Label, Bulk
Brands:
Blossom
Kelling-Kernel Fresh
Peterson's

7807 King Nut Company
31900 Solon Rd
Cleveland, OH 44139-3536 440-248-8484
Fax: 440-248-0153 800-860-5464
info@kingnut.com www.kingnut.com
Manufacturer and packager of nuts and snacks including; almonds, banana chips, apricots, beef jerky and cajun party mix
President/CEO: Martin Kanan
Chairman: Michael Kanan
VP Sales/Marketing: Matthew Kanan
Estimated Sales:$35 Million
Number Employees: 100-249
Sq. footage: 86000
Type of Packaging: Consumer, Food Service, Private Label, Bulk
Brands:
KINGS
SUMMER HARVEST BRANDS

7808 King Soopers Bakery
60 Yuma St
Denver, CO 80223-1204 303-778-3128
Fax: 303-871-9260 www.kingsoopers.com
Manufacturer of bread and pastries
President: Russ Dispense
Plant Manager: Dave Higgins
Estimated Sales:$100 Million
Number Employees: 250-499
Parent Co: Kroger

7809 King's Command Foods
7622 S 188th St
Kent, WA 98032-1021 425-251-6788
Fax: 425-251-0523 800-247-3138
info@kingscommand.com
www.kingscommand.com
Processor of further processed beef, veal, pork and chicken products
President: Ronald Baer
Vice President: Grant Lorsung
CFO: Greg Arend
Plant Manager: Mark Wallace

Estimated Sales:$299900000
Number Employees: 100-249
Type of Packaging: Consumer, Food Service

7810 King's Cupboard
P.O.Box 27
Red Lodge, MT 59068-0027 406-446-3060
Fax: 406-446-3070 800-962-6555
sales@kingscupboard.com
www.kingscupboard.com
All natural dessert sauces and hot chocolate mixes
Owner: Richard Poore
Estimated Sales:$ 5 - 10 Million
Number Employees: 50-99
Type of Packaging: Consumer, Food Service, Private Label, Bulk
Brands:
Beartooth Kitchens

7811 King's Hawaiian
19161 Harborgate Way
Torrance, CA 90501-1316 310-533-3250
Fax: 310-533-8732 800-800-5461
consumer@kingshawaiian.com
www.kingshawaiian.com
Hawaiian sweet bread and rolls
CEO: Mark Taira
CEO: Mark Tiara
Estimated Sales:$ 10-20 Million
Number Employees: 250-499
Sq. footage: 150000
Brands:
King's Hawaiian

7812 King's Meat & Seafood
1515 Harvard Street
Houston, TX 77008-4216 713-923-6868
Fax: 713-346-2688 eddiehsi@aol.com
Pork products, beef and chicken, food service
President: Eddie Hsieh
Quality Control: Erika Zastillo
Estimated Sales:$ 100-500 Million
Number Employees: 60

7813 Kingchem
5 Pearl Ct
Allendale, NJ 07401-1656 201-825-9988
Fax: 201-825-9148 800-211-4330
p.sivolella@kingchem.com www.kingchem.com
Processor of herbal supplements
Manager: Carmine Covino
VP: Austin Bishop
Marketing Manager: Frank Fortuna
Director/Sales: Patrick Sivolella
Director Of Purchasing: Lillian Wu
Estimated Sales:$ 10-20 Million
Number Employees: 10-19
Sq. footage: 2500
Brands:
Kingchem

7814 Kingfish
7400 New Lagrange Rd # 405
Louisville, KY 40222-4870 502-339-0565
Fax: 502-339-0230
President/CEO: James Cowgill
CEO: Kyle Noltmeyer
Estimated Sales:$10,000,000
Number Employees: 5-9

7815 Kingly Heirs
PO Box 283
Elkhart, IN 46515 527-296-1166
Fax: 527-296-1188 info@kinglyheirs.com
www.kinglyheirs.com/
Manufacturer and distributor of gourmet cake mixes.
Founder/Owner/President: Kingly Heirs

7816 Kings Canyon Corrin
1750 S Buttonwillow Avenue
Reedley, CA 93654-4400 559-638-3571
Fax: 559-638-6326 sales@kccfruit.com
www.kccfruit.com
Peaches, apricots and other fruits
President: Steve Kenfield
VP Sales: Fred Berry

7817 Kings Delight
P.O.Box 5935
Gainesville, GA 30504-0935 770-532-2395
Fax: 770-531-1603 www.kingsdelight.com

Processor of processed poultry including chargrilled nuggets, hot wings, boneless skinless breast filets, breaded chicken rings and fries, breaded fritters, tenders, breakfast patties, etc
  CEO: Barry Jan Cooley
  Sales/Marketing VP: Randal Cochran
  OS Operations Director: Michael Farmer
Estimated Sales: $ 20-50 Million
Number Employees: 500-999

7818 Kings Food Products
12 N 35th St
Belleville, IL 62226-6202   618-233-0400
                    Fax: 618-233-0497
Processor of barbecued meat products and sauces
  President: Tom Siegel
  Vice President: Dan Siegel
Estimated Sales: $ 5 - 10 Million
Number Employees: 10-19
Parent Co: Deli Star Ventures
Type of Packaging: Consumer, Food Service, Private Label, Bulk

7819 Kings Processing
188 Marshall Street
Middleton, NS B0S 1P0
Canada   902-825-2188
                    Fax: 902-825-2180
Processor of fresh salads and vegetables
  Pres.: Richard Melven
Number Employees: 20-49
Type of Packaging: Consumer, Food Service

7820 Kingsburg Apple Sale
PO Box 456
Kingsburg, CA 93631-0456   559-897-5132
  Fax: 559-897-4532 sales@kingsburgapple.com
                    www.kingsburgapple.com
Apples, Asian pears, peaches, nectarines, persimmons, pluots
  President: John Hein
Estimated Sales: $100+ Million
Number Employees: 100-249

7821 Kingsbury Country Market
5001 S Us 35
Kingsbury, IN 46345   219-393-3016
Processor of beef, hog, rabbit, ostrich and lamb; custom butchering available
  Pres.: Jerry Winter
  Secy./Treas.: Sandra Winter
Number Employees: 5-9
Brands:
  Butcher Boy

7822 Kingsville Fisherman's Company
PO Box 37
Kingsville, ON N9Y 2E8
Canada   519-733-6534
                    Fax: 519-733-6959
Processor and exporter of fresh and frozen perch and pickerel
  Sls. Mgr.: John Murray
  Pres.: Carl Fraser
Number Employees: 50-99
Type of Packaging: Bulk

7823 Kinnikinnick Foods
10940-120 Street
Edmonton, AB T5H 3P7
Canada   780-424-2900
      Fax: 780-421-0456 877-503-4466
  info@kinnikinnick.com www.kinnikinnick.com
Manufacturer of gluten free bakery products
  President: Ted Wolf
  CEO: Jerry Bigam
  CFO: Lynne Bigam
  VP: Jay Bigam
Number Employees: 60
Number of Products: 120
Sq. footage: 30000
Type of Packaging: Consumer, Food Service
Brands:
  Kinnikinnick Foods, Inc.

7824 Kintetsu World Express
100 Jericho Quadrangle
Sutie 326
Jericho, NY 11753
                    800-275-4045
                    www.kweusa.com

  Manager: Yasuo Tanaka

7825 Kiolbassa Provision Company
1325 S Brazos St
San Antonio, TX 78207-6931   210-226-8127
  Fax: 210-226-7464 800-456-5465
  link@kiolbassa.com www.kiolbassa.com
Manufacturer of sausage products including smoked, polish and jalapeno flavored sausage and Mexican style chorizo; also a meat packing industry.
  President: Michael Kiolbassa
  CEO: Robert Kiolbassa
  Vice President: Sandra Kiolbassa
  Secretary/Treasurer: Barbara Kiolbassa
Estimated Sales: $ 20 - 50 Million
Number Employees: 50-99
Type of Packaging: Consumer

7826 Kiona Vineyards Winery
44612 N Sunset Rd
Benton City, WA 99320-7500   509-588-6716
  Fax: 509-588-3219 info@kionawine.com
                    www.kionawine.com
Wines and wine grapes
  Owner: John Williams
  Owner: Ann Williams
  Manager/Winemaker: Scott Williams
Estimated Sales: Below $ 5 Million
Number Employees: 5-9
Number of Brands: 1
Number of Products: 16
Type of Packaging: Private Label
Brands:
  Kiona

7827 Kirby & Holloway Provisions
P.O.Box 222
Harrington, DE 19952-0222   302-398-3705
  Fax: 302-398-4088 800-995-4729
                    www.kirbyandhollowayinc.com
Processor of sausage and scrapple; wholesaler/distributor of meat and cheese products
  President: Russell Kirby
  Ownr.: Rudy Kirby
  Finance Manager: Mike Davis
Estimated Sales: $6400000
Number Employees: 20-49
Type of Packaging: Consumer, Food Service, Private Label, Bulk

7828 Kirigin Cellars
11550 Watsonville Rd
Gilroy, CA 95020-9434   408-847-8827
  Fax: 408-847-3820 folks@kirigincellars.com
                    www.kirigincellars.com
Manufacturer of wines
  Manager: Allen Kreutzer
  Winemaker: Allen Kreutzer
Estimated Sales: Below $5 Million
Number Employees: 1-4
Brands:
  Kirigin Cellars

7829 Kirkland Custom Seafoods
P.O.Box 2040
Kirkland, WA 98083-2040   425-822-1891
      Fax: 425-889-9248 800-321-3474
Processor of salmon, albacore tuna, rainbow trout, oysters, dungeness crab, shrimp, pates and mousses
  President: Thad Pound
  Sales Manager: Lindsay Turner
Estimated Sales: $1000000
Number Employees: 1-4
Sq. footage: 10000
Type of Packaging: Consumer, Private Label, Bulk
Brands:
  ALDER COVE

7830 Kirsco/Kay Packing
2800 Standish Street
Detroit, MI 48216-1539   313-963-2900
                    Fax: 313-237-0040
Processor of boneless beef, pork and poultry
  President: David Kirsch
Estimated Sales: $ 50 - 100 Million
Number Employees: 20-49
Parent Co: KBD
Type of Packaging: Food Service, Bulk

7831 Kiska Farms
P.O.Box 4707
Pasco, WA 99302-4707   509-547-7765
  Fax: 509-547-7746 kathy@kiskafarms.com
                    www.kiskafarms.com

Potatos
  Co-Owner: Kathy Blasdel
  Co-Owner: Judy Johnston

7832 Kistler Vineyards
4707 Vine Hill Rd
Sebastopol, CA 95472-2236   707-823-5603
      Fax: 707-823-6709 abc@kistlerwine.com
                    www.kistlerwine.com
Wines
  President: Stephen Kistler
  CEO: Stephen Kistler
Estimated Sales: $ 20-50 Million
Number Employees: 50-99
Brands:
  Durell Vineyard
  Dutton Ranch
  Hyde Vineyard
  McCrea Vineyard
  Sonoma Coast

7833 Kitch'n Cook'd Potato Chip Company
1703 W Beverley St
Staunton, VA 24401-3007   540-886-4473
      Fax: 540-886-0558 800-752-1535
  kitncook@ntelos.net www.kitchncookd.com
Processor of potato chips
  President: George Raymond Curry
Estimated Sales: $1100000
Number Employees: 10-19
Type of Packaging: Consumer

7834 Kitchen Basics
PO Box 41022
Brecksville, OH 44141   440-838-1344
  Fax: 440-838-5841 info@kitchenbasics.net
                    www.kitchenbasics.net
cooking stocks

7835 Kitchen Kettle Foods
P.O.Box 380
Intercourse, PA 17534-0380   717-768-8261
      Fax: 717-768-3614 800-732-3538
                    info@continentalinn.com
                    www.kitchenkettle.com
Manufacturer of jams, jellies and relishes
  President: Michael Burnley
  VP: Joanne Ladley
  CEO: Pat Burnley
Estimated Sales: $ 50 - 100 Million
Number Employees: 100-249

7836 Kitchen Pride Mushroom Farms
P.O.Box 585
Gonzales, TX 78629-0585   830-540-4516
  Fax: 830-540-4556 sales@kitchenpride.com
                    www.kitchenpridemushrooms.com
Grower of mushrooms
  President: Darrell Mc Lain
  Sls.: Phil McLain
Estimated Sales: $2300000
Number Employees: 50-99
Sq. footage: 100000
Type of Packaging: Consumer, Food Service, Private Label, Bulk
Brands:
  Kitchen Pride Farms

7837 Kitchen Products
18 Rackliffe Street
Gloucester, MA 01930-4151   978-283-1384
  President: William O'Connor
Estimated Sales: $ 1-2.5 Million
Number Employees: 5

7838 Kitchen Table Bakers
41 Princeton Drive
Syosset, NY 11973   516-931-5113
      Fax: 516-932-5467 800-486-4582
                    info@kitchentablebakers.com
                    www.kitchentablebakers.com
gourmet, wheat, gluten and sugar free wafer crisps
  President/Owner: Barry Novick

7839 Kitchens Seafood
1001 E Baker St
Plant City, FL 33563-3700   813-750-1888
      Fax: 813-750-1889 800-327-0132
                    sales@kitchensseafood.com
                    www.kitchensseafood.com

Manufacturer, packer and importer of frozen seafood including lobster, crab, shrimp, shrimp meat and langostinos
President: Dan La Fleur
Estimated Sales:$51 Million
Number Employees: 1-4
Type of Packaging: Consumer, Food Service, Private Label, Bulk
Other Locations:
Kitchens Seafood - Production
Jacksonville FL

7840 Kittery Lobster Company
P.O.Box 304
Kittery, ME 03904-0304   207-439-6035
Fax: 207-763-3861
Lobster
Owner: Hugh Reynolds
Estimated Sales:$1 Million
Number Employees: 5-9

7841 (HQ)Kittling Ridge Estate Wines & Spirits
297 S Service Road
Grimsby, ON L3M 1Y6
Canada   905-945-9225
Fax: 905-945-4330 www.kittlingridge.com
Processor and exporter of alcoholic beverages including liqueurs, whiskey, rum, vodka, brandy, bitters, wines, icewine and ready-to-drink cocktails
V.P. Fin.: Peter Kosacky
V.P. Sls.: Tim Burrows
CEO/Pres.: John Hall
Number Employees: 100-249
Brands:
Canadian
Kingsgate

7842 Kittridge & FredricksonFine Coffees
2801 SE 14th Ave
Portland, OR 97202-2203   503-234-7788
Fax: 503-231-9827 800-558-7788
info@kfcoffee.com   www.kfcoffee.com
Coffees
President: Don Dominguez
Founder: Bud Dominguez
Estimated Sales:$ 10 - 20 Million
Number Employees: 10-19
Brands:
K&F

7843 Kitts Meat Processing
P.O.Box 8
Dedham, IA 51440-0008   712-683-5622
Processor of bologna
Partner: David Kitt
Partner: Shawn Kitt
Estimated Sales:$190,000
Number Employees: 5-9

7844 Kitty Clover Snacktime Company
6916 N 97th Cir
Omaha, NE 68122-3037   402-342-7342
Potato chips and snack foods

7845 Klaire Laboratories
10439 Double R Boulevard
Reno, NV 89521-8905   888-488-2488
Fax: 858-350-7883 888-488-2488
http://www.klaire.com
Processor and exporter of allergen-free nutritional supplements
President: Cary Fereuson
Vice President: Jeffrey Mersky
Number Employees: 20-49
Parent Co: Kek Industries
Brands:
VITAL LIFE

7846 Klamath River Barbeque
PO Box 711
Montague, CA 96064   530-459-5629
Fax: 530-459-3612 klamathbbq@aol.com
Wholesale and retail consumer products, foodservice products, private labeling, co-packing, PFR, cannery license, pH controlled processing.
Owner: Kendra Gill
Vice President: Francis Gill
Plant Manager: Linda Oliver
Estimated Sales:$30,000
Number of Products: 7
Sq. footage: 2000

Type of Packaging: Consumer, Food Service, Private Label
Other Locations:
Klamath River Barbeque
Yreka CA
Brands:
Klamuth River BBQ
Nucci's Restaurant
Pat's Pimentos
RWB Mt Ranch Foods
Wildfire Foods

7847 (HQ)Klein Family Vintners
P.O.Box 6010
Healdsburg, CA 95448-6010   707-433-6511
Fax: 707-433-8635 www.rodneystrong.com
Processor of wines
President: Tom Klein
Pres. (Windsor): Dennis Colbert
CFO: Cobin Tinter
Estimated Sales:$ 20 - 50 Million
Number Employees: 100-249
Type of Packaging: Consumer, Private Label
Brands:
Rodney Strong

7848 Klein Foods
P.O.Box 656
Marshall, MN 56258-0656   507-532-3127
Fax: 507-537-1940 800-657-0174
honey@starpioint.net
Honey and honey products
President: Stephen Klein
Estimated Sales:$5-9.9 Million
Number Employees: 5-9
Type of Packaging: Private Label

7849 Klein Pickle Company
4118 W Whitton Ave
Phoenix, AZ 85019-3625   602-269-2072
Fax: 602-269-2069
Pickles and condiments
Owner: Byron Arnold
Estimated Sales:$ 1-2.5 Million
Number Employees: 20-49

7850 Klein's Kosher Pickles
4118 W Whitton Ave
Phoenix, AZ 85019-3625   602-269-2072
Fax: 602-269-2069 sales@kleinpickles.com
www.kleinpickleco.com
Processor of kosher pickles
President: Byron Arnold
VP: Mark Arnold
Estimated Sales:$ 1-2.5 Million
Number Employees: 20-49
Sq. footage: 300000
Type of Packaging: Consumer, Food Service
Brands:
Mrs. Klein's

7851 Kleinpeter Farms Dairy
14444 Airline Hwy
Baton Rouge, LA 70817-6899   225-753-2121
Fax: 225-752-8964 www.kleinpeterdairy.com
Milk, cream, cottage cheese
President: Jeff Kleinpeter
CEO: D Kleinpeter
Estimated Sales:$ 20-30 Million
Number Employees: 100-249

7852 Klement Sausage Company
207 E Lincoln Ave
Milwaukee, WI 53207-1593   414-744-2330
Fax: 414-744-2438 800-553-6368
tomajack@klements.com   www.klements.com
Sausage and beef products
President: James T Klement
Co-President: Roger Klement
Vice President: Tim Gibbons
Director: Dan Lipke
Plant Manager: Bryan DuCharme
Estimated Sales:$ 50-75 Million
Number Employees: 100-249
Sq. footage: 220000

7853 Klemme Cooperative Grainery
122 W Main Street
Klemme, IA 50449-9053   641-444-4262
Plant Manager: Darryl Schweers
Estimated Sales:$ 2.5-5 Million
Number Employees: 20

7854 Klingshirn Winery
33050 Webber Rd
Avon Lake, OH 44012-2330   440-933-6666
Fax: 440-933-7896
contactus@klingshirnwine.com
www.klingshirnwine.com
Wines
President: Allan Klingshirn
Director Manufacturing: Lee Kingshirn
*Estimated Sales:*Below $ 5 Million
Number Employees: 5-9
Brands:
Klingshirn Winery

7855 Klinke Brothers Ice Cream Company
2450 Scaper St
Memphis, TN 38114-6546   901-743-8250
Fax: 901-743-8254
Processor of ice cream and frozen yogurt
President: John Klinke
Estimated Sales:$ 20 - 50 Million
Number Employees: 50-99
Type of Packaging: Consumer, Food Service
Brands:
Angel Food

7856 Klomar Ship Supply Company
2200 Perimeter Rd
Mobile, AL 36615-1131   251-471-1153
Transportation company providing ocean transport
Owner: Mike Kloumassis

7857 Klondike Cheese
P.O.Box 234
Monroe, WI 53566-0234   608-325-3021
Fax: 608-325-3027   www.klondikecheese.com
Processor of cheese
President: Ron Bulholzer
Marketing Director: Ron Buholzer
Estimated Sales:$ 10 - 20 Million
Number Employees: 20-49
Type of Packaging: Consumer, Private Label

7858 Klondike Cheese Factory
P.O.Box 234
Monroe, WI 53566-0234   608-325-3021
Fax: 608-325-3027 ron@klondikecheese.com
Manufacturer of cheese
President: Ron Bulholzer
Estimated Sales:$10-20 Million
Number Employees: 20-49

7859 Kloss Manufacturing Company
7566 Morris Ct # 310
Allentown, PA 18106-9247   610-391-3820
Fax: 610-391-3830 800-445-7100
questions@klossfunfood.com
www.klossfunfood.com
Processor and exporter of flavoring extracts for Italian ices and slushes; also, concession equipment and supplies, fountain syrups, popcorn, cotton candy, nachos and waffles; wholesaler/distributor serving the food service market
President: Richard C Kloss
Vice President: Stephen Kloss
Estimated Sales:$ 3 - 5 Million
Number Employees: 10-19
Sq. footage: 30000
Type of Packaging: Food Service, Private Label, Bulk
Brands:
Kloss

7860 (HQ)Klosterman Baking Company
4760 Paddock Rd
Cincinnati, OH 45229-1079   513-242-1109
Fax: 513-242-3151
comments@klostermanbakery.com
www.klostermanbakery.com
Processor of bread and hard rolls
Chairman: Kenneth Klosterman
President: Chip Klosterman
President: Kenneth Klosterman Jr
Sales Director: Dennis Wiltshire
Purchasing Manager: Larry Wright
Estimated Sales:$47900000
Number Employees: 20-49
Type of Packaging: Consumer, Food Service

7861 Klosterman Baking Company
508 W Main St
Springfield, OH 45504-2662   937-322-9588
Fax: 937-322-6733 www.klostermanbakery.com
Processor of bread
Chairman of the Board: Kenneth Klosterman
President: Chip Klosterman
Plant Manager: John Tucker
Estimated Sales:$47900000
Number Employees: 100-249
Parent Co: Klosterman Baking Company
Type of Packaging: Consumer, Food Service

7862 Kluge Estate Winery & Vineyard
100 Grand Cru Dr
Charlottesville, VA 22902-7763   434-977-3895
Fax: 434-977-0606 info@klugeestate.com
www.klugeestateonline.com
Wines
President: Patricia Kluge
COO: John Beckman
Vineyard Manager: Tom Child
Estimated Sales:$ 3 - 5 Million
Number Employees: 5-9

7863 Knapp Vineyards
2770 Ernsberger Rd
Romulus, NY 14541-9757   607-869-9271
Fax: 607-869-3212 800-869-9271
winery@knappwine.com www.knappwine.com
Wines
Owner: Gene Pierce
Vice President: Susanna Knapp
*Estimated Sales:*Below $ 5 Million
Number Employees: 20-49
Type of Packaging: Private Label
Brands:
Knapp

7864 Knappen Milling Company
P.O.Box 245
Augusta, MI 49012-0245   269-731-4141
Fax: 269-731-5441 800-562-7736
wheat@knappen.com www.knappenmilling.com
Manufacturer of soft wheat, cereal bran, wheat and
flour
President: Charles Knappen III
CFO: Darrell Roese
CEO: C B Knappen Iii
Sales Director: Todd Wright
Plant Manager: John Shouse
Number Employees: 20-49
Type of Packaging: Private Label, Bulk
Brands:
100% FLAKED WHEAT
ARBUTUS FLOUR
HEAVY BRAN
SATIN WHITE FLOUR
SOTAC

7865 Knese Enterprise
P.O.Box 20475
Floral Park, NY 11002-0475   516-354-9004
Fax: 516-354-9004 bradstasteofny@aol.com
Spicy gourmet mustard, kettle potato chips, pretzels
and pretzel dip
President: Brad Knese
Estimated Sales:$ 1 - 3 Million
Number Employees: 5-9
Type of Packaging: Consumer
Brands:
Brad's Pretzel Dip
Kettle Chips
Pretzels

7866 (HQ)Knight Seed Company
12550 W Frontage Road
Suite 203
Burnsville, MN 55337-2402   952-894-8080
Fax: 952-894-8095 800-328-2999
ksc@knightseed.com www.knightseed.com
Processor, importer and exporter of soybeans, dried
beans, peas and buckwheat; exporter of lentils
President/CEO: Dave Dornacker
Manager: Jeff Pricco
VP: Tom Kennelly
Marketing: Tim Kukowski
Sales: Dan Dahlquist
Estimated Sales:$ 3 - 5 Million
Number Employees: 5-9
Sq. footage: 3000
Other Locations:
Knight Seed Co.
Vanscoy SK

Brands:
KNIGHT
KSC
LEGACY

7867 (HQ)Knights Appleden Fruit
RR 3
Colborne, ON K0K 1S0
Canada   905-349-2521
Fax: 905-349-3129
Processor, importer and exporter of apples
Pres.: Roger Knight

7868 Knipschildt Chocolatier
12 South Main Street
Norwalk, CT 06854   203-838-3131
Fax: 203-838-3137 info@knipschildt.com
www.knipschildt.com
chocolates
President/Owner: Fritz Knipschildt

7869 Knoll Creek Dairy
104 Osborn Rd
Harrison, NY 10528-1304   718-892-4500
Fax: 718-823-7441
Manufacturer of milk, buttermilk, cheese, cream,
cottage cheese, ice cream and sour cream
Vice President: Norman Marrow
Estimated Sales:$1-2.5 Million
Number Employees: 10-19
Type of Packaging: Consumer, Food Service

7870 Knott's Berry Farm Foods
200 Boysenberry Lane
Placentia, CA 92870-6422   714-579-2400
Fax: 714-579-2490 800-289-9927
info@knottsberryfarmfoods.com
www.knottsberryfarmfoods.com
Processor of jams, jellies and preserves; also, pan-
cake and fruit syrups, spaghetti sauces, salad dress-
ings, specialty foods and gift packs
President/CEO/Chairman: Bruce Rohde
EVP/CFO: Frank Sklarsky
Senior VP Corporate Affairs/CCO: Michael
Fernandez
Senior VP/Controller: John Gehring
Number Employees: 100-249
Sq. footage: 250000
Parent Co: ConAgra Grocery Products
Type of Packaging: Consumer, Food Service

7871 Knotts Wholesale Foods
125 N Blakemore St
Paris, TN 38242-4283   731-642-1961
Fax: 731-644-1962 joshknott@knottsfoods.com
www.knottsfoods.com
Processor of refrigerated sandwiches and sandwich
spreads; wholesaler/distributor of specialty foods;
rack jobber services available
President: Jerry Knott
VP Operations: Greg Dawson
VP Sales: BJ Knott
Estimated Sales:$5000000
Number Employees: 20-49
Sq. footage: 60000
Brands:
Knott's
Knott's Meat Snacks
Knott's Novelty Candy
Knott's Salads

7872 (HQ)Knouse Foods
800 Peach Glen Idaville Rd
Peach Glen, PA 17375-0001   717-677-8181
Fax: 717-677-7069 sriley@pg.knouse.com
www.knouse.com
Manufacturer and exporter of apple products, pie
fillings, juices, cider and vinegar; also, cheese
sauces and puddings available
President/CEO: Ken Guise
Marketing Manager: Ken Millage
Manager Special Markets: Rick Esser
Estimated Sales:$229 Million
Number Employees: 500-999
Type of Packaging: Consumer, Food Service, Pri-
vate Label, Bulk
Brands:
APPLE TIME
COBBLER
LINCOLN
LUCKY LEAF
MUSSLEMAN'S
SPEAS FARM

7873 Knouse Foods Cooperative
815 S Kalamazoo St
Paw Paw, MI 49079-9230   269-657-5524
Fax: 269-657-7512 www.knouse.com
Manufacturer and exporter of processed apple,
cherry and other fruit products including sauces, pie
fillings, juices, cider and vinegar
Manager: Bill Jensen
Dir. of Private Label: Lee Esser
Estimated Sales:$16800000
Number Employees: 100-249
Parent Co: Knouse Foods Cooperative
Type of Packaging: Consumer, Food Service, Bulk

7874 Knouse Foods Cooperative
421 Grant St
Chambersburg, PA 17201-1675   717-263-9177
Fax: 717-263-6262
Processor of canned and jarred apples and apple
sauce
President: Kenneth E Guise Jr
Plant Manager: Chet Amick
Estimated Sales:$ 50-100 Million
Number Employees: 100-249
Parent Co: Knouse Foods Cooperative
Type of Packaging: Consumer

7875 Knouse Foods Cooperative
P.O.Box 308
Orrtanna, PA 17353-0308   717-642-8291
Fax: 717-642-5096 www.knouse.com
Processor of canned and jarred apples and apple
sauce
Manager: Greg Monn
Plant Manager: Mike Binkley
Estimated Sales:$ 50-100 Million
Number Employees: 250-499
Parent Co: Knouse Foods Cooperative
Type of Packaging: Consumer

7876 Knox Mountain Farm
RR 1
Franklin, NH 03235   603-934-9826
800-943-2822
President: Cynthia Huber
Estimated Sales:$ 2.5-5 Million
Number Employees: 5

7877 Knoxage Water Company
227 9th Avenue
San Diego, CA 92101-7403   619-234-3333
Fax: 858-530-2529
Water
Manager: Hank Adair
President: Doug Reed
Director Manufacturing: Robert Wagner
Estimated Sales:$ 1-2.5 Million appx.
Number Employees: 18

7878 Knudsen's Candy
25067 Viking Street
Hayward, CA 94545-2703   800-736-6887
Fax: 510-293-6890 anyone@knudsens.com
www.knudsens.com
Dessert toppings, caramel topping, wrapped cara-
mels, boxed chocolates all homemade ice cream and
candy
President: Gary Love
CEO: Gary Love
Sales Director: Gina Quiriconi
Estimated Sales:$2.5-5 Million
Number Employees: 10-19
Sq. footage: 20000
Brands:
Gramms Bep's Gourmet Ffoods
Grand Finale

7879 Koa Trading Company
P.O.Box 1031
Lihue, HI 96766-5031   808-245-6961
Fax: 808-245-8036 info@koatradingcoinc.com
www.koatradingcoinc.com
Food and beverage products.
President: Peter Yukimura
Estimated Sales:$300,000-500,000
Number Employees: 1-4

7880 Koala Moa Char Broiled Chicken
94-059 Leokane St # 2
Waipahu, HI 96797-2249   808-677-0126
Fax: 808-671-3527 koalamoa@inix.com
www.koala-moa.com

Broiled chicken
President: Gerald Shimabukuro
VP: Kristana Speach
Estimated Sales: $ 1-2.5 Million
Number Employees: 5-9

7881 Kobricks Coffee Company
693 Luis Munoz Marin Boulevard
Jersey City, NJ 07310-1225   201-656-6313
Fax: 201-656-3665   800-562-3662
info@kobricks.com   www.kobricks.com
Italian espresso and other coffees
President: Lee Kobrick
Co-Owner: Steve Kobrick
Estimated Sales: $ 10-24.9 Million
Number Employees: 30-50
Brands:
Kobricks Coffee Company
La San Marco
Leodoro Espresso Com
Shearer
Tazo Teas
Torani Italian Syrup

7882 Koch Food
P.O.Box 749
Chattanooga, TN 37401-0749   423-266-0351
Fax: 423-266-8833   dannuc@kochfoods.com
www.kochfoods.com
Processor of poultry
Manager: Don Davis
Estimated Sales: $ 50 - 100 Million
Number Employees: 250-499
Parent Co: Koch Foods
Type of Packaging: Consumer

7883 (HQ)Koch Foods
1300 Higgins Rd # 100
Park Ridge, IL 60068-5766   847-384-5940
Fax: 847-384-5961   800-837-2778
www.kochfoods.com
Manufacturer and exporter of frozen, portion control
and specialty chicken
CEO: Joseph C Grendys
Operations Manager: Mike Rogers
Estimated Sales: $1 Million
Number Employees: 20-49
Type of Packaging: Consumer, Food Service
Other Locations:
Koch Foods Export Office
Gainesville GA
Koch Foods Sales Office
Morton MS
Brands:
Bc Rogers

7884 Koch Foods
P.O.Box 603
Morristown, TN 37815-0603   423-586-5722
Fax: 423-586-5710   www.kochfoods.com
Processor of dressed poultry
President: Joe Grundy
Co-Partner: Don Atkinson
Sales Manager: George Harrison
Plant Manager: Danny Smith
Estimated Sales: $60000000
Number Employees: 5-9
Sq. footage: 45000
Type of Packaging: Consumer, Food Service, Private Label, Bulk

7885 Koch Foods
1835 Kerr St
Chattanooga, TN 37408-2017   423-266-0351
Fax: 423-266-8833   dannuc@kochfoods.com
www.kochfoods.com
Manufacturer and exporter of fresh, raw and frozen
chicken
Manager: Nick Strange
Communications Director: Todd Womack
General Manager: R Pendergraft
Manager: Nick Nuckolls
Estimated Sales: $1 Billion
Number Employees: 250-499
Parent Co: Koch Poultry
Type of Packaging: Food Service

7886 Koch Poultry
4404 W Berteau Ave
Chicago, IL 60641-1907   773-286-4343
Fax: 773-286-8952   800-837-2778
www.kochfoods.com

Processor of fresh and frozen chicken breasts
President, Koch Meats: Joe Grendys
Plant Manager: Jim Dunbar
Plant Manager: Tyler Davis
Estimated Sales: $ 20-50 Million
Number Employees: 250-499
Type of Packaging: Consumer, Food Service

7887 Koda Farms
P.O.Box 10
South Dos Palos, CA 93665-0010   209-392-2191
Fax: 209-392-6558   info@kodafarms.com
www.kodafarms.com
Processor of rice and rice flour
President: Edward K Koda
Estimated Sales: $ 50 - 100 Million
Number Employees: 100-249
Type of Packaging: Consumer
Brands:
Blue Star Mockiko
Diamond K
Kokuho Rose
Sho Chiku Bai

7888 Kodiak Salmon Packers
PO Box 38
Larsen Bay, AK 99624-0038   907-847-2250
Fax: 907-847-2244   grant@kspi.net
www.kspi.net
Processor of frozen and canned wild Alaskan
salmon
President: Alan Beardsley
Executive VP: John Lotzgesell
Production Manager: Van Johnson
Estimated Sales: $750000
Number Employees: 3

7889 Koegel Meats
3400 W Bristol Rd
Flint, MI 48507-3199   810-238-3685
Fax: 810-238-2467   questions@koegelmeats.com
www.koegelmeats.com
Processor and packer of sausage, natural casing and
long frankfurters, bratwurst, bockwurst and smoked
specialties
President: John Koegel
Vice President: Kathryn Koegel
Sales Director: Tom Lakies
Operations Manager: Jim Lay
Estimated Sales: $21840933
Number Employees: 50-99
Number of Products: 35
Sq. footage: 100000
Type of Packaging: Consumer, Food Service

7890 (HQ)Koehler Bakery Company
5902 Warden Road
North Little Rock, AR 72120-6041   501-835-4946
Fax: 501-835-6857   800-262-5900
Processor of frozen bakery desserts, cakes, muffins,
etc
CEO: Walter Koehler
V.P. Sls.: Ralph Koehler
President: Bob Koehler
President: Bob Koehler
Sales Director: Ralph Koehler
Director Engineering: Don Pepper
Plant Manager: Marty Green
Number Employees: 85
Sq. footage: 75000
Type of Packaging: Consumer, Food Service, Private Label, Bulk
Brands:
Kitty Koehler Kitchens
Kitty Koehler's Kitchens

7891 Koepplinger Bakery
535 Griswold Street
Suite 2600
Detroit, MI 48226-3687   248-967-2020
Fax: 248-967-0722
Breads and rolls
President: John Mather
Estimated Sales: $ 10-24.9 Million
Number Employees: 100-150

7892 Koeze Company
2555 Burlingame Ave SW
Wyoming, MI 49509-2237   616-724-2620
Fax: 616-243-5430   800-555-3909
service@koezedirect.com   www.koeze.com

Processor of nut candies including peanut, tree nuts,
and candy
President: Scott Koeze
CEO: Jeff Koeze
Sales Director: Tom Lakos
Purchasing Manager: John Feenstra
Estimated Sales: $9672287
Number Employees: 20-49
Sq. footage: 80000
Type of Packaging: Consumer, Bulk

7893 Koffee Kup Bakery
436 Riverside Ave
Burlington, VT 05401-1452   802-863-2696
Fax: 802-860-0116   c52345arol@aol.com
www.koffeekupbakery.biz
Bread and doughnuts
President: Ronald Roberge Sr
CEO: Andrew Mathews
Quality Control: Tom Beauregard
Vice President: Carol Roberge
CFO: Eddie Matthews
VP: James Kokinos
General Manager: Mattson Davis
Purchasing Manager: Steve Hebert
Estimated Sales: $ 10-20 Million
Number Employees: 50-99
Type of Packaging: Private Label
Brands:
Koffee Kup

7894 Koha Food
500 Alakawa St # 104
Honolulu, HI 96817-4576   808-845-4232
Fax: 808-841-5398
Oriental foods
President: Paul Kim
Estimated Sales: $ 5 - 10 Million
Number Employees: 20-49

7895 Kohler Mix Specialties
4041 Highway 61 N
White Bear Lake, MN 55110-4631   651-426-1633
Fax: 651-426-7876 www.deanfoods.com
Processor of dairy products including ice cream
mixes, ice milk, shakes, etc
Director National Sales: Mark Johnson
VP Procurement: Lee Groehler
Plant Manager: Matt Mensink
Estimated Sales: $100+ Million
Number Employees: 100-249
Parent Co: Michael Foods
Type of Packaging: Consumer, Food Service

7896 Kohler Mix Specialties
100 Milk Ln
Newington, CT 06111-2242   860-666-1511
Fax: 860-667-9274   fabbri@michaelfoods.com
www.michaelfoods.com
Processor of soft serve ice cream and shake mix
President: Gregg Ostrander
Plt. Mgr.: Peter Fabbri
Plant Manager: John Lacombe
Estimated Sales: $ 50 - 100 Million
Number Employees: 50-99
Parent Co: Michael Foods
Type of Packaging: Food Service

7897 Kokinos Purity Ice CreamCompany
PO Box 31
Monroe, LA 71210-0031   318-322-2930
Processor of ice cream
President: Henry Kokinos
Number Employees: 10-19
Type of Packaging: Consumer, Food Service

7898 Kokopelli's Kitchen
9116 N Cave Creek Rd
Phoenix, AZ 85020-2525   602-943-8882
Fax: 602-943-8740   888-943-9802
kokopellis@mindspring.com
www.kokopelliskitchen.com
Manufacturer of wide array of gourmet Southwest
dry-mixes: bread, muffins, pancakes, bean and
soups, rice dishes, salad dressings, salsas, enchilada
sauce and cocoas
President: Cheryl Joseph
Estimated Sales: $ .5 - 1 million
Number Employees: 1-4
Number of Products: 45
Sq. footage: 3000
Parent Co: Kokopelli's Kitchen
Type of Packaging: Consumer, Bulk

Brands:
KOKOPELLI'S KITCHEN

7899 Kolatin Real Kosher Gelatin
325 Second Street
Lakewood, NJ 08701   732-364-8700
Fax: 732-370-0877   info@koshergelatin.com
www.koshergelatin.com
Supplier of real kosher gelatin used in confectionary products, meats, pates and as a thickener and emulsifier in soups, gravies and sauces.
Parent Co: Glatech Productions

7900 (HQ)Kolb-Lena Cheese Company
3990 N Sunnyside Rd
Lena, IL 61048-9613   815-369-4577
Fax: 815-369-4914
Manufacturer of cheese including camembert, baby and bay Swiss, brie, feta and soft; also, gourmet foods
Manager: Tom Dahmen
Estimated Sales: $35.7 Million
Number Employees: 50-99
Parent Co: BC USA
Type of Packaging: Consumer, Food Service
Brands:
DELICO

7901 Kollar Cookies
PO Box 502
Woodbridge, NJ 07095-0502   732-229-3364
Fax: 732-750-1960   ibn@home.com
www.kollarcookies.com
Cookies
Owner: Janice Kollar
Estimated Sales: $ 1-2.5 Million
Number Employees: 5
Brands:
Kollar

7902 Kombucha King International
PO Box 44203
Phoenix, AZ 85064-4203   602-263-0792
Fax: 602-263-0792   800-896-9676
President: John Gutowski

7903 Kombucha Wonder Drink
P.O.Box 4244
Portland, OR 97208-4244   503-224-7331
Fax: 503-224-2295   877-224-7331
info@teaports.com   www.wonderdrink.com
Tea and herbal infusions
Founder/Owner: Steve Lee
CEO: Craig Decker
Research & Development: Koei Kudo
Marketing Director: Koei Kudo
Sales Director: Todd Hager
Estimated Sales: $650,000
Number Employees: 5-9
Type of Packaging: Private Label
Brands:
Empire
Teaports

7904 Kona Brewing
75-5629 Kuakini Hwy
Kailua Kona, HI 96740-1664   808-334-2739
Fax: 808-329-8869   808-334-2739
pub@konabrewingco.com
www.konabrewingco.com
Beer
President: Mattson Davis
CFO: Keith Kinsey
Quality Control: Rich Tucciarone
Marketing Director: Steve Cole
Estimated Sales: $ 30-50 Million
Number Employees: 50-99
Type of Packaging: Private Label
Brands:
Kona Brewing

7905 Kona Coffee Council
P.O.Box 9002
Kealakekua, HI 96750-9002   808-323-2911
inquiries@kona-coffee-council.com
www.kona-coffee-council.com
Coffee
Manager: Barry Gitelson
VP: Bob Foerster
Estimated Sales: $ .5 - 1 million
Number Employees: 1-4

7906 Kona Cold Lobsters Ltd
73-4460 Queen Kaahumanu Hy 103
Kailua Kona, HI 96740-2637   808-329-4332
Fax: 808-326-2882
Lobsters
President: Joseph Wilson
Estimated Sales: Less than $300,000
Number Employees: 5-9

7907 Kona Kava Coffee Company
PO Box 168
Philo, CA 95466-0168   707-985-3913
Fax: 707-895-3913
Coffee
Owner: Jonathan O Bergin
Estimated Sales: Under $500,000
Number Employees: 1-4

7908 Kona Premium Coffee Company
75 Keke St
Keauhou, HI 96739   808-322-9550
Fax: 808-322-9275   888-322-9550
info@konapremium.com
www.konapremium.com
Commercial and retail coffee
Owner: Robert Millslagle
CFO: Jeff Woode
Director of Sales: James Lenhart
VP Operations: Peter Donovan
Estimated Sales: $ 20-50 Million
Number Employees: 20-49
Type of Packaging: Private Label
Brands:
Kona Coffee
Royal Konaccino

7909 Konetzkos Market
P.O.Box 341
Browerville, MN 56438-0341   320-594-2915
Processor of smoked meat and sausage
Owner: Jim Becker
Estimated Sales: Less than $500,000
Number Employees: 1-4
Type of Packaging: Consumer

7910 Konto's Foods
P.O.Box 628
Paterson, NJ 07544-0628   973-278-2800
Fax: 973-278-7943   info@kontos.com
www.kontos.com
Manufacturer of hand stretched flat bread and Kontos fillo dough and fillo products.
Founder/President: Evripides Kontos
Vice President/Director of Sales: Steve Kontos
Estimated Sales: $ 50-100 Million
Number Employees: 50-99
Sq. footage: 65000
Type of Packaging: Food Service
Brands:
Konto's

7911 Kookaburra Liquorice Co
17461 147th Street SE
#14A
Monroe, WA 98272   360-805-6858
Fax: 360-805-6859   sales@kookaburrapacific.com
www.kookaburrapacific.com
licorice
President/Owner: Donald Cook
CEO: Bradley Cook
Number Employees: 5

7912 Kool Ice & Seafood Company
110 Washington St
Cambridge, MD 21613-2804   410-228-2300
Fax: 410-228-1027
www.freshmarylandseafood.com
Seafood
Owner: Dave Nickerson
Estimated Sales: $ 5 - 10 Million
Number Employees: 20-49

7913 Kopali Organics
8101 Biscayne Blvd
#609
Miami, FL 33138-4668   305-751-7341
Fax: 305-751-7344   www.kopaliorganics.com
organic foods
COO: Norman Brooks

7914 (HQ)Kopper's Chocolate Specialty Company
39 Clarkson St
New York, NY 10014-3605   212-243-0220
Fax: 212-243-3316   800-325-0026
info@kopperschocolate.com
www.kopperschocolates.com
Processor, importer and exporter of confectionery items including chocolate covered espresso beans, chocolate covered gummy bears and Danish mint lentils.
President: Jeffrey Alexander
Estimated Sales: $7800000
Number Employees: 1-4

7915 Koppert Cress USA
23423 Middle Rd
Route 48
Cutchogue, NY 11935   516-437-5700
Fax: 516-437-5703   info.usa@koppertcress.com
www.koppertcress.com
micro-vegetables

7916 Korbs Baking Company
540 Pawtucket Avenue
Pawtucket, RI 02860-6098   401-726-4422
Fax: 401-726-4446
Baked goods
President: Edmund Korb
Estimated Sales: $ 1-2.5 Million
Number Employees: 50

7917 Korinek & Company
4828 W 25th St
Cicero, IL 60804-3432   773-242-1917
Fax: 773-242-1917
Processors of jams and jellies for bakeries
President: George F Korinek
Estimated Sales: $1800000
Number Employees: 5-9
Type of Packaging: Food Service

7918 Kornfections
14516 Lee Rd # C
Chantilly, VA 20151-1638   703-930-5795
Fax: 703-817-9560   800-469-8886
kornfections@verizon.net
www.kornfections.com
Gourmet popcorn and confections.
President: Jay Yang
Marketing/Public Relations: Jerry Lerner
Estimated Sales: $ 3 - 5 Million
Number Employees: 5-9
Number of Brands: 1
Number of Products: 22
Sq. footage: 2400
Type of Packaging: Consumer, Food Service, Private Label, Bulk

7919 Korte Meat Processors
810 Deal St
Highland, IL 62249-1313   618-654-3813
Fax: 618-654-8207
Processor of beef and pork
Owner: Dave Korte
Estimated Sales: $ 3 - 5 Million
Number Employees: 5-9
Type of Packaging: Consumer, Bulk

7920 Koryo Winery Company
13719 Alma Ave
Gardena, CA 90249-2513   310-532-3240
Fax: 310-532-3240
Wines
President: Sarah Kym
Operations Manager: Roy Kym
Estimated Sales: Less than $500,000
Number Employees: 20-49
Type of Packaging: Private Label
Brands:
Dong Dong Joo Rice Wine
Mackoly Rice Wine
Sochu Distilled Rice

7921 Kosher French Baguettes
683 McDonald Ave
Brooklyn, NY 11218-4913   718-633-4994
Baguettes
Owner: Paul Gima
Estimated Sales: $300,000-500,000
Number Employees: 5-9

7922 Kossar's Bialystoker Kuchen Bakery
367 Grand St
New York, NY 10002-3951   212-473-4810
          Fax: 212-253-2146   877-424-2597
          kossarsmail@kossarsbialys.com
                www.kossarsbialys.com
Bakery products
     Owner: Danny Cohen
     Owner: Danny Cohen
Estimated Sales: $500,000-$1 Million
Number Employees: 10-19
Brands:
     Bialy
     Kashruth

7923 Kosto Food Products Company
1325 N Old Rand Rd
Wauconda, IL 60084-3302   847-487-2600
     Fax: 847-487-2654 www.kostofoods.com
Processor and exporter of salad dressings, food col-
orings, pudding and ice cream mixes; importer of
colorants, stabilizers, ice cream mixes, drink crys-
tals, meat extenders and puddings
     President: Donald F Colby
     CEO: Steve Colby
     Sales Director: Richard Gray
Estimated Sales: $1300000
Number Employees: 10-19
Type of Packaging: Consumer, Food Service, Pri-
vate Label, Bulk
Brands:
     Dari Pride
     Food Pak
     Freezerta
     Kosto
     Mack's
     Mrs Slaby's
     Slushade

7924 Kotarides Baking Company of Virginia
PO Box 2056
Norfolk, VA 23501-2056   757-461-1000
                Fax: 757-622-1260
Processor of bread and rolls
     Dir./Human Resources: Walt Basnight
Estimated Sales: $ 10 - 20 Million
Number Employees: 450
Brands:
     GOLDEN GRAIN
     MARY JANE
     NATURAL GRAIN

7925 Kowalski Sausage Company
2270 Holbrook St
Hamtramck, MI 48212-3487   313-873-8200
          Fax: 313-873-4220   800-482-2400
                www.kowality.com
Processor and packer of sausage
     President: Michael Kowalski
Estimated Sales: $32800000
Number Employees: 100-249
Number of Products: 75
Type of Packaging: Consumer, Food Service

7926 Koyo Foods
2410 Santa Clara Street
Richmond, CA 94804-5622   510-527-7066
                Fax: 510-527-0178
Rice cakes

7927 Kozlowski Farms
5566 Hwy 116
Forestville, CA 95436-9697   707-887-1587
          Fax: 707-887-9650   800-473-2767
          koz@kozlowskifarms.com
                www.kozlowskifarms.com
Manufacturer of natural and specialty food products,
including: 100% fruit spreads, jams, mustards, preserves, chutneys, jellys, fruit butters, dessert sauces,
steak and BBQ sauces, fruit vinegar, salad dressings
and chipotle sauces.CCOF apples on Pinot Noir
grapes are farmed on the property. Visitors are also
welcomed to visit the farm and try fresh, homemade
fruit tarts, pies and cookies from the bakery. Most
products certified Kosher.
     President: Carmen Kozlowski
     CEO: Perry Kozlowski
     CFO: Cindy Kozlowski-Hayworth
     VP: Carol Kozlowski-Every
Estimated Sales: $1,000,000
Number Employees: 20-49

Number of Brands: 1
Number of Products: 90
Sq. footage: 20000
Type of Packaging: Consumer, Private Label
Brands:
     Kozlowski Farms
     Sonoma County Classics

7928 Kozy Shack
83 Ludy St
Hicksville, NY 11801-5114   516-870-3000
     Fax: 516-870-3001 www.kozyshack.com
Manufacturer and exporter of ready-to-eat puddings
including rice, tapioca, chocolate, vanilla, banana;
also, flan
     Chairman: Vincent Gruppuso
     President/CEO: Lenny Pippin
     Marketing Manager: Diana Gruppuso
     VP Business Development: John Rooney
Estimated Sales: $100 Million
Number Employees: 250-499
Sq. footage: 70000
Type of Packaging: Consumer, Food Service, Bulk
Brands:
     KOZY SHACK

7929 Kraemer's Wisconsin Cheese
1173 N 4th St
Watertown, WI 53098-3201   920-261-6363
          Fax: 920-261-9606   800-236-8033
          kwcheese@kraemercheese.com
                www.kraemercheese.com
Cheese
     President: Richard Kraemer
Estimated Sales: Below $ 5 Million
Number Employees: 5-9

7930 Kraft
7 Campus Dr
Parsippany, NJ 07054-4413   973-292-1755
          Fax: 973-682-2153 www.nabisco.com
Processor of cookies, crackers, cereals, sauces, mus-
tard, nuts, snacks, candy, gum, condiments, baking
powder, pasta, dessert mixes, puddings, etc
     President: Samer Chebib
     CIO/EVP: Doreen Wright
Estimated Sales: $100+ Million
Number Employees: 250-499
Parent Co: Kraft Foods
Type of Packaging: Consumer, Food Service, Pri-
vate Label, Bulk
Brands:
     BARNUM'S ANIMAL
     CHEESE CHIPS
     CHIPS AHOY!
     CREAM SAVERS
     CREAM SAVERS SOFT CANDY
     FUNFRUITS
     HANDY SNACKS
     HONEY MAID
     LIFESAVERS
     LIFESAVERS GUMMIES
     LIFESAVERS KICKERZ
     NABISCO
     NEWTONS
     NILLA
     NUTTER BUTTER
     OREO
     PACK'S 2 GO
     RITZ RITZ BITS
     SNACK WELLS
     TEDDYGRAHAMS
     TERRY'S CHOCOLATE
     TRISCUIT
     TROLLI
     WHEATTHINS

7931 (HQ)Kraft Canada Headquarters
95 Moatfield Drive
Don Mills, ON M3B 3L6
Canada   416-441-5000
          Fax: 416-441-5328   800-268-7808
                www.kraftcanada.com/
Manufacturer and distribution of grocery products;
canned fruits and vegetables, canned soups, pickles,
jam, baking products, seasonings and dressings,
cookies and crackers.
     President Kraft Canada: Fred Schaeffer
     CEO: Wynn Willard
     CFO: Angela Holtham
     VP & General Manager: Dino Bianco
     Manager Export Sales/Marketing: Larry Inglis
     Associate Director Corporate Affairs: Lynne
     Galia

Estimated Sales: $50 Million
Number Employees: 7100
Parent Co: Kraft Foods
Type of Packaging: Consumer, Food Service

7932 (HQ)Kraft Canada Lake ShoreBakery
2150 Lake Shore Blvd W
Toronto, ON M8V 1A3
Canada   416-503-6000
     Fax: 406-503-6100 www.kraftcanada.com/
Manufacturer and distribution of bakery products.
     President Kraft Canada: Fred Schaeffer
     CEO: Wynn Willard
     CFO: Angela Holtham
     VP General Manager: Dino Bianco
     Manager Export Sales/Marketing: Larry Inglis
     Associate Director Corporate Affairs: Lynne
     Galia
Number Employees: 500-999
Parent Co: Kraft Foods
Type of Packaging: Consumer, Food Service

7933 (HQ)Kraft Canada Nabisco Division
10 Park Lawn Road
Toronto, ON M8Y 3H8
Canada   416-253-3200
     Fax: 416-253-3210 www.kraftcanada.com/
Manufacturer and distributor of Nabisco brand prod-
ucts including cookies and crackers.
     President Kraft Canada: Fred Schaeffer
     CEO: Wynn Willard
     CFO: Angela Holtham
     Manager Export Sales/Marketing: Larry Inglis
     Associate Director Corporate Affairs: Lynne
     Galia
Number Employees: 500-999
Parent Co: Kraft Foods
Type of Packaging: Consumer, Food Service

7934 Kraft Food Ingredients
8000 Horizon Center Blvd
Memphis, TN 38133-5197   901-381-6500
     Fax: 901-381-6524 www.kraftfoodscompany.com
Processor and exporter of rice and dessert prepara-
tions including coconut, tapioca and gelatin; proces-
sor of maple syrup, dry drink mixes and stuffing
     Sls. Mgr. (Eastern): Bruce Boehmer
     Logistics Assoc.: Sharon Dean
Number Employees: 500-999
Parent Co: Kraft Foods
Type of Packaging: Consumer, Food Service, Pri-
vate Label, Bulk

7935 Kraft Food Ingredients
8000 Horizon Center Blvd
Memphis, TN 38133-5197   901-381-6500
     Fax: 901-381-6524 www.kraftfoodscompany.com
Processor and exporter of food ingredients: natural
and processed cheese, savory flavors, soft cheese,
caramel, marshmallow, mustard cheese powders,
fillings, seasonings and sauces, candy, coconut,
crackers and cookies.
     Chairman/CEO: Irene Rosenfeld
     EVP/Global Business Services & Strategy: David
     Brearton
     EVP/CFO: James Dollive
     EVP/Corporate Legal Affairs: Marc Firestone
     EVP/Global Technology & Quality: Jean Spence
     EVP/Chief Marketing Officer: Jeri Finard
     EVP/Global Human Resources: Karen May
Number Employees: 500-999
Parent Co: Kraft Foods
Type of Packaging: Bulk
Brands:
     A1
     Baker's
     Bulls-Eye
     Chips Ahoy
     Cuisines of the World
     Exceed
     Flavors of Cooking
     Grey Poupon
     Grill Flavor
     Honey Maid
     Kraft
     Miracle Whip
     Nabisco
     Open Pit
     Oreo
     Oscar Mayer
     Philadelphia

Premium Saltine
Ritz

7936 Kraft Foodskery
7300 S Kedzie Ave
Chicago, IL 60629-3595 773-925-4300
Fax: 773-476-6269 800-572-3847
www.kraftfoods.com
Manufacturer and exporter of baked goods including cookies and crackers
Chairman/CEO: Irene Rosenfeld
EVP & CFO: Timothy McLevish
General Manager: Dave Lamy
EVP Chief Marketing Officer: Mary Beth West
EVP Operations & Business Services: David Brearton
Manager: Ray Bazarko
Purchasing Agent: Mike Will
Estimated Sales: $2.3 Billion
Number Employees: 21
Sq. footage: 300000
Parent Co: Kraft Foods
Type of Packaging: Consumer
Brands:
WHOLE GRAIN CHIPS ALOY
WHOLE GRAIN FIG NEWTONS
WHOLE GRAIN WHEAT THINS

7937 Kraft Foods
1400 Murphy Ave SW
Atlanta, GA 30310-4006 404-756-6000
Fax: 404-756-6027 www.kraftfoodscompany.com
Manufacturer of baked goods including biscuits, cookies and crackers.
Chairman/CEO: Irene Rosenfeld
EVP Global Business Services & Strategy: David Brearton
EVP & CFO: James Dollive
EVP Corporate Legal Affairs: Marc Firestone
EVP Global Technology & Quality: Jean Spence
EVP/Chief Marketing Officer: Jeri Finard
EVP Global Human Resources: Karen May
Plant Manager: Jim Diehl
Estimated Sales: $100+ Million
Number Employees: 500-999
Parent Co: Kraft Foods
Type of Packaging: Consumer
Brands:
Breakstones
Breyers
Country Time
Crystal Light
Handi Snacks
Jack's Pizza
Jell-O
Kraft Cooking
Krafts Food
Minute Rice
Post Healthy Classics
Stove Top

7938 Kraft Foods
P.O.Box 300
Albany, MN 56307-0300 320-845-2131
Fax: 320-845-2402 www.kraftfoodscompany.com
Manufacturer of cheese powders
Chairman/CEO: Irene Rosenfeld
EVP Global Business Services & Strategy: David Brearton
EVP/CFO: James Dollive
EVP Corporate Legal Affairs: Marc Firestone
EVP/Global Technology & Quality: Jean Spence
EVP/Chief Marketing Officer: Jeri Finard
EVP/Global Human Resources: Karen May
Plant Manager: Darin Zehr
Estimated Sales: $20-50 Million
Number Employees: 50-99
Parent Co: Kraft Foods
Type of Packaging: Consumer

7939 Kraft Foods
2035 E Bennett St
Springfield, MO 65804-1726 417-881-2701
Fax: 417-881-2139 www.kraftfoods.com

Manufacturer of natural and processed cheese, cream cheese, macaroni and cheese and pasta.
President: W Anthony Vernon
EVP/Global Business Services & Strategy: David Brearton
EVP/CFO: James Dollive
EVP/Corporate Legal Affairs: Marc Firestone
EVP/Global Technology & Quality: Jean Spence
EVP/Chief Marketing Officer: Jeri Finard
EVP/Global Human Resources: Karen May
Plant Manager: Joseph Metzer
Number Employees: 120
Parent Co: Kraft Foods
Type of Packaging: Consumer
Brands:
A1 STEAK SAUCE
ALTOIDS
BAKER'S
BREAKSTONE'S COTTAGE CHEESE
BREYER'S YOGURT
COUNTRY TIME
CRYSTAL LIGHT
DIGIORNO RISING CRUST
GENERAL FOOD INTERNATIONAL COFFEE
GRAPE NUTS
HANDI-SNACKS
HOP ABOARD
JACK'S PIZZA
JACOBS
JELL-O
KNOX
KOOL-AID
KRAFT CHEESE
KRAFT MACARONI AND CHEESE
LUNCHABLES
MAXWELL HOUSE
MILLKA
MINUTE RICE
MIRACLE WHIP
OREO
OSCAR MAYER
PHILADELPHIA
PLANTERS PEANUTS
POLLY-O TRATTORIA
POST HEALTHY CLASSIC
SHAKE 'N BAKE
STOVE TOP
TERRY'S
TOBLERONE
UNEEDA BISCUITS
VELVEETA

7940 Kraft Foods
2340 Forest Ln
Garland, TX 75042-7924 972-272-7511
Fax: 972-485-7706 www.kraftfoodscompany.com
Manufacturer of barbecue sauce, salad dressing, mayonnaise and mustard.
Chairman/CEO: Irene Rosenfeld
EVP/Global Business Services & Strategy: David Brearton
EVP/CFO: James Dollive
EVP/Corporate Legal Affairs: Marc Firestone
EVP/Global Technology & Quality: Jean Spence
EVP/Chief Marketing Officer: Jeri Finard
EVP/Global Human Resources: Karen May
Plant Manager: Wayne Parrish
Estimated Sales: $100+ Million
Number Employees: 100-249
Parent Co: Kraft Foods
Type of Packaging: Consumer

7941 Kraft Foods
261 Delaware St
Walton, NY 13856-1099 607-865-7131
Fax: 607-865-5830 www.kraftfoodscompany.com
Manufacturer of cultured products including sour cream, cottage cheese and flavored dips.
Chairman/CEO: Irene Rosenfeld
EVP/Global Business Services & Strategy: David Brearton
EVP/CFO: James Dollive
EVP/Corporate Legal Affairs: Marc Firestone
EVP/Global Technology & Quality: Jean Spence
EVP/Chief Marketing Officer: Jeri Finard
EVP/Global Human Resources: Karen May
Number Employees: 50-99
Parent Co: Kraft Foods
Type of Packaging: Consumer

7942 Kraft Foods
140 Spring St
Avon, NY 14414-1153 585-226-4400
Fax: 585-226-4306 gmanning@kraft.com
www.kraftfoodscompany.com
Manufacturer and exporter of frozen whipped dessert toppings and packaged lunches including crackers, cheese and cold cuts.
Manager: Greg Manning
EVP/Global Business Services & Strategy: David Brearton
EVP/CFO: James Dollive
EVP/Corporate Legal Affairs: Marc Firestone
Quality Manager: Debbie Grosse
EVP/Chief Marketing Officer: Jeri Finard
EVP/Global Human Resources: Karen May
Estimated Sales: $500 Million to $1 Billion
Number Employees: 450
Sq. footage: 450000
Parent Co: Kraft Foods
Type of Packaging: Consumer, Food Service
Brands:
WHOLE GRAIN WHEAT THINS

7943 Kraft Foods
7352 Industrial Blvd
Allentown, PA 18106-9344 610-398-0311
Fax: 610-366-6560 www.kraftfoodscompany.com
Manufacturer and exporter of cheese and salad dressing.
Chairman/CEO: Irene Rosenfeld
EVP/Global Business Services & Strategy: David Brearton
EVP/CFO: James Dollive
EVP/Corporate Legal Affairs: Marc Firestone
EVP/Global Technology & Quality: Jean Spence
EVP/Chief Marketing Officer: Jeri Finard
EVP/Global Human Resources: Karen May
Plant Manager: Rusty Moore
Estimated Sales: $235.4 Million
Number Employees: 500-999
Parent Co: Kraft Foods
Type of Packaging: Consumer, Food Service, Private Label, Bulk

7944 (HQ)Kraft Foods
3 Lakes Dr
Northfield, IL 60093 847-646-2000
Fax: 847-646-6005 800-323-0768
gec@kraft.com www.kraftfoodscompany.com
Manufacturer of mayonnaise, cheeses, sauces, snacks, meats, cereals, etc.
Chairman/CEO: Irene Rosenfeld
EVP/CFO: Timothy McLevish
Senior Director Corporate Affairs: Renee Zahery
EVP/Global Technology & Quality: Jean Spence
EVP/Chief Marketing Officer: Jeri Finard
EVP/Global Category Development: John Baxter
EVP/Corporate Legal Affairs: Marc Firestone
EVP Operations/Business Services: David Brearton
EVP/Global Supply Chain: Franz Josef Vogelsana

Estimated Sales: $34 Billion
Number Employees: 97,000
Type of Packaging: Consumer, Food Service
Brands:
A.1
ATHENOS
BACK TO NATURE
BAKER'S
BALANCE
BALANCE CARBWELL
BARNUM'S ANIMALS
BOCA
BREAKSTONE'S
CAPRI SUN
CHEESE NIPS
CHEEZ WIZ
COOL WHIP
CORN NUTS
COUNTRY TIME
CREAM OF WHEAT
CRYSTAL LIGHT
DIGIORO
GENERAL FOODS INTERNATIONAL
GEVALIA
GOOD SEASONS
GREY POUPON
HANDI-SNACKS
HONEY MAID
JACK'S
JELL-0
JET-PUFFED

KNOX GELATINE
KNUDSEN
KOOL-AID SLUSHIES
KRAFT
KRAFT DELI DELUXE
LIGHT N' LIVELY
LOUIS RICH
LUNCHABLES
MINUTE
MIRACLE WHIP
NEWTONS
NUTTER BUTTER
OSCAR MAYER
POLLY-O
POST
RITZ
SANKA
STELLA D'ORO
SURE-JELL
TEDDY GRAHAMS
TOMBSTONE
TRISCUIT
VELVEETA
WHEAT THINS
WHOLE GRAIN CHIPS AHOY!
WHOLE GRAIN FIG NEWTONS
WHOLE GRAIN WHEAT THINS
YUBAN

7945 Kraft Foods
100 Deforest Ave
East Hanover, NJ 07936-2813   973-503-2000
    Fax: 201-794-4997 www.kraftfoodscompany.com
Processor of cookies and crackers.
    Chairman/CEO: Samer Chebib
    EVP/Global Technology & Quality: Jean Spence
    EVP/Chief Marketing Officer: Jeri Finard
    EVP/Global Human Resources: Karen May
    Plant Manager: Calvin Reed
    Purchasing Agent: Cathy Connor
Estimated Sales: $ 20 - 50 Million
Number Employees: 1,000-4,999
Parent Co: Kraft Foods
Type of Packaging: Consumer, Food Service
Brands:
    Nabisco

7946 Kraft Foods
100 Deforest Ave
East Hanover, NJ 07936-2813   973-503-2000
                www.kraftfoodscompany.com
Processor of cookies, crackers, biscuits and snacks;
also, ice cream cones, process cheese spreads, gra-
nola bars, pretzels, potato and tortilla chips, pie
crusts, cereal bars, etc
    President: James Postl
Estimated Sales: $ 20 - 50 Million
Number Employees: 500-999
Parent Co: Kraft Foods
Type of Packaging: Consumer, Food Service

7947 Kraft Foods
3 Lakes Dr
Northfield, IL 60093   847-646-2000
        Fax: 847-646-6005 800-323-0768
                www.kraftfoodscompany.com
Processor of macaroni and cheese dinners, pasta sal-
ads, salad dressings, mayonnaise, barbecue sauces,
candies, malted milks, toppings, jellies, preserves,
fruit spreads, cheeses, cream cheese, jams, cottage
cheese, yogurt, etc.
    Chairman/CEO: Irene Rosenfeld
    EVP/CFO: Timothy McLevish
    EVP/Global Technology & Quality: Jean Spence
    EVP/Chief Marketing Officer: Jeri Finard
    EVP Operations: David Brearton
Estimated Sales: $40.4 Billion
Number Employees: 97,000
Parent Co: Kraft Foods
Type of Packaging: Consumer, Food Service, Pri-
    vate Label, Bulk

7948 (HQ)Kraft Foods
3 Lakes Dr
Northfield, IL 60093   847-646-2000
    Fax: 847-646-6005 jeinsiedel@kraft.com
            www.kraftfoodscompany.com

North American food business of Philip Morris
Companies. Packaged food company
    Chairman/CEO: Irene Rosenfeld
    EVP/CFO: Timothy McLevish
    Executive VP: Paula Sneed
    Sales Director: Philip Pellegrino
    Public Relations: Kathy Knuth
    EVP Operations: David Brearton
    Marketing Director: Michael Simmons
    Purchasing Manager: Alene Korby
Estimated Sales: $40.4 Billion
Number Employees: 97,000
Parent Co: Philip Morris Companies
Type of Packaging: Consumer, Food Service, Pri-
    vate Label, Bulk
Brands:
    ATHENOS
    BAKER'S
    BOCA
    BREAKSTONE'S
    BULL'S EYE
    CALUMET
    CERTO
    CHEEZ WHIZ
    CHURNY
    CLAUSSEN
    COOL WHIP
    CRAKER BARREL
    California Pizza
    Capri-Sun
    Carte Noire
    Country Time
    Crystal Light
    D-ZERTA
    DIGIORNO
    DREAM WHIP
    EASY CHEESE
    EVER FRESH
    GOOD SEASON
    GREY POUPON
    General Foods International
    Gevalia
    HANDI-SANCKS
    HARVEST MOON
    HOFFMAN'S
    HONEY MAID
    KNOX GELATINE
    KNUDSEN
    KRAFT 2% MILK SINGLES
    KRAFT DELI DELUXE
    KRAFT DELUXE
    KRAFT FREE SINGLES
    KRAFT SINGLES
    Kool-Aid
    Kool-Aid
    LIGHT N' EASY
    Louis Rich
    MINUTE
    MIRACLE WHIP
    Maxim
    NABISCO
    NILLA
    OLD ENGLISH
    OREO
    Orea
    Oscar Mayer
    PHILADELPHIA CREAM CHEESE
    POLLY-O
    POSTUM
    STOVE TOP
    SURE-JELL
    Sanka
    Starbucks
    TEMP-TEE
    Taco Bell Dinner
    Tang
    VELVEETA
    WOODY'S
    Yuban

**7949 Kraft Foods Biscuit Confections &
Snacks**
100 Deforest Ave
East Hanover, NJ 07936-2813   973-503-2000
                www.kraftfoodscompany.com
    Executive VP: Daryl Brewster
Estimated Sales: $ 20 - 50 Million
Number Employees: 500-999
Brands:
    100-CALORIE
    AIR CRISPS
    ALTOIDS
    ATHENOS

BAKER'S
BALANCE BAR
BARNUM'S ANIMALS
CHEESE NIPS
CHEEZ WHIZ
CHIPS AHOY!
COOL WHIP
CORN NUTS
COUNTRY TIME
CREMESAVERS
CRYSTAL LIGHT
DIGIORNO
GENERAL FOODS INTERNATIONAL COF-
FEES
GEVALIA
GOOD SEASONS
HANDI-SNACKS
HONEY MAID
JACK'S
JELL-O
KOOL-AID
KRAFT CARAMELS
KRAFT MARSHMALLOWS
LIFE SAVERS
LIGHT N' LIVELY
LUNCHABLES
MALLOMARS
MAXWELL HOUSE
MILKA
MINUTE
MIRACLE WHIP
NABISCO FRUIT SNACKS
NABISCO FUN FRUITS
NABISCO GRAHAM
NEWTONS
NILLA
NUTTER BUTTER
OASIS
OSCAR MAYER
PLANTERS
POLLY-0
POST
RITZ
SNACKWELL'S
STARBUCKS
STONED WHEAT THINS
STOVE TOP
SURE-JELL
TACO BELL
TEDDY GRAHAMS
TERRY'S
TOBLER
TOBLERONE
TOMBSTONE
TRISCUIT
TROLLI
VELVEETA
WHEAT THINS
YUBAN

7950 Kraft Foods North America
P.O.Box 1460
Suffolk, VA 23439-1460   757-925-3000
        Fax: 757-925-3082 www.kraftfoods.com
Manufacturer and exporter of peanuts.
    Chairman/CEO: Irene Rosenfeld
    EVP/Global Business Services & Strategy: David
    Brearton
    EVP/CFO: James Dollive
    EVP/Corporate & Legal Affairs: Marc Firestone
    EVP/Global Technology & Quality: Jean Spence
    EVP/Chief Marketing Officer: Jeri Finard
    EVP/Global Human Resources: Karen May
    Plant Manager: Dan Huss
Estimated Sales: $100+ Million
Number Employees: 500-999
Parent Co: Nabisco
Type of Packaging: Consumer
Brands:
    100-CALORIE PACKS
    A1 STEAK SAUCE
    ATHENOS
    BAKERS CHOCOLATE
    BREAKSTONE'S COTTAGE CHEESE
    BREYERS YOGURT
    CAPRI SUN
    CHEEZ WHIZ
    COOL WHIP
    COUNTRY TIME
    CREAM OF WHEAT
    CRYSTAL LIGHT
    GENERAL FOODS INTERNATIONAL COF-
    FEES
    GOOD SEASONS

GREY POUPON
HANDI-SNACKS
IT'S PIZZA ANYTIME
JACK'S PIZZA
JELL-O
JET PUFFED MARSHMALLOWS
KNOX
KOOL-AID
KRAFT DIABETIC CHOICES
KRAFT EASY MAC
KRAFT PARMESAN
LIGHT DONE RIGHT
MAXWELL HOUSE
MINUTE RICE
MINUTE TAPIOCA
MIRACLE WHIP
OSCAR MAYER
PEAK FREENS
POLLY-O
POST CEREAL
POST HEALTHY CLASSICS
RED OVAL FARMS
STELLA DORA
STOVE TOP STUFFING
SUREJELL
TANG
VELVEETA

7951 Kraft Foods/Atlantic Gelatin
1 Hill St # 1
Woburn, MA 01801-4695   781-933-2800
          Fax: 781-935-1566 info@cangel.com
          www.kraftfoods.com
Gelatin and inedible animal oil.
  Chairman/CEO: Richard Lerner
  EVP/Global Business Services & Strategy: Roger
  Deromedi
  EVP/CFO: James Dollive
  EVP/Corporate Legal Affairs: Sanjay Khosla
  EVP/Global Technology & Quality: Jean Spence
  EVP/Chief Marketing Officer: Jeri Finard
  EVP/Global Human Resources: Karen May
  Plant Manager: Kathleen Pigott
Estimated Sales: $ 50-100 Million
Number Employees: 250-499
Number of Brands: 7
Number of Products: 11
Parent Co: Kraft Foods
Brands:
  A Clean Plate Every Time
  A1 Steak Sauce
  Breakfast Made Right
  Breakstone
  Comida Kraft
  Country Time
  Crystal Light
  Hop Aboard
  JELL-O
  Jack's Pizza
  Knox
  Kraft Cooking
  Oh Yeah! Kool-Aid
  Post Healthy Classics
  Stove Top

7952 Kraft Foods/Knudson Products
715 N Divisadero St
Visalia, CA 93291-4607   559-685-0790
      Fax: 559-713-7942 800-323-0768
          www.kraftfoodscompany.com
Processor of powdered milk and butter, cottage
cheese and sour cream.
  Chairman/CEO: Irene C Rosenfeld
  EVP/Global Business Services & Strategy: David
  Brearton
  EVP/CFO: James Dollive
  Finance Executive: Jeff Eddy
  EVP/Global Technology & Quality: Jean Spence
  EVP/Chief Marketing Officer: Jeri Finard
  EVP/Global Human Resources: Karen May
  Plant Manager: Favisto Chavez
Estimated Sales: $ 20-50 Million
Number Employees: 100-249
Parent Co: Kraft Foods
Type of Packaging: Consumer, Food Service, Pri-
  vate Label, Bulk
Brands:
  Crystal Light
  Jacobs House coffees
  Kraft
  Maxwell House coffees
  Oreo cookies
  Philadelphia

Ritz crackers.
Toblerone chocolates

7953 Kraft Foodservices
3110 Cherry Palm Dr # 300
Tampa, FL 33619-8373   813-744-2750
          Fax: 813-744-2675 800-551-2559
          www.kraftfoods.com
Processor of fresh, frozen, canned, pre-portioned
and processed meat and turkey; also, coffee.
  Chairman/CEO: Richard Lerner
  EVP/Global Business Services & Strategy: Roger
  K Deromedi
  EVP/Global Technology & Quality: Jean Spence
  EVP/Chief Marketing Officer: Jeri Finard
  EVP/Global Human Resources: Karen May
Estimated Sales: $ 10 - 20 Million
Number Employees: 20-49
Parent Co: Kraft Foods
Type of Packaging: Food Service
Brands:
  Crystal Light
  Jacobs and Maxwell House
  Kraft
  Oreo
  Philadelphia
  Ritz
  Toblerone

7954 Kraft Pizza & Foodservice
940 S Whelen Ave
Medford, WI 54451-1745   715-748-5550
      Fax: 715-748-7330 800-323-0768
          info@kraftfoodservice.com
          www.kraftfoodservice.com
Frozen pizza and dried beef sticks
  Executive VP: John Baxter
  CEO: Roger K Deromedi
  Director Manufacturing: Mark Grassi
  Chairman: Louis C Camilleri
  Plant Manager: Gary Stanton
Estimated Sales: $ 20-50 Million
Number Employees: 500-999
Parent Co: Kraft Foods
Brands:
  All Life Coffee
  Baker's Cocoa
  Breyers Yogurt
  Caff Origins Coffee
  Calumet Baking Powder
  Kraft Grated Cheese
  Maxwell Coffee
  Maxwell House Tea
  Yuban Coffee

7955 Kraft Pizza Company
401 W North Ave
Little Chute, WI 54140-1012   920-788-0605
      Fax: 920-788-8196 www.kraftfoods.com
Manufacturer of frozen pizza.
  Chairman/CEO: Irene Rosenfeld
  EVP/Global Business Services & Strategy: David
  Brearton
  EVP/CFO: James Dollive
  EVP/Corporate Legal Affairs: Marc Firestone
  EVP/Global Technology & Quality: Jean Spence
  EVP/Chief Marketing Officer: Jeri Finard
  EVP/Global Human Resources: Karen May
Estimated Sales: $100+ Million
Number Employees: 500-999
Parent Co: Kraft Foods
Type of Packaging: Consumer, Private Label
Brands:
  CALIFORNIA PIZZA KITCHEN
  DIGIORNO
  Jack's
  TOMBSTONE

7956 Kramarczuk Sausage Company
215 E Hennepin Ave
Minneapolis, MN 55414-1013   612-379-3018
          Fax: 612-379-7693 www.kramarczuk.com
Sausages
  President: Orest Kramarczuk
Estimated Sales: $500,000-$1 Million
Number Employees: 20-49

7957 Kramer Vineyards
26830 NW Olson Rd
Gaston, OR 97119-8039   503-662-4545
          Fax: 503-662-4033 800-619-4637
  info@kramerwine.com www.kramerwine.com

Wines
  President/CEO/Winemaker: Trudy Kramer
  CEO: Kramer
  VP/Secretary/Vineyard Manager: Keith Kramer
  Marketing VP: Trudy Kramer
Estimated Sales: Less than $500,000
Number Employees: 5-9
Brands:
  Kramer

7958 Kraus & Company
3136 Martin Rd
Commerce Twp, MI 48390-1627   248-960-7555
          Fax: 248-960-7221 800-662-5871
          info@krausecompany.com
          www.krauscompany.com
Flavors, extracts, food colors, fruit preps, variegat-
ing sauces, toppings
  Co-Founder/President: Gerry Kraus
  Co-Founder/CEO: Eva Kraus
  CFO: Saad Alhir
Estimated Sales: $1-$2 Million
Number Employees: 5-9
Type of Packaging: Food Service, Bulk

7959 (HQ)Kreamo Bakers
1910 Lincolnway W
South Bend, IN 46628-2622   574-234-0188
          Fax: 574-287-1839 www.alphabaking.com
Manufacturer of bread and buns
  President: Larry Mitchell
Estimated Sales: $7 Million
Number Employees: 10-19
Type of Packaging: Consumer, Food Service

7960 Krema Nut Company
1000 Goodale Blvd
Columbus, OH 43212-3889   614-299-4131
          Fax: 614-299-1636 800-222-4132
          nuts@krema.com www.krema.com
Processor of peanut butter and nuts including ca-
shews
  President: Mike Giunta
Estimated Sales: Less than $500,000
Number Employees: 5-9
Type of Packaging: Consumer, Food Service, Pri-
  vate Label
Other Locations:
  Krema Nut Company
  Columbus OH
Brands:
  Krema

7961 Kretschmar
71 Curlew Drive
Don Mills, ON M3A 2P8
Canada   416-441-1100
          Fax: 416-441-3386 800-561-4532
  info@kretschmar.com www.kretschmar.com
Processor and exporter of sausage and smoked,
cured and processed beef, pork and poultry prod-
ucts; also, pates; private labeling available
  President: Gerhart Huber
Number Employees: 200
Type of Packaging: Private Label
Brands:
  Karl Kramer
  Kretschmar
  Royal
  Superior

7962 Krier Foods
4555 W Schroeder Dr # 190
Milwaukee, WI 53223-1400   414-355-5400
          Fax: 414-355-5577
Processor of beverages including juice and soda
  Chairman of the Board: B Bruce Krier
  Executive VP: Thoma Bretza
Estimated Sales: $36000000
Number Employees: 5-9
Type of Packaging: Consumer
Brands:
  Fruitland
  Jolly Good

7963 Krinos Foods
4700 Northern Blvd
Long Island City, NY 11101-1017   718-729-9000
          Fax: 718-361-9725 info@krinos.com
          www.krinos.com
Processor, importer and exporter of cheese, olives,
olive oil and pasta
  President: Eric Moscahlaidis
  VP Sales/Marketing: Paul Vertullo

Estimated Sales:$30400000
Number Employees: 1-4
Sq. footage: 160000
Type of Packaging: Consumer, Food Service, Bulk

7964 Krispy Bakery
532 E Lakewood Road
West Palm Beach, FL 33405-2912   561-585-5504
Baked goods
Executive V.P.: Brian Wilson
*Estimated Sales:*Under $500,000
Number Employees: 100-249

7965 Krispy Kernels
2620 Rue Watt
Sainte Foy, QC G1P 3T5
Canada   418-658-1515
Fax: 418-657-5971 info@krispykernals.com
www.krispykernels.com
Peanuts, popcorn, candy and dried fruits and nuts
Owner: Denis Jalbert
CEO: Pierce Rivard
Quality Control: Stephen Jackson
Marketing Director: Renee Maude Jalbert
Sales Director: Stephane Gravel
Plant Manager: Jacques Bieion
Purchasing Manager: Marc Parent
Sq. footage: 100000
Brands:
KRISPY KERNELS

7966 Krispy Kreme Doughnut Company
370 Knollwood St
Winston Salem, NC 27103-1835   336-725-2981
Fax: 336-733-3896 800-457-4779
customer@krispy/creme.com
www.krispykreme.com
Bakery products and coffee
Chairman/President: Scott Livengood
CFO: Michael Phalen
CEO: James H Morgan
Quality Control: Betty Anders
Buyer: Carol Craig
Manufacturing Services Director: Gene Fockman
Plant Manager: Stanley Lowry
Purchasing: Phil Hendrix
Estimated Sales:$670 Million
Number Employees: 1,000-4,999

7967 Kristian Regale
14 Birkmose Park Ln
Hudson, WI 54016-2286   715-386-8388
Fax: 715-386-9295
Manufacturer and Importer of Swedish nonalcoholic
apple and pear juice sparkle
Owner: Nancy Bieraugel
Estimated Sales:$3.4 Million
Number Employees: 7
Type of Packaging: Consumer, Food Service
Brands:
Kristian Regale

7968 Kristin Hill Winery
3330 SE Amity Dayton Hwy
Amity, OR 97101-2003   503-835-4012
Fax: 503-835-4012
Wine
Owner: Eric Aberag
Co-Owner: Eric Aberg
*Estimated Sales:*Under $300,000
Number Employees: 1-4
Type of Packaging: Private Label
Brands:
Kristin Hill

7969 Kristy Kremarie
1218 Memorial Pkwy NW
Huntsville, AL 35801-5940   256-536-7475
Fax: 256-536-7474 gkheath@mindspring.com
www.krispykreme.com
Doughnuts
Manager: Perry Harris
Estimated Sales:$ 5-9.9 Million
Number Employees: 50-99

7970 Kroger Anderson Bakery
433 Sayre St
Anderson, SC 29624-2603   864-226-9135
Fax: 864-224-6531 www.kroger.com

Processor of bakery products; wholesaler/distributor
of general line products and baked goods
Manager: Gerald Spieth
Sls. Mgr.: Jerry Iven
Quality Control: Larry Skagts
Estimated Sales:$100+ Million
Number Employees: 100-249
Parent Co: Kroger Company

7971 (HQ)Kroger Company
1014 Vine St
Cincinnati, OH 45202-1100   513-762-4000
Fax: 513-762-1160 800-576-4377
www.kroger.com
Grocery
President/COO/Director: W Rodney McMullen
Chairman/CEO: David Dillion
SVP/CFO: J Michael Schlotman
Senior VP: Don McGeorge
Manager Bakery Operations: John Masa
Estimated Sales:$76.7 Billion
Number Employees: 334,000
Brands:
Springdale Beverages
Turkey Hill
Wawa

7972 Krohn Dairy Products
N2915 County Road Ab
Luxemburg, WI 54217-7713   920-845-2901
Fax: 920-845-5466 danl@tregafoods.com
www.tregafoods.com
Processor of Italian cheeses including mozzarella
and provolone.
President: Doug Simon
VP: Mike Sipple
Estimated Sales:$ 20 - 50 Million
Number Employees: 50-99
Type of Packaging: Consumer

7973 Kronos Products
4501 W District Blvd
Chicago, IL 60632-3925   773-847-2250
Fax: 773-847-2376 800-621-0099
info@kronos.com www.kronos.com
Greek specialties, frozen
President/CEO: Mike Austin
Chairman of the Board: Joel Jacks
Controller: Margreth Chreiber
VP: Costello Bartiz
VP Operations: George Baumgarten
Estimated Sales:$ 25-49.9 Million
Number Employees: 250-499
Brands:
Kronos

7974 Kruger Foods
22958 Saklan Road
Hayward, CA 94545-1497   510-782-2636
Fax: 510-782-8130 hanskr@aol.com
Processor and exporter of condiments including rel-
ish, pickles and sauerkraut
President: Dennis Kruger
VP: Hans Kruger
Plant Manager: Eric Kruger
Estimated Sales:$22000000
Number Employees: 100
Type of Packaging: Consumer

7975 Krugers
2366 7th St W
St Paul, MN 55116-2825   651-699-1356
Fax: 651-699-9577
Processor of produce
President: William Kruger
Estimated Sales:$3600000
Number Employees: 20-49

7976 Krupka's Blueberries
2647 68th St
Fennville, MI 49408-8623   269-857-4278
Fax: 269-857-4278
Processor of blueberries
Partner: Harold Krupka
Partner: Carmen Krupka
Sales Manager: Connie Krupka
Estimated Sales:$3 Million
Number Employees: 50-99
Type of Packaging: Consumer, Bulk

7977 Kruse & Son
P.O.Box 945
Monrovia, CA 91017-0945   626-358-4536
Fax: 626-303-7349

Processor of meats
President: Dave Kruse
Estimated Sales:$3200000
Number Employees: 100-249
Type of Packaging: Consumer, Food Service

7978 Kruse Meat Products
2100 Kruse Loop
Alexander, AR 72002-8300   501-316-1046
Fax: 501-316-1046
Processor of meat products
President: Jeanne Hutchinson
Estimated Sales:$ 5 - 10 Million
Number Employees: 10-19
Type of Packaging: Consumer

7979 Kubisch Sausage Company
50400 Rizzo Dr
Shelby Twp, MI 48315-3275   586-566-4661
Fax: 586-566-8661
Sausage and other prepared meats
Owner: Vasilj Markovich
*Estimated Sales:*Less than $300,000
Number Employees: 1-4

7980 Kubla Khan Food Company
PO Box 42222
Portland, OR 97242-0222   503-234-7494
Fax: 503-234-7716
Frozen fruits and vegetables
President: Percy Loy
Estimated Sales:$580000
Number Employees: 5
Type of Packaging: Food Service, Bulk
Brands:
KUBLA KHAN

7981 Kuhlmann's Market Gardens & Greenhouses
RR 6
Edmonton, AB T5B 4K3
Canada   780-475-7500
Fax: 780-472-9923
Processor, exporter and packer of cabbage, carrots,
broccoli, peas and potatoes
Pres.: Dietrich Kuhlmann
Number Employees: 50-99
Type of Packaging: Consumer, Food Service

7982 Kulana Foods
590 W Kawailani St # J
Hilo, HI 96720-3173   808-959-9144
Fax: 808-959-8484
Beef and pork slaughtering and processing
President: Brady Yagi
*Estimated Sales:*Below $ 5 Million
Number Employees: 10-19
Type of Packaging: Private Label
Brands:
Fresh Aland Beef and Pork
Kulana Foods

7983 Kunde Estate Winery
P.O.Box 639
Kenwood, CA 95452-0639   707-833-5501
Fax: 707-833-2204 wineinfo@kunde.com
www.kunde.com
Wines
President: Don Chase
CFO: Jim Meredith
Marketing Director: Marcia Kunde Mickelson
Operations Manager: Bill Kunde
Estimated Sales:$ 30-50 Million
Number Employees: 50-99
Type of Packaging: Private Label
Brands:
Estate Cabernet Sauvignon
Estate Chardonnay
Estate Merlot
Estate Syrah
Estate Viognier
Estate Zinfandel (Ce

7984 Kunzler & Company
P.O.Box 4747
Lancaster, PA 17604-4747   717-299-6301
Fax: 717-390-2170 888-586-9537
customerservice@kunzler.com
www.kunzler.com

Manufacturer of meat products: bacon, bologna, ham, hot dogs, scrapple, steaks, luncheon meats
President/CEO: Chris Kunzler III
CEO: Christian C Kunzler Iii
Director Marketing: Rob Kunzler
Director Sales: Tom McCarty
Estimated Sales:$100 Million
Number Employees: 10-19
Type of Packaging: Consumer, Food Service, Private Label, Bulk
Brands:
KUNZLER PRIVATE LABEL

7985 Kunzler/Juniata PackingCompany
P.O.Box 276
Tyrone, PA 16686-0276   814-684-2270
          Fax: 814-684-0210 www.kunzler.com
Processor and packer of meats including pre-sliced, portioned luncheonmeat set-ups, loaves, bacon, sausage, etc.; exporter of bacon
President: Christian C Kunzler Jr III
CEO: John Kunzler
VP/General Manager: David Grazier
Marketing Director: Betty Loht
Sales Director: Tom Coder
Public Relations: Tom Theurer
Plant Manager: Dennis Nevling
Purchasing Manager: Tom Musser
Estimated Sales:$105000000
Number Employees: 100-249
Sq. footage: 42000
Parent Co: Kunzler & Company
Type of Packaging: Consumer, Food Service, Private Label, Bulk
Brands:
Giant Eagle
Juniata
Kunzler
Meadows
Shur Fine

7986 Kupris Home Bakery
23 Williams Road
Manchester, CT 06043-7235   860-649-4746
Household Bakery
Owner: Jeris Kupris

7987 Kurtz Produce
5894 8th Line
Ariss, ON N0B 1B0
Canada   519-824-3279
          Fax: 519-824-4299 kpi@on.aibn.com
Grower and exporter of agricultural products and bottled drinking water.
Pres.: Wilf Kurtz
CEO: Brad Kurtz
VP: Brad Kurtz
Sales: Mike Wilson
Plant Manager: Darren Hedges
Number Employees: 18
Number of Brands: 3
Brands:
Bethune
Black Cat
Superior

7988 Kusha
2332 Barranca Pkwy
Irvine, CA 92606-5017   949-250-1522
          Fax: 949-250-1520 800-550-7423
jerry@kusharice.comm www.kusharice.com
Rice, basmati, jasmine, tea, grape seed oil, cheese
Vice President: Jerry Taylor
*Estimated Sales:*Under $500,000
Number Employees: 10-19
Type of Packaging: Consumer, Food Service, Private Label, Bulk
Brands:
Nasim
Pari
Royal

7989 Kutik's Honey Farm
285 Lyon Brook Road
Norwich, NY 13815-3420   607-336-4105
Fax: 607-895-6298 kutikshoney@mkl.com
          www.kutikshoney.com
Processor of portion packed honey and honey sticks; also, custom gift packs available
President: Charles Kutik
VP: Matt Rideout
Marketing Director: Chuck Kutik
Number Employees: 1-4
Sq. footage: 4685

Type of Packaging: Consumer, Food Service, Private Label, Bulk
Brands:
Kutik's Honey

7990 Kutztown Bologna Company
1500 Oregon Rd # 100
Leola, PA 17540-9753   717-556-0901
          Fax: 717-560-0680 800-723-8824
          info@kutztownbologna.com
          www.actionvideoinc.com
Processor of frozen beef and pork products
President: Gordon Harrower
VP: Gary Landuy
Estimated Sales:$670000
Number Employees: 1-4
Type of Packaging: Consumer, Private Label
Brands:
Kutztown

7991 Kyger Bakery Products
3825 State Road 38 E
Lafayette, IN 47905-5212   765-447-1252
          Fax: 765-447-7989 info@harlanbakeries.com
          www.kygerbakeries.com
Processor of frozen desserts including cream and meringue pies and angel food and sheet cakes; also, retail and institutional packaging available
Executive VP Sales/Marketing: Joseph E Latouf
Type of Packaging: Consumer
Brands:
Kyger

7992 Kyler Seafood
2 Washburn St
New Bedford, MA 02740-7336   508-984-5150
          Fax: 508-991-4664 888-859-5377
info@kylerseafood.com www.kylerseafood.com
Processor of fresh and frozen cod and flounder
Owner: Jeff Manfelt
CFO: Steven Souza
R & D: Paul Poliquinn
Estimated Sales:$ 20-30 Million
Number Employees: 100-249
Type of Packaging: Private Label

7993 Kyong Hae Kim Company
2330 Kalakaua Ave # 85
Honolulu, HI 96815-5001   808-926-8720
          Fax: 808-841-2178
Owner: Kyong Kim

7994 Kyowa Hakko
767 3rd Ave # 9
New York, NY 10017-9023   212-715-0572
          Fax: 212-421-1283 sullivan@kyowa-usa.com
          www.kyowa-usa.com
Manufacturer of amino, nuclei and organic acids; exporter of food ingredients
President: Michinobu Inouc
CEO: Mike Inoue
Sales: Neil Sullivan
Estimated Sales:$ 20-50 Million
Number Employees: 10-19
Parent Co: Kyowa Hakko Kogyo Company
Brands:
Gmp
Imp
Wmp Kyowa

7995 L & S Packing Company
101 Central Ave
Farmingdale, NY 11735-6915   631-845-1717
          Fax: 631-420-7309 877-879-6453
          www.paesana.com
Manufacturer of olives
President: Louis Scaramelli
Estimated Sales:$ 3 - 5 Million
Number Employees: 20-49

7996 L C Good Candy Company
1825 E Tremont St
Allentown, PA 18109-1615   610-432-3290
          Fax: 610-432-7455
Candy and confections
President: Roland R Mink Jr
*Estimated Sales:*Below $200,000
Number Employees: 1-4

7997 L K Bowman & Company
P.O.Box 80
Nottingham, PA 19362-0080   610-932-2240
          Fax: 610-932-4186 800-853-1919
          lkbowman@hanoverfoods.com
          www.hanoverfoods.com
Manufacturer of mushrooms
President: Robert Shelton
Estimated Sales:$10-20 Million
Number Employees: 20-49
Sq. footage: 18139
Parent Co: Hanover Foods Corporation
Type of Packaging: Food Service, Private Label, Bulk
Brands:
GARDEN PATH
MOTHER EARTH
NOTTINGHAM

7998 L&C Fisheries
French River
Kensington, PE C0B 1M0
Canada   902-886-2770
          Fax: 902-886-3003
Processor and exporter of fresh mussels and fresh and frozen lobsters
Owner: Calvin Jollimore
Number Employees: 10-19
Type of Packaging: Consumer, Food Service

7999 (HQ)L&H Packing Company
P.O.Box 831368
San Antonio, TX 78283-1368   210-532-3241
          Fax: 210-532-5033 sales@lhpacking.com
          www.lhpacking.com
Processor of cooked meats, sauces, gravies, patties, fajitas, etc.
CEO: Kenneth E Leonard
Estimated Sales:$100+ Million
Number Employees: 500-999
Type of Packaging: Consumer, Food Service, Private Label, Bulk
Brands:
SURLEAN

8000 (HQ)L&L Packing Company
527 W 41st St
Chicago, IL 60609-2708   773-285-5400
          Fax: 773-285-0366 800-628-6328
          info@worldsbeststeak.com
          www.worldsbeststeak.com
Prime and choice aged beef, pork, veal and lamb
President: Alan Lezak
Sales Manager: Phil Lombardi
Estimated Sales:$24000000
Number Employees: 20-49
Type of Packaging: Private Label

8001 L&M Bakery
203 S Union St
Lawrence, MA 01843-1608   978-687-7346
          Fax: 978-682-4397 www.lm-bakery.com
Processor of fruit squares, nut bread, regular and sour cream coffee cakes and macaroons
Owner: Paul La Plante
VP: Johanne La Plante
Sales Director: Rick Fermoyle
Plant Manager: Andy Stoehrer
Estimated Sales:$ 10 - 20 Million
Number Employees: 10-19
Sq. footage: 10000
Type of Packaging: Consumer, Food Service
Brands:
L & M Bakery

8002 L&M Evans
P.O.Box 81997
Conyers, GA 30013-9428   770-918-8727
          Fax: 847-647-1509
Seafood, clams, fish, fillets
President: L W Bill Evans
Estimated Sales:$300,000-500,000
Number Employees: 1-4

8003 L&M Frosted Food Lockers
P.O.Box 199
Belt, MT 59412-0199   406-277-3522
          Fax: 406-277-3522
Processor of meat and fish
Owner: Steve Serquina
Partner: Jerry Wojtala
Estimated Sales:$200,000+
Number Employees: 1-4
Type of Packaging: Consumer, Food Service

8004 L&M Slaughtering
903 Mill Rd
Georgetown, IL 61846-6341 217-662-6841
abitor@aol.com
Processor of beef, veal, lamb and pork; slaughtering
sevices available
Owner: Todd Green
Estimated Sales: $ 1 - 3 Million
Number Employees: 1-4
Type of Packaging: Consumer

8005 (HQ)L&S Packing Company
101 Central Ave
Farmingdale, NY 11735-6915 631-845-1717
Fax: 631-420-7309 800-286-6487
sales@paesana.com www.paesana.com
Importer of gourmet condiments such as olives, ca-
pers, pickles, cocktail onions, mushrooms, etc.; serv-
ing food service, industrial and private label
markets. Also, high quality authentic pasta sauces
and Chinese sauces, see our ad onthe back cover of
Vol
President: Louis Scaramelli III
Estimated Sales: $ 3 - 5 Million
Number Employees: 20-49
Type of Packaging: Consumer, Food Service, Pri-
vate Label, Bulk
Other Locations:
L&S Packing Co.
Flushing NY
Brands:
Mi-Kee
Paesana
Table Joy

8006 L'Esprit de Campagne
P.O.Box 3130
Winchester, VA 22604-2330 540-955-1014
Fax: 540-955-1018 800-692-8008
lespritfods@hotmail.com
www.lespritdecampagne.com
Dried tomatoes, apples, cherries, blueberries, cran-
berries
President: Joy Lokey
CEO: Carey Lokey
Estimated Sales: Below $ 5 Million
Number Employees: 50-99
Brands:
L'Esprit

8007 L. Craelius & Company
370 N Morgan St
Chicago, IL 60607-1321 312-666-7100
Fax: 312-666-9747
President: Lawrence Craelius
Estimated Sales: $ 20 - 50 Million
Number Employees: 20-49

8008 L. Craven & Sons
1600 N 25th Ave # B
Melrose Park, IL 60160-1868 708-343-0500
Fax: 708-343-6674 800-453-4303
closeouts@lcraven.com www.lcraven.com
Wholesaler/distributor of closeout items including
candy, groceries and snack foods; all quantities and
packaging bought and sold
President: Sam Craven
VP: Barry Craven
VP: Jack Craven
Estimated Sales: $ 20 - 50 Million
Number Employees: 20-49
Sq. footage: 35000

8009 L. East Poultry Company
P.O.Box 6499
Austin, TX 78762-6499 512-476-5367
Fax: 512-476-5360 epoultry@att.net
www.eastpoultry.com
Poultry
President: Ken Aune
Estimated Sales: Below $ 5 Million
Number Employees: 20-49

8010 L. Isaacson
800 W Fulton Market
Chicago, IL 60607-1375 312-421-2444
Fax: 312-421-2736
President: Ben Willner
Estimated Sales: $ 5 - 10 Million
Number Employees: 20-49

8011 L. Mawby Vineyards
4519 S Elm Valley Rd
Suttons Bay, MI 49682-9473 231-271-3522
Fax: 231-271-2927 larry@lmawby.com
www.lmawby.com
Wines
President: Lawrence Mawby
Estimated Sales: $500,000-$1 Million
Number Employees: 1-4
Brands:
L.Mawby
M.Lawrence

8012 L.F. Lambert Spawn Company
1507 Valley Rd
Coatesville, PA 19320-2726 610-384-5031
Fax: 610-384-0390 lambert@lambertspawn.com
www.lambertspawn.com
Processor and exporter of mushroom spawns
President: Hugh McIntyre
General Manager: Joseph Mascrangelo
Estimated Sales: $3300000
Number Employees: 100-249

8013 L.H. Hayward & Company
P.O.Box 23751
New Orleans, LA 70183-0751 504-733-8480
Fax: 504-733-8155 info@camelliabeans.com
www.lhhco.com
Packaging of beans
President: Ken Hayward
CO-Owner: Rick Hayward
Estimated Sales: $ 5-10 Million
Number Employees: 20-49
Type of Packaging: Private Label
Brands:
Camellia

8014 L.H. Rodriguez Wholesale Seafood
3541 S 12th Ave
Tucson, AZ 85713-5914 520-623-1931
Fax: 520-623-0737
Seafood
President: Levi Rodriguez
Treasurer: Albert Rodriguez
Vice President: Joe Rodriguez
Estimated Sales: $ 3 - 5 Million
Number Employees: 5-9

8015 L.I. Cauliflower Association
139 Marcy Ave
Riverhead, NY 11901-3099 631-727-2212
Fax: 631-727-4295 www.licauliflower.com
Manufacturer of cauliflower
President/CEO: Carl Key
Estimated Sales: $5-10 Million
Number Employees: 10-19

8016 L.J. Minor Factory
2621 W 25th St
Cleveland, OH 44113-4794 216-861-8350
Fax: 216-861-0789 www.nestleusa.com
Processor of food bases including meat, poultry, sea-
food and sauce
Plant Manager: Ingolf Nitsch
Plant Manager: Engas Nitch
Estimated Sales: $100+ Million
Number Employees: 250-499
Parent Co: Nestle USA
Type of Packaging: Food Service

8017 L.K. Bowman Company
P.O.Box 80
Nottingham, PA 19362-0080 610-932-2240
Fax: 610-932-4186 800-853-1919
ikbowman@hanoverfoods.com
www.hanoverfoods.com
Processor and exporter of canned, frozen, fresh,
freeze-dried, and refrigerated mushrooms
President: Robert Shelton
Vice President: C Jack Shelton
Quality Control: Jennifer Brickley
Sales Director: Paul Bozzone
Plant Manager: Charles Reed
Estimated Sales: $ 10 - 20 Million
Number Employees: 20-49
Parent Co: Hanover Foods Corporation
Type of Packaging: Food Service, Private Label,
Bulk
Brands:
Garden Path
Nottingham
Wayside

8018 L.L. Curley Packing Company
551 Lafayette St
Colonial Beach, VA 22443-2624 804-224-7544
Fax: 804-224-7035
President: Lloyd L Curley Jr
Estimated Sales: $ 1-2.5 Million
Number Employees: 5-9

8019 LA Dreyfus
3775 Park Avenue
Edison, NJ 08820-2595 732-549-1600
Fax: 732-549-1685 ddiaz@ladreyfus.com
www.ladreyfus.com
Chewing gum base
Estimated Sales: $ 15 - 20 Million
Number Employees: 100-250
Sq. footage: 500000

8020 LA Wholesale Produce Market
1601 E Olympic Blvd
Los Angeles, CA 90021-1936 213-622-8905
Fax: 213-622-7075 888-454-6887
webinfo@lanuthouse.com www.lanuthouse.com
Manufacturer, importer and exporter of tree nuts and
peanuts; also, processor of peanut butter and manu-
factured and coated materials
President: Pat Nakahara
Estimated Sales: $ 3 - 5 Million
Number Employees: 5-9
Sq. footage: 22000
Parent Co: Morven Partners
Type of Packaging: Consumer, Food Service, Pri-
vate Label, Bulk

8021 LBA
18842 13th Pl S
Seatac, WA 98148-2342 206-241-9343
Fax: 206-433-2844 800-522-1185
gsimeon@lba-inc.com www.lba-inc.com
Frozen dough, thaw and serve pastries
President/Owner: Michael Robert
Vice President: Randal Chicoine
Estimated Sales: $ 5-10 Million
Number Employees: 20-49
Type of Packaging: Private Label
Brands:
French Does
LBA

8022 LD Foods
PO Box 1990
Annapolis, MD 21404-1990 410-216-9300
Fax: 410-216-9900
CEO: James Loftis, Jr.

8023 LDI
220 E 4th St
Cincinnati, OH 45202-4102 513-421-1671
Fax: 513-421-1671 www.wendys.com
Manager: Amy Denny
Marketing Director: Bill Still
Estimated Sales: Under $500,000
Number Employees: 20-49

8024 LEF McLean Brothers International
PO Box 128
Wheatley, ON N0P 2P0
Canada 519-825-4656
Fax: 519-825-7374
Processor and exporter of fresh and frozen lake fish
and seafood
President: Robert Ricci
VP Business Development: Danny Ricci
Type of Packaging: Consumer, Food Service, Pri-
vate Label, Bulk

8025 LFI
271 Us Highway 46 # C101
Fairfield, NJ 07004-2495 973-882-0550
Fax: 973-882-0554 lfiinc@aol.com
Imported foods
President: Antonio Lisanti
Marketing Director: Danielle Iannacconi
Public Relations: Carol Lisanti
Estimated Sales: Below $ 5 Million
Number Employees: 5-9
Type of Packaging: Private Label
Brands:
Antonia
Casa Primo

8026 LK Bowman
P.O.Box 80
Nottingham, PA 19362-0080   610-932-2240
Fax: 610-932-4186   800-853-1919
lkbowman@hanoverfoods.com
www.hanoverfoods.com
Mushrooms
President: Robert Shelton
Estimated Sales: $ 10-20 Million
Number Employees: 20-49

8027 LLJ's Sea Products
P.O.Box 296
Round Pond, ME 04564-0296   207-529-4224
Fax: 207-529-4223
Canned and cured fish and seafood.
Owner: Stephen J Brackett
Estimated Sales: $3,000,000
Number Employees: 5-9

8028 LPI
3400 W 35th St
Chicago, IL 60632-3399   773-254-7200
Fax: 773-254-8546 www.lapreferida.com
Distributors of Mexican food
Owner: Richard Steinbarth
Estimated Sales: $ 50-100 Million
Number Employees: 1-4
Type of Packaging: Private Label, Bulk

8029 LPO/ LaDolc
4953 W 135th St
Overland Park, KS 66224-6901   913-681-7757
Fax: 913-681-7757
President: Leslie Oliver

8030 LRM Packaging
41 James St
South Hackensack, NJ 07606-1438   201-342-2530
Fax: 201-342-4351   info@lrmpack.com
www.lrmpackaging.com
Contract packager of snack and dry foods, etc
President: John Natali Jr
Director Sales: John Natali, Jr.
Production Manager: Mike Hoskins
Estimated Sales: Below $ 5 Million
Number Employees: 1-4
Sq. footage: 100000

8031 LSK Smoked Turkey Products
1575 Bronx River Ave
Bronx, NY 10460-3101   718-792-1300
Fax: 718-792-8883 www.smokedmeat.com
Smoked turkey products
President: Dan Salmon
CEO: Owen Grossblatt
Plant Manager: John Garvin
Estimated Sales: $ 9 Million
Number Employees: 10-19
Brands:
LSK

8032 (HQ)LUXCO
5050 Kemper Ave
St Louis, MO 63139-1106   314-772-2627
Fax: 314-772-6021   info@luxco.com
www.luxco.com
Manufacturer, bottler, importer and exporter of quality distilled spirits and wines
President/CEO: Donn Lux
VP Finance/CFO: Steve Soucy
R&D/Quality Manager: John Rempe
VP Sales/Marketing: Dan Streepy
VP Operations: David Bratcher
Production Scheduler: Heather Sokol
Warehouse Manager: Jeff Presson
Purchasing Manager: Daniel Jennings
Estimated Sales: $20-50 Million
Number Employees: 100-249
Sq. footage: 200000
Type of Packaging: Private Label
Brands:
ADMIRAL NELSONS
ARROW CORDIALS
BARBELLA
BOUCHERON
CAFFE' LOLITA
DOS TIRANOS
EVERCLEAR
EZRA BROOKS
INFERNO
JAKOB DENNER
JUAREZ
MARGARITAVILLE

PEARL
PURPLE PASSION
REBEL YELL
ROMERO AMARETTO
SAINT BRENDAN'S
SALVADOR'S
TEQUILA EL MAYOR RESERVE
TVARSCKI
YAGO SANT GRIA

8033 LVO Manufacturing
P.O.Box 188
Rock Rapids, IA 51246-0188   712-472-3734
Fax: 712-472-2203   marilyn_lvo@yahoo.com
www.lvomfg.com
President: Marilyn Mammenga
CFO: Lambert Benno
Estimated Sales: $ 5 - 10 Million
Number Employees: 20-49

8034 LWC Brands Inc
151 Regal Row
Dallas, TX 75247   214-630-9101
Fax: 214-630-7360   ladywalton@ladywalton.com
www.lwcbrands.com
cookies
President/Owner: Mary Alizon-Walton
Estimated Sales: $2.3 Million
Number Employees: 20

8035 La Abra Farm & Winery
1362 Fortunes Cove Ln
Lovingston, VA 22949-2226   434-263-5392
Fax: 434-263-8540
Wines
President: Albert C Weed Ii II
Estimated Sales: Less than $200,000
Number Employees: 1-4

8036 La Bonita Ole Inc
5804 E Columbus Dr
Tampa, FL 33619-1643   813-254-1450
Fax: 813-319-2263   800-522-6648
martha@tamxicos.com   www.tamxicos.com
Manufacturer of tortillas (Tamxicos and Wrapitz).
Founder/Owner/President/CEO: Tammy Young
Executive Administrator: Melanie Bodiford
Director of IT: Gary Macri
VP Operations: Dave Waters

8037 La Boulangerie
7740 Formula Pl
San Diego, CA 92121-2419   858-578-4040
Fax: 858-536-5911
Baked goods
Owner: Gerald Sarnoo
Estimated Sales: Below $ 5 Million
Number Employees: 10-19
Brands:
La Boulangerie

8038 La Brasserie McAuslan Brewing
4850 Rue St Ambroise
Montreal, QC H4C 3N8
Canada   514-939-3060
Fax: 514-939-6136
Processor and exporter of beer and ale including stout
President: Peter McAuslan
Number Employees: 20-49
Type of Packaging: Consumer, Food Service

8039 La Brea Bakery
P.O.Box 7537
Van Nuys, CA 91409-7537   818-742-4242
Fax: 818-742-4276   info@labreabakery.com
www.labreabakery.com
Processor of bread and rolls; also, par-baked and frozen available
President: Nancy Silverton
CEO: John Yamin
Estimated Sales: $100+ Million
Number Employees: 100-249

8040 La Buena Mexican Foods Products
P.O.Box 26626
Tucson, AZ 85726-6626   520-624-1796
Fax: 520-624-1846
Manufacturer of Mexican food products including corn and flour tortillas, tamales and taco and tostado shells
Owner: Carlos Portillo

Estimated Sales: $5-10 Million
Number Employees: 20-49
Type of Packaging: Consumer

8041 La Buena Vida Vineyards
416 E College St
Grapevine, TX 76051-5468   817-481-9463
Fax: 817-421-3635   lbv@labuenavida.com
www.labuenavida.com
Wines
Manager: Adam Artho
Marketing Director: Camille McBee
Estimated Sales: $ 2.5-5 Million
Number Employees: 5-9
Number of Products: 15
Brands:
La Buena Vida Vineyards

8042 La Caboose Specialties
145 S Budd St
Sunset, LA 70584   337-662-5401
Fax: 337-662-5813
Canned fruits, vegetables, preserves, jams and jellies
Owner: Margaret Brinkhaus
Estimated Sales: Under $100,000
Number Employees: 1-4
Type of Packaging: Consumer
Brands:
La Caboose

8043 La Canasta Mexican FoodProducts
P.O.Box 6939
Phoenix, AZ 85005-6939   602-269-7721
Fax: 602-269-7725   www.la-canasta.com
www.la-canasta.com
Flour and corn tortillas and chips
President: Josie Ippolito
CEO: Roger Kelling
Quality Control: Jesus Gonzalez
Sales Director: Hector Quijada
Public Relations: Diane Hamel
Operations Manager: Jesus Castaneda
Plant Manager: Manny Hernandez
Purchasing Manager: Linda Rios
Estimated Sales: $100+ Million
Number Employees: 100-249
Sq. footage: 25000
Type of Packaging: Food Service, Private Label
Brands:
LA CANASTA TORTILLAS
MY NANA'S CHIPS

8044 La Casita's Home Style Mexican Food
100 Lacasita Drive
Holts Summit, MO 65043   573-896-8306
Fax: 573-896-8309
Tortilla chips
Estimated Sales: $ 5-9.9 Million
Number Employees: 6

8045 La Chapalita
1520 Knowles Ave
Los Angeles, CA 90063-1607   323-780-7808
Fax: 323-221-2162   lachapalita@earthlink.net
www.lachapalita.com
Tortillas, Mexican food
Owner: Luis Moya
Estimated Sales: Below $ 5 Million
Number Employees: 20-49

8046 La Chiquita Tortilla Manufacturing
3451 Atlanta Industrial Pkwy
Atlanta, GA 30331-1039   404-351-9822
Fax: 404-351-4446   800-486-3942
stogner-s@yahoo.com
www.lachiquitatortilla.com
Processor of corn and flour tortillas
President: Marcelino Solis
Marketing Director: Jose Solis
Estimated Sales: $ 20 - 50 Million
Number Employees: 50-99
Type of Packaging: Food Service
Brands:
La Chiquita
Provecho

8047 La Chiripada Winery
P.O.Box 191
Dixon, NM 87527-0191   505-579-4437
     Fax: 505-579-4437   800-528-7801
info@lachiripada.com   www.lachiripada.com
Wine
   Owner/President: Michael Johnson
   VP: Michael Johnson
   Tasting Room Manager: Minna Santos
Estimated Sales: Below $ 5 Million
Number Employees: 20-49
Brands:
   La Chiripada

8048 La Cigale Bakery
PO Box 540223
Opa Locka, FL 33054-0223   305-688-7868
   Fax: 305-688-1004   800-333-8578
Processor and exporter of French desserts, breads
and pastries
   Owner/President: Serge Bonvallot
   Sales/Marketing Manager: Serge Bonvallot
Number Employees: 1-4
Parent Co: JSK Trading Corporation
Brands:
   La Cigale Bakery
   La Tarte De Saint-Tropez

8049 La Colonial/Robles Brothers
1700 Rogers Ave
San Jose, CA 95112-1107   408-436-5551
   Fax: 408-441-0430   www.lacolonial.com
Flour tortillas
   President: George Robles
   CEO: George Robles
   Marketing Director: George Robles
Estimated Sales: Below $ 5 Million
Number Employees: 20-49

8050 La Cookie
5700 Savoy Dr
Houston, TX 77036-2226   713-784-2722
   Fax: 713-784-3415
Processor of frozen cookie, muffin and brownie
dough
   Manager: Brian Fung
Estimated Sales: $300,000-500,000
Number Employees: 10-19
Sq. footage: 10000
Parent Co: Pilsner Group
Type of Packaging: Food Service
Brands:
   Neal's

8051 La Cookie
5700 Savoy Dr
Houston, TX 77036-2226   713-784-2722
   Fax: 713-784-3415
Baked goods
   Manager: Brian Fung
   Vice President: Victor Young
Estimated Sales: $ 1-2.5 Million
Number Employees: 1-4

8052 La Costa Coffee Roasting
6965 El Camino Real
Carlsbad, CA 92009-4100   760-434-3233
   Fax: 760-438-5314
Coffee
   President: Doug Novak
Estimated Sales: $ 10-20 Million
Number Employees: 10-19

8053 La Crema Coffee Company
9852 Crescebt Park Drive
West Chester, OH 45069   513-779-6278
   Fax: 513-779-1908
melissa@lacremacoffeecompany.com
   www.lacremacoffeecompany.com
coffee and tea
   President/Owner: Melissa Flohn
   Operations Manager: Cheryl Windhorst

8054 La Flor Spices
25 Hoffman Avenue
Hauppauge, NY 11788-4717   631-885-9601
   Fax: 718-628-4387   www.laflor.com
Manufacturer, importer, exporter and contract
packager of spices, herbs, blends, seasonings and
ground peppers
   President: Ruben La Torre Sr
   VP: Dan La Torre
   Sales/Distribution Manager: Ruben La Torre Jr

Estimated Sales: $5 Million
Number Employees: 45
Sq. footage: 31000
Type of Packaging: Private Label

8055 La Flor Spices Company
25 Hoffman Ave
Hauppauge, NY 11788-4717   631-851-9601
   Fax: 631-851-9606   www.laflor.com
Spices
   President: Reuben Latorre
Estimated Sales: $7.4 Million
Number Employees: 20-49
Type of Packaging: Consumer, Food Service, Bulk
Brands:
   La Flor

8056 La Font Shrimp Company
PO Box 697
Golden Meadow, LA 70357-0697   504-475-5138
   Fax: 504-475-5138
Manufacturers and suppliers of shrimps and
seafoods
   President/CEO: Daniel Lafont
Estimated Sales: $ 20-50 Million
Number Employees: 50

8057 La Francaise Bakery
111 Northwest Ave
Northlake, IL 60164-1603   708-562-0100
   Fax: 708-498-2305   800-654-7220
jimv@lafrancaise.com   www.chefsolutions.com
Processor of croissants, cinnamon rolls, bagels and
danish; also, unbaked frozen croissants and cookie
batter
   President: John Veleris
   COO: Jim Vadevoulis
   Human Resources: Claudia Romo
   Marketing Director: Trudy Lord
   Public Relations: Angel Ray Pimienta
Estimated Sales: $ 20 - 50 Million
Number Employees: 250-499
Type of Packaging: Food Service, Private Label,
Bulk
Brands:
   Spoon-N-Bake

8058 La Fronteriza
6142 American Rd
Toledo, OH 43612-3902   419-729-4070
   Fax: 419-729-9661   800-897-1772
     www.tiarosa.com
Processor of corn and flour tortillas and tortilla chips
   Manager: Jerry Stump
Estimated Sales: $ 20 - 50 Million
Number Employees: 50-99
Parent Co: Bimar Foods
Type of Packaging: Private Label
Brands:
   La Fronteriza

8059 La Have Seafoods
PO Box 100
La Havens, NS B0R 1C0
Canada   902-688-2773
   Fax: 902-688-2766
Processor and exporter of fresh and salted fish in-
cluding pollack, cod, haddock and scallops
   President: Dave Himmelman
Number Employees: 20-49
Type of Packaging: Bulk

8060 La Jota Vineyard Company
1102 Las Posadas Rd
Angwin, CA 94508-9607   707-948-2648
   Fax: 707-965-0324   877-222-0292
     info@lajotawines.com
     www.lajotavineyardco.com
Wines
   Manager: Ed Farver
   VP: Joan Smith
   Sales Manager: John Smith
Estimated Sales: Below $ 5 Million
Number Employees: 10-19

8061 La Malinche Tortilla & Tamale Factory
702 S Port Ave
Corpus Christi, TX 78405-2244   361-884-7883
   Fax: 361-884-9821   lama702@prodigy.net
Processor of Mexican products including tamales,
flour tortillas, taco shells and tostados
   President: Rosario Carrizo
   General Manager: Teresa Hajek

Estimated Sales: $250000
Number Employees: 5-9
Type of Packaging: Consumer

8062 La Mexicana
2703 S Kedzie Ave
Chicago, IL 60623-4735   773-247-5443
   Fax: 773-247-9004   www.lamexicanawraps.com
Processor of tortillas and corn chips
   President: Rudolph Guerrero
Estimated Sales: $4600000
Number Employees: 20-49
Type of Packaging: Consumer

8063 La Mexicana
10020 14th Ave SW
Seattle, WA 98146-3703   206-763-1488
   Fax: 206-768-1050   info@lamexicana.com
     www.lamexicana.com
Mexican foods
   President: Keith Bloxham
   General Manager: William Fry
Estimated Sales: Below $ 5 Million
Number Employees: 50-99
Type of Packaging: Private Label
Brands:
   Habero
   La Mexicana
   Souena

8064 La Mexicana Tortilla Factory
2020 W Clarendon Drive
Dallas, TX 75208-7632   214-943-7770
   Fax: 505-842-0317
     email@lamexicanatortilla.com
Manufacturer of tortillas
Estimated Sales: $ 50 - 100 Million
Number Employees: 35
Sq. footage: 1500
Type of Packaging: Consumer

8065 La Mexicana Tortilla Factory
236 a St
Hayward, CA 94541-4946   510-889-8225
   Fax: 510-889-1080
Processor of corn tortillas
   President: Jesus Villarreal
Estimated Sales: $ 20 - 50 Million
Number Employees: 20-49

8066 La Monegasque
2125 Center Avenue
Fort Lee, NJ 07024-5859   201-585-7877
   Fax: 201-585-8575
Seafood, seafood products

8067 La Monita Mexican Food
2200 E 7th St # B
Austin, TX 78702-3570   512-524-4294
   Fax: 713-692-8217
Mexican food
Estimated Sales: $500,000-$1 Million
Number Employees: 1-4

8068 La Nova Wings
371 W Ferry St
Buffalo, NY 14213-1947   716-881-3355
   Fax: 716-881-3366   800-652-6682
   wingman@ianova.com   www.lanova.com
Processor of frozen chicken wings and tenders
   President/CEO: Joseph Todaro
   Sales, Eastern: Ben Lamonte
   Sales (Midwest): Sam Pantano
   Sales (Western): Joe Pettruzzella
Estimated Sales: $ 1 - 3 Million
Number Employees: 50-99
Type of Packaging: Consumer, Food Service
Brands:
   La Nova

8069 La Panzanella
18475 Olypmic Ave S
Tukwila, WA 98188   206-903-0500
   Fax: 206-903-0698
   croccantini@lapanzanella.com
     www.lapanzanella.com
herb infused rustic crackers
Estimated Sales: $2.7 Million
Number Employees: 25

8070 La Parisienne Bakery
7949 Wellingford Drive
Manassas, VA 20109-2445 301-468-9234
Fax: 301-770-0975 800-727-4790
bonjour@laparisienne.com
www.laparisienne.com
Bakery items
CEO and President: Mark Salman
CFO: Robert Greenblatt
Vice President: George Jermstad
Operations Manager: Glenn Price
Production Manager: Tony Richa
Estimated Sales: $ 20-50 Million
Number Employees: 100-249
Type of Packaging: Private Label
Brands:
Bonjour La Parisienne
Loafin' Around Organ
Planet Bagels

8071 La Patisserie
1317 W McKinley St
Phoenix, AZ 85007-2366 602-254-5868
Fax: 602-253-7430
Bakery products
Owner: Eduardo Teixidor
President: Ed Teixidor
Estimated Sales: Below $ 5 Million
Number Employees: 20-49
Type of Packaging: Private Label
Brands:
La Patisserie

8072 La Paz Products
P.O.Box 459
Brea, CA 92822-0459 714-990-0982
Fax: 714-990-2246 info@lapazproducts.com
www.lapazproducts.com
Processor of cocktail mixes
President: Larry Casey
Estimated Sales: $ 10 - 20 Million
Number Employees: 10-19
Type of Packaging: Consumer, Food Service

8073 La Piccolina
1075 N Hills Drive
Decatur, GA 30033-4220 404-296-1624
Fax: 404-296-2008 800-626-1624
piccola@lapiccolina.com www.lapiccolina.com
Processor and exporter of breadsticks, dips, biscotti, gourmet coffee, cranberry pecan bread, pasta, pasta sauces, olive oil, etc.; manufacturer of biscotti and breadsticks
President: Olympia Manning
VP: Denise Walsh-Bandini
National Sales Manager: Denise Walsh-Bandini
Estimated Sales: $270000
Number Employees: 5
Sq. footage: 3200

8074 La Poblana Tamale Factory
7648 Canal Street
Houston, TX 77012-1198 713-921-4760
Fax: 713-921-1830 lptf1@aol.com
Processor of sausage, tortillas and tamales
President: Maurilio Villareal
Plant Manager: Hector Villareal
Number Employees: 20-49
Type of Packaging: Consumer, Food Service

8075 (HQ)La Preferida
3400 W 35th St
Chicago, IL 60632-3399 773-254-7200
Fax: 773-254-8546 info@lapreferida.com
www.lapreferida.com
Owner: Richard Steinbarth
CFO: Gregory Gondek
Estimated Sales: $11 Million
Number Employees: 20-49
Type of Packaging: Food Service, Bulk
Brands:
La Preferida

8076 La Reina
316 N Ford Blvd
Los Angeles, CA 90022-1121 323-268-2791
Fax: 323-265-4295
sales@lareinafamilybrands.com
www.lareinafamilybrands.com

Processor of flour tortillas
President: Ricardo Robles
CEO: Mauro Robles
VP: Walt Boudreaux
Operations: Francisco Arellano
Purchasing: Luis Farfan
Estimated Sales: $16000000
Number Employees: 1-4
Type of Packaging: Consumer, Food Service, Private Label
Brands:
LA REINA

8077 La Reina
P.O.Box 1349
Monterey, CA 93942-1349 831-372-4003
Owner: Riccardo Giuliano
Estimated Sales: $ 20-50 Million
Number Employees: 50-99

8078 La Rocca Vineyards
P.O.Box 541
Forest Ranch, CA 95942-0541 530-899-9463
Fax: 530-894-7268 800-808-9463
wine@laroccavineyards.com
www.laroccavineyards.com
Wines
President/CEO: Philip La Rocca
Marketing Director: Phaedre LaRocco Morril
Estimated Sales: Under $500,000
Number Employees: 5-9
Brands:
La Rocca Vineyards

8079 (HQ)La Rochelle Winery
5443 Tesla Rd
Livermore, CA 94550-9621 925-243-6442
Fax: 408-270-5881 888-647-7768
smirassou@lrwine.com www.lrwine.com
Processor of vintaged varietal wine
Manager: Janice Fisher
Partner: James Mirassou
Partner: Peter Mirassou
Public Relations: Dave Muret
Sq. footage: 120000
Other Locations:
Mirassou Vineyards
Los Gatos CA
Brands:
Mirassou

8080 La Romagnola
2215 Tradeport Drive
Orlando, FL 32824-7005 407-856-4343
Fax: 407-856-7555 800-843-8359
Processor of fettucine, spaghetti, linguine, angel hair pasta, pasta sheets, tortelloni, ravioli, triangoli and gnocchi; also, noodles including tomato, spinach, black and egg
VP: Peter Fuchs
Sales Director: Cheryl Kuykendall
Number Employees: 50-99
Sq. footage: 34000
Brands:
La Romagnola
Le Patron

8081 La Rosa
1480 W Bernard Drive
Addison, IL 60101-4334 630-916-9552
Fax: 630-916-9561
Gourmet baked goods
President: Joe Verzillo
Estimated Sales: Less than $500,000
Number Employees: 5-9

8082 (HQ)La Rosa Bakery
217 Elizabeth Street
New York, NY 10012-4215 212-281-1500
Processor and baker of rolls and hero bread
Estimated Sales: $300,000-500,000
Number Employees: 1-4
Type of Packaging: Consumer

8083 La Spiga D'Oro Fresh Pasta Co
75 Pelican Way
Suite J
San Rafael, CA 94901 415-453-7000
Fax: 415-453-5574 800-847-2782
sales@lapigadoro.com www.laspigadoro.com
Gourmet fresh and frozen pasta.
President: Robert Clifford
Estimated Sales: Below $ 5 Million
Number Employees: 10

Brands:
La Spiga Doro

8084 La Superior Food Products
P.O.Box 3866
Shawnee Mission, KS 66203-0866 913-432-4933
Fax: 913-432-0121 www.lasuperiorfood.com
Nacho chips, taco shells, flour tortillas, corn tortillas
President: George Young
CFO: Larry O'Brian
R & D: Gordan Grahm
Estimated Sales: $ 2.5-5 Million
Number Employees: 20-49
Type of Packaging: Private Label, Bulk
Brands:
La Superior

8085 La Tang Cuisine Manufacturing
3824 Artdale St
Houston, TX 77063-5246 713-780-4876
Fax: 713-780-4296
Manufacturer of Asian foods including egg rolls, wonton, crab rangoon, spring roll and burritos.
President: Virginia Limbo
CEO: Joey Limbo
Estimated Sales: $250,000-$1 Million
Number Employees: 20-49
Number of Brands: 2
Number of Products: 5
Sq. footage: 10000
Type of Packaging: Food Service, Private Label, Bulk
Brands:
LA TANG
LA VIDA

8086 La Tempesta
439 Littlefield Ave
S San Francisco, CA 94080-6106 650-873-8944
Fax: 650-873-1190 800-762-8330
ltwebinfo@latempesta.com www.latempesta.com
Biscotti
President: Robert Sharp
CFO: Andy Kunkler
VP Marketing: Karen Hunt
Sales/Marketing Coordinator: Jeffrey Miller
Public Relations: Jeff Miller
Plant Manager: Sonia Azar
Estimated Sales: $9000000
Number Employees: 20-49
Type of Packaging: Consumer
Brands:
Amore Bianco
Biscotti Toscani
Panforte

8087 La Tolteca Foods
720 W 8th St
Pueblo, CO 81003-2322 719-543-5733
Fax: 719-543-2128 www.latoltecafoods.com
Processor of fresh and frozen tortillas
Owner: Tom Carpenter
Estimated Sales: $1700000
Number Employees: 20-49
Sq. footage: 50000
Type of Packaging: Consumer, Food Service, Private Label
Brands:
MEXICAN BEAR

8088 La Tortilla Factory
3300 Westwind Blvd
Santa Rosa, CA 95403-8273 707-586-4000
Fax: 707-586-4017 800-446-1516
info@latortillafactory.com
www.latortillafactory.com
Processor and exporter of corn and flour tortillas and healthy and delicious wraps; wholesaler/distributor of Mexican food products including tortilla chips and masa (locally only)
President: Carlos Tamayo
CEO: Stan Mead
Quality Control: Carlos Mojica
Executive Director Sales/Marketing: Jan Remak
Estimated Sales: $8000000
Number Employees: 100-249
Sq. footage: 45000
Type of Packaging: Consumer, Food Service, Private Label, Bulk
Brands:
La Tortilla Factory
Wrap Arounds
Wrappers

8089 La Tourangelle
1145 Harbour Way S
Richmond, CA 94804-3695   510-970-9960
      Fax: 510-970-9964   866-688-6457
contact@latourangelle.com
www.latourangelle.com
Oils
Number Employees: 12

8090 La Vans Coffee Company
158 2nd St
Bordentown, NJ 08505-1837   609-298-5400
Coffees
   Manager: Kostas Halkiadakis
Estimated Sales: Less than $500,000
Number Employees: 1-4

8091 La Vencedora Products
3322 Fowler St
Los Angeles, CA 90063-2594   323-269-7273
      Fax: 323-269-8775   800-327-2572
Processor of fresh salsa, tortilla chips, black bean
and garlic and jalapeno
   President and Owner: Morris Victor
   CEO: Richard Victor
   Vice President: Gregory Victor
Estimated Sales: $ 5 - 10 Million
Number Employees: 10-19
Sq. footage: 8000
Type of Packaging: Consumer, Food Service, Pri-
   vate Label, Bulk
Brands:
   El Rancho
   El Rancho Bean Chips
   El Rancho Salsa Fresca
   El Rancho Tortilla Chips
   Pocos

8092 La Victoria Foods
9200 Whitmore
Rosemead, CA 91770   626-312-2925
      Fax: 626-280-4416   800-423-4450
questions@lavicclub.com   www.lavictoria.com
Manufacturer of salsa, taco sauce, enchilada sauce,
chiles and peppers
   President: R Tanklage
   CEO: R Tanklage
   VP: Jon Tanklage
Estimated Sales: $5-$10 Million
Number Employees: 5-9
Type of Packaging: Private Label
Brands:
   La Victoria
   La Victoria Salsa Su

8093 La Vigne Enterprises
PO Box 2890
Fallbrook, CA 92088-2890   760-723-9997
      Fax: 760-728-2710   helenelv@adelphia.net
www.lavignefruits.com
Gourmet processor of exotic organically grown
fruits. Gained from a single organic source in Cali-
fornia, top varietal fruits are pureed using
state-of-the-art equipment. Packaged frozen in 2 lb.
or 28 lb. pails. Also, dried fruits and gourmet
condiments.
   President: Helene Beck
   Public Relations: Bonnie Carroll
   Operations Manager: Debbie Hampton
   Production Manager: Jim Hampton
Number of Products: 10
Type of Packaging: Food Service, Private Label
Brands:
   LA VIGNS

8094 La Vina Winery
4201 Highway 28
Anthony, NM 88021-8551   575-882-7632
      Fax: 575-882-7632   stark@lavinawinery.com
www.lavinawinery.com
Wine
   Owner/President: Ken Stark
   Co-Owner/CEO: Denise Stark
Estimated Sales: Below $ 5 Million
Number Employees: 1-4
Brands:
   La Vina

8095 LaCrosse Milling Company
P.O.Box 86
Cochrane, WI 54622-0086   608-248-2222
      Fax: 608-248-2221   800-441-5411
jbackus@lacrossemilling.com
www.lacrossemilling.com
Processor of oatmeal and rolled oat flakes; exporter
of milled oat products
   President: Dan Ward
   Sales: Glenn Hartzell
   Plant Manager: Bill Brueger
Estimated Sales: $ 10 - 20 Million
Number Employees: 50-99
Number of Products: 50
Type of Packaging: Food Service, Private Label,
   Bulk
Brands:
   DIAMOND

8096 LaGrander Hillside Dairy
W11299 Broek Rd
Stanley, WI 54768-8215   715-644-2275
      Fax: 715-644-0720
Processor of cheese and dairy products
   Owner: Randy La Grander
Estimated Sales: $3500000
Number Employees: 20-49
Type of Packaging: Consumer

8097 LaMonde Wild Flavors
500 S Jefferson St
Placentia, CA 92870-6617   714-993-7700
      Fax: 714-342-3610   www.wildflavors.com
Natural food, pharmaceutical and cosmetic coloring
blends
Estimated Sales: $ 1-5 Million
Number Employees: 1-4

8098 LaMonica Fine Foods
P.O.Box 309
Millville, NJ 08332-0309   856-825-8111
      Fax: 856-825-9354   info@lamonicafinefoods.com
www.lamonicafinefoods.com
A processor of surf clams and ocean clams from US
certified waters. Serving the fresh, canned and
frozen markets, we produce a complete line of clam
products.
   Owner: Danny La Vecchia
   CFO: Jack Pipala
   VP Operations: Michael LaVecchia
Estimated Sales: $50-100 Million
Number Employees: 20-49
Sq. footage: 90000
Type of Packaging: Consumer, Food Service, Pri-
   vate Label, Bulk
Brands:
   CAPE MAY
   LAMONICA
   MARYLAND HOUSE
   OCEAN CHEF

8099 LaRosa Bakery
79 Newman Springs Road E
Shrewsbury, NJ 07702-4038   732-842-4324
      Fax: 732-842-8029   800-527-6722
www.ecannoli.com
Processor of cannolis, cannoli cream, gourmet but-
ter, cookies and biscotti
   President: Sal Larosa
   VP: Peter LaRosa
   Sales Manager: George Delaney
Estimated Sales: $ 1 - 3 Million
Number Employees: 10-19
Type of Packaging: Consumer, Food Service, Bulk

8100 LaRosa's Bakery
79 E Newman Springs Road
Shrewsbury, NJ 07702-4038   732-842-4324
      Fax: 732-842-8029   800-527-6722
www.ecannoli.com
Cannoli, cannoli cream, biscotti, cookies
   Owner/President: Sal La Rosa, Jr.
   Owner/VP: Peter La Rosa
Estimated Sales: Less than $500,000
Number Employees: 1-4
Brands:
   Larosa's Famous Biscotti
   Larosa's Famous Cannoli
   Larosa's Famous Cookies

8101 Laack Brothers Cheese Company
P.O.Box 182
Greenleaf, WI 54126-0182   920-864-2815
      Fax: 920-864-2867   800-589-5127
lfinic@aol.com
Processor of cold pack cheese spreads and cream
cheese spreads; also, shredded mozzarella and ched-
dar cheeses; wholesaler/distributor of cheeses; serv-
ing the food service market; and retail grocery
markets. Private label packaging also available
   President: Jeff Laack
   VP: Mark Laack
Estimated Sales: $ 10 - 20 Million
Number Employees: 10-19
Sq. footage: 25000
Type of Packaging: Consumer, Food Service, Pri-
   vate Label, Bulk
Brands:
   Laack's Finest

8102 (HQ)Labatt Breweries
181 Bay Street
Suite 200
Toronto, ON M5J 2T3
Canada   416-361-5050
      Fax: 416-361-5200   www.labatt.com
Processor and exporter of beer
   President: Bruce Elliot
   CEO: Hugo Powell
Number Employees: 100-249
Parent Co: Interbrew Company
Type of Packaging: Consumer, Food Service
Brands:
   BLEUE DRY
   BLEUE LEGERE
   BLUE STAR
   BOOMERANG
   BOOMERANG
   BUD LIGHT
   BUDWEISER
   CARLSBERG
   CLUB
   JOHN LABATT CLASSIC
   KOKANEE
   KOKANEE GOLD
   KOKANEE LIGHT
   KOOTENAY BLACK LAGER
   KOOTENAY MOUNTAIN ALE
   KOOTENAY PALE ALE
   KOOTENAY TRUE ALE
   LABATT 50
   LABATT BLUE
   LABATT GENUINE DARFT
   LABATT ICE
   LABATT LIGHT
   LUCKY LAGER
   WILDCAT
   WILDCAT STRONG

8103 Labatt Breweries
50 Labatt Avenue
Lasalle, QC H8R 3E7
Canada   514-366-5050
      Fax: 514-364-8005   www.labatt.com
Processor and exporter of beer
Number Employees: 1,000-4,999
Parent Co: Interbrew Company
Type of Packaging: Consumer, Food Service, Pri-
   vate Label, Bulk

8104 Labatt Breweries
4415 Calgary Trail N
Edmonton, AB T6H 5R7
Canada   780-436-6060
      Fax: 780-436-3656   800-268-2997
www.labatt.com
Processor of domestic beer
   President: Jeff Clark
   Marketing Manager: Lori Owen Turner
   Sales Manager: Trent Carroll
   Brewery Manager: Alann Fernandes
Number Employees: 50-99
Parent Co: Interbrew Company
Type of Packaging: Consumer, Food Service
Brands:
   Bohemia
   Carta Blanca
   Dos Equis
   John Labatt Classic
   Labatt 50
   Labatt Bleue Dry
   Labatt Blue
   Labatt Blue Light
   Labatt Crystal

Labatt Extra Dry
Labatt Genuine Draft
Sol

8105 Labatt Breweries
50 Resources Road
Etobicoke, ON M9N 3N7
Canada   416-248-0751
        Fax: 519-667-7304 800-268-2337
        dale.hill@labatt.com   www.labatt.com
Processor of beer, ale, stout and lager
    President: Carlos Britol
    VP, Supply Chain: Charles Oliver
    Public Affairs Director: Bob Chant
    Plant Manager: Steve Kawai
Number Employees: 500-999
Parent Co: Labatt Breweries
Type of Packaging: Consumer, Food Service
Brands:
    Bed Lies
    Bed Wiser
    Belle-Vue Kriek
    Blue Light
    Classic
    Coconies
    Hoegaarden
    Kittis
    Leffe Blonde
    Stella Artois

8106 Labatt Breweries
PO Box 5050
London, ON N6A 4M3
Canada
                    519-663-5050
        Fax: 519-667-7304 www.labatt.com
Processor and exporter of beer, stout, ale and lager
    Manager: Les Sparling
Number Employees: 500-999
Type of Packaging: Consumer, Food Service

8107 Labrada Nutrition
14850 Woodham Dr # B135
Houston, TX 77073-6134
                    281-209-2137
        Fax: 281-209-2135 www.labrada.com
Sports nutrition products
    President/CEO: Lee Labrada

8108 Lacas Coffee Company
7950 National Hwy # A
Pennsauken, NJ 08110-1412   856-910-8662
        Fax: 856-910-8671 800-220-1133
        info@lacascoffee.com   www.lacas.com
Coffee
    President: John Vastardis
    Treasurer: Michael Vlahos
    R & D: Tony Cigounis
Estimated Sales: $ 10-20 Million
Number Employees: 20-49

8109 Lacassagne's
128 Airline Drive
Metairie, LA 70001-6202   504-834-0900
            Fax: 504-834-6593
Wholesale food distributor
    President: Louis Lacassagne III
Number Employees: 20

8110 Lacey Milling Company
P.O.Box 1193
Hanford, CA 93232-1193   559-584-6634
            Fax: 559-584-9165
Manufacturer of flour
    Owner: Scott Lindrum
    Plant Manager: Steve Verschelden
Estimated Sales: $ 10 - 20 Million
Number Employees: 10-19
Type of Packaging: Bulk
Brands:
    CALIFORNIA SPECIAL
    LACEY

8111 Laci Le Beau Corporation
5533 W San Madele Avenue
Fresno, CA 93722-5077   800-356-0490
Processor of herbal and natural food supplements
and dietary teas including herb, cinnamon spice,
lemon mint, cranberry twist, apricot, irish cream and
amaretto
    CEO: Fred Stine
    VP: Helene Roberson
    VP Sales: Ron Dixon
Number Employees: 20-49
Type of Packaging: Consumer

Brands:
    Cats Claw
    Diet Now
    Energi-2000
    Ginkgo 1000
    Guarana Plus
    Laci Be Beau Super Dieter's
    Laci Le Beau Dieter's Tea
    Laci Le Beau Dietery Suplement
    Laci Le Beau Herbal Specialty Teas
    Melatonin
    Power Time
    Serena Calm
    Super Charge
    Super Diet Now

8112 Lactalis IngredientsSouth Park Plant & Distribution Center
2375 South Park Avenue
Buffalo, NY 14220
                    www.liusa.com
Produces whey products, milk powders, caseins, in-
dustrial butters, nutritional and formulated products.
Number Employees: 500
Parent Co: Lactalis USA
Type of Packaging: Food Service, Bulk

8113 Lactalis USABelmont Plant & Distribution Center
218 South Park Street
Belmont, WI 53510-9639   608-762-5173
                    www.liusa.com
Produces whey products, milk powders, caseins, in-
dustrial butters, nutritional and formulated products.
    CEO: Erick Boutry
    VP & Manager: Lenny Bass
Estimated Sales: $37.5 Million
Number Employees: 150
Parent Co: Lactalis USA
Type of Packaging: Food Service, Bulk

8114 Lactalis USAMerrill Plant
8100 Wighway K South
Merrill, WI 54452   715-675-3326
        Fax: 715-536-3028 888-766-3353
                    www.liusa.com
Manufactures cheeses and cheese products.
Parent Co: Lactalis USA
Type of Packaging: Consumer, Food Service

8115 (HQ)Lactalis USA
950 Third Avenue
22nd Floor
New York, NY 10022   212-758-6666
        Fax: 212-758-7383 888-766-3353
        cheese@lactalis-usa.com www.lactalis-usa.com
Processor, exporter and importer of cheeses includ-
ing brie, Swiss, roquefort, feta, edam, gouda, mozza-
rella, ricotta, shredded, fontina, asiago, grated,
parmesan and romano, as well as snack and spread-
able cheese.
    President: Frederick Bouisset
    VP Sales: Paul Peterson
Estimated Sales: $85000
Number Employees: 765
Sq. footage: 1500
Parent Co: Lactalis American Group
Type of Packaging: Consumer, Food Service, Pri-
vate Label, Bulk
Other Locations:
    Belmont Plant & Distribution Center
    Belmont WI
    Merrill Plant
    Merrill WI
Brands:
    Bridel
    Martin-Collet
    Mozzarella Fresca
    Pere
    Precious
    President
    Rondele
    Societe

8116 Lacto Milk Products Corporation
PO Box 272
Flemington, NJ 08822-0272   908-788-2200
            Fax: 908-788-2737
Processor of yogurt and juices
    General Manager: Edward Steward
Estimated Sales: $100+ Million
Number Employees: 500-999
Parent Co: Johanna Farms
Type of Packaging: Consumer, Private Label, Bulk

8117 Lad's Smokehouse Catering
3731 School St
Needville, TX 77461   979-793-6210
        Fax: 979-793-4220 info@ladssmokehouse.com
                    www.ladssmokehouse.com
Processor of sausage
    President: Robert Case
Estimated Sales: $ 1 - 3 Million
Number Employees: 1-4
Type of Packaging: Consumer
Brands:
    Lad's

8118 Ladish Malting
N5355 Junction Road
Jefferson, WI 53549-9661   920-674-8500
        Fax: 920-674-8570 www.cargill.com
Malt
    President: Sergio Barroso
Estimated Sales: $ 50 - 100 Million
Number Employees: 50-99

8119 Ladoga Frozen Food & Retail Meat
P.O.Box 262
Ladoga, IN 47954-0262   765-942-2225
Processor of frozen meat including beef and pork;
wholesaler/distributor of fruit and vegetables
    President: Harold Lowe
Number Employees: 1-4
Type of Packaging: Consumer, Food Service

8120 Ladson Homemade Pasta Company
3334 W Wilshire Drive
Suite 33
Phoenix, AZ 85009-1455   480-353-0874
                    Fax: 480-661-1156
Macaroni, spaghetti
    President: Gary Capra
Estimated Sales: $ 1-4.9 Million
Number Employees: 3

8121 Lady Gale Seafood
PO Box 58
Baldwin, LA 70514-0058   337-923-2060
                    Fax: 337-923-6909
Processor of fresh and frozen shrimp
    Owner: Wayne Stevens
    CFO: Jessica Burns
Estimated Sales: Below $ 5 Million
Number Employees: 4-10
Type of Packaging: Consumer, Food Service

8122 Lady Walton's Cookies
151 Regal Row # 118
Dallas, TX 75247-5609   214-630-9101
        Fax: 214-630-9101 800-552-8006
        ladywalton@ladywalton.com
                    www.ladywalton.com
    Owner: Susan Walton
Estimated Sales: $ 1 - 3 Million
Number Employees: 20-49

8123 Lady Walton's and Bronco Bob's Cowboy Brand Specialty Foods
151 Regal Row # 118
Dallas, TX 75247-5609   214-630-9101
        Fax: 214-630-9101 800-552-8006
        ladywalton@ladywalton.com
                    www.ladywalton.com
Chipotle sauces
    Owner: Susan Walton
Estimated Sales: $ 1 - 3 Million
Number Employees: 20-49
Brands:
    Bronco Bob's

8124 Laetitia Vineyard
453 Laetitia Vineyard Dr
Arroyo Grande, CA 93420-9701   805-481-1772
        Fax: 805-481-6920 888-809-8463
        info@laetitiawine.com   www.laetitiawine.com
Wine
    Manager: Eric Hickey
    Sales: Mark Newman
    Operations: Dave Hickey
    Production: Eric Hickey
Estimated Sales: Below $ 5 Million
Number Employees: 5-9
Brands:
    Avila

Barnwood
Laetitia

8125 Lafayette Brewing Company
622 Main St
Lafayette, IN 47901-1451   765-742-2591
          Fax: 765-742-3443
mail@lafayettebrewingco.com
www.lafayettebrewingco.com
Processor of ale
  President: Greg Emig
  Brewer: Chris Johnson
  Quality Control: Nancy Emig
Estimated Sales: Below $ 5 Million
Number Employees: 20-49
Type of Packaging: Consumer, Food Service

8126 Lafitte Frozen Foods Corporation
5165 Caroline St
Lafitte, LA 70067-5423   504-689-2041
          Fax: 504-689-3270
Fresh and frozen shrimp processor.
  President: Paul Poon
Estimated Sales: $8.5 Million
Number Employees: 50-99

8127 Lafleur Dairy
617 Hill St
New Orleans, LA 70121-1000   504-464-0812
          Fax: 504-461-8655
Processor of milk and yogurt
  President: Cedric Lafleur
  VP: Tommy Baker
  CFO: Monica Sosta
Estimated Sales: Below $ 5 Million
Number Employees: 40
Parent Co: Borden
Type of Packaging: Consumer, Food Service, Bulk
Brands:
  Borden

8128 Lafollette Vineyard & Winery
64 Harlingen Road
Belle Mead, NJ 08502-5301   908-359-5018
          Fax: 908-874-7884
Wines
  Owner: Miriam Summerskill
Estimated Sales: $68,000
Number Employees: 1
Type of Packaging: Private Label
Brands:
  La Follette

8129 Lafourche Sugar Corporation
141 Leighton Quarters Rd
Thibodaux, LA 70301-6489   985-447-3210
  Fax: 985-447-8728 GN.Lafourche@charter.net
Manufacturer of sugar and blackstrap molasses
  President/CEO: Greg Nolan
Estimated Sales: $1-3 Million
Number Employees: 5-9
Type of Packaging: Consumer

8130 Lago Tortillas International
1700 E 4th St
Austin, TX 78702-4427   512-476-0945
          Fax: 512-476-4931 800-369-9017
          www.ellago.net
Tortillas
  Manager: Luis Centeno
Estimated Sales: $ 5-10 Million appx.
Number Employees: 100-249

8131 Lagomarcino's
1422 5th Ave
Moline, IL 61265-1334   309-764-1814
          Fax: 309-736-5423 lagos@netexpress.net
          www.lagomarcinos.com
Ice cream and confections
  President: Tom Lagomarcino
Estimated Sales: $ 1-2.5 Million
Number Employees: 10-19
Brands:
  Lagomarcino's

8132 Lagorio Enterprises
2771 French Camp Rd
Manteca, CA 95336-9689   209-982-5691
          Fax: 209-982-0235 mail@lagorio.com
          www.lagorio.com
Grower, packer and exporter of fresh tomatoes
  President: Kathy Janssen
  General Manager: Dean Janssen

Estimated Sales: $ 5 - 10 Million
Number Employees: 100-249
Sq. footage: 158943
Brands:
  Ace-Hi

8133 Laguna Beach Brewing Company
422 S Coast Highway
Laguna Beach, CA 92651-2404   949-494-2739
          Fax: 949-497-0659
Processor of ale, stout, lager and porter
  President: Ross Bartlett
  Director Manufacturing: Jack Whybark
Estimated Sales: $ 20-50 Million
Number Employees: 30-50
Type of Packaging: Consumer, Food Service, Private Label, Bulk
Brands:
  Diver's Hole Dunkelweizen
  Festival Light Ale
  Greeter's Pale Ale
  Laguna Beach Blinde
  Main Beach Brown
  Renaissance Red
  Salt Kriek Cherry Be
  Thousand Steps Stout
  Victoria E.S.B.
  Wipe Out

8134 Laguna Cookie & DessertCompany
4041 W Garry Ave
Santa Ana, CA 92704-6315   714-546-6855
          Fax: 714-556-2491 800-673-2473
Cookies and Deserts
  President: Mark McPeak
Estimated Sales: $ 20-50 Million
Number Employees: 250-499

8135 Laird & Company
P.O.Box 7
North Garden, VA 22959-0007   434-296-6058
          Fax: 434-296-0071 877-438-5247
          sales@lairdandcompany.com
          www.lairdandcompany.com
Processor of apple products, wines, spirits, imported
olive oils and balsamic vinegar
  President: Larrie Laird
  General Manager: Lester Clements
Estimated Sales: $10-20 Million
Number Employees: 1-4
Parent Co: Laird & Company
Type of Packaging: Consumer
Brands:
  Captains
  Virginia Fruit

8136 Laird & Company
1 Laird Rd
Eatontown, NJ 07724-9799   732-542-0312
          Fax: 732-542-2244 877-438-5247
          sales@lairdandcompany.com
          www.lairdandcompany.com
Processor and exporter of apple brandy, bourbon,
vodka, gin, blended whiskey and other spirits; im-
porter of wine and bulk alcoholic beverages; also,
contract bottling available
  President: Larrie Laird
  VP Administration: John Laird III
  VP Marketing/Public Relations: Lisa Laird Dunn
Estimated Sales: $ 20 - 50 Million
Number Employees: 50-99
Sq. footage: 155000
Type of Packaging: Private Label, Bulk
Brands:
  Apple Jack
  Bankers Club
  Barrister
  Five Star
  Kasser
  Laird
  Villa Masa

8137 Lake Arrowhead
P.O.Box 11
Twin Peaks, CA 92391-0011   909-337-9228
          Fax: 909-336-1548 877-237-8528
info@lakearrowhead.net www.lakearrowhead.net
  President: Larry Luciano
  Chairman: Richard Teachout
  CFO: Grant Mayne
Number Employees: 5-9
Brands:
  Lake Arrowhead

8138 Lake Champlain Chocolates
750 Pine Street
Burlington, VT 05401-4923   802-864-1808
          Fax: 802-864-1806 800-465-5909
          info@lakechamplainchocolates.com
Specialty chocolate candies
  President/Founder: James Lampman
  Sales Manager: Allyson Brown
Estimated Sales: Less than $500,000
Number Employees: 80
Sq. footage: 24000
Type of Packaging: Consumer, Food Service, Private Label, Bulk
Brands:
  FIVE STAR BARS
  ORIGINAL CHOCOLATES OF VERMONT

8139 Lake Charles Poultry
2808 Fruge St
Lake Charles, LA 70615-3699   337-433-6818
          Fax: 318-433-7855
  President: Danny Bellard
Estimated Sales: $ 5 - 10 Million
Number Employees: 5-9

8140 Lake City Foods
5183 General Road
Mississauga, ON L4W 2K4
Canada   905-625-8244
          Fax: 905-625-8245
Processor and exporter of drink mixes, jelly pow-
ders, soup bases and mixes, army rations, nondairy
coffee creamers and camping and trail foods
  Owner: David Reichmann
  Owner: Andrew Wiseberg
Number Employees: 10-19
Parent Co: Eden Manufacturing Company
Type of Packaging: Consumer, Food Service, Private Label, Bulk
Brands:
  Anytime
  Camp Rite
  Gibbons
  Quickset

8141 Lake Country Foods
132 S Concord Rd
Oconomowoc, WI 53066-3555   262-567-5521
          Fax: 262-567-5714 mthomas5@execpc.com
          www.lcfoods.com
Processor of malted milk, malt extract, dry blended
foods, etc
  Owner: Dave Erdman
  National Accounts Manager: John Markan
  VP Technical Services/Quality Assurance:
  Michael Thomas
  VP Sales: Myron Jones
  National Sales Manager: Myron Jones
Estimated Sales: $ 20-30 Million
Number Employees: 50-99
Sq. footage: 150000

8142 Lake Erie Frozen Foods Company
1830 Orange Rd
Ashland, OH 44805-1335   419-289-9204
          Fax: 419-281-7624 800-766-8501
          mbuckingham@leffco.net www.leffco.net
Manufacturer of breaded cheese and vegetables
  President: William Buckingham
Estimated Sales: $2.4 Million
Number Employees: 20-49
Type of Packaging: Consumer, Food Service, Private Label

8143 Lake Helen Sprout Farm
145 W Michigan Avenue
Lake Helen, FL 32744-2935   386-228-2871
Processor, packer and wholesaler/distributor of
sprouts
  Assistant Manager: N Hazen
Number Employees: 5-9
Sq. footage: 6000
Type of Packaging: Food Service, Private Label, Bulk
Brands:
  Lake Helen Sprout Farm

8144 Lake Packing Company
755 Lake Landing Dr
Lottsburg, VA 22511-2503   804-529-6101
          Fax: 804-529-7374 lapco@sylvaninfo.net

Processor of frozen oysters and canned tomatoes, tomato juice and hominy
President: Sameul Lake Cowart
Estimated Sales: Under $ 1 Million
Number Employees: 20-49
Parent Co: Cowart Seafood
Type of Packaging: Consumer, Food Service, Private Label

8145 Lake Shore Frozen Foods
P.O.Box 409
Lake City, PA 16423-0409   814-774-3131
          Fax: 814-774-3136   877-774-3668
          www.lakeshorefrozenfood.com
Frozen donuts, pie shells, unfinished donuts, waffles
Chairman: Bruce MacLeod
CEO: Nat Burnside
Estimated Sales: $ 10-20 Million
Number Employees: 50-99

8146 Lake Sonoma Winery
340 Healdsburg Ave
Healdsburg, CA 95448-4106   707-473-2999
          Fax: 707-431-8356   877-850-9463
info@lswinery.com   www.lakesonomawinery.net
Wines
President: Gary Heck
CEO: Gary Heck
Sales: Pat Paulson
Marketing Director: Gary Heck
Estimated Sales: $1-$2.5 Million
Number Employees: 5-9
Brands:
  LAKE SONOMA WINERY

8147 Lake St. George Brewing
RR 1
Box 2505
Liberty, ME 04949   207-589-4690
WINES
President: Marilyn Beer
Estimated Sales: Under $500,000
Number Employees: 1-4

8148 Lake States Yeast
515 W Davenport Street
Rhinelander, WI 54501   918-535-2676
          Fax: 715-369-4034   vbond@wausaupaper.com
          www.wplakestates.com
Manufacturer and exporter of yeasts including inactive dried, torula, autolyzed, formulated and specialty grades that inlcudes smoked, roasted, and grill flavors.
Sales Director: Vernon Bond
Operations Manager: Stuart Bacon
Production Manager: Rick Bishop
Plant Manager: Linda Fox
Number Employees: 20-49
Parent Co: Rhinelander Paper Company
Type of Packaging: Private Label, Bulk
Brands:
  Lake States

8149 Lake Titus Brewery
Hc 1
Box 58b
Malone, NY 12953   518-483-2337
Brewers
Owner: Fred Ruvola
Estimated Sales: $500,000-$1 Million
Number Employees: 20-49

8150 Lakefront Brewery
1872 N Commerce St
Milwaukee, WI 53212-3701   414-372-8800
Fax: 414-372-4400   info@lakefrontbrewery.com
          www.lakefrontbrewery.com
Processor of beer
Owner: Russ Davis
Marketing Director: Orlando Segura
Estimated Sales: Below $ 5 Million
Number Employees: 5-9
Type of Packaging: Private Label
Brands:
  River West Stein

8151 Lakeport Brewing Corporation
201 Burlington Street E
Hamilton, ON L8L 4H2
Canada   905-523-4200
          Fax: 905-523-6564 www.lakeportbrewing.ca
Processor and exporter of beer, ale, lager and stout
President: Teresa Cascioli
Sales/Marketing Executive: Ian McDonald

Number Employees: 200
Type of Packaging: Consumer, Food Service
Brands:
  BRAVA
  LAKEPORT HONEY LAGER
  LAKEPORT ICE
  LAKEPORT LIGHT
  LAKEPORT PILSENER
  LAKEPORT STRONG
  MONGOOSE
  STEELER LAGER
  WEE WILLY

8152 Lakeridge Winery & Vineyards
19239 Highway 27
Clermont, FL 34715-9025   352-394-8627
          Fax: 352-394-7490   800-768-9463
lakeridgew@aol.com   www.lakeridgewinery.com
Wines
President: Geary Cox
Estimated Sales: $ 10-20 Million
Number Employees: 20-49
Brands:
  Lakeridge

8153 Lakeshore Winery
5132 State Route 89
Romulus, NY 14541-9779   315-549-7075
          Fax: 315-549-7102   info@lakeshorewinery.com
          www.lakeshorewinery.com
Farm winery
President/CEO/CFO: John Bachman
Estimated Sales: $ 5-9.9 Million
Number Employees: 2
Brands:
  Lakeshore

8154 Lakeside Foods
1055 W Broadway
Plainview, MN 55964-1059   507-534-3141
          Fax: 507-534-3005 www.lakesidefoods.com
Manufacturer and exporter of frozen and canned vegetables including corn, peas and lima beans; also, meat
Manager: Bill Arendt
VP Human Resources: Tom Reilly
Director Operations: Jim Schwarzhoff
General Manager: Bill Arendt
Estimated Sales: $100 Million
Number Employees: 20-49
Type of Packaging: Consumer
Other Locations:
  Lakeside Foods - Manufacturing
  Manitowoc WI
  Lakeside Foods - Manufacturing
  Belgium WI
  Lakeside Foods - Manufacturing
  Random Lake WI
  Lakeside Foods - Manufacturing
  Reedsburg WI
  Lakeside Foods - Manufacturing
  Seymour WI
  Lakeside Foods - Manufacturing
  Plainview MN
  Lakeside Foods - Manufacturing
  Brooten MN
  Lakeside Foods - Manufacturing
  Owatoona MN
  Lakeside Foods - Manufacturing
  New Richmond WI
  Lakeside Foods - Manufacturing
  Eden WI
  Lakeside Foods - Distribution
  Manitowoc WI
  Lakeside Foods - Distribution
  Plainview MN
  Lakeside Foods - Distribution
  Belgium WI
Brands:
  EUREKA
  HOBBY
  LAKESIDE

8155 Lakeside Foods
P.O.Box 1327
Manitowoc, WI 54221-1327   920-684-3356
Fax: 920-686-4033   jferguson@lakesidefoods.com
          www.lakesidefoods.com
Canned vegetables, frozen vegetables, canned meats, organic vegetables and meal starters
President/COO: David Yanda
CEO/Chairman: J. Douglas Quick
Human Resources VP: Thomas Reilly
Processed Food Sales SVP: Jeff Lund
Operations VP: Jim Schwarzhoff

Estimated Sales: $200 Million
Number Employees: 50-99
Sq. footage: 400000
Type of Packaging: Consumer, Food Service, Private Label
Other Locations:
  Lakeside Foods Processing Plant
  Manitowoc WI
  Lakeside Foods Processing Plant
  Belgium WI
  Lakeside Foods Processing Plant
  Random Lake WI
  Lakeside Foods Processing Plant
  Reedsburg WI
  Lakeside Foods Processing Plant
  Seymour WI
  Lakeside Foods Processing Plant
  Planview MN
  Lakeside Foods Processing Plant
  Brooten MN
  Lakeside Foods Processing Plant
  New Richmond WI
  Lakeside Foods Processing Plant
  Eden WI
  Lakeside Foods Processing Plant
  Owatonna MN
Brands:
  Festal
  Read
  Tendersweet

8156 Lakeside Foods
P.O.Box 1327
Manitowoc, WI 54221-1327   920-684-3356
Fax: 920-686-4033   jferguson@lakesidefoods.com
          www.lakesidefoods.com
Canner of peas, corn and lima beans
President: J Douglas Quick
Senior VP: Jeff Lund
VP: James Ferguson
CEO: David J Yanda
Senior VP Sales: David Yanda
Senior VP Operations: Jim Schwarzhoff
Estimated Sales: $301,200,000
Number Employees: 250-499
Type of Packaging: Consumer

8157 Lakeside Foods
P.O.Box 5
Seymour, WI 54165-0005   920-833-2371
          Fax: 920-833-7504 www.lakesidefoods.com
Processor of canned vegetables including peas, carrots, beets, corn, etc
General Manager: John Selmer
Marketing Manager: James Farley
Estimated Sales: $ 10 - 20 Million
Number Employees: 20-49
Sq. footage: 170000
Parent Co: Lakeside Foods
Type of Packaging: Consumer, Food Service, Private Label, Bulk

8158 Lakeside Foods
P.O.Box 196
New Holstein, WI 53061-0196   920-898-5702
          Fax: 920-898-5705 www.lakesidesystems.com
Processor and canner of corn and peas
President: Tim Honigschmitt
Estimated Sales: $10-20 Million
Number Employees: 20-49
Type of Packaging: Private Label

8159 Lakeside Foods
P.O.Box 430
Brooten, MN 56316-0430   320-346-2900
          Fax: 320-346-2903 www.lakesidefoods.com
Processor of frozen vegetables including corn, peas and lima beans
General Manager: Jeff Griep
Estimated Sales: $ 20-50 Million
Number Employees: 100-249
Sq. footage: 65000
Parent Co: Lakeside Foods
Type of Packaging: Bulk

8160 Lakeside Foods
457 Canal St
Mondovi, WI 54755-1603   715-926-5075
          Fax: 715-926-5076 www.lakesidefoods.com

Manufacturer of canned and frozen vegetables, canned dry beans, jellies and preserves, frozen and shelf stable meals, canned meats and stew, organic products, health beverage supplements, non-dairy frozen dessert toppings, salsas andother sauces
President/CEO: Doug Quick
SVP Processed Food Sales: Jeff Lund
SVP Operations: Dan Cavanaugh
Plant Manager: Jim Kern
Estimated Sales: $20-50 Million
Number Employees: 100-249
Type of Packaging: Private Label
Other Locations:
Lakeside Foods - HQ
Manitowoc WI

8161 Lakeside Mills
P.O.Box 230
Rutherfordton, NC 28139-0230   828-286-4866
Fax: 828-287-3361 sales@lakesidemills.com
www.lakesidemills.com
Processor of corn meal, hush puppy mix and breadings; importer of peppers and spices
VP: Aaron King
Number Employees: 10-19
Parent Co: Lakeside Mills
Type of Packaging: Consumer, Food Service, Private Label, Bulk
Brands:
Blue Ribbon
Kings Old Fashion

8162 Lakeside Packing Company
667 County Road #50
Harrow, ON N0R 1G0
Canada   519-738-2314
Fax: 519-738-3684 www.lakesidepacking.com
Processor of peppers, sauerkraut, relishes and olives; wholesaler/distributor and importer of jams and apple juice
President: Don Woodbridge
Type of Packaging: Consumer, Food Service

8163 Lakespring Winery
2055 Hoffman Lane
Yountville, CA 94599   707-944-2475
Wines
President: Frank Battat

8164 Lakeview Bakery
6449 Crowchild Trail SW
Calgary, AB T2E 5R7
Canada   403-246-6127
Fax: 403-246-6609 info@organicbaking.com
members.shaw.ca/organicbaking/
Processor of bread, buns and pastries
President: Maureen Hinton
Sales/Distribution: David Hinton
Number Employees: 5-9
Type of Packaging: Consumer, Food Service

8165 Lakeview Farms
P.O.Box 98
Delphos, OH 45833-0098   419-695-9925
Fax: 419-695-9900 800-755-9925
lvfsales@lakeviewfarms.com
www.lakeviewfarms.com
Sour cream, mousse, cheesecake, fruit gelatins, sour cream dip, soy oil dips, imitation sour cream
President: Gene Graves
CEO: Mardy Garlack
VP Sales: Joh Kopilchack
Estimated Sales: $ 30-50 Million
Number Employees: 100-249
Type of Packaging: Bulk
Brands:
Lakeview Farms
Merkt's
Merkt's Bristol Gold
Owl's Nest Cheese
Real Desserts
Winky Foods

8166 Lakewood Juices
P.O.Box 420708
Miami, FL 33242-0708   305-324-5900
Fax: 305-325-9573
newberry@floridabottling.com
www.lakewoodjuices.com
Fruit juices
Manager: Lee Wilson
Sales Manager: Holly Newberry

Estimated Sales: $ 20 - 50 Million
Number Employees: 20-49
Parent Co: Florida Bottling

8167 Lakewood Vineyards
4024 State Route 14
Watkins Glen, NY 14891-9718   607-535-9252
Fax: 607-535-6656
wines@lakewoodvineyards.com
www.lakewoodvineyards.com
Wines
President: Charles Stamp
Estimated Sales: $ 2.5-5 Million
Number Employees: 5-9
Brands:
Lakewood Vineyards
Mystic Mead

8168 Lallemand
PO Box 5512
Petaluma, CA 94955-5512   707-795-1468
Fax: 661-835-4990 800-423-6625
info@lallemand.com www.lallemand.com
Wine industry yeasts
Director: William Pursley
Brands:
Enoferm
Fermaid
Lalvin
Uvaferm

8169 Lallemand/American Yeast
47-00 Northern Boulevard
L.I.C., NY 11101   773-267-2223
Fax: 773-267-4508 gedwards@lallemand.com
www.lallemand.comcurves
Yeast
President: Joanie joans
Estimated Sales: $300,000-500,000
Number Employees: 5-9

8170 Lallemand/American Yeast
1417 Jeffrey Dr
Addison, IL 60101-4331   630-932-1290
Fax: 630-932-1291 mlegel@lallemand.com
www.lallemand.com
Baking enzymes, baking ingredients, dough conditioners, such as bromate replacers, chocolate, cocoa, eggs, nuts, oils, oxidizers, raisins, spices, sweetners, yeast foods, yeast (fresh & dry), starter cultures, baking powder, moldinhibitors
President: Gary Edwards
VP: Merna Legel
Quality Control: Mike Hudson
Sales: Steven Marinella
Estimated Sales: Below $ 5 Million
Number Employees: 20-49
Parent Co: Lallemand, Inc.
Type of Packaging: Food Service, Bulk
Brands:
American Yeast
Eagle
Essential
Fermaid
Lallemand

8171 Lamagna Cheese Company
1 Lamagna Dr
Verona, PA 15147-1137   412-828-6112
Fax: 412-828-6782 info@lamagnacheese.com
www.lamagnacheese.com
Ricotta, feta, shredded mozzarella
President: Rudolph Lamagna
Estimated Sales: $ 10-20 Million
Number Employees: 10-19
Brands:
Lamagana

8172 Lamb-Weston
599 S Rivershore Ln
Eagle, ID 83616-4979   208-938-1047
Fax: 208-658-2202 www.lambweston.com
President: Jeff De Lapp
Number Employees: 50-99
Parent Co: ConAgra Foods
Brands:
HOY PICKS
INLAND VALLEY
SWIFT PREMIUM
SWISS MISS

8173 Lamb-Weston
78153 Westland Rd
Hermiston, OR 97838-9520   541-567-2211
Fax: 541-567-2211 800-766-7783
brian.hersch@lambweston.com
www.lambweston.com
Manufacturer and exporter of frozen French and shoestring fries
Branch Manager: Horst Ellendt
Estimated Sales: $742 Million
Number Employees: 50
Parent Co: ConAgra Foods
Type of Packaging: Consumer, Food Service, Bulk
Brands:
GENERATION 7 FRIES
LAMB'S SUPREME
LW PRIVATE RESERVE
STEALTH FRIES
TIME SAVOR

8174 Lamb-Weston
P.O.Box 1900
Pasco, WA 99302-1900   509-735-4651
Fax: 509-736-0399 800-766-7783
www.lambweston.com
Manufacturer of potato products: French fries (Shoestrings, Twister, CrissCut, Curley QQQ's, seasoned, wedge, crinkle, etc.), mashed, hash browns, chopped and formed products, etc. Also, pizza and snack pockets and fruit turnovers.Foodservice, institutional and retail
President: Jeff Delapp
Number Employees: 5,000-9,999
Parent Co: ConAgra Foods
Type of Packaging: Consumer, Food Service, Private Label
Brands:
Crisscut
Curley Qqq's
Munchers
Twister

8175 Lamb-Weston
103 Depot St
Weston, OR 97886-5020   541-566-3511
Fax: 541-566-2053 800-766-7783
lwinfo@conagrafoods.com
www.lambweston.com
Processor of frozen fruit turnovers and pizza pockets. Specialty potato products.
CFO: Dawnet E Stewart
Plant Manager: Jeff Brasch
Estimated Sales: $ 50 - 100 Million
Number Employees: 100-249
Parent Co: ConAgra Foods
Type of Packaging: Consumer, Food Service, Private Label, Bulk
Brands:
Generation 7 Fries
LW Private Reserve
Lamb's Supreme
Stealth
TimeSavor

8176 Lambent Technologies
7247 Central Park Avenue
Skokie, IL 60076-4045   847-675-3950
Fax: 847-675-3013 800-432-7187
lambent@petrofirm.com www.petrofirm.com
Manufacturer and exporter of nonionic emulsifiers including polysorbates, sorbitan esters and glycerol esters; also, silicone and nonsilicone antifoams and defoamers
President: Michael Hayes
Marketing Manager: Randy Cobb
Sales Manager: Kevin Hrebenar
Estimated Sales: $9800000
Number Employees: 55
Sq. footage: 10000
Parent Co: Petroferm
Brands:
Lambent

8177 Lambert Bridge Winery
4085 W Dry Creek Rd
Healdsburg, CA 95448-9117   707-431-9600
Fax: 707-433-3215 800-975-0555
wines@lambertbridge.com
www.lambertbridge.com
WINE
President: Patricia Chambers
Winemaker: Jill Davis
Estimated Sales: $1.1 Million
Number Employees: 10-19

Type of Packaging: Private Label
Brands:
    Lambert Bridge Winery

8178 Lambrights
P.O.Box 295
Lagrange, IN 46761-0295   260-463-2178
                                Fax: 260-463-7444
Manufacturer of eggs and feed
    Owner and President: Dick Lambright
Estimated Sales:$1-3 Million
Number Employees: 50-99
Type of Packaging: Bulk

8179 Lamesa Cotton Oil Mill
PO Box 2710
Chandler, AZ 85244-2710   806-872-2166
Processor of cottonseed hull and cottonseed oil
Number Employees: 20-49
Parent Co: Chickasha Cotton Oil Company

8180 Lamex Foods
3300 Edinborough Way
Edina, MN 55435-5923   952-844-0585
    Fax: 952-844-0083 usa@lamex-foods.com
                          www.lamexfoods.com
Manufacture of food items
Estimated Sales: $ 50-100 Million
Number Employees: 10-19
Parent Co: Lamex Foods

8181 Lamm Food Service
P.O.Box 2957
Lafayette, LA 70502-2957   337-896-0331
                                Fax: 337-896-9213
    Owner: J D Lively
Estimated Sales:$ 50 - 100 Million
Number Employees: 50-99

8182 Lammes Candies Since 1885
P.O.Box 1885
Austin, TX 78767-1885   512-327-5261
    Fax: 512-310-2280 800-252-1885
                          www.lammes.com
Candy
    Manager: Crystal Bertrand
    VP: Bryan Teich
Estimated Sales: $ 5 - 10 Million
Number Employees: 10-19
Number of Products: 1000
Brands:
    CASHEW CRITTERS
    CHOC-ADILLOS
    LONGHORNS
    PEANUT PAWS
    TEXAS CHEWIE PECAN PRALINE

8183 Lamonaca Bakery
304 7th St
Windber, PA 15963-1343   814-467-4909
Processor of bread products and pizza shells
    President: Mary La Monaca
Estimated Sales: $ 5 - 10 Million
Number Employees: 10-19
Type of Packaging: Consumer, Food Service

8184 Lamoreaux Landing Wine Cellar
9224 State Route 414
Lodi, NY 14860-9641   607-582-6011
    Fax: 607-582-6010 llwc@capital.net
                          www.lamoreauxwine.com
Wines
    Owner: Mark Wagner
    Retail Sales Manager: Susan Whitaker
Estimated Sales: $ 5 -10 Million
Number Employees: 10-19
Type of Packaging: Private Label

8185 Lampasas Locker Plant
PO Box 707
Lampasas, TX 76550-0032   512-556-5121
Processor of pork products and processed beef;
slaughtering services available
    President: Brenda Stephens
Estimated Sales:$280000
Number Employees: 4
Type of Packaging: Consumer

8186 Lampost Meats
805 Shawver Drive
Grimes, IA 50111-1118   515-288-6111
    Fax: 515-288-5727 sglksl@aol.com
                          www.lampostmeats.com

Processor of pork and beef offals
    President: Stanley Lammers
Number Employees: 2
Parent Co: Walking S Farms

8187 Lanaetex Products Incorporated
P.O.Box 6915
Elizabeth, NJ 07202-8915   908-351-9700
                                Fax: 908-351-8753
Processor and exporter of food grade waxes
    President: Mike Gutowski
Estimated Sales:$ 10 - 20 Million
Number Employees: 10-19

8188 Lancaster County Winery
799 Rawlinsville Rd
Willow Street, PA 17584-8700   717-464-3555
                          www.lancastercountywinery.com
Wines
    President: Suzanne Dickel
*Estimated Sales:*Below $ 5 Million
Number Employees: 5-9

8189 Lancaster Packing Company
P.O.Box 7595
Lancaster, PA 17604-7595   717-397-9727
    Fax: 717-397-7744 www.jakeandamos.com
Processor of Pennsylvania Dutch-style pickles, pre-
serves, relishes, syrups, pickled vegetables and
fruits, chow chow and fruit butters packed in glass
canning jars
    President: David Doolittle
    CEO: Sue Doolittle
Estimated Sales: $ 5 - 10 Million
Number Employees: 5-9
Sq. footage: 10000
Type of Packaging: Consumer, Private Label
Brands:
    Jake & Amos

8190 Lance G. Fisher Seafood
P.O.Box 42
Sanford, VA 23426-0042   757-824-3489
                                Fax: 757-824-0529
Processor of fish and seafood
    President: Lance Fisher
Estimated Sales:$2500000
Number Employees: 20-49
Type of Packaging: Consumer

8191 (HQ)Lance Inc
8600 South Blvd
Charlotte, NC 28273   704-554-1421
    Fax: 704-554-5562 800-438-1880
    fresh@lance.com www.lance.com
Manufacturer and exporter of sandwich crackers,
nuts and seeds, captain's wafers, cookies, popcorn,
snack cakes, gold n chees, and 100 calorie packs.
    President/CEO: David Singer
    EVP/CFO/Treasurer/Secretary: Richard Puckett
    SVP/Sales & Marketing: Glenn Patcha
    Senior Vice President/Sales: Frank Lewis
    SVP Human Resources: Earl Leake
    SVP Supply Chain: Blake Thompson
Estimated Sales:$918 Million
Number Employees: 4800
Type of Packaging: Consumer
Other Locations:
    Lance
    Hyannis MA
Brands:
    BLOOPS
    CAN-O-LUNCH
    CAPE COD POTATO CHIPS
    CAPTAIN'S WAFERS
    CHOC-O-LUNCH
    GOLD-N-CHEES
    LANCE
    NEKOT
    NIPCHEE
    OUTPOST
    THUNDER
    THUNDER BOOMERS
    TOASTCHEE
    TOASTY
    VISTA

8192 (HQ)Lanco
350 Wireless Blvd
Hauppauge, NY 11788-3947   631-231-2300
    Fax: 631-231-2731 800-938-4500
    sales@lancopromo.com www.lancopromo.com

Processor of chocolate candy including squares, cir-
cles and triangles
    President: Brian Landow
Estimated Sales:$21900000
Number Employees: 1-4
Type of Packaging: Consumer, Food Service

8193 (HQ)Land O Frost
16850 Chicago Ave
Lansing, IL 60438-1115   708-474-7100
    Fax: 708-474-9329 800-643-5654
Manufacturer and importer of lunch and deli meats
such as; beef, chicken, turkey, ham and meat ingre-
dients
    President: David Van Eekeren
    CEO: Donna Van Eekeren
    CFO: George Smolar
Estimated Sales:$100+ Million
Number Employees: 250-499
Sq. footage: 210000
Type of Packaging: Consumer, Food Service, Pri-
    vate Label
Brands:
    DAGWOOD
    LAND O'FROST
    PREMIUM
    TASTE ESCAPES

8194 Land O Lakes Milk
1200 W Russell St
Sioux Falls, SD 57104-1325   605-330-9526
    Fax: 605-336-7206 www.landolakesinc.com
Manufacturer of beverages including milk, juice,
etc.; wholesaler/distributor of frozen food and dairy
products
    Chairman/CEO: Gregg Engles
    Executive: Steve Sneer
    General Manager: Dana Loseke
Estimated Sales:$36 Million
Number Employees: 100-249
Parent Co: Dean Foods Company
Type of Packaging: Consumer

8195 Land O'Frost
911 Hastings Ave
Searcy, AR 72143-7401   501-268-2473
    Fax: 501-268-0357 800-643-5654
    wnicholson@landofrost.com
                          www.landofrost.com

Processor and importer of ham, beef, chicken and
turkey; also, pre-sliced luncheon meats, pre-por-
tioned julienne meat strips and diced meats
    President: Charles Niementowski
    VP Food Service: F Michael Szabo
    Product Development Director: William
    Nicholson
    VP Retail Sales: Tony Palesotti
Estimated Sales:$100+ Million
Number Employees: 500-999
Sq. footage: 263000
Parent Co: Land O'Frost
Type of Packaging: Consumer, Food Service, Pri-
    vate Label, Bulk
Brands:
    Perfect-O-Portion
    Salad Toppers
    Sandwich Shop

8196 Land O'Lakes
P.O.Box 160
Spencer, WI 54479-0160   715-659-2311
    Fax: 715-659-5990 www.landolakes.com
Processor and exporter of processed, sliced, dried
and loaf cheese.
    President/CEO: Chris Policinski
    Chairman: Pete Kappelman
    SVP/CFO: Dan Knutson
    VP/General Counsel: Peter Janzen
    VP/Strategy & Business Development: Barry
    Wolfish
    EVP/Land O'Lakes Purina Feed: Fernando
    Palacios
    EVP/COO Dairy Foods Value-Added: Steve
    Dunphy
    EVP/COO Dairy Foods Industrial: Alan Pierson
    VP/Public Affairs: Jim Fife
    VP/Human Resources: Karen Grabow
    Plant Manager: Dennis Thomas
    Purchasing Agent: Deanne Luepke
Estimated Sales:$100+ Million
Number Employees: 250-499
Parent Co: Land O'Lakes

Type of Packaging: Consumer, Food Service, Private Label, Bulk

8197 Land O'Lakes
927 8th St
Kiel, WI 53042-4802   920-894-2204
          Fax: 920-894-2956 www.landolakes.com
Processor of cheese
     President/CEO: Chris Policinski
     Chairman: Pete Kappelman
     SVP/CFO: Dan Knutson
     VP/Strategy & Business Development: Barry Wolfish
     VP/General Counsel: Peter Janzen
     EVP Land O'Lakes Purina Feed: Fernando Palacios
     EVP/COO Dairy Foods Industrial: Alan Pierson
     EVP/COO Dairy Foods Value-Added: Steve Dunphy
     VP/Public Affairs: Jim Fife
     VP/Human Resources: Karen Grabow
     Plant Manager: Kevin Schwartz
Estimated Sales: $ 50 - 100 Million
Number Employees: 50-99
Parent Co: Land O'Lakes
Type of Packaging: Consumer
Brands:
     Land O Lakes

8198 Land O'Lakes
405 Park Dr
Carlisle, PA 17015-9270   717-486-7000
          Fax: 717-486-3730 www.landolakes.com
Processor of dry milk, buttermilk, butter and condensed products.
     President/CEO: Chris Policinski
     Chairman: Pete Kappelman
     SVP/CFO: Dan Knutson
     VP/General Counsel: Peter Janzen
     VP/Strategy & Business Development: Barry Wolfish
     EVP/COO Dairy Foods Value-Added: Steve Dunphy
     EVP/COO Dairy Foods Industrial: Alan Pierson
     EVP/Land O'Lakes Purina Feed: Fernando Palacios
     VP/Public Affairs: Jim Fife
     VP/Human Resources: Karen Grabow
     Plant Manager: Alan Vanderneut
Estimated Sales: $100+ Million
Number Employees: 100-249
Parent Co: Land O'Lakes

8199 Land O'Lakes
P.O.Box 64101
St Paul, MN 55164-0101   651-481-2068
          Fax: 218-681-7411 800-328-9680
          lolinfo@nnex.net   www.landolakesinc.com
Processor of dairy products including milk, cream and soft ice cream mixes
     President: Christopher Policinsky
     CFO: Dan Knutson
     COO: Chris Policinski
     Plant Manager: Dan Stelton
Number Employees: 500-999
Parent Co: Land O'Lakes
Type of Packaging: Consumer, Food Service, Private Label
Brands:
     Land O Lakes

8200 Land O'Lakes
2001 Mogadore Rd
Kent, OH 44240-7274   330-678-1578
          Fax: 330-678-2950 800-328-9680
          www.landolakesinc.com
Processor of regular and light butter, margarine and spreads.
     Chairman: Dan Knutson
     CEO: Christopher Policinski
     VP/Strategy & Business Development: Barry Wolfish
     EVP/Land O'Lakes Purina Feed: Fernando Palacios
     EVP/COO Dairy Foods Value-Added: Steve Dunphy
     VP/Public Affairs: Jim Fife
     VP/Human Resources: Karen Grabow
     Plant Manager: Steve Schafer
Number Employees: 100-249
Sq. footage: 85000
Parent Co: Land O'Lakes
Type of Packaging: Food Service, Private Label

8201 Land O'Lakes
P.O.Box 64006
St Paul, MN 55164-0006   651-730-2100
          Fax: 651-730-2111 www.deanfoods.com
Manufacturer of butter, margarine and spreads, cheese, half & half, whip cream, eggs, milk, sour cream cottage cheese, orange juice and yogurt.
     President/CEO Land O'Lakes: Chris Policinski
     Dean Dairy Group: Alan Bernon
     SVP/CFO Land O'Lakes: Dan Knutson
     SVP/COO Dean Dairy Group: Harrald Kroeker
     VP/Business Development Land O'Lakes: Barry Wolfish
     SVP/Planning-Integration Dean Dairy Grp: Pat Ford
     VP/Public Affairs Land O'Lakes: Jim Fife
     SVP/Operations Dean Dairy Group: Kelly Kading

     Plant Manager: Gale Hojer
Estimated Sales: $100-500 Million
Number Employees: 250-499
Type of Packaging: Consumer, Food Service

8202 Land O'Lakes Procurement
1200 W Russell St
Sioux Falls, SD 57104-1325   605-330-9526
          Fax: 605-336-7206 www.landolakesinc.com
Non-fermented uncultured & unflavored milk & cream Products.
     President/CEO: Chris Policinski
     Chairman: Pete Kappelman
     SVP/CFO: Dan Knutson
     Executive: Steve Sneer
     VP/Strategy & Business Development: Barry Wolfish
     EVP/Land O'Lakes Purina Feed: Fernando Palacios
     EVP/COO Dairy Foods Value-Added: Steve Dunphy
     EVP/COO Dairy Foods Industrial: Alan Pierson
     VP/Public Affairs: Jim Fife
     VP/Human Resources: Karen Grabow
Estimated Sales: $300,000
Number Employees: 5-9
Parent Co: Land O'Lakes
Type of Packaging: Consumer, Food Service
Brands:
     Land O'Lakes

8203 (HQ)Land O'Lakes, Inc
4001 Lexington Avenue, North
Arden Hills, MN 55126   651-481-2222
          Fax: 651-481-2000 800-328-9680
          www.landolakesinc.com
Manufacturer of Milk and dairy products including whey blends, butter, margarine, cheese, milk powders, whey powder, whey protein concentrate, whey protein isolate and deproteinized whey powder.
     President/CEO: Christopher Policinsky
     Chairman: Pete Kappelman
     SVP/Chief Financial Officer: Dan Knutson
     Vice President/General Counsel: Peter Janzen
     SVP/Corp. Strategy & Business Dev.: JP Ruiz-Funes
     EVP & COO, Dairy Foods: Steve Dunphy
     SVP/Corporate Marketing & Communications: Barry Wolfish
     EVP/COO Dairy Foods Industrial: Alan Pierson
     Vice President Public Affairs: Jim Fife
     Vice President Human Resources: Karen Grabow
Estimated Sales: $12 Billion
Number Employees: 9,100
Number of Products: 300+
Type of Packaging: Consumer, Food Service, Private Label, Bulk
Other Locations:
     Land O'Lakes
     Gustine CA
Brands:
     4-QUART
     BETTY CROCKER POP SECRET POPCORN
     CAV QUR D
     CHEDDEASE
     CO-JACK
     DAIRY BELT
     DOWNTOWN CAFE ICED CAPPUCINO
     GOLDEN VELVET
     LA CHEDDA
     LAND O'LAKES ALL NATURAL FARM EGGS
     LAND O'LAKES BUTTER
     LAND O'LAKES BUTTERSCOTCH CANDY
     LAND O'LAKES CAPPUCINO CLASSICS
     LAND O'LAKES CHEESE
     LAND O'LAKES COCOA CLASSICS
     LAND O'LAKES DAIRY CASE CHEESE
     LAND O'LAKES DELI CHEESE
     LAND O'LAKES FLAVORED BUTTER
     LAND O'LAKES INTERNATIONAL PASTAS
     LAND O'LAKES MACARONI AND CHEESE
     LAND O'LAKES MARGARINE, SPREADS
     LAND O'LAKES SOUR CREAM
     LAND O'LAKES ULTRA CREAMY BUTTER
     NATURALLY SLENDER
     NEW HOLSTEIN
     NEW YORKER
     NORTHVIEW
     PRIMO

8204 Land O'Pines Company
P.O.Box 1923
Lufkin, TX 75902-1923   936-634-5537
          Fax: 936-634-5875 fwalker@landopines.com
          www.landopines.com
Processor of bottled water and juices
     President/General Manager: Charlie Throckmorton
     Operations: Monia Whinery
     Customer Services & Logistics: Felicia Walker
     Plant Manager: Jerry Hill
Estimated Sales: $ 20 - 50 Million
Number Employees: 50-99
Sq. footage: 35000

8205 Land's End Seafood
38 Landing Road
Swanquarter, NC 27885   252-926-2801
          Fax: 252-926-2801
Shellfish

8206 Land-O-Sun Dairies
P.O.Box 940
O Fallon, IL 62269-0940   618-632-6381
          Fax: 618-628-3309 www.deanfoods.com
Processor of fluid milk and cottage cheese
     Manager: Bill Schaefer
     Operations Manager: Chuck McQuaig
Estimated Sales: $ 10 - 20 Million
Number Employees: 50-99
Parent Co: Suiza Foods
Type of Packaging: Consumer, Food Service, Bulk

8207 (HQ)Land-o-Sun
2900 Bristol Hwy
Johnson City, TN 37601-1502   423-283-5700
          Fax: 423-283-5716 800-283-5765
          www.suizafoods.com
Manufacturer of PET and Flav-O-Rich dairy brands
     President: Rick Fehr
     CEO: Loreen White
     Executive: Rod Barnett
     Sales Director: Fred Myette
Number Employees: 50-99
Parent Co: Suiza Dairy Group
Type of Packaging: Consumer
Other Locations:
     PET 828 322-3730
     Hickory NC
     PET 423 245-5154
     Kingsport TN
     PET 618 632-6381
     O'Fallon IL
     PET 757 397-2387
     Portsmouth VA
     PET 864 576-6280
     Spartanburg SC
     Flav-O-Rich 606 878-7301
     London KY
     Flav-O-Rich 540 669-5161
     Bristol VA
Brands:
     FLAV-O-RICH
     PET

8208 Landies Candies Company
2495 Main St # 350
Buffalo, NY 14214-2154   716-834-8212
          Fax: 716-833-9113 800-955-2634
          www.madeinbuffalo.com
     Owner: Larry Szrama
     VP: Andrew Gaiek
Estimated Sales: $ 3 - 5 Million
Number Employees: 10-19

8209 Landies Candies Company
2495 Main St # 350
Buffalo, NY 14214-2154   716-834-8212
Fax: 716-833-9113   800-955-2634
larrys@landiescandies.com
www.trulysugarfree.com
Processor of boxed chocolates including pecan, peanut, cashew, no sugar, cherry cordials and nut clusters; also, divinity, toffee, taffy, fondant mints, dipped pretzels, peppermint kisses, caramels, truffles and pecan praline desserttopping
President: Larry Szrama
CEO: David Tiech
Vice President: Bryan Tiech
Director Sales: Barbera Kelly
Plant Manager: John Davis
Estimated Sales: $1670977
Number Employees: 10-19
Type of Packaging: Consumer, Private Label, Bulk
Brands:
    Cashew Critters
    Choc Adillos
    Choc'adillos
    Longhorns
    Texas Chewie

8210 Landis Meat Company
PO Box 500
Quakertown, PA 18951-0500   215-536-2150
Fax: 215-538-2409   800-421-1565
dwalls@landismeat.net   www.landismeat.net
Processed meat
President: David Landis
VP: Roland Felix
Vice President: Mark Landis
Quality Control: Robin Moyer
Plant Manager: Wally Huhn
Estimated Sales: $ 10-20 Million
Number Employees: 50-100

8211 Landis Peanut Butter
641 E Cherry Ln
Souderton, PA 18964-1236   215-723-9366
www
Peanut butter
Owner: Raymond Landis
Estimated Sales: $500-1 Million appx.
Number Employees: 1-4

8212 Landlocked Seafoods
PO Box 381
Carroll, IA 51401-0381   712-792-9599
Fax: 712-792-9599
mebner@landlockedseafood.com
Seafood
President: Michael Ebner

8213 Landmark Vineyards
P.O.Box 340
Kenwood, CA 95452-0340   707-833-0053
Fax: 707-833-1164   800-45- 636
info@landmarkwine.com
www.landmarkwine.com
Wines
Owner/CFO: Michael Colhoun
Winemaker: Eric Stern
Public Relations: Mary Colhoun
Estimated Sales: $ 5-10 Million
Number Employees: 10-19
Brands:
    Landmark Damaris Chardonnay
    Landmark Grand Detou
    Landmark Kastania Pi
    Landmark Overlook Ch

8214 Landolfi Food Products
302 Cummings Ave
Trenton, NJ 08611-1195   609-392-1830
Fax: 609-396-6581   www.landolfis.com
Processor of frozen Italian pasta specialties including lasagna, ravioli, manicotti, cavatelli, stuffed shells, gnocchi, tortellini and stuffed rigatoni; also, garlic bread
President: Jack Fu
Director Manufacturing: Paul Melovich
Estimated Sales: $ 10 - 20 Million
Number Employees: 10-19
Type of Packaging: Consumer, Food Service, Private Label, Bulk

8215 Landreth Wild Rice
2320 Industrial Blvd
Norman, OK 73069-8518   405-360-2333
800-333-3533

Processor and exporter of wild rice
Number Employees: 5-9
Type of Packaging: Consumer, Food Service, Private Label

8216 Landrin USA
1000 N West Street
Suite 1200
Wilmington, DE 19801   302-250-4394
Fax: 302-250-4396   info@landrinusa.com
www.landrinusa.com
Confectionery products
CEO: Stan Kissele
Estimated Sales: $3 Million
Number Employees: 10

8217 Landry Armand Company
P.O.Box 623
Cottonport, LA 71327-0623   318-876-2716
Fax: 318-876-2490
Owner: James Bernard

8218 Landry's Pepper Company
1606 Cypress Island Hwy
St Martinville, LA 70582-6013   337-394-6097
Fax: 337-394-7629   landry6097@aol.com
www.cajunhotsauces.com
Hot sauces
President: Toby Bertrand
VP: Toby Bertrand
Estimated Sales: $5-9.9 Million
Number Employees: 5-9
Sq. footage: 50000
Type of Packaging: Consumer, Food Service, Private Label, Bulk
Brands:
    Cajun Gourmet Magic
    Landry's
    Premium

8219 Landshire
9200 W Main St # 1
Belleville, IL 62223-1791   618-398-8122
Fax: 618-398-7627   sales@landshire.com
www.landshire.com
Processor of deli foods including sandwiches; also, coffee and snack foods
President: Joseph Trover
President/CEO: David O'Keefe
CEO: Joseph Trover Jr
Plant Manager: John Viviano
Estimated Sales: $22700000
Number Employees: 250-499
Type of Packaging: Consumer, Food Service, Private Label
Brands:
    Deli Maid
    Landshire

8220 Lane Packing Company
P.O.Box 716
Fort Valley, GA 31030-0716   478-825-3592
Fax: 478-825-0015 www.lanepacking.com
Packer of peaches and pecans
President: Duke Lane Jr
Sales Manager: Bobby Lane
Estimated Sales: $100+ Million
Number Employees: 100-249
Type of Packaging: Bulk
Brands:
    Diamond D

8221 Lane's Dairy
310 N Concepcion St
El Paso, TX 79905-1605   915-772-6700
Fax: 915-772-3097   hjlane3541@aol.com
Manufacturer and exporter of milk and canned and bottled fruit juice
President: John Lane
Production Manager: Chris Lane
Estimated Sales: $2 Million
Number Employees: 20-49
Sq. footage: 15000
Type of Packaging: Consumer
Brands:
    LANES DAIRY

8222 Laney Family Honey Company
25725 New Rd
North Liberty, IN 46554-9379   574-656-8701
Fax: 574-656-8603   info@laneyhoney.com
www.laneyhoney.com

Honey, nuts/honey from America's heartland
President: Dave Laney
Co-Owner: Kay Laney
Estimated Sales: Below $ 500,000
Number Employees: 10-19
Type of Packaging: Consumer
Brands:
    Apple Blossom
    Autumn Wildflower
    Basswood
    Blueberry Blossom
    Buckwheat
    Clover
    Cranberry Blossom
    Michigan Star Thistle
    Orange Blossom
    Spring Blossom
    Wild Blackberry
    Wildflower

8223 Lang Bakery
318 State Avenue
Worthington, MN 56187-2629   507-372-7909
Processor of baked goods
Owner: Charles Lang
Number Employees: 6

8224 Lang Creek Brewery
655 Lang Creek Rd
Marion, MT 59925-9717   406-858-2200
Fax: 406-858-2499   info@langcreekbrewery.com
www.langcreekbrewery.com
Beer and ale
Owner/Brewmaster: John Campbell
Estimated Sales: $ 2.5-5 Million
Number Employees: 5-9
Number of Brands: 1
Number of Products: 8
Brands:
    Tri-Motor
    Windsock

8225 Lang Naturals
20 Silva Ln
Middletown, RI 02842-5638   401-848-7700
Fax: 401-848-7701   david.lang@langnaturals.com
www.langnaturals.com
Processor of salt-free, fat-free and no sugar added sauces including garlic steak, hot, ginger stir fry, thai peanut, honey barbecue, hot wing, sweet and sour, honey mustard and Indian curry; also, low-fat seasoned popcorn and carameled chocolate covered corn. Also offer healthy, organic and nutraceutical foods
Owner: Dave Lang
Vice President: Bruce Lang
Estimated Sales: $$10-20 Million
Number Employees: 20-49
Number of Products: 250
Type of Packaging: Consumer, Food Service, Private Label, Bulk
Brands:
    Enerjuice
    Mr. Spice
    Tangy Bang

8226 Lange Winery
18380 NE Buena Vista Dr
Dundee, OR 97115-9104   503-538-6476
Fax: 503-538-1938   don@langewinery.com
www.langewinery.com
Wines
Owner: Don Lange
Owner/CEO: Wendy Lange
Winemaker: Don Lange
Winemaker: Jesse Lange
General Manager: Jesse Lange
Estimated Sales: $680,000
Number Employees: 5-9
Brands:
    Lange Winery

8227 Langer Juice Company
16195 Stephens St
City of Industry, CA 91745-1718   626-336-3100
Fax: 626-961-2021   bruce@langers.com
www.langers.com
Processor of juices
President: Nathan Langer
CEO: Bruce Langer
National Sales Manager: Tom Bottiaux
Estimated Sales: $39 Million
Number Employees: 100-249
Sq. footage: 140000

Type of Packaging: Consumer, Food Service, Private Label
Brands:
  Dole
  Langers Juice
  Packers Pride
  Tropicana

8228 Langer Juice Company
16195 Stephens St
City of Industry, CA 91745-1718   626-336-1666
    Fax: 626-961-2021   bruce@langers.com
        www.langers.com
Bottled and canned fruit juices, soft drinks
  President: Nathan Langer
  VP: Bruce Langer
  Vice President: David Langer
  National Sales Manager: Tom Bottiaux
Estimated Sales: $30-$50 Million
Number Employees: 20-49
Sq. footage: 140000
Brands:
  Langers

8229 Langtry Estate & Vineyards
21000 Butts Canyon Rd
Middletown, CA 95461-9606   707-987-9127
        Fax: 707-987-9351
    tastingroom@langtryestate.com
        www.langtryestate.com
Wines: Chardonnay, Petite Sirah, Cabernet Sauvignon, Sauvignon Blanc, Merlot, Pinot Grigio
  Manager: Michael Pryor
  Vice President/Winemaker: Bob Broman
  Director Marketing: Karen Melander-Magoon
  National Sales Manager: Greg Brolin
Estimated Sales: $20-50 Million
Number Employees: 5-9
Sq. footage: 72000
Brands:
  Domaine Breton
  Guenoc
  Langtry

8230 Lanthier Bakery
PO Box 640
Alexandria, ON K0C 1A0
Canada   613-525-2435
        Fax: 613-525-2818
Processor of bread and rolls
  President: Marc Lanthier
  CEO: Marc Lanthier
  Marketing Manager: Marc Lanthier
Type of Packaging: Consumer, Food Service
Brands:
  Lanthier

8231 Lantic Sugar
4026 Notre-Dame E
Montreal, QC H1W 2K3
Canada   514-527-8686
    Fax: 514-527-1610   info@lantic.ca
        www.lantic.ca
Processor of sugar including liquid, bulk, soft, icing, granulated, coarse, medium, instant, etc
  President: Gregory Hoskins
  Chairman/CEO: A. Stewart Belkin
  Sr. VP Sales/Marketing: Dennis Hurl
  Director Sales: Normand Dumas
Number Employees: 400
Type of Packaging: Consumer, Food Service, Bulk
Brands:
  Lantic

8232 Lapasta
2727 Pittman Dr
Silver Spring, MD 20910-1807   301-588-1111
    Fax: 301-588-7243   info_lapasta@verizon.net
        www.lapastainc.com
Manufacture fresh, frozen, and shelf-life pasta
  President: Alexis Konownitzine
Estimated Sales: $ 5 - 10 Million
Number Employees: 10-19

8233 Larabar
PO Box 18932
Denver, CO 80218   720-942-1155
    Fax: 720-941-1158   800-543-2147
    info@larabar.com   www.larabar.com
all natural bars

8234 Laredo Mexican Foods
1616 Woodside Ave
Fort Wayne, IN 46816-3942   260-447-2576
    Fax: 219-447-2577   800-252-7336
        http://www.laredomexicanfoods.com
Processor and wholesaler/distributor of Mexican food products including salsa, tortillas and tortilla chips; serving the food service market
  President: Benito Trevino
  General Manager: Raul Trevino
  VP: Reynol Trevino
Number Employees: 5-9
Parent Co: Tregar
Type of Packaging: Consumer, Food Service, Private Label, Bulk
Brands:
  Don Pedro

8235 Laronga Bakery
599 Somerville Ave
Somerville, MA 02143-3296   617-625-8600
    Fax: 617-625-1853   tcono@hotmail.com
        www.larongabakery.com
Bakery products
  President: Michael Ronga
  Owner: Louis Ronga
Estimated Sales: $ 20-50 Million
Number Employees: 50-99
Brands:
  La Ronga Bakery

8236 Larry J. Williams Company
2686 Savannah Hwy
Jesup, GA 31545-5511   912-427-7729
        Fax: 912-427-0611
Shrimp, crab, oysters, scallps, flounder, etc.
  President: Larry Williams
Estimated Sales: $ 1 - 3 Million
Number Employees: 20-49

8237 Larry Matthews Company
P.O.Box 60
Dennysville, ME 04628-0060   207-726-0609
        Fax: 207-726-9571
  Owner: Larry Matthews
Estimated Sales: $ 1 - 3 Million
Number Employees: 1-4

8238 Larry Towns Company
1601 W Douglas Ave
Wichita, KS 67213-4022   316-265-3474
        Fax: 316-262-7770
  Owner: Larry Towns
Estimated Sales: $300,000-500,000
Number Employees: 10-19

8239 Larry's Beans Inc
1507 Gavin Street
Raleigh, NC 27608   919-828-1234
    Fax: 919-833-4567 www.larrysbeans.com
wholesale coffee roaster
  President/CEO: Larry Larson
  CFO: Brad Lienhart
  VP: Kevin Bobal
  Marketing: Kyley Schmidt
  Sales: Erik Iverson
  Plant Manager: Neal England
Estimated Sales: $3.0 Million
Number Employees: 16

8240 Larry's Sausage Corporation
P.O.Box 4
Fayetteville, NC 28302-0004   910-483-5148
        Fax: 910-483-2526
Processor of sausage
  President: Sheila Abe
Estimated Sales: $ 5 - 10 Million
Number Employees: 20-49
Type of Packaging: Consumer

8241 Larry's Vineyards & Winery
1263 Crane Street
Schenectady, NY 12303-1801   518-355-7365
        v1945p@juno.com
Wine
  President/Owner: Larry Brooks
Estimated Sales: Under $500,000
Number Employees: 1-4
Brands:
  Larry's Vineyards

8242 (HQ)Larsen Farms
P.O.Box 188
Hamer, ID 83425-0188   208-662-5501
    Fax: 208-374-5497   IFsales@larsenfarms.com
        www.larsenfarms.com
Dehydrated, prepared potatoes
  Manager: Jan Nel
Estimated Sales: $100-500 Million
Number Employees: 250-499

8243 Larsen Farms
P.O.Box 188
Hamer, ID 83425-0188   208-662-5501
    Fax: 208-374-5497   j_larsen@moment.net
        www.larsenfarms.com
Specialty goat cheese
  Manager: Jan Nel
  Production Manager: Nick Larsen
  Plant Manager: Nick Larsen
Estimated Sales: $ 1-2.5 Million
Number Employees: 5-9
Type of Packaging: Private Label
Brands:
  Larsen Farms Texas Chevre

8244 Larsen Packers
326 W Main Street
Burwick, NS B0P 1E0
Canada   902-538-8060
        Fax: 902-538-8694
Processor and exporter of bologna, salami, pepperoni and pork including fresh, cooked, bacon, ham, sausage and wieners; slaughtering services available; importer of fresh pork
  President: Karl Larsen
Number Employees: 250-499
Sq. footage: 150000
Type of Packaging: Consumer, Food Service, Private Label, Bulk
Brands:
  Brandywine
  Farmland
  Fine Old Tradition
  Fireside
  Larsen
  Light N' Low
  Simons
  Trimcut

8245 Larsen of Idaho
P.O.Box 188
Hamer, ID 83425-0188   208-662-5501
    Fax: 208-662-5568   bdowns@larsenfarms.com
        www.larsenfarms.com
Processor and exporter of dehydrated potato products including flaked, sliced, diced and shredded; also, fresh potatoes available
  President: Blaine Larsen
  Sales Manager: Valynn King
  Director Food Service Sales: Bruce Chamberlain
Estimated Sales: $ 10 - 20 Million
Number Employees: 20-49
Type of Packaging: Consumer, Food Service, Bulk

8246 Larson Potato
7147 137th Ave NE
Park River, ND 58270-9339   701-284-6437
        Fax: 701-284-6580
Processor of produce including potatoes
  President: Gene Larson
Estimated Sales: $350,000
Number Employees: 1-4
Type of Packaging: Consumer

8247 Lartigue Seafood
25802 Chamberlain Drive
Daphne, AL 36526-6083   251-343-3404
        Fax: 251-343-3404
  President: Paul Lartigue
  Vice President: Paul Lartigue III

8248 Larue Pope Company
2713 Abundance Street
New Orleans, LA 70122-5803   504-948-2234
        Fax: 732-270-3033
  Owner: Larue Pope

8249 (HQ)Las Cruces Foods
P.O.Box 98
Mesilla Park, NM 88047-0098   575-526-2352
        Fax: 575-523-5271

Processor of Mexican products including tortillas and taco shells
President: David Grijalva
VP: Miguel Grisalva
Estimated Sales: $461369
Number Employees: 10-19
Other Locations:
Las Cruces Foods
Albuquerque NM

8250 Laska Stuff
132 Griggs Street
Rochester, MI 48307-1414   248-652-8473
President: Steve Sparks

8251 Lassen Foods
5154 Hollister Ave
Santa Barbara, CA 93111-2526   805-683-7696
Fax: 805-683-7627 www.lassens.com
Health food store
Owner: Peter Lassen
Estimated Sales: Under $500,000
Number Employees: 10-19
Sq. footage: 5000
Parent Co: Lassen Foods
Type of Packaging: Consumer, Food Service, Private Label, Bulk
Brands:
Lassen

8252 Latah Creek Wine Cellars
13030 E Indiana Ave
Spokane Valley, WA 99216-1118   509-926-0164
Fax: 509-926-0710 mconway@latahcreek.com
www.latahcreek.com
Wines
President: Mike Conway
VP: Ellena Conway
Estimated Sales: $340,000
Number Employees: 1-4
Type of Packaging: Private Label

8253 Latcham Vineyards
P.O.Box 80
Mt Aukum, CA 95656-0080   530-620-6642
Fax: 530-620-5578 800-750-5591
latcham@directcon.net   www.latcham.com
Wines
President: Frank Latcham
Winemaker: Craig Boyd
Sales Manager: Margaret Latcham
Estimated Sales: $500,000-$1 Million
Number Employees: 10-19
Brands:
Barbera
Port

8254 Late July Organic Snacks
3166 Main Street
Barnstable, MA 02630   508-362-5859
Fax: 508-362-5868 info@latejuly.com
www.latejuly.com
organic snacks
President/Owner: Nicole Dawes

8255 Latonia Bakery
3612 Decoursey Ave
Covington, KY 41015-1438   859-491-8855
Fax: 859-431-4169
Baked goods
President: Bernie Holmer
Estimated Sales: Under $500,000
Number Employees: 5-9

8256 Laura Chenel's Chevre
4310 Fremont Dr
Sonoma, CA 95476-9703   707-996-4477
Fax: 707-996-1816
Goat cheese
Manager: John Van Dyke
Estimated Sales: $ 10-20 Million
Number Employees: 20-49
Brands:
Laura Chenel's

8257 Laura Paige Candy Company
13 Jeanne Drive
Newburgh, NY 12550-1702   845-566-4209
Fax: 845-566-4766 sales@laurapaige.com
www.marshalls.com
Processor of lollipops including hand painted seasonal and regular assortment
President: Elissa Koenig
Chairman: Dr. Louis Korngold
Vice President: Tracey Chalupa

Estimated Sales: Less than $500,000
Number Employees: 30
Sq. footage: 8000
Type of Packaging: Consumer, Food Service

8258 Laura's French Baking Company
6721 S Alameda St
Los Angeles, CA 90001-2123   323-585-5144
Fax: 323-585-0591 888-353-5144
sales@labakery.com   www.labakery.com
Processor of bread, croissants, danish, cakes and pastries
President: Sterling Kim
Estimated Sales: Below $ 5 Million
Number Employees: 20-49
Type of Packaging: Food Service
Brands:
Laura's

8259 Laurel Glen Vineyard
P.O.Box 1419
Glen Ellen, CA 95442-1419   707-526-3914
Fax: 707-526-9801 denise@laurelglen.com
www.laurelglen.com
Wines
Proprietor: Patrick Campbell
Winemaker: Patrick Campbell
Estimated Sales: $ 4 Million
Number Employees: 5-9
Number of Brands: 5
Type of Packaging: Private Label

8260 Laurel Hill
201 Santa Monica Boulevard
Suite 320
Santa Monica, CA 90401-2224   310-395-6630
Fax: 310-917-1205
Manufacturer of bottled and canned soft drinks
President: Ken Miller
Estimated Sales: Less than $200,000
Number Employees: 2
Number of Products: 1
Type of Packaging: Private Label
Brands:
Amazon Mist

8261 Laurent Meat Market
528 Avenue A
Marrero, LA 70072-2117   504-341-1771
Fax: 504-341-0299
Processor and meat packer of fresh and smoked sausages, hogshead cheese, andouille, hamburger and hot patties
Owner: Layton Laurent Sr
Estimated Sales: $500000
Number Employees: 1-4
Type of Packaging: Consumer, Food Service, Bulk

8262 Lava Cap Winery
2221 Fruitridge Rd
Placerville, CA 95667-3700   530-621-0175
Fax: 530-621-4399 lavacap@calweb.com
www.lavacap.com
Wines
President: David Jones
General Manager: Jeanne Jones
National Sales Director: Bill Johnston
Tour Coordinator: Julia Rosenkrantz
Winemaker: Thomas Jones
Vineyard Manager: Charles Jones
Estimated Sales: Below $ 5 Million
Number Employees: 10-19
Number of Brands: 1
Number of Products: 1
Sq. footage: 24000
Type of Packaging: Private Label

8263 Lavash Corporation
2835 Newell St
Los Angeles, CA 90039-3817   323-663-5249
Fax: 323-663-8062
aminassi@westernfiltercor.com
Processor of flatbread
Manager: Edmund Hartounian
Director Marketing: Arthur Minassian
National Sales Manager: Adam Cardenas
Cust./Technical Support Manager: Lori Akian
Estimated Sales: Below $ 5 Million
Number Employees: 10-19
Brands:
Wrap'n Roll

8264 Lavazza Premium Coffee Corporation
3 Park Ave # 28
New York, NY 10016-5902   212-725-8800
Fax: 212-725-9475 800-466-3287
info@lavazzausa.com   www.lavazzausa.com
Lavazza coffees
General Manager: Ennio Ranaboldo
Founder: Luigi Lavazza
Estimated Sales: Below $ 5 Million
Number Employees: 20-49
Brands:
Lavazza

8265 Lawler Foods
P.O.Box 2558
Humble, TX 77347-2558   281-446-0059
Fax: 281-446-3806 desserts@lawlers.com
www.lawlers.com
Processor of frozen cheesecakes, pies, brownies and sheetcakes
President: Bill Lawler
CEO: Carol Lawler
Estimated Sales: $18300000
Number Employees: 100-249
Sq. footage: 110000
Type of Packaging: Consumer, Food Service, Private Label, Bulk

8266 Lawrence Foods
2200 Lunt Ave
Elk Grove Vlg, IL 60007-5685   847-437-2400
Fax: 847-437-2567 800-323-7848
info@lawrencefoods.com
www.lawrencefoods.com
Processor of bakers' and confectioners' supplies including fruit and cream fillings, icings, glazes, preserves and jellies; available in cans, pails and flexible pouches
President: Lester Lawrence
CEO: Lester Lawrence
Estimated Sales: $15800000
Number Employees: 100-249
Sq. footage: 180000
Type of Packaging: Food Service, Private Label, Bulk
Brands:
Lawrence

8267 Lawrences Delights
3126 Oakcliff Industrial St
Doraville, GA 30340-2902   770-451-7774
Fax: 770-451-7623 800-568-0021
aboulos@lawrencedelights.com
www.lddelights.us
Processor and exporter of baked goods including nondairy and sugar-free walnut baklava, chocolate pecan logs and cashew lady fingers
President: Emile Bseibess
Estimated Sales: $ 3 - 5 Million
Number Employees: 10-19
Sq. footage: 5000
Parent Co: Le Liban
Type of Packaging: Food Service, Private Label, Bulk
Brands:
Lawrence's Delights

8268 Lawry's Foods
222 E Huntington Drive
Monrovia, CA 91016-8006   626-930-8870
Fax: 626-930-8851 800-952-9797
bote@usmpagency.com   www.lawrys.com
Processor of prepared gravy and sauce mixes, marinades, seasoned salt and pepper, lemon pepper, garlic spread, etc
President: Thomas Fueling
COO: John Heil
Director Marketing: Joe Scaccia
Estimated Sales: $ 20 - 50 Million
Number Employees: 20-49
Parent Co: Unilever USA
Type of Packaging: Consumer
Brands:
Adolph's Food Seasoning
Lawry's Chicken Saute Sauce
Lawry's Seasonings and Spices
Tio Sancho Mexican Foods

8269 Lax & Mandel Bakery
14439 Cedar Rd
Cleveland, OH 44121-3309   216-382-8877
Fax: 216-382-8875 kosher@laxandmandel.com
www.laxandmandel.com

Cakes, pastries
Co-Owner: Sheldon Weiser
Co-Owner: Helen Weiser
Co-Owner: Jeffrey Weiser
Estimated Sales: $500,000-$1 Million
Number Employees: 10-19

8270 Laxson Provision Company
264 W Lachapelle
San Antonio, TX 78204-1853   210-226-8397
                        Fax: 210-226-0537
President: Gary Laxson
Estimated Sales: $ 20-50 Million
Number Employees: 20-49

8271 Lay Packing Company
3515 Neal Dr
Knoxville, TN 37918-5255   865-922-4320
                        Fax: 865-922-4321
Processor of beef, pork, lamb and veal
Owner: F L Lay
Estimated Sales: $ 1 - 3 Million
Number Employees: 10-19
Parent Co: Lay Packing Company
Type of Packaging: Consumer, Food Service, Private Label, Bulk

8272 Lay's Fine Foods
400 E Jackson Avenue
Knoxville, TN 37915-1103   865-546-2511
        Fax: 865-546-2130 800-251-9636
Processed meat products
President: Joe Lay
Sales Manager: Ferril Maddox
Estimated Sales: $ 20-50 Million
Number Employees: 275
Sq. footage: 175
Type of Packaging: Private Label, Bulk

8273 Laymon Candy Company
276 Commercial Rd
San Bernardino, CA 92408-4149   909-825-4408
                        Fax: 909-825-4693
Processor of candy including brittles, fudge, chocolate creams, chews, nut clusters and taffy. Distributor for thirty-two large candy manufacturers
Owner: Paul T Applen
VP/Owner: Paul Applen
Marketing: Linda Laymon-Applen
Estimated Sales: $ 5 - 10 Million
Number Employees: 20-49
Number of Brands: 2028
Number of Products: 122
Sq. footage: 43000
Brands:
Laymon's

8274 Lazy Creek Vineyard
4741 Highway 128
Philo, CA 95466   707-895-2021
    Fax: 707-895-9226 chandler@lazycreek.com
Estate wines
President: Josh Chandler
VP Marketing: Mary Beth Chandler
Estimated Sales: $ 5-10 Million
Number Employees: 10-19
Brands:
Lazy Creek Vineyards

8275 Lazzaroni USA
299 Market St # 160
Saddle Brook, NJ 07663-5312   201-368-1240
                        Fax: 201-368-1262
Manufacturer and distributor of chocolates and cookies
Executive VP: Kathy Ecoffey

8276 Le Bleu Corporation
PO Box 2093
Advance, NC 27006-2093   336-998-2894
        Fax: 336-998-4167 800-854-4471
    info@lebleu.com www.lebleu.com
Manufacturer and distributor of bottled water
President: Jerry Smith
Executive VP: Keith Hester
VP: Judy Follette
Purchasing Manager: O Bowman
Estimated Sales: $17700000
Number Employees: 115
Sq. footage: 150000
Type of Packaging: Consumer
Brands:
Le Bleu Bottled Water
Nascar Bottled Water

8277 Le Boeuf & Associates
PO Box 932
North Falmouth, MA 02556-0932   508-563-5255
    Fax: 508-884-2040 800-444-5666
        nmleboeuf@msn.com
Wines
President: Normand LeBoeuf
VP: Christopher LeBoeuf
CFO: Chris LeBoeuf
VP: Steve LeBoeuf
VP Marketing: Chris Le Boeuf
Operations Manager: Louise Setterlund
Estimated Sales: $ 20-30 Million
Number Employees: 10
Type of Packaging: Private Label
Brands:
Emerald Bay

8278 Le Chic French Bakery
1043 Washington Ave
Miami Beach, FL 33139-5017   305-673-5522
                        Fax: 305-673-5522
Bakery products including baguettes, buttery croissants, danishes; as well as European style cakes, pies, tarts and pastries
President: Medardo Sanchez
Estimated Sales: $ 2.5-5 Million
Number Employees: 5-9

8279 Le Frois Foods Corporation
56 High St
Brockport, NY 14420-2058   585-637-5003
                        Fax: 585-637-2855
Vinegar
President: Duncan Tsay
Estimated Sales: Under $500,000
Number Employees: 5-9

8280 Le Notre, Alain & MarieBaker
7070 Allensby St
Houston, TX 77022-4322   713-692-0271
    Fax: 713-692-7399 800-536-6873
        lenotre@wt.net www.ciaml.com
Processor, importer and exporter of frozen strudel, muffins, cakes, cookies, danish, etc
Owner: Alain Lenotre
VP: Marie Le Notre
Estimated Sales: $ 20-50 Million
Number Employees: 20-49
Sq. footage: 30000
Type of Packaging: Private Label

8281 Le Pique-Nique
3871 Piedmont Avenue
Oakland, CA 94611-5378   800-400-6454
                        Fax: 510-339-7141
Processor of sausage including chicken, turkey, chicken/apple, cranberries, orange, maple syrup, etc
President: Dennis Donegan
Estimated Sales: Under $500,000
Number Employees: 1-4
Type of Packaging: Consumer, Food Service
Brands:
Calypso Caribbean
Tandoori
Thai Chicken

8282 (HQ)Le Sueur Cheese
P.O.Box 107
Le Sueur, MN 56058-0107   507-665-3353
        Fax: 507-665-2820 800-757-7611
    info@daviscofoods.com www.daviscofoods.com
Manufacturer and exporter of variety of cheese including low-fat, no-fat, enzyme-modified cheeses and other customer specified varieties
President: Mark Davis
VP: Marty Davis
VP: Mitch Davis
VP: Jon Davis
Estimated Sales: $112 Million
Number Employees: 100-249
Other Locations:
Le Sueur Cheese Plant
Jerome ID

8283 LeHigh Valley Dairies
880 Allentown Rd
Lansdale, PA 19446-5298   215-855-8205
                        Fax: 215-855-9834
    www.lehighvalleydairyfarms.com

Processor of milk, cream and juice
Executive Director: James Macri
Sales/Marketing Executive: Frank Mariello
VP Operations: Jim Macrey
Number Employees: 100-249
Parent Co: Suiza Dairy Group
Type of Packaging: Consumer, Food Service

8284 LePage Bakeries
P.O.Box 1900
Auburn, ME 04211-1900   207-783-9161
    Fax: 207-784-4634 lbck@lepagebakeries.com
                        www.barowskys.com
Manufacturer of bread, donuts and english muffins
President: Andrew Barowsky
Chairman: Albert Lepage
VP Marketing: Regis Lepage
Estimated Sales: $300,000-500,000
Number Employees: 500-999
Brands:
Bakers' Select
Barowsky's
Country Kitchen

8285 LeRaysville Cheese
Rr 2 Box 71a
Le Raysville, PA 18829-9621   570-744-2554
        Fax: 570-744-1050 800-595-5196
Cheese
President: James Amory
Estimated Sales: Less than $500,000
Number Employees: 5-9
Type of Packaging: Private Label

8286 Lea & Perrins
15-01 Pollitt Dr
Fair Lawn, NJ 07410-2795   201-265-7400
    Fax: 201-791-8945 800-289-5797
    lpinfo@danone.com www.leaperrins.com
Manufacturer of sauces and condiments
President/CEO: Ralph Abrams
Estimated Sales: $24 Million
Number Employees: 100-249
Parent Co: Danone Group
Type of Packaging: Consumer, Food Service
Brands:
HP
LEA & PERRINS SAUCES

8287 Leach Farms
W1102 Buttercup Ct
Berlin, WI 54923-8327   920-361-1880
                        Fax: 920-361-4474
Processor of fresh and frozen spinach, and celery
President: Thomas Leach
Estimated Sales: $5200000
Number Employees: 100-249
Sq. footage: 10000
Type of Packaging: Food Service, Private Label

8288 Leach Foods Products
W1102 Buttercup Ct
Berlin, WI 54923-8327   920-361-1880
                        Fax: 920-361-4474
Processor of fresh and IQF celery
President: Thomas Leach
CFO: John Zander
Sales Manager: Steve Wahlgreen
Plant Manager: Brian Thiel
Estimated Sales: $ 30-50 Million
Number Employees: 100-249
Sq. footage: 10000
Type of Packaging: Bulk

8289 Leader Candies
132 Harrison Place
Brooklyn, NY 11237-1522   718-366-6900
                        Fax: 718-417-1723
Processor and exporter of candies including hard, caramels, jelly beans, novelties, lollypops, filled, fundraising, hard toffee, starch jellies, bagged and nonchocolate; also, nonfrozen freeze pops available
President: Howard Kastin
Sales: Helen Garfield
VP Manufacturing: Malcom Kastin
Number Employees: 155
Sq. footage: 80000
Type of Packaging: Consumer, Food Service, Private Label, Bulk
Brands:
Beaver Pop
Freez-A-Pops
Kastin's

Leader
Lolly Lo's

8290 Leahy Orchards
1772 Route 209
Franklin, QC J0S 1E0
Canada   450-827-2544
    Fax: 450-827-2470 doug@applesnax.com
                                www.applesnax.com
Processor of apple sauce in cans, jars and portion
packs; also, pie filling
    President: Michael Leahy
    CEO: Michael Leahy
    Chairman: James R Leahy
    Manager Sales/Marketing (USA): Don Keody
Number Employees: 50-99
Type of Packaging: Consumer
Brands:
    Apple Snax

8291 Leams
906 Texas Court
Hutchinson, KS 67502-5136   316-662-4287
                                Fax: 620-662-4287
Sweet and savory flavors
    President: Alice Grigrest
Number Employees: 1-4

8292 Leatex Chemical Company
2722 N Hancock St
Philadelphia, PA 19133-3597   215-739-2000
                                Fax: 215-739-5910
Manufacturer of sulphonated castor oils
    President: Kevin Mc Chesney
    VP Marketing: L Kevin McChesney
Estimated Sales: $5000000
Number Employees: 10-19

8293 Leavenworth Coffee Roast
894 Us Highway 2
Leavenworth, WA 98826-1340   509-548-3313
    Fax: 509-548-4251 800-246-2761
        java@alpinecoffeeroasters.com
        www.alpinecoffeeroasters.com
Processor of coffee including 25 blends
    President: Dale Harrison
    VP: Veronica Harrison
Estimated Sales: $ 1-2.5 Million
Number Employees: 10-19
Type of Packaging: Consumer, Food Service
Brands:
    Chatter Creek

8294 Leaves Pure Teas
7435 E Tierra Buena Lane
Scottsdale, AZ 85260-1608   650-583-1157
    Fax: 650-583-1163 800-242-8807
        teas@leaves.com www.leaves.com
Teas
    President & Chief Operations Officer: Rommie
    Flammer
    Co Founder, Co Chairman, Co CEO: Dan
    Schweiker
    Operations Manager: Jeff Morris
Number Employees: 5-9
Type of Packaging: Private Label
Brands:
    Leaves Pure Tea

8295 (HQ)Leavitt Corporation
P.O.Box 490067
Everett, MA 02149-0002   617-389-2600
    Fax: 617-387-9085 contact@teddie.com
                                www.teddie.com
Processor and exporter of peanut butter and salted
and unsalted cashews and peanuts; importer of raw
cashews
    President/CEO: James Hintlian
    Executive VP: Mark Hintlian
    Quality Control: Christopher Hayes
    Operations Manager: Joseph Saraceno
    Production Manager: Jack Skamarakas
    Purchasing Manager: Frank Ciampa
Estimated Sales: $10-24.9 Million
Number Employees: 50-99
Type of Packaging: Consumer, Food Service, Pri-
    vate Label, Bulk
Brands:
    Americana
    River Queen
    River-Queen
    Teddie

8296 Lebanon Cheese Company
P.O.Box 63
Lebanon, NJ 08833-0063   908-236-2611
    Fax: 908-236-6870 jglotito@blast.net
Cheese
    President: Joe Lotito
Estimated Sales: $3 Million
Number Employees: 5-9
Brands:
    Lebanon Cheese

8297 Lebermuth Company
PO Box 4103
South Bend, IN 46634-4103   574-259-7000
    Fax: 574-258-7450 800-648-1123
    info@lebermuth.com www.lebermuth.com
A world-class fragrance and flavor company that
empowers our passionate and creative team to pro-
vide quality and innovative products using expertise
and technology, which enhances and strengthens our
partners' brand identity.
    President: Robert Brown
    CEO: Irvin Brown
    Vice President: Alan Brown
    VP Marketing/Public Relations: Alan Brown
    Production Manager: Mike Ryan
    Plant Manager: Robert Hall
    Purchasing Manager: Jim Gates
Estimated Sales: $12500000
Number Employees: 50
Sq. footage: 45000
Type of Packaging: Bulk

8298 Lebermuth Company
PO Box 4103
South Bend, IN 46634-4103   574-259-7000
    Fax: 574-258-7450 800-648-1123
    lbrown@lebermuth.com www.labermuth.com
Peppermint processing, fragrances and flavors
    Chairman: Irvin Brown
    President: Rob Brown
    Vice President: Robert Brown
    VP Administration: Alan Brown
Estimated Sales: $ 5-10 Million
Number Employees: 50
Brands:
    The Lebermuth

8299 Leblanc Seafood
PO Box 509
Lafitte, LA 70067-0509   504-689-2631
                                Fax: 504-689-4303
Seafood

8300 Ledonne Brothers Bakery
143 Chestnut St
Roseto, PA 18013-1311   610-588-0423
                                cbath@epix.net
Processor of breads: anchiove, French, Italian, sweet
and Viennese, also; tomato pies
    Co-Owner: Robert Bath
    Co-Owner: Connie Bath
Estimated Sales: Less than $500,000
Number Employees: 1-4
Type of Packaging: Consumer

8301 Lee Anderson's's CovaldaDates
51392 Harrison Street
Coachella, CA 92236-1563   760-398-3441
    Marketing Manager: Ann Jolly
Estimated Sales: Under $500,000
Number Employees: 1-4

8302 Lee Kum Kee
169 Stewart Ave
Brooklyn, NY 11237-1126   718-821-2199
    Fax: 718-821-2989 800-346-7562
    customer-service@lkk.com www.lkk.com
Processor, importer and exporter of condiments and
sauces including chili
    General Manager: Gary Cheung
Estimated Sales: $ 5 - 10 Million
Number Employees: 5-9
Sq. footage: 20000
Parent Co: Lee Kum Kee Company
Type of Packaging: Consumer, Food Service, Pri-
    vate Label, Bulk
Brands:
    Lee Kum Kee
    Panda

8303 (HQ)Lee Kum Kee
14455 Don Julian Rd
City of Industry, CA 91746-3102   626-709-1888
    Fax: 626-709-1899 800-654-5082
    customer_service@lkk.com www.lkk.com
Asian condiments and cooking sauces
    President: Alan Chang
    Marketing Manager: Betty Tsang
Estimated Sales: $ 10-20 Million
Number Employees: 50-99
Type of Packaging: Private Label
Brands:
    Choy Sun
    Full House
    Kum Chun Brand
    Lee Kum Kee
    Lee Kum Kee Premium
    Panda Brand

8304 Lee Seed Company
2242 Iowa 182 Ave
Inwood, IA 51240-7592   712-753-4403
    Fax: 712-753-4542 800-736-6530
    info@soynuts.com www.soynuts.com
Roasted soynuts in 16 flavors
    Co-Owner: Paul Lee
    Co-Owner: Joyce Lee
    Marketing Director: Scott Lee
Estimated Sales: $ 3 - 5 Million
Number Employees: 10-19
Type of Packaging: Consumer, Private Label, Bulk
Brands:
    Super Soynuts

8305 Lee's Century Farms
81356 Lower Dry Creek Road
Milton Freewater, OR 97862-7323   541-938-6532
                                Fax: 541-938-0705
    President: Deborah Lee
    VP Sales/Marketing: John Lee
Estimated Sales: Less than $500,000
Number Employees: 1-4
Brands:
    Lee's

8306 Lee's Food Products
1233 Queen Street E
Toronto, ON M4L 1C2
Canada   416-465-2407
Processor of canned soy sauce and Chinese vegetables including bamboo shoots, water chestnuts and
mushrooms; importer of mushrooms, instant noodles
and mini corn
    President: M Wong
    Secretary/Treasurer: L Wong
Type of Packaging: Consumer, Food Service

8307 Lee's Ice Cream
11431 Cronhill Dr # C
Owings Mills, MD 21117-2269   410-581-0234
    Fax: 410-581-7044 888-669-5337
    info@leesicecream.com www.leesicecream.com
Makers of premium gourmet ice cream products
available in a variety of flavors.
    Founder: Leon Garfield
    Co-Founder: Jaques Rubin
    Co-Founder: Steven Rubin
    CEO: Steve Rubin
Number Employees: 100-249

8308 Leech Lake Reservation
6530 Us Highway 2 NW
Cass Lake, MN 56633   218-335-8200
                                Fax: 218-335-8309
Processor of natural lake and river wild rice
    Manager: Cheryl Dunn
Number Employees: 1-4
Brands:
    Leech Lake

8309 Leech Lake Wild Rice
51664 County Road 137
Deer River, MN 56636   218-246-2746
    Fax: 218-246-2748 877-246-0620
        llwrice@paulbunyan.net
        www.leechlakewildricecompany.com
Wild rice
    Prime Manager: George Donnell
    CFO: Mike Ziemer
    Quality Control: Christine Cummings
    R & D: Steve Mortinson
    Public Relations: Don June
    Production Manager: George Donnell

Estimated Sales: Below $ 5 Million
Number Employees: 5
Type of Packaging: Private Label
Brands:
Leech Lake Wild Rice

8310 Leelanau Fruit Company
2900 S West Bay Shore Dr
Suttons Bay, MI 49682-9614   231-271-3514
Fax: 231-271-4367 info@leelanaufruit.com
www.leelanaufruit.com
Processer and exporter of frozen and brined cherries
and strawberries
President: Glen Lacross
General Manager: Allen Steimel
Estimated Sales: $ 1 - 3 Million
Number Employees: 100-249
Type of Packaging: Consumer, Food Service, Private Label, Bulk

8311 Leelanau Fruit Company
2900 S West Bay Shore Dr
Suttons Bay, MI 49682-9614   231-271-3514
Fax: 231-271-4367 800-431-0718
info@leelanaufruits.com www.leelanaufruit.com
Frozen cherries and strawberries
President: Glenn Lacross
Estimated Sales: Below $ 5 Million
Number Employees: 100-249

8312 Leelanau Wine Cellars
P.O.Box 68
Omena, MI 49674-0068   231-386-5201
Fax: 231-386-9797 800-782-8128
lisa@leelanaucellars.com
www.leelanaucellars.com
Wines
Manager: Tony Lenyth
General Manager: Bob Jacobson
Estimated Sales: $ 5-10 Million
Number Employees: 10-19
Brands:
Leelanau

8313 Lees Sausage Company
1054 Neeses Hwy
Orangeburg, SC 29115-8606   803-534-5517
Fax: 803-531-2809
Manufacturer of sausage, liver pudding, BBQ meat
and sauce, chili, and BBQ hash
President: Walter Lee Jr
Estimated Sales: $18 Million
Number Employees: 20-49
Type of Packaging: Consumer, Private Label

8314 Leeward Resources
401 E Pratt Street
Suite 354
Baltimore, MD 21202-3117   410-837-9003
Fax: 410-837-7527 bbrown@leeward.com
www.leeward.com
Spices, herbal extracts, botanials, essential oils,
fruit juices
President: William Brown
Estimated Sales: $ 3.5 Million
Number Employees: 3

8315 Leeward Winery
2784 Johnson Drive
Ventura, CA 93003-7214   805-656-5054
Fax: 805-656-5092 www.leewardwinery.com
Processor and exporter of table wines
President: Charles A Brigham
Co-Owner: Chuck Gardner
Estimated Sales: $340000
Number Employees: 4
Sq. footage: 8500
Type of Packaging: Consumer, Food Service
Brands:
Leeward

8316 Lef Bleuges Marinor Incorporated
1015 Rg Double
St-Felicien, QC G8K 2M1
Canada   418-679-4577
Fax: 418-679-9602
Processor of frozen blueberries - exports worldwide
President: Jeanne-Pierre Senneville

8317 Lefse House
5014 48th Street
Camrose, AB T4V 1M1
Canada   780-672-7555
Fax: 780-608-2377 info@theLefseHouse.ca
www.thelefsehouse.ca
Processor of Scandinavian all natural baked goods
including potato lefse, flatbread and specialty items
President/CFO: Bernell Odegard
Purchasing Manager: Helen Lien
Estimated Sales: Under $300,000
Number Employees: 1-4
Sq. footage: 1600
Type of Packaging: Consumer, Food Service
Brands:
Lefse House

8318 Left Hand Brewing Company
1265 Boston Ave
Longmont, CO 80501-5809   303-772-0258
Fax: 303-772-9572
brewer@lefthandbrewing.com
www.lefthandbrewing.com
Processor and wholesaler/distributor of English style
ale, stout and porter; also, German style lager and
weiss beer
President: Jon Wallace
Quality Control: Andy Brown
Marketing/Sales/Public Relations: Chris Lennert
Operations Manager: Joe Schiraldi
Estimated Sales: Below $ 5 Million
Number Employees: 20-49
Sq. footage: 13000
Type of Packaging: Food Service, Bulk
Brands:
Deep Cover Brown
Imperial
Juju Ginger
Left Hand Black Jack
Sawtooth
Tabernash

8319 Legacy Soft Gourmet Pretzels
7835 Wilkerson Court
San Diego, CA 92111-3606   858-715-9977
800-916-3260
Processor baked frozen soft gourmet pretzels
CEO/General Manager: Gerald Gaucher
Production Manager: J Martinez
Number Employees: 50-99
Number of Brands: 3
Number of Products: 9
Sq. footage: 13500
Type of Packaging: Food Service, Private Label
Brands:
A La Franchise
Legacy

8320 Legend Brewing Company
321 W 7th St
Richmond, VA 23224-2307   804-232-3446
Fax: 804-231-3417 www.legendbrewing.com
Processor of beer, ale, stout and lager
President: Thomas E Martin
Brewmaster: Brad Mortensen
Estimated Sales: Below $ 5 Million
Number Employees: 20-49
Type of Packaging: Consumer, Food Service
Brands:
Brown Ale
Legand Brown
Legand Pilsner
Porter

8321 Legumes Plus
PO Box 380
Fairfield, WA 99012-0380   509-283-2347
Fax: 509-283-2314 800-845-1349
legumes@nextdim.com www.legumesplus.com
Processor and exporter of soup mixes including lentil and split pea; also, chili
President: Judy Hahner
Marketing Director: Jan Moore
Plant Manager: Gial Ohosen
Number Employees: 5-9
Sq. footage: 8600
Type of Packaging: Consumer, Food Service, Private Label, Bulk
Brands:
Legumes Plus
Lentils of the Palouse

8322 Lehi Roller Mills
P.O.Box 217
Lehi, UT 84043-0217   801-768-4401
Fax: 801-768-4557 800-660-4346
sdejohn@lehirollermills.com
www.lehirollermill.com
Processor of flour, feed and meal; also, mills
President: Sherm Robinson
CFO: Kevin David
Estimated Sales: $20-50 Million
Number Employees: 20-49
Type of Packaging: Private Label
Brands:
Peacock
Turkey

8323 Lehi Valley Trading Company
4955 E McKellips Rd
Mesa, AZ 85215   480-684-1402
Fax: 480-461-1804 info@lehivalley.com
www.lehivalley.com
beans, candy, dried fruit, granola, ice cream mix-ins,
nuts and seeds, popcorn and nuggets, snack items
and trail mix
President/Owner: Lewis Freeman
Estimated Sales: $7.7 Million
Number Employees: 50

8324 Lehr Brothers
12901 Packing House Road
Edison, CA 93220   661-366-3244
Fax: 661-366-1449 spudron1@aol.com
Processor and exporter of potatoes
President: Ronald Lehr
Estimated Sales: $17155306
Number Employees: 50
Type of Packaging: Bulk

8325 Leiby's Dairy
116 Mountain Rd
Tamaqua, PA 18252-5040   570-668-2399
Fax: 570-668-6065
Processor of ice cream including mixes
President: Keith Zimmerman
VP/Secretary: William Parks
Estimated Sales: $ 5 - 10 Million
Number Employees: 10-19
Sq. footage: 30000
Type of Packaging: Consumer, Bulk

8326 Leidenfrost Vineyards
5677 State Route 414
Hector, NY 14841-0221   607-546-2800
Wines
Owner: John Leidenfrost
Estimated Sales: $340,000
Number Employees: 4
Brands:
Leidenfrost Vineyards

8327 Leidenheimer Baking Company
1501 Simon Bolivar Ave
New Orleans, LA 70113-2399   504-525-1575
Fax: 504-525-1596 info@leidenheimer.com
www.leidenheimer.com
Manufacturer of fresh and frozen New Orleans style
French breads and rolls
President: Robert J Whann Iv III
VP: Robert Whann IV
Plant Manager: Terry Park
Estimated Sales: $20 Million
Number Employees: 50-99
Sq. footage: 40000
Type of Packaging: Consumer, Food Service

8328 Leidy's
P.O.Box 64257
Souderton, PA 18964-0257   215-723-4606
Fax: 215-721-2003 800-222-2319
dans@leidys.com www.leidys.com
Pork processing
President: Andrew Leidy
Co-Owner: Terry Leidy
CFO: Scott Schanzembach
Quality Control: John Capra
Sales Manager: Duane Zoscin
Plant Engineer: Denny Gehman
VP Production: Andy Leidy
Estimated Sales: $ 20-50 Million
Number Employees: 100-249
Type of Packaging: Consumer, Bulk
Brands:
Leidy's

8329 Leigh Olivers
PO Box 8346
Tyler, TX 75711   903-245-9183
     Fax: 903-421-1669
customerservice@leigholivers.com
www.leigholivers.com
dips/salsa and cheeses
CEO: Leigh Vickery
VP: Ron Vickery

8330 (HQ)Leighton's Honey
1203 W Commerce Ave
Haines City, FL 33844-3271   863-422-1773
     Fax: 863-421-2299
Manufacturer and packer of honey
President: Harry Posey
Estimated Sales: $22 Million
Number Employees: 10-19
Type of Packaging: Consumer, Food Service, Private Label, Bulk
Brands:
LEIGHTON'S
ORANGE BLOSSOM SPECIAL

8331 Leiner Davis Gelatin
366 N Broadway
Jericho, NY 11753-2025   516-942-4940
     Fax: 516-822-4044
cheryl.michaels@pbleiner.com
www.gelatin.com
Processor, exporter and importer of food grade gelatin including kosher; also, technical service available
NAFTA Sales Manager: Cheryl Michaels
Estimated Sales: $5 - 10 Million
Number Employees: 5-9
Brands:
Leiner Davis

8332 Leiner Health Products
901 E 233rd St
Carson, CA 90745-6204   310-513-2116
     Fax: 310-952-7760   info@leiner.com
www.leiner.com
Manufacturer of vitamins
President: Gale Bansussen
CEO: Bob Kaminski
CEO: Robert R Reynolds
Manager Sales/Marketing: Tom Bovich
Number Employees: 500-999
Brands:
Beneflex
Bumble Bee
Cardio Discovery
LiquiMax
Natural Life
Omega Care
Pharmacist Formula

8333 Leininkugel Brewing Company
1 Jefferson Ave
Chippewa Falls, WI 54729-1318   715-720-1471
     Fax: 715-723-7158   www.leinie.com
Alcoholic malt beverages, beer
President: Bill Leinenkugel
CFO: Dave Kahn
VP Marketing: Richard Leininkugel
Point-of-Sale Manager: John Leininkugel
Operations Manager: Pete Dawson
Estimated Sales: $5-10 Million
Number Employees: 50-99
Brands:
Amber Light
Berry Weiss
Honey Weiss
Leinenkugel Original
Light
Northwoods
Oktoberfest
Red

8334 Leisure Time Ice & Spring Water
P.O.Box 168
Kiamesha Lake, NY 12751-0168   845-794-7040
     Fax: 845-794-0016   800-443-1412
Bottled water
President: Harold Reynolds
Estimated Sales: $10-20 Million
Number Employees: 100-249

8335 Lemate of New England
PO Box 530
Sharon, MA 02067-0530
     781-784-7369

Processor of sweetened cocktail mixes and flavored syrups
President: Kevin Christman
Type of Packaging: Consumer, Food Service, Private Label, Bulk

8336 Lemix
400 Nassau Street W
Canton, OH 44730-1173   330-488-3072
Manufacturer of steak sauce, condiment sauces, cocktail mixes, beverage concentrates and syrups
President: Helmut Chemnitz
Operations: Ron Boni
Estimated Sales: $1 - 3 Million
Number Employees: 1-4
Sq. footage: 16000
Type of Packaging: Consumer, Food Service, Private Label, Bulk
Brands:
Lemix

8337 Lemke Cheese Company
101 Devoe St
Wausau, WI 54403-3228   715-842-3214
     Fax: 715-842-4452   www.greatlakescheese.com
Cheese
COO: Randy Lewis
President Administration: Daniel E Zagzebski
Treasurer: Daniel Zagzebski
Estimated Sales: Below $5 Million
Number Employees: 100-249
Brands:
Great Lakes

8338 Lemke Wholesale
1727 W Poplar Street
Rogers, AR 72758-4146   501-636-3288
     Fax: 501-751-4671
President: Ron Lemke

8339 Lemmes Company
7 Alice Street
Coventry, RI 02816-7300   401-821-2575
Spaghetti sauce, grated cheese, BBQ sauce, relish, jam, mustard
President: Michael Lemme
Estimated Sales: $2.5-5 Million
Number Employees: 1

8340 Lemon Creek Winery
533 E Lemon Creek Rd
Berrien Springs, MI 49103-9714   269-471-1321
     Fax: 616-471-1322   info@lemoncreekwinery.com
www.lemoncreekwinery.com
Wines
President: Tim Lemon
Estimated Sales: $1.8 Million
Number Employees: 20-49
Brands:
Lemon Creek Winery

8341 Lemon-X Corporation
168 Railroad St
Huntington Sta, NY 11746-1540   631-424-2850
     Fax: 631-424-2852   800-220-1061
customerservice@lemon-x.com
www.lemon-x.com
Juices and cocktail mixes
President: James Grassi
Sales Manager: Steve Bogdanos
Purchasing Manager: Stacy Robertson
Estimated Sales: $20-50 Million
Number Employees: 100-249
Type of Packaging: Consumer, Food Service, Private Label, Bulk
Brands:
Growers Fancy Juice Concentrates
Lemon-X Cocktail Mixes

8342 Len Libby's Candy Shop
419 Us Route 1
Scarborough, ME 04074-9705   207-883-4897
     Fax: 207-885-5824   lenlibby@lenlibby.com
www.lenlibby.com
Chocolates and candies
Manager: Shirley Morneault
Vice President: Maureen Hemond
Estimated Sales: $500,000-$1 Million
Number Employees: 10-19

8343 Lena Maid Meats
500 W Main St
Lena, IL 61048-9726   815-369-4522
     Fax: 815-369-2075   www.lenamaidmeats.com

Processor of beef, pork, lamb and venison
Manager: Kevin Koning
Secretary/Treasurer: Suzanne McGiveron
Estimated Sales: $500000
Number Employees: 10-19
Type of Packaging: Bulk
Brands:
Lena Maid

8344 Lenchner Bakery
Unit 1&2
Concord, ON L4K 3G1
Canada   905-738-8811
     Fax: 905-738-3822
Processor and exporter of kosher frozen entrees and dessert pastries including chocolate, almond, cheese, apple, blueberry, cherry, prune, lemon, spinach feta cheese, potato onion, etc.; also, bagels; private labeling available
President: Zeev Lenchner
VP: Angela Ilizarov
Number Employees: 20-49
Sq. footage: 10000
Parent Co: Lechner's
Type of Packaging: Consumer, Food Service, Private Label, Bulk
Brands:
Boueka
Rrrogala

8345 Lender's Bagel Bakery
3801 Dewitt Ave
Mattoon, IL 61938-6616   217-235-3181
     Fax: 217-258-3205
Frozen and refrigertaed bagels.
Quality Control: Mary Young
Plant Manager: Brad Sam
Estimated Sales: $100+ Million
Number Employees: 250-499
Parent Co: Aurora Foods
Type of Packaging: Consumer, Food Service, Private Label, Bulk

8346 Lender's Bagel Bakery
75 Empire Drive
West Seneca, NY 14224-1319   716-668-6761
Frozen and refrigerated bagels.
Manager: Stefon Martin
Plant Manager: Mike Kaldorf
Number Employees: 250-499
Parent Co: Aurora Foods
Type of Packaging: Consumer, Food Service

8347 Lendy's
1581 General Booth Blvd # 101
Virginia Beach, VA 23454-5106   757-491-3511
     Fax: 757-491-8821   lendus@series200.com
www.lendys.com
Processor of sauces including buffalo wing, habanero hot and barbecue
Owner: Kent Von Fecht
Estimated Sales: Less than $500,000
Number Employees: 10-19
Sq. footage: 1250
Type of Packaging: Consumer, Food Service, Private Label, Bulk
Brands:
Buckman's Best
Buckman's Best Snack

8348 Lengacher's Cheese House
5015 Lincoln Highway
Kinzers, PA 17535-9709   717-355-6490
Cheese
President: Arthur Lengacher
Estimated Sales: $500,000 appx.
Number Employees: 1-4

8349 Lengerich Meats
P.O.Box 411
Zanesville, IN 46799-0411   260-638-4123
Processor of beef, pork and lunch meats
Owner: Jim Stephen
Sales Manager: Debbie Woods
Estimated Sales: $670000
Number Employees: 5-9
Type of Packaging: Consumer, Food Service

8350 Lennox Farm
RR 3
Shelburne, ON L0N 1S7
Canada   519-925-6444
     Fax: 519-925-3285   lennoxfarms@huronatio.net

Processor of fresh and frozen rhubarb
President: William French
Number of Employees: 10-19
Type of Packaging: Consumer, Food Service
Brands:
Lennox

8351 Lenny's Bee Productions
403 Wittenberg Road
Bearsville, NY 12409-5635   845-679-4514
lennybee@ulster.net
Processor of smoked trout, bee pollen and honey products
President: Lenny Busciguo
Marketing Manager: Leonardo Busciglio
Vice President: Lynn Duvall
Type of Packaging: Consumer, Food Service, Private Label
Brands:
Lenny's Bee Productions

8352 Lenox-Martell
89 Heath St
Jamaica Plain, MA 02130-1402   617-442-7777
Fax: 617-522-9455 www.lenoxmartell.com
CEO: James Lerner
Sales Director: Howard Segal
Estimated Sales: $ 20 - 50 Million
Number Employees: 20-49

8353 Lenox-Martell
89 Heath St
Jamaica Plain, MA 02130-1402   617-442-7777
Fax: 617-522-9455 jlerner@realcitysoda.com
www.lenoxmartell.com
Processor of colas and juices; wholesaler/distributor of refrigerators and ice and soda machines; serving the food service market; also, installation and maintenance of draft beer systems available
President: James Lerner
Estimated Sales: $5200000
Number Employees: 20-49

8354 Lenson Coffee & Tea Company
PO Box 1103
Pleasantville, NJ 08232-6103   609-646-3003
Fax: 609-646-8606
Processor of coffee; wholesaler/distributor of tea; serving the food service market
Owner: Jimmie Anderson
Estimated Sales: $ 5-10 Million
Number Employees: 20-49
Type of Packaging: Consumer, Food Service, Private Label

8355 Leo G. Atkinson Fisheries
89 Daniel Head Road
South Side
Clarks Harbor, NS B0W 1P0
Canada   902-745-3047
Fax: 902-745-1245
Processor and exporter of fresh, frozen and salted seafood including haddock, cod, halibut and lobster
President: Leo Atkinson
Number Employees: 20-49
Type of Packaging: Consumer, Food Service, Private Label, Bulk

8356 Leo G. Fraboni Sausage Company
1202 13th Ave E
Hibbing, MN 55746-1218   218-263-5074
Fax: 218-263-5074 sales@frabonis.com
www.frabonis.com
Processor of smoked Polish sausages and frozen beef patties
President: Mark Thune
VP: Wayne Thune
Plant Manager: Don Johnson
Estimated Sales: $ .5 - 1 million
Number Employees: 5-9
Type of Packaging: Consumer, Private Label, Bulk

8357 Leo's Bakery
1179 Ocean St
Marshfield, MA 02050-3697   781-837-3300
Fax: 781-837-8949
Bakery products
President: Robert Gagnon
Estimated Sales: $500,000-$1 Million
Number Employees: 10-19

8358 Leon's Bakery
1000 Universal Dr N
North Haven, CT 06473-3151   203-234-3151   203-234-0115
Fax: 203-234-7620   800-223-6844
www.pennantfoods.com
Processor of frozen dough; exporter of wheat and white rolls
President: Luis Alpizar
CEO: John Ruth
CFO: Eric Olson
Sales Manager: Terry Ginn
Plant Manager: Fred Macey
Estimated Sales: $ 5 - 10 Million
Number Employees: 5-9
Sq. footage: 75000
Type of Packaging: Food Service, Private Label, Bulk

8359 Leon's Sausage Company
1143 W Lake St
Chicago, IL 60607-1683   312-829-2250
Fax: 312-829-2098 leons_sba@aol.com
www.sausagesbyamy.com
Processor of specialty sausages including red meat and poultry
CEO: Amy Kurzawski
President: R Chico Kurzawski
Operations Manager: Ed Kleine
Estimated Sales: $ 10 - 20 Million
Number Employees: 20-49
Sq. footage: 32000
Type of Packaging: Consumer, Food Service, Private Label
Brands:
LEON'S
SAUSAGE BY AMY
SLOTKOUSKI
SLOTKOWSKI SAUSAGE

8360 Leon's Texas Cuisine
P.O. Box 1850
McKinney, TX 75070-8160   972-529-2244
Fax: 972-529-2244 scott@texascuisine.com
www.texascuisine.com
Producer of corny dogs and stuffed jalapenos
Owner: Bob Clements
VP Human Resources: Cindy Stephens
Director Sales: Scott Elwonger
SVP Operations: John Vroman
Estimated Sales: $500,000-$1 Million
Number Employees: 100-249
Brands:
Leon's Texas Cuisine

8361 Leona Meat Plant
P.O. Box 156
Troy, PA 16947-0156   570-297-3574
Fax: 570-297-3562 www.leonameatplant.com
Processor of meat including ham, bacon and sausage
President: Charles Debach Ii
Estimated Sales: $1200000
Number Employees: 5-9
Type of Packaging: Consumer

8362 Leonard Fountain Specialties
4225 Nancy St
Detroit, MI 48212-1298   313-891-4141
Fax: 313-892-9200 sales@leonardssyrups.com
www.leonardssyrups.com
Syrups, juices, frozen cocktails
Owner: Leonard Bugajewski
CFO: Maria Cintron
Marketing Director: Leroy Goodall
Production Manager: Tom Niconcher
Plant Manager: John Bamford
Estimated Sales: $ 5-10 Million
Number Employees: 100-249
Sq. footage: 75
Type of Packaging: Food Service, Private Label
Brands:
Bar-Pak
Bulk Co2
Frosty Pak
Lemon Twist
Orange Mist
Polar Pak
Quali-Tea
Thrifty Pak
Tropical Mist

8363 Leonard Mountain Trading
PO Box 67
Leonard, OK 74043   800-822-7700
Fax: 918-366-2800 office@leonardmountin.com
www.leonardmountain.com
Fruit & Veggie Dips, Pasta Salads, Peanuts, Dirty Drink Mixes, Olives and Pickled Vegetables
President: Debbie Berckefeldt
Sales Manager: Fred Berckefeldt
Estimated Sales: $ 10-20 Million
Number Employees: 10
Brands:
Boot Scootin'
Leonard Mountain
Mama Leone's

8364 Leonas Foods
Manzana Center Highway 76
Chimayo, NM 87522   505-351-4660
Fax: 505-351-2189 www.leonas.com
Flour, corn tortillas and tamales
President: Roy Trujillo
Owner: Lila Salazar
Estimated Sales: $10-24.9 Million
Number Employees: 20-49

8365 Leone Provision Company
916 SE 14th Avenue
Cape Coral, FL 33990-3020   941-574-3355
Fax: 941-574-6707
Importer of Italian meats including meat balls and sausages; also, andouille and Polish sausage
President: Rosaria Leone
Type of Packaging: Consumer, Food Service

8366 Leonetti Cellar
1875 Foothills Ln
Walla Walla, WA 99362-9052   509-525-1428
Fax: 509-525-4006 www.leonetticellar.com
Wines
President: Gary Figgins
VP Operations: Chris Figgins
Marketing: Nancy Figgins
Vineyard Manager: Jason Magnaghi
Estimated Sales: $500,000-$1 Million
Number Employees: 5-9
Brands:
Leonetti Cellar

8367 Leonetti's Frozen Food
5935 Woodland Ave
Philadelphia, PA 19143-5919   215-729-4200
Fax: 215-729-7581 leonettifrozenfo@aol.com
www.leonettisfrozenfoods.com
Processor of frozen stromboli and calzones
President: Richard Di Pietro
Plant Manager: Leroy Douglas
Estimated Sales: $1500000
Number Employees: 20-49
Sq. footage: 33000
Type of Packaging: Consumer, Food Service, Private Label, Bulk
Brands:
Leonetti's

8368 Lep Profit International
1950 Spectrum Cir SE
Marietta, GA 30067-8479   770-951-8100
Fax: 770-952-8122

8369 Lepage Bakeries
P.O. Box 1900
Auburn, ME 04211-1900   207-783-9161
Fax: 207-784-4634 lbck@lepagebakeries.com
www.lepagebakeries.com
Processor of bread, rolls and doughnuts
President/Chairman: Albert LePage
CEO: Andrew P Barowsky
Estimated Sales: $5-10 Million
Number Employees: 1-4
Type of Packaging: Consumer

8370 (HQ)Leprino Foods Company
1830 W 38th Ave
Denver, CO 80211-2200   303-480-2600
Fax: 303-480-2605   800-537-7466
cheese@leprinofoods.com
www.leprinofoods.com

Manufacturer of cheese and an exporter of whey products
> President: Larry Jensen
> SVP Administration/CFO: Ron Klump
> SVP QA/R&D: Richard Barz
> SVP Sales/Marketing: Robert Boynton
> SVP Production Operations: Tom Haggerty
Estimated Sales: $21.2 Billion
Number Employees: 2500
Type of Packaging: Food Service, Bulk
Other Locations:
> Leprino Foods
> Allendale MI
> Leprino Foods
> Fort Morgan CO
> Leprino Foods
> Ravenna NE
> Leprino Foods
> Remus MI
> Leprino Foods
> Roswell NM
> Leprino Foods
> Waverly NY
Brands:
> Le-Pro
> Quality-Locked

8371 Leroux Creek Foods
9754 3100 Rd
Hotchkiss, CO 81419-6114   970-872-2256
   Fax: 970-872-2250   877-970-5670
   info@lerouxcreek.com   www.lerouxcreek.com
Processor of organic apple sauce and fruit puree.
> President: Edward Tuft
> Quality Control: Wende Michael
> Marketing: Sarah Tuft
> Operations: Amy Sanders
> Plant Manager: Arturo Mendoza
> Purchasing: Edward Tuft
Estimated Sales: $1500000
Number Employees: 20-49
Number of Products: 14
Type of Packaging: Consumer, Private Label
Brands:
> Leroux Creek

8372 Leroy Hill Coffee Company
3278 Halls Mill Rd
Mobile, AL 36606-2502   251-476-1234
   Fax: 251-476-1296   800-866-5282
   goodtasteiseverything@leroyhillcoffee.com
Processor and wholesaler/distributor of coffee and tea; wholesaler/distributor of general merchandise; serving the food service market
> President: Leroy Hill
Estimated Sales: $18000000
Number Employees: 100-249
Type of Packaging: Consumer, Food Service

8373 Leroy Hill Coffee Company
3278 Halls Mill Rd
Mobile, AL 36606-2502   251-476-1234
   Fax: 251-476-1296   800-866-5282
   goodtasteiseverything@leroyhillcoffee.com
     www.leroyhillcoffee.com
Coffee
> President: Leroy Hill
> Production Manager: Dan Buckley
Estimated Sales: $ 15-20 Million
Number Employees: 100-249
Type of Packaging: Private Label
Brands:
> Leroy Hill

8374 (HQ)Leroy Smith & Sons Inc
P.O.Box 716
Vero Beach, FL 32961-0716   772-567-3421
   Fax: 772-567-8428   www.leroysmith.com
Manufacturer and exporter of citrus fruit including grapefruit and oranges
> President: Elson R Smith Jr
> Vice President: Trey Smith
Estimated Sales: $38 Million
Number Employees: 250-499
Type of Packaging: Consumer
Brands:
> GOLDEN MAGIC
> ISLAND FRUIT
> MAGIC RIVER
> MYSTIC RIVER

8375 Lerro Candy Company
601 Columbia Ave
Darby, PA 19023-2510   610-461-8886
    sales@lerrocandyco.com
    http://www.lerrocandyco.com
Processor of confectionery products including chocolate cherries
> Owner/Manager: John Lerro
Estimated Sales: $$2.5-5 Million
Number Employees: 10-19
Type of Packaging: Consumer

8376 Les Aliments Livabec Foods
95 Rang St Louis
Sherrington, QC J0L 2N0
Canada   450-454-7971
    Fax: 450-454-9100
Processor and exporter of marinated mixed and roasted vegetables and mushrooms in oil; processor of antipasto calabrese, basil and sun-dried tomato pesto; importer of sun-dried tomatoes
> President: Lino Cimagila
> VP: Lino Cimaglia, Jr.
Number Employees: 10-19
Sq. footage: 20000
Brands:
> Livabec
> Livia

8377 Les Aliments Ramico Foods
8245 Rue Le Creusot
St. Leonard, QC H1P 2A2
Canada   514-329-1844
    Fax: 514-329-5096
Processor, canner and exporter of beans, soups, sauces, chicken and meat with beans
> VP: Galal Matta
Number Employees: 10-19
Sq. footage: 12000
Type of Packaging: Private Label

8378 Les Bourgeois Vineyards
P.O.Box 118
Rocheport, MO 65279-0118   573-698-2300
   Fax: 573-698-2170   info@missouriwine.com
     www.missouriwine.com
Wines
> CEO: Curtis Bourgeois
> Marketing Director: Laura Royse
> Office Manager: Sue Good
Estimated Sales: Below $ 5 Million
Number Employees: 50-99
Type of Packaging: Private Label
Brands:
> Les Bourgeois

8379 Les Brasseurs Du Nord
875 Michele Bohec Boulevard
Blainville, QC J7C 5J6
Canada   450-979-8400
   Fax: 450-979-3733   800-378-3733
   info@boreale.com   www.boreale.com
Processor and distributor of beer, ale and stout
> President: Bernard Morin
> Marketing Manager: Bernard Morin
> Vice President: Laura Urtinowski
> CEO: Daniel Lampron
Estimated Sales: $ 5-10 Million
Number Employees: 50-100
Sq. footage: 35000
Type of Packaging: Consumer, Food Service
Brands:
> BER Boreale

8380 Les Brasseurs GMT
5585 De La Rouche
Montreal, QC H2J 3K3
Canada   514-274-4941
   Fax: 514-274-6138   888-253-8330
   info@brasseursrj.com   www.brasseursrj.com
Processor of beer, ale, lager and stout
> Manager: Alain Hudon
> Partner: Brasserie Le Cheval Blanc
> Pioneer: Les Brasseurs GMT
Number Employees: 50-99
Type of Packaging: Consumer, Food Service
Brands:
> Belle Gueule

8381 Les Chocolats Vadeboncoeur
8350 Parkway D'Anjou
Montreal, QC H1K 4S3
Canada   514-493-8504
   Fax: 514-483-3956   800-276-8504

Chocolate

8382 Les Industries Bernard Et Fils
Rue Du Seminaire
St. Victor, QC G0M 2B0
Canada   418-588-6109
    Fax: 418-588-6836
Processor and exporter of pure maple syrup
> President: M Yves Bernard
Type of Packaging: Consumer, Food Service, Private Label, Bulk

8383 Les Salaisons Brochu
183 Route Du President-Kennedy
St. Henri De Levis, QC G0R 3E0
Canada   418-882-2282
   Fax: 418-882-5212   a.lafleur@videotron.ca
Processor of fresh and frozen pork
> Contact: Laurent Brochu
Number Employees: 250-499
Type of Packaging: Consumer, Food Service, Private Label

8384 Les Trois Petits Cochons
453 Greenwich Street
New York, NY 10013-1757   212-219-1230
   Fax: 212-941-9726   800-537-7283
   info@3pigs.com   www.3pigs.com
Processor of natural pates and mousses: meat, poultry, game, vegetable and seafood; also, garlic sausage; importer of cornichons, cepes and petits toasts
> President: Alain Sinturel
> Marketing Director: Valentine Colin
> Sales Director: Maha Freij
Estimated Sales: 6.3 Million
Number Employees: 40
Number of Brands: 2
Type of Packaging: Consumer, Food Service
Brands:
> Coeur De France
> Les Trois Petits Cochons

8385 Les Trois Petits Cochons 3 Little Pigs
453 Greenwich Street
Brooklyn, NY 11232   212-219-1230
   Fax: 212-941-9726   davidh@3pigs.com
     www.3pigs.com
Manufacturer of pates, mini terrines, mousses, vegetable and seafood terrines, charouterie and pork free products.
> President: Alain Sinturel
Estimated Sales: $20-50 Million
Number Employees: 20-49

8386 Les Viandes Or-Fil
2080 Rue Monterey
Laval, QC H7L 3S3
Canada   450-687-5664
    Fax: 450-687-2733
Processor and exporter of fresh and frozen pork
> President: Orlando Filice
Number Employees: 50-99
Type of Packaging: Bulk

8387 Les Viandes du Breton
150 Ch Des Raymond
Riviere-Du-Lup,, QC G5R 5X8
Canada   418-899-6711
   Fax: 418-899-6403   cbreton@quebectel.com
     www.dubreton.com
Processor of fresh and frozen pork; exporter of hams, spare ribs, bellies, etc
> Sales Manager: Gaetan Gauvin
Number Employees: 260
Parent Co: Bose Corporation
Type of Packaging: Consumer, Food Service, Private Label, Bulk
Brands:
> Dubreton Natural

8388 Lesaffre Yeast Corporation
777 E Wisconsin Ave # 11
Milwaukee, WI 53202-5302   414-271-6755
   Fax: 414-347-4795   mail@lesaffre.com
     www.sensient-technologies.com
Yeast
> CEO: Kenneth P Manning
Estimated Sales: $ 20 - 50 Million
Number Employees: 1,000-4,999

8389 Lesley Elizabeth
877 Whitney Dr
Lapeer, MI 48446-2565   810-667-0706
     Fax: 810-667-7287   800-684-3300
          lesley@lesleyelizabeth.com
          www.lesleyelizabeth.com
Gourmet sauces, oils, vinegarettes, pestos and crisps
     President: Lesley Mc Cowen
Estimated Sales: $ 1-5 Million
Number Employees: 10-19
Type of Packaging: Private Label
Brands:
     Lesley Elizabeth
     Lesley Elizabeth's Crisps
     Lesley Elizabeth's Dipping Oils
     Lesley Elizabeth's Dips
     Lesley Elizabeth's Pesto
     Lesley Elizabeth's Vinegarettes
     Lesley Marinara

8390 Leslie Leger & Sons
34 De La Cote
Cap-Pele, NB E4N 3B3
Canada   506-577-4730
          http://www.leslieandsons.com
Processor and exporter of smoked herring and
brined alewife
     President: Leslie Leger
Number Employees: 50-99
Type of Packaging: Bulk

8391 LesserEvil Snacks
95 Lake Avenue
Tuckahoe, NY 10707   914-779-3000
     Fax: 914-779-3099 www.lesserevil.com
all natural snacks
Number Employees: 8

8392 Let Them Eat Cake
3805 S West Shore Blvd # B
Tampa, FL 33611-1047   813-837-6888
          Fax: 813-831-6741
     admin@chocolateismycrayon.com
          www.chocolateismycrayon.com
Processor of custom mini pastries
     President/CEO: Michael Baugh
     Marketing Manager: Michael Baugh
Estimated Sales: Less than $500,000
Number Employees: 1-4

8393 Let's Serve
3 Plattsburgh Avenue
Plattsburgh, NY 12901-4231   518-293-7119
     Fax: 518-293-7119 letsserve@aol.com
Processor of apple butter, apple sauce, peach pre-
serves, jams and fruit spreads
     Owner: Donald Papson
     Co-Owner: Vivian Papson
Estimated Sales: Under $300,000
Number Employees: 400
Sq. footage: 400
Brands:
     Adirondack Orchard
     Heritage Sauces
     Thank the Trees

8394 Let's Serve
3 Plattsburgh Avenue
Plattsburgh, NY 12901-4231   518-293-7119
     Fax: 518-293-7119 letsserve@aol.com
Applesauce, butter, honey cream, jam
     President: Don Papson
     CEO: Don Papson
     Vice President: Vivian Papson
Type of Packaging: Private Label
Brands:
     Let's Serve

8395 Letraw Manufacturing Company
200 Quaker Rd # 2
Rockford, IL 61104-7068   815-987-9670
     Fax: 815-987-9830 rwartell@letraw.com
          www.letraw.com
Manufacture cleaning products
     President: Lane Wartell
     Vice President: Ralph Wartell
Estimated Sales: Less than $500,000
Number Employees: 5-9
Type of Packaging: Bulk
Brands:
     Letraw

8396 Level Valley Creamery
4350 Hurricane Creek Blvd
Antioch, TN 37013-2223   615-641-1027
     Fax: 615-641-7038   800-251-1292
          www.schreiber.com
Processor of dairy products including butter and
cream cheese; also, milk including condensed,
sweetened condensed, nonfat dry, whole powder and
28 1/2% fat; exporter of anhydrous milk fat
     President: Ronald Povinelli
     CFO: Dick Rosenbalm
     VP: David Moss
     Maintenance Engineer: Henry Lorenz
     Plant Manager: Bill Merrick
Estimated Sales: $32000000
Number Employees: 50-99
Sq. footage: 85000
Parent Co: Level Valley Creamery
Type of Packaging: Consumer, Food Service, Pri-
vate Label, Bulk
Brands:
     Country Squire
     Level Valley
     Swift's Brook

8397 Level Valley Creamery
807 Pleasant Valley Road
West Bend, WI 53095-9781   262-377-3073
     Fax: 262-675-2827   800-558-1707
     contact@levelvalley.com www.levelvalley.com
Butter and butter oil, cream cheese, anhydrous milk
and cream
     President: Alexander J Costigan
Estimated Sales: $ 100-500 Million
Number Employees: 200-250

8398 Levonian Brothers
P.O.Box 629
Troy, NY 12181-0629   518-274-3610
     Fax: 518-274-0098 chrispkeller@yahoo.com
          www.2eatcab.com
Manufacturer and exporter of meat products includ-
ing cooked and raw corn beef, pastrami, cooked and
smoked hams, roast beef, natural casing frankfurters
and sausages including Polish, pork and Italian
     President: Robert Nazarian
     Plant Manager: George Lindemann
Estimated Sales: $20-50 Million
Number Employees: 50-99
Type of Packaging: Consumer, Food Service

8399 Lewes Dairy
660 Pilottown Rd
Lewes, DE 19958-1299   302-645-6281
     Fax: 302-645-6290 www.lewesdairy.com
Processor of dairy products
     President/General Manager: Chip Brittingham
Estimated Sales: $ 10 - 20 Million
Number Employees: 20-49
Type of Packaging: Consumer

8400 Lewis Bakeries
200 Albert Street
London, ON N6A 1M1
Canada   519-434-5252
Processor of baked goods including bread, rolls and
pastries
     Asst. General Manager: John Gunn
Estimated Sales: $2800000
Number Employees: 75

8401 Lewis Brothers Bakeries
2792 S Old Decker Rd
Vincennes, IN 47591-7603   812-886-6533
          Fax: 812-886-6921
Manufacturer of raisin bread and fresh and frozen
sweet goods
     President: Jack Lewis Jr.
     VP Finance: Rodger Lesh
     VP Sales: Harry Lincoln
     Plant Engineer: Alan Rister
     Plant Manager: Dan Seyer
Estimated Sales: $ 20 - 50 Million
Number Employees: 100-249
Parent Co: Lewis Brothers Bakeries
Type of Packaging: Consumer, Food Service

8402 Lewis Brothers Bakeries
504 Kendall Street
Sikeston, MO 63801-2742   573-471-1650
          Fax: 573-471-6322
Buns and rolls
     Vice President: Dean Short
     Production Manager: DeWayne Coleman

8403 Lewis Brothers Bakery
P.O.Box 426
La Porte, IN 46352-0426   219-362-4561
     Fax: 219-325-0030 www.lewisbakeries.net
Processor of bread and buns
     Manager: John West
Estimated Sales: $11,500,000
Number Employees: 100-249
Parent Co: Lewis Brothers Bakeries
Type of Packaging: Consumer, Food Service

8404 (HQ)Lewis Brothers Bakery
500 N Fulton Ave
Evansville, IN 47710-1597   812-425-4642
          Fax: 812-425-7609
Manufacturer of low-fat, low-carbohydrate breads.
Products include whole grain and white breads, buns
and several sugar free varieties.
     President: R J Lewis Jr
     CEO: R J Lewis Jr
     VP Finance: Rodger Lesh
     VP Sales: Harry Lincoln
     Buyer: Carol Stratman
Estimated Sales: $ 240 Million
Number Employees: 500-999
Type of Packaging: Consumer, Food Service
Brands:
     Country Hearth

8405 Lewis Brothers Bakery
855 Scott St
Murfreesboro, TN 37129-2735   615-893-6041
          Fax: 615-893-1463
Processor of bread
     Manager: Rick Hardesty Jr
     General Production Manager: Kenneth Burkhart
     General Manager: Rick Hardesty
Estimated Sales: $ 50 - 100 Million
Number Employees: 100-249
Parent Co: Lewis Brothers Bakeries
Type of Packaging: Consumer, Food Service

8406 Lewis Cellars
524 El Cerrito Avenue
Hillsborough, CA 94010-6822   415-445-7884
     Fax: 415-445-7758 wine@lewiscellars.com
          www.lewiscellars.com
Wines
     President: Randy Lewis
Estimated Sales: Below $ 500,000
Number Employees: 1

8407 Lewis Laboratories International
49 Richmondville Ave # 118
Westport, CT 06880-2053   203-226-7343
     Fax: 203-454-0329   800-243-6020
     customerservice@lewis-labs.com
          www.lewis-labs.com
Nutritional supplements
     President: Diana Lewis
Estimated Sales: $500,000-$1 Million
Number Employees: 5-9
Brands:
     Brewer's
     Fabulous Fiber
     Famous Original Formula Staminex
     Lewis Labs RDA
     Super Fabulous Fiber
     Weigh Down

8408 Lewis Packing Company
17480 Shelley Ave
Sandy, OR 97055-8055   503-668-8122
     Owner: Kris Jones
Estimated Sales: Under $500,000
Number Employees: 1-4

8409 Lewis Sausage Corporation
P.O.Box 280
Burgaw, NC 28425-0280   910-259-2642
          Fax: 910-259-9881
Manufacturer of smoked and mild sausage
     President: Edgar Hardy
Estimated Sales: $5-10 Million
Number Employees: 20-49
Type of Packaging: Consumer

Top of column 3 (before 8403):
Estimated Sales: $ 10-24.9 Million
Number Employees: 125

8410 Lewis Smoked Meat Company
9140 S Baltimore Ave
Chicago, IL 60617-4482   773-221-4300
Fax: 773-221-8930   800-648-6328
mail@lewissmoked.com www.lewissmoked.com
Processor of smoked meats and poultry parts including hocks, spare ribs, neck bones, pork skins, turkey wings and tails, dry cured salt pork, etc.; also, private labeling available
President: Willis Myers
Estimated Sales:$3500000
Number Employees: 20-49
Type of Packaging: Bulk

8411 Lewis-Vincennes Bakery
2792 S Old Decker Rd
Vincennes, IN 47591-7603   812-886-6533
Fax: 812-886-6921
Processor of baked goods
President: Jack Louis
Plant Manager: Dan Seyer
Estimated Sales: $ 20 - 50 Million
Number Employees: 100-249
Parent Co: Lewis-Vincennes Bakery
Type of Packaging: Consumer, Food Service, Private Label, Bulk

8412 Lexington Coffee & Tea Company
2571 Regency Rd
Lexington, KY 40503-2920   859-277-1102
Fax: 859-277-6490
Coffee and tea
Owner: Terri Wood
Estimated Sales: $ 5-10 Million
Number Employees: 5-9
Brands:
Lexington Coffee Tea

8413 Li'l Guy Foods
P.O.Box 33662
Kansas City, MO 64120-3662   816-241-2000
Fax: 816-241-2025 800-886-8226
LilGuyFoods@lilguyfoods.com
www.lilguyfoods.com
Manufacturer of Mexican foods including corn tortillas, flour tortillas, flavored tortilla wraps, taco shells, tortilla chips, spices, taco sauce and salsa picante, cheeses and chorizo and chicharones.
President: David Sloan
CFO/Director of Sales: Christina Sloan
VP: Edward Sloan
Sales Manager: Allen Carriere
Office Manager/Customer Service: Jennifer Hart
Plant Manager: Edward Sloan
Estimated Sales:$2000000
Number Employees: 20-49
Sq. footage: 30000
Parent Co: Sloan Acquisition Corporation
Type of Packaging: Consumer, Food Service
Brands:
Li'l Guy
V&V Supremo Cheeses & Meats

8414 Liberty Dairy
530 N River St
Evart, MI 49631-9354   231-734-5592
Fax: 231-734-3880 800-632-5552
www.deanfoods.com
Processor of juice and milk
VP Sales/Marketing: Scott Jacobs
Plant Manager: Gordon Willis
Estimated Sales:$100+ Million
Number Employees: 100-249
Parent Co: Dean Foods Company
Type of Packaging: Consumer, Food Service, Private Label

8415 Liberty Enterprises
PO Box 5250
Stateline, NV 89449-5250   775-588-3656
Fax: 775-588-7366 800-723-3690
jpensec@harland.net
www.libertysite.com/harland
President/CEO: Timothy C Tuff
*Estimated Sales:*Under $500,000
Number Employees: 1-4
Brands:
Altafi
Cavion Plus
Mydas

8416 Liberty Natural Products
8120 SE Stark Street
Portland, OR 97215-2346   503-256-1227
Fax: 503-256-1182 800-289-8427
christy@libertynatural.com
www.libertynatural.com
Processor and exporter of gourmet breath fresheners, natural flavors and oils; processor of vitamins; importer of essential oils and botanical extracts; wholesaler/distributor of gourmet breath fresheners
President: Jim Dierking
Operations Manager: Lonny Lippolo
Estimated Sales:$2500000
Number Employees: 22
Sq. footage: 17000
Type of Packaging: Consumer, Bulk
Brands:
MAX
Natural Gourmet Flavor Oil
TIB

8417 Liberty Orchards Company
P.O.Box C
Cashmere, WA 98815-0485   509-782-2191
Fax: 509-782-1487 800-888-5696
service@libertyorchards.com
www.libertyorchards.com
Processor and exporter of confectionery products including chocolate, holiday and boxed nonchocolate candy
President: Greg Taylor
VP Marketing & Sales: Michael Rainey Sr
Estimated Sales:$12377000
Number Employees: 50-99
Type of Packaging: Consumer, Food Service
Brands:
APLETS
COTLETS
FRUIT CHOCOLATES
FRUIT DELIGHTS
FRUIT FESTIVES
FRUIT PARFAITS
FRUIT SOFTEES
GRAPELETS
HAWAIIAN FESTIVES

8418 (HQ)Liberty Richter
400 Lyster Ave
Saddle Brook, NJ 07663-5910   201-291-8749
Fax: 201-368-3575 lr@mediaetc.com
www.libertyrichter.com
Processor and importer of caviar, mustard, cookies, crackers, olives, breakfast cereals, pasta, rice, anchovies, sardines and dried fruits
President: Lawrence J Lapare
Marketing Director: John Affer
Operations Manager: Kathie Gibbs Forkouski
Estimated Sales: $ 5 - 10 Million
Number Employees: 5-9
Type of Packaging: Consumer
Brands:
Agnesi
Amore
Apollinaris
Arnott's
Arriba
Balanced
Better Than Milk
Chatfield's
Cookie Lovers
Debel
Delacre
Downey's Original
Fazer
Fini
Fre
Harmony Farms
Honeycup
International Collection
Kame
Kitchens of India
Kozlowski Farms
London Fruit & Herb Company
Mazzetti
Melinda's
Mi-Del
Perfect Cup
Rademaker
Sacla
Sapori
Sesmark
Steaz Sparkling Green Tea
Swan Gardens
Tofu Rella

Vegan Rella
Vermont Village Cannery

8419 Liberty Vegetable Oil Company
15306 Carmenita Rd
Santa Fe Springs, CA 90670-5606   562-921-3567
Fax: 562-802-3476
liberty@libertyvegetableoil.com
www.libertyvegetableoil.com
Vegetable oils
President: Irwin Field
VP: Edward Field
Controller: Warren Parr
Executive VP: C Adams
Sales Manager: Ronald Field
Estimated Sales: $ 50 - 100 Million
Number Employees: 50-99
Brands:
Lvo

8420 Libs Candies Downtown
601 Main St
Evansville, IN 47708-1617   812-422-5119
www.libscandies.com
Processor of candy including pecan, flipovers, assorted creams and roasted nut
President: John Libs
Treasurer: R Libs
Number Employees: 10-19
Type of Packaging: Consumer, Private Label, Bulk

8421 Licata Enterprises/World Organics
5242 Bolsa Ave # 3
Huntington Beach, CA 92649-1054 714-893-0017
Fax: 714-897-5677 plicata@prodigy.net
Organic foods
President: Paul Licata
Chairman: Al Licata PhD
Sales: Bernie Luuch
Plant Manager: Peter Reynoso
Estimated Sales: $ 10 - 20 Million
Number Employees: 10-19
Number of Brands: 7
Number of Products: 350
Type of Packaging: Private Label
Brands:
NATURE'S CONCEPT
NU-VISTA
NUTRI-CAL
NUTRITION MASTERS
NUTRITION'S BEST
VITA-VISTA
WORLD ORGANIC

8422 Lichtwer Pharma
61 Broadway
Room 1310
New York, NY 10006-2722   800-226-6227
Fax: 212-292-1542 info@abkit.com
www.lichtwer.com
Processor of dietary supplements in tablet form including garlic, ginseng, ginkgo biloba and St. John's wort (hypericum)
CEO/President: David Illingworth
Director Sales/Marketing: Sasha Taylor
VP Sales: Jim Mellaci
Number Employees: 10-19
Sq. footage: 5000
Parent Co: Lichtwer Pharma AG
Type of Packaging: Consumer
Brands:
Cynara-Sl
Ginkai
Kira
Kwai
Sedonium

8423 Lieber Chocolate & FoodProducts
142 44th Street
Brooklyn, NY 11232-3310   718-499-0888
Fax: 718-499-5636
Chocolates
President: Mark Moskowitz
Estimated Sales: $ 20-50 Million
Number Employees: 20
Brands:
Lieber

8424 Life Extension Foods
P.O.Box 407198
Fort Lauderdale, FL 33340-7198   954-966-4886
Fax: 954-761-9199 800-678-8989
customerservice@lifeextension.com www.lef.org

Owner: William Faloon
Director Nutrition: Ross Pelton
Director, Place for Achieving Total He: Eric R Braverman
Brands:
Life Extension Mixo

8425 Life Force Winery
1055 Saddle Ridge Road
Moscow, ID 83843-8774   208-882-9158
          Fax: 800-497-8258   garric@turbonet.com
Honey wine
President: Garrick Kruse
Estimated Sales: $5-9.9 Million
Number Employees: 8
Brands:
Life Force

8426 Life International
8889 Pelican Bay Boulevard
Suite 301
Naples, FL 34108-7501   239-592-9788
          Fax: 941-592-9787   efgonzalez@prodigy.com
Estimated Sales: Less than $500,000
Number Employees: 5-9

8427 Life-Renewal
Highway 18
Garrison, MN 56450-0092   320-692-4498
          Fax: 320-692-5013   rholmigi00@aol.com
Processor, importer and exporter of herbal products and vitamins; also, spirulina
President: Ronald Holmquist
Number Employees: 1-4
Parent Co: Garrco
Type of Packaging: Consumer, Private Label, Bulk
Brands:
Herbal Slimdown
Life Renewal Herbs
Lr Hp Forte

8428 LifeSpice Ingredients
300 Cherry Lane
Palm Beach, FL 33480   561-844-6334
          Fax: 561-844-6335 www.lifespiceingredients.com
Supplier of spice blends and flavor systems.

8429 LifeTime Nutritional Specialties
1967 N Glassell St
Orange, CA 92865-4320   714-634-9340
          Fax: 714-634-9340
lifetimevitamins@sbcglobal.net
          www.lifetimevitamins.com
Vitamins
President: Tom Pinkowski
Vice President of Sales/Marketing: Tom Pinkowski

8430 Lifeforce Labs LLC
920 Britt Ct
Altamonte Spgs, FL 32701-2080   407-830-0009
          Fax: 407-830-0039   info@lifeforce-labs.com
          www.lifeforce-labs.com
Manufacturer of protein based nutritional drinks.
Managing Partner: Bruce Svetz
Managing Partner: John Sericka

8431 Lifeline Food Company
426 Orange Ave
Sand City, CA 93955-3569   831-899-5040
          Fax: 831-899-0285 www.lifetimecheese.com
Dairy and cheese
President: Jone Chappell
CFO: Greg Chappell
Estimated Sales: Below $ 5 Million
Number Employees: 5-9
Number of Brands: 2
Type of Packaging: Private Label
Brands:
Dairytime
ENERGY BARS
Lifetime
Lifetime Fat Free Cheese
Lifetime Lactose/Fat Free Cheese
Lifetime Low Fat Cheese
Lifetime Low Fat Rice Cheese
SOY CHEESE

8432 Lifestar Millennium
PO Box 5453
Novato, CA 94948-5453   415-457-1400
          Fax: 415-457-8887   800-858-7477
lsmail@lifestar.com   www.lifestar.com

Processor and exporter of natural nutritional supplements; importer of grapeseed oil
President: J Bentley
Operations Manager: K Lindgren
Estimated Sales: $300,000-500,000
Number Employees: 1-4
Type of Packaging: Consumer, Food Service
Brands:
Living Food Concentrates
Multiplex

8433 Lifeway Foods Inc
6431 Oakton St
Morton Grove, IL 60053-2727   847-967-1010
          Fax: 847-967-6558   info@lifeway.net
          www.lifeway.net
Processor and exporter of dairy products including drinkable yogurt, kefir and cheese.
President/CEO: Julie Smolyansky
Founder of Lifeway Foods: Mike Smolyansky
Public/Media Relations: Sarah Ryser
Estimated Sales: $ 4 Million
Number Employees: 100-249
Sq. footage: 60000
Type of Packaging: Consumer
Brands:
BASICS PLUS
FARMER'S CHEESE
KEFIR
KEFIR STARTER
LA FRUTA
SOY TREAT
SWEET KISS

8434 Lifewise Ingredients
350 Telser Rd
Lake Zurich, IL 60047-6701   847-550-8270
          Fax: 847-550-8272   info@lifewise1.com
          www.lifewise1.com
Processor and exporter of health food ingredients including monosodium glutamate replacements, fat replacers, flavor enhancers, flavor maskers
Founder: Richard Share
Sales Director: Richard Share
Lab Manager: Millie Galey
General Manager: Carol Bender
Purchasing Manager: Carol Bender
Estimated Sales: Below $ 5 Million
Number Employees: 5-9
Sq. footage: 3500
Brands:
Bitzels
Lifewise Ingredients
Potentiator Plus
simply rich

8435 Light Rock Beverage Company
9 Balmforth Avenue
Danbury, CT 06810-5908   203-743-3410
          Fax: 203-792-7909
Bottled water, other beverages
President: George Antous
Vice President: Fred Antous
General Manager: Thomas Antous
Estimated Sales: Below $ 5 Million
Number Employees: 18
Brands:
Light Rock

8436 Light Vision Confections
1776 Mentor Avenue
Cincinnati, OH 45212-3554   513-351-9444
          Fax: 253-981-0758   sales@lightvision.com
          www.lightvision.com
Processor of holographic confectionery items including lollypops, hard candy and chocolate
President: Eric Begleiter
CEO: Mike Wodke
CFO: Paul Graham
Estimated Sales: Below $ 5 Million
Number Employees: 20-30
Type of Packaging: Food Service, Private Label
Brands:
HOLOPOP
PopArt

8437 Lightlife Foods
153 Industrial Blvd
Turners Falls, MA 01376-1611   413-774-9000
          Fax: 413-774-9080   800-274-6001
          www.lightlife.com

Processor and exporter of soy-based meat analogs including imitation bacon bits, hamburgers, sausage, frankfurters, cold cuts and dough-wrapped frankfurters; also, tempeh and ground meat substitutes
Manager: Darcy Zbinovec
VP Sales/Marketing: Richard McKelvey
Estimated Sales: $ 20 - 50 Million
Number Employees: 100-249
Parent Co: ConAgra Foods
Brands:
American Grill
Barbecue Grill
Chia's Chili
Classic Sloppy J
Country Breakfast Style
Fakin' Bacon
Fakin' Bacon Bits
Foney Baloney
Garden Vegetable
Gimme Lean Sausage & Beef
Lean Links
Lemon Grill
Lightlife Classics
Lightlife Grills
Lightlife Organic Tempeh
Macro Power Tempeh
Old World Italian Style
Original Soy
Quinoa-Sesame
Smart Dogs
Three-Grain & Soy
Tofu Pups

8438 Lily of the Desert
1887 Geesling Rd
Denton, TX 76208-1411   940-566-9914
          Fax: 940-566-9915   800-229-5459
          custserv@lilyofthedesert.com
          www.lilyofthedesert.com
Processor and exporter of certified organic aloe vera beverages and dietary supplements
President: Don Lovelace
Estimated Sales: $ 1 - 3 Million
Number Employees: 10-19
Type of Packaging: Consumer, Food Service, Private Label, Bulk
Brands:
Lily of the Desert

8439 Lilydale Foods
9620 56th Avenue NW
Edmonton, AB T6E 0B3
Canada   780-435-3944
          Fax: 780-436-6867   800-661-5341
          contactus@lilydale.com   www.lilydale.com
Processor and exporter of fresh and frozen meats, poultry, sausages and sandwiches; also, further processed poultry products including fully cooked, par cooked, breaded and unbreaded
President: Henry Van Zeggalaar
Sales Manager (Food Service): Adrian Feddema
Purchasing Agent: Gerry Doyle
Number Employees: 300
Sq. footage: 80000
Parent Co: Lilydale Cooperative
Type of Packaging: Consumer, Food Service, Bulk
Brands:
Country Fair
Lilydale
Royal Fancy

8440 Limestone Food Service
1516 Industrial Park Drive
Maysville, KY 41056-9691   606-759-7134
          Fax: 606-759-7979
President: Deborah Riggs

8441 Limited Edition
3108 N Big Spring St
Midland, TX 79705-5378   432-686-2008
          Fax: 432-686-2035
Processor of flavored honey butter, dip mixes, jalapenos, pickles and vegetables
Owner: Beverly Vaughan
Controller: Ann Wimberly
Estimated Sales: $300-500,000
Number Employees: 1-4
Sq. footage: 10000
Type of Packaging: Consumer, Food Service, Private Label, Bulk
Brands:
Limited Edition Presents
Udderly Delightful

8442 Limoneria Company
1141 Cummings Rd
Santa Paula, CA 93060-9709   805-933-1455
        Fax: 805-525-8761 info@limoneira.com
                www.limoneira.com
Packinghouse for Sunkist Growers, Inc. citrus fruit.
        President/CEO: Harold Edwards
        VP/Finance & Administration: Don Delmatoff
        Senior Vice President: Alex Teague
        Business Development Manager: David McCoy
        Marketing Director: John Chamberlain
        Director Packing & Sales: Tomas Gonzales
        Director Information Systems: Eric Tovias
        Agritourism Operations Manager: Ryan
        Nasalroad
Estimated Sales: G
Type of Packaging: Food Service

8443 Limpert Brothers
P.O.Box 1480
Vineland, NJ 08362-1480   856-691-1353
        Fax: 856-794-8968 800-691-1353
    limpertbr@aol.com   www.limpertbrothers.com
Processor, importer and exporter of cherries, pro-
cessed fruits, syrups, extracts, flavors, ice cream
bases, marshmallow fluff and bakery ingredients
        President: Pearl Giordano
        R&D: Jim Behringer
        Quality Control: Donna Phrampus
Estimated Sales: $ 10 - 20 Million
Number Employees: 20-49
Number of Brands: 1
Number of Products: 400
Type of Packaging: Food Service, Bulk
Brands:
    LIMPERT BROTHERS

8444 Limur Winery
945 Green Street
5
San Francisco, CA 94133-3601   415-781-8691
                Fax: 415-781-6303
Wines
        Vineyard Manager: Doug Wight
Estimated Sales: $500,000-$1 Million
Number Employees: 1-4

8445 Lin Court Vineyards
1711 Alamo Pintado Rd
Solvang, CA 93463-9712   805-688-8554
        Fax: 805-688-9327 info@lincourtwines.com
                www.lincourtwines.com
Processor of red and white wines
        General Manager: Alan Phillips
Number Employees: 5-9
Sq. footage: 4000
Parent Co: Folly Estates
Type of Packaging: Consumer
Brands:
    Lin Court Vineyards

8446 Lincoln Mills
352 W Side Avenue
Jersey City, NJ 07305-1135   201-433-0070
        President: Jane Jasper
Estimated Sales: Below $ 5 Million
Number Employees: 4

8447 Lincoln Snacks Company
30 Buxton Farm Rd
Stamford, CT 06905-1224   203-329-4545
        Fax: 203-329-4555 800-872-7622
                www.demets.com
Processor of popcorn snacks
        President/CEO: Hendrick Hartong
        CFO: Joanne Prier
        CEO: David Clarke
Estimated Sales: $ 3 - 5 Million
Number Employees: 5-9
Type of Packaging: Consumer
Brands:
    Fiddle Faddle
    Golden Gourmet Nuts
    Poppycock

8448 Linda's Gourmet Latkes
PO Box 491413
Los Angeles, CA 90049   818-705-2364
                888-452-8537
    info@lindasgourmetlatkes.com
    www.lindasgourmetlatkes.com
latkes
        President/Owner: Linda Hausberg

8449 Linda's Lollies Company
54 W 21st St
New York, NY 10010-6908   212-447-6740
        Fax: 212-447-1350 800-347-1545
    info@lindaslollies.com   www.lindaslollies.com
Processor and exporter of gourmet lollypops and
confectionery gifts
        President: Linda Harkavy
        Sales & Marketing: Tammy Demone
        Customer Services: Connie Atticella
Estimated Sales: $1500000
Number Employees: 1-4
Type of Packaging: Consumer, Food Service, Bulk
Brands:
    Linda's Little Lollies
    Linda's Lollies

8450 Lindemann Produce
1111 G Street
Los Banos, CA 93635-3762   209-826-2442
                Fax: 209-826-0787
Exporter and processor of melons including canta-
loupes and honeydews
        General Manager: George Meek
Parent Co: Lindemann Farms
Type of Packaging: Bulk

8451 Linden Beverage Company
3056 Dismal Hollow Rd
Linden, VA 22642   540-635-2118
                Fax: 540-636-4470
    customerservice@alpenglow.net
                www.alpenglow.net
Processor and exporter of sparkling cider
        President: Ben R Lacy Iii III
        Manager: Richard Wadkins
        Sales Manager: Debra Hunter
Estimated Sales: $944344
Number Employees: 20-49
Sq. footage: 25000
Type of Packaging: Consumer
Brands:
    Alpenglow

8452 Linden Cheese Factory
300 Jackson Street
PO Box 439
Linden, WI 53553-0439   608-623-2531
        Fax: 608-623-2567 800-660-5051
Monterey jack, cheddar, colby, longhorn cheese
        President: David Schroeder
Estimated Sales: $ 5-10 Million
Number Employees: 15

8453 Linden Cookies
25 Brenner Dr
Congers, NY 10920-1397   845-268-5050
        Fax: 845-268-5055 800-660-5051
    info@lindencookies.com
    www.lindencookies.com
Cookies and crackers
        President: Paul Sturz
        VP Sales: John Kraemer
        Operation Manager: Paul Sturz
Estimated Sales: $ 10-20 Million
Number Employees: 20-49
Brands:
    Linden's Originals

8454 Lindner Bison
27060 Victoria Lane
Apt 111
Valencia, CA 91355-5139   866-247-8753
        Fax: 661-254-0224 klindner@bisurkey.com
                www.bisurkey.com
Processor of bison/turkey burgers
        President: Kathy Lindner
        COO: Ken Lindner
Number Employees: 1-4
Brands:
    Bison
    Bisurkey

8455 Lindsay Farms
10 Georgia Road SW
Cave Spring, GA 30124-2031   706-777-9797
                Fax: 706-777-0007
Gourmet food
        Owner: Pam Beard
Estimated Sales: Less than $100,000
Number Employees: 1
Type of Packaging: Private Label

Brands:
    Lindsay Farms

8456 Lindsay's Tea
380 Swift Ave # 13
S San Francisco, CA 94080-6232   650-952-5446
        Fax: 650-871-4845 800-624-7031
                www.mouncanostoul.com
Coffee
        Manager: Melanie Mountanos
Estimated Sales: $ 20 - 50 Million
Number Employees: 20-49
Brands:
    Lindsay's Tea

8457 Lindt & Sprungli
PO Box 276
Stratham, NH 03885-0276   603-778-8100
        Fax: 603-778-3102 800-338-0839
    info@lindt.com   www.lindt.com
Chocolate
Estimated Sales: $ 30-50 Million
Number Employees: 650
Brands:
    American Classics
    Lindor Truffles
    Lindt Chocolate

8458 Linette Quality Chocolates
P.O.Box 212
Womelsdorf, PA 19567-0212   610-589-4526
        Fax: 610-589-2706 nutcrckr@ralcorp.com
            www.nutcrackerbrands.com/linette
Candy and confections
        VP Finance: Natalie Denette
        President/CEO: Lars Norgaard
        VP: James P Linette
        Sales Manager: Patti King
Estimated Sales: $ 20-50 Million
Number Employees: 100-249
Brands:
    Linette

8459 Linette Quality Chocolates
P.O.Box 212
Womelsdorf, PA 19567-0212   610-589-4526
        Fax: 610-589-2706 www.ralcorp.com
Chocolate candy
        President: Bill Gatto
        VP: James P Linette
        Marketing Director: Maurice Archambault
        Sales: Ronald Buch
Estimated Sales: $ 25-49.9 Million
Number Employees: 100-249
Brands:
    Linette

8460 Lingle Brothers Coffee
6500 Garfield Ave
Bell Gardens, CA 90201-1897   562-927-3317
                Fax: 562-928-1505
Coffee
        President: Earl Lingle
Estimated Sales: $ 10-20 Million
Number Employees: 20-49

8461 Link Snacks
P.O.Box 397
Minong, WI 54859-0397   715-466-2234
        Fax: 715-466-5151 800-346-6896
                www.linksnacks.com
Snacks
        President/CEO: Jack Link
        Executive VP Marketing: Troy Link
        Executive VP Sales: Jay Link
Estimated Sales: $100+ Million
Number Employees: 250-499
Brands:
    JACK LINK'S
    PICKLED PETE
    TOMAHAWK

8462 Linkmark International
60 Richards Avenue
Paxton, MA 01612-1148   508-753-2797
                Fax: 508-752-7476
Diet Foods
        Chairman: George Abernathy
Estimated Sales: $ 1-2.5 Million
Number Employees: 1-4

8463 Lins International
1601 S Federal Street
Chicago, IL 60616-1229
773-523-4478
Fax: 773-523-3829

President: Su Ju Hsu

8464 Lion Brewery
700 N Pennsylvania Ave
Wilkes Barre, PA 18705-2451
570-823-8801
Fax: 570-823-6686 800-233-8327
info@lionbrewery.com www.lionbrewery.com
Processor of ale, porter, lager and alcoholic and nonalcoholic malt beverages
President: Charles E Lawson Jr
VP: Robert Covert
Estimated Sales:$37349000
Number Employees: 100-249
Type of Packaging: Consumer, Bulk
Brands:
1857
Brewery Hill Black & Tan
Brewery Hill Centennial
Brewery Hill Cherry Wheat
Brewery Hill Pale
Brewery Hill Raspberry
Liebotschauer
Steg Maier
Stegmaier

8465 Lion Brewery
700 N Pennsylvania Ave
Wilkes Barre, PA 18705-2451
570-823-8801
Fax: 570-823-6686 800-233-8327
lorlandini@lionbrewery.com
www.lionbrewery.com
Beer
President: Charles Lawson Jr
CFO: Patrick Belardi
Sales Director: Don Ladhoff
Estimated Sales:$ 30 Million
Number Employees: 100-249
Type of Packaging: Private Label
Brands:
Brewery Hill Black & Tan
Brewery Hill Centennial
Brewery Hill Cherry Wheat
Brewery Hill Pale
Brewery Hill Rasberry
Liebotschauer
Steg Maier

8466 Lion Raisins
PO Box 1350
Selma, CA 93662
559-834-6677
Fax: 559-834-6622 blion@lionraisins.com
www.lionraisins.com
Grower and processor of California raisins and raisin products
President/CEO: Al Lion
CFO: Susan Keller
Operations Manager: Dan Lion
Estimated Sales:$70000000
Number Employees: 400
Sq. footage: 13000
Type of Packaging: Consumer, Food Service, Private Label, Bulk
Brands:
CALIFORNIA GROWN
LION
SUNSHINE CALIFORNIA

8467 (HQ)Lionel Lavallee Company
PO Box 229
Haverhill, MA 01831-0798
978-374-6391
Fax: 978-374-2647 800-343-8292
Manufacturer of meats including beef, pork, lamb, veal, sausage, turkey and chicken
President: Leonard Lavallee
Estimated Sales:$39 Million
Number Employees: 40
Type of Packaging: Food Service

8468 Lioni Latticini, Inc
7803 15th Ave
Brooklyn, NY 11228-2513
718-232-1166
Fax: 718-259-8378 info@lionimozzarella.com
www.lionimozzarella.com
Fresh whole milk mozzarella products
Owner: Michael Virga
Owner/VP: Salvatore Salzarulo
Sales Manager: Michelina Salzarulo
Operations Director: Guiseppe (Sal) Salarulo
Production Supervisor: Salvatore Salzarulo
Plant Supervisor: Salvatore Salzarulo

Estimated Sales:$5,700,000
Number Employees: 1-4

8469 Liono Latticini
555 Lehigh Ave
Union, NJ 07083
908-686-6061
Fax: 908-686-3449 info@lionimozzarella.com
www.lionimozzarella.com
fresh mozzarella products
Estimated Sales:$1.9 Million
Number Employees: 39

8470 Lipsey Mountain Spring Water
P.O.Box 1246
Norcross, GA 30091-1246
770-449-0001
Fax: 770-242-7601 sales@lipseywater.com
www.lipseywater.com
Bottled water
President: Joseph Lipsey Iii III
Estimated Sales:$ 1-2.5 Million
Number Employees: 20-49

8471 Lisa's Salsa Company
2140 University Ave W
St Paul, MN 55114-1820
651-644-4381
Fax: 651-644-1270 contactlisa@salsalisa.com
www.salsalisa.com
Salsa
Owner: Lisa Nicholson
Estimated Sales:$ 5 - 10 Million
Number Employees: 10-19
Brands:
SALSA LISA

8472 Lisbon Sausage Company
433 S 2nd St
New Bedford, MA 02740-5764
508-993-7645
Fax: 508-994-0453
Portuguese sausage
President: Antonio Rodrigues
Vice President: Joan Sparrow
*Estimated Sales:*Below $ 5 Million
Number Employees: 5-9

8473 Lisbon Seafood Company
1428 S Main St
Fall River, MA 02724-2604
508-672-3617
Fax: 508-672-4698
Seafood
Owner: Victor Da Silva
Estimated Sales:$ 1 - 3 Million
Number Employees: 10-19

8474 Litehouse
P.O.Box 1969
Sandpoint, ID 83864-0910
208-263-2030
Fax: 208-263-7821 vbrady@litehouseinc.com
www.litehousefoods.com
Processor of portion controlled refrigerated dressings and dips
Manager: Jennifer Calbert
Estimated Sales:$83473523
Number Employees: 250-499
Type of Packaging: Food Service

8475 Litehouse Foods
1109 N Ella Ave
Sandpoint, ID 83864-2202
208-263-7569
Fax: 208-263-7821 800-669-3169
rlowther@litehouseinc.com
www.litehousefoods.com
Processor and importer of salad dressings, sauces, mustards, dips and horseradish; exporter of salad dressings
President: Dougla Hawkins
CEO: Edward Hawkins Jr
CEO: Edward W Hawkins Jr
Marketing Director: Roxie Lowther
Sales Manager: Allen Wright
Public Relations: Susan Serne
President Operations: Doug Hawkins
Point of Sales Manager: Denise Zagorski
Purchasing Manager: Amy Van Sickle
Estimated Sales:$ 50 - 100 Million
Number Employees: 250-499
Sq. footage: 80000
Parent Co: Meyer Horseradish Company
Type of Packaging: Consumer, Food Service, Private Label, Bulk
Brands:
Chad's
Chadalee Farms
Meyer

8476 Little Amana Winery
P.O.Box 157
Amana, IA 52203-0157
319-668-9664
Fax: 319-668-2853
Wine
Owner: Bob Zuber
Brands:
Ackerman
Breezy Hills
Jasper
Little Swan Lake
Park Farm
Sugar Grove
Summerset
Village

8477 Little Angel Foods
817 Swift Street
Daytona Beach, FL 32114-2000
904-257-3040
Fax: 904-257-1727
Cheesecakes
President: Jim Omeara
Estimated Sales:$ 10-20 Million
Number Employees: 20

8478 Little Crow Foods
P.O.Box 1038
Warsaw, IN 46581-1038
574-267-7141
Fax: 574-267-2370 800-288-2769
customerservice@littlecrowfoods.com
www.littlecrowfoods.com
Manufacturer and contract packager of dry blended products including flour, pancake mixes and breakfast cereals; exporter of flour, cereals and seasoned coating mixes
President: Dennis Fuller
EVP: Kimberly Fuller
VP Operations: Ron Shipley
Estimated Sales:$8 Million
Number Employees: 50-99
Sq. footage: 90000
Type of Packaging: Consumer, Food Service, Private Label, Bulk
Brands:
MIRACLE MAIZE

8479 Little Dutch Boy Bakeries
P.O.Box 240
Draper, UT 84020-0240
801-571-3800
Fax: 801-571-3802
Processor of cookies including shortbread, chocolate chip, coconut, sugar, oatmeal, spice and fudge
President: Frank Bakker
VP: Robert Bakker
Estimated Sales:$ 20 - 50 Million
Number Employees: 50-99
Type of Packaging: Consumer, Private Label
Brands:
Little Dutch Boy Bakeries

8480 Little Freddy's
22151 Us Highway 19 N
Clearwater, FL 33765-2365
727-791-1118
Fax: 727-791-4092 littlefreddys@aol.com
CEO/CFO: Fred Lewis
Estimated Sales:$1-4.9 Million
Number Employees: 5-9
Type of Packaging: Private Label

8481 Little Hills Winery
710 S Main St
St Charles, MO 63301-3443
636-946-6637
Fax: 636-724-1121 877-584-4557
restaurant@little-hills.com www.little-hills.com
Wines
Co-Owner: David Campbell
Co-Owner: Tammy Campbell
Estimated Sales:$8.5 Million
Number Employees: 50-99

8482 Little I
815 3rd Street
Blaine, WA 98230
360-332-3258
Fax: 360-332-3279 sales@littlei.com
www.littlei.com
mints and gums

8483 Little Lady Foods
2323 Pratt Blvd
Elk Grove, IL 60007-5918
847-806-1440
Fax: 847-806-0026 800-439-1440
info@llf.com www.littleladyfoods.com

Customer food creator and manufacturer of premium pizzas, gourmet sandwiches, wraps, paninis grab-n-go items, breakfast items and desserts
President: John Geocaris
CEO: Dan Scales
VP Sales & Marketing: Peter Cokinos
VP Operations: Chris Celeslie
VP Procurement: Bruno Del Rio
Estimated Sales: $350,000,000
Number Employees: 400+
Sq. footage: 50000
Brands:
Bravissimo!
Connie's Pizza
Little Lady
Primerro
Tenaro

8484 Little Miss Muffin
4014 N Rockwell St
Chicago, IL 60618-3721   773-463-6328
Fax: 773-463-7101   800-456-9328
info@littlemissmuffin.com
www.littlemissmuffin.com
Processor of fresh and frozen cakes and pastries
Owner: Staci Minic Mintz
Estimated Sales: $ 20-50 Million
Number Employees: 20-49
Type of Packaging: Consumer, Food Service
Brands:
Little Miss Muffin
Wide Shoulders Bakin

8485 Little Rhody Brand Frankfurts
5 Day St
Johnston, RI 02919-4301   401-831-0815
sales@littlerhodyhotdogs.com
www.littlerhodyhotdogs.com
Manufacturer of sausage, frankfurters, meat products and fast foods
President: Edward Robalisky
Estimated Sales: $3 Million
Number Employees: 1-4
Sq. footage: 10000
Type of Packaging: Consumer, Food Service
Brands:
LITTLE RHODY BRAND

8486 Little River Lobster Company
P.O.Box 507
East Boothbay, ME 04544-0507   207-633-2648
Fax: 604-276-8371
Whole fish/seafood
President: Mike Dalton
Estimated Sales: $810,000
Number Employees: 1-4

8487 Little River Seafood
440 Rock Town Rd
Reedville, VA 22539-3017   804-453-3670
Fax: 804-453-5421   kelly@littleriverseafood.com
www.littleriverseafood.com
Processor of quality crab products.
President: J Gregory Lewis
Estimated Sales: $10026306
Number Employees: 20-49
Type of Packaging: Consumer, Food Service, Private Label, Bulk
Brands:
Little River Seafood

8488 Live A Little Gourmet Foods
37330 Cedar Boulevard
Suite H
Newark, CA 94560-4157   510-744-3683
Fax: 510-744-3684   888-744-2300
info@livealittle.com   www.livealittle.com
Fresh salads dressings and croutons
Owner: Virginia Davis
Estimated Sales: $ 1 - 3 Million
Number Employees: 1-4
Number of Brands: 2
Brands:
Live a Little Dressings
Perfect Croutons

8489 Live Food Products
P.O.Box 7
Santa Barbara, CA 93102-0007   805-968-1020
Fax: 805-968-1001   800-446-1990
info@bragg.com   www.bragg.com

Processor of liquid aminos and organic apple cider vinegar and extra-virgin olive oil
Manager: Sandi Enriquez
Controller: Sandy Gooch
Estimated Sales: $ 5 - 10 Million
Number Employees: 20-49
Brands:
Bragg

8490 Live Oaks Winery
3875 Hecker Pass Road
Gilroy, CA 95020-8805   408-842-2401
Wines
President: Richard Blocher
Estimated Sales: $500-1 Million appx.
Number Employees: 20-49

8491 Livermore Falls Baking Company
49 Gilbert St
Livermore Falls, ME 04254-4238   207-897-3442
Fax: 207-897-6381
Processor of baked goods including rolls and pizza crusts
President: Anthony Maxwell
Estimated Sales: $990000
Number Employees: 5-9

8492 Livermore Valley Cellars
1508 Wetmore Rd
Livermore, CA 94550   925-447-1751
Fax: 925-454-9463   info@lvcwines.com
www.lvcwines.com
Producer of wine
President: Chris Lagiss
CEO: Tim Sauer
Marketing Director: Tim Sauer
Estimated Sales: $1-2.5 Million
Number Employees: 1-4
Brands:
LVC

8493 Living Farms
352 3rd Street E
Tracy, MN 56175-1527   507-629-4431
Fax: 507-629-4258
Food products
Owner: Ardell Anderson
Estimated Sales: Under $500,000
Number Employees: 1-4

8494 Livingston Farmers Association
P.O.Box 456
Livingston, CA 95334-0456   209-394-7611
Fax: 209-394-7952
Processor and exporter of sweet potatoes, peaches and almonds
President: Steve Moler
Estimated Sales: $ 20 - 50 Million
Number Employees: 50-99
Brands:
Yamato Colony

8495 Livingston Moffett Winery
1895 Cabernet Lane
Saint Helena, CA 94574-1605   707-963-2120
Fax: 707-963-9385   800-788-0370
info@livingstonwines.com
www.livingstonwines.com
Winery
President: Diane Livingston
Production Manager: Mark Moffett
Estimated Sales: Below $ 5 Million
Number Employees: 4
Brands:
Gemstone Vineyard
Moffett
Stanley's
Starrey's ion
Syrah

8496 Livingston Provision Company
3701 W Orange Avenue
Tallahassee, FL 32310-5929   850-576-0153
Processor of meat products
Estimated Sales: $ 5 - 10 Million
Number Employees: 1-4
Type of Packaging: Food Service

8497 Livingston's Bull Bay Seafood
P.O.Box 70
Mc Clellanville, SC 29458-0070   843-887-3519
Fax: 843-887-3989

Shrimp and oysters
Co-Owner/President: Bull Livingston
Co-Owner/CEO: Kathy Livingston
Estimated Sales: $1 Million
Number Employees: 5-9

8498 Llano Estacado Winery
P.O.Box 3487
Lubbock, TX 79452-3487   806-745-2258
Fax: 806-748-1674   800-634-3854
info@llanowine.com   www.llanowine.com
Wine
President: Mark Hyman
CFO: Mary McGill
Vice President: James Morris
Operations Manager: Greg Bruni
Estimated Sales: Below $ 5 Million
Number Employees: 20-49
Type of Packaging: Private Label

8499 Lloyd's
P.O.Box 2727
Berwyn, PA 19312-0270   610-293-0516
Fax: 610-293-0689   lloydsofpa@aol.com
www.lloydspa.com
Frozen dessert mixes
President: Barry Jones
Marketing/Sales: Andy Jones
Purchasing Manager: Betty Clark
Estimated Sales: $ 5 -10 Million
Number Employees: 1-4
Number of Brands: 1
Number of Products: 20
Type of Packaging: Food Service, Private Label, Bulk

8500 Lloyd's Barbeque Company
1455 Mendota Heights Rd
Mendota Heights, MN 55120-1002   651-688-6000
Fax: 651-681-1430   www.lloydsbbq.com
Barbeque sauce
President: Stuart Applebaum
President: Lloyd Sigel
Executive VP: Franz Hofmeister
Plant Manager: Jack Goldbach
Estimated Sales: I
Number Employees: 250-499

8501 Loafin' Around
7609 Airpark Road
Suite A
Laytonsville, MD 20879-4165   301-570-4513
Fax: 301-216-1575   loafin@erols.com
Breads
President: John DiLoreto

8502 Lobster Gram International
4664 N Lowell Ave
Chicago, IL 60630-4263   773-777-4123
Fax: 773-777-5546   800-548-3562
www.livelob.com
Lobster
President: Daniel Zawacki
Estimated Sales: $ 1 - 3 Million
Number Employees: 10-19

8503 Lobsters Alive Company
1809 Sunnyside Beach Drive
Johnsburg, IL 60050-6941   815-344-4433
Fax: 815-344-4479
Wholesaler/distributor of lobster tank supplies and parts; also, sales and service of new and reconditioned lobster tanks available; design consultant specializing in large holding systems
General Manager: Joann Baureis
Equipment Specialist: Dennis Baureis
Estimated Sales: $500,000-$1 Million
Number Employees: 1-4
Sq. footage: 2000

8504 Local Tofu
PO Box 333
Nyack, NY 10960-0333   845-727-6393
localtofu@juno.com
Processor of tofu, soy milk, tofu salads, herbal spreads and vegetarian burgers
President: Sam Weinreb
Estimated Sales: Under $500,000
Number Employees: 1-4
Type of Packaging: Consumer
Brands:
Tofu

8505 Lochhead Manufacturing Company
527 Axminister Dr
Fenton, MO 63026-2903 636-326-1222
Fax: 636-326-4447 888-776-2088
sales@lochheadvanilla.com
www.lochheadvanilla.com
Processor and exporter of vanilla extracts including pure, natural and artificial blends.
Member: George Lochhead
Member: John Lochhead
Estimated Sales: $ 10 - 20 Million
Number Employees: 10-19
Type of Packaging: Consumer, Private Label, Bulk

8506 (HQ)Lochhead Manufacturing Company
527 Axminister Dr
Fenton, MO 63026-2903 636-326-1222
888-776-2088
www.lochheadvanilla.com
Produces a variety of vanilla extracts and flavorings available in several blends including both natural and artificial in addition to whole vanilla beans and powders.
President/Co-Owner: George Lochhead
Co-Owner: John Lochhead
Estimated Sales: $ 5 - 10 Million
Number Employees: 5-9
Brands:
Lochhead Vanilla

8507 Lockcoffee
6 Kilmer Road
Larchmont, NY 10538-2636 914-273-7838
Fax: 212-827-0945
Coffee
President: B Brown Lock
Estimated Sales: Under $500,000
Number Employees: 1-4

8508 Lockwood Vineyards
9777 Blue Larkspur Ln # 102
Monterey, CA 93940-6554 831-642-9200
Fax: 831-644-7829 lockwoodoaks@inreach.com
www.lockwoodvineyard.com
Wines
Owner: Paul Toeppen
Estimated Sales: $ 2.5-5 Million
Number Employees: 5-9
Type of Packaging: Private Label

8509 Locus Foods
237 Stanford Parkway
Findlay, OH 45840-1733 419-425-1118
Fax: 419-425-0656
President: Tom Klevay
Estimated Sales: Under $500,000
Number Employees: 1-4

8510 Locustdale Meat Packing
General Delivery
Locustdale, PA 17945-9999 570-875-1270
Processor of sausage, kielbasa, ring bologna and roast chicken and turkey
Owner: Jack Holderman
Estimated Sales: $ 1 - 3 Million
Number Employees: 1-4

8511 Loders Croklaan
24708 W Durkee Rd
Channahon, IL 60410-5249 815-730-5200
Fax: 815-730-5202 800-621-4710
fats.lc@croklaan.com www.croklaan.com
Processor of fats, oils, flavored flakes, emulsifiers, dietary fiber and encapsulates, shortenings
President: Julian Veicht
Marketing Manager: Mary Thomas
Sales: Manuel Laborde
Communications: Ed McIntosh
Estimated Sales: $100+ Million
Number Employees: 100-249
Number of Brands: 25
Parent Co: Loders Croklaan

8512 Lodi Canning Company
P.O.Box 315
Lodi, WI 53555-0315 608-592-4236
Fax: 608-592-4742 bob@lodicanning.com
Manufacturer of canned peas and creamed corn
President: Bob Goeres
Estimated Sales: $2-5 Million
Number Employees: 100-249

Type of Packaging: Private Label
Brands:
DAY BY DAY
IDOL
LODI'S

8513 Lodi Nut Company
1230 S Fairmont Ave
Lodi, CA 95240-5519 209-334-2081
Fax: 209-369-6815 800-234-6887
lodinut@inreach.com www.lodinut.com
Processor of black walnut kernels and nut factory gourmet nuts; also, custom processor and co-packer of English walnut, almond and macadamia kernels
President: Calvin Suess
Executive VP: Virgil Suess
VP Production: Rocky Seuss
Estimated Sales: $7,001,000
Number Employees: 50-99
Type of Packaging: Consumer, Food Service, Private Label, Bulk

8514 Loew Vineyards
14001 Liberty Rd
Mt Airy, MD 21771-9524 301-831-5464
Fax: 301-831-5464 loew@loewvineyard.net
www.loewvineyards.net
Wines
President: William Loew
Estimated Sales: $800,000
Number Employees: 1-4

8515 Loffredo Produce
500 46th St
Rock Island, IL 61201-2129 309-786-0969
Fax: 309-786-0660 800-397-2096
lbeener@loffredo.com www.loffredo.com
Manager: Jerry Moore
Branch Manager: Jerry Moore
Sales: Dave Dalton
Estimated Sales: $ 5-10 Million appx.
Number Employees: 50-99
Parent Co: Lofredo Fresh Produce

8516 Loftshouse Foods
215 N 700 W
A
Ogden, UT 84404-1342 801-317-1480
Fax: 801-392-3015 800-877-7055
investorrelations@ralcorp.com www.ralcorp.com
President: Kevin J Hunt
CEO: David Skarie
Brands:
Bakery Chef
Bremner
Carriage House
Nutcracker Brands
Ralston Foods

8517 Log House Foods
700 Berkshire Ln N
Plymouth, MN 55441-5499 763-546-8395
Fax: 763-546-7339 info@loghousefoods.com
www.loghousefoods.com
Processor of twice-baked cinnamon toast and biscotti, flaked coconut, European-style melting creams for dipping and coating desserts, chocolate chips, candy coatings, etc.
President: Alan Kasdan
VP Operations: Josh Kasdan
Estimated Sales: $17000000
Number Employees: 20-49
Type of Packaging: Consumer, Food Service, Private Label
Brands:
Bella Crema
Jacobsen's Toast
Log House
Log House Candiquik
Plymouth Pantry

8518 (HQ)Loggins Meat Company
1908 E Erwin St
Tyler, TX 75702-6466 903-595-1011
Fax: 903-595-6847 800-527-8610
logginsinc@aol.com www.loggins-meat.com
Manufacturer of pre-portioned beef, pork and chicken items as well as a complete line of ground and breaded products
President: Bobby Loggins
VP Sales/Marketing: George Skinner
Estimated Sales: $ 50 - 100 Million
Number Employees: 250-499
Sq. footage: 75000

Type of Packaging: Consumer, Food Service, Private Label, Bulk
Brands:
Flavor-Best
Grill Sensations
Loggins Legends
Loggins Meat Co.

8519 Lohr Winery
1000 Lenzen Ave
San Jose, CA 95126-2739 408-288-5057
Fax: 408-993-2276 sjwinecenter@jlohr.com
www.jlohr.com
Wines
President: Jerome J Lohr
VP: Jeff Sunquist
Marketing Director: Mark Dirickson
Plant Manager: Dave Mezynski
Estimated Sales: $ 30-50 Million
Number Employees: 50-99
Type of Packaging: Private Label

8520 Lola Savannah
1701 Commerce St # 1a
Houston, TX 77002-2244 713-222-9800
Fax: 713-222-9802 888-663-9166
lola@lolasavannah.com www.lolasavannah.com
Roasted coffee and tea
Owner: Duke Furgh
Vice President: Michael Spencer
Operations Manager: Hank Segelke
Estimated Sales: Less than $500,000
Number Employees: 5-9
Type of Packaging: Consumer, Food Service, Private Label, Bulk

8521 Lolonis Winery
1930 Tice Valley Blvd
Walnut Creek, CA 94595-2203 925-938-8066
Fax: 925-938-8069 sls.mrkting@lolonis.com
www.lolonis.com
Wines
President: Petros Lolonis
Estimated Sales: $600,000
Number Employees: 5-9
Brands:
Ladybug White Old Vines

8522 (HQ)Lombardi Brothers Meat Packers
4720 Tejon Street
Denver, CO 80211-1257 303-458-7441
Fax: 303-458-7444 800-421-4412
Manufacturer of beef, pork, lamb and veal; importer of wild game; wholesaler/distributor of frozen pastas and desserts, soups, health foods, meats and smoked salmon and trout; serving the food service market
President/Owner: Irwin Fishman
VP: George Lombardi
Director Operations: Doug Wax
General Manager: Mike Walters
Estimated Sales: $30 Million
Number Employees: 60
Sq. footage: 30000
Type of Packaging: Food Service
Other Locations:
Lombardi Brothers Meat
Fridley MN
Lombardi Brothers Meat
Le Mars IA

8523 Lombardi's Bakery
177 E Main St
Torrington, CT 06790-5432 860-489-4766
Fax: 860-489-4766
Baked goods
President: Carmen Lombardi
Estimated Sales: Less than $500,000
Number Employees: 1-4
Brands:
Lombardi's

8524 Lombardi's Seafood
7520 Chancellor Dr
Orlando, FL 32809-6919 407-859-1015
Fax: 407-240-2562 800-879-8411
quality@lombardis.com www.lombardis.com
Processor, importer and wholesaler/distributor of fresh and frozen seafood; serving the food service market
Owner: Vince Lomabardi
VP: Vince Lombardi
Supervisor: Mike Lombardi

Estimated Sales:$15400000
Number Employees: 100-249
Type of Packaging: Food Service

8525 Lombardo's Ravioli Kitchen
475 John Downey Dr
New Britain, CT 06051-2909   860-223-7800
    Fax: 860-223-3188
Manufacturer of frozen ravioli, manicotti, lasagna, stuffed shells, tortellini, gnocchi and cavatelli
    Chairman/CEO: Frank Scoleri
    Vice President: Bella Soderi
Estimated Sales:$ 5 - 10 Million
Number Employees: 20-49
Number of Brands: 3
Number of Products: 75
Sq. footage: 25000
Type of Packaging: Consumer, Food Service, Private Label, Bulk
Brands:
    Lombardo's Pasta
    Lombardo's Ravioli Kitchen
    Mr. R'S Ravioli Kitchen

8526 London Farm Dairy
2136 Pine Grove Avenue
Port Huron, MI 48060-3245   810-966-4516
    Fax: 810-984-3139   800-284-5111
Processor of dairy products including ice cream
    CEO: Sharon Spradling III
    District Manager: Larry Harrington
    Sales Manager: Jim O'Brien
Estimated Sales:$ .5 - 1 million
Number Employees: 1-4
Sq. footage: 52000

8527 London Pantry Foods
PO Box 1899
Mt Pleasant, SC 29465-1899   843-761-3890
    Fax: 843-761-3890   888-208-7787
    londonpantry@msn.com
Processor and exporter of pastry puffs, pie dough, poultry pies and meat including pies, processed and English-style banger sausage; also microwavable entrees
    President/CEO: Barrie Jones
Number Employees: 20-49
Number of Brands: 2
Number of Products: 7
Sq. footage: 12000
Type of Packaging: Consumer, Food Service, Private Label, Bulk
Brands:
    L.P. FOODS
    LONDON PANTRY

8528 Lone Elm Sales
N9695 Van Dyne Rd
Van Dyne, WI 54979-9701   920-688-2338
    Fax: 920-688-5233   800-950-8275
    www.loneelm.com
Wholesale distributors
    President: Glen Dedow
    Vice President: Matthew Dedow
Estimated Sales: Below $ 5 Million
Number Employees: 20-49
Type of Packaging: Private Label
Brands:
    Lone Elm

8529 Lone Pine Enterprises
P.O.Box 416
Carlisle, AR 72024-0416   870-552-3217
Processor and exporter rice and soybeans
    Owner/President: Carl Garrich
Estimated Sales:$200,000
Number Employees: 1-4
Type of Packaging: Consumer, Food Service, Bulk

8530 Lone Star Bakery
106 W Liberty St
Round Rock, TX 78664-5122   512-255-3629
    Fax: 512-255-6405   info@roundrockdonuts.com
    www.roundrockdonuts.com
Processor and exporter of pre-baked and frozen buttermilk biscuits, muffins, cinnamon rolls, brownies, sheet cakes, fruit cobblers,pie shells, pecan and fruit pie,and portioned cookie and dough
    Owner: Dale Cohrs
    VP: Bill Scott
    Sales: Rick Perrett
    Operations: Damon Smith
    Plant Manager: Fred Alexander
    Purchasing: Clint Scott

Estimated Sales:$450000
Number Employees: 10-19
Sq. footage: 150000
Type of Packaging: Food Service, Private Label, Bulk
Brands:
    Lone Star

8531 Lone Star Beef Jerky Company
2314 Colgate St
Lubbock, TX 79415-3004   806-762-8833
    Fax: 806-762-8835
Manufacturer of beef jerky and brisket
    President: Don Shobert
Estimated Sales:$200000
Number Employees: 1-4
Type of Packaging: Consumer, Food Service

8532 Lone Star Consolidated Foods
1727 N Beckley Ave
Dallas, TX 75203-1007   214-946-2185
    Fax: 214-946-2286   800-658-5637
    sales@lonestarfunfoods.com
    www.lonestarfunfoods.com
Processor of frozen baked goods including pastries, sweet rolls and yeast raised and cake doughnuts; also, hush puppies
    President: Jim Rader
    CEO: Dolores Burdine
    Sales/Marketing Executive: Dick Melby
    Purchasing Agent: T Griffith
Estimated Sales:$ 20 - 50 Million
Number Employees: 100-249
Sq. footage: 50000000
Parent Co: Burdine Companies
Type of Packaging: Consumer, Food Service

8533 Lone Star Food Products
1727 N Beckley Ave
Dallas, TX 75203-1007   214-946-2185
    Fax: 214-946-2286   www.lonestarfunfoods.com
    President: Burdine Dolores
    Director Marketing: Joe Cabbeneseh
    CEO: Dolores Burdine
    Sales Manager: Dick Melby
Estimated Sales:$ 20 - 50 Million
Number Employees: 100-249
Brands:
    Lone Star

8534 Lone Wolfe Brewing
403 Main Street
Carbondale, CO 81623-2068   970-963-9757
Beer
    Owner: Patricia Cross
    Brewmaster: Donald Wolfe
Estimated Sales: Under $500,000
Number Employees: 1-4

8535 (HQ)Long Beach Seafoods
845 W 16th St
Long Beach, CA 90813-1412   714-995-8901
    Fax: 714-590-0408   honcho2@aol.com
    www.longbeachseafood.com
Processor and exporter of fresh and frozen fish including halibut, salmon, sea bass and swordfish
    President: Tony Delucia
    Vice President: Antonio de Lucia
    Director Manufacturing: Robert Stillwell
    Plant Manager: Tony de Lucia
Estimated Sales:$ 20 - 50 Million
Number Employees: 20-49
Sq. footage: 29000
Type of Packaging: Consumer, Food Service, Private Label, Bulk
Other Locations:
    Long Beach Seafoods
    Del Mar CA
Brands:
    Fan-Sea
    Stars Pride
    Stilwell's

8536 Long Expected Coffee Company
960 Nepperhan Ave
Yonkers, NY 10703-1726   914-969-7933
    Fax: 914-969-8248
Coffee
    Manager: Dean Peialteos
Estimated Sales: Below $ 5 Million
Number Employees: 20-49

8537 Long Food Industries
709 Rock Beauty Road
Fripp Island, SC 29920-7344   843-838-3205
    Fax: 843-838-3918   longfood@isle.net
    www.longfoodindustries.com
Shrimp, cooked/diced chicken, clam (meat and broth), beef (diced/cooked), lobster, fish and pork
    President: Leon Long
Estimated Sales:$ 10-20 Million
Number Employees: 1
Type of Packaging: Food Service

8538 Long Grove ConfectioneryCompany
333 Lexington Dr
Buffalo Grove, IL 60089-6542   847-459-3100
    Fax: 847-459-4871   800-373-3102
    sales@longgrove.com   www.longgrove.com
Processor of confectionery items including chocolates, molded chocolate, apples, novelties, custom molded logos and holiday boxes.
    President: John Mangel Ii II
    Vice President: W David Mangel
    Marketing/Sales: Nick Quartana
    Plant Manager: Barbara Rakestraw
Estimated Sales:$9300000
Number Employees: 50-99
Sq. footage: 25000
Type of Packaging: Consumer, Food Service, Private Label, Bulk
Brands:
    Chicago Mints
    Long Grove Confections
    Myrties
    Myrtles
    Ultimate Apple

8539 Long Kow Foods USA Corporation
369 Can Ness Way
Suite 707
Torrance, CA 90501   310-781-9737
    Fax: 310-212-6768   877-566-4569
    info@crystalnoodle.com   www.crystalnoodle.com
instant noodle soup
    President/CEO: Masaki Mizuhashi

8540 Long Trail Brewing Company
PO Box 168
Bridgewater Corners, VT 05035-0168   802-672-5011
    Fax: 802-672-5012   itales@longtrail.com
    www.longtrail.com
Brewers
    President: Andy Pherson
    Director Manufacturing: Thomas O'Brien
    Purchasing Manager: Mathew Quinian
Estimated Sales:$ 10-20 Million
Number Employees: 20-49
Brands:
    Double Bag
    Harvest
    Hibernator
    India Pale Ale
    Long Trail Ale

8541 Long Vineyards
1535 Sage Canyon Rd
St Helena, CA 94574-9628   707-963-2496
    Fax: 707-963-5016   bob@longvineyards.com
    www.longvineyards.com
Wines
    Co-Owner/President: Robert Long
    Co-Owner: Zelma Long
    Marketing/PR Director: Pat Perini Long
    Winemaking Operations Director: Sandi Belcher
Estimated Sales:$500,000-$1 Million
Number Employees: 1-4
Brands:
    Johannisberg Riesling
    Sangiovese

8542 Longacres Modern Dairy
P.O.Box 69
Barto, PA 19504-0069   610-845-7551
    Fax: 610-845-2041   www.longacresicecream.com
Dairy
    President: Daniel T Longacre Jr
    VP: Newton T Longacre
    Treasurer: Kathryn Longacre
    CFO: Timoty T Longacre
    Plant Engineer: Daniel Longacre
Estimated Sales: Below $ 5 Million
Number Employees: 20-49

Brands:
Longacre

8543 Longbottom Coffee & Tea
4893 NW 235th Ave
Hillsboro, OR 97124-5801   503-648-1271
Fax: 503-681-0944 800-288-1271
info@longbottomcoffee.com
www.longbottomcoffee.com
Processor and importer of specialty coffees including certified organics, espresso, flavored, regionals and blends; wholesaler/distributor of espresso machines and fine teas
President: Michael Baccellieri
Marketing Director: Kerri Harding
Sales Director: Gabrielle Paeson
Operations Manager: Tom Randon
Estimated Sales:$8000000
Number Employees: 50-99
Sq. footage: 8000
Type of Packaging: Consumer, Food Service, Private Label, Bulk

8544 Longford-Hamilton Company
17885 SW Tualatin Valley Hwy
Beaverton, OR 97006-4448   503-642-5661
Fax: 503-649-1321 oldmill566@aol.com
oldmillrum.com
Imported specialty foods and up-scale confectionery products
President: Malarkey Wall
Sales Director: Jan Rudolph
*Estimated Sales:*Below $ 5 Million
Number Employees: 1-4
Number of Brands: 1
Number of Products: 20
Type of Packaging: Consumer
Brands:
Old Mill Brand

8545 Longleaf Plantation
P.O.Box 511
Lumberton, MS 39455-0511   601-794-6001
Fax: 601-794-5052 800-421-7370
longleaf@c-gate.net www.longleafplantation.net
Manufacturers of pecans
President: Warren Hood Jr
Estimated Sales:$ 5-10 Million
Number Employees: 20-49
Brands:
Longleaf Plantation

8546 Longmeadow
20 Williams St
Longmeadow, MA 01106-1950   413-565-4153
Fax: 413-565-4112 http://www.longmeadow.org
Specialty sauces
Manager: Mark Denver
General Manager: Suzie Barton
Estimated Sales:$ 2.5-5 Million
Number Employees: 5-9

8547 Longmeadow Foods
PO Box 1405
Gray, ME 04039-1405   207-529-5879
Fax: 207-529-5813 800-255-8401
jlmeadow@midcoast.com www.fancyfare.com
Gourmet foods
Estimated Sales:$ 2.5-5 Million
Number Employees: 5-9
Brands:
Blackburn's
Death By Chocolate
Downeast Pasta
Kandia
Maine Marinades
Maine Mountain Morni
Nomad Apiaries
Oyster Creek Mushroo
Pemberton's Dessert
Porcupine Island
Raye
Spruce Mountain Blub
Spruce Mountain Blub

8548 Longmont Foods
1935 N Main St
Longmont, CO 80501-2362   303-776-4803
Fax: 303-776-4965 www.longmontarts.com
Processor of fresh and frozen turkey and turkey frankfurters
Owner: Brad Long
Operations Manager: Miguel Ramirez

Estimated Sales:$100+ Million
Number Employees: 1,000-4,999
Parent Co: ConAgra Foods
Type of Packaging: Consumer, Food Service, Private Label

8549 Longo Coffee & Tea
201 Bleecker St
New York, NY 10012-1446   212-477-6783
Fax: 212-979-2303 www.portorico.com
Coffee and tea
President: Peter Longo
Estimated Sales:$ 5-10 Million
Number Employees: 20-49

8550 Longo's Bakery
138 W 21st St
Hazleton, PA 18201-1909   570-454-5825
Fax: 570-454-6246
Breads, rolls, pizza shells
Estimated Sales:$500,000-$1 Million
Number Employees: 10-19

8551 Longview Meat & Merchandise
PO Box 173
Longview, AB T0L 1H0
Canada   403-558-3706
Fax: 403-558-3708 lbj@longviewjerky.com
www.longviewjerky.com
Processor of beef jerky
General Manager: Len Latoski
Plant Manager: Jacky Lau
Type of Packaging: Consumer

8552 Lonz Winery
1965 Fox Road Middle Bass Is
Middle Bass, OH 43446   419-285-5411
Wines
*Estimated Sales:*Under $500,000
Number Employees: 20-49

8553 Look Lobster
P.O.Box 504
Jonesport, ME 04649-0504   207-497-2353
Fax: 207-497-5559
Lobster
President: Bert Sid Look Iii
Vice President: Priscilla Look
Estimated Sales:$ .5 - 1 million
Number Employees: 1-4

8554 (HQ)Look's Gourmet Food Company
1112 Cutler Rd
Whiting, ME 04691-3436   207-259-3341
Fax: 207-259-3343 800-962-6258
office@amlook.com
www.looksgourmetfood.com
Manufacturer of canned clams, crabs, crab meat and lobster, lobster and clam bisque, seafood spreads/dips and clam chowder
President: Michael Cote
President: Jeffrey Look
Estimated Sales:$2.5-5 Million
Number Employees: 10-19
Type of Packaging: Consumer, Food Service, Private Label
Brands:
Atlantic
Bar Harbor
CAP'N JOHN

8555 Lopez Foods
9500 N W Fourth Street
Oklahoma City, OK 73127   405-789-7500
Fax: 405-499-0114
consumerinfo@lopezfoods.com
www.lopezfoods.com
President: Etuardo Sanchez
CFO: Jim English
Plant Manager: Richard Lane
Senior VP: Frank McKee
CFO: Jim English
Quality Control: Keven Nanke
Marketing Director: David Kovirik
Estimated Sales:$ 100-500 Million
Number Employees: 500-999
Brands:
Carneco Foods
Lopez Foods

8556 LorAnn Oils Inc
4518 Aurelius Rd
Lansing, MI 48909   517-822-0215
Fax: 571-822-0807 888-456-7266
customercare@lorannoils.com
www.lorannoils.com
candy oils and flavorings, vanilla extract, food colorings, specialty ingredients, supplies
President/Owner: John Grettenberger Sr
VP: Carl Thalen
Estimated Sales:$4.4 Million
Number Employees: 17

8557 Lora Brody Products
302 Highland Avenue
West Newton, MA 02465-2514   617-928-1005
Fax: 617-558-5383 blanche007@aol.com
www.lorabrody.com
Bread dough enhancer
Brands:
Dough Relaxer
Lora Brody Bread Dou
Sourdough Bread Enha

8558 Lorann Oils
P.O.Box 22009
Lansing, MI 48909-2009   517-882-0215
Fax: 517-882-0507 800-248-1302
customercare@lorannoils.com
www.lorannoils.com
Processor of coffee flavors, cocoa butter, flavoring oils, vanilla extracts, food colorings, fountain syrups, candy making molds and supplies, industrial ingredients, etc
Manager: John Grettenberger
CEO: Carl Thelen
*Estimated Sales:*Below $5 Million
Number Employees: 20-49
Sq. footage: 15000
Type of Packaging: Consumer, Food Service, Bulk
Brands:
Lorann Gourmet
Lorann International

8559 Lords Sausage & CountryHam
P.O.Box 1000
Dexter, GA 31019-1000   478-875-3101
Fax: 478-875-3039 800-342-6002
Manufacturer of fresh and smoked pork sausage and cured country ham
President: Wayne Lord
VP: Britt Lord
Estimated Sales:$10-20 Million
Number Employees: 20-49
Sq. footage: 20000
Type of Packaging: Consumer, Food Service, Private Label, Bulk
Brands:
LORD'S

8560 Loretta's Authentic Pralines
2101 N Rampart St
New Orleans, LA 70116-1627   504-944-7068
Fax: 504-945-5912 loretta.pralines@att.net
www.lorettapralines.com
Pralines and confections
Owner: Loretta Harrison
Estimated Sales:$ 1-2.5 Million
Number Employees: 10-19

8561 Loriva Culinary Oils
601 22nd St
San Francisco, CA 94107-3118   415-401-0080
Fax: 415-401-0087 866-972-6679
info@nspiredfoods.com www.worldpantry.com
Processor and exporter of specialty oils including roasted, infused and toasted sesame, peanut, safflower, walnut, garlic, olive, avocado, hazelnut, macadamia, etc.; also, kosher varieties available
President: Patrick Lee
CEO: David Miller
Consumer Relations: Liz Scatena
Number Employees: 10-19
Parent Co: NSpired Natural Foods
Type of Packaging: Consumer, Food Service, Private Label, Bulk
Brands:
Loriva
Loriva Jazz Roasted Oils
Loriva Supreme Flavored Oils
Loriva Supreme Oils

8562 Los Altos Food Products
15130 Nelson Ave
City of Industry, CA 91744-4334   626-330-6555
Fax: 626-330-6755   info@losaltos.com
www.losaltosfoods.com
Processor and exporter of Mexican and Swiss cheese
President: Raul Andrade
CFO: Alin Andrag
Director Sales/Marketing: Bill Finicle
Estimated Sales: $ 50-100 Million
Number Employees: 100-249
Type of Packaging: Consumer, Food Service

8563 Los Amigos Tortilla Manufacturing
251 Armour Dr NE
Atlanta, GA 30324-3979   404-876-8153
Fax: 404-876-8102   800-969-8226
ruben@losamigos.com   www.losamigos.com
Corn and flour tortillas and chips
President: Zoila Rodriguez
General Manager: Ruben Rodriguez
Plant Supervisor: Carlos Perez
Estimated Sales: Below $ 5 Million
Number Employees: 50-99

8564 (HQ)Los Angeles Nut House Brands
1125 W 6th St # 300
Los Angeles, CA 90017-1894   213-481-0134
Fax: 213-481-0084
Nuts
Executive Director: Azuka Uzoh
Sales Director: Terry McClean
Purchasing Manager: Jon Anderson
Estimated Sales: $ .5 - 1 million
Number Employees: 5-9
Type of Packaging: Private Label

8565 Los Angeles Smoking & Curing Company
1100 West Ewing Street
Seattle, WA 98119   213-628-1246
Fax: 213-614-8857
ron.christianson@oceanbeauty.com
http://www.oceanbeauty.com
Herring, kippers, lox, roe, cod, mackerel, salmon,
shad, caviar and whitefish
President: Howard Klein
VP Sales/Marketing: Richard Schaeffer
Number Employees: 100-249
Parent Co: Ocean Beauty
Type of Packaging: Consumer, Food Service
Brands:
Kodikook
Lascco

8566 Los Arcos Tortillas
2912 N Commerce St
North Las Vegas, NV 89030-3945   702-399-3300
Fax: 702-399-2507 www.tortillasinc.com
Tortillas
Owner: Gus Gutierrez
Partner: Jose Gutierrez
Owner: Salvo Gutierrez
Estimated Sales: $ 2.5-5 Million
Number Employees: 20-49

8567 Los Chileros de Nuevo Mexico
PO Box 6215
Santa Fe, NM 87502   505-768-1100
Fax: 505-242-7513 www.loschileros.com
chiles, corn products, salsa, rubs and mixes
Estimated Sales: $1 Million
Number Employees: 12

8568 Los Gatos Brewing Company
130 N Santa Cruz Ave
Los Gatos, CA 95030-5911   408-395-9929
Fax: 408-395-2769   dine@lgbrewingco.com
www.lgbrewingco.com
Restaurant and brewing center
Owner: Andy Pavicich Jr
Director Manufacturing: Jeff Alexander
General Manager: Randall Bertho
Estimated Sales: $ 2.5-5 Million
Number Employees: 100-249
Brands:
Hefeweizen
Los Gatos Lager
Nut Brown Ale

8569 Los Gatos Tomato Products
P.O.Box 429
Huron, CA 93234-0429   559-945-2700
Fax: 559-945-2661   cwoolf@losgatostomato.com
www.losgatostomato.com
Processor of tomato concentrates
Prsident: Stuart Woolf
Quality Control: Brandon Clement
Sales: David Bodine
Plant Manager: Ray Medeiros
Estimated Sales: $3400000
Number Employees: 20-49
Sq. footage: 50000
Type of Packaging: Bulk

8570 Los Olivos Vintners
P.O.Box 636
Los Olivos, CA 93441-0636   805-688-9665
Fax: 805-686-1690   800-824-8584
Wines
President: Arthur White
Estimated Sales: $ 1-2.5 Million
Number Employees: 5-9
Type of Packaging: Private Label
Brands:
Los Olivos Vintners

8571 Los Pericos Food Products
2301 Valley St
Los Angeles, CA 90057-2113   323-269-5816
Fax: 323-269-1983   sales@lospericosfood.com
www.lospericosfood.com
Mexican tostada shells
Partner: Marcelino Ortega
Estimated Sales: $ 5-10 Million
Number Employees: 20-49
Brands:
Tostada

8572 Lost Coast Brewery
617 4th St
Eureka, CA 95501-1013   707-445-4480
Fax: 707-445-4483   brewbarb@northcoast.com
www.lostcoast.com
Beer
President: Barbara Groom
Sales Director: Briar Bush
Plant Manager: Bill Estles
Estimated Sales: $ 20-50 Million
Number Employees: 50-99
Type of Packaging: Private Label
Brands:
8-Ball Stout
Alleycat Amber
Downtown Brown Ale
Lost Coast Ale
Raspberry Brown Ale
Winter Brown Ale

8573 Lost Hills Winery
3125 E Orange Street
Acampo, CA 95220   209-369-2746
Fax: 209-369-2746
Wines
President: Douglas Charboneau

8574 Lost Mountain Winery
3174 Lost Mountain Rd
Sequim, WA 98382-7918   360-683-5229
Fax: 360-683-7572   888-683-5229
wine@lostmountain.com   www.lostmountain.com
Wine
Co-Owner/Winemaker: Steve Conca
Co-Owner/Winemaker: Sue Conca
Estimated Sales: Less than $500,000
Number Employees: 1-4
Brands:
Lost Mountain Winery

8575 Lost Trail Root Beer Com
PO Box 670
Louisburg, KS 66053-0670   913-837-5202
Fax: 913-837-5762   800-748-7765
lcmill@micoks.net   www.louisburgcidermill.com
Processor, wholesaler/distributor and exporter of ap-
ple cider and root beer; also, apple butter
President: Tom Schierman
Estimated Sales: $500,000-$1 Million
Number Employees: 5-9
Sq. footage: 10000
Type of Packaging: Consumer, Private Label
Brands:
LOST TRAIL
LOUISBURG

8576 Losurdo Creamery
34 Union St
Heuvelton, NY 13654-2200   315-344-2444
Fax: 315-344-2362   www.losurdofoods.com
Processor of Italian cheeses including washed curd,
provolone, mozzarella and ricotta; importer of pec-
orino romano cheese
President: Michael Losurdo, Sr.
VP Sales: Mark Losurdo
Plant Manager: William Muir
Number Employees: 50-99
Sq. footage: 150000
Parent Co: Losurdo Foods
Type of Packaging: Consumer, Food Service, Pri-
vate Label
Brands:
Angustus
Bel-Capri

8577 (HQ)Losurdo Creamery
20 Owens Rd
Hackensack, NJ 07601-3297   201-343-6680
Fax: 201-343-8078   800-245-6787
www.losurdofoods.com
Processor of kosher ricotta cheese
President: Michael Losurdo Sr
Marketing Head: Dincenva Tulibutz
VP: Mark Losurdo
Estimated Sales: $ 20 - 50 Million
Number Employees: 100-249
Type of Packaging: Consumer, Food Service
Other Locations:
Losurdo Creamery
Heuvelton NY
Brands:
Losurdo

8578 Losurdo Foods
20 Owens Rd
Hackensack, NJ 07601-3297   201-343-6680
888-567-8736
marc@losurdofoods.com
www.losurdofoods.com
Providing transportation for cheeses
President: Michael Losurdo Sr
VP Marketing: Marc Losurdo
Number Employees: 10-19

8579 Lotsa Pasta
1762 Garnet Ave
San Diego, CA 92109-3350   858-581-6777
Fax: 858-581-6783   chef@yumm.com
www.lotsapasta.com
Pasta
President: Carol Blomstrom
Estimated Sales: Below $ 5 Million
Number Employees: 20-49
Brands:
Lotsa Pasta

8580 Lotte USA
5243 Wayne Rd
Battle Creek, MI 49037-7323   269-963-6664
Fax: 269-963-6695   lotteusa-inc@yahoo.com
www.lotteusainc.com
Processor of cream-filled cookies, throat drops and
chewing gum
President: T Kaneko
Marketing Manager: Julie Fanning
Sales Manager: Frank Deleo
Operations Manager: Dick Thomason
Purchasing Manager: Ron Parsons
Estimated Sales: $15000000
Number Employees: 20-49
Type of Packaging: Consumer, Food Service
Brands:
FULL BLAST GUM
KOALA NO MARCH COOKIE

8581 Lotus Bakery
3336 Industrial Dr
Santa Rosa, CA 95403-2011   415-238-0791
Fax: 415-526-6377   800-875-6887
sales@lotusbakery.com   www.lotusbakery.com
Bread, cookies and energy bars
Owner: Mark Menning
Estimated Sales: $400,000
Number Employees: 10-19
Type of Packaging: Private Label
Brands:
Spirulina Bee Bar
Spirulina Trail Bar

8582 Lotus Brands

P.O.Box 1008
Silver Lake, WI 53170-1008   262-889-8561
Fax: 262-889-8591   800-824-6396
lotusbrands@lotuspress.com
www.lotusbrands.com
Sells natural products, including teas and herbal supplements
President: Santosh Krinsky
Estimated Sales: $ 1-2.5 Million
Number Employees: 50-99
Number of Brands: 16
Number of Products: 1000
Sq. footage: 38000
Type of Packaging: Consumer, Private Label, Bulk
Brands:
    Ancient Secrets
    Blue Pearl Incense
    Dragon Eggs
    Eco-DenT
    Fuchs Tooth Brushes
    Life Tree Products
    Light Mountain
    Nature's Alchemy
    Neem Aura
    Nirvana
    Paul Penders
    Rainforest Remedies
    Sai Baba Nag Champa
    Smile Brite
    Tifert Aromatherapy
    Yakshi Fragrances

8583 Lotus Foods

921 Richmond St
El Cerrito, CA 94530-2918   510-525-3137
Fax: 510-525-4226   info@lotusfoods.com
www.lotusfoods.com
Rice products
    President/Partner: Kenneth Lee
    CEO: Caryl Levine
    Partner/VP: Caryl Levine
    Marketing Director: Caryl Levine
Estimated Sales: $1 Million
Number Employees: 1-4
Type of Packaging: Consumer, Food Service, Bulk
Brands:
    A World of Rice
    Bhutanese Red Rice
    Cal Riso
    Kaipen
    Kalijira
    Lowell Farms Organic

8584 Lotus Manufacturing Company

529 San Pedro Avenue
San Antonio, TX 78212-5057   210-223-1421
    President: Germino Trevino
Estimated Sales: $ 1-2.5 Million appx.
Number Employees: 1

8585 Lou Ana Foods

P.O.Box 591
Opelousas, LA 70571-0591   337-948-6561
Fax: 337-942-6239   rbiggs@venturafoods.com
www.louana.com
Edible oils
    CFO: Richard Read
    General Manager: William Minor
    CEO: William Minor
Estimated Sales: $ 100-500 Million
Number Employees: 100-249

8586 Lou Pizzo Produce

9660 NW 67th Pl
Parkland, FL 33076-2309   954-941-8830
Fax: 954-941-8870
Produce
    President: Louis Pizzo
    VP: Angelina Pizzo
Estimated Sales: Below $ 5 Million
Number Employees: 1-4
Brands:
    Lou Pizzo

8587 Lou-Retta's Custom Chocolates

3764 Harlem Road
Buffalo, NY 14215-1908   716-833-7111
Fax: 716-689-8113   chocolate@louretta.com
www.lourettas.com
Chocolate laced popcorn, chocolate pretzel nuggets dusted with gold dust and flavored with fresh ground coffee
    President: Loretta Kaminsky
    VP Marketing: Ellen Bradbury
Estimated Sales: Below $ 5 Million
Number Employees: 15
Type of Packaging: Private Label
Brands:
    Buffalo Gold
    Espresso Gold

8588 Lou-Rod Candy

PO Box 197
Lewiston, ME 04243-0197   207-784-5822
Processor of coconut and chocolate covered candies
    President: James Holmes
Number Employees: 10
Sq. footage: 15000000
Type of Packaging: Private Label, Bulk
Brands:
    Down East
    Seavey's
    Sugar Loaf

8589 Lougheed Fisheries

539 2nd Avenue E
Owen Sound, ON N4K 2G5
Canada   519-376-1586
Fax: 519-376-1589
Processor of fresh and frozen fish and seafood
    President: Greg Lougheed
Number Employees: 10-19
Type of Packaging: Bulk

8590 Louis Bakeries

P.O.Box 426
La Porte, IN 46352-0426   219-362-4561
Fax: 219-325-0030
Bread and buns
    Manager: John West
    VP Sales: Dick Barker
Estimated Sales: $ 100-500 Million
Number Employees: 100-249

8591 Louis Dreyfus Citrus

355 9th St
Winter Garden, FL 34787-3651   407-656-1000
Fax: 407-656-1229
Processor of frozen fruit juice concentrates, citrus oils, pulp and purees
    General Manager: Rick Tomlin
    Sales Manager (Bulk): Kenneth Kelly
    District Sales Manager: Robert Toadvine
Estimated Sales: $ 50 - 100 Million
Number Employees: 250-499
Type of Packaging: Consumer, Food Service, Private Label, Bulk
Brands:
    Sunshine State
    Whole Sun
    Winter Gold

8592 Louis Dreyfus Corporation

20 Westport Rd
Wilton, CT 06897-4549   203-761-2000
Fax: 203-761-2275   drh-paris@louisdreyfus.fr
www.louisdreyfus.com
Processor and exporter of long grain milled and brewers' rice, rice bran, beans, wheat, soybeans, etc
    VP Board of Directors: Pierre Louis-dreyfus
    VP Board of Directors: Jean Louis-Dreyus
    CFO: Len Federico
    CEO: William C Reed
    VP Board of Directors: Bernard Baldensperger
    VP Board of Directors: Claude Boquin
    Sr. Executive: Lorraine Bouvier
    Sr. Executive: Patrice De Camaret
    Sr. Executive: Aurelio A.P.Cidade
    Sr. Executive: Peter Griffin
    Sr. Executive: Philippe Louis-Dreyfus
    Sr. Executive: Robert Louis-Dreyfus
Number Employees: 500-999
Parent Co: Louis Dreyfus Corporation
Type of Packaging: Food Service, Private Label, Bulk
Brands:
    Delta Rose
    Missouri's Finest
    Showboat

8593 Louis Dreyfus Corporation - Coffee Division

20 Westport Rd
Wilton, CT 06897-4549   203-761-2000
Fax: 203-761-2275   ldwltsugar@louisdreyfus.com
www.louisdreyfus.com
Coffee
    General Manager: Bernard Baldensperger
    President: Gerard Louis Dreyfus
    CEO: William C Reed
    Sr VP Finance: Leopold Dreyfus
Number Employees: 500-999

8594 Louis J. Rheb Candy Company

3352 Wilkens Ave
Baltimore, MD 21229-4678   410-644-4321
Fax: 410-646-0327   800-514-8293
www.rhebscandy.com
Manufacturer of chocolate candy
    President: Edwin Harger
Estimated Sales: $5-10 Million
Number Employees: 20-49
Type of Packaging: Consumer

8595 Louis Kemp Seafood Company

P.O.Box 188
Motley, MN 56466-0188   218-352-6600
Fax: 218-352-6609   800-325-4732
www.tridentseafoods.com
Processor and exporter of frozen and refrigerated surimi and seafood products
    Quality Control: Suzie Burtels
    VP: Mike Robinson
    Production Manager: Jim Johnson
    Purchasing Manager: Bob Storry
Number Employees: 250-499
Sq. footage: 110000
Parent Co: Bumble Bee Seafoods
Type of Packaging: Food Service, Private Label
Brands:
    Captain Jac
    Louis Kemp
    Pacific Mate
    Seafest

8596 Louis Kemp Seafood Company

2001 Butterfield Road
Downers Grove, IL 60515-1050   218-624-3636
Fax: 218-624-4791
    President: Louis Kemp
    COO: Greg Moore
    Manager: Jim Olson
Estimated Sales: $ 20-50 Million
Number Employees: 100-249

8597 Louis M. Martini

P.O.Box 112
St Helena, CA 94574-0112   707-963-2736
Fax: 707-963-8750   800-321-9463
www.louismartini.com
Wines
    President: Carolyn Martini
    Sales Director: Bob Matheny
    VP Operations/Winemaker: Michael Martini
    Plant Manager: Michael Mullen
Estimated Sales: $100 million +
Number Employees: 100-249

8598 Louis Maull Company

219 N Market St
St Louis, MO 63102-1523   314-241-8410
Fax: 314-241-9840   info@maull.com
www.maull.com
Processor of sauces including barbeque, worcestershire and steak
    President: Louis T Maull Iv
Estimated Sales: $ 5-10 Million
Number Employees: 10-19
Brands:
    Maull's Barbecue Sauce

8599 Louis Severino Pasta

110 Haddon Ave
Westmont, NJ 08108   856-854-7666
Fax: 856-854-6098
Pasta
    President: Peter Severino
Estimated Sales: Below $ 5 Million
Number Employees: 20-49

8600 Louis Sherry

3537 W North Avenue
Chicago, IL 60647-4808   773-486-8243
Fax: 773-486-1620

Ice cream and frozen desserts
Director Operations: Israel Gonzalez

8601 Louis Swiss Pastry
400 Aabc
Aspen, CO 81611-2545   970-925-8592
        Fax: 970-925-1269 karse@packlab.com
Bread and bakery products
    Owner: Felix Tornare
    Owner: Karse Simon
Estimated Sales: $10-20 Million
Number Employees: 10-19

8602 Louis Trauth Dairy
P.O.Box 721770
Newport, KY 41072-1770   859-431-7553
        Fax: 859-431-0349 800-544-6455
info@trauthdairy.com www.trauthdairy.com
Processor of orange juice, spring and distilled water
and cultured dairy products including cottage
cheese, ice cream and nonfat and low-fat sour cream
    Senior VP: Gary Sparks
    Sales Manager Milk Division: Dan Smith
    Operations VP: Steve Trauth
Estimated Sales: $100000000
Number Employees: 250-499
Sq. footage: 100000
Parent Co: Suiza Foods
Type of Packaging: Consumer, Food Service, Private Label, Bulk
Brands:
    Jersey Farms
    Louis Trauth

8603 Louisa Food Products
1918 Switzer Ave
St Louis, MO 63136-3779   314-868-3000
        Fax: 314-868-3014
Processor of frozen Italian foods including ravioli,
cannelloni, tortellini and sauces
    President: John Baldetti
Estimated Sales: $ 50 - 100 Million
Number Employees: 50-99
Type of Packaging: Consumer, Food Service, Private Label, Bulk
Brands:
    Louisa Pastas

8604 Louisburg Cider Mill
14730 Highway K68
Louisburg, KS 66053-8223   913-837-2304
        Fax: 913-837-5762 800-748-7765
        info@louisburgcidermill.com
        www.louisburgcidermill.com
Cider, beverages and a variety of gift items
    President: Shelly Schierman
    Vice President: Tom Schierman
Estimated Sales: $1-2.5 Million
Number Employees: 10-19
Type of Packaging: Private Label
Brands:
    Lost Trail Root Beer
    Louisburg Cider
    Louisburg Farms

8605 Louise Metafora Company
10 Blake Street
Medford, MA 02155-4922   781-871-6918
        Fax: 781-871-3270
    President: John Greeley
Estimated Sales: $ 1-2.5 Million
Number Employees: 1
Brands:
    Espresso Gold

8606 Louise's
1700 Isaac Shelby Drive
Shelbyville, KY 40065-9172   502-633-9700
        Fax: 502-633-3543
Fat free potato chips and crisps
    Quality Assurance Manager: John Lindle
Estimated Sales: $ 5-9.9 Million
Number Employees: 40

8607 Louisiana Coca-Cola Bottling Company
5601 Citrus Blvd
Harahan, LA 70123-5508   504-818-7000
        Fax: 504-826-7212 800-362-6996
Processor of soft drinks
    Manager: Jay Ard
Number Employees: 500-999
Parent Co: Coca-Cola Enterprises
Type of Packaging: Consumer, Food Service, Bulk

8608 Louisiana Crawfish Company
140 Russell Cemetery Road
Natchitoches, LA 71457-2748   318-379-0539
        Fax: 318-379-2816

8609 Louisiana Fish Fry Products
5267 Plank Rd
Baton Rouge, LA 70805-2730   225-356-2905
        Fax: 225-356-8867 800-356-2905
        info@louisianafishfry.com
        www.louisianafishfry.com
Cajun food mixes, breadings, seasonings and sauces
    President: Cliff Pizzolato
    Owner: Anthony Pizzolato
Estimated Sales: $ 10-20 Million
Number Employees: 50-99
Brands:
    Louisiana Fish Fry
    Tony's Seafood

8610 Louisiana Fresh Express
18120 Old Covington Highway
Suite B
Hammond, LA 70403-0652   985-542-1256
        Fax: 985-898-5993
    President: Mark Malkemus

8611 Louisiana Gourmet Enterprises
222 S Hollywood Road
Houma, LA 70360-2717   800-328-5586
        Fax: 985-783-6079 mampapaul@aol.com
Processor of Cajun/Creole sauces, gumbo, piquante,
seasonings and mixes including rice, dinner, cake
and frosting
    Operations Manager: James Bourgeois
    Production Manager: Dave Gilmer
Number Employees: 5-9
Type of Packaging: Consumer, Private Label, Bulk
Brands:
    Lemon Velvet
    Mam Papaul's
    Mama Papaul's
    Mardi Gras King
    Red Velvet

8612 Louisiana Oyster Processors
10557 Cherry Hill Ave
Baton Rouge, LA 70816-4115   225-291-6923
        Fax: 626-571-0613
Processor of fresh oysters
    Owner: Chester Williams
Estimated Sales: $ 5-10 Million
Number Employees: 10-19
Type of Packaging: Consumer, Food Service

8613 Louisiana Packing Company
501 Louisiana St
Westwego, LA 70094-4141   504-436-2682
        Fax: 504-436-1585 800-666-1293
        lapack@iamerica.net www.lapack.com
Processor, importer and exporter of shrimp including
breaded, cooked and IQF
    President: David Lai
    CEO: John Mao
    Plant Manager: David Lai
Estimated Sales: $500,000-$1 Million
Number Employees: 1-4
Sq. footage: 33000
Type of Packaging: Consumer, Food Service, Private Label, Bulk
Brands:
    Bayou Segnette
    Fresh Sea Taste
    Sea Ray
    White Premium

8614 Louisiana Premium Seafoods
P.O.Box 68
Palmetto, LA 71358-0068   337-623-4232
        Fax: 337-623-5852 800-222-4017
        info@louisianaseafood.com
        www.louisianaseafood.com
Frozen alligator meat, blue crabmeat, crawfish meat,
cooked crawfish
    President/CEO: Gregory Benhard
    CFO: Jorge Benhard
    Executive Marketing Assistant: Kathy Johnson
Estimated Sales: $ 50-100 Million
Number Employees: 50-99
Brands:
    Louisiana Premium Seafoods

8615 Louisiana Pride Seafood
2021 Lakeshore Drive Suite 300
New Orleans, LA 70122   504-283-9893
        Fax: 504-283-9468
        http://www.louisianaseafood.com
Seafood
    President: Anthony Lama

8616 Louisiana Rice Company
PO Box 705
Welsh, LA 70591-0705   337- 73-4 44
        Fax: 337- 73-4 41
Rice
    Co-Owner: Paul Guillory
    Co-Owner: Anne Guillory

8617 Louisiana Royal Seafood
1031 Frank Wyatt Road
Henderson, LA 70517-7714   318-228-2988
        Fax: 337-228-2472
Fresh or frozen packaged fish (seafoods)
    President: Alvin Folse
Estimated Sales: $ 10-20 Million
Number Employees: 50-99

8618 Louisiana Royal Seafoods
1031 Frank Wyatt Road
Breaux Bridge, LA 70517-7714   318-228-7506
        Fax: 318-228-2472
Seafood
    President: Alvin Folse

8619 Louisiana Seafood Exchange
2021 Lakeshore Drive Suite 300
New Orleans, LA 70122   504-283-9893
        Fax: 504-283-9468
        http://www.louisianaseafood.com
Processor and exporter of seafood including bass,
garfish, catfish, trout, amberjack, crab, shark and
snapper
    President: Thomas Lusco
    Director Sales: Robert Walker
Estimated Sales: $ 20-50 Million
Number Employees: 50-99
Type of Packaging: Consumer, Food Service, Private Label, Bulk

8620 Louisiana Shrimp & Packing Company
2021 Lakeshore Drive Suite 300
New Orleans, LA 70122   504-283-9893
        Fax: 504-283-9468
        http://www.louisianaseafood.com
Shrimp
    President: Gerard Thomassie

8621 Louisiana Sugar Cane Cooperative
6092 Resweber Hwy
St Martinville, LA 70582-6804   337-394-3255
        Fax: 337-394-3787 info@LASUCA.com
        www.lasuca.com
Processor of sugar
    President: Mike Melancon
Estimated Sales: $ 20 - 50 Million
Number Employees: 50-99
Type of Packaging: Consumer

8622 Louisiana Sugar Cane Cooperation
6092 Resweber Hwy
St Martinville, LA 70582-6804   337-394-3255
        Fax: 337-394-3787 info@lasuca.com
        www.lasuca.com
Processor of sugar and blackstrap molasses
    President: Micheal Melancon
Estimated Sales: $ 20 - 50 Million
Number Employees: 50-99
Type of Packaging: Consumer

8623 (HQ)Lounsbury Foods
11 Wiltshire Avenue
Toronto, ON M6N 2V7
Canada   416-656-6330
        lounsbury@lounsbury.ca
Processor of vinegar, beet relish, mustard and sauces
including regular and extra hot horseradish, seafood
cocktail, mint, tartar, hot and barbecue
    General Manager: Gil Marks
    VP: Tim Higgins
    VP: David Higgins
Type of Packaging: Consumer, Food Service, Private Label, Bulk

Brands:
Cedarvale

8624 Lov-It Creamery
P.O.Box 19010
Green Bay, WI 54307-9010   920-437-7601
          Fax: 920-437-1617 800-344-0333
     whwangerin@yahoo.com   www.schreiber.com
Processor and exporter of butter and butter and mar-
garine blends; also, cream cheese
     President: Larry Ferguson
     Vice President: William Wangerin, Jr.
     VP Sales: Mike La Bouve
Estimated Sales: $3.8 Million
Number Employees: 5,000-9,999
Sq. footage: 181000
Type of Packaging: Consumer, Food Service, Pri-
     vate Label, Bulk
Brands:
     Buttercup
     Lov-It
     Lov-It Butter
     Lov-It Butter Blends
     Lov-It Butterup
     Lov-It Cream Cheese
     Lov-It Margarine
     Lov-It Mascarpone
     Lov-It Neufchatel Cheese
     Lov-It Salted Butter
     Lov-It Sour Cream
     Lov-It Unsalted Butter
     Lov-It Wisconsin Blend
     Seymour
     Wisconsin Blend

8625 Love & Quiches Desserts
178 Hanse Ave
Freeport, NY 11520-4698   516-623-8800
     Fax: 516-623-8817 800-525-5251
          saxelrod@loveandquiches.com
               www.loveandquiches.com
Processor of frozen layer cakes, mousses, tarts, pies,
cheesecakes and quiches; exporter of cakes, cheese-
cakes and brownies
     President: Susan Axelrod
     CEO: Andrew Axelrod
     R&D: Michael Goldstien
     Executive VP: Karen Sullivan
     Marketing Director: Karen Grossman
     Director PR/Buisness Development: Joan A
          Wapner
     Info Systems Manager: Douglas Mendoza
     Production: Olga Thorsell
     Plant Manager: Mike Mazzola
     Purchasing: Bonnie Warstdt
Estimated Sales: $ 50 - 100 Million
Number Employees: 250-499
Sq. footage: 65000
Brands:
     Deep Dish Tiramisu Classico Tray
     Susan's Sweet Talk
     Sweet Singles

8626 Love Creek Orchards
P.O.Box 1401
Medina, TX 78055-1401   830-589-2588
     Fax: 830-589-2880 800-449-0882
          adamsapples@lovecreekorchards.com
               www.lovecreekorchards.com
Grower of apples; processor of apple cider, jams, jel-
lies, butter, sauce and gourmet flavored coffee
     Owner: Baxter Adams
Estimated Sales: $3-5 Million
Number Employees: 20-49
Sq. footage: 2000
Type of Packaging: Consumer, Food Service, Pri-
     vate Label, Bulk
Brands:
     Apple Strudel Coffee Beans
     Love Creek Orchards

8627 Love'n Herbs
70 Deerwood Lane
Apt 8
Waterbury, CT 06704-1665   203-756-4932
     Fax: 203-756-4932 lovenherbs@aol.com
Distributors of all natural salad dressings and mari-
nades that contain Canola oil, vineger, herbs and
spices. No salt, no sugar, no MSG or preservatives.
Also pure canola oil
     President: Maria da Silva-Klanko
     Treasurer: Donald Klanko
     VP: Peter Klanko

Estimated Sales: Under $300,000
Number Employees: 1-4
Sq. footage: 1000
Parent Co: daSilva-Klanko
Type of Packaging: Consumer
Brands:
     All Natural Herbal
     Love'n Herbs

8628 Love's Bakery
P.O.Box 294
Honolulu, HI 96809-0294   808-235-5171
     Fax: 808-841-2646 888-455-6837
          loveshi@gte.net
Breads
     Manager: Donna Ajimine
     Chairman of the Board: Masahide Hosokai
     General Sales Manager: Kevin Takaesu
     Production Manager: Larry Lopes
     Purchasing Manager: Clifford Goya
Estimated Sales: $ 18 Million
Number Employees: 5-9

8629 Lovin' Oven
1072 Harvey Point Road
Suite 115
Hertford, NC 27944   252-426-3003
     Fax: 252-482-5000 888-775-0099
          carol@lovin-oven.com   www.lovin-oven.com
Homemade gingerbread cookies
     Owner: Carol Hammer
Estimated Sales: Less than $500,000
Number Employees: 5-9

8630 Low Country Produce
1919 Trask Parkway
Lobeco, SC 29931   800-935-2792
          Fax: 800-985-0405
          info@lowcountryproduce.com
               www.lowcountryproduce.com
pickles, chutneys & relishes, soups & sauces, salsas
& dips, jellies & preserves

8631 Lowell Farms
4 N Washington St
El Campo, TX 77437-4429   979-543-4950
     Fax: 979-541-5655 888-484-9213
          lowellfm@swbell.net   www.lowellfarms.com
Processor of organic jasmine rice
     Owner: Linda Raun
     VP: Linda Raun
Estimated Sales: Below $ 5 Million
Number Employees: 5-9
Type of Packaging: Consumer, Bulk
Brands:
     Lowell Farms

8632 Lowell Packing Company
P.O.Box 220
Fitzgerald, GA 31750-0220   229-423-2051
     Fax: 229-423-6601 800-342-0313
          sales@lowellpacking.com
               www.lowellpacking.com
Manufacturer of pork; slaughtering services avail-
able
     President: Morris Downing
     VP: Scott Downing
Estimated Sales: $20 Million
Number Employees: 100-249
Sq. footage: 48000
Type of Packaging: Consumer, Food Service
Brands:
     COLONY CITY
     GEORGIA STAR
     LOWELL

8633 (HQ)Lowell Provision Company
23 Aiken Ave
Lowell, MA 01850-1896   978-454-5603
          www.lowellprovisionco.com
Processor of beef, pork, lamb, chicken and veal
     President: Peter Doyle
     Purchasing Manager: Dennis Doyle
Estimated Sales: $ 20 - 50 Million
Number Employees: 10-19
Sq. footage: 6000
Type of Packaging: Consumer, Food Service, Pri-
     vate Label, Bulk
Other Locations:
     Lowell Provision Company
     Chelmsford MA
Brands:
     Doyle's
     Lowell Provision

8634 Lowell-Paul Dairy
14332 County Road 64
Greeley, CO 80631-9317   970-353-0278
          Fax: 970-353-0338
Fluid milk, cream and related products
     President: Margaret Paul
Estimated Sales: $ 5-10 Million
Number Employees: 20-49

8635 Lower Foods
700 S 200 W
Richmond, UT 84333-1209   435-258-2449
     Fax: 435-258-5177 larry@llranch.com
               www.llranch.com
Processor of roast beef, pastrami, corned beef, etc
     President: Larry Lower
     VP: Allan Lower
     Sales: Charles Johnson
     Plant Manager: Mike Mortensen
Estimated Sales: $100+ Million
Number Employees: 20-49
Type of Packaging: Consumer

8636 Lowery's Home Made Candies
6255 W Kilgore Ave
Muncie, IN 47304-4794   765-288-7300
     Fax: 765-747-9662 800-541-3340
          customerservice@loweryscandies.com
               www.loweryscandies.com
Manufacturer of confectionery including caramel,
taffy, chocolate, chocolate covered nuts and choco-
late covered cherries
     President: Michael Brown
     Owner: Thelma Brown
     Owner: Donald Brown
Estimated Sales: $7 Million
Number Employees: 20-49
Type of Packaging: Consumer

8637 Lowery's Premium Roast Coffee
P.O.Box 1858
Snohomish, WA 98291-1858   360-668-4545
     Fax: 360-863-9742 800-767-1783
          jzimm@loweryscoffee.com
               www.loweryscoffee.com
Coffee, wholesale and custom roasters, espresso ma-
chines, espresso accessories
     President: Donald Lowery
     CFO: Jeanette Zimmerman
     Marketing: Mike Lowery
     Roast/Operations Manager: Jerry Lowery
Estimated Sales: Below $ 5 Million
Number Employees: 20-49
Number of Brands: 2
Number of Products: 100
Sq. footage: 5000
Type of Packaging: Private Label
Brands:
     Lowery's Coffee
     Pasano's Syrups

8638 Lowland Seafood
PO Box 66
Lowland, NC 28552-0066   252-745-3751
          Fax: 252-745-5040
Processor of fish, shrimp, crabs and scallops
     President: Carol Potter
Estimated Sales: $1500000
Number Employees: 25
Type of Packaging: Consumer, Food Service, Bulk

8639 Lt Blender's Frozen Concoctions
1202 Post Office St
Galveston, TX 77550-5041   409-765-5666
     Fax: 409-966-1581 orders@ltblender.com
               www.ltblender.com
Manufacturer of frozen concoction drinks in a bag.
Flavors include: margarita; strawberry daiquiri; pina
colada; mudslide; hurricane; mojito; peach bellini
wine freezer; sangria wine freezer; strawberry wine
freezer; and margaritawine freezer.
     Founder/President: Ralph McMorris
     Vice President Marketing: Scott Treadaway

8640 Lu-Mar Lobster & Shrimp
2401 Village Dr
Brownsville, TX 78521-1410   956-546-5525
     Fax: 956-546-0871 www.nationalfish.com
Processor, importer and packer of frozen seafood including shrimp and surimi
     President: Jack Harding
     Sales Director: Jack Harding

Estimated Sales: $ 1 - 3 Million
Number Employees: 1-4
Sq. footage: 2000
Parent Co: Lu-Mar Lobster & Shrimp
Type of Packaging: Consumer, Food Service, Private Label
Brands:
Corona Del Mar
Demerico
Lu-Mar

8641 Luban International
9900 NW 25th St
Doral, FL 33172-2205   305-629-8730
Fax: 305-629-8740 www.fans-usa.com
Cereals
Owner: Luis Banegas

8642 Lubbers Dairy
RR 3
Pella, IA 50219   515-628-4284
Dairy
President: Andy Lubber

8643 Lubbock Cotton Oil Company
2300 E 50th St
Lubbock, TX 79404-4128   806-763-4371
Fax: 806-744-1235
Processor of cottonseed oils
Plant Manager: Frank Sherman
Estimated Sales: $ 50 - 100 Million
Number Employees: 50-99
Parent Co: Archer Daniels Midland Company

8644 Lubec Packing
PO Box 250
Lubec, ME 04652-0250   207-733-5572
Fax: 207-733-2460
Processor of canned sardines
Plant Manager: Peter Boyce
Number Employees: 100-249
Type of Packaging: Consumer

8645 Lubriplate Lubricants
129 Lockwood St
Newark, NJ 07105-4720   973-589-9150
Fax: 973-589-4432   800-733-4755
richardm@lubriplate.com   www.lubriplate.com
Manufacturer and exporter of food grade lubricating
oils and grease
President: Richard Mc Cluskey
VP/General Manager: Jim Girard
Number Employees: 100-249
Parent Co: Fisk Brothers

8646 Lucas Meyer
765 E Pythian Ave
Decatur, IL 62526-2412   217-875-3660
Fax: 217-877-5046   800-769-3660
lecithin@midwest.net   www.lucasmeyer.com
Processor of lecithin and soy flour
President: Peter Rohde
VP: Scott Hagerman
Director Sales/Marketing: Scott Hagerman
Sales Manager: Jack Chenault
Estimated Sales: $600000
Number Employees: 10-19

8647 Lucas Vineyards
3862 County Road 150
Interlaken, NY 14847-9653   607-532-4825
Fax: 607-532-8580   800-682-9463
info@lucasvineyards.com
www.lucasvineyards.com
Processor of wines
President: Ruth Lucas
Marketing Director: Stephanie Lucas
Plant Manager: Ruthie Lucas
Estimated Sales: $ 5 - 10 Million
Number Employees: 10-19
Type of Packaging: Consumer, Food Service
Brands:
Lucas

8648 Lucas Winery
18196 N Davis Rd
Lodi, CA 95242-9280   209-368-2006
Fax: 209-368-4900 www.lucaswinery.com
Fine wines
Owner: David Lucas
Estimated Sales: Less than $500,000
Number Employees: 1-4
Type of Packaging: Private Label

Brands:
Lucas

8649 Lucas World
5709 Springfield Avenue
Laredo, TX 78041-3282   528-625-1000
Fax: 528-625-1099   888-675-8227
www.lucasworld.com
President: Euzondo Alejandro
CEO: Martinez Alejandro
COO: Hugo Martinez
Research & Development: Maru Valdez
Sales Director: Juan Pablo Gonzalez
Parent Co: Lucas World
Brands:
Acidito Lucas
Chorreada
Crazy Hair
Gusano Lucas
Limon Lucas
Muecas
Pelucas
Skwinkles

8650 Lucca Foods
1220 Industrial Way
Sparks, NV 89431-6010   775-356-8611
Fax: 775-356-2180
Manufactures meat and cheese filled frozen pasta
Estimated Sales: $ 1-5 Million
Number Employees: 9

8651 Lucerne Foods
201 42nd Avenue SE
Calgary, AB T2G 1Y3
Canada   403-287-4080
Fax: 403-287-4090
Processor of bread and rolls
Plant Manager: Mike Szewczyk
Number Employees: 100-249

8652 Lucerne Foods
31122 S Fraser Way
Abbotsford, BC V2T 6L5
Canada   604-854-1191
Fax: 604-850-1179 vic.giesbrecht@safeway.com
Processor of frozen fruits and vegetables including
blueberries, cranberries, whole beans, peas and
brussels sprouts; exporter of frozen brussels sprouts,
whole beans and cranberries
Plant Manager: Vic Giesbrecht
Number Employees: 150
Sq. footage: 64000
Type of Packaging: Consumer, Food Service, Private Label, Bulk
Brands:
Bel-Air

8653 Lucerne Foods
5115-57th Street
Taber, AB T1G 1X1
Canada   403-223-3546
Fax: 403-223-2804
Processor of aseptically-packaged juices and drinks;
also, spices
Plant Manager: Loreen Sernowski
Parent Co: Canada Safeway
Type of Packaging: Consumer
Brands:
Edwards
Generic
Town House

8654 Lucerne Foods
131 22nd Street N
Lethbridge, AB T1H 3R6
Canada   403-328-5501
Fax: 403-327-4737
Processor, exporter and importer of frozen vegetables and juice concentrates
Manager: David Jensen
Superintendent: Ed Uyesugi
Production: Vaughn Caldwell
Number Employees: 100-249
Parent Co: Canada Safeway
Type of Packaging: Consumer, Food Service, Private Label, Bulk
Brands:
Party Pride
Safeway
Scotch Bay
Sunny Dawn
Town House

8655 Lucero Olive Oil
2120 Loleta Avenue
PO Box 1018
Corning, CA 96021   916-625-4360
Fax: 916-625-4375   dlucero@luceroliveoil.com
www.luceroliveoil.com
Olive oils

8656 Lucia's Pizza Company
10989 Gravois Industrial Ct
St Louis, MO 63128-2032   314-843-2553
Fax: 314-843-3576
Processor and wholesaler/distributor of frozen pizza
President: Darrell Long
Estimated Sales: $1600000
Number Employees: 20-49
Sq. footage: 25000
Type of Packaging: Consumer, Private Label
Brands:
Lucia's

8657 Lucich Farms
P.O.Box 1266
Delano, CA 93216-1266   661-725-4550
Fax: 661-725-5283   lucich@lightspeed.net
www.grapegift.com
Processor and exporter of table grapes
President: Dave Clyde
CFO: Daril Bishop
VP/Marketing: David Clyde
Sales: Bob Schultz
VP Operations: Mike Ahumada
Controller: Ben Miramontes
Purchasing Manager: Steve Lackey
Estimated Sales: $100+ Million
Number Employees: 100-249
Type of Packaging: Consumer, Bulk
Brands:
Sall-N-Ann

8658 Lucile's Creole Foods
2124 14th St
Boulder, CO 80302-4804   303-442-4743
Fax: 303-939-9848 www.luciles.com
Gourmet Creole foods
Owner: Fletcher Richards
Estimated Sales: $500,000-$1 Million
Number Employees: 20-49
Type of Packaging: Private Label

8659 Lucile's Famous Creole Seasonings
2124 14th St
Boulder, CO 80302-4804   303-442-4743
Fax: 303-939-9848   800-727-3653
info@luciles.com   www.luciles.com
Processor of Creole seasonings and French roast
blend coffee
President: Fletcher Richards III
Sales Manager: Jennifer Fowler
Estimated Sales: $500,000-$1 Million
Number Employees: 20-49
Sq. footage: 4000
Type of Packaging: Consumer, Food Service, Bulk
Brands:
Lucile's

8660 Lucille Farm Products
PO Box 517
Montville, NJ 07045-0517   973-334-6030
Fax: 973-402-6361
lucillefarms@lucille-farms.com
www.lucille-farms.com
Processor and exporter of cheese including mozzarella, provolone and feta
CEO: Alfonso Falivene
VP Sales/Marketing: David McCarthy
Sales Director: David Braff
Operations Manager: Jerry Falivene
Production Manager: Jim Johnson
Estimated Sales: $36691000
Number Employees: 97
Sq. footage: 40000
Brands:
Monte Carlo Premium Mozerella
Mozi Rue Cholesterol Free
Tasty-Lite Cheese Fat Free/Premium

8661 Lucille's Own Make Candies
156 Route 72 E
Manahawkin, NJ 08050-3597   609-597-7300
Fax: 609-597-7393   800-426-9168
jeismann@aol.com   www.lucillescandies.com

Candy and confections
President: Nathaniel Eismann
VP Sales: Janice Eismann
Estimated Sales: $500,000-$1 Million
Number Employees: 5-9

8662 Lucini Italia Company
601 22nd Street
San Francisco, CA 94107   866-972-6879
Fax: 415-401-0087   888-558-2464
renee@lucini.com   www.lucini.com
Extra virgin olive oil
President: Renee Frigo
Estimated Sales: Less than $500,000
Number Employees: 5-9

8663 Lucks Food Decorating Company
3003 S Pine St
Tacoma, WA 98409-4793   206-674-7200
Fax: 206-674-7250   800-426-9778
info@lucks.com   www.lucks.com
Processor and exporter of cake decorations and food colorings; exporter of flavoring extracts
President: Rick Ellison
VP Sales: Rick Ellison
Estimated Sales: $28100000
Number Employees: 50-99
Sq. footage: 100000
Parent Co: Lucks Company
Type of Packaging: Food Service
Brands:
Decons
Edible Image
Lucks
Lucks Roses

8664 Lucks Food Decorating Company
3003 S Pine St
Tacoma, WA 98409-4793   206-674-7200
Fax: 206-674-7250   info@lucks.com
www.lucks.com
Processor of popcorn, canned apples, chicken, vegetables, collard greens and beans
President: Rick Ellison
VP: Darius Luck
Sr. VP Operations: Frank Valdez
Plant Manager: Darius Luck
Number Employees: 100-249
Sq. footage: 198000
Parent Co: International Home Foods
Type of Packaging: Consumer, Private Label

8665 Lucky Seafood Corporation
6203 Jonesboro Road
Morrow, GA 30260-1723   770-960-9889
Fax: 770-968-9400
Seafood
President: David Ng

8666 Lucy's Foods
408 Longs Rd
Latrobe, PA 15650-3506   724-539-1430
Fax: 724-532-0525   zapsausage@aol.com
www.zapsausage.com
Manufacturer of frozen Italian specialties including gnocchi, cavatelli, ravioli, lasagna, manicotti, stuffed shells, stuffed rigatoni, sausage and more. Gift baskets available
President: Nicholas Zappone
Estimated Sales: $6 Million
Number Employees: 1-4
Type of Packaging: Consumer
Brands:
DELGROSSO
DENUNZIO
LOTITO
RIZZO'S
ROSIE'S

8667 Lucy's Sweet Surrender
12516 Buckeye Rd
Cleveland, OH 44120-2652   216-752-0828
Fax: 216-767-0735   mislkel@aol.com
www.lucyssweetsurrender.com
Hungarian pastries and custom European baked goods; including hungarian
President: Michael Feigenbaum
Estimated Sales: $250,000
Number Employees: 5-9

8668 Ludfords
8707 Utica Ave
Rancho Cucamonga, CA 91730-5100 909-948-0797
Fax: 909-948-0597   ludfords@earthlink.com

Processor, importer and exporter of fresh, frozen and canned fruit juices including orange, apple, grape, etc
President: Paul Ludford
Estimated Sales: Below $ 5 Million
Number Employees: 10-19
Sq. footage: 20000
Type of Packaging: Consumer, Food Service, Private Label
Brands:
Ludford's

8669 Ludo LLC
31809 S Roundhead Dr
Cleveland, OH 44139-4739   440-542-6000
Fax: 440-542-9555 www.ludocandytoys.com
Candy
Manager: Stephanie Holmes
Estimated Sales: $300,000-500,000
Number Employees: 1-4
Brands:
BUBBLE CANDY

8670 Ludwick's Frozen Donuts
3217 3 Mile Rd NW
Grand Rapids, MI 49534-1223   616-453-6880
Fax: 616-453-1930   800-366-8816
info@kneadinthedough.com
Processor of frozen doughnuts, fresh cookies, and seafoam candy
President: Thomas Ludwick
CEO: Jack Brown
Estimated Sales: $ 5 - 10 Million
Number Employees: 5-9
Type of Packaging: Consumer, Food Service, Private Label, Bulk
Brands:
Kneadin The Dough

8671 Ludwig Dairy
1309 W 7th Street
Dixon, IL 61021-3307   815-284-7791
Fax: 815-284-7704
Cheese
President: Mirekge Gebaka
Assistant Plant Manager: Duane Hadaway
VP Manufacturing: Mario Jedwabrik
Maintenance Manager: Rich Majewiski
Plant Manager: Michael Imel/ Ed Tomasziewicz
Estimated Sales: $ 5-10 Million
Number Employees: 10
Type of Packaging: Private Label

8672 Ludwig Fish & Produce Company
711 Washington St
La Porte, IN 46350-3337   219-362-2608
Fax: 219-325-8311
Wholesaler/distributor of frozen food, general line products, produce, provisions/meats and seafood; serving the food service market
President: Harold Robinson
Estimated Sales: $3800000
Number Employees: 20-49

8673 Ludwigshof Winery
17533 Highway K4
Eskridge, KS 66423-8975   785-449-2498
Fax: 785-449-2498
Winery
President: Vernon Robinson

8674 Luigino's
525 S Lake Ave
Duluth, MN 55802-2362   218-727-2059
Fax: 218-727-4497 www.michelinas.com
Processor and exporter of frozen pastas, sauces and Oriental and lasagna entrees, pizza and egg rolls and
Manager: Doug Haala
President/COO: Ron Bubar
Sales Director: Charles Pountney
Public Relations: Jim Tills
Operations Manager: Jeff Wilson
Production Manager: Mike Evans
Plant Manager: Joe Scinocca
Number Employees: 50-99
Parent Co: Luigino's
Type of Packaging: Consumer
Brands:
Budget Gourmet
Lean 'n Tasty
Luigino's
Michelina's
Michelina's International
Yu Sing

8675 Luigino's/Michelina Brand
P.O. Box 16630
Duluth, MN 55816-0630   218-628-4800
Fax: 218-624-7019   800-251-7004
www.michelinas.com
Manufacturer and exporter of frozen entrees and snacks including Oriental, low-fat, pizza snack rolls and egg rolls and pizza slices
Chairman/Founder: Geno Paulucci
Plant Manager: Randy Potter
Estimated Sales: $450 Million
Number Employees: 10-19
Number of Brands: 3
Number of Products: 300
Sq. footage: 500000
Type of Packaging: Consumer, Food Service, Private Label
Other Locations:
Luigino's
Jackson OH
Brands:
Budget Gourmet
Luigino's
Michelina's
Michelina's Yu Sing

8676 Lukas Confections
231 W College Ave
York, PA 17401-2103   717-843-0921
Fax: 717-854-9743   lukasclassic@yahoo.com
www.classiccaramel.com
Processor and exporter of sugarless and regular caramel toffee, taffy nougat and caramel including liquid; also salt water taffy and nutraceuticals
President: Robert Lukas
CEO: Robert Lukas
CFO: G Mark Zelinski CPA
Research & Development: Chendran Attepato PhD
Quality Control: Mary Ann Staz
Marketing Director: Robert Lukas
Sales Director: Alan Cotich
Public Relations: R Lukas
Operations Manager: Theresa Braner
Production Manager: Efrain Reyes
Purchasing Manager: Angela Smith
Estimated Sales: $6 Million
Number Employees: 50-99
Number of Brands: 4
Number of Products: 110
Sq. footage: 52000
Type of Packaging: Consumer, Private Label, Bulk
Brands:
Caramel Milk Roll
Classic
Dark Fruit Chews
Dorks
Flipsticks

8677 Lumar Lobster Corporatio
PO Box 433
Lawrence, NY 11559-0433   516-371-0083
Processor of live lobster
President: Stanley Jassem
Estimated Sales: Less than $500,000
Number Employees: 1-4
Type of Packaging: Food Service

8678 Luna's Tortillas
8524 Harry Hines Blvd
Dallas, TX 75235-3013   214-747-2661
Fax: 214-747-5862
Processor of Mexican food products including corn tortillas, flour tortillas, tostadas, taco shells, nacho chips, tamales, hot sauce, pico de gallo, beans, chorizo, masa and hojas.
President: Francisco Luna
Sales/Marketing Executive: Fernando Luna
Purchasing Agent: J Luna
Estimated Sales: $1200000
Number Employees: 10-19
Sq. footage: 10000
Type of Packaging: Consumer, Food Service
Brands:
Luna's

8679 Lund's Fisheries
P.O. Box 830
Cape May, NJ 08204-0830   609-884-7600
Fax: 609-884-0664   info@lundsfish.com
www.lundsfish.com

Processor and exporter of frozen cod, flounder, mackerel, squid, sturgeon, tuna, herring and shad
President: Jeffery Reichle
Sales: Dennis Dowe
Operations: Darren Dowe
Purchasing Manager: Henry Buchianico
Estimated Sales:$21900000
Number Employees: 250-499
Type of Packaging: Consumer, Food Service

8680 Lundberg Family Farm
P.O.Box 369
Richvale, CA 95974-0369   530-882-4551
Fax: 530-882-4500 joe@lundberg.com
www.lundberg.com
Processor of rice and rice products including cereal, flour, dinners, cakes and mixes; also, organic rice
President: Harlan Lundenberg
CEO: Grant Lundberg
VP Sales/Marketing: Tim O'Donnell
Regional Sales Manager: Dirk Burgon
Estimated Sales:$17700000
Number Employees: 100-249
Type of Packaging: Consumer, Food Service, Private Label, Bulk
Brands:
Evergood
Lundberg

8681 Lupi
1801 Bush Street
Baltimore, MD 21230-2044   410-752-3370
President: Lupi Domil

8682 Lupi Marchigiano Bakery
169 Washington Ave
New Haven, CT 06519-1618   203-562-9491
Fax: 203-562-5456
Baked goods
President: Pete Lupi
Estimated Sales: Below $ 5 Million
Number Employees: 20-49

8683 Lusitania Bakery
PO Box 319
Blandon, PA 19510-0319   610-926-1311
Processor of cakes, danish and gourmet muffins
Chairman/CEO: Samuel Chudnovsky
Number Employees: 20-49
Sq. footage: 50000
Type of Packaging: Consumer, Private Label
Brands:
Dutch Kettle Foods
Old Dutch Bakery

8684 Lusty Lobster
10 Portland Fish Pier # A
Portland, ME 04101-4620   207-773-2829
Fax: 207-774-3956
Lobster
President: Doug Douty
Estimated Sales:$ 10 - 20 Million
Number Employees: 10-19

8685 (HQ)Luv Yu Bakery
3410 Bashford Avenue Ct
Louisville, KY 40218-3182   502-451-4511
Fax: 502-451-5510 luvyubrand@aol.com
www.luvyu.com
Chocolate-dipped, buffet and organic cookies, unique snacks, rice crackers and shrimp chips
President: Abel Yu
Vice President: Serena Yu
Sq. footage: 25000

8686 Luxembourg Cheese Factory
12495 N Pleasant Hill Rd
Orangeville, IL 61060-9783   815-789-4227
Fax: 815-789-4434 www.tateandlyle.com
Processor of sodium, calcium and potassium caseinates, milk protein hydrolyzate and hydrolyzed vegetable proteins
President: Mike Ernster
Plant Manager: Frank Furgal
Number Employees: 10-19
Sq. footage: 15000

8687 Luxor California ExportsCorporation
3659 India Street
2nd Floor
San Diego, CA 92103-4767   619-692-9330

Supplier and exporter of agricultural commodities closeouts including dry beans, grains, oils, yeast, dry milk, butter, etc
President: Kamil Kafaji
Estimated Sales:$1000000
Number Employees: 5
Type of Packaging: Bulk

8688 Luyties Pharmacal Company
4200 Laclede Avenue
Department T
Saint Louis, MO 63108-2866   314-533-9600
Fax: 314-535-9600 800-325-8080
luytiesstl@aol.com
Processor and exporter of vitamins and homeopathic products
Director Marketing: Michael Smith
Number Employees: 50-99
Parent Co: Manola Company
Brands:
Luyties

8689 Lykes Meat Group
4611 Lykes Rd
Plant City, FL 33566-0002   813-752-1102
Fax: 813-759-4201 www.smithfield.com
Processor and exporter of sausage, beef, frankfurters and luncheon meats
Human Resources: Shannon Krieger
VP Operations: Paul Brandon
Number Employees: 500-999
Parent Co: Smithfield Foods
Type of Packaging: Consumer, Food Service, Private Label, Bulk

8690 Lyle's Seafoods
PO Box 547
Ocean Park, WA 98640-0547   360-665-4666
Fax: 360-665-4666
Canned salmon, smoked salmon, sturgeon, clams, oysters, crab, oyster products
Owner: Kim Lobry
Brands:
Shoalwater Bay

8691 Lyman Jenkins
PO Box 53
Jericho Center, VT 05465-0053   802-899-3056
Fax: 802-899-3056 800-528-7021
Manufacturer of food products
President: Lyman Jenkins

8692 Lynard Company
15 Maple Tree Ave
Stamford, CT 06906   203-323-0231
Fax: 203-973-0545
snacks and candy
President/Owner: Lillian Flaster
VP: Howard Flaster

8693 Lynard Company
15 Maple Tree Ave
Stamford, CT 06906-2206   203-323-0231
Fax: 203-323-0231 lynardco@aol.com
Chocolates, candies, pretzels, nuts, popcorn, cookies, dried fruits, honey package designing
President: Lillian Flaster
Estimated Sales: Less than $200,000
Number Employees: 5-9

8694 Lynch Foods
72 Railside Road
North York, QC M3A 1A3
Canada   416-449-5464
Fax: 416-449-9165 foodservice@lynchfoods.com
www.lynchfoods.ca
Processor of sauces, soup mixes, drink crystals, dessert powders, preserves, syrups, pie filling and chocolate powders; also, portion pack peanut butter, jams, jellies, salad dressing and pancake syrup
President: Walter J Lynch
CEO: Walter J Lynch
VP Marketing: Peter Henderson
VP Sales: Scott Lynch
Marketing: W Lynch
Number Employees: 100-249
Sq. footage: 120000
Type of Packaging: Consumer, Food Service, Private Label, Bulk

8695 Lynch Supply
15551 W 109th St
Lenexa, KS 66219-1307   913-492-8500
Fax: 913-492-8532 info@fieldmaster.com
www.fieldmaster.com
Manufacturer and exporter of pressure cookers, smokers and roaster ovens; also, seasoning for meat and chicken
President: David Lynch
Estimated Sales:$ 1 - 2.5 Million
Number Employees: 1-4

8696 Lynden Meat Company
1936 Front St
Lynden, WA 98264-1708   360-354-2449
Fax: 360-354-7687
Meat packer; custom slaughtering and packing services available
Owner: Rick Biesheuvel
Estimated Sales:$ 3 - 5 Million
Number Employees: 5-9
Type of Packaging: Consumer

8697 Lynfred Winery
15 S Roselle Rd
Roselle, IL 60172-2043   630-529-9463
Fax: 630-529-4971 888-298-9463
info@lynfredwinery.com
www.lynfredwinery.com
Wines
President: Fred Koehler
CEO: Fred Koehler
CFO: Diane Schramer
Vice President: Valerie Koehler
Sales Manager: Valerie Anderson
Public Relations Officer: Christina Anderson
Estimated Sales:$ 10-20 Million
Number Employees: 20-49
Number of Products: 50
Sq. footage: 24000
Type of Packaging: Private Label
Brands:
LYNFRED

8698 Lynn Dairy
W1929 Us Highway 10
Granton, WI 54436-8899   715-238-7129
Fax: 715-238-7130 lynndairy@tds.net
www.lynndairy.com
Makers of cheese
President: William Schwantes
Marketing Director: Rick Beilke
Estimated Sales:$ 5-10 Million
Number Employees: 100-249
Type of Packaging: Bulk
Brands:
Lynn Dairy
Lynn Protiens

8699 Lynn Springs Water LLC
4325 1st Ave # 562
Tucker, GA 30084-4498   770-572-5928
trthomas@tjafg.com
freewebs.com/xtanaina
Water
President: Tandrias Thomas
CEO: Jocelyn Facen
CFO: Al Thomas
Vice President: Derrick Smith
Estimated Sales:$1-2 Million
Number Employees: 20-49
Number of Brands: 1
Number of Products: 1
Sq. footage: 6000
Type of Packaging: Bulk

8700 Lyo-San
PO Box 598
Lachute, QC J8H 4G4
Canada   450-562-8525
Fax: 450-562-1433
Manufacturer and exporter of freeze-dried yogurt cultures and bifido-bacteria; custom freeze-drying available
Executive VP: Serge Brault
Purchasing: Robert Jacques
Number Employees: 10-19
Sq. footage: 45000
Type of Packaging: Consumer, Food Service, Private Label, Bulk
Brands:
Yogourmet

8701 Lyoferm & Vivolac Cultures
2500 E 46th St
Indianapolis, IN 46205-2427   317-259-5050
        Fax: 317-259-7289   800-844-8649
        vivolac@iquest.net   www.iquest.net
Processor of cultures including dairy, meat and bakery starter, freeze dried/lyophilized and food fermentation; exporter of freeze dried cultures
    President: Wesley Sing
    CEO: Jack Carr
    Marketing Manager: Mike Cigich
Estimated Sales: $ 3 - 5 Million
Number Employees: 20-49
Brands:
    Lyoferm
    Vivolac

8702 (HQ)Lyons-Magnus
3158 E Hamilton Ave
Fresno, CA 93702-4163   559-268-5966
    Fax: 559-233-8249 www.lyonsmagnus.com
Manufacturer and marketer of dessert toppings/sauces, chocolate syrups, hot fudges, fruit fillings, preserves, syrups, juices, and beverages
    President: Robert Smittcamp
    SVP National Sales: Brad Kirk
    Operations Manager: Keith Brantley
Estimated Sales: $100+ Million
Number Employees: 250-499
Sq. footage: 380000
Type of Packaging: Food Service, Private Label, Bulk
Other Locations:
    Lyons-Magnus Plant Facility
    Walton KY

8703 M K Meat Processing Plant
P.O.Box 317
Burton, TX 77835-0317   979-289-4022
        Fax: 978-989-4001
Manufacturer of beef, pork and sausage
    Owner: Jerry Schultz
Estimated Sales: $2.5 Million
Number Employees: 1-4
Type of Packaging: Consumer, Bulk

8704 M&B Fruit Juice Company
955 Home Ave
Akron, OH 44310-4107   330-253-7465
        Fax: 330-253-8401
Processor of fruit drink concentrates including orange, lemonade, pink lemonade, grape, cherry, lime, loganberry, iced tea and punch; also, vanilla and strawberry syrups
    President: James Stone
Estimated Sales: $ 1 - 3 Million
Number Employees: 5-9
Sq. footage: 10000
Type of Packaging: Consumer, Food Service, Private Label, Bulk
Brands:
    Magic-Mix
    Party Punch
    Super-Mix
    Trim-Lite
    WIZ

8705 M&B Products
8601 Harney Rd
Tampa, FL 33637-6600   813-988-2211
        Fax: 813-980-6596   800-899-7255
    rocky@mbproducts.com   www.mbproducts.com
Processor of juice including orange, apple, orange/pineapple, grape, etc.; also, milk, milkshakes and frozen fruit juice bars
    President: Dale McClellan
Estimated Sales: $ 10 - 20 Million
Number Employees: 50-99
Type of Packaging: Consumer

8706 M&CP Farms
3986 County Road Nn
Orland, CA 95963-9810   530-865-9810
    Fax: 530-865-9793   greatolives@greatolives.com
            www.greatolives.com
Products include olive spreads, mixes, cured olives,olive oil, stuffed olives, in addition to spicy beans, and sweet/sour pickles.
    President: Maurice Penna
    Secretary/Treasurer: Cynthia Penna
Estimated Sales: Below $ 5 Million
Number Employees: 5-9
Sq. footage: 15000
Parent Co: D. Beccaris

Type of Packaging: Consumer, Food Service, Private Label, Bulk
Brands:
    Loam Ridge
    M&Cp Farms

8707 M&G Honey Farms
411 S 1st Street
Bushton, KS 67427-9755   316-562-3643
Honey and honey products

8708 M&I Seafood Manufacturers
8805 Kelso Dr
Essex, MD 21221-3112   410-780-0444
        Fax: 410-780-3167
Processor and exporter of frozen seafood crab cakes, crab balls, mushroom caps stuffed with crab imperial, flunder fillets stuffed with crab imperial, breaded fantailed shrimp, fish cakes, flounder fillets, I.Q.F. gulf shrimpshrimpura, shrimp sticks, crab imperial in natural shell, crab meat stuffing, seafood soups and chowders, frozen and pasteurized crab meat
    President: Steve Cohen
    Controller: Mark Stachlorlwski
    Vice President: Ron Kauffman
    General Manager: Steve Cohen
Estimated Sales: $ 20 - 50 Million
Number Employees: 100-249
Sq. footage: 50000
Type of Packaging: Consumer, Food Service, Private Label, Bulk
Brands:
    Chesapeake Bay
    Chesapeake Bay Gourmet

8709 M&L Gourmet Ice Cream
2524 E Monument St
Baltimore, MD 21205-2539   410-276-4880
        Fax: 410-525-8320
Processor and exporter of kosher ice cream
    Owner: Chris Napfel
Estimated Sales: Less than $500,000
Number Employees: 1-4
Type of Packaging: Consumer, Food Service

8710 M&L Ventures
1471 W Commerce Ct
Tucson, AZ 85746-6016   520-884-8232
    Fax: 520-770-9649   info@meritfoods.net
            www.meritfoods.net
Products include produce and groceries, eggs and cheese, deli meats and salad dressings.
    President: Matt Sadowsky
    Secretary/Treasurer: Lynn Sadowsky
    Manager: Bob Richter
    Manager: Paul Rosthenhausler

8711 M&M Fisheries
PO Box 190
Shelburne, NS B0W 2E0
Canada   902-723-2390
        Fax: 902-723-2967
        mm.fisheries@ns.sympatico.ca
Processor and exporter of fresh and frozen haddock, cod, pollack, red fish and silver hake
    President: Gary Goreham
    Manager Sales: Glenn Maxwell
Number Employees: 60
Sq. footage: 14000
Type of Packaging: Consumer
Brands:
    M&M Fisheries
    Novie Fresh

8712 M&M Food Distributors/Oriental Pride
3322 Virginia Beach Blvd
Virginia Beach, VA 23452-5608   757-499-5676
        Fax: 757-499-0807
Ethnic foods
    President: Joan Mallen

8713 M&M Industries Inc
316 Corporate Place
Chattanooga, TN 37419   423-821-3302
        Fax: 423-821-9017   800-331-5305
        cstone@mmcontainer.com
        www.mmcontainer.com/

Manufacturer of Life Latch plastic pails suitable for a variety of purposes including the food industry. Uses include livestock feed and grains; pet food storage; seeds; vitamin supplements; etc.
    VP: Glenn H Morris Jr
    Regional Accounts Manager: Rae Green
    Regional Accounts Manager: Cindy Stone
    Regional Accounts Manager: Tiffany King
    Regional Accounts Manager: Janet Rogers
Estimated Sales: $10-25 Million
Number Employees: 25

8714 M&M Packing Company
PO Box 430
Ballinger, TX 76821-0430   915-365-2227
        Fax: 915-365-2227
Processor of meat including sausage and chili con carne
Estimated Sales: $2 Million
Number Employees: 20
Type of Packaging: Consumer, Food Service

8715 M&M Shrimp Company
408 Lee Street
Biloxi, MS 39530-2455   228-435-4915
        Fax: 228-435-3821
Processor of frozen shrimp
Number Employees: 20-49
Type of Packaging: Consumer, Food Service, Private Label
Brands:
    Captain Joey
    M&M
    Suarez

8716 M&R Company
33 E Tokay St
Lodi, CA 95240-4149   209-369-2725
        Fax: 209-369-7943
Grower, packer and exporter of fruits and vegetables including bell peppers, asparagus, eggplant, beans, cherries, grapes, apples and pears as well as grape juice
    President: Donald Reynolds
    Vice President: Don Reynolds
    Manager Marketing: Craig Lusk
    Sales Director: Andy Foccaci
Estimated Sales: $ 50 - 100 Million
Number Employees: 50-99
Sq. footage: 100000
Type of Packaging: Consumer
Brands:
    Four Aces
    M&R

8717 M&S Tomato Repacking Company
1026 Bay St
Springfield, MA 01109-2427   413-737-4662
    Fax: 413-736-6433   800-343-0371
Packer of tomatoes
    Owner: Laurie Chruscieo
    CFO: Lorrie Chrusrciel
    Assistant Manager: Jim Murphy
Estimated Sales: $ 10 - 20 Million
Number Employees: 20-49
Type of Packaging: Consumer

8718 M-C Dairy Company
106 N Queen Street
Etobicoke, ON M8Z 2E2
Canada   416-231-1491
        Fax: 416-231-1879
Processor and wholesaler/distributor of dairy products including cottage cheese, yogurt, kefir, cream cheese and huslanka
    President: Borys Wrzesnewskyj
Number Employees: 10-19
Sq. footage: 10000
Type of Packaging: Consumer
Brands:
    M.C. Dairy

8719 M-CAP Technologies
3411 Silverside Rd
Wilmington, DE 19810-4812   302-695-5616
        Fax: 302-695-5350   800-641-2001
        jdoncheck@lakefield.net
Processor and exporter of industrial ingredients including bromate replacers, additives and preservatives; also, temperature release vitamins and minerals
    VP Technology: James Doncheck
Parent Co: DuPont Chemical

Brands:
Baker's Label

8720 M-G
P.O.Box 697
Weimar, TX 78962-0697   979-725-8524
Fax: 979-725-9428   800-460-8581
Processor of egg products; wholesaler/distributor of poultry products, frozen foods and seafood; serving the food service market
President: Alvin Mueller
VP: Marvin Hicek
Head Operations: Darryl Dean
Estimated Sales:$ 20 - 50 Million
Number Employees: 20-49
Sq. footage: 10000
Type of Packaging: Food Service
Brands:
Mighty Good

8721 M. Brown & Sons
P.O.Box 188
Bremen, IN 46506-0188   574-546-4942
Fax: 574-258-7468   800-258-7450
info@lebermuth.com   www.lebermuth.com
Botanicals, herbs, and essential oils
President: Larry Brown
Chairman: Irvin Brown
VP: Alan Brown
VP: Robert Brown
Estimated Sales:$ 10-15 Million
Number Employees: 20-49
Parent Co: Lebermuth Company
Type of Packaging: Bulk

8722 M. Licht & Son
P.O.Box 507
Knoxville, TN 37901-0507   865-523-5593
Fax: 865-523-0270   smncs@ix.netcom.com
www.smsweetener.com
Processor and exporter of liquid artificial sweeteners
President: Richard M Licht
VP: Karen McGuire
Estimated Sales:$ 5 - 10 Million
Number Employees: 5-9
Sq. footage: 3200
Type of Packaging: Food Service
Brands:
Smoky Mountain

8723 M. Marion & Company
422 Larkfield Center
Suite 2553
Santa Rosa, CA 95403-1408   707-836-0551
Wine
President: M Dennis Marion
Estimated Sales:$500,000-$1 Million
Number Employees: 1-4

8724 M.A. Gedney
P.O.Box 8
Chaska, MN 55318-0008   952-448-2612
Fax: 952-448-1790   info@gedneypickle.com
www.gedneypickle.com
Processor of condiments, barbecue sauces, vinegars, syrups, pickles, relishes, sauerkraut, salsa, salad dressing, mayonnaise, mustard, etc.; importer of cucumbers
President: Jeffrey Tuttle
CEO: Chuck Weil
VP Sales/Marketing: Ted Forbes
Operations Manager: Thomas Hitch
Estimated Sales:$33000000
Number Employees: 100-249
Type of Packaging: Consumer, Food Service, Private Label, Bulk
Brands:
Devil's Fire
Gedney
Geraldo's
Hiawatha
Max's
Minnesaurus Dill Picklodon
Northland
Northwoods
Pep Fest
State Fair

8725 M.A. Hatt & Sons
RR 3
405 North West Rd
Lunenburg, NS B0J 2C0
Canada   902-634-8407
Fax: 902-634-8407

Processor of sauerkraut
President: Ralph Hatt
VP: Gladys Hatt
Number Employees: 5-9
Type of Packaging: Consumer, Food Service, Bulk
Brands:
Tan Cook

8726 M.A. Johnson Frozen Foods
1912 E Monroe Pike
Marion, IN 46953-2610   800-899-1406
Fax: 800-284-1561
Frozen foods
President: S Allen Johnson
Estimated Sales:$ 5-10 Million appx.
Number Employees: 10

8727 M.A. Patout & Son
3512 J Patout Burns Rd
Jeanerette, LA 70544-7122   337-276-4592
Fax: 337-276-4247 www.mapatout.com
Processor of sugar cane
President: William Patout III
CEO: Craig P Caillier
Estimated Sales:$156451778
Number Employees: 100-249
Type of Packaging: Bulk

8728 M.E. Swing Company
612 S Pickett St # D
Alexandria, VA 22304-4620   703-370-5050
Fax: 703-370-7286   800-485-4019
darren@swingscoffee.com
www.swingscoffee.com
Processor of roasted coffee
Owner: Mark Woarmuth
Executive Vice President: Dwayne Walker
VP Marketing: Dwayne Walker
Director of Operations: Darren Dimisa
*Estimated Sales:*Less than $500,000
Number Employees: 5-9
Sq. footage: 3000
Type of Packaging: Consumer, Food Service, Bulk

8729 M.H. Greenebaum
64 Campbell Avenue
Airmont, NY 10901-6407   973-538-9200
Fax: 973-538-3599
Cheese, cheese products
President: Rasmus Andersen
Estimated Sales:$ 10-20 Million
Number Employees: 5-9

8730 M.H. Zeigler & Sons
1513 N Broad St
Lansdale, PA 19446-1111   215-855-5161
Fax: 215-855-4548 www.zeiglers.com
Processor of apple cider, lemonade and pink lemonade
President: Art Dalzereit
CFO: Timothy Zeigler
Estimated Sales:$$20-50 Million
Number Employees: 50-99
Type of Packaging: Consumer, Food Service, Private Label, Bulk
Brands:
Zeigler's

8731 M.J. Kellner Company
5700 International Pkwy
Springfield, IL 62711-4052   217-529-1663
Fax: 217-529-1715   mjk@mjkellner.com
www.mjkellner.com
Wholesaler/distributor of groceries, meats, produce, frozen foods, baked goods, equipment and fixtures, general merchandise and seafood; serving the food service market
President: Bill Kellner
CFO: S David Rikas
CEO: Chad Nassif
Sales Development Manager: Gary Kelley
Estimated Sales:$ 50 - 100 Million
Number Employees: 50-99

8732 M.M. Bake Shop
444 N 6th Avenue
Laurel, MS 39440-3969   601-428-5153
Bread, rolls
President: Ethel Stewart
*Estimated Sales:*Less than $500,000
Number Employees: 5-9

8733 M.S. Walker
20 3rd Ave
Somerville, MA 02143-4404   617-776-6700
Fax: 617-776-5808 www.mswalker.com
Processor and importer of brandy, liqueurs, wines and spirits
President: Harvey Allen
CEO: Richard Sandler
Estimated Sales:$ 1 - 3 Million
Number Employees: 100-249

8734 M.S. Walker
20 3rd Ave
Somerville, MA 02143-4404   617-776-6700
Fax: 617-776-5808   info@mswalker.com
www.mswalker.com
A wholesale distributor of wines, spirits and cigars, in addition to manufacturing their own brands of spirit products.
CEO: Richard Sandler
Estimated Sales:$ 1-2.5 Million
Number Employees: 100-249

8735 M.W. Milton & Company
P.O.Box 70269
Louisville, KY 40270-0269   502-587-5016
Fax: 502-587-5017
Processor of fresh gourmet salsa, marinades and picante sauces
VP Marketing: Maggie Milton
VP Production: Max Milton
Estimated Sales:$ 3 - 5 Million
Number Employees: 5-9
Sq. footage: 4800
Type of Packaging: Consumer, Bulk
Brands:
Bueno Dia

8736 M/S Smears
701 S Jones St
Pembroke, NC 28372-9696   910-521-1641
Fax: 336-527-4094 www.sweetpotatoes.com
Pies
Manager: Marshall Sherman

8737 (HQ)MAFCO Worldwide Corporation
300 Jefferson St
Camden, NJ 08104-2113   856-964-8840
Fax: 856-964-6029
magnasweet@mafcolicorice.com
www.mafcolicorice.com
Processor and exporter of food ingredients including licorice extracts, flavoring agents and enhancers
President: Steven Taub
Marketing/Sales: J Robinson
Operations: L Gordon
Estimated Sales:$96900000
Number Employees: 100-249
Type of Packaging: Bulk
Brands:
Mafco Magnasweet

8738 MAK Enterprises
37315 26th Street E
Palmdale, CA 93550-6414   661-272-1867
mtaylor1@netport.com
Processor of salsa and hot sauces
CEO: Mark Taylor
CFO: Renee Taylor
Number Employees: 20-49
Brands:
Hell's Furry Fire Hot Sauce
The Salsa Addiction

8739 MAS Sales
11225 W Grand Ave
Northlake, IL 60164-1036   847-451-0005
Fax: 847-451-6563   800-615-6951
pastafactoryusa@juno.com
Frozen spaghetti sauce, lasagna, macaroni, ravioli, spaghetti no meat, spaghetti with meat, manicotti, stuffed shells, tortellini, cannelloni pasta. A full line of fresh frozen string pasta's, frozen extruded shapes, frozen tortellinitortelloni, ravioli, stuffed and regualar gnocchi entrees and frozen sauces
President: Michael Sica
VP: Irene Sica
Quality Control: Jodeph Sica
Marketing: Tom Lichon
Sales: Tom Lichon
Estimated Sales:$ 20 - 50 Million
Number Employees: 20-49
Number of Brands: 1

Number of Products: 1000
Sq. footage: 16000
Type of Packaging: Consumer, Food Service, Private Label, Bulk
Brands:
Pasta Factory

8740 MB Candies
Alternate Route 250
Bridgeport, IL 62417 618-945-7778
888-MBC-ANDY
makinbatch@hotmail.com www.makinbatch.com
Manufacturer of quality hard candy including sugar free varities.
Estimated Sales: $ 1-5 Million
Number Employees: 5-9

8741 (HQ)MBM Corporation
P.O.Box 800
Rocky Mount, NC 27802-0800 252-985-7200
Fax: 252-985-7241 www.mbmfoodservice.com
Processor and exporter of custom cut pork
President: Jerry Wordsworth
Business Development Director: Dennis Parent
Agent: Mitch Brantley
Estimated Sales: $100+ Million
Number Employees: 500-999
Type of Packaging: Consumer, Food Service
Other Locations:
MBM Corp.
Fort Worth TX

8742 MD Foods Ingredients
2840 Morris Avenue
Union, NJ 07083-4851 908-964-4420
Fax: 908-964-6270 800-972-2096
kbolland@earthlink.net
Dairy based ingredients, seasonings, binders and extenders, fat reduced meats, fat replacers, flavor enhancers

8743 MD Labs
3925 E Watkins Street
Suite 200
Phoenix, AZ 85034-8219 602-437-0127
Fax: 602-437-0755 mdlabs@mdlabs.com
www.mdlabs.com
Processor and exporter of decaffeinated and detoxing herbal teas, extracts and capsules
President: Hooman Nikzad
Estimated Sales: $7990930
Number Employees: 26
Sq. footage: 15000
Type of Packaging: Consumer, Food Service, Private Label, Bulk
Brands:
Daily Detox
Daily Detox Ii
Daily Klean
Herbalpathic
Naturally Klean

8744 ME Franks
175 Strafford Ave # 230
Wayne, PA 19087-3333 610-989-9688
Fax: 610-989-8989 www.mefranks.com
M.E. Franks specializes in manufactured milk products such as: non-fat dry milk, whole milk powder, whey powder, whey protein concentrates, functional milk fractions, lactose, buttermilk powder, anhydrous milk fat, cheese, whole milkpowder, casien and caseinates.
President: Don Street
Estimated Sales: $ 10-25 Million
Number Employees: 5-9

8745 MEYENBERG Goat Milk Products
PO Box 934
Turlock, CA 95381-0934 209-634-2731
Fax: 209-668-4753 800-891-4628
info@meyenberg.com www.meyenberg.com
Processor and exporter of goat's milk including evaporated, powdered, and fresh, butter, and goat cheese.
President: Robert Jackson
COO/Marketing: Tracy Plante-Darrimon
Plant Manager: Frank Fillman
Estimated Sales: $18-20 Million
Number Employees: 50
Number of Products: 25
Type of Packaging: Consumer, Bulk

Brands:
MEYENBERG
PROFESSIONAL PREFERENCE

8746 MG Fisheries
PO Box 909
Grand Manan, NB E5G 4M1
Canada 506-662-3471
Fax: 506-662-3779
Products include sea urchin, scallops, shark, monkfish, flounder, pollock-dried, cod-dried, pollock-salted, hake-dried, hake-salted, lobster-live, and cod-salted.
President: Morris Green
Number Employees: 10-19
Type of Packaging: Consumer, Food Service

8747 MGP
100 Commercial St., Cray Business Plz
P.O. Box 130
Atchinson, KS 66002-0130 913-367-1480
Fax: 913-367-0192 www.mgpingredients.com
www.mgpingredients.com
Supplier of dry powders used as binders in chicken patties, meat, and vegetarian burgers.
President, CEO: Tim Newkirk

8748 MGP Ingredients, Inc.
Cray Business Plaza
100 Commercial St., P.O. Box 130
Atchinson, KS 66002-0130 913-367-1480
Fax: 913-367-0192 800-255-0302
www.mgpingredients.com
Process starches and specialty wheat proteins for food and non-food applications.
President/CEO: Tim Newkirk
Number Employees: 195

8749 MIC Foods
8701 SW 137th Avenue
306-308
Miami, FL 33183-4078 786-507-0540
Fax: 786-507-0545 800-788-9335
info@micfood.com www.micfood.com/
Processor and importer of frozen plaintains, yuca, cassava and frozen fruit products.
Marketing VP: Alfredo Lardizabal
Sales VP: Maria Krogh
Estimated Sales: $ 5 - 10 Million
Number Employees: 5-9
Brands:
Big Banana
Costa Clara
Tio Jorge

8750 MJ Barleyhoppers
3030 N Rocky Point Dr W # 820
Tampa, FL 33607-6062 813-287-0907
Fax: 813-282-8158 mjbarleyhoppers@msn.com
www.mjbarleyhoppers.com
Processor of ale, stout and lager
President: Dilip Kanji
General Manager: Jack Noble
Estimated Sales: $ .5 - 1 million
Number Employees: 1-4
Parent Co: Impact Restaurants
Type of Packaging: Consumer, Food Service
Brands:
Oktoberfest

8751 MLO/GeniSoy Products Company
100 W. 5h Street
Suite 700
Tulas, OK 74103 866-606-3829
Fax: 918-278-2850 info@genisoy.com
www.genisoy.com
Powdered beverage mixes, protein bars, sports nutrition products and soy protein bars
President: Tim Bruer
Marketing: Rich Martin
Plant Manager: Jeff Amlin
Estimated Sales: $ .5 - 1 million
Number Employees: 1-4

8752 MNH Erickson Ranch
3916 County Road Mm
Orland, CA 95963-9702 530-865-9587
Fax: 530-865-8637
Co-Owner: Heidi Erickson
Co-Owner: Merritt Erickson

8753 MO Air International
183 Madison Avenue
Suite 1202
New York, NY 10016 212-792-9400
Fax: 212-490-1763 800-247-3131
reservation@moair.com www.moair-usa.com
Manager: Sherry Kawabe

8754 MPK Sonama Corporation
21707 8th Street E
Sonoma, CA 95476-9781 707-996-3931
Fax: 707-996-3999 ginger@mpksonoma.com
www.mpksonoma.com
Sauces, dressings, specialty foods
President: Charles Boles
Plant Manager: Todd Pimentel
Estimated Sales: $ 5-10 Million
Number Employees: 15
Type of Packaging: Private Label

8755 MPK Sonoma Company
21707 8th Street E
Sonoma, CA 95476-9781 707-996-3931
Fax: 707-996-3999
Frozen garlic and ginger, dressings, sauces, dessert toppings, specialty products
President: Charles Boles
Estimated Sales: $ 5 - 10 Million
Number Employees: 5-9
Brands:
Charles Premium
Marinpak

8756 MSRF
2501 N Elston Ave
Chicago, IL 60647-2003 773-227-1115
Fax: 773-227-2031 snejman@msrf.com
Gourmet food gifts
President: David Reich
Estimated Sales: $10-15 Million
Number Employees: 10-19
Brands:
MSRF

8757 MYNTZ!
PO Box 48278
Seattle, WA 98148-0278 253-395-0401
Fax: 253-395-0402 jjabbott@vitechamerica.com
www.myntz.com
MYNTZ! is a confection company that manufactures, packages and distributes up-scale consumer breath mints in a variety of flavors that include vanillamyntblast sugar-free, tropical fruit and orchard fruit.
President/CEO: David Parker
National Sales Director: Robert Kingsley
Customer Service: Diana Klein
Number Employees: 50-99
Brands:
DROPZ
MYNTZ! BREATH MINTS
MYNTZ! INSTASTRIPZ
MYNTZ! LIP BALM
SQYNTZ! SUPERSOURZ

8758 Maat Nutritionals
1875 Century Park E
6th Floor
Los Angeles, CA 90067-2501 310-407-8608
Fax: 310-407-8618 888-818-6228
info@e-maat.com www.e-maat.com
Dietary supplements, vitamins and minerals
President: Rick Mandell

8759 Mac's Donut Shop
P.O.Box 1172
Aliquippa, PA 15001-6172 724-375-6776
Fax: 724-378-2961
Processor of baked goods including doughnuts, cakes, pastries, cookies, muffins, brownies, etc
Owner: Twila Mc Kittrick
VP: Twila McKittrick
Estimated Sales: $1100000
Number Employees: 20-49
Type of Packaging: Consumer

8760 Mac's Farms Sausage Company
P.O.Box 190
Newton Grove, NC 28366-0190 910-594-0095
Fax: 910-594-1812 macfarms@intrstar.net
Sausage, air dried medium and hot, fresh link, fresh patty
Owner: Scott Mc Lamb
CEO: Scott McLamb

Estimated Sales: $700,000
Number Employees: 5-9
Type of Packaging: Bulk
Brands:
    Double D
    Mac's

8761 Mac's Meats Wholesale
1761 W Hadley Ave
Las Cruces, NM 88005-4122   575-524-2751
                                   Fax: 575-526-3826
Processor of meat including pork and beef
    President: Al Guerrero
Estimated Sales: $ 10 - 20 Million
Number Employees: 5-9
Type of Packaging: Consumer, Food Service

8762 Mac's Oysters
Site 7, C2
Fanny Bay, BC V0R 1W0
Canada   250-335-2233
    Fax: 250-335-2065 gordy@macsoysters.com
                       www.macsoysters.com
Processor of clams and fresh shucked oysters
    Managing Director: Gordon McLellan
    General Managaer: Sally Kew
Number Employees: 50-99
Type of Packaging: Consumer, Food Service, Private Label, Bulk

8763 Mac's Snacks
615 N Great Southwest Pkwy
Arlington, TX 76011-5465   817-640-5626
    Fax: 817-649-7832 sales@evansfoods.com
                       www.macssnacks.com
Pork skins and cracklings
    VP: Jim Speake
    Operations Manager: Brad Bothe
Estimated Sales: $ 10-20 Million
Number Employees: 20-49
Parent Co: Evans Food Products
Type of Packaging: Private Label, Bulk

8764 MacDonald Honey Company
RR 2
Box 41
Sauquoit, NY 13456   315-737-5662
Processor of honey
    President: Jon MacDonald
    Owner: Jon MacDonald
Type of Packaging: Consumer, Food Service, Private Label, Bulk
Brands:
    Johnny Mac's

8765 MacEwan's Meats
17 9620 Elbow Drive SW
Calgary, AB T2V 1M2
Canada   403-228-9999
                              Fax: 403-228-9999
Processor of meat pies including chicken, steak and scotch
    President: John Hopkins
    VP: Lynne Hopkins
    Marketing Director: John Hopkins
    Director: John Hopkins
Number Employees: 1-4
Sq. footage: 1500
Type of Packaging: Consumer, Food Service, Bulk
Brands:
    MacEwan's

8766 MacFarlane Pheasants
2821 S Us Highway 51
Janesville, WI 53546-8945   608-757-7881
    Fax: 608-757-7884 877-269-8957
    info@pheasant.com www.pheasant.com
Producer of high quality, young, pheasants; available fresh, frozen, smoked as whole birds or cut down sized products.
    Owner: Bill Mac Farlane
    CFO: Brad Lillie
    Sales: Mary Jo Bergs
    Shipping Manager: David Lennox
    Plant Manager: Bryan Carter
Estimated Sales: $ 1 - 3 Million
Sq. footage: 5000
Type of Packaging: Food Service

8767 MacFarms of Hawaii
89-406 Mamalahoa Hwy
Captain Cook, HI 96704-8941   808-328-2435
    Fax: 808-328-8081 sales@macfarms.com
                       www.macfarms.com

Processor and exporter of chocolate covered macadamia nuts and macadamia nut cookies
    President: Jeff Gilbrech
    VP Sales: Brian Loader
    Manager: Rick Vigden
Estimated Sales: $ 20 - 50 Million
Number Employees: 100-249
Parent Co: Blue Diamond Growers
Type of Packaging: Consumer, Private Label, Bulk
Brands:
    Macfarms of Hawaii

8768 MacGregors Meat & Seafood
265 Garyray Drive
Toronto, ON M9L 1P2
Canada   416-749-5951
    Fax: 416-740-3230 800-268-5953
    graham@macgregors.com www.macgregors.com
Processor of poultry, seafood and meat products; importer of beef and seafood
    CEO: D MacGregor
    Controller/Treasurer: Ed de Vries
Number Employees: 180
Sq. footage: 46000
Brands:
    Macgregors
    Steak King

8769 MacKay's Cochrane Ice Cream
PO Box 250
Cochrane, AB T4C 1A5
Canada   403-932-2455
                              Fax: 403-932-2455
    generalinfo@mackaysicecream.com
           www.mackaysicecream.com
Processor of ice cream, frozen yogurt, sherbet and sorbet
    Manager: Robyn MacKay
    Production Manager: Rhona Mackay
Number Employees: 20-49
Type of Packaging: Consumer, Food Service
Brands:
    Mackay's

8770 MacKinlay Teas
1289 Waterways Dr
Ann Arbor, MI 48108-2783   734-747-9012
    Fax: 734-747-9193 sales@mackinlay.com
                       www.mackinlay.com
Processor of teas; private label packaging is available to selected customers.
    President: Davinder Singh
Estimated Sales: $2.9 Million
Number Employees: 1-4
Type of Packaging: Private Label
Brands:
    MacKinlay Tea's
    Queen Jasmine
    White Tiger Rice
    Wild Blend Rice

8771 MacKnight Smoked Foods
550 NE 185th St
Miami, FL 33179-4513   305-655-0444
    Fax: 305-655-0039 www.macknight.com
Processor and importer of smoked and fresh fish
    President: Jonathan Brown
    General Manager: Alex McMorran
    Plant Manager: Jim Kahlee
Estimated Sales: $ 10 - 20 Million
Number Employees: 20-49
Sq. footage: 10000
Type of Packaging: Consumer, Food Service, Private Label, Bulk

8772 Macabee Foods
140 W Commercial Avenue
Moonachie, NJ 07074-1703   201-489-4343
                              Fax: 201-489-4344
Processor of kosher frozen pizza
    President: Marvin Kochansky
    VP: Jeffery Schmelzer
Number Employees: 5-9
Sq. footage: 4000
Type of Packaging: Consumer, Food Service, Private Label
Brands:
    Macabee

8773 Macco Organiques
100 Rue Mc Arthur
Valleyfield, QC J6S 4M5
Canada   450-371-1066
    Fax: 450-371-5519 macco@maccoca
                       www.macco.ca
Processor and exporter of food preservatives including: calcium acetate; calcium chloride dihy; calcium propionate; potassium acetate; potassium benzoate; sodium acetate anh; sodium benzoate; sodium diacetate; and sodium propionate.
    VP: Jacques Rochon
    Logistics Manager: Simon Rinella
Number Employees: 50-99

8774 Machias Bay Seafood
503 Kennebec Rd
Machias, ME 04654-3449   207-255-8671
                              Fax: 207-255-8243
Seafood
    Owner: Randy Ramsdell
Estimated Sales: $ 1 - 3 Million
Number Employees: 1-4

8775 Mack's Homemade Ice Cream
2731 S Queen St
York, PA 17403-9703   717-741-2027
    Fax: 717-747-0065 www.macksicecream.com
Processor of ice cream
    President: Walter Bloss
Estimated Sales: $ 1 - 3 Million
Number Employees: 20-49
Type of Packaging: Consumer

8776 Mack's Packing
506 E Annabella Rd
Richfield, UT 84701-7085   435-896-4447
Packer of meat products including beef, lamb and pork
    CEO: Jeff Cohen
Estimated Sales: $500,000-$1 Million
Number Employees: 5-9
Type of Packaging: Consumer, Bulk

8777 Mackie International
1900 S Tubeway Ave
Commerce, CA 90040-1612   323-722-0772
    Fax: 323-722-0681 800-733-9762
                       www.mackieinternational.net
Processor of ice pops, fruit flavored drinks and jellies
    President: Ernesto Dacay
    General Manager: Gary Munro
Estimated Sales: $4900000
Number Employees: 50-99
Sq. footage: 60000
Type of Packaging: Private Label, Bulk
Brands:
    Berry Cool
    Snowtime

8778 Macrie Brothers
610 S 1st Rd
Hammonton, NJ 08037-8406   609-561-6822
    Fax: 609-561-6296 bluebuck@bellatlantic.net
                       www.blueblueberries.com
Blueberries
    Owner: Paul Macrie Iii
    CEO: Paul Macrie III
    Operations: Nicholas Macrie
    Production: Michael Macrie
Estimated Sales: Below $ 5 Million
Number Employees: 250-499
Sq. footage: 30000
Type of Packaging: Consumer, Food Service, Private Label, Bulk
Brands:
    Blue Buck

8779 Mad Chef Enterprise
PO Box 321
Mentor, OH 44061-0321   440-951-0846
    Fax: 440-269-2387 800-951-2433
    info@madchef.com www.madchef.com
Products include sauces, seasonings, rubs. Additional products include aprons, grilling mitts, basting brushes, grill lighters, spatulas, grilling baskets, salt & pepper mills, skewers, and mugs.
    President: Michael D'Amico

8780 Mad River Brewing
P.O.Box 767
Blue Lake, CA 95525-0767 707-668-4151
Fax: 707-668-4297 sales@madriverbrewing.com
www.madriverbrewing.com
Beer
President: Robert Smith
CFO: Arlene Rich
Master Brewer: Bob Smith
Estimated Sales: Below $ 5 Million
Number Employees: 20-49

8781 Mad River Farm
100 Ericson Ct # 140
Arcata, CA 95521-8940 707-822-0248
Fax: 707-822-4441 calnorth@humboldt1.com
www.mad-river-farm.com
Mad River Farms produces gourmet food products
such as sunshine marmalade, lemon marmalade,
plum orange jam with brandied raisins and wild
huckleberry jam.
Owner: Marika Mrick
Vice President: Steven Ulrich
Estimated Sales: Below $ 5 Million
Number Employees: 1-4
Number of Brands: 1
Number of Products: 25
Sq. footage: 1000
Type of Packaging: Consumer, Food Service, Private Label, Bulk
Brands:
Mad River Farm

8782 Mad Will's Food Company
2043 Airpark Ct # 30
Auburn, CA 95602-9009 530-823-8527
Fax: 530-823-1756 888-275-9455
orders@madwills.com www.madwills.com
Manufacturer of barbecue sauces, salsas, salad
dressings, mustards, marinades, marinara sauces, hot
sauces, other sauces and specialty food sauces; private label and contract packaging
President: Kim Sullivan
Marketing Director: Tim Sullivan
Operations Manager: Roy Ballard
Purchasing Manager: Jane Demohusado
Estimated Sales: $2700000
Number Employees: 20-49
Number of Products: 70
Type of Packaging: Private Label

8783 Mada'n Kosher Foods
130 SW 3rd Ave
Dania, FL 33004-3656 954-925-0077
Fax: 954-921-8739 info@madankosher.com
www.madankosher.com
Processor of frozen kosher foods including beef, fish
and poultry
President: Samuel Weiss
VP: Richard Marsico
Director Operations: Richard Anthony
Estimated Sales: $210000
Number Employees: 10-19
Sq. footage: 3500
Parent Co: Mada'n Corporation
Type of Packaging: Consumer, Food Service

8784 Made Rite Foods
2229 Sunnybrook Drive
Burlington, NC 27215-4856 336-288-6646
Fax: 336-545-1880
Processor of salads and sandwiches
President: Jerry McMasters
Plant Manager: Alan Harder
Number Employees: 100-249
Parent Co: Made Rite Foods
Type of Packaging: Consumer, Food Service, Private Label, Bulk
Brands:
Made Rite
Sedgefield

8785 Made in Nature
2500 S Fowler Avenue
Fresno, CA 95472-4848 559-445-8601
Fax: 559-445-8601 800-906-7426
info@sonomawestholdings.com
www.madeinnature.com
Organic dried fruits and vegetables
President: Gary Hess
Marketing Manager: Ren Lawrence
Operations: Kimberly Musgrove
Estimated Sales: $ 2.5-5 Million
Number Employees: 10

Brands:
Made In Nature

8786 Made-Rite Sandwich Company
P.O.Box 27
Ooltewah, TN 37363-0027 423-238-5492
Fax: 423-238-5844 800-343-1327
info@GreatAmericanDeli.com
www.greatamericandeli.com
Products include sandwiches, cakes, Hot 2 Go sandwiches, burritos, pocket sandwiches and rollergrill
products.
President: Earl R Sullivan
VP: Steven Corley
Plant Manager: Nelson Shiver
Estimated Sales: $ 10-20 Million
Number Employees: 100-249
Parent Co: Great American Deli

8787 Madelaine Chocolate Novelties, Inc
9603 Beach Channel Dr
Far Rockaway, NY 11693-1398 718-945-1500
Fax: 718-318-4607 800-322-1505
www.madelainechocolate.com
Manufacturers of gourmet chocolate, foiled shapes
for every day and every season; also chocolate covered nuts, fruit and speciality centers. Private labeling. Certified kosher.
President/CFO: Norman Gold
Chairman/CEO: Jorge Farber
Quality Control: Scott Wright
Number Employees: 250-499
Number of Brands: 2
Number of Products: 2000
Sq. footage: 200000
Type of Packaging: Private Label, Bulk
Brands:
MADELAINE CHOCOLATE

8788 Madera Enterprises
32565 Avenue 9
Madera, CA 93636-8346 559-431-1444
Fax: 559-674-8214 800-507-9555
maderaent@aol.com
Processor and exporter of custom fruit juice concentrates and purees including grape, apple, strawberry,
plum, prune, date, raisin, pomegranate, etc.; also,
dried fruits and vinaigrettes
President: Susan Nury
Marketing: Rosanna Andrews-White
Estimated Sales: $ 3 - 5 Million
Number Employees: 5-9
Type of Packaging: Bulk
Brands:
Mina
Zary

8789 (HQ)Madhava Honey
4689 Ute Hwy
Longmont, CO 80503-9127 303-444-7999
Fax: 303-823-5755 800-530-2900
info@madhavahoney.com
www.madhavahoney.com
Processor and exporter of Rocky Mountain honey,
pollen and beeswax
President: Craig Gerbore
Plant Foreman: Harry Hasty
Estimated Sales: $9 Million
Number Employees: 1-4
Sq. footage: 6000
Type of Packaging: Consumer, Food Service, Private Label, Bulk
Other Locations:
Madhava Honey
Parachute CO
Brands:
AGAVE NECTAR
AMBROSIA HONEY
MOUNTAIN GOLD HONEY

8790 Madhouse Munchies
PO Box 946
Colchester, VT 05446-0946 888-623-4687
Fax: 802-655-7711
info@madhousemunchies.com
www.madhousemunchies.com
Low-fat, hand-cooked potato chips
President: J Ehlen
Sales/Marketing Associate: Eric Bleckner
Estimated Sales: $ 740000
Number Employees: 10
Brands:
Madhouse Munchies

8791 Madison Dairy Produce Company
1002 E Washington Ave
Madison, WI 53703-2939 608-256-5561
Fax: 608-256-0985 gstein@maddairy.com
Processor of butter and margarine
Manager: Bob Gettel
VP Sales: Gary Steinhauer
Estimated Sales: $32400000
Number Employees: 50-99
Type of Packaging: Consumer, Food Service, Private Label
Brands:
Creamery Blend
Deerfield
Lady Lee
Red Rose
Roundys

8792 Madison Foods
238 Chester St
St Paul, MN 55107-1207 651-265-8212
Fax: 651-297-6286
Processor of butter substitutes; also, contract
packager of retail and food service sauces
President: Steve Anderson
Estimated Sales: $ .5 - 1 million
Number Employees: 1-4
Type of Packaging: Consumer, Food Service, Private Label, Bulk
Brands:
Better

8793 Madison Vineyard
Hc 72 Box 490
Ribera, NM 87560-9706 575-421-8028
Fax: 575-421-8028 www.madison-winery.com
Wines
Owner: Bill Madison
Owner: Elise Madison
Estimated Sales: $500,000-$1 Million
Number Employees: 1-4

8794 Madonna Estate Mont St John
5400 Old Sonoma Rd
Napa, CA 94559-9708 707-255-8864
Fax: 707-257-2778 mail@madonnaestate.com
www.madonnaestate.com
Wines include Chardonnay, Pinot Noir, Due
Ragazze, Pinot Noir Riserva, Merlot, Cabernet Sauvignon.
President: Andrea Bartolucci
Marketing: Ron Arata
Public Relations: Brette Bartolucci
Vineyard Manager: Andrea Bartolucci
Estimated Sales: $ 2.5-5 Million
Number Employees: 5-9
Brands:
Madonna Estate Mont St John
Poppy Hill

8795 Madrange
85 Division Avenue
Millington, NJ 07946-1316 908-647-6485
Fax: 908-646-8305 mkessler@charter.net
www.fromartharie.com/
Products include cooked hams, goat cheese, dips,
butter, and pates/mousse.
President: Ron Schinbeckler
Vice President: Richard Kessler
Number Employees: 10-19
Type of Packaging: Private Label, Bulk

8796 Madrona Vineyards
PO Box 454
Camino, CA 95709-0454 530-644-5948
Fax: 530-644-7517
winery@madronavineyards.com
www.madronavineyards.com
Products include white wines, red wines, reserve
wines and dessert wines.
President: Richard Bush
Estimated Sales: Below $ 5 Million
Number Employees: 20
Type of Packaging: Consumer

8797 Madys Company
1555 Yosemite Ave
San Francisco, CA 94124-3268 415-822-2227
Fax: 415-822-3673 support@madys.com
www.madys.com

Processor, importer, exporter and wholesaler/distributor of herbal, medicinal and regular teas; also, vitamins, ginseng root, etc
Owner: Sandy Su Wing
General Manager: Marian Hong
Number Employees: 10-19
Sq. footage: 3400
Parent Co: Azeta Brands
Type of Packaging: Consumer, Food Service, Private Label, Bulk
Brands:
Butterfly
Evergreen
Madys
Weiloss

8798 Maebo Noodle Factory
711 W Kawailani St
Hilo, HI 96720-3155   808-959-8763
Fax: 808-959-4404 877-663-8667
sales@one-ton.com www.one-ton.com
Processor of Chinese foods including noodles, wonton chips and saimin
President/Manager: Blane Maebo
VP: Rachel Maebo
Estimated Sales: $550000
Number Employees: 10-19
Type of Packaging: Consumer, Bulk
Brands:
Maebo Noodle Factory, Inc.

8799 Mafco Natural Products
4400 Williamsburg Ave
Richmond, VA 23231-1210   804-222-1600
Fax: 804-226-6325
Manufacturer of herbal powders and teas; also recently added a line of fruit teas.
Manager: Linda Deane
Customer Service: Phyllis Grigg
Estimated Sales: $8200000
Number Employees: 10-19

8800 Mafco Worldwide Corporation
300 Jefferson St
Camden, NJ 08104-2113   856-964-8840
Fax: 856-964-6029
magnasweet@mafcolicorice.com
www.mafcolicorice.com
Manufacturers of licorice
CEO: Stephen Taub
Sales Manager: Jeffrey Robinson
Number Employees: 100-249

8801 Maggie Gin's
127 10th Avenue
San Francisco, CA 94118-1126   415-221-6080
Fax: 415-221-1197 mgin@aol.com
www.goldenwestsf.com
Sauces, marinades
Number Employees: 1-4
Parent Co: Golden West Specialty Foods
Type of Packaging: Private Label
Brands:
Chinese Chicken Salad Dressing
Thai Sauce
Traditional Stir Fry Sauce

8802 Maggie Lyon Chocolatiers
6000 Peachtree Industrial # B
Norcross, GA 30071-1374   770-446-1299
Fax: 770-446-2191 800-969-3500
sales@maggielyon.com
www.sweetinnovations.com
Products include gourmet chocolates, truffles, toffee, caramels, bark and nut clusters, toffee, special occasion and gift baskets, easter selections, bulk chocolates, and promotional products.
President: Jeffery Pollack
VP: Michael Pollack
Estimated Sales: Below $ 5 Million
Number Employees: 20-49
Type of Packaging: Private Label
Brands:
CONNIE'S HANDMADE TOFFEE

8803 Maggie's Salsa
1303 Turley Rd
Charleston, WV 25314   304-550-5460
Fax: 304-881-0289 maggie@maggiesalsa.com
www.maggiesalsa.com
salsa
President/Owner: Maggie Cook

8804 Maggiora Baking Company
1900 Garden Tract Road
Richmond, CA 94801-1219   510-235-0274
Fax: 510-235-2427 info@maggiorabaking.com
www.maggiorabaking.com
Products include sourdoughs, french breads, focaccia, bread sticks, pesto dinner roll clusters, garlic rounds, Hawaiian bread/dinner rolls, Greek rings, egg bread and dinner rolls, and various specialty breads.
President: Dennis Maggiora
Sales Director: Robert Maggiora
General Manager: Don Maggiora
Estimated Sales: $ 5-10 Million
Number Employees: 75

8805 Magic Gumball International
9310 Mason Ave
Chatsworth, CA 91311-5201   818-716-1888
Fax: 818-341-4234 800-576-2020
info@magicgumball.com
www.magicgumball.com
Candy
Owner: Guy Hart
VP: Guy Hat
Estimated Sales: $ 5 - 10 Million
Number Employees: 50-99

8806 Magic Ice Products
1005 E Oak St
Stockton, CA 95205   209-464-8832
Fax: 209-464-0750 800-776-7923
magiciceproducts@attglobal.net
www.magiciceproducts.com
Processor and exporter of gourmet coffee flavor, slush and ice syrups; importer of shave ice machines and equipment
President: Shirley Weist
Warehouse Manager: Stan Heim
Estimated Sales: $1000000
Number Employees: 5-9
Type of Packaging: Consumer, Food Service, Private Label
Brands:
Flavor Magic
Magic Ice

8807 Magic Seasoning Blends
P.O.Box 23342
Harahan, LA 70123   504-731-3590
Fax: 504-731-3576 800-457-2857
info@chefpaul.com www.chefpaul.com
Dry blending in a AIB Superior rated facility. R&D is under the supervision of Chef Paul Prudhomme. 20 years of custom blending experience. Store brands & co-pack a specialty. Contact Camille Collins, Director of Business Developmentccollins@chefpaul.com
President: Shawn Mc Bride
CEO: Shawn McBride
CFO: Paula LaCour
VP: John McBride
R&D: Sean OMeara
Quality Control: Jake Wanda
Marketing: John McBride
Sales Manager: Gregg Villarrubia
Operations Manager: Jeff Hanson
Production Manager: John Alexander
Plant Manager: David Hickey
Purchasing Director: Patricia Cantrelle
Estimated Sales: $ 20 - 50 Million
Number Employees: 50-99
Number of Brands: 3
Number of Products: 29
Sq. footage: 125000
Type of Packaging: Consumer, Food Service, Private Label, Bulk
Brands:
BARBECUE MAGIC
BLACKENED REDFISH MAGIC
BLACKENED STEAK MAGIC
BREADING MAGIC
GRAVY & GUMBO MAGIC
MAGIC PEPPER SAUCE
MAGIC SAUCE & MARINADES
MEAT MAGIC
PIZZA & PASTA MAGIC
PORK & VEAL MAGIC
POULTRY MAGIC
SALMON MAGIC
SEAFOOD MAGIC
SHRIMP MAGIC
SWEETFREE MAGIC
VEGETABLE MAGIC

8808 (HQ)Magic Valley Foods
800 S 9th St
Rupert, ID 83350-9120   208-436-3126
Fax: 208-436-4542 bhuizinga@mr-spud.com
www.mr-spud.com
Processed potatoes-dehydrated and frozen. Also fresh packed potatoes
President: Roger Jones
CFO: William Schow
Marketing: Corey Smith
VP Sales: Bruce Huizinga
Plant Manager: Chuck Tracy
Purchasing Manager: Jerry Grace
Estimated Sales: $ 45 Million
Number Employees: 10-19
Type of Packaging: Consumer, Food Service, Private Label, Bulk
Brands:
Dutch Boilers
Dutchgirl
Idaho Natrually
Magic Valley
Mr. Spud
Top Hat

8809 Magic Valley Fresh Frozen
2100 Trophy Dr
McAllen, TX 78504-4132   956-618-1251
Fax: 956-994-8948
Frozen butter beans, carrots, greens, okra, onions, southern peas
Manager: Ben Bellarrel
Operations Manager: George Calhoon
Estimated Sales: $100+ Million
Number Employees: 100-249

8810 Magic Valley Growers
375 W Avenue D
Wendell, ID 83355   208-536-6693
Fax: 208-536-6695
onions@magicvalleygrowers.com
www.magicvalleygrowers.com
Grower and packer of specialty onions including pearl, boiler, peeled pearl and sets; exporter of pearl and boiler onions
Owner: Robert Reitveld
Marketing/Sales: George Bobango
Estimated Sales: $1,400,000
Number Employees: 20-49
Sq. footage: 53100
Type of Packaging: Consumer, Private Label, Bulk
Brands:
Dutch Boiler
Dutch Girl
Top Hat

8811 Magic Valley Quality Milk Producers
1756 S Buchanan St
Jerome, ID 83338-6146   208-324-7519
Fax: 208-324-7554 mvqmp@lightcom.net
Cooperative selling raw milk to food processors
General Manager: Alan Stutzman
Estimated Sales: $ .5 - 1 million
Number Employees: 1-4

8812 Magna Foods Corporation
16010 Phoenix Drive
City of Industry, CA 91745-1623   626-336-7500
Fax: 626-336-3999 800-995-4394
magnafoods@aol.com
Processor and exporter of confectionery, candy, cookies, crackers and cocoa products
President: Yogi Atmadja
VP: Peter Surjadinata
Estimated Sales: $1500000
Number Employees: 25
Sq. footage: 5000
Parent Co: IBIS
Brands:
Coffeego
Danisa
Roma Marie

8813 Magnanini Winery
172 Strawridge Rd
Wallkill, NY 12589-3905   845-895-2767
Fax: 845-895-9458 www.magwine.com
Wines
Owner: Richard Magnanini
CEO: Galba Magnanini
Estimated Sales: $500,000-$1 Million
Number Employees: 1-4

Type of Packaging: Private Label

8814 Magnetic Springs Water Company
1917 Joyce Ave
Columbus, OH 43219-1029   614-421-1780
          Fax: 614-421-1681   800-572-2990
          www.magneticsprings.com
Processor of drinking, distilled, spring, artesian and infant water
          President: Jeff Allison
          Plant Manager: Tim VanSickle
Estimated Sales: $11900000
Number Employees: 50-99
Sq. footage: 100000
Type of Packaging: Consumer, Food Service, Private Label, Bulk
Brands:
          Magnetic Springs

8815 Magnificent Muffin Corporation
64 Toledo St
Farmingdale, NY 11735-6628   631-454-8022
          Fax: 631-454-8574
Muffins and baked goods
          President: John Schreckinger
Estimated Sales: Below $150,000
Number Employees: 1-4
Type of Packaging: Consumer, Bulk

8816 Magnolia Beef Company
P.O.Box 220
Elizabeth, NJ 07207-0220   908-352-9412
          Fax: 908-352-1576
Processor of beef, veal, lamb and pork
          Owner: Manny Dasilva
Estimated Sales: $6300000
Number Employees: 10-19
Type of Packaging: Food Service, Bulk

8817 Magnolia Citrus Association
1014 E Teapot Dome Ave
Porterville, CA 93257-9766   559-784-4455
          Fax: 559-781-9182
Processor, packer and exporter of Valencia and navel oranges
          Manager: Dominick Arcure
          Manager: Larry Fultz
          Sales: Dominick Arcure
Estimated Sales: $ 10 - 20 Million
Number Employees: 20-49
Type of Packaging: Private Label, Bulk
Brands:
          Magnolia
          Malta
          Memory

8818 Magnolia Meats
1904 Kings Hwy
Shreveport, LA 71103-3693   318-221-2814
Processor of beef, pork and chicken
          President: E Dean
Estimated Sales: $ 3 - 5 Million
Number Employees: 5-9
Type of Packaging: Consumer, Food Service, Bulk

8819 (HQ)Magnotta Winery Corporation
271 Chrislea Road
Woodbridge, ON L4L 8N6
Canada   905-738-9463
          Fax: 905-738-5551   800-461-9463
          mailbox@magnotta.com   www.magnotta.com
Manufacturer, retailer, and exporter of beer, spirits and juice for home winemaking
          CFO: Rossana Magnotta
          CEO: Rossana Magnotta
Number Employees: 99
Sq. footage: 60000
Type of Packaging: Consumer
Other Locations:
          Magnotta Winery Corp.
          Scarborough ON
Brands:
          Magnotta

8820 Magnum Coffee Roastery
16800 Java Blvd
Nunica, MI 49448   616-837-0333
          Fax: 616-837-0777   888-937-5282
          sales@magnumcoffee.com
          www.magnumcoffee.com

Provides a full range of coffee roasting and quality packaging services.
          President: Kevin Kihnke
Estimated Sales: $ 2.5-5 Million
Number Employees: 20-49
Type of Packaging: Private Label
Brands:
          Island Trader
          Magnum Exotic

8821 Mah Chena Company
1416 W Ohio St
Chicago, IL 60642-7156   312-226-5100
          Fax: 312-277-7170
Chinese frozen foods
          President: Heather Shadur
          Sales Manager: Jeffrey Hoffman
          Plant Manager: Willis Yee
Number Employees: 10-19

8822 Mahantongo Game Farms
559 Flying Eagle Rd
Dalmatia, PA 17017-7003   570-758-6284
Processor and exporter of game birds including pheasants and partridges
          President: Lynn Laudenslager
Estimated Sales: $360000
Number Employees: 20-49

8823 Maharishi Ayurveda Products International
1068 Elkton Dr
Colorado Springs, CO 80907-3538   719-260-5500
          Fax: 719-260-7400   800-255-8332
          questions@mapi.com   www.mapi.com
Processor and importer of herbs and herbal products including teas, supplements and seasonings
          President: Prakash Srivastava
          Senior VP: Steven Barthe
          Marketing Director: Russ Guest
          Public Relations: Marsha Bonne
          Operations Manager: Kevin Olson
          Plant Manager: Kishore Nareundkar
Estimated Sales: $280000
Number Employees: 50-99
Number of Brands: 4
Number of Products: 600
Sq. footage: 47000
Type of Packaging: Consumer
Brands:
          Ayurveda
          Clarified Butter
          Maharishi
          Yata, Pilta, Kapha Teas

8824 Maher Marketing Services
1616 Corporate Ct # 140
Irving, TX 75038-2209   972-751-7700
          Fax: 972-751-7777   mmaher@mahermark.com
          www.mahermark.com
Products include imported and domestic cheeses, dairy products, frozen entrees, specialty snacks, crackers and cookies.
          President: Dan Vines
          CEO: Mike Maher
          CFO: Anne Maher
          Marketing Manager: April Tieken
Estimated Sales: $ 5-10 Million appx.
Number Employees: 5-9
Type of Packaging: Bulk

8825 Mahoning Swiss Cheese Cooperative
24062 Route 954 Highway N
Smicksburg, PA 16256-3428   814-257-8884
          Fax: 724-286-9259
Cheese and butter
          President: John Schablach
          Plant Manager: Ralph Juart
Estimated Sales: Below $ 5 Million
Number Employees: 10

8826 Maid-Rite Steak Company
P.O.Box 509
Dunmore, PA 18512-0509   570-343-4748
          Fax: 570-969-2878   800-233-4259
          customerservice@maidritesteak.com
          www.maidritesteak.com

Processor and exporter of frozen portion control meats including beef, hamburger patties, meat balls, veal, pork, lamb and poultry; also, raw and cooked available
          President: Donald Bernstein
          Controller: Alfred Jordano
          VP Marketing: Elaine Herzog
          VP Sales: Mark Golden
          Plant Manager: John Mekilo
          Purchasing Manager: Jerry Davis
Estimated Sales: $41,500,000
Number Employees: 1-4
Sq. footage: 18000
Type of Packaging: Consumer, Food Service, Private Label, Bulk
Brands:
          Chef Italia
          Maid-Rite
          Minit Chef
          Polarized

8827 Main Squeeze
28 S 9th St
Columbia, MO 65201-4814   573-817-5616
          goodfood@main-squeeze.com
          www.main-squeeze.com
Juice concentrates and bar mixes
          Owner: Leigh Lockhart
Estimated Sales: $500,000-$1 Million
Number Employees: 5-9

8828 Main Street Brewery
1203 Main Street
Cincinnati, OH 45202-6326   513-665-4678
Processor of beer, ale and stout, including Woody's American Wheat, Main Street Pale Ale, Abigail's Amber and Steamboat Stout.
          President: Vince Bryant
Number Employees: 50-99
Type of Packaging: Consumer, Food Service

8829 Main Street Custom Foods
170 Muffin Ln
Cuyahoga Falls, OH 44223-3358   330-929-0000
          Fax: 330-920-8329   800-533-6246
          snatoli@mainstreetgourmet.com
          www.mainstreetmuffins.com
Manufacturer of custom and proprietary products including frozen dough, batter, and thaw and serve products. Will create new recipe for your application or match an existing recipe while packaging the product to meet your needs.
          President/CEO: Steven Marks
          President/CEO: Harvey Nelson
          Quality Control: Angela Stoughton
          Marketing: Joe Schaefer
          Sales: Keith Kropp
          Operations: Mike Braun
          Production: Tommie Smith
          Production: Bryan Smith
          Purchasing Director: Jim Braun
Estimated Sales: $15 Million
Number Employees: 100-249
Number of Products: Cust
Sq. footage: 65000
Parent Co: Feature Foods dba Main Street Gourmet
Type of Packaging: Consumer, Food Service, Private Label, Bulk

8830 (HQ)Main Street Gourmet
170 Muffin Ln
Cuyahoga Falls, OH 44223-3358   330-929-0000
          Fax: 330-920-8329   800-533-6246
          snatoli@mainstreetgourmet.com
          www.mainstreetmuffins.com
Manufacturer of gourmet frozen bakery items including an extensive selection of muffin batters, pre-formed cookie dough, thaw and serve muffins, brownies, scones, cinnamon rolls and biscotti. Custom formulations are also available.
          President/CEO: Steven Marks
          President/CEO: Harvey Nelson
          Quality Control: Angela Stoughton
          Marketing: Joe Schaefer
          Sales: Keith Kropp
          Plant Manager/Operations: Mike Braun
          Production: Tommie Smith
          Production: Bryan Smith
          Purchasing Director: Jim Braun
Estimated Sales: $15 Million
Number Employees: 100-249
Number of Brands: 6
Number of Products: 158
Sq. footage: 65000

Type of Packaging: Consumer, Food Service, Private Label, Bulk
Other Locations:
Brands:
Cambritt Cookies
Isabella's Extraordinary Muffins
Main Street Muffins
More Than Moist Muffins
The Softer Biscotti
Wild Fudge Brownies

8831 Main Street Gourmet Fundraising
170 Muffin Ln
Cuyahoga Falls, OH 44223-3358   330-929-0000
Fax: 330-920-8329   800-533-6246
snatoli@mainstreetgourmet.com
www.mainstreetmuffins.com
Manufacturer of muffin batter, cookie dough, strudel, cinnamon rolls and brownies packaged for sale in the fund raising industry.
President/CEO: Steven Marks
President/CEO: Harvey Nelson
Quality Control: Angela Stoughton
Marketing: Joe Schaefer
Sales: Harvey Nelson
Plant Manager/Operations: Mike Braun
Production: Tommie Smith
Production: Bryan Smith
Purchasing Director: Jim Braun
Estimated Sales: $15 Million
Number Employees: 100-249
Number of Products: 10
Sq. footage: 65000
Parent Co: Feature Foods dba Main Street Gourmet
Type of Packaging: Consumer

8832 Main Street Ingredients
P.O.Box 1628
La Crosse, WI 54602-1628   608-781-2345
Fax: 608-781-4667   800-359-2345
information@msing.com   www.msing.com
Processor of hydrocolloids, stabilizers, and dairy ingredients including whey proteins, milk proteins, and milk powders serving the dairy, bakery and nutrition industries; also a private-label contract manufacturer
President: Dave Clark
VP Sales/Marketing: Bill Schmitz
Estimated Sales: $100+ Million
Number Employees: 50-99
Brands:
Cornerstone
Keystone

8833 Main Street Muffins
170 Muffin Ln
Cuyahoga Falls, OH 44223-3358   330-929-0000
Fax: 330-920-8329   800-533-6246
snatoli@mainstreetgourmet.com
www.mainstreetmuffins.com
Manufacturer of gourmet muffins available in both frozen batter and thaw and serve formats. Muffin batters are all natural, preservative free and kosher with an extensive selection that includes fat free, low fat and whole grain. Thaw and serve are available in bulk-packaged format.
President/CEO: Steven Marks
President/CEO: Harvey Nelson
Quality Control: Angela Stoughton
Marketing: Joe Schaefer
Sales: Keith Kropp
Plant Manager/Operations: Mike Braun
Production: Tommie Smith
Production: Bryan Smith
Purchasing Director: Jim Braun
Estimated Sales: $15 Million
Number Employees: 100-249
Number of Brands: 2
Number of Products: 50
Sq. footage: 65000
Parent Co: Feature Foods dba Main Street Gourmet
Type of Packaging: Food Service, Private Label, Bulk
Brands:
Main Street Muffins
More Than Moist Muffins

8834 Main Street's Cambritt Cookies
170 Muffin Ln
Cuyahoga Falls, OH 44223-3358   330-929-0000
Fax: 330-920-8329   800-533-6246
snatoli@mainstreetgourmet.com
www.mainstreetmuffins.com

Manufacturer of frozen gourmet cookie dough in various pre-portioned sizes. The Classic line features all of the standards while the Decadent line is loaded with huge premiums, has great eye-appeal and a variety of unique flavorcombinations.
President/CEO: Steven Marks
President/CEO: Harvey Nelson
Quality Control: Angela Stoughton
Marketing: Joe Schaefer
Sales: Keith Kropp
Plant Manager/Operations: Mike Braun
Production: Tommie Smith
Production: Bryan Smith
Purchasing Director: Jim Braun
Estimated Sales: $15 Million
Number Employees: 100-249
Number of Brands: 1
Number of Products: 45
Sq. footage: 65000
Parent Co: Feature Foods dba Main Street Gourmet
Type of Packaging: Food Service, Private Label, Bulk
Brands:
Cambritt Cookies

8835 Maine Coast Nordic
PO Box 124
Beals, ME 04611-0124   207-497-5910
Processor of fresh salmon
VP: William Groom
Estimated Sales: $ 1-2.5 Million
Number Employees: 5-9
Parent Co: Nordic Enterprises
Type of Packaging: Bulk

8836 Maine Coast Sea Vegetables
3 Georges Pond Rd
Franklin, ME 04634-3320   207-565-2907
Fax: 207-565-2144   info@seaveg.com
www.seaveg.com
Processor of edible seaweed products including candies, sea vegetables, seasonings, chips and pickles; wholesaler/distributor of seaweed including whole and ground
President: Shepard Erhart
General Manager: Carl Karush
Operations Manager: Mary Ellen Lasell
Production Manager: Hannah Russell
Estimated Sales: $5-9.9 Million
Number Employees: 10-19
Number of Products: 40
Sq. footage: 9000
Type of Packaging: Consumer, Bulk
Brands:
Maine Coast Crunch
Maine Coast Sea Vegetables
Sea Cakes
Sea Chips
Sea Seasonings
Sea Vegetables
Wild Crafted Food From the Gulf Of

8837 Maine Freeze
PO Box 189
Lubec, ME 04652-0189   207-733-9715
Fax: 207-733-0936
Seafood
President: Robert Peacock

8838 Maine Lobster Outlet
360 Us Route 1
York, ME 03909-1631   207-363-4449
Fax: 207-363-0613   tea6977aol.com
www.mainelobsteroutlet.com
Lobster
President: Gregory Tsairis
Estimated Sales: $ 1 - 3 Million
Number Employees: 5-9

8839 Maine Mahogony Shellfish
8 Johnson Ln
Addison, ME 04606   207-483-2865
Fax: 207-483-4389 www.mahogany.qpg.com/
Wholesale and retail products include lobster, clams, crab, halibut, mussels, and a wide variety of shellfish.
Manager: Robert Johnson

8840 Maine Seaweed Company
PO Box 57
Steuben, ME 04680-0057   207-546-2875
Fax: 207-546-2875 www.alcasoft.com/seaweed/

Processor of dried seaweed which includes a wide variety of Atlantic seaweeds such as kelp, laminaria, longicruris, alaria, alaria esculenta, digitata, palmaria palmata and fucus vesiculosis.
President: Larch Hanson
Type of Packaging: Consumer

8841 Maine Wild Blueberry Company
P.O.Box 128
Cherryfield, ME 04622-0128   207-255-8364
Fax: 207-255-8341   800-243-4005
mbeal@cherryfieldfoods.com
www.cherryfieldfoods.com
Processor and exporter of canned, dehydrated and frozen wild blueberries
Chairman of the Board: John Bragg
COO: Jeff Vose
Sales Director: Tom Rush
Estimated Sales: $26900000
Number Employees: 20-49
Sq. footage: 100000
Brands:
Maine Wild

8842 Maine Wild Blueberry Company
P.O.Box 128
Cherryfield, ME 04622-0128   207-255-8364
Fax: 207-255-8341   800-243-4005
Frozen, canned and dried fruits
CEO: Regner Kemps
President: John Pragg
COO: Jeff Vose
Sales Manager: Tom Rush
Operations Manager: Earl Wagner
Operations Manager: Ragner Kemp
Plant Manager: Jeff Vose
Estimated Sales: $ 20-50 Million
Number Employees: 100-249
Type of Packaging: Private Label
Brands:
Blue Berry

8843 Maison Le Grand
935 Chemin Principal
St Joseph du Lac, QC J0N 1M0
Canada   450-623-3000
Fax: 450-623-2300   info@maisonlegrand.com
www.maisonlegrand.com
cold-processed sauces (pestos, tapenades, aromatic sauces)

8844 Maisons Marques & Domaines USA
383 4th St # 400
Oakland, CA 94607-4104   510-286-2000
Fax: 510-286-2010 www.mmdusa.net
Maisons, Marques & Domaines is a marketer of family-owned, prestigious producers from the world's great wine regions. Some of the wineries represented by MMD are owned by the House of Louis Roederer, including Porto Ramos-PintoChampagne Deutz, Delas Freres and the Bordeaux properties of Chateau de Pez and also Chateau Haut-Beausejour.
President/CEO: Gregory Ballogh
CFO: Guillaune Fomilleron
CEO: Gregory Balogh
Manager: Heidi Donaldson
Estimated Sales: $ 5-10 Million
Number Employees: 20-49
Brands:
Champagne Deutz
Chateau De Pez
Chateau Haut-Beausejour
Delas Freres
Ramos-Pinto

8845 Maitake Products
1 Madison St # C3
East Rutherford, NJ 07073-1666   973-773-2777
Fax: 973-773-9717   800-747-7418
customerservice@maitake.com
www.maitake.com
Processor and exporter of nutritional mushroom supplements and teas
Owner/President/CEO: Mike Shirota
VP: Joe Carroll
R&D: Dr. Cun Shuang
VP Marketing: Donna Noonan
Production: Masashi Ohara
Estimated Sales: $ 3 - 5 Million
Number Employees: 10-19
Number of Brands: 2

Number of Products: 24
Sq. footage: 4500
Type of Packaging: Consumer, Food Service, Private Label, Bulk
Other Locations:
  Maitake Products
  Ridgefield Park NJ
Brands:
  Grifron
  Grifron D-Fraction
  Grifron Mushroom Emperors
  Grifron Prost Mate
  Mai Green Tea
  Mai Tonic Tea
  Mushroom Wisdom

8846 Maitake Products
1 Madison St # C3
East Rutherford, NJ 07073-1666   973-773-2777
            Fax: 973-773-9717   800-747-7418
            customerservice@maitake.com
                  www.maitake.com
Dietary supplements from medicinal mushrooms
  President: Mike Shirota
  VP: Joe Carroll
Estimated Sales: $ 2.5-5 Million
Number Employees: 10-19
Number of Products: 26
Type of Packaging: Private Label
Brands:
  Grifron
  Grifron D-Fraction
  Grifron Mushroom Emp
  Maigreen Tea
  Maitonic Tea

8847 Majestic Coffee & Tea
2027 San Carlos Ave
San Carlos, CA 94070-1929   650-591-5678
            bobgard@gardfoods.com
Coffee, tea
  President: Bob Gard
Estimated Sales: Less than $400,000
Number Employees: 1-4
Brands:
  Majestic Coffee and Tea

8848 Majestic Distilling Company
P.O.Box 7372
Baltimore, MD 21227-0372   410-242-0200
            Fax: 410-247-7831
            lschuman@majesticdistilling.com
                  www.majesticdistilling.com
Processor and exporter of alcoholic beverages including brandy, scotch, tequila, gin, etc.; importer of brandy, scotch, tequila, whiskey and Canadian rum. Also importing a line of premium spirits
  President/General Manager: Lee Schuman
  Marketing Manager: Corky Graff
  VP National Sales: Corky Graff
Estimated Sales: $ 20 - 50 Million
Number Employees: 20-49
Number of Brands: 8
Number of Products: 15
Sq. footage: 45000
Brands:
  BLACK WATCH
  CANADIAN LEAF
  ODESSE
  OLD SETTER
  PORT ROYAL
  RED BULL
  RED BULL VODKA
  RIKALOFF
  SHAKESPEARE VODKA
  TREVELERS CLUB
  ZELKO

8849 Majestic Flex Pac
1351 Air Wing Road
San Diego, CA 92154   619-710-0207
  Fax: 619-710-0208 sales@majesticflexpac.com
                  www.majesticflexpac.com/
Majestic Flex PAC is a manufacturer and supplier of shrink sleeves, pouches, laminations, and custom bags to numerous industries including that of food and beverage, dairy, bakery and snack, candy and confection.
  President: Leonardo Gutierrez
Type of Packaging: Consumer

8850 Majestic Foods
22 High St # 2
Huntington, NY 11743-7602   631-424-9444
            Fax: 631-424-5874 www.majesticfoods.com
Fruit concentrates, blends, essences and purees, canned fruits and vegetables, frozen fruits, dried fruits, nuts, vegetables and natural colors
  Branch Manager: Ted Farynick
Estimated Sales: $ 20-50 Million
Number Employees: 10-19

8851 Major McGill
5603 Main Street
Flowery Branch, GA 30542-5652   770-967-6001
            Fax: 770-967-3886
Smoked seafood, trout, wali, fresh seafood, prepared foods/entrees
  President: Stephen Major II

8852 Makers Mark Distillery
3350 Burk Spring Rd
Loretto, KY 40037-8027   270-865-2881
            Fax: 270-865-2196 www.makersmark.com
Processor and exporter of whiskey
  President: Bill Samuels Jr
  Master Distiller: David Pickerell
  CEO: Bill Samuels Jr
Estimated Sales: $50-100 Million
Number Employees: 50-99
Parent Co: Hiram Walker & Sons
Type of Packaging: Consumer
Brands:
  Makers Mark

8853 Makers Mark Distillery
3350 Burk Spring Rd
Loretto, KY 40037-8027   270-865-2881
            Fax: 270-865-2196 www.makersmark.com
Processor and exporter of whiskey
  President: Bill Samuels Jr
  CEO: Bill Samuels Jr
Estimated Sales: $24300000
Number Employees: 10-19
Parent Co: Hiram Walker & Sons
Type of Packaging: Consumer
Brands:
  Makers Mark

8854 Malabar Formulas
2716 Lake Arrowhead Road
Lake Arrowhead, CA 92352   800-462-6617
Processor of milk digestants and activated enzyme concentrate
  General Manager: Shirley Partito

8855 Malatchie Farms Pecans
124 Malatchie Road
Fort Valley, GA 31030-8907   912-982-5199
Pecans
  Owner: Walter Forbes
Estimated Sales: $500,000-$1 Million
Number Employees: 10-19

8856 Malcolm Meat Company
2657 Tracy Rd
Northwood, OH 43619-1006   419-666-0702
            Fax: 419-666-2619 800-822-6328
Meat
  President: Jerry R Pasquale
  President: Jeff Savage
Estimated Sales: $ 20-50 Million
Number Employees: 100-249

8857 Malibu Beach Beverage
885 Woodstock Rd
Roswell, GA 30075-2277   770-998-7204
                  877-825-0655
            info@malibubev.com   www.malibubev.com
Manufacturer of nutritional fruit flavored drinks including malibu mango; sunset strawberry; redondo raspberry; oceanside orange; beach peach; and tropical tea.
  Chief Financial Officer: William Wager
  Vice President Corporate Development: Jeff Glattstein Sr
  Chief Operations Officer: Patrick Doran

8858 Malie Kai Hawaiian Chocolates
PO Box 1146
Honolulu, HI 96807   808-599-8600
            Fax: 808-599-8600 info@maliekai.com
                  www.maliekai.com
chocolate bars
  President/Owner: Nathan Sato

8859 Mallard Food Products
708 L Street
Modesto, CA 95354-2240   209-522-1018
            Fax: 209-577-8364
Refrigerated sauces, beef meals, chicken meals, cheese ravioli, meat ravioli, tortellini, fettuccine, ethnic meals
  VP Operations: Pete Rocha
Number Employees: 100-249
Brands:
  Cooking Made Easy
  Mallard's

8860 Mallet & Company
P.O.Box 474
Carnegie, PA 15106-0474   412-276-9000
      Fax: 412-276-9002 800-245-2757
            sales@malletoil.com www.malletoil.com
Manufacturer and exporter of oils, ingredients and custom food processing equipment
  President: Robert Mallet
  EVP: Aaron Mallet
Estimated Sales: $100-500 Million
Number Employees: 50-99
Number of Brands: 10
Number of Products: 70
Sq. footage: 110000
Type of Packaging: Consumer, Food Service, Private Label
Brands:
  EVERITE
  FRY WELL
  FRY'N GOLD
  HIFLEX
  KAKE MATE
  MELLO GOLD
  PAN & GRIDDLE GOLD
  PIC 77
  PRIME FRY
  SATIN DONUT FRY
  SATIN FRY
  SATIN GLO
  SATIN PLUS
  SPARKLE
  SUNNY GOLD
  SUNSHINE
  THRIFTEE GOLD
  TOUCH O'GOLD
  VEGALUBE

8861 Mallorie's Dairy
P.O.Box 720
Silverton, OR 97381-0720   503-873-5346
            Fax: 503-873-2278 www.malloriesdairy.com
Processed milk products include nonfat milk, 1% lowfat milk, 2% reduced fat milk, and vitamin D milk.
  President: Richard Mallorie
  Operations Manager: Terri Mallorie Kilgus
Estimated Sales: $ 10-20 Million
Number Employees: 50-99

8862 Maloney Seafood Corporation
350 Copeland St
Quincy, MA 02169-4030   617-472-1004
            Fax: 617-472-7722 800-566-2837
            info@maloneyseafood.com
                  www.maloneyseafood.com
Importers of seafood
  President: Thomas Maloney
Estimated Sales: $ 10-20 Million
Number Employees: 5-9

8863 Malt Products Corporation
88 Market St
Saddle Brook, NJ 07663-4830   201-845-5337
            Fax: 201-845-9209 800-526-0180
    Info@maltproducts.com   www.maltproducts.com
Manufacturer of malt, molasses, natural sweeteners. We are the largest producer of pure, high quality malts and molasses, liquids and powders, with precisely the characteristics needed for a wide variety of applications. We specialize in prompt and professional service
  Manager: John Johannson
  VP Sales/Marketing: Joe Hickenbottom
Number Employees: 10-19
Type of Packaging: Bulk

8864 Malt-Diastase Company
88 Market St
Saddle Brook, NJ 07663-4830   201-845-3518
            Fax: 201-845-9209 800-772-0416

Processor and exporter of flavoring extracts and syrups
President: Art Levy
Estimated Sales: $ 10 - 20 Million
Number Employees: 10-19
Type of Packaging: Food Service, Bulk

8865 Malt-O-Meal Company
PO Box 631
Northfield, MN 55057   612-338-8551
   Fax: 612-339-5710 www.malt-o-meal.com
Manufacturer and exporter of hot wheat cereal and
ready-to-eat cereals
CEO: Chris Neugent
CFO: John Gappa
Sales Manager: Mike Allen
Estimated Sales: $500 Million
Number Employees: 1400
Type of Packaging: Consumer, Food Service, Private Label, Bulk
Brands:
MALT-O-MEAL

8866 Malt-O-Meal Company
P.O.Box 631
Northfield, MN 55057-0631   612-338-8551
   Fax: 612-339-5710 800-743-3029
   www.malt-o-meal.com
Cereal and grain products
President: John Lettmann
CEO: John Lettmann
CEO: Christopher Neugent
Estimated Sales: $450,000,000
Number Employees: 1,000-4,999
Brands:
Cheerios
Malt-O-Meal Original's
Scooter's
Topso

8867 Mama Amy's Quality Foods
5715 Coopers Avenue
Mississauga, ON L4Z 2C7
Canada
   905-456-0056
   Fax: 905-456-1536
Processor and exporter of pizza and broccoli and
cheese sticks, calzones, jambalaya, etc
Sales/Marketing Director: Aldon Reed
Number Employees: 30
Sq. footage: 7000
Type of Packaging: Consumer, Food Service, Private Label, Bulk
Brands:
Mama Amy's

8868 Mama Del's Macacroni
420 Main St
East Haven, CT 06512-2838   203-469-6255
   Fax: 203-469-6255
Homemade pasta
Owner: Edward Cole
Estimated Sales: Less than $200,000
Number Employees: 1-4
Type of Packaging: Consumer, Food Service, Bulk
Brands:
Mama Del's

8869 Mama Lee's Gourmet Hot Chocolate
9 Music Sq S
157
Nashville, TN 37203-3211   888-626-2533
Fax: 615-226-5763 claycoc@attglobal.com
   www.mamalees.com

Hot chocolate, cappucino, gourmetfoods, desserts
President: Rod Atkins
Production Manager: Wanda Jones
Plant Manager: Richard Allen
Estimated Sales: Under $500,000
Number Employees: 1-4
Type of Packaging: Private Label
Brands:
Mama Lee's Cocoa
Mama Lee's Coffee

8870 Mama Lil's Peppers
832 14th Avenue
Seattle, WA 98122   206-322-8824
   Fax: 206-726-8372 mamalils@zipcon.net
   www.mamalils.com
peppers in oil
President/Owner: Howard Lev

8871 Mama Maria's Tortillas
6898 S 400 W
Midvale, UT 84047-1011   801-566-5150
   Fax: 801-566-7116 mamamarias@mtcon.net
Tortillas and tamales
President: Norbert Martinez
VP: Kenny Martinez
Estimated Sales: Below $ 5 Million
Number Employees: 20

8872 Mama Mucci's Pasta
7676 Ronda Dr
Canton, MI 48187-2430   734-453-4555
   Fax: 734-453-1722 info@mamamuccispasta.com
   www.mamamuccispasta.com
Fresh, dry and frozen filled pastas
President: Vince Mucci
Estimated Sales: $10-20 Million
Number Employees: 10-19
Brands:
Mama Mucci

8873 Mama Rap's & Winery
P.O.Box 247
Gilroy, CA 95021-0247   408-842-5649
   Fax: 408-842-8353 800-842-6262
djciv@garlic.com www.rapazziniwinery.com
Wine
Owner: Charles Larson
Estimated Sales: $ 1-2.5 Million
Number Employees: 5-9

8874 Mama Rose's Gourmet Foods
3434 W Earll Dr # 104
Phoenix, AZ 85017-5284   602-477-8333
   Fax: 602-477-8338 877-325-4477
tonya@mamarosefoods.com
www.mamarosefoods.com
Sixteen years producing gourmet packaged foods ie..
salsa, hot sauce ,jams, jellies, marinara and pizza
sauce, pickled olives, prickly pear products, importing italian pasta and olive oil. Private label and
co-packaging specialists
President: Tonya Greenfield
VP: Al Greenfield
Sales/Marketing Manager: Al Greenfield
Estimated Sales: $5-9.9 Million
Number Employees: 16
Brands:
Mama Rose's

8875 Mama Rosie's Ravioli Company
10 Dorrance St
Charlestown, MA 02129-1027   617-242-4300
   Fax: 617-242-4208 888-246-4300
Frozen pastas
President: Anthony Sardo
CEO: Nicholas Sardo
CFO: Nicholas Sardo
Marketing Director: Bryan Mtnulty
VP Sales: Charles Sardo
Plant Manager: Vicente Tagliamonte
Estimated Sales: $ 5-10 Million
Number Employees: 50-99
Brands:
Mama Rosie's

8876 Mama Tish's Italian Specialties
4800 S Central Avenue
Chicago, IL 60638-1500   708-929-2023
   Fax: 708-458-0027

Italian ice cream and frozen desserts
President/CEO: M Rudasil
Marketing Director: M Wenzell
VP Sales: Fergal Mulchrone
Director Manufacturing: M Wenzell
Plant Manager: I Bidiman
Estimated Sales: $ 5-10 Million
Number Employees: 5

8877 Mama Vida
9631 Liberty Rd # N
Randallstown, MD 21133-2434   410-521-0742
   Fax: 410-521-0785 877-521-0742
miki@mamavida.com www.mamavida.com
Vegetarian chili, eggplant spread, dressings, mustard, sauces, soups, black bean dip, marinade, salsas,
tapenades
President: Toto Mechali
VP: Miki Mechali
Quality Control: Heidi Czakny
Estimated Sales: $1 Million
Number Employees: 5-9
Number of Brands: 30
Number of Products: 18
Type of Packaging: Consumer, Food Service, Private Label, Bulk
Brands:
TOTO'S GOURMET PRODUCTS

8878 Mamma Lina Ravioli Company
6491 Weathers Pl
San Diego, CA 92121-2935   858-535-0620
   Fax: 858-535-5993
Processor of pasta products including ravioli and
frozen lasagna
President: Chick Massullo
Estimated Sales: Less than $500,000
Number Employees: 10-19
Type of Packaging: Consumer, Food Service

8879 Mamma Lombardi's All Natural Sauces
877 Main Street
Holbrook, NY 11741   631-471-6609
infovilla@villalombardis.com
www.mammalombardisauces.com
sauces

8880 Mamma Says
49 Lincoln Road
Butler, NJ 07405-1801   973-283-4463
   Fax: 973-283-2799 877-283-6282
sharyn@mammasays.com www.mammasays.com
Gourmet biscotti in almond pistachio and chocolate
macademia
VP: Jason Cohen
Brands:
Mamma Says

8881 Manchac Seafood Market
131 Bait Alley
Ponchatoula, LA 70454   985-370-7070
   Fax: 985-386-2762
Seafood
President: Duke Robin

8882 Manchac Trading Company
38091 Hope Villa Drive
Prairieville, LA 70769-3850   225-677-8026
   Fax: 225-673-1876
Estimated Sales: $ 3 - 5 Million
Number Employees: 1-4

8883 Manchester Farms
P.O.Box 97
Dalzell, SC 29040-0097   803-469-2588
   Fax: 803-469-8637 800-845-0421
customerservice@manchesterfarms.com
www.manchesterfarms.com
Processor and exporter of frozen quail, turkey and
chicken
President: William J Odom
COO: Gene Tennis
Marketing: Steve Odom
Sales: Bill Odom
Estimated Sales: $6300000
Number Employees: 10-19
Sq. footage: 22000
Type of Packaging: Consumer, Food Service, Private Label
Brands:
Manchester Farms

8884 Mancini Packing Company
P.O.Box 157
Zolfo Springs, FL 33890-0157   863-735-2000
Fax: 863-735-1172   rmancini@mancinifoods.com
www.mancinifoods.com
Manufacturer of peppers and olive oil
   Chairman/President: Frank Mancini
   VP: Alan Mancini
Estimated Sales: $11 Million
Number Employees: 100-249
Type of Packaging: Consumer, Food Service, Private Label, Bulk
Brands:
   MANCINI

8885 Mancuso Cheese Company
612 Mills Rd # 1
Joliet, IL 60433-2897   815-722-2475
   Fax: 815-722-1302   www.mancusocheese.com
Processor of cheese including ricotta, mozzarella, etc.; exporter of pizza supplies; importer of pasta, olive oil, olives and anchovies; wholesaler/distributor of frozen foods, produce, meats, baked goods, general merchandise, etc.
   President: Michael Berta
   VP: Michael Berta
Estimated Sales: $ 5 - 10 Million
Number Employees: 20-49
Sq. footage: 20000
Type of Packaging: Consumer, Food Service, Bulk
Brands:
   Mancuso

8886 (HQ)Manda Fine Meats
P.O.Box 3374
Baton Rouge, LA 70821-3374   225-344-7636
   Fax: 225-344-7647   www.mandafinemeats.com
Processor of beef, ham and sausage
   President: Tommy Yarborough
   Sales Director: Steve Yarboruth
Estimated Sales: $ 20 - 50 Million
Number Employees: 100-249
Type of Packaging: Consumer, Food Service, Private Label, Bulk

8887 Mandarin Noodle Manufacturing Company
3715d Edmonton Tr NE
Calgary, AB T2E 3P3
Canada   403-265-1383
   Fax: 403-264-3038
Processor of rice and wonton noodles, rice rolls and wonton and egg roll wraps
   President: Larry Cheng
Type of Packaging: Consumer, Food Service

8888 Mandarin Soy Sauce
4 Sands Station Rd
Middletown, NY 10940-4415   845-343-1505
   Fax: 845-343-0731   info@wanjashan.com
   www.wanjashan.com
Manufacturer of soy sauce, asian sauce, rice and vinegar
   President: Michael Wu
   VP: Mike Shapiro
Estimated Sales: $16500000
Number Employees: 25
Sq. footage: 100000
Brands:
   Wan Ja Shan

8889 Mandarin Soy Sauce
4 Sands Station Rd
Middletown, NY 10940-4415   845-343-1505
   Fax: 845-343-0731   info@wanjashan.com
   www.wanjashan.com
Manufacturer of naturally brewed soy sauce, regular, lite, clear, nonpreservative, stir-fry, tamari, teriyaki, hoisin and dry soy powder
   President: Michael Wu
Estimated Sales: $ 5 - 10 Million
Number Employees: 20-49
Brands:
   Wan Ja Shan

8890 Manderfield Home Bakery
811 Plank Rd
Menasha, WI 54952-2923   920-725-7794
   Fax: 920-725-7958   www.manderfieldsbakery.com
Bakery products
   President: Jerry Manderfield
Estimated Sales: $ 1-2.5 Million
Number Employees: 20-49

8891 Mandoo
16 Humphrey St
Englewood, NJ 7631-3445   201-568-9337
   Fax: 201-568-9426   mandoo_inc@msn.com
Processor of dumplings
   President: Kyo Lee
Estimated Sales: $ 2.5-5 Million
Number Employees: 10
Type of Packaging: Consumer, Food Service, Bulk
Brands:
   Mandoo

8892 Mane Incorporated
999 Tech Dr
Milford, OH 45150-9535   513-248-9876
   Fax: 513-248-8808   800-595-8936
   webinfo@mane.com   www.maneusa.com
Flavors.
   President: Ken Hunter
   CEO: Kenneth Hunter
   Marketing: Bridget McElfresh
   Sales: Dave Wilson
   Operations: Randy Brown
Estimated Sales: $ 20 - 50 Million
Number Employees: 50-99
Parent Co: V. Fils Mane

8893 Manfred Vierthaler Winery
17136 Highway 410 E
Sumner, WA 98382   888-663-9463
   Fax: 253-863-1633
Wines
Number Employees: 10-19

8894 Manger Packing Company
124 S Franklintown Rd
Baltimore, MD 21223-2036   410-233-0126
   Fax: 410-362-8065   800-227-9262
Manufacturer and packer of meat including pork, beef, chicken, lamb, veal and smoked ham; exporter of beef sausage
   President: Alvin S Manger
Estimated Sales: $9 Million
Number Employees: 10-19
Type of Packaging: Consumer, Bulk

8895 Mangia
23166 Los Alisos Blvd # 228
Mission Viejo, CA 92691-7866   949-581-1274
   Fax: 949-581-2906   866-462-6442
   wmatt@mangiainc.com   www.mangiainc.com
Canned San Marzano tomato products, originally produced in Italy, with no preservatives or added salt
   Owner: Matt Maslowski
   VP: Bob Maruca
Estimated Sales: $ 8 Million
Number Employees: 1-4
Number of Brands: 1
Number of Products: 7
Type of Packaging: Consumer, Food Service
Other Locations:
   Conditalia
   Nocera Superiore, Italy
Brands:
   Carmelia

8896 Manhattan Beach BrewingCompany
124 Manhattan Beach Blvd
Manhattan Beach, CA 90266-5432   310-798-2744
   Fax: 310-798-0365
   www.manhattanbeachbrewingcompany.com
Coffee
   President: David Zislis
   Director Manufacturing: Karol Kmeto
Estimated Sales: $ 1-2.5 Million
Number Employees: 20-49
Brands:
   Dominator Wheat
   Rat Beach Red
   Strand Amber

8897 Manhattan Chocolates
186 E 22nd St
Bayonne, NJ 07002-5005   201-339-6886
   Fax: 201-339-6760
   www.manhattanchocolates.com
Products include premium, deluxe chocolates, jelly rings, truffles, holidayassortments, and a variety of sugar-free products that include chocolate covered nuts and truffles.
   President: David Herzog

Estimated Sales: $ 10-20 Million
Number Employees: 20-49
Type of Packaging: Private Label, Bulk

8898 Manhattan Coffee Company
4333 Green Ash Dr
Earth City, MO 63045-1207   314-731-2500
   Fax: 314-731-1938   800-926-3333
   www.saralee.com
Processor and wholesaler/distributor of coffee
   Manager: Carol Johnson
   Sales Manager: C Wolf
   General Manager: T Allen

8899 Manhattan Special Bottling Corporation
342 Manhattan Ave
Brooklyn, NY 11211-2404   718-388-4144
   Fax: 718-384-0244
   comments@manhattanspecial.com
   www.manhattanspecial.com
Pure Espresso, sodas and iced coffee drinks
   President: Aurora Passaro
Estimated Sales: $ 2.5-5 Million
Number Employees: 5-9

8900 Manhattan Wholesale MeatCompany
P.O.Box 885
Manhattan, KS 66505-0885   785-776-9203
   Fax: 785-776-5940
Wholesaler/distributor of meats; serving the food service market
   President: Stephen D Saroff
Estimated Sales: $ 5 - 10 Million
Number Employees: 20-49

8901 Manildra Milling Corporation
4210 Shawnee Mission Pkwy
Fairway, KS 66205-2506   913-362-0777
   Fax: 913-362-0052   800-323-8435
   info@manildrausa.com   www.manildrausa.com
Processor, exporter and importer of wheat gluten; processor of wheat starch
   President: Gerry Degnan
   VP Sales/Marketing: Jay Piester
Number Employees: 10-19
Parent Co: Manildra Group
Type of Packaging: Bulk
Brands:
   Gembond
   Gemstar

8902 Manitok Food & Gifts
PO Box 97
Callaway, MN 56521-0097   218-375-3425
   Fax: 218-375-4765   800-726-1863
Products include handmade jewelry, dolls, quilts, birch bark baskets, canoes, trays, corporate gift baskets filled with hand-harvested and handmade food products, wild rice, berry jellies and syrups.
Estimated Sales: $ 5-9.9 Million
Number Employees: 4

8903 Manley Meats
302 S 400 E
Decatur, IN 46733-9095   260-592-7313
   Fax: 260-592-6731
   manleymeats@adamwells.com
   www.manleymeats.com
Processor of canned and frozen beef, pork and chicken
   President: Roger Manley
Estimated Sales: $ 10-20 Million
Number Employees: 20-49
Type of Packaging: Consumer, Food Service

8904 Mann Packing
P.O.Box 690
Salinas, CA 93902-0690   831-422-7405
   Fax: 831-422-1131   www.broccoli.com
Processor of produce including mixed vegetables and broccoli; also, broccoli with microwaveable cheese sauce
   President: Joe Nucci
   CEO: Mike Jarrod
   Sales Director: Ron Fuqua
   VP Retail Sales: Craig Enos
Estimated Sales: $30500000
Number Employees: 250-499
Type of Packaging: Consumer, Food Service, Bulk
Brands:
   Broccoli Wokly
   Sugar Valley

Sunny Shores
Sunny Shores Broccoli Wokly

8905 Mann's International Meat Specialties
9097 F St
Omaha, NE 68127-1305   402-339-7000
          Fax: 402-339-1579   800-228-2170
Packer and exporter of precooked roast beef, pastrami, corned beef, smoked meats, frozen prepared soups, entrees, Mexican foods and home meal replacements
    President: Ivan Streit
    VP: Linda Mann
    VP Marketing: John Shipp
    Plant Manager: Bruce Hamilton
Estimated Sales: $11200000
Number Employees: 50-99
Brands:
    El Hombre Hambre
    Gourmet International
    Mann's International

8906 Mannhardt Inc
511 Broadway St
Sheboygan Falls, WI 53085-1500   920-467-1027
    Fax: 773-625-5639   mannhardt1@aol.com
                        mannhardtice.com
Manufacturer of ice storage dispensers and bagging equipment
    President: John Williams
    Sales: Lori Justinger
Number Employees: 10-19

8907 Manor Hill Food Corporation
1200 E Patapsco Ave
Baltimore, MD 21225-2233   410-355-1014
                        Fax: 410-355-1015
Soups
    President: Ed Heil
Estimated Sales: Under $500,000
Number Employees: 100-249

8908 Mansmith Enterprises
P.O.Box 247
San Jn Bautista, CA 95045-0247   831-623-4981
        Fax: 831-623-2150   800-626-7648
        info@mansmith.com   www.mansmith.com
Seasonings and spices
    President: Jon Mansmith
    CEO: Juanita Mansmith
    CFO: John Mansmith
    VP: Jon Mansmith
Estimated Sales: $237,000
Number Employees: 1-4
Type of Packaging: Private Label

8909 Mansmith's Barbecue
P.O.Box 247
San Jn Bautista, CA 95045-0247   831-623-4981
        Fax: 831-623-2150   800-626-7648
        info@mansmith.com   www.mansmith.com
Processor of barbecue products including sauces, seasonings, pastes and grilling spices
    Owner/President: Jon Mansmith
    Owner/Secretary/Treasurer: Juanita Mansmith
Estimated Sales: Less than $250,000
Number Employees: 1-4
Parent Co: Mansmith Enterprises
Type of Packaging: Consumer, Food Service, Private Label
Brands:
    Mansmith's Gourmet

8910 Mantrose-Haeuser Company
1175 Post Rd E
Westport, CT 06880-5431   203-454-1800
        Fax: 203-227-0558   800-344-4229
        Michelle.Frame@Mantrose.com
                        www.mantrose.com
Edible coatings and glazes
    President: William Barrie
    CFO: Sue Ororuee
    Quality Control: Mark Crossman
    Product Manager: Michelle Frame
    Plant Manager: John George
Estimated Sales: $ 10-20 Million
Number Employees: 100-249
Type of Packaging: Private Label
Brands:
    Certicoat
    Certicoat Polishes
    Certified Gum Coats & Glazes
    Certified Shellacs

Certiseal
Confectioners Glaze Thinner
Crystalac
Crystalac Polishing Glazes
Nature Seal
Sparkled Glow

8911 Manuel's Mexican-American Fine Foods
2007 S 300 W
Salt Lake City, UT 84115-1808   801-484-1431
        Fax: 801-484-1440   800-748-5072
Broker of tortilla chips, taco shells, corn tortilla, tostada shells and pre-cut tortillas
    President: Orlando Torres
    VP: Mike Torres
    VP Sales: Paul Torres
Estimated Sales: Below $ 5 Million
Number Employees: 40
Type of Packaging: Consumer, Food Service, Private Label, Bulk

8912 Manuel's Odessa Tortillaand Tamale Factory
1915 E 2nd St
Odessa, TX 79761-5311   432-332-6676
                        Fax: 915-332-6699
Manufacturer of tortillas, canned tamales and tortilla chips
    President: Manuel Gonzalez
Estimated Sales: $10-20 Million
Number Employees: 10-19

8913 Manzana Products Company
P.O.Box 209
Sebastopol, CA 95473-0209   707-823-5313
        Fax: 707-823-5218   manzanaca@aol.com
Manufacturer of applesauce, apple juice, apple cider and apple cider vinegar.
    President: Suzanne C Kaido
Estimated Sales: $ 50 - 100 Million
Number Employees: 100-249
Type of Packaging: Consumer, Private Label, Bulk
Brands:
    North Coast

8914 Manzanita Ranch
4470 Highway 78
Julian, CA 92036-9624   760-765-0102
Grower of apples; processor of fruit juices including apple, grape, cherry and raspberry
    Manager: Jeff Cox
Estimated Sales: $ 3 - 5 Million
Number Employees: 5-9

8915 Maola Milk & Ice Cream Company
P.O.Box S
New Bern, NC 28563-8518   252-638-1131
        Fax: 252-638-2268 www.mdvamilk.com
Processes and packages fluid milk, ice cream, ice cream novelties, juice and other drinks for consumers.
    Manager: Kieth Pardue
Estimated Sales: $94700000
Number Employees: 250-499
Type of Packaging: Consumer, Food Service, Private Label, Bulk

8916 (HQ)Maola Milk & Ice Cream Company
411 E 5th North Street
H
Summerville, SC 29483-5109   803-871-6311
                        Fax: 843-395-1808
Dairy products
    President/CEO: Kenneth Reesman
    Controller: Richard Ruffi
    General Manager: Jim Green

8917 Maple Acres
13900 Campbell Road
Kewadin, MI 49648-9148   231-264-9265
                        Fax: 231-264-8532
Processor of pure Northern Michigan maple syrup in 1/2 pint to one gallon jugs; private label available
    CEO: Chris Luchenbill
    President: Leta Luchenbill
Sq. footage: 6000
Type of Packaging: Consumer, Food Service, Private Label, Bulk
Brands:
    Maple Acres

8918 Maple Donuts
3455 E Market St
York, PA 17402-2696   717-757-7826
        Fax: 717-755-8725   800-627-5348
    charliemaple@aol.com www.mapledonuts.com
Donuts, yeast raised; cake stye, fresh or frozen; pie shells, deep or shallow, organic all products, kosher, tran fat free
    President: Charles Burnside
    CEO: Nat Burnside
    VP/General Manager: Ralph Wooten
    R&D: Jose Rios
    Quality Control: Ann Moates
    Marketing/Sales: Damian Burnside
    Publice Relations: Charles Burnside
    Operations: Luke Burnside
    Production: John Loucks
    Plant Manager: Dan Haines
    Purchasing: Tammy Howard
Estimated Sales: $40-50 Million
Number Employees: 310
Sq. footage: 80000
Parent Co: Maple Donuts LLC

8919 Maple Grove Farms of Vermont
1052 Portland St
St Johnsbury, VT 05819-2815   802-748-5141
        Fax: 802-748-9647   800-525-2540
    maple@maplegrove.com www.maplegrove.com
Pure maple syrup, fruit flavored syrups, sugar free syrup, specialty salad dressings, pancake & waffle mixes, gluten free products, maple candies & spreads.
    VP: Stephen Jones
    Quality Control: Danny Johnson
    Plant Manager: Mark Bigelow
Estimated Sales: $70,000,000
Number Employees: 85
Parent Co: B&G Foods
Type of Packaging: Consumer, Food Service, Private Label, Bulk
Brands:
    Cozy Cottage
    Maple Grove Farms of Vermont
    Up Country Naturals
    Vermont Sugar Free

8920 Maple Hill Farms
P.O.Box 767
Bloomfield, CT 06002-0767   860-242-9689
        Fax: 860-243-2490   800-842-7304
                        www.mhfct.com
Dairy products
    President: William Miller
    Marketing Director: Scott Miller
Estimated Sales: $ 5 - 10 Million
Number Employees: 20-49

8921 Maple Hollow
W1887 Robinson Dr
Merrill, WI 54452-9543   715-536-7251
                www.maplehollowsyrup.com
Processor of maple syrup and sugar; wholesaler/distibutor of maple syrup processing machinery
    Owner: Joe Polak
    Vice President: Barbara Polak
Estimated Sales: $9.9 Million
Number Employees: 5-9
Number of Brands: 5
Number of Products: 4
Sq. footage: 10000
Type of Packaging: Consumer, Private Label
Brands:
    Forest Country
    Maple Gardens
    Maple Hollow

8922 Maple Island
2497 7th Ave E # 105
St Paul, MN 55109-4485   651-773-1000
        Fax: 651-773-2155   800-369-1022
    info@maple-island.com www.maple-island.com
Processor and packager of quality food powders; agglomerate, blend and package into pouches and canisters
    President: Greg Johnson
    Executive VP: Ronald Zirbel
    Director Marketing/Sales: Jim Kelleher
    Plant Manager: Robin Amundson
Estimated Sales: $28675000
Number Employees: 10-19

Type of Packaging: Consumer, Food Service, Private Label, Bulk
Brands:
  Bounce
  Diet Freeze
  Maple Island
  Shakequik

8923 Maple Leaf Bakery
30 St Claire Avenue
Suite 1500
Toronto, ON M4V 3A2
Canada   416-926-2000
        Fax: 416-926-2018 800-805-3460
  slotthm@mapleleaf.ca www.mapleleaf.ca
Bakery products
  President/CEO: Michael McCain
  Corporate Director: Robert Stewart
  Chairman: G. Wallace McCain,O.C.
Estimated Sales: $ 2.5-5 Million
Number Employees: 30-50
Brands:
  California Goldminer
  Eurofresh
  Home Fresh
  Maple Leaf

8924 Maple Leaf Cheesemakers
P.O.Box 974
New Glarus, WI 53574-0974   608-527-2000
        Fax: 608-527-3050 mapleleafl@tds.net
  www.mapleleafcheeseandchocolatehaus.com
Processor and exporter of cheese including
Monterey jack and gouda
  Owner: Barbara Kummerfeldt
Estimated Sales: $500,000-$1 Million
Number Employees: 20-49
Type of Packaging: Consumer, Food Service, Private Label, Bulk
Brands:
  Maple Leaf

8925 Maple Leaf Consumer Foods
7840 Madison Ave # 135
Fair Oaks, CA 95628-3591   916-967-1633
        Fax: 916-967-1690 800-999-7603
  www.mapleleaf.com
Processor of ham and bacon
  President/Owner: ²
  General Manager: Charles Brougher
Estimated Sales: $ 5 - 10 Million
Number Employees: 10-19
Parent Co: Maple Leaf Foods
Type of Packaging: Consumer, Food Service, Private Label, Bulk

8926 (HQ)Maple Leaf Farms
P.O.Box 308
Milford, IN 46542-0308   574-658-4121
        Fax: 574-658-2208 800-384-2812
  consumer@mapleleaffarms.com
  www.mapleleaffarms.com
Produces duck products, supplying retail and food
service markets worldwide. Also produces chicken
patties, strips, nuggets and gourmet entrees.
  Owners & Co-Presidents: John & Scott Tucker
  Owner & Chairman of the Board: Terry Tucker
  VP Finance: Scott Reinholt
  Vice President: Bob Salegna
  Food R&D: Kent Thrasher
  Quality Assurance: Rick Prins
  VP Sales & Marketing: Eric Errig
  VP Operations: Don Ratliff
  VP Live Production: Mike Turk
  Plant Managers: Lee Allen Don Crandall
  Purchasing Managers: Ron Buhr Ronda Morgan
Estimated Sales: $141,000,000
Number Employees: 995
Type of Packaging: Consumer, Food Service, Private Label, Bulk
Brands:
  C&D
  C&D
  Chef Tang
  ECH
  FCH
  Gold Label
  Maple Leaf

8927 Maple Leaf Farms
PO Box 507
Franksville, WI 53126-0507   262-878-1234
Fax: 262-878-3432 rrosdil@mapleleaffarms.com
  www.mapleleaffarms.com

Processor and exporter of fresh and frozen duck
  President: Scott Tucker
  CEO: Terry Tucker
  Plant Manager: Ray Olfzewski
  Purchasing Agent: Sharon Ermi
Estimated Sales: $ 50 - 100 Million
Number Employees: 100-249
Parent Co: Maple Leaf Foods
Type of Packaging: Consumer, Food Service, Private Label

8928 Maple Leaf Foods
1 Warman Drive
Winnipeg, NB R2J 4E5
Canada   204-231-4114
        Fax: 204-231-2944 800-564-6253
  www.mapleleaf.com
Processor of pork
  President: Michael H McCain
  CEO: Michael H McCain
  CFO: Michael H Vels
  Plant Manager: Jeff Parsons
Number Employees: 250-499
Parent Co: Schneider's Dairy
Type of Packaging: Food Service
Brands:
  Burns
  California Goldminer
  Hygrade
  Maison-Cousin
  Nutriwhip
  Shopsy's
  Tenderflake

8929 Maple Leaf Foods
3434 Runge Street
Franklin Park, IL 60131-1315   847-451-8100
        Fax: 847-451-2296 www.mapleleaf.ca
Bagels and French bread
  President: Richard Young
Estimated Sales: $ 50-99.9 Million
Number Employees: 100

8930 Maple Leaf Foods & Scheider Foods
6505 Trans Canada Highway
Saint Laurent, QC H4T 1S3
Canada   514-748-1469
        Fax: 514-748-1630 800-567-1890
  consumer@schneiderfoods.ca
  www.schneiders.ca
Processor of beef and pork
  President: Michael Mc cain
  Sales Manager: Andre des Lauriers
Number Employees: 20-49
Parent Co: J.M. Schneider
Type of Packaging: Consumer, Food Service
Brands:
  Schneider's Frozen Meats
  Schneiders Egg Stuffs
  Schneiders Hot Stuffs
  Schneiders Lean Stuffs

8931 (HQ)Maple Leaf Foods International
Suite 2000
Toronto, ON M4N 3N1
Canada   416-480-8900
        Fax: 416-480-8950 montgomg@mapleleaf.ca
  www.mapleleaf.ca
Processor, importer and exporter of fresh and frozen
meat, seafood, dairy products, produce, potato products and specialty grains
  President: Michael Detlefsen
  Senior VP/Corporate Secretary: Rocco Cappuccitti
  Executive VP/Chief Strategy Officer: Douglas Dodds
  Chief Information Officer: Patrick Ressa
  Chief Financial Officer: Michael Vels
Estimated Sales: $6,365,000
Number Employees: 23,000
Sq. footage: 10500
Type of Packaging: Consumer, Food Service, Private Label, Bulk
Other Locations:
  Maple Leaf Foods Internationa
  Chatham NJ
Brands:
  BITTNER'S
  CALIFORNIA GOLDMINER
  DEMPSTER'S
  HOT & CRUSTY
  HUDRAGE

MAISON COUSIN
MAPLE LEAF
MEDALLION NATURALLY
NATURE'S GOURMET
OLIVIERI
PRIME NATURALLY
PRIME TURKEY
READY CRISP
SHOPSY'S
SLO-ROAST DELI
TENDER FLAKE
TOP DOGS

8932 Maple Leaf Meats
PO Box 70
Winnipeg, NB R3C 2G5
Canada   204-233-2421
        Fax: 204-233-5413
  investorrelations@mapleleaf.com
  www.mapleleaf.com
Processor of meat products
  Director Corporate: James F Hankinson
  President: Chaviva M Hosek
  Controller: John Main
  CEO: Chaviva M Hosek
Number Employees: 400
Sq. footage: 259000
Parent Co: Maple Leaf Foods
Type of Packaging: Consumer, Food Service, Private Label, Bulk
Brands:
  Maple Leaf
  Royale

8933 Maple Leaf Pork
821 Appleby Line
Burlington, ON L7L 4W9
Canada   905-637-2301
        Fax: 905-333-2941 ingrams@mapleleaf.ca
  www.mapleleaf.ca
Processor and exporter of pork
  President: M McCain
  CEO: Michael McCain
  Director Finance: Michael Vels
  VP/General Manager: Wayne Johnson
  VP Sales/Marketing: J Moore
Number Employees: 1000
Parent Co: Maple Leaf Foods
Type of Packaging: Consumer, Food Service

8934 Maple Leaf Pork
4141 1st Avenue
Lethbridge, AB T1J 4P8
Canada   403-328-1756
        Fax: 403-327-9821 info@mapleleaf.ca
  www.mapleleaf.ca
Processor and exporter of fresh and frozen pork including carcass, boxed and by-products
  President: Michael McCain
  Sales: Wilf Fiebich
  General Manager: Ralph Miller
  Plant Manager: Dave Wood
Number Employees: 100-249
Parent Co: Maple Leaf Foods
Type of Packaging: Consumer, Bulk

8935 Maple Leaf Potatoes
2720 2a Avenue N
Lethbridge, AB T1H 5B4
Canada   403-380-9900
        Fax: 403-328-5262 800-268-3708
  info@mapleleaf.ca www.mapleleaf.ca
Processor of Frozen French fries
  General Manager: Lee Gleim
  Production Manager: Joe Thom
Parent Co: Maple Leaf Foods
Type of Packaging: Consumer, Food Service
Brands:
  Snowcap
  York

8936 Maple Mark
148 Route Kennedy
Scott-Junction, QC G0S 3G0
Canada   418-386-2888
        Fax: 418-386-2889 800-261-2881
  mrcpeg@quebectel.com www.maplemark.com
Certifier and authorizer of North America's maple
syrup industry assuring purity and authenticity
  Marketing Director: Annie Burelle
Brands:
  Maple Mark
  Pur Erable

8937 Maple Products
1500 Rue De Pacifique
Sherbrooke, QC J1H 2G7
Canada   819-569-5161
                      Fax: 819-569-5168
Processor and exporter of maple syrup and sugar;
also, kosher grades available
  Production Manager: Ghislain Pare
Number Employees: 10-19
Parent Co: Citadelle
Type of Packaging: Food Service, Bulk
Brands:
  Pride of Canada

8938 Maple Ridge Farms
RR 3 Suite 6, Compartment 4
Prince Albert, SK S6V 5R1
Canada   306-922-8056
  Fax: 306-922-6189 mapleridge@sk.sympatico.ca
                      www.mapleridge.com
Processor for the production and extraction of essen-
tial oils and their fractions. Including caraway seed,
cilantro (coriander foliage), dill seed and foliage.
One hundred tons annually. Serving the bio-organic
industry and ingredientmanufacturers
  President: Martin Gareau

8939 Mapled Nut Company
P.O.Box 116
Montgomery, VT 05470-0116   802-326-4661
        Fax: 802-326-3111 800-726-4661
  nuts@maplenut.com www.maplenut.com
Gourmet maple sugar cashews, almonds, pecans and
walnuts
  Owner: Marsha Phillips
Estimated Sales: $ .5 - 1 million
Number Employees: 1-4

8940 (HQ)Maplehurst Bakeries
50 Maplehurst Dr
Brownsburg, IN 46112-9085   317-858-9000
                      Fax: 317-858-9001
  jbaumann@maplehurstbakeries.com
    www.maplehurstbakeries.com
Bread and other bakery products except cookies and
crackers
  President: Paul Duriacher
  CFO: Joseph Latouf
  CEO: Dave Winiger
  Plant Manager: Tom Nummerdor
Estimated Sales: $ 50-100 Million
Number Employees: 250-499
Type of Packaging: Food Service, Private Label,
  Bulk
Brands:
  Arnie's Bagelicious
  Petrofsky's

8941 Maplehurst Bakeries
62 Adamson Industrial Blvd
Carrollton, GA 30117-9370   770-832-1111
    Fax: 770-834-5589 800-482-4810
  mnorred@maplehurstbakeries.com
    www.maplehurstbakeries.com
Products include cakes, donuts, cookies, bagels,
rolls, breads, pies, danish, cinnamon rolls and crack-
ers.
  President: Paul Durlacher
  CFO: Revin Whitlock
  Vice President: Dave Winiger
  Operations Manager: Tom Nummendor
  Plant Controller: Paul Allen
Estimated Sales: $ 50 Million
Number Employees: 100-249
Number of Products: 200
Parent Co: Maplehurst Bakeries
Type of Packaging: Food Service

8942 Mar Distributing Company
1375 E 6th Street
Suite 8
Los Angeles, CA 90021-1251   213-627-4006
                      Fax: 213-627-7430
Processor, packer and shipper of carrots and produce
  President: Maria Lopez
Estimated Sales: $ 1 - 3 Million
Number Employees: 59
Sq. footage: 8000
Type of Packaging: Private Label
Brands:
  Super Bunny
  Three J'S

8943 Mar-Jac Poultry
P.O.Box 1017
Gainesville, GA 30503-1017   770-531-5000
    Fax: 770-531-5015 800-226-0561
        info@marjacpoultry.com
        www.marjacpoultry.com
Manufacturer and exporter of fresh and frozen
chicken
  CEO: Jamal Al-Barzinji
  VP: Donald Bull
  VP Poultry Operations: Pete Martin
Estimated Sales: $200.3 Million
Number Employees: 1,000-4,999
Type of Packaging: Food Service, Private Label
Brands:
  M-J
  MAR-JAC BRANDS

8944 Mar-K Anchor Bar Hot Sauces
1047 Main Street
PO Box 66
Buffalo, NY 14209-0066   716-853-1791
  Fax: 716-332-4919 sales@buffalowings.com
        www.buffalowings.com
Produces buffalo wings, a variety of sauces, and gift
novelty items.
  Owner/President: Ivano Toscani
Estimated Sales: Below $ 5 Million
Number Employees: 6
Brands:
  Frank & Teressa's Original Anchor
  Frank & Teressa's Wing Sauce

8945 Mar-Key Foods
P.O.Box 603
Vidalia, GA 30475-0603   912-537-4204
  Fax: 912-537-2542 info@markeyfoods.com
        www.markeyfoods.com
Processor of soft drink concentrates, pre-sweetened
drink mixes and freeze pops
  President: Louie Powell
  Secretary: Diane Collins
Estimated Sales: $110000
Number Employees: 20-49
Type of Packaging: Consumer, Food Service, Bulk
Brands:
  Jolly Aid
  Jolly Pops

8946 Mar-Lees Seafood
110 Herman Melville Blvd
New Bedford, MA 02740-7344   508-991-6026
    Fax: 508-990-3468 800-836-0975
  info@marlees.com www.marlees.com
Seafoods
  President: John A Lees
  CEO: John Lees
  CEO: John Lees Jr
  VP Marketing/Sales: Jamie Dwyer
  VP Operations: Dan Canavan
Estimated Sales: $ 20-50 Million
Number Employees: 50-99

8947 (HQ)Maramor Chocolates
1855 E 17th Ave
Columbus, OH 43219-1006   614-291-2244
    Fax: 614-291-0966 800-843-7722
  orders@maramor.com www.maramor.com
Processor and exporter of kosher boxed chocolates,
chocolate covered bagel chips and mints; packaged
for racks and fund raising purposes; contract manu-
facturing available
  President: Michael Ryan
  Sales: Scott Sher
Estimated Sales: $1,600,000
Number Employees: 20-49
Sq. footage: 30000
Type of Packaging: Consumer, Private Label, Bulk
Brands:
  Maramor

8948 (HQ)Marantha Natural Foods
601 22nd St
San Francisco, CA 94107-3118   415-401-0080
    Fax: 415-401-0087 800-299-0048
        www.worldpantry.com

Processor of organic and regular nut and seed but-
ters, trail mixes and dry roasted nuts and seeds; im-
porter of cashews and sesame seeds; exporter of
organic and regular nut and seed butters and trail
mixes
  President: Patrick Lee
  CEO: David Miller
  Production Manager: Vern Niehaus
  Purchasing Manager: Jan Brown
Estimated Sales: $ 10 - 20 Million
Number Employees: 20-49
Sq. footage: 14000
Type of Packaging: Consumer, Food Service, Pri-
  vate Label, Bulk
Other Locations:
  Marantha Natural Foods
  San Leandro CA
Brands:
  Marantha
  Nuttin' Butter

8949 Marathon Cheese
304 E Street
PO Box 185
Marathon, WI 54448-0185   715-443-2211
  Fax: 715-443-3843 www.mcheese.com
Custom packager of cheese
  President: Dan Zastoupil
  Chairman/CEO: John Skoug
  SVP Finance: Gary Peterson
Estimated Sales: $ 500 Million-$ 1 Billion
Number Employees: 2,000
Type of Packaging: Consumer, Food Service, Pri-
  vate Label, Bulk

8950 Marathon Cheese Corporation
500 E Parker Dr
Booneville, MS 38829-5516   662-728-6242
  Fax: 662-728-6267 cbateman@mcheese.com
        www.marathoncheese.com
Manufacturer of cheeses including Swiss, cheddar,
blue and mozzarella
  President: Robert Buchberger
  Human Resource Manager: David Larsen
  Manager: Lisa Trace
  Plant Manager: Lisa Trace
Estimated Sales: $10-20 Million
Number Employees: 250-499
Type of Packaging: Private Label

8951 Marathon Enterprises
9 Smith Street
Englewood, NJ 07631-4607   201-935-3330
    Fax: 201-935-5693 info@sabrett.com
        www.sabrett.com
Processor and exporter of meat products including
ham, turkey, corned beef, tongue, beef, pastrami and
frankfurters
  Chairman of the Board: Gregory Papalexis
  Executive VP: Boyd Edelman
Estimated Sales: $17300000
Number Employees: 100
Type of Packaging: Consumer, Food Service, Pri-
  vate Label, Bulk
Brands:
  Concure
  Golde
  House O'Weenies

8952 Marathon Packing Corporation
1000 Montague St
San Leandro, CA 94577-4332   510-895-2000
                      Fax: 510-895-2022
Cooking oils and shortening
  President: Nelson Chu
Estimated Sales: $10-20 Million
Number Employees: 10-19

8953 Marburger Farm Dairy
1506 Mars Evans City Rd
Evans City, PA 16033-9399   724-538-4800
    Fax: 724-538-3250 800-331-1295
        http://www.marburgerdairy.com
Bottled milk and dairy products
  President: James Marburger
  Quality Control: Bronge Janzki
  Plant Manager: Garrie Wearing
Estimated Sales: $ 10-20 Million
Number Employees: 50-99
Type of Packaging: Private Label

8954 Marburger Foods
1535 N Lancer St
Peru, IN 46970-3601   765-689-5198
Fax: 765-689-5414 info@modernfoods.net
www.modernfoods.net
Processor and exporter of specialty bacon products
including pre-cooked slices and pieces; also, condi-
ments, sauces, relishes and frozen condensed soup
    President: John Marburger
    VP Marketing: Paul Marburger
    Plant Manager: Mike Correll
    Purchasing Manager: Steve Wheeler
Estimated Sales:$61900000
Number Employees: 5-9
Sq. footage: 270000
Parent Co: Armour/Swift-Eckrich
Type of Packaging: Consumer, Food Service, Pri-
    vate Label, Bulk
Brands:
    DWIGHT YOAKAM'S BAKERFIELD
    BSICUITS

**8955 Marcel et Henri Charcuterie
Francaise**
415 Browning Way
S San Francisco, CA 94080-6301   650-871-4230
    Fax: 650-871-5948   800-227-6436
        marcelethenri@sbcglobal.net
        www.marceletehenri.com
Processor of French pate and sausage.
    President: Henri Lapuyade
Estimated Sales:$3 Million
Number Employees: 10-19
Number of Brands: 1
Number of Products: 50
Sq. footage: 15000
Type of Packaging: Consumer, Food Service, Bulk
Brands:
    Marcel Et Henri

8956 Marcetti Frozen Pasta
803 8th St SW
Altoona, IA 50009-2306   515-967-4254
    Fax: 515-967-4147   auntui@auntui.com
        www.marzetti.com
Processor of frozen precooked pasta and dumpling
products.
    VP: Mike Warren
    Point of Sale Manager: Jan Larson
    Public Relations: Suzanne Woodyard
    Operations Manager: Terry Warren
    Production Manager: Chris Carpp
    Plant Manager: Neil Pitman
    Purchasing Manager: Ron Mathis
*Estimated Sales:*F
Number Employees: 100-249
Sq. footage: 100000
Type of Packaging: Consumer, Food Service, Pri-
    vate Label, Bulk
Brands:
    Aunt Vi's
    Warren

8957 Marche Tramsatlantique
4709 Rue St Denis
Montreal, QC H2J 2L5
Canada   514-287-3530
Processor and exporter of fresh and frozen salmon,
eel, mackerel, hake, trout and sturgeon; importer of
caviar
    President: Bruno Marie
Number Employees: 5-9
Type of Packaging: Food Service

8958 Marcho Farms Veal
176 Orchard Ln
Harleysville, PA 19438-1681   215-721-7131
    Fax: 215-721-9719 ltufft@marchofarms.com
Grower and packer of milk fed veal. Processing primal, fresh cuts, portion control, precooked meatballs, meat loaf, bacon and philly steaks
    President: Wayne A Marcho

8959 Marconi Italian Specialty Foods
710 W Grand Ave
Chicago, IL 60654-5574   312-421-0485
    Fax: 312-421-1286 sales@marconi-foods.com
        www.marconi-foods.com

Manufacturers a variety of specialty Italian foods including cheeses; coffees; salad dressings; meats; olive oils; pasta; salads; sauces; seafoods; spices, and
vinegars.
    President: Robert Johnson
    President/CEO/Co-Owner: Robert Johnson
    Co-Owner: Sue Formusa
Estimated Sales:$ 5 - 10 Million
Number Employees: 5-9
Parent Co: V Formusa Company

8960 Marcus Dairy
5 Sugar Hollow Rd
Danbury, CT 06810-7440   203-748-9427
    Fax: 203-791-2759   800-243-2511
        smarcus@marcusdairy.com
        www.marcusdairy.com
Processor of dairy products including butter, cottage
cheese, cream, sour cream, eggs and milk; also, or-
ange juice
    Manager: Fred Sescza
    Vice President: Jeffrey Marcus
    General Manager: Randy Peck
    General Manager: William Fitchett
Estimated Sales:$ 20 - 50 Million
Number Employees: 20-49
Type of Packaging: Consumer, Food Service, Pri-
    vate Label, Bulk
Brands:
    Marcus
    Sun Fresh

8961 Mardale Specialty Foods
1120 Glen Rock Avenue
Waukegan, IL 60085-5458   847-336-4777
                    Fax: 847-336-5030
Processor of portion controlled condiments includ-
ing salad dressing, syrup, jam and mayonnaise
    President: Ronald Tarantino
    Plant Manager: Jim Streiff
Number Employees: 20-49
Type of Packaging: Food Service

8962 Marder Trawling Inc
22 S Water St
New Bedford, MA 02740-7286   508-991-3200
    Fax: 508-990-2901   800-499-3219
    sales@marderbrands.com www.scallopguys.com
Produces a variety of seafood products including sea
scallops, bay scallops, shrimp and scallops
bar-b-skewers.
    President: Brian Marder
    Sales Director: Carlos Santaella

8963 Mardi Gras
150 Bloomfield Ave
Verona, NJ 07044-2711   973-857-3777
    Fax: 973-857-8884 contact@mardigrasfoods.com
        www.mardigrasfoods.com
Gourmet fresh and frozen foods
    Manager: Maria Carrozza
    VP: Kim Newman
*Estimated Sales:*Below $ 5 Million
Number Employees: 10-19
Sq. footage: 2400
Type of Packaging: Consumer

8964 Mareblu Naturals
1151 North Armando Street
Anaheim, CA 92806   714-238-1192
    Fax: 714-238-1246 denise@mbnaturals.com
        www.mbnaturals.com
healthy and natural nuts, healthy and natural nuts
with a tasty crunch
    President/Owner: Michael Kim
Estimated Sales:$2.7 Million
Number Employees: 40

8965 Margarita Man
10818 Gulfdale St
San Antonio, TX 78216-3607   210-979-7191
    Fax: 210-979-0718   800-950-8149
        margman@idworld.net
        www.margaritamansa.com
Processor of frozen drink mixes; wholesaler/distrib-
utor of frozen beverage machines
    President: Chris Murphy
    Plant Manager: Steve Snyder
Estimated Sales:$1 Million
Number Employees: 5-9
Number of Brands: 1
Number of Products: 15
Sq. footage: 2500

Brands:
    Go Bananas
    Go Mango
    Just Add Tequila
    Razzmatazzberry
    The Margarita Man

8966 Mari's New York
195 15th Street
Suite C5
Brooklyn, NY 11215   212-253-2014
    Fax: 615-622-0281 support@marisny.com
        www.marisny.com
brownies

8967 Maria and Son Italian Products
4201 Hereford St
St Louis, MO 63109-1798   314-481-9009
        Fax: 314-481-9109   866-481-9009
Frozen Italian pastas and sauces
    President: John Ard
Estimated Sales:$5-10 Million
Number Employees: 10-19
Brands:
    Maria & Son
    Tita's

8968 Mariani Nut Company
P.O.Box 809
Winters, CA 95694-0809   530-795-3311
    Fax: 530-795-2681 JohnA@marianinut.com
        www.marianinut.com
Processor and exporter of walnuts and almonds
    Partner: Jack Mariani
    Partner: Dennis Mariani
    Partner: Martin Mariani
Estimated Sales:$ 50 - 100 Million
Number Employees: 250-499
Type of Packaging: Consumer, Bulk

8969 Mariani Packing Company
500 Crocker Dr
Vacaville, CA 95688-8706   707-469-6921
    Fax: 707-452-2973   800-672-8655
        productinfo@marianipacking.com
        www.mariani.com
Manufacturer of fresh dried fruit including; plums,
apricots, cranberries, apples, raisins and sun-dried
tomatoes
    Chairman/CEO: Mark Mariani
    President: George Sousa Jr
    EVP: Craig Mackley
    VP Marketing/Sales: Jeff Freeman
    Operations Director: David Drews
Estimated Sales:$110 Million
Number Employees: 100-249
Type of Packaging: Consumer, Private Label, Bulk
Brands:
    MARIANI

8970 Marich Confectionery Company
2101 Bert Dr
Hollister, CA 95023-2562   831-634-4700
    Fax: 831-634-4705   800-624-7055
        sales@marich.com   www.marich.com
Processor of candy including chocolate cherries,
apricots, blueberries, strawberries and nut mixes;
also, mints, toffee and maltballs.
    President: Bradley Van Dam
    Executive VP/COO: Troy van Dam
    VP Marketing/Sales: Michelle van Dam
    Sales Manager: Ellen Filberman
    Plant Manager: Victor Moreno
*Estimated Sales:*Below $ 5 Million
Number Employees: 20-49
Type of Packaging: Consumer
Brands:
    Holland Mints
    Marich
    Wallabeans

8971 Maridee's Country Kitchen Cakes
PO Box 247
Lindsay, OK 73052-0247   800-798-7730
    Fax: 405-756-2702 mdcakes@hotmail.com
        www.marideescakes.com
Cakes
    Co-Owner: Marilou Munn
    Co-Owner: Dee Stout

8972 Marie Brizard Wines & Spirits
2320 Marinship Way
Suite 140
Sausalito, CA 94965-2830   800-878-1123
    Fax: 415-979-0305   info@boissetamerica.com
                www.boissetamerica.com
Processor, importer and exporter of alcoholic beverages including vodka, bourbon, tequila, scotch, brandy, cognac, schnapps, gin, rum, cordials, wines and champagne
    VP/Director Marketing: Michael Avitable
    VP/Director Sales: Robert Bermudez
    Director Operations: Hubert Surville
Number Employees: 20-49
Sq. footage: 6500
Parent Co: Marie Brizard Wines & Spirits USA
Brands:
    Marie Brizard

8973 Marie Callender's Gourmet Products/Goldrush Products
491 San Carlos Street
San Jose, CA 95110-2632   408-288-4090
    Fax: 408-279-3742   800-729-5428
rachel@commissary.com   www.mccornbread.com
Processor of kosher sourdough baking mixes including pancake, biscuit, cornbread, nine-grain and wholewheat bread, etc
    President: Henry Down Jr
Number Employees: 20-49
Parent Co: International Commissary Corporation
Type of Packaging: Consumer, Private Label, Bulk
Brands:
    Goldrush

8974 Marie F
123 Denison Street
Markham, ON L3R 1B5
Canada   905-475-0093
    Fax: 905-475-0038 800-365-4464
                fmarie@ca.inter.net
Manufacturer of beef, butcher supplies and sausage and sheep casings; importer of sausage casings, butcher suppliers and cures; exporter of sausage casings
    President: Sandra Marie Rundle
    Plant Manager: Alaister Sears
Estimated Sales: $1-3 Million
Number Employees: 20-49
Sq. footage: 15000
Type of Packaging: Food Service

8975 Marie's Candies
P.O.Box 766
West Liberty, OH 43357-0766   937-465-3061
    Fax: 937-465-3336 866-465-5781
                info@mariescandies.com
                www.mariescandies.com
Processor of candy including turkins, peanut brittle, toffee, butter creams, peppermint chews and melt-aways
    President: Jay King
    Co-Owner: Kathy King
Estimated Sales: $1,200,000
Number Employees: 20-49
Type of Packaging: Consumer

8976 Marie's Quality Foods
1244 E Beamer Street
Woodland, CA 95776-6002   530-662-9638
                800-544-9516
                www.maries.com
Salad dressing
    President: Richard D Orr
    VP Sales/Marketing: Richard Orr
    Operations Manager: Drew Orr
Number Employees: 20-49
Sq. footage: 100000
Type of Packaging: Consumer, Food Service, Private Label

8977 Marie's Refrigerated Dressings
201 Armory Dr
Thornton, IL 60476-1044   708-877-5150
    Fax: 708-877-1312 800-441-3321
                www.maries.com
Processor of salad dressings
    Plant Manager: Dorothy Munao
    Purchasing Agent: Mike Rhein
Estimated Sales: $ 10 - 20 Million
Number Employees: 20-49
Parent Co: Dean Foods Company
Type of Packaging: Consumer, Food Service

8978 Marietta Cellars
9801 Old River Rd
Hopland, CA 95449-2124   707-433-2747
    Fax: 707-857-4910 www.mendocinohill.com
Producer of wines the list of which includes Angeli Cuvee, Petit Sirah, Cabernet Sauvignon and Zinfandel.
    Manager: Linda Walker
    Office Manager: Suzie Buchignani
    Bookkeeper: Judy Somers
    Marketing Manager: Jake Bilbro
    Facilities Manager: Sarah Herrerra
    Cellar/Bottling Manager: Roman Cisneros
Estimated Sales: $300,000-500,000
Number Employees: 1-4

8979 Marika's Kitchen
106 Old Route 1
Hancock, ME 04640-3448   207-422-2300
    Fax: 207-422-2300 800-694-9400
Processor of almond and walnut baklava and Greek biscota
    Owner: Gloria Day
    Vice President: Michael Savoy
Number Employees: 1-4
Sq. footage: 2500
Type of Packaging: Food Service, Bulk

8980 Marimar Torres Estate
11400 Graton Road
Sebastopol, CA 95472-8901   707-823-4365
    Fax: 707-823-4496 info189@marimarestate.com
                www.marimarestate.com
Wines
    Proprietor/Winegrower: Marimar Torres
    National Sales Manager: Kyle Ray
    Cellar Master: Tony Britton
    Vineyard Manager: Venutra Albor
Estimated Sales: $850,000
Number Employees: 10
Type of Packaging: Private Label
Brands:
    Marimar Torres Estate

8981 Marin Brewing Company
1809 Larkspur Landing Cir
Larkspur, CA 94939-1801   415-461-4677
    Fax: 415-461-4688 brendan@moylans.com
                www.marinbrewing.com
Beer
    General Partner: Brendan Moylan
    Sales Manager: Curtis Cassidy
    Brewmaster: Arne Johnson
Estimated Sales: Below $ 5 Million
Number Employees: 50-99
Brands:
    Albion Amber Ale
    Marin Weiss
    Miwok Weizen Bock
    Mt. Tom Pale Ale
    Old Dipsea Barley Wine
    Point Reyes Porter
    Raspberry Trail Ale
    San Quentin's Breakout Stout

8982 Marin Food Specialties
P.O.Box 609
Byron, CA 94514-0609   925-634-6126
                Fax: 925-634-4647
Processor, importer and exporter of specialty foods including cookies, fig and fruit bars, pasta, trail mixes, marinated vegetables, almond butter, spices and candy; gift baskets available
    President: Joseph Brucia
    VP: Fred Vuylsteke
Estimated Sales: $ 1 - 3 Million
Number Employees: 50-99
Sq. footage: 30000
Type of Packaging: Consumer, Private Label, Bulk
Brands:
    Marin
    Spanky's

8983 Marin French Cheese Company
7500 Red Hill Rd
Petaluma, CA 94952-9438   707-762-6001
    Fax: 707-762-0430 800-292-6001
cheesefactory@marinfrenchcheese.com
                www.marinfrenchcheese.com

Manufacturer of cheeses including camembert cheese, breakfast cheese, brie cheese, schloss cheese and specialty flavored bries; also gift boxes available.
    Owner: Jim Boyce
Estimated Sales: $2500000
Number Employees: 10-19
Type of Packaging: Consumer, Bulk
Brands:
    Rouge Et Noir

8984 Marina Foods
302 NW 1st Street
Dania, FL 33004-2848   954-929-9047
    Fax: 954-925-7833 marinafoods@netzero.com
                www.marinafoods.com
Packers of edible oils and related products
    CFO: Mike Inisinon
Estimated Sales: $ 10-20 Million
Number Employees: 15
Type of Packaging: Private Label, Bulk

8985 Marine MacHines
3 Strawberry Hill Road
Bar Harbor, ME 04609-1206   207-288-0107
    Fax: 207-288-0462 www.acadia.net/marmac/
Company manufactures sea urchin procesing technology and equipment.
    President: Mickey Kestner

8986 Mariner Neptune Fish & Seafood Company
472 Dufferin Avenue
Winnipeg, NB R2W 2X6
Canada   204-589-5341
    Fax: 204-582-8135 800-668-8862
                info@marinerneptune.com
                www.marinerneptune.com
Distributor of fish, seafood and protein food products
    CEO: Russell Page
    VP: Rudi McCowan
    Marketing: Evan Page
    Sales: Doug Chandler
    Plant Manager: Chris Juerson
    Purchasing Director: Evan Page
Number Employees: 20-49
Number of Products: 2000
Type of Packaging: Consumer, Food Service
Brands:
    King Neptune
    Mariner-Neptune

8987 Mariner Seafoods
PO Box 610
Montague, PE C0A 1R0
Canada   902-838-2481
                Fax: 902-838-3735
Processor of fresh and frozen cod, hake, flounder, lobster and crab
    President: Mark Bonnell
    Manager: Mark Bonnell
Number Employees: 100-249
Type of Packaging: Consumer, Food Service, Private Label, Bulk
Brands:
    Mariner Seafoods

8988 Mario's Gelati
88 E 1st Avenue
Vancouver, BC V5T 1A1
Canada   604-879-9411
    Fax: 604-879-0435 info@mariosgelati.com
                www.mariosgelati.com
Processor, importer and exporter of ice cream
    President: Mario Loscerbo
    Vice President: Chris Loscerbo
Estimated Sales: $8000000
Number Employees: 35
Sq. footage: 30000
Brands:
    Mario's Gelati

8989 Marion-Kay Spices
1351 W Us Highway 50
Brownstown, IN 47220-9530   812-358-3000
    Fax: 812-358-3400 800-627-7423
                www.marionkay.com
Processor of spice blends and extracts
    President: John Reid
    CEO: Kordell Reid
Estimated Sales: $2500000
Number Employees: 10-19
Type of Packaging: Consumer, Food Service, Bulk

Brands:
- Claudia Sanders
- Cream of Vanilla
- The House of Flavors

8990 Maris Candy
2266 S Blue Island Ave
Chicago, IL 60608-4345   773-254-3351
Fax: 773-254-3581 mariscandy@msm.com
www.mariscandies.com
Processor of Mexican-style coconut candy
President/CEO: Raul Hernandez
VP/CEO: Maris Elena
VP of Retail: Raul Hernandez Jr.
VP of General Market: Maria Hernandez
VP of Wholesale: Rodrigo Hernandez
Estimated Sales: Below $ 5 Million
Number Employees: 1-4
Type of Packaging: Consumer

8991 Maritime Pacific Brewing Company
P.O.Box 17812
Seattle, WA 98127-1812   206-782-6181
Fax: 206-782-0718 marpacbrew@aol.com
maritimebrewery.citsearch.com/
Micro-brewery
President: George Hancock
Estimated Sales: Below $ 5 Million
Number Employees: 10-19
Number of Brands: s

8992 Mark West Vineyards
7010 Trenton Healdsburg Road
Forestville, CA 95436-9639   707-836-9647
Fax: 707-837-7103
Wine

8993 Mark-Lynn Foods
1090 Pacific Ave
Bremen, GA 30110-2238   770-537-5813
Fax: 770-537-0613 800-327-0162
contact@mark-lynn.com www.hormelfood.com
Contract packagers for dry products
President: Edward Dickinson
VP Operations: Joe Hoffer
Estimated Sales: $35656094
Number Employees: 100-249

8994 Market Day Corporation
555 W Pierce Rd # 200
Itasca, IL 60143-2636   630-285-1470
Fax: 630-285-3340 877-632-7753
chairweb@marketday.com www.marketday.com
Market Day Corporation is a a Fund Raising Food
Cooperative that supports educational institutions in
their fundraising drives by providing a wide selection of high quality foods. Their year-round program offers parents and neighborsthe opportunity to
buy restaurant quality food products through a
school or related organization each month while
contributing a portion of every purchase to their
child's school.
President: Gregory Butler
CEO: Bill Sivak
Number Employees: 100-249

8995 Market Fare Foods
2512 E Magnolia St
Phoenix, AZ 85034-6908   602-275-5509
Fax: 602-220-4462 800-782-9136
dnicklaw@marketfarefoods.com
www.marketfarefoods.com
Processor of pre-frozen and fresh sandwiches
President: Al Carfora
CFO: Barry Brooks
Vice President: Paul Miller
Sales Director: Paul Miller
Production Manager: Darrell Vannier
General Manager: Dave Nicklaw
Purchasing Manager: Bob Parker
Estimated Sales: $85000000
Number Employees: 5-9
Number of Brands: 3
Number of Products: 2
Parent Co: MarketFare Foods
Type of Packaging: Consumer, Private Label
Brands:
- Deli Pride
- Marketfare Allstars
- Select Allstars
- Takeouts

8996 Market Fare Foods
3637 Scarlet Oak Boulevard
Saint Louis, MO 63122-6605   636-225-8808
Fax: 636-825-4514 888-669-6420
customerservice@marketfarefoods.com
www.marketfarefoods.com
Muffins, brownies, cakes, sandwiches, etc
President: Al Carsora
Marketing Director: Toni Belcher
CFO: Barry Brooks
Estimated Sales: $ 20-50 Million
Number Employees: 50
Brands:
- Phoenix

8997 Market Fisheries
7129 S State St
Chicago, IL 60619-1017   773-483-3233
Fax: 773-483-0724
Seafood
President: Haim Brody
Estimated Sales: $ 3 - 5 Million
Number Employees: 10-19

8998 Market Square Food Company
1630 Old Deerfield Rd
Highland Park, IL 60035-3027   847-831-2228
Fax: 847-831-3533 800-232-2299
www.marketsquarefood.com
Specialty food gift items
Founder: James Lockhart
Founder: David Lockhart
Estimated Sales: $ 2.5-5 Million
Number Employees: 5-9
Brands:
- Market Square's
- Twistabout

8999 Marketing & Sales Essentials
PO Box 3748
Blaine, WA 98231-3748   954-452-5191
Fax: 954-452-5141 877-915-5191
m_s_e@bellsouth.net
Manufaturer of gummy candies
Number Employees: 5
Type of Packaging: Consumer, Food Service
Brands:
- EFRUTTI

9000 Marketing Specialists
75 Lane Road
Fairfield, NJ 07004-1044   973-227-7070
Fax: 973-227-7494
Cheese
Marketing Director: Fred D'Agostino
Estimated Sales: $ 100-500 Million
Number Employees: 250-499

9001 Markham Vineyards
P.O.Box 636
St Helena, CA 94574-0636   707-963-5292
Fax: 707-963-4616
admin@markhamvineyards.com
www.markhamvineyards.com
Processor and exporter of wines
President: Bryan Del Bondio
General Manager: Kathryn Fowler
Estimated Sales: $ 5 - 10 Million
Number Employees: 20-49

9002 Markko Vineyard
4500 S Ridge Rd W
Conneaut, OH 44030-9712   440-593-3197
Fax: 440-599-7022 800-252-3197
markko@suite224.net
www.markko.com/mkwinery.html
Wines
President/ Winemaker: Arnie Esterer
Owner: Tim Hubbard
Estimated Sales: $500,000-$1 Million
Number Employees: 1-4

9003 Marks Meat
10290 S Mulino Rd
Canby, OR 97013-9797   503-266-2048
Processor of beef, pork and lamb; custom slaughter-
ing services available
President: Kristie Akin
Estimated Sales: $110000
Number Employees: 5-9
Type of Packaging: Consumer

9004 Marley Orchards Corporation
2820 River Rd
Yakima, WA 98902-1136   509-248-5231
Fax: 509-248-7358
Processor of produce including apples
Chief Financial Officer: Stanley Bostrom
President/Sales & Marketing Staff: William
Gammie
Sales Representative: Tony Bishop
Estimated Sales: $2.8 Million
Number Employees: 75
Type of Packaging: Consumer, Food Service, Bulk

9005 Marlow Candy & Nut Company
65 Honeck Street
Englewood, NJ 07631-4125   201-569-7606
Fax: 201-569-9533 rickyl@marlowcandy.net
Candy and nuts
President: Eric Lowenthal
R & D: Aiden Kirk
Estimated Sales: $ 10-20 Million
Number Employees: 30

9006 Marlow Wine Cellars
Highway 41a-64
Monteagle, TN 37356   931-924-2120
Fax: 931-924-2587
Wines
President: Joe Marlow
Sales Manager: Gena Stevens
Estimated Sales: $ 1-2.5 Million
Number Employees: 1-4

9007 Marnap Industries
225 French St
Buffalo, NY 14211-1586   716-897-1220
Fax: 716-897-1306
dnapora@marnap.comaol.com
www.marnap.com
Processor and exporter of essential oils, spice
blends, seasonings, flavor compounds and oleores-
ins; importer of essential oils and oleoresins
President: Dennis J Napora
VP: Kevin Martin
Sales: Joanne Evans
Production: J Cogley
Estimated Sales: $ 3 - 5 Million
Number Employees: 5-9
Number of Products: 100+
Sq. footage: 12000
Type of Packaging: Bulk
Brands:
- Marnap-Trap

9008 Marquez Brothers International
612 W 5th St
Hanford, CA 93230-5043   559-584-0306
Fax: 559-584-8008
www.marquezbrothers.com/main
www.marquezbrothers.com
Processor of gelatin, sweet and sour cream, Mexican
cheese and liquid yogurt
CEO: Gustave Marquez
VP: Juan Marquez
Plant Manager: Juan Luis De La Torre
Estimated Sales: Less than $500,000
Number Employees: 100-249
Parent Co: Marquez Brothers International
Type of Packaging: Consumer, Food Service

9009 Marrese Cheese Company
N10149 City Trk Ay
Lomira, WI 53048   920-269-4288
Cheese

9010 (HQ)Mars
6885 Elm St
Mc Lean, VA 22101-6031   703-821-4900
Fax: 703-448-9678 www.mars.com
Chocolate, wrigley gum and confections, food,
drinks
President/CEO: Paul Michaels
EVP/CFO: Olivier Goudet
VP: Alberto Mora
VP Supply/R&D/Procurement: Richard Ware
Estimated Sales: $30 Billion
Number Employees: 10,000+
Type of Packaging: Consumer, Bulk
Brands:
- 3 MUSKETEERS
- 5 ACIDITO
- ABOU SIOUF RICE
- ACIDITO
- AIRWAVES

ALTOIDS
AMICELLI
AQUADROPS
BALISTON
BANJO
BIG LEAGUE CHEW
BOMVASO
BOUNTY
CASTELLARI
CELEBRATIONS
COMBOS
CREME SAVERS
DOLMIO
DOUBLEMINT
DOVE
EBLY
ECLIPSE
EXTRA
FLING
FLYTE
GALAXY
GALAXY FLUTE
GENERATION MAX
GUSANO
HUBBA BUBBA
KANTONG
KUDOS
LIFE-SAVERS
LOCKETS
M&M'S
MALTESERS
MARS
MARS DELIGHT
MASTERFOODS
MILKY WAY
MILKY WAY CRISPY ROLLS
MUNCH
MY DOVE
MY M&M'S
NO NAME
ORBIT
RARIS
REVELS
RONDO
ROYCO
SEEDS OF CHANGE
SKITTLES
SNICKERS
STARBURST
SUZI WAN
SWINKLES
TOPIC
TRACKER
TUNES
TWIX
TWIX TOPIX
UNCLE BEN'S
WINTERFRESH
WORLD OF GRAINS
WRIGLEY'S BIG RED
WRIGLEY'S FREEDENT
WRIGLEY'S JUICY FRUIT
WRIGLEY'S BIG RED
WRIGLEY'S FREEDENT
WRIGLEY'S JUICY FRUIT
WRIGLEY'S SPEARMINT

9011 (HQ)Mars Chocolates
800 High St
Hackettstown, NJ 07840-1552   908-852-1000
          Fax: 908-850-2734 www.m-ms.com
Masterfoods USA manufactures and markets Confectionery/Snackfood, Petcare and Food products. This division's confectionery and snackfood brands includes M&M's Chocolate Candies, SNICKERS Bar, TWIX Cookie Bars, STARBURST Fruits Chewsand COMBOS Brand. Masterfoods USA brands also include ETHEL M Chocolates and DOVE Chocolates.
     President/CEO: Paul Michaels
     EVP/CFO: Olivier Goudet
     VP Secretary/General Counsel: Alberto Mora
     VP Supply/R&D/Procurement: Richard Ware
Estimated Sales: $ 16 Billion
Number Employees: 5,000-9,999
Brands:
     CIRKUHEALTH
     DOUBLEMINT
     DOVE
     EXTRA
     FLAVIA
     M&M'S
     MARS
     MILKY WAY

ORBIT
SNICKERS
UNCLE BEN'S

9012 Mars M&M
50 Isleworth Dr
Henderson, NV 89052-6466   702-499-3364
          Fax: 630-850-9021   888-265-6788
                    www.mms.com
Processor of frozen snack foods including ice cream candy bars and specialties
     Owner: Joe Morris
Estimated Sales: $300,000-500,000
Number Employees: 1-4
Parent Co: Mars
Type of Packaging: Consumer
Brands:
     M&M

9013 Marsa Specialty Products
5511 Long Beach Ave
Vernon, CA 90058-3817   323-587-2288
          Fax: 323-587-6729   800-628-0500
                    marsa@earthlink.net
          www.marsaspecialtyproducts.com
Processor of dietetic products including syrups and ketchup
     President: Helga Hanlein
     Secretary/Treasurer: Allen Brown
     Sales Director: James Hanelin
     Operations Manager: Allen Brown
Estimated Sales: $1 Million
Number Employees: 10-19
Type of Packaging: Food Service

9014 (HQ)Marsan Foods
106 Thermos Road
Toronto, ON M1L 4W2
Canada   416-755-9262
          Fax: 416-755-6790   sean@marsanfoods.com
                    www.marsanfoods.com
Processor and exporter of single-series frozen entries and bowls, family size entries, control and private label. Processor and exporter of specialty meal components for healthcare settings
     President: James Jewett
     Director Sales/Marketing: S Lippay
Number Employees: 100
Number of Products: 160
Sq. footage: 75000
Type of Packaging: Consumer, Food Service, Private Label
Brands:
     Balanced Cuisine
     Puree Marsan

9015 Marshakk Smoked Fish Company
6980 75th St
Flushing, NY 11379-2531   718-326-2170
          Fax: 718-384-6661
Specialty foods
     President: Marie Cook
     Vice President: Gary Cook
     Sales Director: Sean Cook
Estimated Sales: $ 10-24.9 Million
Number Employees: 50-99
Type of Packaging: Private Label
Brands:
     Almondina
     Aunt Jenny's
     Babcock
     Boone Maman
     Bovril
     Breadshop
     Brianna's
     Carapelli
     Carr's
     Celestial
     Coco Pazzo
     Colavita
     Consorzio
     Dececco
     Del Verde
     Dell Amore's
     Delouis
     Dessvilie
     Dickinson
     Droste
     Dutch Gold
     Eden
     El Paso
     Finncrisp
     French Market
     Green Mountain

Grielle
Guiltless Gourmet
Hero
Highland Sugar Vermont
Holgrain
Illy
Knorr
Konriko
La Marne Champ
La Posada
La Preferida
Langnese
Lindt
Maille
Marmite
McCann's
Melba
Melitta
Monnini
New York Flatbread
Old Monk
Poell
Pommery
Pritikin
Qugg
Rao's
Romanoff
Spice Hunter
Spice Island
St. Dalfour
Sunbrand
Texmati
Timpone's
Tip Tree
Tropical Bee
Twinings

9016 Marshall Biscuits
100 Jacintoport Blvd
Saraland, AL 36571-3304   251-679-6226
     Fax: 251-679-6227   harris@marshallbiscuits.com
                    www.marshallbiscuits.com
Manufacturer of biscuits including buttermilk, homestyle, brown 'n serve and country style; also, dinner rolls
     President/CEO: Harris Morrissette
Estimated Sales: $95.5 Million
Number Employees: 50-99
Type of Packaging: Consumer, Food Service, Private Label
Brands:
     MARSHALL'S

9017 (HQ)Marshall Durbin Industries
P.O.Box 100755
Irondale, AL 35210-0755   205-956-3505
     Fax: 205-380-5033   sales@marshalldurbin.com
                    www.marshalldurbin.com
Chicken eggs, chicken hatchery, raising, slaughtering and processing of chickens, wholesale poultry.
     President: Melissa Durbin
     Chairman/CEO: Marshall Durbin
     Plant Manager: Robert Poe
Estimated Sales: $ 100-250 Million
Number Employees: 50-99

9018 Marshall Durbin PoultryCompany
1421 Robinwood Cir
Birmingham, AL 35217-1482   205-841-7315
          Fax: 205-841-7346 www.marshalldurbin.com
Chicken eggs, chicken hatchery, raising, slaughtering and procesing of chickens, wholesale poultry.
     Manager: Jimmy Ramia
     Chairman/CEO: Marshall Durbin
Estimated Sales: $ 10-20 Million
Number Employees: 50-99
Other Locations:
     Irondale AL

9019 Marshall Egg Products
P.O.Box 1250
Seymour, IN 47274-3850   812-497-2557
          Fax: 812-497-3311 www.roseacre.com
Processor of eggs
     President: Lois Rust
     Plant Manager: Nick Cary
Estimated Sales: $ 5 - 10 Million
Number Employees: 1,000-4,999
Parent Co: Rose Acre Farms
Type of Packaging: Food Service, Bulk

9020 Marshall Smoked Fish Company
1111 NW 159th Dr
Miami, FL 33169-5807   305-625-5112
Fax: 305-625-5528   info@seaspecialities.com
www.seaspecialities.com
Smoked fish
Manager: Ron Alexander
Controller: Arthur Hom
Manager: Ken Kosierowski
Estimated Sales: $ 50-75 Million
Number Employees: 100-249

9021 Marshall's Biscuit Company
100 Jacintoport Blvd
Saraland, AL 36571-3304   251-679-6226
Fax: 251-679-6227   800-368-9811
harris@marshallbiscuits.com
http://www.marshallbiscuits.com
Breads, rolls
President: A Robert Outlaw Jr
CEO: Harris V Morrissette
Estimated Sales: $ 10-20 Million
Number Employees: 50-99

9022 Marshallville Packing Company
50 E Market St
Marshallville, OH 44645   330-855-2871
Processor of beef, pork including sausage, luncheon
meats, poultry and cheese
President: Frank Tucker
Assistant Manager: John Tucker
Estimated Sales: $3000000
Number Employees: 20-49
Sq. footage: 27000
Type of Packaging: Consumer, Food Service, Bulk

9023 (HQ)Marshmallow Cone Company
5141 Fischer Ave
Cincinnati, OH 45217-1157   513-641-2345
Fax: 513-641-2557   800-641-8551
customerserv@marshmallowcone.com
www.marshmallowcone.com
Manufacturer and exporter of marshmallow filled
ice cream cones and cups and candy
President: John B Arbino
Estimated Sales: $ 10 - 20 Million
Number Employees: 20-49
Sq. footage: 42000
Type of Packaging: Consumer, Food Service, Private Label, Bulk
Brands:
MARPRO

9024 Marshmallow Products
5141 Fischer Ave
Cincinnati, OH 45217-1157   513-641-2345
Fax: 513-641-2557   800-641-8551
customerserv@marshmallowcone.com
www.marshmallowcone.com
Marshmallow-filled ice cream cones and specialty
candies
President: Dan Runk
Vice President: Pamela Arbino
Estimated Sales: $ 5-9.9 Million
Number Employees: 20-49
Brands:
Marpro

9025 Marsyl
308 16th Street
Cody, WY 82414-3214   307-527-6277
Confectionery
Brands:
Birthday Control Pills Candy
Confectionary Expres
Control Pills Candy
Eatable Greetables
Grouch Control Pills
Marsyl Candy
Over the Hill Pills
Passion Control Pill
Spaced Out Candy

9026 Marten's Country Kitchen
PO Box 428
Port Byron, NY 13140-0428   315-776-8821
Fax: 315-776-8201
Potatoes
Estimated Sales: $ 5 - 10 Million
Number Employees: 20-49
Sq. footage: 12500
Type of Packaging: Consumer, Food Service, Private Label, Bulk

9027 Martha Olson's Great Foods
P.O.Box 66
Sutter Creek, CA 95685-0066   209-234-5935
Fax: 209-223-7071   800-973-3966
Customercare@marthasallnatural.com
www.marthasallnatural.com
Processor of all natural baking mixes including pancake, muffin, waffle, bread, cake and scone; also,
chocolate sauce
Owner: Martha Olson
CEO: Margaret Brown
Marketing/National Accounts: Roylene Brown
Production Manager: Harvey Archer
Estimated Sales: $ 2.5-5 Million
Number Employees: 1-4
Brands:
Martha's All Natural
Martha's All Natural Baking Mixes

9028 Martha's Garden
475 Horner Avenue
Toronto, ON M8W 4X7
Canada   416-251-6112
Fax: 416-251-8443   866-773-2887
qvs@marthasgarden.com
www.marthasgarden.com
Processor of fresh onions, cabbage, lettuce, celery,
broccoli, cucumbers, carrots, cauliflower, tomatoes,
zucchini, eggplant, etc
President: Gus Arrigo, Jr.
Quality Assurance Manager: Jefery Musumi
Sales Manager: Richard Sabourin
Number Employees: 20-49

9029 Martin & Weyrich Winery
P.O.Box 7003
Paso Robles, CA 93447-7003   805-238-2520
Fax: 805-238-0887   sales@martinweyrich.com
www.martinweyrich.com
This winery produces a wide selection including
Pinot Grigio, Moscato Allegro, Nebbiolo, Nebbiolo
Vecchio, Insieme, Zinfandel La Primitiva, Cabernet
Etrusco, Vin Santo, in addition to having a fine coffee selection includingcappuccino, espresso, latte
and mochas.
Manager: Katie Stemper
Marketing Director: Larry Persinger
Production Manager: Craig Reed
Purchasing Manager: Cynthia Reed
Estimated Sales: $ 5-10 Million
Number Employees: 20-49
Sq. footage: 6

9030 Martin Brothers Distributing Company
P.O.Box 69
Cedar Falls, IA 50613-0010   319-266-1775
Fax: 319-277-1238   srathbun@martinsnet.com
www.martinnet.com
Wholesaler/distributor of baked goods, dairy items,
frozen food, groceries, meat, produce, seafood, janitorial supplies, equipment, etc.; serving the food service market; also, nutritional services, menu
consulting, layout and designavailable
President: John Martin
Manager Marketing/Merchandising: Diane
Chandler
Director Sales/Marketing: Doug Coen
Estimated Sales: $120000000
Number Employees: 250-499
Sq. footage: 86000

9031 Martin Brothers SeafoodCompany
133 Westwego Expy
Westwego, LA 70094   504-341-2251
Fax: 504-341-2251
Processor of frozen crabmeat and gumbo crabs
President: William Martin
Owner: Donna Martin
Estimated Sales: $5-9.9 Million
Number Employees: 1-4
Type of Packaging: Consumer, Food Service, Bulk

9032 Martin Coffee Company
1633 Marshall St
Jacksonville, FL 32206-6011   904-355-9661
Fax: 904-355-9673   www.martincoffee.com
Manufacturer of coffee
President/Founder: Amy B Martin
VP: Harold Johnson
VP Sales/Marketing: Ben Johnson

Estimated Sales: $15 Million
Number Employees: 10-19
Type of Packaging: Consumer, Food Service, Private Label
Brands:
MARTIN

9033 Martin Farms
337 Magnolia Ave
Patterson, CA 95363-9632   209-892-8653
Fax: 209-892-2652   877-838-7369
info@martinfarms.com   www.martinfarms.net
Processor of sliced, diced and halved sun-dried tomatoes; available in bags and oil
Owner: Joseph Martin
Estimated Sales: Less than $500,000
Number Employees: 1-4

9034 Martin Rosol's
45 Grove St
New Britain, CT 06053-4198   860-223-2707
Fax: 860-229-6690   orders@martinrosols.com
www.martinrosols.com
Processor of cold cuts, hot dogs and kielbasa
President: Robert Rosol
CEO: Eugene Rosol
Vice President: Karen Rosol
Estimated Sales: $ 5 - 10 Million
Number Employees: 20-49
Type of Packaging: Consumer, Private Label

9035 Martin Seafood Company
7901 Oceano Ave # 46
Jessup, MD 20794-9407   410-799-5822
Fax: 410-799-3545   info@martinseafoodco.com
www.martinseafoodco.com
Processor of frozen breaded seafood products;
wholesaler/distributor of raw frozen seafood products; serving the food service market
Owner: Billy Martin
Secretary: Shawn Isaac
Estimated Sales: $3000000
Number Employees: 20-49
Sq. footage: 25000
Type of Packaging: Consumer, Food Service

9036 Martin's Famous Pastries
1000 Potato Roll Ln
Chambersburg, PA 17202-8897   717-263-9580
Fax: 717-263-6687 www.mfps.com
Processor of potato, tortilla and corn chips, pretzels
and extruded snacks
President: Lloyd Martin
Executive VP: James Martin
VP Sales/Marketing: Dennis Wenrick
Estimated Sales: $ 20 - 50 Million
Number Employees: 250-499
Sq. footage: 90000
Parent Co: Consolidated Biscuit Company
Type of Packaging: Consumer, Food Service, Private Label
Brands:
Mr. C'S
Mr. G'S
Nibble With Gibble's

9037 Martin's Potato Chips
P.O.Box 28
Thomasville, PA 17364-0028   717-792-3565
Fax: 717-792-4906   800-272-4477
www.martinschips.com
Processor of potato chips
President: Kenneth Potter
CEO: Kenneth A Potter Jr
cfo: Steve Fitz
Quality Control Manager: Neal Rohrbough
VP Sales/Marketing: Kevin Potter
VP Production: Kenneth Potter Jr
Estimated Sales: $ 50 - 100 Million
Number Employees: 100-249
Sq. footage: 55000
Type of Packaging: Consumer, Food Service, Bulk

9038 Martini & Prati Wines
2191 Laguna Rd
Santa Rosa, CA 95401-3799   707-823-2404
Fax: 707-829-6151   info@martiniprati.com
www.martinraywinery.com
Processor of wines
Manager: Wendi Hawn
VP: Thomas Martini
Estimated Sales: $ 10 - 20 Million
Number Employees: 20-49
Sq. footage: 120000

Type of Packaging: Consumer
Brands:
Fountain Grove
Martini & Prati

9039 Martino's Bakery
335 N Victory Blvd
Burbank, CA 91502-1841   818-842-0715
Fax: 818-842-5111 www.martinosbakery.com
Breads, cakes and related products
Owner: Mario Corradi
CEO: Andy Horvatch
Controller: Kathy Prince
Purchasing Agent: Diana Wang
Estimated Sales: Less than $500,000
Number Employees: 5-9

9040 Martz Vineyards
20799 Highway 128
Yorkville, CA 95494-9201   707-895-2334
Wines
President: Larry Martz
Estimated Sales: Under $500,000
Number Employees: 1-4

9041 Maruchan
15800 Laguna Canyon Rd
Irvine, CA 92618-3103   949-789-2300
Fax: 949-789-2350 maropoulos@worldnet.att.net
Processor and exporter of Oriental foods including
wonton soup and instant ramen noodles
President: Kiyoshi Fukagawa
Estimated Sales: $33200000
Number Employees: 250-499
Parent Co: Toyo Suisan Kaisha
Type of Packaging: Consumer

9042 Marukai Corporation
1740 W Artesia Blvd # 114
Gardena, CA 90248-3238   310-660-6300
Fax: 310-660-6301 info@marukai.com
www.marukai.com
Manufacturer, importer and exporter of Japanese
products
President: Hidejiro Matsu
Estimated Sales: $41 Million
Number Employees: 100-249
Parent Co: Marukai Corporation
Other Locations:
Marukai Corporation
Honolulu HI

9043 Marukan Vinegar (U.S.A.) Inc.
7755 Monroe St
Paramount, CA 90723-5020   562-630-6060
Fax: 562-229-1107 anoble@marukan-usa.com
www.marukan-usa.com
Marukan Vinegar has been brewing natural rice vin-
egars since 1649. Using only selected rice, the vine-
gar is naturally matured by the traditional method
and spends over a month brewing for a richer, more
fully developed flavor.
President: Masahito Kikumoto
CEO: Junichi Oyama
VP Sales/Marketing: Jon Tanklage
Sales/Marketing: Tom McReynolds
Operations: Tosh Zamoto
Production: Toru Saito
Production: Michitsugu Ogawa
Estimated Sales: $7-10 Million
Number Employees: 20-49
Sq. footage: 15000
Parent Co: Marukan Vinegar Co, Ltd
Type of Packaging: Consumer, Food Service, Pri-
vate Label, Bulk
Brands:
Marukan

9044 Marva Maid Dairy
5500 Chestnut Ave
Newport News, VA 23605-2118   757-245-3857
Fax: 757-928-2449 800-544-4439
www.marvamaid.com
Manufacturer and exporter of cottage cheese,
whipped sour cream, whole and low-fat milk and
milk by-products; also, apple, grapefruit and orange
juice
Manager: Danny Lovell
Sales Manager: Ed Boyd
Director Fluid Milk Operations: Bruce Manson
Plant Manager: Rick Meier
Estimated Sales: $397 Million
Number Employees: 1-4

Parent Co: Maryland & Virginia Milk Producers
Association
Type of Packaging: Consumer
Brands:
HARVEST FRESH
MARVA MAID
SLENDO

9045 Marwood Sales
6400 Glenwood St # 308
Shawnee Mission, KS 66202-4025   913-722-1534
Fax: 913-262-9132
Dairy products
President: Mark Woodard
Estimated Sales: $8.2 Million
Number Employees: 1-4
Brands:
Marwood

9046 Marx Brothers
132 32nd St S
Birmingham, AL 35233   205-251-3139
Fax: 205-324-6322 800-633-6376
www.marxbrothersinc.com
Manufacturer of sweetened coconut
President: Edgar Marx Jr
Estimated Sales: $3 Million
Number Employees: 20-49
Type of Packaging: Consumer, Food Service, Pri-
vate Label, Bulk

9047 Mary Ann's Baking Company
8371 Carbide Ct
Sacramento, CA 95828-5636   916-681-7444
Fax: 916-681-7470 www.maryannsbaking.com
Processor of danish and pastries
President: George Demas
General Manager: Bob Burzinski
Plant Manager: Don Lavelle
Estimated Sales: $ 10 - 20 Million
Number Employees: 100-249
Type of Packaging: Consumer

9048 Mary Sue Candies
1786 Union Ave
Baltimore, MD 21211-1417   410-467-9338
Fax: 410-467-1649 info@naroncandy.com
www.marysue.com
Chocolate and soft candy
President: William G Buppert
CFO: Mike Wiss
R & D: Mark Berman
Estimated Sales: $ 5-10 Million
Number Employees: 5-9

9049 Mary of Puddin Hill
P.O.Box 241
Greenville, TX 75403-0241   903-455-6931
Fax: 903-455-4522 800-545-8889
www.puddinhill.com
Processor of pecan fruit cakes and chocolate candy
Owner: Ken Bain
CEO: Ron Massey
Plant Manager: Jerry Davis
Estimated Sales: $1300000
Number Employees: 50-99
Type of Packaging: Private Label

9050 Mary's Candy Shop
238 Main Street
Lewiston, ME 04240-7021   207-783-9824
Processor of confectionery products
President: Luceille Meservier
Estimated Sales: $500,000-$1 Million
Number Employees: 1-4
Type of Packaging: Consumer

9051 Mary's Gone Crackers
PO Box 965
Gridley, CA 95948   530-846-5100
Fax: 530-846-5500 888-258-1250
info@marysgonecrackers.com
www.marysgonecrackers.com
wheat free and gluten free baked goods
President/Owner: Dale Rodrigues
VP of Sales: Mike Quinn
Estimated Sales: $6.8 Million
Number Employees: 57

**9052 Maryland & Virginia Milk
Producers Cooperative**
1985 Isaac Newton Sq W
Reston, VA 20190-5094   703-742-7443
Fax: 703-742-7459 jbryant@mdvamilk.com
www.mdvamilk.com
Processor of milk
President: John D Hardesty
Assistant Secretary: Barbara Riegler
General Manager: George Walgrove
Estimated Sales: $668199064
Number Employees: 20-49
Type of Packaging: Consumer

**9053 Maryland & Virginia Milk
Cooperative Association**
P.O.Box 184
Laurel, MD 20725-0184   301-953-2964
Fax: 301-953-1979 jbryant@mdvamilk.com
www.mdvamilk.com
Milk and dairy products
Manager: David Blake
Manager: William King
Estimated Sales: $ 20-50 Million
Number Employees: 20-49
Brands:
Laurel

9054 (HQ)Maryland Baking Company
951 Glenwood Avenue SE
Atlanta, GA 30316-1886   404-622-1731
Baked goods
Plant Manager: Brooks Mauldin
Estimated Sales: Under $500,000
Number Employees: 50-99

**9055 Maryland Fresh Tomato
Company**
7460 Conowingo Avenue
Building B
Jessup, MD 20794-9361   410-799-5050
Fax: 410-799-1816
Tomatos and vegetables
Estimated Sales: $ 3 - 5 Million
Number Employees: 5-9

9056 Marzipan Specialties
1513 Meridian St
Nashville, TN 37207-5061   615-226-4800
Fax: 615-226-4882 marizapan@isdn.net
www.marzipanspecialties.com
Processor of marzipan candy
Owner: Karl Schoenperger
Estimated Sales: Below $ 5 Million
Number Employees: 5-9
Type of Packaging: Consumer

9057 Masala Chai Company
P.O.Box 8375
Santa Cruz, CA 95061-8375   831-475-8881
Fax: 831-475-5967 masala@masalachaico.com
www.masalachaico.com
Processor and importer of chai teas including bottled
and ready- to-drink, Indian spiced, regular, decaf
and energy tonics
Co-Owner: Raphael Reuben
Co-Owner: Susan Beardsley
Estimated Sales: $240000
Number Employees: 1-4
Sq. footage: 1500
Type of Packaging: Consumer, Food Service, Pri-
vate Label, Bulk
Brands:
Aphroteasiac Chai
Masala Chai

**9058 Mason County Fruit Packers
Cooperative**
3958 W Chauvez Rd # 1
Ludington, MI 49431-8200   231-845-6248
Fax: 231-843-9453 doylefenner@yahoo.com
Processor of frozen cherries and apples, canned ap-
ple juice and sauce, peaches and plums
President: Roy Hackert
CEO: Doyle Fenner
Plant Manager: Joe Bates
Estimated Sales: $82800000
Number Employees: 100-249
Sq. footage: 1000000
Type of Packaging: Consumer, Bulk

9059 Massimo Zanetti Beverage Company
1370 Progress Road
Suffolk, VA 23434   757-538-8083
    Fax: 757-215-7447 www.saralee.com
Roasts and packs coffee
    CEO: Massino Zanetti
    Manager: Chuck Gosstrom
    Plant Manager: Buddy McGuire
Number Employees: 200
Brands:
    CHASE & SANBORN
    CHOCK FULL O'NUTS
    HILLS BROS
    MJB
    SEGAFREDO ESPRESSO

9060 Masson Cheese Corporation
6180 Alcoa Ave
Vernon, CA 90058-3935   323-583-1251
    Fax: 323-585-8765 800-637-7262
    sales@massoncheese.com
    www.massoncheese.com
Natural and processed cheese
    President: Morris Farinella
    Marketing Director: Jean Hendrix
Estimated Sales: $ 10-20 Million
Number Employees: 50-99

9061 Mastantuono Winery
2720 Oakview Rd
Templeton, CA 93465-8798   805-238-0676
    Fax: 805-238-9257
    info@mastantuonowinery.com
    www.mastantuonowinery.com
Wine
    Owner: Pasquale Mastantuono
    Operations Manager: Pasquale Mastantuono
Estimated Sales: Below $ 5 Million
Number Employees: 5-9
Brands:
    Mastantuono Wines

9062 Master Mix
181 W Orangethorpe Avenue
Placentia, CA 92870-6931   714-524-1698
    Fax: 714-524-8540
Processor and exporter of powdered mixes including
soft serve, shake and yogurt; also, syrups, toppings,
water soluable ginseng extract and drink bases
    President: Pat Lagraffe
    VP: Jim LaGraffe
Estimated Sales: $ 1 - 3 Million
Number Employees: 1-4
Sq. footage: 5000
Type of Packaging: Consumer, Food Service, Private Label, Bulk
Brands:
    Chalet Gourmet
    Dairy's Pride
    Master Mix

9063 Master Peace Food Imports
PO Box 36
Pleasantville, NY 10570-0036   914-769-7148
    Fax: 914-769-8944
Health and dietetic foods
    President: John Peace, Jr.
    Secretary: Jolaine Dow Peace
Estimated Sales: Under $500,000
Number Employees: 1-4
Brands:
    Airborne

9064 Master Taste International
1111W Martin Luther King Jr Boulevard
Plant City, FL 33563-5106   813-359-5128
    Fax: 813-757-6060 800-237-7629
    ingredients@crystals-inc.com
    www.crystals-inc.com
Manufacturer, and exporter of a complete spectrum
of fruit and vegetable powders. The value-added vi-
tamins, minerals, and natural qualities of these
unique powders are used for ingredients,
nutraceuticals, colors, and flavors. Organicor
non-GMO available. AIB-certified, kosher, halal
    President: Kevin Lane
Estimated Sales: $20-50 Million
Number Employees: 100
Number of Brands: 10
Number of Products: 450
Sq. footage: 100000
Type of Packaging: Consumer, Food Service, Private Label, Bulk

Brands:
    BAR BLASTER
    Crystal Caps
    Crystalac
    Crystalettes
    Crystals
    Crystals International Food
    JUICE PLUSTOM
    True Crystals

9065 Masterfoods USA
800 High St
Hackettstown, NJ 07840-1552   908-852-1000
    Fax: 908-850-2734 www.m-ms.com
Candy
    Senior VP: Mike Tolkowsky
Number Employees: 5,000-9,999
Brands:
    3 MUSKETEERS
    DOVE CHOCOLATE
    KUDOS
    M&M'S
    MILKY WAY
    SKITTLES
    SNICKERS
    STARBURST
    TWIX BRAND

9066 Masters Gallery Foods
P.O.Box 170
Plymouth, WI 53073-0170   920-893-8431
    Fax: 920-893-6075 800-236-8431
    dmacphee@mastersgalleryfoods.com
    www.mastersgalleryfoods.com
Cheese
    President: Christopher Gentine
    CFO: Catherine Schwartz
    CEO: Jeff Giffin
    Senior VP Marketing: Bob Wilson
Estimated Sales: $ 5-10 Million
Number Employees: 20-49

9067 Masterson Company
4023 W National Ave
Milwaukee, WI 53215-1000   414-647-1132
    Fax: 414-647-1170
    contact@mastersoncompany.com
    www.mastersoncompany.com
Processor of dry ice cream toppings including choc-
olate chips, swirls, almonds, etc.; also, syrup top-
pings including butterscotch, caramel, fudge, etc
    President: Joe Masterson
    Director Sales/Marketing: Irene Grob
    Director Manufacturing: S Burr
    Purchasing Manager: George Guyer
Estimated Sales: $ 50 - 100 Million
Number Employees: 100-249
Type of Packaging: Food Service, Bulk
Brands:
    Masterson

9068 (HQ)Mastertaste
546 Us Highway 46
Teterboro, NJ 7608-1104   888-547-8844
    Fax: 201-329-9801 info@mastertaste.com
    www.mastertaste.com
Flavors, essential oils, oleoresins
    President: Stan McCarthy
Estimated Sales: $40.5 Million
Number Employees: 5-9
Type of Packaging: Food Service, Bulk
Brands:
    Man Heimer
    Mastertaste

9069 Mastertaste
747 Sunpark Drive
Fenton, MO 63026-5315   636-349-0020
    Fax: 636-349-1839 stlfla4douge@aol.com
    www.mastertaste.com
Flavors
    President: Richard Lane
Estimated Sales: $ 10-20 Million
Number Employees: 10
Sq. footage: 20000

9070 (HQ)Mastertaste Company
152 Louis St # A
South Hackensack, NJ 07606-1721   201-641-6555
    Fax: 847-823-9301 www.mastertaste.com

Manufacturer, importer and exporter of flavors, es-
sential oils, oleoresins and fragrances
    Owner: Robert Smith
    North America Communications Director: Nancy Lawrence
Estimated Sales: $100 Million
Number Employees: 100-249
Parent Co: Kerry Group
Type of Packaging: Bulk
Brands:
    MASTERTASTE

9071 Mat Roland Seafood Company
1790 Mayport Rd
Atlantic Beach, FL 32233   904-246-9443
    Fax: 904-241-0645
Processor of fish and shrimp
    President: Brad Roland
Estimated Sales: $2300000
Number Employees: 10
Type of Packaging: Consumer, Food Service, Bulk
Brands:
    Roland Star

9072 Matador Processors
P.O.Box 2200
Blanchard, OK 73010-2200   405-485-3567
    Fax: 405-485-2597 800-847-0797
    matador@matadorprocessors.com
    www.matadorprocessors.com
Processor of frozen foods including chile rellenos
(stuffed peppers), stuffed jalapenos and breaded hors
d'oeuvres including cheese bites, mushrooms, des-
serts, etc.; exporter of chile rellenos, stuffed
jalapenos and mozzarellasticks
    President: Betty Wood
    CFO: Richard Clark
    VP: Ron W Diggs
    R&D: Debbie Funderburk
    Sales: Richard Clark
    Operations: Ron W Diggs
    Plant Manager: Debbie Funderburk
Estimated Sales: $3000000
Number Employees: 50-99
Sq. footage: 27000
Type of Packaging: Food Service, Private Label
Brands:
    Clif's
    Matador

9073 Matangos Candies
S 15th & Catherine St
Harrisburg, PA 17101   717-234-0882
    www.matangoscandies.com
Processor of candy and other confectionery products
    Owner/President: Peter Matangos
Estimated Sales: $100,000
Number Employees: 1-4
Type of Packaging: Consumer
Brands:
    Matangoes

9074 Matanuska Maid Dairy
814 W Northern Lights Blvd
Anchorage, AK 99503-3713   907-561-5223
    Fax: 907-563-7492 info@matmaid.com
    www.matmaid.com
Fluid milk, orange juice and related products
    President: Joe Van Treeck
    Sales Manager: Glenn Soby
    Sales Manager: Linda Bowers
    Plant Manager: Gary Nelson
Estimated Sales: $ 10-20 Million
Number Employees: 20-49
Brands:
    Matanuska Maid

9075 Matanzas Creek Winery
6097 Bennett Valley Road
Santa Rosa, CA 95404-8570   707-528-6464
    Fax: 707-571-0156 800-500-6464
    info@matanzascreek.com
    www.matanzascreek.com
Wines the selection of which includes the Sonoma
County Series: Merlot, Chardonnay, Sauvignon
Blanc, Cabernet Sauvignon and Syrah. Limited Pro-
duction Series wines include 2002 Bennett Valley
Merlot and 2001 Jackson Park Merlot.
    General Manager: Patrick Connelly
    Vice President: William MacIver
    Marketing Director: Peter Kay
    Winemaker: Susan Reed
    Director Operations: Tad Sanders

Estimated Sales: $ 10-20 Million
Number Employees: 20-49
Sq. footage: 20
Type of Packaging: Private Label
Brands:
Journey
Matanzas Creek Winery

9076 Mathews Packing Company
950 Ramirez Rd
Marysville, CA 95901-9444   530-743-9000
Fax: 530-742-6625
Dried prunes, pitted prunes, rice
Owner: Ed Mathews
VP/Marketing: Mark Mathews
Estimated Sales: $1-$2.5 Million
Number Employees: 5-9
Type of Packaging: Private Label

9077 Matilija Water Company
164 W Park Row Ave
Ventura, CA 93001-1838   805-322-7212
Fax: 805-643-3825 www.getpurewater.com
Processor of bottled water; also, wholesaler/distributor of water purification systems; serving the food service market
President: Dom Schakleford
Estimated Sales: $ 1 - 3 Million
Number Employees: 10-19
Type of Packaging: Consumer, Food Service

9078 Matlaw's Food Products
135 Front Ave
West Haven, CT 06516-2837   203-931-9118
Fax: 203-933-8506   800-934-8266
Processor of frozen stuffed clams, pizza, burger and morning bites, egg rolls, pizza and spinach fingers, importer of clam shells
CEO: Eugene Welka
Vice President: Dennis Seffernick
Marketing Director: Jim Delzell
Sales Director: Tim Benevelli
Estimated Sales: $23100000
Number Employees: 100-249
Type of Packaging: Food Service, Private Label, Bulk
Brands:
CHEF ROMEO
CRYSTAL BAY
MATLAW'S

9079 Matrix Health Products
9316 Wheatlands Road
Santee, CA 92071-5644   619-448-7550
Fax: 619-448-2995   888-736-5609
info@earthsbounty.com   www.matrixhealth.com
Manufacturer, importer and exporter of nutritional and herbal supplements including tablets, liquids, powders and capsules - also kosher & organic products. Teas, coffee & vanilla and nonjuice
President: Steven Kravitz
R&D: Stephen Center MD
VP: Judy Kravitz
Number Employees: 10-19
Type of Packaging: Consumer, Private Label, Bulk
Brands:
Colloidal Silver
Dhea
Earth's Bounty
Melatonin
Meno-Select
Noni
Oxy-Caps
Oxy-Cleanse
Oxy-Max
Oxy-Mist
Prosta-Forte
Woman's Select

9080 Matson Fruit Company
P.O.Box 307
Selah, WA 98942-0307   509-697-7100
Fax: 509-697-8168
daryl.matson@matsonfruit.com
www.matsonfruit.com
Processor and exporter of apples and pears
President: Rod Matson
Estimated Sales: $ 50 - 100 Million
Number Employees: 100-249
Type of Packaging: Consumer, Food Service

9081 Matson Vineyards
10584 Arapaho Dr
Redding, CA 96003-7638   530-222-2833
ommatson@snowcrest.com
www.matsonvineyards.com
Wines
President: Oscar Matson
Analyst /Marketing Manager: Kdiko Goto
Winemaker: Roger Matson
Estimated Sales: Under $500,000
Number Employees: 1-4

9082 Matterhorn Ice Cream Company
115 E Plymouth Street
Caldwell, ID 83605-2435   208-459-1635
Fax: 208-459-1965   800-822-1635
customerservice@thematterhorn.com
www.thematterhorn.com
Manufacturer of ice cream novelties
President: Thomas Nist
Estimated Sales: $9,800,000
Number Employees: 85
Type of Packaging: Consumer
Brands:
Big Ed Super Saucer
Matterhorn

9083 Matthew's All Natural
280b Mishawum Rd
Woburn, MA 01801-2062   978-458-7858
Fax: 978-935-5753
Processor and wholesaler/distributor of all-natural breads and English muffins
Manager: Charles Vlahos
Customer Service: Eva Clark
Estimated Sales: $1800000
Number Employees: 5-9
Sq. footage: 9500
Type of Packaging: Consumer
Brands:
Matthew's All Natural

9084 Matthews 1812 House
P.O.Box 15
Cornwall Bridge, CT 06754-0015   860-672-0149
Fax: 860-672-1812   800-662-1812
info@matthews1812house.com
www.matthews1812house.com
Processor of all-natural cakes including apple crumb torte, brandied apricot, chocolate raspberry liqueur, chocolate rum, country spice, fruit and nut, fudge brownie torte, lemon rum, cookies, bar cookies, chocolate explosionbrownies
President: Deanna Matthews
Corporate Secretary: Blaine Matthews
Manager: Cheryl Cass
Estimated Sales: $1 Million
Number Employees: 10-19
Sq. footage: 2000
Type of Packaging: Consumer, Food Service, Private Label
Brands:
Matthews 1812 House

9085 Matthiesen's Deer & Custom Processing
3357 252nd St
De Witt, IA 52742-9223   563-659-8409
Processor of meat products including, beef, lamb, venison, pork and mettwurst
President: Sandy Matthiesen
Estimated Sales: $500,000-$1 Million
Number Employees: 1-4
Type of Packaging: Consumer

9086 Mattus Lowfat Ice Cream
PO Box 311
Glen Cove, NY 11542-0311   718-472-1232
Fax: 718-472-2066   info@mattus.com
www.mattusicecream.com
Ice cream
President: Denis Hurley
CFO: Anthony Rugel
VP: Keven Hurley
General Manager: Joe Lippolis
Estimated Sales: Below $ 5 Million
Number Employees: 20-49

9087 Mauana Loa Macadamia Nut Corporation
1830 Partridge Cir
Florence, SC 29505-3150   843-629-1685
Fax: 843-629-1517
btankersley@maunaloamacs.com
www.maunaloa.com
Macadamia nuts
Estimated Sales: $300,000-500,000
Number Employees: 1-4

9088 Maui Bagel
200 Dairy Rd
Kahului, HI 96732-2978   808-270-7561
Fax: 808-270-7919 www.mauicounty.gov
Bread, rolls, bagels, dounuts, sandwiches
Manager: Jeff Murray
Number Employees: 250-499

9089 Maui Coffee Roasters
444 Hana Hwy # B
Kahului, HI 96732-2315   808-877-2877
Fax: 808-871-2684   800-645-2877
info@hawaiiancoffee.com
www.hawaiiancoffee.com
Roasted coffee
President: Nick Matichyn
CFO: Mike Vaki
Marketing Manager: Cark Musto
VP Sales: Mike Okazaki
Purchasing Manager: Nicky Matichyn
Estimated Sales: $ 1-2.5 Million
Number Employees: 10-19
Type of Packaging: Private Label, Bulk

9090 Maui Pineapple Company
P.O.Box 187
Kahului, HI 96733-6687   808-877-3351
Fax: 808-871-0953   info@mauipineapple.com
www.mauiland.com
Processor and exporter of whole fresh, canned and fresh-cut pineapple; also, pineapple juice and concentrates
President: David Cole
CEO: David Cole
CEO: Robert I Webber
Executive VP Marketing/Sales: James McCann
Estimated Sales: $168666000
Number Employees: 500-999
Type of Packaging: Consumer, Food Service, Private Label, Bulk
Brands:
Hawaiian Gold
King of Hawaii

9091 Maui Pineapple Company
1800 Sutter Street
Suite 850
Concord, CA 94520-2569   925-798-0240
Fax: 925-798-0252
Processor, packer and exporter of pineapple, frozen pineapple juice and pineapple juice concentrate; importer of fresh and processed tropical fruits
President: Arian Nishida
Executive VP Sales/Marketing: James McCann
Director Sales/Service: Bruce Wilson
Estimated Sales: $ 10 - 20 Million
Number Employees: 800
Parent Co: Maui Land & Pineapple Company
Type of Packaging: Consumer, Food Service, Private Label, Bulk
Brands:
Hawaiian Gold

9092 Maui Potato Chips
295 Lalo St
Kahului, HI 96732-2915   808-877-3652
Fax: 808-877-3652
Processor of potato chips
President: Mark Kobayashi
Estimated Sales: $150000
Number Employees: 1-4
Type of Packaging: Consumer
Brands:
Original Maui Kitch'n Cook'd

9093 Maui's Kaanapali EstateCoffee
380 Lahainaluna Road
Lahaina, HI 96761-1460   808-661-1802
Fax: 808-667-0424   kec@maui.net
www.kaanapalicoffee.com
Coffee, tea
Vice President: Barbara Roth

Estimated Sales: $ 10-100 Million
Number Employees: 100
Type of Packaging: Private Label

9094 Mauna Loa Macadamia NutCorporation
16-701 Macadamia Rd
Keaau, HI 96749-8020   808-982-6562
Fax: 808-966-8410   800-832-9993
info@maunaloa.com   www.maunaloa.ocm
Macadamia nuts and various products made with
macadamia nuts including chocolates, cookies and
oils.
　Manager: Darrell Askey
　Plant Manager: Charlie Young
Estimated Sales: $ 50-100 Million
Number Employees: 250-499

9095 Maurice Carrie Winery
34225 Rancho California Rd
Temecula, CA 92591-5054   951-676-1711
Fax: 951-676-8397   800-716-1711
info@mauricecarriewinery.com
www.mauricecarriewinery.com
Wines
　Owner: Buddy Linn
　CFO: Cheri Linn
　Winemaker: Gus Vizgirda
Type of Packaging: Consumer

9096 Maurice French Pastries
4949 W Napoleon Ave
Metairie, LA 70001-2249   504-455-0830
Fax: 504-885-1527   888-285-8261
sales@mauricefrenchpastries.com
www.mauricefrenchpastries.com
Mardi Gras cakes
　Owner: John Luc
Estimated Sales: $ 2.5-5 Million
Number Employees: 50-99
Brands:
　Maurice French Pastries

9097 Maurice Lenell Cooky Company
53 W Jackson Blvd
Chicago, IL 60604-3606   312-322-2222
Fax: 708-456-6552   800-323-1760
www.ecomallbiz.com/lenell/door/
Manufacturer of specialty cookies
　President/Co-Owner: Sonny Cohen
　Co-Owner: Terry Cohen
Estimated Sales: $ 50 - 100 Million
Number Employees: 100-249
Type of Packaging: Consumer, Food Service, Private
　Label, Bulk

9098 Maurice's Gourmet Barbeque
PO Box 6847
West Columbia, SC 29171-6847   800-628-7423
Fax: 803-791-8707   800-628-7423
mail@mauricesbbq.com   www.mauricesbbq.com
Pork, barbeque hams and barbeque products
　President: L Bessinger
　Founder: Maurice Bessinger
Estimated Sales: Less than $500,000
Number Employees: 10-19
Brands:
　Maurice's

9099 Maverick Ranch Natural Meats
5360 Franklin St
Denver, CO 80216-1506   303-294-0146
Fax: 303-294-0623   800-497-2624
info@maverickranch.com
www.maverickranch.com
Beef
　President: Rex Moore
　CEO: Rey Moore, Jr.
　VP of Marketing: Charlie Moore
　Vice President: Charlie Moore
　Marketing Director: Stephanie Schara
　Public Relations: Charlie Moore
　Production Manager: Abel Suarez
Estimated Sales: $ 35 Million
Number Employees: 100-249
Type of Packaging: Consumer, Food Service, Private
　Label
Brands:
　BEEF NATURALITE
　NATURAL CHOICE

9100 Max P.E. Radloff & Sons
PO Box 248
Hustisford, WI 53034-0248   920-349-3266
Fax: 920-349-8537 www.RadloffsCheese.com
Processor of cheese flavors of which include sharp
cheddar, garlic, hot pepper, horseradish, dill, nacho,
port wine, taco, onion, bacon, brick, swiss and
almond.
　President: Rudy Radloff
Estimated Sales: $ .5 - 1 million
Number Employees: 6
Type of Packaging: Consumer, Food Service, Private Label, Bulk

9101 Maxfield Candy
1050 S 200 W
Salt Lake City, UT 84101-3003   801-355-5321
Fax: 801-355-5546   800-288-8002
info@maxfieldcandy.com
www.maxfieldcandy.com
Manufacturer of boxed chocolates, nut logs, cream
sticks, holiday novelties, salt water taffy, cordial
cherries, mint sandwiches, etc.; exporter of boxed
chocolates
　President: Taz Murray
Estimated Sales: $ 5 - 10 Million
Number Employees: 5-9
Sq. footage: 106000
Parent Co: Alpine Confections
Type of Packaging: Consumer
Brands:
　MAXFIELD

9102 Maxim Marketing
6 Journey # 135
Aliso Viejo, CA 92656-5318   949-362-1177
Fax: 949-362-0449   800-476-2257
www.realsnacks.com
　Owner: Terry Kroll
Estimated Sales: $ .5 - 1 million
Number Employees: 1-4

9103 (HQ)Maxim's Import Corporation
2719 NW 24th Street
Miami, FL 33142-7005   305-633-2167
Fax: 305-638-1348   800-331-6652
Processor, importer and exporter of shrimp; proces-
sor of packaged fish; exporter of frozen chicken,
duck, turkey, pork and beef; wholesaler/distributor
of shrimp, pork, beef, poultry, fish, produce and
frozen, specialty and healthfoods
　President: Luis Chi
　CEO: Jeo Chi
Estimated Sales: $4100000
Number Employees: 22
Sq. footage: 35000
Type of Packaging: Bulk
Other Locations:
　Maxim's Import Corp.
　Salvador
Brands:
　Airex
　Alpromar
　Caribe
　De La Marca
　Fish House
　Flodi Pesca
　Golden Star
　Golfo Mar
　Gulf Garden
　Inter Ocean
　Ocean Pac
　Pacific Pride
　Pesaca
　Stefan Mar

9104 Maxin Marketing Corporation
6 Journey # 135
Aliso Viejo, CA 92656-5318   949-362-1177
Fax: 949-362-0449   info@realsnacks.com
www.realsnacks.com
Snack foods
　President: Terry Kroll
Estimated Sales: Less than $500,000
Number Employees: 1-4
Number of Brands: 2
Number of Products: 10
Type of Packaging: Consumer, Private Label, Bulk
Brands:
　Health Creation Caramel Pretzels
　Health Creation Onion Pretzels
　Pocket Pretzels

9105 Maxwell's Gourmet Food
3208 Wellington Ct # L
Raleigh, NC 27615-4121   919-878-4321
Fax: 919-878-4325   800-952-6887
info@maxwellsgourmet.com
www.maxwellsgourmet.com
Peanuts, peanut brittle, chocolate dipped peanut brit-
tle, pecans, chocolate-dipped pecans, pecan brittle,
chocolate dipped pecan brittle, cashews
　Owner: Paxton Kemps
　CEO: Don Kempf
　CFO: Shelia Kempf
　Director Of Marketing: David Chapman
　Director of Sales: Amy Kempf
　Production Manager: Ana Arrendondo
Estimated Sales: $500,000-$1 Million
Number Employees: 5-9
Brands:
　Maxwell's Extraordinary

9106 Maya Maimal Fine IndianFood
PO Box 700
Rhinebeck, NY 12572   845-876-8200
Fax: 845-876-8212   info@mayakaimal.com
www.mayakaimal.com
simmer sauces and spicy ketchup
　President/Owner: Maya Kaimal

9107 Mayacamas Fine Foods
20590 Palmer Ave
Sonoma, CA 95476-7519   707-996-0955
Fax: 707-996-4501   800-826-9621
info@mayacamasfinefoods.com
www.mayacamasfinefoods.com
Processor and exporter of dehydrated soups, salad
dressings, pasta sauces, gravies and seasonings
　President: Vicki Ranzau
　VP: Walter Rahrau
Estimated Sales: $2,400,000
Number Employees: 1-4
Sq. footage: 18000
Type of Packaging: Consumer, Food Service, Private
　Label

9108 Mayacamas Vineyards
1155 Lokoya Rd
Napa, CA 94558-9566   707-224-4030
Fax: 707-224-3979   mayacama@napanet.net
www.mayacamas.com
Processor and exporter of wines including cabernet
sauvignon, chardonnay, sauvignon blanc and pinot
noir
　President: Robert Travers
　Marketing Director: Trina Vaught
Estimated Sales: $88000
Number Employees: 10-19
Brands:
　Mayacamas Vineyards

9109 Mayer Brothers Apple Products
P.O.Box 277
Barker, NY 14012-0277   716-795-9930
Fax: 716-795-3018 www.mayerbrothers.com
Processor of apple juice, fresh and concentrated ap-
ple and fruit drinks and spring water
　General Manager: J Dickinson
　Operation Manager: Michael Gancasz
　Resource Manager: Duane Hoilbrook
　Plant Manager: Peter Wilson
Number Employees: 100-249
Sq. footage: 85000
Parent Co: Mayer Brothers Apple Products
Type of Packaging: Private Label
Brands:
　Mayer Bros

9110 Mayer Brothers Apple Products
3300 Transit Rd
West Seneca, NY 14224-2525   716-668-1787
Fax: 716-668-2437   800-696-2937
www.mayerbrothers.com
Processor of bottled spring water, apple cider and
juices including orange, grapefruit, grape and apple;
also, concentrates including fruit punch, orange,
grape, iced tea and lemonade
　President: John Mayer
　VP: Earl Mayer
　VP/General Manager: Jim Dickinson
　Plant Superintendent: Kent Wakefield
　Plant Manager: John Mayer
　Purchasing Manager: Mike Gancasz

Estimated Sales:$100+ Million
Number Employees: 100-249
Sq. footage: 45000
Type of Packaging: Consumer, Food Service, Private Label, Bulk
Brands:
   Mayer Bros.

9111 Mayer Dairy
N6274 County Road K
Neillsville, WI 54456-8203   715-255-8456
Cheese
   Owner: James Wetzel
   President: Harold Mayer
Estimated Sales:$5-9.9 Million
Number Employees: 5-9

9112 Mayer's Cider Mill
699 Five Mile Line Rd
Webster, NY 14580-2611   585-671-1955
      Fax: 585-671-5269   800-543-0043
                www.mayerscidermill.com
Processor of cider, apples and apple pies; also, beer, grape juice and wine-making supplies
   Owner: David N Bower
*Estimated Sales:*Less than $500,000
Number Employees: 10-19
Parent Co: Mayer's Cider Mill
Type of Packaging: Consumer, Bulk

9113 Mayfair Packing Company
2070 S 7th St
San Jose, CA 95112-6097   408-280-2349
Processor and exporter of dried fruits including peaches, pears, apples, apricots, prunes and cherries; also, apricot kernels, shelled and in-shell walnuts, prune juice and juice concentrates including prune, date, fig, raisin and apricot.
   President: Joseph Melehan
Type of Packaging: Consumer, Food Service, Private Label, Bulk
Brands:
   Farmkist
   Saratoga
   Sugaripe

9114 Mayfair Sales
P.O.Box 40
Buffalo, NY 14217-0040   716-877-0800
      Fax: 716-877-0385   800-248-2881
Candy, gum, snacks
   Director Of Marketing: Chris Tzetzo
   Plant Manager: Steve Tzetzo
Estimated Sales:$ 50 - 100 Million
Number Employees: 100-249
Type of Packaging: Private Label, Bulk

9115 Mayfield Dairy Farms
P.O.Box 310
Athens, TN 37371-0310   423-744-9509
      Fax: 423-745-9118   800-362-9546
                rob-mayfield@deanfoods.com
                www.mayfielddairy.com
Manufacturer of dairy products such as; ice cream, sherbert, cottage cheese, dip, sour cream, milk, whip cream and juices
   President: C S Mayfield Jr
Number Employees: 500-999
Parent Co: Dean Foods
Type of Packaging: Consumer, Food Service
Other Locations:
   Braselton GA

9116 Mayfield Farms
12434 Dixie Road
Brampton, ON L6R 0B2
Canada
                905-846-0506
      Fax: 905-843-2263
Processor of apple products including processed slices, dices, dumplings, fibre powder and juice
   Owner: Ken Speirs
Number Employees: 5-9
Type of Packaging: Consumer, Food Service

9117 Mayo Sausage Company
7120 Charlotte Pike
Nashville, TN 37209-5008   615-742-1162
Sausage
   President: Gerald Hall
Estimated Sales:$500,000-$1 Million
Number Employees: 1-4

9118 Maysville Milling Company
PO Box 716
Maysville, NC 28555-0716   910-743-3481

Manufacturer of feed and cornmeal
   President: Edward Trott Sr
Estimated Sales:$2 Million
Number Employees: 7
Brands:
   MAYCO

9119 Maytag Dairy Farms
P.O.Box 806
Newton, IA 50208-0806   641-792-1133
      Fax: 641-792-1567   800-247-2458
                www.maytagblue.com
Processor of cheeses including blue, cheddar, Swiss, edam, brick and cold pack
   President: Myrna Ver Ploeg
   VP Operations/Production Manager: Jim Stevens
   Plant Supervisor: Robert Wrdzinski
Estimated Sales:$4669423
Number Employees: 20-49
Type of Packaging: Consumer

9120 Mayway Corporation
1338 Mandela Pkwy
Oakland, CA 94607-2055   510-208-3113
      Fax: 510-208-3069   800-262-9929
      info@mayway.com   www.mayway.com
Herbal health foods
   President/CEO: Yvonne Lau
*Estimated Sales:*Below $ 5 Million
Number Employees: 20-49

9121 Mazelle's Cheesecakes Concoctions Creations
PO Box 59345
Dallas, TX 75229-1345   903-737-4315
      Fax: 972-620-0142   sales@mazelles.com
                www.mazelles.com
Processor of cheesecakes and cheesecake petit fours
Estimated Sales:$ 3 - 5 Million
Number Employees: 10-19
Type of Packaging: Consumer, Food Service
Brands:
   Mazelle's

9122 Mazzetta Company
P.O.Box 1126
Highland Park, IL 60035-7126   847-433-1150
      Fax: 847-433-8973   seamazz@mazzetta.com
                www.mazzetta.com
The SeaMazz product line includes a wide variety of seafood and fish such as orange roughy fillets, whiting fillets, greenshell mussels, raw and cooked shrimp, lobster tails, Chilean sea bass fillets, squid and crab meat.
   President: Thomas Mazzetta
Estimated Sales:$ 1 - 3 Million
Number Employees: 10-19

9123 Mazzocco Vineyards
P.O.Box 49
Healdsburg, CA 95448-0049   707-857-3240
      Fax: 707-431-2369   vino@mazzocco.com
                www.mazzocco.com
Wines
   President: Thomas Mazzocco
   Sales/Marketing Manager: Ned Carton
   Winemaker: Antoine Favero
Estimated Sales:$ 1-2.5 Million
Number Employees: 5-9

9124 Mazzoli Coffee
6812 15th Avenue
Brooklyn, NY 11219-6309   718-259-6194
      Fax: 718-234-0928   info@mazzolicoffee.com
                www.mazzolicoffee.com
Coffee
Estimated Sales:$ 5 - 10 Million
Number Employees: 5-9

9125 Mazzoni Brothers
PO Box 297
Minotola, NJ 08341-0297   609-561-6515
                Fax: 609-567-6040
Berries

9126 Mc Jak Candy Company
1087 Branch Rd
Medina, OH 44256-8900   330-722-3531
      Fax: 330-723-4793   www.mcjakcandy.com
Candy products include lollipops in over 20 delicious flavors and also home-style fudge.
   President: Larry Johns
Estimated Sales:$ 3 - 5 Million
Number Employees: 10-19

9127 (HQ)McAnally Enterprises
PO Box 950
Norco, CA 92860   909-797-0144
                800-726-2002
Processor and exporter of cartoned, frozen and liquid eggs and egg products
   President: Carlton Lofgren
   Rep. (S.W.): Glenn Lemley
   Executive VP: James Wyatt
   Marketing Director: John Klien
   Operations Manager: Tom McAnally
   Production Manager: Don Brown
Number Employees: 100-249
Sq. footage: 20000
Type of Packaging: Food Service
Other Locations:
   McAnally Enterprises
   Phoenix AZ

9128 McArthur Dairy
240 NE 71st St
Miami, FL 33138-5528   305-576-2880
      Fax: 305-576-9203 www.deanfoods.com
Manufacturer of grape and prune juice and dairy products including buttermilk, regular, chocolate, low-fat and skim milk
   VP: Brad Abell
Estimated Sales:$50-100 Million
Number Employees: 250-499
Type of Packaging: Consumer, Food Service, Private Label, Bulk

9129 McArthur Dairy
240 NE 71st St
Miami, FL 33138-5528   305-576-2880
      Fax: 305-576-9203   877-803-6565
                www.deanfoods.com
Processor of orange juice, milk, cottage cheese and ice cream
   Treasurer: Richard Hills
   VP: Brad Abell
Estimated Sales:$ 20-50 Million
Number Employees: 50-99
Parent Co: Dean Foods Company
Type of Packaging: Consumer, Food Service

9130 McArthur Dairy
3579 Work Dr
Fort Myers, FL 33916-7535   239-334-1114
      Fax: 239-334-1791 www.mcarthurdairy.com
Dairy products
   Manager: Ray Scribner
Estimated Sales:$ 5-10 Million
Number Employees: 20-49
Brands:
   McArthur Dairy

9131 McCadam Cheese Company
P.O.Box 900
Chateaugay, NY 12920-0900   518-497-6644
      Fax: 518-497-3297   info@mccadam.com
                www.mccadam.com
Processor of a variety of cheeses including aged and waxed cheddars; flavored and reduced fat cheddars; muenster cheese; monterey jack cheese, and extra sharp cheddar cheese in addition to smoked cheeses.
   Chairman: Carl Peterson
   Chief Executive Officer: Paul Johnston
   EVP/Finance & Administration: Margaret Bertolino
   SVP/Information Services: Ralph Viscomi
   SVP/Economics & Legislative Affairs: Robert Wellington
   Director Interational Sales: Peter Gutierrez
   Communications Director: Douglas DiMento
   EVP/Chief Operating Officer: Richard Wellington
   Plant Manager: Ron Davis
Estimated Sales:$ 10 - 20 Million
Number Employees: 100-249
Parent Co: Agri-Mark Inc

9132 McCain Foods
11 Gregg St
Lodi, NJ 07644-2704   201-368-0600
      Fax: 201-368-8771   800-258-1098
                www.ellios.com

Processor of frozen pizza
   Manager: Troy Jemison
   CEO/Mccain Foods USA: Frank Van Schaayk
   VP/Innovation: Charles Gitkin
   VP/Marketing: Patrick Davis
   VP/Sales: Mike Sullivan
   Purchasing Director: Gary Plant
Estimated Sales:$ 20 - 50 Million
Number Employees: 100-249
Parent Co: McCain Foods USA
Type of Packaging: Consumer, Food Service, Private Label, Bulk
Brands:
   BAKE ABLES

9133 McCain Foods
801 Rockwell Ave
Fort Atkinson, WI 53538-2458   920-563-6625
         Fax: 920-563-1394 www.mccain.com
Processor and exporter of frozen appetizers, cheeses, cauliflower, mushrooms, onion rings, onions and peppers
   President/CEO McCain Foods Limited: Dale Morrison
   CEO: Frank Van Schaayk
   VP/Innovation: Charles Gitkin
   VP/Marketing: Patrick Davis
   VP/Sales: Mike Sullivan
   Plant Manager: Scott Chaney
   Purchasing Director: Gary Plant
Estimated Sales:$100+ Million
Number Employees: 250-499
Parent Co: McCain Foods USA
Type of Packaging: Consumer, Food Service
Brands:
   BAKE ABLES

9134 McCain Foods
319 Richardson Rd
Easton, ME 04740-4056   207-488-2561
         Fax: 630-891-6549 www.mccain.com
Potatoes, frozen fries and prepared potato products
   Chairman: Harrison McCain
   President/CEO: Wallace McCain
   Plant Manager: Conrad Caron
Estimated Sales:$ 50-99.9 Million
Number Employees: 500-999
Parent Co: McCain Foods USA
Brands:
   Bake Ables

9135 McCain Foods Canada
9946 Rte 2 Transcanada Hwy
Grand Falls Grand-Sault, NB E3Z 3E3
Canada   506-473-2300
         Fax: 506-473-1008 www.mccain.ca
Manufacturer of a wide range of potato products, beverages, juices, pizzas and desserts.
   Chairman: Allison McCain
   President/CEO: Fred Schaeffer
   Chief Financial Officer: David Sanchez
   VP/Director: B A Fredstrom
Parent Co: McCain Foods Canada
Type of Packaging: Consumer, Food Service

9136 McCain Foods Canada
202 Brownlow Avenue
Dartmouth, NS B3B 1T5
Canada   902-468-3488
         Fax: 902-468-5316 www.mccain.ca
Manufacturer of a wide range of potato products, beverages, juices, pizzas and desserts.
   Chairman: Allison McCain
   President/CEO: Fred Schaeffer
   Chief Financial Officer: David Sanchez
   VP/Director: B A Fredstrom
Parent Co: McCain Foods Canada
Type of Packaging: Consumer, Food Service

9137 McCain Foods Canada
7419 30 Street SE
Calgary, AB T2C 1N6
Canada   403-296-9350
         Fax: 403-279-8366 www.mccain.ca
Manufacturer of a wide range of potato products, beverages, juices, pizzas and desserts.
   Chairman: Allison McCain
   President/CEO: Fred Schaeffer
   Chief Financial Officer: David Sanchez
   VP/Director: B A Fredstrom
Parent Co: McCain Foods Canada
Type of Packaging: Consumer, Food Service

9138 McCain Foods Canada
PO Box 220 Stn Main
Portage La Prairie, MB R1N 3B5
Canada   204-857-9761
         Fax: 204-857-9207 www.mccain.ca
Manufacturer of a wide range of potato products, beverages, juices, pizzas and desserts.
   Chairman: Allison McCain
   President/CEO: Fred Schaeffer
   Chief Financial Officer: David Sanchez
   VP/Director: B A Fredstrom
Parent Co: McCain Foods Canada
Type of Packaging: Consumer, Food Service

9139 McCain Foods Canada
55 Torlake Cres
Toronto, ON M8Z 1B4
Canada   416-259-7851
         Fax: 416-259-0713 www.mccain.ca
Manufacturer of a wide range of potato products, beverages, juices, pizzas and desserts.
   Chairman: Allison McCain
   President/CEO: Fred Schaeffer
   Chief Financial Officer: David Sanchez
   VP/Director: B A Fredstrom
Parent Co: McCain Foods Canada
Type of Packaging: Consumer, Food Service

9140 McCain Foods Canada
PO Box 1479
Coaldale, AB T1M 1N3
Canada   403-345-4418
         Fax: 403-345-4419 www.mccain.ca
Manufacturer of a wide range of potato products, beverages, juices, pizzas and desserts.
   Chairman: Allison McCain
   President/CEO McCain Foods Canada: Fred Schaeffer
   Chief Financial Officer: David Sanchez
   VP/Director: B A Fredstrom
   VP/Marketing: Mark McCauley
   VP/Operations: Bill Adams
   West Canada/Mnfg Manager: David Good
Parent Co: McCain Foods Canada
Type of Packaging: Consumer, Food Service

9141 McCain Foods Canada
225 Lansdowne Road
Lansdowne, NB E7L 4A8
Canada   506-375-5019
         Fax: 506-375-4257 www.mccain.ca
Manufacturer of a wide range of potato products, beverages, juices, pizzas and desserts.
   Chairman: Allison McCain
   President/CEO: Fred Schaeffer
   Chief Financial Officer: David Sanchez
   VP/Director: B A Fredstrom
Parent Co: McCain Foods Canada
Type of Packaging: Consumer, Food Service

9142 McCain Foods Canada
317 Main Street
Florenceville, NB E7L 3G6
Canada   506-392-3036
         Fax: 506-392-8338 www.mccain.ca
Manufacturer of a wide range of potato products, beverages, juices, pizzas and desserts.
   Chairman: Allison McCain
   President/CEO: Fred Schaeffer
   Chief Financial Officer: David Sanchez
   VP/Director: B A Fredstrom
Parent Co: McCain Foods Canada
Type of Packaging: Consumer, Food Service

9143 McCain Foods Canada
PO Box 70
Carberry, MB R0K 0H0
Canada   204-834-2136
         Fax: 204-834-3400 www.mccain.ca
Manufacturer of a wide range of potato products, beverages, juices, pizzas and desserts.
   Chairman: Allison McCain
   President/CEO: Fred Schaeffer
   Chief Financial Officer: David Sanchez
   VP/Director: B A Fredstrom
Parent Co: McCain Foods Canada
Type of Packaging: Consumer, Food Service

9144 (HQ)McCain Foods Canada
107 Main Street
Florenceville, NB E7L 1B2
Canada   506-392-5541
         Fax: 506-392-8156 www.mccain.ca

Processor of frozen foods including beans, broccoli, brussels sprouts, cauliflower, corn, French fried potatoes, prepared dinners and pizza; also, beverage concentrates.
   President/CEO: Fred Schaeffer
   Chairman: Allison McCain
   Chief Financial Officer: David Sanchez
   VP/Director: B A Fredstrom
Number Employees: 4000
Type of Packaging: Consumer, Food Service

9145 McCain Foods Canada
107 Main Street
Florenceville, NB E7L 1B2
Canada   506-392-5541
         Fax: 506-392-6062 pr@mccain.ca
                         www.mccain.ca
Processor of aseptic, frozen and portion-packed juices
   President/CEO: Dale Morrison
   Chairman: Allison McCain
   CFO: David Sanchez
   Director: B A Fredstrom
   Plant Manager: Brian Spencer
Estimated Sales:$4,311,100
Number Employees: 20,000
Parent Co: McCain Foods Limited
Type of Packaging: Consumer, Food Service
Brands:
   MCCAIN

9146 McCain Foods Canada
181 Bay Street
Toronto, ON M5J 2T3
Canada   416-955-1700
         Fax: 416-955-1750 800-363-8516
         pr@mccain.ca   www.mccain.ca
Processor of frozen French fries, appetizers, pizzas and juice concentrates
   President/CEO: Fred Schaeffer
   Chairman: Allison McCain
   Chief Financial Officer: David Sanchez
   VP/Director: B A Fredstrom
   VP Marketing: Mark McCauley
Number Employees: 20-49
Parent Co: McCain Foods USA
Type of Packaging: Consumer, Food Service
Brands:
   Acme
   Boku
   Caterpac
   Dixie
   Ellio's
   FPG
   Golden Citrus
   Golden Fry
   Golden Grown
   Handy Pak
   Junior Juice
   McCain Citrus
   McCain Citrus
   McCain Transport
   McCain U.S.A.
   McCain's
   Squeeze Six
   Valley Farms
   Vita Gold

9147 McCain Foods USA
100 E Lee Rd
Othello, WA 99344-8961   509-488-9611
         Fax: 509-488-3780 800-541-4808
                         www.mccain.com
Processor and exporter of frozen French fries, potato puffs and hash browns
   President/CEO McCain Foods Limited: Dale Morrison
   CEO/Mccain Foods USA: Frank Van Schaayk
   Vice President/Innovation: Charles Gitkin
   Vice President/Marketing: Patrick Davis
   Vice President Sales: Mike Sullivan
   Plant Manager: Ray Cooper
   Purchasing Director: Gary Plant
Estimated Sales:$100+ Million
Number Employees: 500-999
Parent Co: McCain Foods USA
Type of Packaging: Consumer, Food Service, Private Label, Bulk

9148 McCain Foods USA
2629 N Broadwell Ave
Grand Island, NE 68803-2166   308-382-7770
         Fax: 308-389-4481 www.mccainusa.com

Processor of frozen vegetables including cauliflower, okra, onions, peppers, potatoes, sweet potatoes and squash; also, frozen onion rings and apple products.
Manager: Ray Cooper
CEO/Mccain Foods USA: Frank Van Schaayk
Vice President/Innovation: Charles Gitkin
Vice President/Marketing: Patrick Davis
Vice President Sales: Mike Sullivan
Purchasing Director: Gary Plant
Estimated Sales: $100+ Million
Number Employees: 250-499
Parent Co: McCain Foods USA
Type of Packaging: Consumer, Food Service

9149 McCain Foods USA
319 Richardson Rd
Easton, ME 04740-4056   207-488-2561
Fax: 207-488-2829 www.mccain.com
Processor and exporter of frozen French fries, potato puffs and hash browns
President/CEO McCain Foods Limited: Dale Morrison
CEO/Mccain Foods USA: Frank Van Schaayk
VP/Innovation: Charles Gitkin
VP/Marketing: Patrick Davis
VP/Sales: Mike Sullivan
Plant Manager: Conrad Caron
Purchasing Director: Gary Plant
Estimated Sales: $100+ Million
Number Employees: 500-999
Parent Co: McCain Foods USA
Type of Packaging: Consumer, Food Service, Private Label, Bulk

9150 (HQ)McCain Foods USA
2275 Cabot Dr
Lisle, IL 60532-3653   630-955-0400
                                800-258-1098
slfinneg@mccain.ca   www.mccainusa.com
Processor of frozen potato products including French fries, slices, dices, formed and private label brands. Also manufacturer of breaded and battered appetizers
President/CEO McCain Foods Limited: Dale Morrison
CFO: David Sanchez
Chief Human Reources Officer: Janice Wismer
COO: Dirk Van de Put
Purchasing Director: Gary Plant
Estimated Sales: J
Number Employees: 500-999
Brands:
ANCHOR
BEER BUTTERED KING RINGS
BREADED PRETZARELLA STIX
BREW CITY
ELLIO'S
FRYER SAVER
GOLDEN CRISP
MCCAIN
MOORE'S
MOZZALUNA
MOZZAMIA
OLIVENOS
ORE-IDA
POPPERS
PRIMASANO CUBES
PROVAGO WHEELS
QUESO TRIANGOS
SANTA FE
SPICY TORTILLA JUMPIN JACKS
SUN STIX
WRAPPETIZERS

9151 McCain Foods USA
2275 Cabot Dr
Lisle, IL 60532-3653   630-955-0400
Fax: 630-588-5165   www.mccain.com
Manufacturer of frozen foods; french fries and other potato products, vegetables, desserts, pizzas, juices and beverages, oven meals, entrees and appetizers.
Owner: Randy Bartz
CFO: David Sanchez
Estimated Sales: J
Number Employees: 275
Brands:
Flavour Last
Mc Cain

9152 McCain Foods USA
801 Rockwell Ave
Fort Atkinson, WI 53538-2458   920-563-6625
Fax: 920-563-1394   jean.schieffer@mccain.com
                                www.mccain.com
Frozen specialties
Manager: Steve Prater
Plant Manager: Scott Chaney
Estimated Sales: $ 50-99.9 Million
Number Employees: 250-499

9153 McCain Foods USADistribution Center
601 Twin Rail Drive
P.O.Box 489
Minooka, IL 60447-0489   815-467-0455
Fax: 815-467-0460   fyattoni@uscold.com
                                www.uscoldstorage.com
Distribution center for manufacturer that provides a wide range of potato products, beverages, juices, pizzas and desserts.
President/CEO McCain Foods Limited: Dale Morrison
CEO/Mccain Foods USA: Frank Van Schaayk
Vice President/Innovation: Charles Gitkin
Vice President/Marketing: Patrick Davis
Vice President Sales: Mike Sullivan
Manager: Diane Steward
Plant Manager: Brandi Overton
Purchasing Director: Gary Plant
Parent Co: McCain Foods USA
Type of Packaging: Consumer, Food Service

9154 McCain Foods USADistribution Center
2554 Downing Dr
Fort Worth, TX 76106-3023   817-624-1900
Fax: 817-624-7190   fmonroe@uscold.com
                                www.uscoldstorage.com
Distribution center for manufacturer that provides a wide range of potato products, beverages, juices, pizzas and desserts.
Manager: Frank Monroe
CEO/Mccain Foods USA: Frank Van Schaayk
Vice President/Innovation: Charles Gitkin
Vice President/Marketing: Patrick Davis
Vice President Sales: Mike Sullivan
Purchasing Director: Gary Plant
Parent Co: McCain Foods USA
Type of Packaging: Consumer, Food Service

9155 McCain Foods USADistribution Center
1602 Island Drive
PO Box 1903
Laredo, TX 78044   956-722-4329
Fax: 956-722-4325   lguardiola@uscold.com
                                www.mccainusa.com OR
                                www.1800poppers.com
Distribution center for manufacturer that provides a wide range of potato products, beverages, juices, pizzas and desserts.
President/CEO McCain Foods Limited: Dale Morrison
CEO/Mccain Foods USA: Frank Van Schaayk
Vice President/Innovation: Charles Gitkin
Vice President/Marketing: Patrick Davis
Vice President Sales: Mike Sullivan
Purchasing Director: Gary Plant
Parent Co: McCain Foods USA
Type of Packaging: Consumer, Food Service

9156 McCain Foods USADistribution Center
P.O.Box 10
Plover, WI 54467-0010   715-421-3400
Fax: 715-421-7617 www.mccain.com
Distribution center for manufacturer that provides a wide range of potato products, beverages, juices, pizzas and desserts.
President/CEO McCain Foods Limited: Dale Morrison
CEO/Mccain Foods USA: Frank Van Schaayk
Vice President/Innovation: Charles Gitkin
Vice President/Marketing: Patrick Davis
Vice President Sales: Mike Sullivan
Plant Manager: Darek Frye
Purchasing Director: Gary Plant
Parent Co: McCain Foods USA
Type of Packaging: Consumer, Food Service

9157 McCain Foods USADistribution Center
110 Distribution Dr
Hamilton, OH 45014-4257   513-874-6500
Fax: 513-874-6775 www.tippmanngroup.com
Distribution center for manufacturer that provides a wide range of potato products, beverages, juices, pizzas and desserts.
Manager: Larry Tippmann
CEO/Mccain Foods USA: Frank Van Schaayk
Vice President/Innovation: Charles Gitkin
Vice President/Marketing: Patrick Davis
Vice President Sales: Mike Sullivan
Purchasing Director: Gary Plant
Parent Co: McCain Foods USA
Type of Packaging: Consumer, Food Service

9158 McCain Foods USADistribution Center
1845 Westgate Pkwy SW
Atlanta, GA 30336-2851   404-629-2430
Fax: 404-629-0428 www.mccainusa.com OR
                                www.1800poppers.com
Distribution center for manufacturer that provides a wide range of potato products, beverages, juices, pizzas and desserts.
President/CEO McCain Foods Limited: Dale Morrison
CEO/Mccain Foods USA: Frank Van Schaayk
Vice President/Innovation: Charles Gitkin
Vice President/Marketing: Patrick Davis
Vice President Sales: Mike Sullivan
Purchasing Director: Gary Plant
Parent Co: McCain Foods USA
Type of Packaging: Consumer, Food Service

9159 McCain Foods USADistribution Center
218 W Highway 30
Burley, ID 83318-5002   208-678-9431
Fax: 208-678-6722 www.mccain.com
Distribution center for manufacturer that provides a wide range of potato products, beverages, juices, pizzas and desserts.
President/CEO McCain Foods Limited: Dale Morrison
CEO/Mccain Foods USA: Frank Van Schaayk
Human Resources: Linda Langer
Vice President/Innovation: Charles Gitkin
Vice President/Marketing: Patrick Davis
Vice President Sales: Mike Sullivan
Purchasing Director: Gary Plant
Parent Co: McCain Foods USA
Type of Packaging: Consumer, Food Service

9160 McCain Foods USADistribution Center
2629 N Broadwell Ave
Grand Island, NE 68803-2166   308-382-7770
Fax: 308-389-4481 www.mccainusa.com
Distribution center for manufacturer that provides a wide range of potato products, beverages, juices, pizzas and desserts.
Manager: Ray Cooper
CEO/Mccain Foods USA: Frank Van Schaayk
Vice President/Innovation: Charles Gitkin
Vice President/Marketing: Patrick Davis
Vice President Sales: Mike Sullivan
Purchasing Director: Gary Plant
Parent Co: McCain Foods USA
Type of Packaging: Consumer, Food Service

9161 McCain Snack Foods
P.O.Box 2518
Appleton, WI 54912-2518   920-734-0672
Fax: 920-997-7609 www.mccainusa.com
Manufacturers a variety of snack foods including cheese, onion, vegetable, stuffed olives, specialty snacks and pizza.
President/CEO McCain Foods Limited: Dale Morrison
CEO/Mccain Foods USA: Frank Van Schaayk
Executive: Peter Reijula
Vice President/Innovation: Charles Gitkin
Vice President/Marketing: Patrick Davis
Vice President Sales: Mike Sullivan
Purchasing Director: Gary Plant
Parent Co: McCain Foods USA
Type of Packaging: Consumer, Food Service, Private Label, Bulk

9162 McCall Farms
6615 S Irby St
Effingham, SC 29541-3577   843-662-2223
        Fax: 843-665-5234 800-277-2012
                wswink@mccallfarms.com
                www.mccallfarms.com
Processor of canned garbanzo, green and lima beans,
collard greens, kale, spinach, okra, tomatoes, corn,
peas, squash, succotash and peanuts
    President: Henry Swink
    Regional Sales Manager: Woody Swink
    Sales Manager: David Wold
    Director Engineering: Jerry Gulledge
Estimated Sales: $ 5-10 Million
Number Employees: 100-249
Type of Packaging: Consumer, Food Service
Brands:
    Canned Southern Vegetables
    Lord Chesterfield
    Margret Holmes

9163 McCall Farms
6615 S Irby St
Effingham, SC 29541-3577   843-662-2223
        Fax: 843-665-5234 www.mccallfarms.com
Canned beans and soup
    President: Henry M Swink
    Sales Manager: Phil Dunaway
Estimated Sales: $ 10-20 Million
Number Employees: 100-249
Type of Packaging: Private Label
Brands:
    Garcia's
    Lolita's
    Miss Lil's
    Southern Style

9164 McCartney Produce Company
1432 Old Mayfield Rd
Paducah, KY 42003-2947   270-442-2791
        Fax: 270-443-5943 800-522-2791
Fruit and vegetables
    Manager: Jim Pierce
    Manager: Jim Pierce
Estimated Sales: $ 10-20 Million
Number Employees: 5-9

9165 McClancy Seasoning Company
1 Spice Rd
Fort Mill, SC 29707-9501   803-548-2366
        Fax: 803-548-2379 800-843-1968
info@mcclancy.com www.mcclancy.com
Processor and exporter of spices, seasonings and dry
food mixes including salad dressing, dips,
breadings, batters, gravies, soups, sauces and meat
marinades, snack food seasonings, nut and pretzel
coatings, whole and ground spices;custom blending
available.
    President: F Reid Wilkerson Iii III
    Director: Charlie Czagas
    VP: Allen Davis
    VP Sales: Chuck Wiley
Estimated Sales: $21188697
Number Employees: 100-249
Type of Packaging: Consumer, Food Service, Pri-
    vate Label, Bulk

9166 McClane Distribution Center
56 McLane Dr
Fredericksburg, VA 22406-1147   540-374-2000
        Fax: 540-374-2256 www.mclaneco.com
Processor of fresh and frozen sandwiches and pizzas
    President: George Bolts
    VP: Joe Johnson
    Manufacturing/Operations Director: Henry Lopez

    Plant Manager: Henry Lopez
Estimated Sales: $965 Billion
Number Employees: 750

9167 McCleary
P.O.Box 187
South Beloit, IL 61080-0187   815-389-3053
        Fax: 815-389-9842 800-523-8644
                mcclearyshr@mcclearys.com
                www.macscopperkettle.com
Manufacturer and exporter of snack foods including
tortilla chips, potato chips, corn chips, cheese curls,
pretzels, party mix, caramel corn, popcorn, hulless
popcorn, hot snacks and sweet snacks.
    Founder: Eugene McCleary
    VP/General Manager: Jerry Stokely
    VP/Sales & Marketing: Randy Morrow

Estimated Sales: $ 50 - 100 Million
Number Employees: 100-249
Sq. footage: 65000
Type of Packaging: Consumer, Food Service, Pri-
    vate Label
Brands:
    Cheese Twisters
    Corn Chips Ahh's
    Fire Ballz
    MAC'S Copper Kettle
    McCleary's
    Pajeda's
    Potato Blasts
    Pretzel O's Pretzels

9168 (HQ)McCleskey Mills
P.O.Box 98
Smithville, GA 31787-0098   229-846-4110
        Fax: 229-846-4805 mcmills@surfsouth.com
Manufacturer and exporter of shelled peanuts
    President: Jerry Chandler
Estimated Sales: $210 Million
Number Employees: 50-99
Type of Packaging: Consumer, Bulk

9169 McColls Dairy Products
P.O.Box 1313
Sacramento, CA 95812-1313   916-444-7200
        Fax: 916-448-0284 www.crystal-milk.com
Milk and dairy products
    Chairman: Donald K Hansen
    President: Fred Hogan
    Control Assurance: Gina Dezzani
    Marketing Director: Kevin Nagle
    Sales Director: David Walker
    PR Director: Kim Patterson
Estimated Sales: $ 100-250 Million
Number Employees: 500-999
Brands:
    McColl's

9170 McConnell's Fine Ice Cream
815 E Canon Perdido St
Santa Barbara, CA 93103-3007   805-963-2958
        Fax: 805-965-3764
                jimboyoung@mcconnells.com
                www.mcconnells.com
Processor and exporter of ice cream
    Owner: Jimmy Young
    VP: Jimmy Young
Estimated Sales: Below $ 5 Million
Number Employees: 5-9
Type of Packaging: Consumer, Food Service

9171 (HQ)McCormick & Company
18 Loveton Circle
Sparks, MD 21152   410-771-7301
        Fax: 410-771-7462 800-632-5847
                www.mccormick.com
Processor and exporter of herbs, spices, seasonings,
sauces, extracts, mixes, flavors, marinades and
blends
    Chairman/President/CEO: Alan Wilson
    EVP/CFO: Gordon Stetz
    R & D: Hamed Faridi
    VP Sales/Marketing: Mark Timble
    Public Relations: Allen Barrett, Jr.
    VP Corporate Operations: James Radin
    Plant Manager: Mike Novarre
    Purchasing Manager: Len Fischer
Estimated Sales: $ 1.3 Billion
Number Employees: 7,500
Type of Packaging: Consumer, Food Service, Pri-
    vate Label, Bulk
Other Locations:
    McCormick & Co.
    Southhampton
Brands:
    Armanino Farms
    Arte De Dulce
    Bag N' Season
    Bag'n Season
    Bits
    Daregal
    El Toro
    Garden Fare
    Golden Dipt
    La Grille
    McCormick
    McCormick Foods & Spices
    Mojave
    Old Bay
    Produce Partners
    Quick Classic Sauces

    Salad's Dips
    Sierra
    Spice Cargo
    Superherb Farms
    Zebbie's

9172 (HQ)McCormick & Company Inc
18 Loveton Circle
Sparks, MD 21152   410-771-7301
        Fax: 410-527-8289 webmaster@mccormick.com
                www.mccormick.com
Manufacture, markets and distributes spices, herbs,
seasonings, specialty foods and flavors
    Chairman/President/CEO: Alan Wilson
    EVP/CFO: Gordon Stetz
    VP/General Counsel: W Geoffrey Carpenter
    VP Human Relations: Cecile Perich
Estimated Sales: $2,256,200,000 Billion
Number Employees: 5,000-9,999
Type of Packaging: Private Label, Bulk
Brands:
    Armanino Farms
    Arte De Dulce
    Bag N' Season
    Bag'n Season
    Bits
    Daregal
    El Toro
    Garden Fare
    Golden Dipt
    La Grille
    McCormick
    McCormick Foods & Spices
    Mojave
    Old Bay
    Produce Partners
    Quick Classic Sauces
    Salad's Dips
    Sierra
    Spice Cargo
    Superherb Farms
    Zebbie's

9173 McCormick Distilling Company
1 Mc Cormick Ln
Weston, MO 64098-9558   816-640-2276
        Fax: 816-640-3082 888-640-3082
                www.mccormickdistilling.com
Alcoholic beverages
    President: James Zargo
    Vice Chairman: Mike Griesser
    VP Sales: Donald Hammond
Estimated Sales: $ 20-50 Million
Number Employees: 100-249
Type of Packaging: Consumer, Private Label
Brands:
    McCormick

**9174 McCormick Industrial Flavor
Solutions**
P.O.Box 6000
Sparks Glencoe, MD 21152-6000   410-771-7301
        Fax: 410-527-8289 800-632-5847
                www.mccormickflavor.com
McCormick Flavors supplies natural, natural and ar-
tificial, and artificial flavors for industrial formula-
tion needs. Products are available in a variety of
forms, including liquid, paste, and powder; coatings
and condiments; flavors;spices and herbs; and
seasonings.
    Chairman, President & CEO: Alan Wilson
    EVP & CFO: Gordon Stetz
    VP, Human Relations: Cecile Perich
Parent Co: McCormick & Company Inc
Type of Packaging: Consumer, Food Service, Bulk
Brands:
    CHEEZ-ALL FLAVORS
    FLAVORCELL
    FLAVORSPICE FRUIT AND SWEET
    SAVORY SELECT FLAVORS

9175 McCormick Ingredients
211 Schilling Cir
Hunt Valley, MD 21031-1100   410-527-6000
        Fax: 410-527-6001 800-632-5847
                www.mccormick.com

Manufacturer of spices, herbs, extracts, proprietary seasoning blends, sauces and marinades.
Manager: Lawrence Kurziue
President/Chief Operating Officer: Alan Wilson
EVP/Strategic Planning & CFO: Francis Contino Jr
SVP/General Counsel & Secretary: Robert Skelton
VP/Human Relations: Cecile Perich
Estimated Sales: $100+ Million
Number Employees: 250-499
Parent Co: McCormick & Company
Type of Packaging: Consumer, Bulk

9176 McCormick SupHerb Farms
P.O.Box 610
Turlock, CA 95381-0610 209-664-2222
Fax: 209-633-3644 800-787-4372
custserv@supherbfarms.com
www.supherbfarms.com
Processors and marketers of culinary herbs and specialty products the selection of which includes fresh, frozen and freeze-dried varieties.
President: Mike Brem
EVP/Strategic Planning & CFO: Francis Contino
SVP/General Counsel & Secretary: Robert Skelton
VP/Human Relations: Cecile Perich
Parent Co: McCormick & Company Inc

9177 McCoy Matt Frontier International
362 Capistrano Avenue
Pismo Beach, CA 93449-1907 805-773-2994
Fax: 805-773-0378
President: Mat McCoy
Estimated Sales: Under $500,000
Number Employees: 1-4

9178 McCraw Candies
PO Box 731
Farmersville, TX 75442-0731 972-782-7201
Fax: 972-782-6178 800-551-7201
info@countrystorecandy.com
www.countrystorecandy.com
Processor of confectionery products including brittles, taffy, peanut patties, etc
President: Rick Mathews
Estimated Sales: $3 - 5 Million
Number Employees: 12
Sq. footage: 15000
Type of Packaging: Consumer, Private Label, Bulk
Brands:
Country Store Old Fashioned Taffy

9179 McCraw's Candies
PO Box 731
Farmersville, TX 75442-0731 972-782-7201
Fax: 972-782-6178 800-551-7201
Candy
Estimated Sales: $3 - 5 Million
Number Employees: 10-19

9180 McCutcheon's Apple Products
13 S Wisner St
Frederick, MD 21701-5625 301-662-3261
Fax: 301-663-6217 800-888-7537
mrjelly@mccutcheons.com
www.mccutcheons.com
Products include apple juice, apple cider, fruit butters, preserves, jellies, juice sweetened fruit spreads, salad dressings, relishes, hot sauces and more.
President: Robert J Mc Cutcheon III
VP Sales: Vanessa Smith
Estimated Sales: $10 - 20 Million
Number Employees: 20-49
Sq. footage: 63000
Type of Packaging: Consumer, Private Label
Brands:
McCutcheons

9181 McDaniel Fruit Company
P.O.Box 2588
Fallbrook, CA 92088-2588 760-728-8438
Fax: 760-728-4898 camcdan@sbsglobal.net
www.mcdanielavocado.com
Processor, importer and exporter of avocados
Owner: Kay Ahrend
VP Sales/Marketing: Rankin McDaniel
General Sales Manager: Laurie Johnson
Secretary: Larry McDaniel
Estimated Sales: $9300000
Number Employees: 20-49
Sq. footage: 10000

9182 McDonald Dairy
4249 Us Highway 23 S
Alpena, MI 49707-5139 989-354-4212
Fax: 989-356-5749 800-572-5390
Milk and dairy products
Manager: Joe Kensa
Estimated Sales: $5-10 Million
Number Employees: 5-9

9183 McDonald Dairy Company
609 Sb Chavez Dr
Flint, MI 48503-4855 810-232-9193
Fax: 810-232-1899
Processor of fresh milk; wholesaler/distributor of cheese, yogurt and juice; serving the food service market
Sales: Bill Wernet
Estimated Sales: $100+ Million
Number Employees: 250-499
Parent Co: Country Fresh
Type of Packaging: Consumer, Food Service, Private Label

9184 McDowell Fine Meats 2
1719 E McDowell Rd
Phoenix, AZ 85006-3035 602-254-6022
Fax: 602-257-0296
Owner: Matthew Drass
Estimated Sales: $ .5 - 1 million
Number Employees: 1-4

9185 McDowell Valley Vineyards & Cellars
P.O.Box 449
Hopland, CA 95449-0449 707-744-1774
Fax: 707-744-1826
mcdowell@mcdowellsyrah.com
www.mcdowellsyrah.com
Wine
CEO: Bill Crawford
CEO: Gary Leonard
VP: Gary Leonard
Sales Director: Bernadette Byrne
Winemaker/Winegrower: William Crawford
Estimated Sales: $1-2.5 Million
Number Employees: 5-9
Brands:
McDowell

9186 McDuffies Bakery
9920 Main St
PO Box 427
Clarence, NY 14031-2043 716-759-8510
Fax: 716-759-6082 800-875-1598
info@mcduffies.com www.mcduffies.com
Shortbread cookies and biscotti
President: Dave Thomas
VP: Brian Thomas
Operations: Duston Peace
Estimated Sales: $2 Million
Number Employees: 20
Sq. footage: 10000
Type of Packaging: Food Service, Private Label

9187 McFadden Farm
16000 Powerhouse Rd
Potter Valley, CA 95469-8771 707-743-1122
Fax: 707-743-1126 800-544-8230
mcfaddenfarm@pacific.net
www.mcfaddenfarm.com
Processor and exporter of organic herbs including garlic braids and wild rice
Owner: Eugene Mc Fadden
Estimated Sales: $3100000
Number Employees: 20-49
Type of Packaging: Consumer, Food Service, Bulk

9188 McFarland Foods
PO Box 460
Riverton, UT 84065-0460 209-869-6611
www.mcfarlandsfoods.com
Processor and exporter of chicken bacon and ground chicken and turkey; exporter of chicken bacon
President: Gary McFarland
Sales Director: Thomas Mathias
Sales: Mary Bishop
Purchasing Manager: Mike Walker
Number Employees: 20-49
Sq. footage: 13000

Type of Packaging: Consumer, Food Service, Private Label, Bulk
Brands:
Ol' McFarlands

9189 McFarland Foods
PO Box 460
Riverton, UT 84065-0460 801-254-5009
Fax: 801-254-0432 800-441-9596
info@dsi1968.com www.mcfarlandsfoods.com
Chicken and turkey products
President: Stephen Mcfarland
CFO: Barbara McFarland
Quality Control: Justin McFarland
Sales Director: Thomas Mathias
Number Employees: 20-49
Number of Brands: 1
Number of Products: 25
Sq. footage: 12000
Type of Packaging: Consumer, Food Service, Private Label, Bulk

9190 McFarling Foods
333 W 14th St
Indianapolis, IN 46202-2204 317-635-2633
Fax: 317-687-6844 www.mcfarling.com
Wholesaler/distributor of groceries, provisions/meats, frozen foods, produce and seafood; serving the food service market
Chairman of the Board: Donald McFarling
Vice President: R McFarling
VP Sales: G Clay
Purchasing Manager: Leonard McFarling
Estimated Sales: $78000000
Number Employees: 100-249
Sq. footage: 104000

9191 McGlynn Bakeries, LLC
7350 Commerce Lane NE
Minneapolis, MN 55432-3189 763-574-2423
Fax: 763-574-2210 www.c2b.com
Manufacturers of frozen par-baked breads and frozen cookies. Distributors UuS and Canada. Manufactuires & distributes fresh baked goods in Minnesota
President: Kevin Hunt
CEO: Daniel McGlynn
COO: John Prichard
Quality Control: Chrisn Green
R & D: Florent Soisson
VP Marketing: Greg McAfee
VP Operations: Doug Hale
Estimated Sales: $50-60 Million
Number Employees: 200-250
Sq. footage: 150000
Type of Packaging: Consumer, Food Service, Private Label, Bulk

9192 McGrath's Frozen Foods
1 Elizabeth Pl
Streator, IL 61364-1192 815-672-2654
Fax: 815-672-3474
Frozen food
Owner: Kevin Gaede
Estimated Sales: $ .5 - 1 million
Number Employees: 1-4

9193 McGraw Seafood
PO Box 3178
Tracadie Sheila, NB E1X 1G5
Canada 506-395-3374
Fax: 506-395-2821
Processor of fresh and frozen crab, scallops, cod, smelt, mackerel, herring and lobster
General Manager: Paul Boudreau
CEO: Paul Boudreau
Marketing Director: Paul Boudreau
Number Employees: 100-249
Type of Packaging: Consumer, Food Service, Private Label, Bulk
Brands:
Mc Graw

9194 (HQ)McGregor Vineyard Winery
5503 Dutch St
Dundee, NY 14837-9746 607-292-3999
Fax: 607-292-6929 800-272-0192
info@mcgregorwinery.com
www.mcgregorwinery.com
Processor of premium vinifera wines including chardonnay, pinot noir, riesling and gewurztraminer
Owner: John Mc Gregor
Estimated Sales: $5 - 10 Million
Number Employees: 10-19

9195 McHenry Vineyard
330 11th Street
Davis, CA 95616-2010   530-756-3202
    Fax: 530-756-3202 lmchenry@dcn.davis.ca.us
Wines
    Operations Manager: Henry McHenry
    Vineyard Manager: Linda McHenry
Estimated Sales: $30,000
Number Employees: 1-4
Type of Packaging: Private Label

9196 McIlhenny Company
601 Poydras St # 1815
New Orleans, LA 70130-6028   504-523-7370
    Fax: 504-596-6444 800-634-9599
        WhatsCooking@TABASCO.com
            www.tabasco.com
Processor of hot pepper flavors and ingredients
    President: Paul Mc Ilhenny
    Director Marketing: Billy Boswell
Estimated Sales: $500,000-$1 Million
Number Employees: 5-9
Type of Packaging: Bulk
Brands:
    TABASCO® brand Chipotle Pepper Sauc
    TABASCO® brand Garlic
    Tabasco® Green Sauce Miniatures
    Tabasco® Original Red Miniatures
    Tabasco® brand Garlic Pepper Sauce
    Tabasco® brand Habanero Pepper Sauc
    Tabasco® brand Pepper Sauce
    • TABASCO® Bloody Mary Mix – Extra

9197 McIntosh's Ohio Valley Wines
2033 Bethel New Hope Rd
Bethel, OH 45106-9691   937-379-1159
    Fax: 973-379-1962
Wine
    President: Edward Covert
Estimated Sales: $ 1-2.5 Million
Number Employees: 1-4

9198 McJak Candy Company LLC
1087 Branch Rd
Medina, OH 44256-8900   330-722-3531
    Fax: 330-723-4793 800-424-2942
    ljohns@mcjakcandy.com www.mcjakcandy.com
Produces fudge and lollipops
    President: Larry Johns
Estimated Sales: $ 3 - 5 Million
Number Employees: 10-19
Number of Products: 20
Type of Packaging: Consumer, Private Label, Bulk

9199 (HQ)McKee Foods Corporation
10260 McKee Road
PO Box 750
Collegedale, TN 37315-0750   423-238-7111
    Fax: 423-238-7127 mail@littledebbie.com
            www.mckeefoods.com
Manufacturer of cookies, crackers, snack and granola bars, snack cakes and cereal
    President/CEO: Mike McKee
    VP/CFO: Barry Patterson
    Communications/Public Relations Manager: Mike Gloekler
Estimated Sales: $1.1 Billion
Number Employees: 6000
Type of Packaging: Consumer, Food Service, Private Label
Other Locations:
    McKee Foods
    Gentry AR
    Stuarts Draft VA
    Kingman AZ
    Chattanooga TN
Brands:
    FIELDSTONE™ BAKERY
    HEARTLAND®
    LITTLE DEBBIE®
    SUNBELT®

9200 McKenna Brothers
PO Box 70
Cardigan, PE C0A 1G0
Canada   902-583-2951
    Fax: 902-583-2891
    mckenna.bros@pei.sympatico.ca
        www.mckennabrothers.co.uk
Processor and exporter of potato seeds and potatoes
    Director: Peter McKenna
    Director: Shawn McKenna
    Director: Kevin McKenna

Number Employees: 20
Sq. footage: 30000
Type of Packaging: Consumer
Brands:
    PEI

9201 McKenzie of Vermont
160 Flynn Ave
Burlington, VT 05401-5401   802-864-4585
    Fax: 802-651-7335
        www.mckenziecountryclassics.com
Processor, packer and wholesaler/distributor of sausage and smoked meat products
    President: Ray Monkiewicz
    VP Finance and Controller: Arliene Torre
    CEO: Ray Mankiewiecz
Estimated Sales: $ 20 - 50 Million
Number Employees: 10-19
Sq. footage: 25000
Type of Packaging: Consumer, Food Service

9202 McKiever Packing Company
1731 Highway 425 S
Monticello, AR 71655-9795   870-367-6938
Packer of meat including beef and pork
    Owner: Donald McKiever
Estimated Sales: $500000
Number Employees: 5

9203 McKinlay Vineyards
7120 NE Earlwood Road
Newberg, OR 97132-7010   503-625-2534
    Fax: 503-625-2534
Wines
Estimated Sales: $67,000
Number Employees: 1

9204 McKnight Milling Company
15 Cross 138
Hickory Ridge, AR 72347-9268   870-697-2504
    Fax: 870-697-2525
Basmati rice
    Owner: Deloss Mc Knight
    Plant Manager: Walter Pierce
Estimated Sales: $2500000
Number Employees: 1-4
Sq. footage: 5760
Type of Packaging: Consumer, Food Service, Private Label, Bulk
Brands:
    Cache River

9205 McLane Foods
2512 E Magnolia St
Phoenix, AZ 85034-6908   602-275-5509
    www.allstars.marketfarefoods.com/contact.htm
Processor and exporter of frozen sandwiches, burritos and hot dog sauce
    President: Al Carfora
    Controller: Nolin Shaw
    CFO: Todd Monsen
Estimated Sales: $ 5 - 10 Million
Number Employees: 5-9
Parent Co: Market Fair
Type of Packaging: Food Service, Private Label
Brands:
    Casa Buena
    Colonial
    Deli Shoppe
    Sanditos
    Smileys
    Sonritos

9206 McLane's Meats
PO Box 7084
Wetaskiwin, AB T9A 2Y9
Canada   780-352-4321
    Fax: 780-352-8522
Processor of beef and pork sausage and wild game including deer, elk and moose; custom slaughtering services available
    Owner: Robin McLane
Type of Packaging: Private Label

9207 McLaughlin Oil Company
3750 E Livingston Ave
Columbus, OH 43227-2246   614-231-2518
    Fax: 614-231-7431 www.mcglaughlinoil.com
Oils, flavored and pure
    Owner: Steve Theodor
Estimated Sales: $ 5-10 Million
Number Employees: 10-19
Brands:
    Petrol

9208 McLaughlin Seafood
728 Main St
Bangor, ME 04401-6810   207-942-7811
    Fax: 207-947-9176 800-222-9107
    kim@mclaughlinseafood.com
        www.mclaughlinseafood.com
Products include seafood in addition to cookbooks, clothing and kitchenware.
    Owner: Reid Mc Laughlin
Estimated Sales: $300,000-500,000
Number Employees: 1-4

9209 McLemore's Abattoir
1912 Center Dr
Vidalia, GA 30474-9317   912-537-4476
Processor of beef and pork
    Owner: Gene Mc Lemore
Estimated Sales: $1300000
Number Employees: 10-19
Type of Packaging: Consumer

9210 McNasby's Seafood Market
723 2nd Street
Annapolis, MD 21403-3323   410-295-9022
    Fax: 410-280-3707
Seafood

9211 McNeil Specialty Products Company
PO Box 2400
New Brunswick, NJ 08903-2400   732-524-3799
    Fax: 732-524-3303
Processor of nonnutritive sweeteners
    President: Stephen Fanning
    Director Sales (North America): Jim Thornton
    Director International Sales: Joseph Zannoni
Number Employees: 20-49
Parent Co: Johnson & Johnson

9212 McNeill's Brewery
90 Elliot St
Brattleboro, VT 05301-3269   802-254-2553
    Fax: 802-257-1167
Processor of beer, ale, stout, lager and porter
    Owner: Holiday Mc Neill
Estimated Sales: Below $ 5 Million
Number Employees: 10-19
Type of Packaging: Consumer, Food Service
Brands:
    Bucksnort Barleywine
    McNeill's Alle Tage
    McNeill's Champ Ale
    McNeill's Duck's Bre
    McNeill's Extra Spec
    McNeill's Firehouse
    McNeill's Imperial S
    McNeill's Kolsch
    McNeill's Oatmeal St
    McNeill's Old Ringwo
    McNeill's Pulman's P
    McNeill's Ruby Ale
    McNeill's Ruby Ale
    McNeill's Summer IPA
    McNeill's Wassail
    McNeill's Yukon Gold
    Slopbucket Brown

9213 (HQ)McRedmond Brothers
P.O.Box 100902
Nashville, TN 37224-0902   615-361-8997
    Fax: 615-361-5645
Processor of meat and blood meal
    Owner: Stephen Mc Redmond
    VP: Ellen Kade
Estimated Sales: $570000
Number Employees: 5-9
Type of Packaging: Consumer, Bulk

9214 McSteven's
5600 NE 88th St
Vancouver, WA 98665-0971   360-944-5788
    Fax: 360-944-1302 800-838-1056
    sales@mcstevens.com www.mcstevens.com
Processor of beverage mixes including white chocolate, regular and sugar-free cocoa, lemonade, cappuccino, chai, and apple cider; exporter of cocoa mixes
    Owner: Brent Houston
    VP Marketing: Dave Demsky
    VP Operations: Brent Huston
Estimated Sales: $500,000-$1 Million
Number Employees: 20-49

Type of Packaging: Consumer, Food Service, Private Label, Bulk

9215 McTavish Company
10234 NE Glisan St
Portland, OR 97220-4061   503-253-9394
          Fax: 503-254-6616   800-256-9844
                    info@mctavish.biz
          www.mctavishshortbread.com/
Processor of shortbread cookies
    Co-Owner: Denise Pratt
    Co-Owner: Bill Pratt
Estimated Sales: Less than $500,000
Number Employees: 10-19
Type of Packaging: Consumer, Food Service, Bulk
Brands:
    McTavish

9216 McIlhenny Company
601 Poydras St # 1815
New Orleans, LA 70130-6028   504-523-7370
    Fax: 504-596-6444   whatscooking@tabasco.com
                    www.tabasco.com
Manufacturer and exporter of hot, jalapeno and pepper sauces; also, Bloody Mary cocktail mixes
    President: Paul Mc Ilhenny
    CFO: Michael Terrell
    VP Corporate Marketing: Martin Manion
Estimated Sales: $ 5 - 10 Million
Number Employees: 5-9
Sq. footage: 170300
Type of Packaging: Consumer, Food Service, Private Label, Bulk
Brands:
    Tabasco

9217 Mclure's Honey & Maple Products
46 N Littleton Rd
Littleton, NH 03561-3814   603-444-6246
    Fax: 603-444-6659   info@mclures.com
                    www.mclures.com
Processor of pure honey and maple syrup
    Manager: Gordon Hartford
Number Employees: 20-49
Parent Co: Dutch Gold Honey

9218 Mead Containboard
1100 Circle 75 Parkway SE
Suite 500
Atlanta, GA 30339-3079   770-952-7455
          Fax: 770-644-2384
Packaging supplies, corrugated boxes
    President: Mike Snowball

9219 Mead Containerboard
100 SW South Avenue
Blue Springs, MO 64014-3034   501-782-6091
          Fax: 501-783-6003

9220 Mead Johnson Nutrition
2400 W Lloyd Expy
Evansville, IN 47721-0001   812-429-5000
    Fax: 812-429-7714   www.meadjohnson.com
nutritional brands and products for infants and children
    President/CEO: Stephen Golsby
    SVP/CFO: Peter Leemputte
    VP/Controller: Stanley Burhans
    SVP Global R&D: Dirk Hondmann
    SVP Human Resources: Lynn Clark
Estimated Sales: K
Number Employees: 6000
Parent Co: Bristol-Myers Squibb Company
Type of Packaging: Consumer
Brands:
    Boost
    Enfamil
    Lactofree
    Nutramigen
    Pregestimil
    Prosobee

9221 Mead Johnson Nutritional
725 E Main Ave
Zeeland, MI 49464-1331   616-748-7100
          Fax: 616-748-7133   www.meadjohnson.com
Processor of evaporated milk
Estimated Sales: $ 10 - 20 Million
Number Employees: 10-19
Parent Co: Bristol-Myers Squibb Company
Type of Packaging: Consumer

9222 Meadow Brook Dairy
2365 Buffalo Rd
Erie, PA 16510-1459   814-899-3191
    Fax: 814-899-9152   800-352-4010
          www.meadowbrookdairy.com
Processor of milk including whole, skim, 1% and 2%
    Marketing Director: Marty Schwartz
    VP Sales/Marketing: Joseph Martin
    Plant Manager: Rhett Flanders
Number Employees: 100-249
Parent Co: Dean Foods Company
Type of Packaging: Consumer, Food Service
Brands:
    FlavorTight
    Milk Chugs
    Swiss Premium Drinks

9223 Meadow Brook Farms
900 S Keim Street
Pottstown, PA 19465-7736   610-323-3700
          Fax: 610-323-2540
Milk and ice cream
    Vice President: Howard Swavely
    Plant Manager: Tim Lloyd
Estimated Sales: $ 10-20 Million
Number Employees: 20-49

9224 Meadow Gold Dairies
P.O.Box 1880
Honolulu, HI 96805-1880   808-949-6161
    Fax: 808-944-5901   www.meadowgold.com
Processor of cottage cheese, yogurt, sour cream, buttermilk, milk, ice cream, ice cream novelties and juices including orange, guava, passion fruit, etc
    President/General Manager: Glen Muranaka
Estimated Sales: $100+ Million
Number Employees: 100-249
Parent Co: Suiza Dairy Group
Type of Packaging: Consumer, Food Service

9225 Meadow Gold Dairies
P.O.Box 82029
Lincoln, NE 68501-2029   402-434-8400
    Fax: 402-434-8414   800-742-7349
          gsummer@meadowgold.com
          www.meadowgold.com
Processor of milk, cottage cheese, juice and ice cream mix
    General Manager: Bob Lake
    Sales/Marketing Executive: Bill Witt
    Plant Manager: Bill Fralick
    Purchasing Agent: Rick Rodney
Estimated Sales: $100+ Million
Number Employees: 100-249
Sq. footage: 85000
Parent Co: Suiza Dairy Group
Type of Packaging: Consumer, Food Service, Private Label, Bulk

9226 Meadow Gold Dairies
1301 W Bannock St
Boise, ID 83702-5622   208-343-3671
    Fax: 208-345-7697   www.meadowgold.com
Processor of dairy products including milk, sour cream, cottage cheese, cream cheese, yogurt, butter solid & quarters, flavored ice cream, flavored sherbert and fruit drinks
    General Manager: Ralph Hallquist
    Quality Control: Steve Overton
    Sales: Craig Lund
    Production: Chris Cappl
Estimated Sales: $100+ Million
Number Employees: 100-249
Parent Co: Dean Foods
Type of Packaging: Consumer, Food Service, Private Label, Bulk
Brands:
    MEADOW GOLD
    PRIVATE LABELS
    TAMPICO
    VIVA

9227 (HQ)Meadow Gold Dairies
845 S State St
Orem, UT 84097-7025   801-225-3660
    Fax: 801-224-9205   www.meadowgold.com/
Fluid milk, cream, sour cream and related products
    COO: Tom Murray
    Marketing Director: Randy Proctor
    Operations Manager: Mike Koenig
    General Manager: Bruce Williamson
    Plant Manager: Dale Clark

Estimated Sales: $ 50 - 100 Million
Number Employees: 50-99
Brands:
    Meadow Gold
    Viva

9228 Meadow Gold Dairies
P.O.Box 26817
Salt Lake City, UT 84126-0817   801-908-7531
          Fax: 801-973-2750
          jmeenderink@meadowgold.com
          www.meadowgold.com
Fluid milk, cream, sour cream and related products
    Manager: Mike Northrup
    General Manager: Lynn Tuttle
    Plant Manager: Richard Heiler
Estimated Sales: $ 50-99.9 Million
Number Employees: 100-249
Parent Co: Suiza Dairy Group

9229 Meadow Gold Dairy
512 18th Street N
Lewiston, ID 83501-5323   208-746-9006
Distributors-dairy products including butter, ice cream, milk, cheese and yogurt
Estimated Sales: $300,000-500,000
Number Employees: 1-4
Type of Packaging: Consumer, Bulk

9230 Meadowbrook Distributing Corporation
550 New Horizons Blvd
Amityville, NY 11701-1166   631-226-9000
          Fax: 631-226-4233   www.pbg.com
Processor of soft drinks
    President: Richard "Poillon, Jr."
    VP Operations: Tom Fay
    Operations Plant Manager (Garden City): Joe Cacciato
Estimated Sales: $100+ Million
Number Employees: 100-249
Parent Co: PepsiCo
Type of Packaging: Consumer, Food Service

9231 Meadowbrook Farm
2338 Hermany Avenue
Bronx, NY 10473-1198   718-828-6400
          Fax: 718-828-8110
Dairy products
    Manager: Phil Carlson
Estimated Sales: $ 2.5-5 Million
Number Employees: 50-99
Brands:
    Meadowbrook

9232 Meadows Country Products
811 Scotch Valley Road
Hollidaysburg, PA 16648-9693   814-693-9714
    Fax: 814-693-4625   888-499-1001
          jim@meadowscountryproducts.com
          www.meadowscountryproducts.com
Refrigerated desserts, deli salads
    President: James Meadows
    Owner: Margie Meadows
    Secretary/Treasurer: Margie Meadows
    Quality Assurance/Plant Manger: Todd Hill
    General Manager: Jon Thayer
    Sales Manager: Norm Tucker
    Office Manager: Eileen Snyder
    Operations Manager: Jeff Meadows
    Purchasing Director: Mike Ricker
Estimated Sales: Below $ 5 Million
Number Employees: 15
Number of Brands: 1
Number of Products: 60
Sq. footage: 12000
Type of Packaging: Food Service, Private Label, Bulk
Brands:
    MEADOWS COUNTRY PRODUCTS

9233 Meadowvale
109 Beaver St
Yorkville, IL 60560-1797   630-553-0202
    Fax: 630-553-0262   800-953-0201
    Wlsn75@aol.com   www.meadowvale-inc.com
Processor of ice cream, shake and soft serve mixes
    President: Steve Steinwart
    Plant Manager: Ken Baumberger
Estimated Sales: $5000000
Number Employees: 10-19
Sq. footage: 15000
Type of Packaging: Consumer

Brands:
Dairy Queen

9234 Meal Mart
5620 59th St
Flushing, NY 11378-2314   718-894-2000
Fax: 718-326-4642   800-245-5620
eeidlitz@kosherquest.org   www.mealmart.com
Processor of kosher fresh and frozen meat products, entrees and deli meats; private label and co-packing services available
President: Mandal Weinstock
Vice President: Shlomi Pilo
Research & Development: Udi Basis
Plant Manager: Iran Talavera
Purchasing Manager: Zeer Weinstock
Estimated Sales: $ 10-20 Million
Number Employees: 50-99
Sq. footage: 150000
Parent Co: Alle Processing
Type of Packaging: Consumer, Food Service, Private Label, Bulk
Brands:
Meal Mart
Mou Cuisine
New York Kosher Deli

9235 Meat & Fish Fellas
5036 N 54th Ave # 7
Glendale, AZ 85301-7509   623-931-6190
Fax: 623-931-2960
Meat and seafood
Partner: J Tarbell
Partner: Marty Menter
Partner: Inyol Kim
Estimated Sales: $ 3 - 5 Million
Number Employees: 20-49

9236 Meat Center
3035 Fm 822
Edna, TX 77957   361-782-3776
Meat packer
Owner: Eli Salinas
Estimated Sales: $ .5 - 1 million
Number Employees: 5-9
Type of Packaging: Consumer, Bulk

9237 Meat Corral Company
3695 Thompson Bridge Rd
Gainesville, GA 30506-1515   770-536-9188
Fax: 918-622-8003
Meats
President: Richard Webb
Estimated Sales: $ 3 - 5 Million
Number Employees: 5-9

9238 Meat Shop
1225 S Kingshighway Street
Cape Girardeau, MO 63703-8009   573-334-2465
Fax: 573-334-4085   800-791-5104
info@meatshop.com
Processor of cured ham and bacon; also, sausage
President: Bob Osborne
Estimated Sales: $$5-10 Million
Number Employees: 19

9239 Meat-O-Mat Corporation
592 Pacific St
Brooklyn, NY 11217-2077   718-965-7250
Fax: 718-832-1027
Processor and exporter of frozen portion control meats including hamburger, beef, breaded chicken, breaded veal, turkey and ostrich patties; also, full line of Hispanic products including beef patties, taco products and soffrito
President: Ronald Fatato
General Manager: Tony Quaranta
VP Sales/Director Marketing: Freddy Refino
Estimated Sales: $ 20 - 50 Million
Number Employees: 10-19
Type of Packaging: Consumer, Food Service, Bulk

9240 Meatco Sales
5315 54th Street
Mirror, AB T0B 3L0
Canada   403-788-2292
Fax: 403-788-2294
Processor of fresh and frozen beef, pork, wild game and sausage
Manager: Chris Pfisterer
Manager: Steven Pfisterer
Owner: Herman Pfisterer
Type of Packaging: Consumer, Food Service, Private Label, Bulk

9241 Meating Place
185 Grant St
Buffalo, NY 14213-1607   716-885-3623
Fax: 716-885-6328 www.meatingplace.com
Processor of meat products including pork sausage and beef patties
President: Vincent Lorigo
Estimated Sales: $4000000
Number Employees: 20-49
Type of Packaging: Consumer, Food Service

9242 Meatland Packers
3326 15th Avenue SW
Medicine Hat, AB T1B 3W5
Canada   403-528-4321
Fax: 403-529-5986
Processor of fresh and frozen beef, pork, lamb and wild game including elk, moose and deer
President: Frank Noel
Type of Packaging: Consumer, Food Service, Private Label, Bulk

9243 Medallion Foods
3636 Medallion Ave
Newport, AR 72112-9096   870-523-3500
Fax: 870-523-4417 www.medallion-foods.com
Manufacturer of tortilla chips, cheese puffs and extruded corn snacks
President: Rusty Karschner
Number Employees: 100-249
Parent Co: Ralcorp Holdings
Type of Packaging: Consumer

9244 Medallion International
233 W Parkway
Pompton Plains, NJ 07444-1028   973-616-3401
Fax: 973-616-3405 medallionamyb@msn.com
Manufacturer of Flavors: natural and artificial. Edible and essential oils.
President: Michael Boudjouk
Director Sales/Marketing: Paula Boudjouk
Estimated Sales: $18 Million
Number Employees: 10-19
Type of Packaging: Consumer, Food Service, Private Label, Bulk

9245 Medeiros Farms
P.O.Box 102
Kalaheo, HI 96741-0102   808-332-8211
Fax: 808-332-8211
Processor of poultry, eggs, beef and sausage
President: Bernard M Medeiros
Estimated Sales: $ 10 - 20 Million
Number Employees: 10-19
Type of Packaging: Consumer

9246 Meditalia
P.O.Box 1393
New York, NY 10113-1393   212-616-3006
Fax: 212-616-3005 info@peaceworks.net
www.peaceworks.net
Dairy and egg-free jarred sauces
Founder/CEO: Daniel Lubetzky
VP/New Product Development & Marketing: Sasha Hare
VP/Sales: Rami Leshem
VP/Operations: Doris Rivera

9247 Mediterranean Delights
30 Industrial Dr
Bellows Falls, VT 05101-3122   802-460-0033
Fax: 802-869-3559   800-347-5850
info@mediterraneandelights.com
www.mediterraneandelights.com
All natural and certified organic manufacturer of hummus, dips, mediterranean fruit spreads and salads.
President: Joan Day
CEO: Joan Day
Vice President: Nicole Day
Quality Control: David Taclof
Sales: Deanna Wilbur
Plant Manager: David Taclof
Estimated Sales: $ 5 - 10 Million
Number Employees: 20-49
Number of Brands: 4
Number of Products: 33

9248 Mediterranean Gyros Products
1102 38th Ave
Long Island City, NY 11101-6041   718-786-3399
Fax: 718-786-8518

Wholesaler/distributor of Greek specialty items; processor of pita bread
President: Vasilios Memmos
Estimated Sales: $9000000
Number Employees: 20-49

9249 Mediterranean Pita Bakery
9006 132 Avenue NW
Edmonton, AB T5E 0Y2
Canada   780-476-6666
Processor of pita bread
Manager: Ahmed Hagar
Number Employees: 5-9
Type of Packaging: Consumer, Food Service

9250 Meduri Farms Inc
12395 Smithfield Rd
Dallas, OR 97338   503-831-1097
Fax: 503-623-0726 mzobel@diversifiedfood.com
www.medurifarms.com
Processor, importer and exporter of dried cherries, blueberries and strawberries; also, infused cherries with raspberry juice
President: Joe Meduri
Sales: Mike Zobel
Estimated Sales: $18000000
Number Employees: 20-49
Parent Co: Meduri Farms
Type of Packaging: Food Service, Private Label, Bulk
Brands:
Razzcherries

9251 Meeker Vineyard
5375 Dry Creek Rd
Healdsburg, CA 95448-9786   707-433-2500
Fax: 707-431-2549 charlie@meekerwine.com
www.meekerwine.com
Wines the selection of which includes Chardonnay, Dry Rose, Zinfandel, Petite Sirah, Cabernet Sauvignon and Merlot, in addition to others.
President: Charles Meeker
VP Marketing/Operations: John Burtner
Estimated Sales: Less than $500,000
Number Employees: 1-4

9252 Meelunie America
26105 Orchard Lake Rd # 210
Farmington Hills, MI 48334-4578   248-473-2100
Fax: 248-473-2114 info@meelunie-america.com
www.meelunie.com
Starch products: potatos, corn and wheat
Owner: William Lauer
Estimated Sales: $ 3 - 5 Million
Number Employees: 1-4

9253 Mega Blue A Blue
PO Box 950
Tracadie-Sheila, NB E1X 1G7
Canada   506-358-6366
Fax: 506-358-2155
Frozen foods

9254 Mega Pro International
251 Hilton Dr
St George, UT 84770-2320   435-673-1001
Fax: 435-673-1007   800-541-9469
info@mega-pro.com www.mega-pro.com
Processor, importer and exporter of nutritional supplements including vitamins for weight gain and loss
President: Dave Smith
Estimated Sales: $1800000
Number Employees: 20-49

9255 Mehaffie Pies
9338 Dayton Lebanon Pike
Dayton, OH 45458-3839   937-436-2757
Fax: 937-254-4977   937-253-1163
Processor of cheesecake, fresh and frozen pies
President: Robert Columbus
Co-Owner: Jim Columbus
Sales: Mark Berry
Estimated Sales: $500,000-$1 Million
Number Employees: 1-4
Sq. footage: 4000
Type of Packaging: Consumer, Food Service, Private Label, Bulk

9256 Mei Shun Tofu Products Company
523 W 26th St
Chicago, IL 60616-1803   312-842-7000
Fax: 312-791-9429

Canner and exporter of tofu
Owner: Yim Sung
Estimated Sales: Less than $500,000
Number Employees: 5-9
Type of Packaging: Consumer, Food Service, Private Label, Bulk

9257 Meier's Wine Cellars

6955 Plainfield Rd
Cincinnati, OH 45236-3793   513-891-2900
Fax: 513-891-6370   800-346-2941
info@meierswinecellars.com
www.meierswinecellars.com
Processor of fruit juices and wine
President: Edward Moulton
VP: Jack Lucia
Marketing Director: Lynn Lubin
Estimated Sales: $69500000
Number Employees: 20-49
Parent Co: Paramount Distillers
Type of Packaging: Consumer

9258 Meister Cheese Company

P.O.Box 68
Muscoda, WI 53573-0068   608-739-3134
Fax: 608-739-4348   800-634-7837
grandpa@meistercheese.com
www.meistercheese.com
Cheese
President: Scott Meister
Partner: Vicki Thingbold
Partner: Dan Meister
Sales/Marketing: Dan Meister
Estimated Sales: $ 5-10 Million
Number Employees: 20-49
Type of Packaging: Private Label

9259 (HQ)Mel-O-Cream Donuts International

5456 International Pkwy
Springfield, IL 62711-7086   217-483-7272
Fax: 217-483-7744 www.mel-o-cream.com
Donuts, both frozen pre-formed dough and frozen pre-fried
President: Kelly A Grant Jr
CFO: Andrew Williams
VP: Andy Williams
Research & Development: Jim Eck, Jr.
Sales Director: Charlie Lumsdon
Operations Manager: David Waltrip
Production Manager: Dan Alewelt
Estimated Sales: $ 10-20 Million
Number Employees: 50-99
Number of Brands: 1
Number of Products: 200+
Sq. footage: 65000
Type of Packaging: Food Service, Bulk
Brands:
Mel-O-Cream

9260 Melchers Flavors of America

5600 W Raymond Street
Indianapolis, IN 46241-4343   513-858-6300
Fax: 513-858-3110   800-235-2867
sales@melchersflavors.com
www.melchersflavors.com
Food flavorings; including kosher, extracts, syrups and drink mixes
COO: Wolfgang Boehmer
Purchasing Manager: Kellie Hall
Estimated Sales: $ 5-9.9 Million
Number Employees: 20
Type of Packaging: Food Service, Bulk

9261 Mele-Koi Farms

P.O.Box 2987
Newport Beach, CA 92659-0519   949-660-9000
Fax: 949-660-9000
Manufacturer and exporter of powdered tropical drink mixes
Owner: Lloyd L Aubert Jr Jr
Estimated Sales: $400,000
Number Employees: 1-4
Number of Brands: 1
Number of Products: 1
Type of Packaging: Consumer
Brands:
MELE-KOI HAWAIIAN COCONUT SNOW

9262 Meleddy Cherry Plant

1952 Shiloh Road
Sturgeon Bay, WI 54235-8313   920-856-6770

Frozen red tart cherries
President: Melvin Selvick
VP: Eddy Selvick
Estimated Sales: $ 5-10 Million
Number Employees: 20-49

9263 Melissa's/World VarietyPProduce

5325 S Soto St
Vernon, CA 90058-3624   323-588-0151
Fax: 323-588-7841   800-588-0151
hotline@melissas.com   www.melissas.com
Fruits and vegetables
President/CEO: Joe Hernandez
CFO: Bill Schneider
Plant Manager: Mike Stephens
Estimated Sales: $ 10-100 Million
Number Employees: 100-249
Sq. footage: 100000
Brands:
Don Enrique
Jo San
Melissas

9264 Melitta

13925 58th St N
Clearwater, FL 33760-3721   727-535-2111
Fax: 727-535-7376
consumerrelations@melitta.com
www.melitta.com
Processor, importer and exporter of coffee; also, coffee machines and filters
CEO: Marty Miller
CFO: Fred Lueck
CEO: Marty Miller
Marketing: Chris Hillman
Sales: Ed Mitchell
Public Relations: Donna Gray
Operations: Jeff Bridges
Plant Manager: Matthias Bloedorn
Estimated Sales: $ 50 - 100 Million
Number Employees: 100-249
Parent Co: Melitta North America
Type of Packaging: Consumer, Food Service
Brands:
Melitta

9265 Mello's North End Manufacturings

63 N Court St
Fall River, MA 02720-2755   508-673-2320
Fax: 508-675-0893   800-673-2320
info@melloschourico.com   www.mellos.net
Processor and exporter of sausage patties, links and pork
Owner: Eduardo Rego
Sales Manager: Diane Rego
Estimated Sales: $500,000-$1 Million
Number Employees: 1-4
Type of Packaging: Consumer, Food Service, Bulk

9266 Melville Candy Company

70 Finnell Drive
Unit 16
Weymouth, MA 02188   800-638-8063
Fax: 800-466-0516   jmelville8878@aol.com
www.melvillecandycompany.com
gourmet hard candy lollipops
President/Owner: Gary Melville
CFO: Debra Katz
Manufacturing Staff: Liz Mazzilli
Number Employees: 22

9267 Memba

816 Loomis Trail Rd
Lynden, WA 98264-9111   360-354-7708
Fax: 360-354-3906   monte@maberrys.com
www.maberrys.com
Processor of fresh and frozen blueberries, strawberries and raspberries
President: Curt Maberry
Estimated Sales: $ 2.5-5 Million
Number Employees: 20-49
Type of Packaging: Private Label, Bulk

9268 Mendocino Beverages International

10680 Docker Hill Road
Comptche, CA 95427   707-937-0547
Fax: 707-522-2588
Beverages
President: Don Yee
Sales Manager: Nick Carter

Estimated Sales: $ 1-2.5 Million
Number Employees: 10-19
Brands:
Mendocino Sparkling Mineral Water

9269 Mendocino Brewing Company

1601 Airport Rd
Ukiah, CA 95482-6456   707-463-2087
Fax: 797-744-1910   questions@mendobrew.com
www.mendobrew.com
Processor of beer, stout, ale and lager
President: Yashpal Singha
CFO: Jerome Merchant
CEO: Vijay Mallya
Marketing Director: Michael Lovett
Estimated Sales: $4300000
Number Employees: 50-99
Sq. footage: 65000
Type of Packaging: Consumer, Food Service
Brands:
Black Hawk
Blackhawk Stout
Blue Heron
Blue Heron Pale Ale
Eye of the Hawk
Eye of the Hawk Select Ale
Peregrine Golden
Peregrine Pale Ale
Red Tail
Red Tail Ale
Springtide Ale
Yuletide Porter

9270 Mendocino Mustard

1260 N Main St # 11
Fort Bragg, CA 95437-4099   707-964-2250
Fax: 707-964-0525   800-964-2270
info@mendocinomustard.com
mendocinomustard.com
Processor of specialty mustards including hot/sweet and spicy seeded with ale. Foods available in fat-free and sodium-free
President: Devora Rossman
Production Manager: Kathy Silva
Estimated Sales: $255000
Number Employees: 1-4
Number of Brands: 1
Number of Products: 2
Sq. footage: 1600
Type of Packaging: Consumer, Food Service
Brands:
Mendocino
Seeds & Suds

9271 Menemsha Fish Market

P.O.Box 406
Chilmark, MA 02535-0406   508-645-2282
Fax: 508-645-9783
www.menemshafishmarket.com
Processor of fresh and prepared seafood; fish, crabs, scallops and shellfish
Owner: Stanley Larsen
Estimated Sales: $300,000-500,000
Number Employees: 1-4
Type of Packaging: Consumer, Food Service, Private Label, Bulk
Brands:
Menemsha Bites
Poole's

9272 Menghini Winery

P.O.Box 1359
Julian, CA 92036-1359   760-765-2072
Fax: 760-765-2072
Wines
President: Michael Menghini
Estimated Sales: Less than $300,000
Number Employees: 1-4
Type of Packaging: Private Label
Brands:
Menghini

9273 Mennel Milling Company

P.O.Box 806
Fostoria, OH 44830-0806   419-435-8151
Fax: 419-436-5150   800-688-8151
info@mennel.com   www.mennel.com

Processor of flour used in cake mixes, cookies, snack crackers, breadings, batters, gravies, soups, ice cream cones, pretzels and oriental noodles.
President: Donald Mennel
Vice President: Lyle Lahman
CFO: Mark Hall
Quality Control: Jan Levenhagen
VP Sales: Michael Kraus
Operations/Quality Control: Robert Reid
Plant Manager: Joel Hoffa
Estimated Sales: Below $ 5 Million
Number Employees: 100-249
Type of Packaging: Bulk

9274 (HQ)Mennel Milling Company
P.O.Box 806
Fostoria, OH 44830-0806   419-435-8151
      Fax: 419-436-5150   info@mennel.com
               www.mennel.com
Manufacturer of milling soft, hard, spring and specialty wheat flours
President/CEO: Donald Mennel
Plant Manager: Frank Herbes
Estimated Sales: $24 Million
Number Employees: 100-249
Type of Packaging: Consumer, Private Label, Bulk

9275 Mennel Milling Company
P.O.Box 806
Fostoria, OH 44830-0806   419-436-5130
      Fax: 419-435-8737   mmiller@mennel.com
               www.mennel.com
Processor of flour including soft wheat, pastry and cake
President: Donald Mennel
Office Manager: Elizabeth Miller
Plant Manager: Scott Flick
Estimated Sales: $5000000
Number Employees: 10-19
Parent Co: Mennel Milling Company
Type of Packaging: Bulk

9276 Mental Processes
1075 Zonolite Road NE
Atlanta, GA 30306-2013   404-875-7440
      Fax: 319-754-4754   800-431-4018
               mentalprocesses@msn.com
Processor and exporter of dry roasted pumpkin seed snacks
President: Scott Bradford
Estimated Sales: $ 1-2.5 Million
Number Employees: 5-9
Type of Packaging: Consumer, Food Service, Private Label
Brands:
Pumpkorn

9277 Mentone Egg Products
507 N Broadway Street
Mentone, IN 46539-9532   219-353-7691
                  Fax: 219-353-7112
Milk, dairy products
President: Don Strauss
Plant Manager: Mark Casper
Estimated Sales: $ 5-10 Million
Number Employees: 50-99

9278 Menu Meats
17719 Auburn Road
Huntertown, IN 46748-9760   260-432-5596
      Fax: 260-432-5021   800-848-2902
      menumeats@tk7.net   www.menumeatsinc.com
Processor of portion controlled steaks and sausage products; wholesaler/distributor of poultry products including turkey and chicken
President: Donna Fortriede
Sales Manager: Geary Rollins
Estimated Sales: $5.7 Million
Number Employees: 3
Sq. footage: 4600
Type of Packaging: Consumer, Food Service, Private Label

9279 Meramec Vineyards
600 State Route B
St James, MO 65559-1000   573-265-7847
      Fax: 573-265-3453   877-216-9463
               mervine@fignet.com
               www.meramecvineyards.com
Processor of natural grape juice
President: P Meagher
Estimated Sales: $ 3 - 5 Million
Number Employees: 5-9
Type of Packaging: Consumer, Food Service

Brands:
Meramec

9280 Merbs Candies
4000 S Grand Blvd
St Louis, MO 63118-3466   314-832-7117
      Fax: 314-832-0146 www.merbscandy.com
Processor of candy including chocolates and novelties.
President: Terry Bearden
Estimated Sales: $500,000-$1 Million
Number Employees: 10-19
Type of Packaging: Consumer

9281 Mercado Latino
245 Baldwin Park Blvd
City of Industry, CA 91746-1404   626-333-6862
                  Fax: 626-333-5080
Processor of cookies, beans, candy, coconut milk, canned seafood, hominy, corn oil, chile peppers, sauces, spices, charcoal briquettes, brooms and cleaners; importer and exporter of chiles, spices and sauces; wholesaler/distributor of Mexican specialty foods
President: Graciliano Rodriguez
CFO: Jorge Rodriguez
VP/General Manager: Al Mena
Sr. VP/Marketing: Richard Rodriguez
Estimated Sales: $123600000
Number Employees: 100-249
Sq. footage: 225
Brands:
Brillasol
Faraon
Milpas
Ola Blanca
Payaso
Siesta
Sol-Mex
Sun Sun

9282 Mercantile Food Company
PO Box S
Philmont, NY 12565   518-672-0190
      Fax: 518-672-0198   info@mercantilefood.com
               www.mercantilefood.com
Orgainic foods
President and CEO: Michael Marcolla
CFO/R&D/VP Operations: John Whitmer
VP Marketing: Brian Andrew
Estimated Sales: $ 10-100 Million
Number Employees: 10
Type of Packaging: Private Label
Brands:
American Prairie

9283 Mercer Processing
1836 Lapham Dr
Modesto, CA 95354-3900   209-529-0150
      Fax: 209-526-3406   dnoland@mercerfoods.com
               www.mercerfoods.com
Dehydrated fruits, vegetables, soups, shrimp and crab
President: David Noland
Estimated Sales: $ 50 - 100 Million
Number Employees: 50-99
Brands:
Mercer

9284 Merci Spring Water
2 City Center
Suite 200
Saint Louis, MO 63101-1816   314-812-4812
                  Fax: 314-812-4810
Processor and exporter of water including spring, purified and distilled; also, concentrated juices
President: Don Schneeberger
Sales Director: Don Schneeberger
Estimated Sales: $350000
Number Employees: 6
Sq. footage: 22500

9285 Mercon Coffee Corporation
2 Hudson Pl
Hoboken, NJ 07030-5594   201-418-9400
      Fax: 201-418-0306   info@merconcoffee.com
               www.merconcoffee.com
Green coffee
President: Andy Enderlin
President: Andreas Enderlin
CFO/Treasurer: Salvador Rodriguez
Sales Manager: Richard Etkin
Number Employees: 20-49

Brands:
Mercon

9286 Mercury Brewing Company
23 Hayward St
Ipswich, MA 01938-2044   978-356-3329
                  Fax: 450-973-1957
               brewing@mercurybrewing.com
               www.mercurybrewing.com
Manufacture of soda and beer
President: Robert Martin
Estimated Sales: Below $ 5 Million
Number Employees: 10-19
Type of Packaging: Consumer, Food Service
Brands:
Blueberry Ale
Ipswich Ale
Stone Cat Ale

9287 Meredith & Meredith
2343 Farm Creek Rd
Toddville, MD 21672-9729   410-397-8151
                  Fax: 410-397-8130
Frozen soft shell crabs, refrigerated blue crabmeat, oysters
President: Jennings Tolley
VP: Morgan Tolley
Estimated Sales: Below $ 5 Million
Number Employees: 20-49
Type of Packaging: Consumer
Brands:
Meredith's

9288 Meredyth Vineyard
RR 628
Middleburg, VA 20118   540-687-6277
      Fax: 540-687-6288 www.meredythvineyards.com
Wine
Partner: Archie Smith

9289 Meridian Beverage Company
PO Box 941728
Atlanta, GA 31141-0728   770-409-1431
      Fax: 770-263-6960   800-728-1481
               slovinger@meridianclear.com
               www.meridianclear.com
Processor of naturally flavored noncarbonated spring water beverages
President: Steve Lovinger
Convenience Store Manager: Ralph Grasso
Sales Manager: Marilyn Hunter
Number Employees: 20-49

9290 Meridian Nut Growers
1625 Shaw Ave
Clovis, CA 93611-4089   559-458-7272
      Fax: 559-458-7270   jzion@meridiannut.com
               www.meridiannut.com
Grower owned sales and marketing company supporting growers, processors, and buyers of California almonds, pistachios, walnuts, prunes, and raisins as well as South African macadamia nuts. In addition, they handle a full line of various dried fruit and nut products from origins around the world.
Manager: Jim Zion
Grower Relations/Sales Coordinator: Cecilia Kjar
Sales Director: Stacy Dovali
Managing Director: Jim Zion
Accounting Manager: Julie Sawyer
Estimated Sales: $500,000-$1 Million
Number Employees: 20-49
Type of Packaging: Food Service, Private Label, Bulk
Brands:
A&P Growers

9291 Meridian Trading
1136 Pearl St # 201
Boulder, CO 80302-5141   303-442-8683
      Fax: 303-442-8684   meridiantc@qwest.net
               www.meridiantrading.com
Herbal products
President: David Black
Estimated Sales: $ 5 Million
Number Employees: 1-4

9292 Meridian Vineyards
P.O.Box 3289
Paso Robles, CA 93447-3289   805-237-6000
                  Fax: 805-239-5715
               inquiries@meridianvineyards.com
               www.meridianvineyards.com

Wines the selection of which includes Chardonnay Santa Barbara, Sauvignon Blanc, Merlot California, Pinot Noir, Cabernet Sauvignon Blanc, Meridian Shiraz-Cabernet and Cabernet-Merlot.
President: Walter Klenz
Finance Manager: Lisa Cruz
Finance Executive: Lisa Kruse
Marketing Manager: Cath Jager
Estimated Sales: $ 20-50 Million
Number Employees: 100-249
Type of Packaging: Private Label, Bulk

9293 Merkel McDonald
6301 E Stassney Ln # 7-100
Austin, TX 78744-3087   512-385-8822
        Fax: 512-385-8985 800-356-0229
        www.otisspunkmeyer.com
Processor of IQF gourmet cookie dough and thaw/serve cookies and brownies
CEO: Dave Merkel
President: Jeff McDonald
Partner/Sales: Steve Vincent
Marketing Director: Rachel Flesher
Estimated Sales: $ 20 - 50 Million
Number Employees: 50-99
Brands:
    Chippery

9294 Merkley & Sons Packing
3994 W 180n
Jasper, IN 47546-8498   812-482-7020
                Fax: 812-482-7033
Manufacturer of meat products including beef and pork
President/CEO: James Merkley
Estimated Sales: $10-20 Million
Number Employees: 20-49
Type of Packaging: Consumer, Bulk

9295 Merkts Cheese Company
P.O.Box 188
Bristol, WI 53104-0188   262-857-2316
        Fax: 262-857-2276 sales@merktscheese.com
                www.lakeviewfarms.com
Processor of cheese including spreads, pasteurized, processed and cold-pack
President/CEO Lake View Farms: Eugene Graves

VP: Pat Denor
General Manager: Pat Denor
Sales Manager: John Kopilchack
Purchasing Agent: Gary Nies
Estimated Sales: $$20-50 Million
Number Employees: 20-49
Sq. footage: 72000
Parent Co: Bel/Kaukauna USA
Type of Packaging: Consumer, Food Service, Private Label, Bulk
Brands:
    Country Classic
    Merkts
    Owl's Nest

9296 Merlen Foods
2560 Foxfield Road
Suite 300
Saint Charles, IL 60174-5731   630-513-9886
                Fax: 630-377-6691
Syrups
President: Leonard Kolschowsky
Number Employees: 20-49

9297 Merlin Candies
5635 Powell St
Harahan, LA 70123-2223   504-733-5553
        Fax: 504-733-5536 800-899-1549
                www.merlincandies.com
Processor, importer and exporter of confectionery products including custom molded and sugar-free chocolates, seasonal candies and chocolate trolls
President: Jean La Hoste
VP: Mary Crowley
Estimated Sales: $1000000
Number Employees: 5-9
Type of Packaging: Consumer, Food Service, Private Label
Brands:
    Merlin's

9298 Merlino Italian Baking Company
771 Valley St
Seattle, WA 98109-4300   206-284-0744
        Fax: 206-284-0915 800-207-2997
                info@merlinobaking.com
                www.merlinobaking.com
Italian bakery goods, specialty cookies, soy products, organic products, health foods, etc
President: Greg Merlino
Vice President: Basel Nassar
Marketing: Margaret Domer
Sales: Greg Merlino
Operations/Production/Purchasing: Basel Nassar
Plant Manager: Aurelio Coria
Estimated Sales: $ 3 Million
Number Employees: 20-49
Number of Brands: 3
Number of Products: 50
Sq. footage: 10000
Type of Packaging: Consumer, Food Service, Private Label
Brands:
    MERLINO SIGNATURE BRANDS

9299 Merlinos
1330 Elm Ave
Canon City, CO 81212-4499   719-275-5558
        Fax: 719-275-8980 www.den-air.com
Processor of fruit juices including cider-apple, cherry, apple-strawberry, blackberry, red raspberry and grape
President: Michael A Merlino
Estimated Sales: $1127516
Number Employees: 50-99
Type of Packaging: Consumer, Food Service, Private Label, Bulk

9300 Mermaid Spice Corporation
5702 Corporation Cir
Fort Myers, FL 33905-5008   239-693-1986
        Fax: 239-693-2099 mermaid@cyberstreet.com
                www.angelpasta.com
Processor and importer of herbs, spices, seasonings, salt substitutes, rices, soup bases and salad dressings; exporter of spices and soup bases; also, custom blending available
General Manager: Mike Asaad
Estimated Sales: $1-3 Million
Number Employees: 1-4
Sq. footage: 18000
Type of Packaging: Food Service
Brands:
    Mermaid Spice

9301 Merrill Seafood Center
6213 Merrill Rd
Jacksonville, FL 32277-3512   904-744-3132
Seafood
President: Agostinho Arco
Estimated Sales: $500,000-$1 Million
Number Employees: 1-4

9302 Merrill's Blueberry Farms
P.O.Box 149
Ellsworth, ME 04605-0149   207-667-2541
        Fax: 207-667-4052 800-711-6551
        merrblue@merrillwildblueberries.com
                www.merrillwildblueberries.com
Processor, exporter and importer of IQF wild blueberries
President: Delmont Merrill
Vice President: Richard Merrill
Marketing Director: Del Merrill
Plant Manager: Richard Merrill
Estimated Sales: $ 1 - 3 Million
Number Employees: 10-19
Number of Brands: 1
Number of Products: 1
Sq. footage: 50000
Type of Packaging: Private Label, Bulk
Brands:
    MERRILL'S

9303 Merrill's Meat Company
P.O.Box 717
Encampment, WY 82325-0717   307-327-5345
Meat
President: Robert Merrill
Estimated Sales: $500,000-$1 Million
Number Employees: 1-4

9304 Merrimack Valley Apiaries
96 Dudley Rd
Billerica, MA 01821   978-667-5380
                Fax: 978-318-0881
        cardbee@mvabeepunchers.com
                www.mvabeepunchers.com
honey
President/Owner: Andrew Card Jr
Number Employees: 6

9305 Merritt Estate Wines
2264 King Rd
Forestville, NY 14062-9703   716-965-4800
        Fax: 716-965-4800 888-965-4800
        nywines@merrittestatewinery.com
                www.merrittestatewinery.com
Processor and exporter of table wines including red, white, rose, dry, sweet and sparkling
President: William T Merritt
Special Events: Jason Merritt
Estimated Sales: $$1-2.5 Million
Number Employees: 1-4
Sq. footage: 7000
Type of Packaging: Consumer, Food Service, Private Label
Brands:
    Merritt

9306 Merritt Pecan Company
P.O.Box 39
Weston, GA 31832-0039   229-828-6610
        Fax: 229-828-2061 800-762-9152
Processor and exporter of shelled and in-shell pecans
President: John Merritt
President: Richard Merritt
Estimated Sales: $2000000
Number Employees: 20-49
Sq. footage: 27000
Type of Packaging: Consumer, Bulk
Brands:
    Merritt Pecan Co.

9307 Merryvale Vineyards
1000 Main St
St Helena, CA 94574-2011   707-963-2225
        Fax: 707-963-1949 800-326-6069
        info@merryvale.com www.merryvale.com
Wines
President: Jack Schlatter
CFO: Glenn Ochsner
Public Relations: Jean De Luca
Director Winemaking: Stephen Test
Estimated Sales: $ 10-20 Million
Number Employees: 50-99
Brands:
    Merryvale

9308 Mersey Seafoods
24 Bristol Avenue
Liverpool, NS B0T 1K0
Canada   902-354-3467
                Fax: 902-354-2319
Processor and exporter of fresh and frozen cod, flounder, haddock, halibut, herring, mackerel, perch, salted pollack and shrimp
President: William Murphy
Type of Packaging: Consumer, Food Service

9309 Mertz Sausage Company
619 Cupples Rd
San Antonio, TX 78237-4329   210-433-3263
                Fax: 210-433-3218
Processor of smoked, fresh and Italian sausage; also, Mexican chorizo
President: Alejandro Pena
Estimated Sales: $250,000-$290,000
Number Employees: 1-4
Type of Packaging: Consumer
Brands:
    Mertz Sausage

9310 Mesa Cold Storage
9602 W Buckeye Rd
Tolleson, AZ 85353-9101   623-478-9392
        dcouryjr@mesacold.com
        http://www.mesacold.com/
Warehouse providing coooler, freezer and dry storage; wholesaler/distributor of groceries; transportation firm providing local, long and short haul trucking
Owner: Dan Courey
Number Employees: 10-19
Sq. footage: 50000

9311 Messina Hof Wine Cellars & Vineyards
4545 Old Reliance Rd
Bryan, TX 77808-8995 979-778-9463
Fax: 979-778-1729 800-736-9463
winemaker@messinahof.com
www.messinahof.com
Wines
President: Paul Bonarrigo
Co-Owner: Merrill Bonarrigo
Marketing Director: Steve Wiley
Public Relations: Julie Diefenthal
Estimated Sales: $ 10-20 Million
Number Employees: 20-49
Type of Packaging: Private Label, Bulk

9312 Metabolic Nutrition
10450 W McNab Rd
Tamarac, FL 33321-1816 954-720-0806
Fax: 305-945-0804 800-541-2980
info@metabolicnutrition.com
www.metabolicnutrition.com
Processor and exporter of general and sports nutritional supplements
President: Murray Cohen, MD
VP/Sales: Jay Cohen
Estimated Sales: $2,900,000
Number Employees: 5-9
Number of Products: 15
Sq. footage: 14000
Type of Packaging: Private Label
Brands:
ADVANTAGE
CGP
HYDRAVAX
PROTIZYME
SYNEDREX
TAG

9313 Metafoods, LLC
2970 Clairmont Rd NE # 510
Atlanta, GA 30329-4418 404-843-2400
Fax: 404-843-1119 info@metafoods.llc.net
www.metafoodsllc.net
Frozen foods, beef, pork, poultry, frozen seafood, canned goods
President: Joe Wright
CFO: Patricia Smith
Estimated Sales: $ 5 - 10 Million
Number Employees: 20-49

9314 (HQ)Metarom Corporation
11 School Street
Newport, VT 05855 802-334-0117
Fax: 514-375-7953 888-882-5555
accuil@metarom.fr
Processor of natural and artificial flavors and colors; natural extracts
President: Andre Bilodeau
General Manager: Pierre Miclette
CFO: Fernande Dubois
Vice President: John Murphy
Quality Control: Alain Gauther
Estimated Sales: Less than $500,000
Number Employees: 1-4
Parent Co: Metarom Canada
Other Locations:
Metarom Corporation
Granby PQ

9315 Metompkin Bay Oyster Company
P.O.Box 671
Crisfield, MD 21817-0671 410-968-0660
Fax: 410-968-0670 metbay@intercom.net
www.metompkinseafood.com
Fresh and frozen seafood
President: Casey Todd
Co-Owner: Mike Todd
Executive VP: Michael Todd
Estimated Sales: $ 5-10 Million
Number Employees: 100-249
Type of Packaging: Private Label

9316 Metro Mint
PO Box 885462
San Francisco, CA 94188 415-979-0781
Fax: 415-543-2749 info@metromint.com
www.metromint.com
pure water, real mint, no sweeteners
President/Owner: Rio Miura

9317 Metropolis Sambeve Specialty Foods
181 Canal St
Lawrence, MA 01840-1864 978-683-2873
Fax: 978-683-6636 bensmfc@verizon.net
www.metropolisfineconfections.com
Gourmet hard candies, fruit jellies, roasted nuts, chocolates and taffy
Estimated Sales: $ 3 - 5 Million
Number Employees: 5-9
Brands:
Taffy Smooches

9318 Metropolitan Bakery
262 South 19th Street
Philadelphia, PA 19103 215-545-6655
877-412-7323
mail@metropolitanbakery.com
www.metropolitanbakery.com
breads
President/Owner: Jim Lily
President: Wendy Born

9319 Metropolitan Baking Company
8579 Lumpkin St
Hamtramck, MI 48212-3622 313-875-7246
Fax: 313-875-7792 www.metropolitanbaking.com
Bread
Manager: Mike Zrimec
Chairman of the Board: George Kordas
Vice President: Jean Kordas
Estimated Sales: $ 10-20 Million
Number Employees: 50-99
Brands:
Metropolitan

9320 Metropolitan Sausage Manufacturing Company
2908 Alexander Cres
Flossmoor, IL 60422-1704 708-331-3232
Fax: 708-798-2929
Meat and sausage
President: Willard Payne
Estimated Sales: $ 1-2.5 Million
Number Employees: 1-4

9321 Metropolitan Tea Company
4 Bestobell Road
Toronto, ON M8W 4H3
Canada 416-588-0089
Fax: 416-588-7040 800-388-0351
sales@metrotea.com www.metrotea.com
Products include bagged teas, loose teas, gift boxes, tea pots and mugs, tea presses, tea infusers, spoons and squeezers.

9322 Metz Baking Company
1402 N 8th Street
Pekin, IL 61554-2103 309-347-7315
www.saralee.com
Manufacturer of baked goods
CEO: Richard Noll
General Sales Manager: Tom Hicks
Estimated Sales: $200,000
Number Employees: 8
Parent Co: Sara Lee Corporation
Type of Packaging: Bulk
Brands:
BIMBO
EARTHGRAINS
IRONKIDS
RAINBO
Rainbo
SARA LEE

9323 Metzer Farms
26000 Old Stage Rd
Gonzales, CA 93926-9480 831-679-2355
Fax: 831-679-2711 800-424-7755
metzinfo@metzerfarms.com
www.metzerfarms.com
Processor of Asian duck egg products including incubated, salted and fresh; also, whole Chinese geese
President: John Metzer
Estimated Sales: $ 3 - 5 Million
Number Employees: 10-19
Number of Products: 45
Sq. footage: 31000
Type of Packaging: Consumer, Private Label
Brands:
Balut Sa Puti

9324 Metzger Popcorn Company
24197 Road U20
Delphos, OH 45833-9343 419-692-2494
Fax: 419-692-0890 800-819-6072
mail@metzgerpopcorn.com
www.metzgerpopcorn.com
Processor and exporter of popcorn
President: Robert Metzger
Co-Owner: Marilyn Metzger
Production Manager: Todd Gable
Estimated Sales: $860000
Number Employees: 1-4
Sq. footage: 10000
Type of Packaging: Consumer, Food Service, Private Label, Bulk
Brands:
Indian Creek
Mello-Krisp
Metzger Popcorn Co.

9325 Metzger Specialty Brands
250 W 57th Street
Suite 322
New York, NY 10107 212-957-0055
Fax: 212-957-0918 info@tillenfarms.com
www.tillenfarms.com
asparagus (spicy and white), crunchy carrots, dilly beans, hot and spicy beans, maraschino cherries, snappers (snap peas), sweet bells (bell peppers), sunnysides (tomatoes), v-packed green beans
President/Owner: Tim Metzger
Human Resources Manager: Tony Palacios
Warehouse Manager: Robert Stuckey
Estimated Sales: $2 Million
Number Employees: 2

9326 MexAmerica Foods
1037 Trout Run Rd
St Marys, PA 15857-3124 814-781-1447
Fax: 814-834-9042
wecare@mexamericafoods.com
www.mexamericafoods.com
Processor of tortillas including flour, whole wheat and corn; also, tortilla chips including white, yellow, blue and red
President: Gerald B Riddle
Marketing/Sales: Michael Renaud
Operations Manager: Tom Kornacki
Purchasing Manager: Thom Hoffman
Estimated Sales: $5000000
Number Employees: 20-49
Number of Brands: 3-4
Number of Products: 1
Sq. footage: 20000
Type of Packaging: Consumer, Food Service, Private Label, Bulk
Brands:
Mexamerica

9327 Mexi-Frost Specialties Company
37 Grand Avenue
Brooklyn, NY 11205-1309 718-625-3324
Fax: 718-852-8699
Processor and exporter of frozen West Indian, Mexican, Caribbean, Chinese and Italian foods including chicken, meat pies, tamales, burritos, egg rolls, etc
President: Gonzalo Armendariz Jr
VP: Gonzalo Armendariz, Jr.
VP Sales: Mark Armendariz
Plant Manager: Gonzaol Armendariz, Jr.
Estimated Sales: $ 5 - 10 Million
Number Employees: 20-49
Type of Packaging: Consumer, Food Service, Private Label, Bulk
Brands:
Gonzo's Little Big Meat
La Jolla
La Joya
Mexi-Frost

9328 Mexi-Snax
B
1790 W Cortland Ct
Addison, IL 60101-4208 800-974-7629
Fax: 510-786-2119 800-974-7629
http://www.mexisnax.com
Processor and exporter of regular and fat-free baked tortilla chips
President: Frank Schy
COO: Jerry Schy
Sales Manager: Jelli Meyer
Estimated Sales: $$20-50 Million
Number Employees: 20-49
Sq. footage: 35000

Type of Packaging: Private Label
Brands:
 Bake-Stos Tortilla Chips
 Mexi-Snax Tortilla Chips

9329 Mexican Accent
16675 W Glendale Dr
New Berlin, WI 53151-2847   262-784-4422
        Fax: 262-784-5810 marbles33@aol.com
            www.mexicanaccent.com
Processor and exporter of flour and corn tortillas;
processor of tortilla chips; private labeling available
 President: Susan Marvin
 CEO: Jeffrey Ettinger
 CFO: Jody Feragen
 Vice President: William Snyder
 Sales Director: Dennis Lancaster
 Operations Manager: Mike Maglio
 Production Manager: Dennis Johnson
Estimated Sales: $13900000
Number Employees: 50-99
Sq. footage: 120000
Type of Packaging: Consumer, Food Service, Private Label, Bulk
Brands:
 MANNY'S
 MEXICAN ACCENT
 RIO REAL

9330 Mexican Food Products Corporation
1087 Revere Ave
San Francisco, CA 94124-3455   415-648-8550
        Fax: 415-648-0130
Tortillas and tortilla chips
 President: Rosa Rodriguez
 Sales/Marketing: Marco Rodriguez
 Production Manager: Enrique Arellano
Estimated Sales: $ 5-10 Million
Number Employees: 50-99

9331 Mexican Foods
PO Box 42404
Indianapolis, IN 46242-0404   317-236-1090
Processor of tortillas and tortilla and nacho chips
 President: George Bohley
Number Employees: 20-49
Type of Packaging: Consumer, Food Service, Private Label, Bulk
Brands:
 Mardo's

9332 Mexisnax Corporation
6860 El Paso Dr
El Paso, TX 79905-3336   915-779-5709
        Fax: 915-779-4559
Processor of taco shells, tostada chips and flour and
corn tortillas; also, salsa including jalapeno, red
chile and chile con queso
 President: Armando Viescas
 General Manager: Enrique Galindo
 Office Manager: Elvira Martinez
Estimated Sales: $ 5 - 10 Million
Number Employees: 20-49
Sq. footage: 6000
Type of Packaging: Consumer, Private Label
Brands:
 Las Cruces

9333 Meyer Brothers Dairy
5130 Industrial St # 400
Maple Plain, MN 55359-8008   952-473-7343
        Fax: 952-473-8522
CustomerService@MeyerBrosDairy.com
            www.meyerbrosdairy.com
Products include milk, breakfast items, yogurt,
pizza, meat, juices, eggs and bacon, coffee, bottled
water, appetizers, produce and vegetables, butter and
margarine, cheese and bakery items.
 Manager: Jim Otis
 Quality Control Manager: Tom Janas
Estimated Sales: $ 2.5-5 Million
Number Employees: 20-49

9334 (HQ)Meyer's Bakeries
P.O.Box 687
Hope, AR 71802-0687   870-777-9031
        Fax: 870-777-9769 800-643-1542
            www.meyersbakeries.com
Processor of fresh and frozen baked goods including
bread, bagels, rolls, English muffins and waffles
 President: Gerald Hanna
 General Manager: Mike Kraft
 Operations: Rick Ledbetter

Estimated Sales: $51800000
Number Employees: 500-999
Type of Packaging: Consumer, Food Service, Private Label, Bulk
Brands:
 De Wafelbakkers Janssen & Meyer

9335 Meyer's Bakeries
10491 W Battaglia Dr
Casa Grande, AZ 85293-7715   520-466-5491
        Fax: 520-466-5996 800-528-5770
            http://www.meyersbakeries.com
Processor of English muffins
 Manager: Eric Robinson
 Plant Manager: Frank Benefiel
Estimated Sales: $ 10 - 20 Million
Number Employees: 50-99
Sq. footage: 80000
Parent Co: Meyers Bakeries
Type of Packaging: Food Service, Private Label, Bulk

9336 Meyer's Bakeries
850 Mid Florida Dr
Orlando, FL 32824-7020   407-859-2006
        Fax: 407-851-6535 887-859-2006
            www.gwbakeries.com
Processor and exporter of English muffins
 President: Chuck Keeter
 Plant Manager: Wayne Sager
Estimated Sales: $ 20 - 50 Million
Number Employees: 50-99
Parent Co: Meyers Bakeries
Type of Packaging: Consumer, Food Service

9337 Mezza
222 E Wisconsin Avenue
Suite 300
Lake Forest, IL 60045-1723   847-735-2516
        Fax: 415-727-4471 888-206-6054
            sales@emezza.com
Suppliers to the finest kitchens in America with a
worldwide selection of gourmet pantry items
Type of Packaging: Food Service, Private Label

9338 Mi Mama's Tortilla Factory
828 S 17th St
Omaha, NE 68108-3115   402-345-2099
        Fax: 402-345-1059 www.mimamas.com
Tortillas
 General Manager: Paul Sharrar
Estimated Sales: $ 10-20 Million
Number Employees: 20-49

9339 Mi Ranchito Foods
P.O.Box 159
Bayard, NM 88023-0159   575-537-3868
Manufacturer of frozen tamales; also, tortillas, chili
and chili con carne
 President: Joe Ramirez
Estimated Sales: $17 Million
Number Employees: 5-9
Type of Packaging: Consumer, Food Service, Private Label, Bulk
Brands:
 MI RANCHITO

9340 Mi-Lady Bakery
275 Brumby Way
Tifton, GA 31794-4850   229-382-1955
Bakery items
 President: Chip Rhodes
Estimated Sales: Less than $500,000
Number Employees: 5-9

9341 Mia Products
P.O.Box 377
Scranton, PA 18501   570-457-7431
        Fax: 570-457-0915
Processor of frozen juice bars
 General Manager: T Cousins
 President: Gerald Shriber
 VP: Ernest Fogle
Number Employees: 50-99
Parent Co: J&J Snack Foods Company
Type of Packaging: Food Service
Brands:
 Mia

9342 Miami Beef Company
4870 NW 157th St
Hialeah, FL 33014-6486   305-621-3252
        Fax: 305-620-4562 info@miamibeef.com
            www.miamibeef.com

Processor and exporter of frozen and portion control
beef, pork, lamb, hamburgers, cooked roast beef and
ground beef
 President: Michael Young
 Head Sales: Barry Dean
 Plant Manager: Russ Milina
Estimated Sales: $10800000
Number Employees: 50-99
Type of Packaging: Consumer, Food Service, Private Label, Bulk
Brands:
 Miami Beef

9343 Miami Crab Corporation
PO Box 161778
Miami, FL 33116-1778   305-412-4110
        Fax: 305-412-2129 800-269-8395
    sales@miamicrab.com www.miamicrab.com
Crabmeat products
Estimated Sales: $ 5 - 10 Million
Number Employees: 5-9
Type of Packaging: Consumer, Food Service
Brands:
 Flamingo
 Jackpot
 Windy Shoal

9344 (HQ)Miami Purveyors
7350 NW 8th St
Miami, FL 33126-2922   305-262-6170
        Fax: 305-262-6174
Manuafacturer and exporter of frozen foods including beef, pork, ham, poultry, seafood, fruits and vegetables
 Owner: Rick Rothenberg
Estimated Sales: $14.1 Million
Number Employees: 50-99
Type of Packaging: Food Service

9345 Micalizzi Italian Ice
712 Madison Ave
Bridgeport, CT 06606-5511   203-366-2353
            JAYICE712@aol.com
            www.micalizzis.com
Italian ice and ice cream
 Co-Owner: Lucille Piccirillo
 Co-Owner: Jay Piccirillo
Estimated Sales: $500,000-$1 Million
Number Employees: 1-4
Type of Packaging: Consumer, Food Service, Bulk

9346 Miceli Dairy Products Company
2721 E 90th St
Cleveland, OH 44104-3396   216-791-6222
        Fax: 216-231-2504 800-551-7196
            mstorath@miceli-dairy.com
            www.miceli-dairy.com
Processor of Italian cheeses
 President: John Miceli
 CEO: Joseph Miceli
Estimated Sales: $ 20 - 50 Million
Number Employees: 100-249

9347 Miceli's Specialty Foods Company
PO Box 1261
Danbury, CT 06813-1261   203-797-9714
        Fax: 203-743-1420 888-264-2354
    micelis@aol.com www.micelis.com
Pasta sauces, BBQ sauces, salsas, mustards and
caponata
 CEO: Todd Delgadio
Estimated Sales: $300,000-500,000
Number Employees: 1-4

9348 Michael Angelo's Gourmet Foods
200 Michael Angelo Way
Austin, TX 78728-1200   512-218-3500
        512-218-3600 877-482-5486
    customerservice@michaelangelos.com
            www.michaelangelos.com
Premier line of packaged Italian cuisine including
italian entrees, lasagnas, stuffed pasta, snacks and
appetizers, protein dishe
 Owner/CEO: Michael Angelo Renna
 President: Everett Carmody
 VP Retail/Food Service: Joe Keip
 Marketing: Joe Kent
Estimated Sales: $100+ Million
Number Employees: 500-999
Number of Brands: 1
Number of Products: 100
Sq. footage: 132000
Type of Packaging: Consumer, Food Service, Bulk

Brands:
MICHAEL ANGELO'S

9349 Michael D's Cookies & Cakes
11 N Edgelawn Dr # 1
Aurora, IL 60506-4362   630-892-2525
                              Fax: 630-892-2556
Cookies
President: Calvin Gooch
Estimated Sales: Less than $500,000
Number Employees: 5-9
Brands:
  Amazon Basin Brownie
  Conservationist Chip
  Lonesome George Chip
  Okavango Chip
  Savannah Chip
  Stonewall Grant's

9350 (HQ)Michael Foods, Inc.
301 Carlson Pkwy
Suite 400
Minnetonka, MN 55305   952-258-4000
          Fax: 952-258-4911 www.michaelfoods.com
Processor and exporter of frozen and liquid egg
products and microwaveable hash brown potato
products.
President/CEO: James Dwyer
SVP and CFO: Mark Westphal
SVP Operations and Supply Chain: Thomas
Jagiela
Estimated Sales: $1.8 Billion
Number Employees: 3,790
Parent Co: Thomas H Lee Partners
Type of Packaging: Consumer, Food Service, Private Label, Bulk
Other Locations:
  Michael Foods
  Minneapolis MN
Brands:
  ABBOSTFORD FARMS
  ALL DAY CAFE
  ALL WHITES
  BETTER 'N EGGS
  CRYSTAL FARMS
  DINER'S CHOICE
  NORTHERN STAR
  PAPETTI'S
  SIMPLY POTATOES

9351 Michael Granese & Company
640 E Main Street
Norristown, PA 19401-5123   610-272-5099
      Fax: 610-272-1995   elio.camilotto@grande.com
Processor of Italian cheeses including ricotta, mozzarella, scamorza and cream twist
President: John Carfagno Jr
Estimated Sales: $2900000
Number Employees: 10
Sq. footage: 4000
Type of Packaging: Consumer, Bulk
Brands:
  Michael Granese Co.

9352 Michael Holm and Associates
2050 75th St
Woodridge, IL 60517-2307   630-663-1195
          Fax: 630-663-1198   mhajobs@aol.com
                  www.holmandassociates.com
Owner: Michael Holm
Estimated Sales: $ .5 - 1 million
Number Employees: 5-9

9353 Michael's Cookies
10635 Scripps Ranch Blvd # D
San Diego, CA 92131-1087   858-578-0888
      Fax: 858-578-3086   800-822-5384
          info@michaelscookies.com
          www.michaelscookies.com
Processor and exporter of frozen pre-portioned
cookie doughs. Sells nationwide in the US
Manager: Scott Summeril
CFO: Scott Summeril
Estimated Sales: $ 20 - 50 Million
Number Employees: 20-49
Number of Brands: 1
Number of Products: 1
Sq. footage: 30000
Type of Packaging: Food Service, Private Label, Bulk
Brands:
  Bonzers

9354 Michael's Finer Meats &Seafoods
P.O.Box 182700
Columbus, OH 43218-2700   614-527-4900
      Fax: 614-527-4520   800-282-0518
          info@michaelsmeats.com
          www.michaelsmeats.com
Processor and wholesaler/distributor of meat including beef, pork, lamb, veal and wild game
President: Jonathan (John) Bloch
CFO: Betsy Teater
VP: Victor Foreman
Estimated Sales: $100+ Million
Number Employees: 100-249
Sq. footage: 65000
Type of Packaging: Consumer, Food Service, Bulk

9355 Michael's Naturopathic
6003 Randolph Blvd
San Antonio, TX 78233-5719   210-661-8311
      Fax: 210-661-8048   800-525-9643
          staff@michaelshealth.com
          www.michaelshealth.com
Processor of vitamins, minerals and herbal supplements
President: Michael Schwartz
Managing Director: Karen Trabucco
Estimated Sales: $5100000
Number Employees: 20-49
Sq. footage: 13000
Brands:
  Michael's Health Products

9356 Michael's Provision Company
317 Lindsey St
Fall River, MA 02720-1132   508-672-0982
                              Fax: 508-672-1307
Processor of meat products including Portuguese
sausage
President: Ronald Miranda
Owner: Joseph Miranda
Estimated Sales: $ 3 - 5 Million
Number Employees: 5-9
Type of Packaging: Consumer, Food Service, Bulk

9357 Michaelene's Gourmet Granola
7415 Deer Forest Ct
Clarkston, MI 48348-2734   248-625-0156
                              Fax: 248-625-8521
          michaelenes@gourmetgranola.com
              www.gourmetgranola.com
Processor of granola
President: Michaelene Hearn
Estimated Sales: Below $ 5 Million
Number Employees: 5-9
Type of Packaging: Bulk
Brands:
  Michaelene's Gourmet
  Michaelene's Gourmet Granola
  Michaelene's Granola

9358 Michel's Bakery
5698 Rising Sun Ave
Philadelphia, PA 19120-1698   215-725-4328
      Fax: 215-745-1058   info@michelsbakery.com
              www.michelsbakery.com
Danish pastry, muffins, cakes, brownies and pies
President: Jon Liss
Sales Manager: Carl Mauser
CFO: Bill Wagner
CEO: Joseph Liss
Quality Control: Jan Brownlee
Purchasing Manager: Flo Collington
Estimated Sales: $ 20-30 Million
Number Employees: 100-249
Type of Packaging: Private Label
Brands:
  Michele's Family Bakery
  Muffin Tops
  Rittenhouse Food

9359 Michel's Magnifique
35 E 9th Street
New York, NY 10003-6303   212-431-1070
Processor of pates, mousses and sausage including
saucisson
President: Ken Blanchette
Operations Manager: Allan Moss
Number Employees: 5-9
Type of Packaging: Consumer, Food Service

9360 Michel-Schlumberger
4155 Wine Creek Rd
Healdsburg, CA 95448-9112   707-433-7427
      Fax: 707-433-0444   800-447-3060
          winebench@aol.com
          www.michelschlumberger.com
Wine
President: Jacques Schlumberger
CEO: Jerry Craven
President: Jacques Schlumberger
General Manager: Gary Brown
Public Relations: Joy Henderson
VP Operations/Production: Fred Payne
Estimated Sales: Below $ 5 Million
Number Employees: 20-49
Type of Packaging: Private Label
Brands:
  25 Imports From France
  Domaine Michel
  Michel-Schlumberger

9361 Michele's Chocolate Truffles
14704 SE 82nd Dr
Clackamas, OR 97015-9607   503-656-0220
      Fax: 503-656-0440   800-656-7112
          truffles@micheles.com   www.micheles.com
Processor of gourmet hand dipped chocolate truffles,
chews, nut clusters, cordials, toffee and caramel
Owner: Todd Davis
Estimated Sales: $ 3 - 5 Million
Number Employees: 5-9
Number of Brands: 1
Number of Products: 50
Sq. footage: 2500
Type of Packaging: Consumer, Food Service, Private Label, Bulk
Brands:
  MICHELE'S CHOCOLATE TRUFFLES
  VICKI'S ROCKY ROAD

9362 Michele's Family Bakery
2731 S Queen St
York, PA 17403-9703   717-741-2027
      Fax: 717-747-0065 www.macksicecream.com
Ice cream
Owner: Walt Bloss
Manager: Bill Lenick
Estimated Sales: $ 5-9.9 Million
Number Employees: 20-49

9363 Michele's Foods
8855 Ridgeland Ave # 202
Oak Lawn, IL 60453-1074   708-598-6600
      Fax: 708-862-5347   info@michelefoods.com
              www.michelefoods.com
Processor of honey-based syrups
Owner: Michele Wierzgac
VP: Paul Walk
Estimated Sales: $1000000
Number Employees: 10-19
Sq. footage: 100
Type of Packaging: Consumer, Food Service
Brands:
  Michele's Honey Creme

9364 Michele's Original Gourmet Tofu Products
PO Box 28903
Philadelphia, PA 19151-0903   215-922-2588
                              Fax: 215-474-8636
Health foods and sauces
Proprietor: Michael D'Ambrosio
Estimated Sales: $500,000-$1 Million
Number Employees: 1-4
Brands:
  Caesar Dressing
  Humus Tahini
  Tofu Tahini

9365 Michelle Chocolatiers
122 N Tejon Street
Colorado Springs, CO 80903-1406   719-633-5089
      Fax: 719-633-8970   888-447-3654
          customerservice@michellecandies.com
              www.michellecandies.com
Processor, importer and exporter of ice creams and
candy including chocolates and gold coins
VP: Jim Michopoulos
Estimated Sales: $ 5-10 Million
Number Employees: 20-49
Type of Packaging: Consumer, Private Label
Brands:
  Gremlin
  Michelle

9366 (HQ)Michigan Ag Commodities
P.O.Box 488
Breckenridge, MI 48615-0488   989-842-3104
Fax: 989-842-3108   800-472-4629
pfrasco@bwcoop.com www.michag.com
Manfuacturer and exporter of dried beans including
navy, bush cranberry, black, pinto and adzuki
   Manager: Dave Marr
   Marketing Manager - Bean: Patrick Frasco
Estimated Sales:$50-100 Million
Number Employees: 100-249
Sq. footage: 100000
Type of Packaging: Food Service, Private Label,
   Bulk
Brands:
   B&W

9367 Michigan Celery Promotion Cooperative
P.O.Box 306
Hudsonville, MI 49426-0306   616-669-1250
Fax: 616-669-2890 dfrens@iserv.net
www.michigancelery.com
Processor of fresh celery including sliced and diced
   General Manager: Duane Frens
Estimated Sales:$ 1 - 3 Million
Number Employees: 20-49
Type of Packaging: Bulk

9368 Michigan Dairy
29601 Industrial Rd
Livonia, MI 48150-2012   734-367-5390
Fax: 734-367-5391
Processor of dairy products including pasteurized
milk, ice cream, yogurt, cottage cheese and sour
cream
   Manager: Jack Housley
   Plant Manager: Art Shank
Number Employees: 250-499
Parent Co: Kroger Company
Type of Packaging: Consumer

9369 Michigan Dessert Corporation
10750 Capital St
Oak Park, MI 48237-3134   248-544-4574
Fax: 248-544-4384   800-328-8632
sales@midasfoods.com www.midasfoods.com
Specializes in the development and production of
sweet dry mix items. All of our products are dry
blend and either pouch packed for restaurant chains
or bulk packed for our food processing partners.
   President: Richard Elias
   Sr VP Sales/Marketing: Gary Freeman
Estimated Sales:$7 Million
Number Employees: 20-49
Sq. footage: 45000
Parent Co: Midas Foods India
Type of Packaging: Consumer, Food Service, Private Label, Bulk
Brands:
   American Savory
   Michigan Dessert
   Sin Fill

9370 Michigan Farm Cheese Dairy
4295 E Millerton Rd
Fountain, MI 49410-9583   231-462-3301
Fax: 231-462-3805 cheese@andrulischeese.com
www.andrulischeese.com
Processor of cheese including feta and farmer
   President: Lu Andrulis
   Marketing Director: Amanda Andrulis-Preston
   Production Manager: Jim Stankowski
Estimated Sales:$1000000
Number Employees: 10-19
Type of Packaging: Consumer
Brands:
   Farmers

9371 Michigan Freeze Pack
P.O.Box 30
Hart, MI 49420-0030   231-873-2175
Fax: 231-873-3025 www.michiganfreezepack.com
Processor and exporter of asparagus, zucchini
squash, celery, broccoli, peppers, carrots and
eggplant
   President: Gary Dennert
   VP Sales/Finance: John Ritche
   Production Manager: Ronald Clark
   Plant Manager: Mike Ruggles
Estimated Sales:$ 5 - 10 Million
Number Employees: 100-249
Sq. footage: 100000

Type of Packaging: Food Service, Bulk

9372 Michigan Milk ProducersAssociation
P.O.Box 47
Ovid, MI 48866-0047   989-834-2221
Fax: 989-834-2486 Burkhardt@mimilk.com
www.mimilk.com
Milk products include standardized milks, condensed wholemilk, condensed skim milk, sweet condensed milks, instant nonfat dry milk, dried
buttermilk, sweet cream butter, standarized cream,
ice cream mixes, nonfat dry milk and driedwhole
milk.
   President: Eleood Kirkpatric
   Quality Control Manager: Mike Watt
   Member Relations/Public Affairs: Sheila
   Burkhardt
   Operations Manager: Pete O'Connell
   Buyer: Elwood Kirkpatrick
Estimated Sales:$ 20-50 Million
Number Employees: 50-99

9373 Michigan Sugar Company
PO Box 1348
Saginaw, MI 48605-1348   989-799-7300
Fax: 989-799-1263 info@michigansugar.com
www.michigansugar.com
Processor of sweeteners including granulated beet
sugar and molasses, dried beet pulp
   President/CEO: Mark Flegenheimer
   Chairman: Thomas Zimmer
   Vice Chairman: Richard Maurer
   VP/Administration: James Ruhlman
   VP/Marketing: Jerry Coleman
   VP/Sales: Barry Brown
   VP/Commodities & Procurement: Paul
   Pfenninger
   VP/Operations: Herbert Wilson
Number Employees: 20-49
Parent Co: Savannah Foods & Industries
Type of Packaging: Consumer, Food Service, Private Label, Bulk

9374 Michigan Sugar Company
PO Box 1348
Saginaw, MI 48605-1348   989-799-7300
Fax: 989-799-1263 www.michigansugar.com
Manufacturer of beet sugar
   Chairman: Thomas Zimmer
   Secretary: Wayne Hecht
   Treasurer: Chris Grekowicz
   President/CEO: Mark Flegenheimer
   VP Marketing: Jerry Coleman
   VP Operations: Herbert Wilson
Number Employees: 450
Type of Packaging: Consumer, Food Service, Private Label, Bulk
Other Locations:
   Michigan Sugar Factory
   Bay City MI
   Michigan Sugar Factory
   Caro MI
   Michigan Sugar Factory
   Croswell MI
   Michigan Sugar Factory
   Sebewaing MI
Brands:
   Big Chief
   PIONEER

9375 Mickelberry's
810 E 5th St
Falls City, NE 68355   402-245-2461
Fax: 402-245-2404   800-228-0037
www.agr.state.ne.us/tradedir/c0200pre.htm
Refrigerated hams, sliced hams
   Executive VP Sales: Cliff Gaddy
Estimated Sales:$ 20 - 50 Million
Number Employees: 10-19
Brands:
   MICKELBERRY

9376 Microsoy Corporation
300 Microsoy Dr
Jefferson, IA 50129-1228   515-386-2100
Fax: 515-386-3287 www.microsoyflakes.com
Processor and exporter of microsoy flakes used in
soy milk, tofu and other soy based foods
   President: Itaru Tanaka
Estimated Sales:$ 5 - 10 Million
Number Employees: 5-9
Sq. footage: 5000
Parent Co: Mycal Corporation

Type of Packaging: Bulk
Brands:
   Microsoy Flakes

9377 Mid Atlantic Vegetable Shortening Company
125 Sanford Ave
Kearny, NJ 07032-5918   201-467-0200
Fax: 201-991-0765 800-966-1645
jhulihan@midatlanticveg.com
www.midatlanticveg.com
Manufactures a wide variety of shortenings, oils,
margarines, pan releases, zero trans fat shortening
and margarines, and specialty products such as lecithin, garlic spread and spice products. All products
are manufactured under Koshersupervision
   President: Calvin Theobald
   CEO: Perry Theobald
   VP Sales/Marketing: James Hulihan
Estimated Sales:$ 5-10 Million
Number Employees: 20-49

9378 Mid States Dairy
6040 N Lindbergh Blvd
Hazelwood, MO 63042-2804   314-731-1150
Fax: 314-731-1198 express@schnucks.com
www.schnucks.com
Processor of milk, buttermilk, yogurt, cheese, cottage cheese, ice cream, eggnog, sour cream dips, etc
   Manager: Tim Mueller
   Plant Manager: Dale Parsons
Estimated Sales:$ 20 - 50 Million
Number Employees: 100-249

9379 Mid-America Brewing Supply
800 1st Ave W
Shakopee, MN 55379-1148   507-934-4975
Malts and hops, grains dried and liquid malt, filters
and adjuncts
   Manager: J D Demsey
Type of Packaging: Private Label
Brands:
   Briess
   Dewolf-Cosyns
   Gambrinus
   Grain Millers
   Hop Union
   Hugh Baird
   Mn Malting
   Stone Brewery
   Weyermans

9380 Mid-Atlantic Cheese Company
P.O.Box 6342
Parsippany, NJ 07054-7342   973-998-9000
Cheese
   President: Richard Izenberg

9381 Mid-Atlantic Foods
8978 Glebe Park Dr
Easton, MD 21601-7004   410-822-7500
Fax: 410-822-1266   800-922-4688
info@mafi.com www.seaclam.com
Processor and exporter of canned and frozen clams
and seafood chowders, sauces and soups; also, clam
juice
   President: Bob Brennan
   CEO: Steve Gordon
   Marketing Director: Guy Simmons
   Operations Manager: James Kramer
   Plant Manager: William Collins
Estimated Sales:$20000000
Number Employees: 5-9
Sq. footage: 33000
Type of Packaging: Consumer, Food Service, Private Label
Brands:
   Gordon's Chesapeake Classics
   Mid-Atlantic
   Pot O' Gold
   Tucker's Cove
   Worcester

9382 Mid-Eastern Molasses Company
PO Box 100
Oceanport, NJ 07757-0100   732-462-1868
Fax: 732-431-0006
Bulk molasses

9383 Mid-Georgia Processing Company
425 3rd Street Ext
Vienna, GA 31092-1502   229-268-6496
Fax: 229-268-2618 www.goldenpeanut.com

Peanut oil, cake and meal
Manager: James Tinsley
Plant Manager: Dennis Billings
Estimated Sales: $ 20-50 Million
Number Employees: 50-99

9384 Mid-Kansas Cooperative

P.O.Box D
Moundridge, KS 67107-0582   620-345-6328
Fax: 620-345-6330   800-864-4284
webmaster@mkcoop.com   www.mkcoop.com
Cooperative offering grains
President: Dave Christianson
Estimated Sales: Less than $500,000
Number Employees: 20-49

9385 Mid-Pacific Hawaii Fishery

Old Airport Road
Hilo, HI 96720   808-935-6110
Fax: 808-961-6859
Processor and exporter of fresh tuna, marlin and shark
Owner: John Romero
Estimated Sales: $ 2.5-5 Million
Number Employees: 7
Type of Packaging: Consumer, Food Service
Brands:
Mid Pacific

9386 Mid-South Fish Company

P.O.Box 185
Aubrey, AR 72311-0185   870-295-5600
Fax: 870-295-3559
Owner: A L Jolly Jr
Estimated Sales: $ .5 - 1 million
Number Employees: 1-4

9387 Mid-States Dairy Company

P.O.Box 46928
St Louis, MO 63146-6928   314-994-9900
Fax: 314-692-6193 www.schnucks.com
Ice cream, milk, yoghurt, cottage cheese, sour cream, orange juice, specialty Alaskan Classics ice cream
Marketing Manager: Weiny Wedel
President: Sach Sphnuck
CEO: Scott C Schnuck
Owner: Sach Sphnuck
Operations Manager: John Sprangler
Estimated Sales: $ 20-50 Million
Number Employees: 10,000+
Number of Products: 450

9388 Mid-Valley Dairy

199 Red Top Rd
Fairfield, CA 94534-9500   707-864-0502
Fax: 707-864-8203
Dairy products
Plant Manager: Woody Darnell
Estimated Sales: Under $500,000
Number Employees: 100-249

9389 Mid-Valley Nut Company

2065 Geer Rd
Hughson, CA 95326-9614   209-883-4491
Fax: 209-883-2435   info@midvalleynut.com
www.midvalleynut.com
Processor and importer of walnuts
President: John Casazza
Estimated Sales: $4600000
Number Employees: 100-249
Type of Packaging: Consumer, Private Label, Bulk

9390 Mid-Western EnterprisesLimited

9685 S Kean Ave
Palos Hills, IL 60465-1048   708-430-5990
Fax: 708-430-8120   800-222-3032
Olive oil processor
Owner: Peter Zekios
Estimated Sales: $ .5 - 1 million
Number Employees: 1-4

9391 Midamar Corporation

P.O.Box 218
Cedar Rapids, IA 52406-0218   319-362-3711
Fax: 319-362-4111   800-362-3711
www.midamar.com
Halal approved food products includes crescent chicken, ethnic sauces, beef, lamb, shawarma, turkey and pizzas.
President: Bill Aossey
Estimated Sales: $ 20 - 50 Million
Number Employees: 50-99

9392 Middlefield Cheese House

15815 Nauvoo Rd
Middlefield, OH 44062-8501   440-632-5228
Fax: 440-632-5604   800-327-9477
shop@middlefieldcheese.com
www.middlefieldcheese.com
Processor of natural Swiss cheese
President: Ann Rothenbuhler
Estimated Sales: $ 5 - 10 Million
Number Employees: 10-19
Type of Packaging: Bulk
Brands:
Middlefield

9393 Middlesex Sales Company

133 Princeton Street
North Chelmsford, MA 01863-1531   978-459-7776
Processor of closeouts and overstocks including frozen food, dry food, ingredients and related nonfoods
President: Elliot Williams
VP: Brian Williams
Number Employees: 10-19
Type of Packaging: Consumer, Food Service

9394 Middleswarth Potato Chips

250 Furnace Rd
Middleburg, PA 17842-9159   570-837-1431
Fax: 570-837-1731   toddhestor@hotmail.com
Processor of potato chips including regular, barbecue, waffle style, sour cream and onion and salt and vinegar
President: Bob Middleswarth
Estimated Sales: $ 50 - 100 Million
Number Employees: 50-99
Type of Packaging: Consumer, Food Service, Bulk

9395 Midland Bean Company

P.O.Box 118
Cahone, CO 81320-0118   970-562-4235
Fax: 970-677-2219
Manufacturer and wholesaler/distributor of pinto beans
President/Co-Owner: Rod Tanner
Manager: Jack Tanner
Estimated Sales: $20 Million
Number Employees: 1-4
Type of Packaging: Consumer

9396 Midstate Mills

P.O.Box 350
Newton, NC 28658-0350   828-464-1611
Fax: 828-465-5139   800-222-1032
sales@midstatemills.com
www.midstatemills.com
Processor of flour, corn meal, biscuit flour and baking mixes
President: Boyd Drum
Vice President: Steve Arndt
Sales Manager: Don Floyd
Sales Director: Berry Coldwell
VP Operations: Brevard Arndt
Purchasing Manager: Kenny Anderson
Estimated Sales: $27100000
Number Employees: 100-249
Type of Packaging: Consumer, Food Service, Private Label, Bulk
Brands:
Redimix
Southern Biscuit
Tenda Bake

9397 Midstates Dairy

6040 N Lindbergh Blvd
Hazelwood, MO 63042-2804   314-731-1150
Fax: 314-731-1198
Ice cream, milk, yogurt, cottage cheese, sour cream, orange juice, specialty Alaskan Classics ice cream
President: Tim Mueller
Manager: Dale Parsons
Plant Manager: John Spangler
Estimated Sales: $ 20-50 Million
Number Employees: 100-249
Brands:
Schnucks

9398 Midstates Distributor

4001 W Ridge Road
Gary, IN 46408-1849   219-981-1050
Fax: 219-981-2505
President: Charles Simonich

9399 Midway Meats

1721 Airport Rd
Centralia, WA 98531-9069   360-736-5257
Fax: 360-330-2913
Manufacturer and packer of beef and pork
Manager: Denise Hinckley
Estimated Sales: $10-20 Million
Number Employees: 10-19

9400 Midwest Blueberry Farms

13720 Tyler St
Holland, MI 49424-9418   616-399-2133
Fax: 616-399-2133
Blueberries
Owner: Richard Keil
Estimated Sales: Under $300,000
Number Employees: 5-9
Brands:
Midwest Blueberry Farms

9401 Midwest Foods

PO Box 447
Owatonna, MN 55060-0447   507-451-7670
Fax: 507-451-5607
Processor of canned spaghetti dinners and stew including beef, chicken and meatball
Number Employees: 200
Parent Co: Owatonna Canning Company
Type of Packaging: Food Service, Private Label

9402 Midwest Frozen Foods, Inc.

2185 Leeward Ln
Hanover Park, IL 60133-6026   630-784-0123
Fax: 630-784-0424   866-784-0123
sales@frozenvegetables.com
Midwest Frozen Foods provides in house and private label frozen fruits and vegetables to the retail, food services and industrial manufacturing sectors.
President: Zafar Iqbal
VP: Athar Siddiq
Operations: Rob Linchesky
Production: Jose Manjarrez
Estimated Sales: $5 Million
Number Employees: 18
Number of Brands: 2
Number of Products: 100+
Sq. footage: 20000
Type of Packaging: Food Service, Private Label, Bulk

9403 Midwest Seafood

5500 Emerson Way
Suite A
Indianapolis, IN 46226-1477   317-466-1027
Fax: 317-466-1033
Estimated Sales: $ 1 - 3 Million
Number Employees: 5-9

9404 Midwest/Northern

3105 Columbia Ave NE
Minneapolis, MN 55418-1896   612-781-6596
Fax: 612-781-6728   800-328-5502
midwestnut@qwest.net
www.midwestnorthernnut.com
Processor of snack foods including salty and trail mixes and roasted and raw seeds including pumpkin and sunflower; also, confections
President: Laure Rockman
Plant Manager: Tim Fischer
Estimated Sales: $3000000
Number Employees: 20-49
Sq. footage: 40000
Type of Packaging: Consumer, Food Service, Private Label, Bulk
Brands:
Aristo Snacks
Dijon Crunch
Fun Foods
Giant Cashews
Hokey Pokey
Midwest

9405 Miesse Candies

735 Lafayette St
Lancaster, PA 17603-5597   717-392-6011
Fax: 717-392-6142   info@miessecandy.com
www.miessecandies.com
Hard, soft and chocolate candy
Owner: Ryan Dowd
Estimated Sales: Below $ 5 Million
Number Employees: 20-49

9406 Mighty Leaf Tea
136 Mitchell Blvd
San Rafael, CA 94903-2044   415-491-2650
Fax: 415-331-1862 info@mightyleaf.com
www.mightyleaf.com
Whole-leaf tea blends
CEO: Gary Shinner
Estimated Sales: Below $ 5 Million
Number Employees: 5-9

9407 Miguel's Stowe Away
996 S Main St
Stowe, VT 05672-5195   802-253-8900
Fax: 802-253-3946 800-448-6517
mexicanfoods@miguels.com www.miguels.com
Processor and exporter of Mexican food products in-
cluding salsa cruda, blue and white corn tortilla
chips, red chili sauce, flavored salsa and smoked
jalapeno
President: Christopher Pierson
Regional Sales Manager: Tim Couture
Estimated Sales: $ 3 - 5 Million
Number Employees: 1-4
Sq. footage: 5000
Type of Packaging: Consumer, Food Service, Bulk
Brands:
Miguel's

9408 Mikawaya Bakery
800 E 4th St
Los Angeles, CA 90013-1802   213-628-6514
Fax: 213-625-0943 Sales@mikawayausa.com
www.mikawayausa.com
Japanese pastries and ice cream
President: Frances Hashimoto
CFO: Joel Friedman
Estimated Sales: $ 5-10 Million
Number Employees: 20-49
Type of Packaging: Private Label
Brands:
Mikawaya
Mochi Ice Cream

9409 Mike & Jean's Berry Farm
16402 Jungquist Rd
Mt Vernon, WA 98273-8865   360-424-7220
Fax: 360-424-7225 mjberry@fidalgo.net
www.mikeandjeans.com
Processor of fresh cauliflower, strawberries and
raspberries; also, frozen strawberries and raspberries
Owner: Michael Youngquist
Co-Owner: Jeanne Youngquist
Estimated Sales: $ 20-50 Million
Number Employees: 100-249
Type of Packaging: Food Service, Private Label

9410 Mike and Lou's HandmadePizza
43003 Northlake Boulevard
Leesburg, VA 20176   703-669-5636
Fax: 703-669-5635 info@MikeandLous.com
www.mikeandlous.com
Pizza, sandwiches and salads.
Co-Owner: Mike Schumeth
Co-Owner: Lou Schumeth
Type of Packaging: Food Service

9411 Mike's Fish & Seafood
260 Highway 55 N
Glenwood, MN 56334   320-634-5146
Fax: 320-634-3459 800-950-4755
info@lutefiskmike.com www.lutefiskmike.com
Processor and exporter of fresh and frozen lutefish;
also, smoked, cured and pickled herring; importer of
cured herring
President/Owner: Richard Field
Plant Manager: Scott Scoullard
Estimated Sales: $ 1 - 3 Million
Number Employees: 7
Number of Products: 3
Sq. footage: 18000
Type of Packaging: Consumer, Food Service, Pri-
vate Label, Bulk
Brands:
Michael's Classic
Mike's

9412 Mike's Meats
P.O.Box 398
Eitzen, MN 55931-0398   507-495-3336
Processor of meat products including ham, sausage
and dried beef; slaughtering services available
Owner: Don Robley
Estimated Sales: $500,000-$1 Million
Number Employees: 1-4

Type of Packaging: Consumer

9413 Mike's Prime Cut Meats
380 N Main Street
Brigham City, UT 84302-1805   435-723-7333
Manufacturer and packer of beef, pork and lamb
products
Owner: Mike Grimes
Estimated Sales: $7 Million
Number Employees: 22

9414 Mike-Sell's Potato ChipCompany
P.O.Box 115
Dayton, OH 45404-0115   937-228-9400
Fax: 937-461-5707 800-853-9437
info@mike-sells.com www.mike-sells.com
Mike-Sell's Potato Chips include original, groovy,
old fashiioned, reduced fat, and assorted flavors in-
cluding barbecue, cheddar and sour cream, sour
cream, green onion, salt and vinegar and smoked ba-
con. Additional products includepretzels, regular
and cheese puffcorn, cheese curls, corn chips, tortilla
chips, pork rinds and salsa dip.
President: Leslie C Mapp
CFO: Larry Pounds
CEO: David Ray
Quality Control: Troy Lyons
VP Sales & Marketing: L Nat Chandler
Plant Manager: Frank de Moss
Estimated Sales: $ 50-100 Million
Number Employees: 250-499
Parent Co: Mike-Sell's
Type of Packaging: Consumer, Food Service

9415 Miko Meat
230 Kekuanaoa Street
Hilo, HI 96720-4318   808-935-0841
Fax: 808-935-2781
Sausages and hot dogs
President: Ernest Matsumura
General Manager: Matt Asano
Estimated Sales: $ 2.5-5 Million
Number Employees: 5-9

9416 Milan Provision Company
10815 Roosevelt Ave
Flushing, NY 11368-2538   718-899-7678
Fax: 718-335-3354
Manufacturer of Mexican meat
Owner: Salvatore Laurita
Estimated Sales: $1-3 Million
Number Employees: 10-19
Type of Packaging: Consumer, Food Service, Pri-
vate Label, Bulk

9417 Milan Salami Company
1155 67th St
Oakland, CA 94608-1173   510-654-7055
Fax: 510-654-7257
Processor of Italian dry salami and loaf products;
also, sausage and pepperoni
Owner: George Ramsey
Sales: Steven Ramsey
Plant Manager: Greg Ramsey
Estimated Sales: $ 50 - 100 Million
Number Employees: 10-19
Sq. footage: 12000
Type of Packaging: Consumer, Food Service, Pri-
vate Label, Bulk

9418 Miland Seafood
P.O.Box 13569
New Orleans, LA 70185-3569   504-821-4500
Fax: 504-821-4540 www.inlandseafood.com
Seafood
President: Eric Sussman
Estimated Sales: $ 10 - 20 Million
Number Employees: 20-49

9419 Milani Gourmet
2150 N 15th Avenue
Melrose Park, IL 60160-1410   708-216-0704
Fax: 708-216-0709 800-333-0003
www.milanifoods.com
Seasonings, salad dressings, sugar replacements, salt
substitutes and base mixes
Manager of Milani Foods: Linda Fortino
Number Employees: 1-4
Parent Co: Precision Foods
Type of Packaging: Food Service, Bulk
Brands:
Bakers Joy
Charcol-It
Milani

Molly McButter
Mrs Dash Salt Free Seasoning
Sugartwin

9420 Milano Baking Company
433 S Chicago St
Joliet, IL 60436-2268   815-727-4872
Fax: 815-727-3116 milano@uti.com

www.shorewoodchamber.com/milano_bakery.htm
Italian bread and rolls
President: Mario Debenedetti
Estimated Sales: $ 50-100 Million
Number Employees: 50-99

9421 Milano Winery
14594 S Highway 101
Hopland, CA 95449-9708   707-744-1396
Fax: 707-744-1138 800-564-2582
wines@milanowinery.com
www.milanowinery.com
Wines including Cabernet Sauvignon, Petit Verdot,
Carignane, Syrah, Petite Syrah and Merlot.
President: Edward Starr
Vice President: Deanna Starr
Estimated Sales: Below $ 5 Million
Number Employees: 1-4
Number of Brands: 1
Number of Products: 10
Brands:
Milano Family Winery

9422 Milat Vineyards
1091 Saint Helena Hwy S
St Helena, CA 94574-2268   707-963-0758
Fax: 707-963-0168 info@milat.com
www.milat.com
Wines including Chenin Blanc, Chardonnay, Merlot,
Cabernet Sauvignon, Zinfandel, Zivio and dessert
wines.
Owner: Michael Milat
Estimated Sales: $ 1-2.5 Million
Number Employees: 1-4
Brands:
Milat Vineyards

9423 Mild Bill's Spices
PO Box 142
Bulverde, TX 78163   830-980-4124
mildbills@satx.rr.com
http://www.mildbills.com/
Processor and exporter of chili powder, seasoning
blends and barbecue spices, salsa, relish
Owner: Bill Dees
Co-Owner: Tamara Dees
Type of Packaging: Consumer, Food Service
Brands:
Big Bruce's Gunpowder Chili
Fire Marshall's Cajun

9424 (HQ)Miles J H & Company
902 Southampton Ave
Norfolk, VA 23510-1016   757-622-9264
Fax: 757-622-9261 thorp@exportla.com
Processor and exporter of frozen oysters and clams
President: Roy Parker
Director: Jyoti Mukerji
Sales Director: R Miles
Plant Manager: Roy Parker
Purchasing Manager: Ed Miles
Estimated Sales: $18534237
Number Employees: 50-99
Number of Brands: 1
Number of Products: 4
Sq. footage: 70000
Type of Packaging: Food Service, Private Label,
Bulk

9425 Milfico Foods
1350 Greenleaf Ave
Elk Grove Vlg, IL 60007-5521   847-427-0491
Fax: 847-427-0498 milficofoods@msn.com
Frozen catfish, cod, flounder, halibut, perch,
pollock, salmon, tuna, whiting, orange roughy, sole,
red snapper, grouper, swordfish, mahi mahi, tilapia,
pike, lobster tails, oysters, scallops, shrimp, crab,
mussels
President: Ira Gitlin
Estimated Sales: $ 5-10 Million
Number Employees: 20-49
Type of Packaging: Consumer, Food Service, Pri-
vate Label

9426 Milfico Foods
1350 Greenleaf Ave
Elk Grove Vlg, IL 60007-5521   847-427-0491
    Fax: 847-427-0498 milficofoods@msn.com
Frozen fish, seafoods
    President: Ira A Gitlin
    Plant Manager: Steven Goltz
Estimated Sales: $ 5-10 Million
Number Employees: 20-49

9427 Milina's Finest OrganicFood Products
PO Box 1510
Freedom, CA 95019-1510   831-685-6575
    Fax: 831-685-6579
Organic food
    Marketing Director: Kevin Kennedy
    VP: Jennifer Gabriel

9428 Miline Fruit Products
P.O.Box 111
Prosser, WA 99350-0111   509-786-2611
    Fax: 509-786-1724 jharris@milnefruit.com
    www.milnefruit.com
Fruit concentrates
    President: Randy Hageman
    CEO: Dave Wyckoff
    Director of Sales/Marketing: John J Schroeder
Number Employees: 50-99

9429 Milk Specialties Company
260 S Washington St
Carpentersville, IL 60110-2627   847-426-3411
    Fax: 847-426-4121 msc@milkspecialties.com
    www.msccompany.com
Processor of dairy and fat ingredients including
hi-fats and calf milk replacers
    President and COO: Bill Harrington
    CFO: Michael Drennan
    CEO: Trevor Tomkins
    CEO: Trevor Tomkins
    Purchasing: Dave Elsenbast
Estimated Sales: $35200000
Number Employees: 20-49

9430 Milky Whey
910 Brooks St # 203
Missoula, MT 59801-5784   406-542-7373
    Fax: 406-542-7377 800-379-6455
    dairy@themilkywhey.com
    www.themilkywhey.com
Domestic and international wholesaler/distributor of
all whey proteins and dry dairy ingredients including
nonfat dry milk, whole milk, whey powder, butter,
buttermilk powder, caseinates, lactose, nondairy
creamers, whey proteinconcentrates and isolates,
and cheese powders. Custom and private label
blends are available upon request. Please mention
this directory when calling
    President: Curt Pijanowski
    Sales Director: Amy Shay
    Operations Manager: Anita Turnbaugh
    Reception: Tony Cavanaugh
Estimated Sales: $1200000
Number Employees: 5-9
Type of Packaging: Consumer, Private Label, Bulk

9431 Mill City Brewing Company
201 Cabot St
Lowell, MA 01854-3611   978-937-2690
    Fax: 978-934-0097
    info@thebreweryexchange.com
    www.thebreweryexchange.com
Processor of beer, ale, lager, stout and seasonal
brews
    Owner: Frank Hurley
Estimated Sales: Below $ 5 Million
Number Employees: 100-249
Type of Packaging: Consumer, Food Service
Brands:
    Mill City

9432 Mill City Sourdough Bakery
974 7th Street W
Saint Paul, MN 55102-3557   612-224-8871
    Fax: 651-224-8871
Sourdough products
    President: Mary Mattox
Estimated Sales: $ 5-10 Million appx.
Number Employees: 5

9433 Mill Cove Lobster Pound
P.O.Box 280
Boothbay Harbor, ME 04538-0280   207-633-3340
    Fax: 207-633-7206
Processor and wholesaler/distributor of seafood in-
cluding lobster, shrimp, frozen cod, ocean perch,
pollack, clams and oysters
    President: Jeffery Lewis
Estimated Sales: $4-$5 Million
Number Employees: 10-19
Type of Packaging: Consumer

9434 Mill Creek Vineyards
P.O.Box 758
Healdsburg, CA 95448-0758   707-431-2121
    Fax: 707-431-1714 877-349-2121
    brian@mcvonline.com
    www.millcreekwinery.com
Wines
    Proprietor: William Kreck
    General Manager: Yvonne Kreck
    Winemaker: Jeremy Kreck
    Wholesale Sales: John Miller
    Tasting Room: Bruce Thomas
    Bookkeeper: Julie Ricetti
    IT: Brian Kreck
Estimated Sales: Below $ 5 Million
Number Employees: 10-19
Type of Packaging: Private Label
Brands:
    Felta Springs
    Mill Creek Vineyards
    Reflections

9435 Millbrook Vineyard and Winery
26 Wing Rd
Millbrook, NY 12545-5017   845-677-8383
    Fax: 845-677-6186 800-662-9463
    millbrookwinery@millwine.com
    www.millbrookwine.com
Wines the selection of which includes - White
Wines: Pinot Grigio, Gewurztraminer, Tocai
Friulano, Chardonnay and Castle Hill Chardonnay;
Red Wines: Grand Reserve Pinot Noir, Merlot, Hunt
Country Red, Cabernet Franc and Pinot
NoirProprietor's Special Reserve.
    Owner: John Dyson
    CFO: Eric Grans
    General Manager/Sales Manager: Gary Goddard
Estimated Sales: $ 5-10 Million
Number Employees: 10-19
Type of Packaging: Private Label
Brands:
    Millbrook

9436 Mille Lacs Gourmet Foods
P.O.Box 8919
Madison, WI 53708-8919   608-837-8535
    Fax: 608-825-6463 800-843-1381
    customerservice@mille-lacs.com
    www.mille-lacs.com
Processor of gourmet cheeses and chocolates
    President: Jay Singer
    VP: John Manzer
    President: Jay Singer
    Sales Director: David Sandorn
Estimated Sales: $ 5 - 10 Million
Number Employees: 20-49
Brands:
    Degeneve
    Heart of Wisconsin
    Mille Lacs

9437 Mille Lacs MP Company
P.O.Box 8919
Madison, WI 53708-8919   608-837-8535
    Fax: 608-825-6463 800-843-1381
    dsanborn@mille-lacs.com www.mille-lacs.com
Manufacturer and exporter of specialty foods, choc-
olates, cheeses and gift baskets
    President: Jay Singer
    National Broker Manager: David Sanborn
    National Sales Manager: Randy Krause
Estimated Sales: $ 5 - 10 Million
Number Employees: 20-49
Sq. footage: 750000
Parent Co: Wisconsin Cheeseman
Type of Packaging: Consumer, Bulk

9438 Mille Lacs Wild Rice Corporation
P.O.Box 200
Aitkin, MN 56431-0200   218-927-2740
    Fax: 218-927-6124 800-626-3809
    info@canoewildrice.com
    www.canoewildrice.com
Processor and exporter of kosher wild rice; importer
of natural hot breakfast cereals for distribution to
wholesalers/distributors
    President: Chris Ratuski
Estimated Sales: $2500000
Number Employees: 20-49
Parent Co: Shoal Lake Wild Rice
Type of Packaging: Consumer, Food Service, Pri-
vate Label, Bulk
Brands:
    Canoe
    Oh Canada

9439 Millen Fish
P.O.Box 864
Millen, GA 30442-864   478-982-4988
    Fax: 912-982-1746
Fish and fish products
    President: David McMillian
Estimated Sales: $ 3 - 5 Million
Number Employees: 10-19

9440 Millennium Specialty Chemicals
601 Crestwood St
Jacksonville, FL 32208-4455   904-768-5800
    Fax: 904-768-2200 800-231-6728
Processor and exporter of synthetic essential oils,
flavors and fragrances
    President: George Robbins
    VP Materials Management: D Michael Gurkin
    VP Sales/Marketing: Michael Wimberly
Estimated Sales: $100+ Million
Number Employees: 100-249
Parent Co: Hanson Industries
Type of Packaging: Bulk
Brands:
    Arbanex
    Arbanol
    Glidmints
    Zestoral

9441 Millennium Specialty Chemicals
601 Crestwood St
Jacksonville, FL 32208-4455   904-768-5800
    Fax: 904-768-2200 800-231-6728
    www.millenniumchem.com
Aroma organic chemicals, flavors and fragrances
Estimated Sales: $100+ Million
Number Employees: 100-249

9442 (HQ)Miller Brewing Company
3939 W Highland Blvd
Milwaukee, WI 53208-2816   414-931-2000
    Fax: 414-931-2818 www.millerbrewing.com
Processor and exporter of beer including light, ice,
nonalcoholic, lager, ale and malt liquor.
    President/CEO: Norman Adami
    SVP/General Counsel & Secretary: Mike Jones
    SVP/Finance: Gavin Hattersley
    SVP/Miller International: Doug Brodman
    SVP/Strategy & Planning: Kevin Self
    EVP/Chief Marketing Officer: Randy Ransom
    EVP/Sales & Distribution: Tom Cardella
    SVP/Communication & Government Relations:
    Nehl Horton
    COO: Michael Evans
    SVP/Human Resources: Denise Smith
Estimated Sales: $300 Billion
Number Employees: 40
Parent Co: SABMiller
Type of Packaging: Consumer, Food Service
Brands:
    FOSTER'S LAGER
    FOSTER'S SPECIAL BITTER
    HAMM'S
    HAMM'S DRAFT
    HAMM'S SPECIAL LIGHT
    HENRY WEINHARD'S BLUE BOAR PALE
    ALE
    HENRY WEINHARD'S CLASSIC DARK
    HENRY WEINHARD'S HEFEWEIZEN
    HENRY WEINHARD'S NW TRAIL BLOND
    LAG
    HENRY WEINHARD'S PRIVATE RESERVE
    HENRY WEINHARD'S SUMMER WHEAT
    ICE HOUSE 5.5
    ICEHOUSE 5.0
    ICHE HOUSE LIGHT

LEINENKUGEL'S APPLE SPICE
LEINENKUGEL'S BERRY WEISS
LEINENKUGEL'S BIG BUTT DOPPELBOCK
LEINENKUGEL'S CREAMY DARK
LEINENKUGEL'S HONEY WEISS
LEINENKUGEL'S LIGHT
LEINENKUGEL'S OKTOBERFEST
LEINENKUGEL'S ORIGINAL
LEINENKUGEL'S RED LAGER
LEINENKUGEL'S SUNSET WHEAT
MAGNUM MALT LIQUOR
MICKEY'S ICE
MICKEY'S MALT LIQUOR
MILLER GENUINE DRAFT
MILLER GENUINE DRAFT LIGHT
MILLER HIGH LIFE
MILLER HIGH LIFE LIGHT
MILLER LITE
MILWAUKEE'S BEST
MILWAUKEE'S BEST ICE
MILWAUKEE'S BEST LIGHT
OLD ENGLISH 800 MALT LIQUOR
OLDE ENGLISH HG800
OLDE ENGLISH HG800 7.5
PERONI NASTRO AZZURRO
PILSNER URQUELL
RED DOG
SHARP'S NON-ALCOHOLIC BREW
SHEAF STOUT
SOUTHPAW LIGHT
SPARKS
SPARKS LIGHT
SPARKS PLUS 6%
SPARKS PLUS 7%
STEEL RESERVE HIGH GRAVITY
STEEL RESERVE HIGH GRAVITY 6.0
STEEL RESERVE TRIPLE EXPORT 8.1%
STEEL SIX

9443 Miller Brewing Company
863 E Meadow Rd
Eden, NC 27288-3636   336-635-1198
                      www.millerbrewing.com
Processor of beer including light, lager, ice,
nonalcoholic and malt liquor
   Manager: Janice Wangard
   Operations Manager: Jerry Grubb
Number Employees: 4
Parent Co: Miller Brewing Company
Type of Packaging: Consumer
Brands:
   Miller

9444 Miller Brewing Company
13205 Manchester Rd # 410
St Louis, MO 63131-1733   314-822-5483
      Fax: 314-821-0898 tstehr@mbco.com
                      www.millerbrewing.com
Processor of beer including light, ice, lager,
nonalcoholic and malt liquor
   General Manager: Mike Magoulas
   Sales Operations Manager: Dennis Perreault
   Unit Sale Manager: Troy Stehr
Estimated Sales: $ 20 - 50 Million
Number Employees: 20-49
Parent Co: Miller Brewing Company
Type of Packaging: Consumer, Food Service

9445 Miller Brewing Company
13810 SE Eastgate Way
Suite 380
Bellevue, WA 98005-4400   425-641-6775
      Fax: 425-641-7210 www.millerbrewing.com
Processor of beer including light, ice, nonalcoholic,
lager and malt liquor
   Sales/Marketing Executive: Chris Lierman
   Sales Manager: Mike Rhodey
   Sales Administration: Karen Loss
Estimated Sales: $ 20 - 50 Million
Number Employees: 20-49
Parent Co: Miller Brewing Company
Type of Packaging: Consumer, Food Service

9446 Miller Brewing Company
2525 Wayne Madison Rd
Trenton, OH 45067-9799   513-579-8503
      Fax: 513-621-8219 800-944-5483

www.millerbrewing.com/brandsBreweries/trenton.
                                asp

Processor of beer including light, ice, nonalcoholic,
lager and malt liquor
   Manager: Dennis B Puffer
   CEO: Norman Adami
   General Manager Sales: Grant Doster
Estimated Sales: $500 Million to $1 Billion
Number Employees: 500-999
Parent Co: Miller Brewing Company
Type of Packaging: Consumer, Food Service

9447 Miller Brewing Company
3939 W Highland Boulevard
Milwaukee, WI 53208-2816   414-931-2000
      Fax: 414-931-2818 www.millerbrewing.com
Processor of beer including light, ice, nonalcoholic,
lager and malt liquor
   President/CEO: Norman Adami
   COO: Michael Evans
Estimated Sales: K
Number Employees: 40
Type of Packaging: Consumer, Food Service
Brands:
   Miller
   Miller Lite
   Rusty's

9448 Miller Brewing Company
P.O.Box 482
Milwaukee, WI 53201-0482   414-931-2000
      Fax: 414-931-3735 www.millerbrewing.com
Processor of beer including light, ice, lager,
nonalcoholic and malt liquor
   President: Norman J Adami
   Sr. VP: Gavin Hattersley
   CEO: Tom Long
   VP Marketing: Bob Mikulay
Estimated Sales: K
Number Employees: 5,000-9,999
Parent Co: Miller Brewing Company
Type of Packaging: Consumer, Food Service
Brands:
   Genuine Draft
   Miller
   Miller Lite
   Rusty's

9449 Miller Brewing Company
379 Thornall St
Edison, NJ 08837-2225   732-635-1400
                      Fax: 856-489-1454
Processor of beer including ice, light, lager,
nonalcoholic and malt liquor
   Office Manager: Lisa Savage
Estimated Sales: $ 20 - 50 Million
Number Employees: 20-49
Parent Co: Miller Brewing Company
Type of Packaging: Consumer, Food Service, Private Label, Bulk

9450 Miller Brewing Company
P.O.Box 482
Milwaukee, WI 53201-0482   414-931-2000
      Fax: 414-931-3735 800-944-5483
                      www.millerbrewing.com
Processor of beer including ice, light, lager,
nonalcoholic and malt liquor
   President: Norman J Adami
   Executive VP, Worldwide Operations: Virgis W
      Colbert
   CEO: Tom Long
   Sr. VP Finance: Gavin Hattersley
   Sales Manager: Jeff Colbert
Estimated Sales: K
Number Employees: 5,000-9,999
Parent Co: Miller Brewing Company
Type of Packaging: Consumer, Food Service
Brands:
   Miller

9451 Miller Brewing Company
655 Lively Blvd
Elk Grove Vlg, IL 60007-2015   847-758-9941
      Fax: 847-758-9945 www.ornamentaliron.net
Processor of beer including ice, light, lager,
nonalcoholic and malt liquor
   President: Robert Mueller
   General Manager: Sharon Ali
Estimated Sales: $ 1 - 3 Million
Number Employees: 20-49
Parent Co: Miller Brewing Company
Type of Packaging: Consumer, Food Service

9452 Miller Brewing Company
7001 South Fwy
Fort Worth, TX 76134-4097   817-551-3300
      Fax: 817-551-3322 800-645-5376

www.millerbrewing.com/brandsBreweries/ftWorth
                                .asp
Processor of beer including ice, light, lager, non-al-
coholic and malt liquor
   General Manager: Jeff Colbert
   Sales/Marketing Executive: Shaun Brown
   Plant Manager: Jack Jackson
Estimated Sales: $ 1 - 3 Million
Number Employees: 500-999
Parent Co: Miller Brewing Company
Type of Packaging: Consumer, Food Service

9453 Miller Brewing Company
P.O.Box 482
Milwaukee, WI 53201-0482   414-931-2000
      Fax: 414-931-3735 www.millerbrewing.com
Processor of beer including ice, light, lager,
nonalcoholic and malt liquor
   President: Norman J Adami
   Executive VP Marketing: Bob Mikulay
   CEO: Tom Long
   Sr. VP: Gavin Hattersley
Estimated Sales: K
Number Employees: 5,000-9,999
Parent Co: Miller Brewing Company
Type of Packaging: Consumer, Food Service
Brands:
   Miller

9454 Miller Brothers PackingCompany
P.O.Box 337
Sylvester, GA 31791-0337   229-776-2014
                      Fax: 229-776-4728
Manufacturer of beef, sausage, pork, lamb and os-
trich including emu and rhea; slaughtering services
available
   President/Co-Owner: Otis Miller Sr
   VP/Co-Owner: Dan Miller
Estimated Sales: $5-10 Million
Number Employees: 10-19
Type of Packaging: Food Service, Bulk
Brands:
   DAEAB
   GOLD NUGGET

9455 Miller Johnson Seafood
4310 Heron Bay Loop Road S
Coden, AL 36523-3714   251-873-4444
                      Fax: 252-729-1427
Seafood

9456 Miller's Cheese
157 Lee Ave
Brooklyn, NY 11211-8056   718-384-5243
                      Fax: 718-965-0979
Processor of kosher hard cheese
   Owner: David Miller
   Vice President: Max Thurm
   Marketing Director: Meyer Thurm
   Director Marketing: Dov Rapps
Estimated Sales: $1000000
Number Employees: 1-4

9457 Miller's Country Hams
7110 Highway 190
Dresden, TN 38225-2276   731-364-3940
      Fax: 731-364-5338 800-622-0606
   millersham@crunet.com http://www.crunet.com
Country ham
   President: Jan Frick
   Quality Control: Mark Mash
   Vice President: Mark Mash
   CFO: Sharon Burress
   Production Manager: Linda Burcham
   Plant Manager: Barry King
Estimated Sales: $ 5-10 Million
Number Employees: 20-49
Brands:
   Miller's Country Ham

9458 (HQ)Miller's Honey Company
P.O.Box 500
Colton, CA 92324-0500   909-825-1722
      Fax: 909-825-5932 mail@millershoney.com
                      www.millershoney.com
Manufacturer and exporter of honey
   President: Steve Smith
   GM: Richard Barrett

Estimated Sales: $ 5 - 10 Million
Number Employees: 20-49
Type of Packaging: Consumer, Food Service, Private Label, Bulk
Brands:
MILLERS

9459 Miller's Honey Company
P.O.Box 500
Colton, CA 92324-0500   909-825-1722
          Fax: 909-825-5932 800-233-5463
mail@millershoney.com www.millershoney.com
Manufacturer and exporter of honey and beeswax
President: Steve Smith
VP/General Manager: Steven Smith
VP Sales/Marketing: Merrill Paxman
Estimated Sales: $20962713
Number Employees: 20-49
Sq. footage: 70000
Type of Packaging: Consumer, Food Service, Private Label, Bulk
Brands:
Honey Valley
Millers
Rita Miller
Superior

9460 Miller's Meat Market
1524 S Main St
Red Bud, IL 62278-1316   618-282-3334
Fax: 618-282-7799 millermeatman@yahoo.com
          www.redbudchamber.com
Processor of fresh and cured meats including beef, pork, elk, buffalo, sausage, etc.; also, slaughtering services available
Owner: Kevin Miller
Estimated Sales: $300,000-500,000
Number Employees: 5-9
Sq. footage: 5000
Type of Packaging: Consumer, Food Service, Private Label

9461 Miller's Stratford Provision Company
PO Box 654
Southport, CT 06890-0654   203-375-1598
                    Fax: 203-375-7196
Manufacturer of pork and turkey sausage, hot dogs, knockwurst, bratwurst, bologna, kielbasa and ham
President/Partner: John Wunder
VP/Partner: George Wunder
Estimated Sales: $1 Million
Number Employees: 12
Type of Packaging: Consumer, Food Service, Bulk

9462 MillerCoors
405 Cordele Rd
Albany, GA 31705-2109   229-420-5191
          Fax: 229-420-5250 www.millercorrs.com
Processor of beer including light, lager, ice, nonalcoholic and malt liquor
President/Chief Commercial Officer: Tom Long
CEO: Leo Kiely
CFO: Gavin Hattersley
Chief Marketing Officer: Andrew England
Chief Human Resources Officer: Chris Kozina
COO: Dennis Puffer
Plant Manager: Chris Thelen
Estimated Sales: $500 Million to $1 Billion
Number Employees: 600
Parent Co: Miller Brewing Company
Type of Packaging: Consumer
Brands:
COORS
COORS LIGHT
EXTRA GOLD LAGER
HAMM'S
HAMM'S GOLDEN DRAFT
HAMM'S SPECIAL LIGHT
ICEHOUSE
KEYSTONE ICE
KEYSTONE LIGHT
KEYSTONE PREMIUM
MAGNUM MALT LIQUOR
MICKEY'S
MICKEY'S ICE
MILLER CHILL
MILLER GENUNICE DRAFT 64
MILLER GENUINE DRAFT
MILLER HIGH LIFE
MILLER HIGH LIFE LIGHT
MILLER LITE
MILWAUKEE'S BEST ICE
MILWAUKEE'S BEST LIGHT

MILWAUKEE'S BEST PREMIUM
OLD ENGLISH 800 7.5
OLD ENGLISH HIGH GRAVITY 800
OLDE ENGLISH 800
RED DOG
SOUTHPAW LIGHT
STEEL RESERVE HIGH GRAVITY
STEEL RESERVE TRIPLE EXPORT 8.1%
STEEL SIX

9463 MillerCoors
15801 E First Street
Irwindale, CA 91706-2069   626-969-6811
          Fax: 626-969-6365 www.millercoors.com
Processor of beer including light, lager, ice, nonalcoholic and malt liquor
President/Chief Commercial Oficer: Tom Long
CEO: Leo Kiely
CFO: Gavin Hattersley
Chief Marketing Officer: Andrew England
Chief Human Resources Officer: Chris Kozina
COO: Dennis Puffer
Plant Manager: Edward Beers
Estimated Sales: $500 Million to $1 Billion
Number Employees: 75
Parent Co: MillerCoors
Type of Packaging: Consumer
Brands:
AGUUILA
BLUE MOON BELGIAN WHITE
COORS BANQUET
COORS LIGHT
COORS NON-ALCHOLIC
CRISTAL
CUSQUENA
EXTRA GOLD LAGER
FOSTER'S
GEORGE KILLIAN'S IRISH RED
HAMM'S
HENRY WEINHARD'S PRIVATE RESERVE
ICEHOUSE
KEYSTONE LIGHT
LEINENKUGEL'S SUNSET WHEAT
MAGNUM MALT LIQUOR
MGD 64
MICKEY'S
MILLER CHILL
MILLER GENUINE DRAFT
MILLER HIGH LIFE
MILLER LITE
MILWAUKEE'S BEST LIGHT
MOLSON CANADIAN
OLD ENGLISH 800
PERONI NASTRO AZZURRO
PILSNER URQUELL
RED DOG
SHARP'S
SOUTHPAW LIGHT
SPARKS
STEEL RESERVE HIGH GRAVITY
TYSKIE

9464 Millers Blue Ribbon Beef
410 N 200 W
Hyrum, UT 84319-1024   435-245-6456
          Fax: 435-245-6634 800-873-0939
                    www.eamiller.com
Manufacturer of flavors, flavors enhancers, extracts, hydrolyzed proteins and substitutes
President: Ted Miller
Marketing/Sales: Bruce Miller
Personnel Manager: Paul Barnard
Feeder Cattle Procurement: Alan Summers
Cattle Feeding Opportunities: Bryan Summers
Miller Brothers Trucking: Reed Baldwin
Estimated Sales: $ 50 - 100 Million
Number Employees: 250-499

9465 Millers Ice Cream
1918 Center Street
Houston, TX 77007-6105   713-861-3138
Processor of ice cream including novelties, pies, cakes, sandwiches and popsicles
President: Dianne Haren
Estimated Sales: $560000
Number Employees: 4
Type of Packaging: Consumer, Food Service, Private Label, Bulk

9466 Millflow Spice Corporation
800 Plainfield Lane
Valley Stream, NY 11581-3607   631-884-7422
          Fax: 631-884-7806 800-229-6122
info@millflowspicecorp.com
          www.millflowspicecorp.com
Processor, importer and exporter of food colors, flavoring extracts, spices, seasonings and sauces including pesto, worcestershire, soy, barbecue, hot and smoke
President: Zane Moses
Estimated Sales: $2,600,000
Number Employees: 21
Parent Co: Regal Extract Company
Type of Packaging: Consumer, Food Service, Private Label, Bulk
Brands:
Bonton
Growers Company
Millflow
Regal

9467 Milliaire Winery
276 Main St
Murphys, CA 95247-9564   209-728-1658
          Fax: 209-736-1915 wines@milliairewinery.com
                    www.milliairewinery.com
Wines
Manager: Jana Nadler
Estimated Sales: $160,000
Number Employees: 1-4
Brands:
Milliaire Winery

9468 Millie's Pierogi
129 Broadway
Chicopee Falls, MA 01020   413-594-4991
                    800-743-7641
ann@milliespierogi.com
          www.milliespierogi.com
Processor of fully cooked pierogies including cabbage, potato and cheese, cheese, prune and blueberry.
President: Ann Kerigan
Estimated Sales: Less than $500,000
Number Employees: 5-9
Brands:
Millie's Pierogi

9469 Milligan & Higgins
100 Maple Ave
Johnstown, NY 12095-1041   518-762-4638
          Fax: 518-762-7039 milligan@superior.net
                    www.milligan1868.com
Manufacturer, importer and exporter of kosher edible and technical gelatins; protein factory providing gelatin blending and analytical and microbiological laboratories available
President: Lee Kornbluh
Technical Director: Jacob Utzig
Estimated Sales: $20-50 Million
Number Employees: 20-49
Parent Co: Hudson Industries Corporation
Type of Packaging: Bulk

9470 Milling Sausage Company
629 S 10th St
Milwaukee, WI 53204-1316   414-645-2677
                    Fax: 414-645-2679
Processor of sausage and frankfurters
Owner: Matt Miklick
Number Employees: 5-9
Type of Packaging: Bulk

9471 Millrose Brewing Company
45 S Barrington Rd
South Barrington, IL 60010-9508   847-382-7673
          Fax: 847-382-7693 800-464-5576
          manager@millroserestaurant.com
                    www.millroserestaurant.com
Beer
Manager: Lisa Scoville
COO: Mike Sheridan
Director Manufacturing: Thomas Sweeney
Estimated Sales: $ 5-10 Million
Number Employees: 100-249

9472 Mills
375 W Market St
Salinas, CA 93901-1423   831-758-8179
          Fax: 831-424-9475 info@millsfamilyfarms.com
                    www.millsfamilyfarms.com

Grower and exporter of produce including celery, broccoli, cabbage, lettuce, cauliflower and whole leaf and mixed vegetables
    Owner: Roger Mills
    VP/General Manager: Ed Little
Estimated Sales: $ 20 - 50 Million
Number Employees: 20-49

9473 Mills Brothers International
16000 Christensen Rd # 300
Tukwila, WA 98188-2967   206-575-3000
    Fax: 206-957-1362   edmills@ghfoods.com
                                /www.ghfoods.com
Processor, exporter and wholesaler/distributor of specialty and organic grains, dried peas, dried beans, lentils, millet rice and corn products including popcorn kernels, flour, grits, meal and starch; serving the food servicemarket
    President: Eric Mills
Estimated Sales: $36306000
Number Employees: 50-99
Sq. footage: 26000
Type of Packaging: Consumer, Food Service, Private Label, Bulk
Brands:
    Cascade
    Mills Brothers International

9474 Mills Coffee Roasting Company
1058 Broad St
Providence, RI 02905-1600   401-781-7860
    Fax: 401-781-7978   888-781-5282
    info@millscoffee.com   www.millscoffee.com
Coffee
    President: Susan Mills
    Plant Manager: Mike Candy
Estimated Sales: Below $ 5 Million
Number Employees: 5-9
Type of Packaging: Private Label

9475 Mills Seafood
5 Mills Street
Bouctouche, NB E4S 3S3
Canada   506-743-2444
    Fax: 506-743-8497   millsseafood.ca
Seafood processor
    Owner: Steven Mills
    Owner: Marie Allain
    Vice President: Marie Allain
    Quality Control: George Robichaud
    Marketing Manager: Steven Mills
    Marketing: Marie Allain
    Plant Manager: Laurie Allain
Number Employees: 50-99
Type of Packaging: Food Service

9476 Millstream Brewing
P.O.Box 284
Amana, IA 52203-0284   319-622-3672
    Fax: 319-622-6516
    brewery@millstreambrewing.com
            www.millstreambrewing.com
Processor of beers, ales and lagers
    Owner: Chris Priebe
Estimated Sales: Below $ 5 Million
Number Employees: 10-19
Type of Packaging: Consumer, Food Service
Brands:
    Millstream

9477 Milmar Food Group
16 1/2 Station Rd
Goshen, NY 10924   845-294-5400
    Fax: 845-294-6687
Manufacturer of wide variety of value added, OU kosher endorsed, frozen foods including: breakfast selections, vegetarian, chicken, burrito, and pre-plated meal products
    President: Martin Hoffman
    EVP: Roy Makinen
    Marketing Director: Rita O'Connor CMC
    VP Sales: Dov Peikes
Estimated Sales: $14.5 Million
Number Employees: 100-249
Number of Brands: 3
Number of Products: 100
Sq. footage: 60000
Type of Packaging: Consumer, Food Service, Private Label, Bulk
Brands:
    MRS. VEGGIES
    NO FORKS REQUIRED
    SPRING VALLEY

9478 Milne Fruit Products
P.O.Box 111
Prosser, WA 99350-0111   509-786-2611
    Fax: 509-786-1724   rtcallaway@oceanspray.com
                                www.milnefruit.com
Processor and exporter of frozen fruit juice concentrates, and purees including concord grape, strawberry, cranberry, raspberry, blueberry and cherry and others
    President: Randy Hageman
    General Manager: Randall Hageman
    Research & Development: Eric Johnson
    Quality Control: Eric Johnson
    Sales Director: Ryan Callaway
Number Employees: 50-99
Parent Co: Ocean Spray Cranberries
Type of Packaging: Bulk

9479 Milner Milling
P.O.Box 2247
Chattanooga, TN 37409-0247   423-265-2313
                                Fax: 770-358-0120
Flour and grain
    Chairman: Vernon Grizzard Jr
Estimated Sales: $11,100,000
Number Employees: 20-49

9480 Milnot Company
P.O.Box J
Neosho, MO 64850-0560   417-776-2243
    Fax: 417-776-2763   800-877-6455
                                www.milnot.com
Processor of butter, vegetable oil and evaporated milk
    President: Craig Steinke
    CFO: Alain Souligny
Estimated Sales: $ 50 - 100 Million
Number Employees: 50-99
Parent Co: Milnot Company

9481 Milnot Company
120 W Saint John Street
Litchfield, IL 62056-2169   217-324-2146
                                800-877-6455
                                www.milnot.com
Dairy products.
    President: Scott Meader
    Plant Manager: Kevin Brumm
Number Employees: 20-49
Parent Co: Milnot Company
Type of Packaging: Consumer, Private Label, Bulk

9482 (HQ)Milnot Company
100 S 4th Street
Suite 1010
Saint Louis, MO 63102-1823   314-436-7667
    Fax: 314-436-7679   800-877-6455
                                www.milnot.com
Dairy products, baby food, etc
    President: Scott Meader
    CFO: Alain Souligny
    Senior VP Sales: Sal Stazonne
    Purchasing Manager: John Witte
Number Employees: 10-19
Number of Brands: 3
Type of Packaging: Consumer, Private Label
Brands:
    Beech-Nut Baby Food
    Dairy Sweet
    Milnot
    Sunshine

9483 Milo's Whole World Gourmet
94C Columbus Rd
Athens, OH 45701   740-589-6456
    Fax: 740-594-9151   866-589-6456
    info@miloswholeworld.com
            www.miloswholeworld.com
pasta sauces and salad dressings
    President/Owner: Jonathan Milo
    Wholesale Sales Manager: Maryjane Burch
    Production: Jason Cogar

9484 Milone Brothers Coffee
P.O.Box 4367
Modesto, CA 95352-4367   209-526-0865
    Fax: 209-526-1652   800-974-8500
    mbc@milone.com   www.milone.com
Fresh roasted whole bean highest grade coffees.
Custom blending/roasting, espresso and coffee machine experts
    Partner: Joseph Milone

Estimated Sales: $1,000,000
Number Employees: 5-9
Sq. footage: 3000
Type of Packaging: Food Service, Bulk
Brands:
    Milone Brothers

9485 Milos
125 W 55th St
New York, NY 10019-5369   212-245-7400
    Fax: 212-245-4828   www.milos.ca
Frozen potato cakes
    Owner: Costas Spiliadis
Estimated Sales: $ 2.5-5 Million
Number Employees: 10-19

9486 Milroy Canning Company
P.O.Box 125
Milroy, IN 46156-0125   765-629-2221
    Fax: 765-629-2645   milroy@comsys.net
Processor of canned tomatoes
    President: Robert Tobian
    Vice President: Morris Tobian
Estimated Sales: $ 10 - 20 Million
Number Employees: 20-49
Type of Packaging: Consumer

9487 Milsolv Corporation
P.O.Box 444
Butler, WI 53007-0444   262-252-3550
    Fax: 262-252-5250   800-558-8501
    allmilw@milsolv.com   www.milsolv.com
Beverages, confectionery, canned foods, processed cheese, bakery, meat, seafood, dairy
    Chairman: Ed mills
    CEO: Ed Mills
    Sales: Mark Hartung
Brands:
    Milsolv

9488 Milton A. Klein Company
PO Box 363
New York, NY 10021-0006   516-829-3400
    Fax: 516-829-3427   800-221-0248
    allen@miltonklein.com   www.miltonklein.com
    President: Irene Klein
    VP: Allen Klein
Number Employees: 10-19
Sq. footage: 6800

9489 Milwhite
5487 S 14th Hwy
Brownsville, TX 78521   956-547-1970
    Fax: 956-547-1999   www.milwhite.com
Manufacturer and importer of clay, talcs, calcium carbonate, barium sulfate, attapulgite, bentonite and other nonmetallic minerals; exporter of aflatoxin binders
    President: Mike Hughes III
    VP Operations: Mike Hughes
Estimated Sales: $ 20 - 50 Million
Number Employees: 20-49
Type of Packaging: Private Label, Bulk
Brands:
    Blanca
    Gel B
    Milsorb
    Super Gel B
    TDM

9490 Mimac Glaze
271 Glidden Road
Brampton, ON L6W 1H9
Canada   905-457-7737
    Fax: 905-457-7828   877-990-9975
    dave@mimacglaze.com   www.168.144.59.68
Processor of icing stabilizers and ready-to-use icings
    President: David Miles
    Secretary/Treasurer: Marion Miles
    Production Manager: Werner Barduhn
Number Employees: 5-9
Sq. footage: 6600
Type of Packaging: Consumer, Food Service
Brands:
    Paragon
    Supreme

9491 Mims Meat Company
24634 E Freeway
Houston, TX 77229   713-453-0151
                                Fax: 713-453-6714

Manufacturers and Distributors of Beef Patties and Steaks
President: A Mims
Marketing Manager: Phillip Cash
Plant Manager: Dan Mims

9492 Min Tong Herbs
318 7th St
Oakland, CA 94607-4112   510-873-8677
Fax: 510-873-8671   800-562-5777
mintongherbs@hotmail.com
www.mintongherbs.com
Processor and importer of Chinese herbal extracts
President: Charles Chang
Vice President: Susan Chang
Sales: Tiffany Zhon
Estimated Sales: $500,000-$1 Million
Number Employees: 5-9
Number of Brands: 1
Type of Packaging: Consumer, Private Label, Bulk
Brands:
Min Tong

9493 Mincing Overseas Spice Company
10 Tower Rd
Dayton, NJ 08810-1571   732-355-9944
Fax: 732-555-9964   mail@mincing.com
www.mincing.com
Importers, processor of spices, seeds and aromatic herbs
President: Manoj Rupaerlia
CFO: K Jobanputra
Quality Controol: Nagy Beskal
Sales: Dorothy Hollomay
Plant Manager: Charles Armgnti
Purchasing: H Ruparelia
Estimated Sales: $ .5 - 1 million
Number Employees: 1-4
Sq. footage: 50000
Parent Co: Mincing Trading Corporation

9494 Mine & Mommy's Cookies
433 County Road 392
Merkel, TX 79536-7313   915-928-5870
Fax: 915-928-1067   cccookie@prodigy.net
Processor and exporter of prepared flour mixes and doughs
Co-Owner: Monty Tittle
Co-Owner: Marilyn Tittle
Estimated Sales: $1-$2.5 Million
Number Employees: 1-4
Brands:
Mine & Mommy's

9495 Mineo's Pies
1730 Pittston Avenue
Scranton, PA 18505-1630   570-347-8278
Fax: 570-347-5383   monikabakery@aol.com
Baked goods
President: Monika Regger
Estimated Sales: Below $ 5 Million
Number Employees: 8

9496 Mineral & Pigment Solutions
1000 Coolidge St
South Plainfield, NJ 07080-3805   908-561-6100
Fax: 908-757-3488   800-732-0562
customerservice@wcdinc.com   www.wcdinc.com
Manufacturer of high quality minerals, colors, chemicals and additives for the food and pharmaceutical industries
President: Theodore Hubbard
Estimated Sales: $ 50-100 Million
Number Employees: 50-99

9497 Minerva Cheese Factory
P.O.Box 60
Minerva, OH 44657-0060   330-868-4196
Fax: 330-868-7947   info@cheesehere.com
www.cheesehere.com
Processor of dairy products including butter, whey and cheese; also, gift boxes available
Owner: Phil Mueller
Sales Manager: Venae Banner
Sales Representative: Karla Jarvis
Estimated Sales: $15000000
Number Employees: 20-49
Type of Packaging: Consumer, Food Service, Private Label, Bulk

9498 Minerva Dairy
P.O.Box 60
Minerva, OH 44657-0060   330-868-4196
Fax: 330-868-7947   info@minervacheese.com
www.cheesehere.com
Butter, colby and cheddar cheese
President: Phil Mueller
CEO: Adam Mueller
Plant Manager: Dave Saling
Treasurer: Polly Mueller
Marketing Director: Venae Banner
Estimated Sales: $ 25-49.9 Million
Number Employees: 20-49
Brands:
Amish Gourmet
Minerva
Oldworld

9499 Mingo Bay Beverages
721 Seaboard Street
Myrtle Beach, SC 29577-6520   843-448-5320
Fax: 843-448-4162   mingomoe@aol.com
www.iwebtech.com/mingobay
Processor and exporter of coffee, tea and fruit bases, mixes and concentrates
President: Larry Moses
Estimated Sales: $ 1-5 Million
Number Employees: 8
Sq. footage: 80000
Type of Packaging: Consumer, Food Service, Private Label, Bulk
Brands:
Mingo Bay Beverages

9500 Mingo River Pecan Company
2005 Marbabar Ln
Florence, SC 29501   843-662-2452
Fax: 843-664-2338   800-440-6442
jturner@youngpecan.com
Flavored pecans
Executive Director: Chenen Harvey
Estimated Sales: $ 20 - 50 Million
Number Employees: 100-249

9501 Minh Food Corporation
1251 Scarborough Ln
Pasadena, TX 77506-4103   713-740-7200
Fax: 713-740-7205   800-344-7655
Processor of frozen Asian foods
Manager: Cole Lewis
CEO: Ron Minist
Executive VP: Mike Minist
Number Employees: 10-19
Parent Co: Schwan's Sales
Type of Packaging: Consumer, Food Service, Private Label

9502 (HQ)Minn-Dak Farmers Cooperative
7525 Red River Rd
Wahpeton, ND 58075-9698   701-642-8411
Fax: 701-642-6814   www.mdf.coop
Beet sugar manufacturer
President/CEO: David H Roche
Executive VP/CFO: Steven M. Caspers
Plant Manager: Brent Muehlberg
Purchasing: John Nyquist
Estimated Sales: $198,900,000
Number Employees: 500-999
Type of Packaging: Bulk
Other Locations:
Minn-Dak Farmers Coop.
Wahpeton ND

9503 Minn-Dak Growers Limited
P.O.Box 13276
Grand Forks, ND 58208-3276   701-746-7453
Fax: 701-780-9050   info@minndak.com
www.minndak.com
Manufacturer of specialty crop food ingredients
President/GM: Harris Peterson
CFO: Mona Kozojed
Estimated Sales: $ 10 - 20 Million
Number Employees: 20-49
Number of Brands: 3
Number of Products: 9
Sq. footage: 25000
Type of Packaging: Consumer, Food Service, Bulk
Brands:
MDGL
MDM
MINN - DAK

9504 Minn-Dak Yeast Company
18175 Red River Rd W
Wahpeton, ND 58075-9697   701-642-3300
Fax: 701-642-1908
Processor of fresh bakers' yeast
Manager: Richard Ames
Sensient Technologies Sales/Svc. Team: Ravi Arora
Estimated Sales: $7298921
Number Employees: 20-49
Sq. footage: 20000
Parent Co: Minn-Dak Farmers Cooperative
Brands:
Dakota Yeast

9505 Minnehaha Spring Water Company
1906 E 40th Street
Cleveland, OH 44103-3557   216-431-0243
Processor of bottled natural spring water
President: Michael Wright
Number Employees: 20-49
Type of Packaging: Consumer, Food Service, Private Label, Bulk

9506 Minnesota Dehydrated Vegetables
P.O.Box 245
Fosston, MN 56542-0245   218-435-1997
Fax: 218-435-6770   info@mdvcorp.com
www.mdvcorp.com
Processor and importer of dehydrated carrots and potatoes; broker of industrial ingredients; serving processors and wholesalers/distributors
Sales: Karla Holm
Plant Manager: Jim Noyes
Estimated Sales: $ 5-10 Million
Number Employees: 60-100
Type of Packaging: Food Service, Bulk

9507 Minnesota Dehydrated Vegetables
P.O.Box 245
Fosston, MN 56542-0245   218-435-1997
Fax: 218-435-6770   www.mdvcorp.com
Dehydrated vegetables
Manager: Jim Noise
Marketing Director: Jam Moyes
CFO: Jim Noyes
CFO: Jordy Alson
Estimated Sales: $ 5-10 Million
Number Employees: 50-99
Brands:
Minnesota Dehydrated Vegetables

9508 Minnesota Grain
P.O.Box 69
Lake City, MN 55041-0069   651-345-5305
Fax: 651-681-7975   800-535-7405
info@mngrain.com   www.mngrain.com
Processor and exporter of conventional as well as certified organic barley, wheat, rye, grits, specialty grain based food ingredients, meals and quick cooking and whole rolled flakes
Owner: Hudson McMurtrie
CFO: Mark Kucala
Controller: Tom Gastler
VP Marketing/Sales: Mike Mensing
Operations: Mark Kucala
Plant Manager: Rene Patnaude
Estimated Sales: $10000000
Number Employees: 20-49
Type of Packaging: Bulk

9509 Minnesota Malting Company
PO Box 16406
Saint Paul, MN 55116-0406   507-263-3911
Fax: 507-263-5087   rdm@rconnect.com
Manufacturer of barley malt for brewers, distillers and food processors
President/CEO: Richard Mensing
VP/Treasurer: Robert Snook
Estimated Sales: $20-50 Million
Number Employees: 60
Type of Packaging: Bulk

9510 Minnesota Specialty Crops
P.O.Box 320
McGregor, MN 55760-0320   218-768-4917
Fax: 218-768-4413   800-328-6731
minnesotawild@citlink.com

Processor of wild berry syrups, jams, jellies and sauces, maple syrup, honey and whipped honey; also, wild rice pancake mix and organic wild, cultivated long grain and broken wild rice
President: Jack Erckenbrack
General Manager: Lori Gordon
Estimated Sales: $700000
Number Employees: 1-4
Sq. footage: 3200
Type of Packaging: Consumer, Food Service, Private Label, Bulk
Brands:
Minnesota Wild

9511 Minnestalgia
P.O.Box 320
McGregor, MN 55760-0320   218-768-4917
Fax: 218-768-4413 800-328-6731
minnestalgia@citlink.net www.minnestalgia.com
Wines, soup and pancake mixes, berry and maple syrups, honeys, gift baskets and more!
President: Jay Erckenbrack
Estimated Sales: $ 1 - 3 Million
Number Employees: 1-4

9512 Mino Corporation
5406 Sheridan St
Davenport, IA 52806-2260   563-388-4770
Fax: 563-388-4772
President: Jeffrey Melchert
Estimated Sales: $ 10 - 20 Million
Number Employees: 10-19

9513 Minor Fisheries
176 West Street
Port Colborne, ON L3K 4E2
Canada   905-834-9232
Fax: 905-834-5662 minfish@itcanada.com
Processor of whole, dressed, filleted, fresh and frozen fresh water fish including yellow perch, yellow pickerel, white perch, whitefish, smelt, rock bass, silver bass and lingcod
President: Dan Minor
CEO: Dan Minor
Co-Owner: Wray Minor
Marketing Manager: Rodney Minor
Number Employees: 5-9
Sq. footage: 2100
Type of Packaging: Consumer, Bulk

9514 Minter Weisman Company
1035 Nathan Ln N
Minneapolis, MN 55441-5002   952-545-3706
Fax: 612-545-0938 800-742-5655
mmanske@minter-weisman.com
www.minter-weisman.com
Candy
President: Paul Siegel
CEO: Jim Thompson
Controller: Jim Thomson
Marketing Director: Gary Christianson
Estimated Sales: $ 75-100 Million
Number Employees: 100-249
Brands:
Camel
Hersey's
Marlboro

9515 Minterbrook Oyster Company
P.O.Box 432
Gig Harbor, WA 98335-0432   253-857-5251
Fax: 253-857-5521
Info@MinterbrookOysterCo.com
www.minterbrookoyster.com
Processor and exporter of fresh and frozen oysters, Manila clams and mussels
President: Harold E Wiksten
Sales Manager: Mike Paul
Estimated Sales: $8600000
Number Employees: 50-99
Sq. footage: 70
Type of Packaging: Consumer, Food Service, Private Label
Brands:
Minterbrook

9516 (HQ)Minute Maid Company
P.O.Box 2079
Houston, TX 77252   713-888-5000
Fax: 713-888-5959 888-884-8952
www.minutemaid.com

World's leading marketer of premium fruit juices and drinks. Processor of chilled, aseptic and frozen concentrated juices, punches and ades including orange, grape, grapefruit, tangerine, lemon, lime, etc.; also, citrus oils
CEO: E Neville Isdell
COO: Donald Knauss
Senior VP: Mike St John
Public Relations: Ray Crockett
Number Employees: 500-999
Parent Co: Coca-Cola Company
Type of Packaging: Consumer, Food Service
Other Locations:
Minute Maid
Dinuba CA
Apopka FL
Northampton MA
Paw Paw MI
Waco TX
Petersborough ON
Mississauga ON
Brands:
Andifruit
Bacardi Mixes
Bibo
Bright & Early
Cappy
Fruitopia
Hi-C
Juices To Go
Kapo
Minute Maid
Nectar Andina
Odwalla
Odwalla
Samantha
Simply Orange
Sunfill

9517 Minute Maid Company
427 San Christopher Drive
Dunedin, FL 34698-4905   727-733-2121
Fax: 727-733-0212 800-237-0159
www.minutemaid.com / www.cocacola.com
Manufacturer of fruit juice and punch
Chairman/CEO, Coca-Cola: E Neville Isdell
EVP/CFO, Coca-Cola: Gary Fayard
Estimated Sales: $100+ Million
Number Employees: 100-249
Sq. footage: 400000
Parent Co: Coca-Cola Bottling Company
Type of Packaging: Food Service
Brands:
MINUTE MAID

9518 Minute Maid Company
400
2150 Town Square Pl
Sugar Land, TX 77479-1278   713-888-5000
Fax: 609-448-5100 www.minutemaid.com
Manufacturer of orange, grapefruit and apple juices
Chairman/CEO, Coca-Cola: E Neville Isdell
EVP/CFO, Coca-Cola: Gary Fayard
Plant Manager: Allen Vanderneut
Number Employees: 500-999
Parent Co: Coca-Cola Bottling Company
Type of Packaging: Consumer

9519 Minute Maid Company
6900 Lougheed Way
Bombay, BC V6B 4G4
Canada   416-756-8100
Fax: 416-756-8147 800-438-2653
www.cocacola.com
Processor of fresh and frozen orange juice
CEO: Dan McCue
COO: E Neville Isdell
CFO: Gary Fayard
Vice President: Lisa Lowe
Number Employees: 50-99
Parent Co: Coca-Cola Bottling Company
Type of Packaging: Consumer, Food Service
Brands:
Coca Cola

9520 Mira International Foods
11 Elkins Rd
East Brunswick, NJ 08816-2006   732-613-7201
Fax: 732-613-7206 800-818-6472
mirasales@attglobal.net www.miramango.com

Tropical nectars
President: Ramses Awadalla
CEO: Mark Awadalla
Vice President: Pancy Awadalla
Marketing Director: Mariam Gandour
Sales Director: Joseph Awadalla
Public Relations: Mark Awadalla
Estimated Sales: $ 5-10 Million
Number Employees: 5-9
Sq. footage: 24000
Type of Packaging: Private Label
Brands:
Mira Mango Nectar

9521 Miramar Fruit Trading Company
8861 NW 102nd Street
Medley, FL 33178-1338   305-883-4774
Fax: 305-883-4773 miramarfruit.4t.com
Canned guava pulp, mango pulp, grated coconut, papaya chunks, guava shells, orange shells, pina colada mix, black beans, green pigeon peas
President: Carlos Unanue
Manager: Maria Miguel
Estimated Sales: $ 2.5-5 Million
Number Employees: 17
Brands:
Ancel

9522 Miramar Pickles & Food Products
200 NW 20th Ave
Fort Lauderdale, FL 33311-8724   954-351-8030
Fax: 954-462-6862 gr4pickles@aol.com
Sauerkraut, pickles, pickled tomatoes
President: George Bell
Quality Control: Daniel Singer
R & D: Micheal Hirschkorn
Estimated Sales: $ 50-75 Million
Number Employees: 10-19
Brands:
Miramar
Mrs. Nickles

9523 Mirasco
900 Circle 75 Pkwy SE # 200
Atlanta, GA 30339-3075   770-956-1945
Fax: 770-956-0308 atlanta@mirasco.com
www.mirasco.com
Supplier of meats, poultry and seafood
President: Latif Rizk
Estimated Sales: $4.5 Million
Number Employees: 10-19
Type of Packaging: Food Service, Private Label, Bulk

9524 Mirror Polishing & Plating Company Inc
346 Huntingdon Ave
Waterbury, CT 06708-1430   203-574-5400
Fax: 203-597-9448 chromerolls@mpp.net
www.mpp.net
Chromium roll fabricating and surface finishing company that provides rebuilding, grinding, plating and finishing services for all web processing applications used in the manufacturing of plastic sheet & film, paper, non-woven fabricsand food processing industries.
President: Gary Nalband
Vice President Sales & Marketing: Rimas Kozica

9525 Miscoe Springs
89 Northbridge Rd
Mendon, MA 01756-1025   508-473-0550
Fax: 508-473-3971
Processor of bottled spring water
President: Mike Rossi
Estimated Sales: $ 10-20 Million
Number Employees: 20-49
Parent Co: Suiza Foods
Type of Packaging: Consumer, Food Service, Private Label
Brands:
Miscoe Springs

9526 Mishawaka Brewing Company
408 W Cleveland Rd
Granger, IN 46530-9577   574-256-9993
misbrew@aol.com
www.mishawakabrewingcompany.com
Processor of seasonal beer, ale, stout, lager and porter
Owner: Thomas R Schmidt
CEO: Tom Scmidt
Marketing Director: Tom Scmidt

Estimated Sales:$ 1-2.5 Million
Number Employees: 20-49
Type of Packaging: Consumer, Food Service
Brands:
Four Horsemen

9527 Mishler Packing Company
5680 W 100 N
Lagrange, IN 46761-8605   260-768-4156
Fax: 260-768-4354
Manufacturer of meat including beef, pork, cold and luncheon meats
President: Mike Monson
Secretary/Treasurer: Michael Monson
Estimated Sales:$20 Million
Number Employees: 20-49
Type of Packaging: Consumer

9528 Miss Ginny's Orginal Vermont Pickle Works
655 N Main Street
Northfield, VT 05663-6829
Bhutan   802-485-3057
Fax: 802-485-3057
Pickles

9529 Miss Meringue
1709 La Costa Meadows Dr
San Marcos, CA 92078-5105   760-471-4978
Fax: 760-712-7814   800-561-6516
info@missmeringue.com
www.jacquesgourmet.com
Meringues and cookies
Owner: Roland D'Abel
CFO: Rick Lamb
Quality Control: Rom William
Estimated Sales:$ 5-10 Million
Number Employees: 100-249
Brands:
Miss Meringue
Splenda®

9530 Miss Scarlett's
P.O.Box 6729
Chandler, AZ 85246-6729   650-340-9600
Fax: 650-340-9680   800-345-6734
www.missscarlett.com
Marinated and pickled fruits, olives and vegetables; mushrooms, artichokes, asparagus, eggplant, baby corn, grren beans, carrots, Brussel sprouts, snow peas, snap peas, zucchini pickles, sweet baby onions, pickled garlic, cocktialtomatoes, baby okra, cap
Co-Owner: Peggy Luper
Co-Owner: Ralph Luper
Estimated Sales:$2.5-$5 Million
Number Employees: 4
Type of Packaging: Private Label
Brands:
Miss Scarlett

9531 Miss Sophia's Old WorldKits & Gingerbread
1401 Elm St
Dallas, TX 75202-2952   214-741-6800
Fax: 214-741-6807   877-446-4373
plumcreative@att.net   www.misssophia.com
Gingerbread and candy winter village kits
Owner: Jason Osterberger
Brands:
Miss Sophia's Gingerbread

9532 (HQ)Mission Food
PO Box 167847
Irving, TX 75038   469-232-5000
Fax: 972-232-5176   800-424-7862
www.missionfoods.com
Mexican foods including flour and corn tortillas, wraps, tortilla chips, taco shells and tostados, and chicharrones and pork cracklins
Chairman/CEO: Roberto Gonzalez Barrera
CFO: Raul Pelaez Cano
Quality Control: Lucy Gonzalvez
Chief Marketing Officer: Sylvia Hernandez Benitez
VP Sales: Asmia Syed
Estimated Sales:$ 600 Million
Number Employees: 6,610
Type of Packaging: Consumer, Food Service, Private Label, Bulk
Brands:
Diago's
Diane's

Guerrero
Mission

9533 Mission Foods
401 Railhead Rd
Fort Worth, TX 76106-1982   817-624-2123
Fax: 817-624-2964
Processor of Mexican products including taco shells, enchiladas and burritos
Manager: Geraldo Martinez
President: Ernesto Rodriguez
VP: Paul Rodriguez
Estimated Sales:$100+ Million
Number Employees: 250-499
Type of Packaging: Consumer

9534 Mission Foods
P.O.Box 616
Jefferson, GA 30549-0616   706-693-2005
Fax: 706-693-2007   800-240-2447
mission@answers-sys.com
www.missionfoods.com
Manufacturer of taco shells, tortilla chips and flour and corn tortillas
President: Jairo Senise
Estimated Sales:$100+ Million
Number Employees: 250-499
Sq. footage: 4968
Parent Co: Gruma Corporation
Type of Packaging: Consumer, Food Service
Other Locations:
Mission Foods (Southeast)
McMinnville OR
Brands:
MISSION

9535 (HQ)Mission Foods Corporation
P.O.Box 167847
Irving, TX 75016-7847   469-232-5000
Fax: 972-232-5175   800-443-7994
mission@answers-sys.com
www.missionfoodsfsc.com
Processor of flour and corn-based tortillas
Chairman: Roberto Barrera
President/CEO: Jairo Senise
CFO: Joel Suarez
VP/General Manager: Dave Watts
Sr. VP: Robert Smith
VP Sales: Ron Anderson
VP Operations: Felipe Rubino
Number Employees: 500-999
Parent Co: Gruma Corporation
Type of Packaging: Consumer, Food Service, Private Label, Bulk

9536 Mission Foods Corporation
PO Box 2008
Oldsmar, FL 34677-7008   800-443-7994
Fax: 800-272-5207   mission@answers-sys.com
www.missionfoodsfsc.com
Processor of flour and corn tortillas
Sr VP: Robert Smith
Number Employees: 250-499
Parent Co: Gruma Corporation

9537 Mission Foods/Diane's Foods
2046 NE Highway 99w
McMinnville, OR 97128-6290   503-434-5534
Fax: 503-434-6604
Processor and exporter of Mexican foods including tortilla chips
Owner: Kathy Mc Gray
Estimated Sales:$ 3 - 5 Million
Number Employees: 5-9
Sq. footage: 55000
Parent Co: Mission Foods Corporation
Type of Packaging: Consumer, Food Service, Private Label, Bulk
Brands:
Casa De Quesda
Diane's
Mission

9538 Mission Foodservice
PO Box 2008
Oldsmar, FL 34677-7008   800-443-7994
Fax: 800-272-5207   mission@answers-sys.com
www.missionfoodsfsc.com
Manufacturer and exporter of Mexican foods including flour and corn tortillas, tortilla chips, pastries, taco and tostada shells
SVP/GM: Robert Smith
Marketing Director: Robin Tobor
VP Sales: Tom Daley

Number Employees: 1,000-4,999
Sq. footage: 420000
Type of Packaging: Consumer, Food Service, Private Label, Bulk
Brands:
Diago
Dianes
Guerrero
Marias
Mission

9539 Mission Mountain Winery
P.O.Box 100
Dayton, MT 59914-0100   406-849-5524
Fax: 406-849-5524   mmwinery@mountainsky.us
www.missionmountainwinery.com
Wines
President: Thomas Campbell Sr
Estimated Sales:$690,000
Number Employees: 10-19
Brands:
Mission Mountain

9540 Mission Pharmacal Company
P.O.Box 786099
San Antonio, TX 78278-6099   210-696-8400
Fax: 210-696-6010   800-292-7364
www.missionpharmacal.com
Processor of vitamins and nutritional supplements
President: Neill Walsdorf Jr
National Sales Manager (Pharm.): Dan Kibbe
Director Sales: Mike Schwartz
Estimated Sales:$96128979
Number Employees: 50-99
Type of Packaging: Consumer
Brands:
Calcet
Calcet Plus
Citracal
Compete
Fosfree
Iromin
Mission Prenatal

9541 Mission San Juan Juices
32565-B Golden Lantern
#282
Dana Point, CA 92629   949-495-7929
Fax: 949-495-8015   xtremebeverages@cox.net
www.xtremebeverages.com
Manufacturer and Marketer of 100% juices and smoothies in single-serve and mult-serve containers
President: William Quinley
VP: James Moffitt
Estimated Sales:$5 Million
Number Employees: 4
Number of Brands: 3
Number of Products: 20
Type of Packaging: Consumer, Food Service, Private Label
Brands:
Apple Brand Juices
Fruit Ole Smoothies
Mission San Juan Juices

9542 Mission Valley Foods
193 Falcon Crest Road
Middlebury, CT 06762-1526   203-573-0652
Fax: 203-574-5853
General grocery
President: Martin Smith
CFO: Marcia Tejeda
Marketing Director: Linda Ghignone
Public Relations: Janet Williams
Production Manager: David Yurselen
Estimated Sales:$300,000-500,000
Number Employees: 1-4
Type of Packaging: Private Label
Brands:
Brickenridge
Chef Martin

9543 Mississippi Bakery
834 Jefferson St
Burlington, IA 52601-5432   319-752-6315
Fax: 319-752-6233
Processor of bread and sweet goods
Manager: Robert Brookhart
Director Operations/Plant Manager: Rob Brookhard
Estimated Sales:$ 20 - 50 Million
Number Employees: 50-99

9544 Mississippi Blending Company
121 Royal Rd
Keokuk, IA 52632-2028   319-524-1235
Fax: 319-524-9889 800-758-4080
www.alliedstarch.com
Processor and wholesaler/distributor of baking pow-
der, yeast foods, dusting starches. Custom blending,
packaging, private labeling and tolling services
available
President: Randy Schmelzel III
Executive VP: John Hicks
VP Operations: John Hicks
Estimated Sales: $ 20 - 50 Million
Number Employees: 20-49
Sq. footage: 28000
Parent Co: Allied Starch & Chemical
Brands:
Bakers Cream

9545 Mississippi Cheese StrawFactory
342 S Mound St
Yazoo City, MS 39194-4045   662-746-7171
Fax: 662-746-7162 866-830-9415
info@mscheesestraws.com
www.mscheesestraws.com
Processor of specialty foods including cheese,
lemon, and chopped pecan and cinnamon straws and
Mississippi mud puppies, cookies, chocolate chip,
oatmeal, pecan
President: Hunter Yerger
VP: Robbie Yerger
Estimated Sales: $ 10-20 Million
Number Employees: 10-19
Sq. footage: 10000
Type of Packaging: Consumer
Brands:
Mississippi Cheese Straws
Mississippi Mud Pupp
Original Lemon Straw

9546 Missouri Winery Warehouse Outlet
Old Us Highway 66
Cuba, MO 65453   573-885-2168
www.mt-pleasantwines.com
Wines
COO: Sherri Kloppe
Estimated Sales: $5-9.9 Million
Number Employees: 1-4

9547 Mister Bee Potato Chip Company
P.O.Box 1645
Parkersburg, WV 26102-1645   304-428-6133
Fax: 304-428-1291 doug.klein@misterbee.com
www.misterbee.com
Manufacturer of potato chips
President: John Klein
Marketing: John Roth
Sales: Steve Parson
Plant Manager: Marie Licot
Estimated Sales: $ 20 - 50 Million
Type of Packaging: Consumer, Food Service, Bulk
Brands:
MISTER BEE

9548 Mister Cookie Face
1989 Rutgers University Blvd
Lakewood, NJ 08701-4538   732-370-5533
Fax: 732-370-4015 brandy@cookieface.com
www.cookieface.com
Processor of novelty ice cream
Manager: Al Clark
Executive VP: Tammy Shaw
Estimated Sales: $12188199
Number Employees: 100-249
Sq. footage: 40000
Type of Packaging: Consumer, Private Label, Bulk
Brands:
Mr. Cookie Face

9549 Mister Fish
7211 Rolling Mill Rd
Baltimore, MD 21224-2033   410-288-2722
Fax: 410-288-4757
Seafood
Owner: Frank Petilo
Estimated Sales: $ 1 - 3 Million
Number Employees: 20-49

9550 Mister Snacks
PO Box 988
Amherst, NY 14226-0988   716-681-8200
Fax: 716-210-1010 800-333-6393
sales@mistersnacks.com www.mistersnacks.com

Manufacturer of snacks, trail mixes, yogurt, candy
and chocolate coated items
VP: Stephen Stern
President: Micheal Stern
Plant Manager: Ed Lilly
Estimated Sales: $ 10-20 Million
Number Employees: 30
Sq. footage: 14
Type of Packaging: Private Label
Brands:
Stone Mountain Snacks
Sunbird Snacks

9551 Mister Spear
2900 E Harding Way
Stockton, CA 95205   209-464-5365
Fax: 209-464-3846 800-677-7327
misterspear@misterspear.com
www.misterspear.com
Processor and packager of shiitake mushrooms, arti-
chokes, asparagus, avocados, sugar snap peas, toma-
toes, bi-color corn, bing cherries, Fuji apples, etc
President: Chip Arnett Jr
Estimated Sales: $500,000
Number Employees: 5-9
Type of Packaging: Consumer, Food Service
Brands:
MSI
Mister Spear

9552 Misty
6235 Havelock Ave
Lincoln, NE 68507-1279   402-466-8424
Fax: 402-466-7222 www.mistylincoln.com
Processor of all-purpose seasonings and Bloody
Mary mix
Owner: Lisa McMeen
Sales Representative: Dave Walbrecht
Director Operations: Brian Tones
Estimated Sales: $3800000
Number Employees: 10-19
Type of Packaging: Consumer, Food Service

9553 Misty Islands Seafoods
4000 W 50th Avenue
Suite 4
Anchorage, AK 99502-1039   907-248-6678
Fax: 907-279-6228
Seafood
Manager: Robert Melovidov
Manager: Richard Tremaine
Estimated Sales: $ 3 - 5 Million
Number Employees: 5-9

9554 Mitake Trading International
1011 Base Line Road
La Verne, CA 91750-2406   909-596-1981
Fax: 909-596-8231
Squash
President: Mike Amakasu
Estimated Sales: $ 5-10 Million
Number Employees: 5-9

9555 Mitch Chocolate
300 Spagnoli Rd
Melville, NY 11747-3507   631-777-2400
Fax: 631-777-1449 www.misschocolate.com
Processor of hard candy lollypops; wholesaler/dis-
tributor of salt water taffy and fundraising boxed
chocolates; also, re-packing and private labeling
available
President: Lawrence Hirsihheimer
VP Operations: Martin Bloomfield
Estimated Sales: $ 3 - 5 Million
Number Employees: 5-9
Sq. footage: 4000
Type of Packaging: Consumer, Private Label
Brands:
Frolic

9556 Mitchel Dairies
1591 E 233rd Street
Bronx, NY 10466-3336   718-324-6261
Dairy products

9557 (HQ)Mitchell Foods
136 Court Sq
Barbourville, KY 40906-1454   606-546-3586
Fax: 606-546-4190 888-202-9745
sales@mitchellfoods.com
www.mitchellfoods.com

Processor of fresh marinated boneless pork chops,
rib eyes, chicken breast, meat loaf and barbecue
products; also, chili and beer cheese
President: Luanne Mitchell
Owner: Jim Mitchell
VP Quality Control: Greg Mitchell
Estimated Sales: $ 1 - 3 Million
Number Employees: 5-9
Sq. footage: 15000
Type of Packaging: Consumer, Food Service, Pri-
vate Label, Bulk
Other Locations:
Mitchell Foods
Lexington KY
Brands:
Mitchell Foods

9558 Mitchum Potato Chips
P.O.Box 36639
Charlotte, NC 28236-6639   704-372-6744
Fax: 704-339-0066 jwilson@msn.com
Manufacturer of potato chips
President: John Wilson
Marketing Director: Henry Pully
COO: Tommy Thompson
Estimated Sales: $ 10-20 Million
Number Employees: 1-4
Type of Packaging: Bulk
Brands:
MDI
Mitchum Rices
Savealot
Tiggly Wiggly
Ukrop

9559 Mitsubishi Chemical America
1 N Lexington Ave # 15t
White Plains, NY 10601-1712   914-286-3600
Fax: 914-761-0108 webapid@m-chem.com
www.mitsubishichemical.com
Processor of bacteriostatic emulsifiers; also, calcium
suspension, confectionery including chocolate,
low-fat spreads, dairy product analogs and fruit
coatings
President: Hiro Tanaka
Sales: Takazumi Kanekiyo
Number Employees: 1,000-4,999
Parent Co: Mitsubishi Chemical Coorporation
Type of Packaging: Bulk
Brands:
RYOTO SUGAR ESTER

9560 (HQ)Mitsubishi InternationalCorporation
333 S Hope St # 2500
Los Angeles, CA 90071-1407   213-620-8652
Fax: 213-687-2993
Various food commodities
Manager: Osamu Takada
Estimated Sales: $ 7 Million
Number Employees: 10-19

9561 (HQ)Mitsubishi InternationalCorporation
520 Madison Avenue
Floor 18
New York, NY 10022-4327   212-759-5605
Fax: 212-605-1810 800-442-6266
inquire@mitsubishicorp.com www.micusa.com
Food commodities: coffee, cocoa, dairy products,
fruits, vegetables and frozen juice concentrates.
Food ingredients, enzymes, emulsifiers, baking
agents.
President: James Brumm
CFO: Yasuyuki Sugiura
Executive VP/COO: Yoshihiko Kawamura
Sales/Purchasing Representative: Patrick Welch
Number Employees: 250-499
Other Locations:
Seattle WA

9562 Mitsui Foods
35 Maple St
Norwood, NJ 07648-2003   201-750-0500
Fax: 201-750-0150 800-777-2322
www.mitsui-foods.com
Food Service suppliers
President: Dennis Newnham
Estimated Sales: $ 20- 50 Million
Number Employees: 50-99

9563 Mix Industries
22332 Piccadilly Court
Apt 1a
Richton Park, IL 60471-2028   708-339-6692
BarbaraMix@prodigy.net
Manufacturer of Herbal Colon cleanser
President: Barbara Mix
Number Employees: 6

9564 Mix-A-Lota Stuff LLC
4828 N Kings Highway
Pmb 424
Fort Pierce, FL 34951-2203   561-468-4688
brendassauces@aol.com
Sauce
President: Brenda Chinn

9565 Mixerz All Natural Cocktail Mixers
100 Cummings Center
Suite 220B
Beverly, MA 01915   978-922-6497
info@mixerz.com
www.mixerz.com
all natural cocktail mixers
Marketing: Christina Pesente

9566 Mixes By Danielle
615 Pelvedere Street
Warren, OH 44483   330-856-5190
Fax: 330-856-3386   800-537-6499
Urban spices
President: Trissa McClerry

9567 Mixon Fruit Farms
2712 26th Ave E
Bradenton, FL 34208-7427   941-748-5829
Fax: 941-748-1085   800-608-2525
info@mixon.com   www.mixon.com
Manufacturer, packer and exporter of citrus fruits,
vegetables, fudge, honey, jellies, marmalades and
spreads, salsa, dips, pickles and nuts
President: William Mixon Jr
Estimated Sales: $ 50 - 100 Million
Number Employees: 50-99
Sq. footage: 90000
Brands:
MIXON

9568 Miyako Oriental Foods
4287 Puente Ave
Baldwin Park, CA 91706-3420   626-962-9633
Fax: 626-814-4569   877-788-6476
joearai@coldmountainmiso.com
www.coldmountainmiso.com
Processor and exporter of black bean paste and or-
ganic miso including yellow, red and white
President: Noritoshi Kanai
Vice President: Terry Shimizu
Marketing/Sales Manager: Joe Arai
Production Manager: Tetsuo Ishifawa
Estimated Sales: $3000000
Number Employees: 10-19
Sq. footage: 19000
Type of Packaging: Consumer, Food Service, Pri-
vate Label, Bulk
Brands:
Cold Mountain
Yamajirushi

9569 Mizkam Americas
2400 Nicholson Ave
Kansas City, MO 64120-1672   816-483-1700
Fax: 816-483-7448
carolyn-moss@nakanofoods.com
www.mizkam.com
Processor of vinegar and condiments including mus-
tard and hot sauce
Executive VP: Clarice Moore
Marketing Director: Tom Matthews
Operations Manager: Mike Cole
Plant Manager: Wayne Towe
Purchasing Manager: Phyllis Conover
Estimated Sales: $ 10 - 20 Million
Number Employees: 20-49
Type of Packaging: Consumer, Food Service, Pri-
vate Label, Bulk
Brands:
Cushing
Lincoln
Ozark
Rogers
Speas
Springdale

9570 Mizkan Americas
1661 Feehanville Dr # 300
Mt Prospect, IL 60056-6031   847-590-0059
Fax: 847-590-0405   800-323-4358
www.mizkanamericas.com
Manufacturer of Specialty Vinegars, Cooking
Wines, Mustards, Asian Sauces and Dressings, and
other liquid condiments.
President: Craig Smith
Purchasing Manager: Bill Lehman
Estimated Sales: $32,300,000
Number Employees: 50-99
Brands:
Barengo
Four Monks
Mizkan
Nokano

9571 Mo Hotta-Mo Betta
PO Box 4136
San Luis Obispo, CA 93403-4136   800-462-3220
www.mohotta.com
Processor and exporter of hot sauces
President: Tim Eidson
Number Employees: 20-49
Type of Packaging: Consumer, Food Service
Brands:
Hot Sauce For Cool Kids
Mo Hotta - Mo Betta

9572 Mobile Bay Seafood
4680 Smith Road
Coden, AL 36523-3362   251-973-0410
Fax: 706-538-6850
Seafood

9573 Mobile Processing
P.O.Box 501187
Mobile, AL 36605-1187   251-438-6944
Fax: 251-438-6948
Processor of fresh and frozen seafood including
shrimp
Owner: Jim Higdon
Estimated Sales: $2000000
Number Employees: 50-99

9574 Moceri South Western
4909 Pacific Hwy
San Diego, CA 92110-4005   619-297-7900
Fax: 619-297-8900
Beverages and bottling
President: Grace Moceri
Estimated Sales: $ 10 - 20 Million
Number Employees: 10-19
Type of Packaging: Private Label

9575 Model Dairy
P.O.Box 3017
Reno, NV 89505-3017   775-788-7900
Fax: 775-788-7951   800-433-2030
Processor and wholesaler/distributor of a full line of
dairy products including ice cream
Manager: Jim Breslin
Controller: Peggy Baker
VP/General Manager: Jim Breslin
Number Employees: 100-249
Sq. footage: 50000
Parent Co: Suiza Dairy Group
Type of Packaging: Food Service

9576 Model Diary
2515 McKinney Ave. Suite 1200
Dallas, TX 75201   775-788-7900
Fax: 775-788-7940 www.deanfoods.com
Milk
President: Mike Keown
Estimated Sales: $ 50-75 Million
Number Employees: 324

9577 Modern Baked Products
301 Locust Ave
Oakdale, NY 11769-1652   631-589-7300
Fax: 631-589-7383   877-727-2253
www.modernbakedprod.com
Processor of bagels and specialty breads
Owner: James Turco
President: James Turco
Sales Manager (Frozens): John Esposito
Estimated Sales: $100+ Million
Number Employees: 100-249
Type of Packaging: Food Service, Private Label
Brands:
Modern Baked Products

9578 Modern Grocery Company
2055 Eisenhower Pkwy # B
Macon, GA 31206-3140   478-745-3381
Fax: 478-745-3382
Processor of produce including onions and potatoes
Manager: Georgeann Evans
Estimated Sales: $48597147
Number Employees: 10-19
Type of Packaging: Consumer, Food Service

9579 Modern Italian Bakery of West Babylon
301 Locust Ave
Oakdale, NY 11769-1652   631-589-7300
Fax: 631-589-7383 www.modernbakedprod.com
Italian baked goods
President: James Turco
Estimated Sales: $ 10-20 Million
Number Employees: 100-249

9580 Modern Macaroni Company
1708 Mary St
Honolulu, HI 96819-3103   808-845-6841
Fax: 808-845-6841
Processor of dry oriental noodles, shrimp flakes and
soybean flour; wholesaler/distributor of groceries
serving the food service market
Manager: Loraine Okumura
Estimated Sales: $900,000-$1 Million
Number Employees: 10-19
Sq. footage: 2400
Type of Packaging: Consumer, Food Service
Brands:
Hula

9581 Modern Mushroom Farms
P.O.Box 340
Avondale, PA 19311-0340   610-268-3535
Fax: 610-268-3099   info@modernmush.com
www.modernmush.com
Processor of fresh and dried mushrooms including
shiitake, oyster, morel, chanterelle, woodear, porcini
and mixed exotic
President: Chuck Ciarrocchi
VP: K Wood
Human Resource Manager: Jackie Serano
Estimated Sales: $25000000
Number Employees: 500-999
Type of Packaging: Consumer, Food Service, Bulk
Brands:
Dove
Modern
Sherrockee Farms

9582 Modern Packaging
3245 N Berkeley Lake Rd NW
Duluth, GA 30096-3054   770-622-1500
Fax: 770-814-0046
www.modernpackaginginc.com
Contract packager of condiments and liquid food
items; warehouse providing dry, cooler and humid-
ity-controlled storage of foodstuffs, liquid packaging
products and seasonal sales items; also, pick and
pack and rail siding available
President: Herb Sodel
VP: Nancy Sodel
Estimated Sales: $3.6 Million
Number Employees: 50-99
Sq. footage: 100000

9583 Modern Products/Fearn Natural Foods
6425 W Executive Dr
Mequon, WI 53092-4482   262-242-2400
Fax: 262-242-2751   800-877-8935
Seasonings, spices, bake mixes, natural products and
soy products
President: Anthony Palermo
Director Sales/Marketing: Gaylord Palermo
Estimated Sales: Below $ 5 Million
Number Employees: 20-49
Number of Products: 200
Sq. footage: 100000
Type of Packaging: Consumer, Food Service
Brands:
Classique Fare
Rearn Naturefresh
Spice Garden
Spike
Swiss Kriss
Vegeful
Vegit

9584 Modern Tea Packers
P.O.Box 370708
Brooklyn, NY 11237-0708   718-417-1060
                                 Fax: 718-417-6405
Tea and tea bags
    Owner: Julius Medwin
    CEO: Julius Neumann
Estimated Sales:$5-9.9 Million
Number Employees: 20-49

9585 Moderncuts
6425 W Executive Dr
Mequon, WI 53092-4482   262-242-2400
    Fax: 262-242-2751   modernfearn@aol.com
                        www.modernfearn.com
Spices and seasonings
    Chairman: Anthony Palermo
    Marketing Director: Michille Tal
Estimated Sales: Below $ 5 Million
Number Employees: 20-49
Sq. footage: 125
Type of Packaging: Private Label
Brands:
    Fearn
    Spice Garden

9586 Modoc Orchard Company
3050 S Pacific Highway
Medford, OR 97501-8723   541-535-1437
Processor and packer of fresh fruit
    Owner: Don Joseph
Number Employees: 100-249
Type of Packaging: Private Label
Brands:
    Modoc
    Mopac

9587 Moet Hennessy USA
85 10th Ave # 2
New York, NY 10011-4753   212-888-7575
    Fax: 212-251-8388 www.mhusa.com/
Wines and spirits.
    President/CEO: Mark Cornelle
Estimated Sales: $ 500 Million-$ 1 Billion
Number Employees: 50-99
Parent Co: United Distillers & Vintners North
AmericaMA
IL
FL
GA
TX
CA
Brands:
    10 CANE
    ARDBEG
    BELVEDERE
    CAPE MENTELLE VINEYARDS
    CAPEZZANA
    CHANDON
    CHATEAU CHEVAL BLANC
    CHATEAU D'YQUEM
    CHATEAU DE SANCERRE
    CHATEAU LA NERTHE
    CHEVAL DES ANDES
    CHOPIN
    CLOUDY BAY VINEYARDS
    DOM PERIGNON
    ESPERTO
    GLENMORANGIE
    GRAND MARNIER
    GREEN POINT
    HENNESSY
    KRUG
    LAPOSTOLLE
    LIVIO FELLUGA
    MOET & CHANDON
    MONSANTO
    NAVAN
    NEWTON VINEYARD
    NUMANTHIA
    RUINART
    TERRAZAS DE LOS ANDES
    VEUVE CLICQUOT

9588 Mogen David Wine Corporation
Po Box 128
Westfield, NY 14787-0543   716-326-7100
                                  Fax: 716-326-4442
Processor and exporter of kosher and nonkosher
wines including white, rose and red
    Director Of Winery Operations: Don Beebe

Estimated Sales: $ 20 - 50 Million
Number Employees: 50-99
Parent Co: Wine Group/Franzia Wine
Type of Packaging: Consumer

9589 Mohawk Distilled Products
11900 Biscayne Boulevard
North Miami, FL 33181-2743   305-892-3460
                                    Fax: 305-892-3460
Rum
    President/CEO: Marshall Berowitz
Estimated Sales: $ 2.5-5 Million
Number Employees: 1-4
Brands:
    MOHAWK

9590 Mohn's Fisheries
1144 Great River Rd
Harpers Ferry, IA 52146-7565   563-586-2269
                                      Fax: 563-423-1579
Seafood
    Owner: Diane Mohn
Estimated Sales: $300,000-500,000
Number Employees: 1-4

9591 Mojave Foods Corporation
6200 E Slauson Ave
Commerce, CA 90040-3012   323-890-8900
    Fax: 323-890-0910 www.mccormick.com
Manufacturer and exporter of Mexican foods includ-
ing dried chile peppers, produce batter mixes, garlic
products, seasonings and spices
    President: Joseph Nibali
    General Manager: Joseph Nibali
Estimated Sales: $36 Million
Number Employees: 250-499
Sq. footage: 100000
Parent Co: McCormick & Company
Type of Packaging: Consumer, Food Service, Pri-
vate Label, Bulk

9592 (HQ)Mojave Foods Corporation
6200 E Slauson Ave
Commerce, CA 90040-3012   323-890-8900
    Fax: 323-890-0910   infoteam@elguapo.com
                        www.mccormick.com
Manufacturer, importer of dried and dehydrated
foods, packages spice, dry chilies, corn husks, garlic
and produce blends
    President: Joseph Nibali
    Marketing Director: Richard Adlai
Estimated Sales: $23.7 Million
Number Employees: 250-499
Sq. footage: 25000
Brands:
    Camino Real
    El Guapo
    El Primero
    El Rey
    El Royal
    Sol Maduro
    Somberro
    Sunripe

9593 Mojave Foods Corporation
6200 E Slauson Ave
Commerce, CA 90040-3012   323-890-8900
                    Fax: 323-890-0910   800-995-8906
Spices, dry chilies and corn products
    President: Joseph Nibali
    CFO: Jeffrey Glaser
    VP: Joseph Ross
    Marketing Director: Joseph Ross
    Public Relations: Joseph Ross
Estimated Sales: $ 25-49.9 Million
Number Employees: 250-499
Type of Packaging: Private Label

9594 Moka D'Oro Coffee
470 Smith St
Farmingdale, NY 11735-1105   718-387-2373
    Fax: 718-387-1563   888-665-2367
    info@mokadoro.com   www.mokadoro.com
Processor and exporter of espresso, Colombian cof-
fee and mineral water; wholesaler/distributor and
importer of espresso machines; serving the food ser-
vice market
    President: Judith Ruggiero
    VP: Michael Ruggiero
Number Employees: 20-49
Type of Packaging: Consumer, Food Service
Brands:
    Galvania
    Nepi

9595 Molbert Brothers Poultry & Egg Company
415 Avenue D
Lake Charles, LA 70615-6883   337-439-2579
                                     Fax: 337-439-2579
Poultry

9596 Moledina Commodities
5501 Muirfield Court
Flower Mound, TX 75022-6489   817-490-1101
    Fax: 817-490-1105   mohamed@moledina.com
                        www.moledina.com
    President: Mohamed Moledina
    VP: Fidahusein R Moledina
Brands:
    Moledina

9597 Molinaro's Fine ItalianFoods
50-2345 Stanfield Road
Mississauga, ON L4Y 3Y3
Canada   905-275-7400
    Fax: 905-275-6701   800-268-4959
    info@molinarosfinefoods.com
    www.molinarosfinefoods.com
Processor, importer and exporter of pizza, fresh and
frozen pizza shells, fresh pasta, flatbread, focaccia,
pasta sauce, fresh and frozen pasta entrees, meat,
vegetable and cheese lasagna, panzerottis and
calzones
    President: Vince Molinaro
    CEO: Gino Molinaro
    Sales/Marketing: Catherine Pyman
    Purchasing Manager: Frank Molinaro
Number Employees: 140
Sq. footage: 76000
Type of Packaging: Consumer, Food Service, Private Label, Bulk
Brands:
    FAMOSA
    MOLINARO'S
    SUPREMO

9598 (HQ)Molson Breweries
1555 Notre Dame Street E
Montreal, QC H2Y 1B5
Canada   514-521-1786
    Fax: 514-521-5885 www.molson.com
Processor of beer
    Chairman: Kevin Boyce
    President/CEO/Director: Kevin Boyce
    CFO/Executive VP: Brian Burden
    COO North America: Tim Scully
    Chief Marketing Officer: Les Hine
Estimated Sales: $181 Million
Type of Packaging: Consumer, Food Service

9599 Molson Breweries
395 Park Street
Regina, SK S4N 5B2
Canada   306-359-1786
                                     Fax: 306-757-3011
Processor of beer, lager and ale
    Pres/Ceo: Kevin Boyce
    District Sales Manager: Barry Thomson
Number Employees: 15
Parent Co: Molson Companies
Type of Packaging: Consumer, Food Service

9600 Molson Breweries
2 International Drive
Toronto, ON M9W 1A2
Canada   416-675-1786
    Fax: 416-621-8077 www.molson.com
Processor of beer, ale and lager
    President/CEO: Daniel O'Neill
    COO/North America: Kevin Boyce
    Executive VP/CFO: Brian Burden
Estimated Sales: $237,000,000
Number Employees: 100-249
Type of Packaging: Consumer, Food Service
Brands:
    Molson

9601 Molson Breweries
4100 Yonge Street
Suite 200
North York, ON M2P 2E6
Canada   416-226-1786
    Fax: 416-512-3800   800-665-7661
                        www.molson.com

Processor and exporter of beer, ale, stout and lager
Owner/President: Kevin Boyce
Manager Property/Administrative Services: John Young
Number Employees: 50-99
Type of Packaging: Consumer, Food Service
Brands:
Molson

9602 Molson Breweries
175 Bloor Street E
North Tower
Toronto, ON M4W 3S4
Canada   416-975-1786
          Fax: 416-975-4088   800-665-7661
                    www.molson.com
Processor and exporter of beer, ale, stout and lager
CEO/President: Kevin Boyce
Number Employees: 100-249
Type of Packaging: Consumer, Food Service
Brands:
MOLSON CANADIAN ICE
MOLSON CANADIAN LIGHT
MOLSON DIAMOND
MOLSON DRY
MOLSON EXEL
MOLSON EXPORT
MOLSON GOLDEN
MOLSON LIGHT
MOLSON RED JACK
MOLSON STOCK ALE
MOSLON ICE
MOSLON SIGNATURE
MOSLON SPRING ROCK
O'KEEFE
OV
RR

9603 Molson Coors Brewing
1225 17th Street
Suite 3200
Denver, CO 80202   303-279-6565
          Fax: 303-277-5415   800-642-6116
          consumers@coors.com   www.coors.com
Manufacturer of beer
Chairman: Peter Coors
President/CEO: Peter Swinburn
VP: Michael J Gannon
Estimated Sales: $3 Billion
Number Employees: 14,540
Type of Packaging: Consumer
Brands:
ASPEN EDGE
BLACK ICE
BLUE MOON
COORS LIGHT
COORS NON-ALCOHOLIC BEER
COORS ORIGINAL
EXTRA GOLD LAGER
KEYSTONE ICE
KEYSTONE LIGHT
KEYSTONE PREMIUM
KILLIAN'S
RICHARD'S RED ALE
ZIMA
ZIMA CITRUS
ZIMA XXX

9604 Molto Italian Foods
4005 Atlantic Avenue
Wildwood, NJ 08260-4730   609-522-5444
                    Fax: 609-522-5444
Italian foods
President: Joseph "Scrocca, Jr."
Estimated Sales: $ .5 - 1 million
Number Employees: 1-4

9605 Mom 'N Pops
834 Brooks St
New Windsor, NY 12553-4828   845-567-0640
          Fax: 845-567-0652   866-368-6767
          info@momnpops.com   www.momnpops.com
Manufacturers of candy and lollipops
President: Barbara Regenbaum
Sales Director: Stacy Zagon
Estimated Sales: $ 10-20 Million
Number Employees: 20-49
Type of Packaging: Private Label
Brands:
Absolutely Zbest Sweets
Mom 'n Pops

9606 Mom's Bakery
5585 Westfield Dr SW
Atlanta, GA 30336-2680   404-344-4189
          Fax: 404-969-1144   info@momsbakery.com
                    www.momsbakery.com
Manufacturer of buttermilk and yeast raised biscuits
President: Kristi Kay
VP: Daniel Kay
Estimated Sales: $12 Million
Number Employees: 100-249
Sq. footage: 75000
Type of Packaging: Food Service, Bulk

9607 Mom's Barbeque Sauce
591 Treeside Drive
Stow, OH 44224-1111   330-929-7290
Seasonings, sauces
President: Peggy Parson
Vice President: R Parson
Number Employees: 1-4
Brands:
Mom's Barbeque Sauce

9608 Mom's Famous
145 NW 20th St
Boca Raton, FL 33431-7901   561-750-1903
          Fax: 561-750-4105   www.momsfamous.com
Baked goods
President: Tony Danesh
Estimated Sales: $575,000
Number Employees: 10-19
Brands:
Mom's Famous

9609 Mom's Food Company
1308 Potrero Avenue
South El Monte, CA 91733-3013   626-444-4115
          Fax: 626-444-2793   800-969-6667
Processor of pre-baked buttermilk biscuits, corn-bread products and dinner rolls
President: Sam Keith
Estimated Sales: $1100000
Number Employees: 23
Sq. footage: 12000
Type of Packaging: Consumer, Food Service, Private Label, Bulk
Brands:
Mom's

9610 Momence Packing Company
334 W North St
Momence, IL 60954-1157   815-472-6485
                    Fax: 815-472-2459
Processor of frozen sausage
President: Patrick Garinger
Estimated Sales: Below $ 5 Million
Number Employees: 250-499
Type of Packaging: Consumer, Private Label

9611 Mon Ami Champagne Company
3845 E Wine Cellar Rd
Port Clinton, OH 43452-3704   419-797-4445
          Fax: 419-797-9078   800-777-4266
          info@monamiwinery.com
                    www.monamiwinery.com
Champagne
Owner: John Kronberg
Estimated Sales: $500,000-$1 Million
Number Employees: 20-49
Brands:
Mon Ami

9612 Mon Cuisine
5620 59th St
Flushing, NY 11378-2314   718-894-2000
          Fax: 718-326-4642   877-666-8348
          mon@alleprocessing.com
                    www.alleprocessing.com
Manufacturer of kosher vegetarian and vegan entrees and IQF products including cutlets, burgers, steaks, meat balls, pasta, nuggets and stuffed cabbage. Packaged in CPET microwaveable/oven safe trays. Private label and co-packingavailable
Owner: Sruly Weinstock
Co-Owner: Sam Hollander
Vice President: Shlomi Pilo
Research & Development: Udi Basis
Plant Manager: Iran Talavera
Purchasing Manager: Zeer Weinstock
Estimated Sales: $ 20 - 50 Million
Number Employees: 50-99
Sq. footage: 150000
Parent Co: Alle Processing

Type of Packaging: Consumer, Food Service, Private Label, Bulk
Brands:
Mon Cuisine Vegetarian
The Natural Choice

9613 Mon Santo
800 N Lindbergh Blvd
St Louis, MO 63167-0001   314-694-1000
          Fax: 314-694-3057   www.monsanto.com
Produce leading seed brands in large-acre crops like corn, cotton, wheat and oilseed (soybeans and canola), as well as small-acre crops like vegetables.
Chairman/President/CEO: Hugh Grant
EVP/CFO: Carl Casale
SVP: David Snively
EVP Human Resources: Steven Mizell
Estimated Sales: K
Number Employees: 10,000+
Brands:
ACCELERON
ASGROW
DE RUITER SEEDS
DEKALB
DELTAPINE
GENUITY
PRESCRIPTIVE AG SERVICES
ROUNDUP AGRICULTURAL HERBICIDE
ROUNDUP READY
SEMINIS
VISTIVE
WESTBRED WHEAT AND BARLEY VARIETIES
YIELDGARD AND YIELDGARD VT

9614 Mona Lisa Food Products
224 Thompson St # 181
Hendersonville, NC 28792-2806   828-685-2443
          Fax: 828-685-8692   800-982-2546
          info@monalisafoodproducts.com
                    www.monalisafoodproducts.com
Manufacturer of gourmet chocolate products using fine European chocolate.
Owner: Peter Thom
Sales Director: Cecilia Bass
Estimated Sales: $ 20 - 50 Million
Number Employees: 20-49
Number of Products: 50
Sq. footage: 32000

9615 Mona Lisa® Chocolatier
Pob 1632/100426
Arlington, VA 22210
          Fax: 732-203-1690   866-662-5475
          sales@monalisachocolate.com
                    www.monalisachocolate.com
Gourmet chocolates, hard chewable candies and gums. All Mona Lisa®
President/CEO/COB/Dir Int'l Development: James Sarkesian
VP/Gen Corporate Council/Treasurer/CFO: Sean Kidd Esq
General Corporate Council/Board/R&D: Martin Pedata Esq
R&D/QC: James Sarkesian
Quality Control: Martin Pedata
VP/Int'l Sales/Marketing Communications: Scott Bricker
Operations/R&D/QC/Production/Plant Mgr: Ken Mushinskie
Production: James Sankesian
Plant Manager: James Sankesian
Purchasing Director: Sean Kidd Esq
Estimated Sales: $500,000
Number Employees: 1-2
Number of Brands: 1
Number of Products: 22
Sq. footage: 45000
Type of Packaging: Consumer, Private Label
Brands:
CHOCOLATES/MONA LISA®
CHOCOLATIER/MONA LISA®
MONA LISA®

9616 Monaco Baking Company
14700 Marquardt Ave
Santa Fe Springs, CA 90670-5125   562-906-8683
          Fax: 562-906-1823   800-569-4640
          info@monacobaking.com
                    www.monacobaking.com
Manufacturer of gingerbread and shortbread cookies, shortbread and gingerbread cookie mixes.
Sales/Marketing: Philip Moreau

Estimated Sales:$ 20 - 50 Million
Number Employees: 20-49

9617 Monarch Beverage Company
1123 Zonolite Rd NE # 10
Atlanta, GA 30306-2019   404-262-4040
    Fax: 404-262-4001 800-241-3732
        info@monarchbeverages.com
        www.monarchbeverages.com
Manufacturer and exporter of concentrates including
sports and energy drinks, healthy fruit beverages,
enhanced waters, ready-to-drink beverages,
ready-to-drink coffees and soft drinks
    COO: Kevin McClanahan
    CEO: Jacques Bombal
    VP Sales: Bill Lowler
    Business & Procedure Manager: Amy Whitehead
Estimated Sales:$3.2 Million
Number Employees: 20-49
Type of Packaging: Bulk
Brands:
    ACUTE FRUIT™
    AMERICAN COLA®
    COMOTION™
    KICKAPOO JOY JUICE®
    NTRINSIC™
    PLANET COLA®
    REAKTOR®
    RUSH! ENERGY™

9618 Monarch Seafoods
515 Kalihi St
Honolulu, HI 96819-3268   808-841-7877
                    Fax: 808-847-3930
Seafood and seafood products
    President: Thomas Mukaigawa
Estimated Sales:$ .5 - 1 million
Number Employees: 10-19

9619 Mondial Foods Company
P.O.Box 75036
Los Angeles, CA 90075-0036   213-383-3531
Processor and exporter of pineapple and other tropi-
cal juices
    President: Ben Gattegno
Estimated Sales:$210000
Number Employees: 20-49
Type of Packaging: Food Service, Bulk

9620 Mondiv/Division of Lassonde Inc
3810 Alfred Laliberte
Boisbriand, QC J7H 1P8   450-979-0717
    Fax: 450-979-0279 infomondiv@mondiv.vom
                    www.mondiv.vom
tapenades, bruschetta, glass jar gravy, specialty
sauces and dips, glass jar soups and stews,
meat-based pasta sauce, pasta sauce (non-meat), organic pasta sauces, organic glass jar soups, glass jar
(ready-to-serve)meals, pestos andchutneys
    President/Owner: Vito Monopoli

9621 Mondo Baking Company
452 Old Lindale Rd SE
Rome, GA 30161-6947   706-291-8439
    Fax: 706-295-7312 www.kelloggs.com
Bakery products
    President: A D David Mackay
    Manager: Bob Reed
    VP Sales: Jim Owens
Estimated Sales:$ 100-500 Million
Number Employees: 500-999

9622 Money's Mushrooms
#800-1500 W Georgia Street
Vancouver, BC V6G 2Z6
Canada   604-669-3741
    Fax: 604-669-9732 info@moneys.com
                    www.calbur.com
Processor, grower and exporter of canned and pick-
led mushrooms
    President: Keith Potter
    CFO: Cliff Lillicrop
    VP Sales/Marketing: Dean Fleming
Number Employees: 900

Type of Packaging: Consumer, Food Service, Private Label, Bulk
Brands:
    Moneys

9623 Money's Mushrooms
5335-272nd Street
Langley, BC VAW 1P1
Canada   604-857-0477
    Fax: 604-857-0467 800-661-8623
        info@moneys.com www.moneys.com
Processor of mushrooms - fresh or chilled.
    General Manager: Mike Manion
Number Employees: 500-999
Other Locations:
    Money's Mushrooms Ltd.
    Avondale PA

9624 Mongolia Casing Corporation
4706 Grand Ave
Flushing, NY 11378-3007   718-628-3800
    Fax: 718-628-5800 800-221-4887
        casings@worldcasing.com
        www.worldcasing.com
Processor of natural sausage casings
    President: Steven Feinstein
    Controller: Richard Schwartz
    Sales (Midwest Region): Allen Ross
Estimated Sales:$2500000
Number Employees: 20-49

9625 Monin
2100 Range Rd
Clearwater, FL 33765-2125   727-461-3033
    Fax: 727-461-3033 800-966-5225
        monin-usa@monin.com www.monin.com
Processor and exporter of syrups.
    President: Olivier Monin
    CEO: Bill Lombardo
Estimated Sales:$14000000
Number Employees: 50-99
Sq. footage: 32200
Parent Co: George Monin S.A.
Type of Packaging: Consumer, Food Service, Pri-
vate Label, Bulk
Brands:
    Monin

9626 Monini North America
37 North Ave # 201
Norwalk, CT 06851-3827   203-750-0531
    Fax: 203-750-0661 moniniusa@snet.net
                    www.monini.com
Oils
    Chairman: Marco Petrini
*Estimated Sales:*Less than $200,000
Number Employees: 1-4
Type of Packaging: Private Label
Brands:
    Amabile Umbro
    GranFruttato
    Ii Monello
    Il Poggiolo
    Monini

9627 Monk's Bread
P.O.Box 611
Victor, NY 14564-0611   585-243-0660
                    Fax: 585-243-4816
Bread

9628 Monogramme Confections
10630 Midwest Industrial Blvd
St Louis, MO 63132-1221   314-427-4099
    Fax: 314-427-6646 www.ficoninc.com
Confectioneries
    Owner: Charlie Hirschi
Estimated Sales:$ 1-2.5 Million
Number Employees: 5-9

9629 Monroe Cheese Corporation
PO Box 260
Monroe, WI 53566-0260   608-325-5161
                    Fax: 608-325-5168
Cheese
    President: David Rufenacht
    Marketing Director: Dan Pickett
Estimated Sales:$ 50-100 Million
Number Employees: 3

9630 Monsour's
508 N Broadway St
Pittsburg, KS 66762-3920   620-232-7600

Wholesaler/distributor of frozen food, general line
products, health foods, produce, provisions/meats,
etc.; serving the food service market
    Owner: Linda Rybnick
Estimated Sales:$300,000-500,000
Number Employees: 1-4

9631 Monster Cone
8500 Delmeade
Montreal, QC H4T 1L6
Canada   541-636-2022
    Fax: 514-342-0346 800-542-9801
        info@monstercone.com www.monstercone.com
Processor and exporter of waffle bowls and cones
including plain and chocolate dipped
    President: Daniel Mardinger
Number Employees: 50-99
Sq. footage: 20000
Type of Packaging: Consumer, Food Service, Pri-
vate Label, Bulk
Brands:
    MONSTER CONE

9632 Mont Blanc Gourmet
2925 E Colfax Avenue
Denver, CO 80206   303-755-1100
    Fax: 303-283-1100 800-877-3811
        info@montblancgourmet.com
        www.montblancgourmet.com
Processor of chocolate syrup, cocoa powders, chai
mixes, cappuccino, mocha mixes, and powdered hot
cocoa mix. Flavoring: chocolate, white chocolate,
caramel, kahlua
    President: Michael Szyliowicz
    CEO: Irene Szyliowicz
Estimated Sales:$1-$3 Million
Number Employees: 8
Brands:
    Mont Blanc Chocolate Syrups
    Mont Blanc Gourmet H

9633 Montage Foods
885 Providence Rd
Scranton, PA 18508-2558   570-347-2400
    Fax: 570-347-4123 800-521-8325
        www.advance-food.com
Processor of portion-controlled and frozen veal and
lamb
    President: Marv Herman
    Quality Control Manager: Debra Webber
    Operations Manager: Murray Glick
Estimated Sales:$ 50-100 Million
Number Employees: 100-249
Parent Co: Advance Food Compnay Enid, OK
Type of Packaging: Consumer, Food Service, Pri-
vate Label
Brands:
    It's the Veal Thing

9634 Montana Bakery
26 Market Street
Stamford, CT 06902-5834   203-969-7700
                    Fax: 203-969-7440
Baked goods
    President: Gary Zaretsky
    Vice President: Scott Kulkin
Estimated Sales:$ 5-10 Million
Number Employees: 50

9635 (HQ)Montana Coffee Traders
5810 Us Highway 93 S
Whitefish, MT 59937-8414   406-862-7633
    Fax: 406-862-7680 800-345-5282
        traders@coffeetraders.com
        www.coffeetraders.com
Fresh roasted coffee
    Owner: R C Beal
Estimated Sales:$ 20-50 Million
Number Employees: 50-99

9636 Montana Flour & Grain
P.O.Box 517
Fort Benton, MT 59442-0517   406-622-5436
    Fax: 406-622-5439 info@montanaflour.com
        www.montanaflour.com
Manufactures flour and other grain mill products
specializing in organic flours
    President: Andre Giles
*Estimated Sales:*Below $ 5 Million
Number Employees: 10-19
Number of Brands: 3
Number of Products: 15
Type of Packaging: Food Service, Private Label,
Bulk

9637 Montana Legacy Premium Ostrich Products
2105 Central Avenue
Suite 100
Billings, MT 59102-4776   406-656-6444
Fax: 406-656-5077 ostrich@wtp.net
Ostrich products
Owner: David Casagrande
Manager: Clay Watson
Public Relations: Connie Hayes
Estimated Sales: Under $500,000
Number Employees: 5-9

9638 Montana Mountain SmokedFish
10 Elkhorn View Dr
Montana City, MT 59634-9704   406-449-4755
Fax: 406-449-4755 800-649-2959
smkfishqueen@aol.com
www.mysmokedfish.com
Processor of smoked salmon, sockeye salmon, keta salmon, rainbow trout, halibut and salmon spread. All natural, no preservatives
President: Kim Waltee
Estimated Sales: Less than $500,000
Number Employees: 1-4
Type of Packaging: Private Label

9639 Montana Naturals by HealthRite
2307 Morning Star Drive
Park City, UT 84060-6725   406-726-3214
Fax: 406-726-3287 800-872-7218
sales@mtnaturals.com www.mtnaturals.com
Processor and exporter of dietary supplements
General Manager: Sterling Gabbitas
Number Employees: 50-99
Sq. footage: 26000
Parent Co: HealthRite
Type of Packaging: Consumer, Private Label
Other Locations:
Montana Naturals by HealthRit
Arlee MT
Brands:
Pure Energy

9640 Montana Ranch Brand
PO Box 2036
Billings, MT 59103   406-294-2333
Fax: 406-294-2336 www.montanaranchbrand.com
natural piedmontese beef, ranch beef, pioneer pork, prairie lamb, and heritage bison
President/Owner: Ralph Peterson
Number Employees: 3

9641 Montana Soup Company
PO Box 971
Whitefish, MT 59937-0971   406-862-7686
Fax: 406-862-7686 800-862-7687
Soup and soup ingredients
President: Ann Nickerson

9642 Montana Specialty Mills
300 3rd Ave S
Great Falls, MT 59405-1811   406-761-2338
Fax: 406-761-7926
gordon@mtspecialtymills.com
www.mtspecialtymills.com
Primary agricultural processor providing contracting, origination, storage and processing of grain and oilseed-based products to secondary food manufacturers
President: Steve Chambers
Merchandising Manager: Gordon Svenby
Operations: Robert Bender
Estimated Sales: Below $ 5 Million
Number Employees: 20-49
Sq. footage: 20000

9643 Montana Tea & Spice Trading
P.O.Box 8082
Missoula, MT 59807-8082   406-721-4882
Fax: 406-543-1126 montanatea@msn.com
www.montanatea.com
Tea and herbal tea blending, spice blending. Wholesale, retial and mail order
Owner: Sherri Lee
Estimated Sales: $5 Million
Number Employees: 5-9
Number of Brands: 2
Number of Products: 300+
Sq. footage: 4300

9644 Montchevre
916 Silver Spur Rd # 302
Rolling Hls Ests, CA 90274-3828   310-544-0450
Fax: 310-544-1560 info@montchevre.com
www.montchevre.com
Goat cheese
Owner: Arnaud Solandt
Estimated Sales: $ 1 - 3 Million
Number Employees: 5-9

9645 Monte Cristo Trading
14 Harwood Ct
Scarsdale, NY 10583-4121   914-725-8025
Fax: 914-725-0869
General grocery
President: Anton Derosa
Estimated Sales: $530,000
Number Employees: 1-4
Type of Packaging: Consumer, Food Service, Bulk

9646 Monte Vista Farming Company
5043 N Montpelier Rd
Denair, CA 95316-9608   209-874-1866
Fax: 209-874-2024
sales@montevistafarming.com
www.montevistafarming.com
Processor and exporter of almonds
Owner: Jim Crecelius
Marketing Director: Dan Whisenhunt
Estimated Sales: $40,000,000
Number Employees: 50-99

9647 Montebello Brands
1919 Willow Spring Rd
Baltimore, MD 21222-2939   410-282-8800
Fax: 410-282-8809
Processor and exporter of whiskey
President: Leo Conte
Estimated Sales: $24 Million
Number Employees: 20-49
Type of Packaging: Consumer, Food Service

9648 Montebello Kitchens
PO Box 610
Gordonsville, VA 22942   800-743-7687
Fax: 270-209-1371 www.montebellokitchens.com
Spices and rubs, dressing and marinades, sauces, virginia peanuts, coups and milled grains.
President/Owner: Steven Lynch

9649 Montelle Winery
P.O.Box 147
Augusta, MO 63332-0147   636-228-4464
Fax: 636-228-4754 888-595-9463
mervine@fednet.com www.montelle.com
In the late 1960s and early 1970s, a few pioneering souls began to refurbish the old vineyards and winery buildings of Missouri's premier wine-growing regions. One of these pioneers was Clayton Byers, who founded Montelle Vineyards in1970.
Owner: Tony Kooyumjian
Founder: Clayton Byers
Estimated Sales: $ 1-2.5 Million
Number Employees: 1-4
Number of Products: 15

9650 Montello
6106 E 32nd Pl # 100
Tulsa, OK 74135-5495   918-665-1170
Fax: 918-665-1480 800-331-4628
oncall@montelloinc.com www.montelloinc.com
Importer and distributor of emulsifiers and gums
President: Allen Johnson
Estimated Sales: $5,000,000
Number Employees: 5-9

9651 Monterey Fish Company
1222 Merrill St
Salinas, CA 93901-4481   831-755-1923
Fax: 831-775-0156 mntyfish@redshift.com
www.montereyfishcompany.com
Processor of canned and frozen herring, anchovies, herring roe, mackerel, sardines and squid
President: Carmelo J Trinqali
VP: Sal Trinquali
VP Operations: Anthony Trinqali
Plant Manager: Joseph Tringali
Estimated Sales: $1-$2.5 Million
Number Employees: 1-4
Type of Packaging: Consumer, Food Service, Private Label
Brands:
Bono
Seawave

9652 Monterey Mushrooms
260 Westgate Dr
Watsonville, CA 95076-2452   831-763-5300
Fax: 831-763-0700
custserv@mushroomcanning.com
www.montereymushrooms.com
Manufacturer and exporter of canned, frozen and re-frigerated mushroom stems/pieces, slices and buttons
Division Manager: Chris De Gruchy
CEO: Shah Kazmi
Sales Manager: George Temple
Estimated Sales: $100 Million
Number Employees: 1,000-4,999
Sq. footage: 23000
Type of Packaging: Consumer, Food Service, Private Label, Bulk
Other Locations:
Multi Site Fresh Operation Farms
Orlando FL
Multi Site Fresh Operation Farms
Princeton IL
Multi Site Fresh Operation Farms
Royal Oaks CA
Multi Site Fresh Operation Farms
Las Lomas CA
Multi Site Fresh Operation Farms
Morgan Hill CA
Multi Site Fresh Operation Farms
San Miguel, Mexico
Multi Site Fresh Operation Farms
Vancouver, BC Canada
Multi Site Fresh Operation Farms
Arroyo Grande CA
Multi Site Fresh Operation Farms
Madisonville TX
Multi Site Fresh Operation Farms
Loudon TX
Multi Site Fresh Operation Farms
Temple PA
Monterey Processing Facility
Bonne Terre MO
Monterey Product Development
Royal Oaks CA
Brands:
CLEAN N READY
MT LAUREL

9653 (HQ)Monterey Mushrooms
260 Westgate Dr
Watsonville, CA 95076-2452   831-763-5300
Fax: 831-763-0700 800-333-6874
www.montereymushrooms.com
Processor and packer of fresh, frozen and canned mushrooms including shiitake, enoki and oyster
President/CEO: Shah Kazemi
CFO: Ray Selle
CEO: Shah Kazmi
VP Marketing: Joe Cadwell
Estimated Sales: I
Number Employees: 1,000-4,999
Type of Packaging: Food Service
Brands:
Wild Pack

9654 Monterey Mushrooms
P.O.Box 250
Bonne Terre, MO 63628-0250   573-358-3381
Fax: 573-358-2209 800-333-6874
corpmarketing@montmush.com
www.montereymushrooms.com
Processor of small and medium mushrooms including canned, glass-packed, marinated, stemmed, pieced, whole and sliced
President: Shah Kazemi
CFO: Ray Selle
VP Marketing: Carl Fields
Plant Manager: Carl Bennett
Estimated Sales: $7900000
Number Employees: 50-99
Parent Co: Monterey Mushrooms

9655 Monterey Mushrooms Inc.
1108 Beaumont Ave
Temple, PA 19560-1603   610-929-1961
Fax: 610-929-3288 800-763-0700
corpmarketing@montmush.com
www.montereymushrooms.com
Processed mushrooms
Manager: Bruce Debuc
Vice President: Joe Caldwell
VP Sales: Jim Burt
Plant Manager: Terry Schadler
Estimated Sales: $ 2.5-5 Million
Number Employees: 100-249

Brands:
Baby Bella
Clean N Readyo

9656 Monterey Vineyard
800 S Alta Street
Gonzales, CA 93926-9501   831-675-4000
Fax: 831-675-4019
Wines
General Manager/President: Ken Greene
Operations Manager: Ken Greene
Winemaker: Chris Mallar
Production Manager: Noel Vofter
Estimated Sales: Less than $500,000
Number Employees: 5-9

9657 Monterrey Products Company
803 S Zarzamora St
San Antonio, TX 78207-5363   210-435-2872
Fax: 210-435-2877 www.monterreyproducts.com
Manufacturer of Mexican products including mole sauce, candy, spices, chili powder and dry chili mixes
President/Owner: Ernesto De Los Santos
Estimated Sales: $10-20 Million
Number Employees: 10-19
Type of Packaging: Consumer, Food Service

9658 Monterrey Products Company
803 S Zarzamora St
San Antonio, TX 78207-5363   210-435-2872
Fax: 210-435-2877 800-872-1652
www.monterreyproducts.com
Spices, salsa and praline candies
President: Ernest De Los Santos
Estimated Sales: Below $ 5 Million
Number Employees: 10-19
Brands:
Monterrey

9659 Monterrey Provisions
5235 Lovelock St
San Diego, CA 92110-4012   619-294-2222
Fax: 619-294-2220 800-201-1600
information@monprov.com www.monprov.com
Cheese
President: Dick Herrman
Estimated Sales: $ 50-100 Million
Number Employees: 50-99
Brands:
Dietz & Watson
Farmland
Jennie-O
Poorebrothers
Schrieber

9660 Montevina Winery
P.O.Box 100
Plymouth, CA 95669-0100   209-245-6942
Fax: 209-245-6617 cmkenna@tfewines.com
www.montevina.com
Wine
CEO: Louis Trinchero
VP: Jeff Meyers
Estimated Sales: $ 2.5-5 Million
Number Employees: 10-19

9661 Monticello Canning Company
126 Sunset Dr
Crossville, TN 38555-5113   931-484-3696
Fax: 931-484-2095
Manufacturer of canned vegetables including sweet red and green peppers, pimientos, etc
President: Earl Dean
Estimated Sales: $ 3 - 5 Million
Number Employees: 5-10
Type of Packaging: Consumer, Food Service, Private Label, Bulk
Brands:
Betty Ann

9662 Monticello Canning Company
126 Sunset Dr
Crossville, TN 38555-5113   931-484-3696
Fax: 931-484-2095
Peppers, pimentos
President: Earl Dean
COO: Greg Barnwell
Estimated Sales: Below $ 5 Million
Number Employees: 20

9663 Monticello Cellars
4242 Big Ranch Rd
Napa, CA 94558-1396   707-253-2802
Fax: 707-253-1019
Wine@CorleyFamilyNapaValley.com
www.corleyfamilynapavalley.com
Processor of wine and champagne
President: Kevin Corley
Chairman: Jay Corley
Marketing: Stephen Corley
Sales: Stephen Corley
Estimated Sales: $1,300,000
Number Employees: 10-19
Type of Packaging: Consumer

9664 Montione's Biscotti & Baked Goods
123 Union Street
Mansfield, MA 02048-2418   508-285-7004
Fax: 508-695-4471 800-559-1010
mmbiscotti@verizon.net
Baked goods, biscotti
President: Mary Montione
CFO: Dan Mahoney
Estimated Sales: $1 Million
Number Employees: 5-9
Type of Packaging: Private Label

9665 Montmorenci Vineyards
2989 Charleston Hwy
Aiken, SC 29801-8193   803-649-4870
Fax: 803-642-1834 vinonut@aol.com
www.montmorencivineyards.com
Wine
Owner/Winemaker: Robert Scott
Owner: Elaine Scott
General Manager: Stephanie Scott
Operation Manager: Elaine Scott
Estimated Sales: $500,000-$1 Million
Number Employees: 1-4
Type of Packaging: Private Label
Brands:
Blanc du Bois
Chambourcin
De Caradeuc White
Melody
Savannah White
Vin Eclipser

9666 Montreal Chop Suey Company
2100 Moreau Street
Montreal, QC H1W 2M3
Canada   514-522-3134
Fax: 514-522-8074
Processor of Chinese food products including fresh bean and alfalfa sprouts, egg roll and wonton paste, fresh fried noodles and canned bean sprouts
President: Bill Lee
Vice President: David Lee
VP: Robert Lee
Sales Director: John Zielinski
Production Manager: Marc Comtols
Number Employees: 30
Sq. footage: 46000
Type of Packaging: Consumer, Bulk
Brands:
MONTREAL CHOP SUEY

9667 Montrose Potato Growers
PO Box 65
Montrose, CO 81402-0065   970-249-5623
Fax: 970-249-0426
Processor of yellow and Spanish onions and dry pinto beans
President: Herb George
Estimated Sales: $ 1 - 3 Million
Number Employees: 5-9
Type of Packaging: Private Label
Brands:
Colorancho
Out West

9668 Monument Dairy Farms
2107 James Road
Weybridge, VT 05753-9525   802-545-2119
Fax: 802-545-2117
Milk products
Co-Owner: Jon Rooney
Co-Owner: James Rooney
Estimated Sales: $ 10-24.9 Million
Number Employees: 30
Brands:
Monument Dairy Farms

9669 Monument Farms
2107 James Rd
Middlebury, VT 05753-9525   802-545-2119
Fax: 802-545-2117
Milk processor
Manager: Millicent Rooney
Plant Manager: Jonathan Rooney
Estimated Sales: Below $ 5 Million
Number Employees: 20-49
Type of Packaging: Private Label

9670 Moo & Oink
7158 S Stony Island Ave
Chicago, IL 60649-2397   773-493-2755
Fax: 773-493-2042 info@moo-oink.com
www.moo-oink.com
Processor of ready to cook chitterlings, beef and pork hot links; importer of spare ribs.
President: Barry Levy
Vice President: Barry Lezak
Sales Representative: Harvey Lezak
Sales Representative: Wayne McGill
Estimated Sales: $ 20 - 50 Million
Number Employees: 50-99
Sq. footage: 20000

9671 (HQ)Moody Dunbar
P.O.Box 6048
Johnson City, TN 37602-6048   423-952-0100
Fax: 423-952-0289 800-251-8202
esimerly@moodydunbar.com
America's leading manufacturer of bell peppers, flame-roasted peppers and pimientos. From 2 oz. jars to 10# cans and 55 gallon drums, Moody Dunbar offers green, red, and yellow bell peppers in a variety of cuts and styles. Also aleading manufacturer of sweet potatoes and yams.
President/CEO: Stanley Dunbar
CFO: Christy Dunbar
Vice President: Ed Simerly
R&D/Quality Control: Dave Adkins
Marketing: Ed Simerly
Sales: Terri Sams
Public Relations: Tony Treadway
Plant Manager: Ron Austin
Estimated Sales: $ 10 - 20 Million
Number Employees: 20-49
Type of Packaging: Consumer, Food Service
Other Locations:
Saticoy Foods
Santa Paula CA
Brands:
Dromedary
Dunbars
O-Sage
Sunshine

9672 Moody Dunbar
3202 Highway 107
Chuckey, TN 37641-2327   423-257-4712
Fax: 423-952-0289 800-251-8202
Peppers, pimientos
Owner: Stanley Dunbar
President: Ed Simerly
Quality Control: Diva Ajins
R & D: Dawan Dunbar
VP Sales: Ed Simerly
Estimated Sales: $ 10-20 Million
Number Employees: 1-4
Brands:
Cal-Sun
Cannon
Dixie
Dunbars
Nature's Pride

9673 Moon Enterprises
2-11720 Voyager Way
Richmond, BC V6X 3G9
Canada   604-270-0088
Fax: 604-270-8988 thomasleemoon@fido.ca
Processor and exporter of live lobsters, crabs, oysters and geoduck clams, prawn
President: Thomas Lee
Quality Control: Thomas Lee
Plant Manager: Thomas Lee
Number Employees: 10
Type of Packaging: Private Label

9674 Moon Shine Trading Company
1250 Harter Ave # A
Woodland, CA 95776-6106   530-668-0660
Fax: 530-668-6061 800-678-1226
mstco@moonshinetrading.com
www.moonshinetrading.com
Processor and exporter of gourmet chocolate and va-
nilla nut butters cremes, honey and honey products
including fruit spreads and honey straws, bee pollen,
bees wax, royal jelly and propolis; also, gift packs
  Owner: Ishai Zeldner
  Co-Owner: Ishai Zeldner
Estimated Sales: $ 3 - 5 Million
Number Employees: 1-4
Sq. footage: 4000
Type of Packaging: Consumer, Food Service, Pri-
  vate Label, Bulk
Brands:
  Chocolate & Vanilla Nut Spread
  Gourmet Butters & Spreads
  Gourmet Honey Collection
  Honey Fruit Spreads
  Honey In the Straw

9675 Moon's Seafood Company
2513 Woodfield Cir
Melbourne, FL 32904-6657   321-872-0431
Fax: 321-872-0434 800-526-5624
info@moonseafood.com www.moonseafood.com
Shrimp, scallops, clams and crabs
  President: Jay Moon
  Vice President: Rick Madrigal
Estimated Sales: $ 1 - 3 Million
Number Employees: 1-4
Brands:
  Moon's Seafood

9676 MoonLight Kitchen
400 College Sq # 461
Newark, DE 19711-5453   302-266-0558
Fax: 302-266-7810 www.officedepot.com
General grocery
  Manager: Tony Haan
  Public Relations: D Lynn Sinclair
Estimated Sales: Under $500,000
Number Employees: 5-9

9677 Mooney Farms
1220 Fortress St
Chico, CA 95973-9029   530-899-2661
Fax: 530-899-7746 mooneyfarm@aol.com
www.mooneyfarms.com
Processor and exporter of sun dried tomatoes, pesto,
BBQ marinade and tomatoe sauces.
  Partner/Sales: Mary Ellen Monney McConnell
  Partner/Production: Stephen Mooney
  National Sales Manager: Charles Passaro
Estimated Sales: $25,000,000
Number Employees: 50
Sq. footage: 100000
Type of Packaging: Consumer, Food Service, Pri-
  vate Label, Bulk
Brands:
  Bella Sun Luci
  Summer's Choice

9678 Mooney's Packing
7320 Creek Rd
Williamsfield, OH 44093-0135   440-293-7269
Fax: 440-293-7074
Manufacturer of beef and pork
  President: William Mooney
Estimated Sales: $25 Million
Number Employees: 5
Type of Packaging: Consumer, Bulk

9679 Moonlight Brewing Company
2218 Laughlin Road
Windsor, CA 95492-8213   707-528-2537
moonlightguy@comcast.net
www.moonlightbrewing.com
Manufacturer of beer
  President: Brian Hunt
Estimated Sales: $1-3 Million
Number Employees: 1-4
Brands:
  Death and Taxes Black Beer
  Full Moon Light Ale
  Moonlight Pale Lager
  Santa's Tipple
  Twist of Fate Bitter Ale

9680 Moonlite Bar BQ Inn
2840 W Parrish Ave
Owensboro, KY 42301-3312   270-684-8143
Fax: 270-684-8105 800-322-8989
pbosley@moonlite.com www.moonlite.com
Processor of barbecue meats including mutton, pork
and beef; also, bean soup, sauces and chili
  President: Fred Bosley
  VP: Ken Bosley
  Marketing Director: Pat Bosley
  Sales Director: Jim Stroble
  Purchasing Manager: Tracy Philips
Estimated Sales: $ 5 - 10 Million
Number Employees: 100-249
Number of Brands: 1
Number of Products: 48
Parent Co: Wholesale Foods
Type of Packaging: Private Label
Brands:
  Moonlite Bbq Inn

9681 Moore's Candies
3004 Pinewood Ave
Baltimore, MD 21214-1424   410-426-2705
Fax: 410-426-7073
www.moorescandiesmaryland.com
Manufacturer of handcrafted chocolates and candy
including truffles, almond crunch, chocolate-covered
potato chips and pretzels, holiday and wedding
chocolate items and specialty items
  Co-Owner: Jim Heyl Jr
  Co-Owner: Lois Heyl
  VP: Dana Heyl
Estimated Sales: $3 Million
Number Employees: 5-9
Sq. footage: 1250
Type of Packaging: Consumer, Food Service, Pri-
  vate Label, Bulk
Brands:
  MOORES

9682 Mooresville Ice Cream Company
P.O.Box 118
Mooresville, NC 28115-0118   704-664-5456
Fax: 704-663-7829
Manufacturer of ice cream and novelties including
chocolate covered bars, ice cream sandwiches, etc.
  President: Gene Millsaps
Estimated Sales: $5-10 Million
Number Employees: 10-19
Type of Packaging: Consumer, Food Service, Bulk
Brands:
  BIG SCOOP
  DELUXE

9683 Moorhead & Company
PO Box 1850
Loomis, CA 95650-1850   323-873-6640
Fax: 818-787-2010 877-290-2427
mail@moorhead-agar.com
www.moorhead-agar.com
Manufacturer and importer of stabilizers including
agar
  President: Deborah Nichols
  Sales/Marketing: Brenda Franklin
Estimated Sales: $180000
Number Employees: 3
Type of Packaging: Bulk
Brands:
  Agarich
  Agarloid
  Agarmoor

9684 Moosehead Breweries
89 Main Street W
St. John, NB E2K 1H2
Canada   506-635-7000
Fax: 506-635-7029 www.moosehead.ca
Processor and exporter of beer
  Owner/President: Derek Oland
  VP Production: Peter Hennebarry
  Purchasing Agent: Richard Osetchook
Number Employees: 250-499
Type of Packaging: Consumer, Food Service
Brands:
  MOOSEHEAD LAGER

9685 Moosewood Hollow LLC
PO Box 470
Plainfield, VT 05667-0470   802-479-7999
Fax: 802-479-7264 866-463-8733
info@moosewoodhollow.com
www.moosewoodhollow.com
Infused mayple syrup & oat biscotti
  President: Claudia Clark
Estimated Sales: $ 1 - 3 Million
Number Employees: 1-4
Type of Packaging: Consumer

9686 Mootz Candy
220 S Centre St
Pottsville, PA 17901-3501   570-622-4480
Fax: 570-622-1933 mootzweb@dsnow.com
www.mootzcandies.com
Processor of confectionery products including choc-
olate coated creams, caramels and nuts, chocolate
and chocolate chunks
  President: Ned Buckley
  General Manager: Janes Haas
Estimated Sales: $ 3 - 5 Million
Number Employees: 10-19
Type of Packaging: Consumer, Private Label

9687 Morabito Baking Company
757 Kohn St
Norristown, PA 19401-3739   610-275-5419
Fax: 610-275-0358 800-525-7747
www.morabito.com
Manufacturer of specialty breads, bagels and rolls;
wholesaler/distributor of fresh and frozen bakery
products; serving the food service and retail markets
  President/CEO: Michael Morabito Jr
  VP: Michael Angelo Morabito III
Estimated Sales: $10 Million
Number Employees: 100-249
Type of Packaging: Consumer, Food Service, Pri-
  vate Label, Bulk
Brands:
  MORABITO

9688 Moran Coffee Company
P.O.Box 355
Dublin, OH 43017-0355   614-889-2500
Fax: 614-889-6500
Coffee
  President: Thomas Moran
Estimated Sales: $ 5-10 Million
Number Employees: 1-4

9689 Moravian Cookies Shop
224 S Cherry St
Winston Salem, NC 27101-5231   336-748-0230
Fax: 336-748-0501 800-274-2994
sales@salembaking.com
www.moraviancookie.com
Cookies and baked goods
  Operations Manager: Vincent Pellegrino
Number Employees: 10-19

9690 More Than Gourmet
929 Home Ave
Akron, OH 44310   330-762-6652
Fax: 330-762-4832 800-860-9385
info@morethangourmet.com
www.morethangourmet.com
French sauces and stocks.
  President/Owner: Bill Finnegan
  CEO: Bradley Sacks
  VP: Harvey Leff
Estimated Sales: $1.6 Million
Number Employees: 24

9691 More Than Gourmet
929 Home Ave
Akron, OH 44310-4107   330-762-6652
Fax: 330-762-4832 800-860-9385
info@morethangourmet.com
www.morethangourmet.com
Processor of stocks and sauces
  Owner: Brad Sacks
  CFO: Scott Bonnette
Estimated Sales: $500,000-$1 Million
Number Employees: 20-49
Type of Packaging: Consumer, Food Service
Brands:
  Demi-Glace Veal Gold
  Glace De Poulet Gold
  Veggie Glace Gold

9692 Morehouse Foods
760 Epperson Dr
City of Industry, CA 91748-1336   626-854-1655
Fax: 626-854-1656 info@morehousefoods.com
www.morehousefoods.com
Processor, importer and exporter of mustard, horse-
radish and vinegar
  President: David Latter

Estimated Sales: $ 20 - 50 Million
Number Employees: 50-99
Sq. footage: 80000
Type of Packaging: Consumer, Food Service, Private Label, Bulk
Brands:
Chalif
El Rey
Morehouse
Redwood Empire
Rhinegeld

9693 Moresco Vineyards
16865 E Gawne Road
Stockton, CA 95215-9646   209-467-3081
Wine
General Manager: Mark Moresco

9694 Moretti's Poultry
2124 Tremont Ctr
Columbus, OH 43221-3110   614-486-2333
Fax: 614-486-2333 www.morettisofarlington.com
Processor of fresh chicken and turkey
Owner: Tim Moretti
Estimated Sales: $ 1 - 3 Million
Number Employees: 20-49
Type of Packaging: Food Service, Bulk

9695 Morey's Seafood International
1218 Highway 10 S
Motley, MN 56466-8209   218-352-6345
Fax: 218-352-6523 www.moreysmarkets.com
Processor, importer and exporter of fresh and frozen fish including marinated salmon, marinated tilapia and marinated smoked fish as well as many other specialty products.
President: Lynn Girouard
CEO: Dieter Pape
CFO: Gary Ziolkowski
VP/COO: Loren Morey
Marketing Director: Michelle Pape
Sales Director: Brian Augustin
Operations Manager: Robert Thiede
Plant Manager: Patti Zahler
Purchasing Manager: Greg Frank
Estimated Sales: $ 20 - 50 Million
Number Employees: 50-99
Sq. footage: 52000
Parent Co: Morey's Seafood International
Brands:
Morey's

9696 Morgan Food
90 W Morgan St
Austin, IN 47102-1741   812-794-1170
Fax: 812-794-1211   888-430-1780
mfi-web@morganfoods.com
www.morganfoods.com
Manufacturer and exporter of canned foods including condensed soups, baked and refried beans, gravies, condiments and sauces
Chairman/CEO: John Morgan
VP/CFO: Daniel Slattery
VP Marketing: Paul McCaig
Estimated Sales: $50-100 Million
Number Employees: 250-499
Type of Packaging: Consumer, Food Service, Private Label
Brands:
American Beauty
Royal Gem
Scott Country

9697 Morgan Mill
P.O.Box 525
Cherokee, NC 28719-0525   828-497-9227
Fax: 828-497-4330
Rainbow trout
Owner: Dale Owen
Estimated Sales: Less than $200,000
Number Employees: 1-4

9698 Morgan Specialties
1800 S Main Street
Paris, IL 61944-2945   217-465-8577
Fax: 217-463-2844
Lipid-based ingredients
Estimated Sales: $ 10-20 Million
Number Employees: 50-99

9699 Morgan Winery
590 Brunken Ave # C
Salinas, CA 93901-4355   831-751-7777
Fax: 831-751-7780 www.morganwinery.com

Processor and exporter of wine including chardonnay and sauvignon blanc
President: Daniel Lee
Estimated Sales: $850000
Number Employees: 5-9

9700 Morinaga Nutritional Foods
2441 W 205th St # C102
Torrance, CA 90501-1463   310-787-0200
Fax: 310-787-2727 info@morinu.com
www.morinu.com
Processor of aseptically packaged shelf-stable tofu, soy soups, soy smoothies
President: Yasuo Kumoda
Executive VP: Kingi Aoyana
Marketing Director: Susan Bucher
Director Sales: Avis Noble
Estimated Sales: $ 3 - 5 Million
Number Employees: 10-19
Sq. footage: 5000
Parent Co: Morinaga Milk Company
Type of Packaging: Consumer, Food Service, Private Label
Other Locations:
Morinaga Nutritional Foods
Tualatin OR
Brands:
Mori-Nu

9701 Mormac Corporation
P.O.Box 40
North Loup, NE 68859-0040   308-496-4782
Fax: 308-496-4786   800-445-2868
mormac@nctc.net   www.ngtubeholder.com
Processor of popcorn; distributor and exporter of popcorn, popcorn oils, salt and equipment
Manager: Pam Garnick
Vice President: Ted Kastler
Estimated Sales: $2512906
Number Employees: 10-19
Type of Packaging: Consumer, Food Service, Private Label, Bulk

9702 Morning Glory/Formost Farms
PO Box 111
Baraboo, WI 53913-0111   800-289-7787
Fax: 920-336-7165   800-362-9196
commdept@foremostfarms.com
www.foremostfarms.com
Processor of dairy products including fresh sour cream, milk; wholesaler/distributor of ice cream; serving the food service market
President/CEO: David Fuhrmann
General Manager: Jeff Koehler
Manager of Marketing/Sales: Donald Hoff
Manager: Don Mosher
Manager: Wally Heil
Number Employees: 100-249
Number of Products: 10
Parent Co: Foremost Farms USA
Type of Packaging: Consumer, Food Service, Private Label, Bulk
Brands:
Golden Guernsey
Morning Glory

9703 Morning Star Coffee
207 Carter Dr # E
West Chester, PA 19382-4506   610-701-7022
Fax: 610-701-7032   888-854-2233
robin.mars@morningstarcoffee.us
www.morningstarcoffee.us
Coffee roasting
President: Charles Streitwieser
Estimated Sales: $450,000
Number Employees: 5-9
Type of Packaging: Private Label, Bulk
Brands:
Morning Star
Numit

9704 Morning Star Foods
8 Joanna Court
East Brunswick, NJ 08816-2108   800-237-5320
Fax: 732-432-3928
Manufacturer and marketer of consumer packaged goods
President/CEO: Herman Graffinder
CFO: Craig Miller
Sr. VP Marketing: Toby Purdy
Sr. VP Operations: Samuel Hillin
Parent Co: Dean Foods Company
Type of Packaging: Private Label, Bulk

9705 Morning Star Foods
2036 S Hardy Drive
Tempe, AZ 85282-1211   480-966-0080
Fax: 480-966-9456
Aseptic coffee creamers
President: Tom Ernesto
Plant Manager: Ernesto Martinez
Estimated Sales: $ 20-50 Million
Number Employees: 50-99

9706 Morning Star Packing Company
13448 Volta Rd
Los Banos, CA 93635-9785   209-826-8000
Fax: 209-826-8266   kgashaw@morningstarco.com
www.morningstarco.com
Tomatoes and tomato paste
President: Chris Rufer
Quality Control: Tony Manuel
Executive: Ernie Sanchez
Estimated Sales: $ 50-100 Million
Number Employees: 100-249

9707 Morningland Dairy CheeseCompany
6248 County Road 2980
Mountain View, MO 65548-8186   417-469-3817
Fax: 417-469-5086
Processor of gourmet health and raw milk cheeses
President: James Reiners
Estimated Sales: $ 3 - 5 Million
Number Employees: 5-9
Type of Packaging: Consumer, Food Service, Private Label, Bulk
Brands:
Morningland Dairy
Ozark Hills

9708 (HQ)Morningstar Foods
2515 McKinney Ave # 1200
Dallas, TX 75201-1945   214-303-3400
Fax: 214-303-3499 www.deanfoods.com
Manufacturer and distributor of shelf-stable, refigerated and frozen specialty products
Chairman/CEO: Gregg Engles
EVP/COO: John Callahan
COO: Joseph Scalzo
Estimated Sales: K
Number Employees: 27,157
Parent Co: Dean Foods Company
Type of Packaging: Consumer, Food Service, Private Label, Bulk
Brands:
AFFAIR
FROSTIN PRIDE
JAKADA
MOCHA MIX
PASTRY PRIDE
SIGNATURE FLAVORS
TOPPING PRIDE

9709 Morningstar Foods
2515 McKinney Avenue
Suite 1200
Dallas, TX 75201-1945   225-273-2803
www.morningstarfoods.com
Processor and exporter of fresh and frozen nondairy and dairy coffee creamers, frozen nondairy whipped toppings and frozen cakes including cheese, mousse, ice cream and frozen yogurt; also, pancake and waffle batters
President: Miguel Calado
Chairman/CEO: Gregg Engles
Executive VP/Chief Financial Officer: Barry Fromberg
Number Employees: 26.000
Sq. footage: 120000
Type of Packaging: Consumer, Private Label
Other Locations:
Morning Star Foods
Santa Fe Springs CA
Brands:
Affair
Frostin Pride
Jakada
Mocha Mix
Pastry Pride
Signature Flavors By Mocha Mix
Topping Pride

9710 (HQ)Morningstar Foods
P.O.Box 218
Mt Crawford, VA 22841-0218   540-434-7328
Fax: 540-437-7314 www.deanfoods.com

Manufacturer of dairy products including milk and a complete line of UHT products
President/COO: Bing Graffunder
EVP/CFO: Barry Fromberg
Plant Manager: Dean Strobel
Estimated Sales: $100+ Million
Number Employees: 100-249
Sq. footage: 151000
Parent Co: Dean Foods
Type of Packaging: Consumer, Food Service, Private Label, Bulk
Other Locations:
Valley of Virginia Coop. Milk
Salem VA
Brands:
DAIRY FRESH
FOLGERS
HERSHEY'S MILK
JAKADA
MONTICELLO
SHENNANDOAH'S PRIDE
SILK
SUN SOY

9711 Morningstar Foods
299 5th Ave
Gustine, CA 95322-1202   209-854-6461
Fax: 209-854-6412 www.deanfoods.com
Processor and exporter of aerosol whipped cream
Manager: Richard Rosemire
Plant Engineer: Jeff Brock
Production Manager: Richard Rosemire
Plant Manager: Gary Veuve
Estimated Sales: $100+ Million
Number Employees: 100-249
Sq. footage: 125000
Parent Co: Dean Foods Comapny
Type of Packaging: Consumer, Food Service, Private Label

9712 Morningstar Foods
PO Box 657
Richland Center, WI 53581-2829   608-647-6360
Fax: 608-647-8203
Yogurt
President/CEO: Chris Policinski
Chairman: Pete Kappelman
SVP/CFO: Dan Knutson
VP/General Counsel: Peter Janzen
VP/Strategy & Business Development: Barry Wolfish
EVP/Land O'Lakes Purina Feed: Fernando Palacios
EVP/COO Dairy Foods Value-Added: Steve Dunphy
EVP/COO Dairy Foods Industrial: Alan Pierson
VP/Public Affairs: Jim Fife
VP/Human Resources: Karen Grabow
Estimated Sales: K
Number Employees: 50-99
Parent Co: Dean Food

9713 Moroni Feed Company
Pobox 228
West Liberty, IA 52776-0228   435-436-8221
Fax: 435-436-8101 norbest@norbest.com
www.norbest.com/a_moroni_feed.cfm
Processor of fresh and frozen turkeys
President: David Bailey
Estimated Sales: $ 125 Million +
Number Employees: 850
Type of Packaging: Private Label
Brands:
Norbest

9714 Morr-Ad Foodservice
920 Eha St
Wailuku, HI 96793-1426   808-877-2017
Fax: 808-270-9545
Purchasing Manager: Charles Nessel
Number Employees: 20-49

9715 Morre-Tec Industries
1 Gary Rd
Union, NJ 07083-5527   908-688-9009
Fax: 908-688-9005 sales@morretec.com
www.morretec.com
Manufacturer, importer and exporter of magnesium chloride, food grade and potassium bromate; importer and wholesaler/distributor of low sodium substitutes and licorice, spray, dried and powder
President: Leonard Glass
Marketing Director: Michael Fuchs
Operations Manager: Norm Cantoe

Estimated Sales: $ 10 - 20 Million
Number Employees: 10-19
Number of Products: 150
Sq. footage: 25000
Type of Packaging: Consumer, Bulk

9716 Morrione Vineyards
3865 Central Plank Road
Wetumpka, AL 36092-4008   334-567-9957
Wines
President: Tony Morrione
Brands:
Morrione

9717 Morris J. Golombeck
960 Franklin Ave
Brooklyn, NY 11225-2403   718-284-3505
Fax: 718-693-1941 golspice@aol.com
www.golombeckspice.com
Processor, importer and exporter of herbs and spices including basil, cassia, cayenne, garlic, ginger, paprika, etc
President: Hyman Golombeck
Estimated Sales: $ 5 - 10 Million
Number Employees: 10-19
Sq. footage: 120000
Type of Packaging: Bulk

9718 (HQ)Morris National
760 N McKeever Avenue
Azusa, CA 91702-2349   626-334-5114
Fax: 626-334-2577
Importer of specialty foods including gourmet cookies; processor of truffle-filled chocolates and hard candies; importer of specialty foods including gourmet cookies, candies, chocolates, preserves and teas
President: Gerry Morris
VP Operations: Coaute Douesson
Number Employees: 10-19
Sq. footage: 145000
Type of Packaging: Consumer
Brands:
McKeever & Danlee
Very Special Chocolates

9719 Morrison Farms
85824 519th Ave
Clearwater, NE 68726-5239   402-887-5335
Fax: 402-887-4709
morrison@nebraskapopcorn.com
www.morrisonfarms.com
High quality popcorn and dry, edible bean products
President: Frank Morrison
Estimated Sales: $300,000-500,000
Number Employees: 1-4

9720 Morrison Lamothe
2-5240 Finch Ave E
Scarborough
Toronto, ON MIS 5A2
Canada   416-291-6762
Fax: 416-291-5046
headoffice@morrisonlamothe.com
www.profilecanada.com/companydetail.cfm
Manufacturer of frozen prepared entrees, dinners and pot pies including beef, chicken, salisbury steak, macaroni and cheese, cabbage rolls, pasta, etc
Vice President: Ross Sythes
President And Ceo: J.M. Pigott
Estimated Sales: $45 Million
Number Employees: 75
Sq. footage: 38000
Parent Co: Morrison Lamothe
Type of Packaging: Consumer, Private Label
Brands:
CLIFFSIDE
HOLIDAY FARMS
PUB PIES
SAVARIN

9721 Morrison Meat Packers
738 NW 72nd St
Miami, FL 33150-3695   305-836-4461
Fax: 305-836-2750
Processor of ham
Owner: Eduardo Rodriguez
Estimated Sales: $ 20 - 50 Million
Number Employees: 50-99
Type of Packaging: Consumer

9722 Morrison Meat Pies
3403 S 1400 W # C
West Valley, UT 84119-4050   801-977-0181
Fax: 801-977-0448 sales@morrisonmeatpies.com
www.morrisonmeatpies.com
Processor of meat pies and frozen meat pie crust
Owner: Eugene Tafoya
Estimated Sales: $ 3 - 5 Million
Number Employees: 1-4
Type of Packaging: Consumer

9723 Morrison Milling Company
319 E Prairie St
Denton, TX 76201-6109   940-387-6111
Fax: 940-566-5992 800-580-5487
humanresources@morrisonmilling.com
www.morrisonmilling.com
Flour, processed corn, cornmeal, frosting mixes, soups, and gravies
President: Clifton Shoemaker
Chairman: Harry Crumpacker
Treasurer: Rudy Moreno
CEO: Cliff Shoemake
Quality Control: Kenny Newton
Operations Manager: Roger Biete
Purchasing Manager: David Hopkins
Estimated Sales: $ 20-50 Million
Number Employees: 100-249
Type of Packaging: Private Label
Brands:
Morrison Brand

9724 Morrisons Pastries/TurfCheesecake
47 Halstead Avenue
Suite 204
Harrison, NY 10528-4142   914-835-6629
Fax: 914-835-6793 turfcc.com@aol.com
www.turfcc.com
Cheesecake, yogurt and baked goods
Brands:
Baby Watson
Grandpa Morrisons
New York's Turf

9725 Morristown
PO Box 448
Morristown, IN 46161-0448   765-763-6327
Fax: 765-763-7132
Seafood
President: Jim Washburn

9726 Morse's Sauerkraut
3856 Washington Rd
Waldoboro, ME 04572-5502   207-832-5569
Fax: 207-832-2297 866-832-5569
morses@midcoast.com
www.morsessauerkraut.com
Processor of salsa, beet relish, pickled beets and sauerkraut
Owner: David Swetnam
Estimated Sales: Below $ 5 Million
Number Employees: 10-19
Type of Packaging: Consumer, Food Service
Brands:
Morse's

9727 Mortillaro Lobster Company
65 Commercial St
Gloucester, MA 01930-5047   978-282-4621
Fax: 978-281-0579
Lobster
President: Vincent Mortillaro
Estimated Sales: $ 5 - 10 Million
Number Employees: 20-49

9728 Mortimer's Fine Foods
5341 John Lucas Drive
Burlington, ON L7L 6A8
Canada   905-336-0000
Fax: 905-336-0909 mortimer@lara.on.ca
Processor and exporter of frozen beef, prepared and vegetarian entrees and meat pies
VP Sales: Karim Talakshi
Type of Packaging: Consumer, Food Service, Private Label, Bulk
Brands:
Mortimer Fine Foods

9729 Morton & Bassett Spices
84 Galli Dr
Novato, CA 94949-5706   415-883-8530
Fax: 415-883-0813   866-972-6879
mortonbassett@worldpantry.com
www.mortonbassettspices.net
Spices and seasonings
President: Morton Gothelf
Estimated Sales: Below $ 5 Million
Number Employees: 10-19
Number of Products: 70
Brands:
M B Spices

9730 (HQ)Morton Salt
123 N Wacker Dr
Chicago, IL 60606-1760   312-807-2000
Fax: 312-807-2929   800-789-7258
www.mortonsalt.com
Manufacturer of salts, salt substitutes and season-
ings; also, salt shakers and water conditioning salt
President: Walter Becky
CEO: Mark Roberts
CFO: Andy Kotlarz
VP Sales/Marketing: Wayne Carney
Estimated Sales: $500 Million
Number Employees: 2900
Parent Co: Rohn and Haas Company
Type of Packaging: Consumer, Food Service, Pri-
vate Label, Bulk
Brands:
Morton
Star Flake

9731 Morton Salt Company
123 N Wacker Dr
Chicago, IL 60606-1743   312-807-2000
Fax: 312-807-2949 www.mortonsalt.com
Processor and exporter of salt including food grade
and rock
President: Walter W Becky
CEO: Mark Roberts
CFO: Andy Kotlarz
Quality Control: Jim Bazar
Sales: W Lopez
Operations: Jay Tangeman
Production: Bryce Lewis
Plant Manager: Charles Young
Purchasing: Gary Newman
Estimated Sales: 600,000,000
Number Employees: 2900
Parent Co: Rohm & Haas
Type of Packaging: Consumer, Food Service, Pri-
vate Label, Bulk

9732 Mosby Packing Company
P.O.Box 4253
Meridian, MS 39304-4253   601-485-5615
Fax: 601-485-5668   800-844-7225
jmyers@mosbys.net   www.mosbys.net
Processor of smoked pork and pork products
President: Joe Mosby Jr
Marketing Director: Jimmy Maggard
Sales Director: Donny Clearman
Public Relations: J Myers
Accounting Manager: Rita Clearman
Health&Safety Or Human Resources: Dwight
Shumaker
Purchasing Manager: Terri Johnson
Estimated Sales: $ 20 - 50 Million
Number Employees: 50-99
Number of Brands: 4
Number of Products: 85
Sq. footage: 25000
Type of Packaging: Food Service
Brands:
Cedar Grove

9733 Mosby Winery
PO Box 1849
Buellton, CA 93427   800-706-6729
Fax: 805-686-4288   mosbywines@yahoo.com
mosbywines.com
Wines, California and Italian varietals
Estimated Sales: $ 2.5-5 Million
Number Employees: 4
Type of Packaging: Private Label

9734 (HQ)Moscahlades Brothers
30 N Moore St
New York, NY 10013   212-226-5410
Fax: 212-219-8486   g.moscahlades@earthlink.net

Manufacturer and importer of tomatoes, olives, olive
oil and cheeses
President: Nick Moscahlades
Estimated Sales: $ 5 - 10 Million
Number Employees: 5-9
Type of Packaging: Consumer

9735 Moscow Seed Company
PO Box 8983
Moscow, ID 83843-1483   208-882-2324
Fax: 208-882-3312
www.moscowfood.coop.archive/seed.html
Processors of peas, manufacturers of beans peas len-
tils and more.
President: Kimberly Vincent
Vice President: Bill Beck
Sales Manager: Sherri Robson
Estimated Sales: Less than $500,000
Number Employees: 5-9
Type of Packaging: Consumer, Food Service, Pri-
vate Label, Bulk
Brands:
Sun Dried

9736 Mosey's Inc
4 Mosey Drive
Bloomfield, CT 06002-3531   860-243-1725
Fax: 860-243-2806
Processor of meat products including roast, corned
and marinated beef, pastrami and portion controlled
veal and beef patties
VP/General Manager: Russell Pouliot
Number Employees: 100-249
Parent Co: SMG
Type of Packaging: Consumer, Food Service, Pri-
vate Label
Brands:
Davids
Kreip
Mosey's

9737 Mosher Products
PO Box 20549
Cheyenne, WY 82003-7013   307-632-1492
Fax: 307-632-1492   info@wheatandgrain.com
www.wheatandgrain.com
Organic grain
President: Leonard O Mosher
Estimated Sales: Below $ 5 Million
Number Employees: 11
Sq. footage: 60000
Other Locations:
Bushnell NE
Brands:
Mosher Products

9738 Moss Creek Winery
6015 Steele Canyon Rd
Napa, CA 94558-9634   707-252-1295
Fax: 707-254-9327   info@mosscreekwinery.com
www.mosscreekwinery.com
Wines
Owner: Ann Moskowite
Owner: George Moskowite
Winemaker: Nils Venge
Estimated Sales: Less than $500,000
Number Employees: 1-4
Brands:
Moss Creek

9739 Mossholder's Farm Cheese Factory
4017 N Richmond Street
Appleton, WI 54913-9704   920-734-7575
lalomo@athenet.net
www.mossholdercheese.homestead.com
Cheese
Co-Owner: Larry Mossholder
Co-Owner: Lois Mossholder
Estimated Sales: Less than $500,000
Number Employees: 1-4

9740 Mother Earth Enterprises
15 Irving Place
New York, NY 10003-2316   212-777-1250
Fax: 212-614-8132   866-436-7688
denis@hempnut.com   www.hempnut.com
Wholesaler/distributor of hempnuts; hemp oil, meal
and flour; and toasted, sterilized and roasted grain
hemp (seed). Highly adaptable for baking and cooking needs
President: Denis Cicero
Type of Packaging: Food Service

9741 Mother Murphy's Labs
PO Box 16846
Greensboro, NC 27416-0846   800-849-1277
Fax: 336-273-2615   800-849-1277
info@mothermurphys.com
www.mothermurphys.com
Processor of food flavorings and beverage flavors
President: David Murphy
CEO: Kernit Murphy Sr
VP Finance: Tim Hansen
Vice President: Jim Murphy
Directing Lab Manager: Patricia Stressler
Lab Manager: Patricia Batler
Production Manager: Gura Diggs
Plant Manager: John Worsley
Purchasing Manager: Nellie Brown
Estimated Sales: $ 1 - 3 Million
Number Employees: 55
Number of Products: 500
Sq. footage: 65000
Type of Packaging: Food Service, Bulk

9742 Mother Nature's Goodies
13378 California St
Yucaipa, CA 92399-5106   909-795-6018
Fax: 909-795-0748
Processor of granola, seven grain bread, frozen pies
and candy sundrops
President: Albert G Goude
Manager: Ronn Neish
CFO: Learner Guode
Estimated Sales: $ 3 - 5 Million
Number Employees: 20-49
Sq. footage: 8000
Type of Packaging: Private Label
Brands:
Mother Nature's Goodies

9743 Mother Parker's Tea & Coffee
2530 Stanfield Road
Mississauga, ON L4Y 1S2
Canada   905-279-9100
Fax: 905-279-3271 www.mother-parkers.com
Processor and exporter of ground and whole bean
coffees and teas including orange pekoe, regular, de-
caffeinated, black and herbal; importer of green cof-
fee and teas
Co-CEO: Michael Higgins
Co-CEO: Paul Higgins, Jr.
Sr. VP/Finance/Administration: Brian Goard
Vice President: Chris Bklecki
Number Employees: 280
Type of Packaging: Consumer, Food Service, Pri-
vate Label, Bulk
Brands:
Blue Ribbon
Higgins & Burke
Mother Parkers

9744 Mother Teresa's
700 W Plantation Dr
Clute, TX 77531-5248   979-265-7429
Fax: 979-297-0932   888-265-7429
motTfinefoods@cs.com   www.italian-food.us
Vegetables, sauces and dressings
Owner: Teresa Polimano
Estimated Sales: Less than $500,000
Number Employees: 5-9
Brands:
MOTHER TERESA'S FINE FOODS

9745 Mother's Home Bakery
2733 W 8th Avenue
Denver, CO 80204-3707   303-825-3641
Bread
President: Alex Dara
Owner: Sam Palacio
Estimated Sales: $ 5 - 10 Million
Number Employees: 10-19

9746 Mother's Kitchen
499 Veterans Dr
Burlington, NJ 08016-1269   609-387-7200
Fax: 609-386-5329   800-566-8437
smiller@motherskitchen.com
www.motherskitchen.com
Baked goods
President: Donald Butte
CFO: George Lasher
VP Marketing: Steve Shaw
Marketing Director: Vince Mannese
Plant Manager: Andy Cetrone

Estimated Sales: $ 10-20 Million
Number Employees: 100-249
Sq. footage: 105
Type of Packaging: Private Label
Brands:
Baby Watson
Country Club
Creative Bakers
Julf Cheesecake
Mother's Kitchen

9747 Motherland International Inc
8822 Flower Road
Suite 202
Rancho Cucamonga, CA 91730   909-596-8882
Fax: 909-596-8870   800-590-5407
source@motherlandusa.com
www.motherlandusa.com
Processor and exporter of herbs and vitamins in
powder and extract forms used in nutritional supple-
ments; contract manufacturing available
President: Jackson Wen
Marketing: Michael Pinson
Estimated Sales: $ 1 - 3 Million
Number Employees: 20-49
Sq. footage: 25000
Parent Co: Motherland International
Type of Packaging: Consumer, Food Service, Pri-
vate Label, Bulk

9748 Mothers Kitchen Inc
499 Veterans Dr
Burlington, NJ 08016-1269   609-387-7200
Fax: 609-386-5329 www.motherskitchen.com
Processor of kosher frozen baked goods including
breads, cakes and pies
President: Donald Butte
Executive Sales Manager: Luca D'Aiuto
Plant Manager: Gene Finnigan
Estimated Sales: $16400000
Number Employees: 100-249
Sq. footage: 32000
Type of Packaging: Food Service
Brands:
Baby Watson Cheesecake

9749 Mothers Mountain Mustard
2 Mustard Hollow Way
Falmouth, ME 04105   207-781-4658
Fax: 207-781-2121   800-440-9891
sales@mothersmountain.com
www.mothersmountain.com
Mustard, horseradish, ketchup, dill, chili sauce,
creamy horseradish sauce and hot pepper sauce.
Just added - jams and jellies!
President: Carrol Tanner
CFO: Dennis Proctor
Co-Owner: Carol Tanner
Estimated Sales: Below $ 5 Million
Number Employees: 6

9750 (HQ)Motivatit Seafoods
412 Palm Ave
Houma, LA 70364-3400   985-868-7191
Fax: 985-868-7472 msi1@cajunnet.com
www.motivatit.com
Fresh and frozen seafood
Owner: Michael Boisin
Director Manufacturing: Wayne DeHart
Purchasing Agent: Elgin Voisin
Estimated Sales: $ 20-50 Million
Number Employees: 100-249
Brands:
Wine Island Oysters

9751 Mott's
900 King St
Port Chester, NY 10573-1226   914-612-4000
Fax: 914-612-4100   800-964-7842
consumer_relations@dpsu.com
www.cadburyschweppes.com/en
Manufacturer of apple products that include apple
sauce and apple juice
President: Brad Irwin
CEO: Jack Belsito
Marketing VP: Chris Testa
Sr. Product Manager: Amanda Vaughn
Estimated Sales: $ 3 - 5 Million
Number Employees: 100-249
Parent Co: Cadbury Schweppes
Type of Packaging: Consumer, Food Service
Brands:
Mistic

Mistic Carafes
Re Engerize

9752 (HQ)Mott's
900 King St
Port Chester, NY 10573-1226   914-612-4000
Fax: 914-612-4100
www.cadburyschweppes.com/en
Manufacturer of applesauce, cooking wine, cocktail
mixes, fruit drinks, lime juice, apple juice, to-
mato-clam cocktail, fruit drinks, apple juice, to-
mato-clam cocktail, molasses
President/Sales: Michael McGrath
CFO: Dave Gerics
CEO: Jack Belsito
Estimated Sales: $300,000-500,000
Number Employees: 1-4
Parent Co: Cadbury Schweppes PLC
Type of Packaging: Consumer, Food Service, Bulk
Brands:
CLAMATO
GRANDMA'S MOLASSES
HAWAIIAN PUNCH
HOLLAND HOUSE
IBC
MAUNA LA'I
MOTT'S
MOTT'S FRUITSATIONS
MR & MRS T
REALEMON
REALLIME
ROSE'S
YPP-HOO

9753 Motz Poultry
2050 Sportys Drive
Batavia, OH 45103-8704   513-732-1381
Poultry, poultry products
President: Matt Motz
Estimated Sales: $ 2.5-5 Million
Number Employees: 20-49

9754 Mound City Shelled Nut Company
7831 Olive Blvd
St Louis, MO 63130-2039   314-725-9040
Fax: 314-725-9044   800-647-6887
sales@moundcity.com www.nutsgifts.com
Chocolate candy, nut meats, shelled nuts, peanuts
President: Byron Smyrniotis
Vice President: Stacy Smyrniotis
Estimated Sales: $1.8 Million
Number Employees: 10-19
Type of Packaging: Private Label
Brands:
Jordan Almonds

9755 Mount Baker Vineyards
4298 Mt Baker Hwy
Everson, WA 98247-9422   360-592-2300
Fax: 360-592-2526   800-441-8263
www
Wines
President: Randy Finley
Manager: Philippe Renaud
Founder: Al Stratton
Estimated Sales: $ 10 - 20 Million
Number Employees: 20-49
Brands:
Mount Baker Vineyards

9756 Mount Baker Vineyards
4298 Mt Baker Hwy
Everson, WA 98247-9422   360-592-2300
Fax: 360-592-2526
Wine
Owner: Randy Finley
Estimated Sales: $ 5-10 Million
Number Employees: 20-49
Brands:
Mount Baker Vineyards

9757 Mount Bethel Winery
P.O.Box 137
Altus, AR 72821-0137   479-468-2444
Fax: 479-468-2444 www.mountbethel.com
Wines
Owner: Eugene Post
Estimated Sales: $300,000
Number Employees: 5-9

9758 (HQ)Mount Capra Cheese
279 SW 9th St
Chehalis, WA 98532-3313   360-748-4224
Fax: 360-748-3099   800-574-1961
www.mtcapra.com
Processor and exporter of dehydrated powder whey
product and cheese including cheddar, feta and raw
goat milk with no salt
Owner: Frank Stout
General Manager/Marketing Incharge: Arny
Davis
Estimated Sales: $$1-2.5 Million
Number Employees: 10-19
Sq. footage: 5000
Other Locations:
Mount Capra Cheese
Chehalis WA

9759 Mount Claire Spring Water
160 Perkins St
Torrington, CT 06790-6846   860-489-3804
Fax: 860-496-9425   888-525-2473
Water and soft drink
Owner/CEO: Timothy Flynn
Estimated Sales: $500,000-$1 Million
Number Employees: 5-9

9760 Mount Eden Vineyards
22080 Mount Eden Rd
Saratoga, CA 95070-9729   408-867-5832
Fax: 408-867-4329   info@mounteden.com
www.mounteden.com
Wines
President: Jeffrey Patterson
Office Manager: Andrea Kyle
CEO: Neil Hagen
Business Manager: Eleanor Davis Patterson
Estimated Sales: Below $ 5 Million
Number Employees: 5-9
Type of Packaging: Private Label
Brands:
Mount Eden Vineyards

9761 Mount Hope Estate Winery
2775 Lebanon Rd
Manheim, PA 17545-8711   717-665-7021
Fax: 717-664-3466   eduinfo@parenfaire.com
www.parenfaire.com
Wine
President/CEO: Charles Romito
VP: Barbara Lacek
Marketing: Barbara Lacek
Estimated Sales: $ 100-500 Million
Number Employees: 20-49
Brands:
Mazza Vineyards

9762 Mount Olive Pickle Company
P.O.Box 609
Mt Olive, NC 28365-0609   919-658-2535
Fax: 919-658-6296   800-672-5041
mrcrisp@mtolivepickles.com
www.mtolivepickles.com
Manufacturer of pickles, relishes and peppers
President: William Bryan
Human Resources Manager: Chris Martin
Community Relations: Lynn Williams
Estimated Sales: $100+ Million
Number Employees: 500-999
Sq. footage: 970000
Brands:
Mt. Olive

9763 Mount Olympus Waters
P.O.Box 25426
Salt Lake City, UT 84125-0426   801-974-5000
Fax: 801-973-0110   800-628-6056
lynn@mowi.com   www.mowi.com
Manufacturer and supplier of bottler spring water,
cups, water coolers and coffee brewers
Owner: William Bailey
VP/GM: John Andrew
Sales Manager: Dave Albiston
VP Operations: Larry Mulanex
Estimated Sales: $ 5 - 10 Million
Number Employees: 50-99
Type of Packaging: Consumer, Food Service, Pri-
vate Label, Bulk
Brands:
Handi-Tap

9764 Mount Palomar Winery
33820 Rancho California Rd
Temecula, CA 92591-4930   951-676-5047
    Fax: 951-694-5688 800-854-5177
        info@mountpalomar.com
        www.mountpalomar.com
Wines
    President: Peter Poole
    CFO: Beth Raines
    Public Relations: Ami Sansweet
    Director Manufacturing: Etienne Cowper
Estimated Sales: $ 20-50 Million
Number Employees: 50-99
Brands:
    Castelletto
    Mount Palomar
    Rey Sol

9765 Mount Pleasant Winery
5634 High St
Augusta, MO 63332-1652   636-482-9463
    Fax: 636-228-4426 800-467-9463
        mailto@mountpleasant.com
        www.mountpleasant.com
Wines
    President: Phillip Dressel
Estimated Sales: Below $ 5 Million
Number Employees: 20-49

9766 Mount Rose Ravioli & Macaroni Company
157 Gazza Boulevard
Farmingdale, NY 11735-1415   516-694-6940
    Fax: 631-694-2101
Frozen ravioli and tortellini
    President/CEO: Santo Minuto
    Treasurer: Anthony Minuto, Sr.
    Vice President: Thomas Minuto
    Director Manufacturing: Anthony Minuto
Estimated Sales: $ 20-50 Million
Number Employees: 20-49

9767 Mountain City Coffee Roasters
P.O.Box 1058
Enka, NC 28728-1058   828-667-0869
    Fax: 828-667-0869 888-730-0869
        roastmaster@mountaincity.com
        www.mountaincity.com
Coffee
    Owner: Randall Sluder
    Co-Owner: Debra Furr Sluder
Estimated Sales: $1-$2.5 Million
Number Employees: 1-4
Type of Packaging: Consumer, Bulk
Brands:
    Mountain City

9768 Mountain City Meat Company
5905 E 42nd Ave
Denver, CO 80216-4613   303-320-1116
    Fax: 303-320-0449 800-937-8325
        sales@mountaincitymeat.com
        www.mountaincitymeat.com
Manufacturer of fresh, frozen and smoked meat in-
cluding beef, pork, veal and lamb, portion controlled
packaging
    President/Co-Owner: Patrick Boyer
    VP/Co-Owner: Anna Boyer
Estimated Sales: $64.2 Million
Number Employees: 250-499
Type of Packaging: Consumer, Food Service

9769 Mountain Cove Vineyards& Winegarden
1362 Fortunes Cove Ln
Lovingston, VA 22949-2226   434-263-5392
    Fax: 434-263-8540 aweed1@juno.com
        www.mountaincovevineyards.com
Wines
    President: Albert C Weed Ii
Estimated Sales: $ 1 - 3 Million
Number Employees: 1-4

9770 Mountain Crest Brewing SRL LLC
1208 14th Ave
Monroe, WI 53566-2055   608-325-3191
    Fax: 608-325-3198 www.berghoffbeer.com

Processor and exporter of beer and malt liquor in
kegs, bottles and cans; energy drinks and Blumer's
Sodas
    President/Plant Manager: Gary Olson
    CEO: Harry Cumberbatch
    Director of Brewing/Quality Control: Kris Kalav
    Production Manager: Dick Tschanz
Estimated Sales: $10 Million
Number Employees: 50-99
Brands:
    Berghoff Family
    Blumer's Root Beer
    Braumeister
    Braumeister Light
    Huber
    Huber Bock
    Wisi Club

9771 Mountain Fire Foods
2850 Main Road
Huntington, VT 05462-9608   802-434-2685
    Fax: 802-434-2685 karylk@adelphia.net
Marinades and ketchup
    Owner: Karyl Kent

9772 Mountain High Yogurt
1325 W Oxford Ave
Englewood, CO 80110-4429   303-761-2210
    Fax: 303-789-1718
        mountainhigh@mountainhigh.net
        www.mountainhighyoghurt.com
Processor of original and honey style yogurt
    President: Greg Bngles
    Plant Manager: Ralph Lee
Number Employees: 20-49
Parent Co: Borden
Type of Packaging: Consumer, Food Service, Pri-
vate Label
Brands:
    Mountain High

9773 Mountain Lake SpecialtyIngredients Company
PO Box 3100
Omaha, NE 68103-0100   402-595-7463
    Fax: 402-595-5884 sgrisamo@conagra.com
Processor and exporter of food texturizing ingredi-
ents and natural grain based flavors; contract pack-
aging available
    General Manager: Stephen Grisamore
    Plant Manager: Douglas Tenkley
Number Employees: 5-9
Brands:
    Trimchoice

9774 Mountain Orchard Cooperative
1425 Center Mills Road
Aspers, PA 17304-0200   717-677-7155
    Fax: 717-677-9890 800-322-6867
        moc@pa.net
Packer and exporter of fresh fruit including apples,
peaches and pears
    Manager: William Peters
    Sales Manager: George Peters
Number Employees: 10-19
Type of Packaging: Consumer, Food Service, Bulk
Brands:
    Apple Mountain
    Mountain Orchard
    Triangle

9775 Mountain Roastery Coffee Company
1908 Dove Street
Port Huron, MI 48060-6768   416-256-2727
    Fax: 416-256-5622
Coffee, tea
    Director: Eric Shabshore
Estimated Sales: Under $500,000
Number Employees: 5-9

9776 Mountain States Pecan
3801 Country Club Road
Roswell, NM 88201   505-623-2216
    Fax: 505-625-0126 mspstore@pecan.com
        www.pecan.com
Grower and processor of pecans; gift tins available
    Owner: Bruce Haley
    Operations Manager: Reba Haley
Estimated Sales: $2.5-5 Million
Number Employees: 5-9

9777 (HQ)Mountain States Rosen, LLc
355 Food Center Dr # C-16
Bronx, NY 10474-7000   718-842-4447
    Fax: 718-617-4096 800-872-5262
        info@rosenlamb.com www.rosenlamb.com
Processor and wholesaler/distributor of lamb and
veal; serving the food service market
    President/CEO: Bruce Rosen
    Human Resources: Al Montanino
    VP Marketing: Buddy Cooper
Estimated Sales: $120000000
Number Employees: 50-99
Type of Packaging: Food Service
Other Locations:
Brands:
    CEDAR SPRINGS LAMB
    CEDAR SPRINGS NATURAL VEAL
    SHEPHERD'S PRIDE

9778 Mountain Sun Brewery
1535 Pearl St
Boulder, CO 80302-5408   303-546-0886
    Fax: 303-413-1312 www.mountainsunpub.com
Beer
    Owner: Kevin Daly
Estimated Sales: $500,000-$1 Million
Number Employees: 20-49
Brands:
    Colorado Kind Ale
    Quinn's Golden Ale
    Thunderhead Stout

9779 Mountain Sun Organic & Natural Juices
18390 Highway 145
Dolores, CO 81323-9701   970-882-2283
    Fax: 970-882-2270
        mountainsun@mountainsun.com
        www.mountainsun.com
Natural and organic juices
    Owner: William Russel
Estimated Sales: $ 20-50 Million
Number Employees: 50-99
Brands:
    Apple Hill
    Mountain Sun

9780 Mountain Valley Poultry
P.O.Box 6967
Springdale, AR 72766-6967   479-751-7266
    Fax: 479-751-0506 chix@cox-internet.com
Processor of further processed poultry products in-
cluding de-boned, cooked, etc
    Owner: Don Walker
    Owner: Don Walker
Estimated Sales: $ .5 - 1 million
Number Employees: 1-4

9781 Mountain Valley ProductsInc
P.O.Box 246
Sunnyside, WA 98944-0246   509-837-8084
    Fax: 509-837-3481 www.valleyprocessing.com
Processor and exporter of fruit juice concentrates in-
cluding apple and grape; also, apple juice
    Owner: Mary Ann Bliesner
    Maintenance Supervisor: Mark Mulford
    Production/Personnel: David Perez
Estimated Sales: $1150000
Number Employees: 20-49
Sq. footage: 45000
Type of Packaging: Bulk

9782 (HQ)Mountain Valley Spring Company
P.O.Box 1610
Hot Springs, AR 71902-1610   501-624-1635
    Fax: 501-623-5135 800-643-1501
        mvsc@mountainvalleyspring.com
        www.mountainvalleyspring.com

We provide our water under Mountain Valley, Clear Mountain, Diamond, and private brands. In April 2004 we announced the purchase of the assets of Mountain Valley Spring Company. The combined companies will operate under the famousMountain Valley Spring Company name. Mountain Valley Spring Water was established in 1871 and has remained America's premium choice for spring water for 133 years. For more information please visit www.mountainvalleyspring.com

President: Breck Speed
CFO: Brad Fredrge
VP: Jack Henderson
Quality Control: Joe Russellprice
R & D: Asley Tillaway
Marketing: Jim Karrh
Sales: Philip Tappan
Public Relations: Jim Karrh
Operations: Chris Feree
Production: Chris Feree
Plant Manager: Brian Hinds
Estimated Sales: $ 10-20 Million
Number Employees: 100-249
Type of Packaging: Consumer, Food Service, Private Label
Brands:
Carolina Mountain Spring Water
Diamond Spring Water
Mountain Valley Spring Water

9783 Mountain View Fruit Sales
4275 Avenue 416
Reedley, CA 93654-9141   559-637-9933
                         Fax: 559-637-9733
rataide@mountainviewfruit.com
www.mountainviewfruit.com
Necatrines, peaches and plums
President: Randy Ataide
Sales Manager: Mike Thurlow

9784 Mountainbrook of Vermont
P.O.Box 39
Jeffersonville, VT 05464-0039   802-644-1988
Fax: 802-644-6795   lisa@mountainbrookvt.vom
www.mountainbrookvt.com
Dipping oils, fruit spreads, dressings, packaged dry mixes, mustards, and gift packs.
Owner: Lisa Bryan
Estimated Sales: $ 1 - 3 Million
Number Employees: 1-4
Type of Packaging: Consumer

9785 Mountainside Farms Dairy
State Rd
Roxbury, NY 12474   607-326-4161
                         Fax: 607-326-7838
Milk
Estimated Sales: $ 10-24.9 Million
Number Employees: 50-99

9786 (HQ)Mountaire Corporation
204 E 4th Street
North Little Rock, AR 72114   501-372-6524
Fax: 501-372-3972 www.mountaire.com
Poultry
Chairman/CEO: Ronald Cameron
CFO/Secretary: Alan Duncan
EVP/President Mountaire Feeds: DeAnn Landreth

Estimated Sales: $900 Million
Number Employees: 6000
Brands:
Mountaire

9787 Mountaire Farms of Delmarva
P.O.Box 710
Selbyville, DE 19975-0710   302-436-8241
Fax: 302-436-9309 800-441-8263
selby-resume@mountaire.com
www.mountaire.com
Manufacturer of fresh chicken; exporter of frozen poultry products
President/CEO: David Pogge
CFO: Kenneth Barkley
Marketing: Larry Saywell
Sales/Marketing Executive: Larry Saywell
Estimated Sales: $100 Million
Number Employees: 1,000-4,999
Type of Packaging: Consumer, Food Service, Private Label, Bulk
Brands:
LIPMAN POULTRY

9788 Mountaire Farms of North Carolina
17269 NC Highway 71 N
Lumber Bridge, NC 28360   910-843-5942
Fax: 910-843-8840 www.mountaire.com
Manufacturer and exporter of fresh and frozen chicken
Manager: Ralph Seabreaze
Human Resources: Mark Reif
VP Operations: Mike Tirrell
Purchasing Agent: Paul Dietz
Estimated Sales: $600 Million
Number Employees: 1,000-4,999
Parent Co: Mountaire Farms of Del Marva
Type of Packaging: Consumer, Food Service, Private Label

9789 Moutanos Brothers Coffee Company
380 Swift Ave # 13
S San Francisco, CA 94080-6232   650-952-5446
Fax: 650-871-4845   800-624-7031
info@mountanosbros.com
www.mountanosbros.com
Coffee
President: Michael Mountanos
Estimated Sales: Less than $500,000
Number Employees: 20-49
Brands:
Lindsay's Teas
Shade Grown Organic
Straight Coffees

9790 Movie Breads Food
225 Industrial Blouevard
Chateauguay, QC J6J 4Z2
Canada   450-692-7606
Fax: 450-692-1810   trmblaykein05@hotmail.com
Grocery
Brands:
SHEI BRAND
TRADEWINDS

9791 Moweaqua Packing
601 N Main St
Moweaqua, IL 62550-3695   217-768-4714
Processor of beef and pork
Owner: Terry Yoder
Co-Owner: Don Baker
Estimated Sales: $160000
Number Employees: 1-4
Type of Packaging: Consumer

9792 Moyer Packing Company
PO Box 64395
Souderton, PA 18964-0395
Fax: 215-723-5294 800-967-8325
publicrelations@mopac.com   www.mopac.com
Manufacturer and packer of boxed and ground beef; exporter of fresh and frozen boxed beef and offals. Also provides grease recycling bins and services to restaurants
President/CEO: Lee Delp
VP Marketing/Sales: Bruce Blanton
Estimated Sales: $.5 Billion
Number Employees: 1600+
Sq. footage: 85000
Parent Co: Smithfield Foods
Type of Packaging: Consumer, Private Label, Bulk
Brands:
MOPAC

9793 Mozzarella Company
2944 Elm St
Dallas, TX 75226-1509   214-741-4072
Fax: 214-741-4076 800-798-2954
info@mozzco.com   www.mozzco.com
Cow, goat milk and cheeses such as mozzarella, bocconcini, ricotta, mascarpone, mascarpone tortas, queso fresco and blanco, queso oaxaca, scamorza, crescenza, cream cheese, fresh goat cheese, caciotta, montasio and feta
President: Paula Lambert
Estimated Sales: Below $ 5 Million
Number Employees: 10-19
Type of Packaging: Consumer, Food Service
Brands:
Mozzarella Company

9794 Mozzarella FrescaTipton Plant
615 North North Burnett
Tipton, CA 93272   559-752-4823
www.mozzarellafresca.com

Processor and exporter of cheese including mozzarella, mascarpone and ricotta.
President: Andrew Branagh
Branch Manager: Richard Roughton
Number Employees: 140
Sq. footage: 55000
Parent Co: Lactalis USA
Type of Packaging: Consumer, Food Service
Other Locations:
Tipton Plant
Tipton CA
Brands:
MOZZARELL FRESCA

9795 Mozzarella FrescaCorporate & Commercial Headquarters
1800 Gateway Blvd
Suite 100
Concord, CA 94520   925-887-9600
Fax: 925-887-9607   800-572-6818
www.mozzarellafresca.com
Processor and exporter of cheese including mozzarella, mascarpone and ricotta.
President: Andrew Branagh
Estimated Sales: $62.6 Million
Number Employees: 220
Sq. footage: 55000
Parent Co: Lactalis USA
Type of Packaging: Consumer, Food Service
Brands:
MOZZARELLA FRESCA

9796 Mozzicato De Pasquale Bakery Pastry
329 Franklin Ave
Hartford, CT 06114-1890   860-296-0426
Fax: 860-296-8129 info@mozzicatobakery.com
www.mozzicatobakery.com
Bread, pizza, cakes, cookies and ice cream
Owner: Gisella Mozzicato
President: Luigi Mozzicato
COO: Gina Mozzicato
Estimated Sales: Less than $500,000
Number Employees: 20-49

9797 Mozzicato Depasquale Bakery & Pastry Shop
329 Franklin Ave
Hartford, CT 06114-1890   860-296-0426
Fax: 860-296-8129 info@mozzicatobakery.com
www.mozzicatobakery.com
Manufacturer of baked goods such as; breads, cakes, cookies, gelato, pastries and wedding cakes
Owner: Luigi Mozzicato
Estimated Sales: $ 1 - 3 Million
Number Employees: 20-49

9798 Mr Jay's Tamales & Chili
11200 Alameda St
Lynwood, CA 90262-1725   310-537-3932
                         Fax: 310-537-3938
Processor of chili and tamales
President/CEO: Pat Lang
Estimated Sales: Less than $500,000
Number Employees: 1-4
Type of Packaging: Consumer
Brands:
Chicken Link
Chilly

9799 Mr. Brown's Bar-B-Que
3240 N Williams Avenue
Portland, OR 97227-1551   503-274-0966
                         Fax: 503-230-9298
Barbeque sauce
Estimated Sales: Under $500,000
Number Employees: 5-9

9800 Mr. Dell Foods
P.O.Box 494
Kearney, MO 64060-0494   816-628-4644
Fax: 816-628-4633 mliechti@uniteone.net
www.mrdells.com
Processor of IQF vegetables including celery, onions, peppers, carrots and potatoes including pre-cooked, hash brown, diced, sliced and shredded; exporter of IQF hash brown potatoes
President: Kurt Johnsen
VP: Kurt Johnsen
Marketing/Sales Director: Tom Sherrer
Operations Manager: Rick Wilkins
Plant Manager: John Duncan

Estimated Sales:$8445651
Number Employees: 20-49
Sq. footage: 40000
Type of Packaging: Consumer, Food Service, Bulk
Brands:
Mr. Dell's I.Q.F. Country Potatoes
Mr. Dell's I.Q.F. Hash Browns
Mr. Dell's I.Q.F. Herb & Garlic
Mr. Dell's I.Q.F. Santa Fe

9801 Mr. Espresso
696 3rd St
Oakland, CA 94607-3560   510-287-5200
Fax: 510-287-5204   info@mrespresso.com
www.mrespresso.com
Organic coffee
President: Carlo Di Ruocco
CFO: M Di Ruocco
CEO: Marie Francoise
Sales Director: Laura Zambrano
Public Relations: Robert Hunt
Operations Manager: Michael Clarke
Production Manager: John Di Ruocco
Plant Manager: Richard Ocampo
Estimated Sales:$ 10-20 Million
Number Employees: 20-49
Brands:
Faema
Mr. Espresso

9802 Mr. Pickle
44 Brooklyn Terminal Market
Brooklyn, NY 11236-1510   718-251-2500
Fax: 718-763-0503 www.mrpickleinc.com
Pickles
Owner: Alan Neiheis
Owner: Alan Neihaus
Treasurer: Alan Neihaus
Vice President: Scott Wiseman
*Estimated Sales:*Below $ 5 Million
Number Employees: 50-99

9803 (HQ)Mrs Baird's Bakery
14401 Statler Blvd
Fort Worth, TX 76155-2861   817-864-2500
Fax: 817-864-2753 www.mrsbairds.com
Manufacturer of bread, buns, donuts, cinnamon
rolls, honey buns, applie pie and chocolate cup
cakes
President: Reynaldo Reyna
Number Employees: 20-49
Type of Packaging: Consumer, Food Service, Private Label, Bulk
Other Locations:
Mrs Baird's Bakeries
Abilene TX
Mrs Baird's Bakeries
Fort Worth TX
Mrs Baird's Bakeries
Lubbock TX
Mrs Baird's Bakeries
Waco TX
Mrs Baird's Bakeries
Houston TX
Mrs Baird's Bakeries
San Antonio TX
Brands:
BAIRD'S
BIMBO
ENTENMANN'S
MARINELA
OROWEAT
THOMAS'
TIA ROSA

9804 Mrs May's Naturals
860 E 238th Street
Carson, CA 90745-6212   310-830-3130
Fax: 310-830-3045   877-677-6297
info@mrsmays.com   www.mrsmays.com
vegan, non-GMO, cholesterol free, dairy free, wheat
free, gluten free, 0 trans fat and contain no artificial
colors or flavors, nut crunches and bars
President/Owner: Augustine Kim
Estimated Sales:$18 Million
Number Employees: 6

9805 Mrs. Annie's Peanut Patch
1019 B St
Floresville, TX 78114-1947   830-393-7845
Fax: 830-393-9605   mrsanniespeanut@aol.com
www.mrsanniespeanutpatch.com

Processor of home-made peanut brittle, jalapeno
peanut brittle, pecan brittle, peanut patties, pecan
chewies, pecan pralines, flavored peanuts, all natural
peanut butter and raw peanuts
President: Mariano Sanchez
VP: Mary Ann Sanchez
Estimated Sales:$ 1 - 3 Million
Number Employees: 5-9

9806 Mrs. Auld's Gourmet Foods
572 Reactor Way # B4
Reno, NV 89502-4133   775-856-3350
Fax: 775-856-3351   800-322-8537
john@mrs-aulds.com   www.mrs-aulds.com
Processor, importer and exporter of gourmet foods
including brandied cherries, sweet and spicy pickles,
marmalades, preserves, pancake, scone and soda
bread mix, salsa, pasta sauce and bean, red corn and
barbeque chips, chili sausepesto sauce, chestnuts
President/CEO: Evelyn Auld
Sales Manager: Teresa West
Estimated Sales:$ 1 - 3 Million
Number Employees: 5-9
Sq. footage: 3000

9807 Mrs. Baird's Bakeries
7301 South Freeway
Fort Worth, TX 76134   806-763-9304
info@mrsbaird.com
www.mrsbairds.com
Bread and other bakery products except cookies and
crackers.
President: Reynaldo Reyna
Estimated Sales:$1,400,000,000
Number Employees: 1,000-4,999
Parent Co: Bimbo Bakeries USA
Type of Packaging: Consumer, Food Service
Brands:
Mrs. Baird

9808 Mrs. Baird's Bakeries
2701 Palm St
Abilene, TX 79602-5901   325-692-3141
Fax: 325-692-7326 www.mrsbairds.com
Processor of buns, rolls, bread and pies
General Manager: Joe Dangelmaier
Plant Manager: Clarke Flowers
Estimated Sales:$20-50 Million
Number Employees: 100-249
Type of Packaging: Consumer, Food Service, Private Label

9809 Mrs. Baird's Bakeries
225 S 17th St
Waco, TX 76701-1735   254-750-2500
Fax: 254-750-2599 www.mrsbairds.com
Processor of white bread and buns including hamburger and hot dog
Manager: Wesley Steel
Plant Manager: Raymond Kupak
Estimated Sales:$20-50 Million
Number Employees: 20-49
Parent Co: Mrs. Baird's Bakeries
Type of Packaging: Consumer, Food Service, Private Label, Bulk

9810 Mrs. Clark's Foods
740 SE Dalbey Dr
Ankeny, IA 50021-3908   515-299-6445
Fax: 515-964-8397   800-736-5674
info@mrsclarks.com   www.mrsclarks.com

Juices, salad dressings and sauces.

Senior VP of Sales & Marketing: Paul Burmeister

Marketing: Linda Keairns
Director Sales: Pete Knudsen
Director Purchasing: Gary Lukins
Number Employees: 100-249
Number of Brands: 1
Parent Co: Agri Industries

Type of Packaging: Food Service, Private Label
Other Locations:
Alljuice Company
Hendersonville NC
Brands:
Mrs. Clark's

9811 Mrs. Denson's Cookie Company
120 Brush St
Ukiah, CA 95482-3432   707-462-2272
Fax: 707-462-2283   800-219-3199
info@mrsdensonscookies.com
www.mrsdensonscookies.com
Processor and exporter of fruit juice and honey
sweetened cookies including energy, reduced fat,
fat-free, vegan and organic
President/Owner: Mike Bielenberg
Vice President: Desi Ringor
Number Employees: 50-99
Sq. footage: 25000
Type of Packaging: Consumer, Food Service, Private Label, Bulk
Brands:
Monster Cookies
Mrs. Denson's
Total Fit

9812 Mrs. Dog's Products
4320 W El Prado Boulevard
Suite 17
Tampa, FL 33629   616-454-2677
Fax: 616-774-0193   800-267-7364
mrsdogs@mrsdogs.com   www.mrsdogs.com
Processor and exporter of gourmet mustard, Jamaican jerk marinade and habanero pepper sauces; also,
shelled green chile pistachio nuts
Owner: Julie Curtis Applegate
*Estimated Sales:*Less than $500,000
Number Employees: 1-4
Type of Packaging: Consumer
Brands:
Mrs. Dog's

9813 (HQ)Mrs. Fields' Famous Brands
2855 E Cottonwood Pkwy # 400
Salt Lake City, UT 84121-7050   801-736-5600
Fax: 801-736-5970   800-343-5377
srusso@mrsfields.com
www.mrsfieldsfranchise.com
Cookies and baked goods
President: Stephen Russo
VP Operations: Tara Dejpathsh
CFO: Santra Boffa
CEO: John Lauck
Sr. VP Marketing: John Lauck
SVP Operations: Robert Rodriguez
Estimated Sales:$ 100-250 Million
Number Employees: 250-499
Parent Co: Capricorn Investors
Brands:
Mrs. Field's Original Cookies
Pretzel Maker
TCBY

9814 Mrs. Fisher's
1231 Fulton Ave
Rockford, IL 61103-4025   815-964-9114
Fax: 815-964-3880   info@mrsfisherschips.com
www.mrsfisherschips.com
Processor of potato chips including barbecue and
sour cream and onion
Owner: Peter J Di Venti
VP: Chuck Diventi
Estimated Sales:$780000
Number Employees: 10-19
Sq. footage: 10000
Type of Packaging: Consumer
Brands:
Mrs. Fisher
Vita-Sealed

9815 Mrs. Fly's Bakery
608 W Main St
Collegeville, PA 19426-1925   610-489-7288
Fax: 610-489-7488
Bakery products
President: Richard Landis
Estimated Sales:$ 1-2.5 Million
Number Employees: 1-4

9816 Mrs. Grissom's Salad
2500 Bransford Ave
Nashville, TN 37204-2810
615-255-4137
Fax: 615-251-9763 800-255-0571
customerservice@mrsgrissoms.com
www.mrsgrissoms.com
Processor of prepared salad
President: Grace G Grissom
CEO: Kenneth Funger
Plant Manager: Jack McGhee
Estimated Sales: $3100000
Number Employees: 50-99
Sq. footage: 40000
Type of Packaging: Consumer

9817 (HQ)Mrs. Kavanagh's EnglishMuffins
145 N Broadway
Rumford, RI 02916-2801
401-434-0551
Fax: 401-438-0542 800-556-7216
www.homesteadbaking.com
Processor of breads, rolls and English muffins
President: Peter Vican
VP: Bill Vican
Sales Manager: Vinny Palmiotti
Estimated Sales: $ 20 - 50 Million
Number Employees: 50-99
Sq. footage: 40000
Type of Packaging: Food Service, Private Label, Bulk
Brands:
Matthew's All Natural
Mrs. Kavanagh's

9818 Mrs. Leeper's Pasta
4100 N Mulberry Drive
Suite 200
Kansas City, MO 64116-1700
816-502-6000
Fax: 816-584-5100 800-848-5266
mrsleepers@aipc.com www.mrsleeperspasta.com
Processor of flavored dry pasta including shapes, fettucine, angel hair, wheat-free, gluten-free, bulk, organic, kosher and private label
President: Tim Webster
CEO: Ed Muscat
Number Employees: 700
Number of Brands: 6
Type of Packaging: Consumer, Food Service, Private Label, Bulk
Brands:
Eddie's Spaghetti Organic
Fortune Macaroni
Michelle's Organic
Mrs Leeper's Wheat/Gluten Free

9819 Mrs. London's Confections
1 Salem St # 1
Swampscott, MA 01907-1314
781-595-8140
Fax: 781-595-9141
infochoc@chocolatebydesign.com
www.chocolatebydesign.com
Confectionery
Owner: Hope Zabar
Estimated Sales: $500,000-$1 Million
Number Employees: 20-49
Type of Packaging: Private Label
Brands:
Chocolate By Design

9820 Mrs. Malibu Foods
23852 Pacific Coast Highway
Suite 372
Malibu, CA 90265-4876
310-589-2777
Fax: 310-589-2751 800-677-6254
MrsMalibu@aol.com www.mrsmalibu.com
Food
President/Owner: Debra Root
Estimated Sales: $500,000-$1 Million
Number Employees: 5-9
Type of Packaging: Private Label
Brands:
Mrs Malibu

9821 Mrs. Mazzula's Food Products
240 Carter Dr
Edison, NJ 08817-2097
732-248-0555
Fax: 732-248-0442 info@mazzula.com
www.mazzula.com
Sun dried tomatoes, zucchini, salsa, peppers
President: Christopher Lotito
President: Christopher Lotito
Estimated Sales: Less than $500,000
Number Employees: 20-49
Type of Packaging: Bulk

9822 Mrs. McGarrigle's Fine Foods
311 St Lawrence Street
PO Box 163
Merrickville, ON K0G 1N0
Canada
613-269-3752
Fax: 613-269-2736 877-768-7827
info@mustard.ca www.mustard.ca
gourmet mustards, chutneys, preserves and seasonings
President/Owner: Janet Campbell

9823 Mrs. Minnick's Salads
2222 Aisquith Street
Baltimore, MD 21218-6210
410-235-6748
Fax: 410-235-6747 webmaster@minnicks.com
www.minnicks.com
Manufacturer of salads including potato, cole slaw, macaroni, pasta and sauerbraten; also, sauerbraten mix
President: Walter Carew
Estimated Sales: $2 Million
Number Employees: 5
Sq. footage: 14000
Type of Packaging: Food Service
Brands:
MRS MINNICK'S

9824 Mrs. Prindable's Handmade Confections
6300 Gross Point Road
Niles, IL 60714
847-588-2900
Fax: 847-588-0392 888-215-1100
customerservice@mrsprindables.com
www.mrsprindables.com
gourmet caramel apples

9825 Mrs. Rio's Corn Products
215 W Avenue N
San Angelo, TX 76903-8434
325-653-5640
Fax: 325-657-0825 www.mrsrios.earthlink.net
Flour and corn tortillas
President: Armando Martinez
Estimated Sales: $ 20-50 Million
Number Employees: 20-49

9826 Mrs. Smith's Bakeries
7101 Asheville Hwy
Spartanburg, SC 29303-1870
864-503-9588
Fax: 864-503-0219 sales@mrssmiths.com
www.mrssmiths.com
Processor of baked goods including cakes and convenience products
President: David Stanaland
Director Human Resources: Jesse Hobby
Estimated Sales: $ 50 - 100 Million
Number Employees: 250-499
Parent Co: Mrs. Smiths Bakeries
Type of Packaging: Consumer
Brands:
Deep Dish Blueberry
Deep Dish Cherry Crumb
Moose Tracks
No Sugar Added Apple

9827 Mrs. Stratton's Salads
P.O.Box 190187
Birmingham, AL 35219-0187
205-940-9640
Fax: 205-940-9650 www.mrsstrattons.com
Processor of fresh salads including pimiento, potato, cole slaw, chicken and tuna
Chairman of the Board: John Bradford
President: R Vance Fulkerson
Estimated Sales: $ 5-10 Million
Number Employees: 50-99
Type of Packaging: Consumer, Food Service, Private Label
Brands:
Mrs. Stratton

9828 Mrs. Sullivan's Pies
256 Preston St
Jackson, TN 38301-4965
731-427-2101
Fax: 731-422-1045 800-456-2205
sales@mrssullivans.com www.mrssullivans.com
Processor of brownies and pies including coconut, chocolate and pecan
VP: Rodney Myrick
General Manager: Bob Holmes
Production Manager: Melvin Coope
Estimated Sales: $ 10 - 20 Million
Number Employees: 10-19
Sq. footage: 12000
Type of Packaging: Consumer

Brands:
Mrs. Sullivan's

9829 Mrs. T's Pierogies
P.O.Box 606
Shenandoah, PA 17976-0606
570-462-2745
Fax: 570-462-1392 800-233-3170
www.pierogies.com
Processor of low-fat pierogies
President: Tom Twardzik
Vice President: Tim Twardzik
IT Manager: Ted Twardzik Jr
VP Marketing: Gary Loverman
VP Sales: Ron Suchecki
Estimated Sales: $10-20 Million
Number Employees: 100-249
Type of Packaging: Consumer, Food Service
Brands:
Mrs. T'S

9830 Mrs. Weinstein's Toffee
2000 White Settlement Road
Fort Worth, TX 76107-1440
805-965-0422
Fax: 805-965-8123 866-965-0422
toffee@mwtoffee.com www.mwtoffee.com
Processor of toffee covered milk or dark chocolate with almond, hazelnuts, pistachios or pecans
President: Lotte Weinstein's
Brands:
Toffolos

9831 Mrs. Willman's Baking
3732 Canada Way
Burnaby, BC VG5 1G4
Canada
403-250-9105
Fax: 403-250-8706 http://www.mrswillmans.com
Processor of sandwiches, doughnuts, pastries and sausage rolls
CEO: Winston Haffat
President: Eric Olsen
Parent Co: Beaumont Select Corporation
Type of Packaging: Consumer, Food Service
Brands:
ABM
Coral Food
Golden Crust
Prestige

9832 Mt View Bakery
P.O.Box 102
Mountain View, HI 96771-0102
808-968-6353
Processor of bread, cookies, pies, doughnuts, rolls, muffins, etc.
Owner: Russell Sueda
Estimated Sales: Less than $500,000
Number Employees: 5-9
Type of Packaging: Consumer
Brands:
Mt. View Bakery

9833 Mt. Konocti Growers
P.O.Box 365
Kelseyville, CA 95451-0365
707-279-4213
Fax: 707-279-2251 mkg.annette@mchsi.com
Grower, packer and exporter of bartlett pears
Manager: Robert Gayaldo
Number Employees: 5-9
Sq. footage: 85000
Type of Packaging: Bulk
Brands:
Lady of the Lake
Lake Cove
Mt. Konocti

9834 Mt. Nittany Vineyard
300 Houser Rd
Centre Hall, PA 16828-8002
814-466-6373
Fax: 814-466-3066 sales@mtnittanywinery.com
www.mtnittanywinery.com
Wines
President: Joe Carroll
VP: Betty Carroll
Estimated Sales: $ 1-2.5 Million
Number Employees: 5-9
Brands:
Mount Nittany

9835 Mt. Olive Pickle Company
P.O.Box 609
Mt Olive, NC 28365-0609
919-658-2535
Fax: 919-658-6296 800-672-5041
pdenlinger@mtolivepickles.com
www.mtolivepickles.com

Pickles
President/CEO: Bill Bryan
Chairman: E Pope
Marketing Director: Robert "Frye, Sr."
Production Manager: Ken Powell
Plant Manager: Vic Beverage
Estimated Sales: $ 5-10 Million
Number Employees: 500-999
Brands:
Dill Pickles
Little Sister
Majestic
Mt. Olive
No Sugar Added Products
Pepper and Specialty Products
Relishes and Salad Cubes
Sweet Pickles

9836 Mt. Olympus Specialty Foods
1601 Military Road
Buffalo, NY 14217-1205
Fax: 716-839-4006   716-874-0771
info@mtolympusgreeksalad.com
www.mtolympusgreeksalad.com
Processor and exporter of meat, poultry and fish
marinades, Greek salad dressings, pasta sauces and
appetizers, gourmet foods, salsa, hot sauce and sea-
sonings
CEO/President: George Bechakas
Executive VP: Nick Bechakas
Estimated Sales: $ 1 - 3 Million
Number Employees: 20-49

9837 Mucky Duck Mustard Company
1505 Bonner St
Ferndale, MI 48220-1973   248-544-4610
Fax: 248-544-4610   zilkod@aol.com
Processor of gourmet marinades, salad dressings,
mustard, ketchup, and BBQ sauces
President: Dave Zilko
Estimated Sales: Less than $500,000
Number Employees: 1-4
Type of Packaging: Consumer, Food Service
Brands:
American Connoisseur Gourmet
American Moir's
American Mucky Duck
American Special Edition
Mucky Duck

9838 Muir Glen Organic Tomato
424 N 7th Street
Sacramento, CA 95814-0210   916-557-0900
Fax: 916-557-0903
Tomato products
President: Bill Russell
Estimated Sales: $ 2.5-5 Million
Number Employees: 10

9839 Muir-Roberts Company
P.O.Box 26775
Salt Lake City, UT 84126-775   801-363-5809
Fax: 801-355-0221
Packer and exporter of potatoes, onions and frozen
ready-to-process cherries; wholesaler/distributor of
fresh fruits and vegetables; serving the food service
market in the Salt Lake City metropolitan area
President: Phillip Muir
Estimated Sales: $16638274
Number Employees: 70
Sq. footage: 200000
Type of Packaging: Food Service, Private Label,
Bulk
Brands:
Big M

9840 Muirhead Canning Company
5267 Mill Creek Road
The Dalles, OR 97058-8501   541-298-1660
Fax: 541-298-4158   info@muirheadcanning.com
www.muirheadcanning.com
Manufacturer of canned fruits including apricots,
cherries, peaches, pears and plums
Co-Owner: James Barrett Jr
Co-Owner: Dawn Barrett
Estimated Sales: $5-10 Million
Number Employees: 20
Sq. footage: 12000
Type of Packaging: Consumer
Brands:
HOODCREST

9841 Muirhead of Ringoes
43 Us Highway 202 # 31
Ringoes, NJ 08551-1820   908-782-7803
Fax: 908-788-4221   800-782-7803
information@muirheadfoods.com
www.muirheadfoods.com
Specialty foods
President: Edward Simpson
Vice President: Doris Simpson
Marketing Director: Barbara Simpson
Estimated Sales: $500,000 appx.
Number Employees: 5-9
Number of Brands: 1
Number of Products: 25
Sq. footage: 1500
Type of Packaging: Consumer
Brands:
Dragon's Breath
Hazel's
Muirhead

9842 Muller-Pinehurst Dairy C
P.O.Box 299
Rockford, IL 61105-0299   815-968-0441
Fax: 815-961-1625
Manufacturer of dairy products
President: Neal Rosinsky
Estimated Sales: Less than $500,000
Number Employees: 100-249
Parent Co: Prairie Farms Dairy
Type of Packaging: Consumer

9843 Mulligan Sales
P.O.Box 90008
City of Industry, CA 91715-0008   626-968-9621
Fax: 626-369-8452   mulligansales@yahoo.com
www.instantmilk.com
Dairy products
President: Jeff Mulligan
Estimated Sales: $ 10-20 Million
Number Employees: 10-19

9844 Mullins Food Products
2200 S 25th Ave
Broadview, IL 60155-4584   708-344-3224
Fax: 708-344-0153   info@sminty.com
www.controlledair.net
Processor of sauces, condiments and salad dressings
Owner: Jeanne Gannon
CEO: Michael Mullins
Vice President: William Mullins
Marketing Director: Judy Lucas
Sales Director: Shannon Smith
Public Relations: Tom Mullins
Operations Manager: Art Clausen
Plant Manager: Michael Mazur
Purchasing Manager: Ray Johnson
Estimated Sales: $75000000
Number Employees: 250-499
Type of Packaging: Consumer, Food Service, Pri-
vate Label

9845 Multi Foods
19606 NE San Rafael St
Portland, OR 97230-7449   503-666-8998
Fax: 503-661-1698   800-666-8998
www.vistar.com
Pizza products
President: Louis Kirchem
Estimated Sales: $ 50 - 100 Million
Number Employees: 50-99

9846 Multi Marques
3265 Viau Street
Montreal, QC H1V 3J5
Canada   514-255-9492
Fax: 514-255-0150   pheygat@multimarques.com
Manufacturer and distributor of bread, rolls, fruit
cake and sponge cake
Chairman: Michelle Samson-Doel
CEO: Michel Proulx
Regional Plant Director: Francine Henderson
Estimated Sales: $300 Million
Number Employees: 100-249
Parent Co: Canada Bread
Type of Packaging: Consumer, Food Service
Brands:
BON MATIN
CUISINE NATURE
DIANA
DURVIAGE
GAILURON
MAISON COUSIN

PETITE DONCEUR
POM

9847 (HQ)Multiflex Company
455 Braen Ave
Wyckoff, NJ 07481-2949   201-447-3888
Fax: 201-447-1455   marzipanco@aol.com
www.marzipan.com
Processor and exporter of confectionery items in-
cluding marzipan, icing decorations, edible Easter
eggs, chocolate dessert cups, chocolate liqueur cups,
lollypops, sugar decorations and decorated chocolate
covered sandwich cookies
President: Rita Keller
Vice President: Rozie Keller
VP Sales: Royce Keller
Estimated Sales: $1300000
Number Employees: 10-19
Sq. footage: 7500
Type of Packaging: Food Service, Private Label,
Bulk
Brands:
Biermann
Crescent Confections
Keller's
Panorama Easter Eggs
Swissart
Ultra Dark Rondo Kosher

9848 Multnomah Brewing
1603 SE Porter Street
Portland, OR 97202   503-236-3106
Beer
President: Jeff Hendryx
Estimated Sales: Under $500,000
Number Employees: 5-9

9849 Mung Dynasty
2100 Mary St
Pittsburgh, PA 15203-2160   412-381-1350
Grow, pack, ship sprouts; wholesaler/distributor of
Oriental foods, specialty products
Owner: Chris Wahlberg
Estimated Sales: $ 1 - 3 Million
Number Employees: 1-4
Sq. footage: 5000
Brands:
Mori-Nu Tofu
Mung Dynasty

9850 Munroe Dairy
P.O.Box 14287
East Providence, RI 02914-0287   401-438-4450
Fax: 401-438-0035   info@abmunroedairy.com
www.cowtruck.com
Fluid milk
President: Robert Armstrong
Plant Manager: John Sherman
Estimated Sales: $ 10-20 Million
Number Employees: 50-99
Brands:
Munroe Dairy

9851 Munsee Meats
P.O.Box 2843
Muncie, IN 47307-0843   765-288-3645
Fax: 765-282-8076
Beef, beef products
President: Steve Henderixson
President: Rosalyn Selvey
Estimated Sales: $ 20 - 50 Million
Number Employees: 20-49
Brands:
Munsee Meats

9852 Munson's Chocolates
174 Hopriver Rd
Bolton, CT 06043-7444   860-649-4332
Fax: 860-649-7209
munsons@munsonschocolates.com
www.munsonschocolates.com
Processor of chocolate candy
President: Robert Munson
CEO: Karen Munson
Estimated Sales: $10-24.9 Million
Number Employees: 10,000+
Sq. footage: 35000
Type of Packaging: Consumer, Food Service, Pri-
vate Label, Bulk
Brands:
Munson's

9853 Muqui Coffee Company
3398 Grossmont Drive
San Jose, CA 95132-3010
408-929-4405
Fax: 408-929-4505
Coffee
Director: Clyde McMorrow

9854 Murakami Produce Company
P.O.Box 9
Ontario, OR 97914-0009
541-889-3131
Fax: 541-889-2933 800-421-8814
Packer and exporter of dry fresh yellow, red and
white onions
President: Grant Kitamura
Director Marketing: Christopher Woo
Plant Manager: Paul Hopper
Estimated Sales:$19452525
Number Employees: 100-249
Sq. footage: 250000
Type of Packaging: Consumer, Food Service, Private Label

9855 Murdock Farm Dairy
62 Elmwood Rd
Winchendon, MA 01475-1099
978-297-0143
Dairy products
Estimated Sales:$500,000-$1 Million
Number Employees: 1-4

9856 Murphy Goode Estate Winery
20 Matheson St
Healdsburg, CA 95448-4121
707-431-7644
Fax: 707-431-8640
general@murphygoodewinery.com
www.murphygoodewinery.com
A wide selection of wines including chardonay,
cabernet sauvignon, merlot, pinot noir, and
zinfandel.
Manager: Lorri Emmerich
R & D: Lorri Emmerich
Vice President: David Ready
Plant Manager: Lorri Emmerach
Estimated Sales: $ 10-20 Million
Number Employees: 10-19
Number of Brands: 2
Type of Packaging: Private Label
Brands:
Goode & Ready
Murphy Goode

9857 Murphy House
108 S Bickett Blvd
Louisburg, NC 27549-2664
919-496-4173
Fax: 919-496-7101
Processor of deli meats and cheeses
Manager: Margurite Cole
Estimated Sales: $ 1 - 3 Million
Number Employees: 20-49
Type of Packaging: Consumer, Food Service, Bulk

9858 Murphys Creek Brewing
PO Box 1076
Murphys, CA 95247-1076
209-736-2739
Manufacturer of beer
President: Dan Ayala
Director Manufacturing: Micah Millspaw

9859 (HQ)Murray Biscuit Company
4751 Best Road
Suite 140
Atlanta, GA 30337-5616
678-366-7000
Fax: 678-366-7004 800-745-5582
www.murraysugarfree.com
Manufacturer of cookies, crackers and fig bars
President/CEO: Jerry Cavitt
Controller: Bryon Russell
Marketing Director: Scott Chapman
Estimated Sales:$450 Million
Number Employees: 1300
Parent Co: Kellogg Company
Type of Packaging: Consumer, Food Service, Private Label
Brands:
BECKY KAY
BISHOP
FAMOUS AMOS
GREG'S
JACK'S
JACKSON'S
MURRAY
OLD NEW ENGLAND
PLANTATION
SUNNY

9860 Murray Biscuit Company/Kellogg
11475 Great Oaks Way
Alpharetta, GA 30022-2440
678-366-7000
Fax: 678-366-7004 800-745-5582
www.rim.com
Manufacturer of sugar free cookies.
President/CEO: Jerry Cavitt
Controller: Byron Russell
Director Marketing: Scott Chapman
Number Employees: 500-999
Parent Co: Kellogg Company
Type of Packaging: Consumer, Private Label

9861 Murray Biscuit Company/Kellogg Snacks
933 Louise Ave
Charlotte, NC 28204-2131
704-334-7611
Fax: 704-375-6448 www.kellogg.com
Processor and exporter of cookies
President: Jerry Cavitt
Vice President: Dave Greene
Plant Manager: Rob Sweatman
Estimated Sales:$450 Million
Number Employees: 100-249
Parent Co: Kellogg Company
Type of Packaging: Consumer, Private Label

9862 Murray Biscuit Company/Kellogg Snacks
1550 Marvin Griffin Rd
Augusta, GA 30906-3853
706-798-8600
800-776-2667
www.kelloggs.com
Processor and exporter of cookies and crackers
Manager: Tim McGee
Estimated Sales:$450 Million
Number Employees: 500-999
Parent Co: Kellogg Company
Type of Packaging: Consumer, Food Service, Private Label, Bulk
Brands:
Old New England

9863 Murray Biscuit Company/Kellogg Snacks
15500 Lightwave Dr # 100
Clearwater, FL 33760-3505
727-524-6000
Fax: 727-524-6998 www.themurraycompany.com
Processor of cookies and crackers
President: Greg Albers
VP/Marketing Manager: Bill Horton
Estimated Sales:$450 Million
Number Employees: 1-4
Parent Co: Kellogg Company
Type of Packaging: Bulk

9864 Murray Biscuit Company/Kellogg Snacks
1400 N Skokie Highway
Lake Bluff, IL 60044-1131
847-689-8400
Fax: 847-689-8405
Processor of cookies and brownies
General Manager: Charles Turnbull
Estimated Sales:$450 Million
Number Employees: 5-9
Parent Co: Kellogg Company
Type of Packaging: Consumer, Food Service

9865 Murray Cider Company
103 Murray Farm Rd
Roanoke, VA 24019-8102
540-977-9000
Fax: 540-977-1336 www.murraycider.com
Processor of apple juice and cider, also cherry-flavored apple cider
President: Robert Murray
Executive VP: Joseph Murray
Estimated Sales: $ 5 - 10 Million
Number Employees: 10-19
Sq. footage: 30000
Type of Packaging: Consumer, Food Service, Private Label, Bulk
Brands:
Murray's

9866 Murray's Chicken
P.O.Box 13
South Fallsburg, NY 12779-0013
845-436-5001
Fax: 845-436-5001 800-770-6347
info@murryschicken.com
www.murrayschicken.com

All-natural chicken burgers and marinated chicken
breasts
Owner: Murray Bresky
*Estimated Sales:*Below $ 5 Million
Number Employees: 1-4
Brands:
Nature's Kitchen

9867 Muruchan
15800 Laguna Canyon Rd
Irvine, CA 92618-3103
949-789-2300
Fax: 949-789-2350
Instant noodles
President: Kiyoshi Fukagawa
Owner: Mark Horikara
Estimated Sales: $ 100-500 Million
Number Employees: 250-499
Brands:
Muruchan

9868 Murvest Fine Foods
5390 NW 12th Ave
Fort Lauderdale, FL 33309-3153
954-772-6440
Fax: 954-772-7728 murvest@msn.com
www.murvestfoods.com
Pate's and sausages
President: John Murphy
*Estimated Sales:*Below $ 5 Million
Number Employees: 10-19
Brands:
Murvest

9869 Musco Olive Products
17950 Via Nicolo
Tracy, CA 95377-9767
209-836-4600
Fax: 209-836-0518 800-523-9828
sales@muscoolive.com www.olives.com
Processor and exporter of canned olives including
California stuffed green, Sicilian-style, black ripe
and deli, and specialty olives and frozen ripe olives
President: Nicholas Musco
Vice President: Felix Musco
Quality Control: Ben Hall
Marketing Director: Yauna Throne
Sales Director: Fred Ghelardi
Public Relations: Janet Mitchell
Production/Plant Manager: Mike Splitstone
Number Employees: 250-499
Number of Brands: 7
Type of Packaging: Consumer, Food Service, Private Label
Brands:
Black Pearls
Bravo
Early California
Green Pearls
Mediterranean Pearls
Musco

9870 Musco Olive Products
P.O.Box 368
Orland, CA 95963-0368
530-865-4111
Fax: 530-865-5204 www.olive.com
Processor and exporter of pickled mixed vegetables
and olives including Spanish and ripe
President: Dennis Burreson
Sales Manager: Felix Musco
Plant Manager: Dennis Burreson
Estimated Sales: $ 20 - 50 Million
Number Employees: 50-99
Type of Packaging: Consumer, Food Service, Private Label, Bulk

9871 Mushroom Company
902 Woods Rd
Cambridge, MD 21613-9470
410-221-8900
Fax: 410-221-8952
custserv@themushroomcompany.com
www.themushroomcompany.com
Processor and exporter of canned, quick blanched
and frozen mushrooms; also, custom mushroom
sauces, and breaded appetizers
President: Dennis Newhard
Controller: Debbie Timmons
National Sales Manager: Ruth Newhard
Estimated Sales:$16128581
Number Employees: 20-49
Sq. footage: 52000
Type of Packaging: Consumer, Food Service, Private Label, Bulk
Brands:
MGA
Mother Earth

Mushroom Canning Company
Snocap

9872 (HQ)Music Mountain Water Company
PO Box 2252
Birmingham, AL 35246-5195   318-425-4400
Fax: 318-222-6650   800-349-6555
music@musicmountain.com
www.musicmountain.com
Manufacturer of bottled spring water
President: Marcus Wren III
Estimated Sales: $ 1-3 Million
Number Employees: 20
Other Locations:
Music Mountain Spring Water
Alexandria VA
Music Mountain Spring Water
Monroe VA
Music Mountain Spring Water
Lake Charles VA
Music Mountain Spring Water
Ruston VA
Music Mountain Spring Water
Lafayette VA
Music Mountain Spring Water
Natchitoches VA
Music Mountain Spring Water
Austin TX
Music Mountain Spring Water
Tyler TX
Music Mountain Spring Water
Longview TX
Music Mountain Spring Water
Marshall TX
Music Mountain Spring Water
Alto TX
Music Mountain Spring Water
Crockett TX
Music Mountain Spring Water
Glenwood AR

9873 Musicon Deer Farm
Scotchtown Rd
Goshen, NY 10924   845-294-6378
Fax: 516-239-8915   norman@koshervenison.com
www.koshervenison.com
Glatt kosher and venison
President: Norman Schlaff
Estimated Sales: $500,000-$1 Million
Number Employees: 1-4
Type of Packaging: Private Label

9874 Mustard Seed
203 Sanders Road
Central, SC 29630-9349   864-639-1083
877-621-2591
sheltoncj@aol.com
Processor of natural, organic, vegetarian, whole
grain, high fiber, gourmet, heart healthy burger and
protein replacement mixes, burger n' a bag
Owner: Jane Shelton
Brands:
Burgers N'A Bag

9875 Mutchler's Dakota Gold Mustard
445 N 5th Street
Spearfish, SD 57783-2307   605-642-7325
Fax: 605-642-0708   mustard@blackhills.com
Mustard
President: Kelly Hitson
CEO: Betty Lenners

9876 Muth Candies
630 E Market St
Louisville, KY 40202-1117   502-585-2952
Fax: 502-582-2639 www.muthscandy.com
Processor of candy including chocolate, caramel and
peanut brittle
President: Martha Vories
Assistant Manager: Kimberly Bennett
Estimated Sales: Under $500,000
Number Employees: 10-19
Type of Packaging: Consumer
Brands:
Kentucky Tavern
Mojeska's
Muth's Kentucky

9877 Mutiflex Company
455 Braen Ave
Wyckoff, NJ 07481-2949   201-447-3888
Fax: 201-447-1455   marzipanco@aol.com
www.marzipan.com
Marzipan and other candies
President: Royce Keller

Estimated Sales: $ 2.5-5 Million
Number Employees: 20-49

9878 Mutual Fish Company
2335 Rainier Ave S
Seattle, WA 98144-5389   206-322-4368
Fax: 206-328-5889 www.mutualfish.com
Retail/wholesale seafood market that specializes in
the freshest and liveliest seafood, custom seafood
products as well as a complete line of Asian
groceries.
President: Dick Yoshimura
Sales Director: Kevin Yoshimura
Estimated Sales: $1500000
Number Employees: 20-49
Sq. footage: 15000
Brands:
Three Fish

9879 Mutual Flavors
2558 Country Bend Drive
South Jordan, UT 84095-9441   801-231-1354
Fax: 888-343-2922   888-343-2922
sales@mutualflavors.com
www.mutualflavors.com
Exotic tropical flavors and other flavorings
VP: Maureen Glumit
President: James Mungar
VP Sales: Bill Stephens
Account Executive: Jode Hyman
Estimated Sales: $ 10-20 Million
Number Employees: 10-19
Brands:
Mutual Flavors

9880 Mutual Trading Company
431 Crocker St
Los Angeles, CA 90013-2180   213-626-9458
Fax: 213-626-5130 www.lamtc.com
Ethnic foods
President: Noritoshi Kanai
Estimated Sales: $ 50-100 Million
Number Employees: 100-249
Brands:
Miyako
Mizken
My Pizza Raviolis
My Turkey Meatballs
Pizza Pasta, Please
Takara

9881 My Bagel Chips
66 E Walnut Street
Long Beach, NY 11561-3516   516-889-0732
Bagel and bagel products
President: Gerald Golden
Sales Manager: G Golden

9882 My Boy's Baking LLC
1466 Hampton Rd
Allentown, PA 18104-2018   610-759-4552
Fax: 610-759-4525 www.myboysbaking.com
biscotti, cookies and rugelach

9883 My Daddy's Cheesecake
P.O. Box 9
Cape Girardeau, MO 63702-0009   573-335-6660
Fax: 573-335-8258   800-735-6765
sales@mydaddyscheesecake.com
www.mydaddyscheesecake.com
Processor and exporter of confectionery items,
cheesecakes, desserts, wedding and birthday cakes
and gourmet cookies
Owner: Kevin Stanfield
Estimated Sales: Less than $500,000
Number Employees: 5-9
Sq. footage: 2500
Type of Packaging: Consumer, Food Service, Pri-
vate Label
Brands:
Cookie Wedgies
My Daddy's Cheesecake

9884 My Favorite Jerky
2000 5th Street
Apt C
Boulder, CO 80302-4948   303-444-2846
Fax: 303-444-9049 www.myfavoritejerky.com
Beef jerky
President: James David
Brands:
MY FAVORITE JERKY

9885 My Grandma's Coffee Cake of New England
1636 Hyde Park Ave
Hyde Park, MA 02136-2458   617-364-9900
Fax: 617-364-0505   800-847-2636
customerservice@mygrandma.com
www.mygrandma.com
Company makes coffeecakes in a variety of flavors
including Granny Smith Apple, Golden Raspberry,
Cappuccino, New England Blueberry, Chocolate,
Banana Walnut and Cape Cod Cranberry.
President: Robert Katz
Marketing VP: Bruce Mills
National Sales VP: Dan Murphy
Estimated Sales: $ 5-6 Million
Number Employees: 20-49
Sq. footage: 8900
Brands:
My Grandma's of New England

9886 My Grandma's of New England®
1636 Hyde Park Ave
Hyde Park, MA 02136-2458   617-364-9900
Fax: 617-364-0505   800-847-2636
customerservice@mygrandma.com
www.mygrandma.com
Wide variety of homemade gourmet coffee cakes
Owner: Robert Katz
Corporate Account Manager: Joann Keeley
EVP: Dave Katz
Estimated Sales: $ 3 - 5 Million
Number Employees: 20-49

9887 My Sister's Caramels
325 Alabama St
Redlands, CA 92373-8031   909-792-6242
Fax: 909-798-7294
Processor of gourmet caramels including vanilla,
chocolate, praline, peanut butter, holiday mix and
raspberry
Estimated Sales: $ 5 - 10 Million
Number Employees: 5-9
Type of Packaging: Private Label, Bulk
Brands:
My Sister's Caramels

9888 Myers Frozen Food Provisions
P.O.Box 12
St Paul, IN 47272-0012   765-525-6304
Fax: 765-525-9635   info.myers@aol.com
Frozen foods
President: Tony Myers
Sales Manager: Dan Gindling
Production Manager: Mike Myers
Estimated Sales: $ 3 - 5 Million
Number Employees: 5-9
Brands:
Myers Frozen Food

9889 Myron's Fine Foods
1 River St
Erving, MA 01344-4403   413-659-0247
Fax: 413-659-0249   800-730-2820
myrons@chefmyrons.com   www.chefmyrons.com
Processor of natural and kosher cooking sauces in-
cluding tsukeyaki, soy sauce, szechuan, teriyaki,
yakitori, ponzu, wild game and fish
President: Myron Becker
CFO: Lisa Richardson
Vice President: Kathy Becker
Production Manager: Steve Gambino
Plant Manager: Dawn Kennaway
Estimated Sales: Below $ 5 Million
Number Employees: 5-9
Number of Products: 9
Type of Packaging: Consumer, Food Service, Pri-
vate Label, Bulk
Brands:
Chef Myron's Original #1 Yakitori
Chef Myron's Ponzu
Chef Myron's Premium
Chef Myron's Tsukeya
Myron's 20 Gauge Wil

9890 Mystic Coffee Roasters
8 Steamboat Wharf
Mystic, CT 06355-2544   860-536-2999
Coffee, tea
President/Treasurer: Bruce Carpenter
Estimated Sales: $410,000
Number Employees: 10-19

9891 Mystic Lake Dairy
24200 NE 14th Street
Sammamish, WA 98074-3506   425-868-2029
                          Fax: 425-868-0553
Yogurt, bread, muffins and international line of food
    President: Gary Wallace
    CEO: Nellie Wallace
Estimated Sales: Less than $100,000
Number Employees: 2
Brands:
    Mystic Lake Dairy

9892 N.A. Boullon
3280 Glasco Drive
Cumming, GA 30041-8742   770-889-2356
Manufacuter of Grouper, Mahi - Mahi, Snapper, Sea
Bass, Clams, Flounder
    Owner: Bert Boullion

9893 N.B.J. Enterprises
2521 Hillcrest Rd # E
Mobile, AL 36695-3198   251-661-2122
                          Fax: 251-661-6198
Seafood
    Owner: Toni Gulsby
Estimated Sales: $ 1 - 3 Million
Number Employees: 10-19

9894 N.K. Hurst Company
P.O.Box 985
Indianapolis, IN 46206-0985   317-634-6425
        Fax: 317-638-1396   info@nkhurst.com
                          www.hambeens.com
Processor of dried beans
    President: Needham R Hurst
Estimated Sales: $ 20 - 50 Million
Number Employees: 50-99
Type of Packaging: Consumer, Food Service, Bulk

9895 N.Y.K. Line (North America)
377 E Butterfield Rd
Lombard, IL 60148-5615   630-435-7800
        Fax: 630-435-3110   888-695-7447
                          http://www2.nykline.com/
Estimated Sales: $ .5 - 1 million
Number Employees: 5-9

9896 NAYA
1200 High Ridge Road
Stamford, CT 06905-1223   203-321-4800
        Fax: 203-321-4808   800-566-6292
                          www.naya.com
Canadian natural spring water

9897 (HQ)NBTY
2100 Smithtown Avenue
Ronkonkoma, NY 11779   631-200-2000
        Fax: 631-567-7148   800-920-6090
                          www.nbty.com
Manufacturer, marketer and distributor of nutritional
supplements
    President/CFO: Harvey Kamil
    Chairman/CEO: Scott Randolph
    SVP Marketing: James Flaherty
    SVP Operations/Corporate Secretary: Hans
    Lindgren
Estimated Sales: K
Number Employees: 10,000+
Sq. footage: 1200000
Type of Packaging: Consumer, Private Label, Bulk

9898 NC Mountain Water
PO Box 73
Marion, NC 28752-0073   828-756-4090
        Fax: 828-756-4220   800-220-4718
                          ncwater@wnclink.com
                          www.wnclink.com/~ncwater1
Manufacturers of bottled water
    President: Don Freeman
Estimated Sales: $ 1 - 3 Million
Number Employees: 10-19
Type of Packaging: Private Label, Bulk
Brands:
    Natural Mountain Water

9899 ND Labs Inc
202 Merrick Rd
Lynbrook, NY 11563-2622   516-612-4900
        Fax: 516-504-0289   888-263-5227
        sales@ndlabs.com   www.ndlabs.com

Processor of nutritional supplements and foods, in-
cluding fiber and soy products, soy proteins, high-fi-
ber cookies, vegetarian entrees, etc
    President: Diane Altos
    Vice President: Beth Beller
    Marketing/Sales: Michael Allen
    Public Relations: Sherry Shah
Estimated Sales: $2500000
Number Employees: 1-4
Number of Brands: 10
Type of Packaging: Consumer, Food Service, Pri-
vate Label, Bulk
Brands:
    Fiber 7
    Fiber Supreme
    Life Savy
    Nana Flakes
    Soy-Liccous Meals
    Soypro

9900 NECCO
135 American Legion Hwy
Revere, MA 02151-2405   781-485-4500
        Fax: 781-485-4509   800-225-5508
        wafer2wafer@necco.com   www.necco.com
Manufacturer of Bulk and seasonal candy, chocolate
and nonchocolate
    President: Domenic Antonellis
    CEO: Richard S Krause
    VP R&D/Quality Control: Jeff Green
    Marketing Manager: Lory Zimbalatti
    VP Sales/Marketing: Hans Becher
    VP Operations: Stanley Byerly
    Plant Manager: Bruce Grembowitz
Estimated Sales: $ 100 Million
Number Employees: 1,000-4,999
Number of Brands: 17
Number of Products: 500
Sq. footage: 820000
Type of Packaging: Consumer, Food Service, Pri-
vate Label, Bulk
Brands:
    CANADA
    CANDY CUPBOARD
    CANDY HOUSE
    CLARK BAR
    EAGLE BRAND
    HAVILAND
    KETTLE FRESH CARAMEL
    MARY JANE
    MASTERPIECES
    MIGHTY MINTS
    NECCO WAFERS
    SKY BAR
    SLAP STIX
    STINKY FEET
    SWEETHARTSs
    ULTRA MINTS

9901 NOH Foods of Hawaii
1402 W 178th St
Gardena, CA 90248-3202   310-324-6770
        Fax: 310-324-6163   gardena@nohfoods.comm
                          www.nohfoods.com
Manufacturer and exporter of sauces, condiments,
seasonings and Hawaiian coconut pudding and iced
teas
    Founder/CEO: Edwin Noh
    President: Raymond Noh
    Sales Manager: Ricky Ruff
Estimated Sales: $25 Million
Number Employees: 5-9
Sq. footage: 20000
Parent Co: E&M Corporation
Type of Packaging: Consumer, Food Service, Bulk
Other Locations:
    NOH Foods
    Honolulu HI
Brands:
    NOH

9902 (HQ)NORPAC Foods
4350 SW Galewood Street
Lake Oswego, OR 97035   503-635-9311
        Fax: 503-635-7498   www.norpac.com
Frozen vegetables, fruits and juices.
    President/CEO: George Smith
    CFO: Jack Sebastian
    VP Operations: Mark Croeni
Estimated Sales: $400 Million
Number Employees: 4000
Type of Packaging: Consumer, Food Service, Pri-
vate Label, Bulk

Other Locations:
    NORPAC Foods
    Salem OR
Brands:
    FLAV-R-PAC
    NORPAC
    PASTA PERFECT
    SANTIAM
    SOUP SUPREME
    WESTPAC

9903 NORPAC Plant
2325 Madrona Ave SE
Salem, OR 97302-1113   503-581-1426
        Fax: 503-371-8150   800-822-2898
                          www.norpac.com
Manufacturer of frozen vegetables, berry, fruit and
juice products
    President: Erik Jacobson
    Production Manager: Bob Beck
    Plant Manager: Joe Janota
Estimated Sales: $100+ Million
Number Employees: 500-999
Parent Co: NORPAC Foods
Type of Packaging: Consumer, Food Service, Pri-
vate Label, Bulk
Brands:
    FLAV-R-PAC
    NORPAC
    SOUP SUPREME
    WEST-PAC

9904 NOW Foods
395 Glen Ellyn Rd
Bloomingdale, IL 60108-2176   630-545-9098
        Fax: 630-790-8019   888-669-3663
                          www.nowfoods.com
Manufacturer of health foods and supplements
    Owner: Elwood Richard
    Director Sales: Dan Richard

9905 NPC Dehydrators
11761 Highway 770 E
Eden, NC 27288   336-635-5190
        Fax: 336-635-5193   npcmmorales@aol.com
                          www.npcbrewersyeast.com
Dry brewers yeast
    President: R Dean Fullmer
    Executive: Max Selty
    Sales Director: Mike Morales
    Public Relations: Charles Setlif
    Plant Manager: Mike Morales
Estimated Sales: $ 5-10 Million
Number Employees: 30
Type of Packaging: Private Label
Brands:
    Sonic Dried Yeast

9906 NPC Dehydrators
P.O.Box B
Payette, ID 83661-0017   208-642-4471
        Fax: 208-642-4473   npcinc@earthlink.net
                          www.npcbrewersyeast.com
Dry brewers yeast
    Manager: Vicki Swank
Estimated Sales: Less than $500,000
Number Employees: 1-4

9907 NSpired Natural Foods
58 S Service Rd
Melville, NY 11747-4625   631-845-4689
        Fax: 510-686-0126   info@nspiredfoods.com
                          www.nspiredfoods.com
Manufacturer of Natural and organic foods
    Executive Chairman: Charlie Lynch
    President: Patrick Lee
    CFO: Randy Sieve
    Quality Assurance Manager: Fred Tabacchi
    VP Marketing: Robin Robinson
    VP Sales: Marty Hagge
    Customer Service Manager: Liz Scatena
    VP Operations, Ashland: Jeff Williams
Number Employees: 100-249
Brands:
    AH!LASKA
    CLOUD NINE
    COOL FRUITS
    LORIVA
    MARANATHA
    PUMPKORN
    SKINNY
    SUNSPIRE
    TROPICAL SOURCE

9908 NSpired Natural Foods
58 S Service Rd
Melville, NY 11747-4625   631-845-4689
            Fax: 510-686-0126 www.sunspire.com
Processor and exporter of all natural carob and choc-
olate products including baking chips, coated nuts
and raisins, English toffee and organic candies
    President: Patrick Lee
    VP Sales: Tom Tuggle
    Director Operations: Tom Miner
Number Employees: 100-249
Sq. footage: 20000
Parent Co: Green Leaf Natural Foods
Type of Packaging: Consumer, Food Service, Pri-
    vate Label, Bulk
Brands:
    Crystal
    Fruitsource Confections
    Sundrops
    Sunspire
    Sunspire Organics
    Sweets-To-Go

9909 NSpired Natural Foods
58 S Service Rd
Melville, NY 11747-4625   631-845-4689
            Fax: 510-686-0117 www.nspiredfoods.com
Processor of organic iced teas, cocoa and chocolate
syrup; exporter of organic chocolate syrup and
cocoas
    President: Donna Maltz
Estimated Sales: Less than $500,000
Number Employees: 5-9
Type of Packaging: Consumer, Food Service, Bulk
Brands:
    Ah!Laska

9910 NTC Foods Corporation
5680 Main St
Williamsville, NY 14221-5518   716-884-3345
        Fax: 716-884-4680 800-333-1637
    info@ntcmarketing.com   www.ntcmarketing.com
Processor and importer of canned products including
pineapples, pineapple juice and concentrates, man-
darin oranges, olives, mushrooms, tropical fruits and
shrimp
    Owner: Michael Derose
    Operations Manager: David DeRose
Estimated Sales: $ 5 - 10 Million
Number Employees: 10-19
Type of Packaging: Consumer, Food Service, Pri-
    vate Label, Bulk
Brands:
    Libby's
    P/L
    Queen's Pride

9911 NYSCO Products LLC
P.O.Box 725
Bronx, NY 10473-0725   718-792-9000
    Fax: 718-792-7732 Chuck@NYSCO.com
                www.nysco.com
NYSCO Products LLC designs and manufactures
custom and stock displays.
    Owner: Barry Kramer
    Senior Vice President: Chuck Levin

9912 NZMP
1425 Corporate Center Pkwy
Santa Rosa, CA 95407-5434   707-524-6600
    Fax: 707-527-1206 800-358-9096
        www.becomingindependent.org
Processor of dairy based ingredients including high
calcium milk proteins, acid and rennet caseins,
caseinates and stabilizers
    President: Mal Beniston
    CEO: Jack Mc Cue
    Director Technology Marketing: Neil Blazey
Estimated Sales: $50-100 Million
Number Employees: 100-249
Sq. footage: 40000
Type of Packaging: Private Label, Bulk
Brands:
    Alacen
    Alacid
    Alanate
    Alapro
    Alaren

9913 Nabisco Biscuit Company
12000 Roosevelt Blvd
Philadelphia, PA 19116-3001   215-673-4800
            Fax: 215-464-6684 www.nabisco.com

Processor of baked goods including cookies and
crackers
    General Manager: Samer Chebib
    President: Samer Chebib
    CFO: Nick Vaney
    Vice President: John Bodolai
    Sales Director: John Bodolai
    Plant Manager: Larry Campbell
Estimated Sales: $ 20 - 50 Million
Number Employees: 500-999
Parent Co: Kraft Foods
Type of Packaging: Consumer

9914 Nabisco Biscuit Company
6002 S Laburnum Ave
Richmond, VA 23231-5099   804-222-8802
            Fax: 804-226-0906 www.nabisco.com
Processor of baked goods including cookies and
crackers
    President/CEO: Charles Harper
    Plant Manager: Larry Campbell
    Purchasing Manager: Mike Swift
Estimated Sales: $ 20 - 50 Million
Number Employees: 500-999
Parent Co: Kraft Foods
Type of Packaging: Consumer, Food Service
Brands:
    100 CALORIE PACKS
    ARROWROOT
    BARNUM'S ANIMALS CRACKERS
    CAMEO
    CHIPS AHOY!
    CHOCOSTIX
    EASY CHEESE
    FLAVOR ORIGINALS
    GINGER SNAPS
    HONEY MAID
    KRAFT CHEESE NIPS
    KRAFT HANDI-SNACKS
    MALLOMARS
    MIXERS
    NEWTONS
    NILLA WAFERS
    NUTTER BUTTER
    OREO
    PREMIUM
    RITZ
    RITZ BITS SANDWICHES
    SNACKWELLS
    TEDDY GRAHAM
    TOASTED CHIPS
    TRISCUIT
    WHEAT THINS
    WHEATSWORTH
    ZWIEBACK

9915 Nabisco Dry Foods
1 Kraft Court
Glenview, IL 60025-5066   612-331-4325
            Fax: 612-378-2504
Processor and exporter of breakfast cereals includ-
ing regular, quick and instant
    Purchasing Agent: Pat Humphrey
Number Employees: 100-249
Parent Co: Kraft Foods
Type of Packaging: Consumer, Food Service
Brands:
    Life Savers

9916 Nabisco Food Group
151 W Ohio St
Kendallville, IN 46755-2033   260-347-1300
        Fax: 260-347-5590 www.kraftfoodscompany.com
Processor and exporter of candy and confectionery
products
    Manager: Nick Coburn
    Purchasing Manager: Garland LaKamp
Estimated Sales: $100+ Million
Number Employees: 500-999
Parent Co: Kraft Foods
Type of Packaging: Consumer, Food Service, Pri-
    vate Label, Bulk

9917 Nabisco LifeSavers Company
635 E 48th Street
Holland, MI 49423-7801   616-396-1411
            Fax: 616-393-8240
Processor of candy including hard, breath and
sugar-free mints, lollypops and bubble gums
    Plant Manager: Tim Goaley
Number Employees: 600
Parent Co: Kraft Foods
Type of Packaging: Consumer

Brands:
    Life Savers

9918 Nacan Products
60 West Drive
Brampton, ON L6T 4W7
Canada   905-454-4466
        Fax: 905-454-5207 info@nacan.com
                www.nacan.com
Processor of modified starches derived from corn,
waxy maize and tapioca
    President: Roland Sirois
    Vice-Chairman: Jim Grieve
    Business Director (Food Starch): Bill Ruderman
    Executive VP: John Morrell
Parent Co: National Starch & Chemical Company
Brands:
    Nacan

9919 Nafziger Ice Cream Company
515 Independence Drive
#100
Napoleon, OH 43545   419-592-1112
                Fax: 419-592-4069
Ice cream, frozen desserts
    Owner: Dale Nafziger
Estimated Sales: $5-10 Million
Number Employees: 10-19

9920 Nagasako Fish
800 Eha St # 11
Wailuku, HI 96793-1485   808-242-4073
                Fax: 808-244-7020
Seafood
    Owner: Darryl Flinton
Estimated Sales: $ 5 - 10 Million
Number Employees: 10-19

9921 Nagel Veal
1411 E Base Line St
San Bernardino, CA 92410-4113   909-383-7075
                Fax: 909-383-7079
Processor of veal, lamb and beef
    President: Mike Lemler
Estimated Sales: $ 10-20 Million
Number Employees: 50-99

9922 Nagel's Beverages Company
8925 Birch Lane
East Nampa, ID 83706-1287   208-475-1250
        Fax: 208-475-1274 www.nagelbev.com
Manufacturer of beverages
    President/CEO: Ann Matthews
Estimated Sales: $44.8 Million
Number Employees: 105
Type of Packaging: Consumer, Food Service
Brands:
    PEPSI-COLA

9923 Najila's
PO Box 74
Binghamton, NY 13905-0074   607-722-4287
        Fax: 607-773-9012 cookies@najila's.com
Manufacturer of gourmet cookies
    President/CEO: Najla Aswad
Type of Packaging: Food Service, Bulk
Brands:
    NAJLA GONE CHUNKY

9924 Nakano Foods
55 E Euclid Ave
Mt Prospect, IL 60056-1283   847-290-0730
                Fax: 847-590-0482
    dan_baron@nakanofoods.com
                www.nakanofoods.com
Processor and importer of vinegar
    President: Hiroyasu Nakano
    Executive VP: Fred Galyean
    Marketing Manager: Dennis Dedmond
    Sales Director: Shivaun English
Estimated Sales: $32300000
Number Employees: 50-99
Parent Co: Nakano Vinegar
Type of Packaging: Private Label
Brands:
    Barengo
    Four Monks
    Indian Summer
    Lady's Choice
    Nakano
    Paw Paw

9925 Naked Mountain Vineyard& Winery
2747 Leeds Manor Rd
Markham, VA 22643-1715   540-364-1609
nakedmountain@yahoo.com
www.nakedmtn.com
Wines
Co-Owner: Phoebe Harper
Co-Owner: Bob Harper
Marketing/Sales Manager: Drew Hauser
Assistant Winemaker: Don Oldham
Office Manager: Darlene Call
Estimated Sales: Below $ 5 Million
Number Employees: 1-4
Type of Packaging: Private Label
Brands:
Naked Mountain

9926 Naleway Foods
233 Hutchings Street
Winnipeg, MB R2X 2R4
Canada   204-633-6535
Fax: 204-694-4310   800-665-7448
Processor and exporter of frozen foods including
pierogies and panzarotti
VP: Bruce Dorset
Plant Manager: Richard Lyles
Number Employees: 100-249
Type of Packaging: Consumer, Food Service

9927 Nalle Winery
P.O.Box 454
Healdsburg, CA 95448-0454   707-433-1040
Fax: 707-433-6062   doug@nallewinery.com
www.nallewinery.com
Wines
Owner: Lee Nalle
Winemaker: Doug Nalle
Winemaker: Andrew Nalle
Number Employees: 1-4
Number of Brands: 1
Brands:
Nalle

9928 Naman's Meat Company
P.O.Box 88012
Mobile, AL 36608-0012   251-633-2700
Fax: 251-633-2749
Meats
President: Christopher Naman
Estimated Sales: $ 20 - 50 Million
Number Employees: 10-19

9929 Nan Sea Enterprises of Wisconsin
900 Gale St
Waukesha, WI 53186-2515   262-542-8841
Fax: 262-542-4356   www.nanseaofwisc.com
Manufacturer and distributor of fresh frozen king,
dungeness, golden and snow crab; also, lobster and
lobster claws
President: Eric Muehl
VP: Robert Nell
Estimated Sales: $ 10-20 Million
Number Employees: 5-9
Type of Packaging: Food Service, Private Label

9930 Nana Mae's Organics
PO Box 2298
Sebastopol, CA 95473-2298   707-829-7359
Fax: 707-829-7356   appleman@nanamae.com
nanamae.com
Organic apple juice and sauce and vinegar and
honey
Owner: Paul Kolling
R&D: Paul Kolling
Marketing: Paul Kolling
Sales: Kendra Kolling
Public Relations: Kendra Kolling
Estimated Sales: $1,000,000
Number Employees: 15
Number of Brands: 1
Number of Products: 15
Sq. footage: 264000
Type of Packaging: Consumer, Food Service, Private Label, Bulk

9931 Nanci's Frozen Yogurt
1754 N 48th St # 104
Mesa, AZ 85205-3303   480-834-4290
Fax: 480-834-4271   800-788-0808
info@nancis.com   www.nancis.com

Soft serve dessert mixes including frozen yogurt,
fruit freezer sorbet, non-dairy soft serve, no sugar
added mixes, smoothie base mixes, granita mixes
and more than 90 flavors
President/CEO: John Wudel
Spokesperson: Nanci Wudel
Estimated Sales: $ 1 - 3 Million
Number Employees: 10-19
Type of Packaging: Food Service, Bulk
Brands:
Nanci's

9932 Nancy's Candy
171 Electric Rd
Salem, VA 24153   540-986-0550
www.nancyshomemadefudge.com
fudge, chocolates, nut brittles and more

9933 Nancy's Pies
3915 9th St
Rock Island, IL 61201-6721   309-732-4026
Fax: 309-793-0183   800-480-0055
sflorence@nancyspies.com   www.nancyspies.com
Manufacturer of sugar free and no sugar added desserts for diabetics
President: Scott Florence
Quality Control: Susan Stoefen
Marketing Manager: Felicia Carlson
Human Resource Manager: Richard Harper
Manager: Rudy Quick
Estimated Sales: $16 Million
Number Employees: 50-99
Number of Brands: 1
Number of Products: 15
Sq. footage: 60000
Type of Packaging: Bulk

9934 Nancy's Shellfish
91 Falmouth Rd
Falmouth, ME 04105-1841   207-774-3411
Fax: 207-780-0044
Shellfish, seafood
President: Joe Scola
Estimated Sales: $1.4 Million
Number Employees: 5-9

9935 Nancy's Specialty Foods
6500 Overlake Place
Newark, CA 94560-1084   510-494-1100
Fax: 510-494-1140   nsf@nancys.com
www.nancys.com
Processor and exporter of frozen hors d'oeuvres and
quiche
VP Sales: Larry Booth
VP Operations: David Joiner
Plant Manager: Rick Shepherd
Estimated Sales: $19800000
Number Employees: 325
Sq. footage: 86000
Type of Packaging: Consumer, Food Service, Private Label, Bulk
Brands:
Nancy's

9936 Nanka Seimen Company
3030 Leonis Blvd
Vernon, CA 90058-2914   323-585-9967
Fax: 323-585-9969
Processor of Japanese-style and egg noodles, chow
mein, wontons, egg rolls and gyoza skins
President: Shoi Chi Sayano
Estimated Sales: $ 5 - 10 Million
Number Employees: 10-19
Type of Packaging: Consumer, Food Service
Brands:
Golden Dragon
Nanka Udon

9937 Nantucket Nectars
900 King Street
Port Chester, NY 10573-1226   617-868-3600
Fax: 617-868-5490   lorianne@juiceguys.com
www.juiceguys.com
Juices
President: Mark Hellendrung
Chairman: Tom Scott
VP Marketing: Chris Pasta
Public Relations Director: Amy Hornyak
Estimated Sales: $ 20-50 Million
Number Employees: 50-99
Parent Co: Cadbury Schweppes PLC
Type of Packaging: Private Label

9938 Nantucket Off-Shore Seasoning
PO Box 1437
Nantucket, MA 02554-1437   508-994-1300
Fax: 508-257-4533
nantucketseasonings@mediaone.net
BBQ sauce, stuffing blends, BBQ glaze, BBQ marinade

9939 Nantucket Tea Traders
P.O.Box 179
Nantucket, MA 02554-0179   508-325-0203
Fax: 508-325-0203
Tea
President: Judy Kales
Estimated Sales: $120,000
Number Employees: 1-4
Brands:
Nantucket Tea Trader

9940 Nantucket Vineyards
P.O.Box 2928
Nantucket, MA 02584-2928   508-325-5929
Fax: 508-325-5209   jay@ciscobrewers.com
www.ciscobrewers.com
Wine
Owner: Randy Hudson
Founder/Co-Owner: Dean Long
Estimated Sales: $5-9.9 Million
Number Employees: 1-4
Type of Packaging: Private Label
Brands:
Nantucket Vineyard

9941 Nantze Springs
P.O.Box 1273
Dothan, AL 36302-1273   334-794-4218
Fax: 334-712-2899   800-239-7873
cindy@nantzesprings.com
www.nantzesprings.com
Water
President: Malone Garrett
Estimated Sales: $3-5 Million
Number Employees: 50-99
Brands:
Nantze Springs

9942 Napa Cellars
7481 Saint Helena Hwy
Oakville, CA 94562   707-944-2565
Fax: 707-944-9749   800-848-9630
tastingroom@napawineco.com
www.napawineco.com
Wines
Manager: Dean Slattery
Winemaker: Rob Lawson
General Manager: Sheldon Parker
Estimated Sales: $1,600,000
Number Employees: 5-9
Type of Packaging: Private Label
Brands:
Napa Wine

9943 Napa Creek Winery
1001 Silverado Trl S
Saint Helena, CA 94574-9693   707-963-9456
Wines

9944 Napa Valley Kitchens
560 Gateway Dr
Napa, CA 94558-7517   707-254-3700
Fax: 707-254-0742   800-288-1089
contactus@consorzio.com   www.consorzio.com
Manufacturer and exporter of flavored oils, marinades, and dressings
Chairman: John Foraker
Marketing Director: Sarah Bird
Sales Director: Terry Dudley
Production Manager: Mark Osborne
Estimated Sales: $11700000
Number Employees: 50-99
Type of Packaging: Consumer
Brands:
Consorzio
Napa Valley Mustard Co.

9945 Napa Valley Port Cellars
2007 Redwood Rd # 101
Napa, CA 94558-3212   707-257-7777
Fax: 707-257-1497   www.thebankofnapa.com
Wines
President: Shawn Denkler
CEO: M Thomas Lemasters
Estimated Sales: $500-1 Million appx.
Number Employees: 10-19

9946 (HQ)Napa Valley Trading Company
433 Corte Madera Town Center
Suite 487
Corte Madera, CA 94925-1215   415-383-8859
Fax: 415-383-8854 info@napavalleytrading.com
www.napavalleytrading.com
Importer of olive oil, pasta and condiments. Broker of natural and specialty foods
President: Kendall Cook
Sales Director: Norm Peterson
Number Employees: 10-19
Sq. footage: 3000
Type of Packaging: Consumer, Food Service, Private Label, Bulk
Brands:
First Press
Hat Creek
Napa Valley Naturals

9947 Napa Wine Company
P.O.Box 434
Oakville, CA 94562-0434   707-944-8669
Fax: 707-944-9749 800-848-9630
tastingroom@napawineco.com
www.napawineco.com
Wines
Managing Partner: Andrew Hoxsey
General Manager: Sheldon Parker
Winemaker: Rob Lawson
*Estimated Sales:*Under $500,000
Number Employees: 20-49
Type of Packaging: Consumer, Private Label

9948 Napa Wine Company
P.O.Box 434
Oakville, CA 94562-0434   707-944-8669
Fax: 707-944-9749 800-848-9630
retail@napawineco.com   www.napawineco.com
Custom crush wine production
Owner: Andrew Hoxsey
Managing Partner: Andrew Hoxse
General Manager: Sheldon Parker
*Estimated Sales:*Below $ 5 Million
Number Employees: 20-49
Brands:
Napa Wine Company

9949 Napoleon Locker
P.O.Box 38
Napoleon, IN 47034-0038   812-852-4333
Processor of beef and pork; slaughtering services available
Owner: Matt Brancamp
Co-Owner: Kimberly Brancamp
Estimated Sales:$ .5 - 1 million
Number Employees: 10-19
Type of Packaging: Private Label

9950 Napoli Pasta Manufacturers
9719 S Dixie Hwy # 8
Miami, FL 33156-2834   305-666-1942
Fax: 305-254-6139 npmgroup@aol.com
www.worldtrade.org/afb/companies
Pasta products
Owner: Gene Napoli
Plant Manager: Patricia Matuk
Estimated Sales:$5-9.9 Million
Number Employees: 1-4

9951 Nardi Bakery & Deli
12 Connecticut Boulevard
East Hartford, CT 06108-3007   860-289-5458
Fax: 860-289-9012 http://www.nardibakery.com
Bread and rolls
President: Charles Nardi
Estimated Sales:$ 5-9.9 Million
Number Employees: 17

9952 Nardone Brothers BakingPizza Company
420 New Commerce Blvd
Hanover Twp, PA 18706-1445   570-823-0141
Fax: 570-823-2581 800-822-5320
nardone1@ptdprolog.net www.nardonebros.com
Manufacturer of pizza
President: Vinnie Nardone
Secretary: Tom Nardone
CFO: Louis Nardone
Treasurer: Mario Nardone
Estimated Sales:$ 10 - 20 Million
Number Employees: 100-249
Type of Packaging: Consumer

Brands:
NARDONE BROS.
VINCENZO'S

9953 Naron Mary Sue Candy Company
1786 Union Ave
Baltimore, MD 21211-1417   410-467-9338
Fax: 410-467-1649
Manufacturer and importer of gourmet chocolate candy
President: Bill Buppert
VP Production: Mark Berman
Estimated Sales:$10 Million
Number Employees: 5-9
Sq. footage: 68000
Type of Packaging: Consumer, Private Label, Bulk

9954 Nash Finch Company
P.O.Box 490
Statesboro, GA 30459-0490   912-681-4580
Fax: 912-681-1817 www.nashfinch.com
Manager: Preston Benson
Estimated Sales:$ 50 - 100 Million
Number Employees: 50-99

9955 Nash Produce Company
6160 S Nc Highway 58
Nashville, NC 27856-8642   252-443-6011
Fax: 252-443-6746 800-334-3032
nashproduce@aol.com   www.nashproduce.com
Processor of sweet potatoes and cucumbers
President: Thomas Joyner
CEO: Paprica Cooper
Marketing Director: Richard Donna
Sales Manager: Richard Joyner
Estimated Sales:$ 5 - 10 Million
Number Employees: 20-49
Brands:
Nash Produce

9956 Nashoba Valley Winery
92 Wattaquadock Hill Rd
Bolton, MA 01740-1238   978-779-5521
Fax: 978-779-5523 nashoba.winery@gte.net
www.nashobawinery.com
Wines
President: Richard Pelletier
VP: Cindy Rowe Pelletier
*Estimated Sales:*Below $ 5 Million
Number Employees: 20-49
Type of Packaging: Private Label

9957 Nasonville Dairy
10898 Us Highway 10
Marshfield, WI 54449-9772   715-676-2177
Fax: 715-676-3636 www.nasonvilledairy.com
Cheese, cheese products
Owner: Kim Heiman
*Estimated Sales:*Below $ 5 Million
Number Employees: 20-49

9958 (HQ)Nassau Candy Company
530 W John St
Hicksville, NY 11801-1039   516-342-1495
Fax: 516-433-9010 sales@nassaucandy.com
nassaucandy.com
Wholesaler/distributor and importer of confectionery items and specialty food products including pasta, vegetables and salami
Manager: Butch Hurley
Estimated Sales:$ 20 - 50 Million
Number Employees: 100-249
Other Locations:
Nassau Candy Co.
Deer Park NY

9959 Natalie's Orchard Island Juice
330 N Us Highway 1
Fort Pierce, FL 34950-4207   772-465-1122
Fax: 772-465-4303 oijc@gate.net
www.oijc.com
Processor and exporter of fresh squeezed orange, grapefruit, lemon and lime juices; also, lemonade and blended juices
President: Marygrace Sexton
Assistant CEO: John Martinelli
Sales/Logistics Manager: David Cortez
Estimated Sales:$ 20 - 50 Million
Number Employees: 100-249
Type of Packaging: Consumer, Food Service
Brands:
COMPANY FRESHLY SQUEEZED JUICES
NATALIE'S ORCHID ISLAND

9960 Natchez Pecan Shelling Company
P.O.Box 100
Taylorsville, MS 39168-0100   601-785-4333
Pecans
Owner: Harold Bynum
*Estimated Sales:*Less than $500,000
Number Employees: 1-4

9961 Naterl
57 Rabastaliere
St. Bruno, QC J3V 2A4
Canada   450-653-3655
Fax: 450-653-9633 800- 50- 115
www.natrel.com
Processor of milk, butter, ice cream mix, chocolate milk and lemonade
President: Serge Serge Paquette
VP Marketing: Doug Kelly McGregor Gillespie
VP Finance/Administration: Éric Brunelle
Plant Manager: Gerry Verhoef
Number Employees: 100-249
Parent Co: Natrel
Type of Packaging: Consumer
Brands:
Naterl
Quebon
Sealtest
Silk Soy
Ultra'cream

9962 Nathan Seagall Company
1667 Federal Dr # 12
Montgomery, AL 36107-1103   334-279-3174
Fax: 334-279-1751
Manufacturer of produce
Manager: Reid Barnes
Estimated Sales:$3-5 Million
Number Employees: 5-9

9963 Nation Pizza Products
601 E Algonquin Rd
Schaumburg, IL 60173-3803   847-397-3320
Fax: 847-397-9456 drpizza@anationpizza.com
www.nationpizza.com
Frozen pizza sauce and crusts
President: Marshall Bauer
CEO: Marshall Bauer
Estimated Sales:$ 20 - 50 Million
Number Employees: 500-999
Type of Packaging: Consumer
Brands:
Father & Son
My Father's Best
Nation

9964 National Bakers Services
2 S University Drive
Suite 330
Plantation, FL 33324-3307   954-920-7666
Baked goods

9965 (HQ)National Beef Packing
12200 N Ambassador Drive
Suite 500
Kansas City, MO 64163   816-713-8500
Fax: 816-713-8863 800-449-2333
www.nationalbeef.com
Manufacturer of frozen and processed beef
Chairman: Steven Hunt
CEO: Timothy Klein
EVP Operations: Terry Wilkerson
Estimated Sales:$5.4 Billion
Number Employees: 8,900
Parent Co: US Premium Beef, LLC
Type of Packaging: Consumer, Food Service, Private Label, Bulk
Other Locations:
Brawley CA
Brands:
BLACK CANYON® ANGUS BEEF
BLACK CANYON® PREMIUM RESERVE
CERTIFIED ANGUS BEEF®
CERTIFIED ANGUS BEEF® PRIME
CERTIFIED HEREFORD BEEF®
CERTIFIED PREMIUM BEEF®
IMPERIAL VALLEY® PREMIUM BEEF
NATIONAL BEEF®
NATURESOURCE® NATURAL ANGUS
NATUREWELL® NATURAL BEEF
VINTAGE NATURAL BEEF®

9966 National Beverage Corporation
8100 SW Tenth Street
Suite 4000
Fort Lauderdale, FL 33324   954-581-0922
Fax: 954-473-4710 888-462-2349
asknbc@nationalbeverage.com www.nbcfiz.com
Non-alcoholic beverages
President: Joseph Caporella
Chairman/CEO: Nick Caporella
SVP Finance: George Bracken
Estimated Sales:$575 Million
Number Employees: 1200
Parent Co: American Citrus
Type of Packaging: Consumer, Food Service
Brands:
ASANTE
BIG SHOT
CASCADIA ONLY 2 CALORIES
CASCADIA SPARKLING CLEAR
CLEARFRUIT
CRYSTAL BAY
EVERFRESH
FAYGO
LACROIX
MR. PURE
MT. SHASTA
OHANA
RIP IT
RITZ
SHASTA
ST. NICK'S

9967 National Beverage Corporation
8100 SW 10th Streeet
Suite 4000
Fort Lauderdale, FL 33324   954-581-0922
Fax: 954-473-4710 888-462-2349
salesteam@nationalbeverage.com
www.nbcfiz.com
Manufacturer of canned and bottled beverages including soft drinks, juice and spring water
President: Joseph Caporella
Chairman/CEO: Nick Caporella
SVP Finance: George Bracken
Estimated Sales:$575 Million
Number Employees: 1,200
Type of Packaging: Consumer, Food Service
Other Locations:
National Beverage Corp.
Hayward CA
Brands:
ASANTE
BIG SHOT
CASCADIA ONLY 2 CALORIES
CASCADIA SPARKLING CIDER
CLEARFRUIT
CRYSTAL BAY
EVERFRESH
FAYGO
LACROIX
MR PURE
MT. SHASTA
OHANA
RIP IT
RITZ
SHASTA
ST. NICK'S

9968 National By-Products
P.O.Box 7234
Omaha, NE 68107-0234   402-291-2646
Fax: 402-291-4034 bellevue@nbyprod.com
www.nationalby-products.com
Processor of meat
Estimated Sales:$7100000
Number Employees: 50-99
Parent Co: Meat Rendering Company
Type of Packaging: Consumer

9969 National Cheese Company
675 Rivermede Road
Concord, ON L4K 2G9
Canada   905-669-9393
Fax: 905-669-5614
Processor, wholesaler/distributor and importer of cheese
President: Salvatore Lettieri
Vice President: Louis Lettieri
VP: Peter Frangella
Number Employees: 120
Sq. footage: 100000
Type of Packaging: Consumer, Food Service, Private Label, Bulk

Brands:
Tre Stelle

9970 National Egg Products Company
P.O.Box 1377
Social Circle, GA 30025-1377   770-464-2652
Fax: 770-464-2998 www.tyson.com
Processor and exporter of egg products including standard yolk, whole, whites and albumen
Manager: Brad Ginnane
Sales/Marketing Manager: Brad Ginnane
Plant Manager: Terry Anglin
Estimated Sales:$ 1 - 3 Million
Number Employees: 1-4
Sq. footage: 60000
Parent Co: Rose Acre Farms
Type of Packaging: Bulk

9971 National Enzyme Company
P.O.Box 128
Forsyth, MO 65653-0128   417-546-4796
Fax: 417-546-6433 800-825-8545
mail@nzimes.com
www.nationalenzymecompany.com
Manufacturer and exporter of digestive enzymes and nutritional supplements
President: Anthony Collier
Director R&D: Rohit Medhekar PhD
VP Sales/Marketing: Rex Weiss
Marketing Manager: Gary Bennett
Director Manufacturing: Jerry Holvick
Estimated Sales:$ 20 - 50 Million
Number Employees: 50-99
Type of Packaging: Private Label, Bulk
Brands:
EDS
Nozimes

9972 National Fish & OystersCompany
5028 Meridian Rd NE
Olympia, WA 98516-2339   360-491-5550
Fax: 360-438-3681 www.nationaloyster.com
Processor and exporter of fresh and frozen oysters
President: James Bulldis
VP: George Bulldis
Plant Manager: Catherine Gylys
Estimated Sales:$ 5 - 10 Million
Number Employees: 20-49
Sq. footage: 3000
Type of Packaging: Consumer
Brands:
Sea Pearl

9973 National Fish & Seafood
11-15 Parker St
Gloucester, MA 01930-3017   978-282-7880
Fax: 978-282-7882 www.nationalfish.com
Seafood
President: Jack Ventola
Number Employees: 20-49

9974 (HQ)National Fisheries
5151 NW 165th St
Hialeah, FL 33014-6302   305-628-1231
Fax: 305-620-4831
Seafood, seafood products
President: Simon Storn
CFO: Allan Wright
VP: Jack Karson
Purchasing Manager: Enrico Taboado
Estimated Sales:$ 20-50 Million
Number Employees: 50-99
Sq. footage: 35
Type of Packaging: Consumer, Food Service, Private Label

9975 National Fisheries - Marathon
3880 Gulfview Avenue
Marathon, FL 33050-2320   305-743-5545
Fresh seafood including Florida lobster and stone crabs.
President: Simon Storn
Manager: Leo Cooper
Estimated Sales:$10-20 Million
Number Employees: 20-49
Parent Co: National Fisheries

9976 National Food Company
3109 Koapaka St # C
Honolulu, HI 96819-1998   808-839-1118
Fax: 808-839-6866
President: Peter Goo
Estimated Sales:$ 5 - 10 Million
Number Employees: 5-9

9977 National Food Corporation
11725 NW 100th Road
Building 9
Medley, FL 33178-1013   305-884-2020
Fax: 305-884-0303 www.nationalfood.com
Processor, exporter, importer and wholesaler/distributor of plantain, cassava and potato chips, pork rinds, pastries and toast bread
President: Alberto Abrante
VP: Jose Abrante
Number Employees: 10-19
Type of Packaging: Consumer, Food Service, Private Label, Bulk
Brands:
Bananitas
Mariquitas
Rico's
Yuquitas

9978 National Food Corporation
1930 Merrill Creek Pkwy # A
Everett, WA 98203-5897   425-349-4257
Fax: 425-349-4336 www.natlfood.com
Processor and exporter of kosher cream cheese
President: Brian Bookey
Estimated Sales:$ 100-500 Million
Number Employees: 100-249
Type of Packaging: Consumer, Food Service

9979 National Foods
1414 S West Street
Indianapolis, IN 46225-1548   317-634-5645
800-683-6565
Processor and exporter of portion cut meat and frankfurters
President: Steve Silk
Senior VP/General Manager: Martin Silver
Sales/Marketing Executive: Mark Kleinman
Number Employees: 600
Sq. footage: 180000
Parent Co: ConAgra Refrigerated Prepared Foods
Type of Packaging: Consumer, Food Service
Other Locations:
National Foods
Indianapolis IN

9980 National Foods
P.O.Box 978
Liberal, KS 67905-0978   620-624-1851
Fax: 620-626-0624 www.nationalbeef.com
General grocery
President: John Miller
Sales Manager: Mike Sheehan
Parent Co: ConAgra Refrigerated Prepared Foods

9981 National Foods
600 Food Center Drive
Bronx, NY 10474-7037   718-842-5000
Fax: 718-842-5664 800-683-6565
www.higherauthority.com
Processed meats, frankfurters, condiments and relishes. Kosher
President: Steve Silk
CFO: Bob Cahill
Executive VP: Marty Silver
Senior Marketing Manager: Leigh Platte
Sales Director: Scott Jacobs
Operations Manager: Henry Morris
General Manager: Robert Lichtman
Number Employees: 150
Parent Co: ConAgra Refrigerated Prepared Foods
Type of Packaging: Private Label

9982 National Frozen Foods Corporation
P.O.Box 9366
Seattle, WA 98109-0366   206-322-8900
Fax: 206-322-4458 www.nationalfrozenfoods.com
Processor, packer and exporter of frozen foods including fruit and vegetable purees, vegetable blends, peas, corn, carrots, cooked squash, creamed corn, beans, pearl onions, etc
President: S McCaffray
COO: W Rosenbach
CFO: C Gazarek
Human Resources: Bill Wallace
Quality Control: J Bafus
*Estimated Sales:*I
Number Employees: 1,000-4,999
Type of Packaging: Consumer, Food Service, Private Label, Bulk
Brands:
Valamont

9983 National Fruit Flavor Company
935 Edwards Ave
New Orleans, LA 70123-3124   504-733-6757
        Fax: 504-736-0168   800-966-1123
        admin@nationalfruitflavor.com
        www.nationalfruitflavor.com
Beverage concentrates, syrups and mixes
        President: Gene Gamble
        CEO: Eugene Gambel
        VP: Peter Gambel
        Quality Control: Blaine Hill
        Marketing/Sales: Avery Stirratt
        Public Relations: Chris Rooks
        Operations: Peter Gambel
        Quality Control: Blaine Hill
        Plant Manager: Giovanni Galvan
        Purchasing: Mike Ennis
Estimated Sales:$ 10-20 Million
Number Employees: 20-49
Number of Brands: 6
Number of Products: 700
Sq. footage: 41000
Type of Packaging: Consumer, Food Service, Private Label, Bulk
Brands:
        GAMBELINI
        NATIONAL
        OLD COMISKEY
        SNO-BALL
        TASTY
        ZODIAC

9984 National Fruit Product Company
PO Box 916
Lincolnton, NC 28093-0916   704-735-2531
        Fax: 704-732-1779
Processor of vinegar, apple cider, apple juice, juice drinks and apple sauce; also, co-packing available
        President: David Crum
        VP Quality: Jim Zambra
        VP CoPack Sales: L D Shockley
        Operations Manager: Scott MaClean
Number Employees: 100-249
Type of Packaging: Food Service, Private Label
Brands:
        Twelve Oaks
        White House

9985 National Fruit Product Company
P.O.Box 2040
Winchester, VA 22604-1240   540-662-3401
        Fax: 540-665-4671 www.bchn.org
Manufacturer of apple products
        President/COO: Frank Armstrong IV
        CEO: Frank Armstrong Iii
Estimated Sales:$100+ Million
Number Employees: 500-999
Sq. footage: 350000
Type of Packaging: Consumer, Food Service, Private Label, Bulk
Other Locations:
        National Fruit Product Plant
        Winchester NC
        National Fruit Product Plant
        Lincolnton NC
Brands:
        Orchard Boy
        Shenandoah
        Skyland
        White House

9986 National Grape Cooperative
2 S Portage St
Westfield, NY 14787   716-326-5200
        Fax: 716-326-5494   nationalinfo@welchs.com
        www.nationalgrape.com
Fruit and berry juices and jams
        President: Joseph Falcone
        Financial/Accounting Officer: Michael Perda
        General Manager/COO: Brent Roggie
*Estimated Sales:*J
Number Employees: 1,325
Brands:
        Welch's Fruit Juices
        Welch's Jams, Jellie
        Welch's Orchard Froz

9987 National Harvest
PO Box 26455
Kansas City, MO 64196-6455   816-842-9600
        Fax: 816-531-3032   sales@nationalharvest.com
        www.nationalharvest.com/contact

Manufacturer of Baked potato meals and toppings
        President: John Mueller
Estimated Sales:$ 1 - 3 Million
Number Employees: 5-9
Type of Packaging: Food Service, Private Label, Bulk
Brands:
        SUPER STUFFERS

9988 National Importers
1555 Clark Boulevard
Brampton, ON L6T 4G2
Canada   905-791-1322
        Fax: 905-791-6016
Importer of gourmet, Mexican, Chinese, Indian and Thai foods, candy and groceries
        Office Manager: Peggy Hunter
Parent Co: National Importers

9989 National Meat & Provision Company
PO Box 52209
New Orleans, LA 70152-2209   504-525-7224
        Fax: 504-525-4499
Meat
        President: Leonard Lalla

9990 National Noodle Company
741 Commercial Street
San Francisco, CA 94108-1836   415-781-5143
        natlnoodle@aol.com
Processor of Chinese noodles
        Co-Owner: Henry Siu
        Co-Owner: Stacey Siu
Number Employees: 5-9
Sq. footage: 4000
Type of Packaging: Consumer

9991 National Products Company
1206 E Crosstown Pkwy
Kalamazoo, MI 49001-2563   269-344-3640
        Fax: 269-344-1037 www.nationalflavors.com
Syrups, flavoring extracts, processed fruits and oils
        Owner: John Hinkle
Estimated Sales:$ 10-20 Million
Number Employees: 20-49

9992 National Raisin Company
P.O.Box 219
Fowler, CA 93625-0219   559-834-5981
        Fax: 559-834-1055   info@nationalraisin.com
        www.national-raisin.com
Manufacturer and exporter of raisins
        Founder/Co-President: Ernest Bedrosian
        Co-Founder/Co-President: Krikor Bedrosian
        Co-Founder/Co-President: Kenneth Bedrosian
Estimated Sales:$ 50 - 100 Million
Number Employees: 100-249
Type of Packaging: Consumer, Food Service, Private Label, Bulk
Brands:
        Champion

9993 (HQ)National Starch & Chemical Corporate Office
10 Finderne Avenue
Bridgewater, NJ 08807   908-685-5082
        Fax: 908-685-7037   800-366-4031
        nscinquiry@salessupport.com
        www.nationalstarch.com
Manufacturer of specialty starches and fat replacers
        CEO: Walter Schlauch
        CFO: Han Kieftenbeld
        EVP: James Zallie
Estimated Sales:$3 Billion
Number Employees: 2,250
Parent Co: Imperial Chemical Industries
Brands:
        N-Lite
        National
        Purity

9994 National Steak & Poultry
301 E 5th Ave
Owasso, OK 74055   918-274-8787
        Fax: 918-274-0046   800-366-6772
        info@nationalsteak.com   www.nationalsteak.com
Manufacturer of marinated pre-portioned beef and poultry both fully cooked and fresh frozen
        President/CEO: David Albright
        Controller: Bhrent Waddell
        Sales Executive: Dale Lemon
        Plant Manager: Bill Josey

Estimated Sales:$500 Million-$ 1 Billion
Number Employees: 325
Brands:
        NATIONAL STEAK

9995 National Vinegar Company
PO Box 255
Alton, IL 62002-0255   618-465-6532
        Fax: 618-465-7111
Processor of distilled vinegar and sweet cider
        President: Virginia Braun
Estimated Sales:$ 5 - 10 Million
Number Employees: 10-19
Type of Packaging: Consumer, Food Service, Private Label, Bulk
Brands:
        Alton
        Garden Harvest
        Hardin

9996 National Vinegar Company
P.O.Box 2761
Houston, TX 77252-2761   713-223-4214
        Fax: 713-223-4603
        alexwolff@nationalvinegar.com
Manufacturer of distilled white, apple cider, red wine and corn vinegar
        Manager: Joan Weiner
        Vice President: David Wolff
Estimated Sales:$5 Million
Number Employees: 20-49
Type of Packaging: Consumer, Food Service, Private Label, Bulk
Brands:
        National

9997 (HQ)National Vinegar Company
8460 Watson Road
Suite 232b
Saint Louis, MO 63119-5294   314-842-2822
        Fax: 314-842-7298   info@natvin.com
        www.natvin.com
Manufacturer of vinegar
Estimated Sales:$ 1 - 3 Million
Number Employees: 10-19
Type of Packaging: Consumer
Other Locations:
        National Vinegar Company Plant
        Alton IL
        National Vinegar Company Plant
        Olney IL

9998 Nationwide Canning
Effix County Road 34 E
Cottam, ON N0R 1B0
Canada   519-839-4831
        Fax: 519-839-4993
Processor of canned and crushed tomatoes, mushrooms, potatoes, pie fillings, kidney beans and spaghetti and pizza sauce; also, private labeling available
        President and CFO: H Finaldi
        Office Manager: Irene Finaldi
Number Employees: 55
Sq. footage: 50000
Type of Packaging: Private Label
Brands:
        Cottam Gardens

9999 Native American Tea & Cofee
P.O.Box 1266
Aberdeen, SD 57402-1266   605-226-2006
        Fax: 605-226-2414   info@nativeamericantea.com
        www.nativeamericantea.com
Coffee, tea
        Manager: J Almon
*Estimated Sales:*Below $ 5 Million
Number Employees: 5-9
Brands:
        Native American

10000 Native Kjalii Foods
459 Fulton St # 205
San Francisco, CA 94102-4365   415-522-5580
        Fax: 510-686-1757   nativefo@sfsalsa.com
        www.sfsalsa.com
Manufacturer fruit and vegetable salsas, vegetable hummus and tortilla chips
        President/Co-Owner: Bret Jeremy
        Marketing/Co-Owner: Julie Jeremy
Estimated Sales:$ 3 - 5 Million
Number Employees: 1-4
Sq. footage: 4000
Type of Packaging: Consumer, Food Service, Bulk

Brands:
NATIVE KJALII

10001 Native Scents
1040 Dea Ln
Taos, NM 87571-6277   575-758-9656
    Fax: 575-758-5802   800-645-3471
nativescents@starband.net   www.nativescents.net
Processor, importer and exporter of herbal teas and
aromatic products, honey and essential oils, incense,
bath products
President: Marlene Payfoya
CEO: Alfred Savinelli
Estimated Sales: $641,586
Number Employees: 10-19
Number of Products: 127
Sq. footage: 6000
Brands:
Native Scents

10002 Native South Services
Po Box 1157
Fredericksburg, TX 78624   830-997-1431
    Fax: 830-990-9481   800-236-2848
service@nativesouth.com   www.nativesouth.com
Manufacturer of salsas and tortilla chips, vidalia on-
ion cheese biscuits, fried green tomato biscuits and
white chocolate sweet potato biscuits
President/Owner: Lynne Simmons
Estimated Sales: Below $5 Million
Number Employees: 4
Type of Packaging: Food Service, Private Label
Brands:
NATIVE SOUTH

10003 Natra US
1059 Tierra Del Rey #H
Chula Vista, CA 91910-7884   619-397-4120
    Fax: 619-397-4121   800-262-6216
    info@natraus.com
Importer and exporter of cocoa powder, butter and
extract; also, chocolate, caffeine, theobromine and
nutraceuticals
Manager: Maria Dominguez
Vice President: Martin Brabenec
Estimated Sales: $650000
Number Employees: 1-4
Number of Brands: 2
Number of Products: 30
Parent Co: Natra S.A.
Type of Packaging: Consumer, Food Service, Bulk
Brands:
Natra Cacao
Natra US
Natraceutical

10004 Natren
3105 Willow Ln # 100
Thousand Oaks, CA 91361-4919   805-371-4737
    Fax: 805-371-4742   800-992-3323
Processor of yogurt starter and probiotic products
President: Natasha Trenev
CEO: Yordan Trenev
Estimated Sales: $1400000
Number Employees: 50-99
Brands:
Bifido Factor
Bifido Nate
Bio-Nate
D.F.A.
Digesta-Lac
Life Start
Megadophilus
Yogurt Starter

10005 (HQ)Natrium Products
P.O.Box 5465
Cortland, NY 13045-5465   607-753-9829
    Fax: 607-753-0552   800-962-4203
herman@natrium.com   www.natrium.com
Baking Soda/Sodium Biocarbonate manufacturer
President: Tim Herman
Marketing Director: Tim Herman
Estimated Sales: $ 10 - 20 Million
Number Employees: 10-19
Sq. footage: 35000
Type of Packaging: Bulk
Brands:
NATRIUM

10006 Natur Sweeteners, Inc.
11155 Massachusetts Avenue
Los Angeles, CA 90025   310-445-0020
    Fax: 310-473-1086   lmiles@naturresearch.com
    www.cweet.com
Manufacturer of natural intense sweetener; characteristics and other performance qualities similar to
cane sugar

10007 Naturade Inc
1003 N Euclid St
Anaheim, CA 92801-3635   714-535-9178
    Fax: 714-986-7324   800-367-2880
    sales@naturade.com   www.naturade.com
Manufacturer of soy protein powder shake mixes,
herbal-based cough and cold formulas, and
colostrum supplements.
Founder: Nathan Schulman
Executive Vice President Sales: Rick Robinette

10008 (HQ)Natural Balance
383 Inverness Pkwy # 390
Englewood, CO 80112-5864   303-688-6633
    Fax: 303-688-1591   800-624-4260
    service@naturalbalance.com
    www.naturalbalance.com
Processor and wholesaler/distributor of natural nu-
trition supplements for energy, weight loss and
sports
President: Mark Owens
Executive VP: Tim Hinricks
Sales Coordinator: Scott Smith
Plant Manager: John O'Brien
Purchasing Manager: Stephanie McArthur
Estimated Sales: $11400000
Number Employees: 100-249
Sq. footage: 25000
Other Locations:
Natural Balance
Castle Rock CO

10009 Natural By Nature
P.O.Box 464
West Grove, PA 19390-0464   610-268-6962
    Fax: 610-268-4172   www.natural-by-nature.com
Milk, dairy products
Owner: Ned Mac Arthur
Head Sales: Allan Kulick
Estimated Sales: $ 100-500 Million
Number Employees: 100-249

10010 Natural Choice Distribution
5427 Telegraph Ave # U
Oakland, CA 94609-1969   510-653-8212
    Fax: 510-653-8163
Salsa and sandwiches, distribution of natural food
products
Owner: Steve Cutter
Estimated Sales: Below $ 5 Million
Number Employees: 20-49
Type of Packaging: Private Label

10011 Natural Company
8 W Hamilton St
Baltimore, MD 21201-5008   410-628-1262
    Fax: 410-796-3977
    info@thenaturalcompany.com.au
    www.keeper.com.au
Health food, tofu
President: Joan Huang
Estimated Sales: Below $ 5 Million
Number Employees: 6
Brands:
Moon Pads
The Keeper

10012 Natural Enrichment Industries, LLC
1002 South Park
Sesser, IL 62884   618-625-2112
    Fax: 618-625-3112   maryc@neitcp.com
    www.neitcp.com
Manufacturer of Tricalcium Phosphate from a do-
mestically produced lime.
Sales & Marketing Representative: Marci Swartz
Sales Manager: Mary Clark

10013 Natural Exotic Tropicals
450 SW 12th Ave
Pompano Beach, FL 33069-3504   954-783-4500
    Fax: 954-783-8812   800-756-5267
    sales@naturalexotic.com
    www.naturalexotic.com

Sugar-free fruit spreads, jellies, marmalades, butters
and juices
President: Van Herrington
CFO: Jayne Herrington
Estimated Sales: $ 5 - 10 Million
Number Employees: 20-49
Brands:
Natural Exotic Tropicals

10014 Natural Feast Corporation
PO Box 36
Dover, MA 02030-0036   508-984-4230
    Fax: 508-984-1496
Frozen foods
President: Alan Attridge
Estimated Sales: $ 1-2.5 Million
Number Employees: 10

10015 Natural Food Supplements
8725 Remmet Ave
Canoga Park, CA 91304-1519   818-341-3375
    Fax: 818-341-3376
Processor and contract packager of vitamins
President: Elmer Walters
Estimated Sales: $600000
Number Employees: 5-9
Type of Packaging: Bulk
Brands:
Sunshine Valley

10016 Natural Food World
6009 Washington Boulevard
Culver City, CA 90232-7425   310-836-7770
    Fax: 310-836-6454
Health and dietetic foods
President: Anne Stern
Estimated Sales: $ 5-10 Million
Number Employees: 10

10017 Natural Foods
3040 Hill Ave
Toledo, OH 43607-2983   419-537-1711
    Fax: 419-531-6887   800-860-0006
    www.bulkfoods.com
Wholesaler/distributor, importer and packer of dried
fruits including apples, apricots, cherries, papayas,
mangoes, peaches, figs, etc.; also, nuts, candy, bee
pollen, yeast, lecithin, seeds, chocolates, beans, oat
bran, spices, etc
Owner: Frank Dietrich
Estimated Sales: $5,000,000
Number Employees: 20-49
Sq. footage: 450000
Type of Packaging: Food Service, Bulk

10018 Natural Formulas
2125 American Ave
Hayward, CA 94545-1899   510-372-1800
    Fax: 510-782-9793   www.gnld.com
Processor of powdered drink mixes
President: Robert Murphy
Quality Control: Ric Green
Estimated Sales: $ 10 - 20 Million
Number Employees: 50-99

10019 Natural Fruit Corporation
770 W 20th St
Hialeah, FL 33010-2430   305-887-7525
    Fax: 305-888-8208   info@nfc-fruti.com
    www.nfc-fruti.com
Processor and exporter of frozen fruit bars, cocktail
mixes and ice cream novelties
President: Simon Bravo
VP: George Bravo, Sr.
VP Sales/Plant Manager: George Bravo, Jr.
Estimated Sales: $6100000
Number Employees: 20-49
Sq. footage: 20000
Brands:
Allison Jayne
Chunks O'Fruit
Fruti

10020 (HQ)Natural Group
505 South A Street
Second Floor
Oxnard, CA 93030   805-485-3420
    Fax: 805-983-1428
    customerservice@naturalgroup.net
    www.naturalgroup.net
Non-alcoholic beverages, waters, food products
Owner: Kanishka Lal
Executive VP: Judith Keer

Estimated Sales: Below $ 5 Million
Number Employees: 1-4
Type of Packaging: Private Label
Brands:
   AME
   Ame Celebration
   Apres
   Hildon Water
   Purdey's
   Yellow Gold Shelf St

10021 Natural Nectar
196 E Main Street
Huntington, NY 11743   631-367-7280
          Fax: 631-367-7282 www.natural-nectar.com
cracklebred, whole grain wafers, tuiles ice cream
wafers, nectar nugget peanut butter cup, cinnamon
sticks & pretzel cookies, mediterranean sea salt,
chocodream

10022 Natural Oils International
2279 Ward Ave
Simi Valley, CA 93065-1863   805-433-0160
          www.naturaloils.com
Processor, importer and exporter of vegetable oils
   President: Brendon Bonnar
   Sales: Barbara Hardy
   Sales: Jack Phillips
Estimated Sales: $ 1 - 3 Million
Number Employees: 1-4
Sq. footage: 30000

10023 (HQ)Natural Ovens Bakery
4300 County Road Cr
Manitowoc, WI 54220-9263   920-758-2500
          Fax: 920-758-2594 800-558-3535
          www.naturalovens.com
Processor of bread, cookies, rolls and bagels.
   President: Barbara Stitt
   Chairman: Paul Stitt
   CEO: Matt Taylor
   VP Production: Glen Hietpas
Estimated Sales: $ 20 - 50 Million
Number Employees: 100-249
Sq. footage: 28000
Brands:
   100% Whole Grain
   Flax N' Honey
   Nutty All-Natural Wheat
   Sunny Millet

10024 Natural Products
2211 6th Ave
Grinnell, IA 50112-2276   641-236-0852
          Fax: 641-236-4835 npi@npisoy.com
          www.npisoy.com
Roast and mill soybean, flour and grits for food in-
dustry
   General Manager: Paul Lang
   Quality Control: Ray Lang
   Marketing Director: Jon Stratford
Estimated Sales: Below $ 5 Million
Number Employees: 10-19

10025 Natural Quality Company
13805 Llagas Ave
San Martin, CA 95046-9564   408-683-2182
          Fax: 408-683-4249 natqual@aol.com
          www.naturalquality.com
Frozen celery, peppers, chillies
   President: Karen Ash
   COO: Karen Ash
Estimated Sales: $ 50-100 Million
Number Employees: 100-249
Number of Brands: 1

10026 Natural Quick Foods
P.O.Box 25861
Seattle, WA 98165-1361   206-365-5757
          Fax: 206-365-5434 nqf@uswest.net
Vegan, organic pocket sandwiches
   President: Larry Brewer
Estimated Sales: $ 5 - 10 Million
Number Employees: 5-9

10027 Natural Rush
PO Box 421753
San Francisco, CA 94142-1753   415-863-2503
          Fax: 415-431-5763 www.naturalrush.com
Candy, confectionery and honey
   President: Gilles Desaulniers
Estimated Sales: Under $500,000
Number Employees: 1-4
Type of Packaging: Private Label

10028 Natural Spring Water Company
Johnson City, TN 37604   423-926-7905
          Fax: 423-926-8210
Contract packager and bottler of noncarbonated
mountain spring water
   President: Bill Lizzio
   Team Leader: John Gustke
Number Employees: 10-19
Sq. footage: 12000
Type of Packaging: Consumer, Food Service, Pri-
vate Label, Bulk
Brands:
   Laure Pristine

10029 Natural Value Products
14 Waterthrush Ct
Sacramento, CA 95831-2347   916-427-7242
          Fax: 916-427-3784 gary@naturalvalue.com
Processor importer and exporter of organic products
including canned tomatoes, beans, oils, pasta and
pasta and hot sauces; importer of tuna, mandarin or-
anges and artichokes
   President: Gary Cohen
   CEO: Jody Cohen
Estimated Sales: $ 1 - 3 Million
Number Employees: 1-4
Number of Brands: 1
Number of Products: 700
Type of Packaging: Consumer, Food Service, Bulk

10030 Natural Way Mills
24509 390th St NE
Middle River, MN 56737-9367   218-222-3677
          Fax: 218-222-3408 info@naturalwaymills.com
          www.naturalwaymills.com
Processor and exporter of organic wheat,
seven-grain cereal, rye, flax seed, barley, millet,
brown rice, flour and grits; custom milling available;
also, packaging in nitrogen-pack baskets available
   President: Ray Juhl
   CEO: Helen Juhl
   Sales: Rebekah Knapp
   Plant Manager: Charles Knapp
Estimated Sales: $620,000
Number Employees: 5-9
Brands:
   7 Grain Cereal
   Gold N. White Bread Flour

10031 Natural Wonder Foods
1221 45th Street
Brooklyn, NY 11219-2025   718-436-6811
          Fax: 718-972-9708
Processor and exporter of frozen vegetarian burgers,
cutlets and franks
   President: Joseph Grossman
Estimated Sales: $1000000
Number Employees: 6
Type of Packaging: Consumer, Food Service, Pri-
vate Label, Bulk
Brands:
   Frozen Wonders
   Gold

10032 Naturally Delicious
1811 NW 29th St
Oakland Park, FL 33311-2123   954-485-6730
Fax: 954-485-6834 info@naturally-delicious.com
          www.naturally-delicious.com
Breads
   Owner/President: Arthur Price
Estimated Sales: $230,000
Number Employees: 5-9
Brands:
   Naturally Delicious

10033 Naturally Fresh Foods
1000 Naturally Fresh Blvd
College Park, GA 30349-2909   404-765-9000
          Fax: 404-765-9016 800-765-1950
          bdotson@naturallyfresh.com
          www.naturallyfresh.com
Manufacturer and exporter of syrups, sauces, salad
dressings, dips and quiche and bar mixes
   Chairman: Robert Brooks
   President/COO: Jerry Green
   CFO: Pete Rostad
   CEO: Jerry Greene
Estimated Sales: $ .5 - 1 million
Number Employees: 1-4

Sq. footage: 250000
Parent Co: Eastern Foods
Type of Packaging: Consumer, Food Service, Pri-
vate Label, Bulk
Brands:
   JACKAROO
   NATURALLY FRESH
   PROUD PRODUCTS

10034 Naturally Scientific
600 Willow Tree Road
Leonia, NJ 07605-2211   201-585-7055
          Fax: 973-244-0044 888-428-0700
nsilabs@aol.com   www.naturallyscientific.com
Processor of liquid nutritional supplements and food
and beverage ingredients. Produce every vitamin,
mineral or herb in conbinations of up to 200 actives.
Consumables or concentrates. Use a patented highly
bioavailable technology
   President/CEO: Frank Berger
   Executive VP: Marc Pozner
   Marketing Director: Douglas Lynch
   Sales/Group Publisher: Jon Benninger
Estimated Sales: $ 1 - 3 Million
Number Employees: 5-9
Number of Products: 200
Type of Packaging: Consumer, Private Label

10035 Naturally Vitamin Supplements
4404 E Elwood St
Phoenix, AZ 85040-1909   480-991-0200
          Fax: 480-991-0551 800-899-4499
          www.naturally.com
Processor and exporter of health foods and natural
vitamins, minerals and food supplements including
B-complex and C-combination formulas, fish oils,
fiber blends, multi-vitamins and enzymes
   President: Joachim Lehmann
   Export Sales Manager: Mark Wojick
   VP Sales: Don Haygood
Estimated Sales: $ 5 - 10 Million
Number Employees: 10-19
Sq. footage: 20000
Type of Packaging: Food Service, Private Label,
Bulk
Brands:
   All B-100
   All B-50
   Body-Fuel
   Fiber
   Fiber-7
   Ginsen-Rgy
   Hi C-Plex
   Little Vab
   Max-C-Plex
   Mega C-Bio
   Special C-500
   Super Epa
   Super Stress
   Super Vab
   Supreme B 150
   Un-Fad Diet Packs
   Vit-A-Boost

10036 Nature Cure Northwest
PO Box 753
Poulsbo, WA 98370-0753   360-697-8691
          Fax: 360-697-7179 800-957-8048
Processor of bottled bee pollen pills
   President: Allen Schmitt
Estimated Sales: 724,000
Number Employees: 2
Type of Packaging: Food Service
Brands:
   Nature Cure

10037 Nature Kist Snacks
6909 Las Positas Road
Livermore, CA 94551-5143   925-606-4200
          Fax: 925-606-7183
inquiry@naturekistsnacks.com
          www.naturekistsnacks.com
Processor of nut and seed trail mixes; private label-
ing available
   President: Ronald L Mozingo
   Office Manager: Nancy Freitas
   Plant Manager: Rick Dorotheo
Estimated Sales: $ 10 - 20 Million
Number Employees: 20-49
Type of Packaging: Consumer, Private Label

10038 Nature Quality
13805 Llagas Ave
San Martin, CA 95046-9564   408-683-2182
    Fax: 408-683-4249 natqual@aol.com
Processor and exporter of IQF cut celery, olives, onions, garlic and peppers
  President: Karen Ash
  General Manager: Karen Ash
Estimated Sales: $7000000
Number Employees: 100-249
Sq. footage: 20000
Type of Packaging: Food Service, Bulk

10039 Nature Star Foods
15 Spinning Wheel Rd # 314
Hinsdale, IL 60521-2498   630-323-8888
    Fax: 630-323-8988 plockys@aol.com
    www.plockys.com
Manufacturer of Potato sticks, sweet apple chips sticks, sweet nut mixes, tortilla chips
  Owner: Paul Cipolla
Estimated Sales: Below $5 Million
Number Employees: 1-4
Type of Packaging: Private Label
Brands:
  NATURE STAR
  PLOCYY'S APPLE CHIPS

10040 Nature's Apothecary
PO Box 17970
Boulder, CO 80308-0970   970-664-1600
    Fax: 970-664-5106 800-999-7422
    www.naturesapothecary.com
Processor and exporter of fresh organic, medicinal, botanical and herbal liquid extracts
  Director Customer Relations: Nancy Mitchell
Type of Packaging: Consumer, Private Label, Bulk

10041 Nature's Best Food Supplement
195 Engineers Rd
Hauppauge, NY 11788-4020   631-232-3355
    Fax: 631-232-3320 800-345-2378
    info@naturesbest.com www.naturesbest.com
Manufacturer of Sport nutrition products
  President: Hal Katz
  Purchasing Manager: Ernie Geraci
Estimated Sales: $5-10 Million
Number Employees: 20-49
Number of Brands: 4
Number of Products: 150
Type of Packaging: Consumer
Brands:
  DECADES
  ISOPURE
  NO HOLDS BAR
  PERFECT
  PERFECT 1100
  PERFECT ANIMOS
  PERFECT CARBS
  PERFECT Rx
  SOLID PROTEIN

10042 Nature's Bounty
2100 Smithtown Avenue
Ronkonkoma, NY 11779   631-200-2000
    Fax: 631-567-7148 800-433-2990
    info@naturesbounty.com www.nbty.com
Manufaacturer, marketer and distributor of a broad line of high-quality, value-priced nutritional supplements in the United States and throughout the world.
  President/CFO: Harvey Kamil
  Chairman/CEO: Scott Rudolph
  SVP Marketing/Advertising: James Flaherty
  SVP Operations: Hans Lindgren
Estimated Sales: $2.6 Billion
Number Employees: 13,950
Type of Packaging: Bulk
Brands:
  AMERICAN HEALTH®
  DETUINEN®
  ESTER-C(190)
  GNC (UK)®
  GOOD 'N' NATURAL®
  HOLLAND & BARRETT®
  HOME HEALTH™
  JULIAN GRAVES
  LENATURISTE®
  MET-RX®
  NATURE'S BOUNTY®
  PURITAN'S PRIDE®
  REXALL®
  SISU®
  SOLGAR®
  SUNDOWN®

  VITAMIN WORLD®
  WORLDWIDE SPORT NUTRITION®

10043 Nature's Candy
P.O.Box 1429
Fredericksburg, TX 78624-1429   830-997-3844
    Fax: 830-997-6528 800-729-0085
    karen@natural-nut-snacks.com
    www.natural-nut-snacks.com
Processor and wholesaler/distributor of natural and fruit filled candy, maple coated nuts and seasoned nuts and seeds
  President: Michael Zygmunt
  Office Manager: Karen Gold
Estimated Sales: $482000
Number Employees: 5-9
Type of Packaging: Consumer, Private Label, Bulk

10044 Nature's Dairy
5104 S Main St
Roswell, NM 88203-0822   575-623-9640
    Fax: 575-622-1318
Milk, dairy products-noncheese
  President: Gerald Greathouse
Estimated Sales: $ 5 - 10 Million
Number Employees: 20-49
Brands:
  Nature's Dairy

10045 Nature's Finest Products
PO Box 801326
Dallas, TX 75380-1326   773-489-2096
    Fax: 972-960-8760 800-237-5205
    natures@naturesfinest.com
    www.naturesfinest.com
Gourmet foods
  President: Mike Griffin

10046 Nature's Hand
1800 Cliff Rd E # 7
Burnsville, MN 55337-1375   952-890-6033
    Fax: 952-890-6040 www.natureshand.com
Manufacturer and exporter of natural breakfast cereal; also, granola topping and baking ingredients
  Manager: Sean Finney
Estimated Sales: $500,000-$1 Million
Number Employees: 5-9
Number of Brands: 1
Number of Products: 4
Type of Packaging: Consumer, Food Service, Private Label, Bulk
Brands:
  NATURE'S HAND

10047 Nature's Herbs
600 Quality Drive
American Fork, UT 84003-3302   801-363-4060
    Fax: 801-763-0789 800-437-2257
    village@naturesherbs.com
    www.naturesherbs.com
Processor and exporter of dietary supplements and encapsulated herbs
  President/CEO: Ross Blechman
  Executive VP Sales: Dean Blechman
Estimated Sales: $ 5 - 10 Million
Number Employees: 250
Sq. footage: 50000
Parent Co: Twin Laboratories
Type of Packaging: Consumer
Brands:
  Healthcare Naturals
  Herb Masters' Original
  Nature's Herbs
  Power Herbs

10048 Nature's Hilights
1608 Chico River Rd # A
Chico, CA 95928   530-342-6154
    Fax: 530-342-3130 800-313-6454
Processor of baked products including rice crusts, bread, bread sticks, rice pizzas and frozen gluten-free desserts
  President: Gayle Luna
Estimated Sales: $5-9.9 Million
Number Employees: 10-19
Type of Packaging: Food Service, Bulk

10049 Nature's Nutrition
6425 Anderson Way
Melbourne, FL 32940-7467   321-255-5505
    Fax: 321-255-5881 800-242-1115
    info@nothindutherbs.com
    www.nothinbutherbs.com

Processor of organic food and nutritional supplements including vitamins, amino acids, antioxidants and proteins; also, weight loss aids
  President: Dr. Dee Corbitt
Estimated Sales: $500,000-$1 Million
Number Employees: 5-9
Sq. footage: 5000
Brands:
  Harida
  The Capsule

10050 (HQ)Nature's Path Foods
7453 Progress Way
Delta, BC V4G 1E7
Canada   604-940-0505
    Fax: 604-940-0522 dneuman@naturespath.bc.ca
Processor and exporter of organic ready-to-eat cereals and baked goods; also, toaster waffles and vegetarian patties
  President: Arran Stephas
  VP Finance: Robert Patrizio
  VP Marketing/Sales: David Neuman
Estimated Sales: $50 Million
Number Employees: 150
Sq. footage: 79000
Type of Packaging: Consumer, Private Label, Bulk
Other Locations:
  Nature's Path Foods
  Blaine WA
Brands:
  Blueberry Almond Museli
  Eco-Pac
  Evirokidz Creams
  Flaxplus
  Heritage
  Heritage Bites
  Heritage-O's
  Honey'd
  Lifestream
  Ls Flaxplus
  Ls Smart Bran
  Ls Wildberry Muesli
  Manna Bread
  Millet Rice
  Multigrain
  NP Hemp Plus
  NP Kamut Krisp
  NP Soy Plus
  Nature's Path
  Np Mesa Sunrise
  Oaty Bites
  Optimum Power Breakfast

10051 Nature's Plus
2500 Grand Avenue
Long Beach, CA 90815-1764   800-525-0200
    Fax: 800-688-7239 salesinfo@naturesplus.com
    www.naturesplus.com
Processor and exporter of health products including protein weight loss supplements, vitamins and herbs
  Director Marketing: Gerard McIntee
Estimated Sales: $15100000
Number Employees: 60
Parent Co: Natural Organics

10052 Nature's Provision Company
452 Krumville Rd
Olivebridge, NY 12461-5528   845-657-6020
Processor of powdered health food supplements for circulatory improvement; wholesaler/distributor of pH balanced cleansers and lubricants
  President: Clark Jung
Estimated Sales: $ 5 - 10 Million
Number Employees: 5-9
Brands:
  Dr. Rinse Vita Flo Formula

10053 Nature's Select
500 Cascade West Pkwy SE
Grand Rapids, MI 49546-2106   616-956-1105
    Fax: 616-956-0998 888-715-4321
    naturesselect@aol.com www.snackperfect.com
Manufacturer of Premium quality dry roasted soynuts
  President/Owner: Peter Assaly
Estimated Sales: $500,000
Number Employees: 1-4
Number of Brands: 1
Number of Products: 9
Sq. footage: 30000
Brands:
  NATURE'S SELECT

10054 Nature's Sungrown Foods
4340 Redwood Hwy
San Rafael, CA 94903-2121   415-491-4944
    Fax: 415-532-2233   hal@naturessungrown.com
    www.naturessungrown.com
Manufacturer and exporter of natural beef and pork, organic foods (dried fruit, coffee, juice, sauce, tortilla chips, guacamole, jalapeno peppers and Mexican foods
    President: Hal Shenson
Estimated Sales: $5-10 Million
Number of Brands: 2
Type of Packaging: Consumer, Food Service, Private Label, Bulk
Brands:
    NATURE'S SUNGROWN BEEF
    VERA CRUZ MEXICAN FOODS

10055 Nature's Sunshine Products Company
P.O.Box 19005
Provo, UT 84605-9005   801-342-4300
    Fax: 801-342-4305   800-223-8225
    questions@natr.com   www.natr.com
Processor and exporter of health products including vitamins, minerals and herbs
    President: Craig Dalley
    CEO: Douglas Faggioli
Estimated Sales: $258208000
Number Employees: 1,000-4,999
Type of Packaging: Consumer
Brands:
    Nature's Sunshine

10056 (HQ)Nature's Way
P.O.Box 4000
Springville, UT 84663-9007   801-489-1500
    Fax: 801-489-1700   800-962-8873
    sales@naturesway.com   www.naturesway.com
Herbs and vitamins
    CFO: Rich Jones
    CEO: Randy Rose
    Operations Manager: Brian Hufford
    Production Manager: Greg Bone
    Purchasing Manager: Dave Anderson
Estimated Sales: $ 100-500 Million
Number Employees: 100-249
Type of Packaging: Private Label
Brands:
    Chiorofresh
    Echinaguard
    Efamol
    Ginkgold
    Medicine From Nature
    Primadophilus
    Thisilyn

10057 NatureMost Laboratories
60 Trigo Dr
Middletown, CT 06457-6157   860-346-8991
    Fax: 860-347-3312   800-234-2112
    sales@naturemost.com   www.naturemost.com
Manufacturer, importer and exporter of products, vitamins, oils, minerals, herbal supplements; also, contract packaging and private labeling available
    President: Robert Trigo
    Marketing: Sam Schwartz
    Sales: Donna Platnum
    Operations: Fred Wuschner
Estimated Sales: $ 5 - 10 Million
Number Employees: 20-49
Number of Brands: 3
Number of Products: 300
Sq. footage: 20000
Type of Packaging: Consumer, Private Label
Brands:
    Naturemost Labs
    Trigo Labs

10058 Naturel
9339 Foothill Blvd # A
Rancho Cucamonga, CA 91730-3548 909-987-0520
    Fax: 909-390-5453   877-242-8344
    naturelUSA@aol.com   www.naturel.com
Processor of organic agave syrup prepared for 100% agave juice; natural fructose sweetener/flavor enhancer
    Owner: Jong Kee Kim
    National Sales Manager: Oscar Guerrero Whaley
Estimated Sales: Less than $500,000
Number Employees: 1-4
Parent Co: Industrializadora Integral Del Agave, SA DeCV

10059 Natures Best
195 Engineers Rd
Hauppauge, NY 11788-4020   631-232-3355
    Fax: 631-232-3320   800-345-2378
    info@naturesbest.com   www.naturesbest.com
Processor and exporter of athletic supplements and sport drinks
    President: Hal Katz
    Marketing Manager: Delia Mercado
    VP Sales: Ernie Geraci
Estimated Sales: $1500000
Number Employees: 20-49
Brands:
    Decades
    No Holds Bar
    Perfect 1100
    Perfect Aminos
    Perfect Carbs
    Perfect Rx

10060 Naturex
375 Huyler St
South Hackensack, NJ 07606   201-440-5000
    Fax: 201-342-8000   naturex@naturex.com
    www.naturex.com
Naturex is a leading manufacturer of high quality natural antioxidants, colors, herbs & spices oleoresins and essential oils, and botanical extracts for the food, flavor and nutraceutical industries. NATUREX offers all of theseproducts in pure form and also in formulated versions (oil and water soluble versions, liquids or spray dried powders)
    President & CEO: Jacques Dikanksy
    CFO: Thierry Lambert
    VP: Stephane Ducroux
    R&D: Marc Roller
    Quality Control: Nicolas Feuillere
    Marketing: Antoine Dauby
    Sales: Samuel Menard
    Public Relations: Antoine Dauby
    Purchasing Director: Serge Sabrier
Estimated Sales: $ 75 Million
Number Employees: 100-249
Number of Brands: 6
Parent Co: Naturex SA - France
Type of Packaging: Bulk
Brands:
    COLORENHANCE
    OSR
    STABILENCHANCE
    WSR

10061 Naturex (Chart Corp)
375 Huyler St
South Hackensack, NJ 07606-1532   201-440-5000
    Fax: 201-342-8000   naturex@nautrex.us
    www.chartcorp.com
Manufacturer and exporter of botanical extracts, flavoring ingredients and aromatic materials including ethyl vanillin, menthol and vanillin; also, water soluble gums including acacia, guar and locust bean
    President & CEO: Jacques Dikansky
    CFO: Thierry Lambert
Estimated Sales: $ 75 Million
Number Employees: 100-249
Number of Products: 3000
Sq. footage: 40000
Type of Packaging: Bulk

10062 Naumes
P.O.Box 996
Medford, OR 97501-0071   541-772-6268
    Fax: 541-772-3650   juice@naumes.com
    www.naumes.com
Grower of apples, plums, pears, pomegranates, persimmons and Asian pears
    President: Michael D Naumes
Estimated Sales: $100+ Million
Number Employees: 100-249
Type of Packaging: Consumer
Brands:
    Blue Flag
    Cheam of Chelan
    Gold Crest
    Oh Yes
    Pinetree
    Rogue
    Snowcrest

10063 Nautilus Foods
PO Box 1615
Bellevue, WA 98009-1615   425-885-5900
    Fax: 425-885-1900

Frozen fish, fresh and smoked salmon
    President: Thomas Waterer
    Executive VP: Dawn Waterer
    Sales Manager: Joseph Lombardo
    Director Manufacturing: Matt Walton
    Plant Manager: David Kaayk

10064 Navarro Pecan Company
P.O.Box 147
Corsicana, TX 75151-0147   903-872-5641
    Fax: 903-874-7143   800-333-9507
    sales@navarropecan.com
    www.navarropecan.com
Processor and exporter of kosher certified shelled raw and roasted pecans used as ingredients
    Manager: Austin Nixon
    CEO: Mark Frank
Estimated Sales: $ 20 - 50 Million
Number Employees: 100-249
Sq. footage: 185000
Type of Packaging: Consumer, Bulk
Brands:
    Navarro

10065 Navarro Vineyards & Winery
P.O.Box 47
Philo, CA 95466-0047   707-895-3686
    Fax: 707-895-3647   800-537-9463
    sales@navarrowine.com   www.navarrowine.com
Processor of wine and olive oils
    Owner: Deborah Cahn
    VP: Deborah Cahn
Estimated Sales: Less than $500,000
Number Employees: 1-4
Type of Packaging: Consumer, Food Service

10066 Navas Instruments
200 Earnhardt Street
Conway, SC 29526   843-347-1379
    Fax: 843-347-2527   info@navas-instruments.com
    www.navas-instruments.com
Manufacturer of laboratory instruments for testing ash and moisture in food, pet and animal feed, fertilizers, soils and wastewater.

10067 Naya
2500 Rue Naya
Mirabel, QC J7N 3A7
Canada   450-562-7911
    Fax: 450-562-3654   info@naya.com
    www.naya.com
Processor and exporter of bottled spring water
    President: Anita Jarjour
    Executive VP/COO: Stu Levitan
    Director Sales Marketing: Raynald Brisson
    VP Operations: Sylvain Mayrand
Number Employees: 100-249
Sq. footage: 120000
Type of Packaging: Consumer, Food Service, Private Label
Brands:
    Naya

10068 Naylor Candies
P.O.Box 1018
Mt Wolf, PA 17347-0918   717-266-2706
    Fax: 717-266-2706 www.naylorcandies.com
Processor and exporter of confectionery products including butter toffee peanuts, butter mints, cashew crunch, peanut crunch and honey roasted peanuts; importer of cashews and peanuts
    Chairman: Charles Naylor
Estimated Sales: $750000
Number Employees: 10-19
Sq. footage: 8000
Type of Packaging: Consumer, Private Label, Bulk

10069 Naylor Wine Cellars
4069 Vineyard Rd
Stewartstown, PA 17363-8478   717-993-2431
    Fax: 717-993-9460   800-292-3370
    wine@naylorwine.com   www.naylorwine.com
Wines
    President: Richard Naylor
    Winemaker: Ted Potted
Estimated Sales: $ 2.5-5 Million
Number Employees: 10-19
Type of Packaging: Private Label, Bulk
Brands:
    Golden Grenadine
    Naylor

10070 Ne-Mo's Bakery
416 N Hale Ave
Escondido, CA 92029-1496   760-741-5725
Fax: 760-741-0659 800-325-2692
salesadmin@nemosbakery.com
www.nemosbakery.com
Processor and exporter of baked goods including
hand wrapped cake squares, cake slices, cinnamon
rolls, cookies, muffins, mini loaf cakes, danish, cake
breads, coffee cakes, and specialty cakes
Senior VP: Sam Delucca Jr
Senior VP/Sales & Marketing: Sam DeLucca Jr.
Jr
Estimated Sales: $ 10 - 20 Million
Number Employees: 100-249
Sq. footage: 60000
Type of Packaging: Consumer, Food Service, Private Label, Bulk
Brands:
NE-MO'S

10071 Neal's Chocolates
2520 Lynwood Drive
Salt Lake City, UT 84109-1607   801-521-6500
Fax: 801-521-6555 neal@news-chocolates.com
www.neals-chocolates.com
Boxed chocolates
President: Neal Maxfield
Estimated Sales: Less than $500,000
Number Employees: 1-4

10072 Near East Food Products
515 W Main Street
Barrington, IL 60010-4175   847-842-4654
Fax: 847-382-0687 erik_bayer@quakeroats.com
www.neareast.com
Rice, couscous side dishes
Marketing Manager: Erik Bayer
Sales Director: Jim Coy
General Sales Manager/Natural: Erik Bayer
Parent Co: Quaker Oats Company
Brands:
Creative Grains
Near East

10073 Near East Food Products
797 Lancaster Street
Leominster, MA 01453-4551   978-534-3338
800-822-7423
Thrirty different flavors and varieties of pilafs, couscous and grain dishes including taboule
General Manager: Philip Wiggin
Estimated Sales: Under $500,000
Number Employees: 50-99

10074 Nebraska Beef
4501 S 36th St
Omaha, NE 68107-1330   402-734-6823
Fax: 402-733-1624 angelo@nebraskabeef.com
www.nebeef.org
Processor of beef
CFO: Fred Fromi
Partner/VP Finance: Marvin Schrack
COO: Katie Dornhoff
Estimated Sales: $900 Million
Number Employees: 897

10075 Nebraska Popcorn
85824 519th Ave
Clearwater, NE 68726-5239   402-887-5335
Fax: 402-887-4709 800-253-6502
popcorn@nebraskapopcorn.com
www.nebraskapopcorn.com
Experienced grower, processor and packager of
quality popcorn. The fully integrated operation offers microwave, bulk, private label and poly bags of
popcorn to our customers in over 50 countries. Providing premium quality products atcompetitive
prices is the goal of Nebraska Popcorn. Product of
USA.
President: Frank Morrison
Sales: Michelle Steskal
Estimated Sales: $ 10 - 20 Million
Number Employees: 20-49
Number of Brands: 1
Sq. footage: 5000
Type of Packaging: Consumer, Food Service, Private Label, Bulk
Brands:
MORRISON FARMS

10076 Nebraska Salt & Grain Company
115 W 16th St
Gothenburg, NE 69138-1302   308-537-7191
Fax: 308-537-7193
Processor and exporter of corn
President: Norman Geiken
Estimated Sales: $ 3 - 5 Million
Number Employees: 20-49
Type of Packaging: Bulk

10077 Nectar Island
56 5th Ave
St Paul, MN 55128   651-292-9963
Fax: 651-905-1958 sam.hanna@nectarisland.com
www.nectarisland.com
Manufacturer of fruit drinks flavors of which include: pommegranate; pommegranate blueberry;
pommegranate raspberry; mango peach; tropical berries; and guava orange.
Owner: Scott Johnson

10078 Nedlog Company
92 Messner Dr
Wheeling, IL 60090-6448   847-541-0924
Fax: 847-541-1046 800-323-6201
nedlog@nedlog.com www.nedlog.com
Makes and markets over 60 formulas of standard traditional and more exotic juice-based concentrates
such as Strawberry-Apple. Also have an equipment
program based on purchase of our juice concentrates, and a provate label program forconcentrates
and read
Chairman: Grant Golden
CEO: Grant Golden
President/COO: Glenn Golden
CFO: Marilyn Dougal
Research & Development: Gennady Koyfman
Public Relations: Karyl Golden
Estimated Sales: $ 3 - 5 Million
Number Employees: 7
Type of Packaging: Food Service, Private Label
Brands:
BERRY GOOD
CLASSIC BLENDS
FIESTA
HILINE
NEDLOG 100
TROPICAL BLENDS

10079 Neenah Springs
PO Box 9
Oxford, WI 53952-0009   608-586-5605
Fax: 608-586-4509 info@neenahsprings.com
www.neenahsprings.com
Bottler of Artesian water
President: Thomas Rogers
VP: John McFarland
Marketing Director: Dan Revoy
Public Relations: Kathy Payter
Operations Manager: Chris Coates
Plant Manager: Barbara Ravenscroft
Purchasing Manager: Wendy Jankowski
Estimated Sales: $4800000
Number Employees: 52
Sq. footage: 20000
Type of Packaging: Consumer, Food Service, Private Label
Brands:
Glacier Ice
Great Glacier
Mountain Mist
Neenah Springs

10080 Neese Country Sausage
1452 Alamance Church Rd
Greensboro, NC 27406-9430   336-275-9548
Fax: 336-275-0750 800-632-1010
info@neesesausage.com www.neesesausage.com
Processor and packager of country sausage, liver
pudding, c-loaf, souse meat and scraple.
President: Thomas Neese Jr
Plant Manager: Michael Garrett
Estimated Sales: $ 5 - 10 Million
Number Employees: 20-49
Type of Packaging: Consumer, Food Service

10081 Nehalem Bay Winery
34965 Highway 53
Nehalem, OR 97131-9329   503-368-5300
Fax: 503-368-5300 888-368-9463
nbwines@hotmail.com
www.nehalembaywinery.com
Processor of wines including niagara grape, rhubarb,
apple, wildflower honey, chardonnay, white table,
pinot noir and pinot noir blanc
Owner: Ray Schackelford
Estimated Sales: $ 3 - 5 Million
Number Employees: 5-9
Type of Packaging: Consumer

10082 Neighbors Coffee
P.O.Box 54527
Oklahoma City, OK 73154-1527   405-236-3932
Fax: 405-552-2124 800-299-9016
sales@neighborscoffee.com
www.neighborscoffee.com
Manufacturer of coffee; wholesaler/distributor of
tea, cocoa and cappuccino
President: Steve Neighbors
Sales Manager: Phil Huggard
Estimated Sales: $100,000
Number Employees: 50-99
Type of Packaging: Consumer, Food Service, Private Label, Bulk
Brands:
NEIGHBORS

10083 Neilsen-Massey Vanillas
1550 S Shields Dr
Waukegan, IL 60085-8307   847-578-1550
Fax: 847-578-1570 800-525-7873
info@nielsenmassey.com
www.nielsenmassey.com
Producer of the fine vanillas worldwide
President: Camilla Neilsen
VP Finance: David Klemann
CEO: Craig Nielsen
Estimated Sales: $ 10-20 Million
Number Employees: 20-49
Brands:
Madagascar Bourbon Pure Vanilla Bea
Madagascar Bourbon Pure Vanilla Pow
Tahitian Pure Vanilla

10084 Neithart Meats
12862 Foothill Blvd
Sylmar, CA 91342-5330   818-361-7141
Fax: 818-361-7143
Processor and wholesaler/distributor of meats/provisions; serving the food service market
Owner: Jose Macias
Estimated Sales: $30.70 Million
Number Employees: 10-19
Type of Packaging: Food Service

10085 Nekta
17645 Juniper Path
Lakeville, MN 55044-7490   952-898-8020
Fax: 649-573-7988 nektausa@nekta.com
www.nekta.com
All-natural fruit carbohydrate derived from kiwifruit
Director: Adriana Tong
Director: Jonathan Wood

10086 Nell Baking Company
114 County Road 254
Kenedy, TX 78119-4267   830-583-3251
Fax: 830-583-9593 800-215-9190
nellbaking@yahoo.com www.nellbaking.com
Biscotti in ten flavors, gourmet cookies and wafers
President: Lasca Arnold
Estimated Sales: $ 2.5-5 Million
Number Employees: 10
Brands:
Biscotti Di Lasca
Cookies By Lasca

10087 Nellson Candies
5800 Ayala Ave
Baldwin Park, CA 91706-6215   626-334-4508
Fax: 626-812-6525
Manufacturer and exporter of custom formulated
snack, diet/weight loss, sport nutrition and medical
food nutrition bars; contract packaging available
President: W Shieff
Estimated Sales: $100+ Million
Number Employees: 250-499
Sq. footage: 100000
Type of Packaging: Consumer, Food Service, Private Label, Bulk

10088 Nelson Cheese Factory
Highway 35 S
Nelson, WI 54756   715-673-4725
Fax: 715-673-4218 www.nelsoncheese.com

Cheese
President: Edward Greenheck
Estimated Sales:$11,700,000
Number Employees: 10-19
Type of Packaging: Private Label

10089 Nelson Crab
P.O.Box 520
Tokeland, WA 98590-0520   360-267-2911
          Fax: 360-267-2921 800-262-0069
seatreats@techline.com   www.nelsoncrab.com
Processor, importer and exporter of canned, fresh,
smoked and frozen seafood including salmon steaks,
shad, crabs, crab meat and shrimp
President: Kristi Nelson
Plant Manager: Les Candler
Estimated Sales:$ 10 - 20 Million
Number Employees: 50-99
Type of Packaging: Food Service, Private Label
Brands:
Nelson Seatreats

10090 Nelson Ricks Creamery
1755 Fremont Dr
Salt Lake City, UT 84104-4218   801-364-3607
          Fax: 801-364-3600 www.banquetcheese.com
Manufacturer of cheese including cheddar,
Monterey jack and mozzarella
President: Calvin L Nelson
Sales Manager: J Lundgreen
Estimated Sales:$18 Million
Number Employees: 10-19
Sq. footage: 30000
Type of Packaging: Food Service, Private Label,
Bulk
Brands:
BANQUET BETTER FOODS
BANQUET BUTTER
BANQUET CHEESE
GOLD NUGGET BUTTER
GOLD NUGGET CHEESE
GRAND TETON
GRAND TETON CHEESE

10091 Nelson Ricks Creamery Company
1755 Fremont Dr
Salt Lake City, UT 84104-4218   801-364-3607
          Fax: 801-364-3600 www.banquetcheese.com
Manufacturer of natural cheese
President: Cal Nelson
Sales Manager: J Lundgreen
Estimated Sales:$20-50 Million
Number Employees: 20-49
Parent Co: Nelson Ricks Creamery
Type of Packaging: Consumer
Brands:
BANQUET

10092 Nelson's Ice Cream
627 Main St
Royersford, PA 19468-2401   610-948-1282
          Fax: 610-948-3009
Manufacturer of ice cream
Owner: Steve Wisner
Estimated Sales:$300,000-500,000
Number Employees: 10-19
Type of Packaging: Private Label
Brands:
NELSON'S
NELSON'S DUTCH FARMS

10093 Nemac J. Charles, Jr.
Hc
Box 160
Grove, ME 04638   207-454-2674
          Fax: 207-454-7254
Owner: Charles Nemac, Jr.

10094 Nemecek Brothers
300 N Main St
West, TX 76691-1208   254-826-5182
          Fax: 254-826-3719 nemebros@aol.com
Manufacturer of a variety of sausages and smoked
meat products
President: Cindy Hobbs
VP: Sandra O'Connor
Estimated Sales:$ 1 - 3 Million
Number Employees: 5-9
Sq. footage: 6000
Type of Packaging: Consumer, Food Service

10095 Nephi Packing Company
915 N 300 W
Nephi, UT 84648-1162   435-623-0435
          Fax: 435-623-0435
Packer of meat products including beef, lamb and
pork
President: Ted Carlos
Estimated Sales:$92000
Number Employees: 3
Type of Packaging: Consumer, Food Service, Pri-
vate Label

10096 Neptune Fisheries
802 Jefferson Avenue
Newport News, VA 23607-6118   757-893-9200
          Fax: 757-893-9227 800-545-7474
          www.nepfish.com
Processor and importer of frozen, cooked, peeled
and deveined shrimp and scallops; also, lobster tails
President: Robin West
CFO: Richard Costa
National Sales Manager: Aaron Cabral
Sales Director: Sam Weinstein
Plant Manager: Reuben Benkovitz
Number Employees: 5-9
Sq. footage: 60000
Type of Packaging: Consumer, Food Service, Pri-
vate Label, Bulk
Brands:
Neptune

10097 Neptune Foods
4510 S Alameda St
Vernon, CA 90058-2011   323-232-8300
          Fax: 323-232-8833 info@neptunefoods.com
          www.neptunefoods.com
Processor and exporter of frozen cod, perch, pollack,
fish sticks, clams, lobster, oysters, scallops and
shrimp; importer of fish, shrimp and scallops
President: Howard Choi
Executive VP: Hector Poon
Estimated Sales:$ 50-100 Million
Number Employees: 100-249
Sq. footage: 150000
Type of Packaging: Consumer, Food Service, Pri-
vate Label, Bulk
Brands:
CAPTAIN NEPTUNE
MERMAID PRINCESS
NEPTUNE

10098 Nesbitt Processing
End NW 7th Avenue
Aledo, IL 61231   309-582-5183
Processor and wholesaler/distributor of beef, pork,
lamb, goat and deer; slaughtering services available
President/General Manager: Omar Deeds, Jr.
Secretary/Treasurer: Edith Nesbitt
Number Employees: 1-4
Type of Packaging: Consumer

10099 Neshaminy Valley Natural Foods
7614 Dorcas St
Philadelphia, PA 19111-3324   215-745-3773
          Fax: 215-725-3775 nv@orgfood.com
          www.orgfood.com
Gourmet foods
President: Philip S Margolis
COO: Gene Margolis
VP: Gene Margolis
Estimated Sales:$ 5-10 Million
Number Employees: 20-49
Brands:
Neshaminy Valley Natural

10100 Nest Eggs
411 W Fullerton Pkwy # 1402w
Chicago, IL 60614-2849   773-525-4952
          Fax: 773-525-5226 info@fact.cc
          www.fact.cc
Gourmet foods
Executive Director: Richard Wood
VP: Robert Brown
Sales Manager: Steve Roach
*Estimated Sales:*Below $ 5 Million
Number Employees: 5-9

10101 Nestelles's
P.O.Box 329
Tangent, OR 97389-329   503-393-7056
Flavoring extracts and food colors
President: Kathi Jenks
Manager: Oebbe Agee

*Estimated Sales:*Below $ 5 Million
Number Employees: 5

10102 Nestle
30003 Bainbridge Rd
Cleveland, OH 44139-2290   440-349-5757
          Fax: 440-248-6413 www.nestleusa.com
Manufacturer of refrigerated foods including sauces
and cookie doughs; also, ingredients
Chairman/CEO: Brad Alford
Estimated Sales:$10.4 Billion
Number Employees: 25000
Type of Packaging: Consumer, Food Service
Brands:
100 GRAND
ABUELITA
BABY RUTH
BIT-O-HONEY
BUITONI
BUTTERFINGER
CALIFORNIA PIZZA KITCHEN
CARLOS V
CARNATION
CHUNKY
CLASICO
COFFEE-MATE
CRUNCH
DIGIORNO
DOLCE GUSTO
DREYER'S
DRUMSTICK
EDY'S
FROSTY PAWS
GOBSTOPPERS
GOOBERS
HAAGEN-DAZS ICE CREAM
HOT POCKETS
JACK'S
JUICY JUICE
LA LECHERA
LAFFY TAFFY
LEAN CUISINE
LEAN POCKETS
LIBBY'S PUMPKIN
LIK-M-AID FUN DIP
MAGGI SEASONINGS
MAGGI TASTE OF ASIA
MILO
NEASTEA
NERDS
NESCAFE
NESQUIK
NESTLE
NIDO
NIPS
OH HENRY!
OOMPAS
PIXY STIX
PUSH UP
RAISINETS
RUNTS
SNO-CAPS
SPREE
STOUFFER'S
SWEETART'S
TASTER'S CHOICE
THE SKINNY COW
TOLL HOUSE
TOMBSTONE
WONKA

10103 Nestle
3401 Mount Prospect Rd
Franklin Park, IL 60131-1304   847-957-5043
          Fax: 847-957-6362 800-225-2270
          laurie.macdonald@us.nestle.com
          www.nestleusa.com
Processor of chocolate candy
Manager: Jim West
Public Relations/Media: Laurie MacDonald
Manager: Alan Diener
Estimated Sales:$ 100-500 Million
Number Employees: 500-999
Parent Co: Nestle USA
Type of Packaging: Consumer
Brands:
Nestle

10104 Nestle
800 N Brand Blvd
Glendale, CA 91203-1229   818-549-6000
          Fax: 818-549-6952 800-368-5594
          www.nestle.com

Tea and coffee industry creamers
Chairman/CEO: Brad Alford
Estimated Sales: $10 Billion
Number Employees: 500-999
Brands:
Nestle

10105 Nestle Canada Inc
25 Sheppard Avenue W
North York, ON M2N 6S8
Canada 416-512-9000
Fax: 416-218-2654 800-563-7853
corporateaffairs@ca.nestle.com www.nestle.ca
Processor and exporter of frozen and prepared regular and low-fat/low cholesterol dinners, hot cocoa and chocolate milk mixes, instant teas, coffee and candy including chocolate; also, nutritional products.
President: Petraea Heynike
President Food Service: Jaques Meilleur
CFO: Doug Holdt
Public Relations/Media: Catherine O'Brien
Purchasing Agent: Pete Scholtz
Number Employees: 3415
Parent Co: Nestle USA
Type of Packaging: Consumer

10106 Nestle Food Group
72 Sterling Road
Toronto, ON M6R 2B6
Canada 416-535-2181
Fax: 416-535-5545
corporateaffairs@ca.nestle.com
www.nestl,.com
Processor and exporter of chocolate bars
Controller: Bill Paul
Public Relations/Media: Catherine O'Brien
Director Operations: Ursula Wydymus
Number Employees: 400
Parent Co: Nestle USA
Type of Packaging: Consumer, Food Service

10107 Nestle Pizza
940 S Whelen Ave
Medford, WI 54451-1745 715-748-5550
Fax: 715-748-7330 www.nestle.com
Frozen pizza
Chairman/CEO Nestle USA: Brad Alford
CEO: Paul Bulcke
EVP/CFO: James Dollive
EVP/Corporate Legal Affairs: Marc Firestone
EVP/Global Technology & Quality: Jean Spence
EVP/Chief Marketing Officer: Jeri Finard
EVP/Global Human Resources: Karen May
Plant Manager: Gary Stanton
Estimated Sales: $500 Million to $1 Billion
Number Employees: 500-999
Type of Packaging: Consumer
Brands:
CALIFORNIA PIZZA KITCHEN
DELISSIO
DIGIORNO
JACK'S
TOMBSTONE

10108 (HQ)Nestle USA Inc
800 N Brand Boulevard
Glendale, CA 91209-9059 818-549-6000
Fax: 818-549-6952 800-633-2330
www.nestleusa.com
Manufacturer of canned pumpkin, sunflower seeds, coffee, tea, nectar, fruit juices, instant breakfast drinks, nondairy creamer, hot cocoa, and chocolate milk mixes, as well as prepared foods.
Chairman/CEO: Brad Alford
Investor Relations Officer: Anita Baldauf
Business Development Manager: Rich Ingles
Investor Relations Analyst: Silvan Burri
Public Relations & Media: Laurie MacDonald
Estimated Sales: $10 Billion
Number Employees: 25,000
Parent Co: Nestle SA
Type of Packaging: Consumer, Food Service
Brands:
ADDITIONS
AFTER EIGHT BISCUITS & MINTS
ALBERS CORN M GRITS
AQUARI-YUMS
BABY RUTH
BACI
BIT-O-HONEY
BOTTLE CAPS
BUITONI BRAND PASTAS & SAUCES
BUITONI RISOTTO & FOCCACIA MIXES

BUTTERFINGER
CARLOS V
CHEF-MATE
COFFEE-MATE
COFFEE-MATE LATTE
CREATIONS
CROISSANT POCKETS SANDWICHES
CRUCIAL
GLYTROL
GOBSTOPPERS
GOOBERS
GOOD START FORMULAS
HOT POCKETS SANDWICHES
KLIM
LA LECHERA CONDENSED MILK
LAFFY TAFFY
LEAN POCKETS SANDWICHES
LIBBY'S JUICY JUICE
LIBBY'S PUMPKIN
LIK-M-AID FUN DRINKS
MAGGI SEASONINGS
MILO POWDERED DRINK MIX
MINORS
MODULEN IBD
NAN INFANT FORMULA
NERDS
NESCAFE
NESCAFE CAFE CON LECHE
NESCAFE CLASICO
NESCAFE FROT
NESCAFE ICE JAVA
NESQUIK
NESTEA
NESTLE ABUELI CHOCOLATE
NESTLE CARNATION INSTANT
NESTLE CARNATION MALTED MILK
NESTLE CARNATION MILKS
NESTLE CRUNCH
NESTLE DESSERT TOPPINGS
NESTLE EUROPE
NESTLE FOODSERVICES
NESTLE HEALTHCARE NUTRITION
NESTLE HOT COCOA MIX
NESTLE INFANT FORMULAS
NESTLE NIDO 1+, 3+, 6+
NESTLE SIGNA TURTLES
NESTLE SIGNATURES TREASURES
NESTLE TOLL HOUSE CANDY BARS
NESTLE TOLL HOUSE MORSELS
NIPS
NUTREN
NUTRIHEAL
NUTRIHEP
NUTRIRENAL
NUTRIVENT
OH HENRY
OOMPAS
NUTRIVENT
OH HENRY
OOMPAS
ORTEGA
PEPTAMEN
PERUGINA CONFECTIONS

10109 Nestle' Handheld FoodsGroup
345 Inverness Dr S # B2
Englewood, CO 80112-5889 303-790-0303
Fax: 303-790-0214 800-225-2270
laurie.macdonald@us.nestle.com
www.nestleusa.com
Processor of frozen waffles and filled dough pockets.
President/CEO: Stephen Cunliffe
VP: Glenn Lee
Group Marketing Manager: John Becker
Public Relations/Media: Laurie MacDonald
Estimated Sales: $62.7 Million
Number Employees: 100-249
Number of Brands: 3
Type of Packaging: Consumer, Food Service

10110 Neto Sausage Company
1313 Franklin St
Santa Clara, CA 95050-4710 408-296-0818
Fax: 408-296-0538 888-482-6386
netosausage@msn.com www.netosausage.com
Manufacturer of Portuguese, Italian, Mexican, Spanish and chicken sausages
Owner: Deborah Costa
Estimated Sales: $2.5-5 Million
Number Employees: 10-19
Number of Brands: 3
Number of Products: 32
Sq. footage: 16000

Type of Packaging: Consumer, Food Service, Private Label, Bulk
Brands:
LA GRANADA
NETO
ZORRO

10111 Network Food Brokers
355 Lancaster Avenue
Haverford, PA 19041-1547 610-649-7210
Fax: 610-649-0747
Cheese
President: Nate Ostroff
Estimated Sales: $ 2.5-5 Million
Number Employees: 10

10112 Neuchatel Chocolates
461 Limestone Rd
Oxford, PA 19363-1235 610-932-2706
Fax: 610-932-9036 800-597-0759
info@neuchatelchocolates.com
www.neuchatelchocolates.com
Manufacturer of Chocolate confections
President/Chef: Albert Lauber V
Estimated Sales: $ 1 - 3 Million
Number Employees: 20-49

10113 Neuman Bakery Specialties
1405 Jeffrey Dr
Addison, IL 60101-4331 630-916-8909
Fax: 630-916-8919 800-253-5298
blake1@sbcglobal.net www.neumanbakery.net
wholesale bakery
President: George Neuman
CFO: Dan Neuman
VP: George Neuman
R&D: James Neuman
Plant Manager: Bob Barrera
Estimated Sales: Below $5 Million
Number Employees: 25
Sq. footage: 25000
Brands:
NEUMAN

10114 Nevada Baking Company
PO Box 3911
Las Vegas, NV 89127-3911 702-384-8950
Processor of bread and rolls
President: Jim Miller
COO: Robert Mayfield
Sales Manager: Scott Pollock
Number Employees: 100-249
Brands:
Gail's
Roman Meal
Wholesome

10115 Nevada City Brewing
75 Bost Avenue
Nevada City, CA 95959-3024 530-265-2446
Fax: 530-265-2576 ncbrew@oro.net
www.beerme.com
Beer
Co-Owner: Andy Sawdon
Co-Owner: Hans Schillinger
Director Manufacturing: Keith Downing
Estimated Sales: Under $500,000
Number Employees: 1-4
Brands:
Broad St. Brown
Fools Gold Ale

10116 Nevada City Winery
321 Spring St
Nevada City, CA 95959-2420 530-265-9463
Fax: 530-265-6860 800-203-9463
ncwine@ncwinery.com www.ncwinery.com
Wine
President: Wyn Spiller
CEO: Wyn Spiller
Marketing Director: Rod Byers
Sales Director: Rod Byers
Winemaker: Mark Foster
Estimated Sales: $ 2.5-5 Million
Number Employees: 10-19
Brands:
Nevada City Winery

10117 Nevada City Winery
321 Spring St
Nevada City, CA 95959-2420 530-265-9463
Fax: 530-265-6860 800-203-9463
ncwine@ncwinery.com www.ncwinery.com

Wine
President: Wyn Spiller
CEO: Wyn Spiller
Marketing Director: Rod Byers
Sales Director: Rod Byers
Winemaker: Mark Foster
Estimated Sales: $ 2.5-5 Million
Number Employees: 5-9

10118 Nevada County Wine Guild
11372 Winter Moon Way
Nevada City, CA 95959-9694   530-265-3662
bonvino@jps.net
www.ourdailyred.com
Processor of wine
Owner: Tony Norskog
Estimated Sales: Less than $500,000
Number Employees: 1-4
Brands:
Our Daily Red

10119 New Age Canadian Beverage
2503 Baccarat Drive
Hollywood, FL 33026-3741   954-438-1484
VP: John Stubblefield
Estimated Sales: Under $500,000
Number Employees: 1-4

10120 New Bakery Company of Ohio
3005 E Pointe Dr
Zanesville, OH 43701-7263   740-454-6876
Fax: 740-588-5860   800-848-9845
Manufacturer of hamburger buns
Manager: Sam McLaughlin
Plant Manager: Doug Wendeler
Number Employees: 250-499
Sq. footage: 50000
Parent Co: Wendy's International
Type of Packaging: Food Service
Brands:
Sta Fresh
Wendy

10121 New Bedford Linguica
56 Davis St
New Bedford, MA 02746-2495   508-992-9367
Fax: 508-992-9398   877-372-4616
info@fragozo.com   www.fragozo.com
Processor and exporter of Portuguese sausage including linguica, chourico, linguica franks and patties and morcellas
President: Dorothy Anselmo
CEO: Bradford Anselmo
VP: Brad Anselmo
Public Relations: James Davidson
Plant Manager: Alison Anselmo
Estimated Sales: $5-9.9 Million
Number Employees: 5-9
Type of Packaging: Consumer, Food Service, Bulk
Brands:
Chourico
Fragozo
New Bedford Linguica Company
Patties & Franks

10122 New Belgium Brewing Company
500 Linden St
Fort Collins, CO 80524-2457   970-221-0524
Fax: 970-221-0535   888-622-4044
nbb@newbelgium.com   www.newbelgium.com
Beer
CEO: Kimberly Jordan
CFO: Christine Perish
COO: Jennifer Verrier
CFO: Christine Ernst
Marketing Director: Greg Owsley
Public Relations: Meredith Giske
Operations Manager: J Shirosman
Production Manager: Phil Benstein
Estimated Sales: $ 50 Million
Number Employees: 100-249
Sq. footage: 180000
Brands:
Abbey Belgian Style Ale
Blue Paddle Pilsener
Fat Tire Amber Ale
Old Cherry Ale
Porch Swing Style Al
Sunshine Wheat Beer
Trippel Belgian Styl

10123 New Braunfels Smokehouse
P.O.Box 311159
New Braunfels, TX 78131-1159   830-625-7316
Fax: 830-625-7660   800-537-6932
meats@nbsmokehouse.com
www.nbsmokehouse.com
Manufacturer of smoked meats including beef, pork, turkey, ham, chicken and venison; also, jerky
President: Susan Dunbar Snyder
CEO: J Dudley Snyder
VP: Mike Dietert
Estimated Sales: $7.6 Million
Number Employees: 50-99
Type of Packaging: Consumer, Food Service, Private Label, Bulk
Brands:
Dunbar Ranch

10124 New Business Corporation
PO Box 392
East Chicago, IN 46312-0392   800-742-8435
j.thomas.1@att.net
www.gourmetsupreme.com
Processor of ketchup and barbecue, seafood and worcestershire sauces
President: John Thomas
Secretary: Naomi Woods
Estimated Sales: Under $500,000
Number Employees: 1-4
Sq. footage: 1800
Brands:
Gourmet Slim #7
Gourmet Slim Cuisine
Gourmet Supreme

10125 New Canaan Farms
P.O.Box 386
Dripping Springs, TX 78620-0386   512-858-7669
Fax: 512-858-7513   800-727-5267
www.shopncf.com
Processor of gourmet products including jams, salsa, dips and jellies: lemon fig, plum, peach, raspberry, strawberry, blackberry, etc.; also, mustards including jalapeno, honey and German and sauces including jalapeno shrimp, peachpicante, habanero, etc
President: Cindy Figer
Production Manager: Patti Thurman
Estimated Sales: $1200000
Number Employees: 10-19
Type of Packaging: Private Label

10126 New Chapter
20 Technology Dr
Brattleboro, VT 05301-9181   802-257-0018
Fax: 802-257-0652   800-543-7279
info@new-chapter.com   www.new-chapter.com
Processor of natural vitamins and ginger syrups
President: Paul Schulick
Director Sales: Kelli Rooney
Estimated Sales: $ 50 - 100 Million
Number Employees: 50-99

10127 (HQ)New City Packing & Provision Company
P.O.Box 128
North Aurora, IL 60542-0128   630-898-1900
Fax: 630-898-3030   newcty788@aol.com
Manufacturer and exporter of beef, pork and lamb
President/CEO: Marvin Fagel
CEO: Nick Zenneman
Estimated Sales: $50-100 Million
Number Employees: 100-249
Type of Packaging: Consumer

10128 New City Packing Company
P.O.Box 128
North Aurora, IL 60542-0128   630-898-1900
Fax: 630-898-3030
President/CEO: Marvin Fagel
CEO: Nick Zenneman
Estimated Sales: $ 50 - 100 Million
Number Employees: 100-249

10129 New Covent Garden Soup Company
1600 Union Street
San Francisco, CA 94123-4507   415-536-0333
Fax: 415-536-0222
Refrigerated meat soups, seafood soups, vegetable soups
President: Alestair Dorward
VP Sales: Jeff Babikian
VP Operations: John Stapleton

Brands:
Covent Garden

10130 New England Coffee
100 Charles St
Malden, MA 02148-6773   781-324-8094
Fax: 781-397-7580   800-225-3537
consumerrelations@necoffeeco.com
www.newenglandcoffee.com
Product line includes a variety of coffee, whole bean and ground, flavored and regular in addition to decaffeinated blends. Also available is tea, both regular and decaffeinated, flavored and non-flavored and a selection of gift itemsand gift baskets.
President/COO: James Kaloyanides
VP/Finance/Treasurer: Jamie Dostou
VP/Product & Business Development: Michael Kaloyanides
VP/Operations & Human Resources: John Kaloyanides
VP/Purchasing: Stephen Kaloyanides Jr

10131 New England Confectionery Company
135 American Legion Hwy
Revere, MA 02151-2405   781-485-4500
Fax: 781-485-4509   contactus@necco.com
www.necco.com
Processor and exporter of candy including sugar wafers, chocolate bars, caramels, boxed chocolates, chocolate cherries, holiday novelties, taffy, gums, jellies, mints, nougats, coated nuts, lozenges, nonpareils, etc
President: Domenic Antonellis
CFO: Andrew Vosnak
CEO: Richard S Krause
VP Operations: William Leva
Estimated Sales: $100 Million
Number Employees: 1,000-4,999
Parent Co: UIS Industries
Type of Packaging: Consumer, Bulk
Other Locations:
New England Confectionery Co.
Cambridge MA
Brands:
Canada
Candy Cupboard
Candy House
Clark
Deran
Goose Eggs
Haviland
Kettle Fresh
Mary Jane
Masterpieces
Mega Mighty Malts
Mighty Malts
Necco
Sky Bar
Stark
Sweet Talk
Sweethearts

10132 New England Country Bakers
15 Mountain View Rd
Watertown, CT 06795-1648   860-945-9994
Fax: 860-945-9996   800-225-3779
Processor of pound, no-sugar cheesecake and layer cakes, pies and tea breads including apple crumb, maple, banana, blueberry crumb, cranberry, pumpkin and zucchini nut
President: David Spivak
Director Marketing: Donna Spivak
General Manager: Gary Shields
Production: Andrew Kandefer
Estimated Sales: $2000000
Number Employees: 20-49
Number of Brands: 1
Number of Products: 50
Sq. footage: 24000
Type of Packaging: Food Service

10133 New England Cranberry Company
82 Sanderson Ave
Lynn, MA 01902-1974   781-596-0888
Fax: 781-596-0808   800-410-2892
info@newenglandcranberry.com
www.newenglandcranberry.com

Processor and exporter of naturally sweetened dried cranberries, premium suger sweetened dried cranberries, dried wild blueberries, dried cherries, frozen whole cranberries, cranberry jams and jellies, cranberry chutney and pepperjelly, and fine chocolates with sweet cranberries
President: Ted Stux
Sales: Arthur Stock
Estimated Sales:$530000
Number Employees: 10-19
Sq. footage: 1850
Type of Packaging: Consumer, Food Service, Bulk
Brands:
Fresh Pond
New England Cranberry

10134 New England Marketers
22 Fish Pier
PO Box 51545
Boston, MA 02210-1545   617-951-9904
Fax: 617-951-9907 800-688-9904
sara@nemarketers.com OR
info@bayshorechowders.com
www.yankeespecialtyfoods.com OR
www.bayshorechowders.com
Processor of gourmet lobster bisque, New England and Manhattan clam chowders, New England fish chowder, lobster, mussels, etc.
President: Paul Lindquist
VP: Adrienne Lindquist
Estimated Sales:$780000
Number Employees: 4
Type of Packaging: Consumer, Food Service, Bulk
Brands:
BAY SHORE

10135 New England Muffin Company
337 Pleasant St
Fall River, MA 02721-3000   508-675-2833
Fax: 508-675-2833
Processor of fresh and frozen Portuguese muffins in various flavors
Owner: Jose Martin
Estimated Sales:$980000
Number Employees: 5-9
Type of Packaging: Food Service, Bulk

10136 New England Natural Bakers
74 Fairview St E
Greenfield, MA 01301-9654   413-772-2239
Fax: 413-772-2936 800-910-2884
nenb@nenb.com   www.nenb.com
Processor, importer and exporter of breakfast cereals, granolas, muesli, tamari, chocolates and fruit, nut, snack and cracker mixes, and bars; also, private label available
President: John Broucek
Quality Control: Dale Parda
Marketing/Sales: Todd Einig
Operations Manager: Mike Hassay
Purchasing Director: Eric Hassay
Number Employees: 20-49
Number of Brands: 1
Number of Products: 50
Sq. footage: 30000
Type of Packaging: Consumer, Food Service, Private Label, Bulk
Brands:
New England Naturals

10137 New Era Canning Company
4856 1st St
New Era, MI 49446-9677   231-861-2151
Fax: 231-861-4068 www.neweracanning.com
Processor and exporter of canned fruits and vegetables including beans, asparagus and apples; also, canned apple sauce
President/CEO: Rick Ray
Quality Control: Kim Klotz
Sales: Patrick Alger
Production: Jim Merrill
Purchasing: Ron Fekken
Estimated Sales:$ 10 - 20 Million
Number Employees: 100-249
Number of Brands: 3
Number of Products: 65
Sq. footage: 185000
Type of Packaging: Consumer, Food Service, Private Label
Brands:
Good Taste
Necco
New Era

10138 New Generation Foods
5934 S 25th Street
Omaha, NE 68107-4443   402-733-5755
Fax: 402-733-5755 danehodge@hotmail.com
Processor of portion control and breaded foods including beef, chicken, pork and turkey
CFO: Steve McCurdy
National Sales Manager: Dane Hodges
Plant Manager: John Schull
Number Employees: 15

10139 New Glarus Bakery
534 First Street
PO Box 595
New Glarus, WI 53574   866-805-5536
Fax: 608-527-5799 www.newglarusbakery.com
Cookies, breads, pastries, donuts and desserts.
Co-Owner: Howard Weber
Co-Owner: Nancy Weber
Estimated Sales:$500,000-$1 Million
Number Employees: 10-19
Brands:
New Glarus Bakery

10140 New Glarus Brewing
P.O.Box 759
New Glarus, WI 53574-0759   608-527-5850
Fax: 608-527-5855 www.newglarusbrewing.com
Beer
President: Deborah Carey
VP: Deborah Carry
*Estimated Sales:*Below $ 5 Million
Number Employees: 20-49

10141 New Glarus Foods
P.O.Box 549
New Glarus, WI 53574-0549   608-527-2131
Fax: 608-527-2931 800-356-6685
www.nweglarusfoods.com
Processor and exporter of smoked sausage, meat and meat snacks; gourmet gift packs available
President: Rich Nagy
Chairman/CEO: G Woodrow Adkinsld
Executive VP: Michael McDonald
Sales Director: Mike McDonald
Plant Manager: Richard Nagy
Purchasing Manager: G Dombkowski
Estimated Sales:$ 50 - 100 Million
Number Employees: 100-249
Sq. footage: 75000
Type of Packaging: Consumer, Private Label, Bulk
Brands:
Gourmet Preferred
Strickler's
Sugar River

10142 New Grass Bison
PO Box 860033
Shawnee, KS 66286   866-422-5888
sales@newgrassbison.com
www.newgrassbison.com
natural and grassfed bison products

10143 New Harbor Fisherman's Cooperative
P.O.Box 125
New Harbor, ME 04554-0125   207-677-2791
Fax: 207-677-3835 866-883-2922
lobsta@newharborlobster.com
www.newharborlobster.com
Manufacturer of lobster, crab and other seafood
Manager: Linda Vannah
Operations Manager: Ken Tonneson
Estimated Sales:$ .5 - 1 million
Number Employees: 1-4
Type of Packaging: Consumer, Bulk

10144 New Harmony Coffee Roasters
2600 E Tioga Street
Philadelphia, PA 19134-5415   215-925-6770
Fax: 215-925-0821
Coffee
Partner: Sharon Burkard
*Estimated Sales:*Under $500,000
Number Employees: 1-4
Brands:
New Harmony

10145 New Harvest Foods
323 3rd Ave
Pulaski, WI 54162-9033   920-822-2578

Processor of canned vegetables including peas, green beans, sweet corn, carrots, potatoes, sauerkraut and mixed vegetables
President: Timothy Grygield
Production Manager: Tom Wojcik
Plant Manager: Robert Tetzlaff
Estimated Sales:$ 5 - 10 Million
Number Employees: 20-49
Sq. footage: 70000

10146 New Hope Mills
181 York St
Auburn, NY 13021-9009   315-252-2676
Fax: 315-282-0720 sales@newhopemills.com
www.newhopemills.com
Processor of mixes including pancake, bread and cookie; also, milled flour including buckwheat, wheat and pancake
President: Dale Weed
Estimated Sales:$ 3 - 5 Million
Number Employees: 10-19
Number of Products: 20
Sq. footage: 30000
Type of Packaging: Consumer, Food Service, Private Label, Bulk

10147 New Hope Winery
6123 Lower York Rd
New Hope, PA 18938-9620   215-794-2331
Fax: 215-794-2341 800-592-9463
info@newhopewinery.com
www.newhopewinery.com
Red wine
Owner: Sandra Pizza
Estimated Sales:$710,000
Number Employees: 5-9
Number of Products: 25

10148 New Horizon Foods
33440 Western Ave
Union City, CA 94587-3202   510-489-8600
Fax: 510-489-9797 www.tovaindustries.com
Manufacturer of dough conditioners, bread bases, natural mixes, beverage, cake, muffin, pudding, meat spices, spice blends, snack and chip seasonings, custard, ice cream, waffle cone and sauce mixes and bases; exporter of doughconditioners and cake and muffin mixes; contract packaging services available
President: Zach Melzer
Number Employees: 10-19
Parent Co: Tova Industries
Type of Packaging: Consumer, Food Service, Private Label, Bulk

10149 New Horizons Baking Company
PO Box 695
Fremont, IN 46737-0695   260-495-7055
Fax: 219-495-2307 www.newhorizonsbaking.com
Processor of buns and English muffins
President: Tilmon Brown
VP/Director Operations: John Widman
Plant Manager: Joe Gross
Purchasing Manager: Tilmon Brown
Estimated Sales:$ 3 - 5 Million
Number Employees: 50-99
Sq. footage: 40000
Type of Packaging: Food Service, Private Label, Bulk
Other Locations:
New Horizons Baking Company
Norwalk OH

10150 New Jamaican Gold
3536 Arden Rd
Hayward, CA 94545-3908   510-887-4653
Fax: 510-887-7466 800-672-9956
info@jamaican-gold.com
www.jamaican-gold.com
Ready-to-drink coffee/ice cappuccino
CEO: Kenneth Yeung
Sales Director: Kimi Tom
Estimated Sales:$1+ Million
Number Employees: 10-19
Brands:
Jamaican Gold

10151 New Land Vineyard
577 Lerch Rd
Geneva, NY 14456-9238   315-585-4432
Fax: 315-585-9844
Wines
Owner: Dale Nagy

Estimated Sales: Less than $500,000
Number Employees: 1-4

10152 New Meadows Lobster
60 Portland Pier
Portland, ME 04101-4713   207-775-1612
  Fax: 207-874-2456 www.newmeadowslobster.com
Lobster
    Owner: Peter L Mc Aleney
Estimated Sales: $ 5 - 10 Million
Number Employees: 10-19

10153 New Meridian
P.O.Box 155
Eaton, IN 47338-0155   765-396-3344
        Fax: 765-396-3430 www.edenfoods.com
Processor and canner of dry beans; specializing in
private labeling
    Manager: David Morrow
    VP/General Manager: David Brand
Estimated Sales: $ 20 - 50 Million
Number Employees: 20-49
Sq. footage: 45000
Parent Co: Eden Foods
Type of Packaging: Private Label

10154 New Mexico Food Distributors
3041 University Blvd SE
Albuquerque, NM 87106-5040   505-888-0199
      Fax: 505-889-3144 800-637-7084
        www.foodsofnewmexico.com
Processor and wholesaler/distributor of Mexican
food products including enchiladas, corn and flour
tortillas, green chili, roasted and red chili powders,
etc.; serving the food service market
    Owner: Larry Gutierrez
    Sales Manager: Atrian Montoya
Estimated Sales: $ 20 - 50 Million
Number Employees: 20-49
Type of Packaging: Consumer, Food Service

10155 New Morn Foods
4323 Mundy Mill Road
Suite 100
Oakwood, GA 30566-2500   770-536-4561
Processor and exporter of shell eggs
    Sales Manager: Charles Bracket
Number Employees: 20-49
Sq. footage: 20000
Type of Packaging: Consumer, Food Service, Private Label

10156 New Morning
200 Reservoir Street
Suite 200
Needham, MA 02494-3146   781-444-0440
      Fax: 781-444-3411 cdavis@usmillsinc.com
        www.usmillsinc.com
Processor of organic products including pickles, sau-
erkraut, apple sauce, olives, fruit butters, breakfast
cereals and graham crackers; importer of olives; ex-
porter of breakfast cereals and graham crackers
    President: Charles Verde
    VP Marketing/Sales: Carol Pressman
Number Employees: 9
Sq. footage: 25000
Type of Packaging: Consumer, Private Label
Brands:
    Honey Grahams Organic
    New Morning
    New Morning Organic Cereals
    Pickle-Eaters
    Zorba

10157 New Ocean
3077 McCall Dr # 12
Doraville, GA 30340-2832   770-458-5235
        Fax: 770-485-5235
Seafood, shrimp, scallops, king crab, lobster tails,
snow crab
    President: Mei Lin
Estimated Sales: $7,000,000
Number Employees: 5-9

10158 New Orleans Fish House
921 S Dupre St
New Orleans, LA 70125-1343   504-821-9700
  Fax: 504-821-9011 800-839-3474
        www.nofh.com

Processor of fresh and frozen catfish, tilapia, crawfish, softshell crabs, tuna, shark, red snapper, pompano, wahoo, drum, escalor and sheephead
    Owner: Craig Borges
    Co-Owner: Craig Borges
    VP Marketing: Craig Borges
    VP Sales: Cliff Hall
Estimated Sales: $ 20-50 Million
Number Employees: 20-49
Type of Packaging: Consumer, Food Service, Private Label, Bulk

10159 New Orleans Gulf Seafood
9134 Chef Menteur Highway
New Orleans, LA 70127-4134   504-246-7329
                    Fax: 504-246-7415
Seafood
    President: Syed Fakhruddin

10160 New Packing Company
1249 W Lake St
Chicago, IL 60607-1519   312-666-1314
                    Fax: 312-666-8698
Processor of sausage
    President: Kurt Kreuger
Estimated Sales: $1800000
Number Employees: 10-19
Type of Packaging: Consumer

10161 New Salem Tea-Bread Company
837 Daniel Shays Highway
New Salem, MA 01355   978-544-0294
      Fax: 978-544-5643 800-897-5910
    info@teabread.com www.teabread.com
Manufacturer of all natural, kosher teabreads. Flavors: lemon, banana orange cranberry, blueberry vanilla, pumpkin, carrot raisin, almond, apple
cinnamon
    Co-Owner: Steve Verney
    Co-Owner: Kay Verney

10162 New Season Foods
P.O.Box 157
Forest Grove, OR 97116-0157   503-357-7124
                    Fax: 503-357-0419
    mailto:%20info@newseasonfoods.com
        www.newseasonfoods.com
Manufacturer of drum-dried vegetable powders and
other custom ingredients
    President/CEO: Mark Frandsen
Estimated Sales: $5-10 Million
Number Employees: 20-49
Sq. footage: 150000
Type of Packaging: Bulk
Brands:
    FLAVORLAND
    NEW SEASON FOODS

10163 New West Foods
345 California Street
Suite 1150
San Francisco, CA 94104-2664   701-947-2505
      Fax: 701-947-2105 sales@nabison.com
        www.nabison.com
Processor of strawberries, peaches, mixed fruit,
tropicals, blueberries and tropical fruit; exporter of
strawberries; importer of red raspberries, melon
balls, pineapples, grapes and tropical fruit
    President: Dennis Sexus
    CEO: Dieter Pape
    Executive VP: Thomas Riemann
    Sales Manager: Thomas Riemann
    Plant Manager: Milan Ristich
Estimated Sales: $36100000
Number Employees: 147
Parent Co: New West Foods
Type of Packaging: Consumer, Food Service, Pri-
vate Label, Bulk
Brands:
    Golden State
    New West Foods

10164 New West Foods
4324 E Vineyard Avenue
Oxnard, CA 93036-1056   805-485-3745
      Fax: 805-983-1655 sales@nabison.com
        www.newwestfoods.com
Processor and exporter frozen strawberries
    Plant Manager: Rita Castell
Estimated Sales: $ 100-500 Million
Number Employees: 250-499
Type of Packaging: Bulk

10165 New White Palace Bakery
4747 N 11th Street
Philadelphia, PA 19141-3401   215-324-9852
Processor of bread and rolls including rye, wheat
and pumpernickel
    Owner: Norman Tenner
Number Employees: 20-49
Type of Packaging: Consumer, Food Service, Bulk

10166 New World Pasta
P.O.Box 126457
Harrisburg, PA 17112-6457   717-526-2200
  Fax: 717-526-2468 mikehoar@nwpasta.com
                www.newworldpasta.com
Processor of pasta
    CEO: Peter Smith
    General Manager: Del Thacker
Estimated Sales: $5100000
Number Employees: 1,000-4,999
Sq. footage: 300000
Parent Co: New World Pasta
Type of Packaging: Bulk

10167 (HQ)New World Pasta Company7
P.O.Box 126457
Harrisburg, PA 17112-6457   717-526-2200
      Fax: 717-526-2468 800-730-5957
            nwpasta@casupport.com
            www.newworldpasta.com
Pasta and pasta products.
    CEO: Scott Greenwood
    Quality Control: Dan Carlin
    CEO: Peter Smith
    Chif Financial Officer: Ed Lyons
    Sales Director: Alan Geoffrey
    Manager Public Information: Natalie Bailey
Estimated Sales: $ 20-50 Million
Number Employees: 1,000-4,999
Brands:
    American Beauty
    Cremette
    Ideal
    Light 'n Fluffy Nood
    Prince
    Ronzoni
    San Giorgio
    Skinner

10168 New York Apples Sales
1580 Columbia Tpke # 5
Castletn on Hdsn, NY 12033-9531 518-477-7200
                    Fax: 518-477-6770
    mike@newyorkapplesales.com
        www.newyorkapplesales.com
Manufacturer of apples and pears
    President: Kaari Stannard
Estimated Sales: $29 Million
Number Employees: 20-49
Type of Packaging: Consumer, Food Service, Bulk

10169 New York Bagel Boys
P.O.Box 720
West Sacramento, CA 95691-0720 916-739-6540
                    Fax: 916-739-0162
Processor of fresh and frozen bagels
    President: David Levin
Estimated Sales: $600000
Number Employees: 5-9
Sq. footage: 6000
Type of Packaging: Consumer, Food Service

10170 New York Bakeries
261 W 22nd St
Hialeah, FL 33010-1521   305-882-1355
                    Fax: 305-883-0790
Manufacturer exporter of bread, rolls and cakes
    President: Sarah Zimmerman
Estimated Sales: $35 Million
Number Employees: 50-99
Parent Co: New York Bakeries
Type of Packaging: Consumer, Food Service, Pri-
vate Label

10171 New York Bakery & Bagelry
1750 Limetree Lane
Saint Louis, MO 63146-4723   314-731-0080
                    Fax: 314-731-2467
Bagels and baked goods

10172 New York Bottling Company
626 Whittier St
Bronx, NY 10474-6121   718-378-2525
                    Fax: 718-782-6348

Bottled soft drinks
Contact: Zvi Hold
Estimated Sales:$ 5-10 Million
Number Employees: 10-19
Brands:
La Pri Cranberry Apple Drink
La Pri Grapefruit Dr
La Pri Orange Drink

10173 (HQ)New York Coffee & Bagels
109 E 42nd Street
New York, NY 10017-8500   212-986-6116
Fax: 212-986-0057
Coffee
President/CEO: Jason Genussa
Plant Manager: B Hanley
Estimated Sales:$ 10-100 Million
Number Employees: 20

10174 New York Fish House
32-34 Papetti Plz
Elizabeth, NJ 07206-1432   908-351-0045
Fax: 908-351-0021 yashiro@trueworldfoods.com
www.ny-fish.com
Seafood
COO: Jack Sato
CEO: Takeshi Yashiro
CFO: Jack Jewell
Production Manager: Tony Scazzero
Estimated Sales:$ 20-50 Million
Number Employees: 100-249
Brands:
New York Fish House

10175 New York Frozen Foods
25900 Fargo Ave
Cleveland, OH 44146-1369   216-292-5655
Fax: 216-292-5978
Processor of bread and rolls
Executive Director: Mike Mahon
Number Employees: 250-499
Parent Co: T. Marzetti Company
Type of Packaging: Consumer, Food Service

10176 New York International Bread Company
1500 W Church St
Orlando, FL 32805-2408   407-843-9744
Fax: 407-648-2785
Bread and baked products
CEO: Laura Masella
Estimated Sales:$ 5-10 Million
Number Employees: 100-249

10177 New York Pizza
725 E Internatl Speedway Blvd
Daytona Beach, FL 32118-4555   386-257-2050
www.nypizza.ru
Pizza
Owner: Richard Squillante
Estimated Sales: Less than $500,000
Number Employees: 1-4
Brands:
New York Pizza

10178 New York Pretzel
200 Moore St
Brooklyn, NY 11206-3708   718-366-9800
Fax: 718-821-4544 richard@nypretzel.com
www.nypretzel.com
Processor of soft pretzels
Manager: Ron Orfinger
Sales Manager: Russel Orfinger
Number Employees: 50-99
Brands:
New York Pretzel

10179 New York Ravioli & Pasta Company
12 Denton Ave S
New Hyde Park, NY 11040-4904   516-270-2852
Fax: 516-741-5289 888-588-7287
ravkings@nyravioli.com
www.nyravioli.com
Manufacturer of Ravioli and other products
President/Co-Founder: David Creo
VP/Co-Founder: Paul Moncada
Estimated Sales:$ 3 - 5 Million
Number Employees: 10-19
Type of Packaging: Food Service, Private Label, Bulk

10180 (HQ)New Zealand Lamb Company
20 Westport Rd # 320
Wilton, CT 06897-4550   203-529-9100
Fax: 203-529-9101 800-438-5262
shnae@nzlamb.com www.nzlamb.com
Manufacturer of Lamb and lamb products, venison, beef, veal
President: Shane O'Hara
VP Sales/Marketing: Peter Gilligan
Estimated Sales:$10-20 Million
Number Employees: 10-19
Other Locations:
New Zealand Lamb Company
Etobicoke, Ontario,Canada

10181 Newark Meat Supply
PO Box 756
Newark, OH 43058-0756   740-345-6696
Fax: 740-345-0103
Manufacturer and wholesaler/distributor of fresh and frozen meats; wholesaler/distributor of general merchandise, general line, produce and seafood
President: Thomas Hoffman
Estimated Sales:$34 Million
Number Employees: 15
Type of Packaging: Consumer, Food Service

10182 Newburg Corners Cheese Factory
Highway 33
Route 2
Bangor, WI 54614   608-452-3636
Fax: 608-452-3636
Cheese
Owner: Lowell Kitzmann
Owner: Mike Everhart
Number Employees: 1-4

10183 Newburgh Egg Corporation
1255 E 31st Street
Brooklyn, NY 11210-4740   718-692-4392
Fax: 718-677-5909 mbendet@aol.com
Processor of whole eggs, yolks, whipping whites, texture blends and hard-cooked peeled eggs
President/CEO: Mayer Bendit
Number Employees: 10-19

10184 Newburgh Egg Processing
P.O.Box 175
Woodridge, NY 12789-0175   845-434-8115
Fax: 845-434-8216 888-434-8115
newburghegg@cheskill.net
Manufacturer of Eggs
President: Moses Goldstein
VP: Moses Neustadt
*Estimated Sales:*34-40 Million
Number Employees: 20-49

10185 Newburgh Packing Corporation
677 Little Britain Road
New Windsor, NY 12553-6199   845-562-1185
Fax: 845-562-7968
Processor of meat products
President: Henry Scheible
Estimated Sales:$8254264
Number Employees: 40
Type of Packaging: Consumer

10186 Newell Lobsters
PO Box 99
Yarmouth, NS B5A 4B1
Canada   902-742-6272
Fax: 902-742-1542
Processor and exporter of fresh herring roe and lobster
Owner: Robert Newell
Number Employees: 10-19
Type of Packaging: Consumer, Food Service, Private Label

10187 Newfound Resources
PO Box 13695
Saint John's, NL A1B 4G1
Canada   709-579-7676
Fax: 709-579-7668 shrimp@nfld.com
Processor and exporter of frozen shrimp
President: Brian McNamara
Number Employees: 5-9
Type of Packaging: Bulk

10188 Newhart Foods
PO Box 339
Allentown, PA 18105-0339   610-437-5539

Manufacturer of salads
President/CEO: Thomas Bross III
Technical Services Manager: Sandy Erickson
Plant Manager: Don Johnson
Estimated Sales:$15 Million
Number Employees: 50-99
Type of Packaging: Consumer, Food Service, Private Label

10189 Newly Weds Foods
PO Box 1315
Memphis, TN 38101-1315   662-393-3610
Fax: 662-280-5208 800-647-9314
scariker@flavorite.com www.flavorite.com
Manufacturer and exporter of coffee, flavors, spice blends, barbecue sauce, seasonings, teas and dry drink mixes
President: Charles Angell
R&D Manager: Emmett Cook
Estimated Sales:$100 Million
Number Employees: 99
Parent Co: Newly Weds Foods
Type of Packaging: Consumer, Food Service, Private Label, Bulk

10190 (HQ)Newly Weds Foods
4140 W Fullerton Ave
Chicago, IL 60639-2198   773-489-7000
Fax: 773-489-2799 800-621-7521
nwfnorthamerica@newlywedsfoods.com
www.newlywedsfoods.com
Processor and exporter of breadings, batters, seasoning blends, marinades, glazes and capsicum products
President: Charles Angell
CFO: Dan Lechin
Vice President: Bruce Lesinski
R&D: Lynn Theiss
Quality Control: Dave Rey
Sales Director: Jim Chin
Operations Manager: Mike Hopp
Production Manager: Tom Stoll
Plant Manager: Tom Stoll
Purchasing Manager: T Lisack
Number Employees: 1,000-4,999
Other Locations:
Newly Weds Foods
Baldwin Park CA
Brands:
Batter Blends
Blended Breaders
Newly Weds

10191 Newly Weds Foods
70 Grove Street
80
Watertown, MA 02472-2829   617-926-7600
Fax: 617-926-8547 800-621-7521
resumes@newlywedsfoods.com
www.newlywedsfoods.com
Processor of bread crumbs
President: Charles T Angell
General Manager: John Lincoln
Production Manager: Harry Talbot
Estimated Sales:$ 10 - 20 Million
Number Employees: 50-99
Type of Packaging: Bulk

10192 Newly Weds Foods
3306 Central Parkway SW
Decatur, AL 35603-1616   256-350-0602
800-521-6189
Processor of batters, breadings, seasoning blends and marinades
Number Employees: 20-49
Type of Packaging: Bulk

10193 (HQ)Newman's Own
246 Post Rd E
Westport, CT 06880-3615   203-222-0136
Fax: 203-227-5630 www.newmansown.com
Processor and exporter of natural salad dressings, pasta sauces, popcorn, lemonade and salsa
President: Thomas Indoe
COO: Tom Indoe
Vice President: Bill Lee
Sales Director: Linda Rohr
Director Purchasing/Systems: Bill Lee
Estimated Sales:$ 50 - 100 Million
Number Employees: 10-19
Type of Packaging: Consumer, Food Service
Other Locations:
Newman's Own
Aptos CA
Brands:
Newman's Own

Newman's Own Lemonade
Newman's Own Pasta Sauces
Newman's Own Popcorn
Newman's Own Salad Dressing
Newman's Own Salsa

10194 Newmarket Foods
2210 Pine View Way
Petaluma, CA 94954-5687   707-778-3400
Fax: 707-778-3434 info@newmarketfoods.com
www.newmarketfoods.com
VP Sales/Marketing: Tom Mierzwinski
Vice President: Thomas Mierzwinski
Estimated Sales: $ 1-2.5 Million
Number Employees: 1
Type of Packaging: Private Label
Brands:
Butterscotch Bliss
Chocolate Ecstasy
Hot Fudge Fantasy

10195 Newport Flavours & Fragrances
833 N Elm St
Orange, CA 92867-7909   714-628-9894
Fax: 714-771-3588 www.newportflavours.com
Processor of flavor extracts, concentrates, fillings,
icings, glazes, syrups, toppings, oils and fragrances;
also, contract packaging available
President: Bill Sabo
VP: Jeanne Aragon
Estimated Sales: $ 5 - 10 Million
Number Employees: 10-19
Sq. footage: 8800
Type of Packaging: Consumer, Food Service, Private Label, Bulk

10196 Newport Vineyards & Winery
909 E Main Rd
Middletown, RI 02842-5370   401-848-5161
Fax: 401-848-5162 info@newportvineyards.com
www.newportvineyards.com
Wine
Co-Owner: John Nunes
Co-Owner/Vineyard Manager: Paul Nunes
General Manager: John Nunes
Production Manager: George Chelf
Estimated Sales: $ 2.5-5 Million
Number Employees: 10-19
Type of Packaging: Private Label
Brands:
Newport

10197 Newton Candy Company
4912 Airline Dr # G
Houston, TX 77022-3078   713-691-6969
Fax: 713-691-6979
Candy
Manager: Muhammed Nazim
Estimated Sales: $ 2.5-5 Million
Number Employees: 10-19

10198 Newton Vineyard
2555 Madrona Ave
St Helena, CA 94574-2300   707-963-9000
Fax: 707-963-5408 winery@newtonvineyard.com
www.newtonvineyard.com
Wines
President: Dr Su Hua Newton
Sr. EVP: Paolo Mancini
Controller: Tim Lin
Winemaker: Stephen Carrier
Estimated Sales: $20-50 Million
Number Employees: 100-249
Type of Packaging: Private Label
Brands:
Newton Vineyard

10199 Newtown Foods
601 Corporate Dr W
Langhorne, PA 19047-8013   215-579-2120
Fax: 215-579-2129 info@newtownfoods.com
www.newtownfoods.com
Cocoa ingredients, dehydrated fruit, natural extracts,
banana puree, spray-dried ingredients
Owner: John Mc Donald
Estimated Sales: Below $ 5 Million
Number Employees: 1-4
Brands:
Duas Rodas Industrial
Dutch Cocoa BV
Kievit
Schoemaker

10200 Niagara Brewing Company
6863 Lundy's Lane
Niagara Falls, ON L2G 1V7
Canada   905-374-1166
Fax: 905-374-7701 800-267-3392
cri@crivellerbrew.com
www.crivellerbrew.com/cri
Processor of ale and lager
President: Bruce McCubbin
Marketing Director: Matt Johnson
Manager: Barbara Criveller
Production Supervisor/Head Brewer: Kevin Gray
Number Employees: 20-49
Sq. footage: 6000
Type of Packaging: Consumer, Food Service
Brands:
Eisbock
Gritstone
Honey Brown
Millstone
Niagara
Paleao

10201 Niagara Chocolates
3500 Genesee St
Cheektowaga, NY 14225-5015   716-634-4545
Fax: 716-634-4855 800-234-5750
info@niagarachocolates.com
www.niagarachocolates.com
Processor of chocolate novelties including bars, truffles and boxed
President: Phil Terranova
Estimated Sales: $ 10-100 Million
Number Employees: 100-249
Type of Packaging: Consumer
Brands:
Mercken's
Mercken's Chocolate
Sweet Works

10202 Niagara Foods
10 Kelly Ave
Middleport, NY 14105-1210   716-735-7722
Fax: 716-735-9076 www.agvest.com
Processor, importer and exporter of frozen vegetable
products and fruit and vegetable powders and flakes;
also, frozen and dehydrated fruits including apples,
cherries, strawberries, cranberries and wild and cultivated blueberries.
President: Barry Schneider
General Manager: Bob Neuman
Estimated Sales: $14900000
Number Employees: 50-99
Sq. footage: 70000
Parent Co: Agvest
Type of Packaging: Consumer, Food Service, Private Label, Bulk
Brands:
Agvest
Quality

10203 Niagara Milk Cooperative
8450 Buffalo Ave
Niagara Falls, NY 14304-4323   716-692-6543
Fax: 716-283-9782
Milk Producers
President: James Schotz
Estimated Sales: $15-$17 Million
Number Employees: 100-249

10204 Nicasio Vineyards
483 Nicasio Way
Soquel, CA 95073-9782   831-423-1073
Wine
President: Dan Wheeler

10205 (HQ)Niche Import Company
45 Horsehill Rd # 105a
Cedar Knolls, NJ 07927-2041   973-993-8450
Fax: 973-898-0183 800-548-6882
niche@ourniche.com www.ourniche.com
Gourmet foods and beverages
President: Peter Nelson
Media Relations: Barbara Miele
Estimated Sales: $ 2.5-5 Million
Number Employees: 5-9
Type of Packaging: Private Label
Brands:
Asbach Uralt
Stroh
Underberg Bitters

10206 Nichelini Winery
2950 Sage Canyon Rd
St Helena, CA 94574-9641   707-963-0717
Fax: 707-963-3262
nichwine@nicheliniwinery.com
www.nicheliniwinery.com
Wines
Manager: Toni Irwin
Treasurer: Richard Wainright
Wine Maker: Greg Boeger
Estimated Sales: Below $ 5 Million
Number Employees: 1-4
Type of Packaging: Private Label

10207 Nichem Company
619 Ramsey Ave
Hillside, NJ 07205-1009   908-933-0770
Fax: 973-399-8818 sales@nichem.com
www.nichem.com
Processor and importer of ingredients including citric acid, vanillin and sodium citrate; exporter of citric acid
President: Peigeng Lu
Estimated Sales: $700,000
Number Employees: 1-4
Sq. footage: 20000
Type of Packaging: Consumer, Food Service

10208 Nicholas G. Verry
400 1st Street
Parlier, CA 93648-2007   209-646-2785
Wines
Number Employees: 5-9
Sq. footage: 80000
Type of Packaging: Consumer
Brands:
Verry's

10209 Nichols Pistachio
13762 1st Avenue
Hanford, CA 93230-9316   559-688-9463
Fax: 559-688-1603 chuck@nicholsfarms.com.
www.victoriaisland.net
Pistachio nuts
President: Charles Nichols
Marketing Director: Brandon Leslie
Estimated Sales: $ 20 - 50 Million
Number Employees: 100-249
Brands:
Almond Grades
Nichol's Pistachio

10210 Nick Sciabica & Sons
2150 Yosemite Blvd
Modesto, CA 95354-3931   209-577-5067
Fax: 209-524-5367 800-551-9612
sales@sciabica.com www.sciabica.com
Processor of extra virgin olive oil; importer of olive
oil, pasta and tomato products; wholesaler/distributor of wine vinegar, olive oil, canned tomatoes, olives and pasta
President: Daniel Sciabica
CEO: Joseph Sciabica
CFO: Ramesh Singh
VP/Marketing: Johnathan Sciabica
Research & Development: Gemma Sciabica
Quality Control: Nicholas Sciabica
Sales/Public Relations: Dean Cohan
Operations/Production: Nicholas Sciabica
Plant Manager/Purchasing: Nicholas Sciabica
Estimated Sales: $10700000
Number Employees: 20-49
Number of Brands: 6
Number of Products: 150
Sq. footage: 68000
Parent Co: Nick Sciabica & Sons
Type of Packaging: Consumer, Food Service, Private Label, Bulk
Brands:
Marsala
Sciabica's Oil of the Olive

10211 Nickabood's Company
1401 Elwood St
Los Angeles, CA 90021-2812   213-746-1541
Fax: 213-746-1542
Manufacturer of health food products including
sauces, honey, salad dressings, condiments seafood
sauces, baked potato products, miso mayo, and
frozen stuffed potatoes
President: Nick Abood
Estimated Sales: $500,000
Number Employees: 5-9
Number of Brands: 4

Number of Products: 15
Sq. footage: 15000
Parent Co: Fisherman Wharf Foods
Type of Packaging: Consumer, Food Service, Private Label, Bulk
Brands:
DESERT GOLD
FISHERMAN'S WHARF
SO GOOD
SPUD KING

10212 Nickles Bakery of Indiana
604 Harrison St
Elkhart, IN 46516-2706   574-293-0608
Fax: 574-293-0296 www.nicklesbakery.com
Processor of breads including lite 35, midwest grains, bread, buns, rolls, bagels, muffins, breadsticks, snack cakes, pasteries, donuts
Manager: Dan Witticker
Manager: Bill Carter
Estimated Sales: $18300000
Number Employees: 20-49
Parent Co: Alfred Nickles Bakery
Type of Packaging: Consumer, Food Service, Private Label

10213 Nickles Bakery of Ohio
590 N Hague Ave
Columbus, OH 43204-1419   614-276-5477
Fax: 614-276-4699   800-335-9775
www.nicklesbakery.com
Processor of breads and cakes
President: Joe Blake
General Manager: Mark Sponsella
Estimated Sales: $ 50 - 100 Million
Number Employees: 50-99
Parent Co: Nickles Bakery
Type of Packaging: Consumer, Food Service

10214 Nickles Bakery of Ohio
1121 Latham Ave
Lima, OH 45805-2005   419-224-7080
Fax: 419-228-7357 www.nicklesbakery.com
Processor of sandwich buns and bread
Manager: John Nixon
Estimated Sales: $ 3 - 5 Million
Number Employees: 50-99
Type of Packaging: Consumer, Food Service, Private Label
Other Locations:
Alfred Nickles Bakery
Fairmont WV
Alfred Nickles Bakery
Parkersburg WV
Alfred Nickles Bakery
Portage MI
Alfred Nickles Bakery
Elkhart IN
Alfred Nickles Bakery
Kokomo IN
Alfred Nickles Bakery
Plymouth IN
Alfred Nickles Bakery
Fort Wayne IN
Alfred Nickles Bakery
Rochester IN
Alfred Nickles Bakery
Indianapolis IN
Alfred Nickles Bakery
Valpariso IN
Alfred Nickles Bakery
DuBois PA
Alfred Nickles Bakery
Ebensberg PA
Alfred Nickles Bakery
Verona PA

10215 Nickles Bakery of Ohio
1000 Broadway St
Martins Ferry, OH 43935-1972   740-633-1711
Fax: 740-633-6852 www.nicklesbakery.com
Processor of baked goods including bread and buns
CFO: Bill Eisenhower
Plant Manager: Scott Ketter
Estimated Sales: $9,900,000
Number Employees: 100-249
Parent Co: Alfred Nickles Bakery
Type of Packaging: Consumer, Food Service, Private Label

10216 (HQ)Nickles Bakery of Ohio
26 Main Street
Navarre, OH 44662   330-879-5635
Fax: 330-879-5896   800-362-9775
customerservice@nicklesbakery.com
www.nicklesbakery.com

Vendors of bakery products
CFO: Mark Sponseller
Executive Director: David A Gardner
Executive VP: David Gardner
Quality Control: Maryt Brideweser
Marketing Director: Philip Gardner
Purchase Manager: J Kettlewell
Estimated Sales: $ 5-10 Million
Number Employees: 20-49
Brands:
Nickles Bakery

10217 Nicky
223 SE 3rd Ave
Portland, OR 97214-1006   503-234-4263
Fax: 503-234-8268   800-469-4162
info@nickyusa.com   www.nickyusa.com
Distributor of natural game birds and meats including pheasant, poussin, quail, venison, buffalo, rabbit, ostrich, alligator, ducks and wild boar; also, sausage, veal, free range lamb and much more
President: Geoff Latham
VP: Melody Latham
Sales: Brenda Crow
Estimated Sales: Below $ 5 Million
Number Employees: 10-19
Sq. footage: 5000
Type of Packaging: Consumer, Food Service, Private Label, Bulk
Brands:
Cervera
Country Game
Nicky Usa

10218 Nicola International
PO Box 39758
Los Angeles, CA 90039-0758   818-545-1515
Fax: 818-247-8585 nicolain@pacbell.net
www.nicolainternational.com
Finest olives, olives oils and grapes leaves. We specialized in processing tree ripened olives for deli departments, bakery, the pizza industry, salad manufacturers, custom marination and creative gourmet dishes
President: Nicola Khachatoorian
VP: Alice Toomanian
Estimated Sales: $ 20 - 50 Million
Number Employees: 50-99
Type of Packaging: Food Service, Private Label
Brands:
Aiello

10219 Nicola Pizza
8 N 1st St
Rehoboth Beach, DE 19971-2116   302-226-2654
Fax: 302-226-3721 www.nicolapizza.com
Processor of spaghetti sauce
President: Nicholas S Caggiano
VP: Nicolas Caggiano III
CFO: Jaon Caggiano
Estimated Sales: Below $ 5 Million
Number Employees: 20-49
Type of Packaging: Consumer, Food Service
Brands:
Mama Nichola's Sago
Nic-O-Boli

10220 Nicola Valley Apiaries
PO Box 1995
Merritt, BC V1K 1B8
Canada
apaulson@nicolavalley.com   250-378-5208
www.nicolavalleyhoney.com
Processor and packer of liquid, creamed, chunk and comb honey; also, beeswax
CEO: Alan Paulson
CEO: Alan Paulson

10221 Nicole's Divine Crackers
1505 N Kingsbury St
Chicago, IL 60642-2533   312-640-8883
Fax: 312-640-0988 nicolescrackers@msn.com
www.nicolescrackers.com
Crackers
President: Nicole Bergere
Estimated Sales: Below $ 5 Million
Number Employees: 5-9

10222 Niebaum-Coppola Estate Winery
1991 Saint Helena Hwy
Rutherford, CA 94573   707-963-9099
Fax: 707-963-9084 info@niebaumcoppola.com
www.niebaum-coppola.com

Wines
Chairman: Francis Coppola
CEO: Jay Shoemaker
Estimated Sales: $ 5-10 Million
Number Employees: 20-49

10223 Nielsen Citrus Products
15621 Computer Lane
Huntington Beach, CA 92649   714-892-5586
Fax: 714-893-2161 info@nielsencitrus.com
www.nielsencitrus.com
Processor and exporter of frozen, concentrated lemon and lime juice, lemon puree, lime puree, orange puree
President: Chris Nielsen
Vice President: Earl Nielsen
Number Employees: 5-9
Sq. footage: 10000
Type of Packaging: Consumer, Food Service, Private Label, Bulk
Brands:
EZ
Nielsen
Suntree

10224 Nielsen-Massey Vanillas
1550 S Shields Dr
Waukegan, IL 60085-8307   847-578-1550
Fax: 847-578-1570   800-525-7873
info@nielsenmassey.com
www.nielsenmassey.com
Manufacturer and exporter of pure vanilla flavoring extracts and now chocolate extract
President: Camilla Nielsen
CEO/VP: Craig Nielsen
COO: Matthew Nielsen
Retail Sales: Beth Bitzegaio
Estimated Sales: $ 10 - 20 Million
Number Employees: 20-49
Sq. footage: 33500
Type of Packaging: Consumer, Food Service, Private Label, Bulk
Brands:
NIELSEN-MASSEY

10225 Niemuth's Steak & Chop Shop
715 Redfield St
Waupaca, WI 54981-1353   715-258-2666
Processors of meat products including ham, bacon and sausage
President: Robert Niemuth
Sausage Maker: Roger Niemuth
Estimated Sales: $950000
Number Employees: 10-19
Sq. footage: 9000
Type of Packaging: Consumer

10226 Night Hawk Frozen Foods
P.O.Box 867
Buda, TX 78610-0867   512-295-4166
Fax: 512-295-3988   800-580-4166
email@nighthawkfoods.com
www.nighthawkfoods.com
Processor of frozen food including dinners and entrees
President: Charles Hill
Controller: Dale Reistad
Vice President: John Hyde
Operations Manager: Terrell Windham
Purchasing Manager: John Benites
Estimated Sales: $ 20 - 50 Million
Number Employees: 50-99
Number of Products: 25
Sq. footage: 30000
Type of Packaging: Consumer, Food Service
Brands:
Night Hawk

10227 Nikken Foods Company
1820 S 3rd St
St Louis, MO 63104-4040   636-532-1019
Fax: 502-292-3283 nikken@lilar.com
www.nikkenfoods.com
Processor, importer and exporter of soy sauce, fermented soy sauce powders, extracted seafood powders and concentrates and dehydrated mushrooms and oriental vegetables
General Manager: Herb Bench
Parent Co: Nikkens Foods Company
Type of Packaging: Bulk

10228 Nikki's Cookies
2018 S 1st St
Milwaukee, WI 53207-1102   414-481-4899
Fax: 414-481-5222   800-776-7107
info@nikkiscookies.com
www.nikkiscookies.com
Processor and exporter of shortbreads and cookies
President: Nikki Taylor
Estimated Sales: Less than $500,000
Number Employees: 5-9
Sq. footage: 30000
Type of Packaging: Consumer, Food Service
Brands:
English Toffee
Ladybug
Nikki's

10229 Nikola's Biscotti & European Specialties
8300 Grand Ave S
Minneapolis, MN 55420   952-253-5991
Fax: 952-253-5995   888-645-6527
dir@nikolasbiscotti.com
www.nikolasbiscotti.com
Biscotti
Owner: Michael Itskovich
Estimated Sales: $ 15 Million
Number Employees: 10-19
Brands:
Nikola's Biscotti

10230 Nina's Gourmet Dip
6305 Dunaway Court
Mc Lean, VA 22101-2205   703-356-1667
Fax: 703-356-8488
Gourmet and specialty foods
President: Bill Pournaras

10231 Ninety Six Canning Company
109 S Cambridge Street
Ninety Six, SC 29666-1149   864-543-2700
Manufacturer of canned barbecued hash
President/Owner: Jerry Gantt
Estimated Sales: $2.6 Million
Number Employees: 4
Type of Packaging: Consumer

10232 Nino's Enterprises
1301 Carson Drive
Melrose Park, IL 60160-2970   708-344-8082
Processor of frozen pasta
President: Nino Ciccone
VP: Guy Ciccone
Operations Manager: Sebastiano Ciccone
Number Employees: 20-49
Type of Packaging: Consumer, Food Service

10233 Nippon Express USA
3375 Koapaka St # D153
Honolulu, HI 96819-1862   808-833-0202
Fax: 808-833-1333
http://www.nipponexpressusa.com/home.php
Manager: Mamoru Kimura
Estimated Sales: $ .5 - 1 million
Number Employees: 5-9

10234 Nips Potato Chips
806 Pohukaina St
Honolulu, HI 96813-5304   808-593-8549
donnachang@hotmail.com
Potato chips
President: Norman Nip
CEO: Norman Nip
Marketing Director: Norman Nip
Estimated Sales: Less than $500,000
Number Employees: 1-4
Brands:
Nip's Potato Chips

10235 Nisbet Oyster Company
P.O.Box 338
Bay Center, WA 98527-0338   360-875-6629
Fax: 360-875-6684   sales@goosepoint.com
www.goosepoint.com
Processor and exporter of Pacific and farm oysters
President: David Nisbet
Estimated Sales: $4000000
Number Employees: 1-4
Number of Brands: 1
Number of Products: 3
Sq. footage: 3200
Brands:
Goose Point Oysters

10236 Nissin Foods USA Company
2901 Hempland Rd
Lancaster, PA 17601-1386   717-291-5901
Fax: 717-291-9737   export@nissinfoods.com
www.nissinfoods.com
Processor of Asian noodles and noodle soup
Manager: Mike Rehrer
CFO: Howard Wang
Operations Manager: Kaz Nakagawa
Plant Manager: Mike Kirchner
Purchasing Manager: Billie Jo Dangro
Estimated Sales: $33200000
Number Employees: 100-249
Sq. footage: 150000
Parent Co: Nissin Foods USA Company
Type of Packaging: Private Label
Other Locations:
Nissin Foods USA Company
Fort Lee NJ
Brands:
Cup O' Noodles
Oodles of Noodles
Top Ramen

10237 (HQ)Nissin Foods USA Company
2001 W Rosecrans Ave
Gardena, CA 90249-2994   310-327-8478
Fax: 310-515-3751 www.nissinfoods.com
Manufacturer of Ramen and Cup Noodles
President: Ken Sasahara
CFO: Howard Wang
Marketing Manager: Joe Carter
Estimated Sales: $33.20 Million
Number Employees: 500-999
Sq. footage: 150000
Type of Packaging: Private Label
Brands:
CUP NOODLES
TOP RAMEN

10238 Nissley Vineyards
140 Vintage Dr
Bainbridge, PA 17502-9357   717-426-3514
Fax: 717-426-1391   800-522-2387
winery@nissley.com   www.nissleywine.com
Wine
President: Judith Nissley
Vice President: John Nissley
Winemaker: William Gulvin
Estimated Sales: $ 2.5-5 Million
Number Employees: 10-19
Type of Packaging: Private Label
Brands:
Holiday White
Niagara
Rhapsody in Blue
Topaz
Whisper White

10239 Nitta Casings
P.O.Box 858
Somerville, NJ 08876-0858   908-218-4400
Fax: 908-725-2835 www.nittacasings.com
Processor of meat and collagen casings
President: Frank Caroselli
VP Sales/Marketing: George Burt
Marketing Communication: Marchette Johnson
National Sales Manager: Bill Irwin
Estimated Sales: $37700000
Number Employees: 250-499

10240 Nitta Gelatin NA
201 W Passaic St # 402
Rochelle Park, NJ 07662-3127   201-368-0071
Fax: 201-368-0282   800-278-7680
info-g1@nitta-gelatin.co.jp
www.nitta-gelatin.com
Processor of gelatin
President: Guergen Gallert
Office Manager: Tsutomu Takase
General Manager: Jurgen Gallert
Estimated Sales: $ 2.5-5 Million
Number Employees: 1-4
Parent Co: Nitta Gelatin
Type of Packaging: Bulk
Brands:
Nitta Gelatin

10241 No Pudge! Foods
PO Box 387
Wolfeboro Falls, NH 03896-0387   603-230-9858
Fax: 504-539-5427   888-667-8343
customerservice@nopudge.com
www.nopudge.com
Fat free brownie mix
Founder/President: Lindsay Frucci
Estimated Sales: $1-2.5 Million
Number Employees: 2
Type of Packaging: Food Service
Brands:
No Pudge

10242 Noah's Potato Chip Company
P.O.Box 5132
Alexandria, LA 71307-5132   318-445-0283
Snack foods
Owner: Stanley Bohrer
Manager: Stanley Bohrer
Estimated Sales: $ 1-2.5 Million
Number Employees: 1-4

10243 Noble Ingredients
1602 Hylton Road
Pennsauken, NJ 08110   856-486-9292
Fax: 856-486-9202
jacques@noble-ingredients.com
www.noble-ingredients.com
Chocolates, calissons, candies and caramels
President/Owner: Jacques Dahan
Number Employees: 5

10244 Noble Popcorn Farms
P.O.Box 157
Sac City, IA 50583-0157   712-662-4728
Fax: 712-662-4797   800-537-9554
info@noblepopcorn.com
www.noblepopcorn.com
Processor of popcorn including popped, unpopped
and flavored; also, gift sets available
President/CEO: Milo Lines
Plant Manager: Dan Martin
Sales Representative: Gary Witte
Estimated Sales: $ 1 - 3 Million
Number Employees: 10-19
Sq. footage: 8000
Type of Packaging: Consumer, Food Service, Private Label, Bulk
Brands:
Cedar Creek
Noble
Nobleman Popper

10245 Nodine's Smokehouse
P.O.Box 1787
Torrington, CT 06790-1787   860-489-3213
Fax: 860-496-9787   800-222-2059
nodines@snet.net   www.nodinesmokehouse.com
Smoked hams, bacons, chicken, duck, turkey, goose,
sausages, fish and cheeses
President: Ron Nodine
VP: Johanne Nodine
Estimated Sales: $ 3 - 5 Million
Number Employees: 5-9
Type of Packaging: Consumer, Food Service

10246 Noel Corporation
1001 S 1st St
Yakima, WA 98901-3488   509-248-1313
Fax: 509-248-2843   billdalt@noelcorp.com
www.noelcorp.com
Processor and importer of bottled and canned car-
bonated and noncarbonated beverages; also,
bag-in-box juices including orange and apple
President: Rodger Noel
CFO: Larry Estes
VP: Justin Noel
Plant Manager: Mike Trammell
Estimated Sales: $50-75 Million
Number Employees: 50-99
Sq. footage: 200000
Type of Packaging: Consumer, Food Service, Private Label
Brands:
Dr. Pepper
Noel
Pepsi
Seven-Up
Squirt
Tap Juices

10247 Nog Incorporated
P.O.Box 162
Dunkirk, NY 14048-0162   716-366-3322
    Fax: 716-366-8487   800-332-2664
customerservice@noginc.com   www.noginc.com
Manufacturer of ice cream ingredients including
coatings, variegates and background flavors
    President: Bruce Ritenburg Iii III
    R&D Director: Bob Habich
    Plant Manager: Rick Musso
Estimated Sales: $1-3 Million
Number Employees: 10-19
Sq. footage: 24000
Type of Packaging: Bulk

10248 Noh Foods International
220 Puuhale Road
B
Honolulu, HI 96819-2294   808-841-0655
    Fax: 808-841-0830   nohfoods@noh.com
                        www.nohfoods.com
Manufacturer of International seasonings, sauces
and drink mixes
    Chairman: Edwin Noh
    President: Raymond Noh
Estimated Sales: $10-20 Million
Number Employees: 20
Other Locations:
    Noh Foods of Hawaii
    Gardena CA
Brands:
    NOH

10249 Noh Foods International
PO Box 7513
Torrance, CA 90504-8913   310-618-2092
                        Fax: 310-618-0757
Kim Chee dry spice
    President: Raymond Noh
    Chairman of the Board: Edwin Noh
Estimated Sales: $ 5-10 Million appx.
Number Employees: 5

10250 Nolechek's Meats
P.O.Box 599
Thorp, WI 54771-0599   715-669-5580
    Fax: 715-669-7360
nolechek@nolechekmeats.com
        www.nolechekmeats.com
Smoked meats
    Owner: William Nolechek Jr
    VP: Kelly Nolechek
    Production: Leo Hawkeg
Estimated Sales: $ 1 - 3 Million
Number Employees: 5-9

10251 Nomolas Corp-Jarret Specialties
900 Us Highway 9 N
Woodbridge, NJ 07095-1025   732-634-5565
                        Fax: 732-634-5528
Health foods
    President: Mickey Lyons
Estimated Sales: $ 2.5-5 Million
Number Employees: 5

10252 Nomura Tofu Company
2618 S Normal Avenue
Chicago, IL 60616-2512   773-486-7224
Processor of confectionery products and tofu
    President: James Woo
Estimated Sales: $330000
Number Employees: 6
Type of Packaging: Consumer

10253 Nonni's Food Company
601 S Boulder Ave # 900
Tulsa, OK 74119-1303   918-560-4100
    Fax: 918-560-4108   877-295-0289
                        www.nonnis.com
Manufacturer of, pita crisps, biscotti, flatbread bagel
chips, gourmet hand rolled breadsticks, genoa toast
    CEO: Tim Harris
    Finance Executive: Kristi Graham
    Manager Operations: Tammy Breeden
Estimated Sales: $150 Million
Number Employees: 50-99
Type of Packaging: Private Label
Brands:
    New York Style
    Nonni's
    Old London

10254 Nonpareil Corporation
40 N 400 W
Blackfoot, ID 83221-5632   208-785-5880
    Fax: 208-785-3656   800-522-2223
npc@nonparl.com   www.nonparl.com
Processor and exporter of potato products including
sliced, flakes, flour and extract
    President: Christopher Abend
    COO: Walker Gay
    Director Research: Gerry Beck
    Marketing Manager: Robert Weis
    Chairman: Harold Abend
    Plant Manager: Allan White
Estimated Sales: H
Number Employees: 500-999
Type of Packaging: Bulk

10255 Nonpareil Dehydrated Potatoes
40 N 400 W
Blackfoot, ID 83221-5632   208-785-5880
    Fax: 208-785-3656   800-522-2223
nonpar@ida.net   www.nonparl.com
Largest grower and shipper of fresh potatoes, a lead-
ing manufacturer of dehydrated potato pieces and
among the most modern and efficient producers of
potato flakes and flour in the industry.
    President: Christopher Abend
Estimated Sales: H
Number Employees: 500-999
Parent Co: Nonpareil Corporation
Type of Packaging: Consumer

10256 Noodles by Leonardo
1301 5th Ave
Cando, ND 58324-6603   701-968-4464
                        Fax: 701-968-4255
Processor of spaghetti, lasagna, macaroni and
cheese, hamburger dinners and noodles with sauce
    President: Leonard Gasparre
    CFO: Dean Aune
    Quality Control: Marylnn Eleninger
    General Manager: David Speare
Estimated Sales: $ 20 - 50 Million
Number Employees: 50-99
Type of Packaging: Consumer, Food Service
Brands:
    Noodles By Leonardo
    Pasta Louigi

10257 (HQ)Noon Hour Food Products
215 N Desplaines St
Chicago, IL 60661-1140   312-382-1177
    Fax: 312-382-9420   800-621-6636
Processor and importer of salted, canned and pickled
fish, cheese and groceries; wholesaler/distributor of
seafood; serving the food service market
    President: Paul Buhl
    Executive VP: P Scott Buhl
    Marketing Manager: Tyler Swanberg
    Operations Manager: William Buhl
Estimated Sales: $6.7 Million
Number Employees: 20-49
Sq. footage: 155000
Type of Packaging: Food Service
Other Locations:
    Noon Hour Food Products
    Minneapolis MN
Brands:
    Bond Ost
    Briny Deep
    De Mill
    I Will
    Lunds
    Noon Hour
    Swan
    Swan Island
    Viking

10258 Nor-Cal Beverage Company
2286 Stone Blvd
West Sacramento, CA 95691-4097   916-374-2621
    Fax: 916-374-2609   www.ncbev.com
Producer and wholesaler/distributor of beverages
    President: Donald Deary
Estimated Sales: $113300000
Number Employees: 250-499
Sq. footage: 208000

10259 Nor-Cliff Farms
888 Barrick Rd.
Port Colborne, ON L3K 6H2
Canada   905-835-0808
    Fax: 905-892-4011   www.fiddleheadgreens.com
Processor and exporter of fresh, frozen and mari-
nated fiddlehead greens; also, soup mix
    President: Nick Secord

10260 Nor-Tech Dairy Advisors
629 S Minnesota Ave
Sioux Falls, SD 57104-4874   605-338-2404
                        Fax: 605-338-0439
Dairy products marketing and trading
    President: Michael Hines
Estimated Sales: $6 Million
Number Employees: 1-4
Type of Packaging: Food Service, Private Label,
    Bulk
Brands:
    Nor-Tech

10261 NorCal Wild Rice
1550 Drew Ave # 150
Davis, CA 95618-7852   530-758-8550
    Fax: 530-758-8110   nor-calrice@saber.net
                        www.sunwestfoods.com
Grower/packer of processed wild rice; developer of
proprietary wild rice varieties and specialty rices;
processor of quick-cook wild and brown rice. Spe-
cializes in ingredient sales to packers and ingredient
users
    President: James Errecarte
Estimated Sales: $ 5 - 10 Million
Number Employees: 10-19
Sq. footage: 23000
Type of Packaging: Food Service, Private Label,
    Bulk
Brands:
    Nor-Cal

10262 NorQuest Seafoods
5245 Shilshole Ave NW
Seattle, WA 98107-4833   206-281-7022
                        Fax: 206-285-8159
frozensale@norquestseafood.com
                        www.norquest.com
Processor and exporter of salmon, halibut, crab,
shrimp, herring, turbot, cod, spot prawn, sea cucum-
ber, etc
    President: Terry Gardiner
    VP Sales USA & Euorpe: Vic Taggart
    VP Operations: John Sund
Estimated Sales: $12800000
Number Employees: 20-49
Type of Packaging: Consumer, Food Service, Pri-
    vate Label, Bulk
Brands:
    Frigid Zone
    Portlock
    Silver Lining

10263 (HQ)NorSun Food Group
8050 Beckett Center Drive
West Chester, OH 45069-5017   800-886-4326
    Fax: 513-870-0971   800-886-4326
donsmith@norsun.com   www.norsun.com
Processor and exporter of frozen roasted potatoes,
seasoned potatoes, IQF frozen potatos, wedges,
slices, diced, shredded, and whole baked potatos
    President: Linda Pennington
    CEO: Frank Simmons
    Marketing/Sales: Don Smith
Number Employees: 5-9
Sq. footage: 1500
Type of Packaging: Consumer, Food Service, Pri-
    vate Label, Bulk
Other Locations:
    NorSun Food Group
    Rexburg ID

10264 Nora's Candy Shop
321 N Doxtator St
Rome, NY 13440-3121   315-337-4530
    Fax: 315-339-4054   888-544-8224
info@turkeyjoints.com   www.turkeyjoints.com
Manufacturer of candy and other confectionery
products; also chocolate & cocoa products.
    Owner: Spero Haritatos
    Co-Owner: Sharon Haritatos
Estimated Sales: Less than $500,000
Number Employees: 5-9

10265 Norac Technologies
9110-23 Avenue
Edmonton Research Park
Edmonton, AB T6N 1H9
Canada   780-414-9595
        Fax: 780-450-1016 norac@noratech.com
                                                www.noractech.com
Processor and exporter of spice extracts, egg yolk
powder and essential, wheat germ and oat bran oils
        President: Tom Evans
        VP: Uy Nguyen
        Plant Manager: Dan Moser
Number Employees: 10-19
Type of Packaging: Private Label, Bulk
Brands:
    Labex
    SC

10266 Norben Company
P.O.Box 766
Willoughby, OH 44096-0766   440-951-2715
        Fax: 440-951-1366 888-466-7236
            sales@norbencompany.com
                www.norbencompany.com
Established in 1974, Norben Company is a quality
supplier of chemicals and essential raw materials to
the food, pharmaceutical and nutraceutical industries. Distributor of pea protien, pea starch, pea fiber,
bamboo fiber, natural andGMO free ingredients,
nautral fibers, micronized products, low carbohydrate formulations, low fat formulations, custom
blends, nautral flavor enhancers, probiotic and
prebiotic ingredients, and seasoning blends.
        President: B J Kresnye
Estimated Sales:$5,977,123
Number Employees: 5-9

10267 (HQ)Norbest
PO Box 1000
Midvale, UT 84047-1000   801-566-5656
        Fax: 801-255-2309 800-453-5327
    norbest@norbest.com 800-453-5327
Manufacturer and exporter of raw and cooked pro-
cessed turkey products including roasts and deli
breasts; also, luncheon meats including ham, pas-
trami, salami, etc
        President/CEO: Steven Jensen
Estimated Sales:$100+ Million
Number Employees: 20-49
Type of Packaging: Consumer, Food Service, Pri-
    vate Label, Bulk
Brands:
    NORBEST

10268 Norco Ranch
PO Box 910
Norco, CA 92860-0917   951-737-6735
        Fax: 909-737-9405 info@norcoeggs.com
                www.norcoeggs.com
Dairy products
        President: Craig Willardson
Estimated Sales:$ 50 - 100 Million
Number Employees: 250-499
Brands:
    Ranch

10269 Norcrest Consulting
PO Box 400
Divide, CO 80814-0400   719-687-7636
        Fax: 719-687-7635 norcrest@aol.com
Yeast. imports and distributes and markets yeast extracts and Levacan, a baker's yeast glucan. Levapan
yeast extracts find application in soups, snacks,
drinks, frozen and prepared entrees and many low
salt uses
        President: John R Norell
        VP: Beverly Norell

10270 Nordic Group
286 Congress Street
Boston, MA 02110-1009   617-423-3358
        Fax: 617-423-2057 800-486-4002
info@nordic-group.com www.nordic-group.com
Processor and importer of fresh and frozen Norwe-
gian seafood including smoked salmon, cod, had-
dock and fillets
        President: Terje Korsnes
        Finance/Administration VP: Joe Mara
        Regional Sales Manager: Joe Scharon
Estimated Sales:$500,000-$1 Million
Number Employees: 1-4
Parent Co: Nordic Group ASA
Type of Packaging: Food Service, Bulk

Brands:
    Fjord Fresh
    Troll

10271 Nordman of California
4070 S Reed Ave
Sanger, CA 93657-9541   559-638-9923
Wines
        President: James Hansen
Estimated Sales:$ 2 Million
Number Employees: 5-9
Type of Packaging: Bulk
Brands:
    Grape Alpho

10272 Norfolk Hatchery
P.O.Box 132
Norfolk, NE 68702-0132   402-371-5710
Hatchery for baby chicks
        Owner/President: Paula Rasmussen
*Estimated Sales:*Less than $125,000
Number Employees: 1-4
Type of Packaging: Bulk

10273 Norfood Cherry Growers
RR 4
Simcoe, ON M3Y 4K3
Canada   519-426-5784
                            Fax: 519-426-7838
Processor of frozen red pitted cherries
        Director: Marshall Schuyler
Number Employees: 50-99

10274 Norimoor Company
3801 23rd Avenue
2nd Floor
Astoria, NY 11105-1922   718-721-6667
        Fax: 718-721-6668 www.norimoor.com
Manufacturer of Nature made products for health,
vitamins, toothpaste
        President/Owner: Karl Kupka
Estimated Sales:$500,000-$1 Million
Number Employees: 5-9
Brands:
    NORIMOOR
    NORIVITAL VITAMINS

10275 Norpac Fisheries
3140 Ualena St # 205
Honolulu, HI 96819-1965   808-528-3474
        Fax: 808-537-6880 mjbudke@aol.com
Manufacturer of seafood
        Owner: Michael Budke
*Estimated Sales:*10-20 Million
Number Employees: 5-9
Parent Co: T.J. Kraft
Brands:
    MIKARLA'S BEST

10276 Norpaco
30 Peter Ct
New Britain, CT 06051-3545   860-223-4500
        Fax: 860-223-4600 800-252-0222
    dean@norpaco.com www.norpaco.com
Processor and wholesaler/distributor of peppers,
beef jerky, hot and spicy pickled eggs and sausage
        President: Donald Spilka
        VP: Dean Spilka
Estimated Sales:$ 20 - 50 Million
Number Employees: 50-99
Sq. footage: 6000
Type of Packaging: Consumer, Private Label, Bulk
Brands:
    Norpaco

10277 Norris Brothers Syrup Company
P.O.Box 315
West Monroe, LA 71294-0315   318-396-1960
                            Fax: 318-396-2560
Processor of cane syrup
        Owner: Fred Norris
Estimated Sales:$1400000
Number Employees: 10-19
Type of Packaging: Consumer, Food Service, Pri-
    vate Label

10278 Norse Dairy Systems
P.O.Box 1869
Columbus, OH 43216-1869   614-294-4931
        Fax: 614-299-0538 kmcgrath@norse.com
                www.norse.com

Ice cream cones
        President: Scott Fullbright
        R&D: Gunther Brinkman
        CEO: Scot Fulbright
        CFO: Randy Harvey
Estimated Sales:$ .5 - 1 million
Number Employees: 1-4

10279 North Aire Market
689 Canterbury Rd S
Shakopee, MN 55379-1807   952-496-2887
        Fax: 952-496-3444 800-662-3781
            sales@northairemarket.com
                www.northairemarket.com
Manufacturing of Dry soup mixes
        Owner: Maggie Mortensen
        R&D/Co-Owner: Maggie Mortenson
*Estimated Sales:*Below $5 Million
Number Employees: 10-19
Type of Packaging: Consumer, Food Service, Pri-
    vate Label
Brands:
    NORTH AIRE SIMMERING SOUPS

10280 North Alaska Fisheries
PO Box 92737
Anchorage, AK 99509-2737   907-561-2671
                            Fax: 907-561-2748
Seafood and fish
        President: Jack Schulthesis

10281 North American BeverageCompany
901 Ocean Avenue
Ocean City, NJ 08226-3540   609-399-1486
                            Fax: 609-399-1506
        inquiry@northamericanbeverage.com
                www.northamericanbeverage.com
Manufacturer of High energy, low fat premium
chocolate dairy drink
        President: John Imbessi
        Controller: Tom Repichi
Estimated Sales:$ 10 - 20 Million
Number Employees: 10-19
Brands:
    CHOCOLATE MOOSE
    CHOCOLATE MOOSE ENERGY
    HAVANA CAPPUCINO
    RED ROSE ICE
    ROYAL MANDALAY CHAI
    WHITE CHOCOLATE MOOSE

10282 North American Blueberry Council
PO Box 1036
Folsom, CA 95763   916-983-2279
        Fax: 916-983-9370 800-824-6395
    bberry@blueberry.org   www.nabcblues.org
Blueberry
        Chairman: Mark Hurst
        Treasurer: Mike Makara
        Secretary: Henson Barnes
        Executive Director: Mark Villata
Number Employees: 1-4
Brands:
    Blueberry Barbeque Sauce
    Harvest Bar
    Trader Joe's

10283 North American Coffees
14406 Investment Avenue
Laredo, TX 78045-7931   973-359-0300
                            Fax: 973-359-0440
Coffee, tea
        President: Michael Cahill
*Estimated Sales:*Less than $500,000
Number Employees: 1-4

10284 North American Enterprises
4330 N Campbell Ave # 256
Tucson, AZ 85718-5467   520-885-0110
        Fax: 520-298-9733 800-817-8666
                www.capitanelli.com
Importer/distributor of olive oil, oil, balsamic vinegar, pasta sauces, salad dressings and biscotti; importer of Italian dry pasta and gourmet products;
also, specialty gift baskets available
        Owner: Joe Lovallo
        VP Marketing: Grant Lovallo
        National Sales Manager: Tim Champa
        Contact: Lisa Lovallo

Estimated Sales: $ 10 - 20 Million
Number Employees: 10-19
Sq. footage: 2300
Type of Packaging: Consumer, Food Service
Brands:
Caphanelli Fine Foods
Capitanelli Specialty Foods
Capitanelli's
Loison Panetoni
Rummo Gourmet Imported Pasta

10285 North American Reishi/Nammex
PO Box 1780
Gibsons, BC V0N 1V0
Canada   604-886-7799
        Fax: 604-886-9626 info@nammex.com
                www.nammex.com
Processor and exporter of standardized and certified organic mushroom extracts; also, whole dried mushrooms and mushroom mycelia
President: Jeff Chilton
Number Employees: 5-9
Type of Packaging: Bulk

10286 (HQ)North American Salt Company
9900 W 109th St # 600
Overland Park, KS 66210-1436   913-344-9100
        Fax: 913-344-9314 www.compassminerals.com
Full-line salt manufacturer, products include agricultural, water softeners, consumer ice melters, industrial applications, food grade, and rock salt
CFO: Rodney Underdown
CEO: Angelo Brisimitzakis
Sales Director: Nathan Herrman
Estimated Sales: $100+ Million
Number Employees: 100-249
Other Locations:
Ogden UT
Lyons KS
Unity, Saskatchewan
Kenosha WI
Cote Blanche LA
Amherst, Nova Scotia
Goderich, Ontario

10287 North American Seasonings
P.O.Box 1668
Lake Oswego, OR 97035-0868   503-636-7043
        Fax: 503-636-7043 www.geoquest.net
Bulk spices, custom spice blends and food service spices. Also carry a wide variety of ethnic blends, certified organic
Owner: John D Bryan
CFO: Gary Pearce
Research & Development: Camille McKin
Marketing Director: Shawn Simonin
Operations Manager: Kevin Stapleton
Estimated Sales: $ 10-20 Million
Number Employees: 20-49
Number of Products: 500
Type of Packaging: Consumer, Food Service
Brands:
G'S
NAS

10288 North American Water Group
8300 College Boulevard
Overland Park, KS 66210-1841   913-469-1156
                        Fax: 913-451-9418
Bottled water
President: Roger Hood
COO: Lee Dancer
Estimated Sales: $ 5-10 Million
Number Employees: 1

10289 North Atlantic
P.O.Box 682
Portland, ME 04104-0682   207-774-6025
Fax: 207-774-1614 www.northatlanticseafood.com
President: Gerald Knecht
Estimated Sales: $ 10 - 20 Million
Number Employees: 10-19

10290 North Atlantic Fish Company
88 Commercial St # 1
Gloucester, MA 01930-5096   978-283-4121
                        Fax: 978-283-5948

Processor and exporter of frozen catfish, cod, halibut, herring, smelt, squid, shrimp, scallops and whiting; portion controlled breaded and prepared seafood
President: Frank Cefalo
Sales Manager: Joe Bertolino
Operations Manager: James Stuart
Estimated Sales: $4.20 Million
Number Employees: 20-49
Sq. footage: 40000
Type of Packaging: Consumer, Food Service
Brands:
Better Buy
Courageous Captain's
North Atlantic

10291 North Atlantic Products
232 Buttermilk Ln
South Thomaston, ME 4858-3003   207-596-0331
                        Fax: 207-596-0532
Seafood

10292 North Atlantic Seafood
P.O.Box 116
Stonington, ME 04681-0116   207-367-5099
                        Fax: 207-367-2937
Fish and seafood.
President: Delbert Gross
Estimated Sales: $1,600,000
Number Employees: 5-9

10293 North Bay Fisherman's Cooperative
RR 4
Ballantyne's Cove, NS B2G 2L2
Canada   902-863-4988
                        Fax: 902-863-1112
Processor of fresh and frozen lobster, scallops and groundfish; exporter of tuna
Manager: Kim MacDonald
Number Employees: 5-9
Type of Packaging: Consumer, Food Service, Private Label, Bulk

10294 North Bay Produce
P.O.Box 988
Traverse City, MI 49685-0988   231-946-1941
        Fax: 231-946-1902 www.northbayproduce.com
Cooperative, importer and exporter of fresh produce including apples, asparagus, blueberries, cherries, peaches, plums, snow peas, sugar snaps, mangos, raspberries, blackberries, red currants, etc.; also, apple cider
President: Mark Jirardin
Vice President: Richard Bogard
VP Sales/Marketing: Rolo Leyton
Estimated Sales: $19833686
Number Employees: 10-19
Sq. footage: 880
Type of Packaging: Consumer, Food Service, Private Label, Bulk
Brands:
North Bay
Wilderness

10295 North Bay Trading Company
P.O.Box 129
Brule, WI 54820-0129   715-372-5031
                        800-348-0164
                borg@cheqnet.net
Organic and Canadian wild rice, heirloom beans, dehydrated vegetables, dry soup mixes
Owner: Greggar Isaksen
Estimated Sales: $160,000
Number Employees: 5-9
Number of Brands: 2
Number of Products: 6
Type of Packaging: Consumer, Food Service, Bulk
Brands:
BRULE VALLEY
NORTH BAY TRADING COMPANY

10296 North Branch Dairy
6710 Ash St
North Branch, MN 55056-5068   651-674-4414
Milk
Owner: Greg Schneller
Estimated Sales: $ 5-9.9 Million
Number Employees: 1-4

10297 North Coast Processing
P.O.Box 472
North East, PA 16428-0472   814-725-9617
        Fax: 814-725-4374 ncp@ncpusa.com
                www.edsmithusa.com
Processor and contract packager of salad dressings, sauces, marinades and dry seasonings; exporter of salad dressings; private labeling available
President: William Lewis
Operations Manager: Tom Barnes
Plant Manager: Wilson Haller
Estimated Sales: $13800000
Number Employees: 10-19
Sq. footage: 25000
Type of Packaging: Consumer, Food Service, Private Label, Bulk
Brands:
Den
Garden Goodness

10298 North Country Natural Spring Water
PO Box 123
Port Kent, NY 12975-0123   518-834-9400
                        Fax: 518-834-9429
Processor and importer of natural spring water
President: Roger Jakubowski
Estimated Sales: $ 1 - 3 Million
Number Employees: 10-19
Sq. footage: 22000
Type of Packaging: Consumer, Food Service, Private Label, Bulk
Brands:
Loyola Springs
North Country

10299 North Country Smokehouse
P.O.Box 1415
Claremont, NH 03743-1415   603-543-0234
        Fax: 603-543-3016   800-258-4304
                mike@ncsmokehouse.com
                www.ncsmokehouse.com
Smoked meats and cheese
President: Michael Satzow
Estimated Sales: $ 5-9.9 Million
Number Employees: 10-19
Brands:
North Country Smokehouse

10300 North Dakota Mill
P.O.Box 13078
Grand Forks, ND 58208-3078   701-795-7000
        Fax: 701-795-7272   800-538-7721
        khjelden@ndmill.com www.ndmill.com
Processor of flour including semolina, durum, wheat and high-gluten
President: Vance Taylor
Controller/Financial Manager: Ed Barchhenger
Logistics Manager: Mike Jones
Quality Assurance: Bob Sombke
Sales Manager: Steve Sannes
Production Manager: Chris Lemoine
Estimated Sales: $ 50 - 100 Million
Number Employees: 100-249
Type of Packaging: Consumer, Food Service, Private Label, Bulk
Brands:
Dakota Champion
Dakota Queen
Durakota
Empire
Excello

10301 (HQ)North East Foods
1515 Fleet Street
Baltimore, MD 21231-2810   410-558-1050
Baked goods
President/CEO: Danny Amaroso
Secretary: Jerry Grades

10302 North Lake Fish Cooperative
RR 1
Elmira, PE C0A 1K0
Canada   902-357-2572
                        Fax: 902-357-2386
Processor and exporter of fresh and frozen scallops, skate, silversides and lobster
President: Walter Bruce
CEO/General Manager: Mickey Rose
Number Employees: 100-249
Type of Packaging: Bulk

10303 North Pacific Enterprises
4101 Westland Cir
Anchorage, AK 99517-1430   907-243-4398
                                  Fax: 907-243-4399
Estimated Sales: $ .5 - 1 million
Number Employees: 1-4

10304 (HQ)North Pacific Processors
P.O.Box 31179
Seattle, WA 98103-1179   206-726-9900
                                Fax: 206-726-1667
www.northpacificseafoods.com
Canned and cured seafood
   President: Bob Nickinovich
   CFO: Yugi Hanasaki
   VP Administration: James Kudwa
   Sales Director: S Yazawa
   Plant Manager: John Sevier
Estimated Sales: $ 30 -50 Million
Number Employees: 20-49
Type of Packaging: Bulk
Brands:
   SSS
   Sitka

10305 North Pacific Ship Supply
Mile 4 Captain Bay Road
Dutch Harbor, AK 99692   907-581-1700
                                Fax: 907-581-1767

10306 North Peace Apiaries
RR 1
Fort St. John, BC V1J 4M6
Canada   250-785-4808
                                Fax: 250-785-2664
Processor and exporter of honey and bee pollen
   President: Ernie Fuhr
   Secretary/Treasurer: Rose Fuhr
Number Employees: 5-9
Sq. footage: 3780
Type of Packaging: Consumer

10307 North Salem Vineyard
441 Hardscrabble Road
North Salem, NY 10560-1013   914-669-5518
   Fax: 914-669-5079 naumburg@aya.yale.edu
     www.northsalemwine.com
Manufacturer of wines and champagne
   President/Winemaker: George Naumburg Jr
Estimated Sales: Less than $500,000
Number Employees: 1-4
Sq. footage: 6000
Type of Packaging: Consumer
Brands:
   NORTH SALEM DOC'S OWN
   NORTH SALEM RESERVE RED
   NORTH SALEM SEYVAL
   NORTH SALEM SWEET RED
   NORTH SALEM VINEYARD
   RESERVE RED
   RESERVE WHITE

10308 North Shore Bottling Company
1900 Linden Blvd
Brooklyn, NY 11207-6806   718-272-8900
                                Fax: 718-649-2596
   customerservice@nsbottle.com
     www.brooklynbottling.com
Soft drinks
   President: Eric Miller
   VP/General Manager: Tom Deluca
Estimated Sales: $ 20-50 Million
Number Employees: 50-99
Brands:
   Ballantine Ale
   Country Club Malt Liquor
   Gold Crown Lager
   Iberia Malt Liquor
   Laser Malt Liquor
   Pony Malta
   Private Stock Malt Liquor
   Tornado Malt Liquor

10309 (HQ)North Side Foods Corporation
2200 Rivers Edge Dr
Arnold, PA 15068-4540   724-335-5800
   Fax: 724-335-2249 800-486-2201
     www.emberfarms.com

Manufacturer of fully cooked and browned pork,
turkey and specialty flavored sausage products in-
cluding patties, links and crumbles
   President: Robert G Hofmann Ii II
   CFO: Bob Muhl
   VP Sales/Marketing: Ed Fornadel
Estimated Sales: H
Number Employees: 250-499
Parent Co: Smithfield Foods
Type of Packaging: Food Service, Private Label
Brands:
   EMEBR FARMS

10310 North Star Distributing
7934 Ivory Ave
St Louis, MO 63111-3534   314-631-8171
   Fax: 314-631-3315 www.icecreamspecialties.com
Ice creams
   Manager: Greg Winkler
   General Manager: John Kroll
Estimated Sales: Under $500,000
Number Employees: 50-99

10311 North Star Foods
P.O.Box 587
St Charles, MN 55972-0587   507-932-4831
   Fax: 507-932-5624 www.northstarfoods.com
Manufacturer of turkey, beef, pork, chicken and
frozen foods
   President: Brad Arndt
   General Manager: Bruce Christie
Estimated Sales: $30 Million
Number Employees: 100-249
Type of Packaging: Consumer, Food Service, Pri-
vate Label, Bulk

10312 North West Marketing Company
1000 Beacon St
Brea, CA 92821-2938   714-529-0980
                            Fax: 714-577-0985
Processor of dietary supplements and herbal prod-
ucts in tablet and capsule form; manufacturer of soft
gelatin capsule machines and ancillary equipment;
also, custom grinding and granulation available
   President: Jack Brown
   Operations Manager: Margaret Haines
Estimated Sales: $$10-20 Million
Number Employees: 10-19
Sq. footage: 20000
Type of Packaging: Private Label, Bulk

10313 North of the Border
P.O.Box 433
Tesuque, NM 87574-0433   505-982-0681
   Fax: 505-820-2108 800-860-0681
notb@earthlink.net www.gonzodip.com
Manufacturer of Salsa, chile sauce, chile seasoning,
BBQ/Hot sauce, catchup, and soups
   Owner: Gayther Gonzales
Estimated Sales: $ .5 - 1 million
Number Employees: 1-4

10314 North's Bakery California
5430 Satsuma Ave
North Hollywood, CA 91601-2837 818-761-2892
   Fax: 818-763-8637 www.northsbakery.com
Bread and bakery products
   President: Graham North
   CEO: John North
   CFO: Karl North
Estimated Sales: $ 20-50 Million
Number Employees: 50-99

10315 Northampton Brewing Company
11 Brewster Ct
Northampton, MA 01060-3801   413-584-9903
                                    Fax: 413-584-9972
info@northamptonbrewery.com
   www.northamptonbrewery.com
Processor of beer, ale, lager, stout and seasonal
   Manager: Jessica Bellingham
Estimated Sales: Less than $500,000
Number Employees: 50-99
Type of Packaging: Consumer, Food Service
Brands:
   Northampton

10316 Northcenter FoodserviceCorporation
P.O.Box 2628
Augusta, ME 04338-2628   207-623-8451
                                Fax: 207-623-2197

   President: David Crowell
Number Employees: 250-499

10317 Northeast Kingdom Mustard Company
117 Baxter Lane
Brownington, VT 05860-9589   802-754-2813
   Fax: 802-754-2813 nacres@together.net
     www.northeastkingdommustard.com
Manufacturer of Mustard, chutneys, jalapeno pepper
jelly
   Co-Owner: Mark Royer
   Co-Owner: Lynn Royer
Type of Packaging: Bulk

10318 Northeastern Products Company
3500 S Clinton Avenue
South Plainfield, NJ 07080-1318   908-561-1610
                                         Fax: 908-769-9200
Food flavorings
   President: Paul Schiavi
   CEO: Doug Connant
   Controller: Tom Mathern
   Marketing Director: Tina Hatten
Estimated Sales: Below $ 5 Million
Number Employees: 50
Brands:
   Northeastern

10319 Northern Air Cargo
3900 Old International Airport Road
Anchorage, AK 99502   907-243-3331
   Fax: 907-249-5194 800-727-2141
     www.nacargo.com
Transportation company providing air transportation
in Alaska
   CEO: David Karp
Number Employees: 250-499

10320 Northern Breweries
503 Bay Street
Sault St. Marie, ON P6A 1X6
Canada   705-254-7373
   Fax: 705-254-4482 800-461-2258
     sales@northernbreweries.com
     www.northernbreweries.com
Processor of beer, ale and lager
   President: William Sharp
Brands:
   Edelbrau
   Northern Ale
   Northern Extra Light
   Northern Premium light
   Northern Red naple
   Superior Lager
   Thunder Bay Lager

10321 Northern Breweries
185 Lorne Street
Sudbury, ON P3C 4P6
Canada   705-675-7561
   Fax: 705-675-2926 info@northernbreweries.com
     www.northernbreweries.com
Processor of ale
   President: William R Sharp
   Manager: James Kaminski
Number Employees: 10-19
Parent Co: Northern Breweries
Type of Packaging: Consumer, Food Service
Brands:
   Northern

10322 Northern Discovery Seafoods
P.O.Box 310
Grapeview, WA 98546-0310   360-275-7246
   Fax: 360-275-7245 800-843-6921
     seafood@kendaco.telebyte.com
Seafoods

10323 Northern Falls
6812 Old 28th St SE
Grand Rapids, MI 49546-6933   616-954-2061
   Fax: 616-940-0588 www.northernfalls.com
Manufacturer of bottled water including caffeinated
drinking, spring and flavored
   Owner: John Neall
Estimated Sales: $ 1 - 3 Million
Number Employees: 10-19
Type of Packaging: Consumer, Private Label

10324 Northern Feed & Bean Company
P.O.Box 149
Lucerne, CO 80646-0149   970-352-7875
                                Fax: 970-352-7833 nst@frii.com

Manufacturer and exporter of dried pinto beans
Manager: Larry Lande
Sales Manager: Larry Lande
Estimated Sales:$63 Million
Number Employees: 10-19
Parent Co: Helmut Brunner
Type of Packaging: Consumer, Food Service, Private Label
Brands:
FRONTIER

10325 Northern Flair Foods
3247 Gladstone Ln
Mound, MN 55364-9364   952-472-2444
Fax: 952-472-7444   888-530-4453
markgoldberg@yahoo.com
Manufacturer of Gourmet chocolate and candies
President: Mark Goldberg
CEO: Stacy Goldberg
Estimated Sales:$ 5 - 10 Million
Number Employees: 5-9
Brands:
HEAVENLY BEES
MALTO BELLA

10326 Northern Fruit Company
P.O.Box 1986
Wenatchee, WA 98807-1986   509-884-6651
Fax: 509-884-1990 nordic@northernfruit.com
www.northernfruit.com
Processor, packer and exporter of apples, cherries and pears
Co-Owner: James Pauly
Co-Owner: Al Chandler
Co-Owner: James Fullerton
Accounting: Jerry Billingsley
Field and Quality Control: Ryan Vickery
Marketing: Al Chandler
Production: Doug Pauly
Estimated Sales:$15,010,332
Number Employees: 100-249
Sq. footage: 158000
Brands:
Chelan Red
Nordic

10327 Northern Keta Caviar
5720 Concrete Way
Juneau, AK 99801-7813   907-586-6095
Fax: 907-586-6094 caviar@alaska.net
www.northernketa.com
Salmon caviar
President/CEO: Elisabeth Babich
Production Manager: Sean Fansler
Plant Manager: Mark Hiermonymus

10328 Northern Lights BrewingCompany
1701 S Lawson
Airway Heights, WA 99001   509-244-4909
www.nwbrewpage.com
Beer
Owner: Mark Irvin
Estimated Sales:$ 2.5-5 Million
Number Employees: 5-9
Brands:
Chocolate Dunkel
Crystal Bitter

10329 Northern Meats
163 E 54th Ave
Anchorage, AK 99518-1227   907-561-1729
Fax: 907-561-6848
Meats
President: Jerry Urling
Estimated Sales:$ 10 - 20 Million
Number Employees: 1-4

10330 Northern Michigan FruitCompany
7161 NW Bay Shore Drive
Omena, MI 49674   231-386-5142
Fax: 231-386-7626
Processor of regular and sugar-packed IQF apples, cherries, blueberries and strawberries; also, plum and cherry purees
President: Robert Weaver
VP Sales: Tom Hail
Operations Manager: Brian Smith
Number Employees: 100-249
Type of Packaging: Food Service, Private Label, Bulk

Brands:
Iqf Apple Orchard
Iqf Apple Slice
Iqf Sweet Cherry
Iqf Tart Cherry
Sliced Iqf Strawberry
Sugar Cap Block

10331 Northern Neck Bottling Company
15725 Kings Highway
Montross, VA 22520   804-493-8051
Fax: 804-493-9109   800-431-2693
ales@realgingerale.com www.realgingerale.com
Soft drink bottling
President/CEO: Alexander Cummings
CCO: J Alexander Douglas Jr
Chief Marketing Officer: Charles B Fruit
Public Relations: Arthur Carver III
Director Manufacturing: Richard Landon
Estimated Sales:$ 5-10 Million
Number Employees: 20
Brands:
Alive
Aquarious
Carvers Original
Diet Lift
Fanta
Finlay

10332 Northern Ocean Marine
7 Parker St
Gloucester, MA 01930-3025   978-283-0222
Fax: 978-283-5577
Seafood
Owner: Jim Lebouf
Estimated Sales:$1.4 Million
Number Employees: 5-9

10333 Northern Orchard Company
537 Union Rd
Peru, NY 12972-4664   518-643-9718
Fax: 518-643-2751
Wholesaler/distributor, exporter and packer of macintosh apples and honey
President: Albert Mulbury
Estimated Sales:$1950266
Number Employees: 20-49
Type of Packaging: Consumer
Brands:
Champlain Valley

10334 Northern Packing Company
PO Box 582
Brier Hill, NY 13614-0582   315-375-8801
Fax: 315-375-8273
Packer of fresh and frozen beef
President: John Perretta
Estimated Sales:$3300000
Number Employees: 20
Type of Packaging: Consumer

10335 Northern Products Corporation
1932 1st Ave # 705
Seattle, WA 98101-1071   206-448-6677
Fax: 206-448-9664
Processor and exporter of frozen salmon
President: William Dignon
Plant Manager: Terry Barry
Estimated Sales:$ 1 - 3 Million
Number Employees: 1-4
Type of Packaging: Private Label, Bulk

10336 Northern Soy
345 Paul Rd
Rochester, NY 14624-4925   585-235-8970
Fax: 585-235-3753 soyboy@fronteirnet.net
www.soyboy.com
Processor of tofu and soy vegetarian products including burgers, hot dogs, pasta, etc. Certified organic processor
President: Norman Holland
Vice President: Andrew Schecter
Estimated Sales:$ 5 - 10 Million
Number Employees: 20-49
Number of Brands: 1
Number of Products: 24
Sq. footage: 35000
Type of Packaging: Consumer, Food Service, Private Label, Bulk
Brands:
Leaner Wiener
Not Dogs
Soyboy
Tofu Lin

10337 Northern Star Company
3171 5th St SE
Minneapolis, MN 55414-3374   612-339-8981
Fax: 612-331-3434 www.michaelfoods.com
Processor of refrigerated potatoes including hash browns, mashed, diced and sliced
President: Chuck Berry
Estimated Sales:$100+ Million
Number Employees: 250-499
Parent Co: Michael Foods
Type of Packaging: Consumer, Food Service, Private Label
Brands:
Simply Potatoes

10338 Northern Utah Manufacturing
P.O.Box 37
Wellsville, UT 84339-0037   435-245-6014
Fax: 435-245-4542 www.numfg.com
Dry milk
Manager: David Bigelow
Estimated Sales:$ 2.5-5 Million
Number Employees: 20-49

10339 Northern Vineyards Winery
223 Main St N
Stillwater, MN 55082-5021   651-430-1032
Fax: 651-430-1331 northernvineyards@att.net
www.northernvineyards.com
Wines
Manager: Cassie Pittman
VP: Ray Kenow
*Estimated Sales:*Less than $500,000
Number Employees: 5-9
Type of Packaging: Private Label
Brands:
Northern Vineyards

10340 Northern Wind
16 Hassey St
New Bedford, MA 02740-7209   508-997-0727
Fax: 508-990-8792   888-525-2525
info@northernwind.com www.northernwind.com
Processor and exporter of fresh and frozen scallops and lobster
Owner: Ken Melanson
CEO: Ken Melanson
CFO: Craig Henry
Vice President: Craig Weatherly
Quality Control: Rose Perry
CEO: Ken Malenson
VP of Marketing: Betsy Szel
Plant Manager: Lisa Waite
Estimated Sales:$ 50-100 Million
Number Employees: 50-99
Number of Brands: 3
Number of Products: 3
Type of Packaging: Food Service, Private Label, Bulk
Brands:
CAPTAIN'S CALL
MARINER'S CHOICE
OCEAN REQUEST

10341 Northern Wisconsin Cheese Company
1310 Clark St
Manitowoc, WI 54220-5109   920-684-4461
Fax: 920-684-4471
Cheese
Owner: Dave Litterman
Estimated Sales:$ 1 - 3 Million
Number Employees: 10-19
Brands:
Northern Wisconsin Cheese

10342 Northland Cranberries
P.O.Box 1009
Mountain Home, NC 28758-1009   828-693-0711
Fax: 828-697-2984 www.northlandcran.com
Processor and exporter of fruit drinks and juice including apple, cranberry and grape
President: John Swendrouski
Director Sales: Dan Lang
President/Manufacturing: S Klus
Plant Manager: Blake Kehoe
Purchasing Manager: William Haddow
Estimated Sales:$96452346
Number Employees: 100-249
Parent Co: Northland Cranberries
Type of Packaging: Consumer, Food Service, Private Label, Bulk

Brands:
Awake
Meadow Valley
Northland
Seneca
Tree Sweet

10343 Northland Cranberries
20701 Main Street
Jackson, WI 53037   262-677-2221
    Fax: 262-677-3647 info@northlandcran.com
              www.northlandcran.com
Processor of fruit juices
    Chairman/CEO: John Swendrowski
    Plant Supervisor: Dave Carroll
Number Employees: 100-249
Sq. footage: 192000
Type of Packaging: Consumer, Food Service, Private Label
Brands:
    Northland

10344 (HQ)Northland Cranberries
PO Box 8020
Wisconsin Rapids, WI 54495-8020 715-424-4444
    Fax: 715-422-6800 info@northlandcran.com
              www.northlandcran.com
Manufacturer of fruit juice, juice concentrate, fresh and fozen
    Chairman/CEO/Treasurer: John Swendrowski
    President/COO: Ricke Kress
Number Employees: 218
Number of Brands: 5
Number of Products: 250
Type of Packaging: Consumer, Food Service, Bulk
Other Locations:
    Northland Cranberries
    Jackson WI
    Northland Cranberries
    Dundee NY
    Northland Cranberries
    Cornelius OR
    Northland Cranberries
    Wisconsin Rapids WI
Brands:
    Awake
    Meadow Valley
    Northland
    Seneca
    TreeSweet

10345 Northland Frozen Foods
PO Box 359
Sugar City, ID 83448-0359   207-834-3702
    Fax: 207-834-3703 888-667-7837
    lpennington@norsun.com www.norsun.com
Frozen potato food products
    President: Linda Pennington
    Director Manufacturing: Steven Perriault
    Plant Manager: Shawn Lovely
Estimated Sales: $ 20-50 Million
Number Employees: 250-300
Brands:
    Brittany Acres
    Cajun Country
    Northland

10346 Northland Hub
1701 S Cushman St
Fairbanks, AK 99701-6605   907-456-6608
                      Fax: 907-349-3101
    General Manager: Jim Clark
Estimated Sales: $ 5 - 10 Million
Number Employees: 5-9

10347 Northridge Laboratories
20832 Dearborn St
Chatsworth, CA 91311-5980   818-882-5622
    Fax: 818-998-2815 valoreeb@northridgelabs.com
              www.northridgelabs.com
Processor and exporter of vitamins, herbal supplements and protein powders
    President: Brett Richman
Estimated Sales: $6400000
Number Employees: 50-99
Sq. footage: 26000
Type of Packaging: Private Label

10348 Norths Bakery California Inc
5430 Satsuma Ave
North Hollywood, CA 91601-2837 818-761-2892
    Fax: 818-763-8637 www.northsbakery.com
Processor and exporter of English muffins, bread, croissants, danish and crumpets
    President: Graham North

Estimated Sales: $4200000
Number Employees: 50-99
Sq. footage: 17000
Type of Packaging: Food Service, Private Label

10349 Northside Bakery
2923 North Avenue
Richmond, VA 23222-3612   804-329-6851
                      Fax: 804-321-3728
Breads, cakes, pies, pastries
    Owner: Jacky Hatcher
    President: Don Gagliardi
    Vice President: Roseanne Sullivan
Estimated Sales: $500,000-$1 Million
Number Employees: 10-19

10350 Northumberland Cooperative
PO Box 130
Miramichi, NB E1V 3M3
Canada   506-627-7720
    Fax: 506-622-1767 800-332-3328
    info@northumberlanddairy.ca
    www.northumberlanddairy.com
Processor of dairy products including milk and cream; wholesaler/distributor of bottled water, ice cream, ice milk mix, fruit drinks and butter; serving the food service market
    General Manager: Jack Christie
    CEO: Jack Christie
    Marketing Director: Judy McDonald
    Sales Director: Paul Chiasson
Number Employees: 300
Number of Products: 3000
Type of Packaging: Consumer, Food Service, Private Label
Brands:
    FRONTIER WATER
    JUMBO MINISIPS
    MAX CRANBERRY COCKTAIL
    NORTHSHORE BUTTER
    NORTHUMBERLAND

10351 (HQ)Northville Winery
714 Baseline Rd
Northville, MI 48167-1266   248-349-3181
    Fax: 248-349-1165 www.northvillecider.com
Wines
    President: Diane Jones
    Vice President: Cheryl Nelson
Estimated Sales: $10-24.9 Million
Number Employees: 50-99
Type of Packaging: Private Label
Brands:
    Northville Winery

10352 Northwest Candy Emporium
10803 1st Avenue SE
Everett, WA 98208-7059   425-347-7266
    Fax: 425-347-5868 800-404-7266
    candynw@aol.com
    www.qshost.com/northwestcandy
Processor of gourmet candy and cookies
    Owner: Bonnie Reese
    Production Manager: Al Hyde
Number Employees: 20-49
Brands:
    Espress-Umms
    Grandma's Recipe
    Northwest Espresso B

10353 Northwest Chocolate Factory
2162 Davcor Street SE
Salem, OR 97302-1510   503-362-1340
    Fax: 503-362-0186 www.nwchocolate.com
Processor and exporter of chocolate covered hazelnuts
    President: Sam Kaufman
    General Manager: Dan Kaufman
Number Employees: 5-9
Sq. footage: 10000
Type of Packaging: Consumer

10354 Northwest Fisheries
RR 1
Hubbards, NS B0J 1T0
Canada   902-228-2232
                      Fax: 902-228-2116
Processor and exporter of fresh lobster, cod and halibut
    President: Olimpio Martins
Number Employees: 5-9
Type of Packaging: Consumer, Food Service, Private Label, Bulk

10355 Northwest Hazelnut Company
PO Box 276
Hubbard, OR 97032-0276   503-982-8030
    Fax: 503-982-8028 jeff@nwhazelnut.com
              www.nwhazelnut.com
Processor of vacuum-packed hazelnuts
    President: Jeff Kenagy
Estimated Sales: $ 5-10 Million
Number Employees: 4
Type of Packaging: Consumer, Food Service, Private Label
Brands:
    Springhill

10356 Northwest Meat Company
440 N Morgan St
Chicago, IL 60642-6501   312-733-1418
                      Fax: 312-733-1737
Processor of meats
    Owner: Stan Neava
Estimated Sales: $ 5 - 10 Million
Number Employees: 10-19

10357 Northwest Natural Foods
6644 Sexton Dr NW
Olympia, WA 98502-8810   360-866-9661
    Fax: 360-866-0734 nwnfz@yahoo.com
              www.northwestnaturalburgers.com
Fresh and frozen fish/seafood
    Owner: Gene Maltiziffs
Estimated Sales: $1.4 Million
Number Employees: 5-9
Sq. footage: 5
Type of Packaging: Private Label
Brands:
    Medallions

10358 Northwest Naturals
6644 Sexton Dr NW
Olympia, WA 98502-8810   360-866-9661
    Fax: 360-866-0734 nwnx@mailexcite.com
Processor and exporter of ready-to-eat frozen fish patties including salmon, halibut and tuna
    Owner: Gene Maltiziffs
    Sales Manager: Rob Rowley
    Production Manager: Robert Mertic
Estimated Sales: $ 3 - 5 Million
Number Employees: 1-4
Sq. footage: 5000
Type of Packaging: Consumer, Food Service
Brands:
    Medallions

10359 Northwest Naturals Corporation
11805 N Creek Parkway S
Suite A104
Bothell, WA 98011-8803   425-881-2200
    Fax: 425-881-3063 johnb@nwnaturals.com
              www.nwnaturals.com
Processor, importer and exporter of concentrates including juice and iced coffee and fruit beverages and flavors
    President: Gary Maddux
    CEO: Max James
    Sales Director: Stephanie Nicholson
    Public Relations: Terry Bue
    Operations Manager: Danny Shaffer
Estimated Sales: $ 5 - 10 Million
Number Employees: 5-9
Number of Brands: 4
Number of Products: 50
Sq. footage: 30000
Type of Packaging: Consumer, Food Service, Private Label, Bulk

10360 Northwest Packing Company
PO Box 30
Vancouver, WA 98666-0030   360-695-2560
    Fax: 509-575-1541 800-543-4356
    sales@nwpacking.com
    www.neiljonesfoodcompany.com
Processor of canned cherries, pears, plums and apple juice
    CEO: L Neil Jones
    COO: Matt Jones
    National Foodservice Sales Director: Mark Mahoney
Estimated Sales: $500,000-$1 Million
Number Employees: 1-4
Type of Packaging: Private Label

10361 Northwest Pea & Bean Company
P.O.Box 11973
Spokane Valley, WA 99211-1973   509-534-3821
Fax: 509-534-4350 nwpeabean@worldnet.att.net
www.co-ag.com
Processor of dry green and yellow split peas, garbanzo beans and lentils
    Manager: Gary Heaton
    Manager: Gary Heaton
Estimated Sales:$32100000
Number Employees: 10-19
Parent Co: Cooperative Agricultural Producers
Type of Packaging: Food Service, Private Label, Bulk
Brands:
    Empire
    Speedy Cook'n

10362 Northwestern Coffee Mills
30950 Nevers Rd
Washburn, WI 54891-5876   715-373-2122
Fax: 715-747-5405 800-243-5283
order@nwcoffeemills.com
www.nwcoffeemills.com
Processor, importer and exporter of coffee and tea
    Owner: Harry Demorest
*Estimated Sales:*Under $300,000
Number Employees: 1-4
Sq. footage: 2000
Type of Packaging: Consumer, Food Service
Brands:
    American Breakfast Blend
    Backsettler Blend
    Badger Blend
    Baker's Blend
    Broadway Red
    Fancy Dinner Blend
    Ice Road
    Island Blend
    Morning Sun
    North Coast
    Orange Rose
    Sleepeasy
    Stapleton

10363 Northwestern Coffee Mills
PO Box 370
La Pointe, WI 54850-0370   715-747-5555
Fax: 715-747-5405 800-243-5283
nwcoftsp@win.bright.net
www.nwcoffeemills.com
Coffee, tea, spices
    President: Harry Demorest
*Estimated Sales:*Less than $500,000
Number Employees: 1-4
Type of Packaging: Private Label
Brands:
    American Breakfast Blend
    Apostle Islands Organic Coffee
    Brazil Serra Negra
    Ice Road Blend - darkest
    North Coast Tea & Sp
    Northwestern Coffee

10364 Northwestern Extract Company
3590 N 126th St
Brookfield, WI 53005-2411   262-781-6670
Fax: 262-781-0660 800-466-3034
flavors@nwextract.com www.nwextract.com
Manufacturer of flavorings and extracts for the premium food and beverage industry; also flavors, colors, chemicals, syrups, emulsions, oils, brewing extracts and grains, and custom & plain crowns for bottling.
    President: William Peter
    Marketing Director: Patricia Hein
    Sales Director: Patricia Hein
    Purchasing Manager: Michael Peter
Estimated Sales:$ 5 - 10 Million
Number Employees: 5-9
Sq. footage: 10000
Type of Packaging: Consumer, Food Service, Private Label, Bulk
Brands:
    Northwestern
    Sparkle

10365 Northwestern Foods
P.O.Box 14415
St Paul, MN 55114-0415   651-523-0273
Fax: 651-644-8248 800-236-4937
mixes@northwesternfoods.com
www.northwesternfoods.com
Processor of mixes including cocoa, cake, pancake, cappuccino, iced tea, power drinks and pizza dough; broker and wholesaler/distributor of industrial ingredients; serving food processors, food service operators andwholesalers/distributors
    President: Alden Drew
    Vice President: Mimie Pollard
    Sales Manager: Bob Freemore
    Purchasing Manager: Nadine Vandeventer
Estimated Sales:$ 10 - 20 Million
Number Employees: 20-49
Sq. footage: 24000
Type of Packaging: Consumer, Food Service, Private Label, Bulk

10366 Norton Food Distributing
1733 W Broadway St
Idaho Falls, ID 83402-3045   208-524-3631
Fax: 441-818-7711
    Owner: Becky Martin
Estimated Sales:$300,000-500,000
Number Employees: 5-9

10367 Norwalk Dairy
13101 Rosecrans Ave
Santa Fe Springs, CA 90670-4931   562-921-5712
Fax: 562-921-5573
Processor of milk including whole, kosher, reduced, nonfat and chocolate
    VP: Tanya Vanderham
    President: John Vanderham
Estimated Sales:$500,000-$1 Million
Number Employees: 5-9
Type of Packaging: Consumer, Food Service
Brands:
    Norwalk Dairy

10368 Nossack Fine Meats
4951a 78th Street
Red Deer, AB T4P 1N5
Canada   403-346-5006
Fax: 403-343-8066 nossack@delusplanet.net
www.nossack.com
Processor and importer of meat including roast and corned beef, pastrami, sausage and ham; also, garlic rings and pizza products
    President: Karsten Nossack
    Manager: Ingrid Nossack
Number Employees: 50-99
Sq. footage: 22000
Type of Packaging: Consumer, Food Service
Brands:
    Butcher's Pride
    Nossack

10369 Nostalgic Specialty Foods
1440 Coral Ridge Drive
Coral Springs, FL 33071-5433   954-796-1660
Fax: 954-345-1860 800-881-2824
nostalgicfoods@yahoo.com
Gourmet and specialty foods
    CEO: Felder Baun
Number Employees: 1-4

10370 Notre Dame Bakery
PO Box 147
Lewisporte, NL A0G 3T0
Canada   709-535-2738
Fax: 709-535-3406
Processor of bread products, pies, cookies and muffins
    President: John Mullett
    Owner: Larry Mullett
    Owner/Sales: Paula Mullett
    CEO: John Mullett
Number Employees: 5-9
Brands:
    Humpty Dumpty Chips
    Nestle Chocolates

10371 Notre Dame Seafood
PO Box 201
Comfort Cove, NL A0G 3K0
Canada   709-244-5511
Fax: 709-244-3451
Processor and exporter of canned and frozen crab, cod, turbit, capelin, squid, mackerel, lumpfish, roe and lobster
    President: Roger Pike
    VP/General Manager: Rex Eveleigh
Number Employees: 250-499
Parent Co: Provincial Investments
Type of Packaging: Consumer, Food Service

10372 (HQ)Novartis Nutrition Corporation
5320 W 23rd Street
Minneapolis, MN 55416-1657   952-848-6000
Fax: 952-848-6169
rose.underhill@ch.novartis.com
www.novartisnutrition.com
Manufacturer and exporter of nutritional food products including confectionery products, chocolate and malt beverages, dry malt, instant breakfast foods, beverage mixes and mayonnaise
    President: Janet Conneely
Estimated Sales:$121.8 Million
Number Employees: 700
Parent Co: Sandoz Corporation
Brands:
    OVALTINE
    P.D.Q.

10373 Novelty Kosher Pastry
10 Hoffman Street
Spring Valley, NY 10977-4826   845-356-0428
Fax: 845-356-0456
Breads, rolls
Estimated Sales:$300,000-500,000
Number Employees: 5-9

10374 Novelty Specialties
1630 Berryessa Road
Suite D
San Jose, CA 95133-1078   408-927-6682
Fax: 408-259-8633
Candy
Estimated Sales:$300,000-500,000
Number Employees: 1-4

10375 Noveon
9911 Brecksville Rd
Cleveland, OH 44141-3201   216-447-5000
Fax: 216-447-5740 jenny.smith@noveoninc.com
www.noveoninc.com
Synthetic food colors, natural food colors, secondary blends, lakes, solutions
    President: Stephen Kirk
Estimated Sales:$395,800,000
Number Employees: 1,000-4,999
Brands:
    Noveon

10376 Noville
P.O.Box 1876
Wayne, NJ 7474-1876   201-641-2700
Fax: 201-814-1914 llomuntad@noville.com
www.noville.com
Manufacturer and exporter of fragrances, oils and flavors
    CEO: Patrick Firmenich
    General Manager: Daniel Carey
Estimated Sales:$22500000
Number Employees: 150
Parent Co: Firmenich
Type of Packaging: Private Label
Brands:
    Malobates

10377 Novozymes North America
P.O.Box 576
Franklinton, NC 27525-0576   919-494-2014
Fax: 919-494-3450 800-879-6686
enzymesna@novozymes.com
www.novozymes.com
Manufacturer and exporter of enzymes
    President: Thomas Nagy
    Sales/Marketing Executive: Neal Priggi
Estimated Sales:$82300000
Number Employees: 1,000-4,999
Parent Co: Novozymes
Type of Packaging: Bulk

10378 Now & Zen
3 Madrone Park Cir
Mill Valley, CA 94941-1481   415-695-2805
Fax: 415-695-2843 800-335-1959
info@nowandzen.net www.nowandzen.net
Processor of whipped toppings including dairy-free, gluten-free and chocolate; also, vegan cookies, cakes, vegetarian turkey, steak, chicken and barbecue ribs
    President: Miyoko Schinner
    Sales Director: Judy Stoffel
    Operations Manager: Eleese Longino

Number Employees: 10-19
Number of Brands: 1
Number of Products: 15
Type of Packaging: Consumer, Food Service, Bulk
Brands:
    Bbq Unribs
    Chocolate Mousse Hip
    Hip Whip
    Unsteak-Out
    Unturkey

10379 Now Foods
395 Glen Ellyn Rd
Bloomingdale, IL 60108-2176   630-545-9098
    Fax: 630-790-8019 888-669-3663
    jroza@nowfoods.com www.nowfoods.com
Manufacturer, distributor, and exporter of dietary
supplements and whole foods including, vitamins,
minerals, amino acids, herbs, herbal extracts, herbal
teas and essential oils for aromatherapy. NNFA GMP
certified, certified organicby QAI, kosher certified
by the Orthodox Union USA
    Owner: Elwood Richard
    CEO/VP: Al Powers
    Marketing Manager: Jim Ritcheske
    Sales Manager: Dan Richard
    Purchasing Manager: Dave Lendy
Estimated Sales: $100 Million
Number Employees: 100-249
Number of Products: 1500
Sq. footage: 203000
Parent Co: Fruitful Yield Corporation
Type of Packaging: Consumer, Private Label, Bulk
Brands:
    ESTER-C
    NOW

10380 Nspired Natural Foods
58 S Service Rd
Melville, NY 11747-4625   631-845-4689
    www.nspiredfoods.com
Wholesaler/distributor and packager of dried fruits,
nuts and trail mixes.
    President: Gil Pritchard
    CIO: Bob CeVan
Number Employees: 5-9
Sq. footage: 10000

10381 Nu Products Seasoning Company
74 Louis Ct
South Hackensack, NJ 07606-1727 201-440-0065
    Fax: 201-440-0096 800-836-7692
    spice@aol.com www.nuproductsseasoning.com
Suppliers of food seasonings
    President: Henry Goldstein
    Marketing Director: Jim Sandler
    CFO: Celia Hester
Estimated Sales: Below $ 5 Million
Number Employees: 20-49
Type of Packaging: Bulk
Brands:
    Nu

10382 Nu-Tek Foods
501 Krein Avenue
Wapakoneta, OH 45895-2491   419-739-3400
    Fax: 419-739-7783 800-837-0160
Calorie-free sweetener made from acesulfame potassium, preservatives sorbic acid and potassium
sorbate. Specializes in producing a wide variety of
Sun Valley Brand custom cheese products

10383 Nu-Tek Products, LLC
5400 Opportunity Court
Suite 120
Minnetonka, MN 55343   952-936-3600
    Fax: 952-933-1396 info@nu-tekproducts.com
    www.nu-tekproducts.com
Manufacturer and supplier of functional ingredients
which include: soy & dairy protein hydrolysates, reduced sodium salt and modified potassium chloride,
fibers and extracts, and pro-biotic powders

10384 Nu-Way Potato Products
25 Colville Road
Toronto, ON M6M 2Y2
Canada
    416-241-9151
    Fax: 416-241-8274
Manufacturer of fresh potatoes
    Co-Owner: Pat Greco
    Co-Owner: Vincent Greco
Number Employees: 20-49
Type of Packaging: Consumer, Food Service

10385 Nu-World Amaranth
P.O.Box 2202
Naperville, IL 60567-2202   630-369-6851
    Fax: 630-369-6851
    contactus@nuworldfamily.com
    www.nuworldfamily.com
Manufacturer and exporter of amaranth-based prod-
ucts including popped, flour, pre-baked flat bread,
sancks and cereal. Offers foods that are allergy free
and gluten free foods
    Founder/Co-Owner: Larry Walters
    President: Susan Walters-Flood
    CFO: Jim Behling
    Manager/Co-Owner: Diane Walters
    VP Production: Terry Walters
Estimated Sales: Under $500,000
Number Employees: 1-4
Number of Brands: 2
Number of Products: 15
Sq. footage: 2700
Type of Packaging: Consumer, Private Label, Bulk
Brands:
    NU-WORLD AMARANTH

10386 NuGo Nutrition
817 Main Street
Pittsburgh, PA 15215   888-421-2032
    www.nugonutrition.com
nutrition bars
    President/Owner: David Levine
    VP: Steven Smith
Estimated Sales: $1.3 Million
Number Employees: 10

10387 NuNaturals
2220 W 2nd Ave # 1
Eugene, OR 97402-7112   541-344-9785
    Fax: 541-343-0915 800-753-4372
    info@nunaturals.com www.nunaturals.com
Processor of health products including diet nutrients,
odorless garlic, vitamins, minerals, amino acids,
green tea, herbs, extracts, etc
    Owner: Warren Sablosky
    CEO: Warren Sablosky
Estimated Sales: $2,000,000
Number Employees: 5-9
Number of Brands: 17
Number of Products: 78
Sq. footage: 8000
Type of Packaging: Consumer
Brands:
    ALCOHOL FREE STEVIA
    BRAIN HERBS
    BRAIN WELL
    CALM MIND
    CLEAR STEVIA
    DAILY ENERGY
    DAILY SOY
    EXTRA ENERGY
    FAST ASLEEP
    GENTLE CHANGE
    JOINT WELL
    LEVEL RIGHT
    LOSWEET
    MELLOWMIND
    MENTAL ENERGY FORMULA
    PREVENTIN GREEN TEA
    SWEET 'N HEALTHY
    SWEET-X
    THROAT CONTROL SPRAY
    TRAVEL WELL
    WELLNESS DROPS
    WHITE STEVIA

10388 Nuchief Sales
343 Grant Rd
East Wenatchee, WA 98802-5333 509-888-8888
    Fax: 509-884-5197 888-269-4638
    nuchief@nwi.net www.nwi.net
Grower, packer and exporter of apples and pears
    President: Dimitri Mandelis
    VP: Dave Battis
    Quality Control: Ray Vespier
    Sales: Joe Defina
Estimated Sales: $500,000-$1 Million
Number of Brands: 5
Number of Products: 10
Type of Packaging: Consumer, Food Service
Brands:
    BIG CHECK
    CRANE & CRANE
    KEYSTONE

10389 Nueces Canyon Texas Style Meat Seasoning
9501 Highway 290 W
Brenham, TX 77833-9138   979-289-5600
    Fax: 979-289-2411 800-925-5058
    nueces@nuecescanyon.com
    www.nuecescanyon.com
Processor of smoked meats including briskets, hams,
quail, etc., also meat seasonings
    President: George S Caloudas
Estimated Sales: $260000
Number Employees: 20-49
Sq. footage: 10000
Parent Co: Nueces Canyon Ranch
Type of Packaging: Consumer, Food Service

10390 Nueske's Applewood Smoked Meats
Rr 2 Box D
Wittenberg, WI 54499   715-253-2226
    Fax: 715-253-2021 800-386-2266
    info@nueske.com www.nueske.com
Processor of smoked meats including bacon, ham,
sausage and specialty items
    President: Robert Nueske
    VP: James Nueske
Number Employees: 100-249

10391 Nugo Nutrition
817 Main Street
Pittsburgh, PA 15215   888-421-2032
    nugonutrition.com
nutrition bars

10392 Nulaid Foods
200 W 5th St
Ripon, CA 95366-2793   209-599-2121
    Fax: 209-599-5220 www.nulaid.com
Manufacturer of egg products
    President: David Crockett
    CFO: Scott Hennecke
Number Employees: 100-249
Type of Packaging: Consumer, Food Service, Pri-
vate Label, Bulk
Brands:
    NULAID

10393 Nulhegan Brands
PO Box 148
Canaan, VT 05903-0148   802-524-0768
    wgp003@sunfglobal.com
    www.nulheganbrands.com
Manufacturer of gourmet cranberry and wild blue-
berry chutneys

10394 Numi Tea
1050 22nd Ave
Oakland, CA 94606-5205   510-534-6864
    Fax: 510-536-6864 866-972-6879
    info@numitea.com www.numitea.com
Manufacturer of organic teas and teasans
    President/Co-Founder: Ahmed Rahim
    President/Co-Founder: Reem Rahim
Estimated Sales: $ 10 - 20 Million
Number Employees: 10-19
Sq. footage: 25000
Type of Packaging: Consumer, Food Service
Brands:
    NUMI

10395 Nunes Company
P.O.Box 673
Salinas, CA 93902-0673   831-757-1521
    Fax: 831-424-4955 produce@foxy.com
    www.nunescompany.com
Grower and exporter of vegetables
    Owner: F Robert Nunes
    Sales Manager: Tom Nunes, Jr.
    Secretary/Treasurer: Enos Barera
Estimated Sales: $11100000
Number Employees: 50-99
Type of Packaging: Consumer, Food Service, Bulk
Brands:
    Foxy
    Nunes
    Tubby

10396 Nunes Farm Almonds
P.O.Box 311
Newman, CA 95360-0311   209-862-3033
    Fax: 209-862-1038 almonds@nunefarms.com
    www.nunesfarms.com

Processor and exporter of roasted almonds, mixed
nuts and pistachios. candies toffee caramel chews,
chocolate almonds and toffee almonds
President: Arthur Nunes
Estimated Sales: Under $500,000
Number Employees: 20-49
Brands:
Almond Chews
California Crunchies
Caramel Chews
Chocolate Toffee Almonds
Foxy Salads

10397 Nunn Milling Company
4700 New Harmony Rd
Evansville, IN 47720-1721   812-425-3303
                            800-547-6866
Processor of plain and self-rising flour and corn
meal
Manager: Jerry Napp
Estimated Sales: $ 5 - 10 Million
Number Employees: 5-9
Brands:
Nunn-Better

10398 Nuovo Pasta Productions
125 Bruce Avenue
Stratford, CT 06615-6102   203-380-4090
        Fax: 203-336-0656 800-803-0033
        customerservice@nuovopasta.com
                www.nuovopasta.com
Manufacturer of frozen and fresh ravioli, tortelloni,
gnocchi, pasta, and pasta sauces
President: Carl Zuanelli
Production: Joe Dubee
Estimated Sales: Below $ 5 Million
Number Employees: 20
Type of Packaging: Consumer, Food Service

10399 Nurture
28 S Waterloo Rd
Devon, PA 19333-1574   610-293-0718
        Fax: 610-989-0991 888-395-3300
        nurture@nurture-inc.com www.nurture-inc.com
Ingredients for nutritional products
President: H Griffith
Estimated Sales: $1,800,000
Number Employees: 5-9
Brands:
Nurture

10400 Nustef Foods
2446 Cawthra Road
Mississauga, ON L5A 3K6
Canada   905-896-3060
                       Fax: 905-896-4347
Processor and exporter of pizzelle cookies and po-
lenta
CEO: Ces Nucci
Number Employees: 20-49
Sq. footage: 12000
Type of Packaging: Consumer, Food Service, Pri-
vate Label, Bulk
Brands:
Gold'n Polenta
Gold'n Treats
Reko

10401 Nut Factory
P.O.Box 815
Spokane Valley, WA 99016-0815   509-926-6666
        Fax: 509-926-3300 888-239-5288
        nuts@TheNutFactory.com
                www.thenutfactory.com
Processor, packager and importer of nuts and dried
fruits
President: Gene Cohen
Estimated Sales: $1700000
Number Employees: 5-9
Type of Packaging: Consumer
Brands:
Big Value
Old Fashioned
Party Pak
Sunburst

10402 Nut House
558 S Broad St
Mobile, AL 36603-1124   251-433-1689
        Fax: 251-433-3364 800-633-1306
        sales@georges.com www.threegeorges.com

Pecans and chocolates
President: Scott Gonzales
CFO: Gina Barnett
VP: Siophan Gonzalez
Estimated Sales: Under $500,000
Number Employees: 5-9
Type of Packaging: Private Label

10403 Nutfield Brewing Company
P.O.Box 40
Derry, NH 03038-0040   603-434-9678
        Fax: 603-434-1042 general@nutfield.com
                www.nutfield.com
Processor of ale, lager and stout
President: Jim Killeen
Sales Manager: Geoff Tyson
Estimated Sales: Below $ 5 Million
Number Employees: 5-9
Type of Packaging: Consumer, Food Service
Brands:
Nutfield Auburn Ale
Nutfield's Classic Root Beer

10404 Nuthouse Company
558 S Broad St
Mobile, AL 36603-1124   251-433-1689
        Fax: 251-433-3364 www.threegeorges.com
Processor and exporter of pecans and baked goods
President: Scott Gonzales
VP: Sibhan Gonzales
Estimated Sales: $1500000
Number Employees: 50-99
Sq. footage: 30000
Type of Packaging: Consumer
Brands:
3 George
Azalea
Nuthouse

10405 Nutmeg Vineyard
PO Box 146
Andover, CT 06232-0146   860-742-8402
Wine
President: Anthony Maulucci
Estimated Sales: $500,000-$1 Million
Number Employees: 1-4
Type of Packaging: Private Label

10406 Nutorious
2057B Bellevue Street
Green Bay, WI 54311   877-688-6746
        Fax: 866-703-6595 sales@nutoriousnuts.com
                www.nutoriutnuts.com
nut conections
President/Owner: Carrie Liebhauser

10407 Nutra Food Ingredients,LLC
3631 44th Street SE
Suite D
Kentwood, MI 49512   616-656-9928
                Fax: 419-730-3685
        sales@nutrafoodingredients.com
                www.nutrafoodingredients.com
Manufacturer and sellers of high quality ingredi-
ents/products such as protein, gelatin/collagen,
polyols, intensive sweetener, fiber, flavors and organic ingredients

10408 Nutra Nuts
4528 E Washington Blvd
Commerce, CA 90040-1033   323-260-7457
        Fax: 323-260-7459 gocorny@nutranuts.com
                www.nutranuts.com
Manufacturer of Snack mixture of organic popcorn
and soybeans flavored with sea salt or natural spices
or coated with organic sugar
President: Mark Porro
CFO: Michael Porro
Estimated Sales: $300,000-500,000
Number Employees: 1-4
Number of Brands: 1
Number of Products: 3
Sq. footage: 3300
Type of Packaging: Consumer, Food Service, Bulk
Brands:
Grandpa Po's Slightly Spicy
Grandpa Po's Slightly Sweet
Grandpa Po's Slightly Unsalted
Nutra Nuts

10409 NutraSweet Company
200 World Trade Center
Chicago, IL 60654   312-840-5000
        Fax: 312-840-5578 800-535-2656
        ordernow@nutrasweet.com
                www.nutrasweet.com
Sweeteners
President: Craig Petray
CFO: James Stanley
Director Nutritional Science: Maureen Mackey
Purchasing Manager: James Pumphrey
Estimated Sales: $ 100 Million+
Number Employees: 400
Parent Co: JW Childs Associates
Brands:
Equal
Nutrasweet

10410 Nutraceutical Corporation
1400 Kearns Blvd # 2
Park City, UT 84060-7228   435-655-6000
        Fax: 800-767-8514 info@nutraceutical.com
                www.nutraceutical.com
Processor of vitamins, garlic, brewer's yeast and fish
and garlic oils
President: Jeff Hilton
CEO: Frank W Gay Ii
Estimated Sales: I
Number Employees: 500-999
Parent Co: Nutraceutical
Type of Packaging: Consumer, Food Service
Brands:
Bio-Genics

10411 Nutraceutical Corporation
1400 Kearns Blvd # 2
Park City, UT 84060-7228   435-655-6000
        Fax: 435-655-6029 800-669-8877
                www.nutraceutical.com
Processor of teas and nutritional supplements
CEO: Frank W Gay Ii
Director Marketing: Kathryn Riley
Estimated Sales: I
Number Employees: 500-999
Parent Co: Nutraceutical
Type of Packaging: Consumer

10412 Nutraceutical Solutions
6704 Ranger Ave
Corpus Christi, TX 78415-5908   361-854-0755
        Fax: 361-855-8031 800-338-4788
                www.eliquidsolutions.com
Processor of sublingual/liquid vitamins
Owner: Jerry Mc Clure
Estimated Sales: $ 10 - 20 Million
Number Employees: 10-19
Type of Packaging: Consumer

10413 Nutraceutics Corporation
2900 Brannon Avenue
Saint Louis, MO 63139-1440   877-664-6684
        Fax: 314-664-4639 info@nutraceutics.com
                www.nutraceutics.com
Manufacturing , importer and exporter of
nutraceutical tablets, capsules, effervescents,
tropicals and powers
President: Jennifer Jamieson Cherry
Estimated Sales: $500,000-$1 Million
Number Employees: 5-9
Number of Brands: 50
Number of Products: 1000
Type of Packaging: Consumer, Private Label, Bulk
Brands:
DH3
DHEA PLUS
DIET DHEA

10414 Nutranique Labs
398 Tesconi Court
Santa Rosa, CA 95401-4653   707-545-9017
        Fax: 707-575-4611 sales@nutranique.com
Processor and exporter of broccoli sprouts and certi-
fied nutraceutical powders including spinach, wheat
grass juice, tomato, broccoli, garlic, carrot, green
tea, kale and cruciferous blends
General Manager: Mark Martindill
Director Sales/Marketing: Nancy Costa
Operations Manager: Tom Ikesaki
Number Employees: 1-4
Parent Co: FDP USA
Type of Packaging: Bulk
Brands:
Nutranique Labs

10415 Nutrex Hawaii, Inc
73-4460 Queen Kaahumanu Hwy
Kailua Kona, HI 96740-2632   808-326-1353
    Fax: 808-329-4533 800-453-1187
    info@nutrex-hawaii.com
    www.nutrex-hawaii.com
Nutrex Hawaii, Inc, retail/wholesale/distributor products include Hawaiiam Spirulina Pacifica, a nutrient-rich dietary supplement; BioAstin natural astaxanthin, a powerful antioxidant with expanding applications as a humannutraceutical.
    President: Gerald R Cysewski
    Marketing: Bob Capelli
    Sales: Agnes Prehn
Estimated Sales:$500-$1 Million
Number Employees: 50-99
Number of Brands: 2
Parent Co: Cyanotech Corporation
Type of Packaging: Consumer, Private Label, Bulk
Brands:
    Bioastin
    Spirulina Pacifica

10416 Nutri Base
3851 East Thunderhill Place
Phoenix, AZ 85044-6679   480-759-4849
    Fax: 480-759-4079 800-225-3623
    feedback@goldentemple.com
    www.nutribase.com
Cereals
    President: Sat Samtolch Khalsu
    Owner: Guru Simran Singh Khalsa
Type of Packaging: Private Label
Brands:
    Golden Temple
    Rainforest
    Wha Guru Chew

10417 Nutri-Cell
1038 N Tustin Street
Suite 309
Orange, CA 92867-5958   714-953-8307
    Fax: 714-639-0420
    nutricell2100inc@netscape.net
Manufacturer and exporter of animal-free nutritional supplements
    President: Eric Ellison
    CEO: Jeff Ellison
    CFO: Dan Ellison
Number Employees: 1-4
Number of Brands: 2
Number of Products: 7
Sq. footage: 3000
Type of Packaging: Consumer, Private Label
Brands:
    Nutri-Cell

10418 Nutri-Fruit
9212 Riverside Road E
Sumner, WA 98390-8109   253-863-0300
    Fax: 253-863-1939 866-343-7848
    info@nutrifruit.com www.nutri-fruit.com/
Fruit
    President: Chuck Jarrett
Estimated Sales:$ 1-2.5 Million appx.
Number Employees: 10
Brands:
    Nutri-Fruito

10419 Nutri-West
2132 E Richards St
Douglas, WY 82633   307-358-5066
    Fax: 307-358-9208 800-443-3333
    marcia@nutri-west.net www.nutri-west.com
Nutritional supplements
    Owner: Paul White
    Marketing Director: Marcia White
    Vice President: Tiffany Moore
    CFO: Michelle Ediss
    Purchasing Manager: Marc Moore
Estimated Sales:$ 2.5-5 Million
Number Employees: 20-49
Sq. footage: 60
Type of Packaging: Private Label
Brands:
    Nutri West

10420 Nutribiotic
PO Box 238
Lakeport, CA 95453-0238   707-263-0411
    Fax: 707-263-7844 800-225-4345
    info@nutribiotic.com www.nutribiotic.com

Manufacturer and exporter of vitamins and supplements
    President: Richard Perry
    Marketing Manager: Trisca Richardson
    National Sales Manager: Teri Whitestone
    Purchasing Agent: Kenny Ridgeway
Estimated Sales:$6000000
Number Employees: 16
Sq. footage: 30000
Parent Co: Nutrition Resource
Brands:
    Citricidal
    Fruitsnax
    Grapefruit Extract
    Jungle Juice
    Meta Boost
    Meta Rest
    Nutribiotic
    Prozone
    Spectrum Nutritional Shake

10421 Nutricepts
2208 E 117th St
Burnsville, MN 55337-1265   952-707-0207
    Fax: 952-707-0210 800-949-9060
    info@nutricepts.com www.nutricepts.com
Processor and exporter of calcium salts, oxygen consuming agents, oxygen scavengers, mold inhibitors, sodium lactate, humectants, flavor enhancers, etc
    President: Mark Cater
Estimated Sales:$ 3 - 5 Million
Number Employees: 1-4
Type of Packaging: Bulk
Brands:
    Ampliflave
    Oxyvac
    Prop Whey
    Surface Guard

10422 Nutrilabs
1230 Market St # 401
San Francisco, CA 94102-4801   415-863-2363
    Fax: 415-707-2122 800-658-5343
    www.nutrilabs.com
Private label manufacturer vitamins and supplements
    Owner: Etty Motazedi
    VP: Elsie Orell
    Purchasing Director: Argee Davidovici
Estimated Sales: Less than $500,000
Sq. footage: 2800
Type of Packaging: Consumer, Private Label, Bulk
Brands:
    Chromemate
    Citrimax
    Geri-Med
    Renuz-U
    Super B-12 Sublingual
    Valerian Extract
    Virility Plus

10423 Nutrilicious Natural Bakery
5446 Dansher Road
Countryside, IL 60525-3126   708-354-7777
    Fax: 708-354-4797 800-835-8097
    info@nutrilicious.com www.nutrilicious.com
Processor of cookies and doughnuts including plain, old-fashioned, spelt, whole wheat, low-fat baked and wheat-free spelt
    President: Steve Maril
    General Manager: Joe Augelli
Number Employees: 12
Sq. footage: 10000
Type of Packaging: Consumer, Food Service, Private Label

10424 Nutrisoya Foods
4050 Pinard Street
Saint-Hyacinthe, QC J2S 8K4
Canada   450-796-4261
    Fax: 450-796-1837 nutrisoya@citenet.net
Processor and exporter of soy milk and tofu
    President: Nick Feldman
Number Employees: 10-19
Sq. footage: 10000
Type of Packaging: Consumer, Food Service, Private Label, Bulk
Brands:
    Natura
    Nutribio
    Nutrisoy
    Nutrisoya

10425 Nutritech Corporation
719 E Haley St
Santa Barbara, CA 93103-3161   805-963-9581
    Fax: 805-963-0308 800-235-5727
    salesnt@all-one.com www.all-one.com
Manufacturer and exporter of all-in-one multi-vitamin and mineral amino acid powder including rice original and base, green phyto base, active seniors and fruit antioxidant formulas
    President/CEO: Douglas Ingoldsby
    VP Sales: Lori Herman
    VP Operations: Carol Huerta
Estimated Sales:$ 1 - 3 Million
Number Employees: 5-9
Type of Packaging: Consumer
Brands:
    ALL ONE

10426 Nutrition 21
4 Manhattanville Rd
Purchase, NY 10577-2139   914-696-0505
    Fax: 914-696-0860 contactn21@nutrition21.com
    www.nutrition21.com
Organic mineral nutrition includes chromium picolinate, selenium yeast and Cardea salt alternative compound
    President/CEO: Gail Montgomery
    Senior VP: Dean Dimaria
    Marketing Director: K Gwen
*Estimated Sales:*G
Number Employees: 20-49
Brands:
    Chromax

10427 Nutritional Counselors of America
1267 Archie Rhinehart Pkwy
Spencer, TN 38585-4612   931-946-3600
    Fax: 931-946-3602 ncahw@mindspring.com
Vitamins, minerals, herbs, herbal teas, nutritional supplements, and colon cleaners, neutraceuticals and probiotics
    President/CEO: June Wiles
Estimated Sales:$3-$5 Million
Number Employees: 5-9
Sq. footage: 5000
Type of Packaging: Consumer, Private Label
Brands:
    6-N-1
    K-Min
    Min-Col
    NCA

10428 Nutritional International Enterprises Company
P.O.Box 6043
Irvine, CA 92616-6043   949-854-4855
    Fax: 949-854-6170 www.nutrition-intl.com
Processor of nutritionally fortified vitamin supplements; also, nutritional consultation services available
    VP: Cecile Lin
Estimated Sales:$30000000
Number Employees: 20-49

10429 (HQ)Nutritional Laboratories International
1001 S 3rd St W
Missoula, MT 59801-2337   406-273-5493
    Fax: 406-273-5498 info@nutritionallabs.com
    www.nutritionallabs.com
cGMP manufacturer, exporter and contract packager of nutritional and herbal supplements and nutraceuticals including tablets, and capsules
    President: Terry Benishek
    CFO: Mark Richter
    VP Sales/Marketing: Ned Becker
    VP/Sales Marketing: Ned Becker
    Plant Manager: Gary Hiler
    Purchasing Manager: Greg Tomlinson
Estimated Sales:$ 5 - 10 Million
Number Employees: 50-99
Sq. footage: 50000
Type of Packaging: Consumer, Private Label, Bulk

10430 Nutritional Life Support Systems
3650 Hancock St
San Diego, CA 92110-4356   619-294-3954
    Fax: 619-291-1142
Chinese herbal combinations
    Owner: Amador Villanuva
Estimated Sales:$300,000-500,000
Number Employees: 1-4

10431 (HQ)Nutritional Research Associates
P.O.Box 354
South Whitley, IN 46787-0354   260-723-4931
Fax: 260-723-6297 800-456-4931
pookjg@usa.net   www.nutreseassocinc.usrc.net
Processor and exporter of vitamins including caro-
tene, A, D and E
  Manager: Jonathan Pook II
  Acting Manager: Jonathan Pook
Estimated Sales:$979000
Number Employees: 5-9
Sq. footage: 10000
Type of Packaging: Consumer, Bulk
Brands:
  Carex
  Quintrex

10432 Nutritional Specialties
1967 N Glassell St
Orange, CA 92865-4320   714-634-9340
Fax: 714-634-9347 800-333-6168
lifetime@anet.net   www.lifetimevitamins.com
Processor of herbal formulas and nutritional supple-
ments; importer of chlorella powder and tablets; ex-
porter of dietary supplements
  President: Tom Pinkowski
  VP: Tom Krech
  VP: Sale Stauch
Estimated Sales:$ 10 - 20 Million
Number Employees: 20-49
Type of Packaging: Private Label, Bulk
Brands:
  Lifetime
  Tung Hai

10433 Nutritional Supply Corporation
2533 N Carson Street
3127
Carson City, NV 89706-0147   775-888-6900
Fax: 800-671-3144 888-541-3997
nsc24@nsc24.com   www.nsc24.com
Processor and exporter of nutritional supplements,
vitamins and encapsulated herbs
  National Sales VP: Mark Campbell
*Estimated Sales:*Less than $500,000
Number Employees: 1-4
Sq. footage: 15000
Type of Packaging: Consumer, Food Service
Brands:
  Nsc-100
  Nsc-24

10434 (HQ)Nutriwest
2132 E Richards St
Douglas, WY 82633   307-358-5066
Fax: 307-358-9208 800-443-3333
www.nutri-west.com
Processor and exporter of vitamin products and food
and sports drink supplements
  President: Paul White
  VP Marketing: Tony White
  Sales/Marketing: Marcia White
Estimated Sales:$ 20 - 50 Million
Number Employees: 20-49
Sq. footage: 60000
Type of Packaging: Consumer, Private Label
Other Locations:
  Nutriwest
  Alliance NE
Brands:
  Nutriquest
  Nutriwest

10435 Nutro Laboratories
650 Hadley Rd # C
South Plainfield, NJ 07080-2477   908-755-7984
Fax: 908-754-5640 800-446-8876
Processor of vitamins
  President: Michael Slade
  Human Resources: Donna Cirullo
  Sales/Marketing Manager: Chris Burns
Estimated Sales:$25600000
Number Employees: 250-499
Type of Packaging: Consumer

10436 Nuts & Stems
PO Box 39
Rosharon, TX 77583-0039   281-464-6887
Fax: 281-464-7493 nutsandstems@aol.com

Manufacturer of Gourmet flavored pistachios and
cashews

10437 Nutsco Inc
1115 S 2nd St
Camden, NJ 08103-3232   856-966-6400
Fax: 856-966-6544 info@nutsco.com
www.nutsco.com
Cashew nuts in bulk, raw or roasted, and other types
of nuts. Co-packing services for roasting and pack-
ing nuts in bags, can or jars.
  President: Fransisco A Neto
  VP: Patricio Assis
  Marketing: Sueli Vieira
  Sales: Sueli Vieira
  Plant Manager: Steve McCall
Estimated Sales:$ 5-10 Million
Number Employees: 20-49
Number of Brands: 1
Number of Products: 12
Sq. footage: 48000
Parent Co: Usibras (Brazil)
Type of Packaging: Consumer, Private Label, Bulk
Brands:
  Nutsco

10438 Nuttery Farms
PO Box 29
Saint Helena, CA 94574-0029   707-963-1101
Fax: 707-963-5316
Processor, importer and exporter of dried fruits, nuts
and nut meats
  President: Hendrick Smelling
*Estimated Sales:*Less than $500,000
Number Employees: 1-4
Type of Packaging: Consumer, Food Service, Bulk

10439 Nutty Bavarian
305 Hickman Dr
Sanford, FL 32771-6905   407-444-6322
Fax: 407-444-6335 800-382-4788
bruno@nuttyb.com   www.nuttyb.com
Processor of cinnamon nut glaze syrup and fresh
roasted gourmet nuts; Manufacturer of nut roasting
carts and warmers as well as paper and plastic cones
and gift tins for nuts
  President: David Brent
Estimated Sales:$500,000-$1 Million
Number Employees: 10-19
Sq. footage: 7200
Type of Packaging: Consumer, Bulk
Brands:
  NBR 2000
  Nutty Bavarian

10440 Nuvex Ingredients
PO Box 158
Blue Earth, MN 56013-0158   507-526-4331
Fax: 507-526-5026
judy.rogers@nuvexingredients.com
www.nuvexingredients.com
Manufacturer of particulates, inclusions, toppings,
and half products for bars, cereals, fillings, ice
creams, snacks and bakery products.
  President/CEO: Peter Malecka
  EVP Sales: Dave Duffy
  Director Marketing: Grant Gengel
Estimated Sales:$20-50 Million
Number Employees: 200-250
Number of Brands: 2
Number of Products: 45
Sq. footage: 130000
Type of Packaging: Consumer, Food Service, Pri-
vate Label, Bulk
Brands:
  NUCHEWS
  PROTI-OATS

10441 Nylander's Vantage Products
1855 N High Street
Lakeport, CA 95453-3614   916-929-5200
Fax: 916-929-8422
Baked goods
  President: Robert Nylander
*Estimated Sales:*Less than $500,000
Number Employees: 1-4

10442 Nyssa-Nampa Beet Growers
PO Box 2723
Nyssa, OR 97913-0723   541-372-2904
Fax: 541-372-5063 nnbga@microw.net

Cooperative of sugar beet processors
  President: Steve Martineau
  Executive Director: Norma Burbank
  VP: Tom Church
  Executive Director: Rich Turner

10443 O C Lugo Company
99 Main St
Nyack, NY 10960-3109   845-708-7080
Fax: 845-708-7081 info@oclugo.com
www.oclugo.com
Supplier of chemicals, vitamins, minerals, gelatins
and food ingredients. OC Lugo's other division is
Critical Filtration supplies
  President: Richard Lugo
Estimated Sales:$830,000
Number Employees: 5-9

10444 O Chili Frozen Foods Inc
3634 Indian Wells Ln
Northbrook, IL 60062-3102   847-562-1991
Fax: 847-562-1822
Manufacturer of processed frozen meats including
cooked pizza toppings, chopped and formed beef,
veal, pork and poultry, breaded products, entrees,
etc.;
  Owner: J Rothschild
Number Employees: 20-49
Type of Packaging: Consumer, Food Service, Pri-
vate Label, Bulk
Brands:
  CHILLI-O

10445 O Olive Oil
1997 S McDowell Blvd
Suite A
Petaluma, CA 94954   707-766-1755
Fax: 707-763-3782 888-827-7148
info@ooliveoil.com   www.ooliveoil.com
citrus oils, extra virgin, wine vinegars, rice vinegars
and citrus tapenades
Number Employees: 5

10446 O Olive Oil
1997 S McDowell Boulevard Ext
Petaluma, CA 94954-6919   415-460-6598
Fax: 415-460-6599 888-827-7148
mail@ooliveoil.com   www.ooliveoil.com
Manufacturer of Extra virgin citrus olive oils and
oak-aged vinegars
  President/Founder: Greg Hinson
  National Director Sales/Marketing: Shelly
  Haygood
Estimated Sales:$2.5-5 Million
Number Employees: 1-4
Type of Packaging: Private Label
Brands:
  O OLIVE OIL
  O VINEGAR

10447 O&H Danish Bakery
1841 Douglas Ave
Racine, WI 53402-4696   262-637-8895
Fax: 262-631-5395
ohdanish@mohdanishbakery.com
www.ohdanishbakery.com
Danish and pastries
  President: Ray Olesen
  Founder: Christian Olesen
  Co-Owner: Myrna Olesen
Estimated Sales:$ 2.5-5 Million
Number Employees: 50-99
Brands:
  Kringle

10448 O'Boyle's Ice Cream Company
2500 Green Lane & Farragut Avenue
Bristol, PA 19007   215-788-0421
Processor of ice cream, frozen yogurt and frozen
desserts
  Componet: Beverly Boyle
Number Employees: 10-19
Type of Packaging: Consumer, Food Service, Bulk
Brands:
  Country Creamery

10449 O'Brian Brothers Food
PO Box 42382
Cincinnati, OH 45242   513-791-9909
Fax: 513-791-9011 obrian@beamons.com
www.beamons.com
Processor of barbecue sauce and salad dressings in-
cluding French, Italian, honey mustard and ranch
  President/CEO: John O'Brian

Estimated Sales:$500,000-$1 Million
Number Employees: 1-4
Type of Packaging: Consumer, Food Service, Private Label
Brands:
  Beamons

10450 O'Brien & Company
3302 Harlan Lewis Rd
Bellevue, NE 68005-5660   402-291-3600
          Fax: 402-291-0237 800-433-7567
          johnobrien@obrienmeatsnacks.com
Processor of sausage, summer sausage, meat snacks, luncheon meats and frankfurters
  President: John O Obrien
  National Sales Representative: Don Murray
  Plant Manager: David Hascall
Estimated Sales:$6680000
Number Employees: 50-99
Type of Packaging: Consumer, Food Service, Bulk
Brands:
  O'Brien's
  Val-U-Pak

10451 O'Brines Pickling
4103 E Mission Avenue
Spokane, WA 99202-4402   509-534-7255
          Fax: 509-534-5564 ohbrines@spokane.net
          www.ohbrines.com
Pickled products
  President: James Moore
  VP: Marsha Moore
Estimated Sales:$5-9.9 Million
Number Employees: 10-19

10452 O'Danny Boy
1132 Ethel Avenue
Miamisburg, OH 45342-2510   937-866-4638
          Fax: 937-866-8940 888-840-0497
          www.odannyboyicecream.com
Ice cream
  Owner: Robert Haas
  Co-Owner: Kathleen Haas

10453 O'Donnell Formula
1145 Linda Vista Dr # 110
San Marcos, CA 92078-3820   760-471-1182
          Fax: 760-471-1878 800-736-1991
Processor of health food supplements
  President/CEO: Wanda O'Donnell
  CFO: Angela Bongiorno
Estimated Sales:$1-2.5 Million
Number Employees: 5-9
Type of Packaging: Food Service
Brands:
  Flora-Balance
  Latero-Flora

10454 O'Garvey Sauces
1151 Madeline Street
New Braunfels, TX 78132-4725   830-620-6127
          Fax: 830-620-6662
Processor of hot and mild salsas
  President: Norma Garvey
Estimated Sales:$ 1 - 3 Million
Number Employees: 1-4
Type of Packaging: Consumer, Food Service, Private Label, Bulk
Brands:
  Max's Salsa Sabrosa & Design

10455 O'Hara Corporation
120 Tillson Ave # 1
Rockland, ME 04841-3450   207-594-0405
          Fax: 207-594-0407
Processor and exporter of seafood including frozen scallops
  Owner: Frank O'Hara
Estimated Sales:$4100000
Number Employees: 50-99
Type of Packaging: Consumer, Food Service
Brands:
  Cape Ann
  Down East
  Tip Top

10456 O'Mona International Tea
9 Pine Ridge Road
Rye Brook, NY 10573-1414   914-937-8858
          Fax: 914-937-8858
Tea
  President: F Seid
*Estimated Sales:*Under $500,000
Number Employees: 1-4

10457 O'Neal's Fresh Frozen Pizza Crust
122 E College Ave
Springfield, OH 45504-2505   937-323-0050
          redparot@iapdatacom.net
Processor of pizza crust including whole wheat
  Manager: Brian O'Neill
Estimated Sales:$ 1 - 3 Million
Number Employees: 20-49

10458 O'Neil's Distributors
110 S Iroquois Street
Goodland, IN 47948-8004   219-297-4521
          Fax: 219-297-4625
Teas
  Owner: Steven O'Neil
Estimated Sales:$ 2.5-5 Million
Number Employees: 1-4

10459 O'Neill Coffee Company
P.O.Box 245
West Middlesex, PA 16159-0245   724-528-9281
          Fax: 724-528-1566 www.oneillcoffee.com
Processor of coffee; wholesaler/distributor of teas and spices
  CEO: Joseph J Walsh
Estimated Sales:$ 1 - 3 Million
Number Employees: 5-9

10460 O'Neill Packing Company
P.O.Box 7194
Omaha, NE 68107-0194   402-733-1200
          Fax: 402-733-1724
Processor and exporter of beef
  President: Ron O'Neill
  General Production Manager: Brian O'Neill
Estimated Sales:$12200000
Type of Packaging: Consumer, Food Service, Private Label, Bulk

10461 O'Vallon Winery
RR 1
Box 77b
Washburn, MO 65772-9801   417-826-5830
Wine company
  Owner: Frank Huffman
*Estimated Sales:*Under $500,000
Number Employees: 1-4

10462 O-At-Ka Milk Products Cooperative
P.O.Box 718
Batavia, NY 14021-0718   585-343-0536
          Fax: 585-343-4473 800-828-8152
          mpatterson@oatkamilk.com www.oatkamilk.com
Processor and exporter of dairy products including butter, milk powder, condensed milk, milk-based drinks, creams, etc; importer of butter and milk powder
  President: Mac McCampbell
  CFO: Michael Patterson
  VP: David Crisp
  Sales Manager: Richard Edelman
  Operations Manager: Al Smith
  Plant Engineer: Keith Price
Estimated Sales:$145877093
Number Employees: 250-499
Sq. footage: 100000
Type of Packaging: Consumer, Food Service, Private Label, Bulk
Brands:
  Gold Cow
  Spring Farm

10463 O. Malley Grain
P.O.Box 128
Fairmont, NE 68354-0128   402-268-6001
          Fax: 402-268-7241 info@omalleygrain.com
          www.omalleygrain.com
High quality corn supplier to the snack food and tortilla industries
  VP: Dave Waters
  CEO: Rob O'Malley
  Executive VP: James Thomas
Estimated Sales:$ 20-50 Million
Number Employees: 10-19

10464 O.K. Industries
P.O.Box 1119
Fort Smith, AR 72902-1119   479-783-4186
          Fax: 479-784-1358 800-635-9441
          www.okfoods.com

Manufacturer and exporter of chicken parts and further processed chicken products
  Chairman: Collier Wenderoth Jr
  President: Thomas Webb
  CEO: Randy Goins
  Quality Control: John Schuleupner
Estimated Sales:$616 Million
Number Employees: 50-99
Parent Co: OK Industries
Type of Packaging: Consumer, Food Service, Private Label
Brands:
  O.K. FOODS
  TENDERBIRD

10465 OB Macaroni Company
P.O.Box 53
Fort Worth, TX 76101-0053   817-335-4629
          Fax: 817-335-4726 800-555-4336
          www.obpasta.com
Processor of macaroni
  President: Carlo Laneri Jr
Estimated Sales:$ 10 - 20 Million
Number Employees: 20-49
Sq. footage: 50000
Type of Packaging: Consumer, Food Service, Private Label, Bulk
Brands:
  O.B.
  Q&Q

10466 OC Schulz & Sons
P.O.Box 39
Crystal, ND 58222-0039   701-657-2152
          Fax: 701-657-2425 ocschulz@polarcomm.com
Manufacturer of potatoes
  President: Tom Schulz
  Secretary/Treasurer: David Moquist
Estimated Sales:$.5-1 Million
Number Employees: 10-19
Sq. footage: 50000
Type of Packaging: Consumer, Food Service

10467 OCG Cacao
1 Plummers Cor
Whitinsville, MA 01588-2135   508-234-5107
          Fax: 508-234-5495 888-482-2226
          ocggroup@aol.com www.ocgcacao.com
Suppliers of dairy, bakery, confectionery products
  President: Jean Chenal
  General Manager: Roberta White
*Estimated Sales:*Below $ 5 Million
Number Employees: 1

10468 OH Chocolate
600 Manitou Road SE
Calgary, AB T2G 4C5
Canada   403-283-4612
          Fax: 403-287-2117
Processor of baked desserts and Belgian chocolates
  President: Laurie Climan
  Sales Manager: Mark Climan
Number Employees: 10-19
Type of Packaging: Consumer
Brands:
  L'Or Chocolatier
  Ott Chocolate

10469 (HQ)OMEGA Nutrition
6505 Aldrich Rd
Bellingham, WA 98226   360-384-1238
          Fax: 360-384-0700 800-661-3529
          info@omeganutrition.com
          www.omeganutrition.com
Processor of organically pressed oils including borage, flax, hazelnut, sesame, safflower, sunflower, pistachio, almond and canola; also, processor of gluten-free and hazelnut flours; exporter of flax oil
  Owner: Bob Walbert
  Marketing Director: Robert Gaffney
Estimated Sales:$6700000
Number Employees: 20-49
Sq. footage: 16000
Type of Packaging: Food Service, Private Label
Other Locations:
  OMEGA Nutrition U.S.A.
  Vancouver BC
Brands:
  Efa Balanced
  Essential Balance
  Nutriflax
  Omegaflo
  Omegaplus Gla

10470 OSEM USA
333 Sylvan Ave
Englewood Cliffs, NJ 07632-2724   201-871-4433
          Fax: 201-871-8726 mike@osemusa.com
Snacks
    President: Izzet Ozdoga
Estimated Sales: Below $ 5 Million
Number Employees: 5-9
Brands:
    Osem

10471 OSF Flavors
40 Baker Hollow Rd
Windsor, CT 06095-2133   860-298-8350
          Fax: 860-298-8363 800-466-6015
    sales@osfflavors.com www.osfflavors.com
Flavor and colors
    Manager: Doug Nasby
    Marketing Director: Olivier de Botton
    CEO: Olivier DeBotton
    R & D: Linda Foulkner
Estimated Sales: $ 10-20 Million
Number Employees: 20-49
Sq. footage: 10000
Brands:
    OSF Flavors

10472 Oak Creek Brewing Company
2050 Yavapai Dr
Sedona, AZ 86336-4558   928-204-1300
          Fax: 520-204-1361 bestbrew@sedona.net
          www.oakcreekbrew.com
Processor of seasonal beer, ale and lager
    General Manager: Rita Kraus
Estimated Sales: $ 500,000 - $ 1Million
Number Employees: 5-9
Type of Packaging: Consumer, Food Service
Brands:
    Oak Creek

10473 Oak Creek Farms
218 North C Street
Po Box 206
Edgar, NE 68935   402-224-3038
          Fax: 402-224-3536
Processor and exporter of organic grain products including corn chips, flour and masa
    President: Ben Jones
    VP: Jack Horst
Estimated Sales: $200,000
Number Employees: 3
Sq. footage: 3000
Type of Packaging: Consumer, Food Service, Private Label, Bulk
Brands:
    Oak Creek Farms

10474 (HQ)Oak Farm's Dairy
1148 Faulkner Ln
Waco, TX 76704-1916   254-756-5421
          Fax: 254-756-6987 www.oakfarmsdairy.com
Milk
    President: Mackey Willims
    CEO: Mickey Williams
    General Sales Manager: Jerry Przada
    Human Resources: Brad Patten
Estimated Sales: Less than $500,000
Number Employees: 100-249
Other Locations:
    Oak Farms Dairy
    Wichita Falls TX
    Oak Farms Dairy
    Weatherford TX
    Oak Farms Dairy
    Denison TX
    Oak Farms Dairy
    Paris TX
    Oak Farms Dairy
    Houston TX
    Oak Farms Dairy
    Beaumont TX
    Oak Farms Dairy
    Brenham TX
    Oak Farms Dairy
    San Antonio TX
    Oak Farms Dairy
    McAllen TX
    Oak Farms Dairy
    Waco TX
    Oak Farms Dairy
    Austin TX
    Oak Farms Dairy
    Tyler TX
Brands:
    Oak Farm's

10475 Oak Farms
1314 Fredericksburg Rd
San Antonio, TX 78201-5000   210-732-1111
          Fax: 210-737-2534 800-292-2169
          robin-somogyi@deanfoods.com
          www.oakfarmsdairy.com
Processor of milk
    Manager: Matt Conner
    General Sales Manager: Joe Penaloza
    General Manager: Matt Connor
Estimated Sales: $63700000
Number Employees: 250-499
Parent Co: Suiza Dairy Group
Type of Packaging: Consumer, Food Service, Private Label

10476 Oak Farms
P.O.Box 655178
Dallas, TX 75265-5178   214-941-0302
          Fax: 214-941-0309 www.oakfarmsdairy.com
Processors of milk and cream
    General Manager: Craig Roberts
    General Sales Manager: Jerry Przada
    General Manager: Micky Williams
Number Employees: 250-499
Parent Co: Suiza Dairy Group
Type of Packaging: Consumer, Food Service
Brands:
    Oak Farms

10477 Oak Grove Dairy
W10198 Oak Grove Rd
Clintonville, WI 54929-8607   715-823-6226
          Fax: 715-823-6589 oakgrvdy@frontiernet.net
Longhorn, mini longhorn, colby, cheddar, Monterey jack, semi-soft marble and pepper jack cheese
    Co-Owner: David Kust
    Co-Owner: Terry Kust
    Secretary: Theresa Kust
Estimated Sales: $5-9.9 Million
Number Employees: 10-19
Sq. footage: 9300
Type of Packaging: Food Service, Private Label, Bulk

10478 Oak Grove Dairy
1270 Energy Lane
Saint Paul, MN 55108-5225   952-467-2212
          Fax: 952-467-2212
Milk
    Manager: Lonny Saulsbury
Estimated Sales: $ 20-50 Million
Number Employees: 100-249

10479 Oak Grove Orchards Winery
6090 Crowley Road
Rickreall, OR 97371-9706   503-364-7052
Wines
    President: Carl Stevens
Estimated Sales: Under $500,000
Number Employees: 1-4

10480 Oak Grove Smokehouse
17618 Old Jefferson Hwy
Prairieville, LA 70769-3931   225-673-6857
          Fax: 225-673-5757
Manufacturer of seasoned and Cajun/Creole rice mixes, speciality spice mixes, breading and smoked meats
    President: Robert Schexnailder PhD
Estimated Sales: $500,000-$1 Million
Number Employees: 5-9
Number of Brands: 2
Number of Products: 15+
Sq. footage: 17000
Type of Packaging: Consumer, Food Service, Bulk
Brands:
    OAK GROVE SMOKEHOUSE
    SWAMP FIRE SEAFOOD BOIL

10481 Oak Hill Farm
P.O.Box 1989
Glen Ellen, CA 95442-1989   707-996-6643
          Fax: 707-935-6612 800-878-7808
          info@oakhillfarm.net   www.oakhillfarm.net
Organic flowers and produce
    Owner: Anne Teller
Estimated Sales: $ 10-24.9 Million
Number Employees: 5-9
Brands:
    Jim Beam Kentucky Bourbon
    Oak Hill Farms
    Redneck Gourmet

10482 Oak Island Seafood Company
PO Box 947
Portland, ME 04104-0947   207-594-9250
          Fax: 207-594-9281
Seafood
    President: Jay Trenholm

10483 Oak Knoll Dairy
PO Box 443
Windsor, VT 05089-0443   802-674-5426
          Fax: 802-674-9166 oakknoll@earthlink.net
          www.oakknolldairy.com
Manufacturer of 100% goats milk, 2% fat goats milk, chocolate goats milk, and half and half goats milk
    Owner: George Redick
    Owner: Karen Lindbo
Brands:
    OAK KNOLL

10484 Oak Knoll Winery
29700 SW Burkhalter Rd
Hillsboro, OR 97123-9245   503-648-8198
          Fax: 503-648-3377 800-625-5665
          info@oakknollwinery.com
          www.oakknollwinery.com
Manufacturer of Wines
    President: Greg Lint
    President: Greg Lint
    VP Sales/Marketing: John Vuylsteke
    Tasting Room Communications/Founder: Marj Vuylsteke
    Assistant Winemaker: Jim Herinckx
    Cellar Master: Tom Vuylsteke
    Office Manager: Martha Miller
Estimated Sales: Below $5 Million
Number Employees: 10-19
Number of Brands: 2
Number of Products: 8
Type of Packaging: Consumer, Private Label, Bulk
Brands:
    OAK KNOLL

10485 Oak Leaf Confections
440 Comstock Road
Scarborough, ON M1L 2H6
Canada   416-751-0740
          Fax: 416-751-3656 800-338-3631
Processor and exporter of confectionery products including malt balls, gum balls, bubble gum, hard candies and freeze pops
    Owner/President: Philip Terranova
    National Sales Manager: Don Spillane
    Director Finance: Drew MacAskill
Number Employees: 300
Sq. footage: 140000
Type of Packaging: Consumer, Private Label, Bulk

10486 Oak Ridge Winery
P.O.Box 440
Lodi, CA 95241-0440   209-369-4758
          Fax: 209-369-0202 www.oakridgewines.com
Wines
    President: Rudy Maggio
    Quality Control: Juan Cerna
Estimated Sales: $ 10-20 Million
Number Employees: 20-49
Type of Packaging: Private Label

10487 Oak Ridge Winery
P.O.Box 440
Lodi, CA 95241-0440   209-369-4768
          Fax: 209-369-0202 www.oakridgewinery.com
Brandy
    Owner: Rudy Maggio
Estimated Sales: $ 10 - 20 Million
Number Employees: 20-49

10488 Oak Spring Winery
Rr 1 Box 612
Altoona, PA 16601-9449   814-946-3799
          Fax: 814-846-4245 oakspring@keyconn.net
          www.oakspringwinery.com
Wines
    Founder: Sylvia Schraff
    President: Scott Schraff
    Treasurer: John Schraff
Estimated Sales: $5-9.9 Million
Number Employees: 1-4
Brands:
    Oak Spring Winery

10489 Oak State Products

PO Box 549
Wenona, IL 61377   815-853-4348
          Fax: 815-853-4625 www.oakstate.com
Producer of soft cookies, cookie crumbs and top-
pings
    President: David Van Laar
    CFO: Patrick Donnelly
    Vice President: Michael Healy
    Production Manager: Jeff Pickard
    Plant Manager: Jim Shannon
    Purchasing Manager: Anne Newhalfen
Estimated Sales:$22.8 Million
Number Employees: 350
Sq. footage: 160000
Type of Packaging: Consumer, Bulk
Brands:
    Oak State Cookie Jar Delight

10490 (HQ)Oak Valley Farm

1010 Haddonfield Berlin Rd
Voorhees, NJ 08043-3514   856-435-0900
    Fax: 856-435-3019 info@oakvalleyfarms.com
              www.oakvalleyfarms.com
Processor of turkey and turkey products including
raw and fully cooked
    President: Leo Rubin
    CEO: Richard Milbauer
    VP Sales: Bruce Utain
Estimated Sales:$28842984
Number Employees: 5-9
Other Locations:
    El Jay Poultry Corp.
    Watertown SD
Brands:
    All Seasons
    Buttergold
    Chef-Ready
    Oak Valley Farms
    Val-U-Pak

10491 Oak Valley Farms

705 20th Avenue SW
Watertown, SD 57201-7047   605-886-8025
    Fax: 605-882-2895 info@oakvalleyfarms.com
              www.oakvalleyfarms.com
Processor of turkeys
    General Manager: Richard Rogers
    Quality Control: Sarah Hermann
Estimated Sales:$ 50 - 100 Million
Number Employees: 250-499
Parent Co: El Jay Poultry Corporation
Type of Packaging: Consumer

10492 Oakencroft Vineyard & Winery

630 Ivy Ln
Charlottesville, VA 22901-5041   434-296-4188
    Fax: 434-293-6631 mail@aokencroft.com
              www.oakencroft.com
Manufacturer of Wines
    President/Owner: Felicia Warburg Rogan
    Vineyard Manager: Philip Ponton
    Winemaker: Riaan Rossouw
Estimated Sales:$ 1 - 3 Million
Number Employees: 1-4

10493 Oakhurst Dairy

364 Forest Ave
Portland, ME 04101-2092   207-772-7468
    Fax: 207-874-0714 info@oakhurstdairy.com
              www.oakhurstdairy.com
Processor of dairy products including cottage cheese
and sour cream
    President: Stanley Bennett II
    CEO: Stanley Bennett II
    CEO: Stanley T Bennett Ii
    Director of Quality Control: Wendy Donovan
    Landry
    General Sales Manager: John Bennett
    VP Operations: William Bennett
    Production Manager: L Gerry Whiting
Estimated Sales:$ 50 - 100 Million
Number Employees: 100-249
Type of Packaging: Consumer

10494 Oakland Bean Cleaning &Storage

42445 County Road 116
Knights Landing, CA 95645-0518   530-735-6203
                Fax: 530-735-6207
Processor of dry, edible beans including kidney and
pink
    Operations Manager: Frank Anastasi
*Estimated Sales:*Less than $500,000
Number Employees: 1-4

10495 Oakland Noodle Company

P.O.Box 644
Oakland, IL 61943-0644   217-346-2322
                Fax: 217-346-2324
Manufacturer of noodles
    President: Tod Ethington
    Marketing Director: Stephanie Ethington
*Estimated Sales:*Under $500,000
Number Employees: 1-4
Sq. footage: 2000
Brands:
    Oakland Noodle

10496 Oakrun Farm Bakery

PO Box 81070
Ancaster, ON L9G 4X1
Canada   905-648-1818
                Fax: 905-648-8252
Processor and exporter of English muffins and past-
ries
    President: John Voortman
Number Employees: 100-249
Type of Packaging: Consumer, Food Service, Pri-
vate Label

10497 Oasis Breads

440 Venture St
Escondido, CA 92029-1210   760-747-7390
    Fax: 760-747-4854 bread@oasisbreads.com
              www.oasisbreads.com
Processor of flourless sprouted whole grain breads
and deli breads.
    President: Jim Pickell
Estimated Sales:$1300000
Number Employees: 5-9
Sq. footage: 10000
Type of Packaging: Consumer, Private Label
Brands:
    OASIS

10498 Oasis Coffee Company

327 Main Ave
Norwalk, CT 06851-6156   203-847-0554
                Fax: 203-846-9835
Roasting coffee
    President: Ralph Sandolo
    CEO: Veronica Sandolo
    Vice President: Joseph Sandolo
    Marketing Consultant: Martin Blank
Estimated Sales:$ 5-10 Million
Number Employees: 5-9
Brands:
    Oasis Coffee

10499 Oasis Foods

2222 Kirkman St
Lake Charles, LA 70601-7448   337-439-5262
    Fax: 337-437-1174 www.oasisfoodsinc.com
    President: Edward Abrusley
Estimated Sales:$ 10 - 20 Million
Number Employees: 10-19

10500 Oasis Foods

P.O.Box 217
Planada, CA 95365-0217   209-382-0263
                Fax: 209-382-0427
Processor, exporter and canner of fruit including
peaches and Kadota figs
    President: Eric Stephen Bocks
    Operations Manager: Lorraiane Bocks
    Production Manager: Eric Bocks
Estimated Sales:$ 20 - 50 Million
Number Employees: 50-99
Number of Products: 1
Sq. footage: 74000
Type of Packaging: Food Service, Private Label
Brands:
    OASIS
    OREGON FRUIT
    SYSCO

10501 Oasis Foods Company

465 Hillside Ave
Hillside, NJ 07205-1121   908-964-0477
    Fax: 908-688-4375 dickwhite@oasisfoodsco.com
              www.oasisfoodsco.com
Manufacturer of butter blends and substitutes, salad
dressings, shortenings, margarine, edible oils, mayonnaise, sauces, pan and grill oil
    President/CEO: Jeffrey Kuo
    Manager: Allen Savasta
    VP: Anthony Alves

Estimated Sales:$100-500 Million
Number Employees: 100-249
Sq. footage: 300000
Type of Packaging: Consumer, Food Service, Pri-
vate Label, Bulk
Brands:
    ALPINE VALLEY
    EX-SEED
    GARDEN HARVEST
    GOLDEN DELICIOUS
    GOLDEN FRY
    JOLINA
    KLECKNER
    OASIS
    SELECT RECIPE
    TOP FRY
    TOWN & COUNTRY
    TRAIL BLAZIN

10502 Oasis Mediterranean Cuisine

1520 W Laskey Rd
Toledo, OH 43612-2914   419-269-1516
    Fax: 419-324-7777 www.omcfood.com
Mediterranean vegetarian cuisine
    Manager: Mike Francis
    Quality Control: Tonny Obid
Estimated Sales:$ 5-10 Million
Number Employees: 20-49
Brands:
    Non-Dairy Baklava

10503 Oasis Winery

14141 Hume Rd
Hume, VA 22639-1724   540-635-3103
    Fax: 540-635-4653 800-304-7656
    oasiswine@aol.com   www.oasiswine.com
Manufacturer of Wines
    Owner/CEO: Tareq Salahi
    Public Relations: Ann Runyon
Estimated Sales:$5-10 Million
Number Employees: 100-249
Type of Packaging: Private Label
Brands:
    BLEU ROCK VINEYARD WINES
    FIERY RUM CELLARS
    OASIS WINES & SPARKLING WINES

10504 Oberto Sausage Company

P.O.Box 429
Kent, WA 98035-0429   253-854-7056
    Fax: 253-437-6151 877-453-7591
              www.lowreys.com
Processor of beef jerky, salami and sausage includ-
ing cocktail and specialty
    President: Tom Campanile
Estimated Sales:$83200000
Number Employees: 500-999
Type of Packaging: Consumer
Brands:
    Lowery's Meat Snacks
    Oh Boy! Oberto Beef Jerky
    Oh Boy! Oberto Classic
    Pacific Gold
    Smoke Craft

10505 Oberweis Dairy

951 Ice Cream Dr
North Aurora, IL 60542-1475   630-801-6100
    Fax: 630-897-0562 888-645-5868
    hdfeedback@oberweisdairy.com
              www.oberweisdairy.com
Manufacturer of fluid dairy products, premium ice
cream, and ice cream cakes, juice, meat products,
crackers, cookies, salsas
    Chairman: Jim Oberweis
    President/CEO: Robert Renaut
    VP/CFO: Randy Anderson
    VP Marketing: Mark Vance
    VP Route Sales/HR: Mike McCarthy
    VP Supply Chain: Dave Doyle
    VP Retail Operations: Elizabeth Craig
Estimated Sales:$1-2.5 Million
Number Employees: 100-249
Type of Packaging: Food Service, Private Label,
Bulk

10506 (HQ)Obester Winery

12341 San Mateo Rd
Half Moon Bay, CA 94019-7113   650-726-9463
    Fax: 650-726-7074 info@obesterwinery.com
              www.obesterwinery.com
Wines
    Owner: Kendyl Kellogg

Estimated Sales:$ 2.5-5 Million
Number Employees: 5-9

10507 Occidental International Foods
P.O.Box 534
Chester, NJ 07930-0534   908-879-2942
Fax: 908-879-2488   sales@occidentalfoods.com
www.occidentalfoods.com
Manufacturers' representatives and importers of
bulk spices and seeds, including paprika, pure
mancha saffron, chilies dried, crushed and ground,
turmeric, granulated garlic, garlic powder, carda-
mom, annatto, allspice and sesameseeds
President: Scott Hall
CFO: Denise Hall
Estimated Sales:$300,000-500,000
Number Employees: 1-4
Type of Packaging: Food Service, Bulk

10508 Ocean Beauty Seafoods
1100 W Ewing St
Seattle, WA 98119-1321   206-285-6800
Fax: 206-285-9190   info@oceanbeauty.com
www.oceanbeauty.com
Manufacturer of Portion controlled, fresh and frozen
seafood
President: Mark Palmer
CFO: Tony Ross
VP Retail Sales: Ron Christianson
EVP Operations/Sales: Mark Palmer
Plant Manager: Joe Kelso
Estimated Sales:$100+ Million
Number Employees: 1,000-4,999
Type of Packaging: Private Label
Other Locations:
Ocean Beauty - Production
Cordova AK
Ocean Beauty - Processing
Alitak AK
Ocean Beauty
Taunton MA
Ocean Beauty - Plant
Excursion AK
Ocean Beauty - Production
Kodiak AK
Ocean Beauty - Production
Naknek AK
Ocean Beauty - Production
Petersburg AK
Ocean Beauty - Production
Nikiski AK
Brands:
BAY BEAUTY
COMMANDER
DEEP SEA
ECHO FALLS
ICY POINT
LASSCO
MCGOVERN
NATHAN'S
NEPTUNE
OCEAN BEAUTY
OCEAN BONITA
PILLAR ROCK
PINK BEAUTY
PIRATE
PORT CLYDE
RITE
ROYAL ALASKA
SEA CHANCE
SEARCHLIGHT
SOUND BEAUTY
SURF KING
THREE STAR
TRIBE
XIP CAVIAR

10509 Ocean Beauty Seafoods
1100 W Ewing St
Seattle, WA 98119-1321   206-285-6800
Fax: 206-285-9190   info@oceanbeauty.com
www.oceanbeauty.com
Processor of smoked salmon and pickled fish
Owner: Howard Klein
CEO: Bill Terhar
CEO: Mark Palmer
Estimated Sales:$100+ Million
Number Employees: 1,000-4,999
Type of Packaging: Consumer, Food Service
Brands:
Rite Food
Sea Choice

10510 (HQ)Ocean Beauty Seafoods
1100 W Ewing St
Seattle, WA 98119-1321   206-285-6800
Fax: 206-285-9190   info@oceanbeauty.com
www.oceanbeauty.com
Manufacturer and distributor of seafood
President: Mark Palmer
CFO: Tony Ross
National Retail Sales Manager: Kevin Palmer
Estimated Sales:$260 Million
Number Employees: 1,000-4,999
Type of Packaging: Food Service
Other Locations:
Ocean Beauty Seafood Facility
Boston MA
Ocean Beauty Seafood Facility
Cordova AK
Ocean Beauty Seafood Facility
Alitak AK
Ocean Beauty Seafood Facility
Kodiak AK
Ocean Beauty Seafood Facility
Los Angeles CA
Ocean Beauty Seafood Facility
Monroe AK
Ocean Beauty Seafood Facility
Naknek AK
Ocean Beauty Seafood Facility
Petersburg AK
Ocean Beauty Seafood Facility
Seattle WA
Ocean Beauty Seafood Facility
Nikiski AK
Brands:
COMMANDER
ECHO FALLS
ICY POINT
LASCCO
NATHANS
NEPTUNE
OCEAN BONITA
PILLAR ROCK
PINK BEAUTY
PORT CLYDE
RITE FOODS
SEA CHOICE
SEARCHLIGHT
THREE STAR
TRIBE

10511 Ocean Beauty Seafoods
14651 172nd Dr SE
Monroe, WA 98272-1076   425-482-2923
Fax: 425-794-9312   info@oceanbeauty.com
www.oceanbeauty.com
Frozen salmon, smoked salmon, pickled herring,
smoked trout
Manager: Diane Miller
CFO: Tony Ross
VP Sales/Marketing: Ron Christianson
Estimated Sales:$ 20 - 50 Million
Number Employees: 50-99
Brands:
Circle Sea
Echofalls
Icy point
Lascco
Nathan's
Northern Lox
Ocean Bonita
Rite Foods
Scan Fish
Sea Choice
Three Star
Tribe

10512 Ocean Cliff Corporation
362 S Front St
New Bedford, MA 02740-5745   508-990-7900
Fax: 508-990-7950   oceanclf@rcn.com
Processor, importer and exporter of fish and seafood
liquid and powder extracts and spices including
shrimp, clam, crab, fish, lobster and mussel. Pro-
duces seafood flavors both in a liquid and powder
form
Owner: G Gregory White
Estimated Sales:$ 2.5-5 Million
Number Employees: 5-9
Sq. footage: 20000
Type of Packaging: Bulk
Brands:
Ocean Cliff

10513 Ocean Coffee Roasters
259 East Ave
Pawtucket, RI 02860-3800   401-724-6393
Fax: 401-724-0560   800-598-5282
www.excellentcoffee.com
Manufacturer of Coffee, tea
President: William Kapos
*Estimated Sales:*Less than $500,000
Number Employees: 10-19
Brands:
OCEAN COFFEE

10514 Ocean Crest Seafoods
88 Commercial St
Gloucester, MA 01930-5025   978-281-0232
Fax: 978-283-3211 www.neptunesharvest.com
Seafood
President/CEO: Leonard Parco
Estimated Sales:$ 1 - 3 Million
Number Employees: 20-49

10515 Ocean Delight Seafoods
450 Alexander Street
Vancouver, BC V6A 1C5
Canada   604-254-8351
Fax: 604-254-1699
Processor and exporter of fresh fish cakes
President: Shig Hirai
Number Employees: 5-9
Type of Packaging: Consumer, Food Service, Pri-
vate Label, Bulk

10516 Ocean Diamond
20 Potash Road
Oakland, NJ 07436-3100   201-337-9515
Fax: 201-337-0479
Seafood

10517 Ocean Food Company
3 Turbina Avenue
Scarborough, ON M1V 5G3
Canada   416-285-6487
Fax: 416-285-4012   info@oceanfood.ca
Manufactuer of salmon flakes, fish-sausage,
kamaboko, crab-imitation
President: Ken Horisaki
Number Employees: 5-9
Type of Packaging: Consumer, Food Service

10518 Ocean Foods of Astoria
PO Box 626
Astoria, OR 97103-0626   503-325-2421
Fax: 503-325-1770
Seafood
President: Grant Larson
Estimated Sales:$ 10-20 Million
Number Employees: 50

10519 Ocean Fresh Seafoods
4241 21st Ave W # 306
Seattle, WA 98199-1250   206-285-2412
Fax: 206-283-3408 www.oceanfreshsea.com
Processor of fresh and frozen fish and seafood
President: Ted Otness
Plant Manager: Bill Bryant
Estimated Sales:$1,100,000
Number Employees: 5-9
Type of Packaging: Food Service
Brands:
Alaska Fresh

10520 (HQ)Ocean Garden Products
3585 Corporate Ct
San Diego, CA 92123-2415   858-571-5002
Fax: 858-571-2009 www.oceangarden.com
King crab, salmon, shrimp, lobster tails
CFO: Frank Barrancotto
CEO: Javier Corella
Estimated Sales:$33.5 Million
Number Employees: 100-249

10521 Ocean King International
1680 S Garfield Avenue
Alhambra, CA 91801-5413   626-289-9399
Fax: 626-300-8177
Seafood
President/CEO: Jimmie Dang
CFO: Miling Shua
Vice President: Richard Mendelson
Secretary: Jorge Pardinas

10522 Ocean Mist
P.O.Box 1247
Castroville, CA 95012-1247   831-633-2144
    Fax: 831-633-0561 contactus@oceanmist.com
    www.oceanmist.com
Processor/packer/grower of vegetables including spinach, cauliflower, celery, lettuce, artichokes, broccoli, etc.
    President: Ed Boutonnet
    VP Sales: Maggie Bezart
    Sales Director: Joe Feldman
    Sales Manager: Bob Polovneff
    Operations Manager: Les Tottino
    Plant Manager: Mark Rensons
Estimated Sales:$9,200,000
Number Employees: 50-99
Brands:
    MISTER
    OCEAN MIST
    OCEAN MIST MISTEE

10523 Ocean Pride Fisheries
PO Box 330
Lower Wedgeport, NS B0W 2B0
Canada   902-663-4579
    Fax: 902-663-2698
Processor and exporter of smoked salmon, cod and haddock
    President: Dick Feldman
Number Employees: 1-4
Type of Packaging: Consumer, Food Service, Bulk

10524 Ocean Pride Seafood
207 S Richard St
Delcambre, LA 70528-3732   337-685-2336
    Fax: 337-685-2339
Manufacturer of Shrimp and crawfish
    President: Denise Dooley
Estimated Sales:$500,000-$1 Million
Number Employees: 1-4

10525 Ocean Select Seafood
10714 Highway 14
Delcambre, LA 70528-3415   337-685-5315
    Fax: 337-685-6079
Seafood
    President: Mitch Polito
Estimated Sales:$5-$10 Million
Number Employees: 1-4

10526 (HQ)Ocean Spray Cranberries
1 Ocean Spray Dr
Lakeville-Middleboro, MA 02349 508-946-1000
    Fax: 508-946-7704 800-662-3263
ldibiase@oceanspray.com www.oceanspray.com
Manufacturer and exporter of cranberry products including bottled juices, sauces, relish, etc
    President/CEO: Randy Papadellis
    SVP, CFO and Treasurer: Timothy Chan
    SVP/COO: Kenneth Romanzi
    VP Operations: Michael Stamatakos
Estimated Sales:$1.5 Billion
Number Employees: 2000
Type of Packaging: Consumer, Food Service
Other Locations:
    Ocean Spray International
    Palm Harbor FL
    Ocean Spray International
    Lakeville MA
    Ocean Spray International
    Chestney, GBR
Brands:
    CRAISINS
    CRANAPPLE
    CRANCHERRY
    CRANGRAPE
    CRANICOT
    CRANORANGE
    OCEAN SPRAY
    OCEAN SPRAY APPLE JUICE
    OCEAN SPRAY CRANBERRIES
    OCEAN SPRAY CRANBERRY COCKTAIL
    OCEAN SPRAY FRUIT PUNCH
    OCEAN SPRAY FRUIT PUNCH COOLER
    OCEAN SPRAY GRAPEFRUIT JUICE
    OCEAN SPRAY JELLIED CRAN. SAUCE
    OCEAN SPRAY JUICE BLENDS
    OCEAN SPRAY KIWI STRAQ. JUICE
    OCEAN SPRAY LEMONADE
    OCEAN SPRAY ORANGE JUICE
    OCEAN SPRAY PINEAPPLE GRAPEFRUIT
    OCEAN SPRAY PINK GRAPEFRUIT JUICE
    OCEAN SPRAY RUBY RED & MANGO
    OCEAN SPRAY RUBY RED GRAPEFRUIT

OCEAN SPRAY WHOLE BERRY CRANBERRIES
WELLFLEET FARMS
WELLFLEET FARMS CRANBERRY SAUCE
WELLFLEET FARMS SPECIALTY FOODS

10527 Ocean Spray Cranberries
1480 State Route 105
Aberdeen, WA 98520-9524   360-648-2201
    Fax: 360-648-2354 800-662-3263
    www.oceanspray.com
Manufactures fruit juices; manufactures pickles, sauces & salad dressings; manufactures frozen fruits, juices & vegetables
    President: Robert Hawthorne
    CEO: Randy Papadellis
    VP: Michael Stamatakos
Estimated Sales:$ 3 - 5 Million
Number Employees: 5-9
Sq. footage: 130000
Parent Co: Ocean Spray Cranberries
Type of Packaging: Consumer, Food Service
Brands:
    Ocean Spray

10528 Ocean Spray Cranberries
925 74th Ave SW
Vero Beach, FL 32968-9755   772-562-0800
    Fax: 772-562-1215 www.oceanspray.com
Processor of grapefruit concentrate fruit juice
    CFO: Timothy Chan
    Area Manager Citrus Operations: Ted Kucinaky
Estimated Sales:$ 50 - 100 Million
Number Employees: 100-249
Parent Co: Ocean Spray Cranberries
Type of Packaging: Bulk

10529 Ocean Spray Cranberries
104 Park St
Bordentown, NJ 08505-1424   609-298-0905
    Fax: 609-298-8353 www.oceanspray.com
Juice, produce, craisins, sauces and oatmeal
    Manufacturing/Operations Director: Robert Swanson
    Plant Manager: Tim Haggerty
Estimated Sales:$990173000
Number Employees: 300
Parent Co: Ocean Spray Cranberries
Type of Packaging: Consumer, Food Service

10530 Ocean Spray Cranberries
7800 60th Ave
Kenosha, WI 53142-4009   262-694-0621
    Fax: 262-694-5533 www.oceanspray.com
Processor of cranberry products including juices, jelly and sauce
    Plant Manager: George Smedley
Estimated Sales:$100+ Million
Number Employees: 250-499
Parent Co: Ocean Spray Cranberries
Type of Packaging: Consumer, Food Service

10531 Ocean Spray Cranberries
1 Ocean Spray Dr
Middleboro, MA 02349-1000   508-946-1000
    Fax: 508-946-7704 ldibiase@oceanspray.com
    www.oceanspray.com
Processor of cranberry juice and juice concentrate
    CEO: Randy Papadellis
    Chairman: Robert L Rosbe
    CFO: Jr. Tim
    Director: Ryan Walker
Estimated Sales:$ 100-500 Million
Number Employees: 1,000-4,999
Parent Co: Ocean Spray Cranberries
Type of Packaging: Consumer, Food Service, Private Label, Bulk

10532 Ocean Spray Cranberries
1 Ocean Spray Dr
Middleboro, MA 02349-1000   508-946-1000
    Fax: 508-946-7704 800-662-3263
    snewcomb@oceanspray.com
    www.oceanspray.com
Processor of cranberry juice and juice concentrates
    President: Randy Papadellis
    Creative Services: Sharon Newcomb
    CFO: Tim Chan
    Corporate Communications: Denise Perry
    Manager: Marty De Luca
Estimated Sales:$ 20-50 Million
Number Employees: 1,000-4,999
Parent Co: Ocean Spray Cranberries

10533 Ocean Spray Cranberries
1 Ocean Spray Dr
Middleboro, MA 02349-1000   508-946-1000
    Fax: 508-946-7704 800-662-3263
ldibiase@oceanspray.com www.oceanspray.com
Produces fruit juice concentrates and purees—custom blends and premixes, cranberry, concord grape and berry fruit
    President/CEO: Randy Papadellis
    CFO: Tim Chan
    Vice President: Michael Stamatakos
    Board Member: Barbara S Thomas
Estimated Sales:$ 25-50 Million
Number Employees: 1,000-4,999
Brands:
    Craisins
    Ocean Spray
    Ruby

10534 Ocean Spray Ingredient Technology Group
1 Ocean Spray Dr
Middleboro, MA 02349-1000   508-946-1000
    Fax: 508-946-7704 800-662-3263
ing@oceanspray.com www.oceanspray.com
Juice, produce, craisins, sauces and oatmeal
    President/CEO: Randy Papadellis
    VP: Dr Geoffrey Woolford
    CEO: Randy C Papadellis
    VP: Mead Johnson
Estimated Sales:$1.5 Billion
Number Employees: 2,000
Brands:
    Ocean Spray
    Sorbella

10535 Ocean Springs Seafood
608 Magnolia Ave
Ocean Springs, MS 39564-4823   228-875-0104
    Fax: 228-875-0117
mail@oceanspringschambers.com
    www.oceanspringschambers.com
Processor of frozen, fresh, headless and peeled shrimp
    President: Earl Sayard
    VP: Ruby Fayard
    Secretary: Linda Fayard
Estimated Sales:$1500000
Number Employees: 5-9
Type of Packaging: Private Label
Brands:
    Surf Spray
    Tropic

10536 Ocean Union Company
2100 Riverside Pkwy # 129
Lawrenceville, GA 30043-5927   770-995-1957
    Fax: 770-513-8662
Seafood, snapper, grouper, lobster, crab, tuna, eel, mackerel
    President: Jackie Tsai

10537 Oceana Foods
P.O.Box 156
Shelby, MI 49455-0156   231-861-2141
    Fax: 231-861-6351 www.cherrycentral.com
Dried fruit and dried vegetable processing and packaging.
    President: Jeffrey Tucker
    COO: Jeff Tucker
Estimated Sales:$85683203
Number Employees: 50-99
Type of Packaging: Consumer, Food Service, Private Label
Brands:
    McDonald
    P-Royal
    Shelby
    Telephone

10538 Oceanfood Sales
1909 E Hastings Street
Vancouver, BC V5L 1T5
Canada   604-255-1414
    Fax: 604-255-1787 877-255-1414
plathe@oceanfoods.com

Processor and exporter of smoked salmon
President: John Graham
Marketing Manager: David Slate
Production Manager: John Makowhichuk
Number Employees: 50-99
Type of Packaging: Consumer, Food Service, Private Label, Bulk

10539 Oceania Cellars
2204 Corbett Canyon Road
Arroyo Grande, CA 93420-4918   805-481-5434
Wines

10540 Oceanledge Seafoods
138 Rankin Street
Rockland, ME 04841-2318   207-594-4955
Fax: 626-968-0196
Seafood

10541 Oceans Prome Distributing
P.O.Box 2325
Glenview, IL 60025-6325   847-998-5813
Fax: 847-729-5228
President: Jeffrey Burhop
Estimated Sales:$ 5 - 10 Million
Number Employees: 5-9

10542 Oceanside Knish Factory
3445 Lawson Blvd
Oceanside, NY 11572-4903   516-766-4445
Fax: 516-766-2319 www.knishfactory.com
Knishes
President: Leonard Model
*Estimated Sales:*Below $ 5 Million
Number Employees: 20-49

10543 Odell Brewing Company
800 E Lincoln Ave
Fort Collins, CO 80524-2507   970-498-9070
Fax: 970-498-0706 odells@odellbrewing.com
www.odellbrewing.com
Beer
President/CEO: Douglas Odell
Manager Sales/Marketing: John Perant
Treasurer: Wynne Odell
Estimated Sales:$ 10-20 Million
Number Employees: 20-49
Brands:
90 Shilling
Cutthroat Pale Ale
Easy Street Wheat
Easy Street Wheat
Isolation Ale
Levity Golden Amber

10544 Odessa Tortilla & TamaleFactory
1915 E 2nd St
Odessa, TX 79761-5311   432-332-6676
800-753-2445
Processor of Mexican foods including tortillas, pork tamales, chorizo, burritos and shells
President: Manuel Gonzalez
Estimated Sales:$1100000
Number Employees: 10-19
Sq. footage: 6000
Type of Packaging: Consumer, Food Service, Bulk
Brands:
Manuel's
Mito's

10545 Odom's Tennessee Pride Sausage Company
P.O.Box 1187
Madison, TN 37116-1187   615-868-1360
Fax: 615-860-4703 800-327-6269
lmoorer@tnpride.com   www.tnpride.com
Processor of country sausage
President: Larry Odom
Chairman: Richard Odom
President: Larry Odom
Marketing Director: Mark Newell
Plant Manager: Frank Howell
Purchasing Manager: William Truan
Estimated Sales:$66400000
Number Employees: 100-249
Type of Packaging: Consumer, Food Service, Private Label, Bulk
Brands:
Tennessee Pride Country Sausage

10546 Odwalla
1205 S Platte River Dr
Denver, CO 80223-3139   303-282-0500
Fax: 303-282-1199 www.odwalla.com

Processor of fresh citrus juice and co-packer of bottled juice products
Manager: Dennis Dingman
Estimated Sales:$910000
Number Employees: 20-49
Sq. footage: 18000
Parent Co: Coca-Cola Bottling Company
Type of Packaging: Consumer, Food Service, Private Label, Bulk
Brands:
Glorious Morning

10547 (HQ)Odwalla
120 Stone Pine Rd
Half Moon Bay, CA 94019-1783   650-726-1888
Fax: 650-726-4441   800-639-2552
custserv@odwalla.com   www.odwalla.com
Fresh fruit and vegetable juices, geothermal spring water, nutritional bars, soy based drinks and organic soy milk.
President: Shawn Sugarman
COO: Steve McCormick
Senior VP Finance/CFO: James Steichen
Senior VP: James R Steichen
VP Sales: Elizabeth McDonough
Estimated Sales:$146 Million
Number Employees: 500-999
Parent Co: Coca-Cola Bottling Company
Type of Packaging: Consumer
Brands:
A Breath of Fresh
Femme Vitale
Glorious Morning
Juice For Humans
Mango Tango
Mo'beta
Odwalla
Odwalla Cranberry Citrus Bar
Odwalla Fruity C Monster Bar
Odwalla Juices
Odwalla Organic Carrot Bar
Odwalla Peanut Crunch Bar
Serious Ginseng

10548 Oetker Limited
2229 Drew Road
Mississauga, ON L5S 1E5
Canada   905-678-1311
Fax: 905-678-9334   customer_service@oetker.ca
www.oetker.ca
Manufacturer of Cake and muffin mixes, mashed potatoes, drink crystals
Chairman: Dr August Oetker
President: Dr h c August Oetker
Brands:
DR OETKER

10549 Off Shore Seafood Company
P.O.Box 120
Point Lookout, NY 11569-0120   516-432-0529
Seafood, seafood products
President: Robert L Doxsee
*Estimated Sales:*Below $ 5 Million
Number Employees: 20-49
Type of Packaging: Private Label

10550 Office General des EauxMinerales
5260 Avenue Notre-Dame-De-Grace
Montreal, QC H4A 1K9
Canada   514-482-7221
Fax: 514-482-7093   ogem@qc.aira.com
www.saintjustin.ca
Bottler and exporter of carbonated natural mineral water
President: Nicole Lelievre
Number Employees: 23
Type of Packaging: Food Service
Brands:
Saint Justin

10551 Offshore Systems
P.O.Box 920427
Dutch Harbor, AK 99692-0427   907-581-1827
Fax: 907-581-1630 www.offshoresystemsinc.com
VP: Robert Schasteen
Manager: Tiny Schasteen

10552 Oh Boy Corporation
1516 1st Street
San Fernando, CA 91340-2796   818-361-1128
Fax: 818-361-7651   ob1516@aol.com

Manufacturer and exporter of frozen foods including potatoes, pizza and pizza products, garlic bread and tortillas
President: Pietro Vitale
Estimated Sales:$ 50 - 100 Million
Number Employees: 100-249
Type of Packaging: Consumer, Food Service, Private Label

10553 Oh Boy! Corporation
1516 1st Street
San Fernando, CA 91340-2796   818-361-1128
Fax: 818-361-7651   ob1516@aol.com
Pizza, prepared sandwiches, lasagna, meatballs, garlic bread, stuffed potatoes, entrees
President: John Rooney
Chairman of the Board: Concetta Vitale
VP: George Moran
R & D: Chuck Solemon
Quality Control: Luz Aguriie
Accounts/Marketing Director: Tim Lasater
Operations Manager: John Vitale
Plant Manager: Martin Torres
Estimated Sales:$ 10-20 Million
Number Employees: 140
Type of Packaging: Private Label
Brands:
Lola

10554 Oh, Sugar! LLC
1050 Northfield Court
Suite 125
Roswell, GA 30076   678-393-6408
Fax: 678-393-6489 866-557-8427
www.namsbits.com
cookies and candy

10555 Ohana Seafood, LLC
255 Sand Island Access Rd # 2c
Honolulu, HI 96819-2292   808-843-1844
Fax: 808-843-1844
Seafood
Vice President: Jeffrey Yee
Estimated Sales:$570,000
Number Employees: 1-4

10556 Ohio Mushroom Company
1893 N Dixie Hwy
Lima, OH 45801-3255   419-221-1721
Mushrooms

10557 Ohio Packing Company
P.O.Box 30961
Columbus, OH 43230-0961   614-239-1600
Fax: 614-237-0885 800-282-6403
cjones@ohiopacking.com
www.ohiopacking.com
Manufacturer and exporter of fresh smoked and processed ham, bacon, lunch meat, hot dogs and sausage
Manager: Carla Jones Jr
VP: Ronald Wilke
Sales: Christina Wood
VP Operations: Edward Wilke Jr
Estimated Sales:$ 20 - 50 Million
Number Employees: 100-249
Sq. footage: 75000
Type of Packaging: Consumer, Food Service, Private Label, Bulk
Brands:
BAHAMA MAMA
BRUTUS BRATS
BUCKEYE
HARVEST
POPPY'S PRIDE

10558 Ohio Processors Company
244 E 1st St
London, OH 43140-1478   740-852-9243
Fax: 740-488-2536
Processor of whipped topping and nondairy coffee creamers
President: Douglas Smith
Estimated Sales:$ 5 - 10 Million
Number Employees: 20-49
Parent Co: Instantwhip Foods
Type of Packaging: Food Service, Private Label
Brands:
Instant Whip

10559 Ohta Wafer Factory
931 Hauoli St
Honolulu, HI 96826-2655   808-949-2775

Processor of puffed rice cakes and fortune and Japanese tea cookies
President: Herb Ohta
Estimated Sales:$500,000-$1 Million
Number Employees: 1-4
Sq. footage: 3000
Type of Packaging: Consumer, Food Service
Brands:
Ohta's Senbei

10560 Oil-Dri Corporation of America
410 N Michigan Ave # 400
Chicago, IL 60611-4213   312-321-1515
          Fax: 312-321-1271   800-233-9802
          www.oildri.com
Oils
CEO: Daniel Jefrey
President: Daniel Jefrey
CEO: Daniel S Jaffee
*Estimated Sales:*1
Number Employees: 500-999
Brands:
Oil-Dri

10561 Oils of Aloha
P.O.Box 685
Waialua, HI 96791-0685   808-637-5620
          Fax: 808-637-6194   800-367-6010
          info@oilsofaloha.com   www.oilsofaloha.com
Manufactuer of Salad oils and cooking oils
Chairman/Owner: Dana Gray
President: Matthew Papania
Marketing: Barbara Gray
Plant Manager: Matthew Papania
Estimated Sales:$5-10 Million
Number Employees: 10-19
Number of Brands: 1
Sq. footage: 15000
Type of Packaging: Consumer, Food Service
Brands:
OILS OF ALOHA MACADAMIA NUT OIL

10562 Ojai Cook
149 S Barrington Avenue
Los Angeles, CA 90049-3310   310-646-5001
          Fax: 310-839-5135   886-571-1551
          Info@ojaicook.com   www.ojaicook.com
Condiments, sauces and beverages
President/CEO/Marketing Director: Joan Vogel
Brands:
Cocktail Duet
Prickly Pecans
Puckers

10563 Ojai Vineyard
P.O.Box 952
Oak View, CA 93022-0952   805-649-1674
          Fax: 805-649-4651   info@OjaiVineyard.com
          www.ojaivineyard.com
Processor of wine
Owner: Adam Tolmach
Estimated Sales:$590,000
Number Employees: 1-4
Brands:
Ojai

10564 Okahara Saimin Factory
1804 Waiola St
Honolulu, HI 96826-2698   808-949-0588
Fax: 808-949-0375   okaharasf001@hawaii.rr.com
          www.saiminfactory.com
Processor of noodles
President: Kiyoko Okahara
Estimated Sales:$1500000
Number Employees: 20-49
Type of Packaging: Consumer, Food Service

10565 Okanagan Spring Brewery
2808 27th Avenue
Vernon, BC V1T 9K4
Canada
          250-542-2337
          Fax: 250-542-7780   800-663-7037
          people@okspring.com   www.okspring.com
Processor of beer, ale and stout
COO: Richardson Knudson
CEO: John Sleeman
Marketing Director: Paul Meehan
Managing Director: Rick Knudson
Parent Co: Seeman Brewing & Malting Company
Type of Packaging: Consumer, Food Service
Brands:
Okanagan Spring
Shastebury

Sleeman
Strohs Canada

10566 Okeene Milling
P.O.Box 1567
Shawnee, OK 74802-1567   405-273-7000
          Fax: 405-273-7333
          lhammons@shawneemilling.com
          www.shawneemilling.com
Manufacturer of bulk bakery, tortilla and whole wheat flour
CEO: William L Ford
Number Employees: 20-49
Parent Co: Shawnee Milling Company
Type of Packaging: Consumer, Food Service

10567 Oklahoma City Meat
300 S Klein Ave
Oklahoma City, OK 73108-1495   405-235-3308
          Fax: 405-235-9989
Processor of beef, lamb and pork; wholesaler/distributor of chicken
President: Tommy Saunders
Estimated Sales:$ 10 - 20 Million
Number Employees: 20-49
Type of Packaging: Food Service

10568 Okuhara Foods
881 N King St
Honolulu, HI 96817-4554   808-848-0581
          Fax: 808-841-5367   okufood@aol.com
Processor of pre-packaged frozen fish including salted butterfish, salmon and shellfish
President: James N Okuhara
Vice President: Satoru Okuhara
Estimated Sales:$ 10 - 20 Million
Number Employees: 20-49
Type of Packaging: Consumer, Bulk

10569 Oland Breweries
3055 Agricola Street
Halifax, NS B3K 4G2
Canada   902-453-1867
          Fax: 902-453-3847   800-268-2337
          www.labatt.com
Processor of beer, ale, stout and lager
Marketing Director: Brent Qartermain
Number Employees: 100-249
Parent Co: Labatt Breweries
Type of Packaging: Consumer, Food Service
Brands:
Labatt
Oland

10570 Olcott Plastics
602 N 12th St
St Charles, IL 60174-1729   630-584-0555
          Fax: 630-584-5655   888-313-5277
          sales@olcottplastics.com
          www.olcottplastics.com
Manufacturer, importer and exporter of plastic containers, jars and jar closures.
President: Joe Brodner
CEO: Joseph Brodner
Sales: Troy Rusch
Account Manager: Joe Hernandez
Estimated Sales:$ 10 - 20 Million
Number Employees: 50-99
Sq. footage: 80000
Type of Packaging: Consumer, Private Label, Bulk

10571 Old 97 Manufacturing Company
2306 N 35th St
Tampa, FL 33605-4432   813-247-6677
          Fax: 813-247-6259   www.thestephanco.com
Processor of flavoring extracts and over-the-counter pharmaceuticals
Office Manager: Rita Chlau
Plant Manager: Mike Henry
Number Employees: 50-99
Parent Co: Stephan Company

10572 Old Baldy Brewing Company
271 N 2nd Ave
Upland, CA 91786-8327   909-946-1750
          Fax: 909-608-1729
Processor of seasonal beer, ale and stout
President/CEO: Bill Romero
*Estimated Sales:*Less than $500,000
Number Employees: 5-9
Type of Packaging: Consumer, Food Service
Brands:
Old Baldy

10573 Old Cavendish Products
P.O.Box 631
Cavendish, VT 05142-0631   802-226-7783
          Fax: 802-226-7783   800-536-7899
          fruitcakes@tds.net   www.cavendishfruitcake.com
Manufacturer of all natural fruitcake, mustard, herb vinegars
President: Mary Ormrod
Estimated Sales:$ .5 - 1 million
Number Employees: 1-4

10574 Old Chatham Sheepherding
155 Shaker Museum Rd
Old Chatham, NY 12136-2603   518-794-7733
          Fax: 518-794-7641   888-743-3760
          cheese@blacksheepcheese.com
          www.blacksheepcheese.com
Manufacturer of sheep's milk cheese
President/Owner: Thomas Clark
Owner: Nancy Clark
Marketing/Sales: Lorie Appleby
Kleinpeter/Cheesemaker: Benoit Mailloil
Administrative Manager: Sandra Hoehneker
Estimated Sales:$5-10 Million
Number Employees: 20-49
Number of Brands: 1
Number of Products: 14

10575 Old Colony Baking Company
42 Sherwood Ter # 7
Lake Bluff, IL 60044-2230   847-283-9292
          Fax: 847-283-9494   info@ocolony.com
          www.ocolony.com
Manufacturer of Pastries and bag cookie line
President/Owner: Jeffrey Kaufman
Vice President/Owner: Ann Kaufman
Estimated Sales:$ 1 - 3 Million
Number Employees: 1-4
Type of Packaging: Consumer, Food Service, Private Label
Brands:
ANDES CHOCOLATE MINT CHIP COOKIES
BIG TOP ANIMAL COOKIES
CHIQUITA BANANA COOKIES
DIAMOND WALNUT SHORTBREAD COOKIES
MUSSELMAN'S APPLE SAUCE COOKIES
REALEMON LEMON COOKIES

10576 Old Country Bakery
5350 Biloxi Avenue
North Hollywood, CA 91601-3531   818-838-2302
          Fax: 818-838-2307
Cakes and pastry
General Manager: Chris Meyer

10577 Old Country Cheese
5510 County Highway D
Cashton, WI 54619   888-320-9469
          Fax: 608-654-5411   info@oldcountrycheese.com
          www.oldcountrycheese.com
Cheese and jams
President: Kevin Everhart
County Chief: Michael Everhart
Estimated Sales:$ 1-2.5 Million
Number Employees: 20-49
Type of Packaging: Consumer, Private Label, Bulk
Brands:
Old Country Cheese

10578 Old Country Farms
PO Box 921
East Sandwich, MA 02537-0921   508-888-0715
          Fax: 508-833-9261   888-707-5558
          oldctyfarm@aol.com   www.oldcountyfarms.com
Manufacturer of Cranberries, fruits spreads, dried fruit and baking mixes

10579 Old Country Meat & Sausage Company
811 W Washington St
San Diego, CA 92103-1894   619-297-4301
Manufacturer of sausages
President: Manfred Spenner
CEO: Manfred Spenner
Marketing Manager: Manfred Spenner
*Estimated Sales:*Under $500,000
Number Employees: 5-9
Type of Packaging: Bulk
Brands:
Old Country

10580 Old Country Packers
308 Lincoln St
Duryea, PA 18642-1260 570-655-9608
Fax: 570-457-1678
Processor of horseradish including white and red beet, cocktail sauce, chicken wing sauce including mild, hot and honey, sauce and garlic in water and oil
President: Edwarded Orkwis
Estimated Sales: $ .5 - 1 million
Number Employees: 1-4
Sq. footage: 4000
Type of Packaging: Consumer, Food Service, Private Label
Brands:
Old Country
Town Tavern

10581 Old Credit Brewing Company
6 Queen Street W
Port Credit, ON L5H 1L4
Canada 905-271-9888
Fax: 905-274-4154
Manufacturer of amber/red ale and pilsner
President: Aldo Lista
Brewer: Orrin Besko
Number Employees: 5-9
Sq. footage: 6000
Type of Packaging: Consumer, Food Service
Brands:
OLD CREDIT

10582 Old Creek Ranch Winery
10024 Old Creek Rd
Ventura, CA 93001-1002 805-649-4132
Fax: 805-649-9293 winery@oldcreekranch.com
www.oldcreekranch.com
Manufacturer of premium wines
President: John Whitman
Winemaker: Charles Branham
Estimated Sales: Below $5 Million
Number Employees: 5-9
Number of Products: 3
Sq. footage: 4000
Type of Packaging: Private Label
Brands:
OLD CREEK RANCH WINERY

10583 Old Dominion Peanut Corporation
208 W 24th St
Norfolk, VA 23517-1355 757-622-1633
Fax: 757-624-9415 800-368-6887
odpeanuit@aol.com
Processor of candy including hard Christmas, fund raising, cashew and peanut brittle and chocolate covered and butter toffee peanuts
President: William Delchiaro
Estimated Sales: $4500000
Number Employees: 50-99
Sq. footage: 50000
Parent Co: The Virginia Food Group
Type of Packaging: Consumer, Food Service, Private Label, Bulk
Brands:
Old Dominion

10584 Old Dutch Foods
2375 Terminal Rd
Roseville, MN 55113-2577 651-633-8810
Fax: 651-633-8894 800-989-2447
customerservice@olddutchfoods.com
www.olddutchfoods.com
Snack foods including potato chips, popcorn, pretzels, salsa and dips.
President: Steve Aanenson
Estimated Sales: $ 100-500 Million
Number Employees: 250-499
Type of Packaging: Private Label
Brands:
Cocina del Norte
Dutch Crunch
Old Dutch
Ripples

10585 (HQ)Old Dutch Mustard Company
98 Cuttermill Road
Suite 260
Great Neck, NY 11021-3010 516-466-0522
Fax: 516-466-0762

Processor of mustard flour, prepared mustard, vinegar, sauce and juice
President: Paul Santich
Sales Manager: Evan Dobkins
Number Employees: 70
Sq. footage: 100000
Type of Packaging: Consumer, Food Service, Private Label, Bulk
Other Locations:
Brands:
Old Dutch

10586 Old Europe Cheese
1330 E Empire Ave
Benton Harbor, MI 49022-2018 269-925-5003
Fax: 269-925-9560 800-447-8182
www.oldeuropecheese.com
Specialty cheeses
Manager: Francious Capt
Manager: Francois Capt
Packing Manager: Scott Ness
Purchasing Manager: Sam Siriano
Estimated Sales: $ 10 -15 Million
Number Employees: 50-99
Sq. footage: 50
Type of Packaging: Private Label
Brands:
Manchego

10587 Old Fashioned Candy
6210 Cermak Rd
Berwyn, IL 60402-2322 708-788-6669
Processor of chocolate candy
Owner: Theresa Brunslik
Sales Manager: Lynn White
Estimated Sales: $500,000-$1 Million
Number Employees: 5-9
Type of Packaging: Consumer

10588 Old Fashioned Foods Inc
650 Furnace Street
PO Box 111
Mayville, WI 53050 920-387-4444
Fax: 920-387-7929 www.oldfash.com
Cheese spreads, cheese sauce, tex-mex, cheese dips, nacho cheese sauce, squeeze cheese, squeeze salsa, glass cheese spreads, cheese sticks, and aerosol and portion control pouches.
Owner/President: Bernard Youso
Chairman: Gary Youso
CFO: Gary Youso
Quality Control: Ben Lindstrom
Marketing: Bernie Youso
Sales: Jim Clark
Production/Maintenance: Cory Lenhardt
Purchasing: Kathy Emmer
Estimated Sales: $ 5-10 Million
Number Employees: 70
Brands:
Old Faishoned Foods

10589 Old Fashioned Kitchen
1045 Towbin Ave
Lakewood, NJ 08701-5931 732-364-4100
Fax: 732-905-7352 www.oldfashionedkitchen.com
Manufacturer and distributor of specialy frozen foods nationally
President: Jay Conzen
CEO: Elaine Bonugli
CFO: Joann Lemaszewski
R&D: John Kercher
Marketing: Jay Conzen
Sales: Sal Mangiapane
Public Relations: Jay Conzen
Operations: Jay Conzen
Production: Glen Chambers
Plant Manager: John Kercher
Purchasing: Joanne Lemaszewski
Estimated Sales: $ 20 - 50 Million
Number Employees: 100

10590 Old Fashioned Kitchen
PO Box 9097
Newport Beach, CA 92658-1097 949-720-7060
Fax: 732-905-7352 800-833-4635
info@oldfashionedkitchen.com
www.oldfashionedkitchen.com
Blintzes, crepes, pierogies, pancakes
Chairman: Albert Bonugli
Marketing Director: Jeff Brown
Plant Manager: John Kercher
Estimated Sales: $500,000-$1 Million
Number Employees: 1-4
Sq. footage: 31000

Type of Packaging: Food Service
Brands:
Golden
Old Fashioned Kitchen

10591 Old Fashioned Natural Products
2230 Cape Cod Way
Santa Ana, CA 92703-3582 714-835-6367
Fax: 714-835-4948 800-552-9045
www.lalifestyle.com
Processor of vitamins and herbal teas and supplements; also, custom formulations and private labeling available
President: Patricia Logsdon
VP: John Brown
Estimated Sales: $ 10 - 20 Million
Number Employees: 10-19
Sq. footage: 16000
Type of Packaging: Private Label

10592 Old Firehouse Winery
5499 Lake Rd E
Geneva, OH 44041-9425 440-466-9300
Fax: 440-466-8011 800-362-6751
info@oldfirehousewinery.com
www.oldfirehousewinery.com
Ohio wines
Owner: Don Woodward
Estimated Sales: $1-$3 Million
Number Employees: 1-4
Type of Packaging: Consumer

10593 Old Home Foods
370 University Ave W
St Paul, MN 55103-2097 651-312-8900
Fax: 651-312-8901 800-628-8700
info@oldhomefoods.com
www.oldhomefoods.com
Manufacturer of cultured dairy products like cottage cheese, sour cream, yogurt, dips and salsa
President: Geoff Murphy
President: Geoff Murphy
Estimated Sales: $ 20 - 50 Million
Number Employees: 100-249
Type of Packaging: Consumer, Food Service, Private Label, Bulk
Brands:
Old Home

10594 Old House Vineyards
18351 Corkys Ln
Culpeper, VA 22701-4413 540-423-1032
Fax: 540-423-1320 info@oldhousevineyards.com
www.oldhousevineyards.com
Manufacturer of Wines
Owner: Allyson Kearney
Winemaker: Doug Fabbioli
Estimated Sales: $ 3 - 5 Million
Number Employees: 5-9

10595 Old Kentucky Hams
PO Box 443
Cynthiana, KY 41031-0443 859-234-5015
Fax: 859-234-5015
Country hams and bacon
President: Nancy Hisle
Plant Manager: Elizabeth Hunt
Estimated Sales: $1-4.9 Million
Number Employees: 1-4
Sq. footage: 1
Type of Packaging: Private Label
Brands:
Old Kentucky Hams
Traditional Kentucky

10596 Old Mansion Foods
P.O.Box 1838
Petersburg, VA 23805-0838 804-862-9889
Fax: 804-861-8816 800-476-1877
elaina-t@oldmansion.com www.oldmansion.com
Importer and processor of quality spices, seasonings, coffee and teas.
President: Dale Patton
Sales: Tom Mullen
Plant Manager: Kevin Laffoon
Purchasing Director: Wendy Bryant
Number Employees: 20-49
Type of Packaging: Consumer, Food Service, Private Label, Bulk
Brands:
Festiva
Grill Select
Old Mansion
Southern Classic

10597 Old Monmouth Peanut Brittle
627 Park Ave
Freehold, NJ 07728-2351   732-462-1311
Fax: 732-462-6820 sales@oldmonmouth.com
www.oldmonmouthcandies.com
Candy and confections
President: Hal Gunther
Estimated Sales: Below $ 5 Million
Number Employees: 5-9
Brands:
Old Monmouth

10598 Old Neighborhood Foods
37 Waterhill St
Lynn, MA 01905-2134   781-592-0014
Fax: 781-595-7523
Processor of meat and provisions including beef, lamb and pork
Owner: Tom Demarkes
Vice President: John Demakes
Estimated Sales: $50 Million
Number Employees: 100-249
Type of Packaging: Food Service
Brands:
Pleasant

10599 Old Orchard Brands
1991 12 Mile Rd NW
Sparta, MI 49345-9757   616-887-1745
Fax: 616-887-8210 www.oldorchardjuice.com
Previously known as Apple Valley International. A manufacturer of frozen fruit juices including apple
President: Mark Saur
VP Sales/Marketing: Michael McDonald
Estimated Sales: $ 20 - 50 Million
Number Employees: 50-99
Type of Packaging: Consumer

10600 Old Ranchers Canning Company
P.O.Box 458
Upland, CA 91785-0458   909-982-8895
Fax: 909-949-2328
Processor of canned beans, stew, chili, broths and meat and nonmeat soups
President: Donald Graber
Estimated Sales: $ 20 - 50 Million
Number Employees: 50-99
Type of Packaging: Private Label

10601 Old Rip Van Winkle Distillery
2843 Brownsboro Rd # 208
Louisville, KY 40206-1292   502-897-9113
Fax: 502-896-9989
jvanwinkle@oldripvanwinkle.com
www.oldripvanwinkle.com
Manufacturer of bourbon whiskey
Owner: Julian Van Winkle Iii III
Estimated Sales: $1-2.5 Million
Number Employees: 1-4
Brands:
Old Rip Van Wrinkle

10602 Old Sacramento Popcorn Company
1026 2nd St # B
Sacramento, CA 95814-3256   916-446-1980
Fax: 916-442-2676 ospc@concentric.net
www.oldsacramentolivinghistory.com
Processor and exporter of popcorn
Owner: Jim Scott
Estimated Sales: Less than $150,000
Number Employees: 1-4

10603 Old Salt Seafood Company
43 Celestial Drive
Narragansett, RI 02882-1150   401-783-5770
Fax: 401-783-6730
Seafood
President: Ken Loud

10604 Old South Winery
65 S Concord Ave
Natchez, MS 39120-6806   601-445-9924
Fax: 601-442-1215 mailus@newu.net
www.newu.net/
Wines
Owner: Scott O Galbreth Iii
Co-Owner: Edeen Galbreath
Winemaker: Scott Gallbreath III
Estimated Sales: $500,000-$1 Million
Number Employees: 1-4
Type of Packaging: Private Label

Brands:
Old South Winery
Old South Muscadine

10605 Old Tavern Food Products
P.O.Box 438
Waukesha, WI 53187-0438   262-542-5301
Fax: 262-542-5676 888-425-1788
www.oldtaverncheese.com
Cheese, gift packs
President: Jill Strong
VP: Gail Strong
Estimated Sales: $500,000-$1 Million
Number Employees: 5-9
Type of Packaging: Private Label, Bulk
Brands:
Old Tavern Club Cheese

10606 Old Town Coffee & Tea Company
1019 Hillen St
Baltimore, MD 21202-4197   410-752-1229
Fax: 410-528-0369 support@eaglecoffee.com
www.eaglecoffee.com
Processor and importer of coffee and tea
Owner: Nick Constantine
Estimated Sales: Below $ 5 Million
Number Employees: 20-49
Sq. footage: 40000
Type of Packaging: Food Service, Private Label, Bulk

10607 Old Tyme Mill Company
1517 S Kolmar Avenue
21
Chicago, IL 60623-1090   773-521-9484
Fax: 773-521-9486
Waffle, pancake and breading mix
President: John Pontikes
Treasurer: Dorothy Pontikes
Estimated Sales: $ 5-9.9 Million
Number Employees: 5

10608 Old Wine Cellar
4411 220th Trl
Amana, IA 52203-8035   319-622-3116
Fax: 319-622-6162 www.travelenvoy.com/wine
Wines
President: Les Aackermin
Estimated Sales: $ 1-2.5 Million
Number Employees: '5-9
Brands:
Old Wine Cellar

10609 Old Wisconsin Food Products
P.O.Box 8639
Prospect Heights, IL 60070-8639   708-798-0900
Fax: 708-798-3178 800-621-0868
www.buddig.com
Sausage
President: John Buddig
CFO: Roger Buddig
Plant Manager: Charles Belter
Estimated Sales: $200,000
Parent Co: Carl Buddig & Company
Brands:
Carl Budding
Old Wisconsin

10610 Old Wisconsin Sausage Company
5030 Playbird Rd
Sheboygan, WI 53083-1878   920-458-4304
Fax: 920-458-2716 800-558-7840
sales@oldwisconsin.com
www.oldwisconsin.com
Sausage
President: Tom Buddig
Manager: Bob Gielissen
Plant Manager: Bob Gielissen
Estimated Sales: $ 20-50 Million
Number Employees: 100-249
Type of Packaging: Consumer
Brands:
Ends and Curls
Old Wisconsin Mug

10611 Old World Bakery
6210 Eastern Avenue
Baltimore, MD 21224-2906   513-931-1411
Fax: 513-931-3560 owb@fuse.net
www.oldworldbakery.com
Processor of natural breads
Founder: Odette Skally
Public Relations: Cheryl Deleon
Number Employees: 5-9

10612 Old World Spices & Seasonings
4601 Emanuel Cleaver Ii Blvd
Kansas City, MO 64130-2366   816-861-0400
Fax: 816-861-7073 800-241-0070
customerservice@oldworldspices.com
www.oldworldspices.com
Seasoning, spice and sauce packaging
Owner: John Junge
Estimated Sales: $ 1-5 Million
Number Employees: 20-49
Brands:
Old World Creations
Party Creations
Soups For One

10613 Olde Colony Bakery
1391 Stuart Engals Blvd # B
Mt Pleasant, SC 29464-3377   843-216-3232
Fax: 843-216-5553 800-722-9932
OCBenne@aol.com www.oldecolonybakery.com
Manufacturer of gourmet cookies and benne seed wafers
Owner: Peter Rix
Owner: Sheila Rix
Estimated Sales: Less than $500,000
Number Employees: 5-9
Brands:
OLDE COLONY

10614 Olde Country Confections
100 York Street
Gettysburg, PA 17325-1932   717-337-9971
Fax: 717-337-9971 oldecountry@earthlink.net
www.oldecountryconfections.com
Manufacturer of hand made chocolates and other confections

10615 Olde Heurich Brewing Company
1307 New Hampshire Avenue NW
Washington, DC 20036-1507   202-333-2313
Fax: 202-333-9198 lager@foggybottom.com
www.foggybottom.com
Beer
President: Gary Heurich
Estimated Sales: Below $ 5 Million
Number Employees: 5
Brands:
Foggy Bottom Ale
Foggy Bottom Lager
Foggy Bottom Porter
Olde Georgetown Beer
Olde Heurich
Senate Beer

10616 Olde Tyme Food Corporation
PO Box 384
East Longmeadow, MA 01028-0384   413-525-4101
Fax: 413-525-3621 800-356-6533
oldetyme@samnet.net www.oldetymefoods.com
Processor and exporter of snack foods including candy apples, cotton candy, waffles, waffle cones, peanuts, etc.; manufacturer and exporter of concession stand supplies and snack food making machinery including hot dogs
President: David Baker
Sales Director: David Wedderspoon
Estimated Sales: $ 5 - 10 Million
Number Employees: 25
Sq. footage: 25000
Type of Packaging: Consumer, Food Service, Private Label, Bulk
Brands:
Olde Tyme
Ole Style Peanut Butter

10617 Olde Tyme Mercantile
1127 Mesa View Drive
Arroyo Grande, CA 93420-6542   805-489-7991
Fax: 805-481-5578
kevin@oldetymemercantile.com
www.oldetymemercantile.com
Processor of gourmet products including olives, pickles, salad dressings, mustards, mayonnaise and candies
President: Larry Williams
CEO: Kevin Keim
Propietor: Diane Keim
Number Employees: 10-19
Sq. footage: 2000
Type of Packaging: Consumer, Private Label
Brands:
Scully
Wah Maker

10618 Olds Products Company
10700 88th Ave
Pleasant Prairie, WI 53158-2300   262-947-5516
Fax: 262-947-3517   800-233-8064
eamen@oldsfitz.com
Manufacturers prepared mustard and specialty mustard blends and is also the largest bulk ingredient mustard manufacturer.
President: Robert Remien
VP: Timothy McAvoy
Estimated Sales: $6500000
Number Employees: 20-49
Parent Co: Olds Products Company
Type of Packaging: Consumer, Food Service, Private Label, Bulk
Brands:
Koops

10619 Ole Salty's of Rockford
3131 Summerdale Ave
Rockford, IL 61101-3422   815-963-3355
Fax: 815-963-6855 www.olesaltys.com
Potato chips
Manager: Troy Wedeikand
Estimated Sales: Below $ 5 Million
Number Employees: 1-4
Brands:
Ole Salty's

10620 Ole Smoky Candy Kitchen
744 Parkway
Gatlinburg, TN 37738-3206   865-436-4886
Fax: 865-436-0268
Processor of candy
President: Esther J Dych
Estimated Sales: $ 5 - 10 Million
Number Employees: 50-99
Type of Packaging: Consumer

10621 Olive Oil Factory
76 Westbury Park Rd # 101e
Watertown, CT 06795-2780   860-945-9549
Fax: 860-945-8662   info@theoliveoilfactory.com
www.theoliveoilfactory.com
Private labeler of oils including extra virgin olive, flavored and dipping; also, balsamic vinegar
President: David Miller
Estimated Sales: $350,000
Number Employees: 5-9
Sq. footage: 5000
Type of Packaging: Consumer, Food Service, Private Label

10622 Oliver Egg Products
9422 Hungarytown Road
Crewe, VA 23930-4125   804-645-9406
Fax: 804-645-7429   800-525-3447
Processor of frozen and refrigerated egg whites, whole eggs, yolks and scrambled egg mix
Owner: Bill Oliver
Type of Packaging: Food Service, Bulk

10623 Oliver Wine Company
8024 N State Road 37
Bloomington, IN 47404-9449   812-876-5800
Fax: 812-876-9309   800-258-2783
www.oliverwinery.com
Wines
President: William Oliver
Marketing Director: Sarah Villwock
Vice President: Kathleen Oliver
CFO: Kathleen Oliver
Estimated Sales: $ 10-20 Million
Number Employees: 50-99
Brands:
Camelot Mead
Oliver

10624 Oliver Winery
8024 N State Road 37
Bloomington, IN 47404-9449   812-876-5800
Fax: 812-876-9309   800-258-2783
woliver@oliverwinery.com
www.oliverwinery.com
Producer of wines including dry (Sauvignon Blanc, Chardonel, Merlot, Zinfandel, Cabernet Sauvignon, etc.); semi-dry (Gew☐rztraminer, Riesling, Traminette, etc.), and semi-sweet (Harvest Flavors, Catawba, Muscat Canelli, Camelot MeadVidal Blanc Ice Wine, etc.) varieties.
Co-Owner/Winemaker/Vineyard Management: Bill Oliver
Co-Owner/General Manager: Kathleen Oliver

10625 Olives & Foods Inc
13903 NW 67th Avenue
Suite 430
Hialeah, FL 33014-2939   305-821-3444
Processor, importer and exporter of Spanish olives, olive oil, capers, cocktail onions
President: Francisco Orta
VP: Fernando Gazmuri
Sales Director: Andres Reyes
Operations Manager: Ivonne Gazmuri
Number Employees: 1-4
Sq. footage: 800
Parent Co: Acyco, Aceitunas y Conservas S.A.L.
Type of Packaging: Consumer, Food Service, Private Label, Bulk
Brands:
Acyco
Alisa

10626 Olivia's Croutons
1423 North St
New Haven, VT 05472-2035   802-482-2222
Fax: 802-453-7722   888-425-3080
fwc@oliviascroutons.com
www.oliviascroutons.com
Manufacturer of all natural specialty croutons: Butter and garlic, parmesan pepper, vermont cheddar and dill, multi grain with garlic, and gazapach lowfat croutons. Also roasted onion tostini and lemon parsley tostini
President: Francie Caccavo
Estimated Sales: Below $5 Million
Number Employees: 5-9
Type of Packaging: Consumer, Food Service, Private Label, Bulk

10627 Olivier's Candies
2828 54th Ave SE
Calgary, AB T2C 0A7
Canada   403-266-6028
Fax: 403-266-6029   rjefferys@oliviers.ca
Manufacturer of chocolate, hard candy, brittles, barks
President: Wally Marcolin
Secretary: Rick Jeffrey
Number Employees: 10-19
Type of Packaging: Consumer, Bulk

10628 Olmarc Packaging Company
Ste 1100
350 N La Salle Dr
Chicago, IL 60654-1576   708-562-2000
Fax: 708-562-9044   ghansen@olmarc.com
www.olmarc.com
Custom contract packager of cereals, pastas, bakery mixes, confectionery products, etc
CEO: Kenneth Machetti
Director Sales: Laura Grobert
Estimated Sales: $56000000
Number Employees: 900
Type of Packaging: Consumer, Food Service

10629 Olsen Fish Company
2115 N 2nd St
Minneapolis, MN 55411-2204   612-287-0838
Fax: 612-287-8761   800-882-0212
lutefisk@olsenfish.com   www.olsenfish.com
Manufacturef of Lutfisk and pickled herring
President: Chris Dorff
Estimated Sales: $ 3 - 5 Million
Number Employees: 10-19
Type of Packaging: Bulk
Brands:
OLSEN

10630 Olson Livestock & Seed
31921 Rd 711
Haigler, NE 69030-4006   308-297-3283
Fax: 308-297-3284
Processor of popcorn
Owner: Cliff Olson
Owner: Scott Olson
Owner: Steve Olson
Estimated Sales: $ 3 - 5 Million
Number Employees: 1-4

10631 Olson Locker
917 Winnebago Ave
Fairmont, MN 56031-3614   507-238-2563
Fax: 507-238-2564
Processor of meat and meat products
President: Mark Olson

Estimated Sales: $460,000
Number Employees: 1-4
Type of Packaging: Consumer

10632 Olymel
700 Rue Croisetiere
Iberville, QC J2X 4H7
Canada   450-347-1900
Fax: 514-858-5794
Processor, importer and exporter of fresh and frozen chicken, turkey and pork
General Manager: Paul Noiseux
Number Employees: 1,000-4,999
Parent Co: Cooperative Federee of Quebec
Type of Packaging: Bulk
Brands:
Flamingo
Galco

10633 Olympia Candies
11606 Pearl Rd
Strongville, OH 44136   440-572-7747
Fax: 440-572-1819   800-574-7747
sales@olympiacandy.com
www.olympiacandy.com
gourmet treats
President/Owner: Robert McGrath
VP: Celia McGrath
Number Employees: 25

10634 Olympia Frosted Foods
2300 Friendly Grove Road NE
Olympia, WA 98506   360-943-2210
Processor, wholesaler and distributor of frozen fruits and vegetables. Contract Packaging available
Owner/President: Kaiser Huber
Owner/CEO: Caroline Huber
Number Employees: 1-4
Sq. footage: 5400
Type of Packaging: Consumer, Bulk

10635 Olympia International
2166 Spring Creek Road
Belvidere, IL 61008-9507   815-547-5972
Fax: 815-547-5973
Processor, exporter and importer of pickles, mushrooms, horseradish, sweet marinated peppers, beets and salads
President: Greg Bodak
Estimated Sales: $200,000
Number Employees: 1

10636 Olympia Oyster Company
1042 SE Bloomfield Rd
Shelton, WA 98584-7744   360-426-3354
Fax: 360-427-0122   info@olympiaoyster.com
www.olympiaoyster.com
Processor of oysters and clams; also, oyster soup bases
President: Tim McMillin
Estimated Sales: $1500000
Number Employees: 20-49
Type of Packaging: Consumer, Food Service
Brands:
Puget Sound

10637 Olympic Cellars
255410 Highway 101
Port Angeles, WA 98362-9200   360-452-0160
Fax: 360-452-3782   info@olympiccellars.com
www.olympiccellars.com
Wines
Co-Owner: Kathy Charlton
Co-Owner: Molly Rivard
Co-Owner: Libby Sweetser
Winemaker: Benoit Murat
Estimated Sales: Below $ 5 Million
Number Employees: 5-9
Type of Packaging: Private Label
Brands:
Olympic Cellars

10638 Olympic Coffee & Roasting
4907 119th Ave SE
Bellevue, WA 98006-2747   206-244-8305
Fax: 206-244-8323   888-244-8313
olympicscoffee@juno.com
www.olympiccoffee.com
Coffee
Director: Robert Doxsie
Estimated Sales: $ 5 - 10 Million
Number Employees: 5-9
Brands:
Olympic Coffee

10639 Olympic Food Products
519 W Spraker Street
Kokomo, IN 46901-2134 765-452-4008
　　　Fax: 765-452-4086 800-445-6923
Processor of frozen entrees including breaded meat,
breaded veal, prepared pork, stuffed peppers, mush-
rooms, corn dogs and onion rings
　　President: Gary Roberts
　　Plant Manager: Mike Downy
Number Employees: 50-99
Type of Packaging: Consumer, Food Service

10640 Olympic Foods
5625 W Thorpe Rd
Spokane, WA 99224-5309 509-455-8059
　　　Fax: 509-455-8329 salesinfo@olyfoods.com
　　　　　　　　www.olyfoods.com
Processor and exporter of chilled ready-to-drink
fruit juice
　　President: Doug Koffinke
　　Marketing Director: Lindi Larned
　　Public Relations: Teff Erpenbach
　　Purchasing Manager: Brian Steckler
Estimated Sales: $25000000
Number Employees: 50-99
Sq. footage: 87000
Type of Packaging: Consumer, Food Service, Pri-
　　vate Label
Brands:
　　Albertson's
　　Citrus Sunshine
　　Dairyworld
　　Minute Maid
　　Newman's Own
　　Tree Top
　　Washington Natural
　　Western Family

10641 Olympic Specialty Foods
1601 Military Road
Buffalo, NY 14217-1205 716-874-0771
　　　Fax: 716-876-2171
　　info@mtolympusgreeksalad.com
　　www.mtolympusgreeksalad.com
Gourmet foods
　　President: Terry Bechakas
Estimated Sales: Below $ 5 Million
Number Employees: 50

10642 Omaha Meat Processors
6016 Grover St
Omaha, NE 68106-4358 402-554-1965
　　　Fax: 402-554-0224 omahameats@aol.com
Processor, exporter and packer of beef and pork; im-
porter of beef trimmings
　　President: Dave Kousgaard
Estimated Sales: $ 10 - 20 Million
Number Employees: 20-49
Sq. footage: 10000
Type of Packaging: Food Service

10643 Omaha Steaks International
P.O.Box 3300
Omaha, NE 68103-0300 402-597-3000
　　　Fax: 402-597-8252 800-562-0500
　　custserv@omahasteaks.com
　　　　www.omahasteaks.com
Processor, packer and exporter of portion control
meats including sausage, steak, veal and poultry
　　President: Bruce Simon
　　Chairman/CEO: Alan Simon
　　Executive VP: Frede Simon
Number Employees: 250-499
Type of Packaging: Consumer, Food Service
Brands:
　　Omaha Steaks International

10644 Omanga Ice Cream Company
547 Manida St
Bronx, NY 10474-6821 718-617-5922
　　　Fax: 718-617-5927 800-494-6477
Ice cream
　　President: Tony Mohamed
　　General Manager: Robert Haberman
Estimated Sales: $ 10 Million
Number Employees: 20-49
Sq. footage: 12500
Brands:
　　Crab Busters Ice Cream
　　La Salle Ice Cream

10645 Omanhene Cocoa Bean Company
P.O.Box 22
Milwaukee, WI 53201-0022 414-744-8780
　　　Fax: 414-744-8786 800-588-2462
　　topbean@omanhene.com www.omanhene.com
Manufacturer of Hot cocoa mixes, chocolate
　　President: Steven Wallace
Estimated Sales: Below $5 Million
Number Employees: 10-19
Number of Brands: 1
Number of Products: 5
Type of Packaging: Consumer, Private Label, Bulk
Brands:
　　OMANHENE COCOA

10646 Omar Coffee Company
41 Commerce Ct
Newington, CT 06111-2246 860-667-8889
　　　Fax: 860-667-8883 800-394-6627
　　　　info@omarcoffee.com
　　　www.omarcoffeecompany.com
Manufacturer of coffee carts and roasted coffee and
tea
　　Owner: Steve Costas
Estimated Sales: $30,900,000
Number Employees: 20-49
Sq. footage: 30000
Brands:
　　Omar Coffee
　　Omar Flavored Coffee
　　Omar's Gourmet Coffee

10647 Omega Foods
PO Box 21256
Eugene, OR 97402-0402 541-349-0731
　　　Fax: 541-349-0435 800-200-2356
　　info@omegafoods.net www.omegafoods.net
Manufacturer of salmon, tuna, mahi mahi burgers
　　President/Owner: Patrick Sullivan
　　Director Marketing/Administration: Lisa Baker
　　Sales: Lori Johansen
　　Operations: Carl Nelson
　　Plant Manager: Dana Davis
Estimated Sales: $500,000
Number Employees: 9
Number of Brands: 1
Number of Products: 3
Type of Packaging: Consumer, Food Service, Bulk
Brands:
　　OMEGA FOODS
　　OMEGA FOODS SALMON BURGERS
　　OMEGA FOODS TUNA BURGERS

10648 Omega Nutrition
6505 Aldrich Rd
Bellingham, WA 98226 360-384-1238
　　　Fax: 360-384-0700 800-661-3529
　　　　info@omeganutrition.com
　　　　www.omeganutrition.com
Unrefined organic oils
　　Owner: Bob Walbert
　　Marketing Director: Triss Dankin
　　Vice President: Robert Gaffney
　　Co-Founder: Bob Walberg
　　Operations Manager: Andrew Lyman
Estimated Sales: $ 5-10 Million
Number Employees: 20-49
Type of Packaging: Private Label
Brands:
　　Coconut Oil
　　Orange Flax Oil Blend
　　Pumpkin Seed Oil
　　Virgin Coconut Oil
　　Virgin Coconut Oil

10649 Omega Produce Company
P.O.Box 277
Nogales, AZ 85628-0277 520-281-0410
　　　Fax: 520-281-1010 pbomega1@aol.com
　　　　www.omegaproduceco.com
Produce
　　President: George Gotsis
　　Marketing Manager: Nick Gotsis
Brands:
　　Omega

10650 Omega Protein
2105 Citywest Blvd # 500
Houston, TX 77042-2838 713-623-0060
　　　Fax: 713-940-6122 877-866-3423
　　hq@omegaproteininc.com
　　www.omegaproteininc.com
Processor and exporter of menhaden oil for poultry,
red meat and fish
　　President: Joseph L Von Rosenberg III
　　CEO: Joseph L Von Rosenberg
　　Technical Coordinator: Brian Langdon
　　Senior Director Technology: Jane Crowther
Estimated Sales: $117926000
Number Employees: 500-999

10651 (HQ)Omni-Pak Industries
12151 Monarch Street
Garden Grove, CA 92841-2927 714-899-3100
　　　Fax: 714-899-3114
Processor of powdered drinks including diet, muscle
building and fiber
　　VP Sales: Marshall Hugo

10652 Omstead Foods Ltd
5500 North Service Road
10th Floor
Burlington, ON L7L 6W6
Canada 905-315-8883
　　　Fax: 905-315-8493
Processor of breaded and battered cheese, onion
rings and fish including cod, haddock, perch, smelt
and shrimp; also, IQF vegetables, stuffed peppers,
potatoes, peaches, etc.; importer of IQF vegetables
and mushrooms
　　President: Carl Sparkes
　　Marketing Director: Blair Hyslop
　　Sales Director: Eric Longual
　　Sales: Rick Bremner
　　Operations Manager: Mark Tullio
　　Plant Manager: Helari Ansari
Number Employees: 500-999
Parent Co: Snowcrest Packers
Type of Packaging: Consumer, Food Service, Pri-
　　vate Label, Bulk

10653 On Site Gas Systems Inc
35 Budney Rd
Newington, CT 06111-5133 860-667-8888
　　　Fax: 860-667-2222 888-748-3429
　　info@onsitegas.com www.onsitegas.com
On Site Gas designs and manufacturers PSA, mem-
brane and combustion based oxygen and nitrogen
gas generation systems. Applications within the
food industry utilizing food and beverage nitrogen
include that of: beveragemixing/dispensing; coffee
producers/packers; fruit orchards/storage; perishable
transportation; winemakers; and kiln/grain drying.
　　President/Founder: Frank Hursey
　　CEO: Guy Hatch
　　Chief Engineer: Sanh Phan
　　Vice President Sales: Bob Wolff
　　Vice President Manufacturing: Sean Haggerty

10654 On the Verandah
1536 Franklin Rd
Highlands, NC 28741-8557 828-526-2338
　　　Fax: 828-526-4132 otv1@ontheverandah.com
　　　　www.ontheverandah.com
Manufactuer of Sauces
　　Executive Chef: Andrew Figel
　　General Manager: Marlene Figel
Estimated Sales: $300,000-500,000
Number Employees: 10-19
Type of Packaging: Food Service, Bulk
Brands:
　　ALAN'S MANIAC HOT SAUCE

10655 (HQ)On-Cor Foods Products
627 Landwehr Rd
Northbrook, IL 60062-2352 847-205-1040
　　　Fax: 847-205-9592 www.on-cor.com
Processor of frozen foods including chicken and
noodles, hamburgers, lasagna, meat balls, stuffed
peppers, stew, turkey and dumplings
　　President: Howard Friend
　　Controller: John Statis
　　Senior VP: Howard Leafstone
Estimated Sales: $5.20 Million
Number Employees: 10-19
Type of Packaging: Consumer, Food Service
Brands:
　　On-Cor Frozen Entrees

10656 Onalaska Brewing
248 Burchett Road
Onalaska, WA 98570-9405 360-978-4253
Beer
　　Owner: David Moorehead
Estimated Sales: Under $500,000
Number Employees: 1-4

10657 Once Again Nut Butter
P.O.Box 429
Nunda, NY 14517-0429   585-468-2535
Fax: 585-468-5995   888-800-8075
info@onceagainnutbutter.com
www.onceagainnutbutter.com
Processor, importer and exporter of certified organic peanut butter, nut and seed butters and roasted and raw nuts; processor of honey
    Owner: Sandi Alexander
    Sales Director: Mark LaRussa
Estimated Sales: $6200000
Number Employees: 20-49
Type of Packaging: Consumer, Food Service, Private Label, Bulk
Brands:
    Dawes Hill
    Dawes Hill Honey
    Once Again Nut Butter

10658 One Source
300 Baker Ave
Concord, MA 01742-2131   978-318-4300
Fax: 978-318-4690   800-554-5501
Support@onesource.com   www.onesource.com
Seasonings, spices
    President: Philip J Garlick
    VP Marketing: John Brewer
    Sr. VP Global Sales: Philip Garlick
    Accountant: Jason Way
Estimated Sales: $ 1-2.5 Million
Number Employees: 100-249

10659 One Vineyard and Winery
3268 Ehlers Ln
St Helena, CA 94574-9657   707-963-1123
Fax: 707-963-1123 watgongg@aol.com
Table wines
    President: George Watson
Estimated Sales: Less than $500,000
Number Employees: 1-4
Type of Packaging: Private Label

10660 One World Enterprises
1401 Westwood Blvd
Suite 200
Los Angeles, CA 90024   310-802-4220
Fax: 310-477-7077   888-663-2626
www.onenaturalexperience.com
nutritional beverages

10661 Ono Cones of Hawaii
98-723 Kuahao Pl # B3
Pearl City, HI 96782-3103   808-487-8690
Fax: 808-486-5292
Ice cream cones
    Owner: Wayne Howard
    Marketing Manager: Colleen Howard
    Operations Manager: Larry Howard
Estimated Sales: $500,000
Number Employees: 1-4
Brands:
    Ono Cones

10662 Onoway Custom Packers
PO Box 509
Onoway, AB T0E 1V0
Canada
    780-967-2727
Fax: 780-967-2727
Processor of fresh and frozen beef, pork, lamb and wild game including ostrich and bison
    President: David Skinner
Number Employees: 5-9
Type of Packaging: Consumer, Food Service, Private Label, Bulk

10663 Ontario Foods Exports
1200 Aerowood Drive
Unit 14 & 15
Mississauga, ON N1G 4Y2
Canada
    519-826-3768
Fax: 519-826-3460   888-466-2372
karen.edwards@omaf.gov.on.ca
www.omaf.gov.on.ca
Dehydrated and packaged food mixes
    President: David Clarke
    Export Marketing Officer: Diana Campbell
Brands:
    Ontario Foods

10664 Ontario Pork
655 Southgate Drive
Guelph, ON N1G 5G6
Canada
    519-767-4600
Fax: 519-829-1769   877-668-7675
krobbins@ontariopork.on.ca
www.ontariopork.on.ca
Processor of fresh pork
    Executive Director: Jack Silbar
    Director Financial/Operational Services: Lloyd Bauemhuber
    Director Communications/Consumer Mrktg: Keith Robbins
    Director Sales/Logistics: Andrew Marks
Number Employees: 50-99
Type of Packaging: Consumer, Food Service
Brands:
    Ontario Pork

10665 Ontario Produce Company
44 SE 9th Ave
Ontario, OR 97914-0880   541-889-6485
Fax: 541-889-7823 bob@ontarioproduce.net
www.ontarioproduce.us
Manufacturer of red, yellow, red and white onions; warehouse providing dry storage for onions
    President and CEO: Robert A Komoto
    General Manager & Sales: Bob Komoto
    Office Manager & Transportation: Janet Komoto
    Shed Foreman: Arturo Rodriguez
    Inspector: Alan Lovitt
Estimated Sales: $5-10 Million
Number Employees: 10 to 49
Sq. footage: 40000
Type of Packaging: Consumer, Food Service, Private Label, Bulk
Brands:
    A BRAND
    FOPPIANO
    FOX MOUNTAIN
    GOLDEN BIRD
    REAL WEST
    RIVERSIDE
    RODEO
    SILVER SPUR
    WOWIE!

10666 Oogie's Snacks LLC
1932 W 33rd Avenue
Denver, CO 80211   303-455-2107
Fax: 303-496-0153 comments@oogiesnacks.com
www.oogiesnacks.com
flavored gourmet popcorn
Number Employees: 3

10667 Oorganik
PO Box 37305
Houston, TX 77237-7305   281-240-7992
Fax: 281-240-2304
Health and dietetics foods
    President: N Peabody
Estimated Sales: Under $500,000
Number Employees: 1-4

10668 Optima Wine Cellars
P.O.Box 1691
Healdsburg, CA 95448-1691   707-431-8222
Fax: 707-431-7828 info@optimawinery.com
www.optimawinecellars.com
Wines
    Owner/Winemaker: Mike Duffy
    Owner: Nicol Duffy
Estimated Sales: Below $ 5 Million
Number Employees: 1-4
Brands:
    Optima

10669 Optimal Nutrients
1163 Chess Dr # F
Foster City, CA 94404-1119   707-528-1800
Fax: 707-349-1686 timl@optinutri.com
www.optimalnutrients.com
Processor, importer and exporter of finished retail vitamins and supplements including royal jelly, beta carotene, essential fatty acids, etc
    President: Tim Lally
    VP: Darlene Angeli
Estimated Sales: $500,000-$1 Million
Number Employees: 5-9
Sq. footage: 5000
Parent Co: Pegasus Corp

10670 Optimum Nutrition
1756 Industrial Road
Walterboro, SC 29488-9368   843-538-7937
Fax: 843-538-3765   800-763-3444
Manufacturer of sports drinks; wholesaler/distributor of vitamins and supplements
    VP Operations: Bob Baily
    Director Customer Service: Tammie Dew
Estimated Sales: Less than $500,000
Number Employees: 1-4
Brands:
    AMERICAN BODY BUILDING
    OPTIMUM NUTRITION
    SCIENCE FOODS

10671 Opus One
P.O.Box 6
Oakville, CA 94562-0006   707-944-9442
Fax: 707-948-2496   800-292-6787
info@opusonewinery.com
www.opusonewinery.com
Wines
    Manager: David Pearson
    Director Sales/Marketing: Scotty Barbour
    Winemaker: Timothy Mondavi
Estimated Sales: Below $ 5 Million
Number Employees: 20-49
Brands:
    Opus One

10672 OraLabs
2901 S Tejon St
Englewood, CO 80110-1345   303-783-9499
Fax: 303-783-5759   800-290-0577
custsrv@oralabs.com   www.oralabs.com
Breath drops, sour drops and lip balm
    President: Gary Schlatter
    CFO: Ret Jordon
    R & D: Rajendra Agarwal
    Director Sales/Marketing: Roger Casing
    Director International Sales: Doug Kinney
Estimated Sales: $ 5-9.9 Million
Number Employees: 100-249
Brands:
    Leshables

10673 Orange Bakery
17751 Cowan
Irvine, CA 92614-6064   949-863-1377
Fax: 949-863-1932
Processor of frozen dough and baked pastries
    President: Shigeo Ueki
    Marketing/Sales Manager: Joe Galasso
    Production Manager: Truong Hiep
Estimated Sales: $26027689
Number Employees: 50-99
Parent Co: Rheon Automatic Machinery
Type of Packaging: Consumer, Food Service, Private Label, Bulk

10674 Orange Bakery
13400 Reese Blvd W
Huntersville, NC 28078-7925   704-875-3003
Fax: 704-875-3006
Processor of frozen dough products including bread, croissants and pastries
    Plant Manager: Nori Wakita
Estimated Sales: $ 5 - 10 Million
Number Employees: 20-49
Parent Co: Rheon Automatic Machinery
Type of Packaging: Consumer, Food Service

10675 Orange Bang
13115 Telfair Ave
Sylmar, CA 91342-3574   818-833-1000
www.orangebang.com
Processor of fountain and fruit syrups and fruit beverage concentrates
    President: David Fox
Estimated Sales: $6900000
Number Employees: 20-49
Sq. footage: 33000
Type of Packaging: Consumer, Food Service

10676 Orange Cove Sanger Citrus Association
180 South Ave
Orange Cove, CA 93646-9447   559-626-4453
Fax: 559-626-7357
Manufacturer, exporter and packer of oranges
    Manager: Kevin Severns
    General Manager: Jack Cone
Estimated Sales: $50-100 Million
Number Employees: 100-249

Type of Packaging: Consumer, Food Service
Brands:
   ASSURANCE
   LIVEWIRE
   ORDER
   POM POM

10677 Orange Peel Enterprises
2183 Ponce De Leon Cir
Vero Beach, FL 32960-5337   772-562-2766
    Fax: 772-562-9848 800-643-1210
    info@greensplus.com www.greensplus.com
Formulator, processor and exporter of supplements
   President: Jude Deauville
   Director National Sales/Marketing: Todd
   Westover
Estimated Sales: $ 3.5 Million
Number Employees: 20-49
Sq. footage: 15000
Type of Packaging: Consumer, Private Label
Brands:
   Fiber Greens
   Greens
   Pro-Relight
   Protein Greens

10678 Orange-Co of Florida
12010 NE Highway 70
Arcadia, FL 34266-4267   863-494-4939
    Fax: 863-494-2655
Manufacturer and exporter of citrus juices and
nonjuice drinks and bases; packer of citrus juices;
importer of apple and cranberry concentrates
   Chairman/CEO: Ben Griffing III
   CEO: Griffin
   CEO: Steve Ryan
Estimated Sales: $20-50 Million
Number Employees: 100-249
Type of Packaging: Food Service, Private Label,
Bulk
Brands:
   BIRD'S EYE
   CYPRESS GARDENS

10679 Orangeburg Pecan Company
P.O.Box 38
Orangeburg, SC 29116-0038   803-534-4277
    Fax: 803-534-4279 800-845-6970
    uspecans@yahoo.com www.uspecans.com
Processor of shelled pecans
   President: Freddy J D Felder
   Founder: Marion H Felder
Number Employees: 1-4
Type of Packaging: Consumer, Food Service, Bulk

10680 (HQ)Orca Bay Foods
P.O.Box 9010
Renton, WA 98057-9010   425-204-9100
    Fax: 425-204-9200 800-932-6722
info@orcabayfoods.com www.orcabayfoods.com
Manufacturer of Frozen fish and seafood
   President: Ryan Mackey
   Senior Marketing Manager: Richard Mullins
   National Sales Manager: Mark Tupper
   Warehouse Manager: Troy Roy
Estimated Sales: $100+ Million
Number Employees: 100-249
Number of Brands: 1
Number of Products: 20
Sq. footage: 15000
Type of Packaging: Consumer, Food Service, Pri-
vate Label, Bulk
Brands:
   ORCA BAY

10681 Orchard Heights Winery
6057 Orchard Heights Rd NW
Salem, OR 97304-9509   503-391-7308
    Fax: 503-364-1715
    Info@OrchardHeightsWinery.com
    www.islandprincess.com
Wines
   Manager: Carole Wyscaver
   CEO: Carol Wyscaver
   Winemaker: Carol Wyscaver
Estimated Sales: $1-$2 Million
Number Employees: 10-19
Type of Packaging: Private Label
Brands:
   Island Princess
   Orchard Heights

10682 Orchard Island Juice Company
330 N US Highway Drive
Fort Pierce, FL 34950   772-465-1122
    Fax: 772-465-4303 888-373-7444
    www.orchardislandjuice.com
juice
   VP: John Martinelli

10683 (HQ)Ore-Cal Corporation
634 Crocker St
Los Angeles, CA 90021-1002   213-680-9540
    Fax: 213-228-6557 800-827-7474
    mike@ore-cal.com www.ore-cal.com
Manufacturer of shrimp
   President: William Shinbane
   VP: Mark Shinbane
   National Sales Manager: Shelley Gee
Estimated Sales: $148 Million
Number Employees: 100-249
Type of Packaging: Consumer, Food Service, Pri-
vate Label, Bulk
Brands:
   Harvest of the Sea

10684 Ore-Ida Foods
PO Box 57
Pittsburgh, PA 16230   412-237-3450
    www.oreida.com
Processor and exporter of frozen foods including ba-
gels, corn-on-the-cob, pizza, onion rings, pocket
sandwiches, cheese products, pasta, breaded fruits,
squash, zucchini and potato products; also, canned
potatoes
   VP Specialty Products: Nick Tyler
Estimated Sales: $ 20 - 50 Million
Number Employees: 400
Parent Co: H.J. Heinz Company
Type of Packaging: Consumer, Food Service
Brands:
   CHEDDAR BROWNS
   COTTAGE FRIES
   COUNTRY FRIES
   COUNTRY STYLE HASH BROWNS
   COUNTRY STYLE POTATO WEDGES
   COUNTRY STYLE STEAK FRIES
   CRISPERS
   CRISPY CROWNS
   CRISPY CRUNCHIES
   DEEP FRIES CRINKLE CUTS
   DEEP FRIES REGULAR CUTS
   FAST FOOD FRIES
   GOLDEN CRINKLES
   GOLDEN FRIES
   GOLDEN PATTIES
   GOLDEN TWIRLS
   HASH BROWNS
   HOME STYLE POTATO WEDGES
   HOT TOTS
   MICROWAVE HASH BROWNS
   MINI-TATER TOTS
   ORIGINAL, SNACKIN' FRIES
   PIXIE CRINKLES
   POTATO WEDGES W/SKINS
   POTATOES O'BRIEN
   SHOESTRINGS
   SHREDDED POTATO PATTIES
   SHREDDED POTATOES
   SNACKIN' FRIES
   SOUTHERN STYLE HASH BROWN
   STEAK FRIES
   TATER TOTS
   TATER TOTS
   TEXAS CRISPERS
   TOASTER HASH BROWNS
   WAFFLE FRIES
   ZESTIES
   ZESTY TWIRLS
   ZESTY, SNACKIN' TOTS

10685 Oregon Chai
1745 NW Marshall Street
Portland, OR 97209-2420   503-221-2424
    Fax: 503-796-0980 888-874-2424
    nirvana@oregonchai.com www.sellchai.com;
    www.oregonchai.com
Processor amd exporter of chai lattes, blends of tea,
honey, vanilla and spices.
   President: Cory Comstock
   VP Finance: Kurt Peterson
   Senior VP Marketing: Sean Ryan
   VP Marketing: Lori Woolfrey
   Sales Director: Tom Carl
   Production Manager: Emile Gaiera

Estimated Sales: $ 2.5-5 Million
Number Employees: 30
Sq. footage: 9000
Type of Packaging: Consumer, Food Service
Brands:
   Chai Charger
   Herbal Bliss
   Kashmir
   Oregon
   Oregon Chai
   Organic Chai
   Original Chai
   Te Nation Echinacea
   Te Nation Teas
   Te Nation Throat

10686 Oregon Cherry Growers
1520 Woodrow St NE
Salem, OR 97301-0621   503-364-8421
    Fax: 503-585-7710 800-367-2536
    mrm@orcherry.com www.oregoncherries.com
Processor and exporter of fresh, maraschino, froze,
brined, glance, ingredient and canned cherries.
   Quality Control: Lori Waters
   CEO: Edward Johnson
   VP Sales: Bruce Wesche
   National Sales Manager: Wally Van Cleave
   Director Manufacturing: Stephen Travis
Estimated Sales: $ 50 - 100 Million
Number Employees: 100-249
Parent Co: Oregon Cherry Growers
Type of Packaging: Consumer, Food Service, Pri-
vate Label, Bulk
Other Locations:
   Oregon Cherry Growers
   Stockton CA

10687 Oregon Cherry Growers
P.O.Box 1577
The Dalles, OR 97058-8004   541-296-2547
    Fax: 541-296-2509 800-367-2536
    mrm@orcherry.com www.orcherry.com
Processor and wholesaler/distributor of cherries in-
cluding maraschino, canned and frozen; exporter of
fresh cherries and cherry ice cream
   President: Robert Thompson
   Human Resources: Susan Kment
   Quality Control: Lori Waters
Estimated Sales: $53971435
Number Employees: 250-499
Type of Packaging: Consumer, Food Service, Pri-
vate Label, Bulk
Brands:
   Dalles
   Royal Willimette
   Royalette
   The Royal Cherry
   Wy-Am

10688 Oregon Flavor Rack Spice
86319 Lorane Hwy
Eugene, OR 97405-9486   541-342-2085
    Fax: 641-461-3036 800-725-8373
    spice@spiceman.com www.spiceman.com
Spices and seasonings
   Owner: David Johns
Estimated Sales: Less than $500,000
Number Employees: 1-4
Type of Packaging: Food Service
Brands:
   Oregon Flavor Rack

10689 (HQ)Oregon Freeze Dry
P.O.Box 1048
Albany, OR 97321-0407   541-926-6001
    Fax: 541-967-6527 800-547-0245
    industrial-ing@ofd.com www.ofd.com
Manufacturer of freeze-dried meats, poultry, sea-
food, ingredients, entrees, fruit, vegetables, snacks,
desserts, etc.; specializing in freeze-drying, product
development, formulation, mixing and packaging
   President: Herbert Aschkenasy
   SVP: James Merryman
Estimated Sales: $92 Million
Number Employees: 100-249
Sq. footage: 32000
Type of Packaging: Consumer, Food Service, Pri-
vate Label, Bulk
Other Locations:
Brands:
   MOUNTAIN HOUSE

10690 Oregon Fruit Products Company
P.O.Box 5283
Salem, OR 97304-0283   503-378-0255
            Fax: 503-588-9519   800-394-9333
cooking@oregonfruit.com   www.oregonfruit.com
Processor and exporter of canned and frozen fruits
including boysenberries, gooseberries,
marionberries, blackberries, blueberries, red raspber-
ries, strawberries, cherries, kotata berries, figs,
grapes and plums
    President: Paul Gehlar
    Sales Director: Bryan Brown
    Operations Manager: Patti Law
Estimated Sales: $6,100,000
Number Employees: 100-249
Type of Packaging: Consumer, Food Service, Pri-
    vate Label, Bulk
Brands:
    Oregon Fruit

10691 Oregon Hill Farms
32861 Pittsburg Rd
St Helens, OR 97051-9110   503-397-2791
            Fax: 503-397-0091   800-243-4541
    sales@oregonhill.com   www.oregonhill.com
Processor and co-packer of specialty fruit jams, syr-
ups, fruit butters and dessert toppings
    President: Thomas McMahon
Estimated Sales: $ 3 - 5 Million
Number Employees: 10-19
Sq. footage: 17000
Type of Packaging: Consumer, Food Service, Pri-
    vate Label
Brands:
    Oregon Hill
    Swan's Touch

10692 (HQ)Oregon Potato Company
P.O.Box 169
Boardman, OR 97818-0169   541-481-2715
            Fax: 541-481-3443   800-336-6311
opcsales@uci.net   www.oregonpotato.com
Manufacturer of potato products including flakes,
flour and dehydrofrozen diced; also, seasonal packer
of fresh potatoes
    Manager: Steve White
    Director QA/Technical Services: Nick Ross
    Director Global Sales: Barry Stice
Number Employees: 50-99
Sq. footage: 100000
Type of Packaging: Private Label
Other Locations:
    Oregon Potato Co.
    Warden WA
Brands:
    OERGON TRAIL
    REGAL CREST

10693 Oregon Pride
3400 Crates Way
The Dalles, OR 97058-3552   908-537-7539
            Fax: 908-537-2582   888-697-4767
dude@oregonpride.com   www.oregonpride.com
Gourmet kippered beefsteak and beef jerky
    President: James Perkins
Estimated Sales: Below $ 5 Million
Number Employees: 10

10694 Oregon Specialty Company
2624 112th Street S
Suite E2
Lakewood, WA 98499-8867   503-254-7494
            Fax: 503-251-2936   877-254-7494
            info@oregonspecialty.com
            www.oregonspecialty.com
Manufacturer, importer and exporter of hand oper-
ated bottle washers, cappers and fillers; whole-
saler/distributor of wine and beer yeasts, barrel
spigots, liquid and dry beer malts, wine and beer
bottles, bottle brushes, bottle capsfunnels, labels, etc
    President: Henry G Siebens
    Plant Manager: Roger M Schloe
Estimated Sales: $500,000-$1 Million
Number Employees: 5-9
Sq. footage: 10000
Brands:
    Beer-King
    Wine-King

10695 Oregon Spice Company
13320 NE Jarrett St
Portland, OR 97230-1093   503-238-0664
            Fax: 503-238-3872   800-565-1599
kevin@oregonspice.com   www.oregonspice.com
Spices and seasoning blends
    President: Patricia Boday
    Chairman: Larry Black
    Marketing Director: Patricia Boday
Estimated Sales: Below $ 5 Million
Number Employees: 20-49
Brands:
    Oregon Spice

10696 Oregon Trader Brewing
140 NE Hill St
Albany, OR 97321-3002   541-928-1931
            Fax: 541-928-4131   info@oregonbeer.org
            www.calapooiabrewing.com
Beer
    Owner: Mark Martin
    Treasurer: Nancy Coleman
Estimated Sales: Below $ 5 Million
Number Employees: 1-4
Brands:
    Oregon Brewers

10697 Orfila Vineyards
13455 San Pasqual Rd
Escondido, CA 92025-7898   760-738-6500
            Fax: 760-745-3773   info@orfila.com
            www.orfilavineyards.com
Wines
    Owner: Alejandra Orlia
    General Manager: Leon Santoro
    Marketing Manager: Leon Santoro
Estimated Sales: Below $ 5 Million
Number Employees: 20-49
Type of Packaging: Private Label
Brands:
    Mendoza Ridge
    Orfila Vineyards
    Quatre Lepages

10698 Organic By Nature
1542 Seabright Ave
Long Beach, CA 90813-1131   562-901-0119
            Fax: 562-901-9575   800-452-6884
askgrassman@greenkamutcorp.com
            www.organicbynature.com
Organic plant powders
    CEO: David Sandover
    CEO: David Sandoval
    National Sales Manager: Michael Wohlfeld
Estimated Sales: $ 5 - 10 Million
Number Employees: 50-99
Brands:
    Organic By Nature

10699 Organic Cow
PO Box 17577
Boulder, CO 80308-0577   802-685-3123
            Fax: 802-685-4332   800-769-9693
            www.theorganiccow.com
Milk, buttery products
    Owner: Bunny Flint
    Co-Owner: Peter Flint
Estimated Sales: Less than $500,000
Number Employees: 1-4
Brands:
    Organic Cow

10700 Organic Gourmet
4092 Deervale Dr
Sherman Oaks, CA 91403-4609   818-986-3777
            Fax: 818-906-7417   800-400-7772
scenar@earthlink.net   www.organic-gourmet.com
Processor of organic food products including vege-
tarian soups and stocks, yeast extract spreads, bouil-
lon cubes and miso pastes; importer of soups and
sauces
    CEO/Founder: Elke Heitmeyer
    CEO: Elke Heitmeyer
Estimated Sales: $ 1 - 3 Million
Number Employees: 1-4
Number of Brands: 1
Number of Products: 16
Type of Packaging: Consumer, Food Service
Brands:
    Organic Gourmet

10701 Organic India USA
5311 Western Ave
Suite T
Boulder, CO 80301-2746   720-406-3940
            Fax: 720-406-3942   888-550-8332
info_retail@organicindiausa.com
            www.organicindiausa.com

herbal and organic teas
Estimated Sales: $2.8 Million
Number Employees: 12

10702 Organic Milling Company
505 W Allen Ave
San Dimas, CA 91773-1487   909-599-0961
            Fax: 909-599-5180   800-638-8686
            www.organicmilling.com
Processor and exporter of granola and fiber break-
fast cereals
    President: Herish Chopra
    VP Marketing: Tom Bezick
Estimated Sales: $26000000
Number Employees: 100-249
Sq. footage: 100000
Type of Packaging: Private Label
Brands:
    Back To Nature
    Vita Crunch

10703 Organic Planet
231 Sansome St # 3
San Francisco, CA 94104-2304   415-765-5590
            Fax: 415-765-5922   info@organic-planet.com
            www.organic-planet.com
Certified organic ingredients; edible seeds, dried
fruits, tropical fruit, nuts, pulses, sweetners
    President: Hans Schmid
    Sales: Carrie Hueseman
Estimated Sales: $2000000
Number Employees: 5-9
Number of Brands: 1
Number of Products: 50
Brands:
    ORGANIC PLANET

10704 Organic Valley
1 Organic Way
La Farge, WI 54639-6604   608-625-2602
            Fax: 608-625-2600   organic@organicvalley.coop
            www.organicvalley.coop
Processor and exporter of organic dairy products in-
cluding dried and fresh cheeses, eggs, yogurt, milk
and butter; also, organic vegetables and certified or-
ganic pork, beef and chicken; importer of certified
organic bananas
    President: Michael Levine
    CFO: Mike Bedessem
    CEO: George Siemon
    Marketing Director: Theresa Marquez
    National Sales Manager: Eric Newman
Estimated Sales: $100+ Million
Number Employees: 250-499
Sq. footage: 200000
Type of Packaging: Consumer, Food Service, Pri-
    vate Label, Bulk
Brands:
    Organic Valley
    Valley's Family of Farms Meats

10705 Organic Wine Company
1592 Union St # 350
San Francisco, CA 94123-4531   415-256-8888
            Fax: 415-256-8883   888-326-9463
cs@theorganicwinecompany.com
            www.ecowine.com
Organic wines
    CEO: Veronique Raskin
    Vice President: Michelle Ginoulhac
Estimated Sales: $500,000-$1 Million
Number of Products: 45
Brands:
    Bousquette
    Veronique

10706 Organically Grown Company
1800 Prairie Rd # B
Eugene, OR 97402-9722   541-689-5320
            Fax: 541-461-3014   davidl@organicgrown.com
            www.organicgrown.com
Contract packager of fruits and vegetables; importer
of tropical produce and dried fruit; exporter of
squash
    President: David Amorose
    CEO: Josh Hinerfeld
    CEO: Josh Hinerfeld
    Marketing Director: David Lively
    Finance Director: Robbie Vasilinda
Estimated Sales: $23079823
Number Employees: 100-249
Sq. footage: 8000

10707 Oriental Foods
2550 W Main Street
Suite 210
Alhambra, CA 91801-7003   626-293-1994
                              Fax: 626-293-1983
Seafood
    President: Dr Venku Reddy
Estimated Sales:$1,300,000
Number Employees: 5

10708 (HQ)Original American Beverage Company
74 Chester Main Road
North Stonington, CT 06359-1303   860-535-4650
        Fax: 860-535-8545   800-625-3767
Processor of old-fashioned soda and hard apple cider
    President: Donald Benoit
Number Employees: 1-4
Sq. footage: 5000
Type of Packaging: Consumer
Brands:
    Chester's
    Mystic Seaport

10709 Original Cajun Injector
PO Box 97
Clinton, LA 70722-0097   225-683-4490
        Fax: 225-683-4401   800-221-8060
        www.cajuninjector.com
Processor and exporter of liquid injectable marinades for poultry and red meats; also, dry seasonings
    President: Maurice Williams
    Marketing Manager: Leo Honeycott
    Sales: Frank Malta
    Purchasing: Pablo Rodriquez
Estimated Sales:$ 3 - 5 Million
Number Employees: 1-4
Sq. footage: 13600
Type of Packaging: Consumer, Bulk
Brands:
    Cajun Aujus
    Cajun Injector
    Cajun Poultry Marinade
    Cajunshake

10710 Original Chili Bowl
P.O.Box 470125
Tulsa, OK 74147-0125   918-628-0225
    Fax: 918-663-0539 www.windsorfoods.com
Processor of smoked barbecue meats and chili
    COO: Bryan Cather
    Technical Director: Robert Hastings
    Plant Controller: Lil Green
    Plant Manager: John Powers
Estimated Sales:$28600000
Number Employees: 50-99
Parent Co: Windsor Frozen Foods
Type of Packaging: Consumer, Food Service, Bulk
Brands:
    Cripple Creek
    Hickory Hollow

10711 Original Foods, QuebecDivision, Inc.
580 Bechard Avenue
Vanier, QC G1M 2E9
Canada
                              888-440-8880
                    Fax: 866-449-6536
    chantal.langevin@originalfoods.com
    Assistant General Manager: Phillipe Canac-Marquis
    Marketing & Logistics Manager: Kevin Tremblay

    National Sales Manager: Dahna Weber
    Customer Service: Chantal Langevin
Brands:
    ORIGINAL 1957

10712 Original Italian Pasta Poducts Company
36 Auburn Street
Chelsea, MA 02150-1825   617-884-5211
        Fax: 617-884-2563   800-999-9603
Fresh and frozen pasta, sauces
    President: Paul Stevens
    Sales/Marketing: Kathy Burinskas
    Director Operations: Steve Lagasse
    Plant Manager: Jim Dee
    Purchasing Manager: George Hachey
Estimated Sales:$ 5-9.9 Million
Number Employees: 35
Type of Packaging: Private Label

10713 Original Juan
111 Southwest Blvd
Kansas City, KS 66103-2132   913-432-5228
        Fax: 913-432-5880   800-568-8468
    juan@originaljuan.com   www.originaljuan.com
Manufacturer of Specialty foods, snacks, hot sauces, condiments, seasonings, salsas, barbeque sauces
    President: Joe Polo
*Estimated Sales:*Less than $500,000
Number Employees: 20-49
Brands:
    CAJUN BAYOU
    CALIDO CHILE TRADERS
    FIESTA
    JOSE GOLDSTEIN
    ORIGINAL JUAN
    PANISGOOD
    TEXAS LONGHORN
    WILD AND MILD

10714 Original Nut House Brands
11 Leigh Fisher Blvd # B
El Paso, TX 79906-5240   915-772-5871
    Fax: 915-778-0818   800-726-7222
    customerservice@harvestmanor.com
    www.originalnuthouse.com
Processor and exporter of nuts and nut meats including peanuts, almonds, pralines and pecans; also, peanut butter
    President: Richard Kunzig
    Plant Manager: John Cox
Estimated Sales:$50-$100 Million
Number Employees: 5-9
Sq. footage: 200000
Parent Co: Harvest Manor Brands, LLC
Type of Packaging: Bulk
Other Locations:
    Original Nut House Brands
    Gorman TX

10715 Original Nut House Brands
620 E Lime St
Portales, NM 88130   575-356-6691
        Fax: 575-359-0072
    www.originalnuthousebrand.com
Processor and exporter of peanuts
    President: Sam Rigsby
    VP: Levy Polish
    Marketing Manager: Levy Polish
    General Manager: Bill Owen
    Plant Manager: Leonard Stanton
Estimated Sales:$ 20 - 50 Million
Number Employees: 20-49
Parent Co: Original Nuthouse Brands
Type of Packaging: Consumer, Private Label, Bulk

10716 Original Nut House Brands
11 Leigh Fisher Blvd # B
El Paso, TX 79906-5240   915-772-5871
    Fax: 915-778-0818   800-726-7222
    customer.service@harvestnuthouse.com
    www.originalnuthouse.com
Processor of peanuts, pecans, almonds, etc
    Manager Human Resources: Irma M Lopez
    Plant Manager: John Cox
Estimated Sales:$100+ Million
Number Employees: 100-249
Parent Co: Morven Partners
Type of Packaging: Consumer, Food Service, Private Label
Brands:
    Fowler's Everfresh
    Gary's Everfresh
    Hoody's Nut House
    Jimbo Jumbos
    L.A. Nut
    Parnel's
    Pecan
    San Saba

10717 Original Texas Chili Company
P.O.Box 4281
Fort Worth, TX 76164-0281   817-626-0983
        Fax: 817-626-9105   800-507-0009
        sales@texaschilicompany.com
        www.texaschili.com
Frozen chili, taco filling and chili sauce
    President: Danny Owens
    Plant Manager: Rebbca Marlvo
*Estimated Sales:*Below $ 5 Million
Number Employees: 5-9
Type of Packaging: Private Label

Brands:
    Texas Chili

10718 Original Ya-hoo! BakingCompany
5302 Texoma Pkwy
Sherman, TX 75090-2112   903-813-3328
        Fax: 903-893-5036   800-575-9373
        customerservice@yahoocake.com
        www.yahoocake.com
Manufacturer of dessert cakes, cobblers, cookies, cake and pie fillings, bread, frozen dough; custom work is our specialty
    President: Geoffrey Crowley
    R&D: Monette Wible
    Director Sales/Marketing: David Millican
    Sales Administrator: Tanda Wall
    Purchasing Manager: Becky Roberts
Number Employees: 100-249
Sq. footage: 45000
Type of Packaging: Consumer, Food Service, Private Label, Bulk
Brands:
    Ya-Hoo!

10719 Orland Olive Oil Company
7th & Tehama Street
Orland, CA 95963   530-865-4040
        Fax: 530-824-1803   calioz@tco.net
Processor of extra virgin olive oil made from mission variety olives
    Sales Manager/General Manager: Brendan Binder

Estimated Sales:$ 3 - 5 Million
Number Employees: 6
Sq. footage: 3500
Type of Packaging: Food Service, Bulk

10720 Orlando Baking Company
7777 Grand Ave
Cleveland, OH 44104-3099   216-361-1872
        Fax: 216-391-3469   800-362-5504
        customerservice@orlandobaking.com
        www.orlandobaking.com
Manufacturer of specialty breads and rolls including Italian, French, Rye and Wheat breads, a variety of subs, hoagies, kaisers and hamburger rolls
    President: Chester Orlando
    Marketing Director: Sharon Jones
    VP Sales: Nick Orlando Jr
Estimated Sales:$ 20 - 50 Million
Number Employees: 250-499
Sq. footage: 200000
Type of Packaging: Consumer, Food Service, Private Label
Brands:
    ORLANDO

10721 Orlando's Pastries
600 MacDade Boulevard
Collingdale, PA 19023-3804   610-532-9300
        Fax: 610-532-8927   www.orlandospastries.com
Processor of assorted cakes, pastries, cookies and pies including apple, peach and cherry
    President/Co-Owner: Loyd Turner
    Sales Director: David Orlando
Estimated Sales:$500,000-$1 Million
Number Employees: 10-19

10722 Orleans Coffee Exchange
1001 Industry Rd # A
Kenner, LA 70062-6880   504-827-0878
        Fax: 504-827-0818   800-737-5464
    nolajava@bellsouth.net   www.orleanscoffee.com
Manufacturer of coffees including flavored, regular and decaffeinated; also, grinders, coffee makers and tea
    Owner: Bill Siemers
    Owner: Kathleen Siemers
*Estimated Sales:*Less than $500,000
Number Employees: 10-19
Sq. footage: 3000
Type of Packaging: Consumer, Private Label, Bulk

10723 Orleans Food Company
1847 Dock Street
Suite 201
New Orleans, LA 70123-5664   504-733-1311
        Fax: 504-734-7684   800-628-4900
        cook@bumblebee.com
Processor of canned shrimp, crab meat, oysters, clams, sardines, tuna and mackerel; also, bottled clam juice; exporter of canned shrimp; importer of canned seafood
    VP Sales/Marketing: David Cook

Estimated Sales:$ 5 - 10 Million
Number Employees: 5-9
Type of Packaging: Consumer, Food Service, Private Label
Brands:
    Cutcher
    Dejean
    Gulf Belle
    Harris
    Marvelous
    Orleans

10724 Orleans Hill Vineyard Association
PO Box 1254
Woodland, CA 95776-1254   530-661-6538
Wines
    President/Winemaker: James Lapsley

10725 Orleans Packing Company
1715 Hyde Park Ave
Hyde Park, MA 02136-2457   617-361-6611
    Fax: 617-361-2638 www.orleanspacking.com
Importer and packer of olives (26 varieties), capers, Greek pepperoncini, Greek giardiniera, cocktail onions, roasted peppers, artichokes and maraschino cherries (jars, drums and pails); retail, food service, private label and bulk
    President: George Gebelein
Estimated Sales: $ 10 - 20 Million
Number Employees: 10-19
Type of Packaging: Consumer, Food Service, Private Label, Bulk

10726 Orlinda Milling Company
P.O.Box 38
Orlinda, TN 37141-0038   615-654-3633
    Fax: 615-654-4902
Processor of all-purpose and self-rising flour
    President: Ricky Stark
    Vice President: Bryant Stark
    Secretary/Treasurer: Ronnie Stark
Estimated Sales: $470000
Number Employees: 1-4
Type of Packaging: Consumer, Food Service
Brands:
    Crown Jewel
    Kwik Rize

10727 Ormand Peugeog Corporation
PO Box 227155
Miami, FL 33122-7155   305-624-6834
    Fax: 305-624-0911
    www.ormandpeugeog@aol.com
Wine and wine products
    President: Paul Mirengoff.
    CFO: Laura Robledo
    Marketing Director: Olga Robledo
    Plant Manager: Jose Robledo
Estimated Sales: $ 3 Million
Number Employees: 4
Sq. footage: 60
Type of Packaging: Private Label
Brands:
    Cristal
    Frescas
    Gatomax
    Tai Bueno
    This Way Jose

10728 Oroweat Baking Company
480 S Vail Ave
Montebello, CA 90640-4947   323-721-5161
    Fax: 323-720-6015
Processor and exporter of whole grain bread and muffins, French bread, rolls and stuffing mix
    Executive: Kathy Manitsas
    Sales Director: Jim Brennan
    Purchasing: Diana Chovice
Estimated Sales: $100+ Million
Number Employees: 1,000-4,999
Parent Co: Unilever USA
Type of Packaging: Consumer

10729 Orr Mountain Winery
312 8th Ave N # 25
Nashville, TN 37243-1102   615-741-2159
    Fax: 615-741-7225 theorrs@usit.net
    www.tnvacation.com
Wines
    Manager: Susan Whitaker
    Sales Director: Lee Curtis
Estimated Sales: $500,000-$1 Million
Number Employees: 1-4

Brands:
    Orr Mountain Winery

10730 Ortho Molecular Products
3017 Business Park Dr
Stevens Point, WI 54481-8835   715-342-9881
    Fax: 715-342-9866 800-332-2351
    www.orthomolecularproducts.com
Manufacturer and wholesaler/distributor of vitamin supplements
    President: Gary Powers
    Operations Manager: John Pavelski
Estimated Sales: $ 5 - 10 Million
Number Employees: 50-99
Sq. footage: 16000
Parent Co: Ortho Molecular Products

10731 Orval Kent Food Company
120 W Palatine Rd
Wheeling, IL 60090-5823   847-459-9000
    Fax: 847-325-7594
    melissa.willits@chefsolutions.com
    www.orvalkent.com
Processor of refrigerated salads including potato, cole slaw, tuna, chicken, ham, shrimp, crabmeat and fruit; fresh cut fruit; mashed potatoes and side salads and desserts.
    President: Steve Silk
Number Employees: 250-499
Sq. footage: 100000
Type of Packaging: Consumer, Food Service, Private Label, Bulk
Brands:
    Bistro '28
    Chilled Selections
    Citrus Sensations
    Flavor Harvest
    Orval Kent
    Salad Juniors
    Salads Plus
    Signature
    Signature Delight
    Signature Entrees
    Signature Pastas

10732 Orwasher's Bakery Handmade Bread
308 E 78th St
New York, NY 10075-2222   212-288-6569
    Fax: 212-570-2706 info@orwashers.com
    www.orwashers.com
Processor of brick oven baked breads and rolls including black pumpernickel, challah, cinnamon raisin, marble, potato, rye, sour dough, white, and whole wheat.
    President: Aparm Orwasher
Estimated Sales: Less than $500,000
Number Employees: 5-9
Type of Packaging: Consumer, Food Service
Brands:
    Orwasher's

10733 Osage Pecan Company
909 W Fort Scott St
Butler, MO 64730-1204   660-679-6137
    Fax: 660-679-6255
Manufacturer and packer of pecans and other nuts; also dried fruits
    Manager: Teresa Barnes
Estimated Sales: $1-3 Million
Number Employees: 1-4
Number of Products: 100
Sq. footage: 20000
Type of Packaging: Consumer, Food Service, Private Label, Bulk
Brands:
    Osage Chief

10734 Oscar Mayer Foods
910 Mayer
Madison, WI 53704-4256   608-241-3311
    Fax: 608-285-6741 www.oscarmayer.com
Lunch meat, bacon, hot dogs, sandwiches
    President: Nick Meriggioli
    CFO: Irene Rosenfeld
    CFO: Jim Dollive
    Vice President: Sanjay Khosla
    Sales Director: Tom Sampson
    VP Operations: Jose Rojo
Estimated Sales: Over $1 Billion
Number Employees: 5,000-9,999
Parent Co: Kraft Foods
Type of Packaging: Consumer, Food Service, Bulk

Brands:
    Carving Board
    Claussen
    Louis Rich
    Oscar Mayer

10735 Oscars Wholesale Meats
250 W 31st St
Ogden, UT 84401-3899   801-394-6472
    Fax: 801-394-8113
Manufacturer of meat products
    President: Lynn Hartley
Estimated Sales: $25.5 Million
Number Employees: 10-19

10736 Osceola Farms
P.O.Box 679
Pahokee, FL 33476-0679   561-924-4400
    Fax: 561-924-3240
Processor of sugar and syrup
    President: Alexander Fanjul
    Research & Development: Steve Clarke
Estimated Sales: $29000000
Number Employees: 1-4
Parent Co: Florida Crystals
Type of Packaging: Consumer

10737 Oshkosh Cold Storage Company
1110 Industrial Ave
Oshkosh, WI 54901-1105   920-231-0610
    Fax: 920-231-9441 800-580-4680
    ocstg@vbe.com www.cheesesale.com
Cheese, cheese products
    President: Walter Doemel
    Marketing Director: Stan Dietsche
Estimated Sales: $500,000-$1 Million
Number Employees: 5-9
Type of Packaging: Bulk

10738 Oskaloosa Food ProductsCorporation
543 9th Avenue E
Oskaloosa, IA 52577   641-673-3486
    Fax: 641-673-8684 800-477-7239
    info@oskyfoods.com www.oskyfoods.com
Manufacturer and exporter of dried, frozenand liquid egg products.
    President: Blair Van Zetten
    Controller: Brad Hodges
    Sales/Purchasing Director: Jason Van Zetten
    Human Resource Manager: Joyce Wilson
Estimated Sales: $10.6 Million
Number Employees: 82
Type of Packaging: Consumer, Food Service, Private Label, Bulk

10739 Oskri Organics
PO Box 125
Thiensville, WI 53092-0125   414-258-8546
    800-628-1110
    sales@oskri.com www.oskri.com
Processor and exporter of organic coffee, dried fruit and soup bases; also, teas and herbal products; importer of coffee; contract manufacturing available
Estimated Sales: $500,000-$1 Million
Number Employees: 5-9
Type of Packaging: Consumer, Private Label, Bulk

10740 Osman's Pies
4974 Darrow Rd
Stow, OH 44224-1406   330-655-2919
    Fax: 330-655-7824 www.osmanspies.com
Processor of baked products including specialty pies, cakes, cookies, brownies and muffins
    President: Wendy Crowe
    Secretary: Cheryl Crowe
Estimated Sales: $600000
Number Employees: 20-49
Type of Packaging: Consumer

10741 Osowski Farms
33 Gillespie Ave
Minto, ND 58261   701-248-3341
    Fax: 701-248-3341
Processor of sugar beets, grain and dry beans
    Owner: David Osowski
    CEO: Rod Osowski
    Marketing Director: Wayne Osowski
Estimated Sales: $ 1 - 3 Million
Number Employees: 1-4
Type of Packaging: Consumer, Food Service, Bulk
Brands:
    Wayne

10742 Ossian Seafood Meats
P.O.Box 405
Ossian, IN 46777-0405   260-622-4191
    Fax: 260-622-4194
Processor of meats including beef, pork, pork chops, sausage, steak, hamburger and ham
    President: Peter Sorg Jr
Estimated Sales:$ 10 - 20 Million
Number Employees: 20-49
Type of Packaging: Consumer, Food Service, Private Label, Bulk
Brands:
    Hoosier Pride
    Ye Olde Farm Style

10743 Ostrom Mushroom Farms
8323 Steilacoom Rd SE
Lacey, WA 98513-2099   360-491-1410
    Fax: 360-438-2594   info@ostromfarms.com
        www.ostromfarms.com
Manufacturer of mushrooms and mushroom sauce
    President: William Street
Estimated Sales:$100+ Million
Number Employees: 100-249
Type of Packaging: Consumer, Private Label, Bulk

10744 Ota Tofu Company
812 SE Stark St
Portland, OR 97214-1228   503-232-8947
Processor of tofu
    President: Eileen Ota
Estimated Sales:$770000
Number Employees: 10-19
Type of Packaging: Consumer, Bulk

10745 Otis Spunkmeyer
14490 Catalina St
San Leandro, CA 94577-5516   510-357-9836
    Fax: 510-352-5680   800-938-1900
        www.spunkmeyer.com
Manufacturer of Frozen cookie dough, fresh baked muffins, and other gourmet baked goods supplied to food service and retail
    President/CEO: John Schiavo
    CFO: Ahmad Hamade
    Vice President: Jerry Reardon
    VP Marketing: Leslie Steller
Estimated Sales:$100+ Million
Number Employees: 250-499
Type of Packaging: Private Label
Brands:
    OTIS SPUNKMEYER

10746 Otis Spunkmeyer Company
5855 Oakbrook Parkway
Suite F
Norcross, GA 30093-1838   770-446-1860
    Fax: 770-446-2205   800-438-9251
      bhamillton@spunkmeyer.com
        www.spunkmeyer.com
Processor of cookies, muffins, bagels and brownies
    General Manager: Buck Hamillton
    President: John Schievo
Estimated Sales:$ 1-2.5 Million
Number Employees: 20-49
Parent Co: Otis Spunkmeyer
Type of Packaging: Consumer, Food Service
Brands:
    Otis Spunkmeyer

10747 Ott Food Products
705 W Fairview Ave
Carthage, MO 64836-3724   417-358-2585
    Fax: 417-358-4553   800-866-2585
        www.ottfoods.com
Processor of barbecue sauce and salad dressing including French, Italian, ranch and poppy seed
    President: Jack Crede
Estimated Sales:$ 10 - 20 Million
Number Employees: 20-49
Type of Packaging: Consumer, Food Service
Brands:
    Louis Albert & Sons
    Ott's

10748 Ottawa Foods
325 W Williamstown Rd
Ottawa, OH 45875-1845   419-523-3225
    Fax: 419-523-6145   800-837-1631
    info@hirzel.com   www.hirzel.com

Processor of canned tomato products including whole, sliced, crushed, puree and sauce
    President: Karl Hirzel
    Plant Manager: Carl Hirzel
Estimated Sales:$ 2.5-5 Million
Number Employees: 5-9
Parent Co: Hirzel Canning
Type of Packaging: Consumer, Food Service, Private Label
Brands:
    DEI FRATELLI
    SILVER FLEECE
    STAR CROSS

10749 Ottawa Valley Grain Products
PO Box 456
29 Bridge Street
Renfrew, ON K7V 4A6
Canada   613-432-3614
   Fax: 613-432-6148   ronwilson1953@on.aibn.com
        www.ovgp.ca
Manufacturer milled, pearled and pot barley, wheat and barley flow
    President/CEO: Ron Wilson
Number Employees: 10-19
Number of Products: 7
Type of Packaging: Food Service, Bulk
Brands:
    Valley

10750 Ottenberg's Bakers
655 Taylor St NE
Washington, DC 20017-2098   202-281-2578
    Fax: 202-529-3121   800-334-7264
      ottenbergs@ottenbergs.com
        www.ottenbergs.com
Manufacturer of baked goods including breads and rolls
    Owner: Lee Ottenberg
    President: Ray Ottenberg
Estimated Sales:$20 Million
Number Employees: 100-249
Type of Packaging: Food Service

10751 Ottens Flavors
7800 Holstein Ave
Philadelphia, PA 19153-3283   215-365-7801
    Fax: 215-365-7801   800-523-0767
    flavors@ottens.com   www.ottensflavors.com
Manufacturer of spray dry flavorings and imitation and natural confectionary oils and spices; importer and exporter of confectionary flavors and essential oils
    President: George Robinson III
    CEO: Richard Robinson
    Eastern Manager: Sharon D'Alo
    COO: Rudy Dieperink
Estimated Sales:$11.5 Million
Number Employees: 50-99
Sq. footage: 36500
Type of Packaging: Food Service, Private Label, Bulk

10752 Ottens Flavors
7800 Holstein Ave
Philadelphia, PA 19153-3283   215-365-7801
    Fax: 215-365-7801   800-523-0767
    flavors@ottens.com   www.ottensflavors.com
Food flavorings
    President: Joe Robinson
    CEO: Richard Robinson
    R & D: Bob Maxwell
    Quality Control: Ralph Anzano
    CFO: Bob E Amico
    Marketing Manager: Rudy Dieperink
Estimated Sales:$ 75-100 Million
Number Employees: 50-99

10753 Otter Valley Foods
95 Spruce Street
Tillsonburg, ON N4G 5C4
Canada   519-688-3256
    Fax: 519-842-4521   800-265-5731
        www.ottervalley.com
Processor of frozen entrees
    President: John Kelly
    VP: Peter Kelly
    Marketing Director: Doug Yson
Number Employees: 100-249
Type of Packaging: Consumer, Food Service, Private Label
Brands:
    Otter Valley

10754 Ottman Meat Company
315 E 69th St
New York, NY 10021-5527   212-879-4160
    Fax: 212-879-4189 www.greenmarketing.com
Processor and exporter of frozen portion control poultry, veal, hamburgers, roasts and prepared barbecue products
    President: Jacquelyn Ottman
    Sales Manager: Charles Allan
Estimated Sales:$300,000-500,000
Number Employees: 1-4
Parent Co: Long Island Beef Company
Type of Packaging: Consumer, Food Service

10755 Otto & Son
4980 W 9470 S
West Jordan, UT 84081-5691   801-280-0166
    Fax: 801-280-3540   800-453-9462
Manufacturer of meat products including frozen hamburger patties
    Plant Manager: Morgan Robertson
Estimated Sales:$20-50 Million
Number Employees: 100-249
Type of Packaging: Food Service, Bulk

10756 Otto & Son
711 Industrial Dr
West Chicago, IL 60185-1831   630-231-9091
    Fax: 630-231-5441 www.osigroup.com
Processor of meat products
    President: Cristina Gomez
    Vice President: Dale Aden
Estimated Sales:$100+ Million
Number Employees: 100-249
Parent Co: OSI Industries
Type of Packaging: Food Service

10757 Otto W Liebold & Company
1025 Chippewa St
Flint, MI 48503-1548   810-239-1414
    Fax: 810-239-6496   800-999-6328
      rwliebold@lieboldmeat.com
Manufacturer of certified angus beef products and other meat
    Vice President: Dennis Liebold
Estimated Sales:$3 Billion
Number Employees: 20-49
Sq. footage: 25000
Parent Co: Evans Foodservice
Type of Packaging: Consumer, Food Service, Private Label, Bulk
Brands:
    CERTIFIED ANGUS BEEF
    OTTO'S

10758 Ouhlala Gourmet
363 Aragon Avenue 812W
Coral Gables, FL 33134   305-774-7332
      contact@ouhlala.com
        www.ouhlala.com
squeezable fruit to go

10759 Ouma's Bakery
445 Old Lake Road
Poultney, VT 05764-9151   802-287-9310
    Fax: 802-287-2216
      ouma@vermontspringbok.com
        www.vermontspringbok.com
Manufacturer of Brandied cakes
    Owner: Duncan Mcquade
    Owner: Amy Mcquade

10760 Our Best Foods
170 Main St # 210
Tewksbury, MA 01876-1762   978-858-0077
    Fax: 978-858-0052 www.naddif.com
Processor of pork, veal, chicken and beef products
    Owner: Micheal Neddif
Estimated Sales:$ 20 - 50 Million
Number Employees: 20-49
Type of Packaging: Food Service, Private Label
Brands:
    Our Best

10761 Our Cookie
4785 NE 11th Avenue
Oakland Park, FL 33334   954-229-1005
    Fax: 954-229-1009   877-885-2715
    info@ourcookie.com   www.ourcookie.com
cookies

10762 Our Enterprises
8201 N Classen Boulevard
Suite B
Oklahoma City, OK 73114-2136   405-843-1065
Fax: 405-842-0217 800-821-6375
pchase@ourgourmet.com www.ourgourmet.com
Pesto, pickles, fruited honeys, salsas, jellies, sauces,
chow-chow
Estimated Sales:$ 1-2.5 Million
Number Employees: 5-9
Brands:
    Our Gourmet
    Patti's Private Stock

10763 Our Lady of Guadalupe Abbey
PO Box 97
Lafayette, OR 97127-0097   503-852-7148
Fax: 503-852-7742 bakery@trappistabbey.org
www.trappistabbey.org
Fruitcake, date-nut cake

10764 Our Thyme Garden
4017 County Road 424
Cleburne, TX 76031   817-558-3570
Fax: 817-558-3570 800-482-4372
ourthymegarden@yahoo.com
Processor of biscotti, teas and herbal vinegars and
oils. Also herb, fiesta, citrus, renaissance, thyme and
zesty garden
    President: Kimberly Nicholson
    CEO: Mary Doebbeling
Estimated Sales:$300,000-500,000
Number Employees: 1-4
Sq. footage: 1000
Type of Packaging: Consumer, Food Service, Private Label, Bulk
Brands:
    Our Thyme Garden

10765 Out of a Flower
657 Edgewood Drive
Lancaster, TX 75146-1259   214-630-3136
Fax: 214-630-8797 800-743-4696
Processor of ice cream and sorbets made out of edible flowers, herbs and fruits
    President: Jose Sanabria
Estimated Sales:$100000
Number Employees: 2
Brands:
    Chiqui
    Out of a Flower
    Swiss Alp Mineral Water

10766 Outback Kitchens LLC
PO Box 153
Huntington, VT 05462-0153   802-434-5262
Fax: 502-434-5262 natobk@together.net
www.outbackkitchens.com
Chutney
Estimated Sales:$300,000-500,000
Number Employees: 1-4

10767 Outerbridge Peppers
20 Harry Shupe Blvd
Wharton, NJ 07885-1646   973-366-5090
Fax: 973-366-2769 800-989-7007
peppers@ibi.bm
Sherry peppers
    Owner: John Sanacore
Estimated Sales:$ 10 - 20 Million
Number Employees: 100-249

10768 Oven Fresh Baking Company
250 N Washtenaw Ave
Chicago, IL 60612-2014   773-638-1234
Fax: 773-638-1237
Croissants and muffins
    President: George Spanos
    Marketing Director: Steve Sarsitis
Estimated Sales:$ 5-10 Million
Number Employees: 100-249
Brands:
    Oven Fresh

10769 Oven Head Salmon Smokers
101 Oven Head Road
Bethel, NB E5C 1S3
Canada   506-755-2507
Fax: 506-755-8883 877-955-2507
overhead@brunnet.net
www.ovenheadsmokers.com
Manufacturer and exporter of smoked Atlantic
salmon, smoked salmon pate, and jerky
    President: Debra Thorne
    CEO: Joseph Thorne
*Estimated Sales:*Under $1 Million
Number Employees: 4-6
Number of Brands: 1
Number of Products: 3
Brands:
    OVEN HEAD

10770 Oven Poppers
99 Faltin Dr
Manchester, NH 03103-5755   603-644-3773
Fax: 603-669-8646 info@ovenpoppers.com
www.ovenpoppers.com
Processor of frozen seafood entrees
    President: Stacy Kimball
    COO: Andy Desmarais
    Plant Manager: James Carigran
Estimated Sales:$ 5-10 Million
Number Employees: 50-99
Type of Packaging: Consumer, Food Service
Brands:
    Oven Poppers

10771 Oven Ready Products
3-111 Watson Road
Guelph, ON N1E 6X7
Canada   519-767-2415
Fax: 519-823-2196
ovenreadyproducts@on.aibn.com
Manufacturer of frozen unbaked pastry food products, beef rolls, fruit turnovers
    President: Jim Harrison
Number Employees: 1-4
Type of Packaging: Consumer, Food Service
Brands:
    OVEN READY

10772 Over The Moon ChocolateCompany Ltd
2868 W Broadway
Vancouver, BC V6K 2G7
Canada   604-709-9288
Fax: 604-709-9238 800-933-2462
wwww.overthemoon.ca
Manufacturer of Chocolate
    President/Owner: Rob Greehow
Brands:
    OVER THE MOON

10773 Overhill Farms
2727 E Vernon Ave
Vernon, CA 90058-1822   323-582-9977
Fax: 323-582-6122 800-859-6406
sales@overhillfarms.com
www.overhillfarms.com
Processor of frozen and custom prepared entrees,
soups and sauces, poultry, meat, and fish specialties.
    Chairman: James Rudis
    CEO: James Rudis
    Quality Control: Rebecca Smith
    President: James Rudis
    Human Resources Manager: Silvia Ventura
    Plant Manager: Geoff Bickham
*Estimated Sales:*I
Number Employees: 1,000-4,999
Sq. footage: 225000
Parent Co: IBM Foods
Type of Packaging: Consumer, Food Service, Private Label, Bulk
Brands:
    Overhill Farms

10774 Overlake Blueberry Farm
2380 Bellevue Way SE
Bellevue, WA 98004-7327   425-453-8613
Blueberries and related products

10775 Overlake Foods Corporation
PO Box 2631
Olympia, WA 98507-2631   360-352-7989
Fax: 360-352-8076 800-683-1078
info@overlakefoods.com
www.overlakefoods.com
Processor and exporter of frozen blueberries, raspberries, strawberries, blackberries and peaches
    Coo: Rodney Cook
    Sales: Paul Askier
Estimated Sales:$1,518,842
Number Employees: 4
Sq. footage: 1800
Parent Co: Producer Marketing Group
Type of Packaging: Bulk
Brands:
    OVERLAKE

10776 Oversea Fishery & Investment Company
2752 Woodlawn Dr # 5-110
Honolulu, HI 96822-1855   808-847-2500
Fax: 808-836-3308
Seafood
    President: Francis Tsang
Estimated Sales:$ 3 - 5 Million
Number Employees: 1-4

10777 Owens Country Sausage
P.O.Box 830249
Richardson, TX 75083-0249   972-235-7181
Fax: 972-235-2135 800-966-9367
information@Owensinc.com
www.owensinc.com
Processor of pork sausage
    Chairman: Steven Davis
    VP: Terry Russell
    VP Sales: Terry Russell
    Sales Director: Terry Russell
*Estimated Sales:*H
Number Employees: 500-999
Parent Co: Bob Evans Farms
Type of Packaging: Consumer
Brands:
    Owens Original Beef Chili
    Owens Patties
    Owens Roll Sausage
    Owens Smoked Sausage

10778 Owensboro Grain Edible Oils
P.O.Box 1787
Owensboro, KY 42302-1787   270-273-5443
Fax: 270-686-6509 ogcogeo@aol.com
www.louisdreyfus.com
Refined liquid and hydrogenated soybean oil products
    President: Robert Hicks Jr
    CFO: Jeff Erb
    CEO: Robert Hicks Jr Jr
    Sales Director: James Stahler
    Operations Director: Mark Carlyle
Estimated Sales:$ 75-100 Million
Number Employees: 50-99

10779 Owl's Nest Cheese
PO Box 1974
Kaukauna, WI 54130   608-825-6818
Fax: 608-825-3992 www.owlsnestcheese.com
Cheese spreads
    Marketing Director: Larry Hoover
Estimated Sales:$10-24.9 Million
Number Employees: 20-49

10780 Oxford Frozen Foods Limited
4881 Main Street
Oxford, NS B0M 1P0
Canada   902-447-2100
Fax: 902-447-2102
lwillmot@oxfordfrozenfoods.com
www.oxfordfrozenfoods.com
Processor and exporter of frozen blueberries, carrots
and onion rings
    President: John Bragg
Number Employees: 250-499
Type of Packaging: Consumer

10781 Oxford Organics
354 Eisenhower Parkway
Livingston, NJ 07039-1022   908-351-0002
Fax: 908-351-0007 sales@oxorg.com
www.oxorg.com
Natural and synthetic chemicals for flavors and fragrances
Estimated Sales:$ 2.5-5 Million
Number Employees: 1-4

10782 Oxnard Lemon Company
2001 Sunkist Cir
Oxnard, CA 93033-3902   805-483-1173
Fax: 805-486-0595 fdian@oxnardlemon.com
www.oxnardlemon.com

Oxnard Lemon Company is a licensed packer for Sunkist Growers, Inc. and provides packing services for over 100 Sunkist lemon growers, representing over 4,000 acres in the counties of Ventura, Santa Barbara, Monterey, Tulare, KernRiverside, and San Diego.
General Manager: Sam Mayhew
Packinghouse Manager: Frank Diaz
Field Manager: Tom Mayhew
Field Manager: Jose Claudio
Sales Coordinator: Roger Valasco
Office Manager: Rebecca Fetters
Human Resources: Nancy Low
Plant Manager: Jose Claudio
Sq. footage: 250000
Type of Packaging: Food Service

10783 Oyster World
PO Box 1605
Kilmarnock, VA 22482-1605   804-438-5470
Oysters
President: W Cornwell

10784 Ozark Mountain Trading
PO Box 171
Westfield, NJ 07091-0171   908-232-6365
Processor and importer of natural snack foods
President: Jim Forgus
Type of Packaging: Food Service

10785 Ozeki Sake
249 Hillcrest Rd
Hollister, CA 95023-4921   831-630-1101
Fax: 831-637-0953 question@ozekisake.com
www.ozekisake.com
Sake
President: Bunjiro Osabe
COO: Katsuyoshi Yoshida
Estimated Sales: $ 5-10 Million
Number Employees: 20-49
Type of Packaging: Private Label

10786 Ozery's Pita Break
15 Vanley Crescent
Toronto, ON M3J 2B7
Canada
416-630-4224
Fax: 413-630-4217 888-556-5560
mail@pitabreak.com www.pitabreak.com
pita breads
Estimated Sales: $18 Million
Number Employees: 110

10787 Ozone Confectioners & Bakers Supplies
55 Bank St
Elmwood Park, NJ 07407-1146   201-791-4444
Fax: 201-791-2893
Manufacturer and exporter of confectionery products including bagged, licorice, sugar coated jordan almonds, wedding almonds and nonpareil seeds
President: Patrick Lapone
VP: Louis Lapone
Estimated Sales: $ 3 - 5 Million
Number Employees: 10-19
Number of Brands: 1
Type of Packaging: Private Label
Brands:
Lapone's Jordan

10788 Ozuna Food Products Corporation
1260 Alderwood Ave
Sunnyvale, CA 94089-2201   408-400-0495
Fax: 408-727-2029
Processor of corn and flour tortillas; also, plain, salted and flavored tortilla chips
Owner: Vito Ozuna
Estimated Sales: $300,000-500,000
Number Employees: 1-4
Sq. footage: 75000
Type of Packaging: Consumer, Food Service, Private Label, Bulk

10789 P & L Poultry
3821 S Bates Court
Spokane Valley, WA 99206-6348   509-892-1242
Fax: 509-892-1244
Manufacturer of chicken and turkey products including frankfurters
Number Employees: 1-4
Type of Packaging: Consumer, Food Service, Private Label, Bulk

10790 P & M Staiger Vineyard
1300 Hopkins Gulch Rd
Boulder Creek, CA 95006-8632   831-338-0172
pmstaiger@msn.com
Wine
Owner: Paul Staiger
Estimated Sales: Under $300,000
Number Employees: 1-4

10791 P A Menard
P.O.Box 50158
New Orleans, LA 70150-0158   504-620-2022
Fax: 504-592-2784 www.pamenard.com
Contract packager of dairy products, frozen and specialty foods and general line products; wholesaler/distributor of groceries, private label items, frozen and specialty foods, etc.; serving the food service market
President: Mike Menard
CEO: Pamela Boyd
CFO: Al Pearson
Purchasing: Joe Abraham
Estimated Sales: $ 20 - 50 Million
Number Employees: 20-49
Sq. footage: 70000

10792 P&E Foods
2850 Paa St
Honolulu, HI 96819-4440   808-836-8821
Fax: 808-834-8409
Manager: Harry Toywooka
Estimated Sales: $ 5 - 10 Million
Number Employees: 20-49

10793 P&J Oyster Company
1039 Toulouse St
New Orleans, LA 70112-3425   504-523-2651
Fax: 504-522-4960 info@oysterlover.com
www.oysterlover.com
Processor of fresh and frozen oysters
President: Sal Sunseri
President: Alfred Sunseri
Estimated Sales: $ 10 - 20 Million
Number Employees: 20-49
Sq. footage: 10000
Parent Co: P&J Oyster Company
Type of Packaging: Consumer, Food Service
Brands:
Harvest Select
Landlock
P&J
P&J Old New Orleans Seafood House

10794 P&J Oyster Company
1039 Toulouse St
New Orleans, LA 70112-3425   504-523-2651
Fax: 504-522-4960 info@oysterlover.com
www.oysterlover.com
Oysters
General Manager: Alfred Sunseri
Sales Manager: Sal Sunseri Jr
Office Manager: Merri Sunseri-Schneider
Plant Manager: Merri Schneider
Estimated Sales: $ 1-2.5 Million appx.
Number Employees: 20-49
Brands:
Gold Band Products

10795 P&L Seafood of Venice
401 Whitney Ave # 103
Gretna, LA 70056-2500   504-363-2744
Fax: 504-392-3334 www.chartwellsmenus.com
Seafood
Manager: John Duke

10796 P&S Food Trading
4910 W Irving Park Rd
Chicago, IL 60641-2619   773-685-0088
Fax: 773-685-0088
Owner: Edmund Sammando
Estimated Sales: $ .5 - 1 million
Number Employees: 1-4

10797 P&S Ravioli Company
2001 S 26th St
Philadelphia, PA 19145-2598   215-465-8888
Fax: 215-465-3559 support@psravioli.com
www.psravioli.com
Fresh pasta
Owner: Sacondo Di Giacomo
Co-Owner: Secondo Ravioli
Plant Manager: Mariano DiGiacomo
Estimated Sales: Less than $500,000
Number Employees: 20-49
Brands:
P&S Ravioli

10798 P-Bee Products
23011 Moulton Pkwy # F7
Laguna Hills, CA 92653-1226   949-586-6300
Fax: 649-586-6360 800-322-5572
info@pbeeproducts.com www.pbeeproducts.com
Nutritional supplements
President: Raymond Guna
Owner: Steven Kramar
Vice President: Lacey Guna
Estimated Sales: $500,000-$1 Million
Number Employees: 1-4
Type of Packaging: Consumer, Bulk
Brands:
P-Bee

10799 P-R Farms
2917 E Shepherd Ave
Clovis, CA 93619-9152   559-299-0201
Fax: 559-299-7292 robert@prfarms.com
www.prfarms.com
Grower, packer and exporter of apples, apricots, nectarines, oranges, peaches, plums, etc.; also, almonds
General Manager: Pat Ricchiuti
CEO: Pat V Ricchiuti
Sales Director: Robert Rocha
Estimated Sales: $ 10 - 20 Million
Number Employees: 100-249
Sq. footage: 150000
Type of Packaging: Consumer, Food Service, Private Label, Bulk
Brands:
BELLA FRUTTA
P-R FARMS

10800 P. Janes & Sons
PO Box 10
Hant's Harbor, NL A0B 1Y0
Canada
709-586-2252
Fax: 709-586-2870 jgalliford@pjanes.com
www.pjanes.com
Processor and exporter of fresh and frozen seafood
Sales Director: Jeff Galliford
Purchasing Agent: Blair Janes
Type of Packaging: Consumer, Food Service, Private Label, Bulk

10801 P.A. Braunger Institutional Foods
900 Clark St
Sioux City, IA 51101-2000   712-258-4515
Fax: 712-258-1130 braungers@mcleodusa.net
www.braunger.com
Wholesaler/distributor of frozen foods, meats, private label items and general line products; serving the food service market
President: Tony Wald
General Manager: J David
Estimated Sales: $ 10 - 20 Million
Number Employees: 50-99

10802 P.C. Teas Company
882 Mahler Rd # 8
Burlingame, CA 94010-1604   650-697-8989
Fax: 650-697-9016 800-423-8728
info@teastohealth.com www.teastohealth.com
Herbal tea products
Owner: Sunny Wong
Estimated Sales: Below $ 5 Million
Number Employees: 10-19
Type of Packaging: Private Label
Brands:
Natural Green Leaf Brand

10803 P.G. Molinari & Sons
1401 Yosemite Ave
San Francisco, CA 94124-3321   415-822-5555
Fax: 415-822-5834 info@molinarisalame.com
www.molinarisalame.com
Dry salami, sausage
President: Frank Giorgi
Sales Manager: Lou Mascola
Estimated Sales: Below $ 5 Million
Number Employees: 20-49
Type of Packaging: Food Service
Brands:
Finocchiona
Toscano Style

10804 P.J. Lisac & Associates
1815 Red Soils Ct
Oregon City, OR 97045-4139   503-652-1988
Fax: 503-653-1979 www.lisanatti.com

Processor of cheese analogs including soy satin
President: Philip J Lisac
Estimated Sales: $ 5-10 Million
Number Employees: 10-19
Type of Packaging: Consumer, Food Service
Brands:
Lisanatti
Soy-Sation

10805 P.J. Markos Seafood Company
8 1/2 Topsfield Road
Ipswich, MA 01938-2132   978-356-4347
Fax: 978-356-9380
Seafood
Estimated Sales: $ 1 - 3 Million
Number Employees: 5-9

10806 P.J. Merrill Seafood
681 Forest Ave
Portland, ME 04103-4101   207-773-1321
Fax: 207-775-4160
Seafood
President: John Merrill
Estimated Sales: $ 3 - 5 Million
Number Employees: 10-19

10807 P.J. Noyes Company
89 Bridge St
Lancaster, NH 03584-3103   603-788-4952
Fax: 603-788-3873   800-522-2469
info@pjnoyes.com   www.pjnoyes.com
Contract manufacturer and exporter of compressed
tablets and liquids
President: David Hill
Quality Control Manager: Carol Cardinal
Manager Sales/Marketing: James Hoverman
Estimated Sales: $ 10 - 20 Million
Number Employees: 10-19
Type of Packaging: Private Label, Bulk
Brands:
Fishin' Chips
Noyes Precision

10808 P.L. Thomas
4 Headquarters Plz # 203
Morristown, NJ 07960-3963   973-984-0900
Fax: 973-984-5666   plt@plthomas.com
www.plthomas.com
P.L. Thomas, a New Jersey-based ingredient supplier, offers fifty years of innovation in securing reli-
able high quality raw materials for the
food/functional food and nutrition industries. PLT is
a one-stop resource for applicationsolutions, current
industry information and technical service, and spe-
cializes in water-soluble gums and clinically-sup-
ported botanical extracts.
President: Paul Flowerman
Marketing: Paula Nurnberger
Sales: Rodger Jonas
Estimated Sales: $ 5 - 10 Million
Number Employees: 5-9
Brands:
5-Loxin
Ceamgel 1313
Ecoguar
Fenopure
Glisodin
Glocal
Meganatural
Nutralease
Nutraveggie
Nutricran
Ultraguar

10809 P.M. Innis Lobster Company
P.O.Box 85
Biddeford Pool, ME 04006-0085   207-284-5000
Fax: 207-283-3308 www.poollobster.com
Lobster
Owner: Beth Baskin
Estimated Sales: $ 3 - 5 Million
Number Employees: 10-19

10810 P.T. Fish
10b Portland Fish Pier
Portland, ME 04101-4620   207-772-0239
Fax: 907-874-2072
Seafood
Owner: Michael Twiss

10811 P/B Distributors
2450 New York Avenue
Whiting, IN 46394-1959   219-659-7751
Fax: 219-659-7930

President: Jay El-Kareh

10812 PACA Foods
5212 Cone Rd
Tampa, FL 33610-5302   813-628-8228
Fax: 813-628-8426   800-388-7419
pacafoodman@aol.com   www.pacafoods.com
Processor and contract packager of spice blends,
beverage mixes, flour based mixes, seasonings, in-
dustrial premixes, nutrition blends
President: Robert Cabral
VP/CFO: Paul Pritchard
Sales Director: Ed Sullivan
Estimated Sales: $ 5-10 Million
Number Employees: 20-49
Sq. footage: 30000
Type of Packaging: Private Label

10813 PB&S Chemicals
P.O.Box 20
Henderson, KY 42419-0020   270-830-1200
Fax: 270-827-4767   800-950-7267
mid-south.info@brenntag.com
www.brenntagmidsouth.com
Beverage, confectionery, canned foods, processed
cheese, bakery, meat, seafood and dairy applications
President: Joel Hopper
Marketing/Sales: Natalie Vandivier
Number Employees: 100-249
Brands:
Brenntag

10814 PC Teas Company
882 Mahler Rd # 8
Burlingame, CA 94010-1604   650-697-8989
Fax: 650-697-9016   800-423-8728
info@teastohealth.com   www.teastohealth.com
Processor of herbal tea products
President: Sunny Wong
Estimated Sales: Below $ 5 Million
Number Employees: 10-19

10815 PEI Mussel King
PO Box 39
Morrell, PE C0A 1S0
Canada   902-961-3300
Fax: 902-961-3366   800-673-2767
info@peimusselking.com
www.peimusselking.com
Processor of fresh and frozen mussels, oysters and
clams
President: Russell Dockendorff Sr
Co-Owner: Dorothy Dockendorff
Number Employees: 20-49
Type of Packaging: Consumer, Food Service, Pri-
vate Label, Bulk
Brands:
PEI Mussel King

10816 (HQ)PEZ Candy
35 Prindle Hill Rd
Orange, CT 06477-3616   203-795-0531
Fax: 203-799-1679 www.pez.com
Manufacturer and exporter of hard candy and dis-
pensers; importer of wafers and chocolates
President: Joseph Vittoria
CFO: Brian Fry
VP Marketing: Peter Vandall
VP Sales: Dan Silliman
VP Operations: Mark Morrissey
Estimated Sales: $3,100,000
Number Employees: 20-49
Type of Packaging: Consumer
Other Locations:
PEZ Candy
Orange CT
Brands:
PEZ

10817 PFG Milton's Foodservice
3501 Old Oakwood Rd
Oakwood, GA 30566-2802   770-532-7779
Fax: 770-503-9234 www.pfgmiltons.com
President: Danny Berry
Estimated Sales: $ 5 - 10 Million
Number Employees: 5-9

10818 PGP International
P.O.Box 2060
Woodland, CA 95776-2060   530-662-5056
Fax: 530-662-6074   800-233-0110
info@pacgrain.com   www.pacgrain.com

Specialty ingredients
CEO: Zachaey Wochok
CEO: Zachary S Wochok
Research & Development: Jennifer Eastman
Quality Control: Aman Das
Marketing Director: Cary Maigret-Saptiste
Operations Manager: Joe Holbrook
Number Employees: 100-249

10819 PJ's Coffee & Tea
5300 Tchoupitoulas St
New Orleans, LA 70115-1936   504-895-2007
Fax: 504-486-2345   800-527-1055
tmareno@pjscoffee.com   www.pjscoffee.com
Specialty coffee and tea beverages and cafe opera-
tions
Manager: Tom Boudreaux
Owner: Phyllis Jordan
Accounts Manager: Tanya Mareno
Wholesale Manager: Felton Jones
Cafe Operations Manager: Mindy McKnight
Estimated Sales: $ 500,000 - $ 1 Million
Number Employees: 5-9
Type of Packaging: Private Label
Brands:
PJ's Coffee

10820 PM AG Products
17475 Jovanna Drive
Homewood, IL 60430-1020   708-206-2030
Fax: 708-206-1340   800-323-2663
www.pmagproducts.com
Grain, milling, feed
CEO: Pat Mohan
Estimated Sales: $ 20-50 Million
Number Employees: 20

10821 PM Windom
2850 Highway 60 E
Windom, MN 56101-1291   507-831-2761
Fax: 507-831-6216 info@pmglobal.com
www.pmholdings.com
Processor and exporter of meat products including
beef
President: Greg Miller
Plant Manager: Jim Bever
Purchasing Agent: Randy Meyers
Estimated Sales: $ 50 - 100 Million
Number Employees: 250-499
Parent Co: Pm Windom
Type of Packaging: Consumer

10822 PMC Specialties
501 Murray Rd
Cincinnati, OH 45217-1014   513-242-3300
Fax: 513-482-7373   800-228-3673
www.pmcsg.com
Preservatives
Executive: Cory Davids
Estimated Sales: $ 10-20 Million
Number Employees: 250-499

10823 (HQ)PMC Specialties Group
501 Murray Rd
Cincinnati, OH 45217-1014   513-242-3300
Fax: 513-482-7373   800-543-2466
www.pmcsg.com
Manufacturer and exporter of saccharin, BHT,
methyl anthranilate, benzonitrile, etc
President: Rudolph Gulstrand Jr
Executive: Cory Davids
Marketing Manager: Narasimha Rao
Technical Service Contact: Jack Lehner
Number Employees: 250-499
Parent Co: PMC Global
Other Locations:
PMC Specialties Group
Cincinnati OH
Brands:
CAO
SYNCAL

10824 PMP Fermentation Products
900 NE Adams St
Peoria, IL 61603-4200   309-637-0400
Fax: 309-637-9302   800-558-1031
shendrick@pmpinc.com   www.pmpinc.com

Processor of sodium gluconate and erythorbate, calcium gluconate and gluconic acid; importer of glucono-delta-lactone; exporter of sodium erythorbate and gluconate and calcium potassium gluconate
President: Yuzo Kono
Vice President: Dennis Huff
Marketing Manager: Nao Takaoka
Sales Director: Spurgeon Hendrick
Purchasing Manager: Richard Jenks
Estimated Sales:$25000000
Number Employees: 50-99
Parent Co: Fujisawa Pharmaceutical
Type of Packaging: Bulk
Brands:
ERIBATE

10825 POG
PO Box 699
Grand Bend, ON N0M 1T0
Canada   519-238-5704
                                     Fax: 519-238-2424
Processor of onions including frozen, fresh, whole silver skin, pearl vinegar and salt brine
Type of Packaging: Bulk

10826 (HQ)PR Nutrition
3944 Murphy Canyon Road
San Diego, CA 92123-4498   858-576-6488
          Fax: 858-576-9152   800-397-5556
                                     www.prbar.com
Manufacturer of nutritional drink mixes including chocolate, vanilla cream and orange sherbet, supplements
Number Employees: 50
Parent Co: Twinlab Corporation

10827 PRO Refrigeration Inc
P.O.Box 1528
Auburn, WA 98071-1528   253-735-9466
          Fax: 253-735-2631   jimvgst@earthlink.net
                                     www.prochiller.com
Manufacturers of the Pro Chiller System and the Proformer Refrigerated Product Line.
Owner: Jim Vandergiessen Sr
VP/CEO/General Manager: Jim Vander Giessen Jr
Chief Financial Officer: Gary Duim
Operations Manager: Matthew Perala
Inventory Control: Kelly Phelps
Purchasing Manager/Technical Support: Rande Routledge

10828 PaStreeta Fresca
545 Metro Place S
Suite 100
Dublin, OH 43017-5353   800-343-5266
          Fax: 740-342-5068   paStreetafresc@aol.com
Processor of gourmet pastas and sauces
President: Joanne McGonagle
Estimated Sales:$400000
Number Employees: 3
Type of Packaging: Consumer, Food Service
Brands:
Pasta Fresca

10829 (HQ)Pabst Brewing Company
P.O.Box 792627
San Antonio, TX 78279-2627   210-226-0231
          Fax: 210-226-2512   800-935-2337
          products@pabst.com   www.pabst.com
Beer manufacturer
General Manager: John Kanetzke
CEO: Kevin Kotecki
Number Employees: 100-249
Type of Packaging: Consumer
Brands:
Augsberger
Big Bear
Bull Ice
Champale
Clash Malt
Colt 45
Country Club
Falstaff
Goebel
Ice Man
Jacob Best
Laser
Old Milwaukee
Olympia
Pabst Blue Ribbon Beers
Piels
Piels Light

Private Stock
Red Bull Malt Liquor
Red River
Schaefer
Schlitz
Silver Thunder Malt Liquor
Special Brew
St. Ides Special Brew
Stroh's
White Mountain

10830 Pac Moore Products
1844 E Summer St
Hammond, IN 46320-2236   219-932-2666
          Fax: 219-932-3344   solutions@pacmoore.com
                                     www.pacmoore.com
Manufactures kosher foods
President: William Moore
Marketing manager: Bob Lyman
Owner: William Moore
Estimated Sales:$ 10 - 20 Million
Number Employees: 100-249
Brands:
Pac Moore

10831 Pacari Organic Chocolate
6101 Blue Lagoon Drive
Suite 150
Miami, FL 33126   561-214-4726
          Fax: 561-584-6363   info@pacarichocolate.com
                                     www.picarichocolate.com
organic chocolate made in Ecuador

10832 Pace Dairy Foods Company
2700 Valleyhigh Dr NW
Rochester, MN 55901-7601   507-288-6315
          Fax: 507-288-3320   dvalle@packersprovision.com
                                     www.kroeger.com
Natural processed cheese
Manager: Jim Lehman
Controller: Paul Peng
Marketing Manager: Roger Templeton
General Manager: Jim Lehman
Production Manager: Randy Hess
Purchasing Manager: Jim Lehnan
Estimated Sales:$ 50-100 Million
Number Employees: 250-499

10833 Pacheco Ranch Winery
235 Alameda Del Prado
Novato, CA 94949-6657   415-883-5583
                                     Fax: 415-883-6992
          sales@pachecoranchwinery.com
          www.pachecoranchwinery.com
Wines
Manager: Herb Rowland
Head Finance/Distribution: Debbie Rowland
CFO: Debra Rowland
Quality Control: Jamie Mezes
Winemaker: Jamie Meves
Estimated Sales:$ 2.5-5 Million
Number Employees: 1-4
Brands:
Pacheco Ranch

10834 Pacific Alaska Seafoods
219 1st Ave S # 310
Seattle, WA 98104-2551   206-587-0002
                                     Fax: 206-587-0004
Processor, importer and exporter of salmon, halibut, cod, roe, geoduck and herring including fresh, frozen and fillets
President: Tony Cadden
Estimated Sales:$6500000
Number Employees: 1-4

10835 Pacific Blueberries
PO Box 527
Rochester, WA 98579-0527   360-273-5405
                                     Fax: 360-273-5425
Frozen blueberries
COO: Greg McKinney
*Estimated Sales:*Below $ 5 Million
Number Employees: 40

10836 Pacific Cheese Company
21090 Cabot Blvd
PO Box 56598
Hayward, CA 94545-6598   510-784-8800
          Fax: 510-784-8846   info@pacificcheese.com
                                     www.pacific-cheese.com

Cheese
President: Stephen B Gaddis
CFO: Bill Saltzman
Director Plant Operations: Gary Teak
Estimated Sales:$39 Million
Number Employees: 150
Brands:
BELLAFOGLIA
CALIFORNIA SELECT FARMS
CHESWICK
GRAND EUROPEAN
NORTH BEACH
OOMEGA FARMS
PACIFIC BUE

10837 Pacific Choice Brands
4667 E Date Ave
Fresno, CA 93725-2101   559-237-5583
          Fax: 559-237-2078   chris@pcbrands.com
                                     www.pacificchoicebrands.com
Manufacturer and exporter of a variety of products and condiments such as maraschino cherries, garlic, grape leaves, peppers, olives, salsa, sauces, capers and sun dried tomotoes. Kosher and organic products
President: Allan Andrews
VP Sales: Bonifacio Villalobos
Estimated Sales:$39.5 Million
Number Employees: 100-249
Type of Packaging: Consumer, Food Service, Private Label
Brands:
DURANGO GOLD
ORLANDO
PACIFIC CHOICE

10838 Pacific Choice Seafood
1 Commercial St
Eureka, CA 95501-0241   707-442-1113
          Fax: 707-442-2985   sspencer@pacseafood.com
                                     www.pacseafood.com
Seafood
Manager: Frank Dulcich
General Manager: Rick Harris
R & D: Dave Bodiroga
Quality Control: Chuck Corcoran
Estimated Sales:$ 20-50 Million
Number Employees: 100-249

10839 Pacific Coast Brewing Company
906 Washington St
Oakland, CA 94607-4032   510-836-2739
                                     Fax: 510-836-1987
          info@pacificcoastbrewing.com
          www.pacificcoastbrewing.com
Processor of seasonal beer, ale, stout and porter
Owner: Steve Wolff
Owner/Brewmaster: Don Gortemiller
*Estimated Sales:*Below $ 500,000
Number Employees: 20-49
Type of Packaging: Consumer, Food Service
Brands:
Grey Whale
Imperial
Pacific Coast Brewing Co.

10840 Pacific Coast Fruit Company
201 N E Second Avenue -100
Portland, OR 97232   503-234-6411
          Fax: 503-234-0072 www.pcfruit.com
Processor and exporter of frozen fruits, juice concentrates and puree concentrates including strawberry, raspberry, pineapple, cranberry, etc.; importer of frozen elderberries, strawberries and raspberries and peach/apricot puree andberry juice concentrates
President: Dave Nemarnik
Secretary/Treasurer: Ellen McIntyre
Office Manager: Debbie McKee
Number Employees: 5-9
Type of Packaging: Bulk

10841 (HQ)Pacific Coast ProducersCorporate Office
P.O.Box 1600
Lodi, CA 95241-1600   209-367-8800
          Fax: 209-367-1084   pcp@pcoastp.com
                                     www.pcoastp.com
Manufacturer of canned tomatoes, tomato pulp and puree; also, grapes, peaches, pears and apricots
President/CEO: Daniel Vincent
VP Finance/CFO/Treasurer: Mark Wahlman
VP Operations: Daniel Sroufe
*Estimated Sales:*I
Number Employees: 1,000-4,999

Type of Packaging: Consumer, Food Service, Private Label, Bulk
Other Locations:
Pacific Coast Producers Plant
Lodi CA
Pacific Coast Producers Plant
Oroville CA
Pacific Coast Producers Plant
Woodland CA
Brands:
CHOICE
FANCY

10842 Pacific Coast Producers
P.O.Box 32
Oroville, CA 95965-0032   530-533-4311
        Fax: 530-533-2108 www.pcoastp.com
Processor of canned foods including fruit cocktail,
peaches and pears
President/CEO: Daniel Vincent
VP Finance/CFO/Treasurer: Mark Wahlman
VP Operations: Daniel Sroufe
Plant Manager: Chris Ward
Estimated Sales: $ 10 - 20 Million
Number Employees: 20-49
Type of Packaging: Private Label

10843 Pacific Coast Producers
P.O.Box 1600
Lodi, CA 95241-1600   209-367-8800
        Fax: 209-367-1084 pcp@pcoastp.com
        www.pcoastp.com
Canned fruits and vegetables
President: Daniel L Vincent
VP Finance: Mark M Wahlman
Chairman: Anthony Turkovich
Executive VP: Dan Vincent
VP Human Resources: Dick Ehrler
Operations Manager: James Scapace
Estimated Sales: $ 300-500 Million
Number Employees: 1,000-4,999
Type of Packaging: Private Label

10844 Pacific Collier Fresh Company
925 New Harvest Rd
Immokalee, FL 34142-3838   239-657-5283
        Fax: 239-657-4924 800-226-7274
        www.sunripe.com
Manufacturer of beans, cabbage, cucumbers, pota-
toes, squash, tomatos
Manager: Jennifer Levy
Estimated Sales: $ 10 - 20 Million
Number Employees: 20-49
Parent Co: Heller Brothers
Brands:
SUNRIPE

10845 Pacific Echo Cellars
4501 Highway 128
Philo, CA 95466   707-895-2065
        Fax: 707-895-2758 avfizz@pacific.net
        www.pacific-echo.com
Sparkling wine
President: Mineille Guiliano
Manager: Walter Sawitsky
Winery Manager/Winemaker: Tex Sawyer
Vineyard Operations Manager: Bob Nye
Vineyard Manager: Tony Hortlig
Estimated Sales: Below $ 5 Million
Number Employees: 20-49
Type of Packaging: Private Label
Brands:
Pacific Echo
Scharffenberger

10846 Pacific Foods
21612 88th Ave S
Kent, WA 98031-1918   253-395-9400
        Fax: 253-395-3330 800-347-9444
Processor, exporter and importer of flavoring ex-
tracts, seasoning mixes, soup bases, baking powder,
nuts and spices
President: James Hughs
Plant Manager: Brandan Caile
Vice President: Richard Weaver
Plant Manager: Mark Hendrickson
Estimated Sales: $ 5 - 10 Million
Number Employees: 50-99
Type of Packaging: Food Service, Private Label,
Bulk
Brands:
Chef Classic
Crescent

10847 Pacific Foods of Oregon
19480 SW 97th Ave
Tualatin, OR 97062-8505   503-692-9666
        Fax: 503-692-9610 martell@pacificfoods.com
        www.pacificfoods.com
Processor and exporter of aseptic soy milk
President: Jon Gehrs
R&D: Tom Hiatt
CEO: Carolyn Rayback
Sales Director: Tim Ramsey
Operations Manager: Meav Winkle
Production Manager: Kurt Alameda
Estimated Sales: $32200000
Number Employees: 100-249
Sq. footage: 60000
Type of Packaging: Consumer, Food Service, Pri-
vate Label
Brands:
New Moon
Pacific
Pacific Foods
Pacific Foods of Oregon New Moon
Pacific Foods of Oregon Pacific

10848 Pacific Fruit Processors
PO Box 2218
South Gate, CA 90280-9218   323-774-6000
        Fax: 562-630-8392
Processor of dairy fruits for ice cream, yogurt, cakes,
pies, doughnuts, dry mixes and fillings
Chairman: Lee Warner
Plant Manager: Phil Short
Estimated Sales: $8200000
Number Employees: 60
Type of Packaging: Food Service
Other Locations:
Pacific Fruit Processors
Lapham Co
Brands:
Lapham

10849 Pacific Gold Marketing
3451 Yeager Rd
Madera, CA 93637-8728   559-661-6176
        Fax: 559-661-6180 pacgoldinc@aol.com
        www.pacgold.com
Manufacturer of a variety of Nuts, dried fruit and
candy-coated items, including pistachios, almonds,
cashews and dark chocolate pistachios
President: Patricia Locktov
Estimated Sales: Below $5 Million
Number Employees: 100-249
Brands:
PACIFIC GOLD

10850 Pacific Gourmet Seafood
26 Stine Road
Bakersfield, CA 93309-2011   661-533-1260
        Fax: 805-831-9740
Seafood
Partner: Kelly Bowman
Partner: Patsy Bowman

10851 Pacific Harvest Products
13405 SE 30th Ave
Bellevue, WA 98005-4454   425-401-7990
        www.pacificharvestproducts.com
Manufactures dry blends, sauces, dressings, bases.
Custom packaging offers a diverse range of sizes
Number Employees: 20-49
Type of Packaging: Consumer, Food Service, Pri-
vate Label, Bulk
Brands:
FIRMENICH

10852 Pacific Hop Exchange Brewing Company
158 Hamilton Drive
Novato, CA 94949-5630   415-884-2820
        Fax: 415-884-2820
Beer
President: Tom Whelan
CFO: Robert Ankrum
Marketing Director: Tom Whelan
Brewer: Warren Stief
Estimated Sales: Under $500,000
Number Employees: 5-9
Sq. footage: 3
Type of Packaging: Private Label
Brands:
06 Stout
Barbary Coast Barley
Gaslight Pale Ale
Graintrader Wheat Al

Holly Hops Spiced Al
I.P.A.
Irish Stout
Ol' Spout
St. Briogets Strong
Warren's Wonderful W

10853 Pacific International Rice Mills
PO Box 652
Woodland, CA 95776-0652   530-666-1691
        Fax: 530-661-6028 800-747-4764
        www.pirmi.com
Manufacturer, packager and exporter of packaged
and bulk rice and rice bran
President/CEO: Steve Malin
Estimated Sales: $20.4 Million
Number Employees: 100
Number of Products: 10
Parent Co: Anheuser-Busch Companies
Type of Packaging: Consumer, Food Service, Pri-
vate Label, Bulk
Brands:
CALROSE
KAHO MAI
MARUYU
PACIFIC INTERNATIONAL

10854 Pacific Nutritional
P.O.Box 820829
Vancouver, WA 98682-0019   360-253-3197
        Fax: 360-253-6543 michael@pacnut.com
        www.pacnut.com
Processor of tablet, capsule, powder and liquid nutri-
tional formulations. Custom manufacture of vita-
mins and nutritional supplements
President: Michael Schaesser
CFO: Robert Miller
VP: Doug Nielsen
Marketing: Chris Taylor
Sales: Bryce Zehrung
Purchasing Manager: Dianne Herrmann
Estimated Sales: $ 12 Million
Number Employees: 50-99
Sq. footage: 35000
Type of Packaging: Private Label

10855 Pacific Ocean Produce
105 Pioneer St
Santa Cruz, CA 95060-2159   831-423-2654
        Fax: 831-423-2654
Processor of dried seaweed
Owner: Matthew Hodel
Estimated Sales: Less than $300,000
Number Employees: 1-4
Type of Packaging: Consumer, Bulk

10856 Pacific Ocean Producers
1133 N Nimitz Hwy
Honolulu, HI 96817-4522   808-537-2905
        Fax: 808-536-3225
Seafood
Owner: Jim Cook

10857 Pacific Ocean Seafood
P.O.Box 193
La Conner, WA 98257-0193   360-466-4455
        Fax: 360-466-3242
Processor and exporter of salmon, halibut, bottom
fish, black cod and shellfish
Owner: Dong Hwang
Estimated Sales: Less than $200,000
Number Employees: 1-4
Type of Packaging: Consumer, Food Service

10858 Pacific Poultry Company
P.O.Box 15851
Honolulu, HI 96830-5851   808-841-2828
        Fax: 808-842-0872 www.hulihuli.com
Processor of portion controlled poultry products and
barbecue sauce
President: Jaren Hancock
Treasurer: J Cuarisma Jr
VP of Operations: Brent Hancock
Estimated Sales: $ 5 - 10 Million
Number Employees: 50-99
Sq. footage: 10350
Type of Packaging: Consumer, Food Service, Pri-
vate Label
Brands:
EWA
Hawaii's Famous Huli Huli

10859 Pacific Pre-cut Produce
100 W Valpico Rd # A
Tracy, CA 95376-8198   209-835-6300
Fax: 209-833-4525   sales@cutfresh.com
www.cutfresh.com
Manufacturer of fresh-cut salads, fruits and vegetables. As of September 2005 Taylor Fresh Foods acquired a majority interest of the company
President: Alan Applonie
Estimated Sales: $100+ Million
Number Employees: 250-499
Sq. footage: 80000
Parent Co: Taylor Fresh Foods

10860 Pacific Resources International
1021 Mark Ave
Carpinteria, CA 93013-2912   805-684-0624
Fax: 805-684-8624   pri98@earthlink.net
New Zealand grocery products
President: David Noll
Estimated Sales: Under $500,000
Number Employees: 1-4
Type of Packaging: Private Label
Brands:
Arataki
Browns Brushware
Clarus

10861 Pacific Salmon Company
120 W Dayton St
Edmonds, WA 98020-7217   425-774-1315
Fax: 425-774-6856
Processor and exporter of black cod, halibut, salmon, shark, smelt, squid, kosher foods and fish patties
Owner: John Mc Callum
Estimated Sales: $ 5 - 10 Million
Number Employees: 10-19
Brands:
PACIFIC

10862 Pacific Seafood Group
16797 SE 130th Ave
Clackamas, OR 97015-9196   503-905-4500
Fax: 503-905-4228   800-388-1101
lmalony@pacseafood.com   www.pacseafood.com
Processor, wholesaler/distributor and exporter of fresh and frozen albacore, cod, flounder, sole, halibut, herring, mackerel, perch, rockfish, salmon, shad, bass, dogfish, shark, smelt, eel, hagfish, sturgeon, whiting, trout, abaloneclams, mussels, etc
Manager: Avery Evans
Vice President: Dan Obradovich
Manager International Section: Larz Malony
Number Employees: 100-249
Parent Co: Pacific Seafood Company
Type of Packaging: Food Service, Private Label, Bulk

10863 Pacific Seafoods International
10210 Bowerbank Road
Sidney, BC V8L 3X4
Canada   250-656-0901
Fax: 250-656-7615   pacseafoods@home.com
www.pacificseafoods.com
Processor and exporter of fresh and frozen salmon including fillets, smoked wholesides and pre-sliced sides
President: Mick Farup
CEO: Todd Harmon
CFO: Gordon Davies
Quality Control: Georgia Cowell
Number Employees: 20-49
Sq. footage: 12000
Type of Packaging: Consumer, Food Service, Private Label, Bulk
Brands:
St. Laurent
Treasure Island

10864 Pacific Shrimp Company
P.O.Box 1230
Newport, OR 97365-0095   541-265-4215
Fax: 541-265-7164   dwright@pacseafood.com
www.pacseafood.com
Processor and exporter of fresh and frozen fish including albacore tuna, autumn fish, crab, salmon, minced whiting, halibut and herring
Manager: Dave Wright
Vice President: Steve Spencer
Sales Director: Steve Spencer
Manager: Dave Wright
Estimated Sales: $57300000
Number Employees: 20-49

10865 Pacific Spice Company
6430 E Slauson Ave
Commerce, CA 90040-3108   323-726-9190
Fax: 323-726-9442   800-281-0614
Gershon@PacSpice.com   www.pacspice.com
Importer and manufacturer of spices and herbs. Conventional & Organic items, custom blending, private label program. Kosher certified
Owner: Gershon Schlussel
VP: Gershon Schlussel
Sales Manager: Gene Fogel
Estimated Sales: $20-25 Million
Number Employees: 90
Sq. footage: 150000
Type of Packaging: Consumer, Food Service, Private Label, Bulk
Brands:
PACIFIC NATURAL SPICES

10866 Pacific Standard Distributors
34480 SE Colorado Rd
Sandy, OR 97055-8266   503-668-0057
Fax: 650-853-1132 www.modifilan.com
Processor and importer of seaweed food supplements in capsule form
Owner: Vladimir Bajanov
Director: Vladimir Bajanov
Estimated Sales: $ 1 - 3 Million
Number Employees: 1-4
Number of Products: 1
Type of Packaging: Consumer, Food Service, Bulk
Brands:
Modifilan

10867 (HQ)Pacific Surf Food Processors
620 Gladys Avenue
Los Angeles, CA 90021-1004   213-623-3433
Fax: 213-614-0427   800-627-5657
pehuh@pafco.net
Processor, importer and exporter of fresh and frozen seafood including breaded and cooked shrimp and fish fillets and calamari steaks, rings and strips
President: Peter Huh
COO: David Wright
Sales Manager: Buck Boston
Plant Manager: Mike Jamemoor
Estimated Sales: $100000000
Number Employees: 100
Sq. footage: 18000
Type of Packaging: Consumer, Food Service
Brands:
Oceankist
Pacific Surf
Scalone

10868 (HQ)Pacific Tomato Growers
503 10th St W
Palmetto, FL 34221-3801   941-722-3291
Fax: 941-729-5849 www.ptg-eee.com
Processor and wholesaler/distributor of tomatoes
CEO: Joseph Esformes
Estimated Sales: $149756046
Number Employees: 250-499
Parent Co: Heller Brothers
Type of Packaging: Bulk
Brands:
Heller
Roma
SUNRIPE

10869 Pacific Trade International
55 Holomua St
Hilo, HI 96720-5142   808-961-0877
Fax: 808-935-1603 www.hilofish.com
President: Charles Umamoto
Estimated Sales: $ 20 - 50 Million
Number Employees: 20-49

10870 Pacific Trellis
1500 W Manning Ave
Reedley, CA 93654-9211   559-638-5100
Fax: 559-638-5400 www.pacifictrellisfruit.com
Stone fruits and grapes
Manager: Earl Mc Menamin
Estimated Sales: $ 10 - 20 Million
Number Employees: 10-19

10871 Pacific Valley Foods
2700 Richards Rd # 101
Bellevue, WA 98005-4292   425-643-1805
Fax: 425-747-4221   info@pacificvalleyfoods.com
www.pacificvalleyfoods.com
Processor, importer and exporter of french fries/frozen potato products; frozen vegetables; frozen berries; tortillas; dehydrated mashed potato products; and dried peas, lentils, chickpeas.
Co-Owner/Co-Director: Scott Hannah
Co-Owner/Co-Director: Lynn Hannah
Executive VP: John Hannah
Estimated Sales: $2300000
Number Employees: 5-9
Sq. footage: 40000
Parent Co: Pacific Valley Foods
Type of Packaging: Consumer, Food Service, Private Label, Bulk
Brands:
BASIC COUNTRY GOODNESS
CEDAR FARMS
GREAT GUSTO
HI WEST
LYNDEN FARMS
PACIFIC VALLEY

10872 Pacific Westcoast Foods
P.O.Box 219176
Portland, OR 97225-9176   503-636-3520
Fax: 503-636-8582   800-874-9333
gourmet@teleport.com   www.gloriasgourmet.com
Processor of salad dressings, preserves and fruit syrups and fillings; wholesaler/distributor of specialty foods, gift packs, private label items
Owner: Mark Roth
Number Employees: 1-4
Sq. footage: 5000
Type of Packaging: Consumer, Food Service, Private Label, Bulk

10873 Pacific Western BrewingCompany
641 N Nechako Road
Prince George, BC V2K 4M4
Canada   250-562-1131
Fax: 250-562-0799   mail@pwbrewing.com
www.pwbrewing.com
Processor of beer, lager and ale
President: Kazuko Komatfu
CEO: Kazuko Komatfu
Marketing Director: Bruce Clark
Office Manager: Denise Vlanchette
Manager: Thomas Leboe
Number Employees: 50-99
Type of Packaging: Consumer, Food Service
Brands:
Amberale
Iron horse
Lager
Pacific Pilsner

10874 Pacifica Culinaria
PO Box 2409
Temecula, CA 92593-2409   800-622-8880
Fax: 951-695-7593   sales@pacificaculinaria.com
www.pacificaculinaria.com
Infused avacado oils, infused vinegars, agave syrups, wasabi mayonnaise, spiced olives, mayan pearl fresh avacados

10875 Pack Ryt, Inc
P.O.Box 728
Thermal, CA 92274-0728   760-399-5026
Fax: 760-399-0093   info@redidate.com
www.packryt.com
Grower, importer and exporter of dates including organic, dehydrated, diced, pitted, macerated and macerated reground.
President: William Jeffrey
CEO/Owner: George Jeffrey
Financial Manager: Terri Lawrence
Quality Control Manager: Lisa Zeise
Production Manager: Corina Sanchez
Plant Supervisor: Cruz Mendoza
Purchasing Supervisor: Corina Sanchez
Estimated Sales: $20-50 Million
Number Employees: 100-249
Type of Packaging: Consumer, Food Service, Private Label, Bulk
Brands:
CALAVO
PROMEDARY
SUN GLOW

10876 Package Concepts & Materials Inc
1023 Thousand Oaks Blvd
Greenville, SC 29607-5642   864-458-7291
Fax: 864-458-7295 800-424-7264
www.packageconcepts.com
Processor and exporter of cook-in casings for meat and poultry processing
President: Peter Bylenga
Operations Manager: Peter Bylenga
Estimated Sales: $ 10 - 20 Million
Number Employees: 50-99
Sq. footage: 50000
Type of Packaging: Food Service

10877 Packaged Products Division
12395 Belcher Road S
Suite 350
Largo, FL 33773-3096   727-787-3619
Fax: 727-787-3619 888-833-2247
pchampagne@pkgproducts.com
www.pkgproducts.com
Snack foods, nutritious snacks
President: Roger Hoover
Vice President: Jason Brooks
Marketing Director: R Barry Williams
Sales Director: Pat Champagne
Public Relations: Angie Strother
Production Manager: Jerry Adams
Purchasing Manager: Jason Brooks
Estimated Sales: $ 3 Million
Number Employees: 25

10878 Packaging By Design
1460 Bowes Rd
Elgin, IL 60123-5539   847-741-5600
Fax: 847-741-5666
mike@packaging-by-design.com
www.packaging-by-design.com
Flexographic packaging for the food industry product line of which includes roll-stock surface printed films; roll-stock custom laminations; roll-stock reverse printed and laminated; and preformed bags.
VP: Charles Graziano
Sales Manager: Michael Graziano
General Manager: Ira Krakow
Type of Packaging: Consumer

10879 Packers Canning Company
PO Box 907
Lawton, MI 49065-0907   269-624-4681
Fax: 269-624-6009 hbsales@honeebear.com
www.honeebear.com
Processor, canner and exporter of berries, cherries, plums, asparagus, blueberries, etc; importer of asparagus, pie fillings and toppings
President: Robert Packer
Vice President: Steve Packer
Sales Manager: Ronald Armstrong
Director: Toby Fields
Estimated Sales: $ 10 - 20 Million
Number Employees: 50-99
Sq. footage: 150000
Type of Packaging: Consumer, Food Service
Brands:
Michigan Made

10880 Pacsea Corporation
PO Box 898
Aiea, HI 96701-0898   808-836-8888
Fax: 808-836-7888
President: Michael Li

10881 Paddack Enterprises
27052 State Highway 120
Escalon, CA 95320-9502   209-838-1536
Fax: 209-838-8063
Processors of almonds
President: Vernon Paddack
Estimated Sales: $500,000 appx.
Number Employees: 5-9

10882 Paesana Products
101 Central Avenue
PO Box 709
East Farmingdale, NY 11735   631-845-1717
Fax: 631-845-1788 info@paesana.com
www.paesana.com
pasta sauces, stuffed olives, specialty condiments, specialty peppers,marinated artichokes, balsamic vinegars, specialty garlic, specialty mushrooms, extra virgin olive oils, sun dried tomatoes, specialty olives, mediterranean tuna

10883 Page Mill Winery
P.O.Box 2659
Livermore, CA 94551-2659   925-456-7676
info@pagemillwinery.com
www.pagemillwinery.com
Wines
Owner: Dick Stark
Owner: Ome Stark
Vice President: Dane Stark
Sales Director: Gary Brink
Operations Manager: Sue Swartz
Vineyard Manager: Leopoldo Gonzalez
Estimated Sales: Less than $500,000
Number Employees: 1-4

10884 Pahlmeyer Winery
P.O.Box 2410
Napa, CA 94558-0241   707-255-2321
Fax: 707-255-6786 info@pahlmeyer.com
www.pahlmeyer.com
Wines
President: Jayson Pahlmeyer
General Manager: Ed Hogan
Vice President: Michael Haas
General Manager/Director Sales/Marketing: Ed Hogan
Controller: Lynn Gentry
Winemaker: Erin Green
Estimated Sales: Below $ 5 Million
Number Employees: 5-9
Type of Packaging: Private Label
Brands:
Jayson
Pahlmeyer

10885 Pahrump Valley Vineyards
3810 Winery Rd # 1
Pahrump, NV 89048-4898   775-751-7800
Fax: 775-751-7818 800-368-9463
pvw@whrus.com www.pahrumpwinery.com
Wines
Manager: Bill Loken
Estimated Sales: $ 5-10 Million
Number Employees: 20-49
Brands:
Pahrump Valley Winery

10886 Paisano Food Products
261 King Street
Elk Grove Village, IL 60007-1112 773-237-3773
Fax: 773-237-8114
Processor of dried beans and fresh and frozen chicken in gravy
Sales Director: Tom Sibrowski
Plant Manager: Octavio Lopez
Number Employees: 100-249
Parent Co: Cousin Foods
Type of Packaging: Food Service

10887 Paisley Farms
38180 Airport Pkwy
Willoughby, OH 44094-8021   440-269-3920
Fax: 440-269-3929 800-676-8656
Manufacturer of pickled vegetables and relishes; private label, custom packaging, gift boxes and food service available
President: Kenneth Anderson
Estimated Sales: $24 Million
Number Employees: 20-49
Sq. footage: 30000
Type of Packaging: Consumer, Food Service, Private Label, Bulk
Brands:
PAISLEY FARM

10888 Pak Technologies
2730 W Silver Spring Dr
Milwaukee, WI 53209-4222   414-438-8600
Fax: 414-977-1458 www.paktech.com
Contract packager of beverages, dairy products, natural and kosher foods, mixes, oils, sauces, spices, vitamins, spreads, pasta, etc
Owner: Kevin Scheule

10889 Pak-Wel Produce
PO Box 430
Vauxhall, AB T0K 2K0
Canada   403-654-2116
Fax: 403-654-2241
Processor of fresh potatoes and onions; exporter and importer of potatoes
President: Frank Gatto
Manager: Lanze Friesen
Plant Manager: Luke Wyna

Number Employees: 20-49
Type of Packaging: Consumer, Food Service
Brands:
Gourmet
Steakmate

10890 Paklab Products
1315 Gay-Lussac
Boucherville, QC J4B 7K1   450-449-1224
Fax: 450-449-3380 www.paklabproducts.com
premium grape juice and grape juice concentrate

10891 Pal's Homemade Ice Cream
4448 Heatherdowns Blvd
Toledo, OH 43614-3113   419-382-0615
Fax: 419-382-0615
Ice cream, frozen desserts
President: Sebastiano Caniglia
Vice President: Helane Stiebler
Estimated Sales: Less than $500,000
Number Employees: 5-9

10892 Palermo Bakery
1620 Fremont Blvd
Seaside, CA 93955-3607   831-394-8212
Fax: 831-394-0184
Bread and bread products
Owner: Rosario Zito
Estimated Sales: $1.2 Million
Number Employees: 20-49
Type of Packaging: Consumer, Food Service, Bulk
Brands:
Palermo

10893 Palermo's Frozen Pizza
3301 W Canal St
Milwaukee, WI 53208-4137   414-643-0919
Fax: 414-643-1696
customerservice@palermospizza.com
www.palermospizza.com
Manufacturer of frozen pizza products
President: Giacomo Fallucca
CEO: Giacomo Fallucca
Vice President: Angelo Fallucca
Marketing Director: Laurie Fallucca
Brands:
Palermo

10894 Palm Apiaries
P.O.Box 6574
Fort Myers, FL 33911-6574   239-334-6001
Health foods and honey
Owner: Kathleen Cassidy
Estimated Sales: $500-1 Million appx.
Number Employees: 1-4

10895 Palm Bay Imports
5301 N Federal Hwy # 2
Boca Raton, FL 33487-4917   561-893-9998
Fax: 561-893-9975 800-872-5622
pbecker@palmbayimports.com
www.palmbayimports.com
Wine
Manager: David Morrison
Marketing Director: Dana Marks
Sales Manager: Patty Becker
Human Resources Manager: Rosemary Mustacchino
Estimated Sales: $38 Million
Number Employees: 100-249
Type of Packaging: Consumer, Bulk
Brands:
Alexander Grappa
Aneri
Anselmi
Bauchant
Bertani
Blue Fish
Bodegas Campillo
Boissiere
Bottega Vinaia
Boulard
Brown Brothers
Candido
Cavit
Circus
Citra
Col Dorcia
EY
Firstland
Frapin
Frotious
Santana
Sella & Mosca

10896 Palm Springs Baking Company
1196 Montalvo Way
Palm Springs, CA 92262-5441   760-320-7414
                                    Fax: 760-327-0331
Bread and baked goods
    President: David Parker
    Chairman: Robert Penner
    CFO: David Parker
Estimated Sales:$ 10-20 Million
Number Employees: 50-99

10897 (HQ)Palmer Candy Company
P.O.Box 326
Sioux City, IA 51102-0326   712-258-5543
        Fax: 712-258-3224   800-831-0828
vicki@palmercandy.com   www.palmercandy.com
Processor, importer and wholesaler/distributor of
snack foods and confectionery items including
bagged, multi-packs, chocolate bars and vending
    President: Martin Palmer
    Director Of Marketing: Jerry Christenson
    Director Of Sales: Bob O'Neill
    Plant Manager: Bill Kennedy
Estimated Sales:$15.50 Million
Number Employees: 50-99
Sq. footage: 140000
Type of Packaging: Consumer, Food Service, Pri-
    vate Label, Bulk
Other Locations:
    Palmer Candy Company
    Kansas City MO
Brands:
    FAVORITES
    KING BING
    PEANUT BUTTER BING
    TWIN BING

10898 Palmer Packing Company
1315 S 100 E
Tremonton, UT 84337-8727   435-257-5329
Manufacturer and packer of meat products including
ground meat and jerky
    Owner: George Palmer
Estimated Sales:$14 Million
Number Employees: 1-4
Type of Packaging: Consumer, Food Service

10899 Palmer Vineyards
5120 Sound Ave
Riverhead, NY 11901-5533   631-722-9463
        Fax: 631-722-5634   800-901-8783
                palmervineyards@mail.com
                www.palmervineyards.com
Wines
    President: Robert Palmer
    Winemaker: Tom Drozd
Estimated Sales:$ 2.5-5 Million
Number Employees: 10-19
Type of Packaging: Private Label

10900 Palmetto Brewing
289 Huger St
Charleston, SC 29403-4560   843-937-0903
                                    Fax: 843-937-0092
Beer
    President/Brewmaster: Louis Bruce
    Brewer: Ed Falkenstein
*Estimated Sales:*Less than $500,000
Number Employees: 1-4
Brands:
    Palmetto

10901 Palmetto Canning Company
P.O.Box 155
3601 US Highway 41
Palmetto, FL 34220-0155   941-722-1100
                                 Fax: 941-729-1934
                pcanning@palmettocanning.com
                www.palmettocanning.com
Manufacturer and exporter of jams, jellies, pre-
serves, marmalades and barbecue sauce
    Owner: Jonathan C Greenlaw Jr
Estimated Sales:$5-10 Million
Number Employees: 10-19
Sq. footage: 32000
Type of Packaging: Consumer, Private Label
Brands:
    PALMALITO

10902 Palmetto Pigeon Plant
P.O.Box 3060
Sumter, SC 29151-3060   803-775-1204
        Fax: 803-778-2896   palmettopgn@ftc-i.net

Processor of fresh and frozen squab, free range
chicken and poussin
    President: Anthony Barwick
    Office Manager: Sherry Cannon
Estimated Sales:$ 10 - 20 Million
Number Employees: 50-99
Sq. footage: 10800
Type of Packaging: Consumer

10903 Palmieri Food Products
145 Hamilton St
New Haven, CT 06511-5837   203-624-0042
        Fax: 203-782-6435   800-845-5447
                sales@palmierifoods.com
                www.palmierifoods.com
Processor of all-natural gourmet sauces for pasta,
pizza and salsa. Also retail, food service and private
label packaging available
    President: Patrick Palmieri
    Administrative Assistant: Mary Palmieri
Estimated Sales:$ 5 - 10 Million
Number Employees: 10-19
Type of Packaging: Consumer, Food Service, Pri-
    vate Label, Bulk
Brands:
    Andrews
    Palmieri
    Pinders

10904 Palmyra Bologna
P.O.Box 111
Palmyra, PA 17078-0111   717-838-6336
                                Fax: 717-838-5345
        www.seltzerslebanonbologna.com
Manufacturer of smoked bologna
    President: Craig Seltzer
    CFO/Secretary/Treasurer: Peter Stanilla
    VP Sales/Account Executive: Perry Smith
Estimated Sales:$10 Million
Number Employees: 50-99
Type of Packaging: Consumer, Food Service, Pri-
    vate Label, Bulk
Brands:
    PENN DUTCH
    SELTZERS

10905 Pamela's Products
200 Clara Ave
Ukiah, CA 95482-4004   707-462-6605
        Fax: 707-462-6642   info@pamelasproducts.com
                www.pamelasproducts.com
Processor and exporter of wheat and gluten-free
cookies including biscotti; also, wheat and glu-
ten-free pancake, bread and brownie mixes
    Owner: Pamela Sorrells
    Marketing Director: Maureen Eatherly
Estimated Sales:$180000
Number Employees: 5-9
Type of Packaging: Consumer, Bulk
Brands:
    Pamela's
    Wheat-Free & Gluten-Free Biscotti
    Wheat-Free & Gluten-Free Cookies
    Wheat-Free & Gluten-Free Mix
    Wheat-Free Oatmeal Cookies

10906 Pamlico Packing Company
P.O.Box 336
Grantsboro, NC 28529-0336   252-745-3688
        Fax: 252-745-3272   800-682-1113
kingcrab1@hotmail.com   www.bestseafood.com
Processors of fresh and frozen scallops, shrimp,
crabs, crabmeat, flounder, oysters, whiting and trout
    President: W Ed Cross
Estimated Sales:$12,100,000
Number Employees: 50-99
Type of Packaging: Consumer, Food Service, Bulk
Brands:
    Seafood People

10907 Pan American Coffee Company
1614 Willow Ave
Hoboken, NJ 07030   201-795-2434
        Fax: 201-659-1883   800-229-1883
Roasts and sells coffee
    President: Roy Montes
    Quality Control: Edili Jerridy
    General Manager: Ruth Santuccio
Estimated Sales:$ 5-10 Million
Number Employees: 20-49

10908 Pan Pepin
PO Box 100
Bayamon, PR 00960-0100   787-787-1717
        Fax: 787-740-2029 http://www.panpepin.com
Processor of baked goods
    CEO/President: Rafael Rovira
    Marketing Director: Mario Somoza
    VP Finance: Carolina Rodriguez
    VP: Carolina Rodriguez
    General Manager: Miguel Santiago
Number Employees: 300
Type of Packaging: Consumer
Brands:
    Healthy Juice
    Nature Zone
    Pan Pepin

**10909 (HQ)Pan-O-Gold Baking
Company**
P.O.Box 848
St Cloud, MN 56302-0848   320-251-9361
                                 Fax: 320-251-3759
Manufacturer of white and variety bread and buns
    President: Howard Alton Iii III
    President: James Akervik
Estimated Sales:$100 Million
Number Employees: 500-999
Sq. footage: 100000
Type of Packaging: Consumer
Brands:
    BUTTER HEARTH
    COUNTRY HEARTH
    HOLSUM
    LAKELAND
    VILLAGE HEARTH
    VILLAGE INN

10910 Pancho's Mexican Foods
2881 Lamar Avenue
Memphis, TN 38114-5019   901-744-3900
                                Fax: 901-744-0514
Mexican foods
    President: Brenda O'Brien
    VP Manufacturing/Purchasing: Subhash Mehr
Number Employees: 10-19
Type of Packaging: Consumer, Food Service, Pri-
    vate Label, Bulk

10911 Pandol Brothers
401 Road 192
Delano, CA 93215-9598   661-725-3755
        Fax: 661-725-4741   domsls@pandol.com
                www.pandol.com
Grower, importer and exporter of produce including
grapes
    President: Jack Pandol
Estimated Sales:$ 20 - 50 Million
Number Employees: 20-49

10912 Pangburn Candy Company
2000 White Settlement Road
Fort Worth, TX 76107-1467   817-332-8856
        Fax: 940-887-4578 www.pangburn.com
Candy
    President: R Phillips
Estimated Sales:$ 2.5-5 Million
Number Employees: 50

10913 Panoche Creek Packing
3611 W Beechwood Ave # 101
Fresno, CA 93711-0648   559-449-1721
        Fax: 559-431-9970   posobros@aol.com
Processor and exporter of almonds
    President: John Blackburn
    Vice President: Mike Mason
    Marketing Manager: Ross Blackburn
*Estimated Sales:*Less than $500,000
Number Employees: 5-9
Type of Packaging: Private Label, Bulk
Brands:
    Golden

10914 Panola Pepper Corporation
1414 Holland Delta Rd
Lake Providence, LA 71254-5545   318-559-1774
        Fax: 318-559-3003   800-256-3013
panola@bayou.com   www.panolapepper.com
Spices, hot sauce
    President: Grady W Brown
    CFO: Janne Brown
    VP/R & D: Ken Hopkins
    Public Relations: Jim Byrant
    Operations Manager: Danny Morara

*Estimated Sales:*Below $ 5 Million
Number Employees: 20-49
Type of Packaging: Private Label
Brands:
- Gourmet Pepper Sauce
- Gourmet Pepper Sauce
- Panola
- Panola & Private Lab
- Pasta Salad
- Red Pepper Sauce
- Southern Spice
- Steak Sauce

10915 Panos Brands

1 Park 80 Plaza E
Suite 2a
Saddle Brook, NJ 07663   201-843-8900
                    Fax: 201-368-9150
customer.services@panosbrands.com
                www.panosbrands.com
premium, authentic, natural, organic and specialty
foods
- President/Owner: Caroline Ponterio
- VP Finance: John Lennan
- VP: John McLennan
- Sales Manager: Donald Cook
- Human Resources Manager: Jennifer Ricks
- Purchasing: Kathy Burkowski
Estimated Sales:$2.2 Million
Number Employees: 16

10916 Panther Creek Cellars

455 NE Irvine St
McMinnville, OR 97128-4200   503-472-8080
                    Fax: 503-472-5667
info@panthercreekcellars.com
                www.panthercreekcellars.com
Wines
- Owner: Elizabeth Chambers
- Co-Owner: Linda Kaplan
- Sales/Marketing Director: Jack Rovics
- Winemaker: Michael Stevenson
Estimated Sales:$750,000
Number Employees: 1-4
Type of Packaging: Consumer, Private Label

10917 Papa Dean's Popcorn

6484 N New Braunfels Ave
San Antonio, TX 78209-3827   210-822-3625
        Fax: 210-822-2140 deanneu@aol.com
                www.papadeanspopcorn.com
Processor of 30 flavors of gourmet popcorn featured
in bags and/or canisters, several different sizes
avaliable
- Owner: Tara Zaglif
*Estimated Sales:*Less than $500,000
Number Employees: 1-4
Sq. footage: 1200
Type of Packaging: Consumer, Food Service, Private Label, Bulk
Brands:
- Papa Dean's

10918 Papa Leone Food Enterprises

PO Box 6777
Beverly Hills, CA 90212-6777   818-858-0074
                    Fax: 818-858-0134
Manufacturer of Italian and French sauces including
Italian country, fra diavolo, marinara, al'orange,
scampi, Mediterranean and vegetable. Also has
pizzaiola, marinara, pizza, neopolitan, caponata, arti-
choke, arabiata and red clamsauces
- President: Edmond Negari
Number Employees: 1-4
Sq. footage: 2000
Type of Packaging: Consumer, Food Service, Private Label
Brands:
- CHEF ALBERTO LEONE
- MAGIC GOURMET

10919 Pape's Pecan Company

101 S Highway 123 Byp
Seguin, TX 78155-5156   830-379-7442
        Fax: 830-379-9665 888-688-7273
mrpetski@aol.com www.papepecan.com
Processor of pecans
- Owner: Kenneth Pape
- Sales: Harold Pape
Estimated Sales:$ 8 Million
Number Employees: 20-49
Sq. footage: 15000
Type of Packaging: Food Service, Private Label

10920 Paper City Brewery

108 Cabot St
Holyoke, MA 01040-6061   413-535-1588
        Fax: 413-538-5774 info@papercity.com
                www.papercity.com
Processor of ale
- President: Jay Hebert
*Estimated Sales:*Below $ 5 Million
Number Employees: 5-9
Brands:
- Paper City

10921 Papetti's Egg Products

100 Trumbull Street
Elizabeth, NJ 07206-2105   908-351-9618
        Fax: 908-351-7528 800-524-3447
Manufacturer and exporter of egg products includ-
ing dried, diced, pickled, hard and salted, patties,
folded omelets, yolks, whites, etc
- President: Arthur Papetti
- Purchasing Manager: Howard Goodman
Estimated Sales:$300 Million
Number Employees: 550
Sq. footage: 100000
Parent Co: Michael Foods
Type of Packaging: Consumer, Food Service, Private Label, Bulk
Other Locations:
- Papetti's Hygrade Egg Product
  Klingerstown PA
Brands:
- ANGEL WHIP WHITES
- ANGEL WHITE
- BAKER'S 26
- BAKER'S PRIDE
- BAKER'S SUPREME
- BROKE-N-READY
- EASYWAY
- HEALTHY MORN
- HOLTON FOODS
- HYTEX
- LITE-N-HEARTY
- LONG EGG
- QUAKERSTATE FARMS
- SCRAMBLE MIX
- SUGAR YOLK
- TABLE READY
- TABLE READY ASEPTIC PACK

10922 Papita USA

1936 Columbia Avenue
Lancaster, PA 17603-4362   717-392-6376
Food processor of bananas and plantain chips
Estimated Sales:$ .5 - 1 million
Number Employees: 5-9

10923 Pappardelle's Pasta Company

4980 Jackson St
Denver, CO 80216-3018   303-321-4222
        Fax: 303-321-8554 800-607-2782
info@pappardellespasta.com
                www.pappardellespasta.com
Over 100 flavors of dried pasta, fresh-frozen ravioli,
sauces and pestos
- President: Jim Steinberg
- Vice President: Paula Steinberg
*Estimated Sales:*Below $ 5 Million
Number Employees: 10-19
Brands:
- Pappardelle's

10924 Pappy Meat Company

5663 E Fountain Way
Fresno, CA 93727-7813   559-291-0218
        Fax: 559-291-5304 pappy@pappyschoice.com
                www.pappyschoice.com
Processor of spices and seasonings
- President: Marie Papulias
- VP: Edward Papulias
Estimated Sales:$2 Million
Number Employees: 20-49
Type of Packaging: Consumer, Food Service, Private Label, Bulk
Brands:
- Pappy's Choice

10925 Papy's Foods

4131 W Albany St
McHenry, IL 60050-8390   815-385-3313
        Fax: 815-385-3367 custservice@papys.com
                www.pappys.com

Processor of spice blends
- President: Matt Gallimore
- COO: Robert Seul
- VP/Plant Manager: Matthew Gallimore
Estimated Sales:$ 50 - 100 Million
Number Employees: 50-99
Sq. footage: 12000
Type of Packaging: Consumer, Food Service

10926 (HQ)Par-Way Tryson

107 Bolte Lane
Saint Clair, MO 63077-3219   636-629-4545
        Fax: 636-629-1330 800-844-4554
                www.parwaytryson.com
Processor and exporter of release agents and oils
- President: Keyna Koabuzua
- CEO: Dennis Norton
- COO: Mike Abbs
- VP Sales/Marketing: Brad Channing
- VP Sales (Special Markets): John Shively
- Plant Manager: Roe Howelo
Estimated Sales:$20-50 Million
Number Employees: 20-49
Sq. footage: 100000
Type of Packaging: Food Service, Private Label, Bulk
Brands:
- Bak-Klene
- Presidents Cup
- Spray 'n' Cook
- Vegalene

10927 Paradigm Food Works

5875 Lakeview Blvd # 102
Lake Oswego, OR 97035-7047   503-595-4360
        Fax: 503-595-4234 www.paradigmfoodworks.com
Flavoring extracts and syrups, scone mixes and
fudge sauces
- President: Lynne Barra
- CFO: David Barra
Estimated Sales:$ 10-20 Million
Number Employees: 10-19

10928 Paradis Honey

PO Box 99
Girouxville, AB T0H 1S0
Canada   780-323-4283
                    Fax: 780-323-4238
Processor of clover honey, beeswax and pollen
- CEO: Michael Paradis
- Owner/Manager: Jean Paradis
- Secretary/Treasurer: Laura Paradis
Type of Packaging: Bulk
Brands:
- Honey

10929 Paradise

P.O. Box 4230
1200 Dr. Martin Luther King Jr. Blvd.
Plant City, FL 33563-0021   813-752-1155
        Fax: 813-754-3168 800-330-8952
                www.paradisefruitco.com
Manufacturer, importer and exporter of candied
fruits used in fruitcakes and strawberries
- Chairman/CEO: Melvin Gordon
- President/Director: Randy Gordon
- CFO/Treasurer: Jack Laskowitz
Estimated Sales:$21 Million
Number Employees: 250-499
Sq. footage: 275000
Type of Packaging: Consumer, Food Service, Private Label, Bulk
Brands:
- DIXIE
- MOR-FRUIT
- SUN-RIPE

10930 Paradise Fruits

1410 Providence Hwy
Suite 106
Norwood, MA 02062   781-769-4900
                    Fax: 781-769-4910
jbrownbill@paradise-fruits.com
                www.paradise-fruits.com
Free-flowing granulates, pastes, concentrates, juices
and purees.

10931 (HQ)Paradise Island Foods

6451 Portsmouth Road
Nanaimo, BC V9V 1A3
Canada   250-390-2644
        Fax: 250-390-2117 800-889-3370
lthomson@paradise-foods.com

Processor of frozen muffin mixes; packager and importer of cheeses; importer of Mexican, Italian and U.S. foods and pasta; wholesaler/distributor of yogurt, juice, candy, salad dressings and ethnic foods
Owner/President: George Thomson
Sales/Marketing: Len Thomson
Number Employees: 20-49
Sq. footage: 36000
Type of Packaging: Consumer, Private Label, Bulk

10932 Paradise Locker Company
405 SW 208th St
Trimble, MO 64492   816-370-6328
                            Fax: 816-357-1229
Processor of meat products including beef and pork
Owner: Mario Fantasma
Estimated Sales: $ 3 - 5 Million
Number Employees: 10-19

10933 (HQ)Paradise Products Corporation
P.O.Box 325
Roslyn, NY 11576-325   718-378-3554
       Fax: 718-378-3521 800-826-1235
              www.paradiseproductscorp.com
Manufacturer, exporter and importer of marinated foods, condiments, olives, artichokes, pimientos, capers, cauliflower, cherries, corn, kumquats, mushrooms, olive oil, pickled onions, salsa, sauces, etc
President: David Lax
Estimated Sales: $10-20 Million
Number Employees: 60
Sq. footage: 150000
Type of Packaging: Consumer, Food Service, Private Label, Bulk
Brands:
    JULIANA
    PARADISE
    THREE STAR

10934 Paradise Tomato Kitchens
1500 S Brook St
Louisville, KY 40208-1950   502-637-1700
    Fax: 502-637-8060 info@paradisetomato.com
              www.paradisetomato.com
Processor of pouched tomatoes, tomato paste, puree, sauce and pizza sauce
President: Ronald Peters
Research & Development: Arlen Campbell
Quality Control: Justin Uhl
Purchasing Manager: Nathan Cosby
Estimated Sales: $ 10-20 Million
Number Employees: 100-249
Type of Packaging: Food Service, Private Label

10935 Paradise Valley Vineyards
4077 W Fairmount Avenue
Phoenix, AZ 85019-3620   602-233-8727
                            Fax: 602-233-8727
Wines
President: Mark William Stern
Vice President: Tom Dibecco
Sales Director: Jeff Cayton
Estimated Sales: $500-1 Million appx.
Number Employees: 1-4
Type of Packaging: Private Label
Brands:
    Paradise Valley Vineyards
    Paraiso Del Sol

10936 Paragon Laboratories
20433 Earl St
Torrance, CA 90503-2414   310-370-1563
    Fax: 310-370-7354 sales@paralabs.com
              www.paragonlabsusa.com
Custom manufacturer of dietary supplements, vitamins, minerals, herbal products and nutritional supplements; available in tablets, capsules, powders and liquids
President: Jay Kaufman
Estimated Sales: $17900000
Number Employees: 50-99
Type of Packaging: Consumer, Private Label, Bulk

10937 Paragon Vineyards
4915 Orcutt Rd
San Luis Obispo, CA 93401-8335   805-544-9080
              Fax: 805-781-3635
       baileyama@paragonvineyards.com
              www.baileyana.com
Wine
Manager: Michael Blaney
CFO: John R Nevin

Estimated Sales: Below $ 5 Million
Number Employees: 20-49
Brands:
    Ecclestone
    Vintage Port

10938 Parallel Products
401 Industry Rd
Louisville, KY 40208-1692   502-634-1014
       Fax: 813-289-4283 888-883-9100
       CustomerServices@parallelproducts.com
              www.parallelproducts.com
Developer and manufacturer of technologies for the processing of food and beverage wastes. Specific product areas include that of: brewery, winery, distillery services; soft drink, juice services; candy, sugar services; and also thatof pharmaceutical, cosmetic services.
President/Chief Executive Officer: Gene Kiesel
Division Controller: David Kenney
Vice President Sales and Marketing: Ken Reese
National Sales Manager: Ed Stewart
Human Resources/Communications: Hal Park
Chief Operations Officer: David Cogburn
Division Customer Service Manager: Denise Gibson
Plant Manager: Russ Hohn

10939 Paramount Caviar
3815 24th St
Long Island City, NY 11101-3619   718-786-7747
       Fax: 718-786-5730 800-992-2842
              Info@ParamountCaviar.com
              www.paramountcaviar.com
Caviar and smoked salmon
Owner: Hussion Aimami
VP: Amy Arrow
Purchasing Manager: Hossein Aimani
Estimated Sales: $500,000-$1 Million
Number Employees: 5-9
Type of Packaging: Bulk
Brands:
    Canolla Truffles
    Fossen Smoked Salmon
    Manchurian Saffron
    Plantin Dried Mushro

10940 Paramount Chocolates
350 Wireless Blvd
Hauppauge, NY 11788-3947   631-231-2300
       Fax: 631-231-2731 800-842-3000
              www.lancopromo.com
Premium chocolates, truffles, taffy and mints
President: Brian Landow
Estimated Sales: $ 2.5-5 Million
Number Employees: 1-4

10941 Paramount Coffee Company
P.O.Box 13068
Lansing, MI 48901-3068   517-372-5500
       Fax: 517-372-2870 800-968-1222
              www.paramountcoffee.com
Coffees
President: Steve Morris
Sales Director: Steve Morris
Estimated Sales: $25-49.9 Million
Number Employees: 50-99
Sq. footage: 80000
Type of Packaging: Consumer, Food Service, Private Label, Bulk

10942 (HQ)Paramount Distillers
3116 Berea Rd
Cleveland, OH 44111-1596   216-671-6300
              Fax: 216-671-2299
       llubin@paramountdistillers.com
              www.paramountdistillers.com
Processor of distilled spirits and liquors
President: Robert Manchick
VP: Rob Boas
Marketing: Lynn Lubin
VP Sales: Robert Szabo
Plant Manager: Steve Borecky
Estimated Sales: $112300000
Number Employees: 100-249
Other Locations:
    Paramount Distillers
    Cincinnati OH

10943 (HQ)Paramount Farms
11444 W Olympic Blvd
Suite 310
Los Angeles, CA 90064   310-966-4650
       Fax: 310-966-4695 877-450-9493
              www.paramountfarms.com
Grower and processor of almonds and pistachios
President: Stewart Resnick
CFO: Mike Hohmann
Grower Relations Director: Andy Anzaldo
VP/Operations: David Szeflin
Estimated Sales: $150 Million
Number Employees: 1,000
Brands:
    Everybody's Nuts
    Paramount Farms
    Sunkist

10944 (HQ)Paramount Farms
11444 W Olympic Blvd # 250
Los Angeles, CA 90064-1534   310-966-4650
       Fax: 310-966-4695 800-246-6887
       rsmith@paramountfarms.com
              www.paramountfarms.com
Grower and processor of pistachios and almonds
President: Stewart Resnick
Grower Relations Director: Andy Anzaldo
Estimated Sales: $ 250 Million
Number Employees: 20-49
Other Locations:
    Paramount Farms Plant
    Lost Hills CA
Brands:
    ALMOND ACCENTS
    SUNKIST

10945 Parasio Springs Vineyards
38060 Paraiso Springs Rd
Soledad, CA 93960-9517   831-678-0300
    Fax: 831-678-2584 info@paraisovineyards.com
              www.paraisovineyards.com
Manufacturer of Wines
Owner/Grower: Rich Smith
Marketing Director: Dave Muret
Hospitality Director: Jennifer Murphy-Smith
Vineyard Manager: Jason Smith
Production/Winemaker/Sales: David Fleming
Estimated Sales: $1-2.5 Million
Number Employees: 5-9
Number of Brands: 1
Number of Products: 10
Type of Packaging: Private Label
Brands:
    PARAISO

10946 Parco Foods
1 Parco Place
Blue Island, IL 60406-3809   708-371-9200
    Fax: 708-371-5301 jbennett@parcofoods.com
              www.parcofoods.com
Processor of baked, frozen and unbaked cookies, brownies, snack cakes and desserts
President: Thomas A Hoch
Executive VP: J Vincent Kent
VP Sales/Marketing: Doug Davidson
VP Sales: Charles Hoch
Public Relations: C Jekiel
Operations Manager: D Kozlowski
Director Manufacturing: Michael Walz
Purchasing Manager: D Doyle
Estimated Sales: $65500000
Number Employees: 600
Type of Packaging: Consumer, Food Service, Private Label, Bulk
Brands:
    Chuck's Chunky
    Chuck's Snacks
    Party Cookies
    Sweetie Bear Bakery

10947 Parducci Wine Estates
501 Parducci Rd
Ukiah, CA 95482-3015   707-463-5378
       Fax: 707-462-7260 888-362-9463
       info@mendocinowineco.com
              www.mendocinowineco.com
Processor, exporter and wholesaler/distributor of wine
Manager: Tim Thornhill
Owner: Tim Thornhill
Marketing: David Hance
Winemaker: Robert Swain
Estimated Sales: $2700000
Number Employees: 1-4

10948 (HQ)Paris Foods Corporation
1632 Carman St
Camden, NJ 08105-1705 856-964-0915
Fax: 856-964-9719 parisfoods@parisfoods.com
www.parisfoods.com
Supplier of frozen vegetables, frozen French fries, frozen fruit and fruit juices
President: Samuel Rudderow
Estimated Sales:$7200000
Number Employees: 10-19
Type of Packaging: Consumer, Food Service

10949 Paris Frozen Foods
305 Springfield Rd
Hillsboro, IL 62049-1150 217-532-3822
Processor of frozen beef, sausage and pork
President: Allen Hopper
Estimated Sales:$550000
Number Employees: 5-9
Type of Packaging: Consumer

10950 Paris Pastry
1448 Westwood Blvd
Los Angeles, CA 90024-4900 310-474-8888
Fax: 310-470-2097 sales@parispastry.com
www.parispastry.com
Processor of premium baked goods. Packaged ready to ship mousses, chocolate florentine cookies. Private label available; gingerbread houses; French madeleines
President: Raymond Lobjois
Executive Chef: Eric Westphal
Estimated Sales:$260000
Number Employees: 10-19
Sq. footage: 12000
Type of Packaging: Consumer, Food Service, Private Label, Bulk

10951 (HQ)Parish Chemical Company
P.O.Box 277
Orem, UT 84059-0277 801-226-2018
Fax: 801-226-8496 www.parishchemical.com
Processor, exporter, researcher and developer of nutritional food additives, acidulants and preservatives including ferulic acid; also, nutritional supplements including carboxyethylgermanium sesquioxide and indole-3-carbinol
President: W Wesley Parish
Marketing Director: Bill Ellenberger
Estimated Sales:$1200000
Number Employees: 20-49
Sq. footage: 25000
Type of Packaging: Bulk
Other Locations:
Parish Chemical Co.
Orem UT

10952 (HQ)Park 100 Foods
326 E Adams St
Tipton, IN 46072-2001 765-675-3480
Fax: 765-675-3474 800-854-6504
park100@park100foods.com
www.park100foods.com
Manufacturer of custom frozen soups, sauces, chili, side dishes, gravies, fruit toppings, dips, entrees, and portion breaded meats, quick starch component sauces, seafood dishes, pasta and protein kits
Chairman: Jim Washburn
President: Gary Meade
VP: David Alves
Project Manager/National Sales: Robert Orr
Sales: Mike Taft
Estimated Sales:$ 20 - 50 Million
Number Employees: 50-99
Sq. footage: 100000
Other Locations:
Kettle Processed Foods
Morristown IN
Kettle Processed Foods
Kokomo IN
Brands:
PARK 100 FOODS

10953 Park Cheese Company
168 E Larsen Dr
Fond Du Lac, WI 54937-8519 920-923-8484
Fax: 920-923-8485 800-752-7275
info@parkcheese.com www.parkcheese.com
Processor and exporter of Italian specialty cheeses including parmesan, romano, provolone, asiago, fontina and pepato
President: Alfred Liebetrau
Vice President: Eric Liebetrau
Plant Manager: Lewis Blank

Estimated Sales:$ 50 - 100 Million
Number Employees: 50-99
Type of Packaging: Consumer, Food Service, Private Label, Bulk
Brands:
Casaro
Park
Villa

10954 Park Farms
1925 30th St NE
Canton, OH 44705-2501 330-455-0241
Fax: 330-455-5820 800-683-6511
sales@parkfarms.com www.parkfarms.com
Poultry processor of fresh tray pack, bonless, skinless poultry, and whole and cut-up chicken. Distributor of fresh and frozen meat proteins
President: Mike Pastore
CEO: Jim Pastore, Sr.
CFO: Scott Stephens
Quality Control Manager: Paul Storsin
VP Sales: Kim Clark
Public Relations: Carol Capocci
Production Manager: Scott Bucher
Plant Manager: Ron Leeders, Jr.
Purchasing Manager: Scott Hearne
Estimated Sales:$100+ Million
Number Employees: 500-999
Number of Brands: 2
Number of Products: 160
Sq. footage: 150000
Type of Packaging: Consumer, Food Service, Private Label, Bulk
Brands:
Park Farms Fresh'n'natural Chicken

10955 Parker Farm
9405 Holly St NW # B
Minneapolis, MN 55433-5976 763-780-5100
Fax: 763-780-5104 info@parkersfarm.com
www.parkersfarm.com
Cold pack cheese food, peanut butter, cream cheese spread and fresh salsa
President: Rick Etrheim
Estimated Sales:$ 5-9.9 Million
Number Employees: 20-49
Type of Packaging: Private Label

10956 Parker Fish Company
P.O.Box 324
Wrightsville, GA 31096-0324 478-864-3406
Fax: 478-864-9417
Seafood
President: Joe Rowland
Estimated Sales:$ 5 - 10 Million
Number Employees: 10-19

10957 Parker Flavors, Inc
1801 Portal St
Baltimore, MD 21224-6543 410-633-2230
Fax: 410-633-3530 800-336-9113
info@parkerflavors.com www.parkerflavors.com
Manufacturer of vanilla extracts, emulsions, and flavors for bakery, beverage, candy and ice cream
CEO: Tim Parker
Chairman: Malcolm Parker
Estimated Sales:$ 5 - 10 Million
Number Employees: 5-9
Type of Packaging: Private Label, Bulk
Brands:
PARKER

10958 Parker Products
2737 Tillar Street
Fort Worth, TX 76107 817-336-7441
Fax: 817-877-1261 800-433-5749
info@parkerproducts.com
www.parkerproducts.com
candy particulates and other fine ingredients

10959 (HQ)Parker Products
2737 Tillar St
Fort Worth, TX 76107-1395 817-336-7441
Fax: 817-877-1261 800-433-5749
info@parkerproducts.com
www.parkerproducts.com
Processor and exporter of desserts, candy, and confectionery products including ice cream toppings, fudge and flavors; custom-grinding services available
President: Jim Waldroop
CFO: Chris McCrary
CFO: Greg Hodder
Plant Manager: Sandra Perez

Estimated Sales:$ 10-20 Million
Number Employees: 50-99
Sq. footage: 58000
Type of Packaging: Private Label, Bulk
Other Locations:
Parker Products
Andrews TX

10960 Parkers Farm
9405 Holly St NW # B
Minneapolis, MN 55433-5976 763-780-5100
Fax: 763-780-5104 800-869-6685
info@parkersfarm.com www.parkersfarm.com
Processor of cold pack cheese foods and bagel spreads.
President: Rick Etrheim
VP Sales/Marketing: Don Twiford
Office Manager: Marilyn Fisher
Estimated Sales:$ 10 - 20 Million
Number Employees: 20-49
Type of Packaging: Consumer, Food Service, Private Label, Bulk

10961 (HQ)Parkside Candy Company
3208 Main St
Buffalo, NY 14214-1302 716-833-7540
Fax: 716-833-7560
Manufacturer of Lollypops and other candy
President/Owner: Philip Buffamonte
Estimated Sales:$14 Million
Number Employees: 20-49
Type of Packaging: Consumer, Food Service, Private Label, Bulk
Brands:
AUNT ANGIES
OLD FASHIONED

10962 Parma Sausage Products
1734 Penn Ave
Pittsburgh, PA 15222-4385 412-391-4238
Fax: 412-391-7717 877-294-4207
info@parmasausage.com
www.parmasausage.com
Processor of specialty meats including fresh sausage, prosciutto, coppa secca and salami, capicollo, mortadella, salami rosa, kolbassie, andoville, chorizo
President: Rina Edwards
Vice President: Rita Spinabelli
Sales Manager: Erin Schumacher
Purchasing Manager: John Edwards
Estimated Sales:$1300000
Number Employees: 10-19
Type of Packaging: Consumer, Food Service, Private Label, Bulk
Brands:
Gigi
Parma

10963 Parmalat
10th Floor
St George Brant, ON N0E 1N0
Canada 519-448-1311
Fax: 519-448-3134
Processor of spray dried ingredients including, cream, butter, cream cheese, milk and sour cream powders
General Manager: Don Lawrence
Estimated Sales: 1 Billion
Number Employees: 50-99
Parent Co: Parmalat Canada

10964 Parmalat
405 the West Mall
Toronto, ON M9C 5K7
Canada 416-626-1973
Fax: 416-620-3123 www.parmalat.ca
Processor of milk, cheese, juice, cream, sour cream, yogurt and ice cream
VP/General Manager (W Dairy D): Ron Dunsford

Number Employees: 100-249
Parent Co: Parmalat Canada
Type of Packaging: Consumer, Food Service
Brands:
Astro
Beatrice
Parmalat

10965 Parmalat
405 The West Mall
10th Floor
Toronto, ON M9C 5J1
Canada   800-563-1515
          Fax: 514-484-8925   800-363-4393
                              www.parmalat.ca
Processor of whole, skim, 1%, 2% and chocolate
milk
    President: Michael Rosicki
    CEO: Alain lavallee
    Sales/Marketing Executive: Mike Adcock
Number Employees: 250-499
Parent Co: Parmalat Canada
Type of Packaging: Consumer, Food Service
Brands:
    Lactantia

10966 (HQ)Parmalat
405 The West Mall
10th Floor
Toronto, ON M9C 5J1
Canada   416-626-1973
          Fax: 416-620-3666   800-563-1515
                              www.parmalat.ca
Milk and dairy products, fruit juices, cultured prod-
ucts, cheese products and table spreads.
    President/CEO: Alnashir Lakha
    CFO: Michael Rosicki
    Marketing Director: Bill Klump
    Sales Director: Mark O'Toole
    Public Relations: Kathy Coggeshall
    Operations Manager: Peter Lowes
Estimated Sales: $2 Billion
Number Employees: 1000
Type of Packaging: Consumer, Food Service, Pri-
    vate Label, Bulk
Brands:
    ASTRO
    BALDERSON
    BEATRICE
    BLACK DIAMOND
    LACTANIA
    LACTOSE FREE
    PAARKAY
    PARMALAT
    SARGENTO
    SENSATIONAL SOY
    SMART GROWTH
    VITALITE

10967 Parmalat Canada
405 The West Mall
10th Floor
Toronto, ON M9C 5J1
Canada   416-626-1973
          Fax: 416-620-3666   800-563-1515
                              www.parmalat.ca
Manufactures milk and dairy products, fruit juices,
cultured products, cheese products and table spreads.
    President/CEO: Alnashir Lakha
    EVP/CFO: Nash Lakha
    SVP Sales/Marketing: Doug Ettinger
    General Manager: Brad McKay
Estimated Sales: $1.9 Billion
Number Employees: 2900
Parent Co: Parmalat Finanziaria SpA.
Type of Packaging: Consumer, Food Service, Pri-
    vate Label, Bulk
Brands:
    ASTRO
    BALDERSON
    BEATRICE
    BLACK DIAMOND
    BLACK DIAMOND CHEESTRINGS FICELLO
    LACTANTIA
    LACTOSE FREE
    PARKAY
    PARMALAT
    SARGENTO
    SENSATIONAL SOY
    SMART GROWTH
    VITALITE

10968 Parman-Kendall Corporation
PO Box 157
Goulds, FL 33170-7408   305-258-1628
                        Fax: 305-258-2445
Processor, importer and exporter of lime juice, con-
centrate and oil, avocado and mango pulp, citrus ex-
tracts and tropical fruit products
    President: Harold Kendall, Jr.
    Plant Manager: Thomas DeMoss

Estimated Sales: $500,000-$1 Million
Number Employees: 20-49
Type of Packaging: Consumer, Private Label, Bulk
Brands:
    Kendall

10969 Parmx
4117-16 Street SE
Calgary, AB T2G 3R9
Canada   403-237-0707
                        Fax: 403-264-2153
Processor of grated parmesan cheese
    President: Vincent Aiello
    CEO: Vincent Aiello
    Production: Frank Aiello
Number Employees: 10-19
Type of Packaging: Consumer, Food Service
Brands:
    Parmx Cheese

10970 Paron Chocolatier
238 Madison Avenue
New York, NY 10016-2816   212-481-9234
                        Fax: 212-686-5498
Chocolates
    President: Deborah Sessa
    CFO: Harnet Sessa
    Vice President: Dana Sessa
    Operations Manager: Lance Friedman
Estimated Sales: $500-1 Million appx.
Number Employees: 5-9
Sq. footage: 10
Type of Packaging: Private Label

10971 Parrish's Cake Decorating Supplies
225 W 146th St
Gardena, CA 90248-1803   310-324-2253
    Fax: 310-324-8277   800-736-8443
    customerservice@parrishsmagicline.com
            www.parrishsmagicline.com
Manufacturer and exporter of baking supplies in-
cluding custom, aluminum cake pans, cookie cutters,
artificial icing, candy molds and lucite wedding cake
plates and pillars; also, food colors and flavorings;
importer of pastry bagscake decorating tips, etc
    President: Douglas Parrish
    CEO: Robert Parrish
    VP: Norma Parrish
Estimated Sales: $ 1 - 3 Million
Number Employees: 20-49
Number of Products: 4000
Sq. footage: 45000
Type of Packaging: Consumer, Food Service, Pri-
    vate Label, Bulk
Brands:
    Magic Line
    Magic Mist
    Magic Mold
    Perma-Ice

10972 Parthenon Food Products
226 S Main St
Ann Arbor, MI 48104-2106   734-994-1012
    Fax: 734-994-7073 www.parthenonrestaurant.net
Processor of all natural Greek salad dressings and
marinades
    President/Owner: Steve Gavas
    CFO: John Gavas
Estimated Sales: $500,000 appx.
Number Employees: 10-19
Sq. footage: 1000
Type of Packaging: Consumer, Food Service, Pri-
    vate Label, Bulk
Brands:
    Perthenon Greek Salad Dressing

10973 Particle Control
P.O.Box 135
Albertville, MN 55301-0135   763-497-3075
    Fax: 763-497-1773   norm@particlecontrolinc.com
                www.particlecontrolinc.com
Processor of flavors, whey, oat flour, sugar, etc
    Owner/President: Norman Arns
    VP: William Arns
Estimated Sales: $700000
Number Employees: 5-9
Sq. footage: 26000

10974 Particle Dynamics
2601 S Hanley Rd
St Louis, MO 63144-2530   314-968-2376
    Fax: 314-646-3761   800-452-4682
                info@particledynamics.com
                www.particledynamics.com
Manufacturer and exporter of encapsulated and ag-
glomerated vitamins, minerals, flavors, acidulants,
colors, spices as well as other active ingredients
    President: Paul T Brady
    Marketing: Andrea Keith
    Sales VP: Richard Miller
    Purchasing: Jim Cronk
Estimated Sales: $3500000
Number Employees: 20-49
Sq. footage: 45000
Parent Co: KV Pharmaceutical
Type of Packaging: Bulk
Brands:
    Descote
    Destab
    Micromask

10975 Partners Coffee Company
4225 Westfield Dr SW
Atlanta, GA 30336-2651   404-344-5282
    Fax: 404-349-6442   800-341-5282
                jim@partnerscoffee.com
                www.partnerscoffee.com
Processor of coffee
    President: James Gilson
    CEO: Mike Bacco
    Operations Manager: Gerry Larue
    Production Manager: Bob Frazier
    Purchasing Manager: Anne Gilson
Estimated Sales: $2559650
Number Employees: 10-19
Number of Brands: 3
Number of Products: 200
Sq. footage: 20000
Type of Packaging: Consumer, Food Service, Pri-
    vate Label, Bulk
Brands:
    Casa Europa
    H&C
    Partners

10976 Partners, A Tastful Cracker
115 S Brandon Street
Seattle, WA 98108-2231   206-762-4123
    Fax: 206-762-8424   800-632-7477
                service@partnerscrackers.com
                www.partnerscrackers.com
Manufacturer of Low-fat crackers, gourmet granola,
cookies
    President/Owner: Marian Harris
    VP/Owner: Greg Maestretti
    VP Sales/Owner: Cara Figgins
Estimated Sales: $500,000-$1 Million
Number Employees: 10-19
Sq. footage: 12000
Brands:
    BLUE STAR FARMS
    CRACKER SNACKERS
    GET MOVIN SNACK PACKSS
    GOURMET GRANOLA
    PARTNERS
    WISECRACKERS

10977 Party Steak Company
1525 W Sunshine Street
Suite C
Springfield, MO 65807-2311   417-358-9091
Processor of barbecue products including frozen
beef rolls, hamburgers, pork and prepared foods
    President: Robert Faulk
    Production Manager: C Thomas
Number Employees: 10-19
Type of Packaging: Consumer, Food Service, Pri-
    vate Label

10978 Pascal Coffee
960 Nepperhan Ave
Yonkers, NY 10703-1726   914-969-7933
    Fax: 914-969-8248   roaster@optonline.net
                www.pascalcoffee.com
Coffee
    Manager: Dean Peialteos
Estimated Sales: Below $ 5 Million
Number Employees: 20-49
Brands:
    Pascal Coffee

10979 Pasco Beverage
7 Lykes Rd
Lake Placid, FL 33852-9582   863-465-4127
    Fax: 863-465-7111

Chairman: Bob Peiser
Estimated Sales: $ 100-500 Million
Number Employees: 500-999
Parent Co: Vitality Beverages

10980 Pasco Corporation of America
19426 Normandie Ave
Torrance, CA 90502-1013   310-516-1918
    Fax: 310-516-1965

Bakery items
President: Kiyo Kamiyana
Estimated Sales: $ 20-50 Million
Number Employees: 20-49

10981 Pascobel Inc
2066 De La Province
Longueuil, QC J4G 1R7
Canada   450-677-2443
    Fax: 450-677-2899   guy.bouthillier@pascobel.ca
Manufacturer of specialized dairy ingredients including combolak, coverblak, viseolak, culurelak, fractolak and nonfat milk solids
President: Jean Guy Lauziere
Sales Manager: Guy Bouthillier
Technical Director: Pierre Combeaud
Number Employees: 20-49
Sq. footage: 15000
Type of Packaging: Private Label, Bulk
Brands:
BELCOVER
COMBOLIAK
COVERLAK
CULTURELAK
FRACTOLAK
NOLLIBEL
VISCOLAK

10982 Pascucci Family Pasta
4561 Mission Gorge Pl
San Diego, CA 92120-4113   619-285-8000
    Fax: 619-285-0838
Processor of portion controlled fresh and frozen pasta including fettuccine, linguine, ravioli, tortellini and par-baked pizza crusts
President: Fred Doxbeck
Estimated Sales: $500000
Number Employees: 5-9
Sq. footage: 3200
Type of Packaging: Consumer, Food Service, Private Label, Bulk

10983 Pasqualichio Brothers
115 Franklin Ave
Scranton, PA 18503-1935   570-346-7115
    Fax: 570-346-4610   800-232-6233
Processor of beef, veal, lamb, turkey, chicken and pork including picnic and loin
President: Michael Pasqualichio
Vice President: Patrick Pasqualichio
Operations Manager: Don Pasqualichio
Plant Manager: William Pasqualichio
Estimated Sales: $ 20 - 50 Million
Number Employees: 10-19
Sq. footage: 15000
Type of Packaging: Consumer
Brands:
Pasqualichio

10984 Passetti's Pride
923 Hotel Avenue
Hayward, CA 94541-4001   510-728-4969
    Fax: 510-886-6909   800-521-4659
passetti@passettispride.com
www.passettispride.com
Processor of sauces and marinades
Co-Owner: Valentino Passetti
Brands:
Passetti's Pride

10985 Pasta By Valente
P.O. Box 2307
Charlottesville, VA 22902-2307   434-971-3717
    Fax: 434-971-1511   888-575-7670
retail@pastavalente.com   www.pastavalente.com
Produces pasta and marinara sauces
President: Mary F Valente
Estimated Sales: Below $ 5 Million
Number Employees: 5-9

10986 Pasta Del Mondo
27 Seminary Hill Rd # 27
Carmel, NY 10512-1928   845-225-8889
    Fax: 845-225-0900   800-392-8887
Pasta
President: Frank Marrone
Production Manager: Brendan Conboy
Estimated Sales: $300,000-500,000
Number Employees: 1-4
Sq. footage: 6000
Type of Packaging: Consumer, Food Service, Private Label, Bulk
Brands:
Del Mondo

10987 Pasta Factory
11225 W Grand Ave
Northlake, IL 60164-1036   847-451-0005
    Fax: 847-451-6563   800-615-6951
pastafactoryusa@juno.com
www.pastafactoryusa.com
Pasta
President: Michael Sica
VP: Irene Sica
Sales Manager/Marketing: Thomas Lichon
Operations/Purchasing Director: Joseph Sica
Estimated Sales: $2700000
Number Employees: 20-49
Sq. footage: 16000
Parent Co: MAS Sales
Type of Packaging: Consumer, Food Service, Private Label, Bulk
Brands:
Pasta Factory

10988 Pasta International
5715 Coopers Avenue
Mississauga, ON L4Z 2C7
Canada   905-890-5550
    Fax: 905-890-8939   888-607-2782
john@pastainternational.com
www.pastainternational.com
Processor of fresh, prepared and frozen pasta including linguine, fettuccine, spaghetti, ravioli, tortellini, lasagna and cannelloni
Co-President: Rita Liberatore
Co-President: Massimo Liberatore
General Manager: John Liberatore
Number Employees: 5-9
Sq. footage: 29000
Type of Packaging: Consumer, Food Service
Brands:
Pasta International

10989 Pasta Italiana
38 Brooklyn Ave
Massapequa, NY 11758-4815   516-795-9400
    Fax: 516-795-1794   800-536-5611
pasta@pastaitaliana.com
www.pastaitaliana.com
Ravioli, tortelloni, agnolotti, cappelletti, tasca, dry pasta, fresh pasta, short cuts, gnocchi, stuffed pasta and grated chesses
President: Robert Yandolino
Estimated Sales: Below $ 5 Million
Number Employees: 10-19
Number of Brands: 2
Number of Products: 140
Sq. footage: 14000
Type of Packaging: Consumer, Food Service, Private Label, Bulk
Brands:
Alberto
Onestis
Pastaitaliana

10990 Pasta Mami
1600 Roswell St SE # 12
Smyrna, GA 30080-2227   770-438-6022
    Fax: 770-438-9810
Fresh pasta products
President: Mark Portwood
Estimated Sales: $ 2.5-5 Million
Number Employees: 10-19
Type of Packaging: Private Label
Brands:
Pasta Mami

10991 Pasta Mill
12803 149th Street NW
Edmonton, AB T5L 2J7
Canada   780-454-8665
    Fax: 780-454-8668
Processor of fresh and frozen pastas including stuffed tortellini, ravioli and lasagna; also, pasta sauces
President: Steve Parsons
General Manager: Brien Plunkie
Number Employees: 20-49
Type of Packaging: Consumer, Food Service
Brands:
The Pasta Mill

10992 Pasta Montana
1 Pasta Pl
Great Falls, MT 59401-1377   406-761-1516
    Fax: 406-761-1403
comments@pastamontana.com
www.pastamontana.com
Manufactures a line of 24 dry pastas ranging from petite shells and orzo to fettuccine.
President: Yasuhiko Harada
CEO: Yasuhiko Harada
CFO: Craig Smith
Vice President: Randy Gilbertson
Quality Control: John Lacanilao
Marketing Director: Randy Gilbertson
Sales Director: Buzz Weisman
Operations Manager: Kelly Easley
Plant Manager: Stephen SaPerite
Purchasing Manager: Tony Koslosky
Estimated Sales: $ 10-20 Million
Number Employees: 100-249
Sq. footage: 30000
Type of Packaging: Consumer, Food Service, Private Label, Bulk

10993 Pasta Partners
P.O. Box 271097
Salt Lake City, UT 84127-1097   801-977-9077
    Fax: 801-977-8202   800-727-8284
sales@pastapartners.net   www.pastapartners.net
Manufacturer of Handmade pastas in eight flavors, each hand-tied with a miniature bottle of olive oil, dried soup mixes in six flavors and thirteen dried pasta sauce mixes
Owner: Debbie Chidister
VP/Owner: Jody Chidester
Estimated Sales: $ 10 - 20 Million
Number Employees: 20-49
Number of Brands: 2
Number of Products: 45
Sq. footage: 10000
Type of Packaging: Consumer, Private Label
Brands:
PASTA PARTNERS
PLENTIFUL PANTRY

10994 Pasta Quistini
551 Jevlan Drive
Woodbridge, ON L4L 8W1
Canada   905-851-2030
    Fax: 905-856-7555
Processor and exporter of pasta
President: Elena Quistini
Number Employees: 10-19
Type of Packaging: Consumer, Food Service
Brands:
Pasta Al Dente
Pasta Quistini

10995 Pasta Shoppe
2728 Eugenia Ave # 102
Nashville, TN 37211-2172   615-831-0016
    Fax: 615-781-9335   800-247-0188
contactus@pastashoppe.com
www.pastashoppe.com
Manufacturer of pasta, and pasta products, gourmet goodies
Owner: Carey Clarke Aron
VP/Owner: Carey Aron
Estimated Sales: $10-20 Million
Number Employees: 10-19
Type of Packaging: Private Label, Bulk
Brands:
PASTA SHOPPE

10996 Pasta Sonoma
640 Martin Ave # 1
Rohnert Park, CA 94928-7994   707-584-0800
    Fax: 707-584-2332   www.info@pastasonoma.com
www.mendocinopasta.com
Pasta
President: Don Luber
Estimated Sales: $1 Million
Number Employees: 10-19
Type of Packaging: Private Label

10997 Pasta USA
3405 E Bismark Ct
Spokane, WA 99217-6592   509-489-7219
            Fax: 509-489-2848 800-456-2084
      sales@pastausa.com   www.pastausa.com
Processor and exporter of dry pasta for food service,
retail, private label and custom ingredient pasta for
food processors. Also, instant and quick cook pasta,
organic seminola and organic whole wheat pasta.
Macaroni and cheese andother box dinners.
Co-packing is available for all pasta and pasta-re-
lated products. Since 1916
      President: Richard Clemson
      CFO: Mary L Clemson
      Sales: Steve Grayhek
Estimated Sales: $ 20 - 50 Million
Number Employees: 20-49
Sq. footage: 60000
Brands:
      BETTY BAKER
      ITALIAN CHEF
      PRESTO PASTA

10998 Pastene Companies
P.O.Box 256
Canton, MA 02021-0256   781-830-8200
      Fax: 781-830-8225 sales@pastene.com
                  www.pastene.com
Manufacturer of specialty foods including grated
cheese, sauces, oil and vinegar, gourmet vegetables,
fish products, olives, peppers, beans, bread sticks,
pasta, rice and polenta
      President: Mark Tosi
Estimated Sales: $30 Million
Number Employees: 20-49
Type of Packaging: Consumer, Food Service
Brands:
      PASTENE

10999 Pastor Chuck Orchards
PO Box 1259
Portland, ME 04104   207-773-1314
            Fax: 207-871-0117
      pastorchuck@pastorchuckorchards.com
      www.pastorchuckorchards.com
organic applesauce, organic apple salsa and organic
apple butter

11000 Pastorelli Food Products
162 N Sangamon St
Chicago, IL 60607-2210   312-666-2041
      Fax: 312-666-2415 800-767-2829
      info@pastorelli.com   www.pastorelli.com
Processor and exporter of sauces; processor of to-
mato products, vinegars, oils, peppers and pasta; im-
porter of pasta, olive oil and cheeses
      Owner: Richard Pastorelli
Estimated Sales: $ 5 - 10 Million
Number Employees: 10-19
Sq. footage: 45000
Type of Packaging: Consumer, Food Service, Pri-
      vate Label, Bulk
Brands:
      Italian Chef

11001 Pastori Winery
23189 Geyserville Ave
Cloverdale, CA 95425-9724   707-857-3418
Wines
      Owner: Frank Pastori
Estimated Sales: $230,000
Number Employees: 1-4
Brands:
      Pastori

11002 Pastry Chef
112 Warren Avenue
Pawtucket, RI 02860-5604   401-722-1330
                  800-639-8606
Processor of frozen gourmet cakes and pies; ex-
porter of cheesecakes
      President: Per Jensen
      CEO: Paul Meunier
Number Employees: 20-49
Number of Brands: 3
Number of Products: 110
Sq. footage: 20000
Parent Co: Pastry Chef
Type of Packaging: Food Service, Private Label
Brands:
      The Pastry Chef

11003 Pat's Meat Discounter
702 S 6th Avenue
Mills, WY 82604-2532   307-237-7549
Meat
      President: Pat Kaeting
Estimated Sales: $500,000-$1 Million
Number Employees: 1-4

11004 Patak Spices USA
2842 Glen Hollow Drive
Clearwater, FL 33761-3310   727-796-2126
            Fax: 727-797-3414
Processor and importer of Indian condiments including sauces, pastes, pickles, relishes, chutneys, curry,
pappadoms, etc.; also, pickles including mango,
chili, sweet lime, garlic and eggplant
      VP: Raj Pathak
Type of Packaging: Consumer, Food Service
Brands:
      Patak's

11005 Pati-Petite Cookies
1785 Mayview Rd
Bridgeville, PA 15017-1592   412-221-4033
            Fax: 412-221-8711 800-253-5805
Processor of gourmet cookies
      President: Keith Graham
      VP: Bruce Graham
      Production Manager: Keith Graham
Estimated Sales: $1400000
Number Employees: 20-49
Sq. footage: 45000
Type of Packaging: Consumer, Food Service, Bulk

11006 Patisserie Wawel
2541 rue Ontario E
Montreal, QC H2K 1W5
Canada   614-524-3348
Processor of European-style marble sponge cake,
poppy butter strudel and razowy and rye breads;
also, poppy seed, hazelnut and walnut butter fillings
      Owner: Peter Sowa
      Manager: Alina Zych
Number Employees: 10-19
Sq. footage: 3500

11007 Patrick Cudahy
P.O.Box 8905
Cudahy, WI 53110-8905   414-744-2000
      Fax: 414-744-4213 800-486-6900
      charliebrah@patrickcudahy.com
            www.patrickcudahy.com
Manufacturer and exporter of bacon, cooked,
smoked and glazed hams, lard, shortening, pork sau-
sage, pepperoni, hard salami, Genoa salami and bo-
logna, pre-cooked bacon and sausage
      President: William G Otis
      President/COO: William Otis
      SVP: James Matthews
      VP Sales/Marketing: Ramon Aldape
Estimated Sales: $200-300 Million
Number Employees: 1,000-4,999
Sq. footage: 1000000
Parent Co: Smithfield Foods
Type of Packaging: Food Service, Private Label
Brands:
      Agar
      Appleblossom
      Danzig
      Golden Crisp
      Heat & Eat
      La Fortuna
      Patrick Cudahy
      Patricks Pride
      Pavone
      Realean
      Royalean

11008 Patsy's
236 W 56th St
New York, NY 10019-4306   212-247-3491
      Fax: 212-541-5071 sapatsys@aol.com
                  www.patsys.com
Manufacturer of pasta sauces and marinaras, vegeta-
bles, olive oils and vinegars
      President: Joseph Scognamillo
Estimated Sales: $ 1 - 3 Million
Number Employees: 20-49
Brands:
      PATSY'S

11009 Patsy's Brands
236 W 56 Street
New York, NY 10019   212-247-3491
            Fax: 212-541-5071 www.patsys.com
pasta sauces

11010 Patsy's Candies
1540 S 21st St
Colorado Springs, CO 80904-4206   719-633-7215
            Fax: 719-633-6970 866-372-8797
      mike@patsycandy.com   www.patsyscandies.com
Manufacturer of confectionery products including
chocolates, mints, saltwater taffy, fudge, truffles,
roasted nuts, candied popcorn and English toffee
      President: Mike Niswonger
Estimated Sales: $5-10 Million
Number Employees: 10-19
Sq. footage: 12000
Type of Packaging: Consumer, Food Service, Pri-
      vate Label, Bulk
Brands:
      COLORADO PEANUT BUTTER NUGGET
      PRELUDES
      ROSECUP MINTS

11011 Patterson Frozen Foods
P.O.Box 114
Patterson, CA 95363-0114   209-892-2611
            Fax: 209-892-2582
      thomas.ielmini@pattersonfrozenfoods.com
            www.pattersonfrozenfoods.com
Manufacturer of frozen vegetables and fruits
      President: John Ielmini
      VP: Russ Kenerly
      VP Sales: Tom Ielmini
Estimated Sales: $ 50 - 100 Million
Number Employees: 1,000-4,999
Type of Packaging: Consumer, Food Service, Bulk
Other Locations:
      Patterson Frozen Foods Plant
      Monte Alto TX
      Patterson Frozen Foods Plant
      Guatemala
Brands:
      FAIR ACRES
      FRESH PACT
      MICROFRESH
      PAT-SON
      POUR & SAVE
      SPRINGTIME
      THRIFT-T-PAK

11012 Patti's Plum Puddings
15020 Hawthorne Blvd # C
Lawndale, CA 90260-1543   310-376-1463
      Fax: 310-372-4132 www.pattisplumpuddings.com
Manufacturer of Plum pudding, brandied hard sauce
      President/CEO: Patti Garrity
Estimated Sales: $50,000
Number Employees: 1-4
Number of Brands: 1
Number of Products: 2
Sq. footage: 1335
Type of Packaging: Consumer
Brands:
      PATTI'S PLUM PUDDING

11013 Patty Palace
595 Middlefield Road
Unit 16
Scarborough, ON M1V 3S2
Canada   416-297-0510
            Fax: 416-297-4024
Processor and exporter of frozen beef patties
      President: Michael Davidson
Number Employees: 20-49
Type of Packaging: Consumer, Food Service

11014 Paul Piazza & Sons
P.O.Box 52049
New Orleans, LA 70152-2049   504-524-6011
      Fax: 504-566-1322 ppiazza@bellsouth.net
Processor of fresh and frozen shrimp, cod, perch and
lobster
      President: Kristen Baumer
      Plant Manager: Don Schwab
Estimated Sales: $ 10 - 20 Million
Number Employees: 50-99
Sq. footage: 75000
Type of Packaging: Consumer, Food Service, Pri-
      vate Label, Bulk

11015 Paul Schafer Meat Products
343 N Charles St # 3
Baltimore, MD 21201-4326   410-528-1250
Fax: 410-528-1059 FSIS.Outreach@usda.gov
                              www.fsis.usda.gov
Meat products
  Owner: Paul Schaefer
Estimated Sales: $ 1-2.5 Million appx.
Number Employees: 5-9

11016 Paul Stevens Lobster
349 Lincoln St # 32
Hingham, MA 02043-1609   781-740-8001
                              Fax: 781-749-2240
Fish and seafood; lobsters
  Owner: Paul Stevens
Estimated Sales: $870,000
Number Employees: 1-4

11017 Paul de Lima Company
P.O.Box 4813
Syracuse, NY 13221-4813   315-457-3725
        Fax: 315-457-3730 800-962-8864
info@delimacoffee.com   www.delimacoffee.com
Raoster and purveyor of fine coffee
  CEO: W J Drescher Jr
Estimated Sales: $ 50 - 100 Million
Number Employees: 50-99
Number of Products: 2000
Type of Packaging: Consumer, Food Service

11018 Paul's Candy Company
524 W 8360 S
Sandy, UT 84070-6440   801-576-2547
                              Fax: 801-576-1796
Processor of confectionery products
  Owner: Don Roberts
Estimated Sales: Less than $100,000
Number Employees: 3
Type of Packaging: Consumer

11019 Paul's Candy Factory
434 S 300 W
Salt Lake City, UT 84101-1705   801-576-2547
        Fax: 801-363-1294 www.westernut.com
Candy
  Owner: Michael Place
Estimated Sales: Below $ 5 Million
Number Employees: 5-9
Brands:
  Paul's Candy

11020 Paulaur Corporation
105 Melrich Rd
Cranbury, NJ 08512-3589   609-395-8844
        Fax: 609-395-8850 888-398-8844
info@paulaur.com   www.paulaur.com
Processor of bakery and ice cream confectionery toppings and inclusions, liquid sweeteners, specialty sugars and value-added carbohydrates; also, custom blending, granulating, agglomerating, sizing, sieving and milling available
  President: Vincent Toscano
  VP: Larry Toscano
  VP Sales: Lawrence Toscano
Estimated Sales: $6700000
Number Employees: 100-249
Sq. footage: 120000
Type of Packaging: Bulk

11021 Pauline's Pastries
50 Viceroy Road
Concord, ON L4K 3A7
Canada   905-738-5252
  Fax: 905-738-0345 877-292-6826
                        info@paulinespastries.com
                        www.paulinespastries.com
Processor of fresh pastries
  President/CEO: Robyn Perlmutar
  Marketing Director: Pauline Perlmutar
Type of Packaging: Consumer, Food Service
Brands:
  Pauline's

11022 Paumanok Vineyards
P.O.Box 741
Aquebogue, NY 11931-0741   631-722-8800
  Fax: 631-722-5110 info@paumanok.com
                        www.paumanok.com
Wine
  President: Charles Massoud
Estimated Sales: $1,400,000
Number Employees: 20-49

Brands:
  Paumanok Vineyards

11023 Pavero Cold Storage Corporation
P.O.Box 395
Highland, NY 12528-0395   845-691-2992
        Fax: 845-691-2955 800-435-2994
applz25@aol.com   www.paverocoldstorage.com
Grower and packer of apples and pears
  President: Joseph Pavero III
  CEO: Joseph Pavero Iii
  Operations Manager: Jody Pavero
Estimated Sales: $8300000
Number Employees: 50-99

11024 Pavich Family Farms
PO Box 10420
Terra Bella, CA 93270-0420   661-391-1000
  Fax: 661-391-1019 pavich@pavich.com
                        www.pavich.com
Organic produce
  President: Tom Pavich
  CFO: Paul Ostrow
  Director Marketing: William Holbrook
  Purchasing Manager: Clarence Robbins
Estimated Sales: $ 2.5-5 Million
Number Employees: 100
Brands:
  Pavich Thomps
  Pavich Cashews
  Pavich Certified Org
  Pavich Dates
  Pavich Prunes
  Pavich Raisins-Red S

11025 Payne Packing Company
P.O.Box 269
Artesia, NM 88211-0269   575-746-2779
Processor and packer of beef, game and pork
  Partner: Bobby Yates
Estimated Sales: $260000
Number Employees: 1-4
Type of Packaging: Consumer

11026 Pazdar Winery
6 Laddie Road
Scotchtown Branch, NY 10941-1708 845-695-1903
        Fax: 845-695-1903 pazdar@citlink.net
                        www.pazdarwinery.com
Processor of wines
  President/CEO: David Pazdar
  VP Marketing: Tracy Davis-Pazdar
Number Employees: 5-9
Parent Co: Pazdar Beverage Company
Type of Packaging: Consumer, Food Service
Brands:
  PAZDAR WINERY
  SUGARY WINE

11027 Peaberry's Coffee & Tea
5655 College Ave
Oakland, CA 94618-1583   510-653-0450
                              Fax: 510-420-0260
peaberrys@rockridgemarkethall.com
                        www.peaberrys.com
Coffee and tea
  Owner: Lynn Mallard
Estimated Sales: Over $ 1 Million
Number Employees: 20-49
Type of Packaging: Private Label

11028 Peace Mountain Natural Beverages Corporation
P.O.Box 1445
Springfield, MA 01101-1445   413-567-4942
                              Fax: 413-567-8161
peacemountainbeverages@msn.com
        www.peacemountain.com/skinnywater.com
Manufacturer of Bottled water, organic juices, nutraceutical beverages
  Owner: J David
  VP R&D: John Alden
Number Employees: 5-9
Type of Packaging: Private Label
Brands:
  CARDIO WATER
  GIVE YOUR HEART A HEALTHY START
  JANA
  MIRACLE ADE
  MIRACLE JUICE
  MIRACLE JUICE ENERGY DRINK
  PEACE MOUNTAIN
  SKINNY WATER
  SPORTS JUICE

11029 Peace River Citrus Products
582 Beachland Blvd # 300
Vero Beach, FL 32963-1758   772-467-1234
  Fax: 772-492-4056 www.peacerivercitrus.com
Processor and exporter of citrus products
  Manager: Kirsten Besanko
Estimated Sales: $ .5 - 1 million
Number Employees: 100-249
Type of Packaging: Bulk
Other Locations:
  Peach River Citrus Products Plant
  Arcadia FL
  Peach River Citrus Products Plant
  Bartow FL

11030 Peace River Citrus Products
P.O.Box 730
Arcadia, FL 34265-0730   863-494-0440
  Fax: 863-993-3161 www.peacerivercitrus.com
Processor of chilled orange juice
  President: Bill Becker
  Marketing Director: Akira Nagashima
Estimated Sales: $ 20 - 50 Million
Number Employees: 100-249
Type of Packaging: Bulk

11031 Peace Village Organic Foods
76 Florida Avenue
Berkeley, CA 94707-1708   510-524-4420
Organic asian pasta and organic food ingredients
  President: Joel Wollner
Type of Packaging: Consumer, Private Label

11032 Peaceful Bend Vineyard
1942 Highway T
Steelville, MO 65565-5067   573-775-3000
  Fax: 573-775-3001 winery@peacefulbend.com
                        www.peacefulbend.com
Wine
  Owner: Katherine Gill
  CEO: Clyde Gill
  Owner: Clyde Gill
Estimated Sales: $500,000-$1 Million
Number Employees: 1-4
Brands:
  Peaceful Bend

11033 Peaceworks
PO Box 1393
Old Chelsea Station
New York, NY 10113   212-616-3009
        Fax: 212-616-3005 800-732-2321
kind@peaceworks.com   www.peaceworks.com
fruit and nut bars, pesto and tapenades, and sauces
  VP: Sasha Hare
  VP Sales: Rami Leshem
  VP Operations: Doris Rivera
Estimated Sales: $1.3 Million
Number Employees: 8

11034 Peaceworks
444 Park Ave S
New York, NY 10016-7321   212-897-3995
  Fax: 212-831-0982 marketing@peaceworks.net
                        www.peaceworks.com
Processor of basil pesto and pasta sauces; also, sun-dried tomato, olive and smoked eggplant spreads
  CEO: Daniel Lubetzky
  Vice President: Sasha Hare
  Sales Director: Rami Leshem
Estimated Sales: $ 1-2.5 Million
Number Employees: 5-9
Type of Packaging: Consumer, Food Service
Brands:
  Azteca Trading Co.
  Mediterranean Sprate
  Moshe & Ali's Sprat,
  Smoked Eggplant Spra
  Wafa

11035 Peanut Butter & Co
PO Box 2000
New York, NY 10101   212-757-3130
                              Fax: 212-757-3252
customer.service@ilovepeanutbutter.com
                        www.ilovepeanutbutter.com
peanut butter, jams and jellies, snacks and fluff

11036 (HQ)Peanut Corporation of America

2121 Wiggington Road
PO Box 10037
Lynchburg, VA 24506   434-384-7098
          Fax: 434-384-9528 gbparnell@aol.com
                    www.peanutcorp.com
Processor of peanuts
    Owner/President: Stewart Parnell
    Corporate Office Manager: Gloria Parnell
    Sales Director: David Yoth
Estimated Sales: $3-$5 Million
Number Employees: 20-49
Type of Packaging: Consumer, Food Service, Bulk
Other Locations:
    Blakely GA
    Suffolk VA
    Plainview TX
Brands:
    PARNELL'S PRIDE

11037 Peanut Patch

4322 E County 13th St
Yuma, AZ 85365-4631   928-726-6292
          Fax: 928-726-2433 800-872-7688
          thepeanutpatch@thepeanutpatch.com
                    www.thepeanutpatch.com
Peanuts
    Owner: Donna George
Estimated Sales: $ 1 - 3 Million
Number Employees: 10-19

11038 Peanut Patch

P.O.Box 186
Courtland, VA 23837-0186   757-653-2028
          Fax: 757-653-9530 866-732-6883
          feridies@feridies.com
Processor and exporter of gourmet peanuts and pea-
nut candies such as peanut brittle, chocolate covered
peanuts, honey roasted peanuts, cashew brittle, and
chocolate peanut brittle
    President/CEO: Judy Riddick
    CFO: Paul Sheffer
    R&D: Ted Fries
    Quality Control: Ted Fries
    Marketing: Jane Fries
Number Employees: 10-19
Type of Packaging: Consumer, Food Service, Pri-
    vate Label
Brands:
    Peanut Patch

11039 Peanut Processors

P.O.Box 160
Dublin, NC 28332-0160   910-862-2136
          Fax: 910-862-8076 www.peanutprocessors.com
Peanuts
    CEO: Houston Brisson
Estimated Sales: $ 20 - 50 Million
Number Employees: 20-49

11040 Peanut Roaster

394 Zeb Robinson Rd
Henderson, NC 27537-8760   252-431-0100
          Fax: 252-431-0224 800-445-1404
          peanut@peanut.com www.peanut.com
Wholesalers, retailers and manufacturers of peanuts
    President: John Monahan
    Marketing Director: Charles Penick
    CFO: Peanut Roaster
    Quality Control: John William
    Founder: Larry Monahan Sr.
Estimated Sales: Below $ 5 Million
Number Employees: 20-49
Brands:
    The Peanut Roaster

11041 Peanut Shop of Williamsburg

PO Box 250
Portsmouth, VA 23705   757-566-0930
          Fax: 757-566-1605 800-637-3268
          info@thepeanutshop.com
                    www.thepeanutshop.com
Manufacturer of peanuts
    General Manager: Pete Booker
    Operations Mgr: Larry Winslow
    General Manager: Pete Booker
Number Employees: 30
Type of Packaging: Consumer, Food Service, Pri-
    vate Label, Bulk
Brands:
    Peanut Shop of Williamsburg
    Smithfield Tavern

11042 Peanut Shop of Williamsburg

311 Country Street
Suite 201
Portsmouth, VA 23704   800-637-3268
          Fax: 757-673-7006 info@thepeanutshop.com
                    www.thepeanutshop.com
peanuts and peanut products
    Manufacturing Staff Director: Larry Wcislo
    General Manager: Chip Penick
Number Employees: 8

11043 Peanut Wonder Corporation

30 Blank Lane
Water Mill, NY 11976-2134   631-726-4433
          Fax: 631-726-4433 www.peanutwonder.com
Low fat, low calorie peanut butter spread
    President: Lloyd Lasdon
    Vice President: Stuart Lasdon
Estimated Sales: Under $500,000
Number Employees: 1-4
Type of Packaging: Private Label
Brands:
    Peanut Wonder

11044 Pear's Coffee

6171 Grover St
Omaha, NE 68106-4311   402-551-8422
          Fax: 402-551-8401 800-317-1773
          rrb@hermansnuthouse.com
                    www.hermansnuthouse.com
Coffee, nuts
    President: John Larsen
    Operations Manager: Adam Gaines
Estimated Sales: Below $ 5 Million
Number Employees: 20-49
Type of Packaging: Bulk
Brands:
    Pear's Coffee

11045 Pearl Coffee Company

675 S Broadway St
Akron, OH 44311-1099   330-253-7184
          Fax: 330-253-7185 800-822-5282
Manufacturer and packer of roasted regular, flavored
and gourmet coffee; importer of green coffee
    President: John Economou
    VP/Marketing: Johnna Economou
Estimated Sales: $9 Million
Number Employees: 10-19
Sq. footage: 20000
Type of Packaging: Consumer, Food Service, Pri-
    vate Label
Brands:
    Diana

11046 Pearl Reef Oyster Company

PO Box 536
Broussard, LA 70518-0536   318-839-9000
                    Fax: 318-839-8900
Oysters
    President: John Parker

11047 Pearl River Pastry & Chocolates

4 Dexter Plz
Pearl River, NY 10965-2321   845-735-5100
          Fax: 845-735-6434 800-632-2639
          sales@prpastry.com www.prpastry.com
Manufacturer of chocolates, cakes and pastries
    Owner: J Koffman
Estimated Sales: $5-10 Million
Number Employees: 20-49

11048 Pearl Valley Cheese Company

54775 White Eyes Twp Rd 90
Fresno, OH 43824   740-545-6002
          Fax: 740-545-7703 www.pearlvalleycheese.com
Processor of natural cheeses
    President: John Stalder
    General Manager: Chuck Ellis
Number Employees: 10-19
Type of Packaging: Consumer, Food Service, Pri-
    vate Label, Bulk
Brands:
    Pearl Valley

11049 Pearlco of Boston

5 Whitman Rd
Canton, MA 02021-2707   781-821-1010
                    Fax: 781-821-4303
Pickled fruits and vegetables, vegetable sauces and
seasonings, and salad dressings.
    President/Treasurer: Judith Pearlstein

Estimated Sales: $3,100,000
Number Employees: 20-49
Type of Packaging: Food Service, Private Label,
    Bulk
Brands:
    Saratoga

11050 Pearson Candy Company

P.O.Box 64459
St Paul, MN 55164-0459   651-698-0356
          Fax: 651-696-2222 800-328-6507
                    www.pearsoncandy.com
Processor of candy including chocolate and
nonchocolate bagged, bars, multi-packs, mints, holi-
day novelties, vending, nut goodies and nut rolls and
bun bars
    President: Larry L Hassler
Estimated Sales: $ 20 - 50 Million
Number Employees: 100-249
Type of Packaging: Consumer
Brands:
    PEARSON'S BUN BARS
    PEARSON'S MINT PATTIES
    PEARSON'S NUT GOODIE
    PEARSON'S SALTED NUT ROLL

11051 Pearson's Berry Farm

RR 1
Bowden, AB T0M 0K0
Canada   403-224-3011
                    Fax: 403-224-2096
Processor of berry products including jams, pie fill-
ings and dessert toppings
    President: E Leonard Pearson
    Sales Manager: Joyce Park
Number Employees: 20-49
Type of Packaging: Consumer, Food Service
Brands:
    Pearson's Berry Farm

11052 Pearson's Homestyle

RR 1
Bowden, AB T0M 0K0
Canada   403-224-3339
          877-224-3339
          homestyle@homestylebeverage.com
                    www.gordosfoods.com
Processor of gourmet sauces, spices and seasonings;
private labeling and custom liquid filling available.
Produces unique upscale beverages featuring such
natural and wild grown prairie berries as the
Highbush Cranberry, rasberry, wildblack cherries
and the Saskatoon Berry.
    President: Duane Mertin
    Production: Debbie Mertin
Number Employees: 10-19
Sq. footage: 5500
Type of Packaging: Private Label
Brands:
    Gordo's

11053 Pease's Candy Shoppe

1701 S State St
Springfield, IL 62704-4098   217-523-3721
          Fax: 217-523-7581 ILINI83@aol.com
                    www.peasescandy.com
Manufacturer of fine chocolates and salted nuts
    Owner: Robert Flesher
    VP/Treasurer: Robert Flesher
Estimated Sales: $500,000-$1 Million
Number Employees: 5-9
Brands:
    Pease's

11054 Peavey Company

PO Box 52
Ama, LA 70031-0052   225-869-4405
                    Fax: 225-869-4517
Processor and exporter of soybeans, corn, wheat and
feed ingredients
    Plant Manager: Michael Geurtz
Estimated Sales: $9200000
Number Employees: 86
Type of Packaging: Bulk

11055 Pecan Deluxe Candy Company

2570 Lone Star Drive
Dallas, TX 75212-6308   214-631-3669
          Fax: 214-631-5833 800-733-3589
                    www.pecandeluxe.com

Supplier of gourmet cookies and ice creams.
President: Jay Brigham
CFO: Keith Hurd
VP Quality Assurance: Rick Hintermeier
Chief Operating Officer: Tim Markowicz

11056 Pecan Deluxe Candy Company
2570 Lone Star Dr
Dallas, TX 75212-6308   214-631-3669
    Fax: 214-631-5833   800-733-3589
        pdcc_info@pecandeluxe.com
            www.pecandeluxe.com
Processor and exporter of ingredients for frozen desserts and baked goods including toffees, praline nuts, chocolate coated items, flavor bases, sauces, etc.; also, nonfat and nonsugar ingredients available
President: Bennie Brigham
CEO: John Namy
Executive VP: Jay Brigham
R&D Director: Bill Garrison
VP Marketing: Robert Bosma
VP Sales: Robert Bosma
Inventory/Production Coordinator: Wayne Miller
Plant Manager: Mike Cavin
Purchasing Manager: James Mitchell
Estimated Sales: $ 20 - 50 Million
Number Employees: 100-249
Number of Products: 2000
Sq. footage: 63000
Type of Packaging: Bulk

11057 Pechters Baking
840 Jersey St
Harrison, NJ 07029-2056   973-483-3374
    Fax: 973-483-1600   800-525-5779
            www.pechters.com
Processor of baked goods including bread, rolls and bagels
President: George Thomas
Director Operations: Steve Colombo
Estimated Sales: $ 50 - 100 Million
Number Employees: 250-499
Parent Co: Amerifit/Strength Systems
Type of Packaging: Food Service
Brands:
    Pechters

11058 Peco Foods
1020 Lurleen B Wallace Blvd N
Tuscaloosa, AL 35401-2225   205-345-4711
    Fax: 205-366-4533   mhickman@pecofoods.com
            www.pecofoods.com
Processor and exporter of poultry
President: Mark Hickman
CEO: Mark Hickman
CFO: Tommy Elliott
Marketing Director: Bobby Wilburn
Sales Director: Bobby Wilburn
Operations: Courtney Stallings
Processing Director: Holly Dyer
Plant Manager: Tim Daniel
Number Employees: 20-49
Type of Packaging: Consumer, Food Service
Other Locations:
    Peco Foods
    Brooksville MS
    Peco Foods
    Bay Springs MS

11059 Peco Foods
P.O.Box 419
Canton, MS 39046-0419   601-407-1699
    Fax: 601-855-5028   www.pecofoods.com
Processor of fresh and frozen chicken
Plant Manager: Frank Gordon
Estimated Sales: $ 20 - 50 Million
Number Employees: 100-249
Type of Packaging: Consumer
Brands:
    Peco

11060 Peco Foods
P.O.Box 319
Sebastopol, MS 39359-0319   601-625-7432
    Fax: 601-625-0226   swoods@pecofoods.com
            www.pecofoods.com
Manufacturer and exporter of poultry products
President/CEO: Mark Hickman
CFO: Tommy Elliott
COO: Wayne Butler
Sales Manager: Sharon Woods
Plant Manager: Keith Tollett
Estimated Sales: $100+ Million
Number Employees: 500-999

Type of Packaging: Consumer, Food Service

11061 Peconic Bay Winery
P.O.Box 818
Cutchogue, NY 11935-0818   631-734-7361
    Fax: 631-734-5867   info@peconicbaywinery.com
            www.peconicbaywinery.com
Wine
    Manager: Matt Gillies
    Co-Owner: Ursula Lowerre
    Winemaker: Gregory Gove
    General Manager: Matt Gillies
Estimated Sales: Below $ 5 Million
Number Employees: 20-49
Brands:
    Peconic Bay

11062 Pecoraro Dairy Products
904 Erie Blvd W
Rome, NY 13440-2904   315-339-0101
    Fax: 315-339-3008   pcr2c1@aol.com
Processor and exporter of cheeses including feta, ricotta, regular and curd mozzarella, mascarpone and string; also, yogurt and basket cheese
President: Cesare Pecoraro
Operations: Ralph Parlato
Estimated Sales: $ 5 - 10 Million
Number Employees: 5-9
Number of Brands: 4
Number of Products: 12
Sq. footage: 7200
Type of Packaging: Consumer, Food Service, Private Label
Brands:
    Brown Cow Farm East
    Sweet Cheese, Queso Blanco

11063 Pecos Valley Spice Company
500 E 77th Street
Apt 2324
New York, NY 10162-0025   212-628-5374
Spices
    Vice President: G McMeen

11064 Pede Brothers
582 Duanesburg Rd # 1
Schenectady, NY 12306-1096   518-356-3042
            Fax: 518-355-7472
Processor of fresh and frozen pasta
Owner: Romolo Pede
Estimated Sales: $ 20 - 50 Million
Number Employees: 20-49
Type of Packaging: Consumer, Food Service, Private Label

11065 Pedrizzetti Winery
1645 San Pedro Ave
Morgan Hill, CA 95037-9667   408-779-7389
    Fax: 408-779-9083   wines@pedwines.net
            www.pedrizzetti.com
Wines
    President: Michael Sampognaro
Estimated Sales: $500,000-$1 Million
Number Employees: 1-4
Type of Packaging: Consumer, Private Label, Bulk
Brands:
    Barbera
    Sirah

11066 Pedroncelli Winery
1220 Canyon Rd
Geyserville, CA 95441-9639   707-857-3531
    Fax: 707-857-3812   800-836-3894
    service@pedroncelli.com   www.pedroncelli.com
Wines
    President: John Pedroncelli
    VP Marketing: Julie Pedroncelli St. John
    VP Sales: Richard Morehouse
Estimated Sales: $1,500,000
Number Employees: 20-49
Type of Packaging: Private Label
Brands:
    Pedroncelli

11067 Peeled Snacks
530 Third Avenue
Suite 2R
Brooklyn, NY 11215   212-706-2001
    Fax: 646-478-9518   info@peeledsnacks.com
            www.peeledsnacks.com
fruit and nut snacks
    President/Owner: Noha Waibsnaider

11068 (HQ)Peeler's Jersey Farms
706 Leadmine Road
Gaffney, SC 29340-3636   864-487-9996
            Fax: 864-489-2889
Dairy products
Estimated Sales: $ 5-10 Million
Number Employees: 20-49

11069 Peer Foods Inc
1200 W 35th St # 5e
Chicago, IL 60609-1305   773-927-1440
    Fax: 773-927-9859   800-365-5644
    ken@beanplant.com   www.peerfoods.com
Processor of smoked meats including bacon, hams and butts, pigs' feet, sausage and corned beef; also, pickled hocks and Canadian bacon
President: Larry O'Connell
Director Sales/Manufacturing: Harold Dangler
Marketing Manager: Harold Dangler
Director Manufacturing: Bill Froula
Purchasing Manager: N Loose
Estimated Sales: $30000000
Number Employees: 100-249
Type of Packaging: Consumer, Food Service

11070 Peerless Coffee Company
260 Oak St
Oakland, CA 94607-4587   510-763-1763
    Fax: 510-763-5026   800-310-5662
        tellme@peerlesscoffee.com
            www.peerlesscoffee.com
Processor of gourmet coffee
President: Sonja Vukasin
CEO: George Vukasin Sr
Executive VP: George Vukasin Jr
CEO: George Vukasin Sr
Consultant: Michelle Thomas
CFO: Ivan Steves
Estimated Sales: $ 50 - 100 Million
Number Employees: 50-99
Type of Packaging: Consumer, Food Service

11071 Peerless Confection Company
Ste 100
7383 N Lincoln Ave
Lincolnwood, IL 60712-1747   773-281-6100
    Fax: 773-281-5812   sales@peerlesscandy.com
            www.peerlesscandy.com
Manufacturer of hard and filled candy
Chairman: Kathleen Pickens
Estimated Sales: $15 Million
Number Employees: 104
Sq. footage: 170000
Type of Packaging: Consumer
Brands:
    CHIPS N' CHEWS
    LEMAN'S
    ORORA
    PM MIX
    RADIANT MORSELS
    SPRIG-O-MINT
    SUNRAY

11072 Peerless Packing Company
P.O.Box 697
Beckley, WV 25802-0697   304-252-4731
            Fax: 304-255-1290
Processor/packer of fresh meats
Manager: Mark Eye
Estimated Sales: $ 3 - 5 Million
Number Employees: 5-9
Type of Packaging: Consumer, Food Service
Brands:
    Im-Peer-Ial

11073 Peerless Potato Chips
1661 W 11th Ave
Gary, IN 46404-2499   219-885-6843
            Fax: 219-885-7420
Processor of potato chips
Manager: John Hogg
Vice President: John Hogg Jr.
Estimated Sales: $5-9.9 Million
Number Employees: 10-19
Type of Packaging: Consumer, Food Service, Private Label, Bulk
Brands:
    Peerless Potato Chips

11074 Peet's Coffee & Tea
P.O.Box 12509
Berkeley, CA 94712-3509   510-594-2100
    Fax: 510-594-2180   800-999-2132
    amyl@peets.com   www.peets.com

Coffee roaster and tea.
  Chairman: Jean-Michel Valette
  President/CEO: Patrick O'Dea
  CFO/VP: Tom Cawley
  CEO: Patrick J O'Dea
  Quality Control: Jim Reynolds
  Public Relations: Weber Shandwick
  Senior Master Roaster: John Weaver
  Purchasing Manager: Doug Welsh
Estimated Sales: $119 Million
Number Employees: 1,000-4,999

11075 Peetsa Products Company
4828 Stamp Rd
Temple Hills, MD 20748-6715   301-423-3900
                            Fax: 301-423-7301
Foodservices
  President: Ray Seaton
Number Employees: 1-4

11076 Peggy Lawton Kitchens
253 Washington St
East Walpole, MA 02032-1133   508-668-1215
       Fax: 508-660-1636 800-843-7325
Manufacturer of portion packaged brownies and
cookies including preservative-free
  President: William Wolf
  Office Manager: Robert Willis
Estimated Sales: $ 10 - 20 Million
Number Employees: 20-49
Number of Products: 10
Sq. footage: 30000
Type of Packaging: Consumer, Food Service, Private Label, Bulk
Brands:
  PEGGY LAWTON

11077 Pegi
1211 N Harbor Boulevard
Santa Ana, CA 92703-1608   714-554-2110
       Fax: 714-554-2140 800-292-3353
                    pegi@pacbell.com
  President: Corrine Draps
Estimated Sales: Under $500,000
Number Employees: 5-9

11078 Peju Winery
P.O.Box 478
Rutherford, CA 94573-0478   707-963-3600
       Fax: 707-963-8680 800-446-7358
       info@peju.com www.peju.com
Wines
  Owner: Herta Behensky
Estimated Sales: Below $ 5 Million
Number Employees: 20-49
Brands:
  Peju

11079 Pekarna's Meat Market
119 Water St
Jordan, MN 55352-1555   952-492-6101
Manufacturer of meat and meat products including
beef, pork, wild game and sausage
  President: Frank Pekarna
  CEO: Kenny Pekarna
Estimated Sales: $4 Million
Number Employees: 5-9
Type of Packaging: Consumer, Private Label

11080 Pekarskis Sausage
293 Conway Rd
South Deerfield, MA 01373-9663   413-665-4537
Meat and poultry
  Manager: Mike Pekarski
  Marketing Director: Mike Pekarskis
Estimated Sales: $500,000-$1 Million
Number Employees: 1-4
Brands:
  Pekarskis

11081 Peking Noodle Company
1514 N San Fernando Rd
Los Angeles, CA 90065-1282   323-223-2023
       Fax: 323-223-3211 info@pekingnoodle.com
                    www.pekingnoodle.com
Processor and exporter of noodles, egg rolls,
wontons, potsticker wraps, suey gow skins, fortune
cookies and snack foods
  President: Stephen Tong
  Vice President: Frank Tong
  Plant Manager: Maria Gonzalez
Estimated Sales: $2200000
Number Employees: 50-99
Sq. footage: 30000

11082 Pel-Freez
P.O.Box 68
Rogers, AR 72757-0068   479-636-4361
       Fax: 479-636-4282 800-223-8751
       biosales@pelfreez.com www.pelfreez-bio.com
Manufacturer and exporter of frozen and fresh rabbit
  President/CEO: David Dubbell
Estimated Sales: $53 Million
Number Employees: 50-99
Parent Co: Pel-Freez
Type of Packaging: Consumer, Food Service
Brands:
  PEL-FREEZE

11083 Pelican Bay
150 Douglas Ave
Dunedin, FL 34698-7908   727-733-8399
       Fax: 727-734-5860 800-826-8982
       sales@pelicanbayltd.com
       www.pelicanbayltd.com
Processor, wholesaler/distributor and exporter of
baking and drink mixes, spice blends and gourmet
gifts
  President: Char Pfaelzer
  CEO: Linda Pfaelzer
  Executive VP: David Pfaelzer
  Sales: Char Pfaelzer
  Plant Manager: Justin Pfaelzer
  Purchasing: Greg Kathan
Estimated Sales: $ 3 - 5 Million
Number Employees: 20-49
Number of Brands: 1
Number of Products: 200
Sq. footage: 30000
Type of Packaging: Consumer, Private Label, Bulk
Brands:
  Pelican Bay

11084 Pelican Marine Supply
2911 Engineers Rd
Belle Chasse, LA 70037-3150   504-392-9062
                            Fax: 504-394-5528
  President: Peter Bretchel
Estimated Sales: $ 10 - 20 Million
Number Employees: 10-19

11085 Pellegrini Family Vineyards
P.O.Box 546
Fulton, CA 95439-0546   707-575-8463
       Fax: 650-589-7132 800-891-0244
       info@pellegrinisonoma.com
       www.pellegrinisonoma.com
Wines
  Partner/Winemaker: Robert Pellegrini
  Partner/CFO: Richard Pellegrini
  Partner/Property Manager: Jeanne Pellegrini
Estimated Sales: $1 Million
Number Employees: 10-19
Type of Packaging: Private Label
Brands:
  Cloverdale Ranch
  Olivet Lane
  Pellegrini

11086 Pellman Foods
P.O.Box 337
New Holland, PA 17557-0337   717-354-8070
       Fax: 717-355-9944 www.pellmanfoods.com
Processor of frozen cakes and pies
  President: Michael Pellman
  VP: Scott Pellman
  Marketing Director: Deryl Denlinger
  Sales: Roger Carper
  Public Relations: Allen Smoker
  Production: Greg Huber
  Plant Manager: Clair Siegrist
Estimated Sales: $ 20 - 50 Million
Number Employees: 40
Number of Brands: 1
Number of Products: 30
Sq. footage: 50000
Type of Packaging: Consumer, Food Service
Brands:
  PELLMAN

11087 Peloian Packing Company
430 W Ventura St
Dinuba, CA 93618-2651   559-591-0101
                            Fax: 559-591-7584
Manufacturer, packer and exporter of raisins
  President: Edward Peloian

Estimated Sales: $28 Million
Number Employees: 5-9
Type of Packaging: Consumer, Private Label, Bulk

11088 Peluso Cheese Company
429 H St
Los Banos, CA 93635-4113   209-826-3744
                            Fax: 209-826-6782
Mexican style cheese: chihuahua, cotija, freir,
fresco, panela, Quesmo crema
  Manager: Sergio Alvarado
Estimated Sales: $ 20-50 Million
Number Employees: 20-49

11089 Pemaquid Fishermen's Co-Op
P.O.Box 152
New Harbor, ME 04554-0152   207-677-2801
       Fax: 207-677-2818 866-864-2897
       sales@pemaquidlobsterco-op.com
       www.pemaquidlobsterco-op.com
Seafood
  Manager: Wayne Dighton
Estimated Sales: $300,000-500,000
Number Employees: 5-9

11090 Pemberton's Gourmet Foods
32 Lewiston Rd
Gray, ME 04039-7536   207-657-6446
       Fax: 207-657-6453 800-255-8401
       info@pembertongourmet.com
       www.pembertongourmet.com
Sauces, mixes, pancake, scone, muffin mixes and
syrup. Sauces, seasonings, salsa, relish, mustard,
pickles, jams, jellies
  Owner: Jeff Johnson
Estimated Sales: $ .5 - 1 million
Number Employees: 5-9
Sq. footage: 7000

11091 Penauta Products
PO Box 155
Stouffville, ON L4A 7Z5
Canada   905-640-1564
                            Fax: 905-640-8778
Processor and exporter of jarred honey including
raw, liquid and cream; also, bee pollen
  President: Paul Nauta
  Chairman: Henry Nauta
  Production Manager: Martin Nauta
Number Employees: 5-9
Sq. footage: 6000
Type of Packaging: Consumer, Food Service, Private Label, Bulk
Brands:
  Ambrosia
  Meadowview

11092 Pend Oreille Cheese Company
P.O.Box 1969
Sandpoint, ID 83864-0910   208-263-2030
                    www.lighthousefoods.com
Processor of cheese
  Manager: Jennifer Calbert
Estimated Sales: $270000
Number Employees: 1-4
Type of Packaging: Consumer

11093 Pender Packing Company
4520 Nc Highway 133
Rocky Point, NC 28457-9108   910-675-3311
       Fax: 910-675-1625 penderpacking@aol.com
Processor of meat including fresh and smoked sau-
sage, liver pudding, c-loaf, souse loaf, chitterling
loaf, cured sausage, chorizo, fatback and pork
barbecue.
  President: Danny L Baker
Estimated Sales: $4900000
Number Employees: 20-49
Type of Packaging: Consumer

11094 Pendery's
1221 Manufacturing St
Dallas, TX 75207-6505   214-357-1870
       Fax: 214-761-1966 800-533-1870
       email@penderys.com www.pendery.com
Manufacturer of seasonings including bay leaves,
cinnamon, garlic, ginger, paprika, chile pepper and
herb blends
  President/Owner: Patrick Haggerty Jr
Estimated Sales: $1-3 Million
Number Employees: 5-9
Sq. footage: 23000
Type of Packaging: Consumer, Food Service, Private Label, Bulk

Brands:
CHILTOMALINE

11095 Pendery's
1221 Manufacturing St
Dallas, TX 75207-6505   214-357-1870
     Fax: 214-761-1966   800-533-1870
     email@penderys.com   www.penderys.com
Chiles and Spices.
     President: Pat Haggerty
Estimated Sales: Below $ 5 Million
Number Employees: 5-9

11096 Pendleton Flour Mills
P.O.Box 400
Pendleton, OR 97801-0400   541-276-6511
     Fax: 541-276-9151 www.pendleton.or.us
Flour and other grain mill products
     Manager: Greg Loftus
     CFO: Terry Burns
     Marketing Director: Mike McDaniel
     Production Manager: Jean Scott
Estimated Sales: $ 100-500 Million
Number Employees: 50-99

11097 (HQ)Penford Food Ingredients
7094 S Revere Pkwy
Centennial, CO 80112-3932   303-649-1900
     Fax: 303-649-1700   tlengwin@penx.com
         www.penx.com
Manufacturer of Specialty dextrose, potato dextrins, pregelatinized, cook-up potato and tapioca starches; also, modified waxy maize starches and dietary fober, rice starches
     VP/CFO: Steven Cordier
     CEO: Thomas D Malkoski
     Sr Research Team Leader: Dr Ibrahim Abbas PhD
     Director Business Development: Jeff Smith
     Marketing Manager: Ted Lengwin
     Regional Sales Manager: Barbara Howe
Estimated Sales: $50 Million
Number Employees: 500-999
Parent Co: Penford Corporation
Other Locations:
     Penford Food Ingredients - Sales
     Roswell GA
     Penford Food Ingredients - Sales
     Burr Ridge IL
     Penford Food Ingredients
     Newman Lake WA
     Penford Food Ingredients
     Red Wing MN
     PFI - Starch Mfg
     Plover WI
     PFI - Starch Mfg
     Idaho Falls ID
     PFI - Sugar Mfg
     Cedar Rapids IA
     PFI - Starch Mfg
     Richland WA

11098 Penguin Frozen Foods
P.O.Box 1145
Northbrook, IL 60065-1145   847-291-9400
     Fax: 847-291-1588
Processor and exporter of frozen seafood and fish including shrimp, sole, turbot, fillets, lobster, crab meat, etc
     President: Jonathan Appelbaum
Estimated Sales: $2700000
Number Employees: 10-19
Type of Packaging: Consumer, Food Service
Brands:
     Campeche Bay
     Dimo
     Texas Bay

11099 Penguin Natural Foods
6433 Canning St
Commerce, CA 90040-3121   323-727-7980
     Fax: 323-727-7983   800-600-8448
     jgegenhuber@hotmail.com
         www.penguinfoods.com
Ready to serve foods, processed foods
     President: Scott Nairne
     Food Technician: Michael Dunn
     R&D Chef: John Gegenhuber
Estimated Sales: $ 10-20 Million
Number Employees: 20-49

11100 Penhurst Candy Company
995 Greensburg Pike
Pittsburgh, PA 15221-4233   412-271-8880
     Fax: 412-271-1085   800-545-1336

Chocolate candy
Estimated Sales: $ 10-24.9 Million
Number Employees: 50-100

11101 Peninsula Fruit Exchange
2955 Kroupa Rd
Traverse City, MI 49686-9787   231-223-4282
         Fax: 231-223-4299
Manufacturer of frozen cherries
     President: Jim Horton
Estimated Sales: $22 Million
Number Employees: 20-49
Type of Packaging: Consumer, Food Service

11102 Penn Cheese Corporation
7199 County Line Rd
Winfield, PA 17889-9266   570-524-7700
     Fax: 570-523-9691   jon.weber@penncheese.com
         www.penncheese.com
Processor of specialty swiss cheese, including baby and lacey swiss
     President: Michael Price
     Sales Director: Fred Greenberg
     Operations VP: Jonathan Weber
     Production VP: Thomas Weber
Estimated Sales: $ 10 - 20 Million
Number Employees: 10-19
Number of Brands: 2
Number of Products: 2
Sq. footage: 20000
Type of Packaging: Private Label, Bulk
Brands:
     Market Place
     Pennsylvania People

11103 Penn Dutch Food Center
3950 N 28th Ter
Hollywood, FL 33020-1179   954-921-4635
     Fax: 954-921-7448 www.penn-dutch.com
Dutch food
     President: Greg Salsburg
     CEO: George Ronkin
     Secretary/Treasurer: Paul Salsburg
     Managing Director: Kara Boehly
Estimated Sales: $ 20 - 50 Million
Number Employees: 100-249

11104 Penn Herb Company
10601 Decatur Rd # 2
Philadelphia, PA 19154-3212   215-632-6100
     Fax: 215-632-7945   800-523-9971
     info@pennherb.com   www.pennherb.com
Processor and wholesaler/distributor of encapsulated herbs including ginseng and golden seal root; importer of vitamins and supplements
     President: William Betz
     President: Ronald Betz
Estimated Sales: $3500000
Number Employees: 10-19
Sq. footage: 23000
Brands:
     Nature's Wonderland

11105 (HQ)Penn Maid Crowley Foods
10975 Dutton Rd
Philadelphia, PA 19154-3203   215-824-2800
     Fax: 215-824-2820   800-247-6269
         www.hphood.com
Manufacturer of dairy products that include; sour cream, cottage cheese, yogurt, cream cheese, butter, dips, cheese, desserts and condiments
     Controller: Glenn Goenner
     Plant Manager: Ron Nelson
Estimated Sales: $21 Million
Number Employees: 100-249
Sq. footage: 40000
Type of Packaging: Consumer, Food Service, Private Label, Bulk
Brands:
     PENN MAID

11106 Penn Valley Farms
P.O.Box 5935
Gainesville, GA 30504-935   773-685-9929
         Fax: 773-685-8084
Processor of fresh sausage including smoked, steamed, pork, beef, chicken and veal; also, bratwurst, luncheon meats, pizza toppings and pasta. Also offers natural antibiotic free meats
     President: Kurt Penn
Estimated Sales: $7300000
Number Employees: 50
Sq. footage: 15000
Type of Packaging: Consumer, Private Label, Bulk

Brands:
     Hans' All Natural
     Penn Valley Farms

11107 Penn-Shore Vineyards
10225 E Lake Rd
North East, PA 16428-2894   814-725-8688
     Fax: 814-725-8689 www.pennshore.com
Winery
     President: Jeffrey Ore
     Vice President: Cheryl Ore
Estimated Sales: Below $ 5 Million
Number Employees: 5-9
Number of Brands: 23
Type of Packaging: Bulk

11108 Pennant Foods Company
111 Northwest Ave
Northlake, IL 60164-1603   708-562-0100
     Fax: 708-498-2305   800-877-1157
     twellenzohn@pennantfoods.com
         www.chefsolutions.com
Bakery products, including puff pastry and Danish doughs, bakery mixes and bases, fillings, icings and glazes, thaw' n serve cakes and muffins, frozen cookie doughs and other specialties
     CEO: Steve Silk
     CFO: Carl Warchausky
     Human Resources: Claudia Romo
     Chief Information Officer: Michael C Casula
Estimated Sales: $ 20 - 50 Million
Number Employees: 250-499
Brands:
     Chef Solutions
     Pennant

11109 (HQ)Pennfield Corporation
P.O.Box 4366
Lancaster, PA 17604-4366   717-299-2561
     Fax: 717-295-8783 www.pennfield.com
Processor of fresh and frozen chicken, custom cut meats, seafood, frozen food products
     President: Donald Horn
     CEO: Ernest O Horn Iii
     Operations Manager: Fred Keller
     Purchasing Manager: Andy Graybill
Estimated Sales: $200000000
Number Employees: 50-99
Type of Packaging: Consumer, Food Service, Private Label, Bulk
Brands:
     PENFIELD FARMS
     RITTER FOOD

11110 Pennfield Farms
PO Box 70
Lancaster, PA 17608-0070   717-865-2153
     Fax: 717-865-2186   kmith@dolemannatural.com
Processor of egg products and fresh chicken including parts
     President: Mark Mckay
     Plant Manager: Bill Rahn
Number Employees: 400
Parent Co: Pennfield Corporation
Type of Packaging: Consumer, Bulk
Brands:
     COLEMAN

11111 Pennsylvania Brewing Company
800 Vinial St
Pittsburgh, PA 15212-5151   412-237-9400
     Fax: 412-237-9406   pennbrew@hotmail.com
         www.pennbrew.com
Processor and bottler of seasonal beer and ale
     President: Tom Pastorius
     Manager: Rick Brown
Estimated Sales: Below $ 5 Million
Number Employees: 20-49
Type of Packaging: Consumer, Food Service
Brands:
     Penn Dark
     Penn Gold
     Penn Maibok
     Penn Marzen
     Penn Pilsner
     Penn Weizen

11112 Pennsylvania Dutch BirchBeer
67 Buck Pond
Suite 112
Huntingdon Valley, PA 19006   215-396-2012
         Fax: 215-396-2013
     dschwarz@daretogodutch.com
     www.pennsylvaniadutchbirchbeer.com

Manufacturer of soft drinks
President: Michael Geehring
Chairman: Lincoln Warrell
VP Finance: L Lebo
VP: Dwayne Schwartz
Estimated Sales: $1-$2.5 Million
Number Employees: 2
Brands:
Pennsylvania Dutch

11113 (HQ)Pennsylvania Dutch Candies
1250 Slate Hill Road
Camp Hill, PA 17011-3411   866-736-6388
Fax: 717-761-5702   800-233-7082
orderdirect@warrellcorp.com
www.paduteh candies.com
Manufacturer of candies, chocolates and snacks
Chairman: Lincoln A Warrell
President: Dick Billman
SVP Administration/General Manager: Kevin
Silva
Estimated Sales: $20-50 Million
Number Employees: 200
Number of Brands: 3
Sq. footage: 200000
Type of Packaging: Private Label, Bulk
Brands:
KATHERINE BEECHER
MELSTER
PENNSYLVANIA DUTCH CANDIES

11114 Pennsylvania Macaroni Company
2010 Penn Ave
Pittsburgh, PA 15222-4487   412-471-8330
Fax: 412-201-4751   800-223-5928
info@pennmac.com   www.pennmac.com
Pasta
President: David Sunseri
Purchasing Manager: William Sunseri
Estimated Sales: $ 50-100 Million
Number Employees: 50-99

11115 Penny Curtiss Baking Company
P.O.Box 4737
Syracuse, NY 13221-4737   315-454-3241
Fax: 315-455-8244
Processor of fresh and frozen bread, rolls, doughnuts
and cookies
Director Manufacturing: Michael Lawler
Number Employees: 250-499
Sq. footage: 130000
Parent Co: P&C Food Markets
Type of Packaging: Consumer, Private Label
Brands:
Buttermaid
Country Cottage
Tip Top

11116 Penobscot McCrum
28 Pierce St
Belfast, ME 04915-6648   207-338-4360
Fax: 207-338-5742   800-435-4456
sales@penobscotff.com
www.penobscotmccrum.com
Manufacturer, exporter and wholesaler/distributor of
frozen potato productsincluding; potato pancakes,
mashers, skins, wedges and more
Manager: Jay McCrum
Co-Owner: Wade McCrum
Co-Owner: Jay McCrum
Co-Owner: David McCrum
Co-Owner: Darrell McCrum
Estimated Sales: $33 Million
Number Employees: 100-249
Type of Packaging: Consumer, Food Service

11117 Penotti USA
4 Maplegrove Avenue
Westport, CT 06880-4917   203-341-9494
Fax: 203-277-0006   877-720-0896
penottiusa@att.net   www.penotti.com
Chocolate and nut spreads
Director: Stan Rottell
Estimated Sales: $ .5 - 1 million
Number Employees: 1
Type of Packaging: Bulk

11118 Penta Manufacturing Company
50 Okner Pkwy
Livingston, NJ 07039-1604   973-740-2300
Fax: 973-740-1839   sales@pentamfg.com
www.pentamfg.com

Manufacturer, importer and exporter of fructose, rice
starch, nutraceuticals, food and flavor compounds,
specialty chemicals, cooking and essential oils, ex-
tracts, spices, and natural products for food, flavor
and pharmaceuticalcompanies
Owner: Mark Esposito
SVP: George Volpe
Estimated Sales: $ 10 - 20 Million
Number Employees: 20-49
Number of Products: 7000
Sq. footage: 350000
Parent Co: Penta International Corporation
Type of Packaging: Food Service, Private Label,
Bulk

11119 Penta Water Company Inc
2091 Rutherford Road
Carlsbad, CA 92008   760-438-6686
Fax: 760-268-0808   jlupica@pentawater.com
www.pentawater.com
Produces ultra-premium purified drinking water.
New Media Relations: Joe Lupica
Sq. footage: 110000

11120 Penthouse Meat Company
270 Congress Street
Group
Boston, MA 02210-1037   570-563-1153
Fax: 570-563-2665
Frozen beef, veal and pork products
President/CEO: John Attman
Sales Manager: Charles Price
COO: Don Long
Plant Manager: Bob Keen
Estimated Sales: $25-49.9 Million
Number Employees: 100-249
Brands:
Magic Meal
North American
Penthouse

11121 Penwest Foods Company
216 1st St
Richland, WA 99354-5500   509-375-1261
Fax: 509-375-7782 www.penfordfoods.com
Processor and exporter of modified and unmodified
potato starches
President: Greg Horn
Manufacturing Team Leader: Mick Persinger
Plant Manager: Craig Powers
Estimated Sales: $ 3 - 5 Million
Number Employees: 20-49
Sq. footage: 10000
Parent Co: Penwest
Brands:
Penplus

11122 Penwest Foods Company
7094 S Revere Pkwy
Centennial, CO 80112-3932   303-649-1900
Fax: 303-649-1700   Sales@penford.com
www.penx.com
Seasonings, binders and extenders, fat reduced
meats, fat replacers
Chairman: William G Parzybok Jr
General Manager: John R Randall
CEO: Thomas D Malkoski
Estimated Sales: I
Number Employees: 500-999
Brands:
Penwest Foods

11123 Peoples Sausage Company
1132 E Pico Blvd
Los Angeles, CA 90021-2224   213-627-8633
Fax: 213-627-7767
www.peopleschoicebeefjerky.com
Processor of beef jerky
President: Paul Bianchetti
Estimated Sales: $3000000
Number Employees: 10-19
Sq. footage: 5000
Type of Packaging: Consumer, Food Service, Pri-
vate Label, Bulk

11124 Pepe's Mexican Restaurants
1325 W 15th St
Chicago, IL 60608-2107   312-733-2500
Fax: 312-733-2564   bobptak@pepes.com
www.pepes.com
Manufacturer and exporter of frozen Mexican food
products
President: Robert Ptak
General Manager: Mario Dovalina Jr

Number Employees: 1,000-4,999
Sq. footage: 65000
Type of Packaging: Private Label, Bulk
Brands:
Aventura Gourmet
Pepe's, Inc.

11125 Pepes Mexican Foods
122 Carrier Drive
Rexdale, ON M9W 5R1
Canada   416-674-0882
Fax: 416-674-2805   rchen@westonbakeries.com
Processor of corn tortilla chips, flour tortillas,
multi-grain snacks and frozen burritos; importer of
jalapeno peppers, salsa and refried beans; exporter
of multi-grain snacks
VP Sales: Tom Reynolds
National Sales Manager: Tony Kent
Number Employees: 95
Sq. footage: 66000
Parent Co: Signature Brands
Type of Packaging: Consumer, Food Service
Brands:
Casa Del Norte
Gringos
Pepes

11126 Pepper Creek Farms
1002 SW Ard St
Lawton, OK 73505-9660   580-536-1300
Fax: 580-536-4886   800-526-8132
craig@peppercreekfarms.com
www.peppercreekfarms.com
Processor and exporter of jellies, mustards, peppers,
salsa, relish, syrup, mixes, seasonings, etc
President: Susan Weissman
General Manager: Craig Weissman
Estimated Sales: $490000
Number Employees: 10-19
Sq. footage: 7500
Type of Packaging: Consumer, Food Service, Pri-
vate Label
Brands:
Jalapeno
Jalapeno Tnt
Wildfire

11127 Pepper Island Beach
PO Box 484
Lawrence, PA 15055-0484   724-746-2401
Fax: 724-746-1679 www.pepperisland.com
Hot sauce
President: Karen Hasak

11128 Pepper Mill Imports
P.O.Box 775
Carmel, CA 93921-0775   831-393-0244
Fax: 831-393-0801   800-928-1744
sales@peppermillimports.com
www.peppermillimports.com
Processor of extra virgin olive oil. Manufacturer of
pepper & spice mills.
President: William Sterling
Marketing: Amy Paris
Sales: Angel Geil
Estimated Sales: Below $ 5 Million
Number Employees: 10-19
Number of Brands: 2
Number of Products: 112
Sq. footage: 30000
Type of Packaging: Consumer, Food Service, Pri-
vate Label
Brands:
Melina's

11129 (HQ)Pepper Source
2720 Athania Pkwy
Metairie, LA 70002-5904   504-885-3223
Fax: 504-885-3187   sales@peppersource.com
www.peppersource.com
Manufacturer of gourmet sauces, marinades and
glazes
President: Joseph Morse
VP Operations: Paul Liggio
Estimated Sales: $15 Million
Number Employees: 5-9
Type of Packaging: Food Service, Private Label,
Bulk
Other Locations:
Pepper Source
Van Buren AR
Pepper Source
Rogers AR

11130 Pepper Source
5800 Alma Hwy
Van Buren, AR 72956-7202   479-474-5178
    Fax: 479-474-4729   sales@peppersource.com
                www.peppersource.com
Gourmet sauces, marinades and glazes.
    President: Joe Morse
    Director Sales: Mark Watson
    VP Operations: Paul Liggio
    VP Purchasing: Steven Campbell
Estimated Sales: $ 5-10 Million
Number Employees: 100-249
Type of Packaging: Private Label

11131 Pepper Source
11103 N Old Wire Rd
Rogers, AR 72756-9871   479-246-1030
    Fax: 479-246-1061 www.peppersource.com
Gourmet sauces, marinades and glazes.
    VP Marketing: John Bowerman
    Plant Manager: Brad Palmer
Estimated Sales: $ 5-10 Million
Number Employees: 50-99
Type of Packaging: Private Label

11132 Pepper Town
7561 Woodman Street
Van Nuys, CA 91405   800-973-7738
    Fax: 818-909-4785   800-973-7738
            Info@PepperTownUSA.com
                www.peppertownusa.com
Fruity hot sauces
    President: Debbie Sussex
Estimated Sales: $ 90 Million
Number Employees: 2
Type of Packaging: Private Label
Brands:
    Bad Girls In Heat
    Big Top Fantasy
    Fifi's Nasty Little
    Peppergirl
    Sultan's Main Squeez
    Wrong Number

11133 Peppered Palette
3224 Carrington Way
Bellingham, WA 98226-4100   919-468-7101
    Fax: 919-882-9844   866-829-7101
    sweat@toadsweat.com   www.toadsweat.com
Dessert hot sauce
    Owner: Todd Guiton
Estimated Sales: $300,000-500,000
Number Employees: 1-4
Brands:
    Toad Sweat

11134 Pepperidge Farm
P.O.Box 5500
Norwalk, CT 06856-5500   203-846-7000
    203-846-7369   888-737-7374
            www.pepperidgefarm.com
Processor of baked goods including bread and stuff-
ing
    President: Jay Gould
    SVP Strategic Business Development: Pat
    Callaghan
    Director Corporate/Brand Communications: Nan
    Redmond
    Plant Manager: Bart Delaney
Number Employees: 5,000-9,999
Parent Co: Pepperidge Farm
Type of Packaging: Consumer

11135 Pepperidge Farm
P.O.Box 5500
Norwalk, CT 06856-5500   203-846-7000
    Fax: 203-846-7369   888-737-7374
            www.pepperidgefarm.com
Manufacturer of gourmet baked goods including
crackers, cookies, frozen cakes, breads and stuffing
    President: Jay Gould
    Plant Manager: Bart Delaney
Number Employees: 5,000-9,999
Parent Co: Campbell Soup Company
Type of Packaging: Consumer
Brands:
    GOLDFISH
    PEPPERIDGE FARM

11136 Pepperidge Farm
901 N 200 W
Richmond, UT 84333-1499   435-258-2491
    Fax: 435-258-2494   888-737-7374
            info@pepperidgefarm.com
                www.pepperidgefarm.com
Processor of baked goods including cookies, crack-
ers and bread
    President: Douglas R Conant
    Sr. VP: Doreen A Wright
    Plant Manager: Bob Harrison
Estimated Sales: $ 50 - 100 Million
Number Employees: 500-999
Sq. footage: 230000
Parent Co: Pepperidge Farm
Type of Packaging: Consumer
Brands:
    Pepperidge Farm Distinctive Cracke

11137 Pepperidge Farm
230 2nd St
Downers Grove, IL 60515-5249   630-968-4000
    Fax: 630-968-4088   888-737-7374
            www.pepperidgefarm.com
Processor of baked goods including bread, rolls and
stuffing
    President: Mark A Sarvary
    Plant Manager: Paul Caton
Estimated Sales: Less than $500,000
Number Employees: 5-9
Parent Co: Campbell Soup Company
Type of Packaging: Consumer
Brands:
    American Collection
    Distinctive
    Goldfish
    Tahoe

11138 Pepperidge Farm
2222 Interstate Dr
Lakeland, FL 33805-2306   863-688-4000
    Fax: 863-499-8000 www.pepperidgefarm.com
Processor of bakery bread and rolls
    General Manager: Gary Tarr
    President: Tom Martin
Estimated Sales: $ 10 - 20 Million
Number Employees: 100-249
Parent Co: Campbell Soup Company
Type of Packaging: Consumer

11139 Pepperidge Farm
421 Boot Rd
Downingtown, PA 19335-3043   610-269-2500
    Fax: 610-873-4322
    dot_rasiul@pepperidgefarm.com
                www.campbellsoup.com
Processor of baked goods including frozen cakes
and fruit-filled puff pastries
    President: Jay Gould
    Plant Manager: Patrick O'Donnell
    Purchasing Agent: Sheila Wilson
Estimated Sales: $349000000
Number Employees: 250-499
Parent Co: Campbell Soup Company
Type of Packaging: Consumer, Food Service

11140 Pepperidge Farm
5688 Randolph Blvd
San Antonio, TX 78233-6164   210-661-2052
    Fax: 210-590-4262   888-737-7374
            www.pepperidgefarm.com
Processor of bread, stuffing and croutons
    Manager: Darrell Carter
Estimated Sales: $300,000-500,000
Number Employees: 1-4
Parent Co: Pepperidge Farm
Type of Packaging: Consumer, Food Service

11141 Pepperidge Farm
548 Donald St
Bedford, NH 03110-5953   603-623-5821
    Fax: 603-623-6750   800-562-8340
            www.pepperidgefarm.com
Processor of bread, croutons and stuffings
    Manager: Jeff Parker
    Founder: Margaret Rudkin
    President: Jay Gould
Estimated Sales: $300,000-500,000
Number Employees: 1-4
Sq. footage: 2000
Parent Co: Pepperidge Farm
Type of Packaging: Consumer, Food Service
Brands:
    Goldfish

**11142 Pepperidge Farm Bread
Distributor**
4371 S Genesee Rd
Grand Blanc, MI 48439-7958   810-743-9640
    Fax: 810-743-9640 www.pepperidgefarm.com
Processor of bread; warehouse providing storage for
bread
    Owner: Thomas Smith
Estimated Sales: Under $300,000
Number Employees: 1-4
Parent Co: Pepperidge Farms, Inc.
Type of Packaging: Consumer, Food Service

11143 Pepperidge Farms
P.O.Box 5500
Norwalk, CT 06856-5500   203-846-7000
    Fax: 203-846-7369   888-737-7374
            www.pepperidgefarm.com
Processor of bread, stuffing, croutons, cookies and
crackers.
    President: Patrick (Pat) Callaghan
    Plant Manager: Bart Delaney
Estimated Sales: Less than $500,000
Number Employees: 5,000-9,999
Parent Co: Pepperidge Farm
Type of Packaging: Consumer, Food Service, Bulk
Brands:
    Pepperidge

11144 Pepperland Farms
12511 Hammack Road
Denham Springs, LA 70726-7122   225-665-3555
    Fax: 877-296-8683
    pepperlandfarms@earthlink.net
Processor of hot chili peppers including pickled in
vinegar brine
    Owner: Dennis Hall

11145 Peppers
19138 Coastal Hwy
Rehoboth Beach, DE 19971-6110   302-644-6900
    Fax: 302-644-6901   peppers@peppers.com
                www.peppers.com
Hot sauces, specialty hot sauces, wing sauces, jerk,
salsa, BBQ sauces, mustards & dips, marinades &
cajun injectors, peppers, pickles & relishes, olives,
garlic & vegetables, steak sauce, bloody mary &
mixers, chili, soups, pasta &coffee, dry seasoning &
rubs, ketchup, mayonnaise & dressings, thai, curry
& chutney, nuts & snacks, jelly, preserves & peanut
butter.
    President: Chip Hearn
Number Employees: 50-99
Type of Packaging: Consumer, Food Service, Pri-
    vate Label, Bulk

11146 Peppi Chili
2397 Bailey Drive
Norcross, GA 30071-3211   770-449-6149
    Fax: 770-263-1795
Chili and seasonings
    President: Tim Pazdro

11147 Pepsi
555 W Monroe St # 16-01
Chicago, IL 60661-3605   312-821-1000
    Fax: 312-773-4318 www.quakeroats.com
Processor of cookies, oatmeal, corn syrup, baking
mixes, breakfast cereals and sports beverages
    CEO: Steven S Reinemund
    Sr. VP Communications: Tod J MacKenzie
    VP: John Marguardt
    Sr. VP Finance: Matthew M McKenna
Estimated Sales: $ 50-100 Million
Number Employees: 50-99
Parent Co: PepsiCo
Type of Packaging: Consumer, Food Service

11148 Pepsi Bottling Co of Buffalo
2770 Walden Avenue
Buffalo, NY 14225-4747   716-684-4911
    Fax: 716-684-0408   800-235-1131
    podonnel@pepsi.com   www.pepsievents.com
Beverages
    President: Bruce Crair
    CEO: Heath Clarke
    CFO: Douglas Norman
    Vice President: Ralph Kravitz
    COO: Eric J Foss
    Sales Director: Peter Hutto
Estimated Sales: $ 10-100 Million
Number Employees: 100

Brands:
Pepsi

11149 Pepsi Bottling GroupCustomer Service Center
P.O.Box 10
Winston Salem, NC 27102-0010   336-896-4000
Fax: 336-896-6256   PBGPressCenter@pepsi.com
www.pbg
Manufacturer and distributor of sodas, juice drinks and various beverages.
President North American Operations: Robert King
SVP/General Counsel & Secretary: Steven Rapp
SVP/Chief Financial Officer: Alfred Drewes
SVP/Worldwide Operations: Victor Crawford
VP/Strategy: Kathleen Dwyer
SVP/Global Sales/Chief Customer Officer: Brent Franks
SVP/Chief Information Officer: Neal Bronze
SVP/Human Resources: John Berisford
Parent Co: Pepsi Bottling Group
Type of Packaging: Consumer

11150 Pepsi Bottling Group
2770 Walden Ave
Buffalo, NY 14225-4747   716-684-4900
Fax: 716-684-0408   800-235-1131
www.pbg.com
Processor of soft drinks
Manager: Randy Brodsky
SVP/Worldwide Operations: Victor Crawford
SVP/Chief Financial Officer: Alfred Drewes
SVP/General Counsel & Secretary: Steven Rapp
VP/Strategy: Kathleen Dwyer
SVP/Global Sales Chief Customer Officer: Brent Franks
SVP/Chief Information Officer: Neal Bronze
SVP/Human Resources: John Berisford
Estimated Sales: $100+ Million
Number Employees: 250-499
Parent Co: Pepsi Bottling Group
Type of Packaging: Consumer, Food Service
Brands:
Pepsi

11151 Pepsi Bottling Group
5000 Hopyard Road
Pleasanton, CA 94588   925-416-2500
www.pbg.com
Manufacturer of soft drinks
President North American Operations: Robert King
SVP/Worldwide Operations: Victor Crawford
SVP/Chief Financial Officer: Alfred Drewes
SVP/General Counsel & Secretary: Steven Rapp
VP/Strategy: Kathleen Dwyer
SVP/Global Sales/Chief Customer Officer: Brent Franks
SVP/Chief Information Officer: Neal Bronze
SVP/Human Resources: John Berisford
Estimated Sales: $ 50 - 100 Million
Number Employees: 250-500
Parent Co: Pepsi Bottling Group
Type of Packaging: Consumer, Food Service

11152 Pepsi Bottling Group
1300 Cliff Rd E
Burnsville, MN 55337-1419   952-895-1300
Fax: 952-895-1311   800-433-8109
www.pbg.com
Manufacturer of soft drinks
President North American Operations: Robert King
SVP/General Counsel & Secretary: Steven Rapp
SVP/Chief Financial Officer: Alfred Drewes
Sales: Robert Sheehan
VP/Strategy: Kathleen Dwyer
SVP/Global Sales Chief Customer Officer: Brent Franks
SVP/Chief Information Officer: Neal Bronze
SVP/Human Resources: John Berisford
Estimated Sales: $100+ Million
Number Employees: 500-999
Parent Co: Pepsi Bottling Group
Type of Packaging: Food Service

11153 Pepsi Bottling Group
9300 La Porte Fwy
Houston, TX 77017-1989   713-645-4111
Fax: 713-845-3295 www.pbg.com

Manufacturer of soft drinks; wholesaler/distributor of pre-mix and post-mix soda syrups
Chairman/CEO: Robert King
SVP/Worldwide Operations: Victor Crawford
SVP/Chief Financial Officer: Alfred Drewes
SVP/General Counsel & Secretary: Steven Rapp
VP/Strategy: Kathleen Dwyer
SVP/Global Sales Chief Customer Officer: Brent Franks
SVP/Chief Information Officer: Neal Bronzo
SVP/Human Resources: John Berisford
Plant Manager: Gary Burck
Estimated Sales: $100+ Million
Number Employees: 250-499
Parent Co: Pepsi Bottling Group
Type of Packaging: Consumer

11154 Pepsi Bottling Group
4532 Interstate 30
Mesquite, TX 75150-2028   214-324-8500
Fax: 214-324-8525   PBGPressCenter@pepsi.com
www.pbgcareers.com
Processor of soft drinks, fruit punch and bottled water
President North American Operations: Robert King
SVP/Worldwide Operations: Victor Crawford
SVP/Chief Financial Officer: Alfred Drewes
SVP/General Counsel & Secretary: Steven Rapp
VP/Strategy: Kathleen Dwyer
SVP/Global Sales Chief Customer Sales: Brent Franks
SVP/Chief Information Officer: Neal Bronzo
SVP/Human Resources: John Berisford
Plant Manager: Frank Mays
Estimated Sales: $ 10 - 20 Million
Number Employees: 250-499
Parent Co: Pepsi Bottling Group
Type of Packaging: Consumer, Food Service
Brands:
Pepsi

11155 Pepsi Bottling Group
510 W Skelly Dr
Tulsa, OK 74107-9408   918-446-6601
Fax: 918-445-8100   800-963-2424
www.pbg.com
Processor of soft drinks, juices, teas, water and isotonics
President North American Operations: Robert King
SVP/Worldwide Operations: Victor Crawford
SVP/Chief Financial Officer: Alfred Drewes
SVP/General Counsel & Secretary: Steven Rapp
VP/Strategy: Kathleen Dwyer
SVP/Global Sales Chief Customer Officer: Brent Franks
SVP/Chief Information Officer: Neal Bronzo
SVP/Human Resources: John Berisford
Plant Manager: Ray Newman
Estimated Sales: $3000000
Number Employees: 20-49
Parent Co: Pepsi Bottling Group
Type of Packaging: Food Service

11156 Pepsi Bottling Group
6100 NE Loop 410
San Antonio, TX 78218-5499   210-661-5311
Fax: 210-662-3430   800-933-5311
www.pbg.com
Processor of soft drinks
Manager: Steve Milonavitch
SVP/Worldwide Operations: Victor Crawford
SVP/Chief Financial Officer: Alfred Drewes
SVP/General Counsel & Secretary: Steven Rapp
VP/Strategy: Kathleen Dwyer
SVP/Global Sales Chief Customer Officer: Brent Franks
SVP/Chief Information Officer: Neal Bronzo
SVP/Human Resources: John Berisford
Number Employees: 100-249
Parent Co: Pepsi Bottling Group
Type of Packaging: Consumer, Food Service

11157 Pepsi Bottling Group
1480 Beltline Rd
Redding, CA 96003-1410   530-245-2100
Fax: 530-246-2696 www.pbg.com

Processor of soft drinks
Manager: Randy Jensen
SVP/Worldwide Operations: Victor Crawford
SVP/Chief Financial Officer: Alfred Drewes
SVP/General Counsel & Secretary: Steven Rapp
VP/Strategy: Kathleen Dwyer
SVP/Global Sales Chief Customer Officer: Brent Franks
SVP/Chief Information Officer: Neal Bronzo
SVP/Human Resources: John Berisford
Estimated Sales: $ 20 - 50 Million
Number Employees: 50-99
Parent Co: Pepsi Bottling Group
Type of Packaging: Consumer, Food Service

11158 Pepsi Bottling Group
3701 S Zero St
Fort Smith, AR 72908-6914   479-646-7881
Fax: 501-646-4197 www.pbg.com
Processor of soft drinks
Manager: Wes Odegaard
SVP/Worldwide Operations: Victor Crawford
SVP/Chief Financial Officer: Alfred Drewes
SVP/General Counsel & Secretary: Steven Rapp
VP/Strategy: Kathleen Dwyer
SVP/Global Sales Chief Customer Officer: Brent Franks
SVP/Chief Information Officer: Neal Bronzo
SVP/Human Resources: John Berisford
Number Employees: 100-249
Parent Co: Pepsi Bottling Group
Type of Packaging: Consumer, Food Service

11159 Pepsi Bottling Group
7095 Samuel Morse Dr
Columbia, MD 21046-3415   443-285-7476
Fax: 443-285-0446 www.pbg.com
Manufacturer of soft drinks
Manager: Thor Sandell
SVP/Worldwide Operations: Victor Crawford
SVP/Chief Financial Officer: Alfred Drewes
SVP/General Counsel & Secretary: Steven Rapp
VP/Strategy: Kathleen Dwyer
SVP/Global Sales/Chief Customer Officer: Brent Franks
SVP/Chief Information Officer: Neal Bronze
SVP/Human Resources: John Berisford
Number Employees: 250-499
Parent Co: Pepsi Bottling Group
Type of Packaging: Consumer, Food Service

11160 Pepsi Bottling Group
315 Norwood Park S # 5
Norwood, MA 02062-4699   781-501-1600
Fax: 781-501-1604 www.pbg.com
Manufacturer of soft drinks
President North American Operations: Robert King
SVP/Worldwide Operations: Victor Crawford
SVP/Chief Financial Officer: Alfred Drewes
VP: Jim Mitchelle
VP/Strategy: Kathleen Dwyer
SVP/Global Sales/Chief Customer Officer: Brent Franks
SVP/Chief Information Officer: Neal Bronze
SVP/Human Resources: John Berisford
Number Employees: 250-499
Parent Co: Pepsi Bottling Group
Type of Packaging: Consumer, Food Service

11161 Pepsi Bottling Group
7380 W Sand Lake Rd # 230
Orlando, FL 32819-5256   407-354-5800
www.pbg.com
Manufacturer of soft drinks
President North American Operations: Robert King
SVP/Worldwide Operations: Victor Crawford
SVP/Chief Financial Officer: Alfred Drewes
SVP/General Counsel & Secretary: Steven Rapp
VP/Strategy: Kathleen Dwyer
SVP/Global Sales/Chief Customer Officer: Brent Franks
SVP/Chief Information Officer: Neal Bronze
SVP/Human Resources: John Berisford
Number Employees: 250-499
Parent Co: Pepsi Bottling Group
Type of Packaging: Consumer, Food Service

11162 Pepsi Bottling Group
50 W Big Beaver Road
Suite 500
Troy, MI 48084   248-619-3000
www.pbg.com

Manufacturer of soft drinks
President North American Operations: Robert King
SVP/Worldwide Operations: Victor Crawford
SVP/Chief Financial Officer: Alfred Drewes
SVP/General Counsel & Secretary: Steven Rapp
VP/Strategy: Kathleen Dwyer
SVP/Global Sales/Chief Customer Officer: Brent Franks
SVP/Chief Information Officer: Neal Bronze
SVP/Human Resources: John Berisford
Number Employees: 250-499
Parent Co: Pepsi Bottling Group
Type of Packaging: Consumer, Food Service

11163 Pepsi Bottling Group
27717 Aliso Creek Rd
Laguna Beach, CA 92656-3804   949-643-5700
            Fax: 949-643-3163 www.pbg.com
Manufacturer of soft drinks
Manager: Todd Elliott
SVP/Worldwide Operations: Victor Crawford
SVP/Chief Financial Officer: Alfred Drewes
SVP/General Counsel & Secretary: Steven Rapp
VP/Strategy: Kathleen Dwyer
SVP/Global Sales/Chief Customer Officer: Brent Franks
SVP/Chief Information Officer: Neal Bronze
SVP/Human Resources: John Berisford
Number Employees: 250-499
Parent Co: Pepsi Bottling Group
Type of Packaging: Consumer, Food Service

11164 Pepsi Bottling Group
5251 Dtc Pkwy # 1200
Greenwood Vlg, CO 80111-2741   303-713-4900
            Fax: 303-713-4949 www.pbg.com
Manufacturer of soft drinks
Manager: Margaret Gramann
SVP/Worldwide Operations: Victor Crawford
SVP/Chief Financial Officer: Alfred Drewes
SVP/General Counsel & Secretary: Steven Rapp
VP/Strategy: Kathleen Dwyer
SVP/Global Sales/Chief Customer Officer: Brent Franks
SVP/Chief Information Officer: Neal Bronze
SVP/Human Resources: John Berisford
Number Employees: 250-499
Parent Co: Pepsi Bottling Group
Type of Packaging: Consumer, Food Service

11165 Pepsi Bottling Group Canada
5205 Satellite Drive
Mississauga, ON L4W 5J7
Canada   905-212-7377
            Fax: 905-212-7337 800-387-9546
            www.pbg.com/about/canada.html
Processor of soft drinks
President North American Operations: Robert King
SVP/Chief Financial Officer: Alfred Drewes
SVP/General Counsel & Secretary: Steven Rapp
VP/Strategy: Kathleen Dwyer
SVP/Worldwide Operations: Victor Crawford
SVP/Global Sales/Chief Customer Officer: Brent Franks
SVP/Chief Information Officer: Neal Bronzo
SVP/Human Resources: John Berisford
Number Employees: 100-249
Parent Co: Pepsi Bottling Company
Type of Packaging: Consumer, Food Service

11166 Pepsi-Cola Bottling Company
9701 Avenue D
Brooklyn, NY 11236-1919   718-649-2401
            Fax: 718-257-0651
Processor of soft drinks
President: Bill Wilson
Plant Manager: Ron Kimmey
Estimated Sales:$300,000-500,000
Number Employees: 1-4
Parent Co: PepsiCo North America
Type of Packaging: Consumer

11167 Pepsi-Cola Bottling Company
70 Center Dr
St Louis, MO 63120   314-679-7000
            Fax: 314-679-7237 info@pepsiamericas.com
            www.pepsiamericas.com
Processor of regular and diet soft drinks
SVP Supply Chain: Jay Hulbert
SVP Human Resources: Anne Sample
EVP Operations: G Michael Durkin

Estimated Sales:$300,000-500,000
Number Employees: 500-999
Parent Co: PepsiCo North America
Type of Packaging: Consumer, Food Service
Brands:
Pepsi

11168 Pepsi-Cola Canada
1850 Ellice Avenue
Winnipeg, NB R3H 0B8
Canada   204-784-0600
            Fax: 204-783-2173 800-387-9546
            www.pepsi.ca
Processor of bottled soft drinks
President North American Operations: Robert King
SVP/Worldwide Operations: Victor Crawford
SVP/Chief Information Officer: Neal Bronze
Public Relations: Mark Chislett
Type of Packaging: Consumer, Food Service, Bulk

11169 Pepsi-Cola General Bottlers
10 S Dunton Ave
Arlington Hts, IL 60005-1485   847-253-1000
            Fax: 847-394-7231 847-483-6880
            info@pepsiamericas.com
            www.pepsiamericas.com
Processor of soft drinks, fruit juice and tea
CEO: Robert C Pohlad
CFO: Alexander H Ware
President: Kenneth E Keiser
Number Employees: 250-499
Parent Co: Whitman Corporation/Pepsi-Cola General Bottlers
Type of Packaging: Consumer, Food Service
Brands:
Pepsi

11170 PepsiAmericas
383 W 10th St
Reserve, LA 70084-6603   985-536-1191
            Fax: 985-536-2402 info@pepsiamericas.com
            www.pepsiamericas.com
Processor of soft drinks
President: Jack Pezlj
EVP/Chief Financial Officer: Alexander Ware
SVP/Corporate Development: Matthew Carter
SVP/Chief Information Officer: Kenneth Johnsen
SVP/Human Resources: Anne Sample
SVP/Supply Chain: Jay Hulbert
Estimated Sales:$100+ Million
Number Employees: 100-249
Parent Co: PepsiAmericas Inc
Type of Packaging: Consumer, Food Service, Bulk

11171 PepsiAmericas
5733 Citrus Blvd
New Orleans, LA 70123-1662   504-467-3774
            Fax: 504-734-2806 info@pepsiamericas.com
            www.pepsiamericas.com
Processor and wholesaler/distributor of soft drinks, juices, water and malt beverages; serving the food service market
President: Ryan Pelle
President/Chief Operating Officer: Kenneth Keiser
EVP/Chief Financial Officer: Alexander Ware
SVP/Corporate Development: Matthew Carter
SVP/Chief Information Officer: Kenneth Johnsen
SVP/Human Resources: Anne Sample
SVP/Supply Chain: Jay Hulbert
Estimated Sales:$100+ Million
Number Employees: 100-249
Parent Co: PepsiAmericas Inc
Type of Packaging: Consumer, Food Service, Bulk

11172 PepsiAmericas
1207 N Harrison St
Fort Wayne, IN 46808-2761   260-428-9156
            Fax: 260-428-9115 800-388-2235
            info@pepsiamericas.com
            www.pepsiamericas.com
Processor of bottled soft drinks
Manager: Dale Baldwin
President/Chief Operating Officer: Kenneth Keiser
EVP/Chief Financial Officer: Alexander Ware
EVP/US Operations: G Michael Durkins
SVP/Corporate Development: Matthew Carter
EVP/International Operations: James Rogers
SVP/Chief Information Officer: Kenneth Johnsen
SVP/Human Resources: Anne Sample
SVP/Supply Chain: Jay Hulbert

Estimated Sales:$ 50-100 Million
Number Employees: 100-249
Parent Co: PepsiAmericas Inc
Type of Packaging: Consumer, Food Service
Brands:
Pepsi

11173 PepsiAmericas
2221 Democrat Road
Memphis, TN 38132-2043   901-344-7100
            Fax: 901-344-7197 info@pepsiamericas.com
            www.pepsiamericas.com
PepsiAmericas sells a variety of beverages including carbonated soft drinks, waters and juices.
Chairman/CEO: Robert Pohlad
President/Chief Operating Officer: Kenneth Keiser
EVP/Chief Financial Officer: Alexander Ware
EVP/International Operations: James Rogers
SVP/Corporate Development: Matthew Carter
SVP/Human Resources: Anne Sample
SVP/Chief Information Officer: Kenneth Johnsen
EVP/US Operations: G Michael Durkin
SVP/Supply Chain: Jay Hulbert
Estimated Sales:$3.7 Billion
Number Employees: 350
Parent Co: PepsiAmericas Inc
Type of Packaging: Consumer, Food Service

11174 PepsiAmericas
1 Union 70 Center Drive
St Louis, MO 63120-1722   314-679-7000
            Fax: 314-679-7237 info@pepsiamericas.com
            www.pepsiamericas.com
PepsiAmericas sells a variety of beverages including carbonated soft drinks, waters and juices.
Chairman/CEO: Indra Nooyi
CFO: Hugh Johnson
SVP/Chief Information Officer: Robert Dixon
SVP/Chief Procurement Officer: Mitch Adamek
Chief Marketing Officer: Jill Beraud
EVP Sales/Marketing: A Salman Amin
SVP HR/Chief Personnel Officer: Cynthia Trudell

EVP Global Operations: Richard Goodman
SVP/Supply Chain: Jay Hulbert
Estimated Sales:$3.7 Billion
Number Employees: 30
Parent Co: PepsiAmericas Inc
Type of Packaging: Consumer, Food Service

11175 PepsiAmericas
5733 Citrus Blvd
New Orleans, LA 70123-1662   504-467-3774
            Fax: 504-734-2806 info@pepsiamericas.com
            www.pepsiamericas.com
PepsiAmericas sells a variety of beverages including carbonated soft drinks, waters and juices.
CFO: Hugh Hughes
SVP/Chief Information Officer: Robert Dixon
Chief Marketing Offiver: Jill Beraud
EVP Sales/Marketing: A Salman Amin
SVP/Chief Personnel Officer: Cynthia Trudell
EVP Global Operations: Richard Goodman
SVP/Supply Chain: Jay Hulbert
Estimated Sales:$3.7 Billion
Number Employees: 250-499
Parent Co: PepsiAmericas Inc
Type of Packaging: Consumer, Food Service

11176 PepsiAmericas
1400 W 35th St
Chicago, IL 60609-1311   773-893-2285
            Fax: 773-893-2306 info@pepsiamericas.com
            www.pepsiamericas.com
PepsiAmericas sells a variety of beverages including carbonated soft drinks, waters and juices.
Manager: Bill Costillo
President/Chief Operating Officer: Kenneth Keiser
EVP/Chief Financial Officer: Alexander Ware
Manager: Steve Smola
SVP/Corporate Development: Matthew Carter
SVP/Human Resources: Anne Sample
SVP/Chief Information Officer: Kenneth Johnsen
EVP/US Operations: G Michael Durkin
SVP/Supply Chain: Jay Hulbert
Estimated Sales:$3.7 Billion
Number Employees: 50
Parent Co: PepsiAmericas Inc
Type of Packaging: Consumer, Food Service

11177 PepsiAmericas
2121 Sunnybrook Dr
Cincinnati, OH 45237-2107   513-948-5109
     Fax: 513-821-3029 info@pepsiamericas.com
                    www.pepsiamericas.com
PepsiAmericas sells a variety of beverages including
carbonated soft drinks, waters and juices.
   Chairman/CEO: Robert Pohlad
   President/Chief Operating Officer: Kenneth
   Keiser
   EVP/Chief Financial Officer: Alexander Ware
   Manager: Larry Nolte
   SVP/Corporate Development: Matthew Carter
   SVP/Human Resources: Anne Sample
   SVP/Chief Information Officer: Kenneth Johnsen
   EVP/US Operations: G Michael Durkin
   SVP/Supply Chain: Jay Hulbert
Estimated Sales: $3.7 Billion
Number Employees: 250-499
Parent Co: PepsiAmericas Inc
Type of Packaging: Consumer, Food Service

11178 (HQ)PepsiCo
1 Pepsi Way
Somers, NY 10589-2204   914-767-6000
   Fax: 914-767-7761 PBGPressCenter@pepsi.com
                    www.pbg.com
Manufacturer and distributor of sodas, juice drinks
and various beverages.
   Chairman/CEO: Indra Nooyi
   CFO: Hugh Johnston
   SVP/Chief Information Officer: Robert Dixon
   Chief Marketing Officer: Jill Beraud
   EVP Sales/Marketing: A Salman Amin
   SVP HR/Chief Personnel Officer: Cynthia Trudell

Estimated Sales: $35 Billion
Number Employees: 10,000+
Type of Packaging: Consumer
Brands:
   AMP
   AQUAFINA
   AQUAFINA FLAVORSPLASH
   AQUAFINA SPARKLING
   DOUBLESHOT
   FRAPPUCCINO
   LIPTON BRISK
   LIPTON DIET GREEN TEA
   LIPTON ICED TEA
   LIPTON PURELEAF
   LIPTON SPARKLING
   MOUNTAIN DEW
   MUG CREAM
   MUG ROOT BEER
   NO FEAR
   OCEAN SPRAY
   PEPSI
   SEATTLE'S BEST COFFEE
   SIERRA MIST
   SLICE
   SOBE
   SOBE ENERGIZE
   SOBE LEAN
   SOBE LIFEWATER
   SOBE SMOOTH
   SOBE SUGAR FREE
   SOBE VITA-BOOM
   TAZOO
   TROPICANA

11179 PepsiCo
3825 106th St
Urbandale, IA 50322-2043   515-270-1332
     Fax: 515-254-3110 info@pepsiamericas.com
                    www.pepsiamericas.com
PepsiAmericas sells a variety of beverages including
carbonated soft drinks, waters and juices.
   President: Tom Restad
   Chairman/CEO: Robert C Pohland
   EVP/Chief Financial Officer: Alexander Ware
   VP: George Haugo
   SVP/Corporate Development: Matthew Carter
   SVP/Chief Information Officer: Kenneth Johnsen
   EVP/US Operations: G Michael Durkin
   General Manager: Mike Brown
Estimated Sales: $3.7 Billion
Number Employees: 250-499
Type of Packaging: Consumer, Food Service
Brands:
   AMP ENERGY
   AQUAFINA
   AQUAFINA FLAVORSPLASH
   DOUBLESHOT COFFEE DRINK
   DOUBLESHOT ENERGY

   FRAPPUCCINO
   LIPTON BRISK
   LIPTON PURELEAF
   LIPTON SPARKLING
   MOUNTAIN DEW
   MUG CREAM SODA
   MUG ROOT BEER
   NO FEAR
   OCEAN SPRAY
   PEPSI
   SEATTLE'S BEST COFFEE
   SIERRA MIST
   SLICE
   SOBE ADRENALINE
   SOBE ENERGIZE
   SOBE LEAN
   SOBE LIFEWATER
   SOBE SMOOTH
   TAZO
   TROPICANA
   TROPICANA TWISTER SODA

11180 PepsiCo
11701 Roosevelt Blvd
Philadelphia, PA 19154-2183   215-961-4000
          Fax: 215-961-4086 www.pepsico.com
Processor and bottler of soft drinks including cream
soda and root beer
   Chairman/CEO: Indra Nooyi
   SVP/CIO: Robert Dixon
   EVP Sales/Marketing: A Salman Amin
   SVP HR/Chief Personnel Officer: Cynthia Trudell

   EVP Global Operations: Richard Goodman
   Plant Manager: Rich Chominski
Estimated Sales: $500 Million to $1 Billion
Number Employees: 400
Parent Co: Pepsi Bottling Group
Type of Packaging: Consumer, Food Service
Brands:
   Pepsi-Cola

11181 PepsiCo
515 W Main Street
Barrington, IL 60010-4175   847-842-4652
     Fax: 847-382-0687 ronda_shafar@qtgsales.com
                    www.neareast.com
Processor of oatmeal, corn syrup, baking mixes,
breakfast cereal and sports beverages
   VP: Ken Wilcox
Estimated Sales: $ 50-75 Million
Number Employees: 50-100
Parent Co: PepsiCo Beverages & Foods
Type of Packaging: Consumer, Food Service

11182 PepsiCo
800 Fairway Dr
Deerfield Beach, FL 33441-1828   954-725-7000
                    www.pepsico.com
PepsiAmericas sells a variety of beverages including
carbonated soft drinks, waters and juices.
   Chairman/CEO: Indra Nooyi
   CFO: Hugh Johnston
   EVP Sales/Marketing: A Salman Amin
   SVP HR/Chief Personnel Officer: Cynthia Trudell

   EVP Global Operations: Richard Goodman
   Manager: Luis Montoya
Estimated Sales: $3.7 Billion
Number Employees: 250-499
Parent Co: PepsiAmericas Inc
Type of Packaging: Consumer, Food Service

11183 PepsiCo
5411 W 78th St
Indianapolis, IN 46268-4151   317-876-3464
          Fax: 317-876-6945 www.pepsico.com
PepsiAmericas sells a variety of beverages including
carbonated soft drinks, waters and juices.
   Chairman/CEO: Indra Nooyi
   CFO: Hugh Johnston
   VP/Manager: Steve Coston
   EVP Sales/Marketing: A Salman Amin
   SVP HR/Chief Personnel Officer: Cynthia Trudell

   EVP Global Operations: Richard Goodman
   Plant Manager: Tim Donnelly
Estimated Sales: $3.7 Billion
Number Employees: 250-499
Parent Co: PepsiAmericas Inc
Type of Packaging: Consumer, Food Service

11184 PepsiCo
4010 Crittenden Dr
Louisville, KY 40209-1128   502-366-5633
          Fax: 502-375-5223 www.pepsico.com
PepsiAmericas sells a variety of beverages including
carbonated soft drinks, waters and juices.
   Chairman/CEO: Indra Nooyi
   CFO: Hugh Johnson
   VP: Michael Brown
   EVP Sales/Marketing: A Salman Amin
   SVP HR/Chief Personnel Officer: Cynthia Trudell

   EVP Global Operations: Richard Goodman
   Manager: Rick Buonaccorsi
Estimated Sales: $3.7 Billion
Number Employees: 30
Parent Co: PepsiAmericas Inc
Type of Packaging: Consumer, Food Service

11185 PepsiCo
4314 20th Ave SW
Fargo, ND 58103-4434   701-277-0670
          Fax: 701-281-4540 www.pepsico.com
PepsiAmericas sells a variety of beverages including
carbonated soft drinks, waters and juices.
   Chairman/CEO: Indra Nooyi
   CFO: Hugh Johnston
   EVP Sales/Marketing: A Salman Amin
   SVP HR/Chief Personnel Officer: Cynthia Trudell

   EVP Global Operations: Richard Goodman
Estimated Sales: $3.7 Billion
Number Employees: 250-499
Parent Co: PepsiAmericas Inc
Type of Packaging: Consumer, Food Service

11186 PepsiCo
1775 E Kansas City Rd
Olathe, KS 66061-5856   913-791-3000
          Fax: 913-791-3016 www.pepsico.com
PepsiAmericas sells a variety of beverages including
carbonated soft drinks, waters and juices.
   Chairman/CEO: Indra Nooyi
   CFO: Hugh Johnston
   EVP Sales/Marketing: A Salman Amin
   SVP HR/Chief Personnel Officer: Cynthia Trudell

   EVP Global Operations: Richard Goodman
   SVP/Supply Chain: Jay Hulbert
Estimated Sales: $3.7 Billion
Number Employees: 250-499
Parent Co: PepsiAmericas Inc
Type of Packaging: Consumer, Food Service

11187 PepsiCo
671 S Rowlett St
Collierville, TN 38017-2557   901-853-5736
          Fax: 901-853-5728 www.pepsico.com
PepsiAmericas sells a variety of beverages including
carbonated soft drinks, waters and juices.
   Chairman/CEO: Indra Nooyi
   CFO: Hugh Johnston
   EVP Sales/Marketing: A Salman Amin
   SVP HR/Chief Personnel Officer: Cynthia Trudell

   EVP Global Operations: Richard Goodman
Estimated Sales: $3.7 Billion
Number Employees: 250-499
Parent Co: PepsiAmericas Inc
Type of Packaging: Consumer, Food Service

11188 PepsiCo
1999 Enterprise Pkwy
Twinsburg, OH 44087-2207   330-963-5300
     Fax: 330-425-4715 info@pepsiamericas.com
                    www.pepsiamericas.com
PepsiAmericas sells a variety of beverages including
carbonated soft drinks, waters and juices.
   Manager: Richard Bodzenski
   President/Chief Operating Officer: Kenneth
   Keiser
   Finance: Wendy Hurd
   VP: Daniel Hungerman
   SVP/Corporate Development: Matthew Carter
   Human Reources Director: Dave Kalp
   EVP/US Operations: G Michael Durkin
   SVP/Supply Chain: Jay Hulbert
Estimated Sales: $3.7 Billion
Number Employees: 250-499
Parent Co: PepsiAmericas Inc
Type of Packaging: Consumer, Food Service

11189 PepsiCo
3245 Hill Ave
Toledo, OH 43607-2936
419-535-8701
Fax: 419-534-4332 info@pepsiamericas.com
www.pepsiamericas.com
PepsiAmericas sells a variety of beverages including carbonated soft drinks, waters and juices.
Manager: Mike Tournoy
President/Chief Operating Officer: Kenneth Keiser
Finance: Ryan Householder
VP: Michael Hill
SVP/Corporate Development: Matthew Carter
SVP/Human Resources: Anne Sample
Marketing: Mike Collins
SVP/Chief Information Officer: Kenneth Johnsen
EVP/US Operations: G Michael Durkin
SVP/Supply Chain: Jay Hulbert
Estimated Sales:$3.7 Billion
Number Employees: 250-499
Parent Co: PepsiAmericas Inc
Type of Packaging: Consumer, Food Service

11190 PepsiCo
5500 N Lovers Lane Rd
Milwaukee, WI 53225-3008
414-463-4500
Fax: 414-438-2337 info@pepsiamericas.com
www.pepsiamericas.com
PepsiAmericas sells a variety of beverages including carbonated soft drinks, waters and juices.
President: Doug Malnmquist
VP/General Manager: Tim McCarthy
Sales Executive: Marty Latour
SVP/Supply Chain: Jay Hulbert
Estimated Sales:$3.7 Billion
Number Employees: 250
Parent Co: PepsiAmericas Inc
Type of Packaging: Consumer, Food Service

11191 PepsiCo Inc
700 Anderson Hill Rd
Purchase, NY 10577-1444
914-253-2000
Fax: 914-253-2070 www.pepsico.com
Manufacturer of finished soft drinks and concentrates. Also supplies vending machines for restaurants and stores selling Pepsi products.
Chairman/CEO: Indra Nooyi
Chief Executive Officer/Vice Chairman: Michael White
Chief Financial Officer: Richard Goodman
CEO: Dawn E Hudson
SVP/Corporate Strategy & Development: Wahid Hamid
Chief Health/Wellness Innovation Officer: Antonio Lucio
SVP Human Resources: Margaret Moore
SVP/Corporate Communications: Tod MacKenzie

EVP/Operations: Hugh Johnston
SVP/Chief Procurement Officer: Mitch Adamek
Estimated Sales:$43.3 Billion
Number Employees: 198,000
Type of Packaging: Consumer
Brands:
AMP
AQUAFINA
AQUAFINA FLAVORSPLASH
AQUAFINA SPARKLING
DOUBLESHOT COFFEE DRINK
FRAPPUCCINO
LIPTON ICED TEA
LIPTON PURELEAF
LIPTON SPARKLING
MOUNTAIN DEW
MUG
NO FEAR
OCEAN SPRAY
PEPSI
SEATTLE'S BEST COFFEE
SIERRA MIST
SLICE
SOBE
TAZO
TROPICANA

11192 Per-Clin Orchards
4021 13 Mile Rd
Bear Lake, MI 49614-9544
231-889-4289
Fax: 231-889-4810
Manufacturer of cherries and apples; exporter of apples; also, storage and packing facilities available
Owner: Clinton Smeltzer
VP: Donald Smeltzer
Owner: David Smeltzer

Estimated Sales:$35 Million
Number Employees: 1-4
Sq. footage: 50000
Type of Packaging: Consumer
Brands:
CRYSTAL LAKE
FRESH
NORTHERN TREAT

11193 Perdue Farms
PO Box 1656
Horsham, PA 19044-6656
302-422-6681
Fax: 302-424-2654 800-473-7383
www.perdue.com
Manufacturer and exporter of fresh chicken parts
Chairman/CEO/CFO: Jim Perdue
Director Deli Sales: Larry Montuori
Estimated Sales:$270 Million
Number Employees: 20000
Parent Co: Perdue Farms
Type of Packaging: Consumer
Brands:
PERDUE

11194 (HQ)Perdue Farms
31149 Old Ocean City Rd
Salisbury, MD 21804
410-543-3000
Fax: 410-543-3532 800-473-7383
www.perdue.com
Manufacturer and exporter of fresh and frozen chicken and turkey; also, edible oils and fats
Chairman/CEO: James Perdue
SVP/CFO: Eileen Burza
VP/CIO: Sandy Rasel
VP Technical Services: Hank Engster
VP Business Development: Steven Schwalb
SVP Retail/Sales/Marketing: Steve Evans
Logistics Manager: Alan Perry
*Estimated Sales:*K
Number Employees: 20,000
Type of Packaging: Consumer, Food Service, Private Label, Bulk
Other Locations:
Perdue Farms
Monterey TN
Brands:
COOKIN GOOD
COOKIN GOOD CHICKEN
FIT 'N EASY
OVEN STUFFER
PERDUE
PERDUE POULTRY
PRIME PARTS

11195 Perdue Farms
PO Box 1357
Rockingham, NC 28380-1357
910-997-8600
www.perdue.com
Manufacturer of fresh and frozen chicken
Founder: Franklin Perdue
Chairman: Jim Perdue
*Estimated Sales:*100+ Million
Number Employees: 500-999
Type of Packaging: Consumer, Food Service
Brands:
PERDUE

11196 Perdue Farms
200 Savannah Drive
Georgetown, DE 19947-2240
302-855-5555
Fax: 302-855-5655 888-737-3832
chris.whaley@perdue.com www.perdue.com
Processor of fresh chicken
President: Jim Perdue
Vice President: Steve Schwalb
Sales Manager: Nick Notter
Plant Manager: John Evans
Purchasing Agent: Bernadette Halfhill
Number Employees: 1,000-4,999
Parent Co: Perdue Farms
Type of Packaging: Consumer
Brands:
Perdue

11197 Perdue Farms
2300 Industrial Dr
Monterey, TN 38574-3403
931-839-5000
Fax: 931-839-5075 800-473-7383
www.perdue.com
Manufacturer of poultry
Chairman/CEO: Jim Perdue
Estimated Sales:$4.6 Billion
Number Employees: 22,000
Type of Packaging: Consumer, Private Label

Brands:
COOKIN' GOOD
DELUCA
FIT 'N' EASY
GOLPAK
OVEN STUFFER
PRIME PARTS
PURDUE
PURDUE INDIVIDUAL FROZEN
SHAPES
SHENANDOAH
SHORT CUTS

11198 Perdue Farms
P.O.Box 10
Pantego, NC 27860-0010
252-943-3061
Fax: 252-943-3604 www.perdue.com
Processor and exporter of fresh and frozen chicken
Manager: Stephen Fletcher
Plant Manager: Kevin Hurst
Estimated Sales:$ 100-500 Million
Number Employees: 500-999
Parent Co: Perdue Farms
Type of Packaging: Consumer, Food Service, Bulk

11199 Perdue Farms
204 Side Track Dr
Statesville, NC 28625-2565
704-924-5222
Fax: 704-924-5223 800-457-3738
www.perdue.com
Hatcher of fresh chicken; also, feed mill
Manager: Darryl Moore
Sr. VP Retail Sales: Steve Evans
Estimated Sales:$ 5 - 10 Million
Number Employees: 20-49
Parent Co: Perdue Farms
Type of Packaging: Consumer, Food Service
Brands:
Perdue

11200 Perdue Farms
4586 N Us Highway 52
Thorntown, IN 46071-9287
765-436-7990
Fax: 765-436-7919
michael.maroney@perdue.com
www.perdue.com
Breeder of turkey
President: Mike Maroney
Marketing Service Manager: Chris Whaley
Purchasing Agent: Roy Edwards
Estimated Sales:$ 10-20 Million
Number Employees: 50-99
Parent Co: Perdue Farms

11201 Perdue Farms
100 Quality St
Bridgewater, VA 22812-1618
540-828-2581
Fax: 540-828-7768 chris.whaley@perdue.com
www.perdue.com
Processor of fresh and frozen chicken and turkey
Executive Director: Kevin Saxton
Director of Nutrition: Gary Howell
Purchasing Agent: Steve Estep
Estimated Sales:$ 100-500 Million
Number Employees: 500-999
Parent Co: Perdue Farms
Type of Packaging: Consumer, Food Service
Brands:
Perdue

11202 Perdue Farms
PO Box 1656
Horsham, PA 19044-6656
336-679-7733
Fax: 215-672-6988 800-473-7383
joe.forsthoffer@perdue.com www.perdue.com
Processor of fresh and frozen chicken and turkey
President: Jim Perdue
Estimated Sales:$ 1-2.5 Million
Number Employees: 13
Parent Co: Perdue Farms
Type of Packaging: Consumer, Food Service
Brands:
Perdue

11203 Perdue Farms
1835 Us Highway 64a
Nashville, NC 27856-9263
252-459-9763
Fax: 252-459-2331 chris.whaley@perdue.com
www.perdue.com
Processor of fresh and frozen chicken and turkey
Manager: Allen Skinner
Office Manager: John McDanel

Estimated Sales:$ 20-50 Million
Number Employees: 20-49
Parent Co: Perdue Farms
Type of Packaging: Consumer, Food Service
Brands:
Perdue

11204 Perdue Farms
P.O.Box 539
Washington, IN 47501-0539   812-254-4030
        Fax: 812-254-3738   800-654-6972
        www.perdue.com
Processor of fresh and frozen turkey
President: Andy Theine
Manager: Tom Schaffer
Director Live Production: Tom Schaffer
Estimated Sales:$ 5-10 Million
Number Employees: 50-99
Parent Co: Perdue Farms
Type of Packaging: Consumer, Food Service
Brands:
Perdue

11205 Perdue Farms
211 Hicks Road
Candor, NC 27229-8279   410-543-3000
        Fax: 910-673-2711 www.perdue.com
Processor of fresh and frozen chicken
President: Frank Perdue
Number Employees: 100-249
Parent Co: Perdue Farms
Type of Packaging: Consumer, Food Service
Brands:
Perdue

11206 Perdue Farms
9266 Revell Rd
Kenly, NC 27542-9204   919-284-2033
    Fax: 919-284-1923   chris.whaley@perdue.com
        www.perdue.com
Hatchery of fresh and frozen chicken and turkey
Manager: Chris Towne
VP: James Perdue
Manager: Darryl Bryant
Estimated Sales:$ 2.5-5 Million
Number Employees: 20-49
Parent Co: Perdue Farms
Type of Packaging: Consumer, Food Service
Brands:
Perdue

11207 Perdue Farms
P.O.Box 7
Plymouth, NC 27962-0007   252-793-9119
        Fax: 252-793-9383 www.perdue.com
Manufacturer of fresh and frozen chicken and turkey
Manager: Stephen Fletcher
Manager: Stephen Fletcher
Estimated Sales:$10-20 Million
Number Employees: 1-4
Parent Co: Perdue Farms
Type of Packaging: Consumer, Food Service

11208 Perdue Farms
2654 Highway 90 E
Defuniak Springs, FL 32433   850-951-6107
        Fax: 850-951-6126 www.perdue.com
Processor and exporter of fresh chicken parts
Manager: Travis Bowers
Sales Manager: George Bailey
Estimated Sales:$ 100-500 Million
Number Employees: 500-999

11209 Pereg Gourmet Spices
69-66 Main St
Flushing, NY 11367   718-261-6767
    Fax: 718-261-7688   office@pereg-gourmet.com
        www.pereg-gourmet.com
spices, oils, salads and spreads, toppings, bread
crumbs, quinoa, mix for rice, salt, flavored basmati
rice, couscous
President/Owner: Ilan Eshed
Estimated Sales:$1 Million
Number Employees: 9

11210 Perez Food Products
2826 Southwest Blvd
Kansas City, MO 64108-3613   816-931-8761
        Fax: 816-931-2825   perezfoods@birch.net
Processor of Mexican food including tortillas and
taco shells
Owner: Jesse Perez
Sales Manager: Daniel Perez

Estimated Sales:$2500000
Number Employees: 5-9
Type of Packaging: Consumer

11211 Perfect Addition
P.O.Box 8976
Newport Beach, CA 92658-0976   949-640-0220
        Fax: 949-640-0304   perfectadd@aol.com
Frozen foods
President: Constance Grigsby
CFO/VP: Jack Grigsby
CEO/VP Marketing: Connie Grigsby
*Estimated Sales:*Less than $200,000
Number Employees: 1-4
Type of Packaging: Consumer, Private Label
Brands:
Perfect Addition Beef Stock
Perfect Addition Chi
Perfect Addition Fis
Perfect Addition Veg

11212 Perfect Bite Company
747 W Wilson Ave
Glendale, CA 91203   818-507-1527
        Fax: 818-507-1376 www.theperfectbiteco.com
appetizers
President/CEO: Teri Valentine
CFO/Secretary: John Valentine
VP: Joe Forristal
Number Employees: 6

11213 Perfect Foods
4 Hawks Nest Road
Monroe, NY 10950-1801   845-294-8411
        Fax: 845-783-9683   800-933-3288
Manufacturer of fresh wheat grass and sunflower
and buckwheat greens; processor of frozen wheat
grass juice
Owner: Harley Matsil
VP: Alyse Matsil
*Estimated Sales:*Under $500,000
Number Employees: 8
Sq. footage: 6000
Type of Packaging: Consumer
Brands:
GREEN GOLD WHEATGRASS
PERFECT FOODS WHEATGRASS JUICE

11214 Perfection Fine Products
16153 Libby Road
Maple Heights, OH 44137-1219   216-475-5744
        Fax: 216-475-5772
Manufacturer and exporter of fruit juices, beverage
syrups and cocktail mixes
President: Jack Goldberg
Vice President: Bill Overton
Marketing/Sales: Phil Leroy
Public Relations: Connie Rice
Operations Manager: John Stevens
Plant Manager: John Taziros
Purchasing Manager: Bill Overton Jr.
Estimated Sales:$7000000
Number Employees: 18
Parent Co: Great Western
Type of Packaging: Food Service, Private Label
Brands:
ICE & EASY
PERFECTION
SUNNY MORNING

11215 Perfections by Allan
3 Old Creek Ct
Owings Mills, MD 21117-1270   410-581-8670
        Fax: 410-581-0877   800-581-8670
Gourmet dipping cookies and snack foods
President: Allan Taylor
*Estimated Sales:*Under $500,000
Number Employees: 1-4
Type of Packaging: Consumer, Private Label
Brands:
Grandma Taylor's Gourmet Dip

11216 Perfetti
P.O.Box 18190
Erlanger, KY 41018-0190   859-283-1234
        Fax: 859-283-1316 www.perfetti.com
Candy and gum
President: Ronald Korenhof
VP Marketing: Bob Howard
Senior VP Sales: Patrick Cox
Estimated Sales:$ 50 - 100 Million
Number Employees: 100-249
Type of Packaging: Consumer

Brands:
Airheads
Alpenliebe
Bloop
Brooklyn
Chloralit
Daygum
Frisk
Fruitella
Golia
Happydent
Mega Big Babol
Mentos
Morositas
Tabu
Vigorsol
Vivident

11217 Performance Labs
5115 Douglas Fir Rd # M
Calabasas, CA 91302-2597   818-591-9669
        Fax: 818-591-2116   800-848-2537
        info@performancelabs.com
        www.performancelabs.com
Processor and importer of nutritional and herbal sup-
plements including vitamin energizers and garlic,
cardiovascular and antioxidant supplements;
exporter of garlic
Owner: Richard Burke
CEO: David Mercer, Jr.
Purchasing Manager: Allan Suda
Estimated Sales:$3400000
Number Employees: 20-49
Type of Packaging: Consumer
Brands:
Cardiomax
Garlimax
Guardmax
Immumax
Relaxmax
Vitalert

11218 Perham Cooperative Cream
P.O.Box 1388
Savannah, GA 31402-1388   912-233-1167
        Fax: 912-233-1157   800-551-0777
        info@gawine.com   www.gabeer.com
Dairy
CEO: Henry Monsees
Estimated Sales:$ 10 - 20 Million
Number Employees: 50-99

11219 Perino's Seafood
6850 Westbank Expy
Marrero, LA 70072-2523   504-347-5410
        Fax: 504-341-2504
Seafood
Manager: Paul Ocrne
Estimated Sales:$ 3 - 5 Million
Number Employees: 10-19

11220 Perlarom Technology
9133 Red Branch Rd
Columbia, MD 21045-2029   410-997-5114
    Fax: 410-964-9374   leif.kjargaard@danisco.com
        www.perlarom.com
Natural flavors, specialty extracts
Executive VP: Soren Bjerre Nielsen
CEO: Tom Knutzen
Vice President: Philippe Lavielle
Executive VP: Mogens Granborg
Estimated Sales:$ 2.5-5 Million
Number Employees: 20-49

11221 Pernod Ricard USA
777 Westchester Avenue
White Plains, NY 10604-3520   914-539-4500
    Fax: 914-539-4777   tlalla@pernod-ricard-usa.com
        www.pernod-ricardusa.com
Producer and distributor of fine spirits and wines.
The company plans on selling its Seagram's Vodka
brand to Young's Holdings
President: Michel Bord
CFO: Alain Barbet
Estimated Sales:$100+ Million
Number Employees: 685
Brands:
ARAK RAZZOUK
BENRIACH
BLACK BUSH
BOODLES BRITISH GIN
BUSHMILLS
BUSNEL
CANEI

CARRINGTON
CHATEAU DE LIGNERES
CHIVAS REGAL
CORK DRY GIN
ETCHART
GABRIEL BOUDIER
JACOB'S CREEK
JAMESON
MARQUIS DE MONTESQUIO
MARTELL
MIDLETON
MOJITO CLUB
PERNOD
POWERS
RAMAZOTTI
REDBREAST
RICARD
ROYAL CANADIAN
SANDEMAN
SEAGRAM'S GIN
THE GLENLIVET
VIUDA DE ROMERO REPOSADO
WILD TURKEY 101 PROOF
WODKA WYBOROWA WYBOROWA
WYNDHAM ESTATE

11222 Pernod Ricard USA Seagram Lawrenceburg Distillery

7 Ridge Ave
Greendale, IN 47025-1637
812-537-0700
Fax: 812-537-8550
shareholders@pernod-ricard.com
www.pernod-ricardusa.com
Manufacturer and exporter of whiskey and gin
Manager: Richard Brock
VP North American Affairs: Mark Orr
Estimated Sales: $530 Million
Number Employees: 500-999
Parent Co: Pernod Ricard USA
Type of Packaging: Consumer, Food Service
Brands:
ARAK RAZZOUK
ARMAGNAC
BALLANTINE'S
CANADIAN CLUB
CHIVAS REGAL
JACOB'S CREEK
JAMESON
MARQUIS DE MONTESQUIO
MATTEL
PICARD
RICARD
ROYAL CANADIAN
SEAGRAM'S GIN
WILD TURKEY
WYNDHAM ESTATE

11223 Perona Farms Food Specialties

350 Andover Sparta Rd
Andover, NJ 07821-5016
973-729-6161
Fax: 973-729-1097   800-750-6190
info@peronafarms.com   www.peronafarms.com
Manufacturer of Smoked salmon, seafood and seafood products
President: Victor Avondoglio
CFO: Mark Avondoglio
Executive Chef: Kirk Avondoglio
Estimated Sales: $2.5.5 Million
Number Employees: 100-249
Sq. footage: 4100
Brands:
PERONA FARMS

11224 Perricone Juices

550 B St
Beaumont, CA 92223-2672
951-769-7171
Fax: 951-769-7176   frshjus@aol.com
www.perriconejuices.com
Manufacturer of fresh orange, grapefruit, lemon and lime juices; also, lemonade
COO: Tom Carmody
CEO: Tom Carmody
Estimated Sales: $ 50 - 100 Million
Number Employees: 50-99
Type of Packaging: Food Service

11225 Perry Creek Winery

133 Cressman Rd
Telford, PA 18969-1504
215-723-6516
Fax: 215-699-8200   800-880-4026
andrel@perrycreek.com   www.perrycreek.com
Wines
President/CEO: Michael Chazen

Estimated Sales: $1-2.5 Million
Number Employees: 5-9

11226 Perry's Ice Cream Company

1 Ice Cream Plz
Akron, NY 14001-1031
716-542-5492
Fax: 716-542-2544   800-873-7797
www.perrysicecream.com
Manufacturer of frozen desserts including regular, nonfat and sugar-free ice cream, ice milk, sherbet, yogurt and novelties
President: Robert Denning
Estimated Sales: $225 Million
Number Employees: 250-499
Sq. footage: 100000
Type of Packaging: Consumer, Bulk
Brands:
PERRY'S
PERRY'S DELUXE
PERRY'S FREE
PERRY'S LIGHT
PERRY'S PRIDE

11227 Personal Edge Nutrition

275 White Tree Lane
Ballwin, MO 63011-3338
877-982-3343
Fax: 636-394-7067
PEinfo@personaledgeprotein.com
www.personaledgeprotein.com
Manufacturer of Energy and protein bars, granola bars, powdered soy beverages
Parent Co: DuPont Chemical
Brands:
PERSONAL EDGE SUPRO

11228 Personal Health Developm

4115 Transport Street
Ventura, CA 93003-5626
805-644-8596
Fax: 805-644-3511   800-988-4465
diane@thinkproducts.com
www.thinkproducts.com
Processor and exporter of nutritional bars and drinks
CEO: Lizanne Falsetto
National Sales Operations Manager: Tina Payne
Estimated Sales: $ 10-20 Million
Number Employees: 10-19
Parent Co: Prime Health Dietary Supplements
Type of Packaging: Consumer, Food Service, Private Label
Brands:
Think Energy
Think Green
Think Organic
Think Thin

11229 Pestos with Panache by Lauren

176 Johnson Street
Suite 8E
Brooklyn, NY 11201
917-656-3082
Fax: 212-230-7404
lauren@pestoswithpanache.com
www.pestoswithpanachebylauren.com
flavored pestos
President/Owner: Lauren Stewart

11230 Pet Dairy

P.O.Box 4527
Spartanburg, SC 29305-4527
864-576-6280
Fax: 864-574-9605
Processor of dairy products including ice cream and milk
General Manager: Lawrence Ferguson
Quality Control: Lanny McDole
COO: Joe Hogan
Purchasing Agent: Joe Hogan
Estimated Sales: $14500000
Number Employees: 100-249
Parent Co: Land-O-Sun
Type of Packaging: Consumer

11231 Pet Dairy

800 E 21st St
Winston Salem, NC 27105-5354
336-784-1800
Fax: 336-784-1844   800-735-2050
www.petdairy.com
Manufacturer of dairy products
Manager: Dennis Riggs
Division Sales Manager: Don Roland
Operations Manager: Mike Reid
Estimated Sales: $1 Million
Number Employees: 20-49
Parent Co: Dean Foods Company
Type of Packaging: Consumer

11232 Pet Dairy

2320 Turnpike Rd
Portsmouth, VA 23704-2940
757-397-2387
Fax: 757-397-5502
Processor and wholesaler/distributor of fresh dairy products including milk and ice cream
Division Manager: Ken Gardner
Plant Manager: Cliff Raines
Purchasing Agent: Julie Perry
Estimated Sales: $ 10 - 20 Million
Number Employees: 100-249
Parent Co: Land-O-Sun

11233 Pet Milk

P.O.Box 12860
Florence, SC 29504-2860
843-665-6866
Fax: 843-665-4255   800-735-3066
Processor of milk, juice and tea
Key Accounts Manager: John Weston
Sales Manager: Jim Dugger
Division Manager: Lou McCarvy
Plant Manager: James McKnight
Estimated Sales: $660000
Number Employees: 100-249
Sq. footage: 5172
Type of Packaging: Food Service

11234 Petaluma Poultry Processors

P.O.Box 7368
Petaluma, CA 94955-7368
707-763-1904
Fax: 707-763-3924   800-556-6789
petalumareception@petalumapoultry.com
www.petalumapoultry.com
Processor of fresh and antibiotic free chickens
Marketing Director: Brian Starr
Owner: Darrel Freitas
CEO: Matt Junkel
CEO: Darrel Freitas
Estimated Sales: $ 20 - 50 Million
Number Employees: 100-249
Brands:
fresh poultry

11235 Pete & Joy's Bakery

121 E Broadway
Little Falls, MN 56345-3038
320-632-6388
Fax: 320-632-2740
Processor of baked goods
Owner: Peter Kamrowski
Estimated Sales: $8 Million
Number Employees: 20-49

11236 (HQ)Pete's Brewing Company

14800 San Pedro Ave
San Antonio, TX 78232-3733
210-490-9128
Fax: 210-490-9984   800-877-7383
www.petes.com
Processor and exporter of beer including ale, amber ale, lager and raspberry amber ale
President: Scott Barnum
CEO: Jeffrey Atkins
CEO: Carlos Alvarez
VP Sales: Don Quigley
Number Employees: 50-99
Parent Co: Miller Brewing Company
Brands:
Pete's Wicked Ale

11237 Peter Dudgeon International

740 Kopke St
Honolulu, HI 96819-3315
808-841-8071
Fax: 808-842-5093
President: Peter Dudgeon
Estimated Sales: $ 5 - 10 Million
Number Employees: 5-9

11238 Peter Michael Winery

12400 Ida Clayton Rd
Calistoga, CA 94515-9507
707-942-3200
Fax: 707-942-0209   800-354-4459
wineclub@petermichaelwinery.com
www.petermichaelwinery.com
Wines
Owner: Peter Michael
Vice President: Bill Vyenielo
Estimated Sales: $ 1-2.5 Million
Number Employees: 20-49
Brands:
Peter Michael Winery

11239 Peter Pan Seafoods
2200 6th Ave # 10
Seattle, WA 98121-1896   206-728-6000
    Fax: 206-441-9090   sales@ppsf.com
                www.ppsf.com
Processor and exporter of fresh and frozen seafood
including crab, herring and surimi blends; also,
canned salmon; importer of frozen swordfish, mahi
mahi and tuna
    President: Mark Weed
    CEO: Barry D Collier
Estimated Sales: $38000000
Number Employees: 1,000-4,999
Parent Co: Nichiro Corporation
Type of Packaging: Consumer, Food Service, Private Label, Bulk
Brands:
    Deming's
    Double Q
    Gill Netter's Best
    Humpty Dumpty
    Peter Pan
    Seablends
    Seakist
    Unica

11240 Peter Paul Manufacturing Plant
PO Box 310
Naugatuck, CT 06770-0310   203-720-4200
    Fax: 203-720-4205   800-468-1714
                www.hersheys.com
Manufacturer of chocolate candy
    CEO: Richard Lenny
Estimated Sales: $100+ Million
Number Employees: 250
Sq. footage: 254000
Parent Co: Hershey Foods Corporation
Type of Packaging: Consumer, Food Service
Brands:
    Almond Joy
    Mounds
    York

11241 Peter Rabbit Farms
85810 Peter Rabbit Ln
Coachella, CA 92236-1897   760-398-0151
    Fax: 760-398-0972   sales@peterrabbitfarms.com
                www.peterrabbitfarms.com
Processor and exporter of grapefruit, carrots, green
onions, shallots and green and red seedless grapes
    President: John Powell Jr
    CFO: John Powell Jr
Estimated Sales: $100+ Million
Number Employees: 250-499
Type of Packaging: Consumer, Food Service, Private Label, Bulk

11242 Peter's Mustards
PO Box 1036
Sharon, CT 06069-1036   860-364-0842
Mustard
    President: Richard Harris

11243 Petersburg Fisheries
P.O. Box 1147
Petersburg, AK 99833-1147   907-772-4294
    Fax: 907-772-4472   877-772-4294
                krisn@icicleseafoods.com
                www.hookedonfish.com
Manufacturer of fresh, frozen and canned fish and
seafood including Alaskan King crab, Snow crab,
Dungeness crab, Halibut, Sablefish, Rockfish, Herring and Salmon
    President: Don Giles
    Plant Manager: Patrick Wilson
Estimated Sales: $284 Million
Number Employees: 100-249
Parent Co: Icicle Seafood
Type of Packaging: Food Service, Private Label, Bulk

11244 Petersen Ice Cream Company
1104 Chicago Ave # 5
Oak Park, IL 60302-1843   708-386-6130
    Fax: 708-386-6162   info@petersonicecream.com
                www.petersenicecream.com
Processor of ice cream and frozen yogurt
    President and CFO: Robert Raniere
    Treasurer: D Raniere
Estimated Sales: $ 1 - 3 Million
Number Employees: 20-49
Type of Packaging: Consumer, Food Service

11245 Peterson & Sons Winery
9375 E P Ave
Kalamazoo, MI 49048-9762   269-626-9755
                Fax: 616-626-9755
Producer of wine
    Owner: Duane Peterson
    Sales Manager: Tony Peterson
Estimated Sales: $500,000-$1 Million
Number Employees: 1-4

11246 Peterson Farms
250 S Main Street
Decatur, AR 72722   479-752-5000
    Fax: 501-752-5660   800-382-4425
                bayleyh@petersonfarms.com
                www.petersonfarms.com
Poultry and feed
    President: Lloyd E Peterson
    Sr. Sales Director: Bruce Bayley
    CEO and Vice Chairman: Vic Evans
    President: Dan Henderson
    VP Human Resources: Janet Wilkerson
    VP Processing: Richard Ward
Estimated Sales: $ 100-250 Million
Number Employees: 1500
Brands:
    Peterson Farms

11247 Peterson's Ventures
299 S Main St
Salt Lake City, UT 84111-1919   801-359-8880
    Fax: 801-365-0181   info@petersonpartnerslp.com
                www.petersonventures.com
Snack foods
    Managing Partner: Jordan Clements
    Office Manager: Kristi Kruckenberg Kruckenberg

    Associate: Jason Reading
    Manager: Ed Lenamon
Estimated Sales: $ 20-50 Million
Number Employees: 50-99
Brands:
    Cheez Nibbles
    Clover Club
    Grandma Goodwins

11248 Petra International
644 West Street W
Hamilton, ON L8S 1A1
Canada   905-542-2409
    Fax: 905-542-2546   800-261-7226
                petraint@rogers.com   www.petradecor.com
Processor, manufacturer, importer and exporter of
gum paste flowers
    President: Ham Go
Parent Co: Indomex Foods
Type of Packaging: Consumer, Private Label, Bulk
Brands:
    PETRA

11249 (HQ)Petri Baking Products Inc
18 Main St
Silver Creek, NY 14136-1495   716-934-2661
    Fax: 716-934-3054   800-346-1981
                info@petribaking.com   www.petribaking.com
Produces a variety of cookies including molasses,
oatmeal raisin, sugar, chocolate chip and fruit filled.
    President: Richard Cattau
    Founder: Armand Petri
    CFO: Fran Murphy
    Operations Manager: Norm Habib
    Production Manager: Joesph Vogl
    Plant Manager: Joe Vogl
    Purchasing Manager: Michael McFarlane
Estimated Sales: $ 20-50 Million
Number Employees: 100-249
Sq. footage: 75
Type of Packaging: Private Label

11250 Petrie Wholesale
5712 Freemont Drive N
Mobile, AL 36609-7051   251-660-8719
                Fax: 251-660-8719
    Proprietor: Frank Petrie

11251 Petrofsky's Bagels
11800 Borman Drive
Saint Louis, MO 63146-4113   314-432-4177
                Fax: 314-432-5150
Processor of frozen raw dough bagels
    President: Jerry Shapiro
Brands:
    Petrofsky's Bagels

11252 Petrofsky's Bakery Products
701 Fee Fee Road
Maryland Heights, MO 63043-3225   314-432-5101
                Fax: 314-432-0468
Processor and exporter of frozen dough and bagels
    Plant Manager: Eric Brenk
Estimated Sales: $ 10 - 20 Million
Number Employees: 50-99
Parent Co: Maplehurst Bakeries
Type of Packaging: Consumer, Food Service

11253 Petschl's Meats
1150 Andover Park E
Tukwila, WA 98188-3903   206-575-4400
                Fax: 206-575-4463
Processor of meats including beef, lamb, pork, veal
and chicken
    Owner: Bill Petschls
Estimated Sales: $100+ Million
Number Employees: 20-49
Type of Packaging: Consumer, Food Service, Private Label, Bulk

11254 Pett Spice Products
4285 Wendell Dr SW
Atlanta, GA 30336-1632   404-691-5235
    Fax: 404-691-5237   pat@pettspice.net
                www.pettspice.net
Manufacturers and developes wet and dry seasoning
for the meat, poultry, seafood and snack food industries. Specialities include seasonings for dry and injectable marinades, glazes, salad dressings, soups,
sauces, regular and low-fatsnack foods, breading
and many more food products.
    President: Scott Pett
    Plant Manager: Mike Foley
Estimated Sales: $500,000-$1 Million
Number Employees: 5-9
Brands:
    Pett Spice

11255 Pett's Coffee & Tea
P.O.Box 12509
Berkeley, CA 94712-3509   510-594-2100
                Fax: 510-594-2180   www.peets.com
Coffee, tea
    CEO: Patrick J O'Dea
Estimated Sales: I
Number Employees: 1,000-4,999

11256 Pevely Dairy Company
1001 S Grand Blvd
St Louis, MO 63104-1084   314-771-4400
                Fax: 314-771-6695
Processor of dairy products including sour cream,
milk and ice cream
    CFO: Marvin Wulf
    General Manager: Richard Kerckhoff
    Marketing Director: Bob Haberberger
    Operations Manager: Brian Berci
Estimated Sales: $100+ Million
Number Employees: 100-249
Parent Co: Prairie Farms Dairy
Type of Packaging: Consumer, Food Service, Private Label, Bulk

11257 Pez Manufacturing Corporation
35 Prindle Hill Rd
Orange, CT 06477-3616   203-795-0531
                Fax: 203-799-1679   www.pez.com
Manufacturer of Candy and confectionery
    President/CEO: Joseph Vittoria
    CFO/Senior Operating Officer: Louis Falango
    VP Marketing: William Damberg
    Human Resource Manager/Director: Ann
    Hutchinson
Estimated Sales: $20-50 Million
Number Employees: 100-249
Brands:
    MANNER WAFERS & CHOCOLATES
    NAPOLI WAFERS
    PEZ CANDY AND DISPENSERS
    PEZ FUZZY FRIENDS
    PEZ PEPPERMINT

11258 Pfanstiehl Laboratories
1219 Glen Rock Ave
Waukegan, IL 60085-6230   847-623-2645
    Fax: 847-623-9173   pfanstiehl-info@ferro.com
                www.pfanstiehl.com
Processor and exporter of lactic acid
    President: Hector Ortino
    President: Gary Schafer

Estimated Sales: $23900000
Number Employees: 100-249
Type of Packaging: Bulk

11259 Pfeffer's Country Market
411 Sinclair Lewis Avenue
Sauk Centre, MN 56378-1350   320-352-3095
Manufacturer of frankfurters, bologna, sausage and poultry
President: Michael Pfeffer
Estimated Sales: $17 Million
Number Employees: 15
Type of Packaging: Consumer

11260 Pfefferkorn's Coffee
P.O.Box 27007
Baltimore, MD 21230-0007   410-727-3354
Fax: 410-547-1652 800-682-4665
pfeffco@erols.com
Manufacturer of coffee
President: Louis Pfefferkorn
VP/Owner: Samuel Pfefferkorn
Operations Manager: Charles Pfefferkorn
Estimated Sales: $ .5 - 1 million
Number Employees: 5-9
Type of Packaging: Consumer
Brands:
Pfefferkorn's
Pfefferkorn's Coffee
Pfefferkorn's of Federal Hill

11261 Pfeffers Country Market
411 Sinclair Lewis Ave
Sauk Centre, MN 56378-1350   320-352-6490
Fax: 320-352-2206
Meat packing and slaughtering
Owner: Mark Scheefers
Estimated Sales: Below $ 5 Million
Number Employees: 10-19

11262 Pfeiffer's Foods
683 Lake St
Wilson, NY 14172-9702   716-751-9371
Fax: 716-751-6218 tmoje@marzetti.com
www.marzetti.com
Salad dressings
Plant Manager: John Follick
Number Employees: 100-249
Parent Co: T. Marzetti Company
Type of Packaging: Consumer, Private Label
Brands:
Marzetti's
Pfeiffer's

11263 Pfeil & Holing
5815 Northern Blvd
Flushing, NY 11377-2297   718-545-4600
Fax: 718-932-7513 800-247-7955
info@pfeil-verlag.de www.pfeil-verlag.de
Candy
President: Sy Stricker
Estimated Sales: $ 5-10 Million
Number Employees: 20-49

11264 Pfizer
400 Interpace Pkwy # 3
Parsippany, NJ 07054-1118   973-541-5900
Chewing gum and breath mints
Trade Development Manager: Larry Roche
Sales/Marketing Executive: Michael Soriano
Estimated Sales: $ 1 - 3 Million
Number Employees: 1-4
Parent Co: Pfizer
Type of Packaging: Consumer, Food Service
Brands:
Bubbilicious
Certs
Chiclets
Clorets
Cool Mint Drops
Dentyne Ice
Mint*A*Burst
Trident
Vichy

11265 Phamous Phloyd's Barbeque Sauce
2998 S Steele St
Denver, CO 80210-6948   303-757-3285
Fax: 303-757-3373 phloyd@uswest.net
www.phloyds.com

Manufactuter of condiments, Bloody Mary mixes, marinades and hot and barbecue sauces, mustards and dry rubs
President/Owner: Mary Ellen Baran
Estimated Sales: Under $500,000
Number Employees: 1-4
Type of Packaging: Consumer, Bulk
Brands:
PHAMOUS PHLOYD'S BLOODY MARY MIX
PHAMOUS PHLOYD'S DRY RUB
PHAMOUS PHLOYD'S HOT SAUCE
PHAMOUS PHLOYD'S ITALIAN MUSTARD
PHAMOUS PHLOYD'S MARINADE
PHAMOUS PHLOYD'S PEPPER MUSTARD
PHAMOUS PHLOYD'S PHLAMING
PHAMOUS PHLOYD'S PHROG HOT BBQ

11266 Pharmachem Laboratories
130 Wesley Street
Hackensack, NJ 07606-1510   201-343-3611
Fax: 201-343-5807
Manufacturer and exporter of fine chemicals and vitamins including rose hips and acerola extracts
President: David Holmes
Estimated Sales: $ 5 - 10 Million
Number Employees: 5-9
Parent Co: Pharmachem Laboratories

11267 Pharmavite Corporation
P.O.Box 9606
Mission Hills, CA 91346-9606   818-221-6200
Fax: 818-221-6393 800-276-2878
www.pharmavite.com
Processor and exporter of vitamin tablets and ingredients
President: Brent Belly
CEO: Connie Barry
Executive VP Marketing: Catherine Mardesich
Estimated Sales: $300,000-500,000
Number Employees: 1-4
Parent Co: Pharmavite Corporation
Type of Packaging: Bulk
Brands:
Nature Made
Nature's Resources

11268 Pharmline
P.O.Box 291
Florida, NY 10921-0291   845-651-4443
Fax: 845-651-6900 info@pharmlineinc.com
www.pharmlineinc.com
Processor, importer and exporter of nutritional ingredients, herbal extracts, ginseng, ginkgo biloba, lutein, spirulina, royal jelly, lycopene and beta carotene; also, custom blending, granulation, extraction and micronizingavailable
President: John Witterschein
VP Sales/Marketing: Robert Walker
Plant Manager: Christopher Forst
Estimated Sales: $17000000
Number Employees: 100-249
Sq. footage: 50000
Type of Packaging: Bulk
Brands:
Aquamin
Lycopen
Lycosource
Phenalgin
Rhodenol
Rosavin

11269 Pheasant Ridge Winery
3527 E County Road 5700
Lubbock, TX 79403   806-746-6033
Fax: 806-746-6750 billgipson@aol.com
www.pheasantridgewinery.com
Wines
Manager: Bill Blackman
Owner: William Gibson
Estimated Sales: Below $ 5 Million
Number Employees: 5-9
Brands:
Proprietor's Reserve

11270 Phenix Food Service
318 General Colin Powell Pkwy
Phenix City, AL 36869-6953   334-298-6288
Fax: 334-298-6777 www.phenixfoodlocker.com
President: Pat Hardin
Secretary/Treasurer: J Hardin
Executive VP: Jeff Hardin
Estimated Sales: $100+ Million
Number Employees: 20-49

11271 Phenomenal Fudge
4668 Vermont Route 74 W
Shoreham, VT 05770-9689   800-430-5442
Fax: 802-897-7300 800-430-5442
pfudge2000@yahoo.com www.pfudge.com
Manufacturer of fudge
Owner/Fudgemaker: Steve Jackson

11272 (HQ)Phibro Animal Health
65 Challenger Rd # 3
Ridgefield Park, NJ 07660-2110   201-944-6020
Fax: 201-329-7399 888-403-0074
hr@pahc.com www.phibroah.com
Develops, manufactures and markets medicated feed additives as well as marketing animal health and nutrition products.
President: Keith Collins
CFO: Shawn Brosnan
CEO: Gerald K Carlson
Estimated Sales: $100+ Million
Number Employees: 500-999
Brands:
Phibro

11273 Philadelphia Candies
1546 E State St
Hermitage, PA 16148-1823   724-981-6341
Fax: 724-981-6490 pc@phillyc.com
www.phillyc.com
Processor of confectionery items including marshmallow specialties, dietetic, mints, creams, nougats, nuts, fruits and specialty molded holiday, regular and sugar-free chocolates
President: Spyros Macris
Vice President: Georgia Macris
Estimated Sales: $1,100,000
Number Employees: 50-99
Type of Packaging: Bulk
Brands:
Loving Bunny

11274 Philadelphia Cheese Steak Company
520 E Hunting Park Ave
Philadelphia, PA 19124-6009   215-423-3333
Fax: 215-423-3131 800-342-9771
marketing@phillycheesesteak.com
www.phillycheesesteak.com
Processor of frozen cheese steaks
CEO: Nick Karamatsoukas
Founder: Nick Karamatsoukas
Director Marketing: John Karamatsoukas
Estimated Sales: $ 20-50 Million
Number Employees: 50-99
Type of Packaging: Consumer, Food Service
Brands:
Philadelphia Cheese Steak

11275 Philadelphia Macaroni Company
40 Jacksonville Road
Warminster, PA 18974-4804   215-441-5220
www.philamacaroni.com
Manufacturer and supplier of noodles and pasta for private label food service marketplaces. Also a supplier of spring wheat and mills durum flour.
Parent Co: Minot Milling

11276 Philadelphia Macaroni Company
760 S 11th St
Philadelphia, PA 19147-2614   215-923-3141
Fax: 215-925-4298 www.philamacaroni.com
Manufacturer of pasta and noodles
Owner: Luke Marano
Sales/Marketing Director: Joe Viviano
EVP Sales: Bill Stabert
Estimated Sales: $ 20 - 50 Million
Number Employees: 10-19
Type of Packaging: Bulk

11277 Philip Togni Vineyard
PO Box 81
St Helena, CA 94574-0081   707-963-3731
Fax: 707-963-9186 tognivyd@wildblue.net
www.philiptognivineyard.com
Grower and producer of Estate bottled Caberbet only
Partner: Philip Togni
Partner: Birgitta Togni
Partner/Winemaker: Lisa Togni
Estimated Sales: $500,000-$1 Million
Number Employees: 4
Brands:
Philip Togni

11278 Phillips Beverage Company
25 Main St SE
Minneapolis, MN 55414-1061   612-362-7500
                                Fax: 612-362-7501
Processor of cordials and liqueurs
  President: Dean Phillips
  CEO: Edward Phillips
Estimated Sales: $ 10 - 20 Million
Number Employees: 10-19
Type of Packaging: Consumer, Food Service

11279 Phillips Candies
217 Broadway St
Seaside, OR 97138-5805   503-738-5402
        Fax: 503-738-8326 candy@seasurf.net
Processor of candy including fudge and salt water
taffy
  President: Steve C Phillips
Estimated Sales: $2,600,000
Number Employees: 5-9
Type of Packaging: Consumer, Private Label

11280 Phillips Candies of Seas
217 Broadway St
Seaside, OR 97138-5805   503-738-5402
        Fax: 503-738-8326 candy@seasurf.net
Saltwater taffy, chocolaters and fudge
  President: Steven C Phillips
Estimated Sales: $ 1-2.5 Million
Number Employees: 5-9
Brands:
  Phillips Candies

11281 Phillips Farms & Michael David Vineyards
4580 W Highway 12
Lodi, CA 95242-9529   209-368-7384
        Fax: 209-368-5801 888-707-9463
                vintage@lodivineyards.com
                www.lodivineyards.com
Wines
  Partner: Mike Phillips
  Partner: Dave Phillips
Estimated Sales: Below $ 5 Million
Number Employees: 20-49
Brands:
  Michael David Vineyards

11282 Phillips Foods
1027 Wilso Drive
Baltimore, MD 21223-3232   410-837-8523
        Fax: 410-837-8526 800-782-2722
                comments@phillipsfoods.com
                www.phillipsfoods.com
Manufacturer of fresh and pasteurized crabmeat, live
and steamed crabs and fresh and frozen soft crabs
  CEO: Steve Phillips
  President: Mark Sneed
  CFO: Dean Flowers
Estimated Sales: $ 50 - 100 Million
Number Employees: 25
Sq. footage: 3000
Parent Co: Phillips Seafood Restaurants
Type of Packaging: Consumer, Food Service, Bulk
Brands:
  PHILLIPS

11283 Phillips Foods
1215 E Fort Ave
Baltimore, MD 21230-5104   410-547-0220
        Fax: 410-837-8526 888-234-2722
                comments@phillipsfoods.com
                www.phillipsfoods.com
Processor and exporter of refrigerated blue crab
meat, frozen crab cakes, dips, soups and chowders,
in addition to frozen shrimp, appetizers, condi-
ments/seasonings, and salmon cakes.
  CEO: Steven Phillips
  Co-Founder: Shirley Phillips
  Quality Control: Bobby Love
  Plant Manager: Steve Malecki
Estimated Sales: $ 2.5-5 Million
Number Employees: 250-499
Parent Co: Phillips Seafood Restaurants
Type of Packaging: Consumer, Food Service
Brands:
  Crab Slammer
  Phillips Foods

11284 Phillips Foods, Inc. &Seafood Restaurants
1215 E Fort Ave
Baltimore, MD 21230-5104   410-547-0220
        Fax: 410-837-8526 888-234-2722
                comments@phillipsfoods.com
                www.phillipsfoods.com
Manufacturer of seafood and canning
  President: Mark Sneed
  CEO/Owner: Steven Phillips
  CEO: Steven Phillips
  Plant Manager: Steve Malecki
  Purchasing: Newcomb
Estimated Sales: $ 5 - 10 Million
Number Employees: 20-49
Brands:
  E PHILLIPS

11285 Phillips Gourmet
1011 Kaolin Road
PO Box 190
Kennett Square, PA 19348   610-925-0520
        Fax: 610-925-0527 info@phillipsgourmet.com
                www.phillipsmushroomfarms.com
Specializes in the development and production of
proprietary mushroom formulations for multi-unit
restaurant operators and provides a market-leading
variety of ingredients to mmet the needs of virtually
any food manufacturer.
  President: Marshall Phillips
Estimated Sales: $1 Million
Number Employees: 10-19
Type of Packaging: Consumer, Food Service
Brands:
  Bella

11286 Phillips Seafood
1381 Pelican Point Rd NE
Townsend, GA 31331   912-832-4423
                Fax: 912-832-6228
Seafood
  President: Myron Phillips

11287 Phillips Syrup Corporation
1311 Brookpark Road
Cleveland, OH 44109-5874   216-661-4800
                Fax: 216-661-4803
Processor of chocolate, sugar-free, sno-cone, slush
and maple syrups, sundae toppings, fountain drinks,
bar mixes and beverage concentrates. Also
sugar-free for diabetics
  President: Robert Schallman
  Public Relations: Raisa Hawal
  Production/Plant Manager: Joseph Mazak
  Purchasing Manager: Susan Connerton
Estimated Sales: $7000000
Number Employees: 17
Number of Brands: 12
Number of Products: 200
Sq. footage: 15000
Type of Packaging: Food Service, Private Label
Brands:
  Fundae
  Phillips

11288 Phipps Desserts
420 Eglinton Avenue W
Toronto, ON M5V 1E3
Canada   416-481-9111
        Fax: 416-481-5616 www.phippsdesserts.com
Processor of baked gourmet desserts
  Sales Manager: Marjorie Riley
Type of Packaging: Consumer, Food Service
Brands:
  PHIPPS

11289 Phoenicia Patisserie
P.O.Box 13128
Arlington, TX 76094-0128   817-261-2898
                Fax: 817-274-3942
        amerhamedi@phoeniciainternational.com
                www.phoeniciainternational.com
Pastries
  Owner: Amer Hamedi

11290 Phoenician Herbals
7645 E Evans Rd # 3
Scottsdale, AZ 85260-2944   480-368-8144
        Fax: 480-368-2912 800-966-8144
                jbaker4884@aol.com
                www.guardiannutrition.com
Processor and exporter of vitamins, supplements and
herbal teas
  Owner: Redgie Hansen

Estimated Sales: $440,000
Number Employees: 5-9
Brands:
  Phoenician Herbals

11291 Phoenix Agro-IndustrialCorporation
521 Lowell St
Westbury, NY 11590-4422   516-334-1194
        Fax: 516-338-8647 www.phoenixaico.com
International traders of frozen foods
  President: Tomipor Pasto
  Marketing: Julianna Edlyn
  Purchasing Director: Neone Din
Estimated Sales: $ 3 - 5 Million
Number Employees: 5-9
Number of Brands: 28
Number of Products: 45
Sq. footage: 10000
Type of Packaging: Consumer, Private Label, Bulk
Brands:
  Citizen Foods

11292 Phoenix Laboratories
200 Adams Boulevard
Farmingdale, NY 11735-6615   516-822-1230
        Fax: 516-822-1252 800-236-6583
                www.natplus.com
Manufactures of vitamins
  President: Mel Rich
  VP: Steven Stern
Number Employees: 50-99

11293 Phranil Foods
3900 E Main Avenue
Spokane, WA 99202-4737   509-534-7770
                Fax: 509-534-4244
Pies and frozen bakery products
  Owner: Fran Bessermin
  Controller: Bob Clements
Estimated Sales: $ 1-2.5 Million
Number Employees: 20-49

11294 Phyto-Technologies
107 Enterprise Dr
Woodbine, IA 51579-1501   712-647-2755
        Fax: 712-647-2885 877-809-3404
        extracts@phyto-tech.com www.earthpower.com
Nutritional supplements, herbal supplements, ex-
tracts and blends, including chinese herbs
  Founder/President: Albert Leung
  Sales/Marketing: Terry Jinks
Estimated Sales: Below $ 5 Million
Number Employees: 10-19
Sq. footage: 20000
Parent Co: Earth Power
Type of Packaging: Consumer, Private Label
Brands:
  Earth Power's All American
  Earthpower's Phytochi

11295 Phytotherapy Research Laboratory
P.O.Box 627
Lobelville, TN 37097-0627   931-593-3780
        Fax: 931-593-3782 800-274-3727
                newherbs@netease.net
Manufacturer and exporter of certified organic herb
extracts; also, research, development and production
of specialty herbal products in the area of immune
and vital organ support
  President: Brent Davis
Estimated Sales: $500,000-$1 Million
Number Employees: 1-4
Sq. footage: 25000
Type of Packaging: Private Label
Brands:
  Forest Center
  Hahg
  PRL

11296 (HQ)Piantedosi Baking Company
240 Commercial St
Malden, MA 02148-6780   781-321-3400
        Fax: 781-324-5647 800-339-0080
        nikki@piantedosi.com www.piantedosi.com
Processor of specialty breads and rolls
  President: Thomas Piantedosi
  Vice President: Robert Piantedosi
  Research & Development: Lino DiSchino
  Marketing Coordinator: Nikki Hanson
  VP Sales: Joseph Piantedosi Jr

Estimated Sales:$24,254,933
Number Employees: 100-249
Sq. footage: 70000
Type of Packaging: Consumer, Food Service, Private Label, Bulk
Other Locations:
  Piantedosi Baking Co.
  Malden MA
Brands:
  Piantedosi

11297 Piazza's Seafood World
205 James Dr W
St Rose, LA 70087-4036   504-602-5050
      Fax: 504-602-1555   info@cajunboy.net
                  www.cajunboy.net
Processor and exporter of fresh and frozen seafood including crawfish, alligator, catfish, shrimp, crabmeat, softshell crabs
  Manager: Jennifer Champagne
  CFO: Mike Sabolyk
Estimated Sales:$ 5-10 Million
Number Employees: 20-49
Number of Brands: 2
Number of Products: 20
Type of Packaging: Food Service, Private Label
Brands:
  Cajan Boy
  Cajan Delight

11298 (HQ)Picard Peanuts
RR 1
Windham Centre, ON N0E 2A0
Canada   519-443-7779
      Fax: 519-443-6303   888-244-7688
            sales@picardpeanuts.com
            www.picardpeanuts.com
Processor of potato chip covered peanuts
  President: Jim Picard
  CFO: John Picard
  R & D: Lincoln Reid
  Vice President: John Picard
  CFO: John David
  Quality Control: Michael Newsome
  Marketing Director: John Picard
Estimated Sales:$ 5-10 Million
Number Employees: 27
Sq. footage: 32000
Type of Packaging: Consumer, Bulk
Other Locations:
  Picard Peanuts Ltd.
  Waterford ON
Brands:
  Chipnuts

11299 Pickle Cottage
12989 Windy Road
Bucklin, KS 67834-8807   316-826-3502
                        Fax: 316-826-3866
Snack foods and pickles
  President: Barry Stimpert
Estimated Sales:$500,000-$1 Million
Number Employees: 10-19

11300 Picklesmith
P.O.Box 935
Taft, TX 78390-0935   361-528-4953
      Fax: 830-885-4560   800-499-3401
  dsmith@picklesmith.com   www.picklesmith.com
Manufacturer of gourmet pickles and olives
  President: David Smith
Estimated Sales:$ 1-3 Million
Number Employees: 1-4
Sq. footage: 2500
Type of Packaging: Consumer, Food Service
Brands:
  A.P. Smith Canning Co.
  Picklesmith

11301 Pickwick Catfish Farm
4155 Highway 57
Counce, TN 38326-3057   731-689-3805
            KnussK@msn.com
      www.pickwickcatfishfarm.com
Manufacturer of Farm-raised smoked catfish
  Owner: Betty Knussmann
  Co-Owner: Quentin Knussman
*Estimated Sales:*Less than $500,000
Number Employees: 5-9
Brands:
  PICKWICK CATFISH

11302 Pictsweet Frozen Foods
P.O.Box 119
Bells, TN 38006-0119   731-663-7600
      Fax: 800-235-3203   cfarner@pictsweet.com
                  www.pictsweet.net
Processor, importer and exporter of frozen asparagus, beans, broccoli, brussels sprouts, carrots, cauliflower, turnip, mustard and collard greens, okra, peas, spinach, squash, succotash, etc
  President: B Ennis
  President: Mason Leonard
  CEO: James I Tankersley
  Marketing Director: Julia Wells
  Director Manufacturing: Frank Tankersley
Estimated Sales:$$10-20 Million
Number Employees: 1,000-4,999
Number of Products: 100
Parent Co: Pictsweet
Type of Packaging: Consumer, Food Service, Private Label
Brands:
  Dulaney
  Dulany
  Everfresh
  Food Service Packer
  Pictsweet
  Pictsweet Express
  Prime Froz-N
  Tennessee
  Winter Garden

11303 Pidy Gourmet Pastry Shells
90 Inip Dr
Inwood, NY 11096-1011   516-239-6057
      Fax: 516-239-9306   pgps@pidygourmet.com
                  www.pidygourmet.com
Processor and exporter of pastry shells and filled shells
  President: Thierry Demaeck
  General Manager: Philippe Tytgat
  Operations Manager: Michael Lewin-Jacus
  Production Manager: Joanne Lewin-Jacus
Estimated Sales:$ 5-10 Million
Number Employees: 20-49
Sq. footage: 25000
Parent Co: Pidy NV
Type of Packaging: Food Service
Brands:
  Delicaty
  Patibel
  Pidy

11304 (HQ)Pidy Gourmet Pastry Shells
90 Inip Dr
Inwood, NY 11096-1011   516-239-6057
      Fax: 516-239-9306   800-231-7439
                  www.pidygourmet.com
Manufacturer and exporter of pastry shells and filled shells
Estimated Sales:$ 5-10 Million
Number Employees: 20-49
Brands:
  APERI-COEUR
  APERIQUICHE
  BARQUETTE
  CRESCENTGARNITURE
  CROUSTADE 4CM
  CROUSTADE 5CM
  CROUSTADE 7CM
  ESCARCOQUE
  FISHKA
  FLEURETTE
  GAURMANDE
  MIGNARDISE
  MINI-CROUSTADE
  MINI-CROUSTADE SHELL
  MINI-EASRE
  MINI-ROULET
  MINT SHELL
  PUFF PASTRY TARTLET
  QUICHE
  ROULET
  ZAKOUSKI

11305 Pie Piper Products
450 Evergreen Ave
Bensenville, IL 60106-2506   630-595-1550
      Fax: 630-595-1551   800-621-8183
            tbannack@ameritech.net
            www.distinctivefoods.com
Processor and exporter of cakes, cheesecakes and cheesecake on sticks, brownies, quiche and beef frankfurters wrapped in bagel dough
  President: Josh Harris
  Production Manager: Mike Lopardo
Estimated Sales:$ 10-20 Million
Number Employees: 20-49
Sq. footage: 16000
Parent Co: Vienna Manufacturing Company
Type of Packaging: Consumer, Food Service, Private Label
Brands:
  Pie Piper
  Vienna Bageldog
  Wunderbar

11306 Pied-Mont/Dora
176 Saint-Joseph
Ste Anne Des Plaines, BC J0N 1H0
Canada   450-478-0801
      Fax: 450-478-6381   800-363-8003
            info@piedmontdora.com
            www.piedmontdora.coml
Processor, importer and packer of vegetable and fruit dips, jams, jellies and marmalades; also, chocolate spreads, pie fillings, syrups, drink crystals, etc
  President: Louis Limoges
  Representative: Francoise Laplante
Estimated Sales:$5500000
Number Employees: 40
Brands:
  Bensons
  Clancy
  Dora
  Mondial
  Pied-Mont

11307 Piedmont Candy Corporation
404 Market St
Lexington, NC 27292-1293   336-248-2477
      Fax: 336-248-5841   redbirdstk@aol.com
                  www.piedmontcandy.com
Processor of hard, mint, boxed and seasonal candy
  President: Douglas J Reid
  VP: Chris Reid
Estimated Sales:$2,556,054
Number Employees: 20-49
Type of Packaging: Consumer

11308 Piedmont Vineyards & Winery
P.O.Box 286
Middleburg, VA 20118-0286   540-687-5528
      Fax: 540-687-5777   info@piedmontwines.com
                  www.piedmontwines.com
Manufacturer of Wines
  President: Gerhard Von Finck
*Estimated Sales:*Below $5 Million
Number Employees: 5-9
Type of Packaging: Private Label
Brands:
  PIEDMONT

11309 Piedra Creek Winery
6425 Mira Cielo
San Luis Obispo, CA 93401-8395   805-541-1281
            Fax: 805-541-1281   mzuech@fixnet
Wines
  Co-Owner: Margaret Zuech
  Owner/Winemaker: Romeo Zuech
Estimated Sales:$ .5-1 million
Number Employees: 1-4
Brands:
  Piedra Creek Winery

11310 Piemonte Foods
PO Box 9239
Greenville, SC 29604-9239   864-242-0424
      Fax: 864-235-0239   tpl@tpl.com.sg
                  www.tpl.com.sg
Frozen foods
  President/CEO: T P Costello
  CFO: Edward Cathey
  CFO: W E Cathey
  Sales Director: Mary Coleman
  Public Relations: Claire Smith
  Director Manufacturing: Bud Fulder
  Purchasing Manager: Clark McClaskey
Estimated Sales:$ 10-100 Million
Number Employees: 200
Type of Packaging: Private Label

11311 Piemonte's Bakery
1122 Rock St
Rockford, IL 61101-1431   815-962-4833

Processor and wholesaler/distributor of bread including French, Italian, garlic and rye; also, dinner rolls and po-boys
President: Steve McKeever
Secretary: Irene McKeever
Estimated Sales:$2600000
Number Employees: 10-19
Type of Packaging: Private Label
Brands:
Piemonte

11312 Pierceton Foods
P.O.Box 142
Pierceton, IN 46562-0142   574-594-2344
                              Fax: 574-594-2344
Processor of frozen breaded meat products including porkfritters and cheeseburgers; also, steaks, ground beef and grilled tender loins
President: Jerry Wagoner
Plant Manager: Ben Bunyan
Estimated Sales:$1040000
Number Employees: 10-19
Number of Brands: 1
Sq. footage: 6000
Type of Packaging: Food Service
Brands:
Paul's

11313 Pierino Frozen Foods
1695 Southfield Rd
Lincoln Park, MI 48146-2275   313-928-0950
Fax: 313-928-5410 info@pierinofrozenfoods.com
www.pierinofrozenfoods.com
Processor of frozen Italian products including pasta, sauce and gnocchi
President: Pierino Guglielmetti
Operations Manager: Gianni Guglielmetti
Plant Manager: Silvana Gugliemetti
Estimated Sales:$1800000
Number Employees: 20-49

11314 Pierogi Place
8197 W Harrison Road
Mears, MI 49436-9351   231- 87-3 53
Pierogis
President: Marilyn Marciniak

11315 Pierre Foods
9990 Princeton Glendale Rd
Cincinnati, OH 45246-1127   513-874-8741
Fax: 513-874-8395 www.pierrefoods.com
Processor and exporter of specialty foods including pre-cooked and portion controlled beef, pork and poultry, fully baked buns, biscuits and dumplings, and assembled sanwiches
President/CEO: Norb Woodhams
Chairman: Jimmy Richardson
VP Marketing: Jane Nocito
Purchasing: Sam Patton
Estimated Sales:$210 Million
Number Employees: 1,000-4,999
Sq. footage: 223000
Type of Packaging: Consumer, Food Service, Private Label, Bulk
Other Locations:
Pierre Food
Kiawah Island SC

11316 Pierre Foods
9990 Princeton Glendale Rd
Cincinnati, OH 45246-1127   513-874-8741
Fax: 513-874-8395 www.pierrefoods.com
Breads and sandwiches
Production Manager: Tim Starnes
Founder: Samuel Dinerman
CEO: Norbert E Woodhams
Sales Director: Larry Hefner
Estimated Sales:$ 20-50 Million
Number Employees: 1,000-4,999
Sq. footage: 183
Type of Packaging: Private Label
Brands:
Pierre Foods

11317 Pierre's French Bakery
PO Box 14280
Portland, OR 97293-0280   503-233-8871
Fax: 503-233-5060 ifo@acmemad.com
Bakery products
President: Larry McDonald
Estimated Sales:$ 1-2.5 Million appx.
Number Employees: 50

11318 Pierre's French Ice Cream Company
6200 Euclid Ave
Cleveland, OH 44103-3700   216-432-1144
Fax: 216-432-0001   800-837-7342
icecream@pierres.com www.pierres.com
Manufacturer of Ice cream, frozen yogurt, sherbet, sorbet and frosted smoothies
President: Rochelle Roth
Director Marketing: Laura Hindulak
Operations: John Pimpo
Estimated Sales:$20-50 Million
Number Employees: 100-249
Number of Products: 235
Sq. footage: 30000
Type of Packaging: Consumer
Brands:
PIERRE'S
PIERRE'S CARB SUCCESS
PIERRE'S FROSTED SMOOTHIES
PIERRE'S SLENDER

11319 Pierz Cooperative Association
P.O.Box 307
Pierz, MN 56364-0307   320-468-6655
Fax: 320-468-2773 przcoop@pierz.net
Animal feed
Manager: Randy Sullivan
Estimated Sales:$9,032,630
Number Employees: 10-19
Brands:
Farmer Seed

11320 (HQ)Piggie Park Enterprises
1600 Charleston Hwy
West Columbia, SC 29169-5050   803-791-5887
Fax: 803-791-8707   803-628-7423
mail@mauricesbbq.com   www.mauricesbbq.com
Manufacturer of gourmet barbecue sauce and barbecue meat
President: Maurice Bessinger
Estimated Sales:$4.3 Million
Number Employees: 20-49
Type of Packaging: Consumer, Food Service, Bulk
Brands:
Maurice's

11321 Pike Place Brewery
1415 1st Avenue
Seattle, WA 98101-2017   206-622-3373
Fax: 206-622-6648 info@mdv-beer.com
www.pikebrewing.com
Processor of seasonal beer, ale, stout and porter
Owner: Charles Finkel
General manager: Kim Brusco
Director Manufacturing: Allen Fal
Estimated Sales:$ 2.5-5 Million
Number Employees: 100-249
Brands:
Pike

11322 Pikes Peak Vineyards
2910 N Academy Blvd # 102
Colorado Springs, CO 80917-5351   719-576-0075
Fax: 719-226-0639
Wine
President: Bruce Mc Claughlin
Vice President: Taffy McCloughlen
General Manager: Frankie Tuft
*Estimated Sales:*Less than $300,000
Number Employees: 1-4
Brands:
Pikes Peak Vineyards

11323 Pikled Garlik Company
460 Elder Avenue
Suite D
Sand City, CA 93955-3552   831-393-1707
Fax: 831-393-1707   800-775-9788
garlik@zianet.com   www.pikledgarlik.com/
Garlic
President: Judy Knapp
Estimated Sales:$ 1-2.5 Million
Number Employees: 1-4
Brands:
The Pikled Garlik

11324 Piknik Products CompanyInc
PO Box 9388
Montgomery, AL 36108-0008   334-265-1567
Fax: 334-265-9490
contactinfo@piknikproducts.com
www.piknikproducts.com

Processor and exporter of mayonnaise, mustard and salad dressing
President: Herman Richard Loeb
Sales Director: Butch McPherson
Operations Manager: Charles Caraway
Production Manager: Robert Adair
Plant Manager: William Bell
Estimated Sales:$29020184
Number Employees: 205
Type of Packaging: Consumer, Food Service, Private Label
Brands:
Ol' South
Piknik
Salad Queen
Stewart's

11325 Pilgrim Foods
68 Old Wilton Rd
Greenville, NH 03048-3100   603-878-2100
Fax: 603-878-2103 www.pilgrimfoods.net
Juice, vinegar, mustard
President: Paul Santich
Estimated Sales:$ 5-10 Million
Number Employees: 20-49
Type of Packaging: Bulk

11326 Pilgrim's Pride
170 Oneta St
Athens, GA 30601-1862   706-548-5641
Fax: 706-369-5481 www.pilgrimspride.com
Manufacturer and exporter of fresh and frozen chicken
Manager: David Yeary
CEO/Division Manager: Delane Borron
Estimated Sales:$43.8 Million
Number Employees: 500-999
Type of Packaging: Consumer, Food Service
Brands:
GOLD KIST FARMS

11327 Pilgrim's Pride
P.O. Box 747
Boaz, AL 35957-0747   256-593-4223
Fax: 256-593-0336 www.pilgrimspride.com
Processor and exporter of fresh and frozen poultry
Sales Manager: Ronnie Carnes
Plant Manager: Jim Smith
Purchasing Agent: Jerry Haynie
Estimated Sales:$100-500 Million
Number Employees: 1,000-4,999
Type of Packaging: Consumer, Food Service, Bulk

11328 Pilgrim's Pride
330 Co Op Drive
Timberville, VA 22853   540-896-7000
Fax: 540-896-0498 info@pilgrimspride.com
www.prilgrimspride.com
Manufacturer and exporter of fresh and further processed chicken and turkey products including IQF, portioned, C.V.P., ice and tray packed, fresh, frozen, whole, cooked, etc.; also, turkey and chicken luncheon meat, hot dogs, saladsentrees and turkey burgers
President/CEO/COO: David Van Hoose
VP: Robert Hendrix
Purchasing Agent: Jim Ziegler
*Estimated Sales:*K
Number Employees: 5,000-9,999
Type of Packaging: Consumer, Food Service, Private Label, Bulk
Brands:
ROCKINGHAM
WAMPLER FOODS

11329 (HQ)Pilgrim's Pride
4845 US Highway 271 N
Pittsburg, TX 75686-0093   903-434-1000
Fax: 903-856-7505   800-683-1968
www.pilgrimspride.com
Manufacturer and exporter of chicken and turkey.
Chariman: Weesley Mendonca Batista
President/CEO: Don Jackson
EVP/Chief Financial Officer: Richard Cogdill
EVP Operations: Walter Shafer
Estimated Sales:$7 Billion
Number Employees: 41,240
Type of Packaging: Consumer, Food Service, Private Label, Bulk
Other Locations:
Pilgrims Pride Distribution Centers
Phoenix AZ
Chicken Processing - Fresh
Athens AL
Batesville AR

Broadway VA
Canton GA
Carrollton GA
Chattanooga TN
Ellijay GA
Gainesville GA
Guntersville AL
Live Oak FL
Marshville NC
Mayfield KY
Brands:
  GOLD KIST
  PILGRIMS

11330 Pilgrim's Pride
P.O. Box 539
Moorefield, WV 26836-0539   304-538-2381
          Fax: 304-538-1413 800-336-9876
          www.pilgrimspride.com
Manufacturer of Frozen chicken and poultry products
  Manager: Paton Umstot
  EVP/Chief Financial Officer: Richard Cogdill
  Public Relations: Ray Atkinson
  Chief Operating Officer: J Clinton Rivers
Estimated Sales:$100+ Million
Number Employees: 500-999
Type of Packaging: Consumer, Food Service

11331 Pilgrim's Pride
P.O. Box 311267
Enterprise, AL 36331-1267   334-347-0515
          Fax: 334-393-0868 800-633-0908
          www.pilgrimspride.com
Processor and exporter of fresh and frozen chicken
  President/CEO: O B Goolsby Jr
  EVP/Chief Financial Officer: Richard Cogdill
  Chief Operating Officer: J Clinton Rivers
  Plant Manager: Robin Stevens
Estimated Sales:$100-500 Million
Number Employees: 500-999
Type of Packaging: Consumer, Food Service, Private Label, Bulk

11332 Pilgrim's Pride
1129 Old Middleton Road
Elberton, GA 30635-4523   706-283-3821
          Fax: 706-213-3770 www.pilgrimspride.com
Manufacturer of frozen chicken
  General Manager: Skip James
  Controller: Jason Craft
  Manager: Skip James
Estimated Sales:$500 Million-$1 Billion
Number Employees: 600
Type of Packaging: Consumer, Food Service

11333 Pilgrim's Pride
898 Barber St
Athens, GA 30601-2030   706-549-2810
          Fax: 706-548-5121 800-476-6702
info@pilgrimspride.com   www.pilgrimspride.com
Processor of poultry packaged in trays
  Manager: Andy Harris
  Director Corporate Communications: Ray Atkinson
  Vice President: Dan Emery
  Director Sales/Marketing: Dean Wilcox
Estimated Sales:$100+ Million
Number Employees: 1,000-4,999
Parent Co: ConAgra Poultry
Type of Packaging: Consumer
Brands:
  Pilgrims Pride

11334 Pilgrim's Pride
1800 W Frank Ave
Lufkin, TX 75904-3100   936-639-1174
          Fax: 936-639-2179 www.pilgrimspride.com
Processor of prepared and frozen chicken
  CEO: Raplh Simmons
  VP Finance: Scott Wilkins
  SVP: Robert Palm
  Chief Operating Officer: J Clinton Rivers
  Plant Manager: Cecil Jackson
Estimated Sales:$2.6 Billion
Number Employees: 1,500
Type of Packaging: Consumer, Private Label, Bulk

11335 (HQ)Pilgrim's Pride
Route 42 Box S
Broadway, VA 22815   540-896-0607
          Fax: 540-896-3813 www.pilgrimspride.com

Processor and exporter of fresh and frozen chicken
and turkey
  CEO/President: James Keeler
  VP Sales/Marketing: John Turner
  Branch Manager: Ray Powell
  Purchasing Agent: Jim Ziegler
*Estimated Sales:*Over $1 Billion
Number Employees: 60
Type of Packaging: Consumer, Food Service, Private Label, Bulk
Other Locations:
  WLR Foods
  Broadway VA
Brands:
  Rockingham
  Round Hill
  Shen-Valley
  Wampler Foods

11336 Pilgrim's Pride
P.O. Box 630910
Nacogdoches, TX 75963-0910   936-564-6145
          Fax: 936-564-8955 www.pilgrimspride.com
Processor of fresh and frozen chicken
  President/CEO: O B Goolsby Jr
  Chief Financial Officer: Richard Cogdill
  Chief Operating Officer: J Clinton Rivers
  Manager: Ronnie Eddy
  Plant Manager: Robert Garlington
  Purchasing Agent: Randy Crawford
Estimated Sales:$ 100-500 Million
Number Employees: 1,000-4,999
Type of Packaging: Consumer, Food Service, Private Label, Bulk

11337 Pilgrim's Pride
2011 S Good Latimer Expy
Dallas, TX 75226-2297   214-421-9091
          Fax: 214-565-8670 800-824-1159
info@pilgrimspride.com   www.pilgrimspride.com
Processor of fresh and frozen chicken
  President/CEO: O B Goolsby Jr
  Vice President: Dan Emery
  Director of Corporate Communications: Ray Atkinson
  Chief Operating Officer: J Clinton Rivers
  Plant Manager: Rick Rhodes
Number Employees: 1,000-4,999
Parent Co: Pilgrims Pride Corporation
Type of Packaging: Consumer, Food Service, Private Label, Bulk
Brands:
  Pilgrim's Pride

11338 Pilgrim's Pride
2777 N Stemmons Fwy # 850
Dallas, TX 75207-2504   214-920-2200
          Fax: 214-920-2396 800-824-1159
info@pilgrimspride.com   www.pilgrimspride.com
Processor and exporter of fresh and frozen chicken
  Manager: Jerry Wilson
  Vice President: Michael Murray
  Chief Operating Officer: J Clinton Rivers
Estimated Sales:$ 5-10 Million
Number Employees: 50-99
Parent Co: Pilgrims Pride Corporation
Type of Packaging: Consumer, Food Service, Private Label, Bulk

11339 Pilgrim's Pride
898 Barber St
Athens, GA 30601-2030   706-549-2810
          Fax: 706-548-5121 800-824-1159
info@pilgrimspride.com   www.pilgrimspride.com
Poultry processor
  Manager: Andy Harris Jr
  CEO: Andy Haaris
  Sales Director: Marvin Green
  Public Relations: ²
  Chief Operating Officer: J Clinton Rivers
Estimated Sales:$100-499.9 Million
Number Employees: 1,000-4,999
Brands:
  Pilgrima Pride

11340 Pilgrim's Pride
P.O.Box 519
Elberton, GA 30635-0519   706-283-3821
          Fax: 706-213-3770 800-262-7907
info@pilgrimspride.com   www.pilgrimspride.com

Chicken
  Manager: Skip James
  CEO: Basil Botha
  EVP/Chief Financial Officer: Deborah Battiston
  Vice President: Dan Emery
  Sales Director: Darla Knight
  Chief Operating Officer: J Clinton Rivers
  Plant Manager: Michael Buckerus
Estimated Sales:$500,000-$1 Million
Number Employees: 5-9
Brands:
  Pilgrims Pride

11341 Pilgrim's Pride Distribution Center
3420 Avenue F
Arlington, TX 76011-5243   817-640-5508
          info@pilgrimspride.com
          www.pilgrimspride.com
Processor and exporter of fresh and frozen chicken
  President: Knute Klingen
  Chairman: Lonnie Bo Pilgrim
  EVP/Chief Financial Officer: Richard Cogdill
  Vice President Corporate Communications: Gary Rhodes
  Director Corporate Communications: Ray Atkinson
  Chief Operating Officer: J Clinton Rivers
Number Employees: 50-99
Parent Co: Pilgrims Pride Corporation
Type of Packaging: Consumer, Food Service, Private Label, Bulk

11342 Pilgrim's Pride Distribution Center
1010 Pilgrim Street
Mt Pleasant, TX 75455   903-575-3731
          Fax: 903-575-3504 info@pilgrimspride.com
          www.pilgrimspride.com
Processor and exporter of fresh and frozen chicken
  President/CEO: O B Goolsby
  Chairman: Lonnie Bo Pilgrim
  EVP/Chief Financial Officer: Richard Cogdill
  Vice President Corporate Communications: Gary Rhodes
  Director Corporate Communications: Ray Atkinson
  Chief Operating Officer: J Clinton Rivers
  Plant Manager: Curt Beadle
Number Employees: 50-99
Parent Co: Pilgrims Pride Corporation
Type of Packaging: Consumer, Food Service, Private Label, Bulk

11343 Pilgrim's Pride Distribution Center
1972 S 4370 W Unit B
Salt Lake City, UT 84104   801-972-4114
          Fax: 801-974-0981 info@pilgrimspride.com
          www.pilgrimspride.com
Processor and exporter of fresh and frozen chicken
  Manager: Bob Rucker
  Chairman: Lonnie Bo Pilgrim
  EVP/Chief Financial Officer: Richard Cogdill
  Vice President Corporate Communications: Gary Rhodes
  Director Corporate Communications: Ray Atkinson
  Chief Operating Officer: J Clinton Rivers
Number Employees: 50-99
Parent Co: Pilgrims Pride Corporation
Type of Packaging: Consumer, Food Service, Private Label, Bulk

11344 Piller Sausages & Delicatessens
PO Box 338
Waterloo, ON N2J 4A4
Canada   519-743-1412
          Fax: 519-743-7111 www.pillers.com
Processor and exporter of sausage and processed meats
  President: William Huber, Jr.
Number Employees: 100-249
Type of Packaging: Consumer, Food Service, Private Label, Bulk

11345 Pillsbury
1 Red Devil Rd
Hannibal, MO 63401-6312   573-221-9420
          Fax: 573-248-0933 800-775-4777
          www.gmfcu.com

Manufacturer of soup, nacho chips, flour tortillas and taco shells and sauces
CEO: Kent Greff
Project Engineer: Bruce Athman
Plant Manager: Carmen Mazzei
Estimated Sales: $100+ Million
Number Employees: 500-999
Sq. footage: 500000
Parent Co: General Mills
Type of Packaging: Consumer

11346 Pillsbury
2803 NE Orchard Avenue
McMinnville, OR 97128-9378   503-472-5136
Fax: 503-472-1783   800-325-5439
Processor and exporter of frozen doughs and fresh and frozen baked goods including cakes, cookies, breads, rolls, doughnuts, etc
VP/Chief Customer Officer: Christian Berger
Plant Manager: Carolyn Wasson
Number Employees: 100
Sq. footage: 140000
Parent Co: General Mills
Type of Packaging: Food Service, Private Label, Bulk
Other Locations:
Pillsbury
Hazleton PA
Brands:
Hazelwood Farms Bakeries

11347 Pillsbury
3500 Empire Boulevard SW
Atlanta, GA 30354-2638   800-767-4466
Processor of frozen dough
Plant Manager: Gordon Powell
Number Employees: 100-249
Parent Co: General Mills
Type of Packaging: Bulk

11348 Pillsbury
2132 Downyflake Lane
Allentown, PA 18103-4794   610-797-5947
Fax: 610-797-3114   sthierry@diageo-na.com
www.pillsbury.com / www.generalmills.com
Manufacturer of frozen products such as; cookie dough, pie crust, biscuits, breads, rolls and pizza
Plant Manager: John Cervenak
Estimated Sales: $100+ Million
Number Employees: 50
Parent Co: General Mills
Type of Packaging: Consumer, Private Label
Brands:
PILLSBURY

11349 Pillsbury
300 Middlesex Avenue
Medford, MA 02155-5037   781-306-0120
800-289-2732
Processor of par-baked bread
National Accounts Manager: Gary Yarbrough
Number Employees: 100-249

11350 Pillsbury
PO Box 9452
Minneapolis, MN 55440   800-775-4777
Fax: 763-764-8330   800-845-3103
www.pillsbury.com
Processor of bakery mixes and cake flour
General Manager: Alan Rodrigues
Mix Plant Manager: Ray Beckman
Number Employees: 100-249
Parent Co: General Mills
Type of Packaging: Consumer, Food Service, Bulk

11351 Pillsbury Bakeries & Food Services
246 Cree Road
Sherwood Park, AB T8A 3X8
Canada   780-464-1544
Fax: 780-467-5314
Processor and exporter of frozen graham, pie and tart shells
Sales Manager: Bob Grbinsky
Number Employees: 50-99
Type of Packaging: Consumer, Food Service

11352 Pillsbury Canada Limited
675 Cochrane Drive
Suite 700
Markham, ON L3R 0M7
Canada   905-513-8500
Fax: 905-513-9891   800-745-4777
www.pillsbury.z

Manufacturer of pizza, frozen and prepared dough, frozen fruit, taco shells, Mexican dinner kits, seasoning, meat spreads and canned and frozen vegetables including green and wax beans, corn and peas
VP Sales: Blair Ruelens
Parent Co: General Mills
Type of Packaging: Consumer, Food Service

11353 Pillsbury Frozen Foods
2200 Lithonia Industrial Boulevard
Lithonia, GA 30058-4614   770-482-5092
Processor of baking shells and cookies
Sales/Marketing Executive: Cindy Barker
Plant Manager: Vince Venne
Purchasing Agent: Dan Shubert
Number Employees: 100-249
Parent Co: General Mills
Type of Packaging: Consumer

11354 Pilot Meat & Sea Food Company
PO Box 218
Galena, IL 61036-0218   319-556-0760
Fax: 319-556-4131
Meat and seafood
President: Randy Sirk

11355 Pinahs Company
N8w22100 Johnson Dr
Waukesha, WI 53186-1866   262-547-2447
Fax: 262-547-2047   800-967-2447
info@pinahs.com   www.pinahs.com
Manufacturer of Bread and corn based snack chips
Owner: Chris Pinahs
Director Finance: Bill Bruggink
R&D: Peter Sardina
Quality Control: Vicki Dickerson
Director Sales/Marketing: Paul Pearson
Human Resource/Customer Service: Barb Pomierski
Purchasing Manager: Jeff Millar
Estimated Sales: $3 Million
Number Employees: 20-49
Sq. footage: 59000
Type of Packaging: Consumer, Food Service, Private Label, Bulk
Brands:
PINAH'S

11356 Pindar Vineyards
P.O.Box 332
Peconic, NY 11958-0332   631-734-6200
Fax: 631-734-6205 www.pindar.net
Wines
Owner: Herodotus Damianos
VP Sales: Michael Sean Ryan
Estimated Sales: $5-10 Million
Number Employees: 20-49
Brands:
Spring Splendor
Summer Blush

11357 Pine Point Fisherman's Co-Op
P.O.Box 2247
Scarborough, ME 04070-2247   207-883-3588
Fax: 207-883-6772 lobster@maine.rr.com
lobsterco-op.com
A lobsterman's cooperative with a seasonal retail market restaurant and wholesale distribution on the east coast.
Estimated Sales: $ 1 - 3 Million
Number Employees: 5-9

11358 Pine Point Seafood
350 Pine Point Rd
Scarborough, ME 04074-9236   207-883-4701
Fax: 207-883-4797 www.maine-lobster.com
Manufacturer of lobster, lobster tails, clams and steaks
President: B Michael Thurlow
Estimated Sales: $ 1 - 3 Million
Number Employees: 5-9

11359 Pine Ridge Winery
P.O.Box 2508
Yountville, CA 94599-2508   707-253-7500
Fax: 707-253-1493 800-575-9777
info@pineridgewinery.com
www.pineridgewinery.com

Wines
President: George Schlepeler
Marketing Director: Anna Belle
CFO: Eric Grams
CEO: Erle Martin
CFO: David Workman
Sales Director: Nancy Andrus
Public Relations: Sarah Burgess
Operations Manager: Kelvin Morasch
Winemaker: Stacy Clark
Estimated Sales: $ 20 - 50 Million
Number Employees: 50-99
Brands:
Pine Ridge Winery

11360 Pine River Cheese & Butter Company
RR 4
Ripley, ON N0G 2R0
Canada   519-395-2638
Fax: 519-395-4066 800-265-1175
info@pinerivercheese.com
www.pinerivercheese.com
Processor of cheese including cheddar, colby, mozzarella, Monterey Jack, etc
President: Ian Courtney
Number Employees: 30
Sq. footage: 24000
Type of Packaging: Consumer, Bulk

11361 Pine River Pre-Pack
10134 Pine River Rd
Newton, WI 53063-9613   920-726-4216
www.pineriver.com
Manufacturer and processor of cold pack cheese food and pasteurized cheese spreads; also chocolate confections
CEO: Philip Lindemann
Marketing Associate: Mary Lindenann
Estimated Sales: $3004699
Number Employees: 10-19
Sq. footage: 23700
Type of Packaging: Consumer, Private Label
Brands:
PINE RIVER

11362 (HQ)Pine State Creamery Company
500 Glenwood Avenue
Raleigh, NC 27628-6508   919-828-7401
Fax: 919-664-8362
Dairy
President/CEO: John Wiley
Director Manufacturing: L Aldrich
Estimated Sales: $ 100-500 Million
Number Employees: 100

11363 Pines International
P.O.Box 1107
Lawrence, KS 66044-8107   785-841-6016
Fax: 785-841-1252 800-697-4637
pines@wheatgrass.com www.wheatgrass.com
Grower, processor, and exporter of alfalfa, wheat grass, barley grass, rye grass, and oat grass powders and tablets
President: Ron Seibold
CEO: Steve Malone
Sales/Marketing: Allen Levine
Purchasing Director: Jeff Richards
Estimated Sales: $3,635,158
Number Employees: 10-19
Sq. footage: 40000
Type of Packaging: Consumer, Private Label, Bulk
Brands:
MIGHTY GREENS
PINES

11364 Pinnacle Food Products
750 Oakwood Rd
Lake Zurich, IL 60047-1519   847-438-1598
Fax: 847-438-1236
Dry food manufacturer, primarily drink mixes, ingredients, etc.
President: Andy Burke
Estimated Sales: $ 20 - 50 Million
Number Employees: 100-249
Type of Packaging: Food Service, Private Label, Bulk

11365 (HQ)Pinnacle Foods Group
6 Executive Campus # 100
Cherry Hill, NJ 08002-4130   856-969-7100
        Fax: 856-969-7303 877-852-7424
        info@pinnaclefoods.com
        www.pinnaclefoods.com
Manufacturer of pickles, soups, barbeque sauces,
syrup, pancake mix, baking mixes, bagels, frozen
seafood, frozen skillet meals and frozen pizza
    Chairman/CEO: C Dean Metropoulos
    EVP/CFO: N Michael Dion
    CEO: Jeffrey P Ansell
    Business Director, Foodservice: Keith Kandt
Estimated Sales:$511.2 Million
Number Employees: 100-249
Type of Packaging: Consumer
Brands:
    CELESTE
    CHEF'S CHOICE
    COUNTRY KITCHEN
    DUNCAN HINES
    GREAT STARTS
    HUNGRY-MAN
    LENDER'S
    LOG CABIN
    MRS BUTTERWORTH'S
    MRS PAUL'S
    OPEN PIT
    SWANSON
    VAN DE KAMP'S
    VLASIC

11366 Pino's Pasta Veloce
1903 Clove Road
Staten Island, NY 10304-1607   718-273-6660
        Fax: 718-720-5906
Processor of pasta sauce; manufacturer of pasta
heaters for portion control and food preparation
    Manager Marketing: Joe Klaus
    VP Operations: Al Cappillo
Estimated Sales:$ 2.5-5 Million
Number Employees: 1-4
Parent Co: AEI
Type of Packaging: Consumer, Food Service
Brands:
    Pino's Pasta Veloce

11367 Pinocchio Italian Ice Cream Company
12814 160 3rd Street
Edmonton, AB T5V 1Z6
Canada   780-455-1905
        Fax: 780-455-1906
        sales@pinocchioicecream.com
        www.pinocchioicecream.com
Processor of frozen desserts including ice cream and
Italian sorbets
    President: Salvatore Ursino
    VP: Tom Ursino
    Director/Sales Manager: Thomas Ursino
Number Employees: 1-4
Type of Packaging: Consumer, Food Service
Brands:
    Pinocchio

11368 Pinter's Packing Plant
193 S Front St
Dorchester, WI 54425-9559   715-654-5444
        www.pinterspacking.com
Processor of meat including steak, roast, sausage
and buffalo
    President: Daniel Pinter
    VP: Alan Pinter
Estimated Sales:$180000
Number Employees: 5-9
Sq. footage: 6400
Type of Packaging: Consumer

11369 Pinty's Premium Foods
15-17 Seapark Drive
St. Catharines, ON L2M 6S5
Canada   905-688-2412
        Fax: 905-688-1222 800-263-7223
        Retailsales@pintys.com www.pintys.com
Processor of poultry products including chicken fry-
ers, nuggets, burgers, meat balls, wings, stuffed
breasts and pierogies; also, pizza fingers
    Chairman: Fred Williamson
    Vice-Chairman: Ken Thorpe
    VP Marketing: Jon Pintwala
    Sales Manager: W Greer
Number Employees: 100-249
Type of Packaging: Consumer, Food Service

Brands:
    Pinty's

11370 Pintys Delicious Foods
RR 1
Port Colborne, ON L3K 5V3
Canada   905-835-8575
        Fax: 905-834-5093 800-263-9710
Processor and exporter of poultry
    President/Owner: Phil Kudelka
    CEO: Aba Vanderlaan
    CFO: Patricia Bowman
    VP Operations: Jack Vanderlaan
    Sales: Greg Fox
    General Manager: Doug Bowman
Number Employees: 100-249
Sq. footage: 90000
Type of Packaging: Food Service, Bulk
Brands:
    PINTYS DELICIOUS FOODS

11371 Pioneer Confections
1254 W Schubert Ave
Chicago, IL 60614-1247   773-281-6100
        Fax: 773-281-5812
Processor of confectionery products including choc-
olate peanut buttercups, vanilla creams, chocolate
creams, taffy, lollypops and solid chocolates
    President: Russ C Lyman
Estimated Sales:$ 20 - 50 Million
Number Employees: 50-99
Type of Packaging: Consumer

11372 Pioneer Dairy
214 Feeding Hills Road
Southwick, MA 01077-9589   413-569-6132
        Fax: 413-569-3762
Manufacturer of Milk, cream, ice cream
    President: A Colson
    Vice President: Paul Colson
Estimated Sales:$5-10 Million
Number Employees: 30
Number of Brands: 2
Type of Packaging: Food Service, Private Label,
Bulk
Brands:
    MEADOWBROOK CREAMERY
    PIONEER DAIRY

11373 Pioneer Foods Industries
P.O.Box 490
Eudora, AR 71640-0490   870-355-2506
        Fax: 870-355-2507 www.producersrice.com
Soups
    Manager: Jodie Faircloth
*Estimated Sales:*Under $500,000
Number Employees: 10-19

11374 (HQ)Pioneer French Baking
512 Rose Ave
Venice, CA 90291-2606   310-392-4128
        Fax: 310-392-7845
        webmaster@pioneerbakery.com
        www.pioneerbakery.com
Processor of French baked goods including sour-
dough bread; also, wholesale delivery to in-store
bakeries.
    President: Jack Garacochea
Number Employees: 100-249
Sq. footage: 110000
Type of Packaging: Consumer, Food Service, Pri-
vate Label
Brands:
    Goldminer Sourdough
    Pioneer Sourdough

11375 Pioneer Frozen Foods
627 Big Stone Gap Rd
Duncanville, TX 75137-2223   972-298-4281
        Fax: 972-298-0578
Biscuits
    President: Chuck Hanson
Estimated Sales:$ 50-100 Million
Number Employees: 100-249
Brands:
    Pioneer

11376 Pioneer Growers Cooperative
PO Box 490
Belle Glade, FL 33430-0490   561-996-5561
        Fax: 561-996-5703 www.pioneergrowers.com
Processor and exporter of produce including Chi-
nese cabbage, carrots, celery, corn and radishes
    Vice President: Gene Duff

Type of Packaging: Consumer, Bulk
Brands:
    Frontier
    Team
    Well's Ace

11377 Pioneer Live Shrimp
2801 Meyers Road
Oak Brook, IL 60523-1623   847-718-0088
        Fax: 312-226-7376
Shrimp
    President: David Wong

11378 Pioneer Marketing International
188 Westhill Drive
Los Gatos, CA 95032-5032   408-356-4990
        Fax: 408-356-2795 edesoto@jps.net

www.pioneer.com/usa/services/marketing_services
Export and import broker of confectionery products,
snacks and private label items. Consultant in market-
ing, sales and product promotion in England and
Africa
    Partner: Russ Tritomo
    Director Sales: Ed DeSoto
Estimated Sales:$ 1 - 5 Million
Number Employees: 4

11379 Pioneer Nutritional Formulas
304 Shelburne Center Rd
Shelburne Falls, MA 01370-9779   413-625-0169
        Fax: 413-625-9619 800-458-8483
        customerservice@pioneernutritional.com
        www.pioneernutritional.com
Manufacturer of nutritional supplements
    Manager: Sara Rowan
    CEO: Jim Lemkin
Estimated Sales:$ 3 - 5 Million
Number Employees: 10-19
Number of Brands: 1
Number of Products: 23
Brands:
    PIONEER

11380 Pioneer Packing Company
510 Napoleon Rd
Bowling Green, OH 43402-4821   419-352-5283
        Fax: 419-352-7330 wcontris@aol.com
Manufacturer and exporters of Canadian bacon,
smoked meats and pork sausage material
    President: William Contris
Estimated Sales:$5 Million
Number Employees: 20-49
Sq. footage: 50000
Type of Packaging: Consumer, Bulk
Brands:
    AMISH
    COUNTRY
    PIONEER

11381 Pioneer Snacks
30777 Northwestern Highway
Suite 300
Farmington Hills, MI 48334-2594   248-862-1990
        Fax: 248-862-1991 info@pioneersnacks.com
        www.pioneersnacks.com
Meat snacks including smoked meat sticks, beef
jerky, hunter sausage, kippered beef steak, meat &
cheese and turkey jerky.
    Marketing Manager: Craig Thomas
Type of Packaging: Consumer
Brands:
    HOG WILD PORK JERKY

11382 Pioneer Snacks
1829 1st Ave
Mankato, MN 56001-3023   507-388-1661
        Fax: 507-388-5927 www.pioneersnacks.com
Snacks, beef jerky
    President: Robert George
    Maintenance Manager: David Mamagren
    Plant Manager: Rob Andrews
Estimated Sales:$ 50-100 Million
Number Employees: 100-249
Brands:
    Pioneer Snacks

11383 Piper Processing
430 N Main St
Andover, OH 44003-9665   440-293-7170
Processor of beef and pork
    Owner: Terry Orahood
Estimated Sales:$140,000
Number Employees: 1-4

Type of Packaging: Consumer, Bulk

11384 Pippin Snack Pecans
P.O.Box 3330
Albany, GA 31706-3330   229-432-9316
Fax: 229-435-0056   800-554-6887
pipsani@bellsouth.com
Processor and exporter of natural shelled and in-shell pecans including flavored, honey and toasted, amaretto, hickory-smoked, onion-garlic, rum and chocolate covered for gifts; for the wholesale and fundraising markets
Owner: C M Pippin Jr
General Manager: C Pippin, Jr.
Estimated Sales: Less than $500,000
Number Employees: 1-4
Sq. footage: 20000
Type of Packaging: Consumer, Food Service, Private Label, Bulk
Brands:
Pippin Snack

11385 Pippin Snack Pecans Incorporated
P.O.Box 3330
Albany, GA 31706-3330   229-432-9316
Fax: 229-435-0056
Pecans
Owner: C M Pippin Jr
Estimated Sales: $15 Million
Number Employees: 50-99
Type of Packaging: Consumer, Food Service, Bulk

11386 Piqua Pizza Supply Company
1727 W High St
Piqua, OH 45356-9325   937-773-0699
Fax: 937-773-6096   800-521-4442
Processor of frozen pizza crust
President: Diana Creager
VP: Paul Creager
Production Manager: Tom Fahestrock
Estimated Sales: $ 10 - 20 Million
Number Employees: 20-49
Type of Packaging: Consumer, Food Service, Private Label, Bulk
Brands:
Diana's

11387 Pita King Bakery
2210 37th St
Everett, WA 98201-4509   425-258-4040
Fax: 425-258-3366
salesinfo@pitakingbakery.com
www.pitakingbakery.com
Pita Bread
President: Hauss Alaeddine
CEO: Jason Aladdine
Number Employees: 10-19
Sq. footage: 10000
Brands:
PITA KING

11388 Pita Products
30777 Northwestern Highway
Suite 3200
Farmington Hills, MI 48334-2549   734-367-2700
Fax: 734-367-2701   800-600-7482
comments@pitasnax.com   www.pitasnax.com
Baked pita chips
Type of Packaging: Consumer

11389 Pitman & Sons
2103 Atlantic Blvd
Jacksonville, FL 32207-3570   904-768-6888
Fax: 904-768-6888
Manufacturer of produce
President: Jere Pitman
Estimated Sales: $150 Million
Number Employees: 20-49
Type of Packaging: Consumer, Bulk

11390 Pittsburgh Brewing Company
3340 Liberty Avenue
Pittsburgh, PA 15201-1394   412-682-7400
Fax: 412-682-2379
info@pittsburghbrewingco.com
www.pittsburgbrewingco.com
Manufacturer and exporter of alcoholic and nonalcoholic beer
Owner/Brewer: Joseph Piccirilli
Marketing Director: Chris Antone
VP Sales: Tony Ferraro
Brewmaster: Michael Carota
Plant Manager: Bill St Leger

Estimated Sales: $100 Million
Number Employees: 175
Number of Brands: 12
Number of Products: 12
Sq. footage: 450000
Parent Co: Bond Brewing Holdings
Type of Packaging: Consumer
Brands:
AMERICAN
AMERICAN LIGHT
AUGASTINER DARK
AUGASTINER LARGER
AUGASTINER
IC COOLER
IC LIGHT
IRON CITY
MUSTANG
OLD GERMAN
PENNS BEST
PENNS BEST LIGHTING
SIERRA
SIERRA ICE
SIERRA LIGHT

11391 Pittsburgh Snax & Nut Company
2517 Penn Ave # 19
Pittsburgh, PA 15222-4603   412-391-4444
Fax: 412-391-2209   800-404-6887
pghsnax@aol.com
Manufacturer and importer of nuts, dried fruit, trail mixes and confections
Owner: Richard Cuneo
President: Morgan Donato
Estimated Sales: $25 Million
Number Employees: 20-49
Sq. footage: 25000
Type of Packaging: Consumer, Food Service, Private Label, Bulk
Brands:
Earth Delights
Earth Treats
McCunes
Nuts About Pittsburgh

11392 Pittsfield Rye Bakery
P.O.Box 637
Pittsfield, MA 01202-0637   413-443-9141
Fax: 413-499-5331   rickrobbins222@msn.com
Manufacturer of bread, rolls and sweet goods
President: Arnold Robbins
Owner: Linda Robbins
Estimated Sales: $ 5 - 10 Million
Number Employees: 5-9

11393 Pizza Products
38300 W 10 Mile Rd
Farmington Hills, MI 48335-2804   248-474-1601
Fax: 248-474-1608   800-600-7482
comments@pitasnax.com   www.pizzahut.com
Low fat seasoned pizza snack
Manager: Dave Sabol
Marketing Director: Norman Wainwright
Estimated Sales: Below $ 5 Million
Number Employees: 1-4

11394 Pizzas of Eight
1915 Cherokee St
St Louis, MO 63118-3218   314-865-1460
Fax: 314-865-2449   800-422-2901
contact@pizzasofeight.com
www.pizzasofeight.com
Manufacturer of pizza products including dough, cheese and sauce, equipment
President: Chuck McMillen
Estimated Sales: $5-10 Million
Number Employees: 10-19
Number of Brands: 3
Number of Products: 15

11395 Pizzey's Milling & Baking Company
PO Box 132
Angusville, NB R0J 0A0
Canada   204-773-2575
Fax: 204-773-2317   800-804-6433
linda@pizzeys.com   www.pizzeys.com
Processor and exporter of whole and milled flaxseed
President: Linda Pizzey
Managing Partner: Glenn Pizzey
Number Employees: 20-49
Sq. footage: 40000
Parent Co: Glanbia Nutritionals
Type of Packaging: Consumer, Food Service, Private Label, Bulk

11396 Pizzey's NutritionalsA Granbia Company
5951 McKee Road, Suite 100
Fitchburg, WI 53719   608-316-8535
Fax: 608-316-8504   877-804-6444
sales@pizzeys.com   www.pizzeys.com
North America's largest processor of flaxseed ingredients. Created Omega-3 solutions for a range of applications.
R&D: Jessica Marshall
QC: Grant Penn
Marketing: Eric Borchardt
Sales: Jim Lees
Production: Ty Konkright
Plant Manager: Mark Stainer
Parent Co: Granbia Nutritionals
Type of Packaging: Consumer, Private Label, Bulk
Brands:
BEVGRAD
CHOICEGRAD
FORTIGRAD
NUTRIGRAD
PREMIUMGRAD
SELECTGRAD
ULTRAGRAD

11397 Placerville Fruit Growers Association
4600 Missouri Flat Rd
Placerville, CA 95667-6843   530-622-2640
Fax: 530-622-2649   pfgastore@innercite.com
Processor and packer of pears and apples
Manager: John Caswell
Vice President: John Caswell
Estimated Sales: $360000
Number Employees: 1-4
Type of Packaging: Consumer, Food Service, Private Label, Bulk
Brands:
Moutain Bartlett
Placerville Maid

11398 Plaidberry Company
830 Mimosa Avenue
Vista, CA 92081-8146   760-727-5403
dennisdickson@cs.com
www.plaidberry.com
Jams, muffins, pie and cake fillings, juices, confections, yogurt bases, etc
President/Owner: Dennis Dickson
Estimated Sales: Below $ 5 Million
Number Employees: 4
Number of Products: 6
Sq. footage: 37000
Type of Packaging: Consumer, Bulk

11399 Plains Cooperative Oil Mill
P.O.Box 841
Lubbock, TX 79408-0841   806-747-3434
Fax: 806-744-3221 www.pycoindustries.com
Processor of cottonseed oil
President: Gail Kring
Vice President: Gail Kring
Marketing Manager: Robert Lacy
Estimated Sales: $100+ Million
Number Employees: 100-249
Type of Packaging: Consumer

11400 Plains Creamery
P.O.Box 30
Amarillo, TX 79105-0030   806-374-0385
Fax: 806-374-0396 www.plainsdairy.com
Processor of dairy products including ice cream, milk and cream
President: Walter Garlington
Sales Manager: Frank Jones
Estimated Sales: $ 20 - 50 Million
Number Employees: 100-249
Type of Packaging: Consumer

11401 Plains Dairy Products
P.O.Box 30
Amarillo, TX 79105-0030   806-374-0385
Fax: 806-374-0396   800-365-5608
customerservice@plainsdairy.com
www.plainsdairy.com
Milk and milk products
President/CEO: Walter Garlington
R & D: Jeff Covington
CFO: Billy Lindenborn
Marketing Director: Joe Holland

Estimated Sales: $ 50-75 Million
Number Employees: 100-249

11402 (HQ)Plainview Milk ProductsCooperative
130 2nd St SW
Plainview, MN 55964-1394   507-534-3872
　　Fax: 507-534-3992 dmoe@plainviewmilk.com
　　　　　www.plainviewmilk.com
Processor of butter, powdered whey and dry milk including nonfat, whole and buttermilk. Whey protein concentrates, custom agglomeration and spray drying
　　Manager: Dallas Moe
　　Controller: Janna Van Rooyen
　　Sales Manager: Darrell Hanson
　　General Manager: Dallas Moe
　　Plant Manager: Donny Schreiber
Estimated Sales: $ 65 - 75 Million
Number Employees: 50-99
Sq. footage: 180000
Type of Packaging: Consumer, Food Service, Private Label, Bulk
Other Locations:
　　Plainview Milk ProductsCoop.
　　Plainview MN
Brands:
　　Greenwood Prairie

11403 Plainville Farms
7830 Plainville Rd
Memphis, NY 13112   315-689-6384
　　Fax: 315-689-1298 800-724-0206
　　　　mail@plainvillefarms.com
　　　　www.plainvillefarms.com
Turkey products
　　President: Robert W Bitz
　　CEO: Robert W Bitz
　　CFO: Mark Bitz
Estimated Sales: $ 20-50 Million
Number Employees: 100-249
Brands:
　　Heart Liteo
　　Veggie Growno

11404 Plam Vineyards & Winery
3125 Oxbow Place
Solvang, CA 93463-3005   805-688-4446
　　Fax: 805-693-8344 800-978-2633
　　　　ken@plam.com www.plam.com
Wines
　　Co-Owner: Ken Plam
　　Co-Owner: Shirley Plam
　　VP: Shirley Plam
Estimated Sales: Below $ 5 Million
Number Employees: 2
Type of Packaging: Private Label
Brands:
　　Plam Vineyards

11405 Plantation Candies
4224 Bethlehem Pike
Telford, PA 18969-1199   215-723-6810
　　Fax: 215-723-6834 888-678-6468
　　　　chuck@plantationcandies.com
　　　　www.plantationcandies.com
Processor and exporter of hard and filled candy; also, white mint chocolate
　　President: Charles Crawford
　　VP: John Crawford
Estimated Sales: $1500000
Number Employees: 5-9
Type of Packaging: Consumer, Food Service, Private Label, Bulk
Brands:
　　Chocolate Straws
　　Dainties
　　Golden Crunchies
　　Jinglebits
　　Misty Mints

11406 Plantation Coffee
9583 Elk Grove Florin Road
Elk Grove, CA 95624-1803   916-686-2633
　　Fax: 916-686-2755 coffee@plantationcoffee.com
　　　　www.plantationcoffee.com
Coffee
　　President: Dan Davis
　　VP: Dave Davis
　　Production Manager: Richard Walters
Estimated Sales: $ 5-10 Million
Number Employees: 30
Type of Packaging: Private Label

11407 Plantation Foods
P.O.Box 20788
Waco, TX 76702-0788   254-799-6211
　　Fax: 254-412-3409 800-733-0900
　　　　www.cargill.com
Processor and exporter of turkey and chicken
　　Human Resources: Lee Ray
　　VP Marketing/Sales: Jim Jandrain
　　Administration Manager: Carol Lowe
Estimated Sales: $100+ Million
Number Employees: 500-999
Parent Co: Cargill Foods
Type of Packaging: Consumer, Food Service, Private Label, Bulk
Brands:
　　Plantation

11408 Plantation Pecan Company
8695 Highway 65
Waterproof, LA 71375   318-749-5188
　　Fax: 318-749-5535 800-477-3226
　　　　sales@plantation-pecan.com
　　　　www.plantationpecan.com
Distributors of pecan, pies, pralines and fudges
　　President: Harrison Miller
　　Co-Owner: Carol Miller
Estimated Sales: Less than $500,000
Number Employees: 1-4
Brands:
　　Plantation Pecan

11409 Plantation Products
202 S Washington St
Norton, MA 02766-3326   508-285-5800
　　Fax: 508-285-7333 www.plantationproducts.com/
Processor of vegetable seeds, seed packets and seed starting products
　　President: Joseph Raffaele
　　VP: D Sbordon
Estimated Sales: $ 20 - 50 Million
Number Employees: 20-49

11410 Planters LifeSavers Company
4020 Planters Rd
Fort Smith, AR 72908-8438   479-648-0100
　　Fax: 479-646-6842 www.kraft.com
Manufacturer and exporter of nuts including cashews, almonds, peanuts, pistachios, pecans, walnuts, mixed and flavored
　　Manager: Keith Nix
　　CEO: Roger Deromedi
　　Plant Manager: Wayne Parrish
Estimated Sales: $100+ Million
Number Employees: 250-499
Parent Co: Nabisco
Type of Packaging: Consumer

11411 Plantextrakt
119 Cherry Hill Rd # 100
Parsippany, NJ 07054-1114   973-683-1411
　　Fax: 973-257-9351 cswatosch@plantextakt.com
　　　　www.atm1.com
　　President: Bob Morrell
　　Vice President: Werner Baer
　　Operations Manager: Christina Lianos
Estimated Sales: Under $500,000
Number Employees: 1-4

11412 Plantextrakt/Martin Bower
100 Pavonia Avenue
Suite 301
Jersey City, NJ 07310   201-659-3100
　　Fax: 201-659-3180 skim@planetextrakt-inc.com
　　　　www.plantextrakt.com
Produce and process raw materials sold to manufacturers tea, decaf tea & botanicals-core products and tea & botanical extracts.
　　President: Richard Enticott
　　CEO: Werner Baez
Estimated Sales: $20 Million
Number Employees: 3
Type of Packaging: Consumer
Brands:
　　Life Savers
　　Planters

11413 Plastic Container Corporation
2508 N Oak St
Urbana, IL 61802-7207   217-352-2722
　　Fax: 217-352-2822 jgentles@netpcc.com
　　　　www.netpcc.com
Plastic Container Corporation (PCC) manufactures plastic bottles for numerous industries including that of food and beverage. PCC utilizes extrusion blow molding machines to produce containers from any common extrusion blow moldingmaterial.
　　CEO: Ronald Rhoades
　　Sales Manager: Jo Ellen Gentles
　　Sales Representative: John Foote
Sq. footage: 250000
Type of Packaging: Consumer

11414 Platte Valley Creamery
1005 E Overland
Scottsbluff, NE 69361-3702   308-632-4225
Processor of dairy products including ice cream and frozen desserts
　　President: Ron Smith
Estimated Sales: $ 1 - 3 Million
Number Employees: 1-4
Type of Packaging: Consumer

11415 Plaza House Coffee
339 Lincoln Avenue
Staten Island, NY 10306-5001   718-979-9555
　　Fax: 718-667-4394 plazahouse@aol.com
Coffee
　　President: Salvatore Rosso
Estimated Sales: Less than $500,000
Number Employees: 1-4

11416 Plaza Sweets
521 Waverly Ave
Mamaroneck, NY 10543-2235   914-698-0233
　　　　Fax: 914-698-3712
　　customerservice@plazasweetsbakery.com
　　　　www.plazasweetsbakery.com
Processor and exporter of cakes including cognac pumpkin cheese, apple crunch and banana coconut; also, cookies
　　President: Rodney Holder
Estimated Sales: $4300000
Number Employees: 20-49
Type of Packaging: Consumer, Food Service
Brands:
　　Plaza Sweets

11417 Plaza de Espana Gourmet
100 Kings Point Drive
Apt 1004
Sunny Isles Beach, FL 33160-4729   305-971-3468
　　Fax: 305-971-5004 sales@blueskyfoods.com
　　　　www.foodfromspain.com
Specialty food manufacturer and importer of gourmet Spanish foods, extra virgin olive oil, artichokes, asparagus, red roasted piquillo peppers, wine and serrano ham; company vineyards in Rioja, Spain
　　President: Jesus Metias, Sr.
　　Vice President: Serafina Atalaya
　　Marketing Director: Jesus Metias, Jr.
Estimated Sales: $ 2.5-5 Million
Number Employees: '5-9
Parent Co: Plaza De Espana Gourmet Foods
Type of Packaging: Consumer, Food Service, Private Label, Bulk
Brands:
　　Cielo Azul
　　Plaza De Espana
　　Vega Fina
　　Vega Metias

11418 Pleasant Grove Farms
5072 Pacific Ave
Pleasant Grove, CA 95668-9719   916-655-3391
　　　　Fax: 916-655-3699
Grower, processor and exporter of organic almonds, wheat, beans, popcorn and rice
　　President: Thomas Sills
　　VP Sales: Edward Sills
Estimated Sales: $1100000
Number Employees: 5-9
Number of Products: 9
Sq. footage: 10000
Parent Co: Sills Farms
Type of Packaging: Bulk

11419 Pleasant Valley Wine Company
8260 Pleasant Valley Rd
Hammondsport, NY 14840-9514   607-569-6111
　　Fax: 607-569-6135 info@pleasantvalleywine.com
　　　　www.pleasantvalleywine.com
Manufacturer of wines, champagnes, ports and sherries
　　President: Mike Doyle

Estimated Sales:$19 Million
Number Employees: 50-99
Sq. footage: 480000
Type of Packaging: Consumer, Food Service, Private Label, Bulk
Brands:
  Great Western
  Millennium
  Pleasant Valley

11420 Pleasant View Dairy
2625 Highway Ave
Highland, IN 46322-1614   219-838-0155
    Fax: 219-838-1801 www.pleasantviewdairy.com
Processor of dairy products including milk, buttermilk and sour cream
    President: Kenneth Leep
*Estimated Sales:*Less than $500,000
Number Employees: 20-49
Sq. footage: 40000
Type of Packaging: Consumer

11421 Pleasoning Gourmet Seasonings
2418 South Ave
La Crosse, WI 54601-6221   608-787-1030
    Fax: 608-787-1030   800-279-1614
pleason@pleasoning.com   www.pleasoning.com
Manufacturer of seasoning blends-low sodium
    President: Paul Boarman
    Vice President: Lenore Italiano
    Marketing Director: Kathy Boarman
Estimated Sales:$500,000-$1 Million
Number Employees: 1-4
Number of Brands: 1
Number of Products: 30
Sq. footage: 3000
Type of Packaging: Consumer, Food Service, Bulk
Brands:
  PLEASONING GOURMET SEASONING

11422 Plehn's Bakery
3940 Shelbyville Rd
St Matthews, KY 40207-3170   502-896-4438
    Fax: 502-897-9176 www.plehnsbakery.com
Manufacturer of breads, cookies, doughnuts, pastries, pies, cakes and ice cream
    President: Milton Hettinger
Estimated Sales:$6 Million
Number Employees: 20-49
Type of Packaging: Consumer

11423 Plentiful Pantry
PO Box 271097
Salt Lake City, UT 84127   801-977-9077
    Fax: 801-977-8202   800-727-8284
sales@plentifulpantrywholesale.com
    www.plentifulpantry.com
artisan pastas, desserts, dips, dishes, pasta, pasta salads, pizz akits, sauces, and soups
    President/Owner: Debbie Chidester
    VP: Jody Chidester
Estimated Sales:$2.9 Million
Number Employees: 13

11424 Plitt Company
1455 W Willow St
Chicago, IL 60642-1552   773-276-2200
    Fax: 773-276-8537   steve@plittfish.com
    www.plittfish.com
Wholesaler/distributor of fresh and frozen seafood
    President: Steven Wegh
Estimated Sales:$45000000
Number Employees: 100-249
Sq. footage: 110000

11425 Plochman
1333 N Boudreau Rd
Manteno, IL 60950-9384   815-468-3434
    Fax: 815-468-8755 www.plochman.com
Manufacturer of Mustards
    President/CEO: Terry Plochman
Estimated Sales:$6.9 Million
Number Employees: 50-99
Type of Packaging: Consumer, Food Service, Private Label, Bulk
Brands:
  KOSCIUSKO
  PLOCHMAN'S

11426 Plocky's Fine Snacks
15 Spinning Wheel Rd #314
Hinsdale, IL 60521   630-323-8888
    Fax: 630-323-8988   info@plockys.com
    www.plockys.com

specialty tortilla chips, gluten free hummus chips, gluten free hummus, kettle chips, dip strips, and salsa

11427 Pluester's Quality MeatCompany
P.O.Box 68
Hardin, IL 62047-0068   618-396-2224
Processor of meat products; slaughtering services available
    President: Irene Pluester
Estimated Sales:$ 1 - 3 Million
Number Employees: 1-4
Type of Packaging: Bulk

11428 Plum Creek Cellars
3708 G Rd
Palisade, CO 81526-9603   970-464-7586
    Fax: 970-464-0457 www.plumcreekwinery.com
Wines
    Manager: Jenne Baldwin
    Marketing Director: Sue Phillips
    Winemaker: Jenne Bladwin
*Estimated Sales:*Below $ 5 Million
Number Employees: 5-9
Brands:
  Plum Creek

11429 Plumlife Company
10 Northern Blvd
Newbury, MA 01951   978-462-8458
                www.plumlife.co.uk
Plumcakes, bakery products
    President: Jeffrey Freedman
    Founder: Peter Demers
    VP: Donald Laudano
*Estimated Sales:*Under $500,000
Number Employees: 1-4
Brands:
  Plumlife

11430 Plumrose
P.O.Box 1066
East Brunswick, NJ 08816-1066   732-257-6600
    Fax: 732-257-6644   800-526-4909
        consumer@plumroseusa.com
        www.plumroseusa.com
Processor, importer and exporter of sandwich meats and bacon.
    President: John Arends
    Vice President: James Amelang
    Sr. VP Sales: Don Meyer
    Sr. VP Production: Freddy Mortensen
Number Employees: 500-999
Sq. footage: 151443
Parent Co: Vestjyske Slagterier
Type of Packaging: Consumer, Food Service, Private Label, Bulk
Brands:
  DAK
  Danola
  Plumrose

11431 Plumrose USA
P.O.Box 160
Elkhart, IN 46515-0160   574-295-8190
    Fax: 574-294-5335 www.plumroseusa.com
Manufacturer of Pork and ham products
    President/CEO: John Arends
    CFO: Steven Hayman
    Quality Control: Harvey Weston
    VP Sales: Donald Meyer
    SVP Production: Freddy Mortensen
    General Manager: Mike Rozzano
    Plant Manager: Michael Wilfert
Estimated Sales:$295.6 Million
Number Employees: 100-249
Type of Packaging: Consumer, Food Service
Brands:
  DAK FOODS
  DANOLA
  PLUMROSE

11432 (HQ)Plumrose USA
P.O.Box 1066
East Brunswick, NJ 08816-1066   732-257-6600
    Fax: 732-257-6644   consumer@plumroseusa.com
        www.plumroseusa.com
Manufacturer and importer of meats including ham, salami, corned beef, also, cheese
    Owner/President: John Arends
    SVP Sales/Marketing: Don Meyer
Number Employees: 20-49
Parent Co: Danish Crown
Type of Packaging: Consumer, Food Service

Other Locations:
  Plumrose USA
  Council Bluffs IA
Brands:
  DAK
  DANOLA
  PLUMROSE

11433 Plyley's Candies
P.O.Box 8
Lagrange, IN 46761-0008   260-463-3351
    Fax: 260-463-7011   plyley@kuntrynet.com
        www.plyleyscandies.com
Chocolate, hard and sugar free candy
    President: Jack Plyley
    VP: Willard Plyley
*Estimated Sales:*Below $ 500,000
Number Employees: 10-19

11434 Plymouth Beef
415 W 14th Street
New York, NY 10014-1023   718-589-8600
                Fax: 718-860-8930
Processor and exporter of meat products including frozen and fresh beef: burgers, chopped, sliced and stew
    Owner: Jerry Sussman
    Vice President: Andrew Sussman
Type of Packaging: Consumer, Food Service

11435 Plymouth Cheese Counter
3240 County Road Pp
Plymouth, WI 53073-4152   920-892-8781
    Fax: 920-893-5986   888-607-9477
plychzct@excel.com   www.cheesecapital.com
Processor of cheese; gift baskets available
    Owner: Kris Hummes
Estimated Sales:$120000
Number Employees: 1-4
Type of Packaging: Consumer

11436 Plymouth Colony Winery
56 Pinewood Rd
Plymouth, MA 02360-5025   508-747-3334
                Fax: 508-747-4463
pcwinery@plymouthcolonywinery.com
        www.plymouthcolonywinery.com
Wines
    Owner: Charles Caranci
    General Manager: Lydia Carey
Estimated Sales:$ 1-2.5 Million
Number Employees: 1-4
Type of Packaging: Private Label
Brands:
  Plymouth Colony Winery

11437 Plymouth Lollipop Company
145 S Main St # B1-2
Carver, MA 02330-1527   508-866-7409
    Fax: 508-746-5893   800-777-0115
        plimothlollipop@msn.com
        www.plimothlollipop.com
Lollipops and confection ingredients
    President: Bill Johnson
*Estimated Sales:*Less than $500,000
Number Employees: 1-4
Brands:
  Plimoth Lollipop

11438 Po'okela Enterprises
75-5749 Kalawa St
Suite 201
Kailua Kona, HI 96740-1873   808-328-9753
    Fax: 808-328-9753   866-328-9753
    chrys@pookela.com   www.pookela.com
Processor of kona coffee, exporter of roasted kona coffee
    President: Chrystal Yamasaki
Estimated Sales:$100,000
Number Employees: 1-4
Type of Packaging: Private Label, Bulk
Brands:
  100% Kona Coffee
  Po'okela O Honaynau Estate Coffee

11439 Poche's Smokehouse
3015 Main Hwy # A
Breaux Bridge, LA 70517-6347   337-332-2108
    Fax: 337-332-5051   800-376-2437
        info@pochesmarket.com
        www.pochesmarket.com
Meat products
    Owner: Floyd Poche
    Owner: Karen Poche

Estimated Sales: $ 5 - 10 Million
Number Employees: 20-49

11440 Pocino Foods
14250 Lomitas Ave
City of Industry, CA 91746-3014   626-968-8000
Fax: 626-330-8779   800-345-0150
onlythebest@pocinofoods.com
www.pocinofoods.com
Prepared meats
President: Frank Pocino
Vice President: Jerry Pocino
Estimated Sales: $ 10 - 20 Million
Number Employees: 100-249
Type of Packaging: Private Label
Brands:
Pocino

11441 Pocono Cheesecake Factory
Hc 1 Box 95
Swiftwater, PA 18370-9723   570-839-6844
Fax: 570-839-6844 www.cheesecakefactory.net
Processor of cheesecakes
Manager: Alferd Johnson
Estimated Sales: $300,000
Number Employees: 10-19
Sq. footage: 3000
Brands:
Pocono Cheesecake

11442 Pocono Foods
P.O.Box 185
Mt Bethel, PA 18343-0185   570-897-5000
Fax: 570-897-7094 jheilman@noln.com
www.townsends.com
Manufacturer of Frozen chicken products, par-fried, battered, breaded
Manager: Robert Heilman
Vice President: James Heilman
COO: Chuck Dix
Estimated Sales: $17 Million
Number Employees: 50-99
Sq. footage: 40000
Parent Co: Townsends
Type of Packaging: Food Service, Private Label, Bulk
Brands:
A LA HENRI

11443 Pocono Mountain Bottling Company
57 W Chestnut Street
Wilkes Barre, PA 18705-1751   570-822-7695
Bottled spring water and carbonated beverages
President/Treasurer: Veronica Iskra
Estimated Sales: $580,000
Number Employees: 5
Brands:
POCONO MOUNTAIN

11444 Pocono Spring Company
P.O.Box 787
Mt Pocono, PA 18344-0787   570-839-2837
Fax: 570-839-6705   800-634-4584
Bottled water
President/CEO: Michael Melnic
CFO: Bill Fraser
Operations Manager: Tim Fitzgerald
Estimated Sales: $ 1-2.5 Million
Number Employees: 20-49
Brands:
Pocono Spring

11445 Pod Pack International
11800 Industriplex Blvd # 13
Baton Rouge, LA 70809-5185   225-752-1110
Fax: 225-752-1163 tmartin@podpack.com
www.podpack.com
Espresso coffee pods and filter pack. Coffee for hotels, restaurants, and airlines
Owner: Thomas Martin
Quality Control: Gary Kennington
Executive VP/COO: Tom Martin
Estimated Sales: $ 10-20 Million
Number Employees: 10-19
Type of Packaging: Consumer, Food Service, Private Label

11446 Point Adams Packing Company
P.O.Box 162
Hammond, OR 97121-0162   503-861-2226
Fax: 503-861-2312
Processor and exporter of frozen Pacific whiting
Manager: Tom Libby

Estimated Sales: $ 10-20 Million
Number Employees: 100-249
Parent Co: California Shellfish
Type of Packaging: Bulk

11447 Point Adolphus Seafoods
PO Box 63
Gustavus, AK 99826-0063   907-697-2246
Fax: 907-697-2246
Seafood

11448 (HQ)Point Group
1790 Highway A1a
Suite 103
Satellite Beach, FL 32937-5446   321-777-7408
Fax: 321-777-9777   888-272-1249
trump_co@digital.net   www.mmgstock.com
Manufacturer and exporter of coffee, tea and fruit extracts and fruit juices
President: Gary Trump
VP: Roger Koltermann
Type of Packaging: Consumer, Food Service, Private Label, Bulk
Brands:
Mingo Bay Beverages, Inc.

11449 Point Judith Fisherman'sCompany
P.O.Box 730
Narragansett, RI 02882-0730   401-782-1500
Fax: 401-782-1599
Fresh and frozen fish
Manager: Larry Rainey
Sales Manager: John McLaughlin
Estimated Sales: $ 10-20 Million
Number Employees: 50-99

11450 Point Saint George Fisheries
PO Box 1386
Santa Rosa, CA 95402-1386   707-542-9490
Seafood, seafood products
General Manager: Rich Amundson
Estimated Sales: $ 1-2.5 Million appx.
Number Employees: 1

11451 Poiret International
7866 Exeter Boulevard E
Tamarac, FL 33321-8797   954-724-3261
Fax: 954-721-0110 poiretinternatl@bellsouth.net
Processor, importer and exporter of preserves and organic jams
CEO/Purchasing: Ed Kerzner
CFO: Sheila Kerzner
Marketing Director: Stan Margulese
Plant Manager: Frank Bilisi
Number Employees: 20-49
Sq. footage: 25000
Parent Co: Siroper/E. Meurens SA
Type of Packaging: Consumer, Food Service, Private Label, Bulk
Brands:
DELICE
MEURENS
POIRET

11452 Poison Pepper Company
7310 E Shadywoods Court
Floral City, FL 34436-5732   888-539-5540
Fax: 727-894-5540 pure.poison@worldnet.att.net
Sauces
President: Tom Dahl

11453 Pokanoket Ostrich Farm
177 Gulf Rd
South Dartmouth, MA 02748-1514   508-992-6188
Fax: 508-993-5356 pokanokets@aol.com
www.pokanoket.com
Processor of portion control ostrich meat
President: Alan Weinshel
National Sales Manager: Mike Yokemick
Estimated Sales: Below $ 5 Million
Number Employees: 1-4
Type of Packaging: Consumer, Food Service, Private Label
Brands:
Pokanoket Farm

11454 Pokka Beverages
1201 Commerce Blvd
American Canyon, CA 94503-9611   707-557-0500
Fax: 707-557-0100   800-972-5962

Processor of fruit juices, canned iced coffee, iced tea and yogurt flavored drinks
Manager: Willie Peete
Vice President: James Bradney
Marketing Director: Jim Moffitt
Public Relations: Frank Witbeck
Operations Manager: Dan Hancock
Production Manager: Grey Sevey
Estimated Sales: $50000000
Number Employees: 100-249
Sq. footage: 250000
Parent Co: Pokka Corporation
Type of Packaging: Private Label
Brands:
Fruit Ole
Hawaiian Sun
Premium Tea
The Coffee

11455 Pokonobe Industries
2701 Ocean Park Blvd
Santa Monica, CA 90405-5200   310-392-1259
Fax: 310-392-3659   sales@pokonobe.com
www.pokonobe.com
Processor and exporter of expeller pressed, refined and unrefined oils including almond, grapeseed, soy, sunflower, sesame, walnut, corn, olive, linseed, wheat germ, safflower, etc. Rice bran oil, avocado oil, pumkinseed oil, flaxseedoil, hazelnut oil, macademia nut oil, coconut oil, palm oil
General Manager: Robert Grebler
Estimated Sales: $ 5 - 10 Million
Number Employees: 5-9
Type of Packaging: Bulk
Other Locations:
Pokonobe Industries
Santa Monica CA
Brands:
Pokonobe

11456 (HQ)Poland Spring Water
2767 E Imperial Highway
Suite 100
Brea, CA 92821-6713   866-676-1672
800-950-9396
www.polandspring.com
Manufacturer of distilled, sparkling, spring and bottled water
President/CEO Nestle Waters: Kim Jeffrey
Estimated Sales: 1+ Tillion
Number Employees: 250-499
Type of Packaging: Consumer, Private Label

11457 Poland Spring Water
P.O.Box 2313
Greenwich, CT 06836-2313   203-531-4100
Fax: 203-863-0572 www.arrowheadwater.com
Processor, importer and exporter of spring water
President/CEO: Kim Jeffrey
Sr. VP: Jim Waldeck
Marketing Director: Robert DeVino
Public Relations: Jane Lazgin
Estimated Sales: $100 Million+
Number Employees: 250-499
Parent Co: Perrier Group of America
Type of Packaging: Consumer, Food Service
Brands:
Deer Park
Great Bear
Ice Mountain
Perrier
Poland Spring
Vitale

11458 (HQ)Polar Beverage
P.O.Box 15011
Worcester, MA 01615-0011   508-753-4300
Fax: 508-793-0813   800-734-9800
water@polarbev.com   www.polarbev.com
Manufacturer of bottled and canned soft drinks and water
President/CEO: Ralph Crowley Jr
EVP/Treasurer: Chris Crowley
VP Marketing/Sales Planning: Gerald Martin
Estimated Sales: $191 Million
Number Employees: 100-249
Sq. footage: 500000
Type of Packaging: Consumer, Food Service, Private Label
Brands:
A&W
ADIRONDACK BEVERAGES
ADIRONDACK CLEAR N' NATURAL
CAPE COD DRY

DIET RITE3
POLAR
ROYAL CROWN
SEAGRAMS
SEVEN-UP
SILVER SPRING
SQUIRT
SUNKIST COUNTRY TIME
WAIST WATCHER

11459 Polar Foods International
PO Box 2979
Charlottetown, PE C1A 1R6
Canada   902-962-3303
                    Fax: 902-962-3148
            charlottetown@polarfoods.pe.ca
Manufacturer of fresh and frozen seafood including
lobsters, rock and snow crabs, scallops, herring,
mussels, ocean perch, cod, smelt, mackeral, clams,
oysters, flatfish, tuna
    President: Milton MacKay
    VP Marketing/Sales: Ken MacDonald
    VP Special Projects: Garth Jenkins
Estimated Sales: $1+ Million
Number Employees: 600
Type of Packaging: Food Service, Private Label
Brands:
    ABEGWEIT
    BABINEAU
    HOWARD'S COVE
    MERMAID
    POLAR

11460 Polar Water Company
45t Noblestown Road
Carnegie, PA 15106-1655   800-444-7873
                    Fax: 770-739-1884
Bottler of spring and distilled water
    Manager: Woody Godby
Number Employees: 20-49
Parent Co: Sontory Water Group

11461 Polarica
105 Quint St
San Francisco, CA 94124-1403   415-647-1300
            Fax: 415-647-6826 800-426-3872
        info@polarica.com www.polarica.com
Beef, beef products, specialty products
    President: Carlos Tabeira
    Manager: Mitch Niayesh
Estimated Sales: $ 5-10 Million
Number Employees: 5-9
Brands:
    Polarica

11462 Polka Home Style Sausage
8753 S Commercial Ave
Chicago, IL 60617-3221   773-221-0395
                www.polkasausage.com
Processor of sausage
    President: Paul Szczepkowski
    Owner: Ed Szczepkowski
Estimated Sales: Less than $500,000
Number Employees: 1-4
Type of Packaging: Consumer, Food Service
Brands:
    Polka

11463 Pollio Dairy Products
120 Mineola Blvd
Mineola, NY 11501-4064   516-741-8000
        Fax: 516-741-3041 www.kraftfoods.com
Processor of ricotta and mozzarella cheese including
string, grated and smoked
    President: Richard Lerner
    General Manager: Mark Petite
    Marketing Director: John Curran
Number Employees: 20-49
Type of Packaging: Consumer, Food Service

11464 Pollman's Bake Shops
750 S Broad St
Mobile, AL 36603-1197   251-438-1511
    Fax: 251-438-9461 www.pollmansbakeshop.com
Processor of baked goods including cakes, pies and
breads.
    Co-Owner: Charles Pollman
    Co-Owner: Fred Pollman III
Estimated Sales: $ 1 - 3 Million
Number Employees: 20-49
Type of Packaging: Consumer
Other Locations:
    Pollman's Bake Shops
    Mobile AL

11465 Polly's Gourmet Coffee
4606 E 2nd St
Long Beach, CA 90803-5307   562-433-2996
            Fax: 562-439-4119 coffee@pollys.com
                        www.pollys.com
Coffee and tea
    Owner/Roastmaster: Michael Sheldrake
Estimated Sales: Under $500,000
Number Employees: 10-19
Brands:
    Celebes Kalosi
    Colombian Excelso
    Colombian Supremo
    Ethiopian Moka
    Jamaica Blue Mountain
    Java Estate
    Kenya AA
    Kona Hawaii
    La Minita Tarrazu
    Sumatra Mandheling
    Tanzanian Peaberry

11466 Polly-O Dairy Products
120 Mineola Blvd
Mineola, NY 11501-4064   516-741-8000
                    Fax: 516-741-3041
Milk, dairy products, cheese
    Director Marketing: Dave Keefe
Estimated Sales: $ 20-50 Million
Number Employees: 20-49
Brands:
    Polly-O Cheeses

11467 Polypro International
7300 Metro Blvd # 570
Minneapolis, MN 55439-2346   952-835-7717
            Fax: 952-835-3811 800-765-9776
    polypro@polyprointl.com www.polyprointl.com
Processor, importer and exporter of guar and cellu-
lose gums
    President: Mark Kieper
    Vice President: Mark Kieper
Estimated Sales: $ 2.5-5 Million
Number Employees: 1-4
Type of Packaging: Bulk
Brands:
    Procol
    Progum
    Viscol

11468 Pommeraie Winery
10541 Cherry Ridge Road
Sebastopol, CA 95472-9644   707-823-9463
                    Fax: 707-823-9106
Wines
    President: Judith Johnson
Estimated Sales: $500-1 Million appx.
Number Employees: 1-4

11469 Pomodoro Fresca Foods
16 Bleeker Street
Millburn, NJ 07079   973-467-6609
                    Fax: 973-379-1913
Sauces
    President: Lia Battista
Estimated Sales: $ .5 - 1 million
Number Employees: 1-4
Brands:
    Fresca Foods

11470 Pompei Winery
3994 E 89th Street
Cleveland, OH 44105-3962   216-883-9370
Wines
    President: Frederick DePompei
    Sales Manager: Greg Depompei
Estimated Sales: $5-9.9 Million
Number Employees: 1-4

11471 Pompeian
P.O.Box 8863
Baltimore, MD 21224-0863   410-276-6900
            Fax: 410-276-3764 800-638-1224
        fpatton@pompeian.com www.pompeian.com
Processor and importer of Spanish olive oil, red
wine vinegar and artichokes
    President: Frank Patton
    COO: Adolfo Blassino
    CEO: Bill Monroe
    Plant Manager: John Zacot
Estimated Sales: $ 20 - 50 Million
Number Employees: 20-49
Type of Packaging: Consumer, Food Service, Bulk

Brands:
    Avallo
    Laco
    Pompeian Olive Oil
    Romanza

11472 Pon Food Corporation
P.O.Box 747
Ponchatoula, LA 70454-0747   985-386-6941
                    Fax: 985-386-6755
Wholesaler/distributor of groceries, frozen foods,
meats, dairy products and seafood; serving the food
service market
    President: Anthony Berner Jr
    CEO: Anthony Berner, Sr.
Estimated Sales: $15000000
Number Employees: 20-49
Sq. footage: 54000

11473 Pond Brothers Peanut Company
426 County Street
Suffolk, VA 23434-4704   757-539-2356
                    Fax: 757-539-3995
Raw peanuts
    President: Richard L Pond Jr
    CEO: Jeffrey G Pond
    Controller: Ernest Wyatt
Estimated Sales: $ 5-10 Million
Number Employees: 1-4

11474 Pond Pure Catfish
P.O.Box 34
Moulton, AL 35650-0034   256-974-6698
                    Fax: 403-252-3918
Catfish
    Owner: Bobby Norwood
Estimated Sales: $300,000-500,000
Number Employees: 1-4

11475 Ponderosa Valley Vineyard & Winery
3171 Highway 290
Ponderosa, NM 87044-9716   575-834-7487
                    Fax: 505-834-7073
            winemaker@ponderosawinery.com
                    www.ponderosawinery.com
Manufacturer of Red, white and port wines
    Owner: Henry Street
    Owner: Mary Street
    Operations Manager: Henry Street
    Production Manager: Henry Street
Estimated Sales: $150,000
Number Employees: 1-4
Number of Products: 21
Sq. footage: 1000
Type of Packaging: Consumer
Brands:
    CHAMISA GOLD
    JEMEZ BLUSH
    JEMEZ RED
    N.M. RIESLING
    PONDEROSA VALLEY VINEYARDS
    SUMMER SAGE
    VINO DE PATA

11476 Pontchartrain Blue Crab
38327 Salt Bayou Rd
Slidell, LA 70461-1103   985-649-6645
                    Fax: 504-781-5064
        www.pontchartrainbluecrab.com
Pontchartrain Blue Crab Inc is a seafood processor,
importer and exporter with a primary focus on top
quality crab products.
    President/CEO: Gary Bauer Sr
Estimated Sales: $5,000,000
Number Employees: 50-99

11477 Pontiac Coffee Break
2252 Dixie Hwy
Pontiac, MI 48342   248-332-9403
                    Fax: 248-335-0525
        gourmetcoffee@coffeebreakinc.com
                www.coffeebreakinc.com
Coffee
    President: Robert Smith
Estimated Sales: $500,000-$1 Million
Number Employees: 10-19

11478 Pontiac Foods
P.O.Box 25469
Columbia, SC 29224-5469   803-699-1600
                    Fax: 803-699-1649

Coffee
    Manager: John Masa
    General Manager: Joe Girone
    Purchasing Manager: Stan Wilson
Estimated Sales: Under $500,000
Number Employees: 100-249
Brands:
    Kroger
    Pontiac Foods

11479 Pony Boy Ice Cream
211 Middle Road
Acushnet, MA 02743-2017   508-994-4422
                        Fax: 508-995-9459

Ice Cream and frozen yogurt
    President: Raymond White
Estimated Sales: $ 10-20 Million
Number Employees: 10-19
Brands:
    Pony Boy

11480 Ponzi Vineyards
14665 SW Winery Ln
Beaverton, OR 97007-8773   503-628-1227
    Fax: 503-628-0354   info@ponziwines.com
                        www.ponziwines.com
Wines
    President: Richard Ponzi
    Marketing/Sales Director: Maria Ponzi
    Fogelstrom
    Operations Manager: Michel Ponzi
    Winemaker: Luisa Ponzi
Estimated Sales: $ 1 - 3 Million
Number Employees: 10-19
Type of Packaging: Private Label
Brands:
    Ponzi's

11481 Poore Brothers
1898 S Flatiron Ct
Boulder, CO 80301-2875   303-546-9939
    Fax: 303-546-9133 www.boulderchips.com
Marketer and manufacturer of a variety of owned or
licensed brand names products including; T.G.I. Fri-
day's, Cinnabon, Poore Brothers, Texas Style, Boul-
der Canyon Natural Foods, and Tato Skins
    President: Mark Maggio
    Interim CEO: Eric Kufel
    CFO: Steve Weinberger
    Sr. VP Marketing: Steven Sklar
Number Employees: 10-19
Type of Packaging: Consumer, Food Service, Bulk
Brands:
    Boulder Canyon

11482 (HQ)Poore Brothers
5050 N 40th St # 300
Phoenix, AZ 85018-2153   623-932-6200
    Fax: 623-522-2690 800-279-2250
                info@InventureGroup.net
    www.inventuregroup.net/Poore-Brothers.asp
Kettle, batch and continuous cooked potato chips.
    President: Eric Kufel
    Chief Financial Officer: Steve Weinberger
    CEO: Terry McDaniel
    VP Marketing: Scott Fullmar
    VP Manufacturing: Glen Flook
Estimated Sales: $ 50-100 Million
Number Employees: 250-499
Parent Co: The Inventure Group Inc
Type of Packaging: Consumer, Food Service, Pri-
vate Label
Brands:
    Poore Brothers

11483 Poore Brothers
705 W Dustman Road
Bluffton, IN 46714-1178   219-824-9933
    Fax: 219-824-4388   info@amstock.com
                www.poorebrothers.com
Chips
    President/CEO: Eric Kufel
    CFO: Rick Finkbeiner
    CFO: Thomas Freeze
    VP Marketing: Scott Fullmar
    VP Manufacturing: Glen Flook
Number Employees: 100-249
Brands:
    Bob's Texas Style
    Boulder Canyon
    Cinnabon
    Poore Brothers
    TGI Friday's
    Tato Skins

11484 Popchips
550 Montgomery Street
Suite 925
San Francisco, CA 94111   415-391-2211
            Fax: 415-391-2779 866-217-9327
    snackers@popchips.com www.popchips.com
popped potato chips

11485 Popcorn Connection
7615 Fulton Avenue
North Hollywood, CA 91605-1805   818-764-3279
        Fax: 818-765-0578 800-852-2676
    popcornconnection@earthlink.net
            www.popcornconnection.com
Processor and manufacturer of gourmet popcorn
confections and nut; custom labeling is available
    Owner: Kevin Needle
    VP: Ross Wallach
Estimated Sales: $300,000
Number Employees: 3
Number of Brands: 15
Number of Products: 20
Sq. footage: 3500
Type of Packaging: Consumer, Food Service, Pri-
vate Label, Bulk
Brands:
    CORN APPETIT
    CORN APPETIT ULTIMATE
    FRUIT CORN APPETIT
    VIDEO MUNCHIES

11486 Popcorn World
P.O.Box 11283
Kansas City, MO 64119-283   660-359-4471
    Fax: 660-359-4475 800-443-8226
            pam@popcornworld.com
            www.popcornworld.com
Processor of flavored popcorn
    Owner: Pam Kaduce
    CEO: Keith Kaduce
Estimated Sales: $ 1 - 3 Million
Number Employees: 20
Type of Packaging: Consumer, Food Service, Pri-
vate Label, Bulk

11487 Popcorner
1429 N Illinois Street
Swansea, IL 62226-4234   618-277-2676
    Fax: 618-236-9420 popmaster@popcorn.com
Processor of specialty items including gourmet pop-
corn
    Owner: Connie Kimble
Number Employees: 1-4
Sq. footage: 1200
Type of Packaging: Consumer, Private Label, Bulk

11488 Pope Corporation
41180 Vincenti Ct
Novi, MI 48375-1922   248-888-8989
    Fax: 248-888-0765 popecorp@aol.com
            www.setcousa.com
Vegetables
    President: Erminio Parrella
    VP: Dave Kirkpatrick
Estimated Sales: $ 2.5-5 Million
Number Employees: 1-4

11489 Poplar Ridge Vineyards
9782 State Route 414
Hector, NY 14841-9716   607-582-6421
                        Fax: 607-582-6421
Wines
    President: Dave Bagley
Estimated Sales: Less than $200,000
Number Employees: 1-4
Type of Packaging: Private Label
Brands:
    Poplar Ridge Vineyards

11490 Poppa's Granola
473 Grout Road
Perkinsville, VT 05151-9682   802-263-5342
            pappoasgranola@tds.net
Granola
    Co-Owner: Angela Page
    Co-Owner: Jacquelin Antonivich
Type of Packaging: Consumer, Food Service, Bulk

11491 Poppee's Popcorn Company
38727 Taylor Pkwy
Elyria, OH 44035-6275   440-327-0775
    Fax: 440-327-9349   popcorn@jennyspopcorn.com
            www.jennyspopcorn.com

Popcorn, cheese curls, caramel, regular and hot
cheddar cheese corn
    Owner: Tom Mc Guire
    CEO: Bob Shearer
    Sales Manager: Tom McGuire
    Plant Manager: Jay McGuire
Estimated Sales: $ 5-10 Million
Number Employees: 20-49
Type of Packaging: Private Label
Brands:
    Jenny's

11492 Poppers Supply Company
PO Box 90187
Portland, OR 97290-0187   503-239-3792
    Fax: 503-235-6221   info@poppers.com
                www.poppers.com
Processor and exporter of ready-to-eat flavored and
confectioned popcorn and fountain syrup; whole-
saler/distributor of concession equipment and sup-
plies including sno-cone syrup and cotton candy
floss
    President: Vernon Ryles Jr
    Sales Manager: Jody Riggs
Estimated Sales: $1,400,000
Number Employees: 10
Type of Packaging: Consumer, Food Service
Brands:
    Allans
    Poppers

11493 Poppie's Dough
2411 S Wallace
Chicago, IL 60616   312-949-0404
                        Fax: 312-949-0505
    customerservice@poppiesdough.com
                www.poppiesdough.com
cookies, biscotti, brownies and bars, scones and
sconettes
    President/Owner: Ronnie Himmel
Estimated Sales: $1.9 Million
Number Employees: 15

11494 Poppie's Dough
2411 S Wallace St
Chicago, IL 60616-1855   312-640-0404
    Fax: 312-949-0505 888-767-7431
            poppiesdough@interaccess.com
                www.poppiesdough.com
Manufacturer of Cookies in twenty flavors
    Owner: Michelle Garson
Estimated Sales: $5-10 Million
Number Employees: 20-49
Brands:
    POPPIE'S

11495 Poppin Popcorn
933 4th Avenue N
Naples, FL 34102-5814   941-262-1691
                        Fax: 941-262-1691
Popcorns and maize products
    President: Mark Webb
Estimated Sales: Less than $500,000
Number Employees: 1-4

11496 Porinos Gourmet Food
280 Rand St
Central Falls, RI 02863-2512   401-273-3000
    Fax: 401-273-3232 800-826-3938
    porinos@aol.com   www.porinos.com
Processor and exporter of gourmet pasta and barbe-
cue sauces, salad dressings, marinades and pickled
pepper items; importer and wholesaler/distributor of
pastas, olive oils and balsamic vinegars
    Owner: Michael Dressler
    VP Operations: Marshall Righter
Estimated Sales: $1900000
Number Employees: 10-19
Sq. footage: 30000
Type of Packaging: Consumer, Food Service, Pri-
vate Label

11497 Pork Packers International
1001 Prentiss Street
Downs, KS 67437-1835   785-454-3396
Processor of pork
    Plant Manager: Larry Kennedy
Estimated Sales: $$20-50 Million
Number Employees: 50-99
Type of Packaging: Consumer

11498 Pork Shop of Vermont
631 N Pasture Road
Charlotte, VT 05445-9254
Fax: 802-482-2801 802-482-3617
800-458-3441
Smoked sausage and ham
President: Joseph Keenan
Estimated Sales: $ 5-9.9 Million
Number Employees: 7

11499 PorkRubbers BBQ Specialty Products
21w266 Glen Park Road
Lombard, IL 60148-5182
630-424-8200
Fax: 630-424-0231
porkrubbersbbq@prodigy.com
Barbeque specialty products
Owner: Mary Van Petten

11500 Porkie Company of Wisconsin
P.O.Box 100346
Cudahy, WI 53110-6105
414-483-6562
Fax: 414-483-6561 800-333-2588
www.porkiesofwisconsin.com
Processor of pork rinds and cracklings, beef jerky, extruded corn, salted peanuts, pistachios and cashews, olives, pickles, pretzels, potato chips and cheese curls; also, processor and packer of pickled pigs' feet, pork hocks andpickled Polish sausage
President: Gerald Rydeski
Executive VP: Thomas Rydeski
Marketing/Sales: Rick Rydeski
Production: Dan Rydeski
Plant Manager: Mike Sodemann
Estimated Sales: $1600000
Number Employees: 20-49
Number of Products: 50
Sq. footage: 50000
Brands:
JACK'S ALL AMERICAN
PORKIES
SNAK SALES
VINEGAR JOE

11501 Porky's Gourmet
644 Blythe Ave
Gallatin, TN 37066-2226
615-230-7000
Fax: 615-230-2800 800-767-5911
flavor@porkysgourmet.com
www.porkysgourmet.com
Gourmet sauces, seasonings, relishes, jellies and other condiments
President: Ron Boyle
Estimated Sales: $ 5 - 10 Million
Number Employees: 10-19
Type of Packaging: Consumer, Food Service, Private Label

11502 Porrhoff Foods Company
P.O.Box 1502
Des Moines, IA 50305-1502
515-244-5271
Fax: 515-244-7037
President: Craig Potthoff
Estimated Sales: $ 10 - 20 Million
Number Employees: 20-49

11503 Port Chatham Smoked Seafood
1930 Merrill Creek Pkwy
Everett, WA 98203-5897
425-407-4000
Fax: 425-407-4010 800-872-5666
info@norquest.com www.portchatham.com
Processor and exporter of smoked sturgeon, salmon and oysters including frozen, fresh and canned
General Manager: Ken Ng
Sales: Ron Boden
Estimated Sales: $9500000
Number Employees: 50-99
Parent Co: Icicle Seafood
Type of Packaging: Consumer, Food Service
Brands:
Great Northwest
Pacific Select
Portlock

11504 Port Lobster Company
P.O.Box 729
Kennebunkport, ME 04046-0729
207-967-2081
Fax: 207-967-8419 800-486-7029
portlob@gwi.net www.portlobster.com
Manufacturer of Lobster
President: Timothy Hutchins
Estimated Sales: $ 1 - 3 Million
Number Employees: 5-9
Type of Packaging: Consumer

11505 Port Vue Coffee Company
RR 61
Pottsville, PA 17901
570-429-2690
Coffee
President: Randy Palles
Plant Manager: Lori Nora
Estimated Sales: Less than $500,000
Number Employees: 5-9

11506 Porter Creek Vineyards
8735 Westside Rd
Healdsburg, CA 95448-8335
707-433-6321
Fax: 707-433-4245
info@portercreekvineyards.com
www.portercreekvineyards.com
Wine
President: George Davis
Estimated Sales: Under $ 1 Million
Number Employees: 1-4
Brands:
Procter Creek

11507 Porter's Food & Produce
P.O.Box 407
Du Quoin, IL 62832-0407
618-542-2155
Fax: 618-542-2396 www.farefoods.com
President: Ron Porter
Estimated Sales: $ 10 - 20 Million
Number Employees: 20-49

11508 Porter's Pick-A-Dilly
Stw Indstrl Park
Stowe, VT 05672
802-253-6338
Fax: 802-253-6852
President: Lynn Porter
Estimated Sales: Under $500,000
Number Employees: 1-4

11509 Portier Fine Foods
436 Waverly Ave
Mamaroneck, NY 10543-2232
914-381-2549
Fax: 914-381-4045 800-272-9463
portier.finefoods@verizon.net
www.portierfinefoods.com
Processor of smoked salmon, trout, scallops, shrimp, etc.; importer of Caspian sea caviar, grain-fed game and birds and hand-made Belgian chocolates
President: Sean Portier
Sales Director: Patrick Portier
Estimated Sales: Below $ 5 Million
Number Employees: 10-19
Parent Co: Chenoceaux, Inc
Type of Packaging: Consumer, Food Service

11510 Portion Pac
7325 Snider Rd
Mason, OH 45040-9193
513-398-0400
Fax: 513-459-5300 800-232-4829
sales@portionpac.com www.portionpac.com
Manufacturer and exporter of portion control sugar, pepper, salt, ketchup, mustard, sauces, dressings, jams, jellies, syrup, preserves, mayonnaise and artificial sweeteners
Managing Director: Arthur Jack
Executive: Glenn Corbin
GM Administration/Finance/MIS: Susan Al
GM Business Development/Marketing: Bob Ripp
National Sales Manager: Ralph Saltsgaver
Estimated Sales: $356.20 Million
Number Employees: 10,000+
Sq. footage: 130000
Parent Co: H J Heinz USA
Type of Packaging: Food Service, Private Label
Other Locations:
Portion Pac
Stone Mountain GA
Brands:
CHATSWORTH
MADEIRA FARMS
PITCH'R PAK
SALSA DEL SOL
SQUEEZERS
SWEET PLEASERS GOURMET
SWEET PORTION
TASTE PLEASERS GOURMET

11511 Portion Pak
1609 Stone Ridge Dr
Stone Mountain, GA 30083-1109
770-934-3200
Fax: 770-934-7644 www.portionpac.com

Cheese spread, powdered beverages, peanut butter, jelly and icing
President: Barney Rosner
Marketing: Fred Johnson
Plant Manager: John Stephens
Purchasing: Lynn Cooper
Estimated Sales: $ 20-50 Million
Number Employees: 100-249

11512 Portland Brewing Company
2730 NW 31st Ave
Portland, OR 97210-1718
503-226-7623
Fax: 503-226-2702 info@portlandbrew.com
www.macsbeer.com
Processor and exporter of beer, ale, lager, porter and stout
President: Fred Bowman
Vice President: Fred Bowman
Marketing/Public Relations: Eric Starr
Sales Director: Mark Carver
Operations Manager: Bill Wrey
Production Manager: Gary Friedman
Plant Manager: Alan Kornhauser
Estimated Sales: $10266856
Number Employees: 50-99
Type of Packaging: Consumer, Food Service
Brands:
Haystack Black
Mactaranahan's
Oregon Honey
Portland

11513 Portland Shellfish Company
110 Dartmouth St
South Portland, ME 04106-6210
207-799-9290
Fax: 207-799-7179 scout@pshellfish.com
www.portlandshellfish.com
Manufacturer, importer and exporter of fresh and frozen crab
President: Jeff Holden
Human Resources: John Maloney
Estimated Sales: $9 Million
Number Employees: 100-249
Sq. footage: 12000
Type of Packaging: Consumer, Food Service, Private Label, Bulk
Brands:
Portland Lighthouse

11514 Portland Specialty Seafoods
225 Commercial St
Portland, ME 04101-4613
207-699-2989
Fax: 207-774-1614
Seafood
Administrator: Jessica Burton
Estimated Sales: $ 10 - 20 Million
Number Employees: 10-19

11515 Portsmouth Chowder Company
124 Heritage Ave # 1
Portsmouth, NH 03801-8655
603-431-3132
Fax: 603-431-3132
Chowder and seafood products
Owner: Rob Lincoln
Estimated Sales: Below $ 5 Million
Number Employees: 1-4
Brands:
Portsmouth Chowder Company

11516 Portugalia Imports
23 Tremont St
Fall River, MA 02720-4821
508-679-9307
Fax: 508-673-1502
Owner: Fernando Benevides

11517 Portuguese Baking Company
P.O.Box 5550
Newark, NJ 07105-0550
973-589-8875
Fax: 973-589-6510 info@ pbclp.com
www.pbclp.com/
Portuguese rolls
President: Marvin Everseyke
CFO/VP: Louis Pereira
CEO: Steve Latner
Estimated Sales: Under $500,000
Number Employees: 250-499
Type of Packaging: Private Label, Bulk
Brands:
Austin Company
Portuguese Baking Company

11518 Poseidon Enterprises
2351 Adams Drive NW
Atlanta, GA 30318-1919   800-863-7886
                                  Fax: 404-352-0019
Seafood, salmon, tuna, swordfish, grouper, snapper,
live lobster
    President: Richard Lavecchia III

11519 Positively Third StreetBakery
1202 E 3rd St
Duluth, MN 55805-2319   218-724-8619
www.positively3rdstreet.com
Processor of fresh and frozen cookies, bagels, gra-
nola and bread
    Owner: Paul Steklin
Estimated Sales: Less than $500,000
Number Employees: 5-9
Type of Packaging: Consumer, Food Service, Bulk

11520 Post Familie Vineyards
1700 Saint Marys Mountain Rd
Altus, AR 72821-9001   479-468-2741
        Fax: 479-468-2740   800-275-8423
info@postfamilie.com   www.postfamilie.com
Processor of wines, grape juices, jellies, champagne
and table wine grapes
    President: Matthew Post
    VP/Director Marketing: Paul Post
Number Employees: 10-19
Type of Packaging: Consumer, Private Label, Bulk
Brands:
    Aesop's Fable
    Ozark Mountain Vineyards
    Post Familie Vineyards

11521 Pot O'Gold Honey Company
PO Box 1200
Hemingway, SC 29554-1200   843-558-9598
                pollinator@aol.com
Processor of honey
    Co-Owner: David Green
    Co-Owner: Janice Green
Number Employees: 1-4

11522 Potato Services of Michigan
7058 N Wyman Rd
Edmore, MI 48829   989-427-3314
                                  Fax: 989-427-5042
Processor, importer and exporter of potatoes
    President: Tim Wilkes
Estimated Sales: $12072786
Number Employees: 1-4
Type of Packaging: Consumer, Food Service, Pri-
vate Label, Bulk
Brands:
    Spud Pak Choice

11523 Poteet Seafood Company
5067 Blythe Island Hwy
Brunswick, GA 31520-2500   912-264-5340
                                  Fax: 912-267-9695
Seafood
    Owner: Speedy Tostensen
Estimated Sales: $350,000
Number Employees: 1-4

11524 Potomac Farms
P.O.Box 2189
Cumberland, MD 21503-2189   301-722-4410
                                  Fax: 301-722-8433
Milk
    President: David W Gilles
    Manager: David Gilles
Estimated Sales: $ 10-20 Million
Number Employees: 50-99

11525 Pots de Creme
4954 Paris Pike
Lexington, KY 40511-9400   859-299-2254
        Fax: 859-299-4638   www.kyagr.com
Processor of organic produce and herbs, fresh water
prawns, trout and tilapia
    President: Susan Harkins
Number Employees: 1-4
Parent Co: Duntreath Farm
Brands:
    Dubbasue And Company

11526 Potter Siding Creamery Company
P.O.Box 494
Tripoli, IA 50676-0494   319-882-4444
Bakery products and creames
    Owner: Kurt Kortbein

Estimated Sales: Less than $500,000
Number Employees: 1-4

11527 Poudre Valley Creamery
222 La Porte Avenue
Fort Collins, CO 80521-2725   970-482-8475
                                  Fax: 970-482-8475
Processor of ice cream and ice cream novelties;
wholesaler/distributor of milk
    President: Bob McClauskey
Number Employees: 20-49
Type of Packaging: Consumer, Food Service

11528 Poultry Foods Industry
1610 Midland Blvd
Fort Smith, AR 72901-1570   479-783-8996
        Fax: 479-785-4568   www.tyson.com
Poultry, poultry products
    Operations Manager: John Mulson
    Plant Manager: Steve Smalling

11529 Powder Pak
34475 N Circle Drive
Round Lake, IL 60073-9730   847-223-4683
    Fax: 847-223-4685   dcoulter@powderpak.com
                          www.powderpak.com
Packaging and handling powders. Dairy and food ingredients

11530 Powell Bean
313 S Fair St
Powell, WY 82435-2811   307-754-3121
    Fax: 307-754-3936   pbc@directairnet.com
Processor and exporter of dry pinto beans
    Manager: Jamie Franko
Number Employees: 5-9
Type of Packaging: Bulk

11531 Power-Selles Imports
14522 Woodinville Way
Woodinville, WA 98072-6496   425-398-9761
    Fax: 206-783-5836   info@psimports.net
                          psimports.net
Specialty gourmet food products from spain
    Co-Founder: Betsy Power
    Co-Founder: Pere Selles
    General Manager: Monse Alonso
    Sales Manager: Marion Sproul
    Office Manager: Peggy Godfrey
Estimated Sales: $ 3 - 5 Million
Number Employees: 5-9

11532 PowerBar
2150 Shattuck Avenue
10th Floor
Berkeley, CA 94704-1347   510-647-0655
        Fax: 866-574-6420   800-587-6937
                          www.powerbar.com
Health food energy bars and drinks
    General Manager: Cindy Vallar
    VP Sales: Jeff Lozito
    Marketing Manager: Michelle Sitton
Estimated Sales: $ 100-500 Million
Number Employees: 50-99
Parent Co: Nestle USA
Type of Packaging: Private Label
Brands:
    PowerBar
    PowerBar Beverage System
    PowerBar Energy Bites
    PowerBar Essentials
    PowerBar Harvest
    PowerBar Pria
    PowerBar Proteinplus
    Powergel

11533 Powers Baking Company
Ste 141
7771 W Oakland Park Blvd
Sunrise, FL 33351-6736   305-681-7000
        Fax: 305-769-1185   www.powersbaking.com
Breads and rolls.
    President: Dolphus Powers
Estimated Sales: $ 20-50 Million
Number Employees: 80

11534 Poynette Distribution Center
W8070 Kent Rd
Poynette, WI 53955-9713   608-635-4396
                                  Fax: 608-635-7308
www.lakesidefoods.com/poynette1.htm

Processor of canned green beans
    Sr. VP Operations: Daniel C Cavanaugh
    VP Customer Service: James I Ferguson
    General Manager: Ross Moland
    Plant Manager: Mike Hull
Estimated Sales: $ 10 - 20 Million
Number Employees: 20-49
Parent Co: Stokely USA
Type of Packaging: Consumer, Private Label

11535 Prager Winery & Port Works
1281 Lewelling Ln
St Helena, CA 94574-2235   707-963-3720
        Fax: 707-963-7679   800-969-7678
ahport@pragerport.com   www.pragerport.net
Wine
    President: Jim Prager
    CFO: Katie Rooney
Estimated Sales: $1-4.9 Million
Number Employees: 5-9
Brands:
    Prager Winery & Port

11536 Prairie Farms Dairy
722 Broadway St
Anderson, IN 46012-2924   765-649-1261
        Fax: 765-649-8268   www.prairiefarms.com
Milk, dairy products-noncheese
    President: Harry Carter
    CFO: Paul Benne
    Quality Control: Leonardo Otto
    Manager: Doug Banning
Estimated Sales: $ 50-100 Million
Number Employees: 100-249

11537 Prairie Cajun Wholesale
5966 Highway 190
Eunice, LA 70535-8213   337-546-6195
    Fax: 337-546-6400   gatoraid@mindspring.com
                          www.cajunprairie.com
Processor and exporter of frozen seafood and exotic
meats including alligator and nutria
    President: Jeffery Derouen
Estimated Sales: $3100000
Number Employees: 10-19
Type of Packaging: Consumer, Food Service

11538 Prairie City Bakery
100 N Fairway Dr # 138
Vernon Hills, IL 60061-1859   847-573-9640
        Fax: 847-573-9643   800-338-5122
            customerservice@pcbakery.com
                          www.pcbakery.com
Processor of frozen danish, cookies, muffins and
cakes
    President: William Skeens
Estimated Sales: $2,200,000
Number Employees: 5-9
Type of Packaging: Consumer, Food Service, Bulk
Brands:
    Prairie City

11539 (HQ)Prairie Farms Dairy
1100 Broadway
Carlinville, IL 62626-1183   217-854-2547
        Fax: 217-854-6426   icebox@prairiefarms.com
                          www.prairiefarms.com
Processor of dairy products including cottage
cheese, fresh cream, milk, sour cream, yogurt and
ice cream; also, orange juice and fruit drinks
    Chairman: Fred Kuenstler
    CEO: Roger Capps
    VP Finance: Paul Benne
    CEO: Ed Mullins
    VP General Sales: Ed Mullins
    Sales Director: Donald Kullman
    Director Marketing: William Montgomery
Estimated Sales: $50-100 Million
Number Employees: 1,000-4,999
Type of Packaging: Consumer, Food Service, Pri-
vate Label
Brands:
    Prairie Farms

11540 Prairie Farms Dairy
1100 Broadway
Carlinville, IL 62626-1183   217-854-2547
        Fax: 217-854-6426   www.prairiefarms.com
Manufacturer of dairy products and juice that include; milk, orange juice, fruit drinks, cottage
cheese, yogurt, sour cream and dip, ice cream and
sherbet
    General Manager: Kenneth Kuhn
    CEO: Ed Mullins

Estimated Sales:$50-100 Million
Number Employees: 1,000-4,999
Type of Packaging: Consumer, Food Service, Private Label
Brands:
  PRAIRIE FARMS

11541 Prairie Farms Dairy
P.O.Box 338
O Fallon, IL 62269-0338   618-632-3632
  Fax: 618-632-9828 www.prairiefarms.com
Processor of ice cream
  Manager: Patrick Hedger
  Plant Manager: Pat Hedger
Estimated Sales: $ 20 - 50 Million
Number Employees: 20-49
Sq. footage: 50000
Parent Co: Prairie Farms Dairy
Type of Packaging: Consumer

11542 Prairie Farms Dairy
742 N Illinois Ave
Carbondale, IL 62901-1283   618-457-4167
  Fax: 618-549-5608 www.prairiefarms.com
Processor of sour cream, cottage cheese and dips
  CEO: Roger Capps
  Plant Manager: Ron Diuguid
Estimated Sales: $ 10 - 20 Million
Number Employees: 50-99
Parent Co: Prairie Farms Dairy
Type of Packaging: Consumer

11543 Prairie Farms Dairy
415 N 24th St
Quincy, IL 62301-3253   217-223-5530
                    www.prairiefarms.com
Processor of cottage cheese and yogurt
  Plant Manager: Dave Miller
Estimated Sales: $ 5-10 Million
Number Employees: 20-49
Parent Co: Prairie Farms Dairy
Type of Packaging: Consumer, Food Service

11544 Prairie Farms Dairy
1100 Broadway
Carlinville, IL 62626-1183   217-854-2547
  Fax: 217-854-6426 www.prairiefarms.com
Processor of ice cream mixes
  Manager: James Baker
  CEO: Ed Mullins
Estimated Sales: $ 2.5-5 Million
Number Employees: 1,000-4,999
Parent Co: Prairie Farms Dairy
Type of Packaging: Bulk

11545 Prairie Farms Dairy
1800 Adams St
Granite City, IL 62040-3347   618-451-5600
  Fax: 618-451-7251 icebox@prairiefarms.com
                    www.prairiefarms.com
Processor of milk, cottage cheese, orange juice, sour cream and yogurt
  President: Bill Dowling
  CFO: Jim Clancy
  General Manager: Dale Chapman
  Plant Manager: Kevin Mc Clain
Estimated Sales: $ 20-50 Million
Number Employees: 100-249
Parent Co: Prairie Farms Dairy
Type of Packaging: Consumer, Food Service

11546 (HQ)Prairie Farms Dairy
1100 Broadway
Carlinville, IL 62626-1183   217-854-2547
  Fax: 217-854-6426 icebox@prairiefarms.com
                    www.prairiefarms.com
Manufacturers a wide variety of fluid milk products; milk, cottage cheese, sour cream and dips, yogurt, ice cream, butter and creams, frozen treats, and juuices and drinks.
  CEO: Ed Mullins
Estimated Sales: $50-$100 Million
Number Employees: 1,000-4,999
Type of Packaging: Consumer, Food Service
Brands:
  Prairie Farms

11547 (HQ)Prairie Farms Dairy Inc
1100 Broadway
Carlinville, IL 62626-1183   217-854-2547
  Fax: 217-854-6426 icebox@prairiefarms.com
                    www.prairiefarms.com

Manufacturer of dairy products including cottage cheese, fresh cream, milk, sour cream, yogurt and ice cream; also, orange juice and fruit drinks
  CFO: Paul Benne
  GM: Craig Bertrand
  CEO: Ed Mullins
Estimated Sales: $10.5 Million
Number Employees: 1,000-4,999
Type of Packaging: Consumer, Food Service, Private Label, Bulk
Brands:
  PRAIRIE FARMS

11548 Prairie Malt
PO Box 1150
Biggar, SK S0K 0M0
Canada   306-948-3500
  Fax: 306-948-3969 david_klinger@cargill.com
Processor and exporter of barley malt
  General Manager: Bob Chappell
Number Employees: 50-99
Type of Packaging: Bulk

11549 Prairie Mills Company
PO Box 820
Wayzata, MN 55391-0820   612-473-9407
                    Fax: 612-473-9407
Organic flour and cereal
  President: Erik Bruun
Estimated Sales: $500,000-$1 Million
Number Employees: 1-4
Type of Packaging: Private Label
Brands:
  Amaizen Crunch
  Prairie Star

11550 Prairie Mushrooms
53361 Range Road 232
Sherwood Park, AB T8A 4V2
Canada   780-467-3555
                    Fax: 780-467-3893
contact@prairiemushrooms.com
                    www.prairiemushrooms.com
Manufacturer and exporter of mushrooms
  President: George DeRuiter
  Marketing Manager: John Kostelyk
  Sales: Kevin Christman
  Production: Don Kostelyk
Type of Packaging: Consumer, Food Service
Brands:
  PRAIRIE MUSHROOMS

11551 Prairie Sun Grains
Box 2700
Calgary, AB T2P 3C2
Canada   403-290-4618
                    Fax: 403-290-5550 800-556-6807
Processor of organic flour, pancake mixes and hot breakfast cereals; exporter of hot organic breakfast cereals, bars and herbal supplements
  Member: Peggy Lesueur-Brymer
  Broker Sales Manager: Pat Maloney
  Sales Coordinator: Sarah Sanders
Number Employees: 10-19
Type of Packaging: Consumer, Food Service
Brands:
  Golden Loaf
  Prairie Sun
  Rosebud
  Sunny Boy

11552 Prairie Thyme
4363 Center Pl # 3
Santa Fe, NM 87507-1823   505-473-1945
                    Fax: 505-473-0363 800-869-0009
prairiethyme@aol.com   www.prairiethyme.com
Manufacturer of Specialty gourmet condiments, vinegars, flavored cooking oils, fruit salsas, vegetable chutneys
  President/Owner: Gary Hall
Estimated Sales: $300,000-500,000
Number Employees: 1-4
Number of Brands: 1
Number of Products: 4
Sq. footage: 1600
Type of Packaging: Consumer, Food Service, Private Label, Bulk
Brands:
  PRAIRIE THYME
  PRAIRIE THYME GARLIC BASIL OIL
  PRAIRIE THYME PEACH HABANERO
  PRAIRIE THYME RASPBERRY JALAPENO
  PRAIRIE THYME RED RASPBERRY VINEGAR

PRAIRIE THYME ROASTED TOMATO
PRAIRIE THYME TOASTED GARLIC OIL

11553 Praters Foods
2206 114th St
Lubbock, TX 79423-7235   806-745-2727
  Fax: 806-745-9650 dhalsey@praters.com
                    www.praters.com
Processor of smoked meats, breadings, frozen entrees, stuffings, gravies and casseroles
  Owner: Chip Chenowetch
  Sales Manager: Benny Cousatte
  Purchasing Manager: Daryl Halsey
Estimated Sales: $ 10 - 20 Million
Number Employees: 20-49
Type of Packaging: Consumer

11554 Pratzel's Bakery
9263 Dielman Industrial Dr
St Louis, MO 63132-2202   314-993-5511
  Fax: 314-993-0414 pratzel@atdialyahoo.com
                    www.pratzels.com
Bakery products
  President: Ron Pratzel
  CFO/VP: Elaine Pratzel
Estimated Sales: Below $ 5 Million
Number Employees: 20-49
Type of Packaging: Consumer, Food Service, Private Label, Bulk

11555 Precise Food Ingredients
1432 Wainwright Way # 150
Carrollton, TX 75007-4948   972-323-4951
                    Fax: 972-323-5078
Processor of spices and seasonings
  Owner: Ken Stindmire
  Purchasing Agent: Linda Ransom
Estimated Sales: $6000000
Number Employees: 5-9
Type of Packaging: Bulk

11556 Precision Blends
13460 Brooks Drive
Baldwin Park, CA 91706-2292   626-960-9939
  Fax: 626-962-2570 800-836-9979
dwestphal@precisionblends.com
Blend spices
  President: Charles Angell
  Sales Manager: David Alnamva
  Purchasing Manager: Charles Nordell
Estimated Sales: Under $500,000
Number Employees: 20-49
Type of Packaging: Private Label

11557 Precision Foods
11457 Olde Cabin Rd # 100
St Louis, MO 63141-7139   314-567-5408
  Fax: 314-567-7421 800-647-8170
                    www.precisionfood.com
Dry blending and packaging
  President: Jerry Fritz
Estimated Sales: $ 10-20 Million
Number of Brands: 13
Brands:
  Baker's Joy
  DOLE
  Fla*Vor*Ice
  Foothill Farms
  Frostline
  Milani Gourmet
  Molly McButter
  Mrs. Dash
  Otter Pops
  Royal
  Smithers
  Sugar Twin
  Thick-It

11558 Precision Foods
2150 N 15th Avenuue
Melrose Park, IL 60160-1410   708-216-0704
  Fax: 708-216-0709 800-333-0003
                    info@precisionfoods.com
                    www.precisionfoods.com
Salad dressings, desserts, dried beverages, soups, bases and dietetic products
  President: Jerry L Fritz
  CEO: Dennis P Circo
Estimated Sales: $ 10-20 Million
Number Employees: 150
Brands:
  Molly McButter
  Mrs Dash
  Royal

Sugar Twin
Thick It

11559 Precision Plus Vacuum Parts
2055 Niagara Falls Blvd # 4
Niagara Falls, NY 14304-5702   716-297-2039
Fax: 716-297-8210   800-526-2707
info@precisionplus.com   www.precisionplus.com
Manufacturer of vacuum pump replacement parts
Manager: Joseph Miller
Estimated Sales: $7 Million
Number Employees: 50-99
Number of Brands: 15
Number of Products: 2000
Sq. footage: 20000
Parent Co: BOC Group, Inc.
Type of Packaging: Food Service
Brands:
ALCATEL
BOC EDWARDS
BOCE STOKES
BUSCH
EBARA
KINNEY
LEYBOLD
PRECISION SCIENTIFIC
RISTSCHIC
VARIAN
WELCH

11560 Preferred Brands International
9 W Broad Street
Suite 5
Stamford, CT 06902   203-348-0030
Fax: 203-348-0029   800-827-8900
comments@tastybite.com   www.tastybite.com
indian, thai, vegetarian, vegan, kosher and gluten
free foods.
President/Owner: Ravi Nigam
CEO: Ashok Vasudevan
CFO: Sohel Shikari
Executive VP; Sales & Marketing: Meera
Vasudevan
VP/VP Sales & Marketing/Sales Staff: Hans
Taparia
Estimated Sales: $5.7 Million
Number Employees: 10

11561 Preferred Meal Systems
4135 Birney Ave
Scranton, PA 18507-1397   570-457-8311
Fax: 570-457-9241
Processor and exporter of frozen portion control
lunches for airlines and schools
Executive Director: Bob Keen
Director Technology Services: Richard Ludt
Estimated Sales: $4800000
Number Employees: 250-499
Sq. footage: 100000
Type of Packaging: Food Service, Private Label

11562 Preferred Milks
1208 N Swift Rd
Addison, IL 60101-6104   630-678-5300
Fax: 630-678-5311   800-621-5046
info@oxydry.com   www.oxydry.com
Processor and exporter of dairy products including
powdered milk and egg extender blends
Manager: Dan Hoberg
Sales Manager: Donald Kelly, Jr.
Plant Manager: Samuel Vergara
Estimated Sales: $ 20 - 50 Million
Number Employees: 20-49
Sq. footage: 15000
Parent Co: Kelly Flour Company
Type of Packaging: Food Service, Private Label
Brands:
Hi-Bak
Kel-Yolk

11563 Premier Beverages
5301 Legacy Drive
Plano, TX 75024-3109   972-547-6295
Beverages
COO: Robert O'Brien
VP Sales: Scott Corridean
Estimated Sales: Under $500,000
Number Employees: 1-4

11564 Premier Blending
816 E Funston St
Wichita, KS 67211-4309   316-267-5533
Fax: 316-267-6426

Processor of breadings, spice blends and mixes in-
cluding sauce, corn dog, hushpuppy, fritter, funnel
cake, biscuit, muffin, batter, gravy and drink mixes
President/CEO: Peggy Moore
National Sales Manager: Terry Gould
Purchasing Manager: Reatha Stucky
Estimated Sales: $20-50 Million
Number Employees: 50-99
Sq. footage: 90000
Type of Packaging: Food Service, Private Label,
Bulk
Brands:
Tasty Crust

11565 Premier Casing Company
PO Box 7268
Shrewsbury, NJ 07702-7268   732-933-9700
Fax: 732-933-9898   800-933-9766
Processor, importer and exporter of sausage casings
President: Walter Maurer
Number Employees: 6
Type of Packaging: Bulk

11566 Premier Cereals
8621 NE 17th Pl
Clyde Hill, WA 98004-3215   425-451-1451
Fax: 425-451-1451   premierk@nwlink.com
Cereal and cereal flakes
President: Christian F Kongsore
Estimated Sales: $100+ Million
Number Employees: 1-4
Brands:
Premier Cereals

11567 Premier Juices
19321 Us Highway 19 N # 405
Clearwater, FL 33764-3142   727-533-8200
Fax: 727-533-8500
jody.marshburn@premierjuices.com
www.premierjuices.com
Fruit juices
Estimated Sales: $ 2.5-5 Million
Number Employees: 1-4

11568 Premier Malt Products
25760 Groesbeck Hwy
Warren, MI 48089-1589   586-443-3355
Fax: 586-445-4580   www.premiermalt.com
Processor of malt extracts for baking and home
brewing; also, fungal amylase and sequestrants
President: M Stuart Andreas
Estimated Sales: $1500000
Number Employees: 5-9
Type of Packaging: Consumer, Food Service, Bulk
Brands:
Diamalt
Premose

11569 Premier Meats
4013 Brandon Street SE
Calgary, AB T2G 4N5
Canada   403-287-3550
Fax: 403-287-3553
Processor/exporter of boxed, portion-controlled,
fresh and frozen meats including beef, veal and pork
President: E Chaikowski
Number Employees: 20-49
Type of Packaging: Consumer, Food Service, Bulk

11570 Premier Nutrition
6221 Yarrow Dr # A
Carlsbad, CA 92011-1550   760-929-9995
Fax: 760-929-9350   888-836-8972
info@premiernutrition.com
www.premiernutrition.com
Organic nutrition products
Owner: Karry Law
Estimated Sales: $ 5 - 10 Million
Number Employees: 10-19
Type of Packaging: Consumer, Private Label, Bulk
Brands:
Odyssey
Premier Nutrition
Premier Shots
Rocket Shot
Twisted Brand

11571 Premier Pacific Seafoods
111 W Harrison St
Seattle, WA 98119-4111   206-286-8584
Fax: 206-286-8810   johnh@prempac.com
Manufacturer of fresh prepared fish
President: Douglas Forsyth

Estimated Sales: $ 10-20 Million
Number Employees: 10-19
Type of Packaging: Bulk
Brands:
Ocean Phoenix
Premiere Pacific

11572 Premier Packing Company
P.O.Box 81498
Bakersfield, CA 93380-1498   661-393-3320
Fax: 661-392-0799   www.grimmway.com
Grower, packer and shipper of produce including
carrots, citrus, tree fruit, grapes and apples
President: Tom Moore
Plant Manager: Steven Pryor
Number Employees: 250-499
Parent Co: Shell California Products
Type of Packaging: Consumer, Food Service, Pri-
vate Label, Bulk
Brands:
Chef's Delight
Medallion

11573 Premier Roasters
400 Allan Street
Daly City, CA 94014-1637   415-337-4040
Fax: 415-333-7692   info@premierroasters.com
Coffee
President: Dan Wallace
CFO: Jeff Day
VP Marketing: Tom Rector
Operations Manager: Phil Maloney
Estimated Sales: $ 20-50 Million
Number Employees: 20-49
Type of Packaging: Private Label
Brands:
S&W Coffee

11574 Premier Smoked Fish Company
1119 Neshaminy Valley Dr
Bensalem, PA 19020-1222   215-757-0557
Fax: 305-625-5528   800-654-6682
info@seaspecialties.com
www.seaspecialties.com
Processor of fish including smoked salmon, cured
and herring
Owner: J Purner
COO: David Donahue
Controller: John Cicero
Plant Manager: David Sperry
Estimated Sales: $5200000
Number Employees: 5-9
Sq. footage: 24000
Parent Co: SeaSpecialties
Brands:
Mama's
Seaspecialties

11575 Premiere Packing Company
P.O.Box 815
Spokane Valley, WA 99016-0815   509-926-6666
Fax: 509-926-3300   888-239-5288
nuts@thenutfactory.com   www.thenutfactory.com
Snack foods, nuts, chocolates
President: Gene Cohen
Estimated Sales: Below $ 5 Million
Number Employees: 5-9

11576 Premiere Seafood
257 Midland Avenue
Lexington, KY 40508-1978   606-259-3474
Fax: 606-389-9390
Seafood
President: Rex Webb

11577 Premium Brands
P.O.Box 785
Bardstown, KY 40004-0785   502-348-0081
Fax: 502-348-5539
www.kentuckybourbonwhiskey.com
Liquor, beverages
President: Even Kulsveen
Estimated Sales: $290,000
Number Employees: 1-4

11578 Premium Coffee Company
611 Industrial Way W
Eatontown, NJ 07724-2284   732-578-1580
Fax: 732-578-1579   800-524-2743
Processor and packer of coffee including flavored
and espresso; private labeling available
President: Willi Lermer
Estimated Sales: Less than $500,000
Number Employees: 1-4

Type of Packaging: Consumer, Food Service, Private Label, Bulk
Brands:
  Premium

11579 Premium Ingredients International US, LLC
285 E Fullerton Ave
Carol Stream, IL 60188-1886   630-868-0300
                    Fax: 630-868-0310
          sales@premiumingredients.com
          www.premiumingredients.com
Food ingredients and aroma chemicals.
  President: Donald Thorp
  CFO: Donald Cepican
  VP: Daniel Thorp
  Research/Development Director: Suzanne Johnson
  VP Sales/Marketing: Richard Calabrese
Estimated Sales: $30-35 Million
Number Employees: 5-9
Parent Co: AMC Chemicals
Other Locations:
  Premium Ingredients International Holladay UT
  Premium Ingredients International Ellisville MO
  Premium Ingredients International Cranford NJ
  Premium Ingredients Int'l(UK) London, England

11580 Premium Meat Company
1100 W 600 N
Brigham City, UT 84302-4423   435-723-5944
          kdprice@mywebnet.com
Processor of meat including beef, pork and lamb
  President: Douglas W Price
  Sales Manager: David Wells
Estimated Sales: $ 3 - 5 Million
Number Employees: 5-9

11581 (HQ)Premium Standard Farms
805 Pennsylvania Avenue
Suite 200
Kansas City, MO 64105-1340   816-472-7675
  Fax: 816-843-1450 webmaster@psfarms.com
                    www.psfarms.com
Premium pork
  CEO: John Meyer
Number Employees: 4,800

11582 (HQ)Premium Standard Farms
805 Pennsylvania Avenue
Suite 200
Kansas City, MO 64105-1307   816-472-7675
          Fax: 816-843-1450 800-994-7675
                    www.psfarms.com
Processor of pork
  Chairman: Michael Zimmerman
  CEO: John Meyer
  VP & General Counsel: Gerald Schulte
  President: John Meyer
  VP Communications & Public Affairs: Charles Arnot
Estimated Sales: $500 Million to $1 Billion
Number Employees: 300
Type of Packaging: Food Service
Other Locations:
  Milan MO
  Clinton NC
  Princeton MO
  Dalhart TX
Brands:
  Premium Standard

11583 Premium Water
PO Box A
Orange Springs, FL 32182-1003   352-546-2052
          Fax: 352-546-1402 800-243-1163
Manufacturer and exporter of spring and distilled bottled water
  President: Peter Johnson
  GM: Bob McBride
Estimated Sales: $ 5 - 10 Million
Number Employees: 50-99
Sq. footage: 20000
Type of Packaging: Consumer, Food Service, Private Label
Brands:
  Acappella

11584 Premium Waters
2100 Summer St NE # 200
Minneapolis, MN 55413-3068   612-379-4141
          Fax: 612-623-0363 800-332-3332
          custserv@premiumwaters.com
          www.premiumwaters.com
Processor of water including bottled spring, sparkling and distilled.
  President: Greg Nemec
Estimated Sales: $97300000
Number Employees: 500-999
Sq. footage: 16500
Type of Packaging: Consumer, Food Service, Private Label, Bulk
Brands:
  CHIPPEWA
  CHIPPEWA ICED TEA
  CHIPPEWA SPRING WATER
  CRYSTAL GLEN
  EARTH'S PERFECT

11585 Premium Waters
2100 Summer St NE # 200
Minneapolis, MN 55413-3068   612-379-4141
          Fax: 612-623-0363 800-243-1163
          custserv@premiumwaters.com
          www.premiumwaters.com
  President: Grep Nemec
Estimated Sales: $ 2.5-$ 5 Million
Number Employees: 50-99
Brands:
  Aguazul
  Chippewa Spring Water
  Crystal Glen
  Glacier Clear
  Kandiyohi Premium Water

11586 (HQ)Presco Food Seasonings
26 Minneakoning Rd
Flemington, NJ 08822-5725   908-782-4919
          Fax: 908-782-6993 800-526-1713
          info@prescoseasonings.com
          www.prescoseasonings.com
Processor of seasonings and spices for sausage and snacks; also, gravy and sauce mixes
  President: Simon Statter
  VP: Simon Statter
Estimated Sales: $ 20 - 50 Million
Number Employees: 50-99
Type of Packaging: Private Label, Bulk

11587 Prescott Brewing Company
130 W Gurley St # A
Prescott, AZ 86301-3603   928-771-2795
          Fax: 928-771-1115 angpbc1@cableone.net
          www.prescottbrewingcompany.com
Beer
  President: John Nielsen
  CFO: Roxanne Nielsen
  Sales Director: Dave Jacobson
Estimated Sales: $ 1-5 Million
Number Employees: 50-99
Brands:
  Liquid Amber
  Lodgepole Light
  Petrified Porter

11588 President's Choice International
22 St Clair Avenue E
Toronto, ON M4T 2S8
Canada   416-967-2501
          www.presidentschoice.ca
Manufacturer of cookies, cola, biscuits, lasagna, turkey, pizza, coffee, poultry, ice cream and juice
Number Employees: 14
Sq. footage: 5000

11589 Presque Isle Wine Cellar
9440 W Main Rd
North East, PA 16428-2699   814-725-1314
          Fax: 814-725-2092 800-488-7492
          info@piwine.com www.piwine.com
Wine related products
  Owner: Doug Moorhead
  CFO: Douges Moorhead
  Co-Owner: Laury Bouttcher
Estimated Sales: Below $ 5 Million
Number Employees: 20-49
Type of Packaging: Private Label
Brands:
  Presque Isle Wine

11590 Pressed Paperboard Technologies LLC
30400 Telegraph Rd
Bingham Farms, MI 48025-4537   248-646-6500
  Fax: 248-646-6532 donw@papertrays.com OR
                    sales@papertrays.com
          www.papertrays.com/
Manufacturer of press formed, dual-ovenable paperboard trays for the frozen food, school and institutional feeding and pizza industries.
  Owner: Lawrence Epstein
  Vice President Sales: Al Fotheringham

11591 Prestige Proteins
1101 S Rogers Cir # 1
Boca Raton, FL 33487-2748   561-499-6100
          Fax: 561-495-7043 casein@casein.com
                    www.casein.com
Processor and exporter calcium caseinate, sodium caseinate and potassium caseinate
  Owner: Hue Henly
  Sales Manager: Tina Thimlar
Estimated Sales: $18000000
Number Employees: 1-4
Sq. footage: 50000
Type of Packaging: Consumer, Food Service, Private Label, Bulk
Brands:
  Prestige Proteins

11592 (HQ)Prestige Technology Corporation
1101 S Rogers Cir # 1
Boca Raton, FL 33487-2748   561-495-8710
          Fax: 561-495-7043 888-697-4141
          casein@casein.com www.caseinate.com
Processor and importer of regular and rennet casein; also, sodium and calcium caseinates
  President: Hugh Henley
  Director: James Cant
  Director: Godfrey Thomas
Estimated Sales: $18000000
Number Employees: 10-19
Sq. footage: 10000
Other Locations:
  Prestige Technology Corp. Minsk
Brands:
  Prestige Proteins
  Qualcoat

11593 Presto Avoset Group
PO Box 1086
Claremont, CA 91711-1086   909-399-0062
          Fax: 909-399-1162 thigh@rich.com
Nondairy toppings and icings
Brands:
  PASTRY PRIDE
  PASTRY PRO
  POUR N' PERFORMANCE
  POUR N' WHIP
  PRIDE
  QWIP
  TRES CREMAS

11594 Preston Farms
3055 W Bradford Rd NE
Palmyra, IN 47164-7935   812-364-6123
          Fax: 812-364-6105 866-767-7464
  sales@prestonfarms.com www.prestonfarms.com
Growers, processors and packers of specilly selected hybrid popcorn
  CEO: Raymond Preston
  President: Leigh Anne Preston
  Private Label Sales: Charles Shacklette
Estimated Sales: $300,000-500,000
Number Employees: 10-19
Number of Brands: 3
Number of Products: 60
Type of Packaging: Private Label
Brands:
  America's Premium
  Gettelfinger Select
  Heartland U.S.A.
  KY POPPERS
  Spee-Dee Pop

11595 Preston Premium Wines
502 E Vineyard Dr
Pasco, WA 99301-9667   509-545-1990
          Fax: 509-545-1098 info@prestonwines.com
          www.prestonwines.com

Wines
President: Brett Preston
Estimated Sales:$ 5-9.9 Million
Number Employees: 20-49
Brands:
Preston Premium Wines

11596 Preston Vineyards
9282 W Dry Creek Rd
Healdsburg, CA 95448-9134   707-433-3372
          Fax: 707-433-5307   800-305-9707
          retailsales@prestonvineyards.com
          www.prestonvineyards.com
Organic wine, olives, produce and baked goods
Co-Owner: Louis Preston
Co-Owner: Susan Preston
Winemaker: Matt Norelli
Vineyard Manager: Jesus Arzate
Estimated Sales:$ 5-10 Million
Number Employees: 10-19
Brands:
Kuchen

11597 Pretzels
P.O.Box 503
Bluffton, IN 46714-0503   260-824-4838
          Fax: 260-824-0895   800-456-4838
          harvestroad@pretzels-inc.com
          www.pretzels-inc.com/pretzelsinc.htm
Processor and exporter of pretzels and corn extruded
products including cheese curls, corn puffs, crunchy
cheese curls and hot barbecue cheese balls.
President: William Huggins
CEO: William Mann
CEO: William Mann
Marketing Director: Chip Manneson
Sales Director: Marvin Sparks
Operations Manager: John Sommer
Purchasing Manager: Steve Huggins
Number Employees: 100-249
Sq. footage: 200000
Type of Packaging: Consumer, Food Service, Private Label, Bulk
Brands:
Harvest Road
William's Corn

11598 Preuss Bake Shop
107 N State Street
Waseca, MN 56093-2928   507-835-4320
Bakery

11599 (HQ)Price Cold Storage & Packing Company
P.O.Box 4078
Yakima, WA 98904-4078   509-966-4110
          Fax: 509-966-2988   bob@priceapples.com
          www.priceapples.com
Processor, packer and exporter of fresh apples and
pears
President: Robert Price
Vice President: Bob Parsley
Sales Director: Chuck Zgutenhorst
Operations Manager: Norm Weathers
Production Manager: Don Khale
Estimated Sales:$25200000
Number Employees: 100-249
Sq. footage: 200000
Type of Packaging: Consumer, Food Service, Private Label, Bulk
Brands:
Gold Medal
Moon
Naches
Panda
Price
Priceless

11600 Price Seafood
5737 Highway 56
Chauvin, LA 70344-2801   985-594-3067
          Fax: 985-594-7748
Processor of frozen, peeled and dried shrimp
Owner: Norris Price
VP: Norris Price, Jr.
Estimated Sales:$ 10 - 20 Million
Number Employees: 10-19
Sq. footage: 8200
Brands:
Louisiana
Louisiana Cajun
Ocean Blue

11601 Price's Creameries
P.O.Box 3008
El Paso, TX 79923-3008   915-565-2711
          Fax: 915-562-8232 www.pricesmilk.com
Processor of milk, ice cream, sherbet, mellorine,
cream and ice cream and ice milk mixes
General Manager: Gene Carrejo
Plant Manager: Lonnie Williams
Number Employees: 100-249
Parent Co: Dean Foods Company
Type of Packaging: Consumer
Brands:
Price's

11602 Pride Beverages
1887 McFarland Road
Alpharetta, GA 30005-8341   770-663-0990
          Fax: 770-663-0091 www.pridebeverages.com
Juice concentrates
Estimated Sales:$500,000-$1 Million
Number Employees: 1-4

11603 Pride Enterprises Glades
500 Orange Avenue Cir
Belle Glade, FL 33430-5221   561-996-1091
          Fax: 561-996-8559
Sugarcane
Manager: Peter Venables
Facility Manager: Peter Venables
*Estimated Sales:*Under $500,000
Number Employees: 5-9

11604 Pride of Dixie Syrup Company
P.O.Box 1117
Jonesboro, AR 72403-1117   870-935-2252
          Fax: 870-935-9325   800-530-7654
Processor of table syrups for pancakes, waffles and
cooking including maple, honey and crystal white
flavors
President: David Best
Estimated Sales:$180,000
Number Employees: 1-4
Sq. footage: 5000
Type of Packaging: Consumer, Food Service, Private Label
Brands:
Craft's
Pride of Dixie

11605 (HQ)Pride of Italy
1108 56th Street
Kenosha, WI 53140-3669   262-634-2164
          Fax: 262-634-9929
Frozen pizza
President: Joe Gianeselli
President: Joe Gianeselli
Number Employees: 10-19

11606 Pride of Sampson
P.O.Box 289
Clinton, NC 28329-0289   910-592-6188
          Fax: 910-592-1204 www.prideofsampson.com
Processor and exporter of sweet potatoes
Manager: Roger Lane
President: George Wooten
Estimated Sales:$ 50 - 100 Million
Number Employees: 50-99
Parent Co: Wayne E. Bailey
Type of Packaging: Consumer, Bulk

11607 Pride of White River Valley
P.O.Box 106
Gaysville, VT 05746-0106   802-234-9115
          Fax: 802-234-6780
          www.whiterivervalleycamping.com
Owner: Andrew Smith
Estimated Sales:$300,000-500,000
Number Employees: 1-4

11608 Priester Pecan Company
P.O.Box 381
Fort Deposit, AL 36032-0381   334-227-4301
          Fax: 334-227-4294   800-277-3226
          customerservice@priesters.com
          www.priester.com
Processor of pecans, pecan candies and baked goods
President: Ned T Ellis Jr
VP: Ellen Burkett
Public Relations: Faye Hood
Plant Manager: Jim Wheeler
Estimated Sales:$9116910
Number Employees: 50-99
Type of Packaging: Consumer, Private Label, Bulk

Brands:
Cloverland

11609 Prifti Candy Company
106 Green St
Worcester, MA 01604-4141   508-754-5143
          Fax: 508-754-0325   800-447-7438
          info@prifti.com   www.prifti.com
Candies
Owner: Nick Prifti
*Estimated Sales:*Less than $500,000
Number Employees: 1-4
Brands:
Prifti Candy

11610 Prima Foods International
606 SW 13th St
Ocala, FL 34471-0620   352-732-9148
          Fax: 352-732-0625   800-774-8751
          primafoods@worldnet.att.net
          www.primafoods.com
Processor of syrup, cocktail mixes, drink base powder and liquids, tropical fruit purees and fruit juice
concentrates; importer of tropical fruit purees and
juice concentrates; exporter of drink bases and milk
replacers
President: Hector Viale
VP Sales: Mary Lou Sharp
Estimated Sales:$ 5 - 10 Million
Number Employees: 5-9
Sq. footage: 10000
Type of Packaging: Food Service, Private Label, Bulk
Brands:
Flat Wood Farm
Prima Naturals

11611 Prima Kase
PO Box 448
Monticello, WI 53570-0448   608-938-4227
          Fax: 608-938-1227   kase@madison.tds.net
          www.primakase.com
Processor of gouda, fontina, wheel Swiss,
sweet-style Swiss and havarti cheeses
President: Steve McKeon
CEO: Steve McKeon
Estimated Sales:$ 2.5-5 Million
Number Employees: 5-9
Type of Packaging: Consumer, Food Service, Private Label, Bulk
Brands:
Prima Kase

11612 Prime Cut Meat & Seafood Company
2601 N 31st Ave
Phoenix, AZ 85009-1522   602-455-8834
          Fax: 602-455-8711
Meat, seafood
President: Dave Poppen
VP/Treasurer: Linda Poppen
Estimated Sales:$ 50 - 100 Million
Number Employees: 20-49

11613 Prime Food Processing Corporation
300 Vandervoort Ave
Brooklyn, NY 11211-1715   718-963-2323
          Fax: 718-963-3256   888-639-2323
Processor of Chinese dumplings and egg rolls
Owner: Albert Chin
Quality Control: Laymont Dofon
Estimated Sales:$ 20-50 Million
Number Employees: 50-99
Sq. footage: 10000
Type of Packaging: Consumer, Food Service, Private Label, Bulk
Brands:
Prime Food

11614 Prime Ingredients
280 N Midland Ave # U
Saddle Brook, NJ 07663-5708   201-791-6655
          Fax: 201-791-4244   888-791-6655
          info@primeingredients.com
          www.primeingredients.com
Manufacturer of fresh and frozen gourmet dessert,
dips and sauces. Also manufactures cheese, creamers, mixes, glazes, oils, margarines; exporter of olive
oil
Director: Christopher Walsh

Estimated Sales: Below $5 Million
Number Employees: 10-19
Sq. footage: 20000
Type of Packaging: Bulk

11615 Prime Ostrich International
8702a 98th Street
Morinville, AB T8R 1K6
Canada 780-939-3804
Fax: 780-939-4888 800-340-2311
Processor and exporter of ostrich including whole carcasses, jerky, deli and portion controlled cuts and meat pies
President: James Danyluik
Marketing Director: Michelle Danyluik
Number Employees: 5-9
Type of Packaging: Consumer, Food Service, Private Label, Bulk

11616 Prime Pak Foods
2076 Memorial Park Dr
Gainesville, GA 30504-5802 770-536-8708
Fax: 770-536-1638
Processor beef, pork, veal, poultry and barbecue meat products including burgers, patties, meat loaf, breaded choppettes, chicken breasts, chicken and beef fry steak, cubed steaks, chicken tenders and livers, hot wings, etc.; alsochili with beans
President: T Robson
Estimated Sales: $ 50 - 100 Million
Number Employees: 50-99

11617 Prime Pastries
370 North Rivermed Road
Concord, ON L4K 3N2
Canada 905-669-5883
Fax: 905-669-8655 smuchnik@primus.ca
Pastries
President: Steven Muchnik
CFO: Ashley Berman
Brands:
Prime Pastries

11618 Prime Pastry
22 2nd Avenue
Brooklyn, NY 11215-3102 888-771-2464
Fax: 718-237-1988
Processor, importer and exporter of frozen baked goods
VP Sales/Marketing: Russ Slotnick
Estimated Sales: $ 3 - 5 Million
Number Employees: 10-19
Parent Co: Prime Group
Type of Packaging: Food Service, Private Label, Bulk
Brands:
Prime Pastry

11619 Prime Produce
350 N Cypress St
Orange, CA 92866-1028 714-771-0718
Fax: 714-771-0728 yair@prime-produce.com
www.prime-produce.com
Processor of avocados
President: Avi Crane
Business Development Manager: Yair Crane
Sales Manager: Gahl Crane
Operations/Ripening Manager: Miguel Guzman
Estimated Sales: $5-10 Million
Number Employees: 20-49
Type of Packaging: Consumer, Food Service, Private Label, Bulk

11620 Prime Smoked Meats
220 Alice St
Oakland, CA 94607-4394 510-832-7167
Fax: 510-832-4830 www.primesmoked.com
Processor, wholesaler/distributor and exporter of cured and smoked pork products including fresh and frozen
President: Steve Sacks
General Manager: Dave Andes
Office Manager: Ed Pastana
Plt. Mgr.: Dave Andes
Estimated Sales: $5897842
Number Employees: 10-19
Sq. footage: 12000
Type of Packaging: Consumer, Food Service, Private Label, Bulk
Brands:
James
Prime

11621 (HQ)Primer Foods Corporation
P.O.Box 373
Cameron, WI 54822-0373 715-458-4075
Fax: 715-458-4078 sales@primerafoods.com
www.primerafoods.com
Manufacturer of Egg products, encapsulated ingredients, specialty gums, maltodextrins and syrup solids, tomato powders, fudge and carmel concentrates, eggStreme Options
President/CEO: Jon Luikart
Finance Executive: James Anderson
Quality Control: Kristen Zuzek
VP Sales/Marketing: Rolf Rogers
Director Operations: Tom Brown
Estimated Sales: $20-50 Million
Number Employees: 20-49
Sq. footage: 105000
Other Locations:
Primera Foods
Penham MN
Primera Foods
Stockton IL
Primera Foods
Hayfield MN
Primera Foods
Faribault MN
Primer Foods
Altura MN
Brands:
EGGSTREME BAKERY MIX 100
EGGSTREME OPTIONS
EGGSTREME YOLK
EGGSTREME-WE 300
INSTA THICK
MALTA GRAN
PRIME CAP
RICE COMPLETE
RICE PRO 35
RICE TRIN
TAPI
TOMATO MAX

11622 Primera Foods
P.O.Box 373
Cameron, WI 54822-0373 715-458-4075
Fax: 715-458-4078 800-365-2409
sales@primerafoods.com
www.primerafoods.com
Agglomeration, spray drying, eggs, vegetables, encapsulation
President/CEO: Jon Luikart
Finance Executive: James Anderson
Sales Manager: Leslie Rask
Estimated Sales: $ 20-50 Million
Number Employees: 20-49

11623 Primera Meat Service
21649 Stuart Place Rd
Harlingen, TX 78552-1962 956-423-4846
Fax: 956-423-3085
Processor of meat products
Owner: Javier Abundiz
Estimated Sales: $ 3 - 5 Million
Number Employees: 5-9

11624 Primex International Trading Corporation
5777 W Century Blvd
Suite 1484
Los Angeles, CA 90045 310-568-8855
Fax: 310-568-3336 info@primex-usa.com
www.primex-usa.com
grower and processor of pistachios as well as an international trader and exporter of dried fruits and nuts
President/Owner: Ali Amin
COO: Mojgan Amin
Estimated Sales: $184.5 Million
Number Employees: 25

11625 Primo Foods
56 Huxley Rd
Toronto, ON M9M 1H2
Canada 860-573-0134
Fax: 860-657-1487 800-377-6945
uliassm@cox.net www.primofoods.ca
Primo pasta, primo can tomatoes, primo can beans, primo pasta sauces
VP: Tony Gucciardi
Sales: Phil Ulias
Sq. footage: 100000
Type of Packaging: Consumer, Food Service, Private Label

11626 Primo Foods
56 Huxley Road
North York, ON M9M 1H2
Canada 416-741-9300
Fax: 416-741-3766 800-377-6945
Manufacturer of pasta
Plant Manager: Gabe Soffiaturo
Parent Co: Nabisco
Type of Packaging: Consumer, Food Service

11627 Primo Piatto
7300 36th Ave N
Minneapolis, MN 55427-2001 763-531-9194
Fax: 763-536-0100 www.dakotagrowers.com
Pasta, pasta products and services
President: Tim Dodd
Executive: Tom Mac Cani
Estimated Sales: $100+ Million
Number Employees: 100-249

11628 Primos Northgate
2323 Lakeland Dr
Flowood, MS 39232-9514 601-936-3398
Fax: 601-936-3797 don@primocafe.com
www.primoscafe.com
Processor of baked products including pies
Owner: Don Primos
President: Peter Primos
CEO: Peter Primos
Estimated Sales: $500,000 appx.
Number Employees: 20-49
Type of Packaging: Consumer
Brands:
Primos

11629 Primrose Candy Company
4111 W Parker Ave
Chicago, IL 60639-2176 773-276-9522
Fax: 773-276-7411 800-268-9522
shawn@primrosecandy.com
www.primrosecandy.com
Processor and exporter of candy including bagged, filled, fund raising, Halloween, hard and rock; also, lollypops and popcorn specialties
President: Mark Puch
CEO: Mark Puch
VP Sales/Marketing: Richard Griseto
Estimated Sales: $27,800,000
Number Employees: 100-249
Sq. footage: 95000
Type of Packaging: Consumer, Food Service, Private Label, Bulk
Brands:
HUNKEY DOREY
IBC ROOT BEER BARRELS
RICH & CREAMY CARAMELS
TRADITIONAL SALTWATER TAFFY

11630 Prince Michael Vineyards
154 Winery Ln
Leon, VA 22725-2511 540-547-3707
Fax: 540-547-3088 800-869-8242
info@princemichael.com
www.princemichel.com
Wine
Owner: Terry Holzman
Estimated Sales: $ 5-10 Million
Number Employees: 20-49

11631 Prince of Peace Enterprises
3536 Arden Rd
Hayward, CA 94545-3908 510-887-1899
Fax: 510-887-1799 800-732-2328
popsf@popus.com www.popus.com
Processor, importer, exporter and wholesaler/distributor of American ginseng root, instant tea and chocolate covered macadamia nuts; wholesaler/distributor of confectionery items, baked goods and dairy products
President: Kenneth Yeung
VP: Lolita Lim
National Sales Manager: Robert Chan
Purchasing: Maria Wong
Estimated Sales: $11200000
Number Employees: 20-49
Sq. footage: 72000
Brands:
GX POWER
HAZELNUT
JAMAICAN GOLD
MOCHA
NATURE SOOTHE
NEW JAMAICAN GOLD CAPPUCCINO

PRINCE OF PEACE
PRINCE OF PEACE HAWAIIAN
TIGER BALM ANALGESIC OINTMENTS

11632 Princeville Canning Company
606 S Tremont St
Princeville, IL 61559-9468   309-385-4301
Fax: 309-385-2696 www.senecafoods.com
Manufacturer and exporter of canned vegetables including asparagus, pumpkins, green beans, corn and peas; also, salads including German potato, 3/4 bean and garden
Manager: Wally Hochsprung
Plant Manager: David Stoner
Estimated Sales:$10-20 Million
Number Employees: 100-249
Sq. footage: 160000
Parent Co: Owatonna Canning Company
Type of Packaging: Consumer, Food Service, Private Label

11633 Pristine Foods
2508 Gates Cir
Baton Rouge, LA 70809-1028   225-926-4677
Fax: 225-927-3819
General groceries
Estimated Sales:$480,000
Number Employees: 1-4
Type of Packaging: Consumer

11634 Private Brands Coffee &Tea Company
4410 Hunt Avenue
Saint Louis, MO 63110-2112   314-652-0851
Fax: 314-652-5312
Tea and coffee
Sales Manager: Gerald Fratini
*Estimated Sales:*Under $500,000
Number Employees: 1-4

11635 Private Harvest
2617 S Main St
Lakeport, CA 95453-5650   707-263-0694
Fax: 707-263-8362 800-463-0594
info@privateharvest.com
www.privateharvest.com
Gourmet sauces and spreads.
CEO: Bonnie Frese
Vice President: Kurt Frese
Estimated Sales:$ 10-20 Million
Number Employees: 20-49
Type of Packaging: Private Label
Brands:
Bobby Flay
Private Harvest
Private Harvest Bobby Flay
Private Harvest Tuscan Hills
Tuscan Hills

11636 Private Harvest GourmetSpecialities
2617 S Main St
Lakeport, CA 95453-5650   707-263-0694
Fax: 707-263-8362 800-463-0594
info@privateharvest.com
www.privateharvest.com
Produces pasta, BBQ, tartar and steak gourmet sauces
Owner: Kurt Frese
Estimated Sales:$ 50 - 100 Million
Number Employees: 20-49
Type of Packaging: Private Label

11637 Private Label Foods
1680 Lyell Ave
Rochester, NY 14606-2312   585-254-9205
Fax: 585-254-0186 info@privatelabelfoods.com
www.privatelabelfoods.com
Processor and contract packager of barbecue, spaghetti and hot sauces, salad dressings, salsa and marinades
President: Frank Lavorato
VP: Bonnie Lavorato
Estimated Sales:$ 4 Million
Number Employees: 10-19
Sq. footage: 50000
Type of Packaging: Food Service, Private Label

11638 Pro Form Labs
P.O.Box 626
Orinda, CA 94563-0576   925-299-9000
Fax: 925-299-9004 info@proformlabs.com
www.proformlabs.com

Processor and exporter of health products including nutritional supplement powders, vitamins, weight control and sports nutrition tablets, capsules and powders; also, herbal tablets, capsules and powders
President: Doug Gillespie
Customer Service: Kellie Henry
Purchasing Agent: Alex Gillespie
Estimated Sales:$ 3 - 5 Million
Number Employees: 1-4
Sq. footage: 25000
Parent Co: Gillespie & Associates
Type of Packaging: Consumer, Food Service, Private Label, Bulk
Brands:
Healthbody
Juice-Mate
Naturslim

11639 Pro Pac Labs
P.O.Box 9691
Ogden, UT 84409-0691   801-621-0900
Fax: 801-621-0930 888-277-6722
general@propaclabs.com   www.propaclabs.com
Custom contract manufacturer of dietary supplements including herbs, vitamins and minerals
President: Lew Wheelwright
Technology Sales: Zack Bylee
Purchasing Manager: Steven Cherecwich
Estimated Sales:$5193764
Number Employees: 50-99
Type of Packaging: Consumer, Private Label, Bulk

11640 Pro Portion Food
217 N Main Street
Sayville, NY 11782-2512   631-567-4494
Fax: 631-567-1636 elhayes1643@aol.com
Health and dietetics foods
President: Rhoda Rubin
Estimated Sales:$ 5-10 Million
Number Employees: 15

11641 Pro-Pharm
11 N Skokie Hwy
Lake Bluff, IL 60044-1796   847-234-3570
Fax: 847-234-5298 propharrm@ix.netcom.com
Processor, importer and exporter of vitamins, ginseng, herbal products, chlorophyll, amino acids, bee products, powdered extracts, etc
President: Derek Khubchandani
VP: George Edwards
Estimated Sales:$300,000-500,000
Number Employees: 1-4
Sq. footage: 200000

11642 ProSource
PO Box 1058
Alexandria, MN 56308-1058   320-763-2470
Fax: 320-763-7996
Processor and exporter of milk replacers, dairy blends and soy products
President: Donald Crank
Number Employees: 5-9
Type of Packaging: Consumer, Food Service, Private Label, Bulk
Brands:
Custom-Bake
Instapro
Prolait
Proleche

11643 Proacec USA
1158 26th Street
Suite 509
Santa Monica, CA 90403-4621   310-996-7770
Fax: 310-996-7772 proacecusa@proacec.com
www.proacec.com
Produces all natural award winning products from our olive orchards in Andalusia, Spain. In addition to gourmet olives and olive oil we also produce and import to US complimentary food items such as, balsamic vinegars, artichokesanchovies, spices and ca
President: Paul Shortt
*Estimated Sales:*Below $ 5 Million
Number Employees: 10
Number of Brands: 4
Number of Products: 30
Sq. footage: 1000
Type of Packaging: Consumer, Food Service, Bulk
Brands:
CAROLIVA
DON QUIXATE
EL CARMEN
PLANTIO DEL CONDADO

11644 (HQ)Proctor & Gamble Company
1 or 2 Proctor & Gamble Plaza
Cincinnati, OH 45201   513-983-1100
Fax: 513-562-4500 misc.im@pg.com
www.pg.com
Manufacturer of Pringles potato chips, as well as lines of cleaners and paper products.
President & CEO, Proctor & Gamble Corp.: Robert McDonald
President, North America: Steven Bishop
Chief Financial Officer: Jon Moeller
President, Global Snacks & Pet Care: John Goodwin
Estimated Sales:$79 Billion
Number Employees: 135000
Sq. footage: 15000
Type of Packaging: Consumer
Other Locations:
Procter & Gamble Co.
Boca Raton FL
Brands:
100 CALORIE PACKS
ACTONEL
ALWAYS
ARIEL
BOUNTY
CHARMIN
CLAIROL
CREST
DOWNY
FOLGERS
HEAD & SHOULDERS
IAMS
LENOR
OLAY
PAMPERS
PANTENE
PRINGLES
TIDE
WHISPER

11645 Proctor & Gamble Company
767 Winchester Rd
Lexington, KY 40505-3728   859-254-5544
Fax: 859-288-2257 www.pg.com
Processor of peanut butter
Chairman/President: A G Lafley
Vice-Chairman: Bruce L Byrnes
CFO: Clayton Daley
Vice President: Valarie Sheppard
CFO: Clayton C Daley Jr
Plant Manager: Bob White
Estimated Sales:$100+ Million
Number Employees: 100-249
Parent Co: Procter & Gamble Company
Type of Packaging: Consumer

11646 Proctor & Gamble Company
2050 S 35th Ave
Phoenix, AZ 85009-6705   602-269-2171
Fax: 623-269-4107 www.pg.com
Processor of powdered drink mix
Co-Founder: Robert Steele
Co-Founder: James Gamble
CEO: A G Lafley
Estimated Sales:$100+ Million
Number Employees: 100-249
Parent Co: Procter & Gamble Company
Type of Packaging: Consumer, Food Service, Private Label, Bulk
Brands:
Proctor & Gamble

11647 Produce Buyers Company
7201 W Fort St # 93
Detroit, MI 48209-4109   313-843-0132
Manufacturer of produce
President: Salvatore Cipriano
Estimated Sales:$1-3 Million
Number Employees: 1-4

11648 Produce Edge
1125 S Fisher Avenue
Reedley, CA 93654-4218   559-637-9988
Fax: 559-637-9998 edge@produceedge.com
produceedge.com
Growers of tree-ripened peaches, nectarines, plums, apricots, grapes, and persimmons

11649 Producer Marketing Overlake

PO Box 2631
Olympia, WA 98507-2631   360-352-7989
Fax: 360-352-8076 info@overlakefoods.com
www.overlakefoods.com
Manufacturer of blueberries, strawberries, sliced
peaches, Marion blackberries, raspberries
President: Rod Cook
Sales: Paul Askier
General Manager: Bill Whaley
Estimated Sales:$ 5 - 10 Million
Number Employees: 5-9
Parent Co: Overlake Farms
Type of Packaging: Consumer, Food Service, Private Label, Bulk
Brands:
BEE SWEET
OVERLAKE

11650 Producer's Rice

P.O. Box 1248
Stuttgart, AR 72160-1012   870-673-4444
Fax: 870-673-7394 kglover@producersrice.com
www.producersrice.com
Procesor of rice and soybeans
President: Keith Glover
CEO: Keith Glover
VP Marketing, Consumer Products: Gary Reifeiss

Sr VP Rice Sales/Marketing: Marvin Baden
VP Operations: Kenny Dryden
Estimated Sales:$252055279
Number Employees: 500-999
Type of Packaging: Consumer, Food Service

11651 Producers Cooperative

P.O.Box 525
Olathe, CO 81425-0525   970-323-5913
Fax: 970-323-6057 opg@montrose.net
Procesor and exporter of dry edible pinto beans
Manager: Bob Beyer
General Manager: Eob Beyer
Number Employees: 10-19
Sq. footage: 10000
Type of Packaging: Private Label
Brands:
Cowboy
Hub of the Uncompaghre

11652 Producers Cooperative Oil Mill

6 SE 4th St
Oklahoma City, OK 73129-1000   405-232-7555
Fax: 405-236-4887
gconkling@producerscoop.net
www.producerscoop.net
Processor and exporter of cottonseed
Manager: James Graves
Ceo: Gary Conkling
Cfo: Ronda Nault
Marketing Director: Jim Freeman
Sales Director: Cary Crawford
Estimated Sales:$ 50 - 100 Million
Number Employees: 50-99
Number of Products: 1

11653 Producers Dairy Company

222 S Monticello Avenue
Clarksburg, WV 26301-3098   304-623-1831
Dairy products
Owner: Dave Marshall
Estimated Sales:Under $500,000
Number Employees: 5-9

11654 Producers Dairy Foods

P.O.Box 1231
Fresno, CA 93715-1231   559-264-6583
Fax: 559-264-8437
marketing@producersdairy.com
www.producersdairy.com
Dairy food
Chairman: Lawrence Shehadey
Marketing Director: Jacqui Uttrelle
CFO: Frank Sewill
Estimated Sales:$ 100 Million
Number Employees: 100-249

11655 Producers Peanut Company

337 Moore Ave
Suffolk, VA 23434-3819   757-539-7496
Fax: 757-934-7730 800-847-5491
info@producerspeanut.com
www.producerspeanut.com

Processor, importer and exporter of peanut butter
and granulated roasted peanuts
President: James R Pond
Plant Manager: Richard Herto
Estimated Sales:$800,000
Number Employees: 20-49
Sq. footage: 36000
Type of Packaging: Food Service, Private Label,
Bulk
Brands:
America Farms
New Life
Peanut Kids Peanut Butter
Sunny Day
The Peanut Kids

11656 (HQ)Producers Rice Mill

P.O.Box 1248
Stuttgart, AR 72160-1012   870-673-4444
Fax: 870-673-7394 info@producersrice.com
www.producersrice.com
Manufacturer and exporter of packaged rice and par-
boiled rice, bran, screenings, and brewers rice
President/CEO: Keith Glover
VP Finance/Administration: Kent Lockwood
Senior VP Rice Sales/Marketing: Marvin Baden
VP Marketing/Consumer Products: Gary Reifeiss
VP Operations: Kenny Dryden
Estimated Sales:$305 Million
Number Employees: 500-999
Type of Packaging: Consumer, Food Service, Pri-
vate Label, Bulk
Brands:
BUCK GRUB
EQUI-JEWEL
LE GOURMET
PAR EXCELLENCE

11657 Production Techniques Limited

3/39 Sir William Avenue
PO Box 58-874 Greenmount
Auckland,
New Zealand
Email: nick@ptl.co.nz Phone: 64 (09) 274-3561
Fax: 64 (09) 274-3515
www.ptl.co.nz/
Provides manufacturing and processing equipment
for the chocolate, candy, confectionery and bakery
industries. Specialized plant manufacturing covers a
wide range of plant applications including standard
pieces of equipment such asmelters, depositors,
enrobers, moulding plants, cooling tunnels,
temperers and decorators.
President/Chief Executive Officer: Jim Halliday
Sales & Marketing Manager: Nick Halliday

11658 Produits Alimentaire

1186 Rue Du Pont
St Lambert De Lauzon, QC G0S 2W0
Canada   418-889-8080
Fax: 418-889-9730 800-463-1787
Processor of flour, food colors and confectionery
items including hard candies and lollypops; importer
of syrup
Director: Michel Blouin
Number Employees: 20-49
Sq. footage: 8000
Type of Packaging: Consumer, Food Service, Pri-
vate Label, Bulk
Brands:
Blouin
Maltee
Pacha
Supreme

11659 (HQ)Produits Alimentaires Berthelet

1805 Rue Berlier
Laval, QC H7L 3S4
Canada   514-334-5503
Fax: 514-334-3584
Processor of dehydrated foods including soup bases,
sauce mixes, seasonings and beverage crystals; ex-
porter of beverage crystals
President: Guy Berthelet
CEO: Jacques Berthelet
Marketing Manager: Jimmy Berthelet
Number Employees: 100
Sq. footage: 45000
Type of Packaging: Consumer, Food Service, Pri-
vate Label, Bulk
Other Locations:
Produits Alimentaires Berthel
Blainville PQ

Brands:
Berthelet
Juwong
Le Saucier
McLean
Pasta Fiesta
Privilege
St. Hubert

11660 Produits Belle Baie

10 rue du Quai
Caraquet, NB E1W 1B6
Canada   506-727-4414
Fax: 506-727-7166
Packer and exporter of cod, herring, marinated her-
ring roe, ground redfish, shrimp, lobster and crabs
President: Artie Lebouthiller
Number Employees: 250-499
Type of Packaging: Consumer, Food Service

11661 Produits Ronald

200 Rue St Joseph
St. Damase, QC J0H 1J0
Canada   450-797-3303
Fax: 450-797-2389 info@p-ronald.com
www.p-ronald.com
Processor and exporter of vacuum packed and
canned corn-on-the-cob, meat marinades, barbecue
sauces, baked beans and bouillons and sauces for
fondue, dessert fondue
President/General Manager: Jean Messier
Vice President: Daniel Beauregard
Director Quality Control: Julie Legare
Marketing Director: Bernard Belanger
Purchasing Manager: Yvon Martin
Number Employees: 100-249
Sq. footage: 40000
Parent Co: A. Lassonde
Type of Packaging: Consumer, Food Service
Brands:
CAMINO DEL SOL
CANTON
MADELAINE
MONT-ROUGR
ROUGEMONT

11662 (HQ)Proferas Pizza Bakery

1130 Moosic St
Scranton, PA 18505   570-342-4181
Fax: 570-342-4853 www.proferaspizza.com
Processor of frozen pizza including pies, shells and
dough
President: Robert Arvonio
Estimated Sales:$6100000
Number Employees: 50-99
Type of Packaging: Consumer, Food Service, Pri-
vate Label, Bulk

11663 Progenix Corporation

4000 County Road Ww
Wausau, WI 54401-8329   715-675-6021
Fax: 715-675-4931 800-233-3356
progenix@progenixcorp.com
Processor, wholesaler/distributor and exporter of
ginseng and Wisconsin ginseng, bulk whole root, fi-
ber, prong, powder and extract; also, capsules, teas
and gift packaging available
President: Robert Duwe
Number Employees: 20-49
Sq. footage: 13000
Type of Packaging: Consumer, Food Service, Bulk
Brands:
Ameriseng
Wiscon
Wisconsin American Ginseng

11664 Progress Candy

207-209 Jarvis Avenue
Winnipeg, NB R2W 2Z9
Canada   204-586-8027
Fax: 204-586-8028
Manufacturer of confectionery products
President: Ralph Shaff
Secretary: Belva Shaff
Number Employees: 10-15
Number of Products: 120
Sq. footage: 19000
Type of Packaging: Private Label, Bulk
Brands:
PROGRESS CANDY
SARDIS OF CANADA

11665 Progress Industries
270 Sterkel Blvd
Mansfield, OH 44907-1508   419-756-0044
Fax: 419-756-6544
Contract packager of single serving condiment
packs and silverware
President: Eric Weber
CEO: James Schaum
Estimated Sales: $$2.5-5 Million
Number Employees: 50-99
Type of Packaging: Food Service

11666 Progressive Flavors
P.O.Box 517
Hawley, PA 18428-517   805-383-2640
Fax: 805-383-2644 www.progressiveflavors.com
Flavors for food and beverage
President: Norma Schwarz
Estimated Sales: $ 5 - 10 Million
Number Employees: 4
Type of Packaging: Food Service, Bulk

11667 Progresso Quality Foods
500 W Elmer Rd
Vineland, NJ 08360-6314   856-691-1565
Fax: 856-794-1574 800-200-9377
www.generalmills.com
Processor of canned soups, bread crumbs, cooking
oils and spaghetti sauce
Controller: Robert Buchs
Vice President: Anil Arora
Research & Development: Mounir El Hmamsi
Plant Manager: James Ellis
Estimated Sales: $50 Million
Number Employees: 5-9
Sq. footage: 600000
Parent Co: Pillsbury Company
Type of Packaging: Consumer
Brands:
PROGRESSO

11668 Proliant
2425 SE Oak Tree Court
Ankeny, IA 50021-7102   800-369-2672
Fax: 515-289-5110 craig.joy@proliantinc.com
www.proliantinc.com
Protein sciences, including meat stocks, broths, fla-
vors, fats, extracts and enhancers
President: Wally Lauridsen
Regional Sales Manager: Craig Joy
Brands:
Proliant

11669 Proliant Meat Ingredients
2425 SE Oak Tree Court
Ankeny, IA 50021-7102   515-289-5100
Fax: 515-289-5110 800-369-2672
meatingredients@proliantinc.com
www.proliantinc.com/keepitrealTFB
With over 20 years experience in the development
and manufacture of quality protein ingredients for
the food industry, we at Proliant Meat Ingredients
know real. Our ingredients include stocks, broths
and extracts; functional meat andpoultry proteins;
flavor enhancers; savory flavors; animal fats and
tallows and other specialty products. Proliant's in-
gredients are ideal for meat, savory prepared foods
and snack applications. Let us show you the real dif-
ference. Visit us atwww.proliantinc.com
Brands:
MYLOGEL

11670 Prolume Biolume
163 W White Mountain Blvd # D
Lakeside, AZ 85929-7004   928-367-1200
Fax: 928-367-1205 info@prolume.com
www.prolume.com
Food additives that generate their own light, food
bioluminescence ingredients
CEO: Bruce Bryan
Co-Founder: Bruce Bryan
Brands:
Prolume

**11671 Promiseland Meat
PackingCompany**
RR 3
Box 27b
Madill, OK 73446-8916   580-795-3567
Processor of sausage, beef, pork, ham and cold cuts
President: Mike Glenn
Number Employees: 1-4
Type of Packaging: Consumer, Food Service, Pri-
vate Label, Bulk

Brands:
Gregs Old Fashioned

11672 Proper-Chem
46 Arbor Ln
Dix Hills, NY 11746-5128   631-420-8000
Fax: 631-420-8003
Processor and exporter of vitamins and food supple-
ments
President: Emil Backstrom
Estimated Sales: $ 3 - 5 Million
Number Employees: 10-19
Sq. footage: 20000
Type of Packaging: Consumer, Private Label
Brands:
Goubaud
Proper-Care

11673 Prosource
2214 Geneva Road
Alexandria, MN 56308-8995   320-763-2470
Fax: 320-763-7996 www.prosource.net
Bodybuilding and nutritional supplements
Director: Donald Crank
Estimated Sales: $ 2.5-5 Million
Number Employees: '5-9
Brands:
Prosource

11674 Protano's Bakery
2301 N 22nd Ave
Hollywood, FL 33020-2003   954-925-3474
Fax: 954-925-3488 guy@protano.com
www.protano.com
Bakery products
Owner: Guy Protano Jr
Treasurer: Guy Protano
Plant Manager: Bob Woodmancy
Estimated Sales: $ 5-10 Million
Number Employees: 50-99

11675 Protein Palace
7273 W Waterford Road
Hartford, WI 53027-9782   262-673-2698
Cheese

11676 Protein Products Inc
76 Carlton Lane
North Andover, MA 01845-5603   978-689-9083
Fax: 978-975-4325 sales@proteinpro.com
www.proteinpro.com
Processor and exporter of hydrolyzed proteins and
fish gelatin
President: Peter Noble
Sales: Chris Gorski
Type of Packaging: Bulk

11677 Protein Research Associates
1852 Rutan Dr
Livermore, CA 94551-7635   925-243-6300
Fax: 925-243-6308 800-948-1991
info@proteinresearch.com
www.proteinresearch.com
Processor and exporter of nutritional, amino acid
and vitamin/mineral supplements; also, consultant
for new product development specializing in nutri-
tional supplements
President: Robert Matheson
Director: Theodore Aarons
VP Operations: Daniel Aarons
Estimated Sales: $5-10 Million
Number Employees: 5-9
Number of Products: 12
Sq. footage: 33000
Type of Packaging: Private Label, Bulk

11678 Protient
1751 County Road B W # 200
Roseville, MN 55113-4037   651-638-2600
Fax: 651-697-0997 sengler@protient.com
www.protient.com
Manufacturers of quality whey and soy proteins,
protein hydrolysates and proprietary protein blends.
President: K Kachadurian
CFO: Tent Macoy
CEO: Todd Watson
Quality Control: Tom Yezzi
Market Development Specialist: Cheryl Reid
Sr Sales Manager: Kris Hanson
Estimated Sales: $ 5-10 Million
Number Employees: 20-49
Brands:
Protient

11679 Protient (Land O Lakes)
P.O.Box 64101
St Paul, MN 55164-0101   651-481-2068
Fax: 507-334-8695 www.landolakesinc.com
Processor of dry cream powders, margarine and
spreads
President: Christopher Policinsky
Plant Manager: Steve Fiedler
Number Employees: 50-99
Parent Co: Land O'Lakes
Type of Packaging: Consumer

11680 Protos Foods
449 Glenmeade Rd
Greensburg, PA 15601-1170   724-836-1802
Fax: 724-836-3895 protos@protos-inc.com
www.lindwood.com
Manufacturer of Ostrich meats
President: Logan Dickerson
Number Employees: 5-9
Type of Packaging: Food Service, Private Label,
Bulk
Brands:
OSTRIM #1 SPORTS MEAT SNACK
OSTRIM OSTRICH SAUTE

11681 Providence Cheese
49 Rotary Drive
Johnston, RI 02919-4918   401-421-5653
Fax: 401-421-3870
Pasta, cheese
President/Owner: Wayne Wheatley
Estimated Sales: Less than $500,000
Number Employees: 1-4
Type of Packaging: Private Label

11682 Provimi Veal Corporation
W2103 County Road Vv
Seymour, WI 54165-9174   920-833-6861
Fax: 920-833-9850 800-833-8325
chef-bob@provimiveal.com
www.provimifoods.com
Processor and exporter of fresh and frozen veal and
hides
President: Aat Groenvelt
General Manager: Rod MacKenzie
VP: Diane Bunkelman
Sales Director: Mike Wilson
Estimated Sales: $54297827
Number Employees: 100-249
Sq. footage: 130000
Type of Packaging: Consumer, Food Service, Pri-
vate Label, Bulk
Brands:
Provimi

11683 Provost Packers
5340 49th Avenue
Provost, AB T0B 3S0
Canada   780-753-2415
Fax: 780-753-2413 bouma@planet.net.com
Processor of fresh beef and pork
President: Bernard Bouma
Sales Manager: Lyle Bouma
Number Employees: 10-19
Sq. footage: 82000
Type of Packaging: Consumer, Food Service, Pri-
vate Label, Bulk
Brands:
Dutch Brothers
Provost Packers

11684 Pruden Packing Company
336 Carolina Rd
Suffolk, VA 23434-5814   757-539-8773
Fax: 757-925-4971
Packer and exporter of cured ham and pork shoulder
President: Peter Pruden III
General Manager: K Jones
Contact: Kevin Jones
Plant Superintendent: Terry McNitt
Estimated Sales: $3.0 Million
Number Employees: 5-9
Parent Co: Smithfield Companies
Brands:
Champon
Peanut City
Pruden

11685 Pudlo Food Products Company
1651 W Hubbard Street
53
Chicago, IL 60622-6352   312-421-4862

Processor of pickles
President: Walter Pudlo
Estimated Sales: $ 1 - 3 Million
Number Employees: 1-4
Type of Packaging: Bulk

11686 Puebla Foods
75 Jefferson Street
Passaic, NJ 07055-6418   973-473-0201
          Fax: 973-473-3854 pueblafoods@aol.com
Processor of corn tortillas, chips and taco shells; importer of Mexican products including jalapenos, hot sauces, dried peppers, tomatillos, Mexican sodas, etc
President: Felix Sanchez
VP: Carmen Sanchez
Estimated Sales: $11319750
Number Employees: 35
Brands:
El Ranchito
Mipueblito
Pueblafood

11687 Pulakos
2530 Parade St
Erie, PA 16503-2034   814-452-4026
Fax: 814-456-4876 info@pulakoschocolates.com
          www.pulakoschocolates.com
Processor of confectionery including chocolates
President: George Pulakos
VP/Treasurer: J Pulakos
Plant Manager: Pete Skelton
Estimated Sales: $1300000
Number Employees: 20-49
Sq. footage: 16000
Type of Packaging: Consumer, Food Service, Private Label

11688 Pulgini Pasta Products
6600 NW 20th Avenue
Fort Lauderdale, FL 33309-1509   954-973-7458
          Fax: 954-973-7996 pulgini@aol.com
Processor and exporter of specialty pasta including ravioli and noodles
President: Art Tommassetti
Administration Director: Ila Tomassetti
Number Employees: 10-19
Type of Packaging: Consumer, Food Service, Private Label, Bulk

11689 Punch's Nut Company
514 East Avenue
Medina, NY 14103-1655   585-798-3890
          Fax: 585-798-5491
Manufacturer of packaged peanuts
President/Owner: Jack Punch
Estimated Sales: $1-3 Million
Number Employees: 2
Type of Packaging: Consumer, Bulk

11690 Purato's
3235 16th Ave SW
Seattle, WA 98134-1023   206-762-5400
          Fax: 206-767-4088 www.puratos.com
Processor of wheat flour including tortilla, pastry and all purpose
Manager: Steve Picton
Operations Manager: Andy Bebe
Estimated Sales: $ 20 - 50 Million
Number Employees: 20-49
Parent Co: Fisher Mills
Type of Packaging: Food Service, Private Label, Bulk

11691 Puratos Canada
5690 Timberlea Boulevard
Mississauga, ON L4W 4M6
Canada   905-624-7500
          Fax: 905-624-2085 800-668-5537
          info@puratos.ca www.puratos.com
Processor of dough conditioners, bread bases and mixes, pastry mixes, custards, fruit compounds and fillings, glazes and chocolate products including ganache; importer of compounds
President: Robert Fickers
Sales Executive: John McCaffrey
Number Employees: 20-49
Sq. footage: 40000
Parent Co: Puratos NV
Type of Packaging: Food Service, Private Label, Bulk
Brands:
Biopur

11692 Pure Extracts Inc
59 Remington Blvd
Ronkonkoma, NY 11779   631-588-9727
          Fax: 631-588-9729 info@buyextracts.com
          www.pureextracts.us
Manufacturer of herbal extracts
Chairman/President: Gurjeet Bajwa
Manager: Nat Patel
Owner/Sales Exec: Joe Singh
Estimated Sales: $500,000
Number Employees: 5
Number of Products: 42
Sq. footage: 3000
Type of Packaging: Bulk

11693 Pure Food Ingredients
514 Commerce Pkwy
Verona, WI 53593-1841   608-845-9601
          Fax: 608-845-9628 800-355-9601
          stan@itis.com
Processor and importer of canned foods including tomatoes, chiles, jalapenos and olives; also, beeswax and honey
President: Stanley Kanter
Estimated Sales: $1000000
Number Employees: 5-9
Sq. footage: 20000
Type of Packaging: Consumer, Food Service, Private Label, Bulk

11694 (HQ)Pure Foods
P.O.Box 989
Sultan, WA 98294-0989   360-793-2241
          Fax: 360-793-2485
          webmaster@purefoodsinc.com
          www.purefoodsinc.com
Processor and exporter of liquid and dry molasses and honey including table, baking and dry; importer of raw honey
President: Michael Ingalls
CEO: Denice Ingalls
Plant Manager: Dan Johnson
Estimated Sales: $5,000,000
Number Employees: 10-19
Sq. footage: 18000
Type of Packaging: Consumer, Food Service, Private Label, Bulk
Brands:
Bear Mountain
Heins
Miller's
Pure Gold

11695 Pure Sales
660 Baker St # 367
Costa Mesa, CA 92626-4470   714-540-5455
          Fax: 714-540-5974 puresales@aol.com
Pasta and related products
President: James Silver
Estimated Sales: Under $500,000
Number Employees: 1-4

11696 Pure Source
9750 NW 17th St
Doral, FL 33172-2753   305-477-8111
          Fax: 305-477-4002 800-324-6273
          info@thepuresource.com
          www.thepuresource.com
Processor and exporter of vitamins and antioxidants; importer of raw materials; contract packaging and manufacturing
Owner: Joel Meyer
Estimated Sales: Below $ 5 Million
Number Employees: 10-19
Sq. footage: 70000
Type of Packaging: Consumer, Food Service, Private Label, Bulk
Brands:
Pure Source

11697 Pure Sweet Honey Farm
514 Commerce Pkwy
Verona, WI 53593-1841   608-845-9601
          Fax: 608-845-9628 800-355-9601
          psh@chorus.net www.puresweethoney.com
Processor and importer of honey, maple syrup and molasses
President: Stanley Kanter
Sales Director: Mark Pelka
Estimated Sales: $470000
Number Employees: 5-9
Sq. footage: 20000
Type of Packaging: Consumer, Food Service, Private Label, Bulk

Brands:
SPRINGHILL

11698 Pure World Botanicals
375 Huyler St
South Hackensack, NJ 07606-1532   201-440-5000
          Fax: 201-342-8000 custserve@pureworld.com
          www.pureworld.com
Manufacturer, importer and exporter of botanical and natural flavor extracts
President: Qun Yi Zheng
Vice Chairman: Paul Koether
CEO: Jacques Dikansky
Marketing: Monica Johnson
Purchasing Director: Julius Myer
Estimated Sales: $21.7 Million
Number Employees: 250-499
Sq. footage: 150000
Parent Co: Naturex, S.A.
Type of Packaging: Bulk

11699 Pure World Botanicals
375 Huyler St
South Hackensack, NJ 07606-1532   201-440-5000
          Fax: 201-342-8000 custserve@pureworld.com
          www.pureworld.com
Botanical extracts
CFO: Sue Ann Merrill
CEO: Jacques Dikansky
Estimated Sales: $ 10-25 Million
Number Employees: 250-499
Number of Products: 22
Sq. footage: 13000
Brands:
Cascara Sagrada Bark USP
USP NF
Veragel

11700 Pure's Food Specialties
2929 S 25th Ave
Broadview, IL 60155-4529   708-344-8884
          Fax: 708-344-8703 www.puresfood.com
Cookies
President: Elliot Pure
Estimated Sales: Below $ 5 Million
Number Employees: 20-49
Type of Packaging: Bulk

11701 Pure-Flo Water Company
7737 Mission Gorge Rd
Santee, CA 92071-3399   619-448-5120
          Fax: 619-596-4154 800-787-3356
          jodell@pureflo.com www.pureflo.com
Bottled water
President: Bryan Grant
Quality Control: Becky Parker
VP Sales: Douglas Reed
Production Manager: Jerry Linthern
Plant Manager: Duane Anderson
Purchasing Manager: C Grant
Estimated Sales: $ 10-20 Million
Number Employees: 100-249
Sq. footage: 15
Type of Packaging: Consumer, Private Label
Brands:
Pure-Flo Water

11702 Purely American
5635 Raby Road
Suite H
Norfolk, VA 23502   757-466-1312
          Fax: 757-466-3041 800-359-7873
          customerservice@purelyamerican.com
          www.purelyamerican.com
Mixes, sauces and marinades, and peanuts.
President: Ray Leard
Estimated Sales: $500,000
Number Employees: 5
Type of Packaging: Private Label
Brands:
Peter's Beach Sauces
Purely American

11703 Puritan Ice Cream
301 E Wayne St
Kendallville, IN 46755-1457   260-347-2700
          Fax: 260-347-2652 www.atzicecream.com
Ice cream and frozen desserts
President: Terry Atz
Estimated Sales: $ 2.5-5 Million
Number Employees: 10-19

11704 Puritan/ATZ Ice Cream
301 E Wayne St
Kendallville, IN 46755-1457   260-347-2700
Fax: 260-347-2652
customerservice@atzicecream.com
www.atzicecream.com
Processor of ice cream
GM: Terry Atz
GM: Jeff Atz
Estimated Sales: $ 5 - 10 Million
Number Employees: 10-19
Type of Packaging: Consumer, Food Service

11705 Purity Candy Company
422 Market St
Lewisburg, PA 17837-1422   570-524-0823
Fax: 570-524-7793   800-821-4748
www.puritycandy.com
Candy and chocolates
Owner: Margaret Burfeindt
President: Theodore Roosevelt
General Manager Production: Sharon Weiser
Estimated Sales: Less than $500,000
Number Employees: 1-4
Brands:
Purity Candy

11706 Purity Dairies
P.O.Box 100957
Nashville, TN 37224-0957   615-244-1900
Fax: 615-760-2299
Processor of milk, ice cream, yogurt, cottage cheese,
juice, sour cream and heavy cream
Manager: Ann Adcock
Sales Manager: Mike Payne
Number Employees: 250-499
Parent Co: Dean Foods Company
Type of Packaging: Consumer, Food Service

11707 Purity Factories
88-96 Blackmarsh Road
St.John's, NL A1E 1T2
Canada   260-347-2700
Fax: 709-738-2426   800-563-3411
www.purity.nf.ca
Processor and exporter of confectionery products,
jams, fruit syrups and biscuits
General Manager: Doug Spurrell
Sales Manager: Gerry Power
Type of Packaging: Consumer, Food Service, Private Label, Bulk

11708 Purity Farms
14635 Westcreek Road
Sedalia, CO 80135-9783   303-647-2368
Fax: 303-647-9875   800-568-4433
purityfarms@qwest.net   www.purityfarms.com
Processor of organic grade AA clarified butter
President: Kathy Feldenkreis
Number Employees: 1-4
Type of Packaging: Consumer, Food Service, Private Label, Bulk
Brands:
Purity Farms Ghee

11709 Purity Foods
2871 Jolly Rd
Okemos, MI 48864-3586   517-351-9231
Fax: 517-351-9391   800-997-7358
purityfoods@voyager.net   www.purityfoods.com
Processor, importer and exporter of organic baking
mixes, soybeans, dry beans, popcorn, breakfast cereals, flour, buckwheat, spelt, millet, wheat, spelt pasta
and sesame and sunflower seeds; importer of figs,
dried apricots, raisins hazelnuts, etc
President: Donald Stinchcomb
Estimated Sales: $4919431
Number Employees: 5-9
Sq. footage: 12000
Type of Packaging: Consumer, Bulk
Brands:
Erntedank
Purity Foods
Purity Foods Vita-Spelt
Quality America
Vita-Spelt

11710 Purity Foods
2871 Jolly Rd
Okemos, MI 48864-3586   517-351-9231
Fax: 517-351-9391   info@purityfoods.com
www.purityfoods.com

Products include beans, grains, seeds; cereals; cookbooks; flours; granola; pastas; pretzels; and sesame
sticks.
President: Donald Stinchcomb
Regional Sales Manager: Hezeden Graye
Estimated Sales: $5-10 Million
Number Employees: 5-9
Sq. footage: 15000

11711 Purity Ice Cream Company
700 Cascadilla St
Ithaca, NY 14850-3239   607-272-1545
Fax: 607-272-1546   purityice@aol.com
www.purityicecream.com
Processor of ice cream: pints, half gallons and three
gallon tubs
President: Bruce Lane
Estimated Sales: $1000000
Number Employees: 20-49
Type of Packaging: Consumer, Food Service

11712 Purity Products
200 Terminal Dr
Plainview, NY 11803   516-767-1967
Fax: 516-767-1722   888-769-7873
customercare@purityproducts.com
www.purityproducts.com
Processor, importer and exporter of sauces, mayonnaise, vinegar, mustard, salad dressings, vegetable
oils, jellies, pickles, etc.; also; a complete line of
cleaning compounds, flavors, extracts and emulsions
President: William Schroeder
CFO: Bruce Morecroft
Marketing: Al Rodriquez
Sales VP: Al Rodriquez
Operations: Ricky Montejo
Plant Manager: Rick Montejo
Purchasing Director: Charles Menezes
Estimated Sales: $ 1 - 3 Million
Number Employees: 20-49
Sq. footage: 100000
Parent Co: Sea Specialties Company
Type of Packaging: Food Service, Private Label, Bulk
Brands:
Chef's Choice
Cheryl Lynn
Ideal
Purity

11713 Purnell Sausage Company
P.O.Box 366
Simpsonville, KY 40067-0366   502-722-5626
Fax: 502-722-5586   800-626-1512
info@itsgooo-od.com   www.itsgooo-od.com
Manufacturer of sausages
President: Todd Purnell
CEO: Allen Purnell Jr.
CFO: Robert Purnell
Estimated Sales: $100-500 Million
Number Employees: 100-249
Type of Packaging: Consumer, Food Service

11714 Purnell's Old Folks Sausage Company
PO Box 366
Simpsonville, KY 40067-0366   800-626-1512
Fax: 502-722-5586   800-626-1512
www.itsgooo-od.com
Processor of gravy and sausages including whole
hog country, bratwurst, Italian, patties, links, cooked
and biscuit
President: Allen Purnell
Food Service Sales Manager: Todd Purnell
Retail Sales Manager: Bob Sutherhand
Estimated Sales: $100+ Million
Number Employees: 100-249
Type of Packaging: Consumer, Food Service
Brands:
Purnell's Old Folks

11715 Puroast Coffee
P.O.Box 1291
Woodland, CA 95776-1291   530-668-0976
Fax: 530-668-0989   877-569-2243
info@puroast.com   www.pureroast.com
Manufacturer of low acid coffee
President: Carrie Vannuci
CEO: Kerry Sachs
CEO: Kerry Sachs
Public Relations: Beth Goldstene
Operations Manager: Victor Quero
Production Manager: Sally Lopez
Purchasing Manager: Wendy Dial

Estimated Sales: $ 5-10 Million
Number Employees: 10-19
Type of Packaging: Private Label
Brands:
Puroast

11716 Puronics Water Systems Inc
5775 Las Positas Rd
Livermore, CA 94551-7819   925-456-7000
Fax: 925-456-7010   roy.esparza@puronics.com
OR service@puronics.com
www.ionicsfidelity.com
Manufacturer of water treatment systems for the
consumer and commercial markets. Puronics solutions include technologies such as water conditioning, filtering, micro-filtration, filtration, carbon
filtration, reverse osmosis and ultraviolet
disinfection.
Chief Financial Officer: Mark Cosmez II
Director of Commercial Sales: Roy Esparza

11717 Putney Pasta Company
PO Box 445
Chester, VT 05143-0445   802-875-4500
Fax: 802-875-3322   800-253-3683
info@putneypasta.com   www.putneypasta.com
Manufacturer of all-natural frozen pastas inmcluding
tortellini, ravioli, agnolotti, fettucine, linguine, angel
hair and gnocchi; also sauses. Packaged in retail and
food service packs. Branded and private label packer
President: Carol Berry
Plant Manager: Troy Bonnell
Purchasing Agent: Rosemary Stoddard
Estimated Sales: $ 5 - 10 Million
Number Employees: 12
Number of Brands: 1
Number of Products: 35
Sq. footage: 42000
Type of Packaging: Consumer, Food Service, Private Label
Brands:
Putney Pasta

11718 Puueo Poi Factory
265 Kekuanaoa St # D
Hilo, HI 96720-4396   808-935-8435
Fax: 808-934-7762
Processor of Hawaiian food including poi, lau-lau
and kalua
President/Treasurer: Gilbert Chang
VP: Okyo Chang
Business Manager: Shirlene Rayoan
Estimated Sales: $500,000
Number Employees: 1-4
Sq. footage: 2750
Type of Packaging: Consumer, Food Service, Private Label, Bulk
Brands:
Puueo Poi

11719 (HQ)Pyco Industries
P.O.Box 841
Lubbock, TX 79408-0841   806-747-3315
Fax: 806-744-3221   800-289-7266
jtucker@pycoindustries.com
www.pycoindustries.com
Manufacturer fo Cottonseed oil, cake and meal
Manager: Rodney Kuss
SVP Marketing: Robert Lacy
Estimated Sales: $103 Million
Number Employees: 100-249
Type of Packaging: Food Service, Bulk
Brands:
PLAINSMAN COTTON OIL

11720 Pyramid Brewing
1201 1st Ave S
Seattle, WA 98134-1238   206-682-3377
Fax: 206-682-8420   host@pyramidbrew.com
www.pyramidbrew.com
Beer and soda
Manager: Alex Krallis
CFO: Eric Peterson
CFO: Wayne Drury
Chairman: George Hancock
Chairman: Martin Kelly
Director Manufacturing: Jack Schaller
Estimated Sales: Under $500,000
Number Employees: 100-249
Type of Packaging: Private Label
Brands:
Amber Wheat Beer
Best Brown Ale

Hart
Thomas Kemper

11721 Pyramid Juice Company
160 Helman Street
Ashland, OR 97520-1720   541-482-2292
    Fax: 541-482-1002 judd@pyramidjuice.com
        www.pyramidjuice.com
Processor of organic fruit and vegetable juices
    President/CEO: Judd Pindell
    VP: Kim Kemske
Estimated Sales: $5-9.9 Million
Number Employees: 8
Sq. footage: 3500
Brands:
    Mind's Eye Smart Drinks
    Pyramid Juice

11722 Pyrenees French Bakery
717 E 21st St
Bakersfield, CA 93305-5240   661-322-7159
    Fax: 661-322-6713   888-898-7159
        order@pyreneesbakery.com
        www.pyreneesbakery.com
Processor of sour dough bread and rolls; also,
French, nine-grain, squaw, rye, whole wheat bread
and rolls; Sara Lee fresh bagels and bread distributor
    President: Marianne Laxague
    CEO: Juanita Laxague
Estimated Sales: Below $ 5 Million
Number Employees: 20-49
Sq. footage: 21500
Brands:
    Pyrenees
    Sara Lee

11723 Q Bell Foods
PO Box 652
Nyack, NY 10960   845-358-1475
    Fax: 845-353-5680 info@qbellfoods.com
        www.qbellfoods.com
chocolate wafer rolls and chocolate wafer bars

11724 Q Tonic
45 Main Street
Suite 516
Brooklyn, NY 11201   718-398-6642
    Fax: 718-228-8877 info@qtonic.com
        www.qtonic.com
tonic water
    President/Owner: Jordan Sildert

11725 Q.E. Tea
533 Washington Avenue
Bridgeville, PA 15017-2072   412-221-4444
        800-622-8327
        qetea@aol.com
Processor, exporter and importer of coffees and teas
    President: Paul Rankin
    Marketing Manager: Peter Shaffalo
Estimated Sales: $500,000-$1 Million
Number Employees: 5-9
Sq. footage: 12000
Brands:
    Hedley's
    Q.E.

11726 QA Products
1301 Mark St
Elk Grove Vlg, IL 60007-6711   847-595-1003
    Fax: 847-595-1960   800-635-7907
        sales@qaproducts.com   www.qaproducts.com
Manufacturer of custom and standard confectionery
toppings and decorative ingredients for the baking
and ice cream industries.
    President: Russ Campbell
    VP Sales/Marketing: Kevin Fenner
Estimated Sales: $20-50 Million
Number Employees: 100-249
Sq. footage: 86000
Type of Packaging: Bulk
Brands:
    Edible Cake Decorating Scatter

11727 QBI
500 Metuchen Road
South Plainfield, NJ 07080-4810   908-668-0088
    Fax: 908-561-9682 jschortz@4qbi.com
        www.4qbi.com

Processor, importer and exporter of bioflavonoids,
botanical powders and ingredients, herbs,
nutraceuticals, antioxidants, diet and sport supple-
ments, fruit and vegetable powders, concentrated ex-
tracts, bee pollen, etc
    President: Joseph Schortz CPA
    VP Finance: Carlos Mendez
    Marketing: Joan Naso
    Sales Director: Allen Lovitch
    International Account Executive: Rena
    Strauss-Cohen
    Plant Manager: Donald Andrejewski
Number Employees: 50-99
Number of Products: 500
Sq. footage: 56000
Type of Packaging: Bulk
Brands:
    Phytoflow Direct Compression Herbs

11728 QK Corporation
3154 College Drive
Suite F
Baton Rouge, LA 70808-3174   225-753-8292
        Fax: 225-756-2551
Sports and energy drinks
Estimated Sales: $ 2.5-5 Million
Number Employees: 1-4

11729 QST Ingredients, Inc.
9734-40 6th Street
Rancho Cucamonga, CA 91730   909-989-4343
        Fax: 909-989-4334 www.qsting.com
Blended seasonings, ingredients and casings for sausage & pork.
    Office Manager: Jill Mauleon

11730 Quady Winery
P.O.Box 728
Madera, CA 93639-0728   559-673-8068
        Fax: 559-673-0744   800-733-8068
    info@quadywinery.com   www.quadywinery.com
Wines
    President: Andrew Quady
    CFO: Laurel Quady
    Winemaker: Michael Blaylock
    General Manager: Cheryl Russell
Estimated Sales: $ 2.5-5 Million
Number Employees: 10-19
Number of Products: 7
Type of Packaging: Private Label
Brands:
    Electra
    Elysium
    Essensia
    Starbound
    Sweet Dessert Wine

11731 Quail Ridge Cellars & Vineyards
1155 Mee Lane
Saint Helena, CA 94574-9792   707-963-9783
        Fax: 707-963-3593   800-706-9463
        retail@ruthbench.com   www.ruthbench.com
Wine
    President and CEO: Phillip Wade
    CFO: Anthony Bell
    Marketing Director: Michael Stedman
    Public Relations: Victoria Olson
    Production Manager: Jenel Hageman
Estimated Sales: $ 2.5-5 Million
Number Employees: 10-19
Type of Packaging: Private Label
Brands:
    Bell Cellars
    Fox Brook
    Quail Creek

11732 Quaker
515 W Main Street
Barrington, IL 60010-4197   847-382-9860
        Fax: 847-382-0687   800-333-8027
        erik_bayer@qkgsales.com
        www.mothersnatural.com
Hot and cold cereals, rice cakes and all natural foods
    General Sales Manager: Eric Bayer
    Sales Director: Jim Coy
    General Sales Manager, Natural: Erik Bayer
Estimated Sales: $ 50 - 100 Million
Number Employees: 50-99
Parent Co: Quaker Oats Company
Brands:
    Mother's

11733 Quaker Bonnet
175 Allen St
Buffalo, NY 14201-1515   716-884-0435
        Fax: 716-885-7245   800-283-2447
    liz@quakerbonnet.com   www.quakerbonnet.com
Processor of cookies and pastries
    President: Liz Kolken
    Vice President: Benjamin Kolken
Estimated Sales: Less than $500,000
Number Employees: 5-9
Sq. footage: 4300
Type of Packaging: Consumer, Food Service, Pri-
vate Label
Brands:
    BANANA MOON SNACK LINE
    BUFFALO CHIPS
    QUAKER BONNET CELERY SEED FRUIT
    DRE
    QUAKER BONNET DESSERT SHELL
    QUAKER BONNET ELEPHANT EAR DANISH
    QUAKER BONNET SHORTBREAD

11734 Quaker Maid Meats
P.O.Box 350
Shillington, PA 19607-0350   610-376-1500
    Fax: 610-376-2678 www.quakermaidmeats.com
Processor of all beef sandwich steaks, hamburger
patties, breaded veal patties, raw and precooked veal
steaks, and raw and precooked meatballs.
    President: Stanley Szortyka
    Quality Control: Michael May
    VP: Nancy Rubin
    VP Sales: Sergei Szortyka
    Plant Manager: Todd Bray
Estimated Sales: $ 20-50 Million
Number Employees: 100-249
Type of Packaging: Consumer, Food Service, Pri-
vate Label
Brands:
    Gina Lina's Meatballs
    Mama Lucia's Homestyle Meatballs
    Mama Lucia's Italian Style Meatball
    Mama Lucia's Sausage Meatballs
    Quaker Maid Patties
    Quaker Maid Sandwich Steaks

11735 Quaker Oats Company
555 W Monroe St # 16-01
P.O. Box 049003
Chicago, IL 60661-3605   312-821-1000
        Fax: 312-821-1987   800-367-6287
        www.quakeroats.com
Leading manufacturer, processor and exporter of
cookies, oats, oatmeal, farina, granola bars, puffed
wheat, puffed rice, barley, groats, rice, shredded
wheat, pancake syrups and mixes, flour, corn syrups,
baking mixes, pasta and cornmeal.
    Chairman/President/CEO: Robert Morrison
    SVP/Chief Financial Officer: Richard Gunst
Estimated Sales: $1 Billion
Number Employees: 5,000-9,999
Parent Co: PepsiCo North America
Type of Packaging: Consumer, Food Service
Brands:
    KRETSCHMER WHEAT GERM
    QUAKER
    QUAKER RICE SNACKS
    QUISP CEREAL

11736 Quaker Oats Company
418 2nd St NE
Cedar Rapids, IA 52401-1001   319-362-3121
        Fax: 319-398-1692 www.quakeroats.com
Processor and exporter of breakfast cereals including corn, oat, puffed wheat, rice and rolled oats;
also, grits, barley, corn meal and syrups.
    Manager: Roger Vincent
    CEO PepsiCo North America: John Compton
    Chief Financial Officer: Richard Goodman
    SVP/Government Affairs & General Counsel:
    Larry Thompson
    SVP/Corporate Strategy & Development: Wahid
    Hamid
    SVP/Corporate Communications: Tod MacKenzie

    EVP/Operations: Hugh Johnston
    SVP/Human Resources: Margaret Moore
    Plant Manager: Roger Vincent
    Purchasing Agent: Mary Jane Suchan
Number Employees: 300
Parent Co: PepsiCo North America
Type of Packaging: Consumer, Food Service, Pri-
vate Label, Bulk

11737 Quaker Oats Company
1703 E Voorhees St
Danville, IL 61834-6256   217-443-3990
         Fax: 217-443-8622 www.quakeroats.com
Manufacturer and exporter of breakfast cereals and
granola bars
    Manager: Patrick Burke
    CEO/PepsiCo North America: John Compton
    Chief Financial Officer: Richard Goodman
    VP: Magie Lacambra
    SVP/Corporate Strategy & Development: Wahid
    Hamid
    SVP/Corporate Communications: Tod MacKenzie

    EVP/Operations: Hugh Johnston
    SVP/Human Resources: Margaret Moore
    Plant Manager: Steven Brunner
Estimated Sales: $1 Billion
Number Employees: 600
Parent Co: PepsiCo North America
Type of Packaging: Consumer
Brands:
    AUNT JEMINIA
    CAP'N CRUNCH
    KRETSCHMER WHEAT GERM
    LIFE
    MOTHER'S NATURAL FOODS
    NEAR EAST
    QUAKER
    QUISP
    RICE A RONI

11738 Quaker Oats Company
750 Oak Hill Rd
Mountain Top, PA 18707-2112   570-474-3800
         Fax: 570-474-3808 800-367-6287
                        www.quakeroats.com
    President/CEO Quaker Foods: Charles
    Maniscalco
    CEO PepsiCo North America: John Compton
    Chief Financial Officer: Richard Goodman
    SVP/Government Affairs & General Counsel:
    Larry Thompson
    SVP/Corporate Strategy & Development: Wahid
    Hamid
    SVP/Corporate Communications: Tod MacKenzie

    EVP/Operations: Hugh Johnston
    SVP/Human Resources: Margaret Moore
    Plant Manager: Brian Mc Laughlin
Estimated Sales: $ 5 - 10 Million
Number Employees: 100-249
Parent Co: PepsiCo North America
Type of Packaging: Consumer, Food Service
Brands:
    AUNT JEMIMA CORN MEAL
    AUNT JEMIMA SYRUPS & MIXES
    CAP'N CRUNCH
    KRETSCHMER WHEAT GERM
    LIFE CEREAL
    MOTHER'S NATURAL FOODS
    NEAR EAST
    QUAKER 100% NATURAL GRANOLA
    QUAKER GRITS
    QUAKER OATMEAL
    QUAKER OATMEAL SQUARES
    QUAKER OATMEAL TO GO
    QUAKER RICE CAKES
    QUAKER SNACK BARS
    QUAKER SOY CRISPS
    QUAKER TOASTED OATMEAL
    QUAKER TORTILLA MIXES
    QUAKES
    QUISP
    RICE-A-RONI & PASTA RONI

11739 Quaker Oats Company
14 Hunter Street E
Quaker Park
Peterborough, ON K9J 7B2
Canada   705-743-6330
         Fax: 705-876-4125 800-267-6287
                        www.quakeroats.ca

Processor of breakfast cereal
    President/CEO Quaker Foods: Charles
    Maniscalco
    CEO PepsiCo North America: John Compton
    Chief Financial Officer: Richard Goodman
    SVP/Government Affairs & General Counsel:
    Larry Thompson
    SVP/Corporate Strategy & Development: Wahid
    Hamid
    SVP/Corporate Communications: Tod MacKenzie

    EVP/Operations: Hugh Johnston
    SVP/Human Resources: Margaret Moore
Number Employees: 500-999
Parent Co: PepsiCo North America
Type of Packaging: Consumer, Food Service
Brands:
    Quaker

11740 Quaker Oats Company
2822 Glenfield Ave
Dallas, TX 75233-1497   214-330-8681
         Fax: 214-333-1221 www.pepsico.com
Processor of sports beverages
    President/CEO Quaker Foods: Charles
    Maniscalco
    CEO/PepsiCo North America: John Compton
    Chief Financial Officer: Richard Goodman
    SVP/Government Affairs & General Counsel:
    Larry Thompson
    SVP/Corporate Strategy & Development: Wahid
    Hamid
    SVP/Corporate Communications: Tod MacKenzie

    EVP/Operations: Hugh Johnston
    SVP/Human Resources: Margaret Moore
    Plant Manager: Adrian Oliver
Estimated Sales: $ 100-500 Million
Number Employees: 100-249
Parent Co: PepsiCo North America
Type of Packaging: Consumer

11741 Quaker Oats Company
3535 Perlman Drive
Stockton, CA 95206-4203   209-982-5580
         Fax: 209-982-5943 www.quakeroats.com
Processor of oatmeal, baking mixes and breakfast
cereals
    President/CEO Quaker Foods: Charles
    Maniscalco
    CEO PepsiCo North America: John Compton
    Chief Financial Officer: Richard Goodman
    SVP/Government Affairs & General Counsel:
    Larry Thompson
    SVP/Corporate Strategy & Development: Wahid
    Hamid
    SVP/Corporate Communications: Tod MacKenzie

    EVP/Operations: Hugh Johnston
    SVP/Human Resources: Margaret Moore
Number Employees: 50-99
Parent Co: PepsiCo North America
Type of Packaging: Consumer

11742 Quaker Sugar Company
432 Rodney St
Brooklyn, NY 11211-3482   718-387-6500
         Fax: 718-963-2767 info@quakersugar.com
                        www.quakersugar.com
Processor of sugar
    Owner: Harriet Gelfas
    Operations Manager: Adam Wechsler
    Production Manager: Harry Wechsler
Estimated Sales: $1500000
Number Employees: 20-49
Type of Packaging: Consumer, Bulk
Brands:
    Diamond

11743 Quali Tech
318 Lake Hazeltine Drive
Chaska, MN 55318-1093   952-448-5151
                                 800-328-5870
                        www.qualitechco.com
Quali Tech's food division develops and manufacturers high-quality food particulates servicing the
varying needs of the best known food companies in
America and abroad.
    President: Cory Ploen
    CEO: Del Ploen
    VP: Kye Ploen
    Marketing Director: Tim Hennum
    Sales: Jeff Ploen
    Operations Manager: Mike Hodgens

Number Employees: 75
Sq. footage: 45000
Type of Packaging: Bulk
Brands:
    FLAV-R-GRAIN
    FLAVOR-ETTES
    FLAVOR-LITES
    PELL-ETTES
    PEPR
    SEASON-ETTES

11744 Qualifresh Michel St. Arneault
4605 Thibault Avenue
St. Hubert, QC J3Y 3S8
Canada   450-445-0550
         Fax: 450-445-5687 800-565-0550
Processor and exporter of fresh and frozen French
fries
    President: Michelle St. Arneaul
    Sales Manager: Christian Bauzrette
Number Employees: 50-99
Type of Packaging: Consumer, Food Service, Pri-
vate Label
Brands:
    Golden Crop
    Qualifreeze
    Qualifresh

11745 Quality Alaska Seafood
1385 Engineer's Cutoff Road
Juneau, AK 99801   907-789-8495
Seafood
    President: Lloyd Pukis
    Vice President: Brien Pukis

11746 Quality Assured Packing
PO Box 55308
Stockton, CA 95205-8808   209-931-6700
                        Fax: 209-931-0286
         qap@qualityassuredpacking.com
                        www.qualityassured.com
Tomato sauces
    President/CEO: Tom Beard
    COO: Mark Delameter
    VP Finance: Jim Nederostek
    Plant Manager: Angel Aiello
Estimated Sales: $ 10-24.9 Million
Number Employees: 60

11747 Quality Bakery
PO Box 519
Invermere, BC V0A 1K0
Canada   888-681-9977
         Fax: 250-342-4439 888-681-9977
    info@healthybread.com   www.healthybread.com
Processor of extended shelf-life and preserva-
tive-free rye bread
    President: Peter Banga
Number Employees: 20-49
Sq. footage: 7500
Type of Packaging: Consumer, Food Service, Pri-
vate Label, Bulk
Brands:
    Invermere
    Quality Bakery
    Yukon Sourdough Recipe

11748 Quality Bakery Products
888 E Las Olas Blvd
Fort Lauderdale, FL 33301-2272   954-779-3663
         Fax: 954-779-7837 info@qualitybakery.com
Processor of bread crumbs, croutons and stuffings
    President: Harold Hink
    VP: John Hank
Estimated Sales: $$2.5-5 Million
Number Employees: 10-19
Type of Packaging: Consumer, Food Service, Pri-
vate Label, Bulk
Brands:
    Quality Hearth

11749 Quality Bakery/MM Deli
220 W Street
Port Colborne, ON L3K 4E3
Canada   905-834-4911
Processor of baked goods including bread, buns and
cakes
    Owner: Cindy Minor-Gibson
Number Employees: 10-19
Sq. footage: 2000

11750 Quality Beef Company
25 Bath St
Providence, RI 02908-4896   401-421-5668
Fax: 401-421-8570   877-233-3462
info@qualitybeefcompany.com
www.qualitybeefcompany.com
Processor, wholesaler/distributor and broker of ground beef; wholesaler/distributor of frozen foods and seafood
President: Vincent Catauro Jr
Secretary: William Catauro
Estimated Sales: $ 10 - 20 Million
Number Employees: 20-49
Type of Packaging: Food Service

11751 (HQ)Quality Brands
P.O.Box 1450
Deland, FL 32721-1450   386-738-3808
Fax: 386-738-2247   info@qualitybrands.cc
www.qualitybrands.cc
Processor of frozen fruits including apples, blueberries and cherries; also, canned apple juice and fruit and vegetable powders and flakes
Owner: Robbie Roberson
Co-Owner: Joanne Roberson
CFO: Steve Hamilton
VP: Joe Maiz
Estimated Sales: $ 20 - 50 Million
Number Employees: 50-99
Type of Packaging: Food Service
Brands:
Quality Brands

11752 Quality Candy
P.O.Box 070581
Milwaukee, WI 53207-0581   414-483-4500
Fax: 414-483-4137   800-972-2658
jayb@qcbs.com   www.qcbs.com
Processor, exporter and packer of candy including regular and sugar-free boxed, chocolates, brittles, toffees, holiday, mints, molded novelties, etc.; also, nuts, nut mixes and gourmet popcorn
President: Margaret Gile
Number Employees: 50-99
Number of Brands: 2
Number of Products: 2000
Sq. footage: 60000
Parent Co: Quality Candy Shoppes
Type of Packaging: Consumer, Food Service, Private Label, Bulk
Brands:
BUDDY SQUIRREL
FAIRY FOOD
QUALITY CANDY

11753 Quality Candy Company
PO Box 1960
Julian, CA 92036-1960   760-765-1891
Fax: 760-765-1893
customerservice@qcandy.com
www.qcandy.com
Candy
CEO: Pierre Redmond
Estimated Sales: $ 10 - 20 Million
Number Employees: 20-49
Brands:
CHOCO-STARLIGHT
SPI-C-MINT

11754 Quality Candy Shoppes/Buddy Squirrel of Wisconsin
1801 E Bolivar Avenue
St Francis, WI 53235   414-483-4500
Fax: 414-483-4137   800-972-2658
www.qcbs.com
candy
President/Owner: Margaret Gile
CFO: David Reynolds
Estimated Sales: $23.6
Number Employees: 60

11755 Quality Chef Foods
5005 C St SW
Cedar Rapids, IA 52404-7601   319-362-9633
Fax: 319-362-3924   800-356-8307
Processor of frozen soups, sauces and entrees
President: Shannon Ashby
Plant Manager: Steve Maddocks
Estimated Sales: $ 10-20 Million
Number Employees: 10-19
Parent Co: Heinz USA
Type of Packaging: Food Service
Brands:
Quality Chef Foods, Inc.

11756 Quality Chekd Dairies
1733 Park St
Naperville, IL 60563-8478   630-717-1110
Fax: 630-717-1126   mmurphy@qchekd.com
www.qchekd.com
Dairy cooperative with a focus on quality-food safety, dairy training, procurement and marketing
Managing Director: Peter Horvath
CFO: Bruce Tom
Marketing Director: Molly Murphy
Estimated Sales: $ 100-500 Million
Number Employees: 10-19
Brands:
QUALITY CHEKD DAIRY PRODUCTS

11757 Quality Choice Foods
601 Magnetic Drive
Toronto, ON M3J 3J2
Canada   416-650-9595
Processor and importer of specialty stuffed pastas, pesto sauces, garlic spreads and sun-dried tomatoes in oil; exporter of gourmet garlic spreads and pesto sauce
Marketing Manager: Adrian Furman
Number Employees: 10-19
Sq. footage: 4500
Type of Packaging: Consumer, Food Service, Private Label, Bulk

11758 Quality Crab Company
177 Knobbs Creek Dr
Elizabeth City, NC 27909-7002   252-338-0808
Fax: 252-338-6290   888-411-4410
info@nextdayseafood.com
www.nextdayseafood.com
Fresh, processed and canned crab meats
VP: Russell Barclift
Estimated Sales: $ 5-10 Million
Number Employees: 50-99
Type of Packaging: Private Label
Brands:
Jumbo Lump

11759 Quality Croutons
1155 W 40th St
Chicago, IL 60609-2506   773-927-8200
Fax: 773-927-8228   800-334-2796
croutons@interaccess.com
www.qualitycroutons.com
Processor of croutons; packager of portion controlled dry foods
President: David M Moore
Marketing/Sales: Deadra Ashford
Production Manager: Keith Taylor
Estimated Sales: $1900000
Number Employees: 20-49
Sq. footage: 35000
Type of Packaging: Food Service, Private Label, Bulk

11760 Quality Dairy Company
947 Trowbridge Rd
East Lansing, MI 48823-5217   517-319-4114
www.qualitydairy.com
Milk, ice cream and fruit juices
Manager: Swadhyaya Bey
Estimated Sales: Below $ 5 Million
Number Employees: 5-9
Type of Packaging: Private Label

11761 Quality Fisheries
P.O.Box 146
Niota, IL 62358-0146   217-448-4241
Fax: 217-448-4021
Seafood
Owner: Kirby Marsden
Estimated Sales: $1 Million
Number Employees: 1-4

11762 Quality Foods
PO Box 1385
San Pedro, CA 90733-1385   310-833-7890
Fax: 310-833-5424   877-833-7890
info@qualitygoods.com   www.qualityfoods.com
Premium ethnic cuisine, snacks, fried onions, spices, chutneys, teas, pastes, pickles, BBQ sauces, hot sauces, salsa, dressings, marinades, relishes, pepper sauces, steak sauces, mustard and condiments
Estimated Sales: $ 1-2.5 Million
Number Employees: 5-9
Brands:
California Cuisine
Clara's Kitchen

Cummings & York
Hothothot
Jewel of India
Mariachi
Nara
Nonna D'S
Samos
Sarah's Garden
Simple Nevada
Simply
Skull & Bones
Tara Foods
Tomales Bay
Tombstone

11763 Quality Foods Products
172 N Peoria St
Chicago, IL 60607-2311   312-666-4559
Fax: 312-666-7133
President: Chris Aralis
Estimated Sales: $ 10 - 20 Million
Number Employees: 10-19

11764 Quality Foods from the Sea
173 Knobbs Creek Dr
Elizabeth City, NC 27909-7002   252-338-5455
Fax: 252-338-0311
Processor of seafood
President: Marty Martin III
VP: R Martin
Estimated Sales: $11400000
Number Employees: 50-99
Sq. footage: 300000

11765 Quality Ingredients Corporation
14300 Rosemount Dr
Burnsville, MN 55306-6925   952-898-4002
Fax: 952-898-4421   sales@qic.us
www.qic.us
Manufacturer of dehydrated dairy products including; nonfat milk, dry cream, nondairy creamers, powdered shortening, cultured buttermilks, yogurt, sweet whey, cheeses, flavors and grits. Custom Formulation is available.
President: Isabelle Day
Human Resource Manager: Stewart Flanery
Number Employees: 50-99
Type of Packaging: Food Service, Private Label, Bulk
Other Locations:
Quality Ingredients Facility
Marshfield WI

11766 Quality Ingredients Corporation
14300 Rosemount Dr
Burnsville, MN 55306-6925   952-898-4002
Fax: 952-898-4421
tinajamieson@qualityingredients.com
Processor of dehydrated dairy products including nonfat milk, dry cream, nondairy creamers, powdered shortenings, cultured buttermilks, yogurt powders, sweet whey, etc.; also, custom formulation available
President: Isabelle Day
Sales Director: Jane Evans
VP Operations: Elizabeth Maas
Purchasing Manager: Kathey Williams
Estimated Sales: $3600000
Number Employees: 20-49
Sq. footage: 50000
Type of Packaging: Consumer, Food Service, Private Label, Bulk
Brands:
Quali-Cream
Quic Blend
Quic Cheese
Quic Creamer
Quic Whip

11767 Quality Ingredients Corporation
P.O.Box 306
Chester, NJ 07930-0306   908-879-2227
Fax: 908-879-2502   800-843-6314
www.qicusa.com
Wholesale food distributor specializing in liquid malt blends, dry malt blends, mold inhibitors, molasses products, bakery powders, dough conditioners, multi-grain blends, emulsifiers and release agents
President: Tom Schmidt Sr
CEO: Diane Schmidt
VP Operations: Tom Schmidt, Jr.
Number Employees: 10-19
Type of Packaging: Food Service, Private Label, Bulk

Brands:
Attaboy
Hawk
Hawkeye
Qic Rise

11768 Quality Instant Teas
PO Box 1967
Morristown, NJ 07962-1967   973-257-9450
Fax: 973-257-9370 888-283-8327
garyvorsheim@worldnet.att.net
www.qualityinstantteas.com
Tea mixes and concentrates
President: Gary Vorsheim
Estimated Sales: $ 1 Million
Number Employees: 3
Type of Packaging: Private Label

11769 Quality Jersey Products
PO Box 1293
Seaforth, ON N0K 1W0
Canada   519-527-1272
maya@oxford.net
Processor of yogurt, yogurt cheese and buttermilk
porridge with barley
President: Jeff Thorsteinson
Secretary/Treasurer: Janet Thorsteinson
Number Employees: 1-4
Sq. footage: 7500
Brands:
Maya

11770 Quality Kitchen Corporation
131 West St
Danbury, CT 06810-6376   203-744-2000
Fax: 203-791-2875 officemail@salame.com
Processor and exporter of juices and concentrates in-
cluding grapefruit and orange
President: Albert J Salame
VP: Peter Bliss
Sales: Jerry McGuire
Estimated Sales: $5000000
Number Employees: 5-9
Type of Packaging: Consumer, Food Service

11771 Quality Meat Packers
2 Tecumseth Street
Toronto, ON M5V 2R5
Canada   416-703-7675
Fax: 416-504-3756
Processor of fresh and frozen pork
Export Manager: Mike Miller
Number Employees: 500-999
Type of Packaging: Consumer, Food Service, Pri-
vate Label, Bulk

11772 (HQ)Quality Meats & Seafood
P.O.Box 337
West Fargo, ND 58078-0337   701-282-0202
Fax: 701-282-0583 800-342-4250
admin@qualitymeats.com
www.qualitymeats.com
Processor and packer of portion cut smoked ham and
sausage; also, portion controlled seafood
President: Dan Richard
CEO: Cary Wetzstein
CEO: Cary Wetzstein
Sales Manager: Ron Jansen
Director of Purchasing: Lee McCleary
Estimated Sales: $13000000
Number Employees: 50-99
Type of Packaging: Consumer, Food Service, Bulk
Brands:
Valley Maid

11773 Quality Naturally! Foods
18830 San Jose Avenue
City of Industry, CA 91748-1325   626-854-6363
Fax: 626-965-0978 888-498-6986
tangrisani@qnfoods.com www.qnfoods.com
Processor and exporter of bakery mixes, icings, fill-
ings, cappuccino and cocoa drinks; custom dry
blending, co-packing and formulation; AIB,
ISO9001; kosher and organic capabilities
VP: Lincoln Watase
Sales Manager: Jerry Tuma
Number Employees: 50-99
Sq. footage: 56000
Type of Packaging: Food Service, Private Label,
Bulk

11774 Quality Products International
323 Center St
Little Rock, AR 72201-2603   501-372-2121
Fax: 501-614-7900 www.ecosite.com
Owner: Brad Walker
Secretary: Brenda McKown
Treasurer: Caroline Elliott
Estimated Sales: $ .5 - 1 million
Number Employees: 1-4

11775 Quality Sausage Company
1925 Lone Star Dr
Dallas, TX 75212-6300   214-634-3400
Fax: 214-634-2296
Processor, packer, exporter and importer of meat
products including meat balls, taco meat, patties,
pizza toppings and pepperoni
President: Paul A Birinyi
Executive VP: Gene Eisen
Maintenance Manager: Paul Traffard
Operations Manager: Fred Koelewyn
Estimated Sales: $41100000
Number Employees: 100-249
Sq. footage: 165000
Parent Co: H.M. International
Type of Packaging: Food Service

11776 Quality Seafood
399 Market St
Apalachicola, FL 32320-1425   850-653-9696
Fax: 850-653-3375 staceki@yahoo.com
Processor of fresh and frozen shrimp
President: Jako Flowers
Estimated Sales: $140,000
Number Employees: 1-4
Type of Packaging: Private Label
Brands:
Quality

11777 Quality Snack Foods
3750 W 131st St
Alsip, IL 60803-1519   773-548-6140
Fax: 773-285-8662
Processor of pork rinds
President: Victor Sharp
Vice President: Gary Trepina
Plant Manager: Tom Musil
Estimated Sales: $5600000
Number Employees: 70
Sq. footage: 40000
Type of Packaging: Private Label

11778 Quantum Foods
750 S Schmidt Road Bowling Brk
Chicago, IL 60664   630-679-2300
Fax: 630-679-2393 info@quantumfoods.co
www.quantumfoods.com
Producing meat
CEO: Blake Edward
Executive VP: Mike Mianovich
Director Technical Service: Hecto Delgado
VP Production: Bill Kulach
Brands:
Quantum Foods

11779 Quantum Foods LLC
750 S Schmidt Rd
Bolingbrook, IL 60440-4813   630-679-2300
Fax: 630-679-2393 800-334-6328
info@quantumfoods.com
www.quantumfoods.com
Processor of beef into portion-control steaks for
foodservice and retail markets, in addition to pork,
chicken and turkey.
Founder/President/CEO: Edward B Bleka
Marketing Director: Chris Zoltek
Estimated Sales: $ 100-500 Million
Number Employees: 1,000-4,999
Sq. footage: 140000
Type of Packaging: Food Service
Brands:
Quantum Foods

11780 Queen Ann Ravioli & Macaroni Company
7205 18th Ave
Brooklyn, NY 11204-5634   718-256-1061
Fax: 718-256-1189 queenannravioli@aol.com
www.queenannravioliandmacaroni.com
Italian pasta and ravioli
President: George Switzer
Estimated Sales: $ 5-10 Million
Number Employees: 5-9
Type of Packaging: Private Label

11781 Queen Anne Coffee Roaster
900 Queen Anne Ave N # 104
Seattle, WA 98109-3674   206-284-9396
Fax: 206-284-8938
info@metropolitan-market.com
www.metropolitan-market.com
Coffee roasters
Manager: Jim Hill
Director: Eric Stone
Roaster: Susan Hamilton
Estimated Sales: Less than $500,000
Number Employees: 100-249
Brands:
Queen Anne

11782 Queen Bee Gardens
1863 Lane 11 1/2
Lovell, WY 82431-9751   307-548-2543
Fax: 307-548-6721 800-225-7553
spitt@queenbeegardens.com or
www.queenbeegardens.com
Processor and exporter of confectionery products in-
cluding truffles, pralines, English toffee, mints and
turtles with honey
President: Clarence Zeller
Partner: Von Zeller
Vice President: Gene Zeller
Executive Secretary: Bessie Zeller
Estimated Sales: $ 3 - 5 Million
Number Employees: 5-9
Sq. footage: 20000
Type of Packaging: Consumer, Private Label, Bulk
Brands:
Honey Essence
Q-Bee

11783 Queen City Coffee Company
9267 Cincinnati Dayton Rd
West Chester, OH 45069-3839   513-755-1095
Fax: 513-777-5204 800-487-7460
qcccorb@aol.com www.queencitycoffee.com
Coffee beans, products and gift items
President: Robert Badura
Estimated Sales: $ 2.5-5 Million
Number Employees: 1-4
Type of Packaging: Consumer, Food Service, Pri-
vate Label

11784 Queen City Sausage
P.O.Box 25213
Cincinnati, OH 45225-0213   513-541-5581
Fax: 513-541-6182 877-544-5588
www.queencitysausage.com
Processor of sausage and luncheon meats including
bologna and Dutch loaves
President: Elmer Hensler
General Manager: David Dramis
Sales Manager: Patrick Miller
Estimated Sales: $5200000
Number Employees: 1-4
Type of Packaging: Consumer, Food Service, Bulk

11785 Queen International Foods
300 S Atlantic Blvd # 201d
Monterey Park, CA 91754-3228   626-289-0828
Fax: 626-289-7283 800-423-4414
Processor of frozen Mexican foods including
burritos, tacos, taquitos, enchiladas and
chimichangas
Owner: Liza Tang
Controller: Patricia Thistlewhite
National Sales Manager: Douglas Werner
Estimated Sales: $11100000
Number Employees: 1-4
Parent Co: La Reina
Type of Packaging: Consumer, Private Label
Brands:
Anita's
Maria's

11786 Queensboro Farm Products
P.O.Box 227
Canastota, NY 13032-0227   315-697-2235
Fax: 315-697-8267
Processor of dairy products including cottage
cheese, ice cream mix, butter and sour cream;
wholesaler/distributor of milk
President: Allan Miller
General Manager: Don Landry
Plant Manager: Don Landry
Estimated Sales: $ 10 - 20 Million
Number Employees: 20-49
Type of Packaging: Consumer

11787 Queensboro Farm Products
15602 Liberty Ave # 1
Jamaica, NY 11433-1045   718-658-5000
                          Fax: 718-658-0408
Processor and exporter of dairy products including
ice cream mixes, yogurt, farmer and cottage cheese,
sour cream, milk, heavy cream, yogurt drinks, but-
termilk, condensed milk cream and cream cheese
    President: Allan Z Miller
    VP: Lewis Miller
    Sales: Ronalad Silver
Estimated Sales: $22000000
Number Employees: 20-49
Number of Products: 80
Brands:
    Dairy Fresh
    Queensboro

11788 Queensway Foods Company
1611 Adrian Rd
Burlingame, CA 94010-2103   650-697-6666
            Fax: 650-697-9966   info@qfco.com
                                  www.qfco.com
Food products
    Owner: May Huang
    Manager: Tim Yuen
Estimated Sales: $ 5 -10 Million
Number Employees: 5-9
Brands:
    Queensway Foods Company

11789 Quelle Quiche
814 Hanley Industrial Court
Brentwood, MO 63144-1403   314-961-6554
Processor and exporter of frozen and miniature
quiches including lorraine, spinach, broccoli and
crab meat; also, microwaveable and reduced-fat
    President: Eric Victor Cowle
    VP: G Daniella Cowle
Number Employees: 10-19
Sq. footage: 8500
Parent Co: Renaissance Foods
Type of Packaging: Consumer, Food Service, Pri-
vate Label
Brands:
    Les Petites
    Quelle

11790 Quest International Flavors
110 Painters Mill Rd # 6
Owings Mills, MD 21117-4912   410-363-7200
                          Fax: 410-363-0100
    laura.m.singel-scott@questintl.com
                          www.questintl.com
Processor of flavoring extracts
    President: Nancy Trimble
    VP Sales/Marketing: Jack Rush
    Sales Director: William Vanosnabrugg
    Controller: Devin Smith
    Operations Manager: Jim Dechert
    Manager: Bill Ahern
    Plant Manager: George Mathey
    Purchasing Manager: Ed Loreto
Estimated Sales: $300,000-500,000
Number Employees: 1-4
Sq. footage: 175000
Parent Co: Quest International

11791 Quest International Flavors
Hurizerstraatweg 28
1411 GP Naarden,
Netherlands
                          www.questintl.com
Processor of whey solids
    President: William Powell
    Operations Manager: William Ahern
    Communication: Nancy Lawrence
Estimated Sales: $1,540,100,000
Number Employees: 50-99

11792 Quest International Flavors
5115 Sedge Blvd
Hoffman Estates, IL 60192-3708   847-645-7000
        Fax: 847-645-7070 www.questintl.com
Manufacturer of flavor ingredients including savory
flavors, yeast extracts, seasonings, tomato extenders
and drum-dried vegetable products
    President: Jean-Pierre Decosterd
    Manager: Rudy Dieprienk
    Vice President: Ed Ford
Estimated Sales: $100+ Million
Number Employees: 100-249
Sq. footage: 20000

11793 (HQ)Quest International Flavors
5115 Sedge Blvd
Hoffman Estates, IL 60192-3708   847-645-7000
        Fax: 847-645-7070   800-235-6122
                          www.questintl.com
Processor of flavors, emulsifiers, extracts, colors and
enzymes
    President: Jean-Pierre Decosterd
    VP Sales/Marketing: Jack Rush
Estimated Sales: $100+ Million
Number Employees: 100-249

11794 Quest International Fruits & Vegetables
P.O.Box 157
Silverton, OR 97381-0157   503-873-3600
                          Fax: 503-873-7807
    nancie.cinquini@questintl.com
                          www.questintl.com
Drum-dried fruit and vegetables, culinary ingredi-
ents
    President: Timothy Root
    R & D: Joe Wayne
    Quality Control: Shelley White
    Marketing Director: Joe Wayne
Estimated Sales: $ 10-20 Million
Number Employees: 20-49
Type of Packaging: Bulk

11795 Quetzal Company
1234 Polk St
San Francisco, CA 94109-5542   415-673-4181
            Fax: 415-673-4182   888-673-8181
    quetzal@quetzal.org www.coffeeandcocoa.com
Coffee beans
    Owner: Wayne Newman
    Vice President: Wayne Newman
Estimated Sales: Less than $500,000
Number Employees: 5-9
Type of Packaging: Private Label

11796 Quibell Spring Water Beverage
328 E Church Street
Martinsville, VA 24112-2909   540-632-0100
            Fax: 540-344-0311 ieanne@quibell.com
                          www.quibell.com
Bottled water
    President/Chairman: John Franck
    Marketing Director: Dave Vandergrift
    VP: Will Pannill
    Plant Manager: Jeanne Staley
Estimated Sales: $ 1-2.5 Million appx.
Number Employees: 5
Sq. footage: 72
Type of Packaging: Private Label
Brands:
    Quibell Sparkling Water
    Quibell Spring Tea
    Quibell Spring Water

11797 Quiche & Tell
1819 Flushing Ave # 2
Flushing, NY 11385-1002   718-381-7562
            Fax: 718-381-8772 qt1819@aol.com
Quiches and cakes
    President: Larry Italiano
Estimated Sales: $ 1-2.5 Million
Number Employees: 20-49
Type of Packaging: Private Label

11798 Quick's Candy
120 W 2nd Street
Hummelstown, PA 17036-1507   717-566-2211
        Fax: 717-566-5564   800-443-9036
        gladstonecandies@aol.com www.lollies.com
Manufacturer of confectionary products.
    Customer Service: Judy Wojahn
Estimated Sales: Below $ 5 Million
Number Employees: 12
Type of Packaging: Private Label
Brands:
    QUICK'S

11799 Quigley Manufacturing
31 N Spruce St
Elizabethtown, PA 17022-1936   717-367-2441
            Fax: 717-367-4055   800-367-2441
        sales@joelinc.com www.quigleyco.com
Develops and manufacturers high-boiled confections
and lozenges for the branded and private label
market.
    President: David Deck
    VP: David Hess
    Marketing: Libby Moyer
    Plant Manager: Tom Nissley
    Purchasing Director: William Latsha
Estimated Sales: $9500000
Number Employees: 20-49
Sq. footage: 18000
Parent Co: Joel
Type of Packaging: Consumer, Private Label, Bulk
Brands:
    OLD FASHIONED
    SIMON
    SIMONS

11800 Quilceda Creek Vintners
11306 52nd St SE
Snohomish, WA 98290-5727   360-568-2389
    Fax: 360-568-2389 info@quilcedacreek.com
                          www.quilcedacreek.com
Wine
    Partner: Alexander Golitzin
    Partner: Jeannette Golitzin
Estimated Sales: $350,000
Number Employees: 1-4
Type of Packaging: Consumer
Brands:
    Quilceda Creek Vintners

11801 Quillin Produce Company
P.O.Box 225
Huntsville, AL 35804-0225   256-883-7374
                          Fax: 256-536-2456
Processor of produce
    Owner: James Quillin
Estimated Sales: $ 5 - 10 Million
Number Employees: 5-9

11802 Quillisascut Cheese Company
2409 Pleasant Valley Road
Rice, WA 99167-9706   509-738-2011
Processor of goat's milk cheese
    Owner/Purchasing: Rick Misterly
    Owner: Lore Lea
Number Employees: 1-4
Type of Packaging: Food Service
Brands:
    Quillisascut Cheese

11803 Quinalt Pride Seafood
P.O.Box 217
Taholah, WA 98587-0217   360-276-4431
            Fax: 360-276-4880 gensly@quinault.org
                          www.quinaultpride.com
Processor and exporter of precooked, canned and
foil pouched salmon
    Manager: Alan Heather
    CFO: William Parkshurst
Estimated Sales: $ 5 - 10 Million
Number Employees: 20-49
Type of Packaging: Consumer, Food Service, Pri-
vate Label, Bulk

11804 (HQ)Quinlan Pretzels
3rd & Washington
Denver, PA 17517   717-336-7571
Manufacturer of pretzels
    Production Manager: Ken Zvonvheck
Estimated Sales: $20-50 Million
Number Employees: 125
Parent Co: Wise Foods
Type of Packaging: Consumer

11805 Quinoa Corporation
222 E Redondo Beach Blvd # B
Gardena, CA 90248-2302   310-217-8125
        Fax: 310-217-8140 quinoacorp@aol.com
                          www.quinoa.net
Pasta
    President: David Schnorr
Estimated Sales: Below $ 5 Million
Number Employees: 5-9
Type of Packaging: Consumer
Brands:
    ANCIENT HARVEST
    SUPERGRAIN PASTA

11806 Quinoa Corporation
222 E Redondo Beach Blvd # B
Gardena, CA 90248-2302   310-217-8125
Fax: 310-217-8140   quinoacorp@aol.com
www.quinoa.net
A branded product distributor and food merchant
President: Dave Schnorr
Estimated Sales: Below $ 5 Million
Number Employees: 1-4
Type of Packaging: Bulk
Brands:
Ancient Harvest Quinoa
Supergrain Pasta

11807 Quintessential Chocolates Company
P.O.Box 687
Fredericksburg, TX 78624-0687   830-990-9382
Fax: 830-997-0811   qechocolates@juno.com
www.qechocolates.com
Liquid-center chocolates
President: Lecia Duke
Estimated Sales: Less than $500,000
Number Employees: 5-9
Brands:
Canadian Blended Whisky Chocolates
Cutty Sark® Scots Whisky Chocolates
Jack Daniels
Kentucky Bourbon Chocolates
McCallan
Sam Houston Bourbon™ Chocolates
Whidbey's

11808 Quinzani Bakery
380 Harrison Ave
Boston, MA 02118-2281   617-426-2114
Fax: 617-451-8075   800-999-2091
orders@quinzanisbakery.com
www.quinzanisbakery.com
Manufacturer of baked goods including; sandwich
rolls, dinner rolls, French and Italian breads
President: Steven Quinzani
Purchasing Manager: Larry Quinzani
Estimated Sales: $10 Million
Number Employees: 50-99
Type of Packaging: Consumer, Food Service
Brands:
QUINZANI

11809 Quivira Vineyards
4900 W Dry Creek Rd
Healdsburg, CA 95448-9721   707-431-8333
Fax: 707-431-1664   800-292-8339
quivira@quivirawine.com   www.quivirawine.com
Organic wines
Manager: Kris Cuneo
Co-Founder: Henry Wendt
Vineyard Manager: Tony Castellanos
Winemaker/General Manager: Grady Wann
National Sales Manager: Bill Wiebalk
Direct Sales & Inventory: Denise Rose
Assistant Tasting Room Manager: Jana Aitken
Concierge Relations: Pam Jorgensen
Winemaker: Steven Canter
COO: Denise Sanders
Cellar Master: Adam Armstrong
Accounting Manager: Sheila Williams
Office Administrator: Lori-Jo Martin
Estimated Sales: Below $ 5 Million
Number Employees: 10-19
Type of Packaging: Private Label
Brands:
Quivira

11810 Quong Hop & Company
40 Airport Blvd
S San Francisco, CA 94080   650-553-9900
Fax: 650-952-3329   sales@quonghop.com
www.quonghop.com
Manufacturer of soy deli tofu, soy deli baked tofu,
soy deli tofu burger, raquel's hummus and soy deli
tempeh
President/CEO: Frank Stephens
Estimated Sales: $3.1 Million
Number Employees: 42
Sq. footage: 10000
Type of Packaging: Consumer, Food Service, Private Label, Bulk
Brands:
QUONG HOP
RAQUEL'S
SOY DELI

11811 Qzina Specialty Foods
3095 E Patrick Ln
Las Vegas, NV 89120-4932   702-451-3916
Fax: 702-433-7919   qzinalv@flash.net

11812 R & D Sausage Company
15714 Waterloo Rd
Cleveland, OH 44110-1660   216-692-1832
Processor of sausage
Owner: Joseph Zuzak
Estimated Sales: Less than $100,000
Number Employees: 1-4
Type of Packaging: Consumer, Bulk

11813 R & R Seafood
801 1st Avenue
Tybee Island, GA 31328   912-786-5504
Fax: 912-786-5504
Seafood
Owner: Robbie Robertson
Estimated Sales: Less than $100,000
Number Employees: 1-4

11814 R A B Food Group LLC
One Harmon Plaza
10th Floor
Secaucus, NJ   201-553-1100
Fax: 201-333-1809   dross@rabfoodgroup.com
www.rabfoodgroup.com
Manufacturer of processed kosher food products in-
cluding baked goods, pastas, soups, gefilte fish,
grape juice and borscht.
President/CEO: Jeremy Fingerman
Vice President Sales: Kevin O'Brien
Administrator: Deborah Ross

11815 R C Bigelow
201 Black Rock Turnpike
Fairfield, CT 06825-5512   203-334-1212
Fax: 203-334-4751   800-243-5587
info@bigelowtea.com   www.bigelowtea.com
Processor of flavored, herbal, green, decaffeinated
and iced teas; dessert coffees, flavored honey
spreads and full leaf estate teas
President: David Bigelow
President: Robert Crawford
Vice President: Eunice Bigelow
CFO: Donald Janezic
Marketing Director: Robert Kelly
Operations Manager: Cindi Bigelow
Estimated Sales: $ 50 - 100 Million
Number Employees: 170
Type of Packaging: Consumer, Food Service
Brands:
BIGELOW AFTERNOON ASSORTED HERB TEA
BIGELOW APPLE & CINNAMON HERB TEA
BIGELOW ASSORTED BIGELOW TEAS
BIGELOW ASSORTED DECAF TEAS
BIGELOW ASSORTED HERB TEA
BIGELOW ASSORTED STERLING SILVER
BIGELOW BLACK CURRANT
BIGELOW BORPATRA FULL LEAF TEA
BIGELOW CHAMOMILE LEMON HERB TEA
BIGELOW CHAMOMILE MANGO HERB TEA
BIGELOW CHAMOMILE MANGO HERB TEA
BIGELOW CHAMOMILE MINT HERB TEA
BIGELOW CHERRY VANILLA TEA
BIGELOW CHINESE FORTUNE
BIGELOW CINNAMON APPLE HERB TEA
BIGELOW CINNAMON SPICE HERB TEA
BIGELOW CINNAMON STICK
BIGELOW CINNAMON STICK DECAF
BIGELOW CONSTANT COMMENT
BIGELOW CONSTANT COMMENT DECAF
BIGELOW CONSTANT COMMENT LOOSE TEA
BIGELOW COZY CHAMOMILE HERB TEA
BIGELOW CRANBERRY APPLE HERB TEA
BIGELOW DARJEELING BLEND
BIGELOW DARJEELING LOOSE TEA
BIGELOW DRAGONWELL FULL LEAF TEA
BIGELOW EARL GREY
BIGELOW EARL GREY LOOSE TEA
BIGELOW EARLY GREY DECAF
BIGELOW EARLY GREY GREEN TEA
BIGELOW ENGLISH BREAKFAST
BIGELOW ENGLISH BREAKFAST LOOSE TEA
BIGELOW ENGLISH TEATIME
BIGELOW ENGLISH TEATIME DECAF
BIGELOW FRENCH VANILLA
BIGELOW FRUIT ALMOND HERB TEA
BIGELOW GREEN GENMAICHA FULL LEAF

BIGELOW GREEN LOOSE TEA
BIGELOW GREEN TEA WITH LEMON
BIGELOW GREEN TEA WITH MANGO
BIGELOW GREEN TEA WITH MINT
BIGELOW GREEN TEA WITH PEACH
BIGELOW I LOVE LEMON & C HERB TEA
BIGELOW JASMINE FLOWERS FULL LEAF
BIGELOW JASMINE LOOSE TEA
BIGELOW KEEMUN BLACK FULL LEAF
BIGELOW KENILWORTH FULL LEAF TEA
BIGELOW LEMON LIFT
BIGELOW LEMON LIFT DECAF
BIGELOW MINT MEDLEY HERB TEA
BIGELOW ORANGE & SPICE HERB TEA
BIGELOW ORANGE & SPICE HERB TEA
BIGELOW PAI MU TAN FULL LEAF TEA
BIGELOW PEPPERMINT HERB LOOSE TEA
BIGELOW PEPPERMINT HERB TEA
BIGELOW PERFECT PEACH HERB TEA
BIGELOW PLANTATION MINT
BIGELOW PLANTATION MINT DECAF
BIGELOW RASPBERRY ROYALE
BIGELOW RASPBERRY ROYALE DECAF
BIGELOW RED RASPBERRY HERB LOOSE
BIGELOW RED REASPBERRY HERB TEA
BIGELOW RISHEEHAT FULL LEAF TEA
BIGELOW SE CHUNG FULL LEAF TEA
BIGELOW SIX ASSORTED GREEN TEAS
BIGELOW SWEET DREAMS HERB TEA
BIGELOW VANILLA ALMOND TEA
BIGELOW SIX ASSORTED GREEN TEAS
BIGELOW SWEET DREAMS HERB TEA
BIGELOW VANILLA ALMOND TEA
BIGELOW VANILLA CARAMEL TEA
BIGELOW VANILLA HAZELNUT TEA
BIGELOW WILD CHERRY HERB LOOSE TEA

11816 R Four Meats
24 2nd St SW
Chatfield, MN 55923-1208   507-867-4180
Fax: 507-867-4180
Manufacturer and packer of fresh and frozen deer,
beef, pork and lamb, retail sales product shipping
available
Owner: Jeff Remme
Estimated Sales: $1-2.5 Million
Number Employees: 5-9
Type of Packaging: Consumer

11817 R M Lawton Cranberries
221 Thomas St
Middleboro, MA 02346-3321   508-947-7465
Fax: 508-947-0280
Cranberries
Manager: Mark Di Carlo
Estimated Sales: $300,000-$375,000
Number Employees: 5-9
Type of Packaging: Food Service, Bulk
Brands:
R.M. Lawton Cranberries

11818 R&A Imports
P.O.Box 1133
Pacific Plsds, CA 90272-1133   310-454-2247
Fax: 310-459-3218   zonevdka@gte.net
www.raimportsinc.com
Processor and importer of vodka
President: Veronica Pekarovic
Estimated Sales: $1-2.5 Million
Number Employees: 1 to 4
Brands:
Zone

11819 R&B Quality Foods
7755 E Gray Road
Scottsdale, AZ 85260-6980   480-443-1415
Fax: 480-922-1550
Estimated Sales: $ 5 - 10 Million
Number Employees: 5-9

11820 R&F Miller
2521 Mishawaka Ave
South Bend, IN 46615-2263   574-288-6777
Fax: 219-233-9669
President: Michael Miller
Estimated Sales: $ .5 - 1 million
Number Employees: 1-4

11821 R&J Farms
9291 N Elyria Rd
West Salem, OH 44287-9791   419-846-3179
Fax: 419-846-9603 www.rjfarms.com

Processor and exporter of regular and organic soy and dry beans, organic sesame and sunflower seeds, whole and flaked grains, flour, microwaveable popcorn and multi-grain chips and pretzels; importer of garbanzo beans
Owner: Todd Driscoll
Number Employees: 5-9
Sq. footage: 20000
Type of Packaging: Consumer, Private Label, Bulk
Brands:
Country Grown
Whole Earth

11822 R&J Seafoods
P.O.Box 16
King Cove, AK 99612-0016   907-497-3060
                                 Fax: 907-246-4487
Seafood
Plant Manager: Glen Guffey

11823 R&R Homestead Kitchen
3801 Rolling Heights
Oneida, WI 54155   920-869-8244
     Fax: 920-869-1274 888-779-8245
                        www.rnrfudge.com
Hot fudge topping
Owner: Richard Roffers

11824 R&S Mexican Food Products
5818 W Maryland Ave
Glendale, AZ 85301-3909   602-272-2727
     Fax: 602-435-1377 www.rsmexfoods.com
Processor of Mexican products including fruits, vegetables, canned goods, spices, tacos, tamales, tortillas, etc
President: Danny Franks
Sales/Marketing Manager: Mila Cano
Plant Manager: Francisco Ramirez
Estimated Sales: $4415000
Number Employees: 50-99
Sq. footage: 35000
Type of Packaging: Consumer, Food Service

11825 R-K Sausage Company
7700 Harvard Ave
Cleveland, OH 44105-3937   216-341-1251
                                 Fax: 216-341-2389
Processor of sausages, hot dogs and smokies
President: Marty Archacki
General Manager: Donna Stevens
Estimated Sales: $$1-2.5 Million
Number Employees: 5-9
Sq. footage: 3000
Type of Packaging: Consumer, Food Service, Private Label, Bulk

11826 R. Torre & Company
233 E Harris Ave
S San Francisco, CA 94080-6807   650-875-1200
     Fax: 650-875-1600   800-775-1925
     info@torani.com   www.torani.com
Italian syrups
President: Harry Lucheta
CEO: Melania Dulbecco
CEO: Melanie Dulbecco
VP Marketing: Cynthia Eckart
Estimated Sales: $ 50 - 100 Million
Number Employees: 50-99
Type of Packaging: Private Label
Brands:
Caffee Fiori
Frusia
Torani

11827 R.A. Fayard Company
PO Box 343
Biloxi, MS 39533-0343   228-436-6243
                               Fax: 228-436-6243
Shrimp
Estimated Sales: $ 1-2.5 Million
Number Employees: 5-9
Brands:
R.A. Fayard

11828 R.A.B. Food Group LLC
One Harmon Plaza
Secaucus, NJ 07094   201-453-5200
     Fax: 201-333-1809 dross@rabfoodgroup.com
                        www.rabfoodgroup.com

Manufacturer and exporter of kosher foods including matzoth, crackers, cereals, wine, bagel mixes, candy, pickles, gefilte fish, borscht, doughnut mixes, bagel mixes and egg noodles
President/Chief Executive Officer: Jeremy Fingerman
Chairman/Chief Executive Officer: Richard Bernstein
Vice President/Sales: Kevin O'Brien
Public Relations/Media: Deborah Ross
Estimated Sales: $10-20 Million
Number Employees: 20-49
Type of Packaging: Consumer, Food Service, Private Label
Brands:
ASIAN HARVEST
CARMEL
CROYDEN HOUSE
ELITE
GOODMAN'S
GUILTLESS GOURMET
JASON
MANISCHEWITZ
MISHPACHA
MOTHER'S
MRS ADLER'S
ROKEACH
SEASON BRAND
TRADITION

11829 R.B. Morriss Company
1531 Deer Crossing Dr
Diamond Bar, CA 91765-2627   909-861-8671
 Fax: 909-860-5272 rbmorrissco@worldnet.att.net
Environmental and food products
President: Robert Morriss
Estimated Sales: $ 2.5-5 Million
Number Employees: 1-4

11830 R.C. McEntire & Company
P.O.Box 5817
Columbia, SC 29250-5817   803-799-3388
     Fax: 803-254-3540 info@rcmentire.com
                        www.rcmcentire.com
Processor of fresh vegetables including tomatoes, peppers, lettuce, onions, cabbage, salads, tomato repacker, etc
Owner: Buddy Mc Entire Jr
Estimated Sales: $ 10 - 20 Million
Number Employees: 10-19
Sq. footage: 75000
Type of Packaging: Consumer, Food Service, Private Label, Bulk
Brands:
Dinner Reddi
Micro Fast
Salad Pak
Veg Fresh

11831 R.D. Hemond Farms
232 Pottle Hill Road
Minot, ME 04258-4802   207-345-5611
                              Fax: 207-345-5611
Poultry
President: Rolland Hemond
Brands:
Oak Hurst Dairy

11832 R.D. Offutt Company
P.O.Box 7160
Fargo, ND 58106-7160   701-237-6062
     Fax: 701-239-8750 www.rdoequipment.com
Processor of frozen sliced potatoes, French fries, hash browns and patties; also, potato chips
CEO: Ron Offutt
Estimated Sales: $ 20-50 Million
Number Employees: 100-249
Type of Packaging: Consumer, Food Service, Private Label
Brands:
RDO

11833 R.E. Kimball & Company
73 Merrimac Street
Amesbury, MA 01913-4097   978-388-1826
Processor of condiments and preserves
President: Joy Kimball
CEO: Joy Kimeball
Treasurer: Ruth Kimball
Marketing Director: Joy Kimeball
Number Employees: 5-9
Sq. footage: 25000
Type of Packaging: Consumer, Private Label

Brands:
Kimball's
private lable

11834 R.E. Meyer Company
4611 W Adams Street
Lincoln, NE 68524-1444   402-474-8500
     Fax: 402-470-4380 www.meyerbeef.com
Processor and exporter of beef and pork
Number Employees: 100-249
Parent Co: Meyer Holdings
Type of Packaging: Food Service, Private Label, Bulk

11835 R.F.A.
PO Box 717
Newcastle, ME 04553-0717   207-563-2340
                                  Fax: 207-563-2345
President: Justin Braithwaite

11836 R.H. Bauman & Company
P.O.Box 4645
Chatsworth, CA 91313-4645   818-709-1093
                                   Fax: 818-341-8348
General grocery
President: R Bauman
Estimated Sales: Less than $500,000
Number Employees: 1-4
Type of Packaging: Private Label

11837 R.H. Phillips
26836 County Rd
Esparto, CA 95627   530-662-3504
     Fax: 530-662-2880 csutton@rhphillips.com
                        www.rhphillips.com
Wines
Manager: Barry Bergman
CEO: Karl Giguiere
CFO: Bance Schram
Quality Control: David Keim
Public Relations: Lane Giguiere
Wine Maker: Barry Bergman
Plant Manager: Ken Lazzaroni
Estimated Sales: 21,720,000
Number Employees: 100-249
Type of Packaging: Private Label
Brands:
R.H. Phillips

11838 R.I. Provision Company
5 Day St
Johnston, RI 02919-4301   401-831-0815
                                 Fax: 401-274-5508
     sales@littlerhodyhotdogs.com
     www.littlerhodyhotdogs.com
Sausages, franks and toppings
President: Edward Robalisky
Estimated Sales: $ 1-2.5 Million
Number Employees: 10-19
Number of Brands: 1

11839 R.J. Corr Naturals
14028 S McKinley Avenue
Posen, IL 60469   708-389-4200
                         Fax: 708-389-4294
Processor of natural beverages including juice blends, sodas and sparkling mineral water
President: Robert Corr
General Manager: James Corr
VP Operations: Thomas Swan
Number Employees: 10-19
Sq. footage: 16000
Brands:
Gear Up
Ginseng Rush
Natures Flavors
North Star
Rj Corr
Robert Corr

11840 R.L. Albert & Son
19 W Elm St
Greenwich, CT 06830-6452   203-622-8655
     Fax: 203-622-7454 mainmail@albertcandy.com
Candy and confectionery wholesale
President: Lawrence Albert
CFO: Marion Lossick
COO: Robert Cats
Estimated Sales: $ 10-20 Million
Number Employees: 20-49
Brands:
Big Baby
Big Bol
Fortune Bubble

Fun Fruit
Gum Time
Ice Cubes
Mint Balls
Moritz Ice Cubes
Neon Lasers
Pnut Jumbo
So Joao
Stardrops
Stardrops

11841 R.L. Schreiber
1741 NW 33rd St
Pompano Beach, FL 33064-1327   954-972-7102
    Fax: 954-972-4406   800-624-8777
   rlschreiber@rlsinc.com   www.rlschreiber.com
Manufacturer of soup bases, sauces, gravies, spices,
spice blends, custom blending and specialty items
    President: Tom Schreiber
    Sales Director: Joe DeCaro
    Plant Manager: Bernadine Jolley
    Purchasing Manager: Kim Ryan
Estimated Sales: $ 5-10 Million
Number Employees: 50-99
Type of Packaging: Food Service, Private Label

11842 R.L. Schreiber Company
1741 NW 33rd St
Pompano Beach, FL 33064-1327   954-972-7102
    Fax: 954-972-4406   800-624-8777
   rlschreiber@rlsinc.com   www.rlschreiber.com
Processor of soup bases, gravies, sauces and spices
    President: Tom Schreiber
Estimated Sales: $9300000
Number Employees: 50-99
Type of Packaging: Food Service

11843 R.L. Zeigler Company
P.O.Box 1640
Tuscaloosa, AL 35403-1640   205-758-3621
    Fax: 205-758-0185   800-392-6328
   zeigler@zmeats.com   www.zmeats.com
Manufacturer and exporter of lunch meats, bacon
and frankfurters
    President: W Lackey Stephens
Estimated Sales: $ 50 - 100 Million
Number Employees: 20-49
Sq. footage: 100000
Type of Packaging: Consumer, Food Service, Private Label
Brands:
    Talmadge Farms
    Zeigler

11844 R.M. Felts Packing Company
P.O.Box 199
Ivor, VA 23866-0199   757-859-6131
    Fax: 757-859-6381   888-300-0971
    rmfelts@mindspring.com
Processor and exporter of cured and dry salted
smoked ham and picnic hams
    President: Robert M Felts Jr
    CEO: Charles Stallard
Estimated Sales: $ 3 - 5 Million
Number Employees: 10-19
Sq. footage: 17000
Type of Packaging: Consumer, Food Service, Private Label
Brands:
    Southampton

11845 R.M. Palmer Company
P.O.Box 1723
Reading, PA 19603-1723   610-372-8971
    Fax: 610-378-5208   www.rmpalmer.com
Processor and exporter of confectionery products in-
cluding hollow and solid chocolate seasonal novel-
ties, lollypops, everday bag items and novelties.
    President: Richard M Palmer Jr
    CFO: Chuck Shearer
    Quality Control: Tierney Wheaton
    Director of Marketing: David Abrams
    Sales Director: Steve Terroni
    Operations Manager: Mark Schlott
    Production Manager: Mark Schlott
    Plant Manager: Sue Halvonik
    Purchasing Manager: Rich Halliwell
Estimated Sales: $150-200 Million
Type of Packaging: Consumer, Bulk
Brands:
    Bumpkins
    Cookie Dippers

11846 R.R. Fournier & Sons
P.O.Box 732
Biloxi, MS 39533-0732   228-392-4293
    Fax: 228-392-7130
Seafood
    President: Doty A Fournier
    Secretary: Barbara Fournier
Estimated Sales: $ 2.5-5 Million
Number Employees: 20-49

11847 R.R. Lochhead Manufacturing
200 Sherwood Rd
Paso Robles, CA 93446-3546   805-238-3400
    Fax: 805-238-0111   800-735-0545
    cooks@cooksvanilla.com
Processor of vanilla flavoring
    President: R Lochhead
    Manager: S Lochhead
Estimated Sales: $620000
Number Employees: 5-9
Type of Packaging: Consumer, Food Service, Pri-
vate Label, Bulk

11848 R.W. Frookies
PO Box 1649
Sag Harbor, NY 11963-0060   800-913-3663
    800-913-3663
Cookies and baked goods
    President: Ned Parkhouse
Estimated Sales: Under $500,000
Number Employees: 1-4

11849 R.W. Knudsen
P.O.Box 369
Chico, CA 95927-0369   530-899-5000
    Fax: 530-891-6397
   arlene.starkey@jmsmucker.com
    www.jmsmucker.com
Fruit juice
    President: Julia Sabin
    Marketing Assistant: Arlene Starkey
Number Employees: 100-249

11850 RBW & Associates
PO Box 698
Portland, OR 97207-0698   503-223-0843
    Fax: 503-223-2731
Ingredients, yeast products
Number Employees: 5-9

11851 RC Fine Foods
P.O.Box 236
Belle Mead, NJ 08502-0236   908-359-5500
    Fax: 908-359-6957   800-526-3953
   info@rcfinefoods.com   www.rcfinefoods.com
Processor of mixes including soup, gravy, specialty,
salad dressing, dessert and sauce; also, soup bases,
spices, seasonings, extracts, colors and dietetic
products
    President: Elaine Cohen
    Director Sales: Robert Dixon
Estimated Sales: $5500000
Number Employees: 50-99
Sq. footage: 48000
Type of Packaging: Food Service
Brands:
    Rc Fine Foods

11852 RCB Baking
PO Box 6004
Fargo, ND 58108-6004   701-282-2300
    Fax: 701-373-1956
  www.mnstate.edu/busintern/Acct_past_intern.htm
Gingerbread houses and rum cakes
    President: Richard Blajsczak
    Partner: Claire Blajsczak
    Executive VP: Claire Blajszak
    VP Manufacturing: Russ Seely
Number Employees: 50-99
Type of Packaging: Consumer
Brands:
    Effie Marie

11853 RCB International
39878 Turnidge Rd NE
Albany, OR 97321-9556   541-967-3814
    Fax: 450-973-4633   mintbuy@aol.com
Essential oils including spearmint, peppermint,
dillweed, tarragon, parsley, pennyroyal, mentha
citrata, etc
    President: Dana Wendel
    Quality Control: Dana Wendel
    Sales Director: John Wendel

Estimated Sales: $ 5 - 10 Million
Number Employees: 5-9
Type of Packaging: Consumer, Bulk
Brands:
    Mari Mint

11854 RCV Seafood Corporation
556 Riverside Drive
Morattico, VA 22523   804-462-5101
    Fax: 804-462-7401
Processor of seafood including fresh blue crab meat
and crab meal
    President: Weston Conley Jr
Estimated Sales: $917397
Number Employees: 40
Sq. footage: 15000
Type of Packaging: Consumer, Food Service
Brands:
    RCV

11855 RDO Foods Company
4366 24th Ave N
Grand Forks, ND 58203-1304   701-746-0611
    Fax: 701-746-0374   info@rdofoodsco.com
    www.rdofoodsco.com
Snack foods
    Partner: Brian Radi
    CEO: Ronald Offutt
    Quality Control: Jeff Posey
    Marketing Director: Steve Merchant
Estimated Sales: $ 20-50 Million
Number Employees: 50-99

11856 RES Food Products International
PO Box 12511
Green Bay, WI 54307-2511   920-499-7651
    Fax: 920-499-8023   800-255-3768
    sales@edcofood.com   www.edcofood.com
Processor and importer of peppers including
jalapeno, serrano, sport and cascabella; also, cauli-
flower buttons, chipotle powder and pickled vegeta-
bles
    President: James Manning
    VP: Sylvia Roman
    VP: Edward Manning
Estimated Sales: $ 3 - 5 Million
Number Employees: 135
Sq. footage: 16000
Type of Packaging: Food Service, Private Label,
Bulk

11857 REX Pure Foods
P.O.Box 1726
Gonzales, TX 78629-1226   504-822-4141
    Fax: 504-822-4134   800-344-8314
    info@rexfoods.com   www.rexfoods.com
Processor and packer of seafood spices and season-
ings, sauces, liquid and dry blends, vinegar and mus-
tard; also, contract packaging available
    President: J Geldart
    Sales Manager: Marc Gelpi
    VP Production: Al Lefevre
Estimated Sales: $2500000
Number Employees: 115
Type of Packaging: Consumer, Food Service, Bulk
Brands:
    REX

11858 RFI Ingredients
300 Corporate Dr
Blauvelt, NY 10913-1144   845-358-8600
    Fax: 845-358-9003   800-962-7663
    rfi@rfiingredients.com   www.rfiingredients.com
Supplier of natural antioxidants, antimicrobials and
preservatives, natural colors, fruit, vegetable and bo-
tanical extracts and functional food ingredients
    President/CEO: Jeff Wuagneux
    VP Research & Development: Ginny Bank
    Technical Manager: Diyu Hsu
    Marketing: Jennifer Diliddo
    VP Sales: Trisha Devine
    Chief Operations Officer: Drew Luce
    Operations Manager: Neal Cochran
Estimated Sales: $ 10 - 20 Million
Number of Brands: 5
Type of Packaging: Bulk
Brands:
    COLORPURE
    OXYPHYTE
    PHYTBAC
    PHYTONUTRIANCE
    STABILENHANCE

11859 RH Bauman & Company
21021 Devonshire St.
#202
Chatsworth, CA 91311   818-709-1093
Fax: 818-341-8348   877-228-6263
Manufacturer, exporter and importer of coffee flavor
protectors and coffee extenders
President: Russell Bauman
Ceo: Lisa Wong
Estimated Sales:$500000
Number Employees: 6
Number of Brands: 1
Sq. footage: 2500
Type of Packaging: Food Service, Bulk
Brands:
Coffe'a Elite

11860 (HQ)RIBUS
8000 Maryland Ave # 460
St Louis, MO 63105-3910   314-727-4287
Fax: 314-727-1199   info@ribus.com
www.ribus.com
Processor and exporter of natural rice-based food in-
gredients for baked goods, snacks and confectionery
items including chocolate and frosting; also,
nongenetically modified emulsifiers and extrusion
aids
President: Steve Pierce
Sales: Jim Goodall
Estimated Sales:$720000
Number Employees: 5-9
Sq. footage: 10000
Other Locations:
RIBUS
Sabetha KS
Brands:
Nu-Bake
Nu-Rice
Ribus

11861 RJ Balson and Sons Inc
PO Box 4817
Fayetteville, AR 72702   321-281-9473
contact@balsonbutchers.com
www.balsonbutchers.com
sausage

11862 RL Schreiber
1741 NW 33rd St
Pompano Beach, FL 33064-1327   954-972-7102
Fax: 954-972-4406   rlschreiber@rlsinc.com
www.rlschreiber.com
Soups, gravy bases and spices
President: Tom Schreiber
Estimated Sales:$ 5-10 Million
Number Employees: 50-99

11863 RM Palmer Company
P.O.Box 1723
Reading, PA 19603-1723   610-372-8971
Fax: 610-378-5208 www.rmpalmer.com
President: Richard M Palmer Jr
Sales Administrator: Gail Youse
Estimated Sales:$ 20-50 Million
Number Employees: 500-999

11864 ROHA USA, LLC
5015 Manchester Avenue
St. Louis, MO 63110   888-533-7642
Fax: 888-531-0461   roha.usa@rohagroup.com
www.rohagroup.com
Supplier of natural and synthetic food colours.
Production: Rohit Tibrewala

11865 RPM Total Vitality
18032 Lemon Drive
Suite C
Yorba Linda, CA 92886-3386   714-524-8864
Fax: 714-524-3247   800-234-3092
rpmtv.com
Processor and exporter of natural antioxidants in-
cluding flower pollen and dimethylaminoethanol
Owner: Pat McBride
Co-Owner: Roger McBride
Number Employees: 1-4
Sq. footage: 1000
Brands:
Letan

11866 RV Industries
2801 Bankers Industrial Dr
Atlanta, GA 30360-2712   770-729-8983
Fax: 770-729-9428   sales@rvindustries.com
www.rvindustries.com

Processor, importer and exporter of desiccated,
sweetened and toasted coconut, coconut milk pow-
der, aseptic coconut milk and water
President: Andres E Siochi
General Manager: Bob Weschrek
CFO: Bharat Shah
Sales: Robert Santiago
Production: Guillermo Pineiro
Estimated Sales:$14000000
Number Employees: 20-49
Sq. footage: 40000
Parent Co: RV Industries
Type of Packaging: Consumer, Food Service, Pri-
vate Label, Bulk
Brands:
Fiesta
Red V
Tropical

11867 RW Delights
50 Division Ave
Suite 44
Millington, NJ 07946   917-301-5231
866-892-1096
info@heavenlysouffle.com
www.heavenlysouffle.com
individual souffle and creme brulee desserts

11868 RW Garcia Company
P.O.Box 8290
San Jose, CA 95155-8290   408-287-4616
Fax: 408-287-7724   custserv@rwgarcia.com
www.rwgarcia.com
Processor and exporter of organic and commercial
grade tortilla chips; private labeling available
VP: Margaret Garcia
Sales Manager: Jake Stenton
Estimated Sales:$ 10 - 20 Million
Number Employees: 20-49
Sq. footage: 30000
Parent Co: R.W. Garcia Company
Type of Packaging: Private Label
Brands:
Santa Cruz

11869 Rabbit Barn
630 W Clausen Rd
Turlock, CA 95380-9703   209-632-1123
Fax: 209-632-1123   kxva66a@prodigy.com
Processor of rabbit including fresh, frozen, whole
body, cut-up and tray packed
Owner: Larry Sigafoos
CEO: Sherri Sigafoos
Estimated Sales:$ 1 - 3 Million
Number Employees: 1-4
Sq. footage: 4000
Type of Packaging: Private Label
Brands:
Rabbit Barn

11870 Rabbit Creek Products
P.O.Box 1059
Louisburg, KS 66053-1059   913-837-2757
Fax: 913-837-5760   800-837-3073
rcreek@micoks.net
www.rabbitcreekgourmet.com
Processor of muffin, dip, soup, scone, bread,
brownie, and cookie mixes
President: Donna A Cook
Estimated Sales:$ 20 - 50 Million
Number Employees: 20-49
Number of Brands: 1
Number of Products: 120
Type of Packaging: Consumer, Private Label
Brands:
RABBIT CREEK

11871 Rabbit Ridge
3291 Westside Road
Healdsburg, CA 95448-9349   707-431-7128
Fax: 707-431-8018
linda_rabbitridge@yahoo.com
www.rabbitridgewinery.com
Wines
Founder/Winemaker: Erich Russell
President: Joanne James Russell
Compliance/Operations Manager: Sandy James
Director Paso Vineyard Operations: Robert Pierce

Paso Robles Office Manager: Jacqueline Pierce
Paso Robles Assistant to the Director: Mike
Sanford
Healdsburg Operations Director: Linda Garwood
Healdsburg Warehouse Manager: Craig Wisdom

*Estimated Sales:*Below $ 5 Million
Number Employees: 8-20
Brands:
Rabbit Ridge
Rabbit Ridge

11872 Raber Packing
1413 N Raber Rd
Peoria, IL 61604-4790   309-673-0721
Fax: 309-673-6308
Processor of meat products
President: Carroll Wetterauer
Estimated Sales:$ 10 - 20 Million
Number Employees: 20-49
Type of Packaging: Consumer

11873 Raceland Raw Sugar Corporation
175 Mill St
Raceland, LA 70394   985-537-3533
Fax: 985-537-7779
Manufacturer of raw sugar and blackstrap molasses
President/CEO: Dan Duplantis
Estimated Sales:$33 Million
Number Employees: 100-249
Parent Co: M.A. Patout & Son
Type of Packaging: Bulk

11874 Radanovich Vineyards & Winery
3936 Ben Hur Road
Mariposa, CA 95338-9466   209-966-3187
Wines
President: George Radanovich
Estimated Sales:$500,000-$1 Million
Number Employees: 1-4

11875 Radar Farms
P.O.Box 133
Lynden, WA 98264-0133   360-354-6574
Fax: 360-354-7070   info@raderfarms.com
www.raderfarms.com
Processor of frozen rhubarb, red raspberries and
raspberry puree
President: Lyle Rader
Estimated Sales:$ 50-100 Million
Number Employees: 250-499
Type of Packaging: Consumer, Food Service, Pri-
vate Label

11876 (HQ)Radlo Foods
313 Pleasant Street
Watertown, MA 02472-2418   617-926-7070
Fax: 617-923-6440   800-370-1439
info@radlo.com   www.radlo.com
Processor of all natural and organic eggs, 100%
Florida organic orange juice, and all natural beef and
chicken.
President: Jack Radlo
VP: David Radlo
Estimated Sales:$25000000
Number Employees: 25
Type of Packaging: Consumer, Food Service, Pri-
vate Label, Bulk
Brands:
Born Free
Grown Free

11877 Radloff's Cheese
500 W Griffith Street
Hustisford, WI 53034-9768   920-349-3266
Fax: 920-349-8537
Cheese
President: Rudyard Radloff
Treasurer: Wanda Starr
VP Production: Mark Radloff
Estimated Sales:$500,000-$1 Million
Number Employees: 5-9

11878 Radway's Dairy
433 Park Street
New Britain, CT 06051-2730   860-443-8921
Fax: 860-437-7911   800-472-3929
Dairy products and distributors
Estimated Sales:$ 10-20 Million
Number Employees: 25

11879 Raemica
P.O.Box 2408
Running Springs, CA 92382-2408   909-867-7210
Fax: 909-864-0554   800-772-6328
sales@farwestmeats.com

Processor and exporter of meat products including smoked sausage, knockwurst, bologna, salami, bratwurst, frankfurters, kielbasa, beef, pork and smoked pork and turkey parts
- Owner/President: Thomas Serrato III
- VP/General Manager: Wade Snyder
Estimated Sales: Less than $500,000
Number Employees: 50-99
Sq. footage: 25000
Type of Packaging: Consumer, Private Label, Bulk
Brands:
- Far West Meats

11880 Raffetto's Corporation
156 Leroy Street
New York, NY 10014-3301   212-727-8222
   Fax: 212-727-0046
Processor of pasta including macaroni, noodles, tortellini and ravioli
- President: Richard Raffetto
- VP: Andrew Raffetto
Estimated Sales: $ 10 - 20 Million
Number Employees: 20
Type of Packaging: Consumer, Food Service

11881 Raffield Fisheries
P.O.Box 309
Port St Joe, FL 32457-0309   850-229-8229
   Fax: 850-229-8782
raffieldfish@digitalexpress.com
www.raffieldfisheries.com
Processor and exporter of Atlantic thread herring, black drum, black mullet roe, bluefish, blue runner, Jack Crevalle, ladyfish, Spanish sardines, butterfish, goatfish, croakers, crawfish, etc.
- President: William Raffield
- Secretary/Treasurer: Danny Raffield
Estimated Sales: $ 10 - 20 Million
Number Employees: 50-99
Type of Packaging: Consumer, Food Service, Private Label, Bulk

11882 Ragersville Swiss Cheese
2199 Ragersville Rd SW
Sugarcreek, OH 44681   330-897-3055
   Fax: 330-897-0415
Processor of Swiss cheese
- President/Owner: Richard Hicks
- Owner: Diane Hicks
Estimated Sales: $ 3 - 5 Million
Number Employees: 1-4
Sq. footage: 10000
Type of Packaging: Consumer

11883 Raggy-O Chutney
PO Box 1626
Smithfield, NC 27577-1626   919-284-6700
   Fax: 919-284-6706   888-424-8863
raggyo.chutney@simflex.com
Chutney and all-purpose seasoning sauce
Brands:
- B-17
- Raggy-O

11884 Ragold Confections
516 NW 20th St
Wilton Manors, FL 33311-3820   954-566-9092
   Fax: 954-427-0413   rs@ragold.com
www.ragold.com
Candy
- Chairman of the Board: Rainer Schindler
- CFO: Arthur Pauly
Estimated Sales: $ 1.5 Million
Number Employees: 10-19
Type of Packaging: Private Label
Brands:
- Dilbert Mints&Gummies
- Juicefuls Hard Candy

11885 Ragozzino Food
P.O.Box 116
Meriden, CT 06450-0116   203-238-2553
   Fax: 203-235-5158   800-348-1240
nancy@ragozzino.com   www.ragozzino.com
Manufacturer, importer and exporter of soups, pasta's, sauces, entrees and side dishes
- President: Gloria Ragozzino
- VP Business Development: Nancy Ragozzino
- VP: John Ragozzino
- R&D: Susan Ragozzino
- Purchasing Director: Ellen Ragozzino
Estimated Sales: $23 Million
Number Employees: 100-249

Type of Packaging: Consumer, Food Service, Private Label
Brands:
- Sugo
- Zino

11886 Ragsdale-Overton Food Traditions
PO Box 1626
Smithfield, NC 27577-1626   919-284-6700
   Fax: 919-284-6706   888-424-8863
raggy.ochutney@simflex.com
Condiments, chutneys, sauces
- Partner: Sue Overton
- Partner: Carolyn Ragsdale
- Public Relations: Carolyn Ragsdale
Estimated Sales: Under $500,000
Number Employees: 1-4
Type of Packaging: Private Label
Brands:
- B-17 Seasoning/Grilling Sauce
- Raggy-O Apple Chutne
- Raggy-O Cranberry Ch
- Raggy-O Mango Chutne
- Raggy-O Peach Chutne
- Raggy-O Pineapple Ch

11887 (HQ)Rahco International
850 A1a Beach Blvd # 121
St Augustine, FL 32080-6954   904-461-9931
   Fax: 904-461-9932   800-851-7681
rahcoint@aol.com   www.rahcoint.com
Manufacturer of signs, menus and wine lists; importer of wines and gourmet Italian sauces, marmalades and panetone; exporter of Italian style cheeses, signs and wines
- President: Alvin Moser
- Vice President: Olga Lara-Moser
- Operations Manager: David Firch
- Production Manager: Dale Mull
Estimated Sales: $500,000-$1 Million
Number Employees: 5-9
Number of Brands: 12
Number of Products: 60
Sq. footage: 1500
Type of Packaging: Consumer, Food Service, Private Label, Bulk
Other Locations:
- Rahco International
- Agoura Hills CA
Brands:
- DORAL
- PARK CHEESE

11888 Rahr Malting Company
800 1st Ave W
Shakopee, MN 55379-1148   952-445-1431
   Fax: 952-496-7055   frahr@rahr.com
www.rahr.com
Processor and exporter of malt
- President: Gary Lee
- CFO: James Olsen
- R&D: Paul Kramer
Estimated Sales: $43.6 Million
Number Employees: 100-249
Type of Packaging: Bulk

11889 Rahr Malting Company
800 1st Ave W
Shakopee, MN 55379-1148   952-445-1431
   Fax: 952-496-7055   glee@rahr.com
www.rahr.com
Produces and distributes malt and industry related brewing supplies.
- President: Gary Lee
- CFO: James Olsen
- VP Operations: Bob Micheletti
Estimated Sales: $43.6 Million
Number Employees: 100-249
Type of Packaging: Bulk

11890 Rain Sweet
P.O.Box 6109
Salem, OR 97304-0278   503-363-4293
   Fax: 503-585-4657   800-363-4293
gamos@rainsweet.com   www.rainsweet.com

Processor and exporter of frozen blackberries, blueberries, black raspberries, red raspberries, boysenberries; also, IQF and puree cane berries, mushrooms, peppers, onions, pearl onions, bean sprouts
- CEO: George Crispin
- Marketing: Gery Amos
- Sales Manager: Gery Amos
- VP Operations/Production: Mike Harcourt
- Plant Manager: Lynn Mitchell
Estimated Sales: $ 50 - 100 Million
Number Employees: 100-249
Sq. footage: 30000
Type of Packaging: Consumer, Food Service, Private Label, Bulk
Brands:
- RAINSWEET

11891 Rainbow Farms
62 Weatherhead Road
Upper Rawdon, NS B0N 2N0
Canada   902-632-2548
   Fax: 902-632-2434
Processor and exporter of frozen wild blueberries
- President: Ronald Weatherhead
- Vice President: Barbara Hatell
Type of Packaging: Bulk

11892 Rainbow Hill Vineyards
26349 Township Road 251
Newcomerstown, OH 43832-9631   740-545-9305
   www.ravensglenn.com
Wines
- President: Leland Wyse
Estimated Sales: Below $ 5 Million
Number Employees: 5-9
Brands:
- Rainbow Hill Vineyards

11893 Rainbow Light Nutritional Systems
125 McPherson St
Santa Cruz, CA 95060-5818   831-429-9089
   Fax: 831-429-0189   800-635-1233
info@rlns.com   www.rainbowlight.com
Processor of supplements and herbal extracts
- President: Linda Kahler
- Marketing Director: Sara Lovelady
- Sales Director: Monique Wellise
- Public Relations: Julie Dennis
- Operations Manager: Mark Keller
- Production Manager: Mark Keller
- Purchasing Manager: Dee Dee Barrios
Estimated Sales: $6000000
Number Employees: 20-49
Number of Brands: 4
Number of Products: 150
Type of Packaging: Consumer
Brands:
- JUST ONCE NATURAL HERBAL EXTRAS
- RAINBOW LIGHT
- RAINBOW LIGHT HERBAL

11894 Rainbow Pops
45 Benbro Dr
Cheektowaga, NY 14225-4805   716-685-4340
   Fax: 716-685-0810   800-879-7677
jeffbaran@rainbowpops.com
www.rainbowpops.com
Lollipops
- President: Roe Baran
Number Employees: 20-49
Brands:
- POPSTOP
- PREMIUM RAINBOW DROPS
- PREMIUM RAINBOW POPS
- RAINBOW POPS

11895 Rainbow Seafood Market
4303 Maine Ave # 107
Baldwin Park, CA 91706-2395   626-962-6888
   Fax: 626-962-3677
Seafood
- Owner: David Tran
Estimated Sales: $800,000
Number Employees: 1-4
Type of Packaging: Consumer

11896 Rainbow Seafoods
422a Boston St
Topsfield, MA 1983-1216   978-283-5103
   Fax: 978-283-3721   info@rainbowseafood.com
www.rainbowseafood.com

Seafood
President: Frank Powell
Sales: Neil Murphy
Estimated Sales:$2,500,000
Number Employees: 9
Brands:
ALDA
NORTH BREEZE
RAINBOW

11897 Rainbow Slaughtering
2416 E West Salem Road
Creston, OH 44217-9650   330-435-4351
                               Fax: 330-435-4202
Processor of veal
Manager: Dick Rook
Number Employees: 10-19
Parent Co: J&N Vorchheimer
Type of Packaging: Bulk

11898 Rainbow Valley Frozen Yogurt
9444 Shady Grove Court
White Lake, MI 48386   248-760-7577
Fax: 248-353-3466   800-979-8669
All natural soft-serve and hand pack frozen yogurt
mix.
President: William Boyda
VP/Treasurer: Laurel Boyda
Estimated Sales:$500,000-$1 Million
Number Employees: 5-9
Sq. footage: 24000
Type of Packaging: Consumer, Food Service, Private Label, Bulk

11899 Rainbow Valley Orchards
5115 5th St
Fallbrook, CA 92028-9795   760-723-3911
          Fax: 760-723-2144 www.rvoorganic.com
Wholesaler/distributor for organic citrus products
and avocados; processor of organic juices including
orange, grapefruit and raspberry/lemonade; private
label packaging available
President: Richard Hart
VP: Edward Van Hoy
Sales Manager: Patrick Raymond
Estimated Sales:$ 50 - 100 Million
Number Employees: 50-99
Sq. footage: 5000
Type of Packaging: Private Label
Brands:
Rainbow Valley Orchards

11900 Rainforest Company
141 Millwell Drive
Maryland Heights, MO 63043-2509 314-344-1000
                               Fax: 314-344-3044
michaelm@the-rainforest-co.com
www.the-rainforest-co.com
Processor, importer and exporter of gourmet natural
snacks including cashew and Brazil nut crunch and
chew bars; also, popcorn, salad dressings, salsas,
marinades, hot sauces, etc
President: Rick Drevet
Controller: Sherry Dawes
Number Employees: 35
Sq. footage: 20000
Brands:
Jungle Munch
Rainforest Crunch
River Bank

11901 Raja Foods
8110 Saint Louis Ave
Skokie, IL 60076-2925   847-675-4455
Fax: 847-675-4498   800-800-7923
sales@rajafoods.com www.rajafoods.com
Importers of Indian food products
President: Rakesh Patel
VP: Swetal Patel
Estimated Sales:$ 10-20 Million
Number Employees: 10-19
Sq. footage: 92000
Parent Co: Raja Foods

11902 Ralboray
2 Canal Street World Trade Center
Suite 2008
New Orleans, LA 70130   504-524-4800
                               Fax: 504-524-4850

11903 (HQ)Ralcorp Holdings
800 Market Street
St Louis, MO 63101   314-877-7000
          Fax: 314-877-7900   800-772-6757
investorrelations@ralcorp.com www.ralcorp.com
Supplier of private label cereal, producing both
ready-to-eat and hot cereals. Organic cereals, snack
mixes, cereal and nutrition bars and more
President/Co-CEO: Kevin Hunt
President/Co-CEO: David Skarie
CVP/General Counsel & Secretary: Charles
Huber
Estimated Sales:$3.8 Billion
Number Employees: 9,350
Type of Packaging: Consumer, Private Label
Brands:
BREMNER
CARRIAGE HOUSE
NUTCRACKER
RALSTON FOODS

11904 Ralcorp Holdings
420 E Oshkosh St
Ripon, WI 54971-1123   920-748-3151
Fax: 920-748-0233   800-445-8338
RiponFoods@RiponFoods.com
www.ralcorp.com
Cookies
Manager: Allan Orth
CEO: Joe R Micheletto
Plant Manager: Jim Portius
Estimated Sales:$ 10 - 20 Million
Number Employees: 250-499
Type of Packaging: Private Label
Brands:
Bremner
Nut Cracker

11905 Ralph Packing Company
P.O.Box 249
Perkins, OK 74059-0249   405-547-2464
Fax: 405-547-2364   800-522-3979
wbeane1126@aol.com www.ralphspacking.com
Manufacturer of beef, pork and lamb
President: Gary Crane
Estimated Sales:$301 Million
Number Employees: 20-49
Type of Packaging: Consumer, Food Service, Private Label

11906 Ralph Sechler & Son
P.O.Box 152
St Joe, IN 46785-0152   260-337-5461
Fax: 260-337-5771   800-332-5461
lkelsey@sechlerspickles.com
www.sechlerspickles.com
Vegetables
Owner: Max Troyer
Estimated Sales:$ 3-5 Million
Number Employees: 20-49
Brands:
Sechler's

11907 Ralph Sechler & Son Inc
P.O.Box 152
St Joe, IN 46785-0152   260-337-5461
Fax: 260-337-5771   800-332-5461
showroom@sechlerspickles.com
www.sechlerspickles.com
Processor of pickles and peppers
Owner: Max Troyer
VP Technical Services: Karen Sechler-Linn
Sales Manager: Mark Decker
Estimated Sales:$ 10 - 20 Million
Number Employees: 20-49
Sq. footage: 60000
Type of Packaging: Consumer, Food Service, Bulk
Brands:
Sechler's

11908 Ralph's Grocery Company
P.O.Box 54143
Los Angeles, CA 90054-0143   310-884-9000
Fax: 310-884-2601 investors@kroger.com
www.ralphs.com
Manufacturer of bread and bakery products
President: David Hirz
SVP/CFO: Steve McMillan
EVP Store Operations: Dave Hansen
Estimated Sales:$100-500 Million
Number Employees: 500-999
Brands:
RALPHS

11909 Ralph's Italian Ices
2361 Hylan Blvd
Staten Island, NY 10306-3100   718-351-8133
          Fax: 718-448-2005 www.ralphsices.com
Italian ices
Manager: Stephen Lazarra
Owner: Lawerence Silvestro
Owner: Michael Scolaro
Estimated Sales:$300,000-500,000
Number Employees: 5-9
Brands:
Ralph's Italian Ices

11910 Ralphco
P.O.Box 691
Worcester, MA 01613-0691   508-757-8400
Fax: 508-752-7226   800-477-2574
www.ralphco.com
VP: Marc Greenberg
Estimated Sales:$ 3 - 5 Million
Number Employees: 1-4

11911 Ramona's Mexican Food Products
P.O.Box 1275
Gardena, CA 90249-0275   310-323-1950
          Fax: 310-323-4210 info@laflor.com
Manufacturer and exporter of frozen tortillas,
burritos, tamales and Mexican dinners
President: Ramona Banuelos
Estimated Sales:$50-100 Million
Number Employees: 250-499
Type of Packaging: Consumer, Food Service, Bulk

11912 Ramos Orchards
P.O.Box 488
Winters, CA 95694-0488   530-795-4748
                               Fax: 530-795-4148
Processor and exporter of inshell walnuts, dehy-
drated prunes and hulled and shelled almonds
Owner: Fred Ramos
Estimated Sales:$4 Million
Number Employees: 50-99
Type of Packaging: Bulk
Brands:
Ramos Orchards

11913 Ramsen
17725 Juniper Path
Lakeville, MN 55044-9482   952-431-0400
          Fax: 952-275-1926 www.ramsendairy.com
Processor of dry dairy products including nonfat
milk; wholesaler/distributor of food ingredients;
serving the food service market
Owner: Tim Krieger
Vice President: Craig Swanson
Marketing Director: Kathy Stevens
Sales Manager: Dennis Breueur
Estimated Sales:$ 10 - 20 Million
Number Employees: 10-19
Sq. footage: 1800
Type of Packaging: Consumer, Food Service

11914 Ramsey Popcorn Company
5645 Clover Valley Rd NW
Ramsey, IN 47166-8252   812-347-2441
Fax: 812-347-3336   800-624-2060
info@ramseypopcorn.com
www.ramseypopcorn.com
Manufacturer and exporter of microwave, original,
concession, bulk, snack food manufacturer, private
label and international popcorn
President: Wilfred Sieg
VP Operations: Daniel Sieg
Estimated Sales:$5 Million
Number Employees: 20-49
Type of Packaging: Consumer, Food Service, Private Label, Bulk
Brands:
Cousin Willie's

11915 Ramsey/SIAS
6850 Southpointe Pkwy
Cleveland, OH 44141-3260   440-546-1199
          Fax: 440-546-0038   800-477-3788
information@atys-group.us www.atys-group.us
Processor of fruit products including bases, flavors,
extracts, toppings, blends fillings and seasonings;
exporter of processed fruits
President: Robert Prendes
Research & Development: Margaret Whitis
Marketing Director: Emily Redetzki

Estimated Sales: $10-20 Million
Number Employees: 50-99
Parent Co: SIAS MPA
Type of Packaging: Food Service, Private Label, Bulk

11916 Ranaldi Bros Frozen Food Products Inc

111 Commerce Drive
Warwick, RI 02886-2429   401-738-3444
                              Fax: 401-738-4446
Processor of frozen dough, stuffed breads, kosher dairy pastries, private label
    President: Gary Ranaldi
    Vice President: Raymond Ranaldi
    Sales Director: Robin Capraro
    Purchasing Manager: Joseph O'Neil
Estimated Sales: $2500000
Number Employees: 30
Number of Products: 100
Sq. footage: 65000
Type of Packaging: Consumer, Food Service, Private Label, Bulk
Brands:
    Puff Dough Sheets
    Puff Dough Squares

11917 Ranch Oak Farm

3005 Bledsoe St
Fort Worth, TX 76107-2905   817-877-3330
            Fax: 817-877-3742   800-888-0327
    info@RanchOak.com   www.ranchoak.com
Smoked meats
    President: Tom Misfeldt
Estimated Sales: Below $ 5 Million
Number Employees: 5-9
Type of Packaging: Private Label
Brands:
    Ranch Oak Farm

11918 Rancher's Lamb of Texas

1005 City Farm Road
San Angelo, TX 76905-8508   325-659-4004
    Fax: 915-482-8051   sales@rancherslamb.com
            www.rancherslamb.com
Processor of lamb, goat and veal; slaughtering services available
    President: Ken Emrick
    CEO: A Dennis III
    Quality Control: Al Fortier
    Sales Director: Justin Jonas
    Operations Manager: Phillip McQueen
Estimated Sales: $ 30-35 Million
Number Employees: 125
Number of Brands: 2
Number of Products: 10
Sq. footage: 70000
Type of Packaging: Consumer, Food Service, Private Label, Bulk

11919 Rancho De Philo

10050 Wilson Ave
Alta Loma, CA 91737-2314   909-987-4208
                              Fax: 909-987-4208
Dessert wine
    President: Alan Tibbetts
    Co-Owner: Janine Tibbetts
Estimated Sales: $ 1 - 3 Million
Number Employees: 1-4
Type of Packaging: Private Label
Brands:
    Rancho De Philo
    Triple Cream Sherry

11920 Rancho Sisquoc Winery

6600 Foxen Canyon Rd
Santa Maria, CA 93454-9656   805-937-3616
    Fax: 805-937-6601   sisquoc@ranchosisquoc.com
            www.ranchosisquoc.com
Wines
    Manager: Mary Holt
    Marketing Director: Marry Holt
    COO: Edward Holt
Estimated Sales: Below $ 5 Million
Number Employees: 20-49
Brands:
    Rancho Sisquoc

11921 Rancho's

1910 Madison Ave # 724
Memphis, TN 38104-2620   901-276-8820
    Fax: 901-744-0514   www.reinachagency.com
Sauces
    Owner: Deborah Reinach

Estimated Sales: Less than $500,000
Number Employees: 1-4

11922 Randag & Associates Inc

187 Lawndale Avenue
Elmhurst, IL 60126-3523   630-530-2830
            Fax: 630-530-2830   randaginc@aol.com
Contract packager of confectionery products, frozen foods, health foods, industrial ingredients and spices
    President: John Randag
    VP: Nancy Randag
    Purchasing Director: Jennifer Randag
Estimated Sales: $290000
Number Employees: 2
Number of Products: 30
Type of Packaging: Consumer, Food Service, Bulk

11923 Randal Nutritional Products

P.O.Box 7328
Santa Rosa, CA 95407-0328   707-528-1800
    Fax: 707-528-0924   800-221-1697
            www.randalnutritional.com
Processor of vitamins, minerals and nutritional supplements
    President: William Robotham
    Director Marketing/Technical Services: Donald Burns
Estimated Sales: $3200000
Number Employees: 20-49
Sq. footage: 22000
Type of Packaging: Consumer, Private Label, Bulk
Brands:
    Nuturpractic
    Vimco

11924 Randall Food Products

401 S Main St
Tekonsha, MI 49092-9255   517-767-3247
            www.randallbeans.com
Processor and exporter of beans including Great Northern, pinto and mixed
    Plant Manager: Randy Waltz
Estimated Sales: $5 Million
Number Employees: 20-49
Type of Packaging: Consumer, Food Service

11925 Randall Food Products

8050 Hosbrook Rd # 326
Cincinnati, OH 45236-2988   513-793-6525
            info@randallbeans.com
            www.randallbeans.com
Processor of dry beans including mixed, Great Northern and pinto
    President: W Mashburn III
    Office Manager: John Alyward
Estimated Sales: $5 Million
Number Employees: 1-4
Type of Packaging: Consumer, Private Label
Brands:
    Randall

11926 Randall Foods

P.O.Box 2669
Huntington Park, CA 90255-8069   323-587-2383
    Fax: 323-586-1587   800-372-6581
    sales@randallfoods.com   www.randallfarms.com
Processor of poultry
    President: Michal Bloon
    CEO: Ron Potin
    CEO: Stan Bloom
Estimated Sales: $100+ Million
Number Employees: 250-499
Brands:
    Randall Foods

11927 Randol

2320 Kaliste Saloom Rd
Lafayette, LA 70508-6808   337-981-7080
            Fax: 337-981-7083   www.randols.com
    Owner: Frank Randol
    Vice President: Mary Wilson
Estimated Sales: $ 3 - 5 Million
Number Employees: 50-99

11928 Randolph Packing Company

275 Roma Jean Pkwy
Streamwood, IL 60107-2964   630-830-3100
                              Fax: 630-830-1872
Meat
    Owner: Angelo W Carmignani
    Quality Control: Jerry Gasior
    VP: Sandra Biggum
Estimated Sales: $ 20-50 Million
Number Employees: 100-249

11929 Randolph Packing Corporation

403 W Balfour Ave
Asheboro, NC 27203-3247   336-672-1470
                              Fax: 336-672-6545
Processor of meat products
    President: C Donald Hamlet
Estimated Sales: $ 20 - 50 Million
Number Employees: 50-99
Type of Packaging: Consumer

11930 Randy's Frozen Meats

P.O.Box 503
Faribault, MN 55021-0503   507-334-7177
    Fax: 507-334-9210   800-354-7177
            www.randysmeatsandgoodstuff.com
Processor of portion cut meat products; also, frozen pizza and microwaveable deli sandwiches; wholesaler/distributor of meat, dairy items, baked goods, frozen foods, equipment, general merchandise, seafood, etc.; serving the foodservice market
    President and CFO: Randy Creasman
    Owner: Neal Gregg
    Partner: Gary Creasman
Estimated Sales: $ 20 - 50 Million
Number Employees: 20-49
Sq. footage: 10800
Type of Packaging: Consumer, Food Service, Private Label, Bulk

11931 Ranieri Fine Foods

278 Metropolitan Ave
Brooklyn, NY 11211-4006   718-599-0665
                              Fax: 718-599-6457
Italian specialty cheeses
    Manager: Angelo Ronconi
Estimated Sales: $820,000
Number Employees: 1-4
Type of Packaging: Consumer, Food Service, Bulk
Brands:
    Gusparo
    Gusparo
    Madrisicilia
    Ranieri
    Star-Grand Italia

11932 Rao's Specialty Foods

17 Battery Pl # 610
New York, NY 10004-1133   212-269-0151
    Fax: 212-344-1680   info@raos.com
            www.raos.com
Pasta sauces, roasted peppers, premium pasta, olive oil & vinegars, marindaes & dressings, canned tomatoes, and coffee
    Owner: Sharon Straci
    Marketing Manager: Ron Straci
    Sales Manager: Peter Ardigo
Estimated Sales: Below $ 5 Million
Number Employees: 10-19
Number of Brands: 1
Number of Products: 20
Type of Packaging: Private Label

11933 Rapazzini Winery

P.O.Box 247
Gilroy, CA 95021-0247   408-842-5649
    Fax: 408-842-8353   info@rapazziniwinery.com
            www.rapazziniwinery.com
Wine, cooking wines, garlic, jelly, mustard, mayonnaise, spices, salsas and chips
    Owner: Charles Larson
    Owner: Alex Larson
Estimated Sales: Below $ 5 Million
Number Employees: 5-9
Brands:
    Rapazzini Winery

11934 Rapunzel Pure Organics

292 Stonewall Road
Chatham, NY 12037-9780   518-392-8620
    Fax: 518-392-8630   800-207-2814
    info@rapunzel.com   www.rapunzel.com
Organic sugar, organic chocolate, soups and bouillons, seasoned salt, organic vegetable juices, cocoa powder and spreads
    President: Eckhart Kiesel
    Director Sales/Marketing: Dale Kamibayashi
    Sales Director: Jim Douglas
Number Employees: 5-9
Sq. footage: 5000
Type of Packaging: Consumer, Food Service, Bulk
Brands:
    A. Vogel
    Bambu Juices

Biotta Juices
Faqs
Herbamare Juices
Rapunzel Pure Organi

11935 Ratners Retail Foods
138 Delancey St
New York, NY 10002-3325   212-677-5588
www.nycfoods.com/ratners
Dairy products
President: Harold Zankel
VP: Robert Hirmatz
Estimated Sales:$ 2.5-5 Million
Number Employees: 50-99

11936 Raven Creamery Company
3303 NE M L King Boulevard
Portland, OR 97212-2057   503-288-5101
Fax: 503-288-5103
Butter
President: Henry Turner
Marketing Director: Tom Hughes
Estimated Sales:$ 5-10 Million
Number Employees: 10-19

11937 Ravenswood
18701 Gehricke Rd
Sonoma, CA 95476-4710   707-938-1960
Fax: 707-933-2383 800-669-4679
rwwine@ravenswood-wine.com
www.ravenswood-wine.com
Wine
President: Joel Peterson
Wine Club Manager: Cathleen Francisco
CFO: Callie Konno
Executive VP: Justin Faggioli
Assistant Winemaker: Peter Mathis
Estimated Sales:$ 12 Million
Number Employees: 50-99
Brands:
Ravenswood

11938 Ravifruit
140 Prospect Avenue
Hackensack, NJ 07601-2255   201-939-5656
Fax: 201-939-5613

11939 Ravioli Store
75 Sullivan Street
New York, NY 10012-4306   212-925-1737
Processor of fresh, dry and organic pasta including
ravioli, agnolotti, tortellini and gnocchi
President: John A Zaccarro Jr
Estimated Sales:$300,000-500,000
Number Employees: 1-4
Type of Packaging: Consumer, Food Service

11940 Raway Pharmacal
15 Granite Road
Accord, NY 12404-5004   914-626-8133
Processor and exporter of vitamin supplements and
kits
Director: Jack Berman
Number Employees: 1-4
Sq. footage: 5000
Type of Packaging: Consumer, Bulk

11941 Ray Brothers & Noble Canning Company
P.O.Box 314
Hobbs, IN 46047-0314   765-675-7451
Fax: 765-675-7400 renoble@tiptontel.com
www.noblecanning.com
Processor and canner of tomato products including
whole, stewed and diced; also, canned tomato juice
President: Ray Noble
Sales Director: Dan Noble
Director Manufacturing: Mark Noble
Plant Manager: Mark Noble
Estimated Sales:$21.90 Million
Number Employees: 10-19
Sq. footage: 72000
Type of Packaging: Consumer, Food Service, Private Label

11942 Ray's Sausage CompanyInc
3146 E 123rd St
Cleveland, OH 44120-3179   216-921-8782
Fax: 216-921-4736

Fresh pork and beef sausage and links; mild, hot and
extra hot souse, head cheese and beef souse.
President: Renee Cash
CFO/Administrativeexecutive: Leslie Cash Lester

Vice President: Raymond Cash, Jr.
Marketing/Sales: Raymond Hardin
Estimated Sales:$600000
Number Employees: 9
Sq. footage: 700
Type of Packaging: Consumer, Food Service
Brands:
Ray's Headcheese
Ray's Italian Links
Ray's Sausage
Ray's Souse

11943 Raymond Vineyard & Cellar
849 Zinfandel Ln
St Helena, CA 94574-1645   707-963-3141
Fax: 707-963-8498 800-525-2659
hospitality@raymondvineyards.com
www.raymondvineyards.com
Wines
Type of Packaging: Private Label
Brands:
Raymond Vineyard

11944 Raymond-Hadley Corporation
89 Tompkins Street
Spencer, NY 14883-9759   607-589-4415
Fax: 607-589-6442 800-252-5220
www.raymondhadley.com
Importer and contract packager of South and Central
American and African foods, barley, beans, bran,
flour, cereal, dried fruit, grains, rice, spices, starches,
vegetables, etc.; exporter of corn meal
President: Lori Maratea
Sales/Buyer Assistant: Tracy McCutcheon
Sales/Buyer Assistant: Elliot Dutra
Number Employees: 20-49
Sq. footage: 51000
Type of Packaging: Bulk

11945 Rea-D-Pak Foodservices
P.O.Box 279
North Norwich, NY 13814-0279   607-334-3621
Fax: 607-334-5280 800-255-7288
Processor of sauerkraut
Owner: Rita Ashton
Production Manager: Robert Clapp Sr
Plant Manager: Robert Clapp Jr
Number Employees: 20-49
Sq. footage: 45000
Type of Packaging: Consumer, Food Service, Private Label, Bulk
Brands:
Chenango
Delikut
Willie's

11946 Reading Coffee Roasters
316 W Main St
Birdsboro, PA 19508-1900   610-582-2243
Fax: 610-582-3615 800-331-6713
info@thecoffeegourmet.com
www.thecoffeegourmet.com
Gourmet coffee
Owner: Albert Van Maanen
Co-Owner: Rosemary Hartigan
Estimated Sales:$300,000-500,000
Number Employees: 10-19
Type of Packaging: Private Label
Brands:
Jazzy Java Custom Flavored Gourmet
Oscars Flavoring Syrups
Reading Coffee Roast

11947 Readington Farms
P.O.Box 164
Whitehouse, NJ 08888-0164   908-534-2121
Fax: 908-534-5235
Dairy products
President: Donald Merrigan
VP Production: Lawrence Kurz
Production Manager: Doug McDowell
Estimated Sales:$100-$500 Million
Number Employees: 100-249

11948 Ready Bake Foods
2095 Meadowvale Boulevard
Mississauga, ON L5N 5N1
Canada   905-567-0660
Fax: 450-973-1961 www.cor.ca

Processor of frozen baked goods
Chairman: Meyer Feldman Feldman
Vice-Chairman: Martin Maierovits
Secretary: Nathan Bleeman Bleeman
Director Sales: Susan Smith
Number Employees: 100-249
Parent Co: George Weston Foods
Type of Packaging: Consumer, Food Service, Private Label

11949 Ready Foods
2645 W 7th Ave
Denver, CO 80204-4112   303-892-5861
Fax: 303-629-6148
Processor of frozen Mexican foods including tortillas, salsa and taco fillings
Owner and President: Luis Abarca
Estimated Sales:$ .5 - 1 million
Number Employees: 1-4
Type of Packaging: Food Service, Private Label, Bulk
Brands:
Marcos
San Marcos

11950 Ready Portion Meat Company
1546 Choctaw Dr
Baton Rouge, LA 70805-7756   225-355-5641
Fax: 225-355-8895
Wholesaler/distributor of frozen foods, general line
items and meats; serving the food service market
President: Kyle L Beck
Estimated Sales:$5356809
Number Employees: 20-49
Type of Packaging: Bulk

11951 Ready-Pac Produce
P.O.Box 6
Florence, NJ 08518-0006   609-499-1900
Fax: 609-499-0042
Processor of ready-made vegetable salads
Human Resources: Shawn Bray
Director National Accounts: Dave Hughes
Estimated Sales:$ 10 - 20 Million
Number Employees: 50-99
Type of Packaging: Consumer, Food Service, Private Label
Brands:
Ready-Pac

11952 Ready-Pac Produce
4401 Foxdale St
Irwindale, CA 91706-2161   626-856-8686
Fax: 626-856-0088 800-800-7822
www.readypacproduce.com
Fresh-cut produce
Chairman: Antonia Hernández
VP Marketing: Steve Dickstein
CEO: Michael Solomon
Estimated Sales:$ 50-100 Million
Number Employees: 1,000-4,999
Brands:
Ready Pac Aqua Pac
Ready Pac Complete S
Ready Pac European S
Ready Pac Fresh-Cut
Ready Pac Organic Sa
Ready Pac Party Item
Ready Pac Ready Fixi
Ready Pac Ready Snax
Ready Pac Value Pack

11953 Readyfoods
41 Paquin Road
Winnipeg, NB R2J 3V9
Canada   204-661-6955
Fax: 450-973-1960
Processor of turkey, chicken, frozen entrees and
crepe and potato shells
President: Roger Chaoois
National Sales Manager: Brent Beatie
Number Employees: 50-99
Parent Co: Golden Valley Farms
Type of Packaging: Consumer, Food Service
Brands:
Ready Foods

11954 Real Aloe Company
2045 Corte Del Nogal
Carlsbad, CA 92011-1411   805-986-4308
Fax: 805-483-5364 800-541-7809

Processor and exporter of aloe vera products including gel, juice and beverages
Owner: Dan Mundel
VP: M Mundell
Operations Manager: Dan Mundell
Estimated Sales:$1100000
Number Employees: 5-9
Sq. footage: 10500
Type of Packaging: Consumer, Food Service, Private Label, Bulk
Brands:
Cal-Aloe Co.
Real Aloe Co.

11955 Real Cookies
3212 Hewlett Avenue
Merrick, NY 11566-5505   516-221-9300
Fax: 516-221-9561   800-822-5113
realcookies@worldnet.att.net
Frozen chocolate chip cookie dough and cookie mixes including oatmeal raisin, mocha almond, ginger, macadamia, white chocolate, pecan and chocolate chip; exporter of cookie mixes
President: Ellyn Knigin
CFO: Leonard Knigin
Vice President: Marian Knigin
Estimated Sales:$500,000-$1 Million
Number Employees: 5-9
Type of Packaging: Consumer, Food Service, Private Label, Bulk
Brands:
Grandma's Cookie Mix
Real Cookies

11956 Real Food Marketing
201 Wyandotte St # 402
Kansas City, MO 64105-1230   816-221-4100
Fax: 913-671-8083
laura@realfoodmarketinginc.com
www.realfoodbakingco.com
Real Food Marketing, Proprietary Epicurean Food Developers, traditional desserts, breads, meat-filled pastries and ethnic breads and desserts such as; brownies, cookies, muffins, short cake, cakes, low fat and special diet, breads andpot pies. Real Food Marketing - Kanas City, MO & Las Vegas, Nevada. (888)-834-REAL (7325).
President/CEO: Bob Deal
CFO: Tara Cupps
R&D: Bob Deal
Operations: Bill Scott
Purchasing: Clint Scott
Estimated Sales:$ 1 - 3 Million
Number Employees: 1-4
Number of Brands: 2
Number of Products: 50
Sq. footage: 900
Type of Packaging: Consumer, Food Service, Private Label, Bulk

11957 Real Kosher Sausage Company
9 Euclid Ave # B
Newark, NJ 07105-4527   973-690-5394
Fax: 212-598-9011
Manufacturer and exporter of kosher meats including fresh, sausage and deli
President: Jacob Hill
VP: Jonathan Hill
Estimated Sales:$11000000
Number Employees: 5-9
Sq. footage: 15000
Type of Packaging: Consumer, Food Service, Private Label, Bulk
Brands:
999
Real Kosher

11958 Real Sausage Company
2710 S Poplar Ave
Chicago, IL 60608-5909   312-842-5330
Fax: 312-842-5414
Sausage
President: Nicole Makowski
*Estimated Sales:*Below $ 5 Million
Number Employees: 20-49
Brands:
Real Sausage

11959 Reames Foods
P.O.Box 29163
Columbus, OH 43229-0163   614-846-2232
Fax: 614-848-8330   marzetti@ipi.it
www.marzetti.com

Frozen egg noodles; also, pre-cooked lasagna sheets, frozen pot pie crusts and pre-cooked frozen pasta
President: Bruce Rosa
VP Marketing: Dick Anderson
Financial Manager: Doug Sell
Production Manager: Lynn Wehr
Number Employees: 100-249
Parent Co: T. Marzetti Company
Type of Packaging: Consumer, Food Service
Brands:
Reames
Sysco

11960 Reames Foods
803 8th Street SW
Altoona, IA 50009-2306   515-223-6186
Fax: 515-223-0674   800-247-4194
Raw frozen pasta, precooked frozen pasta, raw frozen pie crust
VP: David Hammerberg
Plant Manager: Vernon Chiles
Purchasing Manager: Debbie Chiles
Estimated Sales:$ 20-50 Million
Number Employees: 50-99
Parent Co: Deno Marzetti
Type of Packaging: Bulk
Brands:
Reames Frozen Noodles

11961 Rebec Vineyards
2229 N Amherst Hwy
Amherst, VA 24521-4378   434-946-5168
Fax: 804-946-5168   winery@rebecwinery.com
www.rebecwinery.com
Wines
Manager: Svetlozar Kanev
VP Marketing: Svetlozar Kanev
*Estimated Sales:*Below $ 500,000
Number Employees: 1-4
Type of Packaging: Private Label

11962 Rebecca Ruth Candy
112 E 2nd St
Frankfort, KY 40601-2902   502-223-7475
Fax: 502-226-5854   800-444-3866
info@rebeccaruth.com   www.rebeccaruth.com
Processor of candy including chocolate, filled, mints and bourbon chocolates
President: Charles Booe
Estimated Sales:$380000
Number Employees: 20-49
Type of Packaging: Consumer, Private Label, Bulk
Brands:
100 Bourbon Whiskey
Buffalo Trace
Butter Creams
Classic Liquor Cremes
Creme De Menthe
Rebecca-Ruth

11963 Rebound
1 Pepsi Way
Newburgh, NY 12550-3921   845-562-5400
Fax: 845-562-7840
Beverage manufacturing, water
Owner: Tim Tenney
Estimated Sales:$ 5 - 10 Million
Number Employees: 5-9

11964 Reckitt Benckiser
P.O.Box 225
Parsippany, NJ 07054-0225   973-404-2600
Fax: 973-404-5700   800-333-3899
corpcomms@reckittbenckiser.com
www.reckittbenckiser.com
Processor of canned potatoes and onions
Regional Director: Javed Ahmed
VP Marketing: Alex Whitehouse
VP: Beverly Wilen
VP Sales: Stafford Dow
Technical Director: Paul Siracusa
Estimated Sales:$100-499.9 Million
Number Employees: 10,000+
Parent Co: Reckitt & Colman PLC
Type of Packaging: Consumer, Food Service, Bulk
Brands:
Cattlemen's
Frank's RedHot Sauce
French's

11965 Rector Foods
2280 N Park Drive
Brampton, ON L6S 6C6
Canada   905-789-9691
Fax: 905-789-0989   888-314-7834
rfl@rectorfoods.com   www.rectorfoods.com
Processor and exporter of seasoning blends for meat and poultry and vegetarian industries
President: Eoin Connell
VP Sales: Michael Parry
Lab Services: Andrea Gibson
Purchasing Manager: Donia Tooze
Number Employees: 50
Sq. footage: 53000

11966 (HQ)Red Arrow Products Company LLC
P.O.Box 1537
Manitowoc, WI 54221-1537   920-769-1100
Fax: 920-769-1281   websales@redarrowusa.com
www.redarrowusa.com
Maufactures a wide variety of natural smoke flavors for meat, poultry and food applications. Smoke flavors are complemented by an extensive line of grill flavors, roast flavors and specialty browning. In addition, Red Arrow's equipmentcompany designs and fabricates application equipment to meet specific processing needs
President: Dale Hanke
Sales: Mark Crass
Marketing Coordinator: Kayla Sommer
Sales: Mark Crass
Type of Packaging: Food Service, Private Label, Bulk
Other Locations:
Red Arrow Products Co.
Manitowoc WI
Brands:
ARO-SMOKE
CHAR DEX
CHAR OIL
CHAR SOL
CHAR ZYME
GRILLIN'
MAILLOSE
TOASTIN
TRUE GOLD

11967 Red Bell Brewing
PO Box 681
Foxcroft Square, PA 19046-7081   215-235-2460
Fax: 215-235-2486   888-733-2355
info@redbell.com   www.redbell.com
Beer
Resident: Martin F Spellman
*Estimated Sales:*Less than $500,000
Number Employees: 10-19
Brands:
Philadelphia
Red Bull

11968 Red Chamber Company
1912 E Vernon Ave
Vernon, CA 90058-1611   323-234-9000
Fax: 323-231-8888   info@redchamber.com
www.redchamber.com
Seafood
President: Shu Chin Kou
CFO: Ming Shing Kou
CEO: Ming Bin Kou
Estimated Sales:$ 100-500 Million
Number Employees: 20-49
Brands:
Aqua Star
Mid-Pacific Seafoods
Neptune Foods
OFI Markesa International
Tampa Bay Fisheries

11969 Red Creek Marinade Company
P.O.Box 19875
Amarillo, TX 79114-1875   806-358-3531
Fax: 806-358-1587   800-687-9114
info@red-creek.com   www.red-creek.com
Processor of liquid mesquite-flavored marinades for meats and jerky
Partner: Lawrence E New
Co-Owner: L New
Estimated Sales:$ 1 - 3 Million
Number Employees: 1-4
Number of Brands: 1
Number of Products: 3
Type of Packaging: Consumer, Food Service, Bulk

Brands:
Red Creek

11970 Red Deer Lake Meat Processing
PO Box 38
Calgary, AB T2P 2V5
Canada   403-256-4925
        Fax: 403-256-8882 rdlmeats@telus.net
                                www.rdlmeats.ab.ca
Processor of fresh and frozen beef, hamburgers,
pork, bacon, lamb, goat and sausage including
smoked, pork and beef
    President/General Manager Sales: Brian Barrett
    CEO: Georgina Walker
Number Employees: 20-49
Type of Packaging: Consumer, Food Service, Private Label, Bulk
Brands:
    RDL (Red Deer Lake)

11971 (HQ)Red Diamond
1701 Vanderbilt Rd
Birmingham, AL 35234-1423   205-254-3138
        Fax: 205-254-6062 800-292-4651
                                stevel@reddiamond.com
Manufacturer of coffee; importer of teas and coffees.
Food service distributor; private label tea and coffee
packer
    President: William A Bowron Jr
    President: William Bowron, Jr.
    Assistant VP: Steve Lowry
    Sales Director: Jimmie Lay
Estimated Sales: $58 Million
Number Employees: 100-249
Type of Packaging: Consumer, Food Service, Private Label, Bulk
Brands:
    Red Diamond Coffee & Tea

11972 Red Gold
P.O.Box 83
Elwood, IN 46036-0083   765-754-7527
        Fax: 765-754-3230 877-748-9798
        info@redgold.com www.redgold.com
Manufacturer of tomatoes and tomato products including whole peeled, diced, stewed, crushed, puree,
paste, juice, salsa and ketchup; also, sauces including tomato, pizza, taco, barbecue, chili, seafood
cocktail, marinara andspaghetti
    President/CEO: Brian Reichart
    Finance Manager: Carol Hanna
    Director Marketing/Sales: William Mandler
Estimated Sales: $230 Million
Number Employees: 500-999
Sq. footage: 1000000
Type of Packaging: Consumer, Food Service, Private Label, Bulk
Other Locations:
    Red Gold
    Orestes IN
    Red Gold
    Geneva IN
Brands:
    GLORIETTA
    IL MIGLIORE
    RED GOLD
    RED PACK
    SACRAMENTO
    THERESA
    TUTOROSSO

11973 Red Hot Chicago
4649 W Armitage Ave
Chicago, IL 60639-3405   773-829-3434
        Fax: 312-829-2704 800-249-5226
                                info@redhotchicago.com
                                www.redhotchicago.com
Producer of Chicago style hot dogs
    Owner/President: Scott Ladany
    Founder: Samuel Ladany
Estimated Sales: $ 1 - 3 Million
Number Employees: 1-4
Type of Packaging: Food Service, Bulk
Brands:
    Red Hot Chicago

11974 Red Hot Cooperative
809 Broadway Avenue NE
Redcliff, AB T0J 2P0
Canada   403-548-6453
        Fax: 403-548-7255 laredhot@memlane.com
Cooperative and exporter of greenhouse vegetables
    President: Matt Read
    Sales Manager: John Judge

Number Employees: 50-99
Type of Packaging: Consumer, Food Service

11975 Red Hot Foods
8418 Henderson Road
Ventura, CA 93004-2167   805-659-1614
        Fax: 805-672-2839 redhotfoods2004@yahoo.com
                                www.redhotfoods.com
Condiments, relishes, salsas, bbq sauces, hot sauce,
steak sauce, mixes, olive oil, pesto, bean and chowder mixes.
    President: Butch Baselite
Type of Packaging: Consumer, Food Service, Private Label, Bulk

11976 Red Lake Fisheries Associates
19050 Highway 1 E
Redby, MN 56670   218-679-3513
                                Fax: 218-679-2148
Processor of fish including perch, northern and carp
    Manager: Joel Rohde
Estimated Sales: $ 3 - 5 Million
Number Employees: 500-999
Type of Packaging: Consumer, Food Service, Bulk

11977 Red Lion Spicy Foods Company
420 W Broadway
Red Lion, PA 17356-1908   717-244-0227
        Fax: 717-244-7348 chip@betterthanhot.com
                                www.betterthanhot.com
                                www.redlionspicyfoods.com
Chili mixes, chili powder, original dry rub, serrano
red salsa, serrano red & black salsa, 20 pepper salsa,
20 pepper hot sauce, 20 pepper pickles, 20 pepper
garlic dills, 20 pepper relish, 20 pepper garlic, competition blend chilimix
Type of Packaging: Consumer

11978 Red Mill Farms
290 S 5th St
Brooklyn, NY 11211-6214   718-384-2150
        Fax: 718-384-2988 800-344-2253
        redmill@aol.com www.macaroonking.com
Processor and exporter of macaroons and individually wrapped cakes
    President: Arnold Badner
Estimated Sales: $4,000,000
Number Employees: 20-49
Sq. footage: 30000
Type of Packaging: Food Service
Brands:
    Manhattan Gourmet

11979 Red Oak Farms
PO Box 456
Red Oak, IA 51566-0456   712-623-9224
        Fax: 712-623-4533 info@redoakfarms.com
                                www.redoakfarms.com
Premium USDA certified fresh beef, fresh boxed
beef, portion cut beef, precooked beef, retail and
bulk
    President and CEO: Gordon Reisinger
    CEO: Gordon Reisinger
    CFO: Harley Dillard
    Vice President: Pete Hudgins
    Research & Development: Nancy Pellett
    Sales Director: H Jackson
    Operations Manager: Steve Berendes
Estimated Sales: $ 50 Million
Number Employees: 10
Number of Brands: 3
Number of Products: 12
Type of Packaging: Consumer, Food Service, Bulk
Brands:
    My Favorite Jerky
    Red Oak Farms Hereford Beef

11980 Red Pelican Food Products
5650 Saint Jean Street
Detroit, MI 48213-3415   313-921-2500
Processor and importer of mustard, horseradish, relish, sauerkraut, vinegar, Belgian chocolate and
sauce; importer of cheese
    President: Bernard Cornillie
    Sales Manager: D Cornillie
Number Employees: 5-9
Sq. footage: 14000
Type of Packaging: Consumer, Food Service, Private Label, Bulk

11981 Red River Commodities
P.O.Box 3022
Fargo, ND 58108-3022   701-282-2600
        Fax: 701-282-5325 danh@redriv.com
                                www.redriv.com
Processor and exporter of sunflower seeds, colored
beans, millet, flax, soybeans, and organics
    President/CEO: Robert Majkrzak
    VP Finance/Administration: Randy Wigen
    Quality Control Manager: Erik Barwicki
    VP Marketing: Roger Jaeger
    VP Sales/Marketing: Dan Hofland
Estimated Sales: $137 Million
Number Employees: 100-249
Parent Co: Universal Corporation
Type of Packaging: Food Service, Private Label, Bulk
Brands:
    Brown Flax
    Confection Sunflower Seed
    Goldtex

11982 Red River Foods
9020 Stony Point Pkwy # 380
Richmond, VA 23235-1944   804-320-1800
        Fax: 804-320-1896 800-443-6637
                                www.redriverfoods.com
Nuts, seeds, dried foods and snack foods
    President: James Phipps
Estimated Sales: $ 50-100 Million
Number Employees: 10-19
Number of Products: 30
Parent Co: Universal Corporation

11983 (HQ)Red Rose Trading Company
1237 Trinity North Rd
Wrightsville, PA 17368-9134   717-252-5500
Processor, contract packager and exporter of granola, organic pancake, baking and wheat/gluten-free
mixes; wholesaler/distributor of organic and bulk ingredients, dry mixes and blends; serving the food
service market
    Owner: J Leichter
Estimated Sales: $ 3 - 5 Million
Number Employees: 10-19
Sq. footage: 28000
Type of Packaging: Consumer, Food Service, Private Label, Bulk

11984 Red Star Yeast
777 E Wisconsin Ave # 11
Milwaukee, WI 53202-5302   414-271-6755
        Fax: 414-347-4795 877-677-7000
        carol.stevens@redstaryeast.com
        www.sensient-technologies.com
Yeast, fermentation products
    President: Carol Stevens
    CEO: Kenneth P Manning
Estimated Sales: $ 20-50 Million
Number Employees: 1,000-4,999
Brands:
    Red Star

11985 Red Steer Meats
3812 W Clarendon Ave
Phoenix, AZ 85019-3718   602-272-6677
                                Fax: 602-484-7381
Meat and meat products
    President: Richard Barton
    Vice President: Judy Barton
Estimated Sales: $ 5-10 Million
Number Employees: 5-9
Type of Packaging: Private Label

11986 Red White & Brew
223 Ashley Ct
Redding, CA 96001-3656   530-222-5891
                                www.redwhiteandbrew.com
Beer
    President: Bill Ward
Estimated Sales: $ 5-10 Million
Number Employees: 3
Brands:
    Red White & Brew

11987 Red Willow Natural Foods
205 Country Oaks Road
River Falls, WI 54022-8140   715-425-1489
                                Fax: 715-273-3482
Natural foods
    VP: Miller Rogers
    Manager/COO: Barbara Wickman
    Sales Manager: Jennifer Simon

Brands:
Red Willow Natural Foods

11988 Redco Foods
100 Northfield Dr
Windsor, CT 06095-4730   860-688-2121
          Fax: 860-688-7844   800-645-1190
                              www.greentea.com
Processor of teas.
     President: R Berstynen
     VP: Robert Cassie
     VP Marketing: David Rigg
     Sales Director: Laura Morris
     VP Operations: Doug Farrell
Estimated Sales:$ 5 - 10 Million
Number Employees: 10-19
Type of Packaging: Food Service, Private Label
Brands:
     JUNKET
     RED ROSE
     RED ROSE TEA
     SALADA
     SALADA TEA

11989 Redhawk Vineyard
2995 Michigan City Rd NW
Salem, OR 97304-9704   503-362-1596
     Fax: 503-585-4657 toma@open.org
                    www.redhawkwine.com
Wines
     Owner: John Pataccoli
Estimated Sales:$350,000
Number Employees: 1-4
Type of Packaging: Private Label
Brands:
     Redhawk

11990 Redhook Ale Breweries
35 Corporate Dr
Newington, NH 03801-7852   603-430-8600
     Fax: 603-430-6011 redhook@redhook.com
                    www.redhook.com
Processor of beer and ale
     Manager: Jerry Prial
Estimated Sales:$ 20 - 50 Million
Number Employees: 20-49
Parent Co: Redhook Ale Breweries
Type of Packaging: Consumer, Food Service
Brands:
     Redhook

11991 Redhook Ale Breweries
14300 NE 145th St # 210
Woodinville, WA 98072-6950   425-483-3232
     Fax: 425-485-0761 redhook@redhook.com
                    www.redhook.com
Processor of beer and ale
     President: David Mickelson
     COO: Paul Shipman
     CFO: T. Caldwell
     CEO: Paul S Shipman
     Quality Control: Tuan Liu
     Marketing Manager: Nelson Ray
     Sales Manager: Gerard Prial
Estimated Sales:$ 50-100 Million
Number Employees: 100-249
Parent Co: Redhook Ale Breweries
Type of Packaging: Consumer, Food Service
Brands:
     Ballard Bitter
     Black Hook
     Double Black
     ESB
     Hefeweizen
     Rye
     Wheatbrook
     Winterhook

11992 Redi-Froze
PO Box 4055
South Bend, IN 46634-4055   574-237-5111
                    Fax: 574-234-4162
     Vice President: Jack Enoch

11993 Redi-Serve Food Company
1200 Industrial Dr
Fort Atkinson, WI 53538-2758   920-563-6391
                    Fax: 920-563-3013
Processor of frozen prepared foods including meat
balls, beef patties, chicken patties and breaded veal
cutlets
     President: Jim Bowen
     VP/General Manager: Gary Schimeck

Estimated Sales:$49500000
Number Employees: 250-499
Parent Co: Encore Frozen Foods
Type of Packaging: Consumer, Food Service, Private Label

11994 Redmond Minerals
P.O.Box 219
Redmond, UT 84652-0219   435-529-7402
     Fax: 435-529-7486   800-367-7258
          mail@redmondminerals.com
          www.redmondminerals.com
Manufacturer and exporter of all natural kosher certified sea salt
     President: Rusty Bastain
     Marketing Director: John Peterson
     Sales (RealSalt): Jason Nielson
Estimated Sales:$ 20-50 Million
Number Employees: 50-99
Type of Packaging: Consumer, Food Service, Private Label, Bulk

11995 Redondo's Sausage Factory
94-140 Leokane St
Waipahu, HI 96797-2280   808-671-5444
     Fax: 808-676-7009 www.redondos.com
Sausages
     President: Hitoshi Okada
     VP/General Manager: Yoshi Shinanti
     VP: Toshiyuki Murakane
     Owner: Frank Redondo
Estimated Sales:$ 5-10 Million
Number Employees: 20-49
Brands:
     Pipikaula

11996 Redwood Hill Farm
2064 Gravenstein Hwy N # 130
Sebastopol, CA 95472-2630   707-823-8250
     Fax: 707-823-6976 contact@redwoodhill.com
                    www.redwoodhill.com
Goat and dairy products/cheeses
     Manager: Jennifer Bize
     Marketing Director: Sharon Bice
     CFO: Jennifer Lynn Bice
Estimated Sales:$ 1-2.5 Million
Number Employees: 10-19
Type of Packaging: Private Label
Brands:
     Redwood Hill Farm

11997 Redwood Vintners
12 Harbor Dr
Novato, CA 94945-3507   415-892-6949
                    Fax: 415-892-7469
Distribution and marketing of beverages
     VP Sales: Barney Feinblum
Estimated Sales:$ 20 - 50 Million
Number Employees: 50-99
Brands:
     Redwood Vintners

11998 Reed Corporation
233 W Parkway
Pompton Plains, NJ 07444-1028   973-831-0636
          Fax: 973-831-0791   800-820-REED
Cellulose food fibers
Estimated Sales:$ 2.5-5 Million
Number Employees: 5-9

11999 Reed Lang Farms
P.O.Box 219
Rio Hondo, TX 78583-0219   956-748-2354
                    Fax: 956-748-2888
Ship Ruby Red and Rio Red grapefruits, navel oranges, Lula avacados, pecans, almonds and citrus
blossom honey for gift packages.
     President/Owner: Violet Lang
Estimated Sales:Under $ 300,000
Number Employees: 10-19
Sq. footage: 11025
Type of Packaging: Private Label

12000 Reed's Original Beverage Corporation
13000 S Spring St
Los Angeles, CA 90061-1634   310-217-9400
          Fax: 310-217-9411   800-997-3337
          info@reedsgingerbrew.com
          www.reedsgingerbrew.com

Manufacturer of ginger brewed soft drinks, ginger
candy, and ice cream
     President/CEO: Christopher Reed
     General Manager: Maureen Edwards
     Sales Director: Jeff Ainis
     Brand Manager: Tom Wright
Estimated Sales:$ .5 - 1 million
Number Employees: 20-49
Type of Packaging: Consumer
Brands:
     China Cola
     Reed's Crystalized Ginger Candy
     Reed's Ginger Brews
     Reed's Ginger Ice Cream
     Virgil's Root Beers

12001 Reel Food Service
4482 N Buckboard Pl
Boise, ID 83713-9574   208-376-7972
                    Fax: 208-342-2868
     Owner: Doug Rule
Estimated Sales:$300,000-500,000
Number Employees: 1-4

12002 Reeves Winery
PO Box 1543
Middletown, CA 95461-1543   707-987-9650
Wines

12003 Refined Sugars
1 Federal St
Yonkers, NY 10705-1079   914-963-0206
          Fax: 914-963-1030   800-431-1020
Processor and exporter of sugar
     President: Jack Lay
Estimated Sales:$100+ Million
Number Employees: 250-499
Parent Co: Domino Foods
Type of Packaging: Consumer, Food Service, Private Label, Bulk
Brands:
     4# FLOW-SWEET
     COUNTRY CANE
     JACK FROST

12004 Refrigerated Foods Association
2971 Flowers Rd S # 266
Chamblee, GA 30341-5403   770-452-0660
     Fax: 770-455-3879 info@refrigeratedfoods.org
                    www.refrigeratedfoods.org
Trade association
     Executive Director: Terry Dougherty
Estimated Sales:Less than $500,000
Number Employees: 1-4

12005 Regal Crown Foods
41 Mason St
Worcester, MA 01610-3203   508-752-2679
                    Fax: 508-831-0775
Manufactures vinegar pickles
     President: Douglas Freund
     Public Relations: Monica Freund Kaufman
     Plant Manager: David Giorgio
Estimated Sales:$ 1 - 3 Million
Number Employees: 1-4
Number of Brands: 12
Number of Products: 6
Type of Packaging: Food Service, Private Label

12006 Regal Food Service
P.O.Box 21172
Houston, TX 77226-1172   713-222-8231
     Fax: 713-222-2549 sm11regal@aol.com
Manufacturer of sandwiches and spreads
     Manager: Charles Smith
Estimated Sales:$10 Million
Number Employees: 50-99
Type of Packaging: Consumer, Food Service

12007 Regal Health Foods International
3705 W Grand Ave
Chicago, IL 60651-2236   773-252-1044
     Fax: 773-252-0817 regal_1@prodigy.net
Processor and importer of dried fruits and nuts
     President: Gregory Piatigorsky
     VP Marketing/Sales: Igor Piatigorsky
Estimated Sales:$ 10 - 20 Million
Number Employees: 20-49
Sq. footage: 27000
Type of Packaging: Consumer, Food Service, Private Label, Bulk
Brands:
     Regal

12008 Regco Corporation
10 Avco Road
Haverhill, MA 01835-6935   978-521-4370
    Fax: 978-372-4371   info@regcocorp.com
                www.regenies.com
Crunchy pitas
    President: Regina Ragonese
    Broker Sales Representative: Sheryl Makaron
    Public Relations Director: Peter Ash
    Production Supervisor: Guy Minnick
Number Employees: 14
Brands:
    REGENIE'S CRUNCHY PITAS
    REGENIE'S TREASURE CRISPS

12009 Regency Coffee & VendingCompany
2022 E Spruce Cir
Olathe, KS 66062-5404   913-829-1994
    Fax: 913-393-0097 www.regencycoffee.com
Variety of gourmet coffees, teas, hot beverages, cold beverages and snacks
    Owner: Nancy Robinson
    CEO: William Kirkpatrick
    CFO: Rob Buntun
    Vice President: Kelly Havins
Estimated Sales: $10-24.9 Million
Number Employees: 5-9
Number of Brands: 3
Number of Products: 80
Type of Packaging: Consumer, Food Service, Private Label, Bulk

12010 Regenie's All Natural and Organic Snacks
46 Rogers Rd
Haverhill, MA 01835   978-521-4370
    Fax: 978-372-4371   regina@regenies.com
                www.regenies.com
all natural pita chips
    President/Owner: Regina Ragonese

12011 Regent Champagne Cellars
17 E 74th St
New York, NY 10021-2604   845-691-7296
            Fax: 845-691-7298
Processor of bottled spring and sparkling water, juice, soda and champagne
    President: Herbert Feinberg
    Vice President: Edward Gogel
Estimated Sales: $760000
Number Employees: 10

12012 Regent Confections
111 S Cross Creek Road
Unit B
Orange, CA 92869-5858   714-348-8889
    Fax: 949-794-5517   info@regentconfections.com
                www.regentconfections.com
Manufacturer of candy
    President: Shahid Iqbal
Estimated Sales: $ 20 Million
Number Employees: 4
Type of Packaging: Consumer, Private Label

12013 Regez Cheese & Paper Supply
P.O.Box 312
Monroe, WI 53566-0312   608-325-3417
            Fax: 608-325-3499
Cheese
    President: Michael Einbeck
Estimated Sales: $530,000
Number Employees: 1-4

12014 Reggie Ball's Cajun Foods
501 Bunker Rd
Lake Charles, LA 70615-3875   337-436-0291
            Fax: 337-433-9851
Processor of Cajun seasoning and mixes including rice jambalaya and seafood fry
    Owner/President: Reginald Ball, Jr
Estimated Sales: $300,000-500,000
Number Employees: 1-4
Type of Packaging: Consumer, Food Service, Bulk
Brands:
    Reggie Ball's

12015 Reggie Ball's Cajun Foods
501 Bunker Rd
Lake Charles, LA 70615-3875   337-436-0291
    Fax: 337-433-9851   reggieball@cox-internet.com
                www.ballscajunfoods.com

Processor of cajum seasonings and mixes. Contract packaging and private labeling is available.
    Owner/President: Reginald Ball Jr
Estimated Sales: $500,000-$1 Million
Number Employees: 20-49
Type of Packaging: Private Label

12016 Regis Milk Company
578 Meeting St
Charleston, SC 29403-4537   843-723-3418
            Fax: 843-577-3119
Milk
    President: Thad Mitchum
    Vice President: Eric Shuler
    Plant Foreman: Charlie Green
Estimated Sales: $ 5-10 Million
Number Employees: 20-49
Type of Packaging: Private Label

12017 Register Meat Company
P.O.Box 98
Cottondale, FL 32431-0098   850-352-4269
    Fax: 850-352-2628 www.registermeats.com
Manufacturer of pork products including sausage
    President: Al Kaempfer
Estimated Sales: $10 Million
Number Employees: 5-9
Type of Packaging: Consumer, Bulk

12018 Registry Steaks & Seafood
7661 S 78th Ave # B
Bridgeview, IL 60455-1271   708-458-3100
            Fax: 708-458-3103
Meat, seafood
    President: Rosemarie Migacz
    Vice President: Tony Migacz
Estimated Sales: $ 10 Million
Number Employees: 20-49
Sq. footage: 5000
Type of Packaging: Food Service, Private Label, Bulk

12019 Rego Smoked Fish Company
6980 75th St
Flushing, NY 11379-2594   718-894-1400
            Fax: 718-894-9100
Processor of smoked salmon, sturgeon, trout, sablefish and whitefish; importer of sturgeon
    President: Jason Spitz
    Manager: Sheldon Spitz
    Owner: Conrad Spitz
Estimated Sales: $500,000-$1 Million
Number Employees: 1-4
Sq. footage: 7000
Type of Packaging: Consumer, Bulk
Brands:
    Spibro

12020 Rego's Purity Foods
3049 Ualena St # 415
Honolulu, HI 96819-1946   808-947-9005
            Fax: 808-947-2462
Processor of Portuguese and blood sausage, bologna, frankfurters, hamburger patties and knockwurst
    President: Scott Stevenson
Estimated Sales: $4000000
Number Employees: 1-4
Type of Packaging: Consumer, Food Service

12021 Reheis
235 Snyder Ave
Berkeley Heights, NJ 07922-1150   908-464-1500
    Fax: 908-464-7726   rduffy@reheis.com
                www.reheis.com
Processor, importer and exporter of potassium chloride
    VP R&D: J C Parekh
    VP Sales: D Fondots
    VP Operations: J Bogan
    Plant Manager: Gerry Kirwan
Number Employees: 100-249
Brands:
    KCI

12022 Reid Foods
PO Box 406
Gurnee, IL 60031   847-625-7912
    Fax: 847-625-7913   888-295-8478
    customerservice@reidfoods.com
                www.reidfoods.com
jams, dessert toppings, salsas, soups, pasta, pasta sauces, dips and chili
    President/Owner: Maria Reid
Number Employees: 3

12023 (HQ)Reilly Dairy & Food Company
6603 S Trask St
Tampa, FL 33616-1434   813-839-8458
    Fax: 813-839-0394   info@reillydairy.com
                www.reillydairy.com
Processor and exporter of cream cheese, sour and fresh cream, lactose, casein blends, corn sugar and starches, butter, milk, whey and cheeses
    President: Jerry Reilly
Estimated Sales: $16000000
Number Employees: 50-99
Sq. footage: 100000
Type of Packaging: Consumer, Food Service, Private Label, Bulk
Brands:
    Dixie Fresh
    Wisconsin Gold

12024 Reilly's Sea Products
PO Box 149
South Bristol, ME 04568-0149   207-644-1400
            Fax: 207-644-8192
Seafood
    President: Terry Reilly
Estimated Sales: $ 5 - 10 Million
Number Employees: 20-49

12025 (HQ)Reily Foods Company
640 Magazine St
New Orleans, LA 70130-3406   504-524-6132
    Fax: 504-539-8358   service@luzianne.com
                www.luzianne.com
Manufacturer of mayonnaise, coffee, tea, peanut butter, chili mixes, soups, pasta, beans, hot sauces, Cajun products, salad dressings and cake flours
    Chairman: William Reily III
    President: James McCarthy
    EVP/CFO: Harold Herrmann Jr
    VP: Tony Doughty
    National Broker Sales Manager: Gary Millard
    Corporate Regional Manager: Russ Vanputten
Estimated Sales: $7 Million
Number Employees: 100-249
Parent Co: JFG Coffee
Brands:
    ABITA SPRINGS WATER
    BLUE PLATE
    LA MARTINQUE
    LUZIANNE
    SWANS DOWN

12026 Reily Foods/JFG Coffee Company
3434 Mynatt Ave
Knoxville, TN 37919-4524   865-546-2120
    Fax: 865-524-8725   800-535-1961
    info@reilyfoods.com   www.luzianne.com
Processor of tea, coffee, mayonnaise and peanut butter
    President/CEO: Robert C Maurer
    Sales Manager: Ken Christopher
    VP Operations: Taylor Dulaney
    Plant Manager: Rich Schmader
Number Employees: 100-249
Parent Co: Reily Companies
Type of Packaging: Consumer, Food Service
Brands:
    Blue Plate Mayonnaise
    Luzianne Tea
    Swans Down Cake Flour

12027 Reimann Food Classics
1304 E Cooper Drive
Palatine, IL 60074-7284   847-991-1366
            Fax: 847-359-7528
Processor of pancake and waffle mixes
    President: E Reimann
    Treasurer: L Milkovich
    Vice President: T Milkovich
Number Employees: 5-9
Type of Packaging: Consumer

12028 Reinhart Foods
15 Allstate Parkway Ste. 500
Markham, ON L3R 5B4
Canada   905-754-3503
    Fax: 905-265-9131 www.reinhartfoods.com

Processor of vinegar, bottled maraschino cherries, glace fruit, dates, raisins, coconut, mince meat, pie fillings and apples; exporter of vinegar; importer of maraschino cherries, dates, raisins, coconut and pineapple
President: T Singer
VP/General Manager: D Bell
Assistant General Manager: L Watt
Parent Co: Reinhart Vinegars
Type of Packaging: Consumer, Food Service, Private Label, Bulk
Brands:
Orchard Fresh
Perfec Py
Reinhart

12029 Reinhold Ice Cream Company
800 Fulton St
Pittsburgh, PA 15233-2119   412-321-7600
Fax: 412-321-8456
Processor of ice cream and frozen yogurt
President: Robert Mandell
Vice President: Michael Mandell
Salesman: Diane Beckerman
Plant Manager: Craig Metzgar
Estimated Sales: $7400000
Number Employees: 50-99
Type of Packaging: Consumer, Food Service, Private Label, Bulk

12030 Reist Popcorn Company
P.O.Box 155
Mt Joy, PA 17552-0155   717-653-8078
Fax: 717-653-4121
reistpopcorn@embarqmail.com
reistpopcorn.com
Manufacturer of unpoppped popcorn
President: David Reist
Estimated Sales: $1.3 Million
Number Employees: 5
Type of Packaging: Private Label, Bulk
Brands:
Dutch Country
Hi-Pop

12031 Reiter Dairy
1941 Commerce Cir
Springfield, OH 45504-2011   937-323-5777
Fax: 937-323-2420 www.reiterdairy.com
Processor of whole, skim, 1% and 2% milk, cream and yogurt; also, bottled water and fruit drinks including grapefruit, punch, orange, lemon and lemon/lime
Manager: Brian Riley
Plant Manager: Norris Jackman
Estimated Sales: $100+ Million
Number Employees: 100-249
Parent Co: Dean Foods Company
Type of Packaging: Consumer, Food Service, Private Label

12032 Reiter Dairy
1415 W Waterloo Rd
Akron, OH 44314-1503   330-745-1123
Fax: 330-745-4363 800-362-0825
www.reiterdairy.com
Processor of orange juice and dairy products including ice cream, milk, heavy cream and ice cream mixes
Manager: Bill Riley
Plant Manager: Dave Schirmer
Number Employees: 50-99
Parent Co: Dean Foods Company
Type of Packaging: Consumer, Food Service
Brands:
REITER

12033 Rembrandt Foods
1419 480th Street
Rembrandt, IA 50576-7542   972-847-4421
Fax: 972-746-4545
foodservicesales@rembrandtinc.com
www.rembrandtfoods.com
Egg ingredients and egg products
CEO: David Rettig
CFO: Brad Fullmer
COO: Don Kellen
Number Employees: 275

12034 Renaissance Baking Company
12551 Biscayne Boulevard
North Miami, FL 33181-2522   305-893-2144
Fax: 305-893-3308 renbaking@aol.com
www.renaissancebaking.com

Processor of hearth baked European style sourdough bread, sandwich breads and dinner rolls
President: Steven Bern
Number Employees: 40
Sq. footage: 5000
Type of Packaging: Consumer, Food Service

12035 Renaissance Foods
814 Hanley Industrial Court
Saint Louis, MO 63144-1403   314-961-6554
Fax: 314-961-8731
Baked goods
President: Eric Cowle
Vice President: Daniella Cowle
Plant Manager: Charlene Thurmond
Purchasing Manager: Kathy Ramsey
Estimated Sales: $ 1-2.5 Million appx.
Number Employees: 16
Type of Packaging: Private Label
Brands:
Oven-Bites
Quelle Quiche

12036 Renaissance Vineyard & Winery
P.O.Box 1000
Oregon House, CA 95962-1000   530-692-2248
Fax: 530-692-2497 800-655-3277
sales@rvw.com www.rvw.com
Wines
President: Gideon Beinstock
CFO: Massimo Leotta
VP Distribution: Shawn Robinson
Direct Marketing Manager: Joseph Bruno
Winemaker: Gideon Beinstock
Estimated Sales: $ 10-20 Million
Number Employees: 50-99
Type of Packaging: Private Label
Brands:
RENAISSANCE

12037 Renard's Cheese
248 County Rd S
Algoma, WI 54201-9444   920-487-2825
Fax: 920-487-5042 renards@itol.com
www.renards.com
Cheese
Proprietor: Brian Renard
Proprietor: Gary Renard
Vice President: Chris Renard
Estimated Sales: $ 5-9.9 Million
Number Employees: 5-9
Type of Packaging: Private Label

12038 Renault Winery
72 N Bremen Ave
Egg Harbor City, NJ 08215-3195   609-965-2111
Fax: 609-965-1847 wine@renaultwinery.com
www.renaultwinery.com
Processor of vermouth and wine
President: Joseph Milza
Manufacturing Manager: Raphael Lopez
Estimated Sales: $3649539
Number Employees: 100-249
Type of Packaging: Consumer

12039 Rendulic Packing
800 Manning Ave
McKeesport, PA 15132-3699   412-678-9541
Fax: 412-678-8891 info@nemahalal.com
www.nemahalal.com
Processor and packer of meats including bologna, suckling pig, veal and lamb
Manager: Hasan Ozcan
Estimated Sales: $3300000
Number Employees: 10-19
Type of Packaging: Consumer

12040 Rene Produce Distributors
P.O.Box 1178
Nogales, AZ 85628-1178   520-281-9014
Fax: 520-281-2933 reneprod@dakotacom.net
www.reneproduce.com
Grower and exporter of cucumbers, eggplant, squash, tomatoes and peppers including red, bell and gold
President: Rene Carrillo
Sales Manager: David Kennedy
Sales: George Quintero
Estimated Sales: $ 3 - 5 Million
Number Employees: 10-19
Type of Packaging: Consumer, Food Service
Brands:
Rene

12041 Rene Rey Chocolates Ltd
1119 W 14th Street
North Vancouver, BC V7P 1J9
Canada   604-985-0949
Fax: 604-985-0395 888-985-0949
renerey@axion.net www.chocolate-canada.com
Chocolate, candy
President: Rene Rey
Director Of Marketing: Gerald Pinton
Sq. footage: 20000
Brands:
MAPLE NUTS
NATURE CANADA
SUN MOON STARS

12042 Renfro Foods
P.O.Box 321
Fort Worth, TX 76101-0321   817-336-3849
Fax: 817-336-7910 info@renfrofoods.com
www.renfrofoods.com
Manufacturer of relishes, sauces, peppers and salsas
President: Doug Renfro
CEO: Bill Renfro
Vice President: Becky Renfro
VP Production: James Renfro
Estimated Sales: $12 Million
Number Employees: 20-49
Number of Products: 27
Type of Packaging: Consumer, Food Service, Private Label
Brands:
MRS RENFRO'S

12043 Rentschler's Bakery
245 E Walnut Street
Kutztown, PA 19530-1119   610-683-3506
Processor of pies, cakes and buns
President: Jay Rentschler
VP: Larry Rentschler
Number Employees: 10-19
Type of Packaging: Consumer, Food Service

12044 Renwood Winery
10461 Old Placerville Rd # 150
Sacramento, CA 95827-2525   916-381-9463
Fax: 916-381-9458 800-348-8466
sales@renwood.com www.renwood.com
Wines
President: Robert Smerling
CFO: Bob Moore
VP Marketing: Joe Cusimano
Manager: Abby Bishop
Operations Manager: Bryan Wilkinson
Estimated Sales: $ 5-10 Million
Number Employees: 20-49
Sq. footage: 18
Type of Packaging: Private Label
Brands:
Renwood Wines
Santino Wines

12045 Republic Foods
2633 Swiss Ave
Dallas, TX 75204-5892   214-826-8050
Processor of beef liver including sliced and frozen; also beef offal
President: Don Bagg
Number Employees: 5-9
Type of Packaging: Consumer

12046 Republic of Tea
8 Digital Drive
Suite 100
Novato, CA 94949-8703   415-382-3400
Fax: 415-382-3401 800-354-5530
info@republicoftea.com www.republicoftea.com
Fine full leaf teas and herbs and teaware.
President: Ron Rubin
VP: Stuart Gold
Marketing: Heather Innocenti
Operations: George Phillips
Estimated Sales: $ 2.5-5 Million
Number Employees: 30
Brands:
Daily Green Teas
RED TEA
Republic of Tea

12047 Request Foods
P.O.Box 2577
Holland, MI 49422-2577   616-786-0900
Fax: 616-786-9180 800-748-0378
info@requestfoods.com www.requestfoods.com

Processor of frozen entrees and dinners
President: Jack Dewitt
CFO: Bill Rysdyk
R & D: Jurgen Becker
Quality Control: Tom Muntter
Purchasing Agent: Larry Vanderkolk
Estimated Sales: $ 100-500 Million
Number Employees: 250-499
Type of Packaging: Consumer, Food Service, Private Label

12048 Research Products Company
1835 E North St
Salina, KS 67401-8567   785-825-2181
          Fax: 785-825-8908 800-234-7174
info@researchprod.com   www.researchprod.com
Processor and exporter of flour bleaching premixes, flour maturing premixers,vitamin and mineral ingredients; also, micro-ingredient dispensing system andservices available
President: Monte White
VP: Monte White
Technical Director: Steve Schorn
Estimated Sales: $ 10 - 20 Million
Number Employees: 50-99
Parent Co: McShares
Brands:
    Kurolite
    Oxylite

12049 Reser's Fine Foods
15570 SW Jenkins Rd
Beaverton, OR 97006   503-643-6431
          Fax: 503-646-9233 800-333-6431
                    www.resers.com
Manufacturer of prepared salads, side dishes, dips, Mexican foods and specialty products.
President/CEO: Alvin Reser
CFO: Paul Levy
VP Sales/Marekting: Peter Sirgy
COO: Mark Reser
VP Foodservice: Doug Peck
Estimated Sales: $500 Million
Number Employees: 500-999
Sq. footage: 110000
Type of Packaging: Consumer, Private Label
Brands:
    AMERICAN CLASSICS™ SALADS
    BAJA CAFE® MEXICAN FOODS
    DON PANCHO® TORTILLAS
    MRS KINSER'S® PIMENTO CHEESE
    SENSATIONAL SIDES™
    STONEMILL KITCHES® DIPS

12050 (HQ)Reser's Fine Foods
P.O.Box 8
Beaverton, OR 97075-0008   503-643-6431
          Fax: 503-646-9233 800-333-6431
                    www.resers.com
Processor of salads, sausages, lunch meats, dips, hot buttered rum mix, salad dressings, pasta, pizza, tamales, burritos and tortillas
President: Alvin Reser
COO: Mark Reser
CFO: Paul Leavy
VP Sales/Marketing: Peter Sirgy
Director Marketing: Don Graff
VP Retail Sales: Marty Reser
Estimated Sales: $100+ Million
Number Employees: 500-999
Type of Packaging: Consumer, Food Service
Other Locations:
    Reser's Fine Foods
    Lynchburg VA

12051 Reser's Fine Foods
1811 W 1700 S
Salt Lake City, UT 84104-3841   801-972-5633
          Fax: 801-977-9526 trent@lynnwilson.com
                    www.resers.com
Processor of tortillas, burritos, salads, chili, enchiladas, salsa, tamales and puddings
Manager: Brian Thurlow
COO: Mark Reser
CFO: Paul Leavy
Marketing: Don Graff
Estimated Sales: $ 10 - 20 Million
Number Employees: 100-249
Sq. footage: 100000
Type of Packaging: Consumer, Food Service, Private Label, Bulk
Brands:
    Delseys
    Lynn Wilson's

Mitia
Papa Lynn
Rayo De Sol

12052 Reser's Fine Foods
3167 SE 10th St
Topeka, KS 66607-2508   785-233-6431
          Fax: 785-233-3090 800-333-6431
          bradp@resers.com   www.resers.com/home
President: Alvin Reser
COO: Mark Reser
VP: Tony Kunis
CFO: Paul Leavy
Estimated Sales: $ 100-500 Million
Number Employees: 1-4
Brands:
    Baja Cafe

12053 Resource Trading Company
PO Box 1698
Portland, ME 04104-1698   207-772-2299
                    Fax: 207-772-4709
Processor of frozen lobster, scallops and shrimp; exporter of shrimp and lobster; importer of shrimp
President: Spencer Fuller
Domestic Sales: Tom Keegan
International Sales: Irene Ketalaar-Moon
Type of Packaging: Bulk
Brands:
    Arctic Pride
    Claw Island
    Northern Lights

12054 Restaurant Lulu GourmetProducts
1245 Folsom St
San Francisco, CA 94103-3816   415-255-8686
          Fax: 415-255-8668 888-693-5800
                    leslie@restaurantlulu.com
                    www.restaurantlulu.com
Olive tapenade, specialty honey, balsamic vinegars, herb vinegars, seasonings, sauces, gourmet tomato products
Manager: Tom Ratcliff
Sales Director: Leslie Wilson
Estimated Sales: $ 2.5-5 Million
Number Employees: 1-4
Sq. footage: 4000
Type of Packaging: Private Label

12055 Restaurant Systems International
1000 South Avenue
Staten Island, NY 10314-3430   718-494-8888
          Fax: 718-494-8776 pbrown@restsys.com
                    www.restsys.com
Processor of frozen yogurt
CEO: Richard Nicotra
Number Employees: 20-49
Sq. footage: 10000

12056 Reter Fruit Company
3100 S Pacific Hwy
Medford, OR 97501-8758   541-772-5256
                    Fax: 541-772-5258
Processor and exporter of pears
President: F Baker
Estimated Sales: $380000
Number Employees: 5-9
Type of Packaging: Consumer
Brands:
    Maltese Cross
    Sun-Sugared

12057 Rethemeyer Coffee Company
1711 N Broadway
St Louis, MO 63102   314-231-0990
Coffee
President: A Rethemeyer
Estimated Sales: Less than $500,000
Number Employees: 1-4
Brands:
    Rethemeyer

12058 Retzlaff Vineyards
1356 S Livermore Ave
Livermore, CA 94550-9505   925-447-8941
          Fax: 925-447-9641 retzlaffwinery@gmail.com
                    www.retzlaffwinery.com
Cabernet, sauvignon, chardonnay wines
Owner: Gloria Taylor
Marketing Manager: Connie Vander Vouter
Estimated Sales: Below $ 5 Million
Number Employees: 10-19

Brands:
    Retzlaff Estate Wines

12059 Reutter Candy & Chocolates
4665 Hollins Ferry Road
Baltimore, MD 21227-4601   800-392-0870
                    Fax: 410-510-1222
Candy, chocolate
International Sales: Karl Heigold
Brands:
    CHOCO BERRIES
    FINE MINTS
    THE MINT

12060 Revonah Pretzel Bakery
507 Baltimore St
Hanover, PA 17331-3396   717-630-2883
          Fax: 717-632-3328 www.revonahpretzel.com
Processor of pretzels and potato chips
Owner: Kevin Bidelspach
Estimated Sales: $3900000
Number Employees: 5-9
Sq. footage: 24000
Type of Packaging: Consumer, Food Service, Private Label, Bulk
Brands:
    Bickel
    Sam & Nick's
    Tom Sturgis

12061 Rex Wine Vinegar Company
830 Raymond Blvd
Newark, NJ 07105-2905   973-589-6911
          Fax: 973-589-8988 vcarlesimo@aol.com
Processor of wine and balsamic vinegar, vinegar stock and cooking wines
President: Vincent Carlesimo
Estimated Sales: $2361540
Number Employees: 5-9
Sq. footage: 7500
Parent Co: Regina Wine Company
Type of Packaging: Bulk
Brands:
    Roma-Rex
    Savoia

12062 Rex Wine Vinegar Company
830 Raymond Blvd
Newark, NJ 07105-2905   973-589-6911
                    Fax: 973-589-8988
Manufacturer of Wine vinegar, vinegar stock, and cooking wines
Estimated Sales: $ 3 - 5 Million
Number Employees: 5-9

12063 Rey Food Company
515 Observer Highway
Hoboken, NJ 07030-6552   201-792-1955
                    Fax: 201-792-0236
Meats, cheeses, provisions, poultry
President: Jose Rey
Estimated Sales: $ 10-100 Million
Number Employees: 10

12064 Reynolds Sugar Bush
188572 W Maple Road
Aniwa, WI 54408   715-449-2057
                    Fax: 715-449-2879
Maple syrup and products
President: Juan Reynolds
Estimated Sales: Below $ 5 Million
Number Employees: 4
Type of Packaging: Private Label

12065 Rezolex
2240 Pepper Rd # A
Las Cruces, NM 88007-8036   575-527-1730
                    Fax: 575-527-0221
Seasonings
President: Louis Biad
Plant Manager: Robert Stomp
Estimated Sales: Below $ 5 Million
Number Employees: 20-49

12066 Rhino Foods
79 Industrial Pkwy
Burlington, VT 05401-5435   802-862-0252
          Fax: 802-865-4145 800-639-3350
tcastle@rhinofoods.com   www.rhinofoods.com

Manufacturer of frozen desserts including ice cream novelties, brownies, cookie dough batter, cakes, truffles, low fat, no fat, reduced sugars/NSA, trans fat free
President/Owner: Ted Castle
Director Technical Services: Renita Rodriguez
Marketing Director: John McCarthy
Sales Director: John McCarthy
Estimated Sales: $25 Million
Number Employees: 100-249
Sq. footage: 29000
Type of Packaging: Consumer, Food Service, Private Label, Bulk
Brands:
Chessters
Vermont Velvet

12067 Rhodes Bake-N-Serv
P.O.Box 25487
Salt Lake City, UT 84125-0487   801-972-0122
        Fax: 801-972-0286   800-695-0122
customersatisfaction@rhodesbread.com
www.rhodes-bns.com
Processor of frozen rolls including white and wheat dinner, cinnamon, caramel, orange, sweet dough, pizza crust, pizza dough, biscuits and bread dough.
President: Ken Farnsworth
CEO: Ken Farnsworth Sr
VP Sales/Marketing: Kerry Smith
Number Employees: 50-99
Type of Packaging: Consumer, Food Service, Private Label
Brands:
Dakota Hearth
Rhodes Bake-N-Serv

12068 Rhodes Bean & Supply Cooperative
P.O.Box 338
Tracy, CA 95378-0338   209-835-1284
        Fax: 209-835-1304   ken@beanplant.com
www.beanplant.com
Processor of dried beans
General Manager: Ken Kirsten
Estimated Sales: $500,000-$1 Million
Number Employees: 20-49
Type of Packaging: Bulk
Brands:
Rhodes-Stockton Bean

12069 Rhodes International
P.O.Box 410
Columbus, WI 53925-0410   920-623-5161
        Fax: 920-623-5185   800-876-7333
customersatisfaction@rhodesbread.com
www.rhodesbread.com
Processor of frozen bread and roll dough including white, wheat, raisin, sweet and Italian
President: Ken Farnworth Jr
Operations/Plant Manager: Darryl Campbell
Plant Manager: Darry Campbell
Estimated Sales: $ 20 - 50 Million
Number Employees: 100-249
Sq. footage: 30000
Type of Packaging: Consumer, Food Service, Private Label
Brands:
Dakota Hearth
Rhodes

12070 Rhodes International
P.O.Box 25487
Salt Lake City, UT 84125-0487   801-972-0122
        Fax: 801-972-0286   800-695-0122
customersatisfaction@rhodesbread.com
www.rhodes-bns.com
Frozen bread and roll dough
President/CEO: Kenny Farnsworth
Marketing Director: Bret Sharp
CEO: Ken Farnsworth Sr
CFO: Christina Maybory
VP Sales: Kerry Smith
Plant Manager: Joel Ockerga
Number Employees: 50-99
Type of Packaging: Private Label
Brands:
Rhodes Bake-In-Serve Frozen Dough

12071 (HQ)Rhodia
8 Cedar Brook Drive
CN 7500
Cranbury, NJ 08512   609-860-4000
        Fax: 609-409-8652   800-343-8324
silicones@us.rhodia.com
www.food.us.rhodia.com
Processor, importer and exporter of food and beverage ingredients including phosphates, bicarbonates, hydrocolloids, xanthan, guar and locust bean gum, vanillin, antioxidants, low/no fat systems, emulsifiers, stabilizers, startercultures, colors, etc
President: James Harton
CEO: Jean Clamadieu
CFO: Mark l Dahlinger
SVP/General Counsel: John Donahue
Sales Manager: Scott Marsi
Estimated Sales: $713 Million
Number Employees: 1800
Parent Co: Rhodia SA

12072 Rhodia Inc
8 Cedar Brook Drive
Cranbury, NJ 08512-7500   609-860-4000
        Fax: 609-860-2250 www.rhodia.com
Food ingredient supplier for baking, cereal, snack foods, meat, seafood and poultry
President: James Harton
CFO: Mark Dahlinger
SVP: John Donahue
Estimated Sales: $4 Billion
Number Employees: 1,800

12073 Riba Foods
P.O.Box 630461
Houston, TX 77263-0461   713-975-7001
        Fax: 713-975-7036   800-327-7422
sales@ribafoods.com   www.ribafoods.com
Processor of salsas, pickles, jalapeno peppers, mustards and other sauces, bean dips, quesos and enchilada and pepper sauces
President: Miguel Barrios
Manager Sales/Marketing: Richard Wall
Estimated Sales: $ 5 -10 Million
Number Employees: 10-19
Number of Brands: 2
Number of Products: 45
Sq. footage: 20000
Type of Packaging: Consumer, Food Service, Private Label
Brands:
Arriba
Norte□A
Texas Pepper Works

12074 Ribble Production
1601 Mearns Road
Warminster, PA 18974-1115   215-674-1706
        Fax: 215-674-0123 info@ribbleproduction.com
www.ribbleproduction.com
Manufacturer of decorative toppings including multi/single cell sprinkles, nonpareils, jimmies and mixes; custom manufacturing and packaging
VP: Joseph Van Houten
Number Employees: 20-49
Type of Packaging: Consumer, Food Service, Private Label, Bulk

12075 Ribus
8000 Maryland Ave # 460
St Louis, MO 63105-3910   314-727-4287
        Fax: 314-727-1199   info@ribus.com
www.ribus.com
Specialty ingredients for snack food and extruded products, bakery product performance improvement and beverage system
President: Steve Pierce
Financial Coordinator: Lisa Ennis
Marketing/Customer Service Director: Susie Peters
Estimated Sales: Below $ 5 Million
Number Employees: 5-9
Type of Packaging: Food Service, Private Label, Bulk
Brands:
Ribus

12076 Rice Company
1624 Santa Clara Dr # 120
Roseville, CA 95661-3553   916-787-1084
        Fax: 916-784-7681   jobs@riceco.com
www.riceco.com

Processor, importer and exporter of dry grocery items including rice, popcorn, rice flour, sugar, beans, peas, lentils and ginger
Owner: Duane Kistner
President: J Kapila
Operations Manager: Vicki Manzoli
Estimated Sales: $4500000
Number Employees: 50-99
Type of Packaging: Consumer, Food Service, Private Label, Bulk

12077 (HQ)Rice Deerwood & Grain Processing
21926 County Road 10
Deerwood, MN 56444-8486   218-534-3762
        Fax: 218-534-3802
Manufacturer of wild rice
President: Dan Mohs
Estimated Sales: $1.20 Million
Number Employees: 20-49
Sq. footage: 39000
Type of Packaging: Consumer, Bulk

12078 Rice Foods
5111 Lake Ter NE
Mount Vernon, IL 62864-9666   618-242-0026
        Fax: 618-242-3109
CEO: Lynn Withworth

12079 Rice Fruit Company
P.O.Box 66
Gardners, PA 17324-0066   717-677-8131
        Fax: 717-677-9842   800-627-3359
sales@ricefruit.com   www.ricefruit.com
Processor and exporter of apples, peaches and pears.
President/Manager Plant Operations: David Rice
VP: John Rice
Sales/Marketing: Brenda Briggs
Director of Sales: John Rice
Estimated Sales: $ 50 - 100 Million
Number Employees: 50-99
Type of Packaging: Consumer, Food Service, Bulk

12080 Rice Hull Specialty ProCompany
P.O.Box 188
Stuttgart, AR 72160-0188   870-673-8507
        Fax: 870-673-2116 info@ricehull.com
www.ricehull.com
Processor of parboiled rice hulls which are used as a pressing aid for fruit juice processors
President: John Moore
VP: John Moore
Sales Manager: Greg Crawford
Estimated Sales: $1600000
Number Employees: 10-19

12081 Rice Innovations
8175 Winston Churchill Boulevard
Norval, ON L0P 1K0
Canada   905-451-7423
        Fax: 905-453-8137 info@maplegrovefoods.com
www.maplegrovefoods.com
Processor of organic and gluten-free rice, potato pastas, beverages and other products.
General Manager: Raj Sukul
R&D: Ly Hung
Customer Service: Sally Chee
Number Employees: 47
Type of Packaging: Private Label
Brands:
BODY FUEL
CAFE BONJOUR
CELIFIBR
HERB SCIENCE
MACARIZ
MEDICEA
PASTARISO
PASTATO
RICE REALITY
YING YANG

12082 Rice River Farms/Chieftan Wild Rice Company
P.O.Box 550
Spooner, WI 54801-0550   715-635-6401
        Fax: 715-635-6415   800-262-6368
wildrice@centurytel.net
www.chieftainwildrice.com
Wild rice and wild rice blends
President: Donald Richards
General Manager: Joan Gerland
Operations Manager: Jim Deutsch

Estimated Sales:$ 10 - 20 Million
Number Employees: 20-49
Number of Brands: 1
Type of Packaging: Private Label

12083 Rice Select
P.O.Box 1305
Alvin, TX 77512-1305   281-393-3502
     Fax: 281-393-3532   800-232-7423
     info@riceselect.com   www.ricetec.com
Processor and exporter of rice including Indian-style, brown and white basmati, American jasmine and rice mixes
     President: John Nelson
     VP Sales/Operations: Mark Denman
Estimated Sales:$ 100-500 Million
Number Employees: 50-99
Type of Packaging: Consumer, Food Service, Private Label, Bulk
Brands:
     Chefs Originals
     Jasmati
     Kasmati
     Texmati

12084 Riceland FoodsRice Milling Operations
P.O.Box 927
Stuttgart, AR 72160-0927   870-766-8667
     Fax: 870-766-4368   800-226-9522
     riceland@riceland.com   www.riceland.com
Manufacturer of rice; exporter of rice, rice by-products and rice oil
     Manager: Tom Bracewell
Estimated Sales:$197 Million
Number Employees: 100-249
Parent Co: Riceland Foods Inc
Type of Packaging: Consumer, Food Service, Private Label, Bulk
Brands:
     CHEF-WAY
     DELTA QUEEN
     ORIENTAL HARVEST
     RICELAND
     SAL FRY
     SHUR CHEF
     SUREFRY SOYBEAN MEAL

12085 Riceland FoodsRice Milling Operations
10800 Financial Centre Pkwy
Little Rock, AR 72211-3552   501-225-0936
     Fax: 501-225-9179   888-532-4844
     riceland@riceland.com   www.riceland.com
Manufacturer of a full line of deoiled and fluid lecithin products; Lecigran, Lecisoy, Leciprime. Applications include color and flavor suspension, bakery products, egg replacer/extender, instant powder, icing and fillings, chewing gumbase, chocolate, batters and sauces
Number Employees: 11
Parent Co: Riceland Foods Inc
Type of Packaging: Bulk

12086 Rices Potato Chips
9407 Boyette Road
Biloxi, MS 39532   228-396-5775
     Fax: 228-396-5775
Processor of potato chips and other snack foods
     President: Martha Vergunst
*Estimated Sales:*Less than $250,000
Number Employees: 2
Type of Packaging: Private Label

12087 Ricetec
P.O.Box 1305
Alvin, TX 77512-1305   281-393-3502
     Fax: 281-393-3532   information@ricetec.com
     www.ricetec.com
Processor of aromatic rice; also, researcher and developer of rice varieties
     President: John Nelson
     VP Marketing: R Long
     VP Sales/Operations: Mark Denman
     Operations Manager: M Oenman
Estimated Sales:$23081227
Number Employees: 50-99
Type of Packaging: Consumer, Food Service, Private Label, Bulk
Brands:
     CHEF'S ORIGINAL
     JASMATI RICE

RICE SELECT
TEXMATI RICE

12088 Ricex Company
1241 Hawks Flight Court
El Dorado Hills, CA 95762-9648   916-933-3000
     Fax: 916-933-3232   tbarber@ricex.com
     www.ricex.com
Processor of stabilized rice bran and concentrated rice bran fiber
     President: Terrence Barber
     VP/General Manager: Dan McPeak Jr
Estimated Sales:$3511295
Number Employees: 24
Sq. footage: 20000
Type of Packaging: Bulk
Brands:
     Ricex

12089 Rich Ice Cream Company
2915 S Dixie Hwy
West Palm Beach, FL 33405-1585   561-833-7585
     Fax: 561-655-1952 www.richicecream.com
Processor of ice cream, cream puffs, chocolate eclairs and cakes
     CEO: Jhon Rich
     Marketing Director: Randy Rich
     Controller: Bob Thomas
     VP: Randy Rich
Number Employees: 100-249
Type of Packaging: Consumer, Food Service
Brands:
     Rich Ice Creams

12090 Rich Products Corporation
P.O.Box 631
Fresno, CA 93709-0631   559-486-7380
     Fax: 559-486-0480   duhrich@rich.com
     www.richs.com
Processor of frozen bread
Estimated Sales:$ 50 - 100 Million
Number Employees: 100-249
Parent Co: Rich Products Corporation
Type of Packaging: Consumer, Food Service

12091 Rich Products Corporation
One Robert Rich Way
Buffalo, NY 14213   716-878-8000
     Fax: 716-878-8266   800-356-7094
     www.richs.com
Manufacturer of frozen bread, rolls, cookies and sweet dough
     President/CEO: William Gisel Jr
     EVP/CFO: James Deuschle
*Estimated Sales:*K
Number Employees: 5,000-9,999
Type of Packaging: Consumer, Food Service, Private Label
Brands:
     J.W. ALLEN
     RICH'S

12092 Rich Products Corporation
801 N Kent Street
Winchester, VA 22601-5415   540-667-1955
     Fax: 540-667-1779
Processor of frozen bread, rolls and sweet goods
     CFO: James Pratt
     Production Manager: Jeff Lewallan
     Purchasing Agent: Pamela Maphis
Estimated Sales:$ 50 - 100 Million
Number Employees: 170
Parent Co: Rich Products Corporation
Type of Packaging: Consumer, Private Label

12093 Rich Products Corporation
One Robert Rich Way
Buffalo, NY 14213   716-878-8000
     Fax: 716-878-8266   800-828-2021
     richcanada@rich.com   www.richs.com
Processor of frozen baked products including cookies, breads and muffins
     President/CEO: William Gisel Jr
     EVP/CFO: James Deuschle
*Estimated Sales:*K
Number Employees: 5,000-9,999
Parent Co: Rich Products Corporation
Type of Packaging: Consumer, Food Service, Private Label
Brands:
     Bahama Blast
     Bettercreme
     Byron's Barbecue
     Casa DiBertacchi

Farm Rich
On Top
Rich's Whip Topping
SeaPak

12094 Rich Products Corporation
P.O.Box 388
Claremont, CA 91711-0388   909-621-4711
     Fax: 909-624-6520 www.richs.com
Processor of whipped toppings and coffee creamers
     Manager: Kevin Fisher
     Materials Manager: Kevin Fisher
Estimated Sales:$ 10 - 20 Million
Number Employees: 20-49
Sq. footage: 90000
Parent Co: Rich Products Corporation
Type of Packaging: Consumer, Food Service

12095 Rich Products Corporation
1366 19th Street
Cameron, WI 54822-9591   715-458-4556
     Fax: 715-458-2979
Processor of frozen dough and cookie and cake mixes
     President/CEO: Robert Rich Jr
     Director Marketing: Michael Cannon
     CFO: Charles Trego Jr
     Vice President: William Gisel
     Public Relations: Peter Ciotta
     Operations Manager: Mike Bingham
     Sales Manager: John Wellenzohn
     Purchasing Manager: Jeff Kusche
Number Employees: 3500
Parent Co: Rich Products Corporation
Type of Packaging: Private Label
Brands:
     Bettercreme Frosting & Filling
     Byron's Bronco
     Chocolate Heat N'Ice
     Dutch Brownie Base
     Grand American
     Grand American Ice C
     Jim's
     Mrs. Rich's Cookies
     Pies and Krunchies
     Red Raspberry Bismar
     Rich's Bread and Rol
     Rich's Eclairs
     Rich's Eclairs
     Rich's European Coun
     Rich's Farm Rich
     Rich's Non-Dairy Des
     Rich's Pizza Dough
     Rich's Poly Rich
     Rich's Puddings

12096 Rich Products Corporation
P.O.Box 490
Hilliard, OH 43026-0490   614-771-1117
     Fax: 614-771-8286 www.richs.com
Processor of doughnut mixes, frozen doughnuts, toppings and fillings
     Manager: Mike Calloway
     Managing VP: Brian Townson
     Purchasing Agent: Marylou Bright
Estimated Sales:$100-500 Million
Number Employees: 50-99
Parent Co: Rich Products Corporation
Type of Packaging: Private Label

12097 Rich Products of Canada
PO Box 1008
Fort Erie, ON L2A 5N8
Canada   905-871-2605
     Fax: 905-871-6198   800-263-8174
     RichCanada@Rich.com   www.richs.com
Processor of frozen baked goods, dough, nondairy creamers and whipped topping and Italian specialties
     President: Howard Rich
     CEO: Bill Gisel
     VP Marketing: Nick Stambula
     Purchasing: Paul Furtney
Number Employees: 100-249
Parent Co: Rich Products Corporation
Type of Packaging: Consumer, Food Service, Private Label, Bulk
Brands:
     Allen
     Avoset
     Bahama Blast™
     Byron's Barbecue
     Casa DiBertacchi
     Coffee Rich

Farm Rich
Gold Label Plus Dairy
Jon Donaire
Mother's Kitchen
Presto
Rich's Eclairs
SeaPak
Tres Riches

12098 Rich-Seapak Corporation
P.O.Box 20670
St Simons Island, GA 31522-0670   912-638-5000
Fax: 912-634-3105   800-654-9731
www.richs.com
Processor of shrimp, cheese, French toast and finger
foods
President/CEO: Bruce Major
VP/CFO: Bob Pavone
Number Employees: 100-249
Parent Co: Rich Products Corporation
Type of Packaging: Consumer, Food Service
Other Locations:
Rich-Seapak Corp.
Brownsville TX
Brands:
BYRONS
CASA DE BERTACCHI
FARM RICH
RICHS
SEA PACK

12099 Rich-Seapak Corporation
3555 E 14th St
Brownsville, TX 78521-3235   956-542-0001
Fax: 956-504-4401 www.richs.com
Processor of frozen seafood and vegetables; im-
porter and exporter of frozen shrimp
President: George H Bridger
Operations Manager: Michael Heggie
Director Shrimp Procurement: Bill Hoenig
Estimated Sales: $100+ Million
Number Employees: 250-499
Parent Co: Rich Products Corporation
Type of Packaging: Consumer, Food Service, Pri-
vate Label

12100 Richard Bagdasarian Inc.
P.O.Box 698
Mecca, CA 92254-0698   760-396-2168
Fax: 760-396-2801 rbagdasarian@mrgrape.com
www.bagdasarianinc.com
Grower, shipper and marketer of California Table
Grapes, Citrus and Vegetables for numerous compa-
nies including Sunkist Growers.
Owner: Mike Bozick
VP/Manager: Nick Bozick
VP/Manager: Mike Bozick
VP/Manager: Franz DeKlotz
VP/Manager: Bill Spidell
Type of Packaging: Food Service

12101 Richard Donnelly Fine Chtes
1509 Mission St
Santa Cruz, CA 95060-4740   831-458-4214
Fax: 831-425-0678   888-685-1871
info@donnellychocolates.com
www.donnellychocolates.com
Chocolate, dessert sauces and mixes; gift boxes
available
Owner: Richard Donnelly
Estimated Sales: Less than $500,000
Number Employees: 1-4
Type of Packaging: Private Label
Brands:
Donnelly Chocolates

12102 Richard E. Colgin Company
2230 Valdina St
Dallas, TX 75207-6106   214-951-8687
Fax: 214-951-8668   sales@colgin.com
www.colgin.com
Liquid flavorings
VP: Kerry Thornhill
President: Elizabeth Thornhill
CFO: Sarah Johnson
Estimated Sales: $ 2.5-5 Million
Number Employees: 5-9
Type of Packaging: Private Label
Brands:
Chigarid
Colgin

12103 Richard Green Company
1827 S Meridian St
Indianapolis, IN 46225-1730   317-972-0941
Fax: 317-972-1201 rickg@thepeanutking.com
www.thepeanutking.com
Processor of popcorn and nuts
President: Richard Green
Estimated Sales: $500,000-$1 Million
Number Employees: 5-9
Sq. footage: 24000
Type of Packaging: Consumer, Private Label

12104 Richard L. Graeser Winery
255 Petrified Forest Rd
Calistoga, CA 94515-9795   707-942-4437
Fax: 707-942-4437 richard@graeserwinery.com
www.graeserwinery.com
Wines
Owner: Richard Graeser
Winemaker: Richard Graeser
Estimated Sales: $500,000-$1 Million
Number Employees: 5-9
Type of Packaging: Private Label
Brands:
Graeser

12105 Richard Lanza
847 S 1st Road
Hammonton, NJ 08037-8408   609-561-3984
Fax: 609-561-0187 www.lanzablueberries.com
Package blueberries
Owner: Richard Lanza
Estimated Sales: Under $500,000
Number Employees: 1-4
Type of Packaging: Private Label, Bulk
Brands:
Richard Lanza

12106 Richard's Gourmet Coffee
124 Turnpike St # 10
West Bridgewater, MA 02379-1046 508-587-0800
Fax: 508-587-8139   800-370-2633
sales@richardsgourmet.com
www.richardsgourmet.com
Private label packer of flavored coffees and teas,
lemonade, cappuccino, cocoa, spiced cider, etc
President: Richard Salzman
Estimated Sales: Below $ 5 Million
Number Employees: 10-19
Type of Packaging: Private Label
Brands:
Richard's Gourmet

12107 Richards Maple Products
545 Water St
Chardon, OH 44024-1186   440-286-4160
Fax: 440-286-7203   800-352-4052
sales@richardsmapleproducts.com
www.richardsmapleproducts.com
Processor of maple candy and syrup
President: Debbie Richards
Marketing Director: Debbie Richards
CFO: Annette Polson
Estimated Sales: Under $1 Million
Number Employees: 5-9
Sq. footage: 4160
Type of Packaging: Consumer, Private Label, Bulk
Brands:
Richards' Maple Candy
Richards' Maple Syru

12108 Richards Natural Foods
15213 S Hinman Road
Eagle, MI 48822-9703   517-627-7965
Different kinds of food
President: Richard Osterbeck
Estimated Sales: Under $500,000
Number Employees: 1-4

12109 Richardson Brands Company
7751 SW 62nd Ave # 200
South Miami, FL 33143-4908   305-667-4075
Fax: 305-667-5240   800-839-8938
info@richardsonbrands.com
www.richardsonbrands.com
Processor, importer and exporter of bagged and
boxed confectionery products including color coated
baking chocolate chips, soft and hard mints, chewing gum and chocolate caramel toffees; also, panned
and seasonal candy
Owner: Richard P Anderson
VP Research and Development: Kalman Vadasz
Senior VP Sales & Marketing: Michael Smith

Estimated Sales: $25,000,000
Number Employees: 20-49
Sq. footage: 175000
Parent Co: Agrolimen S.A.
Type of Packaging: Consumer, Food Service, Pri-
vate Label, Bulk
Brands:
After Dinner
Bonkers !
Colombina
Moofus
Numb Drops
Popshots
Sour Chewy Candy
Tattoo Bubble Gum

12110 Richardson Foods Corporation
3268 Blue Heron Dr
Macedon, NY 14502-9343   315-986-2807
Fax: 315-986-5880 www.brfoods.com
Processor of sauces, toppings, crushed fruit, foun-
tain syrups and condiments
CEO: Eric Johnson
Estimated Sales: $ 20 - 50 Million
Number Employees: 100-249
Type of Packaging: Consumer, Food Service, Pri-
vate Label, Bulk

12111 Richardson Vineyards
2711 Knob Hill Road
Sonoma, CA 95476-9560   707-938-2610
Info@richardsonvineyards.com
www.richardsonvineyards.com
Wines
President/CEO: Dennis Richardson
Estimated Sales: Under $500,000
Number Employees: 1-4

12112 Richardson's Ice Cream
156 S Main St
Middleton, MA 01949-2452   978-774-5450
Fax: 978-777-6863
info@richardsonsicecream.com
www.richardsonsicecream.com
Ice cream
President: Paul Richardson
Estimated Sales: $ 5 Million
Number Employees: 5-9
Number of Brands: 1
Number of Products: 1
Type of Packaging: Consumer, Bulk
Brands:
Richardson's Ice Cream

12113 Richelieu Foods
15 Pacella Park Dr # 210
Randolph, MA 02368-1700   781-961-1537
Fax: 781-767-1751 www.richelieufoods.com
Frozen pizzas, meal solutions, salad dressings,mari-
nades and salsas
President/CEO: Vincent Gantergrossi
Sr VP Sales: Anthony Raucci
VP Sales: Phillip Scolley
CEO: Vincent V Fantegrossi
National Director Organic Natural Food: Jon
Deeter
VP Manufacturing Beaver Dam: Colin Swift
General Manager: James Campbell
General Manager: Jason Yoakum
VP Manufacturing Grundy Center: Walt Grineski
Estimated Sales: $100 Million
Number Employees: 250-499
Type of Packaging: Private Label
Brands:
Caterer's Collection
Chef Antonio
Grocer's Garden
Willow Farms

12114 Richfield Foods
800 1st Avenue NE
Cairo, GA 39828-2207   229-377-2102
Fax: 912-377-5797 www.deans.com
Table syrups and boiled peanuts
President: J Roddenberry Jr
Estimated Sales: $ 50-99.9 Million
Number Employees: 130

12115 Richfood Dairy
1505 Robin Hood Road
Richmond, VA 23220-1001   804-746-6206
Fax: 804-746-6057
Milk
Manager: Jeff Clough

*Estimated Sales:*Over $1 Billion
Number Employees: 10

12116 Richland Beverage Associates
2415 Midway Rd # 115
Carrollton, TX 75006-2500   214-357-0248
    Fax: 214-357-9581   sales@texasselectna.com
             www.hphardware.com
Processor and exporter of nonalcoholic malt beverages and beer; also, alcoholic beer
    President: Martha Zelzer
    Sales Manager: Glenn Rogers
*Estimated Sales:*Less than $500,000
Number Employees: 1-4
Sq. footage: 1500
Parent Co: Richland Corporation
Type of Packaging: Consumer, Food Service, Private Label
Brands:
    Texas Select

12117 Richman Festival Ice Cream Company
P.O.Box 389
Paterson, NJ 07543-0389   973-684-8935
              Fax: 973-684-3570
Processor and wholesaler/distributor of ice cream
    President: Mario Calbi
Number Employees: 20-49
Type of Packaging: Consumer
Brands:
    Festival
    Richman

12118 (HQ)Richmond Baking Company
P.O.Box 698
Richmond, IN 47375-0698   765-962-8535
    Fax: 765-962-2253   info@richmondbaking.com
            www.richmondbaking.com
Processor of graham cracker crumbs, cookie crumbs, crushed saltine crackers, cracker meal, packaged cookies, crackers and graham crackers; custom blending of breadings, batters and marinades
    President: Bill Quigg
    Executive VP: Loyce Sherrow
    Operations Manager: Bill Quigg
    Production Manager: Doug Tyree
    Plant Manager: Mike Miller
    Purchasing Manager: Gary Galinger
Estimated Sales:$9200000
Number Employees: 100-249
Sq. footage: 250000
Type of Packaging: Consumer, Food Service, Private Label, Bulk
Other Locations:
Brands:
    Butternut
    Butternut Baked Goods

12119 Richmond Baking Company
P.O.Box 744
Alma, GA 31510-0744   912-632-7213
    Fax: 912-632-7215   info@richmondbaking.com
            www.richmondbaking.com
Processor of batter mixes and breadings for meat, poultry, seafood and vegetables, dessert crumbs
    Manager: Jerry Lady
    Sales: Rick Theidel
Estimated Sales:$ 20 - 50 Million
Number Employees: 100-249
Sq. footage: 84000
Parent Co: Richmond Baking Company
Other Locations:
    Richmond Baking
    Richmond IN
    Richmond Baking
    McMinnville OR

12120 Rick's Picks
195 Chrystie Street
#602E
New York, NY 10002   212-358-0428
    Fax: 212-358-0231 www.rickspicksnyc.com
various types of pickles (sweet, savory and spicy)
    CEO: Rick Field

12121 Rico Foods
578 E 19th St
Paterson, NJ 07514   973-278-0589
    Fax: 973-278-0378   info@expreco.com
            www.ricofood.com
Hispanic foods
    President: Emilio Hernandes
    Vice President: Madeline Fernandez

*Estimated Sales:*Below $ 5 Million
Number Employees: 20-49
Sq. footage: 10
Type of Packaging: Private Label
Brands:
    Delicia
    Rico

12122 Ricos Candy Snacks & Bakery
740 W 28th St
Hialeah, FL 33010-1220   305-885-7392
    Fax: 305-885-7376   sales@ricostostaditos.com
            www.ricosusa.com
Processor of hard candy and snack foods including pork rinds and fried dough
    President: Albertina Padron
    VP: Steven Laderman
*Estimated Sales:*Below $ 5 Million
Number Employees: 10-19
Type of Packaging: Consumer

12123 Riddles' Sweet Impressions
6311 Wagner Road NW
Edmonton, AB T6E 4N4
Canada   780-465-8085
    Fax: 780-468-5929   riddles@telusplanet.net
            www.riddlessweet.com
Processor of candy including lollypop barrels and chocolate
    President: Bill Agnew
    Production Manager: Wendy Agnew
    Quality Control: Wendy Agnew
    VP Sales: Dave Read
Number Employees: 30-50
Sq. footage: 12000
Type of Packaging: Consumer, Food Service, Private Label, Bulk
Brands:
    Riddle's

12124 Ridge Vineyards
17100 Montebello Rd
Cupertino, CA 95014-5435   408-867-3233
    Fax: 408-868-1350   wine@ridgewine.com
            www.ridgewine.com
Wines
    President: Donn Reisen
    Sales Director: Donn Pelsen
Estimated Sales:$50-100 Million
Number Employees: 20-49
Type of Packaging: Private Label
Brands:
    Ridge Vineyards

12125 Rier Smoked Salmon
224 County Rd
Lubec, ME 04652-3611   207-733-8912
    Fax: 207-733-8986   888-733-0807
        rier.com   www.rier.com
Processor of hot and cold smoked, kippered and roasted Atlantic salmon; also, smoked salmon pate and lox, smoked chicken products
    Owner: Vinny Gartmayer
    Sales/Marketing: Frank Rier
Estimated Sales:$450,000
Number Employees: 5-9
Sq. footage: 3500

12126 Riffel's Coffee Company
10821 E 26th St N
Wichita, KS 67226-4524   316-269-4222
    Fax: 316-269-1361   888-399-4567
    riffels@southwind.net   www.riffelscoffee.com
Roast package and private label of arabica beans. Carries four brands of tes, Stasero Italian syrup, coffee jellies
    Administrator: Linda Price
    General Manager: Paul Hawley
    Plant Manager: Lewis Lusk
    Purchasing Manager: Chuck Anderson
*Estimated Sales:*Below $ 5 Million
Number Employees: 10-19
Number of Brands: 15
Number of Products: 700
Sq. footage: 5000
Type of Packaging: Consumer, Food Service, Private Label, Bulk
Brands:
    RIFFELS GOURMET COFFEES

12127 Righetti Specialties
P.O.Box 2513
Santa Maria, CA 93457-2513   805-937-2402
         Fax: 805-937-7243   800-268-1041
  susieq@susieqbrand.com   www.susieqbrand.com
Beans, seasonings, pie mix, sauces & salsas, beef jerky, grilling wood.
    President: Susan Righetti
    VP: Renee Fowler
*Estimated Sales:*Below $ 5 Million
Number Employees: 5-9
Brands:
    Righetti Specialty

12128 Rinehart Meat Processing
P.O.Box 6880
Branson, MO 65615-6880   417-334-2044
              Fax: 417-334-2059
Processor of diet lean ground beef, smoked bacon and ham, sausage and beef jerky
    Owner: Jack Harris
    President: Jack Harris
    Plant Manager: Tim Stewart
Estimated Sales:$ 10 - 20 Million
Number Employees: 20-49

12129 Ringhands' Meat Processing Plant
PO Box 304
Evansville, WI 53536-0304   608-882-5025
              Fax: 608-882-5121
Processor of meat products
    Owner: Larry Ringhand
    Marketing Director: Janis Ringhand
Estimated Sales:$500,000-$1 Million
Number Employees: 5-9
Type of Packaging: Consumer

12130 Rio Grande Valley SugarGrowers
P.O.Box 459
Santa Rosa, TX 78593-0459   956-636-1411
       Fax: 956-636-1449 www.rgvsugar.com
Processor of sugar cane
    President: Randy Rolando
    CEO: Steve Bearden
    Factory Manager: Mark Nittler
Estimated Sales:$79846022
Number Employees: 250-499
Sq. footage: 7000
Type of Packaging: Bulk

12131 Rio Naturals
5050 Robert J. Mathews Parkway
Suite 200
El Dorado Hills, CA 95762   916-719-3924
       Fax: 916-941-3690 www.rionaturals.com
Manufacturer and supplier of calorie free sweeteners.

12132 Rio Syrup Company
2311 Chestnut St
St Louis, MO 63103-2298   314-436-7701
    Fax: 314-436-7707   800-325-7666
    flavors@riosyrup.com   www.riosyrup.com
Manufacturer and exporter of syrups, extracts and concentrates for shaved ice, sno cones, slush flavors and bases and fountain syrups; also manufacturer of liquid food colors
    President: Phillip Tomber
    CEO: Bill Tomber
    Operations/Public Relations: William Tomber
Estimated Sales:$500,000-$1 Million
Number of Brands: 3
Number of Products: 1200
Sq. footage: 23000
Type of Packaging: Consumer, Food Service, Bulk
Brands:
    RIO

12133 Rio Trading Company
4924 Campbell Blvd # 120
Baltimore, MD 21236-5909   443-384-2500
       Fax: 443-384-2525 www2.toad.net
    Owner: Michael Sruanis
Estimated Sales:$500,000-$1 Million
Number Employees: 1-4
Brands:
    Rio Trading

12134 Rio Valley Canning Company
P.O.Box 935
Donna, TX 78537-0935   956-464-7843
              Fax: 956-464-2538

Processor of canned beans, peas, tomatoes, peppers and picante sauce
President: Robert Ault
CEO: Robert Ault
Marketing Director: Robert Ault
Estimated Sales: $ 5-10 Million
Number Employees: 20-49
Type of Packaging: Consumer, Food Service, Private Label
Brands:
Rio Valley

12135 Ripensa A/S
5781 Lee Boulevard
Unit 208
Lehigh Acres, FL 33971-6339   941-561-5882
Fax: 941-561-5885 export@ripensa.dk
www.ripensa.com
Baked goods, cookies, biscuits in boxes, tins, tray packs, containers and acrylic jars
President: Steen Thy Jensen
CEO: Richard Recchia
Estimated Sales: Less than $500,000
Number Employees: 1-4
Type of Packaging: Private Label
Brands:
Ripensa

12136 Ripon Pickle Company
1039 Beier Rd
Ripon, WI 54971-9063   920-748-7110
Fax: 920-748-8092 800-324-5493
odpal@yahoo.com
Manufacturer and exporter of pickles and pickle products
President: Darwin Wiese
Production Manager: Jeffrey Wiese
Estimated Sales: $ 50 - 100 Million
Number Employees: 50-99
Sq. footage: 45000
Type of Packaging: Consumer, Food Service, Private Label, Bulk
Brands:
Pickle O'Pete
Wisconsin Pride

12137 Rippons Brothers Seafood
1814 Hoopersville Rd
Fishing Creek, MD 21634   410-397-3200
Fax: 410-397-3208
Manufacturer of oysters, crabmeat and crabs including soft, steamed and fresh
Owner: Chan Rippons Jr Jr
Estimated Sales: $21 Million
Number Employees: 20-49
Type of Packaging: Consumer, Food Service, Private Label

12138 (HQ)Riser Foods
5300 Richmond Rd
Cleveland, OH 44146-1389   216-292-7000
Fax: 216-591-2640 www.rinirego.com
Ice cream
Manager: Anthony Rego
Estimated Sales: $ 100-499.9 Million
Number Employees: 500-999

12139 Rishi Tea
427 E Stewart St
Milwaukee, WI 53207   414-747-4001
Fax: 414-747-4008 866-747-4483
inquiries@rishi-tea.com www.rishi-tea.com
An award winning loose leaf tea company importing organic and fair trade certified tea fresh each season and direct from origin. Artisan teaware, iced tea and chai concentrate also available.
President/Owner: Joshua Kaiser
VP Sales: Benjamin Harrison
Estimated Sales: $1.3 Million
Number Employees: 9
Sq. footage: 32000
Type of Packaging: Consumer, Food Service, Private Label, Bulk

12140 Rising Dough Bakery
8135 Elder Creek Rd
Sacramento, CA 95824-2307   916-387-9700
Fax: 916-387-9800 orders@risingdough.com
www.risingdough.com
Cakes, pies, muffins, croissants and strudels
Owner: Colette Jamet
Estimated Sales: Below $ 5 Million
Number Employees: 20-49
Brands:
Rising Dough

12141 Rising Sun Farms
5126 S Pacific Hwy
Phoenix, OR 97535-6606   541-535-8331
Fax: 541-535-8350
elizabeth@risingsunfarms.com
www.risingsunfarms.com
Processor and exporter of natural foods including oils, mustard, pesto sauces, dried tomatoes, vinegars, salad vinaigrettes, cheese tortas and marinades
President: Elizabeth Fujas
VP: Richard Fujas
Sales: Jenn Woodward
Public Relations: Jim Woodward
Operations: Chris Hanry
Plant Manager: Richard Fujas
Purchasing Director: Lynn Perkins
Estimated Sales: $1500000
Number Employees: 20-49
Type of Packaging: Consumer, Food Service, Private Label, Bulk
Brands:
Rising Sun Farm Cheese Tortos
Rising Sun Pesto Sauces
Rising Sun Vinagrettes & Marinades

12142 Rit-Chem Company
PO Box 435
Pleasantville, NY 10570-0435   203-769-9110
Fax: 914-769-1408 ritchem@ritchem.com
www.ritchem.com
Artificial sweeteners including Ace K, aspartame, saccharin, xylitol, potassium sorbate and blends
President/Founder: Henry Ritell
CFO: Henry Ritell
VP Sales: Wayne Ritell
VP Purchasing/Logistics: Bruce Ritell
Estimated Sales: $ 10-20 Million
Number Employees: 8

12143 Ritchey's Dairy
2130 Cross Cove Rd
Martinsburg, PA 16662-7619   814-793-2157
Fax: 814-793-0099 800-296-2157
ritcheysdairy@hotmail.com
www.ritcheysdairy.com
Milk, fruit drinks and ice tea
President: Reid Ritchey
Estimated Sales: Below $ 5 Million
Number Employees: 50-99
Type of Packaging: Private Label
Brands:
Ritchey

12144 Ritchie Creek Vineyard
4024 Spring Mountain Rd
St Helena, CA 94574-9773   707-963-4661
Fax: 707-963-4936 rcv@napanet.net
www.ritchiecreek.com
Wines
President: R Minor
Co-Owner: Peter Minor
Estimated Sales: Below $ 5 Million
Number Employees: 5-9

12145 Ritchie Wholesale Meats
527 S West St
Piketon, OH 45661-8042   740-289-4393
Fax: 740-289-4375 800-628-1290
jritchie@zoom.net www.ritchiefoods.com
Processor and pork and beef; wholesaler/distributor of frozen foods, canned and dry groceries, produce and chemicals; serving the food service market
President: James Ritchie
Office Manager: Kevin More
Estimated Sales: $ 20 - 50 Million
Number Employees: 20-49
Type of Packaging: Consumer, Food Service

12146 Rito Mints
PO Box 312
Trio-Rivieres, QC G9A 5G4
Canada   819-379-1449
Fax: 819-379-0344 info@ritomints.com
www.ritomints.com
Candy, mints
President: Maureen Nassif
Number Employees: 20
Type of Packaging: Consumer, Food Service, Private Label, Bulk
Brands:
Ghost Talk

Rito
Sweet Notes

12147 Rito Mints
PO Box 312
Trois Rivieres, QC G9A 5GA
Canada   819-379-1449
Fax: 819-379-0344 info@ritomints.com
www.menthesrito.com
Processor and exporter of candy including mints, conversation hearts and lozenges
President: Morris Masif
General Manager: Peter Nassif
Number Employees: 15
Sq. footage: 16000
Type of Packaging: Consumer, Food Service, Private Label, Bulk
Brands:
Rito
Sweet Notes

12148 Ritts-Chavelle Snack Company
16677 Roscoe Boulevard
North Hills, CA 91343-6109   818-830-3305
Fax: 818-830-0685
Snacks
Owner: Rory Ritts

12149 Rivard Popcorn Products
PO Box 397
Landisville, PA 17538-0397   717-898-7131
Fax: 717-898-7265
Processor of flavored popcorn confections and extruded corn and rice curls and puffs
President: Robert Rivard
National Sales Manager: Joe Guasco
Number Employees: 50-99
Type of Packaging: Consumer

12150 Rivella USA
3100 NW Boca Raton Boulevard
Boca Raton, FL 33431-6650   561-417-5810
Fax: 561-417-5811
Carbonated soft drink
President: Alexander Bart
Estimated Sales: $1.1 Million
Number Employees: 8
Type of Packaging: Food Service, Bulk

12151 Rivendell Winery
P.O.Box 325
New Paltz, NY 12561-325   845-255-2494
Fax: 845-255-2290
rivendellwinery@vintagenewyork.com
www.rivendellwine.com
Wines
President: Robert Ransom
Vice President: Melanie Smith
Estimated Sales: Below $ 5 Million
Number Employees: 10
Brands:
Libertyville Cellars
Rivendell
Soho Cellars

12152 River Market Brewing Company
P.O.Box 901898
Kansas City, MO 64190-1898   816-471-6300
Fax: 816-471-5562 www.rivermarketbrews.com
Processor of beer, ale, lager, stout and seasonal
President: Dvid Pecha
Estimated Sales: $ 1-2.5 Million
Number Employees: 20-49
Type of Packaging: Consumer, Food Service

12153 River One
P.O.Box 5010
Vero Beach, FL 32961-5010   772-770-0432
Fax: 772-770-0858 800-288-6614
river1@aol.com
Grower and exporter of citrus fruits including oranges, tangerines and grapefruit
President: Cody Estes
Sales Manager (North America): Daniel Borer
Estimated Sales: $15000000
Number Employees: 1-4
Sq. footage: 3000
Type of Packaging: Consumer, Bulk
Brands:
Coral
Florida Fresh
Lagoon
Orchid
Tropic

12154 River Road Coffee
PO Box 252
Lake Clear, NY 12945-0252   315-769-9941
                              Fax: 315-769-7130
Coffee
     President: David Copeland
     General Manager: Michelle Yadon
Estimated Sales: $ 2.5-5 Million
Number Employees: 20

12155 River Road Vineyards
5220 Ross Rd
Sebastopol, CA 95472-2158   707-887-2243
                              Fax: 707-887-8160
                  wine@riverroadvineyards.com
                  www.riverroadvineyards.com
Manufacturer of wine; custom labels available
Estimated Sales: Under $500,000
Number Employees: 1-4
Type of Packaging: Private Label
Brands:
     River Road Vineyards

12156 River Run
PO Box 8165
Burlington, VT 05402-8165   802-863-0499
     Fax: 802-863-0377 ian@riverrunsoul.com
                  www.riverrunsoul.com
Sauce and condiments

12157 River Run Vintners
65 Rogge Ln
Watsonville, CA 95076-9418   831-726-3112
     Fax: 831-726-3112 riverrun@cruzio.com
                  www.riverrunwine.com
Wines
     Manager: J P Pawloski
Estimated Sales: Less than $500,000
Number Employees: 1-4
Brands:
     River Run

12158 Riverdale Fine Foods
919 N Main St
Dayton, OH 45405-4694   937-223-3225
     Fax: 937-223-9456 800-548-1304
                  info@daytonnut.com
                  www.riverdalefinefoods.com
Fine chocolates, nuts, snack mixes, cookie mixes,
specialty candy
     President: Stanley Maschino
Estimated Sales: $ 3 - 5 Million
Number Employees: 10-19
Number of Brands: 5
Brands:
     Candy Farm
     Dayton's
     Friesinger's
     Minute Fudge
     Yuletide

12159 Rivere's Seafood Processors
P.O.Box 246
Paincourtville, LA 70391-0246   985-369-6055
     Fax: 985-369-2595 goodfoods@eatel.net
Processor of crawfish, catfish and shrimp
     President/Owner: Darrell Rivere
Estimated Sales: $1-$5 Million
Number Employees: 1-4
Type of Packaging: Consumer, Food Service, Private Label, Bulk
Brands:
     Rivere's

12160 Riverland Vineyards
800 S Alta St
Gonzales, CA 93926-9501   831-675-2481
                              Fax: 831-675-2611
Processor and exporter of wine and sparkling wine
     Owner/President: Jon Moramarco
     General Manager: Wayne Childress
     Sales/Marketing Executive: Mike Jaeger
Number Employees: 100-249
Sq. footage: 800000
Parent Co: Canandaigua Wine Company
Type of Packaging: Consumer, Bulk
Brands:
     Caywood
     Coastal Vitners
     Deer Valley
     Dunnewood
     Mistic Cliff

12161 Riverside Packers
PO Box 2080
Drumheller, AB T0J 0Y0   403-823-2595
Canada   Fax: 403-823-3303
Processor of fresh pork, beef and sausage including
beef, pork and turkey; also, beef patties and jerky
     Owner/President: Grant Spooner
     Co-Owner: Dixie Spooner

12162 Riverton Packing
2515 E Monroe Ave
Riverton, WY 82501-6104   307-856-3838
Processor of meat products
     Owner: Rod Baltes
Estimated Sales: Less than $500,000
Number Employees: 1-4
Type of Packaging: Consumer, Food Service

12163 Rivertown Foods
4601 McRee Ave
St Louis, MO 63110-2239   314-776-5646
     Fax: 314-776-6468 800-844-3210
                  info@rivertownfoods.com
                  www.rivertownfoods.com
Manufacturer of salsas & mexican sauces, marinades, sauces, dressings, and spice blends.
     President: Paul Endraske
     CEO: John Schnoebelen
     General Manager: Monica Holtgreven
Estimated Sales: $500,000-$1 Million
Number Employees: 5-9
Number of Brands: 15
Number of Products: 153
Type of Packaging: Consumer, Food Service, Private Label, Bulk
Brands:
     Taste of the Hill

12164 Riverview Foods
1360 Bethleham Road
Warsaw, KY 41095   859-567-5211
                     Fax: 859-567-5213
Processor of smoked meats and barbecue and tomato
sauces; also, research and development services
available
     President: Bob Weldon
     VP Sales/Marketing: Robert Schroeder
     General Manager: Mike Benton
Number Employees: 50-99
Sq. footage: 25000
Type of Packaging: Consumer, Food Service, Private Label, Bulk
Brands:
     Riverview Foods Authentic

12165 (HQ)Riviana Foods
2777 Allen Parkway
Houston, TX 77019-2141
                     www.riviana.com
Rice and rice products.
     President/CEO: Bastiaan De Zeeuw
     VP/CFO: Gregory Richardson
     VP Marketing: Paul Galvani
     VP Sales: Thomas Forshee
     VP Human Resources: Gerard Ferguson
     VP Manufacturing: Stephen Isaacson
Estimated Sales: $363 Million
Number Employees: 1,000-4,999
Type of Packaging: Consumer, Food Service, Private Label, Bulk
Other Locations:
     Carlisle AR
     Clearbrook MN
Brands:
     CAROLINA
     GOURMET HOUSE
     MAHATMA
     MINUTE
     RIVER
     SUCCESS
     WATER MAIN

12166 Riviana Foods
P.O.Box 369
Memphis, TN 38101-0369   901-948-8556
          Fax: 901-948-3096 www.riviana.com
Processor and exporter of packaged rice products including bran
     Manager: Steve Strong
     Plant Manager: Steve Strong

Estimated Sales: $400 Million
Number Employees: 100-249
Parent Co: Riviana Foods
Type of Packaging: Bulk

12167 (HQ)Riviana Foods
P.O.Box 2636
Houston, TX 77252-2636   713-529-3251
     Fax: 713-529-1866 800-226-9522
     jwraa@gvtel.com www.riviana.com
Processor and exporter of wild rice
     President: W David Hanks
     CEO: Bastiaan De Zeeuw
Estimated Sales: $5-10 Million
Number Employees: 1,000-4,999
Sq. footage: 30000
Type of Packaging: Consumer, Food Service, Private Label, Bulk
Brands:
     Gourmet Grains
     Gourmet House
     Onamia
     Rare Gift
     Simmer 'n Serve

12168 Riviana Foods
30 Mayfield Avenue
Edison, NJ 08837-3821   732-225-7210
          Fax: 732-225-7217 www.riviana.com
Processor of rice including long and short grain,
boxed, white and brown
     Manager: Elton Kennedy Jr
     Marketing Director: Joseph Hafner
     CFO: Wayne Ray
     Vice President: David Hanks
Estimated Sales: $ 10-20 Million
Number Employees: 20-49
Parent Co: Riviana Foods
Type of Packaging: Consumer, Food Service, Private Label, Bulk

12169 Riviana Foods
403 S Washington St
Abbeville, LA 70510-6627   337-893-2236
          Fax: 337-893-1122 www.riviana.com
Processor of rice including boxed, white, brown and
long grain
     Manager: Eddie Gaspard Jr
     President: Joseph Hasner
     Sales/Marketing: Bertha Landry
Estimated Sales: $ 20-50 Million
Number Employees: 50-99
Parent Co: Riviana Foods
Type of Packaging: Consumer, Food Service, Private Label, Bulk

12170 Riviera Ravioli Company
643 Morris Park Ave
Bronx, NY 10460-2597   718-823-0260
          Fax: 718-823-0344 www.rivierapasta.com
Processor of fresh and frozen manicotti, cannelloni,
tortellini, cappelletti, gnocchi, fettuccine, lasagne
and cavatelli
     President: Joseph Giordano
     Plant Manager: Michael Somereve
Estimated Sales: $ 10 - 20 Million
Number Employees: 10-19
Brands:
     Riviera

12171 Road Runner Seafood
586 Rock Road
Colquitt, GA 39837-5905   229-758-3485
                              Fax: 229-758-3991
Catfish, conch, croaker, flounder, full line seafood,
mullet, oysters, shrimp
     President: James Stovall III

12172 Road's End Organics
120 Pleasant Street
Suite E-1
Morrisville, VT 05661-4410   802-888-4130
     Fax: 270-638-2265 877-247-3373
     mkoch@chreese.com www.chreese.com
Dairy free pasta and dip
     President: Matthew Koch
Estimated Sales: $ 3 - 5 Million
Number Employees: 1-4

12173 Roanoke Apple Products
PO Box 1061
Salem, VA 24153-1061   540-375-7341
                              Fax: 540-375-3782
          roanokeappleproducts@msn.com

Processor of vinegar including pure apple cider, white distilled and red wine
President: Glenn Dunville
Marketing Director: Deborah Dunville
Plant Manager: Randy Kesler
Estimated Sales:$1100000
Number Employees: 11
Sq. footage: 22000
Type of Packaging: Food Service, Private Label, Bulk
Brands:
Bandana
Heidecker
Old Kettle

12174 Roanoke City Mills
PO Box 1280
Roanoke, VA 24006-1280   540-343-9383
Processor of flour
President: John Gibson
Number Employees: 20-49
Type of Packaging: Bulk

12175 Roasterie
1204 W 27th St
Kansas City, MO 64108-3555   816-931-4000
Fax: 816-931-4040   800-376-0245
info@theroasterie.com   www.theroasterie.com
Coffee
Owner: Danny O'Neill
Customer Service Manager: Stacy Barter
Quality Control: Norm Killnorm
CFO: Bill Molini
CFO: Carla O'Neill
CFO: Chris Mikuls
Estimated Sales:$ 1-2.5 Million
Number Employees: 20-49
Brands:
Roasterie

12176 Rob Salamida Company
71 Pratt Ave
Johnson City, NY 13790-2255   607-770-7046
Fax: 607-797-4721   info@spiedie.com
www.spiedie.com
Manufacturer and importer of meat marinades, barbecue sauces, and gourmet spice blends.
President: Robert Alan Salamida
Estimated Sales:$4.2 Million
Number Employees: 10-19
Type of Packaging: Consumer, Food Service, Private Label
Brands:
Pinch
Spiedie Sauce
State Fair

12177 Robbie's Natural Products
3191 Grandeur Avenue
Altadena, CA 91001-4301   626-798-9944
Fax: 626-457-8705   info@robbiesnatural.com
www.robbiesnatural.com
Processor of natural and kosher ketchup, salsa, fruit syrup and sauces including barbecue, worcestershire, sweet and sour and garlic
President: Robbie Roberts
Sales Manager: Roberta Fleischer
Estimated Sales:$ 3 - 5 Million
Number Employees: 1-4
Type of Packaging: Consumer, Food Service

12178 Robbins Packing Company
P.O.Box 887
Statesboro, GA 30459-0887   912-764-7503
Fax: 912-489-2823   robbins1@fronhernet.net
Processor and packer of pork, beef, sausage and smoked meats
President: Wayne Paulk
President/Managing Partner: Rodney Poole
Sales Manager: Glen Brown
Plant Manager: Jack Kasses
Estimated Sales:$ 1 - 3 Million
Number Employees: 1-4
Sq. footage: 70000
Type of Packaging: Consumer, Food Service, Private Label, Bulk

12179 Roberian Vineyards
2614 King Rd
Forestville, NY 14062-9723   716-673-9255
Wines
*Estimated Sales:*Under $500,000
Number Employees: 1-4

12180 Robert & James Brands
950 E Maple Road
Birmingham, MI 48009-6408   248-646-0578
Fax: 248-646-6040
Condiments and relishes
Owner: Robert Arnold
Estimated Sales:$ 1-2.5 Million
Number Employees: 5

12181 Robert & Joseph
290 W Bannerman Avenue
Redgranite, WI 54970-9803   920-566-2333
Fax: 920-566-4341
Processed pickles
Partner: Robert Ory
Partner: Joseph Kazda
Number Employees: 20-49

12182 Robert F Pliska & Company Winery
101 Piterra Pl
Purgitsville, WV 26852   304-289-3493
Fax: 304-289-3900   877-747-2737
www.vineyardhome.org
Wines
Owner: Robert Pliska
Wine Maker: Robert F Pliska
Purchasing Manager: TC McGee
Estimated Sales:$ 1 - 3 Million
Number Employees: 1-4
Parent Co: Piterra Farms
Type of Packaging: Consumer
Brands:
101 Piterra Place
Assumption Wines
Mt. Betty
Mt. Mama

12183 Robert J. Preble & Sons
5 Westvale Road
Kennebunkport, ME 04046-6750   207-967-3477
Fax: 207-967-8690
President: Duane Preble

12184 Robert Keenan Winery
P.O.Box 142
St Helena, CA 94574-0142   707-963-9177
Fax: 707-963-8209   rkw@keenanwinery.com
www.keenanwinery.com
Wines
President/CEO: Michael Keenan
Wine Maker: Niles Venge
Estimated Sales:$ 1-2.5 Million
Number Employees: 5-9
Brands:
Robert Keenan Winery

12185 Robert Mondavi Winery
P.O.Box 106
Oakville, CA 94562-0106   707-259-9463
Fax: 707-963-1007   888-766-6328
info@robertmondaviwinery.com
www.robertmondaviwinery.com
Processor and exporter of wines
President/CEO: R Michael Mondavi
Sr VP Business Services: Steve McCarthy
VP Marketing: Martin Johnson
Operations Manager: Greg Evans
Plant Manager: Genevieve Janssens
Estimated Sales:$100+ Million
Number Employees: 100-249
Brands:
MONDAVI

12186 Robert Mondavi Winery
P.O.Box 106
Oakville, CA 94562-0106   707-259-9463
Fax: 707-963-1007   888-766-6238
info@robertmondaviwinery.com
www.robertmondaviwinery.com
Wines
President: Salst Mondavi
Founder: Robert Mondavi
Chairman: Robert Mondavi
Plant Manager: Genevieve Janssens
Estimated Sales:$ 1-2.5 Million
Number Employees: 100-249
Brands:
Robert Mondavi

12187 Robert Mueller Cellars
6301 Starr Rd
Windsor, CA 95492-9653   707-837-7399
Fax: 707-431-8365   www.muellerwine.com
Wines
President: Robert Mueller
CEO: Bruce E Ollodart
Estimated Sales:$ 1-2.5 Million
Number Employees: 1-4
Brands:
Mueller

12188 Robert Pecota Winery
P.O.Box 303
Calistoga, CA 94515-0303   707-942-6625
Fax: 707-942-6671
info@robertpecotawinery.com
www.robertpecotawinery.com
Wines
Co-Owner/Partner: Robert Pecota
Co-Owner/Partner: Kara Pecota Dunn
Co-Owner/Partner: Andrea Pecota White
Marketing: Andrea Pecota White
Sales: Andrea Pecota White
Operations Director/Guest Services: Brenda Wild
Consulting Winemker: Marco DiGiulio
Estimated Sales:$ 1-2.5 Million
Number Employees: 5-9
Type of Packaging: Private Label
Brands:
Robert Pecota

12189 Robert R. Young Sr. Company
P.O.Box 241
Unity, ME 04988-0241   207-948-3254
Fax: 207-338-3498
Owner: Robert Berry
Estimated Sales:$ 3 - 5 Million
Number Employees: 20-49

12190 Robert Rothschild BerryFarm
P.O.Box 767
Urbana, OH 43078-0767   937-653-7397
Fax: 937-652-1044   866-565-6790
customerservice@robertrothschild.com
www.robertrothschild.com
Preserves, mustard, salsas, dips, fruit, dessert toppings, extra virgin olive oil, dressings and herb vinegars
President: Marie O'Donnel
Chairman: Robert Rothschild
CEO: Jim Clegg
CFO: Dominick Maxwell
R & D: Martin Finan
Estimated Sales:$ 10-20 Million
Number Employees: 50-99
Type of Packaging: Consumer, Food Service, Private Label, Bulk

12191 Robert Rothschild Farm
P.O.Box 311
Urbana, OH 43078-0311   614-336-1135
Fax: 937-652-1044   866-565-6790
info@robertrothschild.com
www.robertrothschild.com
Gourmet mustard, vinagrette, sauces and preserves
Chairman: Robert Rothschild
CFO: Don Jones
Marketing/Public Relations: Jill Borering
Production Manager: Diane Oyer
Purchasing Manager: Steve Day
Estimated Sales:$ 10-20 Million
Number Employees: 50-99
Sq. footage: 35
Type of Packaging: Private Label
Brands:
Breadstick Dip & Pizza Sauce
Fiery Raspberry Sals
Honey Mustard Pretze
Raspberry Salsa
Wings-N-Things

12192 Robert Silverman Company
517 N Warwick Avenue
Westmont, IL 60559-1550   630-515-8100
Fax: 630-515-8196
President: Robert Silverman
Estimated Sales:$300,000-500,000
Number Employees: 1-4

12193 Robert Sinskey Vineyards
6320 Silverado Trl
Napa, CA 94558-9747   707-944-9090
      Fax: 707-944-9097 800-869-2030
rsv@robertsinskey.com www.robertsinskey.com
Wines
      Vintner: Rob Sinskey
      Winemaker: Jeff Virnig
      Culinary Director: Maria Helm Sinskey
      Founder: Bob Sinskey
      Sales Manager: Meg Bartley
      Sales Manager: Eric Sother
      Vineyard Manager: Kirk Grace
Estimated Sales: Below $ 5 Million
Number Employees: 20-49
Type of Packaging: Private Label
Brands:
      RSV

12194 Robert's Bakery
17516 Minnetonka Boulevard
Minnetonka, MN 55345-1000   612-473-9719
                          Fax: 612-473-1835
Bakery products
      President: Robert Larson
Estimated Sales: $ 5-9.9 Million
Number Employees: 20

12195 Robertet Flavors
10 Colonial Dr
Piscataway, NJ 08854-4198   732-981-8300
                          Fax: 732-981-1717
robertetflavors@robertetusa.com
                          www.robertet.com
Manufacturer and exporter of beverage and instant
tea mixes, dairy bases, extracts, citrus oils and
flavors
      Deputy Chairman: Peter Lombardo
      SVP R&D: John Scire
      VP Marketing: Steve Wilbur
      Sales Service: Kathy Boyce
Estimated Sales: $50-100 Million
Number Employees: 50-99
Sq. footage: 55000
Parent Co: Robertet
Type of Packaging: Food Service

12196 Roberto A Cheese Factory
7465 Lincoln Street SE
East Canton, OH 44730-9439   330-488-1551
                          Fax: 330-488-1552
Natural cheese
      President: Angelo Roberto
      Co-Owner: Armand Babbo
Estimated Sales: $500,000-$1 Million
Number Employees: 10-19
Brands:
      Roberto Cheese

12197 Roberts Dairy
3805 S Emanuel Cleaver Ii Blvd
Kansas City, MO 64128-2386   816-921-7370
      Fax: 816-921-3437 800-279-1692
                          www.robertsdairy.com
Dairy productss
      President: Jeff Powell
      CEO: Jeff Powell
      General Manager: John Beberneyer
Estimated Sales: $5-10 Million appx.
Number Employees: 250-499
Brands:
      Hiland-Roberts
      Roberts Dairy

12198 (HQ)Roberts Dairy Company
P.O.Box 3825
Omaha, NE 68103-0825   402-344-4321
      Fax: 402-346-0277 www.robertsdairy.com
Manufacturer of fluid milk, culture products includ-
ing sour cream, cottage cheese, and yogurts; also ice
cream
      President/CEO/COO: Jeff Powell
      Controller/CFO: Darrel Cech
Estimated Sales: $200+ Million
Number Employees: 250-499
Type of Packaging: Consumer, Food Service, Pri-
      vate Label, Bulk
Other Locations:
      Roberts Dairy Plant
      Kansas City MO
      Roberts Dairy Plant
      Des Moines IA
      Roberts Dairy Plant
      Iowa City IA

Brands:
      HILAND-ROBERTS
      ROBERTS

12199 (HQ)Roberts Dairy Company
P.O.Box 3825
Omaha, NE 68103-0825   402-344-4321
      Fax: 402-346-0277 gsmith@robertsdairy.com
                          www.robertsdairy.com
Manufacturer of orange juice and dairy products in-
cluding milk and ice milk mixes
      President/CEO/COO: Jeff Powell
      Controller/CFO: Darrell Cech
Estimated Sales: $300 Million
Number Employees: 500-999
Number of Products: 300
Type of Packaging: Consumer, Food Service, Pri-
      vate Label, Bulk
Other Locations:
      Roberts Dairy Company
      Norfolk NE
      Roberts Dairy Company
      Kansas City MO
      Roberts Dairy Company
      Iowa City IA
      Roberts Dairy Company
      Des Moines IA
Brands:
      HILLAD - ROBERTS
      ROBERTS

12200 Roberts Dairy Company
3805 S Emanuel Cleaver Ii Blvd
Kansas City, MO 64128-2386   816-921-7370
      Fax: 816-921-3437 800-279-1692
                          www.robertsdairy.com
Manufacturer of dairy products including milk, sour
cream, yogurt and ice cream specialties
      President/CEO/COO: Jeff Powell
      CFO/Controller: Darrel Cesh
      General Sales Manager: Larry Boudeman
Estimated Sales: $100+ Million
Number Employees: 250-499
Sq. footage: 60000
Type of Packaging: Consumer, Food Service, Pri-
      vate Label, Bulk

12201 Roberts Ferry Nut Company
20439 Yosemite Blvd
Waterford, CA 95386   209-874-3247
      Fax: 209-874-3707 orders@robertsferrynuts.com
                          www.ilikenuts.com
Processor and exporter of almonds and popcorn
      Partner: William Mallory
      Partner: Dorothy Mallory
Estimated Sales: $3135592
Number Employees: 20-49
Type of Packaging: Consumer, Bulk
Brands:
      Roberts Ferry

12202 Roberts Seed
982 22 Rd
Axtell, NE 68924-3618   308-743-2565
      Fax: 308-743-2048 robertsseed@gtmc.net
Processor and exporter of grain, soybeans, popcorn
kernels, wheat, corn and dry edible beans; certified
organic and GMO-free products available
      President: Joe Roberts
Estimated Sales: $950000
Number Employees: 1-4
Sq. footage: 15000
Type of Packaging: Private Label, Bulk

12203 Robertson's Country Meat Hams
P.O.Box 56
Finchville, KY 40022-0056   502-834-7952
      Fax: 502-834-7095 800-678-1521
                          www.finchvillefarms.com
Country ham
      president: William Robertson
      Marketing Director: Jim Robertson
      CFO: Margaret Davis
      CFO: Margaret Davis
Estimated Sales: Below $ 5 Million
Number Employees: 10-19
Type of Packaging: Private Label, Bulk
Brands:
      Finchville Farms

12204 Robichaux's Meat Market
717 W Mill St
Crowley, LA 70526-5505   337-788-4124
                          Fax: 337-788-4108

Meat
      President: Floyd Robichaux
Estimated Sales: Less than $500,000
Number Employees: 5-9

12205 Robin & Cohn Seafood Distributors
3225 Palmisano Boulevard
Chalmette, LA 70043-3633   504-277-1679
                          Fax: 504-277-1679
Seafood
      President: Fay Cohn

12206 Robinson Barbecue SauceCCompany
940 Madison St
Oak Park, IL 60302-4430   708-383-8452
      Fax: 708-383-9486 800-836-6750
      cdell@rib1.com www.rib1.com
Manufacturers of barbecue sauce
      President: Helen Robinson
      CFO: Charlie Robinson
      Marketing Director: Cordell Robinson
      Operations Manager: Bruce Swerdlow
Estimated Sales: $500,000-$1 Million
Number Employees: 20-49
Type of Packaging: Private Label
Brands:
      Robinson Barbecue Sauce

12207 Robinson Cold Storage
24415 NE 10th Avenue
Ridgefield, WA 98642-9449   360-887-3501
Frozen foods
      President/CEO: Allen Nirenstein
      Chairman: Thomas Klein
Estimated Sales: Less than $500,000
Number Employees: 1-4

12208 Robinson Dairy
P.O.Box 5774
Denver, CO 80217-5774   303-825-2990
      Fax: 303-825-8419 800-332-6355
      bward@robinsondairy.com
                          www.robinsondairy.com
Processor of ice cream, yogurt, milk and sour cream
      Plant Manager: Larry Glodek
Estimated Sales: $29400000
Number Employees: 50-99
Parent Co: Suiza Dairy Group
Type of Packaging: Consumer, Food Service

12209 Robinson's Barbecue Sauce Company
940 Madison St
Oak Park, IL 60302-4430   708-383-8452
      Fax: 708-383-9486 www.rib1.com
Processor and exporter of meat seasonings and
sauces including barbecue and hot
      President: Charles Robinson
      VP: Helen Robinson
Estimated Sales: $500,000-$1 Million
Number Employees: 10-19
Sq. footage: 10000
Parent Co: Robinson's #1 Ribs Restaurants
Type of Packaging: Consumer, Food Service, Bulk
Brands:
      Charlie Robinson's
      Charlie Robinson's #1
      Mississippi

12210 Robinsons Sausage Company
701 Robinson Rd
London, KY 40741-9018   606-864-2914
      Fax: 606-864-3252 robinson@mis.net
                          www.robinsonmeats50.com
Processor and wholesaler/distributor of meats in-
cluding whole hog sausage and deli items; whole-
saler/distributor of frozen foods and private label
items
      President: Jimmy Robinson
Estimated Sales: $5500000
Number Employees: 20-49
Sq. footage: 20000
Type of Packaging: Private Label

12211 Robler Vineyard
275 Robbler Vineyard Rd
New Haven, MO 63068-2102   573-237-3986
      Fax: 573-237-3985 info@robblerwines.com
                          www.robblerwines.com

Manufacturer of wine
Owner: Robert Mueller
Owner: Lois Mueller
Estimated Sales: Less than $200,000
Number Employees: 1-4
Brands:
Robller Vineyard and Winery

12212 Roca Food Sales
576 Colonial Park Dr # 130
Roswell, GA 30075-3794   770-993-0030
    Fax: 770-993-0792
Processor of frozen broccoli, carrots, cauliflower, zucchini and squash
Manager: Fred Everett
CEO: Fred Everett
National Sales Manager: Rob Rickerby
Estimated Sales: $ 1-2.5 Million
Number Employees: 5-9
Type of Packaging: Food Service, Private Label, Bulk
Brands:
Roca

12213 Roccas Italian Foods
P.O.Box 150
New Castle, PA 16103-0150   724-654-3344
    Fax: 724-654-4954
Tortellini, Ravioli and pasta products
President: Anthony Rocca
Estimated Sales: Below $ 5 Million
Number Employees: 10-19
Brands:
Roccas

12214 Rocco Enterprises
1 Kratzer Ave
Harrisonburg, VA 22802-4567   540-568-1400
    Fax: 540-568-1401   800-336-4003
info@rocco.com   www.cargill.com
Poultry, poultry products
President: John O'Carroll
CEO: George Pace
Chairman: Donna McCurdy
VP: William Christain Jr
VP Sales: Douglas Lights
Purchasing Manager: C Strickler
Estimated Sales: $ 450 Million appx.
Number Employees: 50-99
Type of Packaging: Private Label
Brands:
Marval
Shady Brook Farms
Valley Chef

12215 Roche Caneros Estate Winry
28700 Arnold Dr
Sonoma, CA 95476-9700   707-935-7115
    Fax: 707-935-7846   800-825-9475
info@rochewinery.com   www.rochewinery.com
Wines
President: Joseph Roche
CFO: Kerstin Kohlstrom
Marketing/Sales: Dino Montalbano
Estimated Sales: $ 5-9.9 Million
Number Employees: 10-19
Type of Packaging: Private Label
Brands:
ROCHE

12216 Roche Fruit
P.O.Box 27
Yakima, WA 98907-0027   509-248-7200
    Fax: 509-453-3835
Fruits
President: John Roche
Estimated Sales: $ 100-500 Million
Number Employees: 250-499
Number of Brands: 1

12217 (HQ)Roche Pharmaceuticals
340 Kingsland Street
Nutley, NJ 07110-1150   973-235-5000
Nutley.medinfo@roche.com
www.rochesusa.com
Manufacturer of vitamins including niacin, biotin, folic acid, beta carotene, sodium citrate, citric acid, pantothenic acid, A, B1, B2, B6, B12, C, D, E, K, etc
President/CEO: George Abercrombie
Estimated Sales: $100-500 Million
Number Employees: 4500-5000
Type of Packaging: Bulk

Other Locations:
Roche Palo Alto
Palo Alto CA
Roche Carolina
Florence SC
Roche Colorado
Boulder CO
Roche/Genetech
S San Francisco CA
Roche/Chugai
San Diego CA

12218 Rochester Cheese
4219 Highway 14 W
Rochester, MN 55901-6672   507-288-6678
    Fax: 507-288-6175   888-288-6678
tomf@rochestercheese.com
www.rochestercheese.com
Fresh grated Parmesan, dehydrated Parmesan and other hard Italian style cheeses. Also produces American style cheeses.
Manager: Greg Anderson
CFO: Sherry Hinkle
VP: Don Roberts
Business Coordinator: Steve Majors
R&D/National Accounts Manager: Harry Appleby
Plant Manager: Gene Enneking
Plant Manager: Paul Domovsky
Plant Manager: Scott Amos
Estimated Sales: $ 20-50 Million
Number Employees: 5-9
Type of Packaging: Private Label

12219 Rock Bottom Brewery
1001 16th St # 100a
Denver, CO 80265-0005   303-534-7616
    Fax: 303-534-2129 www.rockbottom.com
Processor of seasonal beer, ale and stout
Manager: Steve Kominski
Brewmaster: John Clure
President: Frank Day
Senior Managing Partner: Steve Kominsky
Estimated Sales: $ 10-20 Million
Number Employees: 250-499
Type of Packaging: Consumer, Food Service, Bulk
Brands:
Falcon Pale
Red Rock

12220 Rock Point Oyster Company
2182 Chuckanut Drive
Bow, WA 98232-8572   360-765-3765
    Fax: 360-766-6812
Oysters
Estimated Sales: $500,000-$1 Million
Number Employees: 1-4

12221 Rock River Provision Company
P.O.Box 897
Rock Falls, IL 61071-0897   815-625-1195
    Fax: 815-626-0185   800-685-1195
butchershop@rockriverprovision.com
www.rockriverprovision.com
Processor of beef and pork
President: David Hoffman
Estimated Sales: $ 10-20 Million
Number Employees: 20-49

12222 Rock-N-Roll Gourmet
15 Outrigger St
Apt 302
Marina Del Ray, CA 90292   424-228-4901
Fax: 310-751-6397   dan@rocknrollgourmet.com
www.rocknrollgourmet.com
potato chips, cookies and popcorn
President/Owner: Jean Ehrlich
CEO: Dan Ehrlich
CFO: Peter Vermeulen
Number Employees: 10

12223 Rockbridge Vineyard
35 Hillview Ln
Raphine, VA 24472-2403   540-377-6204
    Fax: 888-511-9463   rockwine@cfw.com
www.rockbridgevineyard.com
Wines
Onwer: Shepherd Rouse
Estimated Sales: $ 1 - 3 Million
Number Employees: 1-4
Type of Packaging: Consumer
Brands:
DECHIEL
ROCKBRIDGE VINEYARD

12224 Rocket Products Company
1740 Chase Drive
Fenton, MO 63026-0565   636-343-9110
    Fax: 636-343-0897   800-325-9567
bob.pinkerton@rocketproducts.com
www.rocketproducts.com
Manufacturer of beverage concentrates
Founder/CEO: Charles Lazier, Jr.
General Manager: Robert Pinkerton
Purchasing Director: Barbara Duran
Estimated Sales: $ 5 - 10 Million
Number Employees: 9
Number of Brands: 3
Number of Products: 11
Sq. footage: 15000
Brands:
Dair-E

12225 Rockies Brewing Company
2880 Wilderness Pl
Boulder, CO 80301-5401   303-444-8448
    Fax: 303-444-4796   boulderbeer@aol.com
www.boulderbeer.com
Processor of beer and ale
President: Jeff Brown
Vice President: Diane Greenlee
Marketing Director: Tess Bodine
Operations Manager: David Zuckerman
Production Manager: Eric Grimes
Estimated Sales: $ 20 - 50 Million
Number Employees: 50-99
Number of Brands: 9
Number of Products: 1
Brands:
Boulder
Boulder Amber Ale
Boulder Brews
Boulder Extra Pale
Boulder Pale Ale
Boulder Porter
Boulder Stout
Brown
Buffalo Gold
Cliffhanger
Fall Fest
Igloo
Porter
Rockies Brewing
Rockies Premium Draft
Stout

12226 Rockland Bakery
94 Demarest Mill Rd W
Nanuet, NY 10954-2989   845-623-5800
    Fax: 845-623-6921   800-734-4376
anthony@rocklandbakery.com
www.rocklandbakery.com
Processor of bread, rolls, bagels, cakes, pies and challah; wholesaler/distributor of hot dog rolls and wrapped danish; serving the food service market
President: Sal Battaglai
Sales Manager: Lester Schwartz
Purchasing: Anthony Battaglia
Estimated Sales: $35000000
Number Employees: 250-499
Type of Packaging: Consumer, Food Service

12227 Rockland Boat
20 Park Dr
Rockland, ME 04841-3441   207-594-8181
    Fax: 207-594-8161 www.hamiltonmarine.com
Seafood
President: Leni Gronros
COO: Steve Graebert
Estimated Sales: $ 5 - 10 Million
Number Employees: 10-19

12228 Rockport Lobster
54 Commercial St
Gloucester, MA 01930-5025   978-281-0225
    Fax: 978-281-8578
Lobster
Owner: Craig Babinski
Estimated Sales: $580,000
Number Employees: 1-4

12229 Rockview Farms
P.O.Box 668
Downey, CA 90241-0668   562-927-5511
    Fax: 562-928-9765   800- 42- 247
caroler@rockviewfarms.com
www.rockviewfarms.com

Fluid milk
President: Egbert DeGroot
CFO: Joe Valadez
CEO: Egbert De Groot
Sales Manager: Ken Lee
Plant Manager: Erroll McGowen
Estimated Sales: $ 50-100 Million
Number Employees: 100-249
Type of Packaging: Bulk

12230 Rocky Mountain Coffee Roasters
285 Main Street
Carbondale, CO 81623-2138   780-852-4280
Fax: 780-852-5910   800-666-3465
jrod@rockymountainroasters.com
www.rockymountainroasters.com
Coffee retail/wholesale/roaster
President: Jim Rodkey
CFO: Brad Woods
Vice President: Andy Johnsen
VP Marketing: Andy Johnsen
Operations Manager: Jonathan Kitchensa
Estimated Sales: Under $500,000
Number Employees: 5-9
Brands:
Clipper Foods
Whitney Distributing

12231 Rocky Mountain Honey Company
642 Pugsley St
Salt Lake City, UT 84103-1329   801-355-2054
Fax: 801-355-2054
Manufacturer of beeswax and honey
President: Floyd Meyer
Partner: Melvin Meyer
Estimated Sales: $1-3 Million
Number Employees: 1-4
Parent Co: Meyer Honey Company
Type of Packaging: Consumer, Food Service, Private Label, Bulk

12232 Rocky Mountain Meats
PO Box 2274
Rocky Mountain House, AB T4T 1B7
Canada   403-845-3434
Fax: 780-845-7418
Processor of fresh beef, pork and wild game including deer, elk, moose and bear
Type of Packaging: Consumer, Food Service, Private Label, Bulk
Brands:
Rocky Mountain

12233 Rocky Mountain Natural Meats
9757 Alton Way
Henderson, CO 80640-8496   303-287-7100
Fax: 303-287-7272   800-327-2706
bison@greatrangebison.com
www.greatrangebison.com
Buffalo products
President: Bob Dineen
Marketing Director: Paul Pernarbo
CFO: Bob Dineen
Estimated Sales: $ 10-20 Million
Number Employees: 10-19
Type of Packaging: Private Label
Brands:
Rocky Mountain Natural Meats

12234 Rocky Mountain Packing Company
P.O.Box 2450
Havre, MT 59501-2450   406-265-3401
Fax: 406-265-3401
Processor of meat products
Owner/President: David Swallow
Owner/CEO: Linda Swallow
Estimated Sales: $100,000-$120,000
Number Employees: 1-4
Type of Packaging: Consumer

12235 (HQ)Rocky Mountain Popcorn Company
4875 Ward Rd
Wheat Ridge, CO 80033-1942   303-278-4352
Fax: 303-666-1328   rmpopcorn@msn.com
www.rmpopcorn.com
Processor and exporter of ready-to-eat popcorn
President: Janice Charles
Number Employees: 1-4
Number of Brands: 1
Number of Products: 10
Sq. footage: 20000

Type of Packaging: Consumer, Food Service, Private Label, Bulk
Brands:
Rocky Mountain Popcorn

12236 Rocky Point Shrimp Association
305 E Buchanan Street
Phoenix, AZ 85004-2520   602-254-8041
Fax: 602-523-9637
Shrimp
Estimated Sales: $ 3 - 5 Million
Number Employees: 5-9

12237 Rocky Top Country
4201 Wears Valley Rd
Sevierville, TN 37862-8153   865-428-7311
Fax: 865-428-7524 www.rockytopcountry.com
Fudge
Owner: Robert Glenn
Estimated Sales: $300,000-500,000
Number Employees: 1-4
Type of Packaging: Consumer

12238 Rocky Top Farms
11486 Essex Rd
Ellsworth, MI 49729-9650   231-599-2251
Fax: 231-599-2352   800-862-9303
sales@rockytopfarms.com
www.rockytopfarms.com
Processor and exporter of preserves including raspberry, cherry, strawberry, blackberry and black raspberry; also, butter toppings
President: Tom Cooper
Estimated Sales: $ 3 - 5 Million
Number Employees: 5-9
Type of Packaging: Consumer, Bulk

12239 Rod's Food Products
17380 Railroad St
City of Industry, CA 91748-1023   909-839-8925
Fax: 626-964-5447
Processor and exporter of salad dressings, chip dips, dairy and nondairy sour creams and aerosol whip toppings
Plant Manager: Stuart Saito
Number Employees: 100-249
Parent Co: Dean Foods Company
Type of Packaging: Consumer, Food Service, Private Label, Bulk

12240 Rodda Coffee Company
PO Box 290
Yachats, OR 97498-0290   541-547-4132
Fax: 888-919-2722   ycch@teleport.com
Coffee
President: Tom Rodda
Estimated Sales: Under $500,000
Number Employees: 10-19
Brands:
Rodda Coffee

12241 Rodelle Vanillas
3461 Precision Drive
Fort Collins, CO 80528   970-482-8845
800-898-5457
info@rodellevanilla.com
www.rodellevanilla.com
vanilla, baking essential, herbs and spices

12242 Rodney Strong Vineyards
P.O.Box 6010
Healdsburg, CA 95448-6010   707-433-6521
Fax: 707-433-0939   800-474-9463
info@rodneystrong.com   www.rodneystrong.com
Wines
Proptietor: Tom Klein
VP, Director of Winemaking: Rick Sayre
Estimated Sales: $ .5 - 1 million
Number Employees: 5-9
Type of Packaging: Private Label
Brands:
Rodney Strong

12243 Roelli Cheese Company
15985 State Road 11
Shullsburg, WI 53586   608-965-3779
Fax: 608-965-4510   800-575-4372
www.roellicheese.com
Cheese
President: Dave Roelli
VP: Gary Roelli
Estimated Sales: $ 1 - 3 Million
Number Employees: 10-19

Brands:
Balderson
Bingham Hill Cheeses

12244 Roger Wood Foods
P.O.Box 2926
Savannah, GA 31402-2926   912-964-6335
Fax: 912-964-6367   800-849-9272
david@rodgerwoods.com
www.rogerwoodfoods.com
Sausage
President: David W Solana
CFO: Camille Brown
Director Operations: Bob Lytle
Plant Engineer: Tony Roberts
Estimated Sales: $ 50-100 Million
Number Employees: 100-249
Brands:
Billies

12245 Roger's Recipe
518 Perron Hl
Glover, VT 05839-9735   802-525-3050
Brittle made with maple syrup
Owner: Michael Rogers
Estimated Sales: $300,000-500,000
Number Employees: 1-4
Type of Packaging: Consumer

12246 Rogers Bakery
33 Whiting Street
Plainville, CT 06062-2218   860-747-1686
Manufacturer of breads, rolls, pastries and cookies
President/Co-Owner: Laura Rogers
VP/Co-Owner: Kenneth Rogers
Estimated Sales: $3-5 Million
Number Employees: 20
Type of Packaging: Consumer, Food Service

12247 Rogers Brothers
PO Box 419
Galesburg, IL 61402-0419   309-342-2127
Fax: 309-342-4147
Manufacturer and Wholesaler/distributor of frozen meat and seafood, frozen food, dry goods, dairy products and produce
President: Frank Rogers
VP: George Rogers
Operations Manager: John Rogers
Estimated Sales: $65 Million
Number Employees: 41
Sq. footage: 35000

12248 (HQ)Rogers Sugar
4026 Notre-Dame Street E
Montreal, QC H1W 2K3
Canada   514-527-8686
Fax: 514-527-1610   infos@rogerssugar.com
www.rogerssugar.com
Leading refiner, processor, distributor and marketer of sugar products
President/CEO: Pierre Cote
Sr. VP Sales/Marketing: Dennis Hurl
Sr. VP Operations/Logistics/COO: Yvon Paquin
Number Employees: 325
Type of Packaging: Consumer, Food Service, Bulk
Other Locations:
Vancouver, BC
Taber, Alberta

12249 Rogers Sugar Limited
123 Rogers Street
Vancouver, BC V6A 3N2
Canada   604-253-1131
Fax: 604-253-2517   800-661-5350
infos@rogerssugar.com   www.rogerssugar.com
Processor of dried molasses beet pulp, sugar feed molasses, white granulated sugar and liquid sucrose invert
President/CEO: Pierre Cote
CFO: Daniel Lafrance
Number Employees: 196
Number of Products: 23
Sq. footage: 15
Parent Co: Lantic Sugar Limited
Type of Packaging: Consumer, Food Service, Bulk
Other Locations:
Rogers Sugar Limited
Alberta, Canada
Brands:
Roger's

12250 Rogers' Chocolates Ltd
913 Government Street
Victoria, BC V8W 1X5
Canada
    250-727-6851
Fax: 250-727-6854 800-663-2220
info@rogerschocolates.com
www.rogerschocolates.com
Processor and exporter of confectionery products including boxed cream-filled and dark chocolates, chocolate mint wafers, almond brittles, caramel nutcorn, fudge, etc
President: Jim Ralph
Estimated Sales: $725,100
Number Employees: 110
Sq. footage: 29000
Type of Packaging: Consumer, Private Label
Brands:
   Rogers Imperials
   Victoria Creams

12251 Rogue Ales
2320 SE Osu Dr
Newport, OR 97365-5261
    541-265-3188
Fax: 541-265-7528
Processor and exporter of ale, lager and barley wine
President: Jack Joyce
General Manager: Jim Cline
CEO: Jack Choice
Estimated Sales: $8696522
Number Employees: 50-99
Type of Packaging: Consumer, Food Service

12252 Rogue Creamery
P.O.Box 3606
Central Point, OR 97502-0024
    541-665-1155
Fax: 541-665-1133 info@roguecreamery.com
www.roguecreamery.com
Processor of butter and cheese including cheddar and blue vein cheese.
President/Owner: David Gremmels
CEO: Cary Bryant
Marketing Director: Thomas Vella
Plant Manager: Craig Nelson
Purchasing Manager: Lisa Lawrence
Estimated Sales: $8,000,000
Number Employees: 20-49
Number of Brands: 10
Number of Products: 20
Sq. footage: 40000
Parent Co: Vella Cheese
Type of Packaging: Consumer, Food Service, Bulk

12253 Rohrbach Brewing Company
3859 Buffalo Rd
Rochester, NY 14624-1103
    585-594-9800
Fax: 585-594-1960 info@rohrbachs.com
www.rohrbachs.com
Processor of seasonal beer, ale, stout and lager
President: John Urlaub
CFO: Sam Fletcher
Estimated Sales: $ 1-2.5 Million
Number Employees: 20-49
Type of Packaging: Consumer, Food Service

12254 Rohtstein Corporation
P.O.Box 2129
Woburn, MA 01888-0229
    781-935-8300
Fax: 781-932-3917
Processor of canned pie filling including mince meat
President: Steven A Rohtstein
Executive VP: Eugene Cohen
Sales/Marketing: Barney Butler
Estimated Sales: $ 50 - 100 Million
Number Employees: 50-99
Parent Co: Rohtstein Corporation
Type of Packaging: Food Service

12255 Rohtstein Corporation
P.O.Box 2129
Woburn, MA 01888-0229
    781-935-8300
Fax: 781-932-3917
Canned vegetable and juices
President/Treasurer: Steven Rohtstein
Estimated Sales: $18 Million
Number Employees: 50-99

12256 Rokeach Food Corporation
80 Avenue K
Newark, NJ 07105-3803
    973-589-1472
Fax: 973-589-5298 rokeach@prodigy.com
Ethnic foods
CEO: Victor Ostreicher
Estimated Sales: Less than $500,000
Number Employees: 100-249

Brands:
   Jericho Canyon Red
   Rokeach Food

12257 Roland Industries
2280 Chaffee Drive
Saint Louis, MO 63146-3304
    314-567-3800
Fax: 314-567-5211 800-325-1183
customer.service@abitec-roland.com
www.abitec-roland.com
Processor of breadings, batters, baking powder, fermentation additives, dough conditioners, sausage/meat binders, chocolate milk, baking and cake mixes, etc.; exporter of baking mixes
COO: Ian MacEwan
Vice President: Terry McGuire IV
Plant Manager: Keith Gill
Purchasing Manager: Mary Gajewski
Number Employees: 100-249
Sq. footage: 70000
Parent Co: Abitec Corporation
Type of Packaging: Private Label, Bulk
Brands:
   Best O' the Wheat
   Choice Foods
   Gold N Good
   Golden Meal
   Heritage Hearth

12258 Rolet Food Products Company
70 Scott Ave
Brooklyn, NY 11237-1308
    718-497-0476
Fax: 718-497-0137 rolet@aol.com
www.rolets.com
Sausage and meats, snack foods
President: Mark Turetsky
Executive VP: Charles Littman
Operations Manager: Miles Turetsky
Estimated Sales: $ 10-20 Million
Number Employees: 50-99
Sq. footage: 20
Type of Packaging: Private Label
Brands:
   Delifresh
   Jimmy's
   Potatomania
   Side Show

12259 Roller Ed
1115 Ridgeway Ave # 2
Rochester, NY 14615-3755
    585-458-8020
Fax: 585-458-8169
Manufacturer of Condiments including horseradish and cocktail sauces
Owner: Mike Mendick
Estimated Sales: $1-2.5 Million
Number Employees: 1-4
Number of Products: 2
Sq. footage: 10000
Type of Packaging: Consumer, Food Service, Private Label, Bulk
Brands:
   PRIVATE LABELS
   ROLLERS

12260 Rolling Hills Vineyards
126 Wood Rd
Camarillo, CA 93010-8334
    805-484-8100
Fax: 805-484-8100 www.travelenvoy.com
Wines
President: Ed Pagor
Estimated Sales: Less than $500,000
Number Employees: 1-4
Brands:
   Tempanillo

12261 Rolling Pin Bakery
119 5th Avenue W
Bow Island, AB T0K 0G0
Canada
    403-545-2434
Fax: 403-545-2167
Processor of bread, doughnuts, cakes and pastries
Partner: John Sytsma
Partner: Ineke Sytsma
Number Employees: 1-4
Sq. footage: 1375
Type of Packaging: Consumer, Food Service

12262 Rolling Pin Bakery
2211 Washington Street
Great Bend, KS 67530-2454
    316-793-5381
Baked goods
President: Dave Cooley

Estimated Sales: $500,000 appx.
Number Employees: 1-4

12263 Rolling Pin Manufacturing Corporation
1511 Grandview Dr
S San Francisco, CA 94080-4911
    650-952-7324
Fax: 510-780-1433
Estimated Sales: $ 1 - 5 Million
Number Employees: 5-9

12264 Rollingstone Chevre
P.O.Box 683
Parma, ID 83660-0683
    208-722-6460
Fax: 208-722-6460 chevre@mac.com
www.rollingstonechevre.com
Goat cheese
Owner: Karen Evans
Owner: Charles Evans
Estimated Sales: $150,000
Number Employees: 1-4
Type of Packaging: Consumer, Bulk

12265 Roma
P.O.Box 187
Rice, MN 56367-0187
    320-393-2060
Fax: 320-393-2800 800-328-8514
jefflande@vistarvsa.com www.vistarvsa.com
Natural health food
President: Bill Hanson
Estimated Sales: $ 100-500 Million
Number Employees: 100-249
Brands:
   Assoluti
   Baywood
   Beyond
   Grande
   Hearth Land
   Paincone

12266 Roma & Ray's Italian Bakery
45 Railroad Ave
Valley Stream, NY 11580-6030
    516-825-7610
Fax: 516-887-6866
Italian baked goods
Owner: Robert M De-Giovanni
Estimated Sales: $ 10-20 Million
Number Employees: 10-19

12267 Roma Bakeries
523 Marchesano Dr
Rockford, IL 61102-3596
    815-964-6737
Fax: 815-964-6057
Manufacturer of rolls, bread, danish and pies
President: John Bowler
CFO: Gene Bowler
Vice President: Marilyn Bowler
Estimated Sales: $500,000-$1 Million
Number Employees: 10-19
Type of Packaging: Consumer
Brands:
   Roma Bakeries

12268 Roma Bakery
P.O.Box 348
San Jose, CA 95103-0348
    408-294-0123
Fax: 408-294-0157
Manufacturer of bread, buns and rolls
President: Robert Pera
Secretary: Steven Pera
Estimated Sales: $ 10 - 20 Million
Number Employees: 50-99

12269 Roma Distributing
1937 Windsor Drive
Sierra Vista, AZ 85635-4852
    520-459-8249
Fax: 520-452-8204
Proprietor: Robert Valdez

12270 Roma Packing Company
2354 S Leavitt St
Chicago, IL 60608-4030
    773-927-7371
Fax: 773-927-7370
Processor of sausage including Italian and Polish
President: Steven Lombardi
Owner: Marsha Caputo
Estimated Sales: $ 3 - 5 Million
Number Employees: 5-9
Type of Packaging: Consumer, Private Label, Bulk

12271 Roman Meal Milling Company
P.O.Box 11126
Tacoma, WA 98411-0126
    253-475-0964
Fax: 253-475-1906 www.romanmeal.com

Oats, wheat, barley
President: William Matthaei
Estimated Sales: $ 10 - 20 Million
Number Employees: 50-99

12272 Roman Meal Milling Company
4014 15th Ave N
Fargo, ND 58102-2833   701-282-9656
          Fax: 701-282-9743 877-282-9743
          sales@romanmealmilling.com
          www.dakotaspecialtymilling.com
Processor of whole grain cereals, flour and baking
mixes; also, specialty grain; exporter of baking
mixes and whole grain
VP: Joel Dick
VP Sales/Marketing: Wayne Flood
VP Manufacturing: Joel Dick
Plant Manager: Bill Fletcher
Customer Service: Bernadine King
Estimated Sales: $15000000
Number Employees: 50-99
Type of Packaging: Consumer, Food Service, Pri-
vate Label, Bulk

12273 Roman Packing Company
904 W Omaha Ave
Norfolk, NE 68701-5842   402-371-5990
          Fax: 402-371-5639 800-373-5990
          tydog8@hotmail.com
Processor of meat products including dressed beef,
pork, sausage and luncheon meats
President: Wendell Newcomb
Estimated Sales: $ 10 - 20 Million
Number Employees: 20-49
Type of Packaging: Consumer

12274 Roman Sausage Company
1810 Richard Avenue
Santa Clara, CA 95050-2818   408-988-1222
          Fax: 408-988-0546 800-497-7462
          prima49@aol.com
Processor and importer of patties including sausage,
salmon and tuna; also, salmon fillets
President: Amir Kanji
Estimated Sales: $1,100,000
Number Employees: 10
Sq. footage: 8000
Brands:
Prima Brands

12275 Romanian Kosher Sausage
7200 N Clark St
Chicago, IL 60626-2416   773-761-4141
          Fax: 773-761-9506
Sausages
President: Arnold Loeb
Estimated Sales: Below $ 5 Million
Number Employees: 20-49

12276 Rombauer Vineyards
3522 Silverado Trl N
St Helena, CA 94574-9663   707-963-5170
          Fax: 707-963-5752 800- 62- 220
          sheanar@rombauervineyards.com
          www.rombauer.com
Wines
President: Koerner Rombauer
Sales Director: James Heinemann
General Manager: Dexter Rombauer
CFO: John L
Sales Manager: Joan Rombauer
Estimated Sales: $ 10-20 Million
Number Employees: 20-49
Type of Packaging: Private Label

12277 Romero's Food Products
15155 Valley View Ave
Santa Fe Springs, CA 90670-5323   562-802-1858
          Fax: 562-921-7240
Processor of Mexican sweet bread, tortillas, taco and
tostada shells and tortilla chips
President: Leon Romero Sr
President/Owner: Raul Romero
Estimated Sales: $ 20-30 Million
Number Employees: 100-249
Type of Packaging: Consumer, Food Service, Pri-
vate Label, Bulk
Brands:
Romero's

12278 Ron Tankersley Farms
1300 Factory Pl
Los Angeles, CA 90013-2214   213-622-0724
          Fax: 213-624-2369 www.oceanbeauty.com

Produce
Manager: Donald Rader
Estimated Sales: $ 50 - 100 Million
Number Employees: 100-249

12279 Ron's Produce Company
810 E Market St
Taylorville, IL 62568-2340   217-824-2239
          Fax: 217-824-2230
Produce Wholesalers
Owner: Michael J Nation
Estimated Sales: $ 3 - 5 Million
Number Employees: 5-9

12280 Ron's Wisconsin Cheese
124 Main St
Luxemburg, WI 54217-1102   920-845-5330
          Fax: 920-845-9423
Cheese spreads
Co-Owner: Ron Renard
Co-Owner: Terry Renard
Estimated Sales: Less than $500,000
Number Employees: 5-9
Type of Packaging: Private Label, Bulk

12281 (HQ)Ron-Son Foods
P.O.Box 38
Swedesboro, NJ 08085-0038   856-241-7333
          Fax: 856-241-7338 jim@ronsonfoods.com
          www.ronsonfoods.com
Manufacturer, importer and importer of canned
mushrooms, olives, olive oil, Italian pasta, ancho-
vies, roasted peppers and artichokes
CEO: James Bianco
CEO: James Bianco
VP Sales: James Bianco
Estimated Sales: $2-4 Million
Number Employees: 10-19
Sq. footage: 50000
Type of Packaging: Consumer, Food Service, Pri-
vate Label, Bulk
Brands:
GHIGI
LEONE BIANCO
RON SON
TRIFOGLIO

12282 Ronald Meyer Popcorn Company
P.O.Box 2019
Carnarvon, IA 51450-2019   712-664-2331
          Fax: 712-664-2331
Popcorn
Owner: Milton Meyer
Estimated Sales: $ .5 - 1 million
Number Employees: 5-9
Brands:
Ronald

12283 Ronald Raque Distributing Company
P.O.Box 9048
Louisville, KY 40209-0048   502-267-7400
          Fax: 502-267-8085
President: Ronald Raque
Estimated Sales: $ 3 - 5 Million
Number Employees: 20-49

12284 Rondel, Specialty Foods
8100 Hwy K South
Merrill, WI 54452   715-675-3326
          Fax: 715-536-3028 800-766-3353
          info@rondele.com www.rondele.com
Gourmet spreadable cheese
President: Robert Canstantino
CEO: Bob Constantino
Operations Manager: Don Delago
Estimated Sales: $ 10-20 Million
Number Employees: 50-99
Type of Packaging: Private Label
Brands:
Bread Essentials
Hahn's
Pub Cheese
rondelÃ©
rondelÃ©'s Garlic & Herb's

12285 Roney Oatman
735 Prairie Street
Aurora, IL 60506-5511   630-859-2800
          Fax: 630-859-2935
Manufacturer of ice cream, liquid shake mix
President: John Holmes
Estimated Sales: $20-50 Million
Number Employees: 50

Type of Packaging: Consumer, Food Service, Private Label, Bulk

12286 Ronnoco Coffee Company
4241 Sarpy Ave
St Louis, MO 63110-1704   314-371-5050
          Fax: 314-371-5056 800-428-2287
          info@ronnoco.com www.ronnoco.com
Processor of coffee
Owner: Frank Guyol III
VP Sales: Mark Guyol
Estimated Sales: $8000000
Number Employees: 100-249

12287 Ronnoco Coffee Company
4241 Sarpy Ave
St Louis, MO 63110-1704   314-371-5050
          Fax: 314-371-5056 800-428-2287
          www.ronnoco.com
Coffee
President: Frank Guyol III
Estimated Sales: Below $ 5 Million
Number Employees: 100-249
Brands:
Ronnoco

12288 Ronnybrook Farm Dairy
P.O.Box 267
Ancramdale, NY 12503-0267   518-398-6455
          Fax: 518-398-6464 800-772-6455
          info@ronnybrook.com www.ronnybrook.com
Milk, half & half, cream, chocolate milk, coffee
milk, strawberry milk, drinkable yogurts, yogurt, ice
cream and butter
President: Richard Osofsky
Estimated Sales: $ 1-2.5 Million
Number Employees: 10-19
Type of Packaging: Consumer, Private Label

12289 Ronzoni Foods Canada
185 The West Mall
Suite 1700
Etobicoke, ON M9C 5L5
Canada   416-626-3500
          Fax: 416-626-4569 800-387-5032
Processor of sauce, juice, chowders, condensed milk
and pasta including macaroni
President: Mel Few
Number Employees: 75
Type of Packaging: Consumer, Food Service
Brands:
Catelli
Classico

12290 Roode Packing Company
PO Box 510
Fairbury, NE 68352-0510   402-729-2253
          Fax: 402-477-5743
Processor of beef, sausage and pork including
smoked and cured
President: Tom Roode
Plant Manager: Dwayne Hasselbring
Estimated Sales: $3250000
Number Employees: 33
Type of Packaging: Consumer, Food Service

12291 Roos Foods
P.O.Box 310
Kenton, DE 19955-0310   302-653-0600
          Fax: 302-653-8458 800-343-3642
          roosfoods@aol.com
Processor of cheese, sour cream, exotic drinks, drink
mixes, soy base drinks, and BBQ snacks
President: Anna Roos
Operations Manager: Alex Martin
Plant Manager: Andy Deveza
Estimated Sales: $4900000
Number Employees: 20-49
Number of Brands: 8
Number of Products: 98
Type of Packaging: Consumer, Food Service, Pri-
vate Label
Brands:
Amigo
Mexicana
Roos
Santarosa
Snyapa
Wally's

12292 Rooster Brand Kosher Poultry
13714 Alma Avenue
Gardena, CA 90249-2514   310-719-2390

Poultry products
Sales Manager: Frederik Shadpour

12293 Roquette America
P.O.Box 6647
Keokuk, IA 52632-6647   319-524-5757
     Fax: 319-526-2542   800-553-7035
grain@roquetteamerica.com   www.roquette.com
Manufacturer and exporter of corn, wheat and potato
food ingredients including modified starches, proteins and high fructose and maltose syrups; also, liquid and solid sorbitol, mannitol, maltitol, xylitol,
glucono-delta-lactonemaltodextrins, dextrose, etc
    President: Michael Jurgenson
    VP: Ivan Hasselbusch
    VP Sales/Marketing: Kathy Holsinger
Estimated Sales: $95 Million
Number Employees: 250-499

12294 Rosa Brothers
1100 NW 22nd St
Miami, FL 33127-4528   305-324-1510
     Fax: 305-324-9182
Processor of fresh beef
    Manager: Gene Lamborda
Estimated Sales: $ 20 - 50 Million
Number Employees: 10-19
Type of Packaging: Consumer, Food Service

12295 Rosa Food Products Co Inc
2750 Grays Ferry Ave
Philadelphia, PA 19146-3801   215-467-2214
     Fax: 215-467-6850   rosa@rosafoods.com
             www.rosafoods.com
wholesaler/importer/manufacturer
    Owner: Giacomo Foti
    CEO: Giacomo Foti III
    CFO: Leonardo Foti
    Vice President: Mary Foti
    Research & Development: Angela Foti
    Marketing: Marisa Foti Beckey
    Sales: Dave Greenberg
    Public Relations: Murry Kristol
    Operations/Production: Matthew Foti Beckey
    Plant Manager: Murray Kristol
Estimated Sales: $55+ Million
Number Employees: 33
Sq. footage: 68000
Type of Packaging: Food Service, Private Label
Brands:
    Angela
    Mona
    Rita
    Rosa

12296 Rosalind Candy Castle
1301 5th Ave
New Brighton, PA 15066-2117   724-843-1144
     Fax: 724-847-2008   www.rosalindcandy.com
Processor of confectionery including chocolates
    President: James Crudden
Estimated Sales: $750,000
Number Employees: 10-19
Type of Packaging: Consumer

12297 Rosarita Mexican Foods Company
310 S Extension Road
Mesa, AZ 85210-1292   480-964-8751
            www.conagra.com
Processor of bottled and canned Mexican products
including refried beans, tacos, enchilada and hot
sauces, salsas, chili powder and taco and tostada
shells
    President/Chairman/CEO: Bruce Rohde
    Senior VP/Chief Communications Officer:
    Michael Fernandez
    Executive VP/CFO: Frank Sklarsky
Number Employees: 100-249
Sq. footage: 100000
Parent Co: ConAgra Foods
Type of Packaging: Consumer, Food Service, Pri-
vate Label

12298 Rosati Italian Water Ice
201 E Madison Ave
Clifton Heights, PA 19018-2690   610-626-1818
     Fax: 610-626-0706   srrosati@aol.com
Processor of Italian water ice
    President: Rich Trotter
    VP: David Schumacher
Estimated Sales: $700000
Number Employees: 10-19
Type of Packaging: Consumer

12299 Rose Acre Farms
P.O.Box 1250
Seymour, IN 47274-3850   812-497-2557
     Fax: 812-497-3311   800-356-3447
info2003@goodegg.com   www.roseacre.com
Producer of fresh shell eggs and egg products
    President: Lois Rust
    VP: Mark Whintington
    Marketing Manager: Greg Hinton
    Production Manager: Victor Ritteink
Number Employees: 1,000-4,999
Type of Packaging: Consumer, Food Service, Pri-
vate Label

12300 Rose Brand Corporation
PO Box 380833
Brooklyn, NY 11238-0833   718-789-6400
     Fax: 718-622-2934   800-854-5356
Processor of batch ice cream flavoring, fruit sundae
toppings and fountain syrups
    President: Morris Keller
    Customer Development: Elliot Keller
Estimated Sales: $ 3 - 5 Million
Number Employees: 12
Type of Packaging: Food Service

12301 Rose Brier
5184 NW Springhill Drive
Albany, OR 97321-9150   541-926-4378
     Fax: 541-967-7959   888-926-4378
rosebrier@dnc.net   www.rosebrier.com
Cooking oils, vinegars, olive oils, kitchen art
    President: Lynn Abernathy
Estimated Sales: $300,000-500,000
Number Employees: 1-4
Type of Packaging: Consumer
Brands:
    Abernathy
    Rose Brier

12302 Rose City Pepperheads
1725 SW Multnomah Blvd
Portland, OR 97219-2873   503-226-0862
     Fax: 503-256-8419
susan@rosecitypepperheads.com
    www.rosecitypepperheads.com
Flavored pepper jellies.
    Manager: Moses J Ross
Estimated Sales: $300,000-500,000
Number Employees: 1-4
Type of Packaging: Consumer

12303 Rose Creek Vineyards
226 East Ave N
Hagerman, ID 83332   208-837-4353
     Fax: 208-837-6405
Wines
    Manager: Katie Owsley
    Treasurer: Susan Martin
    Vice President: Stephanie Martin
Estimated Sales: $1-4.9 Million
Number Employees: 1-4

12304 Rose Frozen Shrimp
741 Ceres Avenue
Los Angeles, CA 90021-1515   213-626-8251
     Fax: 213-626-4802
Shrimp
    President: Ken Takiguchi
Estimated Sales: $ 10-20 Million
Number Employees: 20

12305 Rose Hill Distributors
81 Rose Hill Road
Branford, CT 06405-4015   203-488-7231
     Fax: 203-488-2100
Poultry
    President/CEO: Frank Vastola
Estimated Sales: $ 5-10 Million
Number Employees: 20

12306 Rose Hill Seafood
2621 Hamilton Rd
Columbus, GA 31904-8539   706-322-1269
     Fax: 562-220-1575
Frozen foods, canned foods goods, dry goods, poul-
try, seafood, produce, paper goods
    Owner: Jeff Lundsford
Estimated Sales: $ 1 - 3 Million
Number Employees: 20-49

12307 (HQ)Rose Packing Company
65 S Barrington Rd
South Barrington, IL 60010-9589   847-381-5700
     Fax: 847-381-9424   800-323-7363
postmaster@rosepacking.com
    www.rosepacking.com
Manufacturer of fresh, smoked and processed pork
products for the retail and food industries
    CEO: W R Rose
    President: Dwight Stiehl
    Controller: James O'Hara
    VP Sales/Marketing: Jim Vandenbergh
Estimated Sales: $ 50 - 100 Million
Number Employees: 50-99
Type of Packaging: Consumer, Food Service
Other Locations:
    Rose Packing Company Plant
    Chicago IL

12308 Rose Packing Company
4900 S Major Ave
Chicago, IL 60638-1589   708-458-9300
     Fax: 708-458-3248   800-323-7363
postmaster@rosepacking.com
    www.rosepacking.com
Canadian bacon and ham, pork sausage patties, pro-
cessed pork products, ribs, roasts and chops, spiral
slice bone-in and boneless hams, smoked and fresh
pork
    VP: Peter Rose
    Plant Superintendent: Joseph Mihalov
    CEO: W R Rose
    Plant Superintendent: Michael Reiter
Estimated Sales: $ 120 Million
Number Employees: 500-999
Parent Co: Rose Packing Company
Type of Packaging: Consumer, Food Service, Pri-
vate Label
Brands:
    Rose Brands

12309 Rose Trading Company
8457 Eastern Ave
Bell Gardens, CA 90201-6116   562-927-1115
     Fax: 562-927-1185   rosetrading@verizon.net
Wholesale food distributors; fresh and frozen; meat
specialists
    Owner: Neil Keohane
    Purchasing Director: Joey Rose
Estimated Sales: 5 Million
Number Employees: 5-9

12310 Rose Valley Group
P.O.Box 1285
Woodland, CA 95776-1285   530-666-7857
     Fax: 530-666-9568   rosevall@afes.com
Packer and exporter of honeydew melons
    President: Bill Rose
    Sales: Mike Rose
Estimated Sales: $100+ Million
Number Employees: 100-249
Type of Packaging: Consumer, Food Service, Bulk

12311 Rosebud Creamery
Route 3
354 Cornelia Street
Plattsburgh, NY 12901   518-561-5160
     Fax: 518-561-6068
Dairy
    President: Frederick Perras
Estimated Sales: $500-1 Million appx.
Number Employees: 1-4
Brands:
    Rosebud Creamery

12312 Rosebud Farms
525 E 130th St
Chicago, IL 60628-6999   773-928-5331
     Fax: 773-264-6845
Poultry
    President: Jerry Brucer
Estimated Sales: $ 50 - 100 Million
Number Employees: 50-99

12313 Roseland Manufacturing
119 Harrison Ave
Roseland, NJ 07068   973-228-2500
     www.dialpestcontrol.com
Jams, jellies and perserves
    Owner: Jerry Smith
Estimated Sales: $500,000-$1 Million
Number Employees: 5-9

12314 Roselani Tropics Ice Cream
P.O.Box 1170
Wailuku, HI 96793-6170   808-244-7951
          Fax: 808-244-4108 info@roselani.com
                              www.roselani.com
Processor of carbonated beverages and ice cream
    Manager: Todd Assmann
    Sales Manager: Mike Nobriga
Estimated Sales: $15151351
Number Employees: 50-99
Type of Packaging: Consumer, Food Service

12315 Rosell Institute
151 Skyway Avenue
Rexdale, ON M9W 4Z5
Canada   514-522-2133
          Fax: 514-383-4493 human@lallemand.com
                              www.lallemand.com
Manufacturer and exporter of food and dairy microbial cultures, lactobacilli and bifidobacteria; also,
custom formulations available
    President: Oliver Clech
    International Sales/Marketing Manager: Michel
    Ilesco
    Sales Manager (North America): Silvano Arnoldo

Number Employees: 50-99
Sq. footage: 50000
Parent Co: Rougier
Type of Packaging: Consumer, Private Label, Bulk
Brands:
    Ferlac
    Gastro-Ad
    Polylacton
    Probiotic-2000
    Rosell
    Rosellac
    Standard Formulation
    Vitanat

12316 Rosemark Bakery
258 Snelling Ave S
St Paul, MN 55105-2045   651-698-3838
                          Fax: 651-698-0828
Processor of baked goods
    President: Carol Rosemark
Estimated Sales: $ 5 - 10 Million
Number Employees: 20-49

12317 Rosen's Diversified
1120 Lake Ave
Fairmont, MN 56031-1939   507-238-4201
          Fax: 507-238-9966 800-798-2000
                              www.rosens.com
Processor of meat for restaurants, government cus-
tomers and food manufacturers in the U.S.
    President/General Manager: Ivan Wells
    Finance Director: Steve Guetter
    CEO: Thomas J Rosen
Estimated Sales: Nearly $ 1 Billion
Number Employees: 50

12318 Rosenberger's Dairies
P.O.Box 901
Hatfield, PA 19440-0901   215-631-9035
          Fax: 215-855-6486 800-355-9074
    info@rosenbergers.com www.rosenbergers.com
Manufacturer of dairy products including eggs, milk,
cream, sour cream and cheese; also, beverages in-
cluding apple juice, iced tea and fruit drinks
    VP: Marcus Rosenberger
    Production Manager: Jeffery Rosenberger
    Plant Manager: Gerry Whiting
Estimated Sales: $55 Million
Number Employees: 250-499
Type of Packaging: Consumer
Brands:
    ROSENBERGERS

12319 Rosenblum Cellars
2900 Main St # 1100
Alameda, CA 94501-7553   510-865-7007
    Fax: 510-865-9225 drzin@rosenblumcellars.com
                              www.rosenblumcellars.com
Wines
    President: Kent Rosenblum
    CFO: Tim Allen
    Quality Control: Les Horton
    Marketing Director: Kathy Coi
    Operations Manager: Ron Pieretti
Estimated Sales: $ 5-9.9 Million
Number Employees: 20-49
Number of Brands: 1

Number of Products: 40
Sq. footage: 58000
Other Locations:
    Rosenblum Cellars
    Healdsburgh CA
Brands:
    Rosenblum

12320 Roses Ravioli
219 E Walnut Street
Oglesby, IL 61348-1203   815-883-8011
                          Fax: 815-883-8409
Ravioli, tortellini and pasta sauce
    President: Barbara Shields
    Owner: Rose Causa
Estimated Sales: $ 2.5-5 Million
Number Employees: 1-4

12321 Rosetti Fine Foods
3 Railroad Ave
Clovis, CA 93612-1219   559-323-6450
          Fax: 559-323-2022 www.rosettis.com
Biscotti, bark confections
    President: Diane Rosetti
    Secretary/Treasurer: Dan Rosetti
Estimated Sales: $500,000-$1 Million
Number Employees: 5-9
Brands:
    Rosetti Fine Foods

12322 Roseville Corporation
120 Plum Ct
Mountain View, CA 94043-4899   650-592-8988
          Fax: 650-592-8966 888-247-9338
                              www.bigsmiley.com

Candy
Brands:
    BETTY TWIST & MATCH CHOCOLATE
    CANDY
    BIG SMILEY

12323 Rosina Food Products
170 French Rd
Buffalo, NY 14227-2777   716-668-0123
          Fax: 716-668-1132 888-767-4621
    gsetter@rosina.com www.rosina.com
Processor of Italian meat balls, sausage, pizza top-
pings and pasta
    President: Russell Corigliano
    Chairman of the Board: James Corigliano
    Vice President: Frank Corigliano
    CFO: Greg Setter
    Quality Control: Curtis Froevel
    Marketing Director: Mike D'Addieco
    Sales Director: Rich Baran
    Plant Manager: James Stock
Estimated Sales: $ 50-99.9 Million
Number Employees: 250-499
Type of Packaging: Food Service
Brands:
    Rosina

12324 Roskam Baking Company
P.O.Box 202
Grand Rapids, MI 49501-0202   616-574-5757
          Fax: 616-574-1110 www.rothburyfarms.com
Processor of croutons, stuffing, dry mix blends, ce-
reals, and snack components.
    President: Bob Roskam
    Customer Relations: Christina Lehtinen
    General Manager: Perry Kogelschatz
Estimated Sales: $76700000
Number Employees: 100-249
Type of Packaging: Food Service, Private Label,
Bulk

12325 Rosmarino Foods/R.Z. Humbert Company
16216 Turnbury Oak Drive
Odessa, FL 33556-2870   813-926-9053
          Fax: 813-920-0734 888-926-9053
              info@rosmarinofoods.com
              www.rosmarinofoods.com
Speciality award winning foods such as all natural
salad dressings, hearty pasta sauces, flavorful mari-
nades, great grilling sauces, tangy BBQ sauces, and
fiery hot sauces
    President: Rosemary Humbert
    VP Marketing: Roger Humbert
Number Employees: 8
Number of Brands: 3
Number of Products: 50
Sq. footage: 65000

Type of Packaging: Consumer, Food Service, Private Label, Bulk
Brands:
    BONNIES
    LUNA ROSSA
    ROSMARINO

12326 Ross Fine Candies
4642 Elizabeth Lake Rd
Waterford, MI 48328-2831   248-682-5640
                          Fax: 248-682-0457
Processor of candy and other confectionery products
    President: Janet Greaves
Estimated Sales: $300,000
Number Employees: 1-4
Type of Packaging: Consumer, Private Label
Brands:
    Ross Fine

12327 Ross Keller Winery
985 Orchard Rd
Nipomo, CA 93444-9769   805-929-3627
                          Fax: 805-929-4231
Wines
    President/Owner: Jacqueline Tanner
Estimated Sales: Below $ 5 Million
Number Employees: 1-4
Type of Packaging: Private Label
Brands:
    Ross Keller Winery

12328 Ross Laboratories
625 Cleveland Ave
Columbus, OH 43215-1754   614-564-0019
                              www.abbott.com
Processor and exporter of vitamins
    President: Thomas McNally
Number Employees: 5-9
Parent Co: Abbott Laboratories
Type of Packaging: Consumer
Brands:
    Vi-Daylin

12329 Ross Laboratories
901 N Centerville Rd
Sturgis, MI 49091-9302   269-651-0600
          Fax: 269-651-0741 www.abbott.com
Processor and exporter of health products including
health and dietetic foods and medical nutritionals
    Manufacturing/Packaging Manager: Steve
    Vanmol
Estimated Sales: $100+ Million
Number Employees: 500-999
Parent Co: Abbott Laboratories
Type of Packaging: Consumer
Brands:
    Ensure
    Isomil
    Similac

12330 Ross-Smith Pecan Company
107 Plantation Oak Dr
Thomasville, GA 31792-3540   229-859-2225
          Fax: 229-859-2382 800-841-5503
              info@ross-smith-pecans.com
              www.ross-smith-pecans.com
Manufacturer and exporter of nuts including shelled
pecans
    President: Betty McDuffie
Estimated Sales: Less than $500,000
Number Employees: 23

12331 Rossi Pasta
106 Front St
Marietta, OH 45750-3123   740-376-2065
          Fax: 740-373-5310 800-227-6774
    info@rossipasta.com www.rossipasta.com
Gourmet handmade pasta products and sauces
    Manager: Terry St Peter
    Chairman: Frank L Christy
Estimated Sales: Below $ 5 Million
Number Employees: 10-19
Type of Packaging: Private Label

12332 Rostov's Coffee & Tea Company
1618 W Main St
Richmond, VA 23220-4633   804-355-1955
          Fax: 804-355-6963 800-637-6772
    cctea@aol.com www.rostovs.com
Coffee and tea
    President/CFO: Tammy Rostov
    Founder: Jay Rostov
Estimated Sales: Below $ 5 Million
Number Employees: 5-9

Type of Packaging: Consumer
Brands:
    Rostov's Coffee Tea

12333 Rotella's Italian Bakery
6949 S 108th St
La Vista, NE 68128-5703   402-592-6600
    Fax: 402-592-2989 info@rotellasbakery.com
    www.rotellasbakery.com
Processor of hamburger buns, hoagies, bread loaves,
dinner rolls and bread sticks, hot dog buns and brat
buns, and specialty breads.
    CEO: Louis Rotella Sr
    CEO: Louis J Rotella Sr
    Sales Manager: James Rotella
Estimated Sales: $50000000
Number Employees: 250-499
Type of Packaging: Consumer, Food Service

12334 Roth Kase
PO Box 10
Mendham, NJ 07945-0010   608-328-2122
    Fax: 973-543-4566 info@rothkase.com
Processor of havarti, blue, muenster and commodity
cheeses
    CEO: Roth Kase
    Marketing Director: Roth Kase
    Sales Director: Stephen McKeon
Estimated Sales: $ 25-49.9 Million
Number Employees: 53
Type of Packaging: Consumer, Food Service, Bulk
Brands:
    Grand Cru Raclette
    Grand Crue
    Kronenost
    Pesto Havarti
    Rofumo
    Roth Kase
    Roth Kase
    Ustenborg
    Vangogh

12335 Rothman's Foods
4718 Delmar Blvd
St Louis, MO 63108-1706   314-367-5448
Ethnic foods
    President: Arthur Rothman
Estimated Sales: Below $ 5 Million
Number Employees: 5-9

12336 Rotteveel Orchards
6183 Reddick Ln
Dixon, CA 95620-9731   707-678-1495
    Fax: 707-678-1446 info@rotteveel.com
    www.rotteveel.com
Processor and exporter of almonds
    President: Neil Rotteveel
Estimated Sales: $500,000-$1 Million
Number Employees: 5-9
Type of Packaging: Bulk

12337 Roudon-Smith Vineyards
2364 Bean Creek Rd
Scotts Valley, CA 95066-3102   831-438-1244
    Fax: 831-438-4374 sales@roudonsmith.com
    www.roudonsmith.com
Wines
    Owner: Annette Hunt
    Owner: David Hunt
Estimated Sales: $ 1-2.5 Million
Number Employees: 1-4
Brands:
    Roudon Smith Vineyards

12338 Round Hill Vineyards
1680 Silverado Trl S
St Helena, CA 94574-9542   707-963-5252
    Fax: 707-963-0834 800-778-0424
    info@rutherfordwine.com
    www.roundhillwines.com
Wines
    Owner: Morgan Zaninovich
    VP: Mark Fedorchak
    Chairman: Erne Van Asperen
    President: Virginia Van Asperen
    Public Relations: Bonnie Zimmerman
    Production Manager: Keith Groves
    Plant Manager: Bob Iacampo
Estimated Sales: Below $ 5 Million
Number Employees: 20-49
Type of Packaging: Private Label
Brands:
    Round Hill Vineyards

Rutherford Ranch
Van Asperen Vineyard

12339 Round Rock Honey Co, LLC
1308 Chisholm Tr
#107
Round Rock, TX 78681   512-828-5416
    Fax: 512-828-5416 www.roundrockhoney.com
honey

12340 Rousseau Farming Company
P.O.Box 100
Tolleson, AZ 85353-0100   623-936-7100
    Fax: 623-936-7386
Processor of fruits and vegetables
    President: David Rousseau
Estimated Sales: $ 1-2.5 Million
Number Employees: 10-19

12341 Rousselot Gelatin
1231 S Rochester St
Mukwonago, WI 53149-9031   262-363-2789
    Fax: 262-650-8456 www.rousselot.com
Leading manufacturer of gelatins and collegans
    VP: Larry Jeske
Number Employees: 1,000-4,999
Type of Packaging: Bulk

12342 Route 11 Potato Chips
11 Edwards Way
Mt Jackson, VA 22842-2037   540-869-0104
    Fax: 540-869-0176 800-294-7783
    rtl1@shentel.net www.rt11.com
Specialty potato chips and mixed vegetable chips
    President: Sarah Cohen
Estimated Sales: $ 20 - 50 Million
Number Employees: 20-49
Type of Packaging: Consumer, Private Label
Brands:
    Route 11 Potato Chips
    Tabard Farm Potato Chips

12343 Routin America
140 E 80th St
New York, NY 10075-0389   212-772-2500
    Fax: 866-764-1883 800-367-1883
    sales@routin-america.com www.routin.com
Flavored syrups
    President: Jean Cloehte
Estimated Sales: $500,000-$1 Million
Number Employees: 1-4
Type of Packaging: Private Label

12344 Routin America
PO Box 193
Basking Ridge, NJ 07920-0193   908-630-0338
    Fax: 908-953-9216 sales@routin-america.com
    www.routin.com
Tea and coffee syrups
    President: Jean Clochet
Estimated Sales: $ 301 Million
Number Employees: 125
Brands:
    De Philibert Routin
    Ecorange
    Flavours of Summers
    Fruisco
    Fruiss Pet
    Ibiza

12345 (HQ)Rovira Biscuit Corporation
619 Avenue Cuatro Calles
Ponce, PR 00717-1901   787-844-8585
    Fax: 787-848-7176 www.rovirabiscuits.com
Processor of crackers and biscuits; exporter of
crackers
    President and Director: Rafael Rovira
    Executive VP/General Manager: Angel Rodriguez

    Quality Control: Carla Traverso
Number Employees: 100-249
Sq. footage: 45000
Other Locations:
    Rovira Biscuit Corp.
    Pueblo Viejo PR

12346 (HQ)Rowena's
758 W 22nd St
Norfolk, VA 23517-1925   757-627-8699
    Fax: 757-627-1505 800-627-8699
    rowena@rowens.com www.rowenas.com

Processor and exporter of gourmet pound cakes,
jams, curds, dry mixes and sauces
    President: Rowena Fullinwider
    General Manager: Joan Place
    Sales: Ann Cole
    Production: Renee Satterfield
    Warehouse Manager: Dom Tamikk
Estimated Sales: $620000
Number Employees: 20-49
Sq. footage: 13000
Type of Packaging: Consumer, Food Service, Private Label, Bulk
Brands:
    Rowena's
    Rowena's Gourmet Sauces
    Rowena's Jams & Jellies
    Rowena's Pound Cake

12347 Rowland Coffee Roasters
5605 NW 82nd Ave
Doral, FL 33166-3433   305-594-9063
    Fax: 305-594-7603 800-990-9039
    jc@javacabana.com www.medagliadoro.com
Roasted coffee
    President: Jose Souto
Estimated Sales: $ 2.5-5 Million
Number Employees: 5-9

12348 Rox America
P.O.Box 5561
Spartanburg, SC 29304-5561
USA   864-463-4352
    Fax: 864-463-8608 866-476-9872
    info@roxenergy.com www.zimmer-usa.com
Rox energy drink, Rox Aqua power cool drink
    President: Roland Zimmer
    CEO: Amy Rogers
Estimated Sales: $ 1 Million
Number Employees: 5-9
Sq. footage: 3500
Type of Packaging: Private Label
Brands:
    ROX ENERGY DRINK

12349 Roxy Trading
1388 W Foothill Blvd
Azusa, CA 91702-2846   626-610-1388
    Fax: 626-610-1339 roxytrading@earthlink.net
    www.roxytrading.com
Pacific rim, Asian specialty grocery. Products include soy crouton, wonton stripe and vegetarian
bouilion
    President: Elvis Tent
    Purchasing Manager: Paullett Ho
Estimated Sales: $ 10-20 Million
Number Employees: 20-49
Number of Brands: 3
Number of Products: 500
Sq. footage: 45000
Type of Packaging: Consumer

12350 Roy Dick Company
152 Harris Street
Griffin, GA 30223-7017   770-227-3916
    Fax: 770-227-3916
Catfish, shrimp, oysters, chicken
    Owner: Roy Dick

12351 Roy Robin Company
1108 Vincent Berard Rd
Breaux Bridge, LA 70517   337-667-6118
    Fax: 337-667-6059 www.bayoulandseafood.com
    Owner: Adam Johnson
Estimated Sales: $ 3 - 5 Million
Number Employees: 50-99

12352 Roy Stritmatter Company
220 Monroe Street
Hoquiam, WA 98550-1811   360-532-0710
Processor and exporter of frozen seafood including
salmon, smelt and sturgeon
    Owner: Roy Stritmatter
Number Employees: 1-4
Type of Packaging: Consumer, Food Service

12353 Royal Angelus Macaroni
5010 Eucalyptus Ave
Chino, CA 91710-9216   909-627-7312
    Fax: 909-627-7315
    information@royal-angelus.com
    www.royal-angelus.com
Manufacturer and exporter of organic pasta; also,
custom formulas and specialty shapes
    Manager: Glen Macy

Estimated Sales:$43 Million
Number Employees: 50-99
Sq. footage: 48000
Parent Co: Provena Foods
Type of Packaging: Consumer, Food Service, Private Label, Bulk
Brands:
  Royal

12354 Royal Atlantic Seafood
2 Carrie Lane
Gloucester, MA 01930-2328   978-281-6373
    Fax: 978-283-7185

Seafood
  President: Anne Mortillaro

12355 Royal Baltic
9829 Ditmas Ave
Brooklyn, NY 11236-1925   718-385-8300
  Fax: 718-385-4757   royal@royalbalticusa.com
    www.royalbalticusa.com
Smoked fish, gourmet foods, seafood delicacies, cheese, juice, feta, coffee, chocolate candy, and sauces
  President: Alex Kaganovsky
Estimated Sales:$ 10-20 Million
Number Employees: 50-99

12356 Royal Blend Coffee Company
601 NE 1st St
Bend, OR 97701-4742   541-388-8164
  Fax: 541-389-6185   rbsales@royalblend.com
    www.royalblend.com
Processor and importer of specialty roasted coffees
  President: Don Hamon
  Roastmaster: Dona Houtz
Estimated Sales:$ 20 - 50 Million
Number Employees: 50-99
Sq. footage: 6000
Type of Packaging: Consumer, Food Service
Brands:
  Royal Blend

12357 Royal Body Care
P.O.Box 167008
Irving, TX 75016-7008   972-893-4000
    Fax: 972-893-4111
  royalbodycare@royalbodycare.org
    www.rbclifesciences.com
Wholesaler/distributor of health food products and nutritional supplements
  CEO: Clinton Howard
  CFO: Steve Brown
  CEO: John W Price
  Sales Director: Dennis Windsor
*Estimated Sales:*G
Number Employees: 50-99
Sq. footage: 120000
Parent Co: Royal Body Care
Other Locations:
  Royal Bodycare
  Markham ON

12358 (HQ)Royal Caribbean Bakery
620 S Fulton Ave
Mt Vernon, NY 10550-5012   914-668-6868
  Fax: 914-668-5700 888-818-0971
  info@royalcaribbeanbakery.com
    www.royalcaribbeanbakery.com
Processor of Jamaican baked goods and specialty foods including bread, pastries, black fruit cakes, Easter buns, hard dough bread, chicken and vegetable patties, jerk chicken, sausage, ox tail, curried goat, rice and peas
  President/CEO: Jeanette Hosang
Estimated Sales:$5700000
Number Employees: 50-99
Sq. footage: 60000
Type of Packaging: Consumer, Food Service, Private Label, Bulk
Other Locations:
  Royal Caribbean Bakery
  Orlando FL

12359 Royal Caviar
4551 San Fernando Road
Suite 110
Glendale, CA 91204-3234   818-546-5858
    Fax: 818-546-5856 www.royalcaviar.com
Caviar

12360 Royal Center Locker Plant
P.O.Box 250
Royal Center, IN 46978-0250   574-643-3275
    Fax: 574-643-3031

Manufacturer of meat products including beef, pork and lamb
  Owner: Steve Layer
Estimated Sales:$12 Million
Number Employees: 10-19
Type of Packaging: Consumer

12361 Royal Coffee
3306 Powell St
Emeryville, CA 94608-1548   510-652-4256
  Fax: 510-652-3415   royal@royalcoffee.com
    www.royalcoffee.com
Green coffee
  President: Robert Fulmer
  Vice President: Helen Nicholas
Estimated Sales:$ 30-50 Million
Number Employees: 20-49
Type of Packaging: Private Label

12362 Royal Coffee & Tea Company
5900 Ambler Drive
Mississauga, ON L4W 2N3
Canada   800-667-6226
Processor of orange pekoe teas, hot chocolate and coffee including gourmet roasted and ground
  President: Ilia Penek
  VP: Steve Corvese
Number Employees: 10-19
Sq. footage: 10000
Parent Co: Sara Lee Corporation
Type of Packaging: Consumer, Food Service, Private Label, Bulk
Brands:
  Royal Gourmet

12363 Royal Coffee New York
239 Western Ave
Staten Island, NY 10303-1103   718-815-5600
  Fax: 718-815-4363 888-769-2569
  james@royalny.com www.royalny.com
Green coffee
  President: James Schoenhut
  CEO: James Schoenhut
Estimated Sales:$ 2.5-5 Million
Number Employees: 5-9
Brands:
  Brazil Monte Carmelo
  Colombian Huila Especial
  Colombian Pensilvania Supremo
  Colombian Popayan Supremo

12364 Royal Court Cookie Company
10844 Chandler Boulevard
North Hollywood, CA 91601-2937   818-985-1224
  Fax: 818-985-1960 800-730-2545
Processor and exporter of baked goods including pastries, shortbread, biscotti, baked bagel style snack chips and cookies: specialty cinnamon raisin twists, apple cinnamon twists and butter spritz
  Executive VP: Eric Reuveni
Number Employees: 20-49
Type of Packaging: Consumer, Food Service, Private Label, Bulk
Brands:
  California Foodworks
  Royal Court Cookie Co.

12365 Royal Crest Dairy Company
350 S Pearl St
Denver, CO 80209-2098   303-777-3055
  Fax: 303-744-9173 hr@royalcrestdairy.com
    www.royalcrestdairy.com
Fluid milk, cream and related products
  President: Tim Detine
  Founder: Paul Miller
  CFO: Larry Hunt
  Chairman of the Board: Paul R Miller
  CFO: Jack Walter
  Plant Manager: Ron Henke
  Purchasing Manager: Al Martinez
Estimated Sales:$ 20-50 Million
Number Employees: 100-249
Brands:
  Royal Crest

12366 Royal Crown Bottling Company
P.O.Box 1687
Bowling Green, KY 42102-1687   270-842-8106
    Fax: 270-842-2877
Manufacturer of soft drinks and water, waffle and pancake syrups and other flavored vending and fountain syrups in blow-molded plastic containers
  Manager: Mike Trimble
  President/CEO: Nancy Hodge

Estimated Sales:$56 Million
Number Employees: 50-99
Sq. footage: 60000
Parent Co: Nehi-Royal Crown Cola Bottling & Distributing Company
Type of Packaging: Consumer, Food Service, Private Label, Bulk
Brands:
  3 SPRINGS
  BRASS KEG
  SUGAR BARREL
  TEDDY'S

12367 (HQ)Royal Cup Coffee
160 Cleage Dr
Birmingham, AL 35217-1461   205-849-5836
  Fax: 205-271-6071 800-366-5836
  webjava@royalcupcoffee.com
    www.royalcupcoffee.com
Processor of coffee and tea; wholesaler/distributor of coffee equipment; serving the food service market
  President: Hatton C V Smith
  VP Operations: Gene Lewis
  VP Operations: Eugene Lewis
  VP Finance: Lamar Bagby
  Chairman: William Smith Jr
  Quality Control: Bruce Woodall
  Plant Manager: Henry Holden
Estimated Sales:$ 50 - 100 Million
Number Employees: 250-499
Type of Packaging: Food Service
Other Locations:
  Royal Cup
  Birmingham AL

12368 Royal Food Distributors
PO Box 13882
Scottsdale, AZ 85267-3882   602-971-4910
    Fax: 602-971-4910

  President: Bob Ho

12369 Royal Food Products
P.O.Box 33070
Indianapolis, IN 46203-0070   317-782-2660
  Fax: 317-782-2680 sales@royalfp.com
    www.royalfp.com
Processor of salad dressings, mayonnaise, mustard and sauces
  President: Brian King
Estimated Sales:$ 15 Million
Number Employees: 50-99
Type of Packaging: Food Service
Brands:
  Royal

12370 Royal Foods & Flavors
2456 American Ln
Elk Grove Vlg, IL 60007-6204   847-595-9166
    Fax: 847-595-9690
Processor of flavors, seasonings, yeast extracts and hydrolyzed vegetable proteins
  President: Harish Gadhvi
Estimated Sales:$730000
Number Employees: 10-19
Type of Packaging: Bulk

12371 Royal Harvest Foods
55 Avocado St
Springfield, MA 01104-3303   413-737-8392
  Fax: 413-731-9336 sales@royalharv.com
    www.royalharv.com
Frozen prepared chickens, beef, turkey
  President: James Vallides
  Sales: Chris Keller
  Sales Manager: Frank McNamara
Estimated Sales:$ 10-20 Million
Number Employees: 50-99
Sq. footage: 40000
Brands:
  Suffield Poultry

12372 Royal Home Bakery
160 Pony Drive
Newmarket, ON L3Y 7B6
Canada   905-715-7044
Processor of baked goods including bread, buns, biscuits, tarts, cakes and Jamaican patties
  Owner: Harold Chin
  Manager: Doris Chin
  Sales Manager: Hope Chin
*Estimated Sales:*Under $300,000
Number Employees: 4
Sq. footage: 4000

12373 Royal Ice Cream Company
27 Warren St
Manchester, CT 06040-6500　　860-649-5358
　　Fax: 860-647-7376　800-246-2958
　　　　　　sales@royalicecream.com
　　　　　　www.royalicecream.com
Processor of portion packed spumoni, nut roll,
tartufo, fruit sorbet, tortoni, bombe, etc.; also, ice
cream cakes and pies
　　President: James S Orfitelli
　　VP: Cindy Orfitelli
　　Sales/Marketing: John Russo
Estimated Sales: $2000000
Number Employees: 10-19
Sq. footage: 15000
Type of Packaging: Food Service, Private Label

**12374 (HQ)Royal Kedem Food &
WineCompany**
63 Lefante Dr
Bayonne, NJ 07002-5024　　201-437-9131
　　Fax: 718-388-8444　info@royalwines.com
　　　　　　www.kedemwines.com
Processor of grape, cranberry and apple juices, juice
blends, wines and salad dressings; importer of cook-
ies, matzo and wines; exporter of wines
　　President and CEO: David Herzog
　　President: Harry Stern
　　Executive VP: Nathan Herzog
　　Marketing Director: Avi Fertig
　　Sales Director: Jay Buchsbaum
　　Operations Manager: Philip Herzog
　　Production Manager: Michael Herzog
　　Plant Manager: Robert Herzog
Number Employees: 20-49
Sq. footage: 150000
Type of Packaging: Consumer, Food Service, Pri-
vate Label, Bulk
Brands:
　　Baron Herzog
　　Baron Herzog California Wines
　　Kedem
　　Kedem Traditional Wines
　　Savion
　　Shufra
　　Taam Pree

12375 Royal Kraft Company
21258 Wallace King Road
Bush, LA 70431-2601　　504-822-0222
　　　　　　Fax: 504-892-8646

12376 Royal Lagoon Seafood
4720-B Ridgeline Road
Mobile, AL 36619　　251-643-7072
　　　　　　Fax: 251-639-1198
Seafood
　　President: Val Hammond
Estimated Sales: $5,000,000
Number Employees: 6

12377 Royal Madera
7770 Road 33
Madera, CA 93636-8307　　559-486-6666
　　Fax: 559-661-1427　fcvbsales@aol.com
Frozen foods
　　President: Steve Volpe
Estimated Sales: $ 10-20 Million
Number Employees: 20-49

12378 Royal Medjool Date Gardens
PO Box 930
Bard, CA 92222-0930　　760-572-0524
　　Fax: 760-572-2292　rmdates@worldnet.att.net
　　　　　　www.royaldates.com
Grower and exporter of dates and date trees.
　　General Manager: David Nelson
Estimated Sales: $ 10 - 20 Million
Number Employees: 20
Brands:
　　MEDJOOL
　　ROYAL

12379 Royal Moonlight
17719 E Huntsman Ave
Reedley, CA 93654-9205　　559-637-7799
　　　　　　Fax: 559-637-7199
　　russ@moonlightcompany.com
　　　　　　www.royalmoonlight.com
Grapes and other summer fruit
　　President: Russel Tavlan
Estimated Sales: $ 3 - 5 Million
Number Employees: 5-9

Type of Packaging: Consumer, Food Service, Pri-
vate Label, Bulk
Brands:
　　CALIENTE
　　CALIFORNIA COLLECTION
　　MOONLIGHT
　　ROYAL
　　THE RIPE STUFF

12380 Royal Oak Peanuts
13009 Cedar View Road
Drewryville, VA 23844　　434-658-9500
　　Fax: 703-991-8922　800-608-4590
　　　　　　info@royaloakspeanuts.com
　　　　　　www.royaloakspeanuts.com
peanut and peanut products

12381 Royal Pacific Fisheries
Mi 14.5 Kalifornsky Beach Rd
Kenai, AK 99611　　907-283-9370
　　　　　　Fax: 907-283-5974
Fresh, frozen and canned seafood
　　President: Marvin Dragseth
Estimated Sales: $ 5-9.9 Million
Number Employees: 5-9

**12382 Royal Pacific Foods/TheGinger
People**
215 Reindollar Ave
Marina, CA 93933　　831-582-2494
　　Fax: 831-582-2495　800-551-5284
　　info@gingerpeople.com　www.gingerpeople.com
ginger
　　President/Owner: Bruce Leeson
　　VP: Diana Cumberland
Estimated Sales: $9.5 Million
Number Employees: 12

12383 Royal Pacific Tea & Coffee
PO Box 6277
Scottsdale, AZ 85261-6277　　480-951-8251
　　Fax: 480-951-0092　royalpacific@syspac.com
Tea
　　CEO: Art Gartenberg
Estimated Sales: Below $ 5 Million
Number Employees: 20
Type of Packaging: Private Label
Brands:
　　Royal Pacific Coffee
　　Royal Pacific Tea

12384 Royal Packing Company
P.O.Box 82157
Salinas, CA 93912-2157　　831-641-4450
　　Fax: 831-424-0762　www.valdostacpa.com
Grower and packager of lettuce
　　President: David Murdock
　　VP: David Hart
Number Employees: 5-9
Type of Packaging: Consumer, Food Service

12385 Royal Palate Foods
960 E Hyde Park Blvd
Inglewood, CA 90302-1708　　310-330-7701
　　Fax: 310-330-7710　info@koshermeal.com
　　　　　　www.royalpalatefoods.com
Processor, exporter and wholesaler/distributor of ko-
sher foods including chicken, beef, soups, sauces,
frozen entrees, hors d'oeuvres, etc.; serving the food
service market; importer of canned vegetables and
fruits
　　President: William Pinkerson
Estimated Sales: $500,000-$1 Million
Number Employees: 10-19
Sq. footage: 8000
Type of Packaging: Food Service, Bulk
Brands:
　　Royal Palate
　　Sierra Spring Foods

12386 Royal Palm Popcorn Company
100 McGaw Dr
Edison, NJ 08837-3725　　732-225-0200
　　Fax: 732-225-6363　800-526-8865
Gourmet popcorn
　　President: Michael Spitz
Number Employees: 10-19
Brands:
　　Joons Chocolate Popcorn
　　Park Avenue Gourmet
　　Rainbow Popcorn

12387 Royal Pie Bakery
1929 Hancock Street
San Diego, CA 92110-2061　　619-233-6393
Pies and baked goods
　　President: Alex Kuhnel

12388 Royal Products
P.O.Box 13628
Scottsdale, AZ 85267-3628　　480-948-2509
　　Fax: 480-951-0835　service@royalproducts.net
　　　　　　www.royalproducts.net
Processor of health vitamins and supplements
　　President: Johnny Shannon
　　CEO: David Stuart
Estimated Sales: Less than $100,000
Number Employees: 1-4
Type of Packaging: Food Service

12389 Royal Resources
PO Box 24001
New Orleans, LA 70184-4001　　504-283-9932
　　Fax: 504-283-2620　800-888-9932
　　　　　　rrbanfos@bellsouth.net
Salad dressing, jellies, salsas, dessert toppings, hot
sauces and cake mix

12390 Royal Ridge Fruits
13215 Rd F SW
P.O. Box 428
Royal City, WA 99357　　509-346-1520
　　Fax: 509-346-2098　www.royalridgefruits.com
Supplier of dried and frozen cherries, strawberries,
blueberries and raspberries.

12391 Royal Seafood
P.O.Box 1347
Monterey, CA 93942-1347　　831-655-8326
　　　　　　Fax: 831-373-8336
Processor of frozen and fresh fish including cod,
flounder, herring, mackerel, perch, salmon, sole,
squid and tuna
　　Owner/President: Gino Pennisi
　　Owner/VP: Elaine Pennisi
　　Owner/VP: Elaine Pennisi
Estimated Sales: $800,000
Number Employees: 1-4
Type of Packaging: Consumer, Food Service
Brands:
　　Black cod (sablefish
　　CA halibut
　　Channel rockfish (thornyheads
　　Dover sole

12392 Royal Seafood
P.O.Box 1347
Monterey, CA 93942-1347　　831-655-8326
　　　　　　Fax: 831-373-8336
Seafood
　　Owner: Gino Pennisi
　　Marketing Manager: Pennisi Giuseppe
Estimated Sales: $500,000-$1 Million
Number Employees: 1-4
Brands:
　　Royal Seafood

12393 Royal Swedish Classic Coffee
600 E Brook Dr
Arlington Hts, IL 60005-4622　　847-364-9704
　　Fax: 847-364-9702　declan@idbusa.com
Coffee
　　President: Andrew Kramer
Estimated Sales: $100+ Million
Number Employees: 50-99

12394 Royal Touch Foods
315 Humberline Drive
Etobicoke, ON M9W 5T6
Canada　　416-213-1077
　　Fax: 416-213-1055　info@royaltouchfoods.com
　　　　　　www.royaltouchfoods.com
Processor of pork and beef sandwiches
　　Co-Owner: Vince Ruso
　　Production Manager: Dominic Ruso
Number Employees: 50-99
Parent Co: J.M. Schneider
Type of Packaging: Food Service
Brands:
　　Hamish & Enzo
　　Royal Touch

12395 Royal Vista Marketing
100 Willow Plz # 309
Visalia, CA 93291-6215   559-636-9198
          Fax: 559-636-9637 info@royalvista.com
                    www.royalvista.com
Grower and exporter of table grapes, kiwifruit, stone
fruit and figs; importer of stone fruit, kiwifruit and
table grapes
    President: Todd A Steele
    Sales Manager: Patrick Allen
Estimated Sales: $84000
Number Employees: 5-9
Sq. footage: 24000
Parent Co: Atalanta
Type of Packaging: Consumer, Food Service, Bulk
Other Locations:
    Alkop Farms
    Chico CA

12396 Royal Wine Company
63 Lefante Dr
Bayonne, NJ 07002-5024   201-437-9131
                    info@royalwines.com
                    www.royalwines.com
Processor, importer, exporter of wines, grape and
fruit juices, cordials, baked goods, biscuits, wafers,
gourmet foods, chocolates and nuts
    President/CEO: David Herzog
    VP Marketing: Jay Buchsbaum
    Sales: Howard Wang
    Public Relations: Eitan Segal
    Operations: Robert Herzog
    Winemaker/Production: Michael Herzog
Estimated Sales: $70 Million
Number Employees: 10-19
Sq. footage: 183000
Parent Co: Kedem Kosher Wine Company
Type of Packaging: Consumer, Private Label, Bulk
Brands:
    Hi-Five
    Kadem

12397 Royal Wine Company
63 Lefante Dr
Bayonne, NJ 07002-5024   201-437-9131
                    800-382-8299
                    www.kedemwines.com
Processor and exporter of wines, fruit juices, syrups,
gefilte fish, etc.; importer of produce
    President: Michael Herzog
    President/CEO: David Herzog
    Vice President: Herman Herzog
    Public Relations: Mitch Halpert
    Operations Manager: Philip Herzog
    Purchasing Manager: Yidel Kahn
Estimated Sales: $70 Million
Number Employees: 10-19
Parent Co: Royal Wine Corporation
Type of Packaging: Consumer, Private Label

12398 Royale InternationalBeverage Co Inc
5315 Tremont Ave
Davenport, IA 52807-2640   563-386-5222
    Fax: 563-386-1352 royale@netexpress.net
                    www.royalebrands.com
Produce and market frozen beverage products and
equipment
    President: Joe Colombari
Estimated Sales: Less than $500,000
Number Employees: 10-19
Number of Brands: 13
Number of Products: 250
Type of Packaging: Food Service
Brands:
    Cruisin Cool
    Energy Ice
    Royale Smoothie

12399 Royalmark Services
6645 107th Ave
South Haven, MI 49090-9366   269-637-7450
                    Fax: 269-637-2636
Processor and exporter of blueberries; also, custom
packing services available
    President: Vern Adkin
Estimated Sales: $ 3 - 5 Million
Number Employees: 5-9

12400 Royce C. Bone Farms
2913 Sandy Cross Road
Nashville, NC 27856-8633   252-443-3773
    Fax: 252-937-4990 Fbone@rockymountnc.com
                    www.ncsweetpotatoes.com

Processor of sweet potatoes, romaine, tomatoes and
pickles
    President/CEO: David Godwin
    Co-Owner: Fay Bone
    Vice President: Dewey Scott
Number Employees: 10-19
Brands:
    Jean Sweet Potatos

12401 Ruark & Ashton
1548 Taylors Island Road
Woolford, MD 21677-1327   410-221-6076
          Fax: 410-221-6076 800-725-5032
Seafood
    President: Terry Vinson
Estimated Sales: Under $500,000
Number Employees: 1-4

12402 Rubashkin
4308 14th Ave
Brooklyn, NY 11219-1428   718-436-5511
                    Fax: 718-435-4295
Kosher butcher
    President: AA Rubashkin
Estimated Sales: $ 1 - 3 Million

12403 Rubicon/Niebaum-CoppolaEstate & Winery
P.O.Box 208
Rutherford, CA 94573-0208   707-968-1100
          Fax: 707-968-9551 800-782-4266
                    www.niebaum-coppola.com
Wines
    President: John Richburg
    CEO: Jay Shumaker
    Winemaker: Scott McLeod
Estimated Sales: $10 Million
Number Employees: 50-99

12404 Rubino's Seafood Company
735 W Lake St
Chicago, IL 60661-1026   312-258-0020
                    Fax: 312-258-0028
Seafood
    President: James Rubino
Estimated Sales: $ 1 - 3 Million
Number Employees: 5-9
Type of Packaging: Food Service

12405 Rubschlager Baking Corporation
3220 W Grand Ave
Chicago, IL 60651-4194   773-826-1245
                    Fax: 773-826-6619
          mike@rubschlagerbaking.com
                    www.rubschlager.com
Processor and exporter of bread, frozen rolls and
mini-chips.
    President: Paul Rubschlager
    Secretary/Treasurer: Joan Rubschlager
    National Sales Manager: Mike DiCristo
Number Employees: 1-4
Number of Brands: 2
Number of Products: 45
Type of Packaging: Consumer, Food Service
Brands:
    RUBSCHLAGER

12406 Ruby Apiaries
711 5th Avenue
Milnor, ND 58060-4113   701-427-5263
Condiments and relishes
    President: Dick Ruby
    CEO: Doug Ruby
Estimated Sales: Less than $500,000
Number Employees: 1-4

12407 Rucker's Makin' Batch Candies
P.O.Box 278
Hutsonville, IL 62433-0278   618-563-4806
          Fax: 618-563-4663 888-622-2639
    sales@makinbatch.com www.makinbatch.com
Processor of candy including hard, filled and
sugar-free; pre-pack available varities include pea-
nut butter, peppermint, lemon and molasses
    Owner: Rena Smith
Estimated Sales: $95,000
Number Employees: 5-9
Number of Products: 125
Sq. footage: 20000
Type of Packaging: Food Service, Private Label,
    Bulk

12408 Rudd Winery
P.O.Box 105
Oakville, CA 94562-0105   707-944-8577
          Fax: 707-944-2823 info@ruddwines.com
                    www.ruddwines.com
Wines
    President: Leslie Rudd
    COO: Stephen Girard Jr
    Marketing Director: Ellen Hunt
Estimated Sales: $ 5-10 Million
Number Employees: 20-49
Brands:
    Bacigalupi Chardonnay
    Jericho Canyon Red
    Library Wines
    Oakville Estate Red

12409 Rude Custom Butchering
6194 W Pines Rd
Mt Morris, IL 61054-9755   815-946-3795
                    Fax: 815-946-2333
Meats
    President: Kevin Rude
Estimated Sales: $ 10-20 Million
Number Employees: 20-49

12410 Rudi's Organic Bakery
3640 Walnut Street
Unit C
Boulder, CO 80301-2500   303-447-0495
          Fax: 303-447-0516 877-293-0876
                    www.rudisbakery.com
Manufacturer of fresh and frozen certified organic
par baked bread, buns and rolls. Charterhouse Group
has acquired a majority stake in this company
    President: Gary Seaback
    VP: Victoria Smith
Estimated Sales: $ 50 - 100 Million
Number Employees: 150
Sq. footage: 14500
Parent Co: Charterhouse Group
Type of Packaging: Consumer, Food Service, Bulk
Brands:
    Certified Organic Breads
    Certified Organic Buns
    Certified Organic Rolls

12411 Rudolph Foods
3660 Pipestone Rd
Dallas, TX 75212-6109   214-638-2204
    Fax: 214-638-2112 www.rudolphfoods.com
Processor of snack foods including beef jerky and
pork rinds
    Plant Manager: Bob Burns
Number Employees: 50-99
Parent Co: Rudolph Foods
Type of Packaging: Consumer, Food Service, Pri-
    vate Label
Brands:
    Cracklins

12412 Rudolph Foods Company
P.O.Box 509
Lima, OH 45802-0509   419-648-3611
          Fax: 419-648-4087 info@rudolphfoods.com
                    www.rudolphfoods.com
Manufacturer and exporter of pork rinds and related
snacks
    Chairman: John Rudolph
    President: James Rudolph
Estimated Sales: $74 Million
Number Employees: 100-249
Type of Packaging: Consumer, Private Label, Bulk
Brands:
    GRANDPA JOHN'S
    PEPE'S
    RUDOLPH'S
    SOUTHERN RECIPE

12413 Rudolph's Market & Sausage Factory
2924 Elm St
Dallas, TX 75226-1509   214-741-1874
                    Fax: 214-761-2017
    randreason@rudolpmarkets.com
                    www.rudolphmarkets.com
Processor of smoked meats and sausage
    President: Justine M Andreason
Estimated Sales: $ 5 - 10 Million
Number Employees: 10-19
Type of Packaging: Consumer

12414 Rudolph's Specialty Bakery
390 Alliance Avenue
Toronto, ON M6N 2H8
Canada   416-763-4315
Fax: 416-763-4317 rudolph@rudolphsbreads.com
www.rudolphsbreads.com
Processor and exporter of rye and flat breads, tortillas and flan cakes
President: George Paech
Type of Packaging: Consumer, Food Service, Private Label
Brands:
Casa Jorge
Masala Roti
Roti & Chapati
Rudolph's
Taj Mahal
Wwraps

12415 Rudy's Tortillas
535 Regal Row
Dallas, TX 75247-5207   800-878-2401
Fax: 214-638-5317 800-878-2401
lguerra@rudystortillas.com
www.rudystortillas.com
Processor of tortillas, chalupas, tostadas, tacos, flavored wraps, shells and blue, red, yellow and white chips
President: Rudy Guerra Jr
Marketing Director: Louis Guerra
Quality Control: Louis Guerra
VP Operations: Rudy Guerra Jr
Estimated Sales: $ 50-100 Million
Number Employees: 95
Brands:
Rudy's Tortillas

12416 Ruef's Meat Market
P.O.Box 251
New Glarus, WI 53574-0251   608-527-2554
bruef@charter.net
www.ruefsmeatmarket.com
Smoked meats and cheese
Owner: Willy Ruef
CEO: Annette Ruef
Estimated Sales: Less than $300,000
Number Employees: 1-4
Type of Packaging: Consumer, Food Service, Bulk
Brands:
Ruef's Meat Market

12417 Ruffner's
704 W Lancaster Ave
Wayne, PA 19087-2515   610-687-9800
Fax: 610-687-9800 info@ruffners.com
hhtp://www.supercuts.com
Cocktail drink mixes, green tomato salsa
Manager: Steve Costa
Estimated Sales: $300,000-500,000
Number Employees: 1-4
Brands:
Supercuts

12418 Ruggiero Seafood
117 Avenue L
Newark, NJ 07105-3809   973-589-0524
Fax: 973-589-5690 800-543-2110
raquel@ruggieroseafood.com
www.ruggieroseafood.com
Processor, importer and exporter of fresh, frozen and breaded calamari and calamari entrees
President: Rocco Ruggiero
Controller: Connie Dasaliva
Sales Manager: Steve Clemente
Plant Manager: Marcos Fontana
Estimated Sales: $25100000
Number Employees: 100-249
Sq. footage: 25000
Type of Packaging: Consumer, Food Service, Bulk
Brands:
Atlantic Coast
Fisherman's Pride
Fruit of the Sea
Northwind
Ocean Tide

12419 (HQ)Ruiz Food Products
P.O.Box 37
Dinuba, CA 93618-0037   559-591-5510
Fax: 559-591-1969 800-477-6474
contactus@ruizfoods.com www.elmonterey.com

Manufacturer and exporter of frozen foods including burritos, enchiladas, tamales, soft tacos, chili rellenos, flautas and taquitos.
Chairman/CEO: Fred Ruiz
Vice Chairman: Kim Ruiz Beck
CFO: Ricardo Alvarez
Board of Directors: Jack Baker
Board of Directors: Larry Dalicandro
Board of Directors: Bill Henderson
Board of Directors: Wayne Partin
Board of Directors: Terry Peets
Board of Directors: Stuart Woolf
Purchasing Manager: Steve Windh
Estimated Sales: $198.5 Million
Number Employees: 1,000-4,999
Sq. footage: 192000
Type of Packaging: Consumer, Food Service, Private Label, Bulk
Brands:
EL MONTEREY
PRIMA ROSA!
RUIZ FAMILY

12420 (HQ)Ruiz Mexican Foods
2151 E Francis St
Ontario, CA 91761-7723   909-947-7811
Fax: 909-947-2338 tortilla@worldnet.att.net
Processor of die cut and whole wheat flour tortillas; manufacturer of baking equipment including extruders, cooling conveyors and ovens
President: Edward Ruiz Sr
CFO: Uriel Maciaf
CEO: Uriel Macias
R&D: David Rodriguez
Equipment Sales: Ruben Gonzales
Purchasing: Carmen Sandoval
Estimated Sales: $ 50-100 Million
Number Employees: 100-249
Sq. footage: 34000
Type of Packaging: Food Service, Private Label, Bulk

12421 Rumford Baking Powder Company
P.O.Box 150
Terre Haute, IN 47808-0150   812-232-9446
Fax: 812-478-7181 hulman@hulman.com
www.clabbergirl.com
Processor and exporter of baking powder
President: Gary Morris
Director Sales/Marketing: Eric Gloe
Purchasing Manager: Bruce West
Estimated Sales: $ 20 - 50 Million
Number Employees: 100-249
Type of Packaging: Consumer, Food Service, Private Label, Bulk
Brands:
Hearth Club
Rumford

12422 Rumiano Cheese Company
P.O.Box 305
Crescent City, CA 95531-0305   707-465-1535
Fax: 707-465-4141 www.rumianocheese.com
Natural and processed cheese
President: Baird Rumiano
Quality Control: Jus Barrd
Vice President: John Rumiano
Marketing Director: Kirk Olesen
Estimated Sales: $ 10-20 Million
Number Employees: 20-49

12423 (HQ)Run-A-Ton Group
PO Box 2205
Morristown, NJ 07962-2205   973-267-3800
Fax: 973-984-2424 800-247-6580
doon.wintz@runaton.com
www.whollywholesome.com
Manufacturer of conventional and natural baked goods
President/CEO: Doon Wintz
CEO: Robert Wintz
CFO: Linda Hendricks
Vice President: Lynn Nelson
Director Sales Development/Marketing: Janeen Ortega
Estimated Sales: $ 10 - 20 Million
Number Employees: 20-49
Number of Brands: 5
Number of Products: 1000
Sq. footage: 5000
Type of Packaging: Consumer, Food Service, Private Label

Brands:
APPLE VALLEY INN
BUTTERY BAKER
SIMPLE ELEGANCE
WHOLLY WHOLESOME

12424 Rupari Food Service
1208 W Newport Center Dr
Deerfield Beach, FL 33442-7714   954-480-6320
Fax: 954-480-6367 800-578-7274
jmintz@rupari.com www.rupari.com
Snacks and sport drinks
President: Robert Mintz
CFO: Mel Mitchell
VP: Pete Chiappatta
Estimated Sales: $ 12 Million
Number Employees: 20-49
Number of Brands: 2
Number of Products: 7
Type of Packaging: Consumer
Brands:
Bandito's Cheese and Chips
Bandito's Chips
Bandito's Salsa
Mighty Mouse Sports

12425 Rural Route 1 Popcorn
105 E Tama St
Livingston, WI 53554-9537   608-943-8091
Fax: 608-943-8283 800-828-8115
pops@ruralroute1.com www.ruralroute1.com
Popcorn
President: Bradley Biddick
Marketing Director: Nick Solomon
CFO: Bradley Biddick
Estimated Sales: Below $ 5 Million
Number Employees: 20-49
Brands:
Almonds
Creamy Medley of Popcorn
Ivory Almond K'Nuckle

12426 RusDun Farms
2295 Highway 57
Collierville, TN 38017-5329   901-853-0931
Fax: 901-853-0387 mrussel1@midsouth.rr.com
http://www.midsouth.rr.com
Eggs
President: Melvin Russell
Estimated Sales: Below $ 5 Million
Number Employees: 1-4

12427 Ruskin Packaging
910 NW 22nd Street
Miami, FL 33127-4239   305-324-1529
Fax: 305-545-8430 ruskin@bellsouth.net
Processor of dry beans, cole slaw, kale, collard greens, French slaw, salad mixes, spinach, baby lima beans, black-eyed and green peas, red cabbage, julienned carrots, chopped celery and shredded zucchini
President: Cathy Garcia
Sales/Marketing: Andrew Garcia
Estimated Sales: $10000000
Number Employees: 25

12428 Ruskin Redneck Trading Company
1203 1st Street SW
Ruskin, FL 33570-5345   813-645-7710
Fax: 813-641-1979
Sauces
Principal: Sandra Council
Estimated Sales: $ 1 - 3 Million
Number Employees: 2

12429 Russ & Daughters
179 E Houston St # 1
New York, NY 10002-1024   212-475-4880
Fax: 212-475-0345 800-787-7229
info@russanddaughters.com
www.russanddaughters.com
Smoked fish, caviar and specialty foods
Managing Partner: Mark Russ Federman
Estimated Sales: Less than $500,000
Number Employees: 10-19

12430 Russell & Kohne
3444 E Coast Highway
Corona Del Mar, CA 92625-2401   949-675-0994
Fax: 949-675-0994
Baked goods

12431 Russell Brewing Company
202-13018 80th Avenue
Surrey, BC V4A 1A2
Canada   604-599-1190
        Fax: 604-599-1048 info@russellbeer.com
                            www.russellbeer.com
Processor of ale
    President: Mark Russell
    Co-Owner: Peter Russell
Number Employees: 1-4
Type of Packaging: Consumer, Food Service
Brands:
    Russell Cream Ale
    Russell Honey Blonde Ale
    Russell Lemon Wheat Ale
    Russell Oager
    Russell Pale Ale
    Russell Winter Ale

12432 Russell E. Womack
1300 E 42nd St
Lubbock, TX 79404-3516   806-747-2581
        Fax: 806-747-2583 877-787-3559
                rewi@casserolebean.com
                www.casserolebean.com
Processor and packager of dry pinto beans packed in
poly and burlap packs. Casserole Pinto Beans are
available in 1lb, 2lb, 4lb, 10lb, 20lb, and 50lb sizes.
    Owner: Mike Byrne
    Product Managerment/Quality Control: Mike
    Bryne
    Sales Director: Nancy Higginson
    Consumer Affairs: Walter James
    Packaging Plant Manager: Albert Rodriguez
Estimated Sales: $1600000
Number Employees: 10-19
Number of Brands: 1
Number of Products: 1
Sq. footage: 36000
Type of Packaging: Consumer, Food Service

12433 Russell Stover Candies
2212 E Highway 76
Marion, SC 29571   843-423-3022
                        Fax: 843-423-7706
Processor of confectionery products
    Plant Manager: Darryl Ventz
Number Employees: 1,000-4,999
Type of Packaging: Consumer

12434 Russell Stover Candies
1976 Chocolate Dr
Cookeville, TN 38501-2022   931-526-8424
        Fax: 931-528-1391 www.russellstover.com
Manufacturer of chocolate
    Manager: Emma Dillon
    Plant Manager: Gary Opermiller
    Purchasing Agent: Pam Peterson
Estimated Sales: $500 Million
Number Employees: 5-9
Type of Packaging: Consumer

12435 (HQ)Russell Stover Candies
4900 Oak St
Kansas City, MO 64112-2927   816-842-9240
        Fax: 816-561-4350 800-477-8683
                            www.russellstover.com
Chocolate Candy
    President: Scott Ward
    CFO: Dick Masinton
    Research & Development: Wayne Houde
    Quality Control: Chuck Teater
    Marketing Director: Mark Sesler
    Sales Director: Bill Baer
    COO: Dan Trott
    Production Manager: Shawn Chestnut
    Purchasing Manager: Darrin Buehler
Estimated Sales: $500 Million
Number Employees: 5,100
Type of Packaging: Consumer
Brands:
    RUSSELL STOVERS

12436 Russer Foods
665 Perry Street
Buffalo, NY 14210-1384   716-826-6400
        Fax: 716-826-9186 800-828-7021
                            www.russerfoods.com
Processor and exporter of deli foods including
smoked, dried and portioned cut meats
    President: Howard Zemsky
    Sales Manager: Paul Timlan

Estimated Sales: $91700000
Number Employees: 550
Parent Co: IBP
Other Locations:
    Russer Foods
    Boston MA
Brands:
    Russer

12437 Russia
220 Industrial Loop
Staten Island, NY 10304   718-667-8148
                                tsa@varpe.ru
                                www.varpe.ru
Association is united with more than 100 Russian
fishery companies and provides for export of pol-
lack, crab and caviar from Russia.
    President: Alexander Rodin
    R&D: Andrey Tsvetkov
Estimated Sales: $100 Million
Number Employees: 100
Type of Packaging: Consumer, Food Service, Bulk
Other Locations:
    Russia
    Moscow

12438 Russian Chef
40 E 69th St
New York, NY 10021-5016   212-249-1550
        Fax: 212-249-5451 blinihut@aol.com
Processor and packer of fresh and pasteurized ko-
sher caviar including domestic salmon, whitefish,
sturgeon, paddlefish, hackleback and lumpfish; also,
Scottish smoked salmon, tuna and smoked trout; im-
porter of caviar
    President: Simon Kublanov
    Vice President: Lenny Kuvykin
Estimated Sales: $ 1 - 3 Million
Number Employees: 5-9
Sq. footage: 9000
Type of Packaging: Consumer, Food Service
Brands:
    Ivan the Terrible
    Poriloff
    Purepak
    Russian Chef's

12439 Russo Farms
1962 S East Ave
Vineland, NJ 08360-7198   856-692-5942
        Fax: 856-692-8534 drusso@njtripoli.com
                            www.russofarms.com
Processor of fruits and vegetables including green
onions, cabbage, peppers, eggplant, cucumbers,
leafy greens, etc
    President: Damian Russo
Estimated Sales: $12046688
Number Employees: 1-4
Type of Packaging: Consumer
Brands:
    Pat's Best

12440 Russo's Seafood
201 E 40th St
Savannah, GA 31401-9120   912-341-8848
            Fax: 912-234-5703 www.russoseafood.com
Seafood
    Manager: Nolan Mell
Estimated Sales: $ 3 - 5 Million
Number Employees: 10-19

12441 Ruth Ashbrook Bakery
6445 NE M L King Boulevard
Portland, OR 97211-3031   503-240-7437
                        Fax: 503-289-7264
Snack cakes, pies, doughnuts and other goods
    President: Gerald Martinson
    Marketing Director: Glenn Fergeson
    Production Manager: Mark Martinson
    Plant Manager: Gary Taskos
    Purchasing Manager: John Hunter
Estimated Sales: $5-9.9 Million
Number Employees: 20-49

12442 Ruth Hunt Candies
P.O.Box 265
Mt Sterling, KY 40353-0265   859-498-0676
        Fax: 859-498-1556 800-927-0302
                Info@Ruthhuntcandy.com
                www.ruthhuntcandy.com
Confectionary products including pulled cream
candy, bourbon balls, caramels, assorted soft creams,
and sugar free chocolates.
    President: Larry Kezele

Estimated Sales: $790000
Number Employees: 10-19
Number of Products: 70
Sq. footage: 4500
Parent Co: Kezele Corporation
Type of Packaging: Consumer
Brands:
    Blue Monday
    Blue Monday Candybar
    Bourbon Balls
    Official Bourbon Balls
    Ruth Hunt Confections

12443 Rutherford Hill Winery
P.O.Box 427
Rutherford, CA 94573-0427   707-963-1871
        Fax: 707-963-1878 info@rutherfordhill.com
                            www.rutherfordhillwinery.com
Processor of wines
    President: Anthony Terlato
    VP: Willis Blakewell
Estimated Sales: $4500000
Number Employees: 20-49

12444 Rutter Brothers Dairy
2100 N George St
York, PA 17404-1898   717-848-9827
        Fax: 717-845-8751 800-840-1664
                            www.rutters.com
Milk and dairy products
    President: Todd Rutter
    CFO: Tom Jonson
    Treasurer: Stewart Hartman
    CEO: Scott Hartman
    VP: Rey Sendy
    Operations Manager: Todd Rutter
    Plant Manager: Brett Garner
Number Employees: 500-999
Type of Packaging: Private Label
Brands:
    Rutter's

12445 Ryals Bakery
135 S Wayne St
Milledgeville, GA 31061-3439   478-452-0321
Breads, rolls, cakes
    Owner: Jacob Ryals
Estimated Sales: $130,000
Number Employees: 5-9
Brands:
    Ryals Bakery

12446 Ryan Milk
P.O.Box 1175
Murray, KY 42071-0020   270-753-3012
            Fax: 270-753-9474 www.deanfoods.com
Milk and dairy products.
    Group VP: Dan Green
    VP/General Manager: Chuck Harper
    Sr VP Sales/Marketing: Bill Trawick
    Plant Manager: Jeff Kragt
Estimated Sales: $100+ Million
Number Employees: 250-499
Parent Co: Dean Foods Company

12447 Ryan-Parreira Almond Company
21490 Ortigalita Rd
Los Banos, CA 93635-9793   209-826-0272
        Fax: 209-826-3882 rpac@rpacalmonds.com
                            www.rpacalmonds.com
Processor and exporter of almonds
    Owner: Dave Parreira
    Partner: David Parreira
    Shipping Manager: Janet Martin
    Plant Manager: James Smith
Estimated Sales: $4500000
Number Employees: 50-99
Type of Packaging: Bulk

12448 Rye Sales Unlimited
12130 Greenfield Road
Detroit, MI 48227-2021   313-838-1020
Wholesaler/distributor of general line products;
serving the food service market; also, buyer and
seller of closeout inventories
    President: Enrico Rosselli
Number Employees: 5-9
Sq. footage: 55000
Type of Packaging: Consumer, Food Service

12449 Rygmyr Foods
929 Concord Street S
South Saint Paul, MN 55075-5912 651-455-1701
        Fax: 651-455-6058 800-545-3903

Processor of molded popcorn novelties
President: Paul Lattate
Estimated Sales:$ 10 - 20 Million
Number Employees: 30
Sq. footage: 13000
Type of Packaging: Consumer, Private Label
Brands:
Bumpy & Jumpy
Cutie Cupid
Itchy Witchy
Rookie Spookie
Santa Pop

12450 Ryke's Bakery
1788 Terrace St
Muskegon, MI 49442-5697   231-557-8011
                             Fax: 231-728-2162
Processor of cakes, cookies, pies, breads and pastries
Co-Owner: Butch Rouwhorst
Co-Owner: Renee Chiasson-Rouwhorst
Estimated Sales:$720000
Number Employees: 20-49
Sq. footage: 8000
Type of Packaging: Consumer

12451 Ryley Sausage
PO Box 205
Ryley, AB T0B 4A0
Canada   780-663-3990
                             Fax: 780-663-2110
Processor of sausage and deli meatloaf
CEO: Andy Kowalski
President: Andy Kowalski
Marketing Manager: Andy Kowalski
Number Employees: 5-9
Sq. footage: 4500
Type of Packaging: Consumer, Food Service, Private Label, Bulk
Brands:
Ryley
Ryley

12452 Rymer Foods
4600 S Packers Avenue
Suite 400
Chicago, IL 60609-3338   773-254-7530
         Fax: 773-927-7278 800-247-9637
                             www.rymerfoods.com
Processor of hamburgers, steaks, pot roast and meat loaf; also, frozen chicken
CEO: P Edward Schenk
President: Edward Hebert
Marketing Director: John Bormann
Operations Manager: Jose Muguerza
Number Employees: 10-19
Type of Packaging: Food Service

12453 Rymer Seafood
125 S Wacker Drive
Chicago, IL 60606-1702   312-236-3266
                             Fax: 312-236-4169
Seafood
President: Mark Bailin
Estimated Sales:$ .5 - 1 million
Number Employees: 1-4

12454 Ryt Way Industries
21850 Grenada Ave
Lakeville, MN 55044-9076   952-469-1417
    Fax: 952-469-9517 hickeyt@rytway.com
                             www.rytway.com
Exporter and contract packager of cereals and snack foods. Ryt-way Food Products Company is one of the largest contract packagers of its kind in the United States today
President: Glenn Hasse Jr
VP Sales/Marketing: Tim Hickey
VP Operations: Darrell Penning
Number Employees: 500-999
Sq. footage: 200000
Type of Packaging: Private Label

12455 S A Piazza & Associates
15815 SE Piazza
Clackamas, OR 97015-9195   503-657-3123
    Fax: 503-657-1784 spiazza@sapiazza.com
                             www.piazzapizza.com
Processor of coffee including regular and espresso
President: Steve Piazza
National Sales Director: Rick Johnson
Marketing Director: Shari Haworth
Estimated Sales:$ 20 - 50 Million
Number Employees: 50-99
Type of Packaging: Consumer, Food Service
Brands:
Piazza Fine

12456 S&B International Corporation
2815 Dalemead St
Torrance, CA 90505-7039   310-257-0177
                             Fax: 310-543-2168
Seasonings
President: Richard Jones
Estimated Sales:$ 5-10 Million
Number Employees: 1-4

12457 S&D Bait Company
PO Box 3525
Morgan City, LA 70381-3525 504-252-3500
                             Fax: 504-385-5412
Sells live bait.

12458 S&D Coffee, Inc
P.O.Box 1628
Concord, NC 28026-1628   704-339-0917
         Fax: 800-950-4378 www.sndcoffee.com
Coffee
President/CEO: Ron Hinson
Executive Vice President/CFO: Steve Cole
Number Employees: 250-499
Type of Packaging: Food Service, Private Label

12459 S&D Coffee, Inc
P.O.Box 1628
Concord, NC 28026-1628   704-782-3121
    Fax: 704-721-5792 sales@sndcoffee.com
                             www.sndcoffee.com
Coffees
President: Ron Hinson
Executive VP: Steve Cole
Marketing Director: Marcia Brezhear
Number Employees: 500-999
Type of Packaging: Food Service

12460 S&D Import Company
1155 Carolyn Sue Drive
Baton Rouge, LA 70815-4902 504-891-6301
                             Fax: 504-891-0004

12461 S&E Organic Farms
1716 Oak St # 4
Bakersfield, CA 93301-3040 661-325-2644
    Fax: 661-325-2602 seorganic@aol.com
Grower of organic vegetables, dry beans, grains and alfalfa; processor of frozen purees
President: Ed Davis
CEO: Shelley Davis
Manager: Cali Cheek
Estimated Sales:$500,000-$1 Million
Number Employees: 1-4
Type of Packaging: Bulk

12462 S&G Products
P.O.Box 930
Nicholasville, KY 40340-0930   859-885-9411
         Fax: 859-885-3063 800-826-7652
    sgproducts@qc.aibn.com   www.sglocks.com
Processor of bottled and glass and plastic-packed pickled products including beets, cauliflower, onions, olives, pickles, peppers, gherkins, etc.; also, vinegar
Co-Owner: James Sargent
Co-Owner: Halbert Greenleaf
CEO: Jerry A Morgan
Director Sales: Richard Greenberg
Type of Packaging: Consumer, Food Service
Brands:
Lion
Supreme

12463 S&K Industries
9209 Enterprise Ct # C
Manassas Park, VA 20111-4809   703-369-0232
    Fax: 703-369-0875 abuelitask@aol.com
                             www.abuelita.com
Processor of Mexican foods including corn and tortilla chips, tamales, flour and corn tortillas and taco shells; exporter of flour tortilla wraps
President: Eugene Suarez Sr
Director Marketing: Marie Forman
Production Manager: Paul Hammond
Estimated Sales:$ 10 - 20 Million
Number Employees: 50-99
Number of Brands: 3
Number of Products: 45
Sq. footage: 36000

Type of Packaging: Consumer, Food Service, Private Label
Brands:
Abuelita
Casa De Carmen
Nana's Cocina

12464 S&M Communion Bread Company
P.O.Box 40344
Nashville, TN 37204-0344   615-292-1969
                             www.buycommunion.com
Processor of communion bread
President: Barbara Reynolds
Estimated Sales:$ 3 - 5 Million
Number Employees: 10-19
Type of Packaging: Consumer
Brands:
S&M

12465 S&M Fisheries
1272 Portland Road
Kennebunkport, ME 04046-8104   207-985-3456
                             Fax: 207-985-3038
Wholesale distributor of shellfish
President: Stephanie Nadeau
Estimated Sales:$12,000,000
Number Employees: 11

12466 S&N Food Company
1321 Woodthorpe Drive
Mesquite, TX 75181-3519   972-222-1184
                             Fax: 972-222-1184
    sweetpotatodesserts@msn.com
                             www.sandnfood.com
Dessert mixes such as sweet potato pie, sweet potato muffins, sweet potato brownies, chocolate brownies, coffee & chocolate, pumpkin pie, pumpkin brownies, lemon pound cake, chocolate muffin & bread mix, chocolate pound cake, lemonsupreme muffin & bread mix, pumpkin pound cake, pumpkin pancake & waffle mix, sweet potato pound cake, sweet potato pancake & waffle mix, and spiced cider mix.
President: Shirley Peters
*Estimated Sales:*Below $ 500,000
Number Employees: 2
Type of Packaging: Consumer, Private Label
Brands:
SHIRLEY'S

12467 (HQ)S&P
100 Shoreline Hwy # 395
Mill Valley, CA 94941-6608 415-332-0550
    Fax: 415-332-0567 800-935-2337
S&P owns Pabst Brewing, which in 2001 shut down it's 115 year old Texas brewery and it's Pennsylvania plant. The company transferred production of it's brands to Miller Brewing. Pabst pays Miller to brew the beers, but retainsownership of the brands and markets the products.
President/Chairman/CEO/Secretary: Bernard Orsi

Estimated Sales:$ 100-500 Million
Number Employees: 100-249
Brands:
COLT 45
LONE STAR
OLD MILWAUKEE
PABST BLUE RIBBON
PEARL
SCHLITZ

12468 S-Car-Go
1232 Isabel Dr
Sanibel, FL 33957-3510   239-472-1900
                             Fax: 239-472-9180
Processor and importer of prepared frozen escargot
President: Syril Rubin
VP Sales: Maaark Rubin
Estimated Sales:$500,000-$1 Million
Number Employees: 1-4
Brands:
Syril's S-Car-Go

12469 S-W Mills
3646 County Road 22
Archbold, OH 43502-9791   419-445-5206
                             Fax: 419-445-4275 s-wmills@bright.net
Processor and exporter of dehydrated alfalfa pellets and meal
President: Mike Aeschliman
Operator: Martha Wyse
Sales: Ken Vaupel

Estimated Sales: $ 10 - 20 Million
Number Employees: 10-19

12470 S. Abuin Packing
814 2nd Ave
Elizabeth, NJ 07202-3804   908-354-2674
          Fax: 908-354-7170 www.814americas.com
Sausage
     Manager: Michael Patracuolla
     CFO: Michael Patratuolla
Estimated Sales: $ 5-10 Million
Number Employees: 20-49
Brands:
     El Mino
     Riojano

12471 S. Anderson Vineyard
1473 Yountville Cross Rd
Yountville, CA 94599-9471   707-944-8642
     Fax: 707-944-8020 800-428-2259
          savwines@4bubbly.com
          www.clifflledevineyards.com
Processor of wines and champagne
     Owner: Cliff Lede
     CEO: John Anderson
     Owner: Cliff Lede
     Marketing Manager: Alfred Andreson
     Sales Manager: Peter Vanm
Estimated Sales: $430000
Number Employees: 10-19
Type of Packaging: Consumer, Food Service

12472 S. Christina Seafood
527 N Carrollton Avenue
New Orleans, LA 70119-4704   504-486-5301
          Fax: 504-486-5373
Seafood

12473 S. Kennedy Vegetable Lifestock Company
2310 Main Avenue
Clear Lake, IA 50428-2244   641-357-6101
Processor of carrots
     President: Scott Kennedy
Estimated Sales: $600000
Number Employees: 4
Sq. footage: 40000
Brands:
     S.K.

12474 S. Wallace Edward & Sons
PO Box 25
Surry, VA 23883-0025   800-290-9213
     Fax: 757-294-5378 info@virginiatraditions.com
          www.virginiatraditions.com
Virginia hams, sweet hams, bacon & sausage, soups
& stews, specialty meats, desserts, poultry, snacks,
seafood, other good stuff and assortments.
     President: Sammuel Edwards III
     CEO: Wallace Edwards Jr.
     Vice President: Amy Edwards Harte
     Marketing Director: Sammuel Edwards III
     Sales Director: Bob Unterbrink
     Operations Manager: Al Kadons
     Plant Manager: Al Kadons
     Purchasing Manager: Ryan Rowland
Number Employees: 22
Number of Brands: 2
Type of Packaging: Consumer
Brands:
     Colonial Williamsburg
     Edwards
     Surry

12475 S. Zitner Company
3120 N 17th St
Philadelphia, PA 19132-2357   215-229-4990
          Fax: 215-229-9828 zitnermett@aol.com
Candy
     Chairman: M Christine Murphy
     CFO: Matt Mitttelauril
     Quality Control: Joe Martin
Estimated Sales: $ 10-20 Million
Number Employees: 20-49
Brands:
     Zitner's

12476 S.A.S. Foods
2395 Pleasantdale Rd # 2
Doraville, GA 30340-3154   770-263-9312
          Fax: 770-446-9234
Oriental grocery items, seafood, fin fish, shellfish
     President: Goro Iwami

Estimated Sales: $ 5 - 10 Million
Number Employees: 5-9

12477 S.B. Winsor Dairy
18 Clinton St
Johnston, RI 02919-4121   401-231-7832
          Fax: 401-231-7832
Milk and dairy products
     Chef: Alan Winsor
Estimated Sales: $ 2.5-5 Million
Number Employees: 1-4

12478 S.D. Mushrooms
P.O.Box 687
Avondale, PA 19311-0687   610-268-8082
          Fax: 610-268-8644
Processor and importer of mushrooms and mush-
room sauce
     President/Owner: John D'Amico
Estimated Sales: $450,000
Number Employees: 1-4
Type of Packaging: Consumer, Food Service, Pri-
vate Label, Bulk

12479 S.F. Foods Corporation
P.O.Box 913
Evansville, IN 47706-0913   812-428-0888
          Fax: 812-428-0961
     Manager: Jeff Noah
Estimated Sales: $ 10 - 20 Million
Number Employees: 10-19

12480 S.J. McCullagh
245 Swan St
Buffalo, NY 14204-2051   716-856-3473
     Fax: 716-856-3486 800-753-3473
     sjm@buffnet.net   www.mccullaghcoffee.com
Processor, importer and exporter of coffee, tea, non-
dairy creamer and hot chocolate
     President: Warren Emblidge
     Vice President: Roger Van Overstaeten
     Marketing Director: Larry Franko
     Purchasing Manager: Mary Costanzo
Estimated Sales: 9 Million
Number Employees: 50-99
Brands:
     McCullagh-Hatan

12481 S.L. Kaye Company
230 5th Ave
New York, NY 10001-7704   212-683-5600
     Fax: 212-947-7664 kaye230@aol.com
          www.slkaye.com
Candy
     President/Owner: Mitchell Katzman
     Sales Manager: S Handy
Estimated Sales: $ 1-2.5 Million
Number Employees: 1-4
Brands:
     Eskimo Pie Coffeepeaks
     Eskimo Pie Miniatures
     Eskimo Pie Snowpeaks
     Needlers Jersey English Toffee
     Titanic Esm Mints

12482 S.P. Enterprises
1889 E Maule Ave # E
Las Vegas, NV 89119-4603   702-736-4774
     Fax: 702-736-6180 800-746-4774
     spcandy@msn.com   www.espeezcandy.com
Candy
     President: Sam Popowcer
     CEO: Alan Popowcer
Estimated Sales: $ 3 - 5 Million
Number Employees: 5-9
Brands:
     Lillipos
     Money Candy

12483 S.S. Logan Packing Company
P.O.Box 5658
Huntington, WV 25703-0658   304-525-7625
          Fax: 304-529-2516 800-642-3524
Processor of meats
     President: Nester S Logan
     CFO: Richard Logan
Estimated Sales: $20532751
Number Employees: 50-99

12484 S.T. Jerrell Company
802 Labarge Dr
Bessemer, AL 35022-8320   205-426-8930
          Fax: 205-426-8989 www.jerrellpackaging.com

Non-fat dry milk
     CEO: John Lyon
     Vice President: Barry Cornell
Estimated Sales: Below $ 5 Million
Number Employees: 10-19
Sq. footage: 25000
Type of Packaging: Food Service, Private Label,
Bulk
Brands:
     Cloverleaf Farms Peanut Butter
     S. T. Jerrell Nonfat

12485 S.T. Specialty Foods Inc
8700 Xylon Ave N
Brooklyn Park, MN 55445-1817   763-493-9600
          Fax: 763-493-9606
     customerservice@stspecialtyfoods.com
          www.stspecialtyfoods.com
Dry Pasta Dinners
     President/CEO: Dale Schulz
     CFO: Raymond Turcotte
     VP Administration: Barry Calhoon
     VP R&D: Mark Welken
     Quality Control: Nancy Foss
     Seniror VP Sales: Kevin Kollock
     VP Operations: Steve Favro
     Purchasing Manager: Dick Hamblin
Number of Products: 50
Type of Packaging: Private Label
Brands:
     LAND O'LAKE MACARONI & CHEESE
     OUR SPECIALTY PASTA DINNERS

12486 S.W. Meat & Provision Company
2019 N 48th St
Phoenix, AZ 85008-3303   602-275-2000
Processor and wholesaler/distributor of sausage,
ground beef and patties, portion cut steaks and aged
beef sides; also, wholesaler/distributor of grocery
products, frozen foods and general merchandise;
serving the food servicemarket
     President: W David Hart
Estimated Sales: $ 10 - 20 Million
Number Employees: 5-9
Type of Packaging: Food Service

12487 SA Carlson
160 Camfield Rd
Yakima, WA 98908-9684   509-965-8333
     Fax: 509-965-8311 sherm@sacarlson.com
          www.sacarlson.com
Processed fruit ingredients including apple, pear,
peach, grapes, berry fruits, etc.
     President: Sherman Carlson
     Customer Service: Ruffell Carlson
     Quality Control: Carlos Correa
Estimated Sales: $ 5-10 Million
Number Employees: 1-4
Sq. footage: 125000
Type of Packaging: Food Service, Bulk
Brands:
     INVERTEC
     TASTEE

12488 SAF Products
400 S 4th Street
Suite 310
Minneapolis, MN 55415-1418   612-338-0900
     Fax: 414-615-4669 800-641-4615
Processor and exporter of dry yeast including instant
active, active, inactive, etc.
     President: Jack Wheeler
     COO/Executive VP: Sunni Epstein
Number Employees: 20-49
Parent Co: S.I. Lesaffre
Type of Packaging: Consumer, Food Service, Bulk
Brands:
     Saf-Instant
     Saf-Levina
     Saf-Levure

12489 SANGARIA USA
3142 Pacific Coast Hwy # 208
Torrance, CA 90505-6796   310-530-2202
     Fax: 310-530-5335 sangaria@msn.com
Manufacturer, importer and exporter of soft drinks:
Ramune drink, green tea, oolong tea, iced coffee, en-
ergy drink, fruit juices, etc
     Owner: Leona Singer
Estimated Sales: $300,000-500,000
Number Employees: 1-4
Sq. footage: 250000
Parent Co: Japan Sangaria Beverage Company
Type of Packaging: Consumer, Food Service

Brands:
Sangaria

12490 SAS Bakers Yeast
13211 Us Highway 431 S
Headland, AL 36345-6333   334-889-4461
    Fax: 334-889-4529   877-677-7000
    www.lesaffreyeastcorp.com
Baker yeast
   Plant Manager: Dennis Barry
   President: John Reisch
Estimated Sales: $ 20-30 Million
Number Employees: 100-249
Brands:
   SAS Bakers

12491 SASIB Biscuits and Snacks Division
118 W Streetsboro Street
Suite 306
Hudson, OH 44236-2711   330-656-3317
Fax: 330-656-2822   samuelson_sasibna@msn.com
Baked goods, biscuits, snacks

12492 SB Global Foods
1330 N Broad St
Lansdale, PA 19446-1143   215-361-9500
    Fax: 215-361-9323   877-857-1727
    info@sbglobalfoods.com
    www.sbglobalfoods.com
Seasoned filled pretzel nuggets, chocolate covered peanut butter filled pretzel nuggets, and mini marshmellows.
   President: Karl Brown
Estimated Sales: Below $ 5 Million
Number Employees: 5-9
Type of Packaging: Private Label
Brands:
   American Cookie Boy
   Pretzel Pete
   Rocky Mountain Marshmallows
   Rocky Mountain Popcorn

12493 SBK Preserves
1161 E 156th St
Bronx, NY 10474-6226   718-589-2900
    Fax: 718-589-8412   800-773-7378
    info@sarabeth.com   www.sarabeth.com
Processor and exporter of jams, preserves, fruit spreads, syrups and granola cereal
   President: William Levine
   VP: Sarabeth Levine
   Plant Manger: Manuel Padilla
Estimated Sales: $650962
Number Employees: 10-19
Sq. footage: 15000
Parent Co: Sarabeth's Kitchen
Other Locations:
   SBK Preserves
   New York NY
Brands:
   Sarabeth's

12494 SC Enterprises
RR 5
Owen Sound, ON N4K 5N7
Canada   519-371-0456
    Fax: 519-371-5944   sce.d@bmts.com
    www.scdistributors.biz/index.html
Wholesaler/distributor of fresh and frozen fish and wild game; processor of rainbow trout.
   Manager: Winston Jones
Number Employees: 10-19
Sq. footage: 9000

12495 SECO & Golden 100
P.O.Box 323
Deland, FL 32721-0323   386-734-3906
    Fax: 386-738-1378   info@seco-golden100.com
    www.seco-golden100.com
Producer of industrial beverage mixes in liquid and powder for all types of drinks as well as many custom formulations
   President: Ron Edmundson
Estimated Sales: $100+ Million
Number Employees: 20-49
Type of Packaging: Food Service, Private Label, Bulk

12496 SEW Friel
P.O.Box 10
Queenstown, MD 21658-0010   410-827-8841
    Fax: 410-827-9472   jay@sewfriel.com
    www.sewfriel.com

Processor, importer and exporter of canned juices including vegetable, tomato, apple, pineapple, grape and prune; also, canned corn
   President: Michael Foster
   Partner: James Friel Jr
Estimated Sales: $49100000
Number Employees: 1-4
Sq. footage: 240000
Type of Packaging: Consumer, Food Service, Private Label, Bulk
Brands:
   Friel's
   Hudson
   Ole Wye

12497 SFP Food Products
348 Highway 64 E
Conway, AR 72032-9414   501-327-0744
    Fax: 501-327-2808   800-654-5329
    jballard@sfpfoods.com   www.sfpfoods.com
Processor and exporter of waffle, pancake and cone mixes; manufacturer and exporter of waffle and cone irons
   President: Jon Ballard
   VP Marketing/Sales: Jon Ballard
   VP Operations: Ray Ballard
Estimated Sales: $ 3 - 5 Million
Number Employees: 5-9
Sq. footage: 15000
Type of Packaging: Food Service, Private Label

12498 SIF
PO Box 1077
Shelburne, NS B0T 1W0
Canada   902-875-2666
    Fax: 902-875-2706
Processor and exporter of fresh and frozen groundfish
   Manager: Ian Williams
Number Employees: 20-49
Type of Packaging: Consumer, Food Service, Private Label, Bulk

12499 SJH Enterprises
3447 Laura Ln
Middleton, WI 53562-1490   608-831-3001
    Fax: 608-831-3001   888-745-3845
Broker of organic grains and natural colors and flavors
   Manager: Hank Zimmerman
Estimated Sales: $170000
Number Employees: 1-4
Type of Packaging: Consumer, Food Service, Private Label, Bulk

12500 SJR Foods
49 Brook Street
New Bedford, MA 02746-1742   781-821-3090
    Fax: 781-821-5666   rbaras@sjrfoods.com
    www.unholey.com
Processor of cream cheese filled bagels including plain, cinnamon raisin, sesame, poppy and onion
   Owner: Larry Barras
Brands:
   Unholey Bagel

12501 SK Foods
1175 S 19th Ave
Lemoore, CA 93245   559-924-6527
    Fax: 559-924-0178   info@skfoods.com
    www.skfoods.com
Processor of tomato products including paste, sauce, pulp, puree, diced and in juice
   Manager: Randy Yingling
   VP/CFO: Rick Washburn
   VP Marketing: Alan Huey
Estimated Sales: $ 30-50 Million
Number Employees: 5-9
Type of Packaging: Food Service, Bulk

12502 SK Foods International
4666 Amber Valley Parkway
Fargo, ND 58104   701-356-4106
    Fax: 701-356-4102   skfood@skfood.com
    www.skfood.com
Certified organic and conventional non-GMO dry beans, grains, seeds, soybeans, brans/germs, cocoas, flours, oils, meals, and sweetners
   President/CEO: David Skyberg
   VP/Secretary/Treasurer: Beverly Skyberg
   Marketing Director: Jennifer Tesch
Estimated Sales: $3 Million
Number Employees: 17
Type of Packaging: Bulk

12503 SKW Biosystems
1741 Tomlinson Rd
Philadelphia, PA 19116-3847   215-676-3900
    Fax: 215-613-2115   800-223-7073
    www.sweetovation.com
Processor and exporter of fruit preparations
   Plant Manager: Corey Arrick
Number Employees: 100-249
Parent Co: Systems Bio-Industries

12504 SKW Flavor & Fruit Preparation
2021 Cabot Boulevard W
Langhorne, PA 19047-1810   215-702-1000
    Fax: 215-702-1015
Fruits and nonfruit preps for dairy, frozen and refrigerated bakery and food service

12505 SKW Nature Products
2021 Cabot Boulevard W
Langhorne, PA 19047-1810   215-702-1000
    Fax: 215-702-1015
Manufacturer and exporter of cultures, enzymes, edible and industrial gelatins, hydrocolloids, flavors, fragrance raw materials and fruit systems
   VP/General Manager: Kenneth Hughes
   VP/General Manager: George Masson
Number Employees: 500-999
Parent Co: SKW

12506 SKW Nature Products
2350 Kerper Boulevard
Dubuque, IA 52001-2220   563-588-6244
    Fax: 563-588-9063   info@degussa.com
    www.degussa.com
Enzymes and flavor ingredients for food, beverage, dairy and specialties industries
   Head Corporate Communications: Ralph Driever
   Press Relations Officer: Hannelore Gantzer
   Internal Communications: Markus Langer
Number Employees: 100-249

12507 SLB Snacks
420 Lynnway
Lynn, MA 01901-1711   781-593-4422
    Fax: 781-599-8430
Potato chips
   President: William Termano
   Marketing/Sales Manager: David Dugan
   VP Sales: Shehan James
   Plant Manager: Sue Pickering
Estimated Sales: $ 10-24.9 Million
Number Employees: 85

12508 SMG
2890 Chancellor Drive
Crestview Hills, KY 41017-2153   757-952-1100
    Fax: 859-344-3737   www.smgmeats.com
Processor of pre-cooked, prepared and specialty meats including hamburgers, rib eye steaks, luncheon, roast beef, corned and roast beef, wet corn brisket, home meal replacements, etc.; exporter of hot dogs, pastrami and wet cornbrisket
   CEO/President: Joe McCloskey
   VP Sales: Don Mendenhall
Number Employees: 250-499
Parent Co: SMG
Type of Packaging: Consumer, Food Service, Private Label, Bulk
Other Locations:
   S.M.G.
   Flushing NY
Brands:
   FIELD
   FISCHER'S
   KENTUCKY LEGEND
   LIGURIA ITALIAN SPECIALTIES
   MICKELBERRY'S
   MOSEY'S
   NATHAN'S FAMOUS
   SCOTT PETERSEN

12509 SOPAKCO Foods
215 S Mullins St
Mullins, SC 29574-3207   843-464-0121
    Fax: 423-639-7270   800-276-9678
    www.sopakco.com

Processor of pasta sauces; also, retortable pouch manufacturer, canner and contract packager of poultry, meat, fish, pasta, vegetable, bean, fruit and dessert products, flexible, semi-rigid and glass conatiainers
CEO: Al Reitzer
CFO: Steve Keight
R & D: Jim Dukes
Quality Control: Phyllis Calhoun
General Manager: Wynn Pettibone
General Manager: Wynn Pettibone
Plant Manager: Carl Whitmore
Purchasing Director: Beverly Stacey
Estimated Sales:$5-10 Million
Number Employees: 100
Sq. footage: 100000
Parent Co: Unaka Corporation
Type of Packaging: Consumer, Food Service, Private Label

12510 SOUPerior Bean & Spice Company
13115 NE 4th St # 120
Vancouver, WA 98684-5959   360-882-4500
          Fax: 360-694-0862   800-878-7687
                    soupbean@aol.com
Processor of spice blends and mixes including bean soup, pasta salad, bread and broth
Owner: Paul Dendy
VP: Duane Rough Jr
Estimated Sales:$ 5 - 10 Million
Number Employees: 5-9
Sq. footage: 5700
Brands:
Our Counrtry

12511 SP Enterprises
1889 E Maule Ave # E
Las Vegas, NV 89119-4603   702-736-4774
          Fax: 702-736-6180   800-746-4774
          spcandy@msn.com   www.espeezcandy.com
Leading manufacturer of kid's novelty candy including Viper Venom, Viper Vials, Viper Gum, Viper Blast and Aunt Flo's Country Fudge. Also known for Gold Mine Gum, Money Mints, Rock Candy and Jumbo Pops.
President: Sam Popowcer
Estimated Sales:$ 3 - 5 Million
Number Employees: 5-9
Brands:
AUNT FLO'S COUNTRY FUDGE
ESPEEZ
EYE OF THE DRAGON
GOLD MINE GUM
KID WIZARD
MONEY MINTS
USA MINTS
VIPER
VIPER BLAST
VIPER GUM
VIPER VENOM
VIPER VIALS

12512 SPI Foods
805 S Union St
Fremont, NE 68025-6157   402-727-8412
          Fax: 402-727-6327   866-266-1304
          jmilne@spifoods.com   www.spifoods.com
Crisp rice, soy crisp, cereal extrusion, custom extruded ingredients, no boil lasagna and instant pasta
President: Robert Parnow
CEO: John Stout
Controller: Darren Phinney
VP: Jeff Milne Jr.
Research & Development: Shashi Ramaiah
Quality Control: Craig Hammond
Sales Director: Jeff Milne Jr.
Plant Manager: Mark Johnson
Estimated Sales:$ 15 Million
Number Employees: 5-9
Sq. footage: 65000
Parent Co: Plaza Belmont Group
Type of Packaging: Private Label, Bulk
Brands:
Ne-Boil Lasagna
Pasta Defino

12513 SPI Nutritional
222 N Vincent Avenue
Covina, CA 91722-3904   626-915-1151
          Fax: 626-332-7754
Nutritional food
Estimated Sales:$ 5-10 Million appx.
Number Employees: 5

12514 SRA Foods
P.O.Box 12084
Birmingham, AL 35202-2084   205-323-7447
          Fax: 205-323-1772
Wholesale/distributor of meats to restaurants and grocery stores
President: Anthony Anselmo
Estimated Sales:$ 50 - 100 Million
Number Employees: 20-49

12515 SS Lobster Limited
691 River St
Fitchburg, MA 01420-2910   978-342-6135
          Fax: 978-345-7341
Seafood (lobster, clams, shrimp)
President: Mark Strazdas
Estimated Sales:$ 10 - 20 Million
Number Employees: 20-49

12516 SSI Food Service
P.O.Box 700
Caldwell, ID 83606-0700   208-482-7844
          Fax: 208-482-7457
Processes meat to beef patties, fajitas, taco meat and more
President: Kirk Smith
VP Marketing: Jeff Gross
VP Sales: Jeff Gross
VP Operations: Ben Badiola
Purchasing Manager: Neal Waterman
Estimated Sales: 74.80 Million
Number Employees: 500-999

12517 ST Specialty Foods
8700 Xylon Ave N
Brooklyn Park, MN 55445-1817   763-493-9600
          Fax: 763-493-9606 www.stspecialtyfoods.com
Dry pasta dinners, and mix
President/CEO: Dale Schulz
Marketing Director: Kevin Kollock
VP/CFO: Ray Turcotte
CFO: Ray Turcotte
Sales Manager: Kevin Kollock
Operations Manager: Steve Favro
Plant Manager: Paul Westerberg
Purchase Manager: Dick Hamblin
Estimated Sales:$ 10-20 Million
Number Employees: 50-99
Type of Packaging: Private Label

12518 (HQ)SW Red Smith
4145 SW 47th Ave
Davie, FL 33314-4006   954-581-1996
          Fax: 954-581-6775   inquiries@swredsmith.com
                    www.swredsmith.com
Processor, packer and exporter of pickled eggs, sausage and pigs' feet
President: Stephen Foster
Executive VP: David Foster
VP/Sales: Helena Meade
Plant Manager: Michael Sandy
Estimated Sales:$8 Million
Number Employees: 20-49
Number of Brands: 2
Number of Products: 6
Sq. footage: 12000
Parent Co: Red Smith of Florida
Type of Packaging: Consumer
Brands:
Big John
Red Smith

12519 SWELL Philadelphia Chewing Gum Corporation
North Eagle & Lawrence
Havertown, PA 19083   610-449-1700
          Fax: 610-449-2557   sales@swellgum.com
                    www.swellgum.com
Manufacturer and exporter of chewing bubble gum and candy
President: Edward Fenimore
Estimated Sales:$14.5 Million
Number Employees: 100-249
Sq. footage: 200000
Type of Packaging: Private Label, Bulk
Brands:
SWELL

12520 SYFO Beverage Company ofFlorida
7563 Philips Highway
Suite 110
Jacksonville, FL 32256-6824   904-381-9002
          Fax: 904-381-9004
Beverages
President: Cydelle Mendius
Estimated Sales:$ 1-2.5 Million
Number Employees: 1

12521 SYSCO Food Services of Northern New England
P.O.Box 4657
Portland, ME 04112-4657   207-871-0700
          Fax: 207-871-0339   800-632-4446
information@sysconne.com   www.sysconne.com
SYSCO is a marketer and distributor of foodservice products in North America, products of which include a wide variety of fresh and frozen meats, seafood, poultry, fruits and vegetables, plus bakery products, canned and dry foodspaper and disposable products, sanitation items, dairy foods, beverages, kitchen and tabletop equipment.
President/COO: Greg Otterbein
Chairman: Richard Giles
Vice President of Finance: John Rodrigue
Director of Operations: Dain Thomason

12522 SYSCO Foodservice
48811 Warm Springs Boulevard
Fremont, CA 94539-7712   650-494-7200
          Fax: 650-424-9379 www.sysco.com
Manufacturer and exporter of fresh and frozen ground beef and fish; wholesaler/distributor of frozen foods, meat, seafood and specialty foods; serving the food service market
President/CEO: Robert Facciola
Number Employees: 400
Sq. footage: 86000
Type of Packaging: Food Service, Private Label, Bulk
Brands:
FACCIOLA
FMC

12523 Saag's Products
1799 Factor Ave
San Leandro, CA 94577-5617   510-352-8605
          Fax: 510-352-4100   800-352-7224
                    www.saags.com
Processor of meats including traditional sausage, bistro contemporary sausages, frankfurters, roast beef, corned beef, pastrami, turkey breasts, smoked hams and pork products, salamis and dried cured meats, luncheon meats and pates andcondiments
President: Timothy Dam
VP Marketing: Tim Dam
Sales Manager: Andy Burns
VP Operations: Jim Mosle
Estimated Sales:$11300000
Number Employees: 50-99
Type of Packaging: Food Service, Private Label, Bulk
Brands:
Wurstmeister

12524 Sabatino Truffles USA
2212 40th Avenue
Long Island City, NY 11101-4808   718-392-3065
          Fax: 718-392-2357   888-444-9971
                    customer@sabatinostore.com
                    www.sabatinostore.com
Extra virgin olive oil, truffles, truffle butter, truffle oil, pasta, mushrooms, sauces and creams.
President: Frederico Balestra
Estimated Sales:$ 1 - 3 Million
Number Employees: 7
Type of Packaging: Food Service, Private Label

12525 Sabinsa Corporation
121 Ethel Rd W # 6
Piscataway, NJ 08854-5952   732-777-1111
          Fax: 732-777-1443   sabinsa@compuserve.com
                    www.sabinsa.com
Processor of botanical extracts
President: Muhammed Majeed
VP: Mark Sysler
Estimated Sales:$ 20 - 50 Million
Number Employees: 20-49
Brands:
Ashwagandha
Boswellin

Citrin
Citrin K
Curlumin C3 Complex
Digezyme
Gugulidid
Lactospore

12526 Sable & Rosenfeld Foods
12 Lawton Blvd
Toronto, ON M4V 1Z4
Canada   416-929-4214
Fax: 416-929-6727 info@sableandrosenfeld.com
www.sableandrosenfeld.com
cocktail garnishes, appetizers/condiments and sauces.
President/Owner: Myra Sable
VP: Kathy Smith
Sales: Mary O'Neill

12527 Sabra Blue & White FoodProducts
2420 49th St
Astoria, NY 11103-1017   718-389-3800
Manufacturer of Mediterranean dips, spreads, appetizers and gourmet specialities. As of September 2005 Strauss-Elite LTD has acquired a 51% stake in Sabra Salads
CEO: Meiky Tollman
Estimated Sales:$ 20 - 50 Million
Number Employees: 50-99
Parent Co: Strauss-Elite LTD
Type of Packaging: Consumer, Food Service
Brands:
SABRA

12528 Sabra-Go Mediterranean
525 Smith St 535
Farmingdale, NY 11735   631-694-9500
www.sabra.com
Mediterranean style refrigerated dips and spreads that iclude hummus, eggplant dips, babaganoush spreads, and Mediterranean salsa
CEO: Ronen Zohar
CFO: Amit Anand
Executive VP/General Manager: Meiky Tollman
Chief Marketing Officer: Rodrigo Troni
Executive VP Sales: John McGuckin
Human Resources Director: Angela King
Executive VP Operations: Guy Nir

12529 (HQ)Sabroso Company
PO Box 4310
Medford, OR 97501   509-697-7251
www.sabroso.com
Manufacturer of fruit purees, fruit puree concentrates, fruit preparations, fruit flakes, fruit bases and custom fruit solutions.
CEO: James Root
CFO: Mike Molenkamp
VP: John Jaconbsen
Estimated Sales:$ 50 - 100 Million
Number Employees: 300
Parent Co: Tree Top
Type of Packaging: Food Service, Bulk
Other Locations:
Sabroso Co.
Sandy OR

12530 Sacharen Brothers
20 Henri IV Street
Montreal, QC H2S 1V9
Canada   514-277-8205
Fax: 514-277-3283
Processor of sugarless bars including peanut, coconut, carob and sesame; also, halvah, tahini and Passover candies and slices; exporter of halvah, tahini, jelly fruit slices and bars including rice crisp, sesame and snack; importer ofsesame seeds and marshmallows
Co-President: Bryan Abish
Co-President: Lee Shulkin
Number Employees: 20
Sq. footage: 30000
Type of Packaging: Consumer, Food Service, Private Label, Bulk
Brands:
Camel

12531 Sachs Nut Company
P.O.Box 550
Clarkton, NC 28433-0550   910-647-4711
Fax: 910-647-0301 www.sachspeanuts.com

Nuts
President/Owner: Nathan Cox
VP: Sam Cox
Estimated Sales:$ 2.5-5 Million
Number Employees: 50-99
Type of Packaging: Private Label, Bulk
Brands:
Sachs Nut Company

12532 Sacramento Baking Company
9221 Beatty Dr
Sacramento, CA 95826-9702   916-361-2000
Fax: 916-361-0117
Bakery items including cakes
President: Juma Elajou
Marketing Director: Sam Alaclu
Quality Control: Sam Elajou
Estimated Sales:$ 20-50 Million
Number Employees: 20-49
Brands:
Sacramento Baking

12533 Sacramento Cookie Factory
3428 Auburn Blvd
Sacramento, CA 95827   916-482-8222
Fax: 916-482-8222 877-877-2646
www.wafercookie.com
wafer cookies

12534 Saddleback Cellars
P.O.Box 414
Oakville, CA 94562-0414   707-944-8808
Fax: 707-944-2817 www.silveroak.com
Wines
Owner: Ray Duncan
Estimated Sales:$ 20 - 50 Million
Number Employees: 20-49

12535 (HQ)Sadkhin Complex
2306 Avenue U
Brooklyn, NY 11229-4917   718-769-7771
Fax: 718-769-8087 800-723-5446
NYOffice@sadkhin.com www.sadkhin.com
Processor of seasonal herbal formulas and multi-vitamins
Owner: Dr Grigory Sadkhin
Estimated Sales:Less than $500,000
Number Employees: 1-4
Sq. footage: 2200
Type of Packaging: Consumer
Other Locations:
Los Angeles CA
San Francisco CA
Boston MA
Philadelphia PA
Detroit MI
Brands:
The Sadkhin Complex®

12536 Sadler's BBQ Sales
1206 N Frisco St
Henderson, TX 75652-6924   903-657-5581
Fax: 903-655-8404 www.sadlersbbq.com
Processor of barbecued beef and pork, smoked poultry and barbecue sauce; wholesaler/distributor of meats/provisions; serving the food service market
President: Harold Sadler
VP Sales/Marketing: Randy Sadler
VP Operations/General Manager: Jason Flanagan
Purchasing Manager: Brett Hensley
Estimated Sales:$52899000
Number Employees: 250-499
Sq. footage: 100000
Type of Packaging: Consumer, Food Service, Private Label
Brands:
Double S
Sadler's Smokehouse

12537 SafeTrek Foods
315 Edelweiss Dr
Bozeman, MT 59718-3928   406-586-4840
Fax: 406-582-0614 sales@safetrek.com
www.stevequayle.com
Manufacture and exporter of dehydrated, freeze-dried and organic entries, soups, gravies, side dishes
President: Stephen Quayle
CFO: Kathy Madsen
Purchasing Manager: James Young
Estimated Sales:$ 10-20 Million
Number Employees: 10-19
Sq. footage: 50000
Type of Packaging: Consumer, Food Service, Private Label, Bulk

Brands:
SAFETREK

12538 Safeway Beverage
6405 E Stapleton Drive N
Denver, CO 80216-3341   303-320-7960
Fax: 303-322-9309 business.ethics@safeway.com
www.shop.safeway.com
Contract packager of soft drinks
President: Steve Burd
CEO: Steve Burd
Plant Superintendent: Fred Scherrer
Product Control Coordinator: Louise Kimbrough
Chairman: Steve Burd
Plant Manager: Karl Guperian
Estimated Sales:$ 10 - 20 Million
Number Employees: 50-99
Sq. footage: 175000
Parent Co: Safeway Stores
Type of Packaging: Consumer, Private Label
Brands:
Safeway Beverage

12539 Safeway Beverage
1121 124th Ave NE
Bellevue, WA 98005-2101   425-455-6444
Fax: 425-455-6499 www.safeway.com
Processor and exporter of canned and bottled soft drinks
Executive: Greg Sparks
Plant Manager: M Smsith
Estimated Sales:$ 50 - 100 Million
Number Employees: 250-499
Parent Co: Safeway Stores
Type of Packaging: Consumer, Private Label
Brands:
Select Pop

12540 Safeway Dairy Products
4525 Addison Road
Capitol Heights, MD 20743-1002   301-341-9555
www.safeway.com
Processor of ice cream, ice milk, etc
President: Steven Burd
Vice President: Steve Armstrong
Plant Manager: Bruce Bennett
Number Employees: 20-49
Type of Packaging: Consumer, Private Label

12541 (HQ)Safeway Dairy Products
2800 Ygnacio Valley Rd
Walnut Creek, CA 94598-3592   925-944-4000
Fax: 925-467-3230 www.safeway.com
Processor and exporter of dairy and bakery products; also, beverages
President: Steve Burd
Senior VP: Lawrence Jackson
Estimated Sales:$ .5 - 1 million
Number Employees: 1-4
Type of Packaging: Consumer, Private Label

12542 Safeway Inc
P.O.Box 9
Durand, WI 54736-0009   715-672-8911
Fax: 715-672-5017 www.marronfoods.com
Processor of instant nonfat dry milk
Manager: Keith Hall
Superintendent: Dick Hubbard
Estimated Sales:$$2.5-5 Million
Number Employees: 20-49
Parent Co: Safeway Stores
Type of Packaging: Consumer

12543 Safeway Milk Plant
1115 W Alameda Dr
Tempe, AZ 85282-3384   480-894-4391
Fax: 480-929-8025 www.safeway.com
Processor of milk including half and half, skim, whole, 1% and 2%
Plant Manager: Jason Glober
Plant Manager: Jeff Fowler
Number Employees: 50-99
Parent Co: Safeway Stores
Type of Packaging: Consumer, Food Service, Private Label, Bulk

12544 Safeway Stores
1703 W 10th Pl
Tempe, AZ 85281-5254   480-967-9411
Fax: 480-967-9439 877-723-3929
www.safway.com

Processor of ice cream and yogurt
  Manager: Kevin Kluetz
  CEO: Steven A Burd
  CFO: Robert Edwards
  Vice President: Russell Jackson
  Chief Marketing Officer: Brian C Cornell
Estimated Sales:$ 5 - 10 Million
Number Employees: 20-49
Parent Co: Vons Grocery Company
Type of Packaging: Consumer
Brands:
  Safeway

12545 Sagawa's Savory Sauces
8292 SW Nyberg St
Tualatin, OR 97062-9457   503-692-4334
                  Fax: 503-691-0661
Processor and exporter of Hawaiian-style sauces including teriyaki, sweet and sour and Polynesian barbecue; also, salad dressings
  President: Linda Rider
Estimated Sales:$460000
Number Employees: 10-19
Type of Packaging: Consumer, Food Service
Brands:
  Baste & Glaze
  Sweet & Sassy

12546 Sagaya Corporation
3700 Old Seward Hwy
Anchorage, AK 99503-6037   907-561-5173
          Fax: 907-561-2042 www.newsagaya.com
International grocery store offering fresh Alaskan seafood, ethnic cuisine, specialty foods, gourmet groceries, fresh produce, and choice meats
  Manager: Tom Griffin
Estimated Sales:$ 10 - 20 Million
Number Employees: 50-99

12547 Sage Enterprises
6 E Monroe St # 1004
Chicago, IL 60603-2721   847-827-0066
                  Fax: 847-827-6420
  President: Gary Greenberg

12548 Sage V Foods
12100 Wilshire Blvd # 605
Los Angeles, CA 90025-7122   310-820-4496
    Fax: 310-820-2559 sales@sagevfoods.com
                  www.sagevfoods.com
Functional rice ingredients and grains
  President: Pete Vegas
Estimated Sales:$42,173,547
Number Employees: 5-9
Brands:
  Sage V

12549 Sage V Foods LLC
12100 Wilshire Blvd # 605
Los Angeles, CA 90025-7122   310-820-4496
        Fax: 310-820-2559 sales@sagevfoods.com
                  www.sagevfoods.com
Specializes in producing rice based ingredients for use in processed foods. Product line includes rice flour, instant rice, iqf rice, and specially extruded products.
  Owner: Pete Vegas
  Marketing/Sales: Mhari Watanabe
Estimated Sales:$ 5 - 10 Million
Number Employees: 50-99
Type of Packaging: Food Service, Bulk

12550 Saguaro Food Products
1319 N Main Avenue
Tucson, AZ 85705-7235   520-884-8049
        Fax: 520-884-9704 800-732-2447
    sfpchips@flash.net www.saguarofood.com
Southwest gourmet foods, potato, dips and sauces, tortilla and corn chips
  General Manager: Ralph Cortese
  Finance Manager: Laurie Cowan
  Marketing Manager: Sue Heems
  Operations Manager: Raul Ruiz
*Estimated Sales:*Below $ 500,000
Number Employees: 8

12551 Sahadi Fine Foods
4201 1st Ave
Brooklyn, NY 11232-3324   718-768-4790
      Fax: 718-369-0800 800-724-2341
        pwhelan@sahadifinefoods.com
                  www.jdfinefoods.com

Maufacturer of nuts and seeds. Importer of dried fruit, beans, nuts, olives, Mediterranean foods
  President: Morris Elbaz
  VP: Pat Whelan
Estimated Sales:$11 Million
Number Employees: 20-49
Sq. footage: 58000

12552 Sahadi Importing Company
187 Atlantic Ave
Brooklyn, NY 11201-5696   718-624-4550
    Fax: 718-643-4415 sahadis@aol.com
                  www.sahadis.com
Ethnic foods
  President: Charles Sahadi
  VP: Robert Sahadi
*Estimated Sales:*Below $ 5 Million
Number Employees: 20-49
Brands:
  Sahadi

12553 Sahagian & Associates
P.O.Box 997
Oak Park, IL 60303-0997   708-848-5552
          Fax: 708-386-5959 800-327-9273
    sales@sahagianinc.com www.sahagianinc.com
Processor and exporter of bubble gum, licorice, taffy, candy-coated chocolate malted balls, chocolate bites, almonds, chocolate and caramel popcorn; also, multi-colored and tri-colored popcorn, candy coated licorice, chocolate dips andsalami
  President: Linda Sahagian
Estimated Sales:$440000
Number Employees: 5-9
Type of Packaging: Consumer, Private Label, Bulk
Brands:
  A FOOT OF
  A YARD OF
  THE WHOLE 9 YARDS

12554 Sahalee of Alaska
PO Box 104174
Anchorage, AK 99510-4174   907-349-4151
        Fax: 907-349-4161 800-349-4151
                  sahalee@aol.com
Seafood
  President/CEO: Hank Lind
  VP/Secretary/Treasurer: Christa Lind
  Sales Director: Bill Haller

12555 Sahara Coffee
2081 Mountain Vista Way
Reno, NV 89519-6269   775-825-5033
    Fax: 775-825-3190 donna@saharacoffee.com
                  www.saharacoffee.com
Processor and packer of whole leaf loose teas, organic dates and specialty coffees
  Owner: Charles Hubach
*Estimated Sales:*Less than $500,000
Number Employees: 1-4
Brands:
  Sahara

12556 Sahara Natural Foods
14855 Wicks Boulevard
San Leandro, CA 94577-6605   510-352-5111
                  Fax: 510-532-3227
Rice products, soups and organic bulk products
  National Manager: Al Caldwell

12557 Sahlen Packing Company
318 Howard St
Buffalo, NY 14206-2760   716-852-8677
    Fax: 716-852-8684 ron@redlinski.com
                  www.sahlen.com
Manufacturer of meat products that include; sausage, ham, bacon, lard and hot dogs
  President: Joseph Sahlen
Estimated Sales:$18 Million
Number Employees: 20-49
Brands:
  SAHLEN'S

12558 Saint Albans CooperativeCreamy
140 Federal Street
Saint Albans, VT 05478-2000   802-524-6581
    Fax: 802-527-1769 800-559-0343
    stalbanscoop@stalbanscooperative.com
                  www.stalbanscooperative.com
Processor of whole, skim, skim condensed and powdered milk; also, cream
  General Manager: Leon Berthiaume
  Operations Manager: Rob Hirss

Estimated Sales:$192,781,333
Number Employees: 67
Sq. footage: 41500
Type of Packaging: Private Label, Bulk
Brands:
  Orbit

12559 (HQ)Saint Amour/Powerline Foods
12112 Beach Blvd
Stanton, CA 90680-3704   714-827-5366
        Fax: 714-903-2311 sales@rocknrolls.com
                  www.rocksnrolls.com
Processor of cookies including madelines, croquants and teethers; also, snack foods
  Owner: Daniel De St Amour
*Estimated Sales:*Below $ 5 Million
Number Employees: 5-9
Brands:
  Rocks N' Rolls

12560 Saint Armands Baking Company
2811 59th Avenue Dr E
Bradenton, FL 34203-5334   941-753-7494
        Fax: 941-751-1417 sales@sabc.cc
                  www.starbake.com
Processor of bread, rolls and sweet goods
  President: Bernard Vroom
Estimated Sales:$ 1 - 3 Million
Number Employees: 5-9

12561 Saint Arnold Brewing Company
2522 Fairway Park Dr
Houston, TX 77092-7607   713-686-9494
    Fax: 713-686-9474 brewery@saintarnold.com
                  www.saintarnold.com
Processor of seasonal beer, ale, stout, lager and pilsner
  President: Brock Wagner
  Sales Rep: Frank Mancuso
*Estimated Sales:*Below $ 5 Million
Number Employees: 10-19
Type of Packaging: Consumer, Food Service
Brands:
  Amber
  Brown
  Christmas
  Elissa IPA
  Fancy Lawnmower
  Kristall Weizen
  Oktoberfest
  Root Beer
  Spring Bock
  Summer Pils
  Winter Stout

12562 Sainte Genevieve Winery
245 Merchant St
Ste Genevieve, MO 63670-1609   573-883-2800
        Fax: 573-483-3526 800-398-1298
        stgenwinery@hotmail.com
                  www.saintegenevievewinery.com
Wines
  Manager: Elaine Mooney
  CEO: Lineus Hoffmeister
Estimated Sales:$500,000-$1 Million
Number Employees: 1-4
Brands:
  Sainte Genevieve

12563 Saintsbury
1500 Los Carneros Avenue
Napa, CA 94559-9742   707-252-0592
        Fax: 707-252-0595 info@saintsbury.com
                  www.saintsbury.com
Wines
  Managing Partner: Richard Ward
  Managing Partner: David Graves
  Marketing Director: Jonathan Nahrgang
  Sales Director: Jonathan Nahrgang
  Winemaker: Jerome Chery
  Plant Manager: Cian Woods
*Estimated Sales:*Below $ 5 Million
Number Employees: 20
Brands:
  Saintsbury

12564 Sakeone Corporation
820 Elm St
Forest Grove, OR 97116-3041   503-357-7056
        Fax: 503-357-1014 800-550-7253
    talktous@sakeone.com www.sakeone.com

Sake
President/CEO: Steve Boone
Tasting Room Manager: Jennifer Brownstein
Plant Manager: Scott Eagler
Sales Manager: Greg Lorenz
VP Sales: Jim Scalace
Director Marketing: Dewey Weddington
Estimated Sales: Below $ 5 Million
Number Employees: 10-19
Type of Packaging: Private Label
Brands:
G
Momokawa
Moonstone

12565 Sal's Caesar Dressing
PO Box 612
Novato, CA 94948-0612   415-897-0605
Processor of Caesar salad dressings
President: Shirley Lesley
VP: Mark Lesley
Number Employees: 1-4
Type of Packaging: Consumer, Food Service
Brands:
Sal's

12566 Sal-Serve
P.O.Box 501187
Mobile, AL 36605-1187   251-438-6944
                               Fax: 251-438-6948
Salsa
Owner: Jim Higdon
General Manager: Jim Higdon
Estimated Sales: $ 20 - 50 Million
Number Employees: 50-99

12567 Salad Depot
51 Romeo St
Moonachie, NJ 07074-1611   201-507-1980
                                  Fax: 201-507-9001
Vegetables
President/Owner: Dan Zeigler
Marketing Director: John Zeigler
Buyer: Doreen Congo
Estimated Sales: Below $5 Million
Number Employees: 1-4
Brands:
Salad Depot

12568 Salad Oils International Corporation
5070 W Harrison St
Chicago, IL 60644-5141   773-261-0500
Fax: 773-261-7555   saladoiljohn@earthlink.net
Edible oils
President: Rosalie Paris
VP: John Pacente
Estimated Sales: $1,100,000
Number Employees: 10-19
Sq. footage: 15000
Type of Packaging: Private Label
Brands:
Irilla Extra Virgin O.O.
Mi Best Soybean Oil
Onte Verde O.O.
Rgo Mace O.O.
Rosa Canola Oil
Rosa Corn Oil
Rosa Peanut Oil

12569 Salad Ranch/Cattle Canada
PO Box 277
Bentley, AB T0C 0J0
Canada   403-748-3017
                Fax: 403-748-2474
Fresh vegetables, frozen chopped rhubarb, beef jerky, rhubarb juice and more.
President: David Thevenaz
Manager: Brenda Thevenaz
Number Employees: 1-25
Type of Packaging: Consumer, Food Service
Brands:
Alberta Brand
The Salad Ranch

12570 Salad-De-Lites
2997 Westchester Ave
Bronx, NY 10461-4517   718-828-1200
Fax: 718-647-0052 www.chloefoods.com
Processor of salads
CEO: Andrew Themis
Consulting VP: Al Jacobs
Estimated Sales: Less than $500,000
Number Employees: 1-4

Type of Packaging: Consumer, Food Service

12571 Salaison Levesque
500 Beaumont Street
Montreal, QC H3N 1T7
Canada   514-273-1702
                Fax: 514-273-2325
ventes@salaisonlevesque.qc.ca
www.salaisonlevesque.qc.ca
ham products
President/Owner: M Regis Levesque
VP: Mme Annie Levesque
Estimated Sales: $7.1 Million
Number Employees: 30

12572 Salamandre Wine Cellars
108 Don Carlos Drive
Aptos, CA 95003-2912   831-685-0321
newt@cruzio.com
www.salamandrewine.com
Wines
General Partner: Will Shoemaker Md
Winemaker: Wells Shoemaker
Estimated Sales: $170,000
Number Employees: 2
Brands:
Salamndre Wine Cellars

12573 Salamat of Seafoods
P.O.Box 1450
Kenai, AK 99611-1450   907-283-7000
                              Fax: 907-283-8499
Processor of fresh and frozen seafood including salmon, halibut, herring and cod
President: Robert Scott
President/CEO: Robert Scott
Executive VP: Shane Morgan
Director Manufacturing: Roy Bertoglio
Estimated Sales: $ 20-50 Million
Number Employees: 100-249
Type of Packaging: Consumer, Food Service, Bulk

12574 Salem Baking Company
224 S Cherry St
Winston Salem, NC 27101-5231   336-748-0230
          Fax: 336-748-0501 800-274-2994
sales@salembaking.com   www.salembaking.com
Processor of cookies flavors: moravian, spice, sugar, lemon, keylime, black walnut, tangerine-orange and double chocolate.
President: Guy Wilkerson
Estimated Sales: $3500000
Number Employees: 1-4
Parent Co: Dewey's Bakery
Type of Packaging: Consumer, Food Service
Brands:
Moravian Hearth

12575 Salem Food Service
P.O.Box 542
Salem, IN 47167-0542   812-883-2196
     Fax: 812-883-2205 www.salemfoodservice.com
Manufacturer of beef, pork, poultry, ground meat and custom cut steaks
Owner: Jerry Mc Clellan
Estimated Sales: $ 20 - 50 Million
Number Employees: 20-49
Parent Co: Frozen Food Service Corporation
Type of Packaging: Food Service

12576 (HQ)Salem Oil & Grease Company
60 Grove St
Salem, MA 01970-2245   978-745-0585
     Fax: 978-741-4426 thetiger@salemoil.com
Processor and exporter of sulphonated castor oil
President: V Smith III
VP Sales: J Donovan
VP Production: G Hanson
Estimated Sales: $$10-20 Million
Number Employees: 20-49

12577 Salem Old Fashioned Candies
P.O.Box 389
Salem, MA 01970-0489   978-744-3242
                              Fax: 978-745-9459
Processor of candy including bagged, hard, lollypops, mints, rock and taffy
President: Freeman Corkum
Estimated Sales: $950000
Number Employees: 10-19
Type of Packaging: Consumer
Brands:
Chestnut Street

Gems
Jane Stewart
Noah's Treats
Sea Chest
Seabreeze
Spindrift

12578 Salemville Cheese Cooperative
W4481 County Road Gg
Cambria, WI 53923-9304   920-394-3433
Cheese
President: Henry Miller
CFO: William Schrock
Plant Manager: Lavern Miller
Estimated Sales: $ 5-10 Million
Number Employees: 20-49

12579 Salerno Foods
2070 Maple Street
Des Plaines, IL 60018-3019   847-699-3200
          Fax: 847-699-3201   800-247-2848
Processor of cookies and crackers
President/CEO: George Chivari
CFO: Nicola Melilo
Sales Director: Mark O'Toole
Public Relations: Dan Keefe
Operations Manager: Peter Lowes
Parent Co: Parmalat Bakery Group North America
Type of Packaging: Consumer, Food Service
Brands:
LU

12580 Sales Associates of Alaska
1900 Phillips Field Rd
Fairbanks, AK 99701-2707   907-458-0000
          Fax: 907-452-2201 www.qualitysales.net
Wholesale grocers.
President: Gary Nance
Secretary/Treasurer: Carl Olson
Estimated Sales: $ .5 - 1 million
Number Employees: 1-4

12581 Sales USA
220 Salado Creek Road
Salado, TX 76571-5783   254-947-3838
          Fax: 254-947-3338 800-766-7344
                            pompeii1@aol.com
Fruit and vegetable juices.
President: Rusty Justus
CEO: Ronald Cox
CEO: Ronald Seacox
Plant Manager: Lee Simpkins
Estimated Sales: $ 1 - 3 Million
Number Employees: 4
Sq. footage: 15000
Type of Packaging: Consumer, Food Service, Private Label, Bulk

12582 Saletts
27 York Avenue
Randolph, MA 02368-1893   781-961-9900
                                 www.saletts.com
Processor of frozen meat including portion control beef, pork, lamb and veal
President: Glenn Davidson
Vice President: Seymour Salett
Sales Director: Kathleen O'Connor
VP Operations: Jack Bisbitos
Plant Manager: Ken Close
Purchasing Manager: Glenn Davison
Number Employees: 50-99
Sq. footage: 47000
Type of Packaging: Consumer, Food Service, Private Label

12583 Salishan Vineyards
35011 NE North Fork Avenue
La Center, WA 98629-3219   360-263-2713
                                  Fax: 360-263-3675
Wine
President: Joan Wolverton
CFO: Lincoln Wolverton
Estimated Sales: Under $300,000
Number Employees: 1-4
Type of Packaging: Private Label
Brands:
Salishan

12584 Sallock International Foods
27960 Cummings Road
Millbury, OH 43447-9762   419-838-7223
                                 Fax: 419-838-7597

Processor and exporter of American and Lebanese salad dressings, seasonings and soups
Owner: Sly Sallock
Owner: Abraham Sallock
Owner: Manira Sallock
Number Employees: 49
Sq. footage: 5217
Type of Packaging: Consumer, Food Service, Private Label, Bulk

12585 Sally Lane's Candy Farm
2215 Gum Springs Rd
Paris, TN 38242-6362   731-642-5801
Processor of candy including peanut and coconut brittle and hard and sugar-free candies
Owner: Bobby Freeman
Co-Owner/Co-Partner: Jean Peterson
Number Employees: 5-9
Sq. footage: 4000
Type of Packaging: Consumer
Brands:
Sally Lane's

12586 Sally Sherman Foods
300 N MacQuesten Pkwy
Mt Vernon, NY 10550-1093   914-664-6262
Fax: 914-664-2846 vasili.zisis@prodigy.net
Salads
President: Michael Endico
Sales Director: Glene Richards
Estimated Sales: $ 20-50 Million
Number Employees: 50-99

12587 Salmans & Associates
1126 W Chestnut St
Chicago, IL 60642-4111   312-226-1820
Fax: 312-226-6806 sales@salmans.com
Cheese
President: Van Salmans
Estimated Sales: $650,000
Number Employees: 1-4
Brands:
Salmans

12588 Salmolux
P.O.Box 23910
Federal Way, WA 98093-0910   253-874-6570
Fax: 253-874-4042 seafood@salmolux.com
www.salmolux.com
Processor of smoked seafood products; importer and exporter of pates, spreads, salmon burgers, herring, flavored butters and canned seafood salads
President: George Kuetgens
VP/CFO: Kira Kuetgens
Marketing VP: Ed Tropp
Retail Division VP: Steve Hobson
Plant Manager: Ray Crockett
Estimated Sales: $ 20 Million
Number Employees: 100-249
Sq. footage: 60000
Type of Packaging: Consumer, Food Service, Private Label, Bulk
Brands:
Salmolux Anti Pasta
Salmolux Gourmet Smoked Salmon
Salmolux Saute Butters

12589 Salmon River Smokehouse
PO Box 40
Gustavus, AK 99826-0040   907-456-3885
Fax: 907-456-3889
Smoke a variety of fish products.

12590 Salt Lake Macaroni & Noodle Company
5405 W 4700 S
Salt Lake City, UT 84118-6352   801-969-9855
Fax: 801-969-9856
Pasta
Manager: Mike Stover
Estimated Sales: $ 5 - 10 Million
Number Employees: 5-9

12591 Salt River Lobster
PO Box 277
Boothbay, ME 04537-0277   207-633-5357
Fax: 207-633-5357
Sells lobster, shrimp, fish, and various other shellfish.

12592 Saltspring Aqua Farms
107D Meyer Road
Salt Spring Island, BC V8X 1X4
Canada   604-926-3261
Fax: 604-926-5389 www.hatfieldgroup.com
Aquaculture facility raising salmon and producing salmon eggs for export
President: Chris Hatfield
Number Employees: 5-9
Parent Co: Hatfield's Biotechnology

12593 Saluda Meat Center
401 S Main Street
Saluda, SC 29138-1752   864-445-2188
Manufacturer of meat products

Estimated Sales: $4 Million
Number Employees: 18
Type of Packaging: Consumer

12594 Salute Sante! Food & Wine
68 Coombs St # I-2
Napa, CA 94559-3966   707-251-3900
Fax: 707-251-3939 info@grapeseedoil.com
www.grapeseedoil.com
Flavored and regular grapeseed oil
President: Valentin Humer
Estimated Sales: $690,000
Number Employees: 5-9
Type of Packaging: Consumer
Brands:
Salute Sante! Grapeseed Oil

12595 Salvage Sale
1001 McKinney St
Houston, TX 77002-6417   713-223-3100
Fax: 713-286-4602 800-856-7445
customercare@salvagesale.com
www.salvagesale.com
Online marketplace for buyers and sellers of salvage goods
President: Dave Dawson
VP Market Making: Jim Reilly
Marketing Manager: Maria Chamdess
Estimated Sales: $1500000
Number Employees: 20-49
Sq. footage: 30000

12596 (HQ)Salvati Foods
57 N Broadway
Suite 214
Hicksville, NY 11801-2941   516-932-8300
Fax: 516-932-8379 www.salvatifoods.com
Importer, packer and wholesaler/distributor of specialty foods including red and white vinegar, spices, antipasto, stuffed peppers, stuffed eggplant, tomatoes, etc
President: Andrew Benzoni
Sales Director: A Laurino
Production Director: Bruce Leibowitz
Number Employees: 10-19
Sq. footage: 72000
Type of Packaging: Consumer, Food Service, Private Label

12597 (HQ)Salvatore's Pizza Shells
1601 Bleecker Street
Utica, NY 13501-1017   315-735-7919
Processor of pizza shells
President: Salvatore Mott
Co-Owner/Executive VP: Mary Mott
Number Employees: 20-49
Sq. footage: 30000
Type of Packaging: Consumer, Food Service, Private Label, Bulk
Brands:
Salvatore's Bakery
Salvatore's Pizza Shells, Inc.

12598 Sam Hausman Meat Packer
P.O.Box 2422
Corpus Christi, TX 78403-2422   361-883-5521
Fax: 361-883-1003 info@samhausman.com
www.samhausman.com
Processor and exporter of fresh and frozen beef
CEO: Steve R McClure Sr
Operations Manager: Jerry Simpson
Estimated Sales: $ 50-100 Million
Number Employees: 100-249
Type of Packaging: Consumer, Food Service, Bulk

12599 Sam Kane Beef Processors
P.O.Box 9254
Corpus Christi, TX 78469-9254   361-241-5000
Fax: 361-242-2999 jkane@samkanebeef.com
www.samkanebeef.com
Processor and exporter of fresh, frozen and boxed beef.
President: Jerry Kane
Purchasing Agent: Lisa Lopez
Estimated Sales: $ 100-500 Million
Number Employees: 500-999
Type of Packaging: Consumer, Food Service, Bulk

12600 Sam Wylde Flour Company
3235 16th Ave SW
Seattle, WA 98134-1023   206-762-5400
Fax: 206-767-4088 www.puratos.com
Flour
Manager: Steve Picton
Estimated Sales: $ 20-50 Million
Number Employees: 20-49

12601 Sam's Homemade Cheesecake
7666 Miramar Road
San Diego, CA 92126-4202   858-578-3460
Fax: 858-578-3346 etsams@aol.com
Processor of frozen desserts including cheesecake
President: Elizabeth Terris
CEO: Steve Terris
Estimated Sales: $3 Million
Number Employees: 50
Type of Packaging: Consumer, Food Service
Brands:
Sam's Cheesecake

12602 Samadi Sweets Cafe
5916 Leesburg Pike
Falls Church, VA 22041-2202   703- 57-8 06
Fax: 703- 57-8 17
Middle Eastern pastries
Owner: Nora Burgan
Estimated Sales: Less than $500,000
Number Employees: 5-9

12603 Sambets Cajun Deli
8650 Spicewood Spgs Rd # 111
Austin, TX 78759-4323   512-258-6410
Fax: 512-258-6284 800-472-6238
www.sambets.com
Cajun hot sauces, salsas and spices
Owner: Doug Slocombe
Estimated Sales: $300,000-500,000
Number Employees: 1-4

12604 Sambol Meat Company
12405 Bellerive Dr
Kansas City, KS 66109-3173   913-721-2817
Fax: 913-371-7147
Processor of meat products
Owner: Don Sambol
CEO: Bill Kolich
Marketing Manager: Mark Fishman
Estimated Sales: $ .5 - 1 million
Number Employees: 1-4
Type of Packaging: Consumer
Brands:
Sambol

12605 Samjin America
2465 Fruitland Ave
Vernon, CA 90058-2139   213-622-5111
Fax: 213-622-5285 hanmi@wcis.com
General groceries
President: Choong Kang
Estimated Sales: $ 30-50 Million
Number Employees: 20-49

12606 Sampac Enterprises
551 Railroad Ave
S San Francisco, CA 94080-3450   650-876-0808
Fax: 650-876-0338 sales@sampacent.com
www.sampacent.com
Processor, exporter and importer of teas; wholesaler/distributor of herbs, teas, honey, bee pollen, etc
Director: Sammy Ma
Estimated Sales: $2300000
Number Employees: 10-19
Sq. footage: 20000
Type of Packaging: Private Label, Bulk

12607 Sampco
651 W Washington Blvd # 300
Chicago, IL 60661-2138   312-612-5600
          Fax: 312-346-8302   800-767-1689
    info@sampcoinc.com   www.sampcoinc.com
Cooked beef products
    President: David Morrison
    CEO: Dave Morrison
    Vice President: Verna Macintosh
    VP Industrial Sales: Rod McNally
Estimated Sales: $ 5-10 Million
Number Employees: 20-49
Type of Packaging: Private Label
Brands:
    Classico
    Sampco

12608 Sams Food Group
7461 S Sayre Ave
Chicago, IL 60638   708-563-0870
    Fax: 708-563-0789   800-852-0283
          office@samsfoods.com
          www.orringtonfarms.com
Manufacturers soup bases, gravy and sauce mixes,
seasonings and rubs, and dessert mixes for retail,
foodservice and industrial markets.
    President: Alan Levin
Estimated Sales: $ 2.5-5 Million
Number Employees: 10-19
Type of Packaging: Consumer, Food Service, Bulk
Brands:
    Orrington Farms

12609 Sams-Leon Mexican Supplies
5014 S 20th St
Omaha, NE 68107-2925   402-733-3809
Processor of tortillas, taco shells and hot sauce
    Owner: David Murillo
Estimated Sales: Less than $500,000
Number Employees: 1-4
Type of Packaging: Food Service

12610 San Andreas Brewing Company
737 San Benito Street
Hollister, CA 95023-3916   831-637-7074
Fax: 831-637-6170 www.san-andreas-brewing.com
Beer
    President/Brand Manager: Bill Millar
Estimated Sales: Less than $500,000
Number Employees: 5-9
Brands:
    Apricot Ale
    Cranberry Ale
    Earthquake Pale
    Oktoberquake
    Seismic Ale
    Survivor Stout
    Woodruff Ale

12611 San Angel Mexican Foods
668 Worcester Loop Rd
Stowe, VT 05672-4324   802-253-8117
          Fax: 802-253-8090   800-598-6448
          dpeet@pwshift.com

Mexican specialty foods
    President: Donald Peet
Estimated Sales: $300,000-500,000
Number Employees: 1-4
Type of Packaging: Consumer

12612 San Angelo Packing
P.O.Box 1469
San Angelo, TX 76902-1469   325-653-6951
          Fax: 325-658-7272
Packer of beef; slaughtering services available.
    General Manager: Jarrod Stokes
Estimated Sales: Below $ 5 Million
Number Employees: 250-499

12613 San Anselmo's Cookies &Biscotti
PO Box 2822
San Anselmo, CA 94979-2822   415-492-1220
          Fax: 415-492-1282   800-229-1249
    info@sacookies.com   www.sacookies.com
Cookies and biscotti
    Co-Owner: Jane Cloth Richman
    Co-Owner/VP Marketing: Jane Cloth-Richman
Estimated Sales: Below $ 5 Million
Number Employees: 20
Brands:
    San Anselmo's
    San Anselmo's

12614 San Antonio Packing Company
1922 S Laredo St
San Antonio, TX 78207-7093   210-224-5441
          Fax: 210-224-6664
Processor of meats including beef, lamb and pork
    Owner: Rudy Reyes
Estimated Sales: $ 20 - 50 Million
Number Employees: 50-99

12615 San Antonio Winery
737 Lamar St
Los Angeles, CA 90031-2591   323-223-1401
          Fax: 323-221-7261   800-626-7722
          winery@sanantoniowinery.com
          www.maddalenavineyard.com
Processor and importer of varietal and cooking
wines
    President: Steve Riboli Sr
    VP: Tony Tse
    Sales Manager: Rick Rechetnick
Estimated Sales: $12700000
Number Employees: 100-249
Type of Packaging: Consumer, Food Service
Brands:
    Maddalena

12616 San Benito Foods
P.O.Box 100
Hollister, CA 95024-0100   831-637-4434
          Fax: 831-637-7890
Processor of tomato products including ketchup,
paste, sauce, stewed and cooked
    President: Steve Arnoldy
    CEO/CFO: William Scott
    VP Sales/Marketing: Rick Leinenbach
    Sales Manager: Bob Stevens
    Operations Manager/Tech Services: Steve
    Arnoldy
    Production Manager: Chuck Risner
    Plant Manager: Mike Mullin
Estimated Sales: $ 20 - 50 Million
Number Employees: 100-249
Parent Co: Northwest Packing
Type of Packaging: Consumer, Food Service, Pri-
vate Label, Bulk
Brands:
    San Benito

12617 San Benito Foods
PO Box 30
Vancouver, WA 98666-0030   800-453-7832
          Fax: 360-696-3411 www.seedquest.com
Processor and exporter of canned cherries, plums,
pears, tomatoes and fruit juice concentrates includ-
ing pear and apple
    President: L Neil Jones
    VP Sales/Marketing: James Leinenbach
Number Employees: 250-499
Sq. footage: 60000
Type of Packaging: Food Service, Bulk
Brands:
    Oregon Trail
    San Benito

12618 San Diego Soy Dairy
1330 Hill St # B
El Cajon, CA 92020-5758   619-447-8638
          Fax: 619-447-2068   soydairy@aol.com
          www.sandiegosoydairy.com
Processor of soy products including milk, tofu, sal-
ads and salad dressings; also, herbal teas
    Owner: Luke Yam
    CEO: Luke Yam
Estimated Sales: $500,000-$1 Million
Number Employees: 5-9
Sq. footage: 3300
Type of Packaging: Consumer, Food Service
Brands:
    San Diego Soy Dairy
    Waterfall

12619 San Dominique Winery
P.O.Box 2089
Camp Verde, AZ 86322-2089   480-945-8583
          www.garlicparadise.com
Wines
    President: William Staltari
Estimated Sales: Less than $500,000
Number Employees: 1-4
Brands:
    San Dominique

12620 San Fernando Creamery
Farmdale Creamery
1049 W Base Line St
San Bernardino, CA 92411-2310   909-889-3002
    Fax: 909-888-2541   shofferber@linkline.com
          www.farmdale.net
Processor of dairy products including sour cream,
sour cream dressing, buttermilk, cheese, whey,
cream and butter
    Owner: Nick Sibilio
    Manager: Michael Shotts
Estimated Sales: $ 50 - 100 Million
Number Employees: 50-99
Parent Co: Farmdale
Type of Packaging: Consumer, Food Service, Pri-
vate Label, Bulk

12621 San Francisco Bay Coffee
Company
1993 Davis St
San Leandro, CA 94577   510-638-1300
          Fax: 510-632-0839   800-829-1300
          www.rogersfamilyco.com
Processor of coffee including ground, beans, decaf-
feinated and flavored; also, aromatic, herbal and fla-
vored teas. Offer complete private label whole bean
coffee programs
    President: Jon B Rogers
    VP Sales: Jim Rogers
    Co-Founder: Barbara Rogers
    Purchasing Manager: Tom Gerber
Estimated Sales: $ 20-50 Million
Number Employees: 100-249
Sq. footage: 82000
Parent Co: JBR Gourmet Foods
Type of Packaging: Consumer, Food Service, Pri-
vate Label, Bulk
Brands:
    East India Coffee & Tea Co.
    Pastarific Pasta Co.
    San Francisco Coffee

12622 San Francisco Bread Company
1365 N 10th St
San Jose, CA 95112-2804   408-298-6919
          Fax: 408-298-6950 www.specialtybaking.com
Bread
    Manager: Robert Murillo Jr
Estimated Sales: $ 20 - 50 Million
Number Employees: 20-49
Type of Packaging: Private Label

12623 San Francisco Brewing Company
155 Columbus Ave
San Francisco, CA 94133-5114   415-434-3344
          Fax: 415-434-2433   ask@sfbrewing.com
          www.sfbrewing.com
Processor of beer including ale and lager
    Owner: Allan Paul
    Brewmaster: Allan Paul
Estimated Sales: $ 10 - 20 Million
Number Employees: 20-49

12624 San Francisco Fine Bakery
P.O.Box 7114
Redwood City, CA 94063-7114   650-369-8573
          Fax: 650-369-8382   order@sffinebakery.com
          www.sffinebakery.com
Bakery products
    President: Clifford Chen
Estimated Sales: Below $ 5 Million
Number Employees: 20-49
Brands:
    San Francisco Fine Bakery

12625 San Francisco French Bread
580 Julie Ann Way
Oakland, CA 94621-4034   510-638-3252
    sourdoughbread@interstatebrands.com
          www.sourdoughbread.com
Processor and exporter of sourdough bread, rolls and
croutons
    President: Tom Hofmeister
    National Sales Manager: Terry McDonough
Number Employees: 5-9
Parent Co: IBC
Type of Packaging: Consumer, Food Service

12626 (HQ)San Francisco Herb & Natural Food Company
47444 Kato Rd
Fremont, CA 94538-7319   510-770-1215
          Fax: 510-770-9021 800-227-2830
info@herbspicetea.com   www.herbspicetea.com
The ultimate source for organic and conventional bulk herbs, spices, teas, potpourri, capsules, extract oils and accessories. Top quality, widest selection and lowest prices since 1969.
  President/CEO: Barry Meltzer
  VP: Kristi Meltzer
  Quality Control: Uyen Nguyen
  Marketing: Tiffany Nguyen
  Plant Manager: Fahimeh Niroomand
Estimated Sales: $5496793
Sq. footage: 160000
Type of Packaging: Private Label, Bulk
Other Locations:
  San Francisco Herb & Natural
  Culver OR
Brands:
  Bright Eye
  Nature's Herb Company
  Oregon Peppermint
  Relaxing Tea
  Sausalito Spice
  Summer Field Spices

12627 San Francisco Popcorn Works
1028 Revere Avenue
San Francisco, CA 94124-3443   415-822-4744
     Fax: 415-822-3376 800-777-2676
          info@sfpopcornworks.com
          www.sfpopcornworks.com
Popcorn
  President: Joan Adler
Estimated Sales: Below $ 5 Million
Number Employees: 10
Sq. footage: 2
Type of Packaging: Private Label
Brands:
  Naturfood
  San Francisco Popcorn
  Somewhat Sinful

12628 San Francisco Sausage Company
P.O.Box 426
S San Francisco, CA 94083-0426   650-583-4993
     Fax: 650-583-6376 www.rightfoods.com
Columbus salami sausages and meat products
  Owner: Mike Vinnicombe
  CFO: Pete Barale
  Quality Control: Edgard Arriolioga
  Plant Manager: Joe Rosa
Estimated Sales: $ 10-24.9 Million
Number Employees: 50-99
Brands:
  San Francisco

12629 San Francisco Urban Naturals
47444 Kato Rd
Fremont, CA 94538-7319   510-770-1215
          Fax: 510-770-9021
customerservice@herbspicetea.com
          www.herbspicetea.com
Tea and herbs
  President: Barry Meltzer
  CEO: Saye Niroomand
Estimated Sales: $ 5-10 Million
Number Employees: 50-99
Brands:
  San Francisco Herbs

12630 San Gennaro Foods
19255 80th Ave S
Kent, WA 98032-1135   206-723-5089
     Fax: 206-721-5005 800-462-1916
mail@polenta.net   www.polenta.net
Pre cooked polenta. Also mayonnaise, barbeque sauces and salad dressings under Northwest Gourmet brand.
  President: Jerry Mascio
Estimated Sales: $ 1-2.5 Million
Number Employees: 5-9
Type of Packaging: Private Label
Brands:
  NORTHWEST GOURMET
  SAN GENNARO

12631 San Joaquin Figs
3564 N Hazel Ave
Fresno, CA 93722-4912   559-224-4492
Fax: 559-224-4926 rondixon@nutrafig.com
          www.nutrafig.com
Processor of figs including dried, diced and paste; also, fig juice concentrate
  President: Keith Jura
Estimated Sales: $$20-50 Million
Number Employees: 20-49
Brands:
  California Classic
  San Joaquin Supreme
  The Nutra Fig

12632 San Joaquin Valley Dairymen
P.O.Box 2198
Los Banos, CA 93635-2198   209-826-4901
     Fax: 209-826-6717 www.californiadairies.com
Processor and exporter of salted and cultured butter, buttermilk powder, cream and milk including butter, skim, NFDM, condensed, liquid and powder
  President: Richard Cotta
  Marketing Director: Pete Cassinerio
  Operations Manager: Rocky White
Estimated Sales: $100+ Million
Number Employees: 50-99
Sq. footage: 260000
Type of Packaging: Consumer, Food Service, Private Label, Bulk
Brands:
  Valley Queen

12633 San Jose Coffee Company
1500 Cunningham Ave
San Jose, CA 95122-2399   408-272-3311
          Fax: 408-272-7118
Coffee
  Manager: Thomasa Aplha
Estimated Sales: $690,000
Number Employees: 5-9

12634 San Juan Coffee RoastingCompany
P.O.Box 2998
Friday Harbor, WA 98250-2998   360-378-4443
     Fax: 360-378-6658 800-858-4276
          www.rockisland.com/~sjcoffee
Fresh coffee roasted daily
  President: Irene Herring
  Operations Manager: Steve Herring
Estimated Sales: $ 5-10 Million
Number Employees: 5-9

12635 San Luis Sourdough
3877 Long St
San Luis Obispo, CA 93401-7535   805-782-8933
     Fax: 805-543-1279 800-266-7687
info@slodough.com   www.slodough.com
Sourdough bread
  Co-Owner: Dave West
  Co-Owner: Charlie West
  Controller: Ken Fontes
  Marketing Manager: Craig McLaughlin
  Plant Manager: Carol Rounsaville
Estimated Sales: $ 10-20 Million
Number Employees: 5-9
Brands:
  San Luis Sourdough

12636 San Marco Coffee,Inc.
3120 Latrobe Dr # 280
Charlotte, NC 28211-2186   704-366-0533
     Fax: 704-366-0534 800-715-9298
          www.sanmarcocoffee.com
Processor of American coffee, espresso, cappucinno; supplier of coffee machines
  Owner: Marc Decaria
Number Employees: 5-9
Type of Packaging: Consumer, Food Service, Private Label
Brands:
  San Giorgio

12637 San Marzano Foods
218 37th Avenue N
Nashville, TN 37209-4865   615-385-4398
Processor of dried tomatoes and Turkish and Greek olives; manufacturer of olive oil soap; importer of dried fruits, fruit pulp and puree
  President: Ahmet Ozari
  VP: B Waltrip
Number Employees: 5-9
Sq. footage: 10000

12638 San Saba Pecan
2803 W Wallace St
San Saba, TX 76877-3838   325-372-5727
     Fax: 325-372-5171 800-683-2101
          badams@sansabapecan.com
          www.sansabapecan.com
Processor and exporter of pecans
  President: Ranza D Adams
  Vice President: Buddy Adams
Estimated Sales: $11200000
Number Employees: 50-99
Sq. footage: 50000
Type of Packaging: Consumer, Bulk

12639 San-Ei Gen FFI
630 5th Ave
New York, NY 10111-0100   212-315-7840
     Fax: 212-974-2540 contact@saneigen.com
          www.saneigen.com
Processor, importer and exporter of natural colors, flavors and soy dietary fiber
  President: Takashige Shimizu
Estimated Sales: $5 Million
Number Employees: 1-4
Sq. footage: 4400
Parent Co: San-Ei Gen FFI
Type of Packaging: Bulk

12640 San-J International
2880 Sprouse Drive
Richmond, VA 23231   804-226-8333
     Fax: 804-226-8383 800-446-5500
info@san-j.com   www.san-j.com
tamari and shoyu, asian cooking sauces, salad dressing, soups and rice crackers.
  President/Owner: Takashi Sato
  Finance Director: Nancy Boswell
  Marketing Manager: Jennifer Stoltz
  Manufacturing/Distribution Director: Masaki Nakagawa
Number Employees: 40

12641 San-J International
2880 Sprouse Dr
Richmond, VA 23231-6072   804-226-8333
     Fax: 804-226-8383 800-446-5500
sales@san-j.com   www.san-j.com
Manufactures all-natural tamari, a premium soy sauce brewed with more soybeans than ordinary soy sauce. Tamari has a richer, smoother more complex taste than ordinary soy sauce. San-J manufactures a complete line of sauces and saladdressings, soups and crackers. Kosher, organic and all-natural products are available
  President: Takayoshi Sato
  CEO: Takashi Sioto
  Marketing/Public Relations: Kathy Mattisz
  Operations: Masaki Nakagawa
Estimated Sales: $5300000
Number Employees: 20-49
Number of Brands: 1
Number of Products: 22
Parent Co: San Jirushi Corporation
Type of Packaging: Consumer, Food Service, Bulk
Brands:
  SAN-J

12642 Sana Foods
PO Box 10818
Bainbridge Island, WA 98110-0818 206-842-4741
Food Brokers
  President: Tina Nelson
  VP: Paul Lang
  Sales Manager: Bill Poulos
Brands:
  Sana Foods
  Sana Wines

12643 Sanarak Paper & PopcornSupplies
456 Hinman Ave
Buffalo, NY 14216-1098   716-874-5662
          Fax: 716-874-4737
Popcorn
  President: Jim Rogers
Estimated Sales: $500,000-$1 Million
Number Employees: 5-9

12644 Sanborn Sourdough Bakery
5230 S Valley View Blvd # A
Las Vegas, NV 89118-1626   702-795-1030
          Fax: 702-795-8518

Bread and bakery products
President: Donald Sanborn
CFO: Brenda Portela
General Manager: Joe Lazi
Operations Manager: John Klessia
Estimated Sales: $ 20-50 Million
Number Employees: 50-99
Brands:
    Sanborn Sourdough Bakery

12645 Sanchez Distributors
9711 Mid Walk Dr
San Antonio, TX 78230-4075   210-341-1682
                               Fax: 210-341-7470
        asanchez@vineyardbrands.com
Ethnic foods.
    President: Roberto Sanchez
    Sales Manager: Fernando Sanchez
Estimated Sales: $ 5-10 Million
Number Employees: 5-9

12646 Sand Castle Winery
P.O.Box 177
Erwinna, PA 18920-0177   610-294-9181
        Fax: 610-294-9174   800-722-9463
        info@sandcastlewinery.com
        www.sandcastlewinery.com
Wines
    President: Paul Maxian
    CEO: Joseph Maxian
    Marketing/Sales Manager: Stephanie Driver
Estimated Sales: $ 5-10 Million
Number Employees: 10-19
Type of Packaging: Private Label
Brands:
    Johannisberg Riesling
    Sand Castle Winery

12647 Sand Hill Berries
304 Deerfield Rd
Mt Pleasant, PA 15666-9150   724-547-4760
        Fax: 724-547-7319   shberries@aol.com
        www.sandhillberries.com
Processor of raspberries, blackberries, gooseberries,
currants, jostaberries, jams, jellies, vinaigrettes, fruit
sauce and vinegar
    Owner: Susan Lynn
    Co-Partner: Susan Lynn
Estimated Sales: $315000
Number Employees: 1-4
Type of Packaging: Consumer, Private Label

12648 Sand Springs Springwater
160 Sand Springs Rd
Williamstown, MA 01267-2248   413-458-8281
Spring waters
    Owner: Edward Morin
Estimated Sales: $ 2.5-5 Million
Number Employees: 5-9

12649 Sandbar Trading Corporation
408 S Pierce Avenue
Louisville, CO 80027-3018   303-499-7480
                               Fax: 303-527-1727
Herbs and spices
    President: Barry Cowper
    Manager: Dave Halford
Brands:
    Sandbar Trading

12650 Sandco International
151 Union Chapel Rd
Northport, AL 35473-7509   205-339-0145
        Fax: 205-339-8222   800-382-2075
        sandco@uronramp.net   www.sanco.net
Processor and exporter of vitamins and sports sup-
plements, antiaging
    President: Linda Sandlin
    Research & Development: Richard Sandlin
    Marketing: Linda Madison
    Purchasing Manager: Linda Wells
Estimated Sales: $1,100,000
Number Employees: 5-9
Sq. footage: 20000
Type of Packaging: Consumer, Private Label, Bulk

12651 Sanders Candy
23770 Hall Rd
Clinton Twp, MI 48036-1275   586-468-4300
        Fax: 586-478-4795   800-852-2253
        info@sanders-hotfudge.com
        www.sanderscandy.com

Cookies, bread & rolls, danishes, cakes and dough-
nuts
    President/CEO: Judith Brock
    CFO: Joseph Talmage
    Marketing Specialist: Susan Leso
    VP Sales/Marketing: John McGuckin
    Plant Manager: Mike Koch
Estimated Sales: $500,000-$1 Million
Number Employees: 1-4
Parent Co: Country Home Bakers
Type of Packaging: Private Label
Brands:
    Sanders Brand Candy

12652 (HQ)Sanderson Farms
127 Flynt Road
PO Box 988
Laurel, MS 39441-0988   601-649-4030
        Fax: 601-426-1461   800-844-4030
        info@sandersonfarms.com
        www.sandersonfarms.com
Manufacturer and distributor of fresh and frozen
poultry
    President/COO: Lampkin Butts
    Chairman/CEO: Joseph Sanderson
    CFO/Treasurer: D Michael Cockrell
    Director of Development: Bob Billingsley
    Director of Marketing: Bill Sanderson
    Director of Production: Bud West
Estimated Sales: $1.8 Billion
Number Employees: 9,965
Type of Packaging: Consumer, Food Service, Pri-
    vate Label, Bulk
Other Locations:
    Sanderson Farms Production
    Bryan TX
    Collins MS
    Hammond LA
    Hazlehurst MS
    Laurel MS
    McComb MS
    Moultrie GA
    Waco TX
Brands:
    Chef-To-Chef
    Covington Farms
    Happy Home
    Miss Goldy Chicken
    NPF
    Sanderson Farms
    Spring Farms

12653 Sanderson Farms
28163 Highway 28
Hazlehurst, MS 39083-9601   601-894-3721
        Fax: 601-425-0714   www.sanderson.com
Manufacturer of poultry
    Personnel Director: Danny Bullock Jr
    Manager: Larry Lampkin
    Plant Manager: David Brown
Estimated Sales: $395 Million
Number Employees: 300
Parent Co: Sanderson Farms
Type of Packaging: Consumer, Food Service

12654 Sanderson Farms
701 Capitol Parkway
Bryan, TX 77807   979-778-5730
        www.sandersonfarms.com
Processor of frozen foods including chicken, stew
and seafood
    Manager: Karl King
    Plant Manager: Carrie Carter
Estimated Sales: $5 - 10 Million
Number Employees: 1,000
Parent Co: Sanderson Farms
Type of Packaging: Consumer, Food Service, Pri-
    vate Label

12655 Sanderson Farms
1111 N Fir Avenue
Collins, MS 39428   601-765-8211
        Fax: 601-765-1682   www.sandersonfarms.com
Manufacturer of Poultry
    Chairman/CEO: Joe Sanderson Jr
    President/COO: Lampkin Butts
    Plant Manager: Dan Nicovich
Estimated Sales: $100+ Million
Number Employees: 1,000-4,999
Type of Packaging: Consumer, Bulk

12656 Sanderson Farms
Warehouse Drive
Laurel, MS 39441-0988   601-765-2221
        www.sandersonfarms.com

Produces, processes, markets and distributes fresh
and frozen chicken products as well as other processed and prepared food items, including frozen entrees such as chicken and dumplings, lasagna,
seafood gumbo, shrimp creole and corndogs.
    President/COO: Lampkin Butts
    Chairman/CEO: Joe Sanderson Jr
    CFO/Treasurer: D M Cockrell
    CEO: Joe F Sanderson Jr
Estimated Sales: $ 50-100 Million
Number Employees: 5,000-9,999
Parent Co: Sanderson Farms

12657 Sanderson Farms
3640 Highway 190 W
Hammond, LA 70401   985-345-3365
        www.sanderson.com
Manufacturer of poultry
    Sales Manager: Phil Buhler
    Plant Manager: David Brown
Estimated Sales: $395 Million
Number Employees: 900
Parent Co: Sanderson Farms
Type of Packaging: Consumer, Food Service

12658 Sanderson Farms
700 Highway 133
Moultrie, GA 31788   229-891-4061
        www.sanderson.com
Manufacturer of poultry
    Manager: Jeff Black
    Plant Manager: David Brown
Estimated Sales: $395 Million
Number Employees: 1,400
Parent Co: Sanderson Farms
Type of Packaging: Consumer, Food Service

12659 Sanderson Farms
301 Aviation Parkway
Waco, TX 76705   254-741-6605
        www.sanderson.com
Manufacturer of poultry
    Manager: Jeff Black
    Plant Manager: David Brown
Estimated Sales: $395 Million
Number Employees: 1,400
Parent Co: Sanderson Farms
Type of Packaging: Consumer, Food Service

12660 Sandia Shadows Vineyard& Winery
8740 4th Street NW
PO Box 92675
Albuquerque, NM 87199-2675   505-856-1006
        Fax: 505-858-0859   sandiawine@aol.com
        www.sandiawines.com
Wine
    Owner: Phillippe Littot
Estimated Sales: Less than $500,000
Number Employees: 1-4
Brands:
    Sandia Shadows Vineyard & Wine

12661 Sandors Bakeries
2245 W Flagler St
Miami, FL 33135-1522   305-642-8484
                          Fax: 305-643-9358
Breads and other bakery products, except cookies
and crackers.
    President: Orlando Sanchez
Estimated Sales: $237,263
Number Employees: 5-9

12662 Sandra L. Lagrotte
2952 N Webster Ave
Indianapolis, IN 46219-1015   317-549-0073
                                 Fax: 317-549-0177
    Manager: Dick Sawyers
Estimated Sales: $ 20 - 50 Million
Number Employees: 10-19

12663 Sandridge Food Corporation
133 Commerce Dr
Medina, OH 44256-1333   330-725-2348
        Fax: 330-722-3998   jreyn@sandridge.com
        www.sandridge.com

Processor of prepared fresh and refrigerated gourmet salads including vegetable, pasta, protein and potato; also, fresh soups and meatloaf.
  President: Mark Sandridge
  Executive VP: William Frantz
  President: Vincent Sandridge
  VP Sales: Frank Sidari
  Director Research: Suzanne Stachel
  Purchasing Manager: Charles Lacortiglia
Estimated Sales: $ 20 - 50 Million
Number Employees: 250-499
Type of Packaging: Consumer, Food Service, Private Label, Bulk
Brands:
  Sandridge Salads Set Free

12664 Sands African Imports
9 Dey St
Newark, NJ 07103-3609   973-824-5500
      Fax: 973-824-5502 info.sand@aol.com
Oils, seeds
  President: Simon Belfer
  Marketing Director: Michael Sandaua
Estimated Sales: $ 1-2.5 Million appx.
Number Employees: 1-4
Type of Packaging: Private Label
Brands:
  Sands African

12665 Sandstone Winery
P.O.Box 7
Amana, IA 52203-0007   319-622-3081
Homemade wine
  President: Elsie Mattes
  CEO: Joan Stumpff
Estimated Sales: $5-9.9 Million
Number Employees: 10,000+
Type of Packaging: Consumer, Food Service
Brands:
  Sandstone Winery

12666 Sandt's Honey Company
714 Wagener Ln
Easton, PA 18040-8253   610-252-6511
      Fax: 610-252-9069 800-935-3960
Processor and packer of all-natural and kosher certified honey
  President: Lee Sandt
  Vice President: Linda Sandt
Estimated Sales: $1234498
Number Employees: 1-4
Type of Packaging: Consumer, Food Service, Private Label, Bulk
Brands:
  Sandt's

12667 Sandusky Cooperative Milk Producers Association
4601 Maple Avenue
Castalia, OH 44824-9730   419-684-5812
Cooperative selling milk
  Treasurer: Paul Kromer

12668 Sanford Milling Company
P.O.Box 290
Henderson, NC 27536-0290   252-438-4526
      Fax: 252-492-3014 scotthartness@nc.rr.com
Processor of flour
  President: Scott Hartness
Estimated Sales: $ 10 - 20 Million
Number Employees: 10-19
Type of Packaging: Food Service, Private Label, Bulk
Brands:
  Hartness Choice
  Packers Blend
  Snow Flake

12669 Sanford Winery
7250 Santa Rosa Road
Buellton, CA 93427-9787   805-688-3300
      Fax: 805-688-7381
Wines
  Partner: Richard Sanford
  CFO: Stuart Fries
  Marketing Manager: Tom Prendiville
  Operations: Sharon Blewis
  Purchasing Manager: Sharon Blewis
Estimated Sales: Below $ 5 Million
Number Employees: 20
Type of Packaging: Private Label
Brands:
  Sanford

12670 Sangean Enterprises
4627 Illinois Avenue
Louisville, KY 40213-1956   502-459-6556
      Fax: 502-459-4183
  Owner: Patrik Hsu

12671 Sangudo Custom Meat Packers
PO Box 416
Sangudo, AB T0E 2A0
Canada   780-785-3353
      Fax: 780-785-3111 888-785-3353
Processor of frozen beef and pork, pepperoni, bacon and sausage
  President/CEO: Ivan Adams

12672 Sani Dairy
PO Box 160
Johnstown, PA 15907-0160   814-533-2500
      Fax: 814-533-2536
Milk, dairy products-noncheese

12673 Sani-Dairy
425 Locust Street
PO Box 340
Johnstown, PA 15907-0340   412-568-6410
      Fax: 814-533-2536
Dairy products
  President: Wilfred Young
  VP/General Manager: Joe Martin
  Director Marketing/Sales: Paul Bilzor
Estimated Sales: Below $ 5 Million
Number Employees: 2
Brands:
  Mike's Original

12674 Sanitary Bakery
121 E Broadway
Little Falls, MN 56345-3038   320-632-6388
      Fax: 320-632-2740
Cookies
  Owner: Peter Kamrowski
Estimated Sales: Under $500,000
Number Employees: 20-49

12675 Sanitary Tortilla Manufacturing Company
623 Urban Loop
San Antonio, TX 78204-3117   210-226-9209
      Fax: 210-226-9424
Manufacturer of tortillas and other corn products
  Owner: Jesus Villarreal
Estimated Sales: $8 Million
Number Employees: 20-49
Sq. footage: 6000
Type of Packaging: Food Service

12676 Santa Barbara Gourmet
PO Box 779
Buellton, CA 93427-0779   805-686-0951
      Fax: 805-688-6910 gourmet@silcom.com
Natural and alcohol-free wine jelly, snacks and mixes, pickles, grilling sauces
  President: Schloss Bert
  Public Relations Officer: Randie Bert
Number Employees: 1-4
Type of Packaging: Private Label
Brands:
  Breakfast In Bed Snacks and Mixes
  Breakfast Wine Jelly
  Breakfast Wine Sirop
  Vine Star Grilling S

12677 Santa Barbara Olive Company
12477 Calle Real
Goleta, CA 93117-9766   805-562-1456
      Fax: 805-562-1464 800-624-4896
      info@sbolive.com www.sbolive.com
Processor of glass packed vegetables, vinegar, chunky olive pasta sauce, spiced and stuffed olives and salsa; importer and exporter of olives
  President: Craig Makela
  Vice President: Cindy Makela
Estimated Sales: $10000000
Number Employees: 20-49
Type of Packaging: Consumer, Food Service, Private Label, Bulk

12678 Santa Barbara PistachioCompany
P.O.Box 21957
Santa Barbara, CA 93121-1957   805-962-5600
      Fax: 661-766-2436 800-896-1044
      info@sbpistachios.com
      www.santabarbarapistachios.com

Grower and packager of natural flavored pistachios
  President/Owner: Gene Zannon
  CEO: Gail Zannon
  VP Marketing: Josh Zannon
  VP Production: Tristan Zannon
Estimated Sales: Less than $500,000
Number Employees: 1-4
Sq. footage: 4000
Type of Packaging: Consumer, Food Service, Private Label, Bulk
Brands:
  Santa Barbara Pistachio

12679 Santa Barbara Roasting Company
321 Motor Way
Santa Barbara, CA 93101-3436   805-962-5213
      Fax: 805-962-2590 800-321-5282
      help@sbroco.com www.sbroco.com
Coffee
  President: Corey Russell
  Executive Director: Jami Dunlop
  Director Operations: Matthew Moore
Estimated Sales: Below $ 5 Million
Number Employees: 20-49
Type of Packaging: Private Label
Brands:
  Santa Barbara

12680 Santa Barbara Salsa
649 Benet Rd
Oceanside, CA 92058-1208   760-757-2622
      Fax: 760-721-2600 800-748-5523
      info@sbsalsa.com www.sbsalsa.com
Salsa and sauces
  President: Doug Pearson
Estimated Sales: $ 1-2.5 Million
Number Employees: 10-19
Parent Co: California Creative Foods
Type of Packaging: Consumer, Bulk
Brands:
  Chacies®
  Con Gusto®
  San Diego Salsa™
  Santa Barbara Salsa™
  Tio Tio®

12681 Santa Barbara Salsa/California Creative
649 Benet Rd
Oceanside, CA 92058-1208   760-757-2622
      Fax: 760-721-2600 800-748-5523
      info@sbsalsa.com www.sbsalsa.com
Manufacturer of salsa Flavors: artichoke, key lime, garlic; peach; roasted garlic; mango peach; roasted chili; black bean; corn; cheese and salsa; hot pepper and marinades
  President: Doug Pearson
Estimated Sales: $300,000-500,000
Number Employees: 1-4
Brands:
  CHACHIES
  CONGUSTO
  SAN DIEGO SALSA
  SANTA BARBARA SALSA
  TIO TIO

12682 Santa Barbara Winery
202 Anacapa St
Santa Barbara, CA 93101-1887   805-963-3633
      Fax: 805-962-4981 wine@sbwinery.com
      www.sbwinery.com
Wines
  Owner: Pierre Lafond
  Owner: Tierre Iafond
  CFO: Marty-Pooe Winnen
  CEO: Pierre Lafond
  R & D: Jennifer Fredericks
  Marketing Manager: Craig Addis
Estimated Sales: Below $ 5 Million
Number Employees: 20-49
Brands:
  Lafond
  Santa Barbara Winery

12683 Santa Clara Nut Company
1590 Little Orchard St
San Jose, CA 95110-3599   408-298-2425
      Fax: 408-298-0101 santaclaranut@aol.com
Manufacturer and exporter of shelled and in-shell walnuts
  Owner: Jim Pusateri
  VP: Salvatore Pusateri
  Sales Director: Jim Pusateri

Estimated Sales: $15 Million
Number Employees: 5-9
Number of Brands: 1
Number of Products: 1
Sq. footage: 50000
Type of Packaging: Consumer, Food Service, Bulk
Brands:
  Santa Clara

12684 Santa Cruz Brewing Company
516 Front Street
Santa Cruz, CA 95060-4506   831-429-8838
                     Fax: 831-429-8915
Processor of seasonal beer and lager
  Partner: Gerry Turgeon
  President: Gerry Turgeon
  General Manager: Gerry Turgeon
Estimated Sales: $ 10-20 Million
Number Employees: 20-49
Type of Packaging: Consumer, Food Service
Brands:
  Pacific
  Santa Cruz

12685 Santa Cruz Chili & SpiceCompany
P.O.Box 177
Tumacacori, AZ 85640-0177   520-398-2591
    Fax: 520-398-2592   sales@santacruzchili.com
                     www.santacruzchili.com
Processor of chile paste, powder, sauces and spices
  President: Jean Neubauer
  Sales Manager: Armida Castro
Estimated Sales: $500000
Number Employees: 1-4
Type of Packaging: Consumer

12686 Santa Cruz Mountain Vineyard
1395 Felton Quarry Rd
Felton, CA 95018   831-335-4242
                     Fax: 831-335-4242
info@santacruzmountainvineyard.com
          www.scmountainvineyard.com
Wines
  Proprietor: Jeff Emery
Estimated Sales: Below $ 5 Million
Number Employees: 5-9
Brands:
  Santa Cruz Mountain Vineyard

12687 Santa Cruz Valley Pecan
P.O.Box 7
Sahuarita, AZ 85629-0007   520-625-8333
    Fax: 520-719-2853   800-533-5269
        donpecan@greenvalleypecan.com
             www.greenvalleypecan.com
Pecan nuts in multiple sizes, roasted pecans for ice
cream
  President: Richard Walden
  Marketing Director: Bruce Caris
Estimated Sales: $ 3 - 5 Million
Number Employees: 20-49

12688 Santa Elena Coffee Company
550 S Fm 1660 # 5
Hutto, TX 78634-4362   512-846-2908
                     Fax: 512-846-2710
        santa_elena_coffee@msn.com
             www.canincrad.com
Coffee
  Owner: Linda Truong
  Vice President: Astrid Bernstorff
  Marketing Director: Lissette Bernstorff
  Plant Manager: Astrid Bernstorff
  Purchasing Manager: Everardo Bernstorff
Number Employees: 5-9
Sq. footage: 3000
Type of Packaging: Private Label
Brands:
  Santa-Elena Coffee

12689 Santa Fe Bite-Size Bakery
P.O.Box 6530
Albuquerque, NM 87197-6530   505-342-1119
    Fax: 505-891-8740   NCandelaria3@aol.com
                     www.bite-size.com
Bite-size cookies and crackers
  Owner: Lucia Deichmann
Estimated Sales: $ 10 - 20 Million
Number Employees: 10-19
Brands:
  Bite-Size Bakery
  Chocolate Cheesecake Cookies
  Chunky Peanut Butter Cookies

Oatmeal Raisin Cookies
Old Fashion Ginger Snap Cookies
Peppery Wine Bisquit

12690 Santa Fe Bite-Size Bakery
PO Box 1549
Moriarty, NM 87035-1549   505-891-8765
                     Fax: 505-891-8740   800-342-1119
                     www.bite-size.com
Bite-size cookies and crackers, pinon nut chocolate
chip, pistatchio lemon verde, cordoba coffee,
bizcochitos, fiesta wedding and green chile cheddar
cheese
  president: Santa Fe
  Marketing Director: Carolyn Fairman
Estimated Sales: $ 1-2.5 Million
Number Employees: '5-9
Brands:
  Bite-Size

12691 Santa Fe Brewing
Frontage Rd
Santa Fe, NM 87507   505-424-3333
    Fax: 505-474-5573   info@santafebrewing.com
                     www.santafebrewing.com
Brewing of beer
  Owner: David Forester
Estimated Sales: $275,000
Number Employees: 1-4
Brands:
  Santa Fe Brewing

12692 Santa Fe Seasons
34 Uss Thresher Ln
Belen, NM 87002-8233   505-988-1515
          Fax: 505-988-1300   800-264-5535
                     www.santafeseasons.com
Salsa and seasonings
  President: Greg Deneen
  Vice President: Edith Deneen
  Sales Director: Lisa Duck
Estimated Sales: Below $ 5 Million
Number Employees: 20
Brands:
  De Santa Fe
  Santa Fe Seasons

12693 Santa Fe Vineyards
18348 Us 84/285
Espanola, NM 87532-9113   505-753-8100
                     Fax: 505-753-8100
Wines
  Manager: Dan Doughtery
Estimated Sales: $500,000
Number Employees: 1-4
Brands:
  Santa Fe Vineyards

12694 Santa Margarita Vineyard & Winery
33490 Madera De Playa
Temecula, CA 92592-9228   909-676-4431
Wines
  President: Barrett Bird
Estimated Sales: Under $500,000
Number Employees: 1-4
Type of Packaging: Private Label

12695 Santa Maria Foods
10 Armthorpe Rd
Branpton, ON L6T 5M4   416-434-9559
                     Fax: 416-675-7466
prosciutto and mortadella, salami and cured meats,
hams and specialty meats
  President/Owner: Eddie Zilli
  CEO: Frederick Jaques
  CFO: Andrew Linley
  VP Operations: Gordon Maxwell

12696 Santanna Banana Company
P.O.Box 1403
Harrisburg, PA 17105-1403   717-238-8321
                     Fax: 717-238-4480
Manufacturer of Bananas
  President: Ray Santanna
Estimated Sales: $53 Million
Number Employees: 20-49

12697 Santee Dairies
17851 Railroad St
City of Industry, CA 91748-1118   626-923-3000
          Fax: 626-923-3038   www.hartlandfarms.com

Processor of dairy products including butter, cottage
cheese, whipped cream, milk, yogurt, sour cream,
eggnog, ice cream, cream cheese and fruit juices
  President: Paul Bikowitz
  Purchasing Manager: Greg Hackworth
Estimated Sales: $ 75-100 Million
Number Employees: 10,000+

12698 Santini Foods
16505 Worthley Dr
San Lorenzo, CA 94580-1811   510-317-8888
          Fax: 510-317-8343   800-835-6888
                     www.santinifoods.com
Processor of sweetened condensed milk, blended
oils and flavored and natural syrups; importer of ol-
ive oil, wine and pasta; custom formulator of fruit
and flavored drink mixes; testing laboratory provid-
ing food development and USDAtesting services
  President: Bruce Liu
  CFO: Tyler Abbott
  Quality Control: Hal Burgan
  Operations: Roger Tan
Estimated Sales: $ 10-20 Million
Number Employees: 20-49
Sq. footage: 200000
Type of Packaging: Consumer, Food Service, Pri-
vate Label, Bulk
Brands:
  Dairy Hills
  La Vava Blanca
  Lotus Bloom

12699 Sanwa Foods
16505 Worthley Dr
San Lorenzo, CA 94580-1811   510-317-8888
          Fax: 510-317-8343   www.santinifoods.com
Seafoods
  President: Mao-Sheng Liu
  Marketing Manager: N Stewart
Estimated Sales: Below $ 5 Million
Number Employees: 250-499

12700 Sapar
400 S El Camino Real # 630
San Mateo, CA 94402-1705   650-340-8840
                     Fax: 650-344-2053
Fresh vacuum packed pates and mousses, sausages
and foie gras
  Manager: Leland Yee
  CEO: Antonio Pinheiro
  Sales Director: Sebastien Espinasse
Estimated Sales: $2064441
Number Employees: 1-4
Sq. footage: 10000
Type of Packaging: Consumer, Food Service, Pri-
vate Label, Bulk
Brands:
  Fabrique Delices

12701 Sapporo
11 E 44th St # 1710
New York, NY 10017-0050   212-922-9165
          Fax: 212-922-9576   800-827-8234
    info@sapporousa.com   www.sapporousa.com
Processor and importer of beer
  President: Mikio Masawaki
  Chairman: Munekazu Takenishi
Estimated Sales: $ 10 - 20 Million
Number Employees: 10-19
Parent Co: Sapporo
Type of Packaging: Consumer, Food Service

12702 (HQ)Sapudo Cheese
25 Tristate International #250
Lincolnshire, IL 60069-4453   847-267-1100
          Fax: 847-267-1110   stella@stellafoods.com
                     www.saputo.com
Italian and domestic cheese
  President: Terry Brockman
  VP Finance: Steven Hirt
Estimated Sales: $ 100-500 Million
Number Employees: 1,000-4,999
Brands:
  DRAGONE
  FRIGO
  GARDENIA
  LORRAINE
  SAPUTO
  STELLA
  TREASURE CAVE

12703 (HQ)Saputo
6869 Metropolitain Blvd E
Montreal, QC H1P 1X8
Canada   514-328-6662
        Fax: 514-328-3364 saputo@saputo.com
                            www.saputo.com
Cheese, milk, yogurt, dairy ingredients and
snack-cakes
    President & CEO: Lino Saputo Jr
    EVP Finance & Administration: Louis-Philippe
    Carriere
    VP Communications: Claude Pinard
    COO & President, Dairy Products USA: Terry
    Brockman
Estimated Sales: $5.8 Billion
Number Employees: 9600
Parent Co: Agrifoods International
Type of Packaging: Consumer, Food Service, Pri-
    vate Label, Bulk
Other Locations:
    Saputo Dairy Products(Canada)
    Montreal QC
    Saputo Cheese Division
    Lincolnshire IL
    Saputo Dairy Products(Agrentia)
    Buenos Aires
    Saputo Bakery Division(Canada)
    Saint-Leonard QC
Brands:
    ALEX dE PORTNEUF
    ARMSTRONG
    BAXTER
    DAIRYLAND
    DANSCORELLA
    DE LUCIA
    DRAGONE
    DUVILLAGE 1860
    FRIGO CHEESE HEADS
    HOP&GO!
    KINGSEY
    LA PAULINA
    NEILSON
    NUTRILAIT
    RICREM
    RONDEAU
    SAPUTO
    STELLA
    TREASURE CAVE
    VACHON

12704 Saputo
P.O.Box 8
Big Stone City, SD 57216-0008   605-862-8131
        Fax: 605-862-8413 800-824-3373
        info@saputocheese.com www.saputo.com
CHeese
    President: Pierre Bourgie
    Corporate Director: Louis A Tanguay
    Chairman: Lino Saputo
    Plant Manager: Kip Cameron
Estimated Sales: $ 10 - 20 Million
Number Employees: 100-249
Parent Co: Saputo
Type of Packaging: Consumer, Food Service, Pri-
    vate Label, Bulk
Brands:
    Armstrong
    Dairyland
    Hop & Go
    Kingsey
    Lait's Go
    Molfino
    Ricrem
    Senda
    Treasure Cave

12705 (HQ)Saputo
6869 Metropolitan Boulevard E
St Leonard, QC H1P 1X8
Canada   514-328-6662
        Fax: 514-328-3364 saputo@saputo.com
                            www.saputo.com
Cheeses, milk and yogurts, ingredients and bakery
    Chairman: Emanuele Saputo
    President/CEO: Lino Saputo Jr
    Executive VP/Finance & Administrator: Louis
    Philippe Carriere
Estimated Sales: $5.7 Billion
Number Employees: 7,500
Type of Packaging: Consumer, Food Service, Pri-
    vate Label, Bulk
Brands:
    ALEX DE PORTNEUF
    ARMSTRONG

BAXTER
CHEESE HEADS
DAIRYLAND
DANSCORELLA
DE LUCIA
DRAGONE
DUVILLAGE 1860
FRIGO
HOP&GO!
KINGSEY
LA PAULINA
NEILSON
NUTRILAIT
RICREM
RONDEAU
SAPUTO
STELLA
TREASURE CAVE
VACHON

12706 Saputo Cheese
P.O.Box 198
Lena, WI 54139-0198   920-829-5251
        Fax: 920-829-5631 www.saputo.com
Cheese
    Manager: Bruce Unterbrunner
    Plant Manager: John Hoffner
Estimated Sales: $100+ Million
Number Employees: 250-499
Parent Co: Saputo

12707 Saputo Cheese
25 Tristate International #250
Lincolnshire, IL 60069-4453   847-267-1100
        Fax: 847-267-1110 800-558-9714
                            www.saputo.com
Processor and exporter of milk powder and sweet-
ened condensed milk
    President: Terry Brockman
    VP Finances: David Foster
    Director Operations: J McGuinness
Number Employees: 1,000-4,999
Sq. footage: 300
Parent Co: Waterford Foods
Type of Packaging: Bulk
Other Locations:
    Waterford Food Products
    Millville UT

12708 Saputo Cheese
45 E Scott St
Fond Du Lac, WI 54935-2323   920-929-8060
        Fax: 920-929-8069 www.saputo.com
Cheese
    Manager: Tim Hilgers
    Quality Control: Brad Brusky
    Production: Joe Konen
    Plant Manager: Derick Paider
Estimated Sales: $ 10 - 20 Million
Number Employees: 100-249
Parent Co: Saputo
Type of Packaging: Food Service, Private Label,
    Bulk
Brands:
    Dragone
    Frigo
    Gardenia
    Lorraine Cheese
    Stella
    Treasure Cave

12709 Saputo Cheese
1120 Commercial Ave
Reedsburg, WI 53959-2132   608-524-8244
        Fax: 608-524-8091 800-824-3373
                            www.saputo.com
Cheese
    Chairman: Lino Saputo
    President/CEO: Lino Saputo Jr
    President/COO, Cheese Division (USA): Dino
    Dello
    Sales Representative: Cindy Zirngible
    Plant Manager: Kelley Ford
Estimated Sales: $ 20 - 50 Million
Number Employees: 50-99
Parent Co: Saputo
Type of Packaging: Consumer, Food Service, Pri-
    vate Label, Bulk
Brands:
    Dragone
    Frigo
    Lorraine Cheese
    Saputo
    Stella

12710 Saputo Cheese
1052 6th St
Almena, WI 54805-9563   715-357-3775
        Fax: 715-357-6368 www.saputo.com
Cheese
    Plant Manager: Daniel Hubbard
Estimated Sales: $ 50 - 100 Million
Number Employees: 100-249
Parent Co: Saputo
Type of Packaging: Consumer

12711 Saputo Cheese
208 N Miami Street
Peru, IN 46970-2105   765-472-1961
                            Fax: 765-473-5130
Cheese
    Quality Control: Catherine Bernard
    Plant Manager: Richard Jorgenson
Estimated Sales: $ 50 - 100 Million
Number Employees: 80
Sq. footage: 56000
Parent Co: Saputo
Type of Packaging: Consumer, Food Service, Pri-
    vate Label, Bulk
Brands:
    Frigo
    Lorraine
    Stella

12712 Saputo Cheese
10516 Route 116
Hinesburg, VT 05461-8500   802-482-2121
        Fax: 802-482-2115 800-824-3373
        saputo@saputo.com   www.saputo.com
Cheese
    CEO: Lino Saputo Jr
    Executive VP: Louis-Philippe Carrière
    Plant Accountant: Ray Broderick
    COO: Randy Williamson
Estimated Sales: $ 50-100 Million
Number Employees: 50-99
Parent Co: Saputo
Type of Packaging: Food Service, Private Label
Brands:
    Armstrong
    Baxter
    Caron
    Cayer
    Dairyland
    Dragone
    Frigo
    Kingsey
    La Paulina
    Nutrilait
    Ricrem
    Saputo
    Stella
    Treasure Cave
    Vachon

12713 Saputo Cheese
5611 Imperial Hwy
South Gate, CA 90280-7419   562-862-7686
        Fax: 562-861-4265 800-824-3373
        saputo@saputo.com   www.saputo.com
Cheese
    President/CEO: Lino Saputo Jr
    Executive VP: Louis Philippe
    COO: Dino Dello
    Plant Manager: Arthur Sar
Estimated Sales: $100+ Million
Number Employees: 250-499
Parent Co: Saputo
Type of Packaging: Consumer, Food Service
Brands:
    Dragone
    Frigo
    Lorraine
    Saputo
    Stella
    Treasure Cave

12714 (HQ)Saputo Cheese
25 Tristate International #250
Lincolnshire, IL 60069-4453   847-267-1100
        Fax: 847-267-1110 800-824-3373
        knewman@saputocheese.com www.saputo.com
Cheese
    President: Terry Brockman
    Chairman/CEO: Lino Saputo
    Marketing Director: Steve Josen
    Sales Director: Rich Evjen

Number Employees: 1,000-4,999
Parent Co: Saputo
Type of Packaging: Consumer, Food Service, Private Label, Bulk
Other Locations:
Saputo Cheese Div. US Plant
Denmark WI
Saputo Cheese Div. US Plant
Hancock MD
Saputo Cheese Div. US Plant
Monroe WI
Saputo Cheese Div. US Plant
New London WI
Brands:
Cayer
Dragone
Frigo
Lorraime
Saputo
Stella

12715 Saputo Cheese
901 E Levin Ave
Tulare, CA 93274-6525   559-687-9999
   Fax: 559-687-9444   vval@saputo.com
   www.saputo.com
Cheese
President/CEO: Lino Saputo Jr
Chairman: Lino Saputo
Corporate Director: Louis Tanguay
Plant Manager: Bob Timmons
Estimated Sales: $ 100-500 Million
Number Employees: 100-249

12716 Saputo Cheese
340 Tompkins St
Fond Du Lac, WI 54935   920-924-6024
   Fax: 920-922-2509   800-824-3373
   saputo@saputo.com   www.saputo.com
Cheese
President/CEO: Lino Saputo Jr
Executive VP: Louis Philippe
President/COO, Cheese Division (USA): Dino Dello
Number Employees: 50-99
Parent Co: Saputo
Brands:
Dragone
Freego
Lorraine
Saputo
Stella
Treasure Cave

12717 Sara Lee
4649 Le Bourget Drive
Saint Louis, MO 63134-3120   847-956-7575
   Fax: 847-956-7643   www.saralee.com
Salad dressings, barbecue sauce, beverage mixes and pancake syrup
Executive VP: Laurette T Koellner
President: Brenda C Barnes
Chairman: C Steven McMillan
Estimated Sales: $ 25-49.9 Million
Number Employees: 110
Brands:
Ambi Pur
Aoste
Ball Park
Bimbo
BryanIronkids
Kiwi
Sara Lee
Superior

12718 Sara Lee BakeryThe Earth Grains Baking Companies HQ
PO Box 756
Neenah, WI 54957   800-323-7117
   Fax: 605-886-5833   866-613-2784
   www.earthgrains.com
Manufacturer of bakery products including sweet rolls
Controller: Leah Luken
SVP/CIO: George Chappelle
General Manager: Bob Haertel
Production Support: Rod Dilley
Estimated Sales: $ 50 - 100 Million
Number Employees: 60
Parent Co: Sara Lee Bakery Group
Type of Packaging: Consumer

12719 Sara Lee Bakery
3475 S 300 W
Salt Lake City, UT 84115-4341   801-487-4677
   Fax: 801-486-9304   www.saralee.com
Processor of bread, buns, cakes and pies.
Manager: Joe Robinson
EVP/CFO/CAO: L M De Kool
EVP/General Counsel & Secretary: Roderick Palmore
SVP/CIO: George Chappelle
General Manager: Jack Hart
Plant Manager: Joe Robinson
Estimated Sales: $100+ Million
Number Employees: 250-499
Type of Packaging: Consumer, Food Service, Private Label, Bulk
Brands:
Grandma Sycamore
Sara Lee

12720 Sara Lee Bakery
PO Box 756
Neenah, WI 54957-0756   800-323-7117
   www.saralee.com
Producer of croutons, shred, stuffing, and crumbs.
Chairman/CEO: Brenda C Barnes
EVP/CFO/CAO: L M De Kool
EVP/General Counsel & Secretary: Roderick Palmore
SVP/CIO: George Chappelle
Estimated Sales: $ 5 - 10 Million
Number Employees: 137000
Type of Packaging: Consumer, Food Service, Private Label, Bulk
Brands:
AOSTE
BALLPARK
BIMBO
BRYAN
DOUWE EGBERTS COFFEE SYSTEMS
EARTH GRAINS
HILLSHIRE FARM
IRONKIDS
JIMMY DEAN
MAISON DU CAFé)
PICKWICK
SARA LEE
SENSEO
SUPERIOR

12721 Sara Lee Bakery GroupThe EarthGrains - Bakery
2010 Main Street
Jasper, TN 37347-5662   423-837-8856
   www.earthgrains.com
Manufacturer of EarthGrains baked goods including bread
Manager: Larry Ziegler
Number Employees: 12
Parent Co: Sara Lee Corporation
Type of Packaging: Consumer, Food Service, Private Label
Brands:
EARTH GRAINS

12722 Sara Lee Bakery GroupThe EarthGrains - Bakery
298 N Cleveland Street
Memphis, TN 38104-7146
   800-627-0921
   www.earthgrains.com
Manufacturer of Earth Grains bread and buns
Manager: Dan Medlife
Number Employees: 5
Parent Co: Sara Lee Corporation
Type of Packaging: Consumer
Brands:
EARTH GRAINS

12723 Sara Lee Bakery GroupThe EarthGrains - Bakery
425 E Kearney Street
Springfield, MO 65803-3009   417-865-0929
   www.earthgrains.com
Manufacturer of EarthGrains bread and buns
Manager: Gary Pliler
Number Employees: 2
Parent Co: Sara Lee Corporation
Type of Packaging: Consumer, Food Service, Private Label
Brands:
EARTH GRAINS

12724 Sara Lee Bakery GroupThe EarthGrains - Bakery
580 Julie Ann Way
Oakland, CA 94621-4034   510-635-4343
   www.earthgrains.com
Manufacturer of baked goods including breads, buns, muffins and snack cakes
Number Employees: 200
Sq. footage: 122000
Parent Co: Sara Lee Corporation
Type of Packaging: Consumer, Food Service, Private Label
Brands:
EARTH GRAINS

12725 Sara Lee Bakery GroupThe EarthGrains - Bakery
5105 W Cardinal Dr # 2
Beaumont, TX 77705-2634   409-842-9150
   Fax: 409-842-9320   www.earthgrains.com
Manufacturer of fresh and frozen bread, cakes and pastries
Manager: Mike Evans
Number Employees: 11
Parent Co: Sara Lee Corporation
Type of Packaging: Consumer
Brands:
EARTH GRAINS

12726 Sara Lee Bakery GroupThe EarthGrains - Bakery
4808 Leopard St
Corpus Christi, TX 78408-2622   361-884-6311
   Fax: 361-883-2206   www.earthgrains.com
Manufacturer of fresh and frozen bread and buns
Manager: Ernest Aleman
Number Employees: 8
Parent Co: Sara Lee Corporation
Type of Packaging: Consumer, Food Service, Private Label, Bulk
Brands:
COLONIAL/RAINBO
EARTH GRAINS
IRONKIDS
SARA LEE

12727 Sara Lee Bakery GroupThe EarthGrains - Bakery
12027 E 51st Street
Tulsa, OK 74146-6020   918-254-5468
   www.earthgrains.com
Manufacturer of fresh bread and buns
Branch Manager: Larry Spears
Number Employees: 120
Parent Co: Sara Lee Corporation
Type of Packaging: Consumer, Food Service
Brands:
COLONIAL/RAINBO
EARTH GRAINS
GRANT'S FARM
IRONKIDS
SARA LEE

12728 Sara Lee Bakery Group
738 W Van Buren St
Phoenix, AZ 85007-2546   602-252-6881
   Fax: 602-252-9512   www.earthgrains.com
Manufacturer of bread, buns and cakes
Manager: Gary Battenfield
EVP/CFO/CAO: L M De Kool
EVP/General Counsel & Secretary: Roderick Palmore
SVP/CIO: George Chappelle
Estimated Sales: $100-500 Million
Number Employees: 250-499
Parent Co: Sara Lee Corporation
Type of Packaging: Consumer, Food Service, Private Label, Bulk
Brands:
COLONIAL/RAINBO
EARTH GRAINS
GRANT'S FARM
IRONKIDS
SARA LEE

12729 Sara Lee Bakery GroupThe EarthGrains - Bakery
2401 W 13th Street N
Wichita, KS 67203-1930   316-943-3176
   www.earthgrains.com

Manufacturer of baked goods including breads, buns and rolls
Manager: Wanda Wescott
Number Employees: 4
Parent Co: Sara Lee Corporation
Type of Packaging: Consumer
Brands:
COLONIAL/RAINBO
EARTH GRAINS
GRANT'S FARM
IRONKIDS
SARA LEE

12730 Sara Lee Bakery GroupThe EarthGrains - Bakery
4113 Bardstown Road
Suite 101
Louisville, KY 40218-3292   502-491-7499
www.earthgrains.com
Manufacturer of baked goods including bread, buns and rolls
Manager: Lynn Waters
Number Employees: 4
Sq. footage: 108000
Parent Co: Sara Lee Bakery Group
Type of Packaging: Consumer

12731 Sara Lee Bakery GroupBakery
4300 Forest Street
Denver, CO 80216-4505
www.saralee.com
Manufacturer of fresh bread, buns and rolls
Manager: Tim Lee
Number Employees: 38
Parent Co: Sara Lee Corporation
Type of Packaging: Consumer, Food Service, Private Label, Bulk
Brands:
COLONIAL/RAINBO
EARTH GRAINS
GRANT'S FARM
IRONKIDS
SARA LEE

12732 Sara Lee Bakery GroupThe EarthGrains - Bakery
140 Van Ness Ave
Fresno, CA 93721   559-495-3571
www.earthgrains.com
Manufacturer of bread, buns and cakes.
Plant Manager: Chuck Linthicum
Number Employees: 8
Parent Co: Sara Lee Corporation
Type of Packaging: Consumer, Food Service, Private Label
Brands:
COLONIAL/RAINBO
EARTH GRAINS
GRANT'S FARM
IRONKIDS
SARA LEE

12733 Sara Lee Bakery GroupThe EarthGrains - Bakery
2319 Franklin Pike
Nashville, TN 37204-2224   615-298-3001
www.earthgrains.com
Manufacturer of EarthGrains breads and buns
Manager: Doug Crafton
Number Employees: 2
Parent Co: Sara Lee Corporation
Type of Packaging: Consumer
Brands:
COLONIAL/RAINBO
EARTH GRAINS
GRANT'S FARM
IRONKIDS
SARA LEE

12734 Sara Lee Bakery Group
1917 16th St N
Birmingham, AL 35204-1701   205-322-8000
Fax: 205-322-1395 www.saralee.com
Manufacturer of rolls
Plant Manager: Bill Barrett
Number Employees: 10
Sq. footage: 41000
Parent Co: Sara Lee Corporation
Type of Packaging: Consumer
Brands:
COLONIAL/RAINBO
EARTH GRAINS
GRANT'S FARM

IRONKIDS
SARA LEE

12735 Sara Lee Bakery Group
1727 E Anamosa St
Rapid City, SD 57703-6801   605-343-3512
Fax: 605-341-0381 www.saralee.com
Manufacturer of baked goods including bread, snack pies and cakes
Manager: Ken Jaques
EVP/CFO/CAO: L M De Kool
EVP/General Counsel & Secretary: Roderick Palmore
SVP/CIO: George Chappelle
Sales Manager: Kien Jaques
Estimated Sales: $ 50 - 100 Million
Number Employees: 20-49
Parent Co: Sara Lee Bakery Group
Type of Packaging: Consumer, Food Service, Private Label

12736 Sara Lee Bakery GroupThe EarthGrains - Bakery
1040 Hazel Street N
Saint Paul, MN 55119-4800
www.earthgrains.com
Manufacturer of baked goods including breads, buns, rolls, cakes, pies, muffins, etc.
Manager: Dave Lopez
Number Employees: 42
Parent Co: Sara Lee Corporation
Type of Packaging: Consumer, Food Service, Private Label
Brands:
COLONIAL/RAINBO
EARTH GRAINS
GRANT'S FARM
IRONKIDS
SARA LEE

12737 Sara Lee Bakery GroupThe EarthGrains - Bakery
2418 Sybrant Rd
Traverse City, MI 49684-8841   231-922-3296
Fax: 231-922-3296 www.earthgrains.com
Manufacturer of frozen baked goods including pies.
Director, Manufacturing Staff: Doug Corwin
Purchasing Manager: Ken O'Brien
Number Employees: 3
Parent Co: Sara Lee Corporation
Type of Packaging: Consumer, Food Service, Private Label
Brands:
DOUWE EGBERTS
HILLSHIRE
KIWI
SARA LEE

12738 Sara Lee Bakery Group
P.O.Box 29
Hastings, NE 68902-0029   402-462-5105
Fax: 402-462-5239 800-669-4395
www.saralee.com
Manfuacturer of baked goods including breads and buns.
Chairman/CEO: Brenda Barnes
EVP/CFO/CAO: L M De Kool
EVP/General Counsel & Secretary: Roderick Palmore
SVP/CIO: George Chappelle
Manager: Dennis Bumgardner
Plant Manager: Dennis Sample
Estimated Sales: $100+ Million
Number Employees: 1-4
Parent Co: Sara Lee Corporation
Type of Packaging: Consumer, Food Service, Private Label
Brands:
COLONIAL/RAINBO
EARTH GRAINS
GRANT'S FARM
IRONKIDS
SARA LEE

12739 Sara Lee Bakery GroupThe EarthGrains - Bakery
876 Spider Webb Drive SE
Rome, GA 30161-5235   706-295-4499
www.earthgrains.com
Manufacturer of snack cakes, brownies and cookies.
Manager: Jack Bailey
Number Employees: 20
Parent Co: Sara Lee Corporation

Type of Packaging: Consumer, Private Label
Brands:
COLONIAL/RAINBO
EARTH GRAINS
GRANT'S FARM
IRONKIDS
SARA LEE

12740 Sara Lee Bakery Group
272 Broughton Street
Orangeburg, SC 29115-7363   803-534-3535
Fax: 803-533-5117 800-476-3536
www.earthgrains.com
Manufacturer of bread and rolls
Chairman/CEO: Brenda Barnes
EVP/CFO/CAO: L M De Kool
EVP/General Counsel & Secretary: Roderick Palmore
SVP/CIO: George Chappelle
Plant Manager: David Maxwell
Estimated Sales: $50-100 Million
Number Employees: 200
Sq. footage: 180000
Parent Co: Sara Lee Corporation
Type of Packaging: Consumer, Food Service, Private Label, Bulk
Brands:
COLONIAL/RAINBO
EARTH GRAINS
GRANT'S FARMS
IRONKIDS
SARA LEE

12741 Sara Lee Bakery GroupThe EarthGrains - Bakery
9480 Aero Space Drive
St Louis, MO 63134-3826   314-733-0964
800-323-7117
www.earthgrains.com
Wholesale bakery of EartGrains products
Manager: Bill Bell
Number Employees: 500
Parent Co: Sara Lee Corporation
Type of Packaging: Consumer, Food Service, Private Label, Bulk
Brands:
Sara Lee

12742 Sara Lee Bakery GroupThe EarthGrains - Bakery
5680 U S Highway 49
Hattiesburg, MS 39401-7701   601-545-3781
Fax: 601-584-6487 www.earthgrains.com
Processor of buns and rolls
Branch Manager: Warren Stafford
Number Employees: 10
Parent Co: Sara Lee Corporation
Type of Packaging: Consumer

12743 Sara Lee Bakery Group
2651 S Airport Way
Stockton, CA 95206-3522   209-946-0772
Manufacturer of bread and buns
Branch Manager: George Lorenz
Number Employees: 160
Parent Co: Sara Lee Corporation
Type of Packaging: Consumer, Food Service
Brands:
COLONIAL/RAINBO
EARTH GRAINS
GRANT'S FARM
IRONKIDS
SARA LEE

12744 Sara Lee Bakery Group
1916 Piedmont Hwy
Greenville, SC 29605-4830   864-299-0604
Fax: 864-227-9069 www.saralee.com OR
www.earthgrains.com
Processor of frozen bagels
President/Manager: Alex Winston
EVP/CFO/CAO: L M De Kool
EVP/General Counsel & Secretary: Roderick Palmore
SVP/CIO: George Chappelle
Production Manager: Bruce Holland
Plant Director: Alex Hinson
Estimated Sales: $3.2 Billion
Number Employees: 150
Parent Co: Sara Lee Corporation
Type of Packaging: Consumer, Food Service, Private Label

12745 Sara Lee Bakery GroupThe EarthGrains - Bakery
144 Meyers Street
Suite C
Chico, CA 95928-7153   530-343-9631
www.earthgrains.com
Manufacturer of bread and buns
  Branch Manager: Jay Long
Estimated Sales:$100,000
Number Employees: 5
Parent Co: Sara Lee Corporation
Type of Packaging: Consumer, Food Service, Private Label, Bulk
Brands:
  COLONIAL/RAINBO
  EARTH GRAINS
  GRANT'S FARM
  IRONKIDS
  SARA LEE

12746 (HQ)Sara Lee Bakery Group
3470 S Rider Trl
Earth City, MO 63045-1109   314-291-5480
  Fax: 314-259-7131 consumeraffairs@slbg.com
www.earthgrains.com
Manufacturer of EarthGrains and Sara Lee baked goods
  CEO: Richard Noll
  VP/CFO: Ann Ziegler
  VP: David Groce
  Purchasing: William Palmer
Estimated Sales:$2+ Billion
Number Employees: 250
Parent Co: Sara Lee Corporation
Type of Packaging: Consumer, Food Service, Private Label
Brands:
  BIMBO
  SARA LEE

12747 Sara Lee Coffee & Tea
5725 Highway 7
Minneapolis, MN 55416   952-929-0462
  Fax: 612-929-1230   888-246-2598
www.saraleecoffeeandtea.com
Produces coffees; teas; cappucinos; hot cocoas; juices; spices and seasonings; Sara Lee dressings and sauces; soup bases; beverage accompaniments; and vending products.
  Chairman/CEO: Brenda Barnes
  SVP/CEO Sara Lee Food & Beverage: Christopher Fraleigh
  SVP/CEO Sara Lee Coffee & Tea: Frank Van Oers
  SVP/CEO/CAO Sara Lee Food & Beverage: Ann Ziegler
  Plant Manager: Jeff Kozak
Estimated Sales:$3 Billion
Number Employees: 40
Type of Packaging: Consumer, Food Service, Private Label, Bulk
Brands:
  DOUWE EGBERTS
  KAYO
  MARYLAND CLUB
  PARADISE TEAS
  PICKWICK

12748 Sara Lee Coffee & TeaWholesale Coffee & Tea Location
5725 Highway 7
Minneapolis, MN 55416   914-670-3300
  Fax: 319-335-3017   888-246-2598
customerservice@saraleecoffee.com
www.saraleecoffee.com
Processor and exporter of teas, coffee, coffee concentrate and instant hot chocolate
  President: Peter J W Roorda
  Marketing Director: Sylvia Woolfe
  Sales Director: Sheldon Kail
  Operations Manager: Les Cole
  Branch Manager: Roger Fox
  Purchasing Manager: John Kocinski
Number Employees: 60
Parent Co: Sara Lee Corporation
Type of Packaging: Food Service
Brands:
  Chase & Sanborn
  Chock full O'Nuts
  Hill Bros
  MJB
  Superior

12749 Sara Lee Coffee & Tea
4333 Green Ash Drive
Earth City, MO 63045-1207   314-731-2500
www.saraleecoffee.com
Processor of gourmet coffees and teas; also, chocolate drinks
  President: Peter J W Roorda
  VP: Ken Boucher
  General Manager: Lou Wolf
Estimated Sales:$300,000
Number Employees: 6
Parent Co: Sara Lee Corporation
Type of Packaging: Consumer, Food Service, Bulk
Brands:
  Chase & Sanborn
  Chock full O'Nuts
  Hill Bros
  MJB
  Superior

12750 Sara Lee Coffee & Tea
235 N Norwood St
Houston, TX 77011-2311   713-928-6281
  Fax: 713-924-9870   888-246-2598
customerservice@saralee.com
www.saralee.com
Manufacturer of gourmet coffees and teas; also, regular coffee
  Chairman/CEO: Brenda Barnes
  EVP/CFO/CAO: L M De Kool
  EVP/General Counsel & Secretary: Roderick Palmore
  SVP/CIO: George Chappelle
  VP Human Resources: Felix Venezuela
  Production Manager: Jandres Santanos
  Plant Manager: Dan Hickman
Estimated Sales:$3 Billion
Number Employees: 175
Parent Co: Sara Lee Corporation
Type of Packaging: Consumer, Food Service, Private Label, Bulk
Brands:
  CHASE & SANBORN
  CHOCK FULL O'NUTS
  HILL BROTHERS
  MJB

12751 Sara Lee Coffee & Tea
60 Mushroom Blvd
Rochester, NY 14623-3202
www.saralee.com
Coffees; teas; cappucinnos; hot cocoas; juices; spices and seasonings; Sara Lee dressings and sauces; soup bases; beverage accompaniments; and vending products.
  Chairman/CEO: Brenda Barnes
  EVP/CFO/CAO: L M De Kool
  EVP/General Counsel & Secretary: Roderick Palmore
  SVP/CIO: George Chappelle
  Branch Manager: Roland Batista
Estimated Sales:$ 5-10 Million
Number Employees: 46
Parent Co: Sara Lee Corporation
Brands:
  Chase & Sanborn
  Chock full O'Nuts
  Hill Bros
  MJB
  Superior

12752 (HQ)Sara Lee Corporation
3500 Lacey Road
Downers Grove, IL 60515-5424   630-598-8100
  Fax: 630-598-8482 www.saralee.com
Global manufacturer of high quality meats, breads, sweets and baked goods, abd coffees and teas.
  Chairman/CEO: Brenda Barnes
  Interim CEO: Marcel Smits
  Chairman: James Crown
  EVP, CEO Of N. American Retail & Foodsvc: Stephen Cerrone
Estimated Sales:$13 Billion
Number Employees: 41000
Parent Co: Sara Lee/DE
Type of Packaging: Consumer, Food Service, Private Label, Bulk
Other Locations:
  Sara Lee Bakery
  Cincinnati OH
  Sara Lee Bakery
  Decatur GA
  Sara Lee Bakery
  Orangeburg SC

Brands:
  BALL PARK
  ENDUST
  HANES
  JIMMY DEAN
  KIWI
  L'EGGS
  PLAYTEX
  SARA LEE BAKERY GROUP
  WONDERBRA

12753 Sara Lee Food Service
3900 Meacham Blvd
Haltom City, TX 76117-1603   817-427-7700
  Fax: 817-427-7777   800-261-4754
www.saralee.com
Manufacturer and exporter of frozen foods including regular and mini corn dogs, pancake and sausage on a stick and mini pancakes and sausages.
  Chairman/CEO: Brenda Barnes
  EVP/CFO/CAO: L M De Kool
  EVP/General Counsel & Secretary: Roderick Palmore
  SVP/CIO: George Chappelle
  Plant Manager: Bob Taggert
Estimated Sales:$319 Million
Number Employees: 250-499
Sq. footage: 40000
Parent Co: Sara Lee Corporation
Type of Packaging: Consumer, Food Service, Private Label, Bulk
Brands:
  STATE FAIR BRAND CORN DOGS
  STATE FAIR BRAND MINI CORN DOGS
  STATE FAIR BREAKFAST BITES
  STATE FAIR PANCAKE N SAUSAGE

12754 Sara Lee Foods
P.O.Box 756
Neenah, WI 54957-0756   920-982-2611
  Fax: 920-982-1272   800-558-8440
www.saralee.com
Manufacturer of fresh, cured and smoked pork and beef products including bacon and sausage.
  Chairman/CEO: Brenda Barnes
  EVP/CFO/CAO: L M De Kool
  EVP/General Counsel & Secretary: Roderick Palmore
  SVP/CIO: George Chappelle
  General Manager: Nate Leider
  Plant Manager: Phil Ramsey
Estimated Sales:$500 Million-$1 Billion
Number Employees: 1,000-4,999
Parent Co: Sara Lee Corporation
Type of Packaging: Consumer, Food Service
Brands:
  KAHN'S

12755 Sara Lee Foods
8300 96th Ave
Zeeland, MI 49464-9177   616-875-8131
  Fax: 616-875-7591 www.saralee.com
Manufacturer of packaged luncheon meats including ham, turkey and pastrami; also, frankfurters and smoked sausage.
  Chairman/CEO: Brenda Barnes
  EVP/CFO/CAO: L M De Kool
  EVP/General Counsel & Secretary: Roderick Palmore
  SVP/CIO: George Chappelle
  Plant Manager: Ross Myers
Estimated Sales:$ 5 - 10 Million
Number Employees: 1,000-4,999
Parent Co: Sara Lee Corporation
Type of Packaging: Consumer, Food Service

12756 (HQ)Sara Lee Foods
10151 Carver Rd
Cincinnati, OH 45242-4758   513-936-2000
  Fax: 513-936-2170   800-351-7111
www.bests-kosher.com
Processor and exporter of packaged meats including luncheon, smoked sausage, frankfurters and corn dogs
  President: James Hooks
  President Sara Lee Deli: Jerry Laner
  VP Marketing: Nancy Koglmeier
  Group Operations VP: Debra Shankle
  Plant Manager: Dave Ruwe
Estimated Sales:$4 Billion
Number Employees: 100-249
Parent Co: Sara Lee Corporation
Type of Packaging: Consumer, Food Service, Private Label, Bulk

Brands:
Aoste
Ball Park
Best's Kosher
Bryan
Hillshire Farms
Jimmy Dean
Kahn's
Sara Lee

12757 Sara Lee Foods
8000 Centerview Parkway
Suite 300
Cordova, TN 38018-4254   901-756-4051
          Fax: 901-755-9512 www.saralee.com
Processor of beef, pork, ham and turkey
    President/CEO: Robert Kopriva
    President Sara Lee Deli: Jerry Laner
Estimated Sales: $4 Billion
Number Employees: 20-49
Parent Co: Sara Lee Corporation
Type of Packaging: Consumer, Food Service, Bulk
Brands:
    Ambi Pur
    Earth Grains

12758 (HQ)Sara Lee Foodservice
3800 Golf Road
Suite 100
Rolling Meadows, IL 60008   847-595-6000
          Fax: 847-595-6895
    james.mccartney@saralee.com
          www.saralee.com
Specialty coffee, premium cocoa, flavored coffees
and cocoas, teas
    Chairman/CEO: Brenda Barnes
    EVP/CFO/CAO: L M De Kool
    EVP/General Counsel & Secretary: Roderick
    Palmore
    SVP/CIO: George Chappelle
Number Employees: 250-499
Brands:
    Christmas Traditions
    Dutch Velvet
    Paradise Tropical Te
    Sara Lee
    Superior Coffee's

12759 Sara Lee Foodservice
3800 Golf Road
Rolling Meadows, IL 60008   847-595-6000
                    800-261-4754
    customerservice@saraleecoffee.com
          www.saraleefoodservice.com
Produces coffees; teas; cappuccinos; hot cocoas;
juices; spices and seasonings; Sara Lee dressings
and sauces; soup bases; beverage accompaniments;
and vending products.
    President: Thomas Hayes
    VP Marketing: Daryl Gromley
Estimated Sales: $3 Billion
Number Employees: 50-99
Parent Co: Sara Lee/DE
Type of Packaging: Consumer, Food Service
Brands:
    BALL PARK
    BISTRO
    BRIAR STREET MARKET
    BRYAN
    CHEF PIERRE
    DELI D'ITALIA
    DOUWE EGBERTS
    GALILEO
    HEINEMAN & STERN
    HILLSHIRE FARMS
    JAVA COAST
    JIMMY DEAN
    KAHN'S
    KAYO HOT COCOA
    PARADISE TEA
    PICKWICK TEA
    RUDY'S FARM
    SARA LEE
    STATE FAIR
    SUPERIOR

12760 Sara Lee Wholesome Bakery
5711 W 95th Street
Oak Lawn, IL 60453-2344   708-499-5711
          www.saralee.com

Manufacturer of bread, buns, sweet rolls and dough-
nuts
    Chairman/CEO: Brenda Barnes
    EVP/CFO: Marcel Smits
    EVP/General Counsel: Brett Hart
    EVP Human Resources: Stephen Cerrone
Estimated Sales: $3.3 Billion
Number Employees: 80
Parent Co: Sara Lee Corporation
Type of Packaging: Consumer, Food Service, Pri-
vate Label, Bulk
Brands:
    BALL PARK
    BIMBO
    CAFE DO PONTO
    CAFE PILAO
    CAFE PRIMA
    DOUWE EGBERTS
    HILLSHIRE FARM
    JIMMY DEAN
    MAISON DU CAFE
    MARCILLA
    MERRILD
    MOCCONA
    PICKWICK
    SARA LEE
    SENSEO
    STATE FAIR
    ZWITSAL

12761 Sara Lee/Old Home
P.O.Box 337
South Sioux City, NE 68776-0337   402-494-5474
          Fax: 402-494-6986 matt.hall@slbg.com
          www.saralee.com
Processor of restaurant buns and snack pies
    Manager: Noel Simpson
    EVP/CFO/CAO: L M De Kool
    EVP/General Counsel & Secretary: Roderick
    Palmore
    SVP/CIO: George Chappelle
    General Manager: Noel Simpson
Estimated Sales: $ 20 - 50 Million
Number Employees: 100-249
Parent Co: Sara Lee Bakery Group
Type of Packaging: Consumer, Food Service, Pri-
vate Label
Brands:
    Old Home

12762 Sarabeth's Bakery
1161 E 156th St
Bronx, NY 10474-6226   718-589-2900
          Fax: 718-589-8412   800-773-7378
    info@sarabeth.com   www.sarabeth.com
Processor of muffins, cakes, cookies, pastries, pud-
dings, pies, croissants, brownies, tarts and frozen
blintzes
    President: William Levine
    Executive VP: Jennifer Firestone
    Co-Owner: David Case
Estimated Sales: Below $ 5 Million
Number Employees: 20-49
Sq. footage: 4300
Parent Co: Sarabeth's Kitchen
Type of Packaging: Consumer, Food Service
Other Locations:
    Sarabeth's Bakery Ltd.
    New York NY
Brands:
    Sarabeth's

12763 Sarabeth's Kitchen
1161 E 156th Street
Bronx, NY 10474   718-589-2900
          Fax: 718-589-8412 info@saarabeth.com
          www.sarabeth.com
preserves, cakes, cookies
    President/Owner: Bill Scotti
Estimated Sales: $1.2 Million
Number Employees: 50

12764 Sarabeth's Kitchen
1161 E 156th St
Bronx, NY 10474-6226   718-589-2900
          Fax: 718-589-8412   800-773-7378
    info@sarabeth.com   www.sarabeth.com
Manufacturer of jams, jellies, marmalade, preserves,
packages cookies, scone and muffin mixes
    President: William Levine
    CFO: Jeffrey Shapiro
    Co-President: Sarabeth Levine
    Marketing Director: Jason Albucker
    Production Manager: Manuel Padilla

Estimated Sales: Below $ 5 Million
Number Employees: 10-19
Type of Packaging: Private Label

12765 Sarah Lingwood's Kitchen
2920 SW 29th Ct
Cape Coral, FL 33914-3889   360-293-7181
          Fax: 360-299-0828
Processor and exporter of cookies and hand deco-
rated gingerbread
    Owner: Fred McKenzie
Estimated Sales: $500000
Number Employees: 8
Sq. footage: 4200
Type of Packaging: Consumer, Food Service, Pri-
vate Label, Bulk
Brands:
    Sarah Lingwood's Kitchens

12766 Sarah's Vineyard
4005 Hecker Pass Rd
Gilroy, CA 95020-8843   408-842-4278
    Fax: 408-842-3252   sales@sarahsvineyard.com
          www.sarahs-vineyard.com
Wines
    Owner: Tim Slater
Estimated Sales: $500,000-$1 Million
Number Employees: 1-4
Brands:
    SARAH'S VINEYARD

12767 Sarant International Commodities
PO Box 659
Centereach, NY 11720-0659   631-689-2845
          Fax: 631-246-5257   psarant@aol.com
Processor and importer of dehydrated vegetables in-
cluding tomatoes, celery, carrots and red and green
bell peppers
    President: Peter Sarant
    Co-Secretary: Pamela Sarant
Number Employees: 1-4
Type of Packaging: Bulk

12768 (HQ)Saratoga Beverage Group
11 Geyser Rd
Saratoga Springs, NY 12866-9048   518-584-6363
          Fax: 518-584-0380   888-426-8642
          www.saratogaspringwater.com
Processor of sparkling and nonsparkling regular and
flavored spring water, orange and grapefruit juice
and flavored smoothies including raspberry, straw-
berry, blackberry, peach banana, etc
    President: Adam Madkour
    CFO: Robert Braks
    Vice President: Andrew Cook
    Production Manager: Mike Lawson
Estimated Sales: $300,000-500,000
Number Employees: 1-4
Type of Packaging: Consumer, Food Service, Pri-
vate Label
Other Locations:
    Saratoga Beverage Group
    Azusa CA
Brands:
    Saratoga
    Saratoga Splash
    Saratoga Vichy

12769 Saratoga Food Specialties
200 Wrightwood Ave
Elmhurst, IL 60126-1113   630-833-3810
          Fax: 630-833-1932   800-451-0407
    info@saratogafs.com   www.saratogafs.com
Importer, exporter and processor of whole and
ground spices; developer of custom seasoning
blends, seasoned rice, stuffing and gravy mixes.
    Manager: Jim Bejna
    CFO: Ed Herbert
    Vice President: Wade McGeorge
    Research & Development: Paul Maki
    Quality Control: Mark Beattie
    Marketing Director: Kristi Freitager
    Sales Director: George Rackos
    Operations Manager: Jim Benja
    Purchasing Manager: Ron Batzer
Estimated Sales: $30-40 Million
Number Employees: 100-249
Sq. footage: 110000
Type of Packaging: Consumer, Food Service, Pri-
vate Label, Bulk
Other Locations:
    Saratoga Specialties Co.
    Northlake IL

12770 Sardinha Sausage
177 Lepes Rd
Somerset, MA 02726-2635   508-674-2511
    Fax: 508-674-2511   800-678-0178
esardinhs@sardinhas.com   www.sardinhas.com
Processor of gourmet smoked and fresh sausages including chourico, linguica, turkey dogs and kielbasa, breakfast and Italian sausage; private label available
    President: Ed Sardinha
Estimated Sales: $500,000 appx.
Number Employees: 1-4
Sq. footage: 3600
Type of Packaging: Consumer, Food Service, Private Label, Bulk
Brands:
    Francisco's
    Portuguese Sausages
    Sardinha's
    Vincenza's

12771 Sardinia Cheese
312 Roosevelt Drive
Seymour, CT 06483-2128   203-735-3374
    Fax: 203-732-3959   tmavuli@aol.com
Cheese
    CEO/VP: Tony Mavuli
Estimated Sales: $ 5 Million
Number Employees: 3
Type of Packaging: Private Label

12772 Sargeant's Army Marketing
PO Box 82
Bowmanville, ON L1C 1K8
Canada   905-623-2888
Processor of frozen yogurt and waffle cones; manufacturer and exporter of frozen yogurt and ice cream dispensers
    President: Herb Sargeant
Number Employees: 1-4
Type of Packaging: Private Label
Brands:
    Monster
    Whirlywinkles
    Wizard

12773 Sargent's Bear Necessities
321 Guay Farm Road
North Troy, VT 05859-9207   802-988-2903
info@sargentsbearnecessities.com
www.sargentsbearnecessities.com
Jams, jellies, pickles and relishes
    Owner: Michelle Sargent
Number Employees: 1

12774 (HQ)Sargento Foods Inc
1 Persnickety Pl
Plymouth, WI 53073-3544   920-893-8484
    Fax: 920-893-8399   800-243-3737
    www.sargento.com
Manufacturer, importer and exporter of natural and processed cheese
    Chairman/CEO: Lou Gentine
    CFO: George Hoff
    Senior Research Scientist R&D: Craig Hackl
    Senior Packaging Development Manager: Guy Turnbull
    VP Foodservice Sales/Marketing: Sam Colson
    Consumer Products Division Sales Rep: Mike Ruhland
    EVP/COO: Mark Rhyan
    Corporate Chef: Guy Beardsmore
Estimated Sales: $534 Million
Number Employees: 1,000-4,999
Type of Packaging: Consumer, Food Service, Private Label, Bulk
Brands:
    SARGENTO

12775 Sarilii
2110 Chapman Hwy
Knoxville, TN 37920-1904   865-573-1941
    Fax: 865-577-3747   www.saralee.com
Processor of baked goods including bread and rolls
    Plant Manager: Mike Wardell
Estimated Sales: $ .5 - 1 million
Number Employees: 1-4
Parent Co: Cooper Smith
Type of Packaging: Consumer, Food Service, Private Label
Other Locations:
    Kern's Bakery
    London KY

12776 Sarsfield Foods
15 Roscoe Drive
Kentville, NS B4N 3W9
Canada   902-678-2241
    Fax: 902-678-6698
Processor and exporter of frozen pies
    President: Kirk McGrath
Number Employees: 100-249
Sq. footage: 80000
Parent Co: George Weston Foods
Type of Packaging: Food Service, Private Label
Other Locations:
    President Sarsfield Foods Ltd
    Mount Pearl NF

12777 Sartori Food Corporation
P.O.Box 258
107 Pleasant View
Plymouth, WI 53073-0258   920-893-6061
    Fax: 920-892-2732   800-558-5888
info@sartorifoods.com   www.sartorifoods.com
Manufacturer, value-added coverter and marketer of aged Italian cheese, Mexican cheeses, specialty chesses, cheese products and cheese-based flavor systems for the foodservice and food processing marketplace
    President: James C Sartori
    VP: Frederick M Bowes II
    VP of Research & Product Development: Pat Mugan
    Quality Control: Steve Tittl
    Sales: Russ Horneck
    Operations VP: Phillip Kramer
    Production: Mark Thaldorf
    Plant Manager: Jason Schultz
    Purchasing: Helen Cheng
Estimated Sales: $ 50 - 100 Million
Number Employees: 20-49

12778 Sartori Foods
P.O.Box 258
Plymouth, WI 53073-0258   920-893-6061
    Fax: 920-892-2732   800-356-5655
info@sartorifoods.com   www.sartorifoods.com
Manufacturer of specialty cheese: Parmesean, romano, asiago cheeses
    President: James Sartori
Estimated Sales: $20-50 Million
Number Employees: 100-249
Type of Packaging: Private Label

12779 Sarum Tea Company
332 Main Street
Lakeville, CT 06039-1207   860-435-2086
    Fax: 860-435-9304
Tea
    President/CEO: W Harris
    Manager: E Lloyd-Harris
Estimated Sales: Less than $500,000
Number Employees: 1-4
Brands:
    Sarum Tea

12780 Sassafras Enterprises
1622 W Carroll Ave
Chicago, IL 60612-2502   312-226-2000
    Fax: 312-226-0873   800-537-4941
info@sassafrasenterprises.com
www.sassafrasenterprises.com
Gourmet gift baskets, natural pizza and pasta sauces, spices, oils, spreads, bruschettas, mixes, pastas and bread mixes
    Owner: Steven Schwab
    CEO: Steven Schwab
    VP: Nancy Schwab
    Operations Manager: Ron Cahill
Estimated Sales: $ 5 - 10 Million
Number Employees: 20-49
Type of Packaging: Private Label
Brands:
    Superstone

12781 Saticoy Foods Corporation
P.O.Box 4547
Ventura, CA 93007-0547   805-647-5266
    Fax: 805-933-1523
Manufacturer of canned peppers including diced red bell, green strips and halves; also, pimientos
    President: Jerry Hensley
    CEO: Stanley Dunbar
Estimated Sales: $15 Million
Number Employees: 20-49
Parent Co: Moody Dunbar

12782 Saticoy Lemon Cooperative
P.O.Box 46
Santa Paula, CA 93061-0046   805-654-6500
    Fax: 805-654-6510
webmaster@saticoylemon.com
www.saticoylemon.com
Agricultural Cooperative that is owned by the lemon grower members of which the marketing of the fruit is handled through their affiliation with Sunkist Growers, Inc.
    President: Glenn Miller
    Chief Financial Officer: Mike Dillard
    Exchange/Business Development Manager: John Eliot
    Field Manager: David Coert
    Sales Coordinator: Jose Mendez
    MIS Director: Lee Raymond
    Personnel Director: Michael Dennington
    Production Manager: Ron Davis
    Plant Superintendent: Albert Palacio Jr
    Shipping Supervisor: Jose Mares
Type of Packaging: Food Service

12783 Saticoy Lemon Cooperative
348 a St
Fillmore, CA 93015-1905   805-654-6500
    Fax: 805-654-6528
webmaster@saticoylemon.com
www.saticoylemon.com
Agricultural Cooperative that is owned by the lemon grower members of which the marketing of the fruit is handled through their affiliation with Sunkist Growers, Inc.
    Manager: Salvador Ramirez
    Chief Financial Officer: Mike Dillard
    Exchange/Business Development Manager: John Eliot
    Field Manager: David Coert
    Sales Coordinator: Jose Mendez
    MIS Director: Lee Raymond
    Personnel Director: Michael Dennington
    Production Manager: Ron Davis
    Plant Superintendent: Salvador Ramirez
    Shipping Supervisor: Jose Manzano
Type of Packaging: Food Service

12784 Saticoy Lemon Cooperative
103 N Peck Road
Santa Paula, CA 93060   805-654-6515
    Fax: 805-654-6510
webmaster@saticoylemon.com
www.saticoylemon.com
Agricultural Cooperative that is owned by the lemon grower members of which the marketing of the fruit is handled through their affiliation with Sunkist Growers, Inc.
    President: Glenn Miller
    Chief Financial Officer: Mike Dillard
    Exchange/Business Development Manager: John Eliot
    Field Manager: David Coert
    Sales Coordinator: Jose Mendez
    MIS Director: Lee Raymond
    Personnel Director: Michael Dennington
    Production Manager: Ron Davis
    Plant Superintendent: Rene Velasco
    Shipping Supervisor: Juan Martinez
Type of Packaging: Food Service

12785 Saticoy Lemon Cooperative
600 E Third Street
Oxnard, CA 93030   805-654-6543
    Fax: 805-654-6510
webmaster@saticoylemon.com
www.saticoylemon.com
Agricultural Cooperative that is owned by the lemon grower members of which the marketing of the fruit is handled through their affiliation with Sunkist Growers, Inc.
    President: Glenn Miller
    Chief Financial Officer: Mike Dillard
    Exchange/Business Development Manager: John Eliot
    Field Manager: David Coert
    Sales Coordinator: Jose Mendez
    MIS Director: Lee Raymond
    Personnel Director: Michael Dennington
    Production Manager: Ron Davis
    Plant Superintendent: Albert Rivera
    Shipping Supervisor: Albert Palacio Sr
Type of Packaging: Food Service

12786 Satiety
1027 Maple Ln
Davis, CA 95616-1720   530-757-2699
Wines, wine vinegars, table grapes, wine grapes
  Owner: Sterling Chaykin
Estimated Sales:$270,000
Number Employees: 1-4
Brands:
  Ambrosia
  Satiety

12787 Satnam Overseas Limited
400 Apgar Dr # E
Somerset, NJ 08873-1154   732-868-3141
            Fax: 732-868-3143
  webmaster@kohinoorbasmati.com
  www.neicorporation.com
Rice
  CEO: Ganesh Skandan
Estimated Sales:$ 2.5-5 Million
Number Employees: 10-19
Brands:
  Kohinoor
  Satman Overseas

12788 Satori Teas
825 W Market Street
Salinas, CA 93901-1404   831-753-0511
    Fax: 831-753-0541   800-444-7286
            satoritea.com
Processor, importer and exporter of herbal teas including spearmint blend, amino acid/mineral blend, rose hip, chamomile, cinnamon, peppermint/licorice, red clover, lemon grass, oatstraw, etc
  President: Steven Steigman
  Manager: Josie Steigman
Estimated Sales:$ 20 - 50 Million
Number Employees: 50-99
Parent Co: Business Development Labs
Type of Packaging: Consumer, Food Service, Private Label, Bulk
Brands:
  Eternal
  Ginseng Power
  Googol
  Gourmet Dieter
  Infinity Spice
  Long Life
  Original C
  Satori
  Sleeper

12789 Sattwa Chai
P.O.Box 805
Newberg, OR 97132-0805   503-538-4715
    Fax: 503-538-5125   info@sattwac.com
            www.sattwachai.com
Tea, chai
  Owner: Juanita Crampton
  Owner: David Fields
  CFO/VP Operations: Juanita Crampton
  Purchasing Manager: Jan Rhine
Estimated Sales:$ 2.5-5 Million
Number Employees: 1-4
Parent Co: Sattwa Chai
Type of Packaging: Food Service, Private Label, Bulk
Brands:
  Black Tea Chai
  SATTWA SUN CHAI
  Sattwa Chai Concentrate
  Sattwa Kovalam Spice Chai
  Sattwa Shanti Herbal Chai
  Sattwa Sun Chai

12790 Sau-Sea Foods
303 S Broadway # 32
Tarrytown, NY 10591-5410   914-631-1717
            Fax: 914-631-0865
Processor of shrimp and sauces including cocktail, tartar and horseradish
  President: Antonio Estadella
  National Sales Manager: Edward Cauley
Estimated Sales:$1300000
Number Employees: 5-9
Type of Packaging: Consumer, Food Service, Private Label, Bulk
Brands:
  Sea Maid
  Seagull Bay

12791 Sauces 'n Love
86 Sanserson Ave
Suite 130
Lynn, MA 01902   781-595-7771
    Fax: 781-595-7799   866-772-8237
  info@saucesnlove.com   www.saucesnlove.com
scarpetta, sauces, pesto, bruschetta, spreads and dips
  CEO: Paolo Volpati-Kedra

12792 Saucilito Canyon Vineyard
3080 Biddle Ranch Rd
San Luis Obispo, CA 93401-8320   805-543-2111
    Fax: 805-543-2111   info@saucelitocanyon.com
            www.saucelitocanyon.com
Wines
  Owner: Bill Greenough
  Owner: Nancy Greenbough
  Marketing/Sales Manager: Nancy Greenbough
  Winemaker: Amy Freeman
*Estimated Sales:*Less than $500,000
Number Employees: 1-4
Type of Packaging: Private Label
Brands:
  Saucelito Canyon

12793 Saugy
30 Cross Street
Providence, RI 02904-2605   401-640-1879
    Fax: 401-383-9374   866-467-2849
  saugy@cox.net   www.saugy.net
Manufacturer of frankfurters
  President: Maureen O'Brien
  VP/Treasurer: Joanne Burton
  General Manager: Joe McGuire
  General Manager: Ted Burton
Estimated Sales:$5-10 Million
Number Employees: 10-19
Type of Packaging: Consumer, Food Service, Bulk

12794 Saunders Provision Company
1107 E Princess Anne Road
Norfolk, VA 23504-2834   757-627-5611
    Fax: 757-627-9017   800-486-5611
            saunder@exis.net
Manufacturer and exporter of portion control meats including beef, lamb, veal, pork and chicken
  President: Edwin Salomonsky
Estimated Sales:$20-50 Million
Number Employees: 30
Sq. footage: 25000
Type of Packaging: Consumer, Food Service, Private Label, Bulk

12795 Sausage Kitchen
18893 SE McLoughlin Blvd
Oak Grove, OR 97267-6756   503-656-9766
            Fax: 503-656-0567
Sausage and smoked salmon
  President: Nicholas Allick
  Plant Manager: David Parker
Estimated Sales:$350,000
Number Employees: 5-9

12796 Sausage Shoppe
4501 Memphis Ave
Cleveland, OH 44144-1912   216-351-5213
  cheinle@sausageshoppe.com
            www.sausageshoppe.com
Processor of sausage and luncheon meat
  President/Owner: Norm Heinle
  VP/Owner: Carol Heinle
  Plant Manager: Alan Heinle
Number Employees: 1-4
Type of Packaging: Consumer, Bulk
Brands:
  Sheffler Ham

12797 Sausages by Amy
1143 W Lake St
Chicago, IL 60607-1618   312-666-6989
    Fax: 312-829-2098   www.sausagesbyamy.com
Sausages
  President: Amy Kurzawski
  President: Chico Kurzawski
Estimated Sales:$ 5-10 Million
Number Employees: 50-99

12798 Sausal Winery
7370 Highway 128
Healdsburg, CA 95448-8018   707-433-2285
    Fax: 707-433-5136   800-500-2285
            www.sausalwinery.com
Wines
  President: David Demostene
*Estimated Sales:*Below $ 5 Million
Number Employees: 10-19
Brands:
  Sausal Wines

12799 Sausalito Expresso
27 Braun Court
Sausalito, CA 94965-1174   415-331-5407
            Fax: 415-331-5435
Tea and coffee flavors

12800 Saval Foods
P.O.Box 8630
Elkridge, MD 21075-8630   410-379-5100
    Fax: 410-379-8068   800-527-2825
            www.savalfoods.com
Manufacturer of fine quality delicatessen products such as processed roast beef, corn beef, pastrami and products for home meal replacement
  President: Paul Saval
  EVP: Howard Saval
Estimated Sales:$100+ Million
Number Employees: 100-249
Sq. footage: 57000
Type of Packaging: Food Service, Private Label, Bulk
Brands:
  Elite
  Saval

12801 Savannah Bee Company
PO Box 10914
Savannah, GA 31412   912-234-0688
    Fax: 912-234-0125   info@savannahbee.com
            www.savannahbee.com
honey
  President/Owner: Ted Dennard
Estimated Sales:$1.1 Million
Number Employees: 8

12802 Savannah Chanelle Vineyards
23600 Congress Springs Rd
Saratoga, CA 95070-9755   408-741-2934
    Fax: 408-867-4824   www.savannahchanelle.com
Wines
  Owner: Gregg Gorham
  Co-Owner: Kellie Ballard
  Winemaker: Tony Craig
Estimated Sales:$ 5 - 10 Million
Number Employees: 10-19
Brands:
  Savannah Chanelle Vineyards

12803 Savannah Cinnamon & Cookie Company
2604 Gregory St
Savannah, GA 31404-1426   912-233-1433
    Fax: 912-233-3004   800-288-0854
  savcinn@aol.com   www.savannahcinnamon.com
Cinnamon and other liquid flavors for coffee, tea and juices
  Owner: Brian Wiggins
Estimated Sales:$ 1-2.5 Million
Number Employees: 10-19
Type of Packaging: Consumer
Brands:
  Savannah Cinnamon Mix
  Savannah Squares

12804 Savannah Foods & Industries
2 Oxnard Dr
Port Wentworth, GA 31407-2406   912-234-1261
    Fax: 912-651-4905   800-241-3785
Processor and exporter of sugar and artificial sweeteners.
  President: Bob Peiser
  CEO: W Sprague III
  VP Sales: Joe Herb
  Plant Manager: Phillip Rowland
Estimated Sales:$100+ Million
Number Employees: 250-499
Parent Co: Imperial Holly Corporation
Type of Packaging: Consumer, Food Service, Private Label, Bulk
Other Locations:
  Savannah Foods & Industries
  Bremen GA

12805 Savannah Foods Industrial
P.O.Box 4225
Port Wentworth, GA 31407-4225   912-964-1361
            Fax: 863-983-9210

Processor and exporter of sugar including granulated, powdered, brown, cubes and in envelopes
    Manager: Phillip Rowland
    Purchasing Agent: Larry Dykes
Number Employees: 5-9
Parent Co: Savannah Foods & Industries
Type of Packaging: Consumer, Food Service, Private Label, Bulk

12806 (HQ)Savino's Italian Ices
1126 S Powerline Road
Deerfield Beach, FL 33442-8121   954-426-4119
Processor of frozen Italian ice fruit desserts
    CEO: Sal Savino
Number Employees: 1-4
Type of Packaging: Bulk

12807 Savoia Foods
85 Independence Dr
Chicago Heights, IL 60411-4198   708-754-6950
    Fax: 708-754-2133   800-867-2782
    jbamonti@msn.com   www.savoiafoods.com
Processor and exporter of pasta
    President/Owner: Rudolph Bamonti
Estimated Sales: $500,000-$1 Million
Number Employees: 5-9
Type of Packaging: Consumer, Food Service
Brands:
    Savoia

12808 Savoie Industries
P.O.Box 69
Belle Rose, LA 70341-0069   225-473-9293
    Fax: 225-473-9294
Processor of blackstrap molasses and sugar
    President: Michael Daigle
Estimated Sales: $ 10 - 20 Million
Number Employees: 50-99
Type of Packaging: Consumer

12809 Savoie's Sausage & FoodProducts
1742 Highway 742
Opelousas, LA 70570-0549   337-948-4115
    Fax: 337-948-9571   sales@savoiesfoods.com
    www.savoiesfoods.com
Manufacturer of sausage including hog's headcheese, boudin, andouille and tasso; also, barbecue sauce, roux and dressing mix
    President/Owner: Eula Savoie
    Marketing Manager: Frederick Lafleur
    Operations Manager: Gerald Boullion
Estimated Sales: $9 Million
Number Employees: 50-99
Sq. footage: 25000
Type of Packaging: Consumer, Private Label
Brands:
    CAJUN HOUSE
    REAL CAJUN
    SAVOIE'S

12810 Savory Foods
P.O.Box 1604
Portsmouth, OH 45662-1604   740-354-6655
    Fax: 740-353-2482   savory@zoomnet.net
Processor and exporter of pork rinds
    President: Marcia Sanderlin
    VP Sales/Production: K Sanderlin
    Safety Manager: Adam Dengel
    Production Manager: Ed Thompson
    Plant Manager: Rigel Olmos
Number Employees: 20-49
Sq. footage: 60000
Type of Packaging: Food Service, Private Label
Brands:
    Porkies
    Savory
    Southern Style

12811 Sawtooth Winery
13750 Surrey Ln
Nampa, ID 83686-9128   208-467-1200
    Fax: 208-468-7934   www.sawtoothwinery.com
    www.sawtoothwinery.com
Wines
    Winemaker/General Manager: Brad Pintler
    President: Ken McCabe
    Partner: Charles Pintler
    Retail Manager/Events Coordinator: Ina DeBoer
Estimated Sales: $1-2.5 Million
Number Employees: 1-4
Brands:
    Sawtooth

12812 Saxby Foods
4120 98th Street NW
Edmonton, AB T6E 5A2
Canada   780-440-4177
    Fax: 780-440-4480   jon@saxbyfoods.com
    www.saxbyfoods.com
Processor and exporter of frozen desserts including cakes and cheesecakes. Co-packer of private label in Canada, USA, Carribean
    President: Jonathan Avis
    Quality Control: Ana Avalos
    Public Relations: Thea Avis
    Plant Manager: Sean Gillis
    Purchasing: Rhys Amatori
Number Employees: 120
Sq. footage: 50000
Brands:
    Albertson's
    Safeway
    Walmart

12813 Saxon Chocolates
21 Coleville Rd
Toronto, ON M6M 2Y2
Canada   416-675-6363
    Fax: 416-675-2777   sales@saxonchocolates.com
    www.saxonchocolates.com
belgian chocolates
    President/Owner: Johan DeGrees
Estimated Sales: $2.3 Million
Number Employees: 20

12814 Saxon Creamery
855 Hickory Street
Cleveland, WI 53015   920-547-4108
    Fax: 480-393-4478   info@saxoncreamery.com
    www.saxoncreamery.com
cheeses

12815 Say Ying Leong Look Funn Factory
1028 Kekaulike St
Honolulu, HI 96817-5007   808-537-4304
Ethnic foods
    Owner: Fooying Chee
Estimated Sales: $ 2.5-5 Million
Number Employees: 1-4

12816 Sayklly's Candies& Gifts
910 2nd Ave N
Escanaba, MI 49829-3811   906-786-3092
    Fax: 906-786-3096 http://www.saykllyscandy.com
Processor of candy including brittles, butterscotch, caramels, chocolate, coconut, taffy, etc.
    President: Michael F Kobasic
    Owner: Cheryl Kobasic
Estimated Sales: $170000
Number Employees: 5-9
Type of Packaging: Consumer

12817 Sazerac Company
P.O.Box 52821
New Orleans, LA 70152-2821   504-831-9450
    Fax: 504-831-2383   800-899-9450
    info@sazerac.com   www.sazerac.com
Distilled spirits
    President: Mark Brown
    CFO: Kent Broussard
    VP: Jay Cummins
    VP: Stephen Camisa
    Sales/Marketing Manager: William Pananos
    Point of Sales Manager: Debbie Ledet
    Plant Manager: Dubois
Estimated Sales: $ 50-100 Million
Number Employees: 100-249
Type of Packaging: Private Label
Brands:
    Old Charter Bourbon

12818 Scala Packing Company
707 N Orleans Street
Chicago, IL 60610-3572   312-944-3567
    Fax: 312-944-4716
Manufacturer of roast beef and hot and sweet Italian sausage
    President: Pat Scala
Estimated Sales: $20-50 Million
Number Employees: 150
Type of Packaging: Food Service, Private Label, Bulk

12819 Scally's Imperial Importing Company Inc
4354 Victory Blvd
Staten Island, NY 10314-6733   718-983-1938
    Fax: 718-259-2195   scallyimperial@aol.com
Importers, packers and distributors of food products including canned tomato products, olives, mushrooms, beans, peppers, pickles, giardiniera, artichokes, canned clams, canned shrimp, canned crab meat, canned tuna, and edibleoils.
    President/Sales/Plant Manager: Alex Scarselli
    CEO: Alessandre Scarselli
    VP/Purchasing Director: Christine Scarselli
Estimated Sales: $ 5 Million
Number Employees: 20-49
Sq. footage: 10000
Type of Packaging: Consumer, Food Service, Private Label
Brands:
    LA PERLA
    PRIMA DONNA
    SCALLI

12820 Scan American Food Compampany
1410 80th Street SW
Suite F
Everett, WA 98203-6200   425-514-0500
    Fax: 425-514-0400
    scanamerican@scanamerican.com
    www.scanamerican.com
Processor, importer and exporter of natural food flavors and extracts, aroma materials, proteins, fish oils and freeze dried seafood
    President: Svein Bjorge
Estimated Sales: $ 5 - 10 Million
Number Employees: 5-9

12821 Scandia Seafood Company
130 Tillson Avenue
Rockland, ME 04841-3424   207-596-7102
    Fax: 207-596-7105
Crabs, cold water shrimp, America lobster, Atlantic herring
    President: Asger Jorgensen
Sq. footage: 25000

12822 (HQ)Scandinavian Formulas Inc
140 E Church St
Sellersville, PA 18960-2402   215-453-2500
    Fax: 215-257-9781   800-288-2844
    info@scandinavianformulas.com
    www.scandinavianformulas.com
Manufacturer, importer and exporter of vitamins and supplements, chemicals and ingredients
    President: Catherine Peklak
    Marketing: Sylvie Millet
    Purchasing Director: Denise Covelens
Estimated Sales: $1005000
Number Employees: 5-9
Number of Brands: 7
Number of Products: 7
Sq. footage: 9000
Type of Packaging: Consumer, Private Label, Bulk
Other Locations:
    Scandinavian Natural Health &
    Perkasie PA
Brands:
    ALKYROL
    BILBERRY EXTRACT
    DHEA
    LYCOPENE
    MELATONIN
    SALIX SST
    SINCERA SKIN CARE PRODUCTS

12823 Scandinavian Laboratories
794 Sunrise Blvd
Mt Bethel, PA 18343-6004   570-897-7735
    Fax: 570-897-7732   scanlabs@epix.net
    www.oceanaproducts.com
Processor of nutritional products including shark liver and fish oils, essential fatty acids, effervescent tablets and liquid emulsions; importer and exporter of nutritional supplements including shark liver oils; also, contractpackaging available
    President: Olav Sandnes
Estimated Sales: $500,000
Number Employees: 5-9
Type of Packaging: Private Label, Bulk
Brands:
    Calcitrace
    Ecomega

Glycomarine
Oceana
Pedia-Vit
Promega
Squalene

12824 Scanga Meat Company
9250 County Road 156
Salida, CO 81201-9588   719-539-3511
          Fax: 719-539-6344   rlscanga@vanion.com
Manufacturer and packer of beef, poultry, seafood
     President: Ralph Scanga Jr
Estimated Sales: $29 Milion
Number Employees: 10-19
Sq. footage: 20000
Type of Packaging: Consumer, Food Service, Private Label, Bulk

12825 Scarborough Meat Packers
29 Skagway Avenue
Scarborough, ON M1M 3T9
Canada   416-269-7758
                    Fax: 416-269-8944
Processor and exporter of fresh and frozen chicken, pork and beef products
     General Manager: Daniel Sham
Number Employees: 50-99
Type of Packaging: Consumer, Food Service, Private Label, Bulk

12826 Scenic Fruit Company
7510 SE Altman Rd
Gresham, OR 97080-8808   503-663-3434
          Fax: 503-663-7095 800-554-5578
     sales@scenicfruit.com   www.scenicfruit.com
Processor of frozen berries
     Manager: Joe Mc Michael
     Plant Manager: John Vasquez
Estimated Sales: $18000000
Number Employees: 100-249
Type of Packaging: Food Service, Bulk

12827 Scenic Valley Winery
P.O.Box 395
Lanesboro, MN 55949-0395   507-467-2958
     Fax: 507-467-2640 www.scenicvalleywinery.com
Wines
     Owner: Karrie Ristau
Estimated Sales: $470,000
Number Employees: 5-9

12828 Schadel's Bakery
212 N Bullard Street
Silver City, NM 88061-5308   505-538-3031
Bakery
     President/CEO: Dexter Seay
Estimated Sales: $500,000 appx.
Number Employees: 5-9

12829 Schaefer Packing
P.O.Box 589
Mundelein, IL 60060-0589   847-949-2820
                    Fax: 847-949-0045
Wholesaler/distributor and packer of meats/provisions
     President: Craig Schaefer
     Vice President: Heidi Schuster
     Sales Manager: Kristin Dehlkek
Estimated Sales: $ 10 - 20 Million
Number Employees: 20-49
Brands:
     Blitz Power Mints

12830 Schafer Fisheries
21985 Waller Rd
Fulton, IL 61252-9780   815-589-3368
          Fax: 815-589-3369 www.schaferfish.com
Seafood
     Manager: Margaret Hattan
Estimated Sales: $ 3 - 5 Million
Number Employees: 10-19

12831 Schafley Tap Room
2100 Locust St
St Louis, MO 63103-1616   314-241-2337
          Fax: 314-241-8101 gimmes@schlafly.com
                    www.schlafly.com
Processor of beer, ale, lager, stout and seasonal beers
     President: Tom Schlafly
     Marketing Director: Mitch Turner
     VP: Dan Kopman
     CFO: D J Jean
Estimated Sales: $ 20-50 Million
Number Employees: 50-99

Type of Packaging: Consumer, Food Service
Brands:
     Schlafly

12832 Schaller & Weber
2235 46th St
Long Island City, NY 11105-1305   718-721-5480
          Fax: 718-956-9157   800-847-4115
               info@schallerweber.com
               www.schallerweber.com
Processor of meat including ham and German-style sausage, poultry, cold cuts, cooked and smoked products, salami and cervelat and seafood
     President: Ralph Schaller
Estimated Sales: $12800000
Number Employees: 50-99
Type of Packaging: Consumer

12833 Schaller's Bakery Inc
826 Highland Ave
Greensburg, PA 15601-4316   724-837-3660
          Fax: 724-837-6764 800-241-1777
Manufacturer of baked goods
     President: Warren Schaller
Estimated Sales: $2 Million
Number Employees: 20-49
Sq. footage: 21000
Type of Packaging: Consumer, Food Service, Private Label, Bulk

12834 Schaller's Packers
430 State Route 8
Cassville, NY 13318   315-822-3924
                    Fax: 315-822-3924
Processor of ham, bacon, kielbasa, jerky, salami, sausage, frankfurters, pepperoni, bologna, bratwurst, liverwurst, bockwurst, weisswurst, etc
     Owner: Ken Barrows
     VP: Betty Schaller
Estimated Sales: $ 5 - 10 Million
Number Employees: 10-19
Sq. footage: 7000
Type of Packaging: Consumer, Food Service, Private Label, Bulk

12835 Schapiro's Kosher Winery
400 E 57th St
New York, NY 10022-3019   212-755-5066
          Fax: 212-755-3210 www.schapiro-wine.com
Processor of kosher wines
     Manager: Ramon Sanchez
Estimated Sales: $300,000-500,000
Number Employees: 1-4
Type of Packaging: Consumer, Food Service

12836 Scharffen Berger Choclate Maker
914 Heinz Ave
Berkeley, CA 94710   510-981-4050
          Fax: 510-981-4051 www.scharffenberger.com
dark chocolate
     CEO: John Scharffenberger
     CFO/COO: Jim Harris
     Marketing: Norm Shea

12837 Scharffen Berger Chocolate Maker
914 Heinz Ave
Berkeley, CA 94710-2717   510-981-8495
          Fax: 510-981-4051 800-930-4528
               pr1@scharffenberger.com
               www.scharffenberger.com
Semi-sweet chocolates, bittersweet chocolates, unsweetened chocolates, cocoa powder, chocolate bars
     Founder: Dr Robert Steinberg
     Founder: John Scharffenberger
Estimated Sales: Below $ 5 Million
Number Employees: 10-19
Brands:
     Cocoa Powder
     Home Chef Bars
     Mocha Bars
     Nibby Bars
     Scharffen Berger

12838 Schat's Dutch Bakeries
763 N Main St
Bishop, CA 93514-2427   760-873-7156
                    Fax: 760-872-4932
               schatsbakery@mindspring.com
               www.erickschatsbakery.com
Baked goods
     Owner: Erick Schat
     CFO: Mirika Marijke

Estimated Sales: Below $ 5 Million
Number Employees: 50-99
Brands:
     Erick Schat

12839 Schenk Packing Company
1321 S 6th St
Mt Vernon, WA 98273-4919   360-336-2128
                    Fax: 360-336-3092
Processor and exporter of meat products; custom slaughtering available.
     Manager: Steve Lenz
Estimated Sales: $ 50 - 100 Million
Number Employees: 20-49
Type of Packaging: Consumer, Food Service

12840 Schenkel's All Star Dairy
P.O.Box 642
Huntington, IN 46750-0642   260-356-4225
                    Fax: 260-359-5045
Processor of dairy products
     Manager: Larry Brown
Estimated Sales: $ 50 - 100 Million
Number Employees: 100-249
Parent Co: Suiza Dairy Group
Type of Packaging: Consumer
Other Locations:
     Schenkel's Dairy
     Fort Wayne IN
Brands:
     Pure Sealed

12841 Schepps Dairy
P.O.Box 279000
Dallas, TX 75227-9600   214-824-8163
          Fax: 214-824-1526 800-428-6455
     schdfwjobs@suizafoods.com   www.schepps.com
Processor of juice, milk, cheese and sour cream; wholesaler/distributor of cottage cheese and butter
     Chairman: Pat Ford
     President/CEO: Pete Schenkle
     CFO: Eddie Tollison
     VP: Pat Boyle
     Quality Control: Pat Moore
Estimated Sales: $ 50-100 Million
Number Employees: 1,000-4,999
Sq. footage: 60000
Parent Co: Suiza Dairy Group
Type of Packaging: Consumer, Food Service, Private Label, Bulk
Other Locations:
     Schepps Dairy
     Harlingen TX
Brands:
     Schepps Dairy

12842 Schiavone's Casa Mia
1907 Tytus Avenue
Middletown, OH 45042-2367   513-422-8650
          Fax: 513-422-8602 http://www.schiavones.com
Sauces
     President: Michael Schiavone
Estimated Sales: $500,000-$1 Million
Number Employees: 20-49

12843 Schiff Food Products
7401 W Side Ave
North Bergen, NJ 07047-6430   201-861-2503
          Fax: 201-861-2503 schifffood@aol.com
Manufacturer, importer and exporter of spices, seeds, herbs and dehydrated vegetables
     President: David Deutscher
Estimated Sales: $17 Million
Number Employees: 20-49
Sq. footage: 78000
Type of Packaging: Consumer, Private Label
Brands:
     SCHIFF FOOD

12844 (HQ)Schiff Nutrition International
2002 S 5070 W
Salt Lake City, UT 84104-4726   801-975-5000
          Fax: 801-972-2223 www.schiffnutrition.com
Manufacturer and distributor of vitamins, nutritional supplements and sports nutrition products
     President/CEO: Bruce Wood
     EVP/CFO: Joesph Baty
     EVP Operations: Tom Elitharp
Estimated Sales: I
Number Employees: 250-499
Sq. footage: 418000
Type of Packaging: Consumer, Private Label

Other Locations:
 Weider Nutrition Internation
 Salt Lake City UT
Brands:
 FI-BAR
 SCHIFF
 TIGER'S MILK

12845 Schiltz Foods
7 W Oak St
Sisseton, SD 57262-1440   605-698-7651
          Fax: 605-698-7112 877-872-4458
          jschiltz@schiltzfoods.com
          www.schiltzfoods.com
Processor and exporter of dressed geese and goose products
 President: Richard Schiltz
 VP/Director of Sales: James Schiltz
Estimated Sales: $2,100,000
Number Employees: 100-249
Number of Brands: 4
Number of Products: 20
Sq. footage: 34000
Type of Packaging: Consumer, Food Service, Private Label, Bulk
Brands:
 All American Holiday Goose
 Whetstone Valley

12846 Schirf Brewing Company
P.O.Box 459
Park City, UT 84060-0459   435-649-0900
          Fax: 435-649-4999 www.wasatchbeers.com
Processor of beer
 President: Greg Schirf
Estimated Sales: $ 20 - 50 Million
Number Employees: 50-99
Brands:
 Wasatch

12847 Schisa Brothers
4886 Edgeworth Dr
Manlius, NY 13104-2107   315-463-0213
          Fax: 315-463-0248 Info@schisabrothers.com
          www.schisabrothers.com
Baked goods
 President: Bruce Dew
 CFO: Bryan Touchstone
 Director Sales: Ched Cummings
Estimated Sales: $ 10-20 Million
Number Employees: 20-49
Brands:
 All Kitchen
 Great Lakes
 Hereford Beef
 Hormel
 Tyson

12848 Schleswig Specialty Meats
P.O.Box 399
Schleswig, IA 51461-399   712-676-3324
          Fax: 712-676-3936 ssmeats@iowatelecom.net
Manufacturer and packer of pork
 President: Richard Beatty
 Plant Manager: Phil Smith
Estimated Sales: $5-10 Million
Number Employees: 25
Sq. footage: 20000
Type of Packaging: Private Label

12849 Schloss & Kahn
P.O.Box 117
Montgomery, AL 36101-0117   334-288-3111
          Fax: 334-286-5295 www.usfoodservice.com
 President: Rick Combs

12850 Schloss Doepken Winery
9177 Old Route 20
Ripley, NY 14775-9510   716-326-3636
          shdwines@cecomet-net.com
Wines
 President: John Watso
Estimated Sales: $500,000-$1 Million
Number Employees: 1-4
Brands:
 Schloss Doepken

12851 Schlotterbeck & Foss Company
P.O.Box 8609
Portland, ME 04104-8609   207-772-4666
          Fax: 207-774-3449 800-777-4666
          info@schlotterbeck-foss.com
          www.schlotterbeck-foss.com

Processor of salad dressings, chutneys/relishes, jams, jellies and fruit spreads, fish sauces, stir fry oils, glazes, mustards, table syrups, salsas, barbecue sauces, dry blend mixes, caosting and batters, ice cream toppings, flavorsand extracts, dairy drink bases, toppings and fruit sauces.
 President: Peter Foss
 CEO: Richard Foss
 VP Finance: Ray Farnham
 CEO: Clif Foss
 Marketing Manager: Charles Foss
 Sales Director: Arthur Kyncos
 Plant Manager: Richard Raymond
 Purchasing Manager: Annmarie Bruns
Estimated Sales: $5200000
Number Employees: 20-49
Sq. footage: 30000
Type of Packaging: Consumer, Food Service, Private Label, Bulk
Brands:
 Foss
 Mos-Ness

12852 Schmidt Baking Company
7801 Fitch Ln
Baltimore, MD 21236-3998   410-668-8200
          Fax: 410-882-2051 800-456-2253
          comments@schmidtbaking.com
          www.schmidtbaking.com
Processor of baked goods including white and grain breads.
 President: John Paterakis
 VP: Tom Beardsley
 Marketing Director: Steven Favazza
 Sales Manager: Thomas Lewis
Estimated Sales: $76700000
Number Employees: 500-999
Type of Packaging: Consumer
Brands:
 Blue Ribbon
 Old Tyme
 Sunbeam

12853 Schmidt Baking Company
511 Cumberland Valley Place
Martinsburg, WV 25401-2666   304-262-0867
          Fax: 304-263-0963 800-456-2253
          bbarnes@schmidtbaking.com
          www.schmidtbaking.com
Processor of bread and rolls
 President/CEO: Pete Smith
 Branch Manager: Bill Cave
 Plant Manager: Dennis Schwartz
Estimated Sales: $ 1 - 3 Million
Number Employees: 20-49
Parent Co: Schmidt Baking Company
Brands:
 Schmidt's Blue Ribbon White Bread
 Schmidt's Butter Bread
 Schmidt's Italian Bread
 Schmidt's Potato Bread
 Sunbeam Bread

12854 Schmidt Brothers
2425 S Fulton Lucas Rd
Swanton, OH 43558-9658   419-826-3671
          Fax: 419-826-8696
          lawrence@schmidtbrosinc.com
          www.schmidtbrosinc.com
Grower of produce including pumpkins
 President: Lawrence Schmidt
 VP: Robert Schmidt
Estimated Sales: $3500000
Number Employees: 50-99
Sq. footage: 375000
Type of Packaging: Bulk

12855 Schneider Cheese
N4085 County Road M
Waldo, WI 53093-1513   920-467-3351
          Fax: 920-467-6184
Cheese
 President: John Schneider
 CFO: Thomas Paul
 Quality Control: Jane Gau
Estimated Sales: $ 10-20 Million
Number Employees: 130

12856 (HQ)Schneider Foods
PO Box 130
Kitchener, ON N2G 3X8
Canada   519-741-5000
          Fax: 519-749-7400

Processor and exporter of frozen and refrigerated frankfurters, meat pies, sausage, ham, bacon, deli meats and poultry; fat and calorie reduced products available
 President: Douglas Dodds
 President (Cust. Foods): Paul Lang
 VP Business: John Howard
 Quality Control: Judy Tetker
 R & D: Tim Gorgon
Number Employees: 1800
Sq. footage: 730000
Type of Packaging: Consumer, Food Service, Private Label, Bulk
Other Locations:
 Schneider Corp.
 Ayr ON
Brands:
 Deli-Best
 Lifestyle
 Lunchmate
 Mini-Sizzlers
 Olde-Fashioned
 Red Hots
 Schneider's

12857 Schneider Foods
180 Northumberland Street
Ayr, ON N0B 1E0
Canada   519-632-7416
          Fax: 519-632-8850 www.schneiderfoods.ca
Processor of frozen, breaded and fully cooked fried chicken
 Plant Manager: Lou Cappa
Number Employees: 150
Parent Co: J.M. Schneider
Type of Packaging: Food Service

12858 Schneider Foods
Perth County Road 139
Saint Marys, ON N4X 1C4
Canada   519-229-8900
          Fax: 519-229-8953 800-567-1890
          cwehniai@schneiderfoods.ca www.schneiders.ca
Processor of frozen and fresh poultry
 Founder: John Metz Schneider
 Plant Manager: Cheryl Firby
Number Employees: 250-499
Parent Co: J.M. Schneider
Type of Packaging: Consumer, Food Service, Private Label

12859 Schneider Foods
5523 176th Street
Surrey, BC V3S 4C2
Canada   604-576-1191
          Fax: 604-576-6762
Processor of fresh sausage
 President: Doug Dodds
 Sales/Marketing Executive: Mike McRae
 General Manager: Jeff Parker
 Purchasing Agent: Dean Rybchuk
Number Employees: 250-499
Parent Co: J.M. Schneider
Type of Packaging: Consumer, Food Service

12860 Schneider Foods
362 Laird Road
Guelph, ON N1G 3X7
Canada   519-837-4848
          Fax: 519-837-2533
Processor of packaged and frozen luncheon meats including beef, pork and chicken
 Plant Manager: Brian Keller
 Purchasing Agent: Don Drury
Number Employees: 50-99
Parent Co: J.M. Schneider
Type of Packaging: Consumer, Food Service, Private Label

12861 Schneider Foods
550 Kipling Avenue S
Etobicoke, ON M8Z 5E9
Canada   416-252-5790
          Fax: 416-252-6215 cwehniai@schneiderfoods.ca
          www.schneiders.ca
Processor of fresh and frozen beef
 President/General Manager: Ron Flaury
 CEO: Rick Young
 Marketing Director: Doug Gingrich
 Purchasing Agent: Carmela Cieri
Number Employees: 100-249
Parent Co: J.M. Schneider
Type of Packaging: Consumer, Food Service

Brands:
Schneider Foods

12862 Schneider Foods
550 Kipling Avenue S
Etobicoke, ON M8Z 5E9
Canada   905-542-6800
Fax: 905-542-0911   800-268-0634
www.schneider.ca
Processor of fresh and frozen beef and pork
CEO: Doug Dodds
President: Doug Dodds
Sales Manager: George Muller
Number Employees: 20-49
Parent Co: J.M. Schneider
Type of Packaging: Consumer, Food Service
Brands:
Schneider

12863 Schneider Valley Farms Dairy
1860 E 3rd St
Williamsport, PA 17701-3923   570-326-2021
Fax: 570-326-2736
Processor of milk including whole, low-fat, flavored
and skim, buttermilk, ice cream products, sherbet,
ice cream mixes, sour cream, dips, fruit juices/drinks
and iced teas; wholesaler/distributor of whipped top-
ping, cottage cheeseyogurt, butter, etc
President: William Schneider
Sales/Marketing Director: Edward Schneider Jr
VP Sales: Edward Schneider Sr
Estimated Sales: H
Number Employees: 100-249
Parent Co: Schneider's Dairy
Type of Packaging: Food Service

12864 Schneider's Dairy Holdings Inc
726 Frank St
Pittsburgh, PA 15227-1299   412-881-3525
Fax: 412-881-7722 www.schneidersdairy.com
Processor of dairy products including milk, cream,
cheese, ice cream mixes, whipped topping, eggs,
butter, etc.; also, iced tea, fruit drinks, juices and
water
President: William Schneider
Manager: Tom Arnold
Vice President: Edward Schneider
Operations Director: William Schneider
Estimated Sales: $82000000
Number Employees: 250-499

**12865 Schobert's Cottage Cheese
Corporation**
586 Seiberling Street
Akron, OH 44306-3237   216-733-6876
Cottage cheese
President: Mike Barr
Estimated Sales: $ 2.5-5 Million
Number Employees: 5

12866 Schoep's Ice Cream Company
P.O.Box 3249
Madison, WI 53704-0249   608-249-6411
Fax: 608-249-7900   800-236-0032
www.schoepsicecream.com
Manufacturer of ice cream, frozen yogurt, light ice
cream, frozen custard, sherbert and novelties.
President: Paul Thomsen
Data Processing: Roger Bunders
Sales: Paul Hagen
Operations: Dale Christensen
Purchsing: Bruce Moltumyr
Estimated Sales: $ 20 - 50 Million
Number Employees: 100-249
Number of Brands: 12
Number of Products: 332
Sq. footage: 62500
Type of Packaging: Consumer, Food Service, Pri-
vate Label, Bulk
Brands:
Schoep's

12867 Schokinag North America
5301 Office Park Dr # 200
Bakersfield, CA 93309-0652   661-322-4020
Fax: 661-322-1156   info@schokinagna.com
www.schokinagna.com
Cocoa powder and chocolate from Ivory Coast co-
coa beans
Manager: Cheri Butler
Marketing Director: Lisa Blizzard
Estimated Sales: $ 1-2.5 Million
Number Employees: 1-4
Sq. footage: 12000

Type of Packaging: Consumer, Food Service, Bulk
Brands:
Schokinag North America

12868 Schoppaul Hill Winery at Ivanhoe
301 S Locust Street
Denton, TX 76201-6055   940-380-9463
Fax: 940-387-5471
Wines
President: John Anderson
CFO: Gary Anderson
Estimated Sales: $ 5-9.9 Million
Number Employees: 3

12869 Schott's Bakery
P.O.Box 7568
Houston, TX 77270-7568   713-869-5701
Fax: 713-869-6530 mturner@flowersfoods.com
www.flowersfoods.com
Processor of breads, buns and rolls
President: Andy Brown
Quality Control: Kim Kleinituizen
VP: Mike Lawson
Operations Manager: Wayne Bristow
Estimated Sales: $43 Million
Number Employees: 100-249
Parent Co: Flowers Baking Company
Type of Packaging: Consumer

12870 (HQ)Schramsberg Vineyards
1400 Schramsberg Rd
Calistoga, CA 94515-9624   707-942-6668
Fax: 707-942-4336   800-877-3623
info1@schramsberg.com   www.schramsberg.com
Processor of sparkling wine
President: Jamie Davies
General Manager/Winemaker: Hugh Davies
Marketing: Laurent Sarazin
Estimated Sales: $3000000
Number Employees: 20-49
Number of Brands: 2
Number of Products: 7
Other Locations:
Schramsberg Vineyards
Alijo
Brands:
J. SCHRAM
MIRABELLE
SCHRAMSBERG

12871 Schreiber FoodsPlant
208 Dykeman Road
Shippensburg, PA 17257-8700   717-530-5000
www.sficorp.com
Processor of Raskas cream cheese for foodservice
industry
Quality Control Director: Barb Wisor
Branch Manager: Dave Pilgert
Number Employees: 195
Parent Co: Schreiber Foods
Type of Packaging: Food Service, Bulk
Brands:
RASKAS

**12872 Schreiber FoodsPlant/Distribution
Center**
2321 Jefferson St
Wisconsin Rapids, WI 54495-1918   715-422-7500
Fax: 715-422-7539
schreiberweb@schreiberfoods.com
www.schreiberfoods.com
Processor of cheese
President & CEO: Larry Ferguson
Co-Founder: L D Schreiber
Co-Founder: Merlin Bush
Co-Founder: Daniel Nusbaum
Manager: Nicholas Destain
Number Employees: 200
Parent Co: Schreiber Foods
Type of Packaging: Consumer, Food Service

12873 Schreiber FoodsPlant
885 N 600 W
Logan, UT 84321-3195   435-787-8490
Fax: 435-752-5257
schreiberweb@schreiberfoods.com
www.schreiber.com

Processor of cheese
Chairman: John Meng
President/CEO: Larry Ferguson
Co-Founder: L D Schreiber
Co-Founder: Merlin Bush
Co-Founder: Daniel Nusbaum
SVP Foodservice Sales: Mike Haddad
Branch Manager: Mike Moehlmann
Number Employees: 300
Parent Co: Schreiber Foods
Type of Packaging: Consumer, Food Service

12874 Schreiber FoodsPlant
116 E Oak Street
Clinton, MO 64735-1553   660-885-6133
schreiberweb@schreiberfoods.com
www.sficorp.com
Processor of cheese
Manager: Galen Carter
Purchasing Director: Linda Plumlee
Number Employees: 200
Parent Co: Schreiber Foods
Type of Packaging: Consumer, Food Service

12875 Schreiber FoodsPlant
502 N Madison Street
Green Bay, WI 54301-5125   920-455-6741
800-344-0333
schreiberweb@schreiberfoods.com
www.sficorp.com
Processor of cheese
Branch Manager: Wayne Whiting
Number Employees: 27
Parent Co: Schreiber Foods
Type of Packaging: Consumer, Food Service
Brands:
American Heritage
Clearfield Deli
Cooper

12876 Schreiber FoodsPlant
10 Dairy Street
Monett, MO 65708-2502   417-235-6061
Fax: 417-235-4188
schreiberweb@schreiberfoods.com
www.sficorp.com
Processor of cheese
Number Employees: 175
Parent Co: Schreiber Foods
Type of Packaging: Consumer, Food Service

12877 Schreiber FoodsPlant
2255 White Sulphur Rd
Gainesville, GA 30501-3903   770-534-2239
Fax: 770-538-0590
schreiberweb@schreiberfoods.com
Manufacturer of shredded, chuck and sliced cheeses,
pimento spread.
Plant Superintendent: Mike Welborn
Estimated Sales: $20-50 Million
Number Employees: 200
Sq. footage: 146000
Brands:
DEEP SOUTH

12878 (HQ)Schreiber Foods Inc
425 Pine Street
Green Bay, WI 54301   920-437-7601
Fax: 920-437-1617   800-344-0333
schreiberweb@schreiberfoods.com
www.schreiberfoods.com
Natural cheese, proces cheese, cream cheese, spe-
cialty cheese, substitute/imitation cheese, string
cheese, yogurt and butter blends
President/CEO: Mike Haddad
VP Finance/CFO: Matt Mueller
VP Foodservice Sales: John O'Connor
Estimated Sales: $3+ Billion
Number Employees: 5,500
Type of Packaging: Consumer, Food Service, Pri-
vate Label, Bulk
Other Locations:
Tempe AZ
Gainesville GA
Carthage MO
Clinton MO
Monett MO
Mt Vernon MO
Ravenna NE
Shippensburg PA
Nashville TN
Stephenville TX
Logan UT

Smithfield UT
Green Bay WI
Brands:
AMERICAN HERITAGE
CLEARFIELD
COOPER
LAFERIA
LOV-IT
MENU
RASKAS
READY-CUT
SCHOOL CHIOCE
SCHREIBER

12879 Schreier Malting Companypecialty Malt Division
P.O.Box 59
Sheboygan, WI 53082-0059   920-458-6126
Fax: 920-458-9034   800-669-6258
specialtymalts@specialtymalts.com
www.schreiermalt.com
Processor and exporter of brewers' malt
Estimated Sales:$ 10 - 20 Million
Number Employees: 10-19
Type of Packaging: Bulk

12880 Schug Carneros Estate Winery
602 Bonneau Rd
Sonoma, CA 95476-9749   707-939-9365
Fax: 707-939-9364   800-966-9365
info@schugwinery.com   www.schugwinery.com
Wines
Founder: Walter Schug
Owner: Gertrud Schug
Sales/Marketing Director: Alex Schug
Winery Chef: Kristine Schug
Winemaker: Michael Cox
Estimated Sales:$ 5 -10 Million
Number Employees: 5-9
Brands:
Schug

12881 Schuil Coffee Company
3679 29th St SE
Kentwood, MI 49512-1811   616-956-1881
Fax: 616-956-7928   sales@schuilcoffee.com
www.schuilcoffee.com
Coffee
President/CEO: Greta Schuil
Estimated Sales:$500,000-$1 Million
Number Employees: 20-49
Type of Packaging: Private Label
Brands:
Coppets
IBC
Schuil Coffee

12882 Schultz Provisions Company
14 Loon Hill Road
Dracut, MA 01826-4015   800-272-0030
Fax: 207-771-2460   800-932-7477
Processor of meat products
General Manager: Donald Schultz
Brands:
Schultz

12883 (HQ)Schulze & Burch BiscuitCompany
1133 W 35th St
Chicago, IL 60609-1485   773-927-6622
Fax: 773-376-4528 www.toastem.com
Manufacturer of toaster pastries, cereal bars, crackers and fruit snacks
Chairman/CEO: Patrick Boyle
President: Kevin Boyle
VP Sales/Marketing: Bill Stuart
Estimated Sales:$75 Million
Number Employees: 500-999
Sq. footage: 500000
Type of Packaging: Consumer, Food Service, Private Label, Bulk
Brands:
POP UPS
SNACKIN FRUITS
TOAST'EM

12884 (HQ)Schumacher Wholesale Meats
1114 Zane Ave N
Golden Valley, MN 55422-4679   763-546-3291
Fax: 763-546-0053   800-432-7020
ms@schumeats.com   www.schumeats.com

Processor and wholesaler/distributor of meat
President: John F Schumacher
Sales/Marketing Manager: Matt Schumacher
Operations Manager: Bob Timm
Purchasing: Bob Timm
Estimated Sales:$6700000
Number Employees: 20-49
Type of Packaging: Consumer, Food Service, Private Label, Bulk
Brands:
Crown
Great Meats
Valley

12885 Schuster Marketing Corporation
6251 W Forest Home Ave
Milwaukee, WI 53220-1916   414-543-2999
Fax: 414-543-5588   888-254-8948
www.blitzpowermints.com
Ann innovative tablet pressing manufacturer that also has the ability to manufacture tablet pressed chewing gum with or without active ingredients such as nutraceuticals.
President: Stephen P Schuster
VP Sales: Heidi Schuster
Estimated Sales:$ 5 - 10 Million
Number Employees: 5-9
Brands:
BLITZ POWER MINTS

12886 Schwab & Company
1111 Linwood Blvd
Oklahoma City, OK 73106-7039   405-235-2376
Fax: 405-236-4694   800-888-8668
ron@schwabmeat.com   www.schwabmeat.com
Processor of fresh and frozen beef and pork
President: W Schwab
Marketing Director: Ron Walton
CFO: Gail Anderson
Estimated Sales:$ 10-20 Million
Number Employees: 20-49
Type of Packaging: Consumer, Food Service, Private Label, Bulk
Brands:
Schwab

12887 (HQ)Schwan's Consumer Brands North America
8500 Normandale Lake Blvd
Bloomington, MN 55437-3813   952-832-4300
www.mrssmiths.com
Classic pies, deep dish pie shells, deep dish pies and classic cobblers
President: J Ronald Frump
CEO: Calvin Brink
VP: William Strenglis
VP Product Development: Karen Gunderson
VP Marketing/Sales: Mark Courtney
Operations: Mike Bramlett
Purchasing: Brian Palmer
Estimated Sales:$600 Million
Number Employees: 120
Number of Brands: 200
Sq. footage: 5
Parent Co: Swan Food Company
Type of Packaging: Consumer, Food Service, Private Label, Bulk
Other Locations:
Atlanta GA
Crossville TN
Montgomery AL
Pembroke NC
Brands:
Mrs. Freshley's
Mrs. Smith's
Stilwell Oregon Farms

12888 Schwan's Sales Enterprises
115 W College Dr
Marshall, MN 56258-3810   507-532-3274
Fax: 507-537-8226   800-533-5290
www.schwans.com
Main dishes, sandwiches, sauces, appetizers, snacks, pizzas, fruits, vegetables, breads, ice cream, desserts, treats, breakfast, beverages
President/CEO: Lenny M Pippin
Executive VP/Finance/CFO: Tracy Burr
Executive VP: John M Beadle
Estimated Sales:$ 12 Million
Number Employees: 10,000+
Type of Packaging: Consumer, Food Service
Brands:
ARCTIC EXPRESS
ASIAN SENSATIONS

CHICAGO TOWN
COYOTE GRILL
EDWARDS
FRESCHETTA
GLACIER MOUNTAIN CREAMERY
HEIDI'S GOURMET DESSERTS
IMPROMPTU GOURMET
LARRY'S
MINH
MRS SMITH'S
PROOF PERFECT
RED BARON
SABATASSO'S
SCHWAN'S
TONY'S
WESTERN COUNTRY PIES
ZINGS

12889 Schwans Bakeries
P.O.Box 432
Stilwell, OK 74960-0432   918-696-8325
Fax: 918-696-5691
Processor of breaded and battered vegetables, ready-to-bake cobblers, pies and pie shells
Plant Manager: Jason Blake
Estimated Sales:$100+ Million
Number Employees: 500-999
Sq. footage: 630000
Type of Packaging: Consumer, Food Service

12890 (HQ)Schwans Food Company
6875 Jimmy Carter Blvd
Norcross, GA 30071-1237   770-449-4900
Fax: 478-482-3450   800-241-0559
franklin@edwardsbaking.com
www.schwansbakeryfs.com
Processor of frozen ready-to-serve and pre-baked fruit pies, cold set pies, layer cakes, cheesecakes, etc
President: Jerry Hanna
CFO: Tom Mannion
Research & Development: George Krubert
Quality Control: Sara Cook
Marketing Director: Polly Johnson
Sales Director: Henry Gonzalez
Sales: Jeff Crowley
Operations Manager: Joe Leonardo
VP Purchasing: Eric Mathis
Number Employees: 100-249
Sq. footage: 500000
Type of Packaging: Consumer, Food Service, Private Label
Other Locations:
Edwards Fine Foods
Tucker GA
Heidi Gourmet
Atlanta GA
Western Country Pie
Salt Lake City UT
Brands:
Edwards Family Recipe
Edwards Gourmet
Gourmet Concepts
Mother Butler
Oven Art
Peachtree
Western Country

12891 Schwans Frozen Foods
115 W College Dr
Marshall, MN 56258   507-532-3274
Fax: 507-537-8226   800-533-5290
www.schwans.com
Frozen prepared meal; fruits and vegetables; snacks; ice cream and desserts; also beverages
President/CEO/COO/Director: Gregory Flack
EVP Finance/CFO: James Dollive
Executive VP: John M Beadle
Sales: Steve Deaton
Estimated Sales:$3.5 Billion
Number Employees: 18,000
Type of Packaging: Consumer, Food Service, Private Label, Bulk
Brands:
Cisco

12892 Schwartz Meat Company
P.O.Box 1000
Sophia, WV 25921-1000   304-683-4595
Fax: 304-683-3257 www.threadsaver.com
Manufacturer of frozen pizza toppings and meat crumbles
Owner: Ray Lambert
Number Employees: 5-9
Type of Packaging: Food Service, Private Label, Bulk

12893 Schwartz Pickle Company
4401 W 44th Pl
Chicago, IL 60632-4305   773-927-7700
        Fax: 773-927-3750 800-621-4273
                www.bayvalleyfoods.com
Processor of pickles including sweet and kosher dill;
also, sauerkraut
    President: Gary Newman
    Executive VP: Gary Bergsma
    Plant Manager: Michael Timm
Estimated Sales: $ 20 - 50 Million
Number Employees: 100-249
Type of Packaging: Consumer, Food Service, Private Label, Bulk

12894 Schwebel Baking Company
P.O. Box 6018
Youngstown, OH 44501-6018   330-783-2860
        Fax: 330-782-1774 www.schwebels.com
Manufacturer of Bagels, variety, hearth baked and
enriched breads, buns, rolls, pita bread, english muffins and tortillas for the consumer food industry.
    President: Joseph M Schwebel
    EVP: Paul Schwebel
    VP Operations/Manufacturing: Michael Elenz
    VP Operations: Tom Shannon
Estimated Sales: $120 Million
Number Employees: 250-499
Type of Packaging: Consumer

12895 Schwebel Baking Company
P.O. Box 6018
Youngstown, OH 44501-6018   330-783-2860
        Fax: 330-782-1774 800-860-2867
todd-bruinsma@pnwb.com   www.schwebels.com
Processor of bread and rolls
    President: Joseph Schwebel
    Plant Manager: Jim Ervin
Estimated Sales: $120 Million
Number Employees: 250-499
Parent Co: Schwebel Baking Company
Type of Packaging: Consumer, Food Service, Private Label

12896 Schweigert Foods
702 E 13th St
Albert Lea, MN 56007-3250   507-377-2526
        Fax: 507-377-6692 www.wbfoods.com
Manufacturer of sausage, chicken, turkey, luncheon
meats, wieners, ham, pork
    Manager: Terry Conroy
    VP: Dennis Porter
    Human Resources: Ann Christensen
    General Manager: Jean Pestorious
    Plant Manager: Charles Hanson
Estimated Sales: $100 Million
Number Employees: 250-499
Parent Co: Willow Brook
Type of Packaging: Consumer, Food Service

12897 Scialo Brothers
257 Atwells Ave
Providence, RI 02903-1521   401-421-0986
        Fax: 401-274-6117 877-421-0986
info@scialosbakery.com   www.scialobakery.com
Italian bread, bakery products, pastries, cakes, pies,
cookies and wedding cakes
    Co-Owner: Lois Ellis
    Co-Owner: Carol Gaeta
Estimated Sales: $500,000-$1 Million
Number Employees: 10-19

12898 Sconza Candy Company
1 Sconza Candy Ln
Oakdale, CA 95361-7899   209-845-1890
        Fax: 510-638-5792 877-568-8137
        customerservice@sconzacandy.com
                www.sconzacandy.com
Processor and exporter of candy including brittles,
panned, butterscotch, hard, filled, mints, butter toffee nuts and seasonal; available for fund raising;
also, bagged and boxed
    President: James Sconza
Estimated Sales: $6 Million
Number Employees: 50-99
Sq. footage: 50000
Type of Packaging: Consumer, Food Service, Private Label, Bulk
Brands:
    Bean Heads
    Bruiser
    Fruit Breaker
    Jordanettes
    Meteorites
    Pip Squeaks
    Sconza
    Screamer
    Wizbanger
    Zoygs

12899 Scooty's Wholesome Foods
PO Box 18898
Boulder, CO 80308-1898   303-440-4025
                Fax: 970-663-6013
Gourmet and specialty foods
    President: Scott Silverman
Estimated Sales: Under $500,000
Number Employees: 1-4

12900 Scot Paris Fine Desserts
537 Greenwich Street
New York, NY 10013-1000   212-807-1802
Processor of cheesecakes, pies, tarts, cakes, etc; importer of baking ingredients including cocoa, vanilla, ginger, chocolate and IQF fruits
    Owner: Scot Paris
    Sales Director: Michael Camerman
    Sales: Mark Conway
Sq. footage: 500

12901 Scotian Gold Cooperative
2900 Lovett Road
Coldbrook, NS B4R 1A6
Canada   902-679-2191
    Fax: 902-679-4540 scotian@scotiangold.com
                www.scotiangold.com
Processor and packer of apples and pears; also, apple cider
    President: David Cudmore
    Vice President: David Parrish
Number Employees: 70
Type of Packaging: Consumer, Private Label
Brands:
    Scotian Gold

12902 Scotsburn Dairy Group
PO Box 768
Truro, NS B2N 5E8
Canada   902-895-4412
                Fax: 902-893-1136
Processor of dairy products including butter, milk,
ice cream and cottage cheese; wholesaler/distributor
of frozen foods, strawberries, vegetables, meat,
chicken, etc.; serving the food service market
    CEO/President: Jim McConnell
Parent Co: Scotsburn Cooperative Services
Type of Packaging: Consumer, Food Service, Private Label

12903 Scott Adams Foods
288 Newton Sparta Rd
Newton, NJ 07860-2749   973-300-2091
                www.pdifoods.com
Vegan meat alternative and vegetarian wraps
    President: Jack Parker
    CEO: Scott Adams
Estimated Sales: $ 1 - 3 Million
Number Employees: 1-4
Type of Packaging: Private Label
Brands:
    DILBERITO
    PROTEIN CHEF

12904 Scott Farms
7965a Simpson Rd
Lucama, NC 27851-9371   919-284-4014
        Fax: 919-284-4872 877-284-4030
scottfarms@cocentral.com www.scottfarms.com
Grower and shipper of sweet potatoes
    Owner: Linwood Scott
Estimated Sales: Below $ 5 Million
Number Employees: 5-9
Brands:
    Sonny's Pride

12905 Scott Hams
1301 Scott Rd
Greenville, KY 42345-4683   270-338-3402
        Fax: 270-338-6643 800-318-1353
scotthams@scotthams.com www.scotthams.com
Processor and exporter of country cured and fully
cooked hams, bacon, smoked sausage, turkey, jams
and fruit butters, sorghum molasses, honey, dried apples, relish, bean soup mix, biscuits, pork cracklins
and dog biscuits
    President: Leslie Scott

Estimated Sales: Less than $500,000
Number Employees: 1-4
Brands:
    Scott's

12906 Scott's Auburn Mills
117 S Lincoln St
Auburn, KY 42206   270-542-4101
        Fax: 270-542-4103 800-962-7857
Manufacturer of white and yellow corn meal and
wheat flour
    President: Ray Clark
Estimated Sales: $2 Million
Number Employees: 20-49
Sq. footage: 20000
Type of Packaging: Consumer, Food Service, Private Label, Bulk

12907 Scott's Candy
301 Broadway Dr
Sun Prairie, WI 53590-1742   608-837-8020
        Fax: 608-837-0763 800-356-2100
Processor and exporter of boxed and tinned chocolates
    CEO: Gary Ricco
    National Sales Manager: James Regan
Estimated Sales: $ 3 - 5 Million
Number Employees: 20-49
Parent Co: Wisconsin Cheeseman
Type of Packaging: Consumer, Private Label
Brands:
    Classic Choice
    Scott's

12908 Scott's Sauce Company
1205 N William St
Goldsboro, NC 27530-2163   919-734-0711
                                800-734-7282
        info@scottsbarbequesauce.com
                www.scottsbarbequesauce.com
Processor of barbecue sauces
    President: A Martel Scott Jr III
Estimated Sales: Less than $500,000
Number Employees: 5-9
Sq. footage: 7000
Parent Co: Scott's Barbecue
Type of Packaging: Consumer
Brands:
    Scott's Barbeque Sauce

12909 Scott's of Wisconsin
301 Broadway Dr
Sun Prairie, WI 53590-1742   608-837-8020
        Fax: 608-837-0763 800-698-1721
        customerservice@wisconsincheeseman.com
                www.wisconsincheeseman.com
Cheese spreads, chocolate candy
    CEO: Holly Berkenstadt
    President: Jay Singer
    CEO: Gary Ricco
    Marketing Director: Charlie Kesler
    Sales Director: Jim Regan
    Purchasing Manager: Mark Pelton
Estimated Sales: $ 1-2.5 Million
Number Employees: 20-49
Type of Packaging: Private Label
Brands:
    Grace Rush
    Nutty Pleasures
    Pecanbacks
    Scott's
    Scott's of Wisconsin
    Scottie
    Trinkets

12910 Scott-Bathgate
PO Box 765
Winnipeg, NB R3C 2G1
Canada   204-943-8525
                Fax: 204-957-5902
Processor and importer of snack foods, food colorings, mustard, peanut butter, candy and shelled and
in-shell sunflower seeds
    National Director: Vic Homyshyn
    Office/Credit Manager: D Sheridan
    Production Manager: Jens Fieting
Type of Packaging: Food Service
Brands:
    Food Club
    Nutty Club

12911 Scotty Wotty's Creamy Cheescake
216 Us Highway 206
Suite 14
Hillsborough, NJ 08844-4384   908-281-9720
                                   Fax: 908-281-9720
Cheesecake
    President: Scott Discount
    Marketing Director: Scott Discount
Brands:
    Scotty Wotty's

12912 Scray's Cheese Company
2082 Old Martin Rd
De Pere, WI 54115-8015   920-336-8359
                              Fax: 920-336-0553
Cheese
    President: Jim Scray
    Marketing Manager: Jim Scray
Estimated Sales:$500,000-$1 Million
Number Employees: 5-9
Type of Packaging: Private Label
Brands:
    Scray's Cheese

12913 Scripture Candy
PO Box 386
Adamsville, AL 35005-0386   205-250-8001
    Fax: 888-444-4775   888-317-7333
                    www.scripturecandy.com
Candy
    Owner: Brian Adkins

12914 Sculli Brothers
1114 S Front St
Philadelphia, PA 19147-5598   215-336-1223
                                   Fax: 215-336-1225
Processor of beef, veal, Italian sausage, ham and salami
    President: Robert Sculli
Estimated Sales:$ 5 - 10 Million
Number Employees: 1-4
Type of Packaging: Private Label, Bulk
Brands:
    Bari

12915 Sea Best Corporation
PO Box 753
Ipswich, MA 01938-0753   978-768-7475
                              Fax: 314-241-1377
Seafood

12916 Sea Breeze Fruit Flavors
441 Us Highway 202
441 Main Rd
Towaco, NJ 07082-1201   973-334-7777
    Fax: 973-334-2617   800-732-2733
                    info@seabreezesyrups.com
                    www.seabreezesyrups.com
Processor and exporter of syrups including chocolate, pancake and fountain; also, sundae toppings, bar mixes, juice concentrates and beverage dispensing equipment
    President: Steven Sanders
    Technical Director: Frank Maranino
Estimated Sales:$25-49.9 Million
Number Employees: 50-99
Type of Packaging: Consumer, Food Service, Private Label
Brands:
    Bosco
    Sea Breeze
    Tropic Beach

12917 Sea Dog Brewing Company
26 Front St
Bangor, ME 04401-6418   207-947-8004
    Fax: 207-947-8720   larry.k@seadogbrewing.com
                    www.seadogbrewing.com
Beer
    General Manager: Larry Killam
    Director Operations: Jim Bunting
    CFO: Kimberly Simons
    Accounts Department: Kathy Young
    General Manager: Zobeida Peters
Estimated Sales:$ 50-100 Million
Number Employees: 50-99
Type of Packaging: Consumer, Food Service
Brands:
    Sea Dog

12918 Sea Farm & Farmfresh Importing Company
PO Box 3427
Alhambra, CA 91803-0427   323-265-7075
                               Fax: 323-265-9578
Seafood products.
    CEO: Hooi Eng Ooi
    VP Operations: S Tan
Estimated Sales:$ 5 - 10 Million
Number Employees: 10-19

12919 Sea Fresh Alaska
1620 Larch Street
Kodiak, AK 99615-6207   907-486-6226
                             Fax: 907-486-6222
Seafood

12920 Sea Fresh USA
11 Portland Fish Pier
Portland, ME 04101-4620   207-773-6799
                               Fax: 207-773-7804
Seafood
    Manager: Jesse Wendell
Estimated Sales:$ 20 - 50 Million
Number Employees: 20-49

12921 Sea Garden Seafoods
100 Amason Ave
Meridian, GA 31319   912-832-4437
    Fax: 912-832-6834   andy@snowsouth.com
                    www.snowsouth.com
Manufacturer of Crab meat and shrimp products
    President/CEO: Andrew Amason
    Purchasing Agent: Carol Amason
Estimated Sales:$100 Million
Number Employees: 50-99
Parent Co: Snowsouth
Type of Packaging: Bulk

12922 Sea Gold Seafood Products
38 Blackmer St
New Bedford, MA 02744-2614   508-993-3060
    Fax: 508-993-3070   seagold01@msn.com
                    www.seagolddips.com
Processor of dips including gourmet seafood and crab dip, buttered seafood and lobster dip, seafood and jalapeno crab dip, spicy shrimp dip, seafood and shrimp scampi dip, cajun seafood and crab dip, clams casino clam dip, and seafoodnewburg dip.
    Owner: Micheal Trazzra
    Operations Manager: Wendy Harwood
*Estimated Sales:*Below $ 5 Million
Number Employees: 10-19
Number of Brands: 1
Number of Products: 9
Sq. footage: 5000
Type of Packaging: Consumer, Food Service
Brands:
    Sea Gold

12923 Sea Horse Wharf
245 W Point Rd
Phippsburg, ME 04562-5127   207-389-2312
                                 Fax: 207-389-1005
Seafood.
    Owner: Douglas Scott
Estimated Sales:$300,000-500,000
Number Employees: 1-4

12924 Sea K Fish Company
225 Sigurdson Ave
Blaine, WA 98230-4004   360-332-5121
                             Fax: 360-332-8785
Processor and exporter of seafood including halibut
    Manager: Mike Ordal
    General Manager: Sam Henley
    VP: George Costello
Estimated Sales:$ 20 - 50 Million
Number Employees: 20-49
Type of Packaging: Consumer, Food Service

12925 Sea Level Seafoods
P.O.Box 2085
Wrangell, AK 99929-2085   907-874-2401
                               Fax: 907-874-2158
Seafood
    Manager: Vern Phillips
Estimated Sales:$ 20 - 50 Million
Number Employees: 20-49

12926 Sea Lyons
9093 Springway Court
Spanish Fort, AL 36527-5522   251-626-2841
                                   Fax: 251-626-2841

Seafood.
    President: Martha Lyons
    Vice President: Wade Lyons

12927 Sea Nik Food Company
Mile 137 Sterling Highway
Ninilchik, AK 99639   907-567-3980
                           Fax: 907-567-1041
Seafood
Estimated Sales:$ 20 - 50 Million
Number Employees: 50-99

12928 Sea Pearl Seafood
14120 Shell Belt Rd
Bayou La Batre, AL 36509-2308   251-824-2129
    Fax: 251-650-1321   800-872-8804
    info@sea-pearl.com   www.sea-pearl.com
Processor of frozen and breaded shrimp and oysters
    Owner: Joseph G Ladnier
    Plant Manager: Allen Mayfield
Estimated Sales:$3300000
Number Employees: 10-19
Type of Packaging: Consumer, Food Service, Bulk
Brands:
    Neptune Delight
    Sea Pearl Seafood Co., Inc.

12929 Sea Products Company
331 Ford Street
Watsonville, CA 95076-4108   831-768-2600
Processor of frozen fish and seafood including mackerel, sardines, squid, exporter of frozen squid
    VP: A Nobusada
    Sales: Max Boland
Number Employees: 250-499
Sq. footage: 75000
Parent Co: Consolidated Factors
Type of Packaging: Consumer, Food Service, Private Label, Bulk
Brands:
    Red Rose Farm
    Sea Diamond
    Sea Jade
    Sea Pearl

12930 Sea Products Company
PO Box 836
Astoria, OR 97103-0836   503-325-5023
                              Fax: 503-325-2347
Fish and seafoods
    Manager: Judy Zell
    Plant Manager: Terry Miller
Estimated Sales:$ 20-50 Million
Number Employees: 250

12931 Sea Ridge Winery
13404 Dupont Road
Occidental, CA 95465   707-874-1707
Wines
    President: Dan Wickham
Estimated Sales:$500-1 Million appx.
Number Employees: 1-4

12932 Sea Safari
P.O.Box 369
Belhaven, NC 27810-0369   252-943-3091
    Fax: 252-943-3083   800-688-6174
    seasafari@beaufortco.com   www.seasafari.com
Processor and exporter of frozen crawfish and crab meat; also, canned blue crab meat
    Owner/President: Topper Bateman
    Director Marketing: Christine Costley
    Sales Manager: Frances Williams
Estimated Sales:$ 20 - 50 Million
Number Employees: 50-99
Sq. footage: 20000
Parent Co: Sea Safari
Type of Packaging: Consumer, Food Service
Brands:
    Acadian Gourmet
    Ecrevisse Acadienne
    Louisianas Best

12933 Sea Safari
P.O.Box 369
Belhaven, NC 27810-0369   252-943-3091
    Fax: 252-943-3083   seasafari@belhavennc.com
                    www.seasafari.com
Processor of fresh and pasteurized crab meat
    President: Topper Bateman
Estimated Sales:$ 5-10 Million
Number Employees: 50-99
Type of Packaging: Consumer, Food Service

12934 Sea Safari Limited
P.O.Box 369
Belhaven, NC 27810-0369   252-943-3091
          Fax: 252-943-3083   800-688-6174
seasafari@beaufortco.com   www.seasafari.com
Processor of frozen crabs and crab meat
President: Topper Bateman
Estimated Sales: $ 20 - 50 Million
Number Employees: 50-99

12935 Sea Snack Foods
914 E 11th St
Los Angeles, CA 90021-2091   213-622-2204
          Fax: 213-622-7845   seasnack@msn.com
Processor and exporter of cooked IQF shrimp and
seafood cocktails
          President: Fred Ockrim
          Executive VP: Jeff Kahn
          Midwest Sales Manager: Peter Peterson
          Plant Manager: Alfred Dolor
Estimated Sales: $7000000
Number Employees: 50-99
Type of Packaging: Consumer, Food Service
Brands:
          O.K. Brand
          Restaurant Row
          Sea Snack
          Twin Harbors

12936 Sea Stars Goat Cheese
1122 Soquel Ave
Santa Cruz, CA 95062-2106   831-423-7200
          Fax: 831-454-0838
Cheese
          Owner: Nancy Gassney
Estimated Sales: $ 2.5-5 Million
Number Employees: 10-19
Type of Packaging: Private Label

12937 Sea View Fillet Company
15 Antonio Costa Ave
New Bedford, MA 02740-7347   508-984-1406
          Fax: 508-984-1411
Seafood
          Manager: Sandy Harbick
Estimated Sales: $10-24.9 Million
Number Employees: 50-99

12938 Sea Watch International
8978 Glebe Park Dr
Easton, MD 21601-7004   410-822-7500
          Fax: 410-822-1266   sales@seaclam.com
          www.seaclam.com
Processor and exporter of canned and frozen clams,
crab cakes, extruded calamari rings, blue crab meat,
squid, shrimp, soups and seafood chowders
          President: Bob Brennan
          President: Bob Brennan
          Vice President: Bob Redar
          R&D/Quality Control: Larry Hughes
          Marketing Director: Kimberly Scott
          Sales Director: Bob Redar
          Public Relations: Doug Morrow
          Operations Manager: Kenny Carroll
          Purchasing Manager: Susie Jones
Estimated Sales: $ 50 - 100 Million
Number Employees: 20-49
Number of Brands: 4
Type of Packaging: Food Service, Private Label
Brands:
          AMERICAN ORIGINAL
          CAP'NS CATCH
          CAPT. FRED
          EASTERN SHORE FOODS, LLC
          MID-ATLANTIC FOODS
          MR FROSTY
          OLD SALT SEAFOOD
          SAILOR'S CHOICE
          SEAWATCH
          TUCKER'S COVE

12939 Sea-Fresh Seafood Market
2303 Halls Mill Road
Mobile, AL 36606-4603   251-478-3434
          Fax: 251-478-3778
Seafood.
          President: Patrick Meacham
          CFO: Rusty Brennan

12940 SeaBear Smokehouse
605 30th Street
Anacortes, WA 98221   800-454-0023
          Fax: 360-230-2500   wholesale@seabear.com
          www.seabear.com
wild salmon

12941 SeaPerfect Atlantic Farms
PO Box 12139
Charleston, SC 29422-2139   843-762-0022
          Fax: 843-795-6672   800-728-0099
          kgrant@awod.com   seaperfect.com
Processor and exporter of clams; importer of scal-
lops
          President: Carlos Celle
          Sales Director: Michelle Black
          General Manager: Knox Grant
Estimated Sales: $2300000
Number Employees: 45
Sq. footage: 34000
Brands:
          SEAPERFECT

12942 SeaSpecialties
1111 NW 159th Dr
Miami, FL 33169-5807   305-625-5112
          Fax: 305-625-5528   800-654-6682
          info@seaspecialties.com
          www.seaspecialties.com
Seafood
          Manager: Ron Alexander
          Quality Control: Irvin Norss
          CFO: Michael Metzkes
Estimated Sales: $ 20-50 Million
Number Employees: 100-249

12943 Seabear
P.O.Box 591
Anacortes, WA 98221-0591   360-293-4661
          Fax: 360-293-4097   800-645-3474
          smokehouse@seabear.com   www.seabear.com
Processor and exporter of smoked fish and seafoods
          President: Mike Mondello
          General Manager: Kathy Hayward
          Marketing Manager: Barb Hoenselaar
          Director Operations: Cathy Hayward-Hughes
Estimated Sales: $10800000
Number Employees: 1-4
Type of Packaging: Consumer, Bulk

12944 Seaberghs Frozen Foods
200 Westchester Avenue
White Plains, NY 10601-4510   914-948-6377
Frozen foods
          President: Harry Rich
Estimated Sales: $ 1-2.5 Million
Number Employees: 1-4

12945 (HQ)Seaboard Corporation
9000 W 67th St
Shawnee Mission, KS 66202-3698   913-676-8800
          Fax: 913-676-8872   seaboard@seaboardcorp.com
          www.seaboardcorp.com
Processor and exporter of flour, poultry, pork and
produce
          Presdient/CEO: Steven Bresky
          SVP/CFO: Robert Steer
Estimated Sales: $4 Billion
Number Employees: 14000
Type of Packaging: Consumer, Food Service
Other Locations:
          Seaboard Corp.
          Santo Domingo

12946 Seaboard Farms
P.O.Box 1091
Chattanooga, TN 37401-1091   423-756-2471
          Fax: 423-756-2111
          Manager: Leonard Polacek
          Plant Manager: Terry Paschall
Estimated Sales: $ 100-500 Million
Number Employees: 1,000-4,999
Parent Co: Seaboard Farms

12947 Seaboard Foods
9000 W 67th St
Suite 200
Shawnee Mission, KS 66202   913-261-2600
          Fax: 913-261-2626   800-262-7907
          info@seaboardfoods.com
          www.seaboardfoods.com

Produces and sells fresh, frozen and processed pork.
          President: Rodney Brenneman
          VP Finance & Accounting: Kevin Henn
          VP Sales & Marketing: Terry Holton
          VP Plant Operations: Marty Hast
Estimated Sales: $1+ Billion
Number Employees: 6500
Type of Packaging: Consumer, Food Service, Pri-
vate Label, Bulk
Other Locations:
          Processing Plant
          Guymon OK
          Ham Deboning Plant
          Reynosa, MEXICO
          Mount Dora Farms Management
          Houston TX
          Live Production Operations
          Kansas
          Daily's Premium Meats Bacon Plant
          Salt Lake City UT
          Daily's Premium Meats Bacon Plant
          Missoula MT
          Live Production Operations
          Colorado
          Live Production Operations
          Texas
Brands:
          DAILY'S PREMIUM MEATS
          PRAIRIE FRESH PREMIUM PORK
          SEABOARD FARMS

12948 Seabreeze Fish
2311 R Street
Bakersfield, CA 93301-2986   661-323-7936
          Fax: 805-323-7936
Seafood.
Estimated Sales: $300,000-500,000
Number Employees: 1-4

12949 (HQ)Seabrook Brothers & Sons
P.O.Box 5103
Seabrook, NJ 08302-5103   856-455-8080
          Fax: 856-455-9282   seabrob@seabrookfarms.com
          www.seabrookbrothers.com
frozen vegetables
          President/CEO: James Seabrook Jr
          CFO: Barbara Wiler
          Research & Development: Barbara Michalkiewicz

          Quality Control: Barbara Michalkiewicz
          VP Sales/Marketing: Brian Seabrook
          Public Relations: James Seabrook Jr
          Operations: Dave Deon
          Production Manager: Dave Deon
          Plant Manager: Dave Deon
          Purchasing Manager: Joan Wilson
Estimated Sales: $80 Million
Number Employees: 350
Number of Brands: 96
Number of Products: 150
Sq. footage: 372000
Type of Packaging: Consumer, Food Service, Pri-
vate Label, Bulk
Brands:
          SEABROOK FARMS
          SOMERDALE

12950 (HQ)Seabrook Ingredients
103 Westpark Dr # E
Peachtree City, GA 30269-1411   770-487-1230
          Fax: 770-487-3828
          marketing@universalblanchers.com
          www.universalblanchers.com
Pre-cleaning and blanching services, roasted peanuts, granulated peanuts; peanut butter, peanut toppings and variegates, roasted peanut extract
          President: Thomas Beaty
          CEO: Michael Fisher
          CFO: Chuck Davis
          CEO: Michael Fisher
          Quality Assurance: Anne Craig
          VP Sales and Marketing: John Bowen
Type of Packaging: Consumer, Bulk

12951 Seafare Market Wholesale
PO Box 671
Moody, ME 04054-0671   207-646-5160
          Fax: 408-294-3948
Seafood
          President: John Foye
Estimated Sales: $ 10 - 20 Million
Number Employees: 10-19

12952 Seafood & Meat
5681 Highway 90
Theodore, AL 36582-1671
251-653-4600
Fax: 251-653-1109
Seafood and meat distributors.
President: Ruth Summerlin

12953 Seafood & Service Marketing
4470 Chamblee Dunwoody Rd
Dunwoody, GA 30338-6224
770-451-9183
Fax: 770-451-9216 www.servicemark.aol.com
Frozen seafood, full line seafood
President: Paul Kastin
Estimated Sales:$ 20 - 50 Million
Number Employees: 10-19

12954 Seafood Connection
841 Pohukaina St # I
Honolulu, HI 96813-5332
808-591-8550
Fax: 808-591-8445
Suppliers of seafood and gourmet products to customers globally.
President: Stuart Simmons
Estimated Sales:$ 10 - 20 Million
Number Employees: 10 to 19

12955 Seafood Dimension International
P.O.Box 27548
Anaheim, CA 92809-0118
714-692-6464
Fax: 714-282-8997 dmontesai@aol.com
Seafood
Owner: Christi Lang
Estimated Sales:$1.4 Million
Number Employees: 5-9
Number of Brands: 20
Number of Products: 50
Type of Packaging: Food Service
Brands:
20TH CENTURY FOODS
BROOKS STREET BAKING
HARVEST FARM
LIL' FISHERMAN
MIDSHIP
NEPTUNE
SCHONER

12956 Seafood Distributors
420 W Bay Street
Savannah, GA 31401-1115
912-233-6048
Fax: 612-233-3238
Seafood
President: Walter Bryan

12957 Seafood Express
179 Rossmore Road
Brunswick, ME 04011-7745
207-729-0887
Fax: 207-721-9146
Seafood

12958 Seafood Hawaii
875 Waimanu St # 634
Honolulu, HI 96813-5265
808-597-1971
Fax: 808-538-1973
Seafood
President: Jeb Inouye
Estimated Sales:$ 5 - 10 Million
Number Employees: 20-49

12959 Seafood International
P.O.Box 388
Bayou La Batre, AL 36509-0388
251-824-4200
Fax: 251-824-2811
Wholesaler/distributor of fresh and frozen seafood
President: David Robicheaux
Estimated Sales:$ 3 - 5 Million
Number Employees: 1-4

12960 Seafood International Distributor, Inc
1051 Old Henderson Hwy
Henderson, LA 70517-7805
337-228-7568
Fax: 337-228-7573
Seafood
Owner: Roy Robert
Estimated Sales:$3,300,000
Number Employees: 20-49

12961 Seafood Merchants
900 Forest Edge Dr
Vernon Hills, IL 60061-3105
847-634-0900
Fax: 847-634-1351
sales@theseafoodmerchants.com
www.theseafoodmerchants.com

Importer of seafood
President: Roy Axelson
CEO: Bonnie Axelson
Sales: Gayle Janos
Purchasing Director: Bonnie Axelson
Estimated Sales:$ 10-20 Million
Number Employees: 20-49
Sq. footage: 23000
Type of Packaging: Consumer, Food Service, Bulk

12962 Seafood Network
123 Crossbrook Drive
Brunswick, GA 31525-2114
912-267-0422
Fax: 912-267-1918
Crabmeat, shrimp, scallops

12963 Seafood Packaging
2120 Poydras St
New Orleans, LA 70112-1339
504-522-6677
Fax: 504-522-9008
ksharp@seafoodpackaging.com
www.seafoodpackaging.com
Seafood
Owner: Kent Sharp
Estimated Sales:$ 5 - 10 Million
Number Employees: 5-9
Type of Packaging: Consumer

12964 Seafood Plus Corporation
6930 Pershing Road
Berwyn, IL 60402-3937
708-795-4820
Fax: 708-795-7719
Seafood

12965 Seafood Producers Cooperative
2875 Roeder Ave
Bellingham, WA 98225-2063
360-733-0120
Fax: 360-733-0513 spc@spcsales.com
www.spcsales.com
Processor and exporter of salmon, halibut, sablefish and rockfish.
President: Thomas McLaughlin
Sales: Kurt Sigfusson
Estimated Sales:$45,000,000
Number Employees: 5-9
Type of Packaging: Food Service, Bulk
Brands:
Alaska Gold
Longliner
Sitka Gold

12966 Seafood Products Company
2727 Commissioner Street
Vancouver, BC V5K 1A1
Canada
604-255-3141
Fax: 604-255-3196
Processor, importer and exporter of halibut, herring and salmon
VP/General Manager: Daren Hancott
Parent Co: Maple Leaf Foods
Type of Packaging: Consumer

12967 Seafood Services
PO Box D5
Fairhaven, MA 02719-0717
508-999-1502
Fax: 508-993-4001
Seafood
President: David Horton
Estimated Sales:$ 20 - 50 Million
Number Employees: 20-49

12968 Seafood Specialties
155 E Vienna St
Anna, IL 62906-1839
618-833-6083
Fax: 618-833-6083
President: Daniel Lewis
Estimated Sales:$ 1 - 3 Million
Number Employees: 1-4

12969 Seafood Specialties
P.O.Box 665
Coden, AL 36523-0665
251-824-2693
Fax: 251-824-7808
Seafoods
President: Susan Taylor
Human Resources: Bridget Sprinkle
*Estimated Sales:*Under $500,000
Number Employees: 20-49

12970 Seafood Specialty Sales
28 Mulholland Drive
Ipswich, MA 01938-2823
978-356-2995
Fax: 978-356-2275

Seafood

12971 Seafood USA
PO Box 418
Humarock, MA 02047-0418
781-837-7666
Fax: 781-837-7664
President: James Allen

12972 Seaforth Creamery
151 Main Street S
Seaforth, ON N0K 1W0
Canada
519-527-0610
Fax: 519-527-2265 mbarr@seacream.com
www.seacream.com
Processor of regular and light salad dressings
President: Mark Barr
CFO: Murray Mackey
R&D: Clarence Murphy
R&D: Jeff Smith
Estimated Sales:$15100000
Number Employees: 150
Sq. footage: 50000
Type of Packaging: Consumer, Food Service, Private Label, Bulk
Brands:
Village

12973 Seafreeze Pizza
P.O.Box 24978
Seattle, WA 98124-0978
206-767-7350
Fax: 206-763-8514 www.seafreeze.com
Seafood
VP: John Saulnier
Owner: Parry Romani Deconcini
VP: William Bowman
Estimated Sales:$ 10 - 20 Million
Number Employees: 100-249
Brands:
Seafreeze Pizza

12974 Sealand Lobster Corporation
PO Box 423
Tenants Harbor, ME 04860-0423
207-372-6247
Fax: 207-389-1819
Lobster

12975 Sealaska Corporation
1 Sealaska Plz # 400
Juneau, AK 99801-1276
907-586-1512
Fax: 907-586-2304 800-848-5921
russell.dick@sealaska.com www.sealaska.com
Seafood
President: Chris McNeil
CFO: Willian Strafford
CEO: Chris E McNeil Jr
VP: Richard Harris
Estimated Sales:$ 100-200 Million
Number Employees: 20-49
Brands:
Ocean Beauty Seafoods

12976 Seald Sweet Growers & Packers
1991 74th Ave
Vero Beach, FL 32966-5110
772-569-2244
Fax: 772-569-5110 www.sealdsweet.com
Grower, importer and exporter of citrus products including oranges, grapefruit, lemons, clementines, minneolas, tangerines and tangeros.
President/Owner: Hein Deprez
CFO: Christine Wallace
VP: David E Mixon
Marketing Manager: Kim Flores
Estimated Sales:$5-10 Million
Number Employees: 20-49
Sq. footage: 15000
Type of Packaging: Food Service, Bulk
Brands:
Florigold
Seald Sweet

12977 Seapac of Idaho
4074 N 2000 E
Filer, ID 83328-5033
208-326-3100
Fax: 208-326-5935
Processes and packages trout and salmon jerky, smoked rainbow trout, and salmon sausages.
President/General Manager: Ken Ashley
Estimated Sales:$ 7.10 M
Number Employees: 20-49

12978 Seapoint Farms
2183 Fairview Rd
Ste 222
Costa Mesa, CA 92627   949-646-9831
    Fax: 949-646-9851   888-722-7098
        info@seapointfarms.com
        www.seapointfarms.com
importer and manufacturer of edamame products
    President/Owner: Laura Cross
    CEO: Kevin Cross
Estimated Sales: 1.6 Millin
Number Employees: 8

12979 Seapoint Farms
2183 Fairview Rd # 222
Costa Mesa, CA 92627-5674   949-646-9831
    Fax: 949-646-9851   888-722-7098
        info@seapointfarms.com
        www.seapointfarms.com
Manufacturer and distributor of edamame food products
    President: Laura Cross
    CEO: Kevin Cross
Estimated Sales: $ .5 - 1 million
Number Employees: 1-4
Brands:
    Seapoint Farms

12980 Seaside Ice Cream
PO Box 734
Pelham, NY 10803-0734   914-636-2751
    Fax: 631-728-1653
Ice cream
    Owner: Arthur Haas

12981 Season Harvest Foods
556 E Weddell Drive
Suite 2
Sunnyvale, CA 94089   408-749-8018
    Fax: 408-749-7079
        info@seasonharvestfoods.com
        www.seasonharvestfoods.com
Frozen organic and dried ingredients

12982 Seasons' Enterprises
1790 W Cortland Ct
Addison, IL 60101-4208   630-628-0211
    Fax: 630-628-0385   info@seasonssnacks.com
        www.seasonssnacks.com
Processor of organic snack foods including corn
cheese puffs, chocolate covered butter toffee and
tortilla, reduced-fat potato chips, kettle cooked po-
tato chips, peller snacks and popcorn products
    President: Michael Season
    Sales Director: Kelly Garrigan
    Operations Manager: Mark Ruchti
Estimated Sales: $1300000
Number Employees: 5-9
Number of Brands: 2
Number of Products: 35
Sq. footage: 12000
Type of Packaging: Consumer, Food Service, Private Label, Bulk
Brands:
    Butter Toffee Covered Popcorn
    Chocolate Covered Potato Chips
    Chocolate Covered Toffee Popcorn
    Michael Season's Cheese Curls
    Michael Season's Cheese Puffs
    Michael Season's Kettle Potatoes
    Michael Season's Organically Grown
    Michael Season's Sensations
    Sweet Organics

12983 Seaspan Products Corporation
PO Box 663
New York, NY 10150-0663   201-569-9234
    Fax: 201-569-6539
Processor and importer of seafood including frozen
fish, shrimp, lobster tails and whiting fillets
    Owner: Hans Neuman

12984 Seatec
3 Holyoke Wharf
Portland, ME 04101   207-879-7199
    Fax: 207-879-2387
Fresh, dried monkfish, dogfish, and shrimp
    President: Brian Dorman

12985 Seatech Corporation
16825 48th Ave West
Suite 222
Lynnwood, WA 98037   425-835-0312
    Fax: 425-835-0367   johnw@seatechcorp.com
        www.seatechcorp.com
frozen shrimp, crab and scallops
    President: John Wendt
    CFO: Jim Schantz
    Quality Control: Todd Wendt
    Marketing Director: Todd Wendt
    Sales Director: Todd Wendt
Estimated Sales: $6 Million
Number Employees: 3
Number of Brands: 2
Sq. footage: 1000
Type of Packaging: Consumer, Food Service, Private Label, Bulk
Brands:
    CLEAN KITCHEN
    Chiquititos
    Seatech

12986 Seatrade Corporation
P.O.Box 421
Hoboken, NJ 07030-0421   201-963-5700
    Fax: 201-963-0577
    VP: Richard Mendelson
    Sales Manager: Richard Menderlson

12987 Seattle Bar Company
3302 Wallingford Avenue N
Seattle, WA 98103-9039   206-601-4301
    Fax: 206-282-3548 www.seattlebar.com
    Owner: Beth Campbell
Number Employees: 1-4
Brands:
    SEATTLE BAR

12988 Seattle Chocolate Company
1180 Andover Park W
Tukwila, WA 98188-3909   206-624-8989
    Fax: 206-624-0216   800-334-3600
        information@seattlechocolates.com
        www.seattlechocolate.com
Manufacturers of pre-wrapped gifts of natural
meltaway chocolate truffles and truffle bars
    CEO: Jean Thompson
    CEO: Steve Elliot
Estimated Sales: Below $ 5 Million
Number Employees: 10-19
Number of Brands: 1
Number of Products: 11
Type of Packaging: Consumer, Private Label, Bulk
Brands:
    CHICK CHOCOLATES
    SEATTLE CHOCOLATES
    SKINNY TRUFFLES

12989 Seattle Gourmet Foods
19016 72nd Ave S
Kent, WA 98032-1005   425-656-9076
    Fax: 425-656-8059   800-800-9490
        www.seattlegourmetfoods.com
Manufacturer of many of the Pacific Northwest's
specialty food products
    Manager: Tom Means
Estimated Sales: $2.5-5 Million
Number Employees: 10-19
Brands:
    ANNA'S GOURMET
    BIRINGER'S FARM FRESH
    BUCKEYE BEANS AND HERBS
    COY'S COUNTRY NORTHWEST
    FREDERICK'S FINE CHOCOLATES
    INNOVATIVE COOKIES
    MAURY ISLAND FARMS PREMIUM PRE-
    SERVE
    PARADISE FARMS
    QUINN'S
    ST. JEAN'S CANNERY & SMOKEHOUSE
    VICTORIA GOURMET CHOCOLATES

12990 Seattle Gourmet Foods
19016 72nd Ave S
Kent, WA 98032-1005   425-656-9076
    Fax: 425-656-8059   800-800-9490
        sales@seattlegourmetfoods.com
        www.seattlegourmetfoods.com
Chocolate meltaways, coffee spoons, molasses
chews, thin mints, pecan delights, panned nuts, jams,
jellies, fruit toppings, whipped taffy
    President/CEO: Tom Means

12985 (continued - right column)
Estimated Sales: $ 10 - 20 Million
Number Employees: 20-49
Brands:
    ANNA'S
    BIRINGER'S FARM FRESH
    BUCKEYE BEANS & HERBS
    CHOCOLATE NOVELTIES
    COY'S COUNTRY
    MAURY ISLAND FARM
    PARADISE FARMS CONFECTIONS
    QUINN'S

12991 (HQ)Seattle's Best Coffee
2401 Utah Ave S # 400
Seattle, WA 98134-1431   206-903-8010
    Fax: 206-624-3262   sbc@seabest.com
Manufacturer and wholesaler/distributor of ground
coffee and beans; serving the food service market
    Manager: James Strasbaugh
Estimated Sales: $10.9 Million
Number Employees: 100-249
Type of Packaging: Consumer, Food Service

12992 Seavers Bakery
3300 Mayfield Dr
Johnson City, TN 37604-5922   423-928-8131
    Fax: 423-928-8132
Processor of baked goods including pies
    President: Ralph Coomer
    President/CEO: Richard Seaver
    Plant Manager: Richard McKinney
Estimated Sales: $250000
Number Employees: 10-19
Type of Packaging: Consumer

12993 Seavey Vineyard
1310 Conn Valley Rd
St Helena, CA 94574-9624   707-963-8339
    Fax: 707-963-0232   info@seaveyvineyard.com
        www.seaveyvineyard.com
Wines
    President: William Seavey
    Marketing Manager: Nora Bowhay
Estimated Sales: $500,000-$1 Million
Number Employees: 5-9
Brands:
    Seavey Cabernet Sauvignon
    Seavey Chardonnay
    Seavey Marlot

12994 Seaview Lobster Company
P.O.Box 291
Kittery, ME 03904-0291   207-439-1599
    Fax: 207-439-1476   800-245-4997
        orders@seaviewlobster.com
        www.seaviewlobster.com
Seafood
    Owner: Tom Flanagan
Estimated Sales: $ .5 - 1 million
Number Employees: 1-4

12995 Seawatch International
8978 Glebe Park Dr
Easton, MD 21601-7004   410-822-7500
    Fax: 410-822-1266   sales@seaclam.com
        www.seaclam.com
Largest processor of clam products including
canned, fresh and frozen clams, clam and specialty
chowders, clam strips, crab cakes, prepared cala-
mari, and tempura shrimp
    President: Bob Brennan
Estimated Sales: $ 50 - 100 Million
Number Employees: 20-49
Type of Packaging: Food Service

12996 Seaway Company
P.O.Box 868
Fairhaven, MA 02719-0800   508-992-1221
    Fax: 508-992-1253
Seafood.
    Owner: Steve Doonan
Estimated Sales: $ 1 - 3 Million
Number Employees: 1-4

12997 Seawind Trading International
5375 Avenida Encinas # A
Carlsbad, CA 92008-4362   760-438-5600
    Fax: 760-438-5677
Fruits and vegetables
    Executive Director: Rick Rosenquist
Estimated Sales: $860,000
Number Employees: 5-9

12998 Sebastiani Vineyards
P.O.Box Aa
Sonoma, CA 95476-1219   707-933-3200
          Fax: 707-933-3370   800-888-5532
     info@sebastiani.com   www.sebastiani.com
Processor of wines
     Chairman: Richard Cuneo
     President/CEO: Mary Ann Sebastiani Cuneo
     COO: Emma Swain
     CEO: Mary Ann Sebastiani
     VP Marketing: Bob Carroll
     Public Relations: Jim Knapp
     Operations Manager: Paul Bergna
Estimated Sales: $5 Million
Number Employees: 100-249
Type of Packaging: Consumer

12999 Sechrist Brothers
32 E Main St
Dallastown, PA 17313-2206   717-244-2975
                    Fax: 717-244-6532
Processor and packer of meat including bologna,
smoked ham, frankfurters and sausage
     President: George Sechrist
     VP: Jacob Sechrist
Estimated Sales: $910000
Number Employees: 5-9
Sq. footage: 20000
Type of Packaging: Consumer

13000 Seckinger-Lee Company
PO Box 13086
Savannah, GA 31416-0086   912-355-4431
          Fax: 912-355-4431   800-291-2973
     CustServ@ByrdCookieCompany.com
          www.byrdcookiecompany.com
Processor of gourmet bite sized flavored biscuits.
     President/CEO: Benny Curl
     VP: Geoff Repella
     R&D: Shawn Curl
     Marketing: Amy Weddell
     Sales: Shawn Curl
     Public Relations/Human Relations: Amy Waddell

     Operations/Production/Plant Manager: Shawn
     Curl
     Purchasing Manager: Benny Curl
Number Employees: 50
Number of Brands: 3
Number of Products: 74
Sq. footage: 35000
Type of Packaging: Consumer, Private Label
Brands:
     Byrd Basics
     Byrd Cookie Company
     Seckinger-Lee

13001 Seco & Golden 100
P.O.Box 323
Deland, FL 32721-0323   386-734-3906
     Fax: 386-738-1378   info@golden100.com
               www.seco-golden100.com
Processor and exporter of fruit juice and drink con-
centrates; also, centralized purchasing location of
dairy products and juice concentrates
     President: Ron Edmundson
     VP Development: Russ Sager
     Plant Manager: Michael Bowes
Estimated Sales: $219519937
Number Employees: 20-49
Sq. footage: 27000
Type of Packaging: Bulk
Brands:
     Golden 100

13002 Secret Garden
10989 County Road 14
Park Rapids, MN 56470-2119   218-732-4866
          Fax: 218-732-2007   800-950-4409
               sgmorg@wcta.net
          www.secretgardengourmet.com
Manufacturer of gourmet wild rice, bread, entree and
seasoning mixes
     President: Anne Morgan
     Sales/Marketing: Andrea Roberts
     Purchasing Manager: Anne Morgan
Estimated Sales: $550000
Number Employees: 5-9
Sq. footage: 6000
Type of Packaging: Consumer, Private Label
Brands:
     Anne's Country Gourmet
     CONTINENTAL CUISINE
     Creole Classics

Midhaven Farm Cafe
Midheaven Farm
PASTRY PERFECT
Secret Garden
Soup For Singles
Swany White
Swany White Certified Organic
The Secret Garden

13003 Secret House Vineyards
88324 Vineyard Ln
Veneta, OR 97487-9406   541-935-3774
          Fax: 541-935-3774   800-497-1574
     info@secrethousewinery.com
          www.secrethousewinery.com
Wines
     President: Ron Chappel
     CFO: Patty Chappel
Estimated Sales: $ 10-20 Million
Number Employees: 5-9
Brands:
     Secret House

13004 Secret Tea Garden
5559 West Boulevard
Vancouver, BC V6M 3W6
Canada   604-261-3070
     Fax: 604-261-3075   info@secretgardentea.com
                    www.secretgardentea.com
Manufacturers of special varieties of tea
     President: Erin McBeath
     VP: With Kathy

13005 Sedlock Farm
1557 Knoxville Road
Lynn Center, IL 61262-8504   309-521-8284
                    Fax: 309-521-8284
Processor of fresh asparagus and asparagus products
including fettucine; also, vinegars, hot pepper and
jellies
     Owner/CEO: John Sedlock
     VP Manufacturing: Patricia Sedlock
Estimated Sales: Under $300,000
Number Employees: 6
Type of Packaging: Consumer, Food Service, Bulk

13006 See's Candies
3423 S La Cienega Blvd
Los Angeles, CA 90016-4401   310-559-4911
          Fax: 610-604-6255   800-347-7337
     qdordering@sees.com   www.sees.com
Processor and exporter of confectioneries and choc-
olates
     President: Charles Huggins
     CEO: Charles Huggins
     CFO: Ken Scott
     General Manager: Jane Wellsplant
Estimated Sales: $ .5 - 1 million
Number Employees: 5-9
Sq. footage: 220000
Parent Co: See's Candies
Type of Packaging: Consumer
Brands:
     See's Candies

13007 Seed Enterprises
679 19th Rd
West Point, NE 68788-4510   402-372-3238
          Fax: 402-372-2627   888-440-7333
               seedenterprises@alltel.net
Processor and exporter of soybeans
     President: Conrad Reeson
Estimated Sales: $ 1 - 3 Million
Number Employees: 5-9
Sq. footage: 35000
Brands:
     Sunrise

13008 Seeds of Change
P.O.Box 15700
Santa Fe, NM 87592-5700   505-438-8080
          Fax: 505-438-7052   888-762-7333
               www.seedsofchange.com
Organic pasta sauces, grain blends, salsas, salad
dressing, ketchup and dry soup mixes
     Manager: Marc Cool
Estimated Sales: $ 10-20 Million
Number Employees: 20-49
Type of Packaging: Private Label
Brands:
     Seeds of Change

13009 Seeley & Son Apiaries
6527 Waconda Road NE
Brooks, OR 97305-9788   503-792-3523
Processor of honey-filled straws
     Owner: Gary Ceiling
Type of Packaging: Consumer, Food Service, Pri-
vate Label, Bulk
Brands:
     Super Bee Honey Stix

13010 Seenergy Foods
121 Jevlan Drive
Woodbridge, ON L4L 8A8
Canada   905-850-2544
          Fax: 905-850-2563   800-609-7674
               info@seenergyfoods.com
                    www.seenergyfoods.com
Processor and exporter of frozen vegetables includ-
ing vegetable patties and IQF (individually quick
frozen) beans
     President/CEO: Shreyas Ajmer
     Marketing/Sales: Carl McLaughlin
Type of Packaging: Consumer, Food Service, Pri-
vate Label, Bulk
Brands:
     Presidents Choice

13011 Seger Egg Corporation
P.O.Box 265
Farina, IL 62838-0265   618-245-3301
                    Fax: 618-245-3552
Eggs
     President: Larry Seger
     Sales/Marketing: Larry Pemberton
Estimated Sales: $ 10 - 20 Million
Number Employees: 50-99

13012 Seghesio Family Vineyards
14730 Grove St
Healdsburg, CA 95448-4818   707-433-3579
          Fax: 707-433-0545   seghesio@seghesio.com
                    www.seghesio.com
Wines
     CEO: Peter Seghesio
     CFO: Ileana Standridge
     Marketing Director: Cathy Seghesio
     Production Manager/Winemaker: Ted Seghesio
Estimated Sales: $ 10-20 Million
Number Employees: 20-49
Type of Packaging: Private Label
Brands:
     Keyhole Ranch

13013 Segovia Mexican Candy Manufacturer
1837 Guadalupe St
San Antonio, TX 78207-5497   210-225-2102
                    Fax: 210-225-2211
Manufacturer of Mexican confectionery products in-
cluding pralines, divinity, vanilla fudge, sweet pota-
toes, coconut and peanut clusters
     President: Rudy Segovia Jr
Estimated Sales: $3-5 Million
Number Employees: 10-19
Type of Packaging: Consumer, Food Service

13014 Seitz Foods
PO Box 387
Saint Joseph, MO 64502-0387   816-238-1771
          Fax: 816-238-4433   800-383-3128
Processor, exporter and packer of beef, pork, frank-
furters and luncheon meat; also, frozen corn dogs
and chili
     Sales/Marketing Executive: Scott Farris
     VP Operations: Larry Coffman
     Purchasing Agent: Mike Kean
Number Employees: 250-499
Parent Co: Sara Lee Corporation
Type of Packaging: Consumer, Food Service, Pri-
vate Label, Bulk

13015 Sekan Cheese Company
749 Village Court
Girard, KS 66743-2204   316-724-8827
                    Fax: 316-724-4780
Processor of cheese
     President: Richard Buck
Estimated Sales: $430000
Number Employees: 3

13016 (HQ)Select Food Products
120 Sunrise Avenue
Toronto, ON M4A 1B4
Canada   416-759-9316
      Fax: 416-759-9310 800-699-8016
      feedback@selectfoodproducts.com
      www.selctfoodproducts.com
Manufacturers and exporter of salad dressings,
sauces, salsas, relishes, mustard, gravies, canned
dinners, etc; importer of tomatoes and tomato paste
      President: Paul Fredricks
Number Employees: 150
Sq. footage: 116000
Type of Packaging: Consumer, Food Service, Pri-
      vate Label, Bulk
Brands:
      Duthie
      Horne's
      Laing's
      Oxford Inn
      Select

13017 Select Marketing Group
PO Box 66
Huron, OH 44839-0066   419-433-8252
      Fax: 419-627-1582 888-805-0800
      hlandss@msn.com
Processor of wild rice, wholesaler
      President: Hugh Lands
      Marketing/Sales: David Metzger
Estimated Sales: $ 1-2 Million
Number Employees: 5
Number of Brands: 1
Number of Products: 20
Sq. footage: 5000
Type of Packaging: Consumer, Food Service, Pri-
      vate Label, Bulk
Brands:
      Fall River Wild Rice

13018 Select Origins
PO Box 1748
Mansfield, OH 44901-1748   419-924-5447
General groceries
      National Sales Manager: Noel Thompson
Estimated Sales: $ 5-10 Million
Number Employees: 20

13019 Select Supplements, Inc
5800 Newton Dr
Carlsbad, CA 92008-7311   760-431-7509
                                  Fax: 760-804-8073
SSI specializes in the development and manufactur-
ing of nutraceuticlas and other dietary supplement
products.
      Manager: Hector Gudino
      Executive VP: Toshifumi Asada
      QA/QC Manager: David Dean
      Sales: Hector Gudino
      Operations: Hector Gudino
      Production Supervisor: James Morales
      Purchasing Supervisor: Cheryl Moore
Estimated Sales: $990,000
Number Employees: 10-19

13020 Selecto Sausage Company
7119 Avenue F
Houston, TX 77011-3755   713-926-1626
Processor of Mexican products including sausage,
spices and tortillas
      President: Carlos Gonzalez
Estimated Sales: $ 3 - 5 Million
Number Employees: 5-9
Type of Packaging: Consumer

13021 Sellards Winery
6400 Sequoia Cir
Sebastopol, CA 95472-2013   707-823-8293
Wines

13022 Seller Kirk & Company
16 Aspen Way
Schwenksville, PA 19473-1788   215-480-7342
Processor and exporter of chocolate and cocoa prod-
ucts including milk and hot cocoa mix, syrup, dairy
and nondairy flavors and bases
      President: David Sellers
Number Employees: 1-4
Type of Packaging: Consumer, Food Service, Pri-
      vate Label, Bulk
Brands:
      Cloverleaf

13023 Sells Best
P.O.Box 428
Mishawaka, IN 46546-0428   574-255-1910
      Fax: 574-258-6162 800-837-8368
      www.coravent.com
Processor of bakery mixes including breads, dough-
nuts, cakes and muffins including low fat, no choles-
terol or preservatives and sugar free
      President: Gary Sells
      Office Manager: Kathy Campole
      VP Sales: Coleman Caldwell
      Director Manufacturing: Steven Surmay
      Purchasing Manager: James Allen
Estimated Sales: $9000000
Number Employees: 5-9
Sq. footage: 20000

13024 Selma's Cookies
2023 Apex Ct
Apopka, FL 32703-7720   407-884-9433
      Fax: 407-884-6121 800-922-6654
      selmas@selma.com   www.selmas.com
Gourmet cookies, brownies and crispy rice treats.
Estimated Sales: Less than $500,000
Number Employees: 50-99

13025 Seltzer & Rydholm
P.O.Box 1090
Auburn, ME 04211-1090   207-784-5791
                    Fax: 207-784-8685 www.pepsi.com
Bottler of soft drinks
      President: George Cotton
      CFO: George Cotton
      Executive VP: Laurence Pullen
      Quality Control: Bryan Fleweling
      VP Advertising: Cynthia Crocker
      Plant Manager: Ken Mancuso
Estimated Sales: $ 20 - 50 Million
Number Employees: 100-249
Parent Co: PepsiCo
Type of Packaging: Consumer, Food Service, Pri-
      vate Label, Bulk

13026 Seltzer's Smokehouse Meats
P.O.Box 111
Palmyra, PA 17078-0111   717-838-6336
                                  Fax: 717-838-5345
      seltzerssmokehousemeats@att.net
      www.seltzerslebanonbologna.com
Bolognas
      President: Craig Seltzer
      CFO: Peter Stanilla
      Plant Manager: Robert Hartman
Estimated Sales: $ 5-10 Million
Number Employees: 50-99
Type of Packaging: Private Label
Brands:
      Seltzer's Lebanon Bologna
      Seltzer's Sweet Bolo

13027 Selwoods Farm Hunting Preserve
706 Selwood Rd
Alpine, AL 35014-5431   256-362-7595
      Fax: 256-362-3856 www.selwoodfarm.com
Manufacturer of smoked turkey and hams, cakes,
mustards, jams, cookkies, stone ground grits, and
pancake mix
      Owner: Dell Hill
Estimated Sales: $1-3 Million
Number Employees: 5-9
Type of Packaging: Consumer

13028 Seminis Vegetable Seeds
2700 Camino Del Sol
Oxnard, CA 93030-7967   805-351-0106
      Fax: 805-918-2543 info@seminis.com
                                  www.seminis.com
Processor of hybrid vegetable seeds
      VP Marketing: Jorge Christlieb
      CEO: Bruno Ferrari
      CFO: Gaspar Alvarez
Number Employees: 250-499
Parent Co: Seminis Vegetable Seeds
Brands:
      Petoseed
      Royal Sluis

13029 Seminole Foods
P.O.Box 305
Springfield, OH 45501-305   352-245-1171
      Fax: 352-245-8534 800-881-1177
      customerservice@seminolefoods.com
      www.seminolefoods.com

Processor of fresh ground horseradish and fine
sauces.
      President: Robert Schneider
Estimated Sales: Below $ 5 Million
Number Employees: 10
Sq. footage: 19000
Type of Packaging: Consumer, Food Service, Pri-
      vate Label
Brands:
      Seminole

13030 Senape's Bakery
222 W 17th St
Hazleton, PA 18201-2426   570-454-0839
      sfpayer@erols.com
Bread and pizza dough
      President: Mary Lou Marchetti
      Marketing: Mary Lou Marchetti
Estimated Sales: Below $ 5 Million
Number Employees: 20-49

13031 Senba USA
23431 Cabot Blvd
Hayward, CA 94545-1665   510-264-5850
      Fax: 510-264-0938 888-922-5852
      aoki@senbausa.com   www.senbausa.com
Processor of liquid sauces including teriyaki, beef
and tempura; also, miso soup bases; importer of
spray dried alcohol powder and tea extract; also,
contract packaging and dry blending available
      Manager: Hiro Aoki
Estimated Sales: $4,200,000
Number Employees: 20-49
Sq. footage: 13000
Parent Co: Senba Foods Company
Type of Packaging: Consumer, Food Service, Pri-
      vate Label, Bulk

13032 Sencha Naturals
912 E 3rd Street
Building 101
Los Angeles, CA 90013   213-346-9470
      Fax: 213-947-1723 888-473-6242
      inquiry@senchanaturals.com
      www.senchanaturals.com
green tea mints and green tea bars
      President: David Kerdoon
      Operations Manager: Desiree Thomas
Number Employees: 15

13033 Seneca Foods
P.O.Box 250
Clyman, WI 53016-0250   920-696-3331
                                  Fax: 920-696-3566
      consumeraffairs@senecafoods.com
      consumer.senecafoods.com
Processor and exporter of sauces, spaghetti dinners,
corn relish, German potato salad and canned and
glass packed vegetables including beets, red cab-
bage and onions; also, tomato products including
sauces and pulp.
      President/CEO: Kraig H Kayser
      Chief Information Officer: Carl Cichetti
      EVP/Chief Operations Officer: Paul Palmby
      Plant Manager: Virgil Sission
      VP/Procurement: Vincent Lammers
Estimated Sales: $ 10 - 20 Million
Number Employees: 20-49
Parent Co: Seneca Foods Corporation
Type of Packaging: Consumer, Food Service, Pri-
      vate Label

13034 Seneca Foods
418 E Conde St
Janesville, WI 53546-3098   608-757-6000
                                  Fax: 608-752-5042
      consumer-affairs@senecafoods.com
      www.senecafoods.com
Manufacturer of canned vegetables: asparagus, corn,
carrots, mixed vegetables, peas, potatoes, stew
vegetables
      Manager: Paul Palmby
      Chairman: Arthur Wolcott
      Chief Financial Officer: Philip Paras
      General Counsel: John Exner
      Chief Information Officer: Carl Cichetti
      EVP/Chief Operating Officer: Paul Palmby
      VP/Procurement: Vincent Lammers
Estimated Sales: $157 Million
Number Employees: 100-249
Sq. footage: 706400
Parent Co: Seneca Foods Corporation
Type of Packaging: Consumer, Private Label

13035 Seneca Foods
1055 Elm Street
Cumberland, WI 54829-7223   715-822-2181
                                Fax: 715-822-2114
consumer_affairs@senecafoods.com
www.senecafoods.com
Manufacturer of canned and frozen yellow snap
beans and peas.
    Chairman: Arthur Wolcott
    President/CEO: Kraig Kayser
    Controller: Judy Miller
    General Counsel: John Exner
    Chief Information Officer: Carl Cichetti
    EVP/Chief Operating Officer: Paul Palmby
    Manager: Bruce Gonzales
    VP/Procurement: Vincent Lammers
Estimated Sales: $1 Billion
Number Employees: 500
Sq. footage: 223424
Parent Co: Seneca Foods Corporation
Type of Packaging: Consumer

13036 Seneca Foods
3736 S Main St
Marion, NY 14505-9751   315-926-8100
                            Fax: 315-926-8300
consumer_affairs@senecafoods.com
www.senecafoods.com
Processor of apple chips and canned vegetables in-
cluding beets, carrots, corn and mixed; also, frozen
beans including snap, blue lake, wax and green
    President/CEO: Kraig Kayser
    Chairman: Arthur Wolcott
    Senior VP: Cynthia L Fohrd
    Sales/Marketing Executive: Russ Curtis
    EVP/COO: Paul Palmby
Estimated Sales: $1.3 Billion
Number Employees: 3,300
Parent Co: Seneca Foods Corporation
Type of Packaging: Consumer, Food Service, Pri-
    vate Label

13037 Seneca Foods
229 W Waupun St
Oakfield, WI 53065-9741   920-583-3161
                              Fax: 920-583-4315
consumer_affairs@senecafoods.com
www.senecafoods.com
Manufacturer and exporter of canned corn.
    Manager: Gary Collien
    President/CEO: Kraig Kayser
    Chief Financial Officer: Philip Paras
    General Counsel: John Exner
    Chief Information Officer: Carl Cichetti
    EVP/Chief Operating Officer: Paul Palmby
    Plant Manager: Collien Gary
    VP/Procurement: Vincent Lammers
Estimated Sales: $ 20 - 50 Million
Number Employees: 100-249
Sq. footage: 193400
Parent Co: Seneca Foods Corporation
Type of Packaging: Private Label
Brands:
    AUNT NELLIE'S
    BLUE BOY
    DIAMOND A
    FESTAL
    GLACE FRUIT
    LIBBY'S
    LOHMANN
    READ
    STOKELY'S
    TENDERSWEET
    WALLA WALLA

13038 Seneca Foods
PO Box 278
Marion, NY 14505-0278   315-926-8100
                            Fax: 315-926-8300
consumer_affairs@senecafoods.com
www.senecafoods.com
Processor of canned fruits and vegetables
    President: Kraig H Kayser
    Sr. VP: Kraig Kayser
    CFO: Thomas Paulson
    Vice President: Dean Erstad
    CFO: Thomas Paulson
    Sales Director: Dean Erstad
    Plant Manager: Mike Hanchett
Estimated Sales: $ 100-500 Million
Number Employees: 250-499
Parent Co: Seneca Foods Corporation
Type of Packaging: Consumer, Private Label

Brands:
    Seneca Foods

13039 Seneca Foods
P.O.Box 810
Arlington, MN 55307-0810   507-964-2204
                               Fax: 507-964-2441
consumer_affairs@senecafoods.com
www.senecafoods.com
Processor, canner and exporter of peas and whole
kernel corn.
    Chairman: Arthur Wolcott
    President/CEO: Kraig Kayser
    Chief Financial Officer: Philip Paras
    General Counsel: John Exner
    Chief Information Officer: Carl Cichetti
    EVP/Chief Operating Officer: Paul Palmby
    Plant Manager: Doug Schauer
    VP/Procurement: Vincent Lammers
Estimated Sales: $ 50-100 Million
Number Employees: 250-499
Sq. footage: 241236
Parent Co: Seneca Foods Corporation
Type of Packaging: Private Label

13040 Seneca Foods
3736 S Main St
Marion, NY 14505-9751   315-926-4280
                            Fax: 315-926-8300
consumer_affairs@senecafoods.com
www.senecafoods.com
Processor of canned corn and peas
    Manager: Lee Luehring
    Chairman: Arthur S Wolcott
    Senior VP: Cynthia L Fohrd
    Board Member: Thomas Paulson
Estimated Sales: $ 50-100 Million
Number Employees: 1,000-4,999
Parent Co: Seneca Foods Corporation
Type of Packaging: Private Label
Brands:
    Diamond A
    Festal
    Read
    Stokely's
    Tendersweet
    Walla Walla

13041 Seneca Foods
PO Box 232
Buhl, ID 83316-0232   208-543-9350
                          Fax: 208-543-6015
consumer_affairs@senecafoods.com
www.senecafoods.com
Processor and exporter of canned and frozen corn
and sugar snap peas.
    Chairman: Arthur Wolcott
    President/CEO: Kraig Kayser
    Chief Financial Officer: Philip Paras
    General Counsel: John Exner
    Chief Information Officer: Carl Cichetti
    EVP/Chief Operating Officer: Paul Palmby
    VP/Procurement: Vincent Lammers
Estimated Sales: $ 100-500 Million
Number Employees: 750
Sq. footage: 395410
Parent Co: Seneca Foods Corporation
Type of Packaging: Consumer, Food Service, Pri-
    vate Label

13042 Seneca Foods
P.O.Box 35
Blue Earth, MN 56013-0035   507-526-2131
                                Fax: 507-526-4653
consumer_affairs@senecafoods.com
www.senecafoods.com
Processor of canned peas and corn.
    Chairman: Kraig H Kayser
    Chief Financial Officer: Troy Madisky
    Chief Information Officer: Carl Cichetti
    EVP/Chief Operating Officer: Paul Palmby
    Plant Manager: Colleen Gronewold
    VP/Procurement: Vincent Lammers
Estimated Sales: $ 50-100 Million
Number Employees: 250-499
Sq. footage: 145535
Parent Co: Seneca Foods Corporation
Type of Packaging: Consumer, Food Service, Pri-
    vate Label
Brands:
    Aunt Nellie's
    Blue Boy
    Diamond A
    Festal

    Green Giant
    Libbys
    Lohmann
    Read
    Seneca
    Stokley's

13043 Seneca Foods
600 5th St SE
Montgomery, MN 56069-1740   507-364-8641
                                Fax: 507-364-8278
consumer_affairs@senecafoods.com
www.senecafoods.com
Processor of canned and frozen peas and corn.
    Chairman: Kraig H Kayser
    EVP/Chief Financial Officer: Thomas Paulson
    Chief Information Officer: Carl Cichetti
    EVP/Chief Operating Officer: Paul Palmby
    Plant Manager: Paul Hendrickson
    VP/Procurement: Vincent Lammers
Estimated Sales: $ 100-500 Million
Number Employees: 500-999
Sq. footage: 228000
Parent Co: Seneca Foods Corporation
Type of Packaging: Consumer, Food Service, Pri-
    vate Label, Bulk
Brands:
    Seneca Foods

13044 (HQ)Seneca Foods Corporation
3736 S Main St
Marion, NY 14505   315-926-8100
Fax: 315-926-8300   webmaster@senecafoods.com
www.senecafoods.com
Apple chips, canned vegetables, canned potato salad
and canned bean salad.
    President/CEO: Kraig Kayser
    EVP/COO: Paul Palmby
Estimated Sales: $1.3 Billion
Number Employees: 3,300
Type of Packaging: Consumer, Food Service, Pri-
    vate Label, Bulk
Brands:
    AUNT NELLIE'S
    FESTAL
    LIBBY'S®
    READ
    SENECA
    STOKELY'S®

13045 Senor Felix's Gourmet Mexican
4265 Maine Ave
Baldwin Park, CA 91706-3312   626-960-2800
        Fax: 626-560-2855   senorfelix@ffci.us
                            www.senorfelixs.com
Mexican fresh and frozen food, including enchila-
das, burritos, taquitos, tamales, salsa, guacamole dip,
etc
    Owner: Lulu Juco
    Controller: Sam Tabani
    VP Sales/Marketing: Don O'Neill
Estimated Sales: $ .5 - 1 million
Number Employees: 50-99
Type of Packaging: Private Label
Brands:
    Delicioso
    Pacifico
    Senor Felix's

13046 Senor Murphy Candymaker
1904 Chamisa St
Santa Fe, NM 87505-3440   505-988-4311
        Fax: 505-988-2050   877-988-4311
chocolate@senormurphy.com
www.senormurphy.com
Processor of candy
    Owner: Rand Levitt
    VP: Bob Murphy
Estimated Sales: $770000
Number Employees: 5-9
Type of Packaging: Consumer

13047 Senor Pinos de Santa Fe
2600 Camino Entrada
Santa Fe, NM 87507-0491   505-473-3437
        Fax: 505-473-5808   senorpinos@aol.com
                            www.senorpinos.com
Blue-corn flour, southwestern specialties
    Owner: Nate Pino
Estimated Sales: $ 1 Million
Number Employees: 30
Brands:
    Josie's Best Blue Tortilla Chips

13048 Sensational Sweets
355 Sweets Ln
Lewisburg, PA 17837-7759   570-524-4361
  Fax: 570-524-5360 info@sensationalsweets.com
                www.sensationalsweets.com
Chippers the bark with a bite, gourmet fudge, fudge
bites, drizzled popcorn, dipped pretzels, pollylops
  Owner: Virginia Feitner
Estimated Sales: Less than $500,000
Number Employees: 5-9

13049 Sensible Portions
PO Box 753
Wayne, NJ 07474   973-283-9220
  Fax: 973-283-2799 info@gwgourmet.com
              www.sensibleportions.com
all natural and portion control snacks such as multi
grain crisps, mini multi grain crisps, soy crisps, mini
soy crisps, pita crackers, and pita chips.
  President: Jason Cohen
  President: Jerry Bello

13050 Sensient Dehydrated Flavors
P.O.Box 1524
Turlock, CA 95381-1524   209-667-2777
  Fax: 209-634-6235 800-558-9892
        paul.walker@sensient-tech.com
              www.sensient-tech.com
Processes dehydrated vegetable products
  President: Pat Laubacher
  VP Finance: Richard F Hobbs
Estimated Sales: $ 10-25 Million
Number Employees: 250-499
Brands:
  Sensient

13051 Sensient Food Colors
777 E Wisconsine Avenue
Milwaukee, WI 53202-5304   800-558-9892
  corporate.communications@sensient-tech.com
              www.sensient-tech.com
Sensient Technologies is the world's leading sup-
plier of flavors, fragrances and colors used to make a
diverse variety of foods and beverages,
pharmaceuticals, cosmetics, home and personal care
products, specialty printing and imagingproducts,
computer i
  Chairman/President /CEO: Kenneth Manning
  VP CFO/Treasurer: Richard Hobbs
  VP Administration: Richard Carney
  VP Marketing/Technology: Ho-Seung Yang PhD
Estimated Sales: Below $ 5 Million
Number Employees: 15
Brands:
  Sensient

13052 (HQ)Sensient Technologies
777 E Wisconsin Ave # 11
Milwaukee, WI 53202-5302   414-271-6755
  Fax: 414-347-4795 800-558-9892
        info@sensient-tech.com
              www.sensient-tech.com
Manufacturer of flavors, aromas and colors for a va-
riety of food, pharmacetical, cosmetics and house-
hold products
  Chairman/President/CEO: Kenneth Manning
  VP/CFO/Treasurer: Richard Hobbs
  VP/Secretary/General Counsel: John Hammond
Estimated Sales: $100+ Million
Number Employees: 1,000-4,999
Type of Packaging: Consumer, Food Service, Pri-
  vate Label, Bulk
Other Locations:
  Sensient Technologies
  High Ridge MO

13053 (HQ)Sensient Technologies
777 E Wisconsin Ave # 11
Milwaukee, WI 53202-5302   414-271-6755
  Fax: 414-347-4795 800-558-9892
  corporate.communications@sensient-tech.com
              www.sensient-technologies.com
Manfacturers of yeast, colorants, flavorings, addi-
tives, seasonings and toppings
  Chairman: Kenneth Manning
  VP/CFO/Treasurer: Richard Hobbs
  VP Human Resources: Christopher Lawlor
Estimated Sales: $73.9 Million
Number Employees: 1,000-4,999
Brands:
  Fensient Technologies

13054 SensoryEffects Flavor Systems
231 Rock Industrial Park Drive
Bridgeton, MO 63044   314-291-5444
  Fax: 314-291-3289 info@sensoryeffects.com
              www.sensoryeffects.com
Specialty powder flavoring systems, inclusions,
frozen dessert, beverage & dairy systems, creaming
agents, dessert bases and whipped toppings.

13055 Sentry Seasonings

928 N Church Rd
Elmhurst, IL 60126-1014   630-530-5370
                Fax: 630-530-5385
  wayne@sentryseasonings.com
  www.sentryseasonings.com

> **The product development experts
> of Sentry Seasonings are eager to
> offer the assistance and hands-on
> experience to food processors of
> all sizes. Sentry Seasonings will
> ensure the consistent high quality
> and repeat sales of yourproducts,
> whether you choose one of our
> many off-the-shelf Bench Mark
> products or a modified version to
> meet your preferences. Sentry
> Seasonings can also duplicate
> and/or improve your present fla-
> vor profile; formulate, blend and
> package specificallyfor your
> requirements.**

  President: Carla Staniec
  VP: Michael Staniec
Estimated Sales: $730000
Number Employees: 10-19
Sq. footage: 30000
Type of Packaging: Consumer, Food Service, Pri-
  vate Label, Bulk

13056 Seppic
P.O.Box 36272
Newark, NJ 07188-6006   973-882-5597
        Fax: 973-882-5178 877-737-7421
  stephen.oneill@airliquide.com www.seppic.com
Ingredients, minerals and extracts
  President: Jean Marc Giner
  Marketing/Sales: Regis Cazes
Estimated Sales: $ 1-2.5 Million
Number Employees: 20-49
Parent Co: Seppic

13057 Sequoia Grove Vineyards
P.O.Box 449
Rutherford, CA 94573-0449   707-944-2945
  Fax: 707-963-9411 800-851-7841
info@sequoiagrove.com www.sequoiagrove.com
Wines
  President/Winemaker: Michael Trujillo
  CFO: Robert Aldridge
  Vice President: Casandra Knox
  Marketing Director: Anthony Ankers
Estimated Sales: $1-$2.5 Million
Number Employees: 20-49
Type of Packaging: Private Label
Brands:
  Sequoia Grove
  Sequoia Grove

**13058 Sequoia Specialty Cheese
Company**
7000 W Doe Ave # C
Visalia, CA 93291-8623   559-752-4106
  Fax: 559-752-4108 sequoia@inreach.com

Cheese
  Administrator: Ray Chavez
  Production Manager: Greg Moe
Estimated Sales: $1-23 Million
Number Employees: 10-19
Number of Products: 10
Sq. footage: 40000
Type of Packaging: Consumer, Food Service, Pri-
  vate Label
Brands:
  Mt. Whitney

13059 Serenade Foods
P.O.Box 308
Milford, IN 46542-0308   574-658-4121
  Fax: 219-658-2246 www.mapleleaffarms.com
Processor and exporter of poultry
  Manager: Don Crandall
Number Employees: 100-249
Parent Co: Maple Leaf Foods
Type of Packaging: Consumer, Food Service, Pri-
  vate Label, Bulk

13060 Serendipitea
3229 Greenpoint Avenue
Long Island City, NY 11101-2005   718-752-1444
  Fax: 718-752-0333 888-832-5433
  tea@serendipitea.com www.serendipitea.com
Tea; premium grade loose leaf and tisane and accou-
terments.
  Co-Owner: Tomislav Podreka
  Co-Owner: Linda Villano
Number Employees: 5-9
Number of Brands: 1
Number of Products: 100+
Sq. footage: 3000
Type of Packaging: Consumer, Food Service, Pri-
  vate Label, Bulk

13061 Serendipity 3
225 E 60th St
New York, NY 10022-1498   212-838-3531
                800-805-5493
  Cosmeticmall.com www.serendipity3.com
Frozen hot chocolate
  President: Steven Bruce
Estimated Sales: Below $ 5 Million
Number Employees: 50-99
Brands:
  Black & White Mug
  Frrrozen Hot Chocolate Mix

13062 Serendipity Cellars
15275 Dunn Forest Road
Monmouth, OR 97361-9518   503-838-4284
                Fax: 503-838-0067
Wines
  Owner: Glen Longshore
Estimated Sales: $500,000-$1 Million
Number Employees: 1-4

13063 Serengeti Tea
351 W Redondo Beach Blvd
Gardena, CA 90248-2101   310-527-5278
        Fax: 310-527-2154 888-604-2040
  tea@serengetitea.com www.serengetitea.com
Processor of iced teas
  Owner: David Massey
Estimated Sales: $690,000
Number Employees: 5-9
Brands:
  Southern Breeze
  Ticolino

13064 Serra Mission Winery
12 Rolling Rock Lane
Saint Louis, MO 63124-1443   314-991-2559
                Fax: 314-962-3371
Wine
  President: John Bordenhier
Estimated Sales: $500,000-$1 Million
Number Employees: 1-4

13065 Serranos Salsa
632 Ralph Ablanedo Dr # 330
Austin, TX 78748-6619   512-328-9200
  Fax: 512-328-3005 customercare@serranos.com
                www.serranos.com
Soups, ensaladas, tortas
  Owner: Adam Gonzales
  Director: Eric Cross
Estimated Sales: $500-1 Million appx.
Number Employees: 5-9

Brands:
Serranos Salsa

13066 (HQ)Serv-Agen Corporation
1200 S Union Ave
Cherry Hill, NJ 08002-3332   856-663-6966
Fax: 856-663-7016   cwslade1@msn.com
Processor of food colors, flavorings, dehydrated
vegetables, gravy and soup bases, spices, puddings
and sauce mixes including soy and worcestershire
President: Barbara Pearlman
VP: Charles W Slade
Estimated Sales:$989000
Number Employees: 5-9
Sq. footage: 15000
Type of Packaging: Consumer, Food Service, Private Label, Bulk
Brands:
Bennetts
Clawson
Heinle
Key Lime
LEM
Lemon

13067 Serv-Rite Meat Company
2515 N San Fernando Rd
Los Angeles, CA 90065-1325   323-227-1911
Fax: 323-227-9068 www.bar-m.com
Processor of bacon, smoked ham and sausage
President: Gary Marks
Marketing Manager: Anna Cornellius
Estimated Sales:$ 10 - 20 Million
Number Employees: 50-99
Sq. footage: 80000

13068 Service Foods
PO Box 2206
Norcross, GA 30091-2206   770-448-5300
Fax: 770-446-3085
Frozen food and freezer plans
CEO: Keith Cantor
Estimated Sales:$ 5 - 10 Million
Number Employees: 20-49

13069 Service Marketing
4470 Chamblee Dunwoody Rd
Dunwoody, GA 30338-6224   770-451-9183
Fax: 770-451-9216
Seafood, ocean perch, whiting, flounder, trout,
croaker, hake
President: Paul J Kastin
Estimated Sales:$ 20 - 50 Million
Number Employees: 10-19

13070 Service Packing Company
250 Southern Street
Vancouver, BC V6A 2P1
Canada   604-681-0264
Fax: 604-681-9309   service-packing@ttelus.net
Processor, importer, exporter and packer of dates,
currants, raisins, shredded coconut, chocolate chips,
prunes and nuts including walnuts and almonds
President: Ron Huntington
Assistant General Manager: Cathy Vezina
Number Employees: 50-99
Sq. footage: 85000
Type of Packaging: Private Label
Brands:
Martins

13071 Sesaco Corporation
4308 Centergate St
San Antonio, TX 78217-4804   210-590-3352
Fax: 210-590-3665 800-737-2260
www.sesaco.net
Processor, importer and exporter of sesame seeds including white hulled
Executive Director: Ray Langham
Administration: Tina Smith
Operations Manager: Ray Collard
Estimated Sales:$ 3 - 5 Million
Number Employees: 1-4
Type of Packaging: Consumer, Bulk
Brands:
Flour
HP - White Hulled Sesame Seeds
Oil
T2P - Light
T4P - Medium Toasted Hulled Sesame
T5P - Dark
TNP - Toasted Natural Sesame Seeds
Tahini
WNP - Washed Natural Sesame Seeds

13072 Sesinco Foods
54 W 21st Street
New York, NY 10010-6908   212-243-1306
Fax: 212-243-2036
Supplier and exporter of closeout and excess inventory items including frozen and canned foods, beverages, dairy products, etc.; serving retail and food service markets
President: Serbajit Singh
VP: Ann Gaudet
Estimated Sales:$1600000
Number Employees: 7
Type of Packaging: Consumer, Food Service

13073 Sessions Company
P.O.Box 1310
Enterprise, AL 36331   334-393-0200
Fax: 334-393-0240
Manufacturer and exporter of peanut products including butter, meal, cake and refined oil
President: William Ventress
CEO: H Moultrie Sessions Jr
Plant Manager: Chet Faulkner
Estimated Sales:$70 Million
Number Employees: 100-249
Type of Packaging: Consumer, Food Service, Private Label, Bulk
Brands:
PAL
SCHOOL DAY

13074 Seth Ellis Chocolatier
5345 Arapahoe Ave
Suite 5
Boulder, CO 80303   720-470-3257
Fax: 720-565-2462   hey@sethellischocolatier.com
www.sethellischocolatier.com
chocolate
President/Owner: Frederick Levine
Number Employees: 5

13075 Sethness Products Company
P.O.Box 597963
Chicago, IL 60659-7963   847-329-2080
Fax: 847-329-2090   mail@sethness.com
www.sethness.com
Processor, exporter of burnt sugar syrups liquid and
powdered caramel colors
President: Henry Sethness
Estimated Sales:$10,500,000
Number Employees: 50-99
Type of Packaging: Food Service, Bulk

13076 Sethness Products Company
P.O.Box 597963
Chicago, IL 60659-7963   847-329-2080
Fax: 847-329-2090 888-772-1880
mail@sethness.com   www.sethness.com
Manufacturer and exporter of liquid and powdered
caramel colors
Chairman/CEO: Charles Sethness
President: Henry Sethness
Technical Director: Dave Tuescher
Operations Manager: Daniel Sethness
Estimated Sales:$20-50 Million
Number Employees: 50-99
Sq. footage: 95000
Type of Packaging: Food Service, Bulk
Brands:
SETHNESS

13077 Sethness-Greenleaf
1826 N Lorel Ave
Chicago, IL 60639-4376   773-889-1400
Fax: 773-889-0854 800-621-4549
info@sethness-greenleaf.com
www.sethness-greenleaf.com
Processor and exporter of flavorings and extracts
also emulsions
President: Patrick Kearney
National Sales Manager: Tom Schufreider
Operations Manager: John Smyth
Purchasing Agent: Ken Ciokowski
Estimated Sales:$ 20 - 50 Million
Number Employees: 40
Sq. footage: 56000
Type of Packaging: Consumer, Food Service, Bulk

13078 Setton International Foods
85 Austin Blvd
Commack, NY 11725-5701   631-543-8090
Fax: 631-543-8070 800-227-4397
info@settonfarms.com   www.settonfarms.com

Grower, importer, exporter, processor, roaster and
packer of nuts, seeds, dried fruits, candy and snack
foods, specialties include pistachios, cashews, almonds and apricots with an extensive product line,
also, kosher certified andorganic certified
Owner: Joshua Setton
CEO: Joshua Setton
CFO: Stewart Fellner
Vice President: Morris Setton
Quality Control: Harris Cohen
Sales Director: Joseph Setton
COO: Mia Cohen
Production Manager: Otto Hahs
Plant Manager: Joel Ginsberg
Estimated Sales:$ 10 - 20 Million
Number Employees: 20-49
Type of Packaging: Consumer, Food Service, Private Label, Bulk

13079 Setton Pistachio of Terra Bella
P.O.Box 11089
Terra Bella, CA 93270-1089   559-535-6050
Fax: 559-535-6089 800-227-4397
info@settonfarms.com   www.settonfarms.com
Processor and importer of pistachios, bakers' and
confectioners' supplies including carob products,
shredded coconut, dried fruits, crystallized ginger,
nuts, seeds, banana chips, yogurt and chocolate covered products, soy productsetc.
President: Joshua Setton
Executive Vice President: Morris Setton
VP/Sales & Marketing: Joseph Setton
Chief Operations Officer: Mia Cohen
Estimated Sales:$22300000
Number Employees: 100-249
Sq. footage: 50000
Parent Co: Setton International Foods
Type of Packaging: Consumer, Food Service, Bulk

13080 Seven Barrell Brewery
5 Airport Rd
West Lebanon, NH 03784-1658   603-298-5566
Fax: 603-298-5715 www.sevenbarrelbrewery.com
Processor of seasonal beer, ale, stout, lager and
pilsner
President: Nancy Noonan
Manager: Earl Locke
Number Employees: 20-49
Type of Packaging: Food Service
Brands:
Seven Barrell

13081 Seven Brothers Trading
731 N Beach Blvd
La Habra, CA 90631-3657   562-697-8888
Fax: 562-697-8288
General groceries
President: Han Ng
Estimated Sales:$ 2.5-5 Million
Number Employees: 5-9

13082 Seven Hills Coffee Company
11094 Deerfield Rd
Cincinnati, OH 45242-4112   513-489-5220
Fax: 513-489-6888
Coffee
Owner: Andy Timmerman
Director/CFO: Andy Timmerman
Operations Manager: Matthew Kasper
Estimated Sales:$ 2.5-5 Million
Number Employees: 5-9

13083 Seven Hills Winery
212 N 3rd Ave
Walla Walla, WA 99362-1883   509-529-7198
Fax: 509-529-7918 877-777-7870
info@sevenhillswinery.com
www.sevenhillswinery.com
Wines
Owner: Casey McCleann
Founder/Winemaker: Casey McClellan
*Estimated Sales:*Below $ 5 Million
Number Employees: 5-9
Brands:
Seven Hills

13084 Seven K Feather Farm
P.O.Box 485
Taylorsville, IN 47280-0485   812-526-2651
Fax: 812-526-2723
Wholesale/distributor of food
President: Charles Kleinhenz
*Estimated Sales:*Below $ 5 Million
Number Employees: 20-49

13085 Seven Keys Company of Florida
P.O.Box 729
Pompano Beach, FL 33061-0729   954-946-5010
                                      Fax: 954-946-5012
Processor and exporter of tropical jams, jellies, marmalades and coconut toast spreads
    President: Albert Gericke
Estimated Sales:$ 3 - 5 Million
Number Employees: 5-9
Sq. footage: 15000
Type of Packaging: Consumer, Food Service, Private Label
Brands:
    Lapham
    Seven Keys

13086 Seven Lakes Vineyards
1111 Tinsman Road
Fenton, MI 48430-1679   810-629-5686
Wines
    President: Chris Guest
Estimated Sales:$ 5-9.9 Million
Number Employees: 5

13087 Seven Seas Seafoods
901 S Fremont Avenue
Suite 168
Alhambra, CA 91803   626-570-9129
     Fax: 626-570-0079 chris@7seafood.com
                                   7seafood.com
Seafood
    President: Christopher Lin
    VP: Sean Lin
Estimated Sales:$ 5 - 10 Million
Number Employees: 5-9

13088 Seven Up/RC Bottling Company
P.O.Box 859
Paragould, AR 72451-0859   870-236-8765
                                   Fax: 870-236-3781
Processor of soft drinks
    Owner/President: Preston Bland
    Sales/Marketing Executive: John Bland
    Plant Manager: Joe Williams
    Purchasing Agent: Joe Williams
Estimated Sales:$ 20 - 50 Million
Number Employees: 100-249
Type of Packaging: Consumer, Food Service

13089 Severance Foods
3478 Main St
Hartford, CT 06120-1138   860-724-7063
    Fax: 860-527-2045 www.severancefoods.com
Processor of tortilla chips and tortillas including flour and corn
    President: Richard Stevens
Estimated Sales:$3350000
Number Employees: 20-49
Sq. footage: 28000
Type of Packaging: Consumer, Food Service, Private Label, Bulk
Brands:
    Pan De Oro

13090 Severn Peanut Company
P.O.Box 710
Severn, NC 27877-0710   252-585-0838
        Fax: 252-585-1718 800-642-4064
                   www.hamptonfarms.com
Processor, exporter, cleaner, sheller of raw peanuts, Cajun and jalapeno inshell peanuts, raw redskins, raw blanched, roasted snack peanuts, granules, peanut brittle, chocolate coated, peanut bars/squares, butter toffee
    President: Dallas Barnes
    Sales Manager: Rick McGee
    Sales: Carl Gray
Estimated Sales:$80100000
Number Employees: 50-99
Number of Products: 4
Parent Co: Meherrin Agricultural Chemical Company
Type of Packaging: Consumer, Bulk
Brands:
    Northampton
    Sepeco Seed

13091 Seville Olive Company
663 S Anderson St
Los Angeles, CA 90023-1197   323-261-2218
                                   Fax: 323-261-1026
Olives, onions, cherries and peppers
    President: Louis Pavlic Sr

Estimated Sales:$ 10-20 Million
Number Employees: 100-249

13092 Seviroli Foods
601 Brook St
Garden City, NY 11530-6431   516-222-6220
             Fax: 516-222-0534 www.seviroli.com
Italian foods
    President: Joseph Seviroli Sr
    COO: Joseph Seviroli Jr
    Quality Assurance Manager: Nel Reformina
Estimated Sales:$ 5-10 Million
Number Employees: 20-49

13093 Sewell's Fish Market
1178 Lee St
Rogersville, AL 35652-7816   256-247-1378
                                   Fax: 718-617-6851
Seafood
    Owner: Tana Springer
    Public Relations: Tana Springer
Estimated Sales:$ 1 - 3 Million
Number Employees: 1-4

13094 Seydel International
244 John B Brooks Rd
Pendergrass, GA 30567-4609   706-693-2295
        Fax: 706-693-2074 seycoinfo@seydel.com
                                   www.seydel.com
Processor, importer and exporter of starch, dextrin and protein
    President: Scott O Seydel
    Manufacturing Director: Mitch Mullinax
Estimated Sales:$43500000
Number Employees: 50-99
Parent Co: Seydel Company
Type of Packaging: Food Service, Bulk
Brands:
    Emdex
    Emflo
    Emgum
    Emjel
    Emox

13095 Seyfert Foods
1001 Paramount Road
Fort Wayne, IN 46808-1253   219-483-9521
        Fax: 219-484-1508 www.seyfert.com
Processor of salted snack foods; wholesaler/distributor serving the food service market, grocery and convenience stores
    President: Joe Bockerstette
    Senior VP: Cork Sterling
    Controller: Kevin Gould
    Operations Manager: Kevin Kensinger
Number Employees: 100-249
Type of Packaging: Consumer, Food Service

13096 Seymour & Sons Seafood
3201 Saint Charles St
Diberville, MS 39540-5315   228-392-4020
                                   Fax: 228-392-8028
Processor of seafood including frozen catfish and lobster
    President: Paul Seymour
    Plant Manager: David Seymour
Estimated Sales:$1200000
Number Employees: 5-9
Sq. footage: 5000

13097 Sfoglia Fine Pastas & Gourmet
PO Box 921
Freeland, WA 98249-0921   360-331-4080
Gourmet and specialty foods
    President: Stephanie Jushinski
*Estimated Sales:*Less than $500,000
Number Employees: 1-4

13098 Shade Foods
PO Box 6
New Century, KS 66031-0006   913-780-1212
        Fax: 913-780-1720 800-225-6312
                   pvd@shadefoods.com
                   www.kerryingredients.com

Processor liquid chocolate, hard candy, chocolate and yogurt chips, flakes, cereal particles, nuggets, pralines, granola, coated raisins, nuts and candy, etc
    CFO: Yves Gedert
    R&D: Andrew Nelson
    Vice President: Addison Bergfalk
    VP: Jim White
    VP: Bob Blefko
    VP Sales/Marketing: Bob Blefko
    Plant Manager: Miles Miller
    Purchasing Manager: Lynn Christian
Estimated Sales:$ 25 - 49.9 Million
Number Employees: 240
Sq. footage: 145000
Parent Co: Norfoods
Type of Packaging: Private Label, Bulk
Brands:
    Chewy Chunks
    No Boil Pasta
    Shade Icings & Fillings
    Wayfels

13099 Shady Grove Orchards
183 Shady Grove Road
Onalaska, WA 98570-9453   360-985-7033
             shadygrove@myhome.net
             www.chestnutsource.com
Organic American chestnuts and chestnut flour, dried chestnut kernels, seedlings, cookbook
    Co-Owner: Annie Bhagwandin
    Co-Owner: Omroa Bhagwandin
Brands:
    Shady Grove Orchards

13100 Shady Maple Farm
2700 Matheson Boulevard E
Suite 801, East Tower
Mississauga, ON L4W 4V9
Canada   905-206-1455
    Fax: 905-206-1477 info@shadymaple.ca.qc.ca
                   www.shadymaple.ca
Processor and exporter of pure maple syrup products
    President/CEO: Robert Swain
    CFO: Darren Brash
    Marketing Director: Marlene Jolicoeur
    Sales Director: Daniel Neale
Number Employees: 10-19
Sq. footage: 55000
Type of Packaging: Consumer, Food Service, Private Label, Bulk

13101 Shafer Lake Fruit
60643 Red Arrow Hwy
Hartford, MI 49057-9703   269-621-3194
                                   Fax: 269-621-4170
Packers of apples, peaches, plums and asparagus
    President: Dale Drake
Estimated Sales:$ 3 - 5 Million
Number Employees: 1-4
Type of Packaging: Consumer, Bulk

13102 Shafer Vineyards
6154 Silverado Trl
Napa, CA 94558-9748   707-944-2877
    Fax: 707-944-9454 info@shafervineyards.com
                   www.shafervineyards.com
Cabernet sauvignon, chardonnay, merlot, cabernet savignon, sangiovese
    Chairman: John Shafer
    President: Doug Shafer
    Winemaker: Elias Fernandez
Estimated Sales:$ 5-10 Million
Number Employees: 10-19
Brands:
    Firebreak
    Hillside
    Red Shoulder Ranch
    Shafer Vineyards

13103 Shafer-Haggart
21st Floor
Vancouver, BC B63 4E2
Canada   604-669-5512
        Fax: 604-669-9554 888-779-7111
                   info@shafer-haggart.com
                   www.shafer-haggart.com
Processor and importer of canned mushrooms, tomatoes, peaches, tuna and salmon; exporter of frozen poultry and canned corn and fish products
    President: Clive Lonsdale
    Sr. VP: Brian Dougall
Estimated Sales:$55000000
Number Employees: 22

Type of Packaging: Consumer, Food Service, Private Label

13104 Shah Trading Company
3451 McNicoll Avenue
Toronto, ON M1V 2V3   416-292-6927
Fax: 416-292-7932 www.shahtrading.com
rice, spices, beans, peas, and lentils, specialty flours and nuts and dried fruits.

13105 Shahi Food Corporation
2425 Lucknow Drive
Mississauga, ON L5S 1H1
Canada   905-677-4327
Fax: 905-671-2885
Manufacturer and exporter of Indian foods including jams, syrups, basmati rice, chutney and sauces
President: Pal Shah
Administrator/Finance Manager: Margaret Harmsworth
Sales Manager: Bill Dunton
Number Employees: 5-9
Sq. footage: 10000
Type of Packaging: Consumer, Food Service
Brands:
Indian Magic
Shahi

13106 Shaker Valley Foods
3304 W 67th Pl
Cleveland, OH 44102-5243   216-961-8600
Fax: 216-961-8077 cbeefking@yahoo.com
www.shakervalleyfoods.com
Meat processor and food distributor
President: Dean Comber
Estimated Sales: $ 20-50 Million
Number Employees: 20-49

13107 Shakespeare's
3840 W River Dr
Davenport, IA 52802-2412   563-383-0150
Fax: 563-383-0151 800-664-4114
www.shakechocolate.com
Specialty chocolates
Owner: Elisa Shakespeare
Estimated Sales: Less than $500,000
Number Employees: 20-49

13108 (HQ)Shaklee Corporation
4747 Willow Rd
Pleasanton, CA 94588-2740   925-924-2000
Fax: 925-924-2862 800-742-5533
www.shaklee.com
Manufacturer and exporter of nutritional supplements
Chairman/CEO: Roger Barnett
SVP Field Sales: John Earthy
Estimated Sales: $148 Million
Number Employees: 1,000-4,999
Parent Co: Ripplewood Holdings
Type of Packaging: Consumer
Other Locations:
Shaklee Corporation
Norman OK
Brands:
AIRSOURCE
PERFECT PITCHER
SHAKLEE CAROTOMAX
SHAKLEE FLAVOMAX

13109 Shallon Winery
1598 Duane St
Astoria, OR 97103-3707   503-325-5978
paul@shallon.com
www.shallon.com
Fine wines including whey wines and chocolate wines
President: Paul C Vanderveldt
Winemaker: Paul Van Der Veldt
Estimated Sales: Under $300,000
Number Employees: 1-4
Brands:
Shallon Winery

13110 Shallowford Farms
3732 Hartman Road
Yadkinville, NC 27055-5638   336-463-5938
Fax: 336-463-2358 800-892-9539
amanda@shallowfordfarms.com
www.shallowfordfarms.com
Manufacturer of popcorn
President: Amanda Booe
Plant Manager: Caswell Booe

Estimated Sales: $500,000-$1 Million
Number Employees: 10-19
Sq. footage: 21000
Type of Packaging: Consumer, Private Label, Bulk
Brands:
DENNIS
MR SNACK

13111 Shamrock Foods Company
2540 N 29th Ave
Phoenix, AZ 85009-1682   602-233-6400
Fax: 602-233-2791 800-289-3663
azinfo@shamrockfoods.com
www.shamrockfoods.com
Wholesaler/distributor of frozen foods, produce, dairy products, meats, groceries, baked goods and seafood; serving the food service market
President/COO: Kent McClelland
Chairman/CEO: Norman McClelland
SVP/CFO: F Phillips Giltner
VP Human Resources: Robert Beake
Estimated Sales: $1.4 Billion
Number Employees: 2600
Brands:
ASPEN GOLD
BOUNTIFUL HARVEST
BRICKFIRE BAKERY
CHEF MARK
COBBLESTONE MARKET
CULINARY SECRETS
EMERALD VALLEY RANCH
HIDDEN BAY
KATY'S KITCHEN
MARKON FIRST CROP
PIERPORT
PRAIRIE CREEK
PROPAK
READY-SET-SERVE
REJUV
RIDGELINE
SAN PABLO
SHAMROCK FARMS
SILVERBROOK
SMART SOURCE
SOUTHERN PEARL
THE "EVER" FAMILY OF BRANDS
TRESCERRO
TRIFOGLIO
VILLA FRIZZONI
WINDSCAPES
XTREME

13112 Shamrock Slaughter Plant
6400 Us Highway 83
Shamrock, TX 79079-4408   806-256-3241
Processor of meat products
Owner: Larry Cook
Estimated Sales: $500,000-$1 Million
Number Employees: 1-4
Type of Packaging: Consumer

13113 Shane Candy Company
110 Market St
Philadelphia, PA 19106-3066   215-922-1048
Fax: 215-940-0003 www.shanecandies.com
Processor of candy including chocolate, holiday and hard
Owner: Barry Shane
Estimated Sales: $ 5 - 10 Million
Number Employees: 10-19
Sq. footage: 7200
Type of Packaging: Consumer

13114 Shaner's Family Restaurant
193 Main St
South Paris, ME 04281-1697   207-743-6367
Ice cream, frozen desserts
President: John Shaner
Estimated Sales: $ 1-2.5 Million
Number Employees: 20-49

13115 Shanghai Company
2800 SE Division St
Portland, OR 97202-1350   503-235-2527
Fax: 503-235-3842
Processor of canned Chinese noodles
President: Chester Louie Jr
Vice President: David Louie
Estimated Sales: $1100000
Number Employees: 20-49
Type of Packaging: Consumer

13116 Shanks Extracts
350 Richardson Dr
Lancaster, PA 17603-4034   717-393-4441
Fax: 717-393-3148 800-346-3135
jstoner@shanks.com www.shanks.com
Manufacturer, importer and exporter of Spanish saffron, syrups and flavoring extracts including pure vanilla, lemon and almond; contract packaging services available
President: Jeffrey Lehman
Sales Manager: Charley Beck
Operations: Sallie Rhineer
Human Resources: Lydia Zimmerman
Estimated Sales: $ 20 - 50 Million
Number Employees: 50-99
Sq. footage: 90000
Type of Packaging: Consumer, Food Service, Private Label, Bulk
Brands:
Gold Medal
Taste-T

13117 Shapiro Packing Company
1301 New Savannah Rd
Augusta, GA 30901-3843   706-724-6401
Fax: 706-722-2259
Manufacturer and packer of beef and seafood
President: Hebert Shapiro
Estimated Sales: $375,000
Number Employees: 250-499
Type of Packaging: Consumer, Food Service, Private Label, Bulk

13118 Shari Candies
5780 Lincoln Drive
Suite 123-124
Edina, MN 55436-1640   612-935-8953
Fax: 612-935-5170 800-658-7059
info@candyasap.com www.sharicandies.com
Candy and also candy for holidays.
President: Arlen Kitsis
VP: Steve Kitsis
National Sales Manager: Wally Schilf
Type of Packaging: Consumer

13119 Shariann's Organics
734 Franklin Avenue
444
Garden City, NY 11530-4525   800-434-4246
800-434-4246
consumeraffairs@hain-celestial.com
www.shariannsorganic.com
Organic food products
President: Ann Sidchair
VP Marketing: Robert Hunt
Estimated Sales: $ 1-2.5 Million
Number Employees: '1-4
Brands:
Shariann's Italian White Beans
Shariann's Refried P
Shariann's Spicy Veg

13120 Sharkco Seafood International
707 Jump Basin Rd
Venice, LA 70091-4351   504-534-9577
Fax: 504-534-2217
Seafood
President: Khai Nguyen
Estimated Sales: $ 5 - 10 Million
Number Employees: 10-19

13121 Sharon Mill Winery
5701 Sharon Hollow Rd
Manchester, MI 48158   734-971-6337
Fax: 734-971-6386 www.ewashtenaw.org
Wines
Director: Robert Tetens
Estimated Sales: $ 1-2.5 Million
Number Employees: 20-49

13122 Sharp Rock Vineyards
5 Sharp Rock Rd
Sperryville, VA 22740-2333   540-987-9700
Fax: 540-987-9031
jeast@sharprockvineyards.com
www.sharprock.com
Wines
Estimated Sales: $ 1 - 3 Million
Number Employees: 1-4

13123 Shashy's Fine Foods
1700 Mulberry St
Montgomery, AL 36106-1524   334-263-7341
Fax: 334-263-7343

Processor of baked goods
  Co-Owner: Paul Shashy
  Co-Owner: Jimmy Shashy
Estimated Sales:$500,000-$1 Million
Number Employees: 20-49
Type of Packaging: Consumer

13124 Shasta Beverages
9901 Widmer Rd
Shawnee Mission, KS 66215-1282   913-888-6777
          Fax: 913-888-5732 www.shastapop.com
Processor of flavored soft drinks including grape, cola, root beer, orange, kiwi/strawberry, black cherry, etc
  President: Rick Reynolds
  Controller: Charles Reisig
  General Manager: Mike Perez
  Plant Manager: Rick Reynolds
Estimated Sales:$ 20 - 50 Million
Number Employees: 50-99
Parent Co: National Beverage Company
Type of Packaging: Consumer, Food Service, Private Label
Brands:
  Shasta

13125 Shaver Foods
PO Box 1095
Springdale, AR 72765-1095   501-751-7767
                    Fax: 501-751-3578
  President: Tim Owen
  Secretary/Treasurer: Robert Collins

13126 Shaw Baking Company
240 S Algoma Street
Thunder Bay, ON P7B 3C2
Canada   807-345-7327
       Fax: 807-345-7895 http://www.tbaytel.net
Processor of rolls, doughnuts, muffins, Danish pastries and bread including white and whole wheat
  President/General Manager: G Shaw
  Sales Manager: Joe Spina
Number Employees: 100-249
Type of Packaging: Consumer, Food Service
Brands:
  Country Hearth
  Holsum
  Shaw

13127 Shaw's Southern Belle Frozen
P.O.Box 28620
Jacksonville, FL 32226-8620   904-765-4487
  Fax: 904-768-3663 www.shawsouthernbelle.com
Stuffed flounder and deviled crab
  President: Howard Shaw
  Controller: Joanna Zimmerman
  Plant Manager: Robert Wynne
Estimated Sales:$ 10-20 Million
Number Employees: 50-99

13128 Shawmut Fishing Company
PO Box 1986
Anchorage, AK 99508   709-334-2559
                    Fax: 709-596-7189
Processor of frozen crabs
  President: William Berry
  VP: Thomas Caines
Type of Packaging: Consumer, Food Service, Bulk

13129 (HQ)Shawnee Canning Company
P.O.Box 657
Cross Junction, VA 22625-0657   540-888-3429
       Fax: 540-888-7963   800-713-1414
            sales@shawneesprings.com
            www.shawneesprings.com
Manufacturer of apple sauces, apples, peaches, ciders, preserves and jams, fruit butters, apple syrup, apple mixes, honey, pickles, salsa, dressings, relishes and fresh baked pies
  President: William Whitacre
  GM: Lisa Whitacre Johnson
Estimated Sales:$3 Million
Number Employees: 20-49
Sq. footage: 9750
Type of Packaging: Consumer, Private Label
Brands:
  Shawnee Springs

13130 (HQ)Shawnee Milling Company
P.O.Box 1567
Shawnee, OK 74802-1567   405-273-7000
  Fax: 405-273-7333 bford@shawneemilling.com
            www.shawneemilling.com

Manufacturer of flour, cornmeal, complete mixes, custom mixes
  President: William Ford
  VP: Bert Humphreys
  SVP: Sam Garlow
Estimated Sales:$100+ Million
Number Employees: 100-249
Type of Packaging: Consumer, Food Service, Private Label, Bulk
Brands:
  SHAWNEE BEST
  SHAWNEE MILLS

13131 Shearer's Foods
692 Wabash Ave N
Brewster, OH 44613-1020   330-767-5000
       Fax: 330-767-3393   800-428-6843
       info@shearers.com   www.shearers.com
Processor of regular, rippled, flavored and kettle-cooked potato chips
  President: Robert J Shearer
  VP Administration: Patrick McMahon
  VP Purchasing: Jim Allan
  VP: Thomas Shearer
  Sales Director: Coleman Caldwell
  Public Relations: Melissa Shearer
  VP Manufacturing: Steve Surmay
  Plant Manager: Matt Kutschbach
  Purchasing Manager: Jim Allen
Estimated Sales:$ 10 - 20 Million
Number Employees: 250-499
Sq. footage: 75000
Type of Packaging: Consumer, Food Service, Private Label, Bulk
Brands:
  Grandma Shearer's
  Grandma Shearer's Snacks

13132 SheerBliss Ice Cream
2627 Ives Dairy Rd
Suite 100
Aventura, FL 33180   305-692-5800
  Fax: 305-692-8700 info@sheerblissicecream.com
            www.sheerblissicecream.com
ice cream, ice cream bars and ice crea, bites

13133 Shef Products
1518 Scotland Ln
Las Vegas, NV 89102-4814   702-873-2275
                    Fax: 702-873-9375
Processor and wholesaler/distributor of gourmet Italian desserts including ices, gelato, sorbetto, frozen yogurt, ice cream, tartufo, tortoni, biscotti and tiramisu; importer of sorbetto, gelato-frozen yogurt and flavorings; servingthe food service marke
  VP: Chris Philips
  VP Operations: Douglas Guido
Estimated Sales:$ 3 - 5 Million
Number Employees: 1-4
Sq. footage: 5000
Type of Packaging: Consumer, Food Service, Private Label, Bulk

13134 Sheila's Select GourmetRecipe
325 W 600 S
Heber City, UT 84032-2230   435-654-6415
   Fax: 435-654-5449   800-516-7286
       jen@bearcreekfoods.com
       www.bearcreekfoods.com
Soups(bagged and canned), culinary bases, freezies, and salsas.
  President: Kevin Ruda
  CFO: Al Leewen
  Marketing Director: Jeff Hanson
Brands:
  Bear Creek Country Kitchens
  Sheila's Select Gourmet Recipes

13135 Sheinman Provision Company
4192 Viola St
Philadelphia, PA 19104-1093   215-473-7065
                    Fax: 215-473-7038
Processor of sausage, bologna and corned and roast beef
  President: Stan Rultenberg
  Vice President: Richard Sheinman
Estimated Sales:$ 5 - 10 Million
Number Employees: 10-19
Type of Packaging: Consumer, Food Service, Private Label, Bulk
Brands:
  PHILLY MAID
  SHEINMAN

13136 Shekou Chemicals
24 Crescent Street
Waltham, MA 02453-4358   781-893-6878
                    Fax: 781-893-6881
       kimsonchemical@earthlink.net
       www.kimsonchemical.com
Processor, importer and exporter of ingredients including citric acid, ascorbic acid, sodium benzoate, sodium propionate, calcium propionate, ammonium bicarbonate, sodium erythrobate, sodium citrate, potassium citrate and potassiumsorbate
  System Staff: Herb Kimiatek
  Sales/Marketing Executive: Judith Roiva
  Purchasing Manager: Simon Altstein
Estimated Sales:$1100000
Number Employees: 7
Sq. footage: 10000
Type of Packaging: Bulk

13137 Shelburne Farms
1611 Harbor Rd
Shelburne, VT 05482-7671   802-985-8686
                    Fax: 802-985-8123
       lwellings@shelburnefarms.org
       www.shelburnefarms.org
Cheddar cheese
  President: Alexander Webb
  Marketing Manager: Tom Pierce
  Controller: Fred Blythe
Estimated Sales:$ 5-10 Million
Number Employees: 50-99
Brands:
  Vermont

13138 Shell Ridge Jalapeno Project
1432 Highway 35 S
Rockport, TX 78382-3918   512-790-8028
Ethnic foods
  President: Kay Segura Christian
Estimated Sales:$500,000 appx.
Number Employees: 1-4
Brands:
  Kay's Hot Stuff

13139 Shelley's Prime Meats
700 Bergen Avenue
Jersey City, NJ 07306-4890   201-433-3434
                    Fax: 201-433-4549
Processor of provisions/meats including fresh and frozen beef, veal, lamb, pork and poultry
  President: Shelley Geller
  General Manager: Chuck Brennan
Estimated Sales:$11300000
Number Employees: 40
Sq. footage: 10000
Type of Packaging: Food Service

13140 Shelton's Poultry
204 Loranne Ave
Pomona, CA 91767-5731   909-623-4361
   Fax: 909-623-0634   800-541-1833
  trukbaron@sheltons.com   www.sheltons.com
Processor of free range poultry products; also, soups, chili, jerky, sausage, uncured frankfurters, meat balls, etc
  President: Gary Flanagan
Estimated Sales:$ 20 - 50 Million
Number Employees: 20-49
Type of Packaging: Consumer
Brands:
  Shelton's

13141 Shemper Seafood Company
367 Bayview Ave
Biloxi, MS 39530-2502   228-435-2703
                    Fax: 228-432-2104
Seafood, seafood products
  President: Gary Shemper
  CEO: Jeffrey Shemper
Estimated Sales:$600,000
Number Employees: 1-4
Brands:
  Shemper Seafood

13142 Shenandoah Mills
P.O.Box 369
Lebanon, TN 37088-0369   615-444-0841
  Fax: 615-444-0286 donya@shenandoahmills.com
            www.shenandoahmills.com

Processor of dry mixes including biscuit, pancake, corndog, apple fritters, corn meal, corn bread, gravy and hushpuppies; also, breadings including fish, chicken, pork, beef, etc
President: Dale Nunnery
VP: Danny Hodges
Plant Manager: Ike Ladd
Director Sales: George Stonesifer
Public Relations: Linda Carmen
Estimated Sales: $ 5-10 Million
Number Employees: 20-49
Sq. footage: 65000
Type of Packaging: Food Service
Brands:
Shenandoah

13143 Shenandoah Vineyards
12300 Steiner Rd
Plymouth, CA 95669-9503   209-245-4455
    Fax: 209-245-5156   info@sobowine.com
    www.sobonwine.com
Wines
President: Leon Sobon
CEO: Shirley Sobon
Estimated Sales: Below $ 5 Million
Number Employees: 10-19

13144 Shenandoah's Pride
5325 Port Royal Rd
Springfield, VA 22151-2159   703-321-9500
    Fax: 703-321-0573
Milk, dairy products
Manager: Craig Wilson
Plant Manager: Richard Becker
Estimated Sales: $ 30-50 Million
Number Employees: 100-249
Parent Co: Suiza Dairy Group

13145 Shenk's Foods
1980 New Danville Pike
Lancaster, PA 17603-9615   717-393-4240
Fax: 717-393-4240   customerservice@shenks.com
    www.shenks.com
Manufacturer of cheese, butter spreads, jellies, mustards, preserves, relishes and fruit spreads
President: Karl Achtermann
Estimated Sales: $2 Million
Number Employees: 1-4
Sq. footage: 9000
Type of Packaging: Consumer, Private Label
Brands:
Shenk's

13146 (HQ)Shepherd Farms
RR 1
South Beloit, IL 61080-9801   815-389-2997
    Fax: 815-389-1997   800-383-2676
    gshep@seedfarm.com   www.seedfarm.com
Processor and packer of popcorn including yellow, white and specialty hybrids packaged for microwave, air poppers and commercial poppers; also, soybeans and tofu; exporter of soybeans for tofu, miso, natto and shoyu, seed corn and seedsoybeans
Owner: Gene Shepherd
Estimated Sales: $2 Million
Number Employees: 10-19
Sq. footage: 20000
Type of Packaging: Consumer, Food Service, Private Label, Bulk
Other Locations:
Shepherd Farms
Beloit IL
Brands:
Boone County Supreme
Shepherd
Shepherd Supreme

13147 Shepherdsfield Bakery
777 Shepherdsfield Rd
Fulton, MO 65251-5974   573-642-1439
    Fax: 573-642-1439
Processor of frozen gourmet waffles, muffins, breads and whole wheat pancake mixes, pies, cookies and flour
Religious Leader: Thomas Mahaney
CEO: Vicki Staudenmyer
Estimated Sales: $$1-2.5 Million
Number Employees: 20-49
Sq. footage: 40000
Type of Packaging: Consumer, Private Label

13148 Sherm Edwards Candies
509 Cavitt Ave
Trafford, PA 15085-1060   412-372-4331
    Fax: 412-373-8089   800-436-5424
    www.shermedwardscandies.com
Processor of chocolate-covered candy
President: David Golembeski
Estimated Sales: $724000
Number Employees: 20-49
Type of Packaging: Consumer, Bulk

13149 Sherrill Orchards
3265 Valpredo Road
Arvin, CA 93203-9202   661-858-2035
    Fax: 661-858-2035   soprus@aorldnet.att.com
Processor of pomegranate juice, vinegar, apple cider and blends
President: Donna Sherril
Estimated Sales: $340,000
Number Employees: 5
Brands:
Sherrill

13150 Sherwood Brands
1803 Research Blvd # 201
Rockville, MD 20850-6106   301-309-6161
    Fax: 301-309-6162   sales@sherwoodbrands.com
    www.sherwoodbrands.com
Processor and exporter of confectionery products including hard candies, jelly beans, cookies, chocolates, toffee, lollypops and holiday novelties; also, packaged in bags and for fund raising; importer of food containers
President/Chairman/CEO: Uziel Frydman
CFO/Secretary: Christopher Willi
EVP Marketing/Product Develpment: Amir Frydman
Estimated Sales: $45,900,000
Number Employees: 50-99
Sq. footage: 500000
Parent Co: Sherwood Brands
Type of Packaging: Consumer, Private Label
Brands:
Candy Kaleidoscope
Cap'n Poptoy
Cherry & Berry Blast
Creative Gourmet
Tweety
Tweety Pops
Wan-Na-Bes

13151 (HQ)Sherwood Brands
1803 Research Blvd # 201
Rockville, MD 20850-6106   301-309-6161
    Fax: 301-309-6162   orders@sherwoodbrands.com
    www.sherwoodbrands.com
Cookies and candy
Chairman of the Board: Uziel Frydman
Executive VP: Amir Frydman
Estimated Sales: $ 30-50 Million
Number Employees: 50-99
Brands:
Cows Butter Toffee Candies
Demitasse Biscuits
Elana Chocolate
Kastin's Old Fashioned Candies
Ruger Wafers & Cookies
Tongue Tattoo Lollipops
Zed Gum

13152 Sheryl's Chocolate Creations
11 Commercial St
Hicksville, NY 11801-5211   516-681-4060
    Fax: 516-681-4189   888-882-2462
    www.sherylschocolate.com
Hand-dipped chocolate chips, pretzel rods, pretzel twists, sourdough pretzels, mini pretzels, popcorn and assorted cookies
President: Sheryl Simon
Purchasing Manager: Ron Simon
Estimated Sales: $ 1-2.5 Million
Number Employees: 10-19
Sq. footage: 4000
Type of Packaging: Consumer, Private Label, Bulk

13153 Shields Date Gardens
80225 Us Highway 111
Indio, CA 92201-6599   760-347-0996
    Fax: 760-342-3288   800-414-2555
    shieldate@aol.com   www.shieldsdategarden.com
Processor of nuts, dates and fruits including citrus and dried; also, mail order available
Owner: Greg Raumin

Estimated Sales: $ 5 - 10 Million
Number Employees: 20-49
Type of Packaging: Consumer
Brands:
Date Crystals

13154 Shiloh Foods
P.O.Box 1000
Savannah, TN 38372-1000   731-925-1155
    Fax: 731-925-1855   800-795-2550
    sales@shilohfoodsinc.com
    www.savannahclassics.com
Processor of frozen hush puppies, corn bread dressing, vegetable casseroles, gravy and cranberry sauce; packer of dry blends
Owner: John H Bryan Iii
Vice President: J Flatt
Sales Service Director: Larry Moore
Logistics: Gary Austin
Production Manager: Lynn Austin
Purchasing Manager: J Flatt
Estimated Sales: $5600000
Number Employees: 50-99
Sq. footage: 100000
Type of Packaging: Consumer, Food Service, Private Label
Brands:
Neokura
San Like
San Orange
San Red
San Yellow
San-Ei

13155 Shine Companies
4014 Evening Trail Drive
Spring, TX 77388-4936   281-353-8392
    Fax: 281-353-8937   shinecom@aol.com
Processor and exporter of specialty seasonings, artichoke dips and toppings and marinades, salsas and condiments; importer of chile purees
President: Michael Shine
Executive VP: Janet Williams
Number Employees: 6
Sq. footage: 2500
Brands:
Jazzie J
Semdiero

13156 Shine Food
21100 S Western Avenue
Torrance, CA 90501-1700   310-533-6010
    Fax: 310-328-2608   info@shinefood.com
    www.shinefood.com
Processor of dim sum, pot stickers, dumplings, gyoza, shumai and spring rolls
President: Stephen Y Lee
VP: John Freschi
Marketing Manager: Tracy Lee
Estimated Sales: $300,000-500,000
Number Employees: 1-4
Type of Packaging: Private Label, Bulk

13157 Shining Ocean
1515 Puyallup St
Sumner, WA 98390-2234   253-826-3700
    Fax: 206-283-7079   email@kanimi.com
    www.kanimi.com
Processor of frozen surimi and fried seafood
President: Michael Faris
CFO: Howard Frisk
Vice President: C Woods
R & D: Tim Taylor
Quality Control: Raymond McReaey
Production Manager: K Ishiyama
Plant Manager: M Fisher
Estimated Sales: $ 30-50 Million
Number Employees: 100-249
Type of Packaging: Consumer, Food Service, Private Label
Brands:
Emerald Sea
Heathy 1
Kanimi-Tem
Pacific Choice
Sea Farer
Shining Choice

13158 Shionogi Qualicaps
6505 Franz Warner Pkwy
Whitsett, NC 27377-9215   336-449-7300
    Fax: 336-449-3333   800-227-7853
    info@qiallicaps.com   www.qualicaps.com

Processor and exporter of hard gelatin capsules
President: Greg Bowers
Sales: Matt Schappert
CFO: Dennis Stella
CEO: Herb Hugill
Quality Control: Schuck Waldroup
Estimated Sales: $ 5-10 Million
Number Employees: 100-249
Parent Co: Shionogi
Type of Packaging: Bulk

13159 Shipley Baking Company
P.O.Box 10072
Fort Smith, AR 72917-0072   479-452-1933
                          Fax: 479-452-1939
Manufacturer of bread and buns.
President: Frank Shipley
Estimated Sales: $168 Million
Number Employees: 1-4
Type of Packaging: Consumer, Food Service
Brands:
    COUNTRY HEARTH
    HOLSUM
    LESS

13160 Shipmaster USA
8711 E Pinnacle Peak Road
Suite 254
Scottsdale, AZ 85255-3517   480-585-0109
                          Fax: 482-585-0082

13161 Shipyard Brewing Company
86 Newbury St
Portland, ME 04101-4274   207-761-0807
         Fax: 207-775-5567 www.shipyard.com
Processor and exporter of beer, ale and stout
Owner: Fred Forsley
Director Manufacturing: Paul Henry
Estimated Sales: Under $500,000
Number Employees: 20-49
Type of Packaging: Consumer, Food Service
Brands:
    Blue Fin
    Chamberlain
    Goat Island Light
    Longfellow Winter
    Old Thumper Extra Special
    Prelude Christmas

13162 Shirer Brothers Slaughter House
7805 Adamsville Otsego Rd
Adamsville, OH 43802-9732   740-796-3214
Beef, beef products
President: Ronald Shirer
Estimated Sales: $ 1-2.5 Million
Number Employees: 1-4

13163 Shirley Foods
505 Walnut Street
PO Box 457
Shirley, IN 47384-0457   765-738-6511
         Fax: 765-738-6881   800-560-2908
                  www.shirleyfoods.com
Flour and corn tortillas
President: Gary Toth
Estimated Sales: $ 2.5-5 Million
Number Employees: 9
Brands:
    Shirley Foods

13164 Shoei Foods USA
1900 Feather River Blvd
Olivehurst, CA 95961-9627   530-742-7866
         Fax: 530-742-2873   800-527-4712
                  mikem@shoeiusa.com
Grower, packer and seller of prunes
President: Ron Sandage
CFO: Masami Hoki
Vice President: Dick Onyett
Marketing/Sales: Mike Manassero
Plant Manager: Taka Sackamoto
Estimated Sales: $ 50-100 Million
Number Employees: 100-249
Number of Brands: 2
Number of Products: 5
Sq. footage: 30000
Type of Packaging: Consumer, Food Service, Private Label, Bulk

13165 Shoemaker's Candies
PO Box 3345
Santa Fe Springs, CA 90670-1345   562-944-8811
                          Fax: 562-944-1308
                  info@shoemakers-candies.com
                  www.shoemakers-candies.com
Processor of confectionery products including peanut brittle, chocolate nut fudge, chocolate clusters, turtles, etc
President: Mark Shoemaker
VP: Mark Shoemaker
Number Employees: 25
Type of Packaging: Consumer

13166 Shofar Kosher Foods
2365 E Linden Ave
Linden, NJ 07036-1142   908-925-6000
         Fax: 908-925-5331   888-874-6327
                  www.bests-kosher.com
Manufacturer of kosher meats including hot dogs, salami, bologna, corned beef, pastrami, brisket, roast beef and veal
Manager/Sales: Lenny Posnock
Estimated Sales: $3-5 Million
Number Employees: 10-19
Sq. footage: 22000
Type of Packaging: Consumer, Food Service, Bulk
Brands:
    Shofar

13167 Shonan USA
P.O.Box 128
Grandview, WA 98930-0128   509-882-5583
         Fax: 509-882-5890   s.shas@televar.com
Processor of refrigerated fruit juice concentrates including apple, cherry, grape, pear, carrot, strawberry and red raspberry
President: Akira Nozaka
Plant Manager: Robert Briiks
Estimated Sales: $ 5-10 Million
Number Employees: 50-99
Type of Packaging: Bulk
Brands:
    Shonan

13168 Shonfeld's
57 Romanelli Avenue
South Hackensack, NJ 07606-1427   201-883-0100
         Fax: 201-883-0017   800-462-3464
         sales@shonfelds.com   www.shonfelds.com
Gourmet pasta, spices, candies, preserves and honey, oils and vinegar
Founder: Boaz Shonfeld
Estimated Sales: $ 10-20 Million
Number Employees: 250-499
Brands:
    Shonfield's

13169 Shonna's Gourmet Goodies
320 W Center Street
West Bridgewater, MA 02379-1626   508-580-2033
         Fax: 508-580-2044   888-312-7868
Processor of frozen hors d'oeuvres
Owner/President: Howard Sherman
Estimated Sales: Less than $500,000
Sq. footage: 3000
Type of Packaging: Private Label

13170 Shooting Star Farms
P.O.Box 3007
Bartlesville, OK 74006-3007   918-331-0599
         Fax: 888-450-4004   888-850-8540
         imcdonaldA@shootingstarfarms.com
                  www.shootingstarfarms.com
Delightful dips, gift boxes, gracious gourmet salsas, jazzy jellies, marvelous munchies, traditionally tasty salsas.
President: Larry Mc Donald
Estimated Sales: $300,000-500,000
Number Employees: 1-4
Type of Packaging: Consumer

13171 Shore Seafood
P.O.Box 10
Saxis, VA 23427-0010   757-824-5517
         Fax: 757-824-5662   shoresfd@shore.intercom.net
                  www.shoreseafood.com
Seafood
President: Greg Linton
Vice President: Andy Drewer
Estimated Sales: $ 5-10 Million
Number Employees: 20-49
Type of Packaging: Private Label

Brands:
    Chesapeake Bay Delight

13172 Shore Trading Company
665 Union Hill Rd
Alpharetta, GA 30004-5652   770-998-0566
                          Fax: 770-998-0571
Seafood
Owner: Marty Klausner
Estimated Sales: $1 Million
Number Employees: 1-4

13173 Shoreline Chocolates
212 W Shore Rd
Alburg, VT 05440-9780   802-796-3730
         Fax: 802-796-4725   800-310-3730
                  info@lakesendcheeses.com
                  www.lakesendcheeses.com
Produces assorted homemade chocolates.
Operator: Joanne James
Operator: Alton James
Estimated Sales: $300,000-500,000
Number Employees: 1-4

13174 Shoreline Fruit
10850 E Traverse Highway
Suite 4460
Traverse City, MI 49684   585-765-2639
         Fax: 585-765-9443   800-836-3972
                  www.shorelinefruit.com
Grower, processor and marketers of dried fruits and cherry products
CEO: Ken Swanson
CFO: Jason Warren
Marketing Director: Tom Berg
Number Employees: 180

13175 Shreve Meats Processing
200 E McConkey St
Shreve, OH 44676   330-567-2142
Processor of beef and pork
Co-Owner: Ray Haas
Co-Owner: Tim Morris
Estimated Sales: $140000
Number Employees: 5-9

13176 Shreveport Macaroni Company
104 N Common St
Shreveport, LA 71101-2614   318-222-6857
                          Fax: 318-221-7815
Processor of pasta including spaghetti
Plant Manager: Monty Phares
Estimated Sales: $ 20 - 50 Million
Number Employees: 20-49
Parent Co: Arrowhead
Type of Packaging: Consumer, Food Service, Private Label
Brands:
    De Boles

13177 Shrimp World
1020 Hancock Street
Gretna, LA 70053-2321   504-368-1571
                          Fax: 504-368-1573
Shrimp
President: William Chauvin

13178 Shuckman's Fish & Co. Smokery
3001 W Main St
Louisville, KY 40212-1800   502-775-6478
         Fax: 502-775-6470 www.kysmokedfish.com
Smokers of fish & seafood products.
President: Lewis Shuckman
Estimated Sales: $ 3 - 5 Million
Number Employees: 10-19

13179 Shuffs Meat Company
12247 Baugher Rd
Thurmont, MD 21788-2333   301-271-2231
                          Fax: 301-271-1037
Manufacturer of meat products
Owner: Robin Shuff
Estimated Sales: $18 Million
Number Employees: 5-9

13180 Shultz Company
555 Carlisle St
Hanover, PA 17331-2162   717-633-4585
         Fax: 717-637-0487   sales@shultzfoods.com
                  www.shultzfood.com
Pretzels
Owner: Jack Shultz
National Sales Manager: Mark Tralongo
Plant Manager: Joe Semmelman

Estimated Sales: $ 10-20 Million
Number Employees: 1-4
Sq. footage: 135000
Type of Packaging: Consumer, Private Label, Bulk
Brands:
Jake Baked
Pretzel Factory
Salty Stix
Schultz
Shults Pretzels
Zels

13181 Shur-Good Biscuit Co.
11677 Chesterdale Rd
Cincinnati, OH 45246-3917   513-458-6200
Fax: 513-458-6212
Cookies
Manager: Jerry Wallman
CFO: Nicola Melillo
Marketing Director: William Klump
Sales Director: Mark O'Toole
Public Relations: Kathy Coggeshall
Operations Manager: Peter Lowes
Estimated Sales: $ 5 - 10 Million
Number Employees: 100-249
Parent Co: Parmalat Bakery Group North America
Type of Packaging: Consumer

13182 Sidari's Italian Foods
3820 Lakeside Ave E
Cleveland, OH 44114-3891   216-431-3344
Fax: 216-431-6227   siditalian@aol.com
Italian frozen foods
President: Joe Sidari
Estimated Sales: $ 50-100 Million
Number Employees: 50-99

13183 Side Hill Farm
74 Cotton Mill Hl
Brattleboro, VT 05301-7701   802-254-2018
Fax: 802-254-3381
Manfacturer of jams
Owner: Kelt Naylor
Estimated Sales: $ 1 - 3 Million
Number Employees: 1-4
Number of Products: 14

13184 Sieco USA Corporation
9014 Ruland Road
PO Box 55485
Houston, TX 77055-4612   713-464-1726
Fax: 713-464-3323   800-325-9443
amber@sieco-usa.com   www.sieco-usa.com
Processor, importer and exporter of extra virgin and
infused olive oil, and organic olive oil, stuffed olives
and balsamic wine vinegar and white wine vinegar;
processor of sauces; gift packs available.
President: Sherif Cheman
Marketing: Diann Fischer
Number Employees: 3
Number of Brands: 2
Number of Products: 11
Sq. footage: 8600
Type of Packaging: Consumer, Food Service, Private Label, Bulk
Brands:
Amber
Sammy's

13185 Siegel Egg Company
273 Albany Street
Cambridge, MA 02139-4230   617-873-0800
Fax: 617-873-0824   800-593-3447
Manufacturer of fresh and frozen eggs
President: Ken Siegel
Estimated Sales: $102 Million
Number Employees: 59
Type of Packaging: Consumer

13186 (HQ)Siemer Milling Company
P.O.Box 670
Teutopolis, IL 62467-0670   217-857-3131
Fax: 217-857-3092   800-826-1065
siemer@siemermilling.com
www.siemermilling.com
Processor of flour and pasta
President: Rick Siemer
R&D/Technical Sales: Kevin Bodily
VP Quality: Allen Westendorf
VP Production: Vernon Tegeler
Purchasing: Sue Woltman
Estimated Sales: $ 50 - 100 Million
Number Employees: 100-249
Type of Packaging: Consumer, Food Service, Bulk

Brands:
Don's Chuck Wagon
Hodgson Mill
Kentucky Kernel

13187 Siena Foods
16 Newbridge Road
Toronto, ON M8Z 2L7
Canada   416-239-3967
Fax: 416-239-2084   800-465-0422
Processor, importer and exporter of Italian style
meat including Genoa salami, mortadella, cappicola,
prosciutto and hot and mild sausage
General Manager: Enzo DeLuca
Number Employees: 50-99
Type of Packaging: Consumer, Food Service

13188 Sierra Cheese Manufacturing Company
916 S Santa Fe Avenue
Compton, CA 90221-4392   310-635-1216
Fax: 310-639-1096   800-266-4270
sierracheese@aol.com
Processor of Italian cheese including mozzarella,
ricotta, string, tuma, scamorze, requeson, feta, etc
President: John Curran
Vice President: Charlene Franco
Sales Director: Carlos Rivera
General Manager: Charlene Franco
Purchasing Manager: Vince Inga
Number Employees: 20-49
Sq. footage: 15000
Type of Packaging: Consumer, Private Label, Bulk
Brands:
Montebello
Sierra

13189 Sierra Madre Organic Coffee
191 University Blvd
Denver, CO 80206-4613   303-446-0050
Fax: 303-393-8208
organic@sierramadrecoffee.com
www.sierramadrecoffee.com
Organic coffee
President: Mena Moran

13190 Sierra Nevada Brewing Company
1075 E 20th St
Chico, CA 95928-6722   530-345-2739
Fax: 530-893-9358   info@sierranevada.com
www.sierranevada.com
Processor of seasonal beer, ale, stout, lager and
pilsner
Manager: Bob Littell
VP: Steve Harrison
Laboratory Manager: Steven Dressler
Sales Manager: Steve Harrison
Quality Control: Rebecca Newman
Sales Director: W Camusi
Production Manager: Bob August
Estimated Sales: $ 10-20 Million
Number Employees: 100-249
Type of Packaging: Consumer, Food Service
Brands:
Porter & Stout
Sierra Nevada Bigfoo
Sierra Nevada Celebration
Sierra Nevada Pale Ale
Sierra Nevada Stout
Sierra Nevada Summer

13191 Sierra Vista Winery
4560 Cabernet Way
Placerville, CA 95667-8410   530-622-7221
Fax: 530-622-2413   syrah@sierravistawinery.com
www.sierravistawinery.com
Wines
Owner: John Mac Cready
Owner/Winery Office VP: Barbara MacCready
Estimated Sales: Below $ 5 Million
Number Employees: 1-4
Type of Packaging: Private Label
Brands:
SIERRA VISTA

13192 Sifers Valomilk Candy Company
5112 Merriam Dr
Shawnee Mission, KS 66203-2118   913-722-0991
Fax: 913-722-5016   russ@valomilk.com
www.valomilk.com
Valomilk candy cups
President: Russell Sifers
Estimated Sales: $ 2.5-5 Million
Number Employees: 5-9

Number of Brands: 1
Number of Products: 1
Type of Packaging: Private Label
Brands:
SIFERS VALOMILK CANDY CUPS

13193 Sigma International
333 16th Street S
St Petersburg, FL 33705   727-822-1288
Fax: 812-822-6782
Seafood
Estimated Sales: $ 50-100 Million
Number Employees: 20-49

13194 Sigma/Aldrich Flavors &Fragrances
6000 N Teutonia Avenue
Milwaukee, WI 53209-3645   414-273-3850
Fax: 414-273-5793   800-227-4563
www.sigmaaldrich.com
Aroma chemicals, synthetics, certified naturals and
essential oils to redi-packs and pre-packaged samples, also provide raw materials for a wide range of
applications and offer a comprehensive range of kosher certified natural andsynthetic products.
Chairman/President/CEO: Jai Nagarkatti
SVP/CFO/CAO: Rakesh Sachdev
VP Sales: Gerrit J C van den Dool
VP Human Resources: Douglas Rau
Estimated Sales: $2.1 Billion
Number Employees: 6000
Number of Products: 1500
Parent Co: Sigma Aldrich Corporation
Brands:
ALDRICH
FLUKA
SAFC
SIGMA
SUPELCO

13195 Signature Brands
P.O.Box 279
Ocala, FL 34478-0279   352-622-3134
Fax: 352-402-9451   800-456-9573
info@signaturebrands.com
www.signaturebrands.com
Manufacturer, importer and exporter of dessert decorating and specialty baking products. Importer of
preserves.
Chairman/President/CEO: Robert Lawless
EVP/Chief Financial Officer: Francis Contino
CEO: James Schneider
VP/Finance & Treasurer: Paul Beard
VP/Human Relations: Cecile Perich
Estimated Sales: $ 20 - 50 Million
Number Employees: 250-499
Sq. footage: 80000
Parent Co: McCormick & Company
Type of Packaging: Consumer, Food Service, Private Label, Bulk
Brands:
Betty Crocker
Cake Mate
SIGNATURE

13196 Signature Foods
PO Box 557306
Miami, FL 33255-7306   305-264-8768
Fax: 305-264-5076
Rice mixes
President: Oran B Talkington
Estimated Sales: $ 5-10 Million appx.
Number Employees: 3

13197 Signature Fruit
1 Tiffany Point
Suite 206
Bloomingdale, IL 60108-2916   630-980-2481
Fax: 630-980-3211
Processor of canned foods including fruits and vegetables
Director (Central Zone): Bruce Scheer
Business Manager (Midwest): Hank Gergovich
Estimated Sales: $ 3 - 5 Million
Number Employees: 1-4
Parent Co: Tri-Valley Growers
Type of Packaging: Consumer

13198 Signature Fruit
3200 E Eight Mile Road
Stockton, CA 95212-9414   209-931-1531

Processor of maraschino cherries, ketchup and tomatoes including stewed, ripe and cooked
Production Manager: Robert Hancock
Plant Manager: Bill Mortola
Number Employees: 1-4
Sq. footage: 480
Parent Co: Tri-Valley Growers
Type of Packaging: Consumer, Food Service, Private Label, Bulk

13199 Signature Seafoods
4257 24th Ave W
Seattle, WA 98199-1214   206-285-2815
    Fax: 206-282-5938
Processor of salmon
President: William Orr
Estimated Sales: $4,000,000
Number Employees: 10-19
Brands:
H&G Chum
King Salmon
Silver Salmon

13200 Signore Winery
153 White Church Road
Brooktondale, NY 14817-9769   607-539-7935
Wines
Owner: Daniel Signore
Estimated Sales: $ 1-4.9 Million
Number Employees: 1-5

13201 Signorello Vineyards
4500 Silverado Trl
Napa, CA 94558-1100   707-255-5990
    Fax: 707-255-5999
info@signorellovineyards.com
www.signorellovineyards.com
Wines
Owner: Ray Signorello
National Sales Director: Chris Carmichael
Director Marketing: Bruce Donsker
Winemaker: Raymond Signorello Jr
Winemaker: Pierre Birebent
Estimated Sales: Below $ 5 Million
Number Employees: 5-9
Brands:
Signorello

13202 Silani Sweet Cheese
RR 1
Schomberg, ON L0G 1T0
Canada   905-939-2561
    Fax: 905-939-2011   silanicheese@look.ca
Processor and importer of cheese
President: Michael Talarico
CEO/VP: Joe Lanzino
Sq. footage: 25000

13203 Silesia Flavors
5250 Prairie Stone Pkwy
Hoffman Estates, IL 60192-3709   847-645-0270
    Fax: 847-645-0266   info@silesiafl.com
    www.silesia.de
Develops and produces natural, nature identical and artificial as well as process flavours in various forms, plus natural colour extracts and synthetic colours.
President/CEO: Clemens Hanke
Vice President/Executive Officer: Ortwin Winter
VP: Joe Peterkes
Estimated Sales: $ 5-10 Million
Number Employees: 5-9
Parent Co: Silesia Groups
Brands:
Sil-A-Gran
Silarom
Silvanil

13204 Siljans Crispy Cup Company
23 Skyline Crest NE
Calgary, AB T2K 5X2
Canada   403-275-0135
    Fax: 403-275-0061   siljans@telus.net
    www.siljanscrispycup.com
Processor and exporter of edible cups for hors d'oeuvres and desserts
President: B Ersson
CEO: Christina Ersson
Estimated Sales: $500,000
Number Employees: 5
Number of Brands: 1
Number of Products: 1
Sq. footage: 8000

Type of Packaging: Consumer, Food Service, Private Label, Bulk
Brands:
SALMOLUX
SILJANS

13205 Sill Farms Market
50241 Red Arrow Hwy
Lawrence, MI 49064-8781   269-674-3755
    Fax: 269-674-3756
Processor of frozen apples, blueberries, cherries and strawberries
President: Bob Ross
Executive VP: Jean Sill
Plant Manager: Ernest Probin
Estimated Sales: $ 5 - 10 Million
Number Employees: 10-19
Type of Packaging: Consumer, Food Service, Bulk

13206 Sill Farms Market
50241 Red Arrow Hwy
Lawrence, MI 49064-8781   269-674-3755
    Fax: 269-674-3756
Frozen and fresh sliced fruits
President: Bob Ross
Estimated Sales: $5-9.9 Million
Number Employees: 10-19
Brands:
Plowshares
Sunshower

13207 Silliker, Inc
900 Maple Rd # 1w
Homewood, IL 60430-2341   708-957-7878
    Fax: 708-957-8449   888-957-5227
    www.silliker.com
Laboratory providing food testing, microbiological and chemical analysis, technical consulting and audits for HACCP/GMPs employee training services and custom research
President: James Ondyak
VP: Jim Hayes
Marketing Communications Manager: Jessica Sawyer-Lueck
Number Employees: 50-99
Parent Co: BioMerieux Alliance

13208 Silva Farms
PO Box Z
Gonzales, CA 93926-0669   831-675-2327
    Fax: 831-675-2375   silvafarm@inreach.com
Vegetables
Owner: Edward Skua Jr
Estimated Sales: $500,000-$1 Million
Number Employees: 1-4
Type of Packaging: Private Label, Bulk

13209 Silva Harvesting
PO Box Z
Gonzales, CA 93926-0669   831-675-2327
    Fax: 831-675-2375   silva@inreach.com
Processor, packer and exporter of lettuce, broccoli, cabbage and celery in food service packs and cartons
President: John Silva
Estimated Sales: $500,000-$1 Million
Number Employees: 1-4
Sq. footage: 30000
Type of Packaging: Consumer, Food Service, Private Label, Bulk
Brands:
Silva
Titanic
Very Best

13210 Silva International
523 N Ash Street
Momence, IL 60954   815-472-3535
    Fax: 815-472-3536   kdevries@silva-intl.com
    www.silva-intl.com
Dehydrated vegetables, ingredients, herbs and fruits.
President: Peter Schmidt
VP: Kent DeVries
Quality Assurance Manager: Ed Bove
General Manager: Steve DeYoung
Estimated Sales: $ 2.5-5 Million
Number Employees: 20-49

13211 Silvan Ridge
27012 Briggs Hill Rd
Eugene, OR 97405-9767   541-345-1945
    Fax: 541-345-6174   info@silvanridge.com
    www.silvanridge.com

Wines
President: Carolyn Chambers
CEO: Elizabeth Chambers
CFO: Jim Plumber
Quality Control: Bryan Wilson
Marketing: Phil Cowles
Sales: Ryan Shockley
Public Relations: Angela Bennett
Operations: Haley Smith
Estimated Sales: Below $ 5 Million
Number Employees: 5-9
Number of Brands: 2
Brands:
Hinman Vineyards
Silvan Ridge

13212 Silver Creek Distillers
134 N 3300 E
Rigby, ID 83442-5630   208-754-0042
    Fax: 208-754-4758
Beverage grade alcohol
Manager: Bill Scott
Plant Manager: Bill Scott
Estimated Sales: $3,200,000
Number Employees: 5-9
Brands:
Teton Glacier Vodka

13213 Silver Creek Farms
450 Locust St S
Twin Falls, ID 83301-7848   208-736-0829
    Fax: 208-736-0725
Smoked fruit and salmon

13214 Silver Creek Specialty Meats
P.O.Box 3307
Oshkosh, WI 54903-3307   920-232-3581
    Fax: 920-232-3589
    www.silvercreekspecialtymeats.com
Processor of natural casing sausage
President: William Kramlich Sr
CEO: Bill Kramlich Jr
Estimated Sales: $4500000
Number Employees: 10-19
Type of Packaging: Food Service, Private Label, Bulk

13215 Silver Ferm Chemical
2226 Queen Anne Ave N # C
Seattle, WA 98109-2372   206-282-3376
    Fax: 206-282-0105   info@silverfernchemical.com
    www.silverfernchemical.com
Food chemicals and ingredients
President: Sam King
Number Employees: 5-9

13216 Silver Fox Vineyard
4683 Morning Star Ln
Mariposa, CA 95338-9361   209-966-4800
    Fax: 209-966-4369   enjoy@sti.net
    www.silverfoxvineyards.com
Wines
Co-Owner/Co-Operator: Marvin Silver
Co-Owner/Co-Operator: Karen Silver
Estimated Sales: Below $ 5 Million
Number Employees: 5-9
Brands:
Silver Fox Vineyard

13217 Silver Lake Cookie Company
141 Freeman Ave
Islip, NY 11751-1427   631-581-4000
    Fax: 631-581-4510   info@silvercookies.com
    www.silverlakecookie.com
Processor and exporter of baked goods including crackers, cookies and biscuits
President: Joseph Vitarelli
Executive VP: Rocco Vitarelli
Sales: Doug Wainscott
Estimated Sales: $15375669
Number Employees: 250-499
Sq. footage: 140000
Type of Packaging: Consumer, Food Service, Private Label, Bulk

13218 Silver Lake Sausage Shop
80 Ethan St
Providence, RI 02909-5327   401-944-4081
Sausage
President: Erminia Santilli
Estimated Sales: Less than $500,000
Number Employees: 1-4

13219 (HQ)Silver Lining Seafood
P.O.Box 6092
Ketchikan, AK 99901-1092   907-225-6664
          Fax: 907-225-3891 www.tridentseafoods.com
Processor and exporter of fresh, smoked and canned seafood.
          Plant Manager: Leigh Gerber
Estimated Sales: $500,000-$1 Million
Number Employees: 5-9
Type of Packaging: Consumer, Food Service, Bulk

13220 Silver Mountain Vineyards
P.O.Box 3636
Santa Cruz, CA 95063-3636   408-353-2278
          Fax: 408-353-1898   info@silvermtn.com
                              www.silvermtn.com
Wine
          President: Jerold O'Brien
Estimated Sales: $ 1-2.5 Million
Number Employees: 1-4
Type of Packaging: Private Label
Brands:
          Silver Mtn Vineyards

13221 Silver Oak Cellars
P.O.Box 414
Oakville, CA 94562-0414   707-944-8808
          Fax: 707-944-2817   800-273-8805
          info@silveroak.com   www.silveroak.com
Processor of cabernet sauvignon red wine
          President: Raymond Duncan
          General Manager: Dave Cofran
Estimated Sales: $ 20 - 50 Million
Number Employees: 20-49

13222 Silver Palate Kitchens
211 Knickerbocker Rd
Cresskill, NJ 07626-1830   201-568-0110
          Fax: 201-568-8844   800-872-5283
                    www.silverpalate.com
Processor and exporter of vinegars, oils, chutneys, mustards, savories, sweet sauces, preserves, brandied fruits, salad dressings, pasta, oatmeal, etc
          Owner: Peter Harris
          VP: Tom Buro
Estimated Sales: $ 20 - 50 Million
Number Employees: 20-49
Type of Packaging: Consumer, Food Service, Private Label, Bulk
Brands:
          Silver Palate

13223 Silver Sea Sales Company
810 S Caton Avenue
Baltimore, MD 21229-4210   410-644-4661
                              Fax: 410-646-7569

          President/CEO: Thomas Rea

13224 Silver Spring Gardens
P.O.Box 360
Eau Claire, WI 54702-0360   715-832-9739
          Fax: 715-832-9915   800-826-7322
          orders@silverspringfoods.com
                    www.ssfoods.com
Processor of horseradish, mustard, cocktail and tartar sauces; also, chopped garlic, and portion control items
          President: Ed Schaefer
          Marketing Manager: Rita Schrantz
          VP Sales/Marketing: Tom Geheran
          Purchasing: Jeff Holden
Estimated Sales: $36449975
Number Employees: 100-249
Parent Co: Huntsinger Companies
Type of Packaging: Consumer, Food Service, Private Label, Bulk
Brands:
          Atlantic Meyers
          Bookbinder'S
          Good
          Silver Spring

13225 Silver Springs Citrus
P.O.Box 155
Howey In Hills, FL 34737-0155   352-324-2101
          Fax: 352-324-2033   800-940-2277
          ppatrick@silverspringscitrus.com
                    www.silverspringscitrus.com
Manufacturer, importer and exporter of juices
          President: John Rees
          VP/Sales: Pat Patrick
          Operations: Bill Roscoe

Estimated Sales: $75 Million
Number Employees: 100-249
Sq. footage: 960000
Type of Packaging: Consumer, Food Service, Private Label, Bulk

13226 Silver Star Meats
PO Box 393
Mc Kees Rocks, PA 15136-0393   412-771-5539
                              Fax: 412-771-0568
          germony@silverstarmeats.com
                    www.silverstarmeats.com
Processor of bologna, liverwurst, kielbasa, bratwurst, ham and sausage including country, smoked, sweet and link
          President: Robert Germony
          Plant Manager: Bovalina Domanic
Estimated Sales: $11000000
Number Employees: 70
Type of Packaging: Consumer, Food Service, Private Label
Brands:
          Rzaca

13227 Silver State Foods
3725 Jason St
Denver, CO 80211-2624   303-433-3351
          Fax: 303-433-2883   800-423-3351
          tom@silverstatefoods.com
                    www.silverstatefoods.com
Processor of canned and frozen foods including prepared, spaghetti sauce and egg noodles
          Manager: Tom Ernst
Estimated Sales: $600,000
Number Employees: 1-4
Number of Brands: 2
Number of Products: 2
Sq. footage: 5600
Type of Packaging: Consumer, Food Service, Private Label, Bulk
Brands:
          Aiellos
          Salvatore's

13228 Silver Streak Bass Company
PO Box 99
Danevang, TX 77432   979-543-8989
          Fax: 979-543-8840   eksent@wcnet.net
Producer of farm-raised hybrid striped bass
          Owner: Jim Ekstrom
Number Employees: 1-4
Parent Co: Ekstrom Enterprises
Type of Packaging: Bulk
Brands:
          Silver Streak

13229 Silver Sweet Candies
522 Essex St
Lawrence, MA 01840-1242   978-688-0474
                              Fax: 978-683-6636
Candy and confections
          Owner: Robert Burkinshaw
Estimated Sales: Below $ 5 Million
Number Employees: 5-9

13230 Silver Tray Cookies
6861 SW 196th Avenue
Suite 203
Fort Lauderdale, FL 33332-1628   305-883-0800
          Fax: 305-888-8438   info@silvertraycookies.com
                    www.silvertraycookies.com
Cookies, sugar free pound cake and fruit flavored cream cakes
          President: Perry Burk
Estimated Sales: Below $ 5 Million
Number Employees: 2
Brands:
          Silver Tray Cookies

13231 SilverLeaf International
13003 Murphy Rd # M9
Stafford, TX 77477-3937   281-495-1250
          Fax: 281-499-5505   800-442-7542
          info@4garlic.com   m   www.4garlic.com
Marinated garlic hors d'oeuvres, blue cheese and feta cheese stuffed olives, olive oils, dips and salsa, spices and seasonings, jams and jellies, sauces, Italian pasta
          President: Neal McWeeney
          VP: Adriane McWeeney
Estimated Sales: $1-2.5 Million
Number Employees: 1-4
Number of Brands: 1
Number of Products: 50

Type of Packaging: Consumer, Private Label

13232 Silverado Hill Cellars
PO Box 2640
Napa, CA 94558-0263   707-253-9306
          Fax: 707-253-9309   shc@napanet.net
Wine
          President: Yuichiro Terada
Estimated Sales: $ 1-2.5 Million
Number Employees: 5

13233 Silverado Vineyards
6121 Silverado Trl
Napa, CA 94558-9415   707-257-1770
          Fax: 707-257-1538 www.silveradovineyards.com
Wine
          President: Diane D Miller
          Quality Control: Elina Franceschi
Estimated Sales: Below $ 5 Million
Number Employees: 20-49

13234 Silverbow Honey Company
1120 E Wheeler Rd
Moses Lake, WA 98837-1866   509-765-6616
          Fax: 509-765-6549   866-444-6639
          customer.service@silverbowhoney.com
                    www.silverbowhoney.com
Specialty honey, table honey, gourmet honey, sweet mustard, hot honey mustard, honey butter, gift sets, beeswax, beeswax candles and both colored and natural beeswax.
          President: Gary Grigg
Estimated Sales: $7207423
Number Employees: 20-49
Sq. footage: 38000
Type of Packaging: Consumer, Food Service, Private Label, Bulk
Brands:
          Silverbow

13235 Silverston Fisheries
1507 N 1st St
Superior, WI 54880-1146   715-392-5551
                              Fax: 715-392-5586
Fish
          Owner: Stuart Sivertson
Estimated Sales: $ 10-20 Million
Number Employees: 20-49

13236 Simco Foods
1180 S Beverly Dr # 509
Los Angeles, CA 90035-1157   310-284-9050
          Fax: 310-284-8221   info@simco.us
                    www.simco.us
Wholesaler/distributor and exporter of groceries, canned fruits and vegetables, cereals, jams, jellies, peanut butter, macaroni & cheese and french fries; specializing in closeouts, excess inventory, pack changes and short codedmerchandise and opportunity buys
          President: David Sims
          CEO: Aman Simantob
Estimated Sales: $ 10 - 20 Million
Number Employees: 10-19
Number of Brands: 3
Sq. footage: 8000
Type of Packaging: Food Service
Brands:
          FIRST HARVEST
          SIMCO
          STELLA

13237 Simeus Foods International
812 S 5th Ave
Mansfield, TX 76063-2210   817-473-1562
          Fax: 817-473-0591   888-772-3663
                    www.simeusfoods.com
Manufacturer of appetizers, breaded products, pork products, pre-cooked meats, soups, sauces and side dishes
          President: Kelly Hansen
Estimated Sales: $100+ Million
Number Employees: 100-249
Type of Packaging: Food Service
Other Locations:
          Simeus Foods Plant Facility
          Forest City NC

13238 Simeus Foods International
1233 N Church Street
Rocky Mount, NC 27804-2812   817-473-1562
          Fax: 817-473-0591   888-772-3663
                    www.simeusfoods.com

Processor and exporter of chicken, frankfurters, ham, seafood and frozen dinners
President: Winslow Goins
Executive VP: Jim Hutcheson
Number Employees: 50-99
Parent Co: Simeus Foods International

13239 (HQ)Simeus Foods International
812 S 5th Ave
Mansfield, TX 76063-2210   817-473-1562
Fax: 817-473-0591   888-772-3663
rartzer@simeusfoods.com
www.simeusfoods.com
Manufacturer of customized food products for national chain restaurants such as; appetizers, pork products, ready-to-cook breaded products, sauces and side dishes
President: Kelly Hansen
Estimated Sales: $100-500 Million
Number Employees: 100-249
Type of Packaging: Food Service
Other Locations:
Simeus Foods Plant
Forest City NC
Simeus Foods Plant
Mansfield TX

13240 SimmaLoosa Company
203 W Saint Mary Drive
Covington, LA 70433-7428   985-892-1400
Processor of natural fruit juice bases and flavors; serving food processors
President: Roy Allison
CEO: Wayne Allison
Type of Packaging: Bulk

13241 Simmons Foods
P.O.Box 430
Siloam Springs, AR 72761-0430   479-524-8151
Fax: 479-524-6562 www.simmonsfoods.com
Manufacturer of poultry products
President/COO: Todd Simmons
CFO: Mike Jones
VP Marketing: Jerry Laster
Estimated Sales: $50-100 Million
Number Employees: 100-249
Type of Packaging: Consumer, Food Service, Private Label, Bulk
Other Locations:
Simmons Foods
Jay OK
Simmons Foods
Southwest City MO

13242 (HQ)Simmons Foods
P.O.Box 430
Siloam Springs, AR 72761-0430   479-524-8151
Fax: 479-524-6562 webmaster@simfoods.com
www.simmonsfoods.com
Manufacturer and exporter of fresh and frozen chicken
Chairman: Mark Simmons
President/CEO: Todd Simmons
CFO: Mike Jones
VP Marketing: Jerry Laster
Director Puchasing: Brett Garton
Estimated Sales: $460 Million
Number Employees: 100-249
Sq. footage: 30000
Type of Packaging: Consumer, Food Service, Private Label, Bulk
Brands:
MANU MAKER
SIMMONS
TOWN & COUNTRY
WATER VALLEY FARMS

13243 Simmons Foods
10700 S State Highway 43
South West City, MO 64863-7272 417-762-3271
Fax: 417-762-3278 comments@simfoods.com
www.simmonsfoods.com
Chicken in various ways such as fully cooked, ready to cook, frozen or fresh, marinated, glazed, grill marked, breaded and more.
Chairman: Mark Simmons
General Manager: Donald Felder
Plant Manager: Bryce Landers
Director Purchasing: Ronald Horn
Estimated Sales: $ 100-500 Million
Number Employees: 1,000-4,999

13244 Simmons Hot Gourmet Products
22 Greenview Close
Lethbridge, AB T1H 4K8
Canada   403-327-9087
Fax: 403-328-9589 info@firenbrimstone.com
www.firenbrimstone.com

13245 Simon Hubig Company
2417 Dauphine St
New Orleans, LA 70117-7801   504-945-2181
Fax: 504-945-2328 www.hubigs.com
Processor of baked goods
Owner: Otto F Ramsey
VP: Otto Bamsey Jr
Production Manager: Mike Tricou
Estimated Sales: $ 20 - 50 Million
Number Employees: 20-49

13246 Simon Levi Cellars
9380 Sonoma Hwy
Kenwood, CA 95452-9032   707-833-5070
Fax: 707-833-1355   888-315-0040
info@slcellars.com   www.slcellars.com
Wines
President: Brad Jacobs
Estimated Sales: $ 1-2.5 Million
Number Employees: 10-19
Brands:
Maboroshi
SLC

13247 Simon's Specialty Cheese
P.O.Box 223
Little Chute, WI 54140-0223   920-788-6311
Fax: 920-788-1424   800-444-0374
simonchz@athenet.net www.simonscheese.com
Cheese
President: Dave Simon
Cheese Maker: Roger Krohn
CFO: Doug Simon
Cheesemaker: Terry Lensmire
Operations/R & D: Chris Simon
Estimated Sales: $ 25-49.9 Million
Number Employees: 50-99
Type of Packaging: Private Label
Brands:
Simon's

13248 Simple Foods
116 Killewald Ave
Tonawanda, NY 14150-2312   716-743-8850
800-234-8850
simplefoodsusa@yahoo.com
www.simplefoodsusa.com
Processor of natural snacks including oat bars and carob items made with dairy free and nonhydrogenated oils including peanut butter, almond and mint cups, rice cakes and carob squares
President: Karen Pease
Estimated Sales: $ 5 - 10 Million
Number Employees: 5-9
Type of Packaging: Consumer, Bulk
Brands:
Annie's
Magic Munchie

13249 Simplot Food Group
PO Box 27
Boise, ID 83707   208-336-2110
Fax: 208-384-8022   800-572-7783
jrs_info@simplot.com   www.simplotfoods.com
Distributor of avocado pulp, frozen potatoes, frozen fruit, frozen vegetables and frozen cornados
Chairman/President/CEO: Jeffrey Ettinger
SVP/CFO/Director: Jody Feragen
Estimated Sales: + $ 3 Billion
Number Employees: 1,000-4,999
Parent Co: J.R. Simplot Company
Type of Packaging: Food Service
Brands:
ROASTWORKS
SPUDSTERS

13250 Simply Delicious
8411 Highway N Carolina 86 N
Cedar Grove, NC 27231   919-732-5294
Fax: 919-732-5180
Sauces, dressings
President: John Troy

13251 Simply Divine
623 E 11th St # 2
New York, NY 10009-4111   212-541-7300
Fax: 212-541-5444 jmarlowsd@aol.com
www.simplydivine.com
Processor of kosher gourmet soups, sauces, entrees, salads and desserts
Owner: Judith Geller Marlow
Estimated Sales: $500,000-$1 Million
Number Employees: 20-49
Type of Packaging: Consumer, Food Service
Brands:
Simply Divine

13252 Simply Gourmet Confections
PO Box 50141
Irvine, CA 92619   714-505-3955
Fax: 714-505-3957 info@simplyscrumptious.com
www.simplyscrumptious.com
gourmet confections and cookies
President/Owner: Debra Formaneck

13253 Simply Lite Foods Corporation
P.O.Box 9000
Commack, NY 11725-9000   631-543-9600
Fax: 631-543-8283   800-753-4282
questions@simplylite.com
www.sweetnlowcandy.com
Products and sugar free hard candy
President: Sal Asaro
Estimated Sales: $ 50-100 Million
Number Employees: 5-9
Brands:
Sweet'n Low

13254 Simpson & Vail
P.O.Box 765
Brookfield, CT 06804-0765   203-775-0240
Fax: 203-775-0462   800-282-8327
info@svtea.com   www.svtea.com
Processor, exporter and importer of coffee and gourmet tea
President: Jim Harron Jr
CEO: Joan Harron
Estimated Sales: $ .5 - 1 million
Number Employees: 5-9
Sq. footage: 8000
Type of Packaging: Food Service

13255 Simpson Spring Company
P.O.Box 328
South Easton, MA 02375-0328   508-238-4472
Fax: 508-238-5691 sales@simpsonspring.com
www.simpsonspring.com
Processor of flavoring extracts for carbonated beverages
President: William Bertarelli
Estimated Sales: $2900000
Number Employees: 10-19

13256 Sims Wholesale
540 River St
Batesville, AR 72501-7141   870-793-1109
Fax: 870-793-2230 grocer@inbco.net
Wholesaler/distributor of general line products; serving the food service market
Manager: Mike Hanson
General Manager: Kenneth Thornton

13257 Sinbad Sweets
2509 W Shaw Avenue
Fresno, CA 93711-3308   559-298-3700
Fax: 559-298-9194   800-350-7933
Processor of pastries including baklava, strudel, tarts and fillo; exporter of baklava
President: Michael Muhawir
CEO: Edwina Aquino Seidel
COO: Anita Reina
Vice President: John Seidel
Public Relations: Sascha Muhawi
Operations Manager: Larry Burrow
Production Manager: Klaus Gernet
Number Employees: 50-99
Sq. footage: 30000
Type of Packaging: Consumer, Food Service, Private Label, Bulk
Brands:
Oliver Twist
Sinbad Sweets

13258 Singer Extract Laboratory
13301 Inkster Rd
Livonia, MI 48150-2226   313-345-5880
Fax: 313-345-8686 singerextract@msn.com
www.singerextract.com
Manufacturer of extracts, flavorings and food colorings
Plant Manager: Mike Letourneau
Estimated Sales: $ 1 - 3 Million
Number Employees: 1-4
Number of Brands: 7
Number of Products: 50
Sq. footage: 5000
Type of Packaging: Consumer, Food Service, Private Label
Brands:
SEELY

13259 Singer Extract Laboratory
13301 Inkster Rd
Livonia, MI 48150-2226   313-345-5880
Fax: 313-345-8686 singerextract@msn.com
www.singerextract.com
Extracts and flavorings, food colorings, bar specialties and syrups.
President: Mike Letourneau
Estimated Sales: Below $ 5 Million
Number Employees: 3
Number of Brands: 3
Number of Products: 50
Sq. footage: 5000
Brands:
4%
Belmo
Seely

13260 Singleton Seafood
P.O.Box 2819
Tampa, FL 33601-2819   813-247-5366
Fax: 813-247-1782 800-553-3954
seafoodretail@conagrafoods.com
www.conagraseafood.com
Processor of frozen shrimp, breaded fish and shrimp, peeled and deveined shrimp, cooked shrimp, shrimp specialties
President: Dennis Reeves
CFO: Andr, Hawaux
Vice President: Rob Sharpe
Research & Development: Nina Burt
Quality Control: Don Toloday
Marketing Director: Dan Davis
Sales Director: Doug Knudsen
Production Manager: Bill Jacks
Plant Manager: Mike Pent
Purchasing Manager: Bill Stone
Estimated Sales: $300,000-500,000
Number Employees: 1-4
Number of Brands: 8
Number of Products: 200
Sq. footage: 200000
Parent Co: ConAgra Foods
Type of Packaging: Consumer, Food Service, Private Label, Bulk

13261 Sini Fulvi U.S.A.
3636 33rd Street
Suite 200
Long Island City, NY 11106-2329   718-267-8325
Fax: 718-361-6999 sinifulvi@aol.com
www.sinifulvi.com
Importer of Italian, Spanish and Portuguese cheeses and Italian cured meats
President: Agostino Sini
Vice President: Pierluigi Sini
Marketing Director: Michele Buster
Estimated Sales: $ .5 - 1 million
Number Employees: 5-9
Parent Co: Sini Fulvi
Type of Packaging: Consumer, Food Service, Bulk
Brands:
Cacio De Roma
Cacio De Roma Cheese
Crotonese
Drunken Goat Cheese
Genuine
Genuine Fulvi Romano Cheese
I Buonatarula Sini
Pasture Sini
Rustico Cheese
Sfizio Crotonese
Sini Fulvi
Spizzico Pepato Aged
Triggi

13262 Sinton Dairy Foods Company
5151 Bannock St
Denver, CO 80216-1850   303-292-0111
Fax: 303-294-9215 800-666-4808
ruf51@aol.com www.sintondairy.com
Processor of dairy products including milk and cottage cheese
General Manager: Joel Midkiff
Marketing Manager: Randy Furstenau
Estimated Sales: $ 20 - 50 Million
Number Employees: 20-49
Type of Packaging: Consumer
Brands:
Lite Time
Quality Chekd
Sinton's
Watts-Hardy

13263 (HQ)Sinton Dairy Foods Company
P.O.Box 578
Colorado Springs, CO 80901-0578   719-633-3821
Fax: 719-633-4376 800-388-4970
mmaloney@sintondairyfoods.com
www.sintondairy.com
Manufacturer of dairy products including milk, ice cream, butter, sour cream, dips and dressings, cheese, eggs, cottage cheese, drinkable yogurts and drinks and mixes
GM: Joel Midkiff
VP: Scott Lewis
Quality Assurance Manager: Amanda Moore
Marketing Manager: Randy Furstenau
Operations Manager: Bill Keating
Plant Manager: Mike Maloney
Estimated Sales: $ 50 - 100 Million
Number Employees: 250-499
Type of Packaging: Consumer
Brands:
SINTON

13264 Sioux Honey Association/Sue Bee
511 E Katella Ave
Anaheim, CA 92805-6608   714-776-4112
Fax: 714-776-6481 www.suebee.com
Processor and exporter of honey including clover, orange, sage, natural and raw
CEO: Gary Evans
Sales Manager (Western Region): Leo Martinkus
Plant Manager: Carl Kayl
Estimated Sales: $110 Million
Number Employees: 10-19
Type of Packaging: Consumer, Food Service, Private Label, Bulk
Brands:
Aunt Sue
Clover Maid
Natural Pure
North American
Sue Bee

13265 Sioux Honey Association/Sue Bee
P.O.Box 388
Sioux City, IA 51102-0388   712-258-0638
Fax: 712-258-1332 ronsuebee@aol.com
www.suebee.com
Processor and exporter of honey
Chairman: L John Milam
CEO: Gary Evans
CEO: Dave Allibone
VP Marketing/Sales: Jim Powell
Assistant VP Sales/Marketing: Ron Junck
Estimated Sales: $110 Million
Number Employees: 50-99
Type of Packaging: Consumer, Food Service, Private Label, Bulk
Brands:
Aunt Sue
Clover Maid
Natural Pure
North American
Sue Bee

13266 Sioux-Preme Packing Company
P.O.Box 255
Sioux Center, IA 51250-0255   712-722-2555
Fax: 712-722-2666 garym@siouxpreme.com
www.siouxpreme.com
Manufacturer and exporter of pork products
President/CEO: Gary Malenke
CFO: Richard White
VP Sales: Jose Gonzalez

Estimated Sales: $77 Million
Number Employees: 100-249
Type of Packaging: Consumer, Private Label, Bulk

13267 SipDisc
30 E 60th St
New York, NY 10022-1008   212-688-8778
Fax: 212-319-9778 sales@sipdisc.com
www.sipdisc.com
Manufacturer of the SipDisc Straw for the food and beverage industry.
President: Alex Greenburg Ph.D

13268 Siptop Packaging Inc
450 Export Boulevard
Mississauga, ON L5S 2A4
Canada   905-670-8381
Fax: 905-670-8325 info@siptop.com
www.siptop.com/
Siptop Packaging's product line includes beverage packaging technology that utilizes a form, fill and seal machine that produces an innovative stand-up drink pouch that is low cost, environmentally friendly and has a built in strawthat is convenient and eliminates the mess that is created with typical pouch straws.
Sales Representative: Grant Joyce
Senior Director Operations: Jack Vanderdeen
Type of Packaging: Consumer

13269 Sir Real Foods
50 Hazelton Drive
White Plains, NY 10605-3816   914-948-9342
Fax: 914-948-9342 sirrealjuice@verizon.net
www.sirreal.com
Juices, beverages
President: Michael Albert
Vice President: Douglas Albert
Estimated Sales: Under $500,000
Number Employees: 10-19
Brands:
Americus Natural Spring Water

13270 Sirocco Enterprises
228 Industrial Ave
Jefferson, LA 70121-2904   504-834-1549
Fax: 504-837-7762 www.siroccoenterprises.com
Manufacturer and exporter of ready-to-use liquid cocktail mixers
President: Tony Muto
VP: Anthony Muto
Production: Benny Peel
Estimated Sales: $1 Million
Number Employees: 5-9
Number of Brands: 1
Number of Products: 10
Sq. footage: 13000
Type of Packaging: Food Service
Brands:
PAT O'BRIEN'S COCKTAIL MIXES

13271 Sisler's Ice & Ice Cream
102 S Grove Street
Ohio, IL 61349   815-376-2913
Fax: 815-766-33 888-891-3856
sisler@sisler.com www.sislers.com
Processor of ice, ice cream
Owner/Operator: Bill Sisler
Manager: Dan Thompson
Estimated Sales: $500,000-$1 Million
Number Employees: 5-9
Sq. footage: 18000
Type of Packaging: Consumer, Food Service
Brands:
Sisler's Dairy

13272 Sister's Gourmet
P.O.Box 1550
Dacula, GA 30019-0027   678-425-9242
877-338-1388
sales@sistersgourmet.com
www.sistersgourmet.com
One bowl easy to bake gourmet cookie mixes and other excellent gourmet gifts.
Owner: Lisa Sorensen
Estimated Sales: $ 5 - 10 Million
Number Employees: 50-99

13273 Sister's Kitchen
3 Westview Ave
Rutland, VT 05701-3733   802-775-2457
Fax: 802-775-2457 dufdecer@sover.net
www.sisterskitchen.net

Maple flavored vinegar and mixes

13274 Sitka Sound Seafoods
329 Katlian St
Sitka, AK 99835-7596   907-747-6662
Fax: 907-747-6268   employment@ssssitka.com
                                      www.ssssitka.com
Processor and exporter of fresh and frozen seafood
from Alaska including abalone, black cod, halibut,
herring, rockfish, Pacific salmon and king and snow
crabs
    President: Harold Thompson
    Plant Manager: Jon Hickman
Estimated Sales: $ 20-50 Million
Number Employees: 100-249
Sq. footage: 30000
Parent Co: North Pacific Seafoods

13275 Sivetz Coffee
349 SW 4th St
Corvallis, OR 97333-4622   541-753-9713
Fax: 541-757-7644   info@sivetzcoffee.com
                                      www.sivetzcoffee.com
Roasted coffee beans, extracts, almond kernels, ha-
zelnut kernels, and coffee roasting machines
    President: Mike Sivetz
Number Employees: 1-4
Type of Packaging: Consumer, Bulk
Brands:
    Sivetz Coffee Essence

13276 Six Mile Creek Vineyard
1551 Slaterville Rd
Ithaca, NY 14850-6335   607-272-9463
Fax: 607-277-7344   800-260-0612
info@sixmilecreek.com   www.sixmilecreek.com
Wines
    Co-Owner: Nancy Battistella
    Co-Owner: Roger Battistella
Estimated Sales: $ 1 - 3 Million
Number Employees: 1-4
Type of Packaging: Private Label
Brands:
    Six Mile Creek

13277 Skim Delux Mendenhall Laboratories
715 Morton St
Paris, TN 38242-4296   731-642-9321
Fax: 731-644-3398   800-642-9321
info@deluxmilk.com   www.deluxmilk.com
Processor and exporter of dairy analogs, formulas
and flavors for calcium-fortified milk, juice and fruit
drink beverages; also, chocolate milkshake mixes
    Owner: David Travis
    Sales Assistant: Melissa Taylor
Estimated Sales: $500,000-$1 Million
Number Employees: 5-9
Type of Packaging: Bulk

13278 Skinners' Dairy
24741 Deer Trace Drive
Ponte Vedra Beach, FL 32082-2114 904-733-5440
Milk, dairy products
    President: Denny Gaultney
Estimated Sales: $ 10-20 Million
Number Employees: 100

13279 Skjodt-Barrett Foods
2395 Lucknow Drive
Mississauga, ON L5S 1H9
Canada
                                       905-671-2884
Fax: 905-671-2885   877-600-1200
                                      www.skjodt-barrett.com
Processor of fruit fillings, icings, glaze, sauces, mar-
inades and caramel.
    President: Dan Skjodt
    R&D: Pal Shah
    VP Research & Innovation: Pal Shah
    VP Sales/Marketing: Mike Durham
    Human Resources Manager: Elizabeth Sarginson
    Operations Manager: Gulzar Dabass
Estimated Sales: $13.3 Million
Number Employees: 10-19
Sq. footage: 25000
Type of Packaging: Food Service, Private Label,
Bulk
Brands:
    Skjodt-Barrett

13280 Sky Haven Farm
4871 Shepherd Creek Rd
Cincinnati, OH 45223-1015   513-681-2303
                                      Fax: 513-681-8305

Cured hams
    President: Edward J Dreyer
Estimated Sales: $ 1-2.5 Million
Number Employees: 1-4

13281 Sky Vineyards
4352 Cavedale Road
Glen Ellen, CA 95442-9767   707-935-1391
Fax: 510-540-8442   infoatskyvineyards.com
                                      www.skyvineyards.com
Wines
    Owner: Lore Olds
    COO: Linn Brinier
    Sales: Matt Gerloff
Estimated Sales: $ 3 - 5 Million
Number Employees: 5-9
Brands:
    Sky Vineyards

13282 Skylark Meats
4430 S 110th St
Omaha, NE 68137-1235   402-592-0300
          Fax: 402-592-1414   800-759-5275
                                      www.skylarkmeats.com
Processor and exporter of portion control steaks and
liver; wholesaler/distributor of meat products; serv-
ing the food service market
    President: James Leonard
    VP (Retail Sales): Steve Giroux
    VP Ground Beef Sales: James Binder
    VP Foodservice Sales: John Bauer
    VP Liver Sales: Robert Elliott
    VP Vending & Convenience Store Sales: John
    O'Brien
Estimated Sales: $41100000
Number Employees: 250-499
Sq. footage: 185000
Parent Co: Rosen's Diversified
Type of Packaging: Consumer, Food Service

13283 Slap Ya Mama Cajun Seasoning
1103 W Main Street
Ville Platte, LA 70586   337-363-6904
          Fax: 337-363-6608   sales@slapyamama.com
                                      www.slapyamama.com
seasonings

13284 Slate Quarry Winery
460 Gower Road
Nazareth, PA 18064-9219   610-759-0286
                                      Fax: 610-746-9684
                                      winery@slatequarrywines.com
Wines
    General Manager: M Eleanor Butler
    Production Manager: Sidney Butler
Estimated Sales: $ 1-2.5 Million
Number Employees: 5-9

13285 Slathars Smokehouse
RR 1
Box 52bb
Lake City, MN 55041-9312   507-753-2080
Beef
Estimated Sales: $300,000-500,000
Number Employees: 1-4

13286 Sleeman Breweries
7989 82nd Street
Delta, BC V4G 1L7
Canada
                                       604-940-2887
                                      www.sleeman.com
Ale
    CEO: Rick Knudson
    Chairman: John W Sleeman
    CFO: Paul Renaud
    Vice President: Paul Renaud
Number Employees: 20-49
Type of Packaging: Consumer, Food Service
Brands:
    Sleeman

13287 Sleeman Brewing & Malting Company
551 Clair Road W
Guelph, ON N1L 1E9
Canada
                                       519-822-1834
          Fax: 519-822-0430   800-268-8537
                                      www.sleeman.com
Beer, ale and lager
    President: Rick Knucson
    CFO: Dan Camrogozynski
Number Employees: 300
Type of Packaging: Consumer, Food Service

Brands:
    Sleeman Amber
    Sleeman Clear
    Sleeman Cream Ale
    Sleeman Honey Brown Lager
    Sleeman Original Dark
    Sleeman Origial Draught
    Sleeman Premium Light
    Sleeman Silver Creek Lager
    Sleeman Steam

13288 Slim Fast Foods Company
PO Box 3625
West Palm Beach, FL 33402-3625   561-833-9920
                Fax: 561-822-2876 www.slim-fast.com
Meal replacement drinks and bars
    President: Marc Covent
    CFO: Carl Tsang
    COO: Art Peters
Estimated Sales: $ 50 - 100 Million
Number Employees: 50-99
Type of Packaging: Consumer
Brands:
    SLIM FAST

13289 Smart & Final
P.O.Box 512377
Los Angeles, CA 90051-0377   323-869-7500
                                      Fax: 323-869-7858
          customerrelations@smartandfinal.com
                                      www.smartfoodservice.com
Food service suppliers
    President: Etienne Snollaerts
    CFO: Richard N Phegley
    CFO: Rick Phegley
    CEO: George Golleher
    Chairman: Ross E Roeder
Estimated Sales: $ 1 Billion+
Number Employees: 5,000-9,999
Brands:
    Smart & Final

13290 Smart Ice
3340 Royalston Ave
Fort Myers, FL 33916-1623   239-334-3123
                                      Fax: 239-332-4628
Processor and wholesaler/distributor of coolers,
shelf stable freezer pops, flavored drinks and filled
Easter baskets and Christmas stockings
    Owner: David Radford Jr
    Sales Manager: Arnold Bonn
Estimated Sales: $1.4 Million
Number Employees: 10-19
Type of Packaging: Consumer
Brands:
    Ice Age
    Smart Drinks
    Smart Ice
    Smarty Bats

13291 Smart Juices
52 E Union Blvd
Bethlehem, PA 18018   484-257-7080
          Fax: 484-727-7425 www.smartjuice.com
organic 100% juice

13292 Smeltzer Orchard Company
6032 Joyfield Rd
Frankfort, MI 49635-9163   231-882-4421
Fax: 231-882-4430   info@smeltzerorchards.com
                                      www.smeltzerorchards.com
Processor and exporter of frozen apples, apple juice,
asparagus and cherries; also, dried blueberries, cher-
ries, apples, strawberries and cranberries
    President: Tim Brian
    Plant Manager: Mike Henschell
Estimated Sales: $9305725
Number Employees: 50-99
Type of Packaging: Food Service

13293 Smiling Fox Pepper Company
610 Cherrywood Drive
North Aurora, IL 60542-1032   630-337-3734
          info@sfoxpepco.bizland.com
                                      www.sfoxpepco.com
Relishes and jellies
    Co-Owner: Mary Patterson
    Co-Owner: Scott Patterson
Type of Packaging: Consumer

13294 Smith & Son Seafood
P.O.Box 2118
Darien, GA 31305-2118   912-437-6471
                                      Fax: 912-437-3553

Shrimp
President: Jean Smith

13295 Smith Dairy Products Company
1381 Dairy Ln
Orrville, OH 44667-2503   330-683-8710
          Fax: 330-683-1079   800-776-7076
          ikegraham@smithdairy.com
          www.smithdairy.com
Processor of cheese, cottage cheese, ice cream and
milk; also, fruit drinks and juices
President: Steve Schmid
Marketing: Bill McCabe
VP Sales: Brian Defelice
VP Production: Eddie Steiner
Purchasing: John Schmid
Estimated Sales: $100+ Million
Number Employees: 250-499
Sq. footage: 75000
Type of Packaging: Consumer, Food Service, Private Label
Brands:
Moovers
Ruggles
Smith's

13296 Smith Enterprises
1953 Langston St
Rock Hill, SC 29730-3385   803-366-7101
          Fax: 803-366-1958   800-845-8311
Candy
Chairman of the Board: Jacob D Smith
Sales Director: Tony Morgan
Estimated Sales: $ 30-50 Million
Number Employees: 250-499

13297 (HQ)Smith Frozen Foods
P.O.Box 68
Weston, OR 97886-0068   541-566-3515
          Fax: 541-566-3707
          webactivity@smithfrozenfoods.com
          www.smithfrozenfoods.com
Processor and exporter of frozen vegetables including baby lima beans, diced and sliced carrots, kernel corn, corn-on-the-cob and peas
CEO: Sharon Smith
CEO: Gary Crowder
Quality Control Specialist: Traci Jensen
Sales Manager: David Stoddard
Purchasing Manager: Corry Zenger
Estimated Sales: $55000000
Number Employees: 500-999
Type of Packaging: Consumer, Food Service, Private Label, Bulk
Brands:
Smith

13298 Smith Frozen Foods
P.O.Box 68
Weston, OR 97886-0068   541-566-3515
          Fax: 541-566-3707   800-547-0203
          kellybrown@smithfrozenfoods.com
          www.smithfrozenfoods.com
Processor and exporter of frozen produce including peas, carrots, baby lima beans and cut and cob corn
Account Executive: Sharon Smith
Quality Control: Traci Jensen
CEO: Gary Crowder
Sales Manager: Dave Stoddard
Estimated Sales: $ 1 - 3 Million
Number Employees: 5-9
Type of Packaging: Consumer, Food Service, Private Label, Bulk

13299 Smith Meat Packing
1420 Thomas St
Port Huron, MI 48060-3311   810-985-5900
          Fax: 810-985-4504
Packer of smoked and cured pork
President: Anthony Peters
Estimated Sales: $ 5 - 10 Million
Number Employees: 10-19
Sq. footage: 15000
Type of Packaging: Bulk

13300 (HQ)Smith Packing Regional Meat
P.O.Box 446
Utica, NY 13503-0446   315-732-5125
          Fax: 315-732-1166   www.smithpacking.com

Manufacturer and exporter of meat products including fresh and frozen beef, pork, veal, lamb, chicken and turkey; also, US grade AA eggs, a full line of processed meats including ham, bacon, frankfurters, sausage, kielbasa, turkeybreast, etc
President: Wesley Smith
VP: Mark Smith
Estimated Sales: $12.6 Million
Number Employees: 1-4
Sq. footage: 50000
Type of Packaging: Private Label
Brands:
EVERGOOD
HONEST JOHN'S

13301 Smith Provision Company
2251 W 23rd St
Erie, PA 16506-2916   814-452-2525
          Fax: 814-452-3142   800-334-9151
Processor of smoked luncheon meats and ham, frankfurters, roast beef and sausage
Chairman of the Board: Magnus Weber
VP: John Weber
Estimated Sales: $8198187
Number Employees: 20-49
Sq. footage: 25863
Type of Packaging: Consumer, Food Service, Private Label, Bulk
Brands:
Smith's

13302 Smith Vineyard & Winery
13577 Dog Bar Rd
Grass Valley, CA 95949-8379   530-273-7032
          Fax: 530-273-0229   christina@smithwine.com
          www.smithwine.com
Wines
Manager: Christina Smith
Estimated Sales: $500-1 Million appx.
Number Employees: 5-9

13303 Smith's Bakery
P.O.Box 16389
Hattiesburg, MS 39404-6389   601-288-7000
          Fax: 601-584-6487   www.forrestgeneral.com
Bakery
President: William C Oliver
Estimated Sales: $ 1-2.5 Million appx.
Number Employees: 1-4

13304 Smith, Weber & Swinton Company
6250 Camp Industrial Rd
Cleveland, OH 44139-2750   440-248-1500
          Fax: 440-248-1500   www.schwebels.com
Breads and buns
Manager: Pat Lobb
Marketing Director: Thomas Steve
Estimated Sales: $10-24.9 Million
Number Employees: 5-9

13305 Smith-Coulter Company
8579 Lakeport Rd
Chittenango, NY 13037-9577   315-687-6510
          Fax: 315-687-6637
Processor and exporter of produce including onions and turf grass
Owner: Chris Coulter
Estimated Sales: $ 3 - 5 Million
Number Employees: 5-9
Brands:
Bulls Eye

13306 Smith-Madrone Vineyards& Winery
4022 Spring Mountain Rd
St Helena, CA 94574-9773   707-963-2283
          Fax: 707-963-2291   contact@smithmadrone.com
          www.smithmadrone.com
Wines
Manager: Stuart Smith
Manager: Charles Smith
Winemaker: Charles Smith
Estimated Sales: $ 1-2.5 Million
Number Employees: 5-9
Brands:
Smith-Madrone

13307 Smithfield Foods
424 E Railroad Street
Clinton, NC 28328-4360   910-592-2104
          Fax: 910-299-3036
          donnie.stephenson@psfarms.com
          www.smithfield.com

Processor and exporter of meat products including pork and ham
Manager: Ken Wilson
Chairman/CEO: John Meyer
VP: Jere Null
Operations VP: George Nelms
Operations VP: Glenn Clark
Estimated Sales: $500 Million to $1 Billion
Number Employees: 1500
Sq. footage: 600000
Parent Co: Premium Standard Farms
Type of Packaging: Consumer, Private Label, Bulk
Brands:
Lundy's
Pig & Banner
Tomahawk

13308 (HQ)Smithfield Foods
200 Commerce St
Smithfield, VA 23430-1204   757-365-3000
          Fax: 757-365-3017   888-366-6767
          information@smithfieldfoods.com
          www.smithfieldfoods.com
World's largest pork processor and hog producer
President/CEO: C Larry Pope
EVP/CFO: Robert Manly IV
EVP: Joseph Luter IV
Estimated Sales: $11.2 Billion
Number Employees: 48,000
Type of Packaging: Consumer, Food Service, Private Label, Bulk
Brands:
Cumberland Gap Provision
Farmland Foods Inc
Gwaltney of Smithfield
John Morrell & Co
Kraukus Foods International
North Side Foods
Patrick Cudahy
Quick-to-Fix
Smithfield
Smithfield Beef Group
Smithfield Deli Group
Smithfield Foodservice Group
Smithfield Innovation Group
Smithfield RMH Foods Group
Stefano Foods

13309 Smithfield Packing Company
111 Commerce Street
Smithfield, VA 23430-1201   757-357-4321
          Fax: 757-357-1339   www.smithfield.com
Processor and exporter of pork including ham
Manager: Jospeh W Luter Iii III
President: Lewis Little
CFO: Dan Sabin IV
Vice President: Steve Canale
Sales/Marketing: Susan Carr
Estimated Sales: K
Number Employees: 4636
Type of Packaging: Consumer, Food Service, Private Label
Other Locations:
Smithfield Packing Company
Kingston NC

13310 Smoak's Bakery & Catering Service
2058 Walton Way
Augusta, GA 30904-2302   706-738-1792
          Fax: 706-733-8979   tomt3@bellsouth.com
          www.smoaksbakery.com
Cakes, cookies and breads
President: Steve Pierce
General Manager: Audery Hawn
Owner: Dan Smoak
Estimated Sales: $ 1-2.5 Million
Number Employees: 20-49
Type of Packaging: Private Label

13311 Smoke & Fire Natural Food
35 Railroad Ave
Great Barrington, MA 01230-1510   413-528-8008
          Fax: 413-528-7997   tofu@smokeandfire.com
          www.smokeandfire.com
Smoked and flavored tofu
Owner: Robert Harvey
Co-Founder: Mona Young
Estimated Sales: Under $500,000
Number Employees: 5-9
Brands:
Smoke & Fire

13312 Smoke House
20 Smokehouse Rd
Sagle, ID 83860-8698   208-263-6312
                          Fax: 208-762-8979
Smoked meats
    Owner: Dick Struntz
Estimated Sales: $ .5 - 1 million
Number Employees: 1-4

13313 Smoked Fish Factory
501 Garyray Drive
Weston, ON M9L 1P9
Canada   416-745-4323
                          Fax: 416-745-5297
Processor and exporter of smoked salmon including
sockeye, coho and Atlantic; processor of smoked
chub, whitefish, carp, ciscoe, rainbow, sable and
mackerel
    President: Ron Daiter
    VP: Stephen Daiter
Number Employees: 10-19
Sq. footage: 15000
Brands:
    Epic-Cure
    Party-Pak

13314 Smokehouse Winery
10 Ashby Rd
Sperryville, VA 22740-2243   540-987-3194
                          Fax: 540-987-8189
smokehousewinery@earthlink.net
www.smokehousewinery.com
Wines
    Owner: John Hallberg
Estimated Sales: $300,000-500,000
Number Employees: 1-4

13315 Smokey Denmark Sausage
3505 E 5th St
Austin, TX 78702-4913   512-385-0718
    Fax: 512-385-4843 info@smokeydenmark.com
www.smokeydenmark.com
Processor of beef, pork and venison sausage
    President: Johnathan Pace
Estimated Sales: $2500000
Number Employees: 10-19
Type of Packaging: Consumer

13316 Smokey Farm Meats
Box 434
Carbon, AB T0M 0L0
Canada   403-272-6587
    Fax: 403-272-6587 beeffarm@telus.net
Processor of beef jerky, pepperoni and sausage
    President: Tracy Smith
    CEO: Sylvia Schmidt
Number Employees: 1-4
Type of Packaging: Consumer, Food Service, Private Label, Bulk
Brands:
    Smokey Farm Meats

13317 Smolich Brothers
760 Theodore St
Crest Hill, IL 60403-2380   815-727-2144
Processor of sausage including hot, mild, smoked,
pork and bratwurst
    President: Rudy Smolich
    Co-Owner: Joe Smolich
Estimated Sales: Less than $500,000
Number Employees: 1-4
Type of Packaging: Consumer

13318 Smothers Winery/Remick Ridge
1976 Warm Springs Rd
Glen Ellen, CA 95442-8717   707-833-1010
    Fax: 707-833-2313 800-795-9463
    sales@smobro.net
www.smothersbrothers.com/remick
Wines
    President/Owner: Thomas Smothers
    Owner: Marcy Smothers
Estimated Sales: Below $ 5 Million
Number Employees: 5-9
Brands:
    Smothers/Remick Ridge

13319 Smucker Quality Beverages
P.O.Box 369
Chico, CA 95927-0369   530-899-5000
    Fax: 530-891-6397 www.jmsmucker.com

Processor and exporter of natural juice and soda
    President: Julia Sabin
    Marketing Manager: Arlene Starkey
    Sales Manager: Kevin Cobb
Number Employees: 100-249
Parent Co: J.M. Smucker Company
Type of Packaging: Consumer, Private Label
Brands:
    After the Fall
    Natural Brew
    Rocket Juice
    Rw Knudsen
    Santa Cruz

13320 Smucker Quality Beverages
340 Old Bay Ln
Havre De Grace, MD 21078-4013   410-939-1403
    Fax: 410-942-1400 smqb5@apply.nationjob.com
www.jmsmucker.com
Processor of natural fruit juices including apple,
pear, grape, cranberry lemonade, punch, mango, pas-
sion, banana/pineapple and apple blends; also, peach
vanilla and vanilla bean cream and strawberry drinks
    Manager: Doug Arington
    Chairman/Co-Chief Executive Officer: Timothy
    Smucker
    Senior VP/ Consumer Market: Vincent Boyd
    Senior VP/Special Markets: Fred Duncan
Estimated Sales: $9,900,000
Number Employees: 20-49
Parent Co: J.M. Smucker Company
Type of Packaging: Consumer, Food Service

13321 Smuggler's Kitchen
PO Box 570
Dundee, FL 33838-0570   800-604-6793
    tnischan@smugglerskitchen.com
www.smugglerskitchen.com
Processor of dehydrated foods including Irish potato
soup, vegetable dips, Cajun and chili sauces, etc
    Co-Owner: Tom Nischan
    Co-Owner: Pat Nischan
Number Employees: 1-4

13322 Smuttynose Brewing
225 Heritage Ave # 2
Portsmouth, NH 03801-5610   603-436-4026
    Fax: 603-433-1247 info@smuttynose.com
www.smuttynose.com
Beer
    President: Peter Egelston
    Executive Brewer: David Yarrington
    CFO: Gale Merrigan
    Head Brewer: Greg Blanchard
    Sales Manager: Kevin Love
    National Sales Manager: Anka Jacobs
    Marketing: Jaime Pruzansky
    Office Manager: Deb Fitt
Estimated Sales: Below $ 5 Million
Number Employees: 10-19
Type of Packaging: Private Label
Brands:
    Big Beer Series
    Old Brown Bag
    Portsmouth Lager
    Smuttynose Belgian W
    Smuttynose Robust Po

13323 Snack Appeal
3601 Old Post Road
Fairfax, VA 22030-1807   540-383-0561
                          Fax: 540-383-0576
Processor and exporter of snack foods including
low-fat potato chips and low-fat sandwich products
Type of Packaging: Consumer, Food Service

13324 Snack Factory
PO Box 3562
Princeton, NJ 08543-3562   609-683-5400
    Fax: 609-683-9595 888-683-5400
    info@pretzelcrisps.com www.pretzelcrisps.com
Manufacturer of pretzel crisps-all natural and fat
free; available in garluc, original and everything
flavors.
    President: Warren Wilson
    VP: Sara Wilson
Estimated Sales: $ 5 Million+
Number Employees: 9
Sq. footage: 200000
Type of Packaging: Consumer, Food Service, Private Label, Bulk
Brands:
    Snack Factory

13325 Snack King Corporation
16150 Stephens St
City of Industry, CA 91745-1718   626-336-7711
                          Fax: 626-336-3777 800-748-5566
    info@snakking.com www.snakking.com
Manufacturer of snack foods, tortilla chips and
cheese puffs (extruded food snack)
    CEO: Berry Levin
    CEO: Barry C Levin
Estimated Sales: $100+ Million
Number Employees: 500-999

13326 Snack Works/Metrovox Snacks
6116 Walker Avenue
Maywood, CA 90270-3447   323-771-3221
    Fax: 888-865-3639 888-224-7110
    sales@giftbasketsupplies.com
www.giftbasketsupplies.com
Popcorn, pretzels, chocolates, and gift boxes.
    Owner: Paul Voxland
Estimated Sales: $500,000-$1 Million
Number Employees: 5-9

13327 SnackMasters
P.O.Box 70
Ceres, CA 95307-0070   209-537-9770
    Fax: 209-669-3240 800-597-9770
    jerky@snackmasters.com
www.snackmasters.com
Meat snacks
    President: James Rekoutis
Estimated Sales: $ 10-20 Million
Number Employees: 50-99
Type of Packaging: Bulk

13328 Snackerz
6351 Chalet Dr
Commerce, CA 90040-3705   562-928-0023
    Fax: 562-928-8923 888-576-2253
www.snackerz.com
Candy and nuts
    Owner: Ron Emrani
Estimated Sales: $ 10 - 20 Million
Number Employees: 20-49
Type of Packaging: Consumer

13329 (HQ)Snak King Corporation
16150 Stephens St
City of Industry, CA 91745-1718   626-336-7711
    Fax: 626-336-3777 info@snakking.com
www.snakking.com
Processor and exporter of snack foods, caramel corn,
tortilla and corn chips, popcorn, beef jerky, pork
rinds, cheese and rice puffs, nut meats and candy.
    President/CEO: Barry Levin
    Quality Control: Rudy Molinar
    VP Marketing: Bruce Waterworth
Estimated Sales: $100+ Million
Number Employees: 500-999
Sq. footage: 175000
Type of Packaging: Consumer, Food Service, Private Label, Bulk
Other Locations:
    Snak King Corp.
    City Industry CA
Brands:
    CARMENS
    EL SABROSO
    HEALTHY BITES
    JENSEN'S ORCHARD
    SNAK KING

13330 Snake River Brewing Company
P.O.Box 3317
Jackson, WY 83001-3317   307-739-2337
    Fax: 307-739-2296 brewpub@rmisp.com
www.snakeriverbrewing.com
Processor of seasonal beer, ale, stout, lager and
pilsner
    President/CEO: Albert E Upsher
Estimated Sales: $ 20 - 50 Million
Number Employees: 50-99
Type of Packaging: Consumer, Food Service
Brands:
    Snake River

13331 (HQ)Snapple Beverage Group
900 King St
Port Chester, NY 10573-1226   914-612-4000
    Fax: 914-612-4100 800-762-7753
    rlibonate@snapbevgrp.com
www.cadburyschweppes.com/en

Processor of beverages including iced tea, fruit juice, etc.
President: Jack Belsito
CEO: Gerrit Schoen
Vice President: Marc Hechema
SVP Operations: Joe Holland
Estimated Sales: $15,510,000
Number Employees: 1-4
Parent Co: Cadbury Schweppes PLC
Type of Packaging: Consumer, Food Service
Brands:
DIET RITE
MISTIC
NEHI
RC COLA
SNAPPLE
STEWART'S

13332 Snappy Popcorn Company
P.O.Box 160
Breda, IA 51436-0160   712-673-2347
          Fax: 712-673-4611   800-742-0228
          jon@snappypopcorn.com
          www.snappypopcorn.com
Manufacturer, wholesaler/distributor and exporter of popcorn and supplies
Owner: Alan Tiefenthaler
CEO: Alan Tiefanthaler
VP Sales: Jon Tiefenthaler
Estimated Sales: $5 Million
Number Employees: 20-49
Sq. footage: 25000
Type of Packaging: Food Service, Bulk

13333 Snelgrove Ice Cream Company
850 E 2100 S
Salt Lake City, UT 84106-1832   801-486-4456
          Fax: 801-486-3926   800-569-0005
          www.dreyers.com
Processor, exporter and wholesaler/distributor of ice cream and ice cream novelties
President: Scott West
Estimated Sales: Less than $500,000
Number Employees: 50-99
Parent Co: MKD Distributing
Type of Packaging: Consumer, Food Service, Private Label, Bulk

13334 Sno Pac Foods
521 Enterprise Dr
Caledonia, MN 55921-1844   507-725-5281
          Fax: 507-725-5285   800-533-2215
          snopac@snopac.com   www.snopac.com
Processor of frozen organic vegetables including soy and eda mame beans, green peas, whole kernel corn, cut green and mixed
President: Peter Gengler
VP: Darlene Gengler
Estimated Sales: $3527129
Number Employees: 50-99
Type of Packaging: Consumer, Food Service, Bulk
Brands:
Sno Pac

13335 Sno-Co Berry Pak
1518 4th Street
Marysville, WA 98270-5012   360-659-3555
Fruit
President: Christie Monroe
Treasurer: Barbara Clark
Estimated Sales: $ 10-20 Million
Number Employees: 20-49

13336 Sno-Shack
109 S 2nd W
Salt Lake City, UT 84115   801-466-1771
          Fax: 801-466-1790   sales@snoshack.com
          www.snoshack.com
Processor and exporter of flavors, thickeners and sweeteners; also, shaved ice equipment including shavers, bottles, racks and yogurt flavoring, carts, concession trailers, etc
Owner: Jared Sommer
Owner: Cheryl Lewis
Sales Director: Peter Orr
Manager: Bud Orr
Purchasing Manager: Brooke Anstine
Estimated Sales: $ 1 - 3 Million
Number Employees: 1-4
Sq. footage: 9000
Type of Packaging: Consumer, Food Service, Private Label
Brands:
Carts

Concessions
Kiosks

13337 SnoWizard Extracts
101 River Rd
New Orleans, LA 70121-4222   504-832-3901
          Fax: 504-832-1646   800-366-9766
          info@snowizard.com
Snowball, snowcone and shaved ice machines and flavorings
President: Ronald Sciortino
Estimated Sales: $ 5 - 10 Million
Number Employees: 10-19
Sq. footage: 5000
Type of Packaging: Consumer, Food Service, Bulk
Brands:
Ronald Reginald's
SnoLite
Snowizard

13338 Snokist Growers
P.O.Box 1587
Yakima, WA 98907-1587   509-457-8444
          Fax: 509-453-9359   800-377-2857
          info@snokist.com   www.snokist.com
Processor of fresh apples, pears and cherries; also, canned apple rings and sauces, fruit purees, pears and plums
President: Valerie Woener
CEO: Valerie Woener
CFO: Jim Davis
CEO: Valerie Woerner
Sales Director: Rich Boldoz
Sales: Neil Galone
Operations Manager: Doug Schreiler
Estimated Sales: $100,000
Number Employees: 500-999
Number of Products: 10
Sq. footage: 50000
Type of Packaging: Consumer, Food Service, Private Label, Bulk
Brands:
BLUE RIBBON
COHORT
DEAR LADY
NU HOUSE
RED RIBBON
SNOKIST
TRI OUR

13339 Snokist Growers
P.O.Box 1587
Yakima, WA 98907-1587   509-457-8444
          Fax: 509-453-9359 www.snokist.com
Berries
Manager: Eric Strutzel
CEO: Valerie Woerner
Estimated Sales: $ 20-50 Million
Number Employees: 100-249

13340 (HQ)Snow Ball Foods
P.O.Box 70
Fredericksburg, PA 17026-70   856-629-4081
          Fax: 856-875-7311   800-360-7669
          info@snowballfoods.com
          www.snowballfoods.com
Manufacturer and exporter of fresh and frozen turkey and chicken products
President: Jerry Colt
VP Marketing/Sales: Don O'Brien
Estimated Sales: $ 25 Million
Number Employees: 250
Number of Brands: 3
Number of Products: 110
Sq. footage: 150000
Type of Packaging: Consumer, Food Service, Private Label, Bulk
Brands:
Executive Chef
Snow-Ball
Sunbird

13341 Snow Beverages
928 Broadway
Suite 504
New York, NY 10010   212-353-3270
          Fax: 646-219-7559   info@snowbeverages.com
          www.snowbeverages.com
natural soda plus vitamins
CEO: Stuart Strumwasser
Number Employees: 3

13342 Snow Dairy
119 W 800 S
Springville, UT 84663-9416   801-489-6081
          Fax: 801-489-6081
President: Mark Snow
Estimated Sales: Less than $500,000
Number Employees: 1-4

13343 Snow's Ice Cream Company
80 School St
Greenfield, MA 01301-2410   413-774-7438
          Fax: 413-774-5406   gary@bartshomemade.com
          www.bartshomemade.com
Processor and wholesaler/distributor of ice cream, sorbet and frozen yogurt; wholesaler/distributor of frozen food, candy, snack foods, sauces, mustards and salsa's
Owner: Gary Schaefer
CFO/Sales: Gary Schaefer
Estimated Sales: Below $ 5 Million
Number Employees: 5-9
Sq. footage: 16000
Parent Co: Another Roadside Attraction
Type of Packaging: Consumer, Food Service, Private Label, Bulk
Brands:
Bart's Homemade
Snow's Nice Cream

13344 SnowBird Corporation
379 Broadway
Bayonne, NJ 07002-3631   201-858-8300
          Fax: 201-451-5000   800-576-1616
          sales@snowbirdwater.com
          www.snowbirdwater.com
Manufacturer of bottled filtered, spring, and distilled water, coffee makers and hot foods; wholesaler/distributor of water fountains and bottled water coolers; repair services available
President: Diane Drey
Vice President: Gerald Giannangeli
Estimated Sales: $ 3 - 5 Million
Number Employees: 5-9
Sq. footage: 66000
Brands:
Snowbird

13345 Snowbear Frozen Custard
620 W Stadium Avenue
Lafayette, IN 47906-2668   765-743-8024
          rick@snowbearfc.com
          www.snowbear.com
Retailers of frozen desserts
Partner: Richard Lodde
Partner: Kirk Lodde
Partner: William Lodde
Partner: Tom Lodde
Estimated Sales: $500,000-$1 Million
Number Employees: 10-19
Number of Products: 50

13346 Snowcrest Packer
1925 Riverside Road
Abbotsford, BC V2S 4S8
Canada   604-859-4881
          Fax: 604-859-1426   info@snowcrest.ca
          www.snowcrest.ca
Processor and importer of frozen apples, blueberries, cherries, cranberries, raspberries, strawberries, asparagus, beans, broccoli, brussels, sprouts, cauliflowers, corn, peas, peppers, rhubarb, spinach, squash and turnips
President: Tom Smith
Quality Control: Lim Lee
Sales: Pascal Countant
Operations Manager: Rob Christl
Number Employees: 120
Sq. footage: 110000
Parent Co: Omstead Foods
Type of Packaging: Consumer, Food Service, Private Label, Bulk
Other Locations:
Snowcrest Packer Ltd.
Burnaby BC
Brands:
Bonniebrook
Brentwood
Delnor
Pennysaver
Snowcrest

13347 Snowizard Extracts
101 River Rd
New Orleans, LA 70121-4222   504-832-3901
            Fax: 504-832-1646   800-366-9766
    info@snowizard.com www.snowizard.com
Snoballs, snowcones and shaved ice
    President: Ronnie Sciortino
Estimated Sales: $ 5 - 10 Million
Number Employees: 10-19
Type of Packaging: Private Label
Brands:
    Snowizard

13348 Snyder Foods
15350 Old Simcoe Road
Port Perry, ON L9L 1A6
Canada   905-985-7373
            Fax: 905-985-7289
Processor and exporter of meat and fruit pies, sausage rolls, quiche, stuffed sandwiches and pie and tart shells
    General Manager: Dave Jackson
Number Employees: 125
Sq. footage: 55000
Type of Packaging: Consumer, Food Service, Private Label
Brands:
    J.M. Schneider
    Maple Leaf
    Marks & Spencer
    Pillsbury
    Red-L
    Richs

13349 Snyder's Ice Cream
2114 Centre St
Ashland, PA 17921-1015   570-875-3320
Processor of ice cream
    Owner: Jim Freed
Estimated Sales: $ 1 - 3 Million
Number Employees: 20-49
Type of Packaging: Consumer

13350 Snyder's of Hanover
P.O.Box 6917
Hanover, PA 17331-0917   717-632-4477
            Fax: 717-632-7207
    consumeraffairs@snyders-han.com
    www.snydersofhanover.com
Manufacturer and exporter of snack foods including pretzels, flavored pretzel pieces and potato, tortilla and corn chips.
    Chairman: Michael Warehime
    CEO: Carl Lee
    CEO: Carl Lee
Estimated Sales: $240 Million
Number Employees: 500-999
Number of Products: 45
Type of Packaging: Consumer
Brands:
    SNYDER'S OF HANOVER

13351 SoBe Beverages
40 Richards Ave
Norwalk, CT 06854-2327   203-899-7111
            Fax: 203-899-7177   800-588-0548
            www.sobebev.com
Healthy fruit and herb beverages with vitamins and minerals
    President: Scott Mossitt
    CEO: Jessica Lee
    CFO: Norm Snyder
    VP: Pamela Woods
    Marketing: Bill Bishop
Estimated Sales: $ 75-100 Million
Number Employees: 50-99
Brands:
    Sobe

13352 Sobaya
PO Box 40
Cowansville, QC J2K 3H1
Canada   450-266-8808
        Fax: 450-266-4750   800-319-8808
        info@sobaya.ca www.sobaya.ca
Natural pasta, organic pasta, Kamut organic pasta and Spelt organic pasta.
    President: Jacques Petit
    Marketing: Sandra Prevost
    Sales Representative: Sandra Prevost
Number Employees: 5
Number of Brands: 1
Number of Products: 14

Sq. footage: 5000
Parent Co: Eden Foods
Type of Packaging: Consumer, Private Label, Bulk
Brands:
    GENMAI UDON
    SOBA
    SOMEN
    UDON

13353 Sobon Estate
12300 Steiner Rd
Plymouth, CA 95669-9503   209-245-4455
        Fax: 209-245-5156 info@sobonwine.com
                www.sobonwine.com
Wine
    Co-Owner: Leon Sobon
    Co-Owner: Shirley Sobon
    Assistant Winemaker/Vineyard Manager: Paul Sobon
    Coordinator of Computer/Business Systems: Robert Sobon
    Sales/Marketing: Tom Quinn
Estimated Sales: $ 5 - 10 Million
Number Employees: 10-19
Brands:
    Shenandoah Vineyards
    Sobon Estate

13354 Societe Cafe
10768 Rue Salk
Montreal-Nord, QC H1G 4Y1
Canada   514-325-9130
        Fax: 514-325-6398 parent@sympatico.ca
            www.intermatch.qc.ca/cafe
Processor and exporter of aroma coffee; importer of green coffee beans and cocoa; custom blending available
    President: M Claude Parent
    Sales/Marketing Executive: Andre Richer
    Purchasing Agent: Linda McGail
Number Employees: 12
Sq. footage: 6000
Type of Packaging: Consumer, Food Service, Private Label, Bulk
Brands:
    Altima
    Aroma
    Bourbon Excelso

13355 Society Hill Snacks
8845 Torresdale Ave
Philadelphia, PA 19136-1510   215-708-8500
        Fax: 215-288-4117   800-595-0050
        info@societyhillsnacks.com
        www.societyhillsnacks.com
Gourmet sweet roasted nuts, snack mixes and great munchies.
    President: Ronna Schultz
Estimated Sales: $ 1 - 3 Million
Number Employees: 1-4
Type of Packaging: Consumer, Food Service, Private Label, Bulk
Brands:
    Afrique
    Cinnful Coco
    Cravin Asian
    Hot Stuff
    Loco Coco
    Love That
    Society Hill Gourmet Nut Company
    Tres Toffee
    Tropical Honey Glace

13356 Sofo Foods
253 Waggoner Blvd
Toledo, OH 43612-1988   419-476-4211
        Fax: 419-478-6104   800-447-4211
        sales@sofofoods.com www.sofofoods.com
Manufacturer of fresh produce, meats, cheeses, disposables, appetizers
    President/CEO/Owner: Tony Sofo
    Marketing: Liz Sofo
    Public Relations: Kim Nevel
Estimated Sales: $ 20-50 Million
Number Employees: 250-499
Type of Packaging: Food Service
Brands:
    A&M Cheese

13357 Soft Gel Technologies
6986 Bandini Blvd
Commerce, CA 90040-3326   323-726-0700
        Fax: 323-726-7065   800-360-7484
        sales@soft-gel.com www.soft-gel.com

Processor of herbal and nutritional supplements
    President: Ron Udell
    VP Sales Administration: Diane Hembree
Type of Packaging: Private Label, Bulk
Brands:
    Coqsol
    SGTI

13358 Soho Beverages
8075 Leesburg Pike
Suite 760
Vienna, VA 22182-2739   703-689-2800
Soft drinks
    President: Tom Cox
Estimated Sales: $ 5-10 Million
Number Employees: 5
Type of Packaging: Private Label
Brands:
    Soho Natural Lemonades
    Soho Natural Soda &

13359 Sokol & Company
5315 Dansher Rd
Countryside, IL 60525   708-482-8250
        Fax: 708-482-9750   800-328-7656
    bparoubek@solofoods.com www.solofoods.com
Cake and pastry fillings, almond paste and marzipan, pie and dessery fillings, marshmallow and toasted marshmallow creme, fruit butters, Asian dipping sauces and marinades, seasoning mixes.
    Chairman: John Sokol Novak
    President: John Novak Jr
    CEO: John Novak Jr
    Research & Development: Larry Lepore
    Quality Control: Galina Mann
    Marketing Director: Eva Karnezis
    Sales Director: Bobby Paroubek
    Plant Manager: Mark Kiefhaber
    Purchasing Manager: Andy Kaminski
Estimated Sales: $16 Million
Number Employees: 50-99
Number of Brands: 5
Sq. footage: 25000
Type of Packaging: Consumer, Food Service, Private Label
Brands:
    BAKER
    BOHEMIAN KITCHEN
    DOBLA
    SIMON FISCHER
    SOLO

13360 Sokol Blosser Winery
P.O.Box 399
Dundee, OR 97115-0399   503-864-2282
        Fax: 503-864-2710   800-582-6668
    info@sokolblosser.com www.sokolblosser.com
Wines
    Manager: Michael Brown
    Marketing Director: Alex Sokol Blosser
    CFO: Alison Sokol Blosser
    Winemaker: Russ Rosner
Estimated Sales: Below $ 5 Million
Number Employees: 10-19
Number of Products: 7
Brands:
    Evolution
    Medetrina
    Sokol Blosser

13361 Solae
4300 Duncan Avenue
St. Louis, MO 63110   314-659-3000
        Fax: 314-629-5749   800-325-7108
                www.solae.com
Develops innovative soy technologies and ingredients for food, meat and industrial products.
    Chairman: Craig Binetti
    CEO: Torkel Rhenman
    CFO: Steve Fray
    VP/General Counsel: Cornel Fuerer
    Senior Director Research & Development: Phil Kerr PhD
Estimated Sales: $1 Billion
Number Employees: 2,400
Other Locations:
    Central Soya Company
    Fort Wayne IN

13362 (HQ)Solae Company
4300 Duncan Avenue
St Louis, MO 63110   314-659-3000
        Fax: 314-982-1121   800-325-7108
                www.solae.com

Manufacturer and exporter of soy ingredient products including textured vegetable proteins, textured and functional soy concentrates and isolates, specialty lecithins and polymers
CEO: Torkel Rhenman
CFO: Steve Fray
VP/General Counsel: Cornel Fuerer
Senior Director R&D: Phil Kerr PhD
VP Marketing/Global Strategy: Michele Fite
Estimated Sales: $1 Billion
Number Employees: 3,500
Parent Co: DuPont & Bunge Limited
Type of Packaging: Bulk
Other Locations:
Solae Manufacturing Plant
Louisville KY
Solae Manufacturing Plant
Bellevue OH
Solae Manufacturing Plant
New Bremem OH
Solae Manufacturing Plant
Remington IN
Solae Manufacturing Plant
Gibson City IL
Solae Manufacturing Plant
Pryor OK
Solae Manufacturing Plant
Memphis TN
Solae Manufacturing Plant
Mexico D.F.
Brands:
Proplus
Supro
Suproplus
Suprosoy

13363 Solana Beach Baking Company
5920 Pasteur Ct
Carlsbad, CA 92008-7317   760-931-0148
Fax: 760-444-9883   info@solanabaking.com
www.solanabaking.com
Breads and pastries
President: David Wells
Quality Control: Kim Hogan
R & D: David Mears
Estimated Sales: $ 30-50 Million
Number Employees: 250-499

13364 Solana Gold Organics
P.O.Box 1340
Sebastopol, CA 95473-1340   707-829-1121
Fax: 707-829-4715   800-459-1121
www.solanagold.com
Processor of organic apples and apple products including kosher, dried, sauce, vinegar, juice, etc
Owner: John Kolling
Sales Director: Chris Blackburn
Estimated Sales: $630000
Number Employees: 1-4
Type of Packaging: Consumer, Private Label, Bulk
Brands:
Solana Gold
Solana Gold Organics

13365 Solgar Vitamin & Herb
500 Willow Tree Rd
Leonia, NJ 07605-2232   201-944-2311
Fax: 201-944-7351
productinformation@solgar.com
www.solgar.com
Manufacturer of natural dietary and nutritional supplements
President/CEO: Allen Skolnick
Estimated Sales: $ 100-500 Million
Number Employees: 250-499
Number of Products: 400
Sq. footage: 50000
Parent Co: NBTY
Type of Packaging: Consumer
Brands:
Kangavites
Natural Bouncin' Berry
Nature's Bounty
Rexall
Solgar
Sundown

13366 Solnuts
P.O.Box 450
Hudson, IA 50643-0450   319-988-3221
Fax: 319-988-4647   800-648-3503
nnewton@kerrygroup.com   www.kneygroup.com

Processor of dry roasted soy nuts and all natural full fat soy flour
Manager: Mike Patterson
Vice President: Michael Healy
Marketing Director: Jim Andrews
Sales/Marketing: Nancy Newton
Operations Manager: Dave Zanchetti
Production Manager: Mike Patterson
Plant Manager: Mike Devine
Estimated Sales: $ 3 - 5 Million
Number Employees: 5-9
Sq. footage: 16000
Parent Co: B.V. Solnut
Type of Packaging: Food Service, Private Label, Bulk
Brands:
Solnuts

13367 Solo Worldwide Enterprises
5683 Columbia Pike
Suite 205
Falls Church, VA 22041-2891   703-845-7072
Fax: 703-560-5744   soloworld@aol.com
General grocery
President, US Division: Eyob Mamo
Estimated Sales: $500,000-$1 Million
Number Employees: 5-9
Brands:
Solo

13368 Soloman Baking Company
3820 Revere St # A
Denver, CO 80239-3464   303-371-2777
Fax: 303-375-9162   sbcinc@att.net
Processor of pita bread, bagel and pita chips, snack mixes and tortillas greek pita
President: Sam Soloman
CEO: Andy Soloman
CFO: Malik Soloman
Estimated Sales: $ 5 - 10 Million
Number Employees: 10-19
Number of Products: 8
Sq. footage: 12000
Type of Packaging: Consumer, Private Label

13369 Soloman Baking Company
3820 Revere St # A
Denver, CO 80239-3464   303-371-2777
Fax: 303-375-9162
Bakery products
President: Sam Soloman
Marketing Director: Hian Soloman
CFO: Annas Soloman
Quality Control: Hiam Soloman
R & D: Max Soloman
Estimated Sales: $ 5-10 Million
Number Employees: 5-9
Brands:
Soloman

13370 Soluble Products Company
480 Oberlin Ave S
Lakewood, NJ 08701-6997   732-364-8855
Fax: 732-364-6689   sales@spcus.com
www.solubleproducts.com
Manufacture of supplements for every lifestyle, including diet, bodybuilding, sports nutrition, nutraceutical and children's products
President: Stephen Hoffman
CEO: Stephen Hoffman
VP: Stewart Hoffman
Sales Manager: Thomas A Flora
Sales Manager: Thomas Flora
Estimated Sales: $ 2.5-5 Million
Number Employees: 20-49
Sq. footage: 50000
Type of Packaging: Private Label
Brands:
Soluble Products

13371 Solvang Bakery
460 Alisal Rd
Solvang, CA 93463-2726   805-688-4939
Fax: 805-686-4407   800-377-4253
www.solvangbakery.com
Processor and exporter of bread, cake and Danish tarts
President: Susan Halme
General manager: Melissa Redell
Estimated Sales: $ 3 - 5 Million
Number Employees: 20-49
Type of Packaging: Consumer, Food Service

13372 Solvay Chemicals
3333 Richmond Ave
Houston, TX 77098   713-525-6500
Fax: 713-525-7800   800-765-8292
david.calvo@solvay.com
www.solvaychemicals.com
Manufacturer of food grade hydrogen peroxids, IXPER® Calcium Peroxide, and BICAR® Sodium Bicarbonate for use in bleaching/decolorization, dough conditioning, leavening, sulfite reduction, microbial sterilization and productpurification.
President: Richard Hogan
Marketing: David Calvo
Number Employees: 100-249
Parent Co: Solvay America

13373 Somerset Food Service
P.O.Box 799
Somerset, KY 42502-0799   606-274-4858
Fax: 606-274-5141   info@somersetfoods.com
www.somersetfoods.com
Food distributor.
President/CEO: Tim Williams
Co-Owner: Mac Goodby
Estimated Sales: $ 20 - 50 Million
Number Employees: 100-249

13374 Somerset Industries
901 North Bethlehem Pike
Spring House, PA 19477-0927   215-619-0480
Fax: 215-619-0489   800-883-8728
benc@somersetindustries.com
www.somersetindustries.com
Wholesaler/distributor, importer and exporter of closeout items bought and sold. The correctional food specialist. Warehouse and transportation services provided
President: Jay Shrager
CFO: Carole Shrager
VP: Alan Breslow
Marketing Director: Candace Shrager
Sales Manager: Ben John McVay
General Manager: Ben Caldwell
Number Employees: 20-49
Type of Packaging: Food Service, Private Label, Bulk
Brands:
21st CENTURY
ANNAMARIA
BOBBIE
SOMERSET
TINY'S TREATS

13375 Somerset Syrup & Beverage
100 McGaw Dr
Edison, NJ 08837-3725   732-225-0209
Fax: 732-225-6363   800-526-8865
www.eatfunfood.com
Confection products
President: Robert Spitz
Estimated Sales: Below $ 5 Million
Number Employees: 20-49

13376 Sommer Maid Creamery
Route 313
Doylestown, PA 18901   215-345-6160
Fax: 215-345-4945
sextonmaid@sommermaid.com
www.sommermaid.com
Processor of cheese, eggs, butter and margarine
President: Frank Sexton
CFO: John T Poprick
VP/General Manager: Harry Mattern
Estimated Sales: $ .5 - 1 million
Number Employees: 5-9
Type of Packaging: Consumer, Food Service, Private Label, Bulk
Brands:
State

13377 Sommer's Food Products
106 W 7th Street
Salisbury, MO 65281-1108   660-388-5511
Potato chips
President: Jack Richardson
Estimated Sales: $ 5-9.9 Million
Number Employees: 7
Brands:
Sommer's Food

13378 Sona & Hollen Foods
3712 Cerritos Avenue
Los Alamitos, CA 90720-2481   562-431-1379
Fax: 562-598-6207   800-200-7662

Processor of portion control products including condiments, ketchup, pickle relish, salsa, jelly, oils, salad dressings and sauces; exporter of salsa and sauce; importer of water chestnuts
President: John Kidde
VP Sales/Marketing: Wes Stroben
Plant Manager: Frank DeAnda
Purchasing Manager: Sevoca Glass
Number Employees: 20-49
Sq. footage: 30000
Parent Co: Ventura Foods, LLC
Type of Packaging: Consumer, Food Service, Private Label, Bulk
Brands:
Homade
Lindy's
Sona

13379 Sonne
896 22nd Ave N
Wahpeton, ND 58075-3026   701-642-3068
Fax: 701-642-9403 800-727-6663
info@dakotagourmet.com
www.dakotagourmet.com
Processor of roasted sunflower seeds, trail mixes and toasted corn and soybeans
Manager: Lucy Spiekermeier
Manager: Lucy Spiekermeier
Estimated Sales:$3000000
Number Employees: 20-49
Sq. footage: 20550
Type of Packaging: Consumer, Food Service, Private Label, Bulk
Brands:
Dakota Gourmet
Dakota Gourmet Heart Smart
Dakota Gourmet Toasted Korn

13380 Sonoco
1 N 2nd St
Hartsville, SC 29550-3300   843-383-7000
Fax: 843-383-7008 800-377-2692
corporate.communications@sonoco.com
www.sonoco.com
Global manufacturer of consumer and industrial packing products and provider of packaging services.
Chairman/President/CEO: Harris Deloch Jr
Owner: Dennis Close
SVP/CFO: Charles Hupfer
Senior Vice President: Jim Brown
VP/Chief Information Officer: Bernard Campbell
Vice President Corporate Planning: Kevin Mahoney
Senior Vice President Human Resources: Cynthia Hartley
Estimated Sales:$3.7 Billion
Number Employees: 16,500

13381 Sonoco Wholesale Grocers
P.O.Box 4319
Houma, LA 70361-4319   985-851-0727
Fax: 985-872-2251 www.sontheimeroffshore.com
Provide offshore catering for people on drilling rigs.
President: John Sontheimer

13382 Sonoita Vineyards
Hc 1 Box 33
Elgin, AZ 85611-9730   520-455-5893
Fax: 520-455-5893 www.sonoitavineyards.com
Wines
Owner/Winemaker: Gordon Dutt
General Manager: Mike Duppost
VP: Jack Strolline
Estimated Sales:$ 1-2.5 Million
Number Employees: 5-9

13383 Sonoma Gourmet
4668 Primero Court
Cotati, CA 94931   707-792-7613
Fax: 707-792-7614
tauceboy@fonomagourmet.com
www.fonomagourmet.com
Gourmet pasta, pasta sauces, marinades/cooking sauces and Tuscan olive spreads
Co-Partner: William Weber
Co-partner: Roger Declerq
Estimated Sales:$ 3 - 5 Million
Number Employees: 10-19

13384 Sonoma Gourmet
466-A Primero Court
Cotati, CA 94931-3020   707-792-7613
Fax: 707-792-7614
sauceboys@sonomagourmet.com
www.sonomagourmet.com
Specialty sauces and condiments
Co-Owner: William Weber
Co-Owner: Roger Declercq
Estimated Sales:$ 2.5-5 Million
Number Employees: 9
Number of Brands: 30
Number of Products: 200
Type of Packaging: Private Label
Brands:
Pometta's
Sonoma Gourmet

13385 Sonoma Seafoods
2 E Spain St
Sonoma, CA 95476-5729   707-996-1931
Fax: 707-935-8846 877-411-2123
sgray@sonomaseafoods.com
www.gypsyboots.com
Stuffed entree products include fish and stuffed seafood in addition to a recently introduced new product line including poultry, pork, beef and vegetables.
Owner: Pete Vivani
Partner: Scott Gray
Sales Manager: Georgine Drees
Estimated Sales:$ 5-9.9 Million
Number Employees: 20-49

13386 Sonoma Wine Services
PO Box 207
Vineburg, CA 95487-0207   707-996-9773
Fax: 707-996-0145
Wines: shipping, storage. Controlled environment bonded warehouse
President: Warren McCambridge
CFO: Denise McCambridge
*Estimated Sales:*Under $500,000
Number Employees: 1-4
Brands:
Sonoma Wine

13387 Sonoma-Cutrer Vineyards
P.O.Box 9
Fulton, CA 95439-0009   707-528-1181
Fax: 707-528-1561 info@sonomacutrer.com
www.sonomacutrer.com
Wines
Managing Director: Keith Levine
Owner: H Jabarin
CFO: Marilo Calabuig
Corporate Communications: James Caudill
Estimated Sales:$ 1-2.5 Million
Number Employees: 50-99
Brands:
Alban Viognier
Chateau Montelena
Hartwell Cabernet
Louis Roederer
MacPhail Pinot
Oberschulte Syrah
Worthy Cabernet

13388 Sonstegard Foods Company
707 E 41st St # 107
Sioux Falls, SD 57105-6050   605-338-4642
Fax: 605-338-8765 800-533-3184
info@sonstegard.com www.sonstegard.com
Sonstegard Foods Company is a major wholesaler of powdered, liquid, and frozen egg products. We sell egg products to food processors, mix manufacturers, schools, food distributors, and industries including the salad dressing industrycandy industry, pasta industry, and others.
President: Philip Sonstegard
Estimated Sales:$ 75-100 Million
Number Employees: 5-9

13389 Soolim
154 Woodstone Drive
Buffalo Grove, IL 60089-6704   847-357-8515
Fax: 847-357-8517 soolimltd@aol.com
Processor and importer of Oriental herbal products
President: Seung Shin
CFO: Chang Jin Lee
Vice President: Gina Lee
Plant Manager: Sang Hoon Shin
Estimated Sales:$500,000 appx.
Number Employees: 5-9
Sq. footage: 12000

Type of Packaging: Consumer

13390 Sopacko Packaging
P.O.Box 827
Bennettsville, SC 29512-0827   843-479-3811
Fax: 843-479-3725 www.sopacko.com
Processor of canned vegetables, beef, pork, stews and poultry; also, pouches of barbecue pork and beef, beef stew, meatballs, tuna with noodles and pasta with sauce
President: Lonnie Thompson
VP: Bill McCreary
Plant Manager: Vera Hahn
Purchasing Manager: Stewart Clark
Estimated Sales:$ 20-50 Million
Number Employees: 100-249
Parent Co: Sopacko
Type of Packaging: Consumer, Food Service, Private Label
Brands:
Sopakco

13391 (HQ)Sopakco Foods
P.O.Box 1047
Mullins, SC 29574-1047   843-464-7851
Fax: 843-464-2096 sfernald@sopakco.com
www.sopakco.com
Sauces, dressings
President/CEO: Lonnie Thompson
Manufacturing Director: William Pettibone
Plant Operations: Bill Jennings
Purchasing: Gene Gasque
Estimated Sales:$ 5-10 Million
Number Employees: 250-499

13392 Sophia's Sauce Works
2533 N Carson Street
Carson City, NV 89706-0147   916-315-3584
Fax: 916-315-9372 800-718-7769
ssw@lanset.com www.ssw-inc.com
Processor of all natural sauces, spreads and dressings
Chairman: Sophia Fridas
President: Jim Fridas
Number Employees: 5-9
Sq. footage: 2000
Parent Co: Sophia's Sauce Works
Type of Packaging: Consumer
Brands:
SOPHIA'S AUTHENTIC
SOPHIA'S SAUCE WORKS

13393 Sopralco
6991 W Broward Blvd
Plantation, FL 33317-2907   954-584-2225
Fax: 954-584-3271 sopralco@aol.com
Processor and importer of ready-to-drink espresso; manufacturer and importer of espresso dispensing equipment; also, fiberglass carts
Owner: Peter Marciante
VP: Arcelia De Battisti
Marketing: Ana Ordaz
Estimated Sales:$ 1-2.5 Million
Number Employees: 1-4
Sq. footage: 1250
Parent Co: Sopralco
Type of Packaging: Consumer, Food Service
Brands:
Espre
Espre-Cart
Espre-Matic

13394 (HQ)Sorbee International
9990 Global Rd
Philadelphia, PA 19115-1006   215-677-5200
Fax: 215-677-7736 800-654-3997
www.sorbee.com
Processor of confectionery items including sugar hard candy, low-fat candy bars and sugar-free items
President: Elliot Stone
VP Sales: Barry Sokol
Estimated Sales:$31200000
Number Employees: 20-49
Other Locations:
Sorbee International Ltd.
Philadelphia PA
Brands:
DREAM CANDY
GLOBAL BRANDS
SORBEE

13395 Sorrenti Family Farms
14033 Steinegul Road
Escalon, CA 95320-9512   209-838-1127
Fax: 209-838-7809   888-435-9490
wildrice@sonnet.com
Wild rice, blended rices, quick-cook rice mixes,
pasta and wild rice mixes, soup mixes, muffin
mixes, focaccia mix and pizza kits
Estimated Sales: $ 2.5-5 Million
Number Employees: 1-4
Brands:
Cucina Sorrenti
Mighty Wild
Rising Star Ranch
Sorrenti Family Farm
Urban Delights

13396 Sorrento LactalisCorporate & Commercial Headquarters
2376 S Park Ave
Buffalo, NY 14220-2670
Fax: 716-823-6454   800-828-7031
fsinfo@sorrentolactalis.com
www.sorrentocheese.com
Manufactures and exports mozzarella, provolone,
mascarpone and ricotta cheeses.
President/CEO: Frederick Bouisset
CFO: John Zielinski
VP Sales & Marketing: John Alfieri
Estimated Sales: $800+ Million
Number Employees: 1,500
Sq. footage: 143872
Parent Co: Lactalis American Group
Type of Packaging: Consumer, Food Service, Private Label, Bulk
Other Locations:
Nampa Plant & Distribution Center
Nampa ID
NJ Distribution Center
Little Ferry NJ
Brands:
PRECIOUS®
SORRENTO®

13397 Sorrento Lactalis
2376 S Park Ave
Buffalo, NY 14220-2670   800-828-7031
Fax: 716-823-6454 www.sorrentolactalis.com
World reknowned cheese brands made available to
the foodservice industry, as well as marketing,
menu, and customer profiling information.
President/CEO: Frederick Bouisset
CFO: John Zielinski
VP: Charles Hylkema
VP Sales/Marketing: John Alfieri
Estimated Sales: $14 Billion
Number Employees: 1,500
Number of Brands: 8
Parent Co: Sorrento Lactalis
Type of Packaging: Food Service
Brands:
BELMONT GOAT CHEESE
GALBANI
MOZZARELLA FRESCA
PRECIOUS
PRESIDENT
RONDELE
SORRENTO
VALBRESO FETA

13398 Sorrento LactalisPlant & Distribution Center
4912 E Franklin Rd
Nampa, ID 83687-8400   208-467-4424
Fax: 208-467-9987 agerard@sorrentolactalis.com
www.sorrentolactalis.com
Cheese, cheese products
Manager: Alain Gerared
Plant Manager: Jean Claude Bruneau
Estimated Sales: $ 10-20 Million
Number Employees: 600
Parent Co: Lactalis American Group
Type of Packaging: Consumer, Food Service
Brands:
Precious
Sorrento Cheese

13399 Sorrento LactalisNJ Distribution Center
33 Ludwig Street
Little Ferry, NJ 08+57-8400   201-440-8383
www.sorrentolactalis.com

Cheese, cheese products
Manager: Mark Quinpoalo
Estimated Sales: $10-20 Million
Number Employees: 10
Parent Co: Lactalis American Group

13400 Sorrento Lobster
P.O.Box 124
Sorrento, ME 04677-0124   207-422-9082
Fax: 207-422-9033
Seafood.
Manager: Rick Freeman Jr
Estimated Sales: $2,100,000
Number Employees: 5-9

13401 Soteria
180 Kite Lake Road
Fairburn, GA 30213-9608   404-768-5161
Fax: 404-768-3704
heavenlyseason@mindspring.com
Processor of natural and dry seasoning blends with
no salt, MSG or calories
CEO: Lee Armstrong
Executive VP: Denise Armstrong
VP Operations: Keith Jackson
Number Employees: 1-4

13402 Source Consumer Products
25 Sylvan Road S
Suite Q
Westport, CT 06880-4637   203-222-3881
Fax: 203-222-3883
Chewing gum
President: John Weiss

13403 Source Food Technology
2530 Meridian Parkway
Suite 300, Research Triangle Park
Durham, NC 27713   919-806-4545
Fax: 919-806-4842   866-277-3849
www.sourcefoodtechnology.com
Processor of cholesterol-free shortenings, fats and
oils; also, cholesterol reduced egg and dairy products
CEO: Henry Cardello
VP Sales: Patrick Halliday
Number Employees: 5-9

13404 Source Food Technology
12235 Nicollet Avenue
Burnsville, MN 55337-1650   612-890-6366
Fax: 612-890-5748
Nutritionally enhanced food ingredients
Estimated Sales: $ 10-25 Million
Number Employees: 19

13405 Source Naturals
23 Janis Way
Scotts Valley, CA 95066-3506   831-438-1144
Fax: 831-438-7410   800-815-2333
heidib@thresholdent.com
Manufacturer and wholesaler/distributor of dietary
supplements
Founder/CEO: Ira Goldberg
Estimated Sales: $100+ Million
Number Employees: 250-499
Parent Co: Threshold Enterprises
Brands:
SOURCE

13406 Souris Valley Processors
PO Box 460
Melita, NB R0M 1L0
Canada   204-522-8210
Fax: 204-522-8210
Processor of beef and pork
President: Larry Danyluk
Number Employees: 5-9
Sq. footage: 4000
Type of Packaging: Consumer, Food Service

13407 Sourthern Tea
1267 Cobb Industrial Dr
Marietta, GA 30066-6699   770-428-3528
Fax: 770-425-6188   800-241-0896
www.tetley.com
Processor and exporter of tea bags
Manager: John Langston
Plant Manager: Paul Scell
Estimated Sales: $ 20 - 50 Million
Number Employees: 100-249
Parent Co: Tetley USA

Type of Packaging: Consumer, Food Service, Private Label, Bulk

13408 South Beach Coffee Company
975 Arthur Godfrey Road
Miami Beach, FL 33140-3329   305-576-9696
Fax: 305-532-0409 info@discoverourtown.com
www.southbeachcoffee.com
Coffee for wholesale and retail customers
President: Hagai Gringarten
Vice President: Droma Gringarten
Marketing Director: Karen Kong
Operations Manager: Ruben Meoqui
Estimated Sales: $ 1-5 Million
Number Employees: 13
Type of Packaging: Consumer, Private Label
Brands:
LINCOLN ROAD BLEND
OCEAN DRIVE BLEND
OCEAN ROAD BLEND

13409 South Beach Novelties &Confectionery
44 Robin Rd
Staten Island, NY 10305-4799   718-727-4500
Fax: 718-448-4108 johnl4244@AOL.com
Confections
Owner: John Lagana
Purchasing Manager: John Lagana
Estimated Sales: $ 10 - 20 Million
Number Employees: 5-9
Brands:
Gator Ade
Polar Spring Water

13410 South Bend Chocolate
3300 W Sample St
South Bend, IN 46619-3079   574-233-2577
Fax: 574-233-3150   800-301-4961
orders@sbchocolate.com www.sbchocolate.com
Distinctive chocolates
President: Mart Tarner
Marketing Director: Kristina Pier
Estimated Sales: $ 20 - 50 Million
Number Employees: 50-99
Brands:
South Bend Chocolate

13411 South Ceasar Dressing Company
PO Box 612
Novato, CA 94948-0612   415-897-0605
Fax: 415-897-0605
Salad dressing
Partner: Shirley Lesley
Partner: Mark Lesley
Estimated Sales: Under $500,000
Number Employees: 1-4
Type of Packaging: Private Label
Brands:
South Ceasar Dressing Company

13412 South Exotic Foods
2605 Camino Del Rio S # 220
San Diego, CA 92108-3749
USA   619-491-0438
Fax: 619-294-6750
rolando@southexoticfoods.com
Tamales, burritas & variety of authentic mexican
foods plus hot chocolate
Owner: Elizabeth La Shure
VP: Rolando Espinosa
Sales: Michael Spinner
Estimated Sales: $300,000-500,000
Number Employees: 1-4

13413 South Georgia Pecan
P.O.Box 5366
Valdosta, GA 31603-5366   229-244-1321
Fax: 229-247-6361   800-627-6630
info@georgiapecan.com www.georgiapecan.com
Manufacturer and exporter of shelled pecans
Co-Owner: Jim Worn
Co-Owner: Ed Crane
Estimated Sales: $ 20 - 50 Million
Number Employees: 100-249
Type of Packaging: Consumer
Brands:
DASHER PECAN

13414 South Georgia Pecan Company
P.O.Box 5366
Valdosta, GA 31603-5366   229-244-1321
Fax: 229-247-6361   800-627-6630
info@georgiapecan.com www.georgiapecan.com

Processor and exporter of nut meats and pecans including shelled and in-shell
President/Owner: Jim P Worn
Owner: Ed Crane
VP: Jimmy Colwell
Purchasing: Gary Peters
Estimated Sales:$10,700,000
Number Employees: 100-249
Type of Packaging: Bulk
Brands:
South Georgia
Southland's

13415 South Louisiana Sugars
PO Box 67
Saint James, LA 70086-0067   225-265-4056
Fax: 225-265-4060   info@slscoop.com
www.SLSCoop.com
Processor of sugar including raw, turbinado granulated and clarified syrup
President: Ronald Blanchard
Vice President: John Thigaut
General Manager: Jan Bergeron
Production Manager: Walter Simoneaux
Plant Manager: Keith Guedry
Purchasing Manager: Andrew Robertson
Estimated Sales:$20 Million
Number Employees: 50
Type of Packaging: Consumer, Private Label
Brands:
Cajun Crystals
Cajun Gold

13416 (HQ)South Mill Distribution
649 West South Street
PO Box 1037
Kennett Square, PA 19348-0424   610-444-4800
Fax: 610-444-1338   info@southmill.com
www.southmill.com
Grower, processor and distributor of mushrooms, (fresh, canned, blanched, value-added and dried, etc) and produce with the ability to deliver to 36 states overnight. Warehouse offering cooler storage for produce; transportationservices include LTL
President: Michael Pea
Sales Manager New Orleans: Jay Joyce
Sales Manager Dallas: Shawn Weidman
Sales Manager Houston: Dennis Smith
Estimated Sales:$ 20 - 50 Million
Number Employees: 500-999
Sq. footage: 120000
Parent Co: Kaolin Mushroom Farms
Type of Packaging: Consumer, Food Service, Private Label, Bulk
Other Locations:
South Mill Distribution:Forest Park
Atlanta GA
South Mill Distribution:Haraham
New Orleans LA
South Mill Distribution:Houston
Houston TX
South Mill Distribution:Dallas
Dallas TX
Brands:
Brown King
South Mill Mushroom Sales

13417 South Pacific Trading Company
15052 Ronnie Dr # 100
Dade City, FL 33523-6011   352-567-2200
Fax: 352-567-2257   888-505-4439
scot@nonipacific.com   www.nonipacific.com
Private label, dietary supplements, import/export bulk noni juice (certified organic), cocnut oil (certified organic)
President: Scot Vallantyne
Sales Director: Susan Ballantyne
Operations Manager: Brenda Rossbach
Plant Manager: James Dean
Estimated Sales:$1 Million
Number Employees: 5-9
Number of Brands: 2
Number of Products: 8
Sq. footage: 17000
Type of Packaging: Consumer, Private Label, Bulk
Brands:
CHERRY NONI
COCONUT PACIFIC
NONI "C"LECT
NONI PACIFIC

13418 South Shores Seafood
1822 E Ball Rd
Anaheim, CA 92805-5936   714-956-2722
Fax: 714-956-0277

Seafood
President: Michael Armstrong
Estimated Sales:$2,000,000
Number Employees: 5-9

13419 South Texas Spice Company
2106 Castroville Rd
San Antonio, TX 78237-3516   210-436-2280
Fax: 210-436-6658
Spices
Partner: Zeferino Menchaca
Estimated Sales:$390,000
Number Employees: 5-9
Brands:
Menchaca
South Texas Spice
Yellow Rose

13420 South Valley Citrus Packers
P.O.Box 10055
Terra Bella, CA 93270-0055   559-906-1033
Fax: 559-525-4206   vcpg@vcpg.com
www.vcpg.com/gvh.htm
Packinghouse and licensed shipper of Sunkist Growers Inc. citrus products.
Manager: Cliff Martin
Grower Service Representative: Maribel Nenna
General Manager Visalia Citrus Packing: Bob Walters
Parent Co: Visalia Citrus Packing Group
Type of Packaging: Food Service

13421 South Valley Farms
15443 Beech Ave
Wasco, CA 93280-7604   661-391-9000
Fax: 661-391-9012   hmemmott@fmc-slc.com
www.southvalleyfarms.com
Grower and exporter of almonds and pistachios; processor of hulled and shelled almonds
President: John Creer
VP: Daryl Wilkendors
Processing Manager: Jonathan Meyer
Estimated Sales:$ 2.5-5 Million
Number Employees: 100-249
Sq. footage: 80000
Parent Co: Farm Management Company
Type of Packaging: Bulk

13422 South West Foods Tasty Bakery
P.O.Box 1411
Tyler, TX 75710-1411   903-877-3481
Fax: 903-877-6903   dennisprice@brookshires.com
www.brookshires.com
Baked goods
Manager: Sheila Vickery
Brands:
South West

13423 Southchem
2000 E Pettigrew St
Durham, NC 27703-4049   919-596-0681
Fax: 919-596-6438   800-849-7000
Beverages, confectionery, canned foods, processed cheese, bakery, meat, seafood, dairy
President: Gil D Steadman
Number Employees: 100-249

13424 Southeast Alaska SmokedSalmon Company
550 S Franklin St
Juneau, AK 99801-1330   907-463-4617
Fax: 907-463-4644
Smoked salmon
President: Sandro Lane
CEO: Giovanni Gallizio
Estimated Sales:$ 50 - 100 Million
Number Employees: 100-249

13425 Southeast Baking Corporation
49 Batesville Ct
Greer, SC 29650-4800   864-627-1380
Fax: 864-627-1381
Processor of bread
President: Mario Romano
Estimated Sales:$500,000-$1 Million
Number Employees: 10-19

13426 Southeast Canners
7607 Veterans Pkwy
Columbus, GA 31909-2503   706-324-0040
Fax: 706-324-6404

Processor of canned and bottled soft drinks
President: Sheyenne Bradford
Plant Manager: Don Hambrick
CFO: Robert Heurich
Controller: Pat Barnes
Quality Control: Malinda Delradge
Estimated Sales:$ 20-50 Million
Number Employees: 50-99
Parent Co: PepsiCo
Type of Packaging: Consumer, Food Service
Brands:
Pepsi

13427 Southeast Dairy Processors
3803 E Columbus Dr
Tampa, FL 33605-3220   813-621-3233
Fax: 813-626-1516   info@instantwhip.com
www.instantwhipflorida.com
Milk and dairy products
President: William Tiller
Estimated Sales:$ 5-10 Million
Number Employees: 20-49
Type of Packaging: Private Label

13428 Southeastern Meat Association
131 W Broadway St # A
Oviedo, FL 32765-6302   407-365-5661
Fax: 407-365-8945   info@southeasternmeat.com
http://www.southeasternmeat.com
Processor and packer of frozen portion controlled beef, pork, veal and chicken
Executive Director: Anna Ondick
Estimated Sales:$20-50 Million
Number Employees: 1-4
Type of Packaging: Consumer, Food Service

13429 Southeastern Meats
PO Box 8325
Birmingham, AL 35218-0325   205-785-3194
Fax: 205-780-8517
Meat
Chairman/CEO: Lester Newby Jr
CFO: Trecia Franks

13430 Southeastern Mills
P.O.Box 908
Rome, GA 30162-0908   706-291-6528
Fax: 706-295-5411   800-334-4468
customerservice@semills.com   www.semills.com
Processor of flour, corn meal & grits, sauce & gravy mixes, specialty baking mixes, batters & breadings, seasonings & marinades
President: Robert Ugrizzard
CEO: Vernon Grizzard
Director Sales: Michael O'Connor
Plant Manager: David Neff
Purchasing Manager: Chris Wheeler
Estimated Sales:$100+ Million
Number Employees: 100-249
Type of Packaging: Consumer, Food Service, Private Label, Bulk
Brands:
Four Roses
Good Loaf
Southeastern Mills
Stivers Best
Strong Boy

13431 Southeastern Sales
PO Box 467
Hixson, TN 37343-0467   423-877-3781
Fax: 423-877-3784
Processor and exporter of poultry and poultry products
President: M Wilson, Jr.
*Estimated Sales:*Less than $500,000
Number Employees: 1-4
Sq. footage: 5000
Type of Packaging: Consumer, Food Service, Bulk

13432 Southeastern Wisconsin Products Company
500 W Edgerton Ave
Milwaukee, WI 53207-6029   414-482-1730
Fax: 414-482-2812   www.campbellsoup.com
Processor of yeast, sage oil and dairy flavoring extracts
President: Del Nirode
Quality Manager: Michael Malencore
Production Manager: Raymond Miller
Plant Manager: Bill Blue
Purchasing Manager: John Schmidt

Estimated Sales:$ 20 - 50 Million
Number Employees: 20-49
Parent Co: Campbell Soup Company

13433 Southern Bar-B-Que
PO Box 206
Jennings, LA 70546   337-824-3877
          Fax: 337-824-6678   866-612-2586
          www.southernbbqsauce.com
bbq sauce, basting sauce, crawfish, shrimp and crab
boil, frying oil, grill-n-que rub, grill-n-que sauce,
pepper sauce, roux, salsa, seasoning and spray
basters

13434 Southern Bell Dairy
607 Bourne Ave
Somerset, KY 42501-1919   606-679-1131
          Fax: 800-441-8931   800-468-4798
          mike.chandler@southernbelledairy.com
          www.southernbelledairy.com
Dairy
     President: Mike Chandler
     President: Martin Shearer
     Marketing Manager: Doug Wade
     VP Sales: Glenn Carlyle
     General Sales Manager: Gene Kennedy
     Manager Information Systems: Dan/Judy Hall
     Plant Manager: Kevin Randolf
Estimated Sales:$ 50-99.9 Million
Number Employees: 100-249

13435 Southern Belle SandwichCompany
1969 N Lobdell Ave
Baton Rouge, LA 70806-1726   225-927-4670
          Fax: 225-928-5661   800-344-4670
          www.southernbellesandwich.com
Processor of fresh sandwiches
     President: Lloyd Bearden Jr
     VP: Homer Miller
     Sales Manager: Rick Bearden
Estimated Sales:$ 5 - 10 Million
Number Employees: 100-249
Sq. footage: 10000
Parent Co: Bearden Sandwich Company
Type of Packaging: Consumer

13436 Southern Beverage Packers
P.O.Box 560
Appling, GA 30802-0560   706-541-9222
          Fax: 706-541-1730   800-326-2469
          qch2o@cs.com
Processor of water and marketer of crystalline soft
drink and fruit drinks
     President: David Byrd
     Vice President: Stephen Byrd
     Marketing Director: Jeff Millick
     Production Manager: Lynn Hebbard
     Plant Manager/Purchasing: Richard Maddox
Estimated Sales:$7200000
Number Employees: 20-49
Number of Brands: 2
Number of Products: 50
Type of Packaging: Consumer, Bulk
Brands:
     Carolina Choice
     Flowing Wells
     Flowing Wells Natural Water
     Kist
     Spingtime
     Springtime Natural Artesian Water

13437 Southern Brown Rice
P.O.Box 185
Weiner, AR 72479-0185   870-684-2354
          Fax: 870-684-2239   800-421-7423
          office@hoguefarms.com
          www.southernbrownrice.com
Processor of organically grown rice bran and flour;
also, long, medium and short grain rice including
basmati, brown, wild and wild blend
     Manager: Bill Weeks
Estimated Sales:$740000
Number Employees: 5-9
Sq. footage: 14000

13438 Southern California Brewing Company
833 Torrance Blvd # 105
Torrance, CA 90502-1733   310-329-8881
          Fax: 310-516-7989
          thebrewer@angelcitybrewing.com
          www.angelcitybrewing.com

Processor of seasonal beer, ale, stout, lager and
pilsner
     President/CEO: Michael Bowe
Estimated Sales:$3-$5 Million
Number Employees: 1-4
Type of Packaging: Consumer, Food Service
Brands:
     Bear Country Bavarian
     Bock
     California Light Blonde
     Old Red Eye
     Winter Wonder

13439 Southern Delight Gourmet Foods
1621 Scottsville Rd
Bowling Green, KY 42104-3244   270-782-9943
          Fax: 270-843-7544   866-782-9943
          info@southern-delight.com
          www.southern-delight.com
Gourmet sauces, gourmet marinades, gourmet salsas,
gourmet seasonings, gourmet gift sets
     Owner: Bart Anderson
Estimated Sales:$ 3 - 5 Million
Number Employees: 1-4
Type of Packaging: Consumer

13440 Southern Farms Fish Processors
103 W 26th Avenue
Kansas City, MO 64116-3060   870-355-2594
          Fax: 870-355-4024   800-264-2594
Processor of frozen catfish fillets, nuggets, strips,
tidbits and breaded
     President: John Gentry
Type of Packaging: Consumer, Food Service
Brands:
     Springwater Farms

13441 Southern Fish & Oyster Company
1 Eslava St
Mobile, AL 36603   251-438-2408
          Fax: 251-432-7773
Seafood, oysters
     Owner: Ralph Atkins
Estimated Sales:$ 1 - 3 Million
Number Employees: 10-19

13442 (HQ)Southern Flavoring Company
1330 Norfolk Ave
Bedford, VA 24523-2223   540-586-8565
          Fax: 540-586-8568   800-765-8565
          service@southernflavoring.com
          www.southernflavoring.com
Processor of liquid food flavorings
     President: E Thomas Messier
     VP Marketing: John Messier
Estimated Sales:$5000000
Number Employees: 10-19
Sq. footage: 35000
Parent Co: Southern Flavoring
Type of Packaging: Consumer, Private Label, Bulk
Brands:
     Clapier Mill
     Happy Home

13443 Southern Gardens CitrusProcessing
1820 County Road 833
Clewiston, FL 33440-9222   863-983-3030
          Fax: 863-983-3060 www.southerngardens.com
Processor of citrus juices, concentrates, blends and
ingredients
     President: Robert Baker Jr
     Finance Executive: Ginny Pena
     VP Marketing: Charles Lucas
Number Employees: 100-249
Parent Co: US Sugar Corporation
Type of Packaging: Bulk

13444 Southern Gold Honey CompAny
3015 Brown Rd
Vidor, TX 77662-7902   409-768-1645
          Fax: 409-768-1009   808-899-2494
Processor, exporter and wholesaler/distributor of
honey and specialty items including pecan cream
honey and fruit flavored honeys; also, beeswax and
candles; gift items available
     Owner: Gretchen Horn
*Estimated Sales:*Less than $500,000
Number Employees: 20-49
Type of Packaging: Consumer, Private Label
Brands:
     Southern Gold Honey

13445 Southern Heritage Coffee Company
6555 E 30th St # F
Indianapolis, IN 46219-1133   317-543-2080
          Fax: 317-543-0757   800-486-1198
          kevin@heritage-coffee.com
          www.coppermooncoffee.com
Processor, importer, exporter and contract roaster of
coffee including house blends and gourmet, liquid
concentrate, espresso, instant cappuccino, pads, ho-
tel in-room filter packed coffees
     Manager: Doug Bachman
     CEO: Kevin Daw
     Sales Director: Kevin Daw
     Operations Manager: Dick Middleton
     Purchasing Manager: Tom Oldridge
Number Employees: 20-49
Sq. footage: 52000
Type of Packaging: Consumer, Food Service, Pri-
vate Label, Bulk
Brands:
     Coffee Scapes
     Espresso Caruso
     Espresso Maria
     Heritage Espresso Pods
     Heritage Select
     Mugshots
     SORENGETI COFFEES
     Safari Blend Liquid Coffee
     Santa's Favorite
     Select Blend In-Room Coffee
     Southern Heritage
     World Coffee Safari Gourmet

13446 Southern Ice Cream Specialties
1058 King Industrial Dr
Marietta, GA 30062-2492   770-428-0452
          Fax: 770-426-5441
Processor of ice cream novelties
     Manager: Craig McDufie
     Plant Manager: Kevin Vondusaar
Number Employees: 100-249
Parent Co: Kroger Company
Type of Packaging: Consumer, Private Label
Brands:
     Healthy Indulgence
     Texas Gold

13447 Southern Minnesota BeetSugar Cooperative
P.O.Box 500
Renville, MN 56284-0500   320-329-8305
          Fax: 320-329-3252   info@smbsc.com
          www.smbsc.com
Manufacturer of molasses and sugar. The company
has acquired Holly Sugar Corporation
     President: John Richmond
     VP Finance: Jeff Plathe
     Operations: Darvin Hauptli
     VP Operations: Mark Suhr
Estimated Sales:$202.7 Million
Number Employees: 500-999
Type of Packaging: Consumer, Bulk

13448 Southern Minnesota BeetSugar Cooperative
P.O.Box 500
Renville, MN 56284-0500   320-329-8305
          Fax: 320-329-3252   info@smbsc.com
          www.smbsc.com
Manufacturer of sugar beets.
     President: John Richmond
     Operations: Darvin Hauptli
*Estimated Sales:*Under $500,000
Number Employees: 1-4

13449 Southern Packing Corporation
4004 Battlefield Blvd S
Chesapeake, VA 23322-2431   757-421-2131
          Fax: 757-421-3633
Processor and packer of beef, pork and veal
     President: H Brooke
     VP: B Brooke
Estimated Sales:$ 50 - 100 Million
Number Employees: 20-49
Type of Packaging: Consumer, Food Service, Bulk
Brands:
     Cavalier

13450 Southern Peanut Company
P.O.Box 160
Dublin, NC 28332-0160 910-862-2136
Fax: 910-862-8076 www.peanutprocessors.com
Processor of peanuts including in shell, raw shelled, blanched redskins, peanut granules, oil & dry roasted peanuts and peanut butter.
President: Houston Brisson
Plant Manager: Luke Clearman
Estimated Sales:$11098380
Number Employees: 10-19
Sq. footage: 180000
Parent Co: Peanut Processors
Type of Packaging: Consumer, Food Service, Bulk

13451 Southern Popcorn Company
1892-C East Brooks Road
Memphis, TN 38118-6608 901-362-5238
Fax: 901-888-0230 murrey@mindspring.com
Popcorn, jellies, dessert toppings
President: Murrey Watkins
Estimated Sales:$5-9.9 Million
Number Employees: 10-19

13452 Southern Pride Catfish Company
Ste 900
2025 1st Ave
Seattle, WA 98121-3123 334-624-4021
Fax: 334-624-8224 800-343-8046
info@americanprideseafoods.com
www.southernpride.net
Processor and exporter of farm-raised catfish
President: Joe Glover
Quality Control: Alice Moore
VP Sales: Randy Rhodes
Public Relations: Mary Hand
Operations Manager: Bobby Collins
Number Employees: 500-999
Type of Packaging: Consumer, Food Service, Private Label
Brands:
SOUTHERN PRIDE

13453 Southern Ray's Foods
PO Box 402552
Miami Beach, FL 33140-0552 800-972-8237
Fax: 914-833-5009 ray@southernrays.com
www.southernrays.com
Processor and exporter of apple wine and maple teriyaki marinades; also, barbecue sauces including southern style, three pepper, honey and orange, island pepper, roasted and smoked garlic and ginger, etc
Owner: Steve Hasday
Type of Packaging: Consumer, Food Service, Private Label
Brands:
Southern Ray's

13454 Southern Roasted Nuts
PO Box 508
Fitzgerald, GA 31750-0508 912-423-5616
Fax: 912-423-6550
Roasted nuts
President: Allen Conger
Estimated Sales:$ 10-24.9 Million
Number Employees: 40

13455 Southern Seafood Distributors
26400 Buford Creel Rd
Franklinton, LA 70438-6324 985-839-6220
Fax: 985-839-6297
Seafood
Owner: Jackie Creel
Estimated Sales:$ 1 - 3 Million
Number Employees: 1-4

13456 Southern Shell Fish Company
P.O.Box 97
Harvey, LA 70059-0097 504-341-5631
Fax: 504-341-5635
Processor, canner and exporter of crabmeat, oysters and shrimp
Manager: Dennis Skrmetta
Sales Manager: H Burke Jr
Plant Manager: Golden Boutte
Estimated Sales:$1400000
Number Employees: 1-4
Parent Co: Deepsouth Packing Company
Type of Packaging: Consumer, Food Service, Private Label
Brands:
Blue Plate
Dunbar
Gulf Kist
House of Windsor
Pride New Orleans

13457 Southern Shellfish
120 Johnny Mercer Boulevard
Savannah, GA 31410-2142 912-897-3650
Fax: 912-897-6036
Seafood, shellfish

13458 Southern Snow Manufacturing
103 W W St
Belle Chasse, LA 70037-1111 504-393-8967
Fax: 504-393-0112 snowmfg@gs.net
www.southernsnow.com
Manufacturer and exporter of artificial concentrates including colors and flavors; also, ice block shavers
President: Bubby Wendling
Marketing: Danielle Havnen
Estimated Sales:$1500000
Number Employees: 10-19
Sq. footage: 10000
Brands:
Southern Snow

13459 Southern Star Seafood
301 N 25th St
Fort Pierce, FL 34947-3306 561-461-5787
Fax: 561-468-6929
Processor of seafood including trout; also, canned and frozen shellfish including lobster and lobster meat
President: William Hudgins
Type of Packaging: Consumer, Food Service

13460 Southern Style Nuts
2419 Meadows Ln
Sherman, TX 75092-3021 903-893-7704
Fax: 903-463-0102 800-624-8242
info@squirrelbrand.com
www.southernstylenuts.com
Processor of roasted and blended nuts including snack mixes, hot and honey roasted peanuts, confectionery pecans and almonds and sweet and salty cashews
President: Michael Kurilecz
VP: Virgil Williamson
Estimated Sales:$6200000
Number Employees: 20-49
Type of Packaging: Consumer, Food Service, Private Label, Bulk
Brands:
Roann's Confections
Southern Style Nuts
Squirrel Brand

13461 Southern Tea Company
1267 Cobb Industrial Dr
Marietta, GA 30066-6699 770-428-3528
Fax: 770-427-7019
Tea
Manager: John Langston
VP Sales/Marketing: Bruce Klodt
*Estimated Sales:*Under $500,000
Number Employees: 100-249
Type of Packaging: Private Label, Bulk

13462 Southernfood Specialties
4300 Bankers Cir # A
Atlanta, GA 30360-2738 770-447-4600
Fax: 770-447-0406 800-255-5323
customerservice@southernfoodspecialties.
www.southernfoodspecialties.com
Cookies, biscuits, cheese dips and toffee
Estimated Sales:$ 5 - 10 Million
Number Employees: 20-49
Brands:
Cheese Tabs
Delicias Toffee
Southernfood Specialties
Tabasco
Wesley's Kitchen
Willingham Manor

13463 Southington Packing Company Inc
553 Mount Vernon Road
Southington, CT 06489 860-628-9544
Processor of meat products including beef, goat, pork and lamb; slaughtering services available
President: David Hubeny
Estimated Sales:$150000
Number Employees: 4
Type of Packaging: Consumer, Food Service

13464 Southside Seafood Company
1544 Forest Pkwy
Morrow, GA 30260-3555 404-366-6172
Fax: 404-366-6178 www.southsideseafood.com
Seafood
President: Robert Lee
Estimated Sales:$ 3 - 5 Million
Number Employees: 10-19

13465 Southtowns Seafood & Meats
P.O.Box 1956
Blasdell, NY 14219-0156 716-824-4900
Fax: 716-822-8216
Processor and of beef, pork, lamb, veal, poultry and frozen seafood; serving the food service market
Manager: David Norton
Director (Meat): William Mutton
Estimated Sales:$ 50 - 100 Million
Number Employees: 20-49
Type of Packaging: Food Service, Private Label

13466 Southwest Canners of Texas
617 Industrial Dr
Nacogdoches, TX 75964-1291 936-569-9737
Fax: 936-569-7019 www.swcanners.com
Canner of soft drinks
President/CEO: Jack Tigner
Chairman of the Board: Don Mapel
CFO: Jennifer Morris
Quality Control: Keith Thompson
Plant Manager: Rodman Reed
Estimated Sales:$ 30-50 Million
Number Employees: 50-99
Type of Packaging: Consumer, Food Service
Brands:
Coke

13467 Southwest Nut Company
825 W. Main Street
Fabens, TX 79838 915-764-4949
Fax: 888-593-1262 info@southwestnut.com
www.southwestnut.com
Pecans
Sq. footage: 50000

13468 Southwest Specialty Food
700 N Bullard Ave
Goodyear, AZ 85338-2506 623-931-3131
Fax: 623-931-9931 800-536-3131
southwest@asskickin.com www.asskickin.com
Makers of gourmet hot sauce and other fine products such as hot sauces, salsas, snacks, gift sets, marinades/sauces, chili mixes/spices, beverages and condiments.
Owner: Jeff Jacobs
*Estimated Sales:*Below $ 5 Million
Number Employees: 5-9
Type of Packaging: Private Label
Brands:
Banditos Salsas
Candy Ass
Habanero Products From Hell
Seasonings From Hell
Spontaneous Combustion

13469 Southwest Spirit
701 Buford Drive
Socorro, NM 87801-4019 800-838-0773
Fax: 505-838-0177 info@swspirit.com
www.swspirit.com
Salsas
Co-Owner: Cynthia Fowler
Co-Owner: Jim Fowler
Type of Packaging: Consumer

13470 Southwestern Wisconsin Dairy Goat Products
P.O.Box 103
Mt Sterling, WI 54645-0103 608-734-3151
Fax: 608-734-3810 mtsterling@mwt.net
www.buygoatcheese.com
Processor of raw goat's milk cheeses including cheddar, feta, pasteurized country jack and pasteurized no salt cheddar; also, goat's milk butter; raw milk sharp cheddar; raw milk mild cheddar; pasteurized cheddar; rae milk organiccheddar; fresh Jack flavors: tomato and basil, jalapeno pepper, chive, dill, garlic, onion
Manager: Shannon Adams
Marketing/Sales: Patricia Lund
Plant Manager: Al Bekkum
Estimated Sales:$1946722
Number Employees: 10-19

Number of Brands: 1
Number of Products: 13
Sq. footage: 2450
Type of Packaging: Consumer, Food Service, Private Label, Bulk
Brands:
  Kickapoo of Wisconsin
  Mt. Sterling Cheese Co.

13471 Sovena USA
1 Olive Grove Street
Rome, NY 13441   315-797-7070
    Fax: 315-797-6981
customerservice@sovenausa.com
www.sovenausa.com
Manufacturer of domestic edible oils including olive, corn, soybean, peanut and salad; importer of olive oil
  CEO: Steve Mandia
  CFO: Dave Lofgren
  VP: Bert Mandia
  VP Sales/Marketing: Mark Mottit
Estimated Sales:$12.7 Million
Number Employees: 80
Sq. footage: 15000
Brands:
  CLIO POMACE
  CLIO PURE
  GEM 100%
  GEM BLENDED
  GEM EXTRA

13472 Sow's Ear Winery
303 Coastal Rd
Brooksville, ME 04617-3705   207-326-4649
Wines
  President: Thomas Hoey
Estimated Sales:$20,000
Number Employees: 5-9

13473 Soy Vay Enterprises
P.O.Box 452
Felton, CA 95018-0452   831-335-3824
    Fax: 831-335-3589   800-600-2077
support@soyvay.com   www.soyvay.com
Teriyaki, salad dressing and marinade, hoisin and garlic-based sauce
  President/Owner: Eddy Scher
Estimated Sales:$ 1 - 3 Million
Number Employees: 1-4
Type of Packaging: Consumer, Food Service, Private Label
Brands:
  Cha-Cha Chinese Chicken Dressing
  Chinese Marinade
  Island Teriyaki
  Soy Vay Veri-Veri Teriyaki

13474 SoyLife Division
3300 Edinborough Way # 712
Edina, MN 55435-5963   952-920-7700
    Fax: 952-920-7704   soylife@schoutenusa.com
www.frutarom.com
Soy isoflavone, nutraceutical ingredients
  President: Laurent Leduc
*Estimated Sales:*Less than $500,000
Number Employees: 5-9

13475 SoyTex
609 Eagle Rock Ave
West Orange, NJ 07052-2903   973-243-1899
    Fax: 973-243-0800   888-769-8391
soytexinfo@soytex.com   soytex.com
Manufacturer and sell meat substitution products made from high quality soy protein concentrate using modern extrusion technology.
  President: Joseph Nazarian
  VP: Tirdad Zandieh

13476 Soyfoods of America
1091 Hamilton Rd
Duarte, CA 91010-2743   626-358-3836
    Fax: 626-358-4136   www.soyfoodsusa.com
Processor of soy milk and yuba; also, regular and marinated tofu, cultured soy beverage, bulk soymilk
  Owner: Kanin Lee
  Sales Director: Harry Tanikawa
Estimated Sales:$ 20 - 50 Million
Number Employees: 20-49
Sq. footage: 15000
Type of Packaging: Consumer, Food Service, Private Label, Bulk

Brands:
  Furama
  Soywise

13477 Soylent Brand
PO Box 165475
Irving, TX 75016-5475   972-255-4747
pinegap@flashnet.com
www.solvent.com
Salsa
  President/CEO: Jack Veach
  CFO: Fred Harper
  Vice President: Morris Woodall
  Research & Development: R Michael MacGregor
  Quality Control: James Valikont, Jr.
  Sales Director: Dana Davidson
  Operations/Production: Lynne Wainman
  Plant Manager: Robert Roggers
Number Employees: 10-19
Number of Brands: 1
Number of Products: 6
Sq. footage: 5500
Parent Co: Solvent Interntional
Type of Packaging: Private Label
Brands:
  Guacamole Salad
  Salsa Picante
  Tex-Mex
  Verde

13478 Spanarkel Company
72 W Sylvania Ave # B
Neptune City, NJ 07753-6733   732-775-4144
    Fax: 732-775-3598   info@aol.com
Manufacturer of gourmet sauces, broker of packaging components
  President: John Spanarkel
  VP: James Spanarkel
Estimated Sales:$500,000-$1 Million
Number Employees: 10-19
Parent Co: Sparks Sales Company
Type of Packaging: Private Label, Bulk
Brands:
  Spanarkel

13479 (HQ)Spangler Candy Company
P.O.Box 71
Bryan, OH 43506-0071   419-636-8992
    Fax: 419-636-3695   888-636-4221
info@spanglercandy.com
www.spanglercandy.com
Makes lollipops, candy canes and circus peanuts
  President: Kirk Vashaw
  CEO: Dean Spangler
  CFO: Bill Martin
  CEO: Dean L Spangler
  Marketing Director: Jim Knight
  VP Sales: Denny Gunter
  Operations Manager: Steve Kerr
Number Employees: 500-999
Sq. footage: 500000
Other Locations:
  Spangler Candy Co.
  Bryan OH
Brands:
  ASTRO POPS
  CANE CLASSICS
  DUM DUM POPS
  PICTURE POPS
  SAF-T-POPS
  SPANGLER CANDY CANES
  SPANGLER CHOCOLATES
  SPANGLER CIRCUS PEANUTS

13480 Spangler Vineyards
491 Winery Ln
Roseburg, OR 97471-9365   541-679-9654
    Fax: 541-679-3888   info@spanglervineyards.com
www.spanglervineyards.com
Wines
  Co-Owner: Patrick Spangler
  Co-Owner: Loree Spangler
  Winemaker: Leonard Postles
*Estimated Sales:*Less than $500,000
Number Employees: 1-4
Type of Packaging: Private Label
Brands:
  Spangler Vineyards

13481 Spanish Gardens Food Manufacturing
2301 Metropolitan Ave
Kansas City, KS 66106-5599   913-831-4242
www.spanishgardens.com

Processor of taco shells, sauce, spices, tortilla chips and corn and flour tortillas
  President: Norma Jean Miller
  VP: Jean Miller
Estimated Sales:$1300000
Number Employees: 20-49
Sq. footage: 40000
Type of Packaging: Consumer, Food Service, Bulk

13482 Sparboe Companies
2183 E 11th Street
Los Angeles, CA 90021-2802   213-626-7538
info@sparboe.com
www.sparboe.com
Processor of fresh and frozen eggs; exporter of eggs and butter; wholesaler/distributor of butter, frozen fruits, cheeses and oils; serving the food service market
  President: Bob Sparboe
  Vice President: Beth Fechnell
Estimated Sales:$20-50 Million
Number Employees: 20-49
Sq. footage: 50000
Type of Packaging: Food Service, Private Label, Bulk
Brands:
  Bes Tex
  Except Mix

13483 Sparkling Spring Water Company
700 N Deerpath Drive
Vernon Hills, IL 60061-1802   847-247-5359
    Fax: 847-247-5800   800-772-7554
kknuth@sswc.com   www.sparklingspring.com
Bottled water-drinking, distilled, spring, fluoridated and infant
  President: Warner Tillman
  Vice President: George Lucas
  Marketing Director: Mark Hollingsworth
  Operations Manager: Ray Branaman
Estimated Sales:$ 10-100 Million
Number Employees: 50
Type of Packaging: Consumer, Food Service, Private Label, Bulk
Brands:
  Baby's Own
  Pure Distilled
  Sparkling Spring

13484 Sparkling Water Distributors
PO Box 695
Merrick, NY 11566-0695   516-867-8291
    Fax: 516-377-1228   800-277-2755
waterp0wer@aol.com
Processor of sparkling and spring water, root beer and black cherry and cream soda
  President: Mark Eisenberg
  VP: Rebecca Scott
  Sales Manager: Richard Stern
Number Employees: 5-9
Sq. footage: 5000
Type of Packaging: Food Service, Private Label

13485 Sparrer Sausage Company
4325 W Ogden Ave
Chicago, IL 60623-2925   773-762-3334
    Fax: 773-521-9368   800-666-3287
info@sparrers.com   www.sparrers.com
Purveyor of high quality gourmet, deli, appetizer and snack sausage products.
  President: Brian Graves
  VP: Daniel Coyle
  National Accounts Manager: Duane Dudek
  Operations: Brian Graves
  Purchasing: Daniel Sala
Estimated Sales:$22772607
Number Employees: 50-99
Type of Packaging: Consumer, Food Service, Private Label, Bulk

13486 Sparta Foods
1565 1st Ave NW
New Brighton, MN 55112-1948   651-697-5500
    Fax: 651-697-0600   800-700-0809
www.thsinc.com
Corn chips, salsa, tortillas and barbecue sauce
  VP: Eric Stack
  Quality Control: Cris Hold
  COO: Jose Flores
  CEO: John Johnson
  CFO: John Smith
  Marketing Director: Rob Wood
Estimated Sales:$ 25-49.9 Million
Number Employees: 100-249

Type of Packaging: Private Label, Bulk

13487 Spartan Imports
1305 Monroe St
Endicott, NY 13760   607-748-7557
Wholesalers of food and groceries
    President: George Anastos
Estimated Sales:$500,000 appx.
Number Employees: 1-4

13488 Spaten Beer
4621 Little Neck Parkway
Little Neck, NY 11362   718-281-1912
             sna@spatennorthamerica.com
                      www.spatenusa.com
beer

13489 Spaten West
284 Harbor Way
S San Francisco, CA 94080-6816   650-794-0800
    Fax: 650-794-9567   spaten@spatenusa.com
                      www.spatenusa.com
Beer
    President: Chris Hildebrandt
    CFO: Erfried Besch
Estimated Sales: $ 10-20 Million
Number Employees: 20-49
Brands:
    Spaten

13490 Spaulding Sales
8700 N 2nd St # 202
Brighton, MI 48116-1296   810-229-4166
                      Fax: 810-227-4218
Cheese
    President: Pat Spaulding
Estimated Sales:$500,000-$1 Million
Number Employees: 1-4

13491 Spear Packing
25 Home News Row
New Brunswick, NJ 08901-3645   732-247-4212
Beverages
    President: John Ciullo
Estimated Sales: $ 50-100 Million
Number Employees: 50

13492 SpecialTeas
2 Reynolds Street
Norwalk, CT 06855-1015   203-866-1522
        Fax: 203-375-6820 888-365-6983
    service@specialteas.com www.specialteas.com
Gourmet tea
    Managing Director: Juergen Link
Estimated Sales:$ 5-10 Million
Number Employees: 5-9

13493 (HQ)Specialty Bakers
P.O.Box 130
Marysville, PA 17053-0130   717-957-2131
        Fax: 717-957-0156 800-233-0778
        ladyfingers@specialtybakers.com
             www.sbiladyfingers.com
Manufacturer and exporter of sponge, snack and an-
gel food cakes, lady fingers, dessert shells, French
twirls and jelly rolls
    President: John Piotrowski
    COO: James Wilson
    CEO: John Plotrowski
Estimated Sales:$100+ Million
Number Employees: 100-249
Type of Packaging: Consumer, Private Label
Other Locations:
    Specialty Bakers
    Marysville PA
    Specialty Bakers
    Lititz PA
    Specialty Bakers
    Dunkirk NY
Brands:
    Specialty

13494 Specialty Baking Products
653 Brigham Road
Dunkirk, NY 14048-2361   716-366-0938
Processor of baked goods including cream horns and
puff pastry products
    President: Jan Phillips
    Sales Manager: Frank Nappo
    Plant Manager: Gerry Hamilton
Estimated Sales: $ 50 - 100 Million
Number Employees: 50-99
Sq. footage: 23000
Parent Co: Petri Baking Products

13495 Specialty Beverages
75403 Desert Park Dr
Indian Wells, CA 92210-8355   626-963-5536
                      Fax: 626-335-2148
Processor of ginseng soft drinks including ginger
ale, cola, apple soda, sarsaparilla and chocolate cola
    President: James Towery
    VP/Sales Manager: James Towery
Estimated Sales:$1200000
Number Employees: 1
Type of Packaging: Consumer
Brands:
    Barons

13496 Specialty Brands
4200 Concours
Ontario, CA 91764-4981   909-477-4700
        Fax: 909-477-4600 800-782-1180
                      www.joseole.com
Processor of frozen foods including tortillas, tama-
les, burritos, taquitos, appetizers and pastas
    President: Patrick O'Ray
    Senior VP: Chris Meyer
    Quality Control: Mike Cramer
    Marketing: Tim Shea
    Sales: Mark Dueshane
    Operations: Jim Meiers
Estimated Sales: $ 20 - 50 Million
Number Employees: 50-99
Parent Co: FoodBrands America
Type of Packaging: Consumer, Food Service, Pri-
vate Label, Bulk
Brands:
    BUTCHER BOY
    FRED'S FOR STARTERS
    JOSE OLE
    POSADA
    ROTANELLI'S

13497 Specialty Brands
P.O.Box 796
Carthage, MO 64836-0796   417-358-8104
        Fax: 417-358-5323 www.windsorfoods.com
Processor of frozen Italian specialties including lasa-
gna, meat balls, ravioli and spaghetti sauce
    Manager: Charlie Smith
    Plant Manager: Joe Henry
    Purchasing Agent: Arthur Meneola
Estimated Sales: $ 50 - 100 Million
Number Employees: 100-249
Sq. footage: 47000
Parent Co: FoodBrands America
Type of Packaging: Consumer, Food Service
Brands:
    Rotanelli

13498 Specialty Brands of America
1400 Old Country Rd # 103
Westbury, NY 11590-5119   516-997-6969
        Fax: 516-997-7299 info@sbamerica.com
                      www.sbamerica.com
Sugar-free syrup, pure maple syrup, flatbreads,
crackers, chowder, all-natural coating mix
    President: Dominique Bastien
    Sales Director: Mischell Amarado
Estimated Sales: $ 10-20 Million
Number Employees: 20-49
Sq. footage: 15000
Parent Co: Specialty Brands of America
Type of Packaging: Consumer, Food Service, Bulk
Brands:
    Cary's
    Dixie Fry
    New York Flatbreads
    O.T.C.
    Thelma's

13499 Specialty Cheese Company
430 N Main St
Reeseville, WI 53579-9790   920-927-3888
        Fax: 920-927-3200 800-367-1711
        scci@specialcheese.com
             www.specialcheese.com
Cheese packaging
    President: Paul Scharfman
Estimated Sales: $ 2.5-5 Million
Number Employees: 50-99
Type of Packaging: Private Label
Brands:
    Hem
    Lavacarica
    Rich Cow

13500 Specialty Coffee Roasters
901 NW 133rd Ave
Miami, FL 33182-1809   561-278-0003
        Fax: 800-805-4422 800-253-9363
        sales@specialtycoffeeroasters.com
             www.specialtycoffeeroasters.com
Processor, packer and importer of gourmet coffees;
exporter of gourmet coffees
    President: Gabriela Harvey
Estimated Sales:$300,000
Number Employees: 3
Sq. footage: 5000
Parent Co: MGH Holdings Corporation
Type of Packaging: Consumer, Food Service, Pri-
vate Label, Bulk
Brands:
    Shalina

13501 Specialty Commodities
1530 47th Street NW
Fargo, ND 58102-2858   701-282-8222
             www.specialtycommodities.com
Supplier of dried fruits, legumes, nuts, seeds and
spices.

13502 Specialty Enzymes
13591 Yorba Ave
Chino, CA 91710-5071   909-613-1660
        Fax: 909-613-1663 info@specialtyenzymes.com
             www.specialtyenzymes.com
Enzymes and enzyme blends
    President: Vasant Rathi
    Marketing Director: Gabrielle Sill
    Vice President: Larry Schwartz
    Technical Service Manager: Vickie Lentner
*Estimated Sales:*Below $ 1 Million
Number Employees: 20-49
Type of Packaging: Bulk

13503 Specialty Food America
5055 Huffman Mill Rd
Hopkinsville, KY 42240-9162   270-889-0017
                      888-881-1633
        customerservice@specialtyfoodamerica.com
             www.specialtyfoodamerica.com
Processor of herbs and spices; cooking related sup-
plies and contract packaging
    Owner: Tom Marshall
*Estimated Sales:*Below $ 5 Million
Number Employees: 1-4
Sq. footage: 1200
Type of Packaging: Consumer, Private Label
Brands:
    Lucini Honestete
    Sonoma Syrups

13504 (HQ)Specialty Foods Corporation
520 Lake Cook Road
Suite 550
Deerfield, IL 60015-5634   847-405-5300
                      Fax: 847-405-5310
Processor of breads, cookies and cakes
    CFO: Robert L Fishbune
Number Employees: 5-9
Type of Packaging: Consumer, Food Service, Pri-
vate Label
Other Locations:
    Specialty Foods Corp.
    Deerfield IL

13505 (HQ)Specialty Foods Group
603 Pilot House Dr # 4
Newport News, VA 23606-1904   757-952-1200
        Fax: 757-952-1201 800-238-0020
             www.smgmeats.com
Manufacturer of meat
    President: Thomas Davis
    CEO: Bonita Then
Estimated Sales: $ 10 - 20 Million
Number Employees: 1,000-4,999
Number of Products: 12
Type of Packaging: Consumer, Food Service, Pri-
vate Label, Bulk
Other Locations:
    SFG Production Plant
    Owensboro KY
    SFG Production Plant
    Humboldt IA
    SFG Production Plant
    Chicago IL
    SFG Production Plant
    Williamston NC
Brands:
    ALPINE LACE

FIELDS
FISCHERS
LIGURIA
MICKELBERRY
MOSEY'S
NATHAN'S FAMOUS
SWIFT PREMIUM
WILLIAM FISCHER DELI MEATS

13506 Specialty Foods International
304 Eureka Drive NE
Atlanta, GA 30305-4256 404-816-8268
Fax: 404-844-9155
jpeters@specialtyfoodsintl.com
www.specialtyfoodsintl.com
Olive oil

13507 Specialty Foods South
P.O.Box 13615
Charleston, SC 29422-3615 843-766-2580
Fax: 843-766-2580 800-538-0003
www.charlestonfavorites.com
Gourmet foods
Owner: James Hagood
Estimated Sales: Under $500,000
Number Employees: 1-4
Type of Packaging: Private Label, Bulk

13508 Specialty Industrial Products
PO Box 18390
Spartanburg, SC 29318-8390 864-579-4530
Fax: 864-579-6818 800-747-9001
garyd@siproducts.com www.siproducts.com
Processor of chemicals including surfactants and
emulsifiers
VP/General Manager: Gary Dowell
VP Sales: Jim Heyward
Estimated Sales: $$10-20 Million
Number Employees: 50-99
Sq. footage: 60000

13509 Specialty Ingredients
1130 W. Lake Cook Road
Suite 320
Buffalo Grove, IL 60089 847-419-9595
Fax: 847-419-9547 sales@ingredientsinc.com
www.ingredientsinc.com
Dehydrated/whole/starch potato products, soy based
ingredients, dairy ingredients, food acids and salts,
and frozen & dehydrated vegetables.
Sales: Jim Stewart

13510 Specialty Ingredients
P.O.Box 474
Watertown, WI 53094-0474 920-261-4229
Fax: 920-261-0443
Processor of liquid sugar
Manager: Lonnie Schuett
Estimated Sales: $ 3 - 5 Million
Number Employees: 10-19
Type of Packaging: Bulk

13511 Specialty Minerals
35 Highland Ave
Bethlehem, PA 18017-9482 610-882-8725
Fax: 610-882-1570 800-801-1031
jayesty@SpecialtyMinerals.com
www.mineralstech.com
Manufacturer, sellers and exporters of food and
pharmaceutical grades of precipitated calcium car-
bonate, ground limestone and talc
Chairman: Paul Saueracker
Human Resources: Gary Duckwall
Commercial Manager: Jay Esty
Number Employees: 50-99
Parent Co: Minerals Technologies
Type of Packaging: Private Label
Other Locations:
SMI Mineral Plant
Adams MA
SMI Mineral Plant
Canann CT
SMI Mineral Plant
Barretts MT
SMI Mineral Plant
Lucerne Valley CA
Brands:
ALBAGLOS
JETCOAT
OPACARB
PCC

13512 Specialty Products
13525 Hummel Rd
Cleveland, OH 44142-2597 216-362-1050
Fax: 216-362-6506 luis.granja@gortons.com
www.gortons.com
Processor and exporter of breading batter
Manager: Luis Granja
Controller: Sue Spisak
Specialty Products: Luis Granja
Plant Manager: Luis Granja
Estimated Sales: $10-20 Million
Number Employees: 20-49
Parent Co: Gorton's
Type of Packaging: Food Service, Private Label,
Bulk

13513 Specialty Rice Marketing
1000 W 1st St
Brinkley, AR 72021-9000 870-734-1233
Fax: 870-734-1237 800-467-1233
info@dellarice.com www.dellarice.com
Processor, miller and exporter of five types of rice
Manager: Ojus Ajmara
General Manager: Glenda Hilsdon
Estimated Sales: $800,000
Number Employees: 10-19
Sq. footage: 8000
Brands:
Della
Della Gourmet Rice
Gourmet Basmati Rice
Jasmine

13514 Specialty Steak Service
P.O.Box 797
Erie, PA 16512-0797 814-452-2281
Fax: 814-459-1213 comments@curtze.com
www.curtze.com
Processor of meat
President: Bruce Kern Sr
President: Scott Keim
Estimated Sales: $88900000
Number Employees: 100-249
Sq. footage: 75000
Parent Co: C.A. Curtze Company
Type of Packaging: Food Service

13515 Speco
3946 Willow St
Schiller Park, IL 60176-2311 847-678-4240
Fax: 847-678-8037 800-541-5415
sales@speco.com www.speco.com
Manufacturer and exporter of meat cutting equip-
ment including meat and mincer knives and bone
collector systems
President: Craig Hess
Sales Manager: Steve Jacob
Production Manager: Clarence Hoffman
Estimated Sales: $ 10-20 Million
Number Employees: 50-99
Sq. footage: 25000
Brands:
Superior
Triumph

13516 Spectrum Organic Products
1105 Industrial Ave
Petaluma, CA 94952-1141 707-778-8900
Fax: 707-765-1026 800-995-2705
spectrumorganics@worldpantry.com
www.spectrumorganics.com
Manufacturer of natural oils and condiments. The
Hain Celestial Group plans to merge with this
company
President/CEO: Neil Blomquist
VP: Randall H Sias
Founder/Chairman: Jethren Phillips
Estimated Sales: $20-50 Million
Number Employees: 50-99
Type of Packaging: Private Label
Brands:
Spectrum Naturals

13517 Spence & Company
160 Manley Street
Brockton, MA 02301-5509 508-427-1627
Fax: 508-427-5557 salmon@spenceltd.com
www.spenceltd.com
Processor of smoked fish; importer of fish ingredi-
ents
President: Alan Spence
Estimated Sales: $4500000
Number Employees: 25
Type of Packaging: Consumer, Food Service

13518 Spencer Packing Company
P.O.Box 753
Washington, NC 27889-0753 252-946-4161
Fax: 252-946-4162
spencerpacking@earthlink.net
www.spencersausage.com
Processor and packer of pork
President: Harold Spencer
Estimated Sales: $1,250,000
Number Employees: 10-19

13519 Sperry Apiaries
15750 Highway 46
Kindred, ND 58051-9561 701-428-3000
Honey
President: Mark Sperry
Estimated Sales: Under $500,000
Number Employees: 1-4
Number of Brands: 1
Number of Products: 1

13520 Spice & Spice
655 Deep Valley Dr # 125d
Rolling Hls Ests, CA 90274-3615 310-265-2914
Fax: 310-265-2934 866-729-7742
info@spicenspice.com www.spicenspice.com
Direct manufacturers/importers/wholesalers of bulk
line of whole and ground spice products: black pep-
per, white pepper, cumin, cinnamon, crush chili, cin-
namon stick, chili powder, granulated garlic, dry
chili pods (Arbol, JaponesIndian S4's)
Owner: Anthony Dirocco
CEO: Mukesh Thakker
R & D: Nitul Unekekett
Quality Control: Nina Lukamanje
Estimated Sales: $ 5-10 Million
Number Employees: 1-4
Number of Brands: 1
Number of Products: 25
Sq. footage: 50000
Type of Packaging: Food Service, Bulk
Brands:
BOAT BRAND

13521 Spice Advice
2301 SE Tones Dr
Ankeny, IA 50021-8887 515-965-2711
Fax: 515-965-2801 800-247-5251
spiceadvice@achfood.com www.tones.com
Processor and exporter of spices, seasonings, dry
blends and mixes including datenut rolls, cakes,
sauces and gravies; importer of spices and herbs.
Manager: Doug Aldrige
Chief Information Officer: Donnie Steward
Chief Financial Officer: Jeffrey Atkins
SVP General Counsel/Corporate Secretary:
Carmen Sciackitano
VP Product Development/Quality Mgmt: Pete
Friedman
VP Sales/Marketing: Kenny Shortsleeve
VP Strategy & Development: Jack Straton
SVP Human Resources: Deborah Murdock
VP Operations: Bill Wells
Estimated Sales: $48,900,000
Number Employees: 500-999
Sq. footage: 750000
Parent Co: Philp Burns & Company
Type of Packaging: Consumer, Food Service, Pri-
vate Label, Bulk
Brands:
Blue Ribbon
Chef's Taste
Chocolate Decors Sprinkle
Dec-A-Cake
Dromedary
Dromedary Cake Mixes
Durkee
Egg Shade Food Coloring
Fluff Marshmallow Toppings
French's
French's Dry Mixes
Good Harvest
Guiltless Gourmet
Heart-Loc
Lawler's
Lepak
Perc
Presti's
San Jacinto Spice Ranch
Spice Islands
Tone's

13522 Spice House International Specialties

46 Bethpage Rd
Hicksville, NY 11801-1512   516-942-7248
Fax: 516-942-7249   spicehouse@hotmail.com
www.spicehouseint.com
Manufacturer, wholesaler/distributor, exporter and
importer of spices and blends, specialty foods, hot
sauces, dried fruits and nuts; serving the food ser-
vice market from around the world; Asia, Middle
East, Europe, Thai and China.
President: Anthony Provetto
Estimated Sales: $ 5 - 10 Million
Number Employees: 5-9
Sq. footage: 4600
Type of Packaging: Consumer, Food Service, Pri-
vate Label, Bulk

13523 Spice Hunter

P.O.Box 8110
San Luis Obispo, CA 93403-8110   805-544-6632
Fax: 805-544-9046   800-444-3061
cr@spicehunter.com   www.spicehunter.com
Processor of dried bean soups, entree seasonings,
dips, salad seasonings, Asian soups, spices and drink
mixes
President: Conrad Sauer
VP Administration: John Doyle
VP: John Doyle
Marketing Director: Trish Bellrose
Sales Director: Joe Leonard
Operations Manager: John Doyle
Plant Manager: Tim Ewen
Estimated Sales: $18435754
Number Employees: 50-99
Number of Products: 200
Sq. footage: 113000
Parent Co: C.F. Sauer Company
Type of Packaging: Private Label, Bulk
Brands:
Oriental Noodle Soup
Quick & Natural Soup
Quick Pot Pasta
Savory Smoke
Simmer Kettle
Spice Hunter
Spice Hunter Spices & Herbs

13524 Spice King Corporation

438 El Camino Drive
Beverly Hills, CA 90212-4222   310-836-7770
Fax: 310-836-6454
Processor, importer and exporter of custom formu-
lated natural spices and seasonings; also, dehydrated
vegetables and fruits
General Manager: James Stephens
VP: A Stern
Marketing Director: Anne Stern
Number Employees: 20-49
Sq. footage: 25000

13525 Spice Market

5 Dwight Place
Fairfield, NJ 07004-3405   201-876-9111
Fax: 201-876-9002   800-223-3502
pepper4@ix.netcom.com   www.spicemarket.com
Importer of incense sticks, potpourri, oils and gifts
President: Joel Bahr
Vice President: Bob Friedman
Plant Manager: Ed Diaz
Purchasing Manager: Norma Galbraith
Number Employees: 50-99
Type of Packaging: Consumer
Brands:
SPICE RITE

13526 Spice O' Life

PO Box 70406
Seattle, WA 98127-0406   206-789-4195
Fax: 206-782-9339   spiceguy@spiceolife.com
www.spiceolife.com
Processor of custom blended spices
Owner: Scotty McDonell
Account Manager: Judith Jager
Advertising Manager: David Barker
Number Employees: 1-4

13527 Spice Rack Chocolates

10908 Courthouse Rd
Suite 102 #264
Fredericksburg, VA 22408   540-847-2063
Fax: 416-757-5183 www.spicerackchocolates.com

dark chocolates infused with hers and spices
President/Owner: Mary Schellhammer
CFO: Paul Schellhammer

13528 Spice Time Foods/Julius& Joe's

15 Farview Ter
Paramus, NJ 07652-2703   201-291-4200
800-345-9225
Processor, importer and exporter of spices, herbs and
seasonings; processor of gravy mixes, sauces and
bouillon cubes
Manager: Simon Makhlouf
VP Sales/Marketing: John Stapleton
VP Operations: Joseph Mandel
Estimated Sales: $ .5 - 1 million
Number Employees: 1-4
Sq. footage: 100000
Type of Packaging: Consumer, Food Service, Pri-
vate Label, Bulk

13529 Spice World

8101 Presidents Dr
Orlando, FL 32809-9113   407-851-9432
Fax: 407-857-7171   800-433-4979
sworld@spiceworldinc.com
www.spiceworldinc.com
Processor and exporter of nuts, custom seasoning
blends and garlic including minced, chopped and
packed in olive oil or water
President: Andrew Caneza
General Manager: Gary Caneza
Sales: Eric Dutreil
Sales/Purchasing: Louis Hymel
Estimated Sales: $ 5 - 10 Million
Number Employees: 100-249
Sq. footage: 120000
Type of Packaging: Consumer, Food Service, Pri-
vate Label, Bulk
Brands:
3-SONS
CAJUN CLASSIQUES
CHEF CUISINE
CHUBS
SPICE WORLD
SPICY-GEE

13530 Spice of Life

2195 S Courtenay Parkway
Merritt Island, FL 32952-4013   321-453-5727
Fax: 321-454-4482   harlanddon@aol.com
Processor and exporter of custom and standard sea-
soning blends for poultry, meat and seafood
President: Donna Adams
CEO: Harland Adams
Estimated Sales: Below $ 5 Million
Number Employees: 20
Sq. footage: 15000
Type of Packaging: Consumer, Food Service, Pri-
vate Label, Bulk

13531 Spiceco

6c Terminal Way
Avenel, NJ 07001-2228   732-499-9070
Fax: 732-499-9139 www.spice-co.com
Manufacturer of spices including basil, bay leaves,
garlic, oregano, paprika, pepper, etc
President: Andy Barna
Estimated Sales: $11.2 Million
Number Employees: 50-99
Type of Packaging: Consumer, Food Service, Pri-
vate Label, Bulk
Brands:
PRIDE OF MALABAR
PRIDE OF SHANDUNG
PRIDE OF SZEGED

13532 Spiceland

6604 W Irving Park Rd
Chicago, IL 60634-2435   773-736-1000
800-352-8671
Spices
Co-Owner: Doris Stockwell
Co-Owner: Jim Stockwell
Estimated Sales: Less than $500,000
Number Employees: 1-4
Brands:
Spiceland

13533 Spiceman

86319 Lorane Hwy
Eugene, OR 97405-9486   541-342-2085
Fax: 541-342-2085   800-725-8373
www.spiceman.com

Manufacturer of spice blends, marinades, relishes,
catsups, gift sets.
President/Owner: David Johns
Number Employees: 20-49

13534 (HQ)Spices of Life Gourmet Coffee

4135 Dr Martin Luther King Bl
Fort Myers, FL 33916-4809   239-334-8004
Fax: 941-549-9041
Coffee
Owner: Cheryl Dejonghe
Vice President: Edward Miller
Estimated Sales: $300,000-500,000
Number Employees: 1-4

13535 Spiceworld

11290 Interchange Circle N
Miramar, FL 33025-6000   954-436-9148
Fax: 954-436-9280   800-433-4980
Processor, exporter and wholesaler/distributor of
peanuts and minced, chopped and peeled garlic
President: Gary Caneza
General Manager: Richard Kearns
Estimated Sales: $9500000
Number Employees: 60
Sq. footage: 10000
Parent Co: Spiceworld
Type of Packaging: Consumer, Bulk

13536 (HQ)Spilke's Baking Company

290 S 5th St
Brooklyn, NY 11211-6214   718-384-2150
Fax: 718-384-2988   redmill@aol.com
www.macaroonking.com
Processor of individually packaged macaroons and
cakes including kosher
President: Arnold Badner
Estimated Sales: $ 10 - 20 Million
Number Employees: 10-19
Sq. footage: 30000
Type of Packaging: Consumer, Food Service
Brands:
Jennie
Manhattan Gourmet
Red Mill Farms

13537 Spinelli Coffee Company

3100 Airport Way S
Seattle, WA 98134-2116   415-821-7100
Fax: 415-821-7199
Coffee
President: Christophe Calkins
Number Employees: 10

13538 Spinney Creek Shellfish

2 Howell Ln
Eliot, ME 03903   207-439-2719
Fax: 207-439-7643   877-778-6727
customerservice@spinneycreek.com
www.spinneycreek.com
Seafood
President: Thomas Howell
Estimated Sales: $ 10 - 20 Million
Number Employees: 10-19

13539 Spitz USA

1775 Horseshoe Drive
Loveland, CO 80538-7201   970-613-9319
Fax: 970-613-9320
National Sales Manager: Roger Shantz

13540 Splendid Specialties

23 Pimentel Ct # B
Novato, CA 94949-5661   415-506-3000
Fax: 415-506-3002   info@tornranch.com
www.tornranch.com
Manufacturer and purveyor of gourmet specialty
foods that include the finest chocolates and baked
goods, and famous dried fruit and nuts from Califor-
nia's lush, fertile valleys.
President: Dean Morrow
Estimated Sales: $ 20 - 50 Million
Number Employees: 50-99
Brands:
Cafe Time
GiGi Baking Company
Mashuga Nuts & Cookies
Splendid Specialties Chocolates

13541 Splendid Spreads

1483 Auburn Court
Eagan, MN 55122   877-632-1300
Fax: 651-688-7630 www.splendidpreads.com

gouret salmon spreads and toppings
President/Owner: Judy Tucker

13542 Spoetzl Brewery
PO Box 368
Shiner, TX 77984-0368   361-594-3383
            Fax: 361-594-4334   shiner@shiner.com
                www.shiner.com
Shiner Bock, Shiner Blonde, Shiner Hefeweizer,
Shiner Light, Shiner Bohemian Black Lager, Shiner
Kosmos
    Manager: Carlos Alvarez
    Director Finance: Jim Bolz
    Quality Control: Peter Takacs
    Brewmaster: Jimmy Mauric
    Brewmaster: John Hybner
Estimated Sales: $ 20 - 50 Million
Number Employees: 50-99
Parent Co: Gambrinus Company
Type of Packaging: Consumer
Brands:
    Shiner Blonde
    Shiner Bock
    Shiner Dunkelweizen
    Shiner Hefeweizen
    Shiner Kolsch
    Shiner Light

13543 Spohrers Bakeries
600 MacDade Boulevard
Collingdale, PA 19023-3804   610-532-9959
                    Fax: 610-532-8927
Pastries
    Owner: David Olandi
    Manager: Derek Everstyke
Brands:
    Spohrers Bakeries

13544 Spokandy Wedding Mints
1412 W 3rd Ave
Spokane, WA 99201-7024   509-624-1969
        Fax: 509-624-2017 www.spokandy.com
Chocolates, wedding mints, brittles, barks, saltwater
taffy
    President: Todd Davis
    Plant Manager: Mary Ellithorp
Estimated Sales: Below $ 5 Million
Number Employees: 5-9
Type of Packaging: Private Label

13545 Spokane Seed Company
6019 E Alki Ave
Spokane Valley, WA 99212-1019   509-535-3671
    Fax: 509-535-0874   spokseed@spokaneseed.com
                www.spokaneseed.com
Processor and exporter of peas and lentils
    President: Peter Johnstone
    CFO: Jeff White
    Sales: Nelson Fancher
Estimated Sales: $3900000
Number Employees: 20-49
Type of Packaging: Consumer, Food Service, Bulk
Brands:
    Greenpod
    Rumba

13546 SportPharma USA
1915 Mark Court
Suite 150
Concord, CA 94520-8502   925-686-1451
Brands:
    SPORTPHARMA

13547 Sportabs International
PO Box 492118
Los Angeles, CA 90049-8118   310-451-2625
        Fax: 310-207-8526   888-814-7767
                www.sportabs.com
Processor and exporter of multi-vitamin tablets
    President: Richard Griswold
Estimated Sales: Under $500,000
Number Employees: 1-4
Type of Packaging: Consumer
Brands:
    Spor Tabs

13548 Sporting Colors LLC
315 Southwind Pl
Manhattan, KS 66503-3137   785-539-7500
        Fax: 785-539-7522   888-394-2292
                www.panerabread.com
    Manager: Jillyn Schmidt
    CEO: S Jeff Schroeder

Estimated Sales: $ 1 - 3 Million
Number Employees: 20-49

13549 Sportsmen's Cannery
P.O.Box 1011
Winchester Bay, OR 97467-0800   541-271-3293
        Fax: 541-271-9381   800-457-8048
    karch@presys.com www.sportsmenscannery.com
Gourmet canned seafood products including smoke-
house and gift boxes
    Manager: Brandy Roelle
    Secretary: Mikyale Karcher
Estimated Sales: Below $ 1 Million
Number Employees: 10-19
Brands:
    Sportsmen's Cannery

**13550 Sportsmen's Cannery &
Smokehouse**
P.O.Box 1011
Winchester Bay, OR 97467-0800   541-271-3293
        Fax: 541-271-9381   karch@presys.com
                www.sportsmenscannery.com
Processor and canner of salmon, albacore tuna, stur-
geon and shellfish
    Manager: Brandy Roelle
    Owner: Mikayle Karcher
Number Employees: 1-4
Type of Packaging: Consumer, Private Label
Brands:
    Winchester

13551 Sportsmen's Sea Foods
1617 Quivira Rd
San Diego, CA 92109-7801   619-224-3551
    Fax: 619-224-1646   www.sportsmensseafood.com
Processor of canned fish including albacore, bonito,
marlin, tuna and yellow tail
    President: Tom Busalacchi
Estimated Sales: $300,000-500,000
Number Employees: 10-19

13552 Spot Bagel Bakery
1401 2nd Avenue
Suite 211
Seattle, WA 98101-2007   206-623-0066
                    Fax: 206-623-0069
Baked goods

**13553 Spotted Tavern Winery &Dodd's
Cider Mill**
PO Box 175
Hartwood, VA 22471-0175   540-752-4453
                    Fax: 540-752-4611
Wine, sparkling cider, Virginia hard cider and fresh
apple cider in season.
    Owner: Cathy Harris

13554 Spottswoode Winery
1902 Madrona Ave
St Helena, CA 94574-2354   707-963-0134
                    Fax: 707-963-2886
    spottswoode@spottswoode.com
                www.spottswoode.com
Wines
    Owner: Mary Novak
    VP: Peah Armstrong
    National Sales/Marketing: Lindy Novak Lahr
    Consumer Sales/Tours: Shanyn McDaera
    Winemaker: Rosemary Cakebread
Estimated Sales: Below $ 5 Million
Number Employees: 5-9

13555 Sprague Foods
385 College Street E
Belleville, ON K8N 5S7
Canada   613-966-1200
    Fax: 613-962-8600   info@spraguefoods.com
                www.spraguefoods.com
Processor of beans, soups, beans in sauce, pasta in
tomato sauce, salad dressings, and other items.
    President: Roger Sprague
Number Employees: 20-49
Type of Packaging: Consumer, Food Service

13556 Spray Dynamics
108 Bolte Ln
St Clair, MO 63077-3218   636-629-7366
        Fax: 636-629-7455   800-260-7366
    spray@usmo.com   www.spraydynamics.com

Manufacturer and exporter of liquid and dry ingredi-
ent applicators and dispensers for food processing
machinery.
    Owner: Dave Holmeyer
    Accounts Payable: Melanie Booher
    Marketing Coordinator: Stephanie Butenhoff
    Sales Representative: George Wipperfurth
    Service Manager: Craig Booher
Estimated Sales: $2.5-5 Million
Number Employees: 20-49
Brands:
    CLOG-FREE SLURRY SPRAY ENCOATER
    DELTA DRY
    DELTA LIQUID
    ECONOFLO
    ENHANCER
    MASTER SERIES
    METER MASTER
    MICRO-METER AIRLESS
    POWDER XPRESS
    SOFT FLIGHT
    UNISPENSE

13557 Sprecher Brewing
701 W Glendale Ave
Milwaukee, WI 53209-6509   414-964-7837
        Fax: 414-964-2462   888-650-2739
            beer@sprecherbrewery.com
                www.sprecherbrewery.com
Beer
    President: Randal Sprecher
    Production Manager: Tom Bosch
Estimated Sales: $ 20-50 Million
Number Employees: 20-49

13558 (HQ)Spreda Group
PO Box 378
Prospect, KY 40059-0378   502-426-9411
        Fax: 502-423-7531   spredausa@aol.com
                www.spredausa.com
Processor, importer and exporter of fruit and vegeta-
ble powder, tomato paste, colors, spray and vacuum
dried and dehydrated fruits and vegetables, etc.; pro-
cessor of apple pectin and apple juice concentrate
    President: George Falk
    Secretary: Carolyn Sharpe
    VP: James Falk
Number Employees: 100-249
Type of Packaging: Food Service, Bulk
Brands:
    Elmasu
    Obi Pektin
    Puccinelli
    Spreda

13559 Spring Acres Sales Company
1280 Macedonia Rd
Spring Hope, NC 27882-8368   252-478-5127
        Fax: 252-478-5266   800-849-5436
            springacres@mindspring.com
Processor of sweet potatoes including medium, large
and jumbo
    Owner: Cindy Joyner
    VP/Sales: Norman Brown
Estimated Sales: $500,000-$1 Million
Number Employees: 1-4
Type of Packaging: Bulk
Brands:
    Hernandez
    Spring Acres
    Tarheel

13560 Spring Creek Apiaries
206 9th Street NW
Beulah, ND 58523-6240   701-873-4450
Processor of honey
    Owner: Don Wetzel
Number Employees: 3
Type of Packaging: Consumer, Bulk

13561 Spring Creek Natural Foods
212c E Main Street
Spencer, WV 25276-1602   304-927-3780
        Fax: 304-927-1815   scnf@kvinet.com
                www.springcreeknaturalfood.com
Tofu
    President: Donald Carpenter
Estimated Sales: $ 2.5-5 Million
Number Employees: 15

13562 Spring Glen Fresh Foods
P.O.Box 518
Ephrata, PA 17522-0518   717-733-2201
Fax: 717-738-4335   800-641-2853
www.springglen.com
Processor of soup and stew including meat, poultry and seafood; also, potato, pasta and macaroni salad, coleslaw, entrees and desserts including cobblers, parfaits, cheese, puddings, gelatin and custards
President: John Warehime
Sales Manager: Thomas Soderberg
Plant Manager: Tom Schauer
Purchasing Agent: Rich Paulukow
Estimated Sales:$19200000
Number Employees: 100-249
Parent Co: Hanover Foods Corporation
Type of Packaging: Consumer, Food Service, Private Label
Brands:
Deli Direct
Spring Glen

13563 Spring Grove Foods
312 S 3rd St
Miamisburg, OH 45342-2933   937-866-4311
Fax: 937-866-1410
Manufacturer of cheese, beef, pepperoni, ham, salami, sausage and bologna
President: Jerry Beale
Estimated Sales:$10 Million
Number Employees: 5-9
Sq. footage: 10000
Type of Packaging: Food Service, Private Label, Bulk

13564 Spring Hill Farm Dairy
136 Neck Rd
Haverhill, MA 01835-8028   978-373-3481
Fax: 978-521-0870 www.springhillwater.com
Dairy products
President: Dale F Rogers
*Estimated Sales:*Below $ 5 Million
Number Employees: 20-49

13565 Spring Hill Meat Market
P.O.Box 38
Spring Hill, KS 66083-0038   913-592-3501
Processor of meat products
Owner: William Madison
Estimated Sales:$ 1 - 3 Million
Number Employees: 1-4
Type of Packaging: Consumer

13566 Spring Ledge Farms
5438 State Route 14
Dundee, NY 14837-8804   607-678-4038
Fax: 607-243-7214
Processor of fresh grapes
President: Earl Andrews
Estimated Sales:$ .5 - 1 million
Number Employees: 1-4

13567 Spring Mountain Vineyards
2805 Spring Mountain Road
Saint Helena, CA 94574-1798   707-967-4188
Fax: 707-967-2753   877-769-4637
info@springmtn.com   www.springmtn.com
Processor and exporter of wines
General Manager: Tom Ferrell
Director of Marketing: Leah McEachern
Director of Sales: Brian Boswick
Director Manufacturing: Craig Becker
Estimated Sales:$2500000
Number Employees: 35
Type of Packaging: Consumer

13568 Spring Mountain Vineyard
2805 Spring Mountain Road
Saint Helena, CA 94574-1775   707-967-4188
Fax: 707-963-2753   877-769-4637
info@springmtn.com   www.springmtn.com
Wines
President: Gil Nickel
Co-Owner: John Nickel
Estimated Sales:$ 3 - 5 Million
Number Employees: 5-9
Brands:
Chateau Chevalier

13569 Spring Tree Maple Products
28 Vernon St
Brattleboro, VT 05301-3666   802-254-8784
Fax: 802-254-8648   info@sbamerica.com
www.springtree.com

Supplier of pure maple syrup, sugar-free syrup, sugar-free honey substitute, canola margarines, cocoa products, cashew nuts, almonds, pistachios, walnuts, dried fruits and other commodities. Maple syrup available for private label
President: Don Basian
VP: Dom Pastrien
Customer Service: Sandee Kabaniec
Estimated Sales:$ 20 - 50 Million
Number Employees: 5-9
Sq. footage: 6000
Parent Co: Specialty Brands of America
Type of Packaging: Consumer, Food Service, Private Label, Bulk
Brands:
Canola
Canoleo
Spring Tree

13570 Spring Tree Maple Products
28 Vernon St
Brattleboro, VT 05301-3666   802-254-8784
Fax: 802-254-8648   info@sbamerica.com
www.springtree.com
Spring Tree Maple Products, Brattleboro, Vermont is the Export and Industrial Division of Specialty Brands of America, Inc. selling pure maple syrup to corporations and major distributors.
President: Don Bastien
Estimated Sales:$ 20-50 Million
Number Employees: 5-9
Brands:
Spring Tree

13571 Spring Water Company
925 Cavalier Blvd
Chesapeake, VA 23323-1549   757-485-3200
Fax: 757-487-4970   800-832-0271
mdfrancesco@perriergroup.com
deerparkwater.com
Processor of bottled spring and distilled water
CFO: Kim Jefferies
General Manager: Michael Difrancesco
Plant Manager: Edgar Gaskins
Estimated Sales:$ 3 - 5 Million
Number Employees: 20-49
Sq. footage: 36500
Type of Packaging: Consumer, Food Service
Brands:
A&D Water Care
Culligan
Diamond Springs
H2o To Go
Hydrologix
Miller's
The Water Fountain
Water & Health
Water Fountain of Edenton
Yoder Dairies

13572 Springbank Cheese Company
PO Box 1204
Woodstock, ON N4S 8P6
Canada   519-539-7411
Fax: 519-539-0294   800-265-1973
spcheese@oxford.net   www.springbankcheese.ca
Processor and packer of cheese
President: Tom Hamsworth
Estimated Sales:$ 5-9.9 Million
Number Employees: 5
Sq. footage: 6500
Brands:
Gjetost Ekte
Wensleydale Blueberry

13573 Springdale Cheese Factory
19104 Highway EE
Richland Center, WI 53581-0238   608-538-3213
Fax: 608-538-3212   ltorkelson@aol.com
Processor of muenster and brick cheese
President: Thomas Torkelson
Estimated Sales:$6100000
Number Employees: 35
Type of Packaging: Consumer, Food Service

13574 Springdale Ice Cream & Beverages
11801 Chesterdale Rd
Cincinnati, OH 45246-3407   513-671-2790
Fax: 513-671-2864
Ice cream
Human Resources: Stacey Rose
Plant Engineer: Mike Smith
Number Employees: 100-249

13575 Springfield Creamery
29440 Airport Rd
Eugene, OR 97402-9537   541-689-2911
Fax: 541-689-2915   sue@nancysyogurt.com
www.nancysyogurt.com
Processor and exporter of cultured dairy products including yogurt, cottage cheese, sour cream, cream cheese and kefir; also, soy yogurt
President: Joe Kesey
Estimated Sales:$9508040
Number Employees: 20-49
Number of Brands: 1
Number of Products: 13
Sq. footage: 20000
Type of Packaging: Consumer, Food Service, Private Label, Bulk
Brands:
Nancy's
Nancy's Cottage Cheese
Nancy's Cream Cheese
Nancy's Sour Cream
Nancy's Yogurts

13576 Springfield Smoked FishCompany
150 Switzer Avenue
Springfield, MA 01109-1096   413-737-8693
Fax: 413-747-7360   800-327-3412
Alan@SpringfieldSmokedFish.com
www.ssfish.com
Processor of kosher foods including cream cheese spreads, pickled herring, smoked fish and whitefish, salmon and herring salads; exporter of pickled herring and smoked fish
President: Bob Axler
VP: Alan Axler
Number Employees: 38275
Sq. footage: 8000
Type of Packaging: Consumer, Food Service, Private Label, Bulk
Brands:
AXLER'S
SPRINGFIELD

13577 Springhill Cellars
2920 NW Scenic Drive
Albany, OR 97321-9827   541-928-1009
Fax: 541-928-1009   springhill@proaxis.com
www.springhillcellars.com
Wines
President: Michael Lain
*Estimated Sales:*Less than $500,000
Number Employees: 3
Brands:
Springhill

13578 Springhill Farms
PO Box 10000
Neepawa, NB R0J 1H0
Canada   204-476-3393
Fax: 204-476-3791
Processor of fresh and frozen pork
General Manager: William Teichroew
Number Employees: 400
Type of Packaging: Bulk
Brands:
Spring Hill Farms

13579 Springville Meat & ColdStorage
268 S 100 W
Springville, UT 84663-1804   801-489-6391
Fax: 801-491-3399
Processor of domestic and game meats including ground beef and patties, beef, poultry, lamb and buffalo; also, custom processing available
President: David Cope
VP: Ray Cope
Estimated Sales:$ 5 - 10 Million
Number Employees: 10-19
Sq. footage: 25000
Type of Packaging: Consumer, Food Service

13580 Sprout House
17267 Sundance Drive
Ramona, CA 92065-6951   760-788-7979
Fax: 760-788-4800   800-777-6887
info@sprouthouse.com   www.sprouthouse.com
Sprouting seeds
President: Richard Kohn
Marketing Director: Steve Meyerowitz
Estimated Sales:$500,000
Number Employees: 1-4
Type of Packaging: Private Label

Brands:
    Hemp Sprout Bag
    Sprout House & Salad
    Sproutman's Organic

13581 Spruce Foods
800 S El Camino Real
Suite 210
San Clemente, CA 92672-4274   949-366-9457
    Fax: 928-443-9216 bobbreen@sprucefoods.com
                    www.sprucefoods.com
Importer of organic grocery products
    President: Bob Breen
Estimated Sales:$ 5 - 10 Million
Number Employees: 4
Number of Brands: 3
Number of Products: 160
Brands:
    Lapas
    Massetti
    Montebello

13582 Spruce Mountain Blueberries
PO Box 68
West Rockport, ME 04865-0068   207- 23-6 35
    Fax: 207- 23-6 85 sprucemtn@worldnet.att.net
Wild blueberry chutney, blueberry topping, cran-
berry chutney, conserves, jam, and blueberry vinegar
    Owner: Molly Sholes
Estimated Sales:$70,000
Number Employees: 1-4
Number of Brands: 1
Number of Products: 7
Type of Packaging: Consumer, Food Service

13583 Sprucewood Handmade Cookie Company
PO Box 430
Warkworth, ON K0K 3K0
Canada   877-632-1300
    Fax: 705-924-2626 sprucewood@bellnet.ca
            www.sprucewoodbrands.com
flavored shortbread cookies and nuts
    President/Owner: Mark Pollard

13584 Spurgeon Vineyards & Winery
16008 Pine Tree Rd
Highland, WI 53543-9602   608-929-7692
    Fax: 608-929-4810 800-236-5555
            info@SpurgeonVineyards.com
            www.spurgeonvineyards.com
Manufacturer of wines in the following flavors;
honey, cranberry, grape, sweet cherry, white and
juice blend
    Co-Owner: Glen Spurgeon
    Co-Owner: Mary Spurgeon
    Vice President: James Spurgeon
Estimated Sales:$1 Million
Number Employees: 1-4
Type of Packaging: Consumer, Private Label, Bulk
Brands:
    Spurgeon Vinyards

13585 Squab Producers of California
409 Primo Way
Modesto, CA 95358-5721   209-537-4744
    Fax: 209-537-2037 squabbob@aol.com
                www.squab.com
Processor and exporter of fresh and frozen squab,
pheasant, quail, poussin and partridge
    President: Robert Shipley
Estimated Sales:$ 5 - 10 Million
Number Employees: 20-49
Sq. footage: 10000
Type of Packaging: Consumer, Food Service, Pri-
vate Label, Bulk
Brands:
    King-Cal
    Mendes Farms
    SIERRA GOURMET

13586 Squair Food Company
1418 Newton Street
Los Angeles, CA 90021-2726   213-749-7041
                    Fax: 213-749-3591
Mexican foods
    President: Jerry Karrizer
    Vice President: Morris Kharrazi
Estimated Sales:$1-4.9 Million
Number Employees: 1-4

13587 Square-H Brands
2731 S Soto St
Vernon, CA 90058-8026   323-267-4600
                    Fax: 323-261-7350
Pork, sausage, ham and bacon
    President/ CEO: Henry Haskell
    Marketing Director: Randy Strelioff
    CFO: Bill Hanniegan
    Quality Control: Robert Jarne
Estimated Sales:$ 50-100 Million
Number Employees: 100-249
Number of Brands: 2
Number of Products: 200

13588 Squire Boone Village
406 Mount Tabor Rd
New Albany, IN 47150-2207   812-941-5900
    Fax: 812-941-5920 888-934-1804
                www.squireboone.com
Snacks
    Owner: Rick Conway
Number Employees: 50-99

13589 Squirrel Brand Company
113 Industrial Blvd # D
McKinney, TX 75069-7233   214-585-0100
    Fax: 214-585-0880 800-624-8242
info@squirrelbrand.com www.squirrelbrand.com
Nuts
    President: Brent Meyer Jr
Estimated Sales:$ 5-9.9 Million
Number Employees: 1-4
Sq. footage: 40
Type of Packaging: Private Label
Brands:
    Coconut Zipper
    Squirrel
    Squirrel Nut Caramel
    Squirrel Nut Chew
    Squirrel Nut Zippers

13590 St Charles Trading
650 N Raddant Rd
Batavia, IL 60510-4207   630-377-0608
    Fax: 630-406-1936 stc-trading@worldnet.att.net
                www.stcharlestrading.com
Supplier and broker of surplus, obsolete and
off-spec food ingredients, nuts, oils, sugar, sauces,
juices, spices and dairy, tomato and confectionery
products
    President: Charles H Wetzel
    VP: Kevin Coe
    CEO: William Manns
Estimated Sales:$15000000
Number Employees: 10-19
Sq. footage: 12000

13591 St Mary's & Ankeny Lakes Wild Rice Company
PO Box 3667
Salem, OR 97302-0667   800-225-9453
    Fax: 503-371-9080 800-555-5380
            info@wildriceonline.com
            www.wildriceonline.com
Grower and processor of certified organic wild rice;
also, nonorganic and wild rice blends available
    Co-Owner: Larry Payne
    Co-Owner: Sharon Jenkins-Payne
    CEO: Sharon Jenkins-Payne
Number Employees: 1-4
Sq. footage: 3000
Parent Co: Wild & Ricey Northwest
Type of Packaging: Consumer, Food Service, Pri-
vate Label, Bulk
Brands:
    St. Mary's

13592 St. Charles Trading
330 Freymuth Road
Lake Saint Louis, MO 63367-1814   636-625-1500
    Fax: 636-625-4930 800-336-1333
            stc-trading@worldnet.att.net
                www.stctrading.com
Food ingredients including buttermilk powder, casein, cheese, cocoa powders, jams and jellies,
freeze-dried fruits, chocolate chips, vitamins, vanilla, whey protein, nuts, ice cream mixes and dried
eggs
    President: Charles Wetzel
Estimated Sales:$ 10-20 Million
Number Employees: 10

13593 St. Clair Ice Cream Company
155 Woodward Ave
Norwalk, CT 06854-4731   203-853-4774
    Fax: 203-857-4099 office@stclairicecream.com
                www.stclairicecream.com
Special occasion ice cream and sorbet molded into a
variety of shapes.
    Manager: Kay Gelsman
*Estimated Sales:*Below $ 5 Million
Number Employees: 5-9
Brands:
    St. Clair Ice Cream

13594 St. Clair Industries
3067 E Commercial Boulevard
Fort Lauderdale, FL 33308-4311   954-491-0400
                    Fax: 954-351-9082
Processor and exporter of catalyst altered water
    President: Saul Rubinoff
    CEO: Anne Rubinoff
    Vice President: Anne Rubinoff
*Estimated Sales:*Less than $100,000
Number Employees: 2
Sq. footage: 5000
Type of Packaging: Consumer, Bulk
Brands:
    BRIZ
    WILLARD

13595 (HQ)St. Cloud Bakery
1408 W Saint Germain St
St Cloud, MN 56301-4128   320-251-8055
                    Fax: 320-253-3693
Manufacturer of pies, cookies and pastries
    President: Jeffery Westerlund
Estimated Sales:$29 Million
Number Employees: 10-19
Sq. footage: 2200
Type of Packaging: Consumer, Food Service, Pri-
vate Label, Bulk
Brands:
    LAKELAND
    LAKELAND BAKED COOKIES
    ST CLOUD BAKERY

13596 St. Croix Beer Company
PO Box 16545
Saint Paul, MN 55116-0545   651-387-0708
    Fax: 651-439-0221 info@stcroixbeer.com
                www.stcroixbeer.com
Processor and wholesaler/distributor of lager and
regular, maple and pepper ale
    President: Karl Bremer
*Estimated Sales:*Less than $500,000
Number Employees: 1-4
Type of Packaging: Consumer, Food Service
Brands:
    Serrano
    St. Croix

13597 St. Francis Pie Shop
PO Box 847
Clayton, CA 94517-0847   510-655-0136
                    Fax: 510-655-2585
Bakery
    President/CEO: John Buschini
    Sales Manager: Michael Combs
Estimated Sales:$ 20-50 Million
Number Employees: 50-99

13598 St. Francis Vineyards
100 Pythian Rd
Santa Rosa, CA 95409-6529   707-833-2148
    Fax: 707-833-1394 info@stfranciswine.com
                www.stfranciswine.com
Wines
    President: Joseph Martin
    CFO: Patti Smith
    CEO: Lloyd Canton
    Marketing Director: Nan Fontaine
    Production Manager: Dennis Borell
*Estimated Sales:*Below $ 5 Million
Number Employees: 100-249
Brands:
    Claret
    Reserve Cabernet Sauvignon
    Reserve Merlot
    Reserve Zinfandel

13599 St. Innocent Winery
5657 Zena Rd NW
Salem, OR 97304-9722   503-378-1526
    Fax: 503-378-1041 www.stinnocentwine.com

Wines, still and sparkling
Owner: Mark Velossak
Winemaker: Mark Vlossak
Estimated Sales: Below $ 5 Million
Number Employees: 5-9
Type of Packaging: Private Label
Brands:
St. Innocent

13600 St. Jacobs Candy Company
Brittles 'n More
1441 King Street N
St. Jacobs, ON N0B 2N0
Canada   519-884-3505
Fax: 519-884-9854 sales@brittles-n-more.com
www.brittles-n-more.com
Candy manufacturer; brittles, fudges, beernuts, caramel, turkish delight, sponge toffee, hard candy drops &Æshapes, hard candy suckers and batter crunch.
President: Michael McEachern
Operations: Deana Pfanner
Production: Rhys Carter
Estimated Sales: $750,000
Number Employees: 25
Number of Products: 9
Sq. footage: 2500
Type of Packaging: Consumer, Private Label, Bulk

13601 St. James Sugar Cooperative
PO Box 67
Saint James, LA 70086-0067   225-265-4056
Fax: 225-265-4060 info@slscoop.com
www.slscoop.com
Processor of blackstrap syrup and sugar
Sales Representative: Mr. Bourgeois
Estimated Sales: $ 10 - 20 Million
Number Employees: 50-99
Type of Packaging: Consumer

13602 St. James Winery
540 Sidney St
St James, MO 65559-1071   573-265-7912
Fax: 573-265-6200 800-280-9463
info@stjameswinery.com
www.stjameswinery.com
Wines and grape juice
President: Andrew Hofherr
CFO: Andrew Hofherr
Vice President: John Hofherr
Purchasing Manager: Peter Hofherr
Estimated Sales: $ 5-10 Million
Number Employees: 20-49
Sq. footage: 300
Type of Packaging: Bulk
Brands:
St. James Winery

13603 St. John Levert
6142 Resweber Hwy # A
St Martinville, LA 70582-6805   337-394-9694
Fax: 337-394-9624
Manufactures raw cane sugar; sugar cane refining
Owner: Lawerence Levert
Estimated Sales: $ 3 - 5 Million
Number Employees: 5-9
Type of Packaging: Bulk
Brands:
Farmers

13604 (HQ)St. John's Botanicals
P.O.Box 100
Bowie, MD 20719-0100   301-262-5302
Fax: 301-262-2489 info@stjohns.com
www.stjohnsbotanicals.com
Processor and exporter of spice blends, herb teas, essential oils, ginseng products, nutritional supplements, etc.; wholesaler/distributor of herbs, spices, etc.
Owner: Sydney Vallentyne
Ceo: Sydney Vallentync
Estimated Sales: $500,000-$1 Million
Number Employees: 1-4
Type of Packaging: Private Label, Bulk
Brands:
ROSE HILL
SCENT-O-VAC
THE PREFUME GARDEN

13605 (HQ)St. Julian Wine Company
P.O.Box 127
Paw Paw, MI 49079-0127   269-657-5568
Fax: 269-657-5743 800-732-6002
wines@stjulian.com   www.stjulian.com

Processor and exporter of grape beverages including champagne, wine and juice
President: David Braganini
Executive VP: Chas Catherman
Marketing Director: Kim Babcock
VP Sales: Joe Zuiderueen
Wine Maker: David Miller, Ph.D.
Estimated Sales: $9216001
Number Employees: 50-99
Type of Packaging: Consumer, Food Service

13606 St. Laurent Brothers
1101 N Water St
Bay City, MI 48708-5625   989-893-7522
Fax: 989-893-6571 800-289-7688
www.stlaurentbrothers.com
Processor of peanuts including salted, roasted and candy coated; also, peanut butter
President: Keith Whitney
Co-Owner: Steve Frye
Estimated Sales: $1900000
Number Employees: 20-49
Type of Packaging: Consumer, Food Service, Bulk

13607 St. Lawrence Starch
141 Lakeshore Road E
Mississauga, ON L5G 1N7
Canada   905-274-3671
Fax: 905-271-1258
Processor of starches and corn sweeteners including glucose and fructose
CEO: Nick Lacivita
Sales Manager: Howard Low
Parent Co: Cargill Foods

13608 St. Martin Sugar Cooperative
6092 Resweber Hwy
St Martinville, LA 70582-6804   337-394-3255
Fax: 337-394-3787 info@lasuca.com
www.lasuca.com
Sugar and condiments
President: Mike Melancon
General Manager: Michal Comb
Estimated Sales: $ 30-50 Million
Number Employees: 50-99
Brands:
St. Martin

13609 St. Mary Sugar Cooperative
P.O.Box 269
Jeanerette, LA 70544-0269   337-276-6761
Fax: 337-276-4297
Sugar and condiments
President: Raphael Rodriguez
Plant Manager: Ronald Guilotte Jr
Estimated Sales: $500,000-$1 Million
Number Employees: 50-99

13610 St. Maurice Laurent
Rang 6 Nord
St. Bruno, QC G0W 2L0
Canada   418-343-3655
Fax: 418-343-2996
Processor of cheese and butter
President: Luc St Laurent
Number Employees: 25
Sq. footage: 10000

13611 St. Ours & Company
P.O.Box 566
Norwell, MA 02061-0566   781-331-8520
Fax: 781-331-8628
Processor of frozen shellfish including lobster, crab, clam and dehydrated seafood broths; wholesaler/distributor of seafood and specialty foods; serving the food service market
President: Fred St Ours
Sales: John Christian
Director Manufacturing: Richard St. Ours
Estimated Sales: $ 3 - 5 Million
Number Employees: 5-9
Type of Packaging: Consumer, Food Service, Bulk
Brands:
St. Ours

13612 St. Simons Seafood
5598 Altama Ave
Brunswick, GA 31525-2205   912-265-5225
Fax: 912-264-3181
Seafood and fish.
President: Chuck Egeland
Estimated Sales: $1,500,000
Number Employees: 5-9

13613 St. Stan's Brewing Company
821 L Street
Modesto, CA 95354-0837   209-524-2337
Fax: 209-524-4827
stanislausbrewco@st-stans.com
www.st-stans.com
Beer
President/CEO: Garith Helm
CFO: Romy Angle
Plant Manager: Eric Kellner
Estimated Sales: $ 20-50 Million
Number Employees: 35
Type of Packaging: Private Label
Brands:
Red Sky Ale
St. Stan's Alt Beer

13614 Stacey's Famous Foods
10334 N Taryne Street
Hayden, ID 83835-9807   650-261-9912
800-782-2395
crabcakes@staceysfoods.com
www.staceysfoods.com
Frozen seafood, seafood products such as; sauces, appetizers, quiches, pot pies, potatoe
Owner/President: Stacey James
Estimated Sales: Less than $500,000
Number Employees: 1-4
Brands:
Stacey's

13615 Stacy's Pita Chip Company
663 North St
Randolph, MA 02368-4317   781-961-7799
Fax: 781-961-2830 888-332-4477
stacy@pitachips.com   www.pitachips.com
Manufacturer and distributor of pita and soy-based chips.
President: Stacy Madison
CEO: Mark Andrus
Estimated Sales: $ 5 - 10 Million
Number Employees: 10-19

13616 Stadelman Fruit
P.O.Box 445
Zillah, WA 98953-0445   509-829-5145
Fax: 509-829-5164 http://www.stadelmanfruit.com
Processor and exporter of produce including apples, cherries, nectarines, pears, plums and prunes
President: Peter Stadelman
CEO: Rob Stewart
Number Employees: 500-999
Type of Packaging: Consumer, Food Service, Private Label, Bulk

13617 Staff of Life Natural Foods
1305 Water St
Santa Cruz, CA 95062-1517   831-423-8632
Fax: 831-423-8065 staflife@pacbell.net
www.staffoflifemarket.com
Natural foods
President: Richard Josephson
VP: Gary Bascou
Estimated Sales: $ 5-10 Million
Number Employees: 100-249
Brands:
Beckmann
Imagine Foods
Natures Path
R.W.Knudsen

13618 Stafford County Flour Mills Company
P.O.Box 7
Hudson, KS 67545-0007   620-458-4121
Fax: 620-458-5121 800-530-5640
admin@flour.com   www.hudsoncream.com
Bread flour
President: Alvin A Brensing
Estimated Sales: $ 25-30 Million
Number Employees: 20-49
Type of Packaging: Consumer
Brands:
Hudson Cream Flour

13619 Stage Coach Sauces
3829 Reid St
Palatka, FL 32177-2509   386-328-6330
Fax: 386-328-6330 www.stagecoachsauces.com

Contract packager and exporter of sauces and condiments including steak, barbecue, pepper, chicken wing and seafood; also, contract packaging of wet and dry products available
President: Terry Geck
VP Marketing: Lisa Marie Geck
Plant Manager: Terry Geck
Estimated Sales: $ 3 - 5 Million
Number Employees: 5-9
Sq. footage: 10000
Type of Packaging: Consumer, Food Service, Private Label
Brands:
Stage Coach Sauces

13620 Stagnos Bakery
233 Auburn Street
East Liberty, PA 15206-3209   412-441-3485
Processor of bread and hoagie buns.
President: Anthony Stagno
President: Frances Stagno
Estimated Sales: $ 20 - 50 Million
Number Employees: 20-49
Type of Packaging: Consumer, Food Service, Bulk

13621 Stags' Leap Winery
6150 Silverado Trl
Napa, CA 94558-9748   707-944-1303
Fax: 707-944-9433   800-640-5327
stagsleap@beringerblass.com
www.stagsleap.com
Wines
Manager: Kevin Morrisey
Director Operations: Kevin Morrisey
Marketing Director: Bob Janis
Estimated Sales: $ 10-20 Million
Number Employees: 20-49
Brands:
Stags

13622 Stahlbush Island Farms
3122 SE Stahlbush Island Rd
Corvallis, OR 97333-2709   541-753-8942
Fax: 541-754-1847   barry@stahlbush.com
www.stahlbush.com
Processor of IQF broccoli, carrots, green beans, peas, pumpkins, sweet potatoes, spinach, corn, asparagus, strawberries, cranberries, apples and pears; also, frozen fruit and vegetable purees
President: William Chambers
VP: Karla Chambers
Marketing: Tracy Miedema
Sales Manager: Barry Westfall
Plant Manager: Kim Baglien
Estimated Sales: $ 20 - 50 Million
Number Employees: 100-249

13623 Stahmann Farms
22500 S Highway 28
La Mesa, NM 88044-9531   575-526-2453
www.stahmanns.com
Pecans
Owner: Sally Stahmann-Solis
Vice-CEO: Deane Stahmann
Number Employees: 100-249
Type of Packaging: Bulk

13624 Stallings Headcheese Company
2314 Portsmouth St
Houston, TX 77098-3902   713-523-1751
Manufacturer of headcheese and boudin
Owner: Fred Chu
Estimated Sales: $1-3 Million
Number Employees: 1-4
Sq. footage: 2000

13625 Stampede Meat
7351 S 78th Ave
Bridgeview, IL 60455-1185   773-376-4300
Fax: 773-376-9349   800-353-0933
raym@stampedemeat.com
www.stampedemeat.com
Specializes in custom made center of the plate beef and pork entrees for the needs of the restaurant and hospitality industry.
President: Edward Ligas
VP Marketing/Sales: Ray McKiernan
Estimated Sales: $ 100-500 Million
Number Employees: 250-499
Type of Packaging: Food Service

13626 Stan-Mark Food Products
1100 W 47th Pl
Chicago, IL 60609-4302   773-847-1761
Fax: 773-847-6253   800-651-0994
stan@stanmark.net   www.stanmark.biz
Processor, importer and exporter of pickles, spices, grains and seeds; importer of herring
CEO and President: Stanley Opechowski
R&D: Mark Kongrecki
Estimated Sales: $ 20 - 50 Million
Number Employees: 20-49
Sq. footage: 60000
Type of Packaging: Consumer, Private Label, Bulk

13627 Stanchfield Farms
73 Medford Road
Milo, ME 04463-1515   207-732-5173
Fax: 207-732-5173   sales@stanchfieldfarms.com
www.stanchfieldfarms.com
Sweet and spicy pickles, pure fruit jams and jellies, bouron barbeque sauce and marinades, fruit chutneys, and pickled vegetables
Type of Packaging: Consumer

13628 Standard Bakery
P.O.Box 341
Kealakekua, HI 96750-0341   808-322-3688
Fax: 808-322-2462
Processor of cakes, pies and pastries
President: Lloyd Fujino
Estimated Sales: $ .5 - 1 million
Number Employees: 10-19
Type of Packaging: Consumer, Food Service

13629 Standard Beef Company
216 Food Terminal Plz
New Haven, CT 06511-5910   203-787-2164
Fax: 203-752-1703
Processor and wholesaler/distributor of beef, pork, lamb, poultry, veal, cold cuts, dairy products and fish; importer of goat and bull beef; wholesaler/distributor of equipment and fixtures and frozen foods
President: Henry Bawarsky
VP: William Dober
vp: Steven Wildstein
Estimated Sales: $100+ Million
Number Employees: 20-49
Sq. footage: 15000

13630 (HQ)Standard Candy Company
715 Massman Dr
Nashville, TN 37210-3787   615-889-6360
Fax: 615-889-7775   800-226-4340
sales@standardcandy.com   www.googoo.com
Manufacturer, exporter and contract packager of candy including bars, boxed, log rolls and caramel corn
President: James W Spradley Jr
VP: Thomas Drummond
Director: Anthony Olberding
Director Of Marketing: Joanne Barthel
Sales: Brian Fitzpatrick
Public Relations: Joanne Barthel
Operations: Dennis Adcock
Plant Manager: Gary Baker
Purchasing: Brian Hillman
Estimated Sales: $57604250
Number Employees: 50-99
Sq. footage: 200000
Type of Packaging: Private Label, Bulk
Brands:
COCONUT WAVES
CUMBERLAND RIDGE
GOO GOO CLUSTER

13631 Stangl's Bakeries
1210 Merchant Street
Ambridge, PA 15003-2252   724-266-5080
Baked foods
President: Suzanne Mickey
Estimated Sales: Less than $500,000
Number Employees: 1-4

13632 Stanislaus Food Products
1202 D Street
Modesto, CA 95354-2407   209-522-7201
Fax: 209-527-0227   800-327-7201
www.stanislausfoodproducts.com
Manufacturer of canned tomato paste and sauces
Owner/President: Dino Cortopassi
President: Thomas Cortopassi
President: Robert Ilse
Estimated Sales: $500 Million to $1 Billion
Number Employees: 105

Type of Packaging: Food Service
Brands:
7/11
74-40
80-40
AL DENTE
ALTA CUCINA
FULL RED
PIZZAIOLO
PIZZALETTO
POMAROLA
SAPORITO
TOMATO MAGIC
TRATTORIA
VALOROSO

13633 Stanley Drying Company
P.O.Box 157
Stanley, WI 54768-0157   715-644-5827
www.adm.com
Processor of honey and molasses
Manager: Rick Troyer
Plant Manager: Donald Marquardt
Estimated Sales: $ 5 - 10 Million
Number Employees: 10-19
Parent Co: DEC International
Type of Packaging: Consumer

13634 Stanley Orchards
5 Orchard Dr
Modena, NY 12548   845-883-7351
Fax: 845-883-5077   sales@stanleyorchards.com
www.stanleyorchards.com
Fruits, berries
President/CEO: Ronald Cohn
VP/Plant Manager: Stanley Cohn
Controller: Susan Surprise
Sales Manager: Anthony Maresca
Treasurer/Shipping Manager: Barry Cohn
Sales/Transportation: Randy Wolfe
Estimated Sales: $ 10-20 Million
Number Employees: 10-19
Number of Brands: 7
Type of Packaging: Private Label
Brands:
A & J
Family Ties
Gourmet Apple
Grand Prix
Liberty Empire
Northern Orchard
Stanley

13635 Stanley Provision Company
50 Batson Drive
Manchester, CT 06042-1657   860-649-0656
888-688-6347
Processor of sausage, kielbasa and ground beef
President: Stephen Wisniewski
Number Employees: 10-19
Sq. footage: 10000
Type of Packaging: Consumer, Food Service

13636 Stanley's Best Seafood
7475 Patruski Road
Coden, AL 36523-3181   251-824-2801
Fax: 919-734-1201
Seafood
Owner: Robert Stanley

13637 Stanz Foodservice
P.O.Box 24
South Bend, IN 46624-0024   574-232-6666
Fax: 574-236-4169 www.stanz.com
Cheese
President: Mark Harman
Estimated Sales: $100+ Million
Number Employees: 100-249
Sq. footage: 10000

13638 Stapleton-Spence PackingCompany
1530 the Alameda # 320
San Jose, CA 95126-2303   408-297-8815
Fax: 408-289-5480   800-297-8815
www.stapleton-spence.com
Processor and canner of dried fruits, seeds and nuts; exporter of dried prunes
CEO: Bradley Stapleton
VP: S Stapleton
Sales Manager: M Stapleton
Estimated Sales: $15000000
Number Employees: 10-19
Sq. footage: 100000

Type of Packaging: Consumer, Food Service, Private Label
Brands:
County Fair
Monta Vista

13639 Star Creek Brewing Company
1901 N Akard Street
Dallas, TX 75201-2305   214-999-0999
                              Fax: 214-999-1001
Beer
Estimated Sales: $500,000-$1 Million
Number Employees: 1-4

13640 Star Fine Foods
4652 E Date Ave
Fresno, CA 93725-2123   559-498-2900
                              Fax: 559-498-2910
postmaster@starfinefoods.com
www.starfinefoods.com
California's leading importers, processors, packers and distributors of Mediterranean specialty food products.
President: Patti Andrade
VP Finance: Brian Staggs
Vice President: David Prats
Quality Control: Debbie Verboort
Marketing Director: Patti Andrade
Operations Manager: Joe Cusimano
Estimated Sales: $4600000
Number Employees: 20-49
Sq. footage: 75000
Parent Co: S.A. Borges
Type of Packaging: Consumer, Food Service, Private Label, Bulk
Brands:
Golden Gate
Italian Kitchen
San Francisco Salad
Star

13641 Star Foods
PO Box 22185
Cleveland, OH 44122-0185   216-831-0992
Fax: 216-831-4368 800-837-0992
ritz@starfoods.com www.starfoods.com
President: Mark Lackritz
CEO: Cliff Sobol
Estimated Sales: $ 1 - 3 Million
Type of Packaging: Food Service, Private Label, Bulk

13642 Star Hill Winery
1075 Shadybrook Lane
Napa, CA 94558-4047   707-255-1957
                              Fax: 707-252-1976
Wines
President: Jacob Goldenberg
Estimated Sales: Under $500,000
Number Employees: 1-4

13643 Star Kay White
P.O.Box 147
Congers, NY 10920-0147   845-268-6304
Fax: 845-268-3572 800-874-8518
inquiry@starkaywhite.com
www.starkaywhite.com
Processor and exporter of flavoring syrups and extracts.
President: Walter Katzenstein
CEO/General Manager: Theodore Van Leer
CFO: Martin Hettinger
VP: Jim Katzenstein
R&D: Richard Sroka
Quality Control: Chris Sheridan
Marketing: Stephen Platt
Sales: Jim Taft
Production: Simon Rodriguez
Plant Manager: George Granada
Purchasing Manager: Judy Beaman
Estimated Sales: $ 20 - 50 Million
Number Employees: 50-99
Number of Brands: 1
Number of Products: 750
Sq. footage: 45000
Type of Packaging: Bulk

13644 Star Packaging Corporation
453 Circle 85 St
Atlanta, GA 30349-6085   404-763-2800
Fax: 404-763-5435 www.starpackagingcorp.com

Specializes in the printing, lamination, and conversion of flexible packaging materials in the form of roll stock, pouches and bags.
President: Michael Wilson
Estimated Sales: $ 20 - 50 Million
Number Employees: 100-249

13645 Star Ravioli Manufacturing Company
2 Anderson Ave
Moonachie, NJ 07074-1678   201-933-6427
Fax: 201-933-0484 sales@starravioli.com
www.starravioli.com
Producers of more than thirty varieties of ravioli, as well as other italian specialties including manicotti, stuffed shells, gnocchi, cavatelli, tortellini, fettuccini and much more.
President: Laurence Piretra
CFO: Laurence Piretra
R&D: Rick Pisani
Quality Control: Rick Pisani
Estimated Sales: $ 3 - 5 Million
Number Employees: 10-19
Sq. footage: 12000
Type of Packaging: Consumer, Food Service, Private Label, Bulk

13646 Star Route Farms
95 Olema Bolinas Rd
Bolinas, CA 94924-9710   415-868-1658
Fax: 415-868-9530 warrenweber@earthlink.net
www.starroutefarms.com
Produce
Owner: Warren Weber
Estimated Sales: Below $ 5 Million
Number Employees: 20-49

13647 Star Seafood
PO Box 118
Bayou La Batre, AL 36509-0118   251-824-3110
                              Fax: 251-824-4199
Seafood

13648 Star Snacks Company
105 Harbor Drive
Jersey City, NJ 07305-4505   201-200-9820
Fax: 201-200-9827 800-775-9909
Processor, packer and exporter of dried fruits and nuts including cashews, peanuts, mixed, almonds, filberts, apricots, banana chips, etc.; also, sunflower seeds
President: Andre Engel
Executive VP: Mendel Brachfeld
Estimated Sales: $ 20 - 50 Million
Number Employees: 50-99
Sq. footage: 30000
Parent Co: Gel Spice Compnay
Brands:
Harbor View
Imperial Label
Manhattan Nut
Star

13649 Star Union Brewing Company
PO Box 282
Hennepin, IL 61327-0282   815-925-7400
Beer

13650 Star Valley Cheese
P.O.Box 436
Thayne, WY 83127-0436   307-883-2510
Fax: 307-883-2410 svcheese@silverstar.com
Processor of cheese including mozzarella and provolone
Manager: Tami Luthi
Vice President: Frank Dana
Estimated Sales: $5700000
Number Employees: 20-49
Type of Packaging: Consumer, Food Service, Private Label
Brands:
Bell
Star

13651 Star of the West
162 N Water St
Kent, OH 44240-2419   330-673-2941
                              Fax: 330-673-2439
Miller of soft wheat flour
Sales Manager: Charles Williams III
Plant Manager: Steve Michel
Estimated Sales: $ 5 - 10 Million
Number Employees: 20-49

13652 Star of the West MillingCompany
P.O.Box 146
Frankenmuth, MI 48734-0146   989-652-9971
                              Fax: 989-652-6358
art.loeffler@starofthewest.com
www.starofthewest.com
Processor and exporter of soft wheat flours and bran; processor of beans including black, red, dry navy, soy and colored
President: Art Loeffler
VP: Mike Fassezke
Marketing: Joe Cramer
CFO: Eric Bushey
Estimated Sales: $ 50 - 100 Million
Number Employees: 50-99
Type of Packaging: Bulk

13653 (HQ)Star of the West MillingCompany
P.O.Box 146
Frankenmuth, MI 48734-0146   989-652-9971
Fax: 989-652-6358 www.starofthewest.com
Manufacturer of flour, cearal bran and wheat germ
President: Art Loeffler
CFO: Eric Bushey
Plant Manager: Kenneth Schuman
Estimated Sales: $144 Million
Number Employees: 50-99
Type of Packaging: Private Label, Bulk

13654 Star-Kist
375 N Shore Dr
Pittsburgh, PA 15212-5836   412-222-2200
Fax: 412-222-4050 www.delmonte.com
Processor, canner and exporter of tuna
Marketing: Barry Shepard
Media Relations: Melissa Murphy
Estimated Sales: $ .5 - 1 million
Number Employees: 1-4
Parent Co: Del Monte Foods
Brands:
CHUNK LIGHT TUNA
GOURMET'S CHOICE TUNA FILLETS
LOW SODIUM TUNA
SOLID WHITE ALBACORE TUNA
STARKIST FLAVOR FRESH POUCH
STARKIST LUNCH TO-GO
STARKIST SELECT
STARKIST TUNA CREATIONS

13655 Star-Kist Caribe
3051 Road 64
Mayaguez, PR 00680   787-834-2424
                              Fax: 787-834-3175
Processor, canner and exporter of tuna
General Manager: Alfredo Archilla
Number Employees: 1,000-4,999
Parent Co: Star-Kist Foods
Type of Packaging: Consumer, Food Service

13656 Starbrook Industries Inc
325 S Hyatt St
Tipp City, OH 45371-1241   937-473-8135
Fax: 937-473-0331 Richard@StarbrookInd.com
www.starbrookind.com/
Product line includes forming and non-forming food packaging films designed for Bi-Vac, Dixie Pak and Multi Vac machines.
Sales Manager: Richard Anderson

13657 (HQ)Starbucks Coffee Company
2401 Utah Ave S
Seattle, WA 98134   206-447-1575
Fax: 206-447-0828 800-782-7282
www.starbucks.com
Whole bean coffees and rich-brewed Italian style espresso beverages, a variety of pastries and confections, coffee-related accessories and equipment. Also a processor of ice cream and coffee drinks including blended and flavored; alsononfat and dairy-free blended juiced teas; roaster of whole bean coffees
Chairman/President/CEO: Howard Schultz
CFO/CAO/EVP: Troy Alstead
Estimated Sales: $5 Billion
Number Employees: 10,000+
Type of Packaging: Consumer, Private Label, Bulk
Brands:
Brazil Ipanema Bourbon
Caffe Verona
Double Shot
Ethos Water
Frappuccino

Gold Coast Blend
Lightnote Blend
Milder Dimensions
Serenade Blend
Siren's Note Blend
Starbucks
Tazo
Tiazzi
Yukon Blend

13658 Starich
28490 2nd Street
Daphne, AL 36526-7150   251-626-5037
Seafood

13659 Stark Candy Company
P.O.Box 65
Pewaukee, WI 53072-0065   262-691-0600
        Fax: 262-691-2947   800-558-2300
        www.necco.com
Manufacturer of candy including wafers, hard, peanut butter chews, salt water taffy, caramel apple dip, gummies, candy raisins, lollypops, mints, etc.; packaged for racks and theatre vending; also, holiday novelties available
    President/CEO: Domenic Antonellis
    VP/CFO: Stan Byerly
    VP R&D: Jeff Green
    Marketing Manager: Lory Zimbalatti
    VP Research: Bruno Mastrodicasa
    Plant Manager: Patricia A Raap
Estimated Sales: $ 20 - 50 Million
Number Employees: 100-249
Parent Co: New England Confectionery Company
Type of Packaging: Consumer, Bulk
Brands:
    CANADA
    CANDY CUPBOARD
    CANDY HOUSE
    CLARK BAR
    EAGLE BRAND
    KETTLE FRESH CARAMEL
    MARY JANE
    MASTERPIECES
    MIGHTY MINTS
    NECCO WAFERS
    SKY BAR
    SLAP STIX
    STINKY FEET
    SWEETHARTS
    ULTRA MINTS

13660 (HQ)Stark Candy Company
135 American Legion Highway
Revere, MA 02151-2405   985-446-1354
        Fax: 985-448-1627   800-621-1983
Manufacturer and exporter of candy
    President: Dominic Antonellis
    General Manager: Bobby Folfe
    VP Sales: Tom Drummond
Number Employees: 30
Type of Packaging: Consumer

13661 Starkel Poultry
PO Box 73340
Puyallup, WA 98373-0340   253-845-2876
    Fax: 253-841-1004   starkel@starkelpoultry.com
        www.starkelpoultry.com
Processor and exporter of bagged fowl including fresh and frozen
    President: Elsie Starkel
    Quality Control: Susan Mazza
    Owner: Susan Mazza
Estimated Sales: $4400000
Number Employees: 45
Type of Packaging: Consumer, Bulk

13662 Starport Foods
P.O.Box 22366
San Francisco, CA 94122-0366   714-525-5810
    Fax: 415-731-0663   866-206-9343
        sales@starportfoods.com
        www.starportfoods.com
Ethnic specialty sauces, dressings and seasonings
    Owner/VP: Cheryl Tsang
Estimated Sales: $500,000-$1 Million
Number Employees: 5-9
Number of Products: 40
Type of Packaging: Consumer, Food Service, Private Label, Bulk

13663 Starr & Brown
10610 NW Saint Helens Road
Portland, OR 97231-1048   503-287-1775

Wine
    President: Eric Brown
Estimated Sales: Less than $500,000
Number Employees: 1-4

13664 Startup's Candy Company
P.O.Box 589
Provo, UT 84603-0589   801-373-8673
        Fax: 801-373-7312
        customerservice@startupcandy.com
        www.startupcandy.com
Manufacturer of candy and confectionery products
    President: Harry W Startup
    Vice President: Jon Startup
Estimated Sales: $2,000,000
Number Employees: 5-9
Type of Packaging: Consumer

13665 Starwest Botanicals
11253 Trade Center Dr
Rancho Cordova, CA 95742   916-638-8100
    Fax: 916-853-9673   888-273-4372
        www.starwest-botanicals.com
Processor, importer and exporter of herbs and herbal extracts, spices and essential and vegetable oils; also, custom milling, blending and formulating available
    Owner/President/CEO: Van Joerger
    VP Finance: Mark Wendley
    SVP R&D/Production Manager: Dawn Bennett
    Marketing/Product Development: Daniela Nelson
    VP Sales: Richard Patterson
    Purchasing: Bonnie Sadkowski
Estimated Sales: $9.7 Million
Number Employees: 60
Sq. footage: 50000
Type of Packaging: Bulk
Brands:
    Nature Actives
    Starwest

13666 Stasero International
2001 S Plum Street
Seattle, WA 98144-4536   206-328-0690
    Fax: 206-324-4586   888-929-2378
        info@stasero.com   www.stasero.com
Italian-style syrups, shakable toppings, blended ice coffee mixes
    President: Sabru Kabani
    VP Marketing: Aisha Kabani
    CFO: Joann Watts
    Vice President: Mel Moomjean
Estimated Sales: $ 20 - 50 Million
Number Employees: 20-49
Type of Packaging: Private Label
Brands:
    Stasero

13667 Stash Tea Company
P.O.Box 910
Portland, OR 97207-0910   503-684-4482
    Fax: 503-684-4424   800-547-1514
        stash@stashtea.com   www.stashtea.com
Processor of hot and cold tea including green, black, herbal, decaffeinated and iced
    President: Tom Lisicki
    Marketing Director: Dorothy Arnold
    Manager: Susan Brown
    Public Relations: Konnie Turney
Estimated Sales: $8,300,000
Number Employees: 50-99
Type of Packaging: Consumer, Food Service, Bulk
Brands:
    Exotica
    Stash
    Stash Premium Organic Teas
    Yamamotoyama 1690

13668 Stassen North America
408 S Pierce Ave
Louisville, CO 80027-3018   303-527-1700
    Fax: 303-527-1702   sales@snatea.com
        www.coopertea.com
General grocery
    President: Mike Fitzgerald
Estimated Sales: $ 2.5-5 Million
Number Employees: 10-19

13669 State Fish Company
2194 Signal Pl
San Pedro, CA 90731-7288   310-832-2633
    Fax: 310-831-2402   888-658-3474
        calsquid@aol.com   www.statefish.com

Processor, importer and exporter of fish and seafood including shellfish
    President: John Deluca
    Vice President: Vanessa De Luca
    Marketing Director: Janet Esposito
    Domestic Sales: Klaus Brittinger
Estimated Sales: $21900000
Number Employees: 100-249
Type of Packaging: Private Label, Bulk
Brands:
    Calamari of California
    Fiesta Del Mar
    Nautilus

13670 State Fish Distributors
4513 S Halsted Street
Chicago, IL 60609-3413   773-451-0500
        Fax: 773-225-4660
Seafood
    President: Donald Nathan

13671 State of Maine Cheese Company
461 Commercial St
Rockport, ME 04856-4455   207-236-8895
    Fax: 207-236-9591   800-762-8895
        infoA@cheese-me.com   www.cheese-me.com
Cheese
    President: Cathe Morrill
Estimated Sales: $500,000-$1 Million
Number Employees: 5-9

13672 Stateline Boyd
PO Box 550
Lynn, MA 01903-0650   781-593-4422
        Fax: 781-599-8430
Snack foods
    President: Steven Jakubowski
    CFO: W Duncan Reed
    COO: Michael Schena
    VP Sales: Donald LaDouceur
Estimated Sales: $ 50-100 Million
Number Employees: 250

13673 Statewide Meats & Poultry
211 Food Terminal Plz
New Haven, CT 06511-5997   203-777-6669
        Fax: 203-492-4073
Processor and wholesaler/distributor of meat
    President: Stephen Falcigno
Estimated Sales: $7900000
Number Employees: 20-49

13674 Stauber Performance Ingredients
4120 N Palm St
Fullerton, CA 92835-1026   714-441-3900
    Fax: 714-441-3909   888-441-4233
        customerservice@stauberusa.com
        www.stauberusa.com
Leading supplier of bulk ingredients to the nutritional products, food and cosmetic industries
    Owner: Danny Stauber
    CEO: Dan Stauber
    Diretor/Quality Assurance: Pat Wratschko
Number Employees: 50-99
Sq. footage: 50000
Type of Packaging: Bulk

13675 Stauffer Biscuit Company
360 S Belmont St
York, PA 17403-2616   717-843-9016
    Fax: 717-843-0592   800-673-2473
        mlcarione@stauffers.net   www.stauffers.net
Manufacturer of cookies, crackers and snack products
    President: Marc Garrett
Estimated Sales: $ 50 - 100 Million
Number Employees: 500-999

13676 Stauffer's
8670 Farnsworth Rd
Cuba, NY 14727-9720   585-968-2700
        Fax: 585-968-2722
Manufacturers of cookies.
    Manager: John Fletcher
Estimated Sales: $ 2.5-5 Million
Number Employees: 20-49
Brands:
    Stauffer's

13677 Stavis Seafoods
212 Northern Avenue
Boston, MA 02210-2049   617-482-6349
    Fax: 617-482-1340   800-390-5103
        fish@stavis.com   www.stavis.com

Importer, exporter and wholesaler/distributor of
fresh and frozen seafood. Fresh seafood includes
cod, haddock, pollock, tuna, swordfish, mahi, snap-
per, grouper and seabass fillets, rockshrimp and
baby scallops
President: Richard Stavis
CFO: Mary Fleming
Marketing: Ruth Levy
Sales: David Lancaster
Operations: Emily Stavis
Purchasing Manager: Robert Landy
Estimated Sales: $121350000
Number Employees: 98
Number of Brands: 5
Number of Products: 700
Sq. footage: 40000
Type of Packaging: Food Service, Private Label,
Bulk
Brands:
Bos'n
Boston Pride
Foods From the Sea
Prince Edward

13678 Stawnichy Holdings
PO Box 18
Mundare, AB T0B 3H0
Canada   780-764-3912
Fax: 780-764-3765 888-764-7646
shltd@telusplanet.net www.mundaresausage.com
Processor of pepperoni, frankfurters, Ukrainian-style
sausage, bologna, garlic rings, cooked and pressed
ham, salami, ham and bacon loafs, macaroni and
cheese loafs, corned beef, pastrami, beef jerky, ba-
con, veal cutlets, ground beefpierogies, etc
VP/General Manager: E Stawnichy
Secretary: Jeanette Stawnichy
Number Employees: 20-49
Sq. footage: 11500
Brands:
Stawnichy's

13679 Ste. Chapelle Winery
19348 Lowell Rd
Caldwell, ID 83607-9502   208-453-7830
Fax: 208-453-7831 877-783-2427
info@stchappelle.com www.stechapelle.com
Wines
Manager: Mary Sloyer
Estimated Sales: Below $ 5 Million
Number Employees: 20-49
Parent Co: Canandaigua Wine Company
Type of Packaging: Private Label

13680 Steak Specialists
PO Box 33465
Atlanta, GA 30332-1001   404-874-8073
steak@netspace.net.au
Meat
Executive VP: Morris Taylor
Purchasing Manager: M Rose

13681 Steak-Umm Company
P.O. Box 350
Shillington, PA 19607-0350   860-928-5900
Fax: 860-928-0351 http://www.steakumm.com
President: Dennis Newnham
Marketing: Evan Tetreault
Sales: Mark Wojcik
Estimated Sales: $14100000
Number Employees: 120
Sq. footage: 176000
Brands:
Red.L
Spare-The-Ribs
Steak-Umm
Steak-Umm Sandwich To Go

13682 Stearns & Lehman
30 Paragon Pkwy
Mansfield, OH 44903-8074   419-522-2722
Fax: 419-522-1152 800-533-2722
slinfo@kerrygroup.com www.kerryamericas.com
Processor and exporter of Italian syrups, specialty
sugars and powdered toppings for coffees; also, cof-
fee and tea flavors and extracts; private labeling
available
Manager: Jim Powers
Executive VP: Sally Stearns
Regional Sales Manager: Jody Hastings
Plant Manager: Phyllis Thomas
Purchasing Manager: Dee Porter

Estimated Sales: $7900000
Number Employees: 20-49
Sq. footage: 50000
Type of Packaging: Private Label
Brands:
Dinatura
Dolce
Flavor-Mate
Gift of Bran
My Hero
Paradise Bay
Select Origins
Senza
Stearns & Lehman

13683 Stearns Wharf Vintners
217 Stearns Wharf # G
Santa Barbara, CA 93101-3582   805-966-6624
Fax: 805-966-6624
www.stearnswharfvintners.com
Wines
President: Candy Scott
Estimated Sales: $ 2.5-5 Million
Number Employees: 5-9
Brands:
Stearns Wharf

13684 Steckel Produce
905 State Highway 16
Jerseyville, IL 62052-2834   618-498-4274
Fax: 618-498-4780
Fruits and vegetables
President: Dennis Steckel
Estimated Sales: $3 Million
Number Employees: 5-9

13685 Steel's Gourmet Foods
55 E Front St # D175
Bridgeport, PA 19405-1489   610-520-9780
Fax: 610-277-1228 800-678-3357
info@steelsgourmet.com
www.steelsgourmet.com
Processor and exporter of gourmet, sugar free des-
sert toppings, jams, sweetners, syrups and condi-
ments; also organic salad dressings, condiments,
fruit spreads and low sugar fudge sauces.
President: Elizabeth Steel
Plant Manager: Carlos Short
Estimated Sales: Over $500,000
Number Employees: 5-9
Number of Products: 60
Sq. footage: 10000
Parent Co: Clack-Steel
Type of Packaging: Consumer, Private Label
Brands:
Charlie Trotter Foods
Daven Island Trade
Steel's Gourmet

13686 Steelback Brewery
88 Farrell Drive
Tiverton, ON N0G 2T0
Canada   519-368-3663
Fax: 519-368-5676 800-879-0541
bafi@primeline.net
Processor of apple juice concentrate
Production Manager: Jay Paul
Type of Packaging: Bulk

13687 Steep & Brew Coffee Roasters
855 E Broadway
Monona, WI 53716-4012   608-223-0707
Fax: 608-223-0355 800-876-1986
coffee@steep-n-brew.com www.cafefair.org
Coffee
President: Mark Ballering
VP/Sales Manager: Mark Mullee
Estimated Sales: Below $ 5 Million
Number Employees: 20-49
Type of Packaging: Private Label
Brands:
Cafe Fair

13688 Steese Ice Cream
433 Blacktown Road
Grove City, PA 16127-4303   724-748-4115
Processor and wholesaler/distributor of ice cream;
serving the food service market
Owner: Robert Steese
Number Employees: 10-19
Type of Packaging: Consumer, Food Service, Bulk

13689 Stefano Gourmet A Tasteof Italy
PO Box 8
Rural Ridge, PA 15075-0008   412-781-4104
Fax: 412-781-4210 888-781-4104
chefsteff@chefsteff.com www.chefsteff.com
Italian specialty food products
President/CEO: Steff Tedeschi
Sales Director: Bill Acker
Plant Manager: Gabriel Negri
Purchasing Manager: Emma Tedeschi
Estimated Sales: $ 10-20 Million
Number Employees: 5-9
Type of Packaging: Private Label
Brands:
Steff Gourmet Italia
Steff Gourmet Italian Sauces

13690 Stegall Smoked Turkey
6608 E Marshville Blvd
Marshville, NC 28103-1198   704-624-6628
Fax: 704-624-2510 800-851-6034
info@stegallsmokedturkey.com
www.stegallsmokedturkey.com
Processor of frozen hickory-smoked turkey and
honey-glazed ham
President: Don Stegall
Marketing Director: Don Stegall
VP: Marceil Stegall
Estimated Sales: $500,000-$1 Million
Number Employees: 5-9
Sq. footage: 110000
Type of Packaging: Private Label
Brands:
Stegall Smoked Turkey

13691 Stehlin & Sons Company
10134 Colerain Ave
Cincinnati, OH 45251-4902   513-385-6164
Fax: 513-385-6165
Processor of beef and pork
President: John Stehlin
Estimated Sales: $1300000
Number Employees: 10-19
Type of Packaging: Consumer, Bulk

13692 Steinbach Provisions Company
741 W 47th St
Chicago, IL 60609-4409   773-538-1511
Fax: 773-538-3131
Processor of beef
Owner: Thomas Steinbach
VP: Jack Steinback
Estimated Sales: $ 3 - 5 Million
Number Employees: 5-9
Type of Packaging: Bulk

13693 Steiner Cheese
PO Box 280
Baltic, OH 43804-0280   330-897-5505
Fax: 330-897-6911
Processor of Swiss cheese
President: James Sommers
VP: Dale Lendon
Estimated Sales: $ 5 - 10 Million
Number Employees: 5
Type of Packaging: Consumer, Bulk

13694 (HQ)Steiner, S.S.
655 Madison Ave # 17
New York, NY 10065-8043   212-515-7200
Fax: 212-593-4238 sales@hopsteiner.com
www.hopsteiner.com
Processor, importer and exporter of hops extracts,
pellets and oils
Owner: Louis S Gimbel Iii
VP: Louis Gimbel IV
VP: Martin Ungewitter
Estimated Sales: $ 20 - 50 Million
Number Employees: 20-49
Type of Packaging: Food Service
Other Locations:
Steiner, S.S.
Salem OR
Brands:
Hopsteiner

13695 Steinfurth IncElectromechanical Measuring Systems
530 Means Street
Suite 120
Atlanta, GA 30318   404-586-6817
Fax: 404-586-6824
info@steinfurthinstruments.com
www.steinfurth.com/

Steinfurth is a producer of specialist measuring devices for the beverage industry, the food industry, pharmaceuticals and mining.
Marketing & Sales Manager North America: Yvonne Harper

13696 Steinfurth Instruments
530 Means Street
Suite 120
Atlanta, GA 30318   404-588-6817
Fax: 404-586-6824
info@steinfurthinstruments.com
www.steinfurthinstruments.com
Steinfurth Instruments is a producer of specialist measuring devices for the beverage industry, the food industry, pharmaceuticals and mining.
Marketing and Sales Manager: Yvonne Harper

13697 Stella Baking Company
2901 11th Street
Rockford, IL 61109-1207   815-398-5191
Processor of baked goods including crackers, cookies, biscuits and pizza shells; also, lard
Owner: Frank Geroci
Estimated Sales: $150000
Number Employees: 5
Type of Packaging: Consumer, Food Service, Bulk

13698 Stella D'Oro Biscuit Company
184 W 237th St
Bronx, NY 10463-4102   718-549-3700
Fax: 718-884-6494   stephen.spaner@kraft.com
www.stelladoro.com
Processor and exporter of cookies, bread sticks and biscuits
President: Michele Abo
Estimated Sales: $75,000,000
Number Employees: 20-49
Parent Co: Nabisco
Type of Packaging: Consumer

13699 Stello Foods
PO Box 413
Punxsutawney, PA 15767-0413   814-938-8611
Fax: 814-938-8769   800-849-4599
stellofoods@hotmail.com   www.stellofoods.com
Processor of peppers, mustards, sauces, salsas, vinegars, spreads, salad dressings and brined products
President: Nickki L Stello
Vice President: James Stello
Estimated Sales: $2.5 Million
Number Employees: 30
Sq. footage: 60000
Type of Packaging: Consumer, Food Service, Private Label, Bulk
Brands:
PINKS
RAPES
ROSIE'S

13700 Steltzner Vineyards
5998 Silverado Trl
Napa, CA 94558-9416   707-252-7272
Fax: 707-252-2079   wines@steltzner.com
www.steltzner.com
Bottled wine
President: Richard M Steltzner
Marketing Director: Alison Steltzner
Co-Founder: Dick Steltzner
General Manager: Kim Gish
Estimated Sales: $ 10-20 Million
Number Employees: 20-49
Brands:
Steltzner Vineyards

13701 Stengel Seed & Grain Company
14698 Sd Highway 15
Milbank, SD 57252-5452   605-432-6030
Fax: 605-432-6064   gstengel@tnics.com
Processor of organic grains. Services include cleaning, dehulling, packaging, warehousing and shipping.
President: Doug Stengel
Estimated Sales: Less than $500,000
Number Employees: 5-9
Sq. footage: 30000

13702 Stepan Company
100 W Hunter Ave
Maywood, NJ 07607-1088   201-845-3030
Fax: 201-712-7235   800-523-3614
food.health@stepan.com   www.stepan.com

Processor and exporter of medium chain triglycerides and structured lipids
President/CEO: F Quinn Stepan Jr
CFO: James Hurlburt
Research & Development: Jenifer Haydinger Galante PhD
Quality Control: Parul Vyas
Marketing: James Butterwick
Plant Manager: Don Watson
Purchasing Director: Ed Sebastian
Estimated Sales: $ 20 - 50 Million
Number Employees: 50-99
Sq. footage: 11000
Parent Co: Stephan Company
Type of Packaging: Bulk
Brands:
NEOBEE 1053
NEOBEE 1095
NEOBEE 895
NEOBEE M-20
NEOBEE M-5
WECOBEE FS
WECOBEE M
WECOBEE S

13703 Stephany's Chocolates
P.O.Box 1088
Grand Junction, CO 81502-1088   303-421-7229
Fax: 303-421-7256   800-888-1522
customerservice@stephanyschocolates.com
www.stephanyschocolates.com
Bulk and boxed chocolates, toffee, mints, toffee, creams, nuts and chews, mint meltaways and cherry cordials.
President: Hal Strottan
Quality Control: Cathy Warner
Estimated Sales: $ 10-20 Million
Number Employees: 170
Brands:
Colorado Almond Toffee
Denver Mint
Stephany's Chocolates

13704 Stephen's Gourmet Kitchens
P.O.Box 10
Farmington, UT 84025-0010   801-974-0198
Fax: 801-974-0166   800-845-2400
sdejohn@hotcocoa.com   www.hotcocoa.com
Processor of hot cocoa and cappuccino
Owner: David Cowley
Estimated Sales: $ 3 - 5 Million
Number Employees: 5-9
Type of Packaging: Consumer, Food Service
Brands:
Cafe Tiamo

13705 Sterigenics International
PO Box 30667
Los Angeles, CA 90030-0667   510-770-9000
Fax: 510-770-1499   800-472-4508
info@sterigenics.com   www.sterigenics.com
Irradiator of spices, dehydrated vegetable ingredients and seasoning blends
CEO: David E Meyer
CFO: Fred Ruegsegger
Deputy CEO: Marc Markey
Number Employees: 20-49
Brands:
Sterigenics

13706 Sterling Candy
595 S Broadway
Hicksville, NY 11801-5036   516-932-8300
Fax: 516-932-8392
Candy
President/CEO: Edward Greenberg
Public Relations: Stacey Greenberg
Estimated Sales: $ 10-24.9 Million
Number Employees: 50

13707 Sterling Extract Company
10929 Franklin Ave # V
Franklin Park, IL 60131-1430   847-451-9728
Fax: 847-451-9745
www.sterlingextractcompany.com
Processor of pure and artifical vanilla flavoring extracts, flavors for ice cream, candy and bakery products.
President: Craig Wakefield
Vice President: Lynn Wakefield
Marketing Director: John Wakefield
Sales Director: Deborah Pavone
Estimated Sales: $1500000
Number Employees: 5-9

Type of Packaging: Bulk
Brands:
Bourbonil
Star-Van
Sterling Old Fashion Flavors
Vanaleigh 6b

13708 Sterling Foods
1075 Arion Pkwy
San Antonio, TX 78216-2883   210-490-1669
Fax: 210-490-7964
cdietzel@sterlingfoodusa.com
www.sterlingfoodsusa.com
Processor of shelf stable bakery products and snack foods.
President: John Likovich
CEO: John Likovich
Sr VP/COO: Nick Davis
Director of Research & Development: John Brahm
Director of Quality Assurance: Andy Lobmeyer
Sr VP Sales/Marketing: Fred Friend
Director of Sales/Marketing: Christie Dietzel
Manager of Human Resources: Jim Kuehl
Director of Operations: Mike Sides
Director of Plant Services: Mike Brehm
Estimated Sales: $7900000
Number Employees: 100-249
Sq. footage: 85000

13709 Sterling Pacific Meat Company
PO Box 2637
Los Angeles, CA 90051-0637   310-274-7635
Fax: 323-643-8292   www.sterlingmeat.com
Processor of chicken, lamb, beef and pork products
Owner: Jim Asher
Estimated Sales: $100 - 499 Million
Number Employees: 100

13710 Sterzing Food Company
1819 Charles St
Burlington, IA 52601-2201   319-754-8467
Fax: 319-752-7195   800-754-8467
sterzing2@lisco.com   www.sterzingchips.com
Manufacturer of potato chips and sour cream and dip
President: Tom Blackwood
Vice President: Thomas Blackwood
Estimated Sales: $2 Million
Number Employees: 20-49
Type of Packaging: Consumer
Brands:
Sterzing's

13711 Stettler Meats
PO Box 1495
Stettler, AB T0C 2L0
Canada   403-742-1427
Fax: 403-742-1429
Fresh meats, processed meats, wild game, custom cutting & wrapping, pork, beef, and bison.
Manager: Randy Cherewko
Sales: Kelly Greenwood
Number Employees: 1-25
Type of Packaging: Consumer, Food Service

13712 Steuk's Country Market &Winery
165 E Washington Row
Sandusky, OH 44870-2610   419-625-8324
Fax: 419-625-9007
Wines
President: Charles Sprigg
Estimated Sales: $ 2.5-5 Million
Number Employees: 1-4

13713 Steve Connolly Seafood Company
34 Newmarket Sq
Roxbury, MA 02118-2601   617-427-7700
Fax: 617-427-7697   800-225-5595
Fresh and frozen seafood, lobster, shellfish, smoked fish, prepared foods
President: Stephan Connolly
Marketing Director: Willy Warner
CFO: John Curley
Quality Control: Donald Putney
CFO: Michel Zukowki
CFO: Mike Zukowski
Operations Manager: Walter Peary
Production Manager: William Blenn
Estimated Sales: $ 28 Million
Number Employees: 50-99
Type of Packaging: Bulk
Brands:
Steve Connolly

13714 Steve's Doughnut Shop
4 Winslow Ave
Somerset, MA 02726-2318   508-672-0865
Doughnuts
 Owner: Mario Gulinello
Estimated Sales: $ 1-2.5 Million
Number Employees: 10-19

13715 Steve's Mom
200 Food Center Dr
Bronx, NY 10474-7030   718-842-8090
        Fax: 718-832-6302   800-362-4545
ruggiebake@aol.com   www.steves-mom.com
Processor of kosher dessert strudels, vegetable stru-
dels, rugelach, coconut macaroons, brownies, and
cheesecake
 President: Suellen Schussel
 Vice President: Erwin Schussel
Estimated Sales: $664696
Number Employees: 5-9
Sq. footage: 2500
Type of Packaging: Consumer, Food Service, Pri-
vate Label, Bulk
Brands:
 Fudgeroons
 Scotcheroons
 Steve's Mom

13716 Stevenot Winery & Imports
2690 San Domingo Rd
Murphys, CA 95247-9646   209-728-0638
 Fax: 209-728-3710 info@stevenotwinery.com
        www.stevenotwinery.com
Wines
 Owner: Barden Stevenot
 Winemaker: Chuck Hovey
Estimated Sales: $ 5-10 Million
Number Employees: 5-9
Type of Packaging: Bulk
Brands:
 Shephard Ridge
 Stevenot Winery

13717 Stevens Point Brewery
2617 Water St
Stevens Point, WI 54481-5248   715-344-9310
 Fax: 715-344-8897   800-369-4911
        www.pointbeer.com
Processor and exporter of beer
 President: Jim Weichman
 CEO: Joe Martino
 Brewing: John Zappa
 Operations Manager: Art Oksuita
Estimated Sales: $ 20 - 50 Million
Number Employees: 20-49
Parent Co: Barton Beers

13718 Stevens Sausage Company
P.O.Box 2304
Smithfield, NC 27577-2304   919-934-3159
 Fax: 919-934-2568   800-338-0561
tstev25536@aol.com   www.stevens-sausage.com
Processor of fresh ham, pork, frankfurters and sau-
sage
 President: N Stevens
 Plant Manager: Tim Stevens
Estimated Sales: $7327743
Number Employees: 50-99
Type of Packaging: Consumer, Food Service, Bulk

13719 Stevens Tropical Plantation
6550 Okeechobee Blvd
West Palm Beach, FL 33411-2798   561-683-4701
        Fax: 561-683-4993
Processor and importer of syrups, fruit juices, nectar
and beverage bases
 President: Henry Stevens Jr
Estimated Sales: $ 1 - 3 Million
Number Employees: 5-9
Sq. footage: 10000
Type of Packaging: Consumer, Food Service
Brands:
 Parkway
 Sunny Isle

13720 Stevens Tropical Plantation
6550 Okeechobee Blvd
West Palm Beach, FL 33411-2798   561-683-4701
        Fax: 561-683-4993   800-785-1355
        www.stevenstropicalplantation.com
Bottled fruit juices
 Owner: Henry W Stevens Jr Jr

Estimated Sales: $990,000
Number Employees: 5-9
Brands:
 Stevens

13721 Stevenson-Cooper
P.O.Box 46345
Philadelphia, PA 19160-6345   215-223-2600
 Fax: 215-223-3597 waxcooper@aol.com
        www.stevensoncooper.com
Manufacturer and exporter of oils including cotton-
seed and palm oils; also, manufacturer of paraffin
and sealing wax
 President: Dennis Cooper
 R&D: Tammy Pullins
Estimated Sales: Below $ 5 Million
Number Employees: 5-9

13722 Stevia LLC
PO Box 80311
Valley Forge, PA 19484-0311   610-265-7102
 Fax: 610-265-7102   888-878-3842
admin@SteviaDessert.com   www.sweevia.com
 President: Lisa Jobs
Brands:
 Sweetvia
 Sweevia

13723 Stevison Ham Company
P.O.Box 219
Portland, TN 37148-0219   615-323-7315
 Fax: 615-325-5914   800-844-4267
sales@stevisonham.com   www.stevisonham.com
Smoked ham, ribs, BBQ pork
 President: Michael Stevison
 VP Marketing: Sean Stevison
 Vice President: John White
 CFO: Oara Stevison
Estimated Sales: $ 20-30 Million
Number Employees: 50-99
Brands:
 Stevison's

13724 Stewart Candy Company
400 Bonneyman Rd
Waycross, GA 31501   912-283-1970
 Fax: 912-285-0228 deens@stewartcandy.com
        www.stewartcandy.com
Candy and confections
 President: Jimmy Stewart Iii
 CFO: Deen J Stewart
 Sales Director: Sam Stewart
Estimated Sales: $ 20-50 Million
Number Employees: 20-49

13725 Stewart's Beverages
709 Westchester Avenue
White Plains, NY 10604-3103   914-397-9200
Processor of soft drinks
 President: Samuel M Simpson
 CFO: Myron D Stadler
Number Employees: 20-49
Parent Co: Triarc Companies
Type of Packaging: Consumer, Food Service

13726 Stewart's Ice Cream
P.O.Box 435
Saratoga Springs, NY 12866-0435   518-581-1000
 Fax: 518-581-7076 www.stewartsshops.com
Processor of whole, 2% and skim milk; also, regular
and low-fat ice cream
 Manager: John Bottisti
Estimated Sales: $300,000-500,000
Number Employees: 50-99
Type of Packaging: Consumer

13727 Stewart's Private BlendFoods
4110 W Wrightwood Ave
Chicago, IL 60639-2172   773-489-2500
 Fax: 773-489-2148   800-654-2862
        info@stewarts.com   www.stewarts.com
Processor, importer and exporter of coffees includ-
ing flavored, decaffeinated and roasted; also, fla-
vored and blended teas
 President: Donald Stewart
 CEO: Robert Stewart
 Vice President: William Stewart Jr
 Production Manager: Elita Pagan
 Plant Manager: Ed Fabro
Estimated Sales: $2,000,000
Number Employees: 20-49
Sq. footage: 48000
Type of Packaging: Consumer, Food Service, Pri-
vate Label, Bulk

Brands:
 Stewarts

13728 Stewarts Market
17821 State Route 507 SE
Yelm, WA 98597-9654   360-458-2091
        Fax: 360-458-3150
Meat and homemade sausage
 President: Dorthy Carlson
 Vice President: Stewart Carlson
Estimated Sales: $ 3 - 5 Million
Number Employees: 20-49

13729 Stewarts Seafood
8401 Highway 188
Coden, AL 36523-3059   251-824-7368
        Fax: 251-824-7369
Seafood
 President: Janice Stewart
Estimated Sales: $ 10 - 20 Million
Number Employees: 20-49

13730 Stichler Products
1800 N 12th St
Reading, PA 19604-1545   610-921-0211
 Fax: 610-921-0294 spicandy@aol.com
Processor of confectionery products including deco-
rative and ornamental
 President: Martin Deutschman
 Vice President: Brad Deutschman
 Public Relations: Kathy Paules
Estimated Sales: $4700000
Number Employees: 20-49
Sq. footage: 62000
Type of Packaging: Consumer, Food Service, Pri-
vate Label, Bulk
Brands:
 CANDY FARMS

13731 Stickney & Poor Company
157 Berkeley Road
North Andover, MA 01845-5265   508-261-8967
Processor and exporter of portion-controlled prod-
ucts including ketchup, relish, nondairy coffee
creamers, honey, artificial sweeteners, jams, jellies,
marmalades, preserves, mayonnaise, mustard, salt,
pepper, vinegar, salad dressingsand dipping sauces
 President: H Sandy Brown
 VP: Chuck Lavery
Number Employees: 50-99
Type of Packaging: Food Service, Private Label,
Bulk
Brands:
 Harvest Selects
 Stickney & Poor

13732 Sticky Fingers Bakeries
420 Columbus Avenue
San Francisco, CA 94133-3902   800-458-5826
        Fax: 509-922-7102
        sales@stickyfingersbakeries.com
        www.stickyfingersbakeries.com
English Scones. Delete this entry it is a duplicate
entry - the correct entry is 14374 with the Spokane,
Washington address.

13733 Sticky Fingers Bakeries
PO Box 14533
Spokane Valley, WA 99214-0533   509-922-1985
 Fax: 509-922-7102   800-458-5826
        sales@stickyfingersbakeries.com
        www.stickyfingersbakeries.com
Bakery mixes, English Scones, gourmet breads,
brownies, quick breads, jams, and curds.
 President/CEO: Tom Owens
 Vice President: Ted Vogelman
 Sales Director: Tom Owens
Number Employees: 1-4
Type of Packaging: Private Label
Brands:
 Sticky Fingers Bakeries Eng Muffin
 Sticky Fingers Bakeries Jams
 Sticky Fingers Bakeries Scones

13734 Stiebs
11767 Road 27 1/2
Madera, CA 93637   559-661-0031
 Fax: 559-661-0032 pominfo@stiebs.com
        www.stiebs.com
Concentrates, extracts, arils, powders, blending and
formulation.
 Partner: Jerry Pantaleo
 Partner: Brad Miller
Number Employees: 10

13735 Stilwell Foods
P.O.Box 432
Stilwell, OK 74960-0432   918-696-8325
                        Fax: 918-696-5691
gwen.fletcher@schwansbakery.com
www.flowersindustries.com/flowers
Frozen fruit, breaded vegetables, fruit pies
President: Michael Taffer
Controller: Greg Jones
VP Sales: Jack Lundberg
VP Operations: Jim Gross
Plant Manager: Jason Blake
Purchasing Manager: Travis Gregory
Estimated Sales: $ 100-500 Million
Number Employees: 500-999
Brands:
Premium Pak
Starr Springs
Stilwell

13736 Stimson Lane Vineyards &Estate
P.O.Box 1976
Woodinville, WA 98072-1976   425-488-1133
        Fax: 425-415-3657 800-267-6793
info@ste-michelle.com www.stimson-lane.com
Processor, exporter and importer of wines
President/CEO: Allen Shoup
CEO: Theodor P Baseler
Executive VP Marketing: Ted Baseler
Senior VP Sales: Glen Yaffa
Estimated Sales: $ 10 - 20 Million
Number Employees: 250-499
Parent Co: UST
Type of Packaging: Consumer, Food Service, Private Label, Bulk
Other Locations:
Stimson Lane Vineyards & Esta
Woodinville WA

13737 Stimson Lane Winery
660 Frontier Road
Prosser, WA 99350-5507   509-882-3928
                        Fax: 509-882-3808
Processor and exporter of red and white wines
Cellar Master: Ped Baseler
Red Wine Maker: Gordy Hill
Number Employees: 20-49
Parent Co: Stimson Lane
Type of Packaging: Consumer, Food Service

13738 Stinson Seafood Company
P.O.Box 69
Prospect Harbor, ME 04669-0069   207-963-7331
        Fax: 207-963-2328 www.connors.ca
Manufacturer of canned herring products, sardines
President/CEO: Chris Lischewski
General Manager: Roger Webber
Plant Manager: Peter Colson
Estimated Sales: $100 Million
Number Employees: 500-999
Parent Co: Connor Bros
Type of Packaging: Consumer, Food Service, Private Label
Brands:
ADMIRAL
BEACH CLIFF
BULLDOG
COMMANDER
NEPTUNE
POSSUM

13739 Stinson Seafood Company
66 Bowery Street
Bath, ME 04530-2817   207-963-7331
                        Fax: 207-775-7965
Prepares tasty and nutritious canned sardine products.
Plant Manager: Chris Anderson
Number Employees: 1-4
Parent Co: Stinson Seafood
Type of Packaging: Consumer, Private Label
Brands:
BEACH CLIFF

13740 Stirling Foods
P.O.Box 569
Renton, WA 98057-0569   425-251-9293
        Fax: 425-251-0251 800-332-1714
stirling@stirling.net www.stirling.net
Processor and exporter of gourmet beverage flavors and syrups
President: Mark Greiner
CEO: Earl Greiner

Estimated Sales: $1,300,000
Number Employees: 5-9
Type of Packaging: Consumer, Food Service, Private Label
Brands:
Stirling Gourmet Flavors

13741 Stock Popcorn Company
P.O.Box 830
Lake View, IA 51450-0830   712-657-2811
        Fax: 712-657-2550 stockpop@netins.net
www.stockpopcorn.com
Processor and exporter of yellow and white popcorn including processed unpopped and microwaveable; also, feed sack fashion packaging for popcorn
President: James Stock
Number Employees: 5-9
Type of Packaging: Consumer, Private Label, Bulk
Brands:
Lil' Chief
Lil' Chief Popcorn

13742 Stock Yards Packing Company
340 N Oakley Blvd
Chicago, IL 60612-2216   312-733-6050
        Fax: 312-733-0738 800-621-1119
customerservice@stockyards.com
www.stockyards.com
Processor and exporter of beef, pork, veal and lamb
President: Dan Pollack
Plant Manager: Oscar Moore
Estimated Sales: $ 10 - 20 Million
Number Employees: 100-249
Sq. footage: 60000

13743 Stockmeyer North America
170 Beaverbrook Rd # 2
Lincoln Park, NJ 07035-1441   973-628-7330
                        Fax: 973-628-2919
customerservice@stockmeyer.net
www.stockmeyer.net
Candy
President: Maarten Moog
Estimated Sales: $ 5-10 Million
Number Employees: 5-9

13744 Stockpot
22505 State Route 9 SE
Woodinville, WA 98072-6010   425-415-2000
        Fax: 425-415-2004 800-468-1611
stockpotinfo@stockpot.com www.stockpot.com
Manufacturer of fresh refrigerated soups and chowders, entrees and stews, gravies, chilies, sauces, specialty products, vegan and vegetarian, and marinades.
President: Kathleen Horner
CFO: Art Olson
Marketing/Public Relations: Gary Merritt
Operations Manager: George Andrews
Estimated Sales: $ 20-50 Million
Number Employees: 100-249
Parent Co: Campbell Soup Company
Type of Packaging: Private Label
Brands:
STOCKPOT

13745 Stockton Cheese
300 W Railroad Ave
Stockton, IL 61085-1500   815-947-3361
        Fax: 815-947-2768 cloehr@stocktoncheese.com
www.stocktoncheese.com
Processor of Swiss cheese
Manager: Chuck Loehr
Plant Manager: Chuck Loehr
Estimated Sales: $ 20 - 50 Million
Number Employees: 50-99
Parent Co: Brewster Dairy
Type of Packaging: Bulk

13746 Stockton District Kidney Bean
PO Box 338
Tracy, CA 95378-0338   209-887-3420
                        Fax: 209-887-2107
Processor of dry beans
Manager: Robert Maulhardt
Number Employees: 5-9
Sq. footage: 78000
Type of Packaging: Bulk

13747 Stockton Graham & Company
4320 Delta Lake Dr
Raleigh, NC 27612-7000   919-881-8271
        Fax: 919-881-0746 800-835-5943
info@stocktongraham.com
www.stocktongraham.com
Wholesale specialty beverages
President: Jeff Vojta
Estimated Sales: $500,000-$1 Million
Number Employees: 10-19
Brands:
Stoktin Grahan

13748 Stoffle Meat Company
PO Box 546
Topeka, KS 66601-0546   785-234-2683
                        Fax: 785-234-5614
Processor of meat products
Owner: Mary Lou Lewis
Number Employees: 5-9

13749 Stokes Canning Company
10700 E Geddes Ave
Englewood, CO 80112-3800   303-790-0623
                        Fax: 303-292-4364
www.centennialspecialtyfoods.com
Soups
CFO: Douglas L Evans
COO: Jeffery Nieder
Sales/Marketing Director: Robert A Beckwith Jr.
Estimated Sales: $ 10-100 Million
Number Employees: 100-249
Brands:
Ellis
Strokes

13750 Stoller Fisheries
P.O.Box B
Spirit Lake, IA 51360-0127   712-336-1750
        Fax: 712-336-4681 www.stollerfisheries.com
President: Larry Stoller
Estimated Sales: $ 20 - 50 Million
Number Employees: 20-49

13751 Stoller Fisheries
P.O.Box B
Spirit Lake, IA 51360-0127   712-336-1750
        Fax: 712-336-4681 stollerfisheries@mchsi.com
www.stollerfisheries.com
Processor and exporter of fresh fish including carp, buffalo, sheepheads and suckers
President: Larry Stoller
Executive VP: Thomas Opheim
Estimated Sales: $ 20 - 50 Million
Number Employees: 20-49
Parent Co: Progressive Companies
Type of Packaging: Bulk

13752 Stolt SeaFarm
9149 E Levee Rd
Elverta, CA 95626-9559   916-991-4420
        Fax: 916-991-4334 800-525-0333
www.sterlingcaviar.com
Processor of white sturgeon including fresh, cold smoked and frozen
Manager: Peter Struffenegger
CFO: Joeseph Ruffo
R&D: Richard Helfrich
Quality Control: Richard Helfrich
Estimated Sales: $ 10 - 20 Million
Number Employees: 20-49
Sq. footage: 55000
Type of Packaging: Food Service

13753 Stone Cellar Kitchens
5821 Wilderness Avenue
Riverside, CA 92504-1004   951-352-5713
                        Fax: 909-352-5710
Processor of jams, jellies, marmalades, syrups, apple butter and apple sauce; private labeling available
President: Thomas Harris
Co-Owner: Richard Harris
Estimated Sales: $10900000
Number Employees: 49
Sq. footage: 15000
Parent Co: Triple H Food Processors
Type of Packaging: Consumer, Food Service, Private Label, Bulk
Brands:
Stone Cellar

13754 Stone Crabs
11 Washington Ave
Miami Beach, FL 33139-7395   305-534-8788
        Fax: 305-532-2704 800-260-2722
        www.joesstonecrabs.com
Processor of fresh and frozen stone crabs, whole
lobsters and lobster tails
    President: Stephen Sawitz
    CFO: Marc Fine
    Marketing Director: Tracie Gordon
    Operations Manager: James McClendon
    Plant Manager: Ron Pressley
Estimated Sales: $ 10 - 20 Million
Number Employees: 20-49
Type of Packaging: Consumer, Food Service
Brands:
    SCI

13755 (HQ)Stone Hill Wine Company
1110 Stone Hill Hwy
Hermann, MO 65041-1280   573-486-2221
        Fax: 573-486-3828
    hermann-info@stonehillwinery.com
        www.stonehillwinery.com
Manufacturer of grape juice, wine and champagne
    President: James Held
    VP: Betty Held
    Sales Director: Thomas Held
    Production Manager: Jon Held
Estimated Sales: $ 50 - 100 Million
Number Employees: 100-249
Number of Brands: 1
Number of Products: 20
Other Locations:
    Stone Hill Winery
    New Florence MO
    Stone Hill Winery
    Branson MO
Brands:
    Stone Hill Winery

13756 Stone Meat Processor
1485 Stonefield Way
Ogden, UT 84404-1211   801-782-9825
        Fax: 801-782-1109
Processor of ground beef
    President: Frank Stone
Estimated Sales: $ 10 - 20 Million
Number Employees: 20-49
Type of Packaging: Consumer, Food Service

13757 Stone Mountain Pecan Company
1781 Highway 78 NW
Monroe, GA 30655-5227   770-266-6659
        Fax: 770-207-4403 800-633-6887
        smpc1@mindspring.com
        www.stonemountainpecan.com
Processors of pecans
    President: Robby E Coker
Estimated Sales: $3200000
Number Employees: 5-9
Type of Packaging: Consumer, Food Service, Pri-
    vate Label, Bulk

13758 Stone Mountain Vineyards
1376 Wyatt Mountain Rd
Dyke, VA 22935-1371   434-990-9463
    info@stonemountainvineyards.com
        www.stonemountainvineyards.com
Wines
    Founder: Alfred Breiner
Estimated Sales: $ 3 - 5 Million
Number Employees: 5-9

13759 Stone's Home Made CandyShop
145 W Bridge St
Oswego, NY 13126-1440   315-343-8401
        Fax: 315-343-8401 888-223-3928
        information@oswego.com
Candy and confectionery products
    Owner: Jan Stachowicz
Estimated Sales: $300,000
Number Employees: 5-9
Sq. footage: 4500
Type of Packaging: Consumer, Food Service

13760 Stonegate
2300 Lower Chiles Valley Rd
St Helena, CA 94574-9632   707-603-2203
    Fax: 707-603-2209 info@stonegatewinery.com
        www.stonegatewinery.com
Wines
    President: Paul D Croft Croft
    CFO: Cathy del Fava

Estimated Sales: $ 5-10 Million
Number Employees: 10-19

13761 Stoneridge Winery
13862 Ridge Rd
Sutter Creek, CA 95685-9652   209-223-1761
Wines
    Owner: Gary Porteous
Estimated Sales: Below $ 5 Million
Number Employees: 5-9

13762 (HQ)Stonewall Kitchen
2 Stonewall Ln
York, ME 03909-1665   207-351-2713
        Fax: 207-351-2715 800-207-5267
        info@stonewallkitchen.com
        www.stonewallkitchen.com
Processor and exporter of jam, mustard, sauces, rel-
ish, dessert toppings and salad dressing
    VP: Jonathan King
    CFO: Lori King
    Vice President: Jim Stott
    Research & Development: Bruce Doty
    Marketing Director: Natalie King
    Production Manager: Joe Fuller
Estimated Sales: $ 10-24.9 Million
Number Employees: 250-499
Sq. footage: 30000
Type of Packaging: Consumer
Brands:
    Stonewall Kitchen

13763 Stonies Sausage Shop Inc
1507 Edgemont Blvd
Perryville, MO 63775-1230   573-547-2540
        Fax: 573-547-1747 888-546-2540
        contact@stoniessausageshop.com
        www.shopstonies.com
state and national champion smoked meats and sausages, retail store, wholesale, mail order, deer processing, private label, 50 years in business, federal
inspection
    President/Partner: Roger Wibbenmeyer
    Co-Owner: Tyson Wibbenmeyer
Estimated Sales: $1-1.5 Million
Number Employees: 20
Sq. footage: 15000
Type of Packaging: Food Service, Private Label

13764 Stonington Lobster Cooperative
P.O.Box 87
Stonington, ME 04681-0087   207-367-2286
        Fax: 207-367-2802
Lobster
    Manager: Steve Robins Iii
Estimated Sales: $ 5 - 10 Million
Number Employees: 10-19

13765 Stonington Vineyards
P.O.Box 463
Stonington, CT 06378-0463   860-535-1222
        Fax: 860-535-2182 800-535-1222
        info@stoningtonvineyards.com
        www.stoningtonvineyards.com
Processor of table wines including chardonnay, sea-
port white, fume vidal, white and bush, cabernet
franc and gewurztraminer
    President: Cornelius H Smith
    General Manager/Winemaker: Mike McAndrew
    Marketing Director: Nick Smith
Estimated Sales: $400000
Number Employees: 5-9
Sq. footage: 10000
Type of Packaging: Consumer
Brands:
    Seaport Blush
    Seaport White
    Seaport Wines
    Stonington
    Stonington Vineyards

13766 Stony Hill Vineyard
P.O.Box 308
St Helena, CA 94574-0308   707-963-2636
    Fax: 707-963-1831 info@stonyhillvineyard.com
        www.stonyhillvineyard.com
Wines
    President: Peter Mc Crea
    Office Manager: Willinda McCrea
    Vineyard and Winery Operations: Mike Chelini
    Vineyard Foreman: Alejandro Salomon
    Customer Relations: Mary Burklow
Estimated Sales: $500,000-$1 Million
Number Employees: 10-19

Brands:
    Stony Hill Vineyard

13767 Stony Ridge Winery
4948 Tesla Rd
Livermore, CA 94550-9530   925-449-0458
        Fax: 925-449-0646
    bacchus@stonyridgewinery.com
        www.crookedvine.com
Wines
    Owner: Rick Corbett
    Winemaker: Dale Vaughn-Bowen
Estimated Sales: Below $ 5 Million
Number Employees: 10-19
Brands:
    Orobianco-California NV

13768 Stonyfield Farm
10 Burton Dr
Londonderry, NH 03053-7436   603-437-4040
        Fax: 603-437-7594 www.stonyfield.com
Processor of fresh, frozen and soy yogurt including
plain and fruit flavored
    President: Gary Hirshberg
    CFO: Diane Carhart
    Marketing Director: Karen Billings
    Sales Director: Carter Elenz
    Public Relations: M Viederman
    Operations Manager: John Daigle
    Production Manager: Herb Berwald
    Purchasing Manager: Steve Inamorathi
Estimated Sales: $300,000-500,000
Number Employees: 1-4
Type of Packaging: Consumer, Food Service
Brands:
    Stonyfield Farm Frozen Yogurt
    Stonyfield Farm Ice Cream
    Stonyfield Farm Refrig Yogurt
    Yo Baby Yogurt

13769 Stop & Shop Manufacturing
104 Meadow Road
Readville, MA 02136-2349   617-361-8400
        Fax: 781-364-2012
Processor and wholesaler/distributor of milk, juices
and sodas
    Marketing Director: William Sress
Estimated Sales: $ 3 - 5 Million
Number Employees: 20-49
Parent Co: Stop & Shop Supermarket Company
Type of Packaging: Consumer

13770 Storck
325 N Lasalle St # 400
Chicago, IL 60654-6467   312-467-5700
        Fax: 312-467-9722 800-621-7772
    info@us.storck.com   www.storck.com
Processor of confectionery items including butter-
scotch, toffee, chocolate and chocolate/caramel: bars
and bags
    President: Liam Killeen
    VP Marketing: Ralf Hilpuesch
    VP Sales: Steve Meisinger
Estimated Sales: $9,000,000
Number Employees: 50-99
Type of Packaging: Consumer
Brands:
    MAMBA
    MILKFULS
    PEANUT RIESEN
    RIESEN
    TOFFIFAY
    WERTHER'S CHOCOLATES
    WERTHER'S ORIGINAL
    WERTHER'S ORIGINAL CHEWY CARA-
    MELS

13771 Storck Canada
1 City Centre Drive
Mississauga, ON L5B 1M2
Canada   905-272-4480
        Fax: 905-272-6899 800-305-7551
        www.storck.com
Candy
    VP: Terry Dennis
Number Employees: 20-49
Brands:
    CAMPINO
    KNOPPERS
    MERCI
    MERCI CROCANT
    MERCI PUR
    MINI DICKMANN'S
    SUPER DICKMANN'S

TOFFIFEE
WERTHER'S ORIGINAL

13772 Storer Meat Company
PO Box 6242
Cleveland, OH 44101-1242   216-621-7538
Fax: 216-621-9230   800-355-7537
www.fivestarbrandmeats.com
Wholesaler/distributor of Five Star brand hand-
crafted sausages and hams
President: Robert Gutwein
VP: Brad Herdman
Estimated Sales:$3 Million
Sq. footage: 30000
Type of Packaging: Consumer, Food Service
Brands:
Five Star

13773 Storheim's
1596 Arapahoe Trl
Green Bay, WI 54313-6761   920-498-2343
Fax: 920-592-0897
Gourmet foods
Owner: Ray Kern
Manager: Nate Kern

13774 Storrs Winery
303 Potrero St # 35
Santa Cruz, CA 95060-2782   831-458-5030
Fax: 831-458-0464   salesmgr@storrswine.com
www.storrswine.com
Wines
Owner/President: Stephen Storrs
Owner/VP: Pamela Bianchini-Storrs
Operations Manager: Aaron Storrs
Production Manager: Morgan Storrs
Estimated Sales:$1-2.5 Million
Number Employees: 5-9
Brands:
Storrs

13775 Story Winery
10525 Bell Rd
Plymouth, CA 95669-9516   209-245-6208
Fax: 209-245-6619   800-712-6390
storyzin@cdepot.net   www.zin.com
Wines
Owner: Bruce Tichneor
CEO: Jan Tichenor
Marketing Director: Jan Tichenor
Estimated Sales:$500,000-$1 Million
Number Employees: 1-4
Brands:
Story Wine

13776 Story's Popcorn Company
P.O.Box 247
Charleston, MO 63834-0247   573-649-2727
Fax: 314-649-3374
Popcorn
President: A Story III
Estimated Sales:$ 10-20 Million
Number Employees: 1-4

13777 Storybook Mountain Winery
3835 State Highway 128
Calistoga, CA 94515-9739   707-942-5282
Fax: 707-942-5334
sigstory@storybookwines.com
www.storybookwines.com
Wines
President: Jerry Seps
Estimated Sales:$540,000
Number Employees: 5-9
Brands:
Storybook Mountain Winery

13778 Stoudt Brewing Company
P.O.Box 880
Adamstown, PA 19501-0880   717-484-4387
Fax: 717-484-4182   beernet@stoudtsbeer.com
www.stoudtsbeer.com
Processor of seasonal beers, ale, stout, lager and
pilsner
President: Carol Stoudt
CFO: Edward Stoudt
Estimated Sales:$ 5-10 Million
Number Employees: 50-99
Type of Packaging: Consumer, Food Service

13779 Strasburg Provision
172 Rosanna Ave
Strasburg, OH 44680-9719   330-878-5557
Fax: 330-878-5558   800-207-6009
www.strasburgprovision.com
Processor of meat products and catering
President: Rudolf M Klapper
Sales: Herb Gritzan
Production: Frank H Klapper
Estimated Sales:$3000000
Number Employees: 20-49
Type of Packaging: Consumer, Food Service, Pri-
vate Label, Bulk

13780 Strathroy Foods
PO Box 188
Strathroy, ON   N7G 3J2
Canada   519-245-4600
Fax: 519-245-3661
Processor and exporter of frozen vegetables includ-
ing peas and carrots and other vegetable varieties
President: Craig Richardson
Type of Packaging: Consumer, Food Service, Pri-
vate Label
Brands:
Red Valley

13781 Straub Brewery Industries
303 Sorg St
St Marys, PA 15857-1592   814-834-2875
Fax: 814-834-7628   sales@straubber.com
www.straubbeer.com
Manufacturer of beer
President: Daniel Straub
Brewmaster: Thomas Straub
Estimated Sales:$ 20 - 50 Million
Number Employees: 20-49
Brands:
Straub
Straub Light

13782 Straub's
8282 Forsyth Blvd
Clayton, MO 63105-1626   314-725-2121
Fax: 314-725-2123   888-725-2121
straubs@anet-stl.com   www.straubs.com
Processor of steaks, seafood including lobster tails
and gift baskets
President: Jack Straub
Founder: William A Straub
CEO: Jack W Straub Jr
Owner: J W Straub
Number Employees: 100-249
Brands:
Straubs

13783 Straus Family Creamery
P.O.Box 768
Marshall, CA 94940-0768   415-663-5464
Fax: 415-663-5465   800-572-7783
family@strausmilk.com
www.strausfamilycreamery.com
Producers of organic milk and dairy products.
President: Albert Straus
Estimated Sales:$ 5 - 10 Million
Number Employees: 50-99

13784 Strauss Bakeries
1615 W Lexington Avenue
Elkhart, IN 46514-1943   219-295-4373
Fax: 219-522-2137
Bakery products
President: Steve Strauss
Sales Manager: John Macley
Estimated Sales:$ 5-10 Million
Number Employees: 100-249

13785 Strauss Veal & Lamb International
P.O.Box 342
Hales Corners, WI 53130-0342   414-421-5250
Fax: 414-421-6059   800-562-7775
info@straussveal.com   www.straussveal.com
Veal
President: Randy Strauss
Estimated Sales:$ 50-100 Million
Number Employees: 100-249

13786 Streamline Foods
6018 W Maple Rd
West Bloomfield, MI 48322-4404   248-851-2611
Fax: 248-737-2035   info@streamlinefoods.com
www.streamlinefoods.com

Grain, flour, sugars and syrups, dry blends, starches,
chemicals, soy products, dairy products salt, peanut
butter products
Manager: Dave Owens
VP Manufacturing Services: Don Gordon
Sales Rep: Teddy Kertis
Operations Manager: Doug Vause
Estimated Sales:$ 50-100 Million
Number Employees: 5-9
Brands:
Chocolate Mousse Maker

13787 Strebin Farms
28245 SE Division Dr
Troutdale, OR 97060-9486   503-665-8328
Fax: 503-669-7783   strebin@strebin.com
www.strebin.com
Processor of fresh and frozen red raspberries
President: William Strebin
CEO: William P Strebin
Marketing Director: William P Strebin
Estimated Sales:$ 5-10 Million
Number Employees: 50-99
Type of Packaging: Food Service
Brands:
Strebin Farms

13788 Streblow Vineyards
PO Box 233
Saint Helena, CA 94574-0233   707-963-5892
Fax: 707-963-5835
streblowvineyards@earthlink.net
Wine
President/Owner: Bruce Streblow
Co-Owner: Ana Canales
Brands:
Streblow Vineyards

13789 Streit Matzo Company
150 Rivington St
New York, NY 10002-2411   212-475-7000
Fax: 212-505-7650
AronStreit@StreitsMatzos.com
www.streitsmatzos.com
Manufacturer of matzos and other fine kosher foods.
President: Aron Yagoda
Executive VP: Aron Yogoda
Sales: Mel Gross
Production: Alan Adler
Estimated Sales:$5-10 Million
Number Employees: 50-99
Brands:
ETHNIC DELIGHTS
STREITS

13790 Stretch Island Fruit
P.O.Box 1099
Allyn, WA 98524-1099   360-275-6050
Fax: 360-275-6184   info@stretchislandfruit.com
www.stretchislandfruit.com
Processor and exporter of organic and natural fruit
leather snacks
President: Ron Sagerson
CEO: Bob Sagerson
Quality Control: Michael Doehm
R&D: Michael Doehm
Director Sales/Marketing: Gerry Thygesen
Estimated Sales:$ 20 - 50 Million
Number Employees: 50-99
Sq. footage: 12000
Type of Packaging: Consumer, Food Service
Brands:
STRETCH ISLAND

13791 Striplings
1401 West Blvd
Moultrie, GA 31768-4223   229-985-4226
Manufacturer of beef and pork products including
smoked sausage
Manager: Clint Goss
Co-Owner: Lisa Hardin

Number Employees: 5-9
Sq. footage: 14000
Type of Packaging: Consumer
Other Locations:
  Stripling's General Store
  Cordele GA
Brands:
  DUNN'S

13792 Stroehmann Bakeries

3996 Paxton St
Harrisburg, PA 17111-1423   717-564-1891
        Fax: 717-564-9231   800-220-2867
                www.stroehmann.com
Processor of baked goods including pan breads and
rolls.
  President: Gary J Prince
  Executive Chairman: Galen Weston
  EVP/Finance: Richard Mavrinac
  Director Sales: Richard Adams
  Chief Operating Officer: Dalton Phillips
  Plant Manager: Larry Valentine
  Chief Merchandising Officer: Mark Foote
Estimated Sales: $ 50 - 100 Million
Number Employees: 250-499
Sq. footage: 200000
Parent Co: George Weston Bakeries
Type of Packaging: Consumer, Food Service, Pri-
  vate Label

13793 Stroehmann Bakeries

P.O.Box 976
Horsham, PA 19044-0976   215-672-8010
        Fax: 215-672-6988   800-984-0989
                www.stroehmann.com
Processor of sliced breads, buns and rolls and stuff-
ing
  CEO: Gary Prince
  Director Marketing: Francis Strazzella
Number Employees: 1,000-4,999
Parent Co: George Weston Foods
Brands:
  D'Italiano
  Dutch Country
  Stroehmann
  Sunbeam
  Taystee

13794 Stroehmann Bakeries

P.O.Box 976
Horsham, PA 19044-0976   215-672-8010
        Fax: 215-672-6988 www.stroehmann.com
Processor of baked products
  President: Antonio Leta
  CFO: Bill Petersen
  CEO: Gary Prince
Estimated Sales: $24,900,000
Number Employees: 1,000-4,999

13795 Stroehmann Bakeries

325 Kiwanis Blvd
West Hazleton, PA 18202-1180   570-455-2066
        Fax: 570-455-0003 www.stroehmann.com
Manufacturer of baked goods
  Manager: Guy Ball
  CFO: Bill Peterson
  VP Sales: Tom Delapine
Estimated Sales: $100+ Million
Number Employees: 250-499
Parent Co: George Weston Foods
Type of Packaging: Consumer

13796 Stroehmann Bakeries

P.O.Box 110
Norristown, PA 19404-0110   610-825-1140
        Fax: 610-825-5896   800-984-0989
                www.stroehmann.com
Processor of baked products including breads, rolls,
snack cakes and cookies
  Director Sales: Tom Delapine
  Owner: Harold J Stroehmann Jr
Estimated Sales: $ 20 - 50 Million
Number Employees: 250-499
Type of Packaging: Consumer, Food Service, Pri-
  vate Label
Brands:
  D'Italiano
  Maier's Country
  Maier's Country Rolls
  Maier's Deli Rolls
  Maier's Italian

13797 Stroehmann Bakery

P.O.Box 976
Horsham, PA 19044-0976   215-672-8010
        Fax: 215-672-6988   800-984-0989
  info@stroehmann.com   www.stroehmann.com
Manufacturer of sliced breads, buns and rolls, and
stuffing.
  President: W Galen Weston
  CFO: Richard P Mavrinac
  CEO: Gary Prince
  Sr. VP: Louise M Lacchin
Estimated Sales: Less than $500,000
Number Employees: 1,000-4,999
Brands:
  Arnold
  Boboli
  Brownberry
  D'Italiano
  Dutch Country
  Entenmanns'
  Freihofers
  Maier's
  Thomas'

13798 Strom Products Ltd

1500 Lakeside Dr # 110
Bannockburn, IL 60015-1234   847-236-9676
        Fax: 847-267-1404   800-862-3311
  noyolks@stromproducts.com   www.noyolks.com
Processor and exporter of cholesterol-free egg noo-
dles, vegeatable macaroni, macaroni and cheese
dinners.
  Owner/CEO: Robert Strom
  President: Gary Henke
Estimated Sales: $35 Million
Number Employees: 10-19
Type of Packaging: Consumer
Brands:
  No Yolks
  Wacky Mac

13799 Strossner's Bakery

21 Roper Mountain Rd
Greenville, SC 29607-4125   864-233-3996
        Fax: 864-232-2819 www.strossners.com
Processor of prepared European bread mixes, cakes,
tortes, fancy pastries, danish and baked/partially
baked breads
  Owner: Richard Strossner
  Sales Manager: Mary Michalsky
  Production Manager: Connie Jud
Estimated Sales: $2,000,000
Number Employees: 50-99
Sq. footage: 14000
Type of Packaging: Consumer, Food Service

13800 Strub Pickles

100 Roy Boulevard
Brantford, ON N3R 7K2
Canada   519-751-1717
        Fax: 519-752-5540 info@strubpickles.com
                www.strubpickles.com
Processor of sauerkraut, hot peppers, sweet
pimientos, horseradish, herring, jalapeno peppers,
kosher dill pickles and relish; exporter of pickles, re-
frigerated and shelf stable foods, zucchini relish and
chili sauce
  President: Leo Strub
  CEO: Martin Strub
  CFO: Arnold Strub
  Vice President: Anoy Strub
Number Employees: 100-249
Number of Brands: 2
Number of Products: 250
Sq. footage: 106000
Type of Packaging: Consumer, Food Service, Pri-
  vate Label, Bulk
Brands:
  Strub's
  Willie's

13801 Strube Packing Company

PO Box 36
Rowena, TX 76875-0036   325-442-2851
                        Fax: 325-442-2018
Manufacturer of lamb, goat, veal, and mutton; also,
slaughtering services available
  President: Al Strube III
  Sales/Marketing Manager: Brian Strube
  Human Resource Manager: George Correa
Estimated Sales: $10 Million
Number Employees: 40
Number of Products: 61
Type of Packaging: Consumer, Food Service, Bulk

13802 Strube Vegetable & Celery Company

2404 S Wolcott Ave
Chicago, IL 60608-5300   312-226-6888
        Fax: 312-226-7644 www.strube.com
Manufacturer of produce
  President/Owner: Robert Strube
  CEO: Janet Fleming
Estimated Sales: $67.4 Million
Number Employees: 100-249

13803 Struthious Ostrich Farm

386 Extonville Road
Allentown, NJ 08501-1503   609-208-0702
        Fax: 609-208-0703   ostrichfm@aol.com
Processor of ostrich meat and eggs; also, chicks
Number Employees: 10-19

13804 Stryker Sonoma Winery Vineyards

5110 Highway 128
Geyserville, CA 95441-9422   707-433-1944
        Fax: 707-433-1948   800-433-1944
  info@strykersonoma.com
                www.strykersonoma.com
Wine
  Owner: Craig Mac Donald
  Owner: Karen Naley
  Owner: Kat Stryker
Estimated Sales: Below $ 5 Million
Number Employees: 5-9
Brands:
  Stryker Sonoma Winery Vineyards

13805 Stuart Hale Company

4350 W Ohio St
Chicago, IL 60624-1051   773-638-1800
        Fax: 773-638-1888   info@grandwarehouse.com
                www.grandwarehouse.com
Processor of bakers' supplies including bakery pan
grease and pan and white mineral oils
  President: David Schulman
  General Manager: Stuart Schulman
Estimated Sales: $170000
Number Employees: 10-19
Type of Packaging: Private Label, Bulk

13806 Stuart Seafoods

1520 W Marine View Drive
Everett, WA 98201-2067   425-258-2546
Seafoods

13807 Stubb's Legendary Kitchen

811 Barton Springs Rd
Austin, TX 78704-8702   512-480-0203
        Fax: 512-476-3425   800-883-3238
  info@jelly.com   www.ilovestubbs.com
Processor of salsas, salad dressings, pastas and spa-
ghetti and pesto sauce; exporter of salsa; importer of
extra virgin olive oil
  President: Scott Jensen
  VP Operations: Robert Varley
Estimated Sales: $ 5 - 10 Million
Number Employees: 10-19
Sq. footage: 12000
Type of Packaging: Consumer

13808 Stubb's Legendary Kitchen

811 Barton Springs Rd
Austin, TX 78704-8702   512-480-0203
        Fax: 512-476-3425   800-227-2283
  customerservice@stubbsbbq.com
                www.ilovestubbs.com
Rubs, sauces and marinades
  Founder: C B Stubblefield
Estimated Sales: $ 5 - 10 Million
Number Employees: 10-19
Brands:
  Stubb's

13809 Sturgis Pretzel House

219 E Main St
Lititz, PA 17543-2011   717-626-4354
        Fax: 717-627-2682   info@sturgispretzel.com
                www.sturgispretzel.com
Processor of hard pretzels
  Manager: Aerin Sturgis
  VP: Michael Tshudy
  Owner: Barbara Tshudy
Estimated Sales: $500000
Number Employees: 10-19
Sq. footage: 20000

Type of Packaging: Consumer, Food Service, Private Label, Bulk
Brands:
America's Original
Sturgis Pretzel House

13810 Sturm Foods
P.O.Box 287
Manawa, WI 54949-0287   920-596-2511
          Fax: 920-596-3040   800-347-8876
info@sturminc.com   www.sturmfoods.com
Manufacturer and exporter of hot wheat cereal, powdered drink mixes, grits, rice & sauce side dishes, pasta & sauce side dishes, seasoning & coating mix, stuffing mix, onion soup & recipe mix, nonfat milk, pancake & waffle mix, hotcocoa mix, instant oatmeal, sugar-free instant oatmeal, canister oats, sugar-free drink mixes and sugar-free stix.
President: Mike Upchurch
CFO: Robert Ruegger
Export Sales Manager: Jim Sturm
Estimated Sales: $77400000
Number Employees: 250-499
Sq. footage: 400000
Type of Packaging: Consumer, Food Service, Private Label, Bulk
Brands:
Sturm's Village Farm

13811 Stutz Candy Company
400 S Warminster Rd
Hatboro, PA 19040-4097   215-675-2632
          Fax: 215-675-1438   888-692-2639
Processor of candy including boxed chocolates
President: John Glaser
Estimated Sales: $3100000
Number Employees: 20-49
Sq. footage: 21000
Type of Packaging: Consumer

13812 Su Bee's Discount Foods
1401 SE Morrison Street
Portland, OR 97214-2645   503-234-2000
Buyer of salvaged/close-out foods
Co-President: Herbert Hochfeld
Number Employees: 10-19
Sq. footage: 15000
Type of Packaging: Consumer, Bulk

13813 Subco Foods Inc
4350 S Taylor Dr
Sheboygan, WI 53081-8479   920-457-7761
          Fax: 920-457-3899   800-676-5188
mkhan@subcofoods.com   www.subcofoods.com
Contract packager/ Private label manufacturer products include: drink mixes, iced tea mixes, hot chocolate, gelatins, puddings, cappuccino mixes, coffee creamers, instant gravies, soup bases, spice/spice blends, cake mixes andnutraceuticals
President: Mas Khan
Estimated Sales: $13100000
Number Employees: 50-99
Sq. footage: 125000
Type of Packaging: Food Service, Private Label
Other Locations:
Subco Foods Inc
West Chicago IL
Brands:
New Image

13814 Subco Foods Inc
1150 Commerce Dr
West Chicago, IL 60185-2680   630-231-0003
          Fax: 630-231-0678   info@subcofoods.com
          www.subcofoods.com
Contract packager of dry mixes, cappuccino, cocoa, cake mixes, soup bases, spices, coffee creamers, rice products, etc
President: Mas Khan
Plant Manager: J McGrath
Purchasing Agent: Syed Zaidi
Estimated Sales: $23000000
Number Employees: 100-249
Sq. footage: 55000
Other Locations:
Subco Foods
Sheboygan WI
Brands:
New Image

13815 Sucesores de Pedro Cortes
PO Box 363626
San Juan, PR 00936-3626   787-754-7040
          Fax: 787-764-2650   cortesco@tld.net

Processor of chocolate and cocoa products; private labeling available; importer of chocolate, milk drinks and crackers; wholesaler/distributor of confectionery items, beverages and biscuits
President: Ignacio Cortes Del Valle
VP: Ignacio Cortes Gelpi
Number Employees: 50-99
Number of Brands: 11
Sq. footage: 50000
Type of Packaging: Consumer, Private Label, Bulk
Brands:
Chocolate Cortes
Choki
Semi-Industrialized

13816 Sudbury Soups and Salads
40 Walker Farm Rd
Sudbury, MA 01776-2442   978-443-7715
          Fax: 978-443-7715   888-783-7687
sudsoup@ultranet.com   www.sudburysoup.com
Natural foods, dry soup mixes, lentils
CEO: Susan Sullivan
Brands:
Sudbury

13817 Sudlersville Frozen Food Locker
P.O.Box 203
Sudlersville, MD 21668-0203   410-438-3106
          Fax: 410-438-3121   info@sudlersville.org
          www.sudlersville.org
Processor of frozen meat products including beef and pork
Owner: Dwayne Nickerson
Bookkeeper: Marge Messner
Estimated Sales: Less than $500,000
Number Employees: 5-9
Type of Packaging: Consumer
Brands:
Sudlersville

13818 Sudwerk Privatbrauerei Hubsch
2001 2nd St
Davis, CA 95618-5474   530-758-8700
          Fax: 530-753-0590   contact@sudwerk.com
          www.sudwerk.com
Beer
Owner: Tim Mc Donald
VP: Dean Unger
Quality Assurance: Candace Whalin
Marketing Director: Dave Sipes
Plant Manager/Purchasing Director: Neil Jensen
Estimated Sales: Below $ 5 Million
Number Employees: 50-99
Brands:
Hubsch Doppel Bock
Hubsch Dunkel
Hubsch Lager
Hubsch Marzen
Hubsch Pilsener
Suderwerk Doppel
Suderwerk Dunkel
Suderwerk Lager
Suderwerk Mai Bock
Suderwerk Marzen
Suderwerk Pilsenser

13819 Sugai Kona Coffee
P.O.Box 783
Kealakekua, HI 96750-0783   808-322-7717
          Fax: 808-322-4008   kona@kona.net
          www.sugaikonacoffee.com
Producers of Sugai Kona coffee
Manager: Lee Sugai
CEO: Lee Sugai
Estimated Sales: $1 Million
Number Employees: 1-4
Number of Brands: 5
Number of Products: 30
Sq. footage: 15000
Type of Packaging: Consumer, Food Service, Private Label, Bulk
Brands:
SUGAI KONA GROVE COFFEE
Sugai Kona Coffee Emporium

13820 Sugar Bowl Bakery
1963 Sabre St
Hayward, CA 94545-1021   510-782-2118
          Fax: 510-782-2119   info@sugarbowlbakery.com
          www.sugarbowlbakery.com

Processor of baked goods, gourmet cakes and pastries.
President: Andrew Ly
CFO: Bradsord Stette
Manager: Larry Sato
R & D: Stephanie Vu
Sales Manager: Wilson Seet
Purchasing Agent: Kevin Ly
Estimated Sales: $300,000-500,000
Number Employees: 5-9
Sq. footage: 20000

13821 Sugar Cane Growers Cooperative of Florida
P.O.Box 666
Belle Glade, FL 33430-0666   561-996-5556
          Fax: 561-996-4780   info@scgc.org
          www.scgc.org
Manufacturer of sugar and blackstrap molasses
President/CEO: George Wedgworth
Estimated Sales: $285 Million
Number Employees: 500-999
Type of Packaging: Consumer

13822 Sugar Cane Industry Glades Correctional Institution
500 Orange Avenue Cir
Belle Glade, FL 33430-5221   561-829-1400
          Fax: 561-992-1355   www.dc.state.fl.us
Grower of sugar cane, oranges and grapefruit
Manager: Shannon Robert
Number Employees: 1-4
Parent Co: PRIDE of Florida
Type of Packaging: Bulk

13823 Sugar Creek Packing
2101 Kenskill Ave
Washington Ct Hs, OH 43160-9404   740-335-7440
          Fax: 740-335-7443   800-848-8205
Sales@sugarcreek.com   www.sugar-creek.com
Manufacturer of meat products including sausage and bacon
Chairman: John Richardson
Estimated Sales: $20 Million
Number Employees: 100-249
Type of Packaging: Consumer, Food Service, Bulk
Other Locations:
Sugar Creek Packing Plant
Bloomington IL
Sugar Creek Packing Plant
Cincinnati OH
Sugar Creek Packing Plant
Dayton OH
Sugar Creek Packing Plant
Frontenac KS
Brands:
SUGAR CREEK

13824 Sugar Creek Winery
125 Boone Country Ln
Defiance, MO 63341-3103   636-987-2400
          Fax: 636-987-2051   info@sugarcreekwines.com
          www.sugarcreekwines.com
Wines
President: Ken Miller
President: Wesley Wissman
Estimated Sales: $ 5-10 Million
Number Employees: 20-49

13825 Sugar Creek/Eskimo Pie
301 N El Paso Ave
Russellville, AR 72801-3721   479-968-1005
          Fax: 479-968-5651   800-445-2715
cwhiteside@eskimo.com   www.yogenfruz.com
Processor of ice cream and frozen smoothie and frozen yogurt mix
President: Scott Vanhorn
Director Business Development: Fred Fullerton Jr

Operations Manager: Scott Van Horn
Estimated Sales: $ 20 - 50 Million
Number Employees: 20-49
Sq. footage: 25000
Parent Co: Eskimo Pie Corporation
Type of Packaging: Private Label

13826 Sugar Flowers Plus
601 Vine Street
Glendale, CA 91204   818-545-3592
          Fax: 818-545-7459   800-972-2935
sugarflowersplus@earthlink.net
          www.sugarflowersplus.com

hand made gum paste and royal icing cake decorations
    President/Owner: Terry Becker
Number Employees: 4

13827 Sugar Flowers Plus
601 Vine St
Glendale, CA 91204-1417   818-247-5521
          Fax: 818-545-7459 800-972-2935
          sugarflowersplus@earthlink.net
          www.sugarflowers.com
Manufacturer of cake decorations including gum paste flowers
    Owner: Terry Becker
    R&D: Anna Becker
    Sales: Garrick Wright
    Plant Manager: Gary Roundtree
Estimated Sales: $ .5 - 1 million
Number Employees: 1-4
Type of Packaging: Consumer, Food Service
Brands:
    Sugar Flowers

13828 Sugar Foods
950 Raco Drive
Lawrenceville, GA 30045-4307   770-339-0184
Processor of portion controlled sugar and sugar substitutes
    President: Stephan O'Dell
Number Employees: 100-249
Type of Packaging: Food Service

13829 Sugar Foods
P.O.Box 1220
Sun Valley, CA 91353-1220   818-768-7900
    Fax: 818-768-7619 info@sugarfoods.com
          www.sugarfoods.com
Contract packager and exporter of dry entrees, side dishes, mixes including snack, nondairy creamer, sugar and sugar substitutes and croutons in bags, pouches, cups, cartons and canisters
    President: Stephen O'Dell
    Operations Manager: Brian Thomson
Estimated Sales: $8500000
Number Employees: 250-499
Sq. footage: 350000
Parent Co: Sugar Foods Corporation

13830 Sugar Foods Corporation
950 3rd Ave # 21
New York, NY 10022-2786   212-753-6900
    Fax: 212-753-6988 info@sugarfoods.com
          www.sugarfoods.com
Products include sweetners, non dairy creamers, croutons, stuffing mixes, crumbs/cracker meal, snacks & snack mixes, specialty items, and almonds.
    Chairman/Co-CEO: Donald G Tober
    Executive VP: Jim Walsh
    VP Communications: Rick Ticknor
Estimated Sales: 1
Number Employees: 500-999
Type of Packaging: Consumer, Food Service
Brands:
    ALMOND TOPPERS
    BLUE DIAMOND
    C&H
    CRISP 'N FRESH
    FRESH GOURMET
    NATRATASTE
    NON DIARY TOPPINGS
    SUGAR IN THE RAW
    SUPERSNAX
    SWEET 'N LOW
    TRUE LEMON

13831 Sugar Kake Cookie
570 Fillmore Ave
Tonawanda, NY 14150-2509   716-693-4715
    Fax: 716-693-0575 800-775-5180
          www.bremnercookies-crackers.com
Processor and exporter of fig bars and cookies including sandwich cremes, shortbread and sugar wafers
    President: Rick Wilsman
    Finance Executive: Rick Karnath
    Sales Manager: David Boyce
Estimated Sales: $23600000
Number Employees: 100-249
Parent Co: Bremner
Type of Packaging: Consumer, Private Label
Brands:
    Sugar Kake

13832 Sugar Plum
88 Dilley St
Kingston, PA 18704-3437   570-288-0559
          Fax: 570-288-1710 800-447-8427
          customerservice@sugar-plum.com
          www.sugar-plum.com
Chocolate covered potato chips, chocolate covered pretzels and chocolate covered popcorn.
    Owner: Frann Edley
Estimated Sales: Less than $500,000
Number Employees: 1-4
Brands:
    Dip Sticks
    Get Popped
    Supremes

13833 Sugar Plum Farm
P.O.Box 136
Plumtree, NC 28664-0136   828-766-6272
    Fax: 828-765-0019 888-257-0019
          sugarplumfarm@boone.net
          www.sugarplumfarm.com
Processor of gourmet foods including dried fruits, fruit confections and apricot syrup; gift packages available
    Owner: James Pitts
    Owner: Helen Pitts
Estimated Sales: Less than $500,000
Number Employees: 1-4
Sq. footage: 8000
Brands:
    Ceder House

13834 Sugarbush Farm
591 Sugarbush Farm Rd
Woodstock, VT 05091-8089   802-457-1757
          Fax: 802-457-3269 800-281-1757
    Sugarbsh@sower.net www.sugarbushfarm.com
Waxed cheeses and Pure Vermont Maple Syrup
    President: Elizabeth Luce
Estimated Sales: $ .5 - 1 million
Number Employees: 5-9

13835 Sugardale Foods
P.O.Box 8440
Canton, OH 44711-8440   330-455-5253
    Fax: 330-430-7660 www.sugardalefoods.com
Manufacturer of hams, deli meats, bacon, wieners and smoked sausage
    Chairman: Neil Genshaft
    President: Harry Valentio
    CFO: Kevin Bender
    Sales Director: Don Dimaid
    Plant Manager: Rick Hawley
    Purchasing Manager: Lee Poludniak
Estimated Sales: $ 100-500 Million
Number Employees: 500-999
Parent Co: Fresh Mark

13836 Sugarman of Vermont
P.O.Box 1060
Hardwick, VT 05843-1060   802-472-9891
          Fax: 802-472-8526 800-932-7700
          www.sugarmanofvermont.com
Processor and exporter of jams, jellies, marmalades and preserves; processor and exporter of maple syrup
    President: Anthony Sedutto
Number Employees: 20-49
Sq. footage: 40000
Type of Packaging: Consumer, Food Service, Private Label, Bulk
Brands:
    Sugarman

13837 Sugarwoods Farm
2287 Glover St
Glover, VT 05839-9356   802-525-3718
          Fax: 802-525-4103 800-245-3718
          office@sugarwoods.com
          www.sugarwoodsfarm.com
Produces Vermont maple syrup, maple candy, maple cream and all natural pancake mixes.
Estimated Sales: $ 1 - 3 Million
Number Employees: 5-9
Type of Packaging: Consumer, Food Service, Private Label

13838 Suity Confection Company
PO Box 558943
Miami, FL 33255-8943   305-639-3300
    Fax: 305-591-9886 mailcenter@suity.com
          www.suity.com

Wholesaler/distributor, importer and exporter of candy, chocolate and snack foods
    CFO: Jose Garrido
    VP: Jose Garrido Jr
    Quality Control: Luis Perez
Estimated Sales: $ 20-50 Million
Number Employees: 2
Brands:
    Bubble Gum
    Fruiticas Lollipops
    Fruity Ball
    Party Snacks
    Salty Snacks

13839 Suiza Dairy Corporation
Avenue San Patricio Esquina D
Rio Piedras, PR 00921   787-792-7300
                    Fax: 787-782-8120
Processor of dairy products and fruit drinks/juices
    President: Carmen Laura Marrero
Number Employees: 20-49
Parent Co: Suiza Foods
Type of Packaging: Consumer
Brands:
    Quik
    Suiza

13840 Sukhi's Gourmet Indian Food
23682 Clawaiter Rd
Hayward, CA 94545   510-264-9265
          Fax: 510-264-1236 888-478-5447
          info@sukhis.com www.sukhis.com
gourmet indian food
    President/Owner: Sukhi Singh

13841 Sullivan Harbor Farm
P.O.Box 96
Sullivan, ME 04664-0096   207-422-2209
          Fax: 207-422-8229 800-422-4014
          sullivanharborfarm@verizon.net
          www.sullivanharborfarm.com
Smoked salmon
    Owner: Joel Franzman
Estimated Sales: $300,000-500,000
Number Employees: 1-4

13842 Sullivan Vineyards Winery
P.O.Box G
Rutherford, CA 94573-0907   707-963-9646
          Fax: 707-963-0377 877-277-7337
          www.sullivanwine.com
Wines
    CEO: Joanna C Sullivan
    CFO: Sean Sullivan
    VP Marketing: Kelleen Sullivan
    Operations Manager: Ross Sullivan
Estimated Sales: Below $ 5 Million
Number Employees: 5-9
Type of Packaging: Private Label
Brands:
    Sullivan Cabernet Sauvignon
    Sullivan Chardonnay
    Sullivan Coeur De Vigne
    Sullivan Merlot

13843 Sumida Fish Cake Factory
1332 Launa Street
Hilo, HI 96720-3234   808-959-9857
Fish cakes
    President: Masayuki Sumida
Estimated Sales: $500,000-$1 Million
Number Employees: 20-49

13844 Sumida Pickle Products
1001 Dillingham Boulevard
Honolulu, HI 96818   808-841-4227
Processor of pickles and pickled vegetables
    President: Marion Ku
    VP: Steve Ku
Number Employees: 1-4
Sq. footage: 2000
Type of Packaging: Consumer

13845 Summer In Vermont Jams
686 Davis Rd
Hinesburg, VT 05461-9359   802-453-3793
          norrisberryfarm@qmavt.net
Homegrown, homemade jams and jellies
    President: Norma Norris
Estimated Sales: $ .5 - 1 million
Number Employees: 1-4

13846 Summercorn Foods
1410 W Cato Springs Road
Fayetteville, AR 72701-6752   501-521-9338
Fax: 501-443-5771   888-328-9473
info@summercorn.com   www.summercorn.com
Processor of whole grain baked goods and soy foods; wheat free and yeast free
Owner: David Druding
Sales Manager: Hillary Goodman
Plant Manager: Jason Shabatura
Purchasing Manager: Richard Stawffacher
Estimated Sales: $500,000-$1 Million
Number Employees: 1-4
Sq. footage: 5000
Type of Packaging: Consumer, Bulk

13847 Summerfield Farm Products
4206 Twymans Mill Rd
Orange, VA 22960-4850   540-547-9600
Fax: 540-547-9628   800-898-3276
jamienicoll@summerfieldfarm.com
www.summerfieldfarm.com
Free-range veal, venison, salmon and condiments
President: Jamie Nicoll
Marketing Manager: Mary Thornton
Financial Manager: Carolyn Mills
Accounts Receivable: Barbara Frazier
Estimated Sales: Below $ 5 Million
Number Employees: 10
Brands:
Summerfield Farms

13848 Summerfield Foods
335 Shiloh Valley Ct
Santa Rosa, CA 95403-8085   707-579-3938
Fax: 707-579-8442
claudia@summerfieldfoods.com
www.summerfieldfoods.com
Contract packager and exporter of canned vegetarian foods including refried beans, soups and chili; also, cookies and cakes; private labeling available
President: Roland Au
Executive VP: John Stanghellini
Estimated Sales: $2000000
Number Employees: 10-19
Type of Packaging: Consumer, Private Label
Brands:
Summerfield's

13849 Summerland Sweets
RR2 S69
Summerland, BC V0H 1X2
Canada   250-494-0377
Fax: 250-494-7432   800-577-1277
ssweets@cnx.net   www.summerlandsweets.com
Canner of fruit candy/pectin jelly including apricot, cherry and apple; also, fruit leather, gourmet jam, fruit syrup and fruit pulp
President: Frances Beulah
Estimated Sales: $1,200,000
Number Employees: 10
Number of Brands: 2
Number of Products: 40
Type of Packaging: Food Service, Private Label

13850 Summit Brewing Company
910 Montreal Circle
Saint Paul, MN 55102-4246   651-265-7800
Fax: 651-265-7801   info@summitbrewing.com
www.summitbrewing.com
Brewer of beer
President: Mark Stutrud
Operations Manager: Christopher Seitz
Production Manager: Jon Lindberg
Number Employees: 20-49
Sq. footage: 58000
Brands:
Summit

13851 Summit Hill Flavors
253 Lackland Drive West
Middlesex, NJ 08846   732-805-0335
Fax: 732-805-1994   www.summithillflavors.com
Natural flavorings for dry and liquid applications used for marinating meats and poultry. Flavorings for soups, gravies, sauces, food bases and pasta dishes.

13852 Summit Lake Vineyards &Winery
2000 Summit Lake Dr
Angwin, CA 94508-9778   707-965-2488
Fax: 707-965-2281
www.summitlakevineyards.com

Wines
President: Robert Brakesman
CEO: Heather Griffin
Marketing Director: Heather Griffin
Estimated Sales: $200,000-$300,000
Number Employees: 1-4
Number of Brands: 3
Number of Products: 3
Brands:
Clair Riley Zinfandel Port
Emily Kestral Cabern
Summit Lake Vinyards

13853 Summit Point Raceway Orchards
P.O.Box 190
Summit Point, WV 25446-0190   304-725-8444
Fax: 304-728-7124   800-927-7531
office@bsr-inc.com
www.summitpointorchards.com
Fresh apples, specialty varieties
President: William Scott
Marketing Director: Barbara Scott
Operations Manager: Maria Orsini
Production Manager: Park Fifer
Estimated Sales: $ 2.5-5 Million
Number Employees: 20-49
Type of Packaging: Private Label

13854 Summum Winery
707 Genesee Ave
Salt Lake City, UT 84104-1460   801-355-0137
Fax: 801-366-9081   orderinfo@summum.org
www.summum.org
Wines
Manager: Bernie Aua
Founder: Amen Ra
Estimated Sales: $ 1-2.5 Million
Number Employees: 5-9
Brands:
Summum

13855 Sumptuous Selections
51 Belamose Avenue Rocky Hl
Rocky Hill, NJ 08553   860-563-6390
Fax: 860-563-0178
Pickled crudites, infused vinegars and oils, spirited hors d'oeuvre preserves, savory fruit butter, hand-packed salsas

13856 Sun Empire Foods
P.O.Box 376
Kerman, CA 93630-0376   559-846-8208
Fax: 559-846-9488   800-552-4786
www.sunempirefoods.com
Hand made coated delicacies.
Co-Owner: Phil Dee
Co-Owner: Sandy Dee
Plant Manager: Philip Dee
Estimated Sales: $ .5 - 1 million
Number Employees: 5-9
Number of Products: 100
Type of Packaging: Consumer

13857 Sun Garden Growers
1455 Hagberg Road
PO Box 190
Bard, CA 92222-0190   760-572-0088
Fax: 760-572-0577   800-228-4690
Grower, processor and exporter of organic dates including whole, coconut roll, almond roll, chopped and pitted, oat flour coated, medjool, halawi, dayri, zahidi, etc
Estimated Sales: $3 Million
Number Employees: 50
Number of Brands: 2
Number of Products: 10
Sq. footage: 30000
Type of Packaging: Consumer, Private Label, Bulk
Brands:
Sun Garden Growers

13858 Sun Garden Sprouts
820 E 20th St
Cookeville, TN 38501-1451   931-526-1106
Fax: 931-526-8338   www.sproutnet.com
Bean sprouts
President: Robert Rust
Marketing: Kelly Warren
Estimated Sales: $ 5 - 10 Million
Number Employees: 20-49
Brands:
Sun Garden Sprouts

13859 Sun Groves
3393 State Road 580
Safety Harbor, FL 34695-4931   727-726-8484
Fax: 727-726-7158   800-672-6438
www.sungroves.com
Fruit, berries
Marketing Manager: Joe Sevars
Estimated Sales: $ 20-50 Million
Number Employees: 20-49
Brands:
Sun Groves

13860 Sun Harvest Foods
3085 Beyer Boulevard
Suite A-105
San Diego, CA 92154-3479   619-690-1128
Fax: 619-690-1173   artshf@msn.com
Processor, importer and exporter of IQF entrees, canned vegetables, jalapenos, tomatillo, sauces, salsa, broccoli, cauliflower, vegetable blends and fruit; kosher items available
President: George Gonzalez
Estimated Sales: $20-50 Million
Number Employees: 300
Sq. footage: 160000
Parent Co: Productos Frugo S.A. de C.V.
Type of Packaging: Consumer, Food Service, Private Label, Bulk
Brands:
Frugo
Products Frugo Sa de CV

13861 Sun Hing Foods
271 Harbor Way
S San Francisco, CA 94080-6811   650-583-8188
Fax: 650-583-8188   800-258-6669
sunhing@sunhingfoods.com
www.sunhingfoods.com
Processor of ethnic foods
Owner: Trung Dang
Sales: Rosenda Chan
Estimated Sales: $ 20 - 50 Million
Number Employees: 20-49
Number of Brands: 9
Brands:
Black & White Brand
Cow & Mill Brand
Dairy Girl
Flower
Fortune
Fuyuki
Hoa Lan
Longevity Brand
Parrot Brand

13862 Sun Olive Oil Company
150 Vaquero Road
Templeton, CA 93465-9632   805-434-0626
Fax: 805-434-0626   rory@sunoliveoil.com
www.sunoliveoil.com
Olive oil
President: Rory Muniz
Brands:
Sun Olive Oil

13863 Sun Opta Ingredients
100 Apollo Dr
Chelmsford, MA 01824-3605   781-276-5100
Fax: 781-276-5101   800-353-6782
customer-service@sunopta-food.com
www.sunopta.com
World's largest producer of oat fiber for the food industry. The company also offers; a line of stabilized bran (wheat, oat, corn), wheat germ, novelty starches, custom stabilizer blends, Cellulose Gel and Konjac flour. In addition, ifoffers a broad range of food processing services
President: Douglas Shreve
R&D: Jim Podolske
Marketing: Rudi Van Mol
Sales: Doug Shreves
Estimated Sales: $300,000-500,000
Number Employees: 1-4
Parent Co: Sun Opta Inc
Type of Packaging: Bulk
Brands:
Crystalean
Opta Oat Fiber
Optafil
Optaglaze
Optagrade
Optamist
Optex

13864 Sun Orchard
P.O.Box 27508
Tempe, AZ 85285-7508   480-966-1770
Fax: 480-921-1426 800-505-8423
info@sunorchard.com www.sunorchard.com
Processor of juices including orange, grapefruit, lemon and lime; also, apple cider, lemonade, margarita mix and granita slushes
President/CEO: Marc Isaacs
VP, Grower Relations: Chris Hess
Marketing Director: Bob Corlett
VP Sales: Israel Vargas
Estimated Sales:$ 20-50 Million
Number Employees: 50-99
Sq. footage: 40000
Type of Packaging: Consumer, Food Service, Private Label, Bulk
Brands:
Sun Orchards Labels

13865 Sun Orchard of Florida
P.O.Box 2008
Haines City, FL 33845-2008   863-422-5062
Fax: 863-422-5176 www.sunorchard.com
Processor and exporter of citrus fruit
President: Isao Yokote
VP: Troy Gamble
Estimated Sales:$ 50 - 100 Million
Number Employees: 100-249
Parent Co: Gilco Fruits Corporation
Type of Packaging: Bulk

13866 Sun Orchard of Florida
P.O.Box 2008
Haines City, FL 33845-2008   863-422-5062
Fax: 863-422-5176 877-875-8423
www.sunorchard.com
Citrus juice
President: Marc Isaacs
CEO: Marc Isaacs
VP: Troy Gamble
Estimated Sales:$ 20-50 Million
Number Employees: 100-249
Type of Packaging: Private Label
Brands:
Rendezvous Bay

13867 (HQ)Sun Pac Foods
10 Sun Pac Boulevard
Brampton, ON L6S 4R5
Canada   905-792-2700
Fax: 905-792-8490 info@sunpac.com
Processor and contract packager of canned fruit juices, drinks and concentrates, bread crumbs, croutons and tortilla chips; importer of canned seafood and mandarin orange sections; exporter of juices and drinks
President: J Riddell
VP Finance: Vince McEwan
VP Imports/Exports: Cathy Knowles
Number Employees: 135
Sq. footage: 355000
Type of Packaging: Consumer, Food Service, Private Label, Bulk
Brands:
Featherweight
Fiesta
McDowell Ovens
Saico
Sun Crop
Sun Pac

13868 Sun Pacific Shippers
P.O.Box 217
Exeter, CA 93221-0217   559-592-7121
Fax: 559-592-3308 www.sunpacific.com
Grower, exporter and shipper of produce
CEO: Robert W Reniers
Sales Manager: Steve Nelson
Estimated Sales:$100+ Million
Number Employees: 100-249
Brands:
Hershey

13869 Sun Pure
5200 Us Highway 98 S
Lakeland, FL 33812-4203   863-619-2222
Fax: 863-453-2224 www.sunpure.com
Flavors
Manager: Francisco Vega
Sales/Marketing: Primo Bader
VP Technical Services: Bill DuBose

Estimated Sales:$ .5 - 1 million
Number Employees: 1-4
Type of Packaging: Private Label

13870 Sun Ray International
1260 Lake Blvd
Davis, CA 95616   530-758-0088
Fax: 530-758-0089 sales@sunraygroup.net
www.sunraygroup.net
Agricultural food ingredients such as dehydrated onion, garlic, tomato and other vegetable products.

13871 Sun Ridge Farms
1055 17th Avenue
Santa Cruz, CA 95062-3033   831-462-1280
Fax: 831-462-9431 800-655-3252
info@sunridgefarms.com
www.sunridgefarms.com
Manufacturer, processor, and exporter of organic and natural foods including pastas, trail mixes, candies, cereals, grain/bean blends, nuts, seeds and dried fruit blends. Also racks, bins, and labels for bulk food dispensing systems
President: Morty Cohen
Marketing: Mark Deverencazi
Sales: Gregg Armstrong
Public Relation: Kai Conner
Operations: Ron Giannini
Production: Franknce Taberas
Purchasing Agent: Trish Gregg
Estimated Sales:$500,000-$1 Million
Number Employees: 140
Parent Co: Falcon Trading Company
Type of Packaging: Consumer, Private Label, Bulk
Brands:
Sunridge Farms

13872 Sun State Beverage
2442 Pleasant Hill Rd
Atlanta, GA 30349   770-451-3990
Fax: 770-813-0065
Beverages
President: John Son
Estimated Sales:$ 2.5-5 Million
Number Employees: 1-4

13873 Sun States
PO Box 25965
Charlotte, NC 28229-5965   704-821-0615
Fax: 704-821-0616
Cheese
Marketing Director: Marty Crosby

13874 Sun Sun Food Products
14415 115th Avenue NW
Edmonton, AB T5M 3B8
Canada   780-454-4261
Processor of Oriental foods including bean sprouts, steamed noodles and wonton and egg roll wrappers
Manager: Ken Nhan
Type of Packaging: Food Service
Brands:
Sun Sun

13875 Sun Valley
P.O.Box 351
Reedley, CA 93654-0351   559-591-1515
Fax: 559-591-1616 sunvaly@mobynet.com
www.sunvalleypacking.com
Plums, peaches and nectarines
Owner: Walter Jones
Brands:
KAY PAK

13876 Sun Valley Mustard
731 1st Ave N
Hailey, ID 83333-5024   208-578-0078
Fax: 208-785-0216 800-628-7124
bstuns@cs.com www.sunvalleymustard.com
Mustard
President: Latham Williams
General Manager: Barbara Stuns
*Estimated Sales:*Under $500,000
Number Employees: 1-4
Brands:
Sun Valley Mustard

13877 Sun Wellness/Sun Chlorel
3914 Del Amo Boulevard
Torrance, CA 90503-2159   310-371-5515
Fax: 310-371-0094 800-829-2828
www.sunwellness.com

Processor, wholesaler/distributor, importer and exporter of ginseng and chlorella including tablets, liquid extract and green single cell algae with broken cell walls
President: George Higashida
Director Marketing: Rose Straub
Marketing Manager: Susan Arboua
Public Relations: Janise Zantine
Number Employees: 10-19
Sq. footage: 5000
Parent Co: YSK International Corporation
Brands:
Green Magician
Sun Chlorella
Sun Siberian Ginseng
Wakasa

13878 Sun West
2281 W 205th Street
Torrance, CA 90501-1450   310-320-4000
Fax: 310-320-8444 info@upperlimit.biz
www.upperlimit.biz
Distributor of rice based sweeteners and rice based proteins
President: Qasim Habib
Estimated Sales:$ 2.5-5 Million
Number Employees: 5

13879 Sun World International
P.O.Box 80298
Bakersfield, CA 93380-0298   661-392-5000
Fax: 661-392-5092 info@sun-world.com
www.sun-world.com
Fresh fruits and vegetables ranging from apricots, peaches, nectarines and grapes to tangerines, grapefruit, lemons and oranges to sweet colored peppers and seedless watermelon. Also Medjool dates and Deglet Noor dates.
CEO: Timothy Shaheen
CFO: Stan Speer
CEO: Allen Vangelos
Quality Control: David Aquino
Sr VP Sales/Marketing: Mike Aiton
Sr VP Sales/Marketing: Mike Aiton
Sr VP Operations: Kevin Andrew
Estimated Sales:$ 100-250 Million
Number Employees: 5,000-9,999

13880 Sun-Brite Canning
PO Box 70
Ruthven, ON N0P 2G0
Canada   519-326-9033
Fax: 519-326-8700 jiacobel@sun-brite.com
Tomato canners
President: Henry Lacobelli
Director Marketing/Logistics: John LaCobelli
Number Employees: 50-99
Type of Packaging: Consumer, Food Service, Private Label

13881 Sun-Glo of Idaho
P.O.Box 300
Sugar City, ID 83448-0300   208-356-7346
Fax: 208-356-7351 bruce@sunglo-idaho.com
www.sungloidaho.com
Processor and exporter of potatoes including baked, cubed, diced and IQF hash browns
CEO: Jerry Hastings
CEO: George M Crapo
Sales Manager (Frozens): Frank Simmons
Estimated Sales:$ 50 - 100 Million
Number Employees: 100-249
Sq. footage: 100000
Type of Packaging: Consumer, Food Service, Private Label, Bulk
Brands:
Sun Supreme
Sun-Glo
Top Bakes

13882 Sun-Maid
P.O.Box 9106
Pleasanton, CA 94566-9105   925-463-7400
Fax: 925-463-7521 800-246-4849
smaid@sunmaid.com www.sunmaid.com
Fruit
Marketing Director: Rob Miller Muller
President: Barry Kriebel
VP: John Slinkard
CFO: Richard Emde
Estimated Sales:$ 10-20 Million
Number Employees: 1-4
Brands:
Sun-Maid Raisins

Sunsweet Prunes
Valley Fig

13883 Sun-Maid Growers of California
13525 S Bethel Ave
Kingsburg, CA 93631-9212   559-896-8000
Fax: 559-897-6348 800-272-4746
smaid@sunmaid.com   www.sun-maid.com
Manufacturer of sun-dried fruits including raisins,
peaches, apricots and pears; also, raisin paste and
juice concentrate; exporter of raisins
President: Barry Kriebel
Chairman: Jon Marthedal
Estimated Sales: $309.6 Million
Number Employees: 550
Sq. footage: 650000
Type of Packaging: Consumer, Food Service, Pri-
vate Label, Bulk
Brands:
Sun-Maid

13884 Sun-Re Cheese
178 Lenker Ave
Sunbury, PA 17801-2902   570-286-1511
Fax: 570-286-5123
Processor of Italian cheeses including pizza, mozza-
rella and ricotta
Owner: Thomas Aiello Jr
Plant Manager: Gary Deates
Estimated Sales: $ 20 - 50 Million
Number Employees: 20-49
Type of Packaging: Consumer, Food Service, Pri-
vate Label, Bulk

13885 Sun-Rise
3423 Casa Marina Road NW
Alexandria, MN 56308-9058   320-846-5720
Beverages
President: John Sherman
Brands:
Sun-Rise Beverages

13886 Sun-Rype Products
1165 Ethel Street
Kelowna, BC V1Y 2W4
Canada   250-860-7973
Fax: 250-762-3611 888-786-7973
investor@sunrype.com   www.sunrype.com
Manufacturer of juice and fruit snacks and also or-
ganic fruit snacks.
President: Eric Sorensen
CFO: Robert McGowan
Vice President: Brad Bucharan
R & D: Barb Clarke
Quality Control: Lynn Tamaki
Marketing Director: Cam Johnston
Sales Director: Derek Brown
Public Relations: Magda Kapp
Estimated Sales: $ 104 Million
Number Employees: 350
Type of Packaging: Consumer, Food Service, Pri-
vate Label, Bulk
Brands:
Energy-To-Go
Fruit-To-Go
Sun-Rype

13887 SunOpta Grains
P.O.Box 128
Hope, MN 56046-0128   507-451-8201
Fax: 507-451-8201 800-297-5997
foodinfo@sunopta.com   www.sunopta.com/foods
Organic, non-GMO & IP soy, corn, whole grains, in-
gredients and consumer products
President: Allan Routh
CFO: Rick Johnson
CFO: Rick Johnson
Estimated Sales: Below $ 5 Million
Number Employees: 20-49
Type of Packaging: Consumer, Food Service, Bulk
Brands:
NFD
Nordic
Sunrich

13888 SunOpta Sunflower
P.O.Box 331
Breckenridge, MN 56520-0331   218-643-8467
Fax: 218-643-4555 800-654-4145
sunflower@sunopta.com
www.sunopta.com/foods

Specializes in bringing identity preserved,
non-GMO and organic soybeans, sunflower and corn
products to market utilizing vertically integrated
business models.
President: Allan Routh
General Manager: Steve Arnhalt
Quality Control: Amanda Amundson
Sales Director: Nancy Nelson
Plant Manager: John Bontjes
Estimated Sales: $44 Million
Number Employees: 100-249
Sq. footage: 100000
Parent Co: SunOpta, Inc
Type of Packaging: Consumer, Food Service, Pri-
vate Label, Bulk
Brands:
Sl Sunflowers

13889 SunPure
5200 Us Highway 98 S
Lakeland, FL 33812-4203   863-619-2222
Fax: 863-453-2224 pcheatham@sunpure.com
www.sunpure.com
Processor, importer and exporter of essence, oils,
citrus flavors, natural chemicals and aromas and
pulp concentrate
Manager: Francisco Vega
VP Marketing/Finances: Kim James
Director Sales (Beverages): Rick Plank
Estimated Sales: $1600000
Number Employees: 1-4
Sq. footage: 136200
Type of Packaging: Bulk

13890 (HQ)SunRich
P.O.Box 128
Hope, MN 56046-0128   507-451-4724
Fax: 507-451-2910 800-297-5997
sueklem@sunrich.com   www.sunrich.com
Processor and exporter of soy products including
milk, tofu powder and frozen green soybeans; also,
corn products including grits and flour
President: Allan Routh
Sales Director: Kate Leavitt
Estimated Sales: $65040181
Number Employees: 20-49
Type of Packaging: Food Service, Private Label,
Bulk
Other Locations:
SunRich
Cresco IA
Brands:
SOY SUPREME
SUNRICH
SWEET BEANS

13891 SunRise Commodities
140 Sylvan Ave
Englewood Cliffs, NJ 07632-2514   201-947-1000
Fax: 201-947-7667 www.foodimportgroup.com
Supplier and importer of nuts and dried fruits
President: Robert Feuerstein
Estimated Sales: $ 50 - 100 Million
Number Employees: 50-99

13892 SunStar Heating Products,Inc
306 W Tremont Ave
Charlotte, NC 28203-4946   704-372-3486
Fax: 704-332-5843 888-778-6782
info@sunstarheaters.com
www.sunstarheaters.com
Manufacturers of Heavy Duty Patio Heating Prod-
ucts, Mushroom Type Patio Heaters, Tube-Type
Infared Gas Heaters, High Intensity Ceramic Infared
Natural Gas Heater, Heavy Duty Infared Heater and
many more products
President: Frank L Horne Jr Jr.
Parent Co: Gas-Fired Products, Inc

13893 SunWest Organics
1550 Drew Ave # 150
Davis, CA 95618-7852   530-758-8550
Fax: 530-758-8110 www.sunwestfoods.com
Organic brown, pilaf, wild mix, and crisp rice.
President: James Errecarte
Estimated Sales: $ 20 - 50 Million
Number Employees: 10-19
Sq. footage: 30000

13894 Sunbeam
229 Coffin Avenue
New Bedford, MA 02746-2299   508-997-9401
Fax: 508-993-6324 800-458-8407
petracca_bart@interstatebrands.com
www.interstatebrands.com
Breads, rolls
Director Product Development: Kenneth Newman

Estimated Sales: $ 20-50 Million
Number Employees: 500-999
Brands:
Health O Meter
Mr. Coffee
Oster
Sunbeam

13895 Sunbeam Baking Company
301 Dallas Street
El Paso, TX 79901-1821   915-533-8433
Fax: 915-534-0043 800-328-6111
Processor of baked products including bread, rolls,
buns and cake
VP Sales: Jef Dunigan
VP Sales: Tony Ruiz
Number Employees: 100-249
Sq. footage: 80000
Parent Co: Flowers Industries
Brands:
Sunbeam

13896 Sunburst Foods
1002 Sunburst Dr
Goldsboro, NC 27534-8667   919-778-2151
Fax: 919-778-9203 info@sunburstfoods.com
www.sunburstfoods.com
Processor and wholesaler/distributor of prepacked
sandwiches
President: A Ray Lewis
Chairman: B Darden
VP: Chuck Darden
Estimated Sales: $13 Million
Number Employees: 100-249
Sq. footage: 50000
Type of Packaging: Consumer

13897 Sunchef Farms
4722 Everett Avenue
Vernon, CA 90058-3133   323-588-5800
Fax: 323-588-2285
Processor of portion-controlled chicken including
marinated and flavored products
President: Steve Tsatas

13898 Suncoast Foods Corporation
1929 Hancock Street
San Diego, CA 92110-2061   619-299-0475
Fax: 619-299-0464
Baked goods

13899 Suncrest Farms
97 Minnisink Rd
Totowa, NJ 07512-1945   973-595-0214
Fax: 973-595-0214 suncrest@wightman.ca
www.suncrestfarms.com
Ham
Owner: E L Scott
Estimated Sales: Less than $500,000
Number Employees: 1-4
Brands:
Suncrest Farms

13900 Sundance Industries
P.O.Box 1446
Newburgh, NY 12551-1446   845-565-6065
Fax: 845-562-5699 sundanceind@verizon.net
www.sundanceind.com
Manufacturer of Wheateena wheatgrass juicers.
President/CEO: Alden Link
VP Marketing: Alden Link
Office Manager: Valerie Lynn
Estimated Sales: $1-3 Million
Number Employees: 1-4
Number of Brands: 1
Number of Products: 9
Sq. footage: 14000
Type of Packaging: Consumer
Brands:
WHEATEENA

13901 Sundance Roasting Company
PO Box 1886
Sandpoint, ID 83864-0904   208-265-2445

Manufacturer and exporter of organic brewable coffee alternative
> Owner: Barbara Veraniam
Estimated Sales: Under $500,000
Number Employees: 1-4
Sq. footage: 600
Type of Packaging: Consumer, Bulk
Brands:
> Sundance Barley Brew

13902 Sundial Gardens
59 Hidden Lake Rd
Higganum, CT 06441-4441   860-345-4290
> Fax: 860-345-3462   sundial9@localnet.com
> www.sundialgardens.com
Processor of spices, herb blends, tea cake and scone mixes including hazelnut, pumpkin-ginger, cranberry and traditional; importer of rare and herbal teas
> Owner: Ragna Goddard
> VP: Thomas Goddard
Estimated Sales: Less than $500,000
Number Employees: 1-4
Sq. footage: 2500
Type of Packaging: Consumer
Brands:
> Ceylon Teas
> China Teas
> Herbal Teas
> India Teas
> Mulling Cider
> Sundial Blend Teas
> Sundial Gardens

13903 Sunergia Soyfoods
PO Box 1186
Charlottesville, VA 22902-1186   434-970-2798
> Fax: 801-437-3484   800-693-5134
> info@sunergiasoyfoods.com
> www.sunergiasoyfoods.com
Makers of healthy and delicious seasoned tofu. Includes ten delicious flavors such as italian herb, savory portabella, peanut & ginger, indian masala, spicy thai, garlic shitake, porcini herb, spinach jalapeno, pesto and spicyindian.
> President: Jon Kessler
> Vice President: John Raphaelidis
> Sales Manager: Marsha Burger
> Operations Manager: Jon Kessler
Estimated Sales: $200,000
Number Employees: 3
Number of Brands: 2
Number of Products: 13
Type of Packaging: Consumer, Food Service, Private Label, Bulk
Brands:
> More-Than-Tofu
> Sunergia Breakfast Style Sausage
> Sunergia More Than Tofu Garlic
> Sunergia More Than Tofu Herbs
> Sunergia More Than Tofu Porcinis
> Sunergia More Than Tofu Savories
> Sunergia More-Than-Tofu
> Sunergia Organic Soy Sausage
> Sunergia Smoked Portabella Sausage

13904 Sunflower Food and Spice Company
4114 NW Riverside St
Riverside, MO 64150-9668   816-741-1600
> Fax: 913-599-3787   800-377-4693
> info@sunflowerfoodcompany.com
> www.sunflowerfoodcompany.com
Honey toasted sunflower nuts, bagel spread mixes, farmer's popcorn cob, sunflower seed cookies, sunny seed drops, sunflower seed granola, and sunflower seed vinaigrette.
> Owner: Casey O'Sullivan
> Vice President: Mike Meier
Estimated Sales: $ 5-10 Million
Number Employees: 5-9
Sq. footage: 6000
Type of Packaging: Consumer, Food Service, Bulk
Brands:
> BBQ Pretzel Snack
> Cinnamon Pretzel Twists
> Dip@Stick
> Farmer's Popcorn Cob
> Lost Trail
> Lucky Twist Choc Peanut Butter
> Original Bagel Spread
> Say Cheese!Pretzel Bits
> Sunflower Nutty Nuggets

13905 Sunflower Restaurant Supply
P.O.Box 1277
Salina, KS 67402-1277   785-823-6394
> Fax: 785-823-5512   norman@sunflowersrs.com
> www.sunflowersrs.com
> President: Leroy Baumberger
> CEO: W Baumberger
Estimated Sales: $5568263
Number Employees: 20-49
Sq. footage: 36000
Brands:
> Lyon

13906 (HQ)Sunfresh
376 Road 12 SW
Royal City, WA 99357-0400   509-346-9438
> sunfresh@atnet.net
Processor, packer, shipper and exporter of fresh produce including potatoes, onions, pinto beans, asparagus, apples and cherries
> President: Randal Niessner
> Sales Director: Larry Sieg
Estimated Sales: $20-$25 Million
Number Employees: 85
Type of Packaging: Consumer, Food Service, Private Label
Brands:
> DOLE
> FRESH ONE
> GREEN GIANT
> SUN FAIR
> SUNFRESH
> SUNGEN

13907 Sunfresh Foods
125 S Kenyon St
Seattle, WA 98108-4207   206-764-0940
> Fax: 206-764-0960   800-669-9625
> jam@freezerves.com   www.freezerves.com
Uncooked freezer jams and fruit sauces
> President: Reed Hadley
> VP Marketing: Jerry Brozowski
Estimated Sales: Below $ 5 Million
Number Employees: 5-9
Type of Packaging: Food Service, Private Label
Brands:
> President's Choice
> Sunfresh Freezerves
> Western Classics

13908 Sungarden Sprouts
820 E 20th St
Cookeville, TN 38501-1451   931-526-1106
> Fax: 931-526-8338   bob@sproutnet.com
> www.sproutnet.com
Grower, packer and exporter of fresh and frozen alfalfa and bean sprouts
> Owner: Robert Rust
Estimated Sales: $2300000
Number Employees: 20-49
Parent Co: International Specialty Supply
Type of Packaging: Consumer, Food Service, Private Label, Bulk

13909 Sungold Foods
2624 Vermont Avenue
PO Box 3022
Fargo, ND 58504-3022   701-250-6895
> Fax: 701-282-5325   866-798-4786
> www.sunbutter.com
Manufacturers Sunbutter, a nut spread made from sunflower seeds available in a variety of flavors including creamy, natural, honey crunch, natural crunch, and organic in addition to whole sunflower seeds and trail mixes.
> CEO: Rob Majkrzak
> CFO: Randy Wigen
> VP Marketing: Dan Hofland
> Operations Manager: Brad Newton
Number Employees: 50-99
Type of Packaging: Consumer, Food Service, Private Label, Bulk

13910 Sunja's Oriental Foods
40 Foundry St
Waterbury, VT 05676-1525   802-244-7644
> Fax: 802-244-6880   sunjas@madriver.com
> www.sunja.com
Oriental foods, kimchee, all natural sauces, frozen specialties, sushi
> President: Sunja Hayden
Estimated Sales: $ 5 - 10 Million
Number Employees: 5-9

13911 SunkiStreet Growers
616 E Sunkist St
Ontario, CA 91761-1721   909-983-9811
> Fax: 909-933-2409   800-225-3727
> www.sunkist.com
Processor and exporter of citrus juice
> President: Henry Asseldt
> VP: Ted Leaman
> Director Sales/Marketing: Michael Staudt
Estimated Sales: $17400000
Number Employees: 100-249
Parent Co: Sunkist Growers
Type of Packaging: Bulk

13912 Sunkist Almond Accents
2140 W Olympic Blvd # 400
Los Angeles, CA 90006-2276   213-252-9422
> Fax: 310-966-4695   pr@almondaccents.com
> www.paramountfarms.com
Grower and processor of sliced, flavored almonds that are packed by Paramount Farms, Inc., for Paramount Growers Cooperative, Inc. under a trademark license from Sunkist Growers, Inc., the product of which is marketed and distributedthrough the Sunkist brand name.
> Owner: Sun Kim
> President/CEO Sunkist Growers: Timothy Lindgren
> Chief Financial Officer Paramount Farms: Gregg Dunn
> VP/Global Licensing Sunkist Growers: Gregory Combs
> SVP/Corporate Relations Sunkist Growers: Michael Wootton
> Grower Relations Paramount Farms: Andy Anzaldo
> VP/Operations Paramount Farms: David Szeflin
Estimated Sales: $150 Million
Number Employees: 1,000-4,999

13913 Sunkist California Pistachios and Almonds
11444 W Olympic Blvd # 250
Los Angeles, CA 90064-1534   310-966-4650
> Fax: 310-966-4695
> corporate.communications@sunkistgrowers.com
> www.paramountfarms.com
Processor of Sunkist Pistachios and Sunkist Almonds grown in California.
> President Paramount Farms: Stewart Resnick
> President/CEO Sunkist Growers: Timothy Lindgren
> Chief Financial Officer Paramount Farms: Gregg Dunn
> VP/Global Licensing Sunkist Growers: Gregory Combs
> SVP/Sales & Marketing Sunkist Growers: Russell Hanlin
> SVP/Corporate Relations Sunkist Growers: Michael Wootton
> Grower Relations Paramount Farms: Andy Anzaldo
> VP/Operations Paramount Farms: David Szeflin
Type of Packaging: Food Service

13914 Sunkist Candyc/o Jelly Belly Candy Company
1 Jelly Belly Ln
Fairfield, CA 94533-6741   707-428-2800
> Fax: 707-428-2863   800-323-9380
> International.sales@jellybelly.com
> www.jellybelly.com
Jelly Belly Candy Company, the makers of Sunkist Fruit Gems and Fruit Slices, is a licensee of Sunkist Growers, Inc. and manufacturers the fruit pectin treats which are available in a variety of flavors including orange, lemongrapefruit and lime/raspberry.
> President/CEO Sunkist Growers: Timothy Lindgren
> President/COO Jelly Belly Candy Company: Robert Simpson
> Chairman/CEO Jelly Belly Candy Company: Herman Rowland Sr
> CEO: Herman Rowland
> SVP/Sales & Marketing Sunkist Growers: Russell Hanlin
> VP/Fresh Fruit Sales Sunkist Growers: John McGuigan
> SVP/Corporate Relations Sunkist Growers: Michael Wootton
Type of Packaging: Food Service

13915 Sunkist Dispensed Juices
400 N Tampa St # 1700
Tampa, FL 33602-4716   813-301-4600
Fax: 813-301-4230 888-863-6726
jdesmond@vitalityinc.com
www.vitalityfoodservice.com
Vitality Beverages is a manufacturer that offers a complete line of frozen 100% juices, juice blends and juice drinks featuring Sunkist brand orange juice and Sunkist lemonade.
President/CEO Sunkist Growers: Timothy Lindgren
CEO: Gary Viljoen
Vitality Beverage Service Contracts: Russ Heady
VP/Canadian Sales Vitality Beverages: Bing Smith
VP/U.S. Sales Vitality Beverages: Jerry Desmond

SVP/Corporate Relations Sunkist Growers: Michael Wootton
National Account Mgr Vitality Beverages: Rich Connor
Customer Service Vitality Beverages: Tracy Menetre
Number Employees: 500-999
Type of Packaging: Consumer, Food Service

13916 Sunkist Fresh Fruit Sales/Domestic-International Markets-Food Se
P.O.Box 7888
Van Nuys, CA 91409-7888   818-986-4800
Fax: 818-379-7522 www.sunkist.com OR
www.sunkist.com/merchandising/sales.asp
Processor and marketer of citrus fruits including oranges, tangerines, lemons and grapefruit.
Manager: Olivia Bautista
VP/Law and General Counsel: Thomas Moore
VP/Chief Financial Officer: Richard French
VP/Fresh Fruit Sales: John McGuigan
VP/Global Licensing: Gregory Combs
SVP/Sales & Marketing Corporate Office: Russell Hanlin
SVP/Corporate Relations & Administration: Michael Wootton
Parent Co: Sunkist Growers
Type of Packaging: Consumer, Food Service, Bulk

13917 (HQ)Sunkist Growers
14130 Riverside Drive
Sherman Oaks, CA 91423   818-986-4800
Fax: 818-379-7405 info@sunkistgrowers.com
www.sunkist.com
Sunkist Growers Trademark Licensing Operations Division provides branded products services. Sunkist licensed products are available in the following categories: Fruit Juices, Fruit Drinks, Healthy Snacks, Baking Mixes, CarbonatedBeverages, Confections, Vitamins, Frozen Novelties, Salad Toppings, Freshly Peeled Citrus, Chilled Jellies and even Nonfood products.
President/CEO: Tim Lindgren
VP/Chief Financial Officer: Richard French
VP/Law & General Counsel: Thomas Moore
VP/Global Licensing: Gregory Combs
VP/Fresh Fruit Sales: John McGuigan
SVP/Sales & Marketing: Russell Hanlin
SVP/Corporate Relations & Administration: Michael Wootton
VP/Citrus Juice & Oil Business: Frank Bragg
VP/Chief Operations Officer: James A Padden
Vice Chairman: Craig Armstrong
Plant Manager: Robert Eldridge
VP/Marketing & Sales Promotions: Robert Verloop
Estimated Sales: $ 1+ Billion
Number Employees: 500
Type of Packaging: Food Service, Private Label

13918 Sunkist Growers
80 Everett Avenue
Suite 305
Chelsea, MA 02150   617-884-9750
Fax: 617-889-0136 www.sunkist.com

Processor of oranges, tangerines, lemons and grapefruit.
President/CEO Corporate Office: Timothy Lindgren
Sales & Marketing Manager Chelsea Office: Michael Ieradi
SVP/Corporate Sales & Marketing: Russell Hanlin
VP/Corporate Fresh Fruit Sales: John McGuigan
SVP/Corporate Relations & Administration: Michael Wootton
Estimated Sales: $ 1-2.5 Million
Number Employees: 3
Parent Co: Sunkist Growers
Type of Packaging: Consumer, Food Service, Bulk

13919 Sunkist Growers
616 E Sunkist St
Ontario, CA 91761-1721   909-983-9811
Fax: 909-933-2459 800-798-9005
www.sunkist.com
Processor of oranges, tangerines and lemons.
President/CEO Corporate Office: Timothy Lindgren
VP: Ted Leaman
SVP/Corporate Sales & Marketing: Russell Hanlin
VP/Corporate Fresh Fruit Sales: John McGuigan
SVP/Corporate Relations & Administration: Michael Wootton
Estimated Sales: $ 1-2.5 Million
Number Employees: 500-999
Parent Co: Sunkist Growers
Type of Packaging: Consumer, Food Service, Bulk

13920 Sunkist Growers
110 Tulliallan Ln
Cary, NC 27511-5670   410-663-2967
Fax: 410-997-2317 bschrott@sunkistgrowers.com
www.sunkist.com
Processor and marketer of citrus fruits including oranges, tangerines, lemons and grapefruit.
President/CEO Corporate Office: Jeffrey D Gargiulo
Vice President: James A Padden
SVP/Sales & Marketing Corporate Office: Russell Hanlin
SVP/Corporate Relations & Administration: Michael Wootton
Sales Representative Columbia Office: Bob Roberts
Estimated Sales: $ 1-5 Million
Number Employees: 10-20
Parent Co: Sunkist Growers
Type of Packaging: Consumer, Food Service, Bulk
Brands:
Sunkist

13921 Sunkist Growers
1000 Ridc Plz # 103
Pittsburgh, PA 15238-2923   412-967-9801
Fax: 412-967-9804 www.sunkist.com
Processor of oranges, tangerines, lemons and grapefruit.
Manager: Lex Revetta
SVP/Sales & Marketing Corporate Office: Russell Hanlin
Sales Representative Pittsburgh Office: Lex Revetta
SVP/Corporate Relations & Administration: Michael Wootton
Sales Representative Pittsburgh Office: Tony Greco
Estimated Sales: $ 1 - 3 Million
Number Employees: 1-4
Parent Co: Sunkist Growers
Type of Packaging: Consumer, Food Service, Bulk

13922 Sunkist Growers
59 Carol Dr
Buffalo, NY 14215-3601   716-895-3744
Fax: 716-895-3744
corporate.communications@sunkistgrowers.com
www.sunkist.com
Processor of citrus fruits including oranges, tangerines, lemons and grapefruit.
Manager: Lynn Groblewski
SVP/Sales & Marketing Corporate Office: Russell Hanlin
Sales Representative Buffalo Office: Lynn Groblewski
SVP/Corporate Relations & Administration: Michael Wootton

Estimated Sales: $500,000-$1 Million
Number Employees: 1-4
Parent Co: Sunkist Growers
Type of Packaging: Consumer, Food Service, Bulk
Brands:
Sunkist

13923 Sunkist Growers
10707 Corporate Drive
Suite 124
Stafford, TX 77477   281-240-6446
Fax: 281-240-4080 www.sunkist.com
Processor of fresh and canned oranges, tangerines, lemons and grapefruit.
President/CEO Corporate Office: Timothy Lindgren
Sales Representative Stafford TX Office: Mark Imming
Sales Representative Stafford TX Office: Jeff Horan
Sales Representative Stafford TX Office: Joe Padilla
SVP/Sales & Marketing Corporate Office: Russell Hanlin
SVP/Corporate Relations & Administration: Michael Wootton
Estimated Sales: $ 1-2.5 Million
Number Employees: 1-5
Parent Co: Sunkist Growers
Type of Packaging: Consumer, Food Service, Bulk

13924 Sunkist Growers
2929 W Main St
Visalia, CA 93291-5700   559-739-8392
Fax: 559-739-0856 www.sunkist.com
Processor of oranges, tangerines, lemons and grapefruit.
President/CEO Corporate Office: Timothy Lindgren
VP/Chief Financial Officer Corporate: Richard French
SVP/Sales & Marketing Corporate Office: Russell Hanlin
SVP/Corporate Relations & Administration: Michael Wootton
Estimated Sales: $ 5-10 Million
Number Employees: 20-49
Parent Co: Sunkist Growers
Type of Packaging: Consumer, Food Service, Bulk

13925 Sunkist Growers
9003 Bishops View Cir
Cherry Hill, NJ 8002-3465   856-663-2343
Fax: 856-633-3560 www.sunkist.com
Processor of oranges, tangerines, lemons and grapefruit.
President/CEO Corporate Office: Timothy Lindgren
VP/Chief Financial Officer Corporate: Richard French
Sales Representative Pennsauken Office: Bill Givens
Sales Representative Pennsauken Office: Karen Smith
SVP/Sales & Marketing Corporate Office: Russell Hanlin
SVP/Corporate Relations & Administration: Michael Wootton
Estimated Sales: $1-2.5 Million
Number Employees: 1-4
Parent Co: Sunkist Growers
Type of Packaging: Consumer, Food Service, Bulk
Brands:
Sunkist

13926 Sunkist Growers
5711 Golf Crest Dr
West Chester, OH 45069-1703   513-741-9494
Fax: 513-741-8608 www.sunkist.com
Processor of oranges, lemons, tangerines and grapefruit.
Manager: Tom Burkett
SVP/Sales & Marketing Corporate Office: Russell Hanlin
District Sales Manager Cincinnati Office: John Young
SVP/Corporate Relations & Administration: Michael Wootton
Estimated Sales: $2.$5-5 Million
Number Employees: 5-9
Parent Co: Sunkist Growers
Type of Packaging: Consumer, Food Service

13927 Sunkist Growers
7201 W Fort Street
Building Office 59
Detroit, MI 48209-2977   313-843-4160
                            Fax: 313-843-7411
Shipper of fresh oranges, tangerines, lemons and grapefruit
   Manager: Aaron Swerling
   Assistant Manager: John Leslie
Estimated Sales: $ 1-2.5 Million
Number Employees: 1-4
Parent Co: Sunkist Growers
Type of Packaging: Consumer, Food Service, Bulk

13928 Sunkist Growers
43 Old Farmers Rd
Long Valley, NJ 07853-3149   908-876-9500
                            Fax: 973-316-0266 www.sunkist.com
Processor and marketer of citrus fruits including oranges, tangerines, lemons and grapefruit.
   Manager: Brad Blaine
   SVP/Sales & Marketing Corporate Office: Russell Hanlin
   Sales Representative Parsippany Office: Brad Blaine
   SVP/Corporate Relations & Administration: Michael Wootton
   Sales Representative Parsippany Office: Jeff Savage
Parent Co: Sunkist Growers
Type of Packaging: Consumer, Food Service, Bulk

13929 Sunkist Growers
15849 S 40th Pl
Phoenix, AZ 85048-7459   602-956-1238
                            Fax: 602-956-5043 www.sunkist.com
Processor and marketer of citrus fruits including oranges, tangerines, lemons and grapefruit.
   Manager: Aaron Leeming
   SVP/Sales & Marketing Corporate Office: Russell Hanlin
   Sales Representative Phoenix Office: Ron Carbone
   SVP/Corporate Relations & Administration: Michael Wootton
   Sales Representative Phoenix Office: Debra Roesch
Parent Co: Sunkist Growers
Type of Packaging: Consumer, Food Service, Bulk

13930 Sunkist Growers
11841 SE Mountain Sun Dr
Clackamas, OR 97015-9247   503-655-3803
                            Fax: 503-655-4221 www.sunkist.com
Processor and marketer of citrus fruits including oranges, tangerines, lemons and grapefruit.
   President/CEO Corporate Office: Timothy Lindgren
   SVP/Sales & Marketing Corporate Office: Russell Hanlin
   Sales Representative Portland Office: Tom Bauer
   SVP/Corporate Relations & Administration: Michael Wootton
   Sales Representative Portland Office: Karen Lary
Parent Co: Sunkist Growers
Type of Packaging: Consumer, Food Service, Bulk

13931 Sunkist Growers
7077 Beaubien East #206
Anjou, QC H1M 2Y2
Canada   514-354-8181
                            Fax: 514-354-8345 www.sunkist.com
Processor and marketer of citrus fruits including oranges, tangerines, lemons and grapefruit.
   President/CEO Corporate Office: Timothy Lindgren
   SVP/Sales & Marketing Corporate Office: Russell Hanlin
   Sales Representative Montreal Office: John Lemarguand
   SVP/Corporate Relations & Administration: Michael Wootton
Parent Co: Sunkist Growers
Type of Packaging: Consumer, Food Service, Bulk

13932 Sunkist Growers
210 Ontario Food Terminal
165 The Queensway
Toronto, ON M8Y 1H8
Canada   416-259-5491
                            Fax: 416-259-4960 www.sunkist.com
Processor and marketer of citrus fruits including oranges, tangerines, lemons and grapefruit.
   President/CEO Corporate Office: Timothy Lindgren
   SVP/Sales & Marketing Corporate Office: Russell Hanlin
   Sales Representative Toronto Office: Natalie Lewicky
   SVP/Corporate Relations & Administration: Michael Wootton
   Sales Representative Toronto Office: Jim Van Dusen
Parent Co: Sunkist Growers
Type of Packaging: Consumer, Food Service, Bulk

13933 Sunkist Growers
201-827 Belgrave Way
Annacis Business Park
New Westminster, BC V3M 5R8
Canada   604-524-5001
                            Fax: 604-524-0660 www.sunkist.com
Processor and marketer of citrus fruits including oranges, tangerines, lemons and grapefruit.
   President/CEO Corporate Office: Timothy Lindgren
   SVP/Sales & Marketing Corporate Office: Russell Hanlin
   Sales Representative Vancouver Office: Walt Cieslukowski
   SVP/Corporate Relations & Administration: Michael Wootton
   Sales Representative Vancouver Office: Natalie Eng
Parent Co: Sunkist Growers
Type of Packaging: Consumer, Food Service, Bulk

13934 Sunkist Growers
1501 42nd Street
Suite 470
West Des Moines, IA 50266   515-226-9005
                            Fax: 515-226-9726 www.sunkist.com
Processor and marketer of citrus fruits including oranges, tangerines, lemons and grapefruit.
   President/CEO Corporate Office: Timothy Lindgren
   SVP/Sales & Marketing Corporate Office: Russell Hanlin
   Sales Representative Des Moine Office: Kevin Pratt
   SVP/Corporate Relations & Administration: Michael Wootton
Parent Co: Sunkist Growers
Type of Packaging: Consumer, Food Service, Bulk

13935 Sunkist Growers
101 East Park Boulevard
NCNB Tower Suite 467
Plano, TX 75074   972-516-8824
                            Fax: 972-578-9036 www.sunkist.com
Processor and marketer of citrus fruits including oranges, tangerines, lemons and grapefruit.
   President/CEO Corporate Office: Timothy Lindgren
   SVP/Sales & Marketing Corporate Office: Russell Hanlin
   Sales Representative Plano Office: Tom Welter
   SVP/Corporate Relations & Administration: Michael Wootton
   Sales Representative Plano Office: Tim Rogers
Parent Co: Sunkist Growers
Type of Packaging: Consumer, Food Service, Bulk

13936 Sunkist John P Newman Research and Development Center
760 East Sunkist Street
Ontario, CA 91761   909-983-5852
                            Fax: 909-822-2125 800-383-7141
corporate.communications@sunkistgrowers.com
                            www.sunkistresearch.com/
The Sunkist John P. Newman Researh and Development Center, located in Ontario, California, conducts research and houses expertise in fruit and vegetable packing, sorting, labeling, conditioning, storage, and transportation.
   President/CEO Corporate Office: Timothy Lindgren
   VP/Law and General Counsel: Thomas Moore
   SVP/Corporate Sales & Marketing: Russell Hanlin
   VP/Corporate Fresh Fruit Sales: John McGuigan
   SVP/Corporate Relations & Administration: Michael Wootton
Parent Co: Sunkist Growers

13937 Sunland Inc/Peanut Better
PO Box 1059
Portales, NM 88130   575-356-6638
                            Fax: 575-356-6630
customerservice@sunlandinc.com
                            www.sunlandinc.com
peanuts, peanut butter and flavored infused peanut
   President/CEO: Jimmie Shearer

13938 Sunlike Juice
91 Finchdene Square
Scarborough, ON M1X 1A7
Canada   416-297-1140
                            Fax: 416-297-5703
Processor and exporter of fruit juices and drinks including apple, apple/strawberry, cranberry cocktail, grapefruit, mango, orange juice, orange/pineapple, peach, pineapple, fruit punch, grape, papaya, pink lemonade, black cherry andiced tea
   President: Terry Topos
   Consultant: Tim Britton
Brands:
   Sunlike

13939 Sunline Brands
8100 Water Street
Saint Louis, MO 63111-3689   314-638-5770
                            Fax: 314-638-0820
Manufacturer of candy and confectionery including hard, taffy, seasonal, vending, bagged, multi-packs, etc
   VP: Sandy Hagerman
Parent Co: Sunmark Companies
Type of Packaging: Consumer, Bulk
Brands:
   Chewy Zaps
   Lik-m-aid Fun Dip
   Pixy Stix
   Spree
   Sunsations
   SweetTarts
   Tangy Taffy

13940 Sunmaid Growers
5568 Gibraltar Drive
Pleasanton, CA 94588-8544   925-463-8200
          Fax: 925-463-7521 800-752-9277
smaid@sunmaid.com   www.sunmaid.com
Dried fruits
   President: Berry Kriebel
   Marketing Director: Mark Bagley
   CFO: Richard Emde
   Purchasing Manager: Dan Little
Estimated Sales: $ 183 Million approx.
Number Employees: 150
Type of Packaging: Private Label
Brands:
   Sunmaid
   Sunsweet Prune Juice
   Sunsweet Prunes
   Sunsweet/Sun-Gold

13941 Sunmet
PO Box 509
Del Rey, CA 93616-0509   559-445-1574
          Fax: 559-445-0572 sales@sunmet.com
Processor and exporter of Granny Smith apples, peaches, plums, nectarines and table grapes
Type of Packaging: Consumer, Food Service, Private Label, Bulk
Brands:
   Sunmet

13942 Sunny Avocado
20872 Deerhorn Valley Road
Jamul, CA 91935-7937   619-479-3573
          Fax: 619-479-2960 800-999-2862
sunnyavocado@sunny-avocado.com
                            www.sunny-avocado.com
Provides extra chunky avocado pulp, original mild qualcomole and spicy blends; guac, salsa and guacamaya drink
   President: Enrique Bautista
   VP: Ana Rosa Bautista
   VP Sales/Marketing: Michael Spinner
Estimated Sales: $120000
Number Employees: 2
Type of Packaging: Food Service, Private Label, Bulk
Brands:
   Sunny Avocado

13943 Sunny Cove Citrus LLC
440 Anchor Ave
Orange Cove, CA 93646-2200   559-626-4085
Fax: 559-626-7210
customer.service@sccitrus.com
www.sccitrus.com
Packinghouse and licensed shipper of citrus products for Sunkist Growers Inc.
President: Tom Clark
Field Manager: Justin Kulikov
Controller: Warren Lee
Office Manager: Vera Fast
Sq. footage: 170000
Type of Packaging: Food Service

13944 Sunny Delight Beverage Company
7000 Lagrange Blvd SW
Atlanta, GA 30336-2820   404-349-7480
Fax: 404-267-4488   800-395-5849
Service.Fin@SunnyD.com
www.proctorandgamble.com
Fruit drinks
President/CEO: Wayne William
CFO: James (Jim) Dahmus
Operations/Production: Robert Rutkowski
VP Sales: John Crossetti
Plant Manager: Amir Ghanaad
Estimated Sales: $ 50-99.9 Million
Number Employees: 100-249
Brands:
Sunny D

13945 Sunny Dell Foods
135 N 5th Street
Oxford, PA 19363   610-932-5164
Fax: 610-932-9479 sunnydell.com
Mushrooms (canned, marinated, refrigerated, glass and specialty)
Finance Manager: Lori Caligiuri
Sales Manager: Bobby Fella
Purchasing Manager: Monica Philistine
Estimated Sales: $14.5 Million
Number Employees: 75

13946 Sunny Fresh Foods
206 W 4th St
Monticello, MN 55362-8524   763-271-5600
Fax: 763-271-5711   800-872-3447
www.sunnyfreshfoods.com
Processor of eggs including fresh, liquid, mixes, omelets, diced, hard-cooked and pre-cooked
President: Michael Luker
Director Sales/Marketing: Dale Jenkins
Marketing Manager: Rebecca Hanf
Number Employees: 250-499
Parent Co: Cargill Foods
Type of Packaging: Food Service, Private Label

13947 Sunny South Pecan Company
P.O.Box 1400
Statesboro, GA 30459-1400   912-764-5337
Fax: 912-489-1391   800-764-3687
Processor and grower of pecans
Owner: Garland L Nessmith
VP: Steve Rushing
Estimated Sales: $500,000-$1 Million
Number Employees: 1-4
Sq. footage: 15600
Type of Packaging: Consumer
Brands:
Savannah
Sunny South

13948 Sunny's Seafood
19 Wedgewood Street
Everett, MA 02149-1515   617-261-7123
Fax: 617-261-6492
Seafood
President: Steven Dulock Sr

13949 Sunnydale Meats
165 Hyatt St
Gaffney, SC 29341-1558   864-489-6091
Fax: 864-489-6092
Manufacturer of beef, pork, chicken, turkey, bacon, sausage and wieners
President: Anthony Hopper Jr Jr
Estimated Sales: $15 Million
Number Employees: 10-19

13950 Sunnyland Farms
P.O.Box 8200
Albany, GA 31706-8200   229-436-5654
Fax: 229-888-8332   800-999-2488
www.sunnylandfarms.com
Nuts, mixed nuts, pecans, dried fruits and specialty products.
Sales Manager: Beverly Willson
Purchasing: Larry Willson
Estimated Sales: $ 10 - 20 Million
Type of Packaging: Consumer, Bulk
Brands:
Sunnyland Farms

13951 Sunnyland Mills
4469 E Annadale Ave
Fresno, CA 93725-2221   559-233-4983
Fax: 559-233-6431   800-501-8017
mike@sunnylandmills.com
www.sunnylandmills.com
Leading manufacturer of premium quality organic and traditional bulgur wheat, pearled soft white wheat, and Grano
President: Steve Orlando
VP: Mike Orlando
Plant Manager: Steve Orlando
Number Employees: 10-19
Sq. footage: 18000
Type of Packaging: Food Service, Bulk
Brands:
Sunnyland

13952 Sunnyrose Cheese
PO Box 93
Diamond City, AB T0K 0T0
Canada   403-381-4024
Fax: 403-381-3838
FLACOSTE@AGROPUR.COM
www.milkingredients.ca
Processor of cheeses including cheddar, colby, mozzarella, Monterey jack, gouda, havarti, marble, parmesan and specialty
President Sales: Emanuela Leoni
Number Employees: 10-19
Parent Co: Agropur
Type of Packaging: Consumer, Food Service
Brands:
Sunnyrose Cheese

13953 Sunnyside Farms
PO Box 164
Neligh, NE 68756-0164   402-791-2210
Fax: 402-791-2210
Produce
President: James McNally
Estimated Sales: Under $500,000
Number Employees: 1-4

13954 Sunnyside Organics
PO Box 478
Washington, VA 22747-0478   540-675-2627
Fax: 540-675-1135
Family owned farm that produces eggs, prime meats, and 200 kinds of fruits, vegetables and herbs.

13955 Sunnyside Vegetable Packing
730 Lebanon Road
Millville, NJ 08332-9773   856-451-5077
Fax: 856-451-4388
Vegetables
President: Vic Sammartano
Estimated Sales: Under $500,000
Number Employees: 50-99

13956 (HQ)Sunnyslope Farms Egg Ranch
9845 Nancy Avenue
Cherry Valley, CA 92223-3599   951-845-1131
Processor and exporter of fresh shell and frozen eggs
President: Stefan Illy
General Manager: Bill Ingram
Estimated Sales: $20-50 Million
Number Employees: 20-49
Sq. footage: 300000

13957 Sunray Bakery Corporation
50 Northwestern Drive
6
Salem, NH 03079-5811   603-898-3079
Baked goods
Manager: Joe Ceppecelli
Estimated Sales: $ 10-20 Million
Number Employees: 10

13958 Sunray Food Products Corporation
3441 Kingsbridge Ave
Bronx, NY 10463-4003   718-548-2255
Fax: 718-548-2313 www.zenobianut.com
Processor of nuts including cashews and pistachios; also, nut mixes, pumpkin and sunflower seeds
Manager: Agustine Morales
Manager: Dave Brechner
Estimated Sales: $423177
Number Employees: 10-19
Parent Co: Zenobia Company
Type of Packaging: Consumer, Food Service, Private Label, Bulk
Brands:
Private Stock
Zenobia

13959 Sunridge Farms
P.O.Box 4273
Salinas, CA 93912-4273   831-755-1430
Fax: 831-755-1429 www.coastlineproduce.com
Bulk and packaged organic and natural foods, snacks, dried fruits, nuts and trail mixes; natural candies; granolas and cereals; grain and bean blend; pastas
President: Milton Henderson
VP: Pelsh Adrian
Marketing Director: Vivian Guajardo
Sales: Dave Adrian
Estimated Sales: $ 2.5-5 Million
Number Employees: 20-49
Type of Packaging: Consumer, Food Service, Bulk
Brands:
Coastline

13960 Sunrise Confections
1800 Northwestern Dr
El Paso, TX 79912-1122   915-877-1172
Fax: 915-877-1198   800-685-1475
www.sunriseconfections.com
Manager: Beth Podol
CEO: Richard Harshman
Director Of Marketing: Grant Bassett
VP Sales/Marketing: Alex Chimens
Estimated Sales: $300,000-500,000
Number Employees: 1-4

13961 Sunrise Growers
701 W Kimberly Ave # 210
Placentia, CA 92870-6354   714-630-2170
Fax: 714-630-0920   stcircle@sunrisegrowers.com
www.frozsun.com
Processor and exporter of fresh strawberries, cauliflower, broccoli, lettuce, bell peppers, artichokes, green beans and cabbage
President: Douglas Circle
CEO: Edward Haft
Estimated Sales: $ .5 - 1 million
Number Employees: 1-4
Type of Packaging: Consumer, Food Service, Bulk
Brands:
Sunrise
Sunshine
Touchdown

13962 Sunrise Markets
300 Powell
Vancouver, BC V6A 1G4
Canada   604-685-8019
Fax: 604-685-4043
Processor of tofu and soy milk
General Manager: Peter Joe
Operations Manager: Shirley Joe
Plant Manager: Jimmy Cuan
Number Employees: 50-99
Sq. footage: 25000
Type of Packaging: Consumer, Food Service

13963 Sunrise Winery
1418 Shasta Avenue
San Jose, CA 95126-2531   408-741-1310
Wines
President: Rolayne Storz
Estimated Sales: $500-1 Million appx.
Number Employees: 1-4

13964 Suns Noodle Company
2415 Weaver Way
Atlanta, GA 30340-1532   770-448-7799
Fax: 770-446-7599
Noodles
President: Allen Sun

*Estimated Sales:*Below $ 5 Million
Number Employees: 50

13965 Sunset Farm Foods
P.O.Box 963
Valdosta, GA 31603-0963 229-242-9973
Fax: 229-242-3389 800-882-1121
webinfo@sunsetfarmfoods.com
www.sunsetfarmfoods.com
Processor of smoked sausage, fresh sausage, smoked meats, cooked products (souse, chitterling loaf, liver pudding, chili)
President: J D Carroll
VP: T Carroll
Sales: Charles Harrell
Plant Manager: Ricky Lightsey
Estimated Sales:$ 20 - 50 Million
Number Employees: 50-99
Number of Brands: 6
Number of Products: 250
Sq. footage: 40000
Type of Packaging: Consumer, Food Service, Private Label, Bulk
Brands:
FLAVORITY
GEORGE MAID
GEORGIA REDS
GEORGIA SPECIAL
QUEEN OF DIXIE
SOUTHERN CHEF
SUNSET FARM

13966 Sunset Specialty Foods
PO Box 1360
Sunset Beach, CA 90742-1360 562-592-4976
Fax: 562-592-3806
Processor and exporter of specialty frozen items including pizza, chocolate chip cookies, etc
Number Employees: 20-49
Sq. footage: 27000
Type of Packaging: Consumer, Food Service, Private Label, Bulk
Brands:
Amelia's
Deli
Dina
Maestro Giovanni

13967 Sunset Wholesale
1650 N 7th St # 1
Lebanon, PA 17046-2159 717-272-4906
Fax: 717-270-4323 800-876-2123
Supplier of closeout and salvage foods, toys and gifts
President: Terry Longenecker
Estimated Sales:$ 20 - 50 Million
Number Employees: 50-99

13968 Sunshine Burger Company
P.O.Box 888
Fort Atkinson, WI 53538-888 845-647-2700
Fax: 845-647-2065
www.organicandnaturalnews.com/guide/cat41.htm
1
Processor of vegetarian burgers made with sunflower seeds, brown rice, carrots, sea salt and spices
Owner: Carol Debberman
Owner: John Hiler
Estimated Sales:$500,000-$1 Million
Number Employees: 1-4
Sq. footage: 7000
Type of Packaging: Consumer, Food Service
Brands:
Organic Sunshine
Sunshine

13969 Sunshine Dairy
584 Coleman Rd
Middletown, CT 06457-6117 860-346-6644
Fax: 860-346-5246
Milk, dairy products
President: Nancy A Guida
Estimated Sales:$ 10-20 Million
Number Employees: 20-49
Brands:
Guida

13970 Sunshine Dairy Foods
801 NE 21st Ave
Portland, OR 97232-2280 503-234-7526
Fax: 503-233-9441
parbuthnot@sunshinedairyfoods.com
www.sunshinedairyfoods.com

Processor of dairy products including ice cream, yogurt, fresh milk and cultures
Owner: Sam Karmounas
Estimated Sales:$ 20 - 50 Million
Number Employees: 100-249
Sq. footage: 75000
Type of Packaging: Consumer, Food Service, Private Label, Bulk
Brands:
Albertson's
Quality Chekd
Tillamook
Western Family

13971 Sunshine Farm & Gardens
Rr 5
Renick, WV 24966 304-497-2208
Fax: 304-497-2698 barry@sunfarm.com
www.sunfarm.com
Processor, importer and exporter of organic fruits including apples and pawpaws; also, organic herbs and seeds
President: Barry Glick
VP: Zak Glick
Estimated Sales:$400000
Number Employees: 100-249
Sq. footage: 65000

13972 Sunshine Farms
N8873 Currie Rd
Portage, WI 53901-9218 608-742-2016
Fax: 608-742-1577 considine@jvlnet.com
www.sunshine-farms.com
Processor and wholesaler/distributor of cheese and goat milk; wholesaler/distributor of health foods
President: Dan Considine
Estimated Sales:$ 3 - 5 Million
Number Employees: 1-4
Type of Packaging: Consumer
Brands:
Sunshine Farms

13973 Sunshine Farms
1680 Horse Pasture Road
Roseboro, NC 28382-7110 910-564-2421
Fax: 910-564-5302
Processor of pumpkins and pecans
Estimated Sales:$ .5 - 1 million
Number Employees: 1-4

13974 Sunshine Farms Dairy
123 Gateway Boulevard N
Elyria, OH 44035-4999 440-322-6301
Processor of dairy products including buttermilk, whipped cream, cottage cheese, sour cream and ice cream; also, dips, sherbet and soft-serve mixes, fruit drinks, orange juice, etc
President: Denis Walter
Service Manager/Secretary: Dennis Walter
Estimated Sales:$33874611
Number Employees: 475
Parent Co: Consun Food Industries
Type of Packaging: Consumer, Food Service, Private Label, Bulk
Brands:
Sunshine Farms

13975 Sunshine Farms Poultry
PO Box 10595
West Palm Beach, FL 33419-0595 561-881-4500
Fax: 561-881-9252
Poultry, poultry products
Estimated Sales:$ 5-10 Million
Number Employees: 5-9

13976 Sunshine Food Sales
2900 NW 75th St
Miami, FL 33147-5946 305-696-2885
Processor and importer of fresh and frozen fish including mackerel, kingfish, lobster and crabs
President: Carlos Sanchez
Co-Owner: David Dossi
Plant Manager: Jesus Alonsa
Number Employees: 1-4
Type of Packaging: Bulk

13977 Sunshine Fresh
20 W End Road
Totowa, NJ 07512-1406 973-812-4777
Fax: 973-812-4988
Processor of pickles; wholesaler/distributor of deli products; serving the food service market
President: Michael Rosenblum

Estimated Sales:$8100000
Number Employees: 45
Type of Packaging: Food Service

13978 Sunshine Seafood
P.O.Box 136
Stonington, ME 04681-0136 207-367-2955
Fax: 207-367-6394
Fish, seafood and shellfish.
President: James Eaton
Estimated Sales:$2,600,000
Number Employees: 10-19

13979 Sunstates Refrigerated
PO Box 910
Moultrie, GA 31776-0910 912-985-8918
Fax: 912-985-8959
Cold storage

13980 Sunstone Vineyards & Winery
125 N Refugio Rd
Santa Ynez, CA 93460-9303 805-688-9463
Fax: 805-686-1881 800-313-9463
jeff@sunstonewinery.com
www.sunstonewinery.com
Wines
President: Bion Rice
CEO: Linda Rice
VP: Ashley Rice
Marketing Director: Jeff Munsey
Estimated Sales:$1-$2 Million
Number Employees: 1-4

13981 Sunsweet Growers
901 N Walton Ave
Yuba City, CA 95993-9370 530-674-5010
Fax: 530-751-5395 800-417-2253
sunsweet@casupport.com www.sunsweet.com
Largest handler of dried tree fruits such as prunes, apricots, peaches, pears and apples. Also manufactures juices and specialty fruits.
President/CEO: Arthur Driscoll
CFO: Ana Spyres
VP North American Marketing: Steve Riccardelli
VP Global Sales/Marketing: Dane Lance
VP Operations: Gene Dodson
Purchasing Angent: Traci Vaniszeski
Estimated Sales:$262.4 Million
Number Employees: 600
Type of Packaging: Consumer, Food Service, Private Label, Bulk

13982 (HQ)Suntory International
7 Times Sq # 21
New York, NY 10036-6524 212-891-6600
Fax: 212-891-6601 www.suntory.com
Bottled water and beverages
President/CEO: Seishi Ueno
EVP/CFO: Tsuyoshi Nishizaki
Sales/Marketing Director: Satoru Shimizu
Estimated Sales:$1,594,400,000
Number Employees: 2199
Brands:
Artesian Spring
Belmont Spring Disti
Belmont Spring Water
Hinckley & Schmitt N
Hinckley Springs
Hinckley-Schmitt
Isotonic
Kentwood Premium Coffee
Kentwood Springs
Kidz Water
Mountain Spring
Nursery Drinking Wat
Nursery Drinking Wat
Sierra Spring Nurser
Sierra Springs
Suntory Bottled Wate
Suntory Oolong Tea

13983 Suntory Water Group
5660 New Northside Dr NW # 500
Atlanta, GA 30328-5826 770-933-1400
Fax: 770-956-9495 www.suntorywatergroup.com
Bottled water, assorted beverages
President: David Krishock
Contoller: Rick Puckett
VP: Patrick Goguillon
Sales Director: Steve Bayliss
Public Relations: Elizabeth Weinmann
VP Operations: Mike Chandler
Purchasing Manager: John Houser

Estimated Sales: $ 400 Million
Number Employees: 1,000-4,999
Parent Co: Suntory International Corporation

13984 (HQ)Sunwest Foods
1550 Drew Ave # 150
Davis, CA 95618-7852 530-758-8550
Fax: 530-758-8110
jhasbrook@sunwestfoods.com
www.sunwestfoods.com
Processor and exporter of regular, organic and wild
rice; also, walnuts, almonds, pistachios and pecans
President: James Errecarte
Director Specialty Rice Division: John Hasbrook
Estimated Sales: $ 20 - 50 Million
Number Employees: 10-19
Sq. footage: 100000
Brands:
Nutririte
SunNuts
SunWest

13985 SupHerb Farms

P.O.Box 610
Turlock, CA 95381-0610 209-633-3600
Fax: 209-633-3644 800-787-4372
custserv@supherbfarms.com
www.supherbfarms.com

CrEATe! Get ready-to-use fresh
flavor with SupHerb Farms'
all-natural fresh frozen culinary
herbs, specialty vegetables, culinary herb pastes, vegetable purees
and creative blends. Complete microbiological testing ensures food
safety. We set the standard for outstanding customer service, inspired culinary support,
collaborative customer partnerships and innovative custom
products.

President: Mike Brem
CFO: Joe Ford
R&D: Mike Lehman
Quality Control: Susan Spafford England
Marketing: Laurel Place
Sales VP: Don Douglas
Estimated Sales: $40-50 Million
Number Employees: 100-249
Sq. footage: 75000
Type of Packaging: Food Service, Bulk
Brands:
SUPHERB FARMS

13986 Super Bakes
1700 Cushman Dr
Lincoln, NE 68512-1238 402-423-1234
Fax: 402-423-4586 800-222-3276
wandas@neb.rr.com www.superbakes.com
Processor and exporter of organic grain mixes
President: Susan Zink
Chairman: Dwaine Rogge
VP Sales/Marketing: Shari Rogge-Fidler
Estimated Sales: $2311332
Number Employees: 20-49
Brands:
Wanda's

13987 Super Nutrition Life Extension
1100 W Commercial Blvd # 100
Fort Lauderdale, FL 33309-3748 954-766-8433
Fax: 954-202-7745 800-678-8989
customerservice@lifeextension.com www.lef.org

Processor of supplements including nutritional,
anti-aging and sport supplements; also, vitamin
formulas
Owner: William Flannon
Marketing/Design: Kathy Mooney
National Sales Manager: Michael Mooney

13988 Super Smokers BBQ
1711 W Us Highway 50
O Fallon, IL 62269-1668 618-624-6742
terry@supersmokers.com
www.supersmokers.com
Sauces

**13989 Super Snooty Sea Food
Corporation**
37 Fish Pier
Boston, MA 02210-2054 617-426-6390
Processor and wholesaler/distributor of frozen sea-
food including round and filleted flat fish
General Manager: Paul Sousa
Number Employees: 5-9
Type of Packaging: Consumer

13990 Superbrand Dairies
9 Wax Myrtle Ct
Montgomery, AL 36117-3770 334-277-6010
Fax: 334-279-6964
Processor of frozen pizza
Owner: Dennis Houde
Plant Manager: J Parsons
Number Employees: 50-99
Parent Co: Winn Dixie
Type of Packaging: Private Label

13991 Superbrand Dairies
3000 NW 123rd Street
Miami, FL 33167-2517 305-685-8079
Fax: 305-687-1703
Processor of milk and juice: orange, grapefruit and
apple
Assistant Manager: Mark Holston
Plant Manager: Dwight Moore
Number Employees: 50-99
Parent Co: Winn Dixie
Type of Packaging: Consumer

13992 Superior Bakery
PO Box 898
North Grosvenordale, CT 06255-0898 860-923-9555
Fax: 860-923-2087
Processor of baked goods including hearth breads
and rolls
President: Louis Faucher
Plant Manager: Raymond Faucher, Jr.
Estimated Sales: $ 50 - 100 Million
Number Employees: 50
Sq. footage: 50000
Type of Packaging: Consumer, Food Service, Pri-
vate Label, Bulk
Brands:
Green-Freedman
Kasanofs's
Superior

13993 Superior Baking Company
176 N Warren Avenue
Brockton, MA 02301-3431 508-586-6601
Fax: 508-580-4056 800-696-2253
sbaking1@comcast.net
Processor of breads, rolls, bagels, pastries and wraps
President: Michael DeBenedictis
VP Sales: Joseph Ferrini
Vice President: Robert DeBenedictis
Marketing Director: Joseph Ferrini
Sales Director: Joseph Ferrini
Estimated Sales: Below $ 5 Million
Number Employees: 60
Sq. footage: 16000
Type of Packaging: Consumer, Food Service, Pri-
vate Label, Bulk

13994 Superior Bean & Spice Company
PO Box 753
Brush Prairie, WA 98606-0753 360-694-0819
Fax: 360-883-6915
Vegetables, soup mixes
President: Duane Rough

13995 Superior Cake Products
105 Ashland Ave
Southbridge, MA 01550-2803 508-764-3276
Fax: 508-765-5344

Processor of cakes and snack cakes including carrot
spice rolls, Boston cream pie, etc
President: Chris Smith
CEO: Chris Smith
VP Finance: Michael Faucher
VP: Karo Mc Hugh
Marketing Manager: Chris Smith
VP Sales: Christopher Smith
VP Operations: Raymond Faucher Jr
Type of Packaging: Consumer, Food Service, Pri-
vate Label
Brands:
Superior Cake

13996 Superior Dairy
4719 Navarre Rd SW
Canton, OH 44706-2300 330-477-4515
Fax: 330-477-5908 800-683-2479
Processor of dairy products
President: Joseph Sorhnlen
President/COO: Daniel Sorhnlen
CEO: Joseph P Soehnlen
Sales Manager: Jeff Bouequin
Estimated Sales: $ 50 - 100 Million
Number Employees: 100-249
Type of Packaging: Consumer, Private Label

13997 Superior Farms
1477 Drew Ave
Davis, CA 95618-4881 530-297-7299
Fax: 530-758-3152 800-228-5262
maymikej@aol.com www.superiorfarms.com
Processor of lamb
CEO: Dennis "Breen,"
Sales Manager: Mike Burke
CEO: Les Oesterreich
General Manager Manufacturing: Martin Ducken
Brands:
Superior Farms

13998 Superior Farms
1477 Drew Ave
Davis, CA 95618-4881 530-297-7299
Fax: 530-758-3152 800-228-5262
thiinc@superiorfarms.com
www.superiorfarms.com
Processor of lamb, venison, buffalo and veal
President: Les Oesterriech
Marketing Director: Patty Crippen
CEO: Les Oesterreich
Corporate Food Service Sales Manager: Geof
Lambert
Corporate Retail Sales Manager: Mike Burns
Estimated Sales: $ 100-500 Million
Number Employees: 20-49
Brands:
Superior Farms

13999 Superior Foods
275 Westgate Dr
Watsonville, CA 95076-2470 831-728-3691
Fax: 831-722-0926 cindy@superiorfoods.com
www.superiorfoods.com
Importer, exporter, packer and wholesaler/distributor
of frozen fruits and vegetables including broccoli,
pea pods, sugar snap peas and asparagus
President: Mateo Lettunich
CEO: D Moore
Sales Director: Mark Colendich
Operations/Production: Neil Happee
Estimated Sales: $12500000
Number Employees: 20-49
Sq. footage: 11000
Brands:
Asian Pride
Garden Fresh
Orchard Park
Superior Foods
Superior Pride

14000 Superior Frozen Vegetables
Rr 3 Box 162
Cornell, MI 49818-9405 906-384-6466
Processor of frozen vegetables
President: Michael Van Damme
Co-Owner: Mike Van Damme
CEO: James Leininger
Estimated Sales: $ 5 - 10 Million
Number Employees: 50-99
Parent Co: Paul Van Damme & Sons
Type of Packaging: Consumer

14001 Superior Meat Company
480 N 500 E
Vernal, UT 84078-1808   435-789-3274
Processor of meat products
    Owner: D J Reynolds
    Sales Manager: D Reynolds
Estimated Sales: Less than $500,000
Number Employees: 1-4
Type of Packaging: Consumer, Food Service

14002 Superior Mushroom Farms
52557 Range Road
Suite 215
Ardrossan, AB T8E 2H6
Canada   780-922-2535
    Fax: 780-922-2078 866-687-2242
        crimini@telusplanet.net
Grower of fresh mushrooms
    President/CEO: Brent Schwabe
    Marketing/Sales Director: Wanda Ziober
    Production Manager: Norman Schwabe
Number Employees: 50
Type of Packaging: Consumer, Food Service, Bulk

14003 (HQ)Superior Nut & Candy Company
1111 W 40th St
Chicago, IL 60609-2506   773-254-7900
    Fax: 773-254-9171 800-843-2238
Processor of nuts including honey roasted, salted
meats and trail mixes; also, fund raising programs
available
    President: Anthony Mastrangelo
    VP: Mona Mastrangelo
Estimated Sales: $16068865
Number Employees: 20-49
Sq. footage: 33000

14004 Superior Nut Company
225 Monsignor Obrien Hwy
Cambridge, MA 02141-1249   617-876-3808
    Fax: 617-876-8225 800-251-6060
        info@superiornutstore.com
        www.superiornut.com
Nuts
    President: Harry Hintlian
Estimated Sales: $1-2.5 Million
Number Employees: 1-4
Type of Packaging: Consumer, Food Service, Bulk
Brands:
    Superior Nut Company

14005 Superior Nutrition Corporation
601 N Market Street
Wilmington, DE 19801-3006   302-655-5762
    Fax: 302-655-5760 info@sncorp.com
        www.sncorp.com
Baked onion pieces
Estimated Sales: $ 2.5-5 Million
Number Employees: 1-4

14006 Superior Ocean Produce
4423 N Elston Ave
Chicago, IL 60630-4418   773-283-8400
    Fax: 773-561-0139 www.fishguy.com
Seafood
    Owner: William Dugan
Estimated Sales: $ 1 - 3 Million
Number Employees: 10-19

14007 Superior Packing Company
PO Box 277
Ellensburg, WA 98926-0277   509-925-1495
    Fax: 509-925-1497
Processor and exporter of fabricated lamb
    Sales Manager: Gary Ekiss
Estimated Sales: $ 10 - 20 Million
Number Employees: 1-4
Type of Packaging: Consumer, Food Service

14008 Superior Pasta Company
905 Christian St
Philadelphia, PA 19147-3807   215-922-7278
    Fax: 215-922-7114
Pasta products
    Owner: Joe Lonanno
Estimated Sales: $1,300,000
Number Employees: 10-19
Type of Packaging: Private Label

14009 Superior Pecan
303 Britt Place
Eufaula, AL 36027-1605   334-687-2031
    Fax: 334-687-2075 800-628-2350
        superiorpecan@earthlink.net
        www.superiorpecan.com
Manufacturer of pecans
    President/Owner: Georgia Hamm
Estimated Sales: $4 Million
Number Employees: 15
Sq. footage: 18000
Type of Packaging: Consumer

14010 Superior Quality Foods
2355 E Francis St
Ontario, CA 91761   909-923-4733
    Fax: 909-947-7065 800-300-4210
        service@superiortouch.com
        www.superiortouch.com
Processor of soup bases, beef extracts, dried season-
ings and sauce mixes
    President: Barbara Lyster
    General Manager: Albert Barriga
    VP Sales/Marketing: Jim Wallace
Estimated Sales: $22.3 Million
Number Employees: 67
Type of Packaging: Food Service, Bulk

14011 Superior Seafood & MeatCompany
623 S Olive Street
South Bend, IN 46619-3309   574-289-0511
    Fax: 574-289-0919
Seafood and meat
    President: Joe Neary Sr

14012 Superior Seafoods
P.O.Box 5596
Tampa, FL 33675-5596   813-248-2749
    Fax: 813-247-4539
Seafood
    President: Ernest Donini
Estimated Sales: $500,000-$1 Million
Number Employees: 1-4

14013 Superior Trading Company
837 Washington St
San Francisco, CA 94108-1290   415-982-8722
    Fax: 415-982-7786 super837@aol.com
        www.superiortrading.com
Processor, importer and exporter of herbal teas,
herbs, soaps and loquat syrups; processor of ginseng
products; wholesaler/distributor and importer of
sports drinks
    President: Michael Chung
    Manager: Anna Lee
    Vice President: Luke Chung
Estimated Sales: $ 5 - 10 Million
Number Employees: 5-9
Sq. footage: 5000
Type of Packaging: Bulk
Brands:
    Nin Jiom
    Superior Herb & Ginseng

14014 Superior's Brand Meats
P.O.Box 571
Massillon, OH 44648-0571   330-830-0356
    Fax: 330-830-3174 www.freshmark.com
Processor of meat products including beef, pork and
luncheon and smoked meat
    President: Neil Gunshaft
    CEO: Neil Genshaft
Estimated Sales: $ 20 - 50 Million
Number Employees: 250-499
Parent Co: Fresh Mark
Type of Packaging: Consumer, Bulk

14015 (HQ)Supermarket Productions
657 Tamagon Drive
PO Box 6124
San Rafael, CA 94903-0124   415-479-0211
    Fax: 415-479-0211 adlman@pacbell.net
Manufacturer of IQF roasted vegetables, also garlic
puree, ginger puree, roasted garlic, jalapeno puree,
frozen entrees and soups; broker of industrial ingredients; serving food processors. A new item now
manuafactured; sweet sliceplantains
    President: Jeffrey Adlman
    CEO: B F Deal
    CFO: L Adlman
    Research & Development: Chef Lisa
    Purchasing Director: Scott Pryor

Number Employees: 12
Sq. footage: 50000
Brands:
    DELIVAMEX
    FRESHLINE FOODS
    FRUVEMEX MEXICALI

14016 Supermoms
625 2nd St
St Paul Park, MN 55071-1807   651-459-2253
    Fax: 651-459-0804 800-944-7276
        www.supermoms.com
Bakery products
    President: Doug Muchow
    Quality Control: Rhonda Brueur
Estimated Sales: $ 10-20 Million
Number Employees: 250-499

14017 Superstore Industries
199 Red Top Rd
Fairfield, CA 94534-9500   707-864-0502
    Fax: 707-864-8203 www.ssica.com
Processor of dairy products including milk, cottage
cheese, yogurt and ice cream; also, orange juice
    Facility Manager: Ron Harris
    Plant Manager: Woody Darnell
Estimated Sales: $ 50 - 100 Million
Number Employees: 100-249
Brands:
    Superstore

14018 Suprema Specialties
14253 S Airport Way
Manteca, CA 95336-8641   209-858-9696
    Fax: 209-858-9599
Milk, cheese, cheeses include mozzarella, parmesan,
ramano, Monterrey jack and chedder cheese
    Owner: Ming Shin-Kou

14019 (HQ)Suprema Specialties
P.O.Box 39
Paterson, NJ 07543-0039   973-684-2900
    Fax: 973-684-8680 800-543-2479
Processor of Italian cheese including parmesan,
romano, mozzarella and ricotta
    Chairman of the Board: Mark Cocchiola
    CEO: Douglas Hopkins
    CFO: Thomas Reed
    VP Sales: Tom Egan
    Plant Manager: William Robles
Estimated Sales: $ 20 - 50 Million
Number Employees: 50-99
Sq. footage: 25000
Type of Packaging: Consumer, Food Service, Pri-
vate Label, Bulk
Other Locations:
    Suprema Specialties
    Manteca CA
Brands:
    Suprema

14020 Supreme Beef
5219 S 2nd Avenue
Dallas, TX 75210-3302   214-428-1761
    Fax: 214-421-3950
Beef
    President/CEO: Steve Spiritas
Estimated Sales: $ 100-500 Million
Number Employees: 250-499

14021 Supreme Chocolatier
1150 South Ave
Staten Island, NY 10314-3404   718-761-9600
    Fax: 718-761-5279
        customerservice@superiorconfections.com
        www.superiorconfections.com
Processor and exporter of chocolate novelties in foil
    President: George Kaye
    VP Marketing: Wayne Stottmeister
Estimated Sales: $6,100,000
Number Employees: 100-249
Type of Packaging: Consumer
Brands:
    Superior Chocolatier
    Superior Confections, Inc.
    The Chocolate Factory

14022 Supreme Dairy Farms Company
111 Kilvert St
Warwick, RI 02886-1083   401-739-8180
    Fax: 401-739-8230 supreme.dairy@verizon.net
        www.supremedairyfarms.com

Processor and importer of tomato products; also, mozzarella and ricotta cheese
President: Paul Areson
Estimated Sales: $7000000
Number Employees: 10-19
Sq. footage: 14000
Type of Packaging: Food Service, Private Label
Brands:
AVANTI
SUPREME DAIRY FARMS

14023 Supreme Frozen Products
5813 W Grand Avenue
Chicago, IL 60639-2812   773-622-3336
Fax: 773-622-3350   johnp@supremetamale.com
www.supremetamale.com
Processor of Mexican food including tamales, chili, fajitas and burritos
President: John Paklaian
Estimated Sales: $ 5 - 10 Million
Number Employees: 5-9

14024 Supreme Frozen Products
5813 W Grand Ave
Chicago, IL 60639-2812   773-622-3777
Fax: 773-622-3350   888-643-0405
johnp@supremetamale.com
www.supremetamale.com
Beef tamales, been and bean burritos, beeh chili with beans, crispy pizza fluffs
Owner: John Pak
Estimated Sales: $ 5-10 Million
Number Employees: 10-19

14025 Supreme Rice Mill
P.O.Box 490
Crowley, LA 70527-0490   337-783-5222
Fax: 337-783-3204   staff@supremerice.com
www.supremerice.com
Manufacturer and exporter of white and brown rice and quick-cooking white and brown rice
Chairman: Gordon Dore
President/CEO: William Dore
VP: Georgette Dugas
Estimated Sales: $100 Million
Number Employees: 50-99
Brands:
SOFGRAIN
SUPREME

14026 Suram Trading Corporation
2655 S Le Jeune Rd # 1006
Coral Gables, FL 33134-5844   305-448-7165
Fax: 305-445-7185 www.suram.com
Frozen seafood-shrimp
President: Guido Adler
CFO: Ana Adler
Marketing Director: José Pelaez Pelaez
Estimated Sales: $ 50-100 Million
Number Employees: 5-9
Brands:
Suram

14027 Sure Fresh Produce
1302 W Stowell Rd
Santa Maria, CA 93458-9730   805-349-2677
Fax: 805-349-2674   888-423-5379
www.surefreshproduce.com
Industrial frozen vegetable ingredient manufacturer of both conventional and organic bulk products
President: Dale Johnson
CFO: Renee Kolding
Quality Control: Corrie Landymore
Marketing Director: Matthew Johnson
Sales Director: Loren Hiltner
Production Manager: Diego Prieto
Plant Manager/Purchasing: Steve Rangel
Estimated Sales: $10-20 Million
Number Employees: 100-249
Number of Products: 750
Sq. footage: 50000
Type of Packaging: Food Service, Bulk
Brands:
Sure Fresh

14028 Sure-Good Food Distributors
6361 Thompson Rd
Syracuse, NY 13206-1448   315-422-1196
Fax: 315-478-5220
Fresh and frozen poultry
President: Jerry Savlov
Estimated Sales: $ 10-20 Million
Number Employees: 10-19

14029 Surface Banana Company
P.O.Box 3153
Bluewell, WV 24701-8153   304-589-7202
Fax: 304-589-7252
Processor of bananas and tomatoes; importer of bananas
Owner: David Surface
Estimated Sales: $300,000-500,000
Number Employees: 1-4

14030 Surlean Food Solutions
1545 S San Marcos
San Antonio, TX 78207-7090   210-227-4370
Fax: 210-226-4208   800-999-4370
dscott@surleanfoods.com
www.surleanfoods.com
Manufacturer of meats, soups, sauces, marinades and more
President: Daryl Scott
VP Sales: Neal Leonard
Estimated Sales: $100+ Million
Number Employees: 250-499
Type of Packaging: Food Service

14031 Susie's South 40 Confections
P.O.Box 4040
Midland, TX 79704-4040   432-570-4040
Fax: 432-682-4040   800-221-4442
CustService@susiessouthforty.com
www.susiessouthforty.com
Toffee, pralines, fudge, gift baskets, gift tins
President/Owner: Susie Hitchcock-Hall
Estimated Sales: $ 3 - 5 Million
Number Employees: 10-19
Type of Packaging: Consumer

14032 Susquehanna Valley Winery
802 Mount Zion Dr
Danville, PA 17821-8613   570-275-2364
Fax: 570-275-5813
Wine
Owner: Miklos Latranyi
Partner: Mark Latranyi
Marketing Manager: Hildetard Latranyi
Estimated Sales: Below $ 5 Million
Number Employees: 1-4
Brands:
Susquehanna Valley

14033 Sustainable Sourcing
PO Box 967
Great Barrington, MA 01230   413-528-5141
Fax: 413-528-5172   sales@himalasalt.com
www.himalasalt.com
organic peppercorns, spices and artisan salt blends
President/Owner: Melissa Kushi
Estimated Sales: $1.5 Million
Number Employees: 10

14034 Suter Company
258 May St
Sycamore, IL 60178-1395   815-895-9186
Fax: 815-895-4814   800-435-6942
www.suterco.com
Processor of canned and refrigerated salads including tuna, chicken, ham, egg and seafood; also, shelf stable lunch kits, deviled egg kits
President: Tim Suter
VP Sales/Marketing: Heidi Wright
Estimated Sales: $ 20 - 50 Million
Number Employees: 100-249
Sq. footage: 75000
Type of Packaging: Consumer, Food Service, Private Label, Bulk
Brands:
Alaska Bay
Suter
Sycamore Farms

14035 Sutherland's Foodservice
P.O.Box 786
Forest Park, GA 30298-0786   404-366-8550
Fax: 404-366-8599   cservice@suthfood.com
www.suthfood.com
Dairy, frozen foods, fresh and frozen meat, fresh and frozen poultry, fresh and frozen seafood, dry grocery, nonfood, and produce. Also represents 100s of brands, for a complete listing see their website.
President: Gene Sutherland Sr
Estimated Sales: $ 20 - 50 Million
Number Employees: 100-249

14036 Sutter Home Winery
P.O.Box 248
St Helena, CA 94574-0248   707-963-3104
Fax: 707-963-2381   legan@suterhome.com
www.tfewines.com
Processor and exporter of wines
CEO: Louis Trinchero
Executive VP: Jim Miller
Marketing Director: Rob Celsi
Public Relations: Stan Hock
Operations Manager: Bob Torres
Plant Manager: Jim Huntsinger
Purchasing Manager: Bryan Lilienthal
Estimated Sales: $250000000
Number Employees: 100-249
Brands:
Sutter Home

14037 Sutton Honey Farms
143 Conn Lane
Lancaster, KY 40444-9706   859-792-4277
Fax: 859-792-4277
Processor and packer of nonfiltered and creamed honey with fruit and cinnamon
President: Rick Sutton
VP: Dianne Sutton
Marketing Director: Dianne Sutton
Sq. footage: 4000
Type of Packaging: Consumer, Private Label, Bulk
Brands:
Sutton's

14038 Suwannee Packing Company
PO Box 490
Live Oak, FL 32064-0490   904-362-1422
Processor and wholesaler/distributor of meat products including beef and pork
Manager: Lavell Croft
Type of Packaging: Consumer, Food Service

14039 Suzanna's Kitchen
4025 Buford Hwy
Duluth, GA 30096-4137   770-476-9900
Fax: 770-476-8899   800-241-2455
www.suzannaskitchen.com
Manufacturer of frozen heat and serve meat products including pork, veal, beef, turkey, barbecue, ribs, corn dogs and chicken breasts, breast strips, chicken patties and wings.
President: Barbara Howard
CEO: Brad Howard
CFO: David Ashton
COO: Brad Howard
Operations Manager: Judith Adams
Estimated Sales: $20-50 Million
Number Employees: 250-499
Number of Products: 125
Sq. footage: 236000
Type of Packaging: Food Service, Private Label
Brands:
SUZANNA'S

14040 Suzanne's Specialties
421 Jersey Avenue
Suite B
New Brunswick, NJ 08901   732-828-8500
Fax: 732-828-8563   800-762-2135
info@suzannes-specialties.com
www.suzannes-specialties.com
All natural, vegan and organic sweetners, dessert and toppings.
President: Susan Allen-Morano
VP: James Allen
Number Employees: 10-19
Type of Packaging: Consumer, Food Service, Bulk
Brands:
Rice Nectar
Sunrice
Sunshine's
Suzanne's Conserves

14041 Suzanne's Sweets
PO Box 547
Katonah, NY 10536   914-301-5307
Fax: 914-232-1291 www.suzannesweets.com
rugelach

14042 Suzuki's Ice Castle
238 N School Street
Honolulu, HI 96817-3166   808-533-1166
Fax: 808-533-1166   suzuki004@hawaii.rr.com

100% Kona coffee, cookies, gel snacks, hybrid papayas, ice pops, portion pack, portuguese sausage, pours, soft serve, syrups.
President: Dennis Yoshio Suzuki
Estimated Sales: Below $ 5 Million
Number Employees: 2
Number of Brands: 10
Number of Products: 15
Sq. footage: 1000
Parent Co: Suzuki Industries
Brands:
Suzuki's Ice Castle

14043 Svenhard's Swedish Bakery
P.O.Box 24034
Oakland, CA 94623-1034 510-834-5035
Fax: 510-839-6797 800-333-7836
ccare@svenhards.com www.svenhards.com
Manufacturer of pastries such as; cinnamon rolls and danishes
President: Ronny Svenhard
Estimated Sales: 100+ Million
Number Employees: 1-4
Sq. footage: 90000
Type of Packaging: Consumer, Food Service
Other Locations:
Svenhard's Swedish Bakery
Exeter CA
Brands:
SVENHARDS

14044 Swagger Foods Corporation
900 Corporate Woods Pkwy
Vernon Hills, IL 60061-3155 847-913-1200
Fax: 847-913-1263 info@swaggerfoods.com
www.swaggerfoods.com
Supplying the industrial, food service and retail markets as a manufacturer of seasonings, functional foods with vitamins, minerals, omega-3, other micronutrients/nutraceuticals, salt substitutes, soup mixes/bases, rubs, marinadesgravy/sauce mixes, dip/dressing mixes, drink mixes, side dish mixes and other dry blends including Ethnic.
President: Tai Shin PhD
Number Employees: 1-4
Type of Packaging: Consumer, Food Service, Private Label, Bulk
Brands:
BITS O' BUTTER
FANCY PANTRY
HEALTH-FU'D
SPICE SO RITE
SWAGGER

14045 Swan Joseph Vineyards
2916 Laguna Rd
Forestville, CA 95436-3729 707-573-3747
Fax: 707-575-1605 rod@swanwinery.com
www.swanwinery.com
Wines
Owner: Rod Berglin
President: Rod Berglund
CEO: Lynn Swan-Berglund
Estimated Sales: Less than $500,000
Number Employees: 1-4
Brands:
Swan Joseph

14046 Swanson Vineyards & Winery
P.O.Box 459
Rutherford, CA 94573-0459 707-967-3500
Fax: 707-967-3505 800-942-0809
www.swansonvineyards.com
Wines
Owner: W Clarke Swanson
Sales Manager: Michael Opdegraff
Winemaker: Marco Capell
Estimated Sales: $5-9.9 Million
Number Employees: 20-49
Brands:
Swanson Vineyards & Winery

14047 Swanton's Packing
1722 Skunk Hill Road
Fairfax, VT 05454-5416 802-868-4469
Fax: 802-868-4312
Processor and packer of beef and veal
President: Sandy Read
VP Marketing: Frank Read
Number Employees: 32
Type of Packaging: Consumer, Food Service, Bulk

14048 Swatt Baking Company
222 Homer St
Olean, NY 14760-1132 716-372-9480
Fax: 716-373-6019 800-370-6656
www.lacinnamonbread.com
Processor of rolls, regular and cinnamon bread and cinnamon bread sauce
President: Leonard Anzivine
VP: Lee Anzivine
Estimated Sales: $700000
Number Employees: 10-19
Sq. footage: 9400
Type of Packaging: Food Service, Bulk
Brands:
L.A. Cinnamon

14049 Swedish Hill Vineyard
4565 State Route 414
Romulus, NY 14541-9769 315-549-8326
Fax: 315-549-8477 888-549-9463
info@swedishhill.com www.swedishhill.com
Wines
President: Richard Peterson
Quality Control: David Peterson
Estimated Sales: $ 10-24.9 Million
Number Employees: 30
Brands:
Swedish Hill

14050 Sweeney's Gourmet Coffee Roast
671 Middlegate Road
Suite C
Henderson, NV 89011-2628 702-558-0505
Fax: 702-558-3799 www.sweenycoffee.com
Coffee
President: Robert Sweeney
Estimated Sales: $ 2.5-5 Million
Number Employees: 1
Type of Packaging: Private Label, Bulk

14051 Sweenor Chocolate
21 Charles St
Wakefield, RI 02879-3621 401-783-4433
Fax: 401-783-9340 800-834-3123
brian@sweenorchocolates.com
www.sweenorschocolates.com
Processor of chocolates, hard candies, fudge and mints
President: William Sweenor
Vice President: Brian Sweenor
Estimated Sales: $ 5 - 10 Million
Number Employees: 20-49
Type of Packaging: Consumer, Private Label, Bulk

14052 Sweet & Saucy Inc
5974 S Pennsylvania
Centennial, CO 80121 303-807-5132
Fax: 303-798-8258 jane@sweetandsaucy.net
www.sweetandsaucy.net
21 flavors of gourmet caramel and chocolate sauces.
President: Jane Jones
Vice President: Erin Jones
CMO: Robert Jones
COO: Brent Jones
Number of Brands: 1
Number of Products: 21
Type of Packaging: Consumer, Food Service
Brands:
SWEET & SAUCY CARAMEL SAUCES
SWEET & SAUCY CHOCOLATE SAUCES

14053 Sweet Baby Ray's
Po'Box 849
Marlboro, MA 01752 877-729-2229
service@sweetbabyrays.com
www.sweetbabyrays.com
Processor of barbecue and hot and spicy sauce
Estimated Sales: $ 20-50 Million
Number Employees: 13
Parent Co: Ken's Foods
Type of Packaging: Consumer, Food Service
Brands:
Sweet Baby Ray's

14054 Sweet Blessings
23805 Stuart Ranch Rd
Malibu, CA 90265-4856 310-317-1172
Fax: 310-317-1132 www.sweet-blessings.com
Chocolates
President: Dave Singelyn
CEO/Owner: B Wayne Hughes
VP Sales: Mark Bontempo
Estimated Sales: $ 3 - 5 Million
Number Employees: 5-9

Brands:
NOAHS BUDDIES
SWEET BLESSINGS

14055 Sweet Candy Company
P.O.Box 22450
Salt Lake City, UT 84122-0450 801-886-1444
Fax: 801-886-1404 800-669-8669
mail@sweetcandy.com www.sweetcandy.com
Processor of confectionery products including brittles, chocolates, holiday novelties, filled items, jellies, hard candies, jelly beans, marshmallows, mints, nougats, glazed nuts, taffy, etc.; also, in bags
Founder/President: Leon Sweet
VP: Kenneth DuVall
Estimated Sales: $113,000,000
Number Employees: 100-249
Sq. footage: 180000
Type of Packaging: Consumer, Bulk

14056 Sweet City Supply
5908 Thurston Avenue
Virginia Beach, VA 23455-3309 757-456-4800
Fax: 757-456-9980 888-793-3824
candysales@sweetcity.com www.sweetcity.com
A contract manufacturer and national distributor of imported and domestic bulk and packaged candy, nuts, and confections.
President: Ronald Bublick
Type of Packaging: Food Service, Bulk

14057 Sweet Corn Products Company
P.O.Box 487
Bloomfield, NE 68718-0487 402-373-2211
Fax: 402-373-2219 877-628-6115
scpray@bloomnet.com
www.no-nobirdfeeder.com
Processor and exporter of sweet corn products including dry mature for tortilla chips and toasted nuts
General Manager: Raymon Lush
Estimated Sales: $2000000
Number Employees: 1-4
Sq. footage: 23000
Type of Packaging: Consumer, Food Service, Private Label, Bulk
Brands:
Ugly Nut

14058 Sweet Earth Natural Foods
597 Lighthouse Ave
Pacific Grove, CA 93950-2646 831-375-8673
Fax: 831-375-3441 800-737-3311
www.sweetearth.us
Processor of vegetarian foods including soups, salads, burritos, salad dressings, salsa, hummus, vegeburgers, sweet bars, pies and seitan(wheat-meat)
Owner: Russell Hicks
Co-Owner: Caren Hicks
Estimated Sales: $ 3 - 5 Million
Number Employees: 10-19
Sq. footage: 2000
Type of Packaging: Consumer, Food Service, Bulk
Brands:
Awaken Foods
Fiesta Rice
Grand Life Seitan
Heat-N-Eat
Sweet Earth Natural Foods

14059 Sweet Endings
1220 Old Okeechobee Rd
West Palm Beach, FL 33401-6947 561-655-0334
Fax: 561-655-1227 888-635-1177
swtend@aol.com
Processor and exporter of cakes, pies, tortes and crumbles including sugar and fat-free
Owner: Judy Mercur
Estimated Sales: $ 3 - 5 Million
Number Employees: 20-49
Sq. footage: 6000
Type of Packaging: Food Service, Private Label

14060 Sweet Fortunes of America
783a Yerry Hill Road
Woodstock, NY 12498 845-679-7327
Fax: 845-679-7327
Gourmet and specialty foods
President: Carol Lieberman

14061 Sweet Gallery ExclusivePastry
350 Bering Avenue
Toronto, ON M8Z 3A9
Canada   416-232-1539
        Fax: 416-232-1482 sweetg@on.aibn.com
                www.toronto.com/sweetgallery
Processer of sponge cakes, butter cream tortes, pastries, croissants, wedding cakes, danishes and European cakes and pastries
        President: Radi Jelenic
        President: Lidija Jelenic
Number Employees: 20-49
Sq. footage: 5000
Type of Packaging: Consumer

14062 Sweet Green Field LLC
11 Bellwether Way
Unit 305
Bellingham, WA 98225   360-483-4555
        Fax: 360-483-4554 www.sweetgreenfields.com
Sweeteners
        CEO: Dean Francis
        SVP Sales/Marketing: Mike Quin

14063 Sweet Leaf Tea Company
515 South Congress
Suite 700
Austin, TX 78704   512-328-7775
        Fax: 512-328-7725 www.sweetleaftea.com
teas, lemonades, mixers and fixers
        Founder/CEO: Clayton Christopher
        CFO/COO: Brian Goldberg
        Marketing Director: Adi Wilk
        Co-Founder/VP of Sales: David Smith
        Manager Finance/Human Resources: Elizabeth Barber
        VP Operations: Robert Walker
        Production/Logistics Manager: Brian Selensky
Estimated Sales:$1.1 Million
Number Employees: 10

14064 Sweet Life Enterprises
2350 Pullman St
Santa Ana, CA 92705-5507   949-417-3205
        Fax: 949-261-7470 www.sweetlifeinc.com
Processor and exporter of cinnamon rolls and cookies inluding chocolate chip, double fudge chocolate, oatmeal raisin, sugar, peanut butter, white chocolate, snickerdoodle, etc
        CEO: Michael Gray
Estimated Sales:$ 50 - 100 Million
Number Employees: 100-249
Brands:
        The Sweet Life

14065 Sweet Mele's Hawaiian Products
PO Box 218
Kailua, HI 96734
        Fax: 812-537-1971 800-990-8441
        sales@sweetmeles.com   www.sweetmeles.com
Flavored Macadamia nut oil, stir-fry sauces, BBQ sauces, fruit bars, preserves, pancake mix, breakfast gift sets. lemonades, ice tea, coconut chew bars, coconut pineapple butter.
Parent Co: CB International

14066 Sweet Mountain Magic
2131 N Larrabee Street
Apt 6205
Chicago, IL 60614-4422   773-755-4539
                                Fax: 703-437-1031
Ice cream
        President: Stephen Kleiman
        VP Marketing: Ehtel Hammer

14067 Sweet Productions
P.O.Box 275
Jericho, NY 11753-0275   631-842-0548
        Fax: 631-842-0805 sweetsltd@aol.com
                www.sweetproductionsltd.com
Processor and exporter of nutritional bars including fat-free, low-fat coated, meal replacement, high protein, multi-nutrient and herbal composition; also, coatings; custom development services available
        President: Paul Schacher
        CEO: Ben Cohen
        VP: Joseph Pizzo
        Purchasing Manager: Robert Sixnel
Estimated Sales:$60000000
Number Employees: 20-49
Sq. footage: 80000
Type of Packaging: Consumer

14068 Sweet Sam's Baking Company
1049 Zerega Avenue
Bronx, NY 10462-5401   718-822-0599
        Fax: 718-409-0309 richardsklar@hotmail.com
                www.sweetsams.com
Premium all butter bakery products
Estimated Sales:$ 5 - 10 Million
Number Employees: 85

14069 Sweet Shop
1113 Caledonia St
La Crosse, WI 54603-2515   608-784-7724
Processor of ice cream and chocolate
        Owner: Bill Espe
Estimated Sales:$160000
Number Employees: 5-9
Type of Packaging: Consumer

14070 Sweet Shop
625 Stayton Street
Fort Worth, TX 76107-2322   817-332-7941
        Fax: 817-336-9169 800-222-2269
                annan@econfections.com
                www.econfections.com
Processor of confectionery products, handmade chocolates, truffles, nut cluster bars and caramels
        Co-President: James H Webb
        Co-President: Paul Anderson
        VP: Betsy Oldham
        Purchasing Manager: Kenneth Faulk
Estimated Sales:$9,800,000
Number Employees: 110
Type of Packaging: Consumer, Private Label, Bulk

14071 Sweet Shop USA
1316 Industrial Rd
Mt Pleasant, TX 75455-2614   903-575-0033
        Fax: 903-336-9169 dmillican@econfections.com
                www.sweetshopusa.com
Manufacturer of gourmet chocolates
        CEO: Jim Webb
        Marketing/New Product Development: Anna Parker
Estimated Sales:$ 10 - 20 Million
Number Employees: 50-99
Sq. footage: 66000
Type of Packaging: Private Label, Bulk
Brands:
        ANNACLAIRE'S
        PRICE'S FINE CHOCOLATES
        SWEET SHOP

14072 Sweet Shop USA
1316 Industrial Rd
Mt Pleasant, TX 75455-2614   903-575-0033
        Fax: 903-336-9169 800-222-2269
        toffee@mwtoffee.com   www.sweetshopusa.com
Toffee covered in milk chocolate with pecans or almonds
        President: Jim Webb
Estimated Sales:$ 10 - 20 Million
Number Employees: 50-99
Type of Packaging: Consumer, Food Service, Private Label

14073 Sweet Sides
PO Box 8046
Mission Hills, CA 91346-8046   818-832-0174
        Fax: 818-832-0184 bbqsweet@sweetsides.com
                www.sweetsides.com
Berry sauces and condiments
        President: Judy England
Number of Brands: 1
Number of Products: 8
Type of Packaging: Consumer, Food Service, Private Label, Bulk
Brands:
        SWEETSIDES

14074 Sweet Street Desserts
P.O.Box 15127
Reading, PA 19612-5127   610-929-0616
        Fax: 610-921-8195 800-793-3897
        custservice@sweetstreet.com
                www.sweetstreet.com
Variety of coffee bar and desserts: hazelnut cappucino torte, apple crumb cake, chocolate chip crumb cake, sour cream coffee cake
        President: Sandy Solmon
Estimated Sales:$39400000
Number Employees: 5-9
Type of Packaging: Consumer, Food Service
Brands:
        Sweet Street

14075 Sweet Sue Kitchens
106 Sweet Sue Drive
Athens, AL 35611-2181   256-216-0500
                                Fax: 256-216-0531
Processor and exporter of canned poultry products including chicken broth, chunks, stew and dumplings
        Sales/Marketing Executive: Shirley Brown
        Plant Manager: Bob Mahan
        Purchasing Agent: Carol Moore
Number Employees: 250-499
Parent Co: Sara Lee Corporation
Type of Packaging: Consumer, Food Service, Private Label

14076 Sweet Swiss Confections
7821 W Electric Ave
Spokane, WA 99224-9000   509-838-1334
        Fax: 509-456-0824 chocologos@sweetswiss.com
                www.sweetswiss.com
Chocolate truffles, marzipan and personalized chocolate logos
        President: Matt Phillipson
        Controller: Pam Martin
        Vice President: Phina Phillipson
*Estimated Sales:*Below $ 5 Million
Number Employees: 5-9

14077 Sweet Traders
5362 Oceanus Dr # C
Huntington Beach, CA 92649-1000 714-903-6800
        Fax: 714-892-4345 info@sweettraders.com
                www.sweettraders.com
Wine, chocolate, baked goods, and gift baskets; including chocolate wrapped wines and ciders, champagnes and nonalcoholic beverages
        Owner: R Louw
*Estimated Sales:*Under $500,000
Number Employees: 1-4
Sq. footage: 2500
Type of Packaging: Consumer, Private Label

14078 Sweet Water Seafood Corporation
369 Washington Ave
Carlstadt, NJ 07072-2805   201-939-6622
                                Fax: 201-939-4014
Processor of frozen shellfish including squid, conch, clams and mussels
        Manager: Teri Niece
        Chairman: Robert Inglese
Estimated Sales:$500,000-$1 Million
Number Employees: 1-4
Sq. footage: 33000
Type of Packaging: Consumer, Food Service, Private Label, Bulk
Brands:
        Mussel King
        Plumpy

14079 Sweet Works
248 State Road 312
St Augustine, FL 32086-4241   904-825-1700
        Fax: 904-824-0436 877-261-7887
        info@sweetworks.net
                www.whetstonechocolates.com
Manufacturers, sells, and distributes chocolate, candy and gum products in the North American and worldwide confectionery markets.
        Owner: Virigina Whetstone
        CEO: Philip Terranova
        VP Sales: Tom Fox
Number Employees: 250-499
Other Locations:
        Sweetworks
        Buffalo NY
        Sweetworks
        Toronto, Canada
Brands:
        NIAGARA CHOCOLATES
        OAK LEAF CONFECTIONS
        WHETSTONE CANDY

14080 Sweet'N Low
2 Cumberland St
Brooklyn, NY 11205-1000   718-858-4200
        Fax: 718-858-6386 www.cpack.com
        President: Marvin Eisenstadt
        CFO/Director: Stephen Isaacs
        VP Marketing/Sales: Jeffrey Eisenstadt
Estimated Sales:$100+ Million
Number Employees: 250-499
Brands:
        SWEET'N LOW

14081 SweetWorks Inc
3500 Genesee Street
Buffalo, NY 14225   716-634-0880
     Fax: 716-634-4855 www.sweetworks.net
chocolates, candy and gum products
     President/CEO: Philip Terranova
     CFO: Ralph Nicosia
     Marketing Director: Jeanne Palka
     Sales Director: Jerry Tubbs

14082 Sweetbliss by Ilene C Shane
40 W 27th St
Fl 11
New York, NY 10001   212-725-6970
     Fax: 212-725-6976 info@sweetbliss.com
                       www.sweetbliss.com
chocolates
     President/Owner: Ilene Shane
     VP: Iris Libby
Number Employees: 4

14083 Sweetcraft Candies
PO Box 15
Timonium, MD 21094-0015   410-252-0684
                       Fax: 410-252-0352
Candy
     President: George George

14084 Sweetery
1814 E Greenville St
Anderson, SC 29621-2035   864-224-8394
     Fax: 864-224-8469 800-752-1188
thesweetery@carol.net   www.thesweetery.com
Processor of southern comfort baked goods includ-
ing cakes, cheesecakes and pies
     President: Jane Jarahian
Estimated Sales: Under $500,000
Number Employees: 20-49
Type of Packaging: Consumer, Private Label
Brands:
     Southern Special
     Uggly Cake

14085 Sweetwater Brewing Company
195 Ottley Dr NE
Atlanta, GA 30324-3924   404-691-2537
     Fax: 404-691-0936 Steve@sweetwaterbrew.com
                       www.sweetwaterbrew.com
Processor of ale and stout
     President: Freddy Bensch
     Sales: Dave Guender
Estimated Sales: $ 2.5-5 Million
Number Employees: 5-9
Type of Packaging: Consumer, Food Service
Brands:
     Sweetwater
     Sweetwater 42
     Sweetwater Blue

14086 Sweetwater Spice Company
3800 N Lamar Blvd
Suite 730-155
Austin, TX 78756   800-531-6079
     Fax: 512-857-0083 www.sweetwaterspice.com
sauces and marinades

14087 Sweety Novelty
633 Monterey Pass Rd
Monterey Park, CA 91754-2418   626-282-4482
                       Fax: 626-282-2482
Processor of frozen fruit bars and ice cream includ-
ing red bean, mango, green tea, durian, peanut and
taro; also, mocha ice cream including green tea, va-
nilla, strawberry, mango and taro
     President: Tracy Lee
Estimated Sales: $870000
Number Employees: 10-19
Sq. footage: 16000
Type of Packaging: Consumer, Food Service

14088 (HQ)Swift & Company
1770 Promontory Cir
Greeley, CO 80634-9039   970-324-2180
     Fax: 970-506-8307 emailus@swiftbrands.com
                       www.swiftbrands.com
Provides quality beef and pork products to consum-
ers nationwide
     President/CEO: Sam Rovit
     EVP Customers and Supply Chains: Kevin Yost
     EVP Operations: Ted Miller
Number Employees: 10,000+
Parent Co: ConAgra Refigerated Prepared Foods
Type of Packaging: Consumer

14089 Swift & Company
1770 Promontory Cir
Greeley, CO 80634-9039   970-324-2180
     Fax: 970-506-8307 emailus@Swiftbrands.com
                       www.Swiftbrands.com
Processor of brown and serve sausage, hard salami,
pepperoni and mortadella
     Chairman: George Gillet Jr
     CEO/Director: Sam Rovit
     Executive VP/CFO: Danny Herron
     Plant Manager: Jim Brown
Estimated Sales: $100+ Million
Number Employees: 500-999
Parent Co: ConAgra Refigerated Prepared Foods
Type of Packaging: Consumer, Food Service, Pri-
vate Label, Bulk

14090 Swire Coca-Cola
12634 S 265 W
Draper, UT 84020-7930   801-816-5300
                       Fax: 801-816-5342 www.swirecc.com
Processor of soft drinks
     President/CEO: Jack Pelo
     VP/General Manager: Paul Lukanowski
     VP Manufacturing: Kurt Fiedler
Estimated Sales: $100+ Million
Number Employees: 100-249
Sq. footage: 400000
Parent Co: Swire Pacific Holdings
Type of Packaging: Food Service

14091 Swiss American Sausage Corporation
251 Darcy Pkwy
Lathrop, CA 95330-8756   209-858-5555
     Fax: 209-858-1102 info@sasausage.com
                       www.sasausage.com
Processor of sausage, salami and pepperoni
     president: Theodore Arena
     CEO: Theodore Arena
     Human Resources: Heidi Moore
Number Employees: 100-249
Brands:
     Swiss American Sausage

14092 (HQ)Swiss Chalet Fine Foods
9455 NW 40th Street Rd
Doral, FL 33178-2941   305-592-0008
     Fax: 305-592-1651 800-347-9477
     sales@scff.com   www.scff.com
A wide range of quality gourmet products from
sweets to savories
     CEO: Y Hans Baumann
Estimated Sales: $300,000-500,000
Number Employees: 10-19
Brands:
     Felchlin-Swiss
     Haco
     Hero

14093 Swiss Colony
1112 7th Ave
Monroe, WI 53566-1364   608-328-8400
     Fax: 608-328-8457 www.swisscolony.com
Manufacturer of cheese and food gift baskets
     President: John Baumann
Estimated Sales: $50 Million
Number Employees: 1,000-4,999
Sq. footage: 1000000
Brands:
     SWISS COLONY FOODS

14094 Swiss Dairy
12171 Madera Way
Riverside, CA 92503-4849   951-898-9427
                       Fax: 951-734-3786
Processor of milk
     Office Manager: Lorry Olson
Estimated Sales: $ .5 - 1 million
Number Employees: 5-9
Parent Co: Suiza Dairy Group
Type of Packaging: Consumer, Food Service

14095 Swiss Food Products
4333 W Division St
Chicago, IL 60651-1792   773-394-6480
                       Fax: 773-394-6475
     sales@swissfoodproducts.com
                       www.swissfoodproducts.com
Manufacturer and exporter of bases including soup,
gravy, browning, seasoning and sauce; also, flavors
     President: Paul Kalpake
     Vice President: Senya Kalpake

Estimated Sales: $ 5 - 10 Million
Number Employees: 10-19
Sq. footage: 25000
Type of Packaging: Consumer, Food Service, Pri-
vate Label, Bulk
Brands:
     Swiss

14096 Swiss Heritage Cheese
114 E Coates Ave
Monticello, WI 53570-9828   608-938-4455
     Fax: 608-938-1325 www.swissheritagewines.com
Cheese
     President/Treasurer: Paul Rufener
Estimated Sales: $1,600,000
Number Employees: 5-9
Brands:
     Swiss Heritage Cheese

14097 Swiss Valley Farms Company
247 Research Parkway
PO Box 4493
Davenport, IA 52808   563-468-6600
     linda.lee@swissvalley.com
                       www.swissvalley.com
Beverages (dairy and non-dairy), cultured products
(cottage cheese, yogurt, sour cream, dip) and cheese
     CEO: Donald Boelens
     VP Finance: Greg Rexwinkel
     VP Quality/R&D: Jeff Ryan
     VP Sales/Marketing: Jeff Saforek
     VP Human Resources: Deb Sullivan
     VP Operations: Ed Seutter
Estimated Sales: 525,000,000
Number Employees: 20-49
Type of Packaging: Consumer
Other Locations:
     Luana IA
     Mindoro WI

14098 (HQ)Swiss Valley Farms Company
P.O.Box 4493
Davenport, IA 52808-4493   563-468-6600
     Fax: 563-468-6614 www.swissvalley.com
Processor of dry and fresh dairy products including
milk, soft serve ice cream mixes and cheese includ-
ing cheddar, swiss, cream and cottage
     Vice President of Membership: J Gordon Toyne
     CFO: Donald Boelens
     Vice President of Administrative Service: Tom
     Stonz
     Sales/Marketing Executive: Stan Woodworth
Estimated Sales: $525 Million
Number Employees: 20-49
Type of Packaging: Consumer, Food Service, Pri-
vate Label, Bulk

14099 Swiss Valley Farms Company
3510 Central Ave
Dubuque, IA 52001-1182   563-582-7206
     Fax: 563-582-4723 800-397-9156
     webmaster@swissvalley.com
                       www.swissvalley.com
Manufacturer of Milk bottling
     President: J Gordon Toyne
     Co-CEO/CFO: Don Boelens
     Operations: Joe Holbrook
Estimated Sales: $20 Million
Number Employees: 100-249
Sq. footage: 70000
Parent Co: Swiss Valley Farms Company
Type of Packaging: Consumer, Food Service

14100 Swiss Valley Farms Company
133 F Avenue NW
Cedar Rapids, IA 52405-2735   319-364-8153
     Fax: 319-364-3995 www.swissvalley.com
Processor of ice cream mix, milk, cream, cottage
cheese and orange juice
     CEO: J Gordon Toyne
     CFO: Don Boelens
     Plant Manager: Tony Anderson
Estimated Sales: $ 20 - 50 Million
Number Employees: 50-99
Parent Co: Swiss Valley Farms Company
Type of Packaging: Consumer, Private Label

14101 Swiss Way Cheese
1315 Us Highway 27 N
Berne, IN 46711-1031   260-589-3531
     Fax: 219-589-3843 swoss@swissway.com
                       www.swissway.com

Cheese
President: Tim Ehlerding
Operations Manager: Russ Reimer
Estimated Sales: $ 2.5 Million appx.
Number Employees: 5-9
Type of Packaging: Private Label
Brands:
Berne Baby Swiss
Berne Swiss Lace

14102 (HQ)Swiss-American
4200 Papin St
St Louis, MO 63110-1736   314-533-2224
Fax: 314-533-0765 800-325-8150
jweil@swissamerican.com
www.swissamerican.com
Packer, importer and distributor of cheese and fine foods
President: Joseph Hoff
CEO: R Weil
VP: D Boyd
Operations VP: David Boyd
Estimated Sales: $ 5 - 10 Million
Number Employees: 50-99
Sq. footage: 45000
Type of Packaging: Consumer, Bulk
Other Locations:
Swiss-American
North Charleston SC
Brands:
Capricorn
Dutch Garden
Dutch Garden Super Swiss
Epic
Fire Jack
Freshwrap Cuts
Freshwrap Slices
Mr. Sharp
Saint Louis
Verdaccio

14103 Swiss-American Sausage Company
251 Darcy Pkwy
Lathrop, CA 95330-8756   209-858-5555
Fax: 209-858-1102 info@sasausage.com
www.sasausage.com
Processor and exporter of meat pizza toppings including pepperoni, salami, ham, linguica and raw and cooked sausage
President/CEO: Theodore Arena
Human Resources: Heidi Moore
Sales Manager: Paul Sheehan
Estimated Sales: $300,000-500,000
Number Employees: 50-99
Sq. footage: 90000
Type of Packaging: Food Service, Private Label
Brands:
Capo Di Monte

14104 Swissart Candy Company
455 Braen Avenue
Wyckoff, NJ 07481-2949   201-447-0062
Fax: 201-447-1455
Candy
Number Employees: 10-19
Type of Packaging: Private Label
Brands:
Swissart

14105 Swisser Sweet Maple
6242 Swiss Road
Castorland, NY 13620-1244   315-346-1034
Fax: 315-346-1662 swisser@tweny.rr.com
www.swissermaple.com
Pure NY maple syrup, pure maple cream spread, maple candies, maple lollipops, maple granulated sugar, gift arrangements, wedding party favors and corporate gifts. Retail, wholesale and bulk.
Co-Owner: Barbara Zehr
Co-Owner: Jason Zehr
Number Employees: 4-6
Type of Packaging: Consumer, Private Label, Bulk
Other Locations:
Swisser Sweet Maple
Casta-Land NY

14106 Swissland Milk
818 Welty St
Berne, IN 46711-1263   260-589-2761
Fax: 260-589-2761 www.swisslandcheese.com
Milk and yogurt
General Manager: Kirk Johnson

Estimated Sales: $ 1-2.5 Million
Number Employees: 10-19

14107 Swissland Packing Company
3a W Nebraska Street
Frankfort, IL 60423-1417   815-698-2382
Fax: 815-698-2264 800-321-8325
Processor and exporter of fresh and frozen veal
President: Arthur Follenweider IV
VP: David Follenweider
Sales: Stu Bruni
Estimated Sales: $25900000
Number Employees: 118
Brands:
Swiss Class Veal

14108 Switch Beverage
381 Post Rd
Darien, CT 06820   203-202-7383
Fax: 203-202-7386 www.switchbev.com
juice
President/Owner: Mike Gilbert

14109 Switchback Group
3778 Timberlake Dr
Richfield, OH 44286-9187   330-523-5200
Fax: 330-523-5212 info@switchbackgroup.com
www.switchbackgroup.com
Manufacturer of compliance packaging machines, vertical appplications of which include condiments; prepared foods; spices; pre-mixes; salad dresings; dessert toppings; and juice.
Manager: Dave Shepherd
Marketing & Sales Director: David Shepherd

14110 Switzer's
575 N 20th St
East St Louis, IL 62205-1899   618-271-6336
Fax: 618-271-6339
Wholesaler/distributor of frozen foods, groceries, provisions/meats and general merchandise; serving the food service market
President: Carolyn Hundley
President: C Hundley
Estimated Sales: $ 20 - 50 Million
Number Employees: 20-49

14111 Sycamore Creek Company
4974 Bird Drive
Stockbridge, MI 49285-9476   517-851-0049
Fax: 517-851-0019 amcvittie@wgthompson.com
www.sycamorecreek.net
Unsalted, seasoned and confection coated, roasted grains and seeds
President: W G Thompson
Sales Manager: Tina Hernadez
Owner: Leonard Stuttman
Plant Supervisor: Glen Byron
Estimated Sales: $ 2.5-5 Million
Number Employees: 6
Type of Packaging: Private Label
Brands:
Sycamore Creek

14112 Sycamore Vineyards
PO Box 410
Saint Helena, CA 94574-0410   408-779-4738
Fax: 707-963-0554 800-963-9698
wineinfo@freemarkabbey.com
www.freemarkabbey.com
Wines
Director Winemaking: Ted Edwards
Winemaker: Tim Bell
Estimated Sales: Below $ 5 Million
Number Employees: 10

14113 Sylvest Farms Inc
3500 West Blvd
Montgomery, AL 36108-4536   334-281-0482
Fax: 334-284-2915 beth_c@sylvestfarms.com
www.sylvestfarms.com
Manufacturer of poultry
President: Elton Maddox
CEO: Dean Falk
EVP: Lyman Campbell
Estimated Sales: $55 Million
Number Employees: 500-999
Sq. footage: 35000
Parent Co: Wayne Farms
Type of Packaging: Consumer, Food Service, Bulk
Brands:
SYLVEST SUPER

14114 Sylvester Winery
5115 Buena Vista Dr
Paso Robles, CA 93446-8558   805-227-4000
Fax: 805-227-6128 info@sylvesterwinery.com
www.sylvesterwinery.com
Wines
Owner: Sylvia Filippini
Winemaker: Chuck Devlin
Estimated Sales: Below $ 5 Million
Number Employees: 5-9
Brands:
Sylvester

14115 Sylvin Farms Winery
24 N Vienna Ave
Egg Harbor City, NJ 08215-3245   609-965-1548
Wines
Proprietor: Frank Salek
Vineyard Manager: Franklin Salek
Estimated Sales: $500,000-$1 Million
Number Employees: 1-4
Brands:
Sylvin Farms

14116 Symms Fruit Ranch
14068 Sunnyslope Rd
Caldwell, ID 83607-9358   208-459-4821
Fax: 208-459-6932 sfr@symmsfruit.com
www.symmsfruit.com
Processor and exporter of produce including apples, cherries, peaches and plums
President: Richard Symms
Estimated Sales: $12000000
Number Employees: 100-249
Type of Packaging: Consumer, Food Service, Bulk
Brands:
SSS

14117 Symons Frozen Foods
619 Goodrich Rd
Centralia, WA 98531-9336   360-736-1321
Fax: 360-736-6328 www.symonsfrozenfoods.com
Processor and exporter of frozen fruits and vegetables including blackberries, blueberries, red and black raspberries, corn, peas, peas/carrots and succotash
President: William James
Production Manager: Howard McLoughlin
Estimated Sales: $18200000
Number Employees: 50-99
Type of Packaging: Consumer, Food Service, Private Label, Bulk

14118 Symphony Foods
1685 Short Street
Berkeley, CA 94702-1231   510-845-8275
Fax: 510-558-9255
General groceries
Owner: Alan Finkelstein
Number Employees: 1-4
Type of Packaging: Private Label

14119 Symrise
300 North St
Teterboro, NJ 07608   201-288-3200
Fax: 201-288-0843 www.symrise.com
Manufacturer and importer of flavors, fragrances, aroma chemicals
CEO: Dr. Heinz-Jurgen Bertram
CFO: Bernd Hirsch
Estimated Sales: $3+ Billion
Number Employees: 1,000-4,999
Sq. footage: 100000
Parent Co: Symrise GmbH & Co. KG
Brands:
Dariteen
EVOLUTION
Optamint

14120 Synda International
9117 Saint Andrews Place
College Park, MD 20740-4037   301-935-2263
Fax: 301-935-4778
President: Bin Huang

14121 Synergy Flavors Inc
1230 Karl Court
Wauconda, IL 60084-1081   847-487-1011
Fax: 847-487-1066 www.synergytaste.com
Food flavorings and fragrances
President: Roderick W Sowders
VP: Jim Tanger

Estimated Sales:$29 Million
Number Employees: 58
Sq. footage: 40000
Brands:
  Carbery
  Synergy Flavours

14122 Synergy Foods
PO Box 250398
West Bloomfield, MI 48325-0398   313-849-2900
                        Fax: 313-849-2906
Processor of custom made roasted peanuts and peanut products such as butter, flour and oil extracts; also, custom blending, such as, iced tea mix, gelatins and drink mix
  President: Don Soetaert
  CFO: George Lewis
  Operations Manager: Mikhail Adronov
Number Employees: 20-49
Sq. footage: 65000
Type of Packaging: Food Service, Private Label, Bulk

14123 Synergy Plus
500 Halls Mill Rd
Freehold, NJ 07728-8811   732-308-3000
  Fax: 732-761-2878 www.invernessmedical.com
Vitamins
  Manager: Barb McCleer
  Sales Coordinator: Arthur Edell
*Estimated Sales:*Under $500,000
Number Employees: 250-499

14124 Syracuse Casing Company
528 Erie Blvd W
Syracuse, NY 13204-2423   315-475-0309
                        Fax: 315-475-8536
Processor of natural sausage casings
  President: Peter Frey Jr
Estimated Sales:$2200000
Number Employees: 10-19
Sq. footage: 15000
Type of Packaging: Food Service, Private Label, Bulk

14125 Sysco Food Services of Chicago
250 Wieboldt Dr
Des Plaines, IL 60016-3192   847-699-5400
         Fax: 847-299-3048 www.sysco.com
Wholesaler/distributor of groceries, frozen and specialty foods, produce, seafood and meats; serving the food service market
  President: Michael McLoughlin
  CEO: Charles W Staes
*Estimated Sales:*1
Number Employees: 5,000-9,999
Parent Co: Sysco Corporation

14126 Sysco Food Services of Indiana
4000 W 62nd St
Indianapolis, IN 46268-2518   317-291-2020
         Fax: 317-216-9346 www.sysco.com
Wholesaler/distributor of frozen foods, groceries, produce, meats and specialty foods; serving the food service market
  President: Walter Mills
  CEO: L Paul Nasir
Number Employees: 250-499
Parent Co: Sysco Corporation

14127 Sysco I&S Foodservices Inc
8007 127th Avenue NW
Unit N
Edmonton, AB T5C 1R9
Canada   780-478-3451
     Fax: 780-472-8172 www.freshpoint.com
Processor of frozen French fries and peeled and pre-cut vegetables
  President: Richard Pidweberski
  Sales Manager: Gerry Lewis
  Production Manager: Conrad Martin
Number Employees: 100-249
Parent Co: Rosecliff
Type of Packaging: Consumer, Food Service
Brands:
  I&S
  Russbank
  Shur Fresh

14128 Sysco/Louisville Food Service
P.O.Box 32470
Louisville, KY 40232-2470   502-364-4300
    Fax: 502-364-4344 800-669-1236
                        www.sysco.com

Wholesaler/distributor of frozen foods, groceries, produce, meats, dairy and baked products, seafood, specialty foods and general merchandise; serving the food service market
  President: Peter Scatamacchia
  CEO: Steven D Hocker
Number Employees: 500-999
Parent Co: Sysco Corporation

14129 Systems Bio-Industries
2021 Cabot Boulevard W
Langhorne, PA 19047-1810   215-702-1000
         Fax: 215-702-1015 www.skw.de.com
Fruit flavorings and fruit juice concentrates
Number Employees: 50-99

14130 T Hasegawa
14017 183rd St
Cerritos, CA 90703-7000   714-670-1586
  Fax: 714-522-6800 drosson@thasegawa.com
                        www.thasegawa.com
Processor, importer and exporter of custom blended flavors, seasonings and fragrances
  President: Mark Scott
  Sales Manager (Western): Jeff Carlson
  Sales Manager (Eastern): Robert Taylor
Estimated Sales:$8300000
Number Employees: 50-99
Sq. footage: 54000
Parent Co: T. Hasegawa Company
Other Locations:
  T. Hasegawa U.S.A.
  Northbrook IL

14131 T Hasegawa Flavors USA
14017 183rd St
Cerritos, CA 90703-7000   714-670-1586
  Fax: 714-522-6800 salesusa@thasegawa.com
                        www.thasegawausa.com
Flavors and fragances for beverages, cuisine, dairy, salad dressings, sauces and prepared foods
  President: Mark Scott
  Marketing Director: Jeff Carlson
  VP: Hiroyuki Okamura
  CFO: Cindy Hu
Estimated Sales:$ 5-10 Million
Number Employees: 50-99

14132 T O Williams
P.O.Box C
Portsmouth, VA 23705-0080   757-397-0771
       Fax: 757-397-5702 towi@bellatlantic.net
Meat packer
  President: H J Chai
  CEO: Diane Chay
  VP: Peter J Chay
  President: Hyun J Chay
  Marketing: Bridgette McClung
Estimated Sales:$1600000
Number Employees: 20-49
Sq. footage: 13000
Type of Packaging: Food Service
Brands:
  Blue Ribbon Hot Sausage
  Diane's Italian Sausage
  H.C. Smoked Sausage
  Virginia Smoked Sausage

14133 T&A Gourmet
1 Kingsbridge Road
Somerset, NJ 08873-2329   732-828-9565
                        Fax: 732-545-4226
Gourmet and specialty foods
  President: James Morano
*Estimated Sales:*Under $500,000
Number Employees: 1-4

14134 T&J Meat Packing
Rr 1 Box 204
Chicago Heights, IL 60411   708-758-6748
                        Fax: 708-758-8688
Processor of pork
  Owner: Tony Lilovic
  VP Marketing: John Lilovich
Estimated Sales:$ 10 - 20 Million
Number Employees: 20-49
Type of Packaging: Consumer, Bulk

14135 T&T Seafood
14550 Brown Rd
Baker, LA 70714-6522   225-261-5438
                        Fax: 225-261-5260
Seafood
  President: John Tourere

Estimated Sales:$2 Million
Number Employees: 1-4

14136 T. Cvitanovich
1017 W Harimaw Court
Metairie, LA 70001-6231   504-833-6349
                        Fax: 504-833-6458
Processor and distributor of fresh and frozen shrimp
  Owner: Tommy Cvitanovich
Estimated Sales:$ 5 - 10 Million
Number Employees: 10-19

14137 T. Marzetti Company
P.O.Box 29163
Columbus, OH 43229-0163   614-846-2232
       Fax: 614-848-8330 www.marzetti.com
Processor of pancake and waffle syrups, teriyaki and barbecue sauces, condiments and pourable dressings
  President: Bruce Rosa
  Assistant Plant Manager: John Hamstreet
Estimated Sales:$100+ Million
Number Employees: 100-249
Type of Packaging: Food Service, Private Label, Bulk

14138 T. Marzetti Company
P.O.Box 29163
Columbus, OH 43229-0163   614-846-2232
       Fax: 614-848-8330 www.marzetti.com
Processor of low-calorie salad dressings, caviar, barbecue sauce, specialty mustards, egg noodles, marinades, chip dips, gelatin salads, frozen fruit pies, frozen garlic bread, sauces, etc
  President: Bruce Rosa
  Senior VP: Gary Thompson
Number Employees: 100-249
Parent Co: Lancaster Colony Corporation
Type of Packaging: Consumer, Food Service, Private Label, Bulk
Other Locations:
  Marzetti, T., Co.
  Millersburg OH
Brands:
  Allen Dairy
  CARDINI'S ORIGINAL CAESAR
  Cardini
  Frenchette
  Girards
  Inn Maid
  Marzetti
  Mountain Top
  New York
  Pfeiffer
  REAMES
  Romanoff

14139 T. Marzetti Company
P.O.Box 29163
Columbus, OH 43229-0163   614-846-2232
       Fax: 614-848-8330 www.marzetti.com
Processor of salad dressings, sauces and mayonnaise
  President: Bruce Rosa
  National Accounts Manager: Tim Tate
  Sales Manager (Southern Regional): Mary Ann Mitchell-Sainsbury
  Plant Manager: Elden Quilling
Estimated Sales:$ 50 - 100 Million
Number Employees: 100-249
Parent Co: Lancaster Colony Corporation
Type of Packaging: Food Service, Private Label, Bulk

14140 T. Sterling Associates
121 W 4th St
Jamestown, NY 14701-5005   716-483-0769
                        Fax: 716-664-9508
Cheese marketing
  Manager: Spring Martin
Estimated Sales:$ .5 - 1 million
Number Employees: 1-4
Type of Packaging: Private Label

14141 T.B. Seafood
450 Commercial St
Portland, ME 04101-4636   207-871-2420
                        Fax: 207-871-0906
Seafood
  President: Roderick Wintle Jr

14142 T.G. Lee Dairy
P.O.Box 3033
Orlando, FL 32802-3033   407-894-4941
     Fax: 407-896-4757 www.tgleedairy.com

Processor of citrus juices and milk including low-fat, chocolate, whole, skim, 1% and 2%; also, cream and ice cream cones, sandwiches and dixies
Manager: Billy Giovanetti
CEO: Howard Dean
Marketing MAnager: Bill Gilzanetti
VP Sales/Marketing: Bill Giovanetti
Number Employees: 500-999
Parent Co: Dean Foods Company
Type of Packaging: Consumer, Food Service, Private Label, Bulk
Brands:
T.G. Lee Foods

14143 T.J. Blackburn Syrup Works
P.O.Box 928
Jefferson, TX 75657-0928   903-665-2541
Fax: 903-665-7441   800-527-8630
Manufacturer of jams, jellies and syrups
President: Jeffrey Fuquay
Estimated Sales:$40 Million
Number Employees: 50-99
Type of Packaging: Consumer, Bulk
Brands:
BLACKBURN'S
JOHNNIE FAIR

14144 T.J. Kraft
1535 Colburn St
Honolulu, HI 96817-4905   808-842-3474
Fax: 808-842-3475   tkraft@norpacexport.com
www.norpac-export.com
Various types of fresh Hawaiian seafood
President: Thomas Kraft
Estimated Sales:$ 10 - 20 Million
Number Employees: 10-19

14145 T.L. Herring & Company
P.O.Box 3186
Wilson, NC 27895-3186   252-291-1141
Fax: 252-291-1142
Processor and packer of hot dog chili, fresh pork sausage, souse meat, cooked chitterlings. All of these products are produced for Southern tastes
President: Thomas Mark
CFO: Jean Herring
Vice President: Mike Herring
Estimated Sales:$ 5 - 10 Million
Number Employees: 10-19
Sq. footage: 14900

14146 T.M. Duche Company
P.O.Box 845
Orland, CA 95963-0845   530-865-5511
Fax: 530-865-7864 www.duchenut.com
Processor and exporter of almonds
Manager: John Wilson
Plant Manager: Ron Bryant
Estimated Sales:$ 10 - 20 Million
Number Employees: 20-49
Type of Packaging: Consumer, Food Service, Private Label, Bulk

14147 T.S. Smith & Sons
P.O.Box 275
Bridgeville, DE 19933-0275   302-337-8271
Fax: 302-337-8417 www.tssmithandsonsfarm.com
Manufacturer of apples, peaches, nectarines, sweet corn, asparagus, strawberries, soybeans, wheat, barley and broiles; exporter of apples
President: Matthew Smith
Sales (Wholesale/Retail): Thomas Smith
Production Manager: Charles Smith
Estimated Sales:$3-5 Million
Number Employees: 20-49
Type of Packaging: Consumer, Bulk
Brands:
T.S. SMITH & SONS

14148 T.W. Burleson & Son
P.O.Box 578
Waxahachie, TX 75168-0578   972-937-4810
Fax: 972-937-8711 jim@burlesons-honey.com
www.burlesons-honey.com
Processor and exporter of extracted honey
President: T Burleson Jr
Sales Manager: Jim Phillips
Estimated Sales:$ 20 - 50 Million
Number Employees: 20-49
Type of Packaging: Consumer, Food Service, Private Label, Bulk
Brands:
BURLESON'S
NATURAL PURE

14149 T.W. Garner Food Company
P.O.Box 4329
Winston Salem, NC 27115-4329   336-661-1550
Fax: 336-661-1901   800-476-7383
fsherrill@twgarner.com   www.texaspete.com
A leading manufacturer of hot sauce, fresh-ingredient salsa, jams and jellies, and other sauces. The Texas Pete brand of hot sauce products is one of America's top brands. Texas Pete Chicken Wing Sauce is the top-selling brand in theUS.
President: Reg Garner
CFO: Hal Garner
VP: Ann Riddle
R&D/Quality Control: Ann Riddle
Marketing: Glenn Garner
Retail Sales: Jim Frank
Foodservice Sales: Frank Sherrill
Operations: Stan Carroll
Production/Plant Manager: Stan Carroll
Purchasing Director: Stan Carroll
Estimated Sales:$ 10 - 20 Million
Number Employees: 100-249
Type of Packaging: Consumer, Food Service
Brands:
Garner Jams & Jellies
Green Mountain Gringo
Texas Pete

14150 TAIF
600 Kaiser Drive
Suite A
Folcroft, PA 19032-2122   610-631-5544
Processor of frozen pasta and related items
President: Joseph A Talluto
VP: Gus De Nicola
Number Employees: 20-49
Sq. footage: 27000
Type of Packaging: Food Service
Brands:
Talluto's

14151 TCHO Ventures
Pier 17
San Francisco, CA 94111   415-981-0189
Fax: 415-723-7497   info@tcho.com
www.tcho.com
chocolate
President/Owner: Louis Rossetto
Director of Finance: Sam Christian
Estimated Sales:$1.3 Million
Number Employees: 20

14152 TFF Seasoning Division
999 Tech Dr
Milford, OH 45150-9535   513-248-9876
Fax: 513-248-8808   requests@mane.com
www.maneusa.com
Manufacturer of flavors and seasoning blend
President Flavors Division: Ken Hunter
Marketing Manager: Bridget McElfresh
VP Sales/Marketing: Dave Wilson
VP Operations: Philip Lee
Estimated Sales:$ 20 - 50 Million
Number Employees: 50-99
Sq. footage: 65000

14153 TIC Gums
4609 Richlynn Dr
Belcamp, MD 21017-1228   410-273-7300
Fax: 410-273-6469   800-221-3953
info@ticgums.com   www.aragum.com
Oldest supplier of hydrocolloids and all necessary ingredients included gum products
President: Steve Andon
CFO: Mike Dean
VP: Christopher Andon
R & D: Mar Nietl
Marketing: Frances Bowman
Operations: Steve Hartley
Estimated Sales:$ 20-$ 50 Million
Number Employees: 50-99
Type of Packaging: Bulk

14154 TIPIAK INC
45 Church St # 303
Stamford, CT 06906-1733   203-961-9117
Fax: 203-975-9081   laurent.chery@tipiak-e.com
www.tipiak.fr
Processor and importer of couscous, granulated tapioca and tapioca pearls and starches
VP: Laurent Chery
Estimated Sales:$3 - 5 Million
Number Employees: 2

Sq. footage: 1200
Parent Co: TIPIAK SA
Type of Packaging: Consumer, Food Service, Private Label, Bulk
Brands:
Fecularia
Loanoa
Osem
Thai Wah
Tiapak

14155 TKC Vineyards
P.O.Box 759
Plymouth, CA 95669-0759   209-245-6428
Fax: 209-245-4006   888-627-2356
tkcvineyards@outrageous.net
www.tkcvineyards.com
Family winery committed to the production of premium wines. Specialties include Zinfandel, Mourvedre and Cabernet
Owner/CEO: Harold Nuffer
VP/CFO: Monica Nuffer
Marketing Director: Monica Nuffer
*Estimated Sales:*Less than $500,000
Number Employees: 1-4
Type of Packaging: Private Label
Brands:
TKC Vineyards

14156 TNT Crust
P.O.Box 8926
Green Bay, WI 54308-8926   920-431-7240
Fax: 920-431-7249   tntcrust@tyson.com
www.tntcrust.com
Processor and exporter of pre-made, partially baked pizza crusts including thin, thick and raised edge; also, fresh and frozen pizza dough.
President: Roger Lebreck
Vice President: Shreenivas Manthana
VP Sales/Marketing: Larry Kropp
Sales Director: Larry Kropp
VP Operations: Kent Reschke
VP Engineering: Phil Vangsnes
Number Employees: 100-249
Parent Co: FoodBrands America
Type of Packaging: Food Service

14157 TRADE
3409 Babcock Blvd
Pittsburgh, PA 15237-2401   412-366-6332
Fax: 724-452-7030
General grocery
Owner: Chris Trudeau
Estimated Sales:$300,000-500,000
Number Employees: 1-4

14158 TRAINA Foods
PO Box 157
Patterson, CA 95363-0157   209-892-5472
Fax: 209-892-6231   info@traina.com
www.traina.com
Dried apricots, sun dried tomatoes and all dried fruit.
Quality Control Director: Robert Kimball
Marketing Director: Victoria Traina

14159 TRC Nutritional Laboratories
12320 E Skelly Dr
Tulsa, OK 74128-2414   918-437-0555
Fax: 918-492-9546   800-421-7310
www.trccorp.com
Processor of super oxygenated drinking water
President: Rocky D Heinrich
Marketing Director: Sawn Wright
Chairman: Elmer G Heinrich
Estimated Sales:$ 20 - 50 Million
Number Employees: 20-49
Type of Packaging: Consumer
Brands:
Liquidlise
Super Oxy-Pure

14160 TWD
12631 Imperial Highway
Santa Fe Springs, CA 90670-4710   562-404-4110
Fax: 562-404-4150
President/CEO: Othon Cabral
Senior VP Finance: Hector Lozao
Sales Director: Peggy Ahumada
Estimated Sales:$ 1-2.5 Million appx.
Number Employees: 27
Brands:
Mi Rancho

Pepepeno
Ricas

14161 Tabard Farm Potato Chips
PO Box 351
Middletown, VA 22645-0351   540-869-0104
          Fax: 540-869-0176   800-294-7783
          sales@rt11.com   www.rt11.com
Handcooked potato chips, sweet potato chips, mixed
vegetable chips and potato chip cookies.
          President/CEO: Sarah Cohen
Estimated Sales: $ 20 - 50 Million
Number Employees: 20-49
Brands:
          Route 11 Potato Chips

14162 Tabatchnick's Fine Foods
1230 Hamilton St
Somerset, NJ 08873-3343   732-247-6668
          Fax: 732-247-6555   info@tabatchnick.com
          www.tabatchnick.com
Processor of homemade soups, sorbets, icepops and
cheese
          Owner: Ben Tabatchinick
          CFO: Robert Ingebretsen
          VP/National Food Service: Peter Hans
          Institutional Sales: Marc Blake
          Chief Engineer: Bud Barry
          Retail Sales Cooordinator: Claudia Davila
          Commodities Coordinator: Barbara Slicner
          Customer Relations: Michelle Kopitman
          Plant Manager: Cezar Capalong
Estimated Sales: Below $ 5 Million
Number Employees: 20-49

14163 Tabco Enterprises
1906 W Holt Ave
Pomona, CA 91768-3351   909-623-4565
          Fax: 909-623-2605
          www.essentialpharmaceutical.com
Processor and exporter of nutritional food supple-
ments including deep sea fish oil, shark cartilage,
multivitamins and minerals, grape seed extract,
herbal products, spirulina, garlic, etc
          President: Bruce Lin
          Financial Officer: Rebecca Lin
Estimated Sales: $ 5 - 10 Million
Number Employees: 20-49
Sq. footage: 20000
Parent Co: Essential Pharmaceutical
Brands:
          Eden Life
          Essential Elite
          Wonderful Life

14164 Tabernash Brewing Company
1265 Boston Ave
Longmont, CO 80501-5809   303-772-0258
          Fax: 303-772-9572
          brewer@lefthandbrewing.com
          www.lefthandbrewing.com
Processor of seasonal beer and lager
          Owner: Eric Wallace
          CEO: Eric Wallece
          Sales Manager: George Barela
          Director Manufacturing: Mark Luca
Estimated Sales: $5-9.9 Million
Number Employees: 20-49
Type of Packaging: Consumer, Food Service
Brands:
          BlackJack Porter
          Brown Ale
          Deep Cover
          Ginger Ale
          Haystack
          Interial Stout
          Jack Man
          Juju
          Milk stout
          Toleftar Pilfen
          Weat
          Weiss

14165 Table Pride
165 Bailey Street SW
Atlanta, GA 30314-4801   770-455-7464
Processor of baked goods including bread and din-
ner rolls
          President: Wayne Chandler
Number Employees: 50-99
Parent Co: Flowers Baking Company
Type of Packaging: Consumer

14166 Table Talk Pie
120 Washington St
Worcester, MA 01610-2751   508-798-8811
          Fax: 508-798-0848 www.tabletalkpie.com
Processor of pies
          President: Christos Cocaine
          Plant Manager: Jim Cumming
Estimated Sales: $4000000
Number Employees: 50-99

14167 Table de France
2020 S Haven Ave
Ontario, CA 91761-0735   909-923-5205
          Fax: 909-923-7804   info@micheldefrance.com
          www.micheldefrance.com
Processor of specialty bakery goods including
crepes, ice cream wafers, French rolled and wafer
cookies and jelly filled crepes
          President: Herve Le Bayon
          Quality Control: Teresa Aguire
          Sales Director: Erwan Le Bayon
          Plant Manager: Philippe Le Bayon
Estimated Sales: $ 10 - 20 Million
Number Employees: 20-49
Number of Products: 4
Sq. footage: 30000
Type of Packaging: Food Service, Private Label
Other Locations:
          Table De France
          Ontario CA
Brands:
          Krazy
          Michel De France
          Table De France

14168 Tabor Hill/CHI Company
185 Mount Tabor Rd
Buchanan, MI 49107-8326   269-422-1165
          Fax: 269-422-2787 www.taborhill.com
          President: David Upton
Estimated Sales: $ 10-20 Million
Number Employees: 50-99

14169 Tadin Herb & Tea Company
2437 S Eastern Ave
Commerce, CA 90040-1414   323-728-5100
          Fax: 323-837-1455   tadintea@aol.com
          www.tadininc.com
Products include our very successful line of tea bags
and cellophane-packaged herbs and capsules. Products satisfy the growing need for consumers in the
area of herbal remedies. Our products are unique
and well-targeted and serving the Hispanic market.
          President: Jose Gonzalez
          Sales/Marketing: Rafal Lara
Estimated Sales: $ 5-10 Million
Number Employees: 50-99
Brands:
          Tadin

14170 Taffy Town
55 W 800 S
Salt Lake City, UT 84101-2912   801-355-4637
          Fax: 801-355-7664   800-765-4770
          worlds_best_taffy@taffytown.com
          www.taffytown.com
Manufactures taffy, specializes in salt water taffy
          President/CEO: David Glade
          VP Marketing: Jason Glade
          VP Manufacturing: Derek Glade
Estimated Sales: $1-2.5 Million
Number Employees: 20-49

14171 Taft Street Winery
2030 Barlow Ln
Sebastopol, CA 95472-2555   707-823-2049
          Fax: 707-823-8622   taftstreet@sonic.net
          www.taftstreetwinery.com
Wines consisting of Sauvignon Blancs, Chardon-
nays, Zinfadel, Russian river, PEKA Pinot Noir
          President: Michael Tierney
          General Manager/CEO: Mike Martini
          Sales/Marketing Manager: Steve Sack
          Winemaker: Kent Barthman
          Assistant Winemaker: Megan Baccitich
          Cellar Master: Joel Rabune
Estimated Sales: $ 5-10 Million
Number Employees: 10-19
Type of Packaging: Private Label, Bulk

14172 Taftsville Country Store
1471 Cookeville Rd
Corinth, VT 05039-4406   802-439-6575
          800-854-0013
          clwilson@taftsville.com   www.taftsville.com
Supplier of camembert, brie, stilton, gruyere and
parmesan cheese, Vermont maple syrup, Vermont
gourmet foods
          President: Rebecca Loftus
Estimated Sales: $300,000-500,000
Number Employees: 1-4
Type of Packaging: Consumer
Brands:
          Blythedale

14173 Taif Foods
530 Foundry Road
Norristown, PA 19403-3902   610-631-5544
          Fax: 610-631-5439
Macaroni, spaghetti, noodles, ravioli, tortellini and
fettuccini
          President: Joe Talluto
          Vice President: Gus DeNicola
Estimated Sales: $ 5-10 Million
Number Employees: 20-49
Sq. footage: 27000

14174 Tait Farm Foods
179 Tait Road
Centre Hall, PA 16828-7806   814-466-2755
          Fax: 814-466-6561   800-787-2716
          taitfood@earthlink.net   www.taitfarmfoods.com
Specialty jams, jellies, conserves, chutneys, scone
and pan cake mixes, colonial fruit shrubs, interna-
tional fruit sauces and herbal oils
          President: Kim Knorr-Tait
          Production Manager: Pat Althouse
Estimated Sales: Below $ 5 Million
Number Employees: 10
Type of Packaging: Private Label
Brands:
          Raspberry Teriyaki
          Tait Farm Foods
          Tait Farm Foods

14175 Taiyo
5960 Golden Hills Drive
Minneapolis, MN 55416   763-398-3003
          Fax: 763-398-3007   sales@taiyoint.com
          www.taiyointernational.com
Ingredients for the food, beverage and pharmaceuti-
cal industries.
          President: Naganori Yamazaki
Number Employees: 5

14176 Taj Gourmet Foods
190 Fountain Street
Framingham, MA 01702-6213   508-875-6212
          Fax: 508-875-6457   michael@ethnicgourmet.com
          www.ethnicgourmet.com
Processor and exporter of ethnic entrees including
Thai, Indian and Italian
          President: Paul Jaggi
          VP Operations: Harmeet Shanhu
Estimated Sales: $7600000
Number Employees: 25
Sq. footage: 30000
Brands:
          Bravissimo
          TAJ
          Thai Chef

14177 Takara Sake
708 Addison St
Berkeley, CA 94710   510-540-8250
          Fax: 510-486-8758   info@takarasake.com
          www.takarasake.com
Sake - a Japanese alcholic beverage of fermented
rice -
          President/CEO: Kazuyoshi Ito
          CFO: Ken Burd
          VP: Kenzo Shimotori
          Marketing Director: Shuzo Hara
          VP Sales: Yafuifa Tanaka
          Plant Manager: Seizaburo Kawano
Estimated Sales: $ 10-20 Million
Number Employees: 20-49
Type of Packaging: Private Label
Brands:
          Sho Chiku Bai

14178 (HQ)Takasago International Corporation
4 Volvo Dr
Rockleigh, NJ 07647-2508   201-767-9001
          Fax: 201-784-7277 www.takasago.com
Manufacturing and sales of flavors, fragrances, aroma chemicals and fine chemicals.
    President: Horoki Take
    Senior Vice President: Sean Traynor
    SVP Flavor Division & Director: Haruo Nakanishi
    Sales Director: Brian Buck
    Production Manager: Michael DePalma
    Purchasing Manager: Trudy Van Der Wall
Estimated Sales: $160000000
Number Employees: 100-249
Other Locations:
    Takasago International Corpor
    Teterboro NJ

14179 Takasago International Corporation (USA)
4 Volvo Dr
Rockleigh, NJ 07647-2508   201-767-9001
          Fax: 201-784-7277
    aromachemicals@takasagousa.com
          www.takasago.com
Flavors, fragrances, aroma chemicals, and fine chemicals
    President: Sean G Traynor
    CEO: Yoshinari Niimura
Estimated Sales: $50-100 Million
Number Employees: 250-499
Other Locations:
    Northvale NJ
    Teterboro NJ
    New York NY
    Crystal Lake IL

14180 Taku Smokehouse
550 S Franklin St
Juneau, AK 99801-1330   907-463-4617
          Fax: 907-463-4644 800-582-5122
          info@takusmokeries.com
          www.takusmokeries.com
Processor and exporter of Alaskan salmon, halibut, crab and cod including frozen, portion cut, fillet, smoked, salted and packed
    President: Sandro Lane
    Smokehouse Manager: Jeremy LaPierre
    General Manager: Eric Norman
    CEO: Giovanni Gallizio
Estimated Sales: Less than $500,000
Number Employees: 100-249
Sq. footage: 50000
Type of Packaging: Consumer, Food Service, Private Label, Bulk
Brands:
    Taku

14181 Talbott Farms
3782 F 1/4 Rd
Palisade, CO 81526-9330   970-464-5656
          Fax: 970-464-7821 market@talbottfarms.com
          www.talbottfarms.com
Grower and shipper of apples, peaches and pears; processor and shipper of cider
    Principal: Bruce Talbott
    Vice President: C Talbott
Estimated Sales: $20 - 50 Million
Number Employees: 100-249
Sq. footage: 26400
Brands:
    Mountain Gold
    Talbott's

14182 Talbott Teas
3517 N Fremont St
Apt 4
Chicago, IL 60657   312-520-9907
          Fax: 773-404-6420 888-809-6062
          www.talbottteas.com
teas; gourmet, green, black, white, rooibos and more
    CEO: Shane Talbott
Number Employees: 5

14183 Talbott Vineyards
P.O.Box 776
Gonzales, CA 93926-0776   831-675-3000
          Fax: 831-675-3120 info@talbottvineyards.com
          www.talbottvineyards.com

Wines - specializing in Chardonnay and Pinot Noir
    Manager: Sam Balderas
    General Manager: Sam Balderas
    Marketing/Sales: Lee Codding
    Marketing Manager: Ross Allen
    Customer Service: Cindy Garza
Estimated Sales: Below $5 Million
Number Employees: 10-19
Number of Brands: 3
Number of Products: 7
Type of Packaging: Consumer
Other Locations: Sleepy Hollow Vineyard
    Gonzales CA
    River Road Vineyard
    Sant Lucia Highlands CA
    Del Mar Vineyard
    Dalinas Valley CA
Brands:
    KALI HART CHARDONNAY
    LOGAN CHARDONNAY
    TALBOTT CHARDONNAY
    TALBOTT DIAMOND T CHARDONNAY

14184 Talenti
9019 Governors Row
Dallas, TX 75247   214-526-3600
          comments@talentigelato.com
          www.talentigelato.com
gelato and sorbetto
Number Employees: 30

14185 Talisman Foods
3324 S 200 E
Salt Lake City, UT 84115-4502   801-487-6409
          Fax: 801-487-6409
Processor of turkey
    President: Chad Maddox
    VP: Ben Maddox
Estimated Sales: $1-2.5 Million
Number Employees: 5-9

14186 Talk O'Texas Brands
1610 Roosevelt Street
San Angelo, TX 76905-6235   325-655-6077
Manufacturer of pickled okra, liquid hickory smoked flavor
    President: Lawrence Ricci
    VP: Lisa Ricci
    VP Operations: Dan Herrington
Number Employees: 7
Sq. footage: 60000
Type of Packaging: Consumer

14187 Talking Rain Beverage Company
P.O.Box 549
Preston, WA 98050-0549   425-222-4900
          Fax: 425-222-4901 800-734-0748
    events@talkingrain.com   www.talkingrain.com
Beverages including five healthy thirst quenching product lines - spring water, oxygenated water, sparkling water, diet flavored non-carbonated water and flavored non-carbonated water. Some products are enhanced with fruit flavorsenriched with natural herbal supplements and infused with vitamins.
    Owner: Doug Mac Lean
    Technical Service: James Fecteau
    VP Marketing/R & D: Nina Morrison
    VP: Michael Fox
    Quality Control: Sam Samia
    VP Sales: Wayne King
    National Accounts Manager: John Stevens
    Plant Manager: Chuck Park
    Purchasing Manager: Monica Runyon
Estimated Sales: $5-10 Million
Number Employees: 50-99
Brands:
    Diet Ice Botanicals
    Sparkling Ice
    Talking Rain
    Talking Rain Biotonical

14188 Tall Grass Toffee
14406 W 100th Street
Lenexa, KS 66215   913-599-2158
          Fax: 913-599-2160 877-344-0442
          info@tallgrasstoffee.com
          www.tallgrasstoffee.com
toffee

14189 Tall Talk Dairy
11961 S Emerson Road
Canby, OR 97013-9311   503-266-1644
Dairy products
    Marketing Director: Harlent Peterson
    Sales Director: Esther Peterson

14190 Talley Farms
P.O.Box 360
Arroyo Grande, CA 93421-0360   805-489-2508
          Fax: 805-489-5201 talley@talleyfarms.com
          www.talleyfarms.com
Grower and exporter of produce including sugar peas, bell peppers, nappa, cabbage, romaine lettuce, zucchini, Blue Lake beans, spinach and cilantro
    President: Brian Talley
    CEO: Todd Talley
    Sales Director: Jeff Halfpenny
    Operations Manager: Ryan Talley
    Plant Manager: Arturo Ibarra
Estimated Sales: $10 - 20 Million
Number Employees: 250-499
Number of Brands: 2
Number of Products: 12
Type of Packaging: Consumer, Food Service, Bulk
Brands:
    ARROYO GRANDE
    TALLEY FARMS

14191 Talley Vineyards
P.O.Box 360
Arroyo Grande, CA 93421-0360   805-489-2508
          Fax: 805-489-5201 info@talleyvineyards.com
          www.talleyfarms.com
Estate wines such as Chardonnay and Pinot Noir
    President: Don Talley
    Marketing Director: David Block
    CFO: Brain Caley
Estimated Sales: Below $5 Million
Number Employees: 10-19
Brands:
    Talley Vineyards

14192 Tamarack Farms Dairy
1701 Tamarack Rd
Newark, OH 43055-1390   740-522-8181
          Fax: 740-522-9235 866-221-4141
    investors@kroger.com   www.kroger.com
Processor of milk and juices including fruit and vegetable
    Chairman/CEO: David B Dillon
    VP Operations: Mark Prestidge
    President: Don McGeorge
    Plant Engineer: Tony Neely
Number Employees: 100-249
Parent Co: Kroger Company
Type of Packaging: Consumer, Food Service, Private Label, Bulk
Brands:
    City Market
    Dillons
    Food4Less
    Gerbes
    King Soopers
    Owen's
    QFC
    Ralphs
    Smith's

14193 Tamarind Tree
518 Justin Way
Neshanic Station, NJ 08853-4270   908-369-6300
          800-432-8733
Processor of shelf stable, all-natural and preservative, wheat and gluten-free Indian vegetarian entrees, snack foods, condiments and spicy lentil crisps; exporter of shelf stable and all-natural Indian vegetarian entrees
    President: Harshad Parekh
Number Employees: 1-4
Sq. footage: 2000
Brands:
    Pappadums
    The Taste of India

14194 Tamashiro Market
802 N King St
Honolulu, HI 96817-4513   808-841-8047
          Fax: 808-845-2722
Japanese foods
    President: Cyrus Tamashiro
Estimated Sales: $10 - 20 Million
Number Employees: 20-49

14195 Tami Great Food
22 Briarcliff Dr
Monsey, NY 10952-2503   718-788-4200
          Fax: 718-788-4326

Manufactures quick frozen & cold pack vegetables, excluding. potato products; manufactures frozen food products
President: Martin Rosenberg
VP: Renee Rosenberg
Estimated Sales: $1.7 Million
Number Employees: 10
Sq. footage: 6000

14196 Tampa Bay Copack
15052 Ronnie Dr # 100
Dade City, FL 33523-6011   352-567-7400
      Fax: 352-567-2257   scot@tampabaycopack.com
      www.tampabaycopakc.com
Contract manufacturing beverage bottling, pastuerizer, formulation, private label, product development.
President: Scot Ballantyne
Research & Development: Vince Curetto
Number Employees: 5-9
Sq. footage: 17000
Type of Packaging: Private Label

14197 Tampa Bay Fisheries
P.O.Box 750
Dover, FL 33527-0750   813-752-8883
      Fax: 813-752-3168   800-234-2561
      info@tbfish.com   www.tbfish.com
Manufacturer, exporter and importer of frozen seafood including crab cakes, lobster, oysters, scallops and shrimp including breaded, headless, etc.
President: Rob Paterson
Estimated Sales: $25 Million
Number Employees: 250-499
Sq. footage: 245000
Type of Packaging: Consumer, Food Service

14198 (HQ)Tampa Farm Services
14425 Haynes Rd
Dover, FL 33527-4412   813-659-0605
      Fax: 813-659-0197   info@tampafarms.com
      www.4-grain.com
Processor, packer, exporter and distributor of shell eggs
President: Mike Bynum
Executive VP: Sam Bynum
VP: Blair Bynum
Estimated Sales: $ 20 - 50 Million
Number Employees: 100-249
Sq. footage: 70000
Type of Packaging: Consumer, Food Service, Private Label, Bulk
Other Locations:
Tampa Farm Services
Indiantown FL
Brands:
4-Grain All-Natural
Indiantown
Tampa Farm Service

14199 Tampa Maid Foods
P.O.Box 3709
Lakeland, FL 33802-3709   863-687-4411
      Fax: 863-683-8713   800-237-7637
      info@tampamaid.com   www.tampamaid.com
Processor, importer and exporter of frozen prepared seafood including breaded, peeled and deveined shrimp, stuffed flounder, oysters, scallops and appetizers
President/CEO: George Watkins
CFO/Senior VP: Edward Smith
Data Processing: Gene Gerstmeier
Production Manager: Kevin Stallworth
Purchasing Manager: Tim Moore
Number Employees: 250-499
Sq. footage: 140000
Type of Packaging: Consumer, Food Service, Private Label, Bulk

14200 Tampico Beverages
3106 N Campbell Ave
Chicago, IL 60618-7921   773-296-0190
      Fax: 773-296-0191   877-826-7426
      comments@tampico.com   www.tampico.com
Processor, exporter and importer of beverage bases and citrus blends
CEO: John Carson
CEO: Scott Miller
VP Marketing: Tracey Schroeder
Number Employees: 1-4
Type of Packaging: Bulk
Brands:
Tampico Punches

14201 Tampico Spice Company
P.O.Box 1229
Los Angeles, CA 90001-0229   323-235-3154
      Fax: 323-232-8686   info@tampicospice.com
      www.tampicospice.com
Processor of spices and seasoning blends
President: Jesus Martinez
Estimated Sales: $8,500,000
Number Employees: 20-49
Type of Packaging: Consumer, Food Service, Private Label, Bulk
Brands:
Tampico

14202 Tamuzza Vineyards
111 Cemetry Road
Hope, NJ 07844   908-459-5878
      Fax: 908-459-5560   info@tamuzzavineyards.com
      www.tamuzzavineyards.com
Wines
President: Al Ivory
Owner: Paul Tamuzza
Winemaker: Paul Tamuzza
Estimated Sales: $ 5-9.9 Million
Number Employees: 10

14203 Tandem Enterprises
PO Box 2470
Darien, CT 06820-0470   203-852-1406
      Fax: 203-852-1426   800-779-3276
      www.middlesexfarm.com
Processor of hot mustards, hot pepper jellies, grilling glazes and jams
Co-Owner/Partner: Bobbi Stuart
Co-Owner/Partner: Susan Coyne
Number Employees: 1-4
Type of Packaging: Consumer, Food Service
Brands:
Ginger Jazz
Orange & Hot
Pepper Pizzaz
Sweet & Hot

14204 Tanglewood Farms
297 Riverdale Rd
Warsaw, VA 22572-4020   804-394-4505
      Fax: 804-333-0422
Produce products such as cantaloupe, squash, tomatoes
President: Earl Lewis
VP: John E Lewis
Marketing: Ken Taylor
Estimated Sales: $ 2.5-5 Million
Number Employees: 5-9

14205 (HQ)Tanimura & Antle
P.O.Box 4070
Salinas, CA 93912-4070   831-455-2255
      Fax: 831-455-3913   www.taproduce.com
Processor and exporter of cauliflower, broccoli, broccoflower, celery, lettuce, scallions, green onions and value-added products
President: Ken Silveira
CEO: Rick Antle
CEO: Rick Antle
Sales Director: Shiro Higashi
Estimated Sales: $214200000
Number Employees: 100-249
Type of Packaging: Consumer
Other Locations:
Tanimura & Antle
Salinas CA
Brands:
Brian
Salad Time
T & A
Tanbro

14206 Tankersley Food Service
3203 Industrial Park Rd
Van Buren, AR 72956-6109   479-471-6800
      Fax: 479-471-6851   800-726-6182
Distributor of general grocery
President: Danny Lloyd
Marketing Director: Rick Climer
CFO: David Wilson
Estimated Sales: $ 1-2.5 Million
Number Employees: 1-4
Brands:
Dolmany
Simplex

14207 Tanks Meat
P.O.Box 31
Elmore, OH 43416-0031   419-862-3312
      www.tanksmeats.com
Manufacturer of beef and pork
President: Alois W Amstutz
Estimated Sales: $5-10 Million
Number Employees: 10-19
Type of Packaging: Consumer, Food Service, Bulk

14208 Tantos Foods International
227 Lanastaff Road
Richmond Hill, ON L4C 6N1
Canada   905-763-9994
      Fax: 905-731-5881   info@tantos.com
      www.tantos.com
Processor, exporter and importer of hot sauce, frozen fruit pulp, plantain, cassava and taro chips, annatto seeds, powder norbixin and ackees
Co-President: Jorge Donato
Sales Director: Ayaaz Merali
Manager: Konrad Lutz
Estimated Sales: $$1-3 Million
Number Employees: 35
Sq. footage: 7000
Parent Co: Mejores Alimentos de Costa Rica/Alina Foods C.A.
Type of Packaging: Consumer, Food Service, Private Label, Bulk
Brands:
Banana Gold
Tantos

14209 Taos Brewing Supply
1416 4th Street
Santa Fe, NM 87505-3422   505-983-0505
      Fax: 505-983-0505
Designer, packager and distributor of natural flavor soft drinks and root beer
President: Jonathan Riebli
Number Employees: 5-9
Sq. footage: 4000

14210 Taos Trails Brewery
PO Box 1480
Ranchos De Taos, NM 87557-1480   505-758-0099
Brewing of root beer

14211 Tapatia Tortilleria
104 E Belmont Ave
Fresno, CA 93701-1403   559-441-1030
      Fax: 559-441-1712   800-219-7329
      customerservice@latapatiaca.org
      www.tortillas4u.com
Corn and flour tortillas
Owner: Hellen Chavez-Hansen
Sr. VP: John Hansen
Senior VP: John Hansen
Export Director: Dan Soleno
Estimated Sales: $ 100-500 Million
Number Employees: 100-249
Type of Packaging: Private Label
Brands:
Tapatia Tortilleria

14212 Tapatio Hot Sauce
4685 District Blvd
Vernon, CA 90058-2731   323-587-8933
      Fax: 323-587-5266   info@tapatiohotsauce.com
      www.tapatiohotsauce.com
Processor and exporter of hot sauce
Owner/President: Luis Saavedra
Estimated Sales: $ 5 - 10 Million
Number Employees: 20-49
Type of Packaging: Consumer, Food Service
Brands:
TAPATIO

14213 Tapper Candies
15637 Neo Parkway
Cleveland, OH 44128-3150   216-825-1000
      Fax: 330-825-1010
Candy
Estimated Sales: $ 5 - 10 Million
Number Employees: 5-9

14214 Taqueria El Milagro
1923 S Blue Island Ave
Chicago, IL 60608-3014   312-433-7620
      Fax: 773-650-4692
Cuisine: Mexican
VP: Rafael Lopez
Marketing/Sales: Raulinda Fierria

Estimated Sales: $ 20-50 Million
Number Employees: 5-9

14215 Tara Foods
801 Virginia Ave
Atlanta, GA 30354-1913   404-559-0605
    Fax: 404-559-9090   DON@TARAELITE.COM
      www.taraelite.com
Processor of peanut butter and flavoring extracts - nut spreads
    Owner: Debra Theall
    VP: Julie Davis
    Plant Manager: Richard Barnhill
Estimated Sales: $300,000-500,000
Number Employees: 5-9
Parent Co: Kroger Company
Type of Packaging: Consumer, Food Service, Private Label
Brands:
    Tara Foods

14216 Tarara Winery
13648 Tarara Ln
Leesburg, VA 20176-5236   703-771-7100
    Fax: 703-771-8443   winesales@tarara.com
      www.tarara.com
Wine specialties such as Chardonnay, Pinot Gris, Viognier, Cabernet Franc
    Executive Director: Heather Akers
    Operations Manager: Margaret Russell
    Production Manager: Daniel Alcorso
    Winemaker: Rob Warren
Estimated Sales: $ 5-10 Million
Number Employees: 20-49
Number of Products: 12
Brands:
    Varietals
    Viognier

14217 Tarazi Specialty Foods
13727 Seminole Dr
Chino, CA 91710-5515   909-628-3601
    Fax: 909-590-4869   nabil@terazifoods.com
      www.tarazifoods.com
manufacturer of premium quality tahini and falafel dry mix
    Owner: Nabil Huleis
    CFO: J Huleis
    VP: J Huleis
Estimated Sales: $2-5 Million
Number Employees: 10
Sq. footage: 11800
Type of Packaging: Consumer, Food Service, Private Label, Bulk
Brands:
    Tarazi

14218 Target Flavors
7 Del Mar Dr
Brookfield, CT 06804-2401   203-775-4727
    Fax: 203-775-2147   800-538-3350
info@targetflavors.com   www.targetflavors.com
Processor and exporter of flavorings and extracts
    Owner: John Mac Lean
    General Manager: Bill McLean
Estimated Sales: $2100000
Number Employees: 10-19
Sq. footage: 25000

14219 Tarpoff Packing Company
PO Box 6
Granite City, IL 62040-0006   618-452-8180
Processor/packer of beef
    President: John Tarpoff
Number Employees: 10-19
Type of Packaging: Consumer, Bulk

14220 Tartan Hill Winery
4937 S 52nd Ave
New Era, MI 49446-8023   231-861-4657
      tartanhill@usawines.com
A family-operated winery specializing in estate wines made from French hybrid grapes, with a range from dry reds and whites to sweet, late harvest styles
    Owner: Paul Goralski
Estimated Sales: Less than $500,000
Number Employees: 1-4

14221 Tarzai Specialty Foods
13727 Seminole Dr
Chino, CA 91710-5515   909-628-3601
    Fax: 909-590-4869   tarazifoods@tarazifoods.com
      www.tarazifoods.com

Sesame seeds - raw or roasted, Garbanzo beans, Tahini-a savory sesame paste, Falafel mix, and Tabouli
    CFO: Johnny Huleis
    President: William Huleis
    Marketing Director: Christine Huleis
Estimated Sales: $ 2.5-5 Million
Number Employees: 1-4
Brands:
    Falafel Dry Mix
    Tabouli
    Tahini

14222 Tase-Rite Company
1211 Kingstown Rd
Wakefield, RI 02879-2441   401-783-7300
      Fax: 401-789-2889
General grocery and meats
    President: Wesley Lessard
    Marketing Director: Gary Lessard
    Vice President: Gary Lessard
    CFO: Wesley Lessard
Estimated Sales: $ 5-10 Million
Number Employees: 5-9

14223 Taste It Presents
200 Sumner Ave # A
Kenilworth, NJ 07033-1319   908-241-0672
    Fax: 908-241-9410   sales@tasteitpresents.com
      www.tasteitpresents.com
Processor of frozen ethnic pastries including tiramisu
    President: John Alair
Estimated Sales: $ 50 - 100 Million
Number Employees: 20-49
Type of Packaging: Consumer, Food Service, Private Label

14224 Taste Maker Foods
1415 E McLemore Ave
Memphis, TN 38106-3470   901-274-4407
    Fax: 901-272-1088   800-467-1407
      custsvc@tastemakerfoods.com
      www.tastemakerfoods.com
Spcies, seasonings, bakery mixes and dry blends
    President: Robert Reed
    VP: Justin Reed
    Quality Control: Stacey Castleman
    Director Operations: Bill Tomlinson
    Plant Manager: Justin Dukes
Estimated Sales: $ 5 - 10 Million
Number Employees: 10-19
Sq. footage: 25000
Parent Co: Reed Food Technology
Type of Packaging: Consumer, Food Service, Private Label, Bulk
Brands:
    Old Hickory
    Taste Maker

14225 Taste Teasers
6910 Northwood Rd
Dallas, TX 75225-2436   214-750-6334
    Fax: 214-696-3316   800-526-1840
Processor and exporter of jalapeno based condiments and confections
    President: Susanne Hilou
    VP: Eddie Michel
Estimated Sales: $100000
Number Employees: 1-4
Type of Packaging: Consumer, Food Service, Bulk
Brands:
    Hot Chocolate-Fine Chocolate
    Pepper Chicks

14226 Taste of Gourmet
P.O.Box 540
Indianola, MS 38751-0540   662-887-2522
    Fax: 662-887-5547   800-833-7731
      jennifer@tasteofgourmet.com
      www.tasteofgourmet.com
Processor and exporter of catfish pate and capers; also, fudge and lemon pie mixes including fat-free
    President: Evelyn Roughton
Estimated Sales: $885603
Number Employees: 20-49
Type of Packaging: Consumer
Brands:
    Antique Crown Foods
    Mississippi Delta Fudge
    Mississippi Mousse
    The Crown Restaurant Gourmet

14227 Taste of Nature
400 S Beverly Dr
Beverly Hills, CA 90212-4424   310-396-4433
    Fax: 310-396-4432   info@candyasap.com
      www.candyasap.com
Candy
    Manager: Scott Samet
Estimated Sales: $ 3 - 5 Million
Number Employees: 5-9
Brands:
    Care Bears Gummi Bears
    Cat in the Hat Cotton Candy
    Cat in the Hat Sour Gummies
    Cookie Dough Bites
    Cotton Candy Swirl
    HULK Candies
    Jolt Cola Energy Rush
    Muddy Bears
    Shari Candies
    Sour Cotton Candy Swirl
    SpiderMan Cotton Candy
    SpiderMan Sour Gummi Mutant Spiders
    Sqwiggles
    TINY TARTS

14228 Tastee Apple Inc
60810 County Road 9
Newcomerstown, OH 43832-9638   740-498-8316
    Fax: 740-498-6108   800-262-7753
      customerservice@tasteeapple.com
      www.tasteeapple.com
Processor of apple products including chocolate covered apples; caramel apples; apple cider; and apple powder, in addition to jelly apples, candy apples and wild apples.
    President: Greg Hackenbracht
    Director Manufacturing: Jerry Herbert
    Purchasing Manager: Steve Barker
Estimated Sales: $100+ Million
Number Employees: 250-499
Sq. footage: 65000
Type of Packaging: Consumer, Food Service, Private Label, Bulk
Brands:
    Tastee

14229 Tastee Fare
P.O.Box 192070
Little Rock, AR 72219-2070   501-568-7870
      Fax: 501-568-7876
Processor of waffle mixes; manufacturer of waffle bakers
    President: Ron Munsey
    Marketing Director: Brad Munfey
    Manager National Sales: Tom McVey
    VP Sales: Bob Polyister
Estimated Sales: $ 50 - 100 Million
Number Employees: 250-499
Brands:
    Wassle Mix

14230 Tasty Baking Company
2801 W Hunting Park Ave
Philadelphia, PA 19129-1392   215-221-8500
    Fax: 215-223-3288   800-338-2789
      mary.borneman@tastykake.com
      www.tastykake.com
Manufacturer of baked goods and snack cakes
    Chairman: James Ksansnak
    President/CEO: Charles Pizzi
    SVP/CFO: David Marberger
    CEO: Charles P Pizzi
Estimated Sales: $250+ Million
Number Employees: 500-999
Type of Packaging: Private Label
Brands:
    JUNIORS
    KANDY KATES
    KREAMIES
    SENSABLES
    TASTYKAKE

14231 Tasty Mix Quality Foods
88 Walworth St
Brooklyn, NY 11205-2808   718-855-7680
    Fax: 718-855-7681   866-TAS-TYMX
      tastymx@aol.com   www.tastymix.com
Manufacturer of dough conditioners and stabilizers for the pasta and bakery industries
    Manager: Sal Ballarino Jr Jr
    Co-Owner: Louis Ballarino
Estimated Sales: $5-9.9 Million
Number Employees: 5-9
Sq. footage: 5000

Type of Packaging: Consumer, Food Service, Private Label, Bulk
Brands:
DOUGH STABILIZER
GOLD-TEX FLOUR
SHELF-AID

14232 Tasty Seeds Ltd
130 Market Street
Winkler, NB R6W 4A3
Canada   204-331-3480
          Fax: 204-325-6832   888-632-6906
admin@tastyseed.com   www.tastyseeds.com
Salted, seasoned and cajun sunflower seeds, and pumpkin seeds
Owner: Wayne Nestibo
Owner: Bryan Tyerman
Owner/Sales/Marketing Manger: Brad Edwards

14233 Tasty Selections
350 Creditston Road
Suite 102
Concord, ON L4K 3Z2
Canada   905-760-2353
       Fax: 905-660-4858 www.tastyselections.com
Processor/manufacturers of frozen proportioned cookie dough, frozen muffin batters and a broad selection of thaw and serve cakes.
President: Alan Greenspoon
Number Employees: 20-49
Sq. footage: 25000
Type of Packaging: Consumer, Food Service, Bulk

14234 Tasty Tomato
PO Box 6984
San Antonio, TX 78209-0984   210-822-2443
       Fax: 210-822-2538 www.worldtrade.org
Spaghetti sauce
President/CEO: Rollin King
Estimated Sales: $ 2.5-5 Million
Number Employees: 5

14235 Tasty-Toppings
P.O.Box 728
Columbus, NE 68602-0728   402-564-1347
        Fax: 402-563-1469   800-228-4148
Manufacturer of salad dressings
President: Gordon Hull
Estimated Sales: $50 Million
Number Employees: 20-49
Sq. footage: 65000
Type of Packaging: Consumer, Food Service, Private Label
Brands:
DOROTHY LYNCH
DOROTHY LYNCH SALAD DRESSING

14236 Tastybaby
23852 Pacific Coast Highway
#748
Malibu, CA 90265   310-317-4404
       Fax: 310-317-4404   866-588-8278
info@tastybaby.com   www.tastybaby.com
frozen organic baby food
President/Co-Founder: Shannan Swanson
CEO/Co-Founder: Liane Weintraub

14237 Tastykake
2801 W Hunting Park Ave
Philadelphia, PA 19129-1392   215-221-8500
       Fax: 215-223-3288 www.tastykake.com
Processor of baked goods including snack cakes, doughnuts, cookies, pies, etc
Chairman: James E Ksansnak
President: Charles P Pizzi
Senior VP/CFO: David Marberger
CEO: Charles P Pizzi
CEO: Charles P Pizzi
VP Sales: Dan Nagle
Estimated Sales: I
Number Employees: 500-999
Parent Co: Tasty Baking Company
Type of Packaging: Consumer
Brands:
Tastykake

14238 Tata Tea
1001 Dr Martin L King Jr Blvd
Plant City, FL 33563-5150   813-754-2602
       Fax: 813-754-2272   tatainc@tatainc.com
                            www.tata.com

Tea
President: Ashok Bhardwha
Chairman: Patrick McGoldrick
Quality Control: Ivey Campbell
Estimated Sales: $ 2.5-5 Million
Number Employees: 20-49
Brands:
Tata Tea

14239 Tatangelo's Wholesale Fruit & Vegetables
80 Hanlan Road
12-13
Vaughan, ON L4L 3P6
Canada   905-850-0545
       Fax: 905-850-2241   877-328-8503
Processor of frozen fruit and vegetables
President/CEO: John Tatangelo
VP: Rocco Tatangelo
Number Employees: 10-19
Type of Packaging: Food Service
Brands:
Tatangelo

14240 Tate & Lyle North American Sugars
95 Queen's Quay E
Toronto, ON M5E 1A3
Canada   416-366-3561
       Fax: 416-366-7550 800-361-1657
                   info@tlna.com   www.tlna.com
Manufacturer and exporter of refined white sugar; exporter of iced tea, drink crystals and gelatin mixes; importer of raw sugar
President/CEO: Andrew Ferrier
VP Sales/Marketing: Barry McEwen
Estimated Sales: $100 Million
Number Employees: 350
Type of Packaging: Consumer, Food Service, Bulk
Other Locations:
Redpath Sugars
St. Laurent PQ
Brands:
RED PATH

14241 Tate & Lyle North American Sugars
95 Queen's Quay E
Toronto, ON M5E 1A3
Canada   416-366-3561
       Fax: 416-366-7550   800-267-1517
                                   www.tlna.com
Manufacturer of sugar including brown, fondant, invert, liquid, etc.; also, molasses
President/CEO: Andrew Ferrier
Chief Executive: Iain Ferguson
Number Employees: 400
Parent Co: Tate & Lyle North American Sugars
Type of Packaging: Consumer, Bulk
Brands:
REDPATH
STALEY
TATE & LYLE CITRIC ACID

14242 Tate & Lyle North American Sugars
301 State Rt 17
Rutherford, NJ 07070-2575   201-842-7723
Processor of sugar
VP Specialty Ingredients: Christopher Cumero
Marketing: Josephine Anguili
VP Sales/Marketing: Robert Martinelly
Number Employees: 5-9
Parent Co: Tate & Lyle North American Sugars
Type of Packaging: Consumer, Food Service, Private Label, Bulk
Brands:
Domino
Quik-Flo

14243 Tate & Lyle Staley Company
2200 E Eldorado St
Decatur, IL 62525   217-423-4411
       Fax: 217-421-2216 www.tateandlyle.com
Processor of dextrin, dextrose, polydextrose, proteins, soy sauce, corn starch, high fructose corn syrup, fat replacers and thickeners; exporter of starches and sweeteners
President: Matthew Wineinger
Corporate Secretary: J P Mohan
Sales/Marketing Executive: Gary Augustine

Estimated Sales: Over $1 Billion
Number Employees: 2,098
Parent Co: Tate & Lyle North American Sugars
Type of Packaging: Bulk
Brands:
Binasol
Canners Pfp
Confectioners' F&G
Consista
Dress'n 400
Dura-Jel
Freezist
Fruitfil
Hi-Jel
Isosweet
Kol-Guard
Krystar
Lo-Temp
Maxi-Gel
Maximaize
Mira Sperse
Mira-Bake
Mira-Cleer
Mira-Gel
Mira-Quik
Mira-Set
Mira-Thik
Neto
Nu-Col
Nu-Star
Perma-Flo
Redi-Tex
Redisol
Rezista
Shur-Fil
Soft-Set
Sta-Lite
Sta-Mist
Sta-O-Paque
Sta-Rx
Sta-Slim
Staclipse
Stadex
Staleydex
Star-Dri
Starco
Stellar
Sweetose
Tender-Jel
Tenderfil
Thin N' Thik
Vico

14244 Tate Cheese Company
PO Box 1040
Valley City, IL 62340   217-833-2314
       Fax: 217-833-2226 www.worldtrade.org
Dairy products and processed cheese
President: Hamer Tate
Controller: Richard Krueger
Marketing Director: Joe Cline
Production Manager: Paul Ruble
Purchasing Manager: Becky Killebrew
Estimated Sales: $ 25-49.9 Million
Number Employees: '5-9

14245 Tate's Bake Shop
43 N Sea Rd
Southampton, NY 11968-2001   631-283-9830
       Fax: 631-283-9844 info@tatesbakeshop.com
                               www.tatesbakeshop.com
All pastries and rolls made fresh daily - all wholesome ingredients - pies, cakes, chocolate chip cookies, breads, and brownies
Owner: Kathleen King
Estimated Sales: $ 1 - 3 Million
Number Employees: 20-49

14246 Tate's Bake Shop
43 N Sea Rd
Southampton, NY 11968   631-283-9830
       Fax: 631-283-9844 info@tatesbakeshop.com
                               www.tatesbakeshop.com
cookies, cakes, brownies and squares.
President/Owner: Kathleen King

14247 Tatra Herb Company
222 Grove St
Morrisville, PA 19067-1235   215-295-5476
       Fax: 215-736-3089   888-828-7248
tatraherb@comcast.net   www.tatraherb.com
Processor of herbal teas
President: George Zofchak
CEO: George Zofchak

Estimated Sales: Less than $500,000
Number Employees: 1-4
Type of Packaging: Consumer

14248 Taurus Foods
6908 E 30th Street
Indianapolis, IN 46219-1105   317-545-7425
                              Fax: 317-549-9553
Meat purveyor
    President: Ronald Stein

14249 Taylor All Star Dairy Foods
337 Merchant St
Ambridge, PA 15003-2523   724-266-2370
                          Fax: 724-266-6650
Dairy products
    President: Joseph Taylor
Estimated Sales: $ 10-100 Million
Number Employees: 5-9

14250 Taylor Cheese Corporation
P.O.Box 639
Weyauwega, WI 54983-0639   920-867-2337
                           Fax: 920-867-2360
Custom cheese cut, slice and wrap services for private label or conversion needs. Shingled slice packaging gift box components.
    President: Robert Ehrenberg
    Marketing Director: Bob Ehrenberg
Estimated Sales: Below $ 5 Million
Number Employees: 10-19

14251 Taylor Farms
911 Blanco Cir # B
Salinas, CA 93901-4449   831-754-0471
    Fax: 831-794-0473 tsalisbury@taylorfarms.com
                       www.taylorfarms.com
Processor of fresh cut fruit and vegetables including cantaloupe, honeydew, pineapple, onions, lettuce, peppers, garlic, cabbage and tomatoes
    President: Bruce Taylor
    Chairman/CEO: Bruce Taylor
    CFO: Tom Brain
    VP Production: Vikki Chandley
Number Employees: 5,000-9,999
Sq. footage: 50000
Type of Packaging: Consumer, Food Service, Private Label, Bulk

14252 Taylor Meat Company
P.O.Box 670
Taylor, TX 76574-0670   512-352-6357
    Fax: 512-352-9426 taylormc@swbell.net
                       www.taylormeat.com
Manufacturer of beef and pork
    President: Ron Ivy
Estimated Sales: $38 Million
Number Employees: 20-49
Type of Packaging: Consumer, Food Service, Bulk
Brands:
    TIP TOP

14253 Taylor Orchards
P.O.Box 975
Reynolds, GA 31076-0975   478-847-4186
    Fax: 478-847-4464 gafruit@gnat.net
                       www.taylororchards.com
Processor, packer and exporter of peaches
    Owner: Jeff Wainwright
    Owner/Sales Manager: Walter Wainwright
Estimated Sales: $7215000
Number Employees: 10-19
Sq. footage: 4000
Type of Packaging: Consumer, Bulk

14254 Taylor Packing Company
PO Box 188
Wyalusing, PA 18853   570-746-3000
    Fax: 570-746-1298 info@taylorpacking.com
                       www.cargill.com
Coarse and fine ground beef, case-ready ground beef, vacuum-packed boxed beef, fresh vacuum-packed and frozen variety meat items
    Manager: Andy Ripic Jr.
Estimated Sales: $500 Million to $1 Billion
Number Employees: 1,000-4,999

14255 Taylor Packing Company
182 Wilkie Ave
Yuba City, CA 95991-9437   530-671-1505
    Fax: 530-751-1514 www.taylorbrosfarms.com

Processor and exporter of prune concentrate and dried prunes including Ashlock pitted and whole
    President: Richard Taylor
    VP: John Taylor
Estimated Sales: $ 20 - 50 Million
Number Employees: 20-49
Sq. footage: 25000
Type of Packaging: Food Service, Private Label, Bulk
Brands:
    Cal Gold
    California Gold
    Taylor Brothers Farms

14256 Taylor Provisions Company
63 Perrine Ave
Trenton, NJ 08638-5197   609-392-1113
    Fax: 609-392-1354 www.taylorprovisions.com
Processor of meat products
    President: John T Cumbler
    VP: G Cumbler
Estimated Sales: $100+ Million
Number Employees: 50-99

14257 (HQ)Taylor Shellfish Farms
130 SE Lynch Rd
Shelton, WA 98584-8615   360-426-6178
    Fax: 360-427-0327 orders@taylorshellfish.com
                       www.taylorshellfish.com
Manufacturer of fresh and frozen oysters, clams, mussels, scallops and crabs
    President: Jeff Pearson
    Human Resources: John Fogo
Estimated Sales: $16 Million
Number Employees: 100-249
Type of Packaging: Consumer
Other Locations:
    Taylor Shellfish Farms
    Bow WA
Brands:
    Taylor Shellfish

14258 Taylor's Frozen Foods
20 Atlantic St
Charleston, SC 29401-2730   843-723-1878
                            Fax: 843-723-5115
Processor of frozen flounder, squid, scallops and deviled crabs
    President: Carolyn G Torlay
    VP: L Fraser Torlay
    Director Manufacturing: Gwendolyn Hamilton
Estimated Sales: $ 3 - 5 Million
Number Employees: 10-19
Type of Packaging: Consumer, Food Service
Brands:
    Colony Garden

14259 Taylor's Mexican Chili
116 S West Street
Carlinville, IL 62626-1758   217-854-8713
                             800-382-4454
    dave@taylorschili.com www.taylorschili.com
Chili, sauce, beans
    Owner: Joe Gugger
    Operations VP: Dave Tucker
    Production VP: Dave Tucker
Estimated Sales: Less than $500,000
Number Employees: 1-4
Brands:
    Taylor's Mexican Chili

14260 Taylor's Poultry Place
4701 Augusta Rd
Lexington, SC 29073-9197   803-356-3431
Processor of poultry
    President: Luther Taylor
Estimated Sales: Less than $500,000
Number Employees: 1-4

14261 Taylor's Sausage Company
1822 N Grand Blvd
St Louis, MO 63106-1299   314-652-3476
Sausages
    President: Bettie Taylor
Estimated Sales: Below $ 5 Million
Number Employees: 5-9

14262 Tayse Meats
1979 W 25th St
Cleveland, OH 44113-3455   216-664-1799
Beef
    Owner: Keith Tayse
Estimated Sales: Less than $500,000
Number Employees: 1-4

14263 Taystee Bakeries
855 W Washington St
Marquette, MI 49855-4139   906-226-2587
                           Fax: 906-226-2954
Bakery items
    Plant Manager: David Edgren
Estimated Sales: $ 2.5-5 Million
Number Employees: 100-249

14264 Tazo Tea
PO Box 66
Portland, OR 97207-0066   503-736-9005
    Fax: 503-231-8801 800-299-9445
    dhanson@tazo.com   www.tazo.com
Premium teas, bottled tea and juice, organic chai and full leaf teas
    President: Tal Johnson
    R & D: Michael De La Cruz
    Quality Control: Teri Gass
    Marketing Director: Suzanne Baird
    Sales Director: Tom Clemente
    Operations Manager: Rick Lelli
    Production Manager: Tom Jones
    Purchasing Manager: Chris O'Leary
Estimated Sales: $ 10-24.9 Million
Number Employees: 20-49
Number of Brands: 1
Parent Co: Starbucks Coffee Company
Type of Packaging: Private Label

14265 Tea Aura
234 Dunview Avenue
Toronto, ON M2N 4J2
Canada   416-225-8868
          info@teaaura.com
          www.teaaura.com
shortbread cookies infused with tea

14266 Tea Beyond
PO Box 1911
West Caldwell, NJ 07007   973-226-0327
    Fax: 973-226-0327 info@teabeyond.com
                       www.teabeyond.com
authentic teas

14267 Tea Forte
23 Bradford St
Concord, MA 01742   978-369-7777
    Fax: 978-369-3427 info@teaforte.com
                       www.teaforte.com
whole leaf teas with rough-cut herbs and flowers
    President/Owner: Peter Hewitt
Estimated Sales: $10 Million
Number Employees: 30

14268 Tea Needs Inc
3000 Banyon Road
Boca Raton, FL 33432   561-237-5237
    mark@teaneeds.com
    www.teaneeds.com
Disposable instant cup of tea. The teabag is inside of each cup. Three lines are available: tea, fruit tea, and Chinese herb tea.
    President & Owner: Mark Reiman
    VP: Alla Kartel
    Marketing: Ed Camargo
    Operations: Joyce Liang
Estimated Sales: $ 10 Million
Number Employees: 20-49
Number of Brands: 6
Number of Products: 18
Sq. footage: 10000
Type of Packaging: Consumer, Private Label, Bulk
Brands:
    HAPPY CUP TEA

14269 Tea Room
110 C Mezzetta Court
American Canyon, CA 94503   707-561-7080
    Fax: 707-561-7081 866-515-8866
    info@thetearoom.biz www.thetearoom.biz
artisan organic chocolate truffles, organic chocolate bars, tea-infused, french macaroons
    President/Owner: Heinz Rimann

14270 Tea-n-Crumpets
252 Coleman Dr
San Rafael, CA 94901-1209   415-457-2495
    Fax: 415-457-1893 tcrumpets@aol.com
                       www.tea-n-crumpets.com

Organic crumpets, superior quality teas, jams, tea accessories and gift items from around the world.
President: Norman Barahona
CEO: Jena Rose
Estimated Sales:$ 1 - 3 Million
Number Employees: 1-4

14271 Teawolf Industries, Ltd
25 Riverside Drive
Pine Brook, NJ 07058   973-575-4600
Fax: 973-575-4601 www.teawolf.com
Supplier of vanilla products for ice cream & frozen gelato's, yogurts and bakery applications. Chocolate and coffee extracts, sweeteners and teas.

14272 Tebay Dairy Company
Lubeck Rd
Parkersburg, WV 26101   304-863-3705
Fax: 304-863-8712
Processor of dairy products including ice cream
Owner: Robert Kent Tebay Jr
Estimated Sales:$3,200,000
Number Employees: 10-19
Type of Packaging: Consumer
Brands:
Tebay

14273 Tech Pak Solutions
85 Bradley Drive
Westbrook, ME 04092-2013   207-878-6667
Fax: 425-883-9455
Temperature controlled management for food products.
Vice President: Richard Brown

14274 Techni-Brew International
19730 NE Sandy Blvd
Portland, OR 97230-7310   503-666-4545
Fax: 503-669-2223 800-454-4077
info@boyds.com www.boydscoffee.com
The equipment division of Boyd Coffee Company. The mission is to develop and introduce new, innovative and technologically advanced coffee brewing and related equipment to the North American coffee industry. Also manufacturers anddistributes coffee and espresso carts, airpots & servers, and other related items.
Co-President: Richard Boyd
Co-President: David Boyd
R&D: Mike Johnson
Marketing: Jason Chin
Sales: Jeff Snyder
Estimated Sales:$ 20 - 50 Million
Number Employees: 250-499
Sq. footage: 150000
Parent Co: Boyd Coffee Company
Type of Packaging: Food Service
Brands:
Boyds Coffee
Coffee House Roasters
Island Mist Iced Tea
Italia D'oro
Percival Boyd's Teas of Origin
Today
Viaggio

14275 Technical Oil
1 Adamson St
Easton, PA 18042-6184   610-252-8350
Fax: 610-252-9901 ethitech-pa@erols.com
www.technicaloil.com
Processor and exporter of emulsifiers, pan greases and oils and surfactants
Owner: Alan Geisler
Estimated Sales:$ 1-2.5 Million
Number Employees: 5-9
Sq. footage: 30000
Parent Co: Technical Oil
Brands:
Toptex

14276 (HQ)Technical Oil Products
123 Madison St
Boonton, NJ 07005-2153   973-335-0300
Fax: 973-335-1952 orders@technicaloil.com
www.technicaloil.com
Pan release agents, vegetables oil blends, divider and mineral oils, and cake and bread emulsifiers. Available is custom blending services of liquid, dry and paste type products
Owner: Alan Geisler
Number Employees: 5-9
Brands:
SurSweet

14277 Technology Flavors & Fragrances
10 Edison St
Amityville, NY 11701-2875   631-842-7600
Fax: 631-842-8332 flavors@tffi.com
www.tffi.com
Creator and manufacturer of natural and artificial flavors for beverage, food and cosmetics industries
CFO: Joseph A Gemmo
Chairman/CEO: Phil Rosner
CEO: Philip Rosner
Marketing Director: Virginia Bonofligio
Sales Director: Gary Frumberg
Public Relations: Joseph Gemmo
Operations/Production: Ronald Dintemann
Plant Manager: Joseph Piazza
Purchasing Manager: Rose Marotta
Estimated Sales:$15587285
Number Employees: 50-99
Number of Products: 1200
Sq. footage: 52000

14278 Ted Drewes Frozen Custard
6726 Chippewa St
St Louis, MO 63109-2533   314-481-2652
Fax: 314-481-4241 www.teddrewes.com
Frozen custard
President: Ted Jr Drewes
*Estimated Sales:*Below $ 5 Million
Number Employees: 50-99

14279 Ted Shear Associates
1 West Ave
Larchmont, NY 10538-2470   914-833-0017
Fax: 914-833-0233 ted.shear@verizon.net
Honey and vanilla extracts
President: Ted Shear
Estimated Sales:$ 1 - 3 Million
Number Employees: 1-4
Type of Packaging: Private Label

14280 Teddy's Tasty Meats
6123 Mackay St
Anchorage, AK 99518-1739   907-562-2320
Fax: 907-562-1919
Meat
President: Ted Kouris
Secretary/Treasurer: Barbara Kouris
Estimated Sales:$ 50 - 100 Million
Number Employees: 20-49

14281 Tedeschi Vineyards
Hc 1 Box 953
Kula, HI 96790-9304   808-878-6058
Fax: 808-876-0127 info@mauiwine.com
www.mauiwine.com
Wines
President: Pardee Erdman
COO: Paula Hegele
Sales Manager: James McLean
Estimated Sales:$ 20-50 Million
Number Employees: 20-49
Type of Packaging: Private Label
Brands:
Maui Blanc
Maui Blush
Maui Brut
Maui Splash
Maui Ulupalakua Red

14282 Tee Lee Popcorn Corp
P.O.Box 108
Shannon, IL 61078-0108   815-864-2363
Fax: 815-864-2388 800-578-2363
www.teeleepopcorn.com
Processor and exporter of microwaveable popcorn
President: James D Weaver
Sales Director: Wayne Vock
Estimated Sales:$ 20 - 50 Million
Number Employees: 20-49
Sq. footage: 40000
Type of Packaging: Consumer, Private Label, Bulk
Brands:
Prime Time
Tee Lee

14283 Tee Pee Olives
P.O.Box 239
Scarsdale, NY 10583-0239   914-723-6600
Fax: 914-723-2837 800-431-1529
daveco1287@aol.com www.teepeeolives.com

Importer and packer of bulk Spanish green olives in the US.
Owner: Robert Cory
CEO: David Cory
VP/Quality Control: Robert Cory PhD
Marketing Director: Neil Albert
Sales Director: Anthony Gambino
Production Manager: Joseph Fairchild
Plant Manager: Joseph Fairchild
Purchasing Manager: Emil Cairo
Estimated Sales:$ 10 - 20 Million
Number Employees: 10-19
Type of Packaging: Consumer, Food Service, Private Label, Bulk

14284 Teeccino Caffe
P.O.Box 40829
Santa Barbara, CA 93140-0829   805-966-0999
Fax: 805-966-0522 800-498-3434
info@teeccino.com www.teeccino.com
Coffee
President/Founder: Caroline MacDougall
National Sales Manager: Robert Tepper
Estimated Sales:$1,000,800
Number Employees: 5-9
Number of Brands: 1
Number of Products: 7
Type of Packaging: Consumer, Food Service, Private Label, Bulk
Brands:
Balanced Coffee
Teeccino Caffeine-Fr

14285 Teel Plastics
1060 Teel Ct
Baraboo, WI 53913-1069   608-355-3096
Fax: 608-355-3088 800-322-8335
getaquote@teel.com www.teel.com
Teel Plastics is an expert in the extrusion of plastic tubing parts and components for softener and filtration systems. Teel provides value added services such as assembly, chamfering, close tolerance burr-free cutting and punching.
President: Jay Smith
Marketing Director: Bryanna Smith
Sales Director: Randy Thomas
Estimated Sales:$20 Million
Number Employees: 250-499
Sq. footage: 180000

14286 Teeny Foods Corporation
3434 NE 170th Pl
Portland, OR 97230-5072   503-252-3006
Fax: 503-254-3004 www.teenyfoods.com
Processor of pizza, pizza skins and breads including pocket and specialty, including bread sticks, Greek pita, Italian flat bread, foccacia, and dough balls
President: Rick Teeny
VP Sales/General Manager: Darryl Abram
Production Manager: Dave Hermanson
Estimated Sales:$6000000
Number Employees: 50-99
Sq. footage: 24000
Brands:
Teeny Foods

14287 Teff Company
PO Box A
Caldwell, ID 83606-0016   208-455-0375
Fax: 208-454-3330 888-822-2221
info@teffco.com www.teffco.com
Processor of whole grain and flour
President: Wayne Carlson
Marketing Director: Elizabeth Carlson
Secretary: Elizabeth Carlson
Brands:
Maskal Teff

14288 Teixeira Farms
2600 Bonita Lateral Rd
Santa Maria, CA 93458-9703   805-928-3801
Fax: 805-928-9405 www.teixeirafarms.com
Grower of lettuce, broccoli, cabbage, cauliflower and celery
Owner: Allan Texiera
CEO: Chris Wong
Marketing Manager: Grenn Teixeira
Sales Manager: Glenn Teixeira
Estimated Sales:$ 20 - 50 Million
Number Employees: 250-499
Type of Packaging: Consumer, Private Label, Bulk
Brands:
Teixeira

14289 Tejon Ranch
P.O.Box 1000
Lebec, CA 93243-1000   661-248-3000
Fax: 661-248-6209 bzoeller@tejonranch.com
www.tejonranch.com
Processor and exporter of pistachios, walnuts, almonds and wine grapes
President/CEO: Robert Stine
CFO/VP/Corporate Secretary: Allen Lyda
Estimated Sales: Less than $500,000
Number Employees: 100-249
Type of Packaging: Consumer, Private Label, Bulk

14290 Tekita House Foods
6848 El Paso Drive
El Paso, TX 79905-3336   915-779-2181
Fax: 915-775-1857 www.tekitahouse.com
Manufacturer of Mexican food products. Products consist of tortillas, tostadas, pico de gallo salsa, chorizo, tamales, chiles rellenos, taco roll, flautas and pork crackling
President: Nelson Guerra
Estimated Sales: $500,000 appx.
Number Employees: 10-19

14291 Tell Chocolate Corporation
P.O.Box 1017
Waretown, NJ 08758-1017   732-583-8188
Fax: 732-660-8178 tellcorpo1@aol.com
www.store.yahoo.com/tellchocolate
Chocolates
President: Robert Ricci
Co-Owner: Mary Carol
Estimated Sales: Under $500,000
Number Employees: 5-9
Brands:
Marshmallow Chickies
Tell Chocolate

14292 Tell City Pretzel Company
432 Main Street
Tell City, IN 47586-2209   812-547-4631
Fax: 812-547-4850 www.tellcitypretzels.com
Processor of hard pretzels
Owner: Craig Kendall
Plant Manager: Betty Beard
Estimated Sales: $110000
Number Employees: 3
Type of Packaging: Consumer, Bulk

14293 Temo's Candy
495 W Exchange St
Akron, OH 44302-1403   330-376-7229
Processor of confectionery products
President: Lawrence Temo
Estimated Sales: $344051
Number Employees: 5-9
Sq. footage: 10000
Parent Co: Temo's
Type of Packaging: Consumer
Brands:
Temo's

14294 Tempest Fisheries Limited
38 Hassey Street
New Bedford, MA 02740-7209   508-997-0720
Fax: 508-990-2117
Fish and seafood
President: Timothy Mello
Estimated Sales: $ 5 - 10 Million
Number Employees: 5-9

14295 Tempest Vineyards
6000 Karlas Lane
Amity, OR 97101-2321   503-835-2600
Wines
President: Keith Orr
Estimated Sales: Less than $500,000
Number Employees: 1-4

14296 Templar Food Products
571 Central Ave # 114
New Providence, NJ 07974-1546   908-665-9511
Fax: 908-665-9122 800-883-6752
info@icedtea.com
Processor, importer and exporter of organic, black, green, herbal, oolong, chai and iced teas; also, caffeine-free
President: Edward D Reeves
Sales: Susan Brady
Production: Michael Murray
Purchasing Director: Kenneth Flynn

Estimated Sales: $870000
Number Employees: 10-19
Parent Co: Hilltop Tea
Type of Packaging: Private Label
Brands:
Perfect Choice

14297 Temptee Specialty Foods
2011 E 58th Ave
Denver, CO 80216-1517   303-292-1577
Fax: 303-292-1701 tempteeco@aol.com
Processor of portion controlled deli meats including beef; also, specialty processing available
President: Jack Lowe
Sales Manager: Jim Mayworm
Estimated Sales: $3616653
Number Employees: 20-49
Sq. footage: 20000

14298 Ten Ren Tea & Ginseng Company
75 Mott St
New York, NY 10013-4812   212-349-2286
Fax: 212-349-2180 800-292-2049
sales@tenrenusa.com www.tenrenusa.com
Tea
President: Mark Lee
Founder: Ray Ho Lee
Estimated Sales: Below $ 5 Million
Number Employees: 10-19
Brands:
Ten Ren's Tea

14299 Tenn Valley Ham Company
P.O.Box 1146
Paris, TN 38242-1146   731-642-9740
Fax: 731-642-7129 www.cliftyfarm.com
Processor of frozen portion cuts of bacon, ham and barbecue pork and turkey
President: Dan Murphey
Estimated Sales: $ 50 - 100 Million
Number Employees: 100-249
Type of Packaging: Consumer, Food Service
Brands:
Chifty Farm

14300 Tennessee Bun Company
197 Printwood Dr
Dickson, TN 37055-3011   615-441-4600
Fax: 615-441-4627 888-486-2867
www.buncompany.com
Hamburger buns
President: Cordia Harrington
VP Operations: Dave Nemecheck
Plant Manager: Dave Nemecheck
Estimated Sales: Below $ 5 Million
Number Employees: 50-99
Brands:
Tennessee Bun

14301 Tennessee Valley PackingCompany
P.O.Box 709
Columbia, TN 38402-0709   931-388-2623
Fax: 931-388-2624
Processor of meat products including sausages, frankfurters and bologna
President: Richard Jewell Jr
Estimated Sales: $ 3 - 5 Million
Number Employees: 5-9
Type of Packaging: Consumer

14302 Tenth & M Seafoods
1020 M St
Anchorage, AK 99501-3317   907-272-3474
Fax: 907-272-1685 www.10thandmseafoods.com
Processor, exporter and wholesaler/distributor of salmon, halibut, shrimp and bottom fish; importer and wholesaler/distributor of Pacific cod, perch, rockfish, snapper, etc.; serving the food service market
Owner: Skip Winfrey
Co-Owner: Lee Winfree
Estimated Sales: $ 10 - 20 Million
Number Employees: 20-49
Type of Packaging: Consumer, Food Service

14303 Tequila XQ
Placeres #1181 col Chapalita
Guadalajara Jalisco,
Mexico   333-587-7799
Fax: 333-915-3840 sales@tequilaxq.com
www.tequilaxq.com

A 3rd generation, family owned tequila producer based in the heart of the Tequila Region. Casa Tequila XQ was recently awarded 1st place as the best tequila in Mexico by La Academia Mexicana del Tequila.
President: Guillermo Estavillo
Marketing & Sales Director: Yezmin Hawa
Number of Brands: 5
Type of Packaging: Consumer, Food Service
Brands:
AMIGO LOCO
CLIMAX
EXQUISITO
TEQUILA XQ
VODKA ZAR

14304 Terra Botanica Products
268 Saddle Mountain Road
RR 2 Suite 33A, Comp #4
Nakusp, BC V0G 1R0
Canada   250-265-3648
Fax: 250-265-0081 888-410-9977
sales@terrabotanica.com www.terrabotanica.com
Processor of homeopathics, botanical extracts, capsules, gels and vitamins
president: John Miller
CEO: Connie Miller
Marketing Director: John Miller
Sales Director: Paul Peterson
Number Employees: 10,000+
Type of Packaging: Private Label

14305 Terra Harvest Foods
P.O.Box 5764
Rockford, IL 61125-0764   815-636-9500
Fax: 815-636-8400 lbresky@terraharvest.com
www.thfoods.com
Processor and exporter of snack mix items including sesame, corn and rice; also, rice, crackers, chips and snacks
President: Sam Mori
CEO: Terry Jessen
Marketing Director: Lucille Bresky
Sales Director: Jeff Baldwin
Operations Manager: Bob Manzer
Purchasing Manager: Jean Ruthe
Number Employees: 100-249
Sq. footage: 70000
Type of Packaging: Consumer, Private Label, Bulk
Brands:
Sesmark Deli Thins
Sesmark Rice Thins

14306 Terra Sol Chile Company
9415 Burnet Road
Suite 106
Austin, TX 78758-5245   512-836-3525
Fax: 512-502-9112
Chili

14307 Terra's
PO Box 265
Perham, MN 56573-0265   218-346-4100
Beef
President: Rod Osvold
Estimated Sales: Under $500,000
Number Employees: 1-4

14308 Terranetti's Italian Bakery
844 W Trindle Rd
Mechanicsburg, PA 17055-4095   717-697-5434
Fax: 717-697-6815
Processor of fresh rolls and bread including brown, white and rye.
President: Terrance E Mc Mahon
Estimated Sales: $ 20 - 50 Million
Number Employees: 20-49
Sq. footage: 16000
Type of Packaging: Consumer, Food Service
Brands:
Terranetti's

14309 Terrapin Ridge
120 E Clark Street
Freeport, IL 61032-3328   815-232-9708
Fax: 815-232-9768 800-999-4052
info@terrapinridge.com www.terrapinridge.com
Catsup and mustard, sauces, confits, mustard dressings, mustard seed oil, marinated squeezes, dessert squeezes, garnishing sauce, and gift ideas.
President: Martha Furst
Number Employees: 100-249
Parent Co: Furst-McNess Company
Type of Packaging: Private Label

Brands:
Terrapin Ridge

14310 Terrebonne Seafood
6563 Grand Caillou Road
Dulac, LA 70353-2501 985-563-2645
Fax: 985-563-4948
Wholesaler of seafood-shrimp.
President: Larry Authement
Estimated Sales:$7,000,000-$8,000,000
Number Employees: 6

14311 Terrell Meats
1211 E Main Street
Delta, UT 84624-8813 435-864-2600
Fax: 435-864-2600
Processor of beef jerky, beef, pork and lamb
Partner: Clark Terrell
Estimated Sales:$1200000
Number Employees: 6
Type of Packaging: Consumer, Food Service

14312 Terrell's Potato Chip Company
5960 First Avenue South,P.O. Box 84487
Seattle, WA 98124-5787 800-331-5222
Fax: 315-437-2069 800-331-5222
terrellchips@email.msn.com
http://www.email.msn.com
Processor of potato chips including regular, barbecue, onion and sour cream; also, salsa
President: Jack Terrell
Estimated Sales:$6500000
Number Employees: 70
Type of Packaging: Consumer
Brands:
Bachman
Keystone

14313 (HQ)Terri Lynn
1450 Bowes Rd
Elgin, IL 60123-5539 847-741-1900
Fax: 847-741-1912 800-323-0775
sales@terrilynn.com www.terrilynn.com
Manufacturer of Kosher Nuts, Dried Fruits and Chocolates.
President: Terri Schuck
CEO: Joe Graziano Sr
VP: Mark Graziano
Quality Control: Maulek Patel
Marketing: Mark Graziano
Sales: Mark Graziano
Operations: Joe Graziano Jr
Production: Joe Graziano Jr
Plant Manager: Joe Graziano Jr
Purchasing Director: Joe Graziano Jr
Estimated Sales:$ 60,000
Number Employees: 50-99
Number of Brands: 1
Number of Products: 600
Sq. footage: 110000
Parent Co: Terri Lynn, Inc
Type of Packaging: Food Service, Private Label, Bulk
Other Locations:
Terri Lynn-Pecan Shelling Operation
Cordele GA

14314 Terry Brothers
P.O.Box 8
Temperanceville, VA 23442-0008 757-824-3471
Fax: 757-824-3461 inf@terrybrothers.com
www.tyson.com
Processor of clams and oysters
Manager: Bill Ricken
VP: N Terry Jr
Estimated Sales:$2.5-5 Million
Number Employees: 5-9
Type of Packaging: Consumer, Food Service
Brands:
Sewansecott
Terry Brothers

14315 Terry Foods Inc
265 4th Street
Idaho Falls, ID 83401 208-604-8143
nik@terryfoods.com
www.terryfoods.com
Importers and distributors of a wide range of food ingredients, supplying food manufacturers, bakeries and food service companies throughout the USA
CEO: John Gardiner
CFO: Nikolai Terry
Sales Manager: Larry Haws

Estimated Sales:$ 5-10 Million
Number Employees: 1-4
Type of Packaging: Food Service, Bulk

14316 Tessenderlo Kerley
2255 N 44th St # 300
Phoenix, AZ 85008-3279 602-889-8300
Fax: 602-889-8430 800-669-0559
info-tki@tkinet.com www.tkinet.com
Producer of high quality gelatins for the food, pharmaceutical and photoghaphic industry, operating worldwide
CEO: Jordan Burns
Estimated Sales:$ 3 - 5 Million
Number Employees: 250-499
Type of Packaging: Private Label
Brands:
CRYOGEL
INSTAGEL
SOLGEL
SWIFTGEL

14317 Testamints
1248 Sussex Tpke
Unit C-1
Randolph, NJ 07869-2908 973-895-5041
Fax: 973-895-3742 888-879-0400
info@testamints.com www.testamints.com
Confections
President: Al Poe
Estimated Sales:$ 2.5-5 Million
Number Employees: 5-9
Brands:
Promise Pops
Testamints Chewing Gum
Testamints Fruit Flavored Candy
Testamints Sour Fruit Mints
Testamints Sugar Free Mints
Testamints Sugar Mints

14318 Teti Bakery
27 Signal Hill Avenue
Etobicoke, ON M9W 6V8
Canada 416-798-8777
Fax: 416-798-8749 800-465-0123
Processor of pizza, pizza crusts and Italian flat bread; exporter of pizza crusts
President: Franco Teti
VP: Dino Teti
Sales Manager: Tony Saldutto
Number Employees: 20-49
Sq. footage: 14000
Type of Packaging: Consumer, Food Service, Private Label, Bulk
Brands:
San Mario
Teti

14319 (HQ)Tetley Tea
P.O.Box 856
Shelton, CT 06484-0856 203-929-9200
Fax: 203-925-0512 800-728-0084
info@tetleyusa.com www.tetleyusa.com
Tea, coffee and tea bags
President: John Petrizzo
President: Glynne Jones
CFO: John Petrizzo
Sr. VP, Supply Chain: Dan Smith
Number Employees: 500-999
Parent Co: Tata Tea Ltd
Type of Packaging: Private Label
Brands:
Tetley Teas

14320 Teutopolis Lockers Service
312 W Walnut Street
Teutopolis, IL 62467-1024 217-857-3319
Processor of beef and pork
President/Owner: Larry McMahon
Estimated Sales:$500,000-$1 Million
Number Employees: 5-9
Type of Packaging: Consumer, Bulk

14321 Tex-Mex Cold Storage
6665 Padre Island Hwy
Brownsville, TX 78521-5218 956-831-9433
Fax: 956-831-9572 rec@texmexcold.com
www.texmexcold.com
Processor of seafood including shrimp; warehouse providing freezer and dry storage
President: Emilio Sanchez
VP: Norma sanchez
Plant Manager: Nick Sato

Estimated Sales:$6,307,658
Number Employees: 225
Sq. footage: 155000
Type of Packaging: Private Label, Bulk

14322 Tex-Mex Gourmet
PO Box 420963
Houston, TX 77242-0963 713-784-1900
Fax: 713-784-7616 888-345-8467
info@texmexgourmet.com
www.texmexgourmet.com
Sauces
Number Employees: 10-19
Type of Packaging: Consumer, Private Label
Brands:
LOS TIOS
TULDY'S

14323 TexaFrance
PO Box 27228
Austin, TX 78755-2228 512-246-2500
Fax: 512-246-2716 800-776-8937
info@texafrance.com www.texafrance.com
Processor and co-packer of natural pasta and pesto sauces, salad dressings, mustards, chutneys and jellies; private labeling available
President: Jean-Pierre Parant
VP Purchasing: David Griswold
Estimated Sales:$1154099
Number Employees: 7
Sq. footage: 8000
Type of Packaging: Consumer, Private Label

14324 Texas Coffee Company
P.O.Box 31
Beaumont, TX 77704-0031 409-835-3434
Fax: 409-835-4248 800-259-3400
texjoy@texjoy.com www.texjoy.com
Processor of tea, coffee, extracts, spices and seasonings; importer of coffee and tea
President: Carlo Busceme
President/Operations: Carlo Busceme III
VP: Donald Fertitta
Estimated Sales:$ 10 - 20 Million
Number Employees: 20-49
Sq. footage: 45000
Type of Packaging: Consumer, Food Service, Private Label, Bulk
Brands:
Seaport
Texjoy

14325 Texas Crumb & Food Products
3250 Towerwood Dr
Farmers Branch, TX 75234-2315 972-243-8443
Fax: 972-484-9315 800-522-7862
info@dasbrot.com www.dasbrot.com
Processor of bread crumbs, batters, breadings and stuffing and seasoning mixes
President: S Holtsclaw
Vice President: W Holtsclaw
Estimated Sales:$900000
Number Employees: 5-9
Sq. footage: 16000
Parent Co: Das Brot
Type of Packaging: Food Service, Private Label, Bulk

14326 Texas Heat
P.O.Box 33246
San Antonio, TX 78265-3246 210-656-4328
Fax: 210-656-5916 800-656-5916
Processor of picante sauce, chili mix and cheese dip
President: Robert Delgado
Estimated Sales:$ 1 - 3 Million
Number Employees: 1-4
Type of Packaging: Consumer, Food Service

14327 Texas Ladies Composite Organization
PO Box 957
Stephenville, TX 76401-0009 254-968-7446
Fax: 254-968-2161 888-968-2161
Pecans
Manager: Cissy Bramlett
Estimated Sales:$500-1 Million appx.
Number Employees: 5-9

14328 Texas Reds Steak House
P.O.Box 111
Red River, NM 87558-0111 575-754-2964
Fax: 575-754-2309 www.texasreds.com

Steak
President: William Gill
VP: Rik Gill
CFO: Deanna Tapia
Estimated Sales: $ 1-2.5 Million
Number Employees: 20-49
Brands:
Texas Red

14329 Texas Sassy Foods
9600 Great Hills Trail
Suite 150W
Austin, TX 78759   512-215-4022
          Fax: 603-251-0780 www.texas-sassy.com
pickles, relishes, sauces and more

14330 Texas Sausage Company
2915 E 12th St
Austin, TX 78702-2401   512-472-6707
          Fax: 512-472-9360 hotlinks@austin.rr.com
Processor and wholesaler/distributor of sausage;
serving the food service market
President: Gary Tharp
Estimated Sales: $ .5 - 1 million
Number Employees: 5-9
Type of Packaging: Consumer, Food Service

14331 Texas Spice Company
P.O.Box 2133
Cedar Park, TX 78630-2133   512-260-1712
          Fax: 512-260-1713 800-880-8007
          contact@texas-spice.net   www.texasspice.net
Wholesale/Retail custom blending, spices, seasoning
blends, bases, extracts, flavors, coffee & tea
Owner: Beckie Forsyth
Estimated Sales: Below $ 5 Million
Number Employees: 1-4
Type of Packaging: Food Service
Brands:
Texas Spice

14332 Texas Tito's
4611 Wiseman Blvd
San Antonio, TX 78251-4202   210-250-5000
          Fax: 210-250-5055 830-626-1123
          gotexan@agr.state.tx.us   www.gotexan.org
Texas regional food
President: Hiroshi Shimizu
State Marketing Coordinator: Susan Dunn
Deputy Assistant Commissioner Marketing:
Delane Caesar
Estimated Sales: $500,000-$1 Million
Number Employees: 250-499
Brands:
Go Texan

14333 Texas Toffee
5 Santa Fe Place
Odessa, TX 79765-8520   432-563-4105
          Fax: 915-563-4105
Processor and exporter of toffee including milk and
white chocolate, bittersweet, peanut, butterscotch
and sugar-free
President: Susan Leshnower
Number Employees: 1-4
Sq. footage: 32
Type of Packaging: Consumer, Food Service, Pri-
vate Label, Bulk
Brands:
Texas Toffee

14334 Texas Traditions
P.O.Box 2705
Georgetown, TX 78627-2705   512-863-7291
          Fax: 512-869-6212 800-547-7062
          info@texastraditions.com
          www.texastraditions.com
President/Founder: Dianna Howard
Brands:
Texas Traditions

14335 Texas Traditions
P.O.Box 2705
Georgetown, TX 78627-2705   512-863-7291
          Fax: 512-869-6212 800-547-7062
          info@texastraditions.com
          www.texastraditions.com
Processor and exporter of mesquite smoke, jalapeno
pepper, country-style German and black peppercorn
mustard, jalapeno and red chile pepper, prickly pear
cactus jelly, hot salt, seasoning blends and dry dip
mixes
President: Dianna Howard

Estimated Sales: $300,000-500,000
Number Employees: 1-4
Brands:
Texas Hot Salt
Texas Traditions

14336 Thackery & Company
PO Box 58
Bolinas, CA 94924-0058   415-868-1781
          Fax: 415-868-1781 thackrey@earthlink.net
Gourmet foods
President: Sean Thackery
Estimated Sales: Under $500,000
Number Employees: 1-4
Brands:
Thackrey

14337 Thai Kitchen
P.O.Box 13242
Berkeley, CA 94712-4242   510-675-9025
          Fax: 510-675-9045 800-967-8424
          info@thaikitchen.com   www.thaikitchen.com
Thai food
President: Seth Jacobson
Vice President: Dick Neilsen
Estimated Sales: $10-20 Million
Number Employees: 20-49
Type of Packaging: Private Label
Brands:
Thai Kitchen

14338 Thanksgiving Coffee Company
P.O.Box 1918
Fort Bragg, CA 95437-1918   707-964-0118
          Fax: 707-964-0351 800-462-1999
          pkatzeff@thanksgivingcoffee.com
          www.thanksgivingcoffee.com
Processor of vacuum packed coffee including certi-
fied organic, shade grown, regular, decaffeinated
and flavored
CEO: Paul Katzeff
President: Joan Katzeff
Plant Manager: David Gillette
Estimated Sales: $4741877
Number Employees: 50-99
Type of Packaging: Consumer, Food Service, Pri-
vate Label, Bulk
Brands:
Aztec Harvest
Grand Slam
Inca Harvest
Mayan Harvest
Pony Express
Royal Garden Tea
Song Bird
Thanksgiving
ZIP

14339 Thatcher's Special Popcorn
2200 Jerrold Ave # H
San Francisco, CA 94124-1036   415-643-9945
          Fax: 415-643-9948 800-926-2676
          sales@tgsp.com   www.tgsp.com
Gourmet popcorn and snacks
President: Gus Ghassan
Vice President: Ghada Ghassan
Manager: Joe Eidson
Estimated Sales: Less than $500,000
Number Employees: 1-4
Type of Packaging: Private Label
Brands:
Joy's Gourmet Snacks
Thatcher's
Thatcher's Special Popcorn

14340 (HQ)The Bama Company
5377 E 66th St N
Tulsa, OK 74117-1813   918-592-0778
          Fax: 918-732-2902 800-756-2262
          www.bama.com
Manufacturer and exporter of frozen baked goods
including cookies, pies and biscuits; also, bakers'
and confectioners' supplies including dough, pastry
and crumb crust pie shells
President/CEO: Paula Marshall-Chapman
CEO: Paula Marshall
QC Manager: Maurice Lawry
Director Brand Sales: Gary Wilson
Number Employees: 100-249
Type of Packaging: Consumer, Food Service

14341 The Cheesecake Factory
26901 Malibu Hills Road
Calabasas Hills, CA 91301   818-871-3000
          Fax: 818-871-3001 www.cheesecakefactory.net
Cheesecakes
President: Michael Jannini
Chairman/CEO: David Overton
Senior VP Finance/CFO: Michael Dixon
Senior VP Marketing/Public Relations: Howard
Gordon
COO: David Gordon
Estimated Sales: $1.6 Billion
Number Employees: 5-9
Brands:
Cheesecake Factory

14342 The Lollipop Tree, Inc
319 Vaughan St
Portsmouth, NH 03801   603-436-8196
          Fax: 603-436-0282 800-842-6691
          info@lollipoptree.com   www.lollipoptree.com
A family-owned specialty food manufacturer of all
natural baking mixes, condiments and jams, as well
as exclusive products prepared for private label spe-
cialty retailers. Lollipop Tree's line of Good Simple
Food® includes pepperjellies, organic baking mixes,
cookie mixes, dessert bread mixes and dessert
sauces, grilling sauces, pancakes mixes, jams, scone
mixes, and syrups.
President: Robert Lynch
CEO: Laurie Lynch
CFO: Bob Lynch
R&D: Collen Smith
Marketing Manager: Melissa Lawton
Sales: Luke Morton
Public Relations: Sue Downey
Operations: Robert Lynch
Production: Adam Podolec
Plant Manager: Adam Podolec
Purchasing: Adam Podolec
Estimated Sales: $ 20 - 50 Million
Number Employees: 50-99
Number of Products: 90
Sq. footage: 68000
Type of Packaging: Consumer, Private Label
Brands:
Harborside
Lollipop Tree
Quick Loaf
The Lollipop Tree

14343 The Long Life Beverage Company
P.O.Box 7802
Mission Hills, CA 91346-7802   661-259-5575
                    800-848-7331
          info@long-life.com   www.long-life.com
Processor, importer and exporter of organic herbal
black and green teas, currently offer over 40 boxed
varieties and 11 ready to drink bottled iced teas, and
a variety of enhanced waters
Owner: Troy Long
Sales Director: Mark Cook
Operations Manager: Lori Kwoka
Purchasing Manager: Beth Kreoll
Estimated Sales: $$7.5 Million
Number Employees: 1-4
Number of Brands: 3
Number of Products: 52
Sq. footage: 11000
Parent Co: Consac Industries
Type of Packaging: Consumer, Private Label
Brands:
Enhance Vitamin/Waters
Long Life Black Teas
Long Life Green Teas
Long Life Herbal Teas
Long Life Iced Teas

14344 (HQ)The Scoular Company
2027 Dodge Street
Omaha, NE 68102   402-342-3500
          wwilms@scoular.com
          www.scoular.com
Merchandise a full range of agricultural products:
traditional and specialty crops, food and feed ingre-
dients, and even freight. Market over 100 products
on 5 continents, and growing.
Chairman of the Board: Marshall Faith
CEO: Chuck Elsea
President: David Faith
COO: Bob Ludington
COO: Bob Ludington
Estimated Sales: $4.3 Billion
Number Employees: 250-499

Number of Products: 100+
Parent Co: Scoular Company

14345 (HQ)The Solae Company
4300 Duncan Avenue
St Louis, MO 63188   314-982-1000
Fax: 260-425-5301 800-325-7108
www.solae.com
Manufacturer of soybean ingredient products, including textured vegetable proteins, textured and functional soy concentrates and isolates, specialty lecithins, polymers
CEO: Torkel Rehnman
CFO: Steve Fray
VP/General Counsel: Cornel Fuerer
Senior Director R&D: Phil Kerr PhD
VP Global Operations: Paul Bossert Jr
Estimated Sales: $1+ Billion
Number Employees: 3500
Type of Packaging: Consumer, Bulk
Other Locations:
Central Soya Company - Processing
Decatur IN
Central Soya Company - Processing
Gibson City IL
Central Soya Company - Processing
Marion OH
Central Soya Company - Grain Plant
Indianapolis IN
Central Soya Company - Processing
Bellevue OH
Central Soya Company - Grain Plant
Cincinnati OH
Central Soya Company - Processing
Delphos OH
Central Soya Company - Mfg
Remington IN
Central Soya Company - Processing
Morristown IN
Central Soya Company - Grain
Jeffersonville OH
Central Soya Company - Grain
Waterloo IN
Central Soya Company - Bulk Oil
Pawtucket RI
Central Soya Company - Mfg
New Bremen OH
Brands:
FIBRIM
SOLAE

14346 Theo Chocolate
3400 Phinney Ave N
Seattle, WA 98103   206-632-5100
Fax: 206-632-0413 info@theochocolate.com
www.theochocolate.com
chocolate
Founder: Joe Whinney
Number Employees: 10

14347 Theoworld
P.O. Box 18071
Fairfield, OH 45018-0071   773-268-2800
Fax: 773-268-2850 http://www.theoworlds.com
President: Ted Mitsakopoulos
Estimated Sales: $ 5 - 10 Million
Number Employees: 10-19

14348 Theriaults Abattoir
P.O.Box 314
Van Buren, ME 04785-0314   207-868-3344
Fax: 207-868-2866
Processor of meat products and hydrogenated fats
President: Reynold A Theriault
Estimated Sales: $36000
Number Employees: 1-4
Type of Packaging: Consumer

14349 Thermice Company
1445 E Putnam Avenue
Old Greenwich, CT 06870-1379   203-637-4500
General grocery
President: Dave Herman
Estimated Sales: $ .5 - 1 million
Number Employees: 5-9

14350 Thiel Cheese & Ingredients
N7630 County Hwy BB
Attn: Kathy Pitzen
Hilbert, WI 54129   920-989-1440
Fax: 920-989-1288 kathyp@thielcheese.com
www.thielcheese.com

Manufacturer and custom formulator of processed cheeses that are used primarily as ingredients in other food products
President: Steven Thiel
Sales: Kathy Pitzen
Number Employees: 50-99
Type of Packaging: Consumer, Food Service, Private Label, Bulk
Brands:
Thiel

14351 Thirs-Tea Corporation
18522 NE 2nd Ave
Miami, FL 33179-4427   305-651-4350
Fax: 305-652-4478 sales@thirs-tea.com
www.thirs-tea.com
Processor and exporter of liquid iced tea bases and concentrates
President: Steve Bragg
Estimated Sales: $500,000-$1 Million
Number Employees: 10-19
Type of Packaging: Consumer, Food Service, Private Label, Bulk
Brands:
THIRS-TEA

14352 Thiry Daems Cheese Factory
RR 2
Box 21
Luxemburg, WI 54217-9802   920-845-2117
Fax: 920-845-2629
Cheese
Estimated Sales: $ 1-2.5 Million
Number Employees: 20

14353 Thistledew Farm
Rr 1 Box 122
Proctor, WV 26055-9608   304-455-1728
Fax: 304-455-1740 800-854-6639
thistle@ovis.net www.thistledewfarm.com
Processor of honey, hot pepper butter, hot honey mustard, wild wing and rib sauce, garden gourmet salad dressing, original honey mustard, red raspberry, and red raspberry honey vinegar, candles, cosmetics, gift boxes and cratesbaskets, and other great products.
President: Ellie Conlon
CEO: S Conlon
Estimated Sales: $200,000
Number Employees: 1-4
Number of Brands: 2
Number of Products: 7
Sq. footage: 5000
Type of Packaging: Consumer, Food Service, Private Label, Bulk
Brands:
Thistledew Farm's
West's Best

14354 Tholstrup Cheese
6366 Norton Center Dr
Muskegon, MI 49441-6032   231-798-4371
Fax: 231-798-4374 800-426-0938
Cheese
Manager: Torben Siggaard
VP: Hans Lund
Vice President: Vincent Staiger
Plant Manager: Ernst Siggaard
Estimated Sales: $500,000 appx.
Number Employees: 20-49
Brands:
Saga

14355 Thoma Vineyards
11975 Smithfield Rd
Dallas, OR 97338-9339   503-623-6420
Fax: 503-623-4310 www.vanduzer.com
Wines
Manager: Jim Kakacek
Estimated Sales: $300,000-500,000
Number Employees: 5-9

14356 Thomas Brothers Ham Company
1852 Gold Hill Rd
Asheboro, NC 27203-4291   336-672-0337
Fax: 336-672-1782 thomasbros@sheboro.com
Processor and packer of country hams; wholesaler/distributor of frozen and specialty foods and meats; serving the food service and retail markets in the southeast
President/CFO: Howard M Thomas
Quality Control: Don Thomas
Sales/Plant Manager: Don Thomas
Plant Manager: Don Thomas

Estimated Sales: $ 10 - 20 Million
Number Employees: 20-49
Number of Brands: 10
Number of Products: 300
Type of Packaging: Consumer, Private Label
Brands:
Farmer Dons Country Ham
Private Labels
Thomas Brothers Country Ham

14357 Thomas Canning/Maidstone
Rural Route 1
Maidstone, ON N0R-1K0
Canada   519-737-1531
Fax: 519-737-7003 thomasca@mnsi.com
Processor and canner of tomatoes and tomato juice
President: Bill Thomas
Type of Packaging: Food Service, Private Label
Brands:
UTOPIA

14358 Thomas Dairy
P.O.Box 519
Rutland, VT 05702-0519   802-773-6788
Fax: 802-747-7121 sales@thomasdairy.com
www.thomasdairy.com
Fluid milk
President: Richard Thomas Jr
Founder: Orin Thomas
Marketing Director: John Thomas
Estimated Sales: $ 5-10 Million
Number Employees: 20-49
Brands:
Thomas

14359 Thomas Fogarty Winery
3270 Alpine Rd
Portola Valley, CA 94028-7523   650-851-6777
Fax: 650-851-5840 800-247-4163
info@fogartywinery.com
www.fogartywinery.com
Wines
Executive Director: Anne Krolczyk
Winemaker: Michael Martella
Director Sales/Marketing: Anne Krolczyk
Office Administrator: Melissa Baker
Tasting Room Manager: Rick Davis
Assistant Winemaker: Nathan Kandler
Office Manager: Carrie Larkin
Events Coordinator: Dana Miller
Events Planner: Becky Thatcher
Estimated Sales: Below $ 5 Million
Number Employees: 10-19
Brands:
Thomas Fogarty Winery

14360 Thomas Gourmet Foods
P.O.Box 8822
Greensboro, NC 27419-0822   336-299-6263
Fax: 336-299-7852 800-867-2823
info@thomasgourmetfoods.com
www.thomasgourmetfoods.com
Sauce, marinade, dressing, cocktail sauce, tartar sauce, Bloody Mary mix, marinara and pasta sauce
Owner: Dwight Thomas
CEO: Brian Thomas
Estimated Sales: $ 3 - 5 Million
Number Employees: 5-9
Number of Brands: 1
Type of Packaging: Consumer, Private Label, Bulk
Brands:
Thomas

14361 Thomas Kemper Soda Company
91 S Royal Brougham Way
Seattle, WA 98134   206-381-8712
host@tksoda.com
www.tksoda.com
Beverages
Owner: Thomas Kemper
Chairman: Laura Bracken-Clough
President: T Maxwell Clough
Estimated Sales: $ 5-10 Million
Number Employees: 1
Brands:
Thomas Kemper Birch Soda
Thomas Kemper Cola
Thomas Kemper Cream

14362 Thomas Kruse Winery
3200 Dryden Ave
Gilroy, CA 95020-9072   408-842-7016
Fax: 408-842-7016 krusewine@aol.com
www.thomaskrusewinery.com

Manufacture of wine
President/CEO: Thomas Kruse
Marketing Director: Thomas Kruse
Estimated Sales: Below $ 5 Million
Number Employees: 1-4
Brands:
Thomas Kruse Winery

14363 Thomas Lobster Company
PO Box 77
Islesford, ME 04646-0077 207-244-5876
Fax: 808-244-7020

Lobster

14364 Thomas Packing Company
4643 Farley Dr
Columbus, GA 31907-6342 706-689-3513
Fax: 770-227-2166 800-729-0976
jon@crouch.com www.thomasgourmet.com
Processor and packer of meat products including
cured ham, bacon, smoked, andouille and frankfurt-
ers; also, smoked turkeys and hams for holiday gift
boxes
President: Lee Thomas
CEO: Billy Thomas
Estimated Sales: $ .5 - 1 million
Number Employees: 5-9
Sq. footage: 26000
Type of Packaging: Consumer, Food Service, Bulk
Brands:
Thomas
Treasure

14365 Thomasson's Potato ChipCompany
265 Bowman St
Mansfield, OH 44903-1699 419-529-9424
Fax: 419-529-6789 800-466-9424
chips@joneschips.com www.joneschips.com
Manufacturer and exporter of potato chips, pretzels
and cheese puffs
President: Robert Jones
Director of Sales: Don Markov
Production Manager: Roy Kehl
Estimated Sales: $ 10 - 20 Million
Number Employees: 20-49
Sq. footage: 22000
Type of Packaging: Consumer, Private Label
Brands:
Thomasson's

14366 Thompson Candy Company
80 S Vine St
Meriden, CT 06451-3823 203-235-2541
Fax: 203-630-2492 800-648-4058
custsvc@thompsoncandy.com
www.thompsoncandy.com
Processor and exporter of chocolate molded prod-
ucts including organic, foiled novelties, bars and
filled cups
President: Bill Losust
Estimated Sales: $ 20 - 50 Million
Number Employees: 100-249
Sq. footage: 114000

14367 Thompson Packers
550 Carnation St
Slidell, LA 70460-1899 985-641-6640
Fax: 985-645-2112 800-989-6328
support@thompack.com www.thompack.com
Manufacturer and exporter of frozen beef, pork, veal
and lamb; processor of frozen ground beef and ham-
burger patties
President: Mary Thompson
CEO: M Thompson
Estimated Sales: $21 Million
Number Employees: 1-4
Sq. footage: 50000
Type of Packaging: Consumer, Food Service, Pri-
vate Label

14368 Thompson Seafood
P.O.Box 1057
Darien, GA 31305-1057 912-437-4649
Processor of shrimp, trout and flounder
Partner: Rita Young
Estimated Sales: $575000
Number Employees: 1-4
Type of Packaging: Food Service, Bulk

14369 Thompson's Fine Foods
5973 Pheasant Dr
Shoreview, MN 55126-4692 651-481-0374
Fax: 651-482-1944 800-807-0025
muclijoh@msn.com
Processor of mild/sweet, medium/spicy, hot/spicy
and hot/hot barbecue dipping sauces for meats,
sandwiches and appetizers
Owner: John Thompson
Owner/President: John Thompson
Estimated Sales: Under $500,000
Number Employees: 1-4
Type of Packaging: Consumer, Food Service, Pri-
vate Label, Bulk
Brands:
Thompson's Black Tie

14370 Thoms-Proestler Company
P.O.Box 7210
Rock Island, IL 61204-7210 309-787-1234
Fax: 309-787-1248 upchurchj@tpcinfo.com
www.tpcinfo.com
Wholesaler/distributor of groceries, meats, produce,
dairy products, seafood, frozen foods, equipment
and fixtures and general merchandise; serving the
food service market
President: Michael Wiedower
Sales/Marketing Manager: Bill Brownson
Purchasing Manager: Bryan Marley
Estimated Sales: $97300000
Number Employees: 500-999
Sq. footage: 236000

14371 Thomson Food
4435 Venture Avenue
Duluth, MN 55811-5705 218-722-2529
Fax: 218-722-2743 info@thomsonfoods.com
www.thomsonfoods.com
Produces jams, jellies, preserves, syrups, salsas,
marinades, barbecue, pizza, spaghetti sauces, fla-
vored vinegars, vinaigrettes, and salad dressings.
President: Joel Kozlak
VP: Kan Kalligher
Plant Manager: Mike Lonetto
Estimated Sales: $ 1-5 Million
Number Employees: 14
Number of Brands: 2
Number of Products: 40
Sq. footage: 16000
Type of Packaging: Consumer, Food Service, Pri-
vate Label
Brands:
Mama Cella's
Thomson Berry Farms

14372 Thomson Meats
618 Hamilton Avenue W
Melfort, SK S0E 1A0
Canada 306-752-2802
Fax: 306-752-4674 sales@rascalsfoods.com
www.rascalsfoods.com
Processor of value added meat products including
fresh and frozen pork, beef and chicken
CEO: Paul Marciniak
CFO: Wendy Welsch
R&D: Daryl Durell
Marketing: Donna Walton
Sales: Ron Andrujek
Plant Manager: Gerard Kiefe
Number Employees: 42
Sq. footage: 30000
Type of Packaging: Private Label, Bulk

14373 Thor Incorporated
1280 W 2550 S
Ogden, UT 84401-3238 801-393-3312
Fax: 801-621-3298 888-846-7462
inquirie@thorincorporated.com
www.thorincorporated.com
Custom formulating and contract packaging for vita-
mins and supplements in liquids, capsules and
powders
President: Allen Glanville
Estimated Sales: $ 10-20 Million
Number Employees: 10-19
Type of Packaging: Private Label

14374 Thor-Shackel HorseradishCompany
16w224 Shore Ct
Burr Ridge, IL 60527 630-986-1333
Fax: 630-986-0125

Processor of fresh grated horseradish and sauces in-
cluding cocktail, horseradish, etc
Owner: Michael Dogan
General Manager: Michael Dogan
General Manager: Joe Dogan
Estimated Sales: $ 3 - 5 Million
Number Employees: 10-19
Sq. footage: 30000
Type of Packaging: Consumer, Food Service, Pri-
vate Label, Bulk
Brands:
Thor's

14375 Thornbury Grandview Farms
PO Box 538
Thornbury, ON N0H 2PO
Canada 519-599-2225
Fax: 519-599-3550 dvt.grandview@dmts.com
Processor and exporter of game meats including bi-
son, venison, wild boar, caribou, ostrich, musk-ox
and emu; importer of alligator and rattlesnake
President: Desmond Von Teichman
Plant Manager: Bob Hutchinson
Number Employees: 12
Sq. footage: 7500
Type of Packaging: Food Service, Private Label
Brands:
Grandview Farms

14376 Thornton Bakery
4244 Elvis Presley Boulevard
Memphis, TN 38116-6424 901-324-2118
Baked goods
Estimated Sales: Under $500,000
Number Employees: 50-99

14377 Thornton Foods Company
8590 Magnolia Trl # 121
Eden Prairie, MN 55344-7645 952-944-1735
Fax: 952-944-2083 thorntonfoods@aol.com
Manufacturer of low-fat and fat-free dairy based
food products including pasta and cheese sauces
President/CEO: Barbara Thornton
Estimated Sales: $5-10 Million
Number Employees: 5-9
Type of Packaging: Consumer, Food Service, Pri-
vate Label, Bulk
Brands:
LIVING LIGHT
LIVING LIGHT DAIRY BLEND

14378 Thornton Winery
P.O.Box 9008
Temecula, CA 92589-9008 951-699-0099
Fax: 951-699-5536 info@thorntonwine.com
www.thorntonwine.com
Wines, champagne
President: John Thornton
Co-Owner: Steve Thornton
CFO: Tim Kelly
Quality Control: Cheryl Rolph
Public Relations Manager: Jan Schneider
Production Manager: Jon McPherson
Estimated Sales: $ 5-10 Million
Number Employees: 50-99
Brands:
Thornton

14379 Thorough Fare Gourmet
PO Box 490
Marlboro, VT 05344-0490 802-257-5612
thoroughfare@amtraders.com
Salad dressing, marinades, and baking mixes

14380 Thorpe Vineyard
8150 Chimney Heights Blvd
Wolcott, NY 14590-9201 315-594-2502
Fax: 315-594-2502 winery@thorpevineyard.com
www.thorpevineyard.com
Wine
President: Fumie Thorpe
Estimated Sales: Less than $500,000
Number Employees: 1-4
Type of Packaging: Private Label
Brands:
Thorpe Vineyard

14381 Those Hersey Brothers
495 N Main St
Casnovia, MI 49318-9405 616-675-4641
Fax: 616-675-4110 800-289-2767

Processor and exporter of apples and peaches
Owner: Burnett Hersey II
Bookkeeper: Sheila Wamser
Sales: Cindy Stockwell
Estimated Sales: $ 20 - 50 Million
Number Employees: 50-99
Type of Packaging: Consumer, Food Service, Bulk

14382 Three Lakes Winery
P.O.Box 37
Three Lakes, WI 54562-0037   715-546-3080
                Fax: 715-546-8148   800-944-5434
     info@fruitwine.com   www.fruitwine.com
Processor of wine including cranberry, apricot, cran-
berry/apple, cranberry/raspberry, blackberry, straw-
berry, wild plum, strawberry-rhubarb, red raspberry,
rhubarb, Italian plum and kiwi
President: Mark Mc Cain
Advertising/Marketing: Marla Shane
Sales/Distribution: Mark McCain
Wine Maker: Scott McCain
Production Manager: Scott Foster
Estimated Sales: $720000
Number Employees: 5-9
Sq. footage: 4000
Type of Packaging: Consumer
Brands:
Fruit of the Woods

14383 Three Rivers Fish Company
P.O.Box 668
Simmesport, LA 71369-0668   318-941-2467
                Fax: 318-941-2467
Fresh and frozen seafood/fish
Owner: William Arnouville
Estimated Sales: $730,000
Number Employees: 1-4

14384 Three Springs Farm
RR 1
Box 128
Prospect, VA 23960   804-574-2314
                Fax: 804-574-7248
Processor and contract packager of garlic seed and
elephant garlic cloves
Owner: Garrett Doering
Number Employees: 5-9
Type of Packaging: Consumer, Private Label, Bulk

14385 Three Springs Water Company
1800 Pine Run Rd
Laurel Run, PA 18706-9419   570-823-7019
                Fax: 570-822-6177   800-332-7873
Processor and bottler of low-mineral and so-
dium-free spring water
President: Jim Tosh
Estimated Sales: $ 3 - 5 Million
Number Employees: 20-49
Sq. footage: 40000
Type of Packaging: Consumer, Food Service, Pri-
vate Label
Brands:
3 Springs

14386 Three Vee Food & Syrup Company
110 Bridge St
Brooklyn, NY 11201-1575   718-858-7333
                Fax: 718-858-7371   800-801-7330
     info@3vee.com   www.3vee.com
Processor and exporter of liquid meat tenderizers,
dessert toppings, fruit concentrates, pulps, syrups
and juices including orange, papaya, black raspberry,
mango, guava, cranberry, coconut, etc.; importer of
juice concentrates and purees
Owner: Elshi Gambo
VP: Clara Stark
Marketing/Sales Manager: Bruce Borwick
Estimated Sales: $ 20 - 50 Million
Number Employees: 20-49
Sq. footage: 21000
Type of Packaging: Consumer, Food Service, Pri-
vate Label, Bulk

14387 Threshold RehabilitationServices
1000 Lancaster Ave
Reading, PA 19607-1699   610-777-7691
                Fax: 610-777-1295   trsincmail@trsinc.org
                www.trsinc.org
Contract packagers
President: Ronald Williams
Sales/Marketing: Nancy Benjamin

Estimated Sales: $ 20 - 50 Million
Number Employees: 250-499
Sq. footage: 20000

14388 Thrifty Ice Cream
9200 Telstar Ave
El Monte, CA 91731-2814   626-571-0122
                Fax: 626-280-2905 www.riteaid.com
Processor and exporter of ice cream
Manager: Larry Crosby
Export Director: Bob Dwyer
CFO: Mary Salmons
Quality Control: Lory Irias
Plant Manager: Ron Simmer
Estimated Sales: $ 20-50 Million
Number Employees: 100-249
Parent Co: Thrifty
Type of Packaging: Consumer, Food Service, Bulk

14389 Thrifty Vegetable Company
728 Crocker St
Los Angeles, CA 90021-1412   213-485-8804
                Fax: 213-629-2253 media@thriftyfoods.com
                www.thriftyvegetable.com
Manufacturer of produce
President: George Abadjian
Estimated Sales: $45 Million
Number Employees: 20-49

14390 (HQ)Thumann's
670 Dell Rd # 1
Carlstadt, NJ 07072-2292   201-935-3636
                Fax: 201-935-2226 sales@thumanns.com
                www.thumanns.com
Manufacturer and packer of delicatessen products
that include; ham, roast beef, corned beef, pastrami,
turkey, liverwurst, bologna, hot dogs, breakfast
meats and sausages, cheeses, soups, salads, condi-
ments and frozen products
Owner: Bob Burke Sr
Estimated Sales: $ 50 - 100 Million
Number Employees: 250-499
Brands:
THUMANN'S

14391 Thyme & Truffles Hors D'oeuvres
135 Miranda Avenue
Toronto, ON M6B 3W8
Canada   416-256-0275
                Fax: 416-256-1697   877-489-8636
                tandt@thymeandtruffles.com
                www.thymeandtruffles.com
Processor of frozen oven-ready hors d'oeuvres with
assorted fillings including canapes; also, frozen veg-
etarian entrees
President: Rhonda Richer
QA/QC Specialist: Santi Vicente
Sales Manager: Tim Lipa
Director of Operations: Gino Giansante
Production Manager: Alfred Meth
Number Employees: 50-99
Number of Products: 40
Sq. footage: 12500
Type of Packaging: Food Service, Private Label,
Bulk
Brands:
Thyme & Truffles

14392 Thymly Products
1332 Colora Road
Colora, MD 21917-1422   410-658-4820
                Fax: 410-658-2899 vincer@thymlyproducts.com
                www.thymlyproducts.com
Food baking additives, flavors, specialty blends
President: Harry T Muller
Vice President: Shirley Wiest
Sales Manager: Paul Canfient
Plant Manager: Chuck Osterrider
Purchasing Agent: Vince Reynolds
Estimated Sales: $3.5 Million
Number Employees: 37
Type of Packaging: Private Label
Brands:
Baker's Cremes
Bread Glaze
Brew Buffers
Glalcto
Parve Plain Muffin

14393 Tianfu China Cola
2 Brady Ln
Katonah, NY 10536-2502   914-232-3102
                Fax: 914-232-9184 davorganic@aol.com

Processor of natural soft drinks; importer of herbs
President: David Robinov
Estimated Sales: $500,000-$1 Million
Number Employees: 1-4
Brands:
China Cola

14394 Tic Gums
4609 Richlynn Dr
Belcamp, MD 21017-1228   410-273-7300
                Fax: 410-273-6469   800-899-3953
     svandenheuvel@ticgums.com   www.aragum.com
Ingredients and mixes
President: Scott Riesler
Director Field Technical Services: Ted Benic
CFO: Mike Dean
CEO: Steven Andon
R & D: Mar Nieto
Quality Control: Ian Sklar
Marketing Manager: Frances Bowman
Operations Manager: Steve Hartley
Technical Services Manager: Marceliono Nieto
Estimated Sales: $ 20-50 Million
Number Employees: 50-99

14395 Tichon Seafood Corporation
7 Conway St
New Bedford, MA 02740-7205   508-999-5607
                Fax: 508-990-8271
Processor of fresh and frozen fish including squid,
scallops and fish sticks
President: Daniel Tichon
VP: R Tichon
Executive VP: Ronald Tichon
Estimated Sales: $1200000
Number Employees: 20-49
Sq. footage: 60000
Type of Packaging: Consumer
Brands:
Tichon

14396 TideWays
750 Seashore Avenue
Peaks Island, ME 04108-1252   207-766-0062
                Fax: 312-787-6070
Seafood crackers, lobster bites with onion, clam
bites with garlic, shrimp bites with cajun spices
Brands:
Clambites With Garlic
Lobsterbites With On
Shrimpbites With Caj

14397 Tideland Seafood Company
P.O.Box 99
Dulac, LA 70353-0099   985-563-4516
                Fax: 985-563-4296
Manufacturer of prepared fresh shrimp; fish & sea-
food canning and curing.
President: Judith Gibson
Estimated Sales: $ 5 - 10 Million
Number Employees: 5-9

14398 Tiger Meat Provisions
1445 NW 22nd St
Miami, FL 33142-7741   305-324-0083
                Fax: 305-324-1570
Packer of fresh pork
President: Jose Requejo
Estimated Sales: $ 10 - 20 Million
Number Employees: 20-49
Type of Packaging: Food Service
Brands:
Tiger

14399 Tiger Mushroom Farm
PO Box 909
Nanton, AB T0L 1R0
Canada   403-646-2578
                Fax: 403-646-3767
Processor of mushrooms
President: Tiger Goto
Operations Manager: Jack Trinn
Number Employees: 20-49
Sq. footage: 16500
Type of Packaging: Consumer, Food Service
Brands:
Tiger

14400 (HQ)Tillamook County Creamery Association
4175 Highway 101 N
Tillamook, OR 97141-7770   503-842-4481
                Fax: 503-842-6039 www.tillamookcheese.com

Manufacturer of dairy butter, cheese, nonhygroscopic cheddar cheese whey powder and ice cream; exporter of dried whey, sour cream, yogurt, fluid milk
Chairman: George Allen
President/CEO: Jim McMullen
CEO: Jim McMullen
VP Sales/Marketing: Jay Allison
VP Operations: Cliff Brady
Estimated Sales: $270 Million
Number Employees: 250-499
Type of Packaging: Consumer, Food Service, Private Label, Bulk
Brands:
TILLAMOOK

14401 Tillamook Meat Company
405 Park Avenue
Tillamook, OR 97141-2524   503-842-4802
Fax: 508-342-2330
Manufacturer of meat products including beef, lamb, pork and poultry, jerky
President/Co-Owner: Laurel Travis
VP/Co-Owner: Mark Travis
Estimated Sales: $1-3 Million
Number Employees: 7
Type of Packaging: Consumer, Food Service, Bulk

14402 (HQ)Tiller Foods Company
967 Senate Dr
Dayton, OH 45459-4017   937-435-4601
Fax: 937-435-1408
Processor of portion controlled dairy products including sour cream, half and half, nondairy creamers, whipped cream and toppings
President: Donald Tiller Jr
Sales Manager: David Yost
Estimated Sales: $5 - 10 Million
Number Employees: 5-9
Type of Packaging: Consumer, Food Service, Private Label, Bulk
Other Locations:
Tiller Foods Co.
Tampa FL

14403 Tillie's Gourmet
173 Ash Way
Doylestown, PA 18901   215-272-8326
Fax: 215-348-2192   danielle@tilliesgourmet.com
www.tilliesgourmet.com
dressings, marinades and blue crab salsas

14404 Tim's Cascade Chips
1150 Industry Dr N
Algona, WA 98001-6552   253-833-0255
Fax: 253-939-9411   800-533-8467
consumer_affairs@birdseyefoods.com
www.birdseyefoods.com
Processor and exporter of snacks including mixes, caramel corn, potato chips and corn curls
President: Dennis M Mullen
COO: Jeff Leichleiter
Sales/Marketing Executive: George Masiello
Estimated Sales: $ 20 - 50 Million
Number Employees: 50-99
Sq. footage: 130000
Parent Co: Agrilink Foods
Type of Packaging: Consumer, Food Service, Private Label

14405 Timber Crest Farms
4791 Dry Creek Rd
Healdsburg, CA 95448-9714   707-473-9765
Fax: 707-433-8255   888-374-9325
tcf@timbercrest.com   www.sonic.net
Manufacturer of organic and preservative free dried fruits, nuts, tomatoes and specialty food products
Co-Owner: Ronald Waltenspiel
Co-Owner: Ruth Waltenspiel
Public Relations: Ruth Waltenspiel
Estimated Sales: $4.5 Million
Number Employees: 250-499
Number of Brands: 2
Number of Products: 50
Sq. footage: 30000
Type of Packaging: Consumer, Food Service, Private Label, Bulk
Brands:
Sonoma
Timber Crest Farm

14406 Timber Lake Cheese Company
PO Box A
Timber Lake, SD 57656   605-865-3605
Fax: 605-865-3605
Cheese
President: Virgil Johnson
Estimated Sales: Less than $500,000
Number Employees: 1-4

14407 Timber Peaks Gourmet
6180 N Hollowview Ct
Parker, CO 80134-5808   303-841-8847
Fax: 303-805-0174   800-982-7687
www.mountainhousekitchen.com
Cocoa, bean soups, dessert mixes, bread mixes, trail mixes, and dried salsa
President: Laurie Yankoski
Estimated Sales: $100,000
Number Employees: 1-4
Number of Brands: 1
Number of Products: 41
Sq. footage: 1500
Type of Packaging: Consumer, Bulk
Brands:
MUD
Mountain House Kitchen

14408 Timeless Traditions
4943 Us Route 7
Pittsford, VT 05763-9824   802-483-6024
dethbysauc@yahoo.com
www.piecesofvermont.com/timeless
Dessert sauces

14409 Tin Wistle
954 W Eckhardt Avenue
Penticton, BC V2A 2C1
Canada   250-770-1122
Fax: 250-770-1122   tindrew@telus.net
Processor of ale
President: Lorraine Nagy
Number Employees: 5-9
Type of Packaging: Consumer, Food Service
Brands:
Black Widow
Coyote
Ratle Snack

14410 Tina's
1401 N Kraemer Boulevard
Anaheim, CA 92806-1405   714-630-4123
Fax: 714-630-0650
customerservice@tinasinc.com
www.tinasinc.com
Baked goods
President: Tina Wilson
CEO: Tian Wilson
Estimated Sales: $ 75-100 Million
Number Employees: 50-100
Brands:
Tina's

14411 Tip Top Canning Company
P.O.Box 126
Tipp City, OH 45371-0126   937-667-3713
Fax: 937-667-3802   tiptop@woh.rr.com
Manufacturer of canned tomatoes and tomato products; whole peeled tomatoes, stewed tomatoes, diced tomatoes, Mexican stewed tomatoes, Italian stewed tomatoes, tomato sauce, pizza sauce, Italian diced tomatoes, Italian diced tomatoesspices, diced chili ready tomatoes, whole peeled and onion tomatoes, sloppy joe, Italian crushed tomatoes, paste, tomato juice, vegetable juice, ketchup
President: George Timmer
Account Executive: Beth Metzler
National Sales Manager: Cynthia Timmer
Estimated Sales: $ 10 - 20 Million
Number Employees: 20-49
Number of Products: 60
Sq. footage: 150000
Type of Packaging: Consumer, Food Service, Private Label, Bulk

14412 Tip Top Poultry
P.O.Box 6338
Marietta, GA 30065-0338   770-973-8070
Fax: 770-973-6897   www.tiptoppoultry.com
Processor and exporter of poultry
President: Robin Burruss
VP: Lee Bates
Technical VP: Mitch Forstie
Production Manager: Steve Moore

Estimated Sales: $126930394
Number Employees: 250-499
Type of Packaging: Consumer, Bulk

14413 Tipiak
45 Church St # 303
Stamford, CT 06906-1733   203-961-9117
Fax: 203-975-9081   laurent.chery@tipiak-e.com
www.tipiak.fr
Specialty rices and beans, tapioca flour and pearls, frozen appetizers and desserts.
CEO: Laurent Cherry
VP: Laurent Cherry
Estimated Sales: Below $ 5 Million
Number Employees: 1-4

14414 Tipp Distributors
1477 Lomaland Dr # E5
El Paso, TX 79935-4704   915-594-1618
Fax: 915-590-1225   888-668-2639
www.novamex.com
Condiments and relishes
President: Ramon Carrasco
CEO: Luis Fernandez
Estimated Sales: $ 1-2.5 Million
Number Employees: 100-249
Brands:
Chata
Cholula
D'Gari
Ibarra
Jarritos
Mineragua
Rogelio Bueno
San Marcos
Sangria Seorial
Sidral Mundet
Tuny

14415 Titterington's Olde English Bake Shop
48 Cummings Park
Woburn, MA 01801-2123   781-938-7600
Fax: 781-938-7676   dkrane@titteringtons.com
www.titteringtons.com
Baked goods
Owner: Richard Foster
Estimated Sales: $ 20 - 50 Million
Number Employees: 20-49

14416 Titusville Dairy Products
P.O.Box 186
Titusville, PA 16354-0186   814-827-1833
Fax: 814-827-2510   800-352-0101
tdpc@online.net   www.titusvillepa.com
Processor of ice cream mixes, dairy products, juices, fruit drinks and bottled water
Manager: Ralph Kerr
Plant Manager: Chester Anthony
Estimated Sales: $9300000
Number Employees: 20-49
Sq. footage: 28565
Type of Packaging: Consumer, Private Label
Brands:
Blossom Time
Natural Harvest
Titusville Dairy Products

14417 To Market-To Market
4880 Ireland Ln
West Linn, OR 97068-2953   503-657-9192
Fax: 503-655-3390
kathy@tomarket-tomarket.com
tomarket-tomarket.com
Processor of natural spice blends
President: Kathy Parson
Number Employees: 1-4
Type of Packaging: Consumer, Food Service

14418 Today's Traditions
2560 Dominic Drive
Suite A
Chico, CA 95928-7185   530-893-2646
Fax: 530-893-9344   800-816-6873
info@todaystraditions.com
www.todaystraditions.com
Processor of chicken, turkey, beef, ham and vegetable flavored meat analogs, frozen and freezed dried meat extenders and vegetarian tamales; importer of tofu
President: Karen Goodwin
Estimated Sales: Below $ 5 Million
Number Employees: 15
Sq. footage: 4000

Type of Packaging: Consumer, Food Service, Private Label, Bulk
Brands:
No Bones Wheat-Meat
Today's Tamales
Tofurky

14419 Todd's
P.O.Box 4821
Des Moines, IA 50305-4821   515-266-2276
          Fax: 515-266-1669 800-247-5363
          sales@toddsltd.com www.toddsltd.com
Food product manufacturer (wet and dry). KOsher and organic certified.
President/CEO: Alan Niedermeier
Quality Control: Diana Burzloff
Public Relations: Alissa Douglas
Operations: Duane Hettkamp
Production: Jeff Sullivan
Plant Manager: John Routh
Purchasing: Danielle Robinson
Estimated Sales: $ 1 - 3 Million
Number Employees: 30
Number of Brands: 40
Number of Products: 200
Sq. footage: 80000
Type of Packaging: Consumer, Food Service, Private Label, Bulk
Brands:
BUTCHER'S FRIEND
PAPA JOE'S SPECIALTY FOOD

14420 Todd's
6055 Malburg Way
Vernon, CA 90058   323-585-5900
          Fax: 323-585-5900 800-938-6337
          sales@todds.com www.todds.com
Processor, importer and exporter of nuts and nut meats, dried fruit, trail mixes, candy, etc
President: Todd Levin
Estimated Sales: $ 5 - 10 Million
Number Employees: 5-9
Type of Packaging: Consumer, Food Service, Private Label, Bulk
Brands:
DR JERKYLL & MR HIDE
HUCKLEBERRY'S FARM
JUST SNAK-IT
LUCY'S SWEETS
TODD'S TREATS

14421 Todd's Enterprises
2450 White Rd
Irvine, CA 92614-6250   949-250-4080
          Fax: 949-724-1338 toddsaz@aol.com
          www.toddsfoods.com
Processor and exporter of soups, sauces, chili and salad dressings
President: Phil De Carion
Marketing Director: Ed Stokes
Manufacturing Manager: Roger McFarland
Plant Manager: Dan Foss
Purchasing Manager: Dan Foss
Number Employees: 100-249
Parent Co: Todd's Central Commissary
Type of Packaging: Food Service, Private Label
Brands:
Todd's

14422 Toddville Seafoods
2345 Farm Creek Road
Toddville, MD 21672-9729   410-397-8129
Manufacturer of crab meat
President: Morgan Tolley
Vice President: Jennings Tolley
Estimated Sales: $5 Million
Number Employees: 20-49
Type of Packaging: Consumer

14423 (HQ)Toddy Products
1206 Brooks St
Houston, TX 77009-8809   713-225-2066
          Fax: 713-225-2110 toddy@toddyproducts.com
          www.toddycafe.com
Processor and exporter of liquid concentrates including coffee, tea, mocha, chai, etc.; also, espresso pecan brittle; manufacturer of cold brew coffee makers
Owner: Strother Simpson
Vice President: Scott Schroer
Estimated Sales: $1500000
Number Employees: 10-19
Sq. footage: 20000
Type of Packaging: Consumer, Food Service, Private Label, Bulk

Brands:
Toddy
Toddy Cappuccino
Toddy Coffee Crunch
Toddy Coffee Maker
Toddy Gourmet Iced Tea Concentrate
Toddy Mocha

14424 Todhunter Foods
PO Box 1447
Lake Alfred, FL 33850-1447   863-956-1116
          Fax: 863-956-3979
          humanresources@todhunter.com
          www.todhunter.com
Processor of vinegar and cooking wine; contract packager of fruit juices and carbonated/flavored beverages; importer of alcoholic beverages and juice concentrates; exporter of alcoholic beverages and vinegar
President: Jay Maltby
Research & Development: Ron Call
National Sales Manager: Jimk Polansky
Senior VP Manufacturing: Ousik Yu
Number Employees: 100-249
Sq. footage: 450000
Parent Co: Todhunter International
Type of Packaging: Consumer, Food Service, Private Label, Bulk

14425 Todhunter Foods & Monarch Wine Company
222 Lakeview Avenue
Suite 1500
West Palm Beach, FL 33401-6174 561-655-8977
          Fax: 561-655-9718 800-336-9463
          jpolansky@cruzoninc.com www.todhunter.com
Processor of cooking wines, powdered wine flavors, denatures spirits, vinegar and wine reductions.
President: Jay Maltby
CFO: Ezra Shashoua
Vice President: D Chris Mitchell
Sales Director: Jim Polansky
Plant Manager: Ousik Yu
Purchasing Manager: Frank Dibling
Number Employees: 410
Parent Co: Todhunter International
Type of Packaging: Consumer, Food Service, Private Label, Bulk

14426 (HQ)Todhunter International
PO Box 4057
West Palm Beach, FL 33402-4057 561-655-8977
          Fax: 561-655-9718 sales@todhunter.com
          www.todhunter.com
President: Jay S Maltby
CEO: Jay Maltby Jr
Sales Manager: James Polansky
Public Relations: Dennis Mitchell
VP Manufacturing: Ousik Yu
Purchasing: Frank Dibling
Estimated Sales: $90444293
Number Employees: 410
Parent Co: Angostura International
Type of Packaging: Consumer, Food Service, Private Label, Bulk
Other Locations:
Todhunter International
U.S. Virgin Islands
Brands:
Cruzan
Ron Carlos

14427 Toe-Food Chocolates andCandy
2500 Milvia Street
Suite 216
Berkeley, CA 94704-2636   510-649-9250
          Fax: 510-849-3810 888-863-3663
          sales@toefood.com www.toefood.com
Chocolate and candy in the shape of feet.
Founder/CEO: Mark Wolpa
Estimated Sales: $300,000-500,000
Number Employees: 8
Brands:
TOE-RIFIC CANDY

14428 Toffee Company
4550 Post Oak Place Dr # 220
Houston, TX 77027-3139   713-840-9696
          Fax: 713-840-8786 BBurk924@aol.com
          www.taaffeassoc.com
Toffee, candy
Owner: Peter Taaffe
Estimated Sales: $ 1 - 3 Million
Number Employees: 5-9

14429 Tofield Packers
5020 50th Avenue
Tofield, AB T0B 4J0
Canada   780-662-4842
          Fax: 780-662-4842
Processor of fresh and processed meats including sausage and wild game; also, custom slaughtering available
President: Dale Erickson
Number Employees: 10-19
Type of Packaging: Consumer, Bulk

14430 Toft Dairy
P.O.Box 2558
Sandusky, OH 44871-2558   419-625-4376
          Fax: 419-621-2010 800-521-4606
          info@toftdairy.com www.toftdairy.com
Processor of milk, ice cream, frozen yogurt, fruit drinks and orange juice
President: Eugene Meisler
VP: Tom Meisler
Food Processor Packer: Chuck Meisler
Plant Manager: Dennis Meisler
Estimated Sales: $16310930
Number Employees: 50-99
Type of Packaging: Consumer, Food Service, Private Label, Bulk

14431 Tofu Shop Specialty Foods
65 Frank Martin Ct
Arcata, CA 95521-8930   707-822-7401
          Fax: 707-822-7401 info@tofushop.com
          www.tofushop.com
Manufacturer of fresh tofu, smoked tofu, fresh soymilks, international spiced tofu, seasoned and baked tofu including cutlets, patties and sausage patties, and fresh tofu spreads.
President: Matthew Schmit
Estimated Sales: $ 10 - 20 Million
Number Employees: 20-49
Number of Products: 22
Sq. footage: 4500
Type of Packaging: Consumer, Bulk
Brands:
Snack Fu
Tofu Shop

14432 Tofutti Brands
50 Jackson Dr
Cranford, NJ 07016-3504   908-272-2400
          Fax: 908-272-9492 tofuttibrands@aol.com
          www.tofutti.com
Processor and exporter of nondairy food products including imitation cream cheese, no-cholesterol egg products made of egg whites and tofu with added vitamins and minerals and frozen tofu desserts
CEO: David Mintz
CFO: Steven Kass
CEO: David Mintz
Estimated Sales: $19014000
Number Employees: 10-19
Type of Packaging: Consumer, Food Service, Bulk
Brands:
Lite Lite Tofutti
Tofutti
Tofutti Better Than Cheesecake

14433 Toho America Corporation
9751 Ikena Cir
Honolulu, HI 96821   808-395-5885
          Fax: 808-395-5242
Fish and seafood broker
President: Toyoki Higashishiba

14434 Tokunaga Farms
12019 S Highland Avenue
Selma, CA 93662-9003   559-896-0949
Farm products
President: George Tokunga

14435 Tom & Dave's Specialty Coffee
3095 Kerner Blvd # A
San Rafael, CA 94901-5420   415-454-3064
          Fax: 415-454-3281 800-249-5050
          siteorders@tomanddaves.com
          www.tomanddaves.com
Coffee
Owner: Christopher Rygg
Estimated Sales: Below $ 5 Million
Number Employees: 5-9
Type of Packaging: Private Label
Brands:
Columbian

House Blend
Moka-Java

14436 Tom & Sally's Handmade Chocolates
P.O.Box 600
Brattleboro, VT 05302-0600   802-254-4200
Fax: 802-254-5518   800-827-0800
tom@tomandsalys.com   www.tomandsallys.com
Processor of gourmet chocolate products including
old-fashioned creams, foil-wrapped coins, spoons,
nut patties, lollypops, almond bark, dessert toppings
and molded
Chairman: Thomas E Fegley
Estimated Sales:$ 3 - 5 Million
Number Employees: 10-19
Sq. footage: 11700
Type of Packaging: Consumer, Private Label
Brands:
Cowlicks
Dog-Gones
Reindeer Pies
Vermont Meadow Muffins
Vermont Pasture Patties

14437 Tom Cat Bakery
P.O.Box 7139
Long Island City, NY 11101-9139   718-786-4224
Fax: 718-472-0310   info@tomcat-bakery.com
www.tomcat-bakery.com
French and Italian breads, rolls, baguettes
President: Noel Labat-Comess
Estimated Sales:$ 50-100 Million
Number Employees: 50-99
Brands:
Tom Cat Bakery

14438 Tom Clamon Foods
2220 W Reagan St
Palestine, TX 75801-2247   903-729-3932
Fax: 903-723-3573
Beef
Owner: Gene Hamon
Estimated Sales:$ 20-50 Million
Number Employees: 20-49

14439 Tom Davis & Sons Dairy Company
21631 Meyers Rd
Oak Park, MI 48237-3105   248-399-6970
Fax: 248-399-6196   800-399-6970
adim@tomdavisdairy.com
www.prairiefarms.com
Dairy products distributers
President: Gary Davis
CEO: Tom Davis
Marketing Director: Jim Davis
Estimated Sales:$ 50 - 100 Million
Number Employees: 50-99
Type of Packaging: Private Label
Brands:
Prairie Farms

14440 Tom Ringhausen Orchards
P.O.Box 201
Hardin, IL 62047-0201   618-576-2311
Processor and grower of fruits and vegetables in-
cluding apples, peaches, plums, pears, nectarines,
blackberries, squash, pumpkins, melons and turnips.
Also cider
President: Tom Ringhausen
*Estimated Sales:*Under $300,000
Number Employees: 5-9
Sq. footage: 3000
Type of Packaging: Consumer
Brands:
Tom Ringhausen

14441 Tom Sturgis Pretzels
2267 Lancaster Pike
Reading, PA 19607-2498   610-775-0335
Fax: 610-796-1418   800-817-3834
www.tomsturgispretzels.com
Pretzels
President: Bruce Sturgis
Founder: Tom Sturgis
Vice President: Barbara Sturgis
Sales Director: Timothy Snyder
Operations Manager: Jean Harms
Production Manager: David Amour
Plant Manager: Mike Kappenstein
Estimated Sales:$ 5 Million
Number Employees: 20-49

Number of Brands: 3
Sq. footage: 75000
Type of Packaging: Private Label
Brands:
Cousin Rachel Pretzels
Mr. C'S Pretzels
Tom Sturgis Pretzels

14442 Tom Tom Tamale Manufacturing
4750 S Washtenaw Ave
Chicago, IL 60632-2096   773-523-5675
Processor of tamales
President: Nick Petros
Estimated Sales:$500,000-$1 Million
Number Employees: 10-19
Type of Packaging: Consumer

14443 Tom's Foods
3001 E State Highway 31
Corsicana, TX 75109-9048   903-874-6553
Fax: 903-874-7831 www.tomsfoods.com
Processor of baked extruded products, corn and po-
tato chips
Plant Manager: Arbie Thomas
Estimated Sales:$100+ Million
Number Employees: 100-249
Sq. footage: 86000
Parent Co: Tom's Food
Type of Packaging: Consumer
Brands:
Tom's

14444 Tom's Foods
P.O.Box 60
Columbus, GA 31902-0060   706-323-2721
www.tomsfoods.com
Processor of snack foods including potato chips
Manager: Jack Warden
Plant Manager: John Rothenfluh
*Estimated Sales:*I
Number Employees: 1,000-4,999
Type of Packaging: Private Label

14445 Tom's Ice Cream Bowl
532 McIntire Ave
Zanesville, OH 43701-3342   740-452-5267
Fax: 740-452-0931 www.tomsicecreambowl.com
Processor of ice cream
Owner: William Sullivan
Estimated Sales:$ 1 - 3 Million
Number Employees: 20-49
Type of Packaging: Consumer

14446 Tom's Snacks Company
8600 S Boulevard
Charlotte, NC 28273   706-323-2721
Fax: 706-323-8231   800-995-2623
bsmith@tomfoods.com   www.tomsfoods.com
Manufacturer of snack foods; potato chips, pork
skins, corn chips, tortilla chips and fries
Supply Chain VP, Lance Inc.: Blake Thompson
Estimated Sales:$ .5 - 1 million
Number Employees: 50-100
Parent Co: Lance, Inc.
Type of Packaging: Consumer
Brands:
Tom's

14447 Tomahawk Farms Meat Packers
603 S Wilson Ave
Dunn, NC 28334-5832   910-892-3155
Manufacturer of country cured ham
President: Barry Hulet
Estimated Sales:$10-20 Million
Number Employees: 1-4
Parent Co: Lundy Packing
Type of Packaging: Consumer

14448 (HQ)Tomanetti Food Products
631 Allegheny Avenue
Oakmont, PA 15139-2003   412-828-3040
Fax: 412-828-2282   800-875-3040
sales@tomanetti.com   www.tomanetti.com
Pizza shells, breadsticks and focaccia.
President: George Michael
COO: Robert Finlay
Sales Manager: Chris Presutti
Production Supervisor: Bill Vidra
Plant Manager: Paul Sypolt
*Estimated Sales:*Below $ 5 Million
Number Employees: 30

14449 Tomaro's Bakery
411 N 4th St
Clarksburg, WV 26301-2004   304-622-0691
Manufacturer of bread, rolls and pizza crusts
President: Janice Brunett
Estimated Sales:$6 Million
Number Employees: 10-19
Type of Packaging: Consumer

14450 Tomasello Winery
225 N White Horse Pike
Hammonton, NJ 08037-1868   609-561-0567
Fax: 609-561-8617   800-666-9463
wine@tomasellowinery.com
www.tomasellowinery.com
Wines
President: Charles J Tomasello Jr
Owner: Jack Tomasello
Vice President: Jack Tomasello
*Estimated Sales:*Below $ 5 Million
Number Employees: 5-9
Brands:
Tomasello Winery

14451 Tomasinos Sausage
3819 Columbus Rd NE
Canton, OH 44705-4428   330-454-4171
Fax: 330-454-3835
Processor of sausage including mild, pork and
smoked
President: Mark V Prestier
Estimated Sales:$ 20 - 50 Million
Number Employees: 10-19
Type of Packaging: Consumer, Food Service, Bulk

14452 Tomasso Corporation
20425 Clark Graham
Baie D'Urfe, QC H9X 3T5
Canada   514-325-3000
Fax: 514-457-5107 www.tomassocorp.com
Manufacturer of frozen Italian entrees including
meat lasagna, chicken lasagna, meat sauce,
vegeatble lasagna, cannelloni, macaroni and cheese
Chairman/CEO: J-Rene Ouimet
CFO/Treasurer: Peter Thomas
VP/Sales & Marketing: Bruce Blyth
VP/Operations: Jose Chagnon
Number Employees: 120
Sq. footage: 53000
Type of Packaging: Food Service, Private Label
Brands:
BUONA CUCINA
GUSTO ITALIA
PIAZZA TOMASSO

14453 Tommaso's Fresh Pasta
2680 Nova Dr
Dallas, TX 75229-2219   972-869-1111
Fax: 972-869-9937
Pasta and sauces
Owner: Jack Rayome
Director Research: Ray Etheridge
Estimated Sales:$ 5-9.9 Million
Number Employees: 20-49
Sq. footage: 12000
Type of Packaging: Consumer, Food Service, Pri-
vate Label, Bulk

14454 Tommy Tang's Thai Seasonings
7313 Melrose Avenue
Los Angeles, CA 90046-7512   323-937-5733
Fax: 323-937-5781 www.tommytangs.net
Seasonings, spices
President: Sandi Tang
Owner: Tommy Tang
Estimated Sales:$ 1-2.5 Million
Number Employees: '10-19

14455 Tomorrow Enterprise
5918 Spanish Trl W
New Iberia, LA 70560   337-783-2666
Fax: 337-233-9514
Hot sauces
President: Tony Morrow

14456 Tone Products Company
2129 N 15th Ave
Melrose Park, IL 60160-1406   708-681-3660
Fax: 708-681-2368 www.toneproducts.com

Processor and exporter of fountain syrups, soup bases, toppings, pancake syrup and beverage concentrates
President: Tim Evon
Secretary/Treasurer: Tom Evon
VP: Mike Evon
Estimated Sales: $ 20 - 50 Million
Number Employees: 50-99
Sq. footage: 46000
Type of Packaging: Consumer, Private Label, Bulk
Brands:
Bonnie
Bonnie Maid
Hi-Tone
Maple Wood
Rainbo-Rich
Sno-Bal

14457 Tonex
27 Park Row
Wallington, NJ 07057-1629   973-773-5135
       Fax: 973-916-1091   tonexinc@aol.com
       www.tonexinc.com
Processor of cappuccino, nondairy creamers, instant coffee and tea and chocolate covered nuts; importer and exporter of beer, vodka, candy, fresh and dried fruits, tea, instant cappuccino, juice and juice concentrates, etc
Owner: Bogdan Torbus
President: Grace Torbus
Marketing Director: Angela Torbus
Type of Packaging: Consumer, Food Service, Private Label, Bulk
Brands:
Chocolate Covered Nuts
Instant Cappuccino
Instant Tea

14458 Tony Chachere's Creole Foods
PO Box 1639
Opelousas, LA 70571-1639   337-948-4691
       Fax: 337-948-6854   800-551-9066
       creole@tonycachere.com
       www.tonychachere.com
Seasonings and rice dinner mixes
President/CEO: Donald Chachere Jr
Marketing Director: Christopher Roch
CFO: William Pollingue
CFO: Donald Chachere Jr
VP Sales: Mona Campbell Jr
Public Relations: Janice LeBlanc
Production Manager: Alex Chachere II
Plant Manager: Carl Trahan
Purchasing Manager: Christy Bernard
Estimated Sales: Below $ 5 Million
Number Employees: 2
Type of Packaging: Consumer, Food Service, Private Label, Bulk
Brands:
Instant Roux & Gravy
More Spice Seasoning
Tony Chachere's Orig

14459 Tony Downs Foods Company
P.O.Box 28
Madelia, MN 56062-0028   507-642-3203
       Fax: 507-642-3397
       mforstie@downsfoodgroup.com
       www.tonydownsfoods.com
Processor of poultry: fully cooked, diced-frozen and commercial and retail canned chicken
President: David Sawyer
CEO/Chairman: Richard Downs
CFO: Patty Anderson
VP: Mitch Forstie
Sales: Leo Zachman
Estimated Sales: $22800000
Number Employees: 250-499
Sq. footage: 100000
Type of Packaging: Consumer, Food Service, Private Label, Bulk

14460 Tony Downs Foods Company
P.O.Box 28
St James, MN 56081-0028   507-375-3111
       Fax: 507-375-3048   rkrull@tonydownsfoods.com
       www.tonydownsfoods.com
Frozen foods
Co-President: Richard Downes
CFO: Patty Anderson
CEO: Dick Downs
Plant Manager: Jeff Hinkle
Estimated Sales: $ 20-50 Million
Number Employees: 50-99

Brands:
Downsfare
Infrared Foods

14461 Tony Packo Food Company
1902 Front St
Toledo, OH 43605-1292   419-691-6054
       Fax: 419-691-8358   866-472-2567
       shop@tonypacko.com   www.tonypackos.com
Pickles, relishes
Owner: Tony Packo
Estimated Sales: Less than $500,000
Number Employees: 50-99
Brands:
Tony Packo's

14462 Tony V'S Oyster House
PO Box 1052
Amite, LA 70422-1052   504-748-8110
Seafood

14463 Tony Vitrano Company
P.O.Box 2001
Jessup, MD 20794-2001   410-799-7444
       Fax: 410-799-8917
Processor of apples, oranges, cucumbers, onions, lettuce and squash
Executive Director: Anthony Vitrano
Estimated Sales: $ 20 - 50 Million
Number Employees: 50-99
Type of Packaging: Consumer, Food Service

14464 Tony's Fine Foods
3575 Reed Ave
Broderick, CA 95605-1628   916-374-4000
       Fax: 916-372-0727   scott@tonysfinefoods.com
       www.tonysfinefoods.com
Different kind of foods
Executive VP/CFO: Scott Berger
COO: Jerry Walsh
President: Karl Berger
Estimated Sales: $ 10-100 Million
Number Employees: 250-499
Brands:
Tony's

14465 Tony's Ice Cream Company
604 E Franklin Blvd
Gastonia, NC 28054-7111   704-867-7085
Processor of ice cream
President: Robert Coletta
VP: Louis Coletta
Estimated Sales: $ 10 - 20 Million
Number Employees: 20-49
Type of Packaging: Consumer

14466 Tony's Seafood
5215 Plank Rd
Baton Rouge, LA 70805-2730   225-357-9669
       Fax: 225-355-5451   www.tonysseafood.com
Seafood
President: William Pizzolato
Estimated Sales: $ 20 - 50 Million
Number Employees: 100-249

14467 Too Goo Doo Farms/Easy Tray LLC
8761 Dorchester Road
Suite 100
North Charleston, SC 29420-7320   843-767-0196
       Fax: 843-552-8045   info@easytrayllc.com
       www.toogoodoofarms.com
Manufacturer of pre-packaged peppers and sweet onions
Chairman: Daniel Stevenson
CFO/Treasurer: Lloyd Pearson
Secretary: Douglas Pratt-Thomas
Estimated Sales: $300,000-500,000
Number Employees: 1-4
Sq. footage: 32000
Type of Packaging: Consumer, Food Service, Bulk
Other Locations:
Easy Tray Southeastern Plant
North Charleston SC
Brands:
Too Goo Doo Farms

14468 Too Good Gourmet
2380 Grant Ave
San Lorenzo, CA 94580-1806   510-317-8150
       Fax: 510-317-8755   877-850-4663
       info@toogoodgourmet.com
       www.toogoodgourmet.com

Gourmet cookies packed in whimsical toy boxes
Owner: Amie Watson
Marketing/Sales: Katie Bidstrup
Estimated Sales: $ 5 - 10 Million
Number Employees: 5-9
Type of Packaging: Consumer, Food Service, Private Label, Bulk

14469 Tooele Valley Meat
P.O.Box 476
Grantsville, UT 84029-0476   435-884-3837
       Fax: 435-884-6781
Processor of beef, pork, veal and lamb
President: Edward Roberts
Estimated Sales: $800000
Number Employees: 5-9
Type of Packaging: Consumer, Food Service

14470 (HQ)Tootsie Roll Industries
7401 S Cicero Ave
Chicago, IL 60629-5885   773-838-3400
       Fax: 773-838-3435   800-877-7655
       www.tootsie.com
Manufacturer and exporter of confectionery products including chocolate, gum drops, chewy candies, candy bars, licorice, jelly beans, lollypops, mints, etc
Chairman/CEO: Melvin Gordon
President/COO/Director: Ellen R Gordon
VP: George Rost Jr
VP Marketing/Sales: Thomas Corr
VP Manufacturing: John Newlin Jr
Estimated Sales: $464.4 Million
Number Employees: 500-999
Type of Packaging: Consumer, Food Service, Bulk
Brands:
ANDES
BLOW POP
BLUE RAZZ
CARMEL APPLE POPS
CELLA CHERRIES
CHARLESTON CHEW
CHARM'S
CHILD'S PLAY
CRY BABY
DUBBLE BUBBLE
FLUFFY STUFF
FROOTIES
JUNIOR MINT
MASON CROWS
MASON DOTS
NIK-L-NIP
RAZZELS
SUGAR BABY
SUGAR DADDY
TOOTSIE ROLL
TOOTSIE ROLL POPS
ZIP-A-DEE-DOO-DA POPS

14471 Top Choice Meat Processing
68 E Fetterman Street
Buffalo, WY 82834-1940   307-684-7741
Meat packers
President: Patricia Tanner
Number Employees: 1-4
Type of Packaging: Consumer, Food Service

14472 Top Hat Company
P.O.Box 66
Wilmette, IL 60091-0066   847-256-6565
       Fax: 847-256-6579   info@tophatcompany.com
       www.tophatcompany.com
Processor of sauces including raspberry, hot, mocha and mint fudges, butterscotch, caramel, Mayan legacy, prince of orange and Southern sin; also, double chocolate fondue and bittersweet chocolate
President: Marla Murray
Estimated Sales: Less than $1,000,000
Number Employees: 20-49
Type of Packaging: Consumer, Food Service, Private Label, Bulk
Brands:
Top Hat Dessert Sauces

14473 (HQ)Topco
7711 Gross Point Rd
Skokie, IL 60077-2697   847-676-3030
       Fax: 847-676-4949   webmaster@topco.com
       www.topco.com
Grocery, frozen, dairy, bakery, general merchandise, health & beauty care, pharmacy, branded meat, equipment and supplies, business services, world brands and diverting.
President: Steve Lowery
CEO: Steve K Lauer

Estimated Sales: $ 50 - 100 Million
Number Employees: 250-499
Type of Packaging: Consumer, Food Service, Private Label
Other Locations:
Topco
Skokie IL
Brands:
CLEAR VALUE
DINING IN
FOOD CLUB
FULL CIRCLE
PAWS
PRICE SAVER
SHUR FINE
TOP CARE
TOP CREST
VALU TIME
WORLD CLASS

14474 Topolos at Russian River Vine
PO Box 358
Forestville, CA 95436-0358   707-887-1575
Fax: 707-887-1399   topolos@topolos.com
www.topolos.net
Wine and gourmet foods
President: Michael Topolos
Estimated Sales: $ 5-10 Million
Number Employees: 6
Brands:
Topolos at Russian River Vine

14475 Topor's Pickle Company
2800 Standish St
Detroit, MI 48216-1539   313-237-0288
Fax: 313-981-4249
Pickles, dill green tomatoes, hot pickles with red peppers, Hungarian hot banana peppers
President: Larry Topor
Estimated Sales: $ 3 - 5 Million
Number Employees: 1-4

14476 Topper Food Products
20 Williamsburg Court
East Brunswick, NJ 08816-3251   732-238-1225
800-377-2823
Processor of sauces including marinara, Creole, pesto, salsa picante, primavera, white clam and alfredo; also, sugar-free, fat-free and low sodium varieties available
President: Lou Topper
Number Employees: 5-9
Type of Packaging: Consumer, Food Service, Private Label, Bulk
Brands:
Papa Lomagi

14477 Topper Meat Company
26400 State Road 80
Belle Glade, FL 33430   561-996-6541
Fax: 561-996-8021
Beef
Director: Eduardo Recio
Estimated Sales: $ 10-100 Million
Number Employees: 100-249

14478 Topps Company
1 Whitehall St
New York, NY 10004-3612   212-376-0300
Fax: 212-376-0573   www.thetoppsvault.com
Gum, candy
Chairman/President/CEO: Arthur T Shorin
VP/CFO: Catherine K Jessup
CEO: Scott Silverstein
VP Sales & Marketing: Ron Boyum
VP Internet Options: Warren E Friss
Estimated Sales: $ 290,079,000
Number Employees: 250-499
Brands:
Baby Bottle Pop
Bazooka
Bubble Gum Booster
Juicy Drop Chews
Juicy Drop Pop
Push Pop
Ring Pop
Topps

14479 Topps Company
401 York Ave
Duryea, PA 18642-2035   570-457-6761
Fax: 570-451-2408   candyinfo@topps.com
www.thetoppscompany.com

Processor of confectionery products including sugarless and regular chewing gum and novelty lollypops
President: Arthur Shorin
Human Resources: Bill O Connor
Marketing Manager: John Budd
Sales Director: Ron Boyum
Public Relations: Marty Appel
VP Manufacturing: Michael Drewniak
Estimated Sales: $290079000
Number Employees: 10-19
Brands:
Barfo
Batman
Bazooka Bursts Gum
Big Mouth
Dick Tracy
Memo Book
Push Pops
Ren & Stimpy
Ring Pops
Rocketeer
Super Skates
Superfly
Thumb Fun
Triple Blasts
Tropical Ring Pop
Yo! Street Feet

14480 Topps Meat Company
1161 E Broad Street
Elizabeth, NJ 07201-1006   908-351-0500
Fax: 908-351-0722   info@toppsmeat.com
www.toppsmeat.com
Manufacturer of fresh and frozen hamburgers
Controller: Jay Peskin
EVP/COO: Anthony D'Urso
Quality Assurance/QC Manager: Charlie Chieng
Director Sales/Marketing: Raymond Patnaude
Marketing Coordinator: Janice Dodge
VP/National Sales Manager: Ed Reina
VP Operations: Geoffrey Livermore
Estimated Sales: $40 Million
Number Employees: 50-99

14481 Tops Manufacturing Company
83 Salisbury Rd
Darien, CT 06820-2299   203-655-9367
Manufacturer and exporter of coffee and tea equipment including percolators, knobs, handles, carafes, coffee makers and filters, tea infusers, liquid coffee flavors, glass cups, instant and ground coffee dispensers, measuring spoonsetc
President: Mitch Himmel
VP: Pat Himmel
Sales Manager: Ernie Hurlbut
Estimated Sales: Less than $500,000
Number Employees: 1-4
Sq. footage: 15700
Type of Packaging: Consumer, Food Service
Brands:
Brick-Pack Clip
Fitz-All
Flav-A-Brrew
Kaf-Tan
Measure Fresh
Perma-Brew
Rapid Brew
Tops

14482 Torani Syrups
233 E Harris Ave
S San Francisco, CA 94080-6807   650-875-1200
Fax: 650-875-1600   800-775-1925
www.torani.com
Processor and exporter of Italian flavoring syrups and fruit bases used for sparkling sodas, expresso beverages, specialty drinks and cooking.
CEO: Melanie Dulbecco
CEO: Melanie Dulbecco
VP Marketing: Cindy Eckart
VP Sales: Matt Brandenburger
Estimated Sales: $ 50 - 100 Million
Number Employees: 50-99
Sq. footage: 62000
Type of Packaging: Consumer, Food Service
Brands:
Torani

14483 Torke Coffee Roasting Company
P.O.Box 694
Sheboygan, WI 53082-0694   920-458-4114
Fax: 920-458-0488   800-242-7671
bigbean@torkecoffee.com   www.torkecoffee.com

Manufacturer of coffee
President: Ward Torke
Estimated Sales: $ 20 - 50 Million
Number Employees: 20-49
Brands:
TORKE

14484 Torkelson Cheese Company
9453 W Louisa Rd
Lena, IL 61048-9656   815-369-4265
Fax: 815-369-2302   cheese@aeroinc.net
www.torkelsoncheese.com
Manufacturers Brick, Muenster, Quesadilla and Asadero cheeses.
President/Head Cheesemaker: Duane Torkelson
VP: Cheryl Torkelson
Estimated Sales: $ 10-20 Million
Number Employees: 20-49

14485 Torn & Glasser
1769 Glendale Blvd
Los Angeles, CA 90026-1761   323-661-2332
Fax: 213-688-0941   800-282-6887
Processor of nuts, dried fruit, seeds, granola, beans, rice, dry chili, candy, etc
Owner: Tony Tierno
VP: Greg Glasser
Purchasing Manager: Gus Gutmun
Estimated Sales: $300,000-500,000
Number Employees: 1-4
Type of Packaging: Consumer, Food Service, Private Label, Bulk

14486 Torn Ranch
23 Pimentel Ct # B
Novato, CA 94949-5661   415-506-3000
Fax: 415-506-3002   info@tornranch.com
www.tornranch.com
Manufacturer and purveyor of gourmet specialty foods, dried fruits, roasted nuts, snack foods and shortbreads.
President: Dean Morrow
Vice President: Sue Morrow
Quality Control: Robert Wagner
Estimated Sales: $ 5-10 Million
Number Employees: 50-99
Type of Packaging: Private Label
Brands:
Cafe Time
Gigi Baking Company
Mashuga Nuts & Cookies
Splendid Specialties Chocolate Co

14487 Toro Brewing
17370 Hill Rd
Morgan Hill, CA 95037-9704   408-778-2739
Beer
President: H Geno Acevedo
Estimated Sales: Below $ 5 Million
Number Employees: 1-4

14488 Torre Products Company
479 Washington St
New York, NY 10013-1381   212-925-8989
Fax: 212-925-4627
Manufacturer, importer and exporter of flavoring extracts and essential oils
President: L Raho
Estimated Sales: $10-20 Million
Number Employees: 20-49
Sq. footage: 11000
Brands:
FLAMBE HOLIDAY
LA TORINESE
RUM-BA
SOFT MAC

14489 Torrefazione Barzula & Import
3117 Wharton Way
Mississauga, ON L4X 2B6
Canada   905-625-6082
Fax: 905-625-5741   sales@barzula.com
www.barzula.com
Processor, importer and exporter of coffee beans including green, espresso, Turkish and decaffeinated
President: L Russignan
Treasurer: G Russignan
VP: Phil Cennova
Number Employees: 10-19
Number of Brands: 1
Number of Products: 12
Sq. footage: 24000
Brands:
Barzula

14490 Torrefazione Italia
PO Box 2409
Seattle, WA 98111-2409   206-624-5773
Fax: 206-624-3262   800-827-2333
www.titalia.com
Gourmet/ specialty coffee
President/COO: Dick Holbrook
VP Marketing: Kim Beerli
CFO: Chris December
Founder: Umberto Bizzarri
Sales Director: Tom Danowski
Operations Manager: Jane Albright
*Estimated Sales:*Below $ 500,000
Number Employees: 2
Type of Packaging: Private Label
Brands:
Torrefazione Italia

14491 Torreo Coffee Company
4950 Rhawn St
Philadelphia, PA 19136-2907   215-333-1105
Fax: 215-333-6615   888-286-7736
customerserv@torreo.com   torreo.com
Manufacture a line of premium coffees
President: Eric Patrick
Vice President: H Patrick
Operations Manager: Howard Patrick
Estimated Sales:$500,000-$1 Million
Number Employees: 5-9
Sq. footage: 9600
Parent Co: Torreo Coffee & Tea Company
Type of Packaging: Consumer, Private Label, Bulk
Brands:
TORREO

14492 Tostino Coffee Roasters
4283 S Santa Rita Avenue
Tucson, AZ 85714-1641   520-294-5112
Fax: 520-294-5926   800-678-3519
info@tostino.com   www.tostino.com
Specialty gourmet coffee and teas
President: Jerry Sonenblick
Co-President: Rafael Guerrero
CFO: Michael Bright
Estimated Sales: $ 20-50 Million
Number Employees: 50-99
Type of Packaging: Private Label
Brands:
Cafe Tostino

14493 Total LubricantsKeystone Division
5 N Stiles St
Linden, NJ 07036-4208   908-862-9300
Fax: 908-862-1647   IBU-CSR@total-us.com

http://keystonelubricants.com/keystone/index.htm
Product lines includes food machinery lubricants; air
compressor fluids; metalworking lubricants; and
maintenance lubricants.
Human Resources: Steve Daubert
Food Industry Sales Specialist: Jim Cancila
Food Industry Sales Specialist: Bruce Wolfe
Food Industry Sales Specialist: Rob Stevenson
International Food Industry Specialist: Christine
Richard
*Estimated Sales:*H
Number Employees: 10,000+

14494 Total Ultimate Foods
683 Manor Park Dr
Columbus, OH 43228-9369   614-870-0732
Fax: 614-870-1687   800-333-0732
sales@tuf-inc.com   www.tufinc.com
Dehydrated foods
Manager: Mark Wills
CFO: Terry Weisenstein
Vice President: Terry Weisenstein
R & D: Tim Tomesek
Quality Control: Brian Wilke
Marketing/Sales Manager: Walter Mcnabb
VP Manufacturing: Bill Stone
Estimated Sales: $ 10-20 Million
Number Employees: 20-49
Type of Packaging: Food Service, Private Label
Brands:
Tuf

14495 Totally Chocolate
2025 Sweet Rd
Blaine, WA 98230-9198   360-332-3900
Fax: 360-332-1802   800-255-5506
sales@totallychocolate.com
www.totallychocolate.com
Chocolate manufacturing
Owner: Jeff Robinson
VP Sales: Matt Roth
Plant Manager: Steve Hocker
Purchasing Manager: Christine Danner
Estimated Sales:$ 5-10 Millions
Number Employees: 50-99
Type of Packaging: Private Label
Brands:
Totally Chocolate

14496 Totino's
200 S 6th St # 4000
Minneapolis, MN 55402-1425   612-492-7018
Fax: 612-347-7077
General grocery
*Estimated Sales:*Under $500,000
Number Employees: 10-19

14497 Toucan Chocolates
RR 128
Box 72
Waban, MA 02468   617-964-8696
Fax: 800-816-8696
Chocolate
President: Michael Goldman

14498 Toucan Enterprises
PO Box 1639
Marrero, LA 70073-1639   504-736-9289
Fax: 504-736-9289   800-736-9289
Processor and exporter of powdered juice and cock-
tail mixes
President: David Ervin
Vice President: Kerry Bretz
Plant Manager: Troy Townsend
Number Employees: 1-4
Sq. footage: 6000
Type of Packaging: Consumer, Food Service, Pri-
vate Label, Bulk
Brands:
Daiquiri Factory
Ice Splasher
Toucan

14499 Touch of South
4 Pine Court
Inglewood, CA 90302-2930   310-672-0700
Fax: 310-674-6900   bbqMike@aol.com
www.touchofsouth.com
Barbeque and hot sauce
President: Michael Beatty
CFO: Paul Kidd
Estimated Sales:$150,000
Number Employees: 1-4
Sq. footage: 100
Type of Packaging: Consumer, Food Service, Pri-
vate Label, Bulk

14500 Touche Bakery
384-B Neptune Cres
London, ON N6M 1A1
Canada   518-455-0044
Fax: 519-455-5843   aswartz@touchebakery.com
www.touchebakery.com
Biscotti, cookies, meringues that are all nautral and
nut free
President: Peter Cuddy
CEO: Allan Swartz
Finance/Administration Manager: Pat Gauthier
Sq. footage: 16000
Type of Packaging: Consumer, Food Service, Pri-
vate Label

14501 Touche Bakery
384b Neptune Cr
London, ON N6M 1A1
Canada   519-455-0044
Fax: 519-455-5843   aswartz@touchebakery.com
www.touchebakery.com
biscotti, meringues, cookies, brownies, frozen
cookie dough, muffin and brownie batter
President/CEO: Allan Swartz
Estimated Sales:$1.2 Million
Number Employees: 20

14502 Toufayan Bakeries
3826 Bryn Mawr St
Orlando, FL 32808-4669   407-295-2257
Fax: 407-578-2920   sales@toufayan.com
www.toufayan.com
Processor of pita bread and bread sticks, flatbreads,
bagels, wraps and snack food components.
President: Harry Toufayan
VP Sales: Karen Toufayan
Estimated Sales:$100+ Million
Number Employees: 100-249
Sq. footage: 3500
Parent Co: Toufayan Bakeries
Type of Packaging: Consumer, Food Service

14503 Toufayan Bakeries
175 Railroad Ave
Ridgefield, NJ 07657-2312   201-941-2000
Fax: 201-861-0392   msteve@toufayan.com
Manufacturer of pita bread and bread sticks.
President: Harry Toufayan
Estimated Sales:$ 3 - 5 Million
Number Employees: 50-99
Type of Packaging: Consumer, Food Service

14504 Tova Industries
P.O.Box 24410
Louisville, KY 40224-0410   502-267-7333
Fax: 502-267-7119   888-532-8682
corporate@tovanindustries.com
www.tovaindustries.com
Dry mix food products, spices, table and beverage
syrups
President: Zack Melzer
Sr VP: Yael Melzer
R&D and QA Manager: Chris Matthews
Sales Contract Manager: Mike Northway
Operations Manager: Johan Venter
Purchasing Manager: Chasity Towler
Estimated Sales:$100+ Million
Number Employees: 50-99
Number of Products: 1000
Type of Packaging: Consumer, Food Service, Pri-
vate Label, Bulk
Other Locations:
New Horizon Foods
Union City CA
Brands:
HERITAGE - THE ESSENCE OF TRADITION
LIFESOURCE FOODS
STONEGROUND MILLS
SUPERIOR SPICES
SUPERIOR SYRUPS
TOVA

14505 Town & Country Foods
P.O.Box 88
Greene, ME 04236-0088   207-946-5489
Fax: 207-946-7370 www.tandcfoods.com
Meats and wholesale food distributor.
Owner: Janet Lapin
Estimated Sales:$ 10 - 20 Million
Number Employees: 20-49

14506 Townsend Culinary
P.O.Box 468
Millsboro, DE 19966-0468   302-777-6650
Fax: 302-777-6660 www.townsends.com
Processor of frozen poulty products, soups, etc
CEO: Tom Weisser
*Estimated Sales:*I
Number Employees: 1,000-4,999
Parent Co: Townsends
Type of Packaging: Food Service, Private Label

14507 Townsend Farms
23303 NE Sandy Blvd
Fairview, OR 97024-9618   503-666-1780
Fax: 503-618-8257   jeff@townfend.com
www.townsendfarms.com
Processor, exporter and wholesaler/distributor of
frozen blackberries, boysenberries, loganberries,
raspberries and strawberries; serving the food ser-
vice market; importer of melons, mangos,
pineapples and grapes
President: Mike Townsend
CEO: Jeff Townsend
CFO: Chris Valenti
Estimated Sales:$ 10 - 20 Million
Number Employees: 1,000-4,999
Sq. footage: 150000
Type of Packaging: Consumer, Food Service, Pri-
vate Label, Bulk

14508 Townsend-Piller Packing
719 19 1/4 Avenue
Cumberland, WI 54829   715-822-4910
President: Robert Townsend

14509 Townsends
P.O.Box 730
Pittsboro, NC 27312-0730   919-542-3215
Fax: 919-542-5834 www.townsends.com
Manufacturer of poultry including deboned chicken
President/CEO: P Coleman Townsend
Plant Manager: Don Stone
Estimated Sales: $ 50 - 100 Million
Number Employees: 250-499
Type of Packaging: Bulk

14510 Townsends Inc
22855 Dupont Blvd
Georgetown, DE 19947-8801   302-855-7100
Fax: 302-855-7225 www.townsends.com
Processor and exporter of fresh and frozen poultry
President: Charles Dix
Estimated Sales: $ 10 - 20 Million
Number Employees: 1,000-4,999
Type of Packaging: Food Service, Private Label,
Bulk
Brands:
MARTHA TOWNSEND'S
PERFECT BREAST
PRISTINE CUISINE
RUBY DRAGON
SAUTE SENSATIONS
SPEEDY BIRD
THE AMERICAN SOUP COLLECTION
ULTRA BREAST

14511 Townsends Inc
P.O.Box 709
Siler City, NC 27344-0709   919-663-2050
Fax: 919-663-4153 bbarnes@townsends.com
www.townsends.com
Manufacturer and exporter of fresh and frozen
chicken
President/CEO: P Coleman Townsend
Plant Manager: Steve Fields
Number Employees: 500-999
Parent Co: Townsends Inc
Type of Packaging: Consumer, Private Label, Bulk

**14512 Toxic Tommy's Beef Jerky &
Spices**
PO Box 432
Wadsworth, OH 44282-0432   330-807-7278
Fax: 305-723-7686   866-448-6942
toxictommy@yahoo.com   www.toxictommy.com
Manufacturer of beef jerky and jerky spices
President: Thomas Stabosz
Production: Joe Muscarella
Number Employees: 1-4
Number of Brands: 1
Number of Products: 9
Parent Co: TFS
Type of Packaging: Consumer, Food Service, Pri-
vate Label, Bulk
Brands:
Gold Rush
Grandpa Vals
Toxic Tommy

14513 Trace Mineral Research
P.O.Box 429
Roy, UT 84067-0429   801-731-6051
Fax: 801-731-3702   800-624-7145
infor@traceminerals.com
www.traceminerals.com
Processor of dietary supplements
President: Matt Kilts
Sales Director: Ryan Fisher
Estimated Sales: $4972329
Number Employees: 20-49
Number of Products: 100
Sq. footage: 13000
Type of Packaging: Consumer, Food Service, Pri-
vate Label, Bulk

14514 Tracy-Luckey Company
P.O.Box 880
Harlem, GA 30814-0880   706-556-6216
Fax: 706-556-6210   800-476-4796
ruthtracy@tracy-luckey.com
www.tracy-luckey.com

Processor of shelled pecans and pecan products
President: Francis Tracy
Executive VP: Seaborn Dell
VP Marketing/Sales: Ruth Tracy
Operations/Production/Purchasing: Seaborn Dell
Plant Manager: Homer Gay
Estimated Sales: $ 5 - 10 Million
Number Employees: 50-99
Sq. footage: 80000
Type of Packaging: Bulk
Brands:
SUNBLET

14515 Trade Farm
PO Box 43369
Oakland, CA 94624-0369   510-836-2938
Fax: 510-836-1481   tradefarm@prodigy.net
Frozen, air dehydrated and freeze dried supplier of
Chinese vegetables

14516 Trade Marcs Group
55 Nassau Ave
Brooklyn, NY 11222-3143   718-387-9696
Fax: 718-782-2471
General grocery
Manager: Andi Billow
Estimated Sales: Less than $500,000
Number Employees: 1-4

14517 Trade Winds Pizza
1085 Parkview Road
Green Bay, WI 54304-5616   920-336-7810
Fax: 920-336-2942
Pizzas
Director Operations: Jim Peppich

14518 Trader Joe's Company
604 W Huntington Dr
Monrovia, CA 91016-3297   626-358-8884
Fax: 626-301-4441 www.traderjoes.com
Suppliers of more than 2000 unique grocery and
gourmet items such as bakery, cheeses, chips,
snacks, coffee, fat free or low fat favorites, for your
home, fresh entrees, fresh produce, frozen entrees,
great beers, meatless choices, nutand trail mixes, or-
ganic foods, personal use, pet food, seafod, vita-
mins, and wines.
President: Robin Guentert
CFO: Bryan Palbaum
Manager: Chuck Yarez
Quality Control: Kathy Cipooa
Manager Media Relations: Diane O'Connor
Estimated Sales: $ 1 Billion
Number Employees: 5-9
Brands:
Baker Josef
Charles Shaw
Trader Joe's
Trader Ming

14519 Trader Vic's Food Products
PO Box 8603
Emeryville, CA 94662-0603   510-658-9722
Fax: 510-658-8110   877-762-4824
info@tradervics.com   tradervics.com
Processor and exporter of nonalcoholic cocktail
mixes, syrups, dry spices, sauces and salad dressings
President: Hans Richter
CEO: Hans Richter
VP: Peter Seely
Estimated Sales: $540000
Number Employees: 6
Type of Packaging: Consumer
Brands:
Trader Vic's

14520 Trader's Blend
10378 Main Street
Findley Lake, NY 14736-9708   716-769-7720
General grocery
Owner: Cynthia Bonarigo
Estimated Sales: Less than $500,000
Number Employees: 1-4

14521 Tradeshare Corporation
207 Flushing Avenue
Brooklyn, NY 11205   718-237-2295
Food preparation and general grocery
President: Robert Krasnor
Estimated Sales: $ 2.5-5 Million
Number Employees: 10-19

14522 Tradewinds Coffee Company
5500 Atlantic Springs Rd # 106
Raleigh, NC 27616-1856   919-878-1111
Fax: 919-878-0041   800-457-0406
customerservice@tradwindscoffee.com
www.tradewindscoffee.com
Coffee and coffee flavored candy
President: Art Watkins
Co-Owner: Elaine Watkins
Estimated Sales: Below $ 5 Million
Number Employees: 10-19
Brands:
Trade Winds Coffee

14523 Tradewinds International
PO Box 8
Ellendale, TN 38029-0008   901-385-8884
800-385-8884
Processor and exporter of wild rice
President: John Augustine
Operations Manager: Gwen Augustine
Number Employees: 20-49
Sq. footage: 12000
Type of Packaging: Food Service, Private Label,
Bulk

14524 Tradewinds-Tea Company
635 W 7th St # 403
Cincinnati, OH 45203-1549   513-357-5200
Fax: 513-357-5217   800-599-8434
customerservice@tradewinds-tea.com
www.tradewinds-tea.com
Brewed teas in nine flavors
President: Kenneth Lichtendahl
Marketing Director: Christy Lichtendahl
Estimated Sales: $ 5-10 Million
Number Employees: 5-9
Brands:
Concord Grape
Granny Smith Apple
Ice Tea
Lemon Tea

14525 Traditional Baking
2575 S Willow Avenue
Bloomington, CA 92316-3256   909-421-0391
Fax: 909-877-6728
Baked goods
Estimated Sales: $ 20 - 50 Million
Number Employees: 50-99

14526 Traditional Medicinals
4515 Ross Road
Sebastopol, CA 95472-2250   707-823-8911
Fax: 707-823-1599   800-543-4372
www.traditionalmedicinals.com
Processor of herb teas
President: Drake Sadler
President: Lynda Sadler
Sales Coordinator: Brenda Hodges
Estimated Sales: $3200000
Number Employees: 5
Brands:
Traditional Med Ginger Energy
Traditional Med Gypsy Cold Cure
Traditional Med Organics

14527 Trafalgar Brewing Company
1156 Speers Road
Oakville, ON L6L 2X4
Canada   905-337-0133
Fax: 905-845-2246   info@alesandmeads.com
www.alesandmeads.com
Processor of beer, ale, lager and stout
President: Mike Arnold
Number Employees: 1-4
Type of Packaging: Consumer, Food Service
Brands:
Celtic
Elora ESB
Elora Grand Lager
Elora Irish Ale
Harbour Gold
Paddy's Irish Red
Port Side Amber
Trafalgar

14528 Trail's Best Snacks
3205 Players Club Pkwy
Memphis, TN 38125-8845   605-335-8780
Fax: 605-335-8682   800-852-1863
info@trailsbest.com   www.trailsbest.com

Largest meat snack manufacturer in the United States
Marketing Coordinator: Roxanne Van Loon
Estimated Sales: $ 10 - 20 Million
Number Employees: 5-9
Parent Co: Sara Lee Foods
Type of Packaging: Consumer, Bulk
Brands:
HAPPY TRAILS MEAT SNACK STICKS
TEAM REALTREE
TRAIL'S BEST SNACKS

14529 Trailblazer Food Products
17900 NE San Rafael St
Portland, OR 97230-5930   503-666-5800
Fax: 503-666-6800   800-777-7179
cindy@tbfoods.com   www.tbfoods.com
Preserves, fruit products, quality foods, punches, marinades and syrups
President: Robert Miller
Marketing Director: Mike MIller
Founder: Gary Walls
Estimated Sales: $ 20-50 Million
Number Employees: 20-49
Brands:
Jake's Restaurant
Portland
Trailblazer

14530 Trans Pecos Foods
112 E Pecan St
San Antonio, TX 78205-1512   210-228-0896
Fax: 210-228-0781   pjk@texas.net
www.transpecosfoods.com
Manufacturer, importer and exporter of frozen breaded vegetables
President: Patrick J Kennedy
Plant Manager: Bruce Salcido
Estimated Sales: $3900000
Number Employees: 5-9
Parent Co: Anchor Food Products
Type of Packaging: Consumer, Food Service, Private Label, Bulk

14531 Trans-Ocean Products
10 Charles Street
Needham Heights, MA 02494-2906   508-626-0922
Fax: 508-626-2087
Seafood
Sales Manager: Alan Lipocky

14532 Trans-Ocean Products
350 W Orchard Dr
Bellingham, WA 98225-1769   360-671-6886
Fax: 360-671-0354   888-215-4815
info@trans-ocean.com   www.trans-ocean.com
Processor of imitation crab, lobster and salmon meat
President: Rick Dutton
Executive VP: H Okazaki
VP Sales/Marketing: L Shaheen
Estimated Sales: $ 100-500 Million
Number Employees: 100-249
Sq. footage: 120000
Parent Co: Maruha Corporation
Type of Packaging: Consumer, Food Service, Private Label, Bulk
Other Locations:
Trans-Ocean Products
Salem OR
Brands:
Classic
Pouch Pak
Transocean

14533 Trans-Packers Services Corporation
419 Vandervoort Ave
Brooklyn, NY 11222-5313   718-963-0900
Fax: 718-486-6344   877-787-8837
sales@transpackers.com   www.transpackers.com
Contract packager of food and nonfood products including powders, granules, solids and liquids in glass jars and bottles, etc
President: Selma Weiss
Vice President: Daniel Weiss
Plant Manager: Nester Serrano
Estimated Sales: $4900000
Number Employees: 100-249
Sq. footage: 100000
Type of Packaging: Consumer, Food Service

14534 Transa
704 Florsheim Dr
Libertyville, IL 60048-5002   847-281-9582
Fax: 847-816-6238   sales@hbroch.com
www.hbroch.com
Tomatoes and tomato powder, spices and vegetables
Manager: Donald Swanson
Sales Manager: James Kuzma
Estimated Sales: $ 5 - 10 Million
Number Employees: 5-9

14535 Transamerica Wine Corporation
Brooklyn Navy Yard
Brooklyn, NY 11201   718-875-4017
Fax: 718-625-1180
Wines
Manager: Yeshiah Schwartz
Estimated Sales: $ 5-10 Million
Number Employees: 10-19

14536 Trappe Packing Corporation
P.O.Box 121
Trappe, MD 21673-0121   410-476-3185
Fax: 410-476-3527   ward@parisfoods.com
www.parisfoods.com
Packer and exporter of frozen vegetables including corn, peas, carrots, mixed, succotash, broccoli, cauliflower, potato products, peppers, onions, blends, etc.; also, beans including green, waxed, baby lima and fava
President: Richard Marks
VP: C Johnson
Marketing: Julie Creese
Plant Manager: Anthony Dixon
Estimated Sales: $ 50 - 100 Million
Number Employees: 50-99
Type of Packaging: Food Service, Private Label, Bulk
Brands:
Fine Line
Topmark

14537 Trappey's Fine Foods
PO Box 13610
New Iberia, LA 70562-3610   337-365-8281
Fax: 337-369-7342   www.bgfoods.com
Okra, sauces and ethnic food
CEO: Dave Wenner
CFO: Robert Cantwell
Estimated Sales: $ 10-20 Million
Number Employees: 50-100
Parent Co: B&G Foods
Brands:
Trappey's

14538 Trappist Preserves
167 N Spencer Road
Spencer, MA 01562-1232   508-885-8740
Fax: 508-885-8715   www.monasterygreetings.com
Manufacturer of jellies, jams and marmalades including apricot, peach, strawberry, grape, etc
President: Damian Carr
Purchasing Manager: Henry Scarborough
Estimated Sales: $16 Million
Number Employees: 95
Type of Packaging: Consumer
Brands:
TRAPPIST

14539 Trappistine Quality Candy
300 Arnold Street
Wrentham, MA 02093-1700   508-528-1282
www.trappistinecandy.com
Candy
Number Employees: 20-49

14540 Travel Chocolate
69-20 66th Road
Middle Village, NY 11379   718-841-7030
Fax: 718-228-6440   info@travelchocolate.com
www.travelchocolate.com
organice fair-trade chocolate bars

14541 Traver Ranch
13138 S Bethel Ave
Kingsburg, CA 93631-9216   559-897-4091
Fax: 559-897-1396   lvr3@lightspeed.net
www.traverranch.com
Processor of peaches, nectarines, plums and oranges
President: Harood McBlarly
Plant Manager: Chris Holland
Estimated Sales: $100+ Million
Number Employees: 100-249
Parent Co: LVR Corporation

Brands:
Traver Ranch

14542 Traverse Bay Confections
1025 Industry Dr
Tukwila, WA 98188-4802   206-725-0099
Fax: 203-722-0196
sales@traversebayconfections.com
www.traversebayconfections.com
Gourmet chocolates, cookies and candies.
Owner: Richard Anderson
Estimated Sales: $ 5 - 10 Million
Number Employees: 5-9

14543 (HQ)Travis Meats
7210 Clinton Hwy
Powell, TN 37849-5216   865-938-9051
Fax: 865-938-9211   800-247-7606
wdaletravis@att.net   www.travismeats.com
Processor of frozen veal and pork; also, beef including barbecued, rolls and hamburger patties
President: W Travis
Controller: Brent Atchley
VP Production: Dale Travis
Estimated Sales: $ 20 - 50 Million
Number Employees: 100-249
Sq. footage: 110000
Type of Packaging: Consumer, Food Service
Other Locations:
Travis Meats
Knoxville TN

14544 Treasure Foods
2500 S 2300 W # 11
West Valley, UT 84119-7676   801-974-0911
Fax: 801-975-0553   treasurefoods@hotmail.com
www.honeybutter4u.com
Processor and exporter of whipped honey butter, flavored fruit honey, scones; wholesaler/distributor of frozen foods and general line items; serving the food service market
Owner: Amin Motilla
CFO: Zarina Motiwala
Vice President: Mohamed Motiwala
Marketing Director: Amin Motiwala
Public Relations: Amin Motiwala
Production Manager: Fawad Motiwala
Plant Manager: Fawad Motiwala
Purchasing Manager: Amin Motiwala
Estimated Sales: $450,000
Number Employees: 5
Number of Brands: 3
Number of Products: 3
Sq. footage: 3600
Parent Co: Algilani Food Import & Export
Type of Packaging: Food Service, Private Label, Bulk
Other Locations:
Treasure Foods
Salt Lake City UT
Brands:
HONEY BUTTER TOPPING
RASPBERRY HONEY BUTTER TOPPING
SCONES

14545 Treat Ice Cream Company
11 S 19th St
San Jose, CA 95116-2202   408-292-9321
Fax: 408-298-5859   treaticecream@aol.com
www.treaticecream.com
Processor of gourmet ice cream
Owner: Alfred Mauseth
Vice President: Bob Mauseth
Estimated Sales: $ 3 - 5 Million
Number Employees: 5-9
Sq. footage: 4000
Type of Packaging: Consumer, Private Label, Bulk
Brands:
Treat

14546 Treats Island Fisheries
PO Box 21
Scaly Mountain, NC 28775-0021   207-733-4580
Fax: 207-733-4880
Seafood
President: James English

14547 Treatt USA
4900 Lakeland Commerce Pkwy
Lakeland, FL 33805-7637   863-421-4708
Fax: 863-668-3388   800-866-7704
enquiries@treattusa.com   www.treattusa.com

Processor of food additives including essential oils and aromatic chemicals
Sales: Steve Shelton
VP Sales: Nancy Poulos
Estimated Sales: $ 1 - 3 Million
Number Employees: 50-99
Parent Co: R.C. Treatt & Company
Type of Packaging: Bulk
Brands:
Citreatt
Treattarome

14548 Trebon European Specialties
210 Green St
South Hackensack, NJ 07606-1301 201-343-5161
Fax: 201-343-5102 800-899-4332
info@fratelliberettausa.com
www.fratelliberettausa.com
Italian and Spanish meat specialties
President: Lorenzo Beretta
Estimated Sales: $ 5-10 Million
Number Employees: 20-49

14549 Tree Ripe Products
9 Great Meadow Ln # A
East Hanover, NJ 07936-1703 973-463-0777
800-873-3747
Processor and exporter of nonalcoholic cocktail mixes
President: Joel Fishman
Estimated Sales: $3000000
Number Employees: 1-4
Sq. footage: 10000
Type of Packaging: Consumer, Food Service
Brands:
Frothee Creamy Head
Lem-N-Joy
Tree-Ripe

14550 Tree Tavern Products
PO Box 2545
Paterson, NJ 07509-2545 973-279-1617
Fast food and franchises
President: Louis Francia
Estimated Sales: $ 5-10 Million appx.
Number Employees: 20

14551 (HQ)Tree Top
PO Box 248
Selah, WA 98942-0248 509-697-7251
Fax: 509-698-1421 800-367-6571
faq@treetop.com www.treetop.com
Fruit juices and drinks, applesauce and fruit snacks
President/CEO: Thomas Stokes
VP Finance/CFO: John Wells
Director Quality/Technical Services: Scott Summers
VP Sales: Greg Bainter
VP Public Relations: Julia Stewart Daly
Estimated Sales: $295.4 Million
Number Employees: 1,300
Type of Packaging: Food Service, Private Label, Bulk
Other Locations:
Tree Top
Milton-Freewater OR
Brands:
FIBER RICH
ROVAN
SENECA GRANNY SMITH CONCENTRATE
SENECA JUICES
SENECA ORANGE PLUS BEVERAGE
SENECA R.S.P. TART CHERRY CONCENTRA
TREE TOP
TREE TOP APPLE JUICE
TREE TOP JUICE FIZZ
TREE TOP ORCHARD BLENDS
TREE TOP THREE APPLE BLEND

14552 Tree Top
P.O.Box 248
Selah, WA 98942-0248 509-697-7251
Fax: 509-698-1421 800-542-4055
faq@treetop.com www.treetop.com
Produces grape juice and concentrate, apple juice, apple sauce, apple concentrate and blended juices
CEO: Tom Stokes
Chairman: Dick Olsen
Corporate Communications Manager: Laura Dovey
VP Sales/Marketing: Dave Watkins
Estimated Sales: $ 50-100 Million
Number Employees: 1,000-4,999
Parent Co: Tree Top

Type of Packaging: Consumer, Food Service, Private Label, Bulk
Brands:
Tree Top

14553 Tree of Life
P.O.Box 9000
St Augustine, FL 32085-9000 904-940-2100
Fax: 904-940-2553 Mailbox@TreeofLife.com
www.treeoflife.com
Manufacturer and exporter of natural products including date sweetened chocolates and carob, honey graham and cheddar crackers, gingersnaps, hummus dip, nutritional drinks, soy cheeses, gluten and lactose free products
President: G Palermo
CFO: Belinda Schneader
CEO: Richard Lane
Marketing Director: Karen Waeyenberghe
Estimated Sales: Less than $500,000
Number Employees: 5,000-9,999
Type of Packaging: Consumer, Food Service, Private Label, Bulk
Other Locations:
Elkton FL
Ft Lauderdale FL
Kennesaw GA
North Bergen NJ
Albany NY
Bloomington IN
Milwaukee WI
Minneapolis MN
Dallas TX
Cleburne TX
Los Angeles CA
Clackamas OR
Mississauga, Ontario
Brands:
ANNIE'S HOMEGROWN
BLUE DIAMOND
HAIN PURE
HORIZON ORGANIC
KRAFT FOODS
MANISCHEWITZ
MCCORMICK
NATURADE
NESTLE'
SEEDS OF CHANGE
WORLD FINER FOODS

14554 Tree of Life Albany
4294 Albany St
Albany, NY 12205-4621 518-456-1888
800-691-1880
CustSvcNE@TreeofLife.com
www.treeoflife.com
Wholesale distributor of natural, organic, specialty, ethnic and gourmet food products.
Chairman/President/CEO: Richard Thorne
SVP/Finance/Chief Financial Officer: Tom Wissbaum
COO: Dayne Ryan
SVP/Sales: George Schuetz
Parent Co: Tree of Life
Brands:
ANNIE'S HOMEGROWN
BLUE DIAMOND
HAIN PURE FOODS
HORIZON ORGANIC
KRAFT FOODS
MANISCHEWITZ
MCCORMICK
NATURADE
NESTLE
SEEDS OF CHANGE
WORLD FINER FOODS

14555 Tree of Life Atlanta
2700 Barrett Lakes Blvd NW
Kennesaw, GA 30144-4813 770-218-6020
Fax: 770-218-6030 800-798-5986
CustSvcNE@TreeofLife.com www.treelife.com
Wholesale distributor of natural, organic, specialty, ethnic and gourmet food products.
Chairman/President/CEO: Richard Thorne
SVP/Finance/Chief Financial Officer: Tom Wissbaum
COO: Stacy Hodoh
SVP/Sales: George Schuetz
Parent Co: Tree of Life
Brands:
ANNIE'S HOMEGROWN
BLUE DIAMOND
HAIN PURE FOODS
HORIZON ORGANIC

KRAFT FOODS
MANISCHEWITZ
MCCORMICK
NATURADE
NESTLE
SEEDS OF CHANGE
WORLD FINER FOODS

14556 Tree of Life Canada East
6030 Freemont Blvd
Mississauga, ON L5R 3X4
Canada 905-507-6161
800-263-7054
CustSvcNE@TreeofLife.com
www.treeoflife.com
Wholesale distributor of natural, organic, specialty, ethnic and gourmet food products.
Chairman/President/CEO: Richard Thorne
SVP/Finance/Chief Financial Officer: Tom Wissbaum
SVP/Sales: George Schuetz
Parent Co: Tree of Life
Brands:
ANNIE'S HOMEGROWN
BLUE DIAMOND
HAIN PURE FOODS
HORIZON ORGANIC
KRAFT FOODS
MANISCHEWITZ
MCCORMICK
NATURADE
NESTLE
SEEDS OF CHANGE
WORLD FINER FOODS

14557 Tree of Life Canada West
91 Glacier Street
Coquitlam, BC V3K 5Z1
Canada 604-941-8502
800-661-9655
CustSvcNE@TreeofLife.com
www.treeoflife.com
Wholesale distributor of natural, organic, specialty, ethnic and gourmet food products.
Chairman/President/CEO: Richard Thorne
SVP/Finance/Chief Financial Officer: Tom Wissbaum
SVP/Sales: George Schuetz
Parent Co: Tree of Life
Brands:
ANNIE'S HOMEGROWN
BLUE DIAMOND
HAIN PURE FOODS
HORIZON ORGANIC
KRAFT FOODS
MANISCHEWTIZ
MCCORMICK
NATURADE
NESTLE
SEEDS OF CHANGE
WORLD FINER FOODS

14558 Tree of Life Canada West
2600 61st Avenue SE
Calgary, AB T2C 4V2
Canada 403-279-8988
800-665-1298
CustSvcNE@TreeofLife.com
www.treeoflife.com
Wholesale distributor of natural, organic, specialty, ethnic and gourmet food products.
Chairman/President/CEO: Richard Thorne
SVP/Finance/Chief Financial Officer: Tom Wissbaum
SVP/Sales: George Schuetz
Parent Co: Tree of Life
Brands:
ANNIE'S HOMEGROWN
BLUE DIAMOND
HAIN PURE FOODS
HORIZON ORGANIC
KRAFT FOODS
MANISCHEWITZ
MCCORMICK
NATURADE
NESTLE
SEEDS OF CHANGE
WORLD FINER FOODS

14559 Tree of Life Cleburne
105 Bluebonnet
Cleburne, TX 76031-8956   817-641-8733
          Fax: 817-556-4976   800-800-2155
          CustSvcNE@TreeofLife.com
          www.treeoflife.com
Wholesale distributor of natural, organic, specialty, ethnic and gourmet food products.
  Manager: Clint Wheeler
  SVP/Finance/Chief Financial Officer: Tom Wissbaum
  SVP/Sales: George Schuetz
Parent Co: Tree of Life
Brands:
  ANNIE'S HOMEGROWN
  BLUE DIAMOND
  HAIN PURE FOODS
  HORIZON ORGANIC
  KRAFT FOODS
  MANISCHEWITZ
  MCCORMICK
  NATURADE
  NESTLE
  SEEDS OF CHANGE
  WORLD FINER FOODS

14560 Tree of Life Elkton
4055 Deerpark Blvd
Elkton, FL 32033-2070   904-824-8181
          Fax: 904-825-2012   800-223-2910
          CustSvcNE@TreeofLife.com
          www.treeoflife.com
Wholesale distributor of natural, organic, specialty, ethnic and gourmet food products.
  President: Mike Novak
  SVP/Finance/Chief Financial Officer: Tom Wissbaum
  SVP/Sales: George Schuetz
Parent Co: Tree of Life
Brands:
  ANNIE'S HOMEGROWN
  BLUE DIAMOND
  HAIN PURE FOODS
  HORIZON ORGANIC
  KRAFT FOODS
  MANISCHEWITZ
  MCCORMICK
  NATURADE
  NESTLE
  SEEDS OF CHANGE
  WORLD FINER FOODS

14561 Tree of Life Ft Lauderdale
3225 Meridian Pkwy
Weston, FL 33331-3503   954-384-0904
          Fax: 954-384-0904   800-490-3463
          CustSvcNE@TreeofLife.com
          www.treeoflife.com
Wholesale distributor of natural, organic, specialty, ethnic and gourmet food products.
  Manager: Cliff Ruzzo
  SVP/Finance/Chief Financial Officer: Tom Wissbaum
  SVP/Sales: George Schuetz
Parent Co: Tree of Life
Brands:
  ANNIE'S HOMEGROWN
  BLUE DIAMOND
  HAIN PURE FOODS
  HORIZON ORGANIC
  KRAFT FOODS
  MANISCHEWITZ
  MCCORMICK
  NATURADE
  NESTLE
  SEEDS OF CHANGE
  WORLD FINER FOODS

14562 Tree of Life Los Angeles
5560 E Slauson Ave
Commerce, CA 90040-2921   323-722-2100
          Fax: 323-890-3870   800-899-4217
CustSvcNE@TreeofLife.com   www.a1online.com
Wholesale distributor of natural, organic, specialty, ethnic and gourmet food products.
  Chairman/President/CEO: Richard Thorne
  SVP/Finance/Chief Financial Officer: Tom Wissbaum
  COO: Stacey Hodoh
  SVP/Sales: George Schuetz
Parent Co: Tree of Life
Brands:
  ANNIE'S HOMEGROWN
  BLUE DIAMOND

  HAIN PURE FOODS
  HORIZON ORGANIC
  KRAFT FOODS
  MANISCHEWITZ
  MCCORMICK
  NATURADE
  NESTLE
  SEEDS OF CHANGE
  WORLD FINER FODS

14563 Tree of Life Milwaukee
7225 W Marcia Rd
Milwaukee, WI 53223-3361   414-365-7000
          Fax: 414-365-7049   800-883-1622
          CustSvcNE@TreeofLife.com
          www.treeoflife.com
Wholesale distributor of natural, organic, specialty, ethnic and gourmet food products.
  Chairman/President/CEO: Richard Thorne
  SVP/Finance/Chief Financial Officer: Tom Wissbaum
  SVP/Sales: George Schuetz
Parent Co: Tree of Life
Brands:
  ANNIE'S HOMEGROWN
  BLUE DIAMOND
  HAIN PURE FOODS
  HORIZON ORGANIC
  KRAFT FOODS
  MANISCHEWITZ
  MCCORMICK
  NATURADE
  NESTLE
  SEEDS OF CHANGE
  WORLD FINER FOODS

14564 Tree of Life Minneapolis
860 Vandalia St
St Paul, MN 55114-1305   612-752-6300
                               800-726-7205
          CustSvcNE@TreeofLife.com
          www.treeoflife.com
Wholesale distributor of natural, organic, specialty, ethnic and gourmet food products.
  Manager: Jim Schorzmann
  SVP/Finance/Chief Financial Officer: Tom Wissbaum
  SVP/Sales: George Schuetz
Parent Co: Tree of Life
Brands:
  ANNIE'S HOMEGROWN
  BLUE DIAMOND
  HAIN PURE FOODS
  HORIZON ORGANIC
  KRAFT FOODS
  MANISCHEWITZ
  MCCORMICK
  NATURADE
  NESTLE
  SEEDS OF CHANGE
  WORLD FINER FOODS

14565 Tree of Life North Bergen
P.O.Box 852
North Bergen, NJ 07047-0852   201-662-7200
          Fax: 201-854-8353   800-735-5175
          CustSvcNE@TreeofLife.com
          www.treeoflife.com
Wholesale distributor of natural, organic, specialty, ethnic, and gourmet food products.
  President: Chuck Ramsbacher
  Plant Manager: Frank Powers
Estimated Sales: $ 20-50 Million
Number Employees: 50-99
Parent Co: Tree of Life
Brands:
  ANNIE'S HOMEGROWN
  BLUE DIAMOND
  Bella Good
  HAIN PURE FOODS
  HORIZON ORGANIC
  KRAFT FOODS
  MANISCHEWITZ
  MCCORMICK
  NATURADE
  NESTLE
  SEEDS OF CHANGE
  WORLD FINER FOODS

14566 Tree of Life Portland
12601 SE Highway 212
Clackamas, OR 97015-9036   503-655-1177
          Fax: 503-650-5526   800-437-7297
          CustSvcNE@TreeofLife.com
          www.treeoflife.com
Wholesale distributor of natural, organic, specialty, ethnic and gourmet food products.
  Chairman/President/CEO: Richard Thorne
  SVP/Finance/Chief Financial Officer: Tom Wissbaum
  SVP/Sales: George Schuetz
  Plant Manager: Bryan Singleton
Parent Co: Tree of Life
Brands:
  ANNIE'S HOMEGROWN
  BLUE DIAMOND
  HAIN PURE FOODS
  HORIZON ORGANIC
  KRAFT FOODS
  MANISCHEWITZ
  MCCORMICK
  NATURADE
  NESTLE
  SEEDS OF CHANGE
  WORLD FINER FOODS

14567 Tree of Life Southwest-West Region
5101 Highland Place Dr
Dallas, TX 75236-1449   972-298-2957
          Fax: 972-708-5549   800-869-1650
          CustSvcNE@TreeofLife.com
          www.treeoflife.com
Wholesale distributor of natural, organic, specialty, ethnic and gourmet food products.
  President: Brian Evers
  SVP/Finance/Chief Financial Officer: Tom Wissbaum
  SVP/Sales: George Schuetz
Parent Co: Tree of Life
Brands:
  ANNIE'S HOMEGROWN
  BLUE DIAMOND
  HAIN PURE FOODS
  HORIZON ORGANIC
  KRAFT FOODS
  MANISCHEWITZ
  MCCORMICK
  NATURADE
  NESTLE
  SEEDS OF CHANGE
  WORLD FINER FOODS

14568 Treehouse Farms
6914 Road 160
Earlimart, CA 93219-9627   559-757-4100
          Fax: 559-757-0510
Processor and exporter of almonds including natural, blanched, sliced, roasted, diced and slivered
  President: David Fitzgerald
  Sales Manager: Carol Coffey
Number Employees: 250-499
Sq. footage: 200000
Parent Co: Yorkshire Foods
Type of Packaging: Private Label, Bulk
Brands:
  Treehouse Farms

14569 Treesweet Products
16825 Northchase Drive
Suite 1600
Houston, TX 77060-6099   281-876-3759
          Fax: 281-876-2643
Orange juice and products
  President: Jeffrey Rosenberg
Estimated Sales: $500,000-$1 Million
Number Employees: 5-9
Brands:
  Awake
  Orange Plus
  Treesweet Products

14570 Trefethen Vineyards
PO Box 2460
Napa, CA 94558-0291   707-255-7700
          Fax: 707-255-0793   800-556-4847
winery@trefethen.com   www.trefethen.com

Producer and exporter of wine
President: John Trefethen
VP: David C Whitehouse Jr
Marketing: Terry Hall
Sales: Joe Cusimano
Public Relations: Terry Hall
Production: Richard De Garmo
Estimated Sales: $12000000
Number Employees: 60
Sq. footage: 45000
Brands:
TREFETHEN VINEYARDS

14571 Trega Foods
105 E 3rd Ave
Weyauwega, WI 54983-9067   920-867-2137
Fax: 920-867-2249 doug@tregafoods.com
www.tregafoods.com
Manufacturer of cheese such as cheddar, feta, mozzarella, mozzarella sticks, provolone and dairy ingredients
President: Doug Simon
VP: Richard Wagner
Estimated Sales: $ 5 - 10 Million
Number Employees: 5-9
Type of Packaging: Consumer, Food Service
Other Locations:
Trega Foods Processing Plant
Little Chute WI
Trega Foods Processing Plant
Luxemburg WI
Brands:
TREGA

14572 Treier Popcorn Farms
16793 County Line Rd
Bloomdale, OH 44817   419-454-2811
Fax: 419-454-3983 ptreier@wcnet.org
Manufacturer of popcorn including bagged, natural, buttered and microwaveable; wholesaler/distributor of commercial popcorn poppers and other concession supply equipment; serving the food service market
President: Don Treier
Secretary/Treasurer: Peggy Treier
Estimated Sales: $500,000-$1 Million
Number Employees: 10-19
Number of Brands: 2
Number of Products: 6
Sq. footage: 3000
Parent Co: Treier Family Farms
Type of Packaging: Consumer, Food Service, Bulk
Brands:
LAKE PLAINS
PELTON'S HYBRID POPCORN

14573 Tremblay's Sweet Shop
P.O.Box 228
Hayward, WI 54843-0228   715-634-2785
Fax: 715-634-7830
Candy
President: Dennis Tremblay
Quality Control: Charles Tremblay
Estimated Sales: Below $ 5 Million
Number Employees: 20-49

14574 Trentadue Winery
19170 Geyserville Ave
Geyserville, CA 95441-9528   707-433-3104
Fax: 707-433-5825 888-332-3032
info@trentadue.com www.trentadue.com
Wines
Proprietor: Leo Trentadue
Proprietor: Evelyn Trentadue
General and Vineyard Manager: Victor Trentadue

Winemaker: Miroslav Tcholakov
Estimated Sales: $ 5-10 Million
Number Employees: 10-19
Type of Packaging: Private Label
Brands:
Trentadue

14575 Trenton Bridge Lobster Pound
1237 Bar Harbor Rd
Trenton, ME 04605-6021   207-667-2977
Fax: 207-667-3412 www.trentonbridgelobster.com
Lobster
President: Anthony Pettegrow
Estimated Sales: $ 3 - 5 Million
Number Employees: 10-19

14576 Trenton Processing
120 W Broadway
Trenton, IL 62293-1306   618-224-7383
Fax: 618-224-9038
Processor of meat products
President: Gary Schwend
Purchasing Manager: Judy Kuhn
Estimated Sales: $ 5 - 10 Million
Number Employees: 10-19
Type of Packaging: Consumer

14577 Tres Classique
966 Mazzoni St # 2-1
Ukiah, CA 95482-3475   707-463-2646
Fax: 707-463-2299 888-644-5127
Gourmet cooking, sauces, dipping oils, dessert sauces and herbed wine vinegars
Owner: Thomas Allen
Estimated Sales: Under 500,000
Number Employees: 1-4
Number of Products: 38
Type of Packaging: Food Service, Private Label, Bulk
Brands:
Lemon Splash
Splash

14578 Tri-Boro Fruit Company
2500 S Fowler Ave
Fresno, CA 93725-9308   559-486-4141
Fax: 559-486-7627
Grape grower
President: Chris Fazio
Executive: Tony Fazio
Estimated Sales: $ 5-10 Million
Number Employees: 10-19

14579 Tri-Cost Seafood
13213 Perkins Road
Baton Rouge, LA 70810-2032   225-757-8333
Fax: 225-757-8332
Seafood

14580 Tri-Counties Packing Company
845 Vertin Ave
Salinas, CA 93901-4524   831-422-7841
Fax: 831-422-7856 sales@celeryhearts.com
www.celeryhearts.com
Processor of celery and celery hearts
President/Owner: Jack Baillie
Sales: John Baillie
Estimated Sales: $5 Million
Number Employees: 20-49
Number of Brands: 3
Number of Products: 1
Sq. footage: 46000
Type of Packaging: Consumer
Other Locations:
Tri - Counties Packaging Coompany
Oxnard CA
Brands:
Candy Stick
Snappy
Tri-Sign

14581 Tri-Marine InternationalInc
338 Cannery Street
San Pedro, CA 90731-7310   310-732-6113
www.trimarine-usa.com
Processor, canner, importer and exporter of tuna, mackerel, squid and sardines
President: Renato Curto
COO: Chaiphorn Wangmitayasuk
VP Operations: Ian Boatwood
Number Employees: 500-999
Sq. footage: 500000
Type of Packaging: Consumer, Food Service, Private Label, Bulk
Brands:
American
Bonito
Lucky Strike
Pan Pacific
Sweepstakes
Top Wave

14582 Tri-State Beef Company
2124 Baymiller St
Cincinnati, OH 45214-2208   513-579-1722
Fax: 513-579-1739

Processor of beef
President: Robert Runtz
CEO: Robert Runtz
Secretary/Treasurer: Betty Stout
Marketing Manager: Robert Runtz
Estimated Sales: $ 20 - 50 Million
Number Employees: 50-99
Type of Packaging: Consumer, Food Service, Bulk
Brands:
Soauthter

14583 Tri-State Processing Company
519 W Spraker Street
Kokomo, IN 46901-2197   317-452-4008
Frozen foods
Plant Manager: Calvin Moss
Estimated Sales: $ 10-100 Million
Number Employees: 100

14584 Tri-State Specialties
4430 S Tripp Avenue
Chicago, IL 60632-4321   773-247-0160
Fax: 773-247-0135
Processors and grinders of spices and seasonings; wholesaler/distributor of soy proteins, onion and garlic
President: John Schoenenberger
Technical Services: David Grex
Sales Manager: John Janasko
Number Employees: 20-49
Type of Packaging: Bulk

14585 Tri-States Coca-Cola Bottling Company
5100 Duck Creek Rd
Cincinnati, OH 45227-1450   513-527-6600
Fax: 513-527-6660 800-543-2653
ccemail@na.cokecce.com www.cce.com
Manufacturer and bottler of soft drinks
President: Margy Miller
President/CEO: John Alm
SVP/CFO: William Douglas
VP Information Technology: William Hartman
EVP/General Counsel: John Culhane
VP North American Sales: Mark Schortman
SVP Human Resources: Daniel Bowling III
EVP/COO: G David van Houten Jr
VP Operations Planning/Development: David Katz
Estimated Sales: $100-500 Million
Number Employees: 250-499
Parent Co: Coca-Cola Enterprises
Type of Packaging: Consumer, Food Service, Private Label, Bulk
Brands:
BARQ'S
CAFFEINE FREE COCA-COLA CLASSIC
CAFFEINE FREE DIET COKE
CHERRY COKE
CHIPPEWA WATER
COCA-COLA C2
COCA-COLA CLASSIC
COCA-COLA CLASSIC
COCA-COLA WITH LIME
COCA-COLA ZERO
DANNON
DASANI
DASANI FLAVORED WATERS
DIET BARQ'S
DIET CHERRY COKE
DIET COKE WITH SPLENDA
DIET COKE/COKE LIGHT
DIET MELLO YELLO
DIET NESTEA
DIET NORTHERN NECK
DIET ROCKSTAR
DIET SPRITE ZERO
DIET VANILLA COKE
EVIAN
FANTA
FRESCA
FULL THROTTLE
KMX
MELLO YELLO
MINUTE MAID JUICES/JUICE DRINKS
MINUTE MAID LEMONADE
MINUTE MAID LIGHT
MINUTE MAID LIGHT LEMONADES
PIBB XTRA
POWERADE
POWERADE OPTION
RED FLASH
ROCKSTAR
SEAGRAMS GINGER ALE & MIXERS

SPRITE
SPRITE REMIX
TAB
VANILLA COKE
VAULT

14586 Tri-Sum Potato Chip Company
15 Carter Street
Leominster, MA 01453-3806   978-537-4088
                              Fax: 978-534-5193
Manufacturer of potato chips, popcorn and cheese
puffs
      COO: Richard Gates
Number Employees: 20-50
Type of Packaging: Consumer, Food Service, Private Label, Bulk
Brands:
      Jp's
      Suncrisp

14587 Tri-Sun International
2230 Cape Cod Way
Santa Ana, CA 92703-3582   714-835-6367
      Fax: 714-835-4948   800-387-4786
      customerservice@trisuninternational.com
            www.lalifestyle.com
Processor and wholesaler/distributor of teas and
herbal products
      Owner: Patricia J Logsdon
Estimated Sales: $ 10 - 20 Million
Type of Packaging: Consumer

14588 Tri-Valley Growers
PO Box 1328
Sandy, OR 97055-1328   209-572-5200
                          Fax: 209-572-5987
Packer of canned fruit products
      President/CEO: Joseph Famalette
      VP Marketing: Leon Kreger
      Treasurer: James Eichenberger
      Quality Control: Roy Herman
      Sales Manager: Victor Reed
Number Employees: 250-499
Parent Co: Tri-Valley Growers
Type of Packaging: Consumer, Food Service, Private Label, Bulk
Brands:
      Pik-Nik
      Redwood Inn
      S & W

14589 Tri-Valley Growers
12045 Ingomar Grade
Los Banos, CA 93635-9796   209-827-5000
                          Fax: 209-827-5001
Grower and exporter of tomatoes
      Plant Manager: David Boulware
Number Employees: 100-249
Parent Co: Tri-Valley Growers
Type of Packaging: Consumer, Private Label

14590 Tri-Valley Growers
580 Middletown Blvd
Langhorne, PA 19047-1827   215-702-8131
                          Fax: 215-702-8962
Processor of canned and jarred tomatoes, fruits and
olives
      Business Director: Charles Richie
Number Employees: 5-9
Parent Co: Tri Valley Growers
Type of Packaging: Consumer, Food Service

14591 Triangle Seafood
212 Adams Street
Louisville, KY 40206-1862   502-561-0055
                          Fax: 502-561-0096
Seafood
      President: J Shannon Bouchillon

**14592 Tribe Mediterranean Foods
Company LLC**
110 Prince Henry Drive
Taunton, MA 02780   800-848-6687
                          800-421-3474
      info@ritefoods.com   www.ritefoods.com
Processor and exporter of pickled herring, smoked
salmon, fresh caviar, value-added seafood items and
hummus dips/spreads
      President: Howard Klein
      Executive VP: Harvey Petersiel
      VP Sales/Marketing: Bruce Rubin
Number Employees: 5-9
Sq. footage: 60000

14593 Tribeca Oven
447 Gotham Pkwy
Carlstadt, NJ 07072-2409   201-935-8800
      Fax: 201-935-6685   david@tribecaoven.com
                              www.tribecaoven.com
Processor of breads including rye, white,
wholewheat, etc
      Manager: Jesse Kirsch
Number Employees: 50-99
Type of Packaging: Consumer, Food Service

**14594 (HQ)Trident Seafoods
Corporation**
5303 Shilshole Ave NW
Seattle, WA 98107-4000   206-783-3818
      Fax: 206-782-7195   800-426-5490
      consumeraffairs@tridentseafoods.com
            www.tridentseafoods.com
Processor, importer and exporter of frozen seafood
including halibut, salmon, pollock and king, snow
and Dungeness crabs; also, breaded and battered
seafood and surimi
      President: Charles H Bundrant
      CEO: Steve Okerlund
Estimated Sales: $122300000
Number Employees: 100-249
Type of Packaging: Consumer, Food Service, Bulk
Brands:
      Arctic Ice
      Arctic Ice Rockfish
      Perfectserve Tuna
      Pub House Battered Seafood
      Pubhouse
      Rubenstein's
      Sea Alaska
      Sea Legs
      Trident

14595 Trident Seafoods Corporation
1124 54th Avenue E
Fife, WA 98424-2702   253-922-5577
      Fax: 253-922-2407 www.tridentseafoods.com
Processor of frozen surimi
      General Manager: Jim Bonin
Estimated Sales: $ 20 - 50 Million
Number Employees: 100
Parent Co: Trident Seafood Corporation
Type of Packaging: Food Service
Brands:
      Arctic Ice
      Arctic Ice Rockfish
      Perfectserve Tuna
      Pub House Battered SeafoOD
      Pubhouse
      Rubenstein's
      Sea Alaska
      Sea Legs
      Trident

14596 Trident Seafoods Corporation
P.O.Box 69
Salem, NH 03079-0069   603-893-3368
                          Fax: 603-893-7757
      mikekater@tridentseafoods.com
            www.tridentseafoods.com
Processor of frozen and portion control fish and seafood
      Director Military/Healthcare/Schools: Mike Kater
      Marketing Director: Mike Kater
      Office Manager: Ann Kater
      Purchasing Manager: Mark Kater
Estimated Sales: $ 3 - 5 Million
Number Employees: 1-4
Sq. footage: 1500
Parent Co: Trident Seafood Corporation
Brands:
      Arctic Ice
      Icy Waters
      Interstate Seafoods
      Sea Legs
      Trident Seafoods

14597 Trigo Corporation
PO Box 2369
Toa Baja, PR 00951-2369   787-794-1300
      Fax: 787-794-3110   comprastrigo@prw.net
                              www.prw.net
Processor of rum, vodka, liquor and wine
      Executive Director: Benigno Trigo
      Marketing Director: Mariella Algarin
      Marketing: Eunice Miranva
Number Employees: 20-49
Type of Packaging: Consumer
Brands:
      Ponte Vecckio

**14598 Trinidad Bean & Elevator
Company**
615 5th St
Greeley, CO 80631-2383   970-352-0346
      Fax: 970-571-5256 www.trinidadbenham.com
Manufacturer of dry beans
      Manager: Larry Peterson
      Plant Manager: R J Seader
Estimated Sales: $50-100 Million
Number Employees: 10-19
Type of Packaging: Consumer, Food Service, Private Label, Bulk
Brands:
      Peak

14599 Trinidad Benham Company
3650 S. Yosemite, Suite 300
Po Box 378007
Denver, CO 80237   303-220-1400
      Fax: 303-220-1490   info@trinidadbenham.com
            www.trinidadbenham.com
Manufacturer and exporter of dry beans, rice, popcorn, peas and household aluminum foil
      President/CEO: Carl Hartman
      Plant Manager: Bill Dearmond
Estimated Sales: $50-100 Million
Number Employees: 50-99
Parent Co: Trinidad/Benham Corporation
Type of Packaging: Consumer, Food Service, Private Label, Bulk
Brands:
      Benco-Peak
      CookQuick
      Evans
      Jack Rabbit
      Kings
      Ranch Wagon
      Royal Wrap
      Shamrock

14600 Trinidad Benham Company
PO Box 427
Bridgeport, NE 69336-0427   308-262-1361
                          Fax: 308-586-1058
Manufacturer of dry beans
      President: Bill McCormack
      Area Operations Manager: Dale Eirich
Estimated Sales: $3-5 Million
Number Employees: 25
Type of Packaging: Consumer, Food Service
Brands:
      BENCO PEAK
      COOKQUICK'
      EVANS
      JACK RABBIT
      KINGS
      RANCH WAGON
      ROYAL WRAP
      SHAMROCK

14601 (HQ)Trinidad Benham Company
P.O.Box 378007
Denver, CO 80237-8007   303-220-1400
      Fax: 303-220-1490   info@trinidadbenham.com
            www.trinidadbenham.com
Manufacturer and exporter of dry beans, rice and
popcorn packer and distributor of houshold aluminium foil
      President/CEO: Carl C Hartman
      CFO: Ron Weimer
      EVP: Linda Walasley
      Plant Manager: John Kurtz
Estimated Sales: $229 Million
Number Employees: 50-99
Type of Packaging: Consumer, Food Service, Private Label, Bulk
Other Locations:
      Trinidad/Benham Corp.
      Modesto CA
Brands:
      BENCO PEAK
      COOK QUICK
      EVANS
      JACK RABBIT
      KINGS

RANCH WAGON
ROYAL WRAP
SHAMROCKak

14602 Trinidad Benham Company
P.O.Box 29
Mineola, TX 75773-0029 903-569-2636
Fax: 903-569-2120 www.trinidadbenham.com
Popcorn
President: Carl Hertman
Owner: Trinidad Benham
CFO: Gary Peters
Quality Control: Mark Cantrell
Plant Manager: John Kuntz
Plant Manager: Bill Dearmond
Estimated Sales: $ 20-50 Million
Number Employees: 50-99
Brands:
Peak

14603 Trinidad/Benham Corporation
P.O.Box 1147
Patterson, CA 95363-1147 209-892-9002
Fax: 209-892-7977 info@trinidadbenham.com
www.tbc.com
Processor and exporter of dried beans, rice and popcorn
Manager: Gerry Hazlett
Estimated Sales: $ 1 - 3 Million
Number Employees: 20-49
Parent Co: Trinidad/Benham Corporation
Type of Packaging: Consumer, Food Service, Bulk

14604 Trinity Fruit Sales
9493 N Fork Washington Road
Clovis, CA 93612 559-322-7100
Fax: 559-322-7800 www.trinityfruit.com
Fresh cherries, apricots, peaches, plums, nectarines, kiwi, grapes, apples and pears
President: David White
Number Employees: 16

14605 Trinity Spice
PO Box 3326
Midland, TX 79702-3326 915-683-8333
Fax: 915-683-8333 800-460-1149
southern@marshill.com
www.southerndynamite.com
Gourmet Southern spice blends
President: S Floyd
Type of Packaging: Consumer, Food Service, Private Label, Bulk
Brands:
SOUTHERN DYNAMITE

14606 Trio Foods
310 Industrial Drive
Cabot, AR 72023 501-843-9446
Fax: 501-843-0379
Meat processing
President: Robbie Brown
Operations Manager: Brian Liska
Plant Manager: Larry Tackett

14607 Triple D Orchards
P.O.Box 507
Empire, MI 49630-0507 231-326-5174
Fax: 231-326-5480 866-781-9410
tdo@coslink.net www.tripledorchards.com
Processor and exporter of canned and frozen sweet cherries
President: Travis Keyes
Office Manager: Chance Bunner
Estimated Sales: $ 20 - 50 Million
Number Employees: 100-249
Type of Packaging: Consumer, Food Service, Private Label, Bulk
Brands:
Glen Lake

14608 Triple H
5821 Wilderness Ave
Riverside, CA 92504-1004 951-352-5700
Fax: 951-352-5710 www.triplehfoods.com
Vanillas
President: Tom Harris Jr
Purchasing: Judy Beltinghauser
Estimated Sales: $ 20 - 50 Million
Number Employees: 50-99

14609 Triple H Food Processors
5821 Wilderness Ave
Riverside, CA 92504-1004 951-352-5700
Fax: 951-352-5710 info@triplehfoods.com
www.triplehfoods.com
Processor of barbecue sauces, fruit punch and syrups; also, custom bottling services available
President: Tom Harris Jr
President: Tom Harris
Director of Sales: Joe Crosby
Estimated Sales: $ 10-20 Million
Number Employees: 50-99
Type of Packaging: Private Label
Brands:
Triple H

14610 (HQ)Triple K Manufacturing Company
P.O.Box 219
Shenandoah, IA 51601-0219 712-246-4376
Fax: 712-246-4010 888-987-2824
webmaster@x-tra-touch.com
www.xtratouch.com
Processor and exporter of baking flavorings; dry seasonings; salad dressings; sauces; dietary foods and cleaning products. Contract packaging and private label services also available.
President/Manager: Charles Maxine
VP Sales: B Maxine
Estimated Sales: $1600000
Number Employees: 5-9
Sq. footage: 15600
Type of Packaging: Consumer, Food Service, Private Label
Brands:
DROPS O'GOLD
X-TRA-TOUCH

14611 Triple Leaf Tea
434 N Canal St
S San Francisco, CA 94080-4675 650-588-8255
Fax: 650-588-8406 800-552-7448
triple@tripleleaf-tea.com www.tripleleaftea.com
Processor and exporter of authentic, effective, traditional chinese medicinal teas including green, ginger, ginseng, diet and medicinal; also, American ginseng capsules
President: Johnson Lam
Estimated Sales: $500-$1,000,000
Number Employees: 5-9
Number of Brands: 1
Number of Products: 18
Sq. footage: 5000
Type of Packaging: Consumer, Food Service, Private Label
Brands:
TRIPLE LEAF TEA

14612 Triple Rock Brewing Company
1920 Shattuck Ave
Berkeley, CA 94704-1022 510-549-5999
Fax: 510-843-6920 info@triplerock.com
www.triplerock.com
Beer
Co-Owner: Reid Martin
Co-Owner: John Martin
Estimated Sales: $ 10-20 Million
Number Employees: 10-19
Type of Packaging: Private Label
Brands:
Agate Ale
Black Rock Porter
Bug Juice Ale
Ipax India Pale Ale
Millennium Ale
Pinnacle Pale Ale
Red Rock Ale
Stonehenge Stout
Titanium Ale

14613 Triple Springs Spring Water
199 Ives Ave # 1
Meriden, CT 06450-7179 203-235-8374
Fax: 203-686-0200 www.triplespring.com
Manufacturer of natural spring water
President: George Kuchle
Estimated Sales: $9 Million
Number Employees: 10-19
Type of Packaging: Consumer, Bulk
Brands:
TRIPLE SPRINGS SPRING WATER

14614 Triple T Enterprises
P.O.Box 177
Chauvin, LA 70344-0177 985-594-5869
Fax: 985-594-2168 chris@triple-t-shrimp.com
www.triple-t-shrimp.com
Shrimp
President: Andrew Blanchard
Estimated Sales: $ 20 - 50 Million
Number Employees: 50-99
Brands:
Pride N Joy

14615 Triple U Enterprises
26312 Tatanka Rd
Fort Pierre, SD 57532 605-567-3624
Fax: 605-567-3625 uuubuff@gwtc.net
www.tripleuranch.com
Processor of fresh, smoked, dried and frozen buffalo meat including portion cut
President: Kaye Ingle
CEO: Clint Amiotte
Estimated Sales: $700,000
Number Employees: 1-4
Type of Packaging: Consumer, Bulk

14616 Triple XXX Root Beer Com
2925 Briarpark Drive
Suite 660
Houston, TX 77042-3799 713-780-9203
Fax: 713-780-8764
contact@triplexxxrootbeer.com
www.triplexxxrootbeer.com
Soft drinks
President: Lee Lydick
Estimated Sales: Below $ 5 Million
Number Employees: 1-4
Brands:
Triple XXX

14617 Triple-C
8 Burford Road
Hamilton, ON L8E 5B1
Canada 905-573-7900
Fax: 905-573-7867 800-263-9105
VP Sales & Marketing: Harry Scholtens
Brands:
GUMMY GUY
RACHEL'S
SOUR SIMON

14618 Tripoli Bakery
106 Common St
Lawrence, MA 01840-1633 978-682-7754
Fax: 978-687-8455
Breads, rolls
President: Rosario Zappala
Estimated Sales: $ 1-2.5 Million
Number Employees: 20-49

14619 Tripp Bakers
260 Holbrook Drive
Wheeling, IL 60090-5810 847-541-7040
Fax: 847-537-5240 800-621-3702
trippbakers.com
Processor of fresh and frozen baked goods
President: Greg Goth
Estimated Sales: $ 6 Million
Number Employees: 45
Sq. footage: 45000
Type of Packaging: Consumer, Food Service, Private Label, Bulk

14620 Tripper
PO Box 6450
Malibu, CA 90264-6450 805-988-8851
Fax: 805-988-2992 888-336-8747
info@tripper.com www.tripper.com
Processor and importer of kosher & spices including pepper, nutmeg, cinnamon, and ginger; also, ingredients including vainilla beans and extracts; organic available
President: Patrick Barthelemy
Estimated Sales: $ 1-2.5 Million
Number Employees: 17
Sq. footage: 15000
Type of Packaging: Food Service, Private Label, Bulk
Brands:
Alligator Pepper
Bullfrog Lavander
Chameleon Pepper
Cobra Vanilla
Dragon Cinnamon
Elephant Ginger

Flamingo Pepper
Gorilla Cloves
Leopard Cardamon
Orangutan Mace
Panther Pepper
Rhino Nutmeg
Tiger Pepper
Toro Safron
Tripper

14621 Tristao Trading
116 John St # 500
New York, NY 10038-3316   212-285-8120
        Fax: 212-964-1735 admin@tristaousa.com
Coffee
    Manager: Liz Wagner
    President: Ricardo Tristao
Estimated Sales:$ 5-10 Million
Number Employees: 1-4

14622 Triton Seafood Company
7736 NW 76th Ave
Medley, FL 33166-7540   305-805-3500
        Fax: 305-888-1485 www.neptunes.com
Processor of all-natural conch chowder and conch
fritters
    CEO: Alfredo Alvarez
    Marketing Director: Yvonne Conde
Estimated Sales:$1700000
Number Employees: 10-19
Type of Packaging: Food Service, Private Label
Brands:
    Neptune's

14623 Triton Water Company
P.O.Box 2690
Burlington, NC 27216-2690   336-226-6392
        Fax: 336-229-9768 800-476-9111
        info@alamancefoods.com
        www.alamancefoods.com
Bottled water
    President: William Scott Jr
    Quality Control: Thomas Patricher
    VP Sales: David Willert
Estimated Sales:$ 10-100 Million
Number Employees: 100-249
Brands:
    Big Drinks
    Lil' Drinks
    Lunch Punch

14624 Triumph Brewing Company
138 Nassau St
Princeton, NJ 08542-7011   609-924-7855
        Fax: 609-924-7857 www.triumphbrew.com
Processor of seasonal beer, ale, stout and pilsner
    Manager: Doug Bork
    General Manager: Eric Nutt
*Estimated Sales:*Below $ 5 Million
Number Employees: 50-99
Type of Packaging: Consumer, Food Service

14625 Trochu Meat Processors
PO Box 309
Trochu, AB T0M 2C0
Canada   403-442-4202
        Fax: 403-442-2771 trochumeat@canada.com
        www.trochumeats.com
Processor and exporter of fresh and frozen pork
    President: Ray Price
    Plant Manager: Richard Johnson
Number Employees: 100
Type of Packaging: Food Service

14626 Trophic International
432 W 3440 S
Salt Lake City, UT 84115-4228   801-269-6667
        Fax: 801-269-9666 trophic@bluechipgroup.net
        www.bluechipgroup.net
Lecithins, health foods, wild Mexican yam cream,
colloidal silver
    Owner: Jack Augason
    Sales Director: Jeffrey Augason
    Operations Manager: Mark Augason
    Production Manager: Jeff Hatch
Estimated Sales:$500,000-$1 Million
Number Employees: 5-9
Sq. footage: 10
Type of Packaging: Consumer, Food Service, Pri-
    vate Label, Bulk
Brands:
    Trophic

14627 Trophy Nut Company
P.O.Box 199
Tipp City, OH 45371-0199   937-667-4448
        Fax: 937-667-4656 800-729-6887
    pnieter@trophynut.com www.trophynut.com
Processor and packager of dry and oil roasted nuts
    President: Jeff Bollinger
    VP: Robert Wilke
Estimated Sales:$27964948
Number Employees: 50-99
Sq. footage: 110000
Type of Packaging: Consumer, Food Service, Pri-
    vate Label, Bulk
Brands:
    Nut Barrel
    Trophy Gold Nut Barrel
    Trophy Nut
    True Measures Baking Nuts

14628 Tropic Fish & VegetableCenter
1020 Moana Farmers Market
Honolulu, HI 96814   808-591-2963
        Fax: 808-591-2934
Fish and vegetables
    President: Glenn Tanoue
Estimated Sales:$ 20 - 50 Million
Number Employees: 50-99

14629 Tropical
2208 Austell Rd SW
Marietta, GA 30008-2115   770-805-9248
        Fax: 770-435-1371 800-544-3762
    info@tropicalfoods.com www.tropicalfoods.com
Processor and importer of candy, dried fruits, nuts,
seeds, Oriental rice snacks and dessert toppings
    President: David Williamson
    President: John Bauer
    Sales Director: Debbie Ponton
    Operations Manager: William Stapleton
Estimated Sales:$ 10 - 20 Million
Number Employees: 10-19
Parent Co: Tropical
Type of Packaging: Food Service, Private Label,
    Bulk

14630 (HQ)Tropical
P.O.Box 7507
Charlotte, NC 28241-7507   704-588-0400
        Fax: 704-588-3092 800-220-1413
    info@tropicalfoods.com www.tropicalfoods.com
Processor of snack mixes, dried fruits, roasted nuts,
seeds, candy and confectionery, spices and specialty
foods including oils, vinegars, mustards, artichoke
hearts, roasted bell peppers and pasta
    President: John Bauer
    CEO: Carolyn Bennett
    Sales Director: Rick Ederfield
    Purchasing Manager: Matt Collenberger
Estimated Sales:$24600000
Number Employees: 100-249
Sq. footage: 72000
Type of Packaging: Consumer, Food Service,
    BulkTropical Memphis
    Memphis TN
    Tropical Landover
    Landover MD
Brands:
    CHRISTILLE BAY

14631 Tropical
6580 Huntley Road
Columbus, OH 43229-1029   614-431-7233
        Fax: 614-431-7233 800-538-3941
    tnfcolumbus@aol.com www.tropicalfoods.com
Processor of nut candy, caramels, sesame sticks,
soup mixes and dried fruits
    President: David Williamson
Estimated Sales:$ 10 - 20 Million
Number Employees: 20-49
Sq. footage: 28000
Type of Packaging: Consumer, Food Service, Bulk

14632 Tropical Blossom Honey Company
106 N Ridgewood Ave
Edgewater, FL 32132   386-428-9027
        Fax: 386-423-8469 infO@tropicbeehoney.com
        www.tropicbeehoney.com
honey
    VP: John Ginnis
Estimated Sales:$1.3 Million
Number Employees: 15

14633 Tropical Blossom Honey Company
P.O.Box 8
Edgewater, FL 32132-0008   386-428-9027
        Fax: 386-423-8469 800-324-8843
        info@tropicbeehoney.com
        www.tropicbeehoney.com
Processor, packer and exporter of honey; including
Flordia honey and honey with comb
    VP: John Douglas
    VP: J Douglas Mc Ginnis
    Sales: Michael Hauger
    Operations: Paul Tierney
    Plant Manager: David McGinnis
Estimated Sales:$2597231
Number Employees: 10-19
Number of Brands: 2
Type of Packaging: Food Service, Private Label,
    Bulk
Brands:
    TROPIC BEE
    TROPIC QUEEN

14634 Tropical Cheese Industries
452 Fayette St
Perth Amboy, NJ 08861-3805   732-442-4898
        Fax: 732-442-8227 800-487-7850
        p-kondrup@tropicalcheese.com
        www.tropicalcheese.com
Cheese
    President: Rafael Mendez
    CEO: Michelle Farkas
    CFO: Michelle Farkas
    Executive VP: Robert Fagan
    COO: Martin Allen
Estimated Sales:$ 10-20 Million
Number Employees: 250-499

14635 Tropical Commodities
6606 SW 115th Ct # B
Miami, FL 33173-4732   305-471-9825
        Fax: 305-471-9825 tropicom@direcway.com
Fresh habanero chili peppers and mash as well as
other varieties of chili peppers.
    President: D Douglas Bernard
    Vice President: Robert Kholer
    Marketing: Alberto Beers
Estimated Sales:$1.3-1.5 Million
Number Employees: 5-9
Number of Products: 10
Sq. footage: 15000
Type of Packaging: Private Label, Bulk
Brands:
    Caribbean Hot Peppers

14636 Tropical Fruit ProductsCompany
PO Box 343
San German, PR 00683-0343   787-892-1345
        Fax: 787-264-1045
Processor and exporter of canned fruits, preserves,
jams and jellies
    VP/General Manager: Carmen Fernandes
    Plant Manager: Carmen Lugo
*Estimated Sales:*Under $500,000
Number Employees: 20-49
Sq. footage: 60000
Type of Packaging: Bulk

14637 Tropical Illusions
1436 Lulu Street
PO Box 338
Trenton, MO 64683   660-359-6849
        Fax: 660-359-5347
        tropical@tropicalillusions.com
Processor and exporter of frozen drinks mixes in-
cluding: cocktail, slush and granita, cream base, and
smoothies.
    President: Vance Cox
Estimated Sales:$500,000-$1 Million
Number Employees: 5-9
Sq. footage: 50000
Type of Packaging: Food Service, Private Label
Brands:
    Captain Space Freeze
    Elmeco
    Tropical Illusions

14638 Tropical Nut & Fruit Company
3368 Bartlett Blvd
Orlando, FL 32811-6482   407-843-8141
        Fax: 407-843-4340 800-749-8869
    nutsnorl@aol.com www.tropicalnutandfruit.com

Custom snack mixes, freshly roasted nuts and seeds, baking items, candies, spices, dried fruit, grains and minibar items.
President: Mike Ussery
Estimated Sales: $6000000
Number Employees: 20-49
Type of Packaging: Consumer, Food Service, Private Label, Bulk

14639 Tropical Preserving Company
1712 Newton St
Los Angeles, CA 90021-2710   213-748-5108
Fax: 213-748-4998   sales@tropicalpreserves.com
www.tropicalpreserving.com
Processor and exporter of jams, jellies and apple butter
CEO: Lee S Randall
Estimated Sales: $12,000,000
Number Employees: 20-49
Type of Packaging: Consumer, Private Label
Brands:
Market's Best

14640 Tropical Treets
130 Bermondsey Road
North York, ON M4A 1X5
Canada   416-759-8777
Fax: 416-759-7782   888-424-8229
info@tropicaltreets.com
www.tropicaltreets.com
Processor of tropical ice cream; wholesaler/distributor of tropical food products, drinks and juices
CEO: Rumi Keshavjee
VP Sales/Marketing: Zahir Keshavjee
Number Employees: 15
Sq. footage: 6000

14641 (HQ)Tropicana
1001 13th Ave E
Bradenton, FL 34208   941-747-4461
Fax: 941-747-4461   800-828-2102
www.tropicana.com
Processor and exporter of orange and grapefruit juices; also, frozen concentrates
President: Neil Campbell
Senior VP/CFO: Dennis Hareza
Senior VP Marketing: Ron Coughlin
VP Purchasing: Jim Eicken
Estimated Sales: $3.8 Billion
Number Employees: 3500
Parent Co: PepsiCo
Type of Packaging: Consumer, Food Service
Brands:
LOOZA
TROPICANA

14642 Tropics Beverages
747 N Church Rd
Elmhurst, IL 60126-1420   630-941-7000
Fax: 630-941-7001   800-926-5232
sales@tropicsbeverages.com
www.tropicsbeverages.com
Processor of frozen drink mixes including cappuccino, strawberry, pina colada, margarita, banana, raspberry, passion fruit, peach, mango, rum runner, italian lemonade, four berry, ice cream cocktail mix, non fat yogurt mix and guava.
President: Lee Fayette
Estimated Sales: Less than $500,000
Number Employees: 1-4
Type of Packaging: Food Service
Brands:
Tropics

14643 Troppers
P.O.Box 50211
Santa Barbara, CA 93150-0211   805-969-4054
Baked goods
Manager: Diane Tourney
Estimated Sales: $ .5 - 1 million
Number Employees: 1-4

14644 Trosclair Canning Company
184 Davis Road
Cameron, LA 70631   337-775-5275
Seafood, seafood products
President: Adenise Trosclair
Estimated Sales: Less than $500,000
Number Employees: 1-4

14645 Trotters Imports
6 Maxam Road
Colrain, MA 01340-9501
413-624-0121
800-863-8437

Olives and olive oil

14646 Trout Lake Farm
PO Box 181
Trout Lake, WA 98650-0181   509-395-2025
Fax: 509-395-2645   herbs@troutlakefarm.com
www.troutlakefarm.com
Processor, exporter and importer of certified organically grown medicinal and beverage tea herbs and spices including garlic, oregano, peppermint and spearmint
CEO: Lloyd Scott
Sales Director: Martha-Jane Hylton
Estimated Sales: $3500000
Number Employees: 50
Sq. footage: 40000
Type of Packaging: Bulk
Brands:
1st Sneeze Echinacea
Camus Prarie Tea
Florased Valerian
Trout Lake Farm

14647 Trout of Paradise
P.O.Box 129
Paradise, UT 84328-0129   435-245-3053
Fax: 435-245-4603 www.whitesranch.com
Processor and canner of fresh rainbow trout
President: Grant White
Estimated Sales: $150000
Number Employees: 1-4
Type of Packaging: Consumer, Food Service

14648 Trout-Blue Chelan
P.O.Box 669
Chelan, WA 98816-0669   509-682-2591
Fax: 509-682-4620 www.chelanfruit.com
Processor and exporter of apples
CEO: Reggie Collins
Sales Director: Steve Terry
Estimated Sales: $30067016
Number Employees: 500-999
Type of Packaging: Consumer, Bulk
Brands:
BLUE CHELAN
TROUT

14649 Troy Brewing Company
417 River St
Troy, NY 12180-2822   518-273-2337
Fax: 518-273-4834   info@brownsbrewing.com
www.brownsbrewing.com
Beer
President: Garrett Brown
Estimated Sales: $ 1 - 3 Million
Number Employees: 20-49
Brands:
Ales & Lagers
Brown's Ware
Revolution Hall
Taproom

14650 Troy Frozen Food
404 E Us Highway 40
Troy, IL 62294-2205   618-667-6332
Processor of meat including home cured ham and bacon, frankfurters, bologna and sausage
VP: Donald Nihiser
Estimated Sales: $2000000
Number Employees: 5-9
Type of Packaging: Consumer

14651 Troy Pork Store
36 Pinewoods Ave
Troy, NY 12180-4724   518-272-8291
Fax: 518-272-8291
Processor of fresh, smoked and pickled pork and beef
Owner: Carmen Amedeo
Estimated Sales: $500,000-$1 Million
Number Employees: 1-4
Type of Packaging: Consumer

14652 Troy Winery
3365 Peebles Road
Troy, OH 45373-8437   937-339-3655
Wines
Estimated Sales: $500,000 appx.
Number Employees: 1-4

14653 Troyer Farms
P.O.Box 676
Waterford, PA 16441-0676   724-746-1162
Fax: 724-746-1167   info@troyerfarms.com
Processor of snack foods including pretzels, potato and tortilla chips, popcorn and cheese puffs
President & CFO: Craig Troyer
Estimated Sales: $ 20 - 50 Million
Number Employees: 50-99
Parent Co: Troyer Potato Products
Type of Packaging: Consumer, Food Service, Private Label, Bulk
Brands:
Dan Dee
Troyer Farms

14654 Troyer Foods
P.O.Box 608
Goshen, IN 46527-0608   574-533-0302
Fax: 574-533-3851 www.troyers.com
President: Paris Ball-Miller
Estimated Sales: $100+ Million
Number Employees: 100-249

14655 Troyer Potato Products
P.O.Box 676
Waterford, PA 16441-0676   814-796-2611
Fax: 814-796-6797   info@troyerfarms.com
www.troyerfarms.com
Manufacturer of snack foods including cheese popcorn, potato chips and corn puffs
President: Clifford Troyer
Sales: Sylvia Jones
Estimated Sales: $50 Million
Number Employees: 100-249
Type of Packaging: Consumer, Private Label
Brands:
DAN DEE POTATO CHIPS
DAN DEE PRETZELS
TROYER FARMS
TROYER POTATO PRODUCTS

14656 Troyers Trail Bologna
6552 State Route 515
Dundee, OH 44624-9226   330-893-2414
Fax: 330-893-3058   877-893-2414
Manufacturer of bologna
President: Kenneth Troyer
Estimated Sales: $45 Million
Number Employees: 20-49
Type of Packaging: Consumer, Food Service, Bulk

14657 Tru-Blu Cooperative Associates
PO Box 5
New Lisbon, NJ 08064-0005   609-894-8717
trublucoop@aol.com
Processor of fresh and frozen blueberries
General Manager: Dennis Doyle
Number Employees: 1-4
Type of Packaging: Consumer

14658 Truan's Candies
13716 Tireman St
Detroit, MI 48228-2754   313-584-3400
800-584-3004
info@alinosi.com   www.truanscandiesonline.com
Manufacturer of chocolate's
President: Mark Truan
Estimated Sales: $ 5 - 10 Million
Number Employees: 10-19
Type of Packaging: Private Label

14659 Truchard Vineyards
3234 Old Sonoma Rd
Napa, CA 94559-9701   707-253-7153
Fax: 707-253-7234 www.truchardvineyards.com
Wine
Owner: Anthony Truchard
Estimated Sales: $ 5-10 Million
Number Employees: 20-49
Brands:
Truchard Vineyards

14660 Truckee River Winery
P.O.Box 3393
Truckee, CA 96160-3393   530-587-4626
Fax: 530-550-8809   russ@truckeeriverwinery.com
www.truckeeriverwinery.com
Wines
Co-Owner: Russ Jones
Co-Owner: Joan Jones
Estimated Sales: Under $300,000
Number Employees: 1-4

Type of Packaging: Private Label
Brands:
  Truckee River

14661 True Beverages
2001 E Terra Ln
O Fallon, MO 63366-4434   636-240-2400
      Fax: 636-272-2408 800-325-6152
  truefood@truemfg.com www.truemfg.com
Beverages
  Owner: Bill Smith
Brands:
  True Beverages

14662 True Organic Products International
P.O.Box 523271
Miami, FL 33152-3271   305-885-2619
      Fax: 305-885-1326 800-487-0379
Processor and exporter of organic juices including
orange, apple, pineapple, grape, tangerine, lime, wa-
termelon, blackberry, soursop, lulo and pineapple
blends
  President: Alex Mendez
  VP: Christopher Ramputh
Estimated Sales: $ 3 - 5 Million
Number Employees: 1-4
Sq. footage: 12000
Brands:
  True Organic

14663 True World Foods of Boston
111 E Main St
Gloucester, MA 01930-3860   978-283-1324
      Fax: 978-283-3058 www.trueworldfoods.com
  Manager: Jimmy Watanoide
Estimated Sales: $ 3 - 5 Million
Number Employees: 10-19

14664 True World Foods of Chicago
950 Chase Ave
Elk Grove Vlg, IL 60007-4828   847-718-0088
      Fax: 847-718-0011
  President: Kazuo Sometani
  CEO: Toshio Nishida
Estimated Sales: $ 10 - 20 Million
Number Employees: 50-99

14665 True World Foods of Hawaii
2696 Waiwai Loop
Honolulu, HI 96819-5113   808-836-3222
      Fax: 808-833-4510 www.twfhawaii.com
  President: Jackie Madsuka
Estimated Sales: $ 20 - 50 Million
Number Employees: 20-49

14666 Truesdale Packaging Company
1410 E Veterans Memorial Pkwy
Warrenton, MO 63383-1316   636-456-6800
      Fax: 636-456-6899
Processor and co-packer of canned and bottled bev-
erages including hot pack, cold pack and bag-in-box
soft drinks, root beer, juices, teas and isotonics
  Manager: Tom Williams
  VP/General Manager: Hugh White
Estimated Sales: $$50-100 Million
Number Employees: 100-249
Sq. footage: 201000

14667 Truesoups
26401 79th Ave S
Kent, WA 98032-7321   253-872-0403
      Fax: 253-872-0552 trusoups@uswest.net
              www.truesoups.com
Processor and exporter of fresh or frozen soups;
also, sauces and entrees
  President: Shannon Moshier
  CEO: Bruce Rowe
  VP Marketing: Page Carlsen
  Plant Manager: Mark Rogers
Estimated Sales: $28600000
Number Employees: 250-499
Sq. footage: 55000
Type of Packaging: Consumer, Food Service, Pri-
vate Label, Bulk
Brands:
  Truesoups

14668 Trugman-Nash
19 W 44th St
New York, NY 10036-5902   212-869-6910
      Fax: 212-869-6177 twmayattn@aol.com
              www.trugman-nash.com

Processor and importer of dairy products and tofu
cheese substitute; wholesaler/distributor of cheeses.
Cheesecake manufacturer - private labels and own
brand
  President/CEO: Tom May
  VP: David Aboschinow
Estimated Sales: $ 3 - 5 Million
Number Employees: 1-4
Type of Packaging: Consumer, Food Service, Bulk
Brands:
  Nu-Tofu-C
  Organic Pasta
  Soy Cheese
  UNBELIEVABLE CHEESECAKE

14669 Truitt Brothers Inc
P.O.Box 309
Salem, OR 97308-0309   503-362-3674
      Fax: 503-588-2868 800-547-8712
  truittbros@truittbros.com www.truittbros.com
Manufacturer of canned green beans, cherries, pears
and plums; also, shelf stable entrees
  Co-Owner: Peter Truitt
  Co-Owner: David Truitt
  CFO: Alan Wynn
Estimated Sales: $ 20 - 50 Million
Number Employees: 500-999
Type of Packaging: Consumer, Food Service, Pri-
vate Label
Brands:
  TRUITT BROS.

14670 Trumark
830 E Elizabeth Ave
Linden, NJ 07036-2393   908-486-5900
      Fax: 908-486-5900 800-752-7877
Processor and exporter of sodium and potassium lac-
tate and lactate and acetate blends
  President: Mark Satz
  CEO: Jeff Wales
Estimated Sales: $780000
Number Employees: 10-19

14671 Tsar Nicoulai Caviar
60 Dorman Ave
San Francisco, CA 94124-1807   415-543-3007
      Fax: 415-543-5172 800-952-2842
  info@tsarnicoulai.com www.tsarnicoulai.com
Caviar and smoked fish
  President/CEO: Mats Engstrom
  Co-Owner: Dafne Engstrom
Estimated Sales: $500,000-$1 Million
Number Employees: 10-19
Type of Packaging: Private Label
Brands:
  Tsar Nicoulai Caviar

14672 Tsue Chong Noodle Company
800 S Weller St
Seattle, WA 98104-3014   206-623-0801
      Fax: 206-382-2688
Processor of noodles including egg and chow mein;
also, fortune cookies
  President: Bessie Fan
Estimated Sales: $ 1 - 3 Million
Number Employees: 20-49
Type of Packaging: Consumer, Food Service
Brands:
  Rose

14673 Tualatin Estate Vineyards
10850 NW Seavey Rd
Forest Grove, OR 97116-7703   503-357-5005
      Fax: 503-357-1702 tualatinestate@yahoo.com
              www.tualatinestate.com
Processor and exporter of table wines including
chardonnay, pinot noir, pinot blanc,
gewurztztraminer, riesling and semi-sparkling muscat
  President: William H Malkmus
  Operations Manager/Winegrower: Stirling Fox
  Winemaker: Joe Dobbes
Estimated Sales: $600000
Number Employees: 5-9
Sq. footage: 20000
Parent Co: Willamette Valley Vineyards
Type of Packaging: Consumer
Brands:
  Tualatin Estate

14674 Tucker Cellars
70 Ray Rd
Sunnyside, WA 98944-8412   509-837-8701
      Fax: 509-837-8701 wineman@televar.com
              www.tuckercellars.com

Wines and pickled vegetables
  Co-Owner: Rose Tucker
  Co-Owner: Randy Tucker
Estimated Sales: $1-2.5 Million
Number Employees: 5-9
Brands:
  Tucker

14675 Tucker Packing Company
955 N Mill St
Orrville, OH 44667-1233   330-683-3311
Processor of fresh and frozen beef, pork and lamb
  President: John Tucker
  Plant Manager: Leon Hilty
Estimated Sales: $1600000
Number Employees: 10-19
Type of Packaging: Consumer, Food Service, Bulk

14676 Tucker Pecan Company
350 N McDonough St
Montgomery, AL 36104-3652   334-262-4470
      Fax: 334-262-4690 800-239-4470
              www.tuckerpecan.com
Processor and wholesaler/distributor of pecans
  Manager: David Little
Estimated Sales: $ 5 - 10 Million
Number Employees: 10-19
Sq. footage: 16000
Type of Packaging: Consumer, Food Service, Bulk

14677 Tucson Food Service
P.O.Box 2363
Tucson, AZ 85702-2363   520-622-4605
      Fax: 520-884-0690
  people@tucsonfoodservice.com
              www.tucsonfoodservice.com
Wholesaler/distributor of produce
  President: Thomas M Kusian
  Vice President: James Tooley
  VP Sales: Alfred Thomas
Number Employees: 50-99

14678 Tucson Frozen Storage
6964 E Century Park Dr
Tucson, AZ 85756-9188   520-623-0660
      Fax: 520-624-2869
  laura@tucsonfrozenstorage.com
              www.tucsonfrozenstorage.com
Warehouse providing freezer storage, re-packing and
labeling for frozen foods
  Manager: Laura Levin
  Operations: Alan Levin
Estimated Sales: $500,000-$1 Million
Number Employees: 5 to 9

14679 Tudal Winery
1015 Big Tree Rd
St Helena, CA 94574-9711   707-963-3947
      Fax: 707-968-9691 tudalwinery@aol.com
              www.tudalwinery.com
Wines
  President: Arnold Tudal
  Vice President: John Tudal
  Marketing Director: Susan Greene
Estimated Sales: Less than $500,000
Number Employees: 1-4
Type of Packaging: Private Label
Brands:
  2001 Estate Cabernet Sauvignon
  Flat Bed Red
  Tractor Shed Red

14680 Tufts Ranch
27260 State Highway 128
Winters, CA 95694-9066   530-795-4144
      Fax: 530-795-3844
Grower and packer of apricots, prunes, kiwifruit and
persimmons. Broker of walnuts and almonds
  General Manager: Stan Tufts
  Office Manager: Brad Graf
Estimated Sales: $ 5 - 10 Million
Number Employees: 50-99

14681 Tularosa Vineyards
23 Coyote Canyon Rd
Tularosa, NM 88352-9404   575-585-2260
      Fax: 505-585-2260 800-687-4467
  wine@nmex.com www.tularosavineyards.com
Wines
  Owner: David Wickham
Estimated Sales: $250,000
Number Employees: 5-9
Brands:
  Tularosa Wines

14682 Tulkoff Food Products
1101 S Conkling St
Baltimore, MD 21224-5209   410-327-6585
    Fax: 410-524-0148   800-638-7343
    www.tulkoff.com
Processor of sauces including pesto, cheese, cocktail, tiger and honey mustard; also, horseradish, regular and light breakfast syrups, ginger purees and chopped garlic and shallots
    President: Phillip Tulkoff
    VP Sales: Mark Natale
    Production: Tom Shellooe
    Plant Manager: Dave Maxwell
Estimated Sales: $ 20 - 50 Million
Number Employees: 50-99
Type of Packaging: Food Service, Private Label, Bulk
Brands:
    Snap-Back
    TOP
    Tulkoff

14683 Tull Hill Farms
2264 Hugo Road
Kinston, NC 28501-7173   252-523-4406
    Fax: 252-523-8052
Grower of sweet potatoes
    Sales: Kendall Hill
    Sales: Rob Hill
Number Employees: 20-49
Brands:
    Hill's

14684 Tulocay & Company
P.O.Box 7
Napa, CA 94559-0007   707-252-4727
    Fax: 707-252-8375   888-627-2859
    jane@madeinnapavalley.com
    www.tulocaycemetery.org
Baking mixes, balsamic & champagne vinegars, dessert sauces, dipping and flavored oils, everyday classics, vinaigarettes & dressings, global herbed rubs, herbed rubs, marinades & glazes, mustards, savory sauces, tapenades & savorycondiments, gift sets, and fruit condiments
    Manager: Peter Manasse
    Director Manufacturing: William Cadman
Estimated Sales: Less than $500,000
Number Employees: 1-4

14685 Tulox Plastics Corporation
P.O.Box 984
Marion, IN 46952-0984   765-664-5155
    Fax: 765-664-0257   800-234-1118
    sales@tulox.com   www.tulox.com
Product line for food industry/confectionary items includes Tulox tubes and toppers that are available in rounds, squares, rectangulars, triangulars, and most any other shape imaginable. They are transparent, opaque, colored, orstriped. There are thousands of standard sizes available, but tubes can also be made to fit exact dimensional needs.
    President: John Sciaudone
    National Sales Director: Christopher Sciaudone
Type of Packaging: Consumer

14686 Tumaro's Gourmet Tortillas & Snacks
96 Executive Ave
Edison, NJ 8817-6016   323-464-6317
    Fax: 323-464-6299   800-777-6317
    info@tumaros.com   www.tumaros.com
Manufacturer of Tortillas
    President: Herman Jacobs
    VP: Brian Jacobs
Estimated Sales: $ 10 - 20 Million
Number Employees: 20-49
Type of Packaging: Consumer, Food Service

14687 Tuna Fresh
401 Whitney Ave # 103
Gretna, LA 70056-2500   504-363-2744
    Fax: 504-392-3324   www.chartwellsmenus.com
    Manager: John Duke

14688 Tundra Wild Rice
PO Box 263
Pine Falls, NB R0E 1M0
Canada   204-367-8651
    Fax: 204-367-8309

Processor and exporter of Canadian lake wild rice
    President: Denis Pereux
    CFO: Carol Van Buren
    VP Sales/Marketing: Martin Cyr
Number Employees: 4
Sq. footage: 2840
Type of Packaging: Private Label, Bulk
Brands:
    Tundra

14689 Tupman-Thurlow Company
450 Fairway Dr # 203
Deerfield Beach, FL 33441-1837   954-596-9989
    Fax: 860-658-3001
Processor, importer and exporter of canned meats including beef, luncheon, ham, Vienna sausage and meatballs; also, canned, frozen and aseptic fruit purees, concentrates, particulates and sections
    President: Jeffrey Podell
    Vice President: Greg Silpe
Estimated Sales: $40000000
Number Employees: 5-9
Type of Packaging: Consumer, Food Service, Private Label, Bulk

14690 Turano Pastry Shops
142 N Bloomingdale Rd
Bloomingdale, IL 60108-1017   630-529-6161
    Fax: 630-529-4824 www.chicagopastry.com
Processor of bread including rye, wheat and white; also, pastries, Italian cookies and danish including prune, strawberry and blueberry
    President: Renato Turano
Estimated Sales: $119200000
Number Employees: 20-49
Type of Packaging: Consumer, Food Service

14691 Turano Pasty Shops
6501 Roosevelt Rd
Berwyn, IL 60402-1100   708-788-5320
    Fax: 708-788-3075   info@turano-baking.com
    www.turanobakery.com
Processor of fresh and frozen breads, rolls and pastries
    President: Renato Turano
    Food Service Sales Manager: Bill Carlson
    Plant Manager: Eugenio Turano
Estimated Sales: $ 50-100 Million
Number Employees: 250-499
Type of Packaging: Consumer, Food Service, Private Label
Brands:
    Turano

14692 Turk Brothers Custom Meats
1903 Orange Rd
Ashland, OH 44805-1399   419-289-1051
    Fax: 419-281-8280   800-789-1051
    turkbros@bright.net
Processor and wholesaler/distributor of beef, pork and lamb; wholesaler/distributor of frozen foods, equipment and fixtures and seafood; serving the food service market; also, slaughtering services available
    Owner: Roy Turk
Estimated Sales: $ 5 - 10 Million
Number Employees: 10-19
Type of Packaging: Consumer, Food Service, Bulk

14693 Turkey Creek Snacks
P.O.Box 69
Thomaston, GA 30286-0001   706-647-8841
    Fax: 706-647-3978   info@turkeycreeksnacks.com
    www.turkeycreeksnacks.com
Manufacturer of pork rinds, hard cracklings and hot sauce
    Owner: Laddie Fulcher
Estimated Sales: $ 3 - 5 Million
Number Employees: 20-49
Sq. footage: 25000
Type of Packaging: Consumer, Food Service, Private Label, Bulk
Brands:
    Deli Style
    Sunrise Farms
    Turkey Creek

14694 Turkey Hill Dairy
2601 River Rd
Conestoga, PA 17516-9341   717-872-5461
    Fax: 717-872-4130   800-693-2479
    careers@turkeyhill.com   www.turkeyhill.com

Manufacturer of ice cream, sherbet, frozen yogurt and drinks
    President: Charles Frey
    Marketing Associate: Jason Hean
Number Employees: 500-999
Sq. footage: 107000
Type of Packaging: Consumer, Private Label, Bulk
Brands:
    Turkey Hill

14695 Turkey Hill Sugarbush
10 Waterloo Street
PO Box 160
Waterloo, QC J0E 2N0
Canada   450-539-4822
    Fax: 450-539-1561   nancy@turkeyhill.ca
Processor and exporter of maple products including syrups, cookies, chocolates, coffee, tea, fudge, caramels, butter, soft and hard candies
    President: Michael Herman
    VP: Brian Herman
    Plant Manager: Lloyd Dudley
Estimated Sales: $6 Million
Number Employees: 35
Number of Brands: 1
Number of Products: 85
Sq. footage: 35000
Type of Packaging: Consumer, Private Label, Bulk
Brands:
    TURKEY HILL

14696 Turkey Store Company
116 4th Ave NW
Faribault, MN 55021   507-334-2050
    Fax: 507-332-5349 www.theturkeystore.com
Processor of fresh and frozen whole turkeys
    Director Operations: Steve Williams
    Manager Distribution: Pete Vikeras
Estimated Sales: $ .5 - 1 million
Number Employees: 1-4
Type of Packaging: Consumer, Private Label

14697 Turlock Fruit Company
P.O.Box 130
Turlock, CA 95381-0130   209-634-7207
    Fax: 209-632-4273
Processor and exporter of honeydew melons
    President: Donald Smith
    Treasurer: Stephen Smith
    Secretary: Stuart Smith
Estimated Sales: $500,000-$1 Million
Number Employees: 20-49
Type of Packaging: Consumer, Bulk
Brands:
    King O' The-West
    Oak Flat
    Peacock
    Sycamore

14698 Turn on Beverages Inc
6 Gladwyne Court
Spring Valley, NY 10977-1604   845-354-7720
    Fax: 845-354-5141   866-739-2387
    howard@2turnon.com   www.2turnon.com
A unique adult beverage manufacturer that promises to assist men and women in becoming more sexually aroused.
    President/CEO: Howard Hersh
    R&D/Quality Control: Anton Lintner
    Operations Manager: Cliff Coleman
Estimated Sales: $20 Million
Number Employees: 10+
Number of Brands: 1
Number of Products: 1
Sq. footage: 4000
Type of Packaging: Consumer
Brands:
    Turn On Love Drink

14699 Turnbull Bakeries
3720 Amnicola Highway
Suite 119
Chattanooga, TN 37406-1792   423-265-4551
    Fax: 423-756-3159   800-488-7628
Baked goods
    National Sales Operations Manager: Deris Bagli
Estimated Sales: $ 20 Million
Number Employees: 200

14700 Turnbull Bakeries
PO Box 15149
New Orleans, LA 70175-5149   504-523-5480
    Fax: 504-581-6112

Processor of bread sticks, bread crumbs and melba toast
Estimated Sales: $ 10 - 20 Million
Number Employees: 50-99

14701 Turnbull Bakeries of Lousiana
523 1st St
New Orleans, LA 70130-2004   504-581-5383
Fax: 504-581-6112 turnbula@bellsouth.net
Processor of bread sticks, bread crumbs, and melba toast
President: Elizabeth Turnbull
Vice President: Frank LeCourt
Number Employees: 10,000+
Type of Packaging: Food Service, Private Label, Bulk

14702 Turnbull Cone Baking Company
PO Box 6248
Chattanooga, TN 37401-6248   423-265-4551
Fax: 423-624-8724
Processor of ice cream cones and wafers; also, melba toast
President: Wayne W Turnbull
Director Sales: Deris Bagli
Number Employees: 100-249
Parent Co: Turnbull Bakeries
Type of Packaging: Private Label

14703 Turner & Pease Company
1519 Elliott Avenue W
Seattle, WA 98119-3129   206-282-9535
Fax: 206-282-9633   bowen.bill@comcast.net
www.turnerandpease.com
Manufacturer of butter
President: Milton Turner
National Sales: Bill Bowen
Number Employees: 25
Sq. footage: 18000
Type of Packaging: Consumer, Food Service, Private Label, Bulk
Brands:
CREAMERIE CLASSIQUE
GOLDEN WEST
MEADOWBROOK

14704 Turner Brothers
PO Box 103
Nowata, OK 74048-0103   918-273-1858
Processor of meat products including beef and pork
President: Don Turner
Co-Partner: Ernie Kirby
Number Employees: 1-4

14705 (HQ)Turner Dairies
653 Turner Dairy Rd
Covington, TN 38019-4551   901-476-2643
Fax: 901-476-2761
terencemartin@turnerdairy.com
www.turnerdairy.com
Processor of orange juice and dairy products including milk, low-fat milk, cottage cheese and ice cream
Co-CEO: Jim Turner
Co-CEO: Steve Turner
CFO: Lynn Wall
Sales Manager: Ed Fleming
Plant Manager: Girish Patel
Estimated Sales: l
Number Employees: 100-249
Parent Co: Turner Holdings LLC
Type of Packaging: Consumer, Food Service, Private Label, Bulk
Brands:
Quality Chekd

14706 Turner Dairies
255 Wells Lassiter Road
Jackson, TN 38301-5789   731-427-6012
Fax: 731-424-0963
jimmycrownover@turnerdairy.com
www.turnerdairy.com
Processor of milk, cream and ice cream
Manager: Jim Cronover
owner: Earl Turner
President: Steve Turner
Estimated Sales: $ 5-10 Million
Number Employees: 20-49
Parent Co: Turner Dairy
Type of Packaging: Consumer, Food Service
Brands:
Turner

14707 Turner Dairy Farms
1049 Jefferson Rd
Penn Hills, PA 15235-4700   412-372-2211
Fax: 412-372-0651   800-892-1039
www.turnerdairy.net
Milk
President: Charles H Turner Jr
Estimated Sales: $ 20-50 Million
Number Employees: 100-249

14708 Turner New Zealand
125 Columbia
Aliso Viejo, CA 92656-4101   949-622-6181
Fax: 949-203-2895 www.turner.co.nz
Processor of calamari, mussels, scallops, oysters, chilled fish, venison and lamb; importer of seafood and lamb
Chairman/CEO: Noel Turner
VP Marketing: Daliza Corona
Contact: Michael Hart
Number Employees: 5-9
Sq. footage: 10000
Brands:
Turner New Zealand

14709 Turrentine Salvage Company
3305 Nolensville Pike
Nashville, TN 37211-2995   615-832-3018
Fax: 615-832-3887
Supplier of closeout groceries
President: Rodney Bates
Estimated Sales: $1745292
Number Employees: 15
Sq. footage: 20000

14710 Turris Italian Foods
16695 Common Rd
Roseville, MI 48066-1901   586-773-6010
Fax: 586-773-6851 www.turrisitalianfoods.com
Manufacturer of a full line of Italian specialities including Ravioli, lasagna, manicotti, tortellini and other fine pastas
President: Tom Turri
Sales Manager: Bernard Turri
Plant Manager: John Turri
Estimated Sales: $6.4 Million
Number Employees: 50-99
Sq. footage: 35000
Type of Packaging: Consumer, Food Service, Private Label, Bulk
Brands:
TURRIS

14711 Turtle Island Foods
P.O.Box 176
Hood River, OR 97031-0006   541-386-7766
Fax: 541-386-7754   800-508-8100
info@tofurky.com   www.tofurky.com
Processor, importer and exporter of soy meat analos including tempeh, tofurkey, deli slices, sausages, franks
President: Seth Tibbott
CFO: Sue Tibbott
VP: Bob Tibbott
Quality Assurance Manager: James Athos
Production Manager: Graciela Pulido
Plant Manager: Graciela Pulido
Estimated Sales: $2,398,946
Number Employees: 50-99
Number of Brands: 2
Number of Products: 25
Sq. footage: 10000
Type of Packaging: Consumer, Food Service, Private Label, Bulk
Brands:
SUPER BURGERS
TOFURKY
VEGETABALLS

14712 Turtle Island Foods
P.O.Box 176
Hood River, OR 97031-0006   541-386-7766
Fax: 541-386-7754   800-508-8100
info@tofurky.com   www.tofurky.com
Cheese and vegetable based soups
Founder: Seth Tibbott
CFO: Sue Tibbott
Production Manager: Graciela Pulido
Estimated Sales: Less than $500,000
Number Employees: 1-4
Brands:
SuperBurgers
Tempeh
Tofurky

14713 Turtle Island Herbs
4735 Walnut St # F
Boulder, CO 80301-2553   303-546-6362
Fax: 303-546-0625   800-684-4060
island@earthnet.net   www.earthnet.net
Processor and wholesaler/distributor of organic herbal extracts and syrups
President: Feather Jones
CEO: Bahman Saless
VP Operations: Peter Danielson
Estimated Sales: $300,000-500,000
Number Employees: 1-4
Sq. footage: 1500

14714 Turtle Mountain
330 Seneca Rd
Eugene, OR 97402-2726   541-338-9400
Fax: 541-338-9401 info@turtlemountain.com
www.turtlemountain.com
Processor and exporter of frozen nondairy desserts; also, fat-free
President: Mark Brawerman
CEO: Mark Brawerman
Director Finance: John Giacomelli
VP Technical Services: Doug Furlong
Research & Development: John Tucker
Quality Control: Dan Stethens
Sales: Kevin Brouillette
Estimated Sales: $ 5-10 Million
Number Employees: 5-9
Type of Packaging: Consumer, Food Service, Private Label
Brands:
Carb Escapes
It's Soy Delicious
Organic Lil Buddies
Organic Soy Delicious
Soy Delicious Purely Decadent
Sweet Nothings

14715 Tuscan Bakery
12831 NE Airport Way
Portland, OR 97230-1030   503-256-2099
Fax: 503-256-1929   800-887-2261
www@teleport.com
Processor of biscotti
President/Owner: Michael J Lisac
VP: Wayne Winter
Estimated Sales: Below $ 5 Million
Number Employees: 1-4
Sq. footage: 6000
Type of Packaging: Consumer, Food Service
Brands:
Lawman's

14716 Tuscan Brewing
859 Washington Street
67
Red Bluff, CA 96080-2704   530-529-9318
Fax: 530-529-2001 tuscanbrewery@earthlink.net
tscanbrewery.com
Beer
President: Cathy Conklin
Operations: Phil Conklin
Estimated Sales: $500,000-$1 Million
Number Employees: 5
Type of Packaging: Private Label
Brands:
Paradise Pale Ale
Sundown Brown Ale

14717 Tuscan Dairy Farms
2515 McKinney Ave. Suite 1200
Dallas, TX 75201   908-686-1500
Fax: 908-687-5130   800-526-4416
www.deanfoods.com
Processor of dairy products including extended shelflife ice cream, cottage cheese, fresh milk and sour cream; also contract packaging available
President/CEO: Joseph Scalzo
Sr. VP Finances: Mark Stinson
General Manager: Sam Wolman
Number Employees: 500-999
Parent Co: Suiza Dairy Group
Type of Packaging: Consumer, Food Service, Private Label, Bulk
Brands:
Brown Dairy
Gandys
Louis Trauth
Robinson Dairy
Schepps Dairy

14718 Tuscan Hills
3941 Park Drive
Suite 20-296
El Dorado Hills, CA 95762-4549   916-939-3814
                                   Fax: 916-939-3709
Italian-inspired gourmet foods

14719 (HQ)Tuscan/Lehigh Valley Dais
880 Allentown Rd
Lansdale, PA 19446-5298   215-855-8205
          Fax: 215-855-9834 800-937-3233
               www.lehighvalleydairyfarms.com
Milk, flavored milk, creamers, orange juice.
    Executive Director: James Macri
    President: M Marcus
    CFO: Tim Natole
    CEO: Anthony Ward
    VP Sales: Peter Trigi
    Marketing Director: Brian Kornfield
    Purchasing Manager: Don Gates
Estimated Sales: $ 1-2.5 Million
Number Employees: 100-249

14720 Tuscarora Organic Growers Cooperative
Hc 71
Hustontown, PA 17229   814-448-2173
          Fax: 814-448-2333 info@tog.coop
               www.tog.coop
Cooperative providing fresh fruits and vegetables including certified organic
    Manager: Chris Fullerton
    Sales Manager: Chris Fullerton
    Bookkeeping/Sales: Sherry Meuser
    Office Manager: Christine Treichler
Number Employees: 1-4
Type of Packaging: Bulk
Brands:
    Tuscarora Organic

14721 Tusitala
PO Box 189
Grand Bay, AL 36541-0189   251-865-6240
                             Fax: 251-865-3763
Herbs and herbal supplements
    President: George Spellmeyer
    Secretary: Norma Jean Spellmeyer

14722 Tuterri's/Gaston Dupre
12455 Kerran Street
Suite 200
Poway, CA 92064-8834   858-486-8937
          Fax: 858-486-1770 800-848-5266
               mlpinc@pacbell.net
               www.tuterrisgastondupre.com
Seasoned gourmet pastas
    President: Michelle Muscat
    CFO: Sam Grinuri
    Vice President: Go Muscat
    Marketing Director: Ed Muscat
Brands:
    Gaston Dupr,
    Tuterri's Seasoned P

14723 Tutto Sicilia
241 B6 Ledyard Street
Hartford, CT 06114   860-986-7377
               info@tuttosicily.com
               www.tuttosicily.com
olive oils, bruschetteria, sauces and condiments, cream toppings, marmalades, honey, biscotti

14724 Twang
6255 Wt Montgomery
San Antonio, TX 78252-2227   210-226-7008
          Fax: 210-226-4040 800-950-8095
               info@twang.com www.twang.com
Processor and importer of flavored salts including lemon-lime, traditional and colored margarita, beer, pickle and chili; also, Bloody Mary toppings
    Owner: Roger Trevino Sr
    VP Finance: Patrick Trevino
    Sales/Marketing: Roger Trevino Jr
Estimated Sales: $ 10 - 20 Million
Number Employees: 20-49
Number of Brands: 10
Number of Products: 15
Sq. footage: 12000
Type of Packaging: Consumer, Food Service, Private Label, Bulk
Brands:
    Kid-Tastic

Texican
Twang

14725 Twenty First Century Foods
30 Germania St # A
Jamaica Plain, MA 02130-2315   617-522-7595
                                 Fax: 617-522-8772
Processor of soy products including tofu and tempeh; exporter of tempeh starter
    Owner: Rudy Canale
Estimated Sales: $ .5 - 1 million
Number Employees: 1-4
Sq. footage: 1900
Brands:
    Tofu Cream Chie
    Tofu Pudding

14726 Twenty First Century Snacks
921 S 2nd St
Ronkonkoma, NY 11779-7203   631-588-8000
          Fax: 631-467-3995 800-975-2883
Assortment of nuts, candy and dried fruit
    President: Eddie Bell
Estimated Sales: $ 1-2.5 Million
Number Employees: 10-19
Type of Packaging: Consumer, Food Service, Private Label, Bulk

14727 Twin City Bagels/National Choice Bakery
130 Hardman Ave S
South St Paul, MN 55075-2453   651-554-0200
                                 Fax: 651-554-8383
          shughes@nationalchoicebakery.com
               www.twincitybagels.com
Fresh and refrigerated bagels
    President: Shimon Harosh
    Vice President: Steve Hughes
    Research & Development: Mark Heckel
    Quality Control: Mark Heckel
    Marketing Director: Steve Hughes
    Sales Director: Steve Hughes
    Operations Manager: Steve Hughes
    Production Manager: Jason Holt
    Purchasing Manager: Doug Patten
Number Employees: 100-249
Type of Packaging: Consumer, Private Label

14728 Twin City Foods
P.O.Box 699
Stanwood, WA 98292-0699   206-515-2400
          Fax: 206-515-2499 www.twincityfoods.com
Largest independent processors of frozen vegetables and potatoes.
    President: Roger O Lervick
    Executive VP: John Lervick
    Marketing Director: Mark Lervick
    Plant Manager: William Johnson
Estimated Sales: $120000000
Number Employees: 500-999
Type of Packaging: Consumer, Food Service, Private Label, Bulk

14729 Twin City Wholesale
519 Walker St
Opelika, AL 36801-5999   334-745-4564
          Fax: 334-749-5125 www.tcwholesale.com
    Owner: Johanna Bottoms
    Secretary: Johanna Bottoms
Estimated Sales: $ 10 - 20 Million
Number Employees: 50-99

14730 Twin County Dairy
2206 540th St SW
Kalona, IA 52247-9178   319-656-2776
Manufacturer of white cheddar cheese
    President: John Roetlin Jr
Estimated Sales: $9 Million
Number Employees: 50-99
Type of Packaging: Consumer, Private Label, Bulk

14731 Twin Hens
PO Box 439
Princeton, NJ 08542   908-281-9911
          Fax: 908-281-9908 info@twinhens.com
               www.twinhens.com
chicken pot pies and gluten free beef pot pies
    President/Owner: Linda Twining
    VP: Kathy Herring

14732 Twin Marquis
328 Johnson Ave
Brooklyn, NY 11206-2802   718-386-6868
          Fax: 718-386-0516 800-367-6868
               info@twinmarquis.com
Processor and importer of Asian foods including buns, dumplings, sauces, soups, and noodles; also organic pasta and instant coffee and cappuccino
    President: Joseph Tang
    Executive Director: Terry Tang
    Vice President: Alan But
Estimated Sales: $ 3-4 Million
Number Employees: 50-99
Sq. footage: 22000
Brands:
    Chef One
    Twin Marquis

14733 Twin Valley Products
P.O.Box 42
Greenleaf, KS 66943-0042   785-747-2251
          Fax: 785-747-2278 800-748-7416
               ehenry@grapevine.net
Popped and flavored popcorn and related products
    CEO: Ed Henry
    CEO: Ed Henry
    VP Marketing: Nate Wirrick
    Operations Manager: Carolyn Pinnick
Estimated Sales: $500-1 Million appx.
Number Employees: 20-49
Type of Packaging: Private Label

14734 Twining R & Company
2812 Twining Rd
Greensboro, NC 27406-4615   336-275-8634
          Fax: 336-370-4719 www.twinings.com
Tea
    President: Jim Read
    VP: Russell Karr
    Manufacturing VP: James Read
Estimated Sales: $ 10-20 Million
Number Employees: 50-99
Type of Packaging: Bulk
Brands:
    EARL GREY
    EARL GREY DECAFFEINATED
    EARL GREY GREEN TEA
    IRISH BREAKFAST DECAFF.
    LADY GREY
    LADY GREY DECAFFEINATED
    TWINING BLACKCURRANT
    TWINING CEYLON BREAKFAST
    TWINING CEYLON ORANGE PEKOE
    TWINING DARJEELING
    TWINING DECAFFEINATED GREEN TEA
    TWINING ENGLISH BREAKFAST DECAFF.
    TWINING ENGLISH BREAKFAST GREEN TEA
    TWINING ENGLSIH BREAKFAST
    TWINING GREEN TEA & LEMON
    TWINING GREEN TEA & MINT
    TWINING GUNPOWDER GREEN
    TWINING IRISH BREAKFAST
    TWINING IRISH BREAKFAST DECAFF.
    TWINING JASMINE
    TWINING JAVA GREEN TEA
    TWINING LADY GREY GREEN TEA
    TWINING LAPSANG SOUCHONG
    TWINING LEMON & GINGER HERB TEA
    TWINING LEMON SCENTED
    TWINING MINT GREEN TEA
    TWINING ORANGE & LEMON HERB TEA
    TWINING ORIGINAL GREEN TEA
    TWINING PEACH & PASSION FRUIT TEA
    TWINING PRINCE OF WALES
    TWINING PURE CAMOMILE HERB TEA
    TWINING PURE PEPPERMINT HERB TEA
    TWINING QUEEN MARY
    TWINING STRAWBERRY & MANGO TEA
    TWINING WILD BLACKBERRY HERB TEA

14735 Twinlab
632 Broadway # 11
New York, NY 10012-2614   212-651-8500
          Fax: 631-630-3474 800-645-5626
          international@twinlab.com www.twinlab.com
Processor and importer of vitamins and nutritional supplements
    President: Ross Blechman
    Marketing: David Cohen
Estimated Sales: $100+ Million
Number Employees: 100-249
Type of Packaging: Consumer

Other Locations:
Twin Laboratories
American Fork UT

14736 (HQ)Twinlab
632 Broadway # 11
New York, NY 10012-2614   212-651-8500
          Fax: 631-630-3590   800-645-5626
     product@twinlab.com   www.twinlab.com
Dietary and nutritional food supplements
Chairman: Mark Fox
CFO: Joseph Sinicropi
Marketing: David Cohen
Estimated Sales: $ 100-499.9 Million
Number Employees: 100-249
Brands:
Alvita
Ironman Triathlon
Nature's Herbs
Spring Valley
Twinlab

14737 Two Chefs on a Roll
18201 Central Ave
Carson, CA 90746-4007   310-533-0190
          Fax: 310-436-1722   800-842-3025
          info@twochefsonaroll.com
          www.twochefsonaroll.com
Manufacturer of fresh and frozen gourmet desserts,
dips and sauces
President: Jeffrey Goh
CEO: Eliot Swartz
CFO: Bob Flaharty
Vice President: Montgomery Ward
Sales: Dawn Rasmussen-Hickey
Plant Manager: Camicia Nienberg
Estimated Sales: $ 50 - 100 Million
Number Employees: 100-249
Sq. footage: 91000
Type of Packaging: Food Service, Private Label
Brands:
TWO CHEFS ON A ROLL

14738 Two Chicks and a Ladle
11 G
New York, NY 10010   212-251-0025
          Fax: 914-631-1738   lisafood@aol.com
Fat-free cheesecakes

14739 Two Guys Spice Company
2404 Dennis Street
Jacksonville, FL 32204-1712
          Fax: 904-791-9330   800-874-5656
          products@twoguysspice.com
          www.twoguysspice.com
Broker and wholesaler/distributor of dehydrated on-
ions, garlic and vegetables; also, spices and indus-
trial ingredients
President: Michael Simmons
Vice President: Guy Simmons
Estimated Sales: $2.4 Million
Number Employees: 1-4
Number of Brands: 1
Number of Products: 500
Sq. footage: 5200
Type of Packaging: Food Service, Private Label,
Bulk

14740 Two Leaves and a Bud
23400 Two Rivers Rd #45
Basalt, CO 81621   970-927-9911
     Fax: 970-927-9917   866-631-7973
          support@twoleavesandabud.net
          www.twoleavesandabud.com
teas
President/Owner: Richard Rosenfeld
Estimated Sales: $ 1 Million
Number Employees: 4

14741 Two Rivers Enterprises
490 River St W
Holdingford, MN 56340-4519   320-746-3156
          Fax: 320-746-3158   joeh@stainlesskings.com
          www.stainlesskings.com
Manufacturer of restaurant and food service equip-
ment in addition to providing complete renovations
of processing plants and on-site equipment.
President: Robert Warzecha
Midwest Regional Sales: Joe Herges
Midwest Regional Sales: Mike Gold
Midwest Regional Sales: Steve Bairett

14742 Tyee Wine Cellars
26335 Greenberry Rd
Corvallis, OR 97333-9534   541-753-8754
     Fax: 541-753-0807   merrilee@storypages.com
          www.tyeewine.com
Processor of wine
Owner: Margaret Buchanan
Co-Founder: Nola Moiser
Co-Founder: David Buchanan
Co-Founder: Margy Buchanan
Winemaker: Barney Watson
Estimated Sales: Less than $300,000
Number Employees: 1-4
Type of Packaging: Private Label
Brands:
Tyee

14743 Tyler Candy Company
4337 Dc Dr
Tyler, TX 75701-8416   903-561-3046
          Fax: 903-581-8030   tylercandyco@aol.com
Hard candy
Manager: Ron Sumibek
Estimated Sales: $ 5-10 Million
Number Employees: 20-49
Type of Packaging: Consumer, Private Label
Brands:
Dickies

14744 Tyler Packing Company
P.O.Box 1116
Tyler, TX 75710-1116   903-593-9592
          Fax: 903-593-1273
Manufacturer of beef, pork and veal
President/Owner: Herbert Buie
Estimated Sales: $3-5 Million
Number Employees: 5-9
Type of Packaging: Bulk

14745 (HQ)Tyson Foods
PO Box 2020
Springdale, AR 72764-6999   479-290-4000
          Fax: 479-290-4061   800-643-3410
     tysonir@tyson.com   www.tysonfoodsinc.com
Manufacturer of prepared chicken, beef and pork
products, exporter of chicken and parts.
President/CEO: Donnie Smith
EVP/CFO: Dennis Leatherby
SVP and CIO: Gary Cooper
SVP & Chief Environmental Safety Officer:
Kevin Igli
COO: James Lochner
Estimated Sales: $26.7 Billion
Number Employees: 117,000
Type of Packaging: Consumer, Food Service, Bulk
Other Locations: AK
AZ
CA
GA
HI
ID
IL
IN
IO
KS
KY
LA
Brands:
HOLLY FARMS
LADY ASTER
MCCARTY FOODS
MEXICAN ORIGINAL
PIERRE
SIGNATURE SPECIALTIES
TASTY BIRD
TYSON
WEAVER

14746 Tyson Foods
110 W Freeman Ave
Berryville, AR 72616-3310   870-423-2164
          Fax: 870-423-1681   www.tysonfoodsinc.com
Manufacturer of fresh and frozen poultry products
Chairman: John Tyson
President/CEO: Richard Bond
EVP/CFO: Wade Miquelon
EVP/General Counsel: J Alberto Gonzalez-Pita
SVP/Research & Development: Howell Carper
VP Investor Relations: Ruth Ann Wisener
SVP Human Resources: Kenneth Kimbro
Plant Manager: Craig McDonald
Estimated Sales: $100+ Million
Number Employees: 1,000-4,999
Parent Co: Tyson Foods
Type of Packaging: Consumer, Food Service

14747 Tyson Foods
P.O.Box 2020
Springdale, AR 72765-2020   479-290-4000
          Fax: 479-290-4061 www.tysonfoodsinc.com
chicken, beef and pork
Interim President/Interim CEO: Leland Tollett
EVP/CFO: Dennis Leatherby
SVP/CIO: Gary Cooper
SVP Corporate Research & Development: Craig
Bacon
SVP Food Quality Assurance: Rick Roop
Chief Marketing Officer: Sue Quillin
SVP Sales: Randy Smith
SVP Human Resources: Kenneth Kimbro
SVP/Human Resources: Kenneth Kimbro
Sr Group VP/Chief Development Officer: John
Lea
VP Warehouse/Distribution: Tim McGovern
VP Purchasing: Michael Roetzel
Estimated Sales: $26.8 Billion
Number Employees: 2850
Type of Packaging: Consumer

14748 Tyson Foods
P.O.Box 430
Corydon, IN 47112-0430   812-738-3219
          Fax: 812-738-5831   800-223-3719
          www.tyson.com
Processor of poultry; also, breeding and slaughtering
services available.
Manager: Bill Wood
President/CEO: Richard Bond
EVP/CFO: Wade Miquelon
EVP/General Counsel: J Alberto Gonzalez-Pita
SVP/Research & Development: Howell Carper
VP/Investor Relations: Ruth Ann Wisener
SVP/Human Resources: Kenneth Kimbro
Estimated Sales: $100+ Million
Number Employees: 500-999
Parent Co: Tyson Foods
Type of Packaging: Consumer, Food Service, Bulk

14749 Tyson Foods
5000 N FM 1912
Amarillo, TX 79101   806-335-1531
          Fax: 806-335-7517 www.tysonfoods.com
Manufacturer and exporter of beef
Chairman: John Tyson
President/CEO: Richard Bond
EVP/CFO: Wade Miquelon
EVP/General Counsel: J Alberto Gonzalez-Pita
SVP/Research & Development: Howell Carper
VP/Investor Relations: Ruth Ann Wisener
SVP/Human Resources: Kenneth Kimbro
Plant Manager: Kurt Suther
Estimated Sales: Over $1 Billion
Number Employees: 1,000-4,999
Sq. footage: 580000
Parent Co: Tyson Foods
Type of Packaging: Consumer, Food Service

14750 Tyson Foods
PO Box 2579
Jackson, MS 39207-2579   601-372-7441
          www.tyson.com
Manufacturer and exporter of fresh and frozen
chicken products
President/CEO: Dick Bond
Complex Manager: Richard Evans
Estimated Sales: $200 Million
Number Employees: 800
Parent Co: Tyson Foods
Type of Packaging: Consumer, Food Service, Pri-
vate Label, Bulk

14751 Tyson Foods
1610 Midland Blvd
Fort Smith, AR 72901-1570   479-783-8996
          Fax: 479-785-4568 www.tyson.com
Manufacturer and exporter of fresh and frozen poul-
try.
Chairman: John Tyson
President/CEO: Richard Bond
EVP/CFO: Wade Miquelon
EVP/General Counsel: J Alberto Gonzalez-Pita
SVP/Research & Development: Howell Carper
VP/Investor Relations: Ruth Ann Wisener
SVP/Human Resources: Kenneth Kimbro
Plant Manager: Steve Smalling
Estimated Sales: $10-20 Million
Number Employees: 100-249
Parent Co: Tyson Foods
Type of Packaging: Consumer

14752 Tyson Foods
500 Industrial Dr
Star City, AR 71667-4336   870-628-5733
          Fax: 870-628-5740   800-351-8184
                         www.tyson.com
Processor of poultry
    Manager: Greg Morgan
    President/CEO: Richard Bond
    EVP/CFO: Wade Miquelon
    EVP/General Counsel: J Alberto Gonzalez-Pita
    SVP/Research & Development: Howell Carper
    VP/Investor Relations: Ruth Ann Wisener
    SVP/Human Resources: Kenneth Kimbro
Estimated Sales: $1.2 Million
Number Employees: 20-49
Parent Co: Tyson Foods
Type of Packaging: Consumer, Food Service, Private Label, Bulk

14753 Tyson Foods
P.O.Box 230
Hope, AR 71802-0230   870-777-8646
    Fax: 870-777-7131 www.tysonfoodsinc.com
Processor of fresh and frozen chicken products.
    Chairman: Richard Bond
    SVP/Research & Development: Howell Carper
    VP/Investor Relations: Ruth Ann Wisener
    SVP/Human Resources: Kenneth Kimbro
    Plant Manager: David Keith
Estimated Sales: $100+ Million
Number Employees: 500-999
Parent Co: Tyson Foods
Type of Packaging: Consumer, Food Service, Private Label, Bulk

14754 Tyson Foods
P.O.Box 547
Bloomfield, MO 63825-0547   573-568-2153
    Fax: 573-568-3718 www.tyson.com
Processor of frozen chicken
    President: Richard Bond
    Complex Manager: Richard Bond
    CFO: Wade Miquelon
    Vice President: William Lovette
    Plant Manager: Mark Avery
Estimated Sales: $ 5 - 10 Million
Number Employees: 20-49
Parent Co: Tyson Foods
Type of Packaging: Consumer, Bulk

14755 Tyson Foods
305 Cleveland St
Forest, MS 39074-3200   601-469-1712
    Fax: 601-469-5365 www.tyson.com
Manufacturer of poultry products.
    Manager: Tracy Shannon
    President/CEO: Richard Bond
    EVP/CFO: Wade Miquelon
    EVP/General Counsel: J Alberto Gonzalez-Pita
    SVP/Research & Development: Howell Carper
    VP/Investor Relations: Ruth Ann Wisener
    SVP/Human Resources: Kenneth Kimbro
Estimated Sales: $100+ Million
Number Employees: 500-999
Type of Packaging: Consumer, Private Label

14756 Tyson Foods
P.O.Box 88
Wilkesboro, NC 28697-0088   336-838-2171
    Fax: 336-651-2829 www.tyson.com
Processor of cooked and frozen chicken.
    Chairman: Richard Bond
    President/CEO: Richard L Bond
    SVP/Research & Development: Howell Carpers
    VP/Investor Relations: Ruth Ann Wisener
    SVP/Human Resources: Kenneth Kimbro
    Plant Manager: Mark Wilbur
Estimated Sales: $ 10-20 Million
Number Employees: 100-249
Parent Co: Tyson Foods
Type of Packaging: Consumer, Food Service
Brands:
    Tyson Foods

14757 Tyson Foods
P.O.Box 547
Dexter, MO 63841-0547   573-624-4551
    Fax: 573-624-9834 www.tyson.com

Processor of fresh and frozen chicken.
    Manager: Mark Avery
    President/CEO: Richard Bond
    EVP/CFO: Wade Miquelon
    EVP/General Counsel: J Alberto Gonzalez-Pita
    SVP/Research & Development: Howell Carper
    VP/Investor Relations: Ruth Ann Wisener
    SVP/Human Resources: Kenneth Kimbro
    Complex Manager: Mike Avery
Estimated Sales: $ 100-500 Million
Number Employees: 500-999
Type of Packaging: Consumer, Food Service

14758 Tyson Foods
110 W Freeman Ave
Berryville, AR 72616-3310   870-423-2164
    Fax: 870-423-1681 www.tysonfoodsinc.com
Fresh and frozen chicken
    Manager: Richard Bond
    Complex Manager: Rick Oswald
    Plant Manager: Craig McDonald
    Purchasing Manager: Mirna MacDonald
Estimated Sales: $ 100-500 Million
Number Employees: 1,000-4,999
Brands:
    Tyson Foods

14759 Tyson Foods Plant
5701 McNutt Rd
Santa Teresa, NM 88008-9604   575-589-0100
    Fax: 505-589-1903   800-351-8184
                         www.tyson.com
Chicken slaughtering and processing.
    Chairman: John Tyson
    President/CEO: Richard Bond
    EVP/CFO: Wade Miquelon
    EVP/General Counsel: J Alberto Gonzalez-Pita
    SVP/Research & Development: Howell Carper
    VP/Investor Relations: Ruth Ann Wisener
    SVP/Human Resources: Kenneth Kimbro
Estimated Sales: $ 1 - 3 Million
Number Employees: 5-9
Parent Co: Tyson Foods
Type of Packaging: Consumer, Food Service, Private Label
Brands:
    Deli Gourmet
    Rueben
    TLC

14760 Tyson Fresh Meats
2101 W 6th Ave
Emporia, KS 66801-6323   620-343-3640
    Fax: 620-343-3640 www.tyson.com
Manufacturer and exporter of fresh and frozen beef including carcasses, cuts, by-products and offals.
    President & CEO: Richard Bond
    EVP/CFO: Wade Miquelon
    EVP/General Counsel: J Alberto Gonzalez-Pita
    SVP/Research & Development: Howell Carper
    VP/Investor Relations: Ruth Ann Wisener
    SVP/Human Resources: Kenneth Kimbro
    Manager: Roger Brownrigg
Estimated Sales: $26.4 Billion
Number Employees: 24
Parent Co: Tyson Foods
Type of Packaging: Consumer, Food Service, Private Label, Bulk
Brands:
    TYSON

14761 (HQ)Tyson Fresh Meats
800 Stevens Port Dr
Dakota Dunes, SD 57049-5005   605-235-2061
    Fax: 605-235-2068 www.tyson.com/
Producer of fresh beef, pork and related allied products and supplier of high quality fully prepared meats for the retail and food service industries.
    Chairman: John Tyson
    President/CEO: Richard Bond
    EVP/CFO: Wade Miquelon
    EVP: Noel White
    SVP/Research & Development: Howell Carper
    SVP, Sales International: Roel Andriessen
    VP/Investor Relations: Ruth Ann Wisener
    SVP/Human Resources: Kenneth Kimbro
Estimated Sales: K
Number Employees: 41,000
Parent Co: Tyson Foods
Type of Packaging: Consumer, Food Service, Private Label, Bulk
Brands:
    THOMAS E. WILSON

14762 Tyson Prepared Foods
1320 S University Drive
Suite 600
Fort Worth, TX 76107-5780   817-258-2400
    Fax: 817-258-2438 www.tyson.com
Processor and exporter of pre-cooked food products including pizza toppings, soups, sauces, chili, taco fillings, tacos, taquitos and burritos.
    Chairman: John Tyson
    President/CEO: Richard Bond
    EVP/CFO: Wade Miquelon
    EVP/General Counsel: J Alberto Gonzalez-Pita
    SVP/Research & Development: Howell Carper
    VP/Investor Relations: Ruth Ann Wisener
    SVP/Human Resources: Kenneth Kimbro
Number Employees: 500-999
Parent Co: Tyson Foods
Type of Packaging: Food Service

14763 U Roast Em
16778 W Us Highway 63
Hayward, WI 54843-7214   715-634-6255
    Fax: 715-934-3221   sales@u-roast-em.com
                         www.u-roast-em.com
Supplier of green coffee beans, bulk teas, home roasting supplies and coffee flavorings
Type of Packaging: Consumer
Brands:
    BODUM
    FRESH BEANS

14764 U. Okada & Company
1000 Queen St
Honolulu, HI 96814-4116   808-597-1102
                         Fax: 808-591-6634

    President: Dexter Okada
Estimated Sales: $ 10 - 20 Million
Number Employees: 20-49

14765 U.S. Foodservice
6685 Crescent Dr
Norcross, GA 30071-2934   770-263-4300
    Fax: 770-263-4359   800-554-8050
                         www.usfoodservice.com
Wholesaler/distributor of dry groceries, produce, dairy products, baked goods, general merchandise, private label items, frozen foods, seafood and meats/provisions; serving the food service market
    Manager: Scott Lasalle
    Vice President: Lee Carson
    Warehouse Manager: Greg Kirchner
Estimated Sales: $10-20 Million
Number Employees: 250-499
Parent Co: Alliant Foodservice

14766 (HQ)UAS Laboratories
9953 Valley View Rd
Eden Prairie, MN 55344-3526   952-935-1707
    Fax: 952-935-1650   800-422-3371
    info@uaslabs.com   www.uaslabs.com
Manufacturer and exporter of nutritional supplements including probiotics and antioxidents
    President: S K Dash
    Quality Control: Scot Elert
    Marketing Director: Raj Dash
    Operations Manager: Steven Shack
Estimated Sales: $ 5 - 10 Million
Number Employees: 10-19
Number of Products: 12
Sq. footage: 5400
Type of Packaging: Consumer, Private Label, Bulk
Brands:
    DDS
    DDS Acidophilus
    DDS Junior
    DDS Plus
    UAS Activin Plus
    UAS Coenzyme Q10
    UAS Joint Formula

14767 UDV Canada
401 The West Mall
Suite 800
Etobicoke, ON M9C 5P8
Canada   416-626-2000
    Fax: 416-626-2688 www.diageo.com
Processor and exporter of gin and wine
    President: Stuart Fletcher
    CEO: Paul Walsh
    CFO: Nick Rose
    Vice President: Gary Galanis
Parent Co: Grand Metropolitan
Type of Packaging: Consumer, Food Service

14768 UDV Wines
1160 Battery St # 400
San Francisco, CA 94111-1236   415-835-7300
     Fax: 415-835-8615 www.diageo.com
Processor of wine
     Manager: Mike Wineberger
     VP Marketing: Steve Wyant
Estimated Sales:$ 50 - 100 Million
Number Employees: 50-99
Parent Co: Grand Metropolitan
Type of Packaging: Consumer, Food Service

14769 UFL Foods
450 Superior Boulevard
Mississauga, ON L5T 2R9
Canada   905-670-7776
     Fax: 905-670-7751 pboucek@uflfoods.com
Processor and exporter of custom formulated and
blended ingredients including milk replacers, mus-
tard, seasonings, meat binders, curing preparations,
etc.; also, pasta and rice sauce mixes, soup and sauce
bases, batters andbreadings
     VP: Jack Conway
Number Employees: 100-249
Sq. footage: 110000
Parent Co: Newly Weds Foods
Type of Packaging: Food Service, Private Label,
Bulk

14770 ULDO USA
10 Dewey Road
Lexington, MA 02420-1018   781-860-7800
     Fax: 781-863-1973 productinfo@bakenjoy.com
          www.uldousa.com
Baked goods
Brands:
     Baken Joy

14771 UNOI Grainmill
Route 13-A
Seaford, DE 19973-5749   302-629-4083
Miller of whole wheat flour, white and yellow corn
meal, buckwheat, etc
     Owner: Janice Griffith
     Manager: Charles Willoughby
*Estimated Sales:*Under $300,000
Number Employees: 3
Sq. footage: 10000
Parent Co: United Nation of Islam
Type of Packaging: Private Label
Brands:
     Hearn & Rawlins
     White Dove

14772 US Chocolate Corporation
4801 1st Ave
Brooklyn, NY 11232-4208   718-788-8555
     Fax: 718-788-3311 uschoc@aol.com
Processor and exporter of kosher liquid marble
chocolate and white parve coatings, fudge bases and
flavors.
     President: David Rosenberg
Estimated Sales:$ 10 - 20 Million
Number Employees: 10-19
Sq. footage: 27000
Brands:
     U.S. Brand

14773 US Distilled Products
1607 12th St S
Princeton, MN 55371-2311   763-389-4903
     Fax: 763-389-2549 information@usdp.com
          www.usdp.com
Importer and master distributor, contract bottling,
producer of alcoholic beverages and broker
     President: Bradley P Johnson
     CFO: Pat Pelzer
     General Manager: Todd Geisness
     National Sales Manager: Steve Sullivan
     Production Manager: Kevin Issendorf
Estimated Sales:$ 20-30 Million
Number Employees: 50-99
Sq. footage: 250000

14774 US Durum Products
P.O.Box 10126
Lancaster, PA 17605-0126   717-293-8698
     Fax: 717-293-8699 866-268-7268
          www.usdurum.com
Manufacturer and distributer of couscous throughout
the United States and Canada.
     Manager: Jeffrey Dewey

Estimated Sales:$ 2.5-5 Million
Number Employees: 10-19

14775 US Filter
101 N Park St
East Orange, NJ 07017-1708   973-677-8946
          Fax: 973-678-0444
Processor of bottled spring, distilled and purified
water
     VP: Steve Grossman
Estimated Sales:$ 3 - 5 Million
Number Employees: 5-9
Sq. footage: 40000
Parent Co: Electrified Companies
Type of Packaging: Consumer, Bulk
Brands:
     American Eagle
     Lectrostill

14776 US Food & Pharmaceuticals
313 W Beltline Hwy # 182
Madison, WI 53713-2682   608-278-1293
          Fax: 608-278-9042
Processor of milk minerals, dairy formulations, en-
hanced dairy products and formulations, nutritional
products, nutraceuticals
     President: Rajan Vembu
     VP: James Henderson
     Marketing Director: Richard Nelson
     Public Relations: Kalle Smith
     Operations Manager: Jay Zahom
Estimated Sales:$1500000
Number Employees: 5-9
Sq. footage: 10000
Type of Packaging: Consumer
Brands:
     Dari-Cal
     Infalac
     My-Baby

14777 US Foods
4343 NW 38th St
Lincoln, NE 68524-1909   402-470-2021
     Fax: 402-470-3549 info@u-s-foods.com
          www.u-s-foods.com
Pre-cooked bean, pea & lentil products. Precooked
grain & rice products. Private label ready to eat cere-
als & snacks. contract manufacturing & private label
packaging services
     President: Rick L Williams
     Sales: Medlodie Slaymaker
     Production: Clark Mulder
     Purchasing: Ken Adams
Estimated Sales:$9500000
Number Employees: 50-99
Sq. footage: 80000
Type of Packaging: Private Label, Bulk
Brands:
     Brown's Best
     Crunchee
     Infranized
     Q-C

14778 US Fresh Marketing
2304 Wake Forest Street
Virginia Beach, VA 23451-1458   757-481-2606
     Fax: 757-496-2733 usfresh@pilot.info.net
Processor of hot sauces, pepper powder and flakes;
also, wheat, rice, organic fruit and fresh, canned,
frozen and dehydrated vegetables; importer and ex-
porter of produce
     President: R Battaglia
     CEO: T Battaglia
Estimated Sales:$1-3 Million
Number Employees: 8
Sq. footage: 25000
Type of Packaging: Consumer, Food Service, Pri-
vate Label, Bulk

14779 US Ingredients
P.O.Box 9207
Naperville, IL 60567-0207   630-820-1711
     Fax: 630-820-1883 usingredient@earthlink.net
          www.usingredient@earthlink.net
Seasonings and food flavoring products
     Owner: Eric Maul
Estimated Sales:$ 5-10 Million
Number Employees: 5-9

14780 US Mills
200 Reservoir Street
Needham, MA 02494-3146   781-444-0440
     Fax: 781-444-3411 800-422-1125
          www.usmillsllc.com/

Processor and exporter of natural/organic foods in-
cluding ready-to-eat and hot cereals and graham
crackers.
     President: Charles Verde
     Executive VP: Cynthia Davis
     Sales: William Bunn
Number Employees: 5-9
Number of Brands: 5
Number of Products: 45
Type of Packaging: Consumer
Brands:
     EREWHON
     FARINA MILLS
     NEW MORNING
     SKINNER'S
     UNCLE SAM CEREAL

14781 US Spice Mills
4537 W Fulton St
Chicago, IL 60624-1609   773-378-6800
     Fax: 773-378-0077 usspice@usspice.com
          www.usspice.com
Manufacturer and importer of spices
     President: Nick Patel
Estimated Sales:$600000
Number Employees: 5-9

14782 US Sugar Company
692 Bailey Ave
Buffalo, NY 14206-3003   716-828-1170
     Fax: 716-828-1509 steve@ussugar.net
          www.ussugar.net
Manufacturer of granulated, brown and powdered
sugars; sugar and artificial sweetener packets
     President: William McDaniel
     VP: Steve Ward
     VP Operations: Tom Moran
     Plant Manager: Avery Foy
Estimated Sales:$25 Million
Number Employees: 20-49
Number of Brands: 30
Number of Products: 20
Sq. footage: 300000
Type of Packaging: Consumer, Food Service, Pri-
vate Label
Brands:
     PRIVATE LABEL
     US SUGARS

14783 USA Beverage
1410a E Old Us Highway 40
Warrenton, MO 63383-1316   636-456-5468
     Fax: 636-456-3422 general@usbeverage.com
          www.usbeverage.com
Wines
     President: Hugh White
     CFO: Thomas Nittler
     Marketing Director: Darrell Wiss
     Production Manager: Terre Novell
     Plant Manager: Hugh White
Estimated Sales:$500,000
Number Employees: 20-49
Type of Packaging: Private Label
Brands:
     USA Beverages

14784 USA Fruit
3 North Street
Greenwich, CT 06830-4720   203-661-8280
Fruit
Estimated Sales:$ 3 - 5 Million
Number Employees: 1-4

14785 USA Laboratories
1438 Highway 96
Burns, TN 37029-5030   615-441-1521
     Fax: 615-446-3788 800-489-4872
     usalabs@usalabs.com www.usalabs.com
Processor and exporter of vitamins, minerals, nutri-
tional supplements and weight loss aids
     CEO: Charles Stokes
     CEO: Charles Stokes
     R&D: David Bethshears PhD
     Quality Control: Brad Stokes
     Marketing Director: Erica White
     Sales Director: Shelby Bethsheard
     Operations: Ted Sanders
Estimated Sales:$ 10 - 20 Million
Number Employees: 10-19
Number of Brands: 5
Number of Products: 1000
Sq. footage: 100000
Parent Co: USA Laboratories

Brands:
Burn Off
Jewel Laboratories
Nutreuticals
Power Rangers Chewable Vitamins
USA Best
USA Laboratories Nutrients
USA Sports Labs

14786 USA Sunrise Beverage
I-90 Exit 2 Plaza
S
Spearfish, SD 57783   605-723-0690
Processor and exporter of bottled mineral and spring water and carbonated fruit drinks including papaya, peach, pineapple, etc.; importer of water
President: Omar Barrientos
VP/Secretary: Gene Fairchild
Number Employees: 5-9
Type of Packaging: Consumer, Food Service
Brands:
Dakota Springs
Rushmore Springs
Sunrise

14787 (HQ)UST
P.O.Box 100
Danbury, CT 06813-0100   203-792-4460
          Fax: 203-792-4602 800-650-7411
                    www.ustinc.com
Wines
Owner: Gerald Holton
CEO: John Barr
CFO: James Patracuolla
Vice President: Patricia Dennis
Estimated Sales: $ 10-100 Million
Number Employees: 250-499
Type of Packaging: Private Label
Brands:
Copenhagen
Husky
Rooster

14788 Udi's Granola
6850 N Broadway
Unit G
Denver, CO 80221   303-657-6366
          Fax: 303-657-5373 info@udisgranola.com
                    www.udisgranola.com
flavored granola

14789 Ugo di Lullo & Sons
P.O.Box 126
Westville, NJ 08093-0126   856-456-3700
          Fax: 856-456-7161 dilul8@aol.com
General grocery
Owner: Ugo Di Lullo
Estimated Sales: Below $ 5 Million
Number Employees: 5-9
Brands:
Ugo di Lullo & Sons

14790 Uhlmann Company
1009 Central St
Kansas City, MO 64105-1619   816-221-8200
          Fax: 816-221-5504 800-383-8201
Processor of all-purpose unbleached and wholewheat flour
President: Paul Uhlamnn Iii
Estimated Sales: $ 10 - 20 Million
Number Employees: 10-19
Type of Packaging: Consumer, Food Service
Brands:
Ceresota
Heckers

14791 Uinta Brewing
1722 Fremont Dr
Salt Lake City, UT 84104-4215   801-467-0909
          Fax: 801-463-7151 info@uintabrewing.com
                    www.uintabrewing.com
Beer
President: William Hamill
Public Relations Officer: Steve Kustinec
Estimated Sales: $ 5-10 Million
Number Employees: 10-19
Sq. footage: 26000
Type of Packaging: Private Label
Brands:
Uinta

14792 Ukuva Africa
5210 Carillon Pt
Kirkland, WA 98033-7378   425-828-0609
          Fax: 888-248-7802 888-280-1003
          colleen@tasteofafrica.com
          www.tasteofafrica.com
African spicy sauces
Brands:
Malawi Gold
Swazi Mamma Mamba
Xhosa Umsobo Lyababa

14793 Ulfert Broockmann
611 Burdick Street
Libertyville, IL 60048-3101   847-680-3771
Cheese

14794 Ulker Group
Ferah Cd / Kisiklicesme Sk
2/4 34692 B Camlica
Uskudar / IST / Turkey,
Turkey
          Ph 90(216)5242991 Fx 90(216)3357393 Email:
          cahit.paksoy@ulker.com.tr
          Website: www.ulker.com.tr/ulkerportal/en/
Manufacturer and exporter of numerous food products including chocolate bars; rice crispy bars; cream biscuits; cookies; baby biscuits; crackers; cakes; candies and chewing gum.
Chairman Holding Executive Board/CEO: Murat Ulker
Vice Chairman Holding Executive Board: Orhan Ozokur
President Ulker Division: Ali Ulker
President Trade Division: Mustafa Yasar Serdengecti
President R&D and Business Development: Zeki Ziya Sozen
President Packaging Division: Huseyin Avni Metinkale
President Informatics Division: Murat Inan
President Consumer Division: Taner Karamollaoglu
CEO Packaging Group: Cahit Paksoy Ph.D
Type of Packaging: Food Service

14795 Ultima Foods
2177 Fernand Lafontain
Longueuil, ON J4G 2V2
Canada   450-651-3737
          Fax: 450-651-6868 800-363-9496
                    www.yoplait.ca
Processor of dairy products including regular and drinkable yogurt and fresh cheeses
President/CEO: gerry doutre
CEO: alain David
VP Marketing: Lucie Remillard
VP Sales: Michel Cusson
Number Employees: 4000
Parent Co: Agropur
Type of Packaging: Consumer
Brands:
Minigo
YOP
Yoplait Tubes
creme and fruits
source

14796 Ultimate Bagel
1007 Logan Ave
Altoona, PA 16602-4737   814-942-2435
          Fax: 814-942-2904
          shipping-hhbagels@nyc.rr.com
Processor of bagels
Owner: Doris Doris
Founder: Helmer Toro
CEO: Doris Doris
Estimated Sales: $5-9.9 Million
Number Employees: 10-19
Sq. footage: 2000
Type of Packaging: Consumer, Food Service

14797 Ultimate Biscotti
1000 S Bertelsen Road
Suite 10
Eugene, OR 97402-5448   541-344-8220
          Fax: 541-344-8357 info@ultimatebiscotti.com
                    www.ultimatebiscotti.com
Processor of biscotti including ginger, hazelnut chocolate, citrus, etc.; also, wheat and gluten-free available
President: Heather Kent
Number Employees: 5-9
Sq. footage: 6000

Type of Packaging: Consumer, Food Service, Bulk
Brands:
Ultimate Biscotti

14798 Ultimate Gourmet
P.O.Box 967
Belle Mead, NJ 08502-0967   908-359-4050
          Fax: 908-359-2494
          contact@ultimate-gourmet.com
          www.ultimate-gourmet.com
Bar mixes, jellies, jams, sauces, brandied fruit, barbacue sauces, marinades and rubs
President: Tali Almagor
Estimated Sales: $300,000-500,000
Number Employees: 1-4
Type of Packaging: Consumer, Food Service, Private Label, Bulk
Brands:
Club Tahity
Cramore
Creamy Head
FIREHOUSE
Giroux
Milem
Proud Mary
Raffetto
Tahiti

14799 Ultimate Nut & Candy Company
10665 W Vanowen St
Burbank, CA 91505-1136   818-766-5259
          Fax: 818-762-0462 800-767-5259
          customerservice@ultimatenut.com
          www.ultimatenut.com
Candy, nuts
President: Steve Turner
Quality Control: Theresa Malgonadio
Marketing Manager: Steve Turner
Estimated Sales: $ 50-75 Million
Number Employees: 20-49
Type of Packaging: Private Label
Brands:
Studio Confections
Ultimate Confections

14800 Ultimate Nutrition
161 Woodford Avenue
Plainville, CT 06062-2370   330-405-5008
          Fax: 860-793-5006
          victor.rubino@worldnet.att.net
          www.ultimatenutrition.com
Food processor and exporter of food supplements including capsules, tablets, powders and protein bars; manufacturer and exporter of T-shirts, hats, etc
President: Victor Rubino
Advertising: Seth Darvick
VP Sales: Dean Caputo
Type of Packaging: Consumer

14801 Ultra Enterprises
14108 Lambert Rd
Whittier, CA 90605-2427   626-945-4833
          Fax: 562-698-7362 800-543-0627
          b.kaliultra@verizon.net www.ultraent.com
Processor and sports nutrition of granulars
President/CEO: Bud Thompson
Vice President: Mary Thompson
Number of Products: 50
Type of Packaging: Consumer
Brands:
Sports Nutrition
Ultra Rain Glandulars

14802 Ultra Seal
521 Main St
New Paltz, NY 12561-1609   845-255-2496
          Fax: 845-255-3553 dawnb@ultra-seal.com
                    www.ultra-seal.com
Contract packager of portion controlled products including ketchup, mustard, powder lemonade, fruit juice, iced tea mix, etc
President: Dennis Borrello
Estimated Sales: $8000000
Number Employees: 100-249
Sq. footage: 26000
Type of Packaging: Consumer, Food Service, Private Label, Bulk

14803 Umanoff & Parsons
1704 Boone Ave
Bronx, NY 10460-5400   212-219-2240
          Fax: 718-684-7978 800-248-9993
          service@umanoffparsons.com
          www.umanoffparsons.com

Processor of fresh and frozen all natural kosher dairy cakes, pies, quiches and tarts
President: Simon Seaton
Estimated Sales: $5,200,000
Number Employees: 20-49
Sq. footage: 6500

14804 Umpqua Dairy Products Company
333 SE Sykes Ave
Roseburg, OR 97470-3129   541-672-2638
Fax: 541-673-0256 www.umpquadairy.com
Processor and exporter of ice cream, milk, cottage cheese, sour cream and butter
President: Doug Feldkamp
Executive VP: Steven Feldkamp
Plant Manager: Tom Rise
Estimated Sales: $37591892
Number Employees: 100-249
Type of Packaging: Consumer, Food Service, Private Label

14805 Uncle Andy's Pic & Pay Bakery
171 Ocean St
South Portland, ME 04106-3623   207-799-7199
Fax: 207- 79-9 34
Baked goods
Owner: Dennis Fogg
Estimated Sales: Under $500,000
Number Employees: 10-19

14806 Uncle Ben's
P.O.Box 1737
Greenville, MS 38702-1737   662-335-8000
Fax: 662-378-4370 800-548-6253
www.unclebens.com
Processor of rice
Manager: Ronnie Taylor
Estimated Sales: $100+ Million
Number Employees: 100-249
Parent Co: Mars
Type of Packaging: Consumer
Brands:
UNCLE BEN'S

14807 Uncle Ben's
PO Box 1752
Houston, TX 77251-1752   713-674-9484
Fax: 713-670-2227 www.unclebens.com
Parboiled rice
Number Employees: 50-99

14808 Uncle Bum's Gourmet Foods
5821 Wilderness Ave
Riverside, CA 92504-1004   951-352-5700
Fax: 951-352-5710 800-486-2867
www.triplehfoods.com
Processor and exporter of marinades, sauces, spice mixes, salsas, syrups, bar mixes, dressings, apple sauce, flavored teas, hot sauces, jellies, sports drinks, oils and mustards
President: Tom Harris Jr
Director Sales/Marketing: David Shoemaker
Estimated Sales: $ 20 - 50 Million
Number Employees: 50-99
Sq. footage: 65000
Parent Co: Triple H Food Processors
Type of Packaging: Consumer, Food Service, Private Label, Bulk
Brands:
Hot Jamaican Jerk
Jamaican Jerk Spice Blend
Spanish Style Romesco Sauce
Spicey Caribbean Bbq Sauce
Spicey Teriyaki
Sweet & Spicey

14809 Uncle Charley's SausageCompany
1135 Industrial Park Rd
Vandergrift, PA 15690-6050   724-845-3302
Fax: 724-845-3174
charley@unclecharleyssausage.com
www.unclecharleyssausage.com
Pork, pork products
President: Charles Armitage
Vice President: Charles Armitage Jr
Estimated Sales: $ 5-10 Million
Number Employees: 20-49

14810 (HQ)Uncle Dave's Kitchen
P.O.Box 580
South Londonderry, VT 5155-580   802-824-3600
Fax: 802-824-6033 udk@sover.net
www.uncledaves.com

Processor and exporter of ketchup and honey-horse-radish mustard; also, pasta sauces including marinara, marinara and mushrooms, spicy peanut, sun dried tomato basil and Tex-Mex sauce/salsa with pine nuts
Vice President: J Lyon
Operations Manager: Patricia Romalo
Purchasing Manager: Lynne Andreen
Estimated Sales: $ .5 - 1 million
Number Employees: 5-9
Sq. footage: 3500
Brands:
Corny Salsa
Dippin Mustard
Excellent
Excellent Marinara
Kicken Ketchup
Kickin Cocktail Sauce
Kickin Grill Sauce
Kickin Mustard
Kickin'
Mushroom Marinara
No Fat Spaghetti Sauce
Original Ketchup
Spicey Peanut Sauce
Sundried Tomatoe Basil Pesto
Sunflower Pesto
Tex Mex Sauce
Uncle Dave's

14811 Uncle Fred's Fine Foods
209 N Doughty Street
Rockport, TX 78382-5322   361-729-8320
Processor and importer of habanero ketchup, jelly, hot sweet mustard and chips, salsa, spices, meat rubs and sauces including cocktail, pepper and barbecue
President: Fred Franklin
VP/Co-Owner: Pat Marsh
Manager: Judith Jecmen-Fuhrman
Number Employees: 1-4
Sq. footage: 1600
Parent Co: Island Enterprises
Type of Packaging: Consumer
Brands:
Uncle Fred's Fine Foods

14812 Uncle Grant's Foods
PO Box 210638
San Francisco, CA 94121-0638   415-752-5462
Fax: 415-752-5467 Insanity@hooked.net
Gourmet and specialty foods
President: Dave Schumann
Co-Owner: Lisa Chiapetta
Vice President: Paul Strazulla
Estimated Sales: $ 1-2.5 Million
Number Employees: 1

14813 Uncle Lee's Tea
11020 Rush St
South El Monte, CA 91733-3547   626-350-3309
Fax: 626-350-4364 800-732-8830
contact@unclelee.com www.unclelee.com
Processor, exporter and importer of teas including herb, spiced, traditional and dieter's; co-packing and private label available
President: Kuo-Lin Lee
Vice President: Jonason Lee
Sales Director: James O'Young
Public Relations: Patty Gillno
Plant Manager: Joe Villegas
Estimated Sales: $1400000
Number Employees: 5-9
Parent Co: Ten Ren Tea Company
Brands:
Uncle Lee's Tea

14814 Uncle Ralph's Cookie Company
801 N East St
Frederick, MD 21701-4652   301-695-6224
Fax: 301-695-6327 800-422-0626
sales@uncleralphscookies.com
www.uncleralphscookies.com
Processor of gourmet cookies, brownies, crumb cakes, pound cakes, and quick breads
VP: Ralph Wight
Founder: Peggy Wight
Sales Director: Jamie Mater
Estimated Sales: $ 3 - 5 Million
Number Employees: 50-99
Sq. footage: 30000
Type of Packaging: Consumer, Food Service, Private Label
Brands:
Uncle Ralph's

14815 Uncle Ray's Potato Chips
14245 Birwood St
Detroit, MI 48238-2207   313-834-0800
Fax: 313-834-0443 sandy@unclerays.com
www.unclerays.com
Snack foods without nuts
President: Raymond Jenkins
Purchasing Manager: Jim Coomes
Estimated Sales: $ 50-100 Million
Number Employees: 5-9
Parent Co: Amerifit/Strength Systems
Brands:
Uncle Ray's

14816 Uncle Wiley's
1220 Post Road
Fairfield, CT 06430   203-259-1084
Fax: 203-256-1350 http://unclewileys.com
Makes a variety of packaged seasonings for meats, vegetables, fruits, baking (pies, etc.), salads, etc.
Founder/Owner/President: Wiley Mullins

14817 Uncommon Grounds Coffee
2813 7th St
Berkeley, CA 94710-2702   510-644-4451
Fax: 510-644-2808 800-600-5282
uncommon@uncommongrounds.net
www.uncommongrounds.net
Coffee
Manager: Robert Duque
CFO: Derek Lantner
Operations Manager: Kim Moore
Production Manager: James Spottn
Estimated Sales: $ 1-2.5 Million
Number Employees: 20-49
Type of Packaging: Private Label
Brands:
Double Star Espresso
El Salvador Finca Las Nubes
Ethiopian Organic
Molta Roba

14818 Underground Sauce Network
73 Urbana Street
Cranston, RI 02920-5136   401-464-8508
Fax: 401-942-0061 888-919-6664
info@undergroundsauce.com
www.undergroundsauce.com
Sauces

14819 Une-Viandi
505 Industriel Boulevard
St. Jean Sur Richelieu, NB J3B 5Y8
Canada   450-347-8406
Fax: 450-347-8142 800-363-1955
Processor, importer and exporter of meat products including bone-in and boneless beef, lamb and veal
President: Claude Berni
Export Manager: Lloyd Arshinoff
Number Employees: 50-99
Sq. footage: 22000
Type of Packaging: Consumer, Food Service, Private Label, Bulk

14820 Unette Corporation
88 N Main St
Wharton, NJ 07885-1607   973-328-6800
Fax: 973-537-1010 tsweeney@unette.com
www.unette.com
Contract packager of food colors, condiments, groceries, etc
President: Joseph Hark
Estimated Sales: $4400000
Number Employees: 50-99
Sq. footage: 60000

14821 Ungars Food Products
9 Boumar Pl
Elmwood Park, NJ 07407-2615   201-703-1300
Fax: 201-703-9333 webquery@drpraegers.com
www.drpraegers.com
Veggie burgers, pancakes, breaded fish fillets, fillet fish sticks
President: Peter Praeger
CFO: Jeff Coher
Estimated Sales: $ 2.5-5 Million
Number Employees: 50-99

14822 (HQ)Ungerer & Company
P.O.Box U
Lincoln Park, NJ 07035-0900   973-628-0600
Fax: 973-628-0251 aking@ungerer.org
www.ungererandcompany.com

Manufacturer, importer and exporter of natural and artificial fruit flavors and essential oils including lemon, orange, peppermint, spearmint, ginger, lime and dill
President: K G Voorhees Jr
Estimated Sales:$10 Million
Number Employees: 100-249
Type of Packaging: Consumer, Private Label, Bulk
Other Locations:
Ungerer & Company Plant
Bethlehem PA
Ungerer & Company Plant
Oaxaca, Mexico

14823 Uni-President
PO Box 910
La Puente, CA 91747-0910   626-961-1671
Fax: 626-369-7126 mfwu@unipresidentusa.com
www.unipresidentusa.com
Processor and exporter of Oriental noodles and dry soups
President: Mao Sheng Liu
Sales/Marketing Executive: Jeffrey Hsich
Purchasing Agent: Diane Mo
Estimated Sales:$4200000
Number Employees: 65
Sq. footage: 175845
Parent Co: Uni-President
Type of Packaging: Consumer, Food Service, Private Label

14824 Unibroue/Unibrew
80 Rue Des Carriers
Chambly, QC J3L 2H6
Canada   450-658-7658
Fax: 450-658-9195 www.unibroue.com
Processor and exporter of gourmet beer
President: Andre Dion
Number Employees: 100-249
Type of Packaging: Consumer, Food Service
Brands:
Unibrew
Unibroue

14825 Unica
23w101 Kings Ct # 100
Glen Ellyn, IL 60137-7215   630-790-8107
Fax: 630-790-8117 www.x-it-dk.com
Sugar free confectionary
President: Peter Zeuthen
Estimated Sales:$ 5 - 10 Million
Number Employees: 5-9
Brands:
UNICA

14826 Unicof
102 Executive Dr # D
Sterling, VA 20166-9555   703-904-0777
Fax: 703-904-7817 ted@unicof.com
General grocery
President: Hanif Moledina
President: Kyle B Klyman
Estimated Sales: $ 10-100 Million
Number Employees: 5-9
Brands:
Unicof

14827 Uniconfis Corporation
5901c Peachtree Dunwoody Road NE
Suite 125
Atlanta, GA 30328-5382   770-481-0440
Fax: 770-481-0340
Candy
Sales Coordinator: Alison Parham
*Estimated Sales:*Under $500,000
Number Employees: 5-9

14828 Unified Foods
145 Vallecitos De Oro # 208
San Marcos, CA 92069-1459   760-744-7225
Fax: 760-744-7215
Processor, exporter and importer of dehydrated vegetables including bell peppers, carrots, celery, peas, corn, mushrooms, garlic, etc
Owner: Dan Stouder
VP: Dan Stouder
Sales Manager: Simone Grunewald
Estimated Sales:$ 1 - 3 Million
Number Employees: 1-4
Sq. footage: 10000
Type of Packaging: Bulk

14829 Unified Western Grocers
3626 11th Ave
Los Angeles, CA 90018-3601   323-731-8223
Fax: 323-731-6821 www.ubgrocers.com
Processor of milk including whole, 1% and 2%; wholesaler/distributor of yogurt, cottage cheese, orange juice, fruit punch and sour cream
Manager: John Jackson
Sales/Marketing: Jeffrey Quintana
Estimated Sales:$100+ Million
Number Employees: 100-249
Parent Co: Certified Grocers of California
Type of Packaging: Consumer

14830 Unified Western Grocers
457 E Martin Luther King Jr
Los Angeles, CA 90011-5650   323-232-6124
Fax: 323-234-7381 grocers@aol.com
www.uwgrocers.com
Bread and rolls
President: Alfred Plamann
Chief Engineer: Floyd Smith
Sales Manager: Norm Bowers
General Manager: John Bedrosian
Plant Manager: Jim Teague
Estimated Sales:$ 50-100 Million
Number Employees: 100-249
Type of Packaging: Private Label, Bulk

14831 Unilever
523 S 17th St
Harrisburg, PA 17104-2220   717-234-6215
Fax: 717-231-5419 www.bestfoods.com
Processor of pasta
Manager: James Pagano
President Americas: Bill Fertenbaugh
President Europe: Rudy Markham
President Foods: Manvinder Singh Banga
President Asia Africa: Harish Manwani
Chief Human Resources Officer: Sandy Ogg
Chief Financial Officer: Rudy Markham
Deputy Chief Financial Officer: John Ripley
Group Treasurer: Pascal Visee
Estimated Sales:$ 10 - 20 Million
Number Employees: 50-99
Sq. footage: 300000
Parent Co: Unilever USA
Type of Packaging: Bulk
Brands:
Lipton Foods

14832 Unilever
5430 Cote De Liesse Road
Mont-Royal, QC H4P 1A6
Canada   514-735-1141
Fax: 514-733-7499
denis.labattaglia@unilever.com
www.unilever.com
Processor of tea
President: Ralph Kugler
Regional Sales Manager: Don Boudreau
Plant Manager: Dennis Labattaglia
Number Employees: 100-249
Parent Co: Unilever USA
Type of Packaging: Consumer
Brands:
Dove
Herbal Lipton
Red Rose
Salada
Sunlight

14833 Unilever
Ste 200
2200 Cabot Dr
Lisle, IL 60532-914   847-678-1241
Fax: 847-671-2290 877-995-4483
www.unileverusa.com
Manufacturer and exporter of frozen and canned soups and concentrated soup bases.
Group Chief Executive: Patrick Cescau
President Americas: John Rice
President Europe: Kees Van Der Graaf
President Home & Personal Care: Ralph Kugler
President Foods: Manvinder Singh Banga
President Asia Africa: Harish Manwani
Chief Human Resources Officer: Sandy Ogg
Chief Auditor: Alan Johnson
Chief Financial Officer: Rudy Markham
Deputy Chief Financial Officer: John Ripley
Group Treasurer: Pascal Visee
Number Employees: 500
Type of Packaging: Consumer, Food Service, Bulk

14834 (HQ)Unilever
390 Park Avenue
New York, NY 10022-4609   212-888-1260
Fax: 212-318-3600 www.unilever.com
Culinary products, frozen foods, ice cream, tea-based beverages, spreads and cooking products and general grocery
President: John W Rice
CFO: Robert Gillespie
VP/Treasurer: R Gluck
President Bestfoods Affiliates: John Moorhead
Public Relations: Stephen Milton
VP Operations/Business Development: Steve Driver
Food Technologist: Aaron Yang
Estimated Sales:$ 5 -10 Billion
Number Employees: 15500
Brands:
BEN & JERRY'S
BERTOLLI
BREYERS
GOOD HUMOR
HELLMAN'S
I CAN'T BELIEVE IT'S NOT BUTTER
KLONDIKE
KNORR
KNORR (LIPTON) SIDES
LIPTON
POPSICLE
PROMISE
RAGU
SHEDD'S SPREAD COUNTRY CROCK
SKIPPY
SLIM-FAST
WISH-BONE

14835 Unilever Bertolli USA, Inc.
800 Sylvan Ave
Englewood Cliffs, NJ 07632-3201   201-894-4000
Fax: 201-871-8257
MediaRelations.USA@unilever.com
www.unileverus.com
Processor and importer of olive oil and olive oil products including salad dressings and aerosol sprays; also, balsamic vinegar
President: Michael Polk
Marketing Manager: Paul Barrett
Estimated Sales:$20-50 Million
Number Employees: 10,000+
Parent Co: Unilever Canada
Type of Packaging: Consumer, Food Service, Private Label, Bulk
Brands:
Bertolli
Tirreno

14836 Unilever Bestfoods
800 Sylvan Ave
Englewood Cliffs, NJ 07632-3201   201-894-4000
Fax: 201-871-8257 corpaffairs.usa@unilever.com
www.bestfoods.com
Manufacturer and processor of salad dressings, noodles, macaroni, soups and iced tea mixes; herbal, regular and lemon flavored teas; well-known US grocery, specialty, and baking brands as well as food service
General Manager: Tony Santoro
VP: Gregory Phillips
Sales/Marketing Executive: Dave Landers
Media Relations: Jennifer Stalzer
Purchasing Agent: Bob Talbot
Number Employees: 10,000+
Parent Co: Unilever USA
Type of Packaging: Consumer, Food Service
Brands:
BEN & JERRY'S
BEST FOODS
BETOLLI
BREYER'S
BRUMMEL AND BROWN
FIVE BROTHERS
GOOD HUMOR
HELLMANN'S
I CAN'T BELIEVE IT'S NOT BUTTER
IMPERIAL
KNORR
LAWRY'S
LIPTON
PROMISE
RAGU
SHEDD'S
SKIPPY

TAKE CONTROL
WISH-BONE

14837 Unilever Bestfoods
1785 Ashby Road
Merced, CA 95348-4302   209-723-8831
Fax: 209-383-0988 877-995-4483
www.unileverusa.com
Processor of canned spaghetti sauces and tomato pastes
President: John Rice
Estimated Sales: $100+ Million
Number Employees: 500-999
Parent Co: Unilever USA
Type of Packaging: Consumer, Food Service
Brands:
Axe
Bertolli
Caress
Dove
Good Humor
Hellmann's
Lipton
Lwary's
Ponds
Promise

14838 Unilever Canada
160 Bloor Street E
Suite 1500
Toronto, ON M4W 3R2
Canada   416-964-1857
Fax: 416-963-5197
unilevercanada.foundation@unilever.com
www.unilever.ca
Manufacturer of a variety of products for the food industry, health and beauty industry as well as household products.
President/CEO: David Blanchard
VP/General Counsel & Corporate Secretary: John Coyne
VP/Chief Financial Officer: Paulo De Castro
VP/General Manager Foods: Mark Olney
VP/Customer Development: Stephen Kouri
VP/Brand Development HPC: Geoff Craig
Director Human Resources: Michael White
Number Employees: 250-499
Parent Co: Unilever USA
Type of Packaging: Consumer, Food Service
Brands:
Becel
Breyers
Hellmann's
Knorr
Lipton
Red Rose
Slim-Fast

14839 Unilever Foods
1400 Waterloo Rd
Stockton, CA 95205-3743   209-466-9580
Fax: 209-466-0937 info@unilever.com
www.unilever.com
Processor of tomatoes including paste, diced and crushed.
Group Chief Executive: Patrick Cescau
President Americas: John Rice
President Europe: Kees Van Der Graaf
President Home & Personal Care: Ralph Kugler
President Foods: Manvinder Singh Banga
President Asia Africa: Harish Manwani
Chief Human Resources Officer: Sandy Ogg
Chief Auditor: Alan Johnson
Chief Financial Officer: Rudy Markham
Deputy Chief Financial Officer: John Ripley
Group Treasurer: Pascal Visee
Number Employees: 100-249
Parent Co: Unilever USA
Type of Packaging: Consumer, Food Service, Private Label, Bulk
Brands:
Becel
Bertolli
Blue Band
Flora

14840 Unilever United States
800 Sylvan Ave
Englewood Cliffs, NJ 07632-3201   201-567-8000
Fax: 201-871-8257
MediaRelations.usa@unilever.com
www.unilever.com

Processor of salad dressing, seasonings and tea powder.
Group Chief Executive: Patrick Cescau
President Americas: John Rice
President Home & Personal Care: Ralph Kugler
President Foods: Manvinder Singh Banga
President Asia Africa: Harish Manwani
President Europe: Kees Van Der Graaf
Chief Human Resources Officer: Sandy Ogg
Chief Auditor: Alan Johnson
Chief Financial Officer: Rudy Markham
Deputy Chief Financial Officer: John Ripley
Group Treasurer: Pascal Visee
Plant Manager: Rich Germinder
Number Employees: 250-499
Sq. footage: 350000
Type of Packaging: Consumer, Food Service

14841 Unimark Group Inc
124 McMakin Road
Bartonville, TX 76226-8400   817-491-2992
Fax: 817-491-1272
Processor and importer of chilled fruits
President/CEO: Jakes Jordaan
Sales: Ira Heid
Estimated Sales: $ 50-100 Million
Number Employees: 1000-1500
Type of Packaging: Food Service, Bulk
Brands:
Circle R
Flavor Fresh
Fruits of Four Seasons
Sunfresh
Sunfresh Brand

14842 Union
14522 Myford Rd
Irvine, CA 92606-1000   714-734-2200
Fax: 714-734-2223 800-854-7292
marisela@unionfoods.com www.unionfoods.com
Processor and exporter of Oriental ramen noodles
President: Sang Mook Lee
CEO: Victor Sim
Sales Manager: Bob Hicks
Estimated Sales: $10900000
Number Employees: 100-249
Sq. footage: 100000
Type of Packaging: Consumer, Private Label
Brands:
Noodle Plus
Smack Cup-A-Ramen
Smack Ramen
Snoodles

14843 Union Beverage Company
2600 W 35th Street
Chicago, IL 60632-1602   773-254-9000
Fax: 773-890-8039 800-685-6868
contact@nwscorp.com www.nwscorp.com
Alcoholic beverages, wine and spirits
Chairman: James E Lacrosse
Executive VP: John H Baker
VP Sales/Marketing: Greg Mauloff
Purchasing Manager: Jan Schaver
Estimated Sales: $ 100-500 Million
Number Employees: 400
Parent Co: National Wine and Spirits
Type of Packaging: Private Label

14844 Union Dairy Fountain
1252 Woodside Dr
Freeport, IL 61032-6722   815-233-2233
Fax: 815-233-2233
Dairy products
President: Barbara Groves
Estimated Sales: Less than $500,000
Number Employees: 5-9

14845 Union Fisheries Corporation
6186 N Northwest Hwy
Chicago, IL 60631-2126   312-738-0448
Fax: 773-763-8775
Prepared fresh or frozen fish and seafood
Owner: Jim Gubrow
Estimated Sales: $ 3 - 5 Million
Number Employees: 5-9

14846 Union Seafoods
2100 W McDowell Rd
Phoenix, AZ 85009-3011   602-254-4114
Fax: 602-254-4117
Seafood
President: Ernest Linsenmeyer

Estimated Sales: $4,000,000
Number Employees: 1-4

14847 Unipro/Ethical Nutrients
100 Avenida La Pata
San Clemente, CA 92673-6304   949-366-0818
Fax: 949-366-2859 800-621-6070
Processor of vitamins, supplements and sports nutrition products
Brand Manager: Mike Katke
Marketing Manager: Tim Katke
Number Employees: 100-249
Parent Co: Metagenics
Brands:
Ethical Nutrients
Metagenics
Unipro

14848 Unique Bakery Company
16 Dohme Avenue
Toronto, ON M4B 1Y9
Canada   416-751-8200
Fax: 416-751-0712 info@uniquebakery.com
www.uniquebakery.com
Processor and exporter of fresh and frozen baked goods including fruit and meat pies, tea biscuits, fruit turnovers, squares, tarts and danish, muffins, loaf/pound cakes, croissants and angel food cakes
President: John Siotas
Number Employees: 20-49
Sq. footage: 16000
Type of Packaging: Consumer
Brands:
Unique Bakery

14849 Unique Foods
3221 Durham Dr # 107
Raleigh, NC 27603-3507   919-779-5600
Fax: 919-779-3766
Processor of canned and exotic mushrooms
Owner: Lou Deangelis
CEO: Louis De Angelis
Marketing Head: Louis De Angelis
Estimated Sales: $3700000
Number Employees: 20-49
Sq. footage: 7500

14850 Unique Ingredients
PO Box 483
Naches, WA 98937-0483   509-653-1991
Fax: 509-653-1992 oly@werunique.com
www.werunique.com
Dried apples in a variety of cuts, styles and varieties; offering air dried, drum dried and upon request, freeze dried fruits and vegetables, specializing in apples, apricots, cherries, peaches, plums, raisins, bananas and all tropicalfruits. Certified organic.
Finance Director: Dave Olsen
Sales: Matt Gibbs
Sales: Karen Bentz
Estimated Sales: $13 Million
Number Employees: 1-4
Number of Products: 100
Sq. footage: 500
Type of Packaging: Private Label, Bulk
Brands:
Unique Ingredients

14851 Unique Vitality Products
P.O.Box 1003
Agoura Hills, CA 91376-1003   818-889-7739
Fax: 818-889-4895 uniquevitality@sbcglobal.net
Processor and exporter of vitamins
President: Pierre Van Wessel
CEO: Robert Van Wessel
CFO: Wendy Van Wessel
Quality Control: Ashwin Patel
Production: Hasmuck Patec
Estimated Sales: $ .5 - 1 million
Sq. footage: 400000
Type of Packaging: Private Label, Bulk
Brands:
HYPO FORM
KIDNEY RINSE
LIVER RINSE
UNIQUE COLONIC RINSE
VASCUSTREM

14852 Uniquely Together
Apt 3
2000 W Estes Ave
Chicago, IL 60645-2452   847-675-1555
     Fax: 847-675-4049   800-613-7276
     info@uniquelytogether.com
     www.uniquelytogether.com
Cocktail biscuit collection, line of chocolates, line of
sandwich creme cookies; all natural
     Owner: Mark Callahan
     Owner: Anne Callahan
Number Employees: 5-9
Number of Brands: 1
Number of Products: 22
Sq. footage: 5500
Type of Packaging: Consumer, Private Label
Brands:
     Heavenly Cluster
     Heavenly Clusters Collection
     Martini Biscuit
     Sweet Savory Cocktai

14853 Unison
15902a Halliburton Road
Pmb 192
Hacienda Heights, CA 91745-3505   626-917-3668
     Fax: 626-917-7468   unisonincorp@hotmail.com
Processor, importer and exporter of dried fruits and
vegetables including apricots, peaches, pears, ber-
ries, apple rings, etc
     President: Xifu Wang
Number Employees: 5-9
Type of Packaging: Consumer, Bulk

14854 United Apple Sales
124 Main St # 5
New Paltz, NY 12561-1552   845-256-1500
     Fax: 845-256-9550   uasales@aol.com
     www.unitedapplesales.com
Grower, importer and exporter of apples
     COO: Chuck Andola
     Domestic/Export Sales: Dean Decker
Estimated Sales: $360,000
Number Employees: 1-4
Type of Packaging: Consumer, Food Service
Brands:
     AMERICA'S FRUIT
     STORM KING

14855 United Canadian Malt
843 Park Street S
Peterborough, ON K9J 3V1
Canada   705-876-9110
     Fax: 705-876-9118   800-461-6400
Processor, exporter and importer of dried and cus-
tom liquid brewing extracts, malt syrups and liquid
malt
     President/General Manager: JM Smith
     Operations: L Pecoskie
Number Employees: 15
Sq. footage: 124900
Type of Packaging: Bulk
Brands:
     BRU-MIX
     CANADIAN GRAND
     MASTER BAKER
     MASTER BREWER

14856 United Canning Corporation
11991 South Ave
North Lima, OH 44452-9744   330-549-9807
     Fax: 330-549-9808
Processor of canned mushrooms
     Owner: Andrew Dibacco
     Plant Manager: Richard Innocenzi
Number Employees: 10-19
Sq. footage: 45000
Type of Packaging: Consumer, Food Service, Pri-
vate Label
Brands:
     Frankies
     Masterbrand
     Sno-Top

14857 United Citrus Products
244 Vanderbilt Ave # 1
Norwood, MA 02062-5052   781-769-7300
     Fax: 781-769-9492   800-229-7300
     ksmith@unitedscitrus.net   unitedcitrus.net

manufacturer of bulk dry blends and liquid food
products including: cocktail mixes, cocktail
rimmers, beverage juices, energy drinks, hydration
beverages, frozen carbonated beverages, superfruit
beverages and dry blended specialtydesserts
     President: Richard Kates
     VP/General Manager: Kenneth Smith
     R&D: Linda Halik
     Quality Control: Cheryl Senato
     Sales: Robert Labrie
     Public Relations: Sherox Creative
     Purchasing: Carole Johanson
Estimated Sales: $5 Million
Number Employees: 20
Type of Packaging: Consumer, Food Service, Private Label, Bulk
Brands:
     ALL-IN-ONE
     BEST WAY
     FLORIDA'S OWN
     GOOD SPIRITS
     JOLLIE JUAN
     SIR CITRUS
     THE LAST WORD

14858 United Dairy
P.O.Box 280
Martins Ferry, OH 43935-0280   740-633-1451
     Fax: 740-633-6759   800-252-1542
     dlongentte@uniteddairy.com
     www.uniteddairy.com
Full line of dairy products including fluid milk, low
fat milks, chocolate, skim, half & half, buttermilk,
dairy smart, ultra skim, juices and drinks. Also, cot-
tage cheese, sour cream and dips, sterile products,
yogurt and icecream.
     President: Joseph Carson
Estimated Sales: $110000000
Number Employees: 250-499
Type of Packaging: Consumer

14859 United Dairy
P.O.Box 1247
Uniontown, PA 15401-1247   724-438-8581
     Fax: 724-438-1197   800-966-6455
     www.uniteddairy.com
Manufacturer of ice cream, milk and juice; whole-
saler/distributor of yogurt, sour cream and cottage
cheese; serving the food service market
     Manager: Ed Evans
     Operations Manager: Tim Griglack
Estimated Sales: $50-100 Million
Number Employees: 100-249
Parent Co: Martins Dairy
Type of Packaging: Consumer, Food Service, Pri-
vate Label, Bulk
Other Locations:
     United Dairy - Manufacturing Plant
     Martins Ferry OH
     United Dairy - Manufacturing Plant
     Charleston WV
     United Dairy
     Lancaster OH
     United Dairy
     Portsmouth OH
     United Dairy
     Latrobe PA
     United Dairy
     Beckley WV
     United Dairy
     Fairmont WV
     United Dairy
     Richmond KY

14860 United Dairy Farmers
3955 Montgomery Rd
Cincinnati, OH 45212-3798   513-396-8700
     Fax: 513-396-8736
     consumerrelations@udfinc.com
     www.udfinc.com
Milk and ice cream
     President: Brad Lindner
     Marketing Director: David Lindner
     CFO: Marilyn Mitchell
     R & D: Arlene Higgins
     COO: Marilyn Mitchell
Estimated Sales: $ 50-99.9 Million
Number Employees: 1,000-4,999
Brands:
     UDF

14861 United Dairymen of Arizona
P.O.Box 26877
Tempe, AZ 85285-6877   480-966-7211
     Fax: 480-829-7491   info@uda.com
     www.uda.org
Cooperative offering milk, butter and powdered
dairy products
     CFO: Scott H Benson
     Director Plant Operations: Dermot Carey
Estimated Sales: $366854098
Number Employees: 100-249

14862 (HQ)United Distillers & Vintners
801 Main Avenue
Norwalk, CT 06851-1127   203-323-3311
     Fax: 203-359-7402 www.UnitedDistillers.com
Distilled liquors, spirits and wines
     President: Charles Phillips
     Senior VP: John Adams
     Marketing Manager: James Thomson
Number Employees: 500-999
Brands:
     Asbach Brandy
     Bell's Scotch
     Black & White
     Canard Duchene
     Cardhu
     Classic Malts
     Dewar's White Label
     Dom Perignon
     George Dickel Whiske
     Glen Ord Scotch
     Gordon's Gin
     Gordon's Vodka
     Gordon's Vodka
     Haig
     Hennessy Cognacs
     Hine Cognac
     I.W. Harper Bourbon
     Johnny Walker Scotch
     Mercier Champagnes
     Safari
     Scoresby Scotch
     Tanqueray Gin
     The Dimple
     Vat 69
     Veuve Cliquot
     Weller Bourbon
     White Horse

14863 United Fishing Agency Limited
1131 N Nimitz Hwy # 38
Honolulu, HI 96817-4522   808-536-2148
     Fax: 808-526-0137
Seafood
     Manager: Frank Goto
Estimated Sales: $ 20 - 50 Million
Number Employees: 50-99

14864 United Fruit Growers
205 W 8th St
Palisade, CO 81526-8662   970-464-5671
     Fax: 970-464-7922
Cooperative packer and seller of fresh peaches
     Public Relations Officer: Ed Whitman
Estimated Sales: $500,000-$1 Million
Number Employees: 5-9
Sq. footage: 36000
Parent Co: Fruita Consumers Cooperative
Type of Packaging: Consumer, Private Label, Bulk

14865 United Fruits Corporation
2811 Wilshire Boulevard
Santa Monica, CA 90403-4803   310-829-0261
     Fax: 310-829-0265
Processor and exporter of fruit including apples,
apricots, cherries, grapefruit, grapes, lemons, honey-
dew lemons, nectarines, oranges, pears, plums, etc
     President: James Peterson
     Manager Sales: Melanie Harris
Estimated Sales: $ 20 - 50 Million
Number Employees: 5-9
Type of Packaging: Bulk

14866 United Intertrade
PO Box 821192
Houston, TX 77282-1192   800-969-2233
     Fax: 713-827-7881   800-969-2233
     info@mitalenacoffee.com
     www.mitalenacoffee.com
Coffee
     President: Burhan Ajouz
     VP/CFO: Misako Ajouz

Estimated Sales:$ 1.5 Million appx.
Number Employees: 19
Type of Packaging: Private Label
Brands:
    Bluebonnet Coffee
    Cafe Don Pedro
    Cafe Orleans-Coffee
    Cafe Unico-Espresso
    Divian Coffee
    Diwan Coffee
    Imperial Choice Coff
    Mediterranean Coffee
    Mitalena Coffee
    Unico

14867 United Intertrade Corporation

PO Box 821192
Houston, TX 77282-1192   713-827-7799
    Fax: 713-827-7881 800-969-2233
    info@mitalenacoffee.com
    www.mitalenacoffee.com
Processor and canner of green and roasted coffee beans
    President: Bob Ajouz
    VP: Misako Ajouz
Number Employees: 5-9
Sq. footage: 10000
Type of Packaging: Private Label, Bulk
Brands:
    Bluebonnet
    Cafe Dondedro
    Cafe Orleans
    Cafe Unico
    Imperial Choice
    Mediterranean

14868 United Marketing Exchange

215 Silver St
Delta, CO 81416-1517   970-874-3332
    Fax: 970-874-9525 mike@umefruit.com
    www.umefruit.com
Processor and exporter of fresh fruits and onions
    President: Harold Broughton
    Sales Manager: Mike Gibson
Estimated Sales:$1089000
Number Employees: 1-4
Parent Co: Hi Quality Packing
Type of Packaging: Consumer
Brands:
    Burrow
    OWL
    Tom-Tom

14869 United Meat Company

1040 Bryant St
San Francisco, CA 94103-4485   415-864-2118
    Fax: 415-703-9061
Manufacturer, exporter and importer of frozen portion controlled lamb, venison, veal and beef
    President: Phil Gee Jr
    VP: Michael Chu
Estimated Sales:$20-50 Million
Number Employees: 20-49
Sq. footage: 19430
Type of Packaging: Food Service
Brands:
    UMC

14870 United Natural Foods

P.O. Box 301
Chesterfield, NH 03443-0301   603-256-3000
    Fax: 603-256-6959 800-451-2525
    ghogan@unfi.com www.unfi.com
Natural foods
    President: Steven Townsend
    CFO: Jackie Hartwell
    Sales: Mark Bushway
    Purchasing Manager: Thomas Nunziata
Estimated Sales:$ 100-500 Million
Number Employees: 250-499
Parent Co: Hershey Import Company

14871 United Natural Foods

P.O. Box 999
Dayville, CT 06241-0999   860-779-2800
    Fax: 860-779-5678 800-877-8898
    info@unfi.com www.unfi.com
Vegetables
    President: Steven H Townsend
    Sr. VP Marketing: Daniel V Atwood
    CEO: Steven Spinner
    CFO: Rick Puckett
Estimated Sales:$ 5-10 Million
Number Employees: 5,000-9,999

Brands:
    UNFI
    United Natural Foods

14872 United Noodle Manufacturing Company

511 W 500 N
Salt Lake City, UT 84116-3414   801-485-0951
Manufacturer of Chinese noodles and fortune cookies
    Owner: Rufus Spraug
Estimated Sales:$$1-2.5 Million
Number Employees: 1-4
Type of Packaging: Consumer, Food Service

14873 United Packing

113 Gano St
Providence, RI 02906-3822   401-751-6935
    Fax: 401-223-0125
Processor of Portuguese sausages
    President: Tony Cabral
Estimated Sales:$510,000
Number Employees: 5-9

14874 (HQ)United Pickle Products Corporation

4366 Park Ave
Bronx, NY 10457-2494   718-933-6060
    Fax: 718-367-8522 info@pickle.com
    www.unitedpickle.com
Processor and exporter of condiments, chow chow, horseradish, relishes, cucumbers, sauerkraut and pickle products: importer of olives.
    Owner: Stephen Leibowitz
    Owner: Marvin Weishaus
    Plant Manager: Jose Torrez
*Estimated Sales:*25 Million
Number Employees: 1-4
Type of Packaging: Consumer, Food Service, Bulk
Other Locations:
    United Pickle Products Corp.
    Rosenhayn NJ
Brands:
    Leibo
    Leibowitz
    Nathan's Famous
    Teddy's
    United
    United Brand
    Upco
    Upzo

14875 United Pie Company

1016 Middlebury St
Elkhart, IN 46516-4510   574-294-3419
Manufacturer of baked products including pies
    President: Blanche Nichols
Estimated Sales:$10 Million
Number Employees: 5-9
Type of Packaging: Consumer

14876 United Poultry Company

742 N Broadway
Los Angeles, CA 90012-2820   213-620-9948
Processor of chicken
    President: Frank Fogarty
Number Employees: 50-99
Type of Packaging: Consumer, Food Service

14877 United Provision Meat Company

156 S Ohio Ave
Columbus, OH 43205-1359   614-252-1126
    Fax: 614-252-1127 unitedmeats@cs.com
    www.unitedprovisionmeatco.com
Manufacturer of portion controll meats including cooked prime rib, meatballs, meatloaf, beef roasts, pork roasts, london broil, chicken, turkey, geese, duck, cornish hens, sloppy joes and corned beef and pastrami
    President: Allen Scott
Estimated Sales:$5 Million
Number Employees: 5-9
Sq. footage: 12000
Type of Packaging: Food Service

14878 United Pulse Trading

1720 Burnt Boat Drive
Suite 104
Bismarck, ND 58503
        701-751-1623
    Fax: 701-751-1626 info@uspulses.com
    www.uspulses.com

red split lentils, yellow split peas, green split peas, chickpeas, laird/eston/richlea lentils, whole red lentils, kabuli chickpeas and split desi chickpeas
    President/Owner: Murad Katib
    CFO: Lory Island
    VP: Gaepan Bourassa
Number Employees: 3

14879 United Salt Corporation

4800 San Felipe St
Houston, TX 77056-3908   713-877-2600
    Fax: 713-877-2609 800-554-8658
    uscinfo@tum.com www.unitedsalt.com
Processor and exporter of salt including plain, iodized, agricultural and water conditioning
    President: Jim O'Donnell
    VP: Theresa Feldman
Estimated Sales:$16,100,000
Number Employees: 50-99
Parent Co: Texas United Corporation
Type of Packaging: Consumer, Food Service, Private Label, Bulk
Brands:
    Flavor House
    Gulf
    Ranch House

14880 United Shellfish Company

P.O.Box 146
Grasonville, MD 21638-0146   410-827-8171
    Fax: 410-827-7436 sales@unitedshellfish.com
    www.unitedshellfish.com
Processor and wholesale/distributor of fresh and frozen seafood including fresh fish fillet, poultry, fresh pasta, steamer clams, oysters and mussels, frozen squid, shrimp, scallops, fresh steak fish, whole fish, frozen fish, lobsterfrozen crab, frying clams, hardshell clams, misc clams and other products.
    Manager: Dave Messenger
    Sales Manager: John Walker
Estimated Sales:$19600000
Number Employees: 50-99
Sq. footage: 30000
Parent Co: Ipswich Shellfish Group
Type of Packaging: Food Service

14881 United Society of Shakers

707 Shaker Rd
New Gloucester, ME 04260-2652   207-926-4597
        888-624-6345
    usshakers@aol.com www.shaker.lib.me.us
Herbal teas, culinary herbs, herb mixes
    Executive Director: Leonard Brooks
*Estimated Sales:*Less than $200,000
Number Employees: 5-9
Type of Packaging: Consumer, Food Service, Bulk
Brands:
    United Society of Shakers

14882 (HQ)United States Bakery

P.O.Box 14769
Portland, OR 97293-0769   503-731-5679
    Fax: 503-731-5680 www.usbakery.com
Manufacturer of baked goods including bread, buns, rolls and pastries
    Chairman/CEO: Robert Albers
    President/COO: Mark Albers
    CFO: Jerry Boness
Estimated Sales:$275 Million
Number Employees: 1,000-4,999
Type of Packaging: Consumer, Food Service
Brands:
    BAY CITY
    KATE'S
    MCKENZIE FARMS
    SEATTLE INTERNATIONAL
    SVENHARD'S

14883 United States Bakery

P.O.Box 14769
Portland, OR 97293-0769   503-731-5679
    Fax: 503-731-5680 www.usbakery.com
Processor of bread, buns, rolls and doughnuts
    Chairman: Marc Albers
    CEO: Bob Albers
    CFO: Jerry Boness
    Vice President: Todd Cornwell
    President: mark Albers
    Sales Director: Ron McKnight
    Operations Manager: William Zimmerman
    Purchasing Manager: Ken Waltos
*Estimated Sales:*I
Number Employees: 1,000-4,999

Type of Packaging: Consumer, Food Service, Private Label
Brands:
  Franz

14884 United Universal Enterprises Corporation
7747 N 43rd Ave
Phoenix, AZ 85051-5712   623-842-9691
  Fax: 623-842-4605   univenterp@cs.com
Wholesaler/distributor, importer and exporter of general merchandise, frozen seafood, canned fruits, grains, meat, cooking oils and powdered milk; serving the food service market
  Manager: Louis Galvac
  Vice President: Linda Kirschner
Estimated Sales: $ 3 - 5 Million
Number Employees: 10
Sq. footage: 7000
Type of Packaging: Food Service, Private Label

14885 United Valley Bell Dairy
508 Roane St
Charleston, WV 25302-2091   304-344-2511
  Fax: 304-344-2518
Fluid milk
  Manager: John Duty
  Marketing Director: Halan Varley
Estimated Sales: Less than $500,000
Number Employees: 100-249
Type of Packaging: Private Label

14886 Universal Beef Products
3511 Canal St
Houston, TX 77003-1835   713-224-6043
  Fax: 713-224-0716
Beef products
  President: Neil Brody
Estimated Sales: $ 2.5-5 Million
Number Employees: 20-49

14887 Universal Beverages
P.O.Box 448
Ponte Vedra Bch, FL 32004-0448   904-280-7795
  Fax: 904-280-7794   ubisyfocorp@aol.com
                      syfobeverages.com
Processor and exporter of bottled water including purified and sodium free; also, regular and flavored seltzer and naturally sparkling water
  President: Jonathan O Moore
  CEO: Jonathan Moore
  Plant Manager: Justin Jones
Estimated Sales: $ $2.5-5 Million
Number Employees: 20-49
Sq. footage: 100000
Parent Co: Universal Beverages Holding Corporation
Type of Packaging: Consumer, Food Service, Private Label
Brands:
  Syfo

14888 (HQ)Universal Beverages
3301 W Main St
Leesburg, FL 34748-9714   352-315-1010
Fax: 352-315-1009 info@universalbeverages.com
                   www.universalbeverages.com
Bottled water
  Manager: Justin Jones
Estimated Sales: $1.6 Million
Number Employees: 5-9
Type of Packaging: Private Label
Brands:
  100% Purified Non Carbonated Water
  Naturally Flavored S
  Syfo Brand Original

14889 Universal Blanchers
62 Hightower Road
Blakely, GA 39823-9445   229-723-4181
  Fax: 912-723-8887
Processed peanuts
  President: Thomas Baty
Estimated Sales: $ 25-49.9 Million
Number Employees: 150

14890 Universal Commodities
141 Parkway Rd # 20
Bronxville, NY 10708-3618   914-779-5700
  Fax: 914-779-5742   universaltea@uctt.com
                      www.uctt.com
Tea importers
  President: Domenick Ciaccia
  Director: Paul Strader

Estimated Sales: $ 5-10 Million
Number Employees: 5-9

14891 Universal Concepts
1608 NW 34th Ter
Lauderhill, FL 33311-4210   918-367-0197
  Fax: 954-792-4502
Meat tenderizers
Estimated Sales: Under $500,000
Number Employees: 1-4

14892 Universal Flavor Corporation
5600 W Raymond St
Indianapolis, IN 46241-4343   317-243-3521
  Fax: 317-240-1524
Manufacturer and exporter of flavors and fragrances including fruit, beverage, dairy, coffee, tea, vanilla and frozen dessert for bottlers, canners, dairies, food processors, etc
  President: Michael du Bois
  Marketing Executive: Bob Burns
  CEO: Ken Manning
Number Employees: 1,000-4,999
Parent Co: Universal Foods
Type of Packaging: Private Label, Bulk

14893 Universal Flavors
5600 W Raymond St
Indianapolis, IN 46241-4343   317-243-3521
  Fax: 317-240-1524   800-325-3826
  uniflavor@primary.net   www.unifoods.com
Manufacturers of flavorings
  President: Pat Spurgeon
  CEO: Ken Manning
  Senior Food Technologist: Jennifer Burke
  Marketing Manager: Eric Dick
  Product Manager: Greg McClatchy
Estimated Sales: $ 100-500 Million
Number Employees: 1,000-4,999
Type of Packaging: Bulk

14894 Universal Formulas
10123 Roger Street
Portage, MI 49002-7111   616-383-3340
  Fax: 616-383-3449   800-342-6960
Processor of enzymes, minerals and herbs
  President: Ralf Ostertag
Estimated Sales: $ $2.5-5 Million
Number Employees: 4

14895 Universal Laboratories
3 Terminal Rd
New Brunswick, NJ 08901   732-545-3130
  Fax: 732-214-1210   800-872-0101
  info@universalnutrition.com
  www.universalnutrition.com
Processor and exporter of vitamins, powdered proteins and confections including candy bars
  President: Clyde Rockoff
  Director Marketing: Steve Patton
Estimated Sales: $100+ Million
Number Employees: 100-249
Sq. footage: 120000
Brands:
  Animal Pak
  Forza
  Hardfast
  Natural Sterols
  Yohimbe Bar

14896 Universal Meat Products
1111 Greenwood Road
Pikesville, MD 21208-3607   410-484-3900
  Fax: 410-486-7713
Processor of meat products
  President: kevin gaipher
Estimated Sales: $ 3 - 5 Million
Number Employees: 5-9
Type of Packaging: Consumer, Food Service

14897 Universal Poultry Company
1769 Old West Broad Street
Athens, GA 30606-2867   706-546-6767
  Fax: 706-546-6790
Poultry
  Manager: Robert Harris
Estimated Sales: $500,000-$1 Million
Number Employees: 5-9

14898 Universal Preservachem Inc
33 Truman Drive S
Edison, NJ 08817-2426   732-777-7338
  Fax: 732-777-7885   laurie@upichem.com
                      www.upichem.com

Wholesaler/distributor of chemicals and ingredients. Vitamins sweeteners preservatives, antioxidants, acidulants, etc
  Chairman of the Board: Herbert Ravitz
  VP Sales: Mike Ravitz
Estimated Sales: $4100000
Number Employees: 20
Sq. footage: 60000
Type of Packaging: Private Label, Bulk

14899 Unruh's Quality Meats
195 Crumpler Road
Deridder, LA 70634-5574   337-463-7688
Processor of beef, pork, lamb and pork sausage; also, custom slaughtering available
  Owner: Dewayne Unruh
Number Employees: 5-9
Sq. footage: 32000
Type of Packaging: Consumer, Food Service, Private Label, Bulk

14900 Upcountry Fisheries
85 Kino Pl
Makawao, HI 96768-8891   808-871-8484
  Fax: 808-871-6071
Seafood
  Owner: Richard Samsing
Estimated Sales: $ .5 - 1 million
Number Employees: 1-4

14901 Upper Crust Bakery
3655 W Washington St
Phoenix, AZ 85009-4759   602-255-0464
  Fax: 602-255-0433   pmiller@ucbakery.com
                      www.uppercrustbakeryusa.com
Bread and bakery products
  President: Tab Navidi
  Sales/Marketing: Pat Navidi
Estimated Sales: $ 20-50 Million
Number Employees: 100-249
Type of Packaging: Private Label

14902 Upper Crust Baking Company
P.O.Box 203
Pismo Beach, CA 93448-0203   805-543-1295
  Fax: 805-543-1284   800-676-1691
  contact@uppercrustbaking.com
  www.uppercrustbaking.com
Biscotti, cookies and crostini
  President: Tracey Aumiller
Estimated Sales: $ 5-9.9 Million
Number Employees: 5-9
Type of Packaging: Consumer
Brands:
  Upper Crust Biscotti

14903 Upper Crust Biscotti
P.O.Box 203
Pismo Beach, CA 93448-203   800-676-1691
  Fax: 805-543-1284   866-972-6879
  uppercrustbiscotti@worldpantry.com
  www.uppercrustbiscotti.com
Manufacturer of flavored Biscotti, flavored Tyni Biscotti, flavored Itti Bittie Cookies, and flavored Wine Crostini.
  Owner: Terez Tyni
Estimated Sales: $ 500,000 - $ 1Million
Number Employees: 11
Sq. footage: 4500
Brands:
  Itty-Bittie Biscotti
  Itty-Bittie Cookies
  Upper Crust Biscotti

14904 (HQ)Upstate Farms Cooperative
25 Anderson Rd
Buffalo, NY 14225-4905   716-892-3156
  Fax: 716-892-3157   emailus@upstatefarms.com
                      www.upstatefarmscoop.com
Processor of dairy products and meat including pepperoni, Genoa and hard salami, mortadella, roast beef and Italian sausage.
  CEO: Bob Hall
Estimated Sales: $260 Million
Number Employees: 20-49
Parent Co: Upstate Milk Cooperative
Type of Packaging: Consumer, Food Service, Private Label, Bulk
Brands:
  BISON
  BREAKSTONE'S
  INTENSE MILKS
  MILK FOR LIFE
  UPSTATE FARMS

14905 Upstate Farms Cooperative
25 Anderson Rd
Buffalo, NY 14225-4905   716-892-3156
Fax: 716-892-3157 866-874-6455
emailus@upstatefarms.com
www.upstatefarmscoop.com
Processor of milk and juice and cultured dairy products
CEO: Bob Hall
Estimated Sales: $260 Million
Number Employees: 20-49
Number of Brands: 5
Number of Products: 100
Type of Packaging: Consumer, Food Service, Private Label, Bulk
Brands:
    BISON
    BREAKSTONES
    Upstate Farms

14906 Upstate Farms Cooperative
45 Fulton Ave
Rochester, NY 14608-1032   585-458-1880
Fax: 585-458-2887 www.upstatefarms.com
Processor of milk
CEO: Bob Hall
Sales Manager (Eastern): Jerry Malne
Account Manager: Dick Pearce
Plant Manager: Stephen Hranjec
Estimated Sales: $260 Million
Number Employees: 100-249
Parent Co: Upstate Farms
Type of Packaging: Consumer, Food Service, Private Label, Bulk

14907 Uptown Bakers
318 I Street NE
Washington, DC 20002-4342   202-546-6500
Fax: 703-243-4050 www.uptownbakers.com
Processor of European pastries and breads including scones, cinnamon bread, muffins, cookies, danish and cakes
President: Frank Sciacca
Number Employees: 100-249
Type of Packaging: Consumer, Food Service

14908 Urban Accents
4241 N Ravenswood Ave
Chicago, IL 60613-1199   773-528-9515
Fax: 773-528-9533 877-872-7742
customerservice@urbanaccents.com
www.urbanaccents.com
Processor of snack crakers and distinctive spices
President: Tom Knibbs
Vice President: Jim Dygas
Estimated Sales: Below $ 5 Million
Number Employees: 5-9
Type of Packaging: Private Label
Brands:
    Bloody Mary Blend

14909 Urban Oven
910 S Hohokam Drive
Suite 101
Tempe, AZ 85281   480-921-2476
Fax: 480-921-2477 866-770-6836
gene@urbanoven.com www.urbanoven.com
crackers
Owner: Gene Williams
Director of Sales: Linda Anne Marty
Number Employees: 7

14910 Urbani Truffles
8657 Hayden Place
Culver City, CA 90232-2901   310-842-8850
Truffles
Estimated Sales: Below $ 5 Million
Number Employees: 10

14911 Ursula's Island Farms
6321 Corgiat Drive S
Suite A
Seattle, WA 98108-2862   206-762-3113
Fax: 206-762-0658
Dry fruit

14912 Usine de Congelation St. Bruno
698 Rue Melancon, Cp 160
St. Bruno, QC G0W 2L0
Canada
418-343-2206
Fax: 418-343-2513

Processor and exporter of blueberry products including frozen, concentrate and puree; also, cranberry products including whole and sliced and frozen fava beans
General Manager: Jeannot Cote
Number Employees: 100-249
Type of Packaging: Food Service
Brands:
    Quebec Wild Blueberries, Inc.

14913 (HQ)Utz Quality Foods
900 High St
Hanover, PA 17331   717-637-6644
Fax: 717-633-5102 800-367-7629
info@utzsnacks.com www.utzsnacks.com
Manufacturer of potato chips, pretzels, popcorn, tortilla chips, cheese curls, pub fries, sunflower chips, prok rinds, etc.
President: Tom Dempsey
Chariman/CEO: Mike Rice
VP/CFO: Todd Staub
EVP Sales/Marketing: Dylan Lissette
VP Public Relations: Jane Rice
VP Manufacturing: Paul Schaum
Estimated Sales: $165 Billion
Number Employees: 1,800
Sq. footage: 550000
Type of Packaging: Consumer, Food Service, Bulk
Other Locations:
    Utz Distribution Centers
    East Hartford CT
    Patterson NY
    Laurel DE
    Newark DE
    Auburn ME
    West Springfield MA
    North Easton MA
    South Yarmouth MA
    Wilmington MA
    Shrewsbury MA
    Cumberland MD
    Waldorf MD
    Hanover PA
Brands:
    GRANDMA UTZ'S
    HANOVER
    KETTLE KRISP

14914 Uvalde Meat Processing
508 S Wood St
Uvalde, TX 78801-5653   830-278-6247
Fax: 830-278-6245
Manufacturer of sausage, venison, goat, beef, lamb and pork; also, game birds; slaughtering services available
President/Co-Owner: Pat Jackowski
VP/Co-Owner: Gail Jackowski
Estimated Sales: $1-3 Million
Number Employees: 10-19

14915 V Chocolates
3590 South Via Terra Street
Salt Lake City, UT 84115   801-269-8444
Fax: 801-269-8449 vmail@vchocolates.com
www.vchocolates.com
chocolates
Number Employees: 12

14916 V L Foods
70 W Red Oak Lane
White Plains, NY 10604-3602   914-697-4851
Fax: 914-697-4888
President: Paul Pruzan
Brands:
    PICCADELI

14917 V&E Kohnstamm
882 3rd Ave # 7
Brooklyn, NY 11232-1902   718-788-6320
Fax: 718-768-3978 800-847-4500
flavorinfo@virginiadare.com
Processor and exporter of flavors, masking agents, bases, extracts, vanilla, orange oils and colors
President: Howard Smith
Executive VP: Howard Smith Jr
Estimated Sales: $21100000
Number Employees: 100-249
Type of Packaging: Private Label, Bulk
Brands:
    Veko

14918 V&V Supremo Foods
2141 S Throop St
Chicago, IL 60608-4410   312-421-1020
Fax: 312-421-7359 800-547-8773
www.vvsupremo.com
Processor, importer and wholesaler/distributor of Mexican-style cheese, chorizo, sour cream, etc. serving the food service and retail markets
President: Gilberto Villasenor
Estimated Sales: $71700000
Number Employees: 100-249
Type of Packaging: Consumer, Food Service
Brands:
    V&V Supremo Chihuahua
    V&V Supremo Del Caribe
    V&V Supremo Queso Fresco

14919 V-Link
299 Stone Valley Way
Alamo, CA 94507-1248   925-552-7088
Fax: 925-552-7092
President: K Chang
CFO: Tina Hsieh
Estimated Sales: $300,000-500,000
Number Employees: 1-4

14920 V. Sattui Winery
1111 White Ln
St Helena, CA 94574-1599   707-963-7774
Fax: 707-963-4324 800-799-8888
info@vsattui.com www.vsattui.com
Processor of wines
Owner: Daryl Sattui
CEO: Tom Davies
Sales Manager: Chester Sattui
Estimated Sales: $19061626
Number Employees: 50-99
Type of Packaging: Consumer

14921 V.G. Buck California Foods DB
PO Box 1037
Kenwood, CA 95452-1037   707-833-6548
Fax: 707-833-5725 vgbuckcal@aol.com
General grocery
Sales Director: John Landsdale
Point of Sales Manager: V Buck
Operations Manager: Deborah Rogers
Number Employees: 10-19
Type of Packaging: Private Label

14922 V.W. Joyner & Company
PO Box 387
Smithfield, VA 23431-0387   757-357-2161
Fax: 757-357-0184 www.smithfield-company.com
Processor and exporter of smoked cured country hams, picnics and bacon for distribution to wholesale, retail and restaurant markets
VP/General Manager: Larry Santure
Plant Manager: R Howell
Number Employees: 10-19
Sq. footage: 40000
Parent Co: Smithfield Companies
Type of Packaging: Consumer, Food Service, Private Label, Bulk
Brands:
    Joyner's
    Red Eye Country Picnic
    V.W. Joyner Genuine Smithfield

14923 VANCO Trading
50 Old Kings Hwy N # 101
Darien, CT 06820-4609   203-656-2800
Fax: 203-655-8307 janvaneck@vancotrading.com
www.vancotrading.com
Food chemicals and ingredients
Owner: J Vaneck
Estimated Sales: $500,000-$1 Million
Number Employees: 1-4
Brands:
    Quinine

14924 VIOBIN
226 W Livingston St
Monticello, IL 61856-1673   217-762-2561
Fax: 217-762-2489 888-473-9645
info@viobinusa.com www.viobinusa.com
Defatted wheatgerm, refined and unrefined wheat germ oil
Manager: Roger Moore
Sales Manager: Geni Heide
Estimated Sales: $ 10-20 Million
Number Employees: 20-49
Brands:
    Viobin

14925 (HQ)VIP Foods
1080 Wyckoff Ave
Flushing, NY 11385-5757　　718-821-3942
　　Fax: 718-497-7110　vipfoods@aol.com
　　www.vipfoodsinc.com
Processor and exporter of soups, instant lunches, low-calorie sweeteners and mixes including dessert, pasta, tea, hot chocolate, pasta, pudding, cake and cake mixes, sauce and chicken coating
　　Owner: Mendel Freund
　　Sales Manager: Esther Freund
Estimated Sales: $ 10 - 20 Million
Number Employees: 20-49
Sq. footage: 45000
Type of Packaging: Consumer, Food Service, Private Label, Bulk
Brands:
　　Kojel
　　Minute Lunch
　　Soup Bowl
　　VIP

14926 VIP Foodservice
P.O.Box 517
Kahului, HI 96733-7017　　808-877-5055
　　Fax: 808-877-4960 www.vipfoodservice.com
Wholesaler/distributor of grocery products, meat, produce, dairy items, frozen foods, baked goods, seafood and equipment and fixtures; serving the food service market
　　President/VP Sales: Nelson Okumura
　　Marketing Manager: Lynne Marie
　　VP Operations: Brian Tokeshi
　　VP Purchasing: Steve Smith
Estimated Sales: $100+ Million
Number Employees: 100-249
Sq. footage: 60000

14927 VIP Sales Company
2395 American Ave
Hayward, CA 94545-1807　　918-252-5791
　　Fax: 918-254-1667　sbeck@vipfoods.com
　　www.vipfoods.com
Packer and exporter of frozen fruits, vegetables and Chinese entrees and prepared foods; importer of raspberries, blueberries and broccoli
　　President: Guy Lewis
　　CEO: G Lewis
　　Sr. VP/COO: Lee Turman
　　VP Sales/Marketing: Steve Beck
　　Public Relations: Mick Lewis
　　Plant Manager: Don Avera
　　VP Purchasing: Fred Meyer
Estimated Sales: $5900000
Number Employees: 30
Number of Brands: 5
Number of Products: 180
Type of Packaging: Consumer, Food Service, Private Label, Bulk
Brands:
　　BASIC VALUE
　　FOOD PAC
　　FOOD TREND
　　TAI PAN
　　VIP

14928 VLR Food Corporation
510 Oyster Lane
Unit 2
Concord, ON L4K 2C1
Canada　　905-669-0700
　　Fax: 905-669-9829　800-387-7437
　　sales@tgfnet.com　www.jonathant.com
Processor of fillo dough, hors d'ouvres and fillo pastry entres
　　President: Victor Fradkin
　　CEO: Larry Hoffman
　　Marketing: Erin Hoffman
　　VP Sales: Bob Duncan
　　VP Production: Karl Bauernfreund
Number Employees: 100-249
Number of Brands: 3
Number of Products: 20
Type of Packaging: Food Service
Brands:
　　Jonathan T.
　　TGF

14929 VMI Corporation
13838 Industrial Road
Omaha, NE 68137-1104　　402-334-8100
　　Fax: 402-334-9280　800-228-2248

Variety meats including liver, portion cuts, retail and food service
　　President: Robert Elliott
　　Comptroller: Jim Pearson
　　Plant Manager: Robert Matton
　　Purchasing Manager: Dan Roulette
Estimated Sales: $ 10-25 Million
Number Employees: 100
Sq. footage: 20
Type of Packaging: Private Label
Brands:
　　Coast
　　Le Cort
　　Prime International
　　Tender Yam

14930 VOD Gourmet
3 Stormy Circle
PO Box 4922
Greenwich, CT 06831-0418　　203-531-5172
　　Fax: 203-532-4883　vodost@optonline.net
　　www.vodgourmet.com
Swedish cheese with peppercorn vodka, juniper berries, pre-cooked/frozen
　　President: Ulla Nylan
Estimated Sales: $300,000-500,000
Number Employees: 1-4
Type of Packaging: Private Label, Bulk
Brands:
　　VOD

14931 VT Made Richard's Sauces
471 Bushey Road
Saint Albans, VT 05478-9604　　802-524-3196
　　Fax: 802-524-4224　sauce@vtmadebbqu.com
　　www.vtmadebbqu.com
BBQ sauce, game sauce and marinades, gift favors and hot sauce.
　　Co-Owner: Steve Rocheleau
　　Co-Owner: Martha Rocheleau
Estimated Sales: $150,000+
Number Employees: 2
Number of Products: 5
Type of Packaging: Consumer, Food Service, Private Label, Bulk

14932 Vac Pac Manufacturing Company
P.O.Box 6339
Baltimore, MD 21230-0339　　410-685-5181
　　Fax: 410-332-4536　800-368-2301
　　vacpac@pobox.com　www.vpmfg.com
Manufacturer and exporter of heat shrinkable polyethylene cook-in bags for meat, poultry, etc
　　President: Aron Perlman
　　VP: Hessa Tary
Estimated Sales: $4114713
Number Employees: 20-49

14933 Vacaville Fruit Company
830 Eubanks Dr # D
Vacaville, CA 95688-8765　　707-448-5292
　　Fax: 707-447-1085　info@vacavillefruit.com
　　www.vacavillefruit.com
Processor importer and exporter of kosher dried fruit and fruit pastes; serving the food service market
　　President: Richard Nola
　　Director Sales/Marketing: Nicole Nola
　　Plant Superintendent: Gary De La Rosa
Estimated Sales: $4200000
Number Employees: 50-99
Type of Packaging: Consumer, Food Service, Bulk

14934 Val Verde Winery
100 Qualia Dr
Del Rio, TX 78840-7697　　830-775-9714
　　Fax: 830-775-5394 www.valverdewinery.com
Wines
　　Owner: Thomas Qualia
　　Operations Manager: Thomas Qualia
Estimated Sales: $300,000
Number Employees: 5-9
Type of Packaging: Private Label
Brands:
　　Val Verde Winery

14935 Val's Seafood
3437 Winford Drive
Mobile, AL 36619-4309　　251-639-1103
　　Fax: 251-639-1198
Seafood
　　President: Val Hammond

14936 Valdez Food
1815 N 2nd St
Philadelphia, PA 19122-2305　　215-634-6106
　　Fax: 215-634-8645
Processor of Chinese food products including wonton soup, chow mein, fish cakes, shrim, egg & pizza rolls.
　　President: Perfecto Valdez Jr
　　Treasurer: Juanito Valdez
Estimated Sales: $500,000-$1 Million
Number Employees: 10-19
Sq. footage: 4500
Type of Packaging: Consumer

14937 Valenie Packers
PO Box 255
Colinton, AB T0G 0R0
Canada　　780-675-5881
　　Fax: 780-675-5581
Processor of pork including sausage, cured hams and bacon, packers
　　President: Joe Erbach
Number Employees: 5-9
Type of Packaging: Consumer, Food Service

14938 Valentine Enterprises
940 Collins Hill Rd
Lawrenceville, GA 30043-4409　　770-995-0661
　　Fax: 770-995-0725　info@valentine.com
　　www.veiusa.com
Processor and exporter of powdered products including diet meal replacements, protein, fiber, sport fitness products, lecithin granules, etc.; contract filler of fiber composite cans, plastic bottles and packets
　　President: Donald McDaniel
　　CEO: Don Mc Daniel
Estimated Sales: $25000000
Number Employees: 20-49
Sq. footage: 50000

14939 Valentine Sugars
129 Valentine Dr
Lockport, LA 70374-3969　　985-532-2541
　　Fax: 985-532-6806 www.valentinechemicals.com
Processor of sugar
　　President: Hugh Caffery
Estimated Sales: $500,000-$1 Million
Number Employees: 20-49
Type of Packaging: Consumer
Brands:
　　Valentine Sugars

14940 Valhrona
1801 Avenue of the Stars
Suite 600
Los Angeles, CA 90067-5908　　310-277-0401
　　Fax: 310-277-7304　bjduclos@pacbell.net
　　www.valhrona.com
Candy and baking chocolate
　　President: Bernard Duclos
　　Founder: Monsieur Guironnet
Estimated Sales: $300,000-500,000
Number Employees: 1-4
Type of Packaging: Private Label
Brands:
　　Valrhona

14941 Valley Bakery
1438 Main St
Rock Valley, IA 51247-1224　　712-476-5386
Processor of cookies, breads, rolls and pastries
　　Owner: Ted Triezenberg
Estimated Sales: $150000
Number Employees: 20-49
Type of Packaging: Consumer

14942 Valley Dairy Fairview Dairy
3200 Graham Avenue
Windber, PA 15963-2599　　814-467-5537
　　Fax: 814-467-5538
Processor and wholesaler/distributor of ice cream; serving the food service market
　　President: Joseph Greubel
　　Vice President: Melissa Blystone
　　Marketing Director: Virgina Greubel
　　Plant Manager: Ray Sneets
Number Employees: 20
Sq. footage: 12000
Parent Co: Fairview Dairy
Type of Packaging: Consumer, Food Service
Brands:
　　ICE CREAM JOE
　　VALLEY DAIRY

14943 Valley Fig Growers
2028 S Third St
Fresno, CA 93702-4156   559-237-3893
     Fax: 559-237-3898   lcain@valleyfig.com
     www.valleyfig.com
Manufacturer and exporter of figs including whole, diced, extruded, powder and paste; also, fig juice and juice concentrate
     President: Michael Emigh
     VP Finance/Secretary/Treasurer: James Gargiulo
     VP Industrial Sales: Gary Jue
Estimated Sales: $19.5 Million
Number Employees: 100-249
Sq. footage: 150000
Type of Packaging: Consumer, Food Service, Private Label, Bulk
Brands:
     BLUE RIBBON
     ORCHARD CHOICE
     SUN-MAID

14944 Valley Fruit & Vegetable
312 Toronto Avenue
Apt 44
McAllen, TX 78503-2951   956-686-8056
     sales@valleyfruit.com
     www.valleyfruit.com
Processor and exporter of Texas-grown citrus fruits including grapefruits and oranges; importer of limes and melons; also, cold storage available
     President: Dan Seitz Jr
     Office Manager: Billy Davis
Estimated Sales: Below $ 5 Million
Number Employees: 5
Sq. footage: 200000
Type of Packaging: Consumer, Food Service, Private Label
Brands:
     Better 'n Ever
     Gold Mine
     Grand Prize

14945 Valley Grain Products
23865 Avenue 18
Madera, CA 93638-9644   559-675-3400
     Fax: 559-675-0723
Processor of corn flour, tortilla chips and taco shells
     Manager: Barry Runyon
Number Employees: 50-99

14946 Valley Institutional Foods Company
36080 N Expressway 281
Edinburg, TX 78541-5112   956-687-6211
     Fax: 956-687-8845
Processor of meat; wholesaler/distributor of meat and frozen food; serving the food service market
     President: Luis Flores III
Estimated Sales: $ 50 - 100 Million
Number Employees: 10-19
Type of Packaging: Food Service

14947 Valley Lahvosh Baking Company
502 M St
Fresno, CA 93721-3013   559-485-2700
     Fax: 559-485-0173   800-480-2704
     customerservice@valleylahvosh.com
     www.valleylahvosh.com
Processor of Valley Lahvosh, America's premier brand of crackerbreads, and Valley Wraps, flatbreads for wraps. Also manufacture a line of natural crackerbread under the Stone Street Bakery brand name
     President: Janet Saghatelian
     Vice President: Agnes Saghatelian
     Marketing Coordinator: Jenni Bonsignore
     Sales Director: Chip Muse
     Operations Manager: Danny Olosa
     Production Manager: Brian Sperling
Estimated Sales: $3877239
Number Employees: 50-99
Number of Brands: 2
Number of Products: 33
Sq. footage: 40000
Type of Packaging: Consumer, Food Service
Brands:
     CALLEY LAHVOSH
     HEARTS
     LAHVOSH
     ROUND LAHVOSH
     SOFT SQUARE
     STONE STREET
     VALLEY BAKERY

     VALLEY LAHVOSH CRACKERBREAD
     VALLEY LAHVOSH FLATBREAD
     VALLEY WRAPS

14948 Valley Maid Ice Cream
1115 Molitor Road
Aurora, IL 60505-1117   630-851-2241
Processor of ice cream products including sherbet, novelties, sandwiches, drum sticks and dixie cups
     President: F James Steinwart
Number Employees: 5-9
Type of Packaging: Consumer

14949 Valley Meat Company
217 Daly Ave
Modesto, CA 95354-3901   209-544-8950
     Fax: 209-522-5892   800-222-6328
     sales@valleymeat.com   www.valleymeat.com
Manufacturer of hamburger patties and ground beef
     President/CEO: Russell Heffner
Estimated Sales: $10 Million
Number Employees: 20-49
Type of Packaging: Consumer, Food Service, Bulk

14950 Valley Milk Products
412 E King Street
Strasburg, VA 22657-2433   540-465-5113
     Fax: 540-645-4042
Milk and specialty dried food ingredients
     President: Don Utz
     CFO: Jeff Mank
Estimated Sales: $ 10-24.9 Million
Number Employees: 35

14951 Valley Packing Company
50 Albany Avenue
Hartford, CT 06120-2899   860-522-3805
     Fax: 860-247-8601
Processor and wholesaler/distributor of meats
     Owner: Micheal Pane
Number Employees: 3
Type of Packaging: Bulk

14952 Valley Packing Company
55324 National Road
Lansing, OH 43934   740-635-0154
Processor of fresh and frozen meat including beef, pork, lamb and veal
     President: Kermit Kull
Estimated Sales: $810000
Number Employees: 5
Type of Packaging: Consumer, Food Service, Bulk

14953 Valley Pie Company
739 E Dunlap Avenue
Phoenix, AZ 85020-2917   602-943-4512
Manufacturer of pies
     President: George Pabst Sr
     Sales Manager: Pete Pabst
Estimated Sales: $10-20 Million
Number Employees: 13
Type of Packaging: Consumer

14954 Valley Pride Pack
P.O. Box 227
Norwalk, WI 54648-0227   608-823-7445
     Fax: 608-823-7862
Packer of beef; slaughtering services available
     President: Rick Stewart
     Sales Manager: Chuck Hartzell
     Sales: Lee Campisi
Estimated Sales: $100+ Million
Number Employees: 50-99
Brands:
     Valley Pride Pack

14955 Valley Queen Cheese Factory
200 E Railway Ave
Milbank, SD 57252-1813   605-432-4563
     Fax: 605-432-9383   cheese@vqcheese.com
     www.vqcheese.com
Processor of whey and cheese
     CEO: Mark Leddy
     Co-CEO: Dave Gonzenbach
     Vice President: Max Gozenbach
     Quality Control: Jody Kuper
     Plant Engineer: Dave Gozenbach
     Operations Manager: Lance Johnson
Estimated Sales: $ 10 - 20 Million
Number Employees: 100-249
Type of Packaging: Consumer
Brands:
     Valley Queen

14956 Valley Research
3502 N Olive Rd
South Bend, IN 46628-8407   574-232-5000
     Fax: 574-232-2468   800-522-8110
     sales@valleyenzymes.com
     www.valleyenzymes.com
Processor and exporter of standard and custom blended enzymes for starch hydrolysis, fruit juice processing, baking, meat tenderizing, nutritional supplements and waste treatment.
     President: Arthur Sears
     Executive VP: Michael Gorbitz
     Quality Controll: Johnna Klute
Estimated Sales: $ 20 - 50 Million
Number Employees: 20-49
Type of Packaging: Bulk
Brands:
     Bio Tab
     Crystalzyme
     Flavareze
     Validase
     Valley AP

14957 Valley Rich Dairy
RR 2
Box 354a
Clarksburg, WV 26301-9641   304-472-7899
     Fax: 304-472-2009
Manufacturer of dairy products
     President: Donnie Underwood
     VP: Rick Meier
Estimated Sales: $5-10 Million
Number Employees: 7
Type of Packaging: Consumer

14958 Valley Sun Products of California
3324 Orestimba Rd
Newman, CA 95360-9628   209-862-1200
     Fax: 209-862-1100   888-786-3743
     ranaya@valleysun.com   www.valleysun.com
Sun-dried tomatoes, plain and in oil
     CEO: Robert Benech
     VP: Chuck Perry
Estimated Sales: $100+ Million
Number Employees: 250-499
Type of Packaging: Consumer, Food Service, Private Label, Bulk

14959 Valley Tea & Coffee
1101 W Valley Blvd # 103
Alhambra, CA 91803-2470   626-281-5799
     Fax: 626-281-5799
Tea and coffee
     Manager: Ted Lee
     CEO: Ted Lin
Estimated Sales: Under $300,000
Number Employees: 1-4
Type of Packaging: Food Service

14960 Valley Tomato Products
P.O. Box 31390
Stockton, CA 95213-1390   209-982-4586
     Fax: 209-982-5280   www.campbellsoup.com
Processor of canned tomato paste
     CEO: Douglas Conant
     CEO: Douglas Conant
     CFO: Robert Schiffner
     Vice President: Mark Sarvary
     VP: Mark Sarvary
     Plant Manager: Brian Dunning
Number Employees: 100-249
Brands:
     Campbell's
     Pace
     Pepperidge
     Prego
     Swanson

14961 Valley View Blueberries
21717 NE 68th St
Vancouver, WA 98682-9060   360-892-2839
     valley.view@comcast.net
Processor of dried blueberries and strawberries, jams, syrups, glazes, honeys, trail mixes, pancake and corn bread mixes and chocolate covered blueberries; also, no-sugar products available
     President: Vicki Duchesneau
Estimated Sales: $86,000
Number Employees: 1-4
Sq. footage: 4000
Type of Packaging: Consumer, Food Service, Private Label, Bulk

Brands:
Valley View Blueberries

14962 Valley View Cheese Company
6028 Route 62
Conewango Vly, NY 14726-9730   716-296-5821
                            Fax: 716-296-5822
Cheese
President: Rick Binder
Marketing Manager: Linda Bates
Plant Manager: Linda Bates
Estimated Sales: $500,000-$1 Million
Number Employees: 20-49
Brands:
Valley View Cheese

14963 Valley View Packing Company
P.O.Box 5699
San Jose, CA 95150-5699   408-289-8300
    Fax: 408-289-8897 www.valleyviewpacking.com
Manufacturer and exporter of dried fruits and fruit
juices and concentrates
President: Sal Rubino
Estimated Sales: $17 Million
Number Employees: 5-9
Type of Packaging: Consumer, Food Service, Private Label, Bulk

14964 Valley View Winery
1000 Upper Applegate Rd
Jacksonville, OR 97530-9175   541-899-8468
    Fax: 541-899-8468 800-781-9463
    valleyviewwinery@charter.net
    www.valleyviewwinery.com
Wines
Owner: Ann Wisnovsky
CFO: Mark Wisnovsky
Vice President: Michael Wisnovsky
Estimated Sales: $380,000
Number Employees: 5-9
Type of Packaging: Private Label
Brands:
Anna Maria
Valley View

14965 Valley of Mexico
PO Box 62
Norwalk, CT 06853-0062   203-348-0402
    Fax: 203-323-9926
Processor and wholesaler/distributor of Mexican
food products including salsas, black bean dip and
tortilla chips; serving the consumer and food service
markets; importer of bottled water
President: Stephen Bowling
Number Employees: 1-4
Sq. footage: 10000
Type of Packaging: Consumer, Food Service, Private Label
Brands:
Valley of Mexico

14966 Valley of the Moon Winery
P.O.Box 1951
Glen Ellen, CA 95442-1951   707-996-6941
    Fax: 707-996-5809
    luna@valleyofthemoonwinery.com
    www.valleyofthemoonwinery.com
Wines
Manager: Randy Meyer
Marketing Manager: Paul Young
President: Harold Duncan
Production Manager: Pat Henderson
Estimated Sales: $ 10-20 Million
Number Employees: 20-49
Brands:
Valley of the Moon

14967 Valley of the Rogue Dairy
PO Box 1327
Grants Pass, OR 97528-0319   541-476-2020
    Fax: 541-476-4014
Manufacturer of milk
President: Palmer Zottola
Estimated Sales: $16 Million
Number Employees: 13
Type of Packaging: Consumer, Food Service, Private Label, Bulk

14968 Vallos Baking Company
1800 Broadway
Bethlehem, PA 18015-3802   610-866-1012
    Fax: 610-866-1012

Bread, donuts and rolls
Owner: Tina Hanushack
Co-Owner: Gus Skoutelas
Estimated Sales: $ 10-20 Million
Number Employees: 10-19
Type of Packaging: Consumer, Food Service

14969 (HQ)Van Bennett Food Company
101 N Carroll St
Reading, PA 19611-1697   610-374-8348
    Fax: 610-374-6714 800-423-8897
    sales@vanbennett.com   www.vanbennett.com
Processor of potato salad, rice pudding and tapioca;
wholesaler/distributor of meats, frozen food, general
line items and specialty foods, produce and
dairyitems; serving the food service market
President: P B Emmett
CEO: J R Marcinko
Estimated Sales: $ 20 - 50 Million
Number Employees: 20-49
Sq. footage: 18000
Brands:
Betty's

14970 Van De Kamp Frozen Foods
PO Box 10367
Erie, PA 16514-0367   814-898-1500
    Fax: 814-898-4186 www.pinnaclefoodscorp.com
Processor of frozen battered and breaded fish fillets
and sticks
Marketing Director: Eric Grosgogeat
Plant Manager: Howard Tuefel
Estimated Sales: $100+ Million
Number Employees: 250-499
Sq. footage: 120000
Parent Co: Pinnacle Foods
Type of Packaging: Consumer
Brands:
VAN DE KAMP

14971 Van De Walle Farms
5310 W Old Us Highway 90
San Antonio, TX 78227-2243   210-436-5551
    Fax: 210-436-6766
    www.sanantoniofarmsonline.com
Processor of Mexican fajita marinade, pico de gallo,
salsa, enchilada and picante sauce and peppers including jalapeno, serrano and chile
Manager: Michael Knuth
VP: Elaine Thompson
Sales/Marketing Director: Don Johnson
Estimated Sales: $ 20 - 50 Million
Number Employees: 50-99
Sq. footage: 45000
Type of Packaging: Consumer, Food Service, Bulk
Brands:
Van De Walle Farms

14972 Van Der Heyden Vineyards
4057 Silverado Trl
Napa, CA 94558-1113   707-257-0130
    Fax: 707-257-3311 800-948-9463
    talig@vanderheydenvineyards.com
    www.vanderheydenvineyards.com
Wine
Manager: Andrea Vander Heyede
Estimated Sales: $1-2.5 Million
Number Employees: 1-4
Type of Packaging: Private Label
Brands:
Van Der Heyden

14973 Van Drunen Farms
300 W 6th St
Momence, IL 60954-1136   815-472-3100
    Fax: 815-472-3850 idorn@vandrunen.com
    www.vandrunenfarms.com
Food ingredient manufacturer
President: Edward Van Drunen
CFO: Deb Drunen
R&D: Jeff Van Drunen
Sales: Irv Dorn
Operations: Rick Ouwenga
Purchasing: Mike Cialdella
Estimated Sales: $80,000,000
Number Employees: 250-499
Number of Brands: 4
Number of Products: 1100
Sq. footage: 120000
Type of Packaging: Consumer, Food Service, Private Label, Bulk
Brands:
Van Drunen Farms

14974 Van Dyke Ice Cream
145 Ackerman Ave
Ridgewood, NJ 07450-4205   201-444-1429
Ice cream, frozen desserts and novelties
Owner: Demetrios Kotrokas
Estimated Sales: $ 2.5-5 Million
Number Employees: 10-19

14975 Van Dykes Chesapeake Seafood
P.O.Box 221
Cambridge, MD 21613-0221   410-228-9000
    Fax: 410-228-5957
Seafood
Owner: Eleanor Van Dyke
Estimated Sales: $ 1 - 3 Million
Number Employees: 5-9

14976 Van Ekris & Company
61 Broadway
New York, NY 10006-2701   212-898-9600
    Fax: 212-514-9234 info@vanekris.com
                    www.vanekris.com
General grocery
Owner: Anthonie Van Ekris
Sr. VP: John Proctor
VP: Marie Barbato
Estimated Sales: $ 10 - 20 Million
Number Employees: 20-49

14977 Van Leer Chocolate Corporation
1301 Sinatra Dr
Hoboken, NJ 07030-5632   201-798-8080
    Fax: 201-798-0138 800-826-2462
    custsrvc@vanleerchocolate.com
            www.shipyardmarina.com
Chocolate
Manager: Scott Applegate
CFO: Anthony Forns
Operations Manager: Robert Mohn
Plant Manager: Tom Jones
Purchasing Manager: Tom Thoelen
Estimated Sales: $ 25-49.9 Million
Number Employees: 100-249

14978 Van Oriental Foods
4828 Reading Street
Dallas, TX 75247-6705   214-630-0333
    info_vanfoods@yahoo.com
            www.vaneggrolls.com
Processor of frozen foods including regular and
low-fat egg rolls, fried wontons, crab rangoon, enchiladas, burritos and spring rolls
Owner: Kimberly Durnan
Co-Owner: Gretchen Perrenot
Corporate Treasurer: Theresa Motter
Sales Manager: Carl Motter
Plant Engineer: Apollo Nguyen
Type of Packaging: Consumer, Food Service, Private Label, Bulk

14979 Van Otis Chocolates
341 Elm St
Manchester, NH 03101-2708   603-627-1611
    Fax: 603-627-0781 800-826-6847
    feedback@vanotis.com   www.vanotis.com
Chocolates
Owner: Dave Quin
Co-Owner: Frank Bettencourt
Estimated Sales: Less than $500,000
Number Employees: 1-4
Sq. footage: 20000
Type of Packaging: Private Label
Brands:
Foiled Chocolate
Swiss Fudge Sampler Tier
Van Otis Swiss Fudge

14980 Van Peenans Dairy
978 Valley Rd
Wayne, NJ 07470-2997   973-694-2551
    Fax: 973-696-3854
Dairy
Owner: Tunis Van Peenan
Estimated Sales: $ 5-10 Million
Number Employees: 20-49

14981 Van Roy Coffee
4569 Spring Rd
Cleveland, OH 44131-1023   216-749-7069
    Fax: 216-749-7039 877-826-7669
    awatterson@cheslergroup.com
            www.vanroycoffee.com

Processor of roasted coffee and tea; also, spices
President/CEO: Jeffrey Miller
Vice President: John Schanz III
Estimated Sales: $1,400,000
Number Employees: 10-19
Sq. footage: 38000
Type of Packaging: Food Service, Private Label, Bulk
Brands:
DE-KAFFO
VAN ROY

14982 Van Tone Creative Flavors Inc
200 Metro Dr
Terrell, TX 75160-9169   972-563-2600
          Fax: 972-563-2640 800-856-0802
                    david-hinds@airmail.net
Processor of food, ice cream, bakers, dairy and beverage flavoring concentrates, food colors, slush concentrates and syrups including sno-cone, FCB, granita, smoothie, fruit drink and fountain
Owner: Joe Gibbs
VP Marketing: Steve Myrlin
VP Sales: Joe Gibbs
Estimated Sales: $3494044
Number Employees: 20-49
Sq. footage: 36000
Type of Packaging: Food Service, Private Label, Bulk
Brands:
Allez
Cyclone
Van Tone

14983 Van Waters & Roger
PO Box 446
Summit, IL 60501-0446   708-728-6830
          Fax: 708-728-6801 jim.lacey@vwr-inc.com
                    www.vopakusa.com
Distributor of chemicals and food ingredients
President: Terry Irvine
President: James Lacey
Chief Marketing Department: Mark Buntin
Head Sales Department: Mike Clary
Number Employees: 250-499
Brands:
Van Waters & Roger

14984 Van de Kamp's
225 W Vine Street
Chambersburg, PA 17201-1164   570-263-4127
          Fax: 570-263-8975
Processor and exporter of pies, fish and vegetables
Plant Manager: James Frey
Number Employees: 100-249
Parent Co: Van de Kamps
Type of Packaging: Consumer, Food Service, Private Label

14985 Van's International Foods
20318 Gramercy Place
Torrance, CA 90501-1511   310-320-9559
          Fax: 310-320-8805
customerservice@vansintl.com
                    www.vansintl.com
Processor of round, square, toaster, mini and jumbo frozen waffles including original, whole grain, wheat-free, organic and gluten-free
President: James Kelly
Sales Director: Kim Fernandez
Operations Manager: Frank Copenhaver
Estimated Sales: $4600000
Number Employees: 40
Sq. footage: 10000
Type of Packaging: Private Label
Brands:
VAN'S

14986 Van-Lang Foods
88 Eisenhower Lane N
Lombard, IL 60148-5414   630-268-1953
          Fax: 630-268-1954 info@vanlangfoods.com
                    www.vanlangfoods.com
Processor of frozen hors d'oeuvres and appetizers
President: Hien Lam
Estimated Sales: Below $ 5 Million
Number Employees: 15
Type of Packaging: Food Service
Brands:
Van-Lang

14987 (HQ)Vance's Foods
PO Box 627
Gilmer, TX 75644   800-497-4834
          Fax: 800-497-4329 800-497-4834
                    www.vancesfoods.com
Processor and exporter of nondairy and fat-free potato-based milk substitutes including dry and liquid, and dry soy-based milk substitutes
President: Vance Abersold
VP: Glenn Abersold
Director Marketing: Frederick Mattos
Type of Packaging: Consumer, Food Service, Bulk
Brands:
NotMilk
Sno-E Tofu
Vance's Darifree

14988 Vanco Products Company
1 Mt Vernon St
Dorchester, MA 02125-1604   617-265-3400
Processor of bakery supplies
President: Chris Anton
Production Manager: Carl Hogenda
Estimated Sales: $ 5 - 10 Million
Number Employees: 10-19
Sq. footage: 15000
Parent Co: Johnson's Food Products Corporation
Type of Packaging: Consumer

14989 Vanco Products Company
2916 Delafield Street
Houston, TX 77023-5890   713-921-0234
          Fax: 713-921-7862 800-231-9564
                    vancospices.com
Packer and distributor of garlic, spices and peanuts
President: Owen Nelson
Manager Inside Sales: Robert Arriaga
Production Manager: Owen Nelson
Estimated Sales: $710000
Number Employees: 7
Type of Packaging: Consumer, Food Service, Private Label, Bulk

14990 Vancouver Island Brewing Company
2330 Government Street
Victoria, BC V8T 5G5
Canada   250-361-0007
     Fax: 250-360-0336 info@vanislanbrewery.com
                    www.vanislandbrewery.com
Brewer of lager and ale
President: Barry Fisher
CFO: Hugh Mitchell
Marketing/Sales Manager: Jennifer Little
Brewmaster: Ralf Pitroff
Number Employees: 20-49
Sq. footage: 28000
Parent Co: Island Pacific Brewing Company
Type of Packaging: Consumer
Brands:
BLONDE ALE
HERMANN'S DARK LAGER
HERMANNATOR ICE BOCK
PIPER'S PALE ALE
VANCOUVER ISLANDER LAGER
VICTORIA LAGER
WOLF'S SCOTTISH CREAM ALE

14991 Vande Walle's Candies
400 N Mall Dr
Appleton, WI 54913-8569   920-738-7799
          Fax: 920-738-3280
Processor of candy including boxed, fund raising, Easter, Valentine, bars, brittles, caramels, chocolates, toffee, fudge, caramel corn and popcorn specialties. Baked goods-pound cakes, plum pudding cakes and cookies
President: Jay Vande Walle
Estimated Sales: $ 5-10 Million
Number Employees: 20-49
Sq. footage: 40000

14992 Vanee Foods Company
5418 McDermott Dr
Berkeley, IL 60163-1299   708-449-7300
          Fax: 708-449-2558 jackridge@vaneefoods.com
                    www.vaneefoods.com
Manufacturer of gravies and canned entrees; custom formulation and co-packing also available
President: Aloysius Van Eekeren
VP: Ron Vanee
Plant Manager: Fred Hansen
Estimated Sales: $17000000
Number Employees: 100-249

Type of Packaging: Food Service

14993 Vanlab Corporation
86 White Street
Rochester, NY 14608-1435   585-232-6647
          Fax: 585-232-6168 bmarchetti@vanlab.com
Flavoring supplies, flavors
President: David A Patton
VP: Diane Merritt
General Manager: William Marchetti
R & D: Florent Montagne
VP: Jim Abraham
Marketing/Sales: Kim Kubach
Operations/Production: Jim Abraham
Plant Manager: Hank Rankowsky
Estimated Sales: $ 10-20 Million
Number Employees: 30-50
Sq. footage: 35000
Type of Packaging: Food Service, Private Label, Bulk

14994 (HQ)Vanlaw Food Products
P.O.Box 2388
Fullerton, CA 92837-0388   714-870-9091
                    Fax: 714-870-5609
Processor and exporter of refrigerated and shelf stable salad dressings, pancake syrup, syrup concentrates, flavorings, extracts, colorings, ice cream toppings and barbecue and teriyaki sauces; importer of romano and parmesan cheeseolive oil and balsamic vinegar
President: Matthew Jones
VP: Michael Bilyk
Director of Sales: John Gilbert
Estimated Sales: $ .5 - 1 million
Number Employees: 1-4
Sq. footage: 130000
Type of Packaging: Consumer, Food Service, Private Label
Brands:
California Classics
Sunfruit
Zito

14995 Vanns Spices
6105 Oakleaf Ave
Baltimore, MD 21215-3316   410-358-3007
          Fax: 410-358-1780 800-583-1693
sales@vannsspices.com www.vannsspices.com
Spices and seasonings
President: Ann Wilder
Executive VP: Erhan Kurany
Estimated Sales: $ 5-10 Million
Number Employees: 20-49
Type of Packaging: Private Label, Bulk

14996 Vantage USA
4740 S Whipple St
Chicago, IL 60632-2024   773-247-1086
          Fax: 708-401-1565 www.VantageUSA.net
Organic/natural & commodity wholesaler consolidator/supplier and logistics provider. Specializing in natural and private label products planning & development.
Owner: Dan Gash
Type of Packaging: Food Service, Private Label, Bulk
Brands:
APPLEGATE FARMS
CARGILL
COLAVITA
CUCINA VIVA
EBERLY
EXCALIBUR
EXCEL
GOTHAM
GREAT PLAINS
HONEYSUCKLE
NORBEST
PRAIRIE GROVE
REICHERT
ROMA
SMART CHOICE
TASTE IT
TURANO

14997 Varco Brothers
1832 N Burling Street
Chicago, IL 60614-5104   312-642-4740
Noodles, spaghetti and macaroni
President: John Varco
Estimated Sales: $ 1-2.5 Million
Number Employees: 1-5

14998 Varda Chocolatier
41 S Spring St
Elizabeth, NJ 07201-2608   908-354-9090
          Fax: 908-354-9091   800-448-2732
          vardachoco@aol.com
          www.vardachocolatier.com
Processor of chocolate confectionery products including truffles, dessert cups, novelties and creative chocolate presentation
     Owner: Varda Shandan
     Director Sales: Liz Lopez
Estimated Sales:$5500000
Number Employees: 50-99

14999 Varet Street Market
99 Varet St
Brooklyn, NY 11206-4016   718-387-5452
          Fax: 718-302-0560
Tropical fruit
     President: Alfonzo Estevez
     CEO: Lely Estevez
*Estimated Sales:*Less than $400,000
Number Employees: 1-4
Type of Packaging: Food Service, Bulk
Brands:
     Reyes Mares

15000 Varied Industries Corporation
905 S Carolina Ave
Mason City, IA 50401-5813   641-423-1460
          Fax: 641-423-0832   800-654-5617
          vi-cor@vi-cor.com   www.vi-cor.com
Manufacturer and exporter of lactic acid fermentation and yucca extracts for food, feed and litter products
     President: Mark Holt
     Vice President International Business: Gerry Keller
     Director Marketing: Jodi Ames
     Plant Manager: Brad Davis
Estimated Sales:$ 10 - 20 Million
Number Employees: 10-19
Sq. footage: 15000
Parent Co: International Whey Technics
Brands:
     Desert Gold Dry
     Kulactic
     Kulsar

15001 Variety Foods
7001 Chicago Rd
Warren, MI 48092-1615   586-268-4900
          Fax: 586-268-6627 www.champenes.com
Processor of baked cheese curls and jumbos, fried cheese twists, popcorn, tortilla chips, baking and salted nuts, trail mixes, candies and Easter and gift baskets
     President: James Champane
     VP Internal Operations: George Champane
Estimated Sales:$ 20 - 50 Million
Number Employees: 50-99
Type of Packaging: Consumer, Food Service, Private Label, Bulk
Brands:
     Cha Cha's
     Champane's
     Cheese-A-Roos
     Munch-A-Roos
     Old Favorite
     Pic-A-Nut
     Sun Ray
     Zappers

15002 Varni Brothers/7-Up Bottling
400 Hosmer Ave
Modesto, CA 95351-3920   209-521-1777
          Fax: 209-521-5922   water@noahs7up.com
          www.noahs7up.com
Processor and exporter of soft drinks, purified water, etc
     President: John Varni
     CEO: Fred Varni
Estimated Sales:$37000000
Number Employees: 50-99
Sq. footage: 120000
Parent Co: Dr. Pepper/7-UP Bottling Companies
Type of Packaging: Food Service, Private Label

15003 Vassilaros & Son
2905 120th St
Flushing, NY 11354-2505   718-886-4140
          Fax: 718-463-5037   info@vassilaroscoffee.com
          www.vassilaroscoffee.com

Coffee, tea and cocoa.
     President: John Vassilaros
Estimated Sales:$ 5-10 Million
Number Employees: 20-49

15004 Vatore's Italian Caramel
PO Box 2861
Salisbury, MD 21802-2861   410-341-3177
          Fax: 410-341-4674   877-828-6737
          vatores@aol.com   www.vatores.com
Candy
     Owner: Tim Beyer
     VP: Janet Beyer
Estimated Sales:$500,000-$1 Million
Number Employees: 1-4
Brands:
     Vatore's

15005 Vaughn Rue Produce
1217 Peachtree Rd NW
Wilson, NC 27896-2058   252-237-6710
          Fax: 252-237-7662   800-388-8138
Processor of sweet potatoes, butternut squash and pickles
     President: Vaughn Rue
*Estimated Sales:*Below $ 5 Million
Number Employees: 1-4
Brands:
     Rue's Choice
     Steakhouse

15006 Vaughn-Russell Candy Kitchen
1624 Augusta St
Greenville, SC 29605-2924   864-271-7786
     Fax: 704-484-8326   vaughnrussell@bellsouth.net
          www.vaughnrussell.com
Candy
     Owner: Betty Hartman
     Plant Manager: Helen Gibson
*Estimated Sales:*Less than $500,000
Number Employees: 5-9
Brands:
     Vaughn Russell

15007 Vauxhall Foods
PO Box 430
Vauxhall, AB T0K 2K0
Canada   403-654-2771
          Fax: 403-654-2211   info@potatopower.com
          www.potatopower.com
Processor and exporter of dehydrated potato granules
     President: Frank Gatto
     CFO: Frank Inaba
     Research & Development: Gordon Packer
     General Manager: Ken Tamura
     Production Manager: Ken Franz
Number Employees: 50-99
Sq. footage: 50000
Type of Packaging: Food Service, Private Label, Bulk
Brands:
     CHIPPER
     GOURMET
     V.G. BLUE

15008 Vaxa International
600 N West Shore Blvd # 800
Tampa, FL 33609-1197   813-870-2904
          Fax: 888-734-4154   800-248-8292
          Customerservice@vaxa.com   www.vaxa.com
Processor of dietetic chocolate and vanilla powdered shake mixes
     President: Bill Harper
     VP: Chris Behan
Estimated Sales:$ 1 - 3 Million
Number Employees: 20-49
Parent Co: Direct Access Network
Type of Packaging: Consumer, Private Label, Bulk
Brands:
     Vaxa

15009 Vega Food Industries
80 Stamp Farm Rd
Cranston, RI 02921-3400   401-942-0620
          Fax: 401-942-5760   800-973-7737
          www.vegafoods.com
Processor of gourmet stuffed and sliced cherry peppers, olives, peppers and packed salads in oil and garlic
     Owner: Dennis Tofaro
     VP: Anthony Cippola
     Operations Manager: Frank Bisignano
     Plant Manager: Carrie Zamborano

Estimated Sales:$1900000
Number Employees: 10-19
Sq. footage: 5000
Type of Packaging: Consumer, Food Service, Private Label, Bulk
Brands:
     Vega's Gourmet

15010 (HQ)Vege-Cool
2100 Orestimba Road
Newman, CA 95360-9788   209-862-2360
Processor of lima beans and peas
     Owner: William Cerutti
     Manager: Steve Lewis
Estimated Sales:$400,000
Number Employees: 3
Type of Packaging: Bulk

15011 Vegetable Juices
7400 S Narragansett Ave
Chicago, IL 60638-6022   708-924-9500
          Fax: 708-924-9510   888-776-9752
          contactus@vegetablejuices.com
          www.vegetablejuices.com
Known for turning fresh ingredients into innovative solutions, our juices, purees and diced vegetables have been our specialty for over 70 years. These products provide fresh natural flavors, textures and color to many different flavorsystems. And our Innovation Center is available for creative collaboration, sound advice and technical expertise.
     CEO: James Hurley
     CFO: Michael Brunson
     Sr VP Sales/Marketing: Barry Horne
     R&D: Anthony Popielarz
     Quality Control: Paul Bollinger
     Operations: Mike O'Hara
Estimated Sales:$10-20 Million
Number Employees: 100-249
Type of Packaging: Food Service, Bulk

15012 VeggieLand
222 New Rd # 2a
Parsippany, NJ 07054-5626   973-808-1540
          Fax: 973-882-3030   888-808-5540
          russgrabow@aol.com   www.veggieland.com
Processor and exporter of vegetarian foods including burgers, meat balls, frankfurters, sausage, sandwiches and chili
     Manager: Len Torine
     Executive VP: Len Torine
*Estimated Sales:*Below $ 5 Million
Number Employees: 20-49
Sq. footage: 16000
Brands:
     Veg-T-Balls
     Veggieland

15013 Vegi-Deli
17 Paul Drive
San Rafael, CA 94903-2043   415-526-1450
          Fax: 415-526-1453   888-473-3667
          info@vegideli.com   www.vegideli.com
Vegetarian meat alternative deli products including pepperoni, cold cuts and pizza toppings and vegi-jerky, pepperoni snack sticks.
     General Manager: Debra Ventura
Estimated Sales:$ 3-5 Million
Number Employees: 8
Sq. footage: 6000
Type of Packaging: Consumer, Food Service, Private Label
Brands:
     Quick Stix
     Vegetarian Slice of Life

15014 (HQ)Velda Farms
402 S Kentucky Ave # 500
Lakeland, FL 33801-5337   863-686-4441
          Fax: 863-686-7792   800-279-4166
          www.veldafarms.com
Dairy products
     President: Glen Herrington
     Marketing Director: Robin Chaddick
     CFO: Tim Long
Number Employees: 500-999
Parent Co: Suiza Dairy Group
Brands:
     Velda Farms

15015 Velda Farms
501 NE 181st St
North Miami Bch, FL 33162-1067   305-525-8228
Fax: 305-651-2766   800-795-4649
www.veldafarms.com
Processor of juice and dairy products including milk,
cream and ice cream
President: James Dintaman
VP/CFO: Niell Larsen
General Sales Manager: Bill Aaronson
Estimated Sales: $ 50 - 100 Million
Number Employees: 250-499
Parent Co: Suiza Dairy Group
Type of Packaging: Consumer, Food Service, Private Label, Bulk
Brands:
Sunnydell
Velda

15016 Velda Farms
402 S Kentucky Ave # 500
Lakeland, FL 33801-5337   863-686-4441
Fax: 863-686-7792   800-279-4166
customerserviceteam@veldafarms.com
www.veldafarms.com
Processor of juices and dairy products including ice
cream
President: Glen Herrington
VP Manufacturing: Norm Rasmussen
Branch Manager: Frank Mondello
Plant Manager: Vince Porter
Purchasing Manager: Vince Vitale
Estimated Sales: $$5-10 Million appx.
Number Employees: 500-999
Parent Co: Suiza Dairy Group
Type of Packaging: Consumer
Brands:
Barricini
Bassetts
Sunnydell

15017 Velda Farms
1000 6th St SW
Winter Haven, FL 33880-3334   863-298-9742
Fax: 863-294-3851   800-279-4166
www.veldafarms.com
Processor of dairy products
Executive Director: Glen Harrington
Marketing Director: Frank Mardello
Sr. Financial Officer: Jerry Harper
Plant Manager: Terry Witt
Estimated Sales: $ 20 - 50 Million
Number Employees: 100-249
Parent Co: Suiza Dairy Group
Type of Packaging: Consumer
Brands:
Velda Farms

15018 Vella Cheese
P.O.Box 191
Sonoma, CA 95476-0191   707-938-3232
Fax: 707-938-4307   800-848-0505
vella@vellacheese.com   www.vellacheese.com
Processor of cheese including Monterey jack,
asiago, cheddar, dry jack and Italian-style table
President: Sarah Vella
Estimated Sales: $2,000,000
Number Employees: 10-19
Sq. footage: 10740
Type of Packaging: Consumer
Brands:
Asiago
Bear Flag
Dry Sack
High Moisture Fresh Jack
Mezzo
Seasoned Cheddar Cheese
Seasoned Jack Cheese
Sello
Vella

15019 Velvet Creme Popcorn Company
4710 Belinder Rd
Westwood, KS 66205-1883   913-236-7742
Fax: 913-236-9631   888-553-6708
customerservice@velvetcremepopcorn.com
www.velvetcremepopcorn.com
Processor of popcorn
President: Jerry Wright
Estimated Sales: $1 Million-1.5
Number Employees: 5-9
Sq. footage: 30000
Type of Packaging: Consumer

15020 Velvet Freeze Ice Cream
7355 W Florissant Ave
St Louis, MO 63136-1348   314-381-2384
Fax: 314-381-2384   800-589-5000
info@velveticecream.com
www.velveticecream.com
Ice cream, yogurt and sherbet
Owner: John Mc Guinness
Founder: Joe Dager
Executive VP: Matt Mueller
Estimated Sales: Below $ 5 Million
Number Employees: 5-9
Brands:
Velvet

15021 Velvet Ice Cream Company
P.O.Box 588
Utica, OH 43080-0588   740-892-3921
Fax: 740-892-4339   800-589-5000
info@velveticecream.com
www.velveticecream.com
Processor of ice cream and frozen desserts.
President: Joseph Dager
VP: Michael Dager
Sales Manager: Luconda Dager
Estimated Sales: $ 50 - 100 Million
Number Employees: 100-249
Type of Packaging: Consumer

15022 Velvet Milk
309 Sutton Lane
Owensboro, KY 42301-0370   270-683-4561
Fax: 270-683-4562
Milk
Estimated Sales: $ 5-10 Million
Number Employees: 5-9

15023 Venice Maid Foods
PO Box 1505
Vineland, NJ 08362-1505   856-691-2100
Fax: 856-696-1295   800-257-7070
sales@venicemaid.com   www.venicemaid.com
Manufacturer of canned pasta, sauces, gravies, and
meat entrees
President: John Kelly
VP of Finance: Rick Kebler
VP: Darrel Wunderlich
R & D: Rich Gibbs
Quality Control: Cecelia Monkata
Marketing/Sales: Donna George
Operations: Ed Leibrand
Production: Debbie Volk
Plant Manager: Dave Bernier
Purchase Executive: Terry Hannah
Estimated Sales: $ 5-10 Million
Number Employees: 20-49
Type of Packaging: Private Label

15024 Venice Spumoni/Spring Valley Ice Cream
1216 S Carlisle St
Philadelphia, PA 19146-3121   215-467-0311
Fax: 215-467-1668   800-784-0312
veniceice1@aol.com
Processor of Italian ices and ice cream including all
natural and kosher and distributor of Good Humor-Breyers novelties
CEO: Arlene Klein Weir
Operations: Jon R Swezey
Number Employees: 20-49
Sq. footage: 20000
Type of Packaging: Consumer, Food Service, Private Label, Bulk
Brands:
Jazzy Juice
Spumoni
Venice

15025 Venison America
494 County Road a # B
Hudson, WI 54016-4510   715-386-6628
Fax: 715-386-6613
venisonamerica@sbcglobal.net
www.venisonamerica.com
Marketer and processor of fresh and frozen farm
raised game meat from alligator to yak; gourmet
items, corporate gift boxes, etc.
President/Owner: Steve Loppnow
VP: Kent Phillips

Estimated Sales: $ 5-10 Million
Number Employees: 1-4
Sq. footage: 2000
Type of Packaging: Consumer, Food Service

15026 Ventana Vineyards Winery
2999 Salinas Hwy # 10
Monterey, CA 93940-5706   831-372-7415
Fax: 831-655-1855   800-237-8846
info@ventanawines.com
www.ventanawines.com
Wines
Owner: Randy Pura
VP/Marketing Director: LuAnn Meador
Bookkeeper: Christy Florez
Vineyard Foreman: David Rodriguez
Production Manager: Reggie Hammond
Winemaker: Miguel Martinez
National Sales Manager: Terry Lannon
California Sales Manager: Sarah Robinson
Sales/Marketing: Gerre Calderon
Tasing Room Manager: Rosemary
Hermans-Walls
Estimated Sales: $ 1 - 3 Million
Number Employees: 10-19
Type of Packaging: Private Label
Brands:
Ventana Wines

15027 Ventre Packing Company
6050 Court Street Rd
Syracuse, NY 13206-1711   315-463-2384
Fax: 315-463-5897   enrico@enrics-ventre.com
www.ventre.com
Manufacturer and exporter of low sodium, organic
and fat-free sauces including meat, mushroom, marinara, barbecue, etc.; also, dips including cheese,
pinto, black bean and salsa; importer of tomatoes;
contract packager of nonorganictomato products and
salsas
Chairman: John Ventre Jr
Persident/CEO: Martin Ventre
EVP: Jacqueline Papai
Estimated Sales: $10-20 Million
Number Employees: 10-19
Sq. footage: 100000
Type of Packaging: Consumer, Food Service, Private Label
Brands:
ENRICO
ENRICO MEXICAN
ENRICO'S
GIANNI
LA CASA
MCDEI
MEDEI

15028 Ventura Coastal Corporation
2325 Vista Del Mar Dr
Ventura, CA 93001-3700   805-653-7000
Fax: 805-653-7777
Manufacturer and exporter of citrus concentrates
and single strength juices; contract packager of
frozen pectin products
President: William Borgens
Estimated Sales: $44 Million
Number Employees: 100-249
Type of Packaging: Consumer, Food Service, Private Label, Bulk

15029 Ventura Foods
650 W Sedgley Ave
Philadelphia, PA 19140-5528   215-223-8700
Fax: 215-225-4204   www.venturafoods.com
Manufacturer of mayonnaise, salad dressings, sauces
and syrups for private label and food service.
Manager: Melissa Castle
Estimated Sales: $100 Million
Number Employees: 7
Parent Co: Ventura Foods LLC
Type of Packaging: Food Service, Private Label
Other Locations:
ventura Foods Foodservice/Retail
Portland OR
Ventura Foods
Salem Foodservice OR
Ventura Foods Retail/Export
Los Angeles CA
Ventura Foods Foodservice/Export
City of Industry CA
Ventura Foods Foodservice
Albert Lea MN
Ventura Foods Foodservice
Waukesha WI
Ventura Foods Foodservice

St Joseph MO
Ventura Foods Foodservice
Chambersburg PA
Ventura Foods SE Distribution Ctr
Bingmingham AL
Ventura Foods Retail/Foodservice
Opelousas LA
Ventura Foods Foodservice
Dallas, Ft Worth TX
Brands:
   CHEF SUPREME
   CHEF'S PRIDE
   GOURMAY
   HIDDEN VALLEY POURABLE DRESSINGS

15030 Ventura FoodsProduction Plant
633 South Mission Road
Los Angeles, CA 90023-1010   323-265-4300
                        www.venturafoods.com
Manufactures margarines under the Saffola and
Gold-N-Sweet brands, butter blends, as well as pri-
vate lables in these product catergories.
Number Employees: 14899
Parent Co: Ventura Foods LLC
Type of Packaging: Consumer, Food Service, Pri-
   vate Label, Bulk
Other Locations:
   Ventura Foods Plant
   Portland OR
   Ventura Foods Plant
   Salem OR
   Ventura Foods Plant
   Albert Lea MN
   Ventura Foods Plant
   Ontario CA
   Ventura Foods Plant
   St Joseph MO
   Ventura Foods Plant
   Ft Worth TX
   Ventura Foods Plant
   Waukesha WI
   Ventura Foods Plant
   Thornton IL
   Ventura Foods Plant
   Chambersburg PA
   Ventura Foods Plant
   Opelousas LA
   Ventura Foods Plant
   Brimingham AL
   Custom Pack & Export
   City Of Industry CA
Brands:
   CHEF'S PRIDE
   CINEMA GOLD
   CITATION
   CLASSIC GOURMET
   COCO POP BARS
   DEAN'S
   GOLD-N-SOFT
   GOLDEN TOP
   GRANDIOSO
   HIDDEN VALLEY
   LOUANA
   MARIE'S
   MOR GOLD
   PERFECTO PEANUT POPPING OIL
   PHASE
   POP-ALL
   POPPIN' TOPPIN'
   SALAD BISTRO
   SMART BALANCE
   SUNBURST
   SUNGLOW
   VENTURA
   VO-POP
   WHITE CAP

15031 Ventura Foods
715 N Railroad Ave
Opelousas, LA 70570-4335   337-948-6561
   Fax: 337-942-6239 mbates@venturafoods.com
                        www.louana.com
Ventura's oil refining facility produces Lou Ana
brand retail/foodservice oils and concession prod-
ucts. It also supplies private label oil to customers.
   CEO/General Manager: Bill Minor
   VP: Richard Biggs
   Plant Manager: Bill Hausman
Estimated Sales: $1 Billion
Number Employees: 183
Parent Co: Ventura Foods LLC
Type of Packaging: Consumer, Food Service, Pri-
   vate Label, Bulk
Brands:
   Coco-Pop
   Lou Ana

Mermaid
Mor Gold Plus
Perfecto
Pop 'n Lite
Triumph

15032 Ventura Foods
2900 Jurupa St
Ontario, CA 91761-2915   714-257-3700
                        www.venturafoods.com
Produces extensive line of branded and private label
products, inlcuding: syrups, mayonnaise, salad
dressings, oils, shortenings, and sauces. It also pro-
vides contract packaging services for a variety of
products sold to retail andfoodservice customers.
   General Manager: Wayne Kess
   Manager: Wayne Kess
Estimated Sales: $1 Billion
Number Employees: 80
Parent Co: Ventura Foods LLC
Type of Packaging: Consumer, Food Service, Pri-
   vate Label, Bulk
Brands:
   GOLD-N-SWEET
   SAFFOLA
   TABLE MAID

15033 Ventura FoodsFoodservice/Export/Custom Pack
14970 Don Julian Rd
City of Industry, CA 91746-3111   626-961-8911
   Fax: 626-336-3229 800-327-3906
                        www.venturafoods.com
Produces and extensive line of branded and private
label products including: shortenings; oils; marga-
rine; salad dressings; mayonnaise; sauces and syr-
ups. Also contract packaging and export site.
   Plant Manager: John Collie
Estimated Sales: $1 Billion
Number Employees: 300
Parent Co: Ventura Foods LLC
Type of Packaging: Consumer, Food Service, Pri-
   vate Label
Brands:
   Gold N Sweet
   LouAna
   Saffola

15034 Ventura Foods
1100 Defiel Road
Ft Worth, TX 76179-5601   817-232-5450
   Fax: 817-232-4230 www.venturafoods.com
Shortenings, oils, margarines, salad dressings, may-
onnaise, and sauces.
   President: Vinced Vincent
   Plant Manager: Tim Davis
Estimated Sales: $1 Billion
Number Employees: 89
Parent Co: Ventura Foods LLC
Type of Packaging: Food Service, Private Label
Brands:
   Extend
   Savory

15035 Ventura FoodsFoodservice
3371 Portland Rd NE
Salem, OR 97301-8415   503-585-6423
   Fax: 503-585-1286 www.venturafoods.com
Produces a full line of branded and private label
products for the foodservice market, including mar-
garine, oils, and shortening.
   President/COO: Richard Mazer
   CFO: Craig Moore
   Senior VP: Peter DeBartolomeo
   VP Western Sales: Jim Dunn
Estimated Sales: $1 Billion
Number Employees: 70
Sq. footage: 100000
Parent Co: Ventura Foods LLC
Type of Packaging: Food Service, Private Label
Brands:
   Chef's Pride
   Gold-N-Sweet

15036 Ventura FoodsFoodservice/Retail/Export
9000 Ne Marx Drive
Portland, OR 97220-1339   503-255-5512
   Fax: 503-253-6357 www.venturafoods.com

Manufactures a variety of branded and private label
products for foodservice and retail customers, in-
cluding margarine, mayonnaise, salad dressings and
sauces.
   Manager: Allen Taylor
   President/COO: Richard Mazer
   VP Western Sales: Jim Dunn
   Plant Manager: Martin Sutliffe
Estimated Sales: $ 20-50 Million
Number Employees: 50-99
Parent Co: Ventura Foods LLC
Type of Packaging: Consumer, Food Service

15037 (HQ)Ventura FoodsHeadquarters
Brea, CA   714-257-3700
   Fax: 714-257-3702 877-836-8872
                        www.venturafoods.com
Manufactures margarines under the Saffola and
Gold-N-Sweet brands, butter blends, as well as pri-
vate lables in these product catergories.
   CEO: Richard Mazer
   CFO: Craig Moore
   SVP, Corporate Business Development: B Kelly
   Brintle
Estimated Sales: $364 Million
Number Employees: 2,099
Parent Co: CHS & Mitsui Co - Joint Venture
Type of Packaging: Consumer, Food Service, Pri-
   vate Label, Bulk

15038 Venture Vineyards
PO Box 185
Lodi, NY 14860-0185   607-582-6774
                              888-635-6277
venturev@capital.net   www.vineyards4sale.com
Grower of asparagus, raspberries and grapes includ-
ing concord, Niagara, Catawaba, and Delaware.
Also a processor of grape juice and importer and ex-
porter of concord grapes
   President: Melvin Nass
   VP: Phyllis Nass
   Operations Manager: Andrew Nass
Number Employees: 5-9
Sq. footage: 10000
Brands:
   Venture For the Best

15039 Venus Wafers
70 Research Rd
Hingham, MA 02043-4341   781-740-1002
   Fax: 781-749-7195 800-545-4538
saf@venuswafers.com   www.venuswafers.com
Processor and exporter of crackers including
fat-free, toasted onion, garden vegetable, garlic and
herb, multigrain, cracked pepper and gourmet:
toasted wheat and garden vegetable; also, stoned
wheat and multigrain available in giftbaskets.
   CFO: Edward Barmakian
Estimated Sales: $ 5 - 10 Million
Number Employees: 20-49
Type of Packaging: Consumer
Brands:
   Deli-Catessen
   Old Brussels
   Venus Wafers

15040 Veramar Vineyard
905 Quarry Rd
Berryville, VA 22611-4222   540-955-5510
   Fax: 540-955-0404 info@veramar.com
                        www.veramar.com
Wines
   Co-Owner: James Bogaty
   Co-Owner: Della Bogaty
Number Employees: 5-9

15041 Verdelli Farms
7505 Grayson Rd
Harrisburg, PA 17111-5146   717-561-2900
   Fax: 717-561-2941 800-422-8344
                        www.verdelli.com
Processor of fresh fruits and vegetables
   CFO: Dan Verdelli
   President: Albert Verdelli
   CFO: Ron Miller
   VP: Daniel Verdelli
   President: Albert Verdelli
   Marketing Head: Joanne Verdelli
Estimated Sales: $100+ Million
Number Employees: 500-999
Sq. footage: 13500
Type of Packaging: Consumer, Food Service, Bulk

15042 Verhoff Alfalfa Mills
2404 N Summit St
Toledo, OH 43611-3508 419-726-2655
Fax: 419-726-6629 800-834-8563
verhoffalfalfa@bright.net
www.alfagreensupreme.com
Processor of dehydrated alfalfa
Manager: Ken Vaupel
VP/General Manager: Donald Verhoff
CEO/General Manager: Ken Vaupel
Corporate Controller: Cortney Schaefer
Logistics Coordinator/Customer Service: Andrea Grant
Quality Control/Operations: Michael Wood
Estimated Sales: $2274776
Number Employees: 5-9
Type of Packaging: Bulk

15043 Veritas Chocolatier
1816 Johns Drive
Glenview, IL 60025 847-729-8787
Fax: 847-729-8879 800-555-8331
info@veritaschocolatier.com
www.veritaschocolatier.com
chocolate truffles

15044 Veritas Vineyards & Winery
145 Saddleback Farm
Afton, VA 22920-2324 540-456-8000
Fax: 540-456-8483 contact@veritaswines.com
www.veritaswines.com
Wines
Owner: Andrew Hodson
Estimated Sales: $ 3 - 5 Million
Number Employees: 5-9

15045 Vermilion Packers
4825-47 Avenue
Vermilion, AB T9X 1J4
Canada 780-853-4622
Fax: 780-853-4623
vermillionpacker@hotmail.com
Processor of fresh and cured meats including sausage
President: Rick Bozak
Estimated Sales: Below $ 5 Million
Number Employees: 14
Type of Packaging: Consumer, Food Service
Brands:
Vermilion

15046 Vermints
PO Box 196
Saxtons River, VT 05154-0196 802-869-2233
Fax: 802-869-1100 jon@vermints.com
www.vermints.com
Manufacturer of all natural breath mints
Estimated Sales: $300,000-500,000
Number Employees: 1-4
Parent Co: Ohare Enterprises

15047 Vermont BS
373 Hayden Hill Road W
Hinesburg, VT 05461-9533 802-482-2152
Fax: 802-482-2152 bpmjec@aol.com
Butterscotch sauce

15048 Vermont Bread Company
P.O.Box 1217
Brattleboro, VT 05302-1217 802-254-4600
Fax: 802-257-0165 dianep@vermontel.com
Manufacturer of baked goods including organic whole grain and French sourdough breads, baguettes and rolls. Charterhouse Group acquired the company
President: Hy Lerner
Human Resources: Susan Bitelli
Estimated Sales: $10 Million
Number Employees: 50-99
Parent Co: Charterhouse Group
Type of Packaging: Consumer

15049 Vermont Bread Company
P.O.Box 1217
Brattleboro, VT 05302-1217 802-254-4600
Fax: 802-257-0165 dianep@vermontel.com
Processor of all-natural, organic and premium bread
President: Lisa Lorimer
Human Resources: Susan Bitelli
Plant Manager: Susan Vitelly
Estimated Sales: $10 Million
Number Employees: 50-99
Sq. footage: 22000

Type of Packaging: Consumer, Food Service, Private Label
Brands:
Vermont
Windham Hearth

15050 Vermont Butter & CheeseCompany
40 Pitman Rd
PO Box 95
Websterville, NY 05678 802-479-9371
Fax: 802-479-3674
info@vtbutterandcheeseco.com
www.vtbutterandcheeseco.com
cow's milk cheeses, goat's milk cheeses and signature aged artisanal cheeses
President/Owner: Bob Reese
Estimated Sales: $6.6 Million
Number Employees: 28

15051 Vermont Chocolatiers
9 East St
Northfield, VT 05663-6719 802-485-5181
Fax: 802-485-5191 877-485-4226
info@cermontchocolatiers.com
www.vermontproductsmall.com
Chocolate and shortbread
Co-Owner: Walter Delia
Co-Owner: Jane Delia
Estimated Sales: $300,000-500,000
Number Employees: 1-4

15052 Vermont Confectionery
P.O.Box 380
Shaftsbury, VT 05262-0380 802-447-2610
Fax: 802-447-2610 800-545-9243
vtcandy@sover.net www.vermontcandy.com
Chocolate
Owner: George Mc Cain
Estimated Sales: $ 3 - 5 Million
Number Employees: 5-9

15053 Vermont Country Naturals
PO Box 238
Charlotte, VT 05445-0238 802-425-5445
Fax: 802-425-5444 800-528-7021
vcn5@yahoo.com
Processor of kosher, wildcrafted maple sugar (powder and granules) and maple syrup
President: Joan Savoy
CEO: Jeffrey Madison
Estimated Sales: $300,000-500,000
Number Employees: 3
Sq. footage: 3500
Parent Co: Vermont Country Maple Mixes
Brands:
MAPLE SPRINKLES

15054 Vermont Country Store
PO Box 1108
Manchester Center, VT 05255-1108 802-362-8460
Fax: 802-362-8288
customerservice@vermontcountrystore.com
www.vermontcountrystore.com
Authentic New England foods; cheeses, maple syrups, etc
President: Bill Sholice
Marketing Director: Cyndy Marshall
CFO: Penny Jhonson
Estimated Sales: $ 20-50 Million
Number Employees: 100-249
Type of Packaging: Private Label, Bulk
Brands:
Vermont Country Store

15055 Vermont Family Farms Milk
140 Federal Street
Saint Albans, VT 05478-2015 802-524-6581
Fax: 802-527-1769 800-559-0343
stalbanscooperative@stalbanscooperative.com
Whole, 2%, 1%, and skim milk
Estimated Sales: $100+ Million
Number Employees: 50-99

15056 Vermont Food Experience
PO Box 943
Shelburne, VT 05482-0943 802-985-8101
Fax: 802-885-2040
Gourmet and specialty foods
President: Richard Hurlburt
Estimated Sales: Under $500,000
Number Employees: 1-4

15057 Vermont Harvest Speciality Foods
1733 Mountain Rd
Stowe, VT 05672 802-253-7138
Fax: 802-253-7139 800-338-5354
info@vtharvest.com www.vtharvest.com
Jams, jellies, chutneys and breads
Founder: Patty Foltz
Estimated Sales: $ 1 - 3 Million
Number Employees: 1-4

15058 Vermont Liberty Tea Company
1 Derby Ln # 1
Waterbury, VT 05676-8926 802-244-6102
Fax: 802-244-6102 jmvt@pshift.com
www.vermontlibertytea.com
Herbal, green and black tea
Owner: John McConnell
Estimated Sales: $ .5 - 1 million
Number Employees: 1-4

15059 Vermont Natural Company
RR 112
Jacksonville, VT 05342 802-368-2231
Fax: 802-368-7556
Gourmet and specialty foods
Principal: Robert Moses
Estimated Sales: $300,000-500,000
Number Employees: 12
Sq. footage: 17
Type of Packaging: Private Label

15060 Vermont Nut Free Chocolates
10 Island Cir
Grand Isle, VT 05458-4408 802-372-4654
Fax: 802-372-4654 888-468-8373
vtnutfree@aol.com www.vermontnutfree.com
Nut free chocolates
Owner: Gail Elvidge
Estimated Sales: $ 1 - 3 Million
Number Employees: 10-19

15061 Vermont Pepper Works
PO Box 282
Fairfax, VT 05454-0282 802-888-5311
Fax: 802-888-1711
sales@vermontpepperworks.com
www.vermontpepperworks.com
Manufacturer of pepper sauces
Co-Owner: Jeff Mitchell
Co-Owner: Julie Mitchell

15062 Vermont Pretzel
PO Box 524
Bellows Falls, VT 05101-0524 802-869-2837
Fax: 802-869-2837 888-671-4774
pretzels@sover.net www.vermontpretzel.com
Stuffed and soft pretzels, cookies and bars
President: Christine Holtz

15063 Vermont Specialty Food Association
Freedom Foods
24 Pleasant Street
Randolph, VT 05060 802-728-0070
Fax: 802-728-0071 www.freedom-foods.com
fruit infused maple syrups, vermont gift baskets, vermont mustards, vermont granola & mixes

15064 Vermont Sprout House
25 Mountain View Street
Bristol, VT 05443-1312 802-453-3098
Fax: 802-453-2132
Sprouts, soups and side dishes
President: Susan Tomasi
Sales Manager: Blaine Sprout
General Manager: Joe MacWilliams
Estimated Sales: $ 5-10 Million
Number Employees: 10-19
Brands:
Vermont Sprout

15065 Vermont Sweetwater Bottling Company
1075 Vermont Route 30 N
Poultney, VT 05764-9633 802-287-9897
Fax: 802-287-9230 800-974-9877
york@sover.net www.vtsweetwater.com
Soda
Co-Owner: Robert Munch
Co-Owner: Richard Munch
Estimated Sales: $ 3 - 5 Million
Number Employees: 5-9

15066 Vermont Tea & Trading Company
P.O.Box 1050
Middlebury, VT 05753-5050   802-388-4005
        Fax: 802-388-4005   tea@together.net
Loose leaf teas
    Co-Owner: Curron Malhotra
    Co-Owner: Bruce Malhotra
Estimated Sales: $ 1 - 3 Million
Number Employees: 1-4

15067 Vern's Cheese
312 W Main St
Chilton, WI 53014-1312   920-849-7717
    Fax: 920-849-7883   info@vernscheese.com
                www.vernscheese.com
Cheese
    President: Vern Knoespel
Estimated Sales: $ 20-50 Million
Number Employees: 20-49

15068 Veronica Foods Company
1991 Dennison St
Oakland, CA 94606-5225   510-535-6833
        Fax: 510-532-2837 800-370-5554
    mandvbrad@attbi.com www.evoliveoil.com
Olive oil manufacturers and importers
    President: Michael Bradley
    CEO: Mike Bradley
    CFO: Leah Bradley
    VP: Veronica Bradley
    Marketing: Arnie Kaufman
    VP Retail Sales: Arnie Kaufman
    Operations: Fred Johnson
    Production: Myron Manown
    Plant Manager: Dave Fitzgerald
    Purchasing: Fred Johnson
Estimated Sales: $16200000
Number Employees: 20-49
Sq. footage: 228000
Brands:
    Dainty Pak
    Delizia
    Italia
    Panther
    Purn Life

15069 Very Best Foods
PO Box 521894
Miami, FL 33152-1894   305-824-9165
                Fax: 305-824-9156
Processor and exporter of frozen foods and plantain,
cassava, taro and banana chips
    President: Isidoro Rodriguez
Estimated Sales: Under $500,000
Number Employees: 5-9
Brands:
    Chicharritas
    Costa Rica Yuca
    Malanguitas
    Old San Juan
    Pepitos

15070 Veryfine Products
P.O.Box 8005
Littleton, MA 01460-8005   978-486-3522
        Fax: 978-952-6245 800-837-9346
    donna.sitkiewicz@kraft.com www.veryfine.com
Fruit juice drinks
    President/CEO: Roger Deromedi
    Purchasing Manager: Sam Bowden
Estimated Sales: $ 150 Million
Number Employees: 1-4
Sq. footage: 350000
Parent Co: Kraft Foods
Brands:
    Balsams Baby Water
    Balsams Springwater
    Fruit2O
    Juice-Ups
    Veryfine Apple Quenchers
    Veryfine Chillers Tea & Lemonade
    Veryfine Juices

15071 Vessey & Company
P.O.Box 28
Holtville, CA 92250-0028   760-352-6376
    Fax: 760-352-7645   kevinolson@redshift.com
                www.vessey.com

Grower of cabbage including red, green, bok choy
and napa; also, red and yellow onions, red and yukon potatoes, sweet corn, cantaloupes and garlic including fresh, whole, peeled, minced and chopped;
importer and exporter of garlic
    President: Jon Vessey
    Sales Manager: David Grimes
    Sales: Eric Pompa
Estimated Sales: $3100000
Number Employees: 10-19
Type of Packaging: Food Service, Bulk

15072 Vetter Vineyards Winery
8005 Prospect Station Rd
Westfield, NY 14787-9630   716-326-3100
    Fax: 716-326-3100   wine@cecomet.net
                www.vettervineyards.com
Wines
    Co-Owner: Mark Lancaster
    Co-Owner: Barbara Lancaster
Estimated Sales: $300,000-500,000
Number Employees: 1-4
Type of Packaging: Private Label
Brands:
    Vetter Vineyards

15073 Vi-Gor Cup Corporation
2740 Grand Avenue
Bellmore, NY 11710-3556   516-431-7722
                Fax: 516-997-4471
Processor and exporter of health foods including salt
substitutes, soup ingredients, vegetable powders and
condiments
    President: William Cantor
    Sales Director: Bernard Cuttler
Estimated Sales: $ 1 - 3 Million
Number Employees: 5-9
Parent Co: Henesco Corporation
Type of Packaging: Consumer, Food Service, Pri-
vate Label, Bulk

15074 Via Della Chiesa Vineyards
413 Church Street
Raynham, MA 02767-1008   508-822-7775
                Fax: 508-880-0500
        www.capecodcranberrywine.com
Wines
    President: Robert DiCroce
    CFO: Sharon Tweedy
    Marketing Manager: Kate Desmond
    Public Relations Officer: Lidm Piwa
    Winery Manager: Dolly Tulsiani
    Production Manager: Matyas Vogel
Estimated Sales: Below $ 5 Million
Number Employees: 10
Type of Packaging: Private Label
Brands:
    Cranberry Blush Wine
    Dry-Atlantic Coastal
    Raspberry Rave Wine

15075 Viader Vineyards & Winery
1120 Deer Park Rd
Deer Park, CA 94576-9715   707-963-3816
    Fax: 707-963-3817   info@viader.com
                www.viader.com
Vineyards and Winery
    Owner/Winemaker: Delia Viader
    Executive Assistant: Valaree Martinez
    Shipping Manager: Blanca Avina
    Sales/Marketing Director: Janet Viader
    Vineyard Manager/Winemaker: Alan Viader
    Winemaker: Delia Viader
Number Employees: 10
Type of Packaging: Consumer, Food Service, Pri-
vate Label
Brands:
    Viader

15076 Viamar Foods
27 Carpenter St
Glen Cove, NY 11542-2398   516-759-0652
                Fax: 516-759-5752
Processor of pasta
    President: Victor Ghini
    CFO: Robert Ghini
Estimated Sales: $120,000
Number Employees: 1-4
Type of Packaging: Food Service, Private Label,
Bulk
Brands:
    Papagallo

15077 Viano Winery
150 Morello Ave
Martinez, CA 94553-3598   925-228-6465
    Fax: 925-228-5670   info@vianovineyards.com
                www.vianovineyards.com
Wines
    Partner: Clement Viano
    President: Paula Viano
Estimated Sales: Less than $400,000
Number Employees: 1-4
Brands:
    Viano Winery

15078 Viansa Winery
25200 Arnold Dr
Sonoma, CA 95476-9222   707-935-4700
        Fax: 707-935-5654 800-995-4740
    tuscan@viansa.com www.viansa.com
Wines
    President: John Bryan
    CEO: Vicki Sebastiani
    CFO: Russ Jay
    Co. Founder: Sam Sebastiani
    Winemaker: Michael Sebastiani
Estimated Sales: $ 5-10 Million
Number Employees: 50-99
Brands:
    Nebbiolo
    Vernaccia

15079 Viau Foods
6625 Ernest Cormier
Montreal, QC H7C 2V2
Canada   450-665-6100
        Fax: 450-665-7100 800-663-5492
                www.viausila.com
cooked or dry cured pepperoni, italian cooked
meats, sausages, pizza toppings and meatballs.

15080 Vic Rossano Incorporated
2102 Cabot Street
Montreal, QC H4E 1E4
Canada   514-766-5252
                Fax: 514-765-3959
Manufacturer of peanut butter regular and natural al-
mond and cashew butter, tahini, new product=
soypeanut butter
    President: Rosette Rossano
    VP: Deborah Abecassis
Estimated Sales: $$4-10 Million
Number Employees: 15
Sq. footage: 45000
Type of Packaging: Consumer, Private Label, Bulk
Brands:
    Simply Nuts
    Yum Nature

15081 Vic's Gourmet Popping Corn Company
11213 E Cir
Omaha, NE 68137-1243   402-331-2822
    Fax: 402-331-2507 www.barrelofunsnacks.com
Popcorn
    President: Ken Nelson
Brands:
    Vic's

15082 Vichy Springs Mineral Water Corporation
2605 Vichy Springs Rd
Ukiah, CA 95482-3507   707-462-9515
    Fax: 707-462-9516 vichy@vichysprings.com
                www.vichysprings.com
Processor and exporter of naturally carbonated bot-
tled mineral water
    President: Gilbert Ashoff
    VP: Marjorie Ashoff
Estimated Sales: $500,000 appx.
Number Employees: 10-19
Number of Products: 1
Sq. footage: 7000
Type of Packaging: Private Label
Brands:
    Vichy Springs
    Vichy Springs Mineral Water

15083 Vickey's Vittles
16420 Gledhill St
North Hills, CA 91343-2807   818-841-1944
    Fax: 818-841-1191   vickeysvittles@msn.com
                www.vickeysvittles.com

Processor of specialty cookies, bundt cakes, brownies, dessert bars, pies and cobblers; also, gift baskets, fat-fee and low-fat items available
President: Vickey Conover
Estimated Sales:$300,000-500,000
Number Employees: 5-9
Brands:
    Vickey's Vittles

15084 Victor Allen Coffee Company
1401 12th St NW
Albuquerque, NM 87104-2117   505-856-5282
          Fax: 505-856-5588   800-662-2575
                email@avaloncoffee.com
                    www.avaloncoffee.com
Coffee and tea
    Manager: Aaron Simpson
    Marketing Specialist: Kathryn Utterback
    VP Sales: Liz Kollar
    Operations Manager: Andy Wieczorek
Estimated Sales: Below $ 5 Million
Number Employees: 5-9
Type of Packaging: Private Label
Brands:
    Avalon Organic Coffee
    Bosque Tea Co
    High Desert Roasters
    Rio Grande Roasters

15085 Victor Allen's Coffee and Tea
P.O.Box 307
Little Chute, WI 54140-0307   920-788-1252
                    800-394-5282
    lwolters@victorallen.com   www.victorallen.com
Coffee, tea
    Owner: Scott Dercks
Estimated Sales: $ 20-50 Million
Number Employees: 5-9
Type of Packaging: Private Label

15086 Victor Ostrowski & Son
524 S Washington St
Baltimore, MD 21231-3030   410-327-8935
    Fax: 410-252-9372 www.ostrowskisausage.com
Polish garlic bologna, liver sausage, stuffed cabbage and horseradishes
    Owner/President: John Ostrowski
Estimated Sales: $ 1 - 3 Million
Number Employees: 5-9
Type of Packaging: Consumer

15087 Victor Packing Company
11687 Road 27 1/2
Madera, CA 93637-9440   559-673-5908
    Fax: 559-673-4225   victor@victorpacking.com
                www.victorpacking.com
Manufacturer, and exporter of currants and raisins including organic, natural, golden and seedless; also, raisin juice concentrate and raisin paste available
    Owner: Victor Sahadtjain
    VP: Margaret Sahatdjian
Estimated Sales:$20-50 Million
Number Employees: 50-99
Number of Products: 10
Sq. footage: 150000
Type of Packaging: Consumer, Food Service, Private Label, Bulk
Brands:
    LIBERTY BELL
    MADERA
    NATURAL THOMPSON
    VICTOR

15088 Victor Preserving Company
P.O.Box 482
Ontario, NY 14519-0482   315-524-2711
    Fax: 315-524-7040   onedavid@aol.com
Processor of sauerkraut
    President/CEO: David Tobin
Estimated Sales: $ 3 - 5 Million
Number Employees: 10-19
Sq. footage: 45000
Type of Packaging: Private Label

15089 Victoria Fancy Sausage
6508 118th Avenue NW
Edmonton, AB T5W 1G6
Canada
                    780-471-2283
                Fax: 780-477-5381
Processor of fresh beef, pork, chicken and wild game including venison, elk and moose
    President: John Snyder
Number Employees: 5-9
Sq. footage: 3500

Type of Packaging: Bulk
Brands:
    Victoria Fancy

15090 Victoria Gourmet
17 Gill St
Woburn, MA 01801-1720   781-935-2100
          Fax: 781-935-9979   866-972-6879
                info@vgourmet.com   www.vgourmet.com
Blended seasonings
    President: Victoria Taylor
Estimated Sales:$500,000-$1 Million
Number Employees: 1-4

15091 (HQ)Victoria Packing Corporation
443 E 100th St
Brooklyn, NY 11236-2103   718-649-2180
                    Fax: 718-649-7069
    victoria@victoriapacking.com
            www.victoriapackingcorp.org
Manufacturer, importer and exporter of condiments, canned vegetables, edible oils, sauces, condiments, and dips
    President/CEO: Benjamin Aquilina
    VP Finance/CFO: Robert Haberman
    VP Sales: William Paskowski
Estimated Sales:$31.3 Million
Number Employees: 100-249
Number of Brands: 5
Number of Products: 300
Sq. footage: 250000
Type of Packaging: Consumer, Food Service, Private Label, Bulk
Brands:
    VICTORIA

15092 Victoria's Catered Traditions
1240 Eastridge Place
Manteca, CA 95336   209-823-8213
    Fax: 208-823-8213   877-272-5208
        www.victoriascateredtraditions.com
chocolate covered popcorn
    President/Owner: Victoria Costa

15093 Victory Seafood
208 W Elina St
Abbeville, LA 70510-8239   337-893-9029
                    Fax: 337-898-0614
Fresh and frozen crabmeat
    Owner: Kevin E Dartez
Estimated Sales: $ 5 - 10 Million
Number Employees: 20-49

15094 Vidalia Brands
Highway 121
Reidsville, GA 30453   912-654-2726
        Fax: 912-654-9135   800-752-0206
                becky@vidaliabrands.com
                www.vidaliabrands.com
Vidalia sweet onions, gourmet treats, peach salsa, blossom kit, salad dressings, relishes, BBQ sauce, chow-chow
    President/CEO: Sandra Bland
    Marketing Director: Wendy Moore
    Vice President: Sandra Bland
    Public Relations: Susan Lynch
    Plant Manager: Mike Gulbranson
Number Employees: 50-99
Type of Packaging: Private Label
Brands:
    Vidalia

15095 (HQ)Vidalia Sweets Brand
818 Ga Highway 56 W
Lyons, GA 30436-5945   912-565-8881
    Fax: 912-565-0199   vsbrelish@cybersouth.com
                www.vidalialabs.com
Processor of fresh and pickled onions, onion relish, barbecue sauce, etc.; wholesaler/distributor of vidalia onions and specialty food products; serving the food service market
    President: Jim P Cowart
Estimated Sales:$210000
Number Employees: 1-4
Type of Packaging: Consumer, Food Service
Brands:
    Vidalia Sweets

15096 Vie de France Bakery
4507 Mills Pl SW # R
Atlanta, GA 30336-1826   404-696-5486
        Fax: 404-699-1612   800-933-5486
                www.viedefrance.com

Processor of bread and rolls
    Manager: Ken Graham
    Marketing Director: Laura Fezouati
    Sales/Marketing Executive: Scott Kennedy
Estimated Sales:$ 10 - 20 Million
Number Employees: 50-99
Parent Co: Vie de France Yamazaki
Type of Packaging: Consumer, Food Service
Brands:
    Vie De France

15097 Vie de France Bakery
1049 Industrial Dr
Bensenville, IL 60106-1216   630-595-9521
        Fax: 630-595-3686 www.viedefrance.com
Processor of bread; wholesaler/distributor of cakes, cookies, muffins and danish
    President: Sado Yasumura
    Plant Manager: Tom O'Donnell
Estimated Sales:$ 3 - 5 Million
Number Employees: 50-99
Parent Co: Vie de France Yamazaki

15098 Vie de France Bakery
2070 Chain Bridge Rd # 500
Vienna, VA 22182-2588   703-442-9205
        Fax: 703-821-2695   800-446-4404
                www.viedefrance.com
Bakery products
    President: Sadao Yasumura
Estimated Sales: $ 5-9.9 Million
Number Employees: 1,000-4,999

15099 Vie de France Yamazaki
2070 Chain Bridge Rd # 500
Vienna, VA 22182-2588   703-442-9205
        Fax: 703-821-2695   800-446-4404
                www.viedefrance.com
Processor of baked goods including croissants, pastries and danish
    President: Sadao Yasumura
Estimated Sales: $ 3 - 5 Million
Number Employees: 1,000-4,999
Parent Co: Vie de France Yamazaki
Type of Packaging: Bulk

15100 Vie de France Yamazaki
2070 Chain Bridge Rd # 500
Vienna, VA 22182-2588   703-442-9205
        Fax: 703-821-2695   800-393-8926
                www.viedefrance.com
Processor of breads, rolls and pastries
    President: Sadao Yasumura
Estimated Sales:$90000000
Number Employees: 1,000-4,999
Sq. footage: 27000
Parent Co: Vie de France Yamazaki
Type of Packaging: Consumer, Food Service, Private Label, Bulk

15101 Vie de France Yamazaki
3046 E 50th Street
Vernon, LA 71270   323-582-1241
                    Fax: 323-585-7532
Processor of frozen dough and French bakery products
    General Manager: Driss Goulhiane
    Distribution Manager: Doug Cassenelli
    Production Manager: Jerry Gorne
Estimated Sales:$4700000
Number Employees: 70
Sq. footage: 50000
Parent Co: Vie de France Yamazaki
Type of Packaging: Food Service

15102 Vie de France Yamazaki
5060 Nome St
Denver, CO 80239-2726   303-371-6280
        Fax: 303-371-5646 www.viedefrance.com
Processor of French breads, croissants, European cakes and pastries
    General Manager: Mike Digan
Estimated Sales: $ 1 - 3 Million
Number Employees: 20-49
Sq. footage: 13000
Parent Co: Vie de France Yamazaki
Type of Packaging: Consumer, Food Service
Brands:
    Vie De France

15103 Vie-Del Company
11903 S Chestnut Ave
Fresno, CA 93725-9618   559-834-2525
        Fax: 559-834-1348 /www.vinarium-medien.com

Processor and exporter of fruit concentrates including grape; also, wine and brandy
President: Dianne Nury
Vice President: Richard Watson
Customer Service: Janel Cook
Purchasing Manager: Robert Reiter
Estimated Sales:$18800000
Number Employees: 100-249

15104 Vienna Bakery
10032 81st Avenue NW
Edmonton, AB T6E 1W8
Canada   780-436-8211
                          Fax: 780-439-2140
Processor of gourmet bread and pastries
President: Bernie Jager
CEO: Bernie Jager
Marketing Manager: Bernie Jager
Number Employees: 10-19
Type of Packaging: Consumer, Food Service
Brands:
   Vienna

15105 Vienna Beef
2501 N Damen Ave
Chicago, IL 60647-2101   773-278-7800
      Fax: 773-278-4759   info@kingkold.com
                          www.viennabeef.com
Meats
CEO: Dennis Vignieri
VP: Jane Lustig
CEO: James W Bodman
Estimated Sales:$100+ Million
Number Employees: 500-999
Brands:
   Bistro
   Chipico
   King Kold
   Pie Piper
   WonderBar

15106 (HQ)Vienna Beef
2501 N Damen Ave
Chicago, IL 60647-2101   773-278-7800
      Fax: 773-278-4759   800-621-8183
            foodservice@viennabeef.com
                          www.viennabeef.com
Manufacturers and distributors of beef
Chairman: James Bodman
VP Finance: Richard Steele
Estimated Sales:$ 75-100 Million
Number Employees: 500-999
Type of Packaging: Private Label
Brands:
   Bistro
   Chipico
   King Kold
   Pie Piper
   Vienna
   Wunderbar

15107 Vienna Meat Products
170 Nugget Avenue
Scarborough, ON M1S 3A7
Canada   416-297-1062
      Fax: 416-297-0836   800-588-1931
Processor and importer of ham, sausage, cold cuts, turkey products, roast beef, corned beef and pastrami.
President: Michael Latifi
Director Retail Sales: Vince Romano
Number Employees: 50-99
Brands:
   Austrian Crown
   Grand Chef De Paris
   Vienna

15108 (HQ)Vienna Sausage Company
2501 N Damen Ave
Chicago, IL 60647-2199   773-278-7800
      Fax: 773-278-4759   800-326-6652
                          www.viennabeef.com
Processor of pickles; processor and exporter of cured meat, soups, kosher specialties and desserts.
Co-CEO and Co-Chairman: James Bodman
Co-CEO and Co-Chairman: James Eisenberg
CFO: Richard Steele
SVP/Sales & Marketing: Thomas McGlade
VP/Human Resources: Jane Lustig
SVP/Operations: Jack Bodman
VP/Purchasing: Richard Ewert
Estimated Sales:$99,000,000
Number Employees: 250-499

Type of Packaging: Consumer, Food Service, Private Label
Brands:
   BISTRO
   CHIPICO
   KING KOLD
   PIE PIPER
   VIENNA
   WUNDERBAR

15109 (HQ)Vienna Sausage Company
6033 Malburg Way
Vernon, CA 90058-3969   323-583-8951
      Fax: 323-585-7580   800-733-6063
                          www.viennabeef.com
Processor of pickles; processor and exporter of cured meat, soups, kosher specialties and desserts.
Co-CEO and Co-Chairman: James Bodman
Co-CEO and Co-Chairman: James Eisenberg
CFO: Richard Steele
SVP/Sales & Marketing: Thomas McGlade
VP/Human Resources: Jane Lustig
SVP/Operations: Jack Bodman
VP/Purchasing: Richard Ewert
Number Employees: 100-249
Type of Packaging: Consumer, Food Service, Private Label

15110 Vietti Foods Company Inc
P.O.Box 40464
Nashville, TN 37204-0464   615-244-7864
      Fax: 615-242-7055   800-240-7864
            jjacobs@viettifoods.com
                          www.viettifoodsinc.com
Processor and canner of pork and beef with barbecue sauce, chili spaghetti, regular chili and beef stew; also, sauces including hot dog, spaghetti and Creole.
President: Philip Connelly
Chief Financial Officer: Mark Johnson
Director of Technical Services: Dee Folmar
National Sales Manager: Voyne Stepp
Director Operations: Frank Baltz
Purchasing Manager: Trent Baker
Estimated Sales:$ 20 - 50 Million
Number Employees: 20-49
Type of Packaging: Consumer, Food Service, Private Label
Brands:
   SOUTHGATE
   VIETTI

15111 Vigneri Confections
810 Emerson St
Rochester, NY 14613-1804   585-254-6160
      Fax: 585-254-6872 /www.vigneri.com
Processor and importer of European desserts and pastries including panettones, tortes, bignolara, tartufo, cassata, tiramisu, etc; also, chocolate Easter eggs
President: Filippo Vigneri
Office Manager: Lucy Turrisi
Estimated Sales:$ 5 - 10 Million
Number Employees: 5-9
Sq. footage: 8000
Type of Packaging: Consumer, Private Label
Brands:
   Vigneri

15112 Vigo Importing Company
P.O.Box 15584
Tampa, FL 33684-5584   813-884-3491
      Fax: 813-884-7139   info@vigo-alessi.com
                          www.vigoalessi.com
Processor and exporter of seasoned rice dinners, paella and bread crumbs; importer of olives, peppers, sundried tomatoes, olive oil, cheese, pasta, balsamic vinegar, bread sticks, pine nuts, coffee, vegetable pates, porcini mushrooms,artichokes, etc
President: Anthony Alessi Sr
CEO: Sam Ciccarello
Estimated Sales:$ 50 - 100 Million
Number Employees: 100-249
Sq. footage: 280000
Type of Packaging: Consumer, Food Service, Private Label, Bulk

15113 Vigor Cup Corp
630 Shore Road
Apt 704
Long Beach, NY 11561-4669   516-785-6352
                          Fax: 516-997-4471
Dehydrated soups and seasonings
President: William Kantor

*Estimated Sales:*Below $ 5 Million
Number Employees: 6
Brands:
   Vigor Cup

15114 Viking Distillery
1101 E Broad Ave
Albany, GA 31705-2872   229-436-0181
                          Fax: 229-434-1768 www.bartonbrands.com
Manufacturer of bourbon blends, gin and vodka
President: Alexander Burk III
Plant Manager: Julius Drakes
Estimated Sales:$6 Million
Number Employees: 10-19
Parent Co: Barton Brands
Type of Packaging: Consumer

15115 Viking Seafoods Inc
50 Crystal St
Malden, MA 02148-5919   781-322-2000
      Fax: 781-397-0527   800-225-3020
            jcovelluzzi@vikingseafoods.com
                          www.vikingseafoods.com
Processor of frozen seafood including fish cakes, fish and chips, cod, fish flake, halibut, perch, fish sticks, fish patties, scallops and shrimp; also, value-added products including Nordica and bake n'broil style.
President: Charles Gulino
CEO: James Covelluzzi
CEO: James Covelluzzi
Sales Manager: Douglas Farrell
Plant Manager: Joseph Novello
Estimated Sales:$8200000
Number Employees: 50-99
Type of Packaging: Consumer, Food Service
Brands:
   Kitchens of the Sea
   Viking

15116 Viking Trading
2375 John Glenn Drive
Atlanta, GA 30341-1900   770-455-8630
                          Fax: 770-455-9632
Blue crab, caviar, conch, crab, crawfish, kingfish, lobster meat
President: Juan Vales

15117 Villa Helena/Arger-Martucci Winery
1455 Inglewood Ave
St Helena, CA 94574-2219   707-963-4334
      Fax: 707-963-4748 www.arger-martucci.com
Wines
President: Carol Martucci
Marketing Director: Katarena Arger
Estimated Sales:$500,000-$1 Million
Number Employees: 1-4
Type of Packaging: Private Label
Brands:
   Villa Helena

15118 Villa Milan Vineyard
7287 E County Road 50 N
Milan, IN 47031-8946   812-654-3419
            vineyard@seidata.com
                          www.seidata.com/villa-milan
Wines
President: John Garrett
CEO: Marc A McNeece
Estimated Sales:$ 2.5-5 Million
Number Employees: 10-19
Brands:
   Villa Milan

15119 Villa Mt. Eden Winery
8711 Silverado Trl S
St Helena, CA 94574-9577   707-944-2414
                          Fax: 707-963-7840
            jessica.cope@ste-michelle.com
                          www.villamteden.com
Processor and exporter of wines
Manager: Jeff Mc Bride
Estimated Sales:$ 10 - 20 Million
Number Employees: 10-19
Parent Co: Stimson Lane
Type of Packaging: Consumer

15120 Villa Parks Orchards Cooperative
P.O.Box 307
Fillmore, CA 93016-0307   805-524-0411
      Fax: 805-524-4286   888-524-4402
            frank@vpoa.net OR villapark@vpoa.net
                          www.vpoa.net

Packinghouse for the processing of Sunkist Growers Inc. citrus fruit.
President/General Manager: Brad Leichtfuss
Field Mgr/Grower Relations Orange Cty: Mike Leichtfuss
Field Superintendent District 1: Hector Moreno
Field Mgr/Grower Relations District 1: Jim Cleland
Field Mgr/Grower Relations Ventura: Bruce Leichtfuss
Sales & Packing Coordinator: Frank Martinez
Grower Relations/Consultant: Don Clift
Type of Packaging: Food Service

15121 Village Imports
211 S Hill Dr
Brisbane, CA 94005-1255   415-562-1120
   Fax: 415-562-1131   888-865-8714
    info@villageimports.net   www.eiltd.com
French specialty foods and wine, vinegars, condiments, vinagrettes, and sparkling lemonade
Owner: Larry Binstein
Marketing: Thierry Foucaut
Estimated Sales: $ 20 - 50 Million
Number Employees: 20-49
Parent Co: MIF San Francisco
Type of Packaging: Consumer
Brands:
LE VILLAGE

15122 Village Roaster
9255 W Alameda Avenue
Lakewood, CO 80226-2802   303-238-8718
   Fax: 303-233-4370   800-237-3822
    contact@villageroaster.com
     www.villageroaster.com
Coffee
President: Jim Curtis
VP: Kathleen Curtis
CFO: Kathleen Curtis
Estimated Sales: Under $500,000
Number Employees: 1-4
Brands:
Village Roaster

15123 Villar Vintners of Valdese
4950 Villar Ln NE
Valdese, NC 28690-8706   828-879-3202
     Fax: 828-879-3202
Wines
President: Joel Talmas
CEO: Ernest Jahier
Estimated Sales: $ 3 - 5 Million
Number Employees: 5-9
Brands:
Villar Vintners

15124 Vilore Foods Company
8220 San Lorenzo Dr
Laredo, TX 78045-8704   956-726-3633
   Fax: 956-728-8383   info@vilore.com
     www.vilore.com
Wholesaler/distributor of Mexican foods including jalapeno peppers, fruit nectars, hot sauce, chicken bouillon, powdered drinks and nopalitos; exporter of canned Mexican foods and fruit nectars; importer of Mexican salsas, fruitnectars and jalapeno peppers
President: Marco Mena
CEO: Glen Leonard
Marketing Director: Luis Menchero
Operations Manager: Jose Luis Murillo
Estimated Sales: $10400000
Number Employees: 20-49
Sq. footage: 260000
Type of Packaging: Consumer, Food Service, Private Label

15125 Vilotti & Marinelli Baking Company
755 S 11th Street
Philadelphia, PA 19147-2698   215-627-5038
Bread and rolls
President: Daniel Pisanelli
Estimated Sales: Below $ 5 Million
Number Employees: 30

15126 Vina Vista Vineyard & Winery
925 Buckland Ave
San Carlos, CA 94070-1809   707-857-3722
   Fax: 707-857-3602   www.navarrowine.com
Wines
President: Keith Nelson
Estimated Sales: Less than $300,000
Number Employees: 1-4

15127 Vinalhaven Fishermens Co-Op
P.O.Box 366
Camden, ME 04843-0366   207-236-0092
   Fax: 207-236-7733   fewx2@foxislands.net
Seafood
Owner: John R Long
Estimated Sales: $ 1 - 3 Million
Number Employees: 5-9

15128 Vince's Seafoods
1105 Lafayette St
Gretna, LA 70053-6345   504-368-1544
   Fax: 504-368-1545   bjimenez1@cox.net
Processor and exporter of frozen and boiled seafood; shrimp, crabs, oysters, crawfish, catfish, tuna, trout, flounder and tilapia. Also available; gumbo and soups
President: Barbara Jimenez
Estimated Sales: $500,000-$1 Million
Number Employees: 1-4
Sq. footage: 8000

15129 Vincent Arroyo Winery
2361 Greenwood Ave
Calistoga, CA 94515-1031   707-942-9231
     Fax: 707-942-0895
   wine@vincentarroyowinery.com
     www.vincentarroyo.com
Wines
President: Vincent Arroyo
Estimated Sales: Below $ 5 Million
Number Employees: 5-9
Type of Packaging: Bulk

15130 Vincent B. Zaninovich &Son
P.O.Box 1000
Richgrove, CA 93261-1000   661-725-2497
   Fax: 661-725-5153   www.vbzgrapes.com
Processor and exporter of grapes
President: Andrew Zaninovich
Estimated Sales: $11600000
Number Employees: 10-19
Type of Packaging: Bulk
Brands:
Mr Z
Richgrove King
VBZ

15131 Vincent Formusa Company
710 W Grand Ave
Chicago, IL 60654-5574   312-421-0485
   Fax: 312-421-1286   sales@marconi-foods.com
     www.marconi-foods.com
Processor of vinegar and hot sport and serrano peppers; also, oils including salad, soybean, corn, cottonseed, olive and vegetable; importer of olives, olive oil and pasta; exporter of giardiniera
President: Robert Johnson
President: Formusa Johnson
Estimated Sales: $ 5 - 10 Million
Number Employees: 5-9
Sq. footage: 15000
Type of Packaging: Consumer, Food Service, Bulk
Brands:
Digiovanni
Marconi

15132 Vincent Giordano Corporation
2600 Washington Ave
Philadelphia, PA 19146-3834   215-467-6629
   Fax: 215-467-6339   www.vgiordano.com
Italian ices, frozen fruit and juice novelties
President: Guy Giordano
Vice President: Bruce Belack
Sales Director: Mike Bosse
Plant Engineer: Jerry Little
Estimated Sales: $ 50-75 Million
Number Employees: 50-99

15133 Vincent Piazza Jr & Sons
5736 Heebe St
Harahan, LA 70123-5505   504-734-0012
   Fax: 504-734-8752   800-259-5016
    packages@piazzaseafood.com
     www.piazzaseafood.com
Processor of shrimp; wholesaler/distributor of crab, crawfish, alligator, conch, octopus, clams, lobster, frog legs, scallops, turtle, gumbo, etc
Owner: Vincent Piazza Jr
Sales and Inventory Control: Nicholas Piazza
Computer Systems and Purchasing: Bryan Piazza

Estimated Sales: $ 2.5-5 Million
Number Employees: 20-49
Sq. footage: 24000
Type of Packaging: Food Service
Brands:
Lucky Star
Papa Piazza Brand
Papa's Fresh Catch
Tri Dragon

15134 Vincent Potato Chip Company
5 Beacon Heights Lane
Marblehead, MA 01945-1579   978-745-1505
Processor of potato chips
President: Thomas Voyer
Sales Manager: David Dugan
Number Employees: 50-99
Type of Packaging: Consumer

15135 Vincent's Food Corporation
669 Knollwood Dr
West Hempstead, NY 11552-3139   516-481-3544
     Fax: 516-742-4579
Manufacturer of sauces
President: Anthony Marisi
Estimated Sales: $ 5 - 10 Million
Number Employees: 5-9

15136 Vincor International
441 Courtneypark Drive E
Mississauga, ON L5T 2V3
Canada   905-564-6900
   Fax: 905-564-6909   800-265-9463
     www.vincorinternational.com
Wine and vodka cooler importer, marketer and distributor.
President: Donald Triggs
Number Employees: 2000
Type of Packaging: Consumer, Food Service
Brands:
Camarad
Goundry Fine Wine
Hogue
Inniskillin
Jackson-Triggs
Kim Crawford Wines
Kumala
Loiseau Bleu
Pallenque
Toasted Head

15137 Vine Village
4059 Old Sonoma Rd
Napa, CA 94559-9702   707-255-4099
   Fax: 707-255-8431   mikeker@napanet.net
     www.vinevillage.org
Wine
Executive Director: Michael Kerson
Estimated Sales: Below $ 5 Million
Number Employees: 20-49
Type of Packaging: Private Label
Brands:
Carneros Chardonnay

15138 Vineland Ice & Storage
544 E Pear St
Vineland, NJ 08360-3743   856-692-3990
     Fax: 856-692-3992
Warehouse providing frozen storage; manufacturer of ice
Owner: Mark Di Meo
Estimated Sales: $ 1 - 3 Million
Number Employees: 5-9
Type of Packaging: Food Service, Bulk

15139 Vino's
923 W 7th St
Little Rock, AR 72201-4005   501-375-8466
   Fax: 501-375-8468   vinos@vinosbrewpub.com
     www.vinosbrewpub.com
Beer and pizza
President: Henry Lee
CEO: Dan O'Byrne
Estimated Sales: Below $ 5 Million
Number Employees: 20-49
Type of Packaging: Private Label
Brands:
7th Street Pale
Big House Ale
Lazy Boy Stout

15140 Vinoklet Winery & Vineyard
11069 Colerain Ave
Cincinnati, OH 45252-1425   513-385-9309
Fax: 513-385-9379 vinokletwinery@fuse.net
www.vinokletwines.com
Wine manufacturer and restaurant service
Owner/Winemaker: Kreso Mikulic
Estimated Sales: $500,000 appx.
Number Employees: 10-19
Type of Packaging: Food Service
Brands:
Vinoklet

15141 (HQ)Vinquiry
7795 Bell Rd
Windsor, CA 95492-8519   707-838-6312
Fax: 707-838-1765 info@vinquiry.com
www.vinquiry.com
Manufacturer of wine industry yeasts and supplements
Owner/CEO: Marty Bannister
President: John Schilter
Estimated Sales: $ 5 - 10 Million
Number Employees: 20-49
Sq. footage: 10400
Type of Packaging: Private Label, Bulk
Other Locations:
Vinquiry Central Coast Office
Santa Maria CA
Vinquiry Napa Office
Napa CA

15142 Vintage Chocolate Imports
461 Frelinghuysen Ave
Newark, NJ 07114-1426   908-354-9304
Fax: 908-354-9265   800-207-7058
information@echocolates.com
www.echocolates.com
Chocolate
President: Pierrick Chouard
Operations Manager: Bryan Sargent
Estimated Sales: Below $ 5 Million
Number Employees: 5-9
Type of Packaging: Private Label
Brands:
Dagoba Organic Chocolate
Fritz Knipschildt

15143 Vintage Produce Sales
PO Box 977
Kingsburg, CA 93631-0977   559-897-1622
Fax: 559-897-8793
Peaches, nectarines, blueberries, apricots, plums and grapes
Brands:
RIVER ISLAND
RIVER VALLEY FARMS

15144 Viobin USA
226 W Livingston St
Monticello, IL 61856-1673   217-762-2561
Fax: 217-762-2489 info@rex-oil.com
www.viobinusa.com
Processor and exporter of defatted wheat germ and wheat germ oil
Manager: Roger Moore
Quality Control: Carol Wintersteen
Marketing/Sales: Geni Heider
Production: Jerry Sample
Plant Manager: Roger Mohr
Estimated Sales: $ 10 - 20 Million
Number Employees: 20-49
Sq. footage: 100000
Parent Co: McShares
Type of Packaging: Private Label, Bulk
Other Locations:
VioBin Corp.
Salinas KS
Brands:
Rex Oil
Viobin

15145 Viola's Gourmet Goodies
P.O.Box 351075
Los Angeles, CA 90035-9475   323-731-5277
Fax: 323-731-6898 violasgg@pacbell.net
www.violasgourmet.com
Gourmet relish, jelly, zinger and rim shot
Owner: Nancy Rowland
Estimated Sales: $ .5 - 1 million
Number Employees: 1-4
Type of Packaging: Bulk
Brands:
Viola's

15146 Violet Packing
123 Railroad Ave
Williamstown, NJ 08094-1699   856-629-7428
Fax: 856-629-6340 info@donpepino.com
www.donpepino.com
Manufacturer of peppers, tomatoes and sauces including spaghetti and pizza
President/Owner: Rob Ragusa
VP Operations: Chip Sclafani
GM: Lou Sclafani
Estimated Sales: $10-20 Million
Number Employees: 50-99
Parent Co: Don Pepino Company
Type of Packaging: Consumer, Food Service
Brands:
Don Pepino
Sclafani
Violet

15147 Violore Foods Company
8220 San Lorenzo Dr
Laredo, TX 78045-8704   956-726-3633
Fax: 956-728-8383 info@vilore.com
www.vilore.com
Jalapeno peppers
President: Marco Mena
Estimated Sales: $ 2.5-5 Million
Number Employees: 20-49

15148 Virgil's Root Beer
13000 S Spring Street
Los Angeles, CA 90061-1634   800-997-3337
information@virgils.com
www.virgils.com
Processor of root beer
Owner: Chris Reed
Parent Co: Reed's Ginger Brew
Type of Packaging: Consumer, Food Service
Brands:
Virgil's

15149 Virginia & Spanish Peanut Company
260 Dexter St
Providence, RI 02907-2798   401-421-2543
Fax: 401-421-2557   800-673-3562
www.vspnutco.com
Processor of salted nuts, peanuts and peanut butter
President/CFO: Robert Kalocstian
VP/Treasurer: Candale Kaloostain
Estimated Sales: $ 10 - 20 Million
Number Employees: 5-9
Sq. footage: 16000
Type of Packaging: Consumer, Food Service, Private Label, Bulk
Brands:
Anchor
Brown Bear

15150 Virginia Chutney Company
195 Piedmont Avenue
PO Box 511
Washington, VA 22747   540-675-1984
Fax: 540-675-1985 sales@virginiachutney.com
www.virginiachutney.com
chutneys

15151 Virginia Dare
822 Third Avenue
Brooklyn, NY 11232   718-788-1776
Fax: 718-768-3978   800-847-4500
flavorinfo@virginiadare.com
www.virginiadare.com
Liquid and dry flavors; vanilla, tea, coffee and cocoa extracts and concentrates; Prosweet flavor inprovers and masking agents and flavor emulsions
President: Howard Smith Jr
International VP: Lee W Kohnstamm
VP Marketing: Paul Graffigna
Purchasing: Christina Smith
Estimated Sales: $211 Million
Number Employees: 175
Type of Packaging: Bulk
Brands:
Contrasweet
G-Brew
Gourmet Brew
Prosweet
Superfex
Superfreeze
Tre Cafe
Vidarome

15152 Virginia Diner
322 West Main Street
Wakefield, VA 23888   757-899-6213
Fax: 757-899-2281   888-823-4637
custservice@vadiner.com www.vadiner.com
peanuts (gourmet, seasoned, in-the-shell and raw), cashews, almonds, etc., peanut brittle, nutty candies and snacks
President/Owner: Christine Epperson

15153 Virginia Honey Company
PO Box 1915
Inwood, WV 25428-1915   800-974-4778
Fax: 304-263-0946 info@virginiabrand.com
www.virginiabrand.com
Honey, salad dressings, including Vidalia Onion Vinagarette salad dressing, sauces, jams and jellies, herring products, salmon products, condiments, horseradish, cream cheese, party platers
CEO: Terry Hess
Parent Co: Vita Food Products
Type of Packaging: Consumer, Food Service, Private Label, Bulk
Brands:
VIRGINIA BRAND
VITA BRAND

15154 Virginia Trout Company
PO Box 128
Monterey, VA 24465-0128   540-468-2280
Fax: 540-468-2279
Manufacturer of fresh and frozen mountain trout
President: David Johnston
Estimated Sales: $3 Million
Number Employees: 6
Type of Packaging: Food Service
Brands:
ALLEGHENY
MOUNTAIN TROUT

15155 Visalia Produce Sales Inc
201 W Stroud Ave
Kingsburg, CA 93631-9531   559-897-6652
Fax: 559-897-6650 george@visaliaproduce.com
www.visaliaproduce.com
California fruits and vegetables
Owner: Stan Shamoon
Sales Representative: Stan Shamoon
Sales Representative: Aron Gularte
Sales Representative: George Matoian
Estimated Sales: $ 1 - 10 Million
Number Employees: 100-249

15156 Vision Pack Brands
531 Main Street #513
El Segundo, CA 90245   877-477-8500
Fax: 866-825-1808 visionpack@verizon.net
www.visionpackbrands.com
products for gift baskets (gourmet crackers, snacks and dip, candy, confections and beverages

15157 Vision Seafood Partners
41 Summer Street
Kingston, MA 02364-1418   781-585-2000
Fax: 773-561-0139
Seafood

15158 (HQ)Vista Bakery
P.O.Box 888
Burlington, IA 52601-0888   319-754-6551
Fax: 319-752-0063   800-553-2343
sales@vistabakery.com www.vistabakery.com
Manufacturer and exporter of sandwich cookies and crackers
VP: Tyler Cooke
VP Sales: Tyler Cook
Manufacturing Director: Jim Hartschuh
Plant Manager: Jeff Schuster
Estimated Sales: $200 Million
Number Employees: 500-999
Parent Co: Lance
Type of Packaging: Consumer, Food Service, Private Label, Bulk
Brands:
VISTA
VISTA CHOICE

15159 Vita Coco
39 West 14t Street
#404
New York, NY 10011
Fax: 800-407-0439   877-848-2262
info@vitacoco.com www.vitacoco.com/

Vita Coco is a nutritional drink containing only 100% natural coconut water from Brazil.
Co-Founder: Michael Kirban
Co-Founder: Ira Liran
Type of Packaging: Food Service

15160 Vita Food Products
2222 W Lake St
Chicago, IL 60612-2210   312-738-4500
Fax: 312-738-3215 www.vitafoodproducts.com
Processor and exporter of smoked and pickled herring and salmon; also, frozen cod and salmon
President: Stephen Rubin
CEO: Clifford K Bolen
Production Manager: Robert Godwa
Plant Manager: Barry Wineberg
Purchasing Manager: Louis Lyrla
Estimated Sales: H
Number Employees: 100-249
Type of Packaging: Consumer, Food Service
Brands:
Vita

15161 Vita Specialty Foods
PO Box 1915
Inwood, WV 25428   304-267-8500
Fax: 304-263-0946   800-974-4778
www.vitafoodproducts.com
seafood, barbecue ribs and spices, barbecue sauces, condiments, dressings, dessert toppings, honey and syrups, hot sauces, jim beam steak sauce, jim beam marinades, marinades, salsas, scorned woman hot sauce, snacks, tea concentratesvisalia onion vinaigrette, wing sauces

15162 Vita Specialty Foods
P.O.Box 1915
Inwood, WV 25428-1915   304-267-8500
Fax: 304-263-0946   800-974-4778
www.vitaspecialtyfoods.com
Manufacturer of condiments, including salad dressings, sauces, marinades, mustards, honey and teas
Manager: Chuck Martin
CEO: Terry Hess
Director Marketing: Douglas Horn
Sales: Valerie McCaffrey
Number Employees: 100-249
Number of Brands: 9
Number of Products: 200
Type of Packaging: Consumer, Food Service
Brands:
Artie Bucco
Artie Bucco Gourmet Foods
Courvoisier
Drambuie
Jim Beam Gourmet Foods
Kahlua
Oak Hill Farms
Scorned Woman
Virginia Brand

15163 Vita-Pakt Citrus Company
355 S Harvard Avenue
Lindsay, CA 93247-9700   559-562-6008
Fax: 559-562-1014   sales@vita-packcitrus.com
Processor and exporter of sweetened and unsweetened citrus peels, pulps and bases including orange, lemon, grapefruit and tangerine
General Manager: Paul Gottschall
Office Manager: James Benner
Sales Manager: Doug Peterson
Number Employees: 80
Sq. footage: 36000
Type of Packaging: Consumer, Food Service, Bulk

15164 Vita-Pakt Citrus Company
P.O.Box 309
Covina, CA 91723-0309   626-332-1101
Fax: 626-966-8196 www.vita-pakt.com
Producer of fruit juices, concentrates, purees, specialty citrus peel products and dehydrated fuits and vegetables.
President: James Boyle
VP: Abe Rodriguez
Quality Control: Armon J Abhajian
Estimated Sales: $32900000
Number Employees: 20-49
Other Locations:
Vita-Pakt Citrus Products Co.
Lindsay CA
Brands:
Bireleys
Cold Gold
Vita Pak

15165 Vita-Plus
953 E Sahara Ave # 21b1
Las Vegas, NV 89104-3012   702-733-8805
Fax: 702-369-8597   info@lifelinevitaplus.com
www.lifelinevitaplus.com
Dairy
Owner: Roop Rache
Co-Owner: Eddie Molina
Estimated Sales: $ 5-10 Million
Number Employees: 10-19
Brands:
Cortilite
Life Line Vita Plus
Vita-Plus

15166 Vita-Pure
410 W 1st Ave
Roselle, NJ 07203-1047   908-245-1212
Fax: 908-245-1999   JCampis@prodigy.net
Food/dietary supplements, vitamins, nutritional supplements
President: Achyut Sahasra
Vice President: Jaqueline Schauffler
Marketing Director: Joseph Campis
Operations Manager: Sheldon Tannebaum
Production Manager: Angelo Padilla
Estimated Sales: $ 5-10 Million
Number Employees: 20-49
Sq. footage: 17500
Type of Packaging: Private Label

15167 VitaTech International
2802 Dow Ave
Tustin, CA 92780-7212   714-832-9700
Fax: 714-731-8482   vitatech@vitatech.com
www.vitatech.com
Manufacturer of nutritional supplements including vitamins, enzymes, herbs, botanicals, glandulars and minerals
President: Thomas Tierney
VP Sales: Greg Williford
Estimated Sales: $23200000
Number Employees: 250-499
Sq. footage: 140000
Type of Packaging: Private Label

15168 Vital Products
8 Brown Avenue
Blackwood, NJ 08012-4810   856-228-1150
Fax: 856-228-0665   bobvitol@yahoo.com
www.musclebuildingproducts.com
Processor of health foods, vitamins and supplements
Owner: Val Vasilef
Sales Director: Robert Giacoboni
Estimated Sales: Less than $500,000
Number Employees: 1-4
Type of Packaging: Consumer, Bulk
Brands:
Russian Bear

15169 Vitale Poultry Company
800 E Cooke Rd
Columbus, OH 43214-2804   614-267-1874
Fax: 614-267-7824
Poultry processing
Co-Owner: Mark Cecutti
Co-Owner: Dan Cecutti
President: Rose Vitale
Estimated Sales: $ 5-9.9 Million
Number Employees: 10-19

15170 Vitalicious
11 Broadway
New York, NY 10004   212-233-6030
Fax: 212-233-6031   877-848-2877
customerservice@vitalicious.com
www.vitalicious.com
100 calorie VitaTops, VitaMuffins, VitaBrownies, VitaMixes, VitaCakes

15171 Vitality Foodservice
400 N Tampa St # 1500
Tampa, FL 33602   813-301-4600
Fax: 813-301-4230   888-863-6726
jdoan@vbeverages.com
www.vitalityfoodservice.com

Fruit juices, coffees, teas, hot chocolate and cappuccinos, sports drinks, cocktail mixes, smoothies, thickened beverages for healthcare, enhanced flavored waters, carbonated soft drinks, sugar-free beverages and more.
President/CEO: Gary Viljoen
EVP/CFO: Kimberly Johnson
EVP/COO: John Minton
Estimated Sales: $700 Million
Number Employees: 500-999
Sq. footage: 90000
Parent Co: Pride Beverages
Type of Packaging: Food Service, Private Label, Bulk
Brands:
Diamond Grove
Ocean Spray
Pride of B.C.
Sunsational

15172 Vitality Foodservice
28 Mollard Court
Barrie, ON L4N 8Y1
Canada   705-722-9049
Fax: 705-722-9533   800-668-5463
bmsmith@vbeverages.com
www.pridebeverages.com
Processor, importer and exporter of fruit juices and frozen fruit drink concentrates; also, coffee
President/CEO: Al Oddis
VP Sales/Marketing: Randy Larson
Operations Manager: Rick Silver
Purchasing Agent: Jane Axt
Estimated Sales: $700 Million
Number Employees: 58
Sq. footage: 9700
Parent Co: Vitality Foodservice
Type of Packaging: Food Service, Private Label, Bulk

15173 Vitality Life Choice
PO Box 21133
Carson City, NV 89721-1133   775-882-7186
Fax: 775-882-6686   800-423-8365
wwww.vitality-corp.com
Candy

15174 Vitamer Laboratories
17802 Gillette Ave
Irvine, CA 92614-6582   949-863-0340
Fax: 949-859-3523   800-432-8355
customerservice@vitamer.com
www.vitamer.com
Processor of dietary supplements and herbal products
President: Steve Brown
VP: Jane Drinkwalter
Marketing: Gene Nacagawa
Sales: Bob Norman
Estimated Sales: $ 20 - 50 Million
Number Employees: 100-249
Parent Co: Anabolic
Type of Packaging: Private Label

15175 Vitamilk Dairy
4141 Agate Road
Bellingham, WA 98226-8745   206-529-4128
Fax: 206-524-7070 www.vitamilk.com
Processor of dairy products including milk, sour cream and ice cream
President: E Gerald Teel
VP Sales: Larry Burns
Plant Manager: Paul Nelson
Number Employees: 100-249
Type of Packaging: Consumer, Food Service, Private Label, Bulk

15176 (HQ)Vitamin Power
39 Saint Marys Pl
Freeport, NY 11520-4634   516-378-0900
Fax: 516-378-0919   800-645-6567
info@vitaminpower.com
www.vitaminpower.com
Produces nutritional supplements, distributed exclusively through independent dealers, individual retailers and professional healthcare offices.
President: David Henry Friedlander
Estimated Sales: $2 Million
Number Employees: 10-19
Sq. footage: 20000
Type of Packaging: Consumer
Brands:
Vitamin Power

15177 (HQ)Vitaminerals
1815 Flower St
Glendale, CA 91201-2024   818-500-8718
                              Fax: 818-240-2785
Processor and exporter of food supplements and vitamins
   Owner: Michael Gorman
   President: John Gorman III
   VP: Mike Gorman
Estimated Sales: $ 5 - 10 Million
Number Employees: 20-49
Sq. footage: 35000
Brands:
   Hampshire Laboratories
   Vitaminerals

15178 Vitamins
200 E Randolph St # 5130
Chicago, IL 60601-6535   312-861-0700
          Fax: 312-861-0708 www.vitamins-inc.com
Processor of nutritional ingredients including
defatted wheat germ, wheat germ oil and soluble
vitamins
   President: James F Carozza
   President: J Carozza
   VP Operations: Darin Salyer
Estimated Sales: $4100000
Number Employees: 1-4

15179 Vitarich Ice Cream
572 Highway One
Fortuna, CA 95540   707-725-6182
   Fax: 707-725-6186 info@humboldtcreamery.com
                   www.humboldtcreamery.com
Manufacturer of ice cream, sherbet, frozen yogurt
and ice cream mixes and novelties
   President: Rich Ghilarducci
Number Employees: 20-49
Type of Packaging: Consumer, Food Service, Private Label, Bulk
Other Locations:
   Vitarich Ice Cream Co.
   Seattle WA
Brands:
   VITARICH

15180 (HQ)Vitarich Laboratories
4365 Arnold Ave
Naples, FL 34104-3390   239-430-2266
   Fax: 239-430-4930 800-817-9999
                   v.decock@planetinternet.be
                   www.vitarichlabs.com
Processor, importer and exporter of vitamins,
nutraceuticals and food supplements including
herbal, whole leaf wheat, barley and algae
   President: Kevin Thomas
   Marketing: Bill Foley
   Sales Director: Frank Guzzo
Estimated Sales: $ .5 - 1 million
Number Employees: 5-9
Sq. footage: 20000
Type of Packaging: Consumer, Private Label, Bulk
Other Locations:
   Vitarich Laboratories
   Bainbridge GA
Brands:
   Hydra-Green

15181 Vitasoy USA
1 New England Way
Ayer, MA 01432-1514   978-772-6880
          Fax: 978-772-6881 info@vitasoy-usa.com
                   www.vitasoy-usa.com
Soy foods and Asian pasta; also soy drinks
   President/CEO: Walter Riglian
   Quality Control: Rick Baum
   VP Marketing: Susan Rolnick
   Operations: John Wareham
Estimated Sales: $150 Million
Number Employees: 160
Sq. footage: 42000
Parent Co: Vitasoy International Holdings
Type of Packaging: Consumer, Food Service, Private Label
Brands:
   Nasoya

15182 Vitatech International
2802 Dow Ave
Tustin, CA 92780-7212   714-832-9700
          Fax: 714-731-8482 vitatech@vitatech.com
                   www.vitatech.com

Manufacturer of vitamins
   President: Thomas Tierney
   VP Sales/Client Services: Greg Williford
Estimated Sales: $20-50 Million
Number Employees: 250-499
Type of Packaging: Private Label

15183 (HQ)Vitech America Corporation
833 1st Avenue S
Kent, WA 98032-6139   253-859-5985
   Fax: 253-859-5912 jjabbott@vitechamerica.com
                   vitechamerica.com
Processor, packager and exporter of nutritional sup-
plements, vitamin C, multiple vitamins, lactase en-
zyme caplets, calcium tablets, confections, breath
mint, energy drinks and cosmetics
   President: David Parker
   VP Operations: Donald Parker
   Purchasing Manager: Mike Harris
Estimated Sales: $11503924
Number Employees: 75
Sq. footage: 20000
Type of Packaging: Private Label, Bulk
Brands:
   Body Dynabolics
   Clinic
   Flexon C2g
   Lactzyme
   MYNTZ
   SQYNTZ
   Swisscal 500
   Theragar
   Theraprin
   Vitarite Nutritionals
   Vitergy
   Zincguard

15184 Vity Meat & Provisions Company
1418 N 27th Avenue
Phoenix, AZ 85009-3603   602-269-7768
                              Fax: 602-269-0044
   President: Michael Brown
   VP Finance: Gary Rasmussen
Estimated Sales: $ .5 - 1 million
Number Employees: 1-4

15185 Vivienne Dressings
P.O.Box 16072
St Louis, MO 63105-0772   314-994-7549
          Fax: 636-947-1123 800-827-0778
   ttucker@vivienne.com www.vivienne.com
Gourmet dressings and marinades
   President: Thomas A Tucker
Estimated Sales: Below $ 5 Million
Number Employees: 1-4
Brands:
   Vivienne

15186 Vivion
929 Bransten Rd
San Carlos, CA 94070-4073   650-595-3600
          Fax: 650-595-2094 800-479-0997
   mpoleselli@vivioninc.com www.vivioninc.com
Acids, sweeteners, preservatives, gums, vitamins,
antioxidants and fibers
   President: Edward Poleselli
   Vice President: Michael Poleselli
Estimated Sales: $ 15 Million
Number Employees: 5-9

15187 Vivolac Cultures Corporation
3862 E Washington St
Indianapolis, IN 46201-4470   317-356-8460
          Fax: 317-356-8450 sales@vivolac.com
                   www.vivolac.com
Manufacturer and exporter of dairy, meat and bread
starter cultures in pelletized, frozen and freeze-dried
form
   President: Wesley Sing
   Technical Sales: David Winters
Estimated Sales: $1.4 Million
Number Employees: 20-49
Type of Packaging: Private Label, Bulk
Brands:
   Bioflora
   Vivolac

15188 Vlasic Foods
17950 Via Nicolo
Tracy, CA 95377-9767   559-734-7455
                              Fax: 559-734-3095
Processor of canned olives
   Controller: Lubbert Van Dellen
Parent Co: American Rice

Type of Packaging: Consumer, Food Service, Private Label
Brands:
   Early California

15189 Vocatura Bakery
695 Boswell Ave
Norwich, CT 06360-2826   860-887-2220
Breads
   President: John Vocatura
Estimated Sales: $500,000-$1 Million
Number Employees: 10-19
Brands:
   Vocatura

15190 Vogel Popcorn
2683 350th St
Lake View, IA 51450-7536   712-657-8561
                              Fax: 712-657-2152
Processor of popcorn
   Manager: Dave Brpelcing
Estimated Sales: $ 10 - 20 Million
Number Employees: 20-49
Type of Packaging: Consumer, Private Label, Bulk

15191 Vogel Popcorn
2301 Washington St
Hamburg, IA 51640-1835   712-382-2634
          Fax: 712-382-1357 800-831-5818
                   www.vogelpopcorn.com
Processor and exporter of popcorn and popping oils;
importer of popcorn and popcorn seeds
   President: Kelly Madden
   Quality Assurance Supervisor: John Kirschbaum
   Operations Manager/Director Agronomics: Mark
   Schleisman
   Purchasing: Kelly Madden
Estimated Sales: $ 20 - 50 Million
Number Employees: 50-99
Parent Co: Golden Valley Microwave Foods
Type of Packaging: Consumer, Food Service, Private Label, Bulk
Brands:
   Act Ii
   Cowboy
   Vogel

15192 Voget Meats
P.O.Box 26
Hubbard, OR 97032-0026   503-981-6271
   Fax: 503-981-0220 www.vogetmeats.com
Smoked meats, sausages
   CEO: Merle Stutzman
   Vice President: Grace Stuzman
Estimated Sales: $ 2.5-5 Million
Number Employees: 10-19
Type of Packaging: Private Label
Brands:
   Voget Meats

15193 Vogue Cuisine
4163 Jasmine Avenue
Culver City, CA 90232-3406   310-391-1053
          Fax: 310-390-0883 888-236-4144
                   voguecuisine@comcast.net
                   www.voguecuisine.com
Processor of natural dehydrated low sodium and or-
ganic instant soup bases and mixes including
chicken, beef, onion and vegetable vegetar-
ian-chicken
   CEO: Carol Schlanger
   Vice President: Clinton Helvey
   Public Relations: Carol Helvey
Number Employees: 1-4
Type of Packaging: Private Label
Brands:
   VOGUE BEEF BASE
   VOGUE CHICKEN BASE
   VOGUE ONION BASE
   VOGUE VEGEBASE
   VOGUE VEGETARIAN CHICKEN BASE

15194 Volcano Island Honey Company
46-4013 Puaono Rd
Honokaa, HI 96727-7028   808-775-1000
          Fax: 808-775-0412 888-663-6639
                   info@volcanoislandhoney.com
                   www.volcanoislandhoney.com
Gourmet honey
   Manager: Candice Choy
Estimated Sales: Under $500,000
Number Employees: 5-9
Brands:
   Rare Hawaiian

15195 Vollwerth & Company
P.O.Box 239
Hancock, MI 49930-0239   906-482-1550
Fax: 906-482-0842   800-562-7620
topdog@vollwerth.com   www.vollwerth.com
Processor of sausage and meat products; wholesaler/distributor of hotel and restaurant supplies; serving the food service market
President: Robert Vollwerth
VP: Jim Schaf
Sales Representative: Richard Vollwerth
Production Manager: Adam Manderfield
Estimated Sales: $100+ Million
Number Employees: 20-49

15196 Volpi Italian Meats
5258 Daggett Ave
St Louis, MO 63110-3026   314-772-8550
Fax: 314-772-0411   billh@volpifoods.com
Italian specialty meats, salami, proscuitto ham, pancetta, coppa, rotola
CEO: Armando Pasetti
President: Lorenza Pasetti
Quality Control: Cort Ballard
Marketing: Adiasa Seomanobic
Sales Director: Christine Illuminato
Operations Manager: Butch Duggan
Estimated Sales: $ 20-50 Million
Number Employees: 100-249
Brands:
Volpi

15197 Von Gal
3101 Hayneville Rd
Montgomery, AL 36108-3900   334-261-2700
Fax: 334-261-2801   800-542-6570
jason.bennett@vongal.com   www.vongal.com
Manufacturer of palletizers for industries such as baking, bottling, brewing, and pet food.
Manager: Paul Probst
Sales Manager: Jason Bennett

15198 Von Stiehl Winery
115 Navarino St
Algoma, WI 54201-1246   920-487-5208
Fax: 920-487-5108   800-955-5208
vonstiehl@itol.com   www.vonstiehl.com
Manufacturer of wine
President: William Schmiling
Estimated Sales: $5 Million
Number Employees: 20-49
Type of Packaging: Consumer

15199 Von Strasser Winery
1510 Diamond Mountain Rd
Calistoga, CA 94515-9669   707-942-0930
Fax: 707-942-0454   888-359-9463
wines@vonstrasser.com   www.vonstrasser.com
Wines
Owner/Executive Winemaker: Rudy Von Strasser
Director National Sales/Marketing: John Schulz
Vice President: Rita Von Strasser
Vineyard Manager: Gerardo Alfaro
Assistant Winemaker: Jason Bull
Vineyard Manager: Gerardo Alfaro
Estimated Sales: $ 2.5-5 Million
Number Employees: 5-9
Type of Packaging: Private Label
Brands:
Von Strasser
Von Strasser

15200 Voortman Cookies
4455 N Service Road
PO Box 5206
Burlington, ON L7L 4X7
Canada   905-335-9500
Fax: 905-332-5499   info@voortman.com
Manufacturers a variety of cookies including prepackaged family packs and seasonal cookies.
President: Harry Voortman
Founder: William Voortman
VP Sales: Adrian Voortman
Number Employees: 250-499
Sq. footage: 171339
Type of Packaging: Consumer, Bulk
Brands:
Voortman

15201 Voortman Cookies
2575 S Willow Ave
Bloomington, CA 92316-3256   909-877-8471
Fax: 909-877-6728
voortman@voortmancookies.com
www.voortmancookies.com
Manufacturers a variety of cookies including prepackaged family packs and seasonal cookies.
President: Kathleen Voortman-Cunni
Founder: William Voortman
Sq. footage: 42000
Brands:
Voortman
Zero Trans Fats

15202 Vosges Haut-Chocolat
2211 N Elston Ave
Suite 203
Chicago, IL 60614   773-388-5560
Fax: 773-772-7917   888-309-866
www.vosgeschocolate.com
chocolate truffles and gourmet gifts
Owner: Katrina Markoff

15203 Voyager South
8440 Sterling Dr
Mobile, AL 36695-3618   251-634-0450
Fax: 318-388-4539
Estimated Sales: $ 1 - 3 Million
Number Employees: 1-4

15204 Vrymeer Commodities
PO Box 545
St Charles, IL 60174-0545   630-584-0069
Fax: 630-377-5521
Processor, exporter and importer of cocoa powder, liquor and butter; also, chocolate drops, candies and coatings
VP Worldwide Distribution: Andrew Nold
Number Employees: 100
Sq. footage: 30000
Parent Co: Ronstadt Group Companies
Type of Packaging: Bulk
Brands:
Vrymeer

15205 Vynecrest Vineyards andWinery
172 Arrowhead Ln
Breinigsville, PA 18031-1462   610-398-7525
Fax: 610-398-7530   800-361-0725
wines@vynecrest.com   www.vynecrest.com
Wines
Co-Owner: Janice Landis
Co-Owner: John Landis
Estimated Sales: Less than $200,000
Number Employees: 1-4
Type of Packaging: Private Label
Brands:
Vynecrest Vineyards

15206 Vyse Gelatin Company
5010 Rose St
Schiller Park, IL 60176-1023   847-678-4780
Fax: 847-678-0329   800-533-2152
info@vyse.com   www.vyse.com
Manufacturer, exporter and importer of food grade gelatins
President: Gary Brunet
R&D: Rick Rossini
VP: John Deane
Sales: Margaret Miller
Estimated Sales: $ 3 - 5 Million
Number Employees: 10-19
Type of Packaging: Food Service, Private Label, Bulk
Brands:
150 Bloom
225 Bloom
610-D
710-D
Atlas
Celero
Economix
Finemix
Flour Fine
Hypowr
Pbc-210
Protector
Seeclear
Stabilo
Superclear
Superla
Supertex
Superwhip

Textura
Vee Gee
Velvatex
Viscomix
X-Fine

15207 Vyse Gelatin Company
5010 Rose St
Schiller Park, IL 60176-1023   847-678-4780
Fax: 847-678-0329   800-533-2152
info@vyse.com   www.vyse.com
Gelatin; all grades and types
President: Gary Brunet
Sales Director: Joel Ayres
Estimated Sales: $ 10-15 Million
Number Employees: 10-19
Type of Packaging: Food Service, Private Label, Bulk
Brands:
VYSE Gelatin

15208 (HQ)W&G Flavors
11110 Pepper Rd # A
Hunt Valley, MD 21031-1204   410-771-6606
Fax: 410-771-6608   jwaynewheeler@sun-ripe.com
http://sun-ripe.com/wg/
Processor and exporter of bakery and confectionary supplies and mixes including dry bar, salad dressings and sauces
President: J W Wheeler
Production Manager: Tim Wheeler
Estimated Sales: $1,000,000
Number Employees: 10-19
Type of Packaging: Food Service, Bulk
Brands:
COAG-U-LOID
CONDEX
PIE RITE
SUN-RIPE
T.H. ANGERMEIER
VEG-A-LOID

15209 W&G Marketing Company
P.O.Box 1742
Ames, IA 50010-1742   515-233-4774
Fax: 515-233-4773 www.wgmarketing.com
Processor and exporter of roasting pigs including whole and frozen; also, meat and poultry by-products and fully cooked barbecue turkey, beef and pork
President: Darren Dies
President Sales/Marketing: Darren Dies
VP Operations: Robert Olinger
Estimated Sales: $ 5 - 10 Million
Number Employees: 1-4
Sq. footage: 20000
Type of Packaging: Consumer, Food Service, Private Label
Brands:
Hickory Grove
W&G's

15210 W&W Meats
7493 Shadowbrook Drive
Willoughby, OH 44094-9742   216-621-7846
Processor of beef, pork, lamb, breaded veal and pork; also, frozen fish and vegetables
President: Sheldon Weiser
Vice President: Jeff Weiser
Number Employees: 20-49
Type of Packaging: Food Service
Brands:
Elnore

15211 W. Forrest Haywood Seafood Company
431 Messick Rd
Poquoson, VA 23662-1815   757-868-6748
Fax: 757-868-1111
Fresh crabmeat
President: Laura Hornsby
VP: Delores Forrest
Estimated Sales: $ 2.5-5 Million
Number Employees: 1-4

15212 W. Roberts
1300 Forest Dr
Annapolis, MD 21403-1436   410-269-5380
Fax: 410-263-0805
Manager: Maurice Jones
Estimated Sales: $ 5 - 10 Million
Number Employees: 20-49

15213 W.A. Cleary Products
P.O.Box 10
Somerset, NJ 08875-0010   732-247-8000
Fax: 732-247-6977   800-238-7813
www.waclearyproducts.com
Manufacturer and exporter of lecithin and release agents for the bakery, chocolate and confectionery industries
President: John Christman
Estimated Sales: $ 20 - 50 Million
Number Employees: 20-49
Sq. footage: 15000
Parent Co: W.A. Cleary Corporation
Brands:
Clearlubes
Clearoil
Clearote Lecithins
Kettubes
Panlube
Tabl-Eze 350

15214 W.F. Cosart Packing Company
1145 E Firebaugh Ave
Exeter, CA 93221-9701   559-592-2821
Fax: 559-592-6259
Fresh fruits and vegetables
President: Keith Cosart
Estimated Sales: $ 50 - 100 Million
Number Employees: 50-99

15215 W.H. Harris Seafood
PO Box 145
Chester, MD 21619-0145   410-827-8104
Fax: 410-827-9057   whh@dmv.com
www.harriscrabhouse.com
Crabs and oysters
Chairman: William Jerry Harris
Vice President: Art Oertel
Estimated Sales: $ 5-10 Million
Number Employees: 50
Type of Packaging: Consumer
Brands:
Bay Shore

15216 W.J. Clark & Co
350 N La Salle Dr # 900
Chicago, IL 60654-5136   312-329-0830
Fax: 708-626-4064
Canned and packaging products,cold cereals, hot cereals, soya sauces, seasoning mixes
President: Bill Clark
VP Sales: Dorie Vedas
Estimated Sales: $ 20-50 Million
Number Employees: 5-9
Brands:
W.J. Clark

15217 W.J. Stearns & Sons/Mountain Dairy
50 Stearns Road
Storrs Mansfield, CT 06268-2701   860-423-9289
Fax: 860-423-3486 www.mountaindairy.com
Processor and wholesaler/distributor of dairy products including cream and milk
President: W Stearns
Vice President: James Stearns
Plant Manager: James Stearns
Estimated Sales: $3 Million
Number Employees: 35
Type of Packaging: Consumer, Private Label

15218 W.L. Halsey Grocery Company
P.O.Box 6485
Huntsville, AL 35813-0485   256-772-9691
Fax: 256-461-8386   sales@halseyfoodservice.com
www.halseygrocery.com
Wholesaler/distributor of groceries, provisions/meats, produce, dairy products, frozen foods, baked goods, etc.; serving the food service market
President: Cecilia Halsey
Estimated Sales: $56471684
Number Employees: 100-249
Sq. footage: 90000

15219 W.L. Petrey Wholesale Company
P.O.Box 68
Luverne, AL 36049-0068   334-335-6582
Fax: 334-335-2422   mail@petrey.com
www.petrey.com
Wholesaler/distributor of frozen food, general merchandise, general line products, provisions/meats and seafood
CEO: James Jackson Sr
CEO: James W Jackson

Number Employees: 250-499

15220 W.O. Sasser
135 Johnny Mercer Blvd
Savannah, GA 31410-2118   912-898-9504
Fax: 912-897-0331
Owner: W O Sasser
Estimated Sales: $ .5 - 1 million
Number Employees: 5-9

15221 W.R. Delozier Sausage Company
12350 Chapman Highway
Seymour, TN 37865-6231   865-577-5907
Sausages
President: W Delozier
Estimated Sales: Less than $500,000
Number Employees: 1-4

15222 W.S. Wells & Sons
P.O.Box 109
Wilton, ME 04294-0109   207-645-3393
Fax: 207- 64-5 33
Canned fiddleheads and dandelions, green beans, baked beans, soup mixes
Owner: Adrian Wells
Estimated Sales: $ 2.5-5 Million
Number Employees: 10-19

15223 W.T. Ruark & Company
P.O.Box 99
Fishing Creek, MD 21634-0099   410-397-3133
Fax: 410-397-2007   wtruark@intercom.net
Manufacturer of seafood including oysters, crabs and crabmeat
President: William Ruark
Estimated Sales: $21 Million
Number Employees: 20-49
Type of Packaging: Consumer

15224 WA Bean & Sons
229 Bomarc Rd # 1
Bangor, ME 04401-2678   207-947-0364
Fax: 207-990-4211   800-649-1958
sales@beansmeats.com   www.beansmeats.com
Processor of natural casing frankfurters and sausages, hams, tri-cooked meats, haggis and mincemeat.
President: David Bean
Treasurer: Elizabeth Bean
Sales Director: Gordon Brasslett
Estimated Sales: Under $5 Million
Number Employees: 20-49
Sq. footage: 4
Type of Packaging: Consumer, Food Service, Private Label, Bulk

15225 WA Cleary Products
P.O.Box 10
Somerset, NJ 08875-0010   732-247-8000
Fax: 732-247-6977   800-238-7813
waclearycorp@aol.com
www.waclearyproducts.com
Lecithin, release products for the baking and candy industries
President: John Christman
Marketing Director: John Chirstion
Estimated Sales: $ 50-100 Million
Number Employees: 20-49
Brands:
WA Cleary

15226 (HQ)WCC Honey Marketing
636 Turnbull Canyon Rd
City of Industry, CA 91745-1119   626-855-3086
Fax: 626-855-3087   info@wcommerce.com
www.wcommerce.com
Processor and exporter of natural sweeteners, syrups and nutritional supplements including honey, comb honey, molasses, blackstrap molasses, corn syrup, agave nectar and royal jelly; importer of honey, barley malt sweetener, rice syrupand juice concentrate
Owner: Anthony Li
General Manager: Chuck Burkholder
National Sales Manager: Norma Robinson
Purchasing Manager: James Littlejohn
Estimated Sales: $ 5 - 10 Million
Number Employees: 5-9
Sq. footage: 29700
Type of Packaging: Consumer, Food Service, Private Label, Bulk
Other Locations:
Western Commerce Corp.
Kansas City MO
Brands:
Cucamonga

El Panal
Fruitsweet
Hawaiian Gold
Lo Han
Pot O' Gold
Powers

15227 WFI
1209 W Saint Georges Ave
Linden, NJ 07036-6117   908-925-9494
Fax: 908-925-9537 www.waldenfarms.com
Sauces
President: Paul Berko
Sales Director: Mitchell Berko
Operations Manager: V Naccarato
Estimated Sales: $500,000-$1 Million
Number Employees: 20-49
Type of Packaging: Private Label
Brands:
Walden Farms

15228 WG Thompson & Sons
PO Box 250
Blenheim, ON N0P 1A0
Canada   519-676-5411
Fax: 519-676-3185   srobert@wgthompson.com
Manufacturer, importer, exporter and wholesaler/distributor of soya and dry beans, corn, seeds and cereal grains; wholesaler/distributor of groceries, produce, general merchandise, private label/generic items, etc.; serving the foodservice market
President: Wes Thompson
Secretary: Andrew McVittie
Food Products Manager: John O'Brien
Contact: Sue Robert
Estimated Sales: $100 Million
Number Employees: 350
Type of Packaging: Consumer, Food Service, Private Label, Bulk
Brands:
C&G
HYLAND

15229 WILD Flavors
1261 Pacific Ave
Erlanger, KY 41018-1260   859-342-3600
Fax: 859-342-3610   info@wildflavors.com
www.wildflavors.com
Develops, manufactures, and distributes flavors, flavor systems, colors, health ingredients and systems to the food and beverage industry.
Owner: Dr Hans-Peter Wild
CEO: Michael Ponder
CFO: Gary Massie
CEO: Michael H Ponder
Senior Director, Quality Control: Karen Eberts
Senior Director, Marketing: Donna Hansee
VP Sales: Reed Lynn
Senior Director, Public Relations: Donna Hansee
VP Operations: David Haase
Director, Operations: Dan Holtzleiter Sr
Senior Director, Procurement: Tony Sizemore
Number Employees: 250-499
Sq. footage: 350000
Type of Packaging: Consumer, Food Service, Private Label, Bulk

15230 WILD Flavors
PO Box 75204
Cincinnati, OH 45275-0204   513-771-5904
888-945-3352
info@wildflavors.com   www.wild-group.de
Processor and exporter of flavors, colors and other ingredients for food and beverage
Marketing Manager: Oliver Hodapp
Estimated Sales: $ 5 - 10 Million
Number Employees: 5-9
Type of Packaging: Food Service, Private Label

15231 WILD Flavors (Canada)
7315 Pacific Circle
Mississauga, ON L5T 1V1
Canada   905-670-1108
Fax: 905-670-0076   800-263-5286
www.wildflavors.com
Processor of flavors, colors, seasonings, spray-dried ingredients, sauces, batters, coatings, marinades; also, custom blending; exporter of cheese powders
Acting Director: Tim Husted
Director Finance: Tamara Robichaud
R & D: Allison Berridge
Operations Director: Tim Husted
Plant Manager: Dave Oldroyd
Purchasing Manager: Leigh Bailey

Number Employees: 30-50
Number of Products: 200
Sq. footage: 60000
Parent Co: WILD Flavors
Type of Packaging: Food Service, Bulk

15232 WK Eckerd & Sons
5067 Blythe Island Hwy # B
Brunswick, GA 31520-2500   912-265-0332
           Fax: 912-261-8460   eckerd@thebest.net
Seafood
    President: William Eckerd
Estimated Sales: Below $ 5 Million
Number Employees: 1-4

15233 WMFB
Apt 94
209 Webster St
Beaver Dam, WI 53916-3074   920-887-1771
                      Fax: 920-887-3683
Processor of frozen pasta
    President: Steve Baldwin
    Vice President: Roger Dusso
    CFO: Dan Gartland
    Vice President: Roger Dusso
    Quality Control: Sandra Saunders
    Operations Manager: Jerry Klawitter
Estimated Sales: $ 10-20 Million
Number Employees: 20-49
Type of Packaging: Food Service, Private Label,
    Bulk
Brands:
    WMFB

15234 WSI
223 Rodeo Ave
Caldwell, ID 83605-6714   208-459-0777
                      Fax: 208-455-4859
Processor of dry pinto beans and seed grain
    General Manager: Leeon Martineau
    Purchasing Agent: Tammy Gaviola
Estimated Sales: $100+ Million
Number Employees: 100-249
Parent Co: J.R. Simplot Company
Type of Packaging: Consumer, Private Label, Bulk

15235 WSMP
P.O.Box 399
Claremont, NC 28610-0399   828-459-7626
           Fax: 828-459-3131   www.pierrefoods.com
Processor of cured ham and baked goods
    President: Tim Starnes
    COO: David R Clark
    VP Sales: Larry Hefner
Estimated Sales: $100+ Million
Number Employees: 500-999
Type of Packaging: Consumer, Food Service
Brands:
    Country
    Mom & Pop's

15236 WSU Creamery
101 Food Quality
Pullman, WA 99164-0001   800-457-5442
           Fax: 509-335-7525   800-457-5442
    salvadalena@wsu.edu   www.wsu.edu/creamery
Processor of cheddar cheese and ice cream
    WSU Creamery Manager: Russ Salvadalena
    Assistant Manager: John Haugen
Number Employees: 50
Sq. footage: 20000
Type of Packaging: Consumer, Food Service
Brands:
    Cougar Gold
    Viking

15237 WTI, Inc.
281 Martin Luther King Jr. Avenue
Jefferson, GA 30549-1477
           Fax: 706-387-5159   800-827-1727
                      www.wtiinc.com
Marinades and flavorings for meat.
    President: Wolf Ludwig
    Sr. Vice President: Michael Crump

15238 WWS
4032 Shoreline Dr # 2
Spring Park, MN 55384-4503   952-541-9001
                      Fax: 952-541-9206
Merchandiser of feed and food grade, fats, oils,
    meals, lard, tallow, etc.
    President: Wendy Storlie
    Southwest Area Manager: Alec Shellum
    West Coast Manager: Tony Trowbridge

Estimated Sales: $$10-15 Million
Number Employees: 5-9
Sq. footage: 1800

15239 Wabash Coffee
P.O.Box 576
Vincennes, IN 47591-0576   812-882-6066
    Fax: 812-882-8371 www.wabashfoodservice.com
Coffee
    President/CEO: Robert Bierhaus
    CEO: Jayne Young
Estimated Sales: $ 50 - 100 Million
Number Employees: 100-249

15240 Wabash Heritage Spices
2525 N 6th St
Vincennes, IN 47591-2405   812-895-0059
           Fax: 812-895-0064   info@knoxcountyarc.com
                      www.knoxcountyarc.com
Spices, powders
    President: Michael Carney
    Research & Development: John TRUE
    Quality Control: John TRUE
    Plant Manager: Leroy Douffron
Number of Brands: 1
Number of Products: 90
Sq. footage: 240000
Type of Packaging: Consumer, Food Service, Pri-
    vate Label, Bulk
Brands:
    WASBASH HERITAGE

15241 Wabash Seafood Company
2249 W Hubbard St
Chicago, IL 60612-1613   312-733-5070
                      Fax: 312-733-2798
Seafood
    President: John Rebello
Estimated Sales: $ 10 - 20 Million
Number Employees: 20-49

15242 Wabash Valley Farms
6323 N 150 E
Monon, IN 47959-8010   219-253-6650
           Fax: 219-253-8172   800-270-2705
                      charlotte@wfarms.com
                      www.popcornpopper.com
Processor and exporter of popcorn and popper gift
baskets including seasonings, spices, oils and drink
mixes
    President: Dani Paluchniak
    Vice President: Joe Dold
    Sales Manager: Steve Dold
    Purchasing Manager: Joe Dold
Estimated Sales: $4041306
Number Employees: 5-9
Parent Co: Felknor International
Type of Packaging: Consumer
Brands:
    Theater II
    Wasbash Valley Farm
    Whirley Pop

15243 Wabash Valley Produce
P.O.Box 127
Dubois, IN 47527-0127   812-678-3131
                      Fax: 812-678-5931
Processor of bulk liquid egg products including pas-
teurized and raw whole eggs, egg whites and egg
and salt yolks
    President: Larry Seger
Estimated Sales: $100+ Million
Number Employees: 100-249
Sq. footage: 25000
Type of Packaging: Bulk

15244 Wabi Fishing Company
14608 Smokey Point Boulevard
Marysville, WA 98271-8946   360-659-9474
           Fax: 360-659-9093   888-536-7696
    wabi@silvernet.net   www.leosown.com
Wild Pacific smoked salmon available in five flavors
    President: Leo Palmer
Brands:
    King Nova
    Leo's
    Sockeye Nova

15245 Wachusett Brewing Company
175 State Rd E
Westminster, MA 01473-1208   978-874-9965
           Fax: 978-874-0784   info@wachusettbrew.com
                      www.wachusettbrew.com

Processor of flavored ales.
    Owner: Ned La Fortune
    Sales Manager: Peter Quinn
    Plant Engineer: Kevin Buckler
Estimated Sales: Below $ 5 Million
Number Employees: 10-19
Type of Packaging: Consumer, Food Service
Brands:
    Wachusett

15246 Wachusett Potato Chip Company
759 Water St
Fitchburg, MA 01420-6499   978-342-6038
                      Fax: 978-345-4894
Processor of potato chips including regular, rippled,
flavored and no-salt added
    President: Edward Krysiak
Estimated Sales: $10 Million
Number Employees: 50-99
Sq. footage: 56000
Type of Packaging: Consumer, Food Service, Pri-
    vate Label
Brands:
    Wachusett

15247 Waco Beef & Pork Processors
523 Precision Dr
Waco, TX 76710-6972   254-772-4669
                      Fax: 254-772-4579
Manufacturer of fresh portion controlled beef,
chicken and pork including sausage, chorizo and
bratwurst; importer of beef skirts; wholesaler/dis-
tributor of meat and general merchandise; serving
the food service market
    Manager: Sara Jones
Estimated Sales: $2.2 Million
Number Employees: 5-9
Sq. footage: 10000
Type of Packaging: Food Service
Brands:
    PRECISION

15248 Wagner Excello Food Products
2625 Gardner Rd
Broadview, IL 60155-4499   708-338-4488
    Fax: 708-338-4495   peter.mail@wagnerfoods.com
                      www.wagnerfoods.com
Bar mixes, maple syrups, juices and water
    Owner: Harry Berger
    VP: Peter Fisher
Estimated Sales: $ 10-20 Million
Number Employees: 10,000+
Number of Brands: 1
Type of Packaging: Food Service, Private Label

15249 Wagner Gourmet Foods
10618 Summit St
Shawnee Mission, KS 66215-2050   913-469-5411
                      Fax: 913-469-1367
    customerservice@wagner-gourmet.com
                      www.hicks-ashby.com
Processor of spices, preserves, jams, ice cream
sauces, seasoned rice and gift pack assortments; im-
porter of tea; wholesaler/distributor of snack foods
including cookies
    President: James T Baldwin
Estimated Sales: $ 3 - 5 Million
Number Employees: 5-9
Sq. footage: 120000
Parent Co: Wagner Gourmet Foods
Type of Packaging: Consumer, Private Label

15250 Wagner Seafood
9626 S Pulaski Rd
Oak Lawn, IL 60453-3391   708-636-2646
                      Fax: 843-559-1156
Seafood
    President: Robert Wagner
Estimated Sales: $300,000-500,000
Number Employees: 1-4

15251 Wagner Vineyards
9322 State Route 414
Lodi, NY 14860-9641   607-582-6976
           Fax: 607-582-6446   866-924-6378
    d.wagner@wagnervineyards.com
                      www.wagnervineyards.com
Processor of wines and beer; exporter of wines
    President: Stanley Wagner
    Retail Manager: Carol Voorhees
    COO: John Wagner
    Public Relations: Laura Lee

Estimated Sales: $2,762,368
Number Employees: 50-99
Sq. footage: 36000
Type of Packaging: Consumer
Brands:
  Wagner Brewing Co.
  Wagner Vineyards

15252 Wah Yet Group
28301 Industrial Blvd # C
Hayward, CA 94545-4429   510-887-3801
          Fax: 510-887-3803   800-229-3392
Processor and exporter of dieters' and ginseng teas;
importer of health drinks
  President: Ying Lau
  Manager: Judy Lau
Estimated Sales: $ 1 - 3 Million
Number Employees: 1-4
Sq. footage: 2000
Type of Packaging: Consumer
Brands:
  Chinese Ginseng
  Green Leaf

15253 Wainani Kai Seafood
2126 Eluwene St # A
Honolulu, HI 96819-2348   808-847-7435
      Fax: 808-841-7536   lpang00@yahoo.com
Seafood
  President: Lance Pang
Estimated Sales: $ 3 - 5 Million
Number Employees: 5-9

15254 Waken Meat Company
1015 Boulevard SE
Atlanta, GA 30312-3809   404-627-3537
                  Fax: 404-624-3191
Beef, pork, chicken, frozen seafood
  President: Charles Waken
Estimated Sales: $300,000-500,000
Number Employees: 5-9

15255 Wakunaga of America
23501 Madero
Mission Viejo, CA 92691-2764   949-855-2776
      Fax: 949-458-2764   800-421-2998
      info@wakunaga.com   www.kyolic.com
Manufacturer of nutritional supplements.
  Manager: Jay Levy
Estimated Sales: $ 20 - 50 Million
Number Employees: 50-99
Number of Brands: 5
Number of Products: 70
Sq. footage: 42000
Parent Co: Wakunaga Pharmaceutical
Brands:
  BESURE
  ESTRO LOGIC
  KYO-CHLORELLA
  KYO-DOPHILUS
  KYO-GREEN
  KYO-GREEN HARVEST BLEND
  KYOLIC
  MODUCARE
  MODUCHOL
  MODUPROST

15256 Walcan Seafood
PO Box 429
Heroit Bay, BC V0P 1H0
Canada   250-285-3361
          Fax: 250-285-3313 www.walcan.com
Salmon

15257 Walden Farms
1209 W Saint Georges Ave
Linden, NJ 07036-6117   908-925-9494
      Fax: 908-925-9537   800-229-1706
  info@waldenfarms.com   www.waldenfarms.com
Processor and exporter of salad dressings, dips, bbq
sauces, pancake syrups, fruit spread jams and jellies,
fruit syrups, ketchup and seafood sauces, bruschetta
and chocolate syrup.
  President: Mitchell Berko
  Vice President: Paul Berko
  Operations: Brian Sherwood Ph.D
Number Employees: 20-49
Sq. footage: 16000
Type of Packaging: Consumer, Food Service
Brands:
  Walden Farms

15258 Walden Foods
660 N Loudoun St
Winchester, VA 22601-4986   540-722-6165
          Fax: 540-622-2840   800-648-7688
                walden@waldenfoods.com
                www.waldenfoods.com
Processor of all natural and gourmet applewood
smoked seafood and poultry
  President: John P Good Jr
  VP Marketing: Christine Hyre
Number Employees: 5-9
Sq. footage: 12500
Type of Packaging: Consumer, Food Service
Brands:
  The Farm At Mt. Walden

15259 Waldensian Bakeries
320 Main St E
Valdese, NC 28690-2812   828-874-2136
      Fax: 828-874-4910 www.saralee.com
Processor of white and rye bread, cakes, snacks and
pound cakes, groceries and related products
  VP Marketing: Bill Mitchell
  Plant Manager: Andy Lopez
Estimated Sales: $ 5 - 10 Million
Number Employees: 5-9
Parent Co: Sara Lee
Type of Packaging: Consumer, Food Service, Private Label

15260 Walker Foods
237 N Mission Rd
Los Angeles, CA 90033-2103   323-268-5191
          Fax: 323-268-7812   800-966-5199
      info@walkerfoods.net   www.walkerfoods.net
Walker Foods established in 1914 is the home of El
Pato salsas, (hot tomato sauce) the famous yellow
and red can with the DUCK on the label. Walker
Foods also produces Enchilada sauce, yellow chilies
and jalapeno peppers and twopicante sauces for the
retail and food service trade. The food service division
supplies the trade with its award winning
Golden State Yellow mustard and also manufactures
white distilled vinegar under the Golden State label.
  President: Robert Walker
  Director Food Service/Industrial Sales: Craig
    Wendel-Smith
  Production Manager: Alfred Heredia
  Plant Manager: Fernando Montano
Estimated Sales: $10-20 Million
Number Employees: 50-99
Sq. footage: 120000
Type of Packaging: Consumer, Food Service, Private Label, Bulk
Brands:
  El Pato
  Golden State

15261 Walker Meats Corporation
821 Tyus Carrollton Rd
Carrollton, GA 30117-9609   770-834-8171
                  Fax: 770-834-2208
Beef, pork, poultry, produce, seafood
  President: Donald Walker
Estimated Sales: $ 10 - 20 Million
Number Employees: 20-49

15262 Walker Valley Vineyards
PO Box 24
Walker Valley, NY 12588-0024   845-744-3449
Wines
  Owner: Gary Dross
Estimated Sales: $ 5-9.9 Million
Number Employees: 4
Brands:
  Walker Valley Vineyards

15263 Walker's Seafood
312 Southwest Sq
Jonesboro, AR 72401-5984   870-932-0375
                  Fax: 870-935-8697
Seafood
  President: Darrell Walker
  Secretary/Treasurer: Patricia Walker

15264 Walkers Shortbread
170 Commerce Drive
Hauppauge, NY 11788-3944   631-273-0011
          Fax: 631-273-0438   800-521-0141
                cs@walkersshortbread.com
                www.walkersshortbread.com
Importer of shortbread and cookies
  President: Norman Barnes
  Marketing: Karen Riley

Estimated Sales: $2800000
Number Employees: 19
Parent Co: Walkers Shortbread
Type of Packaging: Consumer, Bulk
Brands:
  Duchy Originals
  Kambly
  Walker's
  Walkers

15265 Wall Meat Processing
P.O.Box 408
Wall, SD 57790-0408   605-279-2348
Manufactures slab & sliced bacon and other meat
products
  Owner: Oliver Carson
Estimated Sales: $ 1 - 3 Million
Number Employees: 1-4
Type of Packaging: Private Label

15266 Wall-Rogalsky Milling Company
416 N Main St
Mc Pherson, KS 67460-3404   620-241-2410
          Fax: 620-241-7167   800-835-2067
                www.cerealfood.com
Miller of flour including, bakery, bread, all-purpose
and self-rising; also, pancake and waffle mix, wheat
bran and mill feeds
  President/CEO: J Brent Wall
  Plant Superintendent: Kendall Allison
  Vice President: Wayne Ford
  Plant Manager: Max Streit
Estimated Sales: $ 10 - 20 Million
Number Employees: 20-49
Sq. footage: 41270
Type of Packaging: Consumer, Food Service, Private Label, Bulk
Brands:
  America's Best
  Bake-Rite H & R
  Kansas Sun
  Utility
  W-R

15267 Walla Walla Gardeners' Association
205 N 11th Ave
Walla Walla, WA 99362   509-525-7070
          Fax: 509-529-4170   800-553-5014
      wwga@wwsonion.com   www.wwsonion.com
Processor and exporter of yellow and sweet onions,
spinach, asparagus and radishes
  General Manager: Bryon Magnaghi
  Production Manager: Steve Hendrickson
Estimated Sales: $100+ Million
Number Employees: 100-249
Number of Brands: 3
Sq. footage: 15000
Type of Packaging: Consumer, Private Label
Brands:
  Gloria
  Top Choice
  Walla Walla

15268 Wallaby Yogurt Company
110 Mezzetta Ct # B
American Canyon, CA 94503-9691   707-553-1233
      Fax: 707-553-1293   info@wallabyyogurt.com
                www.wallabyyogurt.com
  Manager: Jerry Chou
  CEO: Claudia Suh
Estimated Sales: $ 1 - 3 Million
Number Employees: 20-49
Brands:
  Wallaby

15269 Wallace Edwards & Sons
11455 Rolfe Highway
Surry, VA 23883   757-294-3121
      Fax: 757-294-5378   edwardsham@aol.com
Virginia hams, hickory smoked bacon, dry cured
duck, sausage, turkey, and Virginia peanuts
  President/CEO: Bob Anderson

15270 Wallace Fisheries
PO Box 2046
Gulf Shores, AL 36547-2046   251-986-7211
                  Fax: 251-987-5127
Seafood

15271 Wallace Grain & Pea Company
PO Box 218
Palouse, WA 99161-0218   509-878-1561
          Fax: 509-878-1671   dave@wallacegrain.com

Processor and exporter of chickpeas, barley, lentils and peas
President: Joe Hulett
Assistant Manager: Gary Heaton
Estimated Sales: $500,000-$1 Million
Number Employees: 1-4
Type of Packaging: Consumer, Food Service, Private Label, Bulk
Brands:
Palouse

15272 Wallace Plant Company
201 High St
Bath, ME 04530-1677   207-443-2640
Fax: 207-386-0268
Seafood
Owner: Wallace Plant
Estimated Sales: $1 Million
Number Employees: 5-9
Type of Packaging: Consumer

15273 Wallingford Coffee Company
P.O.Box 603267
Cleveland, OH 44103-0267   216-241-3267
Fax: 216-694-2150   800-714-0944
Coffee
Manager: Joe Negrelli
CFO: Michael Hoban
Manager: Joe Negrelli
Estimated Sales: $ 1-2.5 Million
Number Employees: 5-9
Type of Packaging: Private Label, Bulk
Brands:
Wallingford

15274 Wallingford Coffee Mills
11401 Rockfield Ct
Cincinnati, OH 45241-1971   513-771-4570
Fax: 513-771-3138   800-533-3690
sales@wallingfordcoffee.com
www.wallingfordcoffee.com
Coffee
President: Gary Weber
Operations Manager: Gary Davis
Estimated Sales: $ 50-100 Million
Number Employees: 50-99
Brands:
Wallingford

15275 Wally Biscotti
4850 E 39th Ave
Denver, CO 80207-1010   303-320-9969
Fax: 303-320-9966   866-659-2559
wallybicotti@aol.com   www.wallybiscotti.com
Biscotti
President: Wally Friedlander
Marketing Manager: Waally Biscotti
Operations Manager: Jamey Biscotti
Estimated Sales: $1-$1.3 Million
Number Employees: 20-49
Type of Packaging: Consumer, Food Service, Private Label, Bulk
Brands:
Wally Biscotti

15276 Walpex Trading Company
1320 S Dixie Highway
Suite 700
Coral Gables, FL 33146-2954   305-662-9744
Exporter of raisins, soy meal, corn, sugar, beans and pistachio nuts
VP: Frank Piraino
Number Employees: 5-9

15277 Walsh's Coffee Roasters
273 Baldwin Avenue
San Mateo, CA 94401-3914   650-347-5112
Fax: 650-347-0569
Coffee
Owner/President: John Walsh
Estimated Sales: Less than $500,000
Number Employees: 1-4

15278 Walsh's Seafood
Rr 1
Gouldsboro, ME 04607   207-963-2578
Fax: 207-963-2578
Seafood
Owner: Craig Walsh

15279 Walt Koch
315 W Ponce De Leon Ave # 500
Decatur, GA 30030-2448   404-378-3666
Fax: 404-378-8492 www.waltkoch.com

Poultry frozen foods, meats, seafood
Owner: Keith Steinberg
Cfo: Cindy Groover
Sales Manager: Keith Steinberg
Estimated Sales: $ 5 - 10 Million
Number Employees: 5-9
Type of Packaging: Consumer, Food Service

15280 Walter P. Rawl & Sons
824 Fairview Road
Pelion, SC 29123-9433   803-359-3645
Fax: 803-359-8850 www.rawl.net
Grower of green onions, collards, mustard greens, turnip greens and roots, zucchini, kale and yellow summer squash
President: Howard Rawl
Director of Sales: Ashley Rawl
Head General Manager: Marshall Sherman
Estimated Sales: $24323805
Number Employees: 110
Type of Packaging: Consumer, Food Service

15281 Waltham Beef Company
18 Food Mart Road
Boston, MA 02118-2802   617-269-2250
Fax: 617-269-8183
Processed beef, pork, poultry
President: Douglas Atamian
President: Wesley Atamian
Type of Packaging: Private Label

15282 Waltkoch
315 W Ponce De Leon Ave # 500
Decatur, GA 30030-2448   404-378-3666
Fax: 404-378-8492 www.waltkoch.com
Poultry, frozen foods, meats, seafood
Owner: Keith Steinberg
Estimated Sales: $15,200,000
Number Employees: 20-49
Type of Packaging: Consumer

15283 Wampler Foods
2777 Stemmons Freeway,Suite 850
Dallas, TX 75207-2268   717-624-2191
Fax: 717-624-3687 www.wampler.com
Processor and exporter of turkey products including whole birds, breasts, legs, thighs, livers, burgers, smoked, rolls, ham, bologna, etc
Manager: David Boyer
Purchasing Agent: Patty Ziegler
Estimated Sales: $100+ Million
Number Employees: 500-999
Sq. footage: 120000
Parent Co: Wampler Foods
Type of Packaging: Consumer, Food Service

15284 Wampler's Farm Sausage Company
781 Highway 70 W
Lenoir City, TN 37771-7659   865-986-2056
Fax: 865-988-3280   800-728-7243
tedjr@wamplersfarm.com
www.wamplersfarm.com
Processor, packer and exporter of sausage
President: Ted Wampler
Vice President: John Ed Wampler
Sales Manager: Doug Young
Operations Manager: Darrell Griffis
Plant Supervisor: Mike Marney
Plant Manager: Jim Wampler
Estimated Sales: $24000000
Number Employees: 100-249
Type of Packaging: Consumer, Food Service, Private Label, Bulk
Brands:
Wampler's Farm

15285 Wan Hua Foods
804 6th Ave S
Seattle, WA 98134-1304   206-622-8417
Fax: 206-622-7088 info@wanhuafoods.com
www.wanhuafoods.com
Processor of fresh cooked noodles including udon, yaki soba, miki and chow mein; also, wonton and pot sticker wrappers
President: Sui-Ming Tam
VP: Judy Tam
Estimated Sales: $1700000
Number Employees: 10-19
Sq. footage: 12000
Brands:
Miki
Phillipino's

U-Don
Yakisoba

15286 Wanchese Fish Company
2000 Northgate Commerce Pkwy
Suffolk, VA 23435-2142   757-673-4500
Fax: 757-653-4550 www.wanchese.com
Processor and exporter of fresh and frozen seafood including flounder, bass, scallops, trout, tuna, dolphin, etc.; importer of scallops
Owner: Sam Daniels
VP: Ken Daniel
Estimated Sales: $6400000
Number Employees: 20-49
Sq. footage: 40000
Parent Co: Daniels Enterprises
Type of Packaging: Consumer, Food Service, Private Label, Bulk
Other Locations:
Wanchese Fish Co.
Hampton VA

15287 Wanda's Nature Farm
1700 Cushman Dr
Lincoln, NE 68512-1238   402-423-1234
Fax: 402-423-4586   wandas@neb.rr.com
www.superbakes.com
Processor and exporter of natural mixes including bread, cake, muffin, pancake, pasta, pizza, bagels, etc
President: Susan Zink
Vice President: David Eisner
Marketing Director: Shari Rogge-Fidler
Estimated Sales: $2311332
Number Employees: 20-49
Type of Packaging: Consumer, Food Service

15288 Wapsie Produce
P.O.Box 378
Decorah, IA 52101-0378   563-382-4271
Fax: 563-382-8210   info@capons.com
www.capons.com
Processor and exporter of frozen capons and fowl
President: Marc Nichols
VP: Paul Nichols
Estimated Sales: $ 10 - 20 Million
Number Employees: 50-99
Type of Packaging: Consumer, Private Label
Brands:
Ioma
Minowa
Thrift

15289 Wapsie Valley Creamery
P.O.Box 391
Independence, IA 50644-0391   319-334-7193
Fax: 319-334-4914
Manufacturer of Monterey and marble pepper jack, cheddar and colby cheese; processor and exporter of kosher reduced lactose whey, edible dried delactose and lactose
President: Mark Nielsen
VP: Wilbur Nielsen
Public Relations Manager: Bob Hill
Estimated Sales: $20-50 Million
Number Employees: 50-99
Sq. footage: 78000
Type of Packaging: Consumer, Private Label, Bulk

15290 War Eagle Mill
11045 War Eagle Road
Rogers, AR 72756-7544   479-789-5343
Fax: 479-789-2972   info@wareaglemill.com
www.wareaglemill.com
Processor and miller of stone burr corn meal and wholewheat flour and mixes
President: Zoe Caywood
Type of Packaging: Consumer

15291 Ward Cove Packing Company
88 E Hamlin St
Seattle, WA 98102-3144   206-323-3200
Fax: 206-323-9165   wrdscove@msn.com
www.wardscove.com
Processor and exporter of canned and frozen salmon and crab; also, exporter of surimi
President: Bill Weissfield
Estimated Sales: $ 50 - 100 Million
Number Employees: 100-249
Parent Co: Ward Cove Packing Company
Type of Packaging: Consumer, Food Service
Other Locations:
Ward Cove Packing Co.
Seattle WA

Brands:
Northern Pride
Pirate

15292 Warden Peanut Company
620 E Lime St
Portales, NM 88130   575-356-6691
      Fax: 575-359-0072
Snack foods
VP: Sam Rigsey
General Manager: Bill Owen
Plant Manager: Leonard Stanton
Estimated Sales: Under $500,000
Number Employees: 20-49

15293 Warner Candy
Ste A
1240 Don Haskins Dr
El Paso, TX 79936-7887   847-928-7200
     Fax: 847-928-2115 www.warnercandy.com
Candy
Estimated Sales: $ 10 - 20 Million
Number Employees: 20-49

15294 (HQ)Warner Vineyards Winery
706 S Kalamazoo St
Paw Paw, MI 49079-1558   269-657-3165
    Fax: 269-657-4154 800-756-5357
     kevins@warnerwines.com
     www.warnerwines.com
Wines
President: Patrick Warner
Estimated Sales: $500,000
Number Employees: 5-9
Type of Packaging: Consumer, Private Label
Brands:
Warner Vineyards

15295 (HQ)Warner-Lambert Confections
810 Main St
Cambridge, MA 02139-3588   617-491-2500
     Fax: 617-547-2381
Candy
President/CEO: J Craig
Plant Manager: Gerald Chesser
Estimated Sales: Under $500,000
Number Employees: 100-249

15296 Warrell Corporation
1250 Slate Hill Rd
Camp Hill, PA 17011-8011   717-761-5440
     Fax: 717-761-2206 800-233-7082
     sales@warrellcorp.com
     www.padutchcandies.com
Processor, importer and exporter of confectionery products
President: Patrick Huffman
Marketing Director: Richard Warrell
Number Employees: 50-99
Sq. footage: 200000
Parent Co: Pennsylvania Dutch Company
Type of Packaging: Consumer, Food Service

15297 Warren & Son Meat Processing
7585 State Route 821
Whipple, OH 45788-5164   740-585-2421
     Fax: 740-585-2073
Processor of beef, pork, lamb, specialty meats and smoked sausage and ham
Owner/Sales: Danny Warren
Marketing Director: Kathryn Warren
Estimated Sales: $ 3 - 5 Million
Number Employees: 5-9
Type of Packaging: Consumer, Bulk

15298 Warren Cheese Plant
PO Box 686
Warren, IL 61087-0686   815-745-2627
     Fax: 815-745-2843 applejack@aeroinc.net
     www.applejackcheese.com
Mozzarella, string and apple jack cheese
Cheesemaker: Duane Torkelson
Estimated Sales: $ 20-50 Million
Number Employees: 20-49
Brands:
Apple Jack

15299 Warren Laboratories
1656 Ih 35 S
Abbott, TX 76621-3014   254-580-9990
     Fax: 254-580-9944 800-421-2563
     karenk@warrenlabsaloe.com
     www.warrenlabsaloe.com

Processor of refined aloe vera beverages
Manager: Tony Tustejovsky
Estimated Sales: $2100000
Number Employees: 10-19

15300 Warwick Ice Cream Company
743 Bald Hill Rd
Warwick, RI 02886-0713   401-821-8403
     Fax: 401-821-8404
Manufacturer of ice cream cakes, pies and popsicles
Owner: Gerard Bucci Sr Jr
Estimated Sales: $1-3 Million
Number Employees: 20-49
Type of Packaging: Consumer, Food Service, Bulk

15301 Wasatch Meats
926 Jefferson St
Salt Lake City, UT 84101-2983   801-363-5747
     Fax: 801-363-5759 christy@wasatchmeats.com
     www.wasatchmeats.com
Processors of meat including beef, pork and poultry.
President: Rich Broadbent
VP: Scott Rich
VP Marketing: Mark Broadbent
VP Sales: Mark Broadbent
Operations Manager: Roger Rausch
Production Foreman: Dave Burke
Estimated Sales: $15914424
Number Employees: 20-49
Type of Packaging: Food Service

15302 (HQ)Washburn Candy Corporation
PO Box 3277
Brockton, MA 02304-3277   508-588-0820
     Fax: 508-588-2205 www.fbwashburncandy.com
Candy
President: James Gilson
Estimated Sales: $ 10-20 Million
Number Employees: 30-50
Sq. footage: 150000
Type of Packaging: Private Label
Brands:
Sevigny
Waleeco
Washburn

15303 Washington Beef
P.O.Box 832
Toppenish, WA 98948-0832   509-865-2121
     Fax: 509-865-2827 800-289-2333
     info@wabeef.com   www.wabeef.com
Packer of beef; slaughtering services available
President: Robert Rebholtz
CEO: Gayland Pedhirney
Estimated Sales: $ 100-500 Million
Number Employees: 500-999

15304 Washington Crab Producers
P.O.Box 1488
Westport, WA 98595-1488   360-268-9161
     Fax: 360-268-9410 cwhitney@pacseafood.com
     www.pacseafood.com
Processor and exporter of fresh and frozen Dungeness crab, cod, sole, bottomfish and shrimp meat; processor of fresh and frozen halibut
President: Frank D Dulcich
Assistant Manager: Glen White
Plant Manager: Bill Wideman
Estimated Sales: $100+ Million
Number Employees: 100-249
Parent Co: Pacific Coast Seafoods
Type of Packaging: Consumer, Food Service, Private Label, Bulk
Brands:
Pacific Fresh
Sea Haven
Sea Rock

15305 Washington Fruit & Produce Company
401 N 1st Ave
P.O.Box 1588
Yakima, WA 98907-1588   509-457-6177
     Fax: 509-452-8520 information@washfruit.com
     www.washfruit.com
Processor and exporter of fresh fruits including apples, pears, and cherries.
Manager: Tom Hanses
Estimated Sales: Less than $500,000
Number Employees: 1-4
Type of Packaging: Consumer, Bulk

15306 Washington Potato Company
P.O.Box 2248
Warden, WA 98857-2248   509-349-8803
     Fax: 509-349-2362 opcsales@ucinet.com
Processor and exporter of frozen and dehydrated potatoes
CEO: Frank Tiegs
Plant Manager: Mel Savage
Estimated Sales: $ 50 - 100 Million
Number Employees: 100-249
Parent Co: Oregon Potato
Type of Packaging: Food Service, Bulk

15307 Washington Quality FoodProducts
P.O.Box 308
Ellicott City, MD 21041-0308   410-465-5800
     Fax: 410-750-0163 800-735-3585
Baking mixes, flour, cornmeal, batters and breadings
President/CEO: Samuel Rogers III
CFO: James Koehnlein
CEO: Sam Rogers Jr
R&D/Quality Control: Michael Loverde
Marketing/Sales/Public Relations: Steve Friesner
Operations/Production: Thomas Rogers
Plant Manager: Robert Windsor
Purchasing Manager: Samuel Rogers III
Estimated Sales: $100+ Million
Number Employees: 100-249
Type of Packaging: Consumer, Food Service, Private Label, Bulk
Brands:
INDIAN HEAD
RAGA MUFFINS
WASHINGTON

15308 Washington Rhubarb Growers Association
P.O.Box 887
Sumner, WA 98390-0160   253-863-7333
     Fax: 253-863-2775 800-435-9911
     rhubarb@blarg.net
Cooperative of Washington rhubarb growers; also, manufacturer of IQF rhubarb
Manager: Matt Celis
General Manager: Cindy Moore
Estimated Sales: $19 Million
Number Employees: 5-9
Sq. footage: 12000
Type of Packaging: Bulk
Brands:
First Pick
Sumner

15309 Washington State Juice
10725 Sutter Ave
Pacoima, CA 91331-2553   818-899-1195
     Fax: 818-899-6042
Manufactures and processes fruit concentrates, blends and natural flavors. Custom blending is available
President: Fred Farago
Estimated Sales: $ .5 - 1 million
Number Employees: 100-249
Type of Packaging: Food Service, Private Label, Bulk

15310 Wasson Brothers Winery
17020 Ruben Ln
Sandy, OR 97055-9276   503-668-3124
     Fax: 503-668-3124
     www.wassonbrotherswinery.com
Wines
Partner: James Wasson
Partner: John Wasson
Estimated Sales: $ 1-2.5 Million
Number Employees: 1-4
Brands:
Wasson

15311 (HQ)Water Concepts
1700 E Higgins Rd # 420
Des Plaines, IL 60018-3883   847-699-9797
     Fax: 847-699-9889 waterjoe@waterjoe.com
     www.waterconcepts.com
Processor of caffeine enchanced natural artesian water.
Owner: Steve Rodgers
Marketing: Joe Brumfield
Estimated Sales: $300,000-500,000
Number Employees: 1-4
Type of Packaging: Consumer, Food Service

Brands:
Water Joe

15312 Waterfield Farms
500 Sunderland Road
Amherst, MA 01002-1038   413-549-3558
          Fax: 413-549-9945 bioshelter@aol.com
          www.bioshelters.com
Processor of tilapia fish, basil, tomatoes and pesto sauces
     President: John Reid
     Vice President: Tracy Hightower
     Director of Aquaculture: Dr Jose Llobrera
Estimated Sales: $500-1 Million appx.
Number Employees: 20-49
Type of Packaging: Consumer, Food Service
Brands:
     Hydroponic Sweet Basil
     Tilapia
     Waterfield Farms

15313 Waterfront Seafood
14358 Shell Belt Rd
Bayou La Batre, AL 36509-2330   251-824-2185
          Fax: 251-824-4307
Seafood
     President: Norwood Cain
     Vice President: Nor Cain

15314 Waterfront Seafood Market
2900 University Ave # A4
West Des Moines, IA 50266-1251   515-223-5106
     Fax: 515-224-9665 waterfrontseafood@msn.com
          www.waterfrontseafoodmarket.com
Seafood
     President: Ted Hanke
Estimated Sales: $ 3 - 5 Million
Number Employees: 50-99

15315 Watermark Innovation
400 Noyac Rd
Suite A-1
Southampton, NY 11968   201-693-8285
     Fax: 631-259-2329 inquiries@purecool.com
          www.purecool.com
flavored water

15316 Watermill Foods
1565 S Main Street
Milton Freewater, OR 97862-1228 541-938-6601
     Fax: 541-938-6449 fruit@watermillfoods.com
Processor and exporter of frozen fruits including apples, cherries and prune plums
     CEO/Executive VP: Bill Albee
     Operations Manager: Dennis Mettler
     Raw Products Manager: Mike Hendricks
Number Employees: 100-249
Parent Co: Tree Top
Type of Packaging: Consumer, Food Service, Bulk
Brands:
     Mountain Fresh
     Watermill

15317 (HQ)Watson Foods Company
301 Heffernan Dr
West Haven, CT 06516-4139   203-932-0528
     Fax: 203-932-8266 800-388-3481
          keith.clemens@watsonfoods.com
          www.watsonfoods.com
Processor, exporter and importer of nutritional additives, vitamin-mineral blends, food fibers and functional additives in bulk, tablets and water soluble packets
     President: John Watson
     VP Sales: Bill Murphy
Estimated Sales: $19700000
Number Employees: 100-249
Sq. footage: 127000
Type of Packaging: Bulk
Other Locations:
     Watson Foods Co.
     Rockville CT
Brands:
     Oven Spring

15318 Watson Nutritional Ingredients
301 Heffernan Drive
West Haven, CT 06516-4151   203-932-3000
          Fax: 203-932-8266
     mary.watson@watsonfoods.com
          www.watsonfoods.com
Hops, malt, brewers yeast
Estimated Sales: $ 20 - 50 Million
Number Employees: 100-249

15319 Watson's Quality Food Products
P.O.Box 215
Blackwood, NJ 08012-0215   856-227-0594
     Fax: 856-228-6756 800-257-7870
          sales@watsonsquality.com
          www.watsonsquality.com
Processor and packer of poultry and meat
     President: Raymond Buseman
     Executive Vice President: David Buseman
     General Sales Manager: Eddie Skee
     Director of Manufacturing: Bill Levis
Estimated Sales: $21000000
Number Employees: 100-249
Type of Packaging: Consumer, Food Service

15320 Waugh Foods
P.O.Box 2807
East Peoria, IL 61611-0807   309-427-8000
     Fax: 309-694-3115 www.waughfoods.com
Wholesaler/distributor of frozen and refrigerated food, fresh dairy and produce; serving the food service market in Central Illinois
     President: Joe Waugh
     CEO: Joe Waugh Sr
Estimated Sales: $18600000
Number Employees: 50-99

15321 Waverly Crabs
3400 Greenmount Ave
Baltimore, MD 21218-2823   410-243-1181
          Fax: 410-243-0348
Crab
     Owner: Jane Gordon
Estimated Sales: $ 3 - 5 Million
Number Employees: 10-19

15322 Wawa Food Market
260 Baltimore Pike
Media, PA 19063-5699   610-283-9292
     Fax: 610-358-8878 800-444-9292
          www.wawa.com
Milk and dairy products
     Chairman/CEO: Richard D Wood Jr
     President/COO: Howard B Stoeckel
     Executive VP: There du Pont
     Plant Manager: Dennis Shea
Estimated Sales: $ 100-499.9 Million
Number Employees: 500-999
Brands:
     Wawa

15323 Wawona Frozen Foods
100 W Alluvial Ave
Clovis, CA 93611-9176   559-299-2901
     Fax: 559-299-1921 peaches@wawona.com
          www.wawona.com
Processor and exporter of IQF and syrup packed frozen fruits including peaches, strawberries and mixed fruit; also a variety of fruit-based portion controlled products; importer of frozen fruits including melons, grapes and pineapple
     President: William Smittcamp
     Marketing Director: Bill Astin
     Industrial Sales: Sheila Woodward
     VP Operations: Albert Petersen
     Production Manager: Ruben Paraga
     Plant Manager: Tim Finley
     Purchasing Manager: Ken Cole
Estimated Sales: $55429138
Number Employees: 100-249
Type of Packaging: Consumer, Food Service, Private Label, Bulk
Brands:
     SUMMER PRIZE
     WAWONA FROZEN FOODS

15324 Wawona Packing Company
12133 Avenue 408
Cutler, C9 93615-2056   559-528-4000
     Fax: 559-528-4696 sales@wawonapacking.com
          www.wawonapacking.com
Apricots, plums, figs, grapes, peaches, and nectarines
     President: Brent Smittcamp
     Sales Manager: Tony Supino
Estimated Sales: $35 Billion
Number Employees: 1400
Brands:
     SWEET 2 EAT

15325 Wax Orchards
22744 Orchard Road SW
Vashon Island, WA 98070   206-463-9735
     Fax: 206-463-9731 800-634-6132
          customerservice@waxorchards.com
          www.waxorchards.com
Fat-free, fruit-sweetened preserves and toppings
     President: Anna Sestrap
Estimated Sales: $400,000
Number Employees: 5
Sq. footage: 15
Brands:
     Wax Orchards

15326 Way Baking Company
2100 Enterprise St
Jackson, MI 49203-3410   517-787-6720
     Fax: 517-787-3021 800-347-7373
          www.perfectionbakeries.com
Processor of baked goods
     President: John Pop
     Senior VP: Mark Porter
Estimated Sales: $ 20 - 50 Million
Number Employees: 100-249
Brands:
     Aunt Millie

15327 Wayco Ham Company
506 N William St
Goldsboro, NC 27530   919-735-3962
     Fax: 919-734-4080 800-962-2614
          tworrell@waycohams.com
          www.waycohams.com
Processor of country ham and smoked turkey
     President: Tony Worrell
     VP: George Howell
Estimated Sales: $4300000
Number Employees: 20-49
Type of Packaging: Consumer, Food Service, Private Label

15328 Wayfield Foods
5145 Welcome All Rd SW
Atlanta, GA 30349-2551   404-559-3200
     Fax: 404-559-3206 webmaster@teamtatham.com
          www.wayfieldfoods.com
General grocery items, frozen foods, meats, dairy, deli items, seafood, produce
     President: Ronald Edenfield
Estimated Sales: H
Number Employees: 500-999

15329 Waymouth Farms
5300 Boone Ave N
New Hope, MN 55428-4034   763-533-5300
     Fax: 763-533-9890 800-527-0094
          service@waymouth.com
          www.goodsensesnacks.com
Processor of sunflower and soynut milk chocolate and yogurt flavored nuts fruits and pretzels; also, trail mixes, frosted raisins, milk balls, peanut brittle, salted nut mixes, salted pretzels and seasoned snacks. Organic dried fruitsnuts and trail mixes
     President: Gerard Knight
     Chief Financial Officer: Dan Amundson
     VP Development and Planning: Julie Cotton
     Director Of Quality Assurance: Dean Giroux
     VP Operations: Dave Cleland
     General Manager: Bernie Fashingbauer
     Purchasing Manager: Louis Keenan
Estimated Sales: $35,700,000
Number Employees: 100-249
Number of Brands: 6
Sq. footage: 100000
Type of Packaging: Consumer, Food Service, Private Label, Bulk
Brands:
     FruitzeLs
     Good Sense
     Salad Pizazz
     Waymouth Farms' Organic

15330 Wayne Dairy Products
1590 NW 11th St
Richmond, IN 47374-1404   765-935-7521
     Fax: 765-935-2184 800-875-9294
          www.smithdairy.com
Processor of dairy products including milk, soft serve and hard ice cream and shake mixes
     President: Steve Schmid
     VP: Ron Them
     Sales Manager: Mike Grenert

Estimated Sales:$ 20 - 50 Million
Number Employees: 100-249
Parent Co: Smith Dairy
Type of Packaging: Consumer, Food Service, Bulk
Brands:
Smith Dairy

15331 Wayne E. Bailey ProduceCompany
P.O.Box 467
Chadbourn, NC 28431-0467   910-654-5163
Fax: 910-654-4734   800-845-6149
web@sweetpotatoes.com
www.sweetpotatoes.com
Processor of sweet potatoes
CEO/Owner: George Wooten
CFO: Stuart Hill
CEO: George Wooten
Estimated Sales:$ 3 - 5 Million
Number Employees: 5-9
Brands:
Girlwatcher
Playboy
Pride of Samspon

15332 Wayne Estay Shrimp Company
317 Oak Streetreet
Grand Isle, LA 70358-0946   985-787-3237
Fax: 985-787-2296
Fish/Seafood
President: Wayne Estay
Sales Manager: Wayne Estay
Estimated Sales:$300,000
Number Employees: 6

15333 Wayne Farms Decatur Fresh
254 Ipsco Street
Decatur, AL 35601   256-353-0312
www.waynefarmsllc.com
Manufacturer and exporter of fresh and frozen poultry
Branch Manager: Clark Dotts
Marketing/Sales Manager: Kerry Fohner
Estimated Sales:$100 Million
Number Employees: 814
Sq. footage: 42500
Parent Co: ContiGroup Companies, Inc.
Type of Packaging: Consumer

15334 Wayne Farms Decatur Further Processing West
112 Plugs Drive
Decatur, AL 35601   256-552-4873
www.waynefarmsllc.com
Manufacturer and exporter of fresh and frozen poultry
Manager: Heath Loyd
Estimated Sales:$100 Million
Number Employees: 849
Sq. footage: 42500
Parent Co: ContiGroup Companies, Inc.
Type of Packaging: Consumer

15335 Wayne Farms Decatur Further Processing East
100 Plugs Drive
Decatur, AL 35601   256-584-7010
www.waynefarmsllc.com
Manufacturer and exporter of fresh and frozen poultry
Manager: Doug Anderson
Director: Sandy Bishop
*Estimated Sales:*I
Number Employees: 440
Sq. footage: 42500
Parent Co: ContiGroup Companies, Inc.
Type of Packaging: Consumer

15336 (HQ)Wayne Farms, LLC
4110 Continental Dr
Oakwood, GA 30566-2800   678-450-3100
Fax: 770-538-2121   800-392-0844
www.waynefarmsllc.com
Manufacturer of poultry
President/CEO: Elton Maddox
CFO: Courtney Fazekas
VP Quality Assurance/Food Safety: Bryan Miller
VP Sales/Marketing/Business Development: Jack Coleman
VP Human Resources: David Malfitano
VP Operations: Guy Hinton
VP Purchasing: Gary Niedfeldt

Estimated Sales:$1.3 Billion
Number Employees: 9,200
Sq. footage: 100000
Parent Co: ContiGroup Companies, Inc.
Type of Packaging: Consumer, Food Service, Private Label
Other Locations:
Wayne Farms
Danville AR
Albertville AL
Union Springs AL
Oakwood GA
Pendergrass GA
Dobson NC
Laurel MS
Wayne Farms Decatur Fresh
Decatur AL
Wayne Farms Decatur Processing East
Decatur AL
Wayne Farms Decatur Processing West
Decatur AL
Brands:
DUTCH QUALITY HOUSE
PLATINUM HARVEST
WAYNE FARMS

15337 Wayne Farms, LLC
1020 County Road 114
Jack, AL 36346   334-897-3435
www.waynefarmsllc.com
Manufacturer and exporter of fresh and frozen poultry
Manager: Justin Jayroe
Manager: Jack Sherwood
Number Employees: 950
Sq. footage: 42500
Parent Co: ContiGroup Companies, Inc.
Type of Packaging: Consumer
Brands:
DUTCH QUALITY HOUSE
PLATINUM HARVEST
WAYNE FARMS

15338 Wayne Farms, LLC
3456 Old Oakwood Rd
Oakwood, GA 30566-2907   678-989-3900
www.waynefarmsllc.com
Processor, exporter and packager of fresh and frozen chicken
General Manager: Jimmy Kemp
Number Employees: 41
Parent Co: ContiGroup Companies, Inc.
Type of Packaging: Consumer, Food Service

15339 Wayne Farms, LLC
444 Baskin Street South
Union Springs, AL 36089-0470   334-738-2930
Fax: 334-738-2039 www.waynefarmsllc.com
Processor and exporter of poultry
Manager: Craig Vallentine
*Estimated Sales:*I
Number Employees: 980
Parent Co: ContiGroup Companies, Inc.
Type of Packaging: Bulk

15340 Wayne Farms, LLC
977 Wayne Poultry Road
Pendergrass, GA 30567   706-693-2271
www.waynefarmsllc.com
Processor of fresh and frozen chicken including parts, strips, portion control, appetizers, etc
Manager: Alane Ivory
Number Employees: 1,300
Parent Co: ContiGroup Companies, Inc.
Type of Packaging: Consumer, Food Service, Private Label
Brands:
Dutch Quality House Products
Platinum Harvest Products
Wayne Farms Products

15341 Wayne Farms, LLC
525 Mississippi Avenue
Laurel, MS 39440   601-425-4721
www.waynefarmsllc.com
Manufacturer and exporter of fresh and frozen poultry
Manager: Benny Bishop
Estimated Sales:$100 Million
Number Employees: 811
Sq. footage: 42500
Parent Co: ContiGroup Companies, Inc.
Type of Packaging: Consumer

15342 Wayne Farms, LLC
Highway 10 East
Danville, AR 72833   479-495-4400
www.waynefarmsllc.com
Manufacturer and exporter of fresh and frozen poultry
Finance/Plant Manager: Art Callahan
Operations/Production/Mfg Manager: Steve Nolin

Purchasing Director: Eddy Bruce
*Estimated Sales:*I
Number Employees: 1,028
Sq. footage: 42500
Parent Co: ContiGroup Companies, Inc.
Type of Packaging: Consumer

15343 Wayne Farms, LLC
700 McDonald Avenue
Albertville, AL 35950   256-878-3404
www.waynefarmsllc.com
Manufacturer and exporter of fresh and frozen poultry
Director: Scott Cromley
Manager: Tim Holmes
Operations Manager: Charlie Peacock
*Estimated Sales:*I
Number Employees: 1,011
Sq. footage: 42500
Parent Co: ContiGroup Companies, Inc.
Type of Packaging: Consumer

15344 Wayne Farms, LLC
802 East Atkins Street
Dobson, NC 27017   336-386-8151
www.waynefarmsllc.com
Manufacturer and exporter of fresh and frozen poultry
Director: Tammy Bush
Purchasing Director: Joe Best
Number Employees: 850
Sq. footage: 42500
Parent Co: ContiGroup Companies, Inc.
Type of Packaging: Consumer

15345 Weathervane Foods
15 Linscott Road
Woburn, MA 01801-2001   781-935-5458
Fax: 781-932-4191
General grocery
President: Howard Smillie
Estimated Sales:$340,000
Number Employees: 3

15346 Weaver Brothers
417 Dearborn Street
Berne, IN 46711-2012   219-589-2869
Fax: 219-589-3038
Cheese
Marketing Director: Wayne Amstutz

15347 Weaver Nut Company
1925 W Main St
Ephrata, PA 17522-1112   717-738-3781
Fax: 717-733-2226   info@weavernut.com
www.weavernut.com
Processor importer and distributor of nuts, dried fruits, candies, confectionery items, snack mixes, gourmet coffees and teas, beans and spices; custom roasting and contract packaging available
President: E Paul Weaver Iii III
Vice President: Michael Reis
Sales Director: Tom Flynn
Estimated Sales:$18000000
Number Employees: 20-49
Number of Products: 3500
Sq. footage: 58000
Type of Packaging: Consumer, Private Label, Bulk
Brands:
Arcor
Asher's
Hershey Chocolate
Jaret
Jelly Belly
Nabisco
Wilbur Chocolate

15348 (HQ)Weaver Popcorn Company
9850 West Point Drive,Suite 100
Indianapolis, IN 46256   765-934-2101
Fax: 765-934-4052   800-999-2365
consumercare@popweaver.com OR
webmaster@weaverpopcorn.com
www.popweaver.com

Processor and exporter of regular and microwave popcorn; also, caramel popcorn specialties including caramel with almonds and pecans and fat-free.
President: Dyveke Cox
Director Operations: Will Weaver
Estimated Sales: $ 20 - 50 Million
Number Employees: 100-249
Type of Packaging: Consumer, Food Service, Private Label, Bulk
Brands:
Bonnie Lee
Pop Weaver
Weaver Original

15349 Weaver Popcorn CompanyManufacturing Facilty
P.O.Box 395
Van Buren, IN 46991-0395   765-934-2101
        Fax: 765-934-4052   800-999-2365
        consumercare@popweaver.com OR
        webmaster@weaverpopcorn.com
        www.popweaver.com
Processor and exporter of regular and microwave popcorn; also, caramel popcorn specialties including caramel with almonds and pecans and fat-free.
President: Michael E Weaver
Founder: Ira Weaver
Director Operations: Will Weaver
Estimated Sales: $ 20 - 50 Million
Number Employees: 100-249
Type of Packaging: Consumer, Food Service, Private Label, Bulk

15350 Weaver Potato Chip Company
1600 Center Park Rd
Lincoln, NE 68512-1228   402-423-6625
        Fax: 402-423-0492
        sjackson@affinitymanagementco.com
        www.affinitysnakcs.com
Processor and exporter of popcorn and potato, corn and tortilla chips; also, wholesaler/distributor of pretzels, salsa and jerky
President: Dan Koch
VP Finance: Pat Weaverson
Operations Manager: Mike Eisenhower
Estimated Sales: $ 20 - 50 Million
Number Employees: 50-99
Type of Packaging: Consumer, Food Service, Private Label, Bulk

15351 Weaver R. Apiaries
16495 County Road 319
Navasota, TX 77868-6513   936-825-2333
        Fax: 936-825-3642   rweaver@tca.net
        www.rweaver.com
Processor of honey
President: Richard Weaver
Office Manager: Risa Davis
Estimated Sales: $ .5 - 1 million
Number Employees: 10-19
Sq. footage: 10000
Type of Packaging: Consumer, Food Service, Private Label, Bulk
Brands:
Weaver's

15352 Webbpak
P.O.Box 188
Trussville, AL 35173-0188   205-655-3500
        Fax: 205-655-3500   800-655-3500
        past40@aol.com   www.webbpak.com
Processor of vinegar, syrups, sauces, drink mixes and flavorings
President: Peter Calzone
Estimated Sales: $660,000
Number Employees: 1-4
Sq. footage: 10000
Type of Packaging: Consumer, Food Service, Private Label
Brands:
Diamond Joe
Farmers Favorite
Flowing Gold
Formula 18
Johnny Boy Vanilla
Webb's

15353 Webbs Citrus Candy
38217 Highway 27
Davenport, FL 33837-7886   863-422-1051
        Fax: 863-422-6214   www.citruscandy.com

Processor of mints, lemon drops, taffy, toffee, nougats, glazed and coated nuts, fudge, vanilla and chocolate candies, etc
President: John Webb
Estimated Sales: $1200000
Number Employees: 5-9
Type of Packaging: Consumer, Food Service, Bulk

15354 Webco Foods
8225 NW 80th St
Miami, FL 33166-2160   305-633-0100
        Fax: 305-639-6052   richard@webcofoods.com
        www.webecofoods.com
Food
Owner: Luis Teijeiro
Marketing: Richard de la Torre
Estimated Sales: $ 10-20 Million
Number Employees: 20-49
Brands:
Ferrarini

15355 Weber Flavors
562 Chaddick Dr
Wheeling, IL 60090-6056   847-215-1980
        Fax: 847-215-2073   800-558-9078
        info@weberflavors.com   www.weberflavors.com
Vanilla, natural and artificial flavors, color selections, cocoa blends
President: Andrew G Plennert
Founder: Edgar A Weber
Estimated Sales: $ 25-50 Million
Number Employees: 50-99
Brands:
Blue Moon
Hy Van
Hy Van Supreme
Simply Natural
Simply Natural Like
Whol-Bean

15356 Weber-Stephen Products Company
200 E Daniels Rd
Palatine, IL 60067-6266   847-934-5700
        Fax: 847-407-8900   800-446-1071
        support@weberstephen.com   www.weber.com
Processor of meat products
Owner: Paul Weber
Owner: Evelyn Weber
CEO: James C Stephen Sr
Estimated Sales: $ 50 - 100 Million
Number Employees: 500-999
Brands:
Weber

15357 Webster City Custom Meats
P.O.Box 280
Webster City, IA 50595-0280   515-832-1130
        Fax: 515-832-5515   888-786-3287
        wccm@webstercitycustommeats.com
        www.webstercitycustommeats.com
Processor of smoked ham, smoked bacon, smoked turkeys, fresh sausage products, boneless ham roasts, and smoked pork loins.
President: Dean Bowden
Partner/Secretary/Treasurer: Terry Reaman
Estimated Sales: $24000000
Number Employees: 100-249
Sq. footage: 57000
Type of Packaging: Food Service, Private Label

15358 Webster Distributing Company
2911 8th Avenue
Chattanooga, TN 37407-1544   423-622-1428
        Fax: 423-622-5309
Supplier of closeouts of food products
President: Barry Webster
Estimated Sales: $2671699
Number Employees: 10
Sq. footage: 50000
Type of Packaging: Food Service

15359 Webster Farms
Unit 1
Cambridge Station, NS B0P 1G0
Canada   902-538-9492
        Fax: 902-538-7662   webfarm@ca.inter.net
Processor of frozen strawberries and rhubarb; also, dry beans
President: Greg Webster
Number Employees: 20-49
Type of Packaging: Consumer, Food Service

15360 Wechsler Coffee Corporation
10 Empire Boulevard
Moonachie, NJ 07074-1380   201-440-9311
        800-800-2633
Processor of gourmet coffee, tea and drink bases; importer of green coffee; wholesaler/distributor of general merchandise and groceries including coffee and tea; serving the food service market
President: Mike O'Donnell
VP Finance: Jim Pypen
Estimated Sales: $300,000-500,000
Number Employees: 10-19
Sq. footage: 100000
Parent Co: Superior Coffee & Foods
Type of Packaging: Food Service, Private Label

15361 Wedding Cake Studio
7373 Stanhope Kell Road
Williamsfield, OH 44093   440-667-1765
        Fax: 440-293-5573   charity@thecakeloft.net
        www.thecakestudio.cc
Cakes and candy
President: Craig Harvey
Estimated Sales: Under $500,000
Number Employees: 1-4
Brands:
Ther Cake Loft

15362 Wedemeyer's Bakery
314 Harbor Way
S San Francisco, CA 94080-6900   650-873-1000
        Fax: 650-873-3170   www.wedemeyersbakery.com
Processor of bread and rolls
President: Larry Strain
Estimated Sales: $ 5 - 10 Million
Number Employees: 20-49
Type of Packaging: Consumer, Food Service
Brands:
Better Way

15363 Weems Brothers Seafood Company
320 Bayview Avenue
Biloxi, MS 39530-2601   228-432-5422
        Fax: 228-374-4834
Processor and exporter of headless and peeled frozen shrimp
Co-Owner: Laddie Weems
Co-Owner: Ronnie Weems
Estimated Sales: $990000
Number Employees: 5
Sq. footage: 75000
Type of Packaging: Consumer, Food Service
Brands:
Gulfstar
Gulfview

15364 Weetabix Company
20 Cameron St
Clinton, MA 01510-3700   978-368-0991
        Fax: 978-365-7268   800-343-0590
        info@weetabixusa.com   www.weetabixusa.com
Processor of breakfast cereals and specialty grain-based ingredients
President: John Carver
VP: Chuck Marble
VP Marketing/Sales: Ned Boundy
Director Sales (Ingredient Division): Jack Lane
Operations Manager: Richard Zieba
Estimated Sales: $26900000
Number Employees: 250-499
Parent Co: Weetabix
Type of Packaging: Consumer, Food Service, Private Label, Bulk
Brands:
ALPEN
GRAINSFIELD'S
MINIBIX
WEETABIX

15365 Weetabix of Canada
PO Box 2020
Cobourg, ON K9A 5P5
Canada   905-372-5441
        Fax: 905-372-7261   www.weetabix.com

Processor and exporter of breakfast cereals and ingredients
CEO: K Wood
VP Finance: Jeff Bakker
Executive VP: C Marble
R&D: S Abel
VP Marketing: Kent Spalding
Sales/Customer Service: Laura Nistor
VP Operations: B Grosskopf
Plant Manager: Paul Whitehead
Number Employees: 200
Number of Brands: 3
Number of Products: 90
Parent Co: Weetabix, Ltd
Type of Packaging: Consumer, Food Service, Private Label, Bulk
Brands:
Alpen
Grain Shop
Weetabix

15366 Wege Pretzel Company
116 N Blettner Avenue
Hanover, PA 17331-9209   717-843-0738
Fax: 717-632-4190   wege@wege.com
www.wege.com
Processor of pretzel products including sourdough hard pretzels, sourdough nugget pretzels, butter flavored little pretzels, unsalted honey whole wheat pretzels with sesame seeds, party stick pretzels, cruncher style sourdough specialsand sourdough thin pretzels.
President: Ike Laughman
VP Marketing: William Still
Estimated Sales: $8200000
Number Employees: 85
Sq. footage: 110000
Parent Co: LDI
Type of Packaging: Consumer, Food Service, Private Label, Bulk
Brands:
Dutchie
Wege

15367 Wei-Chuan
6655 Garfield Ave
Bell Gardens, CA 90201-1807   562-927-6681
Fax: 562-927-0780   kittyw@weichuanusa.com
www.weichuanusa.com
Processor, importer and exporter of egg and spring rolls, dumplings and sauces including stir fry, sweet and sour, barbecue, oyster, plum, lemon, soy and hoisin; importer of bamboo shoots, mushrooms, pineapple and baby corn
President: Steve Lin
VP: Ben Chang
Dairy Division Manager: Chiao-hua Chang
Sales Director: Jesse Valdez
VP Production: James Chang
Purchasing Manager: Ming-huang Chiang
Estimated Sales: $ 20 - 50 Million
Number Employees: 250-499
Type of Packaging: Consumer, Food Service, Private Label
Brands:
Farmer King
Golden Foods
Ho-Tai
Lotus
Wei-Chaun
Wei-Chuan

15368 Weibel Champagne Vineyards
PO Box 3398
Fremont, CA 94539-0398   510-656-2340
Fax: 510-656-0109
Wines
President: Fred Weibel Jr
Sales: Douglas Richards
Operations Manager: Gary Habletzel
Estimated Sales: $ 6 Million
Number Employees: 65
Sq. footage: 100
Type of Packaging: Private Label

15369 Weil's Food Processing
483 Erie Street N
Wheatley, ON N0P 2P0
Canada
                    519-825-4572
                    Fax: 519-825-7437
Processor of asparagus, canned tomatoes and potatoes
President: Henry Weil
Sales Administration: Mark Weil

Number Employees: 10-19
Type of Packaging: Consumer, Food Service, Private Label

15370 Weinberg Foods
11410 NE 124th Street
Suite 264
Kirkland, WA 98034-4305   800-866-3447
Fax: 310-230-9057
weinberg@weinbergfoods.com
www.weinbergfoods.com
Processor of kosher egg products, dry milk and vegetable powders; importer of kosher vegetable powders; exporter of kosher egg products
President: David Weinberg
Sales: Ashley Hester
Number Employees: 1-4
Sq. footage: 3000
Type of Packaging: Bulk

15371 Weir Sauces
773 Magellan Way
Napa, CA 94559-4747   415-884-5849
Fax: 707-265-2801   kim@weirsuaces.com
www.weirsauces.com
Sauces

15372 Weisenberger Mills
P.O.Box 215
Midway, KY 40347-0215   859-254-5282
Fax: 859-254-0294   800-643-8678
flourusa@te.net   www.weisenberger.com
Processor and exporter of wheat flour, cornmeal and baking mixes including biscuit, pancake, pizza dough, cornbread and hush puppies; exporter of fish batter breading
President: Mac Weisenberger
Vice President: Philip Weisenberger
Estimated Sales: $900000
Number Employees: 5-9
Sq. footage: 16000
Type of Packaging: Consumer, Food Service, Private Label

15373 Weiser River Packing
P.O.Box 773
Weiser, ID 83672-0773   208-549-0200
Fax: 208-549-0503
Processor and exporter of onions
President: Calvin Hickey
Estimated Sales: $1000000
Number Employees: 10-19
Type of Packaging: Consumer, Food Service, Private Label, Bulk
Brands:
Burger Buddies
Head of the Class
Sun Lovin
Weiser River Whoppers

15374 Weiss Brothers Smoke House
132 Norton Rd
Johnstown, PA 15906-2906   814-539-4085
Fax: 814-536-3951
Processor of smoked and Italian sausage, bacon, frankfurters and bologna
President: Walter Grata
Quality Control: Joseph Miller
Estimated Sales: Below $ 5 Million
Number Employees: 5-9

15375 Weiss Homemade Kosher Bakery
5011 13th Ave
Brooklyn, NY 11219-3519   718-438-0407
Fax: 718-438-1872   800-498-3477
Processor of kosher breads, cakes, pastries, rugulach and wedding cakes
President: Abe Weiss
Estimated Sales: $ 1 - 3 Million
Number Employees: 20-49

15376 (HQ)Weiss Noodle Company
31313 Aurora Road
Solon, OH 44139-2705   440-248-4550
Fax: 440-542-7977
Noodles
President: James Price
Estimated Sales: $ 5-10 Million appx.
Number Employees: 20
Brands:
Weiss Noodle

15377 Weiss Provisions
2840 Smallman St
Pittsburgh, PA 15222-4787   412-434-1262
Fax: 412-434-6822   800-458-6328
Processor of beef, lamb, pork, poultry, corned beef and deli meats
President: Bill Wedner
Estimated Sales: $$10-20 Million
Number Employees: 20-49
Brands:
Weiss

15378 Welch's Foods Inc
400 Walker St
Lawton, MI 49065-9726   269-624-1308
Fax: 269-624-6696   jcallahan@welchs.com
www.welchs.com
Manufacturer and exporter of juices, jellies, jams, fruit drinks and frozen concentrates.
President/Chief Executive Officer: David Lukiewski
SVP/Chief Financial Officer: Albert Wright III
VP/Marketing: Chris Heye
VP/Operations: David Engelkemeyer
VP/Human Resources & Administration: Thomas Gettig
Plant Manager: Bill Rungaitis
SVP/Supply Chain & Technology: Peter Martin
Estimated Sales: $579 Million
Number Employees: 250-499
Parent Co: Welch Foods
Type of Packaging: Consumer

15379 Welch's Foods Inc
139 S Lake St
North East, PA 16428-1209   814-725-4577
Fax: 814-725-1087   support@welchs.com OR
jcallahan@welchs.com
www.welchs.com
Manufacturer and exporter of fruit jellies, jams, juices, drinks and frozen concentrates.
President/Chief Executive Officer: David Lukiewski
SVP/Chief Financial Officer: Albert Wright III
VP/Marketing: Chris Heye
Corporate Communications Director: Jim Callahan
VP/Operations: David Engelkemeyer
VP/Human Resources & Administration: Thomas Gettig
Plant Manager: Chuck Evans
SVP/Supply Chain & Technology: Peter Martin
Estimated Sales: $579.4 Million
Number Employees: 250-499
Sq. footage: 530000
Parent Co: Welch Foods
Type of Packaging: Consumer, Food Service

15380 (HQ)Welch's Foods Inc
575 Virginia Road
3 Concord Farms
Concord, MA 01742-9101   978-371-1000
Fax: 978-371-3855   800-340-6870
jcallahan@welchs.com   www.welchs.com
Processor of jams, jellies, marmalades, preserves, beverage and frozen dessert bases, juice concentrates, frozen dessert pops and juice including grape, tomato, apple cider, cranberry and cranberry blends.
President/Chief Executive Officer: Bradley Irwin
VP/Corporate Controller: Robert McMillen III
SVP/Chief Financial Officer: Albert Wright III
CEO: Brad Irwin Esq
VP/International: William Hewins
VP/Corporate Planning: Judy Carr
Vice President Marketing: Chris Heye
VP/Sales: Damon Hart
Corporate Communications Director: Jim Callahan
VP Operations: David Engelkemeyer
VP/Human Resources & Administration: Thomas Gettig
VP/Supply Chain: Andrew Staniar
SVP/Supply Chain & Technology: Peter Martin
Estimated Sales: J
Number Employees: 1,000-4,999
Parent Co: National Grape Cooperative
Type of Packaging: Consumer, Food Service
Brands:
Welch's

15381 Welch's Foods Inc
10 E Brunean Avenue
PO Box 6067
Kennewick, WA 99336-6067   509-582-2131
        Fax: 509-586-8882   jcallahan@welchs.com
                www.welchs.com
Processor and exporter of grape juice, jellies and
jams
    President/Chief Executive Officer: David
    Lukiewski
    SVP/Chief Financial Officer: Albert Wright III
    VP/Marketing: Chris Heye
    SVP/Supply Chain & Technology: Peter Martin
    Corporate Communications Director: Jim
    Callahan
    VP/Operations: David Engelkemeyer
    VP/Human Resources & Administration: Thomas
    Gettig
    Assistant Plant Director: Marty Gardner
    Purchasing Agent: Jim Goatchner
Estimated Sales: $ 50 - 100 Million
Number Employees: 100-249
Parent Co: Welch Foods
Type of Packaging: Consumer, Food Service

15382 Welch's Foods IncCorporate Research & Technology Center
749 Middlesex Tpke
Billerica, MA 01821-3900   978-663-3966
                jcallahan@welchs.com
                www.welchs.com
Research and Technology Center features product,
process and package development laboratories along
with a pilot plant, product sensory testing facilities
and microbiological laboratories in addition to hous-
ing all of the Company'sresearch and development,
corporate quality assurance and corporate
engineering staff.
    President/Chief Executive Officer: David
    Lukiewski
    VP/Corporate Controller: Robert McMillen III
    SVP/Chief Financial Officer: Albert Wright III
    VP/Legal & General Counsel/Secretary: Vivian S
    Y Tseng Esq
    VP/International: William Hewins
    VP/Corporate Planning: Judy Carr
    Vice President Marketing: Chris Heye
    VP/Sales: Damon Hart
    Corporate Communications Director: Jim
    Callahan
    Vice President Operations: David Engelkemeyer
    VP/Human Resources & Administration: Thomas
    Gettig
    VP/Supply Chain: Andrew Staniar
    SVP/Supply Chain & Technology: Peter Martin
Number Employees: 100-249
Sq. footage: 40000
Parent Co: Welch's Foods Inc
Type of Packaging: Consumer, Food Service

15383 Welch's Foods Inc
504 Birch Ave
Grandview, WA 98930-1601   509-882-9943
        Fax: 509-882-1623   jcallahan@welchs.com
                www.welchs.com
Processor and exporter of grape juice, jellies and
jams.
    President/Chief Executive Officer: David
    Lukiewski
    SVP/Chief Financial Officer: Albert Wright III
    VP/Marketing: Chris Heye
    SVP/Supply Chain & Technology: Peter Martin
    Corporate Communications Director: Jim
    Callahan
    VP/Operations: David Engelkemeyer
    VP/Human Resources & Administration: Thomas
    Gettig
Number Employees: 100-249
Parent Co: Welch's Foods Inc
Type of Packaging: Consumer, Food Service

15384 Welch's Foods Inc
100 N Portage St
Westfield, NY 14787-1054   716-326-5252
        Fax: 716-326-5494   jcallahan@welchs.com
                www.welchs.com

Bulk grape juice concentrate
    President/Chief Executive Officer: David
    Lukiewski
    SVP/Chief Financial Officer: Albert Wright III
    VP/Marketing: Chris Heye
    Corporate Communications Director: Jim
    Callahan
    VP/Operations: David Engelkemeyer
    VP/Human Resources & Administration: Thomas
    Gettig
    SVP/Supply Chain & Technology: Peter Martin
Estimated Sales: $10-20 Million
Number Employees: 100-249
Parent Co: National Grape Cooperative

15385 Welch, Home & Clark Company
7 Avenue L
Newark, NJ 07105-3805   973-465-1200
    Fax: 973-465-7332   whc@welch-holme-clark.com
                www.welch-holme-clark.com
Sells and distributes: refined, USP/NF, crude and
kosher vegetable oils.
    President: William Dugan
Estimated Sales: $ 10 - 20 Million
Number Employees: 10-19
Type of Packaging: Bulk

15386 Welcome Dairy
H4489 Maple Rd
Colby, WI 54421-0497   715-223-2874
        Fax: 715-223-3958   800-472-2315
                info@welcomedairy.com
                www.welcomedairy.com
Manufacturer of cheese, sauces, spreads and smoked
products
    President: Terry Eggebrecht
Estimated Sales: $ 50 - 100 Million
Number Employees: 50-99
Type of Packaging: Consumer
Brands:
    WELCOME DAIRY

15387 Weldon Ice Cream Company
2887 Canal Dr
Millersport, OH 43046-9701   740-467-2400
                mgmt@weldons.com
                www.weldons.com
Processor of ice cream including novelties, sand-
wiches, creamsicles and fudgecicles
    Owner: David Pierce
Estimated Sales: $460000
Number Employees: 5-9
Type of Packaging: Consumer, Food Service, Bulk

15388 Well Dressed Food Company
PO Box 1207
Tupper Lake, NY 12986   866-567-0845
                Fax: 518-618-3147
        salesA@welldressedfoods.com
                www.welldressedfoods.com
breakfast mixes, sweet & savory jams, crunchy granola, dessert mixes, sauces/rubs and honey & toppings
    President/Owner: David Tomberlin

15389 Well Pict Berries
209 Riverside Rd
Watsonville, CA 95076-3656   831-722-3871
        Fax: 831-722-6041   dan@wellpict.com
                www.well-pict.com
Packer and grower of strawberries
    President: Timothy Miyasaka
    CFO: George Schaaf
    General Manager: Eric Miyasaka
    Quality Control: Keith Bungo
Estimated Sales: $ 30-50 Million
Number Employees: 20-49

15390 Well-Bred Loaf
201 Route 303
Valley Cottage, NY 10989-2018   845-268-3500
        Fax: 845-268-8811   800-444-5623
Processor of pound cakes, brownies, muffins, danish
and blondies
    Owner: John Stiloski
    General Manager: Frank Greenberg
    Director Sales: Arnie Lichtenstein
Number Employees: 20-49
Sq. footage: 41000
Type of Packaging: Consumer, Food Service

15391 Wellington Brewing
950 Woodlawn Road W
Guelph, ON N1K 1G2
Canada   519-837-2337
        Fax: 519-837-3142   800-576-3853
                mail@wellingtonbrewery.ca
                www.wellingtonbrewery.ca
Processor of beer, ale, lager and stout
    Office Manager: Faith Laird
    President: Michael Stiirrup
    CEO: Doug Darkens
Number Employees: 10-19
Type of Packaging: Consumer, Food Service
Brands:
    Beehive
    Black Knight
    Countryale
    Iron Uke
    Spa
    Trailhead

15392 Wellington Foods
3250 E 29th St
Long Beach, CA 90806-2321   562-989-0111
                Fax: 562-989-9322
        tharnacksr@wellingtonfoods.com
                www.wellingtonfoods.com
Health foods and institutional foods
    Owner: Anthony Harnack Sr
Estimated Sales: $ 2.5-5 Million
Number Employees: 20-49
Brands:
    Wellington Foods

15393 (HQ)Wells' Dairy
1 Blue Bunny Drive
Le Mars, IA 51031   712-546-4000
        Fax: 712-548-3011   800-942-3800
                www.wellsdairy.com
Manufacturer of frozen novelties, milk, sour cream,
yogurt, sherbert, juice, cottage cheese, and snack dip
    President/CEO: Michael Wells
    SVP/CFO: Mark Garth
    SVP Marketing/R&D: Jim Reynolds
    SVP Sales: Mike Crone
    SVP Human Resources: Jeff Stanley
    SVP Operations: David Lyons
Estimated Sales: $1 Billion
Number Employees: 2,800
Type of Packaging: Consumer, Food Service, Bulk
Other Locations:
    Ice Cream Plant
    St. George UT
Brands:
    BLUE BUNNY®
    BOMBPOP

15394 Welsh Farms
205 Spruce St
Newark, NJ 07108-2627   973-642-3000
        Fax: 732-918-8253   800-221-0663
Processor of powdered milk, buttermilk, ice cream
and juice
    President: Scott Korman
    General Manager: Robert Pailillo
    Purchasing Manager: John Bakman
Estimated Sales: $ 5 - 10 Million
Number Employees: 5-9
Sq. footage: 90000
Parent Co: Welsh Farms
Type of Packaging: Consumer, Food Service
Brands:
    Welsh Farms - Ice Cream

15395 Welsh Farms
1330 Main Ave
Clifton, NJ 07011-2215   973-772-2388
                Fax: 973-403-0180
Processor of ice cream and frozen yogurt
    Owner: Atul Patel
    General Manager: Robert Pailillo
    Plant Manager: Joe Marscovetta
Number Employees: 20-49
Type of Packaging: Consumer, Food Service

15396 Welsh Farms
205 Spruce St
Newark, NJ 07108-2627   973-642-3000
                Fax: 732-918-8253
Dairy
Estimated Sales: Under $500,000
Number Employees: 5-9

15397 Wendy's International
4288 W Dublin Granville Rd
Dublin, OH 43017-1442   614-764-3100
Fax: 614-785-4100   800-937-5449
www.wendys.com
Grocery
Project Manager: Stacey Resnick
CFO: Jay Fitzsimmons
VP: Dennis Farraw
Investor Shareholder Relations Specialis: Marsha Gordon
Estimated Sales: $ 20 - 50 Million
Number Employees: 500-999

15398 WendySue & Tobey's
15530 Broadway Center St
Gardena, CA 90248-2137   310-516-9705
Fax: 310-516-0876   info@wendysue-tobeys.com
www.wendysue-tobeys.com
Bakery
President: John Roberts
Plant Manager: John Roberts
Estimated Sales: Below $ 5 Million
Number Employees: 20-49
Type of Packaging: Private Label

15399 Wenger's Bakery
900 N 10th St
Reading, PA 19604-2302   610-372-6545
info_wenger's@aol.com
Buns, pies, cakes, breads, cookies and pastries
Owner: Javiar Martinez
Marketing Director: Peter Menicucci
Estimated Sales: $500,000
Number Employees: 20-49
Type of Packaging: Consumer

15400 Wengers Springbrook Cheese
538 Baintree Road
Davis, IL 61019-9440   815-865-5855
Fax: 815-865-5977   wengers@statelineisp.com
Processor of Swiss and muenster cheeses
President: Fred Wenger
Secretary/Treasurer: Phillis Wenger
CFO: John Wenger
Vice President: Fred Wenger
Estimated Sales: $ .5 - 1 million
Number Employees: 5-9
Type of Packaging: Consumer, Private Label, Bulk

15401 (HQ)Wengert's Dairy
2401 Walnut St
Lebanon, PA 17042-9444   717-273-2658
Fax: 717-273-2794   800-222-2129
Processor of milk including 2% and skim; also,
chilled orange juice, iced tea and fruit drinks
General Manager: Mike Eiceman
Co-President: John Wengert
Chairman: Harlan Wengert
Estimated Sales: $500,000-$1 Million
Number Employees: 100-249
Sq. footage: 30000
Type of Packaging: Consumer, Food Service, Private Label
Other Locations:
Wengert's Dairy
Camp Hill PA
Brands:
Swiss 2
Swiss Premium
Swiss Premium

15402 Wenk Foods Inc
PO Box 368
Madison, SD 57042-0368   605-256-4569
Fax: 605-256-3204   wfi@hcpd.com
www.wenkfoods.com
Processor and exporter of frozen and dried egg products; also, frozen whole geese
President: William Wenk
Sales Director: Norbert Moldan
Number Employees: 50-99
Sq. footage: 30000
Type of Packaging: Consumer, Food Service, Private Label, Bulk
Brands:
Wenk

15403 Wenner Bread Products
33 Rajon Rd
Bayport, NY 11705-1101   631-563-6262
Fax: 631-563-6546   800-869-6262
sales@wennerbread.com
www.wenner-bread.com
Processor of frozen unbaked bread products including egg twist rolls, Italian bread, bagels, hard rolls, challah and specialty breads; also, par-baked breads and rolls.
CEO/General Manager: Richard Wenner
VP National Sales: Andrew Pisani
Technical Sales Manager: Nancy Cappola
Estimated Sales: $100+ Million
Number Employees: 250-499
Sq. footage: 72000
Type of Packaging: Food Service, Private Label, Bulk
Brands:
Rustica
Wenner

15404 Went's Dairy
8450 Buffalo Ave
Niagara Falls, NY 14304-4395   716-692-6543
Fax: 716-283-9782
Processor of milk and cream
Manager: James Miklinski
Plant Engineer: Bryan Ziemendorf
Assistant Plant Manager: Frank Buzelli
General Manager: Jim Miklinski
Number Employees: 100-249
Parent Co: Niagara Milk Cooperative
Type of Packaging: Consumer, Food Service, Private Label

15405 Wente Brothers Estate Winery
5565 Tesla Rd
Livermore, CA 94550-9149   925-456-2300
Fax: 925-456-2301   info@wentevineyards.com
www.wentevineyards.com
Wines
President: Peter Chouinard
CEO: Eric Wente
CFO: Gary Ventling
Executive VP: Philip Wente
Marketing Manager: Christine Wente
Operations Manager: Antonio Zaccheo
Production Manager: William Joslin
Estimated Sales: $ 50-100 Million
Number Employees: 250-499
Brands:
Crane Ridge Merlot
Riva Ranch Chardonnay

15406 Wenzel's Bakery
125 E Broad Street
Tamaqua, PA 18252-2007   570-668-2360
Baked goods
President: George Wenzel Jr
Estimated Sales: $76,000
Number Employees: 3
Type of Packaging: Consumer

15407 Werling & Sons Slaughterhouse
P.O.Box 148
Burkettsville, OH 45310-0148   419-375-4186
Fax: 419-375-4187   www.werlingandsons.com
Processor of meat products and hydrogenated fats;
custom slaughtering available
Treasurer: Jim Werling
Estimated Sales: $ 5 - 10 Million
Number Employees: 20-49
Type of Packaging: Consumer, Bulk

15408 Wermuth Winery
3942 Silverado Trl
Calistoga, CA 94515-9611   707-942-5924
Wines
Estimated Sales: $500,000-$1 Million
Number Employees: 1-4

15409 Wesco Foods Company
1014 Vine St
Cincinnati, OH 45202-1141   513-762-4139
Processor of fruits, vegetables, floral and natural foods
VP: Reggie Griffin
Merchandising/Procurement: Mike Ross
Number Employees: 5-9
Parent Co: Kroger Company
Type of Packaging: Consumer

15410 Wesco International
PO Box 7870
Alhambra, CA 91802-7870   626-441-3879
Fax: 626-441-8087

15411 Wessanan
420 W Broadway Avenue
Minneapolis, MN 55411   612-331-3775
Fax: 612-378-8398
Milk, dairy products-noncheese
President: Tim Green
VP Sales: Pat Graiziger
Plant Manager: John Gronholm
Number Employees: 100-249
Brands:
Clover Leaf

15412 West Bay Fishing
RR 1
Box 752
Gouldsboro, ME 04607-9753   207-963-2392
Fax: 207-963-7403
Seafood
President: Richard Noble

15413 West Brothers Lobster
830 Pigeon Hill Rd
Steuben, ME 04680-3905   207-546-3622
Fax: 207-255-3987
Lobster
Owner: Blair West
Estimated Sales: $300,000-500,000
Number Employees: 1-4

15414 West Central Turkeys
704 N Broadway
Pelican Rapids, MN 56572-4147   218-863-6800
Fax: 218-863-3171
Processor and exporter of turkey
Superintendent: Roger Stephenson
Plant Manager: Don Cole
Estimated Sales: $$20-50 Million
Number Employees: 500-999
Parent Co: Jennie-O Foods
Type of Packaging: Consumer, Bulk

15415 West Coast Products Corporation
717 Tehama St
Orland, CA 95963-1248   530-865-3379
Fax: 530-865-1581   800-382-3072
www.westcoastproducts.net
Manufacturer and exporter of specialty olives and olive oil
President: Estelle Krackov
Estimated Sales: $2.5 Million
Number Employees: 10-19
Type of Packaging: Food Service, Bulk
Brands:
OLINDA

15416 West Coast Specialty Coffee
71 Lost Lake Ln
Campbell, CA 95008-6642   650-259-9308
Fax: 650-259-8024   rh@specialtycoffee.com
www.specialtycoffee.com
Coffee and coffee equipment and supplies
President: Robert Hensley
Number Employees: 1-4
Type of Packaging: Consumer, Food Service, Bulk

15417 West Field Farm
28 Worcester Rd
Hubbardston, MA 01452-1139   978-928-5110
Fax: 978-928-5745   877-777-3900
info@chevre.com   www.chevre.com
Processor of surface ripened and fresh goat cheese
President: Robert Stetson
Estimated Sales: $500,000-$1 Million
Number Employees: 5-9
Sq. footage: 3000
Type of Packaging: Consumer, Food Service
Brands:
Capri
Classic Blue
Hubbardson Blue

15418 West India Trading Company
2086 Route 950
Petit-Cap, NB E4N 2J7
Canada   514-849-6031
Fax: 514-499-8449   witco@qc.aibn.com
Processor of smoked herring with bones and boneless
President: A. De Vasconcelos
VP: A De Montbrun
Parent Co: West India Trading Company
Type of Packaging: Bulk
Brands:
Wico

15419 (HQ)West Liberty Foods
P.O.Box 318
West Liberty, IA 52776-0318   319-627-7285
          Fax: 319-627-6334 888-511-4500
wlfsales@wlfoods.com www.wlfoods.com
Co-Manufacturer of ready-to-eat sliced processed
meat, poultry and protein products
    Manager: Carolyn Aranday
    Chairman: Paul Hill
    VP Business Development: Charles Cook
Estimated Sales:$100+ Million
Number Employees: 1,000-4,999
Sq. footage: 270000
Parent Co: Iowa Turkey Growers Cooperative
Type of Packaging: Consumer, Food Service, Private Label
Other Locations:
    West Liberty Foods Plant
    Mt Pleasant IA
    West Liberty Foods Plant
    Sigourney IA

15420 West Meat & Locker Company
121 Zinser Place
Washington, IL 61571-2553   309-444-8475
Processor of beef and pork; slaughtering services
available
    President: Harold B West
Estimated Sales:$200000
Number Employees: 10
Type of Packaging: Consumer, Food Service, Private Label, Bulk

15421 West Pac
9671 N 5th E
Idaho Falls, ID 83401-5637   801-973-7400
          Fax: 801-973-7436 801-973-7407
Processor of cake mixes, barbecue sauces and
spices; contract packager of liquid and dry mixes in
cans, bottles and boxes
    President: Hal Havens
Number Employees: 5-9
Sq. footage: 20000
Type of Packaging: Consumer, Private Label
Brands:
    Gourmet Spices

15422 West Pak Avocado
42322 Avenida Alvarado
Temecula, CA 92590-3445   951-296-5757
          Fax: 951-296-5744 800-266-4414
matt@westpakavocado.com www.wpavo.com
Importer, exporter and packer of avocados; importer
of Mexican and Chilean fruits; processor of persim-
mons and kumquats
    Owner: Galen Newhouse
    Import Export Director: Dave Culpeper
    VP/General Manager: Galen Newhouse
Estimated Sales:$ 3 - 5 Million
Number Employees: 50-99
Sq. footage: 22000
Type of Packaging: Consumer, Food Service, Bulk
Brands:
    Asian Star
    West Pak

15423 West Park Wine Cellars
P.O.Box 280
West Park, NY 12493-0280   845-384-6709
          Fax: 845-384-6709 www.westparkwinery.com
Wines
    President: Louis Fiore
*Estimated Sales:*Under $300,000
Number Employees: 1-4
Type of Packaging: Private Label
Brands:
    Full Service Caterin

15424 West Point Dairy Products
412 E Elk St
West Point, NE 68788-1065   402-372-5551
          Fax: 402-372-5061 info@westpointdairy.com
                    www.westpointdairy.com
Dairy products including butter
    President: Susan Peckham
    Vice President: Mark Peckham
    Production Manager: Valen Neesen
Estimated Sales:$ 20-50 Million
Number Employees: 50-99
Type of Packaging: Private Label
Brands:
    COUNTRY CREAM BUTTER

15425 West Virginia Sausage Company
P.O.Box 329
New Haven, WV 25265-0329   304-882-3194
          Fax: 304-882-3194
Manufacturer of sausage
    Manager: Tammy Paugh
Estimated Sales:$1.7 Million
Number Employees: 5-9
Type of Packaging: Consumer, Bulk

15426 WestFarm Foods
618 N Allumbaugh St
Boise, ID 83704-9213   208-375-3062
          Fax: 208-378-7101
Processor of milk
    Manager: Alan Shrader
    Sales Manager: Dave Wisenor
    Purchasing Agent: Jack Ring
Estimated Sales:$ 50 - 100 Million
Number Employees: 100-249
Parent Co: West Farm Foods
Type of Packaging: Consumer, Food Service, Private Label, Bulk

15427 WestFarm Foods
P.O. Box 79007
Seattle, WA 98119   425-392-6463
          Fax: 425-391-6458 800-333-6544
westfarm@westfarm.com www.darigold.com
Processor of butter, yogurt, cottage cheese and sour
cream
    President: John Underwood
    CFO: Steve Boyd
    Director Manufacturing Products: Joe Portman
    Plant Manager: Kim Niino
Estimated Sales:$ 100-500 Million
Number Employees: 100-249
Parent Co: West Farm Foods
Type of Packaging: Consumer, Food Service
Brands:
    Darigold Brand
    Lucerne Brand
    Safeway
    Single Serve Milk

15428 WestFarm Foods
PO Box 79007
Seattle, WA 98119-7907   206-286-6832
          Fax: 206-281-3456
contact.westfarm@westfarm.com
                    www.westfarm.com
Processor of milk and fruit drinks
    President/CEO: John Underwood
    Chairman: Rod DeJong
    Plant Manager: Bruce Hodges
Estimated Sales:$ 5 - 10 Million
Number Employees: 5-9
Parent Co: West Farm Foods
Type of Packaging: Consumer, Food Service, Private Label, Bulk
Brands:
    Fred Meyer
    Haggen
    Safeway
    Western Family

15429 WestFarm Foods
P.O. Box 79007
Seattle, WA 98119   509-837-8000
          http://www.darigold.com
Processor of milk and hard cheese
    Plant Manager: David Puckett
    CEO: John Underwood
Estimated Sales:$100+ Million
Number Employees: 100-249
Parent Co: West Farm Foods
Type of Packaging: Consumer, Food Service, Private Label, Bulk
Brands:
    Dairygold

15430 Westar Nutrition Corporation
1239 Victoria St
Costa Mesa, CA 92627-3933   949-645-6100
          Fax: 949-645-9131 800-645-1868
cs@vivalife.com www.vivalife.com
Processor of nutraceuticals and nutritional supple-
ments
    President: David Fan
    National Sales Manager: Cheryl Cartwright
    Technical Director: Simon Hsia PhD
Estimated Sales:$29800000
Number Employees: 20-49

15431 Westbend Vinyards
5394 Williams Rd
Lewisville, NC 27023-8278   336-945-5032
          Fax: 336-945-5294 866-901-5032
westbendvineyards@alltel.net
                    www.westbendvineyards.com
Wine
    Owner: Jack Kroustalis
    Manager: Steve Shepard
Estimated Sales:$500,000-$1 Million
Number Employees: 10-19

15432 (HQ)Westbrae Natural Foods
734 Franklin Avenue
Suite 444
Garden City, NY 11530-4525   800-434-4246
          800-434-4246
                    www.westbrae.com
Processor, importer and exporter of natural and or-
ganic soy and rice beverages, tortilla and potato
chips, soups, beans, chili, condiments, sauces, rice
cakes, popcorn, pretzels, licorice, cookies, spreads
and Oriental foods
    President: Andrew Jacobson
    CEO: B Allen Lay
    CFO: Ira Lamel
Number Employees: 20-49
Sq. footage: 39000
Type of Packaging: Consumer, Private Label
Brands:
    Bearitos
    Little Bear Organic
    Westbrae Natural
    Westsoy

15433 Westbrook Trading Company
3410b Odgen Road SE
Calgary, AB T2G 4N5
Canada   403-290-0860
          Fax: 403-264-3017 800-563-5785
Processor and exporter of fresh, frozen and boxed
beef and pork
    President: Michael Nutik
    Sales Manager: Daren Uens
Number Employees: 100-249
Type of Packaging: Consumer, Food Service, Bulk

15434 Westco Bakemark
7351 Crider Ave
Pico Rivera, CA 90660-3705   562-949-1054
          Fax: 562-948-2655 800-695-5061
bakemark@bakemark.com www.bakemark.com
Baked goods
    President: Larry Sullivan
    Marketing Coordinator: Mitchelle Munguia
    VP: Bruce Reynolds
    Marketing/Sales Manager: James Parker
    Operations Manager: Don Roby
    Manufacturing Manager: Allan Schmidt
Estimated Sales:$ 20-50 Million
Number Employees: 250-499
Type of Packaging: Private Label
Brands:
    Aloha Dandy
    Apricot Dandy
    Brite White Icing Bay
    Carribean Bouquet
    Ellison Moist Muffin
    No Time Bread Base
    No Time Bread Condit
    Pie Do Aid
    Reserve Cabernet Sauvignon
    Supreme Date

15435 Westco-Bake Mark
7351 Crider Ave
Pico Rivera, CA 90660-3705   562-949-1054
          Fax: 562-948-2655 www.westco.com
Processor, importer and exporter of ingredients and
supplies including mixes, fillings, icings and frozen
products for the baking, food processing and food
service industries
    Owner/President: Brett Weaver
    VP: Bruce Reynolds
    Sales: Tim Williams
    Plant Manager: John Kupniewski
Estimated Sales:$ 20 - 50 Million
Number Employees: 250-499
Parent Co: CSM
Type of Packaging: Food Service, Bulk
Other Locations:
    Westco-BakeMark
    Oklahoma City OK

15436 Westdale Foods Company
14541 S 88th Ave
Orland Park, IL 60462-2752   708-458-7774
Fax: 708-458-1298 westdalefoods@AOL.com
www.westdalefoods.com
Candy
Owner: Tom Vandervliet
Estimated Sales: $ 5-10 Million
Number Employees: 10-19
Brands:
Sachers
Schluckwerder
Schumann's
Schwarteau
Siljans
Simpkins
Smooth & Melty
Soldans

15437 Western Alaska Fisheries
1111 3rd Ave # 3200
Seattle, WA 98101-3264   206-447-4400
Fax: 206-447-9700
Processor, importer and exporter of fresh and frozen
fish including cod, halibut, herring and shellfish
President: Fumito Kawa
Estimated Sales: $112000000
Number Employees: 1-4
Parent Co: Maruha Corporation
Type of Packaging: Food Service, Bulk

15438 Western Bagel Baking Corporation
7814 Sepulveda Blvd
Van Nuys, CA 91405-1062   818-786-5847
Fax: 818-787-3221 wbinfo@westernbagel.com
www.westernbagel.com
Processor and exporter of fresh and frozen bagels.
President: Steve Ustin
Vice President: Skip Scheidt
Operations Manager: Jim Schultz
Estimated Sales: $29280131
Number Employees: 250-499
Sq. footage: 30000
Brands:
Western

15439 Western Beef Jerky
7209b 101 Avenue NW
Edmonton, AB T6A 0H9
Canada   780-469-4817
Fax: 780-468-5006
Processor of beef jerky
President: Danny Ljubsa
Number Employees: 1-4
Type of Packaging: Consumer

15440 Western Dairy Products
3625 Westwind Boulevard
Santa Rosa, CA 95403-1067   707-524-6770
Fax: 707-524-6777 800-433-2479
Dairy products
President: Graeme Honeyfield
Estimated Sales: $500,000-$1 Million
Number Employees: 5-9

15441 Western Dairymen Corporation
6350 N 2150 W
Smithfield, UT 84335-9700   435-563-3281
Fax: 435-563-3388 www.dfamilk.com
Cheese
Manager: Don Hansen
Estimated Sales: $ 50 - 100 Million
Number Employees: 100-249

15442 Western Dressing
PO Box 276
Grundy Center, IA 50638-0276   319-824-3304
Fax: 319-824-3304
Desserts
President: Emmet O'Sullivan
Estimated Sales: $ 5-10 Million
Number Employees: 50

15443 Western Flavors & Fragrances
4555 Las Positas Road
Livermore, CA 94551-8866   925-373-9433
Fax: 925-373-6257 info@wffsensory.com
www.wffsensory.com
Processor and exporter of flavors including vanilla,
citrus and vegetable extracts for use in dairy, bever-
ages, health foods, confectionery, cereals, etc
President: Richard Grame
COO: Adib Nassar
vp: Gary Pryor
Marketing Director: Robert Gabriel
Public Relations: Nicki Turrin
Purchasing Manager: Roberta Kashiwase
Estimated Sales: $ 50 - 100 Million
Number Employees: 25
Sq. footage: 20000

15444 Western Foods
P.O.Box 194060
Little Rock, AR 72219-4060   501-562-4646
Fax: 501-568-3447
thuffman@western-foods.com
western.foodorderentry.com
Wholesaler/distributor of groceries, frozen foods,
meats, cleaning supplies, disposables, table top
needs, etc.; serving the food service market
President: Tony Huffman
Vice President: Ed Fason
Estimated Sales: $51987685
Number Employees: 50-99

15445 Western Meats
P.O.Box 4185
Rapid City, SD 57709-4185   605-342-0322
Fax: 605-342-5375 bando@rapidnet.com
Processor of meat including beef and buffalo
President: Bruce Anderson
Secretary: Gail Hise
Plant Manager: Al Holzer
Estimated Sales: $ 10 - 20 Million
Number Employees: 20-49
Sq. footage: 8000
Type of Packaging: Consumer, Food Service, Pri-
vate Label, Bulk

15446 Western Meats
4101 Capitol Blvd SW
Tumwater, WA 98501-4069   360-357-6601
Processor of beef and pork
President: Dennis Mydlar
Estimated Sales: $500,000-$1 Million
Number Employees: 10-19
Type of Packaging: Consumer, Food Service

15447 Western New York Syrup Corporation
P.O.Box 334b
Lakeville, NY 14480-0910   585-346-2311
Processor of liquid sweeteners
Manager: Tim Calway
Assistant Manager: Lee Robinson
Estimated Sales: $ 5 - 10 Million
Number Employees: 1-4
Parent Co: Archer Daniels Midland Company
Type of Packaging: Bulk

15448 Western Pacific Commodities
3960 Howard Hughes Parkway
5th Floor
Las Vegas, NV 89169-5972   702-312-8080
Fax: 702-320-8889
info@westernpacificcommodities.com
www.wpcommodities.com
Importer of Asian food products, including rice, ex-
porter of rice and ingredients, plus agricultural com-
modities such as beef, poultry, wheat, corn, barley,
rice, coffee, sorghum and soybean
President: Kevin Lougheed
Estimated Sales: $ 22 Million
Number Employees: 10-19
Number of Brands: 15
Number of Products: 220
Sq. footage: 24000
Type of Packaging: Consumer, Food Service, Pri-
vate Label, Bulk
Brands:
Bushel In A Box
Emperor's Choice
Lucky Triple 888
Royal Pacific Foods

15449 Western Sugar Company
2100 E Overland
Scottsbluff, NE 69361-7734   308-632-4155
Fax: 308-632-3388 www.westernsugar.com
Manufacturer of beet sugar
Manager: Steve Howlette
CEO: Larry Steward
Estimated Sales: $100 Million
Number Employees: 500-999
Parent Co: Western Company
Type of Packaging: Food Service, Bulk

15450 Western Sugar Cooperative
7555 E Hampden Ave # 600
Denver, CO 80231-4837   303-830-3939
Fax: 303-830-3941 www.westernsugar.com
Processor of beet sugar
CEO: Inder Mathur
CFO: Greg Huff
CEO: Indur Mathur
Sales Director: Frank Bush
Operations Manager: Gary Price
Estimated Sales: $251,100,000
Number Employees: 500-999
Type of Packaging: Consumer, Private Label, Bulk
Brands:
GW

15451 Western Syrup Company
13766 Milroy Pl
Santa Fe Springs, CA 90670-5131   562-921-4485
Fax: 562-921-5170
Processor and exporter of custom formulated bever-
age bases, concentrates, flavors and flavor emul-
sions for carbonated beverages, slushes, sno-cones,
etc.; also, dessert toppings including chocolate
syrup, fudge and fruit
President: Pushpa Sastry
Sales Director: Ken Molder
Plant Manager: Marlon King
Estimated Sales: $ 3 - 5 Million
Number Employees: 5-9
Sq. footage: 55000
Parent Co: Western Syrup Company
Brands:
Bartenders Pride
High Mountains
Rooster
Western Syrup

15452 Westfield Farm
28 Worcester Rd
Hubbardston, MA 01452-1139   978-928-5110
Fax: 978-928-5745 877-777-3900
info@chevre.com www.chevre.com
Goat and cow cheeses
President: Robert Stetson
VP Marketing: Debby Stetson
Marketing Director: Bob Stetson
Sales Director: Debby Stetson
Estimated Sales: $500,000-$1 Million
Number Employees: 5-9
Brands:
Capri Goat Cheese
Hubbardston Blue

15453 Westfield Foods
19 Lark Industrial Pkwy # F
Greenville, RI 02828-3003   401-949-3558
Fax: 401-949-3738 info@milliessoups.com
www.milliessoups.com
Processor of dry soup and rice mixes; also, chili
President: John Pezzillo
Estimated Sales: $130000
Number Employees: 1-4
Sq. footage: 8500
Type of Packaging: Consumer, Food Service
Brands:
Millie's

15454 Westhill Dairy
60 Brisbane Road
North York, ON M3J 2K2
Canada   416-661-0580
Fax: 416-661-0587
Processor and wholesaler/distributor of cultured
dairy products including sour cream, yogurt, cream
and pressed cottage cheese and buttermilk; whole-
saler/distributor of beverages; serving the food
service market
General Manager: Paul Roach
Secretary: Abe Gomel
Number Employees: 50-99
Sq. footage: 30000
Type of Packaging: Consumer, Food Service, Bulk
Brands:
Bird's Hill
Blue Bell
Old Country
Western
Western Creamery

15455 (HQ)Westin
11808 W Center Rd # 1
Omaha, NE 68144-4435   402-691-8800
          Fax: 402-691-7920   800-228-6098
                    www.westininc.com
Processor of bacon bits, imitation bacon bits, leci-
thin, onion rings, breaded cheese, sunflower seeds,
soy products, corn starch, salad dressings, sauces,
etc.; importer of olives; exporter of frozen breaded
vegetables
    President: R Westin
    CEO: Scott Carlson
Number Employees: 100-249
Type of Packaging: Consumer, Food Service, Pri-
    vate Label, Bulk
Other Locations:
    Westin
    Wahoo NE
Brands:
    BIG RED
    FAIRBURY
    FEASTER FOODS
    GREAT AMERICAN

15456 Westlam Foods
P.O.Box 1987
Chino, CA 91708-1987   909-627-7535
    Fax: 909-628-1030   800-722-9519
Manufacturer of dry and dehydrated beans, rice and
popcorn
    President: Carl Hartman
Estimated Sales: $50-100 Million
Number Employees: 20-49
Sq. footage: 80000
Parent Co: Trinidad/Benham Corporation
Type of Packaging: Consumer, Food Service, Pri-
    vate Label, Bulk
Brands:
    EVANS
    PEAK COOKQUIK
    VALLEY FARMS

15457 Westnut
PO Box 905
Cornelius, OR 97113-0905   503-538-2161
    Fax: 503-538-8924   sales@westnut.com
                    www.westnut.com
Nuts, hazelnuts
Estimated Sales: $ 5-10 Million
Number Employees: 40

15458 Weston Bakeries
1425 the Queensway
Etobicoke, ON M8Z 1T3
Canada
                    416-252-7323
          Fax: 416-252-8941
Processor and exporter of bread, rolls, English muf-
fins and stuffings
    President: Ralph Robinson
Number Employees: 250-499
Parent Co: George Weston Foods
Type of Packaging: Consumer, Food Service

15459 Weston Bakeries
5819 2nd Street SW
Calgary, AB T2H 0H3
Canada
                    403-259-1500
          Fax: 403-259-6494
    Customer_Service@weston.ca
          www.foodsfortrade.com
Processor of bread, rolls and stuffing
    General Manager: Ed Holik
    VP Sales/Distribution: Norm Skelton
    Production/Technical Manager: Pat Boswell
Number Employees: 100-249
Parent Co: Weston Bakeries
Brands:
    Casa Mendosa
    Country Harvest
    D'Italiano
    Deli-World
    Wonder

15460 Weston Bakeries
83 Railway Street
Kingston, ON K7K 2L7
Canada
                    613-548-4434
          Fax: 613-548-8480   800-267-0229
Processor of bread and rolls
    Branch Manager: Larry Brandt
    Plant Manager: Larry Brandt

Number Employees: 50-99
Sq. footage: 50000
Parent Co: Weston Bakeries
Type of Packaging: Consumer, Food Service
Brands:
    Weston

15461 Weston Bakeries
1425 The Queens Way
Toronto, ON M8Z 1T3
Canada   416-252-7323
          Fax: 416-252-6573   800-590-6861
    customer_service@weston.ca   www.weston.ca
Processor of bread, rolls and English muffins
    President: Ralph Robinson
    National Commosion Manager: Julian Franklin
    Plant Coordinator: Jim Hennessey
    Purchasing Agent: Colin Bellenger
Number Employees: 250-499
Parent Co: Weston Bakeries
Type of Packaging: Consumer, Food Service
Brands:
    Weston

15462 Weston Bakeries
695 Martindale Road
Sudbury, ON P3E 4H6
Canada   705-673-4185
          Fax: 705-673-5695   www.gwbakeries.com
Processor of bread and rolls
    VP: Geoffrey H. Wilson
    Owner: George Weston
    Sales/Marketing: Serge Veilleux
    Plant Manager: Ed Scopazzi
Number Employees: 100-249
Parent Co: Weston Bakeries
Type of Packaging: Consumer, Food Service
Brands:
    Arnold
    Thomas

15463 Westport Locker Service
707 S West St
Westport, IN 47283-9116   812-591-3033
                    877-265-0551
Processor of meat products including beef, lamb and
pork
    Owner: Ben Davis
Estimated Sales: $ 3 - 5 Million
Number Employees: 5-9

15464 Westport Rivers Vineyard& Winery
417 Hixbridge Rd # C
Westport, MA 02790-1316   508-636-3423
          Fax: 508-636-4133   800-993-9695
          retail@westportrivers.com
                    www.westportrivers.com
Wine jellies, wine ketchup, wine mustards, wines,
champagne
    President: Robert Russell
    Vice President: Carol Russell
    Owner: Carol Russell
    Sales Director: Jan Potts
Estimated Sales: $ 1.5 Million
Number Employees: 10-19
Number of Brands: 2
Number of Products: 15
Sq. footage: 2700
Type of Packaging: Private Label
Brands:
    Westport Farms Sparkling
    Westport Farms Specialty Foods
    Westport Farms White & Rose
    Westport Rivers Vine

15465 Westside Brewing Company
340 Amsterdam Ave
New York, NY 10024-6932   212-721-2161
          Fax: 212-721-2017   www.westsidebrewingco.com
Processor of seasonal beer, ale, stout, pilsner and
porter
    Owner: Steve Wiebe
    CEO: Mark Pahna
    Marketing Manager: Steve Wiebi
Estimated Sales: Below $ 5 Million
Number Employees: 20-49
Type of Packaging: Consumer, Food Service
Brands:
    Westside

15466 Westway Trading Corporation
16450 36th St SE
Mapleton, ND 58059-9740   701-282-5010
          Fax: 701-281-2695   www.westwaytrading.com
Processor and exporter of molasses
    Manager: Jeff Olson
Estimated Sales: $ 5 - 10 Million
Number Employees: 10-19
Type of Packaging: Bulk

15467 Westwood Winery
11 E Napa St
Sonoma, CA 95476-6708   707-935-3246
          Fax: 707-935-3286   info@westwoodwine.com
                    www.westwoodwine.com
Wines
    Founder: Umbert Urch
    Co-Owner: Betty Urch
Estimated Sales: $ 3 - 5 Million
Number Employees: 5-9
Brands:
    Stanley's
    Westwood Winery

15468 Wet Planet Beverage
130 Linden Oaks # C
Rochester, NY 14625-2834   585-381-3560
          Fax: 585-381-4025   donna@joltcola.com
                    www.wetplanet.com
Processor of root beer, spring water and colas; also,
sports, guaranas and ginseng drinks
    President: C J Rapp
    coo: Lowell Patric
    CEO: Christopher Annesi
    VP Marketing: Brian Creary
    Sales Director: Brian Creary
    Operations Manager: Shirley Mellor
Estimated Sales: $ 5 - 10 Million
Number Employees: 5-9
Type of Packaging: Consumer, Food Service
Brands:
    Blubotol
    Blue Bottle
    Cronk 2 O
    First Tec
    Jolt
    Jolt-Cola
    Pirate's Keg
    Pirates Keg
    XTC

15469 Wetherby Cranberry Company
3365 Auger Rd
Warrens, WI 54666-7517   608-378-4813
          Fax: 608-378-3157   wetherby@mwt.net
                    www.freshcranberries.com
Processor of cranberries
    Owner: Nodji Van Wichen
    Owner/CEO: James Van Wychen
Estimated Sales: $ .5 - 1 million
Number Employees: 1-4
Type of Packaging: Consumer, Bulk
Brands:
    Wetherby

15470 Wetta Egg Farm
2909 N 263rd Street W
Andale, KS 67001-9647   316-445-2231
          Fax: 316-444-2468
Processor of eggs and egg products
    President: Louis Wetta
    Vice President: Earl Wetta
Estimated Sales: $ 1 - 3 Million
Number Employees: 5-9
Type of Packaging: Consumer, Food Service

15471 Wexler Meat Company
5750 Old Orchard Road
Suite 520
Skokie, IL 60077-1081   773-927-5656
          Fax: 773-927-1853
Processor of beef carcasses
    President: Michael Gitelman
    VP: Barry Chudnow
    Vice President: Anne Hierman
    VP Sales: John Alexander
Estimated Sales: $76600000
Number Employees: 275
Type of Packaging: Bulk

15472 Weyand Fisheries
471 Biddle Ave
Wyandotte, MI 48192-2703   734-284-0400
          Fax: 734-284-2671 800-521-9815
carolyn@weyandfish.com   www.weyandfish.com
Processor of fresh, frozen and batter-dipped fish
    President: David Blume
    Vice President: Carolyn Smith
    Plant Manager: Richard Weyand
Estimated Sales: $5932554
Number Employees: 5-9
Type of Packaging: Consumer, Food Service, Private Label, Bulk

15473 Weyauwega Star Dairy
P.O.Box 658
Weyauwega, WI 54983-0658   920-867-2870
    Fax: 920-867-3325 www.wegastardairy.com
Cheese
    President: James Knaus
    Sales Director: Debby Stetson
Estimated Sales: $ 10-20 Million
Number Employees: 50-99
Brands:
    Weyauwega Star Dairy

15474 Weyhaupt Brothers Packing
703 Schlueter Germaine Rd
Belleville, IL 62220-5237   618-233-0452
          Fax: 618-233-0454
Processor and packer of meat products including
bone-in ham, smoked bacon, smoked sausage, Polish
sausage, bologna, braunschweiger, liver sausage,
head cheese and blood sausage; also, Spanish-style
sausage including chorizo, sashashonand butifara
    President: Amy Voubet
Estimated Sales: $ 10 - 20 Million
Number Employees: 20-49
Sq. footage: 22000
Parent Co: Wards Cured Meats
Type of Packaging: Consumer
Brands:
    Valencia Espanol Style
    Weyhaupt Bros. Packing

15475 Whaler Vineyard Winery
6200 Old River Rd
Ukiah, CA 95482-9657   707-462-6355
          Fax: 707-462-6353
Wines
    President: Russ Nyborg
    CFO: Tara Larwood
    VP Marketing/VP Operations: Ann Nyborg
Estimated Sales: $500,000-$1 Million
Number Employees: 1-4
Type of Packaging: Private Label
Brands:
    Flagship Shiraz
    Flagship Zinfandel
    Whaler Vineyard Flag

15476 Whaley Pecan Company
P.O.Box 609
Troy, AL 36081-0609   334-566-3504
          Fax: 334-566-9336 800-824-6827
info@whaleypecan.com   www.whaleypecan.com
Processors of shelled pecans and some exports
    President: Robert Whaley
Estimated Sales: $5,000,000
Number Employees: 20-49
Sq. footage: 40000
Type of Packaging: Consumer, Food Service, Bulk
Brands:
    Whaley's
    Whaley's Fancy Shelled

15477 Wham Food & Beverage
519 S 21st Avenue
Hollywood, FL 33020-5015   954-920-7857
    Fax: 954-449-0628 Jon@whamfoods.com
          www.whamfoods.com
Liquidator of food and beverage closeouts by the
truckload
    President/CEO: Jonathon Auspitz
    VP: Adam Busch
    Marketing/Sales: Adam Busch
Estimated Sales: $5,220,000
Number Employees: 8
Number of Brands: 40
Number of Products: 248
Type of Packaging: Consumer, Food Service, Private Label, Bulk

15478 Wharton Seafood Sales
P.O.Box 440
Paauilo, HI 96776-0440   808-776-1087
          Fax: 877-591-8944 800-352-8507
Seafood
    President: Bailey Wharton
Estimated Sales: Less than $100,000
Number Employees: 1-4

15479 What's Brewing
1807 Tierra Mesa
San Antonio, TX 78263-3941   210-648-6470
          Fax: 210-308-6522
Beer
    President: Roger Chbeir
Estimated Sales: Less than $500,000
Number Employees: 1-4

15480 Wheat Montana Farms & Bakery
P.O.Box 647
Three Forks, MT 59752-0647   406-285-3614
          Fax: 406-285-3749 800-535-2798
          info@wheatmontana.com
          www.wheatmontana.com
Grain, flour, bread
    President: Dean Folkvord
    Marketing Director: Rita DeAngelis-Kockl
    Production Manager: Randall Larson
Estimated Sales: $ 5-10 Million
Number Employees: 100-249
Type of Packaging: Consumer, Food Service, Private Label, Bulk

15481 Wheeling Coffee & SpiceCompany
13 14th St
Wheeling, WV 26003-2833   304-232-0141
    Fax: 304-232-0162 800-500-0141
    whgcoffee@wheelingcoffeeco.com
          www.wheelingcoffeeco.com
Processor of roast coffee and spices
    President: Mary Ann Lokmer
    CEO: Stephanie Ann Lokmer
Estimated Sales: $5-9.9 Million
Number Employees: 10-19
Type of Packaging: Consumer, Food Service, Bulk
Brands:
    Paramount Coffee

15482 Whetstone Candy Company
2 Coke Road
St Augustine, FL 32086-5764   904-825-1710
    Fax: 904-824-0436 sales@whetstonecandy.com
          www.whetstonecandy.com
Candy and confectionery
    Chairman: Hank Whetstone
    President: Philip Terranova
Estimated Sales: $ 50-99.9 Million
Number Employees: 400
Brands:
    Wheatstone

15483 Whipple Company
PO Box 275
Natick, MA 01760-0275   508-653-2660
          Fax: 508-653-2662 800-345-2925
Processor of mince meat, fruit and cream pie fill-
ings, preserves, marmalades, sweet relishes, ice
cream toppings, pancake syrup, fountain syrups, pri-
vate label and custom packing available
    President: Andrew Crain
    Marketing Director: Max Pesa
    Production Manager: Steven Molind
    Purchasing: Ken Ostrowski
Number Employees: 20-49
Sq. footage: 40000
Type of Packaging: Consumer, Food Service, Private Label, Bulk
Brands:
    Grandmother's

15484 Whispering Gardens Gourmet Foods
1411 Edgehill Place
Pasadena, CA 91103-1130   626-795-7334
Fax: 626-795-4013 jam@millicentspreserves.com
          www.millicentspreserves.com
Preserves
Brands:
    MILLICENT'S PRESERVES

15485 Whistler Brewing Company
302 - 1505 West 2nd Avenue
Vancouver, BC V6H 3Y4
Canada   604-932-6185
    Fax: 604-932-7293 http://www.whistlerbeer.com
Processor and exporter of ale and lager
    President: Trevor Khoe
Number Employees: 10-19
Type of Packaging: Consumer, Food Service

15486 Whistler Brewing Company
4355 Canada Way
Burnaby, BC V5G 1J3
Canada   604-438-2337
    Fax: 604-437-3292 whistlerbrewery@sprint.com
Processor of ale and lager
    President: Trevor Khoe
    Marketing: Joseph Tan
Estimated Sales: $ 1 Million
Number Employees: 11
Sq. footage: 1600
Type of Packaging: Consumer, Food Service

15487 Whitaker Foods
P.O.Box 3278
Evansdale, IA 50707-0278   319-234-3056
    Fax: 319-234-7734 800-553-7490
          sales@whitakerfd@aol.com
          www.whitakerfoods.com
Manufacturer of frozen meat including sausage,
breaded pork and pork slices
    President: Ron Bright
    Co-President: Shari Bright
Estimated Sales: $50 Million
Number Employees: 20-49
Type of Packaging: Consumer, Food Service, Private Label, Bulk

15488 Whitcraft Wines
36A S Calle Cesar Chavez
Santa Barbara, CA 93109-2128   805-730-1680
    Fax: 805-730-1086 whitcraftwinery@cox.net
          www.whitcraftwinery.com
Wines
    Owner: Chris Whitcraft
Estimated Sales: $ 1-2.5 Million
Number Employees: 1
Number of Brands: 1
Number of Products: 12
Sq. footage: 2500
Brands:
    Whitcraft Winery

15489 White Cap Fish Company
120 Montauk Hwy
Islip, NY 11751-3431   631-581-0125
    Fax: 631-277-6578 www.whitecapfish.com
Processor of seafood including tuna
    Owner: V Russo
    VP: Jim Joeckel
Estimated Sales: $ 1 - 3 Million
Number Employees: 10-19

15490 White Castle System
P.O.Box 1498
Columbus, OH 43216-1498   614-228-5781
          Fax: 614-464-0596 866-272-8372
          www.whatyoucrave.com
Bakery and meat products
    VP: John S Kobacker
    President: Bill Ingram
    VP Marketing: Kim Kelly Bartley
    CEO: Edgar W Ingram Iii
    Marketing Director: Jamie Richardson
    VP Manufacturing: Robert Johns
Estimated Sales: 491995000
Number Employees: 10,000+
Brands:
    White Castle Cheeseburgers
    White Castle Hamburg

15491 White Cloud Coffee
199 E 52nd St
Boise, ID 83714-1479   208-322-1166
    Fax: 208-322-6226 800-627-0309
          info@whitecloudcoffee.com
          www.whitecloudcoffee.com
Roasted coffee
    President: Jerome Eberharter
    CEO: Jerome Eberharter
    Director Marketing: Ron Thompson
    VP Sales/Operations: Roger Daub
Estimated Sales: $ 5-10 Million
Number Employees: 20-49

Brands:
Buckaroo
Cowboy
Kona Island

15492 White Coffee Corporation
1835 Steinway Pl
Long Island City, NY 11105-1076   718-204-7900
Fax: 718-956-8504   800-221-0140
joan@whitecoffee.com   www.whitecoffee.com
Processor, importer and exporter of cocoa, coffee, tea, soup mixes and bases and gelatin
President: Carole White
Owner: Jonathan White
Marketing Director: Gregory White
Plant Manager: Tom Tolfree
Estimated Sales:$18800000
Number Employees: 100-249
Brands:
Melitta
Parker House
White House

15493 White Fence Farm Chicken
1376 Joliet Rd
Romeoville, IL 60446-4078   630-739-1720
Fax: 630-739-4466   www.whitefencefarm.com
Poultry
President: Robert Hastert Jr
Estimated Sales:$ 5 - 10 Million
Number Employees: 100-249

15494 White Hall Vineyards
5190 Sugar Ridge Rd
Crozet, VA 22932-2200   434-823-8615
tastingroom@whitehallvineyards.com
www.whitehallvineyards.com
Wines
Co-Owner: Antony Champ
Co-Owner: Edith Champ
Estimated Sales:$ 3 - 5 Million
Number Employees: 5-9

15495 White Lily Foods Company
129 E Guenther
San Antonio, TX 78204-1402   865-546-5511
Fax: 865-521-7725   800-264-5459
www.whitelily.com
Manufacturer of flour, corn flour meal and baking and gravy mixes
President: Ken Danton
Estimated Sales:$ 50 - 100 Million
Number Employees: 750
Type of Packaging: Consumer, Food Service, Private Label, Bulk
Brands:
WHITE LILY

15496 White Oak Farms
343 Main St
Sandown, NH 03873-2101   603-887-2233
Fax: 603-887-2880   800-473-8869
info@macaroons.com   www.macaroons.com
Macaroons
President: James Price
*Estimated Sales:*Below $ 5 Million
Number Employees: 5-9
Brands:
St. Julien Macaroons

15497 White Oak Vineyards & Winery
7505 Highway 128
Healdsburg, CA 95448-8020   707-433-8429
Fax: 707-433-8446
tastingroom@whiteoakwinery.com
www.whiteoakwinery.com
Wines
Owner: Bill Meyers
Marketing Director: Jerry Baker
CEO: Don Grogh
Public Relations: Denise Gill
Production Manager: Steve Ryan
*Estimated Sales:*Below $ 5 Million
Number Employees: 5-9
Type of Packaging: Private Label
Brands:
White Oak Chardonnay
White Oak Merlot
White Oak Sauvignon

15498 White Packing Company
PO Box 7067
Fredericksburg, VA 22404-7067   540-898-2029

Manufacturer of Meat
President: Karl White
Estimated Sales:$21 Million
Number Employees: 150
Type of Packaging: Consumer

15499 White Rock Distilleries
P.O.Box 1829
Lewiston, ME 04241-1829   207-783-1433
Fax: 207-783-8409 www.threeolives.com
Alcoholic beverages
CEO: Paul Coulombe
CFO: Robert Payne
Quality Control: Mona Bilodeau
Plant Manager: Dennis Coulombe
Estimated Sales:$ 50-100 Million
Number Employees: 100-249
Brands:
White Rock

15500 White Rock Products Corporation
1722 Whitestone Expressway
Whitestone, NY 11357-3013   718-746-2217
Fax: 718-767-0413   800-969-7625
info@whiterockbev.com
www.whiterockbeverages.com
Processor and exporter of carbonated and noncarbonated soft drinks; also, mixes, iced teas, fruit drinks and spring water
President: Alfred Morgan III
Marketing Director: Larry Bodkin
Estimated Sales:$9000000
Number Employees: 10
Number of Brands: 6
Type of Packaging: Consumer, Food Service
Brands:
Chocolate Delight
Delicious
Kentucky Nip
Kentucky Nip Cherry Julep
La Cascade Del Cielo
Lemon Licious Lemonade
Punch 'n Fruity
Pure Rock
Rock Pop Carbonated Beverages
Sarsaparilla
Sioux City
Sioux City Sarsaparilla
Southern Swirl
TNT Chocolate
Tealicious Iced Tea
Western Style Soft Drinks
White Rock
White Rock Orchards
Workout Energy Drinks

15501 White Rock Vineyards
1115 Loma Vista Drive
Napa, CA 94558-9752   707-257-7922
Fax: 707-257-7922
caves@whiterockvineyards.com
www.whiterockvineyards.com
Wines
Owner: Henry Vandendries
Winemaker: Christopher Vandendriessche
Estimated Sales:$450,000
Number Employees: 5-9
Brands:
White Rock Vineyards
White Rock Vineyards

15502 White Swan Fruit Products
P.O.Box Y
Plant City, FL 33564-9022   813-752-1155
Fax: 813-754-3168 www.paradisefruitco.com
Processor and exporter of candied fruit and peels; manufacturer of custom plastic molders
Executive VP: Eugene Weiner
CEO: Melvin S Gordon
*Estimated Sales:*G
Number Employees: 250-499
Parent Co: Paradise Beverages
Type of Packaging: Consumer, Food Service, Private Label, Bulk
Brands:
Queen Anne
White Swan

15503 White Toque
536 Fayette Street
Perth Amboy, NJ 08861-3742   201-863-2885
Fax: 201-863-2886   800-237-6936
info@whitetoque.com   www.whitetoque.com

Importer of IQF fruits and vegetables and specialty and broad-line food service distributors with a wide selection of imported European high quality frozen and dry goods
President/CEO: Gigier Memmel
Sales Director: Graham Taylor

15504 White Wave
12002 Airport Way
Broomfield, CO 80021-2546   303-635-4490
Fax: 303-443-3952   800-488-9283
questions@whitewave.com   www.whitewave.com
Processor of vegetarian products including soymilk, nondairy yogurt, tofu, baked tofu, tempeh and seitan (wheat based meat analog)
President/CEO: Steve Demos
CFO: Pat Calhoun
Marketing Director: James Terman
Sales Director: Steve Hughes
Estimated Sales:$1 Million
Number Employees: 50-99
Number of Brands: 3
Number of Products: 40
Sq. footage: 30000
Parent Co: Dean Foods Company
Type of Packaging: Consumer, Food Service, Private Label, Bulk
Brands:
Silk
White Wave

15505 White Wave Foods
PO Box 2768
Jacksonville, FL 32203-2768   904-354-8256
Fax: 904-353-5837   800-874-6765
Processor of milk including whole, skim, 1% and 2%; also, cream and specialty dairy fluids
VP Sales: David Roger
Estimated Sales:$ 50-100 Million
Number Employees: 100-249
Parent Co: Dean Foods Company
Type of Packaging: Consumer, Food Service, Private Label

15506 White's Meat Processing
1700 Portsmouth Rd
Peebles, OH 45660-9702   937-587-2930
Processor of beef, pork and lamb
Owner: Don White
Estimated Sales:$490000
Number Employees: 1-4
Type of Packaging: Consumer, Bulk

15507 White-Stokes Company
3615 S Jasper Pl
Chicago, IL 60609-1399   773-523-0742
Fax: 773-523-0767   800-978-6537
nick@whitestokes.com   www.whitestokes.com
Processor of pie fillings; also, marshmallow, butterscotch and bittersweet hot fudge toppings, nougats, caramel creams, pectin, coconut paste, etc
President: Nicholas Tzakis
VP: George Tzakis
Customer Relations: Melissa Pagan
Estimated Sales:$1400000
Number Employees: 20-49
Type of Packaging: Bulk

15508 Whitefish Brewing
PO Box 1949
Whitefish, MT 59937-1949   406-862-2684
Fax: 406-862-9684
Beer
Owner: Gary Hutchison
*Estimated Sales:*Below $ 5 Million
Number Employees: 3

15509 Whitehall Lane Winery
1563 Saint Helena Hwy S
St Helena, CA 94574-9775   707-963-9454
Fax: 707-963-7035
greatwine@whitehalllane.com
www.whitehalllane.com
Wines
Proprietor: Tom Leonardini Sr
Winemaker: Dean Sylvester
*Estimated Sales:*Below $ 5 Million
Number Employees: 10-19
Brands:
Whitehall Lane

15510 Whitehall Specialties
P.O.Box 677
Whitehall, WI 54773-0677   715-538-2326
Fax: 715-538-4723 888-755-9900
wsisales@triwest.net
www.whitehall-specialties.com
Imitation cheese, cheese food slices, blended cheese products, dried, grated
President: Steven Fawcett
R&D: Terry Holliday
Quality Control: Ron McKernon
Marketing/Sales: Michelle Sonsalla
Plant Manager: Scott Kulig
Purchasing: John Liska
Estimated Sales: $ 50-100 Million
Number Employees: 100-249
Sq. footage: 50
Type of Packaging: Food Service, Private Label, Bulk
Brands:
Ridgeview Farms
Whitehall

15511 Whitey's Ice Cream Manufacturing
2525 41st St
Moline, IL 61265-5017   309-762-2175
Fax: 309-762-0053 888-594-4839
whiteys@whiteysicecream.com
www.whiteysicecream.com
Processor of ice cream, ice milk, frozen yogurt and novelties
Co-Owner: Jon Tunberg
Co-Owner: Jefff Tunberg
Estimated Sales: $7500000
Number Employees: 250-499
Sq. footage: 20000
Type of Packaging: Consumer, Private Label

15512 Whitfield Foods
P.O.Box 791
Montgomery, AL 36101-0791   334-263-2541
Fax: 334-262-4203 800-633-8790
tdensmore@whitfieldfoods.com
www.whitfieldfoods.com
Manufacturer of maple products including butter and maple-citrus products; also, syrup including butter maple, cane, honey and corn
President: Les Massey
Estimated Sales: $50-100 Million
Number Employees: 100-249
Sq. footage: 1200003
Type of Packaging: Consumer, Food Service, Private Label
Brands:
ALAGA
PLOW BOY
YELLOW LABEL

15513 Whitford Cellars
4047 E 3rd Ave
Napa, CA 94558-4011   707-942-0840
Fax: 707-942-0840 whitford@napanet.net
www.whitfordcellars.com
Winery of chardonnay, pinot noir and syrah
Co-Owner: Duncan Haynes
Co-Owner: Patricia Haynes
Estimated Sales: $500-1 Million appx.
Number Employees: 1-4
Number of Brands: 2
Number of Products: 4
Sq. footage: 2500
Type of Packaging: Private Label
Brands:
OLD VINES
WHITFORD

15514 Whitley's Peanut Factory
P.O.Box 647
Hayes, VA 23072-0647   804-642-7688
Fax: 804-642-7658 800-470-2244
customercare@whitleyspeanut.com
www.whitleyspeanut.com
Processor and exporter of snack nuts in cans, jars and bags including peanuts, almonds, cashews, mixed, pecans and honey-roasted; importer of raw cashews, brazil nuts and filberts. Also Virginia hams.
President: Craig Smith
VP Sales: James Scannell
Estimated Sales: $590000
Number Employees: 20-49
Type of Packaging: Consumer, Food Service, Private Label, Bulk
Brands:
Flavor Crunch
The Peanut Factory

15515 Whitney & Son SeaFoods
814 East St # 3
Pittsfield, MA 01201-5367   413-445-4586
Fax: 413-445-4447 800-414-6223
Processor of produce
President: Peter Whitney
General Manager: John Hajjar
Estimated Sales: $ 5 - 10 Million
Number Employees: 10-19

15516 Whitney Foods
15504 Liberty Ave
Jamaica, NY 11433-1000   718-291-3333
Fax: 718-291-0560
Dairy products
President: Kenneth Schlossberg
Marketing Director: Bill Masterson
VP Sales: Robert Zak
Marketing: Brian Lee
Estimated Sales: $ 2.5-5 Million
Number Employees: 20-49
Brands:
Whitney Yogurt

15517 Whittaker & Associates
1794 Charline Ave NE
Atlanta, GA 30306-3128   404-266-1265
Fax: 678-285-0547 jobs@whittakersearch.com
www.mwhitaker.com
Wholesale food manufacturing, dairy, beverage, bakery, meat, poultry, ingredients
Owner: Peggy Whitaker
Estimated Sales: Less than $500,000
Number Employees: 1-4

15518 Whole Earth Bakery
130 Saint Marks Pl # 1009
New York, NY 10009-5843   212-677-7597
Processor of baked goods
Owner: Peter Slyvestri
Estimated Sales: $110000
Number Employees: 1-4

15519 Whole Herb Company
19800 8th St East
PO Box 1203
Sonoma, CA 95476   707-935-1077
Fax: 707-935-3447
sales@wholeherbcompany.com
www.wholeherbcompany.com
Raw material supplier of herbs, spices, botanicals, spice blends, extracts and essential oils
President: Gillian Bleimann
CEO: James Thrower
General Manager: George Blasiola
Sales: Brian Babbini
Operations Manager: Holly Sherwood
Plant Manager: Joe Nagy
Purchasing: Rena Janacek
Estimated Sales: $10 Million
Number Employees: 20
Number of Products: 500+
Sq. footage: 65000
Type of Packaging: Food Service, Bulk
Brands:
Jasmine Green
Mango Sunrise Tea
Peach Ambrosia
Somaguard
Somaguard Premium Grape Extract
Summer Berry Delight

15520 Whole Life Nutritional Supplements
13340 Saticoy St # B
North Hollywood, CA 91605-7643   818-255-5357
Fax: 818-255-5307 800-748-5841
wholelife2@aol.com
Wholesaler/distributor and contract packager of vitamins
Manager: Rajen Patel
Director Sales: Irma Arroyo
Estimated Sales: $ 1 - 3 Million
Number Employees: 5-9
Sq. footage: 5000
Type of Packaging: Private Label

15521 Whole in the Wall
43 S Washington St
Binghamton, NY 13903-1711   607-722-5138
Fax: 607-722-4237 info@wholeinthewall.com
www.wholeinthewall.com
Premium quality natural pesto, whole wheat bread and bagels, mushroom soup.
President: Elliot Fiks
CFO: Stacey Gould
Estimated Sales: Less than $500,000
Number Employees: 10-19
Type of Packaging: Consumer, Food Service, Private Label, Bulk

15522 Wholesale Pizza Company
1605 County Hospital Road
Nashville, TN 37218-2503   615-242-1655
Pizza
Estimated Sales: Under $500,000
Number Employees: 1-4

15523 Wholesome Classics
44 Redding Rd
Campbell, CA 95008-6736   408-292-2392
Fax: 408-292-2394
carol@wholesomeclassics.com
www.wholesomeclassics.com
Low fat and wheat free baking mixes; private labeling available
Research & Development: Carol Zelinski
Number Employees: 1-4
Type of Packaging: Consumer, Private Label
Brands:
N-Dur-Enzo

15524 Wholesome Sweeteners
PO Box 339
Savannah, GA 31402-0339   912-651-4820
Fax: 912-964-0227 800-680-1896
info@wholesomesweeteners.com
www.wholesomesweeteners.com
Processor and exporter of organic evaporated cane juices and molasses
President: David Montgomery Jr
Brand Manager: Pamela Lalumiere
Director Marketing: Nancy Barbee
Number Employees: 5-9
Sq. footage: 15000
Parent Co: Imperial Holly Corporation
Brands:
Sucanat
Wholesome Foods

15525 Whyte's Food Corporation
1700 Aimco Boulevard
Mississauga, ON L4W 1B1
Canada   905-624-5065
Fax: 905-624-4033 dboloten@whytes.ca
www.whytes.ca
Processor of refrigerated and shelf-stable pickles, peppers, horseradish, sauerkraut, pickled herring and sauces including spaghetti, pizza and entree; importer and packer of olives, maraschino cherries and capers; exporter ofpickles
VP: Antonio Arruda
Pres.: Paul Kawaja
VP Finance: Andrew Anderson
Number Employees: 100-249
Sq. footage: 160000
Type of Packaging: Consumer, Food Service, Private Label, Bulk
Brands:
Grand Prix
Mrs. Whyte's
Trans-Alpine
Uni-Chef
Via Italia

15526 Wiard's Orchards
5565 Merritt Rd
Ypsilanti, MI 48197-9367   734-482-7744
Fax: 734-482-7753 www.wiards.com
Cherries
President: Jay Wiard
Estimated Sales: $ 20-50 Million
Number Employees: 100-249

15527 Wichita Packing Company
1315 W Fulton St
Chicago, IL 60607-1123   312-421-0606
Fax: 312-421-0696
information@wichitapacking.com
www.wichitapacking.com

Processor of baby back and St. Louis style ribs
Owner: Robert Golang
VP: Gerald Guon
Estimated Sales:$22697783
Number Employees: 20-49

15528 (HQ)Wick's Pies
P.O.Box 268
Winchester, IN 47394-0268   765-584-8401
Fax: 765-584-3700   800-642-5880
wickspies@wickpies.com   www.wickspies.com
Processor of frozen pies and pie shells
President/Owner: D E Wickersham
VP: Clark Loney
Quality Control: Sue Bone
Marketing/Sales: Marsha Welch
Purchasing: Steve Burge
Estimated Sales:$9 Million
Number Employees: 50-99
Sq. footage: 20000
Type of Packaging: Consumer, Food Service
Brands:
Wick's

15529 Wicker's Food Products
P.O.Box 129
Hornersville, MO 63855-0129   573-737-2416
Fax: 573-737-2113   800-847-0032
wickers@vip1.net   www.wickersbbq.com
Marinades
Manager: Misty Edmonston
*Estimated Sales:*Less than $500,000
Number Employees: 5-9
Brands:
Wicker

15530 Wicklund Farms
3959 Maple Island Farm Road
Springfield, OR 97477-9404   541-747-5998
Fax: 541-747-7299
spicedgreenbeans@wicklundfarms.com
www.wicklundfarms.com
Processor and exporter of spiced green beans and
bean relish
President: Larry Wicklund
Estimated Sales:$1600000
Number Employees: 6
Type of Packaging: Consumer, Food Service, Pri-
vate Label, Bulk

15531 Widman Popcorn Company
1173 10th Road
Chapman, NE 68827-2716   308-986-2293
Fax: 308-986-2386   wpopcorn@kdsi.net
Processor and exporter of popcorn including white,
yellow, high expansion and mushroom
President: Darrell Widman
Estimated Sales:$500-1 Million appx.
Number Employees: 10-19
Type of Packaging: Consumer, Food Service, Pri-
vate Label, Bulk
Brands:
Widman's Country

15532 Widmans Candy Shop
116 S Broadway
Crookston, MN 56716-1955   218-281-1487
Chocolate-covered potato chips, peanut butter
candy, cow pies
President: George Widman
*Estimated Sales:*Less than $500,000
Number Employees: 1-4

15533 Widmer Brothers BrewingCompany
929 N Russell St
Portland, OR 97227-1733   503-281-2437
Fax: 503-281-1496   webmail@widmer.com
www.widmer.com
Beer
President: Kurt Widmer
CFO: Terry Michaelson
CEO: Terry Michaelson
Quality Control: Mike Domenghini
Sales Director: Tim McFall
Public Relations: Marty Wall
Director Manufacturing: Sebastian Pastore
Estimated Sales:$ 50-100 Million
Number Employees: 100-249
Number of Brands: 3
Type of Packaging: Private Label
Brands:
Hefeweizer

OKIO
Widmer Brothers

15534 Widmer's Cheese Cellars
P.O.Box 127
Theresa, WI 53091-0127   920-488-2503
Fax: 920-488-2130   888-878-1107
info@widmerscheese.com
www.widmerscheese.com
Brick, colby cheese and extra sharp cheddar
President: Joseph Widmer
*Estimated Sales:*Below $ 5 Million
Number Employees: 20-49
Number of Brands: 1
Number of Products: 10
Sq. footage: 16000
Type of Packaging: Consumer, Bulk
Brands:
Widmer's Cheese

15535 Widmer's Wine Cellars
1 Lake Niagara Ln
Naples, NY 14512-9799   585-374-6311
Fax: 585-374-3266 www.widmerwine.com
Processor and exporter of wine and grape juice
President: Clenn Curtiss
Maintenance Supervisor: Mack Baxter
Estimated Sales:$ 50 - 100 Million
Number Employees: 100-249
Parent Co: Canandaigua Wine Company
Type of Packaging: Consumer, Food Service, Pri-
vate Label, Bulk
Brands:
Great Western
Lake Niagara
Taylor
Widmer's

15536 Widoffs Modern Bakery
129 Water St
Worcester, MA 01604-5080   508-752-7200
Fax: 508-756-6365
Bakery products
President: Jerry Ducas
*Estimated Sales:*Below $ 5 Million
Number Employees: 20-49
Brands:
Hearth

15537 Widow's Mite Vinegar Company
1309 P Street NW
Apt 6
Washington, DC 20005-3750   202-462-3669
Fax: 202-462-3669   877-678-5854
jimdc@worldnet.att.net
www.widowsmitevinegar.com
Salad dressing mix and Creole vinegar
President: John Allen Franciscus
Vice President: James Franciscus
Type of Packaging: Consumer, Bulk

15538 Wiederkehr Wine Cellars
3324 Swiss Family Dr
Altus, AR 72821-9037   479-468-3551
Fax: 479-468-4791   800-622-9463
info@wiederkehrwines.com
www.wiederkehrwines.com
Wines
Manager: Gary Wiederkehr
WineMaster: Al Wiederkehr
President: Gary Wiederkehr
CFO: Beverly Morrow
Estimated Sales:$ 10-20 Million
Number Employees: 50-99
Brands:
Wiederkehr Wine

15539 Wiegardt Brothers
P.O.Box 309
Ocean Park, WA 98640-0309   360-665-4111
Fax: 360-665-4950
Manufacturer and exporter of fresh oysters
President: Lee Wiegardt
Estimated Sales:$10-20 Million
Number Employees: 50-99
Type of Packaging: Consumer
Brands:
JOLLY ROGER
TIDEPOINT

15540 Wiggin Farms
6590 Hillgate Road
Arbuckle, CA 95912-9712   530-476-2288
Fax: 530-476-2856   wiggin@wigginfarms.com
www.colusanet.com/wigginfarms
Flavored and roasted nuts and almonds including
shelled, in-shell, diced, etc.; also, almond butter and
butter toffee
President: Sharon Wiggin
Marketing Director: Janice Rhodd
Operations Manager: Brent Wiggin
Production Manager: Jim Wiggin
Estimated Sales:$5-9.9 Million
Number Employees: 20-49
Type of Packaging: Consumer, Food Service, Pri-
vate Label, Bulk
Brands:
Taste Adventure

15541 Wilbur Chocolate
48 N Broad St
Lititz, PA 17543-1005   717-626-3249
Fax: 717-626-3487   800-233-0139
jan_o'brien@cargill.com   www.wilburbuds.com
Processor of chocolate and confectionery coatings,
drops and chips for the dairy, bakery and food indus-
try
President/CEO: William J Shaughnessy
Inside Sales: Amy Weik
Estimated Sales:$283,000,000
Number Employees: 250-499
Parent Co: Cargill Foods
Type of Packaging: Food Service, Bulk
Brands:
Brandywine
Bronze Medal
Platinum 2000
R-346 Milk Chocolate Flavored
R-346 Milk Chocolate Flavored
Scarlet
Windsor

15542 Wilbur Chocolate Company
48 N Broad St
Lititz, PA 17543-1005   717-626-1131
Fax: 717-626-3487   800-448-1063
chocolate@cargill.com   www.wilburbuds.com
Manufacturer of chocolate and cocoa products in-
cluding cocoa powder, ice cream coatings, chocolate
drops, cream coatings, confectionary coatings, choc-
olate coatings, sugar-free chocolate, chocolate
chunks, compound drops, cocoa butterand chocolate
liquor
President: William Shaughnessy
Sales: Mark Freeman
Estimated Sales:$100 Million
Number Employees: 250-499
Parent Co: Cargill Incorporated
Brands:
Gerkins Cocoa
Peter's Chocolate
Wilbur Chocolate

15543 Wilcox Farm
40400 Harts Lake Valley Rd
Roy, WA 98580-9182   360-458-7774
Fax: 360-458-6950   tbuti@wilcoxfarms.com
www.wilcoxfarms.com
Milk
President/CEO: Barrie Wilcox
Marketing Director: Brent Wilcox
Estimated Sales:$ 100-500 Million
Number Employees: 250-499
Type of Packaging: Bulk
Brands:
Wilcox

15544 Wild Bill's Foods
2316 Norman Rd
Lancaster, PA 17601-5960   717-390-1978
Fax: 717-295-9722   800-848-3236
wildbill@wildbillsfoods.com
www.wildbillsfoods.com
Manufacturer of beef jerky
General Manager/Public Relations: Michael Kane

CFO: Steve Woelkers
CEO: Phil Clemmens
R&D/Quality Control: Greg Rhinier
Marketing Director: John Connell
Sales Manager: Teresa Musser
Operations/Plant Manager: Steve Groff Jr
Production Manager: Armando Torres Jr

Estimated Sales: $10-15 Million
Number Employees: 100-249
Parent Co: Clemens Family Coporation
Type of Packaging: Consumer, Bulk

15545 Wild Blueberry Companies
PO Box 1130
Kennebunkport, ME 04046-1130   207-967-5024
        Fax: 207-967-5023   wildblueberries@qwi.net
                www.wildblueberrries.com
Blueberries
    Executive Director: John Sauve
Number Employees: 1-4

15546 Wild Fruitz Beverages
270 Ridings Way
Ambler, PA 19002-5246   718-909-0819
        Fax: 973-742-7634   888-688-7632
        sales@wildfruitz.com   www.wildfruitz.com
Carbonated natural fruit juices
    President/CEO: Trev Warshauer
    Chairwoman: Sally Watt
    CFO: Jon Jensen
Estimated Sales: $ 3.3 Million
Number Employees: 6
Brands:
    Wild Fruitz

15547 Wild Hog Vineyard
P.O.Box 189
Cazadero, CA 95421-0189   707-847-3687
    Fax: 707-847-3160   info@wildhogvineyard.com
                www.wildhogvineyard.com
Processor of wine
    Owner: Daniel Schoenseld
    Co-Owner: Marion Schoenfeld
Estimated Sales: Less than $500,000
Number Employees: 1-4
Sq. footage: 2000
Brands:
    Wild Hog Vineyard

15548 Wild Horse Winery
P.O.Box 910
Templeton, CA 93465-0910   805-434-2541
    Fax: 805-434-3516   info@wildhorsewinery.com
                www.wildhorsewinery.com
Wine
    President: Scott Welcher III
    Winemaker: Mark Cummins
Estimated Sales: $ 10-20 Million
Number Employees: 20-49
Brands:
    Wild Horse

15549 Wild Planet Foods
1585 Heartwood Drive
Suite F
McKinleyville, CA 95519   707-840-9116
        Fax: 707-839-3260   800-998-9945
        elizabeth@wildplanetfoods.com
                www.wildplanetfoods.com
seafood
    President/Owner: Bill Carvalho
    CEO: Terry Hunt
    Sales: Justin Desiderio

15550 (HQ)Wild Rice Exchange
1277 Santa Anita Ct
Woodland, CA 95776-6122   530-669-0150
    Fax: 530-668-9317   800-223-7423
    thewildriceexch@aol.com   www.wildrice.org
Processor, importer and exporter of wild rice, products and blends including basmati, arborio, red gourmet rices, organic, brown and polished white; also, quick-cook, frozen and pre-mixed pilaf; large line of specialty beans; customprocessing
    Manager: Carlos Zambello
    Sales: Carlos Zambello
    Production: Golnar Emam
Type of Packaging: Consumer, Food Service, Private Label, Bulk
Brands:
    Gourmet Valley
    Gourmet Valley Foods
    Great Valley

15551 Wild Things
344 S Clark Drive
Beverly Hills, CA 90211-3608   310-412-4139
                Fax: 310-412-4991

Flavored vinegars and olive oils in decorative bottles
    President: Penni Haradon
    CFO: Mike Haradon
    Vice President: Hollie Wasserman
Estimated Sales: $500,000-$1 Million
Number Employees: 5-9
Number of Products: 130
Type of Packaging: Consumer, Food Service, Private Label

15552 Wild Thyme Cottage Products
127-B Donegani
Pointe Claire, QC H9R 5E9
Canada   514-695-3602
    Fax: 514-695-3602   wild.thyme@sympatice.ca
Processor and exporter of jams, jellies, marmalades, relishes and chutneys
    President: David Ranlings
    Sales/Production: Dorothea McNiver
Number Employees: 1-4
Number of Brands: 1
Number of Products: 50
Sq. footage: 700
Type of Packaging: Consumer, Food Service
Brands:
    Wild Thyme Cottage Products

15553 Wild Thymes Farm
643 County Route 403
Greenville, NY 12083-1703   518-966-5990
        Fax: 518-966-5998   800-724-2877
    info@wildthymes.com   www.wildthymes.com
Chutneys, salad dressings, fruit spreads, sauces/marinades, mustards, balsamic vinegars
    Owner: Enid Stettner
    Owner: Ann Stettner
    Research & Development: Enid Stettner
    Quality Control: Enid Stettner
    Marketing Director: Ann Stettner
    Public Relations: Ann Stettner
Estimated Sales: $1-$2.5 Million
Number Employees: 10-19
Number of Brands: 1
Number of Products: 50
Type of Packaging: Consumer, Food Service, Private Label, Bulk

15554 Wild West Spices
P.O.Box 471
Cody, WY 82414-0471   307-587-8800
        Fax: 307-587-8800   888-587-8887
        info@wildwestspices.com
                www.wildwestspices.com
Manufacturer of western-style spice blends, grilling spices and rubs, all natural dry mixes and dips
    President: Bonnie Dallinger
    VP: Bonnie Dallinger
Estimated Sales: Less than $500,000
Number Employees: 1-4
Brands:
    Wild West Spices, Inc.

15555 Wild Winds Farms
1 Lake Niagara Ln
Naples, NY 14512-9799   585-374-6311
        Fax: 585-374-3266   800-836-5253
Wine and wine coolers
    President: Clenn Curtiss
Estimated Sales: $ 25-49.9 Million
Number Employees: 100-249

15556 Wildcat Produce
PO Box 5224
McGrew, NE 69353   308-783-2438
                Fax: 308-783-1054
Cucumbers, green beans, onions, potatoes and pumpkins
    President: Mike Chrisman
    CEO: Ruftin Rahmig
Brands:
    Wildcat Produce Garden

15557 Wildhurst
P.O.Box 1310
Kelseyville, CA 95451-1310   707-279-0548
        Fax: 707-279-1913   800-595-9463
        info@wildhurst.com   www.wildhurst.com
Wines
    President: Myron Holdenried
    Winemaker: Mark Burch
Estimated Sales: Below $ 5 Million
Number Employees: 5-9
Type of Packaging: Private Label

Brands:
    Reserve Chardonnay
    Reserve Fume Blanc
    Wildhurst Cabernet F
    Wildhurst Chardonnay
    Wildhurst Merlot
    Wildhurst Zinfandel

15558 Wildlife Cookie Company
PO Box 1158
Saint Charles, IL 60174-7158   630-377-6196
        Fax: 630-377-6321   sales@wildlifecookie.com
                www.wildlifecookie.com
Cookies

15559 Wildly Delicious
47 Railside Rd
Toronto, ON M3A 1B2
Canada   416-444-2011
        Fax: 416-444-0010   888-545-9995
        feedback@wildlydelicious.com
                www.wildlydelicious.com
dip, mix and spread, seasoning, spices and salts, premium oils and vinegars, gourmet sauces, pastes and mustards.
    CEO: Michelle Muscat
    Operations: Austin Muscat

15560 Wildtime Foods
P.O.Box 1471
Eugene, OR 97440-1471   541-726-9081
        Fax: 541-747-5067   800-356-4458
    info@wildtime.com   www.grizzliesbrand.com
Bulk and packaged cereals
    President: Genevieve Averill
    Marketing Director: Whit Hemphill
Estimated Sales: Below $ 5 Million
Number Employees: 10-19
Sq. footage: 4500
Brands:
    Grizzliesh

15561 Wildwood Natural Foods
416 E Riverside Dr
Watsonville, CA 95076-5015   831-728-4448
        Fax: 831-728-4445   800-464-3915
        tofurus@aol.com   www.pmo.com
Natural foods
    Director: John Breen
    Quality Control: Hiti Uojas
    Marketing Director: Janet Taylor
    Operations Manager: Jeremiah Ridenour
    Production Manager: Robyn Shurbet
    Plant Manager: Dolly Gianni
    Purchasing Manager: Doug Porter
Estimated Sales: $ 10-20 Million
Number Employees: 100-249
Type of Packaging: Private Label
Brands:
    Grilled & Marinated Tofu
    Plain Tofu
    Smoked Tofu
    Soy Sour Cream
    Soymilk
    Soymill
    Soyogurt
    Wildwood Baked Tofu

15562 Wileman Bros & Elliott,Inc
P.O.Box 309
Cutler, CA 93615-0309   559-732-5321
        Fax: 559-528-2456   andrew@mr-sunshine.com
                www.mr-sunshine.com
Offers a full line of California citrus products
    President: Frank Elliott Iii
    CEO: Tommy Elliott
    CFO: Brian Johnson
    Research & Development: Brad McCord
    Quality Control: Raul Lopez
    Sales Director: Andrew Felts
    Public Relations: Truman McGuire
    Operations Manager: Manuel Guillen
    Production Manager: Mark Savage
    Plant Manager: Jon Hornburg
Estimated Sales: $50 - 100 Million
Number Employees: 100-249
Sq. footage: 5000
Type of Packaging: Consumer, Food Service, Private Label, Bulk

15563 Wilhelm Foods
116 S Elliott Rd
Newberg, OR 97132-2120   503-538-2929
                Fax: 503-538-1992

Plaidberries and plaidberry products
President: Charles Cox
Estimated Sales:$ 5 - 10 Million
Number Employees: 10-19

15564 Wilke International
14321 W 96th Ter
Shawnee Mission, KS 66215-4709   913-438-5544
Fax: 913-438-5554   800-779-5545
whw@wilkeinternational.com
www.wilkeinternational.com
Processor, importer, exporter and wholesaler/distributor of lactic acid, lactates, sports nutrition and dietary supplements
President: Wayne Wilke
Director Administration: John Veazey
General Manager: James France
Estimated Sales:$ 5 - 10 Million
Number Employees: 10-19
Type of Packaging: Bulk
Brands:
Createam
Nutrasense

15565 (HQ)Wilkins-Rogers
P.O.Box 308
Ellicott City, MD 21041-0308   410-465-5800
Fax: 410-750-0163
info@washingtonqualityfoods.com
www.washingtonqualityfoods.com
Processor and exporter of flour, corn meal, baking
mixes, breading and batters
President: Samuel Rogers Jr
Joint CEO: Samual Rogers III
Joint CEO: Tom Rogers III
CEO: Sam Rogers Jr
Estimated Sales:$27,900,000
Number Employees: 100-249
Sq. footage: 180000
Type of Packaging: Consumer, Food Service, Private Label, Bulk
Brands:
Crutchfield
Indian Head
Raga Muffins
Spanglers
Velvetx
Washington

15566 Wilkinson-Spitz
705 Bronx River Road
Suite 204
Yonkers, NY 10704-1752   914-237-5000
Fax: 914-237-7295
Candy
Manager: Joel Miller
VP: Jim Koehlein
Sales Director: Leon Gleaves
Estimated Sales:$ 1-2.5 Million appx.
Number Employees: 1

15567 Will Poultry Company
P.O.Box 1146
Buffalo, NY 14240-1146   716-853-2000
Fax: 716-853-2011 www.chickenwings.org
Fresh and frozen institutional poultry, seafood and
meats
President: Donald Will
Estimated Sales:$ 50-100 Million
Number Employees: 100-249
Brands:
Will

15568 Will-Pak Foods
3350 Shelby Street
Suite 200
Ontario, CA 91764-5556   909-945-4554
Fax: 909-945-4545   800-874-0883
taste_adv@earthlink.net
www.tasteadventure.com
Manufacturer of all-natural foods including soups,
beans, chilies, and side dishes
President: Gary Morris
Estimated Sales:$1300000
Number Employees: 10
Sq. footage: 10000
Type of Packaging: Food Service, Private Label,
Bulk
Brands:
TASTE ADVENTURE

15569 Willamette Valley Walnuts
475 NE 17th St
McMinnville, OR 97128-3326   503-472-3215
www.walnutcitywineworks.com
Processor and exporter of shelled walnuts and English walnut meats
Owner: Zac Spence
VP: Todd Heidgerken
Estimated Sales:$500,000-$1 Million
Number Employees: 1-4
Type of Packaging: Consumer, Food Service, Private Label, Bulk

15570 Willcox Packing House
P.O.Box 122
Willcox, AZ 85644-0122   520-384-2015
Processor of meat products including beef, lamb and
pork
Owner: David Harris
Estimated Sales:$870000
Number Employees: 5-9
Type of Packaging: Consumer, Food Service, Private Label, Bulk

15571 William Atwood Lobster Company
P.O.Box 202
Spruce Head, ME 04859-0202   207-596-6691
Fax: 207-596-6958   support@atwoodlobster.com
www.atwoodlobster.com
Fresh and frozen lobster meat, shrimp, crabmeat,
frozen lobster tails, fresh crabs and whole lobsters
President: William Atwood
CEO: William McGonagle
R & D: David Atwood
Sales Manager: Sandy Cox
Estimated Sales:$ 10-20 Million
Number Employees: 50-99
Brands:
William Atwood

15572 (HQ)William B. Reily & Company
3501 Duncanwood Lane
Baltimore, MD 21213-4093   410-675-9550
Fax: 410-327-1214
Beer
Manager: Maxim Hoffmann
CEO: Platner Reily
President: William Reily
Estimated Sales:$ 10-20 Million
Number Employees: 30
Parent Co: Reily Companies
Type of Packaging: Consumer, Food Service, Private Label, Bulk
Brands:
Blue Plate Mayonnaise
Jfg Products
Luzianne Tea

15573 William Bolthouse Farms
7200 E Brundage Ln
Bakersfield, CA 93307-3099   661-366-7205
Fax: 661-366-7289 www.bolthouse.com
Grower, shipper and packer of fresh carrots, carrot
products and carrot juice concentrate
President: Andre Radandt
Sales Manager: Yannick Le Mintier
VP: Tim McCorkle
Director Sales/Marketing: Tim McCorkle
Sales Manager: Scott Reade
Estimated Sales:$100+ Million
Number Employees: 1,000-4,999
Type of Packaging: Bulk
Brands:
Coldwater Creek
Green Giant
Look Mom
Shortcuts

15574 William Bounds
3737 W 240th St
Torrance, CA 90505-6003   310-375-0505
Fax: 310-375-0756   800-473-0504
customerservice@wmboundsltd.com
www.wmboundsltd.com
Spices, flavored chocolate, colored sugars.
President: Helen Bounds
*Estimated Sales:*Below $ 5 Million
Number Employees: 20-49

15575 William E. Caudle Company
6443 E Twin Creek Drive
Idaho Falls, ID 83401-5868   208-523-6637
Fax: 208-523-9586

15576 William E. Martin & Sons Company
9341 170th St
Jamaica, NY 11433   718-291-1300
Fax: 718-291-0331   mail@martinspices.com
www.martinspices.com
Processor, wholesaler/distributor, exporter and importer of spices, seasonings, salts, herbs and herbal
supplements, seeds, powders and raisins. Wholesaler/distributor of dehydrated onion and garlic
products, full line of ground spicesand bakery seeds
Owner: William Martin Jr
VP: Spencer Martin
Sales: Sy Schwartz
Estimated Sales:$ 10 - 20 Million
Number Employees: 20-49
Sq. footage: 60000
Type of Packaging: Bulk
Brands:
W.E.M.

15577 William Grant & Sons
350 5th Ave # 3005
New York, NY 10118-3005   212-594-4848
Fax: 212-643-8884   webmaster@wmgrant.com
www.grantusa.com
Wines
President: William Aron
Manager: Carol Louis
VP Administration & Finance: Steven Klauber
Executive VP Fine Wine: Richard Carrretta
VP Marketing: Mark Teasdale
Sales Director: Joel Gosler
Estimated Sales:$ 120 Million
Number Employees: 100-249
Brands:
Armida
Balvenie
Berentzen
Borgianni
Brolio
Castello Di Volpaia
Clan Macgregor
Colombo
Dry Sack
Fonterutoli
Frangelico Liqueur
Glenfiddich
Glenfiddich
Grant's
Licor 43
Luis Felipe Edwards
Marques De Murrieta
McDowell
Metaxa

15578 William Harrison Vineyar
1443 Silverado Trl S
St Helena, CA 94574-9798   707-963-8310
Fax: 707-963-4552   800-913-9463
info@harrisonvineyards.com
www.harrisonvineyards.com
Processor of garlic dill pickles
Manager: Bruce Bradley
CEO: Lyndsey Harrison
*Estimated Sales:*Less than $500,000
Number Employees: 1-4
Type of Packaging: Consumer
Brands:
Aceto D'Oro
Kirk and Glotzer New
New York Deli

15579 William Harrison Vineyards & Winery LLC
1443 Silverado Trail
St Helena, CA 94574   707-963-8762
Fax: 707-963-8762 www.whwines.com
Wines
Owner: William Harrison
Marketing/Sales: Rob Monaghan
Winemaker/General Manager: Bruce Bradley
Brands:
Mario Perelli-Minetti
Miriam

15580 William Hill Winery
1761 Atlas Peak Rd
Napa, CA 94558-1251   707-224-5424
Fax: 707-224-4484
whw_info@williamhillwinery.com
www.williamhillwinery.com

Wine
President: Bill Newlands
Vice President: Glenn Salva
Public Relations: George Rose
Production Manager: Jill Davis
Plant Manager: Calvin Chase
Estimated Sales: $ 10-20 Million
Number Employees: 20-49
Type of Packaging: Private Label
Brands:
William Hill Winery

15581 William Karas & Sons
2436 Griffin Road
Churchville, NY 14428-9557   585-757-2751
Grower and packer of onions and potatoes
Co-Partner: Larry Karas
Co-Partner: William Karas
Number Employees: 5-9
Sq. footage: 34000
Type of Packaging: Consumer, Private Label, Bulk
Brands:
W.K.

15582 William Poll
1051 Lexington Ave
New York, NY 10021-3294   212-288-0501
Fax: 212-288-2844 800-993-7655
wpollny@aol.com   www.williampoll.com
Baked potato thins, dips, sauces, dip indulgencs
President: Stanley Poll
Estimated Sales: Less than $500,000
Number Employees: 5-9
Type of Packaging: Consumer
Brands:
Baked Potato Thins
Dip Indulgence

15583 William R. Clem Company
181 Virginia Ave
Lexington, KY 40508-3238   859-233-0821
Fax: 859-233-0868
President: William Clem
Estimated Sales: $ 10 - 20 Million
Number Employees: 20-49

15584 William Turner
6335 Knollwood Drive
Frederick, MD 21701-5828   301-620-1135
Fax: 301-620-1560
Coffees

15585 William's Pork
1027 US Highway 74 East
Lumberton, NC 28358   910-608-2226
Fax: 910-628-0081 william@britishbacon.com
www.britishbacon.com
bacon, hams, sausages, pork chops, ribs

15586 Williamette Filbert Growers
14875 NE Tangen Rd
Newberg, OR 97132-6890   503-538-9256
Fax: 503-538-9256 benmitchell@wifi-nw.com
Processor and exporter of hazelnuts including
in-shell, kernels, raw, roasted, sliced, diced and
blanched
Owner: Ben Mitchell
Manager: Benson Mitchel
Estimated Sales: $3 Million
Number Employees: 10-19
Sq. footage: 36000
Type of Packaging: Private Label, Bulk
Brands:
Willamette

15587 Williams Candy Company
18 Main St
Somerville, MA 02145-1496   617-776-0814
Fax: 617-776-0816
Chocolate candy
President: Ron Cataldo
Estimated Sales: Below $ 5 Million
Number Employees: 5-9
Type of Packaging: Bulk

15588 Williams Cheese Company
P.O.Box 249
Linwood, MI 48634-0249   989-697-4492
Fax: 989-697-4203 800-968-4462
jim@williamscheese.com
www.williamscheese.com

Processed and flavored cheese
President: James A Williams
Marketing Manager: Jay Williams
Sales Director: Todd Williams
Operations Manager: Mike Williams Sr
Purchasing Manager: Ladd Williams
Estimated Sales: $ 9 Million
Number Employees: 50-99
Sq. footage: 20
Type of Packaging: Private Label
Brands:
Amish Country
Cheese Rounds and Bricks
Cheese Spreads
Williams

15589 Williams Creek Farms
PO Box 292
Williams, OR 97544-0292   541-846-6481
Grower of organic produce including berries, apples,
garlic, onions and lettuce; packer of organic sun
dried cherry tomatoes and sun dried apples
Owner/Manager: Randy Carey
Number Employees: 5-9

15590 (HQ)Williams Foods Inc
13301 W 99th St
Lenexa, KS 66215-1348   913-894-1348
Fax: 913-888-0727 800-255-6736
info@williamsfoods.com
www.williamsfoods.com
Processor of custom blended seasonings, gravy
mixes and sauces including spaghetti and alfredo;
also, fruit pectin.
Chairman/President/CEO: Conrad Hock Jr
Board of Directors: Robert Aders
Board of Directors: John Cairns
Finance Executive: Annie Woodward
Board of Directors: Maurice Charlat
Board of Directors: Joseph Crocker
Board of Directors: Cordia Harrington
VP Operations: Larry Copus
Estimated Sales: $64000000
Number Employees: 100-249
Sq. footage: 200000
Type of Packaging: Consumer, Food Service, Private Label, Bulk
Other Locations:
Williams Foods
Torrance CA
Brands:
American Beauty
Armour
Creamette
Honeysuckle
Hungry Jack
Jimmy Dean
Ronzoni
San Giorgio
Skinner
Smuckers
Swanson
Williams

15591 Williams Institutional Foods
P.O.Box 233
Douglas, GA 31534-0233   912-384-5270
Fax: 912-384-0533
Wholesaler/distributor of groceries, meat, frozen
foods, bakery goods, equipment and general mer-
chandise; serving the food service market of south-
ern Georgia
President: Carl Williams
VP Distribution: B Williams
Estimated Sales: $37000000
Number Employees: 50-99

15592 Williams Packing Company
P.O.Box 856
Goldsboro, NC 27533-0856   919-735-0262
Fax: 919-735-0277
Processor of sausage
Manager: Steve Lipscomb
Sales Manager: Merle Sullivan
Estimated Sales: $ 3 - 5 Million
Number Employees: 10-19
Type of Packaging: Consumer

15593 Williams Seafood Market& Wines
10627 E Sprague Ave
Spokane Valley, WA 99206-3633   509-922-4868
Manufactuer of seafoods and wine
Owner: Vince Ofield

Estimated Sales: $300,000-500,000
Number Employees: 1-4

15594 Williams of Vermont
P.O.Box 7452
Portland, ME 04112-7452   207-774-3355
Fax: 207-828-4489
Wines
President: Steve Amadon
Estimated Sales: $ 100-500 Million
Number Employees: 1-4

15595 Williams-Carver Company
P.O.Box 3140
Kansas City, KS 66103-0140   913-236-4949
Fax: 913-236-9331 800-763-4411
sales@williamscarver.com
www.williamscarver.com
Provides quality design, sales, installation, and ser-
vice
President: Rich F Carver
Estimated Sales: $ 1 - 3 Million
Number Employees: 10-19

15596 Williams-Selym Winery
6575 Westside Rd
Healdsburg, CA 95448-8323   707-433-6425
Fax: 707-431-4862 contact@williamsselym.com
www.williamsselyem.com
Wines
Manager: Bob Cabral
Proprietor: Kathe Dyson
Marketing Director: Mark Malpiede
Executive Winemaker: Bob Cabral
Winemaker: Lynn Krausmann
Assistant Winemaker: Mark Ray
Estimated Sales: $ 1-2.5 Million
Number Employees: 5-9
Brands:
Williams-Selym Winery

15597 Williams-West & Witt Products
212 Cook St
Michigan City, IN 46360-2412   219-879-8236
Fax: 219-879-8237 wwwsoup@adsnet.com
www.williamswestandwitts.com
Processor of dry gravy mixes, cooking sauces, sea-
sonings and soup bases including chicken, beef,
ham, onion, garlic, turkey, pork, crab, salmon,
shrimp, lobster, vegetable, mushroom, etc.; also
available, vegetarian, natural, GMO freebases and
low sodium bases
President: Victor Palmer
VP: Brian Quealy
R&D Manager: John True
Sales Manager: Georgeann Quealy
Controller: Brian Quealy
Estimated Sales: $1100000
Number Employees: 5-9
Type of Packaging: Consumer, Food Service, Pri-
vate Label, Bulk
Brands:
COOKS DELIGHT

15598 Williamsburg Chocolatier
P.O.Box 1712
Williamsburg, VA 23187-1712   804-966-9000
Fax: 804-966-9025 wmsbgchoc@aol.com
www.williamsburgchocolate.com
Processor of confectionery products, pound cakes,
chocolate lollypops, dessert toppings, fudge and sea-
sonal chocolate specialties
Owner: Maryann Boho
Marketing: Lee Boho
Estimated Sales: Under 500,000
Number of Products: 50
Sq. footage: 1200
Type of Packaging: Consumer

15599 Williamsburg Foods
8012 Hankins Industrial Park
Toano, VA 23168-9259   757-566-0930
Fax: 757-673-7006
sales@williamsburgfoods.com
www.thepeanutshop.com
Processor of Virginia peanuts and specialty nut
meats. Processor of cocoa mixes including choco-
late, raspberry, traditional and chocolate hazelnut
VP: Pete Booker
Sales Director: Jeff Armbruster
Plant Manager: Larry Winslow
Number Employees: 20-49
Type of Packaging: Consumer

Brands:
Amber Brand Deviled Smithfield Ham
Colonial Williamsburg
King's Arms Tavern
Nut Case Collection
Peanut Shop of Williamsburg
Smithfield Tavern

15600 Williamsburg Winery
5800 Wessex Hundred
Williamsburg, VA 23185-8063   757-229-0999
Fax: 757-229-0911   wine@wmbgwine.com
www.williamsburgwinery.com
Wines
President: Patrick Dufseler
Estimated Sales: $3.7 Million
Number Employees: 20-49
Type of Packaging: Private Label
Brands:
Donmir Wine Cellars
La Donaings De Franc
Williamsburg Winery

15601 Willies Smoke House
562 S Main St
Harrisville, PA 16038-1626   724-735-4184
Fax: 724-735-4184 800-742-4184
williespa@pathway.net
Processor of hickory smoked meat products including ham, bacon, sausage, poultry, dried beef, jerky, pork loins, etc
Owner: John Mc Kee
Estimated Sales: $500,000 appx.
Number Employees: 1-4
Sq. footage: 1900
Type of Packaging: Consumer

15602 Willmar Cookie & Nut Company
P.O.Box 88
Willmar, MN 56201-0088   320-235-0600
Fax: 320-235-0659 www.gurleysfoods.com
Cookies and crackers. Salted and roasted nuts and seeds
President: Michael Mickelson
CEO: Michael Mickelson
General Manager: Steve Loy
Vice President: Tom Taunton
Estimated Sales: $ 10-24.9 Million
Number Employees: 100-249
Sq. footage: 140000
Type of Packaging: Private Label
Brands:
Gurley's

15603 Willmark Sales Company
P.O.Box 444
West Hempstead, NY 11552-444   718-388-7141
Fax: 718-963-3924
Processor and exporter of bakery ingredients
President: Robert Leibowitz
Technical Director: Beryl Berkinsky
Estimated Sales: $ 10 - 20 Million
Number Employees: 50-99

15604 Willoughby's Coffee & Tea
550 E Main St # 27
Branford, CT 06405-2948   203-481-1700
Fax: 203-481-1777 800-388-8400
www.willoughbyscoffee.com
Coffee
President: Barry Levine
CEO: Robert Williams
Estimated Sales: $500,000-$1 Million
Number Employees: 10-19
Brands:
Willoughby's

15605 Willow Foods
7774 SW Nimbus Ave
Beaverton, OR 97008-6423   503-641-6602
Fax: 503-641-6899 800-338-3609
willowfood@luckyfood.com
www.luckyfood.com
Processor of egg rolls, spring rolls, chow mein and fried rice
Owner: Tammy Jo
Sales Director: Peter Yu
Estimated Sales: $ 5 - 10 Million
Number Employees: 20-49
Number of Brands: 1
Number of Products: 20
Type of Packaging: Consumer, Food Service, Private Label, Bulk

Brands:
Willow

15606 Willow Hill Vineyards
5460 Loudon Street
Johnstown, OH 43031-9261   740-587-4622
Fax: 740-587-0999
Wines
Owner: Dave Rechsteiner
Estimated Sales: Less than $500,000
Number Employees: 1-4
Brands:
WILLOW HILL

15607 Willow Tree Poultry Farm
997 S Main St # 2
Attleboro, MA 02703-6299   508-222-2479
Fax: 508-222-8258
comments@willowtreefarm.com
www.willowtreefarm.com
Processor of poultry products
President: Chester Cekala
Estimated Sales: $14,500,000
Number Employees: 50-99

15608 WillowOak Farms
P.O.Box 388
Woodland, CA 95776-0388   530-662-1983
Fax: 530-662-0907 888-963-2767
wiloakfarm@aol.com www.willowoakfarms.com
All-natural hors d'oeuvre spreads, sauces and salad dressings
President: Kevin Sanchez
Research & Development: Massimo Di Sciullo
Director of Marketing: Kevin Sanchez
Estimated Sales: $ 1-2.5 Million
Number Employees: 1-4
Number of Brands: 3
Number of Products: 30
Sq. footage: 20000
Type of Packaging: Consumer, Food Service
Brands:
L'Ortolano
Willow Oak Farms

15609 Willowbrook Foods
P.O.Box 2519
Wichita, KS 67201-2519   800-423-2362
Fax: 417-837-1675 800-423-2362
info@wbfoods.com www.wbfoods.com
Processor and exporter of fresh and frozen turkey
President: Mike Briggs
VP Deli Sales: Gordon Day
Operations Manager: Greg Abbiatti
Estimated Sales: $ 100-500 Million
Number Employees: 1900
Parent Co: Promise Land Foods
Type of Packaging: Consumer, Food Service, Private Label, Bulk

15610 Willowcroft Farm Vineyards
38906 Mount Gilead Rd
Leesburg, VA 20175-6721   703-777-8161
Fax: 703-777-8157 willowine@aol.com
www.willowcroftwine.com
Wine
Owner: Lewis Parker
Estimated Sales: $ 1 - 3 Million
Number Employees: 1-4

15611 Willy Wonka Candy
1445 Norwood Ave
Itasca, IL 60143-1199   630-773-0267
Fax: 630-773-1467 888-694-2656
info@hometownfavorites.com
www.hometownfavorites.com
Candy
President/CEO: David Kewer
Plant Manager: Ann Haffron
Purchasing Manager: L Glen
Estimated Sales: $ 50-100 Million
Number Employees: 250-499
Brands:
Willy Wonka

15612 Willy Wonka Candy Factory
1445 Norwood Ave
Itasca, IL 60143-1199   630-773-0267
Fax: 630-773-1467
Manufacturer of Interactive chocolate bar
CFO: Bill Rasmussen
CEO: David Kewer
Number Employees: 250-499
Parent Co: Nestle USA

Type of Packaging: Consumer
Brands:
XPLODER

15613 Willy's Pickle Products
20280 Bathurst Street N
Holland Landing, ON L9N 1N3
Canada   905-836-6532
Fax: 905-954-1092
Processor of pickles, peppers and sauerkraut
President: Richard Lehmann
VP: Kurt Lehmann
Sq. footage: 28000
Type of Packaging: Private Label, Bulk
Brands:
New York
Willy's

15614 Wilson Candy Company
408 Harrison Ave
Jeannette, PA 15644-1997   724-523-3151
Fax: 724-523-5959
Processor of boxed and bulk chocolates
President: Doug Wilson
VP: Kay Wilson
Production Manager: Rob Kane
Estimated Sales: $870000
Number Employees: 10-19
Sq. footage: 9600
Type of Packaging: Consumer, Private Label, Bulk
Brands:
Wunder Bar

15615 Wilson Corn Products
P.O.Box 97
Rochester, IN 46975-0097   574-223-3177
Fax: 574-223-3414
Flour and other grain mill products.
President: Thomas Wilson
CEO: John Cory
Estimated Sales: $ 10-20 Million
Number Employees: 20-49

15616 Wilson's Fantastic Candy
384 Greenway Rd
Memphis, TN 38117-4338   901-767-1900
Fax: 901-398-1375
wilsonfoods@mindspring.com
www.wilsonfoods.com
Processor of candy including caramels, chocolates, coconut, fudge, corn, bagged, fundraising, theater and vending; also, fat-free and sugar-free cookies and glazed nuts
Owner: Robert Wilson
VP/General Manager: Jerry Adams
Number Employees: 5-9
Sq. footage: 15000
Parent Co: Kemmons Wilson Companies
Type of Packaging: Consumer, Bulk
Brands:
Wilson Foods

15617 Wilson's Oysters
1981 S Van Ave
Houma, LA 70363   985-857-8855
Fax: 985-857-8139 wilson@wilsonsoysters.com
www.wilsonsoysters.com
Oysters
President: Wilson Voisin Jr
Estimated Sales: $5-10 Million
Number Employees: 20-49

15618 Wilsonhill Farm
141 Poker Hill Road
Underhill, VT 05489-9639   802-899-2154
Fax: 802-899-2154
Processor of mixes including bread, pancake and muffin; also, apple butter
President: Amy Dandurand
VP: Luc Dandurand
Number Employees: 1-4
Sq. footage: 3500
Type of Packaging: Consumer, Food Service, Private Label
Brands:
Wilsonhill

15619 Wimberley Valley Winery
2825 Lone Man Mountain Rd
Driftwood, TX 78619-9313   512-847-2592
Fax: 281-288-8298
info@wimberleyvalleywinery.com
www.wimberleyvalleywinery.com

Wines
   President: Howard Pitman
   VP: Dean Valentine
Estimated Sales:$500,000-$1 Million
Number Employees: 1-4
Type of Packaging: Bulk
Brands:
   Wimberley Valley

15620 Wimmer's Meat Products

P.O.Box 286
West Point, NE 68788-0286   402-372-2437
    Fax: 402-372-5659 800-358-0761
        lou@wimmersmeats.com
        www.wimmersmeats.com
Processor of natural casing weiners, skinless
weiners, natural casing link sausages,
brauschweiger, summer sausage, smokies, sliced
lunchmeats and deli meats.
   President: Dave Wimmer
   Chariman: Harold Wimmer
Estimated Sales:$ 20 - 50 Million
Number Employees: 100-249
Type of Packaging: Consumer, Food Service, Private Label, Bulk
Brands:
   Ambassador
   Bassetts
   Fairbury's

15621 Winans Chocolates & Coffees

308 W Water St
Piqua, OH 45356-2238   937-773-1981
    Fax: 937-773-2388 www.winanscandies.com
Processor of candy
   President: Joe Reiser
Estimated Sales:$ 10 - 20 Million
Number Employees: 20-49
Type of Packaging: Consumer

15622 Winchester Cheese Company

32605 Holland Rd
Winchester, CA 92596-9696   951-926-4239
   Fax: 951-926-3349 sales@winchestercheese.com
        www.winchestercheese.com
Processor of gouda cheese
   Manager: Jeff Floot
*Estimated Sales:*Less than $500,000
Number Employees: 5-9
Sq. footage: 3650
Type of Packaging: Consumer, Food Service, Private Label, Bulk
Brands:
   Cumin Gouda
   Herb Gouda
   Jalapeno Gouda
   Mild Gouda
   Sharp Gouda
   Super Aged Gouda

15623 Winchester Farms Dairy

675 Rolling Hills Ln
Winchester, KY 40391-8102   859-745-5500
       Fax: 859-745-5547 www.kroger.com
Processor of milk including chocolate, 2%, whole
and skim; also, buttermilk
   President: Bill McCarthy
   CFO: Mike McGuire
   VP: Michael Schlotman
Estimated Sales:$500,000-$1 Million
Number Employees: 100-249
Parent Co: Kroger Company
Type of Packaging: Consumer, Private Label
Brands:
   Kroger

15624 Windatt Farms

1481 County Road #12
Picton, ON K0K 2T0
Canada
             613-393-5289
         Fax: 613-393-5289
Processor and exporter of frozen rhubarb and cherries
   President: Reg Windatt
Number Employees: 10-19
Sq. footage: 3500
Brands:
   Windatt Farms

15625 Windcrest Meat Packers

1350 Scugog 3rd Line
Port Perry, ON L9L 1B3
Canada
             905-985-7267
             800-750-2542

Processor of meat products including beef, pork,
lamb, goat and veal
   President: Victor DiMinno
   Operations Manager: Michael DiMinno
Type of Packaging: Consumer, Private Label

15626 Winder Dairy

P.O.Box 70009
West Valley, UT 84170-0009   801-224-8686
    Fax: 801-969-2223 800-946-3371
Processor of bread, pastries, cakes, rolls, milk, fruit
juices, cottage cheese, sour cream and yogurt
   Manager: Jake Smith
   Executive VP: Kent Winder
   Plant Manager: Dan Lukes
Estimated Sales:$44100000
Number Employees: 100-249
Sq. footage: 50000
Type of Packaging: Consumer, Food Service, Private Label
Brands:
   Valley Farms
   Winder

15627 Windham Winery

14727 Mountain Rd
Purcellville, VA 20132-3638   540-668-6464
   Fax: 540-668-7679 info@windhamwinery.com
        www.windhamwinery.com
Wines
   Owner: George Bazaco

15628 Windmill Candy

3331 70th Street
Lubbock, TX 79413-6130   806-785-4688
        Fax: 806-794-1512
Candy
   President: Michele Adams

15629 Windmill Water

2042 Hwy 333
Edgewood, NM 87015-6740   505-281-9287
   Fax: 505-286-9669 Windmillwater@comcast.net
        www.windmillwater.com
Bottled spring water
   President: Leon Ricter
   Plant Manager: Leon Ricter
   Office Manager: Diana Ricter
Estimated Sales:$ 1 - 3 Million
Number Employees: 1-4

15630 Windsor Confections

4632 Telegraph Ave
Oakland, CA 94609-2022   510-653-3703
   Fax: 510-653-3755 800-860-0021
     sales@windsorconfections.com
     www.hooperschocolate.com
Produces a variety of chocolate confections including chocolate dipped strawberries and gift baskets.
Windsor Confections is a unique social venture - a
division of the California Autism Foundation, sales
of their chocolate providesupport to autism services
and public awareness campaigns.
   President: Jeff White LCSW
Estimated Sales:$ 5 - 10 Million
Number Employees: 10-19
Parent Co: California Autism Foundation
Brands:
   ANYTIME CANDY
   BREAK UP
   CALIFORNIA FINEST
   CHEWEY KISSES
   CHOCOLATE JOLLIES
   HOOPEE DOOPS
   MY SELECTION
   OLD FASHIONED
   PATIO SQUARES
   ROYAL GIFT
   SMOOTH AND MELTIES

15631 (HQ)Windsor Foods

3355 W Alabama St # 730
Houston, TX 77098-1866   713-843-5200
        Fax: 713-960-9709
     rgutierrez@windsorfoods.com
     www.windsorfoods.com
Processor of frozen Chinese finger food
   President: Greg Geib
   R&D: Jean Lee
Estimated Sales:$10-24.9 Million
Number Employees: 1,000-4,999
Sq. footage: 12000
Brands:
   Golden Tiger

15632 Windsor Frozen Foods

3355 W Alabama St # 730
Houston, TX 77098-1866   713-843-5200
    Fax: 713-960-9709 800-437-6936
        awright@windsorfoods.com
        www.windsorfoods.com
Manufacturer of frozen Italian specialties including
ravioli, tortellini, lasagna, stuffed shells, manicotti,
cannelloni, gnocchi, rotini, customized pastas and
Italian sauces
   President/CEO: Oreste Boscia
   CEO: Greg Geib
Estimated Sales:$20-50 Million
Number Employees: 1,000-4,999
Type of Packaging: Consumer, Food Service, Bulk
Brands:
   BERNARDI
   GOLDEN TIGER
   THE ORIGINAL CHILI BOWL

15633 Windsor Vineyards

P.O.Box 368
Windsor, CA 95492-0368   707-836-5000
    Fax: 707-836-5900 800-333-9987
     webamster@windsorvineyards.com
     www.windsorvineyards.com
Producer and retailer of wines and champagnes
   President: Tammy Boatright
   Executive VP: Donna Elias
   Sales: Howard Smith
Estimated Sales:$ 50 - 100 Million
Number Employees: 100-249
Number of Brands: 1
Number of Products: 42
Parent Co: Klein Family Vinters
Type of Packaging: Consumer
Brands:
   Windsor Vineyards

15634 Windsor Vineyards

P.O.Box 368
Windsor, CA 95492-0368   707-836-5000
    Fax: 707-836-5900 800-992-4233
     webmaster@windsorvineyards.com
     www.windsorvineyards.com
Processor of wines
   President: Tammy Boatright
   General Manager: J B Winkler
   VP Operations: Pat McDowell
Estimated Sales:$ 50 - 100 Million
Number Employees: 100-249
Sq. footage: 10000
Brands:
   Windsor Vineyards

15635 Windwalker Vineyards

7360 Perry Creek Rd
Somerset, CA 95684-9207   530-620-4054
   Fax: 530-620-5224 windwalkerinfo@gotsky.com
        www.windwalkervineyard.com
Wines
   Owner: Jim Taff
   Operations: Alanna Taff
*Estimated Sales:*More than $500,000
Number Employees: 3
Brands:
   Windwalker

15636 Windward Trading Company

125 Larkspur Street
San Rafael, CA 94901-4711   415-457-2411
    Fax: 415-457-4916 800-858-8119
General grocery
   Owner: Richard Rein
   Owner: Rena Rein
*Estimated Sales:*Under $500,000
Number Employees: 1-4

15637 Wine Country Chef LLC

PO Box 1416
Hidden Valley Lake, CA 95461   707-322-0406
   Fax: 800-306-2660 chef@winecounrtychef.net
        www.winecounrtychef.net
Organic spice blends and all natural marinades &
sauces
   President/Owner: Harold Imbrunetti
Estimated Sales:$250,000
Number Employees: 2
Number of Brands: 4
Number of Products: 4
Type of Packaging: Consumer, Food Service, Bulk
Brands:
   WINE COUNTRY CHEF GOURMET MARI-

NADE
WINE COUNTRY CHEF LEMON PEPPER
RUB
WINE COUNTRY CHEF SPICED MUSTARD
WINE COUNTRY CHIEF SPICED BBQ RUB

15638 Wine Country Kitchens
511 Alexis Ct
Napa, CA 94558-7526   707-252-9463
                          Fax: 707-252-9424
wck@winecountrykitchens.com
www.winecountrykitchens.com
Manufacturer of gourmet oils, wine vinegars, pasta
suaces and salad dressings
    Owner: John Mc Intosh
    Quality Control: Brian Witbracht
    Marketing Director: Marilyn Moe Asmuth
Estimated Sales: $ 20-50 Million
Number Employees: 20-49
Type of Packaging: Private Label
Brands:
    Napa Valley Barbeque Co.
    Napa Valley Harvest
    Wine Country Kitchens

15639 Wine Country Pasta
201 W Napa St
Sonoma, CA 95476-6643   707-935-1366
Pasta
    Owner: Joe Wade
Estimated Sales: Below $ 5 Million
Number Employees: 1-4

15640 Wine Group
240 Stockton Street
Suite 800
San Francisco, CA 94108-5325   415-986-8700
                          Fax: 415-986-4305
Processor of wines
    President: David Mackesey
Number Employees: 5-9
Type of Packaging: Consumer
Brands:
    FRANZIA WINE
    GLEN ELLEN
    MG VALLEJO
    MOGEN DAVID

15641 Wine-A-Rita
31 Knotty Pine Place
Texarkana, TX 75503   903-832-7309
    Fax: 903-838-7803 info@wineglace.com
                          www.wineglace.com
frozen wine drinks
    President/Owner: Donna Griffin
    CEO: Judy Smith

15642 Winfrey Fudge & Candy
40 Newburyport Tpke
Rowley, MA 01969-2106   978-948-7448
        Fax: 978-948-7088 888-946-3739
    info@winfreys.com www.winfreys.com
Chocolates and fudge
    Owner: Chris Winfrey
    CFO: Christine Winfrey
Estimated Sales: Below $ 5 Million
Number Employees: 10-19
Brands:
    Winfrey's

15643 Wing Candy Company
504 Brown Street
Branson, MO 65616-2801   417-334-3238
    Fax: 417-334-3238 www.wingcandycompany.com
Processor of confectionery, honey, sorghum, relishes
and jellies
    President: Ebb Johnson
    Vice President: Macie Johnson
Estimated Sales: $ 1 - 3 Million
Number Employees: 1-4
Type of Packaging: Consumer

15644 Wing Hing Noodle Company
1642 E 23rd St
Los Angeles, CA 90011-1804   323-235-5432
    Fax: 323-231-9022 888-223-8899
    kenny@winghing.com www.winghing.com
Processor and importer of fresh, dry and pre-cooked
noodles; also, fortune cookies, tofu products and egg
roll, wonton and potsticker wrappers
    President: Kenny Yee
Estimated Sales: $1800000
Number Employees: 20-49

Brands:
    Wing Hing Gold Coin
    Wing Hing Panda

15645 Wing It
PO Box 673
Falmouth, MA 02541-0673   508-540-9860
    Fax: 508-540-9861 wingitinc@aol.com
                          www.wingit.com
Processor of buffalo wing sauce
    President: Steven Robinson
Type of Packaging: Consumer, Food Service, Pri-
vate Label, Bulk
Brands:
    Wing It

15646 Wing Nien Company
30560 San Antonio St
Hayward, CA 94544-7102   510-487-8877
    Fax: 510-489-6666 ghall@wnfoods.com
                          www.wnfoods.com
Processor and packager of sauces, oils, salsa, mus-
tard and syrups; exporter of organic oils and sauces;
also, custom blending and packaging in portion
packs, glass bottles and plastic containers available
    Manager: Linda Lee
    Plant Superintendent: Jon Choy
Estimated Sales: $ 10 - 20 Million
Number Employees: 20-49
Sq. footage: 45000
Parent Co: US Enterprise Corporation
Type of Packaging: Consumer, Food Service, Pri-
vate Label
Other Locations:
    Wing Nien Co.
    Vancouver BC

15647 Wing Seafood Company
1850 S Canal St
Chicago, IL 60616-1502   312-942-9930
                          Fax: 312-942-0391
    Owner: Wing Ng
Estimated Sales: $1.2 Million
Number Employees: 5-9

15648 (HQ)Wing Sing Chong Company
390 Swift Ave # 13
S San Francisco, CA 94080-6221   415-552-1234
                          Fax: 415-552-3812
Manufacturer, importer and wholesaler/distributor of
Oriental foods
    Owner: Roberta Woo
Estimated Sales: $15 Million
Number Employees: 1-4
Sq. footage: 50000
Brands:
    LANTERN

15649 (HQ)Wing's Food Products
50 Torlake Crescent
Toronto, ON M8Z 1B8
Canada   416-259-2662
    Fax: 416-259-3414 custserv@wings.ca
                          www.wings.ca
Processor of portioned controlled foods including
ketchup, mustard, relish, vinegar, soy and plum
sauce and steam cooked noodles; manufacturer of
egg roll wrappers
    president: Neal Lee
    General Manager: Neal Lee
    Finance Manager: Cynthia Lee
Parent Co: Wing's Food Products
Type of Packaging: Food Service, Private Label,
Bulk
Other Locations:
    Wing's Food Products
    Edmonton AB
Brands:
    Wing's
    Wing's

15650 Wing-Time
P.O.Box 775003
Steamboat Spgs, CO 80477-5003   970-871-1198
    Fax: 970-871-1215 info@wingtime.com
                          www.wingtime.com
Buffalo wing and barbecue sauces available in six
varieties
    President: Terence Brown
Estimated Sales: Below $ 5 Million
Number Employees: 1-4
Number of Brands: 1
Number of Products: 6
Type of Packaging: Consumer, Food Service, Pri-
vate Label

15651 (HQ)Winger Cheese
P.O.Box 238
Towner, ND 58788-0238   701-537-5463
    Fax: 701-537-5854 www.wingercheese.com
Manufacturer of cheese
    Owner: Pete Winger
Number Employees: 1-4
Type of Packaging: Food Service, Bulk
Brands:
    Winger

15652 Wings Foods of Alberta
2959 Parsons Road
Edmonton, AB T6N 1B8
Canada   780-433-6406
    Fax: 780-431-1026 custserv@wingsalberta.com
                          www.wingfood.com
Processor of noodles, condiments and fortune cook-
ies
    President: Barry Lee
    Sales Manager: Doug Petrie
    Production Manager: Chris Hambley
Number Employees: 50-99
Sq. footage: 85000
Type of Packaging: Private Label
Brands:
    PC
    Wing's

15653 Winkler
500 Main St.
Winkler, MB R6W 4B3   812-937-2044
    Fax: 812-937-2044 http://www.winklertimes.com
    President: Tom Winkler
Number Employees: 100-249

**15654 (HQ)Winmix/Natural Care
Products**
7466 Cape Girardeau Street
Englewood, FL 34224-8004   941-475-7432
    Fax: 941-475-7432 soyflax5000@ewol.com
                          www.naturalsoyproducts.net
Processor and exporter of soft serve ice cream and
sorbets, meat analogs, fruit juice and beverage bases,
low-fat replacers and nonfat mixes. Importer of juice
and coffee bases. Research and development ser-
vices available for icecream, sorbet and meatless
analogs and health care products
    Owner: Winsor Eveland
    CEO: Martha Efird
Estimated Sales: $100000
Number Employees: 2
Number of Brands: 4
Number of Products: 350
Sq. footage: 2000
Type of Packaging: Consumer, Food Service, Pri-
vate Label, Bulk
Brands:
    Multy Grain Foods
    Soy Flax 5000
    Winmix

15655 Winn-Dixie Dairies
PO Box 639
Hammond, LA 70404-0639   985-549-6870
                          Fax: 985-549-6879
Processor of milk, fruit punch, juices, teas and water
    Plant Manager: J Thornton
Number Employees: 50-99
Parent Co: Winn Dixie
Type of Packaging: Consumer

15656 (HQ)Winn-Dixie Stores
5050 Edgewood Court
Jacksonville, FL 32254   904-783-5000
        Fax: 904-783-5294 800-946-6349
    info@winndixie.com www.winndixie.com
Coffee and tea
    President/CEO: Peter Lynch
    SVP/CFO: Bennett Nussbaum
Estimated Sales: $7.4 Billion
Number Employees: 50,000
Parent Co: Harris Teeter, Inc
Brands:
    Astor
    THRIFTY MAID
    WINN & LOVETT
    WINN-DIXIE

15657 (HQ)Winning Solutions
P.O.Box 5408
Pagosa Springs, CO 81147-5408   970-264-2949
            Fax: 970-731-6706   800-899-2563
winningin@aol.com   www.miracleofaloe.com
Processor and exporter of aloe vera gel drinks, juice blends, etc
      President: JC Clarke Jr
Estimated Sales:$500,000-$1 Million
Number Employees: 5-9
Sq. footage: 2000
Type of Packaging: Consumer, Food Service
Other Locations:
      Winning Solutions
      Westport CT

15658 Winnsboro Beverage Packers
P.O.Box 515
Winnsboro, LA 71295-0515   318-435-9404
            Fax: 318-435-5221
Processor of carbonated soft drinks
      Owner: Marcy Thompson
      Plant Manager: D Richards
Number Employees: 100-249
Parent Co: Winnsboro Beverage Packers
Type of Packaging: Consumer, Private Label

15659 Winona Packing Company
P.O.Box 745
Winona, MS 38967-0745   662-283-4317
            Fax: 662-283-4799
Processor of beef and pork; also, fresh and smoked sausage
      President: Bill Graves Jr
      Vice President: Vicky Stiemann
Estimated Sales:$ 10-20 Million
Number Employees: 20-49
Type of Packaging: Consumer, Food Service

15660 Winslow B. Whitley
405 N Center Avenue
Oakley, ID 83346   208-862-3229
Vegetables

15661 Winter Garden Citrus
P.O.Box 770069
Winter Garden, FL 34777-0069   407-656-4423
            Fax: 407-656-1007
Frozen citrus beverages
      President: Steven Beckenmeyer
      General Manager: Everette Fisher
      CFO: Floyd Skipper
      CEO: Everett Fischer
      General Manager: Eberette Fischer
      Sales Manager: Peter Hann
      Operation Manager: Mary Turner
      Plant Manager: Paul Ballentine
Estimated Sales:$ 50-100 Million
Number Employees: 100-249
Type of Packaging: Private Label
Brands:
      Winter Garden

15662 Winter Harbor Co-Op
P.O.Box 69
Winter Harbor, ME 04693-0069   207-963-5857
            Fax: 207-963-7275
Whole fish and seafood
      Manager: Randy Johnson
Estimated Sales:$600,000
Number Employees: 1-4

15663 Winter Sausage Manufacturing Company
22011 Gratiot Avenue
Eastpointe, MI 48021-2294   586-777-9080
            Fax: 586-777-7996
dw.wintersausage@sbcglobal.net
            www.wintersausage.com
Manufacturer of sausages, premium deli meats and spiral hams. Proprietary and private label
      President: Rosemary Wuerz
      Founder: Eugene Winter
      VP/Sales: Ron Eckert
      R&D/Marketing: Dorianne Wuerz
      Quality Control: Mary Ellen Menard
      Production/Purchasing Director: Eugene Wuerz
      Plant Manager: Greg Van Hazenbrouck
Estimated Sales:$4.7 Million
Number Employees: 40
Type of Packaging: Consumer, Private Label, Bulk
Brands:
      Farmer Jack

Kroger
Lipary

15664 Winterbrook Beverage Group
2000 Schenley Place
Greendale, IN 47025-1593   812-537-7348
Bottled water
      President: Raymond Smith
Brands:
      Cascadia
      Lacroix Sparkling Wa
      Lacroix Spring Water
      Winterbrook Seltzer

15665 Wintergreen Winery
P.O.Box 648
Nellysford, VA 22958-0648   434-361-2519
Fax: 434-361-1510   info@wintergreenwinery.com
            www.wintergreenwinery.com
Wine
      Co-Owner: Jeff Stone
      Co-Owner: Tamara Stone
Estimated Sales:$ 1 - 3 Million
Number Employees: 1-4

15666 Winters Winery
15 Main St
Winters, CA 95694-1722   530-795-3201
            Fax: 916-795-1119
Wine
Estimated Sales:$ 1-2.5 Million
Number Employees: 1-4

15667 Wisconsin Cheese
1931 N 15th Ave
Melrose Park, IL 60160-1402   708-450-0074
      Fax: 708-450-1670   wiscon@wisconcorp.com
            www.wisconcorp.com
Processor of romano and parmesan cheese, oil, white and red wine vinegar, spices and tomatoes; importer of cheese, oil, tomatoes and pasta
      President: Natale Caputo
      Marketing Director: Jerry Jack
      Purchasing Manager: Joy Baker
Estimated Sales:$ 20 - 50 Million
Number Employees: 50-99
Sq. footage: 52000
Parent Co: Wiscon Corporation
Type of Packaging: Consumer, Food Service, Private Label, Bulk
Brands:
      Caputo
      Grate Wiscon
      Red Cow
      Red Sheep

15668 Wisconsin Cheese
200 University Ave
Westwood, MA 02090-2307   781-320-0288
            Fax: 781-320-0108
Cheese
      Manager: Ralph Panico
      Marketing Director: Ralph Panico
*Estimated Sales:*Less than $500,000
Number Employees: 5-9

15669 Wisconsin Cheese Group
P.O.Box 228
Monroe, WI 53566-0228   608-325-2012
      Fax: 608-329-2381   800-332-6518
            info@wisconsincheesegroup.com
            www.wisconsincheesegroup.com
Cheese
      Manager: Arthur Stickley
Estimated Sales:$ 10-24.9 Million
Number Employees: 50-99
Brands:
      U Viajero
      Wisconsin Cheese

15670 Wisconsin Cheeseman
P.O.Box 1
Madison, WI 53701-0001   608-837-5166
            Fax: 608-837-5493
customerservice@wisconsincheeseman.com
            www.wisconsincheeseman.com
Processor and exporter of cheese and chocolate specialties
      President: Gary Ricco
Estimated Sales:$60600000
Number Employees: 250-499
Type of Packaging: Consumer, Food Service, Private Label, Bulk

15671 Wisconsin Dairy State Cheese
P.O.Box 215
Rudolph, WI 54475-0215   715-435-3144
            Fax: 715-435-3146
Cheddar cheese
      President: Mike Moran
Estimated Sales:$ 20-50 Million
Number Employees: 20-49
Brands:
      Black River
      Hennings

15672 Wisconsin Dairyland Fudge Company
216 Broadway
Wisconsin Dells, WI 53965-1565   608-254-4136
      Fax: 608-254-7771   wisconsin@dellsfudge.com
            www.dellsfudge.com
Dairy farm products
      Manager: Roj Rosen
*Estimated Sales:*Below $ 5 Million
Number Employees: 20-49
Brands:
      Dairyland
      Swiss Made

15673 Wisconsin Farmers' Union Cheese Company
Highway 18
Montfort, WI 53569   608-943-6771
      Fax: 608-943-6769   shop@wfucheese.com
            www.wfucheese.com
Manufacturer of aged, curd, fresh cheese; gift boxes are available
      Owner: Doug Peterson
      Plant Manager/Production: Tim Tehl
Estimated Sales:$500,000-$1 Million
Number Employees: 1-4
Brands:
      Montforte

15674 Wisconsin Packing Company
4700 N 132nd St
Butler, WI 53007-1603   262-781-2400
            800-558-2000
Processor of hamburger patties, chili and diced beef
      President: Justin Segel
      VP Sales/Operations: Frank Vignieri
      Plant Manager: Rick Chamber
Number Employees: 250-499
Sq. footage: 140000
Type of Packaging: Consumer, Food Service, Private Label, Bulk

15675 Wisconsin Spice
P.O.Box 190
Berlin, WI 54923-0190   920-361-3555
      Fax: 920-361-0818 www.wisconsinspice.com
Manufacturer and exporter of gourmet spices and herbs, seasoning blends, dry mustard products and prepared liquid mustards
      President: Phillip Sass
Estimated Sales:$7 Million
Number Employees: 20-49
Type of Packaging: Consumer, Food Service, Private Label, Bulk
Brands:
      Uncle Phil's

15676 Wisconsin Whey International
N2689 County Road S
Juda, WI 53550-9714   608-233-5101
            Fax: 608-934-1044   wiswhey@tds.net
Processor and exporter of kosher and HALAL approved whey products including edible lactose and whey protein concentrate
      President: Linda Smith
      Sales Manager: Doug Clairday
Number Employees: 50-99
Sq. footage: 23900
Type of Packaging: Bulk
Brands:
      LACTOSE PHARMA
      WISCONSIN WHEY INTERNATIONAL
      WPC 34
      XL 2000
      XL 440
      XL 480

15677 Wisconsin Wilderness Food Products

101 W Capitol Dr
Milwaukee, WI 53212-1120   414-964-6466
Fax: 414-964-6675   800-359-3039
www.wisconsinwilderness.com
Processor of bread and dessert mixes including cranberry cinnamon, date nut and apple crisp; also, cranberry mustard and chutney, honey mustard and preserves
President: Margaret Gunn
Plant Manager: Christina Grohmann
Estimated Sales: $1000000
Number Employees: 10-19
Number of Brands: 2
Number of Products: 30
Sq. footage: 21000
Type of Packaging: Consumer, Food Service, Private Label, Bulk

15678 Wisdom Natural Brands

1203 W San Pedro St
Gilbert, AZ 85233-2406   480-921-1373
Fax: 480-966-3805   800-899-9908
wisdom@wisdomnaturalbrands.com
www.wisdomnaturalbrands.com
Herbal teas
President: James May
Vice President: Steve May
Quality Control: Mike Small
Operations Manager: Mike Small
Estimated Sales: $ 1 - 3 Million
Number Employees: 10-19
Type of Packaging: Consumer, Private Label, Bulk
Brands:
LA MERCED ORGANIC
STEVIA PRODUCTS
SWEET AND SLENDER NATURAL SWEETENER
SWEET LEAF
WISDOM NUTRITION
WISDOM OF THE ANCIENTS HERBAL TEAS

15679 (HQ)Wise Foods

245 Townpark Dr NW # 75
Kennesaw, GA 30144-5887   770-426-5821
Fax: 770-528-0971   snackmaster@wisesnacks.com
www.wisesnacks.com
Manufacturer of salty snack foods
President/CEO: Richard Robertson
CFO: Thomas Van Autreve
CEO: Ed Lambert
Marketing VP: Terry McDaniel
Sales VP: Terry McDaniel
Number Employees: 1,000-4,999
Type of Packaging: Private Label
Other Locations:
Wise Foods Inc
Berwick PA
Wise Foods Inc
Bristol VA
Wise Foods Inc
Spartanburg SC
Brands:
BRAVOS
KRUNCHERS
NEW YORK DELI
QUINLAN
RIDGIES

15680 Wise Foods

228 Rasely St
Berwick, PA 18603-4533   570-759-4000
Fax: 570-759-4001
snackmaster@wisesnacks.com
www.wisesnacks.com
Manufacturer of salty snack foods
Manager: Tony Kennedy
CFO: Tom Mannion
Operations: Bruce Roberts
Number Employees: 1,000-4,999
Other Locations:
Wise Foods Inc
Bristol VA
Wise Foods Inc
Spartanburg SC

15681 Wise Foods

100 Amor Ave # 3
Carlstadt, NJ 07072-2100   201-507-2100
Fax: 973-898-1840   corporate@wisesnacks.com
www.wisesnacks.com

Manufacturer of salty snacks foods
Executive Director: John Mc Ginnis
CEO: Richard Robertson
President: Edward M Lambert
Sales Director: Marc Atkinson
Estimated Sales: $ 1 - 3 Million
Number Employees: 5-9
Parent Co: Palladium Equity Partners
Type of Packaging: Private Label
Brands:
BRAVOS
CHEEZ DOODLES
KETTLE COOKED POTATO CHIPS
RIDGIES
WISE POTATO CHIPS

15682 Wise Foods

2233 Weaver Pike
Bristol, TN 37620-5615   864-585-9011
Fax: 864-594-6628
Manufacturer of salty snacks foods.
President/Owner: Bo Savage
Director Manufacturing: Dewey Armstrong
Estimated Sales: $50-99.9 Million
Number Employees: 250-499
Other Locations:
Wise Foods Inc
Bristol VA
Wise Foods Inc
Berwick PA

15683 Wish List/Good Fortunes

6754 Eton Ave
Canoga Park, CA 91303-2813   818-595-1555
Fax: 818-595-1550   800-644-9474
orders@goodfortunes.com
www.corporatecandyworks.com
Fortune cookies
Owner: Karen Staitman
VP: Steven Staitman
Estimated Sales: Below $ 5 Million
Number Employees: 10-19
Brands:
Good Fortunes

15684 Wishnev Wine Management

2125 Oak Grove Rd # 120
Walnut Creek, CA 94598-2537   925-930-6374
Fax: 925-930-6388
Wines
Owner: Sanford Wishnev
Estimated Sales: $300,000-500,000
Number Employees: 1-4
Type of Packaging: Private Label

15685 Wisner Minnow Hatchery

681 Pete Haring Rd
Wisner, LA 71378-4653   318-724-6133
Fax: 318-724-6138 www.haringspridecatfish.com
Catfish
President: Carl Haring
Estimated Sales: $ 20 - 50 Million
Number Employees: 250-499

15686 Wissahickon Spring Water International

10447 Drummond Rd
Philadelphia, PA 19154-3897   215-824-3300
Fax: 215-824-3180   800-394-3733
tedh@wspringwater.com
www.wspringwater.com
Bottled water
General Manager: Ted Hertz
CFO: Mike Pessiki
Director of Sales: Joe Panichelli
Estimated Sales: $ 20-50 Million
Number Employees: 50-99
Type of Packaging: Private Label
Brands:
Wissahickon Spring Water

15687 Wisteria Candy Cottage

P.O.Box 985
Boulevard, CA 91905-0085   619-766-4453
800-458-8246
www.candycottage.com
Candy
Owner: Dana Eascobellis
Co-Owner: LuzCelia Rankin
Estimated Sales: Less than $500,000
Number Employees: 1-4
Type of Packaging: Private Label

15688 Witness Tree Vineyard

7111 Spring Valley Rd NW
Salem, OR 97304-9777   503-585-7874
Fax: 503-362-9765   888-478-8766
info@witnesstreevineyard.com
www.witnesstreevineyard.com
Wines
President: Carolyn Devine
CEO: Carolyn Devine
Vice President: Dennis Devine
Marketing Manager: Carolyn Devine
National Sales Director: Mark Pape
Winemaker/Vineyard Manager: Steven Westby
Estimated Sales: $ 2.5-5 Million
Number Employees: 5-9
Type of Packaging: Private Label
Brands:
Witness Tree Vineyard

15689 Wixon/Fontarome

1390 E Bolivar Ave
St Francis, WI 53235-4521   414-769-3000
Fax: 414-769-3024   chuck-ehemann@wixon.com
www.wixon.com
Processor and packer of natural spices, seasoning blends for meat products, flavors, food chemicals, etc
President: A Peter Gottsacker
Executive VP: Chuck Ehemann
VP Sales/Marketing: Jerry Morgan
Estimated Sales: $46675000
Number Employees: 100-249
Parent Co: Fontarome
Type of Packaging: Consumer, Food Service, Private Label, Bulk
Brands:
Flavor Shaker
French Flavor Maker
Licorics Granules

15690 Wixson Honey

4937 Lakemont Himrod Rd
Dundee, NY 14837-8820   607-243-8583
Fax: 607-243-7143 www.wixsonhoney.com
Manufacturer and importer of honey including clover, buckwheat, orange, beeswax and fall flower
Owner: Jerald Howell
Estimated Sales: $3-5 Million
Number Employees: 1-4
Type of Packaging: Consumer, Food Service, Private Label, Bulk

15691 Wizards Cauldron, LTD

878 Firetower Rd
Yanceyville, NC 27379-8110   336-694-5333
Fax: 336-664-5284   ron@wizardscauldron.com
www.wizardscauldron.com
Manufacturer and exporter of natural and organic salad dressing and sauces including barbecue, steak, soy, poultry, stir-fry, hot, table and vegetable
President: Sean Kearney
CEO: John Troy
VP: Glenda Smith
Research & Development: Tina Toney
Quality Control: Jason Dawson
VP Sales and Marketing: Ron Rash
Purchasing Manager: Sean Kearney
Number Employees: 5-9
Sq. footage: 10000
Parent Co: Wizard's Cauldron
Type of Packaging: Consumer, Food Service, Private Label, Bulk
Brands:
Flavor of the Rainforest
Simply Delicious
Troys

15692 Woeber Mustard Manufacturing

1966 Commerce Circle
PO Box 388
Springfield, OH 45501-0388
Fax: 937-323-1679   800-548-2929
raywoeber@woebermustard.com
www.woebermustard.com

Mustard, mayo gourmet, sandwhich pals, mister mustard, woeber's reserve, supreme mustard, organic mustard, crowning touch, horseradish, garlic, vinegars, lemon juice
President: Ray Woeber
Quality Control: Randy Weyant
VP National Sales: Rick Schmidt
Human Resources Manager: Judy Finnegan
Operations Manager: Christopher Woeber
Logistics Manager: Bob Sharp
Purchasing: Joyce Capper
Estimated Sales: $40 Million
Number Employees: 100-249
Type of Packaging: Consumer, Food Service, Private Label, Bulk
Brands:
CROWNING TOUCH
WOEBER

15693 Wohlt Cheese Corporation
P.O.Box 203
New London, WI 54961-0203   920-982-9000
Fax: 920-982-6288   sales@wohltcheese.com
www.wohltcheese.com
Processed cheese
President: Marilyn Taylor
Estimated Sales: $ 10-20 Million
Number Employees: 50-99
Sq. footage: 52000

15694 Wohrles Foods
1619 East St
Pittsfield, MA 01201-3857   413-442-1518
Fax: 413-442-6024   800-628-6114
jon@wohrlesfoods.com   www.wohrlesfoods.com
Meat products, distribute food services
President: Walter Pickwell
VP Marketing: Jon Pickwell
VP Purchasing: Robert Tessler
Estimated Sales: Less than $500,000
Number Employees: 1-4
Type of Packaging: Consumer, Private Label, Bulk

15695 Wolf Canyon Foods
27880 Dorris Drive
Suite 200
Carmel, CA 93923   831-626-1323
Fax: 831-626-1325   info@wolfcanyon.com
www.wolfcanyon.com
Processor and exporter of freeze-dried fruits, vegetables, meat, seafood and dairy products
President: Michael Alaga
VP: Marybeth Frearson
Estimated Sales: $7000000
Number Employees: 3
Sq. footage: 80000
Type of Packaging: Bulk

15696 Wolf Creek Vineyards
2637 Cleveland Massillon Rd
Norton, OH 44203-6417   330-666-9285
Fax: 330-665-1445   800-436-0426
sara@wineryatwolfcreek.com
www.wineryatwolfcreek.com
Wine
President: Andrew Troutman
Estimated Sales: $ 5-10 Million
Number Employees: 10-19
Number of Brands: 1
Number of Products: 15

15697 Wolferman's
P.O.Box 9100
Medford, OR 97501-304   913-888-4499
Fax: 913-492-5195   wolf@wolfermans.com
www.wolfermans.com
Processor of fresh and frozen English muffins, crumpets and tea and toasting bread
President: Micheal Dubois
CFO: Shane Jarvis
CFO: Gary Strub
Estimated Sales: $ 3 - 5 Million
Number Employees: 20-49
Sq. footage: 110000
Parent Co: Sara Lee Corporation
Type of Packaging: Consumer
Brands:
Charlie Trotter's
Wolferman's

15698 Wolff Meat Company
100 Dolorosa # 120
San Antonio, TX 78205-3038   210-335-2626
Fax: 210-335-2926 www.bexar.org

Processor and wholesaler/distributor of beef and pork
Manager: Nelson W Wolff
Number Employees: 1-4
Type of Packaging: Consumer, Food Service

15699 Wolfgang Puck Food Company
1250 4th Street
Suite 310
Santa Monica, CA 90401-1304   310-432-1350
Fax: 310-451-5595
Frozen version of his famous California style pizzas, pastas, canned soups and gourmet specialities
President: Terry Hall
Number Employees: 1-4

15700 Wolfies Gourmet Nuts
130 Olive St
Findlay, OH 45840-5325   419-423-1355
Fax: 419-423-8969   866-889-6887
wolfie@wolfiesnuts.com   www.wolfiesnuts.com
Dry-roasted nut products
Owner: Bill Wolf
Estimated Sales: $5-9.9 Million
Number Employees: 5-9
Type of Packaging: Consumer, Bulk

15701 (HQ)Wolfies Roasted Nuts
130 Olive St
Findlay, OH 45840-5325   419-423-1355
Fax: 419-423-8969   866-889-6887
wolfie@wolfiesnuts.com   www.wolfiesnuts.com
Processor of dry roasted and crisp-coated nuts including cashews, peanuts, almonds and mixes
Owner: Bill Wolf
Estimated Sales: $3000000
Number Employees: 1-4
Sq. footage: 6000
Type of Packaging: Consumer, Food Service, Private Label
Brands:
Totem

15702 Wolfson Casing Corporation
700 S Fulton Ave
Mt Vernon, NY 10550-5014   914-668-9000
Fax: 914-668-6900   800-221-8042
sales@wolfsoncasing.com
www.wolfsoncasing.com
Processor, exporter and importer of sausage casings
Owner: Stephen Bardfield
VP: Stephen Bardfield
Sales Representative: Seth Sommers
Estimated Sales: $26300000
Number Employees: 50-99
Sq. footage: 40000

15703 Wollersheim Winery
P.O.Box 87
Prairie Du Sac, WI 53578-0087   608-643-6515
Fax: 608-643-8149   800-847-9463
info@wollersheim.com   www.wollersheim.com
Wines
President: Philippe Coquard
CFO: Jo Ann Wollersheim
Marketing Director: Julius Coquard
Operations Manager: Phil Coquard
Estimated Sales: Below $ 5 Million
Number Employees: 20-49
Type of Packaging: Private Label
Brands:
Wollersheim Winery

15704 Wolter Farms
7200 Carmel Valley Road
Carmel, CA 93923-9525   831-624-8807
Farm produce

15705 Wolverine Packing
2535 Rivard St
Detroit, MI 48207-2621   313-392-9403
Fax: 313-568-1909
bbartes@wolverinepacking.com
www.wolverinepacking.com
Processor of portion packed lamb, veal and beef
President: Jim Bonahoom
CEO: Alfred J Bonahoom Sr
Estimated Sales: $6 Million
Number Employees: 50-99
Sq. footage: 110000
Type of Packaging: Consumer, Food Service, Private Label, Bulk

15706 Wolverton Seafood
PO Box 1721
Houlton, ME 04730-5721   506-276-4629
Fax: 506-276-1803
Seafood
Owner: Margaret Wolberton

15707 Wonder Bread
1180 W Center St
Provo, UT 84601-3900   801-373-8192
Fax: 801-531-6494
Processor of breads, cakes, cereals and crackers
Manager: Peggy Zobell
Marketing Director: Troy Daw
Estimated Sales: $300,000-500,000
Number Employees: 1-4
Parent Co: Interstate Brands Corporation
Type of Packaging: Consumer, Food Service

15708 Wonder Bread
420 S Dakota Avenue
Tampa, FL 33606-2124   813-253-2813
www.wonderbread.com
Processor of bread, buns and rolls
CFO: Doug Thomas
Plant Manager: Bo Brewer
Number Employees: 100-249
Parent Co: Interstate Brands Corporation
Type of Packaging: Consumer, Food Service

15709 Wonder/Hostess
16823 Douglas Avenue
Jamaica, NY 11433-1241   718-526-3184
Processor of breads, cakes and doughnuts
Manager: Jim Forbes
Estimated Sales: Less than $500,000
Number Employees: 5-9
Parent Co: Interstate Brands Corporation
Type of Packaging: Consumer, Food Service

15710 Wong Wing Foods
1875 Rue Bercy
Montreal, QC H2K 2T9
Canada   514-524-3676
Fax: 514-521-1404   800-361-4820
Processor and exporter of frozen Chinese foods including egg and spring rolls, fried rice, wonton soup, chicken products, entrees, etc.; also, sauces including plum, cherry, garlic, sweet and sour, soya, etc
President: Marcel Wong
CEO: Pauline Wong
President: Erik Yelle
Vice President: Bernard Wong
Marketing/Sales: Colin Prince
Production Manager: Phillipe Cha
Plant Manager: Robert Lee
Purchasing Manager: Victor Lee
Number Employees: 350
Sq. footage: 147337
Type of Packaging: Consumer, Food Service, Private Label
Brands:
Emperors Choice
Pagoda
See Jing
Wong Wing

15711 Wonton Food
222 Moore St
Brooklyn, NY 11206-3744   718-628-7788
Fax: 718-628-1028   800-776-8889
www.wontonfood.com
Processor of fortune cookies, eggroll and wonton skins and dry and fresh noodles including chow mein, lo mein, spinach and wonton; importer of oriental canned and dry goods
President: Sing Lee
CFO: Weilik Chan
Sales/Marketing Manager: Peter Leung
Estimated Sales: $ 20 - 50 Million
Number Employees: 100-249
Type of Packaging: Consumer, Food Service, Private Label

15712 Wood Brothers
P.O.Box 4348
West Columbia, SC 29171-4348   803-796-5146
Fax: 803-796-5291

Processor of mayonnaise, barbecue and tartar sauces, mustard and salad dressings including Thousand Island, French, Italian, blue cheese and slaw
President: Warren C Wood
VP: Douglas Wood
Production Manager: James Wood
Estimated Sales: $110000
Number Employees: 10-19
Type of Packaging: Food Service, Private Label, Bulk
Brands:
Capital
Cardinal
Carolina Chef
Glenwood
Holland

15713 Wood's Sugar Bush
N7845 170th Street
Spring Valley, WI 54767-8101   715-772-4656
Fax: 715-772-4665
Processor of certified organic maple syrup, cream and granulated sugar
President: Scott Wood
Number Employees: 5
Number of Brands: 1
Number of Products: 4
Sq. footage: 3500
Type of Packaging: Consumer, Food Service, Private Label, Bulk

15714 Woodbine
729 Pecan Point Rd
Norfolk, VA 23502-3416   757-461-2731
Fax: 757-461-4704
Manufacturer of beef and pork. Full distribution of food service items
President: Ray Lister
Production Manager: Aubrey Lister
Estimated Sales: $3-5 Million
Number Employees: 10-19
Type of Packaging: Food Service

15715 Woodbury Vineyards
3215 S Roberts Rd
Fredonia, NY 14063-9417   716-679-9463
Fax: 716-679-9464 866-691-9463
woodburyvineyardsginny@hotmail.com
www.woodburyvineyards.com
winery
President: Joseph Carney
Retail Sales Manager: Virginia Bragg
Estimated Sales: $1,700,000
Number Employees: 5
Brands:
Woodbury Vineyards

15716 Wooden Valley Winery
4756 Suisun Valley Rd
Fairfield, CA 94534-3114   707-864-0730
Fax: 707-864-6038 info@woodenvalley.com
www.woodenvalley.com
Wines
President: Richard Lanza
Estimated Sales: $ 1-2.5 Million
Number Employees: 5-9
Brands:
Wooden Valley

15717 Woodfield Fish & OysterCompany
P.O.Box 259
Galesville, MD 20765-0259   410-897-1093
Fax: 410-867-3423
Packaged ice and oyster
Owner: Bill Woodfield
Treasurer: Shirley Day
Vice President: Bill Woddfield
Plant Manager: David Loftice
Purchasing Manager: Ray Hardesty
Estimated Sales: Less than $500,000
Number Employees: 1-4
Type of Packaging: Private Label
Brands:
Woodfield Fish & Oyster
Woodfield Ice

15718 Woodie Pie Company
PO Box 1425
Artesia, NM 88211-1425   505-746-2132
Processor of baked goods including pies
President: D Balencia
Estimated Sales: $500,000-$1 Million
Number Employees: 1-4

Type of Packaging: Consumer
Brands:
Woodie Pie

15719 Woodlake Ranch
21737 Avenue 337
Woodlake, CA 93286   559-564-2161
Fax: 559-564-8120
Grower of olives
President: Everett Kracov
Manager: Randy Childrsh
Estimated Sales: Less than $300,000
Number Employees: 1-4
Type of Packaging: Food Service, Private Label, Bulk

15720 Woodland Foods
2011 Swanson Ct
Gurnee, IL 60031-1221   847-625-8600
Fax: 847-625-5050 sales@woodlandfoods.com
www.woodlandfoods.com
Mushrooms & truffles, chiles, sun-dried tomoatoes, beans, lentils, peas, grains, rice, herbs & spices, asian noodles & seaweed, couscous, polenta & orzo, corn, flours, meals & posoles, dried fruit, nuts & seeds
Owner/President/CEO: David Moore
VP: Ely Quinonez
Quality Assurance Director: Jerry Kruse
Sales Director: Mike Brundidge
COO: Ralph Chor
Product Manager: Paul Suhre
Manager: Andy Gonzalez
Estimated Sales: $10 Million
Number Employees: 50-99
Number of Brands: 4
Number of Products: 500
Sq. footage: 65000
Type of Packaging: Consumer, Food Service, Private Label, Bulk
Brands:
D'allasandro

15721 Woods Fabricators
P.O.Box 167
Taylorsville, GA 30178-0167   770-684-5377
Fax: 770-684-0858 rwoods9595@aol.com
www.woodsfab.com
Equipment Manufacture-cooling tunnels and conveyors
President: Rickey Woods

15722 Woods Smoked Meats
1501 Business Highway 54 W
Bowling Green, MO 63334-1030   573-324-2247
Fax: 573-324-2249 800-458-8426
info@woodssmokedmeats.com
www.woodssmokedmeats.com
Manufacturer of meats including ham, bacon, sausage, poultry, snack food, steaks and bratwurst
Co-Owner: Edward Woods
Co-Owner: Regina Woods
Estimated Sales: $ 5 - 10 Million
Number Employees: 20-49
Number of Brands: 2
Number of Products: 80
Sq. footage: 16000
Type of Packaging: Consumer, Private Label, Bulk
Brands:
Sweet Betsy From Pike
Woods

15723 Woodside Vineyards
340 Kings Mountain Rd
Woodside, CA 94062-3618   650-851-3144
Fax: 650-851-5037
info@woodsidevineyards.com
www.woodsidevineyards.com
Wines
Founder/President: Robert Mullen
Estimated Sales: $1,400,000
Number Employees: 5-9
Type of Packaging: Private Label
Brands:
Woodside Vineyards

15724 Woodsmoke Provisions
1240 Menlo Dr NW
Atlanta, GA 30318-4163   404-355-5125
Fax: 404-355-6850
Salmon and trout
President: Mitchell Gallant
Estimated Sales: $ 3 - 5 Million
Number Employees: 20-49

15725 Woodstock Whole Earth Foods
RR 9
Saugerties, NY 12477   914-247-0777
Gourmet and specialty foods
President: Douglas Bryan
Estimated Sales: Under $500,000
Number Employees: 1-4

15726 Woodward Canyon Winery
11920 W Highway 12
Touchet, WA 99360-9710   509-525-4129
Fax: 509-522-0927 info@woodwardcanyon.com
www.woodwardcanyon.com
Wine
Owner: Rick Small
Production Director: Rick Small
Estimated Sales: Below $ 5 Million
Number Employees: 5-9

15727 Woodworth Honey Company
P.O.Box 247
Halliday, ND 58636-0247   701-938-4647
Fax: 701-938-4657 bon@ndsupernet.com
www.honey.com
Processor and exporter of honey
Owner: Brent Woodworth
Estimated Sales: $ 10 - 20 Million
Number Employees: 10-19
Sq. footage: 6000
Type of Packaging: Bulk

15728 Woody Associates Inc
844 E South St
York, PA 17403-2849   717-843-3975
Fax: 717-843-5829
steven.ziolkowski@woody-decorators.com
www.woody-decorators.com
Founded in 1954, Woody Associates, Inc. is an engineering firm specializing in automatic decorating equipment for the food industry.
President: Harry Reinke
Design Engineer: Steven Ziolkowski

15729 Woody's Bar-B-Q Sauce Company
P.O.Box 66
Waldenburg, AR 72475-0066   870-579-2251
Fax: 870-579-2241 woodybbq@ricebelt.net
Barbeque sauce
President: William Wood
CEO: Cecelia Wood
Estimated Sales: $300,000-500,000
Number Employees: 5-9
Number of Products: 7
Type of Packaging: Consumer, Food Service, Private Label, Bulk

15730 Woolwich Dairy
425 Richardson Road
Orangeville, ON L9W 4Z4
Canada   519-941-9206
Fax: 519-941-9349 877-438-3499
gerhard@woolwichnova.com
www.woolwichdairy.com
Processor and exporter of goat's milk cheeses including cheddar, whole and crumbled feta, mozzarella, gouda, cream and brie
CEO: Tony Dutra
Sales Director: Gerhard Trimmel
Number Employees: 67
Number of Brands: 7
Number of Products: 109
Sq. footage: 4000
Parent Co: Nova Cheese
Type of Packaging: Consumer, Food Service, Private Label, Bulk
Brands:
Chevrai
Gourmet Goat
Madame Chevre

15731 Worden
7217 W Westbow Boulevard
Spokane, WA 99224-5668   509-455-7835
Fax: 509-838-4723 wordenwine@aol.com
Wine
President: Ken Barrett
CEO: Rebecca Chateaubriand
Estimated Sales: $ 1 Million+
Number Employees: 10
Sq. footage: 13000
Type of Packaging: Private Label, Bulk

15732 World Cheese Company
178 28th St
Brooklyn, NY 11232-1604   718-965-1700
                               Fax: 718-965-0979
Producer and importer of kosher cheeses
    President: Leo S Thurm
    VP: Meyer Thurm
    VP Sales: Sam Lonner
Estimated Sales: $20000000
Sq. footage: 25000
Type of Packaging: Consumer, Food Service, Bulk
Brands:
    HAOLAM
    KO-SURE
    MIGDAL
    MILLER'S
    SCHMERLING
    TAAM TOV

15733 World Citrus
2720 University Parkway
Winston Salem, NC 27105-4224   336-723-1861
                               Fax: 336-722-6972
Citrus, fruits and juices
    Manager: Jeanette Cornatzer
    Operations Manager: Henry Tobkin
    Production Manager: Rich Davis
Estimated Sales: $ 2.5-5 Million
Number Employees: 20

15734 World Citrus West
P.O.Box 1111
Lake Wales, FL 33859-1111   863-676-1411
                               Fax: 863-676-0494
Processor and bottler of chilled citrus drinks and
juices including orange and grapefruit
    CEO: Stephen M Caruso
    Sales Manager (Retail): Rod Adamson
Number Employees: 250-499
Parent Co: Florida's Natural Growers'
Type of Packaging: Consumer, Food Service, Private Label, Bulk
Brands:
    Daily Sun
    Donald Duck
    Supersocco

15735 World Confections
185 30th St
Brooklyn, NY 11232-1705   718-768-8100
    Fax: 718-499-4918 info@worldsconfections.com
Manufacturer and exporter of confectionery prod-
ucts including gum, bagged, bars, boxed chocolates,
caramels, lollypops, jaw breakers, peppermint and
lemon twists, seasonal, etc
    President: Mathew Cohen
Estimated Sales: $10 Million
Number Employees: 50-99
Type of Packaging: Consumer, Private Label, Bulk

15736 World Cup Roasters
925 NW Davis Street
Portland, OR 97209-3103   503-228-5503
                               Fax: 503-228-3489
Processor and exporter of coffee and teas; also,
roasting and water filltration services available
    President: Dan Welch
Number Employees: 10-19
Sq. footage: 12500
Type of Packaging: Consumer, Food Service, Bulk
Brands:
    World Cup

15737 World Flavors
76 Louise Dr
Warminster, PA 18974-1588   215-672-4400
    Fax: 215-672-4405 www.worldflavors.com
Processor of custom formulated, manufactured and
packaged ingredients for food processors including
liquid and ground spices, meat, poultry and seafood
seasonings, flavors, breadings, salad dressings and
meat binders, extenders andtenderizing compounds
    President: Robert Holmquist
    VP Sales: Thomas Holmquist
Estimated Sales: $4900000
Number Employees: 50-99
Type of Packaging: Food Service, Private Label,
Bulk

15738 World Ginseng Center
805 Kearny St
San Francisco, CA 94108   415-362-2255
            Fax: 415-362-4859 800-747-8808
            info@worldginsengcenter.com
            www.worldginsengcenter.com
Manufacturer and exporter of ginseng and frozen
seafood
    President: Raymond Chao
    Manager: William Nghe
    Treasurer: Jane Chao
Estimated Sales: $300,000-500,000
Number Employees: 1-4
Type of Packaging: Consumer, Food Service, Pri-
vate Label, Bulk

15739 World Harbors
176 First Flight Dr
Auburn, ME 04210-9055   207-786-3900
        Fax: 207-786-3900 800-355-6221
            sales@worldharbors.com
            www.worldharbors.com
Gourmet specialty foods, sauces and marinades
    President: Steven Arthurs
    CFO: Karen Foust
    Quality Control: Mike Murphy
Estimated Sales: $ 5-10 Million
Number Employees: 20-49
Parent Co: Angostura International
Type of Packaging: Consumer, Food Service
Brands:
    Acadia Naturals
    Angostura
    World Harbors

15740 World Herbs Gourmet Company
PO Box 101
Hadlyme, CT 06439-0101   860-526-1908
                               Fax: 860-526-1908
International seasoning blends for grilling

15741 World Nutrition
7001 N Scottsdale Rd # 2000
Scottsdale, AZ 85253-3666   480-921-1188
        Fax: 480-921-1471 800-548-2710
            www.worldnutrition.info
Processor and importer of vitamins, minerals, or-
ganic grains, fruits, vegetables and dehydrated fruits
and vegetable juices
    President: Ryuji Hirooka
    COO: David Harrington
    Marketing Manager: Pat Buel
    Director Administration: Michele Moose
    Production Manager: Andy Rodriguez
Estimated Sales: $ 50 - 100 Million
Number Employees: 100-249
Sq. footage: 126000

15742 World Organics Corporation
5242 Bolsa Ave
Huntington Beach, CA 92649-1054 714-893-0017
        Fax: 714-897-5677 plicata@prodigy.net
Processor of vitamins, food supplements, herbal ex-
tracts and capsules and chlorophyll liquid and
capsules
    Owner: Paul Licata
    CEO: Al Licata
    Director of Sales: Bernie Lucich
Estimated Sales: Under $500,000
Number Employees: 10-19
Number of Brands: 4
Number of Products: 300
Sq. footage: 8000
Type of Packaging: Private Label
Brands:
    Natural's Concept
    Nu-Vista
    POMA NONI BERRY
    SEAFOOD
    Vita-Vista

15743 World Softgel
1490 W Walnut Parkway
Compton, CA 90220-5002   310-900-1199
                               Fax: 310-900-1192
Processor and exporter of soft gelatin vitamins
    President: Sam Ahn
Type of Packaging: Consumer, Food Service, Pri-
vate Label, Bulk

15744 World Spice
223 E Highland Pkwy
Roselle, NJ 07203-2685   908-245-0600
        Fax: 908-245-0696 800-234-1060
            sales@wsispice.com www.wsispice.com
Processor, importer, exporter and wholesaler/distrib-
utor of spices, seasonings, herbs and dehydrated
vegetables; serving the food service market and
industrial
    President: Bela Lowy
    Vice President: J Lefbowitz
Estimated Sales: $2000000
Number Employees: 5-9
Sq. footage: 15000
Type of Packaging: Food Service, Bulk
Brands:
    WSI

15745 World of Chantilly
4302 Farragut Rd
Brooklyn, NY 11203-6520   718-859-1110
        Fax: 718-859-1303 info@chantilly.com
                           www.chantilly.com
Processor of kosher desserts including cakes, pies,
brownies, tiramisu, tortes, etc
    Owner/President: Alberto Faks
Estimated Sales: $1800000
Number Employees: 5-9
Sq. footage: 10000

15746 World of Coffee
328 Essex Street
Stirling, NJ 07980   908-647-1218
        Fax: 908-647-7827 800-543-0062
    info@worldcoffee.biz www.worldcoffee.biz
coffee roasster

15747 World of Coffee, World of Tea
328 Essex St
Stirling, NJ 07980-1302   908-647-1218
                               Fax: 908-647-7827
Coffee roasting; packaging and labeling services.
    President: Charles Newman
Estimated Sales: $500,000-$1 Million
Number Employees: 5-9
Sq. footage: 7500
Brands:
    World of Coffee
    World of Spices
    World of Tea

15748 World of Spices
328 Essex St
Stirling, NJ 07980-1302   908-647-1218
                               Fax: 908-647-7827
Spices
    President: Charles Newman
Estimated Sales: $ 2.5-5 Million
Number Employees: 5-9

15749 World's Best
163 Morse Street
Norwood, MA 02062-4600   781-762-7778
        Fax: 888-690-8766 888-690-8766
            jim@worldsrealketchup.com
            www.worldsrealketchup.com
All-natural gourmet ketchup
Brands:
    World's Real

15750 World's Finest Chocolate
103 2nd Street
Box 876
Campbellford, ON K0L 1L0
Canada   705-653-3590
        Fax: 705-653-4750 888-821-8452
    customersevice@worldsfinestchoclate.com
            www.wfchocolate.com
Processor of cocoa and chocolate confectionery
products
    Chairman: Edmond F Opler
    VP: Ken Tully
    Host: Linda Milne
    VP Sales/Marketing: Milt Newman
Number Employees: 200
Parent Co: World's Finest Chocolate
Type of Packaging: Consumer
Brands:
    Cook
    Le Meilleur Au Monde
    World Finest

15751 World's Finest Chocolate
4801 S Lawndale Ave
Chicago, IL 60632-3062   773-847-4600
          Fax: 773-847-4006 800-366-2462
          contactus@wfchocolate.com
          www.worldsfinestchocolate.com
Chocolate manufacturer
     President: Howard Zodikoff
     Chairman/CEO: Edmond Opler Jr
     CFO: Mioneal Broz
     CEO: Edmond F Opler
     Research & Development: Bill Goff
     Marketing Mananger: Kate Welbourn
     Sales Director: Larry Vander Meulen
     Production Manager: Ray Deeter
     Plant Manager: Mike Morris
     Purchasing Manager: Bill Erickson
*Estimated Sales:*1
Number Employees: 500-999
Number of Brands: 2
Type of Packaging: Consumer
Brands:
     QUEEN ANNE
     WORLD'S FINEST CHOCOLATE

15752 World's Greatest Ice Cream
P.O.Box 190646
Miami Beach, FL 33119-0646   305-538-0207
          Fax: 305-538-1026 www.thefrieze.com
Ice cream
     President: Lisa Warren
Estimated Sales:$500,000-$1 Million
Number Employees: 10-19

15753 Worldwide Sourcing LLC
584 Lucille Drive
Incline Village, NV 89451-9132   775-833-1480
          Fax: 775-833-1483
     CEO: Seymour Wiessen

15754 (HQ)Wornick Company
1014 Vine St # 2350
Cincinnati, OH 45202-1156   513-621-2825
          Fax: 513-794-0107 800-860-4555
          info@wornick.com OR
     www.foodservice@wornick.com
          www.wornick.com
Processor of shelf stable, refrigerated and frozen en-
trees including baked beans, macaroni and cheese,
lasagna and chicken; exporter of entrees including
chicken breast on rice, pot pie, pot roast, lasagna,
manicotti, tortelliniravioli, turkey, steak, etc.
     President/CEO: Mike Thompson
     Chairman: R Wornick
     Executive Vice President: John McQuay
     Chief Marketing Officer: John Kowalchik
     Director Manufacturing: Diana Mitchell
Estimated Sales:$81800000
Number Employees: 500-999
Sq. footage: 200000
Type of Packaging: Food Service, Private Label
Other Locations:
     Wornick Co.
     McAllen TX

15755 Worthington Foods
1675 Fairview Road
Zanesville, OH 43701-8890   614-885-9511
          Fax: 614-885-2594 800-535-5644
          www.kelloggs.com/brand/worthington
Processor of canned and frozen vegetarian foods
     CEO/President: Dale Twomley
     VP Finance/CFO: William Kirkwood
     Plant Manager: Gene Fluck
*Estimated Sales:*Less than $500,000
Number Employees: 1-4
Sq. footage: 200000
Parent Co: Kellogg Company
Type of Packaging: Consumer, Food Service
Brands:
     Loma Linda
     Morningstar Farms
     Worthington

15756 Worthmore Food Product
1021 Ludlow Ave
Cincinnati, OH 45223-2687   513-559-1473
          Fax: 513-559-0286 worthmore@fuse.net
          www.worthmorefoods.com
Canner of food products including chili con carne,
mock turtle soup, spaghetti sauce, pizza sauce and
mushroom steak sauce
     President: Phil Hock III

Type of Packaging: Consumer, Food Service, Private Label

15757 Wow! Factor Desserts
152 Cree Road
Sherwood Park, AB T8A 3X8
Canada   780-464-0303
          Fax: 780-467-3604 800-604-2253
          info@wowfactorydessert.com
          www.wowfactordesserts.com
Processor of baked goods including cheesecakes,
cakes, tortes and pies for the food service sector
     President: Bryan Yaakov
     VP: Joanne Yaakov
     Purchasing Manager: Dean McMullen
Number Employees: 50-99
Type of Packaging: Consumer, Food Service

15758 Wrangell Fisheries
P.O.Box 908
Wrangell, AK 99929-0908   907-874-3346
          Fax: 907-874-3035
          droberts@wrangellseafoods.com
          www.wrangellseafoods.com
Processor and exporter of canned, fresh and frozen
shrimp, crab, halibut, herring and salmon
     President: Terry Montford
     Vice President: Levi Dow
Estimated Sales:$ 20 - 50 Million
Number Employees: 100-249
Parent Co: J.S. McMillan
Type of Packaging: Food Service, Bulk

15759 Wright Brand Company
P.O.Box 914
Bayou La Batre, AL 36509-0914   251-824-7880
          Fax: 251-824-7880
Processor and distributor of oysters
     President: Stanley Wright
Estimated Sales:$ 1 - 3 Million
Number Employees: 1-4

15760 Wright Brand Foods
700 Wheeler St
Vernon, TX 76384-3431   940-553-1888
          Fax: 940-553-3747 comments@tyson.com
          www.tyson.com
Manufacturer and exporter of smoked ham and ba-
con
     Manager: Jimmy Dennis
Estimated Sales:$120 Million
Number Employees: 500-999
Type of Packaging: Consumer, Food Service, Pri-
vate Label, Bulk
Brands:
     WRIGHT

15761 Wright Enrichment
6428 Airport Rd
Crowley, LA 70526-1604   337-783-3096
          Fax: 337-783-0724 800-201-3096
          wei@wenrich.com
Enriched rice, vitamin mixtures and tablets
     Owner: S L Wright Iv
Estimated Sales:$ 5-10 Million
Number Employees: 100-249

15762 Wright Group
6428 Airport Rd
Crowley, LA 70526-1604   337-783-3096
          Fax: 337-783-0724 800-201-3096
          wei@wenrich.com www.thewrightgroup.net
Processor and exporter of custom vitamin, mineral
and amino acid premixes, microencapsulates and di-
rect compressed granulations
     Owner: S L Wright Iv IV
     Marketing: Monique Roberts
Estimated Sales:$ 10 - 20 Million
Number Employees: 100-249
Type of Packaging: Bulk

15763 Wright Ice Cream
3570 N State Road 63
Cayuga, IN 47928-8156   765-492-3454
          Fax: 765-492-4915 800-686-9561
Ice cream and frozen desserts, dairy products, dried
or canned, and candy and other confectionery prod-
ucts.
     President: Ned Wright
     Marketing Director: Ned Wright
Estimated Sales:$ 3 - 5 Million
Number Employees: 5-9
Type of Packaging: Consumer

Brands:
     Wright Delicious

15764 Wrigley Company
1123 Leslie Street
Don Mills, ON M3C 2I4
Canada   416-449-8600
          Fax: 416-449-1774 www.wrigley.com
Processor of chewing and bubble gum
     CEO/President: Michael McKean
     VP Sales/Marketing: Brian McDonald
     Purchasing Agent: Sandy McCartney
Number Employees: 100-249
Parent Co: William Wrigley, Jr. Company
Type of Packaging: Consumer

15765 (HQ)Wrigley Company
410 N Michigan Ave
Chicago, IL 60611-4287   312-644-4776
          Fax: 312-644-2135 800-824-9681
          www.wrigley.com
Gums, mints, hard and chewy candies, lollipops, and
chocolate.
     President: Dushan Petrovich
     EVP/CFO: Reuben Gamoran
     Executive VP: John Bard
     VP Customer Marketing: Gary Bebee
     VP Information Services: Dennis Mally
Estimated Sales:$ 1 Billion+
Number Employees: 500-999
Parent Co: Mars Inc
Brands:
     5 GUM
     ALTOIDS
     BIG LEAGUE CHEW
     BIG RED
     CREME SAVERS
     DOUBLEMINT
     ECLIPSE
     EXTRA
     FREEDENT
     HUBBA BUBBA
     JUICY FRUIT
     LIFE SAVERS
     ORBIT
     SKITTLES
     SPEARMINT
     STARBURST
     WINTERFRESH

15766 Wrigley Manufacturing Company
P.O.Box 4181
Flowery Branch, GA 30542-2000   770-967-6181
          Fax: 770-967-5666 www.wrigley.com
Manufacturer and exporter of chewing gum
     Chairman/President/CEO: William Wigley Jr
     VP/CFO: Reuben Gamoran
     COO: Ronald Waters
     VP Manufacturing: Donald Balster
Estimated Sales:$100+ Million
Number Employees: 500-999
Parent Co: William Wrigley Jr Company
Type of Packaging: Consumer
Brands:
     AIRWAVES
     ALPINE
     BIG RED
     DOUBLEMINT
     ECLIPSE
     ECLIPSE FRESH
     EXTRA
     FREEDENT
     HUBBA BUBBA
     JUICY FRUIT
     WINTERFRESH
     WRIGLEY SPERARMINT

15767 Wuollet Bakery
2447 Hennepin Ave
Minneapolis, MN 55405-2605   612-381-9400
          Fax: 612-374-0948 www.wuollet.com
Bakers of cakes, desserts, breads and pastries
     Manager: Aaron Wuollet
     CEO: Jim Jurmu
     Operations Manager: Doug Wuollet
Estimated Sales:$ 2.5-5 Million
Number Employees: 20-49

15768 Wurth Dairy
8805 Maple Avenue
Caseyville, IL 62232-2135   217-271-7580
Dairy
     President: Albert Wurth

Estimated Sales: Under $500,000
Number Employees: 1-4

15769 Wy's Wings
PO Box 542
Strasburg, VA 22657-0542   540-465-5355
     800-997-9464
wingking@wyswings.com   www.wyswings.com
Sauces

15770 (HQ)Wyandot
135 Wyandot Ave
Marion, OH 43302-1595   740-383-4031
     Fax: 740-382-5584   800-992-6368
phyllis.hendrix@wyandotsnacks.com
www.wyandotsnacks.com
Manufacturer of snacks including; tortilla, corn and
potato chips. Contract Manufacturing
   Chairman: Joe Donithen
   President/CEO: Nick Chilton
   CFO: Robert Wentz
   CEO: Nick Chilton
   EVP Operations: Rex Parrott
Estimated Sales: $100 Million
Number Employees: 250-499
Type of Packaging: Consumer, Food Service, Private Label

15771 (HQ)Wyandot Inc
135 Wyandot Ave
Marion, OH 43302-1595   740-383-4031
     Fax: 740-382-0115   800-992-6368
www.wyandotsnacks.com
Processor of private label snack foods including
baked cheese puffs and chips including potato, tortilla, nacho and corn.
   President/CEO: Nick Chilton
   VP Finance/CFO: Robert Wentz
   VP Technical Services: Dan McGrady
   Business Strategy Manager: Mitch Newell
   VP Sales: Gary Haugsby
   VP Human Resources: Bryan Hensel
   EVP Operations: Rex Parrott
   VP Supply Chain Management: Tom Shank
Estimated Sales: $28 Million
Number Employees: 350
Sq. footage: 150000
Type of Packaging: Consumer, Food Service, Private Label, Bulk
Brands:
   GRANDADDY'S
   MUCHMATES
   MUNCHRIGHTS
   WYANDOT

15772 Wyandotte Winery
4640 Wyandotte Dr
Gahanna, OH 43230-1258   614-476-3624
   Fax: 614-228-2331   info@wyandottewinery.com
www.wyandottewinery.com
Wines
   President: Jane Scott
   CEO: Joe Reardon
   Marketing Director: Valerie Coolidge
   Winemaker: Robin Coolidge
Estimated Sales: $500,000-$1 Million
Number Employees: 1-4
Brands:
   Wyandotte Graystone Winery
   Wyandotte Winery

15773 Wynn Starr Flavors
5 Pearl Ct
Allendale, NJ 07401-1656   201-934-7800
   Fax: 201-934-6022   800-996-7827
customerservice@wynnstarr.com
www.wynnstarr.com
Flavors, seasonings and natural compound flavors
including chicken broth products, maple glaze for
bacon, sauteed onion flavor system, sauteed garlic
butter oil, natural basil flavor, natural and artificial
bacon flavor (made with realbacon)
   Chairman: Steven Zavagli
   CFO: Gary Raff
Estimated Sales: $ 20-50 Million
Number Employees: 20-49
Brands:
   Wynn Starr

15774 Wynn Starr Foods of Kentucky
4820 Allmond Ave
Louisville, KY 40214-2506   502-368-6345
   Fax: 502-363-4494   800-996-7827
customerservice@wynnstarr.com
www.wynnstarr.com
Processor of flavorings including beef, chicken, turkey, pork, soft drink, fruit and cheese; exporter of
chicken, beef and cheese flavorings
   CEO: Steve Zavagli
   Executive VP Operations: Joseph Zavagli
   VP Operations/Manufacturing: Barry Friedson
   Plant Manager: Barry Friedson
   Purchasing Director: Joann Rakestraw
Estimated Sales: $ 20 - 50 Million
Number Employees: 50-99
Sq. footage: 68000
Parent Co: Wynn Starr Flavors
Type of Packaging: Private Label, Bulk
Brands:
   Wynn Starr Foodservice

15775 Wynnewood Pecan Company
301 S Washita Avenue
Wynnewood, OK 73098-7823   405-665-4102
   Fax: 405-682-2503   800-892-4985
wyrwood@flash.net
Pecans
   President: Jeff Earles
Estimated Sales: Less than $500,000
Number Employees: 1-4

15776 Wysong Corporation
180 N Eastern Rd
Midland, MI 48640   989-631-0009
   Fax: 989-631-8801   800-748-0188
www.wysong.net
Processor of trail mixes, vitamins and potato chips;
also, organic soy, wheat and rice baking items
   President: R Wysong
Estimated Sales: $3100000
Number Employees: 20-49
Brands:
   Wysong

15777 X Cafe
P.O.Box 1100
Princeton, MA 01541-3100   978-464-8010
   Fax: 978-464-8033   877-492-2331
cathy@x-cafe.com   www.x-cafe.com
Processor of coffee extracts and concentrates.
   President: Paul Kalenian
   CFO: Cathy Kalenian
   Sales Director: Michael Bindel
   Plant Manager: Ron Nicholas
Estimated Sales: $ 5 - 10 Million
Number Employees: 10-19
Number of Products: 12
Sq. footage: 16000
Type of Packaging: Food Service, Private Label

15778 XL Beef
4240 - 75th Avenue SE
Calgary, AB T2C 2H8
Canada   403-236-2424
   Fax: 403-236-2489   romashenko@xlfoods.com
www.xlfoods.com
Processor and exporter of beef and beef products
   VP Commodities/Wholesale: Ken Weir
   Sales Manager: Dan Edge
   Plant Superintendent: Barry Fuglsong
Number Employees: 100-249
Sq. footage: 35000
Parent Co: XL Foods
Brands:
   Original Alberta Beef

15779 XL Energy Drink
10 West 33rd Street
Suite 340
New York, NY 10001   212-594-3080
   Fax: 646-514-3189   mr@xl-energy.com
www.xl-energy.com
Manufacturer of energy drink.
   Business Development Director: Michael Raunegger

15780 XL Energy Drink
10 W 33rd Street
Suite 340
New York, NY 10001   212-594-3080
   Fax: 646-514-3189   mr@sl-energy.com
www.xl-energy.com
Energy drink/beverage.
   Business Development Director: Michael Raunegger

15781 Xcell International Corporation
16400 103rd St
Lemont, IL 60439-9667   630-323-0107
   Fax: 630-323-0217   800-722-7751
info@xcellint.com   www.xcellint.com
Seasonings, spices, herbs, teas and mulling spices,
confectionery sprinkles
   President: Dean Henning
   President: Amy Hilliard
   Marketing Director: Leslie Marshall
Estimated Sales: $ 20 - 50 Million
Number Employees: 50-99
Brands:
   Accent's
   Dean Jacob's

15782 Xochitl
17304 Preston Rd
Suite 1240
Dallas, TX 75252   214-800-3551
   Fax: 214-800-3547   info@salsaxochitl.com
www.salsaxochitl.com
all natural and organic salsas, queso dips and corn
chips
   President/Owner: Carlos Salinas

15783 Y Not Foods
1022 Lumbermans Trail
Madison, WI 53716   608-222-2860
   Fax: 608-222-2865   tony@ynotfoods.com
www.ynotfoods.com
Frozen, refrigerated, shelf-stable, dry blends and
mixes.
   Sales Contact: Tony Steinmann

15784 Y&T Packing
P.O.Box 57
Springfield, IL 62705-0057   217-522-3345
   Fax: 217-522-6395   www.turaskymeats.com
Packer/processor of meat
   President: Joseph Turasky
   Co-Owner: Joe Turasky
   Sales Manager: Tom Reilly
Estimated Sales: $1800000
Number Employees: 10-19
Type of Packaging: Consumer

15785 Y&W Shellfish
8725 Us Highway 17
Woodbine, GA 31569   912-729-4814
     Fax: 912-729-1143
Seafood
   Owner: Richard Roberts

15786 YB Meats of Wichita
798 N West St
Wichita, KS 67203-1235   316-942-1213
     Fax: 316-942-1419
Processor of meat products
   President: Ellsworth Kauffman
   CEO: Erik Kaufmann
   Marketing Director: Erik Kaufmann
Estimated Sales: $500,000-$1 Million
Number Employees: 5-9
Type of Packaging: Consumer

15787 YZ Enterprises
1930 Indian Wood Cir
Maumee, OH 43537-4053   419-893-8777
   Fax: 419-893-8825   800-736-8779
almondina@worldpantry.com
www.almondina.com
Processor and exporter of natural almond cookies including low-calorie, no-cholesterol, no-salt, kosher
and parve
   Owner: Yuval Zaliouk
   CFO: Susan Zaliouk
Estimated Sales: $1-5 Million
Number Employees: 10-19
Sq. footage: 16500
Type of Packaging: Consumer
Brands:
   ALMONDINA

15788 Yair Scones/Canterbury Cuisine
P.O.Box 177
Medina, WA 98039-0177   425-486-3334
   Fax: 425-398-0301   800-588-9160
linda.dolstad@fairscones.com
www.conifer-inc.com

Gourmet convenience foods
President: Mike Maher
Operations Manager: Darren Wise
Estimated Sales: $ 10-20 Million
Number Employees: 20-49
Brands:
Canterbury Cusine
Canterbury Naturals
Fisher Fair Scone
Scone Girl

15789 Yakima Brewing Company
1803 Presson Place
Yakima, WA 98903-2200   509-575-1900
                                                Fax: 509-457-6782
Processor and exporter of ales, stout and porter
President: Greg Tranum
Brewmaster: H Grant
Estimated Sales: $3500000
Number Employees: 31
Sq. footage: 40500
Type of Packaging: Consumer
Brands:
Bert Grant's

15790 Yakima Fruit & Cold Storage Company
200 N Frontage Road
Wapato, WA 98951-1180   509-877-0440
                                                Fax: 509-877-0940
stevensmith@yakimaroche.com
www.yakimaroche.com
Manufacturer and exporter of apples, cherries and pears
President: Micheal Wilcox
Estimated Sales: $100 Million
Number Employees: 250-499
Type of Packaging: Consumer, Food Service, Bulk

15791 Yakima River Winery
143302 W North River Rd
Prosser, WA 99350-8228   509-786-2805
                                                Fax: 509-786-3203
redwine@yakimariverwinery.com
www.yakimariverwinery.com
Processor of wine
Co-Owner: John Rauner
Co-Owner: Louise Rauner
Winemaker: John Rauner
Estimated Sales: $500,000-$1 Million
Number Employees: 1-4
Type of Packaging: Private Label
Brands:
Yakima Valley

15792 Yakima Valley Grape Producers
401 Avenue B
Grandview, WA 98930-1622   509-882-1223
                                                Fax: 509-882-1580
Grapes
President: Richard Devis
Estimated Sales: $ 5-10 Million appx.
Number Employees: 50

15793 Yamamotoyama of America
2865 Pomona Blvd
Pomona, CA 91768   909-594-7356
                                                Fax: 909-595-5849
yamamotoyama@yamamotoyama.com
www.yamamotoyama.com
Tea
Chairman: Kahei Yamamoto
Administration Manager/Purchasing: William Yu
Senior VP: Kazumi Ikeda
Estimated Sales: $ 20-50 Million
Number Employees: 100-249

15794 Yamasa Corporation
3655 Torrance Blvd
Suite 240
Torrance, CA 95023   310-944-3883
        Fax: 310-944-3935   made@yamasausa.com
                                www.yamasausa.com
Processor of soy sauce
Manager: Masahiro Ade
VP: K Usukura
National Sales Manager: Michael Grady Loera
Estimated Sales: $ 5 - 10 Million
Number Employees: 4
Type of Packaging: Consumer, Food Service, Bulk
Brands:
Yamasa

15795 Yamasa Fish Cake Company
515 Stanford Ave
Los Angeles, CA 90013-2189   213-626-2211
                                                Fax: 213-627-9018
Processor of fresh and frozen fish cakes
President: Frank Kawana
Estimated Sales: $2900000
Number Employees: 20-49
Type of Packaging: Consumer, Food Service

15796 Yamasho
750 Touhy Avenue
Elk Grove Village, IL 60007-4916   847-981-9342
                                                Fax: 847-981-9347
Estimated Sales: $ 20 - 50 Million
Number Employees: 20-49

15797 Yamate Chocolatier
320 Cleveland Ave
Highland Park, NJ 08904-1845   732-249-4847
        Fax: 732-545-4494   800-433-2462
                                info@YCChocolate.com
                                www.yamatechocolatier.com
Chocolate and confections
Co-Owner: Diane Yamate
Co-Owner: John Cunnell
Estimated Sales: $500,000-$1 Million
Number Employees: 1-4

15798 Yamhill Valley Vineyards
16250 SW Oldsville Rd
McMinnville, OR 97128-8546   503-843-3100
        Fax: 503-843-2450   800-825-4845
                                info@yamhill.com   www.yamhill.com
Wines
President: Stephen Cary
General Manager: David Anderson
Estimated Sales: $ 5-10 Million
Number Employees: 20-49
Brands:
Yamhill Wines

15799 Yangtze Agribusiness Group
PO Box 1071
Great Neck, NY 11023-0071   516-466-1996
                                                Fax: 516-773-0013
                                Newyork@yangtze-China.com
Condiments and relishes

15800 Yankee Specialty Foods
22 Fish Pier
Boston, MA 02210-2054   617-951-9904
        Fax: 617-951-9907   sara@nemarketers.com
                                www.yankeespecialtyfoods.com
Processor and exporter of chili, soup, gumbo and chowder
President: Paul Lindquist
Estimated Sales: $300000
Number Employees: 5
Type of Packaging: Consumer, Private Label
Brands:
Bay Shore

15801 Yarbrough Produce Company
616 16th Ave W
Birmingham, AL 35204   205-323-8651
Manufacturer of salads including fresh vegetables, tossed and cole slaw
President/Co-Owner: June B Yarbrough
VP/Co-Owner: Kenneth Yarbrough Jr
Estimated Sales: $25 Million
Number Employees: 50-99
Sq. footage: 24000
Type of Packaging: Consumer, Food Service
Brands:
GRANNY'S

15802 (HQ)Yarmer Boys Catfish International
5192c Fannett Road
Beaumont, TX 77705-4202   409-842-1962
        Fax: 409-842-1212   vsj42@aol.com
Shrimp
CEO: Glenda Jones
President: Vicky Jones
Sales Director: Trudy Verdine
Number Employees: 100-249
Type of Packaging: Private Label
Brands:
Fishermans Rees

15803 Yarnell Ice Cream Company
P.O.Box 78
Searcy, AR 72145-0078   501-268-2414
        Fax: 501-279-0846   800-766-2414
yarnells@yarnells.com   www.yarnells.com
Processor of frozen products including premium ice creams, frozen treats, guilt free, frozen yogurt, yarnell pints and yarnell sherbert.
President: A Rogers Yarnell II
CEO: Rogers Yarnell
Marketing Director: Cary Sully
Production Manager: Jeff Holtz
Estimated Sales: $21800000
Number Employees: 100-249
Type of Packaging: Consumer, Food Service
Brands:
Guilt Free
Hometown
Yarnell's

15804 Yates Country Hams
430 Nc Highway 49 S
Asheboro, NC 27205-9561   336-629-1795
                                                Fax: 828-459-3138
Processor and exporter of country ham
President/Owner: Milton Yates
Vice President: Roger Yates
Purchasing Manager: Audreu Overman
Number Employees: 10-19
Type of Packaging: Consumer, Food Service, Private Label

15805 Yaya's
515 Acacia Avenue
Corona Del Mar, CA 92625-1906   949-675-7708
Organic and fat-free caramel popcorn
CEO/President: Bob George
VP: Patty George
Estimated Sales: Under $500,000
Number Employees: 1-4
Type of Packaging: Private Label

15806 Yayin Corporation
12725 Hatteras Street
Valley Village, CA 91607-1408   707-829-5686
        Fax: 707-829-0993   ganen@dani.com
Wines
President: Craig Winchell
Estimated Sales: $500,000-$1 Million
Number Employees: 1-4

15807 Ye Olde Pepper Company
122 Derby St
Salem, MA 01970-5646   978-745-2744
        Fax: 978-557-1017   866-393-6533
                                info@yeoldepeppercandy.com
                                www.yeoldepeppercandy.com
Hard and soft candy, chocolates
President: Robert Burkinshaw
Estimated Sales: Below $ 5 Million
Number Employees: 20-49
Brands:
Black Jacks
Salem Gibralters

15808 (HQ)Yellow Emperor
P.O.Box 2631
Eugene, OR 97402-0236   541-485-6664
        Fax: 541-485-0039   877-485-6664
                                info@yellowemperor.com
                                www.yellowemperor.com
Processor of custom herbal extracts, ginseng, teas, tea concentrates and herbal honey
President: Andrew Levine
Estimated Sales: Less than $500,000
Number Employees: 1-4
Sq. footage: 2400
Type of Packaging: Consumer, Private Label, Bulk
Brands:
Honeymoon
Inner Force
Oregon Natural Sportstonic
Phytotherapy
Wild American Herb Co.
Yellow Emperor

15809 Yellow Emperor Pepper Sauce Company
2328 Bullard Avenue
Los Angeles, CA 90032-3505   608-238-2991
                                                Fax: 323-223-1618
Sauces

15810 Yellow Rose Brewing Company
23603 Hartwick Lane
San Antonio, TX 78259-1604   210-496-6669
                        Fax: 210-496-6678
Processor of seasonal beer, ale, stout and pilsner
    President: Glen Fritz
    Sales Manager: Kevin Love
Estimated Sales:$500,000-$1 Million
Number Employees: 5-9
Type of Packaging: Consumer, Food Service
Brands:
    Bubbadog
    Wildcatters Refined
    Yellow Rose Pale

15811 Yeomen Seafoods
P.O.Box 3067
Gloucester, MA 01931-3067   978-283-7422
                        Fax: 978-283-7522
Whole frozen seafood
    President/Treasurer: Thomas Kennedy
Estimated Sales:$4.7 Million
Number Employees: 1-4

15812 Yerba Prima
740 Jefferson Ave
Ashland, OR 97520-3743   541-488-2228
                        Fax: 541-488-2443 800-488-4339
yerba@yerbaprima.com www.yerbaprima.com
Processor and exporter of high quality dietary sup-
plements, specializing in dietary fiber, internal
cleansing aids and herbal products.
    Owner: John Jung
    CEO: John Jung
    Marketing Manager: Shelley Matteson
Estimated Sales:$ 5 - 10 Million
Number Employees: 10-19
Type of Packaging: Consumer, Private Label
Brands:
    Aloe Falls
    Yerba Prima

15813 Yerba Santa Goat Dairy
6850 Scotts Valley Rd
Lakeport, CA 95453-9476   707-263-8131
                        Fax: 707-263-8131
Dairy products
    Owner: Javier Salmon
    Marketing Director: Chris Twohy
*Estimated Sales:*Below $ 5 Million
Number Employees: 1-4

15814 (HQ)Yergat Packing Co Inc
5451 W Mission Avenue
Fresno, CA 93722-5074   559-276-9180
                        Fax: 559-276-2841
Processor and exporter of grapevine leaves
    President: Kirk Yergat
Number Employees: 10-19
Parent Co: Yergat Packing Company
Type of Packaging: Consumer, Private Label

15815 Yewig Brothers Packing Company
P.O.Box 186
Haubstadt, IN 47639-0186   812-768-6208
                        Fax: 812-768-6220 www.dewigmeats.com
Country style meats
    President: Thomas Dewig
Estimated Sales:$ 10-24.9 Million
Number Employees: 20-49

15816 Yick Lung Company
3015 Koapaka Street
Honolulu, HI 96819-1936   808-841-3611
                        Fax: 808-842-4763
Chips, candy and sunflower seeds
    President: Patricia Ching
    Chairman: Gertrude Lee
    COO: Daniel King
Estimated Sales:$5-9.9 Million
Number Employees: 20-49
Brands:
    Yick Lung

15817 Ynrico's Food Products Company
6050 Court Street Rd
Syracuse, NY 13206-1711   315-463-2384
        Fax: 315-463-5897 888-472-8237
nventre@ventre.com www.ventre.com

All natural spaghetti sauce and salsa
    CEO: Martin Ventre
    CFO: Dave Sorensen
    Sales Manager: Rick Alesia
    Production Manager: James Faivre
    VP Purchasing: Jacki Papai
Estimated Sales:$ 10-20 Million
Number Employees: 20-49
Type of Packaging: Private Label

15818 YoCream International
5858 NE 87th Avnue
Portland, OR 97220   503-256-3754
        Fax: 503-256-3976 800-962-7326
info@yocream.com www.yocream.com
Frozen yogurt, ice cream, frozen custard mixes, fruit
and dairy smoothies and frozen beverages.
    Chairman/CEO: John Hanna
    CFO: W Douglas Caudell
    Marketing Director: Suzanne Gardner
    Sales Director: Tyler Bargas
    Operations: Terry Oftedal
    Custom Manufacturing: Matt Hanna
Estimated Sales:$9.9 Million
Number Employees: 60

15819 Yoakum Packing Company
P.O.Box 192
Yoakum, TX 77995-0192   361-293-3541
        Fax: 361-293-2261 gkusak@farmpac.com
                        www.farmpac.com
Processor of smoked and cured pork, beef and poul-
try
    President: Glen Kusak
Estimated Sales:$7,226,707
Number Employees: 20-49
Sq. footage: 30000
Type of Packaging: Consumer, Food Service, Pri-
    vate Label, Bulk
Brands:
    Farm Pac
    Ranch Pac

15820 Yoakum Packing Company
P.O.Box 192
Yoakum, TX 77995-0192   361-293-3541
        Fax: 361-293-2261 www.farmpac.com
    President: Glen Kusak
    Manager: Karin Cockrell
Estimated Sales:$5-10 Million appx.
Number Employees: 20-49

15821 Yoder Dairies
1620 Mount Pleasant Rd
Chesapeake, VA 23322-1219   757-497-3518
        Fax: 757-497-3510 yoderdairies@aol.com
                        www.yoderdairies.com
Processor of milk including standard homogenized,
low-fat, skim, half/half and chocolate; also, cream
buttermilk, whipping cream, eggs, eggnog, spring
water and orange, grapefruit and apple juices, as
well as ice cream.
    President: Kenneth Miller
    VP: L Miller
    General Manager: Maria Dlah
    Plant Manager: Lester Miller
Estimated Sales:$4300000
Number Employees: 31
Type of Packaging: Consumer

15822 Yoder Foods
156 Three Angels Dr
Liberty, KY 42539-5499   606-787-1588
        Fax: 606-845-0038 877-702-0010
Processor of jams, jellies, apple butter, honey and
sorghum; wholesaler/distributor of noodles and
relish
    Owner: Jim Farber
    Secretary: Elmina Miller
    Manufacturing Assistant: Lavina Miller
Number Employees: 1-4
Sq. footage: 2000
Type of Packaging: Consumer
Brands:
    Homestyle Country Jams
    Yoder's Dutch Jams

15823 Yoders
PO Box 249
Grantsville, MD 21536-0249   301-895-5121
    Fax: 301-895-3158 comments@yodermarket.com

Processor and packer of canned, fresh, smoked and
frozen meat products
    President: Ronald Gulledge
    VP/General Manager: Ron Gulledge
Estimated Sales:$9400000
Number Employees: 50
Sq. footage: 50000
Type of Packaging: Consumer, Food Service

15824 Yofarm Company
162 Spring St
Naugatuck, CT 06770-2921   203-720-0000
        Fax: 203-720-0443 www.yofarm.com
Yogurt
    CEO: Thomas G Dixcy
    Plant Manager: Andrew Respondek
Estimated Sales:$ 20-30 Million
Number Employees: 100-249

15825 (HQ)Yohay Baking Company
146 Albany Ave
Lindenhurst, NY 11757-3628   631-225-0300
        Fax: 631-225-4278 www.yohay.com
Processor, importer and exporter of wafer rolls, spe-
cialty cookies, biscotti, and fudge mix, kosher and
all natural products. Retail packaging available
    Owner: Michael Soloman
Number Employees: 20-49
Type of Packaging: Consumer, Food Service, Pri-
    vate Label, Bulk
Brands:
    FUDGE GOURMET
    GOURMET COOKIE PLACE
    SWEETHEART FUDGE

15826 Yokhol Valley Packing Company
P.O.Box 907
Lindsay, CA 93247-0907   559-562-1327
                        Fax: 559-562-6732
Packer of oranges
    Manager: Henry Howison
Estimated Sales:$ 10 - 20 Million
Number Employees: 10-19
Type of Packaging: Bulk

**15827 Yoo-Hoo Chocolate Beverage
Company**
900 King St
Port Chester, NY 10573-1226   914-612-4000
        Fax: 914-612-4100 800-966-4669
        www.cadburyschweppes.com/en
Processor of milk-based beverages
    President: Jack Belsito
    CFO: David Gerics
    Communications Manager: Judy Klym
Estimated Sales:$32,500,000
Number Employees: 1-4
Parent Co: Austin Nichols & Company
Type of Packaging: Consumer
Brands:
    Chocolate Cow
    Devil Shake
    Koko Blanco
    Orangina
    Yoo-Hoo

**15828 Yoo-Hoo Chocolate Beverage
Company**
600 Commercial Ave
Carlstadt, NJ 07072-2607   201-933-0070
                        Fax: 201-933-5360
consumer.relations@brandspeoplelove.com
        www.drinkyoo-hoo.com
Processor of chocolate drinks
    President: Brian O'Byrne
    Marketing Manager: Christine Karumpe
    Plant Manager: Bill Pedeto
Estimated Sales:$16,500,000
Number Employees: 20-49
Parent Co: Yoo-Hoo Chocolate Beverage
Type of Packaging: Consumer

15829 Yoplait USA
1 General Mills Blvd
Minneapolis, MN 55426   763-764-7600
        Fax: 763-764-7384 800-967-5248
        www.generalmills.com
Manufacturer of yogurt
    Chairman/President/CEO: Kendall Powell
    EVP/CFO: Donal Mulligan
    Plant Manager: Dave Towner

Estimated Sales:$14.8 Billion
Number Employees: 10,000+
Parent Co: General Mills
Type of Packaging: Consumer, Food Service
Brands:
COLOMBO
EXPRESSE
GO-GURT
TRIX
YOPLAIT CUSTARD STYLE
YOPLAIT LIGHT
YOPLAIT NOURICHE
YOPLAIT ORIGINAL
YOPLAIT WHIPS

15830 Yoplait-Colombo
PO Box 1113
Minneapolis, MN 55440-1113   763-540-2311
                                Fax: 763-541-5000
Manufacturer of yogurt
Number Employees: 70
Parent Co: General Mills
Type of Packaging: Consumer, Food Service

15831 York Barbell Company
3300 Board Rd
York, PA 17406-8409   717-767-6481
      Fax: 717-764-0044   800-358-9675
info@yorkbarbell.com   www.yorkbarbell.com
Processor of energy bars and food supplements
      Manager: Janis Smith
Estimated Sales:$20000000
Number Employees: 100-249

15832 York Beach Fish Market
15 Railroad Avenue
York Beach, ME 03910   207-363-2763
                          Fax: 302-998-4236
Seafood
      President: Frank Robins
Estimated Sales:$275,000
Number Employees: 5

15833 York Mountain Winery
P.O.Box 7003
Paso Robles, CA 93447-7003   805-238-3925
      Fax: 805-238-0428   hreed@martinweyrich.com
                          www.yorkmountainwinery.com
Processor of red and white wine, dry sherry, champagne and salad dressing
      Owner: David Weyrich
      Manager: Suzanne Redberg
      Wine Maker: Steve Goldman
Estimated Sales:$920000
Number Employees: 5-9
Sq. footage: 3000
Type of Packaging: Consumer
Brands:
      Suzanne's Salad Splash
      York Mountain

15834 Yorktown Baking Company
1700 Front St
Yorktown Heights, NY 10598-4606   914-245-1912
      Fax: 914-243-7138   800-235-3961
Processor of fresh and frozen batter including muffin, scone and cookie. Prpared flour mixes and doughs.
      Owner: Emil Gold
Estimated Sales:$2,600,000
Number Employees: 20-49
Type of Packaging: Consumer, Food Service
Brands:
      Yorktown Baking Company

15835 Yosemite Coffee & Roasting
40879 Highway 41 # C
Oakhurst, CA 93644-9644   559-683-8815
                             Fax: 559-658-8835
Coffee
      Owner: Chris Russell
      President: Chris Russeoo
*Estimated Sales:*Below $ 5 Million
Number Employees: 1-4
Brands:
      Yosemite Coffee

15836 Yosemite Waters
226 South Avenue 54
Los Angeles, CA 90042-4512   323-256-2265
      Fax: 323-256-4707   800-427-8420
            service@yosemitewaters.com
            www.yosemitewaters.com

Processor of bottled and distilled water
      President: Maya Soderstrom
      COO: Genny Kush
      Vice President: Claude Niesen
Estimated Sales:$ 5 - 10 Million
Number Employees: 50-99
Type of Packaging: Consumer, Food Service, Bulk

15837 Yosemite Waters
226 South Avenue 54
Los Angeles, CA 90042-4512   323-256-2265
      Fax: 323-256-4707   800-427-8420
            service@yosemitewaters.com
            www.yosemitewaters.com
Processor of bottled water
      President: Maya Soderstrom
Estimated Sales:$5200000
Number Employees: 50-99
Type of Packaging: Consumer, Food Service

15838 Yoshida Food International
8338 NE Alderwood Rd # 200
Portland, OR 97220-6800   503-872-8450
      Fax: 503-284-0004   888-243-8371
            info@yfintl.com
www.yooshidafoodinternational.comhiyfintl.com
Processor and exporter of non MSG, nonfat and cholesterol-free sauces, marinades, drippings and coatings
      President: Matt Guthrie
      CFO: Tim Sepher
      CEO: Junki Yoshida
      Quality Control: John Hunter
      VP Sales/Marketing: John Moran
      Sales Director: Andy Moberg
      Public Relations: Marti Lucich
      Operations Manager: Eric Rinearson
      Production Manager: Frank Heuschkel
      Purchasing Manager: Ken Hamilton
Estimated Sales:$ 100-500 Million
Number Employees: 50-99
Sq. footage: 65000
Type of Packaging: Consumer, Food Service, Private Label, Bulk
Brands:
      Benihana
      Yoshida Foods International

15839 Yost Candy Company
51 S Cochran St
Dalton, OH 44618-9602   330-828-2777
      Fax: 330-828-8296   800-750-1976
      info@yostcandy.com   www.yostcandy.com
Processor and exporter of lollypops and Halloween candy
      President: Sofie Yost
      Vice President: Joe Yost
      Sales Director: Earl Yost
Estimated Sales:$2000000
Number Employees: 20-49
Type of Packaging: Consumer, Private Label, Bulk
Brands:
      Kiddi Pops
      Licklers
      Lil Kiddies

15840 Yost's Dutch Maid Bakery
809 Scalp Ave
Johnstown, PA 15904-2594   814-266-3191
Processor of baked goods including cupcakes, layer cakes, pies, cookies and breads.
      President: Tim Yost
Estimated Sales:$2400000
Number Employees: 20-49
Brands:
      Dutch Maid

15841 Young Pecan
2455 Entrada Del Sol
Las Cruces, NM 88001-3906   575-524-4321
      Fax: 575-525-3432 www.youngplantations.com
Processor of bagged and boxed pecans
      Manager: Paul Koenig
      Purchasing Agent: Malcolm Burdett
Estimated Sales:$ 2.5-5 Million
Number Employees: 50-99
Parent Co: Young Pecan Company
Type of Packaging: Bulk

15842 Young Pecan Company
1200 Pecan Street
Florence, SC 29501   843-662-8591
      Fax: 843-664-2344   800-829-6864
      sales@youngpecan.com   www.youngpecan.com

Processor of pecans
      President/CEO: James Swink
      EVP: Helen Watts
Estimated Sales:$80 Million
Number Employees: 183
Type of Packaging: Consumer, Food Service, Bulk
Brands:
      Goodbee
      Indian Creek
      Schermer

15843 Young Pecan Company
P.O.Box 5779
Florence, SC 29502-5779   843-662-8591
      Fax: 843-664-2344   800-829-6864
      sales@youngpecan.com   www.youngpecan.com
Pecans
      President: James Swink
      CFO: Murray Garber
      VP: Helen Watts
      Marketing VP: Bob Tankerly
      Plant Manager: Mike Barnes
Estimated Sales:$ 50-100 Million
Number Employees: 10-19
Sq. footage: 155800
Type of Packaging: Consumer, Food Service, Private Label, Bulk
Brands:
      Mingo River
      Pecan Plantations
      Young Pecan Co. Brand
      Young's Golden Sweet

15844 (HQ)Young Winfield
12075 Highway 27
Kleinburg, ON L07 1C0
Canada   905-893-2536
            Fax: 905-893-9682
Manufacturer of onion oil, cajun spice, salt and vinegar seasonings
      General Manager: A Sunderji
Estimated Sales:$3-5 Million
Number Employees: 12
Sq. footage: 27000
Type of Packaging: Consumer, Food Service, Private Label, Bulk
Brands:
      SIMPLY SPICE
      YOU WIN

15845 Young Yoo Company
3539 W Lawrence Avenue
Chicago, IL 60625-5627   773-539-3122
                            Fax: 773-299-9928

15846 Young's Bakery
67 S Gallatin Ave
Uniontown, PA 15401-3540   724-437-6361
Processor of cakes and cookies
      President: Dino Palermo
      Marketing Director: Ruth Palermo
*Estimated Sales:*Less than $500,000
Number Employees: 1-4
Type of Packaging: Food Service

15847 Young's Farm
P.O.Box 13
Paulina, OR 97751-13   928-632-7272
                          Fax: 928-632-7975
      information@youngsfarminc.com
            www.youngsfarminc.com
Poultry and fresh farm products
      President: Dennis Young
Estimated Sales:$ 1-5 Million
Number Employees: 50

15848 Young's Jersey Dairy
6880 Springfield Xenia Rd
Yellow Springs, OH 45387-9610   937-325-0629
      Fax: 937-325-3226   cows@youngsdairy.com
            www.youngsdairy.com
Milk, ice cream, rolls, bread and donuts
      CEO: C Daniel Young
      Human Resource Manager: Ben Young
      Sales Manager: Cathy Young
*Estimated Sales:*Below $ 5 Million
Number Employees: 250-499

15849 Young's Lobster Pound
4 Mitchell St
Belfast, ME 04915   207-338-1160
      Fax: 207-338-5652 www.youngslobsterpound.com

Processor, exporter and importer of fresh and frozen seafood including crabs, lobster, live and shucked clams and mussels, scallops and shrimp; whole-saler/distributor of fresh and frozen seafood
Owner: Raymond Young
Co-Owner: Claire Young
Manager: Raymond Young
Estimated Sales: $ 3 - 5 Million
Number Employees: 20-49
Sq. footage: 2736
Type of Packaging: Consumer, Food Service
Brands:
Young's Lobster Pound

15850 Young's Noodle Factory
1635 Liliha St
Honolulu, HI 96817-3154   808-533-6478
                                 Fax: 808-536-6533
Processor of noodles
Owner: Gordon Kwan
Estimated Sales: $1000000
Number Employees: 10-19
Type of Packaging: Food Service

15851 Young's Shellfish Company
P.O.Box 261
Belfast, ME 04915-0261   207-338-5032
                                Fax: 207-338-1488
Seafood
President: Robert Young
Estimated Sales: $ 3 - 5 Million
Number Employees: 10-19

15852 Yrica's Rugelach & Baking Company
389 4th Street
Brooklyn, NY 11215-2901   718-965-3657
Fax: 718-832-6160 ericasrugelach@aol.com
                   www.ericasrugelach.com
Cookies and rugelach
President: Erica Kalick
CEO: Erica Kalick
Marketing Director: Erica Kalick
Estimated Sales: $500,000-$1 Million
Number Employees: 10-19
Brands:
Erica's Rugelach

15853 Yuengling Brewery
P.O.Box 539
Pottsville, PA 17901-0539   570-622-4141
Fax: 570-622-4011 giftshop@yuengling.com
                   www.yuengling.com
Beer
President: Richard L Yuengling Jr
Quality Control: Joe Frenzy
CFO: Debbie Ferhat
VP Sales/Marketing: David Casinelli
Director Manufacturing: Jim Helmke
Estimated Sales: $ 50-75 Million
Number Employees: 100-249
Type of Packaging: Private Label
Brands:
Lord Chesterfield Al
Original Black & Tan
Traditional Lager
Yuengling Premium Be
Yuengling Premium Li

15854 Yum Yum Potato Chips
40 Du Moulin
Warwick, QC J0A 1M0
Canada   819-358-3600
Fax: 819-358-3687 800-567-5792
yumyum@yum-yum.com www.yum-yum.com
Manufacturer of snack foods including potato chips, cheese sticks, onion rings and fries
President: Pierre Riverd
Director Production: Guy Trudel
Number Employees: 200
Type of Packaging: Consumer, Private Label

15855 Yvonne's Gourmet Sensations
404 Berkshire Way
Marlton, NJ 08053-4222   856-985-7677
                                Fax: 856-810-3798
Gourmet chocolate pretzels, chocolate cookies, chocolate grahams, chocolate waffles
Marketing Manager: Gary Greenberg
Brands:
Yvonne's Gourmet Cho
Yvonne's Gourmet Cho
Yvonne's Gourmet Choc Cookies

15856 Z Foods Inc
9537 Road 29 1/2
Madera, CA 93637   559-673-6368
Fax: 559-673-7508 888-400-1015
customerservice@zfoodsinc.com
www.zfoodsinc.com
dried fruits
President: Daniel Villanueva
VP: Nina Zoria
Number Employees: 2

15857 Z&S Distributing
P.O.Box 27467
Fresno, CA 93729-7467   559-432-1777
Fax: 559-432-2888 800-467-0788
mail@zsfresh.com www.zsfresh.com
Fruits and vegetables.
President: Martin Zaninovich
Estimated Sales: $7,700,000
Number Employees: 10-19
Type of Packaging: Consumer
Brands:
JUST - RIPE

15858 Z.D. Wines LLC
8383 Silverado Trl
Napa, CA 94558-9436   707-963-5188
Fax: 707-963-2640 800-487-7757
info@zdwines.com www.zdwines.com
Processor and exporter of wines including chardon-nay, pinot noir and cabernet sauvignon
President/Partner: Brett DeLeuze
CEO/Partner: Robert DeLeuze
CFO: Julie De Leuze
Marketing Coordinator: Elyse Chambers
VP Sales: Teresa d'Aurizio
Winemaker: Chris Pisani
Estimated Sales: $5-10 Million
Number Employees: 25-50
Number of Brands: 2
Number of Products: 8
Sq. footage: 22732
Type of Packaging: Consumer, Food Service
Brands:
Abacus
Z.D. Wines

15859 ZT Packaging
89-47 Metropolitan Avenue
Rego Park, NY 11374   718-896-8420
Fax: 718-275-9053 800-932-2448
www.ztpackaging.com
plastic bags, custom printed bags, paper bags, boxes

15860 Zaca Mesa Winery
P.O.Box 899
Los Olivos, CA 93441-0899   805-688-9339
Fax: 805-688-8796 800-350-7972
info@zacamesa.com www.zacamesa.com
Wines
President/CEO: Brook Williams
WineMaker: Clay Brock
VP/Finance: Susi English
VP Sales/Marketing: Jim Fiolek
Estimated Sales: $5-10 Million
Number Employees: 20-49
Brands:
Roussanne
Syrah
Z Gris Dry Rose
Zcuvee

15861 Zachary Confections
P.O.Box 219
Frankfort, IN 46041-0219   765-659-4751
Fax: 765-659-1491 800-445-4222
sales@zc-inc.com www.zacharyconfections.com
Processor and exporter of confectionery products in-cluding caramels, boxed chocolates, marshmallows, mints, nougats and holiday novelties.
President/CEO: Patrick Zachary
Senior Vice President: George Anichini
Executive Vice President: Jack Zachary III
Director of Sales: Steve Newman
Estimated Sales: $25-99 Million
Number Employees: 500-999
Type of Packaging: Consumer, Private Label, Bulk
Brands:
ZACHARY

15862 (HQ)Zacky Farms
P.O.Box 12556
Fresno, CA 93778-2556   559-443-2700
Fax: 559-443-2778 800-888-0235
zfsales@zacky.com www.zacky.com
Processor of turkey
Consumer Affairs Director: Lillian Zacky
Estimated Sales: $500,000-$1 Million
Number Employees: 1-4
Type of Packaging: Consumer
Brands:
Culinary Classic Breast of Turkey N
Culinary Classic Slices Breast of T

15863 (HQ)Zacky Farms
2044 Tyler Avenue
South El Monte, CA 91733-3597   626-443-9351
                                       800-888-0235
Processor of turkey products including ham and hot dogs; also, poultry, chicken hot dogs, etc.; whole-saler/distributor of beef, lamb, fish and pork
President: Lillian Zacky
CEO: Bob Zacky
Director Engineering: G Tacheny
Purchasing Manager: R Zacky
Number Employees: 50-99
Type of Packaging: Private Label
Brands:
ZACKY FARMS

15864 Zambezi Organic Forest Honey
5508 Brown Rd
PO Box 751
Oxford, OH 45056   513-523-9209
Fax: 513-523-5351 info@zambezihoney.com
                   www.zambezihoney.com
100% organic, fair trade, raw forest honey from Zambia

15865 Zapp's Chips
307 E Airline Hwy
Gramercy, LA 70052-3019   225-869-9777
Fax: 225-869-9779 800-349-2447
Potato chips
Owner: Roan Zappe
Marketing Director: Richard Gaudry
Estimated Sales: $ 20 - 50 Million
Number Employees: 100-249

15866 Zapp's Potato Chips
307 E Airline Hwy
Gramercy, LA 70052-3019   225-869-8888
Fax: 225-869-9779 800-349-2447
www.zapps.com
Processor and exporter of kosher, kettle style, Cajun and jalapeno flavored potato chips
President: Ron Zappe
Director Sales/Marketing: Richard Gaudry
Estimated Sales: $20-50 Million
Number Employees: 100-249
Type of Packaging: Consumer, Food Service, Bulk

15867 Zarda Bar-B-Q & Catering Company
214 NW State Route 7
Blue Springs, MO 64014-2746   816-229-9999
Fax: 816-224-3171 800-776-7427
info@zarda.com www.zarda.com
Processor of barbecue sauce and baked beans
President: Michael Zarda
Quality Control Manager: Brian Packer
Marketing Director: Terry Hyer
Plant Manager: Ron Dorris
Estimated Sales: $10-24.9 Million
Number Employees: 50-99
Brands:
Zarda

15868 (HQ)Zartic Inc
438 Lavender Dr NW
Rome, GA 30165-2262   706-234-3000
Fax: 706-291-6068 800-241-0516
zartic@zartic.com www.pierrefoods.com

A full service beef, poultry, veal and pork further processor that operates four U.S.D.A. inspected state of the art production facilities and delivers product nationwide via Zartran, Zartic's refrigerated transportation company

Manager: Kenneth Morris
CEO: James Mauer
CFO: Robert Miles
Procurement VP: Francois Gaulin
Sales VP: Mike Wilson
Operations VP: Phillip Morris
Purchasing Agent: Ken Fries
Number Employees: 50-99
Type of Packaging: Consumer
Other Locations:
Zartic Inc (Beef Division)
Cedartown GA
Zartic Inc (Poultry Division)
West Rome GA
Zartic Inc (Pork Division)
Hamilton AL
Brands:
Circle Z
Crispy Steaks
Fryz
Jim's Country Mill Sausage
Shurtenda
Spicy Wings
Vittles
Z-Bird
Zartic
Zartic Beef Bakeables
Zartic Chicken Bakeables
Zartic Chicken Fried Beef Steaks
Zartic Chicken Fryz Flavorz
Zartic Chicken Tenderloins
Zartic Circle Z Beef Burgers
Zartic Crispy Steaks
Zartic Homestyle Meatloaf
Zartic Honey Hugged Chicken
Zartic Pork Bakeables
Zartic Pork Sausage Sampler
Zartic Rockin' Roasted Chicken
Zartic Veal Entree Legends
Zartic Veal Specialties

15869 Zatarain's
82 1st St
Gretna, LA 70053-4745   504-367-2950
Fax: 504-362-2004   800-435-6639
info@zatarain.com   www.zatarain.com
Processor of condiments, flavoring extracts, rice and stuffing mixes, bean seasoning, spices and crab boil.
Manager: James Pearse
CFO: Regina Templet
Research & Development: George Bigner
Quality Control: Karla Schexnader
Customer Service: Valarie Harris
Food Service Sales Manager: Dudley Passman
Account Executive: Robert Ebert
Estimated Sales: $20-50 Million
Number Employees: 250-499
Parent Co: McCormick & Company Inc
Type of Packaging: Consumer, Food Service
Brands:
Zatarain's

15870 (HQ)Zausner Foods
400 S Custer Ave
New Holland, PA 17557-9220   717-355-8505
Fax: 717-355-8561 www.alouettecheese.com
Sauces, dips, pudding, nutritional beverages
President: Frank Otis
COO: Gregg Kenitz
Director Engineering: Scott Whitman
VP Sales: Howard Covenko
Plant Manager: Tim Pent
Estimated Sales: $50 Million+
Number Employees: 50-99
Brands:
Alouette

15871 Zayante Vineyards
420 Old Mount Rd
Felton, CA 95018-9054   831-335-7992
Fax: 831-335-5770 info@zayantevineyards.com
www.zayantevineyards.com
Wines
Owner: Greg Nolten
Co-Owner: Marion Nolten
Co-Owner: Kathleen Starkey-Nolten
Vineyard Manager: Greg Nolten
Estimated Sales: $500,000-$1 Million
Number Employees: 1-4

Type of Packaging: Private Label
Brands:
Zayante

15872 Zazi Baking Company
1360 Industrial Ave
Petaluma, CA 94952-6521   707-778-1635
Fax: 707-778-6991 888-778-6399
support@zazibaking.com www.zazibaking.com
Biscotti and cookies
President: Celeste Longo
VP: Debby Dyar
Sales Director: Phil Walker
Public Relations: Sharon Craig
Plant Manager: Mike Downing
Estimated Sales: $5-10 Million
Number Employees: 10-19
Sq. footage: 6000
Type of Packaging: Food Service, Private Label, Bulk
Brands:
COOKIE BRITTLE
MRS. LITTLE'S
RUNNING RABBIT
SPENDIDO NUGGETS
Splendido Biscotti
ZAZI ORGANICS

15873 Zel R. Kahn & Sons
2 Fifer Ave # 220
Corte Madera, CA 94925-1155   415-924-9600
Fax: 415-924-9690
Wholesaler/distributor and exporter of surplus, salvage and closeout merchandise including dried and canned fruits, vegetables, crackers, cereals, etc
President: Scott Kahn
Executive VP: Joel Jutovsky
Estimated Sales: $300,000-500,000
Number Employees: 5-9
Sq. footage: 40000

15874 (HQ)Zenobia Company
5774 Mosholu Ave
Bronx, NY 10471-2200   718-796-7700
Fax: 718-548-2313 866-936-6242
info@nutsonthenet.com www.nutsonthenet.com
Processor, importer and exporter of pistachios, cashews, pumpkin and sunflower seeds, organic dried fruits, etc
President: Kenneth Bobker
National Sales Manager: Donald DiMatteo
Estimated Sales: $5-10 Million
Number Employees: 1-4
Sq. footage: 25000
Type of Packaging: Consumer, Food Service, Private Label, Bulk
Other Locations:
Zenobia Co.
Bronx NY
Brands:
Indian
Zenobia

15875 Zephyr Hills
10599 NW 67th St
Tamarac, FL 33321-6407   954-597-7852
www.perrier.com
Processor of spring, distilled and drinking water
President/CEO: Kim Jeffries
Number Employees: 50-99
Sq. footage: 25000
Parent Co: Perrier Group of America
Type of Packaging: Consumer, Food Service

15876 Zephyr Hills Bottled Watter Corporation
6403 Harney Rd
Tampa, FL 33610-9349   813-630-5763
Fax: 813-620-6862 800-950-9398
Processor of coffee and bottled spring and distilled water
President: Kim Jeffery
Quality Control Manager: Winnie Louie
Marketing/Sales Development Manager: Monica Kelley
Number Employees: 20-49
Parent Co: Perrier Group of America
Type of Packaging: Consumer
Brands:
Deer Park
Zephyrhillis

15877 Zeppys Bakery
485 S Union St
Lawrence, MA 1843-2811   781-963-7022
Fax: 781-963-6752 zeppy1927@aol.com
Breads, rolls, cakes, cookies, pastries and bagels
President: Doris Zeprun
General Manager: Rochelle Novack
General Manager: Bob Novack
Sales Manager: Eliott Zeprun
Estimated Sales: $10-20 Million
Number Employees: 50-99
Brands:
Zeppys

15878 Zerna Packing
2231 Highway 100
Labadie, MO 63055-2000   636-742-4190
Processor of meat; smoking and curing available
Owner: Carl Zerna Sr
Estimated Sales: $ 1 - 3 Million
Number Employees: 1-4
Type of Packaging: Consumer, Food Service

15879 Zhena's Gypsy Tea
205 Bryant Street
Ojai, CA 93023   805-646-1996
Fax: 805-646-4262 800-448-0803
info@gypsytea.com www.gypsytea.com
teas

15880 Ziegenfelder Company
P.O.Box 6645
Wheeling, WV 26003-0641   304-232-6360
Fax: 304-232-6368 www.budgetsaver.com
Processor of ice cream novelties
CEO: Lisa Allen
Director Sales: Bill Grayzer
Estimated Sales: $20-50 Million
Number Employees: 20-49
Type of Packaging: Consumer

15881 Ziem Vineyards
16651 Spielman Road
Fairplay, MD 21733-1047   301-223-8352
Wines
President: Ruth Ziem
Estimated Sales: Under $500,000
Number Employees: 1-4

15882 Zimmer Custom Made Packaging
P.O.Box 1869
Columbus, OH 43216-1869   614-294-4931
Fax: 614-299-0538 800-338-7465
gbrinkman@norse.com www.norse.com
Sugar cones for ice cream, sleeves, paper tubes and cups for packaging, all-purpose fillers and cup collator that automatically counts, stacks and collates cups
President: Scott Fullbright
CFO: Randy Harvey
CEO: Scot Fulbright
R&D: Gunther Brinkman
Human Resources: Brian McGinney
Estimated Sales: $ 20 - 50 Million
Number Employees: 100-249

15883 Zimmerman Cheese
6853 State Road 78
South Wayne, WI 53587-9724   608-968-3414
Fax: 608-968-3425
Cheese
President: Mark Witke
Marketing Director: Linda Moe
Estimated Sales: $10-24.9 Million
Number Employees: 20-49

15884 Zink & Triest Company
150 Domorah Dr
Montgomeryville, PA 18936-9633   215-469-1950
Fax: 215-469-1951 800-537-5070
abreithaupt@zinktriest.com
Suppliers of vanilla beans, vanillin and ethyl vanillin
President: Henry Todd
Sales Manager: Amie Briethaupt
Estimated Sales: $ 10 - 20 Million
Number Employees: 10-19

15885 Zip-Pak
1800 W Sycamore Rd
Manteno, IL 60950-9369   815-468-6500
Fax: 815-468-6550 info@zippak.com
www.zippak.com

Manufacturer of recloseable zipper products that can be used for storing a variety of products within the food industry.

Chairman/Chief Executive Officer: David Speer
VP/Investor Relations: John Brooklier
SVP/Chief Financial Officer: Ronald Kropp
Finance Executive: Roger Geckner
VP/Research and Development: Lee Sheridan
Senior Vice President: Allan Sutherland
SVP/General Counsel & Secretary: James Wooten
Senior Vice President Human Resources: Sharon Brady
Vice President Patents & Technology: Mark Croll
Parent Co: Illinois Tool Works
Type of Packaging: Consumer

15886 Zipp Manufacturing Company
8300 River Corners Road
Hornerville, OH 44235   440-871-0161
Fax: 440-871-0165   800-521-8700
Manufacturer of flavoring extracts for ice cream and soda fountains; also, chocolate syrup and strawberries

President: James E Zipp
Plant Manager: Tim Swartwood
Estimated Sales: $10 Million
Number Employees: 50
Sq. footage: 15000
Type of Packaging: Consumer, Food Service
Brands:
DOVER

15887 Zippy's
1725 S King St
Honolulu, HI 96826-2134   808-973-0877
Fax: 808-946-6790   customerservice@zippys.com
www.zippys.com
Chili manufacturing
President: Francis Hilga
Number Employees: 50-99
Brands:
Napolean's Bakery
Zippys

15888 Zitner Company
3120 N 17th St
Philadelphia, PA 19132-2357   215-229-4990
Fax: 215-229-9828
Processor of confectionery products including caramel coated apples and Easter candy
Owner: Mc Murphy
Estimated Sales: $10-20 Million
Number Employees: 20-49
Sq. footage: 100000
Type of Packaging: Consumer

15889 Zitos Specialty Foods
129 Cousley Drive SE
Port Charlotte, FL 33952-9149   941-625-0806
Gourmet and specialty foods
Owner: David Smith
Co-owner: Christine Smith
Brands:
Zitos

15890 Zivney Cheese
PO Box 67
Minonk, IL 61760-0067   309-432-2533
Fax: 309-432-2045   800-732-3068
Processor of cheese including Swiss and havarti
President: Jeff Zivney
Plant Manager: Mike Frei
Estimated Sales: $2.5-5 Million
Number Employees: 20-49
Type of Packaging: Consumer, Private Label

15891 Zoelsmanns Bakery & Deli
912 E Abriendo Ave
Pueblo, CO 81004-2598   719-543-0407
Fax: 719-543-4083
Processor of bread, cakes, pies and hard and sweet rolls
Owner: Ron Petkosek
Estimated Sales: $500,000-$1 Million
Number Employees: 5-9
Type of Packaging: Consumer, Food Service, Bulk

15892 Zoll Foods Corporation
15600 Wentworth Ave
South Holland, IL 60473-1271   708-333-3900
Fax: 708-333-3767
Processor of raw and pre-cooked barbeque pork ribs
VP: Al Teska
VP Sales: Matt Galt

Estimated Sales: $100-500 Million
Number Employees: 250-499
Parent Co: ConAgra Foods
Type of Packaging: Food Service

15893 Zone Perfect Nutrition Company
625 Cleveland Ave
Columbus, OH 43215-1754   614-624-7677
Fax: 614-624-9001   800-390-6690
www.zoneperfect.com
Nutrition products, bars, meals, drinks and supplements
President: Gary McCullough
Number Employees: 1,000-4,999
Parent Co: Ross

15894 Zuccaro's Fruit & Produce Company
1000 N 3rd St
Minneapolis, MN 55401-1095   612-333-1122
Fax: 612-333-7511
Processor of produce including cantaloupe, honeydew, watermelon, broccoli, carrots, celery, potatoes, etc.; also, salad mixes available
Owner: John Zuccaro
Estimated Sales: $2.5-5 Million
Number Employees: 20-49

15895 Zumbro
24664 710th St
Hayfield, MN 55940-8739   507-365-8045
Fax: 507-365-8302   800-365-2409
Manufacturer and exporter of food stabilizers, starches, gums, maltodextrins, fat replacers, rice syrups, proteins, etc
President: Eugene Sander
CEO: Eugene Sander
Controller: Maxine Gould
National Sales Manager: Suzanne Williams
Estimated Sales: $25-49.9 Million
Number Employees: 50-99
Sq. footage: 10000
Parent Co: Primera Foods Corporation
Type of Packaging: Bulk
Brands:
Insta*Starch
Insta*Thick
Malta*Gran
Rice Complete
Rice Trin
Z-Coat

15896 Zummo Meat Company
P.O.Box 1688
Beaumont, TX 77704-1688   409-842-1810
Fax: 409-842-5491   zummo@pernet.net
www.zummo.com
Processor of meats including sausage and boudin
President: Frank Zummo
VP: Greg Zummo
Estimated Sales: $5-10 Million
Number Employees: 50-99
Type of Packaging: Consumer
Brands:
Zummo

15897 Zuni Foods
13838 Jones Maltsberger Rd
San Antonio, TX 78247-3904   210-481-3600
Fax: 210-481-3603   800-906-3876
lpickus@dellnet.com   www.momaks.com
Mild table salsa
Owner: John Warlow
Brands:
Zuni Fire Roasted Salsa
Zuni Zalsa Verde

15898 Zweigle's
651 Plymouth Ave N
Rochester, NY 14608-1689   585-546-1740
Fax: 585-546-8721   Zweigles@frontiernet.net
www.zweigles.com
Processor of meat including sausage
President: Roberta Camardo
Treasurer: Michael Keller
Sales Manager: James Vacanti
Plant Manager: Micheal Bidzerkowny
Estimated Sales: $20-50 Million
Number Employees: 50-99
Type of Packaging: Consumer, Food Service, Private Label, Bulk
Brands:
Zweigle's

Annie's, 6636, 13248
Annie's Homegrown, 14553, 14554, 14555,
 14556, 14557, 14558, 14559, 14560,
 14561, 14562, 14563, 14564, 14565,
 14566, 14567
Annie's Macaroni & Cheese, 652
Annie's Naturals, 653
Annie's Naturals Magic Sauces, 653
Annie's Naturals Salad Dressings, 653
Annie's Supreme, 3255
Anniversary Bock, 1806
Ansac Cognac, 6371
Anselmi, 10895
Antelope Valley, 654
Anthony's, 523
Anthony-Thomas Chocolates, 657
Anti Oxidant Edge, 1634
Antioch Farms, 816
Antique Crown Foods, 14226
Antoine's, 15
Antoni Ravioli, 660
Antonia, 8025
Antonio, 2138
Anytime, 8140
Anytime Candy, 15630
Anzio and Sons, 5494
Aoste, 12717, 12720, 12756
Apco, 680
Aperi-Coeur, 11304
Aperiquiche, 11304
Aperossimo, 6009
Apex, 55
Apexo Servo, 158
Apg, 838
Aphroteasiac Chai, 9057
Aplets, 8417
Apollinaris, 8418
Apollo, 851
Apostle Islands Organic Coffee, 10363
Appeteasers, 206
Apple & Eve, 672
Apple Blossom, 8222
Apple Brand Juices, 9541
Apple Cinnamon Pecan Cake, 3089
Apple Corns, 6141
Apple Dandy, 1860
Apple Delight, 5954
Apple Hill, 9779
Apple Jack, 8136, 15298
Apple Jacks, 7676
Apple Mountain, 9774
Apple Ridge, 7286
Apple Royal, 5954
Apple Sidra, 3339
Apple Snax, 8290
Apple Strudel Coffee Beans, 8626
Apple Time, 7872
Apple Valley Inn, 12423
Appleblossom, 11007
Applecreek Orchards, 677
Appledore, 3290
Applegate Farms, 679, 14996
Applerazzi, 3618
Appleton, 680
Appollinaris, 3021
Apres, 10020
Apricot Ale, 3123, 12610
Apricot Dandy, 15434
Apricot Pecan Cake, 3089
Aprikat, 387
Aqua Blox®, 174
Aqua Clara, 683
Aqua Star, 11968
Aquacuisine, 685
Aquadrops, 9010
Aquafina, 687, 11178, 11179, 11191
Aquafina Alive, 687
Aquafina Flavorsplash, 687, 11178, 11179,
 11191
Aquafina Sparkling, 687, 11178, 11191
Aqualon, 6457
Aquamin, 3270, 11268
Aquana, 3021
Aquaresin Spices, 7596
Aquaresins, 7596
Aquari-Yums, 10108
Aquarious, 10331
Aquarius, 3021
Aquaroyale, 3635
Aquavits, 3464
Aquila D'Ora, 6808
Ara, 111

Arak Razzouk, 11221, 11222
Arandas, 6371
Arapahoe, 5896
Arataki, 10860
Arbanex, 9440
Arbanol, 9440
Arbor, 1596
Arbor Crest, 691
Arbor Hill Wine, 693
Arbor Springs Drinking Water, 695
Arbor Springs Purified Water, 695
Arbor Springs Spring Water, 695
Arbuckle, 697
Arbutus Flour, 7864
Arc, 112
Arcadia, 698
Archie Moore's, 705
Archway, 709, 4425
Arco, 614
Arcon, 701
Arcon®, 702
Arcor, 15347
Arcor Premium Hard Filled Candies, 711
Arcor Value Line Hard Candies, 711
Arctic Blast, 7191
Arctic Cape, 5211
Arctic Express, 12888
Arctic Ice, 14594, 14595, 14596
Arctic Ice Rockfish, 14594, 14595
Arctic Iceland, 719
Arctic Pride, 12053
Arctic Seas, 719
Arctic Sprays, 719
Arctica Gardens, 2448
Ardbeg, 9587
Arden Woods, 201
Ardex, 701
Ardmore, 720, 1237
Ardmore Farms, 3387
Ardmore Farms Grove, 3389
Arel, 113
Argo, 57, 58
Argyle Brut, 726
Ariel, 729, 11644
Ariel Blanc, 729
Ariel Brut Cuve, 729
Ariel Cabernet, 729
Ariel Chardonnay, 729
Ariel Merlot, 729
Ariel Rouge, 729
Ariel White Zinfandel, 729
Arista, 732
Aristo Snacks, 9404
Aristocrat, 733
Arizona, 736, 5008
Arizona Fresh Iced Tea, 6105
Arizona Iced Tea, 4758
Arizona Ranch Fresh, 6522
Arizona Vineyards, 747
Arkansas Poly, 749
Arm & Hammer®, 2860
Armagnac, 11222
Armanino, 755
Armanino Farms, 9171, 9172
Armeno, 758
Armida, 15577
Armistead Citrus Products, 759
Armon, 395
Armour, 3175, 3189, 3197, 3206, 15590
Armour and Erickson, 7454
Armour Brown 'n Serve, 3200
Armour Swift-Eckrich, 3211
Armstrong, 12703, 12704, 12705, 12712
Arnie's Bagelicious, 8940
Arnold, 1467, 5494, 13797, 15462
Arnold's, 764
Arnold's Brands, 764
Arnott's, 2263, 8418
Arns, 765
Aro-Smoke, 11966
Arol, 945
Aroma, 13354
Aroma Cuisiner's Choice, 766
Aroma Southern Maison, 766
Aroma Turkish, 766
Aroma Vera, 769
Aroma-Life, 770
Aromahop, 7446
Aromi D'Italia, 774
Arox, 945
Arra Giumarra Vineyards, 5591
Arracado, 5591, 5592

Arriba, 8418, 12073
Arrow, 778
Arrow Cordials, 8032
Arrowhead Crunch, 6141
Arrowhead Mills, 6141
Arrowood, 780
Arrowroot, 1025, 9914
Arroyo Amber Ale, 3494
Arroyo Grande, 14190
Art Coco, 781
Art Fidos Cookies, 781
Art Topo, 781
Art's Tamales, 785
Arte De Dulce, 9171, 9172
Artel, 787
Artesian Spring, 13982
Artezin, 6501
Artho Life, 4527
Arti-Garlico, 5742
Artica, 3261
Artie Bucco, 15162
Artie Bucco Gourmet Foods, 15162
Artuso, 795, 796
Aruero, 4246
Asahi, 6030
Asante, 9966, 9967
Asbach Brandy, 14862
Asbach Uralt, 10205
Aseptilok, 5595
Asgrow, 9613
Ashby's, 13
Ashby's Iced Teas, 3050
Ashby's Teas of London, 3050
Asher, 477, 800
Asher's, 15347
Ashland, 805, 806
Ashman an Original Marinade, 809
Ashman Armbruster's, 809
Ashman Bodean's, 809
Ashman Boli's, 809
Ashman Boulevard Cafe, 809
Ashman Chili Peppers, 809
Ashman Coastal Cactus, 809
Ashman Deathwish, 809
Ashman Edwards Surry Sopping Sauce, 809
Ashman Four Corners, 809
Ashman Fuller's, 809
Ashman George's, 809
Ashman Hog Heaven Sooee Sauce, 809
Ashman Hog Wild Bbq Sauce, 809
Ashman Hot Wing Sauce, 809
Ashman House, 809
Ashman House London Broil Sauce, 809
Ashman Jimmy Sauce, 809
Ashman Joni's, 809
Ashman King Street Blues, 809
Ashman Little Red Raspberry Dijon, 809
Ashman London House, 809
Ashman Magnolia, 809
Ashman Mini Malbon's Bbq Sauce, 809
Ashman Nana's, 809
Ashman Old Hickory Grille & Dip, 809
Ashman Pass Out, 809
Ashman Pigman's, 809
Ashman Red Hot Rooster Sauce, 809
Ashman Rockland's Bbq Sauce, 809
Ashman St. Ann's Bay Jamaican Jerk, 809
Ashman Tailgate, 809
Ashman the Jewish Mother, 809
Ashman Tuscan Gardens Caponata, 809
Ashman Virginia Gentleman, 809
Ashman Whitey's, 809
Ashoka, 6951
Ashwagandha, 12525
Asiago, 15018
Asian Harvest, 11828
Asian Pride, 13999
Asian Sensations, 12888
Asian Star, 15422
Ask Foods, 116
Asp, 5265
Aspen Edge, 9603
Aspen Gold, 13111
Asperzyme, 4494
Aspi-Cor, 6344
Associates, 4157
Assoluti, 12265
Assumption Wines, 12182
Assurance, 10676
Astazanthin, 6343
Astor, 3855, 15656
Astra, 2230

Astral, 55
Astro, 844, 10964, 10966, 10967
Astro Pops, 13479
Atalanta, 846
Atco, 875
Athena's Brownies, 7600
Athena's Cookies, 7600
Athenian, 5937
Athenos, 7944, 7948, 7949, 7950
Athens, 850, 851
Atkins, 853, 854, 855
Atkins Advantage, 855
Atkins Bakery, 855
Atkins Endulge, 855, 4517
Atkins Kitchen, 855
Atkinson's, 858
Atlanta Bread, 859
Atlanta Burning, 861
Atlanta Dairies, 4709
Atlantic, 878, 8554
Atlantic Blueberry, 869
Atlantic Capes, 870
Atlantic Coast, 12418
Atlantic Meat, 876
Atlantic Meyers, 13224
Atlantic Organic, 2503
Atlantic Queen, 881
Atlantic Rose, 2503
Atlantic Seasonings, 886
Atlantic Veal, 888, 889
Atlas, 893, 15206
Atlas Peak, 892
Atomic Fireball, 4761
Attaboy, 11767
Attnetion Span, 6578
Atwater, 897, 898
Atwater Dried Fruits, 898
Au Printemps Gourmet, 902
Auburn, 904
Aubygum, 2382
Audisio & Lori, 7044
Audubon Cellars, 905
Audubon Collection, 905
Auer, 954
Augastiner Dark, 11390
Augastiner Larger, 11390
Augsberger, 10829
August Brothers, 5494
August's Fried, 906, 907
Augustiner, 11390
Ault-Pro, 911
Aunt Aggie De's Pralines, 912
Aunt Angies, 10961
Aunt Bea's, 913
Aunt Bertie's, 2433
Aunt Flo's Country Fudge, 12511
Aunt Gussie's Cookies & Crackers, 914
Aunt Hattie's, 4959, 4975, 6615
Aunt Hattie's Quality Breads, 6615
Aunt Jayne's, 995
Aunt Jemima, 923
Aunt Jemima Corn Meal, 11738
Aunt Jemima Syrups & Mixes, 11738
Aunt Jeminia, 11737
Aunt Jenny's, 9015
Aunt Kitty's, 6191
Aunt Lizzie's, 918
Aunt Millie, 15326
Aunt Millie's, 919
Aunt Nellie's, 13037, 13042, 13044
Aunt Patty's Natural Sweetners, 5650
Aunt Sally's Creamy Pralines, 920
Aunt Sally's Gourmet, 920
Aunt Sue, 13264, 13265
Aunt Vi's, 8956
Aurora Blanc, 1946
Aussie, 5399
Aussie Sauce, 5399
Austin, 7679, 7680, 7681
Austin Company, 11517
Austin Crackers, 7653
Austin®, 7674, 7685
Austinuts, 930
Austrian Crown, 15107
Authentico®, 1316
Author's Choice, 1719
Autin's, 934
Autocrat, 935
Autumn Ale, 1789
Autumn Fest, 4139
Autumn Harvest, 2768
Autumn Leaves, 4680

Basso, 5589
Basswood, 8222
Baste & Glaze, 12545
Batman, 14479
Battaglia, 23
Batter Blends, 10190
Batter-Moist, 4443
Battercrisp, 2382
Batters & Breaders, 5788
Battle Creek, 3337
Bau Maniere, 6009
Bauchant, 10895
Baum's Sweet Bologna, 3707
Baumer, 1197
Bauza Export, 5591
Bavarian, 7190
Bavarian Brand Sausage, 2324
Baxter, 12703, 12705, 12712
Baxters Old Nauvoo, 1203
Bay Beauty, 10508
Bay City, 14882
Bay Shore, 10134, 15215, 15800
Bay State, 4603
Bay State Chowda, 1701
Bayhawk Ipa, 1206
Bayhawk Stout, 1206
Bayou Land Seafood, 1224
Bayou Segnette, 8613
Bayside, 5211
Baywood, 12265
Baywood Cellars, 1227
Baywood Purechoice®, 1228
Baywood Solutions®, 1228
Bazooka, 14478
Bazooka Bursts Gum, 14479
Bazzini, 43
Bbq Pretzel Snack, 13904
Bbq Shack, 993
Bbq Unribs, 10378
Bbq'n Fools, 994
Bbs Bodacious, 995
Bc Rogers, 7883
Be, 634
Be Happy 'n Healthy Snacks, 6205
Bea's Best Corned Beef, 2903
Beach, 5137
Beach Blonde, 1206
Beach Cliff, 13738, 13739
Beachwood, 1234
Beacon Drive-In Iced Tea, 1235
Beakin, 701, 702
Beamons, 10449
Bean Brothers, 3475
Bean Coffee, 982
Bean Forge, 1240
Bean Heads, 12898
Beanos's, 3242
Bear Claw, 7724
Bear Country Bavarian, 13438
Bear Creek Brand, 1244
Bear Creek Country Kitchens, 1242, 13134
Bear Creek Pandhandler Pasta, 1243
Bear Creek Panhandler Brand, 1243
Bear Creek the Texas Two Step, 1243
Bear Flag, 15018
Bear Meadow Farm, 1246
Bear Mountain, 11694
Bear Mush, 6141
Bear Naked®, 7674
Bear Paks, 4680
Bear River, 1776
Beardsley, 4242
Bearitos, 15432
Beartooth Kitchens, 7810
Beat, 3021
Beatrice, 23, 10964, 10966, 10967
Beatrix Potter, 5126
Beattie Brothers, 2831
Beau Jacques, 106
Beaulieu Vineyard, 3956
Beaver, 1261
Beaver Falls, 6293
Beaver Meadow, 1258
Beaver Pop, 8289
Beazur, 2444
Becel, 14838, 14839
Bech, 7232
Beck Cafe, 1263
Beck Farms, 1262
Beck Flavors, 1263
Beck Gourmet, 1262
Beck's, 763

Beck's Dark, 763
Beck's For Oktoberfest, 763
Beckman's, 1267
Beckmann, 13617
Becks Ice Cream, 1264
Becky Kay, 9859
Bed Lies, 8105
Bed Wiser, 8105
Beddy By, 1707
Bedell Cellars, 1271
Bee Gee, 7268
Bee My Honey, 7750
Bee Propolis, 2061
Bee Sting, 5896
Bee Supreme, 3775
Bee Sweet, 11649
Beech-Nut Baby Food, 9482
Beef International, 4648
Beef Master, 3563
Beef Naturalite, 9099
Beef Not, 4033
Beefeater, 6585, 6586
Beefeater Dry, 3320
Beefmate, 3755
Beefsteak, 7095, 7105
Beehive, 1829, 15391
Beehive Botanicals, 1280
Beer Buttered King Rings, 9150
Beer Nuts, 1281
Beer-King, 10694
Beesting, 6152
Beetroot Delights, 1282
Beik's Esb, 607
Beirmeister, 6808
Beit Hashita, 2239
Bekal, 5383
Bekaplus®, 1002
Beko®, 1328
Bel Arbor® Wines, 1897
Bel Normande - Spritzers, 4542
Bel-Air, 8652
Bel-Capri, 8576
Belcolade, 1286
Belcover, 10981
Belgian Ale, 1507
Belgioioso, 1285
Bell, 13650
Bell & Evans the Excellent Chicken, 1289
Bell 'orto, 4513
Bell Bialy, 1032
Bell Cellars, 11731
Bell Mini Bagel, 1032
Bell' Agio, 1104
Bell's Amber Ale, 7590
Bell's Best Brown Ale, 7590
Bell's Kalamazoo Stout, 7590
Bell's Oberon Ale, 7590
Bell's Pale Ale, 7590
Bell's Porter, 7590
Bell's Scotch, 14862
Bella, 11285
Bella Crema, 3050, 8517
Bella Festa, 4549
Bella Frutta, 10799
Bella Good, 14565
Bella Italia, 254
Bella Mercato, 4407
Bella Ravioli, 1303
Bella Rosa, 4513
Bella Rossa, 6399
Bella Sera®, 4226
Bella Sun Luci, 9677
Bella Vista, 1304
Bellafoglia, 10836
Bellati Soy-A-Nuts, 1307
Bellatti Soybeans, 1307
Belle Gueule, 8380
Belle Mead, 6207
Belle of Piru, 4803
Belle River, 1309
Belle-Vue Kriek, 8105
Belleisle, 1312
Bellerose, 1313
Belleweather, 4777
Bellwether, 1318
Belmo, 13259
Belmont Goat Cheese, 13397
Belmont Spring Disti, 13982
Belmont Spring Water, 13982
Belmont Springs, 3520
Belmont Springs®, 3627, 6579
Belvedere, 1324, 3320, 9587

Ben, 2276
Ben & Jerry, 5734
Ben & Jerry's, 1326, 1393, 14834, 14836
Ben & Jerry's Frozen Smoothies, 1326
Ben & Jerry's Ice Cream, 1326
Ben's, 2272
Benbow's, 1332
Bencheley, 4831
Benco Peak, 14600, 14601
Benco-Peak, 14599
Beneflex, 8332
Benevento, 3247
Benihana, 15838
Benley's Irish Creme, 3134
Bennett's, 1213, 1336
Bennetts, 13066
Benriach, 11221
Bensdorp, 1162
Benson's, 1339
Benson's Old Home Kitchens, 1339
Bensons, 11306
Bent's, 5313
Benzel's Brand, 1343
Ber Boreale, 8379
Berardi's, 1346
Berardi's Bodum, 1346
Berardi's Bunn, 1346
Berardi's Effie Mari, 1346
Berardi's Estate Col, 1346
Berardi's Estate-Dir, 1346
Berardi's Harvest Te, 1346
Berardi's Jet Tea Fr, 1346
Berardi's Joe To Go, 1346
Berardi's Melitta, 1346
Berardi's Miniminits, 1346
Berardi's Monin, 1346
Berardi's Nissan, 1346
Berardi's Oregon Cha, 1346
Berardi's Senza, 1346
Berardi's Technibrew, 1346
Berardi's Toddy, 1346
Berardi's Vita-Mix, 1346
Berentzen, 15577
Bergeron, 7264
Berghoff Family, 9770
Berk-Cap, 1359
Berkeley Farms, 3827
Berkley & Jensen, 6876
Berkshire Ale, 1357
Berkshire Ice Cream, 1360
Bermuda Dunes, 3954
Bernadette's Biscotti, 1363
Bernadette's Biscotti Soave, 1363
Bernadette's Cookies, 1363
Bernard, 1365
Bernard Fine Foods, 3818
Bernard Pradel Cabernet, 5782
Bernardi, 15632
Bernardo, 1368
Bernardus, 1369
Berne Baby Swiss, 14101
Berne Swiss Lace, 14101
Bernea Farms, 6851
Bernhardt Peck, 2378
Bernstein's, 1489, 1490
Berry Cool, 8777
Berry Good, 10078
Berry Hill, 7354
Berry Weiss, 8333
Berry White, 7491
Berrylicious, 6995
Bert Grant's, 15789
Bertani, 10895
Bertha's, 4777
Berthelet, 11659
Bertman Raddish Sauce, 7496
Bertolini, 1815
Bertolino, 1815, 1816
Bertolli, 1393, 14834, 14835, 14837, 14839
Berzi, 352
Bes Tex, 13482
Bessie, 1495
Best 501, 1382
Best Brown Ale, 11720
Best Buy, 7761
Best Choice, 5399, 6254
Best Foods, 14836
Best Maid, 3693
Best O' the Wheat, 12257
Best of Brock, 4680
Best of Health, 459
Best of Luck, 6824

Best of Luck Horseshoe Chocolates, 6824
Best Way, 4201, 14857
Best's Kosher, 1387, 12756
Bestovall, 1054
Besure, 6803, 15255
Beta Stab, 7446
Beta-Care, 1365
Beth's, 1396
Beth's Baking Basics, 1396
Bethune, 7987
Betolli, 14836
Bette's Oceanview Diner, 1400
Better, 8792
Better 'n Eggs, 9350
Better 'n Ever, 14944
Better Baked Foods, 1402
Better Buy, 10290
Better Kids, 4517
Better Made, 3483
Better Than Milk, 8418
Better Way, 15362
Bettercreme, 12093
Bettercreme Frosting & Filling, 12095
Betterway Pourers, 2087
Betty, 7491
Betty Ann, 9661
Betty Baker, 10997
Betty Clark's Confections, 2220
Betty Crocker, 5461, 13195
Betty Crocker Pop Secret, 3675
Betty Crocker Pop Secret Popcorn, 8203
Betty Lou's, 1408
Betty Twist & Match Chocolate Candy, 12322
Betty's, 14969
Between Friends Promotional Candy, 5389
Betzios, 3272
Beverly, 4981
Beverly Hills, 7141
Beverly Hills Collection, 5554
Beverly Hills Confection Line, 3226
Beverly International, 1415
Bevgrad, 11396
Bevnet, 1411
Beyond, 12265
Bff, 3817
Bhutanese Red Rice, 8583
Bi-Lo, 3352
Bi-Pro, 3774
Bialy, 7922
Bianchi Vineyards, 1418
Biazzo Brand, 1420
Bib Ulmer Spatz, 1051
Bibo, 9516
Bick's, 1421
Bick's (Canada), 7229
Bickel, 12060
Bickel's, 1422, 1423, 6191
Bickford, 1426
Bickle Snacks, 1424
Biermann, 9847
Biery, 1432
Bifido Factor, 10004
Bifido Nate, 10004
Big B, 1436
Big Baby, 11840
Big Banana, 8749
Big Bear, 10829
Big Beer Series, 13322
Big Blue, 22
Big Bol, 11840
Big Boy, 388
Big Bruce's Gunpowder Chili, 9423
Big Bunny Pop, 358
Big Cajun, 5094
Big Check, 10388
Big Chief, 1438, 2153, 9374
Big Chunks Salsa, 5034
Big City Reds, 1439
Big Drinks, 14623
Big Ed Super Saucer, 9082
Big Fat Toad Pop, 358
Big G Cereals, 5461
Big Heart Pop, 358
Big Horn Premium, 2847
Big House Ale, 15139
Big Hunk, 645
Big John, 12518
Big Juicy, 3640
Big Kahuna, 1876
Big League Chew, 586, 9010, 15765
Big Lips Pop, 358

Big M, 9839
Big Mama, 3175
Big Mama Sausage, 3189
Big Mouth, 14479
Big Onion, 344
Big Papa, 7177
Big Pumpkin Pop, 358
Big Ram, 6014
Big Red, 5886, 15455, 15765, 15766
Big Scoop, 9682
Big Shot, 9966, 9967
Big Skull Pop, 358
Big Sky, 7459
Big Sky Ipa, 1448
Big Smiley, 12322
Big T Burgers, 5461
Big Tex, 4952
Big Time, 2335
Big Top Animal Cookies, 10575
Big Top Fantasy, 11132
Big V, 7223
Big Valley, 7279
Big Value, 10401
Big Y, 624
Big Yummy, 3227
Bigelow, 1452
Bigelow Afternoon Assorted Herb Tea, 11815
Bigelow Apple & Cinnamon Herb Tea, 11815
Bigelow Assorted Bigelow Teas, 11815
Bigelow Assorted Decaf Teas, 11815
Bigelow Assorted Herb Tea, 11815
Bigelow Assorted Sterling Silver, 11815
Bigelow Black Currant, 11815
Bigelow Borpatra Full Leaf Tea, 11815
Bigelow Chamomile Lemon Herb Tea, 11815
Bigelow Chamomile Mango Herb Tea, 11815
Bigelow Chamomile Mint Herb Tea, 11815
Bigelow Cherry Vanilla Tea, 11815
Bigelow Chinese Fortune, 11815
Bigelow Cinnamon Apple Herb Tea, 11815
Bigelow Cinnamon Spice Herb Tea, 11815
Bigelow Cinnamon Stick, 11815
Bigelow Cinnamon Stick Decaf, 11815
Bigelow Constant Comment, 11815
Bigelow Constant Comment Decaf, 11815
Bigelow Constant Comment Loose Tea, 11815
Bigelow Cozy Chamomile Herb Tea, 11815
Bigelow Cranberry Apple Herb Tea, 11815
Bigelow Darjeeling Blend, 11815
Bigelow Darjeeling Loose Tea, 11815
Bigelow Dragonwell Full Leaf Tea, 11815
Bigelow Earl Grey, 11815
Bigelow Earl Grey Loose Tea, 11815
Bigelow Early Grey Decaf, 11815
Bigelow Early Grey Green Tea, 11815
Bigelow English Breakfast, 11815
Bigelow English Breakfast Loose Tea, 11815
Bigelow English Teatime, 11815
Bigelow English Teatime Decaf, 11815
Bigelow French Vanilla, 11815
Bigelow Fruit Almond Herb Tea, 11815
Bigelow Green Genmaicha Full Leaf, 11815
Bigelow Green Loose Tea, 11815
Bigelow Green Tea With Lemon, 11815
Bigelow Green Tea With Mango, 11815
Bigelow Green Tea With Mint, 11815
Bigelow Green Tea With Peach, 11815
Bigelow i Love Lemon & C Herb Tea, 11815
Bigelow Jasmine Flowers Full Leaf, 11815
Bigelow Jasmine Loose Tea, 11815
Bigelow Keemun Black Full Leaf, 11815
Bigelow Kenilworth Full Leaf Tea, 11815
Bigelow Lemon Lift, 11815
Bigelow Lemon Lift Decaf, 11815
Bigelow Mint Medley Herb Tea, 11815
Bigelow Orange & Spice Herb Tea, 11815
Bigelow Pai Mu Tan Full Leaf Tea, 11815
Bigelow Peppermint Herb Loose Tea, 11815
Bigelow Peppermint Herb Tea, 11815
Bigelow Perfect Peach Herb Tea, 11815
Bigelow Plantation Mint, 11815
Bigelow Plantation Mint Decaf, 11815
Bigelow Raspberry Royale, 11815
Bigelow Raspberry Royale Decaf, 11815
Bigelow Red Raspberry Herb Loose, 11815

Bigelow Red Reaspberry Herb Tea, 11815
Bigelow Risheehat Full Leaf Tea, 11815
Bigelow Se Chung Full Leaf Tea, 11815
Bigelow Six Assorted Green Teas, 11815
Bigelow Sweet Dreams Herb Tea, 11815
Bigelow Vanilla Almond Tea, 11815
Bigelow Vanilla Caramel Tea, 11815
Bigelow Vanilla Hazelnut Tea, 11815
Bigelow Wild Cherry Herb Loose Tea, 11815
Bigger Better, 6231
Biggies, 1113
Biladi, 4008
Biladi Tohina, 4008
Bilberry Extract, 12822
Bill Mack's, 1458
Billies, 12244
Billingsgate, 1461
Billy Bock, 1939
Bilopage, 2624
Bimbo, 1465, 1466, 1467, 9322, 9803, 12717, 12720, 12746, 12760
Binasol, 14243
Bingham Hill Cheeses, 12243
Binkert's, 1469
Bio G-3000, 5986
Bio K, 1474
Bio Tab, 14956
Bio-Familia, 7081
Bio-Foods, 1472
Bio-Genics, 10410
Bio-Nate, 10004
Bio-Tech Pharmacal, 1476
Bioallers, 1709
Bioastin, 10415
Bioastin Natural Astaxanthin, 3586
Biobest, 844
Biochem, 3384
Bioflora, 15187
Biogarde, 2382
Biomega, 895
Bionova, 6092
Bionutrient, 706
Biopur, 11691
Biotin Forte, 7013
Biotta Juices, 11934
Birch Bark, 2253
Birch Logs, 2253
Bird's Eye, 1490, 10678
Bird's Eye Voila, 1490
Bird's Hill, 15454
Bird-In-Hand, 1487
Birdie Pak, 1488
Birds Eye, 1489
Birds Eye C&W, 1489
Birds Eye Freshlike, 1489
Birds Eye Steamfresh, 1489
Birdseye, 1492
Bireleys, 15164
Birell, 2633
Biringer's Farm Fresh, 12989, 12990
Birkholm's Jr. Danish, 1496
Birthday Control Pills Candy, 9025
Bis Train, 3033
Bisca, 7081, 7695
Biscotti Di Lasca, 10086
Biscotti Di Roma, 954
Biscotti Di Suzy™, 3504
Biscotti Thins, 530
Biscotti Toscani, 8086
Bishop, 9859
Bison, 8454, 14904, 14905
Bisquick, 5461
Bissett's, 1508
Bisto, 2261
Bistro, 5211, 12759, 15105, 15106, 15108
Bistro '28, 10731
Bistro Faire, 3531
Bistrone, 3021
Bisurkey, 8454
Bit-O-Honey, 10102, 10108
Bitburger, 1320
Bite-Size, 12690
Bite-Size Bakery, 12689
Bits, 9171, 9172
Bits O Honey, 2790
Bits O' Butter, 14044
Bits'n'pops, 589
Bits'o Barley, 6141
Bitter Guard, 1974
Bitterroot Extra Special Bitter, 4880
Bittner's, 8931

Bitzels, 8434
Bj Beer, 2755
Black, 5914
Black & Gold, 2102
Black & Tan, 1320
Black & White, 14862
Black & White Brand, 13861
Black & White Mug, 13061
Black and Tan, 4602
Black Angus Reserve, 513
Black Bear Ale, 1241
Black Bear Stout, 3494
Black Bush, 11221
Black Butte, 3928
Black Canyon® Angus Beef, 9965
Black Canyon® Premium Reserve, 9965
Black Cat, 7987
Black Cherry Royal, 5954
Black Cloud Stout, 3494
Black Cod (Sablefish, 12391
Black Creek Classic, 441
Black Diamond, 1515, 10966, 10967
Black Diamond Cheestrings Ficello, 10967
Black Forest, 3271, 4602
Black Hawk, 9269
Black Hook, 11991
Black Ice, 9603
Black Jacks, 15807
Black Jewell, 1519
Black Jewell®, 1520
Black Knight, 15391
Black Licorice Vines, 528
Black Mesa, 1521
Black Mountain Gold, 1522
Black Pearls, 9869
Black Prince, 1523
Black Ranch Gourmet Grains, 1524
Black River, 15671
Black Rock Porter, 14612
Black Swamp, 6008
Black Swan®, 4226
Black Tea Chai, 12789
Black Tie, 2253
Black Velvet, 1169
Black Watch, 8848
Black Widow, 14409
Black Wolf Blend, 6467
Blackbird Porter, 4880
Blackburn's, 8547, 14143
Blackened Redfish Magic, 8807
Blackened Steak Magic, 8807
Blackening Spice, 2700
Blackhawk Stout, 9269
Blackjack Pasture Cabernet, 5366
Blackjack Porter, 14164
Blanc De Noirs, 4063
Blanc Du Bois, 9665
Blanca, 9489
Blanchard & Blanchard, 7081
Bland Farms, 5722
Blanton's, 1539
Blaser's, 1541
Blasters, 586
Blasting Powder, 3227
Blatin Redfish, 4864
Blazer, 5622
Blazing Star, 202
Blazzin, 1544
Blend Pak, 1545
Blended Breaders, 10190
Blenheim, 1548
Blessing's Mustard, 5034
Bletsoe's Cheese, 1550
Bleu Rock Vineyard Wines, 10503
Bleue Dry, 8102
Bleue Legere, 8102
Bliss Bar, 5816
Blitz Power Mints, 12829, 12885
Blonde Ale, 14990
Blood Building Broth, 150
Blood Building Powder, 150
Blood Cleanse, 6343
Blood Red, 4139
Bloody Mary Blend, 14908
Bloody Mary Juice Burst, 6079
Bloombuilder, 4790
Bloomfield Farms, 1545
Bloomington Brewing, 1558
Bloop, 11216
Bloops, 8191
Blossom, 7806
Blossom Hill, 4204

Blossom Time, 14416
Blouin, 11658
Blount, 1561
Blow Hard Mustard, 6796
Blow Pop, 14470
Blubotol, 15468
Blue Band, 14839
Blue Barn, 803
Blue Bell, 1562, 15454
Blue Berry, 8842
Blue Bird, 1598, 4958, 4959, 4975
Blue Bird Toffe, 6568
Blue Bonnet, 3169, 3175, 3189
Blue Bottle, 15468
Blue Boy, 7058, 13037, 13042
Blue Buck, 8778
Blue Bunny®, 15393
Blue Chelan, 14648
Blue Chip Baker, 1564
Blue Chip Group, 1564
Blue Crab Bay, 1565
Blue Diamond, 1567, 13830, 14553, 14554, 14555, 14556, 14557, 14558, 14559, 14560, 14561, 14562, 14563, 14564, 14565, 14566, 14567
Blue Diamond Almonds, 1567
Blue Diamond Hazelnut, 1567
Blue Diamond Macadamias, 1567
Blue Fin, 13161
Blue Fish, 10895
Blue Flag, 10062
Blue Gold, 1569
Blue Heron, 9269
Blue Heron Pale Ale, 9269
Blue Hill Bay, 172
Blue Jay Orchards, 1573
Blue Light, 8105
Blue Monday, 12442
Blue Monday Candybar, 12442
Blue Moon, 9603, 15355
Blue Moon Belgian White, 9463
Blue Moon Tea, 1576
Blue Moon™, 3313
Blue Paddle Pilsener, 10122
Blue Parrot Aussie-Style Tea, 3036
Blue Pearl Incense, 8582
Blue Plate, 12025, 13456
Blue Plate Mayonnaise, 12026, 15572
Blue Plumb Brandy, 2939
Blue Raspberry, 4680
Blue Razz, 14470
Blue Ribbon, 879, 1584, 3133, 4424, 8161, 9743, 12852, 13338, 13521, 14943
Blue Ribbon Cakes, 7101
Blue Ribbon Golden, 3133
Blue Ribbon Hot Sausage, 14132
Blue Ridge, 5147
Blue Ridge Farms, 1586, 2794, 4648
Blue Ridge Teas, 1589
Blue Runner, 1590
Blue Seal, 2765
Blue Sky, 1591
Blue Sky Artesian Water, 1591
Blue Sky Natural Soda, 1591
Blue Star, 8102
Blue Star Farms, 10976
Blue Star Mockiko, 7887
Blue Water, 5788
Blue Willow, 1594
Blueberry Ale, 9286
Blueberry Almond Museli, 10050
Blueberry Barbeque Sauce, 10282
Blueberry Blossom, 8222
Blueberry Hill, 1596
Blueberry King, 1283
Bluebird, 4952, 5128
Bluebird Restaurant, 1600
Bluebonnet, 14867
Bluebonnet Coffee, 14866
Bluegrass, 6008
Blumer's Root Beer, 9770
Blythedale, 14172
Boar's Head, 1611
Boardwalk, 2335
Boat Brand, 13520
Bob Evans, 1614
Bob Evans Restaurants, 1614
Bob Evans®, 1613
Bob Evans® Restaurant, 1613
Bob's Red Mill, 1623
Bob's Texas Style, 11483
Bobbie, 13374

Grove on the Go, 5346
Grove Street, 1324
Grove Sweet, 2893
Grove, Jr, 5346
Grow-Pac, 6013
Grower's Pack, 6322
Grower's Red, 1946
Growers Blush, 1946
Growers Company, 9466
Growers Fancy Juice Concentrates, 8341
Growers Pride, 5264
Growers White, 1946
Growler, 1320
Grown Free, 11876
Grs, 18
Gruet Winery, 6017
Gsi, 218
Guacamole Salad, 13477
Guarana Plus, 8111
Guardmax, 11217
Guasti Altar Wines, 7498
Guatamalan Antigua, 3301
Guenoc, 8229
Guerrero, 9532, 9538
Guest Chef, 6953
Guflielmo Reserve, 4451
Guggisberg, 6023
Guglielmo, 4451
Guglielmo Vineyard Selection, 4451
Gugulidid, 12525
Guida, 13969
Guida's, 6024
Guido & Sals Old Chicago, 1240
Guido's Serious, 6025
Guidparg Chocolates, 3033
Guilt Free, 15803
Guiltless Gourmet, 6028, 6029, 9015,
    11828, 13521
Guinness, 3956
Guinness Stout, 6030
Guittard, 2806, 3317
Gulden's, 3192, 3194, 7064
Guldener Dutch Sugar Beet Vinegar, 3535
Guldener Fine Ground Mustard, 3535
Guldener Spiced Sugar Beet Vinegar, 3535
Guldener Sweet Coarse Mustard, 3535
Guldener Whole Grain Mustard, 3535
Gulf, 3797, 14879
Gulf Belle, 10723
Gulf Breeze, 1379
Gulf Central, 6033
Gulf City, 6035
Gulf Crown, 6036
Gulf Garden, 9103
Gulf Harvest, 3187
Gulf Kist, 13456
Gulf Pride, 6045
Gulf Star, 6033
Gulf Stream, 7788
Gulf-Maid, 115
Gulfstar, 15363
Gulfview, 15363
Gum Dinger, 4680
Gum Time, 11840
Gummi Alien Invaders, 903
Gummy Guard, 1390
Gummy Guy, 14617
Gummy Squirms, 4680
Gummy Watch, 1390
Gumpert's, 6051
Gun Powder Pearl Pinhead Green Tea, 5825
Gurley, 3244
Gurley Golden Recipe, 3244
Gurley's, 15602
Gurley's Candy, 6057
Gurley's Golden Recipe Nuts, 6057
Gurley's Natures Harvest, 6057
Gusano, 9010
Gusano Grande, 3247
Gusano Lucas, 8649
Gusparo, 11931
Gustafson's, 2537
Gusto Italia, 14452
Guy's, 6061
Guy's Tea, 4461
Guylian, 6062, 7422
Gw, 15450
Gwaltney, 3101, 6063, 6064
Gwaltney of Smithfield, 6065, 13308
Gx Power, 11631
Gyma, 5355
Gyros Usa, 3323

H

H&C, 10975
H&G Chum, 13199
H&H Bagels, 6076
H&K Packers, 6080
H&S Bread Crumbs, 6084
H-O, 5334
H.C. Smoked Sausage, 14132
H2o, 6226
H2o To Go, 13571
H3o, 6110
Haagen Dazs, 5734
Haagen-Dazs, 5461
Haagen-Dazs Ice Cream, 10102
Haake Beck Non-Alcoholic, 763
Habanero Products From Hell, 13468
Habero, 8063
Habersham Estates, 6124
Habitant, 1421, 2261, 4236
Hacienda, 1853, 6127
Haco, 14092
Haddar, 4506
Hadley Date Gardens, 6128
Hafner, 6130
Hagensborg Meltaways Truffles, 6132
Hagerty Foods, 6133
Haggen, 3736, 15428
Hahg, 11295
Hahn's, 5132, 12284
Haig, 14862
Haight Vineyard Wines, 6138
Haiku Teas, 5897
Hain, 6140
Hain Kidz, 4010
Hain Pure, 14553
Hain Pure Foods, 14554, 14555, 14556,
    14557, 14558, 14559, 14560, 14561,
    14562, 14563, 14564, 14565, 14566,
    14567
Hains Celestial, 6141
Hale's Celebration Porter, 6151
Hale's Pale American Ale, 6151
Hale's Special Bitter, 6151
Hall's, 3538
Hallcrest Vineyards, 6159
Hallmark, 6161
Halls, 2107
Ham Nik, 846
Ham Sausage, 2324
Hambrecht Vineyards, 1324
Hamburger Helper, 5461
Hamish & Enzo, 12394
Hamm's, 9442, 9462, 9463
Hamm's Draft, 9442
Hamm's Golden Draft, 9462
Hamm's Special Light, 9442, 9462
Hammond's, 6172
Hammons, 6175
Hampshire Laboratories, 15177
Hamptom Farms, 6179
Hampton House, 6180
Hana-Nori, 154
Hand Made Ball Pop, 358
Handi Snacks, 7937
Handi-Sancks, 7948
Handi-Snacks, 7939, 7944, 7949, 7950
Handi-Tap, 9763
Handy, 7460
Handy Pak, 9146
Handy Snacks, 7930
Hanes, 12752
Hangzhou Sanhe, 6187
Hanna's, 6190
Hannah, 4242
Hannah & Hogg, 3247
Hannah's Delishts, 4406
Hannegan Seafoods, 492
Hanover, 6191, 14913
Hanover Farms, 6191
Hans' All Natural, 11106
Hansen, 6197, 6198
Hansen Apple Juice, 6196
Hansen Fruit Juice B, 6196
Hansen Lemonades, 6196
Hansen Smoothies, 6196
Hansen Sodas, 6196
Hansen Spring Water, 6196
Hansen Tea, 6196
Hansen's Healthy Ant, 6196
Hansen's Healthy Imm, 6196
Hansen's Healthy Int, 6196

Hansen's Healthy Vit, 6196
Hansen-Norge, 6197
Haolam, 15732
Happy Cup Tea, 14268
Happy Day Pops, 6412
Happy Heart Lollipops, 6915
Happy Herberts, 6208
Happy Hive, 6209
Happy Home, 5840, 12652, 13442
Happy Indulgence, 6205
Happy Indulgence Deladent Dips, 6205
Happy Trails Meat Snack Sticks, 14528
Happy Trails T-Shirts, 3110
Happydent, 11216
Harbar's, 6212
Harbor, 6220
Harbor Lighthouse Ale, 1111
Harbor Lights, 1946
Harbor Point, 814
Harbor View, 13648
Harborside, 14342
Harbour Gold, 14527
Hard-E Foods, 6221
Hardcore, 1700
Hardfast, 14895
Hardin, 9995
Hargita, 5680
Hargrave Vineyards, 2491
Hari Om Farms, 6226
Haribo, 1649, 6227
Harida, 10049
Harlan Bakeries, 6231
Harlin Fruit, 6233
Harmon's Gourmet, 2220
Harmony, 5204
Harmony Bay, 3134
Harmony Cellars, 6237
Harmony Farms, 8418
Harmony Snacks, 6238
Harney & Sons, 6241
Harold Food Co., 6243
Harp, 3956
Harp Lager, 6030
Harper Seafood, 6246
Harpoon, 6251
Harrell Nut, 6252
Harrgate, 4542
Harris, 10723
Harris Farms, 6255
Harris Fresh, 6255
Harris Ranch, 6255, 6258
Harrisburg Dairies, 6259
Harrison, 6260
Harrison Golden Goodness, 6261
Harry & David, 6262
Harry London Chocolates, 6264
Harry Ramsden's, 3151
Harry's Choice, 4029
Hart, 11720
Hart Winery, 6266
Hartford, 6269
Hartford Court, 6269
Hartley's, 6271
Hartness Choice, 12668
Hartwell Cabernet, 13387
Harvard, 536
Harvest, 8540, 10557
Harvest Ale British Esb, 4139
Harvest Bakery, 6280
Harvest Bar, 10282
Harvest Delight, 3776
Harvest Delighta, 3696
Harvest Farm, 12955
Harvest Foods, 6283
Harvest Fresh, 9044
Harvest Haven, 4581
Harvest Hearst, 4106
Harvest Moon, 7948
Harvest of the Sea, 10683
Harvest Pasta, 5286
Harvest Road, 11597
Harvest Select, 10793
Harvest Selects, 13731
Harvest Supreme™, 7241
Harvest-Pac, 6288
Hash Browns, 10684
Hat Creek, 9946
Hatfield, 2395, 6293
Hatties, 6413
Hatuey Beers, 1016
Haudecoeur, 4545
Haug, 6295

Haus Barhyte Mustard, 6296
Havana Cappucino, 10281
Haviland, 9900, 10131
Havoc Maker, 6303
Havren, 7335
Hawaii, 4912
Hawaii Coffee Company, 6307
Hawaii Gourmet, 265
Hawaii's Famous Huli Huli, 10858
Hawaiian Delight, 6316
Hawaiian Festives, 8417
Hawaiian Gold, 9090, 9091, 15226
Hawaiian Happy, 7699
Hawaiian Hula Dressing, 7644
Hawaiian Island Crisp, 6305
Hawaiian Island Crisp Cookies, 6305
Hawaiian Joys, 6316
Hawaiian King, 6316
Hawaiian Majesty, 6316
Hawaiian Natural Water, 6317
Hawaiian Princess Smoke, 7135
Hawaiian Punch, 2107, 2277, 4124, 4130,
    9752
Hawaiian Sun, 6320, 11454
Hawk, 11767
Hawkeye, 11767
Hawkhaven, 6322
Hawthorne Valley Farm, 6324
Haystack, 14164
Haystack Black, 11512
Hazel Creek, 6330
Hazel's, 9841
Hazelnut, 11631
Hazelwood Farms Bakeries, 11346
Hazle, 6334
Hazlitt, 6335
Hb Batters, 6845
Hb Breadings, 6845
Hb Pastis, 3464
Head & Shoulders, 11644
Head Country, 6337
Head of the Class, 15373
Health Assure, 5344
Health Best, 5357
Health Concerns, 6341
Health Cookie, 7313
Health Creation Caramel Pretzels, 9104
Health Creation Onion Pretzels, 9104
Health Enhancers, 6342
Health Is Wealth, 6347
Health O Meter, 13894
Health Valley, 4010, 5357, 6140, 6345
Health-Fu'd, 14044
Healthbest, 6349
Healthbody, 11638
Healthcare Naturals, 10047
Healthnut, 1126
Healthseed, 5169
Healthy Bites, 13329
Healthy Choice, 3189, 3194
Healthy Deli, 6195
Healthy Hemp, 5169
Healthy Home, 5494
Healthy Indulgence, 13446
Healthy Juice, 10908
Healthy Morn, 10921
Healthy Oven, 6354
Healthy Request Ready To Serve Soup, 2261
Healthy 'n Fit Nutritionals, 6356
Hearn & Rawlins, 14771
Heart Cleanse, 6343
Heart Liteo, 11403
Heart of Carolina, 1141
Heart of Rye, 2357
Heart of Wisconsin, 9436
Heart-Loc, 13521
Heartex, 6369
Hearth, 15536
Hearth & Kettle, 7802
Hearth Club, 12421
Hearth Land, 12265
Heartland, 812, 6360
Heartland Chocolates, 6264
Heartland Farms, 6365
Heartland Gourmet, 6365
Heartland Mill, 6367
Heartland U.S.A., 11594
Heartland®, 9199
Heartpro, 6369
Hearts, 14947
Heartstar, 6369
Hearttline, 218

Brand Name Index

Intense Milks, 14904
Inter Ocean, 9103
Interial Stout, 14164
Internation Seafood of Alaska, 7074
International Brownie, 7032
International Choice, 846
International Collection, 8418
Interstate Brands, 7088
Interstate Seafoods, 14596
Introvigne's, 624
Invermere, 11747
Invertec, 12487
Invertose Hfcs, 3329
Ioma, 15288
Iowa Quality, 7451
Iowa Quality Meats, 7112
Iowa State, 1760
Ipa, 5781
Ipax India Pale Ale, 14612
Ipswich Ale, 9286
Iqf Apple Orchard, 10330
Iqf Apple Slice, 10330
Iqf Sweet Cherry, 10330
Iqf Tart Cherry, 10330
Irilla Extra Virgin O.O., 12568
Irish Breakfast Decaff., 14734
Irish Mist, 6585, 6586
Irish Stout, 10852
Iromin, 9540
Iron City, 11390
Iron Horse, 7120, 10873
Iron Kettle, 7064
Iron Uke, 15391
Iron-Tek, 3384
Ironkids, 9322, 12720, 12726, 12727,
   12728, 12729, 12731, 12732, 12733,
   12734, 12736, 12738, 12739, 12740,
   12743, 12745
Ironman Triathlon, 14736
Isabella's, 7127
Isabella's Extraordinary Muffins, 8830
Isabo Hearts of Palm, 5066
Isadora, 7600
Isahop, 7446
Island Blend, 10362
Island Fruit, 8374
Island Girl Brand, 1825
Island Mist Iced Tea, 1738, 14274
Island Princess, 7135, 10681
Island Spring, 7140
Island Sweetwater, 7141
Island Teriyaki, 13473
Island Trader, 8820
Island Valley, 3189
Islander, 3265, 4157
Islander's Choice, 4777
Isle De Francis, 1666
Isle of Jura, 6371
Isle of Palms Salad Dressings, 2389
Iso-Sport, 283
Isolation Ale, 10543
Isolone, 7596
Isomalt, 1334
Isomil, 12329
Isopure, 10041
Isosweet, 14243
Isotonic, 6131, 13982
Issimo Celebrations!, 7144
Issimo's Creme Br-L,, 7144
It's A, 3352
It's a Boy, 2834
It's a Girl, 2834
It's a Wrap, 6212
It's It, 7145
It's Pizza Anytime, 7950
It's Soy Delicious, 14714
It's the Veal Thing, 9633
Ital Gelati, 3441
Italia, 7147, 15068
Italia D'Oro, 14274
Italia D'Oro Coffee, 1738
Italian Bread Products, 7275
Italian Chef, 10997, 11000
Italian Gelato Novelties, 3441
Italian Kitchen, 13640
Italian Rose, 7157
Italian Village FoodsÖ, 6535
Itchy Witchy, 12449
Ititropicals, 7077
Itoen, 7163
Itty-Bittie Biscotti, 14903
Itty-Bittie Cookies, 14903

Ivan the Terrible, 12438
Ivanhoe, 7166
Ivanhoe Classics, 7166
Ivanhoe Fresh, 7166
Ives, 1946
Iveta Gourmet, 7168
Ivory Almond K'Nuckle, 12425
Ixima, 7600

J

J & J, 4436, 5549
J Bar B Foods, 7184
J Moreau Fils, 1652
J Nicole Vineyard Pinot Noir, 7181
J Russian River Vall, 7181
J Sparkling Wine, 7181
J&B, 3956
J&J Gourmet, 7327
J&M, 7197
J. Berrie Brown Wine Nuts, 5034
J. Crow's, 7204
J. Filippi, 7206
J. Schram, 12870
J.C. Rivers Gourmet Jerky, 5626
J.F. Braun, 7267
J.J. Nissen, 7083, 7092, 7094
J.M. Schneider, 13348
J.P. Vinhos, 201
J.S. McMillan, 7247
J.S. McMillan Fisheries, 7248
J.T.M. Food Group, 7282
J.W. Allen, 12091
Jack Daniel's, 4831, 6392, 6393, 7287
Jack Daniel's Sauces, 6399
Jack Daniel's® Country Cocktail, 1897
Jack Daniel's® Single Barrel, 1897
Jack Daniel's® Tn Whisky, 1897
Jack Daniels, 11807
Jack Frost, 12003
Jack Link's, 8461
Jack Link's Beef Jerky, 7288
Jack Mackerel, 2763
Jack Man, 14164
Jack Miller, 7289
Jack Rabbit, 14599, 14600, 14601
Jack's, 7944, 7949, 7955, 9859, 10102,
   10107
Jack's All American, 11500
Jack's Pizza, 7937, 7939, 7950, 7951
Jackaroo, 10033
Jackpot, 6014, 9343
Jackson's, 9859
Jackson-Triggs, 15136
Jacob Best, 10829
Jacob's Creek, 11221, 11222
Jacobs, 7939
Jacobs and Maxwell House, 7953
Jacobs House Coffees, 7952
Jacobsen's Toast, 8517
Jacquelynn Cuv'e, 2656
Jacquelynn Syrah, 2656
Jacquins, 4944
Jaffer, 2239
Jager, 7305
Jakada, 9708, 9709, 9710
Jake & Amos, 7312, 8189
Jake Baked, 13180
Jake's Restaurant, 14529
Jakob Denner, 8032
Jalapeanuts, 2155, 2156
Jalapeno, 11126
Jalapeno Gouda, 15622
Jalapeno Tnt, 11126
Jamaica Blue Mountain, 11465
Jamaica Bluemountain, 863
Jamaican Blue Mountain, 3301
Jamaican Gold, 10150, 11631
Jamaican Jerk Spice Blend, 14808
James, 11620
James Chocolate Seal Taffy, 7316
James Cream Mints, 7316
James River, 1957
James Salt Water Taffy, 7316
Jameson, 11221, 11222
Jamesport Vineyards, 7323
Jana, 11028
Janca's, 7325
Jane Dough, 4108
Jane Stewart, 12577
Jane's, 6472
Janes Family Favourites, 7327

Janet Lee, 321
Janet Leigh, 6989
Janta, 6763
Jar-Lu, 6401
Jaret, 15347
Jarritos, 14414
Jashua's Kosher Items, 1585
Jasmati, 12083
Jasmati Rice, 12087
Jasmine, 13513
Jasmine Green, 15519
Jason, 11828
Jason & Son, 7336
Jason Pharmaceuticals, 7337
Jasper, 8476
Jasvine, 7335
Java Coast, 12759
Java Estate, 11465
Java Jelly, 5813
Jaw Busters, 4761
Jaxsons, 7346
Jay & Boots Meats, 7347
Jayson, 10884
Jazz, 7141
Jazz Cola, 6177
Jazzie J, 13155
Jazzy Barbecue Sauce, 992
Jazzy Garlic Jazz, 5742
Jazzy Java, 7354
Jazzy Java Custom Flavored Gourmet,
   11846
Jazzy Juice, 15024
Jb, 7532
Jbr Coffee, 7256
Jc Potter, 879
Jean Sweet Potatos, 12400
Jean-Claude Boisset, 1652
Jecky's Best, 7357
Jekel® Vineyards, 1897
Jell-O, 7944
Jell-O, 7937, 7939, 7949, 7950, 7951
Jelly Bean, 5573
Jelly Belly, 7364, 7365, 15347
Jemez Blush, 11475
Jemez Red, 11475
Jennie-O, 6708, 9659
Jennie-O Turkey Store, 6733
Jenny's, 11491
Jenny's Country Kitchen, 7370
Jensen's Orchard, 13329
Jeremiah's Pick, 7380
Jericho Canyon Red, 12256, 12408
Jero, 1413
Jerry's, 7382
Jerry's Caramel Corn, 7382
Jerry's Cheese Corn, 7382
Jerry's Popcorn, 7382
Jerry's Snack Packs, 7382
Jersey Boardwalk, 6005
Jersey Farms, 8602
Jersey Supreme, 5025
Jerusalem Pita, 4106
Jess Jones Farms, 7388
Jesse's Best, 7389
Jessie Lord, 3381
Jessie Lord, Inc., 3382
Jet Puffed Marshmallows, 7950
Jet Tea, 3317
Jet-Puffed, 7944
Jetcoat, 13511
Jewel Laboratories, 14785
Jewel of India, 11762
Jfg Products, 15572
Jhs - J. Hungerford Smith, 3189
Jif, 7227, 7228, 7229
Jiffy Mix, 2707
Jiffy Pop, 3189, 3201, 7064
Jigg-All, 2087
Jila & Jols, 3726
Jim Beam, 1237, 5070
Jim Beam Gourmet Foods, 15162
Jim Beam Kentucky Bourbon, 10481
Jim Candy, 477
Jim's, 12095
Jim's Country Mill Sausage, 15868
Jimbo Jumbos, 10716
Jimm's, 7400
Jimmy Dean, 7401, 12720, 12752, 12756,
   12759, 12760, 15590
Jimmy's, 12258
Jinglebits, 11405

Jj Nissen, 7095, 7105
Jmh Premium, 7274
Jo Citrus, 7407
Jo San, 9263
Jo's Candies, 7409
Jo's Original, 7409
Joan of Arc, 973, 1553
Jobe's, 2369
Jocko, 2776
Jodar, 7410
Jody Maroni, 7413
Joe Bean Organic Coffee, 5251
Joe Bertman's Ballpark Mustard, 7496
Joe Clark's Candies, Inc., 2916
Joe Corbi's, 7415
Joe Perry's, 807
Joe's Low-Carb, 7057
Joey's, 7426
Johannisberg Riesling, 8541, 12646
John Foster Green, 3149
John Labatt Classic, 8102, 8104
John Morrell, 7451, 7454, 7455
John Morrell & Co, 13308
John O'S, 4644
John West, 6392, 6393, 6395
John Wm. Macy's Cheesecrips, 7462
John Wm. Macy's Cheesesticks, 7462
John Wm. Macy's Sweetsticks, 7462
John Z'S Big City, 6008
Johnnie Fair, 14143
Johnnie Walkers, 3956
Johnny Boy Vanilla, 15352
Johnny Mac's, 8764
Johnny Walker Scotch, 14862
Johnson Concentrates, 7467
Johnson's Alexander Valley, 336
Johnsonville Bratwur, 7476
Johnsonville Country, 7476
Johnston County Hams, 13
Johnston's Winery, 7480
Johr®, 1002
Joint Cleanse, 6343
Joint Maintenance, 3704
Joint Well, 10387
Joker - Fruit Juice, 4542
Joliesse Vineyards, 1652
Jolina, 10501
Jolle Desserts, 2360
Jollie Juan, 14857
Jolly Aid, 8945
Jolly Good, 7962
Jolly Pops, 8945
Jolly Rancher, 6493, 6500
Jolly Rancher Double Blasts, 6497
Jolly Rancher Gummies Candy, 6497
Jolly Rancher Jelly Beans, 6497
Jolly Rancher Lollipops, 6497
Jolly Rancher Soft & Chewy, 6497
Jolly Rancher Sour Blasts, 6497
Jolly Ranchers, 6497
Jolly Roger, 15539
Jolly Rogers, 4139
Jolly Santa Pop, 358
Jolly Time, 537
Jolt, 15468
Jolt Cola Energy Rush, 14227
Jolt-Cola, 15468
Joly Rancher, 6495
Jomints, 7407
Jon Donaire, 7482, 12097
Jonathan International Foods, 4352
Jonathan T., 14928
Jonathan's Organics, 7484
Jonathan's Sprouts, 7484
Jones, 7489
Jones Sausagest, 7487
Jones Soda Carbonated Candy, 1447
Jones Soda Carbonated Sours, 1447
Jones Soda Energy Boosters, 1447
Jones Sours, 1447
Joons Chocolate Popcorn, 12386
Jordan Almonds, 9754
Jordanettes, 12898
Jose Cuervo Margarita Salt Sombrero, 5116
Jose Goldstein, 10713
Jose Ole, 13496
Joseph Farms Cheese, 7500
Joseph Filippi, 7498
Josh & John's Ice Cream, 7511
Joshua's Kosher Kitchen, 1586, 2794
Josie's Best Blue Tortilla Chips, 13047
Joslin, 6119

Mighty Mints, 9900, 13659
Mighty Mouse Sports, 12424
Mighty Wild, 13395
Mightyshakes, 3961
Mignardise, 11304
Miguel's, 9407
Mihel, 2659
Mikarla's Best, 10275
Mikawaya, 9408
Mike, 3124
Mike and Ike, 7546
Mike's, 9411
Mike's Original, 12673
Miki, 15285
Milani, 9419
Milani Gourmet, 11557
Milano, 1995
Milano Family Winery, 9421
Milat Vineyards, 9422
Milcal, 5425
Milcal-Fg, 5425
Milcal-Tg, 5425
Mild Gouda, 15622
Milder Dimensions, 13657
Milem, 14798
Miles River, 1207
Milex®, 751
Milford, 5164
Milk Chugs, 9222
Milk For Life, 14904
Milk Stout, 14164
Milka, 7949
Milkfuls, 13770
Milky Way, 9010, 9011, 9065
Milky Way Crispy Rolls, 9010
Mill City, 9431
Mill Creek Vineyards, 9434
Mill Dance Brand, 846
Millbrook, 5840, 7083, 7084, 7091, 7092, 7094, 7095, 7105, 9435
Mille Lacs, 9436
Millennium, 11419
Millennium Ale, 14612
Millennium Meltaways, 2145
Miller, 9443, 9447, 9448, 9450, 9453
Miller Chill, 9462, 9463
Miller Genuine Draft 64, 9462
Miller Genuine Draft, 9442, 9462, 9463
Miller Genuine Draft Light, 9442
Miller High Life, 9442, 9462, 9463
Miller High Life Light, 9442, 9462
Miller Lite, 9442, 9447, 9448, 9462, 9463
Miller's, 11694, 13571, 15732
Miller's Country Ham, 9457
Millers, 392, 9458, 9459
Millet Rice, 10050
Millflow, 9466
Milliaire Winery, 9467
Millicent's Preserves, 15484
Millie's, 15453
Millie's Pierogi, 9468
Millina's Finest, 6143
Millka, 7939
Mills, 2178
Mills Brothers International, 9473
Millstone, 7227, 7228, 10200
Millstream, 9476
Milnot, 9482
Milo, 10102
Milo Powdered Drink Mix, 10108
Milone Brothers, 9484
Milpas, 9281
Milsolv, 9487
Milsorb, 9489
Milwaukee Rye Bread Mix, 1382
Milwaukee Seltzer Company, 6918
Milwaukee's Best, 9442
Milwaukee's Best Ice, 9442, 9462
Milwaukee's Best Light, 9442, 9462, 9463
Milwaukee's Best Premium, 9462
Mimi's Muffins, 7123
Mimis Cafe, 1613, 1614
Min Tong, 9492
Min-Col, 10427
Mina, 8788
Mind's Eye Smart Drinks, 11721
Mine & Mommy's, 9494
Mineragua, 14414
Minerva, 9498
Minestrone, 3708
Ming Cha, 1707
Mingo Bay Beverages, 9499

Mingo Bay Beverages, Inc., 11448
Mingo River, 15843
Minh, 12888
Mini Babybel, 1284
Mini Dickmann's, 13771
Mini-Croustade, 11304
Mini-Croustade Shell, 11304
Mini-Easre, 11304
Mini-Monsters Candy, 4680
Mini-Roulet, 11304
Mini-Sizzlers, 12856
Mini-Tater Tots, 10684
Mini-Wheats, 7676
Mini-Wheats®, 7674
Minibix, 15364
Minigo, 14795
Minit Chef, 8826
Minn - Dak, 9503
Minnesaurus Dill Picklodon, 8724
Minnesota Dehydrated Vegetables, 9507
Minnesota Heartland, 5252
Minnesota Wild, 9510
Minors, 10108
Minowa, 15288
Mins Plus, 7012
Mint, 11264
Mint Balls, 11840
Mint Coolers, 4680
Mint Lumps, 6412
Mint Pearls, 4680
Mint Puffs, 6412
Mint Shell, 11304
Mint Twists, 857
Mintasure, 6340
Minterbrook, 9515
Mints Jots, 4680
Minute, 7944, 7948, 7949, 12165
Minute Fudge, 12158
Minute Lunch, 14925
Minute Maid, 7189, 9516, 9517, 10640
Minute Maid Juices, 3021
Minute Maid Juices/Juice Drinks, 14585
Minute Maid Lemonade, 14585
Minute Maid Light, 14585
Minute Maid Light Lemonades, 14585
Minute Main Soft Frozen, 5766
Minute Menu, 3940
Minute Rice, 7937, 7939, 7950
Minute Tapioca, 7950
Miprodan®, 751
Mipueblito, 11686
Mira Mango Nectar, 9520
Mira Sperse, 14243
Mira-Bake, 14243
Mira-Cleer, 14243
Mira-Gel, 14243
Mira-Quik, 14243
Mira-Set, 14243
Mira-Thik, 14243
Mirabel, 4864, 4865
Mirabelle, 12870
Mirabo, 2609
Miracle, 286
Miracle Ade, 11028
Miracle Juice, 11028
Miracle Juice Energy Drink, 11028
Miracle Maize, 8478
Miracle Mile, 7629
Miracle Whip, 7935, 7939, 7944, 7948, 7949, 7950
Miramar, 9522
Mirassou, 8079
Mirassou®, 4226
Mirch Masala, 3849
Mirenat, 18
Miriam, 15579
Mirror Pond Pale Ale, 3928
Miscela Bar, 7015
Miscela Napoli, 7015
Miscoe Springs, 9525
Mishpacha, 11828
Miso Master Miso, 5897
Miss Chiquita, 2789
Miss Goldy Chicken, 12652
Miss Lil's, 9163
Miss Love White, 1946
Miss Meringue, 9529
Miss Sally's, 2449
Miss Scarlett, 9530
Miss Sophia's Gingerbread, 9531
Miss Vickie's®, 5214

Mission, 3871, 5706, 9532, 9534, 9537, 9538
Mission Mountain, 9539
Mission Prenatal, 9540
Mission San Juan Juices, 9541
Mississippi, 12209
Mississippi Cheese Straws, 9545
Mississippi Delta Fudge, 14226
Mississippi Mousse, 14226
Mississippi Mud Pupp, 9545
Missouri's Finest, 8592
Mister, 10522
Mister Bee, 9547
Mister Fudge, 2181
Mister Spear, 9551
Mistic, 1411, 9751, 13331
Mistic Carafes, 9751
Mistic Cliff, 12160
Mistic Iced Tea, 4949
Misto, 2138
Misto Dark, 2138
Misty Mints, 11405
Mitalena Coffee, 14866
Mitchell Foods, 9557
Mitchell's, 6191
Mitchum Rices, 9558
Mitia, 12051
Mito's, 10544
Mitoku Macrobiotic, 2825
Miwok Weizen Bock, 8981
Mix-Ups, 589
Mixers, 9914
Mixon, 9567
Miyako, 9880
Miyako, 9880
Mizkan, 9570
Mizken, 9880
Mjb, 9059, 12748, 12749, 12750, 12751
Mlo Sports Nutrition, 5475
Mme Lautrec, 3247
Mn Malting, 9379
Mo Hotta - Mo Betta, 9571
Mo'beta, 10547
Mocafe, 3317
Moccona, 12760
Mocha, 11631
Mocha Bars, 12837
Mocha Magic, 4811
Mocha Marbles, 4811
Mocha Mix, 1213, 9708, 9709
Mocha Mud, 1765
Mocha Mud Cake Mix, 1765
Mochi, 5843
Mochi Ice Cream, 9408
Model Dairy, 3827
Modelo Especial, 5386
Modern, 4111, 9581
Modern Baked Products, 9577
Modern Maid, 7737
Modifilan, 10866
Modoc, 9586
Moducare, 15255
Moduchol, 15255
Modulen Ibd, 10108
Moduprost, 15255
Moet & Chandon, 9587
Moffett, 8495
Mogen David, 15640
Mohawk, 7454, 7455, 9589
Moir's, 207
Moisturlok®, 213
Mojave, 9171, 9172
Mojave Magic, 2194
Mojeska's, 9876
Mojito Club, 11221
Moka-Java, 14435
Moledina, 9596
Molfino, 12704
Molinaro's, 9597
Molly McButter, 319, 9419, 11557, 11558
Molson, 9600, 9601
Molson Canadian, 9463
Molson Canadian Ice, 9602
Molson Canadian Light, 9602
Molson Diamond, 9602
Molson Dry, 9602
Molson Exel, 9602
Molson Export, 9602
Molson Golden, 9602
Molson Light, 9602
Molson Red Jack, 9602
Molson Stock Ale, 9602
Molta Roba, 14817

Mom & Pop's, 15235
Mom 'n Pops, 9605
Mom's, 4843, 9609
Mom's Barbeque Sauce, 9607
Mom's Choice, 6288
Mom's Famous, 9608
Mommy's Choice, 483
Momokawa, 12564
Mon Ami, 9611
Mon Cheri, 4764
Mon Cuisine, 371
Mon Cuisine Vegetarian, 9612
Mona, 12295
Mona Lisa®, 9615
Monadnock Mountain Spring Water, 1572
Monarch, 6682
Monari Federzoni, 7081
Monastery, 3247
Mondavi, 12185
Mondial, 11306
Money Candy, 12482
Money Mints, 12511
Moneys, 9622
Monfort, 3563
Mongo, 5402
Mongoose, 8151
Monica's, 5737
Monin, 3317, 9625
Monini, 9626
Monique's Pasta Sauces, 277
Monnini, 9015
Monsanto, 9587
Monsooned Malabar, 7514
Monster, 3021, 3227, 12772
Monster Chews, 3227
Monster Cone, 9631
Monster Cookies, 9811
Monster Energy Khaos, 6196
Monsters, 5461
Mont Blanc Chocolate Syrups, 9632
Mont Blanc Gourmet H, 9632
Mont Rouge Nature's Best, 33
Mont-Rougr, 11661
Monta Vista, 13638
Montagnolo, 2609
Montalcino, 523
Monte Alban, 1169
Monte Carlo Bake Shop, 1006
Monte Carlo Premium Mozerella, 8660
Montebello, 2209, 13188, 13581
Monterey Cabernet Sauvignon, 2830
Monterey Chardonnay, 2830
Monterey Petite Syrah, 2830
Monterrey, 9658
Montezuma, 1169
Montforte, 15673
Monthaven, 5729
Monticello, 9710
Montmorency, 2719
Montpellier, 1853
Montracheti, 1666
Montreal Chop Suey, 9666
Monument Dairy Farms, 9668
Moo Chew, 1115
Moo-Calcium, 5425
Moo-Mania, 5598
Moofus, 12109
Moon, 11599
Moon Mountain, 6406
Moon Pads, 10011
Moon Pie, 2675
Moon's Seafood, 9675
Moonlight, 12379
Moonlight Mushrooms, 3436
Moonlight Pale Lager, 9679
Moonlite Bbq Inn, 9680
Moonshine Madness, 7724
Moonstone, 12564
Moor, 2885
Moore's, 592, 9150
Moores, 9681
Moose Drool Brown Ale, 1448
Moose Juice, 515
Moose Mountain, 1776
Moose Tracks, 9826
Moosehead Lager, 9684
Moovers, 13295
Mopac, 9586, 9792
Mor Gold, 15030
Mor Gold Plus, 15031
Mor-Fruit, 10929
Morabito, 9687

Naterl, 9961
Nathan's, 5672, 10508, 10511, 14592
Nathan's Famous, 12508, 13505, 14874
Nathans, 10510
Nation, 9963
National, 418, 419, 601, 9983, 9993, 9996
National Beef, 3101
National Beef®, 9965
National Foods, 3211
National Gold, 5722
National One, 5722
National Steak, 9994
Native American, 9999
Native American Foods, 2718
Native Forest, 4354
Native Kjalii, 10000
Native Scents, 10001
Native South, 10002
Natives Pride, 838
Natlans, 5256
Natra Cacao, 10003
Natra Us, 10003
Natrabio, 1709
Natragest, 1843
Natraceutical, 10003
Natrataste, 13830
Natrium, 10005
Natura, 10424
Naturade, 14553, 14554, 14555, 14556,
    14557, 14558, 14559, 14560, 14561,
    14562, 14563, 14564, 14565, 14566,
    14567
Natural, 5214
Natural Bouncin' Berry, 13365
Natural Brew, 7227, 7228, 7229, 13319
Natural Certified Angus Beef, 3807
Natural Choice, 5041, 9099
Natural Country, 3388, 3389
Natural Exotic Tropicals, 10013
Natural Flea Eze, 3704
Natural Gourmet, 6141
Natural Gourmet Flavor Oil, 8416
Natural Grain, 7924
Natural Green Leaf Brand, 10802
Natural Harvest, 11, 14416
Natural Health, 176
Natural High, 3817
Natural Ice, 633, 634
Natural Life, 8332
Natural Light, 633, 634
Natural Lite, 555
Natural Mountain Water, 9898
Natural Personal Care, 3384
Natural Pure, 3239, 13264, 13265, 14148
Natural Sterols, 14895
Natural Thompson, 15087
Natural Touch, 7676
Natural's Concept, 15742
Natural-Source Vitamin E, 91
Naturalcrisp®, 7241
Naturally Aloe, 405
Naturally Delicious, 10032
Naturally Flavored S, 14888
Naturally Fresh, 10033
Naturally Good Fruits & Vegetables, 1489
Naturally Healthy, 5746
Naturally Klean, 8743
Naturally Potatoes®, 1175
Naturally Slender, 8203
Naturalvalves, 5631
Naturaselect™, 1971
Nature Actives, 13665
Nature Canada, 12041
Nature Cure, 10036
Nature Made, 11267
Nature O'S, 6141
Nature Puffs, 6141
Nature Safe, 5986
Nature Seal, 8910
Nature Soothe, 11631
Nature Star, 10039
Nature Valley, 5461
Nature Works, 143
Nature Zone, 10908
Nature's Alchemy, 8582
Nature's Alternative, 5370
Nature's Beauty, 5396
Nature's Best, 1975, 7035
Nature's Blend, 4465
Nature's Bounty, 13365
Nature's Bounty®, 10042
Nature's Burger Mix, 4657

Nature's Choice, 397, 1118
Nature's Classics, 3352
Nature's Concept, 8421
Nature's Dairy, 10044
Nature's Edge, 4317
Nature's Glory, 5396
Nature's Gold, 6688
Nature's Goodness, 1213
Nature's Gourmet, 8931
Nature's Hand, 10046
Nature's Herb Company, 12626
Nature's Herbs, 10047, 14736
Nature's Kitchen, 9866
Nature's Mist, 2349
Nature's Own, 1173, 1174, 1176, 1681,
    1860, 4958, 4959, 4975, 5128
Nature's Own®, 1175
Nature's Partner, 5591
Nature's Path, 10050
Nature's Peak, 7227, 7228
Nature's Plus, 5636
Nature's Pride, 1910, 9672
Nature's Quest, 4561
Nature's Resources, 11267
Nature's Secret, 3124
Nature's Select, 10053
Nature's Sungrown Beef, 10054
Nature's Sunshine, 10055
Nature's Wonderland, 11104
Naturemost Labs, 10057
Natures Club, 43
Natures Flavors, 11839
Natures Fountain, 2044
Natures Path, 13617
Naturesource® Natural Angus, 9965
Naturessence, 1579
Naturewell® Natural Beef, 9965
Naturfood, 12627
Naturox, 7698
Naturslim, 11638
Nautilus, 13669
Navan, 9587
Navarro, 10064
Naya, 10067
Naylor, 10069
Nbr 2000, 10439
Nca, 10427
Ne-Boil Lasagna, 12512
Ne-Mo's, 10070
Neal's, 8050
Near East, 10072, 11737, 11738
Neastea, 10102
Nebbiolo, 15078
Necco, 10131, 10137
Necco Wafers, 9900, 13659
Nectar Andina, 9516
Nectarade, 4927
Nedlog 100, 10078
Needlers Jersey English Toffee, 12481
Neem Aura, 8582
Neenah Springs, 10079
Neera's, 2874
Negra Modelo, 5386
Nehi, 13331
Nehi Flavors, 4949
Neighbors, 10082
Neilson, 12703, 12705
Nekot, 8191
Nelson, 822
Nelson Seatreats, 10089
Nelson's, 1660, 10092
Nelson's Dutch Farms, 10092
Neobee 1053, 13702
Neobee 1095, 13702
Neobee 895, 13702
Neobee M-20, 13702
Neobee M-5, 13702
Neokura, 13154
Neon Beach, 586
Neon Lasers, 11840
Neorom, 4137
Nepi, 9594
Neptune, 10096, 10097, 10508, 10510,
    12955, 13738
Neptune Delight, 12928
Neptune Foods, 11968
Neptune's, 14622
Nerds, 10102, 10108
Nescafe, 10102, 10108
Nescafe Cafe Con Leche, 10108
Nescafe Clasico, 10108
Nescafe Frot, 10108

Nescafe Ice Java, 10108
Neshaminy Valley Natural, 10099
Nesquik, 1895, 6105, 6107, 10102, 10108
Nestea, 3021, 10108
Nestle, 3659, 6763, 10102, 10103, 10104,
    14554, 14555, 14556, 14557, 14558,
    14559, 14560, 14561, 14562, 14563,
    14564, 14565, 14566, 14567
Nestle Abueli Chocolate, 10108
Nestle Carnation Instant, 10108
Nestle Carnation Malted Milk, 10108
Nestle Carnation Milks, 10108
Nestle Chocolates, 10370
Nestle Crunch, 10108
Nestle Dessert Toppings, 10108
Nestle Europe, 10108
Nestle Foodservices, 10108
Nestle Healthcare Nutrition, 10108
Nestle Hot Cocoa Mix, 10108
Nestle Infant Formulas, 10108
Nestle Nido 1+, 3+, 6+, 10108
Nestle Signa Turtles, 10108
Nestle Signatures Treasures, 10108
Nestle Toll House Candy Bars, 10108
Nestle Toll House Morsels, 10108
Nestle', 14553
Neto, 10110, 14243
Neuhaus, 2798
Neuman, 10113
Neutral Slush, 6079
Nevada City Winery, 10116
New Amsterdam® Gin, 4226
New Atlanta, 3665
New Bedford Linguica Company, 10121
New Classics, 5809
New England, 5809
New England Cranberry, 10133
New England Farms Eggs, 3067
New England Naturals, 10136
New England Premium, 6641
New Englander, 7426
New Era, 10137
New Glarus Bakery, 10139
New Granola, 6995
New Harmony, 10144
New Harvest Foods, 2065
New Holstein, 8203
New Holstein Cheese, 2055
New Hoolland, 1665
New Image, 13813, 13814
New Jamaican Gold Cappuccino, 11631
New Life, 11655
New Line Homemade, 5252
New London Eng, 576
New Moon, 10847
New Morning, 10156, 14780
New Morning Organic Cereals, 10156
New Rinkel, 5963
New Season Foods, 10162
New Southern Tradition Teas, 1412
New West Foods, 10163
New World Home Cooking Co., 2513
New York, 14138, 15613
New York Classics, 2796
New York Club, 6316
New York Deli, 15578, 15679
New York Fish House, 10174
New York Flatbread, 9015
New York Flatbreads, 13498
New York Kosher Deli, 371, 372, 9234
New York Pizza, 10177
New York Pretzel, 10178
New York Style, 10102
New York Style Cheesecake, 3089
New York's Turf, 9724
New Yorker, 1734, 8203
Newberry, 6869
Newly Weds, 10190
Newman's Own, 10193, 10640
Newman's Own Lemonade, 10193
Newman's Own Pasta Sauces, 10193
Newman's Own Popcorn, 10193
Newman's Own Salad Dressing, 10193
Newman's Own Salsa, 10193
Newport, 10196
Newport Coffee Traders, 935
Newton Vineyard, 9587, 10198
Newtons, 7930, 7944, 7949, 9914
Next Step Lipil, 1830
Next Step Prosobee Lipil, 1830
Nfd, 13887
Niacin-Time, 7277

Niagara, 1946, 10200, 10238
Niagara Chocolates, 14079
Niagra Seed, 6257
Nibble With Gibble's, 9036
Nibby Bars, 12837
Nic-O-Boli, 10219
Nichol's Pistachio, 10209
Nicholson's Bestea, 6109
Nicholson's Bottlers, 6109
Nicholson's Chok-Nick, 6109
Nickelodeon, 5126
Nickelodeon Ice Cream, 5766
Nickles Bakery, 10216
Nicky Usa, 10217
Nico-Rx, 1709
Nicola, 7141
Nido, 10102
Nielsen, 10223
Nielsen-Massey, 10224
Night Hawk, 10226
Nik Naks, 4680
Nik-L-Nip, 14470
Nikki Bars, 1080
Nikki's, 10228
Nikola's Biscotti, 3317, 10229
Nilla, 7930, 7948, 7949
Nilla Wafers, 9914
Nin Jiom, 14013
Ninja Sticks, 3227
Ninja Trolls, 4680
Nip's Potato Chips, 10234
Nipchee, 8191
Nips, 10102, 10108
Nirvana, 8582
Nissen, 7091
Nitta Gelatin, 10240
Nittany Lion Franks, 7741
No Boil Pasta, 13098
No Bones Wheat-Meat, 14418
No Fat Spaghetti Sauce, 14810
No Fear, 11178, 11179, 11191
No Forks Required, 9477
No Holds Bar, 10041, 10059
No Name, 9010
No Pudge, 4517, 10241
No Sugar Added Apple, 9826
No Sugar Added Products, 9835
No Time Bread Base, 15434
No Time Bread Condit, 15434
No Yolks, 13798
No Yolks Egg Noodles, 5085
No-Cal, 6086
No-Teg, 820
Noah's Spring Water, 203
Noah's Treats, 12577
Noahs Buddies, 14054
Nobadeer Ginger, 2885
Nobella, 6009
Noble, 10244
Nobleman Popper, 10244
Nochebuena, 2102
Nodark, 838
Noel, 10246
Nogurt, 1288
Noh, 9901, 10248
Nojo, 1477
Nokano, 9570
Nolan Porter, 5478
Nollibel, 10981
Nomad Apiaries, 8547
Non Diary Toppings, 13830
Non-Dairy Baklava, 10502
None Such, 4254, 7227, 7228
Noni, 9079, 13417
Noni Nonu, 1404
Noni Pacific, 13417
Nonna D'S, 11762
Nonni's, 10253
Noodle Delights, 2176
Noodle Plus, 14842
Noodles By Leonardo, 10256
Noon Hour, 10257
Noprthern Lites Pancakes, 6644
Nor-Cal, 10261
Nor-Tech, 10260
Norbest, 9713, 10267, 14996
Norchip, 3518
Norden, 2230
Nordic, 10326, 13887
Nordic Pride, 846
Norimoor, 10274
Norivital Vitamins, 10274

Products Frugo Sa De Cv, 13860
Proferm, 3329
Professional Preference, 8745
Progestimil, 1830
Progress Candy, 11664
Progresso, 5461, 11667
Progum, 11467
Prokote, 945
Prolait, 11642
Proleche, 11642
Prolia, 2382
Proliant, 11668
Prolibra®, 5610
Prolume, 11670
Promase, 53
Promedary, 10875
Promega, 12823
Promise, 1393, 14834, 14836, 14837
Promise Pops, 14317
Proof Perfect, 12888
Prop Whey, 10421
Propak, 13111
Proper-Care, 11672
Prophos, 945
Proplus, 13362
Proprietor's Reserve, 11269
Prosante, 2382
Prosobee, 9220
Prosobee Lipil, 1830
Prosource, 11673
Prosperity, 659
Prosta-Forte, 9079
Prostacare, 895
Prostate Cleanse, 6343
Prostavite, 895
Prosweet, 15151
Prosyn, 945
Protech, 945
Protector, 15206
Protein Chef, 12903
Protein Greens, 10677
Protelac, 911
Protflan, 6282
Proti-Oats, 10440
Protient, 11678
Protizyme, 9312
Proto Whey®, 1481
Protrolley, 945
Protykin, 7018
Proud Mary, 14798
Proud Products, 10033
Provago Wheels, 592, 9150
Provecho, 8046
Provimi, 11682
Provimi Veal, 3101
Provon, 5608
Provon®, 5610
Provost Packers, 11683
Prozone, 10420
Pruden, 11684
Prudence, 1957
Psycho Pops, 184
Psycho Psours, 184
Pub Cheese, 12284
Pub House Battered Seafood, 14594, 14595
Pub Pies, 9720
Pubhouse, 14594, 14595
Puccinelli, 13558
Pucker Hustle, 4680
Puckers, 10562
Pueblafood, 11686
Pueblito, 4442
Puff Dough Sheets, 11916
Puff Dough Squares, 11916
Puff Dried, 5568
Puff Pastry Tartlet, 11304
Puff-N-Corn, 1489
Puget Sound, 10636
Pullulan, 7594
Pulp Tex, 2382
Pumpkin Ale, 1939
Pumpkin Seed Oil, 10648
Pumpkorn, 9276, 9907
Punch 'n Fruity, 15500
Pupier, 5675
Puppet Pals, 7707
Pur Erable, 8936
Purdey's, 10020
Purdue, 11197
Purdue Individual Frozen, 11197
Pure & Simple, 555, 5357
Pure Assam Irish Breakfast, 5825

Pure Brand Products, 5375
Pure Breath, 7600
Pure Delivery, 11792
Pure Distilled, 13483
Pure Energy, 9639
Pure Fruite, 2939
Pure Gold, 7804, 11694
Pure Honey, 4121
Pure Maid, 3660
Pure Rock, 15500
Pure Sealed, 12840
Pure Source, 11696
Pure-Bind, 5841
Pure-Cote, 5841
Pure-Dent, 5841
Pure-Flo Water, 11701
Pure-Gel, 5841
Pure-Li Natural, 5631
Puree Marsan, 9014
Purely American, 11702
Purepak, 12438
Purina, 803
Puritan, 1495
Puritan's Pride®, 10042
Purity, 3827, 9993, 11712
Purity Candy, 11705
Purity Foods, 11709
Purity Farms Ghee, 11708
Purity Foods Vita-Spelt, 11709
Purn Life, 15068
Purnell's Old Folks, 11714
Puroast, 11715
Purple Carrot, 7491
Purple Haze, 140
Purple Passion, 8032
Push Pop, 14478
Push Pops, 14479
Push Up, 10102
Put Me Hot, 7418
Putney Pasta, 11717
Putters, 4680
Puueo Poi, 11718
Py-O-My, 5571
Pyett, 4545
Pyramid Juice, 11721
Pyrenees, 11722
Pyridox, 7012
Pyromania, 5402

Q Gel, 3236
Q&Q, 10465
Q-Bee, 11782
Q-C, 14777
Q.E., 11725
Qbr, 6141
Qc Fibers, 3424
Qfc, 14192
Qic Rise, 11767
Qslic, 344
Quail Creek, 11731
Quaker, 1665, 11735, 11737, 11739
Quaker 100% Natural Granola, 11738
Quaker Bonnet Celery Seed Fruit Dre, 11733
Quaker Bonnet Dessert Shell, 11733
Quaker Bonnet Elephant Ear Danish, 11733
Quaker Bonnet Shortbread, 11733
Quaker Grits, 11738
Quaker Maid Patties, 11734
Quaker Maid Sandwich Steaks, 11734
Quaker Oatmeal, 11738
Quaker Oatmeal Squares, 11738
Quaker Oatmeal To Go, 11738
Quaker Rice Cakes, 11738
Quaker Rice Snacks, 11735
Quaker Snack Bars, 11738
Quaker Soy Crisps, 11738
Quaker Toasted Oatmeal, 11738
Quaker Tortilla Mixes, 11738
Quaker®, 5214
Quakerstate Farms, 10921
Quakes, 11738
Qualcoat, 11592
Qualflo, 7049
Quali-Cream, 11766
Quali-Tea, 8362
Qualifreeze, 11744
Qualifresh, 11744
Quality, 146, 257, 10202, 11776
Quality America, 11709

Quality Bakery, 11747
Quality Brand, 1489
Quality Brands, 11751
Quality Candy, 11752
Quality Chef Foods, Inc., 11755
Quality Chek'd, 3557
Quality Chekd, 5379, 13262, 13970, 14705
Quality Chekd Dairy Products, 11756
Quality Cuts, 1584
Quality Hearth, 11748
Quality Minded, 6042
Quality Value, 3352
Quality-Locked, 8370
Quantum Foods, 11778, 11779
Quarrymen Pale, 1558
Quatre Lepages, 10697
Quatro, 2535
Que Pasa Cheese Sauce & Salsa, 1489
Quebec Wild Blueberries, Inc., 14912
Quebon, 9961
Queen Ann, 1141
Queen Anne, 5882, 11781, 15502, 15751
Queen Anne Cordial Cherries, 5881
Queen Anne Jubilees, 5881
Queen Jasmine, 8770
Queen of Dixie, 13965
Queen's Pride, 9910
Queensboro, 11787
Queensway Foods Company, 11788
Quelle, 11789
Quelle Quiche, 12035
Quencher, 2945
Queso Del Sol, 5088
Queso Triangos, 9150
Queso Triangulos, 592
Questias, 5886
Qugg, 9015
Quibell Sparkling Water, 11796
Quibell Spring Tea, 11796
Quibell Spring Water, 11796
Quic Blend, 11766
Quic Cheese, 11766
Quic Creamer, 11766
Quic Whip, 11766
Quiche, 11304
Quick & Natural Soup, 13523
Quick Acid, 344
Quick Chew, 344
Quick Classic Sauces, 9171, 9172
Quick Coat, 344
Quick Cook, 5568
Quick Fibre, 344
Quick Glanz, 344
Quick Gum, 344
Quick Lac, 344
Quick Loaf, 14342
Quick Meals, 787
Quick Oil, 344
Quick Peanut Porridge, 1270
Quick Pot Pasta, 13523
Quick Shine, 344
Quick Start, 1176, 1681
Quick Stix, 15013
Quick's, 11798
Quick-Start®, 1175
Quick-To-Fix, 13308
Quickmash®, 7241
Quickset, 8140
Quik, 13839
Quik Start, 1174
Quik To Fix, 7390
Quik-Flo, 4070, 14242
Quilceda Creek Vintners, 11800
Quillisascut Cheese, 11802
Quinabeer, 2528
Quincy Gold, 1181
Quinine, 14923
Quinlan, 15679
Quinn's, 12989, 12990
Quinn's Golden Ale, 9778
Quinoa Confetti, 2768
Quinoa-Sesame, 8437
Quintessa, 5115
Quintrex, 10431
Quinzani, 11808
Quisp, 11737, 11738
Quisp Cereal, 11735
Quivira, 11809
Quong Hop, 11810
Qwip, 11593

R W Knudsen Family, 7227
R&F, 523
R&R Oatmeal Stout, 1259
R-346 Milk Chocolate Flavored, 15541
R-Own Cola, 4949
R.A. Fayard, 11827
R.H. Phillips, 11837
R.M. Lawton Cranberries, 11817
R.M.Quiggs, 3240
R.W. Knudsen Family, 7228, 7229
R.W.Knudsen, 13617
Rabbit Barn, 11869
Rabbit Creek, 11870
Rabbit Ridge, 11871
Rachel's, 14617
Radeberger, 1468
Rademaker, 8418
Radiant Morsels, 11071
Raffaello, 4764
Raffetto, 14798
Raga Muffins, 15307, 15565
Raggy-O, 11883
Raggy-O Apple Chutne, 11886
Raggy-O Cranberry Ch, 11886
Raggy-O Mango Chutne, 11886
Raggy-O Peach Chutne, 11886
Raggy-O Pineapple Ch, 11886
Raging Cow's, 4130
Ragu, 1393, 14834, 14836
Rail Head Red Ale, 1259
Railroad Ale, 1204
Railyard, 4977
Rain Forest, 5731
Rainberry, 4938
Rainblo®, 4679
Rainbo, 7091, 9322
Rainbow, 11896
Rainbow Coconut, 857
Rainbow Hill Vineyards, 11892
Rainbow Light, 11893
Rainbow Light Herbal, 11893
Rainbow Popcorn, 12386
Rainbow Pops, 3781, 11894
Rainbow Springs, 6892
Rainbow Sticks, 857
Rainbow Valley Orchards, 11899
Rainforest, 6119, 10416
Rainforest Crunch, 11900
Rainforest Organic, 4354
Rainforest Remedies, 8582
Rainsweet, 11890
Raised Right, 3087
Raisin Royales, 7786
Raisinets, 10102
Raisinmate, 3755
Raison D'Etre, 4042
Ralph & Paula Adams Scrapple, 7487
Ralph's Italian Ices, 11909
Ralphs, 11908, 14192
Ralston Foods, 8516, 11903
Ramazotti, 11221
Ramos Orchards, 11912
Ramos-Pinto, 8844
Ranch, 10268
Ranch House, 14879
Ranch Oak Farm, 11917
Ranch Pac, 15819
Ranch Style, 3189, 7064
Ranch Style Brand Beans, 7064
Ranch Wagon, 14599, 14600, 14601
Rancher's Registry Angus Beef, 2369
Ranchero, 2102
Ranchers Registry Angus® Beef, 1278
Rancho De Philo, 11919
Rancho Galante Cabernet, 5366
Rancho Palm Springs, 3954
Rancho Sisquoc, 11920
Rancho Zabaco®, 4226
Randall, 11925
Randall Foods, 11926
Randalls, 3352
Ranieri, 11931
Rao's, 9015
Rapazzini Winery, 11933
Rapes, 13699
Rapid Brew, 14481
Raps Blue Ribbon, 7128
Rapunzel Pure Organi, 11934
Raquel's, 11810

Schranck's, 3247
Schreiber, 371, 12878
Schrieber, 9659
Schrieber Meatless Meats, 372
Schug, 12880
Schuil Coffee, 12881
Schuler, 4680
Schultz, 12882, 13180
Schumann's, 15436
Schwab, 12886
Schwan's, 12888
Schwarteau, 15436
Schweppes, 2107, 2277, 4130
Sci, 13754
Sciabica's Oil of the Olive, 10210
Science Foods, 10670
Sclafani, 15146
Scone Girl, 15788
Scones, 7563, 14544
Sconza, 12898
Scooby Doo, 1699, 5126
Scooby-Doo®, 7685
Scoop-N-Bake, 1054, 7627
Scoopy, 7517
Scooter's, 8866
Scoresby Scotch, 14862
Scorned Woman, 6155, 15162
Scot Pride, 2577
Scotch Bay, 8654
Scotch Maid, 2521, 2522
Scotcheroons, 13715
Scotian Gold, 12901
Scott Country, 9696
Scott Petersen, 12508
Scott's, 12905, 12907, 12909
Scott's Barbeque Sauce, 12908
Scott's of Wisconsin, 12909
Scottie, 12909
Scottish, 1829
Scottsdale Mustard Co, 5341
Scotty Wotty's, 12911
Scramble Mix, 10921
Scramblettes, 3835
Scray's Cheese, 12912
Screamer, 12898
Scully, 10617
Sculptures, 7663
Sea Alaska, 14594, 14595
Sea Breeze, 12916
Sea Cakes, 8836
Sea Chance, 10508
Sea Chest, 12577
Sea Chips, 8836
Sea Choice, 10509, 10510, 10511
Sea Creatures, 4051
Sea Cuisine, 4864, 4865
Sea Devils, 732
Sea Diamond, 3248, 12929
Sea Dog, 12917
Sea Farer, 13157
Sea Fresh, 6533, 6535
Sea Gold, 12922
Sea Haven, 15304
Sea Jade, 3248, 12929
Sea Legs, 14594, 14595, 14596
Sea Life, 874
Sea Maid, 12790
Sea Market, 7259
Sea Mist, 3402
Sea Nuggets, 4864
Sea Pack, 12098
Sea Pearl, 3248, 7371, 9972, 12929
Sea Pearl Seafood Co., Inc., 12928
Sea Ray, 8613
Sea Rock, 15304
Sea Salad, 963
Sea Salt Nuts™, 1566
Sea Seasonings, 8836
Sea Snack, 12935
Sea Strips, 4864
Sea Valley, 6102
Sea Vegetables, 8836
Sea View, 3954
Seablends, 11239
Seaboard Farms, 12947
Seabreeze, 12577
Seabrook Farms, 12949
Seafest, 7064, 8595
Seafood, 15742
Seafood Elite, 4864
Seafood Magic, 8807
Seafood People, 10906

Seafreez, 1163
Seafreez/Shawmut, 1163
Seafreeze Pizza, 12973
Seagram's, 3021
Seagram's Gin, 11221, 11222
Seagrams, 4944, 11458
Seagrams Ginger Ale & Mixers, 14585
Seagull Bay, 12790
Seakist, 11239
Seald Sweet, 6823, 12976
Sealicious, 5916
Sealtest, 9961
Seaman Orchard, 4929
Seapak, 12093, 12097
Seaperfect, 12941
Seapoint Farms, 12979
Seaport, 14324
Seaport Blush, 13765
Seaport White, 13765
Seaport Wines, 13765
Seapro, 4296
Searchlight, 10508, 10510
Seaside, 4674, 6102, 7391
Season Brand, 11828
Season-Ettes, 11743
Seasoned Cheddar Cheese, 15018
Seasoned Delux, 7366
Seasoned Jack Cheese, 15018
Seasonedcrisp®, 7241
Seasoning Complete, 1025
Seasoning Salt, 4542
Seasonings From Hell, 13468
Seasons, 1946
Seaspecialties, 11574
Seastar, 3076
Seastix, 6115
Seatech, 12985
Seattle Bar, 12987
Seattle Chocolates, 12988
Seattle International, 14882
Seattle's Best Coffee, 11178, 11179, 11191
Seavey Cabernet Sauvignon, 12993
Seavey Chardonnay, 12993
Seavey Merlot, 12993
Seavey's, 8588
Seawatch, 12938
Seawave, 9651
Seaway, 3879
Sebeka®, 4226
Sechler's, 11906, 11907
Seckinger-Lee, 13000
Seckinger-Lee Biscuits, 2015
Second Nature, 1213
Secret Garden, 13002
Secret House, 13003
Sedgefield, 8784
Sedna, 7636
Sedonium, 8422
See Jing, 15710
See's Candies, 13006
Seeclear, 15206
Seeds & Suds, 9270
Seeds of Change, 9010, 13008, 14553, 14554, 14555, 14556, 14557, 14558, 14559, 14560, 14561, 14562, 14563, 14564, 14565, 14566, 14567
Seely, 5092, 13258, 13259
Segafredo Espresso, 9059
Segura Viudas, 5162
Seismic Ale, 12610
Seitan Quick Mix, 6141
Select, 3776, 13016
Select Allstars, 8995
Select Blend In-Room Coffee, 13445
Select Origins, 13682
Select Pop, 12539
Select Recipe, 10501
Select Recipe®, 7241
Select White But-R Creme Base, 3776
Selectgrad, 11396
Seline, 2339
Sella & Mosca, 10895
Selleck, 2178
Sello, 15018
Seltzer's Lebanon Bologna, 13026
Seltzer's Sweet Bolo, 13026
Seltzers, 10904
Semdiero, 13155
Semi-Chi, 4942
Semi-Industrialized, 13815
Seminis, 9613
Seminole, 13029

Sen-Sen, 4594
Senate Beer, 10615
Senda, 12704
Seneca, 10342, 10344, 13042, 13044
Seneca Blend, 4816
Seneca Foods, 13038, 13043
Seneca Granny Smith Concentrate, 14551
Seneca Juices, 14551
Seneca Orange Plus Beverage, 14551
Seneca R.S.P. Tart Cherry Concentra, 14551
Senor Felix's, 13045
Sensables, 14230
Sensational Sides™, 12049
Sensational Soy, 10966, 10967
Sensations, 6180
Senseo, 12720, 12760
Sensible Carbs, 3886
Sensible Delights, 2923
Sensient, 13050, 13051
Sentrex, 7076
Senza, 13682
Sepeco Seed, 13090
Sequoia Grove, 13057
Serena Calm, 8111
Serenade Blend, 13657
Serious Ginseng, 10547
Serrano, 13596
Serranos, 4751
Serranos Salsa, 13065
Sesa-Krunch, 6095
Sesame Birch Sticks, 2253
Sesame Seed, 6095
Sesame Street, 672
Sesamin, 4008
Sesmark, 8418
Sesmark Deli Thins, 14305
Sesmark Rice Thins, 14305
Sethness, 13076
Settler's Popcorn, 4829
Seven Barrell, 13080
Seven Hills, 13083
Seven Keys, 13085
Seven Seas, 566
Seven Star, 811
Seven Up, 2277
Seven-Up, 203, 10246, 11458
Sevigny, 4603, 15302
Sewansecott, 14314
Sexpresso, 1014
Seymour, 8624
Seyval Blanc, 1946, 2962
Seyval Blanc Brut Champagne, 1946
Seyval Naturel, 2962
Sfizio Crotonese, 13261
Sgti, 13357
Shabadoo Black and Tan Ale, 1357
Shade Grown Organic, 9789
Shade Icings & Fillings, 13098
Shadow Mountain Foods, Inc., 3107
Shady Brook Farms, 1278, 2369, 12214
Shady Grove Orchards, 13099
Shaeen, 846
Shafer Vineyards, 13102
Shahi, 13105
Shake 'n Bake, 7939
Shake'n'zyme, 3704
Shake-Ups, 6107
Shaken Country Meadows Sweets, 5656
Shakequik, 8922
Shaker Country Meadowsweets, 6568
Shakers Prepackaged Accessories, 2087
Shakespeare Vodka, 8848
Shaklee Carotomax, 13108
Shaklee Flavomax, 13108
Shalina, 13500
Shallon Winery, 13109
Shamiana, 6763
Shamrock, 4538, 14599, 14600
Shamrock Farms, 13111
Shamrockak, 14601
Shana Spice, 2700
Shandy, 1320
Shanghai, 3265
Shape Ups, 7189
Shape-Ups, 7190, 7191
Shapes, 11197
Shari Candies, 14227
Shariann's Italian White Beans, 13119
Shariann's Refried P, 13119
Shariann's Spicy Veg, 13119
Sharp Cheddar Cheese, 918
Sharp Gouda, 15622

Sharp's, 9463
Sharp's Non-Alcoholic Brew, 9442
Shasta, 9966, 9967, 13124
Shastebury, 10565
Shaving Cream Candy Fun Foam, 5467
Shaw, 13126
Shaw's, 624
Shawnee Best, 13130
Shawnee Mills, 13130
Shawnee Springs, 13129
Shea's Black & Tan, 6531
Sheaf Stout, 9442
Shearer, 7881
Shedd's, 14836
Shedd's Spread Country Crock, 1393, 14834
Sheffler Ham, 12796
Shei Brand, 9790
Sheila's Select Gourmet Recipes, 1242, 13134
Sheinman, 13135
Shelby, 10537
Shelf-Aid, 14231
Shelly's Hair Care, 6343
Shelter Pale Ale, 4042
Shelton's, 13140
Shemper Seafood, 13141
Shen-Valley, 11335
Shenandoah, 9985, 11197, 13142
Shenandoah Vineyards, 13353
Shenk's, 13145
Shennandoah's Pride, 9710
Shenson, 6093, 7451
Shephard Ridge, 13716
Shepherd, 13146
Shepherd Supreme, 13146
Shepherd's Pride, 9777
Shephody, 3518
Sher Rockee, 4111
Sheraton, 106
Sherrill, 13149
Sherrockee Farms, 9581
Shiner Blonde, 13542
Shiner Bock, 5386, 13542
Shiner Dunkelweizen, 13542
Shiner Hefeweizen, 13542
Shiner Kolsch, 13542
Shiner Light, 13542
Shiner Premium, 5386
Shining Choice, 13157
Shirley Foods, 13163
Shirley's, 12466
Shirriff (Canada), 7229
Shitake Mushroom Soup Mixes (4), 7305
Sho Chiku Bai, 7887, 14177
Shoalwater Bay, 8690
Shoestrings, 10684
Shofar, 1387, 13166
Shonan, 13167
Shonfield's, 13168
Shop Rite, 6876
Shopsy's, 8928, 8931
Shoregrill, 4864
Shoreline Fruit, 898
Short Cuts, 1665, 11197
Shortbread Housf, 2706
Shortcuts, 15573
Shorty's, 208
Shotskies Gelatin Mixes, 2087
Showboat, 1987, 8592
Showcase Supreme, 7355
Shredded Potato Patties, 10684
Shredded Potatoes, 10684
Shrimp Butler, 7724
Shrimp Magic, 8807
Shrimpbites With Caj, 14396
Shuckers™, 1566
Shufra, 12374
Shults Pretzels, 13180
Shupak, 7609
Shur Chef, 12084
Shur Fine, 7985, 14473
Shur Fresh, 14127
Shur-Fil, 14243
Shurtenda, 15868
Sicilia, 2503
Sicilian Chefs, 2115
Sid and Roxie's, 5956
Side Show, 12258
Sideboard Sweets & Savories, 5737
Sidral Mundet, 14414
Sierra, 9171, 9172, 11390, 13188

Brand Name Index

Sierra Gourmet, 13585
Sierra Ice, 11390
Sierra Light, 11390
Sierra Madre Brand, 4233
Sierra Mist, 11178, 11179, 11191
Sierra Nevada, 1861
Sierra Nevada Bigfoo, 13190
Sierra Nevada Celebration, 13190
Sierra Nevada Pale Ale, 13190
Sierra Nevada Stout, 13190
Sierra Nevada Summer, 13190
Sierra Sausage Co., 7689
Sierra Spring Foods, 12385
Sierra Spring Nurser, 13982
Sierra Springs, 3520, 13982
Sierra Springs®, 3627, 6579
Sierra Vista, 13191
Siesta, 9281
Sifers Valomilk Candy Cups, 13192
Sigma, 3039, 13194
Signal 369, 5955
Signature, 10731, 13195
Signature Delight, 10731
Signature Entrees, 10731
Signature Flavors, 9708
Signature Flavors By Mocha Mix, 9709
Signature Pastas, 10731
Signature Series, 814
Signature Specialties, 14745
Signorello, 13201
Sil-A-Gran, 13203
Silarom, 13203
Siljans, 13204, 15436
Silk, 9710, 15504
Silk Soy, 9961
Silk Soymilk, 3819
Silk Tassel, 3320
Silva, 392, 13209
Silvan Ridge, 13211
Silvanil, 13203
Silver, 7264
Silver Beauty, 170
Silver Creek, 4929
Silver Fleece, 6588, 10748
Silver Floss Sauerkraut, 1489
Silver Fox Vineyard, 13216
Silver King, 2776
Silver Label, 2903
Silver Label Cabernet Sauvigno, 1007
Silver Lake, 4648
Silver Lining, 10262
Silver Mtn Vineyards, 13220
Silver Palate, 13222
Silver Ridge, 1853
Silver Salmon, 13199
Silver Seyual, 1791
Silver Spring, 11458, 13224
Silver Spur, 10665
Silver Streak, 13228
Silver Thunder Malt Liquor, 10829
Silver Tray Cookies, 13230
Silverado Cellars, 2663
Silverbow, 13234
Silverbrook, 13111
Silverland, 849, 7600
Silvers, 4764
Simco, 13236
Simi Ravenswood, 5115
Similac, 12329
Similac Toddler's Best, 131
Simmer 'n Serve, 12167
Simmer Kettle, 13523
Simmonds, 5916
Simmons, 13242
Simon, 11799
Simon Fischer, 13359
Simon's, 4094, 13247
Simons, 8244, 11799
Simpkins, 15436
Simple Elegance, 12423
Simple Nevada, 11762
Simple Serv, 4864
Simpler Life, 6141
Simplesse, 2085
Simplex, 14206
Simplot, 392, 7242
Simplot®, 7241
Simplot® Culinary Fresh™, 7241
Simply, 11762
Simply Chocolate, 6107
Simply Delicious, 15691
Simply Devine, 3941

Simply Divine, 13251
Simply Juices, 3021
Simply Natural, 2708, 4342, 15355
Simply Natural Like, 15355
Simply Natural-Like, 4342
Simply Nuts, 15080
Simply Orange, 9516
Simply Potatoes, 9350, 10337
Simply Rich, 8434
Simply Smart, 1596, 6104
Simply Spice, 15844
Simply Spinach, 7412
Simply Sugar Free, 4423
Simpsons, 5126
Sin Fill, 9369
Sinai Kosher, 1387
Sinatra, 2774, 6370
Sinbad Sweets, 13257
Sincera Skin Care Products, 12822
Sincerity, 1104, 7804
Singel Serving Sundae, 2922
Singers Saving Grace, 6456
Single Origin, 1156
Single Serv, 3961
Single Serve Milk, 15427
Single Vineyard, 4226
Singleto, 3175
Singleton, 3189
Singletree Farms, 7184
Sini Fulvi, 13261
Sinton, 13263
Sinton's, 13262
Sioux City, 15500
Sioux City Sarsaparilla, 15500
Sip, 4487
Sir Citrus, 14857
Sir Francis Stout, 4139
Sir George Fudge, 7715
Siracuse, 4542
Sirah, 11065
Siren's Note Blend, 13657
Sirius Ttr, 4222
Sisler's Dairy, 13271
Sisu®, 10042
Sitka, 10304
Sitka Gold, 12965
Sivetz Coffee Essence, 13275
Six Mile Creek, 13276
Sizzle Heart, 4680
Ski, 4104
Skillet Frittatas, 2369
Skillet Omelets, 2369
Skim Select, 5598
Skincredibles®, 7241
Skincredibles® Plus, 7241
Skinner, 10167, 15590
Skinner Bakery, 7322
Skinner's, 14780
Skinny, 9907
Skinny Truffles, 12988
Skinny Water, 11028
Skipjacks™, 1566
Skippy, 1393, 14834, 14836
Skittles, 9010, 9065, 15765
Skjodt-Barrett, 13279
Skookum, 1598
Skull & Bones, 11762
Skwinkles, 8649
Sky Bar, 9900, 10131, 13659
Sky Vineyards, 13281
Skyland, 9985
Sl Sunflowers, 13888
Slap Stix, 9900, 13659
Slc, 13246
Sleeman, 10565, 13286
Sleeman Amber, 13287
Sleeman Clear, 13287
Sleeman Cream Ale, 13287
Sleeman Honey Brown Lager, 13287
Sleeman Original Dark, 13287
Sleeman Orignial Draught, 13287
Sleeman Premium Light, 13287
Sleeman Silver Creek Lager, 13287
Sleeman Steam, 13287
Sleepeasy, 10362
Sleeper, 12788
Sleepless In Seattle Coffee, 309
Slender, 7141
Slendid, 6457
Slendo, 9044
Slice, 11178, 11179, 11191
Sliced Iqf Strawberry, 10330

Slide Pops, 4660
Slim, 6593
Slim 'n' Trim, 5379
Slim Diez, 7742
Slim Fast, 13288
Slim Jim, 3175, 3189, 3194, 5775
Slim-Fast, 1393, 14834, 14838
Slime Slurps, 400
Slinky Brand Candy, 2293
Slo Poke, 5563
Slo-Roast Deli, 8931
Slopbucket Brown, 9212
Sloppy Joe, 4836
Slotkouski, 8359
Slotkouski Sausage, 8359
Slush Puppie, 2277, 4130
Slush Puppies, 4124
Slushade, 7923
Smack Cup-A-Ramen, 14842
Smack Ramen, 14842
Small Planet Foods, 2475
Small Talk Conversation Hearts, 4433
Smart & Final, 13289
Smart Balance, 15030
Smart Choice, 14996
Smart Dogs, 8437
Smart Drinks, 13290
Smart Growth, 10966, 10967
Smart Ice, 13290
Smart Kids, 6615
Smart Meat Steaks & Hamburgers, 5336
Smart Ones, 6392, 6393, 6394, 6395, 6399
Smart Serve, 208
Smart Source, 13111
Smart Start, 7676
Smart Water, 4473
Smartchocolates, 5288
Smartfood® Popcorn, 5214
Smartfood® Popcorn Clusters, 5214
Smarties, 2532
Smartwater, 3021
Smarty Bats, 13290
Smile Brite, 8582
Smileys, 9205
Smint, 2859
Smirnoff, 3956
Smith, 13297
Smith & Hook Winery, 6136
Smith Brothers Cough Drops, 4594
Smith Dairy, 15330
Smith Home Cured, 188
Smith's, 3352, 13295, 13301, 14192
Smith-Madrone, 13306
Smithers, 11557
Smithfield, 13308
Smithfield Beef Group, 13308
Smithfield Deli Group, 13308
Smithfield Foodservice Group, 13308
Smithfield Innovation Group, 13308
Smithfield Pork, 3101
Smithfield Rmh Foods Group, 13308
Smithfield Tavern, 11041, 15599
Smithwick's, 3956
Smoke & Fire, 13311
Smoke Craft, 10504
Smoked Eggplant Spra, 11034
Smoked Habanero Pretzels, 2770
Smoked Porter, 387
Smoked Salmon, 2348
Smoked Spices, 2348
Smoked Tofu, 15561
Smokehouse, 1567
Smokehouse Favorite, 3475
Smokeless Blackened Seasoning, 2156
Smokersguard, 4594
Smokey Farm Meats, 13316
Smokey Lap-Souchang Vinaigre Det, 5742
Smokey Mesquite, 2711
Smoky Hollow, 1917
Smoky Mountain, 8722
Smoky Mountain Trail Rub, 7724
Smoky Valley, 2711
Smooth & Creamy, 483
Smooth & Melty, 15436
Smooth and Melties, 15630
Smooth-N-Melty, 6031
Smoothie Sparkling Choc.Egg Cream, 2610
Smorz, 7676
Smothers/Remick Ridge, 13318
Smucker's, 7227, 7228, 7229
Smuckers, 15590
Smuttynose Belgian W, 13322

Smuttynose Robust Po, 13322
Snack, 6495
Snack Cafe, 5554
Snack Factory, 13324
Snack Fu, 14431
Snack Pack, 3194
Snack Wells, 7930
Snackin Fruits, 12883
Snackin' Fries, 10684
Snacknut, 1126
Snackwell's, 7949
Snackwells, 9914
Snak King, 13329
Snak Sales, 11500
Snake River, 13330
Snap-Back, 14682
Snapple, 1411, 2107, 4517, 5281, 6677, 13331
Snappy, 14580
Snappy Jack, 6381
Snaps, 527, 528, 529
Snickers, 9010, 9011, 9065
Sno Pac, 13334
Sno-Bal, 14456
Sno-Ball, 9983
Sno-Caps, 10102
Sno-E Tofu, 14987
Sno-Fluf, 7239
Sno-Top, 7039, 14856
Snocap, 9871
Snokist, 13338
Snolite, 13337
Snoodles, 14842
Snoqualmie Falls Lodge, 3275
Snow Cod, 7247
Snow Flake, 12668
Snow Floss, 5164
Snow Goose, 3327
Snow White, 945, 5569
Snow's, 2497
Snow's Nice Cream, 13343
Snow-Ball, 13340
Snowbird, 13344
Snowcap, 8935
Snowcrest, 10062, 13346
Snowden, 3518
Snowite, 2280
Snowizard, 13337, 13347
Snowman, 1776
Snowtime, 8777
Snyapa, 12291
Snyder of Berlin, 1489
Snyder of Berlin Snack Products, 1489
Snyder's of Hanover, 13350
So Good, 10211
So Joao, 11840
So-Good Bar-B-Q Delight, 4093
So-Good Pork Bar-B-Q, 4093
Soauther, 14582
Soba, 13352
Sobe, 11178, 11191, 13351
Sobe Adrenaline, 11179
Sobe Energize, 11178, 11179
Sobe Lean, 11178, 11179
Sobe Lifewater, 11178, 11179
Sobe Smooth, 11178, 11179
Sobe Sugar Free, 11178
Sobe Vita-Boom, 11178
Sobon Estate, 13353
Soccer Pops, 6915
Sochu Distilled Rice, 7920
Societe, 8115
Societe Donatien Bahaud, 201
Society Hill Gourmet Nut Company, 13355
Sockeye Nova, 15244
Soda Fountain, 2092
Sodex, 3765
Sofgrain, 14025
Soft Batch®, 7685
Soft Chews, 5573
Soft Flight, 13556
Soft Mac, 14488
Soft Roll Mix, 3776
Soft Square, 14947
Soft White, 945
Soft-Set, 14243
Soho Cellars, 12151
Soho Natural Lemonades, 13358
Soho Natural Soda &, 13358
Sokol Blosser, 13360
Sol, 8104
Sol Maduro, 9592

Summer Prize, 15323
Summer Sage, 11475
Summer Song, 4938
Summer Sweet, 130
Summer's Choice, 9677
Summerbright Ale, 1789
Summerfield, 5729
Summerfield Farms, 13847
Summerfield's, 13848
Summerlake, 1652
Summerset, 8476
Summit, 13850
Summit Lake Vinyards, 13852
Summum, 13854
Sumner, 15308
Sumptuous Ions, 2095
Sun, 3124
Sun Beauty, 969
Sun Break Scrambled Egg Mix, 2369
Sun Chlorella, 13877
Sun Country, 3511
Sun Crop, 13867
Sun Crop®, 7241
Sun Dried, 9735
Sun Fair, 13906
Sun Fresh, 8960
Sun Garden Growers, 13857
Sun Garden Sprouts, 13858
Sun Glow, 10875
Sun Groves, 13859
Sun King, 7371
Sun Lovin, 15373
Sun Maid, 1339
Sun Meadow, 5307
Sun Moon Stars, 12041
Sun Mountain, 3351
Sun Olive Oil, 13862
Sun Orchards Labels, 13864
Sun Pac, 13867
Sun Ray, 2228, 15001
Sun Siberian Ginseng, 13877
Sun Soy, 9710
Sun Spiced, 5569
Sun Stix, 9150
Sun Sun, 9281, 13874
Sun Supreme, 13881
Sun Valley Mustard, 13876
Sun Vista, 4674
Sun-Dried Tomato Str, 918
Sun-Glo, 13881
Sun-Maid, 33, 13883, 14943
Sun-Maid Fruit, 1339
Sun-Maid Raisins, 13882
Sun-Ripe, 10929, 15208
Sun-Ripened, 1579
Sun-Rise Beverages, 13885
Sun-Rype, 13886
Sun-Sugared, 12056
Sunbeam, 2427, 4958, 4959, 4970, 4975,
   5128, 7092, 12852, 13793, 13894, 13895
Sunbeam Bread, 12853
Sunbelt®, 9199
Sunbird, 13340
Sunbird Snacks, 9550
Sunblet, 14514
Sunbrand, 9015
Sunburst, 10401, 15030
Sunbursts, 7786
Sunchips®, 5214
Suncoast, 5637
Suncrest Farms, 13899
Suncrisp, 14586
Sundance, 5722
Sundance Barley Brew, 13901
Sundial Blend Teas, 13902
Sundial Gardens, 13902
Sundown, 13365
Sundown Brown Ale, 14716
Sundown®, 10042
Sundried Tomatoe Basil Pesto, 14810
Sundrop, 2277, 4124, 4130
Sundrops, 9908
Sunergia Breakfast Style Sausage, 13903
Sunergia More Than Tofu Garlic, 13903
Sunergia More Than Tofu Herbs, 13903
Sunergia More Than Tofu Porcinis, 13903
Sunergia More Than Tofu Savories, 13903
Sunergia More-Than-Tofu, 13903
Sunergia Organic Soy Sausage, 13903
Sunergia Smoked Portabella Sausage, 13903
Sunett, 6595
Sunfill, 9516

Sunflo, 3388
Sunflower Nutty Nuggets, 13904
Sunflower Pesto, 14810
Sunfresh, 13906, 14841
Sunfresh Brand, 14841
Sunfresh Freezerves, 13907
Sunfruit, 14994
Sungen, 13906
Sunglow, 15030
Sunkist, 33, 282, 2277, 4124, 4130, 10943,
   10944, 13920, 13922, 13925
Sunkist Country Time, 11458
Sunkist Flavour Bursts, 5389
Sunkist Fruit First Fruit Snacks, 5389
Sunlight, 14832
Sunlike, 33, 13938
Sunlite, 7239, 7240
Sunmaid, 3730, 7091, 13940
Sunmalt, 7594
Sunmed, 251
Sunmet, 13941
Sunnie, 5955
Sunnuts, 13984
Sunny, 9859
Sunny and Cheese, 2140
Sunny Avocado, 13942
Sunny Boy, 11551
Sunny D, 13944
Sunny Dawn, 8654
Sunny Day, 11655
Sunny Farm, 2448
Sunny Fresh, 2369
Sunny Fresh Free, 2369
Sunny Gold, 8860
Sunny Isle, 13719
Sunny Lea, 3388
Sunny Meadow, 6107
Sunny Millet, 10023
Sunny Morning, 11214
Sunny Shores, 8904
Sunny Shores Broccoli Wokly, 8904
Sunny South, 13947
Sunnydale Farms, 4707, 4709
Sunnydell, 15015, 15016
Sunnyland, 13951
Sunnyland Farms, 13950
Sunnyrose Cheese, 13952
Sunnyside, 6191, 7466
Sunray, 11071
Sunred, 880
Sunrice, 14040
Sunrich, 13887, 13890
Sunridge Farms, 13871
Sunripe, 9592, 10844, 10868
Sunrise, 698, 1104, 1920, 13007, 13961,
   14786
Sunrise 2000, 3124
Sunrise Farms, 14693
Sunsational, 15171
Sunsations, 13939
Sunset, 3247
Sunset Farm, 13965
Sunset Pink, 7672
Sunshine, 379, 7433, 7434, 7654, 8860,
   9482, 9671, 13961, 13968
Sunshine California, 8466
Sunshine Country, 7431, 7436
Sunshine Farms, 13972, 13974
Sunshine Krispy, 7685
Sunshine Spa, 7766
Sunshine State, 8591
Sunshine Valley, 10015
Sunshine Wheat Beer, 10122
Sunshine's, 14040
Sunshower, 13206
Sunspire, 9907, 9908
Sunspire Organics, 9908
Sunsweet Prune Juice, 13940
Sunsweet Prunes, 13882, 13940
Sunsweet/Sun-Gold, 13940
Suntory Bottled Wate, 13982
Suntory Oolong Tea, 13982
Suntree, 10223
Sunwest, 13984
Sunwise, 6191
Suparossa, 1417
Supelco, 13194
Super, 4093
Super Aged Gouda, 15622
Super Antioxidant Blend, 731
Super B-12 Sublingual, 10422
Super Bee Honey Stix, 13009

Super Blue Green Enzymes, 2554
Super Bowl Cleanse, 150
Super Bubble®, 4679
Super Bunny, 8942
Super Burgers, 14711
Super C Active, 150
Super Caffeinated Canned Coffee, 3021
Super Caffeinated Coffee, 3021
Super Charge, 8111
Super Citrimax, 7018
Super Detox, 150
Super Dickmann's, 13771
Super Diet Now, 8111
Super Epa, 10035
Super Fabulous Fiber, 8407
Super Fat Burner, 177, 6343
Super Fine, 6191
Super Gel B, 9489
Super Good, 6849
Super Green, 150
Super Kleaned Wheat, 7804
Super Kmh, 4524
Super Life, 4527
Super Oxy-Pure, 14159
Super Pretzel, 1071
Super Q10, 2554
Super Ropes, 527, 528, 529
Super Salad Oil, 150
Super Skates, 14479
Super Slicer, 2087
Super Soynuts, 8304
Super Stress, 10035
Super Stuffers, 9987
Super Sucker, 903
Super Supreme, 3755
Super Tonic, 150
Super Vab, 10035
Super Vita Vim, 7324
Super-1-Daily, 7277
Super-Mix, 8704
Superb, 92, 701
Superb Select, 92, 701
Superb®, 702
Superburgers, 14712
Superclear, 15206
Supercol, 6457
Supercuts, 12417
Superfex, 15151
Superfine, 6191
Superfly, 14479
Superfreeze, 15151
Supergrain Pasta, 11805, 11806
Superior, 2147, 7961, 7987, 9459, 12717,
   12720, 12748, 12749, 12751, 12759,
   13515, 13992
Superior Cake, 13995
Superior Chocolatier, 14021
Superior Coffee's, 12758
Superior Confections, Inc., 14021
Superior Farms, 13997, 13998
Superior Foods, 13999
Superior Herb & Ginseng, 14013
Superior Lager, 10320
Superior Nut Company, 14004
Superior Pride, 13999
Superior Source, 3278
Superior Spices, 14504
Superior Syrups, 14504
Superjuice, 7190, 7191
Superla, 15206
Superpretzel, 7189, 7190, 7191
Supersnax, 13830
Supersocco, 15734
Superstar Strawberry, 5954
Superstone, 12780
Superstore, 14017
Supertex, 15206
Supervan, 3755
Superwhip, 15206
Supherb Farms, 9171, 9172, 13985
Supper Topper, 215
Suprema, 14019
Supreme, 3755, 6807, 7091, 9490, 11658,
   12462, 14025
Supreme 7, 6449
Supreme B 150, 10035
Supreme Dairy Farms, 14022
Supreme Date, 15434
Supreme Starz, 3185
Supremes, 13832
Supremo, 3423, 9597
Supro, 13362

Suproplus, 13362
Suprosoy, 13362
Suram, 14026
Sure Fresh, 14027
Sure-Jell, 7944, 7948, 7949
Surebond, 3329
Surefresh Foods, 2594
Surefry Soybean Meal, 12084
Surejell, 7950
Surf King, 10508
Surf Spray, 10535
Surface Guard, 10421
Surfax, 2357
Surlean, 7999
Surry, 12474
Sursweet, 14276
Survivor Stout, 12610
Susan Winget, 7123
Susan's Sweet Talk, 8625
Sushi Chef, 1216
Susquehanna Valley, 7741, 14032
Sustagrain®, 3203
Suter, 14034
Sutter Home, 14036
Sutton's, 14037
Suzanna's, 14039
Suzanne's Conserves, 14040
Suzanne's Salad Splash, 15833
Suzi Wan, 9010
Suzuki's Ice Castle, 14042
Svenhard's, 14882
Svenhards, 14043
Swagger, 14044
Swamp Fire Seafood Boil, 10480
Swan, 10257
Swan Gardens, 8418
Swan Island, 10257
Swan Joseph, 14045
Swan's Touch, 10691
Swans Down, 12025
Swans Down Cake Flour, 12026
Swanson, 11365, 14960, 15590
Swanson Broth, 2264
Swanson Vineyards & Winery, 14046
Swanson®, 2263
Swany White, 13002
Swany White Certified Organic, 13002
Swazi Mamma Mamba, 14792
Sweatheart, 7095
Swedish Hill, 14049
Sweepstakes, 14581
Sweet, 822
Sweet & Hot, 14203
Sweet & Sassy, 12545
Sweet & Saucy Caramel Sauces, 14052
Sweet & Saucy Chocolate Sauces, 14052
Sweet & Spicey, 14808
Sweet 'n Healthy, 10387
Sweet 'n Low, 3547, 13830
Sweet 2 Eat, 15324
Sweet and Slender Natural Sweetener,
   15678
Sweet Baby Ray's, 14053
Sweet Basics, 3414
Sweet Beans, 13890
Sweet Betsy From Pike, 15722
Sweet Blessings, 14054
Sweet Blossoms, 2292
Sweet Breath Xtreme Intense Breath, 6348
Sweet Carolina, 5661
Sweet Cheese, Queso Blanco, 11062
Sweet D'Lite®, 1328
Sweet Dessert Wine, 11730
Sweet Earth Natural Foods, 14058
Sweet Factory, 704
Sweet Home Farm, 5731
Sweet Kiss, 8433
Sweet Leaf, 15678
Sweet Meadow Farms, 4768
Sweet Notes, 12146, 12147
Sweet Nothings, 1006, 14714
Sweet Occasion, 4433
Sweet Onion Low Fat Crackers, 1568
Sweet Organics, 12982
Sweet Pepper Low Fat Crackers, 1568
Sweet Pickles, 9835
Sweet Pleasers Gourmet, 11510
Sweet Portion, 11510
Sweet Ripe, 352
Sweet Savory Cocktai, 14852
Sweet Seduction, 5299
Sweet Shells, 6219

White Swan, 5882, 15502
White Tiger Rice, 8770
White Wave, 3317, 15504
White Wings, 2048
Whitefish, 5914
Whitehall, 15510
Whitehall Lane, 15509
Whitehaven®, 4226
Whitewater, 5896
Whitewheat, 4959, 4975
Whitford, 15513
Whitney Distributing, 12230
Whitney Yogurt, 15516
Whol-Bean, 15355
Whole Alternatives, 2517
Whole Earth, 11821
Whole Fruit, 4152, 4517
Whole Grain Chips Ahoy!, 7944
Whole Grain Chips Aloy, 7936
Whole Grain Fig Newtons, 7936, 7944
Whole Grain Wheat Thins, 7936, 7942, 7944
Whole Spectrum, 4526
Whole Sun, 8591
Wholesome, 10114
Wholesome Foods, 15524
Wholesome Valley, 5370
Wholly Wholesome, 12423
Wick's, 15528
Wicker, 15529
Wico, 15418
Wide Shoulders Bakin, 8484
Widman's Country, 15531
Widmer Brothers, 633, 634, 15533
Widmer's, 15535
Widmer's Cheese, 15534
Wiederkehr Wine, 15538
Wilbur Chocolate, 15347, 15542
Wilcox, 15543
Wild & Ricey, 637
Wild American Herb Co., 15808
Wild and Mild, 10713
Wild Blackberry, 8222
Wild Blend Rice, 8770
Wild Crafted Food From the Gulf Of, 8836
Wild Fruitz, 15546
Wild Fudge Brownies, 8830
Wild Goose, 5147
Wild Harvest, 321
Wild Hog Vineyard, 15547
Wild Horse, 5070, 15548
Wild Huckleberry, 5914
Wild Jungle Animal Crackers, 3670
Wild Keta Salmon, 7375
Wild Man, 6155
Wild Olive, 3001
Wild Pack, 9653
Wild Raspberry, 5896
Wild Red King Salmon, 7375
Wild Springs, 1409
Wild Thyme Cottage Products, 15552
Wild Turkey, 11222
Wild Turkey 101 Proof, 11221
Wild Vines®, 4226
Wild West, 1940
Wild West Spices, Inc., 15554
Wild White King Salmon, 7375
Wildcat, 8102
Wildcat Produce Garden, 15556
Wildcat Strong, 8102
Wildcatters Refined, 15810
Wildcraft, 4980
Wilderness, 1489, 1490, 2719, 10294
Wildfire, 11126
Wildfire Foods, 7846
Wildflower, 8222
Wildfruit Fruit Snacks, 5389
Wildhurst Cabernet F, 15557
Wildhurst Chardonnay, 15557
Wildhurst Merlot, 15557
Wildhurst Zinfandel, 15557
Wildwood Baked Tofu, 15561
Will, 15567
Willamette, 15586
Willard, 13594
William Atwood, 15571
William Fischer Deli Meats, 13505
William Hill Estate™, 4226
William Hill Winery, 15580
William Wheeler Winery, 1652
William's Corn, 11597
Williamette Valley Mustard, 6296

Williams, 15588, 15590
Williams-Selym Winery, 15596
Williamsburg Winery, 15600
Williamson's, 3609
Willie's, 11945, 13800
Willingham Manor, 13462
Willoughby's, 15604
Willow, 15605
Willow Farms, 12113
Willow Hill, 15606
Willow Oak Farms, 15608
Willy Wonka, 15611
Willy's, 15613
Wilson Continental D, 3271
Wilson Foods, 15616
Wilsonhill, 15618
Wiltshire, 2548
Wimberley Valley, 15619
Win You, 2952
Winchester, 13550
Wind & Willow Key Lime Cheeseball, 918
Windansea Wheat, 7619
Windatt Farms, 15624
Winder, 15626
Windham Hearth, 15049
Windmill, 432
Windscapes, 13111
Windsock, 8224
Windsor, 2282, 5070, 15541
Windsor Canadian, 1237
Windsor Vineyards, 15633, 15634
Windwalker, 15635
Windy Shoal, 9343
Wine & Pepper, 5804
Wine Country, 6754
Wine Country Chef Gourmet Marinade, 15637
Wine Country Chef Lemon Pepper Rub, 15637
Wine Country Chef Spiced Mustard, 15637
Wine Country Chief Spiced Bbq Rub, 15637
Wine Country Kitchens, 15638
Wine Gift Packaging, 5874
Wine Island Oysters, 9750
Wine-King, 10694
Winemaker's Choice, 6133
Wines, 2535
Winexpert, 616
Winey Keemun English Breakfast, 5825
Winfrey's, 15642
Wing Hing Gold Coin, 15644
Wing Hing Panda, 15644
Wing It, 15645
Wing's, 15649, 15652
Winger, 15651
Wings-N-Things, 12191
Winky Foods, 8165
Winmix, 15654
Winn & Lovett, 15656
Winn-Dixie, 15656
Winston, 4441
Winsuel, 5480
Winter Block, 5784
Winter Brown Ale, 8572
Winter Garden, 11302, 15661
Winter Gold, 8591
Winter Harbor, 4168
Winter Solstice, 607
Winter Stout, 12561
Winter Warlock, 1829
Winter Warmer, 1507
Winter Wonder, 13438
Winterbrook Seltzer, 15664
Winterfest, 3313
Winterfresh, 9010, 15765, 15766
Winterhook, 11991
Winters, 1740
Wintersweet, 2777
Wintrex, 945
Wipe Out, 8133
Wis-Pak Foods, 2369
Wiscon, 11663
Wisconsin American Ginseng, 11663
Wisconsin Blend, 8624
Wisconsin Cheese, 15669
Wisconsin Gold, 12023
Wisconsin Lakeshore, 5252
Wisconsin Pride, 12136
Wisconsin Whey International, 15676
Wisdom & Warter, 1104
Wisdom Nutrition, 15678
Wisdom of the Ancients Herbal Teas, 15678

Wise Potato Chips, 15681
Wisecrackers, 10976
Wiser's Deluxe, 3320
Wiser's Special Blend, 3320
Wiser's Very Old, 3320
Wish-Bone, 1393, 14834, 14836
Wisi Club, 9770
Wisnack, 3894
Wispride, 1284
Wissahickon Spring Water, 15686
Wit, 5896
Witenheim, 2633
Witness Tree Vineyard, 15688
Wiz, 8704
Wizard, 12772
Wizards, 4354
Wizbanger, 12898
Wmfb, 15233
Wmp Kyowa, 7994
Wnp - Washed Natural Sesame Seeds, 13071
Wodka Wyborowa Wyborowa, 11221
Woeber, 15692
Wok Menu, 3904
Wokin'n Tossin', 5742
Wokvel, 5473
Wolf's Scottish Cream Ale, 14990
Wolferman's, 15697
Wolffs, 1495
Wolfgang Puck, 3175
Wolfgang Puck's, 3189
Wolfschmidt, 5070
Wolfschmidt Vodka, 1237
Wollersheim Winery, 15703
Woman's Select, 9079
Womens Bread, 5169
Wonder, 7091, 7095, 7098, 7105, 7264, 15459
Wonder Bread, 3356, 7091, 7092, 7447
Wonder Fry, 7241
Wonder Rice, 3133
Wonderbar, 15105
Wonderbra, 12752
Wonderfood, 4110
Wonderful Life, 14163
Wong Wing, 15710
Wonka, 4660, 10102
Wonka Pixy Stix Mixers, 4660
Woodbury Vineyards, 15715
Woodchuck, 5976
Woodchuck Draft Cider, 5949
Woodchuck Pear Cider, 1320
Wooden Shoe, 432
Wooden Valley, 15716
Woodfield Fish & Oyster, 15717
Woodfield Ice, 15717
Woodford Reserve® Ky Straight, 1897
Woodie Pie, 15718
Woodman's, 1421
Woodruff Ale, 12610
Woods, 15722
Woodside Vineyards, 15723
Woodstock Wheat, 6602
Woody's, 7948
Worcester, 9381
Work Saver, 4507
Workout Energy Drinks, 15500
World Class, 14473
World Classic, 3352
World Coffee Safari Gourmet, 13445
World Cup, 15736
World Finer Fods, 14562
World Finer Foods, 14553, 14554, 14555, 14556, 14557, 14558, 14559, 14560, 14561, 14563, 14564, 14565, 14566, 14567
World Finest, 15750
World Harbors, 15739
World Kitchen's, 1908
World of Coffee, 15747
World of Grains, 9010
World of Spices, 15747
World of Tea, 15747
World Organic, 8421
World Wide, 1402
World Wrestling Fede, 400
World's Best, 6231
World's Finest Chocolate, 15751
World's Real, 15749
Worldfood, 6708
Worldwide Sport Nutrition®, 10042
Worthington, 15755
Worthy Cabernet, 13387

Wos-Wit, 6010
Wowie!, 10665
Wpc 34, 15676
Wrap Arounds, 8088
Wrap'n Roll, 8263
Wrappers, 8088
Wrappetizers, 592, 594, 9150
Wrappy, 6212
Wright, 15760
Wright Delicious, 15763
Wright's, 973
Wrigley Sperarmint, 15766
Wrigley's Big Red, 9010
Wrigley's Freedent, 9010
Wrigley's Juicy Fruit, 9010
Wrigley's Spearmint, 9010
Wrong Number, 11132
Wsi, 15744
Wsr, 10060
Wu Wei, 1594
Wuaconda Orchards, 1763
Wunder Bar, 15614
Wunderbar, 11305, 15106, 15108
Wurstmeister, 12523
Wwrapps, 12414
Wy-Am, 10687
Wyandot, 15771
Wyandotte Graystone Winery, 15772
Wyandotte Winery, 15772
Wychwood, 4542
Wycliff® Sparkling, 4226
Wye River, 2774, 6370
Wylers, 6392, 6395
Wyman's Wild Blueberries, 5570
Wyman's Wild Raspberries, 5570
Wyndham, 106
Wyndham Estate, 11221, 11222
Wynn Starr, 15773
Wynn Starr Foodservice, 15774
Wysong, 15776
Wytase, 7239

X

X-1, 5779
X-Fine, 15206
X-Mix, 6507
X-Tra-Touch, 14610
X-Treme Freeze, 5410
Xanadu Exotic Tea, 3034
Xhosa Umsobo Lyababa, 14792
Xip Caviar, 10508
Xl 2000, 15676
Xl 440, 15676
Xl 480, 15676
Xlnt, 4075
Xploder, 15612
Xtc, 15468
Xtreme, 13111
Xtreme Nerds, 4660

Y

Ya-Hoo!, 10718
Yago Sant Gria, 8032
Yakima Valley, 15791
Yakisoba, 15285
Yakshi Fragrances, 8582
Yamajirushi, 9568
Yamamotoyama 1690, 13667
Yamasa, 15794
Yamato Colony, 8494
Yamhill Wines, 15798
Yami, 904
Yarnell's, 15803
Yata, Pilta, Kapha Teas, 8823
Yaucono, 2132
Ye Olde English, 1250
Ye Olde Farm Style, 10742
Yelkin, 701
Yelkin®, 702
Yellow Emperor, 15808
Yellow Gold Shelf St, 10020
Yellow Label, 15512
Yellow Rose, 13419
Yellow Rose Pale, 15810
Yerba Prima, 15812
Yes!, 3352
Yick Lung, 15816
Yieldgard and Yieldgard Vt, 9613
Yin Yang, 787
Ying Yang, 12081
Yo Baby Yogurt, 13768

African

Gondwanaland, 5754
Honeydrop Foods, 6665
Horriea 2000 Food Industries, 6737
O Chili Frozen Foods Inc, 10444
Omanhene Cocoa Bean Company, 10645
Pots de Creme, 11525
Southern Heritage Coffee Company, 13445
Tantos Foods International, 14208

Arabic

Blue Pacific Flavors & Fragrances, 1579
Choice of Vermont, 2826
Dipasa, 4008
East Wind Nut Butters, 4289
Fillo Factory, 4804
Golden Platter Foods, 5721
Grounds for Thought, 6008
Halal Transactions, 6146
Hommus Factory, 6649
Marantha Natural Foods, 8948
Sacharen Brothers, 12530
Sokol & Company, 13359
Tarazi Specialty Foods, 14217
Tribe Mediterranean Foods Company LLC, 14592
Victoria Packing Corporation, 15091

Argentinean

Blue Pacific Flavors & Fragrances, 1579
Goodheart Brand Specialty Foods, 5777

Asian

A M Todd Company, 10
Acatris, 155
Ajinomoto Food Ingredients LLC, 270
Ajinomoto Frozen Foods USA, 271
Alternative Health & Herbs, 439
American Culinary Gardens, 502
Arctic Seas, 719
Associated Fruit Company, 823
Atlantic Laboratories, 874
Basic Food Flavors, 1177
Baycliff Company, 1216
Boyajian, Inc, 1737
California Style Gourmet Products, 2219
Cathay Foods Corporation, 2510
Chang Food Company, 2616
China Bowl Trading Company, 2774
Chinese Spaghetti Factory, 2781
Chungs Gourmet Foods, 2858
Cinnabar Specialty Foods, 2874
Clements Foods Company, 2952
Clofine Dairy & Food Products, 2964
ConAgra Grocery Products, 3198, 3199
Creme Glacee Gelati, 3441
Cricklewood Soyfoods, 3462
Daerim America, 3635
Dean Distributors, 3817
Delta Food Products, 3904
Dixie USA, 4033
Dong Kee Company, 4086
Eastern Tea Corporation, 4300
Eckert Cold Storage, 4316
Eden Foods Inc, 4338
Edward & Sons Trading Company, 4354
Egg Roll Fantasy, 4366
Erba Food Products, 4506
Flavor House, 4898
Fmali Herb, 4980
Fortella Fortune Cookies, 5062
Franklin Farms, 5131
Frozen Specialties, 5256
Fuji Foods, 5273, 5274
Glacier Fish Company, 5602
Glennys, 5625
Gold Pure Foods Products Company, 5672
Golden Gate Foods, 5704
Golden Whisk, 5742
Great Eastern Sun, 5897
Hain Celestial Canada, 6140
Harvest Food Products Company, 6283
Hawaii Candy, 6305
Health Concerns, 6341
Health is Wealth Foods, 6347
Hormel Foods Corporation, 6709, 6710, 6711, 6712, 6713, 6714, 6715, 6716, 6717, 6719, 6720, 6721, 6722, 6723, 6724, 6725, 6726, 6727, 6728, 6729, 6731

Hormel Foods Pork Division, 6733
House Foods America Corporation, 6757
Hsu's Ginseng Enterprises, 6788
Hung's Noodle House, 6820
Indian Foods Company, 6951
Itoen, 7163
JSL Foods, 7281
JWS Delavau Company, 7283
Kapaa Poi Factory, 7608
Kikkoman International, 7775, 7776
Kraft Food Ingredients, 7934
Kubla Khan Food Company, 7980
L&S Packing Company, 8005
Lawry's Foods, 8268
Lee's Food Products, 8306
Local Tofu, 8504
Mad Will's Food Company, 8782
Maine Seaweed Company, 8840
Mandarin Noodle Manufacturing Company, 8887
Mandoo, 8891
Maruchan, 9041
Metzer Farms, 9323
Michigan Sugar Company, 9373
Millflow Spice Corporation, 9466
Minh Food Corporation, 9501
Mo Hotta-Mo Betta, 9571
Modern Macaroni Company, 9580
Montreal Chop Suey Company, 9666
Moody Dunbar, 9671
Morinaga Nutritional Foods, 9700
Myron's Fine Foods, 9889
Nanka Seimen Company, 9936
Naumes, 10062
Nikken Foods Company, 10227
Nissin Foods USA Company, 10236
Nomura Tofu Company, 10252
NuNaturals, 10387
Ota Tofu Company, 10744
Pacific Ocean Produce, 10855
Pacific Valley Foods, 10871
Paisley Farms, 10887
Pearson's Homestyle, 11052
Peking Noodle Company, 11081
Pharmline, 11268
Premier Pacific Seafoods, 11571
Prince of Peace Enterprises, 11631
Progenix Corporation, 11663
Quong Hop & Company, 11810
San Diego Soy Dairy, 12618
San Francisco Herb & Natural Food Company, 12626
San-J International, 12641
Satori Teas, 12788
Schiff Food Products, 12843
Senba USA, 13031
Shahi Food Corporation, 13105
Shepherd Farms, 13146
Shine Food, 13156
Shining Ocean, 13157
Sno Pac Foods, 13334
Soolim, 13389
Soyfoods of America, 13476
Spice Hunter, 13523
St. John's Botanicals, 13604
Summercorn Foods, 13846
Sun Sun Food Products, 13874
Sun Wellness/Sun Chlorel, 13877
SunRich, 13890
Sunrise Markets, 13962
Superior Trading Company, 14013
Sure Fresh Produce, 14027
Sweet Earth Natural Foods, 14058
Talley Farms, 14190
Tate & Lyle Staley Company, 14243
Timber Crest Farms, 14405
Tofu Shop Specialty Foods, 14431
Tofutti Brands, 14432
Triple Leaf Tea, 14611
Twenty First Century Foods, 14725
Twin Marquis, 14732
Uni-President, 14823
Union, 14842
Van Oriental Foods, 14978
Vessey & Company, 15071
Victoria Packing Corporation, 15091
Vitasoy USA, 15181
Wah Yet Group, 15252
Wan Hua Foods, 15285
Wei-Chuan, 15367
Westbrae Natural Foods, 15432
Willow Foods, 15605

Windsor Foods, 15631
Wing Hing Noodle Company, 15644
Wing Nien Company, 15646
Wong Wing Foods, 15710
World Ginseng Center, 15738
Yamasa Corporation, 15794
Yellow Emperor, 15808

Brazilian

Blue Pacific Flavors & Fragrances, 1579
Chr Hansen, 2833
Cobi Foods, 3009
Corte Provisions, 3336
Country Smoked Meats, 3390
Crofton & Sons, 3475
Gourmet Baker, 5797
Kalustyan Corporation, 7597
Kozy Shack, 7928
McCain Foods USA, 9148
Nielsen Citrus Products, 10223
Northwest Pea & Bean Company, 10361
Odessa Tortilla & Tamale Factory, 10544
Sprague Foods, 13555
Talk O'Texas Brands, 14186
Weyhaupt Brothers Packing, 15474

Cajun

Atlantic Premium Brands, 879
Atlantic Seasonings, 886
Autin's Cajun Cookery, 934
Azar Nut Company, 960
Bayou Land Seafood, 1224
Bear Creek Country Kitchens, 1242
Blue Runner Foods, 1590
Boudreaux's Foods, 1719
Cajun Boy's Louisiana Products, 2152
Cajun Crawfish Distributors, 2154
Cajun Creole Products, 2155
Carnival Brands, 2410
Cheese Straws & More, 2683
Chef Hans Gourmet Foods, 2694
Cooke Aguaculture, 3290
G Di Lullo & Sons, 5310
Gourmet Foods, 5804
Hampton House, 6180
Hollman Foods, 6610
Hummingbird Kitchens, 6814
Kajun Kettle Foods, 7585
Louisiana Gourmet Enterprises, 8611
Magic Seasoning Blends, 8807
Mild Bill's Spices, 9423
Morey's Seafood International, 9695
Oak Grove Smokehouse, 10480
Old Mansion Foods, 10596
Olde Tyme Mercantile, 10617
Raffield Fisheries, 11881
Reggie Ball's Cajun Foods, 12014
Reily Foods Company, 12025
REX Pure Foods, 11857
Savoie's Sausage & Food Products, 12809
Smuggler's Kitchen, 13321
SOUPerior Bean & Spice Company, 12510
Sunset Farm Foods, 13965
Suzanna's Kitchen, 14039
Texas Crumb & Food Products, 14325
Uncle Fred's Fine Foods, 14811
Victoria Packing Corporation, 15091
Woods Smoked Meats, 15722
Yankee Specialty Foods, 15800
Zapp's Potato Chips, 15866
Zummo Meat Company, 15896

Chinese

Acatris, 155
Allied Old English, 393
American Botanicals, 489
American Culinary Gardens, 502
Aristocrat International Corporation, 733
Artel, 787
Basic Food Flavors, 1177
Belleisle Foods, 1312
Calco of Calgary, 2176
Canton Noodle Corporation, 2304
Cathay Foods Corporation, 2510
Chang Food Company, 2616
Chelten House Products, 2708
Chungs Gourmet Foods, 2858
Clements Foods Company, 2952
ConAgra Grocery Products, 3198, 3199
Creative Foodworks, 3433

Dean Distributors, 3817
Delta Food Products, 3904
Dong Kee Company, 4086
Eckert Cold Storage, 4316
Eckroat Seed Company, 4319
Egg Roll Fantasy, 4366
Erba Food Products, 4506
Everfresh Food Corporation, 4563
Favorite Foods, 4730
Fine Choice Foods, 4808
Flavor House, 4898
Fortella Fortune Cookies, 5062
Frozen Specialties, 5256
Fuji Foods, 5274
Gold Pure Foods Products Company, 5672
Golden Gate Foods, 5704
Great Northern Products, 5916
Green Gold Group, 5944
Harvest Food Products Company, 6283
Hawaii Candy, 6305
Health Concerns, 6341
Hong Kong Market Company, 6671
Hong Kong Noodle Company, 6672
Hormel Foods Corporation, 6708
Hung's Noodle House, 6820
JFC International, 7269
JR Laboratories, 7278
Kari-Out Company, 7616
Kelly Gourmet Foods, 7689
Kikkoman International, 7776
L&S Packing Company, 8005
La Tang Cuisine Manufacturing, 8085
Lee Kum Kee, 8302
Lee's Food Products, 8306
Luigino's, 8674
Luigino's/Michelina Brand, 8675
Maebo Noodle Factory, 8798
Mandarin Noodle Manufacturing Company, 8887
Mandarin Soy Sauce, 8888
Marsan Foods, 9014
Maruchan, 9041
Metzer Farms, 9323
Mexi-Frost Specialties Company, 9327
Millflow Spice Corporation, 9466
Min Tong Herbs, 9492
Miyako Oriental Foods, 9568
Montreal Chop Suey Company, 9666
Morinaga Nutritional Foods, 9700
Mung Dynasty, 9849
Nanka Seimen Company, 9936
National Noodle Company, 9990
Nikken Foods Company, 10227
Ohta Wafer Factory, 10559
Paradise Products Corporation, 10933
Peking Noodle Company, 11081
Porkie Company of Wisconsin, 11500
Prime Food Processing Corporation, 11613
Progenix Corporation, 11663
Rosmarino Foods/R.Z. Humbert Company, 12325
San Francisco Herb & Natural Food Company, 12626
Schiltz Foods, 12845
Shanghai Company, 13115
Shine Food, 13156
Sona & Hollen Foods, 13378
Soyfoods of America, 13476
Superior Trading Company, 14013
Sure Fresh Produce, 14027
Tate & Lyle Staley Company, 14243
Texas Coffee Company, 14324
Trade Farm, 14515
Triple Leaf Tea, 14611
Tsue Chong Noodle Company, 14672
Union, 14842
United Noodle Manufacturing Company, 14872
Valdez Food, 14936
Van Oriental Foods, 14978
Victoria Packing Corporation, 15091
Wan Hua Foods, 15285
Wei-Chuan, 15367
Western Pacific Commodities, 15448
Whyte's Food Corporation, 15525
Willow Foods, 15605
Windsor Foods, 15631
Wing Nien Company, 15646
Wing Sing Chong Company, 15648
Wings Foods of Alberta, 15652
Wizards Cauldron, LTD, 15691
Wong Wing Foods, 15710

Whistler Brewing Company, 15485, 15486
Willamette Valley Walnuts, 15569
Wolferman's, 15697
Yakima Brewing Company, 15789
Yellow Rose Brewing Company, 15810
Yorktown Baking Company, 15834

European

Adolf's Meats & Sausage Kitchen, 204
Beck's Waffles of Oklahoma, 1265
Catamount Brewing Company, 2500
Cateraid, 2506
Continental Grain/ContiGroup Companies, 3273
Freezer Queen Foods, 5160
Future Bakery & Cafe, 5300
Legacy Soft Gourmet Pretzels, 8319
Mancini Packing Company, 8884
Milmar Food Group, 9477
Morris National, 9718
Neto Sausage Company, 10110
OH Chocolate, 10468
Orlando Baking Company, 10720
Patisserie Wawel, 11006
Pearson's Homestyle, 11052
Renaissance Baking Company, 12034
Rubschlager Baking Corporation, 12405
Strossner's Bakery, 13799
Uptown Bakers, 14907
Vie de France Yamazaki, 15102
Vigneri Confections, 15111

French

Atlantic Seasonings, 886
Bakehouse, 1050
Bakery Europa, 1076
Breadworks Bakery & Deli, 1782
Brier Run Farm, 1818
Cafe Du Monde, 2121
Carnival Brands, 2410
Cherchies, 2714
ConAgra Grocery Products, 3199
Creme Curls Bakery, 3439
Dufflet Pastries, 4170
Edelweiss Patisserie, 4337
El Segundo Bakery, 4394
Emkay Trading Corporation, 4452
Fiera Foods, 4787
Food Source Company, 5014
Freezer Queen Foods, 5160
G Scaccianoce & Company, 5321
Galassos Baking Company, 5367
Garden Herbs, 5401
General Mills, 5463
Gerard's French Bakery, 5514
Gourmet Baker, 5797
Groezinger Provisions, 6001
Hawaii Star Bakery, 6309
Heluva Good Cheese, 6415
Kolb-Lena Cheese Company, 7900
Kretschmar, 7961
La Brea Bakery, 8039
La Cigale Bakery, 8048
Lactalis USA, 8115
Laura's French Baking Company, 8258
Legacy Soft Gourmet Pretzels, 8319
Les Trois Petits Cochons, 8384
Majestic Distilling Company, 8848
Marcel et Henri Charcuterie Francaise, 8955
Mardi Gras, 8963
Marin French Cheese Company, 8983
Modern Mushroom Farms, 9581
Morabito Baking Company, 9687
Mozzicato Depasquale Bakery & Pastry Shop, 9797
Mrs. Clark's Foods, 9810
Nicky, 10217
Old Fashioned Kitchen, 10589
Orange Bakery, 10674
Oroweat Baking Company, 10728
Out of a Flower, 10765
Palmetto Pigeon Plant, 10902
Papa Leone Food Enterprises, 10918
Piemonte's Bakery, 11311
Pioneer French Baking, 11374
Quelle Quiche, 11789
Rollingstone Chevre, 12264
Royal Wine Company, 12396
S-Car-Go, 12468
Salmolux, 12588

Sapar, 12700
Sarabeth's Bakery, 12762
Savoie's Sausage & Food Products, 12809
Spring Glen Fresh Foods, 13562
Spruce Foods, 13581
T. Marzetti Company, 14138, 14139
Techni-Brew International, 14274
Unique Bakery Company, 14848
Vermont Bread Company, 15048
Vie de France Yamazaki, 15099, 15101
Whyte's Food Corporation, 15525

German

Alle Processing Corporation, 372
Amana Meat Shop & Smokehouse, 453
Aristocrat International Corporation, 733
Athens Pastries & Frozen Foods, 851
Atwood Cheese Company, 900
August Schell Brewing Company, 908
Bay Valley Foods, 1213
Beaverton Foods, 1261
Best Provision Company, Inc., 1389
Big City Reds, 1439
Boesl Packing Company, 1640
Clyde's Italian & German Sausage, 2992
Country Smoked Meats, 3390
Creme Curls Bakery, 3439
David Berg & Company, 3750
Davidson Meat Products, 3761
Del Monte Foods, 3868
Dimpflmeier Bakery, 4001
Dufflet Pastries, 4170
Egon Binkert Meat Products, 4369
El Segundo Bakery, 4394
Elmwood Lockers, 4436
Farmers Meat Market, 4701
Fillo Factory, 4804
Fischer & Wieser Specialty Foods, 4843
Gold Star Sausage Company, 5678
Gourmet Baker, 5797
Gwaltney of Smithfield, 6064, 6065
Hatfield Quality Meats, 6293
Hazle Park Packing Company, 6334
Heidi's Cheese Products, 6381
Kilgus Meats, 7781
Koegel Meats, 7889
Le Notre, Alain & Marie Baker, 8280
Left Hand Brewing Company, 8318
Lightlife Foods, 8437
Little Rhody Brand Frankfurts, 8485
Longmont Foods, 8548
Lykes Meat Group, 8689
Marin French Cheese Company, 8983
Matthiesen's Deer & Custom Processing, 9085
Michigan Farm Cheese Dairy, 9370
Miller's Stratford Provision Company, 9461
Morris National, 9718
Morse's Sauerkraut, 9726
Mrs. Minnick's Salads, 9823
New Canaan Farms, 10125
New Morning, 10156
O'Brien & Company, 10450
Organic Gourmet, 10700
P & L Poultry, 10789
Penn Valley Farms, 11106
Portland Brewing Company, 11512
Purnell's Old Folks Sausage Company, 11714
R.L. Zeigler Company, 11843
Raemica, 11879
Rego's Purity Foods, 12020
Saag's Products, 12523
Schaller & Weber, 12832
Schaller's Packers, 12834
Seneca Foods, 13033
Shelton's Poultry, 13140
Silver Star Meats, 13226
Smith Provision Company, 13301
Smolich Brothers, 13317
Stawnichy Holdings, 13678
Steve's Mom, 13715
Sunnydale Meats, 13949
Thomas Packing Company, 14364
Waco Beef & Pork Processors, 15247
Whole Herb Company, 15519
Willy's Pickle Products, 15613
Wimmer's Meat Products, 15620

Greek

Alimentaire Whyte's Inc, 349
Aslanis Seafoods, 814
Athens Pastries & Frozen Foods, 851
Atlantic Seasonings, 886
Atwood Cheese Company, 900
Bob Gordon & Associates, 1620
Corfu Foods, 3323
Cosmo's Food Products, 3342
Dough Delight, 4106
Fage USA, 4619
Fantis Foods, 4662
Fillo Factory, 4804
Georgia Vegetable Company, 5511
Grecian Delight Foods, 5937
Greek Gourmet Limited, 5938
H&F Food Products Company, 6075
Harlan Bakeries, Inc., 6232
Hommus Factory, 6649
Hormel Foods Corporation, 6719, 6722, 6731
Hye Cuisine, 6846
Kabob's, 7578
Kalustyan Corporation, 7597
Kolb-Lena Cheese Company, 7900
Konto's Foods, 7910
L&S Packing Company, 8005
Lactalis USA, 8115
Lawrences Delights, 8267
Lucille Farm Products, 8660
Marika's Kitchen, 8979
Marsan Foods, 9014
Mediterranean Gyros Products, 9248
Mediterranean Pita Bakery, 9249
Morabito Baking Company, 9687
Mount Capra Cheese, 9758
Mt. Olympus Specialty Foods, 9836
Naumes, 10062
Orleans Packing Company, 10725
Parthenon Food Products, 10972
Pearl Coffee Company, 11045
Pearson's Homestyle, 11052
Pechters Baking, 11057
Purity Foods, 11709
San Joaquin Figs, 12631
San Marzano Foods, 12637
Saputo Cheese, 12712
Sinbad Sweets, 13257
Soloman Baking Company, 13368
Spruce Foods, 13581
Star Fine Foods, 13640
Toufayan Bakeries, 14502
Victoria Packing Corporation, 15091
Woodlake Ranch, 15719

Hawaiian

Aloha Poi Factory, 412
Ames International, 566
Ann's House of Nuts, Inc., 642
AquaCuisine, 685
Barcelona Nut Company, 1126
Cyanotech Corporation, 3586
Dave's Hawaiian Ice Cream, 3749
Diamond Foods, 3963
Garden & Valley Isle Seafood, 5398
Hawaii Candy, 6305
HealthBest, 6349
Healthmate Products, 6351
Honey Acres, 6651
Kapaa Poi Factory, 7608
Kemoo Farm Foods, 7699
King Nut Company, 7807
Lodi Nut Company, 8513
NOH Foods of Hawaii, 9901
Ocean Beauty Seafoods, 10510
Po'okela Enterprises, 11438
Prince of Peace Enterprises, 11631
Puueo Poi Factory, 11718
Rio Grande Valley Sugar Growers, 12130
Sagawa's Savory Sauces, 12545
Setton International Foods, 13078
St. John Levert, 13603
Suzuki's Ice Castle, 14042
Torn & Glasser, 14485

Hispanic

Crown Candy Company, 3493
Energy Club, 4474
Kokopelli's Kitchen, 7898
Moody Dunbar, 9671

Nedlog Company, 10078
Romero's Food Products, 12277
Sierra Cheese Manufacturing Company, 13188
Thiel Cheese & Ingredients, 14350

Hungarian

Boesl Packing Company, 1640
Charlie's Country Sausage, 2645
Chicago 58 Food Products, 2749
E.E. Mucke & Sons, 4237
Erba Food Products, 4506
Famous Specialties Company, 4648
Kajun Kettle Foods, 7585
Olympia International, 10635
Shofar Kosher Foods, 13166
Stawnichy Holdings, 13678
Uncle Dave's Kitchen, 14810
Whole Herb Company, 15519
World Spice, 15744

Indian-Pakistani

Ann's House of Nuts, Inc., 642
Arizona Pistachio Company, 744
Asian Brands, 811
Bear Meadow Farm, 1246
Beetroot Delights, 1282
Blue Jay Orchards, 1573
Bottle Green Drinks, 1714
Brost International Trading Company, 1872
California Fruit & Nut, 2198
California Fruit and Tomato Kitchens, 2201
Chr Hansen, 2833
Cinnabar Specialty Foods, 2874
Cobi Foods, 3009
Commissariat Imports, 3138
Creative Foodworks, 3433
Curry King Corporation, 3560
Deep Foods, 3849
Diamond Foods, 3963
Eastern Tea Corporation, 4300
Eckroat Seed Company, 4319
Fearn Natural Foods, 4735
Ful-Flav-R Foods, 5277
Geetha's Gourmet of India, 5442
Georgia Vegetable Company, 5511
Graves Mountain Cannery, 5879
HealthBest, 6349
Hormel Foods Corporation, 6709, 6719, 6722, 6731
House Foods America Corporation, 6757
House of Spices India, 6763
Indian Foods Company, 6951
Indian Harvest Specialitifoods, 6953
Jardine Organic Ranch Co, 7332
Jay Shah Foods, 7350
Jonathan's Sprouts, 7484
Jyoti Cruisine India, 7554
Kalustyan Corporation, 7597
Kennebec Bean Company, 7712
Kraft Food Ingredients, 7934
Lang Naturals, 8225
Mandoo, 8891
Marsan Foods, 9014
Masala Chai Company, 9057
McKnight Milling Company, 9204
Medallion International, 9244
Moscow Seed Company, 9735
North Bay Produce, 10294
Northumberland Cooperative, 10350
Northwest Pea & Bean Company, 10361
Paramount Farms, 10943
Patak Spices USA, 11004
Raja Foods, 11901
Royal Coffee & Tea Company, 12362
Sahadi Fine Foods, 12551
Schiff Food Products, 12843
Setton International Foods, 13078
Setton Pistachio of Terra Bella, 13079
Shahi Food Corporation, 13105
Silver Palate Kitchens, 13222
Southern Brown Rice, 13437
Specialty Rice Marketing, 13513
Spice Hunter, 13523
Spokane Seed Company, 13545
Spruce Mountain Blueberries, 13582
Stapleton-Spence PackingCompany, 13638
Sunray Food Products Corporation, 13958
Sunwest Foods, 13984
Taj Gourmet Foods, 14176

Bernie's Foods, 1374
Biazzo Dairy Products, 1420
Blue Chip Group, 1564
Blue Mountain Flavors, 1577
Butterball Farms, 1997
Byrne Dairy, 2020
C.F. Sauer Company, 2046
Cache Creek Foods, 2101
Cagnon Foods Company, 2143
Cains Foods/Olde Cape Cod, 2149
Cajun Creole Products, 2155
Calise & Sons Bakery, 2228
Capay Canyon Ranch, 2313
Carmi Flavor & Fragrance Company, 2407
Carole's Cheesecake Company, 2416
Cell Tech International, 2554
Chewys Rugulach, 2742
Chianti Cheese Company, 2747
Chocolate By Design, 2801
Chris Candies, 2835
Ciro Foods, 2884
Cliffstar Corporation, 2959
Coffee Masters, 3050
ConAgra Food Ingredients, 3182
Confection Solutions, 3226
Cooke Aguaculture, 3290
Country Fresh Farms, 3375
Country Pure Foods, 3389
Cricklewood Soyfoods, 3462
Crown Prince, 3498
Dakota Brands International, 3679
Dakota Gourmet, 3681
Dakota Growers Pasta Company, 3682
David's Cookies, 3758
Dawn Food Products, 3777
De-Iorio's Frozen Dough, 3805
Delano Growers Grape Products, 3883
Diehl Food Ingredients, 3985
Dipasa, 4008
Durey-Libby Edible Nuts, 4196
East Coast Fresh Cuts Company, 4278
Eda's Sugarfree Candies, 4333
Elite Bakery, 4413
Empress Chocolate Company, 4464
F&S Produce Company, 4597
F. Gavina & Sons, 4599
First District Association, 4833
Fleischmanns Vinegar, 4923
Flowers Bakery of Winston-Salem, 4969
Foothills Creamery, 5025
Franklin Foods, 5132
French Meadow Bakery, 5169
Garlic Valley Farms Inc, 5419
Gibbons Bee Farm, 5546
Gimbal's Fine Candies, 5573
GKI Foods, 5338
Global Food Industries, 5635
Golden Fluff Popcorn Company, 5702
Golding Farms Foods, 5746
Good Star Foods, 5772
Gorant Candies, 5783
GPR Company, 5350
Great Northern Products, 5916
Haliburton International Corporation, 6154
Harbar Corporation, 6212
Harvest Valley Bakery, 6287
Henningsen Foods, 6426
Hialeah Products Company, 6513
Homestead Mills, 6644
Honey Acres, 6651
Hoopeston Foods, 6688
I Rice & Company, 6852
Instantwhip: Texas, 7010
Isabella's Healthy Bakery, 7127
Ivanhoe Cheese Inc, 7166
Jeremiah's Pick Coffee Company, 7380
Jonathan Lord Corporation, 7483
JR Wood/Big Valley, 7279
Just Born, 7546
Kangaroo Brands, 7605
Kargher Corporation, 7615
Kasilof Fish Company, 7633
Keller's Creamery, 7663
King Nut Company, 7806
Knappen Milling Company, 7864
La Vigne Enterprises, 8093
LaCrosse Milling Company, 8095
Lake Champlain Chocolates, 8138
Lallemand/American Yeast, 8170
Leighton's Honey, 8330
Lukas Confections, 8676
Main Street Custom Foods, 8829

Main Street Gourmet, 8830
Main Street Gourmet Fundraising, 8831
Main Street Muffins, 8833
Main Street's Cambritt Cookies, 8834
Mandarin Soy Sauce, 8888
Martin Farms, 9033
Melchers Flavors of America, 9260
Mendocino Mustard, 9270
Merrill's Blueberry Farms, 9302
MexAmerica Foods, 9326
Mincing Overseas Spice Company, 9493
Moon Shine Trading Company, 9674
Morning Glory/Formost Farms, 9702
Mother Murphy's Labs, 9741
Mrs. Clark's Foods, 9810
Mrs. Leeper's Pasta, 9818
Mushroom Company, 9871
Musicon Deer Farm, 9873
My Grandma's Coffee Cak e of New
    England, 9885
Myron's Fine Foods, 9889
National Fruit Flavor Company, 9983
Natural Wonder Foods, 10031
ND Labs Inc, 9899
New Era Canning Company, 10137
NorSun Food Group, 10263
North American Seasonings, 10287
Northland Cranberries, 10344
Northumberland Cooperative, 10350
Northwest Pea & Bean Company, 10361
Northwestern Foods, 10365
Now & Zen, 10378
Nu-World Amaranth, 10385
Nuvex Ingredients, 10440
Oregon Chai, 10685
Oregon Freeze Dry, 10689
Organic Planet, 10703
Orwasher's Bakery Handmade Bread, 10732
Otis Spunkmeyer, 10745
Ottawa Valley Grain Products, 10749
Pacific Spice Company, 10865
Partners Coffee Company, 10975
Pecoraro Dairy Products, 11062
Peerless Confection Company, 11071
Pellman Foods, 11086
Perfection Fine Products, 11214
Perfections by Allan, 11215
Poiret International, 11451
Porkie Company of Wisconsin, 11500
Premier Blending, 11564
Protein Products Inc, 11676
Queensboro Farm Products, 11787
R.L. Schreiber, 11841
Ranaldi Bros Frozen Food Products Inc,
    11916
Rea-D-Pak Foodservices, 11945
Regal Crown Foods, 12005
Rogers' Chocolates Ltd, 12250
Roller Ed, 12259
Rowena's, 12346
Run-A-Ton Group, 12423
RV Industries, 11866
Santa Barbara Pistachio Company, 12678
Schwan's Consumer Brands North America,
    12887
Scott's Auburn Mills, 12906
Seven Keys Company of Florida, 13085
Sheryl's Chocolate Creations, 13152
Sierra Cheese Manufacturing Company,
    13188
Siljans Crispy Cup Company, 13204
Silver Lake Cookie Company, 13217
Silver Spring Gardens, 13224
Snyder's of Hanover, 13350
Sonne, 13379
Star Kay White, 13643
Steel's Gourmet Foods, 13685
Sterling Extract Company, 13707
Stewart's Private Blend Foods, 13727
Strube Packing Company, 13801
Summit Lake Vineyards & Winery, 13852
Sunnyland Mills, 13951
Supreme Rice Mill, 14025
Templar Food Products, 14296
Thiel Cheese & Ingredients, 14350
Thomas Canning/Maidstone, 14357
Timber Crest Farms, 14405
Top Hat Company, 14472
Tripp Bakers, 14619
Valley Lahvosh Baking Company, 14947
Van Drunen Farms, 14973

Venice Spumoni/Spring Valley Ice Cream,
    15024
Ventre Packing Company, 15027
Victor Preserving Company, 15088
Victoria Packing Corporation, 15091
VIP Foods, 14925
Wachusett Potato Chip Company, 15246
Wawona Frozen Foods, 15323
White Rock Products Corporation, 15500
WILD Flavors (Canada), 15231
Wisconsin Cheeseman, 15670
Woolwich Dairy, 15730
World's Finest Chocolate, 15751
X Cafe, 15777
Yohay Baking Company, 15825

Latin American

Brooklyn Bottling Company, 1860
Erba Food Products, 4506
Felbro Food Products, 4744
Fortitude Brands LLC, 5066
Giumarra Companies, 5592
Goya Foods, 5818
HealthBest, 6349
Mardi Gras, 8963
McDaniel Fruit Company, 9181
Prime Produce, 11619
Schiff Food Products, 12843
T.W. Garner Food Company, 14149

Mediterranean

Choice of Vermont, 2826
Hormel Foods Corporation, 6709, 6719,
    6722, 6731
Mad Will's Food Company, 8782
Near East Food Products, 10072
Papa Leone Food Enterprises, 10918
Shenk's Foods, 13145
Star Fine Foods, 13640

Mexican

Alamo Tamale Corporation, 292
Algood Food Company, 348
Alimentaire Whyte's Inc, 349
Allied Old English, 393
Alvarado Street Bakery, 445
Amigos Canning Company, 569
Anita's Mexican Foods Corporation, 635
Ariza Cheese Company, 735
Arizona Cowboy, 739
Art's Tamales, 785
Artesia Tortilla Factory, 789
Ashman Manufacturing & Distributing
    Company, 809
Atlantic Seasonings, 886
Authentic Specialty Foods, 933
Avo King International, 949
Azteca Foods, 961
B. Martinez & Sons Company, 981
Baja Foods, 1040
Bartush-Schnitzius Foods Company, 1171
BBQ Bunch, 992
Bear Creek Country Kitchens, 1242
Bel/Kaukauna USA, 1284
Bien Padre Foods, 1429
Big B Distributors, 1436
Blue Pacific Flavors & Fragrances, 1579
Border Foods Inc, 1681, 1682
Brooks Tropicals, 1868
Brown-Forman Beverages Worldwide, 1897
Bueno Food Products, 1938
Burke Corporation, 1971
C.J. Vitner Company, 2050
California Creative Foods, 2190
California Fruit and Tomato Kitchens, 2201
California Style Gourmet Products, 2219
Camino Real Foods, 2255
Campbell Soup Company of Canada, 2265
Carmelita Provisions Company, 2406
Carriage House Companies, 2445
Casa Visco Finer Food Company, 2463
Cedarlane Foods, 2546
Chelten House Products, 2708
Chile Today - Hot Tamale, 2770
Choice of Vermont, 2826
Circle R Ranch Gourmet Foods, 2880
City Foods, 2903
Colorado Bean Company/ Greeley Trading,
    3100
Colorado Salsa Company, 3106

Comanche Tortilla Factory, 3128
ConAgra Frozen Foods Company, 3196
ConAgra Grocery Products, 3199
ConAgra Mexican Foods, 3202
Cookies Food Products, 3297
Creative Foodworks, 3433
CW Resources, 2095
Cyclone Enterprises, 3588
Dave's Gourmet, 3748
Dean Distributors, 3818
Del Grosso Foods, 3866
Del Monte Foods, 3868
Del Rey Tortilleria, 3874
Dillman Farm, 3993
Dipasa, 4008
Diversified Avocado Products, 4019
Dolores Canning Company, 4060
Don Miguel Mexican Foods, 4075
Dorina/So-Good, 4093
Double B Foods, 4100
E.D. Smith & Sons, 4236
Edmonds Chile Company, 4347
El Charro Mexican Food Industries, 4380
El Galindo, 4383
El Ranchito, 4392
El Rancho Tortilla, 4393
El Toro Food Products, 4395
El-Milagro, 4396
El-Rey Foods, 4397
Elena's Food Specialties, 4408
Excelline Foods, 4577
Famous Chili, 4646
Father Sam's Syrian Bread, 4725
Fernandez Chili Company, 4756
Fiesta Gourmet of Tejas, 4791
Figaro Company, 4797
Fischer & Wieser Specialty Foods, 4843
Flowers Baking, 4970
Food Products Corporation, 5008
Food Specialties Company, 5016
Foodbrands America, 5022
Fountain Valley Foods, 5088
Franklin Foods, 5132
Frito-Lay, 5215, 5216, 5217, 5218, 5219,
    5221, 5224, 5226, 5227, 5228, 5229
Ful-Flav-R Foods, 5277
Garden Complements, 5399
Genarom International, 5454
George Chiala Farms, 5484
Giumarra Companies, 5592
GNS Spices, 5347
Gold Pure Foods Products Company, 5672
Golden Flake Snack Foods, 5701
Golden Specialty Foods, 5724
Golding Farms Foods, 5746
Goldwater's Food of Arizona, 5748
Gondwanaland, 5754
Goya Foods, 5818
Grande Tortilla Factory, 5854
Great American Appetizers, 5886
Groeb Farms, 6000
Guiltless Gourmet, 6028
Hacienda De Paco, 6127
Hagerty Foods, 6133
Harbar Corporation, 6212
Hartford City Foam Pack aging &
    Converting, 6268
Havoc Maker Products, 6303
Heluva Good Cheese, 6415
Herlocher Foods, 6476
Herr's Foods, 6489
Highwood Distillers, 6549
Hiram Walker & Sons, 6585
Hirzel Canning Company &Farms, 6588
Hormel Foods Corporation, 6708, 6709,
    6710, 6711, 6712, 6713, 6715, 6716,
    6717, 6719, 6720, 6721, 6722, 6723,
    6724, 6725, 6726, 6727, 6728, 6729, 6731
Hormel Foods Pork Division, 6733
Hostess Frito-Lay Company, 6749
Hot Wachula's, 6753
House of Webster, 6774
Hume Specialties, 6811
Humpty Dumpty Snack Foods, 6819
HVJ International, 6119
Iltaco Food Products, 6906
Imus Ranch Foods, 6930
Indel Food Products, 6935, 6936
Interstate Brands Corporation/Wonder Bread
    Bakery, 7093
Jalapeno Foods Company, 7312
Jays Foods, 7351

Elgin Dairy Foods, 4410
Emkay Trading Corporation, 4452
Ener-G Foods, 4469
Erba Food Products, 4506
Faribault Foods, 4674
Fishhawk Fisheries, 4866
Fjord Pacific Marine Industries, 4879
Fremont Company, 5164
Gold Pure Foods Products Company, 5672
H.P. Hood, 6103, 6106
Heaven Hill Distilleries, 6371
Highwood Distillers, 6549
Hiram Walker & Sons, 6585, 6586
Hirzel Canning Company &Farms, 6588
Hood River Distillers, 6682
Horizon Organic Dairy, 6700
Hunter Farms, 6829
Inland Northwest Dairies, 6989
Jessie's Ilwaco Fish Company, 7391
Junuis Food Products, 7543
Kaiser Foods, 7584
Kalustyan Corporation, 7597
Kelchner's Horseradish, 7660
Knoll Creek Dairy, 7869
Kraft Foods, 7941, 7947
Kraft Foods/Knudson Products, 7952
Kruger Foods, 7974
Laird & Company, 8136
Lakeside Foods, 8157
Lakeside Packing Company, 8162
Lifeway Foods Inc, 8433
Litehouse Foods, 8475
Lounsbury Foods, 8623
M.A. Hatt & Sons, 8725
Majestic Distilling Company, 8848
Marcus Dairy, 8960
Marie Brizard Wines & Spirits, 8972
Marva Maid Dairy, 9044
Mike's Fish & Seafood, 9411
Morehouse Foods, 9692
Morrison Lamothe, 9720
New Harvest Foods, 10145
New Hope Mills, 10146
Oakhurst Dairy, 10493
Old Fashioned Kitchen, 10589
Olympia International, 10635
Paisley Farms, 10887
Palmieri Food Products, 10903
Pleasant View Dairy, 11420
Prairie Farms Dairy, 11545
Queensboro Farm Products, 11786, 11787
R&A Imports, 11818
R.A.B. Food Group LLC, 11828
Red Pelican Food Products, 11980
Rego Smoked Fish Company, 12019
Roberts Dairy Company, 12200
Robinson Dairy, 12208
Rod's Food Products, 12239
Roos Foods, 12291
Rosenberger's Dairies, 12318
Roy Stritmatter Company, 12352
San Fernando Creamery Farmdale Creamery, 12620
Santee Dairies, 12697
Schiff Food Products, 12843
Schneider Valley Farms Dairy, 12863
Schneider's Dairy Holdings Inc, 12864
Schwartz Pickle Company, 12893
Setton International Foods, 13078
Sisler's Ice & Ice Cream, 13271

Springfield Creamery, 13575
Stawnichy Holdings, 13678
Stolt SeaFarm, 13752
Strub Pickles, 13800
Sunshine Farms Dairy, 13974
T. Marzetti Company, 14138
Thor-Shackel HorseradishCompany, 14374
Tribe Mediterranean Foods Company LLC, 14592
Trigo Corporation, 14597
Tuscan Dairy Farms, 14717
Umpqua Dairy Products Company, 14804
United Pickle Products Corporation, 14874
Valley Lahvosh Baking Company, 14947
Ventura Foods, 15029
Ventura Foods Production Plant, 15030
Victoria Packing Corporation, 15091
Viking Distillery, 15114
Vitamilk Dairy, 15175
Westhill Dairy, 15454
Willy's Pickle Products, 15613
Woeber Mustard Manufacturing, 15692

Scandinavian

Alimentaire Whyte's Inc, 349
Bella Coola Fisheries, 1299
Bob Gordon & Associates, 1620
Calmar Bakery, 2237
Erba Food Products, 4506
EuroAm, 4541
Fish Brothers, 4847
Flora, 4930
Garden Herbs, 5401
H.J. Heinz Company, 6101
Heinz North America, 6399
Kopper's Chocolate Specialty Company, 7914
Lefse House, 8317
Mersey Seafoods, 9308
Molson Breweries, 9601
Penguin Frozen Foods, 11098
Schiff Food Products, 12843
Star Fine Foods, 13640
Sunnyrose Cheese, 13952
Svenhard's Swedish Bakery, 14043
Victoria Packing Corporation, 15091
Zivney Cheese, 15890

Spanish

Aristocrat International Corporation, 733
Cacique, 2102
California Fruit and Tomato Kitchens, 2201
Canadian Fish Exporters, 2279
Cibao Meat Product, 2866
Conrad Rice Mill, 3240
Corte Provisions, 3336
Country Smoked Meats, 3390
Crofton & Sons, 3475
Dufflet Pastries, 4170
Ecom Manufacturing Corporation, 4326
Elore Enterprises, 4438
Erba Food Products, 4506
Gourmet Baker, 5797
Goya Foods, 5818
Great Northern Products, 5916
H&F Food Products Company, 6075
J&J Snack Foods Corporation, 7191
Kozy Shack, 7928
Kraft, 7930

L&S Packing Company, 8005
Meat-O-Mat Corporation, 9239
Musco Olive Products, 9870
Odessa Tortilla & TamaleFactory, 10544
Olde Tyme Mercantile, 10617
Olives & Foods Inc, 10625
Orleans Packing Company, 10725
Plaza de Espana Gourmet, 11417
Pompeian, 11471
Raffield Fisheries, 11881
Roos Foods, 12291
Royal Wine Company, 12396
Seabrook Brothers & Sons, 12949
Sini Fulvi U.S.A., 13261
Star Fine Foods, 13640
Very Best Foods, 15069
Victoria Packing Corporation, 15091
Weyhaupt Brothers Packing, 15474
Woodlake Ranch, 15719

Swedish

Mike's Fish & Seafood, 9411

Swiss

Atlantic Pork & Provisions, 878
Bellville Meat Market, 1317
C.E. Zuercher & Company, 2043
C.F. Burger Creamery, 2044
Cheese Smokers, 2682
E.E. Mucke & Sons, 4237
East Beauregard Meat Processing Center, 4277
Faber Foods and Aeronautics, 4614
Gaiser's European Style Provisions, 5365
Glanbia Foods, 5608
Glenn's Rabbit & Emu Farm, 5624
Golden Temple, 5731
Guggisberg Cheese, 6023
Heidi's Cheese Products, 6381
Heluva Good Cheese, 6415
Hillsboro Refrigerated Lockers, 6567
Holmes Cheese Company, 6613
Houser Meats, 6776
Indian Valley Meats, 6961
Ivanhoe Cheese Inc, 7166
Kolb-Lena Cheese Company, 7900
Lactalis USA, 8115
Los Altos Food Products, 8562
Marathon Cheese Corporation, 8950
Maytag Dairy Farms, 9119
Middlefield Cheese House, 9392
Morris National, 9718
Mount Capra Cheese, 9758
New England Natural Bakers, 10136
O Chili Frozen Foods Inc, 10444
O'Brien & Company, 10450
Paris Pastry, 10950
Pel-Freez, 11082
Penn Cheese Corporation, 11102
Quality Ingredients Corporation, 11766
Rabbit Barn, 11869
Ragersville Swiss Cheese, 11882
Reilly Dairy & Food Company, 12023
Saag's Products, 12523
Spruce Foods, 13581
Steiner Cheese, 13693
Stockton Cheese, 13745
Swiss Valley Farms Company, 14097
Wengers Springbrook Cheese, 15400

Zivney Cheese, 15890

Thai

Asian Brands, 811
Cinnabar Specialty Foods, 2874
Commodities Marketing, Inc., 3139
Epicurean International, 4500
Golden Whisk, 5742
Lang Naturals, 8225
Mo Hotta-Mo Betta, 9571
Nielsen Citrus Products, 10223
North Bay Produce, 10294
Pastene Companies, 10998
Pearson's Homestyle, 11052
Santa Cruz Chili & SpiceCompany, 12685
Satori Teas, 12788
Setton International Foods, 13078
Star Fine Foods, 13640
Taj Gourmet Foods, 14176
Toddy Products, 14423
Torn & Glasser, 14485
Victoria Packing Corporation, 15091
Western Pacific Commodities, 15448
Whyte's Food Corporation, 15525

Turkish

San Marzano Foods, 12637

West Indian

Bacardi Canada, Inc., 1015
Banana Distributing Company, 1100
Benson's Gourmet Seasonings, 1341
Buffalo Trace Distillery, 1942
California Style Gourmet Products, 2219
California-Antilles Trading Consortium, 2224
Caribbean Food Delights, 2388
Carolyn's Caribbean Heat, 2436
Catskill Mountain Specialties, 2513
Cinnabar Specialty Foods, 2874
Corby Distilleries, 3320
Destileria Serralles, 3935
Erba Food Products, 4506
Highwood Distillers, 6549
Hiram Walker & Sons, 6586
Hood River Distillers, 6682
Kutztown Bologna Company, 7990
Majestic Distilling Company, 8848
Marie Brizard Wines & Spirits, 8972
Matlaw's Food Products, 9078
Mexi-Frost Specialties Company, 9327
National Food Corporation, 9977
Parman-Kendall Corporation, 10968
Royal Caribbean Bakery, 12358
Royal Home Bakery, 12372
Schiff Food Products, 12843
Shahi Food Corporation, 13105
St. John Levert, 13603
Tantos Foods International, 14208
Todhunter International, 14426
Trigo Corporation, 14597
Uncle Bum's Gourmet Foods, 14808
Uncle Fred's Fine Foods, 14811
Very Best Foods, 15069
Victoria Packing Corporation, 15091

Rocky Mountain Meats, 12232
Rolling Pin Bakery, 12261
Ryley Sausage, 12451
Salad Ranch/Cattle Canada, 12569
Sangudo Custom Meat Packers, 12671
Saxby Foods, 12812
Siljans Crispy Cup Company, 13204
Simmons Hot Gourmet Products, 13244
Smokey Farm Meats, 13316
Stawnichy Holdings, 13678
Stettler Meats, 13711
Sun Sun Food Products, 13874
Sunnyrose Cheese, 13952
Superior Mushroom Farms, 14002
Sysco I&S Foodservices Inc, 14127
Tiger Mushroom Farm, 14399
Tofield Packers, 14429
Tree of Life Canada West, 14558
Trochu Meat Processors, 14625
Valenie Packers, 14937
Vauxhall Foods, 15007
Vermilion Packers, 15045
Victoria Fancy Sausage, 15089
Vienna Bakery, 15104
Westbrook Trading Company, 15433
Western Beef Jerky, 15439
Weston Bakeries, 15459
Wings Foods of Alberta, 15652
Wow! Factor Desserts, 15757
XL Beef, 15778

Arizona

Allen & Cowley SpecialtyFoods, 378
American Supplement Technologies, 547
Arizona Brands, 737
Arizona Cowboy, 739
Arizona Institutional Foods, 740
Arizona Natural Products, 741
Arizona Nutritional Supplements, 742
Arizona Pepper Products, 743
Arizona Sunland Foods, 745, 746
Arizona Vineyards, 747
Armistead Citrus Company, 759
Art's Fisheries, 783
Avalon Gourmet, 941
Bakon Yeast, 1078
Bar-S Foods Company, 1113
Bard Valley Medjool Date Growers, 1128
Barone Foods, 1149, 1150
Baywood International, 1228
Beaver Street Brewery, 1259
Biltmore Trading LLC, 1464
Biotec AZ Laboratories, 1482
Black Mountain Brewing Company, 1522
Bob's Texas Style Potato Chip, 1624
C. Gould Seafoods, 2037
Cafe Terra Cotta, 2131
Cave Creek Coffee Company, 2519
CC Pollen Company, 2061
Cheri's Desert Harvest, 2715
Chi & Hing Food Service, 2744
China Mist Tea Company, 2778
Christopher Joseph Brewing Company, 2847
Cinnabar Specialty Foods, 2874
Coffee Reserve, 3057
Consolidated Seafood Enterprises, 3251
Country Estate Pecans, 3371
Crockett-Stewart Honey Company, 3472
Custom Food Service, 3572
Dark Mountain Winery and Brewery, 3740
De Cio Pasta Primo, 3799
Distribution Plus Incorporated (DPI), 4018
E U Blending Company, 4223
East Coast Seafood of Phoenix, 4280
Essentia Water, 4522
Fairytale Brownies, 4632
Farmers Investment Company, 4700
Fiesta Canning Company, 4789
Flagstaff Brewing Company, 4880
Flavorbank Company, 4906
Food Products Corporation, 5008
Frito-Lay, 5224
G & R Food Sales, 5306
Gadsden Coffee/Caffe, 5361
Gecko Gary's, 5440
Gentle Ben's Brewing Company, 5478
Global Nutrition Research Corporation, 5639
Grande Tortilla Factory, 5854
Grantstone Supermarket, 5872
Green Valley Pecan Company, 5960

Gum Technology Corporation, 6049
Gumtech International, 6052
Hobe Laboratories, 6593
Holsum Bakery, 6615
Homestyle Bread, 6646
Honso USA, 6680
Hormel Foods Corporation, 6721
Hosford & Wood Fresh Seafood Providers, 6744
Instantwhip: Arizona, 7007
Ivy Foods, 7170
Janca's Jojoba Oil & Seed Company, 7325
JC's Midnite Salsa, 7262
Karen's Wine Country Cafe, 7614
Karsh's Bakery, 7629
Klein Pickle Company, 7849
Klein's Kosher Pickles, 7850
Kokopelli's Kitchen, 7898
Kombucha King International, 7902
L.H. Rodriguez Wholesale Seafood, 8014
La Buena Mexican Food Products, 8040
La Canasta Mexican Food Products, 8043
La Patisserie, 8071
Ladson Homemade Pasta Company, 8120
Lamesa Cotton Oil Mill, 8179
Leaves Pure Teas, 8294
Lehi Valley Trading Company, 8323
M&L Ventures, 8710
Mama Rose's Gourmet Foods, 8874
Market Fare Foods, 8995
McDowell Fine Meats 2, 9184
McLane Foods, 9205
MD Labs, 8743
Meat & Fish Fellas, 9235
Mesa Cold Storage, 9310
Meyer's Bakeries, 9335
Miss Scarlett's, 9530
Morning Star Foods, 9705
Nanci's Frozen Yogurt, 9931
Naturally Vitamin Supplements, 10035
North American Enterprises, 10284
Nutri Base, 10416
Oak Creek Brewing Company, 10472
Omega Produce Company, 10649
Paradise Valley Vineyards, 10935
Peanut Patch, 11037
Phoenician Herbals, 11290
Poore Brothers, 11482
Prescott Brewing Company, 11587
Prime Cut Meat & Seafood Company, 11612
Proctor & Gamble Company, 11646
Prolume Biolume, 11670
R&B Quality Foods, 11819
R&S Mexican Food Products, 11824
Red Steer Meats, 11985
Rene Produce Distributors, 12040
Rocky Point Shrimp Association, 12236
Roma Distributing, 12269
Rosarita Mexican Foods Company, 12297
Rousseau Farming Company, 12340
Royal Food Distributors, 12368
Royal Pacific Tea & Coffee, 12383
Royal Products, 12388
S.W. Meat & Provision Company, 12486
Safeway Milk Plant, 12543
Safeway Stores, 12544
Saguaro Food Products, 12550
San Dominique Winery, 12619
Santa Cruz Chili & SpiceCompany, 12685
Santa Cruz Valley Pecan, 12687
Sara Lee Bakery Group, 12728
Shamrock Foods Company, 13111
Shipmaster USA, 13160
Sonoita Vineyards, 13382
Southwest Specialty Food, 13468
Sun Orchard, 13864
Sunkist Growers, 13929
Tessenderlo Kerley, 14316
Tostino Coffee Roasters, 14492
Tucson Food Service, 14677
Tucson Frozen Storage, 14678
Union Seafoods, 14846
United Dairymen of Arizona, 14861
United Universal Enterprises Corporation, 14884
Upper Crust Bakery, 14901
Urban Oven, 14909
Valley Pie Company, 14953
Vity Meat & Provisions Company, 15184
Willcox Packing House, 15570
Wisdom Natural Brands, 15678
World Nutrition, 15741

Arkansas

Allen Canning Company, 379
Arkansas Poly, 749
Arkansas Refrigerated Services, 750
Bio-Tech Pharmacal, 1476
Boar's Head Provisions Company, 1607
Brent & Sam's Cookies, 1798
Bright Harvest Sweet Potato Company, 1822
Brinkley Dryer and Storage, 1825
Broadaway Ham Company, 1839
Bryant Preserving Company, 1918
C&C Packing Company, 2025
Cargill Foods, 2375
Coca-Cola Bottling Company, 3020
Coleman Dairy, 3080
ConAgra Frozen Foods Company, 3195
Cormier Rice Milling Company, 3327
Couch's Original Sauce, 3360
Cowie Wine Cellars, 3406
Creative Foods, 3432
Crystal Lake, 3515
Delta Catfish Products, 3902
Diamond Water, 3969
Dunford Bakers, 4185
Eagle Agricultural Products, 4250
Eureka Springs Winery, 4537
Famous Chili, 4646
Fasweet Company, 4721
Fischer Honey Company, 4844
Flowers Baking Company, 4974
G E Hawthorn Meat Company, 5312
George's, 5500
Gold Star Chili, 5677
Good Old Days Foods, 5771
Harris Baking Company, 6254
Hillbilly Smokehouse, 6559
Hiram Walker & Sons, 6585
Hog Haus Brewing Company, 6602
Hot Springs Packing Company, 6752
House of Webster, 6774
Humphreys Dairy, 6817
J&M Foods, 7198
John Garner Meats, 7442
King Kat, 7799
Koehler Bakery Company, 7890
Kruse Meat Products, 7978
Land O'Frost, 8195
Lemke Wholesale, 8338
Lone Pine Enterprises, 8529
McKiever Packing Company, 9202
McKnight Milling Company, 9204
Medallion Foods, 9243
Meyer's Bakeries, 9334
Mid-South Fish Company, 9386
Mount Bethel Winery, 9757
Mountain Valley Poultry, 9780
Mountain Valley Spring Company, 9782
Mountaire Corporation, 9786
O.K. Industries, 10464
Pel-Freez, 11082
Pepper Source, 11130, 11131
Pepsi Bottling Group, 11158
Peterson Farms, 11246
Pioneer Foods Industries, 11373
Planters LifeSavers Com pany, 11410
Post Familie Vineyards, 11520
Poultry Foods Industry, 11528
Pride of Dixie Syrup Company, 11604
Producer's Rice, 11650
Producers Rice Mill, 11656
Quality Products International, 11774
Rice Hull Specialty Pro Company, 12080
Riceland Foods Rice Milling Operations, 12084, 12085
RJ Balson and Sons Inc, 11861
Seven Up/RC Bottling Company, 13088
SFP Food Products, 12497
Shaver Foods, 13125
Shipley Baking Company, 13159
Simmons Foods, 13241, 13242
Sims Wholesale, 13256
Southern Brown Rice, 13437
Specialty Rice Marketing, 13513
Sugar Creek/Eskimo Pie, 13825
Summercorn Foods, 13846
Tankersley Food Service, 14206
Tastee Fare, 14229
Trio Foods, 14606
Tyson Foods, 14745, 14746, 14747, 14751, 14752, 14753, 14758
Vino's, 15139

Walker's Seafood, 15263
War Eagle Mill, 15290
Wayne Farms, LLC, 15342
Western Foods, 15444
Wiederkehr Wine Cellars, 15538
Woody's Bar-B-Q Sauce Company, 15729
Yarnell Ice Cream Company, 15803

British Columbia

Abbotsford Growers Co-operative, 129
Aquatec Seafoods Ltd., 688
Asti Holdings Ltd, 840
Axia Distribution Corporation, 957
Babe's Honey Farm, 1013
Bakemark Ingredients Canada, 1051
Bear Brewing Company, 1241
Bella Coola Fisheries, 1299
Bevco, 1409
Blundell Seafoods, 1603
Brockmann Chocolates, 1846
Brookside Foods, 1870
Butter Baked Goods, 1994
Calkins & Burke, 2230
Canada Bread Company, 2276
Canasoy Enterprises, 2286
Clearly Canadian Beverage Corporation, 2945
Columbia Brewery, 3112
Country Pies, 3386
Dan-D Foods Ltd, 3701
Delta Pacific Seafoods, 3905
Dollar Food Manufacturing, 4058
E-Fish-Ent Fish Company, 4230
Favorite Foods, 4730
Fine Choice Foods, 4808
Fjord Pacific Marine Industries, 4879
Flora Manufacturing & Distributing, 4931
Foley's Candies, 4985
French Creek Seafood, 5167
Ganong Acosta Head Office West, 5387
Ganong Western Canada Division, 5392
GLG Life Tech Corporation, 5340
Golden Valley Foods, 5735
Gourmet Baker, 5797
Great Glacier Salmon, 5900
Hagensborg Foods, 6132
Hain Celestial Canada, 6140
Hampton House, 6180
Healthco Canada Enterprises, 6350
Heritage Salmon Company, 6469
Imperial Salmon House, 6922
Imprint Plus, 6927
Island Farms Dairies Cooperative Association, 7131
Island Scallops, 7136
J.S. McMillan Fisheries, 7247, 7248
Jenport International Distributors, 7371
Jones Soda Vancouver, 7492
Kettle Valley Fruits, 7749
Lucerne Foods, 8652
Mac's Oysters, 8762
Mario's Gelati, 8988
Minute Maid Company, 9519
Money's Mushrooms, 9622, 9623
Moon Enterprises, 9673
Mrs. Willman's Baking, 9831
Nature's Path Foods, 10050
Nicola Valley Apiaries, 10220
North American Reishi/Nammex, 10285
North Peace Apiaries, 10306
Ocean Delight Seafoods, 10515
Oceanfood Sales, 10538
Okanagan Spring Brewery, 10565
Over The Moon Chocolate Company Ltd, 10772
Pacific Seafoods International, 10863
Pacific Western Brewing Company, 10873
Paradise Island Foods, 10931
Pied-Mont/Dora, 11306
Quality Bakery, 11747
Rene Rey Chocolates Ltd, 12041
Rogers Sugar Limited, 12249
Rogers' Chocolates Ltd, 12250
Russell Brewing Company, 12431
Saltspring Aqua Farms, 12592
Schneider Foods, 12859
Seafood Products Company, 12966
Secret Tea Garden, 13004
Service Packing Company, 13070
Shafer-Haggart, 13103
Sleeman Breweries, 13286

Evergreen Juices, 4566
Everson Spice Company, 4569
Excelline Foods, 4577
Excelpro Manufacturing Corporation, 4578
Extracts Plus, 4584
Extreme Creations, 4585
Exxter Trading, 4586
F Gavina & Sons Inc, 4589
F&A Cheese Corporation, 4591
F&A Dairy of California, 4593
F. Gavina & Sons, 4599
Fabe's Natural Gourmet, 4613
Fabio Imports, 4615
Fabrique Delices, 4616
Facciola Meat, 4618
Fall River Wild Rice, 4637
Family Tree Farms, 4645
Fantastic Foods, 4657
Fantasy Cookie Company, 4659
Far Niente Winery, 4664
Far West Rice Inc, 4665
Farallon Fisheries, 4666
Farb's, 4667
Farella-Park Vineyards, 4670
Farm to You, 4689
Farmacopia, 4691
Farmdale Creamery, 4692
Farmer Brothers Company, 4693
Farmers' Rice Cooperative, 4705
Fayter Farms Produce, 4734
FDP, 4606
Felbro Food Products, 4744
Fellom Ranch Vineyards, 4747
Fenestra Winery, 4749
Fentimans North America, 4752
Ferrara Winery, 4762
Ferrari-Carano Vineyards& Winery, 4763
Fess Parker Winery, 4770
Ficklin Vineyards, 4775
Field Stone Winery & Vineyard, 4779
Fieldbrook Valley Winery, 4785
Fiesta Mexican Foods, 4792
Fife Vineyards, 4793, 4794
Fig Garden Packing, 4795
Figamajigs, 4796
Figuerola Laboratories, 4798
Fiji Ginger Company, 4799
Fiji Water LLC, 4801
Fillmore Piru Citrus Association, 4803
Filsinger Vineyards & Winery, 4805
Fine Dried Foods International, 4809
Firestone Vineyard, 4828
Fish Brothers, 4847
Fish Hopper, 4849
Fisher Vineyards, 4858
Fishking Processors, 4868
Fitzpatrick Winery & Lodge, 4872
Flamous Brands, 4885
Flanigan Farms, 4887
Flannery Seafood Company, 4888
Flapjacks, 4889
Flavor Consortium, 4896
Flavor House, 4898
Flavor Specialties, 4902
Flavor Waves, 4904
Flavours Inc, 4916
Flavtek, 4917
Flavurence Corporation, 4918
Fleischmann's Vinegar, 4921
Fleischmanns Vinegar, 4923
Flora Springs Wine Company, 4932
Florence Macaroni Manufacturing, 4934
Florentyna's Fresh Pasta Factory, 4937
Flower Essence Services, 4957
Fmali Herb, 4980
Foley Estates Vineyards & Winery, 4984
Folie a Deux Winery, 4987
Follmer Development/Americana, 4989
Fontazzi/Metrovox Snacks, 4993
Food & Vine, 4996, 4997
Food for Life Baking Company, 5018
Food Mill, 5006
Foppiano Vineyard, 5027
Forman Vineyards, 5056
Fortino Winery, 5064
Fortuna Cellars, 5068
Fortune Cookie Factory, 5071
Forty Second Street Bagel Cafe, 5074
Fosselman's Ice Cream Company, 5075
Foster Farms, 5079
Foster Farms Dairy, 5083, 5084
Fowler Packing Company, 5096

Fox's Fine Foods, 5104
Foxen Vineyard, 5105
Fran's Healthy Helpings, 5111
Franciscan Oakville Estates, 5114
Franciscan Vineyards, 5115
Frank & Dean's Cocktail Mixes, 5117
Frank Capurro & Son, 5118
Frank Family Vineyard, 5119
Frank-Lin Distillers, 5125
Frankly Natural Bakers, 5137
Franzia Winery, 5139
Fratelli Perata, 5140
Frazier Nut Farms, 5142
Freed, Teller & Freed, 5151
Freemark Abbey Winery, 5157
Freeze-Dry Products, 5159
Freixenet, 5162
French Patisserie, 5170
French's Coffee, 5173
Fresh Express, 5178
Fresh Roast Systems, 5188
Fresh Start Bakeries, 5193, 5194, 5195
Freund Baking Company, 5200
Frey Vineyards, 5201
Frick Winery, 5202
Frieda's, 5205
Frisco Baking Company, 5212
Frisinger Cellars, 5213
Frito-Lay, 5230, 5231
Frog's Leap Winery, 5240
Frozfruit Corporation, 5257
Frozsun Foods, 5258
Fruit A Freeze, 5259
Fruit Fillings, 5263
FrutStix Company, 5267
Fudge Fatale, 5272
Ful-Flav-R Foods, 5277
Funkandy Corporation, 5293
Fusion Gourmet, 5299
G B Ratto & Company Int ernational, 5308
G L Mezzetta, 5317
G&G Foods, 5322
G.L. Mezzetta Inc, 5329
Gabriele Macaroni Company, 5357
Gainey Vineyard, 5364
Galante Vineyards, 5366
Galassos Baking Company, 5367
Galaxy Desserts, 5369
Galileo Foods, 5376
Gallands Institutional Foodservice, 5377
Galleano Winery, 5378
Garcoa, 5396
Garden Herbs, 5401
Gardner's Gourmet, 5410
Gardunos Mexican Food, 5412
Garlic Company, 5416
Garlic Festival Foods, 5417
Garlic Survival Company, 5418
Garlic Valley Farms Inc, 5419
Garratt & Gunn, 5422
Garry Packing, 5424
Garuda International, 5425
Gary Farrell Wines, 5426
Gaslamp Popcorn Company, 5429
Gayle's Sweet 'N Sassy Foods, 5438
GCI Nutrients (USA), 5331
Geeef America, 5441
Gelati Celesti, 5445
Gelsinger Food Products, 5450
GEM Cultures, 5333
Gene Belk Fruit Packers, 5456
General Taste Bakery, 5465
Generation Foods Too, 5467
George Chiala Farms, 5484
George Noroian, 5490
Georis Winery, 5513
Gerawan Farming, 5515
Gerhard's Napa Valley Sausage, 5519
Germain-Robin, 5524
Germain-Robin/Alambic, 5525
Gertrude & Bronner's Magic Alpsnack, 5529
Geyser Peak Winery, 5535
GFF, 5335
Ghirardelli Chocolate Company, 5537
Ghirardelli Ranch, 5538
Gibson Wine Company, 5548
Gift Factory/Beverly Hills, 5554
Gil's Gourmet Gallery, 5555
Gill's Onions, 5560
Gilroy, 5567
Gilroy Foods, 5568, 5569

Gimbal's Fine Candies, 5573
Gimbal's Fine Candy, 5574
GINCO International, 5337
Ginco International, 5575
Ginger People®, 5577
Ginkgoton, 5579
Girard Winery/Rudd Estates, 5586
Girard's Food Service Dressings, 5587
Giuliano's Specialty Foods, 5590
Giumarra Companies, 5591, 5592
Giumarra Vineyards, 5593
Giusto's Specialty Foods, 5594
Glacier Foods, 5603
Glen Rose Meat Company, 5616
Glencourt, 5619
Glendora Quiche Company, 5620
Glenoaks Food, 5626
Global Bakeries, 5629
Global Trading, 5641
Gloria Ferrer Champagne, 5644
Gloria Jean's Gourmet Coffees, 5645
GMB Specialty Foods, 5341
GMP Laboratories, 5345
GNS Spices, 5347
GNT USA, 5348
Goglanian Bakeries, 5665
Gold Coast Baking Company, 5666
Gold Coast Ingredients, 5667
Golden Bounty Food Processors, 5686
Golden Boys Pies of San Diego, 5687
Golden Cheese Company of California, 5690
Golden Cheese of California, 5691
Golden Creek Vineyard, 5694
Golden Drop, 5695
Golden Eagle Olive Products, 5696
Golden Foods, 5703
Golden Grain, 5706
Golden Specialty Foods, 5724
Golden State Citrus Packers, 5725
Golden State Foods, 5726, 5727, 5728
Golden State Vintners, 5729
Golden Temple, 5730
Golden Temple, Sunshine & Yogi Tea, 5732
Golden Valley Dairy Products, 5734
Golden Valley Seed, 5736
Golden West Fruit Company, 5738
Golden West Nuts, 5739, 5740
Golden West Specialty Foods, 5741
Golden Whisk, 5742
Goldilocks Bakeshop, 5745
Goldrush Sourdough, 5747
Good Earth® Teas, 5758
Good Fortunes & Edible Art, 5760
Goosecross Cellars, 5782
Gordon Biersch Brewing Company, 5784
Gourmet Foods, 5805
Gourmet Treats, 5810
Gourmet's Secret, 5813
Gourmets Fresh Pasta, 5814
Govadinas Fitness Foods, 5816
Grace Baking Company, 5823
Grain Bin Bakers, 5836
Grainaissance, 5843
Grand Avenue Chocolates, 5846
Granite Springs Winery, 5862
Grant & Janet Brians, 5869
Grapevine Trading Company, 5874
Grating Pacific/Ross Technology Corporation, 5878
Great Cakes, 5894
Great Spice Company, 5922
Great Spring Waters, 5923
Greater Galilee Gourmet, 5933
Greek Gourmet Limited, 5938
Green Foods Corporation, 5942
Green Grown Products, 5945
Green House, 5946
Green House Fine Herbs, 5947
Green Options, 5952
Green Spot Packaging, 5954
Green Valley Apples of California, 5957
Greenberg Cheese Company, 5961
Greenfield Wine Company, 5965
Greenwood Ridge Vineyards, 5972
Grimaud Farms, 5991
Grimmway Farms, 5994
Grimmway Frozen Foods, 5995
Groth Vineyards & Winery, 6007
Guapo Spices Company, 6019
Guayaki Sustainable Rainforest Products, 6020

Guerra Nut Shelling Company, 6021
Guido's International Foods, 6025
Guilliams Winery, 6027
Guittard Chocolate Company, 6031
Gundlach Bundschu Winery, 6053
H Coturri & Sons Winery, 6070
H. Naraghi Farms, 6091
H. Shenson International Export, 6093
H.K. Canning, 6102
Hadley Date Gardens, 6128
Hafner Vineyard, 6130
Hagerty Foods, 6133
Hahn & Company, 6134
Hahn Estates and Smith &Hook, 6136
Hair Fitness, 6144
Half Moon Fruit & Produce Company, 6153
Haliburton International Corporation, 6154
Hallcrest Vineyards, 6159
Hammons Meat Sales, 6174
Handley Cellars, 6185
Hangzhou Sanhe Food Company, 6187
Hansen Beverage, 6196
Hansen's Juices, 6199
Hansen's Natural, 6200
Hanzell Vineyards, 6203
Harbor Food Sales & Services, 6215
Harbor Winery, 6220
Harmony Cellars, 6237
Harold L. King & Company, 6244
Harris Farms, 6255
Harris Freeman & Company, 6256
Harris Moran Seed Company, 6257
Harris Ranch Beef Company, 6258
Harrison Napa Valley, 6260
Hart Winery, 6266
Hartford Family Winery, 6269
Harvest 2000, 6279
Harvest Day Bakery, 6281
Harvest Food Products Company, 6283
Has Beans Coffee & Tea Company, 6290
Haug Quality Equipment, 6295
Hawk Pacific Freight, 6321
Haywood Enterprises, 6329
Health Asure, 6340
Health Concerns, 6341
Health Plus, 6343
Health Valley Company, 6345
HealthBest, 6349
Healthwave, 6352
Healthy Times, 6355
Heaven Scent Natural Foods, 6372
Heck Cellars, 6376
Hecker Pass Winery, 6377
Heinke Industrial Park, 6388
Heinz, 6394
Heitz Wine Cellar, 6403
Helen Grace Chocolates, 6405
Helena View/Johnston Vineyard, 6406
Henry Avocado Company, 6430
Henry Hill & Company, 6435
Herb Tea Company, 6444
Herbal Magic, 6448
Herbal Products & Development, 6449
Heritage Foods, 6464
Hershey Chocolate & Confectionery Division, 6494
Hess Collection Winery, 6501
Hi Ball Energy, 6506
Hi Point Industries, 6507
HiBix Corporation, 6512
Hidden Mountain Ranch Winery, 6521
Hidden Villa Ranch, 6522
Hill of Beans Coffee Roasters, 6556
Hilmar Cheese Company, 6575
Hint, 6582
Hint Mint, 6583
HMC Marketing Group, 6116
Holland American International Specialties, 6607
Homegrown Naturals, 6636
Homestead Fine Foods, 6643
Homestead Ravioli Company, 6645
Homewood Winery, 6648
Honey Rose Baking Company, 6660
HoneyRun Winery, 6663
Honeyville Grain, 6668
Hong Tou Noodle Company, 6674
Honig Vineyard and Winery, 6678
Hop Kiln Winery, 6692
Horizon Winery, 6702
Hormel Foods Corporation, 6714
Hoson Produce, 6746

Hawaii

Idaho

Illinois

Willy Wonka Candy, 15611
Willy Wonka Candy Factory, 15612
Wing Seafood Company, 15647
Wisconsin Cheese, 15667
Woodland Foods, 15720
World's Finest Chocolate, 15751
Wrigley Company, 15765
Wurth Dairy, 15768
Xcell International Corporation, 15781
Y&T Packing, 15784
Yamasho, 15796
Young Yoo Company, 15845
Zip-Pak, 15885
Zivney Cheese, 15890
Zoll Foods Corporation, 15892

Indiana

Abbott's Candy Shop, 132
Accra Pac Group, 157
Advanced Aquacultural Technologies, 209
Agricor, 242
Al Pete Meats, 279
Albanese Confectionery Group, 317
Alpha Baking Company, 420
American Beverage Marketers, 485
American Chemical Service, 497
American Licorice Company, 528
American Ultraviolet Company, 549
AmeriQual Foods, 480
Atkins Elegant Desserts, 853
Aunt Millies Bakeries, 919
B&B Food Distributors, 966
B.N.W. Industries, 988
Baird Dairies, 1039
Beatty Fresh Frozen Meats, 1252
Best Chocolate In Town, 1383
Big B Distributors, 1436
Bloomington Brewing Company, 1558
Bonnie Baking Company, 1668
Bonnie Doon Ice Cream Corporation, 1669
Brightwood Baking Company, 1823
Brook Locker Plant, 1854
Brown County Wine Company, 1883
Browns Dairy, 1901
Butler Winery, 1993
C&G Salsa, 2028
Cadick Poultry Company, 2111
Captain Bob's Jet Fuel, 2342
Carbolite Foods, 2360
Carbon's Golden Malted, 2361, 2362
Cayuga Grain, 2530
Cerestar USA, 2593
Chateau Thomas Winery, 2670
Cheese Factory, 2681
Chester Inc., 2736
Clabber Girl Corporation, 2906
Claeys Candy, 2907
Clover Blossom Honey, 2974
Collins Caviar Company, 3090
Compton Dairy, 3153
Con Agro Food, 3159
ConAgra Dairy Foods, 3169, 3170
Consolidated Biscuit Company, 3245
Cornerstone Floorings & Linings, 3331
Creighton Brothers, 3438
Crossroad Farms Dairy, 3485
Crown Point, 3497
Crystal Lake, 3516
Culture Systems, 3540
Culver Duck, 3543
Dairy Chem Inc, 3644
Dairy Farmers of AmericaGoshen Plant, 3648
Dean Foods Company, 3823
Deutsch Kase Haus, 3938
Diamond Foods, 3963
Dillman Farm, 3993
Dixie Dairy Company, 4028
Doc Miller's Fish & Seafood Company, 4038
Dolly Madison Bakery, 4059
Donaldson's Finer Chocolates, 4083
Dugdale Beef Company, 4172
Easley Winery, 4272
Edy's Grand Ice Cream, 4360
Ellison Bakery, 4425
Empire Tea Services, 4461
Endangered Species Chocolate, 4467
Erbrich-Sewell Products Company, 4507
Farbest Foods, 4668
Farm Boy Food Service, 4682

Food Specialties, 5015
Franklin Supply Company, 5136
Frito-Lay, 5228
Fudge Farms, 5271
Geni, 5473
Ghyslain Chocolatier, 5539
Glover's Ice Cream, 5651
Golden Malted, 5714
Grabill Country Meats, 5822
Graham Cheese Corporation, 5834
Great Western Products Company, 5930
Greenfield Mills, 5963
Harlan Bakeries, 6230, 6231
Harlan Bakeries, Inc., 6232
Harmony Foods Corporation, 6238, 6239
Hartford City Foam Pack aging & Converting, 6268
Heartland Farms, 6361
Henry Davis Company, 6432
Heyerly Bakery, 6505
Holsum Bakery, 6617
Hoople Country Kitchens, 6689
Hulman & Company, 6804
Huber's Orchard Winery, 6792
Huser Paul Company, 6837
Ice Cream Specialties, 6879
Ideal American, 6896
Indiana Beverage 7UP, 6962
Indiana Botanic Gardens, 6963
Instant Products of America, 7006
International Bakers Services, 7029
International Bar-B-Que, 7031
International Food Technologies, 7057
Irani & Company, 7119
J-N-D Company, 7203
John Hene Specialty Meats, 7444
K.B. Specialty Foods, 7566
Kerry Ingredients, 7734
Key III Candies, 7753
Kingly Heirs, 7815
Kingsbury Country Market, 7821
Kreamo Bakers, 7959
Kyger Bakery Products, 7991
Ladoga Frozen Food & Retail Meat, 8119
Lafayette Brewing Company, 8125
Lambrights, 8178
Laney Family Honey Company, 8222
Laredo Mexican Foods, 8234
Lebermuth Company, 8297, 8298
Lengerich Meats, 8349
Lewis Brothers Bakeries, 8401
Lewis Brothers Bakery, 8403, 8404
Lewis-Vincennes Bakery, 8411
Libs Candies Downtown, 8420
Little Crow Foods, 8478
Louis Bakeries, 8590
Lowery's Home Made Candies, 8636
Ludwig Fish & Produce Company, 8672
Lyoferm & Vivolac Cultures, 8701
M. Brown & Sons, 8721
M.A. Johnson Frozen Foods, 8726
Manley Meats, 8903
Maple Leaf Farms, 8926
Maplehurst Bakeries, 8940
Marburger Foods, 8954
Marion-Kay Spices, 8989
Marshall Egg Products, 9019
McFarling Foods, 9190
Mead Johnson Nutrition, 9220
Melchers Flavors of America, 9260
Mentone Egg Products, 9277
Menu Meats, 9278
Merkley & Sons Packing, 9294
Mexican Foods, 9331
Midstates Distributor, 9398
Midwest Seafood, 9403
Milroy Canning Company, 9486
Mishawaka Brewing Company, 9526
Mishler Packing Company, 9527
Morgan Food, 9696
Morristown, 9725
Munsee Meats, 9851
Myers Frozen Food Provisions, 9888
N.K. Hurst Company, 9894
Nabisco Food Group, 9916
Napoleon Locker, 9949
National Foods, 9979
New Business Corporation, 10124
New Horizons Baking Company, 10149
New Meridian, 10153
Nickles Bakery of Indiana, 10212
Nunn Milling Company, 10397

Nutritional Research Associates, 10431
O'Neil's Distributors, 10458
Oliver Wine Company, 10623
Oliver Winery, 10624
Olympic Food Products, 10639
Ossian Seafood Meats, 10742
P/B Distributors, 10811
Pac Moore Products, 10830
Park 100 Foods, 10952
Peerless Potato Chips, 11073
PepsiAmericas, 11172
PepsiCo, 11183
Perdue Farms, 11200, 11204
Pernod Ricard USA Seagram Lawrenceburg Distillery, 11222
Pierceton Foods, 11312
Pleasant View Dairy, 11420
Plumrose USA, 11431
Plyley's Candies, 11433
Poore Brothers, 11483
Praire Farms Dairy, 11536
Preston Farms, 11594
Pretzels, 11597
Puritan Ice Cream, 11703
Puritan/ATZ Ice Cream, 11704
R&F Miller, 11820
Ralph Sechler & Son, 11906
Ralph Sechler & Son Inc, 11907
Ramsey Popcorn Company, 11914
Ray Brothers & Noble Canning Company, 11941
Red Gold, 11972
Redi-Froze, 11992
Richard Green Company, 12103
Richmond Baking Company, 12118
Rose Acre Farms, 12299
Royal Center Locker Plant, 12360
Royal Food Products, 12369
Rumford Baking Powder Company, 12421
S.F. Foods Corporation, 12479
Salem Food Service, 12575
Sandra L. Lagrotte, 12662
Saputo Cheese, 12711
Schenkel's All Star Dairy, 12840
Sells Best, 13023
Serenade Foods, 13059
Seven K Feather Farm, 13084
Seyfert Foods, 13095
Shirley Foods, 13163
Snowbear Frozen Custard, 13345
South Bend Chocolate, 13410
Southern Heritage Coffee Company, 13445
Squire Boone Village, 13588
Stanz Foodservice, 13637
Strauss Bakeries, 13784
Superior Seafood & Meat Company, 14011
Swiss Way Cheese, 14101
Swissland Milk, 14106
Sysco Food Services of Indiana, 14126
Taurus Foods, 14248
Tell City Pretzel Company, 14292
Tri-State Processing Company, 14583
Troyer Foods, 14654
Tulox Plastics Corporation, 14685
Tyson Foods, 14748
United Pie Company, 14875
Universal Flavor Corporation, 14892
Universal Flavors, 14893
Valley Research, 14956
Villa Milan Vineyard, 15118
Vivolac Cultures Corporation, 15187
Wabash Coffee, 15239
Wabash Heritage Spices, 15240
Wabash Valley Farms, 15242
Wabash Valley Produce, 15243
Wayne Dairy Products, 15330
Weaver Brothers, 15346
Weaver Popcorn Company, 15348
Weaver Popcorn Company Manufacturing Facilty, 15349
Westport Locker Service, 15463
Wick's Pies, 15528
Williams-West & Witt Products, 15597
Wilson Corn Products, 15615
Winterbrook Beverage Group, 15664
Wright Ice Cream, 15763
Yewig Brothers Packing Company, 15815
Zachary Confections, 15861

Iowa

Ackerman Winery, 167, 168

Agri Processors, 232
All-States Quality Foods, 368
Allied Blending & Ingredients, 389
Amana Meat Shop & Smokehouse, 453
American Cheesemen, 496
American Pop Corn Company, 537
Anderson Erickson Dairy, 604
Apotheca Naturale, 668
Associated Milk Producers, 826, 833, 836
B&R Quality Meats, 978
Betty Jane Homemade Candies, 1407
Birdsall Ice Cream Company, 1491
Boyd Sausage Company, 1739
Brandmeyer Popcorn Company, 1760
Burke Corporation, 1971
Cargill Texturizing Solutions, 2382
Carriage House Foods, 2446
Casson & Sons, 2488
Cedar Valley Fish Market, 2544
Chocolaterie Stam, 2813
Community Orchard, 3148
Continental Deli Foods, 3271
Cookies Food Products, 3297
Custom Food Processors International, 3570
Dee's All Natural Baking Company, 3845
Devansoy, 3939
Diamond Crystal Specialty Foods, 3962
Dutchland Frozen Foods, 4211
Ehrle Brothers Winery, 4373
Energenetics International, 4471
Energique, 4472
Farmers Hen House, 4699
Farmland Foods, 4710, 4711, 4713
Foreign Candy Company, 5036
Foremost Farms, 5038
Frito-Lay, 5220
Frontier Ingredients, 5250
Frontier Natural Co-op, 5251
Gelita USA, 5448
Gelita/Kind & Knox Gelatine, 5449
Grain Processing Corporation, 5841
Harker's Distribution, 6229
Harvest Innovations, 6284
Heartland Fields, 6362
Heartland Fields, LLC, 6363
Heinz, 6393
Hopson, 6698
Hormel Foods Corporation, 6707, 6710
Humboldt Sausage Company, 6808
Iowa Ham Canning, 7111
Iowa Quality Meats, 7112
J&L Grain Processing, 7195
Jesse's Fine Meats, 7390
Joelle's Choice Specialty Foods LLC, 7423
John Morrell & Company, 7452
Kemin Health, 7698
Kitts Meat Processing, 7843
Klemme Cooperative Grainery, 7853
Lampost Meats, 8186
Landlocked Seafoods, 8212
Lee Seed Company, 8304
Little Amana Winery, 8476
Lubbers Dairy, 8642
LVO Manufacturing, 8033
Marcetti Frozen Pasta, 8956
Martin Brothers Distributing Company, 9030
Matthiesen's Deer & Custom Processing, 9085
Maytag Dairy Farms, 9119
Microsoy Corporation, 9376
Midamar Corporation, 9391
Millstream Brewing, 9476
Mino Corporation, 9512
Mississippi Bakery, 9543
Mississippi Blending Company, 9544
Mohn's Fisheries, 9590
Moroni Feed Company, 9713
Mrs. Clark's Foods, 9810
Natural Products, 10024
Noble Popcorn Farms, 10244
Old Wine Cellar, 10608
Oskaloosa Food Products Corporation, 10738
P.A. Braunger Institutional Foods, 10801
Palmer Candy Company, 10897
PepsiCo, 11179
Phyto-Technologies, 11294
Porrhoff Foods Company, 11502
Potter Siding Creamery Company, 11526
Proliant, 11668
Proliant Meat Ingredients, 11669

Maine

Rainbow Seafoods, 11896
Ralphco, 11910
Regal Crown Foods, 12005
Regco Corporation, 12008
Regenie's All Natural and Organic Snacks, 12010
Richard's Gourmet Coffee, 12106
Richardson's Ice Cream, 12112
Richelieu Foods, 12113
Rockport Lobster, 12228
Rohtstein Corporation, 12254, 12255
Royal Atlantic Seafood, 12354
Royal Harvest Foods, 12371
Salem Oil & Grease Company, 12576
Salem Old Fashioned Candies, 12577
Saletts, 12582
Sand Springs Springwater, 12648
Sardinha Sausage, 12770
Sauces 'n Love, 12791
Schultz Provisions Company, 12882
Sea Best Corporation, 12915
Sea Gold Seafood Products, 12922
Sea View Fillet Company, 12937
Seafood Services, 12967
Seafood Specialty Sales, 12970
Seafood USA, 12971
Seaway Company, 12996
Shekou Chemicals, 13136
Shonna's Gourmet Goodies, 13169
Siegel Egg Company, 13185
Silver Sweet Candies, 13229
Simpson Spring Company, 13255
SJR Foods, 12500
SLB Snacks, 12507
Smoke & Fire Natural Food, 13311
Snow's Ice Cream Company, 13343
Spence & Company, 13517
Spring Hill Farm Dairy, 13564
Springfield Smoked Fish Company, 13576
SS Lobster Limited, 12515
St. Ours & Company, 13611
Stacy's Pita Chip Company, 13615
Stark Candy Company, 13660
Stateline Boyd, 13672
Stavis Seafoods, 13677
Steve Connolly Seafood Company, 13713
Steve's Doughnut Shop, 13714
Stickney & Poor Company, 13731
Stop & Shop Manufacturing, 13769
Sudbury Soups and Salads, 13816
Sun Opta Ingredients, 13863
Sunbeam, 13894
Sunkist Growers, 13918
Sunny's Seafood, 13948
Super Snooty Sea Food Corporation, 13989
Superior Baking Company, 13993
Superior Cake Products, 13995
Superior Nut Company, 14004
Sustainable Sourcing, 14033
Sweet Baby Ray's, 14053
Table Talk Pie, 14166
Taj Gourmet Foods, 14176
Tea Forte, 14267
Tempest Fisheries Limited, 14294
Tichon Seafood Corporation, 14395
Titterington's Olde English Bake Shop, 14415
Toucan Chocolates, 14497
Trans-Ocean Products, 14531
Trappist Preserves, 14538
Trappistine Quality Candy, 14539
Tri-Sum Potato Chip Company, 14586
Tribe Mediterranean Foods Company LLC, 14592
Tripoli Bakery, 14618
Trotters Imports, 14645
True World Foods of Boston, 14663
Twenty First Century Foods, 14725
ULDO USA, 14770
United Citrus Products, 14857
US Mills, 14780
Vanco Products Company, 14988
Venus Wafers, 15039
Veryfine Products, 15070
Via Della Chiesa Vineyards, 15074
Victoria Gourmet, 15090
Viking Seafoods Inc, 15115
Vincent Potato Chip Company, 15134
Vision Seafood Partners, 15157
Vitasoy USA, 15181
Wachusett Brewing Company, 15245
Wachusett Potato Chip Company, 15246

Waltham Beef Company, 15281
Warner-Lambert Confections, 15295
Washburn Candy Corporation, 15302
Waterfield Farms, 15312
Weathervane Foods, 15345
Weetabix Company, 15364
Welch's Foods Inc, 15380
Welch's Foods Inc Corporate Research & Technology Center, 15382
West Field Farm, 15417
Westfield Farm, 15452
Westport Rivers Vineyard& Winery, 15464
Whipple Company, 15483
Whitney & Son SeaFoods, 15515
Widoffs Modern Bakery, 15536
Williams Candy Company, 15587
Willow Tree Poultry Farm, 15607
Winfrey Fudge & Candy, 15642
Wing It, 15645
Wisconsin Cheese, 15668
Wohrles Foods, 15694
World's Best, 15749
X Cafe, 15777
Yankee Specialty Foods, 15800
Ye Olde Pepper Company, 15807
Yeomen Seafoods, 15811
Zeppys Bakery, 15877

Michigan

A.M. Todd Company, 46
Abbott's Meat, 133
Absopure Water Company, 145, 147
Acme Preserve Company, 171
Adkin & Son Associated Food Products, 196
Adm Edible Bean Specialties, 199
Advance Food Brokers, 207
Al Dente, 277
Alinosi French Superfine Candies, 355
Allen's Naturally, 385
AM Todd Company, 104
Amaranth Marketing Group, 458
Amendt Corporation, 473
American Health & Nutrition, 518, 519
American Saucery, 540
American Soy Products, 544
American Spoon Foods, 546
Apple Valley Market, 676
Applewood Orchards, 681
April Hill, 682
Arbor Springs Water Company, 695
Archway Cookies, 709
Aseltine Cider Company, 799
Atwater Block Brewing Company, 897
Awrey Bakeries, 955
Baker's Choice, 1062
Ball Park Franks, 1087
Behm Blueberry Farms, 1283
BelleHarvest Sales, 1310
Ben B. Schwartz & Sons, 1327
Bessinger Pickle Company, 1378
Better Meat North, 1405
Beverage America, 1410
Big Bucks Brewery & Steakhouse, 1437
Blissfield Canning Company, 1552
Blueberry Store, 1597
Boar's Head Provisions Company, 1609
Bob Evans Farms, 1613
Boskydel Vineyard, 1698
Brady Farms, 1751
Brede, 1790
Burnette Foods, 1978, 1979, 1980
Butterball Farms, 1997
Butternut Bread, 2004
C. Roy Meat Products, 2039
C.F. Burger Creamery, 2044
Cadillac Coffee Company, 2112
Cafe Moak, 2124
Carbon's Golden Malted Pancake & Waffle Flour Mix, 2363
Carothers Research Laboratories, 2438
Carson City Pickle Company, 2452
Cateraid, 2506
Cattleman's Meat Company, 2516
Cedar Lake Foods, 2541
Central Michigan Foods, 2577
Chase Farms, 2653
Chateau Grand Traverse, 2660
Cheeze Kurls, 2689
Chef Shells Catering & Roadside Cafe, 2697

Chef Zachary's Gourmet Blended Spices, 2700
Chelsea Milling Company, 2707
Cherry Central Cooperative Inc, 2719
Cherry Growers, 2720, 2721
Cherry Hut, 2723
Chi Company/Tabor Hill Winery, 2745
Chipotle Chile Company, 2785
City Farm/Rocky Peanut Company, 2902
Coastlog Industries, 3005
Coffee Barrel, 3033
Coffee Beanery, 3038
Coffee Express Company, 3047
Cole's Quality Foods, 3077, 3078
Coloma Frozen Foods, 3091
Cooperative Elevator, 3310
Cooperative Elevator Company, 3311
Country Fresh, 3373, 3374
Country Fresh Golden Valley, 3377
Country Home Creations, 3383
Crane's Pie Pantry Restaurant, 3416
Creme Curls Bakery, 3439
Cross & Peters Company, 3483
CSV Sales, 2089
Curtice Burns Foods, 3561
Dairy Fresh Foods, 3660
Dairy Ingredients, 3663
Dawn Food Products, 3777, 3779
De Bruyn Produce Company, 3797
Dean Foods Company/Country Fresh, 3828
Dearborn Sausage Company, 3833
Detroit Chili Company, 3936
Detroit City Dairy, 3937
Dorothy Dawson Foods Products, 4094
Dover Metals, 4114
Drier's Meats, 4155
Dutch Girl Donuts, 4203
E&H Packing Company, 4225
Eastside Deli Supply, 4303
Eden Foods Inc, 4338
Eden Organic Pasta Company, 4339
Elan Nutrition, 4399
Elena's, 4407
Erevia Products, 4508
Everfresh Beverages, 4562
Farmers Co-operative Grain Company, 4694
Farmland Dairies, 4708
Faygo Beverages, 4733
Fenn Valley Vineyards, 4750
Ferris Organic Farm, 4767
Festida Food, 4771
Flamm Pickle & Packing Company, 4884
Four Percent Company, 5092
Franklin Reister & Sons, 5135
Freeland Bean & Grain, 5155
Freestone Pickle Company, 5158
Fresh Roasted Almond Company, 5189
Frito-Lay, 5226
Fruit Acres Farm Market and U-Pick, 5261
Fruit Belt Foods, 5262
Fry Krisp Food Products, 5270
Functional Foods, 5288
Garden Fresh Salsa, 5400
Germack Pistachio Company, 5523
Gielow Pickles, 5550
Giovanni's Appetizing Food Products, 5584
GKI Foods, 5338
Glacial Ridge Foods, 5600
GLCC Company, 5339
Golden Brown Bakery, 5689
Good Harbor Vineyards, 5762
Gordon Food Service, 5785
Graceland Fruit, 5826
Graceland Fruit Inc, 5827
Graminex, 5845
Grand Rapids Brewing Company, 5847
Great Lakes Packing Company, 5910
Great Lakes Tea & Spice Company, 5912
Greenfield Noodle & Specialty Company, 5964
Groeb Farms, 6000
Gunsberg Corned Beef, 6055
Hamilton Quality Convenience Foods, 6169
Happy Hive, 6209
Hausbeck Pickle Company, 6297
Health Enhancers, 6342
Heinz, 6395
Hirsch Brothers & Company, 6587
Hitz Cheese Company, 6591
Hoekstra Meat Company, 6596
Holland-American Wafer Company, 6609
Homestyle Foods Company, 6647

Honeytree, 6667
House of Flavors, 6759
Hudsonville Creamery & Ice Cream, 6797
IBP Foods, 6856, 6857
Independent Dairy, 6939
International Noodle Company, 7069
Interstate Foods, 7107
Inverness Dairy, 7110
J. Rettenmaier, 7212
J.N. Bech, 7232
Jack Brown Produce, 7286
Jenkins Foods, 7367
Jogue Inc, 7427
Joseph Sanders, 7505
Kalamazoo Brewing Company, 7590
Kalamazoo Creamery, 7591
Kalsec, 7596
Kay Foods Company, 7650
Keebler Company, 7653
Kellogg Company, 7676
Kellogg Company Grand Rapids Bakery, 7681
Kellogg Ingredients Company, 7683
Kellogg US Snack Division, 7685
Kent Meats, 7720
Kent Quality Foods, 7721
King Milling Company, 7804
Kirsco/Kay Packing, 7830
Knappen Milling Company, 7864
Knouse Foods Cooperative, 7873
Koegel Meats, 7889
Koepplinger Bakery, 7891
Koeze Company, 7892
Kowalski Sausage Company, 7925
Kraus & Company, 7958
Krupka's Blueberries, 7976
Kubisch Sausage Company, 7979
L. Mawby Vineyards, 8011
Laska Stuff, 8250
Leelanau Fruit Company, 8310, 8311
Leelanau Wine Cellars, 8312
Lemon Creek Winery, 8340
Leonard Fountain Specialties, 8362
Lesley Elizabeth, 8389
Liberty Dairy, 8414
London Farm Dairy, 8526
Lorann Oils, 8558
LorAnn Oils Inc, 8556
Lotte USA, 8580
Ludwick's Frozen Donuts, 8670
MacKinlay Teas, 8770
Magnum Coffee Roastery, 8820
Mama Mucci's Pasta, 8872
Maple Acres, 8917
Mason County Fruit Packers Cooperative, 9058
McDonald Dairy, 9182
McDonald Dairy Company, 9183
Mead Johnson Nutritional, 9221
Meelunie America, 9252
Metropolitan Baking Company, 9319
Michaelene's Gourmet Granola, 9357
Michigan Ag Commodities, 9366
Michigan Celery Promotion Cooperative, 9367
Michigan Dairy, 9368
Michigan Dessert Corporation, 9369
Michigan Farm Cheese Dairy, 9370
Michigan Freeze Pack, 9371
Michigan Milk Producers Association, 9372
Michigan Sugar Company, 9373, 9374
Midwest Blueberry Farms, 9400
Mountain Roastery Coffee Company, 9775
Mucky Duck Mustard Company, 9837
Nabisco LifeSavers Company, 9917
National Products Company, 9991
Nature's Select, 10053
New Era Canning Company, 10137
North Bay Produce, 10294
Northern Falls, 10323
Northern Michigan Fruit Company, 10330
Northville Winery, 10351
Nutra Food Ingredients, LLC, 10407
Oceana Foods, 10537
Old Europe Cheese, 10586
Old Orchard Brands, 10599
Otto W Liebold & Company, 10757
Packers Canning Company, 10879
Paramount Coffee Company, 10941
Parthenon Food Products, 10972
Peninsula Fruit Exchange, 11101
Pepperidge Farm Bread Distributor, 11142

North American Beverage Company, 10281
Northeastern Products Company, 10318
Noville, 10376
Nu Products Seasoning Company, 10381
Nutro Laboratories, 10435
Nutsco Inc, 10437
Oak Valley Farm, 10490
Oasis Foods Company, 10501
Occidental International Foods, 10507
Ocean Diamond, 10516
Ocean Spray Cranberries, 10529
Old Fashioned Kitchen, 10589
Old Monmouth Peanut Brittle, 10597
OSEM USA, 10470
Outerbridge Peppers, 10767
Oxford Organics, 10781
Ozark Mountain Trading, 10784
Ozone Confectioners & Bakers Supplies, 10787
P.L. Thomas, 10808
Pan American Coffee Company, 10907
Panos Brands, 10915
Papetti's Egg Products, 10921
Paris Foods Corporation, 10948
Paulaur Corporation, 11020
Pechters Baking, 11057
Penta Manufacturing Company, 11118
Perona Farms Food Specialties, 11223
Pfizer, 11264
Pharmachem Laboratories, 11266
Phibro Animal Health, 11272
Pinnacle Foods Group, 11365
Plantextrakt, 11411
Plantextrakt/Martin Bower, 11412
Plumrose, 11430
Plumrose USA, 11432
Pomodoro Fresca Foods, 11469
Portuguese Baking Company, 11517
Premier Casing Company, 11565
Premium Coffee Company, 11578
Presco Food Seasonings, 11586
Prime Ingredients, 11614
Progresso Quality Foods, 11667
Puebla Foods, 11686
Pure World Botanicals, 11698, 11699
QBI, 11727
Quality Ingredients Corporation, 11767
Quality Instant Teas, 11768
R A B Food Group LLC, 11814
R.A.B. Food Group LLC, 11828
Ravifruit, 11938
RC Fine Foods, 11851
Readington Farms, 11947
Ready-Pac Produce, 11951
Real Kosher Sausage Company, 11957
Reckitt Benckiser, 11964
Reed Corporation, 11998
Reheis, 12021
Renault Winery, 12038
Rex Wine Vinegar Company, 12061, 12062
Rey Food Company, 12063
Rhodia, 12071
Rhodia Inc, 12072
Richard Lanza, 12105
Richman Festival Ice Cream Company, 12117
Rico Foods, 12121
Riviana Foods, 12168
Robertet Flavors, 12195
Roche Pharmaceuticals, 12217
Rokeach Food Corporation, 12256
Ron-Son Foods, 12281
Roseland Manufacturing, 12313
Roth Kase, 12334
Routin America, 12344
Royal Kedem Food & Wine Company, 12374
Royal Palm Popcorn Company, 12386
Royal Wine Company, 12396, 12397
Ruggiero Seafood, 12418
Run-A-Ton Group, 12423
Russo Farms, 12439
RW Delights, 11867
S. Abuin Packing, 12470
Sabinsa Corporation, 12525
Salad Depot, 12567
Sands African Imports, 12664
Satnam Overseas Limited, 12787
Schiff Food Products, 12843
Scott Adams Foods, 12903
Scotty Wotty's Creamy Cheescake, 12911
Sea Breeze Fruit Flavors, 12916

Seabrook Brothers & Sons, 12949
Seatrade Corporation, 12986
Sensible Portions, 13049
Seppic, 13056
Serv-Agen Corporation, 13066
Shelley's Prime Meats, 13139
Shofar Kosher Foods, 13166
Shonfeld's, 13168
Silver Palate Kitchens, 13222
Snack Factory, 13324
SnowBird Corporation, 13344
Solgar Vitamin & Herb, 13365
Soluble Products Company, 13370
Somerset Syrup & Beverage, 13375
Sorrento Lactalis NJ Distribution Center, 13399
SoyTex, 13475
Spanarkel Company, 13478
Spear Packing, 13491
Spice Market, 13525
Spice Time Foods/Julius & Joe's, 13528
Spiceco, 13531
Star Ravioli Manufacturing Company, 13645
Star Snacks Company, 13648
Stepan Company, 13702
Stockmeyer North America, 13743
Struthious Ostrich Farm, 13803
Summit Hill Flavors, 13851
Sumptuous Selections, 13855
Suncrest Farms, 13899
Sunkist Growers, 13925, 13928
Sunnyside Vegetable Packing, 13955
SunRise Commodities, 13891
Sunshine Fresh, 13977
Suprema Specialties, 14019
Suzanne's Specialties, 14040
Sweet Water Seafood Corporation, 14078
Swissart Candy Company, 14104
Sylvin Farms Winery, 14115
Symrise, 14119
Synergy Plus, 14123
T&A Gourmet, 14133
Tabatchnick's Fine Foods, 14162
Takasago International Corporation, 14178
Takasago International Corporation (USA), 14179
Tamarind Tree, 14193
Tamuzza Vineyards, 14202
Taste It Presents, 14209
Tate & Lyle North American Sugars, 14242
Taylor Provisions Company, 14256
Tea Beyond, 14266
Teawolf Industries, Ltd, 14271
Technical Oil Products, 14276
Tell Chocolate Corporation, 14291
Templar Food Products, 14296
Testamints, 14317
Thumann's, 14390
Tofutti Brands, 14432
Tomasello Winery, 14450
Tonex, 14457
Topper Food Products, 14476
Topps Meat Company, 14480
Total Lubricants Keystone Division, 14493
Toufayan Bakeries, 14503
Trebon European Specialties, 14548
Tree of Life North Bergen, 14565
Tree Ripe Products, 14549
Tree Tavern Products, 14550
Tribeca Oven, 14593
Triumph Brewing Company, 14624
Tropical Cheese Industries, 14634
Tru-Blu Cooperative Associates, 14657
Trumark, 14670
Tumaro's Gourmet Tortillas & Snacks, 14686
Twin Hens, 14731
Ugo di Lullo & Sons, 14789
Ultimate Gourmet, 14798
Unette Corporation, 14820
Ungars Food Products, 14821
Ungerer & Company, 14822
Unilever Bertolli USA, Inc., 14835
Unilever Bestfoods, 14836
Unilever United States, 14840
Universal Laboratories, 14895
Universal Preservachem Inc, 14898
US Filter, 14775
Van Dyke Ice Cream, 14974
Van Leer Chocolate Corporation, 14977
Van Peenans Dairy, 14980

Varda Chocolatier, 14998
VeggieLand, 15012
Venice Maid Foods, 15023
Vineland Ice & Storage, 15138
Vintage Chocolate Imports, 15142
Violet Packing, 15146
Vita-Pure, 15166
Vital Products, 15168
W.A. Cleary Products, 15213
WA Cleary Products, 15225
Walden Farms, 15257
Watson's Quality Food Products, 15319
Wechsler Coffee Corporation, 15360
Welch, Mott & Clark Company, 15385
Welsh Farms, 15394, 15395, 15396
WFI, 15227
White Toque, 15503
Wise Foods, 15681
World of Coffee, 15746
World of Coffee, World of Tea, 15747
World of Spices, 15748
World Spice, 15744
Wynn Starr Flavors, 15773
Yamate Chocolatier, 15797
Yoo-Hoo Chocolate Beverage Company, 15828
Yvonne's Gourmet Sensations, 15855

New Mexico

Amour Chocolates, 575
Artesia Tortilla Factory, 789
Assets Grille & Southwest Brewing Company, 818
Avalon Organic Coffees, 942
Balagna Winery Company, 1079
Binns Vineyards & Winery, 1470
Black Mesa Winery, 1521
Black Shield, 1526
Blue Sky Natural Beverage Company, 1591
Border Foods Inc, 1681
Bueno Food Products, 1938
Cannon's Sweets Hots, 2299
Casados Farms, 2465
Cervantes Foods Products, 2599
Chateau Sassenage, 2667
Cibolo Junction Food & Spice, 2867
Comfort Foods, 3135
Creamland Dairies, 3427
Dee's Cheesecake Factory/Dee's Foodservice, 3846
Deneen Company, 3915
Eagle Rock Food Company, 4255
El Charro Mexican Food Industries, 4380
El Charro Mexican Foods, 4381
Food Processor of New Mexico, 5007
Gallup Sales Company, 5382
Geetha's Gourmet of India, 5442
Gondwanaland, 5754
Gruet Winery, 6017
Herbs, Etc., 6455, 6456
Hurst Vineyards, 6834
Jillipepper, 7396
Joseph's Lite Cookies, 7509
Josie's Best New Mexican Foods, 7513
La Chiripada Winery, 8047
La Vina Winery, 8094
Las Cruces Foods, 8249
Leonas Foods, 8364
Los Chileros de Nuevo Mexico, 8567
Mac's Meats Wholesale, 8761
Madison Vineyard, 8793
Mi Ranchito Foods, 9339
Mountain States Pecan, 9776
Native Scents, 10001
Nature's Dairy, 10044
New Mexico Food Distributors, 10154
North of the Border, 10313
Original Nut House Brands, 10715
Payne Packing Company, 11025
Ponderosa Valley Vineyard & Winery, 11475
Prairie Thyme, 11552
Rezolex, 12065
Sandia Shadows Vineyard & Winery, 12660
Santa Fe Bite-Size Bakery, 12689, 12690
Santa Fe Brewing, 12691
Santa Fe Seasons, 12692
Santa Fe Vineyards, 12693
Schadel's Bakery, 12828
Seeds of Change, 13008
Senor Murphy Candymaker, 13046
Senor Pinos de Santa Fe, 13047

Southwest Spirit, 13469
Stahmann Farms, 13623
Sunland Inc/Peanut Better, 13937
Taos Brewing Supply, 14209
Taos Trails Brewery, 14210
Texas Reds Steak House, 14328
Tularosa Vineyards, 14681
Tyson Foods Plant, 14759
Victor Allen Coffee Company, 15084
Warden Peanut Company, 15292
Windmill Water, 15629
Woodie Pie Company, 15718
Young Pecan, 15841

New York

4C Foods Corporation, 5
A. Bauer's Mustard, 24
A. Stein Meat Products, 37
A.L. Bazzini Company, 43
Abel & Schafer, 136
Abeles & Heymann GourmetKosher Provisions, Inc., 137
Abkit Camocare Nature Works, 143
Accurate Ingredients, 161
Acme Smoked Fish Corporation, 172
Adair Vineyards, 180
ADH Health Products, 64
Adirondack Beverages, 194
Adirondack Maple Farms, 195
Advanced Nutritional Research, Inc., 214
Agger Fish, 226
AGNESI USA, 99
Agrexco USA, 231
Agri-Dairy Products, 234
AgriCulver Seeds, 241
Agro Farma Inc, 248
Ah Dor Kosher Fish Corporation, 258
AIYA, 101
Al Safa Halal, 281
Aladdin Bakers, 287
Alexander International (USA), 335
Alexandra & Nicolay, 337
Alexia Foods, 338
Alkinco, 357
All Round Foods, 365
Alle Processing, 371
Alle Processing Corporation, 372
Allen's Pickle Works, 386
Allied Food Products, 391
Allied Wine Corporation, 395
Amazing Candy Craft Company, 460
Amberg Wine Cellars, 464
Ambrosial Granola, 470
Amcan Industries, 471
America's Best Beverage Company, 481
American Almond Products Company, 484
American Biosciences, 487
American Classic Ice Cream Company, 498
American Health, 517
American Mint, 534
American Tartaric Products, 548
American Vintage Wine Biscuits, 550
Americana Vineyards, 556
Amerol Corporation, 563, 564
Anchor Frozen Foods, 595
Angel's Bakeries, 621
Angelic Gourmet Inc, 622
Anheuser-Busch, 627
ANKOM Technology, 108
Anthony Road Wine Company, 656
Antoni Ravioli, 660
Antonio's Bakery, 662
Aphrodisia Products, 667
Apple & Eve, 672
Apple Acres, 675
Arbor Hill Grapery & Winery, 693
Arbor Mist Winery, 694
Arcadian Estate Winery, 699
Arcee Sales Company, 700
Arctic Glacier, 713, 714, 715, 716, 717
Argo Fine Foods, 724
Arizona Beverage Company, 736
Armenia Coffee Corporation, 757
Arnold's Meat Food Products, 764
Aromachem, 771
Artuso Pastry Foods, 795
Artuso Pastry Shop, 796
Associated Bakers Products, 820
Associated Brands, Inc., 822
Astral Extracts Ltd, 843
At Last Naturals, 845

Healing Light, 6338
Health Products Corporation, 6344
Healthy Oven, 6354
Healthy'N Fit Nutrition als, 6356
Heartland Brewery, 6360
Heavenscent Edibles, 6374
Heintz & Weber Company, 6391
Heinz Bakery Products, 6396
Heisler Food Enterprises, 6402
Heluva Good Cheese, 6415
Hemisphere Associated, 6416
Hena Coffee, 6418
Hendon & David, 6420
Henningsen Foods, 6427, 6428
Henry & Henry, 6429
Heritage Cheese House, 6459
Herkimer Foods, 6474, 6475
Hermann J. Wiemer Vineyard, 6479
Hermann Wiemer Vineyards, 6482
Hermany Farms, 6484
Heron Hill Winery, 6486
Heterochemical Corporation, 6502
Hetty Fair Foods Company, 6503
High Falls Brewing, 6531
High Falls Brewing Company, 6532
High Ridge Foods LLC, 6536
Hilliard Corporation, 6564
Hofmann Sausage Company, 6601
Holey Moses Cheesecake, 6605
Hollow Road Farms, 6611
Homestead Dairies, 6642
Honey Bar/Creme de la Creme, 6653
Honeypot Treats, 6666
Hormel Foods Corporation, 6709
Hornell Brewing Company, 6736
Horstmann Mix & Cream, 6740
House of Spices, 6762
House of Spices India, 6763
Hudson Valley Fruit Juice, 6795
Hudson Valley Homestead, 6796
Hunt Country Vineyards, 6825
Hunt-Wesson Food Service Company, 6826
Hunt-Wesson Foods, 6827
Hurd Orchards, 6832, 6833
Icco Cheese Company, 6876
Icelandic Milk and Skyr Corporation, 6882
Ideal Snacks, 6899
Il Gelato, 6901
Il Tiramisu, 6903
Imagine Foods, 6909
Imperial Foods, 6920
Impromtu Gourmet, 6928
Imus Ranch Foods, 6930
Inca Kola/Golden Kola, 6932
Increda-Meal, 6933
Independent French Manufacturers, 6942
Indo Med, 6969
Interfrost, 7023
International Casein Corporation, 7033
International Fiber Corporation, 7049, 7050
International Flavors & Fragrances, 7051
International Glatt Kosher, 7062
International Harvest, 7063
Irving R. Boody & Company, 7124
Isadore A. Rapasadi & Son, 7128
ISG-Avne Packaging Services, 6871
Italian Foods Manufacturing, 7154
J Freirich Food Products, 7175
J.B. Peel Coffee Roasters, 7217
J.B. Sons, 7218
J.H. Verbridge & Son, 7223
Jamesport Vineyards, 7323
Janowski's Hamburgers, 7329
Java-Gourmet/Keuka Lake Coffee Roaster, 7344
JC World Foods, 7260
Jeryl's Jems, 7387
Jet's Le Frois Foods Corporation, 7392
JF Braun & Sons Inc., 7267
JF Clarke Corporation, 7268
Jianlibao America, 7395
JMP Bakery Company, 7275
Joel Harvey Distributing, 7422
John A. Vassilaros & Son, 7430
Johnson Estate Wines, 7468
Johnston's Winery, 7480
Jonathan Lord Corporation, 7483
Joyva Corporation, 7520
Junior's Cheesecake, 7540
Juniper Valley Farms, 7541
Juno Chef's, 7542
Jurgielewicz Duck Farm, 7544

Kabco, 7577
Karam Elsaha Baking Company, 7612
Karen's Fabulous Biscotti, 7613
Kari-Out Company, 7616
Karl Ehmer, 7618
Katrina's Tartufo, 7641
Kelley Meats, 7669
Kelsen Bisca, 7695
Kemach Food Products Corporation, 7697
King David's All NaturalFood, 7794
Kintetsu World Express, 7824
Kitchen Table Bakers, 7838
Knapp Vineyards, 7863
Knese Enterprise, 7865
Knoll Creek Dairy, 7869
Kopper's Chocolate Specialty Company, 7914
Koppert Cress USA, 7915
Kosher French Baguettes, 7921
Kossar's Bialystoker Kuchen Bakery, 7922
Kozy Shack, 7928
Kraft Foods, 7941, 7942
Krinos Foods, 7963
Kutik's Honey Farm, 7989
Kyowa Hakko, 7994
L & S Packing Company, 7995
L&S Packing Company, 8005
L.I. Cauliflower Association, 8015
La Flor Spices, 8054
La Flor Spices Company, 8055
La Nova Wings, 8068
La Rosa Bakery, 8082
Lactalis Ingredients South Park Plant & Distribution Center, 8112
Lactalis USA, 8115
Lake Titus Brewery, 8149
Lakeshore Winery, 8153
Lakewood Vineyards, 8167
Lallemand/American Yeast, 8169
Lamoreaux Landing Wine Cellar, 8184
Lanco, 8192
Landies Candies Company, 8208, 8209
Larry's Vineyards & Winery, 8241
Laura Paige Candy Company, 8257
Lavazza Premium Coffee Corporation, 8264
Le Frois Foods Corporation, 8279
Leader Candies, 8289
Lee Kum Kee, 8302
Leidenfrost Vineyards, 8326
Leiner Davis Gelatin, 8331
Leisure Time Ice & Spring Water, 8334
Lemon-X Corporation, 8341
Lender's Bagel Bakery, 8346
Lenny's Bee Productions, 8351
Les Trois Petits Cochons, 8384
Les Trois Petits Cochons 3 Little Pigs, 8385
LesserEvil Snacks, 8391
Let's Serve, 8393, 8394
Levonian Brothers, 8398
Lichtwer Pharma, 8422
Lieber Chocolate & Food Products, 8423
Linda's Lollies Company, 8449
Linden Cookies, 8453
Lioni Latticini, Inc, 8468
Local Tofu, 8504
Lockcoffee, 8507
Long Expected Coffee Co mpany, 8536
Longo Coffee & Tea, 8549
Losurdo Creamery, 8576
Lou-Retta's Custom Chocolates, 8587
Love & Quiches Desserts, 8625
LSK Smoked Turkey Products, 8031
Lucas Vineyards, 8647
Lumar Lobster Corporatio, 8677
M.H. Greenebaum, 8729
MacDonald Honey Company, 8764
Madelaine Chocolate Novelties, Inc, 8787
Magnanini Winery, 8813
Magnificent Muffin Corporation, 8815
Majestic Foods, 8850
Mamma Lombardi's All Natural Sauces, 8879
Mandarin Soy Sauce, 8888, 8889
Manhattan Special Bottling Corporation, 8899
Mar-K Anchor Bar Hot Sauces, 8944
Mari's New York, 8966
Marnap Industries, 9007
Marshakk Smoked Fish Company, 9015
Marten's Country Kitchen, 9026
Master Peace Food Imports, 9063
Mattus Lowfat Ice Cream, 9086

Maya Maimal Fine Indian Food, 9106
Mayer Brothers Apple Products, 9109, 9110
Mayer's Cider Mill, 9112
Mayfair Sales, 9114
Mazzoli Coffee, 9124
McCadam Cheese Company, 9131
McDuffies Bakery, 9186
McGregor Vineyard Winery, 9194
Meadowbrook Distributing Corporation, 9230
Meadowbrook Farm, 9231
Meal Mart, 9234
Meat-O-Mat Corporation, 9239
Meating Place, 9241
Meditalia, 9246
Mediterranean Gyros Products, 9248
Mercantile Food Company, 9282
Merritt Estate Wines, 9305
Metzger Specialty Brands, 9325
Mexi-Frost Specialties Company, 9327
Michel's Magnifique, 9359
Milan Provision Company, 9416
Millbrook Vineyard and Winery, 9435
Miller's Cheese, 9456
Millflow Spice Corporation, 9466
Milligan & Higgins, 9469
Milmar Food Group, 9477
Milos, 9485
Milton A. Klein Company, 9488
Mister Snacks, 9550
Mitch Chocolate, 9555
Mitchel Dairies, 9556
Mitsubishi Chemical America, 9559
Mitsubishi InternationalCorporation, 9561
MO Air International, 8753
Modern Baked Products, 9577
Modern Italian Bakery of West Babylon, 9579
Modern Tea Packers, 9584
Moet Hennessy USA, 9587
Mogen David Wine Corporation, 9588
Moka D'Oro Coffee, 9594
Mom 'N Pops, 9605
Mon Cuisine, 9612
Mongolia Casing Corporation, 9624
Monk's Bread, 9627
Monte Cristo Trading, 9645
Morris J. Golombeck, 9717
Morrisons Pastries/Turf Cheesecake, 9724
Moscahlades Brothers, 9734
Mother Earth Enterprises, 9740
Mott's, 9751, 9752
Mount Rose Ravioli & Macaroni Company, 9766
Mountain States Rosen, LLc, 9777
Mountainside Farms Dairy, 9785
Mr. Pickle, 9802
Mt. Olympus Specialty Foods, 9836
Murray's Chicken, 9866
Musicon Deer Farm, 9873
My Bagel Chips, 9881
Najila's, 9923
Nantucket Nectars, 9937
Nassau Candy Company, 9958
National Foods, 9981
National Grape Cooperative, 9986
Natrium Products, 10005
Natural Nectar, 10021
Natural Wonder Foods, 10031
Nature's Best Food Supplement, 10041
Nature's Bounty, 10042
Nature's Provision Company, 10052
Natures Best, 10059
NBTY, 9897
ND Labs Inc, 9899
New Hope Mills, 10146
New Land Vineyard, 10151
New York Apples Sales, 10168
New York Bottling Company, 10172
New York Coffee & Bagels, 10173
New York Pretzel, 10178
New York Ravioli & Pasta Company, 10179
Newburgh Egg Corporation, 10183
Newburgh Egg Processing, 10184
Newburgh Packing Corporation, 10185
Niagara Chocolates, 10201
Niagara Foods, 10202
Niagara Milk Cooperative, 10203
Nog Incorporated, 10247
Nora's Candy Shop, 10264
Norimoor Company, 10274
North Country Natural Spring Water, 10298

North Salem Vineyard, 10307
North Shore Bottling Company, 10308
Northern Orchard Company, 10333
Northern Packing Company, 10334
Northern Soy, 10336
Novelty Kosher Pastry, 10373
NSpired Natural Foods, 9907, 9908, 9909
Nspired Natural Foods, 10380
NTC Foods Corporation, 9910
Nutrition 21, 10426
NYSCO Products LLC, 9911
O C Lugo Company, 10443
O'Mona International Tea, 10456
O-At-Ka Milk Products Cooperative, 10462
Oceanside Knish Factory, 10542
Off Shore Seafood Company, 10549
Old Chatham Sheepherding, 10574
Old Dutch Mustard Company, 10585
Olympic Specialty Foods, 10641
Omanga Ice Cream Company, 10644
Once Again Nut Butter, 10657
Orwasher's Bakery Handmade Bread, 10732
Ottman Meat Company, 10754
Paesana Products, 10882
Palmer Vineyards, 10899
Paradise Products Corporation, 10933
Paramount Caviar, 10939
Paramount Chocolates, 10940
Parkside Candy Company, 10961
Paron Chocolatier, 10970
Pascal Coffee, 10978
Pasta Del Mondo, 10986
Pasta Italiana, 10989
Patsy's, 11008
Patsy's Brands, 11009
Paul de Lima Company, 11017
Paumanok Vineyards, 11023
Pavero Cold Storage Corporation, 11023
Pazdar Winery, 11026
Peaceworks, 11033, 11034
Peanut Butter & Co, 11035
Peanut Wonder Corporation, 11043
Pearl River Pastry & Chocolates, 11047
Peconic Bay Winery, 11061
Pecoraro Dairy Products, 11062
Pecos Valley Spice Company, 11063
Pede Brothers, 11064
Peeled Snacks, 11067
Penny Curtiss Baking Company, 11115
Pepsi Bottling Co of Buffalo, 11148
Pepsi Bottling Group, 11150
Pepsi-Cola Bottling Company, 11166
PepsiCo, 11178
PepsiCo Inc, 11191
Pereg Gourmet Spices, 11209
Perfect Foods, 11213
Pernod Ricard USA, 11221
Perry's Ice Cream Company, 11226
Pestos with Panache by Lauren, 11229
Petri Baking Products Inc, 11249
Pfeiffer's Foods, 11262
Pfeil & Holing, 11263
Pharmline, 11268
Phoenix Agro-Industrial Corporation, 11291
Phoenix Laboratories, 11292
Pidy Gourmet Pastry Shells, 11303, 11304
Pindar Vineyards, 11356
Pino's Pasta Veloce, 11366
Plainville Farms, 11403
Plaza House Coffee, 11415
Plaza Sweets, 11416
Pleasant Valley Wine Company, 11419
Plymouth Beef, 11434
Pollio Dairy Products, 11463
Polly-O Dairy Products, 11466
Poplar Ridge Vineyards, 11489
Portier Fine Foods, 11509
Precision Plus Vacuum Parts, 11559
Prime Food Processing Corporation, 11613
Prime Pastry, 11618
Private Label Foods, 11637
Pro Portion Foods, 11640
Proper-Chem, 11672
Punch's Nut Company, 11689
Pure Extracts Inc, 11692
Purity Ice Cream Company, 11711
Purity Products, 11712
Q Bell Foods, 11723
Q Tonic, 11724
Quaker Bonnet, 11733
Quaker Sugar Company, 11742

Newfoundland and Labrador

North Carolina

Oregon

Prince Edward Island

Washington

West Virginia

Wisconsin

Parent Company Index

John Morrell & Company, 7453, 7454
Pruden Packing Company, 11684
V.W. Joyner & Company, 14922
Smithfield Foods
Gwaltney Food Service, 6063
Gwaltney of Smithfield, 6064, 6065
JBS Packerland, 7258
John Morrell & Company, 7452
Lykes Meat Group, 8689
Moyer Packing Company, 9792
North Side Foods Corporation, 10309
Patrick Cudahy, 11007
Snake River Sugar Company
Amalgamated Sugar Company, 451
Snow Fresh Foods
Endico Potatoes, 4468
Snowcrest Packers
Omstead Foods Ltd, 10652
Snowsouth
Sea Garden Seafoods, 12921
Sobel-Holland
Banner Pharmacaps, 1107
Sokol and Company
Certified Savory, 2598
Solvay America
Solvay Chemicals, 13372
Solvent Interntional
Soylent Brand, 13477
Sonne
Dakota Gourmet, 3681
Sontory Water Group
Polar Water Company, 11460
Sopacko
Sopacko Packaging, 13390
Sophia's Sauce Works
Sophia's Sauce Works, 13392
Sopralco
Sopralco, 13393
Sorrento Lactalis
Sorrento Lactalis, 13397
Southern Flavoring
Southern Flavoring Company, 13442
Sparks Sales Company
Spanarkel Company, 13478
Sparta Foods
Food Products Corporation, 5008
Speaco Foods
Gregory-Robinson Speas, 5978
Specialty Brands of America
Specialty Brands of America, 13498
Spring Tree Maple Products, 13569
Specialty Enzymes and Biochemicals Company
Cal India Foods International, 2160
Spiceworld
Spiceworld, 13535
St. Francis River Farming
Fancy Farms Popcorn, 4649
Star-Kist Foods
Star-Kist Caribe, 13655
Starbucks Coffee Company
Tazo Tea, 14264
Stephan Company
Old 97 Manufacturing Company, 10571
Stepan Company, 13702
Stichting Anheuser-Busch Inbev
City Brewery Latrobe, 2899
Stimson Lane
Stimson Lane Winery, 13737
Villa Mt. Eden Winery, 15119
Stinson Seafood
Stinson Seafood Company, 13739
Stokely USA
Poynette Distribution Center, 11534
Stop & Shop Supermarket Company
Stop & Shop Manufacturing, 13769
Strauss-Elite LTD
Sabra Blue & White Food Products, 12527
Sucocitrico Cutrale Ltd

Cutrale Citrus Juices, 3583
Sugar Foods Corporation
Sugar Foods, 13829
Suiza Dairy Group
Barbe's Dairy, 1119
Borden, 1678
Borden Foods, 1679
Brown's Dairy, 1895
Burger Dairy, 1967
Country Delite, 3370
Country Fresh, 3373, 3374
Dairy Fresh, 3658
Dairymen's, 3676
Frostbite, 5254
Garelick Farms, 5413, 5414, 5415
Land-o-Sun, 8207
LeHigh Valley Dairies, 8283
Meadow Gold Dairies, 9224, 9225, 9228
Model Dairy, 9575
Oak Farms, 10475, 10476
Robinson Dairy, 12208
Schenkel's All Star Dairy, 12840
Schepps Dairy, 12841
Shenandoah's Pride, 13144
Swiss Dairy, 14094
Tuscan Dairy Farms, 14717
Velda Farms, 15014, 15015, 15016, 15017
Suiza Foods
Land-O-Sun Dairies, 8206
Louis Trauth Dairy, 8602
Miscoe Springs, 9525
Suiza Dairy Corporation, 13839
Sun Opta Inc
Sun Opta Ingredients, 13863
Sunkist Growers
Sunkist Fresh Fruit Sales/Domestic-International Markets-Food Se, 13916
Sunkist Growers, 13918, 13919, 13920, 13921, 13922, 13923, 13924, 13925, 13926, 13927, 13928, 13929, 13930, 13931, 13932, 13933, 13934, 13935
Sunkist John P Newman Research and Development Center, 13936
SunkiStreet Growers, 13911
Sunmark Companies
Sunline Brands, 13939
Sunnyland Foods
Brooks County Sausage, 1863
SunOpta
Beta Pure Foods, 1394
SunOpta, Inc
SunOpta Sunflower, 13888
Sunopta, Inc.
Cleugh's Frozen Foods, 2955
Sunset Trails
Circle R Ranch Gourmet Foods, 2880
Suntory International Corporation
Suntory Water Group, 13983
Suntory Water Group
Crystal Springs Water Company, 3520
Crystal Water Company, 3522
DS Waters of America, 3627
Superior Coffee & Foods
Wechsler Coffee Corporation, 15360
Superiors Brand Meats
Fresh Mark, 5185
Suzuki Industries
Suzuki's Ice Castle, 14042
Swan Food Company
Schwan's Consumer Brands North America, 12887
Swire Pacific Holdings
Swire Coca-Cola, 14090
Swiss Colony
Green County Foods, 5941
Swiss Valley Farms Company

Swiss Valley Farms Company, 14099, 14100
Symrise GmbH & Co. KG
Symrise, 14119
Sysco
Fulton Provision Company, 5282
Sysco Corporation
Sysco Food Services of Chicago, 14125
Sysco Food Services of Indiana, 14126
Sysco/Louisville Food Service, 14128
Systems Bio-Industries
SKW Biosystems, 12503

T

T Marzetti Company
Girard's Food Service Dressings, 5587
T. Hasegawa Company
T Hasegawa, 14130
T. Marzetti Company
New York Frozen Foods, 10175
Pfeiffer's Foods, 11262
Reames Foods, 11959
T.A. Ocean Odyssey
Bradye P. Todd & Son, 1752
T.J. Kraft
Norpac Fisheries, 10275
Tallmadge Brothers
Hillard Bloom Packing Co, 6558
Tasty Baking Company
Tastykake, 14237
Tata Tea Ltd
Tetley Tea, 14319
Tate & Lyle North American Sugars
Tate & Lyle North American Sugars, 14241, 14242
Tate & Lyle Staley Company, 14243
Taylor Fresh Foods
Pacific Pre-cut Produce, 10859
TCBY
Americana Foods, 554
Technical Oil
Technical Oil, 14275
Temo's
Temo's Candy, 14293
Ten Ren Tea Company
Uncle Lee's Tea, 14813
Terrace Holdings
Banner Beef & Seafood Company, 1105
Terri Lynn, Inc
Terri Lynn, 14313
Tetley US Holdings Limited
Good Earth® Teas, 5758
Tetley USA
Bustelo Coffee Roasting Company, 1991
Sourthern Tea, 13407
Texas United Corporation
United Salt Corporation, 14879
TFS
Toxic Tommy's Beef Jerky & Spices, 14512
The Inventure Group Inc
Poore Brothers, 11482
The Irving Group
Cavendish Farms, 2522
The Vermont Maple Syrup Company
Butternut Mountain Farm, 2005
The Virginia Food Group
Old Dominion Peanut Corporation, 10583
Thomas H Lee Partners
Michael Foods, Inc., 9350
Threshold Enterprises
Source Naturals, 13405
Thrifty
Thrifty Ice Cream, 14388
Tiller Foods

Instantwhip: Florida, 7009
TIPIAK SA
TIPIAK INC, 14154
Todd's Central Commissary
Todd's Enterprises, 14421
Todhunter International
Todhunter Foods, 14424
Todhunter Foods & Monarch Wine Company, 14425
Tom's Food
Tom's Foods, 14443
Tomanetti Foods
Amberwave Foods, 466
Tony Downs Foods
Butterfield Foods Company, 2000
Tootsie Roll Industries
Cambridge Brands, 2245
Cella's Confections, 2555
Torreo Coffee & Tea Company
Torreo Coffee Company, 14491
Toufayan Bakeries
Toufayan Bakeries, 14502
Tova Industries
New Horizon Foods, 10148
Townsends
Pocono Foods, 11442
Townsend Culinary, 14506
Townsends Inc
Townsends Inc, 14511
Toyo Suisan Kaisha
Maruchan, 9041
Tree of Life
Tree of Life Albany, 14554
Tree of Life Atlanta, 14555
Tree of Life Canada East, 14556
Tree of Life Canada West, 14557, 14558
Tree of Life Cleburne, 14559
Tree of Life Elkton, 14560
Tree of Life Ft Lauderdale, 14561
Tree of Life Los Angeles, 14562
Tree of Life Milwaukee, 14563
Tree of Life Minneapolis, 14564
Tree of Life North Bergen, 14565
Tree of Life Portland, 14566
Tree of Life Southwest-West Region, 14567
Tree Top
Sabroso Company, 12529
Tree Top, 14552
Watermill Foods, 15316
TreeHouse Foods
Bay Valley Foods, 1213, 1214
Tregar
Laredo Mexican Foods, 8234
Treier Family Farms
Treier Popcorn Farms, 14572
Tri Valley Growers
Tri-Valley Growers, 14590
Tri-Union Seafoods
Chicken of the Sea International, 2763
Tri-Valley Growers
Signature Fruit, 13197, 13198
Tri-Valley Growers, 14588, 14589
Triarc Companies
Stewart's Beverages, 13725
Trident Seafood Corporation
Trident Seafoods Corporation, 14595, 14596
Trinidad/Benham Corporation
Trinidad Benham Company, 14599
Trinidad/Benham Corporation, 14603
Westlam Foods, 15456
Triple H Food Processors
Stone Cellar Kitchens, 13753
Uncle Bum's Gourmet Foods, 14808
Tropical
Tropical, 14629
Tropicana
Dole Fresh Vegetable Company, 4052
Troyer Potato Products

General Reference

American Environmental Leaders: From Colonial Times to the Present
An African Biographical Dictionary
Encyclopedia of African-American Writing
Encyclopedia of American Industries
Encyclopedia of Emerging Industries
Encyclopedia of Global Industries
Encyclopedia of Gun Control & Gun Rights
Encyclopedia of Invasions & Conquests
Encyclopedia of Prisoners of War & Internment
Encyclopedia of Religion & Law in America
Encyclopedia of Rural America
Encyclopedia of the United States Cabinet, 1789-2010
Encyclopedia of Warrior Peoples & Fighting Groups
Environmental Resource Handbook
From Suffrage to the Senate: America's Political Women
Global Terror & Political Risk Assessment
Historical Dictionary of War Journalism
Human Rights in the United States
Nations of the World
Political Corruption in America
Speakers of the House of Representatives, 1789-2009
The Environmental Debate: A Documentary History
The Evolution Wars: A Guide to the Debates
The Religious Right: A Reference Handbook
The Value of a Dollar: 1860-2009
The Value of a Dollar: Colonial Era
University & College Museums, Galleries & Related Facilities
Weather America
World Cultural Leaders of the 20th & 21st Centuries
Working Americans 1880-1999 Vol. I: The Working Class
Working Americans 1880-1999 Vol. II: The Middle Class
Working Americans 1880-1999 Vol. III: The Upper Class
Working Americans 1880-1999 Vol. IV: Their Children
Working Americans 1880-2003 Vol. V: At War
Working Americans 1880-2005 Vol. VI: Women at Work
Working Americans 1880-2006 Vol. VII: Social Movements
Working Americans 1880-2007 Vol. VIII: Immigrants
Working Americans 1770-1869 Vol. IX: Revol. War to the Civil War
Working Americans 1880-2009 Vol. X: Sports & Recreation
Working Americans 1880-2010 Vol. XI: Entrepreneurs & Inventors

Bowker's Books In Print®Titles

Books In Print®
Books In Print® Supplement
American Book Publishing Record® Annual
American Book Publishing Record® Monthly
Books Out Loud™
Bowker's Complete Video Directory™
Children's Books In Print®
El-Hi Textbooks & Serials In Print®
Forthcoming Books®
Large Print Books & Serials™
Law Books & Serials In Print™
Medical & Health Care Books In Print™
Publishers, Distributors & Wholesalers of the US™
Subject Guide to Books In Print®
Subject Guide to Children's Books In Print®

Business Information

Directory of Business Information Resources
Directory of Mail Order Catalogs
Directory of Venture Capital & Private Equity Firms
Food & Beverage Market Place
Grey House Homeland Security Directory
Grey House Performing Arts Directory
Hudson's Washington News Media Contacts Directory
New York State Directory
Sports Market Place Directory
The Rauch Guides – Industry Market Research Reports

Statistics & Demographics

America's Top-Rated Cities
America's Top-Rated Small Towns & Cities
America's Top-Rated Smaller Cities
Comparative Guide to American Suburbs
Comparative Guide to Health in America
Profiles of... Series – State Handbooks

Health Information

Comparative Guide to American Hospitals
Comparative Guide to Health in America
Complete Directory for Pediatric Disorders
Complete Directory for People with Chronic Illness
Complete Directory for People with Disabilities
Complete Mental Health Directory
Directory of Health Care Group Purchasing Organizations
Directory of Hospital Personnel
HMO/PPO Directory
Medical Device Register
Older Americans Information Directory

Education Information

Charter School Movement
Comparative Guide to American Elementary & Secondary Schools
Complete Learning Disabilities Directory
Educators Resource Directory
Special Education

TheStreet.com Ratings Guides

TheStreet.com Ratings Consumer Box Set
TheStreet.com Ratings Guide to Bank Fees & Service Charges
TheStreet.com Ratings Guide to Banks & Thrifts
TheStreet.com Ratings Guide to Bond & Money Market Mutual Funds
TheStreet.com Ratings Guide to Common Stocks
TheStreet.com Ratings Guide to Credit Unions
TheStreet.com Ratings Guide to Exchange-Traded Funds
TheStreet.com Ratings Guide to Health Insurers
TheStreet.com Ratings Guide to Life & Annuity Insurers
TheStreet.com Ratings Guide to Property & Casualty Insurers
TheStreet.com Ratings Guide to Stock Mutual Funds
TheStreet.com Ratings Ultimate Guided Tour of Stock Investing

Canadian General Reference

Associations Canada
Canadian Almanac & Directory
Canadian Environmental Resource Guide
Canadian Parliamentary Guide
Financial Services Canada
History of Canada
Libraries Canada

Grey House Publishing
4919 Route 22, PO Box 56, Amenia NY 12501-0056 | (800) 562-2139 | www.greyhouse.com | books@greyhouse.com